THE SERIALS DIRECTORY

AN INTERNATIONAL REFERENCE BOOK

Editorial Advisory Board

Susan A. Cady
Associate Director
for Technical Services
Lehigh University Libraries

Shere Connan
Chief Librarian, Serials Department
Stanford University Libraries

Claude Daris
Serials Librarian
Universite Libre de Bruxelles

Sul H. Lee, Ph.D.
Dean, University Libraries
The University of Oklahoma

Robert W. Gibson, Jr.
Head, Library Department
General Motors Research Laboratories

Peter Gellatly
Senior Editor, LIBRARIANSHIP and
Editor, THE SERIALS LIBRARIAN
The Haworth Press, Inc.

Lois N. Upham, Ph.D.
Assistant Professor
Division of Library and Information Management
Emory University

The Premier Edition of *The Serials Directory: An International Reference Book* was compiled and published by EBSCO Publishing, division of EBSCO Industries, Inc.
    Joe K. Weed, Vice President/General Manager
    Emmy S. Carmichael, Publishing Coordinator
    John Krontiras, Vice President/General Manager—Data Processing
    J. T. Stephens, President—EBSCO Industries, Inc.
The Editorial Staff instrumental in the preparation of *The Serials Directory* includes: Michelle Allen, Jennifer Bellsnyder, Sherry Berry, Susan Emack, Cathy Estes, Leslie McDonald, Lee Ann McWhorter, Cheryl Peterson, Ellen Rice, Glenda Robertson, Lindsey Ryan-Stewart, Kelly Walker.

THE SERIALS DIRECTORY

AN INTERNATIONAL REFERENCE BOOK

PREMIER EDITION 1986

VOLUME II

J-Z

EBSCO PUBLISHING

Division of EBSCO Industries Inc., Birmingham, Alabama

Published by EBSCO Publishing
division of EBSCO Industries, Inc.
P.O. Box 1943, Birmingham, AL 35201

Copyright © 1986 by EBSCO Industries, Inc.

All rights reserved. Reproduction of this directory, in whole or in part, by any method, without permission of the publisher is prohibited.

International Standard Book Number 0-913956-18-X (3-volume set)
International Standard Book Number 0-913956-19-8 (volume 1)
International Standard Book Number 0-913956-20-1 (volume 2)
International Standard Book Number 0-913956-21-X (volume 3)
International Standard Serial Number 0886-4179

Printed and bound in the United States of America.

Every effort has been made to ensure the accuracy of information in *The Serials Directory* and since no payment has been made for the inclusion of any entries, the publisher cannot accept liability for errors or omissions, regardless of the cause.

CONTENTS

Preface vii

User's Guide ix

Filing Rules xv

Subject Headings xvii

Subject Cross References xxi

Tables xxix

    Frequency xxx

    Country of Publication xxxi

    Unit of Currency xxxiii

    Indexes/Abstracts xxxv

Volume 1

    Serials Listing (A-I) 1

Volume 2

    Serials Listing (J-Z) 1487

Volume 3

    Alphabetical Title Index 2993

    Ceased Title Index 4273

    ISSN Index 4293

PREFACE

The Premier Edition of *The Serials Directory: An International Reference Book*, a unique new source of bibliographic and ordering information on more than 113,000 serial titles published around the world, provides easy access to more information on more serial titles than any other printed serials reference source available. The principal reason why this data is so extraordinarily complete is that the information contained in *The Serials Directory* has been drawn from three separate and distinct sources.

To collect the serials data contained in this directory, we looked first to EBSCO's internal title file database. After many years in the subscription service business, EBSCO has compiled an extensive database of information on more than 170,000 serial titles. In developing *The Serials Directory*, this database was useful for the information it contains and also as a guide to identifying titles most often subscribed to by libraries worldwide.

Our second and most noteworthy source of data was the CONSER file. The CONSER file contains information on hundreds of thousands of bibliographic records contributed by the nation's leading libraries. The majority of those title records included in *The Serials Directory* were authenticated by the Library of Congress. CONSER file data has never been published in a directory form before as far as we know. To obtain a good cross section of all types of serial title listings, we matched thousands of the most frequently subscribed to titles from EBSCO's title file database with those from the CONSER file. Next, we established criteria for selecting additional titles which were not so heavily subscribed to and extracted the remaining CONSER data for these titles.

Finally, for information not contained in the EBSCO database nor the CONSER file, we queried publishers directly to obtain answers to many questions that they could best answer. The result is a broad and practical listing of serial titles with significant data. We are proud to offer this new reference tool as a service to librarians, information managers and other professionals around the world.

The information in *The Serials Directory* has been organized in a manner to make researching titles easy. Publications are listed by subject, then alphabetically within each subject category. An alphabetical title index, an ISSN index, and a ceased title index are included for fingertip reference. In addition, currency translations, country of publication abbreviations, frequency abbreviations, and index and abstract abbreviations tables are also included.

The following pages explain how to use *The Serials Directory* for best results. As a supplier of quality subscription services to libraries, businesses, and professionals worldwide, we hope that you will find this new directory to be the most useful reference work of its kind. The goal in developing *The Serials Directory* has been to offer one complete, accurate resource for the most sought after information on serials by librarians and information professionals. We welcome your suggestions for improvement and expansion in future editions. We hope you will continue to trust the name EBSCO for information and management services in the world of serials.

Emmy Carmichael
Publishing Coordinator

Joe K. Weed
Vice President,
General Manager

USER'S GUIDE

USER'S GUIDE

How To Use The Serials Directory

Four major sections comprise The Serials Directory.

- **Serials Listing** (Volumes 1 and 2)
- **Alphabetical Title Index** (Volume 3)
- **Ceased Title Index** (Volume 3)
- **ISSN Index** (Volume 3)

These four parts allow the user to access information simply. The following is an explanation of each section and how to use it.

1. Serials Listing—The serials listing is arranged alphabetically by subject category. The serials listed under each subject heading are in alphabetical order by title. (See Filing Rules—page xv.)

AERONAUTICS, ASTRONAUTICS

THE 99 NEWS. VAT Ninety-Nine News. 0273-608X. Periodical. US. English. mo. $10.00. The 99 News, P O Box 59965, Oklahoma City OK 73159. Tel (405)682-4425.

AAHS JOURNAL. Main/Corp American Aviation Historical Society. VAT American Aviation Historical Society Journal. V. 25- Spring 1980-. 0882-9365. Periodical. US. English. qt. American Aviation Historical Society, 2333 Otis Street, Santa Ana CA 92704. **Ind/Abst** Am. Hist. Life, Hist. Abstr., Part A, Mod. Hist. Abstr., Hist. Abst., Part B, Twent. Century Abstr. **DD** 629. (cum index). *American Aviation Historical Society Journal.*

AAHS NEWSLETTER. Main/Corp American Aviation Historical Society. VAT American Aviation Historical Society Newsletter. Began in 1967. 0300-6875. Periodical. US. English. qt. American Aviation Historical Society, 2333 Otis Street, Santa Ana CA 92704. **LC** TL501.A89. **DD** 629.13009.

This arrangement enables the user to locate easily the relevant subject area and to review at a glance all serial titles relating to that subject. For a list of subject headings and subject cross references, see page xxi.

There are over 20,000 "see notes" throughout the 147 major subject headings and 135 subheadings in the serials listing. These notes refer the user from related subject areas to the primary subject heading under which the full title listing appears.

AMERICAN AGRICULTURE NEWS. 0745-001X. Periodical. US. English. bw. American Agriculture News, PO Box 100, Iredell TX 76649.

AMERICAN AGRICULTURIST. V. 173, No. 4- Apr. 1976-. 0161-8237. Periodical. US. English. mo. $5.00 NY, NJ, PA, and New England, $10.00 all other areas. American Agriculturist, PO Box 516, Ithaca NY 14850. *American Agriculturist, Rural New Yorker, 0002-7219.*

THE AMERICAN FARM & HOME ALMANAC. See Yearbooks, Almanacs, Directories.

AMERICAN JOURNAL OF AGRICULTURAL ECONOMICS. V. 50- Feb. 1968-. 0002-9092. Periodical. US. English. qt. $35.00. John C Redman, Department of Agricultural Economics, University of Kentucky, Lexington KY 40596. **Ind/Abst** Manage. Contents, Sel. Water Resour. Abstr., Coal Abstr., Energy Inf. Abstr., Environ. Abstr., Index Econ. Artic. J. Collect. Vol., GeoRef, Bibliogr. Agric., Biol. Agric. Index, Bus. Period. Index, Energy Res. Abstr., Public Aff. Inf. Serv. Bull. **LC** S560. **DD** 338.105. *Journal of Farm Economics.*

For a description of the contents of the listings, see page xii.

2. Alphabetical Title Index—This index lists, in alphabetical order, the primary title along with main entry, series statement and ceased titles. The additional titles are listed with a "see" note to the primary title.

ACCADEMIA NAZIONALE DE RAGIONERIA *See* PAPERS ON BUSINESS ADMINISTRATION 1617

ACCADEMIE E BIBLIOTECHE D'ITALIA (IT/0001-4451)
[02256885] 2733

Country of Publication, ISSN, and CONSER control number are given with the primary title to aid in further identifying titles for the user. The page number which carries the complete title record is justified to the right of the title. Page numbers which carry references to the title appear directly after the CONSER control number.

ACCELERATION AND PASSING ABILITY (US/0360-6090)
[02244048] 423 2336

---

3. ISSN Index—The ISSN Index contains current as well as preceding ISSN's, arranged in numerical order. The preceding ISSN will appear in italicized typeface in order to distinguish it from the current ISSN.

0737-9285 939
0738-2103 939

---

4. Ceased Title Index—Over 2,000 titles that have ceased publication are included in this index, arranged alphabetically by title.

AMERICAN INDIAN INDEX 1406
AMERICAN INDIAN JOURNAL 1498
ANALES DE FISICA 2841
ANIMAL MORBIDITY REPORT 2799

USER'S GUIDE

SERIAL LISTING CONTENTS

The following data elements (when available) are shown in order of appearance within a listing. Some definitions are taken in part from *MARC Formats for Bibliographic Data*.

Key Title. Key Title is supplied by the National Serials Data Program, or ISDS/Canada, to the CONSER file. The key title is transcribed from title information appearing on the piece and, when necessary, constructed so as to render it unique.

Title Statement. Title Statement is present only when it differs from key title in *any way*. The title statement consists of the short title/title proper, remainder of the title, and the remainder of the title page as well as the number and/or the name of a part/section of a title, if pertinent. The Title Statement, when present, will follow Key Title in uppercase, and will be enclosed in parentheses.

Main Entry—Conference or Meeting. Named conferences or meetings used as main entries. Can contain names of conferences, meetings, religious councils, events, legislative bodies, constitutional conventions, and conventionalized subheadings for state or local elements of American political parties entered subordinately under a political jurisdiction or a corporate body. The Main Entry—Conference or Meeting will be preceded by the prefix "Main/Conf" in boldface.

Main Entry—Corporate Name. Corporate names used as the main entry. Includes associations, institutions, business firms, non-profit enterprises, governments, specific agencies of governments, ships, etc. Main Entry—Corporate Name is preceded by the prefix "Main/Corp" in boldface.

Series Statement—Title. Series statement entered under title. Series Statement—Title is preceded by "Series/Title" in boldface.

Series Statement—Conference/Meeting. Series statement entered under a named conference or meeting. Series Statement—Conference/Meeting is preceded by "Series/Conf" in boldface.

Series Statement—Corporate Name/Title. Series statement entered under a corporate name. Series Statement—Corporate Name/Title is preceded by "Series/Corp" in boldface.

Varying Form of a Title. Titles which may appear on different parts of a serial (or different portions of a title page), different from Key Title and/or Title Statement, and contribute to the further identification of the serial. Parallel titles are also included in this field. Varying Form of a Title is preceded by the prefix "VFOAT" in boldface. Additional titles are separated by commas.

Variant Access Title. Variant form of access to the title when the title contains an initialism, abbreviation, numeral, symbol, nonroman alphabet character, etc. The variant form(s) is given only if this form is not already present by the way of Key Title, Title Statement, or Varying Form of a Title. Variant Access Title is preceded by the prefix of "VAT" in boldface. Additional titles are separated by commas.

Dates of Publication and Volume Information. Beginning (and ending) dates of publication and volume designation. The date may consist of the year, month, or day; month or season and year; or year alone, depending upon the frequency of publication and the usage of the publisher. Designations may appear in the vernacular and/or may be abbreviated.

ISSN. International Standard Serials Number, as assigned by national centers under the auspices of the International Serials Data System (ISDS).

Type of Serial. Indicates if the serial is a periodical, monographic series, or a newspaper.

Country of Publication. Indicated by two letter code—see Country of Publication Table, page xxxi.

Language. If the serial is in more than one language, the predominant language will appear first and any additional languages will follow in parentheses (including languages for translations, summaries, tables of contents, etc.).

Frequency. Indicated by two letter code—see Frequency Table, page xxx.

Price. The list price of the serial at the time information was secured for publication. Any price preceded by a $ symbol is U.S. dollars. If no currency symbol or explanation is present, price is assumed to be in country of publication currency. Unless otherwise noted, rates are for one year library subscriptions. See page xxxiii for Unit of Currency Table.

Publisher Name and Address/Subscription Address. The name and address of the publisher and address for subscription orders, if different.

USER'S GUIDE/SAMPLE LISTING

Telephone Number. Given for both U.S. and foreign serials, when available. Preceded by a prefix of "Tel" in boldface.

Editor(s). Preceded by a prefix of "Ed" in boldface.

Indexes/Abstracts. Specifies the publication(s) in which a serial has been indexed and/or abstracted. Preceded by a prefix of "Ind/Abst" in boldface. See Indexes/Abstracts Abbreviation Table, page xxxv.

Library of Congress Classification. Preceded by prefix of "LC" in boldface.

Dewey Decimal Classification. Preceded by prefix of "DD" in boldface.

Universal Decimal Classification. Preceded by prefix of "UD" in boldface.

National Library of Medicine Classification. Preceded by prefix of "NLM" in boldface.

CODEN Designation. Abbreviation for periodical titles which is assigned by the CODEN section of Chemical Abstracts Service. The abbreviation is a unique identifier for scientific and technical publications. Preceded by prefix of "CODEN" in boldface.

Index Availability. Shows the existence of an index, or a table of contents issued as an index, and the method of acquisition.

Cumulative Index Availability. Specifies if a cumulative index, or a table of contents issued as a cumulative index, is published. Appears in abbreviated form as "cum. index".

Book Reviews. If book reviews are published, the abbreviation "bk rev" will appear.

Advertising. If advertising is accepted, the abbreviation "adv acc" will appear.

Circulation. Annual circulation of publication, unless noted otherwise. Preceded by prefix of "circ" in boldface.

Controlled Circulation. If circulation of serial is controlled by publisher, the abbreviation "ctrl" will appear in parentheses after circulation figures.

Additional Physical Forms Available. Additional media in which serial is published, other than its original, or conventional, form.

Descriptive Listing. Description of content of serial as submitted by publisher. (Descriptions may have been edited for clarity.)

Preceding Entry—Title/Preceding Entry—ISSN. The immediate predecessor or predecessors for the serial title, along with corresponding ISSN, appear in italics. Additional titles and ISSN's are separated by commas.

SAMPLE LISTING

KEY TITLE. (TITLE STATEMENT). **Main/Conf** Main Entry—Conference/Meeting. **Series/Conf** Series Statement—Conference/Meeting. **VFOAT** Varying Form of a Title. **VAT** Variant Access Title. Date of Publication and Volume Designation. ISSN. Type of Serial. Country of Publication. Language(s). Frequency. Price. Publisher Name & Address. **Tel** Telephone Number. **Ed** Editor. **Ind/Abst** Indexes/Abstracts. **LC** Library of Congress Classification. **DD** Dewey Decimal Classification. **UD** Universal Decimal Classification. **NLM** National Library of Medicine Classification. **CODEN** CODEN Designation. Index Availability. cum. index (Cumulative Index Availability). bk rev (Book reviews published). adv acc (Advertising Accepted). **Circ** Circulation. ctrl (Controlled Circulation). Additional Physical Forms Available. Descriptive Listing. *Preceding Entry-Title, Preceding Entry-ISSN.*

FILING RULES

The rules, or guidelines, used in arranging the entries in the *Directory* are outlined on the following page. The use of these rules provides an orderly and consistent arrangement of titles.

FILING RULES

A. General rules
Filing is word by word, with exceptions noted below. The order of characters applies the principle "nothing files before something," with numerals before letters, file A to Z.
1. **Spaces, hyphens, diagonal slashes, and periods** are all filed as blanks:

    Year Book of Design
    Year-Book of Drafting
    Year Book of Engineering
    Yearbook of Architecture

2. **Variant spellings** are filed as written:

    Color World
    Colour and Paint

B. Special Rules and Exceptions.
1. **Modified letters and diacritics**—modified letters are written as their plain English alphabet equivalents.
2. **Punctuation**—punctuation and all non-alphabetic symbols (except those noted in A above) are ignored for filing purposes:

    America and Russia
    America, Washington, and the Revolutionary War
    America (Washington, D.C.: 1983)
    America & Washington Irving
    American Journal
    America's History
    The Americas in World History

3. **Abbreviations**—filed exactly as written with the exception of: Dept., U.S., U.N., Gt. Brit. These are filed as if fully written out:

    Spectroscopy Journal
    St. Louis Dispatch
    Statistical Abstracts

4. **Numerals**—all numerals file character by character according to the numeric value of each **string** of characters.

    Numerals precede letters:

    19th Century Music
    20th Century Studies
    73 Amateur Radio
    291
    25,000 Leading U.S. Corporations

5. **Initials, initialisms, acronyms**—those in which each letter is separated by a space, dash, hyphen, period, or diagonal slash are regarded as a series of separate words. Those in which characters are separated by other marks or symbols, or which are not separated in any way, are regarded as single words:

    C.I.A. Report
    Communications Journal
    CPA Board Exam Report

6. **Initial articles**—the following words are ignored when they appear at the beginning of an entry:

A	Eine	Hio	Na
al	Eit	Hin	Nje
An	el-	Hinar	Nji
As	El	Hinir	O
Az	Els	Hinn	Os
Bir	En	Ho	't
Das	Et	Hoi	Ta
De	Ett	I	The
Dei	Gl'	Il	To
Den	Gli	Ka	Um
Der	ha-	Ke	Uma
Det	Hai	L'	Un
Di	He	La	Un'
Die	He	Las	Una
Dos	he-	Le	Une
Een	Heis	Les	Uno
Eene	Hen	Lo	Y
Egy	Hena	Los	Yr
Ei	Henas	Mia	
Ein	Het	'n	

    Exception—titles composed entirely of words on the list above are filed as written, as well as place names.

    Hence:

    Et Al
    The Journal
    Los Angeles Free Press
    Der Spiegel
    The Una

7. **Names and prefixes**—a prefix that is part of the name of a person or place is treated as a separate word unless it is joined to the rest of the name:

    De Alberti
    De 'Ath, William
    Death, Wilfred

SUBJECT HEADINGS

The following section lists the subject headings used in the *Directory.* The list is arranged alphabetically by subject, with the major topic followed by specific topics within the same category.

SUBJECT HEADINGS

Aeronautics, Astronautics 3	Civil Defense 530	Fish Culture and Fisheries 1124
Agriculture. 22	Classical Studies 531	Folklore 1137
Agricultural Equipment. 72	Clothing and Fashion 534	Food & Drink. .1140
Crop Production and Soil 74	College and School Magazines & Papers 537	Grocery Trade 1155
Dairy & Related Technologies 88		Forestry 1157
Feed Grain and Milling 92	Communication 541	Lumber & Wood 1170
Livestock and Poultry 94	Broadcasting 549	Funeral Service 1174
Anthropology 105	Postal Communications 557	Genealogy and Heraldry 1174
Antiques 115	Telecommunications 560	Archives 1194
Archaeology 117	Computers and Computer Science 568	General Interest 1206
Architecture 130	Conservation & Natural Resources 597	General Interest-Africa 1208
The Arts (General) 140	Consumer Interests 612	General Interest-Asia 1209
Art 155	Copyright, Intellectual Property 616	General Interest-Australia and Oceania 1215
Arts & Crafts, Handicrafts, Decorative Arts. 166	Dance 620	
	Dentistry 622	General Interest-Central America . . .1215
Graphic Arts .170	Drug Abuse and Alcoholism 633	General Interest-Europe 1215
Performing Arts 173	Earth Sciences .639	General Interest-North America 1221
Astrology 176	Geology 645	General Interest-South America 1232
Astronomy 177	Geophysics .666	Geography 1233
Beauty & Cosmetics 183	Hydrology 670	Gifts, Toys 1250
Bibliographies .185	Meteorology .674	Glass and Ceramics 1250
Bicycles and Bicycling 218	Mineralogy 686	Heating, Plumbing, & Refrigeration 1255
Biographies 219	Oceanography 690	History (General) 1258
Biology 225	Petrology 699	History of Africa 1268
Biochemistry 245	Economics 699	History of Asia 1275
Biophysics 251	Cooperatives 726	History of Australia and Oceania 1294
Botany 252	Economic History, Conditions 729	History of Europe 1296
Cytology and Histology 264	Economic Theory 764	History of North, South, and Central America .1316
Genetics 268	Economics: Industry & Production . . .768	
Microbiology 271	Economics: Land 794	Hobbies 1349
Microscopy .277	International Economics 799	Home Economics 1353
Physiology 278	Labor 804	Horses and Horsemanship 1356
Birth Control 285	Education (General) 870	Horticulture and Plant Culture 1360
Boats and Boating 288	Higher Education 916	Florist Trade 1374
Building and Construction 290	School Organization and Administration 951	Hotels/Motels .1374
Carpentry and Woodwork 308		Household Hardware & Appliances 1378
Business 309	Special Aspects of Education 961	Housing and Urban Development 1379
Accounting 341	Theory, Practice of Education 979	Humanities 1397
Advertising & Public Relations 349	Emigration and Immigration 989	Hypnosis 1401
Banking & Finance 355	Encyclopedias & General Reference Books 991	Indexes/Abstracts 1402
Chamber of Commerce 386		Industrial Health & Safety 1452
Commerce 389	Energy 994	Insurance 1458
General Management 413	Engineering 1013	Interior Design 1477
Investments .427	Chemical Engineering 1036	Home Furnishings 1480
Marketing 441	Civil Engineering 1041	International Assistance and Development 1481
Personnel Management 450	Electricity, Electrical Engineering, Electronics 1051	
Public Finance 454		Jewelry 1487
Purchasing 491	Hydraulic Engineering 1076	Clocks and Watches 1488
Chemistry 493	Mechanical Engineering & Machinery.1080	Journalism 1488
Analytical Chemistry 511	Mining Engineering 1093	Law 1493
Crystallography 515	Nuclear Engineering 1104	International Law 1601
Inorganic Chemistry 516	Ethics 1107	Law Enforcement 1609
Organic Chemistry 518	Ethnic 1109	
Physical and Theoretical Chemistry . . .522	Family and Marriage 1117	
Children and Youth Interests 526	Fire Prevention 1121	

SUBJECT HEADINGS

Leather and Fur Industry............1615
Library and Information Science.......1616
Linguistics......................1657
Literary and Political Reviews........1688
Literature......................1700
   Poetry......................1748
Manufacturing...................1756
Mathematics....................1766
Medicine.......................1786
   Allergic, Metabolic, Nutritional
      Diseases..................1845
   Cardiovascular Diseases.........1847
   Dermatology..................1851
   Endocrinology................1853
   Forensic Medicine, Medical
      Jurisprudence..............1856
   Geriatrics....................1857
   Gynecology & Obstetrics.........1859
   Homeopathy..................1865
   Internal Medicine..............1865
   Medical Centers, Hospitals........1870
   Musculoskeletal Diseases........1878
   Neoplasma, Neoplastic..........1880
   Neurology....................1890
   Nursing......................1897
   Ophthalmology................1906
   Orthopedics..................1909
   Otorhinolaryngology............1911
   Pathology....................1913
   Pediatrics....................1917
   Psychiatry, Psychopathology.......1922
   Radiology....................1933
   Respiratory Diseases............1938
   Surgery......................1940
   Toxicology...................1948
   Urology......................1951
Metals & Metallurgy................1953
   Welding......................1967
Metrology and Standardization........1969
Military Science...................1971
Motion Picture...................1986
Motorcycles.....................1994
Museums........................1995
Music..........................2005
Natural History...................2037
Naval Science, Navigation...........2043
Newspapers.....................2051
Numismatics....................2088
Nutrition and Dietetics..............2090
Occupations and Careers...........2095
Office Equipment & Services.........2099
Optometry......................2100
Packaging......................2102

Paints and Painting................2104
Paleontology....................2106
Paper & Pulp Industry..............2108
Parapsychology and the Occult
   Sciences.....................2112
Petroleum and Natural Gas..........2114
Pets...........................2129
Pharmacy......................2130
Philanthropy....................2145
Philately.......................2146
Philosophy.....................2150
Photography & Photographs.........2163
Physical Therapy.................2168
Physical Training.................2170
Physically Impaired...............2173
Physics........................2179
   Analytic and Experimental Mechanics.2192
   Heat........................2194
   Light, Optics, Radiation..........2195
   Magnetism...................2199
   Nuclear Physics................2200
   Sound.......................2204
Plastics........................2204
Political Science..................2208
   Civil Rights...................2230
   International Relations..........2234
   Socialism, Communism, Anarchism,
      Utopianism.................2247
Population Studies................2253
Printing........................2259
Psychology.....................2263
Public Administration..............2283
Public Health and Safety...........2336
Publishing......................2361
   Books and Bookmaking..........2364
Real Estate.....................2371
Recreation, Leisure...............2377
   Games & Amusements...........2382
   Outdoor Life..................2386
   Sports......................2393
Religion, Mythology, Rationalism......2421
   Bible........................2441
   Buddhism....................2444
   Eastern Christian Churches.......2446
   Islam, Bahaism, Theosophy.......2447
   Judaism.....................2449
   Protestantism.................2454
   Roman Catholic Church..........2466
   Theology....................2475
Restaurants.....................2491
Romance and Adventure............2494

Rubber.........................2494
Sanitation, Environmental Technology..2496
Science (General).................2518
Senior Citizens...................2549
Sewing and Needlework............2551
Sexual Life......................2553
Social Sciences (General)...........2555
Societies and Clubs................2574
Sociology: General Works, Theory.....2581
   Manners and Customs...........2597
   Social Pathology, Welfare,
      Criminology................2599
Sound Recordings and Systems......2638
Statistics.......................2641
Technology (General)..............2704
Textiles........................2720
Theater........................2726
Tobacco........................2731
Transportation...................2733
   Automobiles..................2748
   Railroads....................2762
   Roads and Traffic..............2768
   Ships & Shipping..............2775
Travel..........................2783
Veterinary Medicine, Animal Culture...2799
Water Resources..................2811
Women.........................2823
Yearbooks, Almanacs, Directories.....2833
Zoology-Vertebrate and Invertebrate...2970

SUBJECT CROSS REFERENCES

This section combines all subject headings into one alphabetical list, regardless of whether they are a general, main subject or a specific, subordinate subject. Cross references from a subject or topic not used in the *Directory* are made to that which is used. "See also" notes from one subject to a similar subject are included as well.

SUBJECT CROSS REFERENCES

Abortion—See **Birth Control** pg 285; **Ethics** pg 1107
Abstracts—See **Indexes/Abstracts** pg 1402
Accounting—pg 341
Acting—See **Performing Arts** pg 173; **Theater** pg 2726; **Motion Picture** pg 1986
Acupuncture—See **Medicine** pg 1786
Adventure—See **Romance and Adventure** pg 2494
Advertising—See **Advertising & Public Relations** pg 349
Adult Continuing Education—See **Special Aspects of Education** pg 961
Aeronautics, Astronautics—pg 3; see also Transportation pg 2733; Military Science pg 1971
Aesthetics—See **Art** pg 155; **Humanities** pg 1397
Africa—See **General Interest - Africa** pg 1208; **History of Africa** pg 1268
African Studies—See **History of Africa** pg 1268; **Literature** pg 1700
Agricultural Equipment—pg 72
Agriculture—pg 22; see also Food & Drink pg 1140; Horticulture and Plant Culture pg 1360
Air Force—See **Aeronautics, Astronautics** pg 3; **Military Science** pg 1971
Airplanes—See **Aeronautics, Astronautics** pg 3
Alarm/Security Systems—See **Electricity, Electrical Engineering, Electronics** pg 1051
Alcoholism—See **Drug Abuse and Alcoholism** pg 633
Allergic Diseases—See **Allergic, Metabolic, Nutritional Diseases** pg 1845
Almanacs—See **Yearbooks, Almanacs, Directories** pg 2833
Alumni Magazines—See **College and School Magazines & Papers** pg 537
American Studies—See **History of North, South, and Central America** pg 1316
Amusements—See **Games & Amusements** pg 2382
Analytic Mechanics—See **Analytic and Experimental Mechanics** pg 2192
Analytical Chemistry—pg 511
Anarchism—See **Socialism, Communism, Anarchism, Utopianism** pg 2247
Anesthesiology—See **Surgery** pg 1940
Animal Culture—See **Veterinary Medicine, Animal Culture** pg 2799
Anglo-Saxon Studies—See **History of Europe** pg 1296; **Literature** pg 1700
Animal Laboratory Research—See **Veterinary Medicine, Animal Culture** pg 2799
Anthropology—pg 105; see also Archaeology pg 117; Sociology: General Works, Theory pg 2581; Paleontology pg 2106
Antiques—pg 115; see also Museums pg 1995; Hobbies pg 1349
Appliances—See **Household Hardware & Appliances** pg 1378

Archaeology—pg 117; see also Anthropology pg 105; History (General) pg 1258; Paleontology pg 2106
Architecture—pg 130; see also Building and Construction pg 290; Engineering pg 1013; Housing and Urban Development pg 1379; Interior Design pg 1477
Archives—pg 1194; see also Library and Information Science pg 1616; History (General) pg 1258
Army—See **Military Science** pg 1971
Art—pg 155
Arts (General)—pg 140; see also Dance pg 620; Theater pg 2726; Humanities pg 1397
Arts & Crafts, Handicrafts, Decorative Arts—pg 166; see also Glass and Ceramics pg 1250; Gifts, Toys pg 1250; Hobbies pg 1349; Sewing and Needlework pg 2551
Art Galleries—See **Art** pg 155
Arthritis—See **Musculoskeletal Diseases** pg 1878
Arts and Sciences—See **The Arts (General)** pg 140; **Humanities** pg 1397; **Social Sciences (General)** pg 2555
Asia—See **General Interest - Asia** pg 1209; **History of Asia** pg 1275
Asian Studies—See **History of Asia** pg 1275; **Literature** pg 1700
Astrology—pg 176
Astronautics—See **Aeronautics, Astronautics** pg 3
Astronomy—pg 177
Atheism—See **Philosophy** pg 2150
Atlases—See **Geography** pg 1233
Audio-Visual—See **Theory, Practice of Education** pg 979; **Motion Picture** pg 1986; **Art** pg 155
Auditing—See **Accounting** pg 341
Audiology—See **Otorhinolaryngology** pg 1911
Audubon Society—See **Conservation & Natural Resources** pg 597; **Natural History** pg 2037
Australia—See **General Interest - Australia and Oceania** pg 1215; **History of Australia and Oceania** pg 1294
Automobiles—pg 2748; see also Transportation pg 2733
Automobile Racing—See **Sports** pg 2393
Balkan Studies—See **History of Europe** pg 1296
Bahaism—See **Islam, Bahaism, Theosophy** pg 2447
Banking & Finance—pg 355; see also Public Finance pg 454; Cooperatives pg 726; Public Administration pg 2283; Economics pg 699
Bankruptcy—See **Law** pg 1493; **Banking & Finance** pg 355
Baptist—See **Protestantism** pg 2454
Beauty & Cosmetics—pg 183; see also Clothing and Fashion pg 534

Belizean Studies—See **History of North, South, and Central America** pg 1316
Beverage—See **Food & Drink** pg 1140
Bible—pg 2441
Bibliographies—pg 185; see also Library and Information Science pg 1616; Indexes/Abstracts pg 1402
Bicycles and Bicycling—pg 218
Biochemistry—pg 245
Biographies—pg 219
Biology—pg 225; see also Physiology pg 278; Zoology-Vertebrate and Invertebrate pg 2970; Medicine pg 1786
Biophysics—pg 251
Birth Control—pg 285; see also Population Studies pg 2253
Boats and Boating—pg 288
Books and Bookmaking—pg 2364
Botany—pg 252; see also Horticulture and Plant Culture pg 1360; Crop Production and Soil pg 74
Breastfeeding—See **Gynecology & Obstetrics** pg 1859; **Pediatrics** pg 1917
Bride—See **Family and Marriage** pg 1117
British Studies—See **History of Europe** pg 1296
Broadcasting—pg 549; see also Telecommunications pg 560
Buddhism—pg 2444
Budget—See **Public Finance** pg 454; **Banking & Finance** pg 355
Building and Construction—pg 290; see also Architecture pg 130; Civil Engineering pg 1041; Housing and Urban Development pg 1379
Business—pg 309; see also Economics pg 699; Marketing pg 441; Purchasing pg 491
Buying—See **Purchasing** pg 491
Cable Television—See **Broadcasting** pg 549; **Telecommunications** pg 560
Calligraphy—See **Graphic Arts** pg 170
Camping—See **Outdoor Life** pg 2386
Canadian Studies—See **History of North, South, and Central America** pg 1316
Cancer—See **Neoplasma, Neoplastic** pg 1880
Canon Law—See **Theology** pg 2475
Cardiovascular Diseases—1847
Careers—See **Occupations and Careers** pg 2095
Caribbean Studies—See **History of North, South, and Central America** pg 1316
Carpentry and Woodwork—pg 308; see also Building and Construction pg 290; Home Furnishings pg 1480; Hobbies pg 1349
Carpet, Rugs—See **Home Furnishings** pg 1480; **Interior Design** pg 1477; **Textiles** pg 2720
Cartography—See **Geography** pg 1233
Celtic Studies—See **History of Europe** pg 1296; **Literature** pg 1700

SUBJECT CROSS REFERENCES

Central America—See **General Interest - Central America** pg 1215; **History of North, South, and Central America** pg 1316

Ceramics—See **Glass and Ceramics** pg 1250

Chamber of Commerce—pg 386

Chemical Engineering—pg 1036

Chemistry—pg 493

Charities—See **Philanthropy** pg 2145; **Social Pathology, Welfare, Criminology** pg 2599

Chemical Technology—See **Chemistry** pg 493; **Chemical Engineering** pg 1036

Children—See **Children and Youth Interests** pg 526

China, Tableware—See **Glass and Ceramics** pg 1250; **Gifts, Toys** pg 1250

Chinese Studies—See **History of Asia** pg 1275

Chiropractor—See **Physical Therapy** pg 2168

Christianity—See **Religion, Mythology, Rationalism** pg 2421; **Protestantism** pg 2454

Cinema—See **Motion Picture** pg 1986

Cinematography—See **Photography & Photographs** pg 2163; **Motion Picture** pg 1986

City and Regional Planning—See **Housing and Urban Development** pg 1379

Civil Defense—pg 530

Civil Engineering—pg 1041

Civil Service—See **Public Administration** pg 2283

Classical Studies—pg 531; see also Literature pg 1700; Linguistics pg 1657; History (General) pg 1258; Archaeology pg 117

Clocks—See **Clocks and Watches** pg 1488

Clothing and Fashion—pg 534; see also Leather and Fur Industry pg 1615; Textiles pg 2720; Beauty & Cosmetics pg 183

Clubs—See **Societies and Clubs** pg 2574

Coal—See **Mineralogy** pg 686; **Mining Engineering** pg 1093; **Metals & Metallurgy** pg 1953

Coast Guard—See **Naval Science, Navigation** pg 2043

Collectors & Collecting—See **Hobbies** pg 1349; **Philately** pg 2146; **Numismatics** pg 2088; **Antiques** pg 115

College and School Magazines & Papers—pg 537; see also Education (General) pg 870; Higher Education pg 916

Colleges and Universities—See **Higher Education** pg 916; **College and School Magazines & Papers** pg 537

Comics—See **Games & Amusements** pg 2382

Commerce—pg 389; see also Transportation pg 2733

Commercial Art—See **Graphic Arts** pg 170

Communicable Diseases—See **Public Health and Safety** pg 2336

Communication—pg 541

Communism—See **Socialism, Communism, Anarchism, Utopianism** pg 2247

Computer Science—See **Computers and Computer Science** pg 568

Computers and Computer Science—pg 568

Conservation & Natural Resources—See also Natural History pg 2037; Water Resources pg 2811; Economics: Land pg 794; Sanitation, Environmental Technology pg 2496

Construction—See **Building and Construction** pg 290

Consumer Interests—pg 612; see also Economics pg 699

Cookbooks, Cooking—See **Food & Drink** pg 1140; **Home Economics** pg 1353

Cooperative—pg 726; see also Banking & Finance pg 355; Agriculture pg 22

Copyright, Intellectual Property—pg 616

Cosmetics—See **Beauty & Cosmetics** pg 183

Cosmetology—See **Beauty & Cosmetics** pg 183

Cotton—See **Textiles** pg 2720; **Crop Production and Soil** pg 74

Credit Unions—See **Banking & Finance** pg 355

Crime Prevention—See **Law Enforcement** pg 1609

Crime Statistics—See **Statistics** pg 2641; **Law Enforcement** pg 1609; **Social Pathology, Welfare, Criminology** pg 2599

Criminal Law—See **Law** pg 1493

Criminology—See **Social Pathology, Welfare, Criminology** pg 2599

Croatian Studies—See **History of Europe** pg 1296

Crop Production and Soil—pg 74

Crystallography—pg 515

Customs—See **Manners and Customs** pg 2597

Cytology and Histology—pg 264

Dairy & Related Technologies—pg 88

Dance—pg 620; see also Performing Arts pg 173

Data Processing—See **Computers and Computer Science** pg 568

Daycare—See **Social Pathology, Welfare, Criminology** pg 2599; **Special Aspects of Education** pg 961

Decorative Arts—See **Arts & Crafts, Handicrafts, Decorative Arts** pg 166

Defense—See **Military Science** pg 1971

Demography—See **Population Studies** pg 2253

Dentistry—pg 622

Dermatology—pg 1851

Diabetes—See **Endocrinology** pg 1853

Dietetics—See **Nutrition and Dietetics** pg 2090

Directories—See **Yearbooks, Almanacs, Directories** pg 2833

Doctrinal Theology—See **Theology** pg 2475

Dog Racing—See **Sports** pg 2393; **Social Pathology, Welfare, Criminology** pg 2599

Drama—See **Theater** pg 2726; **Performing Arts** pg 173

Drink—See **Food & Drink** pg 1140

Drug Abuse and Alcoholism—pg 633

Early Childhood Education—See **Special Aspects of Education** pg 961

Earth Sciences—pg 639

Eastern Christian Churches—pg 2446

Ecology—See **Biology** pg 225; **Natural History** pg 2037

Economic History, Conditions—pg 729

Economic Theory—pg 764

Economics—pg 699

Economics: Industry & Production—pg 768

Economics: Land—pg 794; see also Real Estate pg 2371

Education (General)—pg 870

Elections—See **Political Science** pg 2208

Electrical Engineering—See **Electricity, Electrical Engineering, Electronics** pg 1051

Electricity, Electrical Engineering, Electronics—pg 1051; see also Energy pg 994; Heating, Plumbing, & Refrigeration pg 1255; Sound Recordings and Systems pg 2638; Public Administration pg 2283

Electronics—See **Electricity, Electrical Engineering, Electronics** pg 1051

Energy—pg 994; see also Petroleum and Natural Gas pg 2114; Electricity, Electrical Engineering, Electronics pg 1051; Public Administration pg 2283; Nuclear Engineering pg 1104; Nuclear Physics pg 2200

Emigration and Immigration—pg 989

Encyclopedias & General Reference Books—pg 991

Endocrinology—pg 1853

Engineering—pg 1013

Entomology—See **Zoology - Vertebrate and Invertebrate** pg 2970

Environmental Studies—See **Sanitation, Environmental Technology** pg 2496

Environmental Technology—See **Sanitation, Environmental Technology** pg 2496

Epilepsy—See **Neurology** pg 1890

Episcopal—See **Protestantism** pg 2454

Estate Planning—See **Law** pg 1493; **Investments** pg 427; **Banking & Finance** pg 355

Ethics—pg 1107

Ethnology—See **Anthropology** pg 105

Europe—See **General Interest - Europe** pg 1215; **History of Europe** pg 1296

European Studies—See **History of Europe** pg 1296

Evangelism—See **Protestantism** pg 2454

Experimental Mechanics—See **Analytic and Experimental Mechanics** pg 2192

Fabric—See **Textiles** pg 2720; **Sewing and Needlework** pg 2551; **Clothing and Fashion** pg 534

Family and Marriage—pg 1117; see also Home Economics pg 1353

Family Planning—See **Birth Control** pg 285

Fashion—See **Clothing and Fashion** pg 534

SUBJECT CROSS REFERENCES

Federal Government—See **Public Administration** pg 2283; **Political Science** pg 2208
Feed Grain and Milling—pg 92
Feminism—See **Women** pg 2823
Films and Film Making—See **Motion Picture** pg 1986
Finance—See **Banking & Finance** pg 355
Fire Prevention—pg 1121
Fish Culture and Fisheries—pg 1124
Fishing—See Fish Culture and Fisheries pg 1124
Florist Trade—pg 1374
Folklore—pg 1137; see also Literature pg 1700; History (General) pg 1258; Religion, Mythology, Rationalism pg 2421; Manners and Customs pg 2597
Food & Drink—pg 1140; see also Restaurants pg 2491; Agriculture pg 22; Home Economics pg 1353
Food Production—See **Economics: Industry & Production** pg 768
Food Technology—See **Food & Drink** pg 1140; **Chemistry** pg 493
Forensic Medicine, Medical Jurisprudence—pg 1856
Forestry—pg 1157
Fraternities—See **Societies and Clubs** pg 2574
French Studies—See **History of Europe** pg 1296; **Literature** pg 1700
Fruit—See **Horticulture and Plant Culture** pg 1360; **Crop Production and Soil** pg 74; **Food & Drink** pg 1140
Fund Raising—See **Philanthropy** pg 2145
Funeral Service—pg 1174
Fur—See **Leather and Fur Industry** pg 1615
Gambling—See **Sports** pg 2393; **Social Pathology, Welfare, Criminology** pg 2599; **Public Administration** pg 2283; **Public Finance** pg 454
Games & Amusements—pg 2382; see also Children and Youth Interests pg 526; Recreation, Leisure pg 2377; Sports pg 2393
Gardening—See **Horticulture and Plant Culture** pg 1360
Gaulliennes Studies—See **History of Europe** pg 1296
Genealogy and Heraldry—pg 1174; see also History (General) pg 1258
General Interest—pg 1206
General Interest-Africa—pg 1208
General Interest-Asia—pg 1209
General Interest-Australia and Oceania—pg 1215
General Interest-Central America—pg 1215
General Interest-Europe—pg 1215
General Interest-North America—pg 1221
General Interest-South America—pg 1232
General Management—pg 413
General Reference Books—See **Encyclopedias & General Reference Books** pg 991
Genetics—pg 268
Geology—pg 645
Geography—pg 1233; see also Travel pg 2783; Economics: Land pg 794
Geophysics—pg 666

Geriatrics—pg 1857; see also Senior Citizens pg 2549
Germanic Studies—See **History of Europe** pg 1296
Gifts, Toys—pg 1250; see also Arts & Crafts, Handicrafts, Decorative Arts pg 166; Glass and Ceramics pg 1250; Games & Amusements pg 2382
Glass and Ceramics—pg 1250; see also Arts & Crafts, Handicrafts, Decorative Arts pg 166
Golf—See **Sports** pg 2393
Government—See **Public Administration** pg 2283; **Political Science** pg 2208
Graphic Arts—pg 170; see also Printing pg 2259
Grocery Trade—1155
Guns—See **Sports** pg 2393; **Military Science** pg 1971
Gynecology & Obstetrics—pg 1859
Handicrafts—See **Arts & Crafts, Handicrafts, Decorative Arts** pg 166
Hearing Disorders—See **Physically Impaired** pg 2173
Heat—pg 2194
Heating, Plumbing, Refrigeration—pg 1255; see also Household Hardware & Appliances pg 1378; Electricity, Electrical Engineering, Electronics pg 1051
Heraldry—See **Genealogy and Heraldry** pg 1174
Herbs and Spices—See **Food & Drink** pg 1140; **Horticulture and Plant Culture** pg 1360
Higher Education—pg 916
Histology—See **Cytology and Histology** pg 264
History (General)—pg 1258
History of Africa—pg 1268
History of Asia—pg 1275
History of Australia and Oceania—pg 1294
History of Europe—pg 1296
History of North, South, and Central America—pg 1316
Hobbies—pg 1349; see also Arts & Crafts, Handicrafts, Decorative Arts pg 166; Numismatics pg 2088; Recreation, Leisure pg 2377; Philately pg 2146; Sports pg 2393; Sewing and Needlework pg 2551
Home Economics—pg 1353; see also Family and Marriage pg 1117; Food & Drink pg 1140
Home Furnishings—pg 1480; see also Interior Design pg 1477; Carpentry and Woodwork pg 308; Household Hardware & Appliances pg 1378
Homeopathy—pg 1865
Homosexuality—See **Sexual Life** pg 2553
Horse Racing—See **Horses and Horsemanship** pg 1356; **Sports** pg 2393; **Social Pathology, Welfare, Criminology** pg 2599
Horses and Horsemanship—pg 1356
Horticulture and Plant Culture—pg 1360; see also Botany pg 252; Crop Production and Soil pg 74
Hospitals—See **Medical Centers, Hospitals** pg 1870

Hotels/Motels—pg 1374; see also Travel pg 2783; Restaurants pg 2491
Household Hardware & Appliances—pg 1378; see also Heating, Plumbing, & Refrigeration pg 1255; Electricity, Electrical Engineering, Electronics pg 1051; Home Furnishings pg 1480
Housing and Urban Development—pg 1379; see also Building and Construction pg 290; Real Estate pg 2371
Human Sexuality—See **Sexual Life** pg 2553
Humanities—pg 1397; see also Social Sciences (General) pg 2555; The Arts (General) pg 140
Hunting—See **Outdoor Life** pg 2386; **Sports** pg 2393
Hydraulic Engineering—pg 1076; see also Hydrology pg 670; Water Resources pg 2811
Hydrology—pg 670; see also Hydraulic Engineering pg 1076; Water Resources pg 2811
Hypnosis—pg 1401
Immigration—See **Emigration and Immigration** pg 989
Income Tax—See **Public Finance** pg 454
Indexes/Abstracts—pg 1402; see also Bibliographies pg 185
Industrial Arts—See **Technology (General)** pg 2704
Industrial Design—See **Engineering** pg 1013; **Manufacturing** pg 1756
Industrial Health & Safety—pg 1452
Inorganic Chemistry—pg 516
Insects—See **Zoology - Vertebrate and Invertebrate** pg 2970
Insurance—pg 1458
Intellectual Property—See **Copyright, Intellectual Property** pg 616
Interior Design—pg 1477; see also Home Furnishings pg 1480; Architecture pg 130
Internal Medicine—pg 1865
International Assistance and Development—pg 1481; see also International Economics pg 799; Social Pathology, Welfare, Criminology pg 2599
International Economics—pg 799
International Law—pg 1601
International Relations—pg 2234; see also Political Science pg 2208; International Law pg 1601; History (General) pg 1258
Investments—pg 427; see also Banking & Finance pg 355
Irish Slavonic Studies—See **History of Europe** pg 1296; **Literature** pg 1700
Irish Studies—See **History of Europe** pg 1296; Literature pg 1700
Irrigation—See **Hydraulic Engineering** pg 1076; Agriculture pg 22
Islam, Bahaism, Theosophy—pg 2447
Jewelry—pg 1487
Journalism—pg 1488; see also Broadcasting pg 549; Literature pg 1700; Publishing pg 2361
Judaism—pg 2449; see also Ethnic pg 1109
Judo/Karate—See **Sports** pg 2393; **Physical Training** pg 2170

SUBJECT CROSS REFERENCES

Kidneys—See **Urology** pg 1951
Korean Studies—See **History of Asia** pg 1275
Labor—pg 804; see also Personnel Management pg 450; Industrial Health & Safety pg 1452
Land—See **Economics: Land** pg 794; **Conservation & Natural Resources** pg 597
Landscape Architecture—See **Horticulture and Plant Culture** pg 1360
Language—See **Linguistics** pg 1657
Language Disorders—See **Physically Impaired** pg 2173; **Special Aspects of Education** pg 961
Latin American Studies—See **History of North, South, and Central America** pg 1316
Laundry—See **Textiles** pg 2720
Law—pg 1493
Law Enforcement—pg 1609; see also Social Pathology, Welfare, Criminology pg 2599; Law pg 1493
Leather and Fur Industry—pg 1615; see also Clothing and Fashion pg 534
Legislation—See **Law** pg 1493; **Public Administration** pg 2283
Leisure—See **Recreation, Leisure** pg 2377
Library and Information Science—See also Archives pg 1194
Life, Death—See **Philosophy** pg 2150
Light, Optics, Radiation—pg 2195
Linguistics—pg 1657; see also Literature pg 1700
Literary and Political Reviews—pg 1688; see also Literature pg 1700; Poetry pg 1748
Literature—pg 1700; see also Literary and Political Reviews pg 1688; Linguistics pg 1657; Poetry pg 1748; Romance and Adventure pg 2494
Livestock and Poultry—pg 94
Local Government—See **Public Administration** pg 2283; **Political Science** pg 2208
Lumber & Wood—pg 1170
Lutheran—See **Protestantism** pg 2454
Machinery—See **Mechanical Engineering & Machinery** pg 1080
Magic—See **Games & Amusements** pg 2382; **Parapsychology and the Occult Sciences** pg 2112
Magnetism—pg 2199
Manners and Customs—pg 2597
Manufacturing—pg 1756
Marines—See **Naval Science, Navigation** pg 2043
Maritime Law—See **Law** pg 1493
Marketing—pg 441
Marriage—See **Family and Marriage** pg 1117
Mathematical Geography—See **Geography** pg 1233
Mathematics—pg 1766
Meat—See **Food & Drink** pg 1140; **Livestock and Poultry** pg 94
Mechanical Engineering & Machinery—pg 1080

Media—See **Communication** pg 541; **Broadcasting** pg 549; **Journalism** pg 1488
Medical Centers, Hospitals—pg 1870
Medical Jurisprudence—See **Forensic Medicine, Medical Jurisprudence** pg 1856
Medicine—pg 1786; see also Public Health and Safety pg 2336
Mental Health—See **Psychiatry, Psychopathology** pg 1922; **Public Health and Safety** pg 2336; **Social Pathology, Welfare, Criminology** pg 2599
Metabolic Diseases—See **Allergic, Metabolic, Nutritional Diseases** pg 1845
Metallurgy—See **Metals & Metallurgy** pg 1953
Metals & Metallurgy—pg 1953; see also Mining Engineering pg 1093
Meteorology—pg 674
Methodist—See **Protestantism** pg 2454
Metrology and Standardization—pg 1969
Microbiology—pg 271
Microscopy—pg 277
Midwifery—See **Gynecology & Obstetrics** pg 1859
Military Administration—See **Military Science** pg 1971
Military Science—pg 1971
Milling—See **Feed Grain and Milling** pg 92
Mineralogy—pg 686
Mining Engineering—pg 1093; see also Metals & Metallurgy pg 1953; Petroleum and Natural Gas pg 2114; Mineralogy pg 686
Motels—See **Hotels/Motels** pg 1374
Motion Picture—pg 1986
Motorcycles—pg 1994
Mountain Climbing—See **Outdoor Life** pg 2386; **Sports** pg 2393
Movies—See **Motion Picture** pg 1986
Musculoskeletal Diseases—pg 1878
Museums—pg 1995; see also Art pg 155; Natural History pg 2037
Music—pg 2005; see also Sound Recordings and Systems pg 2638
Mythology—See **Religion, Mythology, Rationalism** pg 2421
Natural Gas—See **Petroleum and Natural Gas** pg 2114
Natural History—pg 2037; see also Conservation & Natural Resources pg 597; Biology pg 225; Museums pg 1995
Natural Resources—See **Conservation & Natural Resources** pg 597
Naval Science, Navigation—pg 2043; see also Ships & Shipping pg 2775
Navigation—See **Naval Science, Navigation** pg 2043
Navy—See **Naval Science, Navigation** pg 2043
Needlework—See **Sewing and Needlework** pg 2551
Neoplasma, Neoplastic—pg 1880; see also Radiology pg 1933
Nephrology—See **Urology** pg 1951

Neurology—pg 1890; see also Psychiatry, Psychopathology pg 1922; Psychology pg 2263
Newspapers—pg 2051
North America—See **General Interest - North America** pg 1221; **History of North, South, and Central America** pg 1316
Nuclear Engineering—pg 1104
Nuclear Physics—pg 2200
Nuclear Waste—See **Sanitation, Environmental Technology** pg 2496
Numismatics—pg 2088; see also Hobbies pg 1349
Nursing—pg 1897
Nursing Homes—See **Medical Centers, Hospitals** pg 1870
Nutrition and Dietetics—pg 2090; see also Food & Drink pg 1140
Nutritional Diseases—See **Allergic, Metabolic, Nutritional Diseases** pg 1845
Obstetrics—See **Gynecology & Obstetrics** pg 1859
Occult Sciences—See **Parapsychology and the Occult Sciences** pg 2112
Occupational Therapy—See **Psychiatry, Psychopathology** pg 1922; **Occupations and Careers** pg 2095; **Special Aspects of Education** pg 961
Occupations and Careers—pg 2095; see also Labor pg 804; Special Aspects of Education pg 961
Oceania—See **General Interest - Australia and Oceania** pg 1215; **History of Australia and Oceania** pg 1294
Oceanography—pg 690
Office Equipment & Services—pg 2099; see also Computers and Computer Science pg 568
Oil—See **Petroleum and Natural Gas** pg 2114
Ophthalmology—pg 1906
Optics—See **Light, Optics, Radiation** pg 2195
Optometry—pg 2100
Organic Chemistry—pg 518
Oriental Studies—See **History of Asia** pg 1275
Orthodontics—See **Dentistry** pg 622
Orthopedics—pg 1909
Otorhinolaryngology—pg 1911
Outdoor Life—pg 2386; see also Sports pg 2393; Recreation, Leisure pg 2377; Conservation & Natural Resources pg 597; Fish Culture and Fisheries pg 1124
Pacific Studies—See **History of Australia and Oceania** pg 1294
Packaging—pg 2102
Paints and Painting—pg 2104
Paleontology—pg 2106
Paper & Pulp Industry—pg 2108
Parapsychology and the Occult Sciences—pg 2112
Parks—See **Conservation & Natural Resources** pg 597

SUBJECT CROSS REFERENCES

Parliament, House of Commons—See **Public Administration** pg 2283; **Political Science** pg 2208
Patents, Trademarks—See **Copyright, Intellectual Property** pg 616
Pathology—pg 1913
Pediatrics—pg 1917
Performing Arts—pg 173; see also Dance pg 620; Theater pg 2726; Motion Picture pg 1986; Music pg 2005
Personnel Management—pg 450; see also Labor pg 804
Pest Control—See **Sanitation, Environmental Technology** pg 2496; **Forestry** pg 1157
Petroleum and Natural Gas—pg 2114; see also Energy pg 994; Mining Engineering pg 1093
Pharmacy—pg 2130; see also Medicine pg 1786; Toxicology pg 1948
Philanthropy—pg 2145; see also Social Pathology, Welfare, Criminology pg 2599
Philately—pg 2146; see also Hobbies pg 1349
Petrology—pg 699
Pets—pg 2129
Philology—See **Linguistics** pg 1657
Philosophy—pg 2150
Photography & Photographs—pg 2163
Physical Chemistry—pg 522
Physical Education—See **Special Aspects of Education** pg 961; **Physical Training** pg 2170
Physical Therapy—pg 2168
Physical Training—pg 2170; see also Sports pg 2393
Physically Impaired—pg 2173; see also Special Aspects of Education pg 961; Social Pathology, Welfare, Criminology pg 2599
Physicians—See **Medicine** pg 1786
Physiology—pg 278; see also Biology pg 225
Physics—pg 2179
Podiatry—See **Medicine** pg 1786
Poetry—pg 1748; see also Literature pg 1700; Literary and Political Reviews pg 1688
Political Science—pg 2208; see also Public Administration pg 2283; International Relations pg 2234
Pollution—See **Sanitation, Environmental Technology** pg 2496
Population Studies—pg 2253; see also Statistics pg 2641; Birth Control pg 285
Postage Stamps—See **Philately** pg 2146
Pottery—See **Glass and Ceramics** pg 1250
Poverty—See **Social Pathology, Welfare, Criminology** pg 2599
Plant Culture—See **Horticulture and Plant Culture** pg 1360
Plastics—pg 2204
Plumbing—See **Heating, Plumbing, & Refrigeration** pg 1255
Political Reviews—See **Literary and Political Reviews** pg 1688
Postal Communications—pg 557

Poultry—See **Livestock and Poultry** pg 94
Practical Theology—See **Theology** pg 2475
Presbyterian—See **Protestantism** pg 2454
Printing—pg 2259; see also Graphic Arts pg 170
Probation—See **Law Enforcement** pg 1609; **Social Pathology, Welfare, Criminology** pg 2599
Protestantism—pg 2454
Psychiatry, Psychopathology—pg 1922; see also Neurology pg 1890; Psychology pg 2263
Psychology—pg 2263; see also Sociology: General Works, Theory pg 2581
Psychopathology—See **Psychiatry, Psychopathology** pg 1922
PTA—See **School Organization and Administration** pg 951
Public Administration—pg 2283; see also Political Science pg 2208
Public Affairs—See **Public Administration** pg 2283
Public Finance—pg 454; see also Banking & Finance pg 355; Law pg 1493
Public Health and Safety—pg 2336; see also Medicine pg 1786; Sanitation, Environmental Technology pg 2496
Public Relations—See **Advertising & Public Relations** pg 349
Public Utilities—See **Public Administration** pg 2283
Publishing—pg 2361; see also Journalism pg 1488
Pulp Industry—See **Paper & Pulp Industry** pg 2108
Purchasing—pg 491
Radiation—See **Light, Optics, Radiation** pg 2195
Radiology—pg 1933; see also Neoplasma, Neoplastic pg 1880
Railroads—pg 2762
Rationalism—See **Religion, Mythology, Rationalism** pg 2421
Real Estate—pg 2371; see also Housing and Urban Development pg 1379; Economics: Land pg 794
Recreation, Leisure—pg 2377; see also Travel pg 2783; Hobbies pg 1349; Games & Amusements pg 2382; Outdoor Life pg 2386; Sports pg 2393
Refrigeration—See **Heating, Plumbing, & Refrigeration** pg 1255
Reformed Church—See **Protestantism** pg 2454
Regional Planning—See **Housing and Urban Development** pg 1379
Religion, Mythology, Rationalism—pg 2421
Religious Education—See **Special Aspects of Education** pg 961; **Religion, Mythology, Rationalism** pg 2421
Respiratory Diseases—pg 1938
Restaurants—pg 2491; see also Food & Drink pg 1140; Hotels/Motels pg 1374
Retailing—See **Purchasing** pg 491; **Marketing** pg 441
Roads and Traffic—pg 2768

Robotics—See **Computers and Computer Science** pg 568; **Engineering** pg 1013
Roman Catholic Church—pg 2466
Romance and Adventure—pg 2494; see also Literature pg 1700
Rubber— 2494
Safety—See **Industrial Health & Safety** pg 1452; **Public Health and Safety** pg 2336
Sanitation, Environmental Technology—See also Public Health and Safety pg 2336; Conservation & Natural Resources pg 597
School Law/Legislation—See **School Organization and Administration** pg 951
School Organization and Administration—pg 951
Science (General)—pg 2518; see also Technology (General) pg 2704
Secondary Education—See **Education (General)** pg 870
Seismology—See **Geophysics** pg 666
Senior Citizens—pg 2549; see also Geriatrics pg 1857; Social Pathology, Welfare, Criminology—pg 2599
Sewing and Needlework—pg 2551; see also Hobbies pg 1349; Arts & Crafts, Handicrafts, Decorative Arts pg 166
Sexual Life—pg 2553
Ships & Shipping—pg 2775; see also Naval Science, Navigation pg 2043; Commerce pg 389
Shoes—See **Clothing and Fashion** pg 534
Slavery—See **Civil Rights** pg 2230
Slavic Studies—See **History of Europe** pg 1296
Social Pathology, Welfare, Criminology—pg 2599
Social Sciences (General)—pg 2555; see also Humanities pg 1397
Social Security—See **Social Pathology, Welfare, Criminology** pg 2599; **Insurance** pg 1458
Social Service—See **Social Pathology, Welfare, Criminology** pg 2599; **Sociology: General Works, Theory** pg 2581
Socialism, Communism, Anarchism, Utopianism—pg 2247; see also Economic Theory pg 764
Societies and Clubs—pg 2574; see also Higher Education pg 916
Sociology: General Works, Theory—pg 2581; see also Psychology pg 2263
Sound Recordings and Systems—pg 2638; see also Electricity, Electrical Engineering, Electronics pg 1051; Music pg 2005
Soil—See **Crop Production and Soil** pg 74
Sororities—See **Societies and Clubs** pg 2574
Sound—pg 2204
South America—See **General Interest - South America** pg 1232; **History of North, South, and Central America** pg 1316
Special Aspects of Education—pg 961
Spectroscopy—See **Light, Optics, Radiation** pg 2195

SUBJECT CROSS REFERENCES

Speech Pathology—See **Special Aspects of Education** pg 961; **Physically Impaired** pg 2173
Speleology—See **Geophysics** pg 666
Sports—pg 2393; see also Outdoor Life pg 2386; Physical Training pg 2170; Recreation, Leisure pg 2377; Games & Amusements pg 2382
Standardization—See **Metrology and Standardization** pg 1969
State Government—See **Public Administration** pg 2283
Statistics—pg 2641
Surgery—pg 1940
Taxation—See **Public Finance** pg 454
Teaching Materials—See **Theory, Practice of Education** pg 979
Technology (General)—pg 2704; see also Science (General) pg 2518; Engineering pg 1013
Telecommunications—pg 560; see also Broadcasting pg 549
Telegraph—See **Telecommunications** pg 560
Telephone—See **Telecommunications** pg 560
Television and Radio—See **Broadcasting** pg 549
Textbooks—See **Theory, Practice of Education** pg 979
Textiles—pg 2720; see also Clothing and Fashion pg 534
Theater—pg 2726; see also Performing Arts pg 173
Theology—pg 2475
Theoretical Chemistry—See **Physical and Theoretical Chemistry** pg 522
Theory, Practice of Education—pg 979
Theosophy—See **Islam, Bahaism, Theosophy** pg 2447
Tobacco—pg 2731
Tourism—See **Travel** pg 2783; **Economics** pg 699
Toxicology—pg 1948; see also Pharmacy pg 2130
Toys—See **Gifts, Toys** pg 1250
Trade—See **Commerce** pg 389
Trademarks—See **Copyright, Intellectual Property** pg 616
Traffic—See **Roads and Traffic** pg 2768
Transportation—pg 2733; see also Commerce pg 389
Travel—pg 2783; see also Recreation, Leisure pg 2377; Geography pg 1233
Trucks and Trucking—See **Transportation** pg 2733
Ukranian Studies—See **History of Europe** pg 1296
Unions—See **Labor** pg 804
Urban Development—See **Housing and Urban Development** pg 1379
Urology—pg 1951
Utopianism—See **Socialism, Communism, Anarchism, Utopianism** pg 2247
Vacations—See **Travel** pg 2783; **Recreation, Leisure** pg 2377

Veterans—See **Military Science** pg 1971; **Naval Science, Navigation** pg 2043
Veterinary Medicine, Animal Culture—pg 2799; see also Zoology - Vertebrate and Invertebrate pg 2970
Visual Arts—See **Art** pg 155
Vocational Education—See **Special Aspects of Education** pg 961
Volcanoes—See **Geophysics** pg 666
Voting—See **Political Science** pg 2208
Watches—See **Clocks and Watches** pg 1488
Water Resources—pg 2811; see also Hydrology pg 670; Hydraulic Engineering pg 1076; Conservation & Natural Resources pg 597
Water Utilities—See **Public Administration** pg 2283
Weather, Climatology—See **Meteorology** pg 674
Weights and Measures—See **Metrology and Standardization** pg 1969
Welding—pg 1967
Welfare—See **Social Pathology, Welfare, Criminology** pg 2599
Western Australian Studies—See **History of Australia and Oceania** pg 1294
Who's Who—See **Biographies** pg 219
Women—pg 2823
Wood—See **Lumber & Wood** pg 1170
Woodwork—See **Carpentry and Woodwork** pg 308
Workmen's Compensation—See **Labor** pg 804; **Insurance** pg 1458
World Politics—See **Political Science** pg 2208; **International Relations** pg 2234
Writing—See **Journalism** pg 1488; **Literature** pg 1700; **Poetry** pg 1748
Yachts and Yachting—See **Boats and Boating** pg 288
Yearbooks, Almanacs, Directories—pg 2833
Youth—See **Children and Youth Interests** pg 526
Zoology-Vertebrate and Invertebrate—pg 2970; see also Veterinary Medicine, Animal Culture pg 2799

TABLES

Frequency

Country of Publication

Unit of Currency

Indexes/Abstracts

FREQUENCY TABLE

an	Annual
be	Biennial
bm	Bimonthly
bw	Biweekly
ci	Completely irregular
da	Daily
ir	Irregular
mo	Monthly
ni	Normalized irregular
qt	Quarterly
rg	Regular
sa	Semiannual
sm	Semimonthly
sw	Semiweekly
te	Triennial
tm	Three times a month
tw	Three times a week
ty	Three times a year
wk	Weekly

COUNTRY OF PUBLICATION TABLE

The following list of countries and codes has been taken directly from the CONSER/MARC Formats for Bibliographic Data, with the exception being that the United States, Canada, and USSR state and province codes have been grouped under their respective countries, rather than listed individually. For convenience, separate alphabetical lists by country code and by country name are given.

COUNTRY OF PUBLICATION BY CODE

Abbr. Code	Country	Abbr. Code	Country	Abbr. Code	Country
AA	Albania	GR	Greece	PE	Peru
AE	Algeria	GT	Guatemala	PH	Philippines
AF	Afghanistan	GU	Guam	PK	Pakistan
AG	Argentina	GW	Germany, West	PL	Poland
AO	Angola	GY	Guyana	PN	Panama
AT	Australia	HK	Hong Kong	PO	Portugal
AU	Austria	HO	Honduras	PP	Papua New Guinea
BB	Barbados	HT	Haiti	PR	Puerto Rico
BE	Belgium	HU	Hungary	PY	Paraguay
BF	Bahamas	IC	Iceland	QA	Qatar
BG	Bangladesh	IE	Ireland	RE	Reunion
BH	British Honduras (Belize)	II	India	RH	Zimbabwe
		IO	Indonesia	RM	Romania
BL	Brazil	IQ	Iraq	RW	Rwanda
BM	Bermuda	IR	Iran	SA	South Africa
BO	Bolivia	IS	Israel	SG	Senegal
BR	Burma	IT	Italy	SI	Singapore
BS	Botswana	IV	Ivory Coast	SJ	Sudan
BU	Bulgaria	IY	Iraq-Saudi Arabia Neutral Zone	SL	Sierra Leone
CB	Cambodia (Democratic Kampuchea)	JA	Japan	SO	Somalia
		JM	Jamaica	SP	Spain
CC	China, Mainland	JO	Jordan	SQ	Swaziland
CD	Chad	KE	Kenya	SR	Suriname
CE	Ceylon (Sri Lanka)	KN	Korea, North	SU	Saudi Arabia
		KO	Korea, South	SW	Sweden
CG	Congo (Kinshasa) (Zaire)	KU	Kuwait	SY	Syria
CH	China, Republic of (Taiwan)	LB	Liberia	SZ	Switzerland
CK	Colombia	LE	Lebanon	TG	Togo
CL	Chile	LH	Liechtenstein	TH	Thailand
CM	Cameroon	LU	Luxembourg	TI	Tunisia
CN	Canada	LY	Libya	TR	Trinidad and Tobago
CR	Costa Rica	MC	Monaco	TT	Trust Territory of the Pacific Islands
CS	Czechoslovakia	MF	Mauritius	TU	Turkey
CU	Cuba	MG	Malagasy Republic (Madagascar)	TZ	Tanzania
CW	Cook Islands	MK	Muscat and Oman (Oman)	UA	United Arab Republic (Egypt)
CX	Central African Republic (Central African Empire)	ML	Mali	UG	Uganda
		MM	Malta	UI	United Kingdom Misc. Islands
CY	Cyprus	MR	Morocco	UK	United Kingdom
DK	Denmark	MW	Malawi	UR	USSR
DM	Dahomey (Benin)	MX	Mexico	US	United States
DR	Dominican Republic	MY	Malaysia	UV	Upper Volta (Burkina Faso)
EC	Ecuador	MZ	Mozambique	UY	Uruguay
ES	El Salvador	NE	Netherlands	VB	Virgin Islands (British)
ET	Ethiopia	NG	Niger	VC	Vatican City
FI	Finland	NL	New Caledonia	VE	Venezuela
FJ	Fiji	NO	Norway	VI	Virgin Islands (U.S.)
FR	France	NP	Nepal	VM	Vietnam
GE	Germany, East	NQ	Nicaragua	WB	West Berlin
GH	Ghana	NR	Nigeria	YE	Yemen (Yemen (Sana))
GM	Gambia	NU	Nauru	YU	Yugoslavia
GP	Guadeloupe	NZ	New Zealand	ZA	Zambia

COUNTRY OF PUBLICATION TABLE

COUNTRY OF PUBLICATION BY COUNTRY

Country	Abbr. Code	Country	Abbr. Code	Country	Abbr. Code
Afghanistan	AF	Guadeloupe	GP	Pakistan	PK
Albania	AA	Guam	GU	Panama	PN
Algeria	AE	Guatemala	GT	Papua New Guinea	PP
Angola	AO	Guyana	GY	Paraguay	PY
Argentina	AG	Haiti	HT	Peru	PE
Australia	AT	Honduras	HO	Philippines	PH
Austria	AU	Hong Kong	HK	Poland	PL
Bahamas	BF	Hungary	HU	Portugal	PO
Bangladesh	BG	Iceland	IC	Puerto Rico	PR
Barbados	BB	India	II	Qatar	QA
Belgium	BE	Indonesia	IO	Reunion	RE
Bermuda	BM	Iran	IR	Romania	RM
Bolivia	BO	Iraq	IQ	Rwanda	RW
Botswana	BS	Iraq-Saudi Arabia Neutral Zone	IY	Saudi Arabia	SU
Brazil	BL	Ireland	IE	Senegal	SG
British Honduras (Belize)	BH	Israel	IS	Sierra Leone	SL
Bulgaria	BU	Italy	IT	Singapore	SI
Burma	BR	Ivory Coast	IV	Somalia	SO
Cambodia (Democratic Kampuchea)	CB	Jamaica	JM	South Africa	SA
		Japan	JA	Spain	SP
		Jordan	JO	Sudan	SJ
Cameroon	CM	Kenya	KE	Suriname	SR
Canada	CN	Korea, North	KN	Swaziland	SQ
Central African Republic (Central African Empire)	CX	Korea, South	KO	Sweden	SW
		Kuwait	KU	Switzerland	SZ
Ceylon (Sri Lanka)	CE	Lebanon	LE	Syria	SY
		Liberia	LB	Tanzania	TZ
Chad	CD	Libya	LY	Thailand	TH
Chile	CL	Liechtenstein	LH	Togo	TG
China, Mainland	CC	Luxembourg	LU	Trinidad and Tobago	TR
China, Republic of (Taiwan)	CH	Malagasy Republic (Madagascar)	MG	Trust Territory of the Pacific Islands	TT
Colombia	CK	Malawi	MW	Tunisia	TI
Congo (Kinshasa) (Zaire)	CG	Malaysia	MY	Turkey	TU
Cook Islands	CW	Mali	ML	Uganda	UG
Costa Rica	CR	Malta	MM	United Arab Republic (Egypt)	UA
Cuba	CU	Mauritius	MF	United Kingdom	UK
Cyprus	CY	Mexico	MX	United Kingdom Misc. Islands	UI
Czechoslovakia	CS	Monaco	MC	United States	US
Dahomey (Benin)	DM	Morocco	MR	Upper Volta (Burkina Faso)	UV
Denmark	DK	Mozambique	MZ	Uruguay	UY
Dominican Republic	DR	Muscat and Oman (Oman)	MK	USSR	UR
Ecuador	EC	Nauru	NU	Vatican City	VC
El Salvador	ES	Nepal	NP	Venezuela	VE
Ethiopia	ET	Netherlands	NE	Vietnam	VM
Fiji	FJ	New Caledonia	NL	Virgin Islands (British)	VB
Finland	FI	New Zealand	NZ	Virgin Islands (U.S.)	VI
France	FR	Nicaragua	NQ	West Berlin	WB
Gambia	GM	Niger	NG	Yemen (Yemen (Sana))	YE
Germany, East	GE	Nigeria	NR	Yugoslavia	YU
Germany, West	GW	Norway	NO	Zambia	ZA
Ghana	GH			Zimbabwe	RH
Greece	GR				

UNIT OF CURRENCY TABLE

In the serials listing, prices preceded by a $ symbol are in U.S. dollars. All other rates are assumed to be in country of publication currency, unless designated otherwise. Prices given are one-year library subscription rates; exceptions are noted and explained.

Country	Currency	Country	Currency	Country	Currency
Afghanistan	afghanin	Germany, West	mark	Pakistan	rupee
Albania	lek	Ghana	cedi	Panama	balboa
Algeria	dinar	Greece	Greek drachma	Papua New Guinea	kina
Angola	kwanza	Guadeloupe	French franc	Paraguay	guaranies
Argentina	peso argentino	Guatemala	quetzal	Peru	sole
Australia	Australian dollar	Guyana	Guyana dollar	Philippines	peso
Austria	shilling	Haiti	gourde	Poland	zloty
Bahamas	Bahamian dollar	Honduras	lempira	Portugal	eseudo
Bangladesh	taka	Hong Kong	Hong Kong dollar	Qatar	Qatar rival
Barbados	Barbados dollar	Hungary	forint	Reunion	French franc
Belgium	Belgian franc	Iceland	kronur	Romania	lei
Bermuda	Bermuda dollar	Ireland	Irish pound	Rwanda	Rwanda franc
Bolivia	peso	India	rupee	Saudi Arabia	Saudi riyal
Botswana	pula	Indonesia	rupiah	Senegal	CFA franc
Brazil	cruzeiro	Iran	rial	Sierra Leone	leone
British Honduras (Belize)	Beliza dollar	Iraq	Iraqi dinar	Singapore	Singapore dollar
Bulgaria	lev	Israel	shekel	Somalia	Somali shilling
Burma	kyat	Italy	lire	South Africa	SA raud
Cambodia (Democratic Kampuchea)	riel	Ivory Coast	CFA franc	Spain	pesata
Cameroon	CFA franc	Jamaica	Jamaican dollar	Sudan	Sudanese pound
Canada	Canadian dollar	Japan	yen	Suriname	Suriname guilder
Cayman Islands	cordoba/dollar	Jordan	Jordanian dinar	Swaziland	emalangeni
Central African Republic (Central African Empire)	CFA franc	Kenya	Kenya shilling	Sweden	kronor
Ceylon (Sri Lanka)	rupee	Korea, North	won	Switzerland	franc
Chad	CFA franc	Korea, South	won	Syria	Syrian pound
Chile	peso	Kuwait	Kuwaiti dinar	Tanzania	Tanzanian shilling
China, Mainland	renminbi yuan	Lebanon	Lebanese pound	Thailand	baht
China, Republic of (Taiwan)	NT dollar	Liberia	U.S. dollar	Togo	CFA franc
Colombia	peso	Libya	Libyan dinar	Trinidad and Tobago	Trinidad and Tobago dollar
Congo (Kinshasa) (Zaire)	CFA franc	Liechtenstein	Swiss franc	Tunisia	Tunisian dinar
Cook Islands	New Zealand dollar	Luxembourg	Luxembourg franc	Turkey	Turkish lira
Costa Rica	colon	Malagasy Republic (Madagascar)	Malagasy franc	Uganda	Uganda shilling
Cuba	peso	Malawi	Malawi Kwacha	United Arab Republic (Egypt)	Egyptian pound
Cyprus	Cyprus pound	Malaysia	ringgit	United Kingdom	pound sterling
Czechoslovakia	koruna	Mali	CFA franc	United Kingdom Misc. Islands	pound sterling
Dahomey (Benin)	CFA franc	Malta	Maltese pound	United States	U.S. dollar
Denmark	krone	Mauritius	Mauritian rupee	Upper Volta (Burkina Faso)	ruble
Dominican Republic	peso	Mexico	peso	Uruguay	CFA franc
Ecuador	sucre	Monaco	French franc	USSR	new peso
El Salvador	colon	Morocco	dirham	Vatican City	lira
Ethiopia	Ethiopian birr	Mozambique	meticais	Venezuela	bolivare
Fiji	Fiji dollar	Muscat and Oman (Oman)	rial	Vietnam	dong
Finland	fim	Nauru	Australian dollar	West Berlin	mark
France	French franc	Nepal	Nepalese rupee	Yemen (Yemen (Sana))	rial
Gambia	dalasi	Netherlands	guilder	Yugoslavia	dinar
Germany, East	Ostmark	New Caledonia	franc (CFP)	Zambia	Zambian kwacha
		New Zealand	New Zealand dollar	Zimbabwe	Zimbabwean dollar
		Nicaragua	cordoba		
		Niger	CFA franc		
		Nigeria	naira		
		Norway	krone		

INDEXES/ABSTRACTS TABLE

The following is a list of all publications which index, or contain an abstract of, titles in the *Directory*. The column in boldface is the abbreviation of the index or abstract as used in the serial listing. The column opposite is the complete title of the index or abstract.

ABC Pol Sci	ABC Pol Sci: Advance Bibliography of Contents: Political Science and Government	**AID Res. Dev. Abstr.**	A.I.D. Research and Development Abstracts
ABC Pol Sci: bibliogr. contents	ABC Pol Sci: a bibliography of contents: political science and government	**Air Pollut. Titles**	Air Pollution Titles
		Air Univ. Libr. Index Mil. Period.	Air University Library Index to Military Periodicals
ABI/Inform	ABI/Inform	**Alchol Clin. Update**	Alcohol Clinical Update
Abr. Read. Guide	Abridged Readers' Guide to Periodical Literature	**Alcohol. Dig.**	Alcoholism Digest
		Alcohol Drugs Traffic Saf.	Alcohol, Drugs, and Traffic Safety: Current Research Literature
Abstr. Bull. Inst. Paper Chem.	Abstract Bulletin of the Institute of Paper Chemistry	**Altern. Press Index**	Alternative Press Index
Abstr. Iran.	Abstracta Iranica	**Am. Doc.**	American Documentation
Abstr. Anthropol.	Abstracts in Anthropology	**Am. Hist. Life Part A**	America: History and Life. Part A: Article Abstracts and Citations
Abstr. Criminol. Penol.	Abstracts on Criminology and Penology	**Am. Hist. Life Part D**	America: History and Life. Part D: Annual Index
Abstr. Engl. Stud.	Abstracts of English Studies	**Am. Hist. Life Suppl.**	America, History and Life. Supplement
Abstr. Folk. Stud.	Abstracts of Folklore Studies	**Am. Hist. Life**	America, History and Life
Abstr. Health Care Manage. Stud.	Abstracts of Health Care Management Studies	**Am. Hist. Rev.**	American Historical Review
Abstr. Health Environ. Pollutants	Abstracts on Health Effects of Environmental Pollutants	**Am. Humanit. Index**	American Humanities Index
		Am. Indian Index	American Indian Index
Abstr. Hospit. Manage. Stud.	Abstracts of Hospital Management Studies	**Am. Stat. Index**	American Statistics Index
		Amino Acids Pept. Prot. Abstr.	Amino Acids, Peptide & Protein Abstracts
Abstr. Hyg. Commun. Dis.	Abstracts on Hygiene and Communicable Diseases	**Anal. Abstr.**	Analytical Abstracts
Abstr. Mil. Bibliogr.	Abstracts of Military Bibliography	**Anim. Behav. Abstr.**	Animal Behavior Abstracts
Abstr. New World Archaeol.	Abstracts of New World Archaeology	**Anim. Breed. Abstr.**	Animal Breeding Abstracts
Abstr. North Am. Geol.	Abstracts of North American Geology	**Ann. Telecommun.**	Annales des Telecommunications
Abstr. Photogr. Sci. Eng. Lit.	Abstracts of Photographic Science and Engineering Literature	**Annot. Bibliogr. Econ. Geol.**	Annotated Bibliography of Economic Geology
Abstr. Pop. Cult.	Abstracts of Popular Culture	**Annu. Bibliogr. Engl. Lang. Lit.**	Annual Bibliography of English Language and Literature
Abstr. Res. Pastor. Care Couns.	Abstracts of Research in Pastoral Care and Counseling	**Annu. Bibliogr. Mod. Humanit. Res. Assoc.**	Annual Bibliography of the Modern Humanities Research Association
Abstr. Soc. Work.	Abstracts for Social Workers		
Abstr. Trop. Agric.	Abstracts on Tropical Agriculture	**Annu. Index Pop. Music Rec. Rev.**	Annual Index to Popular Music Record Reviews
Abstr. World Med.	Abstracts of World Medicine	**Annu. Leg. Bibliogr.**	Annual Legal Bibliography
Access	Access	**Annu. Romant. Bibliogr.**	Annual Romantic Bibliography
Access Index Little Mag.	Access Index to Little Magazines	**Anthropol. Index**	Anthropological Index
Account. Data Process. Abstr.	Accounting & Data Processing Abstracts	**Anthropol. Lit.**	Anthropological Literature
		APAIS	APAIS: Australian Public Affairs Information Service: A Subject Index to Current Literature
Account. Index. Suppl.	Accountants' Index. Supplement		
Accumu. Vet. Index	Accumulative Veterinary Index		
ACM Guide Comput. Lit.	ACM Guide to Computing Literature		
Acoust. Abstr.	Acoustics Abstracts	**APCA Abstr.**	APCA Abstracts
Adolesc. Ment. Health Abstr.	Adolescent Mental Health Abstracts	**Apic. Abstr.**	Apicultural Abstracts
Afr. Abstr.	African Abstracts	**Appl. Mech. Rev.**	Applied Mechanics Reviews
Agric. Index	Agricultural Index	**Appl. Sci. Technol. Index**	Applied Science & Technology Index
Agricola	Agricola	**Aqualine Abstr.**	Aqualine Abstracts
Agrindex	Agrindex	**Aquat. Sci. Fish. Abstr.**	Aquatic Sciences & Fisheries Abstracts
		Arch. Environ. Health	Archives of Environmental Health

INDEXES/ABSTRACTS TABLE

Abbreviation	Full Title
Archit. Period. Index.	Architectural Periodicals Index
Arct. Bibliogr.	Arctic Bibliography
Art Archaeol. Tech. Abstr.	Art and Archaeology Technical Abstracts
Art Des. Photo	Art, Design, Photo
Art Index	Art Index
Artbibliogr. Mod.	Artbibliographies Modern
Artic. Civ. Eng.	ACE/Articles in Civil Engineering
Arts Humanit. Citation Index	Arts & Humanities Citation Index
ASCE Annu. Comb. Index	ASCE Annual Combined Index
ASCE Publ. Inf.	ASCE Publications Information
Ashers Guide Bot. Period.	Asher's Guide to Botanical Periodicals
Asian Soc. Sci. Bibliogr. Annot. Abstr.	Asian Social Science Bibliography with Annotations and Abstracts
ASTIS Bibliogr.	ASTIS Bibliography
ASTIS Curr. Aware. Bull.	ASTIS Current Awareness Bulletin
Astron. Astrophys. Abstr.	Astronomy and Astrophysics Abstracts
Astronomischer Jahresbericht	Astronomischer Jahresbericht
Aust. Educ. Index.	Australian Education Index
Aust. Leg. Mon. Dig.	Australian Legal Monthly Digest
Aust. Public Aff. Inf Serv.	Australian Public Affairs Information Service: A Subject Index to Current Literature
Aust. Sci. Index	Australian Science Index
Aust. Weld. J.	Australian Welding Journal
Autom. Subj. Citation Alert	Automatic Subject Citation Alert
AV Index	AV Index
Avery Index Archit. Period.	Avery Index to Architectural Periodicals
Avery Index Archit. Period. Second Ed. Revis. Enlarged Suppl.	Avery Index to Architectural Periodicals. Second Edition. Revised and Enlarged Supplement
Bangladesh Agric. Sci. Abstr.	Bangladesh Agricultural Sciences Abstracts
Bank. Lit. Index	American Bankers Association Banking Literature Index
BCIRA Abstr. Foundry Lit.	BCIRA Abstracts of Foundry Literature
BCIRA Abstr. Int. Foundry Lit.	BCIRA Abstracts of International Foundry Literature
Behav. Abstr.	Behavioral Abstracts
Behav. Med. Abstr.	Behavioral Medicine Abstracts
Bell Howell Newsp. Index Houston Post.	Houston Post Index
Ber. Biochem. Biol.	Berichte Biochemie und Biologie
Bibliogr. Agric.	Bibliography of Agriculture
Bibliogr. Bras. Odontol.	Bibliografia Brasileira Odontologia
Bibliogr. Engl. Lit.	Bibliography of English Language and Literature
Bibliogr. Hist. Med.	Bibliography of the History of Medicine
Bibliogr. Index	Bibliographic Index
Bibliogr. Index Geol.	Bibliography and Index of Geology
Bibliogr. Index Geol.	Bibliography and Index of Geology Exclusive of North America
Bibliogr. Index Health Educ. Period	Bibliographic Index of Health Education Periodicals: BIHEP
Bibliogr. Index Micropaleontology	Bibliography and Index of Micropaleontology
Bibliogr. Mission.	Bibliografia Missionaria
Bibliogr. North Am. Geol.	Bibliography of North American Geology
Biblior. Pflanzenschutz-lit.	Bibliographie der Pflanzenschutzliteratur
Bibliogr. Repert. Christ. Inst.	RIC; Bibliographical Repertory of Christian Institutions
Bibliogr. Reprod.	Bibliography of Reproduction: a Classified Monthly List of References Compiled from the Research Literature
Bioeng. Abstr.	Bioengineering Abstracts
Biogr. Index	Biography Index
Biol. Abstr. RRM	Biological Abstracts/RRM
Biol. Abstr.	Biological Abstracts
Biolo. Agric. Index	Biological & Agricultural Index
Biol. Dig.	Biology Digest
Biores. Index	BioResearch Index
Black Inf. Index	Black Information Index
Blind. Vis. Impair. Deaf Blind.	Blindness, Visual Impairment, Deaf-Blindness
Board Cumul. Index Conf.	Board Cumulative Index - Conference
Book Rev. Digest	Book Review Digest
Book Rev. Index	Book Review Index
Book Rev. Index Soc. Sci. Period.	Book Review Index to Social Science Periodicals
Book Rev. Mon.	Book Reviews of the Month
Br. Archaeol. Abstr.	British Archaeological Abstracts
Br. Ceram. Abstr.	British Ceramic Abstracts
Br. Educ. Index	British Education Index
Br. Humanit. Index	British Humanities Index
Br. J. Addict.	British Journal of Addiction
Br. J. Guid. Couns.	British Journal of Guidance & Counselling
Br. Technol. Index	British Technology Index
Bull. Anal. Entomol. Med. Vet.	Bulletin Analytique d'Entomologie Medicale et Veterinarie
Bull. Bibl. Fr.	Bulletin des Bibliotheques de France
Bull. Chem. Thermodyn.	Bulletin of Chemical Thermodynamics
Bull. Inst. Pasteur	Bulletin de l'Institut Pasteur
Bull. Signal.	Bulletin Signaletique

INDEXES/ABSTRACTS TABLE

Abbreviation	Full Title
Bull. Thermodyn. Thermochem.	Bulletin of Thermodynamics & Thermochemistry
Bus. Educ. Index	Business Education Index
Bus. Period. Index	Business Periodicals Index
Cable Video Index	Cable-Video Index
Camb. Sci. Biochem. Abstr., Part 3, Amino-Acids Pept. Prot.	Cambridge Scientific Biochemistry Abstracts. Part 3, Amino Acids, Peptides & Proteins
Can. Bus. Index.	Canadian Business Index
Can. Bus. Period. Index	Canadian Business Periodicals Index
Can. Educ. Index	Canadian Education Index
Can. Environ.	Canadian Environment
Can. Essay Lit. Index	Canadian Essay and Literature Index
Can. Hist. Rev.	Canadian Historical Review
Can. Index Geosci. Data	Canadian Index to Geoscience Data
Can. News. Index	Canadian News Index
Can. Period. Index	Canadian Periodical Index
Canadiana	Canadiana
Canon Law Abstr.	Canon Law Abstracts
Catal. Rev., Sci. Eng.	Catalysis Reviews: Science and Engineering
Cathol. Period. Index	Catholic Periodical Index
Cathol. Period. Lit. Index	Catholic Periodical and Literature Index
CBS News Index	CBS News Index
Ceram. Abstr.	Ceramic Abstracts
Chem. Abstr.	Chemical Abstracts
Chem. Inf. Dienst.	Chemischer Informationsdienst
Chem. Phys. Lipids	Chemistry and Physics of Lipids
Chem. React. Doc. Serv.	Chemical Reaction Documentation Service
Chem. Titles	Chemical Titles
Chicago Psychoanal. Lit. Index	Chicago Psychoanalytic Literature Index
Chicorel Abstr. Read. Learn. Disabil.	Chicorel Abstracts to Reading and Learning Disabilities
Child Dev. Abstr. Bibliogr.	Child Development Abstracts and Bibliography
Child Youth Serv.	Child & Youth Services
Child. Lit. Abstr.	Children's Literature Abstracts
Child. Mag. Guide	Children's Magazine Guide
Chir. Vet. Ref. Abstr.	Chirurgia Veterinaria Referate Abstracts
Christ. Period. Index	Christian Periodical Index
CIS Abstr.	CIS Abstracts
CIS/Index Publ. U.S. Congr.	CIS Index to Publications of the United States Congress
Clarks Dig. Annot.	Clark's Digest-Annotator
Classified Abstr. Arch. Alcohol Lit.	Classified Abstract Archive of the Alcohol Literature
Clin. Behav. Therapy Rev.	Clinical Behavior Therapy Review
Coal Abstr.	Coal Abstracts
Coll. Stud. Pers. Abstr.	College Student Personnel Abstracts
Comb. Cumul. Index Pediatr.	Combined Cumulative Index to Pediatrics
Commer. Fish. Abstr.	Commercial Fisheries Abstracts
Commun. Abstr.	Communication Abstracts
Community Dev. Abstr.	Community Development Abstracts
Community Ment. Health Rev.	Community Mental Health Review
Compumath Citation Index	Compumath Citation Index: CMCI
Comput. Abstr.	Computer Abstracts
Comput. Control Abstr.	Computer & Control Abstracts
Comput. Inf. Syst. Abstr. J.	Computer and Information Systems Abstracts Journal
Comput. Rev.	Computing Reviews
Comput. Rev., Bibliogr. Subj. Index Curr. Comput. Lit.	Computing Reviews: Bibliography and Subject Index of Current Computing Literature
Concr. Abstr.	Concrete Abstracts
Consum. Index Prod. Eval. Inf. Source	Consumers Index to Product Evaluations and Information Sources
Contents Contemp. Math. J.	Contents of Contemporary Mathematical Journals
Contents Curr. Leg. Period.	Contents of Current Legal Periodicals
Contents Pages Manage.	Contents Pages in Management
Contents Recent Econ. J.	Contents of Recent Economics Journals
Corros. Abstr.	Corrosion Abstracts
CRI Abstr.	CRI Abstracts
Crim. Justice Abstr.	Criminal Justice Abstracts
Crim. Justice Period. Index	Criminal Justice Periodical Index
Crim. Penol. Abstr.	Criminology & Penology Abstracts
Crime Delinq. Abstr.	Crime and Delinquency Abstracts
Crime Delinq. Lit.	Crime and Delinquency Literature
CSIRO Abstr.	CSIRO Abstracts
Cumul. Comput. Abstr.	Cumulative Computer Abstracts
Cumul. Index Nurs. Allied Health Lit.	Cumulative Index to Nursing & Allied Health Literature
Curr. Abstr. Chem. Index Chem.	Current Abstracts of Chemistry and Index Chemicus
Curr. Adv. Plant Sci.	Current Advances in Plant Science
Curr. Aust. New Z. Leg. Lit. Index	Current Australian and New Zealand Legal Literature Index
Curr. Aware. Biol. Sci.	Current Awareness in Biological Sciences
Curr. Aware. Bull.	Current Awareness Bulletin
Curr. Awareness Libr. Lit.	CALL; Current Awareness-Library Literature

INDEXES/ABSTRACTS TABLE

Curr. Bibliogr. Aquat. Sci. Fish.	Current Bibliography for Aquatic Sciences & Fisheries
Curr. Book Rev. Citations	Current Book Review Citations
Curr. Contents	Current Contents
Curr. Contents Agric. Biol. Environ. Sci.	Current Contents: Agriculture, Biology, & Environmental Sciences
Curr. Contents Agric. Food Vet. Sci.	Current Contents: Agricultural, Food and Veterinary Sciences
Curr. Contents Behav. Soc. Educ. Sci.	Current Contents: Behavioral, Social, & Educational Sciences
Curr. Contents Behav. Soc. Manage. Sci.	Current Contents: Behavioral, Social & Management Sciences
Curr. Contents Clin. Pract.	Current Contents: Clinical Practices
Curr. Contents Educ.	Current Contents: Education
Curr. Contents, Eng. Tech. Appl. Sci.	Current Contents: Engineering, Technology & Applied Sciences
Curr. Contents Eng. Technol.	Current Contents: Engineering & Technology
Curr. Contents. Life Sci.	Current Contents: Life Sciences
Curr. Contents, Phys. Chem. Earth Sci.	Current Contents: Physical, Chemical & Earth Sciences
Curr. Contents, Soc. Behav. Sci.	Current Contents: Social & Behavioral Sciences
Curr. Dig. Sov. Press	Current Digest of Soviet Press
Curr. Index Commonw. Leg. Period.	Current Index to Commonwealth Legal Periodicals
Curr. Index J. Educ.	Current Index to Journals in Education: CIJE
Curr. Index Stat.	Current Index to Statistics
Curr. Index Stat. Methods Theory	Current Index to Statistics, Methods and Theory
Curr. Law Case Cit.	Current Law Case Citator
Curr. Law Cit.	Current Law Citator
Curr. Law Index	Current Law Index
Curr. Law Statut. Cit. Index	Current Law Statute Citator and Index
Curr. Leather Lit.	Current Leather Literature
Curr. Lit. Aging	Current Literature on Aging
Curr. Lit. Blood	Current Literature of Blood
Curr. Math. Publ.	Current Mathematical Publications
Curr. Pap. Phys.	Current Papers in Physics
Curr. Phys. Index	Current Physics Index
Curr. Surg.	Current Surgery
Curr. Technol. Index	Current Technology Index: CTI
Curr. Titles Electrochem.	Current Titles in Electrochemistry
Curr. U.S. Gov. Period. Microfiche	Current U.S. Government Periodicals on Microfiche
Dairy Sci. Abstr.	Dairy Science Abstracts
Data Process. Dig.	Data Processing Digest
Deep-Sea Oceanogr. Abstr.	Deep-Sea Research and Oceanographic Abstracts
Deep Sea Res. Part B. Oceanogr. Lit. Rev.	Deep Sea Research. Part B. Oceanographic Literature Review
Def. Mark. Technol.	Defense Markets & Technology
Dent. Abstr.	Dental Abstracts
Diabetes Lit. Index	Diabetes Literature Index
Dir. Publ. Proc.	Directory of Published Proceedings
Diss. Abstr.	Dissertation Abstracts
Diss. Abstr. Int.	Dissertation Abstracts International
Doane Inf. Cent. Index. Syst.	DICIS, Doane Information Center Indexing System
Doc. Abstr.	Documentation Abstracts
Doc. Econ.	Documentation Econmique
Doc. Public Adm.	Documentation in Public Administration
Dok. Raumentwickl.	Dokumentation zur Raumentwicklung
DSH Abstr.	DSH Abstracts
Ecol. Abstr.	Ecological Abstracts
Econ. Abstr.	Economic Abstracts
Educ. Adm. Abstr.	Educational Administration Abstracts
Educ. Dig.	Education Digest
Educ. Index	Education Index
Educ. Resour. Inf. Cent. CLGH.	Educational Resources Information Center Clearinghouse
Eight. Century Curr. Bibliogr.	Eighteenth Century: A Current Bibliography
Ekistic Index	Ekistic Index
Electr. Electron. Abstr.	Electrical & Electronics Abstracts
Electr. Eng. Abstr.	Electrical Engineering Abstracts
Electroanal. Abstr.	Electroanalytical Abstracts
Electron. Abstr. J.	Electronics Abstracts Journal
Electron. Commun. Abstr. J.	Electronics and Communications Abstracts Journal
Electron. Publ. Abstr.	Electronic Publishing Abstracts
Elenchus Bibliogr. Bibicus	Elenchus Bibliographicus Biblicus
Employ. Relat. Abstr.	Employment Relations Abstracts
Energy Index	Energy Index
Energy Inf. Abstr.	Energy Information Abstracts
Energy Res. Abstr.	Energy Research Abstracts
Eng. Index	Engineering Index
Eng. Index Annu.	Engineering Index Annual
Eng. Index Bioeng. Abstr.	Engineering Index Bioengineering Abstracts
Eng. Index Energy Abstr.	Engineering Index Energy Abstracts
Eng. Index Mon.	Engineering Index Monthly
Eng. Index Mon. Author Index	Engineering Index Monthly and Author Index
Entertain. Law Report.	Entertainment Law Reporter
Entomol. Abstr.	Entomology Abstracts

INDEXES/ABSTRACTS TABLE

Abbreviation	Full Title
Environ.	Environnement
Environ. Abstr.	Environment Abstracts
Environ. Index	Environment Index
Environ. Period. Bibliogr.	Environmental Periodicals Bibliography
Environ. Qual. Abstr.	Environmental Quality Abstracts
Ephemer. Theologicae Lovanienses	Ephemerides Theologicae Lovanienses
Ergonomics Abstr.	Ergonomics Abstracts
ERIC Abstr.	ERIC Abstracts
ERIC Curr. Index J. Educ.	ERIC Current Index to Journals in Education
Essay Gen. Lit. Index	Essay and General Literature Index
Ethnic Stud. Bibliogr.	Ethnic Studies Bibliography
Eur. Res.	European Research
Exept. Child Educ. Abstr.	Exceptional Child Education Abstracts
Execpt. Child Educ. Resour.	Exceptional Child Education Resources
Excerpta Bot. Sect. A. Taxon. Chorol.	Excerpta Botanica. Sectio A, Taxonomica et Chorologica
Excerpta Bot. Sect. B. Sociol.	Excerpta Botanica. Sectio B, Sociologica
Excerpta Criminol.	Excerpta Criminologica
Excerpta Indonesica	Excerpta Indonesica
Excerpta Med.	Excerpta Medica
Fam. Resour. Database	Family Resources Database
Famli., Fam. Med. Lit. Index	Famli. Family Medicine Literature Index
Farm Gard. Index	Farm and Garden Index
FDA Clin. Exp. Abstr.	FDA Clinical Experience Abstracts
Fed. Tax Artic.	Federal Tax Articles
Fem. Period.	Feminist Periodicals: A Current Listing of Contents
Fert. Abstr.	Fertilizer Abstracts
Field Crop Abstr.	Field Crop Abstracts
Film Lit. Index	Film Literature Index
Fire Res. Abstr. Rev.	Fire Research Abstracts and Reviews
Fluidex	Fluidex
Food Sci. Technol. Abstr.	Food Science and Technology Abstracts
For. Abstr.	Forestry Abstracts
Foreign Lang. Index	Foreign Language Index
Fuel Energy Abstr.	Fuel and Energy Abstracts
Fuel Energy Abstr. Curr. Titles	Fuel Energy Abstracts and Current Titles
Funk Scott Index Corp. Ind.	Funk and Scott Index of Corporations and Industries
Gard. Abstr.	Gardener's Abstracts
Gas Abstr.	Gas Abstracts
Gastroenterol. Abstr. Citations	Gastroenterology: Abstracts & Citations
Gen. Index	General Index
Gen. Sci. Index	General Science Index
Genealogical Period. Annu. Index	Genealogical Periodical Annual Index
Genet. Abstr.	Genetics Abstracts
Geo. Abstr.	Geographical Abstracts
Geol. Abstr.	Geological Abstracts
Geophys. Abstr.	Geophysical Abstracts
Geophys. Tecton. Abstr.	Geophyics & Tectonics Abstracts
GeoRef	GeoRef
GeoSci. Doc.	Geoscience Documentation
Geotech. Abstr.	Geotechnical Abstracts
Geotimes	Geotimes
Gerontol. Abstr.	Gerontological Abstracts
Gesamtverzeichnis Osterreichischer Diss.	Gesamtverzeichnis Osterreichischer Dissertationen
Graphic Arts Abstr.	Graphic Arts Abstracts
Guide Indian Period. Lit.	Guide to Indian Periodical Literature
Guide Perform. Arts	Guide to the Performing Arts
Guide Relig. Period.	Guide to Religious Periodicals
Guide Rev. Books Hisp. Am	Guide to Reviews of Books From and About Hispanic America
Guide Soc. Sci. Relig. Period. Lit.	Guide to Social Science and Religion in Periodical Literature
Health Educ. Bull.	Health Education Bulletin
Help. Person Group	Helping Person in the Group
Herbage Abstr.	Herbage Abstracts
High. Educ. Abstr.	Higher Education Abstracts
Highw. Res. Abstr.	Highway Research Abstracts
Hisp. Press Index	Hispanic Press Index
Hist. Abstr.	Historical Abstracts
Hist. Abstr., Part A, Mod. Hist. Abstr.	Historical Abstracts. Part A. Modern History Abstracts
Hist. Abst., Part B, Twent. Century Abstr.	Historical Abstracts. Part B. Twentieth Century Abstracts
Hortic. Abstr.	Horticultural Abstracts
Hospit. Abstr.	Hospital Abstracts
Hospit. Lit. Index	Hospital Literature Index
Hospit. Manage. Rev.	Hospital Management Review
Hous. Urban Aff. Bibliogr. Guide Microform Collect.	Housing and Urban Affairs: A Bibliographic Guide to the Microform Collection
Hum. Resour. Abstr.	Human Resources Abstracts
Humanit. Index	Humanities Index
Hydata	Hydata
ICSSR Res. Abstr. Q.	ICSSR Research Abstracts Quarterly
ICUIS Abstr. Serv.	ICUIS Abstracts Service

INDEXES/ABSTRACTS TABLE

Abbreviation	Full Name
ICUIS Justice Ministeries	ICUIS Justice Ministeries
IMM Abstr.	IMM Abstracts
Ind. Arts Index	Industrial Arts Index
Ind. Dev. Abstr.	Industrial Development Abstracts
Ind. Hyg. Dig.	Industrial Hygiene Digest
Ind. J. Biochem. Biophys.	Indian Journal of Biochemistry & Biophysics
Index Am. Period. Verse	Index of American Periodical Verse
Index Artic. Jew. Stud.	Index of Articles on Jewish Studies
Index Book Rev. Humanit.	Index to Book Reviews in the Humanities
Index Can. Leg. Period. Lit.	Index to Canadian Legal Periodical Literature
Index Chem.	Index Chemicus
Index. Commonw. Leg. Period.	Index to Commonwealth Legal Periodicals
Index Curr. Urban Doc.	Index to Current Urban Documents
Index Dent. Lit.	Index to Dental Literature
Index Econ. Artic. J. Collect. Vol.	Index of Economic Articles in Journals and Collective Volumes
Index Econ. J.	Index of Economic Journals
Index Fed. Tax Artic.	Index to Federal Tax Articles
Index Foreign Leg. Per. Collect. Essays	Index to Foreign Legal Periodicals and Collections of Essays
Index Free Period.	Index to Free Periodicals
Index Gov. Orders	Index to Government Orders
Index IEEE Publ.	Index to IEEE Publications
Index Indian Period. Lit.	Index to Indian Periodical Literature
Index India	Index India
Index Islam.	Index Islamicus
Index Jew. Period.	Index to Jewish Periodicals
Index Leg. Period.	Index to Legal Periodicals
Index Lit. Am. Indian	Index to Literature on the American Indian
Index Math. Pap.	Index of Mathematical Papers
Index Med.	Index Medicus
Index New Engl. Period.	Index to New England Periodicals
Index New Z. Period.	Index to New Zealand Periodicals
Index Period. Artic. Negroes	Index to Periodical Articles by and about Negroes
Index Period. Artic. Blacks	Index to Periodical Articles by and about Blacks
Index Period. Artic. Relat. Law	Index to Periodical Articles Related to Law
Index Period. Lit. Aging	Index to Periodical Literature on Aging
Index Publies Seperament	Index Publies Seperament
Index Relig. Period.	Index to Religious Periodicals
Index to Relig. Period. Lit	Index to Religious Periodical Literature
Index Sci. Rev.	ISR, Index to Scientific Reviews
Index Soc. Sci. Humanit. Proc.	Index to Social Sciences & Humanities Proceedings
Index South Afr. Period.	Index to South African Periodicals
Index Specif. Stand.	Index Specifications and Standards
Index U.S. Gov. Period.	Index to U.S. Government Periodicals
Index U.S. Gov. Publ.	Index to U.S. Government Publications
Index Vet.	Index Veterinarius
Indexes Publ. Am. Soc. Mech. Eng.	Indexes to Publications-American Society of Mechanical Engineers
Indian Behav. Sci. Abstr.	Indian Behavioural Science Abstracts
Indian J. Radiol.	Indian Journal of Radiology
Indian Libr. Sci. Abstr.	Indian Library Science Abstracts
Indian Psychol. Abstr.	Indian Psychological Abstracts
Indian Sci. Abstr.	Indian Science Abstracts
Indian Sci. Index	Indian Science Index
Indice Agricola Am. Lat. Caribe	Indice Agricola de America Latina y el Caribe
Indice Lit. Dent. Castellano	Indice de la Literatura Dental en Castellano
Indice Lit. Dent. Period. Castellano	Indice de la Literatura Dental Periodica en Castellano
Indice Med. Esp.	Indice Medico Espanol
Indice. Rev. Bibliotecol.	IREBI. Indices de Revistas de Bibliotecologia
Inf. Hotline	Information Hotline
Inf. Rep. Bibliogr.	Information Reports and Bibliographies
Inf. Sci. Abstr.	Information Science Abstracts
Infobank	Infobank
INIS Atomindex	INIS Atomindex
Instrum. Abstr.	Instrument Abstracts
Int. Abstr. Biol. Sci.	International Abstracts of Biological Sciences
Int. Abstr. Oper. Res.	International Abstracts in Operations Research
Int. Aerosp. Abstr.	International Aerospace Abstracts
Int. Afr. Bibliogr.	International African Bibliography
Int. Bibliogr.	International Bibliography
Int. Bibliogr. Book Rev.	International Bibliography of Book Reviews
Int. Bibliogr. Hist. Relig.	International Bibliography of the History of Religions
Int. Bibliogr. Period. Lit.	International Bibliography of Periodical Literature
Int. Bibliogr. Soc. Sci.	International Bibliography of the Social Sciences
Int. Bibliogr. ZeitschriftenLiteratur Allen Gebieten Wissens	Internationale Bibliographie der ZeitschriftenLiteratur aus Allen Gebieten des Wissens

INDEXES/ABSTRACTS TABLE

Int. Build. Serv. Abstr.	International Building Services Abstracts
Int. Bull. Bibliogr. Educ.	International Bulletin of Bibliography on Education
Int. Dev. Abstr.	International Development Abstracts
Int. Exec.	International Executive
Int. Folk. Bibliogr.	International Folklore Bibliography
Int. Guide Classical Stud.	International Guide to Classical Studies
Int. Index	International Index
Int. Index Film Period.	International Index to Film Periodicals
Int. Index Multi Media Inf.	International Index to Multi-Media Information
Int. Index Period.	International Index to Periodicals
Int. J. Rehabil. Res.	International Journal of Rehabilitation Research
Int. Labour Doc.	International Labour Documentation
Int. Labour Rev.	International Labour Review
Int. Nurs. Index	International Nursing Index
Int. Packag. Abstr.	International Packaging Abstracts
Int. Pharm. Abstr.	International Pharmaceutical Abstracts
Int. Polit. Sci. Abstr.	International Political Science Abstracts
Int. Zeitschriftenschan Bibelwissenschaft Grenzgeb.	Internationale Zeitschriftenschan fur Bibelwissenschaft und Grenzgebiete
Interdoc. Co.	Interdocumentation Company
Iowa Drug Inf. Serv.	Iowa Drug Information Service
ISMEC Bull.	ISMEC Bulletin
J. Abstr. Int. Educ.	Journal of Abstracts in International Education
J. Am. Hist.	Journal of American History
J. Am. Med. Assoc.	Journal of the American Medical Association
J. Can. Fict.	Journal of Canadian Fiction
J. Couns. Psych.	Journal of Counseling Psychology
J. Curr. Laser Abstr.	Journal of Current Laser Abstracts
J. Doc.	Journal of Documentation
J. Econ. Abstr.	Journal of Economic Abstracts
J. Econ. Lit.	Journal of Economic Literature
J. Ment. Defic. Res.	Journal of Mental Deficiency Research
J. Read. Writ. Learn. Disabil. Int.	Journal of Reading, Writing, and Learning Disabilities International
JAMA: J. Am. Med. Assoc.	JAMA: The Journal of the American Medical Association
Jazz Index	Jazz Index
Jpn. Period. Index	Japanese Periodicals Index
Key Econ. Sci.	Key to Economic Science
Key Econ. Sci. Manage. Sci.	Key to Economic Science and Managerial Sciences
Key Word Index Wildl. Res.	Key-Word-Index of Wildlife Research
Keyword Index Intern. Med.	Keyword Index in Internal Medicine
Kokunai Igaku Zasshi Kiji Sakuin	Kokunai Igaku Zasshi Kiji Sakuin
Lang. Autom.	Language and Automation
Lang. Lang. Behav. Abstr.	Language and Language Behavior Abstracts: LLBA
Lang. Teach.	Language Teaching
Lang. Teach. Linguist. Abstr.	Language Teaching and Linguistics Abstracts
Landwirtsch. Zentralbl.	Landwirtschaftliches Zentralblatt
Lead Abstr.	Lead Abstracts
Left Index	Left Index
Leg. Contents	Legal Contents
Leg. Inf. Manage. Index	Legal Information Management Index
Leg. Period. Dig.	Legal Periodical Digest
Leg. Resour. Index	Legal Resource Index
Leis. Recreat. Tour. Abstr.	Leisure Recreation and Tourism Abstracts
Leukemia Abstr.	Leukemia Abstracts
Libr. Inf. Sci. Abstr.	Library & Information Science Abstracts
Libr. Lit.	Library Literature
Libr. Sci. Abstr.	Library Science Abstracts
Life Insur. Index	Life Insurance Index
Life Sci. Collect.	Life Sciences Collection
Linguist. Lang. Behav. Abstr.	Linguistics and Language Behavior Abstracts: LLBA
Lit. Crit. Regist.	Literary Criticism Register
Lit. Mod. Art	L.O.M.A. Literature on Modern Art
Litig. Newsl. Table Cases	Litigation Newsletter Table of Cases
Mag. Index	Magazine Index
Manage. Abstr.	Management Abstracts
Manage. Contents	Management Contents
Manage. Index	Management Index
Manage. Market. Abstr.	Management and Marketing Abstracts
Manage. Res.	Management Research
Manage. Rev. Dig.	Management Review & Digest
Mar. Sci. Contents Tables	Marine Science Contents Tables
Mark. Distrib. Abstr.	Marketing & Distribution Abstracts
Mark. Inf. Guide	Marketing Information Guide
Mark. Res. Abstr.	Market Research Abstracts
Marriage Fam. Rev.	Marriage & Family Review
Math. Rev.	Mathematical Reviews
Med. Abstr. J.	Medical Abstracts Journal
Med. Abstr. Serv.	Medical Abstract Service
Med. Care Rev.	Medical Care Review
Med. Res. Index	Medical Research Index

INDEXES/ABSTRACTS TABLE

Abbreviation	Full Title
Pestdoc	Pestdoc
Pet. Abstr.	Petroleum Abstracts
Pet. Energy Bus. News Index	Petroleum/Energy Business News Index
Pharm. News Index	Pharmaceutical News Index
Pharmacognosy Titles	Pharmacognosy Titles
Philip. Abstr.	Philippine Abstracts
Philos. Index	Philosopher's Index
Photogr. Abstr.	Photographic Abstracts
Photogr. Index	Photography Index
Phys. Abstr.	Physics Abstracts
Phys. Briefs	Physics Briefs
Phys. Educ. Index	Physical Education Index
Phys. Med. Biol.	Physics in Medicine & Biology
Pinpointer	Pinpointer
Plant Breed. Abstr.	Plant Breeding Abstracts
Plast. Abstr.	Plastics Abstracts
Point Repere	Point de Repere
Pol. Tech. Abstr.	Polish Technical Abstracts
Pol. Tech. Econ. Abstr.	Polish Technical and Economic Abstracts
Police Sci. Abstr.	Police Science Abstracts
Policy Publ. Rev.	Policy Publications Review
Polit. Sci. Gov. Public Policy Ser.	Political Science, Government & Public Policy Series
Pollut. Abstr. Indexes	Pollution Abstracts with Indexes
Polymer Contents	Polymer Contents
Pooles Index Period. Lit.	Poole's Index to Periodical Literature
Pop. Mag. Rev.	Popular Magazine Review
Pop. Music Period. Index	Popular Music Periodicals Index
Popul. Index	Population Index
Potato Abstr.	Potato Abstracts
Poult. Abstr.	Poultry Abstracts
Pover. Hum. Resour. Abstr.	Poverty & Human Resources Abstracts
Predicasts	Predicasts
Predicasts Forecasts	Predicasts Forecasts
Predicast Overview Mark. Technol.	PROMT, Predicast Overview of Markets and Technology
Prev. Hum. Serv.	Prevention in Human Services
Print. Abstr.	Printing Abstracts
Prop. Liabil. Insur. Index	Property & Liability Insurance Index
Psychedelic Rev.	Psychedelic Review
Psychoanal. Q.	The Psychoanalytic Quarterly
Psychol. Abstr.	Psychological Abstracts
Psychol. Read. Guide	Psychological Reader's Guide
Psychopharmacology Abstr.	Psychopharmacology Abstracts
Public Adm. Abstr. Index Artic.	Public Administration Abstracts and Index of Articles
Public Aff. Inf. Serv. Bull.	Public Affairs Information Service Bulletin
Public Health Rev.	Public Health Reviews
Public Manage. Source	Public Management Sources
Q. Bibliogr. Comput. Data Process.	Quarterly Bibliography of Computers and Data Processing
Qual. Control Appl. Stat.	Quality Control and Applied Statistics
RAPRA Abstr.	RAPRA Abstracts
RCA Tech. Papers Index	RCA Technical Papers Index
Read. Abstr.	Reading Abstracts
Read. Disabil. Dig.	Reading Disability Digest
Read. Guide Period. Lit.	Readers' Guide to Periodical Literature
Recent Publ. Artic.	Recently Published Articles—American Historical Association
Ref. Book Rev. Index	Reference Book Review Index
Ref. Serv. Rev.	Reference Services Review
Ref. Source	Reference Sources
Ref. Z.	Referativnyi Zhurnal
Ref. Z. Fizika	Referativnyi Zhurnal: Fizika
Ref. Z. Math.	Referativnyi Zhurnal: Mathematika
Rehabil. Lit.	Rehabilitation Literature
Relig. Index One, Period.	Religion Index One. Periodicals
Relig. Theol. Abstr.	Religious and Theological Abstracts
Repert. Anal. Artic. Rev. Que.	RADAR: Repertoire Analytique d'Articles de Revues del Quebec
Repert. Bibliogr. Inst. Chret.	Repertoire Bibliographique des Institutions Chretiennes
Repert. Bibliogr. Philos.	Repertoire Bibliographique de la Philosophie
Repert. Int. Litt. Art	RILA, Repertoire International de la Litterature de l'Art
Res. High. Educ. Abstr.	Research into Higher Education Abstracts
Resour. Educ.	Resources in Education
Resumos Indicativos Ind. Pet.	Resumos Indicativos da Industria do Petroleo
Rev. Appl. Entomol.	Review of Applied Entomology
Rev. Fr. Pedagog.	Revue Francaise de Pedagogie
Rev. Hist. Eccles.	Revue D'Histoire Ecclesiastique
Rev. Hist. Litt. Fr.	Revue D'Histoire Litteraire de la France
Rev. Met. Lit.	Review of Metal Literature
Rev. Plant Pathol.	Review of Plant Pathology
Rev. Popul. Rev.	Review of Population Reviews
Rev. Relig. Res.	Review of Religions Research

INDEXES/ABSTRACTS TABLE

Abbreviation	Full Title
Med. Socioecon. Res. Source	Medical Socioeconomic Research Sources
Media Law Report.	Media Law Reporter
Media Rev. Dig.	Media Review Digest
MEDOC	MEDOC
Ment. Health Book Rev. Index	Mental Health Book Review Index
Ment. Retard. Abstr.	Mental Retardation Abstracts
Met. Abstr.	Metals Abstracts
Met. Finishing Abstr.	Metal Finishing Abstracts
Metall. Abstr.	Metallurgical Abstracts
Meteorol. Geoastrophys. Abstr.	Meteorological and Geoastrophysical Abstracts
Methodist Period. Index	Methodist Periodical Index
Microbiol. Abstr.	Microbiology Abstracts
Microcomput. Index	Microcomputer Index
Middle East Abstr. Index	Middle East Abstracts and Index
Middle East J.	Middle East Journal
Mideast File	Mideast File
Mineral. Abstr.	Mineralogical Abstracts
Minproc	Minproc
Mintec, Min. Technol. Abstr.	Mintec : Mining Technology Abstracts
Missionalia	Missionalia
MLA Int. Bibliogr. Books Artic. Mod. Lang. Lit.	MLA International Bibliography of Books and Articles on the Modern Languages and Literatures
MNU, Math. Naturwiss. Unterr.	Mathematische und Naturwissenschaftliche Unterricht
Mod. Lang. Abstr.	Modern Language Abstracts
Mod. Med.	Modern Medicine
Mon. Cat. U.S. Gov. Publ.	Monthly Catalog of United States Government Publications
Mon. Period. Index	Monthly Periodical Index
Multi Media Rev. Index	Multi Media Reviews Index
Multicult. Educ. Abstr.	Multicultural Education Abstracts
Multiple Sclerosis Indicative Abstr.	Multiple Sclerosis Indicative Abstracts
Muscular Dystrophy Abstr.	Muscular Dystrophy Abstracts
Music Artic. Guide	Music Article Guide
Music Index	Music Index
Natl. Newsp. Index	National Newspaper Index
Nav. Abstr.	Naval Abstracts
Neurosci. Abstr.	Neurosciences Abstracts
New Lit. Autom.	New Literature on Automation
New Period. Index	The New Periodicals Index
New Testam. Abstr.	New Testament Abstracts
New York Law J. Dig. Annot.	New York Law Journal Digest-Annotater
Newsearch	Newsearch
Nexis	Nexis
Noise Pollut. Publ. Abstr.	Noise Pollution Publications Abstract
NTA-TIA Bookshelf	NTA-TIA Bookshelf
Nucl. Sci. Abstr.	Nuclear Science Abstracts
Nurs. Allied Health Index	Nursing and Allied Health Index
Nurs. Dig.	Nursing Digest
Nurs. Stud. Index	Nursing Studies Index
Nutr. Abstr. Rev.	Nutrition Abstracts and Reviews
Nutr. Abstr. Rev., Ser. A, Hum. Exp.	Nutrition Abstracts and Reviews. Series A. Human & Experimental
Occup. Ment. Health Notes	Occupational Mental Health Notes
Occup. Saf. Health Abstr.	Occupational Safety and Health Abstracts
Occup. Ther. J. Res.	The Occupational Therapy Journal of Research
Ocean. Abstr.	Oceanic Abstracts
Ocean. Abstr. Indexes	Oceanic Abstracts with Indexes
Oceanogr. Abstr. Bibliogr.	Oceanographic Abstracts and Bibliography
Offshore Abstr.	Offshore Abstracts
Old Testam. Abstr.	Old Testament Abstracts
Onoma	Onoma
Oper. Res. Manage. Sci.	Operations Research Management Science
Ophthalmic Lit.	Ophthalmic Literature
Oral Res. Abstr.	Oral Research Abstracts
Packag. Abstr.	Packaging Abstracts
Pa. Law Finder	Pennsylvania Law Finder
PAIS Foreign Lang. Index	PAIS Foreign Language Index
Pap. Board Abstr.	Paper & Board Abstracts
Park Pract. Des.	Park Practice Design
Park Pract. Grist	Park Practice Grist
Park Pract. Index	Park Practice Index
Park Pract. Prog.	Park Practice Program. Design, Grist, Trends...Index
PASCAL	PASCAL
Pastor. Care Couns. Abstr.	Pastoral Care and Counseling Abstracts
Peace Res. Abstr. J.	Peace Research Abstracts Journal
Peace Res. Rev.	Peace Research Reviews
Percept. Cogn. Dev.	Perceptual Cognitive Development
Period. Guide Comput.	Periodical Guide for Computerists
Periodex	Periodex: Index Analytique de Periodiques de Langue Francaise
Pers. Lit.	Personnel Literature
Pers. Train. Abstr.	Personnel & Training Abstracts
Person. Manage. Abstr.	Personnel Management Abstracts

INDEXES/ABSTRACTS TABLE

Abbreviation	Full Title
Rheol. Abstr.	Rheology Abstracts
RILM Abstr.	RILM Abstracts
Ringdoc	Ringdoc
Romant. Move. Sel. Crit. Bibliogr.	The Romantic Movement: A Selective and Critical Bibliography
Rural Recreat. Tour. Abstr.	Rural Recreation and Tourism Abstracts
Saf. Sci. Abstr. J.	Safety Science Abstracts Journal
Sage Fam. Stud. Abstr.	Sage Family Studies Abstracts
Sage Hum. Stud. Abstr.	Sage Human Studies Abstracts
Sage Public Adm. Abstr.	Sage Public Administration Abstracts
Sage Urban Stud. Abstr.	Sage Urban Studies Abstracts
School Organ. Manage. Abstr.	School Organization & Management Abstracts
School Psych. Rev.	School Psychology Review
Sci. Abstr.	Science Abstracts
Sci. Abstr. Sect. A. Phys. Abstr.	Science Abstracts. Section A. Physics Abstracts
Sci. Cit. Index	Science Citation Index
Sci. Fict. Book Rev. Index	SFBRI: Science Fiction Book Review Index
Sci. Inf.	Sciences de l'Information
Sci. Res. Abstr. J.	Science Research Abstracts Journal
Sci. Res. Abstr. J. Part A.	Science Research Abstracts Journal. Part A: Super Conductivity, Magnetohydrodynamics and Plasmas, Theoretical Physics
Sci. Res. Abstr. J. Part B.	Science Research Abstracts Journal. Part B: Laser and Electro-Optic Reviews, Quantam Electronics and Unconventional Energy Sources
Sci. Tech. Aerosp. Rep.	Scientific and Technical Aerospace Reports
Sel. Rand Abstr.	Selected Rand Abstracts
Sel. Water Resour. Abstr.	Selected Water Resources Abstracts
Seventh Day Adventist Period. Index	Seventh Day Adventist Periodical Index
Ship Abstr.	Ship Abstracts
Sinopse Odontol.	Sinopse de Odontologia
Soc. Behav. Sci.	Social and Behavioral Sciences
Soc. Sci. Citation Index	Social Sciences Citation Index
Soc. Sci. Index	Social Sciences Index
Soc. Welf. Soc. Plan./Policy Soc. Dev.	Social Welfare, Social Planning/Policy & Social Development
Soc. Work Res. Abstr.	Social Work Research & Abstracts
Sociol. Abstr.	Sociological Abstracts
Sociol. Educ. Abstr.	Sociology of Education Abstracts
Sociol. Leis. Sport Abstr.	Sociology of Leisure and Sport Abstracts
Soils Fert.	Soils and Fertilizers
Solid State Abstr. J.	Solid State Abstracts Journal
Solid State Surf. Sci.	Solid State Surface Science
South. Baptist Period. Index	Southern Baptist Periodical Index
Speleol. Abstr.	Speleological Abstracts
Spin	SPIN
Stand. Philip. Period. Index	Standard Philippine Periodicals Index
Stat. Theory Method Abstr.	Statistical Theory and Method Abstracts
Stud. Women Abstr.	Studies on Women Abstracts
Subj. Index Child. Mag.	Subject Index to Children's Magazines
Subj. Index Period.	Subject Index to Periodicals
Subj. Index Sel. Period. Lit.	Subject Index to Select Periodical Literature
Table Gov. Order	Table of Government Orders
Tech. Data Dig.	Technical Data Digest
Tech. Transl.	Technical Translations
Tech. Zentralbl.	Technisches Zentralblatt
Text. Technol. Dig.	Textile Technology Digest
Theatre Drama Speech Index	Theatre Drama & Speech Index
Theol. Literaturzeitung	Theologische Literaturzeitung
Theol. Relig. Bibliogr.	Theological and Religious Bibliographies
Theol. Relig. Index	Theological and Religious Index
Theor. Chem. Eng. Abstr.	Theoretical Chemical Engineering Abstracts
Therm. Abstr.	Thermal Abstracts
Tob. Abstr.	Tobacco Abstracts
Top Manage. Abstr.	Top Management Abstracts
Trade Ind. Index	Trade & Industry Index
Trans. Am. Soc. Civ. Eng.	Transactions of the American Society of Civil Engineers
Transdex	Transdex
Transp. Res. Abstr.	Transportation Research Abstracts
Trends	Trends
Trop. Abstr.	Tropical Abstracts
Trop. Dis. Bull.	Tropical Diseases Bulletin
Twent. Century Lit.	Twentieth Century Literature
U.S. Polit. Sci. Doc.	United States Political Science Documents
United Methodist Period. Index	United Methodist Periodical Index
Urban Aff. Abstr.	Urban Affairs Abstracts
Urban Can.	Urban Canada
Vert. File Index	Vertical File Index
Vet. Bull.	The Veterinary Bulletin
Vetdoc	Vetdoc
Virol. Abstr.	Virology Abstracts
Vis. Index	Vision Index

INDEXES/ABSTRACTS TABLE

Wall Street J. Index	Wall Street Journal Index
Water Pollut. Abstr.	Water Pollution Abstracts
Weed Abstr.	Weed Abstracts
West. Hist. Q.	Western Historical Quarterly
Wildl. Rev.	Wildlife Review
Women Stud. Abstr.	Women Studies Abstracts
Work Relat. Abstr.	Work Related Abstracts
Work Stud. Abstr.	Work Study & O and M Abstracts
World Agric. Econ.	World Agricultural Economics and Rural Sociology Abstracts
World Alum. Abstr.	World Aluminum Abstracts
World Fish. Abstr.	World Fisheries Abstracts
World Surf. Coat. Abstr.	World Surface Coatings Abstracts
World Text. Abstr.	World Textile Abstracts
WRC Inf.	W.R.C. Information
Writ. Am. Hist.	Writings on American History
Years Work Eng. Stud.	Year's Work in English Studies
Zentralbl. Didakt. Math.	ZDM. Zentralblatt fur Didaktik der Mathematik
Zentralbl. Math. Ihre Grenzgeb.	Zentralblatt fur Mathematik und ihre Grenzgebiete
Zool. Rec.	Zoological Record

JEWELRY

AJM. AMERICAN JEWELRY MANUFACTURER. (AMERICAN JEWELRY MANUFACTURER). V. 22, No. 8- Aug. 1977-. 0193-0931. Periodical. US. English. mo. $16.00. American Jewelry Manufacturer, Chilton Way, Radnor PA 19089. **Tel** (215)245-7555. **Ed** Steffan Aletti. bk rev. adv acc. **Circ** 5,200. (ctrl). Technical aspects of jewelry manufacturing and crafting with news of the manufacturing jewelry industry. *American Jewelry Manufacturer.*

AURUM. English. qt. $36.00. International Gold Corporation, PO Box 351, 1211 Geneva 3 Switzerland. **Tel** (022)21 96 66. **Ind/Abst** Art Archaeol. Tech. Abstr., Met. Abstr., World Alum. Abstr. adv acc. **Circ** 7,500. (ctrl). The international review for retailers, manufacturers and designers of gold jewelery.

AUSTRALIAN GEMMOLOGIST. (THE AUSTRALIAN GEMMOLOGIST). 0004-9174. Periodical. AT. English. qt. 12.00. Gemmological Association of Australia, PO Box 35, South Yarra 3141 Victoria Australia. **Tel** (03)2409003. **Ed** W Hicks. **Ind/Abst** GeoRef, Chem. Abstr. **CODEN** AGMLB2. bk rev. adv acc. **Circ** 2,500. Gem material identification original papers, reports, abstracts, book review, published by the Gemmological Association of Australia.

BEDRIJFSGEGEVENS VOOR DE DETAILHANDEL IN UURWERKEN EN GOUDEN EN ZILVEREN WERKEN. **Main/Corp** Economisch Instituut Voor Het Midden- en Kleinbedrijf. Dutch. ir. **LC** HD9747.N4.

BIJOU. V. 1- Jan. 1969. 0006-2316. Periodical. CN. French (English). ir. $19.35. Editions Bijou Ltee, 2950 rue Masson East, Montreal Quebec H1Y 1X4 Canada. **Tel** (728)36-85-86. **Ed** Anne Lussier. bk rev. adv acc. **Circ** 2,100. (ctrl). Read by professional jewelers and watchmakers including jewelry retailers throughout Quebec. *Loupe, 0458-4066; Bijoutier, 0315-5080.*

CANADIAN GEMMOLOGIST. (THE CANADIAN GEMMOLOGIST). No. 1 (Apr. 1976)-. 0226-7446. Periodical. CN. English. ir. The Canadian Gemmologist, Box 1106/Station Q, Toronto Ontario M4T 2P2 Canada. **Tel** (416)652-3137. **Ed** Willow Wight. **DD** 736.205. bk rev. adv acc. **Circ** 500. Official journal of Canadian Gemmological Association* Includes articles of interest to gemmologists plus information about relevant happenings such as international meetings and and about association activities. *News Letter.*

CANADIAN JEWELLER. Began in 1960?. 0008-3917. Periodical. CN. English. mo. $34.83. MacLean Hunter, Circulation Accounting Department, PO Box 100/Station A, Toronto Ontario M5W 1A7 Canada. **Tel** (416)596-5736. **Ed** Simon Hally. **Ind/Abst** Can. Bus. Index. bk rev. adv acc. **Circ** 5,000. (ctrl). Business and product information for jewelers in Canada, primarily aimed at the retail sector. *Trader and Canadian Jeweller, 0315-8802.*

CASTING & JEWELRY CRAFT. VAT Casting and Jewelry Craft. V. 1- May/June 1976-. 0363-5767. Periodical. US. English. bm. $7.50. Alian Publications Inc, 507 Fifth Avenue, New York NY 10017. **LC** TT212. **DD** 739.2705.

CHILTON'S JEWELERS' CIRCULAR/ KEYSTONE. VFOAT Jewelers' Circular/ Keystone. VAT Chilton's Jewelers' Circular Keystone. Vol. 147, No. 9 (June 1977)-. 0194-2905. Periodical. US. English. ir. $42.00. Chilton Company, Chilton Way, Radnor PA 19089. **Tel** (215)964-4000. **DD** 671. *Jewelers' Circular/Keystone, 0021-6267.*

CHILTON'S JEWELERS' CIRCULAR/ KEYSTONE THE GREAT ALL IN ONE DIRECTORY. See Yearbooks, Almanacs, Directories.

DIAMOND NEWS & S.A. JEWELLER. VAT Diamond News and South African Jeweller. Periodical. SA. English. ir. 0.52. Jewelery Council of South Africa, Box 1724, Johannesburg 2000 South Africa. **LC** HD9677.S6. **DD** 338.27820968. *Diamond News and South African Jeweller.*

THE DIAMOND REGISTRY BULLETIN. **Main/Corp** Diamond Registry. 1969. 0199-9753. Periodical. US. English. mo. $90.00. Diamond Registry, 30 West 47th Street, New York NY 10036. **Tel** (212)575-0444. **Ed** Joseph Schlussel. bk rev. adv acc. Important independent insiders information on present and future outlook of the diamond market and a special confidential wholesale price list for all shapes and sizes.

DIAMOND WORLD. Year 1- 1973-. II. English. bm. $12.00. Gem & Jewellery Information Center, A95 Journal House Janta Colony, Jaipur 302 004 India. **Tel** 44398. **Ed** Vidya Vinod Kala. bk rev. adv acc. Covers diamonds trade and industry. Includes market report, technical notes, new equipment, news and notes, etc.

DIAMOND WORLD REVIEW. V. 1- May 1975-. Periodical. IS. English. qt. $20.00. Diamond World Review, PO Box 3237, 52131 Ramat Gan Israel. **Tel** (03)260249. **Ed** Victor Perry. **LC** TS753. **DD** 338.477362305. bk rev. adv acc. **Circ** 5,000. (ctrl). Information from diamond mining, manufacturing and consumer countries for diamantaires, precious stone dealers and jewelers.

EXECUTIVE JEWELER. Vol. 1 (Dec./Jan. 1981)-. 0273-5423. Periodical. US. English. bm. $40.00. Talcott Communications Corporation, 2700 River Road/Suite 409, Des Plaines IL 60018. **Tel** (312)824-7440.

GEMS & GEMOLOGY (GEMOLOGICAL INSTITUTE OF AMERICA : 1967). (GEMS & GEMOLOGY). VFOAT Gems and Gemology. Vol. 12, No. 5 (Spring 1967)-. 0016-626X. Periodical. US. English. qt. $29.50. Gemological Institute of America, 1660 Stewart Street, PO Box 2110, Santa Monica CA 90406. **Tel** (213)829-2991. **Ed** Alice S Keller. **Ind/Abst** GeoRef. **LC** TS753. **DD** 736.205. **CODEN** GEGEA2. bk rev. adv acc. **Circ** 10,000. Comprehensive articles on gemstone identification, synthetics, sources, history, and fashion. Regular sections feature new gems and gem simulants, current news items, and article abstracts. *Gems and Gemology.*

THE GEMSTONE REGISTRY BULLETIN. VFOAT Gemstone Registry. 0882-6269. Periodical. US. English. $90.00. The Gemstone Registry, 30 West 47th Street, New York NY 10036. **Tel** (212)575-0444. **Ed** Joseph Schlussel. bk rev. adv acc. Important independent insiders information on present and future outlook of the gem market. Other information on the jewelry market, special confidential price list for all gem stones.

GOLD + SILBER, UHREN + SCHMUCK. Periodical. GW. German (summaries in English and French). mo. 165.60. Konradin-Verlag, Ptfch 100252 Ernst Mey Str 8, 7022 Leinfelden West Germany. **Tel** 0711-7594-0. **Ed** Klaus Halluass. bk rev. adv acc. **Circ** 10,372. A trade oriented business publication for clocks and watches, gold and silverware, precious stones and costume jewelry.

THE GOLDSMITH. Began with July 1980. 0274-7456. Periodical. US. English. mo. $12.00. Allen-Pacific Company, 41 Sutter Street, San Francisco CA 94104. **LC** HD9747.U5. **DD** 737.2705. *Pacific Goldsmith, 0191-8397.*

HOSEKI GAKKAISHI. (HOSEKI GAKKAI SHI). VFOAT Journal of the Gemmological Society of Japan. Vol. 1, No. 1 (1974/10)-. 0385-5090. Periodical. Japanese (summaries in English). ir. Hoseki Gakkai Nihon, c/o Tohoku Daigaku Rigakubu Ganseki Kobutsu Koshogaku Kyoshitsu Aobayama, Sendai-Shi 980 Japan. **Ind/Abst** GeoRef, Chem. Abstr. **LC** TS750. **CODEN** HOGAD6.

JEWELLERY AND SILVERWARE INDUSTRY. **Main/Corp** Statistics Canada. Manufacturing and Primary Industries Division. Series/Titl Annual Census of Manufacturers : Preliminary Bulletin. VFOAT Fabrication de Bijouterie et d'Orfevrerie. 0384-336X. CN. English (French). an. Receiver General for Canada, Statistics Canada Publications, Ottawa Ontario K1A 0T6 Canada.

JEWELLERY AUCTION - CHARLTON AUCTIONS. (JEWELLERY AUCTION). **Main/ Corp** Charlton Auctions. 0822-4897. Periodical. CN. English. ir. $2.50 Per No. Charlton Auctions, 299 Queen Street West, Toronto Ontario M5V 1Z9 Canada. **DD** 739.27029471354. *Unreserved Public Mini Auction, 0822-7713.*

JEWELLERY AUCTION - TOREX. (JEWELLERY AUCTION). **Main/Corp** Torex. 0822-4935. Periodical. CN. English. ir. $3.50 Per No. Charlton Auctions, 299 Queen Street West, Toronto Ontario M5V 1Z9 Canada. **DD** 739.270294713541.

JEWELLERY JOURNAL. Vol. 4, No. 1 (Spring 1981)-. 0710-4820. Periodical. CN. English. qt. Free to Members. Jewelery Journal, 100 Front Street West, Toronto Ontario M5J 1E3 Canada. **DD** 338.47739270971. *Canadian Jewellery News, 0710-4812.*

JEWELLERY WORLD. V. 1- June/July 1976-. 0383-9818. Periodical. CN. English. bm. $7.00 Canada, $15.00 Foreign. Jewellery World, Box 201, Don Mills Ontario M3C 2S2 Canada. **DD** 338.47739270971.

JEWELRY AD REVIEW. See Business - Advertising & Public Relations.

JEWELRY MAKING GEMS AND MINERALS. VFOAT Gems and Minerals. 0274-8193. Periodical. US. English. mo. $30.00. Jewelry Making Gems, 555 Cajon Street/Suite B, Redlands CA 92373. **Tel** (714)798-3585. **Ed** Jack R Cox. **Ind/Abst** GeoRef, Gen. Sci. Index. **LC** QE351. **DD** 739.2705. bk rev. adv acc. **Circ** 23,000. A how-to publication for those who cut gemstones, make jewelry and collect minerals. Field collecting articles included. *Gems and Minerals, 0016-6278.*

LAPIDARY JOURNAL. (THE LAPIDARY JOURNAL). V. 1- April 1947-. 0023-8457. Periodical. US. English. mo. Lapidary Journal, PO Box 80937, San Diego CA 92138. **Ed** L Quick. **Ind/Abst** Mag. Index, Int. Aerosp. Abstr., GeoRef. **LC** NK7300. **DD** 739.2705. **CODEN** LAJOA6.

LLOYD'S CANADIAN JEWELLERY AND GIFTWARE DIRECTORY. See Yearbooks, Almanacs, Directories.

MODERN JEWELER (KANSAS CITY, MO. : 1981). (MODERN JEWELER). 0744-2513. Periodical. US. English. mo. Hurst House Inc, 15 West 10th Street, Kansas City MO 64105. **LC** HD9747.U5. **DD** 381.4568820973. *Modern Jeweler (National Executive Edition).*

NEWSVIEWS - CANADIAN JEWELLERS INSTITUTE. (NEWSVIEWS). 0824-2194. Periodical. CN. English. qt. Free to Members. Canadian Jewellers Institute, Howard Building, 1491 Yonge Street, Toronto Ontario M4T 1Z4 Canada. **DD** 338.47739270971. *CJI Newsletter.*

THE NORTHWESTERN JEWELER. 0029-3490. Periodical. US. English. mo. $5.00. Northwestern Jeweler, Main Street at Washington, Allrest Lea MN 56007.

THE OFFICIAL PRICE GUIDE TO ANTIQUE JEWELRY. VFOAT Jewelry. 1st Ed. (1982)-. 0742-5805. US. English. an. House of Collectibles Inc, Orlando Central Park, 1900 Premier Row, Orlando FL 32908. **Ed** A G Kaplan. **LC** NK7312. **DD** 739.27075.

OPERATING RESULTS. RETAIL JEWELLERY STORES. VFOAT Retail Jewellery Stores, Resultats de l'Exploitation. Bijouteries au Detail. CN. English (French). an. $7.75 Domestic, $9.30 Foreign. Publication Sales and Services, Statistics Canada, Ottawa Ontario K1A 0V7 Canada. *Operating Results. Independent Retail Jewellery Stores.*

ORNAMENT (LOS ANGELES, CALIF.). (ORNAMENT). Vol. 4, No. 1 (Apr. 1979)-. 0148-3897. Periodical. US. English. qt. $21.00. Ornament, PO Box 35029, Los Angeles CA 90035. **Tel** (213)652-9914. **Ed** Robert K Liv. **Ind/Abst** Art Archaeol. Tech. Abstr. **LC** NK7300. **DD** 739.2705. bk rev. adv acc. **Circ** 7,000. Ancient, ethnic and contemporary jewelry, personal and adornment costume and clothing. *Bead Journal, 0094-2448.*

RETAIL JEWELLER. V. 1- 1963-. Periodical. UK. English. bw. International Thomson Publishing Ltd, 23-29 Emerald Street, London WC1N 3QJ England.

ROCK & GEM. VAT Rock and Gem. V. 1- Mar./ Apr. 1971-. 0048-8453. Periodical. US. English. mo. $14.00 Domestic, $18.00 Foreign. Miller Magazines Inc, 2660 East Main Street, Ventura CA 93003. **Ind/ Abst** GeoRef. **LC** QE420. **DD** 553.

SOUTHERN JEWELER. 0038-4232. Periodical. US. English. mo. $12.00. Ernest H Abernathy Publishing Company, 75 Third Street NW, Atlanta GA 30308. **Tel** (404) 881-6442. **Ed** Roy D Conradi. bk rev. adv acc. **Circ** 8,500. (ctrl). Trade publication for retail jewelers in the Southeastern United States.

Journalism

CLOCKS AND WATCHES

ZEITSCHRIFT DER DEUTSCHEN GEMMOLOGISCHEN GESELLSCHAFT. Main/Corp Deutsche Gemmologische Gesellschaft. Began publication with 1951. Periodical. GW. German. qt. 65.-. E Schweizerbartsche Verlagsbuchhandlung, Johannisstr 3A, D-7000 Stuttgart 1 West Germany. Tel (0711)625001. Ed H Bank and G Lenzen. Ind/Abst Life Sci. Collect., GeoRef. CODEN ZDGGB7. bk rev. adv acc. Circ 2,500.

ALTE UHREN. 1.- Yearly volume. Periodical. German. qt. Verlag Georg D W Callwey, Streitfeldstrasse 35, 8000 Munchen 80 West Germany. Tel 089/ 43 3096. Ed Christian Pfeiffer-Belli. bk rev. adv acc. Circ 5,000. (ctrl). Journal for clock and watch collectors, dealers,museums.

AMERICAN HOROLOGIST AND JEWELER CEASED. Began with issue for June 1946. Ceased with V. 47, No. 12, Dec. 1980. 0002-8797. Periodical. US. English. mo. LC TS540. DD 681.1105. *American Horologist.*

ANTIQUARIAN HOROLOGY. V. 1- Dec, 1953-. Periodical. UK. English. 15.00 Domestic, $33.00 US/Canada. Antiquarian Horological Society, New High Street, Ticehurst Wadhurst Sussex TN5 7AL England. Tel (0580)200155. Ed J M Plowman. LC TS540. DD 681.11309. bk rev. adv acc. Circ 3,000. (ctrl).

ANTIQUARIAN HOROLOGY AND THE PROCEEDINGS OF THE ANTIQUARIAN HOROLOGICAL SOCIETY. VFOAT Antiquarian Horology. V. 1- Dec. 1953-. 0003-5785. Periodical. UK. English. ir. $8.00. Antiquarian Horological Society, New House High Street, Washurst Sussex TN5 7AL England. Tel 0580 200/55. Ed J M Plowman. bk rev. adv acc. Circ 3,000. (ctrl).

ANUARIO DE LA RELOJERIA PARA ESPANA E HISPANOAMERICA. *See* Yearbooks, Almanacs, Directories.

BIENNIAL REPORT OF EXAMINING AND LICENSING BOARDS - MINNESOTA. WATCHMAKERS BOARD. Main/Corp Minnesota. Watchmakers Board. US. English. be. Watchmakers Board, 5th Floor Metro Square Building, Minneapolis MN.

BULLETIN OF THE NATIONAL ASSOCIATION OF WATCH AND CLOCK COLLECTORS. Began with Vol. 1, No. 1, 1943. 0027-8688. Periodical. US. English. bm. National Association of Watch and Clock Collectors, PO Box 33, Columbia PA 17512. LC NK11. DD 681.1106273.

BYTOWN TIMES. 0712-2799. Periodical. CN. English. ir. Free to Members. National Association of Watch and Clock Collectors, Ottawa Valley Chapter # 111, 14 Kinnear Street, Ottawa Ontario K1Y 3R4 Canada. DD 681.110607138.

CLOCKWISE. Vol. 1, No. 1 (Aug. 1979)-. 0199-8579. Periodical. US. English. qt. $62.00. Clockwise, Department AT-10, 1236 East Main Street, Ventura CA 93001. Tel (805)648-6655. LC TS540. DD 681.1105.

THE COMPLETE GUIDE TO AMERICAN POCKET WATCHES. VFOAT Official Guide Book to American Pocket Watches. 1st. Ed. (1981)-. 0730-2924. US. English. an. Overstreet Publications Inc, 780 Hunt Cliff Drive NW, Cleveland TN 37311. Tel (615)472-4135. Ed Walter Presswood. LC NK7492. DD 681.114. adv acc. Circ 15,000. Includes over 10,000 current market prices, rare watch list, over 110 famous watch manufacturers, over 770 illustrations with color, wrist watches and European pocket watches.

EINKAUFSFUHRER UND ADRESSBUCH DER DEUTSCHEN UHREN-, SCHMUCKWAREN- U. METTALWAREN-INDUSTRIE. *See* Metals & Metallurgy.

GOLD + SILBER, UHREN + SCHMUCK. *See* Jewelry.

GUIDE DES ACHETEURS : HORLOGERIE, BIJOUTERIE ET BRANCHES ANNEXES. VFOAT Buyers' Guide. English, French, German, and Spanish. ir. 50.- . H Buchser, Tour-de-l'Ile 4, Geneve Switzerland. Tel (022)288155. Ed Hugo Buchser. LC TS540. adv acc. Circ 4,000. Addresses of watch and clock manufacturers, manufacturers of jewelry, and manufacturers of other trades. *Guide des Acheteurs pour l'Horlogerie et les Branches Annexes.*

HOROLOGICAL DIALOGUES. V. 1- 1979-. 0273-3374. Periodical. US. English. ir. R Stenard, 60 First Street, Garden City NY 11530. LC TS540. DD 681.113075.

HOROLOGICAL TIMES. Vol. 1 Jan 1977-. 0145-9546. Periodical. US. English. mo. $25.00. AWI Central, PO Box 11011, 3700 Harrison Avenue, Cincinnati OH 45214. LC TS540. DD 681.1105. *News of and for the Watchmakers Industry, 0160-2012.*

INDICATEUR SUISSE. French (French, German, English, Italian, and Spanish). an. Indicateur Suisse, Route de la Glane, 1700 Fribourg Switzerland. Tel 037-24 75 75. Ed Marie Dunand. adv acc. Circ 4,000. Provides an address and reference guide to the Swiss watch industry, lists watch manufacturers and retails, periphery industries jewelers, electronics, and components, micro-technology and machine and tools.

JAHRBUCH DER UHRENINDUSTRIE UND IHRER VERWANDTEN ZWEIGE. *See* Yearbooks, Almanacs, Directories.

THE OFFICIAL PRICE GUIDE TO ANTIQUE CLOCKS. VFOAT Antique Clocks. 1st. Ed. (1983)-. 0743-9571. US. English. an. $9.95. House of Collectibles Inc, Orlando Central Park, 1900 Premier Row, Orlando FL 32809. LC NK7492. DD 681.11309730750973.

OPTISCHE EN FOTOTECHNISCHE INDUSTRIE, KLOKKEN- EN UURWERKINDUSTRIE. Series/Titl Produktiestatistieken Industrie. VFOAT Manufacture of Optical and Photo-Technical Products, Manufacture of Clocks and Clockwork. 1980-1981-. NE. Dutch (English). be. 9.25. Centraal Bureau Voor de Statistiek, Prinses Beatrixlaan 428, Postbus 959, 2270 AZ Voorburg Netherlands.

QUID HORLOGER. 81.- Ed. English (French, German or Spanish). $21.95. Croner Publications Inc, 211-05 Jamaica Avenue, Queens Village NY 11428. Tel (212)464-0866. LC TS540. DD 338.47681113025494. *Annuaire de l'Horlogerie Suisse. Guide General de Horlogerie, Bijouterie, Lunetterie et Mecanique de Precision de Suisse.*

REVUE EUROPEENNE DE L'HORLOGERIE-BIJOUTERIE. VFOAT Europaische Uhren und Juwelen Rundschau, European Watchmaking and Jewelry Magazine. Periodical. English (French, German, and Spanish). ir. 30. Revue Europeenne de l'Horlogerie-Bijouterie, rue d'Argent 6, 2500 Bienne Switzerland. LC TS540. DD 681.11094. *Suisse Horlogere, 0039-4874.*

TIMEPIECE. 1981-. UK. English. Brant Wright Associates Ltd, PO Box 22, Ashford England. LC NK7500.L65. DD 681.113075.

UHREN, JUWELEN, SCHMUCK. 10. Jan. 1973-. Periodical. GW. German. sm. $52.59. Bielefelder Verlagsanstalt KG, Postfach 1140, Niederwall 53, D4800 Bielefeld 1 West Germany. LC TS540. *UHR.*

UHREN RUNDSCHAU. VFOAT Revue de la Montre. Periodical. French or German. ir. 50.00. Vogt-Schild Verlag, CH-4500, Solothurn 2 Switzerland. LC HD9999.C6. *Schweizer UHR, Swiss Watch.*

WATCH & CLOCK REVIEW. VAT Watch and Clock Review. Vol. 48, No. 1 (Jan. 1981)-. 0279-6198. Periodical. US. English. mo. $12.00. Roberts Publishing Company, 2403 Champa Street, Denver CO 80205. Tel (303)296-1600. Ed Jayne Barrick. LC TS540. DD 681.1105. bk rev. adv acc. Circ 15,000. (ctrl). Trade journal for the watch and clock industry. *American Horologist and Jeweler, 0002-8797.*

JOURNALISM

30. (LE 30). V. 1- Dec. 1976-. 0384-9325. Periodical. CN. French. mo. $3.00. Federation Professionnelle des Journalistes du Quebec, 1212 rue Panet, Montreal Quebec H2L 2Y7 Canada. DD 070.062714.

ABAKA. V. 1- Sept. 13, 1975-. 0382-9251. Newspaper. CN. English (text in Armenian and French). ir. 32.00. Tikeyan Publication Center, 825 rue Manoogian, Ville St Laurent Quebec H4N 1Z6 Canada. Tel 747-6680. Ed Arsene Mamourian. DD 071.14281. bk rev. adv acc. Circ 1,500. (ctrl). Community and Canadian news, reviews of Armenian life in the diaspora, editorials, articles dealing with Armenian, as well as political issues, book reviews and literary profiles.

THE AEJ NEWSLETTER CEASED. VFOAT A.E.J. Newsletter. VAT Association for Education in Journalism Newsletter. 0278-8179. Periodical. US. English. Association for Education in Mass Communication, University of South Carolina College of Journalism, Columbia SC 29208. Tel (803)777-2005.

AEJMC NEWS. (AEJMC NEWS : THE NEWSLETTER OF THE ASSOCIATION FOR EDUCATION IN JOURNALISM AND MASS COMMUNICATION). VFOAT A.E.J.M.C. News. VAT Association for Education in Journalism and Mass Communication News. Vol. 17, No. 1 (Oct. 1983)-. 0747-8909. Periodical. US. English. mo. Free to Members, $5.00 Nonmembers/Domestic. Association for Education in Journalism and Mass Communication, University of South Carolina, Columbia SC 29208. Tel (803)777-4728. adv acc. Circ 5,000. (ctrl). Contains news and general information on education in journalism and mass communication. Publication is distributed to members of the Association (AEJMC). *AEJMC Newsletter.*

AFRO-ASIAN JOURNALIST. No. 1- Mar. 1964-. Periodical. English. ir. LC PN5450.

AIM REPORT. Main/Corp Accuracy in Media, Inc. VAT Accuracy in Media Report. V. 1- 1972-. 0738-7792. Periodical. US. English. sm. $15.00. Accuracy in Media, 1275 K Street NW/Suite 1150, Washington DC 20005. Tel (202)371-6710. Ed Reed Irvine. Circ 35,000. Exposes media abuse and inaccuracies in print and electronic media.

ALASKA TODAY. 0191-328X. US. English. an. $2.00. Alaska Today, Department of Journalism & Broadcasting, University of Alaska, Fairbanks AK 99701. LC F901. DD 979.8005.

ALBERTA AUTHORS BULLETIN. V. 1- June 1972-. 0707-994X. Periodical. CN. English. ir. Free. Alberta Culture Film and Literary Arts, 12th Floor Cn Tower 10004-104 Avenue, Edmonton Alta T5J 0K5 Canada. Tel 427-2554. Circ 2,600. (ctrl). Organ of Film and Literary Arts Branch - Alberta Culture - market information, news, feature articles, service to Alberta writers.

ALPHABETIZED DIRECTORY OF AMERICAN JOURNALISTS. *See* Yearbooks, Almanacs, Directories.

ALTERNATIVE MEDIA. *See* Political Science.

AMERICAN JOURNALISM. (AMERICAN JOURNALISM : THE PUBLICATION OF THE AMERICAN JOURNALISM HISTORIANS ASSOCIATION). Vol. 1, No. 1 (Summer 1983)-. 0882-1127. Periodical. US. English. qt. $15.00 $10.00. American Journalism, Department of Journalism/ University of Alabama, PO Box 1482, University AL 35486. Tel (205)348-7155. Ed William David Sloan. DD 071. bk rev. adv acc. Circ 250. (ctrl). The refereed journal of the American Journalism Historians Association. It focuses on all aspects of journalism and mass media history.

APF REPORTER. Main/Corp Alicia Patterson Foundation. VAT Alicia Patterson Foundation Reporter. V. 1- June 1978-. 0193-4562. Periodical. US. English. bm. Alicia Patterson Foundation, 122 East 42nd Street, New York NY 10017. LC AP2. DD 051.

ASEAN PRESS YEARBOOK . . . . *See* Yearbooks, Almanacs, Directories.

ASIAN PRESS. (THE ASIAN PRESS). 0304-8667. English. ir. $3.00. Institute for Communication Research, Seoul Nationl University, Readership Research Center, Dong Song Dong, Seoul Korea. LC PN4709. DD 079.5.

ATLAS WORLD PRESS REVIEW CEASED. V. 21, No. 4-V. 27, No. 2. 0161-6528. Periodical. US. English. mo. $16.00. Atlas, PO Box 2250, Boulder CO 80302. Ind/Abst Public Aff. Inf. Serv. Bull., Soc. Sci. Index, Humanit. Index, Read. Guide Period. Lit. LC AP1. DD 051. *Atlas.*

AUSTRALIAN JOURNALISM REVIEW : AJR. VFOAT AJR. 0810-2686. Periodical. English. sa. 6.00. Australian Journalism Review, University of Queensland, St Lucia 4067 Australia. Tel

Journalism

(07)377-4035. Ed John P Henningham. LC PN4701. DD 079.9405. bk rev. adv acc. Circ 600. Articles about various aspects of news media in Australia and overseas.

AYER DIRECTORY OF PUBLICATIONS. See Yearbooks, Almanacs, Directories.

BAMBOO RIDGE. (BAMBOO RIDGE : THE HAWAII WRITERS QUARTERLY). Began with No 1 (Dec. 1978). 0733-0308. Periodical. US. English. qt. $10.00. Bamboo Ridge Press, 990 Hahaione Street, Honolulu HI 96825.

BELL & HOWELL TRANSDEX. VFOAT Bell and Howell Transdex, Transdex Index. Periodical. US. English. mo. Bell & Howell Company, Micro Photo Division, Old Mansfield Road, Wooster OH 44691. NLM Z 6514.T7 T11. Also available in microform. Transdex, 0041-1116.

BERLINER ABHANDLUNGEN ZUM PRESSERECHT. 0409-1949. German. ir. Duncker and Humblot Verlag, Dietrich-Schafer Weg 9, 1000 Berlin 41 West Germany.

BEST NEWSPAPER WRITING. 1979-. 0195-895X. US. English. an. $3.95. Modern Media Institute, 556 Central Avenue, St Petersburg FL 33701. Ed Roy Peter Clark. LC PN4726. DD 081.

THE BEST OF NEWSPAPER DESIGN. 0737-2612. US. English. an. Society of Newspaper Designers, PO Box 17279, Baltimore MD 21203. LC Z253.5. DD 686.2252.

THE BEST OF PHOTOJOURNALISM. See Photography & Photographs.

BRITISH DIRECTORY OF LITTLE MAGAZINES AND SMALL PRESSES. See Yearbooks, Almanacs, Directories.

BROTHER. Series/Titl Bell and Howell Underground Press Collection. 1- Apr. 1971-. Newspaper. US. English.

BULLETIN - AGENCE DE PRESSE LIBRE DU QUEBEC. Main/Corp Agence de Presse Libre du Quebec. No 1- 18/25 Mar. 1971-. 0701-1229. Periodical. CN. French. wk. 5.00. Agence de Presse Libre du Quebec Inc, 3459 rue St-Hubert, Montreal Quebec H2L 3Z8 Canada. DD 070.43509714.

THE BULLETIN - AMERICAN SOCIETY OF NEWSPAPER EDITORS. Main/Corp American Society of Newspaper Editors. No. 546- Nov. 1970-. Periodical. US. English. mo.

BULLETIN - CENTRE FOR INVESTIGATIVE JOURNALISM. (BULLETIN). No. 1 (Oct. 9, 1978)-. 0822-207X. Periodical. CN. English (includes some text in French). qt. 45.00. Centre for Investigative Journalism, c/o Carleton University, St Patrick's College Building, Ottawa Ontario K1S 5B6Canada. Tel (613)564-3891. Ed David Wimhurst and Rod MacDonell. DD 071.1. bk rev. adv acc. Circ 2,000. Tips, opinions and media news for working journalists.

BULLETIN DES JOURNALISTES CEASED. (LE BULLETIN DES JOURNALISTES). V. 1-. 0382-0378. Periodical. CN. French. Federation Professionnelle des Journalistes du Quebec, 1207 rue St-Andre, Montreal Quebec H2L 3S8 Canada. DD 071.14.

THE BULLETIN OF THE AMERICAN SOCIETY OF NEWSPAPER EDITORS. Main/Corp American Society of Newspaper Editors. 0003-1178. Periodical. US. English. ir. $35.00. American Society of Newspaper Editors, PO Box 17004, Washington DC 20041. Tel (703)620-6087. Ed Burl Osborne. LC PN4700. Circ 2,500. The nation's oldest journalism review explores major press controversies and offers practical advice on the nuts-and-bolts of daily newspaper editing.

BURRELLE'S DELAWARE, MARYLAND, VIRGINIA, DISTRICT OF COLUMBIA MEDIA DIRECTORY. See Yearbooks, Almanacs, Directories.

BYLINE. (BYLINE : NORTHWESTERN'S JOURNALISM QUARTERLY). 0731-5449. Periodical. US. English. ty. $10.00. Byline, 1810 Hinman Avenue, Evanston IL 60201. Tel (312)491-7212. Ed Hope Edelman. adv acc. Circ 2,000. (ctrl). Focuses on all aspects of the media. We review and analyze current issues in print and broadcast journalism, advertising and education.

BYLINE. (BYLINE : A MCCARVILLE PUBLICATION). 0744-4249. Periodical. US. English. mo $18.00. Byline Magazine, 1148 South Douglas/Suite E/Boc 30647,

Midwest City OK 73410. Tel (405)733-1129. Ed Mike McCarville. adv acc. Circ 2,500. (ctrl). Focuses on how-to and self-help information; where to sell, how to prepare your material, how to keep going when you want to give up.

A C E Q A C G R INFORMATION. (A C E Q-A C G R INFORMATION). Main/Corp Association Canadienne des Editeurs de Quotidiens. V. 4, No. 2- Feb. 1976-. 0381-1247. Periodical. CN. French. mo. Association Canadienne des Editeurs de Quotidiens, 206 250 Est rue Bloor, Toronto Ontario M4W 1E7 Canada. DD 071.1. C D N P A-C M E C Bulletin, 0381-1239.

C : JET. VFOAT Communication : Journalism Education Today. V. 11- Fall 1977-. 0198-6554. Periodical. US. English. qt. Communication: Journalism Education Today, 4933 17th Place, Lubbock TX 79416. Ind/Abst Curr. Index J. Educ. LC PN4788. DD 373.1897. Communication, 0010-3535.

CAIRO PRESS REVIEW : CPR. Periodical. UR. English. da. FHB, PO Box 1509, Cairo AR Egypt.

CATHOLIC JOURNALIST. 1945. 0008-8129. Periodical. US. English. mo. $10.00. Catholic Journalist, 119 North Park Avenue, Rockville Centre NY 11570. Tel (516)766-3400. Ed James A Doyle. bk rev. adv acc. Circ 2,200. (ctrl). News and information about and for Catholic newspapers, magazines and book publishers and others interested in this field.

CATHOLIC PRESS DIRECTORY. See Yearbooks, Almanacs, Directories.

CENTRAL AMERICAN WRITERS BULLETIN. See Bibliographies.

CHECKLIST OF CURRENT PERIODICALS. See Bibliographies.

CHUNG-KUO HSIN WEN NIEN CHIEN. VFOAT Zhongguo Xinwen Nianjian. 1982-. Chinese. an. 6.00. Chung-Kuo She Hui Ko Hsueh Chu Pan She, 29 Chien Kuo Men Nei Ta Chieh, Pei-Ching China. LC PN4705. DD 079.5.

COLORADO EDITOR. 0162-0010. Periodical. US. English. mo. Colorado Press Association, 1336 Glenarm Place, Denver CO 80204. LC PN4700. DD 070.5.

COLUMBIA JOURNALISM REVIEW. V. 1- Spring 1962-. 0010-194X. Periodical. US. English. bm. Columbia Journalism Review, 200 Alton Place, Marion OH 43305. Tel (212)280-2716. Ind/Abst Energy Inf. Abstr., Environ. Abstr., Film Lit. Index, Book Rev. Index, Humanit. Index, Soc. Sci. Citation Index. LC PN4700. DD 070.05. Index published separately - free - automatically sent. (cum index).

COMMUNICATION ET INFORMATION. See Communication.

COMMUNICATOR. Began with May 1976 issue. 0702-7990. Periodical. CN. English. Royal Navy Communications, B Branch/Whitehall, London SW1 England. DD 071.11.

COMPACTS. Vol. 1, No. 1 (Sept. 82)-. 0714-7457. Periodical. CN. French. mo. 20.00. Union Internationale des Journalistes et de la Presse de Langue Francaise du Quebec Bureau 1010, 10 rue St-Jacques, Montreal Quebec H2Y 1L3 Canada. Tel (514)844-5527. Ed Charles Atala. DD 071.14. bk rev. adv acc. Circ 500. Chronology of important, international events and consequences interpreted for franphone editorialists. Inquiries in journalism and quality of information. Related subjects: cultural, economic, and political.

CONNECTICUT NEWS HANDBOOK. 0277-5956. US. English. an. Connecticut Information Co, Box 2402, Short Beach CT 06405. LC AI21.H37. DD 071.463.

CONTENT. Began with Oct. 1970 issue. 0045-835X. Periodical. CN. English. bm. $15.00. Content, 126-90 Edgewood Avenue, Toronto Ontario M4L 3H1 Canada. Tel (416)461-7742. Ed Dick MacDonald. bk rev. adv acc. Circ 3,000. News, analysis, and comment about journalism in Canada, abroad as practical.

COYOTI PRINTS. Began publication in 1974?. 0700-902X. Periodical. CN. English. mo $3.86. Coyoti Prints, PO Box 257/150 Milehouse, Vancouver British Columbia V0K 2G0 Canada. Tel (604)296-3351. Ed Keith Matthew. DD 301.451970711. bk rev. adv acc. Circ 1,000. (ctrl). A magazine which covers all native events in the surrounding area. We also include reports on national events which affect indigenous people.

CPU : QUARTERLY OF THE COMMONWEALTH PRESS UNION. VFOAT CPU Quarterly. Periodical. UK. English. qt. $15.33. Commonwealth Press Union, Studio House 184 Fleet Street, London ED4A 2DU England.

CURRENT BRITISH JOURNALS. 3rd Ed. (1982)-. UK. English. British Library Lending Division, Boston Spa, Wetherby LS23 7BQ England. Ed David P Woodworth. LC Z6956.G6, PN5124.P4. DD 052.025. NLM Z 6956.G7. Guide to Current Brithish Journals.

THE DEMOCRATIC JOURNALIST. V. 1- Nov. 1953-. 0011-8214. Periodical. English. mo. Artia, PO Box 790, Ve-Smeckack 30, Praha 1 Czechoslovakia. Ed J Knobloch. LC PN4701.

DEMOKRATICHESKII ZHURNALIST. 1961-. Periodical. UR. Russian. ir. $9.00. Victor Kamkin Inc (70241), 12224 Parklawn Drive, Rockville MD 20852. Tel (301)881-5973.

DETROIT FREE PRESS INDEX. See Indexes/Abstracts.

EL DIARIO, LA PRENSA. VFOAT Diario la Prensa. Vol. 16, No. 4,771 (June 14, 1963)-. 0742-9428. Newspaper. US. Spanish. da. El Diario/La Prensa, 143-155 Varick Street, New York NY 10013. LC Newspaper. Diario de Nueva York, La Prensa.

THE DILIMAN REVIEW. Vol. 1, No. 1 (Jan. 1953)-. 0012-2858. Periodical. PH. English. bm. University of the Philippines, College of Social Sciences and Philosophy, Quezon City D55 Philippines. Tel 976061. Ed Francisco Nemenzo. Ind/Abst Abstr. Engl. Stud., MLA Int. Bibliogr. Books Artic. Mod. Lang. Lit. (cum index). bk rev. adv acc. Circ 4,000. (ctrl). Documents and analyses Philippine contemporary history; uses interdisciplinary approach to serve as a forum for ideas; serves to popularize specialized and technical studies in the sciences, social sciences and the arts.

DIRECTORIO DE PERIODISTAS PROFESIONALES DE COLOMBIA. See Yearbooks, Almanacs, Directories.

DIRECTORY - AMERICAN SOCIETY JOURNALISTS AND AUTHORS. See Yearbooks, Almanacs, Directories.

DIRECTORY OF SMALL MAGAZINE-PRESS EDITORS AND PUBLISHERS. See Yearbooks, Almanacs, Directories.

THE DIRECTORY OF SMALL PRESS & MAGAZINE EDITORS & PUBLISHERS. See Yearbooks, Almanacs, Directories.

DIRECTORY - OUTDOOR WRITERS ASSOCIATION OF AMERICA. See Yearbooks, Almanacs, Directories.

DORTMUNDER BEITRAGE ZUR ZEITUNGSFORSCHUNG. 1.- V. 1958-. 0417-9994. Periodical. GW. German. ir. Verlag Dokumentation, Postfach 711009, Possenbacherstr 28, 8000 Muenchen 71 West Germany. LC PN4703. Mitteilungen, Veroffentlichungen.

L'ECHO DE LA PRESSE ET DE LA PUBLICITE. VFOAT EPP, Echo de la Presse et de la Publicite. 1.-30E Year (No 1-937). Periodical. FR. French. wk. $232.82. Editions Jaquemart, 19 rue Pretres St Germain Auxr, 75039 Paris Cedex 01 France. LC PN4702.

EDITOR & PUBLISHER; THE FOURTH ESTATE. VFOAT E & P. VAT Editor and Publisher. V. 1-14, No. 40, June 29, 1901-Mar. 13, 1915. 0013-094X. Periodical. US. English. Ind/Abst Bus. Period. Index.

EDITORIAL EXCELLENCE. Vol. 1-. 0736-1785. Periodical. US. English. an. $5.00. National Conference of Editorial Writers, 6223 Executive Boulevard, Rockville MD 20852. LC PN4778. DD 070.412.

EPIK. VFOAT Journal Epik de Cacouna. VAT Journal Communautaire Epik (1984), Journal Epik du Cacouna (1984). Vol. 10, No. 5 (Jan./Feb. 1984)-. 0828-5977. Periodical. CN. French. ir. Free to Members. Epik, C P 152, Cacouna Quebec G0L 1G0 Canada. DD 071.1476. Journal Communautaire Epik, 0828-5969.

EPP, L'ECHO DE LA PRESSE ET DE LA PUBLICITE. VFOAT Echo de la Presse et de la Publicite. No 938- 10 Feb. 1975-. 0037-209X. Periodical. French. ir. 440.00. Echo de la Presse et de la Publicite, 19 rue des Pretres-Saint-Germain l'Auxerrois, 75039 Paris France. Ed N Jacquemart. LC PN4702. Echo de la Presse et de la Publicite.

FEED-BACK. (FEED/BACK). 1974. 0145-6261. Periodical. US. English. qt. San Francisco State University, Journalism Department, 1600 Holloway Avenue, San Francisco 94132. Tel (415)469-2086 1689. Ed Shannon Bryony. bk rev. adv acc. Circ

Journalism

1,500. Available on microfilm from Xerox University Microfilms. The journalism review for California.

FICTION WRITER'S MARKET. 1st ed. (1981)-. 0275-2123. US. English. an. $19.95. Writers Digest, 9933 Alliance Road, Cincinnati OH 45242. Tel (513)984-0717. Ed Jean M Fredette. LC PN3355. DD 808.02. Circ 19,000. How to write and market your fiction: short stories, novels. Articles, interviews on writing; listings of little magazines, small presses, commercial magazines, publishers, agents, contests, awards.

THE FLORIDA PRESS. Vol. 1, No. 1 (Jan. 1958)-. 0426-5920. US. English. qt. $6.00. Florida Press Association, 306 South Duval, Tallahassee FL 32301.

FOIA UPDATE. VAT Freedom of Information Act Update. Vol. 1, No. 1 (Autumn 1979)-. Periodical. US. English. qt. Superintendent of Documents, U S Government Printing Office, Washington DC 20402. Ind/Abst Index U.S. Gov. Period.

FOLIO, THE MAGAZINE FOR MAGAZINE MANAGEMENT. (FOLIO : THE MAGAZINE FOR MAGAZINE MANAGEMENT). 0046-4333. Periodical. US. English. ir. 58. Folio Magazine Publishing Company, PO Box 697, 125 Elm Street, New Cannaan CT 06840. Tel (203)972-0761. Ed Barbara Love. Ind/Abst Public Aff. Inf. Serv. Bull. LC PN4734. DD 658.91070572. adv acc. Circ 10,000. Available on microfilm from University Microfilms. Contains articles on all aspects of magazine management and protection.

FREELANCE WRITERS REPORT. Vol. 1, No. 1 (March 1982)-. 0731-549X. Periodical. US. English. mo. $30.00 Non-members, $45.00 Membership, (membership includes report). Cassell Communications, 214 Solaz Avenue, Port St Lucie FL 33452.

FREELANCER'S NEWSLETTER. V. 1- 1970-. 0016-0636. Periodical. US. English. mo. Circle Publication Inc, c/o Jo Ann Bardin, 307 Westlake Drive, Austin TX 78746. Tel (512)327-1208. Ed Jo Ann Bardin. bk rev. Articles and news of interest to freelancers, a marketing aid for writers and photographers. Computerized resume service for subscribers.

FURI JANARISUTO NENKAN. 1976-. Japanese. ir. 3800. Masukomi Hyoronshu, 28-8 Maruyama, Shibuya-ku (150), Tokyo Japan. LC PN4705.

GACETA. Main/Corp Federacion Argentina de Periodistas. Vol. 1- 1970-. Spanish. ir. Lavalle 1464, Buenos Aires Argentina. LC PN4705. *Periodista Argentino.*

GAZETTE; INTERNATIONAL JOURNAL OF SCIENCE OF THE PRESS. V. 1- Jan. 1955-. Periodical. NE. English (subtitle in German and French). ir. H E Stenfert Kroese, PO Box 33, Morssingel 9 13, 2312 AZ Leiden Netherlands. LC PN4699. DD 070.5.

GENERAL ASSSEMBLY - INTER AMERICAN PRESS ASSOCIATION. Main/Corp Inter-American Press Association. VFOAT Asamblea General - Sociedad Internamericana de Prensa. US. English (Spanish). an. Interamerican Press Association, 2911 NW 39th Street, Miami FL 33142. LC PN4712. DD 070.0601.

GOOD OLD DAYS. 0046-6158. Periodical. US. English. mo. $18.00. House of White Birches-Tower Press, PO Box 337, Seabrook NH 03874. Tel (603)474-2404. adv acc. (ctrl). A look into the nostalgic past through authentic photos, drawings, cartoons, comics, memories, features, songs, poems, letters, and ads.

GOOD OLD DAYS. SPECIAL ISSUES. (GOOD OLD DAYS). 0160-7510. Periodical. US. English. qt. $10.50. House of White Birches-Tower Press, PO Box 337, Seabrook NH 03874. Tel (603)474-2404. LC E161. DD 917.30305. adv acc. In addition to the 'Good Old Days' monthly, this special issue contains more nostalgia, authentic photos, drawings, cartoons, memories, letters, etc.

THE GPA BULLETIN. VAT Georgia Press Association Bulletin. Issue No. 1 (Dec. 12, 1984)-. 8750-6181. Periodical. US. English. bw. $20.00 Included in Membership Dues. GPA, Georgia Press Building, 1075 Spring Street NW, Atlanta GA 30309.

GRANTA. See Literature.

GRASSROOTS EDITOR. V. 1- Jan. 1960-. 0017-3541. Periodical. US. English. qt. $12.00. International Society of Weekly Newspaper Editors, Department of Journalism, Dekalb IL 60115. Tel (815)753-1925. Ed Donald F Brod. Circ 1,000. Articles relate to the interests and problems of journalists involved with community newspapers.

THE GUARDIAN. V. 20, No. 19- Feb. 10, 1968-. 0017-5021. US. English. wk. $7.00. Institute for Independent Social Journalism Inc, 33 West 17th Street, New York NY 10011. Ind/Abst Altern. Press Index. LC AP2. DD 071.3. *National Guardian, 0362-5583.*

GUIDE TO U.S. BUSINESS, FINANCIAL AND ECONOMIC NEWS CORRESPONDENTS AND CONTACTS. VFOAT Guide to US Business, Financial and Economic News Correspondents and Contacts. 1983-. 0747-7244. US. English. an. $60.00 Nonprofit Organization, $70.00 Others. Larriston Communications, POB 20229, New York NY 10025. Tel (212)864-0150. Ed Craig T Norback. Circ 1,000. A publicity guide listing the national and local media outlets and the editors and correspondents who cover business, finance and economic news.

GUIDE TO U.S. MEDICAL AND SCIENCE NEWS CORRESPONDENTS AND CONTACTS. VFOAT Guide to US Medical and Science News Correspondents and Contacts. 0747-7252. US. English. an. $60.00 Nonprofit Organization, $70.00 Others. Larriston Communications, PO Box 20229, New York NY 10025. Tel (212)864-0150. Ed Craig T Norback. Circ 1,000. A publicity guide listing the national and local media outlets and the editors and correspondents who cover medical, science and health news.

THE GUILD REPORTER. V. 1- Nov. 23, 1933-. 0017-5404. Periodical. US. English. sm. $20.00. Newspaper Guild, 1125 15th Street NW, Washington DC 20005. Tel (202)296-2990. Ed James M Cesnik. LC HD6350.N4. DD 070.5. Circ 33,000. (ctrl). Publishing industry Employee relations, 1st amendment.

HANDS ON (RABUN GAP, GA.). See Education (General).

HANGUK SINMUN PANGSONG YONGAM. VFOAT Korean Press Annual. Began with 1976 Vol. KO. Korean. ir. 16,000. Hanguk Sinmun Yonguso, 31 1-ka Taepyong-No, Chung-ku, Seoul South Korea. LC P92.K6.

HISTORICAL GUIDES TO THE WORLD'S PERIODICALS AND NEWSPAPERS. Began in 1982. 0742-5538. Monographic Series. US. English. ir. Greenwood Press, 88 Post Road West, Westport CT 06881.

HSIN WEN HSUEH YEN CHIU. VFOAT Mass Communication Research. No. 1- 1967-. Chinese. ir. LC PN4705.

HSIN WEN LUN TSUNG. V. 1, (April 1981)-. Periodical. CC. Chinese. ir. $1.10. Hsin Hua Shu Tien Pei-Ching fa hsing So, Peking China Mainland. LC PN5361. DD 079.51.

HSIN WEN TA HSUEH. VFOAT Xin Wen da Xue. Periodical. CH. Chinese. ir. 0.65. Shang-Hai Hsin Hua Shu Tien, Shanghai China. LC PN4722. DD 070.05.

HSIN WEN YEN CHIU TZU LIAO. VFOAT Hsin Wen Yen Chiu Tzu Liao Tsung Kan. V. 1, (August 1979)-. Periodical. CC. Chinese. ir. 0.80. Chung-Kuo She Hui Ko Hsueh Chu Pan She, Hsin Hua Shu Tien Pei-Ching Fa Hsing So, Peking China Mainland. LC PN4705. DD 079.51.

HUDSON'S STATE CAPITAL NEWS MEDIA CONTACTS DIRECTORY. See Yearbooks, Almanacs, Directories.

HUDSON'S WASHINGTON NEWS MEDIA CONTACTS DIRECTORY. See Yearbooks, Almanacs, Directories.

IMPACT. No. 1-. Periodical. US. English. mo. $27.00. Impact Publication Division of Baker and Bowden, PO Box 1896, Evanston IL 60204. Tel (312)475-5748. Ed Robert L Baker. bk rev. Circ 1,200. An in-depth guide on trends, ideas, techniques, and editorial tools in communications for editors, writers, PR execs and communication executives.

IMPRESSUM I. VFOAT Impressum 1. French (German and Italian). an. Burex Medienpublikationen, Niederfeldstrasse 26, 8932 Mettmenstette Switzerland. LC Z6956.S92, PN5334. DD 070.025494.

INDEX DE L'ACTUALITE VUE A TRAVERS LA PRESSE ECRITE. See Indexes/Abstracts.

INDIAN & EASTERN NEWSPAPER SOCIETY PRESS HANDBOOK. Main/Corp Indian and Eastern Newspaper Society. VFOAT I.E.N.S. Press Handbook. II. English. ir. 25.00. IENS Buildings, Rafi Marg 110001, New Delhi India. LC Z6958.I4, PN5374. DD 079.54025.

INDIANA MEDIA JOURNAL. See Library and Information Science.

THE INKLING. 0734-7138. Periodical. US. English. mo. $18.00. The Inkling Journal, PO Box 128, Alexandria MN 56308. Tel (612)762-2020. Ed Marilyn Bailey. bk rev. adv acc. Circ 2,500. A magazine for both beginning and published writers. How-to of writing, book reviews, interviews, markets, business of writing, copyright, word processing, etc.

INTERNATIONAL PRESS BULLETIN. V. 1-2, No. 3. 0020-8361. Periodical. US. English. qt. International Press Bulletin, 4801 09 Second Avenue, Los Angeles CA 90043.

INTERNATIONAL PRESS JOURNAL. Began with Jan./Feb. 1957 issue. Periodical. CN. English. $50.00. Press Journal, PO Box 3285/Station F, Willowdale Ontario M2R 3G6 Canada. Tel (416)491-1201. Ed Bali Sethi. LC PN4699. DD 071.13. bk rev. Circ 1,000. International coverage on serials, who's who, yearbooks, trade directories on all subjects. Review of serial publications from all over the world.

THE INVESTIGATIVE REPORTER. Vol. 1, No. 1 (Jan. 1982)-. 0731-0978. Periodical. US. English. $18.00. The Investigative Reporter, 1401 16 NW, Washington DC 20036. Ed Jack Anderson.

IPI REPORT. V. 1- May 1952-. 0019-0314. Periodical. SZ. English. mo. $56.90. International Press Institute, Dilke House/Malet Street, London WC1E 7JA England. Tel 01-636 0703/4. LC PN4712.

ISSUES IN COMMUNICATIONS. See Communication.

JAPAN ENGLISH MAGAZINE DIRECTORY. See Yearbooks, Almanacs, Directories.

JOHN PETZER ZENGER AWARD FOR FREEDOM OF THE PRESS AND THE PEOPLE'S RIGHT TO KNOW. (THE JOHN PETER ZENGER AWARD FOR FREEDOM OF THE PRESS AND THE PEOPLE'S RIGHT TO KNOW). 1966-. 0146-4957. Monographic Series. US. English. University of Arizona Press, 1615 East Speedway, Order Department, Tuscon AZ 85719. LC PN4738. DD 323.445. *John Peter Zenger Award for Freedom of the Press.*

THE JOURNAL FOR EDUCATION IN PHOTOJOURNALISM. See Photography & Photographs.

JOURNAL HOLDINGS IN THE WASHINGTON-BALTIMORE AREA. 1976-. 0362-4544. US. English. be. $160.00. Metropolitan Washington Council of Government, 1875 Eye Street, Washington DC 20006. Tel (297)223-6800. LC Z6945, PN4801. DD 016.05. NLM Z 6945 J86.

JOURNAL L'ECLAIREUR ABITIBIEN. VFOAT Eclaireur. V. 1 Jan. 1977-. 0384-6784. Periodical. CN. French. mo. 50 Per No. J Albert, Journal l'Eclaireur Abitibien, C P 248 Valdor, Abitibi Quebec J9P 4P3 Canada. DD 071.1413.

JOURNALISM ABSTRACTS. See Indexes/Abstracts.

JOURNALISM DIRECTORY. See Yearbooks, Almanacs, Directories.

THE JOURNALISM EDUCATOR. 0022-5517. Periodical. US. English. qt. $20.00 Domestic, $25.00 Foreign. Association of Journalism and Mass Communications Educators, University of South Carolina/College of Journalism, Columbia SC 29208. Tel (803)777-2005. Ed Thomas A Bowers. Ind/Abst Educ. Index, Curr. Index J. Educ. LC PN4788. adv acc. Circ 2,461. Teaching techniques, new courses and technology, statistical information on students, schools, and careers in journalism.

JOURNALISM HISTORY. V. 1- Spring 1974-. 0094-7679. Periodical. US. English. qt. $15.00. Journalism Department of California State University, Darby Annex 103, Northridge CA 91330. Tel (818)717-5095. Ed Susan Henry. Ind/Abst Am. Hist. Life, Hist. Abstr., Part A, Mod. Hist. Abstr., Hist. Abst.,

Journalism

Part B, Twent. Century Abstr., Writ. Am. Hist., Ref. Source, Humanit. Index, Hist. Abstr. **LC** PN4700. **DD** 071.3. bk rev. adv acc. **Circ** 800. Publish articles on full scope of topics related to mass communications history. Emphasize contextual treatments and new approaches and understanding.

JOURNALISM MONOGRAPHS. No. 1- Aug. 1966-. 0022-5525. Monographic Series. US. English. qt. $25.00. Association for Education in Journalism, University of South Carolina, College of Journalism, Columbia SC 29208. **Tel** (803)777-2005. **Ed** Joe McKerns. **Ind/Abst** Hist. Abstr., Am. Hist. Life. adv acc. **Circ** 2,300. Numbers 1-17 available on microfilm from University Microfilms. In-depth research on a specific topic in the field of journalism.

JOURNALISM SCHOLARSHIP GUIDE. 0449-3354. US. English. an.

JOURNALISM STUDIES REVIEW. V. 1- June 1976-. Periodical. UK. English. an. 1.50. Wale University College, 34 Cathedral Road, Cardiff Wales United Kingdom. **LC** PN4701. **DD** 070.05.

JOURNALISMUS. V. 1- 1960-. GW. German. ir. Rhenisch-Bergische Druckerei und Verlagsgesellschaft, 4 Dusseldorf Schadowstrasse 11 Postfach 1135, Dusseldorf W Germany. **LC** PN4703.

DE JOURNALIST. Vol. 1-. 0022-555X. Periodical. NE. Dutch. sm. Tijl Tijdschriften BV, Postbus 9943, 1006 AP Amsterdam Netherlands. **LC** PN4705. *Katholieke Journalist, Journalist.*

JOURNALIST. V. 1- 1908-. 0022-5541. Periodical. UK. English. mo. $15.33. National Union of Journalists, 314-320 Grays Inn Road, London WC1X 8DP England. **Tel** 01-278 7916. **Ed** Bernie Corbett. bk rev. adv acc. **Circ** 34,000. (ctrl). Journal of the British and Irish National Union of Journalists. Mailed to the vast majority of journalists in newspapers, broadcasting, magazines, book and public relations.

THE JOURNALIST = PAO JEN = WARTAWAN. No. 1- 1978-. SI. Chinese (English and Malay). an. Singapore National Union of Journalists, 17-D Hilton Towers/Leonie Hill, Hsin-Chia-Po Singapore 9. **LC** PN4699. **DD** 079.5957.

JOURNALISTEN-HANDBUCH. German. ir. Wilhelmstrasse 42 62, Weisbaden West Germany. **LC** PN4703. *Wer Schreibt Woruber? Journalisten-Handbuch.*

JOURNALISTS' AFFAIRS. Periodical. English. ir. International Organization of Journalists, Prague 1 Parizska 9, Prague Czechoslovakia. **LC** PN4712.I54. **DD** 070.05.

THE KANSAS PUBLISHER. V. 16- Sept. 1949-. 0022-8737. Periodical. US. English. mo. Kansas Press Association, PO Box 1773, Topeka KS 66601. *Jayhawker Press.*

KIJI NO UCHIGAWA. 1-. JA. Japanese. ir. 250 Single Issue. Asahi Shinbunsha 3-2 Tsukiji 5 Chuo-ku, Tokyo-to 104 Japan. **LC** PN5407.R5.

KIROKU. Edition April 1979-. Periodical. JA. Japanese. ir. 4000. Kirokusha, 26-16 Nakano 5, Nakano-ku 164, Tokyo Japan. **LC** PN5401.

KOKURITSU KOKKAI TOSHOKAN SHOZO WA ZASSHI MOKUROKU. VFOAT National Diet Library Catalog of Japanese Periodicals. 0385-3861. Japanese. ir. **LC** Z6958.J3, PN5407.P4.

LETOPIS ZHURNALNYKH STATEI. 1926-. 0024-1202. Periodical. UR. Russian. wk. $332.00. Victor Kamkin Inc (57603), 12224 Parklawn Drive, Rockville MD 20852. **Tel** (301)881-5973. **Ind/Abst** Math. Rev. (cum index).

LITERARY AGENTS OF NORTH AMERICA MARKETPLACE. (LITERARY AGENTS OF NORTH AMERICA ... MARKETPLACE). 1983/84-. 8756-2219. US. English. an. $14.95 per Vol. Author Aid/Research Associates International, 340-52nd Street East, New York NY 10022. **DD** 070.5202573.

LITERARY AND JOURNALISTIC AWARDS IN CANADA. See Literature.

MAGAZINE QUALITATIVE AUDIENCES. Fall 1979-. 0278-7083. US. English. sa. Magazine Research Inc, 341 Madison Avenue, New York NY 10017. **LC** PN4888.R37. **DD** 051.

MAGAZINE TOTAL AUDIENCES. Fall 1979-. 0278-7075. US. English. sa. Magazine Research Inc, 341 Madison Avenue, New York NY 10017. **LC** PN4888.R37. **DD** 051.

THE MASTHEAD. Began with Spring 1949 issue. 0025-5122. Periodical. US. English. qt. $20.00. National Conference of Editorial Writers, 6223 Executive Boulevard, Rockville MD 20852. **Tel** (301)984-3015. **Ed** Mark A Stuart. **LC** PN4700. bk rev. **Circ** 1,000. Journal devoted to all aspects of producing a daily newspaper editorial page from determining page policy and writing to layout. Journalism education is discussed frequently.

MATTHEWS' LIST. **Main/Corp** Syd Matthews & Partners Limited. V. 1- Jan. 1957-. 0380-4437. Periodical. CN. English (French, Apr. 1978-). ty. Matthew & Partners Ltd, Box CP 1029, Pointe Claire Quebec Canada. **DD** 070.402571.

MEDIA. No. 1- Nov. 1977-. Periodical. HK. English. sm. $60.00. Specialist Publications Ltd, 12/F6 Rhemish Center 248-250 Hennessy Road, Wanchai Hong Kong. **Tel** (617)523-7680.

MEDIA AWARDS HANDBOOK. VAT Media Awards Hand Book. 1968-. 0271-8642. US. English. ir. Media Awards, 621 Sheri Lane, Danville CA 94526. **Tel** (415)837-7562. **Ed** Milton L Levy. **LC** AS8. **DD** 001.44. Directory of contests and awards in newspapers, radio, TV, magazines, advertising. *Honor Awards Handbook.*

MEDIA DATEN, FACHZEITSCHRIFTEN. See Bibliographies.

MEDIA DATEN, ZEITSCHRIFTEN MIT AUSLANDSTEIL. See Bibliographies.

MEDIA GUIDE INTERNATIONAL. EDITION, BUSINESS PUBLICATIONS. (MEDIA GUIDE INTERNATIONAL). 0098-9398. US. English. $110.00. Directories International, 1718 Sherman Avenue, Evanston IL 60201. **LC** Z6941, PN4801. **DD** 070.025. *Newsmedia Guide International.*

MEDIA HISTORY DIGEST. Vol. 1, No. 1 (Fall 1980)-. 0195-6779. Periodical. US. English. qt. $10.00. Editor and Publisher, 11 West 19th Street, New York NY 10011. **Tel** (212)675-4380. **Ed** Hiley Ward. adv acc. **Circ** 1,000. Digest type publication covering the history of news media in short story form.

MEDIA LAW REPORTER. See Law.

MEDIA MAGAZINE. Vol. 1, No. 1 (Nov. 14, 1982)-. 0821-5715. Periodical. CN. English. mo. 25.00. Media Magazine, 643 Yonge Street, Toronto Ontario M4Y 1Z9 Canada. **Tel** (416)927-7200. **Ed** Sherri Craig. **DD** 302.2340971. bk rev. adv acc. **Circ** 10,000. (ctrl). Media magazine reports on the business of the media industry in Canada. *Media Forum, 0228-2925.*

THE MEDIA REPORTER. VFOAT Media Report. 0309-0256. Periodical. UK. English. qt. Brennan Publications, 38 Legh Road, Allestree Derby England. **LC** PN4701. **DD** 072.91.

MEET THE PRESS : AMERICA'S PRESS CONFERENCE OF THE AIR. VFOAT America's Press Conference of the Air. Began with Jan. 6, 1957 issue. 0543-3754. Periodical. US. English. wk. $39.00. Kelly Press Inc, Box 8648, Washington DC 20011. **Tel** (301)386-2800. **Ind/Abst** Mag. Index, Access. **LC** E743.

MEIJI DAIGAKU TOSHOKAN SHOZO CHIKUJI KANKOBUTSU MOKUROKU : WA-OBUNHEN. See Bibliographies.

MEMBERSHIP LIST - INTERNATIONAL PRESS INSTITUTE. **Main/Corp** International Press Institute. English. ir. The Secretariat, 9 Munstergasse, 8001 Zurich Switzerland.

MICROGRAPHICS NEWSLETTER. V. 7 No. 1- Jan. 1975-. 0883-9808. Periodical. US. English. sm. $95.00 US/Canada, $110.00 All Other Countries. Microfilm Publishing Inc, PO Box 313 Wykagyl Station, New Rochelle NY 10804. **Tel** (914)235-5246. **Ed** Mitchell M Badler. **Ind/Abst** Predicasts, Funk Scott Index Corp. **DD** 686. bk rev. adv acc. Issued also in microform by University Microfilms International. News of the micrographics and related industries for users, vendors and other interested parties. *Microfilm Newsletter, 0026-2749.*

MILITARY MEDIA REVIEW. See Military Science.

MOUNTAIN LIBERATOR. V. 3- Oct. 1971-. Periodical. US. English. bw. *Liberator.*

NEUE DEUTSCHE PRESSE. 1-. 04707796. Periodical. SZ. German. sm. Kunst & Wissen Erich Bieber, Dufourstrasse 51, CH-8008 Zurich Switzerland. **LC** PN4703.

NEW JOURNALIST. No. 1-. 0310-365X. Periodical. English. qt. $5.90. New Journalist, PO Box K750, Hay Market 2000 Australia. **Ind/Abst** APAIS, Aust. Public Aff. Inf. Serv.

NEWARK PRESS. Began with issue for Oct. 1982?. 0741-9317. Periodical. US. English. bm. $10.00. Newark Press, 8123 19th Place, Adelphi MD 20783.

NEWSLETTER - CANADIAN SCIENCE WRITERS' ASSOCIATION. **Main/Corp** Canadian Science Writers' Association. Began publication in 1971?. 0703-217X. Periodical. CN. English. ir. Free. B Sheffield, Ontario Research Foundation, Sheridan Park, Mississauga Ontario L5K 1B3 Canada. **DD** 070.4495. (ctrl).

NEWSLETTER - COACH HOUSE PRESS. (NEWSLETTER). Began with Feb. 1977 issue. 0827-3146. Periodical. CN. English. ir. Free. Coach House Press, 401 Huron Street, Toronto Ontario M5S 2G5 Canada. **DD** 070.509713541. (ctrl).

THE NEWSLETTER ON NEWSLETTERS. Began in 1964. 0028-9507. Periodical. US. English. sm. $84.00. Newsletter Clearinghouse, PO Box 311, Rhinebeck NY 12572. **Tel** (914)876-2081. **Ed** Howard Penn Hudson. adv acc. For the newsletter professional—covering world or newsletters-information on management editing graphics promotions-reviews of new NLS.

NEWSWIRE. VFOAT JEA Newswire. **VAT** Journalism Education Association Newswire, News Wire. V. 1- 1973-. 0270-9783. Periodical. US. English. ty. Journalism Education Association, University of Dayton, Dayton OH 45469.

NIEMAN REPORTS. Began with Feb. 1947 issue. 0028-9817. Periodical. US. English. qt. Nieman Reports, PO Box 4951, Manchester NH 03108. **Tel** (617)495-2237. **Ed** Tenney Barbara K Lehman. **LC** PN4700. bk rev. **Circ** 1,800. Provides a forum for discussion of media-related issues by today's leading journalists, educators and public figures.

NOUVELLES - FEDERATION PROFESSIONNELLE DES JOURNALISTES DU QUEBEC. **Main/Corp** Federation Professionnelle des Journalistes du Quebec. 1975-. 0383-8900. Periodical. CN. French. Federation Professionnelle des Journalistes du Quebec, 1212 rue Panet, Montreal Quebec H2L 2Y7 Canada. **DD** 071.14. *Bulletin des Journalistes, 0382-0378.*

OPINION. See Law.

PAGES (CHICAGO, ILL.). (PAGES). 0883-6752. Periodical. US. English. mo. $120.00. Berry Publishing Company, 300 North State Street/Suite 4331, Chicago IL 60610. **DD** 070. *Steam from the Boiler.*

PANDUAN AKHBAR DAN MEDIA. VFOAT Press and Media Guide. English and Malay. ir. Jabatan Penerangan Malaysia, Kementerian Penerangan, Jalan Tun Perak, Kuala Lumpur Malaysia. **LC** Z6958.M3, PN5449.M35.

PAO HSUEH. VFOAT Journalism Magazine. Vol. 1- (1951)-. Periodical. CH. Chinese. sa. $2.00. Chung-Hua Min Kuo Hsin Wen Pien Chi Jen Hsieh Hui, 14-3 Hsi Ning South Road, Taipei Taiwan. **LC** PN4705. **DD** 070.05.

P.C.I. REVIEW. **Main/Corp** Press Council of India. VAT Press Council of India Review. V. 1- Jan. 1972-. Periodical. English. qt. Free. Press Council of India, 10 Janpath, New Delhi 110011 India. **Tel** 388885. **Ed** V P Malik. **LC** PN4705. **DD** 323.445. **Circ** 2,000. Special features on recent events of the press world, articles and adjudications of the council.

PENSEE DE BAGOT. (LA PENSEE DE BAGOT). 0826-2276. Newspaper. CN. French. wk. $25.00. Pensee de Bagot, C P 190, Acton Vale Quebec H0H 1A0 Canada. **DD** 071.14525.

PERS INDONESIA. Dec. 1974-. Periodical. Indonesian. ir. Ditjen PPG Departamen Penerangan, Jalan Veterna 7C (Atas), Jakarta Indonesia. **LC** PN4705.

POET'S MARKETS. 0883-5470. US. English. an. $16.95 Single Issue. Writer's Digest Books, 9933 Alliance Road, Cincinnati OH 45242. **DD** 070.

POLAR STAR. Newspaper. US. English. wk. University of Alaska, Department of Journalism, Fair Banks, AK 99701. **Tel** (907)479-7521.

PRASA POLSKA. Began with June 1947 issue. Periodical. PL. Polish. mo. ARS Polona, Krakowskie Przedmiescie 7, 00-068 Warsaw Poland. **LC** PN5355.P6.

THE PRESS AND THE PEOPLE : ANNUAL REPORT OF THE PRESS COUNCIL. **Main/Corp** Press Council. 0435-2459. UK. English. an. $1.53. The Press Council, No 1 Salisbury Square, London EC4Y BAE England. **LC** PN5111.P73. **DD** 070.05. *Press and the People.*

Journalism

PRESS REVIEW. V. 1- Jan./Feb. 1977-. 0706-9286. Periodical. CN. English. bm. $34.83. Press Review, PO Box 368 Station A, Toronto Ontario M5W 1C2 Canada. Tel (416)368-0512. Ed Sheila Johnston. DD 071.1. bk rev. adv acc. Circ 12,500. (ctrl). A communication national news media magazine covering newspaper, radio and television events, progress and controversy. Public relations and corporate and government relations are featured also.

THE PRESS WOMAN. 1937. 0032-7824. Periodical. US. English. mo. National Federation of Press Women, c/o L L Wolfe, Box 99, Blue Springs MO 64015. Tel (816)229-1666. Ed Lois Lauer Wolfe. adv acc. Circ 5,000. Articles of interest to the journalism profession with major emphasis on women in media careers.

DIE PRESSE DER SOWJETUNION. SZ. German. wk. Kunst & Wissen Erich Bieber, Dufourstrasse 51, CH-8008 Zurich Switzerland. LC AP30.

PRESSE-INFORMATION. Periodical. GW. German. bm. Umschau Verlag, Stuttgrtr Strasse 18-24, Postfach 110262, 6000 Frankfurt 1 West Germany.

PRESSENS ARBOG. See Yearbooks, Almanacs, Directories.

PROBLEMY ZHURNALISTIKI. Vol. 1-. UR. Russian. LC PN5271.

PRO/COMM. See Communication.

PUBLIZISTIK. Began with Jan./Feb. 1956 issue. 0033-4006. Periodical. GW. German. qt. $35.71. Universitatsverlag Konstanz, Postfach 6632, D-7750 Konstanz West Germany. Ind/Abst Recent Publ. Artic., Sociol. Abstr., Lang. Lang. Behav. Abstr. LC PN4703. DD 070.05.

P.W.A.C. NATIONAL NEWSLETTER. VAT Periodical Writers Association of Canada National Newsletter. 0822-4706. Periodical. CN. English. ir. Periodical Writers Association of Canada, 24 Ryerson Avenue, Toronto Ontario M5T 2P3 Canada. DD 070.17506071. P.W.A.C. Newsletter, 0711-5946.

PYONJIBIN HYOPHOE PO. VFOAT Sinmun Pyonjibin Hyophoe po. V. 1-. Periodical. Korean. ir. LC PN4705.

QUARTO POTERE. Yearly V. 1- Oct/Dec. 1973-. IT. Italian. ir. 1000 Single Issue. Sala Stampa, Posta Centrale Piazza Matteotti, Napoli Italy. LC PN4705.

THE QUILL. V. 1-. 0033-6475. Periodical. US. English. an. $18.00. Society of Professional Journalists, 840 North Lake Shore Drive, Chicago IL 60611. Tel (312)649-0060. Ed Ron Dorfman. Ind/Abst Humanit. Index. LC PN4700. DD 070.5. adv acc. Circ 28,000.

QUILL AND SCROLL. 0033-6505. Periodical. US. English. ir. $17.00. Quill and Scroll Society, School of Journalism, State University of Iowa, Iowa IA 52240. Tel (319)353-4475. Ed Richard P Johns. Ind/Abst Curr. Index J. Educ. bk rev. adv acc. Circ 15,000. (ctrl). Publishes articles and information related to secondary schools: Newspapers, yearbooks, and other publications.

R. I. BULLETIN. Main/Corp ANPA Research Institute. VAT Research Institute Bulletin. 0146-1222. US. English. American Newspaper Publishers Association Research Institute, PO Box 598, Easton PA 18044. LC PN4734. DD 338.76107050973.

RASPROSTRANENIE PECHATI. June 1948-. Periodical. UR. Russian. mo. $23.50. Victor Kamkin Inc (70779), 12224 Parklawn Drive, Rockville MD 20852. Tel (301)881-5973.

REAL STORY. (THE REAL STORY). VAT Real Story Newsletter, Newsletter. The Real Story. 0226-6571. Periodical. CN. English. bw. The Real Story, T V Ontario, PO Box 200 Station Q, Toronto Ontario M4T 2T1 Canada. DD 070.172.

REGISTR PERIODICHESKIKH IZDANII STRAN-CHLENOV MTSNTI. CHAST II : VSPOMOGATELNYE UKAZATELI. See Bibliographies.

REPERTOIRE DE LA PRESSE SUISSE. VFOAT Leitfaden der Schweizer Presse. Began with 1969/70 vol. French, German or Italian. ir. Data Information Services, 81 Route de l'Aire, Geneve 1211 26 Switzerland. LC Z6956.S92, PN5334.

RESOURCE-MAG. Vol. 1, No. 1 (Jan. 1982)-. 0712-7243. Periodical. CN. English. mo. 30.18. 18 Van Dusen Boulevard, Toronto Ontario M8Z 3E5 Canada. Tel (416)231-7796. Ed Lynn McFadgen. DD 070.5720688. bk rev. A promotion-oriented newsletter for the magazine trade. Includes promotion tips, news, developments, a professional development article, book review, and around-up of note worthy articles in the trade press.

REVIEW - CENTRE FOR INVESTIGATIVE JOURNALISM. (REVIEW). VFOAT Revue. VAT Centre for Investigative Journalism Review, Revue. Centre pour le Journalisme d'Enquete. 1982-. 0822-2096. CN. English (French). an. Free. Centre for Investigative Journalism, Carleton University, 324 St Patrick's Building, Ottawa Ontario K1S 5B6 Canada. DD 051. (ctrl). Revue Annuelle (Centre for Investigative Journalism), 0826-4732.

ST. LOUIS JOURNALISM REVIEW. (THE ST. LOUIS JOURNALISM REVIEW). VFOAT SJR. VAT Saint Louis Journalism Review. V. 1- (No. 1-). 0036-2972. Periodical. US. English. mo. $13.00 Domestic, $22.00 Foreign. St Louis Journalism Review, 8606 Olive Boulevard, St Louis MO 63132. LC PN4899.S25. DD 071.7866. Focus Midwest.

SAL VUOSIKIRJA. See Yearbooks, Almanacs, Directories.

SALT. V. 1- Jan. 1974-. 0160-7537. Periodical. US. English. ir. Salt, PO Box 1400, Kennebunkport ME 04046. Tel (207)967-3311. Ed Pamela H Wood. LC F26. DD 974.10405. adv acc. Circ 5,000. A cultural journalism field project involving students and professionals using an interdisciplinary perspective in examining and documenting Maine and its people (their lives and work).

SASKATCHEWAN JOURNALIST CEASED. (THE SASKATCHEWAN JOURNALIST). V. 1, No. 4, Feb. 1976-V. 3, No. 6. 0384-0964. Periodical. CN. English. Free to Members, $4.00 Nonmembers. Saskatchewan Journalists' Association, 1964 Park Street, Regina Saskatchewan S4N 2G6 Canada. DD 070.0627124. S J A Newsletter, 0384-0956.

SCHOLASTIC EDITOR'S TRENDS IN PUBLICATIONS. VFOAT Trends in Publications. 1921. 0745-2357. Periodical. US. English. ir. $16.00. University of Minnesota, 620 Rarig Center, 330 21st Avenue South, Minneapolis MN 55455. Tel (612)373-3180. Ed Tom E Rolnicki. DD 070. bk rev. adv acc. Circ 2,200. (ctrl). Scholastic publications. High school and college trends in newspapers, yearbooks, and magazines. Scholastic Editor, 0279-8980.

THE SCHOOL PRESS REVIEW. V. 1- Apr. 1925-. 0036-6730. Periodical. US. English. qt. $12.00. Columbia Scholastic Press Association, Box 11, Columbia University, New York NY 19927-6969. Tel (212)280-3311. Ed Edmund J Sullivan. LC LB3621.A2. DD 371.805. bk rev. adv acc. Circ 3,100. Available in microform from Xerox University Microfilms. How-to articles and general features for student editors of newspapers, magazines and yearbooks in colleges and high schools.

SCIENCE LINK. 0821-7246. Periodical. CN. English. ir. 35.00. Canadian Science Writers Association c/o Jim Steinhart, 559 Deloraine Avenue, Toronto Ontario M5M 2C5 Canada. Tel (416)787-2138. Ed Grant Buckler. DD 070.44950971. bk rev. adv acc. Circ 350. Covers professional development of journalists and public relations people communicating science and technology in Canada. Covers media news and leads on science stories, plus CSWA activities.

SENMON SHINBUN YORAN. JA. Japanese. ir. Nihon Senmon Shinbun Kyokai, 2-12 Toranomon 1 Minato-ku, Tokyo-to 105 Japan. LC Z6958.J3, PN5404.

SESITY NOVINARE. Periodical. CS. Czech. qt. Artia, PO Box 790, Praha 1 Czechoslovakia. LC PN5355.C95.

SHIMBUN RONCHO. 0303-5905. JA. Japanese. mo. 280 Single Issue. Shimbun Geppo Sha, 3-1 Uchisaiwaicho 1-chome Chiyoda-ku, Tokyo Japan. LC PN5401.

SMACKWARM. 0732-1198. Periodical. US. English. sa. $3.50. Smackwarm, Creative Writing Program, Annex 21, University of Nebraska, Omaha NE 68182.

S/N. SPEECHWRITER'S NEWSLETTER. See Communication.

SOURCES CANADA. 1st- Ed. 0381-6400. CN. English. sa. $20.12. Sources, 9 St Nicholas Street Suite 402, Toronto Ontario M4Y 1W5 Canada. Tel (416)964-7799. Ed Barrie Zwicker. DD 338.476871102571. bk rev. adv acc. Circ 11,500. (ctrl). A directory of organizations and their contacts for editors, reporters and researchers. Controlled distribution across Canada to the media.

SOURCES (TORONTO, ONT. : 1981). (SOURCES). Fall 1981-. 0700-480X. Periodical. CN. English. sa. Free to Members. Sources, 91 Raglan Avenue, Toronto Ontario M6C 2K7 Canada. DD 061.105. Content, 0045-835X.

SOUTHERN PROGRESSIVE PERIODICALS DIRECTORY. See Yearbooks, Almanacs, Directories.

SPS NEWSREPORT. Main/Corp Student Press Service. VFOAT Student Press Service News Report. 0274-9777. Periodical. US. English. ir. $36.00. Student Press Service News Report, Cardinal Station, Washington DC 20064. Newsreport - Student Press Service.

STAMM LEITFADEN DURCH PRESSE UND WERBUNG. See Yearbooks, Almanacs, Directories.

STATUS NEWS. Main/Corp Association for Education in Journalism. Committee on the Status of Women in Journalism Education. Sept. 1977-. 0739-9146. Periodical. US. English. bm. $3.00 Members, $4.00 Nonmembers. Status News, School of Journalism, Southern Illinois University, Carbondale IL 62901.

STREUDATEN DER SCHWEIZER PRESSE : ZEITUNGEN, ANZEIGER UND AMTSBLATTER. VFOAT Donnees de Diffusion de la Presse Suisse : Journaux, Feuilles d'Annonces et Feuilles Officielles. French and German. ir. Seestrasse 5 Postfach 623, 8027 Zurich Switzerland. LC PN5337.C5.

THE STUDENT PRESS. 1971-. US. English. an. R Rosen Press, 29 East 21st Street, New York NY 10010. LC LB3621. DD 378.19897.

THE SUBSCRIBER & PRIMARY AUDIENCE STUDY DIGEST. (THE SUBSCRIBER AND PRIMARY AUDIENCE STUDY DIGEST). Fall 1979-. 0197-9892. Periodical. US. English. sa. $25.00. The Media Book Inc, 75 East 5th Street, New York NY 10022. LC PN4888.R37. DD 070.5720688.

SUVREMENNA ZHURNALISTIKA. Periodical. Bulgarian (summaries in English and Russian). qt. 6.00. Bratia Miladinovi No 12, 1000 Sofiia Bulgaria. LC P87.

SYNDICATED COLUMNISTS DIRECTORY. See Yearbooks, Almanacs, Directories.

TAN-CHIANG WEN LI HSUEH YUAN CHUNG WAI CHI KAN PAO CHIH MU LU. VFOAT Tamkang List of Serials. CH. Chinese (English). an. Department of Reader Services, Chueh Shen Memorial Library, Tamkang College of Arts and Sciences, Taipei Taiwan. LC Z6958.T34, PN4832. DD 011.34.

TOWERS CLUB USA NEWSLETTER. Main/Corp Towers Club USA. VAT Towers Club United States of America Newsletter. 0193-4953. Periodical. US. English. mo. $60.00. Towers Club USA Newsletter, PO Box 2038, Vancouver WA 98668-2038. Tel (206)574-3084. Ed Jerry Buchanan. bk rev. adv acc. Circ 4,000. (ctrl). Covers all aspects of writing and marketing how-to-do-it books and reports. Neophytes or professional freelance writers gain tremendous advantage in profit-taking.

TRAINING OF JOURNALISTS. Published in 1959. Periodical. English. qt. Lenseignement du Journalisme, 10 rue Schiller, Strasbourg France.

TRENDS IN COMMUNIST MEDIA. Periodical. US. English. wk. National Technical Information Service, Executive Office of the President, Foreign Broadcast Information Service, 5285 Port Royal Road, Springfield VA 22161.

TRENDS IN COMMUNIST MEDIA. See Political Science - Socialism, Communism, Anarchism, Utopianism.

UKRAJINSKYJ ZURNALIST. (UKRAINSKYI ZHURNALIST). VFOAT Ukrainian Journalist. Began in 1968. 0380-1403. Periodical. CN. Ukrainian. The

Ukrainian Journalist, 140 Bathurst Street, Toronto Ontario M5V 2R3 Canada. **DD** 070.023.

THE UNDERGROUND AND ALTERNATIVE PRESS IN BRITAIN. **VFOAT** Underground Press. 1972-. UK. English. an. Harvester Press, 2 Stanford Terrace, Nr Brighton Sussex, Hassocks England.

U.S. PUBLICITY DIRECTORY. BUSINESS & FINANCE. See Yearbooks, Almanacs, Directories.

U.S. PUBLICITY DIRECTORY. MAGAZINES. See Yearbooks, Almanacs, Directories.

UPEC. **Main/Corp** UPEXC. **VAT** Union de Periodistas de Cuba. **CU.** Spanish. ir. Buro Ejecutive, Union de Periodistas de Cuba, Calle 23, No. 452, Exquina A I Havana Cuba. **LC** PN4705. **DD** 079.7291.

VESTNIK MOSKOVSKOGO UNIVERSITETA. SERIIA X : ZHURNALISTIKA. **Main/Corp** Moscow. Universitet. Began in 1977. Periodical. UR. Russian. bm. Victor Kamkin Inc, 12224 Parklawn Drive, Rockville MD 20852. **Tel** (301)881-5973. **Ind/Abst** Chem. Abstr. **LC** PN4705. Vestnik. Seriia XI: Zhurnalistika.

VICE VERSA (MONTREAL, QUEBEC). (VICE VERSA). V. 1, No. 1 (Summer 1983)-. 0821-6827. Periodical. CN. English (Italian). qt. $1.00 Per No. Vice Versa, PO Box 633 Station N D G, Montreal Quebec H4A 3R1 Canada. **DD** 071.14. Quaderni Culturali, 0712-5186.

VUPROSI NA SUVREMENNATA ZHURNALISTIKA : BIULETIN NA NAUCHNOIZSLEDOVATELSKIIA TSENTUR PO ZHURNALISTIKA PRI SBZH. No. 1-. Periodical. BU. Bulgarian. ir. 6.00. Tsentur, Sofiia, Ul Bratia Miladinovi No 12, Sofiia Bulgaria. **LC** PN4705.

WASHINGTON JOURNALISM REVIEW CEASED. **VFOAT** WJR. V. 1, Oct. 1977. Ceased in 1981. 0149-1172. Periodical. US. English. $22.00. Washington Journalism Review, 2233 Wisconsin Avenue NW/Suite 442, Washington DC 20007. **Tel** (202)333-6800. **LC** AP2. **DD** 051.

WHAT THEY SAID. 1969-. 0512-5804. US. English. an. 32.50. Monitor Book Company Inc, PO Box 3668, Beverly Hills CA 90212. **Tel** (213)271-5558. Ed Alan F Pater and Jason R Pater. **LC** D410. **DD** 901.94. A collection of quotations from speeches, interviews, etc., by persons in all walks of life categorized by subject.

THE WORKING PRESS OF THE NATION. 1945-. 0084-1323. US. English. an. $250.00. National Research Bureau Inc, 424 Third Street, Burlington IA 52601. **Tel** (312)663-5580. Ed Nancy Veatch. **LC** PN4875. **Circ** 1,500. Directory of newspapers, magazines, television and radio stations, and internal corporate reports. Includes data on publicity outlets and personnel in the media industry. Working Press of New York City, Gebbie House Magazine Directory, 0072-0526.

WORLD PRESS DIGEST. V. 1- Oct. 1979-. 0225-5790. Periodical. CN. English. mo. World Press Digest Canada Ltd, 258 Sheppard Avenue East Suite 7, Willowdale Ontario M2N 3B1 Canada. **Tel** (416)225-5013. **DD** 051.

THE WRITER; A MONTHLY MAGAZINE FOR LITERARY WRITERS. See Literature.

THE WRITERS DIRECTORY. See Yearbooks, Almanacs, Directories.

THE WRITER'S HANDBOOK. 1936-. 0084-2710. US. English. an. $21.95. Writer Inc, 120 Boylston Street, Boston MA 02116. **Tel** (617)423-3157. Ed Sylvia K Burack. **LC** PN137. **DD** 029.6. Standard reference book on all writing fields: 100 articles of instruction on writing and selling fiction, nonfiction, plays, poetry, etc., plus over 2,000 markets for manuscripts sales.

WRITER'S LIFELINE. Issue No. 106- Jan. 15, 1979-. 0225-610X. Periodical. CN. English. mo. $40.24. Writers Lifeline, Box 1641, Cornwall Ontario K6H 5V6 Canada. **Tel** (705)679-8375. **DD** 808.0205. Lifeline, 0316-0602.

WRITER'S YEARBOOK. See Yearbooks, Almanacs, Directories.

ZHURNALIST. Jan. 1967-. 0022-5568. Periodical. UR. Russian. mo $24.50. Victor Kamkin Inc (70841), 12224 Parklawn Drive, Rockville MD 20852. **Tel** (301)881-5973. Sovetskaia Pechat.

ZHURNALIST, PRESSA, AUDITORIIA. Began in 1975. 0134-8442. Periodical. UR. Russian. 1.30. **LC** PN4749. **DD** 070.05.

ZHURNALIST UKRAINY. UR. Ukrainian. 0.15 Each issue. Spilka Zhurnalistiv URSR, Brest-Litovskii Prospekt 94, Kyiv USSR. **LC** PN5278.U4.

ZHURNALISTYKA. Began in 1976. 0135-1907. Periodical. UR. Ukrainian (Russian). 1.30. **LC** PN5277.C6.

LAW

1ST READING. **VFOAT** First Reading. 1978. 0744-6748. Periodical. US. English. wk. $25.00 Members, $50.00 Nonmembers. California Hospital Association, PO Box 1100, Sacramento CA 95805. **Tel** (916)443-7401. Ed Ted Fourhas. **Circ** 1,380. Covers legislation affecting the healthcare industry.

20TH CENTURY LEGAL PHILOSOPHY SERIES. V. 1-. 0082-7088. Monographic Series. US. English. ir. Harvard University Press, 79 Garden Street, Cambridge MA 02138. **Tel** (617)661-3761.

ABA JOURNAL. **VFOAT** A.B.A. Journal. **VAT** American Bar Association Journal. Jan. 1984-. 0747-0088. Periodical. US. English. mo. $36.00. American Bar Association, 750 North Lake Shore Drive, Chicago IL 60611. **Tel** (312)988-5555. **Ind/Abst** Women Stud. Abstr., Account. Index. Suppl. **LC** K1. **DD** 349.7305, 347.3005. American Bar Association Journal, 0002-7596.

ABA LAWYERS' TITLE GUARANTY FUNDS NEWSLETTER. **Main/Corp** American Bar Association. Standing Committee on Lawyers' Title Guaranty Funds. **VFOAT** Lawyers' Title Guaranty Funds Newsletter. **VAT** American Bar Association Lawyers' Title Guaranty Funds Newsletter. 0361-3763. US. English. $1.00 Single Issue. American Bar Association Standing Committee on Lawyers' Title Guaranty Funds, 1155 East 60th Street, Chicago IL 60637. **LC** KF1234.A15. **DD** 346.73086.

ABA SECTION OF TAXATION ANNUAL ADVANCED STUDY SESSIONS, ADVANCED TAX PLANNING FOR CLOSELY HELD BUSINESS : ALI-ABA COURSE OF STUDY, MATERIALS. **VFOAT** A.B.A. Section of Taxation Annual Advanced Study Sessions, Advanced Tax Planning for Closely Held Business. US. English. an. 4025 Chestnut Street, Philadelphia, PA 19104. **LC** KF6484.Z9. **DD** 343.73067, 347.30367.

ABA SECTION OF TAXATION ANNUAL ADVANCED STUDY SESSIONS. SELECTED PROBLEMS AND TECHNIQUES IN ESTATE PLANNING. (ABA SECTION OF TAXATION ANNUAL ADVANCED STUDY SESSIONS, SELECTED PROBLEMS AND TECHNIQUES IN ESTATE PLANNING : ALI-ABA COURSE OF STUDY MATERIALS). **VFOAT** A.B.A. Section of Taxation Annual Advanced Study Sessions, Selected Problems and Techniques in Estate Planning. **VAT** American Bar Association Section of Taxation Annual Advanced Study Sessions, Selected Problems and Techniques in Estate Planning. 0732-8184. US. English. an. 4025 Chestnut Street, Philadelphia, PA 19104. **LC** KF6585. **DD** 343.73053, 347.30353.

ABA SOFTWARE REVIEW. **VFOAT** Software Review. **VAT** American Bar Association Software Review, Legal Technology Advisory Council Software Review. Vol. 1, No. 2 I.E. 1 (May 1985)-. 0883-4695. Periodical. US. English. ir. ABA Order Fulfillment, 750 North Lake Shore Drive, Chicago IL 60611. **DD** 001.

ABA/BNA LAWYERS' MANUAL ON PROFESSIONAL CONDUCT. CURRENT REPORTS. **VFOAT** A.B.A./B.N.A. Lawyers' Manual on Professional Conduct. **VAT** American Bar Association, Bureau of National Affairs Lawyer's Manual on Professional Conduct. Began with Vol. 1, No. 1 (Jan. 25, 1984). 0740-4050. US. English. bw. $356.00. Bureau of National Affairs, 1231 25th Street Northwest, Washington DC 20037. **Tel** (202)785-6868. Ed Robert A Robbins. bk rev. **Circ** 2,000. Reports on developments affecting lawyers' professional lives, with accompanying loose-leaf manual that covers full range of ethical and professional topics.

ABCS OF THE CALIFORNIA BOATING LAW. US. English. Department of Navigation and Ocean Developments, 1416 Ninth Street/Room 1336, Sacramento CA 95814. **LC** KFC524.P5. **DD** 343.7940965.

ABINGDON CLERGY INCOME TAX GUIDE. See Business - Public Finance.

ABSTRACTS OF BOOK REVIEWS IN CURRENT LEGAL PERIODICALS. See Indexes/Abstracts.

ABSTRACTS OF SUPREME COURT DECISIONS INTERPRETING THE INTERSTATE COMMERCE ACT. See Indexes/Abstracts.

ACCENT ON COURTS. V. 1- Aug. 1977-. Periodical. US. English. bm. Accent on Courts, Administrative Office of Courts, Frankfort Ky 40601. **Tel** (502)564-7486. **LC** KFK1708.A15. **DD** 347.7690105.

ACCESS REPORTS, PRIVACY. 0191-6688. Periodical. US. English. bw. $127.00. Plus Publications Inc, 2626 Pennsylvania Avenue NW, Washington DC 20037. **LC** KF1262.A15. **DD** 342.730858.

ACCESS REPORTS. REFERENCE FILE. (ACCESS REPORTS REFERENCE FILE). **VFOAT** Reference File. V. 1- 1975-. 0191-6696. Periodical. US. English. mo. $295.00. Washington Monitor, 1301 Pennsylvania Avenue NW/Suite 1000, Washington DC 20004. **Tel** (202)347-7757. Ed R L Plesser.

ACCOUNTANTS' LIABILITY. See Business - Accounting.

ACCOUNTING FOR LAWYERS. See Business - Accounting.

ACCOUNTS FOR THE YEAR ENDED 31ST DECEMBER . . . : AUDITOR-GENERAL'S REPORT. See Business - Public Finance.

ACQUISITIONS AND MERGERS. Series/Titl Corporate Law and Practice Course Handbook Series. 0883-4407. US. English. an. Practising Law Institute, 810 Seventh Avenue, New York NY 10019.

ACROSS THE TABLE. See Economics - Labor.

ACTA JURIDICA (CAPE TOWN, SOUTH AFRICA). (ACTA JURIDICA). 1958-. 0065-1346. Periodical. English. an. $23.10. Juta & Company, P O Box 123, Kenwyn, 7790 South Africa. **Tel** 711181. Ed I Leeman. **Circ** 378. (ctrl). An annual volume of articles and discussions on current legal problems. Butterworths South African Law Review.

ACTAS PROCESALES DEL DERECHO VIVO. V. 1- 1971-. 0254-072X. Periodical. Spanish. mo. Apartado 6593 Carmelitas, Caracas 101 Venezuela. **Ind/Abst** Foreign Lang. Index. **LC** K1.

ACTION (BURLINGAME, CALIF.). See Education (General).

ACTIONS OF THE . . . MINNESOTA LEGISLATURE. **Main/Corp** Minnesota. Office of Revisor of Statutes. Began with Vol. for 1979. US. English. an. $2.50 Per Copy. State Register and Documents Division, State Department of Administration, 117 University Avenue, St Paul MN 55155. **LC** KFM5415. **DD** 348.776026, 347.760826. Actions of the Minnesota Legislature.

ACTIVITE DES COURS ET TRIBUNAUX. STATISTIQUES DIVERSES. See Statistics.

ACTIVITIES AND SUMMARY REPORT OF THE COMMITTEE ON THE DISTRICT OF COLUMBIA, HOUSE OF REPRESENTATIVES. **Main/Corp** United States. Congress. House. Committee on the District of Columbia. 0277-1845. US. English. be. **LC** KF31.8. **DD** 328.7307652.

ACTS FOR THE YEAR . . . SAINT VINCENT AND THE GRENADINES. **Main/Corp** Saint Vincent and the Grenadines. English. an. 32.00. Government Printing Office,

Law

Kingstown St Vincent and The Grenadines. *Laws, Etc. Acts.*

L'ACTUALITE JURIDIQUE : DROIT ADMINISTRATIF. VFOAT AJDA. Periodical. FR. French. mo. $112.41. Actualite Juridique, 17 rue d'Uzes, 75002 Paris France. LC K1. DD 342.440605, 344.402605. *Actualite Juridique.*

L'ACTUALITE JURIDIQUE. PROPRIETE IMMOBILIERE. VFOAT Propriete Immobiliere. 0001-7736. Periodical. French. mo. 335. 17 rue d'Uzes, 75002 Paris France. DD 346.4404305, 344.4064305.

ACUALITE LEGISLATIVE DALLOZ. (ACTUALITE LEGISLATIVE DALLOZ). Vol. 1, No. 1 (Jan. 1983)-. Periodical. FR. French. sm. 11 Rue Soufflot, 75240 Paris Cedex 05 France. DD 349.44 344.4.

ADAMS COUNTY LEGAL JOURNAL. V. 1- 1959/60-. US. English. ir. Gaunt & Sons, 3011 Gulf Drive, Holmes Beach FL 33510. LC Microfilm LL-0171 KFP, KFP52. A3.

ADCA. AMERICAN DIRECTORY OF COLLECTION AGENCIES AND ATTORNEYS. See Yearbooks, Almanacs, Directories.

THE ADELAIDE LAW REVIEW. V. 1- Apr. 1960-. 0065-1915. Periodical. AT. English. sa. Dennis and Company Inc, 251 Main Street, Buffalo NY 14203. Ind/Abst Leg. Resour. Index, APAIS, Aust. Public Aff. Inf. Serv., Index Leg. Period. DD 349.9405, 349.4005. Index published separately - free - automatically sent.

ADELPHIA LAW JOURNAL. Vol. 1, No. 1 (Spring 1982)-. 8756-3630. Periodical. US. English. sa. Adelphia Law Journal, Sigma Nu Phi Legal Fraternity, 9700 Fernwood Road, Bethesda MD 20034. DD 340.

ADIL (KUALA LUMPUR, MALAYSIA). (ADIL). Periodical. English (in Malay). sp. c/o The Attorney General's Chamber, Tingkat 11, Bangunan Bank Rakyat, JL. Tangsi, Kuala Lumpur Malaysia. LC K1. DD 349.59505, 345.95005.

ADMINISTRATION OF JUSTICE MEMORANDA. 0147-3603. US. English. University of North Carolina at Chapel Hill, Institute of Government, Chapel Hill NC 27514. LC KFN7908.A15. DD 347.756.

ADMINISTRATION OF JUSTICE STATISTICS . . . ESTIMATES. See Statistics.

ADMINISTRATION OF PUBLIC LAWS 81-874 & 81-815 - UNITED STATES. DEPT. OF EDUCATION. See Education (General).

ADMINISTRATION PUBLIQUE - INSTITUT BELGE DES SCIENCES ADMINISTRATIVES. Main/Corp Institut Belge des Sciences Administratives. 1.- Yearly Vol. Periodical. French. ir. 1.000. Institut Belge des Sciences Administratives, 98 rue Sainte Bernard, Bruxelles 1060 Belgium. Tel 32.25365922. DD 342.49306. bk rev. adv acc. Circ 600.

ADMINISTRATIVE LAW. 1st- Ed. 0149-3272. US. English. Gilbert Law Summaries, 14415 South Main Street, Gardena CA 90248. LC KF5402.Z9. DD 342.73066.

ADMINISTRATIVE LAW BULLETIN. (THE ADMINISTRATIVE LAW BULLETIN). V. 1- 1973-. 0575-3368. US. English. Office of Administrative Hearings, 915 Capitol Mall/Room 470, Sacramento CA 95814. LC KFC780.A73. DD 342.7940605. *Administrative Law Bulletin.*

ADMINISTRATIVE LAW JUDGE DECISIONS REPORT. Main/Corp United States. Federal Labor Relations Authority. No. 1 (Nov. 27, 1981)-. 0742-616X. US. English. an. F.L.R.A. Office of Administrative Law Judges #416, 1111 20th Street NW, Washington DC 20036. LC KF5365. DD 344.730180264, 347.304180264.

ADMINISTRATIVE LAW NEWS. (THE ADMINISTRATIVE LAW NEWS). Began with: V. 1 Oct. 1974. 0567-9494. Periodical. US. English. qt. 1155 East 60th Street, Chicago IL 60637. Ind/Abst Leg. Resour. Index. *Administrative Law News (American Bar Association. Section on Administration Law : 1961).*

ADMINISTRATIVE LAW NEWSLETTER. 0094-1093. Periodical. US. English. qt. 1510 Fulton National Bank Building, 55 Marietta Street NW, Atlanta GA 30303. LC KFG440.A73. DD 342.7580605.

ADMINISTRATIVE LAW NOTES. 0742-9673. Periodical. US. English. ir. Federal Bar Association, 1815 H Street NW, Washington DC 20006. LC KF5401.A15. DD 342.730605, 347.302605.

ADMINISTRATIVE LAW REPORTS (AGINCOURT, ONT.). (ADMINISTRATIVE LAW REPORTS). V. 1, Pt. 1 (Oct./Nov. 1983)-. 0824-2615. Periodical. CN. English. mo. $65.00. Carswell Legal Publications, 2330 Midlands Avenue, Agincourt Ontario M1S 1P7 Canada. DD 342.71066402642.

ADMINISTRATIVE LAW REVIEW. Vol. 13 Fall 1960-. 0001-8368. Periodical. US. English. qt. $22.00. American Bar Association, 750 North Lake Shore Drive, Chicago IL 60611. Tel (312)988-5555. Ind/Abst Manage. Contents, Trade Ind. Index, Leg. Resour. Index, Index Leg. Period., Soc. Sci. Citation Index, Curr. Law Index, Contents Curr. Leg. Period. (cum index). adv acc. (ctrl) *Administrative Law Bulletin.*

ADMINISTRATIVE REGISTER OF KENTUCKY. 1974. 0096-1493. US. English. mo. $36.00. Legislative Research Commission, State Capital Room 300, Frankfort KY 40601. Tel (502)564-8100. Ed Susan C Harding. LC KFK1236. DD 348.769025. Circ 800. (ctrl). Proposed KY regulations, amendments, emergency regulations, and public hearings scheduled.

ADVANCE ANNOTATION SERVICE TO COLORADO REVISED STATUTES, 1973. Main/Corp Colorado. VFOAT Advance Annotation Service. Began in 1982. 0747-6914. Periodical. US. English. ty. Ed D P Harriman.

ADVANCE ANNOTATION SERVICE TO THE CODE OF ALABAMA 1975. (ADVANCE ANNOTATION SERVICE TO THE CODE OF ALABAMA 1975). 1980-1981, No. 1-. 0747-6612. Periodical. US. English. ty. Michie Company, Bobbs-Merrill Law Publishers, PO Box 7587, Charlottesville VA 22906-7587.

ADVANCED CRIMINAL TRIAL TACTICS FOR PROSECUTION AND DEFENSE. Series/Titl Litigation and Administrative Practice Series. US. English. an. Practising Law Institute, 810 7th Avenue, New York NY 10019. LC KF9656.Z9. DD 354.7307, 347.3057.

ADVANCED IMMIGRATION WORKSHOP. Series/Titl Litigation and Administrative Practice Series. Litigation Course Handbook Series. 8756-873X. US. English. an. Practising Law Institute, 810 7th Avenue, New York NY 10019. LC KF4819.3. DD 342.73082, 347.30282. *Advanced Immigration, 8756-4270.*

ADVANCED REAL ESTATE LAW COURSE. See Real Estate.

ADVANCED WILL DRAFTING. Series/Titl Estate Planning Administration Course Handbook Series** Tax Law and Estate Planning Series. 0732-7579. US. English. an. Practising Law Institute, 810 7th Avenue, New York NY 10019. LC KF755.Z9. DD 346.73054, 347.30654.

ADVANCES IN LAW AND CHILD DEVELOPMENT. Vol. 1 (1982)-. 0732-3565. US. English. ir. $49.50. JAI Press, PO Box 1678, Greenwich CT 06836. Tel (203)661-7602. Ed R L Sprague. Ind/Abst Psychol. Abstr. LC K1. DD 346.730135, 347.306135. NLM W1 AD654F.

ADVERTISING LAW ANTHOLOGY. V. 1- 1973-. 0093-1985. US. English. an. International Library, 3865 Wilson Boulevard/Suite 100-A, Arlington VA 22203. Tel (703)522-8624. LC KF1614.A73. DD 343.73082.

ADVOCACIA DINAMICA : ADV. VFOAT Adv. Periodical. BL. Portuguese. ir. Coad Atualizadora Fiscal Ltda, Av Nove de Julho 3 766, Jardim Paulista, Sao Paulo Brazil. LC KHD72.2. DD 348.81046, 34810846.

ADVOCACIA DINAMICA, SELECOES JURIDICAS : ADV. VFOAT Adv. Periodical. SP. Portueuges. mo. Sistema Coad de Atualizacao Profissional, Avenida Nove de Julho 3 766, Jardim Paulista, CEP 01406, Sao Paulo SP Brazil. LC K1. DD 349.8105, 348.1005.

ADVOCATE. (THE ADVOCATE). V. 1- March 1943-. 0044-6416. Periodical. CN. English. bm. $11.61. Vancouver Bar Association, 4765 Polot House Road, West Vancouver British Columbia Canada V7W 1J2. Tel (604)925-2122. Ed David Roberts. bk rev. adv acc. Circ 6,300. Published by the Vancouver Bar Association and contains legal and educational matter particular reference to the practice of law in British Columbia.

THE ADVOCATE. V. 1- Apr. 1954-. 0400-6216. Periodical. US. English. ir. $10.00. Bronx County Bar Association, 851 Grand Concourse, Bronx NY 10451. LC UNC.

THE ADVOCATE. (THE ADVOCATE : THE SUFFOLK UNIVERSITY LAW SCHOOL JOURNAL). Began publication in 1968. 0568-0425. Periodical. US. English. sa. $6.00. Suffolk University Law School, 41 Temple Street, Boston MA 02114. Tel (617)723-4700. LC KF292.S8414. DD 349.73, 347.3.

ADVOCATE. Began with Jan. 1973 issue. 0199-1876. Periodical. US. English. mo. $25.00. Los Angeles Trial Lawyers Association, 1730 West Olympic Boulevard 306, Los Angeles CA 90015. LC KFC1025.A15. DD 347.794057.

ADVOCATE (FALLS CHURCH, VA.) *CEASED.* (THE ADVOCATE). Began with Mar. 1969. Ceased with Vol. 16, No. 2, Mar./April 1984. 0094-2197. Periodical. US. English. bm. US Government Printing Office, Superintendent of Documents, Washington DC 20402. Ind/Abst Leg. Resour. Index, Index U.S. Gov. Period. LC KF7639.A1. DD 343.730143.

ADVOCATENBLAD. 1.- Vol. Dutch. ir.

ADVOCATES' QUARTERLY (ANNUAL). (ADVOCATES' QUARTERLY). Vol. 1 (1977-78)-. 0704-0288. CN. English. an. Canada Law Book Ltd, 80 Cowdray Court, Agincourt Ontario M1S 1S5 Canada. DD 347.710505.

ADVOCATES' SOCIETY JOURNAL. (THE ADVOCATES' SOCIETY JOURNAL). June 1982-. 0824-3344. Periodical. CN. English. ir. Free to Members, $20.00 Others. The Advocates' Society, 160 Queen Street West, Toronto Ontario M5H 3H3 Canada. DD 347.710505.

O ADVOGADO. Periodical. Portuguese. ir. Rua Coelho Rodrigues, 1.202 1 O Andar Salas 101/2, Teresina Brazil. DD 340.06281.

ADVOKATEN. 0281-3505. Periodical. Swedish. ir. 50.00. Sveriges Advokatsamfund, Laboratoriegatan 4, Stockholm Sweden. *Tidskrift (Sveriges Advokatsamfund).*

A.E. LEGAL NEWSLETTER. (A/E LEGAL NEWSLETTER). VFOAT Legal Newsletter. 0090-2411. Periodical. US. English. ir. V O Schinnerer & Company, 5028 Wisconsin Avenue NW, Washington DC 20016. Tel (202)686-2850. LC K1. DD 344.7301762.

THE AFFILIATE. V. 1- July 1975-. 0360-5485. US. English. bm. American Bar Association, Circulation Department, 1155 East 60th Street, Chicago IL 60637. LC KF325.26. DD 340.05.

AFLTR. AMERICAN FAMILY LAW TAX REPORT. See Business - Public Finance.

AFRICAN LAW DIGEST. Vol. 1, No. 1-. 0002-0052. ET. English. qt. African Law Center, Addis Ababa, University PO Box 1176, Addis Ababa Ethiopia. DD 349.605, 346.005. Index in last issue of volume - attached.

AFRIKA-RECHT & WIRTSCHAFT : ORGAN DER DEUTSCH-SUDAFRIKANISCHEN JURISTEN-VEREINIGUNG E. V. VFOAT Afrika-Recht und Wirtschaft. 1/80-. Periodical. English (German). qt. 120.00. Intrapress, Lortzingstrasse 7, 6200 Wiesbaden West Germany. LC K1. DD 349.6805, 346.8005. *Afrika-Recht.*

AGENCY PUBLICATION - TEXAS WATER QUALITY BOARD. (AGENCY PUBLICATION). Main/Corp Texas Water Quality Board. 0091-0848. US. English. Texas Water Quality Board, PO Box 13246, Austin TX 78711. LC KFT1556.A73. DD 344.7640463.

AGENDA DES PROFESSIONS JUDICIAIRES ET JURIDIQUES. French. ir. 120. 6 rue de Mezieres, Paris France 75006. LC JN2303. DD 347.44013. *Agenda et Annuaire de la Magistrature, du Barreau, du Notariat, des Officiers Ministeriels et de l'Enregistrement.*

AGRARISCH RECHT. 0167-4242. Periodical. Dutch. mo. 195.00. Libresso B V, Distributiecentrum voor Boeken en Tijdsschriften, Postbus 23, 7400 GA Deventer Netherlands. Ind/Abst Excerpta Med. LC K16. *Pacht.*

AGRARRECHT. 0340-840X. GW. German. mo. $61.69. Landwirtschaftsverlag GMBH, Postfach 48 02 10, D-4400 Munster-Hiltrup Germany. Ind/Abst Coal

Abstr., Excerpta Med., Bibliogr. Agric. **LC** K1. **DD** 343.43076.

AHA ILONO. ('AHA' ILONO). 0098-9738. US. English. mo. Hawaii Judiciary Branch, PO Box 2560, Honolulu HI 96804. **LC** KFH510.A73. **DD** 347.96901.

THE AIR AND SPACE LAWYER. Vol. 1, No. 1 (Fall 1983)-. 0747-7449. Periodical. US. English. qt. A.B.A./Forum Committee on Air and Space Law, 1155 East 60th Street, Chicago IL 60637. **LC** KF2400.A15. **DD** 343.73097, 347.30397.

AIR FORCE LAW REVIEW. (THE AIR FORCE LAW REVIEW). Vol. 16, No. 1 (Spring 1974)-. 0094-8381. Periodical. US. English. qt. Superintendent of Documents, US Government Printing Office, Washington DC 20402. **Tel** (202)783-3238. **Ind/Abst** Leg. Resour. Index, Predicasts, Index U.S. Gov. Period., Public Aff. Inf. Serv. Bull., Index Leg. Period., Contents Curr. Leg. Period., Curr. Law Index, Funk Scott Index Corp. Ind. **LC** K25. **DD** 343.730184005. (cum index). *United States Air Force JAG Law Review, 0021-3527.*

AIR LAW. V. 1- 1975-. 0165-2079. Periodical. NE. English. qt. 97.50. Kluwer Law and Taxation Publishers, PO Box 23, Deventer The Netherlands. **Ed** A V Wyk, W Heere, A DuPerron, and I Diederiks. **Ind/Abst** Leg. Resour. Index, Int. Aerosp. Abstr. **LC** K1. **DD** 343.09705. bk rev. adv acc. **Circ** 700. Journal covering topical information on the study and practice of air law, its civil, commerical, administrative and penal aspects as well as aviation policy.

AJS UPDATE. **Main/Corp** American Judicature Society. **VAT** American Judicature Society Update. V. 4- Sept. 1978-. 0190-1427. Periodical. US. English. bm. American Judicature Society, 200 West Monroe Street/Suite 1606, Chicago IL 60606. **LC** KF8700.A15. **DD** 347.73005. *AJS Joint Enterprise, 0362-1057.*

AJURIS. V. 1- July 1974-. BL. Portuguese. ir. Livraria Sulina, Av Borges de Madeiros, Porto Alegre 1030 Brazil. **LC** K1.

AKRON LAW REVIEW. V. 1- Fall 1967-. 0002-371X. US. English. qt. $20.00. University of Akron, College of Law, Akron OH 44304. **Tel** (216)375-7335. **Ed** Michael J Olah. **Ind/Abst** Leg. Resour. Index, Index Leg. Period., Curr. Law Index, Contents Curr. Leg. Period. **LC** K1. **DD** 340.05. (cum index). **Circ** 700. Current developments in law.

AKTUELLE BEITRAGE DER STAATS- UND RECHTSWISSENSCHAFT. 0568-7551. Monographic Series. GE. German. ir. Deutscher Buch Export-Import, Leninstrasse 16, DDR-701 Leipzig East Germany. Comprises studies, monographs, minute-books, omnibus volumes concerning topics of political and legal sciences. *Aktuelle Beitrage zur Staats- und Rechtswissenschaft aus den Sozialistischen Landern (Not in Nal).*

AL-JARIDAH AL-RASMIYAH AL-ITTIHADIYAH. **Main/Corp** Confederation of Arab Republics. V. 1- December 21, 1971-. Arabic. ir.

AL-JARIDAH AL-RASMIYAH, IMARAT ABU ZABY. **Main/Corp** United Arab Emirates. Periodical. Arabic. ir.

AL-JARIDAH AL-RASMIYAH LIL-MAMLAKAH AL-URDUNIYAH AL-HASHIMIYAH. **Main/Corp** Jordan. No. 256- May 25, 1946-. Periodical. US. Arabic. **LC** Microfilm 02156. *Jaridah Al-Rasmiyah Li-Imarat Sharq Al-Urdun.*

AL-KUWAYT AL-YAWM. **Main/Corp** Kuwait. V. 1-. Arabic. ir. Ufilm Al-Kuwayt, SB 15 AL-Safah.

AL-WAQAI AL-IRAQIYAH. **Main/Corp** Iraq. US. Arabic. **LC** Microfilm LL-02149 KPA.

ALA BRIEF. (BRIEF). **VAT** American Lawyers Association Brief. 0162-2986. Periodical. US. English. American Lawyers Association, 292 Madison Avenue, New York NY 10017. **LC** KF200. **DD** 340.06273.

ALABAMA ADMINISTRATIVE MONTHLY. Vol. 1, No. 1 (Oct. 1982)-. US. English. mo. $50.00. Alabama Administrative Monthly Legislative Reference Service, 750 Washington Avenue/Suite 100, Montgomery AL 36130. **LC** KFA36. **DD** 348.76102505, 347.61082505.

THE ALABAMA AND GEORGIA LEGAL DIRECTORY. *See* Yearbooks, Almanacs, Directories.

ALABAMA LAW REVIEW. Began with Fall 1948 issue. 0002-4279. Periodical. US. English. qt. University of Alabama, c/o Law School, Tuscaloosa AL 35486. **Ed** Anita Smith. **Ind/Abst** Leg. Resour. Index, Public Aff. Inf. Serv. Bull., Index Leg. Period., Curr. Law Index, Contents Curr. Leg. Period. **LC** K1. **DD** 340.05. **Circ** 1,300.

THE ALABAMA LAWYER. (THE ALABAMA LAWYER : OFFICIAL ORGAN STATE BAR OF ALABAMA). Vol. 1, No. 1 (Jan. 1940)-. 0002-4287. Periodical. US. English. bm. $15.00. Alabama Lawyer, PO Box 4156, Montgomery AL 36101. **Tel** 0002-7287. **Ed** Robert A Huffaker. **Ind/Abst** Leg. Resour. Index, Index Leg. Period., Curr. Law Index. **DD** 340.05. Index published separately - free - automatically sent. (cum index). bk rev. adv acc. **Circ** 8,000. (ctrl). Official publication of the Alabama State Bar containing association news, court decisions, and other articles of interest to Alabama lawyers. *Alabama Bar Bulletin, 0741-2908.*

THE ALABAMA LEGAL DIRECTORY. *See* Yearbooks, Almanacs, Directories.

THE ALABAMA MESSENGER. 0273-9593. Periodical. US. English. wk. $10.00. Alabama Messenger, 706 Frank Nelson Building, Birmingham AL 35203. **Tel** (205)252-3672.

ALABAMA RULES ANNOTATED. (ALABAMA RULES ANNOTATED : INCLUDING THE RULES OF THE COURTS IN ALABAMA, THE RULES OF THE FEDERAL DISTRICT COURTS, AND THE RULES OF THE ELEVENTH CIRCUIT COURT OF APPEALS OF THE UNITED STATES). 1983 Ed.-. 0747-6620. US. English. an. **LC** KFA529. **DD** 347.761051, 347.610751.

ALABAMA RULES OF COURTS. **Main/Corp** Alabama. Courts. 0198-0319. US. English. West Publishing Company, 50 West Kellogg Boulevard P O Box 3526, St Paul MN 55165. **LC** KFA529. **DD** 347.761051.

ALABAMA STATE BAR FOUNDATION BULLETIN. Began in: 1963?. Periodical. US. English. ir. Alabama State Bar Association, PO Box 671, Montgomery AL 36101. **LC** KF200. **DD** 340.060761.

ALASKA ADMINISTRATIVE JOURNAL. Periodical. US. English. bw. $250.00. AAJ Coordinator/Office of the Lieutenant, Governor Pouch AA, Juneau AK 99811. **LC** KFA1236. **DD** 348.79802505, 347.98082505.

ALASKA BAR BRIEF. 0093-1039. US. English. mo. $12.00. Box 279, Anchorage AK 99510. **LC** KF200. **DD** 340.062798.

THE ALASKA BAR RAG. **VFOAT** Bar Rag. Vol. 1, No. 1 (Sept. 1978)-. 0276-1025. Periodical. US. English. mo. $25.00. Alaska Bar Rag, PO Box 279, Anchorage AK 99510. **LC** KF200. **DD** 349.79805, 347.98005.

ALASKA COURT SYSTEM NEWSLETTER. Periodical. US. English. 303 K Street, Anchorage AK 99501. **LC** KFA1710.A15. **DD** 347.7980105, 347.9807105. *Magistrate Newsletter, Court Reporter.*

ALASKA DIRECTORY OF ATTORNEYS. *See* Yearbooks, Almanacs, Directories.

ALASKA LAW REVIEW. Vol. 1, No. 1 (Summer 1984)-. 0883-0568. Periodical. US. English. sa. $12.00 Domestic, $15.00 Foreign. Alaska Law Review, Duke University, School of Law/Room 006, Durham NC 27706. **Tel** (919)684-5966. **Ed** John Grossbauer. adv acc. **Circ** 2,500. Book reviews and notes pertaining to legal issues of interest to Alaska. *UCLA-Alaska Law Review, 0886-263X.*

ALBANY LAW REVIEW. Vol. 12 June 1948-. 0002-4678. Periodical. US. English. qt. $18.00. Law Review Board, 80 New Scotland Avenue, Albany NY 12208. **Tel** (518)445-2372. **Ind/Abst** Leg. Resour. Index, Index Leg. Period., Curr. Law Index, Contents Curr. Leg. Period. adv acc. **Circ** 800. Law Review. *Albany Law Review of Recent Decisions.*

ALBERTA COURT CALENDAR. July/Dec. 1978-. 0226-4196. Periodical. CN. English. sa. Free. **LC** KEA533. **DD** 347.7123013, 347.1230713, 347.712301.

ALBERTA DECISIONS. CIVIL AND CRIMINAL CASES. (ALBERTA DECISIONS, CIVIL AND CRIMINAL CASES). 1974-. 0319-7980. CN. English. an. 220. Western Legal Publications, 301 - Alexander Street, Vancouver British Columbia V6A 1B2 Canada. **Tel** (604)687-5671. **DD** 348.7123048. All available civil and criminal judgements from Alberta Court of Appeal, Court of Queen's Bench and District Courts of Alberta digested monthly by subjects.

ALBERTA LAW FOR THE 80'S. Vol. 1 (1978)-. 0229-0359. CN. English. an. $80.00. Butterworth & Company Canada Ltd, 2265 Midland Avenue, Scarborough Ontario M1P 4S1 Canada. **DD** 349.712305.

ALBERTA LAW REVIEW. V. 1- Fall 1955-. 0002-4821. Periodical. CN. English. ty. $25.00. University of Alberta, Faculty of Law, Edmonton Alberta T6G 2H5 Canada. **Ed** Mark R Smith. **Ind/Abst** Leg. Resour. Index, Index Leg. Period. bk rev. adv acc. **Circ** 4,600. (ctrl). Law journal-articles, case comments and book reviews. *Alberta Law Quarterly.*

ALBERTA LEGAL TELEPHONE DIRECTORY. *See* Yearbooks, Almanacs, Directories.

ALBERTA REPORTS (FREDERICTON, N.B. : BOUND CUMULATION). (ALBERTA REPORTS). 1 Pt. 1 (Nov. 26, 1976)-. 0703-3109. CN. English. ir. $72.00 Per Vol. Maritime Law Book Ltd, Box 302, Fredericton New Brunswick E3B 4Y9 Canada. **DD** 348.7123043.

ALBERTA, SASKATCHEWAN, MANITOBA CRIMINAL DECISIONS. (ALBERTA SASKATCHEWAN MANITOBA CRIMINAL DECISIONS). **VFOAT** Alberta Saskatchewan Manitoba Criminal Conviction Decisions. 1978-. 0715-3155. CN. English. an. $70.00. Alberta Saskatchewan Manitoba Criminal Decisions, c/o Western Legal Publications, 202-One Alexander Street, Vancouver British Columbia V6A 1B2 Canada. **DD** 345.71002648.

ALBERTA WEEKLY LAW DIGEST. Issue No. 1 (Jan. 7, 1982)-. 0713-892X. Periodical. CN. English. wk. $115.00 Per Vol. Alberta Weekly Law Digest, 2330 Maitland Avenue, Agincourt Ontario M1S 1P7 Canada. **DD** 348.7123046.

ALCOHOL, TOBACCO AND FIREARMS QUARTERLY BULLETIN *CEASED.* **Main/Corp** United States. Bureau of Alcohol, Tobacco, and Firearms. **VFOAT** Alcohol, Tobacco and Firearms Bulletin. No. 1979-1 (Jan./Mar.1979)- No. 1982-4 (Oct./Dec.1982)-. Periodical. US. English. qt. Superintendent of Documents, US Government Printing Office, Washington DC 20402. **Tel** (202)783-3238. *Alcohol, Tobacco and Firearms Bulletin, 0098-0757.*

ALI-ABA CLE REVIEW. **Main/Corp** American Law Institute-American Bar Association Committee on Continuing Professional Education. **VAT** American Law Institute, American Bar Association Continuing Legal Education Review. 0044-7560. Periodical. US. English. ir. free. ALI/ABA, 4025 Chestnut Street, Philadelphia PA 19104. **Tel** (215)243-1656. **Ed** Mark T Carroll. bk rev. **Circ** 80,000. Ads on ALI-ABA CLE courses, books, audio and video-cassettes, and periodicals. *ALI-ABA CLE Review, 0044-7560.*

ALI-ABA CONFERENCE. CONFERENCE ON FEDERAL INCOME TAX SIMPLIFICATION : PAPERS. **Main/Conf** ALI-ABA Conference On Federal Income Tax Simplification. **VAT** American Law Institute-American Bar Association Conference. Conference on Federal Income Tax Simplification: Papers. 0191-3689. US. English. American Law Institute, American Bar Association Committee on Continuing Professional Education, 4025 Chestnut Street, Philadelphia PA 19104. **LC** KF6369.3. **DD** 343.73052.

ALI-ABA COURSE MATERIALS JOURNAL. **VAT** American Law Institute-American Bar Association Course Materials Journal. V. 1-. 0145-6342. Periodical. US. English. bm. $30.00. American Law Institute, American Bar Association, 4025 Chestnut Street, Philadelphia PA 19104. **Tel** (215)243-1656. **Ed** Mark T Carroll. **Ind/Abst** Leg. Resour. Index, Manage. Contents, Curr. Law Index, Contents Curr. Leg. Period. **LC** K1. **DD** 340.0973. **Circ** 8,000. Collection of best outlines and written presentations on legal issues given at ALI-ABA courses.

ALI-ABA COURSE OF STUDY : ABA SECTION OF TAXATION, ADVANCED STUDY SESSIONS, ADVANCED ESTATE PLANNING TECHINIQUES : MATERIALS. **Main/Conf** ALI-ABA Course of Study: Advanced Estate Planning Techniques. 0191-412X. US. English. American Law Institute-American Bar Association Committee on Continuing Professional Education, 4025 Chestnut Street, Philadelphia PA 19104. **LC** KF6585. **DD** 343.73053.

ALI-ABA COURSE OF STUDY. ABA SECTION OF TAXATION, ADVANCED STUDY SESSIONS, ESTATE AND INCOME TAX PLANNING FOR EXECUTIVES AND SMALL BUSINESS OWNERS : MATERIALS. 0191-8249. US. English. American Law Institute-American Bar Association Committee on Continuing Professional Education, 4025 Chestnut

Law

Street, Philadelphia PA 19104. **LC** KF6369.8.E9. **DD** 343.73068.

ALI-ABA COURSE OF STUDY. ABA SECTION OF TAXATION, ANNUAL ADVANCED STUDY SESSIONS, BUSINESS AND ESTATE PLANNING WITH LIFE AND DISABILITY INSURANCE: MATERIALS. (ALI-ABA COURSE OF STUDY : ABA SECTION OF TAXATION, ANNUAL ADVANCED STUDY SESSIONS, BUSINESS AND ESTATE PLANNING WITH LIFE AND DISABILITY INSURANCE : MATERIALS). 0271-3578. US. English. an. ALI-ABA Committee on Continuing Professional Education, 4025 Chestnut Street, Philadelphia PA 19104. **LC** KF1175.Z9. **DD** 346.7308632.

ALI-ABA COURSE OF STUDY. ABA SECTION OF TAXATION, ANNUAL OF TAXATION, ANNUAL ADVANCED STUDY SESSIONS, ADVANCED TAX PLANNING FOR REAL ESTATE TRANSACTIONS: MATERIALS. *See* Real Estate.

ALI-ABA COURSE OF STUDY. ADVANCED BUSINESS TAX PLANNING : MATERIALS. 0191-1651. US. English. American Law Institute, American Bar Association Committee on Continuing Professional Education, 4025 Chestnut Street, Philadelphia PA 19104. **LC** KF6450.Z9. **DD** 343.73068.

ALI-ABA COURSE OF STUDY. ADVANCED TAX PLANNING FOR THE CLOSELY HELD BUSINESS : MATERIALS. US. English. American Law Institute-American Bar Association Committee on Continuing Professional Education, 4025 Chestnut Street, Philadelphia PA 19104.

ALI-ABA COURSE OF STUDY. ALI-ABA CONFERENCE ON ERISA : MATERIALS. Main/Conf ALI-ABA Conference On Erisa. **VAT** American Law Institute-American Bar Association Course of Study. American Law Institute-American Bar Association Conference on Employee Retirement Income Secutity Act: Materials. 0192-821X. US. English. ALI-ABA Committee on Continuing Professional Education, 4025 Chestnut Street, Philadelphia PA 19104. **LC** KF3512.Z9. **DD** 344.7301252.

ALI-ABA COURSE OF STUDY. ATOMIC ENERGY LICENSING AND REGULATION : MATERIALS. 0190-9673. US. English. ALI-ABA Committee on Continuing Professional Education, 4025 Chestnut Street, Philadelphia PA 19104. **LC** KF2138.Z9. **DD** 343.73092.

ALI-ABA COURSE OF STUDY. BANK DEFENSE OF NEGOTIABLE INSTRUMENT CASES: MATERIALS. (ALI-ABA COURSE OF STUDY : BANK DEFENSE OF NEGOTIABLE INSTRUMENT CASES : MATERIALS). 0191-0280. US. English. an. American Law Institute-American Bar Association Committee on Continuing Professional Education, 4025 Chestnut Street, Philadelphia PA 19104. **LC** KF957.Z9. **DD** 346.73096.

ALI-ABA COURSE OF STUDY. BANKING AND COMMERCIAL LENDING LAW : MATERIALS. VFOAT Banking and Commercial Lending Law: Materials. 0271-356X. US. English. an. American Law Institute-American Bar Association Committee on Continuing Professional Education, 4025 Chestnut Street, Philadelphia PA 19104. **LC** KF1035.Z9. **DD** 346.73082.

ALI-ABA COURSE OF STUDY. BASIC ESTATE AND GIFT TAXATION : MATERIALS. 0271-3551. US. English. an. American Law Institute-American Bar Association Committee on Continuing Professional Education, 4025 Chestnut Street, Philadelphia PA 19104. **LC** KF6572.Z9. **DD** 343.73053.

ALI-ABA COURSE OF STUDY. BASIC LAW OF PENSIONS AND DEFERRED COMPENSATION: MATERIALS. (ALI-ABA COURSE OF STUDY : BASIC LAW OF PENSIONS AND DEFERRED COMPENSATION : MATERIALS). 0191-0272. US. English. ALI-ABA Committee on Continuing Professional Education, 4025 Chestnut Street, Philadelphia PA 19104. **LC** KF3512.Z9. **DD** 344.7301252.

ALI-ABA COURSE OF STUDY. BROKER-DEALER REGULATION : MATERIALS. 0271-3535. US. English. American Law Institute-American Bar Association Committee on Continuing Professional Education, 4025 Chestnut

Street, Philadelphia PA 19104. **LC** KF1071.Z9. **DD** 346.730926.

ALI-ABA COURSE OF STUDY. BUSINESS TAX PLANNING : MATERIALS. VFOAT ALI-ABA Course of Study. Advanced Business Tax Planning. **VAT** American Law Institute-American Bar Association Course of Study. Business Tax Planning: Materials. 0193-6905. Periodical. US. English. American Law Institute-American Bar Association Committee on Continuing Professional Education, 4025 Chestnut Street, Philadelphia PA 19104. **LC** KF6450.Z9. **DD** 343.73066.

ALI-ABA COURSE OF STUDY. BUSINESS WORKOUTS : MATERIALS. 0190-9665. US. English. American Law Institute-American Bar Association Committee on Continuing Professional Education, 4025 Chestnut Street, Philadelphia PA 19104. **LC** KF1544.Z9. **DD** 346.73077.

ALI-ABA COURSE OF STUDY. CLASS AND DERIVATIVE ACTIONS AND OTHER MULTIPARTY COMPLEX LITIGATION : MATERIALS. 0191-2011. US. English. ALI-ABA Committee on Continuing Professional Education, 4025 Chestnut Street, Philadelphia PA 19104. **LC** KF8896.Z9. **DD** 347.735.

ALI-ABA COURSE OF STUDY. CONDOMINIUM CONVERSIONS : MATERIALS. **VAT** American Law Institute-American Bar Association Course of Study. Condominium Conversions: Materials. 0191-202X. US. English. ALI-ABA Committee on Continuing Professional Education, 4025 Chestnut Street, Philadelphia PA 19104. **LC** KF581.Z9. **DD** 346.730433.

ALI-ABA COURSE OF STUDY. DOMESTIC TAXATION OF HARD MINERALS : MATERIALS. 0191-2623. US. English. ALI-ABA Committee on Continuing Professional Education, 4025 Chestnut Street, Philadelphia PA 19104. **LC** KF6495.M5. **DD** 343.73055.

ALI-ABA COURSE OF STUDY. EMINENT DOMAIN : MATERIALS. 0190-9339. US. English. American Law Institute-American Bar Association Committee on Continuing Professional Education, 4025 Chestnut Street, Philadelphia PA 19104. **LC** KF5599.Z9. **DD** 343.73025.

ALI-ABA COURSE OF STUDY. ENERGY AND THE LAW, PROBLEMS AND CHALLENGES OF THE LATE 70'S: MATERIALS. (ALI-ABA COURSE OF STUDY : ENERGY AND THE LAW, PROBLEMS AND CHALLENGES OF THE LATE 70'S : MATERIALS). 0191-2585. US. English. ALI-ABA Committee on Continuing Professional Education, 4025 Chestnut Street, Philadelphia PA 19104. **LC** KF2120.Z9. **DD** 343.74092.

ALI-ABA COURSE OF STUDY. ENVIRONMENTAL LAW : MATERIALS. **VAT** American Law Institute-American Bar Association Course of Study Environmental Law: Materials. 0192-0820. US. English. American Law Institute-American Bar Association Committee on Continuing Professional Education, 4025 Chestunt Street, Philadelphia PA 19104. **LC** KF3775.Z9. **DD** 346.73046.

ALI-ABA COURSE OF STUDY. ENVIRONMENTAL LITIGATION : MATERIALS. 0191-166X. US. English. American Law Institute-American Bar Association Committee on Continuing Professional Education, 4025 Chestnut Street, Philadelphia PA 19104. **LC** KF3775.Z9. **DD** 344.730460269.

ALI-ABA COURSE OF STUDY. ERISA AND THE FEDERAL SECURITIES LAWS: MATERIALS. (ALI-ABA COURSE OF STUDY : ERISA AND THE FEDERAL SECURITIES LAWS : MATERIALS). **VAT** American Law Institute, American Bar Association Course of Study. Employee Retirement Income Security Act and the Federal Securities Laws: Materials. 0191-2224. US. English. ALI-ABA Committee on Continuing Professional Education, 4025 Chestnut Street, Philadelphia PA 19104. **LC** KF3512.Z9. **DD** 344.7301252.

ALI-ABA COURSE OF STUDY. ERISA-PHASE II : MATERIALS. **VAT** American Law Institute-American Bar Association Course of Study. Employee Retirement Income Security Act-Phase Two: Materials. 0191-4308. US. English. ALI-ABA Committee on Continuing Professional

Education, 4025 Chestnut Street, Philadelphia PA 19104. **LC** KF3512.Z9. **DD** 344.7301252.

ALI-ABA COURSE OF STUDY. ESTATE PLANNING FOR RETIRING OR DYING CLIENTS: MATERIALS. (ALI-ABA COURSE OF STUDY. ESTATE PLANNING FOR RETIRING OR DYING CLIENTS : MATERIALS). **VAT** American Law Institute-American Bar Association Course of Study. Estate Planning for Retiring or Dying Clients: Materials. 0270-7594. US. English. an. American Law Institute-American Bar Association, Committee on Continuing Professional Education, 4025 Chestnut Street, Philadelphia PA 19104. **LC** KF750.Z9. **DD** 346.73052.

ALI-ABA COURSE OF STUDY. ESTATE PLANNING FOR THE CLOSELY HELD BUSINESS : MATERIALS. 0271-3543. US. English. an. American Law Institute-American Bar Association Committee on Continuing Professional Education, 4025 Chestnut Street, Philadelphia PA 19104. **LC** KF6491.Z9. **DD** 343.73067.

ALI-ABA COURSE OF STUDY. ESTATE PLANNING IN DEPTH : MATERIALS. **VAT** American Law Institute-American Bar Association Course of Study. Estate Planning In Depth: Materials. 0191-8656. US. English. American Law Institute-American Bar Association Committee on Continuing Professional Education, 4025 Chestnut Street, Philadelphia PA 19104. **LC** KF6585. **DD** 343.73053.

ALI-ABA COURSE OF STUDY. ESTATE PLANNING. MATERIALS. (ALI-ABA COURSE OF STUDY. ESTATE PLANNING : MATERIALS). 0270-9694. US. English. an. American Law Institute-American Bar Association Committee on Continuing Professional Education, 4025 Chestnut Street, Philadelphia PA 19104. **LC** KF6585. **DD** 346.73052.

ALI-ABA COURSE OF STUDY. ESTATE PLANNING UNDER THE NEW ESTATE AND GIFT TAX LAW. MATERIALS. (ALI-ABA COURSE OF STUDY : ESTATE PLANNING UNDER THE NEW ESTATE AND GIFT TAX LAW : MATERIALS). 0190-9584. US. English. American Law Institute-American Bar Association Committee on Continuing Professional Education, 4025 Chestnut Street, Philadelphia PA 19104. **LC** KF6572.Z9. **DD** 343.73053.

ALI-ABA COURSE OF STUDY. FEDERAL ELECTION LAW : MATERIALS. 0191-2372. US. English. American Law Institute-American Bar Association Committee on Continuing Professional Education, 4025 Chestnut Street, Philadelphia PA 19104. **LC** KF4886.Z9. **DD** 342.7307.

ALI-ABA COURSE OF STUDY. FEDERAL RULES OF EVIDENCE : MATERIALS. 0191-3859. US. English. American Law Institute-American Bar Association Committee on Continuing Professional Education, 4025 Chestnut Street, Philadelphia PA 19104. **LC** KF8935.Z9. **DD** 347.736.

ALI-ABA COURSE OF STUDY. FRAUD, INSIDE INFORMATION, AND FIDUCIARY DUTY UNDER RULE 10B-5 : MATERIALS. 0191-2178. US. English. American Law Institute-American Bar Association Committee on Continuing Professional Education, 4025 Chestnut Street, Philadelphia PA 19104. **LC** KF9369. **DD** 345.73026.

ALI-ABA COURSE OF STUDY. INVESTMENT ADVISER REGULATION. MATERIALS. (ALI-ABA COURSE OF STUDY. INVESTMENT ADVISER REGULATION : MATERIALS). **VAT** American Law Institute-American Bar Association Course of Study. Investment Adviser Regulation. Materials. 0270-9686. US. English. American Law Institute-American Bar Association Committee on Continuing Professional Education, 4025 Chestnut Street, Philadelphia PA 19104. **LC** KF1072.Z9. **DD** 346.73092.

ALI-ABA COURSE OF STUDY. LAND PLANNING AND REGULATION OF DEVELOPMENT : MATERIALS. **VAT** American Law Institute-American Bar Association Course of Study. Land Planning and Regulation of Development: Materials. 0191-8125. US. English. American Law Institute-American Bar Association Committee on Continuing Professional Education, 4025 Chestnut Street, Philadelphia PA 19104. **LC** KF5698.Z9. **DD** 346.73045.

Law

ALI-ABA COURSE OF STUDY. LAND USE LITIGATION, CRITICAL ISSUES FOR ATTORNEYS, DEVELOPERS, AND PUBLIC OFFICIALS. MATERIALS. (ALI-ABA COURSE OF STUDY : LAND USE LITIGATION, CRITICAL ISSUES FOR ATTORNEYS, DEVELOPERS, AND PUBLIC OFFICIALS : MATERIALS). 0190-9592. US. English. American Law Institute-American Bar Association Committee on Continuing Professional Education, 4025 Chestnut Street, Philadelphia PA 19104. LC KF5698.Z9. DD 346.73045.

ALI-ABA COURSE OF STUDY. LEGAL ASPECTS OF MUSEUM OPERATIONS: MATERIALS. (ALI-ABA COURSE OF STUDY : LEGAL ASPECTS OF MUSEUM OPERATIONS : MATERIALS). 0191-1945. US. English. American Law Institute-American Bar Association Committee on Continuing Professional Education, 4025 Chestnut Street, Philadelphia PA 19104. LC KF4305.Z9. DD 344.73093.

ALI-ABA COURSE OF STUDY. LEGAL ISSUES IN THE COAL INDUSTRY : MATERIALS. 0191-1589. US. English. American Law Institute-American Bar Association Committee on Continuing Professional Education, 4025 Chestnut Street, Philadelphia PA 19104. LC KF1830.Z9. DD 343.73077.

ALI-ABA COURSE OF STUDY. LITIGATION UNDER THE FEDERAL SECURITIES LAWS : MATERIALS. VAT American Law Institute-American Bar Association Course of Study. Litigation Under the Federal Securities Laws. 0191-2046. US. English. American Law Institute-American Bar Association Committee on Continuing Professional Education, 4025 Chestnut Street, Philadelphia PA 19104. LC KF1440. DD 346730920269.

ALI-ABA COURSE OF STUDY MATERIALS. PRACTICE AND PROCEDURE IN FEDERAL TAX CONTROVERSIES: TAX COURT AND ELSEWHERE. (ALI-ABA COURSE OF STUDY : PRACTICE AND PROCEDURE IN FEDERAL TAX CONTROVERSIES, TAX COURT AND ELSEWHERE : MATERIALS). VFOAT Practice and Procedure in Federal Tax Controversies: Tax Court and Elsewhere. VAT American Law Institute-American Bar Association Course of Study Materials. Practice and Procedure In Federal Tax Controversies: Tax Court and Elsewhere. 0190-3888. US. English. an. American Law Institute-American Bar Association Committee on Continuing Professional Education, 4025 Chestnut Street, Philadelphia PA 19104. LC KF6320. DD 343.73040269.

ALI-ABA COURSE OF STUDY : MODERN REAL ESTATE TRANSACTIONS : MATERIALS. 0191-2003. US. English. American Law Institute-American Bar Association Committee on Continuing Professional Education, 4025 Chestnut Street, Philadelphia PA 19104. LC KF665.Z9. DD 346.730436.

ALI-ABA COURSE OF STUDY : OIL SPILLS AND THE LAW : MATERIALS. 0191-2038. US. English. American Law Institute-American Bar Association Committee on Continuing Professional Education, 4025 Chestnut Street, Philadelphia PA 19104. LC KF3790.Z9. DD 344.730463.

ALI-ABA COURSE OF STUDY. PENSION, PROFIT-SHARING, AND OTHER DEFERRED COMPENSATION PLANS : MATERIALS. 0191-3743. US. English. ALI-ABA Committee on Continuing Professional Education, 4025 Chestnut Street, Philadelphia PA 19104. LC KF3509.Z9. DD 344.7301252.

ALI-ABA COURSE OF STUDY. POSTGRADUATE COURSE IN FEDERAL SECURITIES LAW : MATERIALS. 0191-1570. US. English. American Law Institute-American Bar Association Committee on Continuing Professional Education, 4025 Chestnut Street, Philadelphia PA 19104. LC KF1440. DD 346.730666.

ALI-ABA COURSE OF STUDY. PRODUCTS LIABILITY. PREVENTION, LITIGATION, AND LAW REFORM. MATERIALS. (ALI-ABA COURSE OF STUDY. PRODUCTS LIABILITY : PREVENTION, LITIGATION, AND LAW REFORM : MATERIALS). 0272-8982. US. English. an. American Law Institute, 4025 Chestnut Street, Philadelphia PA 19104. LC KF1296.Z9. DD 346.730382.

ALI-ABA COURSE OF STUDY. QUALIFIED PLANS, INSURANCE, AND PROFESSIONAL CORPORATIONS : MATERIALS. VAT American Law Institute, American Bar Association Course of Study. Qualified Plans, Insurance, and Professional Corporations: Materials. 0271-1370. US. English. an. ALI-ABA Committee on Continuing Professional Education, 4025 Chestnut Street, Philadelphia PA 19104. LC KF3512.Z9. DD 343.73052, 347.30352.

ALI-ABA COURSE OF STUDY. REAL ESTATE CONDOMINIUMS AND PUDS : MATERIALS. 0190-9347. US. English. ALI-ABA Committee on Continuing Professional Education, 4025 Chestnut Street, Philadelphia PA 19104. LC KF581.Z9. DD 346.730433.

ALI-ABA COURSE OF STUDY. REAL ESTATE SYNDICATIONS : MATERIALS. (REAL ESTATE SYNDICATIONS : ALI-ABA COURSE OF STUDY, MATERIALS). VFOAT Ali-Aba Course of Study, Materials. VAT American Law Institute-American Bar Association Course of Study. Real Estate Syndications. Materials. 0730-4722. US. English. American Law Institute-American Bar Association, Committee on Continuing Professional Education, 4025 Chestnut Street, Philadelphia PA 19104. LC KF1079.Z9. DD 346.73043, 347.30643.

ALI-ABA COURSE OF STUDY. STATE AND LOCAL TAXATION AND FINANCE: MATERIALS. (ALI-ABA COURSE OF STUDY : STATE AND LOCAL TAXATION AND FINANCE : MATERIALS). 0191-2380. US. English. an. ALI-ABA Committee on Continuing Professional Education, 4025 Chestnut Street, Philadelphia PA 19104. LC KF6730.Z9. DD 343.73043.

ALI-ABA COURSE OF STUDY. TAX AND BUSINESS PLANNING FOR THE SMALL BUT GROWING BUSINESS : MATERIALS. 0190-9355. US. English. American Law Institute, American Bar Association, Committee on Continuing Professional Education, 4025 Chestnut Street, Philadelphia PA 19104. LC KF6491.Z9. DD 343.73068.

ALI-ABA COURSE OF STUDY. THE ECONOMICS OF ANTITRUST : MATERIALS. 0191-2399. US. English. American Law Institute, American Bar Association Committee, 4025 Chestnut Street, Philadelphia PA 19104. LC HD2731. DD 338.47343072.

ALI-ABA COURSE OF STUDY. THE SUPREME COURT AND THE FEDERAL SECURIETIES LAWS, IMPLICATIONS FOR LIABILITIES : MATERIALS. 0190-9975. US. English. American Law Institute-American Bar Association Committee on Continuing Professional Education, 4025 Chestnut Street, Philadelphia PA 19107. LC KF1440. DD 346.730666.

ALI-ABA COURSE OF STUDY. TRIAL EVIDENCE IN FEDERAL AND STATE COURTS, A CLINICAL STUDY OF RECENT DEVELOPMENTS : MATERIALS. 0271-2504. US. English. an. American Law Institute-American Bar Association Committee on Continuing Professional Education, 4025 Chestnut Street, Philadelphia PA 19104. LC KF8935.Z9. DD 347.736.

ALI-ABA COURSE OF STUDY. WATER AND AIR POLLUTION : MATERIALS. 0191-4073. US. English. American Law Institute-American Bar Association Committee on Continuing Professional Education, 4025 Chestnut Street, Philadelphia PA 19104. LC KF3790.Z9. DD 344.730463.

ALI-ABA SYMPOSIUM. REGIONAL SYMPOSIUM ON THE STRUCTURE AND GOVERNANCE OF CORPORATIONS : MATERIALS. VAT American Law Institute-American Bar Association Symposium. Regional Symposium on the Structure and Governance of Corporations: Materials. 0191-3697. US. English. American Law Institute-American Bar Association Committee on Continuing Professional Education, 4025 Chestnut Street, Philadelphia PA 19104. LC KF1414.3. DD 346.73066.

THE ALI REPORTER. Main/Corp American Law Institute. VAT American Law Institute Reporter. V. 1- Oct. 1978-. 0164-5757. Periodical. US. English. qt. American Law Institute, 4025 Chestnut Street, Philadelphia PA 19104. Tel (215)243-1626. Ed Michael Greenwald. LC KF200. DD 349.7305. bk rev. Circ 2,750. (ctrl). Newsletter of the American Law Institute.

ALL-CANADA WEEKLY SUMMARIES. 1977-. 0705-1360. Periodical. CN. English. wk. 650.00. Canada Law Book Ltd, 240 Edward Street, Aurora Ontario L3Y 1B4 Canada. Tel (416)773-6300. Ed Marvin N Goldstein. DD 340.0971. National, civil law summary service that covers every province and territory in Canada. A reporting service, keeping abreast of changes on a weekly basis.

THE ALL ENGLAND LAW REPORTS ANNUAL REVIEW. 1982-. UK. English. an. 12.00. Butterworth Law Publishers, Borough Green, Sevenoaks Kent TN15 8PH England. LC K1. DD 349.42, 344.2.

ALL INDIA CRIMINAL LAW REPORTER. English. mo. 70.00. Manager All India Criminal Law Reporter, Kothi No 108-B Sector 27-A, Chandigarh India. DD 345.46002648, 344.605002648.

ALL INDIA PREVENTION OF FOOD ADULTERATION CASES. VFOAT Prevention of Food Adulteration Cases. II. English. mo. 30.00. International Law Book Company, 1562 Church Road, Kashemere Gate, Delhi-6 India. LC Law. DD 344.54042.

ALLAM- ES JOGTUDOMANY. Vol. 1-. 0002-564X. Periodical. Hungarian. ir.

THE ALLEGHENY LAWYER. Began with Nov. 1958 issue. 0516-7094. Periodical. US. English. mo. $90.00. Allegheny County Bar Association, 920 City-County Building, Pittsburgh PA 15219. Tel (412)261-0518. Ed James I Smith III. LC KF200. DD 340.0974885. Circ 6,200. (ctrl). Newsletter sent to all members of the Bar Association. It informs the lawyers of upcoming educational as well as social events; information of lawyers activities in organizations and communities.

THE ALMANAC OF THE CANNING, FREEZING, PRESERVING INDUSTRIES. See Yearbooks, Almanacs, Directories.

ALPHABETICAL DIRECTORY OF ATTORNEYS IN NEW YORK STATE. See Yearbooks, Almanacs, Directories.

THE ALSA FORUM CEASED. Main/Corp American Legal Studies Association. VAT American Legal Studies Association Forum. V. 2-8, No. 3. 0162-7937. Periodical. US. English. ty. $18.00. Legal Studies Department, Hampshire House University of Massachusetts, Amherst MA 01003. Ind/Abst Leg. Resour. Index. LC K1. DD 340.0973. Newsletter (American Legal Studies Association).

ALTA ADVOCATE. VFOAT A.T.L.A. Advocate. VAT Association of Trial Lawyers of America Advocate. Vol. 9, No. 6 (Oct. 1983)-. 0746-4177. Periodical. US. English. mo. Association of Trial Lawyers of America, 1050 31st Street NW, Washington DC 20007. Alta Bar News, 0164-8160.

ALTERNATIVES TO THE HIGH COST OF LITIGATION. VFOAT Alternatives. Vol. 1, No. 1 (Jan. 1983)-. 0736-3613. Periodical. US. English. mo. $160.00. Law & Business Inc, 757 Third Avenue, New York NY 10017. LC KF9084.A15. DD 347.7377, 347.30777.

THE ALTMAN & WEIL REPORT TO LEGAL MANAGEMENT. See Business - General Management.

ALUMNAE/I DIRECTORY - RUTGERS LAW SCHOOL (NEWARK, N.J.). See Yearbooks, Almanacs, Directories.

ALUMNI DIRECTORY - ALBANY LAW SCHOOL. See Yearbooks, Almanacs, Directories.

ALUMNI DIRECTORY - UNIVERSITY OF CHICAGO LAW SCHOOL. See Yearbooks, Almanacs, Directories.

AMBIENTE Y RECURSOS NATURALES : REVISTA DE DERECHO, POLITICA Y ADMINISTRACION. V. 1, No. 1 (Jan-Mar 1984)-. 0326-422X. Periodical. AG. Spanish (selected English summaries). qt. $30.00. Editorial La Ley Tucuman 1471, 1050 Buenos Aires Argentina. Ind/Abst Life Sci. Collect.

AMC. AMERICAN MARITIME CASES. VFOAT American Maritime Cases. 0160-6786. Periodical. US. English. mo. $285.00. Business Manager AMC, 28 East 21st Street, Baltimore MD 21218.

THE AMERICAN BANKRUPTCY LAW JOURNAL. VFOAT Referee's Journal National Conference of Bankruptcy Judges. Vol. 45, No. 1 (Winter 1971)-. 0027-9048. Periodical. US. English. qt.

$25.00. American Bankruptcy Law, PO Box 983, Lexington KY 40588. **Tel** (606)233-2814. **Ed** Joe Lee. **Ind/Abst** Leg. Resour. Index, Index Leg. Period., Soc. Sci. Citation Index, Curr. Law Index, Contents Curr. Leg. Period. bk rev. **Circ** 3,200. *Journal of the National Conference of Referees in Bankruptcy, 0197-2669.*

AMERICAN BAR ASSOCIATION JOURNAL. V. 1- Jan. 1915-. 0002-7596. Periodical. US. English. American Bar Association, 1155 East 60th Street, Chicago IL 60637. **DD** 340.05.

AMERICAN BAR FOUNDATION RESEARCH JOURNAL. 1976-. 0361-9486. Periodical. US. English. qt. $28.00. American Bar Foundation, 750 North Lake Shore Drive, Chicago IL 60611. **Tel** (312)988-6520. **Ed** Raymand L Solomon and Terence C Halliday. **Ind/Abst** Leg. Resour. Index, Sociol. Abstr., Soc. Welf. Soc. Plan./Policy Soc. Dev., Energy Inf. Abstr., Environ. Abstr., Public Aff. Inf. Serv. Bull., Index Leg. Period., Contents Curr. Leg. Period., Curr. Law Index, Soc. Sci. Citation Index. **LC** K1. **DD** 340.0973. bk rev. adv acc. **Circ** 5,000. A multidisciplinary journal dealing with topics on the legal profession, delivery of legal services, the operation of legal institutions and trends and policy developments in the law.

AMERICAN BAR FOUNDATION RESEARCH REPORTER. **VFOAT** Research Reporter. No. 7-. Periodical. US. English. ir. Free. American Bar Foundation, 1155 East 60th Street, Chicago IL 60623. **Tel** (312)988-6500. **Ed** Bette H Sikes and Richard M Maas. **Circ** 30,000. (ctrl). Discussed the recent works published by the American Bar Foundation and the various activities of the ABF staff. *ABF Research Reporter.*

AMERICAN BAR REFERENCE HANDBOOK. (THE AMERICAN BAR REFERENCE HANDBOOK). 0094-3584. US. English. an. R B Forster & Associates Inc, 3287 Ramos Circle, Sacramento CA 95827. **Tel** (612)871-1395. **DD** 340.02573.

THE AMERICAN BAR, THE CANADIAN BAR, THE INTERNATIONAL BAR. US. English. an. $160.00. R B Forster & Associates Inc, 3287 Ramos Circle, Sacramento CA 95827. **Tel** (916)362-3276. **Ed** David Marcus. **Circ** 33,000. Professional directory of lawyers of the world containing over 64,000 lawyers annually investigated with regard to legal ability, character and diligence.

THE AMERICAN BENCH. 1st- Ed. 0160-2578. US. English. an. $170.00. R B Forster & Associates Inc, 3287 Ramos Cirlce, Sacramento CA 95827. **Tel** (916)362-3276. **Ed** Doreen M de Turo. **LC** KF8700.A19. **DD** 347.7314025 B. Each issue contains an index to its own contents - no vol index - loose. Over 2,500 pages listing current judicial information including 'Bills of Rights' of the United States and each of the fifty states.

AMERICAN BUSINESS LAW JOURNAL. 0002-7766. Periodical. US. English. ty. $16.00 Domestic, $18.00 Foreign. American Business Law Journal, Gettysburg College, J Railing/Box 507, Gettysburg PA 17325-1486. **Tel** (717)334-3131. **Ed** Omar Lee Reed. **Ind/Abst** Manage. Contents, Trade Ind. Index, Leg. Resour. Index, Account. Index. Suppl., ABI/Inform, Bus. Period. Index, Index Leg. Period., Leg. Contents, Soc. Sci. Citation Index, Curr. Law Index, Contents Curr. Leg. Period. **LC** K1. **DD** 346.730705, 347.306705. **CODEN** ABLJAN. bk rev. adv acc. **Circ** 2,300. Available on microfilm. Articles address contemporary legal problems related to business such as contracts, anti-trust and 'whistle-blowers'. *Bulletin - American Business Law Association.*

THE AMERICAN CIVIL LIBERTIES UNION RECORDS AND PUBLICATIONS UPDATE. **Main/Corp** American Civil Liberties Union. 0197-8195. US. English. be. Microfilming Corporation of America, 21 Harristown Road, Glen Rock NJ 07452. **LC** KF4742.3. **DD** 016.32340973.

AMERICAN COMPUTER LAW DIGEST. Vol. 1, No. 1-. 8755-1675. Periodical. US. English. qt. $50.00. American Computer Law Digest Inc, PO Box 39235, Friendship Station, Washington DC 20016. **Tel** (202)232-0800. **Ed** C R Costa and A E Major Jr. **DD** 340. bk rev. **Circ** 2,000. (ctrl). Recent briefs and discussions of court decisions and legislation affecting computer users and marketers.

THE AMERICAN CRIMINAL LAW REVIEW. V. 10- July 1971-. 0164-0364. Periodical. US. English. qt. $27.00. American Bar Association, 750 North Lake Shore Drive, Chicago IL 60611. **Tel** (312)988-5555. **Ind/Abst** Leg. Resour. Index, Index Leg. Period., Soc. Sci. Citation Index, Curr. Law Index. **LC** K1. **DD** 345.73005. *American Criminal Law Quarterly, 0002-8118.*

AMERICAN INDIAN JOURNAL *CEASED.* Began with V. 1-, Oct. 1975-. Ceased with V. 8, No. 1, 1982. 0145-7993. Periodical. US. English. mo. $25.00. Institute for the Development of Indian Law, 927 15th Street NW/Suite 200, Washington DC 20005. **Ind/Abst** Sel. Water Resour. Abstr., Curr. Index J. Educ. **LC** KF8201.A3. **DD** 346.73013. (cum index). *Education Journal of the Institute for the Development of Indian Law, 0090-0958; Legislative Review.*

AMERICAN INDIAN LAW NEWSLETTER. Vol. 1, No. 1 (May 3, 1968)-. Periodical. US. English. bm. $20.00. American Indian Law Center, PO Box 4456, Albuquerque NM 87196. **Tel** (505)277-5462. **Ed** Marc Mannis. **Circ** 500. (ctrl). Contains articles on issues of interest to those concerned with American Indian law.

AMERICAN INDIAN LAW REVIEW. Vol. 1- Winter 1973-. 0094-002X. US. English. an. $10.00. University of Oklahoma College of Law, 300 Timberdell, Norman OK 73019. **Tel** (405)325-2840. **Ed** Dana Simpson. **Ind/Abst** Leg. Resour. Index, Sel. Water Resour. Abstr., Writ. Am. Hist., Index Leg. Period., Curr. Law Index. **LC** K1. **DD** 342.73087. bk rev. adv acc. **Circ** 850. Concentrates on American Indian law, Indian lands, Indian welfare, Indian rights, and the Bureau of Indian Affairs.

THE AMERICAN JOURNAL OF COMPARATIVE LAW. V. 1- Winter/Spring 1952-. 0002-919X. Periodical. US. English. qt. University of California, School of Law, c/o Professor John G. Fleming-Editor, Berkeley, CA 94720. **Ind/Abst** Leg. Resour. Index, Int. Labour Doc., ABC Pol Sci, Women Stud. Abstr., Writ. Am. Hist., Public Aff. Inf. Serv. Bull., Index Leg. Period., Soc. Sci. Citation Index, Curr. Law Index. **LC** K1. Index in last issue of volume - attached. (cum index). Available on microfilm from University Microfilms.

AMERICAN JOURNAL OF CRIMINAL LAW. V. 1- Feb. 1972-. 0092-2315. Periodical. US. English. ty. $15.00. University of Texas, School of Law, 727 East 26th Street, Austin TX 78705. **Tel** (512)471-5151. **Ind/Abst** Leg. Resour. Index, Index Leg. Period., Contents Curr. Leg. Period., Curr. Law Index, Soc. Sci. Citation Index. **LC** K1. **DD** 345.73005.

THE AMERICAN JOURNAL OF JURISPRUDENCE. V. 14- 1969-. 0065-8995. US. English. an. $11.00 Domestic, $12.00 Foreign. Notre Dame Law School, PO Box 486, Notre Dame IN 46556. **Tel** (219)255-2938. **Ed** Charles E Rice. **Ind/Abst** Leg. Resour. Index, ABC Pol Sci, Cathol. Period. Lit. Index, Index Leg. Period., Curr. Law Index, Contents Curr. Leg. Period. **LC** K14. **DD** 340.1. bk rev. adv acc. **Circ** 1,000. Natural law theory and philosophy. *Natural Law Forum, 0199-9702.*

AMERICAN JOURNAL OF LAW & MEDICINE. **VAT** American Journal of Law and Medicine. V. 1- Mar. 1975-. 0098-8588. Periodical. US. English. qt. $40.00. American Society of Law and Medicine, 765 Commonwealth Avenue/16th Floor, Boston MA 02215. **Tel** (617)262-4990. **Ed** Abby Wayne. **Ind/Abst** Leg. Resour. Index, Hospit. Lit. Index, Sociol. Abstr., Soc. Welf. Soc. Plan./Policy Soc. Dev., Excerpta Med., Index Med., Biol. Abstr., Soc. Sci. Citation Index, Curr. Contents, Soc. Behav. Sci., Energy Res. Abstr., Index Leg. Period., Contents Curr. Leg. Period., Curr. Law Index. **LC** K1. **DD** 344.73041. **NLM** W1 AM475. **CODEN** AJLMDN. bk rev. adv acc. **Circ** 9,000. An interdisciplinary law review which contains professional articles, analyses of legislature and judicial developments, and book reviews in the area of health law.

THE AMERICAN JOURNAL OF LEGAL HISTORY. V. 1- Jan. 1957-. 0002-9319. Periodical. US. English. qt. $14.00. American Journal of Legal History, North Broad Street and Montgomery Avenue, Philadelphia PA 19122. **Tel** (215)787-7892. **Ind/Abst** Am. Hist. Life, Hist. Abstr., Part A, Mod. Hist. Abstr., Hist. Abst., Part B, Twent. Century Abstr., Leg. Resour. Index, ABC Pol Sci, Writ. Am. Hist., Soc. Work Res. Abstr., Index Leg. Period., Leg. Contents, Curr. Law Index, Contents Curr. Leg. Period., Hist. Abstr., Soc. Sci. Citation Index, Recent Publ. Artic. **LC** UNC. adv acc.

THE AMERICAN JOURNAL OF TRIAL ADVOCACY. V. 1- Fall 1977-. 0160-0281. Periodical. US. English. ty. $19.00. Cumberland School of Law, Samford University, 800 Lakeshore Drive, Birmingham AL 35229. **Tel** (205)870-2959. **Ed** Charles E Vercelli Jr. **Ind/Abst** Leg. Resour. Index, Index Leg. Period. **LC** K1. **DD** 347.73705. bk rev. adv acc. **Circ** 2,000. Articles, commentaries, and student works with topics focusing exclusively on assisting trial practitioners. Also, selected 'Classic Closings' and light reading useful to the trial attorney.

AMERICAN JURISPRUDENCE PLEADING AND PRACTICE FORMS ANNOTATED. 1956-. Periodical. US. English. ir. Bancroft-Whitney Company, 301 Brannon Street, San Francisco CA 94107. **DD** 347.92.

AMERICAN LAW OF MINING. **Main/Corp** Rocky Mountain Mineral Law Foundation. US. English. an. Matthew Bender & Company Inc, 1275 Broadway, Albany NY 12201. **Tel** (800)833-9844.

AMERICAN LAW REPORTS. ALR 3D. CASES AND ANNOTATIONS *CEASED.* **VFOAT** ALR 3D. Vol. 1-V. 100. US. English. **DD** 345. *American Law Reports Annotated, Second Series.*

AMERICAN LAW REPORTS. ALR 4TH, CASES AND ANNOTATIONS. (AMERICAN LAW REPORTS. ALR 4TH. CASES AND ANNOTATIONS). **VFOAT** ALR 4th. V. 1-. 0730-837X. US. English. Lawyers Cooperative Publishing Company, Aqueduct Building, Rochester NY 14603. **LC** KF132. **DD** 348.7346, 347.3084. *American Law Reports. ALR 3D: Cases and Annotations.*

AMERICAN LAW REPORTS. ALR FEDERAL. CASES AND ANNOTATIONS. (AMERICAN LAW REPORTS. ALR FEDERAL : CASES AND ANNOTATIONS). **VFOAT** ALR Fed. Vol. 1-. US. English. Lawyers Co-Operative Publishing Company, Aqueduct Building, Rochester NY 14603. **LC** KF132. **DD** 34541.

AMERICAN LAW REVIEW (DALLAS, TEX.). (THE AMERICAN LAW REVIEW). V. 16, No. 4 (Jan. 21, 1985)-. 8750-8214. Periodical. US. English. wk. $24.00 Domestic, $50.00 Foreign. The American Law Review, 7616 LBJ Freeway, Dallas TX 75251. **DD** 340. *Financial Trend, 0040-4195.*

THE AMERICAN LAWYER. V. 1- Feb. 1979-. 0162-3397. Periodical. US. English. ir. $125.00. American Lawyer, 205 Lexington Avenue, New York NY 10016. **Tel** (212)696-8900. **Ed** Steven Brill. **Ind/Abst** Leg. Resour. Index. **LC** K1. **DD** 340.0973. bk rev. adv acc. **Circ** 20,000. Serious well-written journalism regarding the business of lawyering. Unique view of people and events shaping the world of law and business highly regarded in those communities.

THE AMERICAN LAWYER. (THE AMERICAN LAWYER. SPECIAL PULL-OUT SUPPLEMENT). Began in 1983. Periodical. US. English. mo. $15.00 Per Issue. American Lawyer, Special Order Department, 205 Lexington Avenue, New York NY 10016. *American Lawyer. Special Pull-Out Section, 0162-3397.*

THE AMERICAN LAWYER GUIDE TO LEADING LAW FIRMS. **VFOAT** Guide to Leading Law Firms. 1983-84-. 8755-4461. US. English. an. $475.00. Am-Law Publishing Corporation, 2 Park Avenue, New York NY 10016. **LC** KF190. **DD** 340.02573. *American Lawyer Guide to Law Firms, 0740-1507.*

AMERICAN SERIES OF FOREIGN PENAL CODES. Vol. 1-. Monographic Series. US. English. ir. Fred B Rothman & Company, 10368 West Centennial Road, Littletown CO 80127. **Tel** (303)979-5657. **Ed** Ed Weiss. US translation of foreign penal codes.

THE AMERICAN UNIVERSITY LAW REVIEW. V. 6- Jan. 1957-. 0003-1453. Periodical. US. English. qt. $15.00. American University Law Review, Washington College of Law, Washington DC 20016. **Tel** (202)885-2651. **Ed** Mitchell E F Plarc. **Ind/Abst** Leg. Resour. Index, Index Leg. Period., Curr. Law Index, Contents Curr. Leg. Period. adv acc. Student and outside author notes and comments on various areas of the law. *American University Intramural Law Review, 0275-1674.*

AMERICANS FOR LEGAL REFORM. Began in 1979. 0739-6813. Periodical. US. English. qt. $15.00 Members. Halt, 201 Massachusetts Avenue Northeast/Suite 319, Washington DC 20002. **Tel** (202)546-4258. **Ed** Richard Herbert. **LC** K1. **DD** 340.30973. bk rev. **Circ** 100,000. (ctrl). Articles on developments in reform of the civil legal system including opinions, news, features, advice on self-help. Strong consumer point of view.

AMICUS. Began with Nov. 1975 issue. 0146-8278. Periodical. US. English. bm. $12.00. National Center for Law and the Handicapped Inc, 211 West Washington Street/Suite 1900, South Bend IN 46601. **LC** KF3738.A15. **DD** 344.73032405.

Law

AMICUS CURIAE. 0360-7739. US. in English. Arkansas Judicial Department, Justice Building/State Capitol Grounds, Little Rock AR 72201. **LC** KFA4108.A15. **DD** 347.7670105.

AMICUS CURIAE (CLARKSVILLE, TENN.). (AMICUS CURIAE). 8756-3428. US. English. an. University of Miami School of Law, P O B 248087, Coral Gables FL 33124.

AMICUS CURIARUM. Main/Corp Maryland. Administrative Office of the Courts. No. 90- Apr. 1976-. 0145-8574. US. English. Administrative Office of the Courts, Court of Appeals Building, PO Box 431, Baltimore MD 21401. **LC** KFM1708.A73. **DD** 347.75205. Newsletter.

AMICUS JURIS. 1st- issue. 0161-0783. Periodical. US. English. sa. Memphis State University, Student Bar Association, Memphis TN 38152. **LC** KF200. **DD** 340.09768.

AMTSBLATT DES BAYERISCHEN STAATSMINISTERIUMS FUR ARBEIT UND SOZIALORDNUNG. Main/Corp Bavaria (Germany). Staatsministerium fur Arbeit und Sozialordnung. 0340-1790. GW. German. sm. 47.50. Staatsministerium fur Arbeit und Sozialordnung, Winzererstrasse 9, 8000 Munchen 40 West Germany. **DD** 344.433. Amtsblatt des Bayerischen Staatsministeriums fur Arbeit und Soziale Fursorge, 0005-7193.

ANAIS DO CONGRESSO BRASILEIRO DE DIREITO ADMINISTRATIVO. Main/Corp Congresso Brasileiro de Direito Administrativo. 1.- 1975-. Portuguese. ir. **DD** 342.8106.

ANAIS FORENSES DO ESTADO DE MATO GROSSO. Main/Corp Mato Grosso, Brazil (State). Tribunal de Justica. Portuguese. ir. $70.00. Tribunal de Justica, Rua Joaquim Murtinho 46 10 Andar Sala 3 Caixa Postal 258, Ciuaba Brazil. **DD** 348.817043.

ANALELE UNIVERSITATII BUCURESTI : DREPT. Main/Corp Universitatea Din Bucuresti. V. 26- 1977-. Periodical. RM. Romanian (French). ir. 12. Universitatii Bucuresti, Ilexim Departamentue Export-Import Presa, PO Box 136-137 Tele 11226 Bucuresti, Str 13 Decembrie Nr 3, Bucuresti Romania. **LC** K2.

ANALES DE DERECHO. See Yearbooks, Almanacs, Directories.

ANALES DE JURISPRUDENCIA. See Yearbooks, Almanacs, Directories.

ANALES DEL FORO. See Yearbooks, Almanacs, Directories.

ANALYSES OF PROPOSED CONSTITUTIONAL AMENDMENTS FOR ELECTION . . . . VFOAT Analyses of Proposed Constitutional Amendments Appearing on . . . Ballot. US. English. Texas Legislative Council, PO Box 12128/Capitol Station, Austin TX 78711. **LC** KFT1601 1876 .A7. **DD** 342.764035, 347.640235.

ANALYSIS OF FEDERAL AND STATE CAMPAIGN FINANCE LAW. US. English. sm. US Federal Election Commission, 1325 K Street NW, Washington DC 20463.

ANALYSIS OF REVISIONS OF THE UNIFORM BUILDING CODE, U.B.C. STANDARDS . . . . Main/Corp International Conference of Building Officials. VFOAT U.B.C. Standards. VAT Analysis of Revisions of the Uniform Building Code, Uniform Building Code Standards. . . Uniform Building Code Standards. 19 -. US. English. an.

ANALYSIS OF WORKMEN'S COMPENSATION LAWS. Main/Corp Chamber of Commerce of the United States of America. 1954-75. 0577-5183. US. English. an. $12.00. Chamber of Commerce of US, 1615 H Street NW, Washington DC 20062. **Tel** (202)463-5509. **Ed** Deborah D Cumberland. **LC** KF3615.Z95. **DD** 344.73021. **Circ** 70,000. Containing charts and accompanying text describing the provisions of workers' compensation laws in the 50 states, the District of Columbia, Guam, Puerto Rico, and Canadian provinces. Analysis of Provisions of Workmen's Compensation Laws and Discussion of Coverages.

ANDHRA LAW TIMES. SUPPLEMENT. VFOAT Alt Acts, Rules, Cent. and AP. English. an. Andhra Law Times, 16-11-418/3 Balaji Sadan Kilsukhnagar, Hyderabad 500-036 India. **DD** 348.5484023, 345.4840823.

ANGELINA COUNTY COURT DIGEST. V. 1- Nov. 8, 1977-. Periodical. US. English. bm. $15.00. 110-112 West Shepherd, PO Box 1487, Lufkin TX 74901. **LC** KFT1799.A53. **DD** 340.09764173.

ANGLO-AMERICAN LAW REVIEW. (THE ANGLO-AMERICAN LAW REVIEW). V. 1- Jan./ March 1972-. 0308-6569. Periodical. UK. English. qt. $76.63. Barry Rose Law Periodicals Limited, East Row Little London Chichester, West Suxxex PO19 1PG England. **Ind/Abst** Leg. Resour. Index, Index Leg. Period., Curr. Law Index. **LC** K1. **DD** 340.05.

ANIMAL RIGHTS LAW REPORTER. Jan. 1980-. 0730-6792. Periodical. US. English. qt. Society for Animal Rights Inc, 421 South State Street, Clarks Summit PA 18411. **LC** KF390.5.A5. **DD** 346.73046954, 347.30646954.

ANNALES AFRICAINES. 1954-. 0066-202X. French. an. Editions A Pedone, 13 rue Soufflot, 75005 Paris France. **Ind/Abst** Am. Hist. Life, Hist. Abstr., Part A, Mod. Hist. Abstr., Hist. Abst., Part B, Twent. Century Abstr. **DD** 349.6605, 346.6005. (cum index).

ANNALES DE DROIT DE LOUVAIN. V. 41, 1-. 0770-6472. Periodical. BE. French. qt. 1,000 Members, 2,100 Others. Secretariat de l'Association des Diplomes en Droit de l'Universite de Louvain, Tienstraat 41, 3000 Louvain Belgium. **LC** K1. **DD** 340.05. Annales de Droit.

ANNALES DE LA FACULTE DE DROIT. Main/Corp Universite Nationale du Zaire. Campus de Kinsahsa. Faculte de Droit. V. 1- 1972-. CG. French. ir. Presses Universitaries du E Zaire, Banque Commerciale Zairoise 923.957/26, Kinshasa Zaire. **LC** K25. **DD** 340.096751.

ANNALI DELLA FACOLTA DI SCIENZE POLITICHE (TRIESTE, ITALY). See Political Science.

ANNALS OF AIR AND SPACE LAW. VFOAT Annales de Droit Aerien et Spatial. V. 1-. 0701-155X. CN. English (French). an. 50.00. Institute of Air & Space Law, McGill University, 3690 Peel Street, Montreal Quebec 43A 1W9 Canada. **Tel** (514)392-6735. **Ed** Nicholas M Matte. **Ind/Abst** Leg. Resour. Index, Index Leg. Period. **LC** K1. **DD** 341.4505. bk rev. **Circ** 1,000. Gathers articles of worldwide prominent scholars, practitioners and other specialists in air and space law. It deals with topics of current interest and problems of growing concern related to emerging air and space activities.

ANNOTATED MANUAL OF STATUTES AND REGULATIONS. Main/Corp United States. Federal Home Loan Bank Board. Periodical. US. English. bm. Superintendent of Documents, US Government Printing Office, Washington DC 20402. **Tel** (202)783-3238.

ANNUAIRE ADMINISTRATIF ET JUDICIAIRE DE BELGIQUE. See Yearbooks, Almanacs, Directories.

ANNUAIRE DE JURISPRUDENCE DU QUEBEC. See Yearbooks, Almanacs, Directories.

ANNUAIRE DES PROFESSIONS JUDICIAIRES ET JURIDIQUES. See Yearbooks, Almanacs, Directories.

ANNUAL ACTIVITIES REPORT OF THE COMMITTEE ON THE JUDICIARY, UNITED STATES SENATE. Main/Corp United States. Congress. Senate. Committee on the Judiciary. 0277-3341. US. English. an. Superintendent of Documents, US Government Printing Office, Washington DC 20402. **LC** KF4987.J8. **DD** 328.7307652.

ANNUAL ADVANCED ANTITRUST WORKSHOP. Main/Corp Advanced Antitrust Workshop. Series/Titl Corporate Law and Practice Course Handbook Series. 1970-. 0194-1127. US. English. an. Practising Law Institute, 810 Seventh Avenue, New York NY 10019. **LC** KF1649.3. **DD** 343.73072.

ANNUAL ADVANCED FAMILY LAW COURSE. Main/Corp State Bar of Texas. Professional Development Program. VFOAT Advanced Family Law Course. 0190-7395. US. English. an. **LC** KFT1294. **DD** 346.764015.

ANNUAL BANKRUPTCY LITIGATION INSTITUTE. Main/Corp Bankruptcy Litigation Institute. VFOAT Bankruptcy Litigation Institute. 1st-. US. English. an. Law & Business Inc, 757 3rd Avenue, New York NY 10017. **LC** KF1527. **DD** 346.730780269, 347.306780269.

ANNUAL BULLETIN - JUDGE ADVOCATE GENERAL'S SCHOOL (U.S.). Main/Corp Judge Advocate General's School (U.S.). US. English. an. Commandant, Judge Advocate General's School US Army, Charlottesville VA 22901. **LC** KF7313.55.J8. **DD** 340.071173.

ANNUAL BUSINESS AND COMMERCIAL LAW SEMINAR FOR LAWYERS IN GENERAL PRACTICE. Main/Conf Business and Commercial Law Seminar For Lawyers in General Practice. 1st (1983)-. 0742-9894. US. English. an. **LC** KFV2605. **DD** 346.7550705, 347.5506705.

ANNUAL CONVENTION REFERENCE MATERIALS - ASSOCIATION OF TRIAL LAWYERS OF AMERICA. Main/Corp Association of Trial Lawyers of America. Convention. VFOAT Reference Materials. 0747-8135. US. English. an. The Association of Trial Lawyers of America, 1050 31st Street NW, Washington DC 20007. **LC** KF8915.A2. **DD** 349.73, 347.3.

ANNUAL DIRECTORY - HAWAII STATE BAR ASSOCIATION. See Yearbooks, Almanacs, Directories.

ANNUAL ENERGY LITIGATION INSTITUTE. EFFECTIVE STRATEGIES & TECHNIQUES. See Energy.

ANNUAL FALL MEETING - AMERICAN BAR ASSOCIATION. SECTION OF LITIGATION. FALL MEETING. (ANNUAL FALL MEETING). Main/Corp American Bar Association. Section of Litigation. Fall Meeting. 0731-4493. US. English. an. ABA Section on Litigation, 1800 M Street NW, Washington DC 20036. **LC** KF8915.A2. **DD** 347.747, 347.3077.

ANNUAL FINANCIAL REPORT FOR YEAR ENDING AUG. 31 . . . - TEXAS. ATTORNEY-GENERAL'S OFFICE. See Business - Public Finance.

ANNUAL FORUM - AMERICAN BAR ASSOCIATION. FORUM COMMITTEE ON AIR AND SPACE LAW. Main/Corp American Bar Association Forum Committee on Air and Space Law. 1st (Feb. 23-25, 1984)-. US. English. an. **LC** KF2400.A75. **DD** 343.73097, 347.30397.

ANNUAL FORUM - AMERICAN BAR ASSOCIATION. FORUM COMMITTEE ON FRANCHISING. ANNUAL FORUM. (ANNUAL FORUM). Main/Corp American Bar Association. Forum Committee on Franchising. Annual Forum. 0739-1323. US. English. an. **LC** KF2023.A75. **DD** 343.730887, 347.303887.

ANNUAL GAMING CONFERENCE : PROCEEDINGS. Main/Corp Gaming Conference. 1st- 1979-. 0272-0736. US. English. an. **LC** KFN985.A75. **DD** 344.7930542, 347.9304542.

ANNUAL GENERAL PRACTICE SECTION SEMINAR COURSE HANDBOOK - INSTITUTE OF CONTINUING LEGAL EDUCATION, ANN ARBOR, MICH. Main/Corp Institute of Continuing Legal Education, Ann Arbor, Mich. 1st- 1977-. 0160-1172. US. English. an. **LC** KFM4281. **DD** 340.9774.

ANNUAL IMMIGRATION AND NATURALIZATION INSTITUTE. See Emigration and Immigration.

ANNUAL IMMIGRATION AND NATURALIZATION INSTITUTE. PROCEEDINGS. See Emigration and Immigration.

ANNUAL INSTITUTE FOR CORPORATE COUNSEL. Main/Corp Institute For Corporate Counsel. Series/Titl Corporate Law and Practice Course Handbook Series. 1st-. 0195-3680. US. English. an. Practising Law Institute, 810 Seventh Avenue, New York NY 10019. **LC** KF1425.Z9. **DD** 346.730664.

ANNUAL INSTITUTE ON EMPLOYMENT LAW. Main/Conf Institute on Employment Law. Series/Titl Litigation and Administrative Practice Series. 12th (1983)-. 0743-4146. Periodical. US. English. an. Practising Law Institute, 810 Seventh Avenue, New York NY 10019. **LC** KF3464.Z9. **DD** 344.7301133, 347.3041133. Annual Institute on Equal Employment Opportunity Compliance, 0198-9022.

ANNUAL INSTITUTE ON SECURITIES REGULATION. Main/Corp Institute on Securities Regulation. Series/Titl Corporate Law and Practice Course Handbook Series. 1st- 1970-. Periodical. US. English. an. Practising Law Institute, 810 Seventh Avenue, New York NY 10019. **Ind/Abst** Index Leg. Period. **LC** KF1440. **DD** 346.7309202636.

ANNUAL JUDICIAL CONFERENCE STATISTICAL REPORT - MISSOURI. See Statistics.

Law

ANNUAL JUDICIAL REPORT - ARIZONA. Main/Corp Arizona. Administrative Office of the Courts. VFOAT Arizona Courts. Began with 1977. US. English. an. Administrative Office of the Courts Supreme Court, State Capitol, Phoenix AZ. LC KFA2908.A73. DD 347.79101, 347.91071. *Report of the Administrative Director of the Supreme Court of Arizona, 0271-4418.*

ANNUAL LAW DIGEST. 1981-. English. an. 150.00. Annual Law Digest Office, Chowk Urdu Bazar, Lahore Pakistan. DD 348.5491046, 345.4910846.

ANNUAL LEGAL BIBLIOGRAPHY - HARVARD UNIVERSITY. LAW SCHOOL. LIBRARY. *See* Bibliographies.

ANNUAL LICENSING LAW AND BUSINESS INSTITUTE. Main/Corp Licensing Law and Business Institute. 1st- 1979-. 0271-3489. US. English. an. Clark Boardman Educational Programs Inc, 435 Hudson Street, New York NY 10013. LC KF3145.A75. DD 346.73048.

ANNUAL MEMBERSHIP TELEPHONE DIRECTORY - ASSOCIATION OF TRIAL LAWYERS OF AMERICA. *See* Yearbooks, Almanacs, Directories.

ANNUAL NOTRE DAME ESTATE PLANNING INSTITUTE. (ANNUAL NOTRE DAME ESTATE PLANNING INSTITUTE : PROCEEDINGS). Main/Corp Notre Dame Estate Planning Institute. Vol. 2 (Sept. 15-16, 1977)-. 0732-8850. US. English. an. $49.00. Callaghen & Company, 3201 Old Glenview Road, Wilmette IL 60091. Ed R W Campfield. LC KF6584.A2. DD 343.73053, 347.30353. *Proceedings, 0278-1840.*

ANNUAL OF INDUSTRIAL PROPERTY LAW. UK. English. an. $40.00. Shepheard-Walwyn, 114 East 23rd Street, New York NY 10016. DD 346.048.

ANNUAL PROCEEDINGS OF THE FORDHAM CORPORATE LAW INSTITUTE. 1974-. 0363-8871. US. English. an. Matthew Bender, 235 East 45th Street, New York NY 10017. LC K1314.6. DD 346.066.

ANNUAL PUBLIC DEFENDERS' WORKSHOP. (ANNUAL PUBLIC DEFENDERS' WORKSHOP HANDBOOK). Main/Corp Public Defenders' Workshop. Series/Titl Criminal Law and Urban Problems Course Handbook Series. 0093-8653. US. English. an. Public Defenders' Workshop, 1133 Avenue of the Americas, New York NY 10036. LC KF9646.A73. DD 345.7305.

ANNUAL REPORT - ADMINISTRATIVE OFFICE OF THE COURTS, COMMONWEALTH OF KENTUCKY. Main/Corp Kentucky. Administrative Office of the Courts. 1976-. US. English. an. Route 8 Twilight Trail, US 127 Lawrenceburg Road, Frankfort KY 40601. LC KFK1708. DD 347.769013. *Docket Reports, 0145-6504 Biennial Report to the General Assembly.*

ANNUAL REPORT - ADMINISTRATIVE OFFICE OF THE COURTS OF GEORGIA CEASED. Main/Corp Georgia. Administrative Office of the Courts. 0363-9320. US. English. an. Georgia Administrative Office of the Courts, 2220 Parklake Drive/Suite 335, Atlanta GA 30345. LC KFG508. DD 353.97580088.

ANNUAL REPORT - ADVISORY COMMITTEE TO THE MINISTER OF JUSTICE ON LEGAL AID. Main/Corp New Brunswick. Adivsory Committee to the Minister of Justice on Legal Aid. CN. English. an. Advisory Committee to the Minister of Justice on Legal Aid, Centennial Building, Fredericton New Brunswick Canada. LC KEN160.A72. DD 347.71501.

ANNUAL REPORT, ALABAMA JUDICIAL SYSTEM. Main/Corp Alabama. Administrative Office of Courts. US. English. an. Administrative Office of Courts, 817 South Court Street, Montgomery AL 36104. LC KFA510. DD 347.76101, 347.61071.

ANNUAL REPORT - ALASKA CODE REVISION COMMISSION. Main/Corp Alaska Code Revision Commission. US. English. an. Alaska Code Revision Commission, Pouch Y State Capitol, Juneau AK 99811. LC KFA1227. DD 353.97980088.

ANNUAL REPORT - ALASKA. COMMISSION ON JUDICIAL CONDUCT. Main/Corp Alaska. Commission on Judicial Conduct. US. English. an. Free. Commission on Judicial Conduct, Boney Memorial Court Building, 303 K Street/Suite 241, Anchorage AK 99501. Tel (907)264-0528. A report published each year to inform the public of the Commission's activities in a calendar year, including yearly statistics.

ANNUAL REPORT - ALASKA COURT SYSTEM. Main/Corp Alaska. Court System. US. English. an. 303 K Street, Anchorage AK 99501. LC KFA1708. DD 347.798013.

ANNUAL REPORT - ALBERTA, LOCAL AUTHORITIES BOARD. (ANNUAL REPORT). Main/Corp Alberta. Local Authorities Board. 0711-2823. CN. English. an. Free. Local Authorities Board, 6th Floor Pacific Plaza 10909 Jasper Avenue, Edmonton Alberta T5J 3L9 Canada. LC KEA477.A72. DD 342.712304, 347.123029.

ANNUAL REPORT - AMERICAN ARBITRATION ASSOCIATION. Main/Corp American Arbitration Association. Began in 1973. US. English. an. American Arbitration Association, 140 West 51st Street, New York NY 10020. LC KF9086. DD 347.739.

ANNUAL REPORT - AMERICAN BAR ASSOCIATION, FUND FOR PUBLIC EDUCATION. Main/Corp American Bar Association. Fund For Public Education. 0197-2634. US. English. an. Office of Resource Development, American Bar Association, 1155 East 60th Street, Chicago IL 60637. LC KF325.1254. DD 349.7306.

ANNUAL REPORT - AMERICAN BAR FOUNDATION. Main/Corp American Bar Foundation. US. English. an. American Bar Foundation, 750 North Lake Shore Drive, Chicago IL 60611. Tel (312)988-6520. Ed Richard H Maas. DD 340.06273. Circ 30,000. (ctrl). Summarizes the research work and staff activities for each calendar year.

ANNUAL REPORT - AMERICAN JUDICATURE SOCIETY. (ANNUAL REPORT). Main/Corp American Judicature Society. 0732-1031. US. English. an. American Judicature Society, 200 West Monroe Street/Suite 1606, Chicago IL 60606. LC KF294.A4. DD 347.73106, 347.307106. *Journal of the American Judicature Society.*

ANNUAL REPORT AND OFFICIAL OPINIONS OF THE ATTORNEY GENERAL OF MARYLAND. Main/Corp Maryland. Dept. of Law. V. 1- 1916-. US. English. an. (cum index).

ANNUAL REPORT - ARKANSAS. JUDICIAL DEPT. Main/Corp Arkansas. Judicial Dept. 1st-. Periodical. US. English. an. LC KFA3671.

ANNUAL REPORT AS REQUIRED BY THE CRIMINAL CODE OF CANADA, SECTION 178.22. (ANNUAL REPORT AS REQUIRED BY THE CRIMINAL CODE OF CANADA, SECTION 178.22, (PROTECTION OF PRIVACY ACT)). Main/Corp Canada. Solicitor General Canada. VFOAT Rapport Annuel Requis par l'Article 178.22 du Code Criminel du Canada, (Loi Sur la Protection de la Vie Privee). 1977-. 0708-3009. CN. English (French, each with title page and separate paging. French text on inverted pages). an. LC KE203. DD 354.710088. *Annual Report to His Excellency the Right Honourable Jules Leger, C.C., C.M.M., C.D., Governor General of Canada as Required by the Criminal Code of Canada, Section 178.22 (Protection of Privacy Act), 0708-3009.*

ANNUAL REPORT - AUSTRALIA. TRADE PRACTICES COMMISSION. Main/Corp Australia. Trade Practices Commission. 0314-0520. English. an. DD 354.9400826.

ANNUAL REPORT BY THE MINISTER FOR BUSINESS AND CONSUMER AFFAIRS ON THE OPERATION OF THE BANKRUPTCY ACT 1966. Main/Corp Australia. Dept. of Business and Consumer Affairs. English. an. LC J905. DD 300.994 S, 354.94008252.

ANNUAL REPORT - CALIFORNIA. OFFICE OF ADMINISTRATIVE LAW. Main/Corp California. Office of Administrative Law. 1980-1981-. US. English. an. Office of Administrative Law 1414 K Street/Suite 600, Sacramento CA 95814. LC KFC780. DD 342.79406, 347.94026.

ANNUAL REPORT - CANADIAN BAR ASSOCIATION. ALBERTA BRANCH. Main/Corp Canadian Bar Association. Alberta Branch. 1981-82-. CN. English. an. Canadian Bar Association Alberta Branch Office, 4th Floor 640 8 Avenue Southwest, Calgary Alberta T2P 1O7 Canada. LC KE366.7.A4. DD 340.0607123.

ANNUAL REPORT - CENTER FOR STATE COURTS. Main/Corp National Center For State Courts. 0196-5433. US. English. an. National Center for State Courts, 300 Newport Avenue, Williamsburg VA 23185. LC KF8736.A16. DD 347.73306, 347.307106.

ANNUAL REPORT - CLEVELAND (OHIO). MUNICIPAL COURT. Main/Corp Cleveland (Ohio). Municipal Court. US. English. an. Cleveland Municipal Court, Justice Center Courts Tower, 1200 Ontario Street, Cleveland OH 44113. LC KFO519.C55. DD 347.7713202, 347.7132072.

ANNUAL REPORT - COMMISSION DES SERVICES JURIDIQUES. Main/Corp Legal Services Commission. 0704-450X. CN. English. Comm des Services Juridiques, 1170 Square Beaver Hall, Montreal Quebec H3B 3C6 Canada. DD 347.714017. *Annual Report Summary, 0225-669X.*

ANNUAL REPORT - CONSUMER PROTECTION DIVISION. Main/Corp Maryland. Consumer Protection Division. US. English. an. Consumer Protection Division, 131 East Redwood Street, Baltimore MD 21202. LC KFM1430. DD 353.97520082.

ANNUAL REPORT - CRIMINAL COURT OF THE CITY OF NEW YORK. Main/Corp New York (City). Criminal Court. 1962-. 0098-1834. US. English. an. Judicial Conference of the State of New York, New York NY 10023. LC KFX2007.3. DD 345.747101.

ANNUAL REPORT - CRIMINAL INJURIES COMPENSATION TRIBUNAL. Main/Corp Ireland (Eire). Criminal Injuries Compensation Tribunal. 1st- 1975-. English. ir. LC KDK471. DD 354.415008488.

ANNUAL REPORT, DISTRICT OF COLUMBIA COURTS. Main/Corp District of Columbia. Joint Committee on Judicial Administration. US. English. an. District of Columbia Courts, 500 Indiana Avenue NW, Washington DC 20001. LC KFD1710. DD 347.75301, 347.53071.

ANNUAL REPORT - FEDERAL ELECTION COMMISSION. (ANNUAL REPORT). Main/Corp United States. Federal Election Commission. Began with 1975. 0145-7284. US. English. an. Federal Election Commission, 1325 K Street NW, Washington DC 20463. LC KF4886. DD 353.091.

ANNUAL REPORT - FEDERAL JUDICIAL CENTER. (ANNUAL REPORT). Main/Corp Federal Judicial Center. 0096-8854. US. English. an. Federal Judicial Center, Dolley Madison House, 1520 H Street NW, Washington DC 20005. LC KF8719. DD 347.732. Vols. for 1982- distributed to depository libraries in microfiche.

ANNUAL REPORT, FISCAL YEAR ... - CONNECTICUT. Main/Corp Connecticut. Superior Court. Family Division. 1978/79-. US. English. an. LC KFC3694.5. DD 346.7460150269, 347.4606150269.

ANNUAL REPORT FOR THE YEAR ENDED - IRELAND. EMPLOYMENT APPEALS TRIBUNAL. Main/Corp Ireland. Employment Appeals Tribunal. 12th (31st Dec. 1979)-. IE. English. an. 0.45. Government Publications Sales Office, GPO Arcade, Dublin 1 Ireland. LC KDK804. DD 354.4150018. *Annual Report.*

ANNUAL REPORT FOR THE YEAR ENDED MARCH 31 - CANADA. RESTRICTIVE TRADE PRACTICES COMMISSION. Main/Corp Canada. Restrictive Trade Practices Commission. 1981-. CN. English. an. LC KE1639.A2. DD 354.710082.

ANNUAL REPORT - ILLINOIS GUARDIANSHIP AND ADVOCACY COMMISSION. Main/Corp Illinois Guardianship and Advocacy Commission. 1980-. US. English. an. Office of Public Information, 123 West Madison/Suite 1700, Chicago IL 60602. LC KFI1565. DD 344.773044, 347.730444.

ANNUAL REPORT - INSTITUTE OF LAW RESEARCH AND REFORM (UNIVERSITY OF ALBERTA). Main/Corp University of Alberta. Institute of Law Research and Reform. CN. English. an. Institute of Law Research and Reform, 402 Law Centre, University of Alberta, Edmonton Alberta Canada. LC KEA149.I56. DD 340.30627123.

ANNUAL REPORT - INTERNATIONAL TELECOMMUNICATIONS SATELLITE ORGANIZATION. *See* Communication - Telecommunications.

Law

ANNUAL REPORT - JOINT COMMITTEE ON PUBLIC HEALTH AND SAFETY OF THE CONNECTICUT GENERAL ASSEMBLY (CONNECTICUT). Main/Corp Connecticut. General Assembly. Joint Committee On Public Health and Safety. US. English. an. Joint Committee on Public Health and Safety, Connecticut General Assembly, State Capitol, Room 503A, Harford CT 06115. LC KFC3611.6. DD 344.74604.

ANNUAL REPORT - JOINT LEGISLATIVE COMMITTEE ON THE PROBLEMS OF PUBLIC HEALTH, MEDICARE, MEDICAID AND COMPULSORY HEALTH AND HOSPITAL INSURANCE (NEW YORK STATE). Main/Corp New York (State). Legislature. Joint Legislative Committee on the Problems of Public Health, Medicare, Medicaid and Compulsory Health and Hospital Insurance. 1968-. 0548-815X. US. English. an. New York State Legislature, RD Box 196 East, Albany NY 12203. LC KFN5010.6. DD 344.747041. *Annual Report of the Joint Legislative Committee on the Problems.*

ANNUAL REPORT. JUDGES OF THE PROVINCIAL COURT SUPERANNUATION FUND. Main/Corp Saskatchewan. VFOAT Judges of the Provincial Court Superannuation Fund. 1978/79-. 0711-2807. CN. English. an. LC KES539.A72. DD 354.7124014, 347.1240714.

ANNUAL REPORT - JUDGES' RETIREMENT SYSTEM, STATE OF ARIZONA. Main/Corp Arizona. Judges' Retirement System. US. English. an. Public Safety Personnel Retirement System, Room 411/3113 North Central, Phoenix AZ 85012. LC KFA2925.5.S3. DD 347.791014.

ANNUAL REPORT - JUSTICE DEVELOPMENT COMMISSION (BRITISH COLUMBIA). See Public Administration.

ANNUAL REPORT - JUSTICE INSTITUTE OF BRITISH COLUMBIA. Main/Corp Justice Institute of British Columbia. 1978/79-. 0709-9983. CN. English. an. Justice Institute of British Columbia, 4180 West 4th Avenue, Vancouver British Columbia V6R 4J5 Canada. DD 874.013.

ANNUAL REPORT - KENTUCKY PRETRIAL SERVICES AGENCY. Main/Corp Kentucky. Pretrial Services Agency. 1st- 1976/77-. US. English. an. Administrative Office of the Courts Route 8 Twilight Trail, Frankfort KY 40601. LC KFK1776.6. DD 347.769072.

ANNUAL REPORT - LAW REFORM COMMISSION (AUSTRALIA). Main/Corp Australia. Law Reform Commission. 1975-. English. ir. DD 340.30994.

ANNUAL REPORT - LAW REFORM COMMISSION OF CANADA. Main/Corp Law Reform Commission of Canada. VFOAT Rapport Annuel. 1st- 1971/72-. 0382-1463. CN. text in English and French. an. Receiver General for Canada, Supply & Services, Ottawa Ontario K1A 0S9 Canada.

ANNUAL REPORT - LAW REFORM COMMISSION OF WESTERN AUSTRALIA. Main/Corp Western Australia. Law Reform Commission. 1972/73-. 0311-2276. AT. English. ir. Law Reform Commission, R&I Bank Building, 593 Hay Street, Perth Australia. DD 340.309941.

ANNUAL REPORT - LAWYERS COMMITTEE FOR INTERNATIONAL HUMAN RIGHTS. (ANNUAL REPORT). Main/Corp Lawyers' Committee for International Human Rights. 8755-1462. US. English. an. The Lawyers Committee for International Human Rights, 36 West 44th Street, New York NY 10036. LC K3236.2. DD 341.48105.

ANNUAL REPORT - LEGISLATIVE PROGRAM REVIEW AND INVESTIGATIONS COMMITTEE (CONNECTICUT). Main/Corp Connecticut. General Assembly. Legislative Program Review and Investigations Committee. US. English. an. Room 404 State Capitol, Hartford CT 06115.

ANNUAL REPORT - LOUISIANA STATE BAR ASSOCIATION. (ANNUAL REPORT). Main/Corp Louisiana State Bar Association. 0882-9845. US. English. an. Louisiana State Bar Association, 21 O'Keefe Avenue/Suite 600, New Orleans LA 70112.

ANNUAL REPORT - MARYLAND COMMISSION ON INTERGOVERNMENTAL COOPERATION. (ANNUAL REPORT - MARYLAND, COMMISSION ON INTERGOVERNMENTAL COOPERATION). Main/Corp Maryland Commission on Intergovernmental Cooperation. 0098-8766. US. English. an. Old Armory Building, PO Box 231, Annapolis MD 21404. LC KFM1609. DD 353.97529.

ANNUAL REPORT - MASSACHUSETTS ADVOCACY CENTER. Main/Corp Massachusetts Advocacy Center. 1st- 1974-. 0362-1383. US. English. an. Massachusetts Advocacy Center, 2 Park Square, Boston MA 02116. LC KFM2840. DD 353.9744.

ANNUAL REPORT - MASSACHUSETTS LABOR RELATIONS COMMISSION. See Economics - Labor.

ANNUAL REPORT - MICHIGAN. DEPT. OF MENTAL HEALTH. OFFICE OF RECIPIENT RIGHTS. See Public Health and Safety.

ANNUAL REPORT - MICHIGAN OFFICE OF CRIMINAL JUSTICE PROGRAMS. (ANNUAL REPORT). Main/Corp Michigan. Office of Criminal Justice Programs. 0092-2773. US. English. an. Office of Criminal Justice Programs, Lewis Cass Building, Second Floor, Lansing MI 48913. LC HV7272. DD 364.

ANNUAL REPORT - MINISTRY OF THE ATTORNEY-GENERAL (BRITISH COLUMBIA). (ANNUAL REPORT). Main/Corp British Columbia. Ministry of the Attorney-General. Began in 1976. 0704-6022. CN. English. an. LC KEB475.A72. DD 354.711065. *Annual Report.*

ANNUAL REPORT - MINISTRY OF THE ATTORNEY GENERAL (ONTARIO). Main/Corp Ontario. Ministry of the Attorney General. 1974/75-. 0382-1803. CN. English. an. Ministry of the Attorney General, 18 King Street East, Toronto Ontario M5C 1C5 Canada. LC KEO855.A72. DD 354.713065.

ANNUAL REPORT, MINNESOTA BOARD ON JUDICIAL STANDARDS FOR THE CALENDAR YEAR . . . . Main/Corp Minnesota Board on Judicial Standards. Began in 1975. US. English. an. 202 Minnesota State Bank Building, 200 South Robert Street, St Paul MN 55107. LC KFM5925.5.D5. DD 347.776014, 347.760714.

ANNUAL REPORT - NATIONAL DISTRICT ATTORNEYS ASSOCIATION. Main/Corp National District Attorneys Association. US. English. an. Suite 1432/666 North Lakeshore Drive, Chicago IL 60611.

ANNUAL REPORT - NEW JERSEY. ADMINISTRATIVE OFFICE OF THE COURTS. Main/Corp New Jersey. Administrative Office of the Courts. VFOAT New Jersey Judiciary Annual Report. US. English. an. Administrative Office of the Courts, State House Annex CN-037, Trenton NJ 08625. LC KFN1871. DD 347.749013, 347.490713. *Annual Report of the Administrative Director of the Courts.*

ANNUAL REPORT - NEW JERSEY JUDICIARY. Main/Corp New Jersey. Administrative Office of the Courts. 0149-0494. Periodical. US. English. an. *Annual Report of the Administrative Director of the Courts.*

ANNUAL REPORT - NEW MEXICO. ATTORNEY GENERAL'S OFFICE. Main/Corp New Mexico. Attorney General's Office. US. English. an. Office of the Attorney General, PO Drawer 1508, Santa Fe NM 87504. LC KFN4040. DD 353.97890088. *Report of the Attorney General of New Mexico, 0749-2065.*

ANNUAL REPORT - NEW YORK STATE COMMISSION ON JUDICIAL CONDUCT. Main/Corp New York State Commission on Judicial Conduct. US. English. an. New York State Commission on Judicial Conduct, 801 Second Avenue, New York NY 10017. LC KFN5984.5.D57. DD 347.747014.

ANNUAL REPORT - NEW YORK (STATE). DEPUTY ATTORNEY GENERAL FOR MEDICAID FRAUD CONTROL. Main/Corp New York (State). Deputy Attorney General for Medicaid Fraud Control. 4th (1979)-. US. English. an. LC KFN5617. DD 353.974700841.

ANNUAL REPORT - NEW YORK (STATE). LEGISLATURE. ASSEMBLY. STANDING COMMITTEE ON CODES. Main/Corp New York (State). Legislature. Assembly. Standing Committee on Codes. US. English. an. Legislative Office Building/Room 659, Albany NY 12248. LC KFN6100. DD 345.74705, 347.470505. *Annual Report to the People from the New York State Assembly, Standing Committee on Codes.*

ANNUAL REPORT - NEW YORK (STATE). LEGISLATURE. ASSEMBLY. STANDING COMMITTEE ON LABOR. Main/Corp New York (State). Legislature. Assembly. Standing Committee on Labor. VFOAT Annual Report of the Assembly Standing Committee on Labor. 1979-. US. English. an. The Assembly, State of New York Standing Committee on Labor, Albany NY 12248. LC KFN5556. DD 353.97470083. *Annual Report of the Standing Committee on Labor.*

ANNUAL REPORT - NORTH DAKOTA JUDICIAL COUNCIL. Main/Corp North Dakota. Judicial Council. 1976-. US. English. an. State Capitol, Bismarck ND 58505. LC KFN8671. DD 347.78401.

ANNUAL REPORT OF NEBRASKA PUBLIC COUNSEL. Main/Corp Nebraska. Office of the Public Counsel. 10th (1980)-. US. English. an. LC KFN441.O5. DD 353.97820091. *Annual Report and Brochure of the Nebraska Ombudsman.*

ANNUAL REPORT OF THE ATTORNEY GENERAL OF THE UNITED STATES. Main/Corp United States. Dept. of Justice. 0148-5229. US. English. an. US Department of Justice, Office of the Attorney General, Washington DC 20430. DD 353.5.

ANNUAL REPORT OF THE BOARD OF TRUSTEES. Main/Corp Judges Retirement System of Illinois. Board of Trustees. US. English. an. Judges Retirement System of Illinois, 415 Iles Park Place, Springfield IL 62718. LC KFI1725.5.A6. DD 331.252909773. *Annual Statement of the Board of Trustees.*

ANNUAL REPORT OF THE CASELOADS AND OPERATIONS OF THE COURTS OF WASHINGTON. 1981-. US. English. an. LC KFW71. DD 347.797013, 347.970713. *Report On Caseloads and Operations of the Courts of Washington.*

ANNUAL REPORT OF THE CHIEF ADMINISTRATOR OF THE COURTS. Series/Tlt State of New York Legislative Document. VFOAT Report of the Chief Administrator of the Courts. Jan. 1, 1978-Dec. 31, 1978-. US. English. an. Office of Court Administration, 270 Broadway, New York NY 10007. LC KFN5950.A73. DD 347.747013, 347.470713.

ANNUAL REPORT OF THE COLORADO JUDICIARY. Main/Corp Colorado. Office of the State Court Administrator. VFOAT Annual Report, Colorado Judiciary. July 1, 1979 to June 30, 1980-. 0731-3195. US. English. an. Office of the State Court Administrator, 2 East 14th Avenue, Denver CO 80203. LC KFC1871. DD 347.788013, 347.880713.

ANNUAL REPORT OF THE COMMISSION ON JUDICIAL DISCIPLINE, STATE OF HAWAII (FOR PERIOD JUNE 1, . . . TO JUNE 30, . . .). Main/Corp Hawaii. Commission on Judicial Discipline. 1st (June 1, 1979-June 30, 1980)-. US. English. an. PO Box 2560, Honolulu HI 96804. LC KFH525.5.D5. DD 347.969014, 349.690714.

ANNUAL REPORT OF THE CONNECTICUT LAW REVISION COMMISSION. Main/Corp Connecticut Law Revision Commission. US. English. an. Connecticut Revision Commission/University of Connecticut School of Law, 1800 Asylum Avenue, West Hartford CT 06117. LC KFC3627.L38. DD 340.3.

ANNUAL REPORT OF THE DIRECTOR - ADMINISTRATIVE OFFICE OF THE UNITED STATES COURTS. (ANNUAL REPORT OF THE DIRECTOR FOR THE TWELVE MONTH PERIOD ENDING . . .). Main/Corp United States. Administrative Office of the United States Courts. VFOAT Annual Report of the Director. 0095-7836. US. English. an. Superintendent of Documents, US Government Printing Office, Washington DC 20402. LC KF8732. DD 347.7313.

Law

ANNUAL REPORT OF THE DISTRICT OF COLUMBIA COMMISSION ON JUDICIAL DISABILITIES AND TENURE. Main/Corp District of Columbia. Commission on Judicial Disabilities and Tenure. Apr. 1975-Sept. 1976-. 0735-4827. US. English. an. Building A Room 312/505 5th Street NW, Washington DC 20001. LC KFD1725. DD 347.753014, 347.530714.

ANNUAL REPORT OF THE IMMIGRATION AND NATURALIZATION SERVICE. See Emigration and Immigration.

ANNUAL REPORT OF THE JOINT LEGISLATIVE COMMITTEE ON CHILDREN (SOUTH CAROLINA). Main/Corp South Carolina. Joint Legislative Committee on Children. US. English. an. Joint Legislative Committee on Children, Blatt Building/Suite 118, PO Box 11867, Columbia SC 29211. LC KFS1891.M5. DD 346.7570135, 347.5706135.

ANNUAL REPORT OF THE JUDICIAL COUNCIL OF NEW MEXICO. Main/Corp New Mexico. Judicial Council. 0360-4659. US. English. an. University of New Mexico School of Law, Judicial Council, 117 Stanford NE, Albuquerque NM 87131. LC KFN4108. DD 347.789.

ANNUAL REPORT OF THE JUDICIAL COUNCIL OF THE STATE OF WASHINGTON. Main/Corp Washington (State). Judicial Council. 26th- 1977-. US. English. an. Seattle Judicial Council, 508 Condon Hall, 1100 NE Campus Parkway, Seattle WA 98195. LC KFW508.A73. DD 347.79701. Report.

ANNUAL REPORT OF THE LAW FOUNDATION (SASKATCHEWAN). Main/Corp Law Foundation (Saskatchewan). 1973/74-. CN. English. an. Law Foundation, 2236 Albert Street, Regina Saskatchewan S4P 2V4 Canada. DD 338.47340097124.

ANNUAL REPORT OF THE LAW REFORM COMMISSION OF BRITISH COLUMBIA. Main/Corp Law Reform Commission of British Columbia. Series/Titl LRC. 1970-. 0381-2510. CN. English. an. Law Reform Commission of British Columbia, Parliament Building, Victoria British Columbia V8V 4S6 Canada. LC Law. DD 340.309711.

ANNUAL REPORT OF THE LEGISLATIVE ANALYST (CALIFORNIA). Main/Corp California. Legislature. Joint Legislative Budget Committee. Legislative Analyst. US. English. an. Legislative Analyst/State of California, 925 L Street/Suite 650, Sacramento CA 95814. LC HJ11. DD 328.79407658.

ANNUAL REPORT OF THE MASSACHUSETTS COMMISSION ON JUDICIAL CONDUCT. Main/Corp Massachusetts. Commission on Judicial Conduct. US. English. an. Commission on Judicial Conduct, 14 Beacon Street/Suite 102, Boston MA 02108. LC KFM2925.5.D5. DD 347.744014, 347.440714.

ANNUAL REPORT OF THE MASSACHUSETTS TRIAL COURT. Main/Corp Massachusetts. Trial Court. Office of the Chief Administrative Justice. 1980-. 8756-1034. US. English. an. Office of the Chief Administrative Justice/Trial Court, 317 New Court House, Boston MA 02108. DD 347.

ANNUAL REPORT OF THE PRESIDENT OF THE UNITED STATES ON THE TRADE AGREEMENTS PROGRAM. Main/Corp United States. President. Began with 21st, 1976. 0190-3098. US. English. an. Office of the US Trade Representative, 1800 G Street NW, Washington DC 20506. LC HF1731. DD 343.73087. Trade Agreements Program, Annual Report, 0192-3013.

ANNUAL REPORT OF THE PROSECUTOR COUNCIL (TEXAS). Main/Corp Texas. Prosecutor Council. 1981-. US. English. an. Texas Law Center, 1414 Colorado Suite 602, Austin TX 78711. LC KFT1777. DD 353.97640088.

ANNUAL REPORT OF THE SECRETARY-GENERAL'S ACTIVITIES. Main/Corp International Association of Legal Science. UK. English. an. International Association of Legal Science, High Cliff Eden Park, Lancaster England. DD 341.0621.

ANNUAL REPORT OF THE SELECT COMMITTEE ON SMALL BUSINESS, UNITED STATES SENATE CEASED. (ANNUAL REPORT OF THE SELECT COMMITTEE ON SMALL BUSINESS, UNITED STATES SENATE FOR THE . . . CONGRESS . . . SESSION). Main/Corp United States. Congress. Senate. Select Committee on Small Businesses. Began in 1950. Ceased with 31st, 96th Congress, 2nd Session. 0360-5523. US. English. an. LC KF31.3.

ANNUAL REPORT OF THE SUBCOMMITTEE TO INVESTIGATE THE ADMINISTRATION OF THE INTERNAL SECURITY ACT AND OTHER INTERNAL SECURITY LAWS OF THE COMMITTEE ON THE JUDICIARY, UNITED STATES SENATE. See Public Administration.

ANNUAL REPORT OF THE SUPREME COURT (PHILIPPINES). Main/Corp Philippines. Supreme Court. English. an. DD 347.599035, 345.990735.

ANNUAL REPORT OF THE WORKERS' COMPENSATION COURT OF OKLAHOMA. Main/Corp Oklahoma. Workers' Compensation Court. 1978-. 0272-8354. US. English. an. Workers' Compensation Court of Oklahoma, Jim Thorpe Building, Oklahoma City OK 73105. LC KFO1542.A152. DD 344.7660210269, 347.6604210269. Report.

ANNUAL REPORT - OFFICE OF THE FARMERS' ADVOCATE (ALBERTA). Main/Corp Alberta. Office of the Farmers' Advocate. 0318-5044. CN. English. an. Office of the Farmers' Advocate, 1101 Agriculture Building, 9718-107 St Edmonton Alberta Canada. DD 343.71230760269.

ANNUAL REPORT - OHIO LEGAL RIGHTS SERVICE. Main/Corp Ohio. Legal Rights Service. US. English. an. Ohio Legal Rights Service, Atlas Building 5th Floor/8 East Long Street, Columbus OH 43215. LC KF337.O5. DD 347.771017.

ANNUAL REPORT - OKLAHOMA CRIME VICTIMS COMPENSATION BOARD. Main/Corp Oklahoma Crime Victims Compensation Board. 1st (Oct. 19, 1981-June 30, 1982)-. Periodical. US. English. an. Oklahoma Crime Victims Compensation Board, 3033 North Walnut/Suite 100 West, Oklahoma City OK 73105. LC KFO1400. DD 344.76603288, 347.66043288.

ANNUAL REPORT ON HAZARDOUS MATERIALS TRANSPORTATION : HAZARDOUS MATERIALS TRANSPORTATION ACT (TITLE I, PUBLIC LAW 93-633). Main/Corp United States. Materials Transportation Bureau. 10th (calendar year 1979)-. US. English. an. US Department of Transportation, Research and Special Programs Administration, Washington DC 20590. Vols. for (1983-) distributed to depository libraries in microfiche.

ANNUAL REPORT ON THE COURTS OF KANSAS. Main/Corp Kansas. Office of the Judicial Administrator. 1st- 1977/78-. US. English. an. LC KFK71. DD 347.781023. Statistical Report on the District Courts of Kansas, 0453-2295.

ANNUAL REPORT ON THE LEGISLATIVE COUNCIL RULES CLEARINGHOUSE. VFOAT Legislative Council Rules Clearinghouse. Began in 1979. US. English. an. Room 147 North State Capitol, Madison WI 53702.

ANNUAL REPORT ON THE WORK OF THE GEORGIA COURTS. Main/Corp Georgia. Administrative Office of the Courts. July 1, 1981 to June 30, 1982-. 0739-8247. US. English. an. Georgia Justice Center, Suite 500/84 Peachtree Street, Atlanta GA 30361. LC KFG508 .A813. DD 353.97580088. Annual Report, 0363-9320.

ANNUAL REPORT ON TITLE I, PUBLIC LAW 89-313 (ILLINOIS). Main/Corp Illinois. Office of Education. Program Evaluation and Assessment Section. US. English. an. State Board of Education/ Illinois Office of Education, 100 North First Street, Springfield IL 62777. LC LA267. DD 371.20709773.

ANNUAL REPORT - ONTARIO LABOUR RELATIONS BOARD. (ANNUAL REPORT). Main/Corp Ontario Labour Relations Board. 1980/81-. 0711-849X. CN. English. an. Ontario Labour Relations Board, 400 University Avenue, Toronto Ontario Canada. LC KEO641.A72. DD 354.7130083.

ANNUAL REPORT OPINIONS - VERMONT LABOR RELATIONS BOARD. Main/Corp Vermont Labor Relations Board. VFOAT Vermont Labor Relations Board Opinions. US. English. an. LC KFV332.8.P77. DD 344.74301890413539, 347. 43041890413539. Opinions.

ANNUAL REPORT - OREGON STATE BAR. (ANNUAL REPORTS). Main/Corp Oregon State Bar. VFOAT Oregon State Bar Annual Reports. 1979-. 0739-6627. US. English. an. Oregon State Bar, 1776 SW Madison, Portland OR 97205. LC KF332.O7. DD 340.060795. Committee Reports . . . Annual Meeting.

ANNUAL REPORT - PHILADELPHIA. DEPT. OF RECORDS. Main/Corp Philadelphia. Dept. of Records. US. English. an. LC JS1274.A13. DD 352.1640974811.

ANNUAL REPORT REGARDING THE NEED FOR ADDITIONAL SUPERIOR COURT JUDGESHIPS IN GEORGIA. Main/Corp Georgia. Administrative Office of the Courts. US. English. an. 55 Marietta Street/Suite 2000, Atlanta GA 30303. LC KFG515. DD 347.7580234.

ANNUAL REPORT - REGINALD HEBER SMITH COMMUNITY LAWYER FELLOWSHIP PROGRAM. (ANNUAL REPORT). Main/Corp Reginald Heber Smith Community Lawyer Fellowship Program. 8755-2442. US. English. an. 2900 Van Ness Street NW, Washington DC 20008. DD 344.

ANNUAL REPORT RELATING TO JUDICIAL ADMINISTRATION IN THE COURTS OF OREGON. Main/Corp Oregon. Office of the State Court Administrator. 0731-0528. US. English. an. Office of the State Court Administrator, Supreme Court Building, Salem OR 97301. LC KFO2471. DD 347.795013, 34790713.

ANNUAL REPORT - REPUBLIC OF ZAMBIA, LAW DEVELOPMENT COMMISSION. Main/Corp Zambia. Law Development Commission. ZA. English. ir. 20. Department of Legal Affairs, Law Development Commission, PO Box 136, Lusaka Zambia. DD 340.3096894. Annual Report For the Year . . . .

ANNUAL REPORT - RESTRICTIVE PRACTICES COMMISSION (IRELAND). Main/Corp Ireland (Eire). Restrictive Practices Commission. English. ir. LC KDK552. DD 354.41700827.

ANNUAL REPORT - SASKATCHEWAN HUMAN RIGHTS COMMISSION. (ANNUAL REPORT). Main/Corp Saskatchewan Human Rights Commission. 0826-953X. CN. English. an. Free. Saskatchewan Human Rights Commission, 8th Floor Canterbury Towers 224 4th Avenue South, Saskatoon Saskatchewan S7K 5M5 Canada. Tel 933-5952. Ed Rene Roy. LC KES458.A72. DD 354.712400811. Circ 500. Report of the Saskatchewan Human Rights Commission which enforces human rights legislation in Saskatchewan.

ANNUAL REPORT - SRI LANKA. NITI KOMISAN DEPARTAMENTUVA. Main/Corp Sri Lanka. Niti Komisan Departamentuva. English. an. 1.85. Government Publications Bureau, PO Box 500, Colombo Sri Lanka. DD 340.3095493.

ANNUAL REPORT - STATE OF DELAWARE, DEPARTMENT OF JUSTICE. Main/Corp Delaware. Dept. of Justice. 0098-7832. US. English. an. State of Delaware, Department of Justice, Dover DE 19901. LC KFD427.5.A8. DD 353.97515.

ANNUAL REPORT - STATE OF MAINE, ADMINISTRATIVE OFFICE OF THE COURTS. Main/Corp Maine. Administrative Office of the Courts. 1976-. US. English. an. State of Maine/Administrative Office of the Courts, PO Box 4820 DTS, Portland ME 04112. LC KFM510. DD 347.741013, 347.410713.

ANNUAL REPORT - STATE OF NEW JERSEY, DEPARTMENT OF LAW & PUBLIC SAFETY. Main/Corp New Jersey. Dept. of Law and Public Safety. VAT Annual Report - State of New Jersey, Department of Law and Public Safety. 1963-. 0548-5290. US. English. an. Department of Law and Public Safety, State House Annex, Trenton NJ 08625. LC KFN2227. Annual Report of the

Law

Violent Crimes Compensation Board, 0092-3079; Report.

ANNUAL REPORT - THE JUDICIAL STANDARDS COMMISSION, STATE OF NORTH CAROLINA. Main/Corp North Carolina. Judicial Standards Commission. 1st- 1973-. US. English. an. Judicial Standards Commission, State of North Carolina, PO Box 1122, Raleigh NC 27602. LC KFN7925.5.D5. DD 347.756014.

ANNUAL REPORT - THE SOUTHWESTERN LEGAL FOUNDATION. Main/Corp Southwestern Legal Foundation. Began with 1957/58 report. 0561-1784. US. English. an. Free. Southwestern Legal Foundation, PO Box 830707, Richardson TX 75083-0707. Tel (214)690-2373. Circ 2,000. Describes activities and programs sponsored by one of foundation's five centers. In 1983, 26 programs were held for 2,800 students, 44 US states, 47 foreign countries.

ANNUAL REPORT TO THE GENERAL ASSEMBLY ON THE ILLINOIS JUDICIAL CONFERENCE, WITH RECOMMENDATIONS. Main/Corp Illinois. Supreme Court. US. English. an. Illinois Supreme Court, Supreme Court Building, Springfield IL 62706. LC KFI1710. DD 347.7730105, 347.7307105.

ANNUAL REPORT TO THE GOVERNOR AND THE LEGISLATURE ON THE FREEDOM OF INFORMATION LAW (NEW YORK (STATE)). Main/Corp New York (State). Committee on Public Access to Records. 1st- 1978-. US. English. an. Department of State, 162 Washington Avenue, Albany NY 12231. LC KFN5827. DD 342.7470853, 347.4702853.

ANNUAL REPORT TO THE LEGISLATURE - CALIFORNIA. PUBLIC EMPLOYMENT RELATIONS BOARD. Main/Corp California. Public Employment Relations Board. 1979-. US. English. an. LC KFC562.P8. DD 344.7940189041353, 347.9404189041353.

ANNUAL REPORT TO THE LEGISLATURE ON CHAPTER 383 LAWS OF 1975, THE SMALL BUSINESS PROCUREMENT ACT (MINNESOTA). Main/Corp Minnesota. Dept. of Economic Development. VFOAT Annual Report, Small Business Procurement Act. 1975/76-. US. English. an. 480 Cedar Street, St Paul MN 55101. LC KFM5551.5. DD 346.7760652.

ANNUAL REPORT TO THE LEGISLATURE, Z'BERG-NEJEDLY FOREST PRACTICE ACT OF 1973 (CALIFORNIA). Main/Corp California. State Board of Forestry. VAT Annual Report to the Legislature, Z'Berg Nejedly Forest Practice Act of 1973. 0195-4385. US. English. an. LC KFC396. DD 353.974940082338.

ANNUAL REPORT TO THE SUPREME COURT OF ILLINOIS. Main/Corp Illinois. Administrative Office of Illinois Courts. 0536-3713. US. English. an. Administrative Office of Illinois Courts, Supreme Court Building, Springfield IL 62706. LC KFI1708. DD 347.7730353.

ANNUAL REPORT - UNITED STATES. FOREIGN CLAIMS SETTLEMENT COMMISSION. Main/Corp United States. Foreign Claims Settlement Commission. VFOAT F.C.S.C. Ann. Rep, FCSC Ann. Rep. 0739-5353. US. English. an. Foreign Claims Settlement Commission, 1111 20th Street NW, Washington DC 20579. LC KF6074. DD 346.730360264 347.306360264. *Annual Report to the Congress for the Period . . .*, 0565-5587.

ANNUAL REPORT, UTAH COURTS CEASED. Main/Corp Utah Judicial Council of Utah. 1973/74-1982/83. 0098-9045. US. English. an. LC KFU510. DD 347.79201.

ANNUAL REPORT - UTAH JUVENILE COURT. See Sociology: General Works, Theory - Social Pathology, Welfare, Criminology.

ANNUAL REPORT - WESTERN AUSTRALIA. SUPREME COURT. LAW LIBRARY. See Library and Information Science.

ANNUAL REPORT WITH STATISTICS AND RELATED DATA - JUDICIAL COUNCIL OF THE SUPREME COURT OF LOUISIANA. See Statistics.

ANNUAL REPORTS FOR THE YEARS . . . - ZAMBIA. INDUSTRIAL RELATIONS COURT. Main/Corp Zambia. Industrial Relations Court. English. an. 30 Per Issue. Industrial Relations Court, Government Printer, POB 30136, Lusaka Zambia. DD 344.6894010269, 346.8940410269.

ANNUAL REPORTS OF COMMITTEES - AMERICAN BAR ASSOCIATION. SECTION OF ADMINISTRATIVE LAW. Main/Corp American Bar Association. Section of Administrative Law. V. 1- 1964-. US. English. an. American Bar Association, Department of Administrative Law, 1155 60th Street, Chicago IL 60637. LC KF325.124. DD 342.7306.

ANNUAL REVIEW, NORTH CAROLINA. (ANNUAL REVIEW, NORTH CAROLINA). VFOAT Annual Review, N.C. 3rd (1982)-. 0738-0798. US. English. an. Wake Forest-Cle, PO Box 7206 Reynolds Station, Winston Salem NC 27109-7206. LC KFN7481. DD 349.756, 347.56. *Annual Review Institute, North Carolina*, 0277-2345.

ANNUAL REVIEW OF BANKING LAW. Vol. 1 (1982)-. 0739-2451. US. English. an. Ind/Abst Index Leg. Period. LC K1. DD 346.73082, 347.30682.

ANNUAL REVIEW OF CRIMINAL LAW. VFOAT Criminal Law. 1982-. 0821-7912. CN. English. an. $28.00 Per Vol. Annual Review of Criminal Law, c/o Carswell Company, 2330 Midland Avenue, Agincourt Ontario M1S 1P7 Canada. LC KE8807.7. DD 345.71, 347.105.

ANNUAL REVIEW OF OPERATIONS - SUPERIOR COURT OF THE DISTRICT OF COLUMBIA. Main/Corp District of Columbia. Superior Court. US. English. an. LC KFD1715. DD 347.753023.

ANNUAL REVIEW OF POPULATION LAW. 1974-. 0364-3417. US. English. an. $26.00. Fund For Population Activities, 485 Lexington Avenue Room 1820, New York NY 10017. Tel (212)850-5648. LC K2000.A53. DD 344.048. NLM WA 33.1 A615.

ANNUAL SECURITIES REGULATION INSTITUTE. Main/Corp Securities Regulation Institute. Series/Titl Corporate Law and Practice Course Handbook Series. 1st- 1969-. US. English. an. Practicing Law Institute, 810 7th Avenue, New York NY 10017. LC KF1440. DD 346.73092.

ANNUAL SECURITIES SEMINAR COURSE HANDBOOK. Main/Corp Institute of Continuing Legal Education, Ann Arbor, Mich. 0160-1555. US. English. an. LC KFM4414.A1. DD 346.7740666.

THE ANNUAL STATEMENT OF THE SENATE OF THE INNS OF COURT AND THE BAR. Main/Corp Senate of the Inns of Court and the Bar. 1974/75-. UK. English. an. Senate of the Inns of Court and the Bar, 11 South Square Gray's Inn, London WC1 England. LC KD500. DD 340.06242. *Annual Statement.*

ANNUAL STATISTICAL REPORT, IOWA JUDICIARY. See Statistics.

ANNUAL SURVEY OF AMERICAN LAW. 1942-. 0066-4413. US. English. qt. $18.00 Domestic, $19.00 Foreign. Annual Survey Office, 137 MacDougal Street/Room 23, New York NY 10012. Tel (212)598-2505. Ed Joseph Profaci. Ind/Abst Leg. Resour. Index, Index Leg. Period., Curr. Law Index, Contents Curr. Leg. Period. LC KF178. DD 340.0973. adv acc. Circ 2,000. Provides a perceptive analytic account of the year's legal development, covering legal trends and important recent decisions and legislation.

ANNUAL SURVEY OF BANKRUPTCY LAW. 1st- 1979-. 0270-1464. US. English. an. Callaghan & Company, 3201 Old Glenview Road, Wilmette IL 60091. Ed W L Norton. LC K1. DD 346.73078.

ANNUAL SURVEY OF COLORADO LAW. 0160-5658. US. English. an. $7.50. Continuing Legal Education in Colorado, 200 West 14th Avenue, Denver CO 80204. Tel (303)753-3351. Ind/Abst Leg. Resour. Index. LC KFC1870. DD 340.09788.

ANNUAL SURVEY OF INDIAN LAW. II. English. an. 100.00. Indian Law Institute, Opposite the Supreme Court, New Delhi India. Tel 389429. Ed V S Deshpande. Circ 1,000. (ctrl). Contains a sufficent analysis of major developments and decisions of the supreme court and high courts each year in the principal fields of Indian law.

ANNUAL SURVEY OF MASSACHUSETTS LAW. 1954-. 0570-2674. US. English. an. $24.50. Boston College Law School, 885 Centre Street, Newton Centre MA 02159. Tel (617)552-8557. Ed Renee Landers. Ind/Abst Leg. Resour. Index, Curr. Law Index. (cum index). Circ 500. Survey of Massachusetts law developed or changed during the year.

ANNUAL SURVEY OF SOUTH AFRICAN LAW. 1947-. SA. English. an.

ANNUARIO DI STATISTICHE GIUDIZIARIE (ITALY). See Yearbooks, Almanacs, Directories.

ANTIOCH LAW JOURNAL. Vol. 1 (Fall 1981)-. 0735-0384. US. English. an. $10.00. Antioch School of Law, 1624 Crescent Circle, Washington DC 20009. Tel (202)639-2697. Ed Frederica Miller. LC K1. DD 340.05. bk rev. adv acc. Circ 300. The purpose is to present meritorious views on current legal issues that reflect Antioch School of Law's committment to social and economic justice.

ANTITRUST. V. 1- Winter 1978-. 0162-7996. Periodical. US. English. American Bar Association, 750 North Lake Shore Drive, Chicago IL 60611. Tel (312)988-5555. LC KF1632. DD 353.7307205.

ANTITRUST ADVISOR. 1st- Ed. US. English. ir. $85.00. Shepards McGraw Hill, PO Box 1235, Colorado Springs CO 80901. Tel (800)525-2474. Includes complete discussion of the Sherman Act, the Clayton Act, the Robinson-Patman Act and the Federal Trade Commission Act organized to help practitioners.

ANTITRUST BULLETIN. V. 1- Apr. 1955-. 0003-603X. Periodical. US. English. qt. Federal Legal Publications, 157 Chambers Street, New York NY 10007. Ind/Abst Manage. Contents, Trade Ind. Index, Leg. Resour. Index, ABI/Inform, Index Leg. Period., Index Econ. Artic. J. Collect. Vol., Public Aff. Inf. Serv. Bull. LC K1. DD 343.7307205. CODEN ATBUAU. (cum index).

ANTITRUST DIVISION MANUAL. Main/Corp United States. Dept. of Justice. Antitrust Division. 1979-. US. English. ir. US Department of Justice, Antitrust Division, Washington DC 20402.

ANTITRUST LAW & ECONOMICS REVIEW. VAT Antitrust Law and Economics Review. V. 1-. 0003-6048. Periodical. US. English. qt. $54.50. Antitrust Law & Economics Review, PO Box 6134, Washington DC 20044. Ind/Abst Index Leg. Period., Manage. Contents, Leg. Resour. Index, ABI/Inform, Public Aff. Inf. Serv. Bull., Bus. Period. Index.

ANTITRUST LAW HANDBOOK. Series/Titl Antitrust Law Library. VFOAT Antitrust Law Hand Book. 1983-84-. 0738-5919. US. English. an. Clark Boardman Company Ltd, 435 Hudson Street, New York NY 10014. LC KF1632.5. DD 343.73072, 347.30372.

ANTITRUST LAW SYMPOSIUM. Main/Corp New York State Bar Association. Section on Antitrust Law. 0066-4901. US. English. an. $7.50. New York State Bar Association, 1 Elk Street, Albany NY 12207. Tel (518)463 3200. Ind/Abst Index Leg. Period.

ANTITRUST LAWS AND TRADE REGULATION. US. English. bm. $455.00. Matthew Bender & Company Inc, 1275 Broadway, Albany NU 12201. Tel (800)833-9844.

ANTITRUST REPORT (NATIONAL ASSOCIATION OF ATTORNEYS GENERAL). (ANTITRUST REPORT). Began in Dec. 1980. Periodical. US. English. mo. $95.00. National Association of Attorneys General, 444 North Capitol Street, Washington DC 20001. Tel (202)628-0435. Antitrust Bulletin (National Association of Attorneys General).

ANUARIO CONSULTIVO DE TRABAJO. See Yearbooks, Almanacs, Directories.

ANUARIO DA PROPRIEDADE INDUSTRIAL. See Yearbooks, Almanacs, Directories.

ANUARIO DE DERECHO ADMINISTRATIVO. See Yearbooks, Almanacs, Directories.

ANUARIO DE DERECHO AMBIENTAL. See Yearbooks, Almanacs, Directories.

Law

ANUARIO DE DERECHO CIVIL. See Yearbooks, Almanacs, Directories.

ANUARIO DE HISTORIA DEL DERECHO ESPANOL. See Yearbooks, Almanacs, Directories.

ANUARIO DE JURISPRUDENCIA LABORAL. See Yearbooks, Almanacs, Directories.

ANUARIO DE LA FACULTAD DE DERECHO. See Yearbooks, Almanacs, Directories.

ANUARIO DEL MINISTERIO DE JUSTICIA. See Yearbooks, Almanacs, Directories.

ANUARIO HISTORICO JURIDICO ECUATORIANO. See Yearbooks, Almanacs, Directories.

ANUDANOM KI MANGEM (INDIA. MINISTRY OF LAW AND JUSTICE). Main/Corp India (Republic). Ministry of Law and Justice. VFOAT Demands For Grants. II. Hindi and English. ir. Government of India Press, Ministry of Law & Justice, Minto Road, New Delhi India. DD 354.54065.

ANWALTSBLATT. Periodical. German. ir. Deutscher Anwaltverein, 5300 Bonn 1 Adenauerallee 106, Bonn West Germany. LC K1. DD 340.0943.

APPLICATION AND INSTRUCTIONS FOR INTERNATIONAL REGISTRATION PLAN. US. English. an. Free. Secretary of State, Commercial & Farm Truck Division, Springfield IL 62756. Tel (217)782-4815. Trucking registration. *International Registration Plan, Application and Instructions.*

AQUINAS LAW JOURNAL CEASED. V. 1- 1972-. English. ir. 15.00. Aquinas University College, Colombo-8 Ceylon. LC K1. DD 340.05.

ARBEIT UND RECHT. 1.- Yearly Vol. 0003-7648. Periodical. GW. German. mo. Bund Verlag GMBH, Postfach 90 08 40, 5 Koln 90 West Germany. Ind/Abst Foreign Lang. Index.

ARBEITS- UND SOZIALRECHTLICHE SCHRIFTENREIHE. See Economics - Labor.

DAS ARBEITSRECHT DER GEGENWART. Vol. 1 1963-. 0066-586X. GW. German. an. Erich Schmidt Verlag GMBH, POB 7330, Viktoriastr 44-A, D4800 Bielefeld 1 West Germany. Tel 0521/66061. Ed G Muller. bk rev. Yearbook labour law. *Jahrbuch des Arbeitsrechts Und der Damit ZusammenhAngenden Teile der Sozialpolitik.*

ARBEJDSRETLIGE KENDELSER. DK. Danish. an. Juristforbundets Forlag, Gothersgade 133, 1123 Kbenhavn K Denmark.

ARBITRATION. Main/Corp National Academy of Arbitrators. 0148-4176. US. English. ir. Bureau of National Affairs Inc, 1231 25th Street NW, Washington DC 20037. Tel (301)258-1033.

ARBITRATION & THE LAW. (ARBITRATION & THE LAW : AAA GENERAL COUNSEL'S ANNUAL REPORT). Main/Corp American Arbitration Association. Office of the General Counsel. VFOAT Arbitration and the Law. 1981-. 0733-6160. US. English. an. $50.00. American Arbitration Association, 140 West 51st Street, New York NY 10020. Tel (212)484-4000. Ed Linda M Miller. LC KF9085.A15. DD 347.739, 347.3079. Highlights the most significant legal developments in dispute resolution during the year.

THE ARBITRATION JOURNAL. V. 1-6, Jan. 1937-Autumn 1942. 0003-7893. Periodical. US. English. qt. $40.00. American Arbitration Association, 140 West 51st Street, New York NY 10020. Tel (212)484-4000. Ed Linda Miller. Ind/Abst Manage. Contents, Trade Ind. Index, Leg. Resour. Index, Int. Labour Doc., ABI/Inform, Index Leg. Period., Contents Curr. Leg. Period., Soc. Sci. Index, Bus. Period. Index, Soc. Sci. Citation Index, Curr. Law Index, Am. Hist. Life, Hist. Abstr. DD 380.12605. bk rev. (ctrl) Digest of court decisions in labor, commercial commercial construction, maritime, medical malpractice and insurance arbitration- lists important books and periodicals in dispute resolutions.

ARBITRATION NEWSLETTER. No. 71 (May 1, 1955)-. Periodical. US. English. ir. Cornelius Printing Company, USWA Circulation Department, 2457 East Washington Street, Indianapolis IN 46201.

ARBITRATION TIMES. (ARBITRATION TIMES : NEWS AND VIEWS FROM THE AMERICAN ARBITRATION ASSOCIATION). Spring 1982-. 8756-5455. Periodical. US. English. qt. American Arbitration Association, 140 West 51st Street, New York NY 10020. Tel (212)484-4000. Ed Betty Blaisdell Berry and Linda M Miller. LC HD5503. DD 331.891430973. Circ 70,000. (ctrl). A newspaper containing the latest information on alternative methods of dispute resolution. Contains articles, columns by dispute resolution specialists, people, conference listings. *News and Views,* 0093-6979.

ARCHIV FUR RECHTS- UND SOZIALPHILOSOPHIE. See Genealogy and Heraldry - Archives.

ARCHIVES DE POLITIQUE CRIMINELLE. See Genealogy and Heraldry - Archives.

ARCHIVES PARLEMENTAIRES DE 1787 A 1860. See Genealogy and Heraldry - Archives.

ARCHTYPE. See Physically Impaired.

ARIZONA ADVOCATE. 0004-1386. Periodical. US. English. ir. University of Arizona, College of Law, Tucson AZ 85721. Tel (602)626-5554.

ARIZONA BAR BRIEFS. Began in 1982. 0745-4384. Periodical. US. English. mo. $15.00. State Bar of Arizona, 234 North Central/Suite 858, Phoenix AZ 85004. LC KF200. DD 340.060791. *Arizona Bar News Notes.*

THE ARIZONA BAR JOURNAL. (ARIZONA BAR JOURNAL). Began with June 1965 issue. 0004-1424. Periodical. US. English. qt. $11.00. 243 North Central Avenue, Phoenix AZ 85004. Ind/Abst Leg. Resour. Index. LC K1. DD 340.05.

ARIZONA CAPITOL TIMES. Vol. 83, Issue 22 (June 2, 1982)-. 0744-7477. Periodical. US. English. wk. $28.00. Arizona Capitol Times, PO Box 2260, Phoenix AZ 85002. Tel (602)258-7026. Ed Brad Christensen. adv acc. Circ 2,100. Weekly wrap-up of state legislative, political, and government affairs. All legislation introduced is described and tracked. Attorney General opinions published monthly; agency rules and regulations hearings published monthly. *Arizona Legislative Review.*

ARIZONA LAW REVIEW. V. 1- Spring 1959-. 0004-153X. Periodical. US. English. qt. $12.00. College of Law, University of Arizona, Tucson AZ 85721. Tel (602)621-1764. Ed Scott Hill-Kennedy. Ind/Abst Index Leg. Period., Curr. Law Index, Leg. Resour. Index, Contents Curr. Leg. Period. bk rev. adv acc. Circ 2,000. (ctrl). Publishes articles and commentary on topics of interest to the legal community.

ARIZONA LEGISLATIVE SERVICE. VFOAT ARS Legislative Service. 0094-4246. US. English. West Publishing Company, Box 3526, 50 West Kellogg Boulevard, St Paul MN 55166. LC KFA2431. DD 348.79102.

ARIZONA STATE LAW JOURNAL. 1974-. 0164-4297. Periodical. US. English. bm. $15.00. Arizona State University, College of Law, Tempe AZ 85781. Tel (602)965-6287. Ed James L Wright. Ind/Abst Leg. Resour. Index, Public Aff. Inf. Serv. Bull., Index Leg. Period., Contents Curr. Leg. Period., Curr. Law Index. LC K1. DD 340.05. bk rev. adv acc. Circ 2,000. (ctrl). *Law and the Social Order.*

ARKANSAS COURT RULES. 1983 Ed.-. 0747-6884. US. English. an.

ARKANSAS LAW NOTES : REPORTS TO THE ARKANSAS BAR. 1983-. Periodical. US. English. an. University of Arkansas/ School of Law, Waterman Hall, Fayetteville AR 72701. LC K1. DD 349.767, 347.67.

ARKANSAS LAW REVIEW. V. 22- Spring 1968-. 0004-1831. Periodical. US. English. qt. $7.00. Arkansas Law Review & Bar Association Inc, Fayetteville AR 72701. Ind/Abst Leg. Resour. Index, Index Leg. Period. LC K1. DD 340.05. (cum index). *Arkansas Law Review and Bar Association Journal.*

ARKANSAS LAW REVIEW AND BAR ASSOCIATION JOURNAL. 0004-1831. Periodical. US. English. qt. Arkansas Law Review, University of Arkansas/ Waterman Hall, Fayetteville AR 72701. Tel (501)575-5601. Ind/Abst Index Leg. Period., Curr. Law Index, Leg. Resour. Index, Contents Curr. Leg. Period.

THE ARKANSAS LAWYER. (ARKANSAS LAWYER). V. 1- June 1967-. Periodical. US. English. qt. $15.00. Arkansas Bar Association, West Markham, Little Rock AR 72201. Tel (501)375-4605. Ed Ruth Williams. Ind/Abst Leg. Resour. Index, Curr. Law Index. LC KF200. DD 340.09767. bk rev. adv acc. Circ 3,500. The official publication of the Arkansas Bar Association. Presents a broad spectrum of bar issues, from an historical, innovative and informational perspective.

THE ARKANSAS LEGAL DIRECTORY. See Yearbooks, Almanacs, Directories.

ARKANSAS, LOUISIANA, AND MISSISSIPPI LEGAL DIRECTORY. See Yearbooks, Almanacs, Directories.

THE ARKANSAS REGISTER. V. 1- Aug. 1977-. Periodical. US. English. mo. $40.00. Arkansas Register, 507 Capitol Hill Building, Little Rock AR 72201. Tel (501)371-3684. Ed Joseph Franklin. LC KFA3636. DD 348.767028. Index published separately - free - automatically sent. Circ 302. Publishes rules and regulations of state agencies of Arkansas, opinions of the Attorney General and proclamations of the Governor and the state agencies.

THE ARMY LAWYER. Began with Aug. 1971. 0364-1287. Periodical. US. English. mo. US Government Printing Office, Superintendent of Documents, Washington DC 20402. Tel (202)783-3238. Ind/Abst Leg. Resour. Index, Index U.S. Gov. Period., Curr. Law Index, Index Leg. Period., Contents Curr. Leg. Period. LC KF7209.A1. DD 3437301. *Advocate (Falls Church, VA.),* 0094-2197.

ARQIOVPS DPS TROBIMAOS DE ALCADA : ORGAO OFICIAL DOS TRIBUNAIS DE ALCADA DO ESTADO DO RIO DE JANEIRO. VFOAT A.T.A. 1 (Jan./June 1983)-. Portuguese. sa. Jura Editora, Av Visconde de Guarapuava 2435 1O. Andar, CEP 80.000 Curitiba Parana Brazil. LC KHD8105. DD 348.8153043, 348.1530843.

ARQUIVOS DO INSTITUTO DE DIREITO SOCIAL. Main/Corp Instituto de Direito Social (Sao Paulo, Brazil). BL. Portuguese. ir. Instituto de Direito Social, Avenida Paulista No 726, Sao Paulo Brasil. LC K9. DD 344.81.

ARQUIVOS DO MINISTERIO DA JUSTICA. Main/Corp Brazil. Ministerio da Justica. 0100-1213. Portuguese. ir. rua Mexico 128 60. Andar, Rio de Janeiro Brazil. Ind/Abst Foreign Lang. Index. LC K2. DD 340.0981. *Arquivos.*

ARS AEQUI. 0004-2870. Periodical. NE. Dutch. mo. $8.45. Stichting Ars Aequi, Bijleveldsingel 72, 6524 AE Nijmegen Netherlands. Ind/Abst Excerpta Med.

ART & THE LAW. See The Arts (General).

ASBESTOS LITIGATION REPORTER. Began in Feb. 1979. 0273-3048. Periodical. US. English. sm. $800.00. Andrews Publishing Inc, PO Box 200, Edgemont PA 19028. Tel (215)353-2565. Ed Leonard E B Andrews. The national journal of record for asbestos litigation.

ASIAN LAW FORUM. V. 1- 1976-. 0145-0220. US. English. an. $1.25. Temple University, Department of Sociology, Philadelphia PA 19122. DD 340.095.

ASSESSMENT AND VALUATION LEGAL REPORTER. V. 1- July 1971-. 0090-6352. US. English. mo. $135.00. International Association Assessing Officer, PO Box 94573, Chicago IL 60690-4573. Tel (312)947-2053. LC KF6759.5.A59. DD 343.73042. Circ 700. Summaries of court decisions dealing with questions of valuation, property taxation, etc.

ASSICURAZIONE. See Insurance.

ASSUNTOS EUROPEUS. VFOAT Asseur. Vol. 1, No. 1 (Feb. 1982)-. Periodical. English (French and Portuguese). ty. $35.00. Assuntos Europeus Secretario, C P 21302, 1100 Lisboa Portugal. Ind/Abst Foreign Lang. Index, Public Aff. Inf. Serv. Bull. LC K1. DD 349.405, 342.05.

ASSURANCES, BANQUES, TRANSPORTS. Began publication in 1965. Periodical. French. mo. DD 346.569207, 345.692067.

AT ISSUE; HIGHLIGHTS OF THE LEGISLATIVE SESSION. Main/Corp Illinois. General Assembly. House of Representatives. Republican Staff. US. English. an. House Republican

Law

Staff, 300 State Capitol Building, Springfield IL 62706. **LC** KFI1215. **DD** 348.77301, 347.73081.

ATLA LAW REPORTER. Main/Corp Association of Trial Lawyers of America. **VAT** Association of Trial Lawyers of America Law Reporter. V. 20- Feb. 1977-. 0364-8125. Periodical. US. English. mo. $100.00. Association of Trial Lawyers of America, 1050 31st Street NW, Washington DC 20007. **Tel** (202)965-3500. **LC** KF294.A8. **DD** 347.737. *News Letter - Association of Trial Lawyers of America, 0093-1160.*

ATLA MASTERS AT WORK. **VAT** American Association of Trial Lawyers Masters at Work. 1-. 8755-9390. US. English. an. Association of Trial Lawyers of America, 1050 31st Street Northwest, Washington DC 20007-4499. **DD** 347.

ATLA PRODUCTS LIABILITY LAW REPORTER. **VFOAT** A.T.L.A. Products Liability Law Reporter. **VAT** Association of Trial Lawyers of America Products Liability Law Reporter. Vol. 1, No. 1 (Jan. 1982)-. 0745-2926. Periodical. US. English. mo. $75.00. Association of Trial Lawyers of America, 1050 31st Street NW, Washington DC 20007. **Tel** (202)965-3500. Ed Jeffrey Robert White. **LC** KF1296.A15. **DD** 346.73038205, 347.3063805.

ATLANTIC PROVINCES REPORTS. Vol. 1 (1975)-. 0713-8970. CN. English. ir. Maritime Law Book Ltd, Box 302, Fredericton New Brunswick E3B 4Y9 Canada. **DD** 348.715042.

ATLANTIC REPORTER DIGEST. V. 1- 1930-. US. English. West Publishing Company, 1413 K Street NW, St Paul MN 55165. **DD** 345.415.

ATLANTIC REPORTER. SECOND SERIES. V. 1- A.2D. 8750-2631. Periodical. US. English. wk. $105.00. West Publishing Company, 50 West Kellogg Road, St Paul MN 55102. **LC** KF135.A7. **DD** 348.73422, 347.308422. *Atlantic Reporter.*

THE ATTORNEY-CPA. (THE ATTORNEY-CPA : A PUBLICATION OF THE AMERICAN ASSOCIATION OF ATTORNEY-CERTIFIED PUBLIC ACCOUNTANTS, INC). **VFOAT** Attorney-C.P.A. 0571-8279. Periodical. US. English. qt. $20.00. American Association of Attorney-Certified Public Accountants Inc, PO Box 3561, Tulsa OK 74135. **Ind/Abst** Account. Index. Suppl. **LC** KF297.A1. **DD** 349.73, 347.3.

ATTORNEY EMPLOYMENT FACT BOOK. *See* Economics - Labor.

ATTORNEY FEE AWARDS REPORTER. Vol. 5, No. 4 (June 1982)-. 0732-7552. Periodical. US. English. bm. $120.00. Law & Business Inc, 855 Valley Road, Clifton NJ 07013. **Tel** (201)472-7400. Ed Harvey Miller and Andrea Grumfest. **LC** KF8995.A59. **DD** 347.7377, 347.30777. bk rev. **Circ** 500. Information and analysis of current fee awards to attorneys by state and federal courts. *Federal Attorney Fee Awards Reporter, 0193-3353.*

THE ATTORNEY GENERAL'S DIGEST. Periodical. US. English. qt. Maryland Office of Attorney General, 1 S Calvert Street, Baltimore MD 21202. **Tel** (301)659-4095. **LC** KFM1761.A59.

ATTORNEY GENERAL'S MESSENGER. Main/Corp Minnesota. Attorney General's Office. V. 1- Apr. 1976-. US. English. Office of the Attorney General State of Minnesota, 102 Capitol Building, St Paul MN 55155. **LC** KFM5840. **DD** 342.77606.

ATTORNEY GENERAL'S OPINIONS. Main/Corp Kentucky. Attorney General's Office. 0455-0315. US. English. Kentucky Department of Education, Bureau of Administration and Finance, 1923 Capital Plaza, Frankfort KY 40601. **LC** KFK1590. **DD** 344.76907.

ATTORNEY GENERAL'S REPORT ON FEDERAL LAW ENFORCEMENT AND CRIMINAL JUSTICE ASSISTANCE ACTIVITIES. Main/Corp United States. Dept. of Justice. **VFOAT** Report on Federal Law Enforcement and Criminal Justice Assistance Activities. 0161-6307. US. English. be. US Department of Justice, Attorney General, Washington DC 20530. **LC** KF9223. **DD** 364.973. *Attorney General's Annual Report: Federal Law Enforcement and Criminal Justice Assistance Activities.*

ATTORNEYS AND AGENTS REGISTERED TO PRACTICE BEFORE THE U.S. PATENT AND TRADEMARK OFFICE. **VAT** Attorneys and Agents Registered to Practice Before the United States Patent and Trademark Office. 0361-3844. US. English. an. Superintendent of Documents, US Government Printing Office, Washington DC 20402. **LC** KF3165.A3. **DD** 346.730486025. Vols. for 1982- distributed to depository libraries in microfiche. *Attorneys and Agents Registered to Practice Before the U.S. Patent Office.*

THE ATTORNEY'S DIRECTORY OF FORENSIC PSYCHIATRISTS IN THE UNITED STATES AND CANADA. *See* Yearbooks, Almanacs, Directories.

ATTORNEYS' DIRECTORY OF SAN DIEGO COUNTY. *See* Yearbooks, Almanacs, Directories.

THE ATTORNEYS GENERAL OF THE STATES AND OTHER JURISDICTIONS. US. English. an. $7.50. The Council of State Governments, PO Box 11910, Iron Works Pike, Lexington KY 40578.

THE ATTORNEY'S MANAGEMENT REPORT. *See* Business - General Management.

ATTORNEYS MARKETING REPORT. Vol. 1, No. 1 (July 1982)-. 0745-1369. Periodical. US. English. mo. $96.00. Professional Publications Inc, PO Box 81067, Atlanta GA 30366. **Tel** (404)455-7600. Ed Suzanne Verity. bk rev. In-depth information on how law firms can market their services. Practical advice on what some inventive firms are doing.

ATTORNEYS PERSONNEL REPORT. Began with Aug. 1984 issue. 8750-2763. Periodical. US. English. mo. $149.00. Attorneys Personnel Report, PO Box 80280, Atlanta GA 30366. **Tel** (404)455-7600. Ed Norman Crampton. adv acc. Directed to the particular personnel needs of the law office: interviewing, recruiting, compensation and general management.

AUCKLAND UNIVERSITY LAW REVIEW. Vol. 1, No. 1 (1968)-. 0067-0510. NZ. English. an. 12.00. Auckland University Law Students Society, Private Bag, Auckland New Zealand. **Tel** 737-999. Ed Leslie Olsen and Rosemary Tobin. **Ind/Abst** Leg. Resour. Index, Index Leg. Period. **LC** K1. **DD** 340.05. bk rev. adv acc. **Circ** 1,600. (ctrl). Law, both civil and criminal, expecially common law and the law relating to New Zealand.

AUDIT REPORT, ATTORNEY GENERAL'S OFFICE. Main/Corp Texas. Attorney General's Office. Began with Vol. for 1950/52. US. English. an. **LC** KFT1627.5.A8. **DD** 353.9764505. *Audit Report: Attorney General's Department.*

AUDIT SUSPENSE DIGEST. Main/Corp United States. Internal Revenue Service. 0362-1790. US. English. US Treasury Department/ Internal Revenue Service, 15th Street & Pennsylvania Avenue NW, Washington DC 20220. **LC** KF6314.A59. **DD** 353.00724.

AUSTRALIAN BUSINESS LAW REVIEW. V. 1- Mar. 1973-. 0310-1053. Periodical. AT. English. ir. Law Book Company, 301-305 Kent Street, Sydney Australia. **Ind/Abst** Manage. Contents, Leg. Resour. Index, ABI/Inform, APAIS, Aust. Public Aff. Inf. Serv. **LC** K1. **DD** 346.940705. **CODEN** ABRVDO.

AUSTRALIAN COMPANY LAW CASES. AT. English. ir. CCH Australia Ltd, PO Box 230, North Ryde NSW 2113 Australia. **DD** 346.94066.

AUSTRALIAN COMPANY LAW REPORTS. Vol. 1 (1974-1976)-. 0313-8445. AT. English. an. Butterworths, North Sydney New South Wales 2060 Australia. Ed W E Paterson and H H Ednie. **DD** 346.9406602648, 349. 4066602648.

THE AUSTRALIAN CRIMINAL REPORTS. Vol. 1, Pt. 1 (Aug. 1980)-. English. ir. Ed Fiori Rinaldi. **DD** 345.94002642, 349.405002642.

AUSTRALIAN JOURNAL OF LAW AND SOCIETY. **VFOAT** Australian Journal of Law & Society. Vol. 1, No. 1-. 0729-3356. Periodical. English. sa. $20.66. Macquarie University School of Law, Balaclava Road, North Ryde New South Wales 2113 Australia. **Tel** (02)88-9380. **LC** K1. **DD** 340.11505. bk rev. adv acc. **Circ** 300. Seeks to provide a forum to reflect the growing awareness that law cannot be properly studied in isolation from society.

AUSTRALIAN LAW JOURNAL. (THE AUSTRALIAN LAW JOURNAL). V. 1- May 5, 1927-. 0004-9611. Periodical. AT. English. ir. Methuen Law Book Company Limited, 35 Mitchell Street, c/o EBSCO Bennett, North Sydney New South Wales 2600 Australia. **Ind/Abst** Leg. Resour. Index, APAIS, Aust. Public Aff. Inf. Serv., Energy Res. Abstr., Index Leg. Period., Curr. Law Index. **DD** 347.05.

AUSTRALIAN LAW REPORTS. 0310-0014. US. English. ir. D & S Publishers, PO Box 5105, Clearwater FL 33518. **Tel** (800)237-9707. **DD** 348.9404. *Australian Argus Law Reports.*

AUSTRALIAN LEGAL DIRECTORY. *See* Yearbooks, Almanacs, Directories.

AUSTRALIAN LEGAL MONTHLY DIGEST. 0004-9646. Periodical. AT. English. mo. Methuen Law Book Company Limited, 35 Mitchell Street, c/o EBSCO Bennett, North Sydney New South Wales 2600 Australia.

AUSTRALIAN MINING AND PETROLEUM LAW ASSOCIATION YEARBOOK. *See* Yearbooks, Almanacs, Directories.

AUSTRALIAN PLANNING APPEAL DECISIONS. Vol. 1, No. 1 (June 1982)-. 0728-6309. English. ir. Methuen Law Book Company Ltd, 35 Mitchell Street, c/o Bennett EBSCO, North Sydney New South Wales 2006 Australia. Ed Kenneth H Gillford and Brian Robert Michael Hayes.

AUSTRALIAN TRADE PRACTICES. **VFOAT** Australian Trade Practices Reporter. 0310-7469. AT. English. ir. CCH Australia Ltd, PO Box 230, North Ryde New South Wales 2113 Australia. **DD** 343.9408.

AUTEURSRECHT. V. 1-. Periodical. Dutch. ir. 40.00. Vereniging voor Auteursrecht, Marius Bauerstraat 30, Amsterdam 1017 Netherlands. **LC** K1.

AUTOMOTIVE LITIGATION REPORTER. 0278-4726. Periodical. US. English. sm. $700.00. Andrews Publications, PO Box 200, Edgemont PA 19028. **Tel** (215)353-2565. Ed Leonard E B Andrews. **LC** KF1297.A8. **DD** 346.730382, 347.306382. The national journal of record covering automotive litigation including autos, trucks, motorcycles, ATVs and tires.

AVIATION CASES. **VFOAT** CCH Aviation Cases. **VAT** Commerce Clearing House Aviation Cases. Vol. 1 (1822-1945)-. US. English. Commerce Clearing House, 4025 West Peterson Avenue, Chicago IL 60646. **Tel** (312)583-8500. **LC** KF2400. Bound volumes of cases on federal aviation regulation, insurance and liability problems.

AVIATION LITIGATION REPORTER. May 23, 1983-. 0737-7746. Periodical. US. English. sm. $700.00. Andrews Publications Inc, POB 200, Edgemont Pa 19028. **Tel** (215)353-2565. Ed L Andrews. **LC** KF2454.A59. **DD** 346.730322, 347.306322. Journal of record of aviation related litigation.

THE AVISO. 1979-. US. in English. an. $7.95. **LC** KF193.D3. **DD** 349.7642811025, 347. 62428110025.

AWARD NUMBERS. Main/Corp Great Britain. Central Arbitration Committee. UK. English. Her Majesty's Stationery Office, 49 High Holborn, London WC1V 6HB England. **LC** KD3070.A44. **DD** 344.41018902648, 344. 10418902648.

BACKGROUND PAPER - INSTITUTE OF LAW RESEARCH AND REFORM. UNIVERSITY OF ALBERTA. (BACKGROUND PAPER - INSTITUTE OF LAW RESEARCH AND REFORM, UNIVERSITY OF ALBERTA). Main/Corp University of Alberta. Institute of Law Research and Reform. Series Corp University of Alberta. Institute of Law Research and Reform. Residential Tenancies Project. No. 1- 1975-. 0382-5744. Monographic Series. CN. English. Institute of Law Research and Reform, University of Alberta, Edmonton Alberta T6G 2H5 Canada. **DD** 346.7104342.

BALANCING THE SCALES. Began publication with: V. 1, No. 1 (July/Aug. 1979). 0734-1822. Periodical. US. English. bm. Legal Services of Northeastern Wisconsin, 221 Cherry Street, Green Bay WI 54301.

BALDWIN'S OFFICIAL EDITION KRS KENTUCKY REVISED STATUTES AND RULES SERVICE. Main/Corp Kentucky. **VFOAT** Baldwin's Official Edition K.R K.R.S. Kentucky Revised Statutes and Rules Service. US. English. ir. $535.00. Banks-Baldwin Law Publishing, PO Box 1974, University Center, Cleveland OH 44106. **Tel** (216)721-7373. Contains the full text of all Kentucky statute law of a general and permanent nature currently in effect, with effective dates and complete legislative histories.

Law

BALDWIN'S OHIO LEGISLATIVE SERVICE. VFOAT Ohio Legislative Service. 1971-. 0092-0959. US. English. mo. $210.00. Banks-Baldwin Law Publishing Company, PO Box 1974 University Center, Cleveland OH 44106. Tel (216)721-7373. LC KFO15. DD 348.771026. Full text of all laws enacted by the General Assembly, complete with purpose clauses and effective dates.

BALDWIN'S OHIO TAX LAW AND RULES. Main/Corp Ohio. VFOAT Ohio Tax Law and Rules. 1st- Ed. US. English. ir. $125.00. Banks-Baldwin Law Publishing Company, PO Box 1974 University Center, Cleveland OH 44106. Tel (216)721-7373. (cum index). Published in cooperation with state tax agencies, this is the official guide to Ohio taxation.

BALDWIN'S OHIO TAX SERVICE. VFOAT Ohio Tax Service. Began with Vol. for 1978. 0739-1234. US. English. qt. $120.00. Banks Baldwin Law Publishing Company, PO Box 1974 University Center, Cleveland OH 44106. Tel (216)721-7373. Ed Maryann B Gall. LC KFO470.A6. DD 343.77104, 347.71034. Issues cover current developments by providing: status of bills, full text of official acts, tax agency rules, illustrative forms and decisions and opinions both reported and unreported.

BALTIMORE COUNTY GUIDE TO LAWS COVERING TENANT-LANDLORD RELATIONS IN THE CITY I.E. COUNTY AND THE STATE. Main/Corp Baltimore Neighborhoods, Inc. 1975-. US. English. an. Baltimore Neighborhoods Inc, 319 East 25th Street, Baltimore MD 21218. LC KFM1799.B32. DD 346.752710434.

BANGLADESH LABOUR CASES. See Economics - Labor.

BANKA VE TICARET HUKUKU DERGISI. Turkish. ir. 40.00. Batider, Banka ve Ticaret Hukuku Arastrma Enstitusu, Hukuk Fakultesi, Cebeci/Ankara, Ankara Turkey. LC K2.

THE BANKERS LETTER OF THE LAW. 0005-5433. Periodical. US. English. mo. $131.25. Warren Gorham Lamont Inc, 210 South Street, Boston MA 02111. Tel (800)225-2363 Outside Massachusetts.

BANKING, CORPORATION & BUSINESS LAW NEWSLETTER. VAT Banking, Corporation and Business Law Newsletter. 0148-3684. Periodical. US. English. New York State Bar Association, 1 Elk Street, Albany NY 12207. LC KFN5225.A15. DD 346.73066.

BANKING LAW ANTHOLOGY. Series/Titl National Law Anthology Series. Vol. 1 (1983)-. 0737-2159. US. English. an. $59.95. International Library Book Publishers, 3865 Wilson Boulevard/Suite 100-A, Arlington VA 22203. LC K2. DD 346.73082, 347.30682.

THE BANKING LAW JOURNAL. Vol. 1, No. 1 (May 15, 1889)-. 0005-5506. Periodical. US. English. bm. $71.40. Warren Gorham & Lamont Inc, 210 South Street, Boston MA 02111. Tel (800)225-2363. Ind/Abst Manage. Contents, Leg. Resour. Index, ABI/Inform, Index Leg. Period., Public Aff. Inf. Serv. Bull., Soc. Sci. Citation Index, Curr. Law Index, Contents Curr. Leg. Period. DD 346.7308205, 347.3068205. Available on microfilm from University Microfilms International. *Business Law Journal, Bankers Magazine, 0730-4080.*

BANKING LAW JOURNAL DIGEST. 1889-. 0271-6909. US. English. ir. Warren Gorham & Lamont, 1633 Broadway, New York NY 10019. *Digest of the Banking Law Journal.*

BANKING LAW JOURNAL DIGEST. FEDERAL SUPPLEMENT CEASED. 0147-4715. US. English. an. Warren Gorham & Lamont, 1633 Broadway, New York NY 10019. LC KF971.3. DD 346.73082.

BANKING LAW. NEW YORK BANKING LAW. (BANKING LAW : NEW YORK BANKING LAW). Main/Corp New York (State). 0198-9251. US. English. ir. Matthew Bender & Company Inc, 1275 Broadway, Albany NY 12202. Tel (800)833-9844. LC KFN5250.A333. DD 346.74708202632.

BANKING LAW REPORT. Vol. 1, No. 1 (Mar. 1984)-. 0742-3942. Periodical. US. English. mo. Free to Members, $120.00 Others. Executive Enterprise Publications, 333 West 60th Street, New York NY 10023. LC KF967. DD 346.7308205, 347.3068205.

BANKING LEGISLATION IN THE CONGRESS. Main/Corp American Bankers Association. 0094-7555. US. English. 112 Connecticut Avenue NW, Washington DC 20036. LC KF969.78. DD 346.73082.

BANKING LEGISLATION IN THE ... SESSION, ... CONGRESS. Main/Corp American Bankers Association. Federal Legislative Committee. US. English. an.

BANKRUPTCY LAW LETTER. V. 1, No. 1 (JAN. 1981)-. 0744-7671. Periodical. US. English. mo. $88.20. Warren Gorham & Lamont Inc, 210 South Street, Boston MA 02111. Tel (617)432-2020.

THE BANKRUPTCY STRATEGIST. Vol. 1, No. 1 (Nov. 1983)-. 0747-8917. Periodical. US. English. mo. $95.00. Leader Publications, 111 Eighth Avenue, New York NY 10011. Tel (800)221-8195. Ed Herbert S Schlagman. LC KF1507. DD 346.7307805, 347.3067805. Reports on legislative and judicial developments in bankruptcy law; includes articles on pretrial and trial strategy, as well as accounting and financial issues.

BAR. 0092-3877. Periodical. US. English. mo. State Bar of Texas, Colorado at 15th Street, Austin TX 78701. LC KF200. DD 340.062764.

BAR BRIEF. (BAR BRIEF : THE NEWSLETTER OF THE BEVERLY HILLS BAR ASSOCIATION). Main/Corp Beverly Hills Bar Association. 0749-0615. Periodical. US. English. $30.00. Beverly Hills Bar Association, 300 South Beverly Hills Avenue/Suite 201, Beverly Hills CA 90212. Tel (213)553-664. Ed David M Shacter. LC KF200. DD 340.060794. adv acc. Circ 2,600. (ctrl). Legal articles on all substantive law issues.

BAR BULLETIN (AUGUSTA, ME.). (BAR BULLETIN). 0738-0364. Periodical. US. English. bm. $12.00 Members. Maine State Bar Association, 124 State Street, PO Box 788, Augusta ME 04330. LC KF200. DD 340.060741. *Maine Bar Bulletin, 0542-1314.*

THE BAR EXAMINER. V. 1- Nov. 1931-. 0005-5824. US. English. qt. National Conference of Bar Examiners, 333 North Michigan Avenue, Chicago IL 60601. Ind/Abst Leg. Resour. Index. DD 347.069.

BAR LEADER. Began with March/April 1975 issue. 0099-1031. Periodical. US. English. bm. $17.00. American Bar Association, 750 North Lake Shore Drive, Chicago IL 60611. Tel (312)988-5555. Ind/Abst Leg. Resour. Index, Curr. Law Index. LC KF200. DD 340.06273. *Bar Activities, Bar Keys; Communications Coordinator.*

THE BAR LIST OF THE UNITED KINGDOM CEASED. 1977-1985. UK. English. an. 10.00. Stevens & Sons, 11 New Fetter Road, London EC4P 4EE England. LC KD336. DD 340.02541.

BAR NEWS. Main/Corp Illinois State Bar Association. 1- Sept. 1960-. 0445-4200. Periodical. US. English. ir. Illinois State Bar Association, Illinois Bar Center, Springfield IL 62701. DD 340.

BAR NOTES. Main/Corp North Carolina Bar Association. VFOAT Barnotes. Began in 1950?. 0546-4714. Periodical. US. English. bm. North Carolina Bar Association, 1312 Annapolis Drive, PO Box 12806, Raleigh NC 27605. LC KF200. DD 340.060756. (cum index).

BAR REPORT. Main/Corp District of Columbia Bar. 0271-2024. US. English. The District of Columbia Bar, 1426 H Street NW 8th Floor, Washington DC 20005. LC KF200. DD 349.75306.

BAR TOPICS. VFOAT Westchester Bar Topics. Began with issue for: Oct. 1956. Periodical. US. English. qt. $6.00. Westchester Bar Association, 65 Court Street, White Plains NY 10601. Tel (914)761-3707.

BARBADOS LAW REPORTS. Vol. 1 (1948-57)-. English. ir. LC KGL1012. DD 348.72981043, 347.29810843.

BARCLAYS CALIFORNIA LAW MONTHLY. Vol. 6, No. 6 (June 1984)-. 8755-772X. Periodical. US. English. mo. $185.00. Matthew Bender & Company Inc, 1275 Broadway, Albany NY 12201. LC K2. DD 349.79405, 347.94005. *Barclays Law Monthly, 0164-3835.*

BARNOTES. Periodical. US. English. ir.

BARREAU. V. 1- Sept. 1969-. 0381-7016. Periodical. CN. Multilingual (text also in English). mo. Barreau du Quebec, Palais de Justice, 9th Floor/1 rue Notre Dame Est, Montreal Quebec H2Y 1B6 Canada.

BARRISTER. (THE BARRISTER). Began in 1967. 0331-0086. Periodical. English. ir. LC K2. DD 3401.09669. *Law Student.*

BARRISTER BULLETIN. 0094-310X. US. English. Los Angeles County Bar Association, 606 South Olive Street/Suite 1212, Los Angeles CA 90014. LC KF200. DD 340.06279493.

BARRISTER (CHICAGO, ILL.). (BARRISTER). V. 1- Feb. 1974-. 0094-5277. US. English. qt $5.00. American Bar Association, 750 North Lake Shore Drive, Chicago IL 60611. Tel (312)988-6047. Ed Anthony Monahan. Ind/Abst Index Leg. Period., Contents Curr. Leg. Period., Curr. Law Index, Leg. Resour. Index. LC K2. DD 340.05. adv acc. Circ 150,000. (ctrl). The magazine for the young lawyer, reporting on law, the practice of law and law-firm management. *Law Notes (American Bar Association. Young Lawyers Section), 0732-8370.*

BARRISTER (PHILDADELPHIA, PA.). (THE BARRISTER). 0739-2494. Periodical. US. English. qt. PTLA, PO Box 889, 111 North Front Street, Harrisburg PA 17108. LC KF200.

BARRISTER (UNIVERSITY OF MIAMI. SCHOOL OF LAW). (THE BARRISTER). 0408-6007. Periodical. US. English. an. University of Miami, School of Law, Coral Cables FL 33124.

BARRISTERS NEWSLETTER. Main/Corp Los Angeles County Bar Association. Vol. 1, No. 1 (Jan. 1985)-. 0883-8682. Periodical. US. English. qt. $1.00 Members. Los Angeles County Bar Association, PO Box 55020, Los Angeles CA 90055. DD 340.

BATAS AT KATARUNGAN. Vol. 1, No. 1 (Feb. 1982)-. Periodical. English. sa. $20.00. University of the Philippines, Law Center/Bocobo Hall Diliman, Quezon City Philippines. LC K2. DD 349.59005, 345.99005.

BAURECHT. VFOAT Droit de la Construction. Periodical. French (German). ir. Seminar fur Schweizerisches Baurecht, Universitat, 1700 Freiburg West Germany. Ind/Abst Energy Res. Abstr. LC K2. DD 343.49407869005, 344. 94037869005.

BAYLOR LAW REVIEW. V. 1- Summer 1948-. 0005-7274. Periodical. US. English. qt. $20.00. Baylor University, Box 6262, Waco TX 76706. Ind/Abst Leg. Resour. Index, Women Stud. Abstr., Public Aff. Inf. Serv. Bull., Index Leg. Period., Curr. Law Index, Contents Curr. Leg. Period. bk rev. adv acc. Circ 1,250. Articles treat all areas of Texas and federal law, with articles by leading authorities and comments and casenotes by student authors.

B.C. CROWN COUNSEL NEWSLETTER. (B. C. CROWN COUNSEL NEWSLETTER). VAT British Columbia Crown Counsel Newsletter. V. 1- 1979-. 0709-2598. Periodical. CN. English. British Columbia Crown Counsel Association, 420-700 West Georgia Street, Vancouver British Columbia V7Y 1C6 Canada. DD 345.7105.

BCBA NEWS. VFOAT B.C.B.A. News. Periodical. US. English. Bucks County Bar Association, 135 East State Street, Doylestown PA 18901.

THE BEAVER COUNTY LEGAL JOURNAL. V. 1- Mar. 25, 1939/Mar. 16, 1940-. 0277-3856. Periodical. US. English. ir. Robert Ogden Davis, 325 Commerce Street, Beaver PA 15009.

BEHAVIORAL SCIENCES & THE LAW. VFOAT Behavioral Sciences and the Law. Vol. 1, No. 1-. 0735-3936. Periodical. US. English. qt. John Wiley & Sons Inc, 605 Third Avenue, New York NY 10158. Ind/Abst Leg. Resour. Index, Excerpta Med., Psychol. Abstr. LC K2. DD 344.7304405, 347.3044405. NLM W1.

BEITRAGE ZUM AUSLANDISCHEN OFFENTLICHEN RECHT UND VOLKERRECHT. No. 1-. 0172-4770. Monographic Series. German. ir. Springer Verlag-New York Inc, 175 5th Avenue, New York NY 10010. Tel (212)460-1500. Numbered series.

BELLI LAW JOURNAL. V. 1, Issue 1 (Winter 1984)-. 0741-2088. Periodical. US. English. qt. $35.00. Belli Law Journal, 26701 Quail Creek No 295, Laguna Hills CA 92653. LC K2. DD 347.73705, 347.307705.

BENCH & BAR INTERIM. VFOAT Interim. VAT Bench and Bar Interim. May 20, 1981-. 0731-8855. Periodical. US. English. Minnesota State Bar Association, 100 Minnesota Federal Building, Minneapolis MN 55402.

Law

BENCH AND BAR OF MINNESOTA. (BENCH & BAR OF MINNESOTA). Vol. 24, No. 17-18 (May-June 1968)-. 0276-1505. US. English. mo. $20.00. Minnesota State Bar Association, Suite 403/ 430 Marquette Avenue, Minneapolis MN 55401. **Tel** (612)333-1183. Ed Judson Haverkamp. **Ind/Abst** Leg. Resour. Index, Curr. Law Index. bk rev. adv acc. **Circ** 11,500. (ctrl). Official publication of Minnesota State Bar Association. Editorial focus on substantive law, legal profession. *Bench and Bar of Minnesota, 0276-1505.*

BENCHMARK. Main/Corp South Dakota. Supreme Court. Office of the Court Administrator. 1976/77-. US. English. an. South Dakota Unified Judicial System, State Court Administrator's Office, State Capitol, Pierre SD 57501. **LC** KFS3570. **DD** 347.78301.

BENCHMARK. (BENCHMARK : A BIMONTHLY REPORT ON THE CONSTITUTION AND THE COURTS). V. 1, No. 1 (Jan./Feb. 1984)-. 0743-0310. Periodical. US. English. bm. $20.00. Benchmark, PO Box 15449, Washington DC 20003. **LC** KF4546.A3. **DD** 342.73005, 347.302005.

BENDER'S DICTIONARY OF 1040 DEDUCTIONS. See Encyclopedias & General Reference Books.

BENDER'S FEDERAL PRACTICE MANUAL. Main/Corp United States. Courts. 1953-. US. English. ir. Matthew Bender & Company Inc, 1275 Broadway, Albany NY 12201. **Tel** (800)833-9844.

BENDER'S PAYROLL TAX GUIDE. (BENDER'S . . . PAYROLL TAX GUIDE). **VFOAT** Payroll Tax Guide. 0732-6564. US. English. Matthew Bender, 235 East 45 Street, New York NY 10017. **LC** KF6436. **DD** 343.7305242, 347.3035242.

BENDER'S UNIFORM COMMERCIAL CODE SERVICE. US. English. ir. Matthew Bender & Company Inc, 1275 Broadway, Albany NY 12201. **Tel** (800)833-9844.

BENEFITS TODAY. Vol. 1, No. 1 (July 20, 1984)-. 0747-9131. Periodical. US. English. bw. RSPD, 1231 25th Street Northwest, Washington DC 20037. **DD** 346.

BERETNING - FORBRUGEROMBUDSMANDEN. Main/Corp Denmark. Forbrugerombudsmanden. **VFOAT** Forbrugerombudsmandens Beretning. DK. Danish. ir. J H Schultz Boghandes, Mntergade 19, 1116 Kbenhavn K Denmark.

BERITA BADAN PEMBINAAN HUKUM NASIONAL. Main/Corp Badan Pembinaan Hukum Nasional. V. 1.- Jan. 1975-. Indonesian. ir. Pusat Dokumentasi Hukum Bphn, Jalan Medan Merdeka 9, Jakarta Indonesia.

BERKELEY-KOLNER RECHTSSTUDIEN. (1- 1961)-. 0409-1264. Periodical. GW. German. ir. CF Muller Juristischer Verlag, Postfach 102640, D69 Heidelberg 1 West Germany.

BERKS COUNTY LAW JOURNAL. V. 1- 1908/09-. 8750-3379. US. English. wk. $26.00. Berks County Bar Association, 544-548 Court Street, Reading PA 19603. **Tel** (215)375-4593. Ed Michael J Connolly. **DD** 348. Each issue contains an index to its own contents - no vol index - loose. adv acc. **Circ** 627. Reporting of local court opinions and the publishing of local legal advertising.

BERLINER JURISTISCHE ABHANDLUNGEN. 0523-0209. German. ir. Duncker und Humblot Verlag, Dietrich-Schafer-Weg 9, 1000 Berlin 41 West Germany.

THE BEST OF LAW AND MEDICINE. US. English. ir. American Medical Association, 535 North Dearborn Parkway, Chicago IL 60610. **Tel** (312)645-4927.

BEST'S DIRECTORY OF RECOMMENDED INSURANCE ATTORNEYS. See Yearbooks, Almanacs, Directories.

DER BETRIEB. 1- 1948-. 0005-9935. Periodical. GW. German. wk. Handelsblatt GMBH, Postfach 1102/Kasernenstr 67, 4000 Duesseldorf West Germany. **Tel** 0211/8388. **Ind/Abst** Coal Abstr., Energy Res. Abstr.

BEVERLY HILLS BAR ASSOCIATION JOURNAL. VFOAT Beverly Hills Bar Journal. V. 11, No. 4 (July/Aug. 1977)-. Periodical. US. English. qt. $30.00. Beverly Hills Bar, 300 South Beverly Drive, Beverly Hills CA 90212. **Tel** (213)553-6644. Ed David Shacter. **LC** K2. **DD** 340.05. adv acc. **Circ** 3,000. (ctrl). Deals with legal topics, both substantive and procedural. *Journal of the Beverly Hills Bar Association.*

BIBLIOGRAPHIC GUIDE TO LAW. See Bibliographies.

BIBLIOGRAPHIE JURISTISCHER FESTSCHRIFTEN UND FESTSCHRIFTENBEITRAGE : DEUTSCHLAND, SCHWEIZ, OSTERREICH. See Bibliographies.

BIBLIOGRAPHIE : STAAT UND RECHT. See Bibliographies.

BIBLIOGRAPHIE : STAAT UND RECHTDER DEUTSCHEN DEMOKRATISCHEN REPUBLIK. See Bibliographies.

A BIBLIOGRAPHY ON FOREIGN AND COMPARATIVE LAW. See Bibliographies.

BIBLIOGRAPHY SERIES - UNITED STATES. DEPT. OF JUSTICE. See Bibliographies.

BIBLIOGRAFIA IDG. A, DIRITTO COMMERICALE. Series/Titl Collana di Documentazione Giuridica. 1979-. IT. Italian. an. 9,000. Case Editrice Giuffre, Via Statuto 2, 20121 Milano Italy. **DD** 016.3464507, 016.3445067.

BIENNIAL REPORT OF THE DEPARTMENT OF LAW TO . . . GOVERNOR, COMMONWEALTH OF KENTUCKY FOR THE BIENNIAL PERIOD . . . AS REQUIRED BY KRS 15.080. Main/Corp Kentucky. Dept. of Law. US. English. be. **LC** KFK1627.5.A8. **DD** 353.97690088. *Biennial Report of the Attorney General to the General of the Commonwealth of Kentucky for the Biennial Period . . . as Required by KR 15.080.*

BIENNIAL REPORT OF THE WISCONSIN DEPARTMENT OF JUSTICE. Main/Corp Wisconsin. Department of Justice. **VFOAT** Attorney-General's Biennial Report to the Legislature. US. English. be. State of Wisconsin/ Department of Justice, 819 North 6th Street/Room 520, Wilwaukee WI 53203. **LC** KFW2827.5.A8. **DD** 353.97750088.

BIENNIAL REPORT - STATE OF ILLINOIS, LEGISLATIVE ADVISORY COMMITTEE ON PUBLIC AID. Main/Corp Illinois. General Assembly. Legislative Advisory Committee on Public Aid. 1973/75-. US. English. be. Room 4 C/State Office Building, Springfield IL 62767.

BIENNIAL REPORT - STATE OF WISCONSIN, DEPARTMENT OF REGULATION AND LICENSING. Main/Corp Wisconsin. Dept. of Regulation and Licensing. 0145-8647. US. English. be. Department of Regulation and Licensing, 201 East Washington Avenue, Madison WI 53702. **LC** KFW2725. **DD** 353.9775008243.

BIENNIAL REPORT TO THE LEGISLATURE - MONTANA LEGISLATIVE ASSEMBLY. ADMINISTRATIVE CODE COMMITTEE. Main/Corp Montana. Legislative Assembly. Administrative Code Committee. US. English. be. Montana Legislative Council, State Capitol, Helena MT 59601. **LC** KFM9011.6. **DD** 342.7860605.

BIHAR BAR COUNCIL JOURNAL. Main/Corp Bihar State Bar Council. Periodical. English. ir. .30/-. Bihar State Bar Council, High Court Building, Patna - 1 India. **DD** 348.5412046.

BILE, BOLETIN DE INFORMACION LEGAL. Periodical. AG. Spanish. ir. $25.00. Instituto Para la Integracion de America Latina, Casilla de Correo 39 - Suc 1, 1401 Buenos Aires Argentina. **DD** 346.807.

BILL OF RIGHTS JOURNAL. (THE BILL OF RIGHTS JOURNAL). Vol. 1, No. 1 (Dec. 1968)-. 0006-2499. US. English. an. National Emergency Civil Liberites Comittee, 175-5th Avenue, New York NY 10010. **Ind/Abst** Leg. Resour. Index, Altern. Press Index. **LC** K2. **DD** 323.40973.

BILLS AND LAWS OF THE NATIONAL STATE ASSEMBLY. Main/Corp Sri Lanka. 1972-. CE. English. ir. $0.50. Government Publications Bureau, PO Box 500, Colombo Sri Lanka. **DD** 348.5493022. *Acts of Ceylon.*

BIOTECHNOLOGY LAW REPORT. Vol. 1, No. 1 (Jan. 1982)-. 0730-031X. Periodical. US. English. mo. $343.00. Mary Ann Liebert Inc, 157 East 86th Street, New York NY 10028. **Tel** (212)289-2300. Ed Gerry Elman. **LC** KF3827.G4. **DD** 344.73095, 347.30495. bk rev. adv acc. Newsmagazine covering advances and developments in patent, regulatory biomedical, licensing, and international law as they relate to biotechnology.

BIRK'S. VFOAT Birk's Register of Commercial Attorneys. 0091-4002. US. English. 3539 Hennepin Avenue, Minneapolis MN 55408. **LC** KF195.C57. **DD** 346.7307025.

BIULLETEN VERKHOVNOGO SUDA SSSR. Main/Corp Russia (1923- U.S.S.R.). Verkhovnyi Sud. 1942-. 0557-5257. Periodical. UR. Russian. bm. $10.00. Victor Kamkin Inc (70078), 12224 Parklawn Drive, Rockville MD 20852. **Tel** (301)881-5973.

THE BLACK LAW JOURNAL. V. 1- Spring 1971-. 0045-2181. Periodical. US. English. ty. $25.00. University of California at Los Angeles, School of Law/Room 1242, Los Angeles CA 90024. **Tel** (213)825-7941. Ed Linda Fraser. **Ind/Abst** Leg. Resour. Index, Index Leg. Period., Curr. Law Index, Contents Curr. Leg. Period. **LC** K2. **DD** 340.5. bk rev. adv acc. **Circ** 750. Publishes articles addressing legal issues of relevance to blacks and other minority communities. Past article subjects include desegregration, civil rights, affirmative action, police abuse and apartheid.

BLAIR COUNTY LAW REPORTER. V. 1-2, Feb. 1898-1903. Periodical. English. ir.

BLATTER FUR EIN NEUES BODENRECHT. Periodical. SZ. French (German). qt. 2.50 Each Issue. Schweizerische Gesellschaft fur Ein Neues Bodenrecht, Postfach 2276, 3001 Bern Switzerland. **LC** K2. **DD** 346.4940432, 344.9406432.

BNA'S LAW REPRINTS. CRIMINAL LAW SERIES. VFOAT Criminal Law Series. **VAT** Bureau of National Affairs Law Reprints. Criminal Law Series. Vol. 12, No. 1-. 0275-6986. Monographic Series. US. English. ir. $250.00. Bureau of National Affairs, 1231 25th Street NW, Washington DC 20037. *Law Reprints. Criminal Law Series.*

BNA'S LAW REPRINTS. LABOR LAW SERIES. See Economics - Labor.

BNA'S LAW REPRINTS. SECURITIES REGULATION SERIES. VFOAT Securities Regulation Series. **VAT** Bureau of National Affairs Law Reprints. Securities Regulation Series. Vol. 5, No. 1-. 0275-696X. Monographic Series. US. English. an. $248.00. Bureau of National Affairs Inc, 1231 25th Street NW, Washington DC 20037. **Tel** (301)258-1033. *Law Reprints. Securities Regulation Series.*

BNA'S LAW REPRINTS. TAX SERIES. VFOAT Tax Series. **VAT** Bureau of National Affair's Law Reprints. Tax Series. Vol. 13, No. 1-. 0275-6951. Monographic Series. US. English. ir. $248.00. Bureau of National Affairs Inc, 1231 25th Street NW, Washington DC 20037. **Tel** (301)258-1033. *Law Reprints. Tax Series.*

BOARD OF CONTRACT APPEALS DECISIONS. See Military Science.

THE BOCA BASIC HOUSING- PROPERTY MAINTENANCE CODE. See Building and Construction.

THE BOCA BASIC MECHANICAL CODE. See Building and Construction.

THE BOCA BASIC/NATIONAL BUILDING CODE. See Building and Construction.

BOILER AND PRESSURE VESSEL SAFETY ACT AND RULES AND REGULATIONS. Main/Corp Illinois. 1978-. US. English. Superintendent of Boiler and Pressure Vessel Safety, 302 Amory Building, Springfield IL 62706. **LC** KFI1580.5.S7. **DD** 344.7710472, 347.7104472. Index in last issue of volume - attached. *Boiler Safety Act, and Boiler Rules and Regulations Formulated and Published by Authorization of the Board of Boiler Rules.*

BOLETIM - CENTRO DE ESTUDOS, PROCURADORIA GERAL DO ESTADO. Main/Corp Sao Paulo, Brazil (State). Procuradoria Geral do Estado. Centro de Estudos. V. 1- 1/15 Jan. 1977-. Portuguese. ir. Praca da Liberdade, 272-3 Andar, 01503 Sao Paulo Brazil.

BOLETIM DA BIBLIOTECA. Main/Corp Petroleo Brasileiro, S.A. Servico Juridico. Biblioteca. BL. Portuguese. ir. Sejor, Av Republica do Chile 65 170, S/1751 Rio de Janeiro Brazil. **DD** 016.34981.

Law

BOLETIM DA PROCURADORIA GERAL. Main/Corp Rio de Janeiro (State). Departamento de Estradas de Rodagem. PRocuradoria Geral. Yearly V. 1- (No. 1-). Portuguese. ir. Praca Fonseca Ramos S/No., Edificio Sede do DER/RJ, 6 Pavimento, Porto Alegre Brazil. DD 343.8150494.

BOLETIM DA REPUBLICA. Main/Corp Mozambique. Portuguese. ir. DD 340.09679. *Boletim Oficial.*

BOLETIM DA SUSEP. Main/Corp SUSEP (Government Agency : Brazil). VFOAT Boletim da S.U.S.E.P. BL. Portuguese. ir. Superintendencia de Seguros Privados/Departamento de Servicos, Gerais Av Rio Branco 109/210. Andar GR 2104 Rio de Janeiro RJ Brazil. LC KHD1212. DD 346.8108605, 348.1068605.

BOLETIM DE REFERENCIA LEGISLATIVA. Main/Corp Universidade Federal Fluminense. Secao de Referencia Legislativa. Portuguese. ir. Univeridade Federal Fluminense, R Miguel de Frias 9, Caixa Postal 1108, Niteroi Brazil. DD 348.81028.

BOLETIM DO TRABALHO E EMPREGO. 2A I.E. SEGUNDA SERIE. Main/Corp Portugal. Ministerio do Trabalho. Servico de Informacao Cientifica e Tecnica. English. ir. 600.00. Ministerio do Trabalho, Praca de Londres 2 10 Sala 1, Lisboa Portugal. DD 344.46901.

BOLETIM ELEITORAL. Main/Corp Brazil. Tribunal Regional Eleitoral de Sao Paulo. Portufuese. ir. Tribunal Regional Editorial de Sao Paulo, rua Francisca Miquelina 123-9 PO S Andar, 01381 Sao Paulo Brazil. DD 342.8107.

BOLETIM INFORMATIVO ADUANEIRAS. BL. Portuguese. ir. $2150. Edicoes Aduaneiras Ltda, Cx P 30.280, Sao Paulo Brazil. DD 343.8105605, 348.1035605.

BOLETIM INFORMATIVO MENSAL (PORTO ALEGRE, BRAZIL). (BOLETIM INFORMATIVO MENSAL : BIM). VFOAT BIM. Periodical. Portuguese. mo. Corregedoria-Geral de Justica Palacio da Justica, 4O. Andar, Porto Alegre Brazil. LC KHD8330.A15. DD 347.8165005, 348.16507005.

BOLETIM INFORMATIVO - PROCURADORIA GERAL DO ESTADO. Main/Corp Bahia, Brazil (State). Procuradoria Geral do Estado. Portuguese. ir. Procuradoria Geral do Estado, Travessa da Ajuda No 2 - 20 Andar, Salvador Brazil. LC K2. DD 340.09814.

BOLETIM OFICIAL. PARTE I. Main/Corp Rio de Janeiro (Brazil : State). Yearly V. 1- 18 March 1975-. Portuguese. ir. Rua do Lavradio 34, Rio de Janeiro Brazil.

BOLETIN ANGLOHISPANO. Vol. 1, No. 1 (Oct. 1980)-. 0731-8111. Periodical. US. English (Spanish). bm. $15.00. Bola Publications, 8769 Devon Avenue, Hesperia CA 92345. Ed Ricardo Nance. LC KFC81. DD 349.79405, 347.94005. bk rev. Circ 500. English-Spanish-English glossary of Mexican Spanish.

BOLETIN - COLEGAS. (COLEGAS). Main/Corp Colegio Antioqueno de Abogados. VAT Boletin - Colegio Antioqueno de Abogados. 0302-802X. Spanish. ir. Colegio Antioguevo de Abogados, Edificio Bolsa de Medellin CRA 50 No 50-48 of 700, Medellin Colombia.

BOLETIN DE INFORMACIONES JURIDICAS : ORGANO DE INFORMACION DEL CENTRO DE INVESTIGACION JURIDICA DE LA FACULTAD DE DERECHO Y CIENCIAS POLITICAS DE LA UNIVERSIDAD DE PANAMA. PN. Spanish. sa. DD 348.728731026, 347.287310826.

BOLETIN DE INFORMACIONES SOCIO-JURIDICAS. Main/Corp Colombia. Ministerio de Justicia. Yearly V. 1- Nov. 1971-. Spanish. ir.

BOLETIN DE JURISPRUDENCIA Y RESOLUCIONES ADMINISTRATIVAS SOBRE URBANISMO Y VIVIENDA. See Housing and Urban Development.

BOLETIN DE LEGISLACION DE LAS COMUNIDADES AUTONOMAS : BCA. See Public Administration.

BOLETIN DE LOS COLEGIOS DE ABOGADOS DE ARAGON. Yearly V. 18- (No. 71-). Periodical. SP. Spanish. ir. Colegio de Abogados de Zaragoza, Coso 1, Zaragoza Spain. LC K3. DD 340.094655.

BOLETIN DEL INSTITUTO DE DERECHO PRIVADO. Periodical. Spanish. ir. LC K600.A2. DD 346.005, 342.605.

BOLETIN DEL MINISTERIO DE JUSTICIA. V. 1, No. 1 (Jan-March 1980)-. Periodical. AG. Spanish. qt. Direccion General do Coordinacion, Gral Gelly y Obes 2289 - 4O. Picso, 1425 Buenos Aires Argentina. DD 349.8205.

BOLETIN INFORMATIVO DEL DEPARTAMENTO DE DERECHO POLITICO. 3 (Spring 1979)-. Periodical. SP. Spanish. qt. 900. Secretario del Boletin, Departamento de Derecho Politico, Universidad Nacional de Educacion A, Education A Distancia Ciudad Universitaria, Madrid 3 Spain. LC K2. DD 349.4605, 344.6005. *Boletin Informativo del Departamento de Derecho Politico e Internacional.*

BOLETIN INFORMATIVO - INSTITUTO DE FILOSOFIA DEL DERECHO. Main/Corp Universidad del Zulia. Instituto de Filosofia del Derecho. Yearly V. 4, No. 7-. Periodical. VE. Spanish. ir. Universidad Del Zulia, Apartado 1490, Maracaibo Venezuela. DD 340.1. *Boletin Informativo - Centro de Estudios de Filosofia del Derecho.*

BOLETIN JUDICIAL DE LA PROVINCIA DE BUENOS AIRES. Main/Corp Buenos Aires (Argentine : Province). VFOAT Diario de Jurisprudencia de la Provincia de Buenos Aires. Yearly V. 1- (No. 1). Periodical. US. Spanish.

BOLETIN JUDICIAL (PUERTO RICO. OFFICE OF COURT ADMINISTRATION.). (BOLETIN JUDICIAL). Yearly V. 1, No. 1 (Jan.-March 1979)-. Periodical. PR. Spanish. qt. Oficina de Administracion de los Tribunales, Area de Relaciones y Coordinacion Interagencial, Calle Vela Parada 35 1/2 Hato Rey Station Call Box 22A, Hato Rey Puerto Rico 00919. LC K2. DD 349.729505, 347.295005.

BOLETIN MEXICANO DE DERECHO COMPARADO. NEUVA SERIE. Vol. 1 1968-. 0041-8633. Periodical. MX. Spanish. ty. $35.00. Institute of Investigaciones Juridicas, Torre Human 3er/Cludad University, Mexico DF Mexico. Ind/Abst ABC Pol Sci.

BOLETIN OFICIAL DE LA PROVINCIA DE SAHARA. Main/Corp Spanish Sahara. Spanish. ir.

BOLETIN OFICIAL DEL ESTADO. Main/Corp Spain. Yearly V. 1-26. SP. Spanish. ir. $65.40. Boletin Oficial del Estado, Trafalgar 27, Madrid 10 Spain. *Boletin Oficial de la Junta de Defensa Nacional de Espana.*

BOLETIN OFICIAL, MINISTERIO DE EDUCACION. ACTOS ADMINISTRATIVOS. See Education (General).

BOLETIN OFICIAL, MINISTERIO DE EDUCACION Y CIENCIA. ACTOS ADMINISTRATIVOS. See Education (General).

BOSTON BAR JOURNAL. Vol. 1, No. 1 (Jan. 1957)-. 0524-1111. Periodical. US. English. $25.00. Boston Bar Association, 16 Beacon Street, Boston MA 02108. Ind/Abst Leg. Resour. Index, Curr. Law Index. LC UNC. DD 347. *Bar Bulletin (Boston, Mass.).*

THE BOSTON BARRISTER. 0197-1921. Periodical. US. English. Boston Bar Association, 16 Beacon Street, Boston MA 02108. LC KF200. DD 340.06074461.

BOSTON COLLEGE ENVIRONMENTAL AFFAIRS LAW REVIEW. Main/Corp Boston College. Law School. VFOAT Environmental Affairs Law Review. V. 7- 1978-. 0190-7034. Periodical. US. English. qt. $22.00. Environmental Law Center, Boston College 885 Centre Street, Newton MA 02159. Tel (617)552-8001. Ind/Abst Electron. Commun. Abstr. J., ISMEC Bull., Pollut. Abstr. Indexes, Saf. Sci. Abstr. J., Leg. Resour. Index, Life Sci. Collect., Can. Environ., Sel. Water Resour. Abstr., Coal Abstr., Energy Inf. Abstr., Environ. Abstr., GeoRef, Biol. Abstr., Public Aff. Inf. Serv. Bull., Energy Res. Abstr., Index Leg. Period., Soc. Sci. Index, Ocean. Abstr., Contents Curr. Leg. Period., Curr. Law Index, Bibliogr. Index Geol. LC K5. DD 344.7304605. CODEN BCERDX. bk rev. Circ 1,500. *Environmental Affairs, 0046-2225.*

BOSTON COLLEGE INDUSTRIAL AND COMMERCIAL LAW REVIEW. V. 1- Fall 1959-. Periodical. US. English. LC Microfilm LL-095, K2.

BOSTON COLLEGE LAW REVIEW. V. 19- Nov. 1977-. 0161-6587. Periodical. US. English. ir. Boston College Law School, 885 Centre Street, Newton Centre MA 02159. Tel (617)552-8557. Ind/Abst Manage. Contents, Leg. Resour. Index, Index Leg. Period., Public Aff. Inf. Serv. Bull. LC K2. DD 340.05. adv acc. Circ 1,000. *Boston College Industrial and Commercial Law Review.*

BOSTON UNIVERSITY JOURNAL OF TAX LAW. VFOAT Journal of Tax Law. Vol. 1 (Mar. 1983)-. 0741-8477. Periodical. US. English. an. $10.00. Boston University Ulumni Center, 765 Commonwealth Avenue, Boston MA 02215. Tel (617)353-2000. DD 343.

BOSTON UNIVERSITY LAW REVIEW. Main/Corp Boston University. School of Law. V. 1- Jan. 1921-. 0006-8047. Periodical. US. English. ir. $22.00. Boston University of Law Review, 765 Commonwealth Avenue, Boston MA 02215. Tel (617)353-3166. Ed Margaret C Jenkins. Ind/Abst Manage. Contents, Leg. Resour. Index, Public Aff. Inf. Serv. Bull., Index Leg. Period., Soc. Sci. Citation Index, Curr. Law Index, Contents Curr. Leg. Period. bk rev. adv acc. Circ 4,000. A legal journal containing up-to-date articles by law professors and practicing attorneys, professional quality notes and case comments by student members.

BOWKER'S LAW BOOKS AND SERIALS IN PRINT UPDATE. (BOWKER'S LAW BOOKS AND SERIALS IN PRINT UPDATE : MATERIALS ON LAW AND LAW RELATED TOPICS RECENTLY PUBLISHED AND TO BE PUBLISHED). VFOAT Law Books and Serials in Print Update. Vol. 2, No. 2 (Feb. 1984)-. 0000-0760. US. English. mo. R R Bowker Company, 205 East 42nd Street, New York NY 10017. LC KF1. DD 016.34005. *Law Information Update, 0000-0728.*

BOYCOTT LAW BULLETIN. VFOAT Middle East Monthly. 0162-1726. Periodical. US. English. mo. $445.00 Domestic, $525.00 Foreign. Boycott Law Bulletin, PO Box 73326, Houston TX 77273. LC KF1987.A15. DD 343.73087. *Anti-Boycott Bulletin, 0149-3310.*

BRACTON LAW JOURNAL. (THE BRACTON LAW JOURNAL). V. 1- 1965-. 0308-4574. Periodical. UK. English. sa. University of Exeter, Amory Building/Rennes Drive, Exeter EX4 4RJ England. Ind/Abst Leg. Resour. Index, Index Leg. Period. LC K2. DD 349.4105.

THE BRIEF. V. 9, No. 3- May, 1980-. 0273-0995. Periodical. US. English. qt. $15.00. American Bar Association, 750 North Lake Shore Drive, Chicago IL 60611. Tel (312)988-6046. Ed Anne Mendelson and James Carr. adv acc. Circ 22,000. (ctrl). Recent trends and how-to articles for tort and insurance lawyers. *INCL Brief.*

THE BRIEF TIMES REPORTER. 0164-789X. Periodical. US. English. wk. $135.00. The Public Record Corporation, 1666 Lafayette Street, Denver CO 80218. Tel (303)832-8262.

BRIEF/CASE CEASED. (THE BRIEF CASE). Vol. 1, No. 1 (Sept. 1950)-V. 23, No. 2 (March/April 1973)-. 0520-9633. Periodical. US. English. mo.

BRIEFLY SPEAKING. (BRIEFLY SPEAKING : A MONTHLY REPORT FOR MEMBERS OF THE CANADIAN BAR ASSOCIATION-ONTARIO). Vol. 1, No. 1 (Sept. 1980 I.E. 1979)-. 0715-3759. Periodical. CN. English. mo. Free. Briefly Speaking, CBAO Centre, Suite 1000/120 Adelaide Street West, Toronto Ontario M5K 1T1 Canada. DD 340.060713. (ctrl).

BRIGHAM YOUNG UNIVERSITY LAW REVIEW. 1975-. 0360-151X. US. English. ty. $50.00. Brigham Young University, 453 JRCB, Provo UT 84602. Tel (801)378-3580. Ed Allen Haynie. Ind/Abst Leg. Resour. Index, ABI/Inform, Index Leg. Period., Curr. Law Index, Contents Curr. Leg. Period. LC K2. DD 340.05. adv acc. Circ 650. Articles and student pieces reviewing laws and cases relating to the legal system.

BRITISH COLUMBIA DECISIONS, STATUTE CITATOR. 0715-4798. Periodical. CN. English. mo. British Columbia Desicions Statute Citator, 301-1 Alexander Street, Vancouver British Columbia V6A 1B2 Canada. DD 348.

Law

BRITISH COLUMBIA DECISIONS WEEKLY HEADNOTES. Issue No. 1 (Mar. 12/82)-. 0715-4550. Periodical. CN. English. wk. 110.00. British Columbia Decisions Weekly Headnotes, Suite 301/1 Alexandra Street, Vancouver British Columbia V6A 1B2 Canada. **DD** 348.711044.

BRITISH COLUMBIA GAZETTE. PART II. REGULATIONS. (THE BRITISH COLUMBIA GAZETTE. PART II, REGULATIONS. V. 1, No. 1 (Apr. 17, 1958)-. 0824-7986. CN. English. bw. $19.35. Queens Printer, Parliament Building, Victoria BC Canada. **DD** 348.71102505. Available on microfilm as: British Columbia. The British Columbia Gazette, Toronto: Micromedia, British Columbia. The British Columbia Gazette.

BRITISH COLUMBIA LABOUR RELATIONS BOARD DECISIONS. See Economics - Labor.

BRITISH COLUMBIA LAW REPORTS. V. 1- 1977-. 0703-3060. Periodical. CN. English. ir. Burroughs, 201 513-8th Avenue SW, Calgary Alberta T2P 1G3 Canada. **LC** KEB104. **DD** 348.711043.

BRITISH COLUMBIA SUCCESSION DUTY AND GIFT TAX LEGISLATION. Main/Corp British Columbia. 1st- Ed. 0317-0551. Periodical. CN. English. an. CCH Canadian Ltd, 6 Garamond Court, Don Mills Ontario M3C 1Z5 Canada. **DD** 343.71105302633.

BRITISH COLUMBIA WEEKLY LAW DIGEST. Issue No. 1 (Jan. 6, 1982)-. 0713-8865. Periodical. CN. English. wk. British Columbia Weekly Law Digest, 2330 Maitland Avenue, Agincourt Ontario M1S 1P7 Canada. **DD** 348.711046.

BRITISH JOURNAL OF LAW AND SOCIETY CEASED. V. 1-8, No. 2. 0306-3704. UK. English. $15.00. 6 1/2 Suffolk Street. **Ind/Abst** Soc. Welf. Soc. Plan./Policy Soc. Dev., Sociol. Abstr. **LC** K2. **DD** 340.11505.

BROADCASTING AND THE LAW. See Communication - Broadcasting.

BROKEN BENCH REVIEW. See Business.

THE BRONX COUNTY BAR JOURNAL. Vol. 1, No. 1 (Winter 1983)-. 8755-6081. Periodical. US. English. qt. Bronx County Bar Association, 851 Grand Concourse, Bronx NY 10451. **LC** KF200. **DD** 340.060747275.

BROOKLYN LAW REVIEW. V. 1- Apr. 1932-. US. English. qt. $15.00. Brooklyn Law Review, 250 Joralemon Street, Brooklyn NY 11201. **Tel** (718)780-7968. **Ed** Kenneth M Koprowicz. **Ind/Abst** Index Leg. Period., Curr. Law Index, Leg. Resour. Index, Contents Curr. Leg. Period. **LC** MICROFILM LL-096 K2. bk rev. **Circ** 800. Legal periodical on topics of current interest to the legal community; annual review of important second circuit cases.

BRUNSWICK TAX REPORT. (THE BRUNSWICK TAX REPORT). Began with issue for Mar. 1984 V. 5, No. 3). 0828-5365. Periodical. CN. English. mo. $95.00 Per Year. Brunswick Tax Report, 130 Adelaide Street/Suite 2400, West Toronto Ontario M5H 3C2 Canada. **DD** 343.7104. Gage/MacMillan Tax Report, 0228-4170.

BUDAPESTI EOTVOS LORAND TUDOMANYEGYETEM ALLAM ES JOGTUDOMANYI KARANAK ACTAI. (A BUDAPESTI EOTVOS LORAND TUDOMANYEGYETEM ALLAM ES JOGTUDOMANYI KARANAK ACTAI). Main/Corp Budapest. Tudomany-Egyetem. Allam- es Jogtodomanyi Kar. **VFOAT** Acta Facultatis Politico-Iuridicae Universitatis Scientiarum Budapestinensis de Rolando Eotvos Nominatae. 1.- Vol. 0524-904X. Hungarian (summaries in Russian and French or German). ir. **Ind/Abst** Am. Hist. Life, Hist. Abstr., Part A, Mod. Hist. Abstr., Hist. Abst., Part B, Twent. Century Abstr.

BUFFALO LAW JOURNAL. 0197-4955. Periodical. US. English. sw. $60.00. Buffalo Publishing Company, 125 Broadway, Buffalo NY 14203. **Tel** (716)852-4919. **LC** K2. **DD** 349.74705.

BUFFALO LAW REVIEW. V. 1- Spring 1951-. 0023-9356. Periodical. US. English. qt. $18.00. Buffalo Law Review, State University of New York Buffalo, Amherst Campus, 605 John Lord O' Brien Hall, Buffalo NY 14226. **Tel** (716)636-2059. **Ed** Karen Hassett. **Ind/Abst** Leg. Resour. Index, Sociol. Abstr., Soc. Welf. Soc. Plan./Policy Soc. Dev., Index Leg. Period. **LC** K2. **DD** 340.05. (cum index). bk rev. **Circ** 600. (ctrl). A compilation of legal research regarding every facet of the law, of interest to practicing attorneys and legal scholars.

BUILDING PERMITS : ANNUAL SUMMARY. See Building and Construction.

BUILDING PERMITS FOR MAJOR CITIES. See Building and Construction.

BUILDING PERMITS. PERMIS DE BATIR. See Building and Construction.

BUILDING PERMITS (STATISTICS CANADA). See Building and Construction.

BUILDING REGULATION. See Building and Construction.

BULETINUL OFICIAL AL REPUBLICII SOCIALISTE ROMANIA. PARTEA A II-A. Main/Corp Romania. RM. Romanian. ir. Ilexim Press Department, PO Box 1-136-1-137, Bucharest-Romania. Buletinul Oficial.

BULETINUL OFICIAL AL REPUBLICII SOCIALISTE ROMANIA. PARTEA A III-A. Main/Corp Romania. RM. Romanian. ir. Ilexim Press Department, PO Box 1-136-1-137, Bucharest-Romania. Buletinul Oficial.

BULETINUL OFICIAL AL REPUBLICII SOCIALISTE ROMANIA. PARTEA A III-A. SUPLIMENT. Main/Corp Romania. 1975-. Romanian. ir. 6.00 Single Issue. Buletinul Oficial Biroul de Publicitate Si Difuzare, Pentru Buletinul Oficial, Str Mendeleev Nr 7 Sectorul 1, Bucuresti Romania.

BULETINUL OFICIAL AL REPUBLICII SOCIALISTE ROMANIA. PARTEA I. Main/Corp Romania. Year 1- Aug. 21, 1965-. RM. Romanian. ir. Ilexim Press Department, PO Box 1-136-1-137, Bucharest-Romania. Buletinul Oficial.

BULETINUL OFICIAL AL REPUBLICII SOCIALISTE ROMANIA. SUPLIMENT A. Main/Corp Romania. Year 1- 15 May 1974-. RM. Romanian. ir. 2.00. Serviciul Buletinului Oficial Si Al Publicatiilor, Ct Virament BNRSR 30.73.03.00 Filiala, Sector 4 Buracrest Romania.

BULLETIN ADMINISTRATIF DES ASSURANCES. See Insurance.

BULLETIN DE DROIT IMMOBILIER. Vol. 1, No. 1 (1 June 1985)-. 0829-1802. Periodical. CN. French. mo. $65,00. Editions Yvon Blais, Case Postale 180, Cowansville Quebec J2K 3H6 Canada. **Ed** Lise Szmigielski. **DD** 346.71404305.

BULLETIN DES ARRETS DE LA COUR DE CASSATION. Main/Corp Belgium. Cour de Cassation. **VFOAT** Arrets de la Cour de Cassation de Belgique. FR. French. mo. $99.78. Imprimerie Nationale, BP 637, 59506 Douai Cedex France. bk rev. Deals mostly with the decisions rendered by the Civil Court of France (Commercial and Social Courts).

BULLETIN DES TRANSPORTS INTERNATIONAUX PAR CHEMINS DE FER. **VFOAT** Zeitschrift fur den Internationalen Eisenbahnverkehr. Year 1-. Periodical. SZ. French (German). mo. 30.00. Office Cent Transports Internationaux par Chemins de fer a Berne, Gryphenhubeliweg 30, 3006 Berne Switzerland. **Tel** (031)43 17 62. bk rev. **Circ** 800. Studies judgements and important information for the interpretation, application and development of railway transport law.

BULLETIN D'INFORMATION. RETAIL SALES TAX ACT. LOI SUR LA TAXE DE VENTE AU DETAIL. (BULLETIN D'INFORMATION). No. 1/77- April 1977-. 0226-3033. Periodical. CN. French. ir. Retail Sales Tax Act, Loi Vente Taxe Detail, Toronto Ontario Canada. **DD** 343.713055205.

BULLETIN D'INFORMATION SUR LES ACTIVITES JURIDIQUES AU SEIN DU CONSEIL DE L'EUROPE ET DANS LES ETATS MEMBRES: BULLETIN D'INFORMATION DE LA DIRECTION DES AFFAIRES JURIDIQUES DU CONSEIL DE L'EUROPE. **VFOAT** Bulletin d'Information de la Direction des Affaires Juridiques du Conseil de l'Europe. US. French. ir. Manhattan Publishing Company, 80 Brook Street, PO Box 650, Croton NY 10520. **DD** 349.405, 344.005.

BULLETIN DU CENTRE DE DOCUMENTATION D'ETUDES JURIDIQUES, ECONOMIQUES ET SOCIALES. French. ir. C E D E J, 22 rue El Fawakeh - Mohandessin-Dokki, Le Caire United Arab Republic. **LC** K2. **DD** 349.6205, 346.2005.

BULLETIN HUKUM. Day 1, No. 1-. Periodical. English (Indonesian). qt. JL Tanah Abang Timur, No 7, Jakarta Pusat Indonesia.

BULLETIN INDEX-DIGEST SYSTEM. SERVICE FOUR. EXCISE TAX. See Indexes/Abstracts.

BULLETIN INDEX-DIGEST SYSTEM. SERVICE THREE. EMPLOYMENT TAXES. See Indexes/Abstracts.

BULLETIN INDEX-DIGEST SYSTEM. SERVICE TWO. ESTATE AND GIFT TAX. See Indexes/Abstracts.

BULLETIN JURIDIQUE - ASSOCIATION DE LA CONSTRUCTION DE MONTREAL ET DU QUEBEC. Main/Corp Association de la Construction de Montreal et du Quebec. V. 1- May 1975-. 0701-0303. Periodical. CN. French. mo. Association de la Construction de Montreal et du Quebec, 4970 Place de la Savane, Montreal Quebec H4P 1Z6 Canada. **DD** 352.99209714.

BULLETIN LEGISLATIF BELGE. No. 1- 1931-. Periodical. BE. French. wk. Maison F Larcier SA, 39 rue des Minimes, B-1000 Bruxelles Belgium.

BULLETIN (NEBRASKA. WORKMEN'S COMPENSATION COURT). (BULLETIN). Periodical. US. English. Nebraska Workmen's Compensation Court, State Capitol Building, Lincoln NE 68509. **LC** KFN342.A15. **DD** 344.78202105, 347.82042105.

BULLETIN OF COMPARATIVE LABOUR RELATIONS. See Economics - Labor.

BULLETIN OF LAW, SCIENCE & TECHNOLOGY. VAT Bulletin of Law, Science and Technology. No. 1- Jan. 1976-. 0362-3769. Periodical. US. English. bm. American Bar Association, Section of Science and Technology, 1155 East 60th Street, Chicago IL 60637. **Ind/Abst** Leg. Resour. Index. **LC** KF325.188. **DD** 344.73095062.

BULLETIN OF LEGAL DEVELOPMENTS. No. 1- Jan. 21, 1966-. 0007-4969. Periodical. UK. English. sm. $95.77. British Institute of International and Comparative Law, Charles Clore House 17/Russell Square, London WC1B 5DR England. **Tel** 01-636 5802-3-4. **Ed** Celia Hampton. Index published separately - free - automatically sent. **Circ** 350. News of developments in law worldwide and internationally.

BULLETIN OF PROCEEDINGS TAKEN IN THE SUPREME COURT OF CANADA. Main/Corp Canada. Supreme Court. **VFOAT** Bulletin des Procedures Devant la Cour Supreme du Canada. 0384-2487. Periodical. CN. English (text in French).

BULLETIN OF THE AMERICAN ACADEMY OF PSYCHIATRY AND THE LAW. See Medicine - Psychiatry, Psychopathology.

BULLETIN OF THE EUROPEAN COMMUNITIES. V. 1- Jan. 1968-. 0007-5116. Periodical. English. ir. 36.00. European Communities Information Service, Mrs Sloan, 2100 M Street NW/Suite 707, Washington DC 20037. **Tel** (202)862-9547. **Ind/Abst** World Text Abstr., GeoRef, Int. Packag. Abstr. **LC** HC241.2. **DD** 940.05. CODEN BEUCBC. Covers milestones in the implementation of common policies, the development of external relations, and activities of the different institutions. Bulletin from the European Community for Coal and Steel, Bulletin of the European Economic Community, 0531-3430.

BULLETIN OFFICIEL DES ANNONCES CIVILES ET COMMERCIALES (FRANCE). Periodical. FR. da. Direction Journax Officiels, 26 rue Dessaix, 75732 Paris Cedex 15 France. **DD** 346.440705. Bulletin Officiel des Annonces Commerciales.

BULLETIN OFFICIEL DES ASSURANCES - FRANCE. MINISTERE DE L'ECONOMIE. Main/Corp France. Ministere de l'Economie. French. ir. 22.00 Single Issue. Ministere de l'Economie, Direction des Assurances, 54 rue de Chateaudun, Paris 9E France. **DD** 346.44086, 344.40686. Bulletin Administratif des Assurances.

BULLETIN OFFICIEL DU MINISTERE DE LA JUSTICE (FRANCE). Main/Corp France. Ministere de la Justice. 0750-0416. FR. French. qt. 105.00. 27 rue de la Convention, 75732 Paris Cedex 15 France.

BULLETIN OFFICIEL DU MINISTERE DE L'ENVIRONNEMENT ET DU CADRE DE VIE ET DU MINISTERE DES TRANSPORTS (FRANCE). Main/Corp France. Ministere de l'Environnement et du Cadre de Vie. FR. French. an. Direction Journaux

Law

Officiels, 26 rue Desaix, 75727 Paris Cedex 15 France. **DD** 344.44046, 344.40446.

BULLETIN OFFICIEL DU MINISTERE DE L'EQUIPEMENT ET DE L'AMENAGEMENT DU TERRITOIRE (FRANCE). Main/Corp France. Ministere de l'Equipement et de l'Amenagement du Territoire. FR. French. ir. 132.00. Direction des Journaux Officiels, 26 rue Desaix, 75727 Paris Cedex 15 France. **DD** 344.4406. *Bulletin Officiel du Ministere de l'Equipement.*

BULLETIN OFFICIEL DU MINISTERE DES TRANSPORTS MARINE MARCHANDE (FRANCE). Main/Corp France. Ministere des Transports. French. tm. Service des Ventes de l'Imprimerie Nationale, 2 rue Paul-Hervieu, 75732 Paris Cedex 15 France. **DD** 343.4409602636, 344. 4039602636.

BULLETIN OFFICIEL DU SECRETARIAT D'ETAT AUX DEPARTEMENTS ET TERRITOIRES D'OUTRE-MER (FRANCE). Main/Corp France. Secretariat d'Etat aux Departements et Territoires d'Outre-Mer. May/June 1974-. French. ir. Secretariat d'Etat aux Departements et Territoires d'Outre-Mer, 27 rue Oudinot, Paris 7E France. **DD** 342.4406. *Bulletin Officiel du Secretaire d'Etat Aupres du Premier Ministre Charge des Departements et Territoires d'Ou.*

BULLETIN OFFICIEL. TEXTES LEGISLATIFS ET REGLEMENTAIRES. US. English (French or Spanish).

BULLETIN - ORANGE COUNTY BAR ASSOCIATION. (BULLETIN). 0279-9243. Periodical. US. English. mo. $24.00. Orange County Bar Association, 17291 Irvine Boulevard #309, Tustin CA 92680. **Tel** (714)838-9200.

BULLETIN SSQ RESPECTING SOCIAL LAWS. VAT Bulletin Services de Sante du Quebec Respecting Social Laws. Vol. 12 (Jan. 1983)-. 0822-5699. CN. English. an. Free. SSQ Mutuelle d'Assurance, 2525 Boulevard Laurier, CP 10500, Sainte-Foy Quebec G1V 4H6 Canada. **Tel** (418)651-7000. **DD** 344.71402. **Circ** 80,000. Resume of ten most important social laws - federal and province of Quebec. Reflects situation of January first of current year. *Bulletin SSQ sur les Lois Sociales. English,* 0713-8458.

BULLETIN - TEXAS. PUBLIC UTILITY COMMISSION. Main/Corp Texas. Public Utility Commission. Began with Mar. 15, 1976 Issue. US. English. sm. $35.00. State Treasurer, Accounting Division, Public Utility Commission, 7800 Shoal Creek Boulevard, Austin TX 78757. **LC** KFT1485. **DD** 343.764090262, 347.640390262. (cum index).

BUNDESGESETZBLATT - GERMANY (WEST). Periodical. German (text of international treaties or agreements also in English and French). German Language Publishing Inc, 560 Sylvan Avenue, Englewood Cliffs NJ 07632. **Tel** (212)736-7455. **Ind/Abst** Energy Res. Abstr., Coal Abstr. *Reichsgesetzblatt, Verordnungsblatt fur die Britische Zone; Getetzblatt der Verwaltung des Vereinigten Wirtschaftgebietes.*

BUNDESGESETZBLATT. TEIL 1 - GERMANY (FEDERAL REPUBLIC, 1949-). GW. German. $19.47. Bundesanzeiger, Postfach 108006, 5 Koln 1 West Germany.

BUNDESGESETZBLATT. TEIL 2 - GERMANY (FEDERAL REPUBLIC, 1949-). GW. German. $19.47. Bundesanzeiger, Postfach 108006, 5 Koln 1 West Germany.

BURNS INDIANA STATUTES ANNOTATED. ADVANCE ANNOTATION SERVICE. VFOAT Burns Indiana Statutes. Vol. 1, No. 1 (Nov. 1981)-. 0747-7007. Periodical. US. English. ir. Michie Bobbs Merrill, PO Box 7587, Charlottesville VA 22906. **Tel** (804)295-6171.

BUSINESS ACCOUNTING FOR LAWYERS NEWSLETTER. *See* Business - Accounting.

THE BUSINESS ADVOCATE. 0193-4414. Periodical. US. English. mo. $40.00. Chamber of Commerce of US, 1615 H Street NW, Washington DC 20062. **Tel** (202)463-5606. **LC** KF1409. **DD** 346.73066.

THE BUSINESS ADVOCATE. (THE BUSINESS ADVOCATE : A U.S. CHAMBER OF COMMERCE PUBLICATION). Vol. 1, No. 1 (Sept. 26, 1983)-. 0746-3669. Periodical. US. English. bw. The Business Advocate, 4940 Nicholson Street, Kensington MD 20895. **LC** HC101. **DD** 330.973005. *Washington Report (Chamber of Commerce of the United States),* 0043-0714.

BUSINESS & THE LAW. VAT Business and the Law. Vol 1, No. 1 (Apr. 1984)-. 0825-4982. Periodical. CN. English. mo. $145.00. R de Boo Publishers, 81 Curlew Drive, Don Mills Ontario M3A 3P7 Canada. **DD** 346.710705.

BUSINESS LAW LETTER (BOCA RATON, FLA.). (THE BUSINESS LAW LETTER). **VFOAT** B.L.L. Vol. 1, No. 1 (Apr. 1983)-. 0737-8157. Periodical. US. English. mo. Business Law Letter, 10076 Boca Entrada Boulevard, Boca Raton FL 33433. **LC** KF1355.A15. **DD** 346.730705, 347.306705.

BUSINESS LAW MEMO. Vol. 1, No. 1 (Sept. 1980)-. 0271-9045. Periodical. US. English. American Bar Association, 720 North Lake Shore Drive, Chicago IL 60611. **Tel** (312)988-5555. **LC** KF872. **DD** 346.730705.

BUSINESS LAW REPORTER. Vol. 1, No. 1 (Aug. 1981)-. 0277-1713. Periodical. US. English. mo. $150.00. Litigation Research Group, 651 Brannan Street, San Francisco CA 94915. **LC** KF884. **DD** 346.730702648, 347.306702648.

BUSINESS LAW REPORTS. V. 1- Apr. 1977-. 0703-5551. Periodical. CN. English. mo. Carswell Company, 2330 Midland Avenue, Agincourt Ontario M1S 1P7 Canada. **LC** KE915.8. **DD** 346.7107. (cum index).

BUSINESS LAW REVIEW CEASED. (BUSINESS LAW REVIEW : AN OFFICIAL PUBLICATION OF THE NATIONAL ASSOCIATION OF BUSINESS LAW TEACHERS, INC). V. 8-14, No. 1. 0145-9074. Periodical. US. English. sa. $5.00 Members, $6.00 Nonmembers. National Association of Business Law Teachers, West Virginia University, Armstrong Hall, Morgantown WV 26506. **Ind/Abst** Public Aff. Inf. Serv. Bull. *Eastern United States Business Law Review.*

BUSINESS LAW REVIEW. *See* Business.

BUSINESS LAWYER. V. 1- 1946-. 0007-6899. Periodical. US. English. qt. $27.00. American Bar Association, 750 North Lake Shore Drive, Chicago IL 60611. **Tel** (312)988-5555. **Ind/Abst** Manage. Contents, Leg. Resour. Index, Energy Inf. Abstr., Environ. Abstr., Account. Index, Suppl., ABI/Inform, Public Aff. Inf. Serv. Bull., Index Leg. Period. (cum index). adv acc. (ctrl)

BUSINESS REGULATION LAW REPORT. WAGE AND PRICE CONTROLS. (BUSINESS REGULATION LAW REPORT : WAGE AND PRICE CONTROLS). 0094-2502. US. English. sm. $60.00. Warren Gordon & Lamont Inc, 89 Beach Street, Boston MA 02111. **LC** KF6067.A73. **DD** 343.7307.

BUSINESS REORGANIZATIONS UNDER THE BANKRUPTCY CODE. (BUSINESS REORGANIZATIONS UNDER THE BANKRUPTCY CODE : ALI-ABA COURSE OF STUDY MATERIALS). **VFOAT** ALI-ABA Course of Study Materials. 0733-4613. Periodical. US. English. an. 4025 Chestnut Street, Philadelphia PA 19104. **LC** KF1544.Z9. **DD** 346.7306626, 347.3066626.

BUSINESS TAX STRATEGIST. Vol. 1, No. 1 (Nov. 1981)-. 0730-3165. US. English. mo. Business Tax Strategist, 10076 Boca Entrada Boulevard, Boca Raton FL 33433. **LC** KF6450.A15. **DD** 343.7306805, 347.3036805.

BUTTERWORTHS CURRENT LAW. 0110-070X. NZ. English. ir. D & S Publishers, PO Box 5105, Clearwater FL 33518. **Tel** (800)237-9707. **LC** Law. **DD** 340.09931.

BUTTERWORTHS ORANGE TAX HANDBOOK. 1st- Ed. UK. English. an. Butterworth & Company Publishers Inc, 19 Cummings Park, Woburn MA 01801. **LC** KD5415. **DD** 343.4104.

BUTTERWORTHS YELLOW TAX HANDBOOK. 15th- Ed. UK. English. an. Butterworth and Company Publishers Inc, 19 Cummings Park, Woburn MA 01801. **LC** KD5423.99. **DD** 343.4204. *Butterworths Tax Handbook.*

BVR, BERNISCHE VERWALTUNGSRECHTSPRECHUNG. JAB, JURISPRUDENCE ADMINISTRATIVE BERNOISE. VFOAT Bernische Verwaltungsrechtsprechung. Periodical. German (summaries in French). ir. 58.00. Genossenschafts-Buchdruckerei AG, 3000 Bern 16 Switzerland. **DD** 348.4945025.

BYGNINGSREGLEMENT (DENMARK). Main/Corp Denmark. Byggestyrelsen. 0107-119X. Danish. ir. *Bygningsreglement for Kbstaederne og Landet.*

CABLE TELEVISION LAW. MUNICIPAL LAW OFFICERS EDITION. (CABLE TELEVISION LAW : MUNICIPAL LAW OFFICERS EDITION). 0161-6811. Periodical. US. English. mo. Communications Law Publishers, 1819 H Street Northwest, Washington DC 20006. **LC** KF2844.A15. **DD** 343.730994.

CABLE T.V. LAW & FINANCE. VFOAT Cable TV Law and Finance. Vol. 1, No. 1 (Mar. 1983)-. 0736-489X. Periodical. US. English. mo. $125.00. Leader Publications Inc, 111 8th Avenue/Suite 900, New York NY 10011. **LC** KF2844.A15. **DD** 343.7309946, 347.3039946.

CABLE TV LAW REPORTER. VFOAT Cable T.V. Law Reporter, Cable Television Law Reporter. No. 1 (Sept. 6, 1984)-. 0749-7652. Periodical. US. English. sm. Paul Kagan Associates Inc, 26386 Carmel Rancho Lane, Carmel CA 93923. **LC** KF2844.A59. **DD** 343.7309946 347.3039946. Newsletter on the latest and most important legal cases, including antitrust, first amendment, franchising, taxation, copyright, rate regulation, privacy and international law.

CADERNO DE DIREITO ECONOMICO. No. 1-. Periodical. Portuguese. ir. Centro de Estudos de Extensao Universitaria Avenida, Professor Alfonso Bovero 175, 01254 Sao Paulo Brazil. **LC** K3. **DD** 348.103805.

CADERNO DE PESQUISAS TRIBUTARIAS. No. 1-. Portuguese. ir. Centro de Estudos de Extensao Universitaria, Av Prof Alfonso Bovero 175, 01254 Sao Paulo Brazil. **LC** K3. **DD** 343.810405.

CADERNOS DE ALTOS ESTUDOS DO CENTRO BRASILEIRO DE DIREITO TRIBUTARIO. No. 1-. Periodical. Portuguese. ir. **LC** K3. **DD** 343.810405, 348.103405.

CADERNOS DE DIREITO PRIVADO. V. 1-. Periodical. BL. Portuguese. ir. Departamento de Direito Privado da Faculdade de Direito da Universidade Federal Fluminese, R President Pedreira, No 54, Niteroi Brazil. **LC** K3. **DD** 346.81005.

CAHIERS DE DROIT. (LES CAHIERS DE DROIT). Vol. 1, No. 1 (Dec. 1954)-. 0007-974X. Periodical. CN. French (English). qt. 45.00. Wilson & Lafleur, CP 24 Place d'Armes, Montreal Quebec H24 3L2 Canada. **Tel** 656-7884. Ed Henri Brun. **Ind/Abst** Index Leg. Period., Point Repere, Leg. Resour. Index, Curr. Law Index. (cum index). bk rev. **Circ** 1,600. The review seeks to promote the juridicial science and informs in a critical manner about the condition of law in the province of Quebec.

CAHIERS DE DROIT EUROPEEN. 1965-. 0007-9758. Periodical. French. bm. $72.63. Mausib F Larcier SA, 39 rue des Minimes, B-1000 Bruxelles Belgium. **Tel** 02/ 512-47-12. **Ind/Abst** Int. Labour Doc.

LES CAHIERS DE DROIT FAMILIAL. Periodical. French. ir. S A Ferd Larcier, rue des Mimines 39, 526 FB-CCP, 000-0042375-83, Bruxelles Belgium. **DD** 346.49301505. *Revue de Droit Familial.*

CAHIERS DE LA DIRECTION DE LA RECHERCHE ET DE L'INFORMATION. (LES CAHIERS DE LA DIRECTION DE LA RECHERCHE ET DE L'INFORMATION). **Main/Corp** Chambre des Notaires du Quebec. Direction de la Recherche et de l'Information. V. 1- April 1978-. 0708-644X. Periodical. CN. French. ir. Free. Chambre des Notaires du Quebec, Bureau 1658/630 Ouest Boulevard Dorchester, Montreal Quebec H3B 1T6 Canada. **DD** 347.714016.

LES CAHIERS DE L'IQAJ : PUBLICATION DE L'INSTITUT QUEBECOIS D'ADMINISTRATION JUDICIAIRE. VAT Cahiers de l'Institut Quebecois de l'Administration Judiciaire. Vol. 1, No. 1 (May 1984)-. 0824-9814. Periodical. CN. French. ir. Free to Members of l'IQAJ. Institut Quebecois d'Administration Judiciaire, 5E Etage 1200 Route de l'Eglise, Saint-Foy Quebec G1V 4M1 Canada. **DD** 347.714016.

CALIFORNIA BUSINESS LAW REPORTER. VFOAT California Continuing Education of the Bar. V. 1- Jan. 1980-. 0199-669X. Periodical. US. English. ir. $91.00. California

Law

Continuing Education of the Bar, 2300 Shattuck Avenue, Berkeley CA 94704. **Tel** (415)642-5340. **Ed** Hale Kronenberg. Features informative articles; emphasizes how new developments relate to or change prior law, how they can be used in your practice; what pitfalls to avoid and more.

CALIFORNIA COMMISSIONER OF CORPORATIONS CURRENT OFFICIAL OPINIONS ISSUED PURSUANT TO THE CORPORATE SECURITIES LAW OF 1968. Main/Corp California. Dept. of Corporations. 0360-0955. US. English. California Continuing Education of the Bar, 2300 Shattuck Avenue, Berkeley CA 94704. **LC** KFC350. **DD** 346.79409202646.

CALIFORNIA COMMISSIONER OF CORPORATIONS CURRENT OFFICIAL OPINIONS ISSUED PURSUANT TO THE FRANCHISE INVESTMENT LAW. Main/Corp California. Dept. of Corporations. 0362-1804. US. English. California Continuing Education of the Bar, 2300 Shattuck Avenue, Berkeley CA 94704. **LC** KFC442. **DD** 343.794088.

CALIFORNIA CONTRACTORS LICENSE LAW AND REFERENCE BOOK. 1st- Ed. Periodical. US. English. an. Contractors State License Board, 1020 North Street, Sacramento CA 95814. **DD** 692.9.

CALIFORNIA FAMILY LAW MONTHLY. Vol. 1, No. 1 (Aug. 1984)-. 0882-7842. Periodical. US. English. mo. $160.00. Matthew Bender & Company Inc, PO Box 2077, Oakland CA 94604. **Tel** (415)446-7100. **Ed** Steven Revell. Analysis of new California court cases and statutes relating to family law matters such as divorce, community property, etc.

CALIFORNIA FAMILY LAW REPORT. VFOAT CFLR. Began in 1977?. 0164-7040. Periodical. US. English. mo. $195.00. California Family Law, 107 Caledonia #E, Sausalito CA 94965. **Tel** (415)332-9000.

CALIFORNIA GOVERNMENT CONTRACTS. V. 1- Aug. 1979-. 0271-2741. Periodical. US. English. mo. $45.00. California Procurement Publications, 980 University Avenue/ Suite 201, Sacramento CA 95825. **LC** KFC224.A15. **DD** 346.79402305.

CALIFORNIA LAW REVIEW. Vol. 1, No. 1 (Nov. 1912)-. 3278-1221. US. English. bm. Ind/Abst Leg. Resour. Index, ABC Pol Sci, Women Stud. Abstr., ABI/Inform, Curr. Law Index, Index Leg. Period., Public Aff. Inf. Serv. Bull. **LC** K3. **DD** 340.05. CODEN CLARDJ. (cum index). Available on microfilm.

CALIFORNIA LAWS FOR PSYCHOTHERAPISTS. 1980-. US. English. an. Law Distributors, 14415 South Main Street, Gardena CA 90248. **LC** KFC31. **DD** 349.794024616.

CALIFORNIA LAWS RELATING TO YOUTHFUL OFFENDERS, *INCLUDING THE YOUTH AUTHORITY ACT, THE JUVENILE COURT LAW, ... LEGISLATIVE CHANGES. US. English. **LC** KFC1177.A29. **DD** 345.79408, 347.94058. *California Juvenile Court Law.*

CALIFORNIA LAWYER. Vol. 1, No. 1 (Sept. 1981)-. 0279-4063. Periodical. US. English. mo. $12.00. State Bar of California, 555 Franklin Street, San Francisco CA 94102. **Tel** (415)561-8280. **Ed** Jonathan Maslow. Ind/Abst Leg. Resour. Index, Index Leg. Period. **LC** KF200. **DD** 349.79505, 347.95005. bk rev. adv acc. **Circ** 105,000. (ctrl). Official publication of the State Bar of California. Ariticles and features pertaining to the personal and professional lives of attorneys. *California State Bar Journal, 0161-9241.*

THE CALIFORNIA LEGAL DIRECTORY. See Yearbooks, Almanacs, Directories.

CALIFORNIA LIBRARY LAWS. Main/Corp California State Library. 1974-. 0097-9902. US. English. an. California State Library, PO Box 2037, Sacramento CA 95814. **LC** KFC675.A29. **DD** 344.794092.

CALIFORNIA PHARMACY LAWS, WITH RULES AND REGULATIONS. US. English. Board of Pharmacy, 1021 O Street, Sacramento CA 95814. **LC** KFC546.5.P4. **DD** 344.794042. *Pharmacy Laws of California and Administrative Rules of Board of Pharmacy.*

CALIFORNIA REAL PROPERTY LAW REPORTER. 0146-7530. US. English. mo. $144.00. California Legal Publications, 100 Bush Street/Suite 2712, San Francisco CA 94104. **LC** KFC140.A59. **DD** 346.794043.

CALIFORNIA SCHOOL LAW DIGEST. 0094-2057. US. English. mo. $50.00. California School Law Digest, PO Box 1752, Fresno CA 93717-1752. **Tel** (209)486-4590. **Ed** Mary Beth de Goede and Brian J. McCully. **LC** KFC648.A59. **DD** 344.7940705. **Circ** 500. Covers legal developments (appellate court and perb decisions) affecting California public schools (student rights, employment discrimination and teacher dismissals).

CALIFORNIA STATE BAR JOURNAL CEASED. Main/Corp State Bar of California. V. 45-56, No.8. 0161-9241. Periodical. US. English. mo. $5.00. 1230 West Third Street, Los Angeles CA 90017. **Ind/Abst** Index Leg. Period. Index in last issue of volume - attached. *Journal (State Bar of California), 0039-002X; Reports (State Bar of California), 0585-1017.*

CALIFORNIA SUPERIOR COURT CRIMINAL TRIAL JUDGES' BENCHBOOK. VFOAT California Criminal Trial Judges Benchbook. 1973-. 0743-0477. US. English. an. **Ed** Richard F C Hayden and William B Keene. **LC** KFC1155. **DD** 345.79405, 347.94055.

CALIFORNIA SUPREME COURT SERVICE. V. 1- Sept. 29, 1978-. 0164-3339. Periodical. US. English. sm. $150.00. American Institute of Continuing Legal Education, PO Box 71526/350 South Figueroa Street, Los Angeles CA 90071. **LC** KFC45.1. **DD** 348.794043.

CALIFORNIA WESTERN LAW REVIEW. Vol. 1, No. 1 (Spring 1965)-. 0008-1639. Periodical. US. English. ty. $10.50. California Western Law Review, California WSCH Law, 350 Cedar Street, San Diego CA 92101. **Tel** (619)232-1716. **Ed** Paul E Lacy. Ind/Abst Leg. Resour. Index, Index Leg. Period., Public Aff. Inf. Serv. Bull., Curr. Law Index, Contents Curr. Leg. Period. (cum index). bk rev. adv acc. **Circ** 1,400. (ctrl). Informative, in-depth articles by experts in their field of the law, as well as case notes and comments on particular points of the law written by law students.

CALIFORNIA WORKERS' COMPENSATION REPORTER. V. 3, No. 7- Aug. 1975-. 0363-129X. Periodical. US. English. mo. $155.00. PO Box 975, Berkeley CA 94701. **Tel** (415)654-8221. **Ed** Melvin S Witt. **LC** KFC592.A15. **DD** 344.7942005. bk rev. **Circ** 1,250. Key developments in workers' compensation in California including reports and comments on appellate cases and WCAB decisions, legislative changes, and news of interest. *California Workmen's Compensation Reporter, 0091-5211.*

CAMBRIAN LAW REVIEW. (THE CAMBRIAN LAW REVIEW). Began with 1970 issue. 0084-8328. UK. English. an. 14.00. University College of Wales, Department of Law, Aberystwyth Wales United Kingdom. **Tel** Aberystwyth 31111. **Ed** J E Trice. Ind/Abst Leg. Resour. Index, Index Leg. Period., Curr. Law Index. **LC** K3. **DD** 340.05. bk rev. adv acc. **Circ** 700. A law review covering articles of a general academic interest both British and comparative and with British legal history bibliography and book reviews.

CAMBRIDGE LAW JOURNAL. (THE CAMBRIDGE LAW JOURNAL). Vol. 1, No. 1 (1921)-. 0008-1973. Periodical. UK. English. sa. $53.00. Cambridge University Press, 510 North Avenue, New Rochelle NY 10801. **Tel** (914)235-0300. **Ed** L S Sealy. Ind/Abst Manage. Contents, Leg. Resour. Index, Ref. Source, Index Leg. Period., Contents Curr. Leg. Period., Curr. Law Index. **DD** 340.05. Index published separately - free - automatically sent. (cum index). bk rev. Publishes articles on all aspects of private and public law, with special emphasis on contemporary developments. Influential in matters of law reform, judicial thinking and in legal scholarship.

CAMBRIDGE STUDIES IN ENGLISH LEGAL HISTORY. Monographic Series. UK. English. ir. Cambridge University Press, 510 North Avenue, New Rochelle NY 10801. **Tel** (914)235-0300.

CAMP RESORT LAW REPORT. Vol. 1, No. 1 (May 1984)-. 0748-2396. Periodical. US. English. qt. Land Development Institute, 1401 16th Street NW, Washington DC 20036. **Tel** (202)232-2144. **Circ** 125. (ctrl). News on federal, state and local laws regarding campground development; court and administrative decisions.

CAMPAIGN LAW REPORTER. V. 1- Feb. 1974-. 0094-1921. US. English. mo. $245.00. Pacific Communications Group, 1225 Eighth Street/Suite 105, Sacramento CA 95814. **Tel** (916)444-0329. **LC** KFC710.A73. **DD** 342.7940705.

CAMPAIGN PRACTICES REPORTS. VFOAT CP Reports. V. 1- June 17, 1974-. 0361-056X. Periodical. US. English. bw. Congressional Quarterly, 1414 22nd Street NW, c/o C Ryan, Washington DC 20037. **Tel** (202)335-0444. **LC** KF4885.A15. **DD** 342.730705.

CAMPBELL LAW REVIEW. V. 1-. 0198-8174. Periodical. US. English. sa. Campbell College School or Law, PO Box 1165, Buis Creek NC 27506. **Tel** (919)893-8552. **Ed** Paul Ridgeway. Ind/Abst Leg. Resour. Index, Index Leg. Period., Curr. Law Index. **LC** K3. **DD** 349.75605, 347.56005. bk rev. adv acc. **Circ** 700. Law Review.

CAMPBELL'S LIST; THE LAWYERS' GUIDE TO OUT-OF-TOWN COUNSEL. 97th- 1976-. US. English. an. $10.00. Campbells List Inc, 100 East Ventris Avenue, PO Box 428, Maitland FL 32751. **Tel** (305)644-8298. **Ed** John A Campbell Jr. **Circ** 6,500. (ctrl). A directory of selected lawyers since 1879. Will accept referrals from out-of-town lawyers and clients. All are in general practice and most handle collections. *Campbell's List.*

CANADA BUSINESS CORPORATIONS ACT WITH REGULATIONS. 1st- Ed. 0317-6649. Periodical. CN. English. CCH Canadian, 6 Garamond Court, Don Mills Ontario M3C 1Z5 Canada. **DD** 346.7106602633.

CANADA FEDERAL COURT REPORTS. VFOAT Recueil des Arrets de la Cour Federale du Canada. 1971-. 0384-2568. Periodical. CN. Multilingual (text in English and French in parallel columns). mo. 92.00 Domestic, 110.40 Foreign. Receiver General for Canada, Supply & Services, Ottawa Ontario K1A 0S9 Canada. *Canada Exchequer Court Reports, 0384-255X.*

CANADA GAZETTE. PART 2. (CANADA GAZETTE. PART II MICROFORM). VFOAT La Gazette du Canada. Partie II. 0045-4206. Periodical. CN. English (French). Micromedia Limited, 144 Front Street West, Toronto Ontario M5J 1G2 Canada. **DD** 348.710205.

THE CANADA GAZETTE. PART I. VFOAT La Gazette du Canada. Partie I. Periodical. CN. text in English and French. wk. 135.00 Domestic, 162.00 Foreign. Receiver General for Canada, Supply and Services, Ottawa Ontario K1A 0S9 Canada.

CANADA LEGAL DIRECTORY. See Yearbooks, Almanacs, Directories.

CANADA SUPREME COURT REPORTS. VFOAT Recueil des Arrets de la Cour Supreme du Canada. 1970-. 0045-4230. Periodical. CN. English (French). mo. 93.00 Domestic, 111.60 Foreign. Receiver General for Canada, Supply and Services, Ottawa Ontario K1A 0S9 Canada.

CANADA. TAX APPEAL BOARD CASES. INDEX. SUPPLEMENT. See Indexes/Abstracts.

THE CANADIAN ABRIDGMENT. APPENDIX. 1969-. Monographic Series. CN. English. Carsell Company Ltd, 2330 Midland Avenue, Agincourt Ontario M1S 1P7 Canada. **DD** 348.71046.

CANADIAN ALTERNATIVES. V. 1- Spring 1979-. 0227-8049. Periodical. CN. English. Prepaid Legal Services Program of Canada, Faculty of Law, University of Windsor, Windsor Ontario N9B 3P4 Canada. **DD** 368.

CANADIAN-AMERICAN LAW JOURNAL. VFOAT Canadian American Law Journal. Vol. 1, Issue 1 (Spring 1982)-. 0740-7084. Periodical. US. English. sa. $16.00 US, $18.00 Canada. Gonzaga University School of Law, Spokane WA 99220. **LC** K3. **DD** 349.7105, 347.1005.

CANADIAN BAR ASSOCIATION CONTINUING EDUCATION SEMINARS. VFOAT CBA Continuing Education Seminars. 0316-876X. Monographic Series. CN. English. Canada Law Book Ltd, 80 Cowdray Court, Agincourt Ontario M1S 1S5 Canada. **DD** 340.0971.

CANADIAN BUSINESS LAW JOURNAL. See Business.

CANADIAN CASES ON EMPLOYMENT LAW. Vol. 1, Pt. 1 (Oct./Nov. 1983)-. 0824-2607. Periodical. CN. English. mo. $65.00. Carswell Legal Publications, 2230 Midlands Avenue, Agincourt Ontario M1S 1P7 Canada. Ind/Abst Index Can. Leg. Period. Vit. **DD** 344.710102642.

CANADIAN CASES ON THE LAW OF INSURANCE. See Insurance.

Law

CANADIAN CASES ON THE LAW OF TORTS. V. 1- Oct. 1976-. 0701-1733. Periodical. CN. English. ir. $35. The Carswell Company Ltd, 2330 Midland Avenue, Agincourt Ontario M1A 1P7 Canada. LC KE1231.A45. DD 346.7103.

CANADIAN COMMUNICATIONS LAW REVIEW. See Communication - Telecommunications.

CANADIAN COMMUNITY LAW JOURNAL. VFOAT Revue Canadienne de Droit Communautaire. Vol. 1 (1977)-. 0704-0857. CN. English (French). an. 7.50. University of Windsor, Faculty of Law, Windsor Ontario N9B 3P4 Canada. Tel (519)253-4232. Ed Jason P Howie. Ind/Abst Leg. Resour. Index. LC K3. DD 340.071071. bk rev. adv acc. Circ 500. (ctrl). The journal is a bilingual publication committed to areas of law that affect the community as a whole.

CANADIAN COMPUTER LAW REPORTER. See Computers and Computer Science.

CANADIAN CRIMINAL CASES (BOUND CUMULATION). (CANADIAN CRIMINAL CASES). New Ser., V. 1 (1963)-V. 5 (1970). 0008-3348. CN. English. wk. 548.00. Canada Law Book, 240 Edward Street, Aurora Ontario L3Y 1B4 Canada. Tel (416)773-6300. Ed E L Greenspan. (cum index). adv acc. National series of law reports containing full text of all important decisions rendered in criminal and quasi-criminal cases from all Canadian courts and jurisdictions. Canadian Criminal Cases Annotated.

CANADIAN CUSTOMS AND EXCISE REPORTS. V. 1-. 0228-3409. CN. English. an. Butterworths, 6 Thorncliffe Park Drive, Toronto Ontario M4H 1H3 Canada. DD 343.7105602648.

CANADIAN DEPRECIATION GUIDE. Main/Corp CCH Canadian Limited. 3rd- Ed. 0068-8649. Periodical. CN. English. ir. CCH Canadian Ltd, 6 Garamond Court, Don Mills Ontario M3C 1Z5 Canada. DD 343.71052. The New Depreciation System, 0316-828X.

CANADIAN DOCTOR. Began in 1935. 0008-3429. Periodical. CN. English. mo. 39.00. Southam Communications Ltd, 1450 Don Mills Road, Don Mills Ontario M3B 1X2 Canada. Tel (416)445-6641. Ed Kim Coffman. Ind/Abst Hospit. Lit. Index. NLM W1 CA55. adv acc. Circ 34,000. (ctrl). Medical law and ethics including malpractice case studies as well as the politics in medicine stress management for physicians.

CANADIAN ENVIRONMENTAL LAW REPORTS. V. 7, No. 2- April 1978-. Periodical. CN. English (or French). bm. $42.56. Canadian Environment Research Foundation, 243 Queen Street West 4th Floor, Toronto Ontario M5V 1Z4 Canada. Tel (416)977-2410. LC KE3612. DD 344.7104602642, 344'. 71'04602642. Canadian Environmental Law News, 0317-6517.

CANADIAN INSURANCE LAW REPORTER. VFOAT Canadian Insurance Law Reports. 1951/55-. 0588-6562. Periodical. CN. English. CCH Canadian, 6 Garamond Court, Don Mills Ontario M3C 1S5 Canada. DD 346.71086. Prompt reporting of insurance decisions from all Canadian courts. Insurance Law Reporter.

CANADIAN JOURNAL OF INSURANCE LAW. See Insurance.

CANADIAN LAW LIST. (THE CANADIAN LAW LIST). Began with 1883 issue. 0084-8573. Periodical. CN. English. an. Canada Law Book Ltd, 80 Cowdray Court, Agincourt Ontario M1S 1S5 Canada. DD 340.02571. Carswell's Directory of Canadian Lawyers, 0411-1508.

CANADIAN LAWYER. Began with Issue for Oct. 1977. 0703-2129. Periodical. CN. English. ir. $18.58. Canadian Lawyer Magazine Ltd, 401-56 The Esplanade, Toronto Ontario M5E 1A7 Canada. Tel (416)368-7746. Ed Paul T Heron. Ind/Abst Leg. Resour. Index. DD 340.0971. bk rev. adv acc. Circ 34,000. (ctrl). A magazine about lawyers, not about the law. Highlights personalities, trends, developments. Regular articles on management and economics.

CANADIAN LEGAL & LEGISLATIVE BENEFITS REPORTER. VFOAT Canadian Legal and Legislative Benefits Reporter. Vol. 1, No. 1 (Oct. 1983)-. 0740-1043. Periodical. US. English. qt. International Foundation of Employee Benefit Plans, 18700 West Bluemound Road, PO Box 69, Brookfield WI 53005. LC KE3298.A13. DD 344.7101255.

CANADIAN NATIVE LAW REPORTER. Began publication in 1979. 0225-2279. Periodical. CN. English (French). qt. 40.00. University of Saskatchewan, Native Law Centre, Diefienbaker Centre, Saskatoon Saskatchewan S7N 0W0 Canada. Tel (306)966-6189. Ed Zandra MacEachern. DD 346.7101'3. bk rev. Circ 300. Specialized quarterly law report series providing a combination of articles and reported and previously unreported judgments. Each part (4 in total) contains a subject index. Canadian Native Law Bulletin, 0706-9790.

CANADIAN OCCUPATIONAL SAFETY AND HEALTH LAW MONTHLY REPORT. See Industrial Health & Safety.

CANADIAN UNEMPLOYMENT INSURANCE LEGISLATION. See Insurance.

CANADIAN WORKMEN'S COMPENSATION. (CANADIAN WORKMEN'S COMPENSATION : ACTS, REGULATIONS AND COMPARATIVE SUMMARY). 1958-. 0069-004X. Periodical. CN. English. an. CCH Canadian Ltd, 6 Garamond Court, Don Mills Ontario M3C 1Z5 Canada. DD 344.710210263.

CANNONS OF CONSTRUCTION. (THE CANNONS OF CONSTRUCTION). Began in 1970?. 0319-7085. Periodical. CN. English. The Cannons of Construction Law Centre, University of Alberta, Edmonton Alberta T6G 2H5 Canada.

CANTERBURY LAW REVIEW. (THE CANTERBURY LAW REVIEW). Vol. 1, No. 1 (1980)-. 0112-0581. Periodical. English. an. Ind/Abst Leg. Resour. Index. LC K3. DD 349.93105, 349.31005.

CAPITAL CASES. No. 1 (Nov. 30, 1981)-. 0748-6286. US. English. LC KF9227.C2. DD 345.730773, 347.305773.

CAPITAL PERSPECTIVES. Vol. 1, No. 1 (Nov. 1981)-. 0278-9027. US. English. bm. National District Attorneys Association, 708 Pendleton Street, Alexandria VA 22314. LC KF9640.A15. DD 345.7301, 347.3051.

CARBON COUNTY LAW JOURNAL. (THE CARBON COUNTY LAW JOURNAL). 0090-8789. US. English. Carbon County Bar Association, Box 6, Jim Thorpe PA 18229. LC KFP52.C37. DD 348.74826043.

CARDIOLOGISTS' LEGAL LETTER. Vol. 1, No. 1 (Feb. 1983)-. 0741-515X. Periodical. US. English. mo. Free. Merck Sharp & Dohme, Division of Merck Sharp & Company Inc, West Point PA 19486. LC KF2910.C37. DD 346.73033205, 347.30633205.

CARDOZO ARTS & ENTERTAINMENT LAW JOURNAL. VFOAT Cardozo Arts and Entertainment Law Journal. Vol. 1 (Spring 1982)-. 0736-7694. Periodical. US. English. sa. $10.00. Benjamin N Cardozo School of Law, Room 121/55th Avenue, New York NY 10003. Tel (212)790-0292. Ed Elana Gershen. LC K3. DD 344.7309705, 347.3049705. bk rev. adv acc. Circ 300. (ctrl). Arts and entertainment law.

CARDOZO LAW REVIEW. V. 1- Spring 1979-. 0270-5192. Periodical. US. English. qt. $15.00. Cardozo Law Review, Room 533/ 55 5th Avenue, New York NY 10003. Ind/Abst Leg. Resour. Index, Index Leg. Period. LC K3. DD 349.74705.

THE CARIBBEAN LAW LIBRARIAN : BULLETIN OF THE CARIBBEAN ASSOCIATION OF LAW LIBRARIES. See Library and Information Science.

CARSWELL'S FAMILY LAW DIGESTS. CUMULATIVE SUPPLEMENT. 2nd-. 0229-7299. CN. English. ir. DD 346.7101502648.

CARSWELL'S PRACTICE CASES ANNOTATED. V. 1- June 15, 1976. Periodical. CN. English. bw. Carswell Company, 2330 Midland Avenue, Agincourt Ontario M1S 1P7 Canada. LC KEO1115.8. DD 347.71105.

CARTA DE DERECHO DE FAMILIA. Periodical. Spanish. ir. LC K3. DD 346.86101505.

CASE & COMMENT (ROCHESTER, N.Y.). (CASE & COMMENT). VFOAT Case and Comment. Vol. 71, No. 4 (July-Aug. 1966)-. 0008-7238. Periodical. US. English. bm. $7.50. Case & Comment, 50 Broad Street East, Rochester NY 14694. Tel (716)546-5530. Ed Joseph J Marticelli. Ind/Abst Energy Inf. Abstr., Environ. Abstr. adv acc. Circ 110,077. (ctrl). Regular features include recent case summaries, legal humor and new product news and variety of how-to articles. Case and Comment, 0008-7238.

CASE COMMENTARIES AND BRIEFS. Vol. 1, No. 1 (July 1981)-. 0736-8240. Periodical. US. English. mo. National District Attorney's Association, 708 Pendleton Street, Alexandria VA 22314. LC KF9614. DD 345.730502648, A 347. 305502648.

CASE UPDATE. Vol. 1, No. 1 (Fall 1983)-. 0749-7709. Periodical. US. English. qt. Eastern Mineral Law Foundation, West Virginia University College of Law, PO Box 6130, Morgantown WV 26506. Tel (304)293-2470. Ed William C Williams. DD 346. Circ 700. (ctrl). Concise summary of pertinent legal decisions related to mineral law in the Eastern United States.

CASE WESTERN RESERVE LAW REVIEW. V. 19- Nov. 1967-. 0008-7262. Periodical. US. English. qt. $16.00. Case Western Reserve University, School of Law, 11075 East Boulevard, Cleveland OH 44106. Tel (216)368-3312. Ind/Abst Leg. Contents, Index Leg. Period., Curr. Law Index, Leg. Resour. Index, Contents Curr. Leg. Period. LC K3. DD 349.7305.

CASELOAD STATISTICAL REPORT . . . FOR SUPREME COURT OF ALABAMA, COURT OF CRIMINAL APPEALS, COURT OF CIVIL APPEALS, CIRCUIT COURTS, DISTRICT COURTS. See Statistics.

CASES DECIDED IN THE SUPREME COURT OF VIRGINIA. Main/Corp Virginia. Supreme Court. VFOAT Virginia Reports. V. 212-. US. English. Supreme Court of Virginia, Office of The Executive Secretary, 100 North Ninth Street/Third Floor, Richmond VA 23219. LC KFV2445. DD 348.755043. Cases Decided in the Supreme Court of Appeals of Virginia.

CAT FAMILY. (THE CAT FAMILY). No. 1- Oct. 1977-. 0705-1565. Periodical. CN. English. ir. Westminster Legal Services Society, 445 Columbia Street, New Westminster British Columbia V3L 1A9 Canada. DD 340.0222.

CATALOGO COLETIVO DE PERIODICOS EM DIREITO. V. 1- 1975-. Portuguese. ir. Universidade de Sao Paulo Faculdade de Direito Biblioteca Central, Largo de Sao Francisco, 95 Sao Paulo 01005 Brazil. DD 016.34005.

CATALOGUE - NATIVE AMERICAN RIGHTS FUND. (CATALOGUE). Main/Corp National Indian Law Library. V. 1- 1973/74-. 0092-3419. US. English. an. National Indian Law Library, 1506 Broadway, Boulder CO 80302. Tel (303)447-8760. LC KF8201.A1. DD 016.342701087. Circ 1,000. An index to legal materials on Federal Indian Law of the National Indian Law Library.

THE CATHOLIC LAWYER. V. 1- Jan. 1955-. 0008-8137. Periodical. US. English. qt $5.00. St Johns University School of Law, Grand Central and Utopia Parkway, Jamaica NY 11439. Tel (718)990-6654. Ed Edward T Fagan. Ind/Abst Leg. Resour. Index, Cathol. Period. Lit. Index, Index Leg. Period., Cathol. Period. Index, Curr. Law Index, Contents Curr. Leg. Period. LC UNC. (cum index). Circ 1,700. Magazine devoted to timely legal problems having ethical, canonical, or theological implications.

CATHOLIC UNIVERSITY LAW REVIEW (1975). (CATHOLIC UNIVERSITY LAW REVIEW). V. 25- Fall 1975-. 0008-8390. Periodical. US. English. qt. $18.00. Catholic University of America, 620 Michigan Avenue NE, Washington DC 20064. Tel (202)635-5157. Ed Catherine T Clarke. Ind/Abst Index Leg. Period., Soc. Sci. Citation Index, Leg. Contents, Curr. Law Index, Leg. Resour. Index, Contents Curr. Leg. Period. LC K3. DD 340.05. bk rev. adv acc. Circ 1,200. A legal publication of professional and student-authored articles. Special issues include: communications law and D.C. survey-focusing on legal developments in the District of Columbia. Catholic University of America (1972).

CAVEAT. 1- 1956?-. 0411-3012. Periodical. US. English. ir. University of Illinois, College of Law, Urbana IL 61801.

CAVEAT VENDOR. 0197-193X. Periodical. US. English. Caveat Vendor, PO Box 12487 Capitol Station, Austin TX 78711. LC KFT1430.A59. DD 343.7307105.

Law

CAYMAN GAZETTE. No. 1- Jan. 6, 1975-. 0376-7779. English. bw. $20.00. Cayman Islands Government Information Services, 3rd Floor Tower Building, Grand Cayman British West Indies. **Tel** (809)94-97999. **DD** 340.0972921.

CBAO SECTIONEWS CEASED. **Main/Corp** Canadian Bar Association. Ontario Branch. **VAT** Canadian Bar Association-Ontario Sectionews. Began July/Aug. 1983. Ceased with issue for Mar./Apr. or May/June 1985. 0828-6531. Periodical. CN. English. bm. Free to Members. Canadian Bar Association Ontario, 120 Adelaide Street West/Suite 1000, Toronto Ontario M5H 1T1 Canada. **DD** 340.060713.

CCH ESTATE PLANNING GUIDE. VFOAT C.C.H. Estate Planning Guide. **VAT** Commerce Clearing House Estate Planning Guide. 1976 Ed.-. 0733-6144. US. English. $25.00 V. 1-4. Commerce Clearing House Inc, 4025 West Peterson Avenue, Chicago IL 60646. **Tel** (312)583-8500. Ed Sidney Kess and Bertil Westlin. LC KF750. **DD** 343.73053, 347.30353. This comprehensive handbook is a 'must' for the estate owner and his advisers when planning and formulating a successful estate plan.

CELA NEWSLETTER. (THE CELA NEWSLETTER). **Main/Corp** Canadian Environmental Law Association. **VFOAT** Section Nouvelles de l'A C D E. **VAT** Canadian Environmental Law Association Newsletter, Section Nouvelles de l'Acde, Section Nouvelles de l'Association Canadienne du Droit de l'Environnememt. V. 1- Feb. 1976-. 0707-7866. Periodical. CN. English. bm. $10.00 Includes Membership in CELA. Canadian Environmental Law Research Foundation, Suite 301/1 Spadina Crescent, Toronto Ontario M2S 2J5 Canada. LC KE3612. **DD** 344.7104602642.

CEMETERY BUSINESS & LEGAL GUIDE. See Funeral Service.

CENTRAL SCHOOL LAW DIGEST. V. 1- Feb. 1976-. 0363-7980. US. English. mo. $45.00. School Law Digest Corporation, S56W23674 Maplewood Terrace, Waukesha WI 53186. LC KF4114. **DD** 344.770705.

CENTRE COUNTY LEGAL JOURNAL. V. 1- 1960-. Periodical. English. be. LC Microfilm 0181 (LL). Each issue contains an index to its own contents - no vol. index - loose.

CERL FORUM. See Economics - Labor.

CHAPTER 11 REPORTER. VFOAT Chapter Eleven Reporter. Vol. 1, No. 1 (Aug. 1983)-. 0748-562X. Periodical. US. English. mo. $60.00. Roth Publishing Group, 485 Fifth Avenue, New York NY 10017. **DD** 346.

CHECKLISTS OF BASIC AMERICAN LEGAL PUBLICATIONS. VFOAT Checklists Basic American Legal Publications. US. English. ir. Fred B Rothman Company, 10368 West Centennial Road, Littleton CO 80127. **Tel** (303)979-5657. Ed Marcia Zubrow. A checklist of basic American legal publications i.e. state session laws, state reports, etc. Very useful for law libraries.

CHEMICAL & RADIATION WASTE LITIGATION REPORTER. See Sanitation, Environmental Technology.

CHEMICAL REGULATION REPORTER. **Main/Corp** Bureau of National Affairs (Washington, D.C.). V. 1- Mar. 18, 1977-. 0148-7973. Periodical. US. English. $820.00. Bureau of National Affairs Inc, 1231 25th Street NW, Washington DC 20037. **Tel** (301)258-1033. LC KF3958.A15. **DD** 344.73042.

CHEMICAL SUBSTANCES CONTROL. See Chemistry.

CHICAGO BAR RECORD. V. 16- Oct. 1934-. 0009-3505. Periodical. US. English. bm. $9.00. Chicago Bar Association, 29 La Salle Street, Chicago IL 60603. **Ind/Abst** Leg. Resour. Index, Index Leg. Period. *Chicago Bar Association Record.*

CHICAGO-KENT LAW REVIEW. VFOAT Chicago Kent Law Review. V. 17- Dec. 1938-. 0009-3599. US. English. qt. $18.00. Illinois Institute of Technology-Law Review, 77 South Wacker Drive, Chicago IL 60657. **Ind/Abst** Leg. Resour. Index, Index Leg. Period., Curr. Law Index, Contents Curr. Leg. Period. LC K3. **DD** 340. *Chicago-Kent Review.*

CHICAGO LAWYER. Began with Nov. 1, 1978. 0199-8374. Periodical. US. English. mo. $27.00. Chicago Lawyer, Room 800, 220 South State Street, Chicago IL 60604. **Tel** (312)939-7150. Ed Rob Warden. LC K3. **DD** 349.77305, 347.73005. bk rev.

adv acc. **Circ** 8,000. (ctrl). A newspaper geared toward the Cook county legal community.

CHICANO LAW REVIEW. V. 1- Summer 1972-. 0090-3620. Periodical. US. English. $12.00. Chicano Law Student Association, 405 Hilgard Avenue, Los Angeles CA 90024. **Ind/Abst** Leg. Resour. Index. LC K3. **DD** 340.05.

CHILD SUPPORT REPORT. Vol. 1, No. 1 (Jan. 1979)-. Periodical. US. English. mo. US Department of Health and Human Services, Office of Child Support Enforcement, National Child Support Enforcement Reference Center, 6110 Executive Boulevard, Rockville MD 20852. **Tel** (301)443-5106. Ed Free. bk rev. **Circ** 10,000. (ctrl). Information on child support enforcement programs, policies and regulations at federal, state, and local levels.

CHILDREN'S LEGAL RIGHTS JOURNAL. Vol. 1, No. 1 (July/Aug 1979). 0278-7210. Periodical. US. English. qt. $32.50. William S Hein, 1285 Main Street, Buffalo NY 14209. **Tel** (716)882-2600. **Ind/Abst** Leg. Resour. Index, Curr. Law Index. LC KF479.A15. **DD** 346.73013505, 347.30613505. **Circ** 550. The leading journal on children's legal rights.

CHINA: INTERNATIONAL TRADE. (CHINA, INTERNATIONAL TRADE). 0734-9599. Periodical. US. English. qt. Document Expediting Project, Exchange & Gift Division Library of Congress, Washington DC 20540. **Ind/Abst** Am. Stat. Index. LC HF3836.5. **DD** 382.095100212. *China, International Trade Quarterly Review, 0197-3398.*

CHINA LAW REPORTER. VFOAT Chung-Kuo fa lu Chi Kan. Vol. 1, No. 1 (Summer 1980)-. Periodical. US. English. qt. $27.00. American Bar Association, 750 North Lake Shore Drive, Chicago IL 60611. **Tel** (312)988-5555. Ed Tao-Tai Hsia and Thomas J Pasmussen. **Ind/Abst** Leg. Resour. Index. LC K3. **DD** 349.5105, 345.1005. (ctrl). Concerned mainly with practical issues facing lawyers and scholars.

CHINESE LAW AND GOVERNMENT. Began with Spring 1968 issue. 0009-4609. Periodical. US. English (Chinese). qt. $178.50. M E Sharpe Inc, 80 Business Park, Armonk NY 10504. **Tel** (914)273-1800. Ed Michael Y M Kau. **Ind/Abst** Curr. Contents Behav. Soc. Educ. Sci., Curr. Contents, Soc. Behav. Sci., Public Aff. Inf. Serv. Bull., Soc. Sci. Citation Index. LC K3. **DD** 340.0951. adv acc. **Circ** 300. Significant scholarly works and policy documents in the fields of politics and government. Works of major significance from Japanese, Russian, and Taiwan sources sometimes included.

CHITTY'S LAW JOURNAL. Began publication in Nov. 1950. 0009-4889. Periodical. CN. English. mo. $30.95. 535 Glengarry Avenue, Toronto Ontario M5M 1G2 Canada. **Tel** (416)787-0383. **Ind/Abst** Leg. Resour. Index, Curr. Law Index, Contents Curr. Leg. Period. *Fortnightly Law Journal, 0701-3051.*

CHROSTWAITE'S PENNSYLVANIA MUNICIPAL LAW REPORTER. V. 48-. US. English. an. Local Government Service, RD No 3, Mechanicsburg PA 17055. *Municipal Law Reporter.*

CHUKAI JIDOSHA ROPPO. VFOAT Jidosha Roppo. Periodical. JA. Japanese. ir. 2200. Daiichi Hoki, 1-17 Minami Aoyama 2-chome, Minato-ku 107, Tokyo Japan.

CHUNG WEN FA LU LUN WEN SO YIN. VFOAT Index to Chinese Legal Periodicals. CH. Chinese. an. Soochow University Press, Wai Shuang Hsi Shih Lin, Taipei Taiwan Republic of China. Ed Tung Wu Ta Hsueh Tu Shu Kuan. LC K33. **DD** 349.51016, 345.10016.

CIENCIA PENAL. Periodical. Portuguese. ir. $30.00. Editora Convivio, Alameda Eduardo Prado 705, CEP 01218 Sao Paulo Brazil. LC K3.

CIENCIA PENAL. Began in 1973. Periodical. BL. Portuguese. ir. Companhia Editora Forense, Av Erasmo Braga 299, 1 E 2 Andares, 20020 Rio de Janeiro Brazil. LC K3. **DD** 345.005, 342.5005.

CIJL BULLETIN. VFOAT C.I.J.L Bulletin. No. 4 (Oct. 1979)-. English. sa. $8.00. American Association for the International Commission of Jurists, 777 United Nations Plaza, New York NY 10017. **Tel** (212)972-0883. Ed Ustinia Dolgepol. LC K115.A2. **DD** 340.05. Worldwide case studies of independence of judiciary and state repression against judges, lawyers and judicial organisms. *Bulletin of the Centre for the Independence of Judges and Lawyers (CIJL).*

CIS FEDERAL REGISTER INDEX. See Indexes/Abstracts.

CIS FOUR-YEAR CUMULATIVE INDEX. See Indexes/Abstracts.

THE CITATION. Began May 9, 1958. 0009-7446. Periodical. US. English. sm. $25.00. American Medical Association, 555 North Dearborn Street, Chicago IL 60610. **Tel** (312)645-4927. Ed Nancy Lou Watson. NLM W1 CI961. **Circ** 2,400. Summaries of the latest court decisions affecting physicians and other health professionals.

CITIZENS' FORUM ON THE COURT. (CITIZENS' FORUM ON THE COURTS : A NEWSLETTER OF THE AMERICAN JUDICATURE SOCIETY). Vol. 1, No. 1 (Summer 1984)-. 0748-2000. Periodical. US. English. qt. Free. American Judicature Society, 25 East Washington Street/Suite 1600, Chicago IL 60602. LC KF8712. **DD** 347.73105.

CITIZENS LAW ADVISOR. 0270-8299. Periodical. US. English. qt. $12.00. Citizens Law Library, 7 South Wirt Street, PO Box 1745, Leesburg VA 22075. LC K3. **DD** 349.7305, 347.3005.

CITY OF CHICAGO BUILDING CODE. **Main/Corp** Chicago. 1977-. US. English. $16.50. Index Publishing Corp, 308 West Randolph Street, Chicago IL 60606. LC KFX1242. **DD** 343.7731107869. *City of Chicago Building Code and Contractors Register.*

CITY OF LONDON LAW REVIEW. (CITY OF LONDON LAW REVIEW : JOURNAL OF THE MANSFIELD LAW CLUB, CITY OF LONDON POLYTECHNIC). Michaelmas 1974-. 0306-9788. Periodical. UK. English. sa. $15.00. City of London Polytechnic, Law Department, 84 Moorgate, London E1 7NT England. **Tel** (02)283-1030. Ed Frank Webb. **Ind/Abst** Leg. Resour. Index, Curr. Law Index. LC K3. **DD** 349.4205, 344.2005. bk rev. adv acc. **Circ** 300. The journal contains articles and case notes of topical interest. The contributors are predominantly academics, practitioners and members of the English judiciary.

CIVIL & MILITARY LAW JOURNAL. V. 1- Jan./March 1965-. 0045-7043. Periodical. English. qt. $20.00. Civil & Military Law Journal, D-1-24 Rajouri Garden, New Delhi 110027 India. **Tel** 584498.

CIVIL CAUSE (BOTSWANA). **Main/Corp** Botswana. High Court. English. ir. Botswana Government High Court, PO Box 87, Government Printer, Gaborone Botswana Africa. **DD** 348.681041.

CIVIL CODE (CALIFORNIA). VFOAT West's California Codes. 1978-. Periodical. US. English. an. Civil Code, 50 West Kellogg Boulevard, St Paul MN 55102.

CIVIL DIGEST. (THE CIVIL DIGEST). **Main/Corp** Virginia. Office of the Attorney General. 0097-790X. US. English. Office of the Attorney General, Supreme Court Building, 1101 East Broad Street, Richmond VA 23219. LC KFV2840. **DD** 348.75505.

CIVIL JUDICIAL STATISTICS. See Statistics.

CIVIL JUSTICE QUARTERLY. Vol 1 (Jan. 1982)-. 0261-9261. Periodical. UK. English. qt. 44.00. Sweet & Maxwell Ltd, North Way Andover, Hampshire SP10 5BE England. **Tel** 01-583-9855. Ed Carol Tullo. **Ind/Abst** Leg. Resour. Index. LC K3. **DD** 347.0505, 342.7505. bk rev. adv acc. **Circ** 500. A practical forum for debate and discussion in matters of litigation practice and procedure.

CIVIL LAW OPINIONS OF THE JUDGE ADVOCATE GENERAL, UNITED STATES AIR FORCE. **Main/Corp** United States. Air Force. Judge Advocate General. Vol. 1 (1961/1977). 0748-7657. US. English. Judge Advocate General, Department of the Air Force, The Pentagon, Washington DC 20330. LC KF7405. **DD** 343.730184, 347.303184.

CIVIL LITIGATION REPORTER. VFOAT CEB Civil Litigation Reporter. V. 1- July 1979-. 0199-0802. Periodical. US. English. bm.

CIVIL PRACTICE ANNUAL OF NEW YORK. **Main/Corp** New York (State). 1923-. US. English. an. Matthew Bender & Company Inc, 1275 Broadway, Albany NY 12201. **Tel** (800)833-9844.

CIVIL PROCEDURE. **Main/Corp** Bay Area Review Course, Inc. 0099-1244. US. English. an. Bay Area Review Course Inc, 5900 Wilshire Boulevard, Los Angeles CA 90036. LC KF8841. **DD** 347.735.

Law

CIVIL RICO REPORT. VFOAT BNA Civil Rico Report. VAT Civil Racketeer Influenced and Corrupt Organizations Act Report. Vol. 1, No. 1 (June 5, 1985)-. 0884-0032. US. English. wk. $345.00. Buraff Publications, 1231 25th Street NW, Washington DC 20037. DD 347.

THE CIVIL SERVICE COURT DIGEST. V. 1- Jan. 1980-. 0272-006X. Periodical. US. English. mo. $20.00. Civil Service Court Digest, 1860 Broadway, New York NY 10023. LC KF5390.A59. DD 342.7306802643.

CLAIMS FORUM. V. 1- March/April 1976-. 0364-3603. Periodical. US. English. bm. $18.00. J R Hendee, PO Box 322, Medina NY 14103. LC KF2258.A15. DD 343.73093.

CLASS ACTION REPORTS. V. 1-. 0746-7168. Periodical. US. English. qt. Class Action Reports Inc, 6900 Wisconsin Avenue, Bethesda MD 20815. LC K3.

CLASSIFIED INDEX OF DECISIONS OF THE REGIONAL DIRECTORS OF THE NATIONAL LABOR RELATIONS BOARD IN REPRESENTATION PROCEEDINGS. See Indexes/Abstracts.

CLASSIFIED INDEX OF NATIONAL LABOR RELATIONS BOARD DECISIONS AND RELATED COURT DECISIONS. See Indexes/Abstracts.

CLASSIFIED INDEX, TRULY AGREED TO AND FINALLY PASSED HOUSE AND SENATE BILLS (MISSOURI). See Indexes/Abstracts.

CLE BULLETIN. Main/Corp West Virginia. University. College of Law. V. 1-. 0148-4346. Periodical. US. English. West Virginia University Law Center, Morgantown WV 26506. LC KFW1257. DD 340.09754.

THE CLE REGISTER. See Education (General).

CLEARINGHOUSE REVIEW. Began in Sept. 1967. 0009-868X. Periodical. US. English. mo. $75.00. National Clearinghouse for Legal Services, 407 South Dearborn/Suite 400, Chicago IL 60605. Tel (312)939-3830. Ed Lucy Moss. Ind/Abst Leg. Resour. Index, Public Aff. Inf. Serv. Bull., Index Leg. Period. LC UNC. DD 349.7305, 347.3005. bk rev. adv acc. Circ 8,700. Articles on poverty law, including health, welfare, employment, youth and consumer law; developments of currently litigated cases; and reviews of related documents and manuals.

CLEVELAND BAR JOURNAL. 0160-1598. Periodical. US. English. mo. $10.00. Cleveland Bar Association, 118 St Clair - 2nd Floor, Cleveland OH 44114-1253. Tel (216)696-3525. Ed Thomas J Brady. LC KF200. DD 340.0977132. adv acc. Circ 5,000. Journal for lawyers who are members of the Cleveland Bar Association. Journal.

CLEVELAND-MARSHALL LAW NOTES. 0145-1545. Periodical. US. English. Cleveland-Marshall College of Law, 1801 Euclid Avenue, Cleveland Ohio 44115. LC KF292.C514. DD 340.071177132.

CLEVELAND STATE LAW REVIEW. V. 18, No. 3- Sept. 1969-. 0009-8876. US. English. qt. Cleveland State University, Cashiers Office, 1983 East 24th Street, Cleveland OH 44115. Ind/Abst Leg. Resour. Index, Index Leg. Period., Contents Curr. Leg. Period., Curr. Law Index. LC K3. DD 340.05. Cleveland-Marshall Law Review.

CLIC ABSTRACTS ON PUBLIC LEGAL EDUCATION AND INFORMATION (PLEI) RESEARCH. See Indexes/Abstracts.

CLIC'S LEGAL MATERIALS LETTER. (C L I C 'S LEGAL MATERIALS LETTER). Main/Corp Canadian Law Information Council. VFOAT Bulletin d'Information Juridique. VAT Canadian Law Information Council's Legal Materials Letter. No. 1- Oct. 1977-. 0704-0393. Periodical. CN. English (French). bm. $5.03. Canadian Law Information Council, 161 Laurier Avenue West/5th Floor, Ottawa Ontario K1P 5J2 Canada. Tel (613)236-9766. DD 340.0971.

CLIENT COUNSELING UPDATE. (CLIENT COUNSELING UPDATE : CCU). VFOAT CCU. Vol. 1, No. 1 (Oct. 1980)-. 0276-752X. Periodical. US. English. $1.00. American Bar Association Law Student Division, 750 North Lake Shore Drive, Chicago IL 60611. Tel (312)988-5622. Ed Glenda A Berg. LC KF311.A15. DD 340.02373. Newsletter contains news articles concerning client counseling.

CLINICAL LAW JOURNAL & NEWSLETTER. VFOAT Clinical Law Newsletter (Apr. 1977). VAT Clinical Law Journal and Newsletter. 0147-8605. Periodical. US. English. $4.00. Clinical Newsletter, Pepperdine University, School of Law, 1520 South Anaheim Boulevard, Anaheim CA 92805. LC KF282.A15. DD 340.071173.

CLM, CONSUMER LAW MONTHLY. VFOAT Consumer Law Monthly. Periodical. US. English. mo. PO Box 3496, Walnut Creek CA 94598. LC KFC375.A15. DD 343.7940705.

CLR NEWSLETTER. Main/Corp North Dakota. University. School of Law. Central Legal Research. V. 1- April 1977-. Periodical. US. English. mo. University of North Dakota, School of Law, Grand Forks ND 58202. LC KFN8675. DD 345.7840072.

CMI NEWS LETTER. VFOAT C.M.I. News Letter. Periodical. English. qt. 300. Comite Maritime International, Borzestraat 17, B-2000 Antwerp Belgium. LC K1150.A13. DD 343.09605, 342.39605.

COASTAL LAW MEMO. Issue 1 (Aug. 1980)-. 0730-6822. Periodical. US. English. University of Oregon, Law School Ocean & Coastal Law Center, Eugene OR 97403. Tel (503)686-3845. Ed Richard G Hildreth. LC KFO2851.8.A15. DD 346.795046917, 347.950646917. Circ 1,500. Provides single-topic, substantive analysis of current issues in coastal law to all members of the ocean-oriented community and the interested public at large.

CODE ADMINISTRATIF. Main/Corp France. 1. Ed. French. ir. Dalloz, 11 rue Soufflot, Paris France.

CODE CIVIL. Main/Corp France. Series/Titl Petits Codes Dalloz. FR. French. an. Fundacao do Desenvolvimento Admistrativo, 11 rue Soufflot, 75420 Paris France.

CODE CIVIL DE LA PROVINCE DE QUEBEC CEASED. Main/Corp Quebec (Province). VFOAT Civil Code of the Province of Quebec. Began publication in 1919? Ceased 1980. 0317-0837. Periodical. CN. English (French). an. Wilson & Lafleur Ltd, 39 Notre Dame Street West, Montreal Quebec H2Y 1S5 Canada. DD 346.714002632.

CODE OF FEDERAL REGULATIONS : 1, GENERAL PROVISIONS. VFOAT General Provisions. US. English. an. US Government Printing Office, Superintendent of Documents, Washington DC 20402. Vols. for (1985-) distributed to some depository libraries in microfiche.

CODE OF FEDERAL REGULATIONS. 16, COMMERCIAL PRACTICES. VFOAT Commercial Practices. US. English. an. US Government Printing Office, Superintendent of Documents, Washington DC 20402. Vols. for (1984-) distributed to some depository libraries in microfiche.

CODE OF FEDERAL REGULATIONS. 20, EMPLOYEES BENEFITS. VFOAT Employees' Benefits. US. English. an. US Government Printing Office, Superintendent of Documents, Washington DC 20402. Vols. for (1984-) distributed to some depository libraries in microfiche.

CODE OF FEDERAL REGULATIONS. 21, FOOD AND DRUGS. VFOAT Food and Drugs. US. English. an. US Government Printing Office, Superintendent of Documents, Washington DC 20402. NLM KF 70.A3 C66. Vols. for (1984-) distributed to some depository libraries in microfiche.

CODE OF FEDERAL REGULATIONS. 23, HIGHWAYS. Main/Corp United States. Dept. of Transportation. VFOAT Highways. US. English. an. US Government Printing Office, Superintendent of Documents, Washington DC 20402. Vols. for (1984-) distributed to some depository libraries in microfiche.

CODE OF FEDERAL REGULATIONS. 26, INTERNAL REVENUE. Main/Corp United States. Internal Revenue Service. VFOAT Internal Revenue. US. English. an. US Government Printing Office, Superintendent of Documents, Washington DC 20402. Vols. for (1984-) distributed to some depository libraries in microfiche.

CODE OF FEDERAL REGULATIONS. 27, ALCOHOL, TOBACCO PRODUCTS AND FIREARMS. Main/Corp United States. Dept. of the Treasury. VFOAT Alcohol, Tobacco Products and Firearms. US. English. an. Superintendent of Documents, US Government Printing Office, Washington DC 20402.

CODE OF FEDERAL REGULATIONS. 29, LABOR. VFOAT Labor. US. English. an. Superintendent of Documents, US Government Printing Office, Washington DC 20402. Vols. for (1984-) distributed to some depository libraries in microfiche.

CODE OF FEDERAL REGULATIONS. 44, EMERGENCY MANAGEMENT AND ASSISTANCE. VFOAT Emergency Management and Assistance. US. English. an. US Government Printing Office, Superintendent of Documents, Washington DC 20402. Vols. for (1984-) distributed to depository libraries in microfiche.

CODE OF FEDERAL REGULATIONS. CFR INDEX AND FINDING AIDS. See Indexes/Abstracts.

CODE OF FEDERAL REGULATIONS. LSA, LIST OF CFR SECTIONS AFFECTED. VFOAT L.S.A., List of C.F.R. Sections Affected. Began with Aug. 1977. US. English. mo. US Government Printing Office, Superintendent of Documents, Washington DC 20402. NLM KF 70.A3 C675. Code of Federal Regulations. Cumulative List of CFR Sections Affected, 0363-8839.

CODE OF GEORGIA ANNOTATED, ADVANCE ANNOTATION SERVICE. US. English. 3110 Crossing Park, Norcross GA 30071. LC KFG39. DD 348.758026.

CODE OF GEORGIA, UNANNOTATED EDITION. US. English. ir. $149.95. Harrison Company Publishers, 3110 Crossing Park, Norcross GA 30091. Tel (800)241-3561.

CODE OF LAWS OF SOUTH CAROLINA. ANNOTATED. (CODE OF LAWS OF SOUTH CAROLINA; ANNOTATED). US. English. Lawyers Co-Operative Publishing Company, Aqueduct Building, Rochester NY 14603.

CODE PENAL - (FRANCE). Series/Titl Petits Codes Dalloz. FR. French. an. Jurisprudence Generale Dalloz, 11 rue Soufflot, 75240 Paris Cedex 05 France.

CODE RURAL; CODE FORESTIER - (FRANCE). See Forestry.

CODIFICATION OF PRESIDENTIAL PROCLAMATIONS AND EXECUTIVE ORDERS. VFOAT Presidential Proclamations and Executive Orders. Began with 1961/77. 0191-4839. US. English. Superintendent of Documents, US Government Printing Office, Washington DC 20403. LC KF70. DD 348.731. NLM KF 70 .A473.

COGITATIONS. (COGITATIONS : ON LAW AND GOVERNMENT). VFOAT Cogitations on Law and Government. Vol. 1, No. 1 (Summer 1983)-. 0741-9333. Periodical. US. English. qt. Cogitations on Law and Government, Box 35, Gifford IL 61847. LC K3. DD 349.7305, 347.3005.

COLECTANEA DE JURISPRUDENCIA CANONICA. Main/Corp Salamanca. Pontificia Universidad Eclesiastica. Facultad de Derecho Canonico. Spanish. ir.

COLECTIA DE LEGI SI DECRETE. Main/Corp Romania. RM. Romanian. qt. Ilexim Press Department, PO Box 1-136-1-137, Bucharest Romania.

COLETANEA DA LEGISLACAO DA EDUCACAO E CULTURA. Main/Corp Brazil. BL. Portuguese. ir. Departamento de Documentacao e Divulgacao, Brasilia Brazil. DD 344.8107.

COLETANEA DA LEGISLACAO TRIBUTARIA. Main/Corp Parana (Brazil : State). Vol. 1-. Portuguese. ir. LC KHD7877.A27. DD 343.8162040263, 348. 1620340263.

COLETANEA DE DECRETOS NUMERADOS. Main/Corp Coias, Brazil (Statel). Secretaria do Governo. Portuguese. ir. Instituto Butantan Av Vital Brazil, CP 65 Butantan, Sao Paulo Brazil.

COLETANEA DE LEGISLACAO. Main/Corp Brazil. Secretaria de Planejamento. Setor de Documenta Cao. Portuguese. ir. Presidencia da Republica, Secretaria de Planejamento, Diretoria de Administracao, Av Presidente Antonio Carlos 375, 60 Andar S/637, Rio de Janeiro Brazil.

Law

COLETANEA DE REGIMENTOS E ESTATUTOS DA ADMINISTRACAO DO DISTRITO FEDERAL. Main/Corp Distrito Federal (Brazil). V. 1- 1974-. Portuguese. ir.

COLETANEA DE RESOLUCOES DO CONSELHO DELIBERATIVO. COLETANEA DE ATOS DA PRESIDENCIA. Main/Corp Instituto do Acucar e do Alcool (Brazil). 1972-. BL. Portuguese. ir. Instituto do Acucar e do Alcool, Caixa Postal 420, Rio de Janeiro Brazil. LC Law. Coletanea de Atos, Coletanea de Atos da Presidencia.

COLLECTION AGENCY ACT WITH RULES AND REGULATIONS - (CALIFORNIA). Main/Corp California. US. English. Bureau of Collection and Investigative Services, 1430 Howe Avenue, Sacramento CA 95825. LC KFC446.C6. DD 346.794077.

A COLLECTION OF LEGAL OPINIONS. Main/Corp United States. Environmental Protection Agency. Office of General Counsel. V. 1- Dec. 1970/73-. 0361-6673. US. English. an. US Environmental Protection Agency, Office of Public Affairs, Washington DC 20460. LC KF3775. DD 344.7304602646.

THE COLLEGE ADMINISTRATOR AND THE COURTS. V. 1- April 1978-. 0192-1371. US. English. qt. College Administration Publications Inc, Box 8492, Asheville NC 28804. Tel (704)252-0883. Ed Bickel. LC KF4225.A59. DD 344.73074. Circ 2,000. Briefs prepared expressly for college administrators involving higher court decisions affecting administration of institutions of higher education.

COLLEGE LAW BULLETIN. Vol. 1, Nov. 1968-. 0010-101X. Periodical. US. English. mo. United States National Student Association, 2115 South Street NW, Washington DC 20008.

COLLEGE LAW DIGEST. Jan. 15, 1970-. 0045-737X. Periodical. US. English. bm. National Association of College and University Attorney, 1 Dupont Circle NW/Suite 650, Washington DC 20036. LC KF4225.A59. DD 344.73074. West's Education Law Reporter. Special Pamphlet.

THE COLLEGE STUDENT AND THE COURTS. 0145-1472. US. English. qt. College Administration Publication, PO Box 8492, Asheville NC 28804. Tel (704)252-0883. Ed Young and Gehring. LC KF4243.A59. DD 344.73079, 347.30479. Circ 2,800. Briefs of higher court decisions involving student institutional relationships in higher education.

COLLIER BANKRUPTCY CASES. V. 1- Sept. 1974-. 0099-1848. US. English. bw. $325.00. Matthew Bender & Company Inc, 1275 Broadway, Albany NY 12201. Tel (800)833-9844. LC KF1515.A2. DD 346.7307802648.

COLLIN COUNTY COMMERCIAL RECORD. VFOAT Commercial Record. 0745-5909. Newspaper. US. English. wk $300.00. Daily Commercial Record Inc, 202 West Louisiana/Suite 207, McKinney TX 75069. LC K3. DD 340.05.

COLORADO COURT RULES. 0741-4145. US. English. $22.00. West Publishing Company, 50 West Kellogg Boulevard, Box 3526, St Paul MN 55165. LC KFC2329. DD 347.788051, 347.880751.

COLORADO COURT RULES ANNOTATED. Main/Corp Colorado. Supreme Court. VFOAT Colorado Court Rules. 1983 Ed.-. 0747-6922. US. English. an. LC KFC2329. DD 347.788051, 347.880751.

COLORADO COURTS. 0731-7964. Periodical. US. English. mo. Colorado Judicial Department, 2 East 14th Avenue, Denver CO 80203. LC KFC2310. DD 347.7880105, 347.8807105.

COLORADO LAWYER. V. 1, No. 1- Jan. 1972-. 0363-7867. Periodical. US. English. mo. $30.00. Colorado Bar Association, 1900 Grant Street/Suite 940, Denver CO 80203. Tel (303)860-1118. Ed Arlene Abady. Ind/Abst Leg. Resour. Index, Index Leg. Period., Curr. Law Index. LC K3. DD 340.09788. bk rev. adv acc. Circ 9,000. Professional journal for members of the Colorado Bar Association. Articles of interest to attorneys: court opinions ads, court business and other items.

COLORADO LEGISLATIVE COUNCIL RECOMMENDATIONS. Main/Corp Colorado. General Assembly. Legislative Council. VFOAT Report to the Colorado General Assembly, Recommendations For . . . . US. English. an. Room 46, State Capitol, Denver CO 80203. LC KFC1820, KFC1806. DD 300.9788 S, 348.78801, 300. 9788 S, 347.88081.

COLORADO REPORTER COLORADO CASES REPORTED IN PACIFIC REPORTER, SECOND SERIES. VFOAT Colorado Reporter. 0744-9828. US. English. wk. $60.00. West Publishing Company, 50 West Kellogg Boulevard, PO Box 3526, St Paul MN 55165. DD 340.

COLUMBIA JOURNAL OF ENVIRONMENTAL LAW. V. 1- Fall 1974-. 0098-4582. Periodical. US. English. sa. $32.00. Columbia University School of Law, Box B-28, 435 West 116th Street, New York NY 10027. Tel (212)280-2539. Ed Linda Gordon. Ind/Abst Electron. Commun. Abstr. J., ISMEC Bull., Pollut. Abstr. Indexes, Saf. Sci. Abstr. J., Leg. Resour. Index, Sel. Water Resour. Abstr., Energy Inf. Abstr., Environ. Abstr., Index Leg. Period., Curr. Law Index. LC K3. DD 344.7304605. bk rev. adv acc. Circ 1,000. Publishes articles, notes, comments, and book reviews on subjects of importance to the environmental-legal community.

COLUMBIA JOURNAL OF LAW AND SOCIAL PROBLEMS. V. 1- June 1965-. 0010-1923. Periodical. US. English. qt. $24.00 Domestic, $26.00 Foreign. Columbia University School of Law, 435 West 116th Street, New York NY 10027. Tel (212)280-3738. Ed Florence A Fredman. Ind/Abst Leg. Resour. Index, ABC Pol Sci, Public Aff. Inf. Serv. Bull., Index Leg. Period., Soc. Sci. Citation Index, Curr. Law Index, Contents Curr. Leg. Period. (cum index). bk rev. adv acc. Circ 800. A law journal focusing on general legal issues and their impact on pressing social concerns.

COLUMBIA LAW ALUMNI BULLETIN (NEW YORK, N.Y. : 1980). (COLUMBIA LAW ALUMNI BULLETIN). Vol. 13, No. 4 (Fall 1980)-. US. English. qt. Law Alumni Bulletin, Columbia Law School, 435 West 116th Street, Box 3, New York NY 10027. LC KF292.C6. DD 340.07117471. Law Alumni Bulletin (Columbia Law School Alumni Association).

COLUMBIA LAW ALUMNI OBSERVER. (THE COLUMBIA LAW ALUMNI OBSERVER). VFOAT Observer. 0093-304X. Periodical. US. English. qt. Columbia Law Alumni Observer, 435 West 116 Street, New York NY 10027. LC KF292.C6. DD 340.07117471. Columbia Law Observer.

COLUMBIA LAW REVIEW. V. 1- Jan. 1901-. 0010-1958. Periodical. US. English. mo. $32.00. Columbia Law Review, 435 West 116th Street, Box 1026, New York NY 10027. Tel (212)280-4398. Ind/Abst Manage. Contents, Leg. Resour. Index, Account. Index. Suppl., ABC Pol Sci, Women Stud. Abstr., Public Aff. Inf. Serv. Bull., Index Leg. Period. LC MICROFILM LL-0100 K3. DD 340.05. NLM W1 CO285. (cum index). bk rev. adv acc. Circ 3,200. (ctrl). Current legal issues. Usually several by students and 2-3 by judges, lawyers, practitioners, or professors.

COMM/ENT: A JOURNAL OF COMMUNICATIONS AND ENTERTAINMENT LAW. V. 1, No. 1- Fall 1977-. 0193-8393. Periodical. US. English. qt. $20.00. University of California Hastings College of Law, 198 McAllister Street, San Francisco CA 94102. Tel (415)565-4731. Ed Kenneth Wilton. Ind/Abst Index Leg. Period., Curr. Law Index. LC K3. DD 343.7309905, 347.3039905. bk rev.

COMMENTARIES. Began in 1968. 0147-6696. US. English. qt. Boston University School of Law, 765 Commonwealth Avenue, Boston MA 02215. LC KF1. DD 340.

THE COMMERCIAL BAR. 0098-4957. US. English. an. Commercial Publishing Company, 740 South Fulton Avenue, Mt Vernon NY 10550. LC KF195.C57. DD 346.07025.

COMMERCIAL LAW CASE REPORTS. V. 74: Sept. 9, 1974-. US. English. mo. $3.00. Parker Publishing, Box 936, Duncan OK 73533. LC KF880.A2. DD 346.78107.

COMMERCIAL LAW. GOLD BOOK. BENDER PAMPHLET EDITION. NEW YORK UNIFORM COMMERCIAL CODE, GENERAL OBLIGATIONS LAW. (COMMERCIAL LAW). Main/Corp New York (State). VFOAT Commercial Law UCC-GOL. 0277-3643. US. English. an. Matthew Bender, 235 East 45th Street, New York NY 10017. LC KFN5225.A29. DD 346.74707, 347.47067.

COMMERCIAL LAW JOURNAL. V. 35, No. 8- Aug. 1930-. 0010-3055. Periodical. US. English. ir. $35.00. Commerical Law League of America, 222 West Adams Street/Suite 599, Chicago IL 60603. Tel (312)236-4942. Ed Leo E Smith. Ind/Abst Manage. Contents, Leg. Resour. Index, Index Leg. Period., Contents Curr. Leg. Period. bk rev. adv acc. Circ 7,000. Articles on business and commercial law, credit, finance, banking law, and insolvency law. Commercial Law League Journal.

COMMERCIAL LAWS OF EUROPE. V. 1- April 1978-. Periodical. UK. English (Multilingual). mo. $214.54. European Law Centre, Elm House, 4 Bloomsbury Square, London WC1A 2RL England. Tel 01-404-4300. Ed Lusia Ten Kate. DD 346.407. adv acc. Full text in English plus original language of laws from countries of Western Europe together with their legislative histories, explanatory notes and other essential information.

COMMERCIAL LEASE LAW INSIDER. 0736-0517. Periodical. US. English. mo. $145.00. Brownstone Publishers Inc, PO Box 4177, Grand Central Station, New York NY 10163. Tel (212)473-8200. Circ 3,500. Practical legal information for lessors and lessees of commercial property.

COMMITTEE DIRECTORY OF THE SECTION OF CORPORATION, BANKING AND BUSINESS LAW OF THE AMERICAN BAR ASSOCIATION. See Yearbooks, Almanacs, Directories.

COMMITTEE REPORTS - LOCAL GOVERNMENT LAW SECTION OF THE AMERICAN BAR ASSOCIATION. Main/Corp American Bar Association. Section of Local Government Law. 0587-2936. US. English. an. The American Bar Association, 1155 East 60th Street, Chicago IL 60637. LC KF5300.A73. DD 342.7309.

COMMITTEE REPORTS - SECTION OF LABOR AND EMPLOYMENT LAW, AMERICAN BAR ASSOCIATION. Main/Corp American Bar Association. Section of Labor and Employment Law. 1979-. 0270-4889. US. English. an. American Bar Association, Division of Professional Service Activities, 1155 East 60th Street, Chicago IL 60637. LC KF3353. DD 344.7301. Committee Reports - Section on Labor Relations Law, American Bar Association.

COMMODITIES LAW LETTER. 0277-2930. Periodical. US. English. mo. $168.00. Commodities Law Press Association, 900 Third Avenue, 20th Floor, New York NY 10022. Tel (212)935-0638. Ed Richard A Miller. Ind/Abst Leg. Resour. Index. LC KF1085.A15. DD 343.730805, 347.303805. bk rev. Report and analysis of legal developments affecting commodities/futures industry. For lawyers, accountants, and executives.

THE COMMON LAW LAWYER. 0160-659X. Periodical. US. English. bm. International Common Law Exchange Society, PO Box 51, Palo Alto CA 94302. Tel (415)962-8073. LC K110.l53. DD 340.205.

COMMON MARKET LAW REVIEW. Vol. 1, No. 1 (June 1963)-. 0588-7453. Periodical. UK. English. qt. 130.00. Kluwer Academic Publishing Group Distribution Center, PO Box 322, 3300 AH Dordrecht Netherlands. Tel 078-334248. Ed H G Schermers. Ind/Abst Leg. Resour. Index, Soc. Sci. Citation Index, Curr. Law Index. DD 349.405, 344.005. (cum index). bk rev. adv acc. A review of common market law published in cooperation with the British Institute of International and Comparative Law, and the Europe Institute of the University of Leiden.

COMMONWEALTH ARBITRATION REPORTS. Main/Corp Australia. Commonwealth Conciliation and Arbitration Commission. V. 122- Jan./May 1968-. AT. English. ir. Australian Government Publishing Service, PO Box 84, Canberra Australian Capital Territory 2600 Australia. DD 344.9401890264. Commonwealth Arbitration Reports.

COMMONWEALTH CARIBBEAN LAW LIST. (THE COMMONWEALTH CARIBBEAN LAW LIST). 1976-. 0703-9212. CN. English. an. Canada Law Book Ltd, 80 Cowdray Court, Agincourt Ontario M1S 1S5 Canada. DD 340.025729.

COMMONWEALTH COURT REPORTS. Main/Corp Pennsylvania. Commonwealth Court. VFOAT Pennsylvania Commonwealth Court Reports. V. 1- 1970/71-. Periodical. US. English. ir. Murrelle Printing Company Inc, Box 100, Sayre PA 18840. Tel (717)888-2244. Ed William Wilks. LC KFP49. DD 348.748043. Circ 1,000. Opinions of the Commonwealth Court of Pennsylvania.

COMMONWEALTH LAW BULLETIN. No. 1- July 1974-. 0305-0718. Periodical. UK. English. qt. 10. Commonwealth Secretariat, Marlborough House

Law

Pall Mall, London SW1Y 5HX England. **Tel** 839-3411. **Ed** Jeremy Pope. **DD** 348.009171241. bk rev. adv acc. **Circ** 2,500. Up-to-date notes on recent legislation, case law and law reform proposals, in the 49 commonwealth independent countries, and at the international level.

COMMONWEALTH OF AUSTRALIA GAZETTE. GENERAL. Main/Corp Australia. Periodical. AT. English. wk. Australia Government Public Service, PO Box 84, Canberra Australian Capital Territory 2600 Australia. **DD** 340.0994. *Australian Government Gazette.*

COMMONWEALTH OF AUSTRALIA GAZETTE. PERIODIC. Main/Corp Australia. AT. English. ir. **DD** 340.0944. *Australian Government Gazette.*

COMMONWEALTH OF AUSTRALIA GAZETTE. PUBLIC SERVICE. Main/Corp Australia. July 7, 1977-. Periodical. AT. English. wk. $258.25. Australia Government Public Service, PO Box 84, Canberra Australian Capital Territory 2600 Australia. **DD** 340.0994. *Australian Government Gazette.*

COMMUNICATIONS AND THE LAW. V. 1- Winter 1979-. 0162-9093. Periodical. US. English. bm. $60.00. Meckler Publishers, 11 Ferry Lane West, Westport CT 06880. **Tel** (203)226-6967. **Ed** Theodore R Kupferman. **Ind/Abst** Leg. Resour. Index, ABI/Inform, Index Leg. Period. **LC** K3. **DD** 343.7309905. **CODEN** COMLDE. bk rev. adv acc. **Circ** 750. Discussions and studies of the impact of communications issues on legal and judicial affairs.

COMMUNICATIONS LAW (NEW YORK, N.Y. : 1982). (COMMUNICATIONS LAW). **Series/Titl** Patents, Copyrights, Trademarks, and Literary Property Course Handbook Series. 1982-. US. English. an. Practising Law Institute, 810 Seventh Avenue, New York NY 10019. **LC** KF4774. **DD** 343.730998, 347.303998. *Annual Communications Law Institute.*

COMMUNICATIONS LAWYER. (COMMUNICATIONS LAWYER : PUBLICATION OF THE FORUM COMMITTEE ON COMMUNICATIONS LAW, AMERICAN BAR ASSOCIATION). Vol. 1, No. 1 (Winter 1983)-. 0737-7622. Periodical. US. English. qt. American Bar Association, Forum Committee on Communications Law, 1155 East 60th Street, Chicago IL 60637. **LC** KF2750.A15. **DD** 343.73099, 347.30399.

THE COMMUNICATOR. 0573-1046. Periodical. US. English. bm. Chicago Bar Association, 29 South LaSalle Street, Chicago IL 60603.

COMMUNIQUE - LAW SOCIETY OF MANITOBA. (COMMUNIQUE). Sept. 1982-. 0824-2186. Periodical. CN. English. mo. Free to Members. Law Society of Manitoba, 1400 One Lakeview Square, 155 Carlton Street, Winnipeg Manitoba R3C 3H8 Canada. **Tel** 942-5571. **Ed** Graeme Garson. **DD** 340.0607127. **Circ** 2,000. (ctrl). Publication goes to law society membership to keep them current with operations of society, rule changes, new governing body to members and any matters of general interest to membership.

COMMUNIS SCRIPTURA. 0730-6970. Periodical. US. English. The Missouri Bar, PO Box 119, Jefferson City MO 65102. **LC** KFM8195.7.L38. **DD** 340.0712778.

COMMUNITY ASSOCIATION LAW REPORTER. Jan. 1978-. 0190-1192. Periodical. US. English. mo. $78.00. Community Associations Institute, 3000 South Eads Street, Arlington VA 22202. **Tel** (703)548-8600. **Ed** Emily Baumgardner. **LC** KF581.A15. **DD** 346.73043305. **Circ** 3,000. (ctrl).

COMMUNITY EDUCATION SERIES. Began publication in 1972?. 0317-3585. Monographic Series. CN. English. John Howard Society of Ontario, 168 Isabella Street, Toronto Ontario M4Y Canada. **DD** 345.71.

COMMUNITY PROPERTY JOURNAL. V. 1- Winter 1974-. 0196-4453. Periodical. US. English. qt. $86.00. Panel Publishers, 14 Plaza Road, Greenvale NY 11548. **Tel** (516)484-0006. **Ed** Leo Kornfeld. **Ind/Abst** Leg. Resour. Index, Account. Index. Suppl., Curr. Law Index, Contents Curr. Leg. Period. **LC** K3. **DD** 347.30642. **Circ** 1,200. (ctrl). A quarterly publication zeroing in on the effects of community property on taxes, estate planning, marital dissolution, probate, pensions, insurance, creditors rights, tort, etc.

COMPANY LAW DIGEST (NEW DELHI, INDIA). (COMPANY LAW DIGEST). Periodical. II. English. qt. 50.00. Company Law Digest, ASAF Ali Road, PO Box 717, New Delhi 110 002 India. **DD** 346.5406605 345.4066605.

COMPANY LAW JOURNAL (NEW DELHI, INDIA). (THE COMPANY LAW JOURNAL). Periodical. English. mo. 347 Domestic, $95.00. Company Law Journal, 66/2230 Gurdwara Road Karol Bagh, PO No 2693, New Delhi 11005 India. **Tel** 572-0678. **Ed** L M Sharma. bk rev. adv acc. **Circ** 2,100. (ctrl). Indian corporate laws: practice and procedure, acts and bills of Indian parliament, rules notifications circulars by government, and reports of Indian/English superior courts.

COMPARATIVE JURIDICAL REVIEW. Vol. 1 (1964)-. 0069-7893. US. English (Spanish). ir. Rainforth Foundation, 3001 Ponce de Leon Boulevard, Coral Gables FL 33134. **Tel** 446-7856. **Ed** Mario Diaz-Cruz. **Ind/Abst** Leg. Resour. Index, Curr. Law Index, Recent Publ. Artic. **DD** 340. (cum index). bk rev. **Circ** 1,000.

COMPARATIVE LABOR LAW. V. 1- Spring 1976-. 0147-9202. Periodical. US. English. qt $10.00 Domestic, $12.50 Foreign. Comparative Labor Law, University of California, School of Law, Los Angeles CA 90024. **Ind/Abst** Manage. Contents, Int. Labour Doc., Public Aff. Inf. Serv. Bull. **LC** K3. **DD** 344.0105. *Bulletin - International Society for Labor Law and Social Legislation, United States National Committee, 0146-0234.*

COMPARATIVE LAW SERIES. Main/Corp British Institute of International and Comparative Law. 0068-2160. Monographic Series. UK. English. ir. British Institute of International and Comparative Law, Charles Clore House/17 Russell Square, London WC1B 5DR England. **Tel** 01-405-4051-2-3.

COMPENDIO TEORICO Y PRACTICO - ALALC. Main/Corp Asociacion Latinoamericana de Libre Comercio. AG. Spanish. an. Peru 707 Cap Casilla C Central, Buenos Aires Argentina. **DD** 343.805605, 348.035605.

COMPENDIUM OF GRIEVANCE ARBITRATION DECISIONS. 1980-. 0226-3890. CN. English. **LC** KEN7804.A54. **DD** 344.7160189143, 3471604189143. *Compendium of Grievance Arbitration Decisions, 0226-3890.*

COMPENDIUM OF LAWS AND JURISPRUDENCE OF THE REPUBLIC OF LEBANON. English or French. ir. PO Box 539, Damascus Syria. **DD** 340.095692.

COMPENDIUM OF LAWS OF THE FEDERATION OF ARAB REPUBLICS. English. ir. PO Box 539, Damascus Syria. **DD** 340.0962.

COMPETITION LAW IN THE EUROPEAN COMMUNITIES. Periodical. UK. English. mo. Centre for Legal & Business Information, Rectory Road, Great Waldingfield, Sudbury Suffolk CO10 0TL England. **DD** 341.753.

COMPILATION OF BAR EXAMINATION QUESTIONS. Main/Corp Institute for Bar Review Study. US. English. an.

COMPILATION OF PRESIDENTIAL DECREES - (REPUBLIC). Main/Corp Philippines. V. 1- (No. 1/245-). 0115-2203. English. ir. Rural Bankers Legal Reference Center, 317 Samanillo Building, Manila Phillipines. **DD** 348.59901.

COMPILATION OF RULES OF STATE AGENCIES - (RHODE ISLAND). Main/Corp Rhode Island. Dept. of State. US. English. **LC** KFR40. **DD** 348.745025.

COMPILATION OF STATE AND FEDERAL PRIVACY LAWS. VFOAT Compilation of State & Federal Privacy Laws. 1977-78 Ed.-. 0882-9136. US. English. an. $14.50. Privacy Journal, PO Box 15300, Washington DC 20003.

THE COMPLEAT LAWYER. Vol. 1, No. 1 (Winter 1984)-. 0741-9066. Periodical. US. English. qt. $12.00 ABA Section of General Practice Members, Included in Dues, $20.00 Non-Members, Continental US, $25.00 Non-Members, Foreign. American Bar Association, 1155 East 60th Street, Chicago IL 60637. **LC** K3. **DD** 349.7305, 347.3005.

COMPLETE BOOK OF TAX DEDUCTIONS. 1985 Ed.-. 0743-2224. US. English. an. Barnes and Noble Books, 10 East 53rd Street, New York NY 10022. **Ed** Robert S Holzman.

LC HJ4653.D4. **DD** 343.73052305 347.30352305. *Take It Off, 0193-3094.*

COMPREHENSIVE INDEX, CALIFORNIA ADMINISTRATIVE CODE. See Indexes/Abstracts.

COMPUTER LAW & PRACTICE : THE JOURNAL OF COMPUTER AND COMMUNICATIONS LAW. VFOAT Computer Law and Practice. Vol. 1, No. 1 (Sept./Oct. 1984)-. 0266-4801. Periodical. UK. English. bm. Frank Cass and Company, 11 Gainsborough Road, London E11 1RS England.

COMPUTER LAW AND TAX REPORT. V. 1- Aug. 1974-. 0361-7203. Periodical. US. English. mo. $81.90. Warren Gorham & Lamont, 210 South Street, Boston MA 02111. **Tel** (800)225-2363 Outside MA. **LC** KF1890.C6. **DD** 343.73070285.

COMPUTER LAW INSTITUTE. Series/Titl Patents, Copyrights, Trademarks, and Literary Property Course Handbook Series. 1983-. US. English. an. Practising Law Institute, 810 Seventh Avenue, New York NY 10019.

THE COMPUTER LAW MONITOR. Vol. 1, No. 1 (Aug. 1983)-. 0741-8809. Periodical. US. English. qt. $79.50. Research Publications Inc, PO Box 9267, Asheville NC 28815. **Tel** (704)298-8291. **Ed** Patricia A Hollander. **LC** KF390.5.C6. **DD** 343.73078004, 347.30478004. **Circ** 250. (ctrl). Briefs of selected significant higher court decisions affecting the field of computer related systems.

COMPUTER LAW (NEW YORK, N.Y. : 1981). (COMPUTER LAW). Series/Titl Commercial Law and Practice Course Handbook Series. 1981-. US. English. an. Practising Law Institute, 810 Seventh Avenue, New York NY 10019.

COMPUTER LAW REPORTER. Vol. 1, No. 1 (July 1982)-. 0739-7771. Periodical. US. English. bm. $575.00. Computer Law Reporter, 1519 Connecticut Avenue NW/Suite 200, Washington DC 20036. **Tel** (202)462-5755. **Ed** Neil J Cohen. bk rev. **Circ** 300. (ctrl). A publication including 150 pages in each issue of articles, decisions and documents in various areas of computer-related law.

COMPUTER LAW STRATEGIST. Vol. 1, No. 1 (May 1984)-. 0747-8933. Periodical. US. English. mo. $125.00. Leader Publications, 111 8th Avenue, Suite 900, New York NY 10011. **Tel** (800)221-8195. **Ed** Julian S Millstein. **LC** KF390.5.C6. **DD** 343.7307800164, 347. 3037800164. Reports on judicial, legislative and regulatory developments in computer law, including copyright, licensing, contracts, computer crime, warranties, and financing.

COMPUTER LAW (TORONTO, ONT.). (COMPUTER LAW). Vol. 1, No. 1 (Jan. 1984)-. 0824-4790. Periodical. CN. English. mo. $495.00. Computer Law, 12th Floor/34 King Street East, Toronto Ontario M5C 1E5 Canada. **DD** 346.7107.

THE COMPUTER LAWYER. Vol. 1, No. 1 (Feb. 1984)-. 0742-1192. Periodical. US. English. mo. $195.00. Law & Business Inc, 855 Valley Road, Clifton NJ 07013. **Tel** (201)472-7400. **Ed** Iles Gilburne, Ronald Johnston, Allen Grogan, and Andrea Hirsch. **LC** KF390.5.C6. **DD** 343.730780016405, 347. 303780016405. bk rev. **Circ** 1,500. The autoritative report by 'hands-on', nationally known computer lawyers with action oriented.

COMPUTER/LAW JOURNAL. VAT Computer Law Journal. V. 1- Spring 1978-. 0164-8756. Periodical. US. English. qt. $72.00 US/Canada/Mexico, $76.00 all other countries. Center for Computer/Law, PO Box 3549, Manhattan Beach CA 90266. **Tel** (213)372-0198. **Ed** Michael D Scott. **Ind/Abst** Electron. Commun. Abstr. J., ISMEC Bull., Pollut. Abstr. Indexes, Saf. Sci. Abstr. J., Manage. Contents, Leg. Resour. Index, Comput. Control Abstr., Electr. Electron. Abstr., Sci. Abstr. Sect. A. Phys. Abstr., Index Leg. Period. **LC** K3. **DD** 340.02854. **CODEN** COLJD3. bk rev. **Circ** 1,000. An international journal on the legal problems of the computer, telecommunications, and information industries.

CONCILIATION COURTS REVIEW. Vol. 1 Mar. 1963-. 0588-9774. Periodical. US. English. sa. Association of Family Conciliation Court, 1217 Shadybrook Drive, Beverly Hills CA 90210. **Tel** (804)253-2000. **Ind/Abst** Public Aff. Inf. Serv. Bull.

CONDENSED CPA TAX REVIEW. See Business - Accounting.

CONDOMINIUM LAW AND PRACTICE, FORMS. US. English. be. Matthew Bender & Company Inc, 1275 Broadway, Albany NY 12201. **Tel** (800)833-9844.

Law

CONFLICTS OF LAW. Main/Corp Bay Area Review Course, Inc. 0099-0418. US. English. an. Bay Area Review Course Inc, 5900 Wilshire Boulevard, Los Angeles CA 90036. LC KF412. DD 342.73042.

CONGRES - ASSOCIATION QUEBECOISE DE PLANTIFICATION FISCALE ET SUCCESSORALE. (CONGRES). Main/Corp Association Quebecoise de Planification Fiscale et Successorale. Congres. 1979-. 0713-7486. CN. French. an. $33.00 Per Vol. Association Quebecoise de Planification Fiscale et Successorale, Bureau X24/1455 Peel, Montreal Quebec H3A 1T5 Canada. DD 343.714053. *Congres, 0713-7478.*

CONGRESSIONAL RECORD. (CONGRESSIONAL RECORD : PROCEEDINGS AND DEBATES OF THE . . . CONGRESS). Main/Corp United States. Congress. 43rd Congress, Special Session of the Senate of the United States (Mar. 4 to 26, 1873)- Vol. 1-. 0883-1947. US. English. US Government Printing Office, Superintendent of Documents, Washington DC 20402. LC KF35. DD 328.7302. NLM KF 35 U58. Vols. for June 16-21, 1980- are distributed to some depository libraries in microfiche. *Congressional Globe.*

CONGRESSIONAL RECORD (DAILY EDITION). (CONGRESSIONAL RECORD; PROCEEDINGS AND DEBATES OF CONGRESS). Main/Corp United States. Congress. 43rd Congress-March 4, 1873-. 0363-7239. Periodical. US. English. da. Superintendent of Documents, US Government Printing Office, Washington DC 20402. Tel (202)783-3238. Ind/Abst Chem. Abstr. LC KF35. DD 328.7302. CODEN CGLRB3. Available on microfilm from University Microfilm Library Service.

CONNECTICUT BAR JOURNAL. VFOAT CBJ. V. 1- Jan. 1927-. 0010-6070. Periodical. US. English. bm. Connecticut Bar Association, 101 Corporate Place, Rocky Hill CT 06067. Tel (203)721-0025. Ind/Abst Leg. Resour. Index, Index Leg. Period., Curr. Law Index. DD 347.05. (cum index).

CONNECTICUT CIRCUIT COURT REPORTS. CASES ARGUED AND DETERMINED IN THE APPELLATE DIVISION OF THE CIRCUIT COURT, AND MEMORANDA FILED IN THE CIRCUIT COURT OF THE STATE OF CONNECTICUT. Began with V. 1, 1961/63. 0589-3577. Periodical. US. English. Circuit Court of the State of Connecticut, Hartford CT 06115.

THE CONNECTICUT FAMILY LAW JOURNAL. Vol. 1, No. 1 (Oct. 1982)-. 0737-920X. Periodical. US. English. bm. $59.95. Butterworth Legal Publishers, 381 Elliot Street, Newton Upper Falls MA 02164. LC KFC3700.A15. DD 346.74601505, 347.46061505.

THE CONNECTICUT INSURANCE LAW REVIEW. 1981-. 0742-924X. US. English. an. R B Yules Esq, Attorney at Law, PO Box 3597, Hartford CT 06103. LC KFC3785. DD 346.7460865, 347.4606865.

CONNECTICUT LAW JOURNAL. VFOAT Connecticut Law Journals . . . Advance Sheets of the Connecticut Supplement. V. 1- Jan. 1935-. 8750-0973. US. English. ir. Commission on Official Legal Publications, 78 Meadow Street, East Hartford CT 06108. Ed J J Sweeney.

CONNECTICUT LAW REVIEW. Vol. 1, No. 1 (June 1968)- issue in June 1968. 0010-6151. Periodical. US. English. qt. $16.00. University of Connecticut, School of Law, 65 Elizabeth Street, Hartford CT 06105-2290. Tel (203)241-4607. Ed Ellen Aho. Ind/Abst Leg. Resour. Index, Index Leg. Period., Curr. Law Index, Contents Curr. Leg. Period. bk rev. adv acc. Circ 1,600. (ctrl). Publishes articles, book reviews and casenotes on current legal topics by scholars, practitioners and students.

THE CONNECTICUT LAW TRIBUNE. Began with Nov. 4, 1975 issue. 0198-0289. Periodical. US. English. wk. $175.00. Connecticut Law Tribune, 106 Ann Street, Hartford CT 06103. Tel (203)525-3436. Ed Theodore B Epstein. LC K3. DD 071.463. (cum index). bk rev. adv acc. Circ 1,800. Publishes significant decisions of Connecticut courts and agencies, summaries of new legislation, and articles on developments affecting the legal profession.

CONNECTICUT LAWYER. Periodical. US. English. ir. Connecticut Bar Association, 101 Corporate Place, Rocky Hill CT 06067. Tel (203)721-0025.

THE CONNECTICUT LEGAL DIRECTORY. *See Yearbooks, Almanacs, Directories.*

CONNECTICUT SCHOOL OF LAW ANNUAL. (CONNECTICUT SCHOOL LAW ANNUAL : CSLA). VFOAT CSLA. 0749-131X. US. English. an. $4.50 Per Copy. J F D'Angelo Editor, Connecticut School Law Annual, CCSU Foundation, 1615 Stanley Street, New Britain CT 06050. LC KFC3990.A15. DD 344.730705, 347.304705.

CONNECTICUT WORKER'S COMPENSATION REVIEW OPINIONS. (CONNECTICUT WORKERS' COMPENSATION REVIEW OPINIONS : OPINIONS OF THE COMPENSATION REVIEW DIVISION OF THE WORKER'S COMPENSATION COMMISSION OF THE STATE OF CONNECTICUT). Main/Corp Connecticut. Workers' Compensation Commission. Compensation Review Division. Vol. 1, No. 1-. 0732-0833. US. English. qt. Butterworth Legal Publishers, 381 Elliot Street, Newton Upper Falls MA 02164. LC KFC3942. DD 344.746021, 347.460421.

CONSEILLER JURIDIQUE CEASED. (LE CONSEILLER JURIDIQUE). Aug. 1974-May/June 1979. 0316-0777. Periodical. CN. French. mo. Free. Etude Legale Service de Police de la Communaute Urbaine de Montreal, Bureau 491/750 rue Bonsecours, Montreal Quebec H2Y 3C7 Canada. DD 340.09714.

CONSTITUTION, JEFFERSON'S MANUAL, AND RULES OF THE HOUSE OF REPRESENTATIVES OF THE UNITED STATES. Main/Corp United States. Congress. House. 0195-5888. US. English. Superintendent of Documents, US Government Printing Office, Washington DC 20402. LC KF4992. DD 328.7305. *Constitution of the United States, Jefferson's Manual, the Rules of the House of Representatives, and a Digest and Manual of the Rules and Practice of the House of Representatives.*

CONSTITUTIONAL AMENDMENTS PROPOSED BY THE LEGISLATURE AND ARGUMENTS FOR AND AGAINST - (NEW MEXICO). Main/Corp New Mexico. Legislative Council Service. US. English. New Mexico Legislative Council Service, 334 State Capitol, Santa Fe NM 87503. LC KFN4001 1911 .A7. DD 342.789035, 347.890235.

CONSTITUTIONAL LAW. Main/Corp Bay Area Review Course, Inc. 0098-7638. US. English. an. Bay Area Review Course Inc, 5900 Wilshire Boulevard, Los Angeles CA 90036. LC KF4550.Z9. DD 342.73.

CONSTITUTIONALLY SPEAKING. CN. English. Nancy Allan, Department of Attorney-General, Room 104/Legislative Building, 450 Broadway, Winnipeg Manitoba R3C 0V8 Canada. LC KEM454.A13. DD 342.7127005, 347.12702005.

CONSTITUTIONS OF THE UNITED STATES, NATIONAL AND STATE. Main/Corp Columbia University. Legislative Drafting Research Fund. 1962-. 0572-8274. US. English.

CONSTRUCTION AND DESIGN LAW DIGEST. July 1984-. 8755-7568. Periodical. US. English. mo. $395.00. Michie Company, PO Box 7587, Charlottesville VA 22906-7587. Tel (804)295-6171. DD 343. Comprehensive legal analysis of 1,500 plus construction and design cases each year in US. Includes expert critical commentary, practice tips and useful advice.

CONSTRUCTION & SURETY LAW DIVISION NEWSLETTER. Main/Corp New York State Bar Association. Construction & Surety Law Division. VFOAT Construction and Surety Newsletter. VAT Construction and Surety Law Division Newsletter. 0148-933X. Periodical. US. English. Free. Publications Department, New State Bar Association, One Elk Street, Albany NY 12207. Tel (518)463-3200. Ed Eugene Goldberg. LC KFN5230.B8. DD 343.747078. Circ 500. (ctrl). Newsletter of section, current related legal issues and cases discussed dealing with construction law.

THE CONSTRUCTION CLAIMS CITATOR. V. 1, No. 1 (Sept./Oct. 1982)-. 0742-0889. US. English. bm. $315.00. Construction Industry Press, 1105F Spring Street, Silver Springs MD 20910. Tel (301)589-4884. Ed Bruce Jeruls. LC KF90L.A53. DD 343.730786902648, 347. 303786902648. Synopsis of court and board of contract appeals decisions involving the construction industry.

CONSTRUCTION CONTRACT MODIFICATIONS; COURSE MANUAL. US. English. an. Federal Publications Inc, 1725 K Street NW, Washington DC 20006. LC KF865. DD 343.73078.

CONSTRUCTION CONTRACTS. Series/Titl Real Estate Law and Practice Course Handbook Series. 0277-9323. US. English. an. $40.00. Practising Law Institute, 810 7th Avenue, New York NY 10019. Tel (212)765-5700. LC KF902.Z9. DD 343.73078624, 347.30378624. Covers rights and liabilities of owners, contractors, subcontractors, and sureties; the practicalities of drafting the construction contract, litigating claims, and avoiding litigation.

CONSTRUCTION INDUSTRY LITIGATION REPORTER. March 13, 1984-. 0743-0299. Periodical. US. English. sm. $700.00. Andrews Publications Inc, PO Box 200, Edgemont PA 19028. DD 346.

CONSTRUCTION LAW LETTER. Vol. 1, No. 1-. 0827-3480. Periodical. CN. English. bm. $38.00. Build/Law Publications, c/o University of Toronto, Department of Architecture, 230 College Street, Toronto Ontario M5S 1A1 Canada. DD 343.7107869005.

CONSTRUCTION LAW REPORTS. (CONSTRUCTION LAW REPORTS : ANNOTATED). V. 1, Pt. 1, (Oct./Nov. 1983)-. 0824-2593. Periodical. CN. English. mo. $65.00. Carwell Company, 2330 Midland Avenue, Agincourt Ontario M1S 1P7 Canada. DD 343.7107869002642.

THE CONSTRUCTION LAWYER. V. 1- Spring 1980-. 0272-0116. Periodical. US. English. Forum Committee on the Construction Industry, Suite 1700/69 West Washington Street, Chicago IL 60602. Ind/Abst Leg. Resour. Index. LC KF1950.A15. DD 343.73078690025, 347. 30378690025.

CONSTRUCTION LITIGATION REPORTER. Vol. 1, No. 6 (Sept. 1980)-. 0279-1102. Periodical. US. English. mo. Litigation Research Group, PO Box 77903, San Francisco CA 94107. Tel (415)543-5433. Ed Marc Schneier. Circ 875. Summaries of judicial and agency decisions in construction law together with articles discussing contemporary litigation topics; subject index. *Architects, Engineers & Contractors Litigation Reporter.*

CONSUMER CREDIT. Series/Titl Commercial Law and Practice Course Handbook Series. 0098-048X. US. English. an. Practising Law Institute, 810 Seventh Avenue, New York NY 10019. LC KF1040.Z9. DD 346.73073.

CONSUMER CREDIT AND TRUTH-IN-LENDING COMPLIANCE REPORT. Began with Nov. 1969 issue. 0300-6034. Periodical. US. English. mo. $100.80. Warren Gorham & Lamont, 210 South Street, Boston MA 02111. Tel (800)225-2363 Outside MA. LC KF1039.A15.

CONSUMER DEBTORS AND THE BANKRUPTCY CODE. (CONSUMER DEBTORS AND THE BANKRUPTCY CODE : ALI-ABA COURSE OF STUDY, MATERIALS). VFOAT ALI-ABA Course of Study, Materials. 0732-863X. US. English. an. ALI-ABA Committee on Continuing Professional Education, 4025 Chestnut Street, Philadelphia PA 19104. LC KF1526. DD 346.73078, 347.30678.

CONSUMER DISPUTE RESOLUTION. VFOAT Consumer Dispute Resolution, Exploring the Alternatives. 0736-2226. US. English. $25.00. American Bar Association, 1800 M Street NW, Washington DC 20036.

CONSUMER FINANCE LAW BULLETIN. V. 4, No. 4- Dec. 1950-. Periodical. US. English. wk. National Consumer Finance Association, 1000 Sixteenth Street Northwest, Washington DC 20036. *Bulletin of the Law Forum.*

CONSUMER FINANCE LAW QUARTERLY REPORT. VFOAT Quarterly Report. Vol. 38, No. 3 (Summer 1984)-. 0883-4555. Periodical. US. English. qt. $15.00. 100 Beneficial Center, Peapack NJ 07977. *Personal Finance Law Quarterly Report, 0362-6342.*

CONSUMER PROTECTION NEWSLETTER. 0191-8567. Periodical. US. English. $25.00. The Committee on the Office of Attorney General, National Association of Attorneys General Foundation, 3901 Barrett Drive, Raleigh NC 27609. LC KF1602. DD 343.7307.

Law

CONTENTS OF CURRENT LEGAL PERIODICALS. See Indexes/Abstracts.

CONTRACT MANAGEMENT. 0190-3063. Periodical. US. English. mo. $20.00. National Contract Management Association, 6728 Old McLean Village Avenue, McLean CA 22101. Tel (703)442-0137. Ind/Abst Manage. Contents. LC KF842. DD 353.0071105. *Newsletter.*

CONTRACTS. Main/Corp Bay Area Review Course, Inc. 0098-762X. US. English. an. Bay Area Review Course Inc, 5900 Wilshire Boulevard, Los Angeles CA 90036. LC KF801.Z9. DD 346.7302.

CONTROLLED WILDLIFE SERIES. US. English. ir. Association of Systematics Collections, University of Kansas, Musuem of Natural History, Lawrence KS 66045. Tel (913)864-4867. Lists state and federal wildlife laws and protected species.

CONVEYANCER AND PROPERTY LAWYER. (THE CONVEYANCER AND PROPERTY LAWYER). N.S. V. 1- Sept. 1936-. 0010-8200. Periodical. UK. English. bm. $44.45. Sweet & Maxwell Ltd, North Way Andover, Hampshire SP10 5BE England. Tel 01-583 9855. Ed Carl Tullo. Ind/Abst Leg. Resour. Index, Index Leg. Period. (cum index). bk rev. adv acc. Circ 3,000. A comprehensive approach to conveyancing and allied topics. *Conveyancer.*

COOLEY LAW REVIEW. Vol. 1, No. 1 (Trinity Term 1982)-. 0733-3501. Periodical. US. English. ty. $20.00. Thomas Cooley Law School, 217 Capital Avenue, PO Box 13038, Lansing MI 48901. Tel (517)371-5140. Ed Amy Bertani. LC K3. DD 349.7305, 347.3005. adv acc. Circ 476. Contains articles on interesting, current legal topics of interest. Features the distinguished Brief Award Competition designed to recognize and promote effective appellate advocacy.

CORNELL LAW FORUM (ITHACA, N.Y. : 1974). (CORNELL LAW FORUM). Vol. 1, No. 1 (Jan. 1974)-. 0010-8839. US. English. Cornell Law School, Myron Taylor Hall, Ithaca NY 14853. Tel (607)256-7590. Ind/Abst Leg. Resour. Index, Curr. Law Index. LC KF292.C6914. DD 340.05. *Cornell Law Forum (Ithaca, N.Y. : 1949).*

CORNELL LAW REVIEW. V. 53- Nov. 1967-. 0010-8847. Periodical. US. English. bm. $22.00. Cornell Law Review, Cornell University, Ithaca NY 14853. Tel (607)256-3387. Ed Benjamin Marcus. Ind/Abst Manage. Contents, Leg. Resour. Index, Hospit. Lit. Index, Account. Index. Suppl., ABC Pol Sci, Soc. Work Res. Abstr., Public Aff. Inf. Serv. Bull., Index Leg. Period., Soc. Sci. Citation Index, Curr. Law Index, Contents Curr. Leg. Period. LC K3. DD 340.05. NLM W1 CO8597. bk rev. Circ 3,500. (ctrl) *Cornell Law Quarterly, 8755-2213.*

CORPORATE AND PERSONAL TAXATION IN THE ARAB WORLD. 0160-4732. US. English. $12.50. Subscription Department, Harvard Square, Box 92, Cambridge MA 02138. DD 343.05209174927.

THE CORPORATE COUNSEL. V. 3, No. 2- March/April 1978-. 0193-4880. Periodical. US. English. bm. $295.00. Executive Press c/o L V Croft, PO Box 3895, San Francisco CA 94119. Tel (415)955-6217. LC KF1397. DD 346.7306605. *Corporate Executive.*

CORPORATE COUNSEL REVIEW. V. 1- Oct. 1978-. Periodical. US. English. qt. State Bar of Texas, Corporate Counsel Section, PO Box 3725, Houston TX 77001. Ind/Abst Leg. Resour. Index. LC K3. DD 346.7306605.

CORPORATE COUNSEL : STATE BAR SECTION REPORT. Main/Corp State Bar of Texas. Corporate Counsel Section. V. 1- Nov. 1975-. Periodical. US. English. State Bar of Texas, PO Box 12487 Capitol Station, Austin TX 78711. LC KFT1413.A15. DD 346.764066.

CORPORATE COUNSEL'S ANNUAL. Began publication in 1966. 0589-784X. US. English. Matthew Bender, 1275 Broadway Albany NY 12201.

CORPORATE LAW AND PRACTICE COURSE HANDBOOK SERIES. Main/Corp Practising Law Institute. No. 1- 1968-. US. English. ir. $550.00. Practising Law Institute, 810 7th Avenue, New York NY 10019. Tel (212)765-5700. Offers the busy practitioner a quick and economical way to keep up with the current trends, developments, and problems in corporate law and practice.

THE CORPORATE LEGAL LETTER. Periodical. UK. English. mo. $99.61. Centre for Legal & Business Information, Rectory Road, Great Waldingfield, Sudbury Suffolk CO10 OTL England. Tel 0787 78607. LC KD2072. DD 346.4106605.

CORPORATE PRACTICE COMMENTATOR. V. 1- May 1959-. 0010-8995. Periodical. US. English. qt. Callaghan & Company, 201 Old Glenview Road, Wilmette IL 60091. Ed F H O'Neal. (cum index).

CORPORATE PRACTICE SERIES. Main/Corp Bureau of National Affairs (Washington, D.C.). No. 1 (1978)-. 0162-5691. Periodical. English. wk. Bureau of National Affairs Inc, 1231 25th Street NW, Washington DC 20037. Tel (301)258-1033. Monographic Series.

CORPORATE PRACTICE SERIES. WASHINGTON MEMORANDUM. VFOAT Washington Memorandum. No. 130 (April 28, 1981)-. 0883-5489. Periodical. US. English. wk. The Bureau of National Affairs Inc, 1231 25th Street Northwest, Washington DC 20037. LC KF1397. DD 343.730705, 347.303705. *BNA's Washington Memorandum, 0162-5683.*

THE CORPORATION JOURNAL. Began with V. 2. 0045-8597. US. English. ir. C T Corporation System, 277 Park Avenue, New York NY 10019. LC KF1397. DD 346.73066, 347.30666. *Corporation Trust Company Journal.*

CORPORATION LAW AND TAX REPORT (1975). (CORPORATION LAW AND TAX REPORT). Began with May 1975 issue. 0147-1619. Periodical. US. English. sm. $88.20. Warren Gorham & Lamont Inc, 210 South Street, Boston MA 02111. Tel (800)225-2363 Outside MA. LC KF1397. DD 346.7306605. *Corporation Counsel's Law and Tax Report.*

THE CORPORATION LAW REVIEW. V. 1- Winter 1978-. 0149-8827. Periodical. US. English. qt. $71.40. Warren Gorham & Lamont Inc, 210 South Street, Boston MA 02111. Tel (800)225-2363 Outside MA. Ind/Abst Manage. Contents, Trade Ind. Index, Leg. Resour. Index, Account. Index. Suppl., ABI/Inform, Index Leg. Period. LC K3. DD 346.7306605.

CORPORATIONS. Main/Corp Bay Area Review Course, Inc. 0099-1236. US. English. an. Bay Area Review Course Inc, 5900 Wilshire Boulevard, Los Angeles CA 90036. LC KF1414.3. DD 346.73066.

THE CORRECTIONS COURT DIGEST. 0360-196X. US. English. mo. $20.00. Juridical Digests International, 1860 Broadway, New York NY 10023. LC KF9728.A59. DD 344.730356.

COUNSELING CLIENTS IN THE ENTERTAINMENT INDUSTRY. 0271-2385. Periodical. US. English. an. Practising Law Institute, 810 Seventh Avenue, New York NY 10019. LC KF390.E57. DD 343.73078791.

COUNTY BAR UPDATE. Vol. 1, No. 1 (Jan. 1981)-. 0279-9626. Periodical. US. English. mo. $1.00 Members with dues, $2.00 Nonmembers. Los Angeles County Bar Association, PO Box 55020, Los Angeles CA 90055. LC KF200. DD 340.06079493.

COURS DE PERFECTIONNEMENT DU NOTARIAT. No. 1- 1975-. 0316-1234. Periodical. CN. French. $10. Chambre des Notaires du Quebec, 630 Ouest Boul Dorchester, Montreal Quebec H3B 1S6 Canada. DD 346.7140024349. *Cours de Perfectionnement.*

COURT. V. 1- Spring 1976-. Periodical. UK. English. qt. 6.00. Court and Judicial Publishing Company, 117 Hatfield Road, St Albans AL1 4JS England. LC KD7302. DD 347.42025.

COURT CASES OF SPECIAL INTEREST TO THE OMBUDSMAN INSTITUTION. July 14, 1980- . -. 0227-6178. CN. English. an. $10.00. International Ombudsman Institute, Faculty of Law University of Alberta, Edmonton Alberta T6G 2H5 Canada. DD 342.06670264.

COURT COMMENTARIES. 0731-7972. Periodical. US. English. qt. Court Commentaries, Supreme Court of Virginia, 11 South 12th Street, Richmond VA 23219. LC KFV2910.A15. DD 347.75501, 347.55071.

COURT CRIER. 0098-8871. US. English. qt. National Association for Court Administration, 1132 Waukegan Road, Glenview IL 60025. LC KF200. DD 347.7313062.

COURT DECISIONS. V. 1- Dec. 1974-. 0701-1482. Periodical. CN. English. Institute of Municipal Assessors of Ontario, 9 Clintwood Gate, Don Mills Ontario M3A 1M3 Canada. DD 343.71304202643.

COURT DECISIONS AND LEGAL OPINIONS. (COURT DECISIONS AND LEGAL OPINIONS, SUMMARIZED FOR WASHINGTON CITIES). 0093-3023. US. English. an. $2.00. Municipal Research and Service Center of Washington, 4719 Brooklyn Avenue NE, Seattle WA 98105. LC JS303.W2, KFW431. DD 342.79709.

COURT DECISIONS - FEDERAL TRADE COMMISSION. (COURT DECISIONS). Main/Corp United States. Federal Trade Commission. Began with V. 10, 1976. 0190-1184. US. English. an. Superintendent of Documents, US Government Printing Office, Washington DC 20402. LC KF1605.A2. DD 343.73080269. *Statutes and Court Decisions, Supplement of Statutes and Court Decisions.*

COURT DECISIONS RELATING TO THE NATIONAL LABOR RELATIONS ACT. See Economics - Labor.

COURT IMPROVEMENT BULLETIN. No. 1 (Spring 1981)-. 0731-3624. Periodical. US. English. American Judicature Society, 200 West Monroe/Suite 606, Chicago IL 60606. LC KF8712. DD 347.73105, 347.307105.

COURT JUDGEMENT REPORT. VFOAT Rapport sur Jugement de Cour. V. 1- March 1978-. 0706-7178. Periodical. CN. English (French). mo. $85. Kolectal-Info Ltd, 95A Botsford Street, Moncton New Brunswick E1C 4X2 Canada. DD 347.715077.

COURT JUDGEMENT REPORT. VFOAT Nova Scotia Court Judgement Report. V. 1- Apr. 1978-. 0705-6672. Periodical. CN. English. ir. $85. Kolectal Information, 95A Botsford Street, Moncton New Brunswick E1C 4X2 Canada. DD 346.716077.

COURT MANAGEMENT JOURNAL. Began with 1978 Vol. 0276-1661. Periodical. US. English. an. $8.25. National Center State Courts, 300 Newport Avenue, Williamsburg VA 23187. Tel (804)253-2000. Ed Steve Otto. Ind/Abst Leg. Resour. Index. LC KF8732.A15. DD 347.7301305, 347.3071305. adv acc. Circ 2,000. (ctrl) CMJ'S aim is to provide organizations of court management a forum for exchanging knowledge and experiences. It features an up-to-date directory of national, court-related organizations.

COURT NEWS. Periodical. US. English. qt. Administrative Office of the State Courts, 250 Benefit Street/Room 705, Providence RI 02903. LC KFR510. DD 347.7450105, 347.4507105.

COURT REVIEW. 1961. 0011-0647. Periodical. US. English. qt. $25.00. American Judges Association, 300 Newport Avenue, Williamsburg VA 23185. Tel (804)253-2000. Ed Edward W Pliska and Amy Rausch. LC K3. DD 340.0973. bk rev. adv acc. Circ 2,000. Issues of current interest to judges, judicial salary tables, book reviews and schedules of judicial education courses. *Municipal Court Review (Denver, Colo.).*

COURT STATISTICS, TASMANIA. See Statistics.

COURTROOM MEDICINE. 0590-0301. Monographic Series. US. English. ir. Matthew Bender & Company Inc, 1275 Broadway, Albany NY 12201. Tel (800)833-9844.

COURTS & CLE BULLETIN. VAT Courts and CLE Bulletin. V. 1- Aug. 1965-. 0544-4993. Periodical. US. English. mo. Missouri Bar Association, 326 Monroe Street, Jefferson MO 65101. LC UNC.

CRACKNELL'S LAW STUDENTS' COMPANION. Began with 1, 1966. 0590-0441. Periodical. UK. English. ir. D & S Publishers, PO Box 5105, Clearwater FL 33518. Tel (800)237-9707.

CRAWFORD COUNTY LEGAL JOURNAL. V. 1- 1960/61-. 0574-3869. US. English. an. Crawford County Bar Association, New Wilmington PA 16142.

CREDIT MANUAL OF COMMERCIAL LAWS FOR . . . . VFOAT War Edition of Credit Manual of Commerical Laws. 0070-1467. US. English. an. $49.50. National Association of Credit Management, 520 Eighth Avenue, New York NY 10018. Tel (212)947-5070. Ed James J Andover. Easy-to-use reference work. Covers all aspects of commerical law. Includes most recent rules and

Law

legislation enacted by congress and state legislatures. *Credit Manual of Commercial Laws with Diary.*

CREIGHTON LAW REVIEW. Vol. 1, No. 1 (Spring 1968)-. 0011-1155. Periodical. US. English. qt. $25.00. Creighton Law Review, 2200 California Street, Omaha NE 68178. **Tel** (402)280-2980. Ed Peter R Bulmer. **Ind/Abst** Leg. Resour. Index, Index Leg. Period., Curr. Law Index, Contents Curr. Leg. Period. **LC** K3. **DD** 340.05. (cum index). bk rev. adv acc. **Circ** 1,100. (ctrl). Publishes articles by students, the bench, and the bar, covering a widespectrum of legal topics.

CRIM. COMMITTAL. **Main/Corp** Botswana. High Court. English. ir. Botswana Government Printer, High Courts PO Box 87, Gaborone Botswana Africa. **DD** 348.68194.

THE CRIMINAL APPEAL REPORTS. **Main/Corp** Great Britain. Court of Appeal. UK. English. 22.00. Sweet & Maxwell, 11 Fetter Lane, London EC4P 4EE England. **LC** KD7865.A2. **DD** 345.41002643. *Criminal Appeal Reports.*

THE CRIMINAL APPEAL REPORTS *CEASED.* **Main/Corp** Great Britain. Court of Criminal Appeal. V. 1-49. UK. English. ir. $123.92. Sweet & Maxwell Ltd, 11 New Fetter Lane, London EC4 4EE England.

THE CRIMINAL APPEAL REPORTS. (SENTENCING). **Main/Corp** Great Britain. Court of Appeal. V. 1- 1979-. 0144-3321. UK. English. ir. $64.36. Sweet & Maxwell Ltd, North Way Andover, Hampshire SP10 5BE England. **Tel** 01-583-9855. Ed Santha Rasaih. bk rev. adv acc. **Circ** 700. A series of law reports devoted solely to matters of sentencing.

CRIMINAL DEFENSE. Began with Dec. 1973 issue. 0093-8610. Periodical. US. English. qt. $5.00. University of Houston/Bates College of Laws, 3801 Cullen, Houston TX 77004. **Ind/Abst** Public Aff. Inf. Serv. Bull. **LC** KF9240. **DD** 345.7301.

CRIMINAL DEFENSE NEWSLETTER. Began with Nov. 1977 issue. 0731-082X. Periodical. US. English. mo. State Appellate Defender, Office Legal Resources Project, Third Floor/North Tower, 1200-6th Avenue, Detroit MI 48226. **LC** KFM4775. **DD** 345.7740504405, 347. 7405504405.

CRIMINAL DIVISION. (CRIMINAL DIVISION : ANNUAL REPORT). **Main/Corp** United States. Dept. of Justice. Criminal Division. 1983-84-. 0747-8542. US. English. an. US Department of Justice Criminal Division, 10th and Constitution NW, Washington DC 20530. **LC** KF9223. **DD** 353.0088.

CRIMINAL JUSTICE. V. 1- Spring 1973-. 0092-2498. US. English. qt. American Bar Association/Criminal Law, 1155 East 60th Street, Chicago IL 60637. **LC** KF9619.A1. **DD** 345.7305.

CRIMINAL JUSTICE JOURNAL. V. 1- Spring 1976-. 0145-4226. US. English. sa. $16.00. Western State University, College of Law, 2121 San Diego Avenue, San Diego CA 92110. **Tel** (619)298-3111. Ed Thomas Burger. **Ind/Abst** Index Leg. Period., Contents Curr. Leg. Period., Leg. Resour. Index, Curr. Law Index. **LC** K3. **DD** 345.730505. bk rev. adv acc. **Circ** 600. Features articles of current interest to those involved in criminal justice. A law review published by the students of Western State University, San Diego.

CRIMINAL JUSTICE LEGISLATIVE BULLETIN. **Main/Corp** University of North Carolina at Chapel Hill. Institute of Government. 0360-0173. US. English. bw. North Carolina Institute of Government, University of North Carolina, Chapel Hill NC 27514. **LC** KFN7962. **DD** 345.75605.

CRIMINAL JUSTICE QUARTERLY. (THE CRIMINAL JUSTICE QUARTERLY). 0092-3907. US. English. qt. Editor Division of Criminal Justice Appellate Section, 7 Glenwood Avenue, East Orange NJ 07017. **Ind/Abst** Public Aff. Inf. Serv. Bull. **LC** K3. **DD** 345.730505.

THE CRIMINAL LAW *CEASED.* 1967-1980. Periodical. US. English. mo.

CRIMINAL LAW. **Main/Corp** Bay Area Review Course, Inc. 0098-8049. US. English. Legal Book Corporation, 316 West 2nd Street, Los Angeles CA 90012. **Tel** (213)626-3494. **LC** KF9219.3. **DD** 345.73.

CRIMINAL LAW. **Main/Corp** New York (State). VFOAT Criminal Law P.L.-C.P.L. US. English. an. Matthew Bender & Company Inc, 1275 Broadway, Albany NY 12201. **Tel** (800)833-9844. **LC** KFN6100.A29. **DD** 345.747, 347.4705.

CRIMINAL LAW BULLETIN. V. 1- Feb. 1965-. 0011-1317. Periodical. US. English. bm. $71.40. Warren Gorham & Lamont Inc, 210 South Street, Boston MA 02111. **Tel** (800)225-2363. **Ind/Abst** Leg. Resour. Index, Public Aff. Inf. Serv. Bull., Index Leg. Period., Curr. Law Index, Contents Curr. Leg. Period. **LC** K3.

CRIMINAL LAW COMMENTATOR. 0093-4674. Periodical. US. English. bm. $15.00. Federal Legal Publications, 95 Morton Street, New York NY 10014.

CRIMINAL LAW DIGEST. (CRIMINAL LAW DIGEST. SUPPLEMENT). 1982-. 0824-7544. CN. English. an. **DD** 345.71002648. *Criminal Law Digest. Cummulative Supplement (Toronto, Ont.), 0712-1407.*

CRIMINAL LAW INDEX. SUPPLEMENT. *See Indexes/Abstracts.*

CRIMINAL LAW JOURNAL. 0011-1325. Periodical. II. English. mo. $60.00. All India Reporter Limited, Medows HS Nagindas/Master Road, Bombay 400 023 India.

CRIMINAL LAW JOURNAL. Vol. 1, No. 1 (Feb. 1977)-. 0314-1160. Periodical. AT. English. bm. Methuen Law Book Company Ltd, 35 Mitchell Street c/o Bennett-EBSCO, North Sydney New South Wales 2060 Australia. **Ind/Abst** APAIS, Aust. Public Aff. Inf. Serv., Index Leg. Period. **LC** K3. **DD** 349.405005.

CRIMINAL LAW LEGISLATIVE NEWSLETTER. **Main/Corp** New York State Bar Association. Criminal Justice Section. 0192-589X. Periodical. US. English. New York State Bar Association, One Elk Street, Albany NY 12207. **LC** KFN6100.A15. **DD** 345.747005.

CRIMINAL LAW MONTHLY (HOUSTON, TEX.). (CRIMINAL LAW MONTHLY). Vol. 1, No. 1 (Mar. 1981)-. 0278-1816. Periodical. US. English. mo. $125.00. c/o Patrick Bishop, PO Box 740504, Houston TX 77274. **Tel** (713)479-4189. Ed Patrick Bishop. **LC** KF9214. **DD** 345.73002648, 347.305002648. bk rev. adv acc. **Circ** 450. Synopses of reported criminal law cases, including US Supreme Court cases, other federal court cases, and state cases. *Nedrud, The Criminal Law, 0272-7625.*

CRIMINAL LAW OUTLINE. 0145-7322. US. English. an. $10.00. National Judicial College, Judicial College Building University of Nevada Reno, Reno NV 89557. **Tel** (702)784-6747. Ed George B Richter. **LC** KF9210.3. **DD** 345.73. **Circ** 6,000. Annotated outline of criminal law and procedure confined to federal constitutional laws; emphasis on 4th, 5th, 6th, and 8th amendments and miscellaneous due process problems.

THE CRIMINAL LAW REPORTER. V. 1- Apr. 19, 1967-. 0011-1341. US. English. $263.00. Bureau of National Affairs, 1231-25th Street NW, Washington DC 20037. **LC** KF9615. **DD** 343.0973.

CRIMINAL LAW REVIEW. (THE CRIMINAL LAW REVIEW). Jan. 1954-. 0011-135X. Periodical. UK. English. mo. 58.23. Associated Book Publishers Limited, North Way Andover, Hampshire SP10 5BE England. **Tel** (01)583-9855. Ed J Belford. **Ind/Abst** Index Leg. Period., Curr. Law Index, Leg. Resour. Index, Soc. Sci. Citation Index. (cum index). bk rev. adv acc. **Circ** 6,000. A wide range of articles by experts in criminal law for everyone involved in the practical problems of the criminal process.

CRIMINAL LAW REVIEW (CLARK BOARDMAN COMPANY). (CRIMINAL LAW REVIEW). 1 (1979)-. 0192-3323. US. English. ir. Clark Boardman Company Ltd, 435 Hudson Street, New York NY 10014. **Ind/Abst** Soc. Sci. Citation Index, Curr. Law Index. **LC** K3. **DD** 345.73005, 347.305005.

CRIMINAL PROCEDURE. **Main/Corp** Bay Area Review Course, Inc. 0099-1228. US. English. Legal Book Corporation, 316 West 2nd Street, Los Angeles CA 90012. **Tel** (213) 626-3494. **LC** KF9619.3. **DD** 345.7305.

CRIMINAL PROCEDURE HANDBOOK. 1984-. 0743-4626. US. English. an. Clark Boardman Company Ltd, 435 Hudson Street, New York NY 10014. **LC** KF9602.5. **DD** 345.7305, 347.3055.

CRIMINAL TRIAL MANUAL, CALIFORNIA. SUPPLEMENT. 0732-0930. US. English. bm. Hanford Publishing Company, 1284 Wheatland Avenue, Lancaster PA 17603.

CRIMINAL TRIAL MANUAL. MARYLAND. 0732-7293. US. English. qt. Hanford Publishing Company, 1284 Wheatland Avenue, Lancaster PA 17603.

CRIMINAL TRIAL MANUAL. TEXAS. 0732-7242. US. English. qt. Hanford Publishing Company, 1284 Wheatland Avenue, Lancaster PA 17603.

CRITICA GIUDIZIARIA. Yearly V. 1- Jan./Feb. 1976-. Periodical. Italian. ir. $10.00. C.C.P.N. 10511400 Intestato A Casa Editrice Patron, Via Badini 12, 40127 Bologna Italy. **LC** K3.

CROWN'S NEWSLETTER. May 1972-. 0319-8510. Periodical. CN. English. mo. Ontario Crown Attorneys' Association/Crown's Newsletter, c/o Kenneth Chasse Crown Attorney's Office, The Court House, Toronto M5G 1V1 Canada. **LC** KE8802. **DD** 345.71005.

CUADERNO DE DERECHO INTERNACIONAL PRIVADO. No. 1-. Monographic Series. UY. Spanish. ir. Fundacion de Cultura Universitaria, 25 de Mayo 537, Montevideo Uruguay. **LC** K13. **DD** 340.9.

CUADERNO DEL INSTITUTO URUGUAYO DE DERECHO PROCESAL. **Main/Corp** Instituto Uruguayo de Derecho Procesal. VFOAT Cuaderno de Derecho Procesal. Spanish. ir. **LC** K9.

CUADERNOS. **Main/Corp** Valencia (City). Universidad. Catedra de Derecho del Trabajo. Yearly V. 1- June 1971-. Spanish. ir. Paseo Al Mar 24, Valencia Spain. **LC** K26.

CUADERNOS AGRARIOS. 1- June 1977-. Periodical. Spanish. ir. Instituto Peruano de Derecho Agrario, Apartado No 11549, Jesus Maria, Lima Peru. **LC** K3.

CUADERNOS DE BIBLIOGRAFIA ESPANOLA. SERIE A : DERECHO. *See Bibliographies.*

CUADERNOS DE FAMILIA. Vol. 1, No. 1 July/Sept. 1981-. Periodical. Spanish. qt. Abeledo-Perrot Sociedad Anonima Editora e Impresora, Lavalle 1280, 1048 Buenos Aires Argentina. **LC** KHA480.A15. **DD** 346.8201505, 348.2061505.

CUADERNOS JURIDICOS. Periodical. Spanish. ir. Facultad de Ciencias Juridicas y Politcas, Universidad Nacional Pedro Herquez Urena, Edificio No 3, Locales 217 y 218, Campus, Autopista Duarte, Santo Domingo Dominican Republic. **LC** K3. **DD** 340.097293.

CUADERNOS JURIDICOS. 1- August 1977-. Periodical. CL. Spanish. ir. Arzobispado de Santiago, Plaza de Arms 44, Casilla 30-D Santiago Chile. **LC** K3. **DD** 340.0983.

CUMBERLAND LAW REVIEW. V. 6- Spring 1975-. 0360-8298. Periodical. US. English. bm. $17.00. Samford University, Box 2268, Lakeshore Drive, Birmingham AL 35209. **Tel** (205)870-2757. Ed W Benjamin Johnson. **Ind/Abst** Leg. Resour. Index, Index Leg. Period., Curr. Law Index, Contents Curr. Leg. Period. **LC** K3. **DD** 340.05. (cum index) bk rev. **Circ** 2,000. A scholarly legal periodical published three times per year which examines new developments in the legal field. *Cumberland-Samford Law Review, 0045-9275.*

THE CUMBERLAND LAWYER. V. 1- 1966-. 0590-3378. Periodical. US. English. ty. Cumberland School of Law, 800 Lakeshore Drive, Birmingham AL 35209.

CUMBERLAND-SAMFORD LAW REVIEW. V. 1-5, No. 3. Periodical. English. ty. **LC** Microfilm(O.

CURRENT AUSTRALIAN AND NEW ZEALAND LEGAL LITERATURE INDEX. *See Indexes/Abstracts.*

CURRENT CENTRAL LEGISLATION. Periodical. English. mo. 70.00. Eastern Book Co, 34 Lalbagh, Lucknow - 226 001 India. **Tel** 43171. **LC** Law. **DD** 348.54022, 345.40822. bk rev. adv acc. **Circ** 4,000. Contains central acts, ordinances, regulations, rules and notifications and also notifications of the Supreme Court of India.

CURRENT INDEX TO COMMONWEALTH LEGAL PERIODICALS. *See Indexes/Abstracts.*

CURRENT INDEX TO LEGAL PERIODICALS. *See Indexes/Abstracts.*

Law

CURRENT LAW CASE CITATOR. UK. English. Sweet & Maxwell, 11 New Fetter Lane, London England. **Tel** (01)583-9855. Ed Kevan Norris. LC KD296. DD 348.42047. Circ 6,000. (ctrl) Indicies of all case law developments since 1947.

CURRENT LAW CITATOR. UK. English. an.

CURRENT LAW INDEX. See Indexes/Abstracts.

CURRENT LAW STATUTE CITATOR. UK. English. Ed J Burke.

CURRENT LAW STATUTE CITATOR AND INDEX. See Indexes/Abstracts.

CURRENT LAW STATUTES ANNOTATED. 1947-. Periodical. UK. English. ir. Sweet and Maxwell, 11 New Fetter Lane, London England.

CURRENT LEGAL BIBLIOGRAPHY. See Bibliographies.

CURRENT LEGAL FORMS. US. English. qt. Matthew Bender & Company Inc, 1275 Broadway, Albany NY 12201. **Tel** (800)833-9844.

CURRENT LEGAL PROBLEMS. VFOAT Legal Problems. 1968-. Monographic Series. UK. English. an.

CURRENT PROBLEMS IN FEDERAL CIVIL PRACTICE. 0748-7592. Periodical. US. English. Practising Law Institute, 810 7th Avenue, New York NY 10019. LC KF8840. DD 347.735, 347.3075.

CURRENT PUBLICATIONS IN LEGAL AND RELATED FIELDS. V. 1- 1953-. 0011-3859. US. English. ir. $115.00. Fred B Rothman & Company, 10368 West Centennial Road, Littletown CO 80127. **Tel** (303)979-5657. A bibliographic source containing a listing of books and materials in law and related fields.

CURRENT TAX INTELLIGENCE. UK. English. an. LC KD5352. DD 343.4104, 344.1034.

CUSTOMS BULLETIN AND DECISIONS. (CUSTOMS BULLETIN AND DECISION : REGULATIONS, RULINGS, DECISIONS, AND NOTICES CONCERNING CUSTOMS AND RELATED MATTERS OF THE UNITED STATES COURT OF CUSTOMS AND PATENT APPEALS AND THE UNITED STATES CUSTOMS COURT). 0162-6442. Periodical. US. English. wk. US Government Printing Office, Superintendent of Documents, Washington DC 20402. **Tel** (202)783-3238. LC KF6687.A2. DD 343.73056. Customs Bulletin, 0011-4146.

CUSTOMS REGULATIONS OF THE UNITED STATES. Main/Corp United States. Customs Service. Periodical. US. English. ir. Superintendent of Documents, Attn SSO, US Government Printing Office, Washington DC 20402. **Tel** (202)783-3238.

CUYAHOGA CRIMINAL DEFENSE LAWYERS ASSOCIATION NEWSLETTER. VFOAT CCDLA Newsletter. Vol. 7, No. 1 (Fall 1984)-. 0882-9853. Periodical. US. English. qt. Cuyahoga Criminal Defense Lawyers Association, Greene & Hennenberg Company LPA, 801 Bond Court Building, Cleveland OH 44114. Cuyahoga County Criminal Courts Bar Association Newsletter.

CYLA QUARTERLY. VAT California Young Lawyers Association Quarterly. Vol. 1, No. 1 (Aug. 1984)-. 8750-944X. Periodical. US. English. qt. CYLA, The State Bar of California, 555 Franklin Street, San Francisco CA 94102.

CZASOPISMO PRAWNO-HISTORYCZNE. VFOAT Annales d'Histoire du Droit. V. 1- 1948-. 0070-2471. Periodical. PL. Polish (French). sa. ARS Polona, Krakowski Przedmiescie 7, Warszawa Poland. Ind/Abst Am. Hist. Life, Hist. Abstr., Part A, Mod. Hist. Abstr., Hist. Abst., Part B, Twent. Century Abstr. Przewodnik Historyczno Prawny.

DAILY BULLETIN - INSTITUTE OF GOVERNMENT, UNIVERSITY OF NORTH CAROLINA AT CHAPEL HILL. Periodical. US. English. da. $35.00. State Legislative Building, PO Box 7294, Raleigh NC 27611. **Tel** (919)733-2484. Ed Robert P Joyce. LC JK4166. DD 328.756005. Circ 2,200. (ctrl) Comprehensive record of activities of North Carolina General Assembly while it is in session; digest explanation of each bill introduced; and current status of all bills.

THE DAILY RECORDER'S SACRAMENTO COUNTY LEGAL DIRECTORY. See Yearbooks, Almanacs, Directories.

THE DAILY REPORT. 0276-5926. Periodical. US. English. ir. The Daily Report, PO Box 637, Bakersfield CA 93302. **Tel** (805)322-3226.

THE DAILY REPORTER. 0360-9510. Periodical. US. English. ir. $96.00. Sioux City Daily Reporter, 706 Pierce Street, Sioux City IA 51101. **Tel** (712)255-8829. Ed Jeffrey S Scotsky. LC K4. DD 340.09777. adv acc. Circ 500. Includes court and commercial news.

THE DAILY WASHINGTON LAW REPORTER. V. 1- Jan. 13, 1874-. US. English. da. $61.20. 1625 Eye Street NW, Washington DC 20006.

DAITO HOGAKU. Main/Corp Daito Bunka Daigaku Hogakkai. VFOAT Journal of Law and Politics. Ed.1974-. Japanese. ir. Daito Bunka Daigaku Hogakkai, 9-1 Takashimadaira 1 Itabashi-ku, Tokyo Japan. LC K4. DD 340.0952.

DALHOUSIE LAW JOURNAL. V. 1- Sept. 1973-. 0317-1663. Periodical. CN. English (French). $4.50. Dalhousie University, Faculty of Law, Halifax Nova Scotia B3H 4J2 Canada. Ind/Abst Leg. Resour. Index, Index Leg. Period. LC K4. DD 340.05.

DALIL AL-KUWAYT AL-YAWM. Main/Corp Markaz Al-Kuwayt Lil-Malumat Wa-al-mikrufilm. Arabic. qt. Wizarat Al-Takhtit Markaz Al-Kuwayt Lil Malumat Wa-Al-Mikrufilm, S B 15 Al-Safah, Al-Kuwayt.

DAMAGES FOR PERSONAL INJURY AND DEATH IN CANADA. SUPPLEMENT. (DAMAGES FOR PERSONAL INJURY AND DEATH IN CANADA, 1958-1972. SUPPLEMENT). 1973-. 0317-9532. Periodical. CN. English. an. Carswell Company, 2330 Midland Avenue, Toronto Ontario Canada. Ed Immanuel Goldsmith. DD 346.710302643.

DAR ES SALAAM UNIVERSITY LAW JOURNAL. Periodical. TZ. English. ir. .27. Faculty of Law, University of Dar Es Salaam, PO Box 35034, Dar Es Salaam Tanzania. LC K4. DD 340.09678. Journal of the Denning Law Society.

DARMA HUKUM. Periodical. Indonesian. mo. LC K4.

DATA AND MATERIALS FOR THE FISCAL YEAR . . . : FINANCE COMMITTEE REPORT UNDER THE CONGRESSIONAL BUDGET ACT. US. English. an. LC KF6221.A55. DD 353.007222. Vols. for (1982-) distributed to some depository libraries in microfiche. Data and Materials for the Finance Committee Report Under the Congressional Budget Act.

DATA JURIDICA. Periodical. NE. Dutch. mo. 182.86. U Kluwer bv, Postbus 23, 7400 GA Deventer Netherlands. **Tel** 05700-91225. Ed H R W Gokkel. LC K4. bk rev. adv acc. Circ 700. Review of legal literature; abstracts of books and magazine articles.

DATALINE (DALLAS, TEX.). (DATALINE). VFOAT Law School Computer Group Dataline. Vol. 1, No. 1-. 8755-2361. Periodical. US. English. qt. $5.00. Law School Computer Group, Southern Methodist University School of Law, Dallas TX 75275. DD 340.

DATENSCHUTZ UND DATENSICHERUNG. Periodical. GW. German. qt. 158,-. Friedr Vieweg Verlag, PTFH 5829/Faulbrunnenstrasse 13, D6200 Wiesbaden 1 West Germany. **Tel** (06121)534-1. Ed Ing K Rihaczer. LC K4. DD 342.430853, 344.302853. bk rev. adv acc. Circ 2,300. Deals with the interpretation of the law, the steps of following the BDGS and the introduction problems attaching there to the brief information, original reports and empirical surveys.

DATENVERARBEITUNG IM RECHT. Vol. 1- June 1972-. 0301-2980. Periodical. French or German with English summaries. qt. Walter de Gruyter Inc, 200 Saw Mill River Road, Hawthorne NY 10532. **Tel** (914)747-0110. Ind/Abst Comput. Control Abstr., Electr. Electron. Abstr., Sci. Abstr. Sect. A. Phys. Abstr., Comput. Rev. LC K4. CODEN DRECDD.

DAUPHIN COUNTY REPORTS. VFOAT Dauphin County Reporter. V. 1- 1898-. US. English. ir. Ed G R Barnett. Each issue contains an index to its own contents - no vol index - loose.

D.C. CIRCUIT HANDBOOK. VFOAT Legal Times of Washington D.C. Circuit Handbook. 0270-0506. US. English. an. $50.00. Law & Business Inc, 757-3rd Avenue, New York NY 10017.

D.C. CODE UPDATER. VFOAT DC Code Updater. 0740-1744. US. English. Wilkes & Artis, 1666 K Street North West/Suite 600, Washington DC 20006. LC KFD1240. DD 348.753028, 347.530828.

THE DE PAUL LAW REVIEW. (DE PAUL LAW REVIEW). VFOAT DePaul Law Review. Vol. 1, No. 1 (Autumn-Winter 1951)-. 0011-7188. US. English. qt. $15.00. De Paul University, College of Law, 25 East Jackson Boulevard, Chicago IL 60604. **Tel** (312)341-8554. Ed Thomas Donnelly. Ind/Abst Leg. Resour. Index, Index Leg. Period., Curr. Law Index, Contents Curr. Leg. Period. LC UNC. (cum index). bk rev. (ctrl). Law review.

DEBTOR & CREDITOR. BENDER PAMPHLET EDITION. (DEBTOR & CREDITOR). Main/Corp New York (State). VAT Debtor and Creditor. 0147-3719. US. English. Matthew Bender and Company, 235 East 45th Street, New York NY 10017. LC KFN5364.A29. DD 346.747077.

THE DECALOGUE JOURNAL. V.1- Sept. 1950-. Periodical. US. English. 180 West Washington Square, Chicago IL 60602.

THE DECALOGUE JOURNAL : A PUBLICATION OF THE DECALOGUE SOCIETY OF LAWYERS. Vol. 1, No. 1 (Sept., 1950)-. 0011-7250. Periodical. US. English. ir. $2.00. Decalogue Society of Lawyers, 180 West Washington Street, Chicago IL 60602. **Tel** (312)263-6493. Ed Elmer Gertz. Ind/Abst Leg. Resour. Index, Curr. Law Index. bk rev. adv acc. Circ 2,000. (ctrl). A journal of interest to the practicing jewish lawyer or law student. Articles of legal interest also for the general legal community.

DECISIONES DE PUERTO RICO. Main/Corp Puerto Rico. Supreme Court. Vol. 1- Sept. 25, 1899-. US. Spanish. ir. Equity Publishing Corporation, Main Street, Orford NH 03777. **Tel** (603)353-4351. Each issue contains an index to its own contents - no vol index - loose.

DECISIONS. Main/Corp United States. Maritime Subsidy Board. VFOAT Reports. V. 1- Aug. 1961-Sept. 1964-. 0565-6893. US. English.

DECISIONS AND ORDERS. See Industrial Health & Safety.

DECISIONS AND ORDERS OF THE NATIONAL LABOR RELATIONS BOARD. See Economics - Labor.

DECISIONS DE LA COMMISSION DES LOYERS CEASED. Main/Corp Quebec (Province). Commission des Loyers. VFOAT Recueil de Jurisprudence. Began 1975-1980. Discontinued with No 1, 1980. 0382-3571. CN. French (English). an. $5.00. Commission de Loyers, Quebec Quebec Canada.

DECISIONS OF THE FEDERAL MARITIME COMMISSION. Main/Corp United States. Federal Maritime Commission. VFOAT Federal Maritime Commission Reports. Began with V. 7, Sept. 1961/Feb. 1964. US. English. Superintendent of Documents, US Government Printing Office, Washington DC 20402. LC KF2606. DD 343.73096402646. Decisions of the Federal Maritime Board, and Maritime Administration, Department of Congress.

DECISIONS OF THE UNITED STATES MERIT SYSTEMS PROTECTION BOARD. Main/Corp United States. Merit Systems Protection Board. Vol. 1 (Jan. 11, 1979-Mar. 19, 1980)-. 0731-4450. US. English. ir. Superintendent of Documents, US Government Printers Office, Washington DC 20402. LC KF5336. DD 342.7306802646, 347. 3026802646. (cum index).

DECISIONS - WORKERS COMPENSATION BOARD (VICTORIA). Main/Corp Victoria, Australia. Workers Compensation Board. V. 1- 1938/45-. English. ir.

DECRETOS LEYES DICTADOS POR LA JUNTA DE GOBIERNO DE LA REPUBLICA DE CHILE. Main/Corp Chile. 1-. Spanish. ir. Editorial Juridica de Chile, Av R Lyon 946 Casilla 4256, Santiago Chile. DD 343.8301.

DECRETOS-LEYES PARA GOBIERNO DE UN PAIS A TRAVES DE UNA JUNTA DE GOBIERNO DE RECONSTRUCCION NACIONAL. Main/Corp Nicaragua. Began in 1979. Spanish. sa. LC KGG35. DD 348.7285023, 347.2850823.

Law

DECRETOS REFERENTES A REFORMAS ADMINISTRATIVAS. Main/Corp Sao Paulo, Brazil (State). BL. Portuguese. ir. Governador do Estado de Sao Paulo, Avenida Casper Libero 464, Sao Paulo Brazil. DD 342.816106.

THE DEFENDER. 0270-3432. Periodical. US. English. mo. The Defender, Room 519/8 East Long Street, Columbus OH 43215. LC KFO578.A15. DD 345.77101.

DEFENDER NEWSLETTER. Vol. 1 Oct. 10, 1963-. 0011-751X. Periodical. US. English. American Bar Center, 750 North Lake Shore Drive, Chicago IL 60611.

DEFENSE LAW JOURNAL. Vol. 1 (1957)-. 0011-7587. US. English. ir. $55.00. Allen Smith & Company Publishers, 1435 North Meridian Street, Indianapolis IN 46202. Tel (317)634-4098. Ed R Patterson. Ind/Abst Leg. Resour. Index, Curr. Law Index. LC K4. DD 346.730323 347.306323. (cum index). Articles on trial preparation and practice, products liability, medical and legal malpractice, workers' compensation, medical evidence, economists' testimony, settlement strategy and other topics of interest to defense lawyers.

DEFERRED GIVING. 8756-1255. US. English. an. Taswise Giving, PO Box 299/13 Arcadia Road, Old Greenwich CT 06870. LC KF6449.A65. DD 343.7305.23, 347.303523.

THE DELAWARE JOURNAL OF CORPORATE LAW. Vol. 1-. Periodical. English. ty. $32.00. Delaware Law School of Widener College, 2001 Washington Street, Wilmington DE 19802. Tel (302)478-3000. Ed Arthur L Dent. Ind/Abst Manage. Contents, Leg. Resour. Index, Index Leg. Period. LC K4. DD 346.75106605. bk rev. adv acc. Circ 900. (ctrl). Law journal with corporate focus; anti-trust, banking, commercial, securities and general corporate law.

THE DELAWARE LAW MONTHLY. V. 1- Dec. 1978-. 0193-4007. Periodical. US. English. mo. $200.00. The Delaware Law Monthly, PO Box 262, Wilmington DE 19899. LC KFD57. DD 348.751046.

DELAWARE LAWYER. (DELAWARE LAWYER : A PUBLICATION OF DELAWARE BAR FOUNDATION). Vol. 1, No. 1 (Spring 1982)-. 0735-6595. Periodical. US. English. ty. $6.00. Delaware Lawyer, 113 West 18th Street, Wilmington DE 19801. Tel (302)658-8045. Ed William E Wiggins. Ind/Abst Leg. Resour. Index. LC KF200. DD 340.060751. bk rev. adv acc. Circ 2,500. Each issue covers a principal topic from varying viewpoints. Themes: environment, professional competence, lawyers in politics, and how the criminal justice system functions for lawyers and laymen.

DELAWARE REPORTER. 220 A.2D/236 A.2D- 1969-. 0091-5564. US. English. West Publishing Company, 1413 K Street NW, St Paul MN 55165. LC KFD47. DD 348.751043. *Delaware Chancery Reports, Delaware Reports.*

DELHI LAW REVIEW. V. 1- 1972-. II. English. ir. 25 Domestic, 5 UK, $10.00 others. University of Delhi, Faculty of Law, Delhi 7 India. Tel 2518483. Ed M P Singh. LC K4. DD 340.0954. bk rev. adv acc. Circ 200. Current legal developments including issues of jurisprudential and philosophical nature in any branch of law.

DELIKT EN DELINKWENT. Began with Nov. 1970 issue. Periodical. Dutch. ir. 51.00. Postbus 1148, Arnhem Netherlands. LC K4. *Tijdschrift voor Strafrecht.*

DELTIO PHOROLOGIKES NOMOTHESIAS. Periodical. GR. Greek, Modern. ir. 6.000. Hodos Akademias 71-73, Athena 106 78 Greece. *Deltion Phorologikes Nomothesias.*

DELTION AUTOKINETISTIKES NOMOTHESIAS KAI NOMOLOGIAS. Greek, Modern. ir. 2000. Datianes, Patision 14 Stoa Phexe, Athenai Greece. Tel 3623206. Ed Maria Dalians. Circ 2,000. Automobile law in Greece and abroad.

DENVER LAW JOURNAL CEASED. V. 43-61. 0011-8834. Periodical. US. English. qt. $15.00 Domestic, $16.00 Foreign. Denver Law Journal Association, 200 West 14th Avenue, Denver CO 80204. Ind/Abst Leg. Resour. Index, Sel. Water Resour. Abstr., Coal Abstr., Public Aff. Inf. Serv. Bull., Energy Res. Abstr., Index Leg. Period. LC K4. DD 340.05. (cum index). *Denver Law Center Journal, 0734-0737.*

DEPRECIATION GUIDE, INCLUDING ADR SYSTEM, SYSTEM FOR PRE-1971 ASSETS. Main/Corp Commerce Clearing House. VAT Depreciation Guide, Including Asset Depreciation Range System, System for Pre-1971 Assets. 0271-2016. US. English. $7.00. Commerce Clearing House Inc, 4025 West Peterson Avenue, Chicago IL 60646. LC KF6386.Z9. DD 343.7305234.

DERECHO. Spanish. ir. Colegio de Abogados de Medellin, Apartado Nacional 3446, Medellin Colombia. LC K4.

DERECHO COMPARADO. No. 1- Dec. 1977-. Periodical. AG. Spanish (summaries in English and French). sa. Asociacion Argentina der Comp, Chacabuco 78, Piso Oficina 9, 1069 Buenos Aires Argentina. LC K4. DD 340.205.

DERECHO DEL TRABAJO. Began publication in 1941. Periodical. AG. Spanish. mo. La Ley SA, Tucuman 1471, 89 Buenos Aires Argentina. Tel 49 5481. (cum index).

DERECHO FINANCIERO. Vol. 1- 2. Half 1975-. CK. Spanish. ir. Calle 35 No.4-89, Apartado Aereo 29677, Bogata Columbia. LC K4. DD 346.8610705.

DERECHO LABORAL. Vol. 1- (No. 1-). Periodical. UY. Spanish. qt. Cerrito 420-ESC, 404 Montevideo Uruguay.

DERECHO PENAL Y CRIMINOLOGIA. V. 1 (No. 1-). Periodical. Spanish. ir. LC K4. DD 345.861005.

DERECHO PESQUERO. No. 1 (Oct. 1981)-. Periodical. MX. Spanish. ir. Academia Internacional de Derecho Pesquero, Dr Jimenez No 336-302, Mexico 06720 DF Mexico. LC K4. DD 343.0769205, 342.3769205.

DERECHO SOCIAL. Yearly V. 1- Sept. 1978-. Periodical. PY. Spanish. ir. 250.- Per Issue. Instituto Paraguayo de Derecho del Trabajo, Casilla de Correo No 853, Asuncion Paraguay. DD 344.89201, 348.92041.

DERECHO Y CIENCIAS SOCIALES (UNIVERSIDAD AUTONOMA DE NUEVO LEON. FACULTAD DE DERECHO Y CIENCIAS SOCIALES). (DERECHO Y CIENCIAS SOCIALES). Periodical. MX. Spanish. bm. Facultad de Derecho Y Ciencias Sociales Ciudad Universitaria, San Nicolas de los Garza, Nuevo Leon, Monterrey Mexico. LC K4. DD 349.7205, 347.20005.

DERECHO Y POLITICA. Began with Jan.-Apr. 1977 Issue. Periodical. Spanish. ir. LC K4. DD 349.729305, 347.293005.

DERECHOS SOCIALES. No. 1- Nov. 1973-. Spanish. ir. Asociacion Peruna de Derechos, Jiron de la Union No 1011, Of. 3, 3er Piso, Lima Peru.

DES LITIGATION REPORTER. VFOAT D.E.S. Litigation Reporter. VAT Diethylstilbestrol Litigation Reporter. June 9, 1981-. 0276-5675. Periodical. US. English. sm. $700.00. Andrews Publishing Inc, PO Box 200, Edgemont PA 19028. Tel (215)353-2565. Ed Leonard E B Andrews. LC KF1297.D7. DD 346.730382, 347.306382. The national journal or record of diethylstilbestrol litigation.

DESIGN LAWS AND TREATIES OF THE WORLD. US. English. ir. Bureau of National Affairs Inc, 1231-25th Street NW, Washington DC 20037. Tel (301)258-1033.

DESKBOOK ENCYCLOPEDIA OF AMERICAN SCHOOL LAW. See Encyclopedias & General Reference Books.

DETAILED DEMAND FOR GRANTS OF LAW DEPARTMENT. Main/Corp Jammu and Kashmir. Law Dept. 0376-8287. II. English. ir. Ranbir Government Press, Jammu and Kashmir/Law Department, Jammu India. DD 354.5460088.

DETENTION REPORTER. Began in 1983. 0742-552X. Periodical. US. English. mo. $30.00. CRS Inc, Box 234, Kents Hill ME 04349. LC KF9730.A15. DD 349.7305, 347.3005.

DETERMINATIONS OF THE NATIONAL MEDIATION BOARD. Main/Corp United States. National Mediation Board. Began with V. 6, July 1, 1976/June 30, 1979. 0270-4196. US. English. an. $8.00. National Mediation Board, 1425 K St NW, Washington DC 20572. Tel (202)523-5335. LC KF3386.A2. DD 344.7301880264. *Determination of Craft or Class of the National Mediation Board.*

DETERMINATIONS OF THE NEW YORK STATE COMMISSION ON JUDICIAL CONDUCT. Main/Corp New York State Commission on Judicial Conduct. Vol. 1 (1978-1979)-. US. English. be. LC KFN5984.5.D57. DD 347.747014, 347.470714.

DETROIT COLLEGE OF LAW ALUMNI NEWS. Periodical. US. English. be. Detroit College of Law, 130 East Elizabeth Street, Detroit MI 48201. Tel (313)965-0150. Ed Thomas E Reynolds. LC KF292.D47. DD 340.071177434. bk rev. adv acc. Circ 6,500. (ctrl). Interpretation and analysis of current legal issues. Trends in education.

DETROIT LAWYER. V. 1- June 1931-. 0011-9652. Periodical. US. English. mo. (cum index).

DEUTSCHE RICHTERZEITUNG. Vol. 28 No. 10 (Oct 1950)-. Periodical. German. mo. $29.90. Carl Heymanns Verlag KG, Gereonstrasse 18-32, 5000 Koln 1 West Germany. Index in last issue of volume - attached.

DEUTSCHES VERWALTUNGSBLATT. (DEUTSCHES VERWALTUNGSBLATT : MIT VERWALTUNGSARCHIV). 0012-1363. Periodical. German. sm. 360.-. Carl Heymanns Verlag KG, Gereonstrasse 18-32, 5000 Koln 1 West Germany. Tel (0221)134022. Ed Werner Hoppe. Ind/Abst Energy Res. Abstr. bk rev. adv acc. Circ 3,650. (ctrl). Decisions and sentences, treaties and statements according to the German administration on law. *Reichsverwaltungsblatt, Deutsche Verwaltung.*

DEVELOPMENTS IN CORPORATE, BANKING AND SECURITIES LAW. (DEVELOPMENTS IN CORPORATE, BANKING, AND SECURITIES LAW). Summer 1972-. 0093-1829. US. English. State Bar of Georgia, Section of Corporate and Banking Law, 84 Peachtree Street, Atlanta GA 30303. LC KFG210.A73. DD 346.758066.

DEVELOPMENTS IN TORTS PRACTICE SOUND RECORDING. US. English. an.

DIARI OFICIAL DE LA GENERALITAT DE CATALUNYA. Main/Corp Catalonia (Spain). SP. Spanish. ir. 3000. Diari Oficial del Generalitat, Palau de la Generalitat, Barcelona Spain. DD 349.46705, 344.67005.

DIARIO DA JUSTICA. Main/Corp Santa Catarina, Brazil. Portuguese. ir. $200. Imprensa Oficial do Estado de Sanat Catarina, Caixa Postal 138, Florianopolis Brazil.

DIARIO DA JUSTICA. Main/Corp Goias (Brazil : State). Consorcio de Empresas de Radio Difusao E Noticias do Estado. Portuguese. da. Consorcio de Empresas de Radiodifusao E Noticias do Estado, Av Presidente Costa E Silva Esq, c/rua d Abel, Jardim Bela Vista, Goiana Goias Brazil. LC KHD7104.3. DD 348.8173043, 348.1730843.

DIARIO DA JUSTICA DO ESTADO DE MATO GROSSO. Portuguese. da. Imprensa Oficial do Estado - IOMAT, Caixa Postal No 80, Cuiaba Mato Grosso Brazil. DD 349.817205, 348.172005.

DIARIO DA REPUBLICA. Main/Corp Portugal. Portuguese. ir. 1600. Portugal, rua de d'Francisco Manuel de Melo 5, Lisbon Portugal. *Diario do Governo.*

DIARIO DA REPUBLICA. Main/Corp Sao Tome and Principe. Portuguese. ir. 330. Impr Nacional, Caixa Postal No 28, Sao Tome E Principe. DD 349.6699305, 346.6993005.

DIARIO DE CENTRO AMERICA. Main/Corp Guatemala. Spanish. ir. 18 Calle 6-72 Zona 1, Guatemala Guatemala. DD 340.097281. *Guatemalteco.*

DIARIO OFICIAL, ESTADO DE SAO PAULO : DIARIO DA JUSTICA. Main/Corp Sao Paulo, Brazil (State). Portuguese. ir. $500. rua da Mooca, 1921 Cep 03103-SP, Sao Paulo Brazil. DD 340.09816.

DIARIO OFICIAL, ESTADO DE SAO PAULO : INEDITORIAIS. Main/Corp Sao Paulo, Brazil (State). Portuguese. ir. $500. rua da Mooca, 1921 Cep 03103-SP, Sao Paulo Brazil. DD 340.09816.

DIARIO OFICIAL, ESTADO DE SAO PAULO. PODER JUDICIARIO. Main/Corp Sao Paulo (Brazil : State). Imprensa Oficial do Estado. BL. Portuguese. ir. $5100. Imprensa Oficial do Estado, rua Maria Antonia 294, Sao Paulo Brazil. DD 348.8161046, 348.1610846. *Diario Oficial, Estado de Sao Paulo. Diario da Justica.*

DIARKES KODIX NAUTERGATIKES & NAUTILAKES NOMOTHESIAS. VFOAT Diarkes Kodix Nautergatikes Kai Nautilakes Nomothesias. Greek, Modern. ir. Tzortz 20-22, Athenai Greece.

Law

DICKINSON LAW REVIEW. V. 1- Jan. 1897-. 0012-2459. Periodical. US. English. qt. $20.00. Dickinson School of Law, 15 South College Street, Carlisle PA 17013. Tel (717)243-4611. **Ind/Abst** Leg. Resour. Index, Index Leg. Period. DD 347.05. (cum index). adv acc. **Circ** 1,500. (ctrl). Publishing legal articles by outside authors and law school students. Forum.

DICTA; A COMPILATION FROM THE VIRGINIA LAW WEEKLY. Main/Corp Virginia Law Weekly. V. 1- 1948/49-. US. English. ir. University of Virginia Law School, WL Brown Hall-North Grounds, Charlottesville VA 22901.

DICTA : HARVARD LAW SCHOOL MAGAZINE. Vol. 1 (Spring 1982)-. Periodical. US. English. Harvard Law School, Mail Room, 1563 Massachusetts Avenue, Cambridge MA 02138.

DICTA; NEWSLETTER FOR ATTORNEYS OF SAN DIEGO COUNTY. 1- 1952-. 0417-4569. Periodical. US. English. mo. $10.00. San Diego County Bar Association, 1434 Fifth Avenue, San Diego CA 92101. Tel (714)231-0781.

DICTIONARY CATALOG OF THE COLUMBIA UNIVERSITY LAW LIBRARY. SUPPLEMENT. See Library and Information Science.

DICTIONNAIRE PERMANENT FISCAL. See Encyclopedias & General Reference Books.

DIE. Main/Corp Germany (Federal Republic, 1949-). GW. German. ir. IDW-Verlag, Postfach 320580, D 4 Dusseldorf West Germany. DD 343.4305402632.

LA DIFESA PENALE. V. 1, No. 1 (April/June 1983)-. Periodical. Italian. ty. 44.000. Edizioni Bucalo, 04100 Latina, Casella Postale 51, C C P 1027404.

DIGEST AND INDEX OF LAWS ENACTED. See Indexes/Abstracts.

DIGEST BUSINESS & LAW JOURNAL. See Business.

DIGEST, HOUSE AND SENATE BILLS AND RESOLUTIONS. Main/Corp South Carolina. General Assembly. US. English. Legislative Information Systems, 112 Blatt Building, 1105 Pendleton Street, Columbia SC 29201. LC KFS1815. DD 348.75701, 347.579081. Digest of Action on Bills and Resolutions.

DIGEST OF ACTS OF THE GENERAL ASSEMBLY OF VIRGINIA. Main/Corp Virginia. General Assembly. Session 1980-. US. English. an. Commonwealth of Virginia, Division of Legislative Automated Systems, PO Box 654, Richmond VA 23205. LC KFV2438. DD 348.755026, 347.550826. Digest of Acts of Assembly.

DIGEST OF BILLS ENACTED BY THE GENERAL ASSEMBLY. Main/Corp Colorado. General Assembly. 0160-1377. US. English. 30 State Capitol Building, Denver CO 80203. LC KFC1807. DD 348.788026.

DIGEST OF CITY LAWS. Main/Corp Municipal Research and Services Center of Washington. **Series Corp** Its Information Bulletin. 0090-175X. US. English. $2.00 Single Issue. Municipal Research and Service Center of Washington, 4719 Brooklyn Avenue NE, Seattle WA 98105. LC JS303.W2, KFW430. DD 352.0797 S, 342.79709.

DIGEST OF COMMISSION POLICIES AND COURT DECISIONS. WATER AND SEWER. Vol. 1, No. 1 (1970-1980)-. US. English. an. James J Konish, PO Box 385, Gainesville FL 32601. LC KFF289.A59. DD 343.7590924, 347.5903924.

DIGEST OF COUNCIL BILLS. Main/Corp Wisconsin. Legislative Council. 0272-832X. US. English. Wisconsin Legislative Council, 147 North State Capitol, Madison WI 53702. LC KFW2415. DD 348.77501, 347.75081. Digest of Legislative Council Bills in the Legislature.

DIGEST OF COURT DECISIONS. Began with Mar. 15, 1973 issue. 0516-9011. Periodical. US. English. qt. American Arbitration Association, 140 West 51st Street, New York NY 10020. LC KF9085.A59. DD 346.73070269, 347.30670269. Arbitration Law, 0518-2611.

DIGEST OF DECISIONS OF THE COURT. Main/Corp Kenya. Court of Appeal. Nov./Dec. 1977-. English. ir. PO Box 30087, Nairobi Kenya. DD 348.6762046, 346.7620846. Digest of Decisions of the Court.

DIGEST OF ENACTMENTS, GENERAL ASSEMBLY. Main/Corp Ohio. Legislative Service Commission. 0160-0915. US. English. Columbus OH 43215. LC KFO15. DD 348.771026.

DIGEST OF GENERAL LAWS ENACTED BY THE REGULAR SESSION AND SPECIAL SESSION OF THE FLORIDA LEGISLATURE. Main/Corp Florida. Legislature. Joint Legislative Management Committee. Statutory Revision Division. 1978-. US. English. an. Statutory Revision Division, Room 726/The Capitol, Tallahassee FL 32304. LC KFF38. DD 348.759026. Digest of General Laws Enacted by the Regular Session of the Florida Legislature, 0364-8249.

DIGEST OF GENERAL LAWS ENACTED BY THE REGULAR SESSION OF THE FLORIDA LEGISLATURE. Main/Corp Florida. Legislature. Joint Legislative Management Committee. Division of Statutory Revision and Indexing. 0364-8249. US. English. Holland Building/Room 25 Tallahassee FL 32304. LC KFF38. DD 348.759026.

DIGEST OF KUWAIT OFFICIAL GAZETTE. Main/Corp Cultural & Publishing Bureau. English. wk. Cultural & Publishing Bureau, PO Box 24582, Kuwait. DD 348.5367024, 345.3670824.

DIGEST OF MOTOR LAWS. See Transportation - Automobiles.

DIGEST OF OFFICIAL OPINIONS - ATTORNEY GENERAL. (DIGEST OF OFFICIAL OPINIONS). Main/Corp Florida. Attorney General. 0092-0843. US. English. Free. Florida Attorney General, The Capitol, Tallahassee FL 32301. Tel (904)488-4374. LC KFF440. DD 348.75905. Circ 1,200. (ctrl). Digest of official opinions of Florida's attorney general.

DIGEST OF OFFICIAL OPINIONS - ATTORNEY GENERAL. (DIGEST OF OFFICIAL OPINIONS). Main/Corp Arkansas. Attorney General's Office. 0364-0817. US. English. Office of the Attorney General, Justice Building, Little Rock AR 72201. LC KFA4040. DD 348.76705.

DIGEST OF OPINIONS OF THE ATTORNEY GENERAL. Main/Corp Oklahoma. Attorney General's Office. V. 1- Jan. 15/ Mar. 15, 1963-. 0012-2777. Periodical. US. English. mo. $5.00. Office of Attorney General, 112 Capitol, Oklahoma City OK 73105. Tel (405)521-3921.

DIGEST OF OPINIONS, THE JUDGE ADVOCATES GENERAL OF THE ARMED FORCES. See Military Science.

DIGEST OF OREGON LAWS. (DIGEST OF OREGON LAWS, WITH TABLES). Main/Corp Oregon. Legislative Assembly. Legislative Counsel Committee. 0095-1161. US. English. be. Oregon Legislative Assembly, Legislative Counsel Committee, S420 State Capital, Salem OR 97310. LC KFO2438. DD 348.795026.

DIGEST OF RICO INVESTIGATIONS. VAT Digest of Racketeer Influenced and Corrupt Organizations Statute Investigations. 0276-0150. US. English. US Department of Justice, Federal Bureau of Investigation, Washington DC 20535. LC KF9375.A59. DD 345.7305, 347.3055.

DIGEST OF SENATE JOURNAL OF THE STATE LEGISLATURE OF WYOMING. Main/Corp Wyoming. Legislature. Senate. Began with vol. for 1975. US. English. be. LC KFW4218. DD 348.747022, 347.470822. Digest of Senate and House Journals of the State Legislature of Wyoming.

THE DIGEST OF STATE LAND SALES REGULATIONS. See Real Estate.

DIGEST OF UNREPORTED DELAWARE DECISIONS. US. English. Delaware Legal Press, 132 Nassau Street, New York NY 10038. LC KFD47.1. DD 348.751046.

DIGEST - PARLIAMENT OF WESTERN AUSTRALIA. (THE PARLIAMENT OF WESTERN AUSTRALIA DIGEST). Main/Corp Western Australia. Parliament. 0312-6862. AT. English. ir. Government Printer, Parliament House Harvest Terra, Perth Western Australia 6000 Australia. DD 348.94101.

DIGEST - UNITED STATES. MERIT SYSTEMS PROTECTION BOARD. (DIGEST). Main/Corp United States. Merit Systems Protection Board. 0737-2671. US. English. $26.00. Superintendent of Documents, US Government Printing Office, Washington DC 20402. Tel (202)783-3238. LC KF5336.A75. DD 342.7306802648, 347. 3026802648. Digest, 0731-3454.

DIRECT INVESTMENT LAW REPORT. Vol. 1, No. 1 (Apr. 1980)-. 0270-4552. Periodical. US. English. mo. $175.00 US and Canada, $195.00 Elsewhere. Transnational Investments Ltd, 1101 Connecticut Avenue NW/Suite 600, Washington DC 20036. LC KF1575.A15. DD 346.730705, 347.306705.

DIRECT RESPONSE MARKETING LAW REPORTS. V. 1, No. 1 (May 15, 1982)-. 0732-9261. Periodical. US. English. sm. $330.00. Direct Response Marketing Law Reports, 1629 K Street NW, Washington DC 20006.

DIRECTORIO DEL ABOGADO. See Yearbooks, Almanacs, Directories.

DIRECTORY - AMERICAN BAR ASSOCIATION. FORUM COMMITTEE ON COMMUNICATIONS LAW. See Yearbooks, Almanacs, Directories.

DIRECTORY - AMERICAN BAR ASSOCIATION. FORUM COMMITTEE ON THE CONSTRUCTION INDUSTRY. See Yearbooks, Almanacs, Directories.

DIRECTORY - AMERICAN BAR ASSOCIATION. FORUM COMMITTEE ON THE ENTERTAINMENT AND SPORTS INDUSTRIES. See Yearbooks, Almanacs, Directories.

DIRECTORY - AMERICAN BAR ASSOCIATION. SECTION OF TORT AND INSURANCE PRACTICE. See Yearbooks, Almanacs, Directories.

DIRECTORY - AMERICAN BAR ASSOCIATION. YOUNG LAWYERS DIVISION. See Yearbooks, Almanacs, Directories.

DIRECTORY - AMERICAN BAR ASSOCIATION. YOUNG LAWYERS DIVISION. See Yearbooks, Almanacs, Directories.

DIRECTORY - CANADIAN ASSOCIATION OF LAW LIBRARIES. See Yearbooks, Almanacs, Directories.

DIRECTORY - FEDERAL COMMUNICATIONS BAR ASSOCIATION. See Yearbooks, Almanacs, Directories.

DIRECTORY - FORUM COMMITTEE ON FRANCHISING. See Yearbooks, Almanacs, Directories.

DIRECTORY - FORUM COMMITTEE ON HEALTH LAW, AMERICAN BAR ASSOCIATION. See Yearbooks, Almanacs, Directories.

DIRECTORY - INTERNATIONAL ASSOCIATION OF LAW LIBRARIES. See Yearbooks, Almanacs, Directories.

DIRECTORY OF BAR ACTIVITIES. See Yearbooks, Almanacs, Directories.

DIRECTORY OF CANADIAN GRADUATE PROGRAMMES IN LAW. See Yearbooks, Almanacs, Directories.

DIRECTORY OF COUNTY OFFICIALS (ANNAPOLIS, MD.). See Yearbooks, Almanacs, Directories.

DIRECTORY OF JUSTICE RELATED SERVICES, CAPITAL REGION DISTRICT. See Yearbooks, Almanacs, Directories.

DIRECTORY OF LAW LIBRARIES. See Yearbooks, Almanacs, Directories.

DIRECTORY OF LEGAL EMPLOYERS (1985). See Yearbooks, Almanacs, Directories.

DIRECTORY OF LIFE INSURANCE LAWYERS. See Yearbooks, Almanacs, Directories.

DIRECTORY OF MEMBERS - AUSTRALASIAN UNIVERSITIES LAW SCHOOLS ASSOCIATION. See Yearbooks, Almanacs, Directories.

Law

DIRECTORY OF MEMBERS - STATE BAR OF ARIZONA. See Yearbooks, Almanacs, Directories.

DIRECTORY OF MEMBERS - THE SOCIETY OF PUBLIC TEACHERS OF LAW. See Yearbooks, Almanacs, Directories.

DIRECTORY OF OFFICERS, COUNCIL AND COMMITTEES. See Yearbooks, Almanacs, Directories.

DIRECTORY OF REGISTERED PATENT ATTORNEYS AND AGENTS. See Yearbooks, Almanacs, Directories.

DIRECTORY OF SAN FRANCISCO ATTORNEYS. See Yearbooks, Almanacs, Directories.

DIRECTORY OF THE KANSAS BAR ASSOCIATION. See Yearbooks, Almanacs, Directories.

DIRECTORY OF THE NEW MEXICO BENCH AND BAR. See Yearbooks, Almanacs, Directories.

DIRECTORY OF THE OFFICERS, BOARD OF MANAGERS, COMMITTEES AND SECTIONS AFFILIATED AND COOPERATING ORGANIZATIONS. See Yearbooks, Almanacs, Directories.

DIRECTORY OF WOMEN ATTORNEYS IN THE UNITED STATES. See Yearbooks, Almanacs, Directories.

DIRECTORY - STATE BAR OF GEORGIA. See Yearbooks, Almanacs, Directories.

DIRECTORY - THE SECTION OF LITIGATION. See Yearbooks, Almanacs, Directories.

DIREITO ADMINISTRATIVO (COIMBRA, PORTUGAL). (DIREITO ADMINISTRATIVO). Yearly V. 1, No. 1, (Jan./Feb. 1980)-. Periodical. Portuguese. ir. Centelha Promocao do Livro, S.A.R.L., Apartado 241, 3003 Coimbra Portugal. DD 342.469060, 344.6902605.

DIREITO & JUSTICA : REVISTA DA FACULDADE DE DIREITO DA PONTIFICIA UNIVERSIDADE CATOLICA DO RIO GRANDE DO SUL. V. 1, No. 1 (1st. Semester 1979)-. Periodical. BL. Portuguese. sa. Faculdade de Direito da Pucrs Cidade Universitaria, Avienda Ipiranga 6681, Predio 9 90.000, Porto Alegre RS Brazil. LC K4. DD 349.8105, 348.1005.

DIREITO E AVESSO : BOLETIM DA NOVA ESCOLA JURIDICA BRASILEIRA. Yearly V. 1, No. 1, (Jan./June 1982)-. Periodical. Portuguese. sa. $1000. Edicoes Nair Ltda, Caixa Postal 13-1957, CEP 70.259 Brasilia DF Brazil. LC K4. DD 340.05.

DIREITO NUCLEAR. Yearly V. 1- July 1979-. Periodical. BL. Portuguese. ir. Associacao Brasileira de Direito Nuclear, rua General Severiano No 90, Rio de Janeiro CEP 22290 Brazil. Ind/Abst Energy Res. Abstr. LC K4. DD 343.092505, 342.392505.

DIREITO TRIBUTARIO. Portuguese. ir. J Bushatsky, rua Riachuelo 195, Sao Paulo Brazil. LC K4.

DIRITTO AEREO. See Aeronautics, Astronautics.

DIRITTO COMUNITARIO E DEGLI SCAMBI INTERNAZIONALI. Periodical. French or Italian. ir. 17.000. Sedit, C.C.P. 3/48819, Milano Italy. Diritto Negli Scambi Internazionali.

IL DIRITTO DEGLI ITALIANI. 1978-. Periodical. IT. Italian. ir. Giuffre, Via Statuto 2, 20121 Milano Italy. DD 349.4505.

DIRITTO DEL LAVORO. (IL DIRITTO DEL LAVORO). V. 1- Jan./Feb. 1927-. 0012-3404. Periodical. IT. Italian. bm. 105.000 Domestic, 200.000 Foreign. Fondazione Diritto del Lavoro, 14 Via Gramsci, 00197 Rome Italy. Tel 360.66.49. Ind/Abst Foreign Lang. Index, PAIS Foreign Lang. Index. bk rev. Circ 1,500. Collective bargaining, regulation of strikes, trade unions, industrial relations, dismissment and all the most important aspects of Italian labor law, through articles and cases.

IL DIRITTO DELLE RADIODIFFUSIONI E DELLE TELECOMUNICAZIONI. Vol. 1- 1969-. Periodical. IT. Italian. ir. Eri Edizioni Rai, Via Arsenale, 10121 Torino Italy. Tel 6-36862216. adv acc. All aspects of law concerning the distribution of radio and telecommunications in Italy and the world.

DIRITTO DELL'IMPRESA. 83/1-. Periodical. Italian. qt. 60.000. Via Chiatamon 7, 80121 Napoli Italy. LC K4. DD 343.08, 342.38.

DIRITTO DI FAMIGLIA E DELLE PERSONE. Began in 1972. IT. Italian. qt. 65.000 Domestic, 100.000 Foreign. Casa Editrice Dr A Giuffre SPA, Via Statuto 2 Periodical Department, 20121 Milano Italy. Tel 02/652341. Ed Vincenzo Lojacono. bk rev. adv acc. Circ 2,600. This journal deals with the most diverse rulings of jurisprudence and doctrine on the many problems arising in family law.

DIRITTO E GIURISPRUDENZA. Periodical. IT. Italian. qt. Casa Editrice Dott Eugenio Jov, Via Mezzocannone 109, 80134 Napoli Italy. Dritto e Giurisprudenza.

DIRITTO E SOCIETA. Yearly V. 1-. Periodical. IT. Italian. qt. G C Sansoni, Via Benedetto Varchi 47, 50121 Firenze Italy. LC K4. DD 340.11505.

IL DIRITTO ECCLESIASTICO E RASSEGNA DI DIRITTO MATRIMONIALE. Vol. 82- Jan./Mar. 1971-. 0012-3455. Periodical. IT. Italian. qt. 60.000 Domestic, 90.000 Foreign. Casa Editrice Dr A Giuffre SPA, Via Statuto 2 Periodical Department, 20121 Milano Italy. Tel 02/652341. Ed Sergio Bianconi. bk rev. adv acc. Circ 700. The magazine publishes studies on relations between the state and the Catholic Church, as well as verdicts on matrimonial questions.

DISCHARGED WORKER. VFOAT D.W. Aug. 1982-. 8755-822X. Periodical. US. English. mo. Quinlan Publishing Company Inc, 131 Beverly Street, Boston MA 02114. DD 344. Unemployment Compensation Law Bulletin.

DISPUTE RESOLUTION. 0271-2709. US. English. qt. Free. ABA Public Service Activities Division, 1800 M Street Northwest, Washington DC 20036. Tel (202)331-2258. Ed Lawrence Freedman. LC KF9084.A15. DD 347.739, 347.3079. bk rev. Circ 7,000. A newsletter which features latest happenings in the dispute resolution field emphasizing legislation, community and court-based programs, school-based programs, seminars and publications. Alternative Update Bulletin.

DISPUTE RESOLUTION PAPERS SERIES. VFOAT Dispute Resolution Papers. Began in 1982. 0741-3793. Monographic Series. US. English. ir. American Bar Association Order Fulfillment, 1155 East 60th Street, Chicago IL 60637. LC UNC.

DISPUTE RESOLUTION PROGRAM DIRECTORY. See Yearbooks, Almanacs, Directories.

DISPUTE RESOLUTION RESOURCE DIRECTORY. See Yearbooks, Almanacs, Directories.

DISTRICT ATTORNEY LEGAL INFORMATION NOTEBOOK : DALINE. VFOAT DALINE. Vol. 1, Issue 1 (Jan. 1984)-. US. English. qt. LC KFC1155.A15. DD 345.79405, 347.94055.

DISTRICT COUNCIL JOURNAL. See Public Administration.

DISTRICT LAWYER. 1976. 0147-7943. Periodical. US. English. bm. $20.00. District of Columbia Bar, 1426 H Street NW/Suite 840, Washington DC 20005. Tel (202)638-1500. Ed Jane Ottenberg. Ind/Abst Leg. Resour. Index. LC KF200. DD 340.09753. adv acc. Circ 42,000. (ctrl). Information of interest to lawyers.

DISTRICT OF COLUMBIA CODE ENCYCLOPEDIA. See Encyclopedias & General Reference Books.

DISTRICT OF COLUMBIA COURT RULES ANNOTATED. VFOAT DC Court Rules Annotated. 1981 Ed-. 0747-6949. US. English. an. Michie Company, Box 7587, Charlottesville VA 22906. LC KFD1729. DD 347.753051, 347.530751.

DIZIONARIO BIBLIOGRAFICO DELLE RIVISTE GIURIDICHE ITALIANE. See Bibliographies.

DJF BLADET. VFOAT D.J.F. Bladet. Jan. 8, 1982-. Periodical. Danish (text in English). bw. 300.00, Free to Members. Danmarks Jurist- OG, Konomforbund Gothersgade 133, 1123 Kbenhavn K Denmark. LC K4.

DJF HANDBOGEN. 1983-. 0108-3627. DK. Danish. ir. Danmarks Jurist- OG, Konomforbund Gothersgade 133, 1123 Kbenhavn K Denmark.

D.O., DIARIO OFICIAL, ESTADO DO RIO DE JANEIRO. PARTE I. Main/Corp Rio de Janeiro (Brazil : State). BL. Portuguese. ir. $338. rua Sao Jose, No 35/222/224, Rio de Janeiro Brazil. Diario Oficial do Estado do Rio de Janeiro. Parte I.

D.O., DIARIO OFICIAL, ESTADO DO RIO DE JANEIRO. PARTE III. Main/ Corp Rio de Janeiro (Brazil : State). BL. Portuguese. ir. $338. rua Sal Jose No 35/222/224, Rio de Janeiro Brazil. Diario Oficial do Estado do Rio de Janeiro. Parte III.

D.O., DIARIO OFICIAL, ESTADO DO RIO DE JANEIRO. PARTE IV. Main/ Corp Rio de Janeiro (Brazil : State). VAT Diario Ofical, Diario Oficial, Estado do Rio de Janeiro. Parte Cuatro. Periodical. Portuguese. ir. $260. Imprensa Oficial do Estado do Rio de Janeiro, rua Marques de Olinda S/N Niteroi, Rio de Janeiro Brazil. DD 340.09815.

D.O., DIARIO OFICIAL, ESTADO DO RIO DE JANEIRO. PARTE V. Main/Corp Rio de Janeiro (Brazil : State). Portuguese. ir. 260.00. Imprensa Oficial do Estado do Rio de Janeiro, rua Marques de Olinda, 29 Centro Niterio, CEP 24.030, Rio de Janeiro Brazil. Tel 722.8955/719.1122. Circ 24,000. (ctrl).

DOCKET. (THE DOCKET : THE NEWSLETTER OF THE NATIONAL INSTITUTE FOR TRIAL ADVOCACY). 0739-3210. Periodical. US. English. qt. Legal Education Center, Suite 104/William Mitchell College of Law/40 North Milton, St Paul MN 55104. LC KF8911.A3. DD 347.7350405, 347.30750405.

DOCKET CALL CEASED. Began in July 1966-V. 18, No. 3 (Fall 1983). 0569-3160. Periodical. US. English. qt. 1155 East 60th Street, Chicago IL 60637. Ind/Abst Leg. Resour. Index. LC UNC. DD 347.73504, 347.307504.

DOCKET REPORT - CENTER FOR CONSTITUTIONAL RIGHTS. Main/Corp Center For Constitutional Rights. 0148-5997. US. English. sa. Center For Constitutional Rights, 835 Broadway, New York NY 10003. Tel (212)674-3303.

THE DOCKET SHEET. V. 1- Dec. 1959-. Periodical. US. English. bm. The Supreme Court of the United States, Washington DC 20543.

DOCTRINA PENAL. Yearly V. 1, No. 1 A 4-. Periodical. AG. Spanish. qt. Talcahuano 494, Buenos Aires Argentina. LC K4. DD 345.005, 342.5005.

DOCTRINA Y LEGISLACION ADUANERA. Periodical. Spanish. ir. $7. Ciudadela 1387 -Esc 2, Montevideo Uruguay. LC K4. DD 343.89505605.

DOCUMENTA. Portuguese. ir. $180.00. Ministero da Educacao E Cultura, Departemento de Documentacao E Divulgacao, Esplanada dos Ministerios Bloco H Terreo, Brasilia Brazil.

DOCUMENTACION: COLECCION NACIONAL DE DISPOSICIONES. Spanish. ir. Amalio M Fernandez Libreria Editorial, 25 De Mayo 477 P Baja OF 11, Montevideo Uruguay.

DOCUMENTACION JURIDICA. No. 1- Jan./March 1974-. Spanish. ir. Secretaria General Technica del Ministerio de Justica, Gabinete de Documentacion Y Publicaciones, Calle de San Bernardo 66-2. B, Madrid Spain. LC K4. Informacion Juridica.

DOCUMENTATION JURIDIQUE ETRANGERE. Volume 1-. Periodical. French. ir. rue Defacqz, 1-1050 Bruxelles Belgium. Textes Legislatifs Etrangers.

DOMANVERKET. Main/Corp Sweden. Domanverket. Swedish. an. Domanverket, Pelle Bergs Backe 3, Falun Sweden.

DOMINION LAW REPORTS. 4TH SERIES. A WEEKLY SERIES OF REPORTS OF CASES FROM ALL THE COURTS OF CANADA. V.1 (1984)-. Periodical. English. ir.

Law

DOMINION LAW REPORTS. ANNOTATION SERVICE. (DOMINION LAW REPORTS. ANNOTATION SERVICE (SECOND AND THIRD SERIES)). 1970-. 0316-652X. Periodical. CN. English. an. Canada Law Book, 80 Cowdray Court, AgIncourt Ontario M1S 1S5 Canada. DD 348.71047.

DOMINION LAW REPORTS. FOURTH EDITION. Vol. 1 (Feb. 12, 1984)-. 0012-5350. CN. English. *Dominion Law Reports. Third Series.*

DOMME FOR OVERTRDELSE AF ARBEJDSMILJLOVGIVNINGEN. Danish. ir.

DONNELLEY SEC HANDBOOK. Main/Corp R.R. Donnelley and Sons Company. Financial Printing Division. VAT Donnelley Securities and Exchange Commission Handbook. Feb. 1974-. 0273-3633. US. English. R R Donnelley & Sons Company, 350 East Twenty-Second Street, Chicago IL 60616. LC KF1433.99. DD 346.730666, 347.306666.

DOSSIER - CANADIAN LAW INFORMATION COUNCIL. (DOSSIER : AN INVENTORY OF CURRENT LEGAL RESEARCH IN CANADA). VFOAT L'Inventaire des Activites de Recherches Juridiques Courantes au Canada. 1984-. 0825-4672. CN. English (includes some text in French). an. 15.00. Canadian Law Information Council, 5th Floor/161 Laurier Avenue West, Ottawa Ontario K1P 5J2 Canada. Tel (613)236-9766. Ed Lorna K Rees-Potter. DD 340.072071. Circ 250. An inventory supplying detailed information on legal research currently underway in Canada.

DRAKE LAW REVIEW. Vol. 1, No. 1 (Nov. 1951)-. 0012-5938. Periodical. US. English. qt. $15.00. Drake University Law School, James H Dinan, Des Moines IA 50311. Tel (515)271-2930. Ed James H Dinan. Ind/Abst Leg. Resour. Index, Sociol. Abstr., Soc. Welf. Soc. Plan./Policy Soc. Dev., Index Leg. Period., Curr. Law Index, Lang. Lang. Behav. Abstr., Contents Curr. Period. adv acc. Circ 1,700.

DRINKING/DRIVING LAW LETTER. VFOAT Drinking, Driving Law Letter. Vol. 1, No. 1 (Jan. 15, 1982)-. 0730-2568. Periodical. US. English. bw. $120.00. Callaghan & Company, 3201 Old Glenview Road, Wilmette IL 60091. Tel (800)323-1336. Ed Donald H Nichols. LC KF2231.A15. DD 345.730247, 347.305247. Circ 2,500. Summarizes literature and court opinions regarding driving while under the influence of intoxicating beverages.

DRIVER LICENSING LAWS ANNOTATED. SUPPLEMENT. Main/Corp United States. National Highway Traffic Safety Administration. VFOAT Driver Licensing Laws Annotated. 1981-. 0740-9788. US. English. an. National Highway Traffic Safety Administration, Washington DC 20590.

DROIT AFRICAIN DU TRAVAIL. FR. French. sm. $279.37. Editions d'Iena, 17 rue Thiers, 78110 le Vesinet France. DD 344.60102648, 346.04102648.

DROIT ET CULTURES : CAHIERS DU CENTRE DE RECHERCHE DE L'U.E.R. DE SCIENCES JURIDIQUES. 0247-9788. Periodical. French. ir. 2 rue de Rouen, 92001 Nanterre France. LC K4. DD 340.2, 342.

DROIT ET PRATIQUE DU COMMERCE INTERNATIONAL. VFOAT International Trade Law and Practice. V. 1- Jan. 1975-. 0335-5047. Periodical. US. English or French with summaries in the other language. qt. Masson Publ USA Inc, 211 East 43rd Street/Room 1306, New York NY 10017. Tel (212)370-1937. Ind/Abst Foreign Lang. Index, Public Aff. Inf. Serv. Bull. LC K4. DD 343.087.

DROIT INTERNATIONAL PRIVE : TRAVAUX DU COMITE FRANCAIS DE DROIT INTERNATIONAL PRIVE. Began with Vol. for 1979-1980. Periodical. FR. French. ir. 55. 15 Quai Anatole-France, 75700 Paris France. LC K7001. DD 340.9.

LE DROIT MARITIME FRANCAIS. 0012-642X. FR. French. mo. Le Droit Maritime Francais, 190 Boulevard Haussmann, Paris 75008 France.

DROIT POLONAIS CONTEMPORAIN. VFOAT Contemporary Polish Law. Vol. 1 1963-. 0070-7325. PL. French (English or Russian). qt. ARS Polona, Krakowskie Przedmiescie 7, 00-068 Warsaw Poland. Ind/Abst Foreign Lang. Index.

DROIT SOCIAL. V. 1- 1938-. 0012-6438. Periodical. FR. French. ir. 532.69 Domestic, 602.00 Foreign. Librairie Sociale Economique, 3 rue Soufflot, 75005 Paris France. Tel 634 1030. Ind/Abst Int. Labour Doc. NLM W1 DR39E.

DRUG LAW REPORT. Vol. 1, No. 1 Jan.-Feb. 1983. 0734-6166. Periodical. US. English. bm. $75.00. Clark Boardman Company Ltd, 435 Hudson Street, New York NY 10014. Tel (800)221-9428. LC KF3890.A15. DD 345.73027705, 347.30527705.

DRUG LAW REPORTER. Vol. 1, No. 1 (Aug. 1981)-. 0278-176X. Periodical. US. English. mo. $275.00 Includes Binder. National College for Criminal Defense, PO Drawer 14007, Houston TX 77021. LC KF3890. DD 345.730277, 347.305277.

DUKE LAW JOURNAL. V. 7- 1957-. 0012-7086. Periodical. US. English. bm. $28.00 Domestic, $30.00 Foreign. Duke University School of Law, Room 006, Durham NC 27708. Tel (919)684-5966. Ed Steven Lynch. Ind/Abst Leg. Resour. Index, Hospit. Lit. Index, Soc. Sci. Citation Index, Index Leg. Period., Curr. Law Index, Contents Curr. Leg. Period. LC K4. (cum index). bk rev. adv acc. Circ 1,400. Administrative and general law reviews, comments and notes. *Duke Bar Journal.*

DUNHILL INSURANCE LAW REPORT. *See* Insurance.

DUNHILL LIABILITY LOSS REPORT. Oct. 1977-. 0706-8964. Periodical. CN. English. mo. $75.00. Dunhill Research & Development Ltd, Drawer 637, Yarmouth Nova Scotia Canada. DD 346.7103202642.

DUNHILL PRODUCTS LAW REPORT. Mar. 1982-. 0820-7291. Periodical. CN. English. mo. Dunhill Products Law Report, Drawer 520, Yarmouth Nova Scotia B5A 4B6 Canada. DD 346.71038. *Dunhill Products Liability Law Report, 0709-891X.*

DUQUESNE LAW REVIEW. V. 7- 1968/69-. 0093-3058. Periodical. US. English. qt. $15.00. Duquesne University, School of Law, 900 Locust Northwest, Pittsburgh PA 15282. Tel (412)434-5020. Ed Louis E Wagner. Ind/Abst Leg. Resour. Index, Energy Inf. Abstr., Environ. Abstr., Writ. Am. Hist., Index Leg. Period., Coal Abstr., Contents Curr. Leg. Period., Curr. Law Index. LC K4. DD 340.05. bk rev. adv acc. Circ 1,500. (ctrl). The review publishes scholarly writings dealing with current legal topics. *Duquesne University Law Review, 0012-7213.*

DVIVEDI'S ANNUAL DIGEST FOR MADHYA PRADESH. 1970-. II. English. ir. Law Journal Publications, Jayendragan J, Gwalior 1 India. Ed Harihat Nivas Dvivedi. DD 347.54010264.

DWELLING CONSTRUCTION UNDER THE UNIFORM BUILDING CODE. *See* Building and Construction.

DZIENNIK URZEDOWY MINISTERSTWA PRACY, PAC I SPRAW SOCJALNYCH. Main/Corp Poland. Ministerstwo Pracy, Pac I Spraw Socjalnych. R. 1- (No. 1-). Polish. ir. 40.00. Ministertwo Pracy, PAC I Spraw Socjalnych, Centrala Korportazu Prasy I Wydawnictw Ruch, Warszawa Poland.

EARTHBOND. V. 4- Feb. 1975-. 0098-9479. Periodical. US. English. mo. Migrant Legal Action Program, 1910 K Street Northwest, Washington DC 20006. LC KF3580.A4. DD 344.7301544. *MLAP Monthly Report.*

EASTERN AFRICA LAW REVIEW. V. 1- Apr. 1968-. 0012-8678. Periodical. English. ty. University of Dar Es Salaam, Faculty of Law, PO Box 35093, Dar Es Salaam Tanzania. LC K5. DD 340.05.

EASTERN LAW REPORTS. Pt. 1 (Aug. 9, 1982)-. II. English. mo. Eastern Law House, 54 Ganesh Chunder Avenue, Calcutta India 700013. DD 348.541042, 345.410842.

THE ECCLESIASTICAL COURT DIGEST. V. 1- Jan. 1963-. 0424-2068. Periodical. US. English. mo $15.00. Juridical Digests Institute, 1860 Broadway, New York NY 10023. LC UNC.

ECHO DE LA COUR. BOTTIN. *See* Yearbooks, Almanacs, Directories.

ECHO DE LA COUR. DISTRICT JUDICIAIRE TERREBONNE. (ECHO DE LA COUR). VFOAT Court House Echo. Began publication in Apr.? 1977. 0218-7771. Periodical. CN. English (text in French). mo. Court Echo Newspaper, Suite 222/1400 Sauve Street West, Montreal Quebec H4N 1C5 Canada. DD 348.714048.

ECOLOGICAL ILLNESS LAW REPORT. VFOAT E.I.L.R. Vol. 1, No. 1 (Nov./Dec. 1982). 8755-9013. Periodical. US. English. bm. $20.00. Ecological Illness Law Report, PO Box 1796, Evanston IL 60204-1796. Tel (312)256-3730. Ed Earon S Davis. DD 363. bk rev. adv acc. Circ 600. News journal on chemically induced illnesses, legal cases and governmental actions affecting those made ill at work, outdoors and/or indoors. For both professionals and laymen. *Ecological Health Law Report.*

ECOLOGY LAW QUARTERLY. Began publication with V. 1, Winter 1971. 0046-1121. Periodical. US. English. qt $25.00. University of California, School of Law, Berkeley CA 94720. Tel 642-0457. Ed Denise Antolini. Ind/Abst Electron. Commun. Abstr. J., ISMEC Bull., Pollut. Abstr. Indexes, Saf. Sci. Abstr. J., Leg. Resour. Index, Life Sci. Collect., Sel. Water Resour. Abstr., Excerpta Med., Coal Abstr., Energy Inf. Abstr., Environ. Abstr., GeoRef, Energy Res. Abstr., Index Leg. Period. LC K5. DD 344.7304605. (cum index). bk rev. adv acc. Circ 2,000. The nation's leading environmental law journal, published by the students of Boalt Hall School of Law, University of California. Publishes articles on a range of environmental law topics.

EDUCADORES; REVISTA LATINOAMERICANA DE EDUCACION. *See* Education (General).

EDUCATION FOR THE HANDICAPPED LAW REPORT. 1976. 0744-4117. US. English. sm. CRR Publishing Co, 421 Kind Street/PO Box 1905, Alexandria VA 22313. Tel (703)684-0510. Ed S James Rosenfeld. Circ 1,000. Current information on special education law and policy— includes judicial decisions interpreting P.L. 94-142, SEP policy letters, DAS bulletins, OCR letters of finding and SEA decisions.

EDUCATION LAW AND THE PUBLIC SCHOOLS. BULLETIN AND UPDATE SUBSCRIPTION SERVICE. VFOAT Bulletin and Update Subscription Service. V. 1, No. 1 (Feb./Mar. 1980)-. 0196-6715. Periodical. US. English. qt. $24.95. Allyn and Bacon Inc, 470 Atlantic Avenue, Boston MA 02210.

EDUCATION LAW BULLETIN. Began with Mar. 1975 issue. 0276-718X. Periodical. US. English. ir. Center for Law & Education Inc, Gutman Library 6 Appin Way, Cambridge MA 02138. Tel (617)495-4666. LC KF4114. DD 344.730702648, 347.304702648.

EDUCATIONAL FREEDOM. 0013-1741. Periodical. US. English. sa. $5.00. Educational Freedom Foundation, 20 Parkland Glendale, St Louis MO 63122. LC KF4124.A15. DD 344.730705, 347.304705.

EDUCATIONAL STATUTES ENACTED IN SOUTH CAROLINA. Main/Corp South Carolina. 1976-. US. English. LC KFS2190.

EDUCATOR'S LEGAL SERVICE BRIEFS. 0148-3048. Periodical. US. English. sm. $96.00. Institute for Learning, 161 Saybrook Industrial Park, Old Saybrook CT 06475. LC KF4108.7. DD 344.7307.

EDUCATOR'S LEGAL SERVICE REPORTS. 0148-4206. Periodical. US. English. sm. Connecticut Institute for Learning, 171 Saybrook Industrial Park, Old Saybrook CT 06475. LC KF4102. DD 344.730705.

L'EGALE. 1976-. 0384-062X. Periodical. CN. English (French). L'Egale, PO Box 6471 Station A, Toronto Ontario M5W 1X3 Canada. DD 346.71013.

L'EGYPTE CONTEMPORAINE. *See* Economics.

EHS LAW BULLETIN SERIES, JAPAN. Main/Corp Japan. Laws, Statutes, etc. JA. English. ir. Eibun Horei Sha, 18-14 Nakano 4 chome, Nakano ku Tokyo Japan.

EINKOMMENSTEUER-RICHTLINIEN, EINKOMMENSTEUERGESETZ, EINKOMMENSTEUER-DURCHFUHRUNGSVERORDNUNG. Main/Corp Germany (West). Bundesministerium der Finanzen. VFOAT Einkommensteuergesetz Mit. German. ir. DD 343.4305202632.

EKPAIDEUTIKE NOMOTHESIA. GR. Greek, Modern. ir. 200.00. N Drikakes, G Staruou 6, Athenai T T 121 Greece.

Law

ELC. Main/Corp Education Law Center. VAT Education Law Center. V. 1- Winter 1975/76-. 0364-118X. Periodical. US. English. qt. Education Law Center, Suite 800/605 Broad Street, Newark NJ 07102. LC KF4102. DD 344.74907105.

ELECTION ADMINISTRATION REPORTS. VFOAT EA Reports. Began with issue for Jan. 7, 1976. 0145-8124. Periodical. US. English. bw. $111.00. Plus Publications Inc, 2626 Pennsylvania Avenue Northwest, Washington DC 20037. LC KF4886.A45. DD 342.7307. *Electionews.*

EMENTARIO DE JURISPRUDENCIA. Main/Corp Espirito Santo (Brazil : State). Tribunal de Justica. Yearly V. 1, No. 1/2 (Jan./Feb. 1980)-. Portuguese. ir. LC KHD6904.2. DD 348.8152043, 348.1520843.

EMENTARIO DE JURISPRUDENCIA DO TRIBUNAL DE JUSTICA DO ESTADO DO RIO DE JANEIRO. Main/Corp Rio de Janeiro (Brazil : State). Tribunal de Justica. Yearly V. 1, (1980)-. BL. Portuguese. an. Editora Liber Juris Ltda, rua da Assembleia 36, 20 Andar, Rio de Janeiro RJ Brazil. DD 348.8153043, 348.1530843.

EMENTARIO DO TRIBUNAL FEDERAL DE RECURSOS. VFOAT Ementario da Jurisprudencia do Tribunal Federal de Recursos. Yearly V. 1, No. 1 (July/79)-. Portuguese. mo. DD 348.81041, 348.10841.

EMENTARO DA LEGISLACAO ESTADUAL. Main/Corp Para, Brazil (State). V. 1- 1947/57-. BL. Portuguese. ir. DSG/DISA Setor de Comunicacoes, rua 13 de Maio N PO S89, Altos 66.00 Belem Brazil. DD 348.811028.

EMORY LAW JOURNAL. Vol. 12- Winter 1974-. 0094-4076. US. English. qt. $8.00. Emory University School of Law, 1722 North Decatur Road, Atlanta GA 30322. Ind/Abst Leg. Resour. Index, ABC Pol Sci, Index Leg. Period. LC K10. DD 340.05. *Journal of Public Law.*

EMORY LAW JOURNAL. V. 23- Winter 1974-. Periodical. US. English. qt. Emory University School of Law/Gambrell Hall, Atlanta GA 30322. Tel (404)329-6830. LC Microfilm O. *Journal of Public Law.*

EMPLOYEE BENEFIT PLANS. See Economics - Labor.

EMPLOYEE BENEFIT PLANS UNDER ERISA. (EMPLOYEE BENEFIT PLANS UNDER ERISA : FEDERAL REGULATIONS). 0882-5580. US. English. an. Prentice-Hall Inc, Englewood Cliffs NJ 07632. LC KF3512.A329. DD 344.7301252, 347.3041252.

EMPLOYEE BENEFITS REPORT. 0884-478X. Periodical. US. English. mo. Warren Gorham & Lamont Inc, 210 South Street, Boston MA 02111. DD 344. *Executive Compensation & Employee Benefits Report, 0273-9046.*

EMPLOYEE EMPLOYER FEDERAL EMPLOYMENT TAX GUIDE. Aug. 1980 Ed.-. 0278-8039. US. English. Agsten Foundation, PO Box 649, Bluefield WV 24701. LC KF6436.A15. DD 343.73052044, 347.30352044.

EMPLOYEE RELATIONS LAW JOURNAL. V. 1- Summer 1975-. 0098-8898. Periodical. US. English. qt. Executive Enterprises Publishing Co, 33 West 60th Street, New York NY 10023. Tel (212)489-2670. Ind/Abst Manage. Contents, Trade Ind. Index, Leg. Resour. Index, Hospit. Lit. Index, ABI/Inform, Bus. Period. Index, Index Leg. Period., Contents Curr. Leg. Period., Soc. Sci. Citation Index, Curr. Law Index. LC K5. DD 344.730105. CODEN ERLJDC.

EMPLOYER'S GUIDE TO LAW SCHOOLS. 1984-. 8755-0695. US. English. an. NALP Administrative Office, Tulane Law School, 6325 Freret Street, New Orleans LA 70118. DD 340. *Employers' Guide to NALP Member ABA-Approved Law Schools.*

EMPLOYMENT-AT-WILL REPORTER. Vol. 1, No. 1 (May 1983)-. 0745-9653. Periodical. US. English. mo. $245.00. New England Legal Publishers, PO Box 48, Boston MA 02101.

EMPLOYMENT DISCRIMINATION DIGEST. V. 1- Dec. 1977-. 0148-107X. Periodical. US. English. qt. $18.00. Employment Discrimination Digest, Management Information Associates, PO Box 887, 641 Longview Street, Montgomery AL 36102. LC KF3464.A15. DD 344.730113305.

EMPLOYMENT LAW REPORT. (THE EMPLOYMENT LAW REPORT). Vol. 1, No. 1 (Oct. 1980)-. 0228-5266. Periodical. CN. English. mo. $297.93. Concord Publishing Ltd, 70 Yorkville Avenue, Toronto Ontario M5R 1B9 Canada. Tel (416)964-2758. DD 344.7101.

EMPLOYMENT LAW UPDATE. 0270-2479. Periodical. US. English. mo. $60.00. C & A Publishing Company, PO Box 971, Tulsa OK 74101. LC KF3302. DD 344.730105.

EMPLOYMENT PRACTICES DECISIONS. See Economics - Labor.

END OF SESSION REPORT : HIGHLIGHTS OF THE ... LEGISLATIVE SESSION. VFOAT Highlights of the ... Legislative Session. 1981-. US. English. an. Illinois House of Representatives, 300 State Capitol Building, Springfield IL 62706. LC KFI1215. DD 348.77301, 347.73081. *At Issue (Springfield, Ill.).*

ENERGY LAW JOURNAL. V. 1-. 0270-9163. Periodical. US. English. sa. Secretary Federal Energy Bar Association, 1666 K Street Northwest, Washington DC 20006. Ind/Abst Leg. Resour. Index, Energy Inf. Abstr., Environ. Abstr., Int. Aerosp. Abstr., Public Aff. Inf. Serv. Bull., Index Leg. Period. LC K5. DD 346.730467905.

ENERGY LEGISLATIVE SERVICE. 0149-5550. Periodical. US. English. sm. McGraw Hill, 1221 Avenue of the Americas, New York NY 10020. Tel (202)624-7500. LC KF2120.A15. DD 343.73092.

ENERGY REGULATION DIGEST. 0190-1516. Periodical. US. English. bw. Capital Energy Letter, Box 1096, Tulsa OK 74101. LC KF2120. DD 346.730467.

THE ENERTAINMENT AND SPORTS LAWYER. (THE ENTERTAINMENT AND SPORTS LAWYER : PUBLICATION OF THE FORUM COMMITTEE ON THE ENTERTAINMENT AND SPORTS INDUSTRIES). Vol. 1, No. 1 (Spring 1982)-. 0732-1880. Periodical. US. English. qt. American Bar Association, Forum Committee on the Entertainment and Sports Industries, 1155 East 60th Street, Chicago IL 60637. LC KF4290.A15. DD 344.73099, 347.30499.

ENTERTAINMENT & SPORTS LAW JOURNAL. VFOAT Entertainment and Sports Law Journal. Vol. 1, No. 1 (Spring 1984)-. Periodical. US. English. Managing Editor, Entertainment, Sports Law Journal, University of Miami School of Law, PO Box 248087, Coral Gables FL 33124.

ENTERTAINMENT LAW & FINANCE. VFOAT Entertainment Law and Finance. Vol. 1, No. 1 (Apr. 1985)-. 0883-2455. Periodical. US. English. mo. $95.00. Leader Publications Inc, 111 Eighth Avenue/ Suite 900, New York NY 10011. Tel (800)221-8195. Ed Stan Soocher. DD 344. Reports on legal and financial developments in entertainment industry, including case decisions, legislation, tax rulings, contract drafting, strategy in litigation and representation. *Entertainment Legal News, 0747-8593.*

ENTERTAINMENT LAW JOURNAL (LOYOLA OF LOS ANGELES SCHOOL OF LAW). (ENTERTAINMENT LAW JOURNAL). VFOAT Loyola of Los Angeles Entertainment Law Journal. Vol. 1 (1981). 0273-4249. US. English. an. $15.00. Loyola of Los Angeles, Attn: D M Carpenter 1441 West Olympic Boulevard, Los Angeles CA 90015. Tel (213)736-1114. Ind/Abst Leg. Resour. Index. LC K5. DD 344.73099, 347.30499.

ENTERTAINMENT LAW REPORTER. V. 1- June 1, 1979-. 0270-3831. Periodical. US. English. mo. $125.00. Entertainment Law Reporter Publishing Company, 2210 Wilshire Boulevard/Suite 311, Santa Monica CA 90403. Tel (213)736-1089. Ed Lionel S Sobel. LC KF4290.A59. DD 344.73099. bk rev. adv acc. Circ 900. Legal developments in motion pictures, television, radio, music, sports, and the arts.

ENTSCHEIDUNGEN DES BUNDESARBEITSGERICHTS. Main/ Corp Germany (Federal Republic, 1949-). Bundesarbeitsgericht. 0433-7050. German. ir. *Entscheidungen.*

ENTSCHEIDUNGEN DES BUNDESGERICHTSHOFES IN ZIVILSACHEN. Main/Corp Germany (West) Bundesgerichtshof. Vol-. German. ir. Carl Heymanns Verlag KG, Gereonstrasse 18-32, 5000 Koln 1 West Germany. Tel (303)979-5657. (cum index). *Entscheidungen des Reichsgerichts in Zivilsachen.*

ENTSCHEIDUNGEN DES BUNDESVERFASSUNGSGERICHTS. Main/Corp Germany (West). Bundesvarfassungsgericht. Vol-. GW. German. ir. JCB Mohr, Paul Siebeck, Postfach 2040, 7400 Tuebingen West Germany. (cum index).

ENTSCHEIDUNGEN DES BUNDESVERWALTUNGSGERICHT. Main/Corp Germany (Federal Republic, 1949-). Bundesverwaltungsgericht. 0013-9106. German. ir. Carl Heymanns Verlag KG, Gereonstrasse 18-32, 5000 Koln 1 West Germany.

ENTSCHEIDUNGEN DES PREUSSISCHEN OBERVERWALTUNGSGERICHTS. Main/Corp Prussia. Oberverwaltungsgericht. German. ir. Carl Heymanns Verlag KG, Gereonstrasse 18-32, 5000 Koln 1 West Germany.

ENTSCHEIDUNGEN DES SCHWEIZERISCHEN BUNDESGERICHTS. AMTLICHE SAMMLUNG. ARRETS DU TRIBUNAL FEDERAL SUISSE. RECUEIL OFFICIEL. Main/Corp Switzerland. Bundesgericht. VFOAT Arrets du Tribunal Federal Suisse. V. 1-. SZ. German. ir. Imprimeries Reunies SA, 33 Avenue de la Gare, 1001 Lausanne Switzerland. (cum index).

ENTSCHEIDUNGEN IN ARBEITSRECHTSSACHEN. Main/Corp Germany (Democratic Republic, 1949-). Oberstes Gericht. German. ir. 13.00. Staatsverlag der Deutschen, Demokratischen Republik, Berlin East Germany. DD 348.431041.

ENVIRONMENTAL AND PLANNING LAW JOURNAL. Vol. 1, No. 1 (Apr. 84). 0813-300X. Periodical. AT. English. ir. The Law Book Company Ltd, 44-50 Waterloo Road, North Ryde New South Wales 2113 Australia. LC K5. DD 344.9404605 349.4044605.

ENVIRONMENTAL LAW AND PRACTICE. Series/Titl Litigation and Administrative Practice Series. Criminal Law and Urban Problems Course Handbook Series. US. English. an. Practising Law Institute, 810- 7th Avenue, New York NY 10019. LC KF3775.Z9. DD 344.73046, 347.30446.

ENVIRONMENTAL LAW HANDBOOK. 0147-7714. US. English. ir. $51.00. Government Institutes Inc, PO Box 1096, Rockville MD 20850. Tel (301)251-9250. LC KF3775. DD 344.73046.

ENVIRONMENTAL LAW NEWSLETTER. 0163-545X. Periodical. US. English. qt. $10.00. Texas State Bar, PO Box 12487 Capitol Station, Austin TX 78711. Tel (713)651-2496. LC KFT154.A15. DD 344.76404605.

ENVIRONMENTAL LAW (NORTHWESTERN SCHOOL OF LAW). (ENVIRONMENTAL LAW). Began publication with Vol. 1 (Spring 1970). 0046-2276. Periodical. US. English. ty. $20.00. Northwestern School of Law, 10015 Southwest Terwilliger Boulevard, Portland OR 97219. Tel (503)244-1181. Ed Bruce Weyhrauch. Ind/Abst Life Sci. Collect., Excerpta Med., Int. Aerosp. Abstr., Index Leg. Period., Energy Inf. Abstr., Environ. Abstr., GeoRef, Leg. Contents, Curr. Law Index, Leg. Resour. Index, Ocean. Abstr. Indexes, Bibliogr. Index Geol., Contents Curr. Leg. Period., Pollut. Abstr. Indexes, Ocean. Abstr. LC K5. DD 344.7304605, 347.3044605. bk rev. adv acc. Circ 1,100. Articles covering hazardous waste pollution, nuclear power, federalism and the environment, public land management, Indian treaties fishing rights.

ENVIRONMENTAL LAW REPORTER. V. 1- 1971-. 0046-2284. US. English. mo. $595.00. Environmental Law Institute, 1616 P Street Northwest/Suite 200, Washington DC 20036. Tel (202)328-5150. Ed Phillip D Reed. Ind/Abst Leg. Resour. Index, Curr. Law Index, Public Aff. Inf. Serv. Bull. Circ 1,300. Reporting service - 5 looseleaf volume - 12 monthly releases - 12 issues of news and analysis - updates issued weekly. Keeps you informed of major judicial, legislative and regulatory developments. Provides quick access to all major federal statutes and regulations.

ENVIRONMENTAL LAW SECTION JOURNAL. 8756-9280. Periodical. US. English. New York State Bar Association, One Elk Street, Albany NY 12207. LC KFN5610.A15. DD 344.74704605, 347.47044605. *Newsletter (New York*

Law

State Bar Association. Environmental Law Section), 0736-7104.

ENVIRONMENTAL LAW SYMPOSIUM. Vol. 1 (1981)-. Periodical. US. English. an. Ed Peter W Schroth. LC K5. DD 344.046, 342.446.

ENVIRONMENTAL LAW (WASHINGTON, D.C.). (ENVIRONMENTAL LAW). Began with Winter 1978. 0748-8769. Periodical. US. English. qt. American Bar Association's Standing Committee on Environmental Law, 1800 M Street NW, Washington DC 20036. LC KF3775.A15. DD 344.7304605, 347.3044605. *Environmental Law Newsletter.*

ENVIRONMENTAL LEGISLATION. Periodical. US. English. wk. University of Pittsburgh, 228 Parran Hall, University of Pittsburgh, Pittsburgh PA 15260.

ENVIRONMENTAL LEGISLATION REPORTER. No. 1- Jan. 9, 1976-. 0362-5400. Periodical. US. English. wk. Virginia Water Resources Center, 225 Norris Hall, Blacksburg VA 24061. LC KFV2754.A15. DD 344.75504605.

ENVIRONMENTAL POLICY AND LAW. V. 1- June 1975-. 0378-777X. Periodical. NE. English. bm. $87.59. Elsevier Science Publishers, PO Box 211, 1000 AE Amsterdam Netherlands. Tel (020)5803911. Ind/Abst Life Sci. Collect., Excerpta Med., Energy Inf. Abstr., Environ. Abstr., GeoRef, Bibliogr. Agric., Energy Res. Abstr., Soc. Sci. Citation Index, Pollut. Abstr. Indexes, Bibliogr. Index Geol. DD 344.04605.

ENVIRONMENTAL PROTECTION : THE LEGAL FRAMEWORK. US. English. ir. $80.00. Shepards McGraw Hill, PO Box 1235, Colorado Springs CO 80901. Tel (800)525-2474. (cum index). Extensive analysis of current law as it affects environmental issues.

ENVIRONMENTAL RIGHTS AND REMEDIES. CUMULATIVE SUPPLEMENT. Began with 1973-1976. US. English. an. Ed Steven G Davison and Bernard S Cohen.

ENVIRONMENTAL UPDATE. 0743-9083. Periodical. US. English. Wolf Block, Schorr and Solis-Cohen/Twelfth Floor Packard Building, Philadelphia PA 19102. LC KFP354.A15. DD 344.74804605, 347.48044605.

ENVIRONS. 0193-6387. Periodical. US. English. Environmental Law Society, King Hall/University of California, Davis CA 95616. LC KFC610.A15. DD 344.794046.

EPHEMERIS HELLENON NOMIKON. VFOAT Greek Lawyers' Journal. Periodical. Greek, Modern. mo. Arsake 6, Athens Greece. LC K5. *Ephemeris Ton Hellinon Nomikon.*

EPITHEORESIS NAUTILIAKOU DIKAIOU. Year 1- (No. 1-). Greek, Modern. ir. 500.00. I N Serges, Zoodochou Peges 3, Athenai T T 142 Greece. LC K5.

EPLB, EMERGENCY PHYSICIAN LEGAL BULLETIN. (EPLB. EMERGENCY PHYSICIAN LEGAL BULLETIN). VFOAT Emergency Physician Legal Bulletin. V. 1- 1975-. 0098-1524. Periodical. US. English. qt. $25.00. Medical Publishers Inc, PO Box 293, Westville NJ 08093. Ed James E George. NLM W1 E51. (ctrl). Covers medical legal aspects of emergency care.

THE EQUAL EMPLOYER. 0146-6488. Periodical. US. English. bw. $156.00. Federal Publications Inc, 1725 K Street Northwest, Washington DC 20006. LC KF3464.A15. DD 344.7301133.

EQUAL EMPLOYMENT COMPLIANCE UPDATE. V. 1- Aug. 1977-. 0160-435X. Periodical. US. English. mo. Callaghan and Company, 165 North Archer Avenue, Mundelein IL 60060. LC KF3464.A15. DD 344.7301133. *Equal Employment Compliance Special Report,* 0160-4368.

EQUAL EMPLOYMENT OPPORTUNITY COMPLIANCE. Series/Titl Corporate Law and Practice Course Handbook. 1972-. 0161-4541. US. English. Practising Law Institute, 810 Seventh Avenue, New York NY 10019. LC KF3464.Z9. DD 344.7301133.

EQUAL EMPLOYMENT OPPORTUNITY IN THE FEDERAL COURTS. *See* Economics - Labor.

EQUIPMENT LEASING. Main/Corp New York (City). Practising Law Institute. US. English. Practising Law Institute, 810 7th Avenue, New York NY 10019. LC KF946.Z9. DD 346.73047.

EQUITABLE DISTRIBUTION JOURNAL. Vol. 1, No. 1 (Jan. 1984)-. 0743-247X. Periodical. US. English. mo. $75.00. National Legal Research Group, 2421 Ivy Road/Box 7187, Charlottesville VA 22906. LC KF532.7.A15. DD 346.73040269, 347.30640269.

ESTADISTICAS JUDICIALES DE ESPANA. *See* Statistics.

ESTATE AND FINANCIAL PLANNING FOR THE CLOSELY HELD CORPORATION. Series/Titl Tax Law and Estate Planning Series. Began with Vol. for 1978. 0732-9296. US. English. an. Practising Law Institute, 810 Seventh Avenue, New York NY 10019. LC KF1466.Z9. DD 346.730668, 347.306668.

ESTATE PLANNERS ALERT. (ESTATE PLANNING & TAXATION COORDINATOR. ESTATE PLANNERS ALERT). VAT Estate Planning and Taxation Coordinator. Estate Planners Alert. 0163-9986. Periodical. US. English. mo. Research Institute of America, 589-5th Avenue, New York NY 10017.

ESTATE PLANNING. V. 1- Autumn 1973-. 0094-1794. Periodical. US. English. bm. $30.00. Warren Gorham & Lamont, 210 South Street, Boston MA 02111. Ind/Abst ABI/Inform, Account. Index. Suppl. LC KF750.A1. DD 346.7305205.

ESTATE PLANNING. Main/Corp Institute for Business Planning, Inc. 0014-1216. US. English. bm. $72.00. Warren Gorham & Lamont, 210 South Street, Boston MA 02111. Ind/Abst Curr. Law Index, Leg. Resour. Index, Contents Curr. Leg. Period.

ESTATE PLANNING & CALIFORNIA PROBATE REPORTER. VFOAT CEB Estate Planning & California Probate Reporter. VAT Estate Planning and California Probate Reporter. V. 1- Oct. 1980-. 0273-7027. Periodical. US. English. bm. $96.00. California Continuing Education Bar, 2300 Shattuck Drive, Berkeley CA 94704. Tel (415)642-5340. Ed Edward Halbach. Features practice-oriented articles in each issue, digests of the latest developments (including legislation and court cases), extensive editorial comments analyzing the significance of developments, and more.

ESTATE PLANNING CHECKLISTS-FORMS. 0014-1224. Periodical. US. English. qt. Institute for Business Planning Inc, IBP Plaza, Englewood Cliffs NJ 07632.

ESTATE PLANNING (LOS ANGELES, CALIF.). (ESTATE PLANNING). 0278-4009. US. English. an. California Continuing Education of the Bar, 2300 Shattuck Avenue, Berkeley CA 94704. LC KF750.A2. DD 343.73053, 347.30353.

ESTATE PLANNING REVIEW. V. 1-6, Sept. 1974-Dec. 1980. 0098-2873. Periodical. US. English. mo. $48.00. Commerce Clearing House, 4025 West Peterson Avenue, Chicago IL 60646. Tel (312)583-8500. Ed Sidney Kess and Bertil Westlin. LC KF746.A3. DD 346.73052. Covers new estate planning developments and cases. Real-life facts and figures show how to keep estate taxes at 'legal vows'.

ESTATE TAX TECHNIQUES. US. English. an. Matthew Bender and Company Inc, 1275 Broadway, Albany NY 12201. Tel (800)833-9844.

ESTATES AND TRUSTS QUARTERLY. V. 1- Sept. 1973-. 0381-8888. Periodical. CN. English. qt. $62.00 Domestic, $65.00 Foreign. Canada Law Book Ltd, 240 Edwards Street, Aurora Ontario L4G 359 Canada. Tel (416)773-6300. Ed Robert C Dick. DD 346.71052. bk rev. adv acc. Articles on new insights and innovative approaches to estate and trust planning and administration. Also solutions to problems unique to the drafting of wills and trusts.

ESTATES & TRUSTS REPORTS. V. 1- 1977-. 0706-5655. Periodical. CN. English. mo. $35/Bound Vol., including monthly parts. 2330 Midland Avenue, Agincourt Ontario M1S 1P7 Canada. DD 346.'71'0502642.

ESTIMATES. PART III, ADMINISTRATION OF FEDERAL JUDICIAL AFFAIRS (CANADA). VFOAT Budget des Depenses. CN. English (French). $3.00 Domestic, $3.60 Foreign. Canadian Government Publishing Centre, Supply and Services Canada, Ottawa Ontario K1A 0S9 Canada. LC KF8226.A72. DD 354.710088.

ESTIMATES. PART III, CANADA LABOUR RELATIONS BOARD. VFOAT Budget des Depenses. CN. English (French). $3.00 Domestic, $3.60 Foreign. Canadian Government Publishing Centre, Supply and Services Canada, Ottawa Ontario K1A 0S9 Canada. LC KE3153.A72. DD 354.710083.

ESTIMATES. PART III, DEPARTMENT OF JUSTICE CANADA, CANADIAN UNITY INFORMATION OFFICE PROGRAM. VFOAT Budget des Depenses. CN. English (French). $3.00 Domestic, $3.60 Foreign. Canadian Government Publishing Centre, Supply and Services Canada, Ottawa Ontario K1A 0S9 Canada. LC KE4752.A72. DD 354.710088.

ESTIMATES. PART III, FEDERAL COURT OF CANADA. VFOAT Budget des Depenses. CN. English (French). $3.00 Domestic, $3.60 Foreign. Canadian Government Publishing Centre, Supply and Services Canada, Ottawa Ontario K1A 0S9 Canada. LC KE8265.A72. DD 347.71010681, 347.10710681.

ESTIMATES. PART III, LAW REFORM COMMISSION OF CANADA. VFOAT Budget des Depenses. CN. English (French). $3.00 Domestic, $3.60 Foreign. Canadian Government Publishing Centre, Supply and Services Canada, Ottawa Ontario K1A 0S9 Canada. LC KE430.A72. DD 354.710088.

ESTIMATES. PART III, RESTRICTIVE TRADE PRACTICES COMMISSION OF CANADA. VFOAT Budget des Depenses. CN. English (French). $3.00 Domestic, $3.60 Foreign. Canadian Government Publishing Centre, Supply and Services Canada, Ottawa Ontario K1A 0S9 Canada. LC KE1639.A2. DD 354.710082.

ESTIMATES. PART III, SOLICITOR GENERAL CANADA. VFOAT Budget des Depenses. CN. English (French). $6.00 Domestic, $7.20 Foreign. Canadian Government Publishing Centre, Supply and Services Canada, Ottawa Ontario K1A 0S9 Canada. LC KE8813.A72. DD 354.710088. *Estimates. Part III, Solicitor General Secretariat.*

ESTIMATES. PART III, SUPREME COURT OF CANADA. VFOAT Budget des Depenses. CN. English (French). $3.00 Domestic, $3.60 Foreign. Canadian Government Publishing Centre, Supply and Services Canada, Ottawa Ontario K1A 0S9 Canada. LC KE8244.A72. DD 347.710350681, 347.107350681.

ESTIMATES. PART III, TARIFF BOARD. VFOAT Budget des Depenses. CN. English (French). $3.00 Domestic, $3.60 Foreign. Canadian Government Publishing Centre, Supply and Services Canada, Ottawa Ontario K1A 0S9 Canada. LC KE6096.A72. DD 354.007246.

ESTUDIOS DE DERECHO. V. 1- 1952?-. 0014-1461. Periodical. CK. Spanish. sa. $26.00. Universidad de Antioquia, Apartado Aereo 1226, Medellin Columbia. Ind/Abst Foreign Lang. Index.

ESTUDOS DE DIREITO PUBLICO : EDP. VFOAT EDP. Yearly V. 1, No. 1, Jan./June 1982)-. Periodical. Portuguese. ir. Associacao dos Advogados da Prefeitura do Municipio de, Sao Paulo rua Maria Paula 96-6 O Andar, CEP 01319 Sao Paulo SP Brazil. LC K5. DD 342.0905, 342.2905.

ESTUDOS LEGISLATIVOS. *See* Public Administration.

ETHICS IN GOVERNMENT REPORTER. 1980-. 0279-2869. US. English. mo. $175.00. Washington Service Bureau Inc, 655-15th Street NW, Washington DC 20005. Tel (202)833-9200. Ed Linda Peterson. Circ 200. (ctrl). Full text of ethics in government act of 1978 executive order 11,222 regulations advisory opinions case ruling and selected bar association rules.

ETUDES DE LOGIQUE JURIDIQUE. Periodical. French, English, or German. ir. E Bruylant, rue de la Regence 67, Bruxelles Belgium. Ed CH Perelman.

EUROPARECHT. Periodical. GW. German. qt. $53.00. Nomos Verlagsgesellschaft, Postfach 610, Waldseer Strasse 3-5, D-757 Baden-Baden West Germany. Tel 0 72 21/34 41.

EUROPE. BASIC OIL LAWS AND CONCESSION CONTRACTS. ORIGINAL TEXTS. SUPPLEMENT. (EUROPE : BASIC OIL LAWS AND CONCESSION CONTRACTS. ORIGINAL TEXTS. SUPPLEMENT).

Law

Main/Corp Petroleum Legislation, New York. 0093-5018. US. English. qt. $4,500.00. Barrows Company Inc, 116 East 66th Street, New York NY 10121. **DD** 343.73077.

EUROPEAN COMMERCIAL CASES. V. 1- Apr. 1978-. Periodical. UK. English. an. European Law Centre, Elm House 10-16 Elm Street, London WC1X 0BP England. **DD** 341.754.

EUROPEAN LAW DIGEST. V. 1- Jan. 1973-. 0305-8476. UK. English. mo. $214.54. European Law Centre Ltd, 4 Bloomsbury Square, London WCIA 2RL England. **Tel** 01-404 4300. Ed Irene D Snook. **DD** 348.4026. adv acc. Finding guide to legal developments in Europe in case law and legislation with emphasis on economic law, human rights law, private and public international law.

EUROPEAN LAW NEWSLETTER. Periodical. UK. English. mo. $130.00. The Financial Times, Circulation Department Bracken House/10 Cannon Street, EC4P 4BY London England. **LC** K5. **DD** 340.05.

EUROPEAN LAW REVIEW. V. 1- Nov. 1975-. 0307-5400. Periodical. UK. English. bm. $114.93. Sweet & Maxwell Ltd, North Way, Andover Hants SP105BE England. **Ind/Abst** Leg. Resour. Index, Index Leg. Period., Curr. Law Index. **LC** K5. **DD** 341.242.

EUROPEAN TRANSPORT LAW. VFOAT Droit Europeen des Transports, Europaisches Transportrecht, Diritto Europeo dei Trasporti, Europees Vervoerrecht. Vol. 1, No 1-. Periodical. BE. English. bm. 5.200.-. European Transport Law, Maria Henriettalei 1, 2018 Antwerpen Belgium. **Tel** 032313655. Ed Robert Wyffels. bk rev. **Circ** 2,500. Publishes regular series of articles, comments, and principal judgements of all countries about judicial international transportation matters in six languages.

EUSKAL HERRIKO AGINTARITZAREN ALDIZKARIA. **Main/Corp** Pais Vasco (Spain). VFOAT Boletin Oficial del Pais Vasco. Basque (Spanish). ir. Duque de Wellington 2, Vitoria-Gasteiz Spain.

EVIDENCE. **Main/Corp** Bay Area Review Course, Inc. US. English. ir. Legal Book Corporation, 316 West 2nd Street, Los Angeles CA 90012. **Tel** (213)626-3494. **LC** KF8935.Z9. **DD** 347.736.

EVIDENTIA. 0161-3138. Periodical. US. English. qt. $10.00. Criterion Inc, 13140 Coit Road/Suite 318, Dallas TX 75240. **LC** KF1600.A15. **DD** 340.0973.

EXAMENS - FORMATION PROFESSIONNELLE DU BARREAU DU QUEBEC. (EXAMENS). **Main/Corp** Barreau du Quebec. Formation Professionelle. 1975/1979-. 0828-6272. CN. French. an. Editions y Blais, CP 180, Cowansville Quebec J2K 3H6 Canada. **DD** 349.714076.

EXAMINING COURT DECISIONS AND OPINIONS OF THE ATTORNEY GENERAL CONSTRUING ALASKA STATUTES. 1980-81-. US. English. an. Legislative Affairs Agency, Pouch Y State Capitol, Juneau AK 99801. **LC** KFA1607. **DD** 347.798014, 347.980714. Report of Examination of Court Decisions Construing Alaska Statutes Rendered by the Supreme Court of Alaska.

EXCISE NEWS. VFOAT Nouvelles de l'Accise. No. 9- May 1973-. 0708-9031. Periodical. CN. English (text in French). qt. Free. Receiver General for Canada, Supply & Services, Ottawa Ontario K1A 0S9 Canada. **Tel** (613)995-2946. **Circ** 60,000. Newsletter containing information on Canadian federal sales and excise tax laws and on the administrative policy of the Department of National Revenue (Canada) regarding these laws. Federal Sales Tax News, 0708-9023.

EXECUTIVE COMPENSATION AND EMPLOYEE BENEFITS REPORT. 0273-9046. Periodical. US. English. mo. $75.60. Warren Gorham & Lamont, 210 South Street, Boston MA 02111. **LC** KF1424.A15. **DD** 344.7301252, 347.3041252. Executive Compensation Report, 0162-7503.

EXECUTIVE LEGAL GUIDE. 0730-9856. Periodical. US. English. mo. Bureau of Business Practice, 24 Rope Ferry Road, Waterford CT 06386. **LC** KF1600.A15. **DD** 343.730705, 347.303705.

EXECUTIVE ORDER - CALIFORNIA. US. English. **LC** KFC34. **DD** 342.794002636, 347.940202636.

EXECUTIVE ORDER (CONNECTICUT). US. English. State of Connecticut, Governors Office, Hartford CT 06115. **LC** KFC3634.A2. **DD** 348.74601.

EXECUTIVE ORDER (LIBERIA). English. ir. **DD** 348.666201, 346.662081.

EXECUTIVE ORDER - VIRGINIA. US. English. Commonwealth of Virginia, PO Box IB, Richmond VA 23201. **LC** KFV2434.A2. **DD** 348.75501.

AN EXECUTIVE SUMMARY OF THE KANSAS JUDICIAL BRANCH. **Main/Corp** Kansas. Office of Judicial Administration. US. English. an. Office of Judicial Administration, 301 West 10th, Topeka KS 66612. **LC** KFK510. **DD** 347.781 347.81071.

EXECUTIVE'S COURT WATCH. 0164-2901. Periodical. US. English. mo. Bureau of Business Practice, 24C Rope Ferry Road, Waterford CT 06386. **LC** KF1600.A59. **DD** 343.7307.

EXECUTIVE'S TAX REVIEW. V. 1- Mar. 1976-. 0363-2407. Periodical. US. English. mo. $65.00. Commerce Clearing House, 4025 West Peterson Avenue, Chicago IL 60646. **LC** KF6369.8.E9. **DD** 343.73052.

EXPENSES AND APPROPRIATIONS OF THE MISSISSIPPI LEGISLATURE. 0363-0919. US. English. **LC** JK4670. **DD** 328.762076.

THE EXPERT AND THE LAW. (THE EXPERT AND THE LAW : A PUBLICATION OF THE NATIONAL FORENSIC CENTER). Vol. 1, No. 1 (Dec. 7, 1981) -. 0737-8726. Periodical. US. English. bm. $55.00. National Forensic Center, PO Box 3161, Princeton NJ 08540. **Tel** (800)526-5177. Ed Linda Field. **LC** KF8961.A15. **DD** 347.7367, 347.30767. bk rev. adv acc. **Circ** 1,000. (ctrl). The application of scientific medical and technical knowledge to litigation.

EXPERT WITNESS JOURNAL. (EXPERT WITNESS JOURNAL : ILLUSTRATES EI'S EXPERT WITNESS ASSISTANCE). 0277-0555. Periodical. US. English. an. $5.00. Expertise Institute, Box 38-1494Y, Miami FL 33138. **LC** KF8961.A15. **DD** 347.7366, 347.30766. Lawlab Journal.

EXPIRING LEGISLATION WITH BUDGETARY IMPACT. See Business - Public Finance.

EXPORT ADMINISTRATION REGULATIONS. **Main/Corp** United States. Office of Export Administration. Began with 1974. 0094-8411. US. English. an. US Government Printing Office, Superintendent of Documents, Washington DC 20402. **Tel** (202)783-3238. **LC** KF1987.A329. **DD** 343.73087. Export Control Regulations, 0094-842X.

EXPORT REBATES. See Business - Commerce.

EXPORTS UNDER THE CONCESSIONAL SALES PROGRAM : TITLE I, PUBLIC LAW 480. US. English. US Department of Agriculture, Foreign Agricultural Service, Washington DC 20250. Vols. for Apr. 1983- distributed to depository libraries in microfiche.

EXTERNADO (UNIVERSIDAD EXTERNADO DE COLOMBIA). (EXTERNADO : REVISTA DE LA UNIVERSIDAD EXTERNADO DE COLOMBIA). VFOAT Revista de la Universidad Externado de Colombia. No. 1 (Oct. 1981)-. Periodical. CK. Spanish. ir. La Universidad, Calle 12 No 1-17, Bogota Colombia. **LC** K19. **DD** 340.05. Revista de la Universidad Externado de Colombua.

EXTERNAL AFFAIRS SERVICE LIST. **Main/Corp** Malta. Ministry of Foreign Affairs. English. ir. Ministry of Foreign Affairs, Palazzo Parizio Merchant Street, Valletta Malta. **LC** JX1802.7. **DD** 354.458500892.

F M COMPILATION OF THE STATUTES OF CANADA. **Main/Corp** Canada. VFOAT Recueil F M des Statuts du Canada. 1970/72-. 0380-2639. CN. text in English and French. an. Municipal Forms Ltd, Farnham Quebec J2N 2R6 Canada. **DD** 348.71022.

FA CHIH HSUEH KAN. VFOAT Law & Society. Periodical. CH. Chinese or German. ir. $50.00 per copy, $1.50 US. 2nd Floor No 5-9, Lane 6 Han-Chow South Road Sec, 1 100 Taiwan, Tai-Pei Republic of China. **Ind/Abst** Soc. Work Res. Abstr. **LC** K6.

FACTUM : BOLETIN OFICIAL DEL COLEGIO DE ABOGADOS DE PUERTO RICO. Periodical. Spanish. ir. Factum, Apartado 1900, San Juan Puerto Rico 00903. **LC** KGV235.C65. **DD** 340.0607295.

FAIR EMPLOYMENT COMPLIANCE. See Economics - Labor.

FAIRSHARE. VFOAT Fair Share. VAT Fair Share. 0273-3560. Periodical. US. English. mo. $98.00. Law Business Inc, 855 Valley Road, Clifton NJ 07013. **Tel** (201)472-7400. Ed Henry H Foster Jr and Ronald L Brown. **LC** KF506.A3. **DD** 346.73016305, 347.30616305. bk rev. **Circ** 1,200. Review of legal decisions affecting divorce, child support and custody, spousal maintenance, alimony, and visitation.

FAMILY ADVOCATE. V. 1- Summer 1978-. 0163-710X. Periodical. US. English. qt. $27.00. American Bar Association, 750 North Lake Shore Drive, Chicago IL 60611. **Tel** (312)988-5555. **Ind/Abst** Leg. Resour. Index. **LC** KF501.A3. **DD** 346.7301505. (ctrl). Family Law Newsletter, 0427-9638.

FAMILY LAW. BENDER PAMPHLET EDITION. (FAMILY LAW). **Main/Corp** New York (State). 0099-1988. US. English. Matthew Bender, 1275 Broadway, Albany NY 12201. **LC** KFN5115.A29. **DD** 346.747015.

FAMILY LAW (CHICHESTER, WEST SUSSEX). (FAMILY LAW). Vol. 1, No. 1 (Jan./Feb. 1971). 0014-7281. UK. English. ir. 27.50. Jordan & Sons Limited, POB 260-15, Pembroke Road, Bristol BS8 3BA England. **Tel** 0272 732861. Ed M M McColl. **Ind/Abst** Curr. Law Index, Leg. Resour. Index. **LC** K6. **DD** 346.4101505, 344.1061505. bk rev. adv acc. **Circ** 4,000. Essential information on the latest developments in every branch of the law relating to the family.

FAMILY LAW COMMENTATOR. V. 1- Oct./Nov. 1971-. 0093-4682. Periodical. US. English. bm. $17.50. Federal Legal Publishing Inc, 157 Chambers Street, New York NY 10007. **Tel** (212)619-4949. Ed Richard M Weiner. **LC** KFN5115.A73. **DD** 346.747015. Explores the fast moving and complex practice of domestic relations law.

FAMILY LAW FINANCE REPORT. (THE FAMILY LAW FINANCE REPORT). Vol. 1, No. 1 (Mar. 1981)-. 0228-4197. Periodical. CN. English. mo. $135.42. Canada Publishing Corporation, 164 Commander Boulevard, Agincourt Ontario M1S 3C7 Canada. **Tel** (416)293-8141. **DD** 346.7104.

FAMILY LAW QUARTERLY. V. 1- Mar. 1967-. 0014-729X. Periodical. US. English. qt. $27.00. American Bar Association, 750 North Lake Shore Drive, Chicago IL 60611. **Tel** (312)988-5555. **Ind/Abst** Leg. Resour. Index, Women Stud. Abstr., Index Leg. Period., Soc. Work Res. Abstr., Soc. Sci. Citation Index, Curr. Law Index, Abstr. Soc. Work., Contents Curr. Leg. Period. (ctrl). Proceedings of the Section, 0270-1685.

FAMILY LAW REFORM ACT CASES. Vol. 1-. CN. English. Ed James C MacDonald. **LC** KEO213.A45. **DD** 346.713015, 347.130615.

FAMILY LAW REFORM REPORTER. V. 1- July 1978-. 0706-5647. Periodical. CN. English. mo. $46.43. Family Law Reform Reporter, 2 Bloor Street West/Suite 1902, Toronto Ontario M4W 358 Canada. **Tel** (416)920-7422. **DD** 346.71301502648.

THE FAMILY LAW REPORTER. V. 1- Nov. 12, 1974-. 0148-7922. Periodical. US. English. wk. $308.00. Bureau of National Affairs Inc, 1231 25th Street NW, Washington DC 20037. **Tel** (202)452-4995. Ed Randy P Auerbach. **LC** KF501.A3. **DD** 346.7301505. bk rev. Digests and summaries of litigation and legislation concerning domestic relations.

FAMILY LAW REVIEW. V. 9, No. 2- July 1977-. 0149-1431. Periodical. US. English. Free. New York State Bar Association, 1 Elk Street, Albany NY 12207. **Tel** (518)463-3200. Ed Elliot D Samuelson. **LC** KFN5115.A15. **Circ** 3,100. (ctrl). Section newsletter-current section information and family law issues discussed. Family Law Section Newsletter, 0148-3692.

FAMILY LAW REVIEW. V. 1- Jan. 1978-. 0705-1131. Periodical. CN. English. qt. 30.00. Jonah Publications Limited, 620 Sheppard Avenue West, Downsview Ontario M3H S21 Canada. **LC** K6. **DD** 346.7101505.

FAMILY LAW TRIAL SUMMARIES. V. 1, No. 1 (June 15, 1982)-. Periodical. US. English. mo. $65.00. Family Law Trial Summaries, 2554 Lincoln Boulevard/Suite 211, Marina Del Rey CA 90291. **LC** KFC1199.L62. **DD** 346.79493016602648, 347.94930616602648.

FAR EASTERN LAW REVIEW. V. 4, No. 3 (Sept. 1956)-. 0046-3272. Periodical. PH. English. sa. $20.00. Far Eastern University, Institute of Law Nreyes SR ST, Manila Philippines. FEU Law Quarterly.

Law

FCL NEWSLETTER. Main/Corp Friends Committee on Legislation of California. VAT Friends Committee on Legislation Newsletter. 0532-7091. Periodical. US. English. mo. $15.00. Friends Committee on Legislation of California, 926 J St #1214, Sacramento CA 95814. Tel (916)443-3734. *California Report.*

THE F.E.D. LETTER. (THE FED LETTER). Began in 1975. 0363-9371. Periodical. US. English. sm. $24.00. L A Holley, Box 188, Bainbridge Island WA 98110. LC KF5336.A15. DD 342.73085.

FEDERAL AID FACT BOOK. 1974-. 0094-7296. US. English. an. National School Public Relations Association, 1801 North Moore Street, Arlington VA 22209. LC KF4137.A45. DD 379.1210973.

FEDERAL AND STATE JUDICIAL CLERKSHIP DIRECTORY. *See* Yearbooks, Almanacs, Directories.

FEDERAL BANKING LAW REPORT. 0744-8791. Periodical. US. English. ir. $121.00. Federal Banking Law Service, 1117 North 19th Street/Suite 400-A, Arlington VA 22209-0655.

FEDERAL BAR JOURNAL. (THE FEDERAL BAR JOURNAL). V. 1- Sept. 1931-. 0014-9039. Periodical. US. English. qt.

FEDERAL BAR NEWS & JOURNAL. VFOAT Federal Bar News and Journal. Vol. 28, No. 9 (Sept. 1981)-. 0279-4691. Periodical. US. English. mo. $23.00. Federal Bar Association, 1815 H Street NW/Suite 408, Washington DC 20006. Tel (202)638-0252. Ed Lynn P Weidberg. Ind/Abst Leg. Resour. Index, Index Leg. Period. LC K6. DD 349.7305, 347.3005. bk rev. adv acc. Circ 16,000. A 48 to 56 page journal describing Federal Bar Association activities and various law topics of interest to the federal legal profession. *Federal Bar News, 0014-9047; Federal Bar Journal, 0014-9039.*

FEDERAL CARRIERS CASES. Main/Corp Commerce Clearing House. 1936/40-. 0093-2108. US. English. Commerce Clearing House, 4025 West Peterson Avenue, Chicago IL 60646. Tel (312)583-8500. LC KF1091. DD 343.73093. (cum index). Federal controls over motor and water carriers, freight forwarders.

FEDERAL COMMUNICATIONS COMMISSION REPORTS. (FEDERAL COMMUNICATIONS COMMISSION REPORTS. CUMULATIVE INDEX DIGEST OF DECISIONS AND REPORTS OF THE FEDERAL COMMUNICATIONS COMMISSION OF THE UNITED STATES). Main/Corp United States. Federal Communications Commission. VFOAT Cumulative Index Digest of Decisions and Reports of the Federal Communications Commission of the United States. 0098-3942. US. English. ir. Superintendent of Documents, US Government Printing Office, Washington DC 20402. LC KF2763.35. DD 343.73099402646.

FEDERAL COMMUNICATIONS LAW JOURNAL. V. 30- Winter 1977-. 0163-7606. Periodical. US. English. ty. $18.00. Federal Communications Law Journal, UCLA School of Law, 405 Hilgard Avenue, Los Angeles 90024. Tel (213)825-3712. Ed Gil Aronow. Ind/Abst Manage. Contents, Leg. Resour. Index, Index Leg. Period. LC K6. DD 343.73099405. bk rev. adv acc. Circ 2,500. The journal carries articles on broadcast communications, satellite telecommunications, and entertainment law. It is the oldest scholarly journal in the country, exclusively devoted to communications law and related fields. *Federal Communications Bar Journal.*

FEDERAL CONTRACTS REPORT. Main/Corp Bureau of National Affairs (Washington, D.C.). Began with Feb. 24, 1964 issue. 0014-9063. Periodical. US. English. Bureau of National Affairs Incorporated, 1231 25th Street Northwest, Washington DC 20037. Tel (301)258-1033. LC KF849.A1. DD 346. Index published separately - free - automatically sent.

THE FEDERAL COURT CLERKS' NEWS. 0428-111X. Periodical. US. English. bm. $12.00 Clerks, $6.00 Ch. Dep. Clerks, $1.20 Dep. Clerks. Federal Court Clerks Association, 1834 U.S. Courhouse, 3rd Street and Constitution Avenue North West, Washington DC 20061.

FEDERAL COURT MANAGEMENT STATISTICS. *See* Statistics.

FEDERAL COURT OF APPEAL DECISIONS. VFOAT Canada Federal Court of Appeal Decision. 1981-. 0227-0390. Periodical. CN. English. an. $73.52. Western Legal Publications Ltd, 301 Alexander Street, Vancouver British Columbia 4A6 1B2 Canada. Tel (604)687-5671. DD 348.71046.

FEDERAL COURT PROCUREMENT DECISIONS. V. 1, No. 1 (Oct. 1982)-. 0734-9513. Periodical. US. English. mo. $400.00. Federal Publications Incorporated, One Lafayette Centre, Washington DC 20036.

FEDERAL EXCISE TAX REPORTER: CODE, REGULATIONS, RULINGS, DECISIONS, ORGANIZED BY CODE SECTIONS AND ANNOTATED, THOROUGHLY INDEXED. *See* Indexes/Abstracts.

FEDERAL FINANCIAL REGULATORY DIGEST. 0730-5028. US. English. mo. Capitol Reports Inc, 1750 Pennsylvania Avenue NW, Washington DC 20006. LC KF1039.A15. DD 346.73073, 347.30673.

FEDERAL GOVERNMENT LEGAL CAREER OPPORTUNITIES. *See* Occupations and Careers.

FEDERAL INCOME, GIFT, AND ESTATE TAXATION. *See* Business - Public Finance.

FEDERAL INCOME TAX PROCEDURES. *See* Business - Public Finance.

FEDERAL JUDICIAL WORKLOAD STATISTICS. *See* Statistics.

THE FEDERAL LAND POLICY AND MANAGEMENT ACT; AN INTERIM REPORT. Main/Corp United States. Bureau of Land Management. US. English. US Department of the Interior, Bureau of Land Management, 18th & E Street NW, Washington DC 20240. LC KF5605. DD 353.008232.

FEDERAL LAW JOURNAL. (THE FEDERAL LAW JOURNAL). V. 1-. 0273-3641. Periodical. US. English. $36.00. Federal Law Journal, 995 Westwood Square, Box 837, Oviedo FL 32765. LC K6. DD 349.7305, 347.3005.

FEDERAL LAW REVIEW. V. 1- 1964-. Periodical. English. Methuen Law Book Company Ltd, 35 Mitchell Street, North Sydney New South Wales 2060 Australia. Ind/Abst Leg. Resour. Index, APAIS, Aust. Public Aff. Inf. Serv., Index Leg. Period., Curr. Law Index, Leg. Resour. Index.

FEDERAL LITIGATION SECTION NEWSLETTER. Feb. 15, 1984-. 0742-9754. Periodical. US. English. ir. Federal Bar Association, Federal Litigation Section, 1815 H Street NW, Washington DC 20006. LC KF8840.A2. DD 347.37505, 347.307505.

FEDERAL LOCAL COURT RULES. Main/Corp United States. District Courts. 0745-2306. US. English. bm. $175.00. Callaghan & Company, 3201 Old Glenview Road, Wilmette IL 60091. DD 347.

FEDERAL MERIT SYSTEMS REPORTER. VFOAT FMSR. Began in 1981. 0746-035X. US. English. mo. $475.00. Labor Relations Press, PO Box 579, Fort Washington PA 19034. Ed Jim Campion. Full-text reporter of MSPB and court decisions. Includes abstracts, full-text, many access points, cite tracker, statute tracker, citator, articles, and parallel database.

FEDERAL OFFENDERS IN THE UNITED STATES DISTRICT COURTS. VFOAT Federal Offenders in the US District Courts, Federal Offenders in the United States Courts. Began with 1962/63. 0503-471X. US. English. an. Administrative Office of the United States Court, Washington DC 20001. LC KF183. DD 345.7302, 347.3052.

FEDERAL PAROLE DECISION-MAKING : SELECTED REPRINTS. Began with V. 1, 1974/77. US. English. US Parole Commission Research Unit, Bethesda MD 20014.

FEDERAL PERSONNEL MANUAL SYSTEM. FPM SUPPLEMENT 990-1. CIVIL SERVICE LAWS, EXECUTIVE ORDERS, RULES AND REGULATIONS. VFOAT Civil Service Laws, Executive Orders, Rules and Regulations. Periodical. US. English. ir. Superintendent of Documents, Attn SSO US Government Printing Office, Washington DC 20402. Tel (202)783-3238.

FEDERAL REGISTER. Began with V. 1, No. 1, March 14, 1936. 0097-6326. Periodical. US. English. $305.00. US Government Printing Office, Superintendent of Documents, Washington DC 20402. Tel (202)783-3238. Ind/Abst Hospit. Lit. Index, Coal Abstr., Chem. Abstr., Energy Inf. Abstr., Environ. Abstr., Pollut. Abstr. Indexes, Ocean. Abstr. LC KF70. NLM KF 70.A2 F292. CODEN FEREAC. Vols. for 1985- distributed to some depository libraries in microfiche.

FEDERAL REGULATION OF EMPLOYMENT NEWSLETTER. Feb. 10, 1983-. 0746-5653. Periodical. US. English. bw. $66.00. Research Institute of America Incorporated, 589 5th Avenue, New York NY 10017. LC KF3315. DD 344.730105, 347.304105. *FRES Newsletter, 0192-0839.*

THE FEDERAL RESERVE ACT OF 1913, WITH AMENDMENTS AND LAWS RELATING TO BANKING. Main/Corp United States. 1920- Ed. US. English. US Government Printing Office, Washington DC 20402. DD 332.11.

FEDERAL RULES OF EVIDENCE NEWS. V. 1- Jan. 1976-. 0364-3581. Periodical. US. English. mo. Callaghan and Company, 6141 North Cicero Avenue, Chicago IL 60646. LC KF8931.A3. DD 347.73605.

FEDERAL RULES SERVICE. V. 1-25. 0164-4564. US. English. mo. Callaghan & Company, 3201 Old Glenview Road, Wilmette IL 60091. Ed J A Pike, H G Fischer, J W Willis and Jane A Pike. DD 347.

FEDERAL TAX COMPLIANCE MANUAL. *See* Business - Public Finance.

FEDERAL TAX COURSE (STUDENTS ED.). (FEDERAL TAX COURSE). 1980-. 0737-8718. US. English. an. Prentice-Hall Inc, Englewood Cliffs NJ 07632. LC KF6289. DD 343.7304, 347.3034. *Prentice-Hall Federal Tax Course (Students Edition).*

FEDERAL TAXATION (HOUSTON, TEX.). (FEDERAL TAXATION). 1984 Ed.-. 0742-7816. US. English. an. $29.95. Dame Publications, 7800 Bissonnet/Suite 415, Houston TX 77074. LC KF6289. DD 343.7304, 347.3034.

FEDERAL TRADE COMMISSION DECISIONS. *See* Business - Commerce.

FEDERAL TRIAL NEWS. Vol. 1, No. 1 (June 1982)-. 0739-2109. US. English. National Conference of Federal Trial Judges, American Bar Association, 1155 East 60th Street, Chicago IL 60637. LC KF8775.A15. DD 347.7314, 34730714.

FEDERATION OF INSURANCE & CORPORATE COUNSEL QUARTERLY. VFOAT Federation of Insurance and Corporate Counsel Quarterly. Vol. 36, No. 1 (Fall 1985)-. 0887-0942. Periodical. US. English. qt. $26.00. 117 North Linn Street, Iowa City IA 52240. LC PAR. *Federation of Insurance Counsel Quarterly, 0430-2583.*

FEDERATION OF INSURANCE COUNSEL QUARTERLY. VFOAT F.I.C. Quarterly. Vol. 1, No. 1 (Oct. 1950)-. 0430-2583. Periodical. US. English. qt. Federation of Insurance Counsel, 117 North Linn Street, Iowa IA 52240. Ind/Abst Leg. Resour. Index, Index Leg. Period. LC K6. DD 346.7308605, 347.3068605. (cum index).

F.E.P. GUIDELINES. *See* Business - Personnel Management.

FICHERO DE JURISPRUDENCIA. Spanish. ir.

FIDUCIARY REPORTER. Began in 1951. Periodical. US. English. mo. Geo T Bisel Company, 710 South Washington Square, Philadelphia PA 19106.

FIDUCIARY TAX RETURN GUIDE. Began with Vol. for 1977. 0736-0975. US. English. an. $3.50. Research Institute of America Inc, 589 Fifth Avenue, New York NY 10017. LC KF6443.Z9. DD 343.730532, 347.303532.

FINAL BUDGET SUMMARY. Main/Corp California. US. English. an. $1.00. Bill Room State Capitol, Sacramento CA 95814. LC KFC842. DD 353.97940072253.

Law

FINAL COMPREHENSIVE ANNUAL SERVICE PLAN FOR THE COMMONWEALTH OF MASSACHUSETTS UNDER TITLE XX OF THE SOCIAL SECURITY ACT. See Sociology: General Works, Theory - Social Pathology, Welfare, Criminology.

FINAL REPORT - TEXAS LEGISLATIVE SERVICE. (FINAL REPORT, LEGISLATURE). Main/Corp Texas Legislative Service. 0093-1381. US. English. Texas Legislative Service, PO Box 100, Austin TX 78767. LC KFT1215. DD 348.76401.

FINAL REPORTS OF INTERIM JOINT AND SPECIAL COMMITTEES. Main/Corp Kentucky. General Assembly. Legislative Research Commission. 1974/75-. US. English. an. Legislative Research Commission, State Capitol/Room 300, Frankfort KY 40601. LC KFK1227, KFK1220. DD 300.9769 S, 328.76907657053. *Joint Legislative Committees Final Report, . . . Iterim.*

FINAL TABLES AND INDEX TO LEGISLATIVE MEASURES. See Indexes/Abstracts.

FINANCIAL SERVICES LAW REPORT. V. 1, No. 1 (May 1985)-. 0883-2447. Periodical. US. English. mo. $165.00. Leader Publications, 111 Eighth Avenue/Suite 900, New York NY 10011. DD 343.

FINANZ JOURNAL. See Business - Public Finance.

FINDING AIDS ANNUAL. US. English. an. $3.00 Individual or Additional Copies, Free of charge to all State Register subscribers. State of Minnesota, Department of Administration, State Register and Public Documents Division, 177 University, St Paul MN 55155. LC KFM5438. DD 348.776025, 347.760825.

FINE PRINT (ATHENS, GA.). (THE FINE PRINT). V. 1, No. 1 (Jan. 1981)-. 0273-2661. Periodical. US. English. mo. Editor the Fine Print, 1294 E Broad Street, Athens GA 30601. LC KF292.G414. DD 349.75805, 347.58005.

FIREARMS LITIGATION REPORTER. Vol. 1, No. 1 (July/Sept. 1983)-. 0741-3807. Periodical. US. English. qt. $30.00. Foundation for Handgun Education, Box 72, 110 Maryland Avenue NE, Washington DC 20002. Tel (202)544-7227. Ed Michael Hancock. LC KF3941.A15. DD 344.73053305, 347.30453305. Circ 300. Newsletter reporting recent developments in firearms litigation and related matters.

FIRST PAYMENTS, WEEKS COMPENSATED AND BENEFITS PAID TO WOMEN, BY INDUSTRIAL GROUP UNDER OHIO UNEMPLOYMENT COMPENSATION LAW. US. English. Division of Research and Statistics, Ohio Bureau of Employment Services, Columbus OH 43216. LC HD7096.U6. DD 368.440088042.

F.J., REVISTA DE LA FACULTAD DE JURISPRUDENCIA Y CIENCIAS SOCIALES. Main/Corp Quito. Universidad Central. Facultad de Jurisprudencia y Ciencias Sociales. Periodical. Spanish. ir. Facultad de Jurisprudencia y Ciencias Sociales, Casilla Postas 23-11, Quito Spain. LC K17.

FLEET STREET REPORTS OF INDUSTRIAL PROPERTY CASES FROM THE COMMONWEALTH AND EUROPE. Periodical. UK. English. mo. LC KD1365.A2. DD 346.420486. *Fleet Street Patent Law Reports.*

FLETCHER. Main/Corp Fletcher School of Law and Diplomacy. V. 1- Spring 1978-. 0161-8350. Periodical. US. English. ty. Free. Fletcher School of Law and Diplomacy, Tufts University, Medford MA 02155.

FLITE NEWSLETTER. (FLITE NEWSLETTER : FEDERAL LEGAL INFORMATION THROUGH ELECTRONICS). VAT Federal Legal Information Through Electronics Newsletter. Began with V. 3, No. 3, Oct./Dec. 1974. 0364-6785. Periodical. US. English. qt. Flite Department of the Air Force, Denver CO 80279. LC KF242.A1. DD 349.73072. *Lite Newsletter.*

FLORIDA ADMINISTRATIVE LAW REPORTS. VFOAT FALN. V. 1- Jan. 15, 1979-. 0194-4800. Periodical. US. English. bw. $275.00. Judicial & Administrative Research Associates, 1327 North Adams Street, PO Box 4284, Tallahassee FL 32303. LC KFF440. DD 348.759025.

THE FLORIDA BAR CASE SUMMARY SERVICE. Main/Corp Florida Bar. 0164-6427. Periodical. US. English. wk. $95.00. The Florida Bar, Case Summary Service, Tallahassee FL 32301. Tel (904)222-5286. Ed Edith Sheeks. Circ 1,200. Provides summaries of selected opinions from the Florida Supreme Court and District Court of Appeals.

THE FLORIDA BAR JOURNAL. (FLORIDA BAR JOURNAL). V. 27, No. 7- July 1953-. 0015-3915. Periodical. English. ir. $25.00. The Florida Bar Association, Tallahassee FL 32301-8226. Tel (904)222-5286. Ed Linda H Yates. Ind/Abst Leg. Resour. Index, Index Leg. Period., Curr. Law Index. LC KF200. DD 340.05. bk rev. adv acc. Circ 38,500. (ctrl). Contains how-to articles which strive to help advance the education, competence, ethical practice, and public responsibility of lawyers. Official publication of the Florida Bar. *Florida Law Journal.*

FLORIDA BAR NEWS. 0360-0114. Periodical. US. English. sm. $12.00. Florida Bar Association, Tallahassee FL 32301. Tel (904)222-5286. Ed Linda H Yates. LC KF200. DD 340.062759. adv acc. (ctrl). Official publication of the Florida Bar. General topics of interest, actions affecting the legal profession by the courts, legislature, and the Board of Governors.

FLORIDA CASES REPORTED IN SOUTHERN REPORTER, SECOND SERIES. VFOAT Florida Cases. 0744-981X. US. English. wk. $60.00. West Publishing Company, 50 West Kellogg Boulevard, PO Box 3526, Saint Paul MN 55165. DD 340.

FLORIDA DIGEST. US. English. ir. West Publishing Company, 50 West Kellogg Boulevard, PO Box 64526, St Paul MN 55164.

FLORIDA DIGEST, 1846 TO DATE. 1936- V. 1, 1937. US. English. LC KFF57.

THE FLORIDA LAW WEEKLY. 0274-8533. Periodical. US. English. wk. $240.00. Florida Law Weekly, PO Box 4284, 1327 North Adams Street, Tallahassee FL 32315. Tel (904)222-3171. Ed E Neil Young. Circ 3,000. Complete opinions- Florida Supreme Court and district courts of appeal within 1-10 days of filing. Index/tables each issues; cumulative indexes quarterly. Binders included.

THE FLORIDA LEGAL DIRECTORY. See Yearbooks, Almanacs, Directories.

FLORIDA LEGISLATURE, . . . SUBJECT INDEX. See Indexes/Abstracts.

THE FLORIDA REAL ESTATE BROKER & THE LAW. See Real Estate.

FLORIDA RULES OF COURT. (FLORIDA RULES OF COURT : CONTAINING AMENDMENTS). 0735-6838. US. English. an. LC KFF529. DD 347.759051, 347.590751.

FLORIDA STATE UNIVERSITY LAW REVIEW. V. 1- Winter 1973-. 0096-3070. Periodical. US. English. qt. $20.00. Florida State University, College of Law, Tallahassee FL 32306-1034. Tel (904)644-2045. Ed Alan B Fields. Ind/Abst Leg. Resour. Index, Index Leg. Period., Curr. Law Index, Contents Curr. Leg. Period. LC K6. DD 340.05. (cum index). bk rev adv acc. Circ 1,200. Features articles by legal authorities analyzing and critiquing major court decisions and legal developments affecting economic, political and social activities.

FLORIDA STATUTES. US. English. be. Florida Legislature, The Capitol/Room 804, Tallahassee FL 32304.

FLORIDA STATUTES ANNOTATED. US. English. ir. Harrison Company Publishers, 3110 Crossing Park, Norcross GA 30091.

FLRA REPORT OF CASE DECISIONS AND FSIP RELEASES. See Economics - Labor.

FOCUS. 0148-026X. Periodical. US. English. American Bar Association Fund for Public Education, 1155 East 60th Street, Chicago IL 60637. LC KF200. DD 340.06273.

FOCUS ON SPECIAL EDUCATION LEGAL PRACTICES. 0747-959X. Periodical. US. English. qt. National Information Center For Handicapped Children and Youth, Box 1942, Washington DC 20013. LC KF4210.A15. DD 344.73079105, 347.30479105.

THE FOLIO. PUBLIC RELATIONS. 1979-. 0198-7143. Periodical. US. English. mo. $15.95. National Academy Code Administration, 6861 Elm Street Road, McLean VA 22101. LC KF5701.A15. DD 343.7307869005.

FOLK OG FORSKNING. 1977, No. 1-. 0105-712X. Periodical. Danish. ir. 50.00. Universitetsforeningens Sekretariat, Puggardagade 7 6760 Ribe Denmark.

FOOD AND DRUG ADMINISTRATION AND THE CONGRESS. Main/Corp United States. Food and Drug Administration. Office of Legislative Affairs. VFOAT FDA and the Congress. 95th- Congress. 0194-0597. US. English. be. Department of Health Education & Welfare, 5600 Fishers Lane, Rockville MD 20852. LC KF3869. DD 344.7304205. NLM W2 A F7FC. *FDA and the Congress.*

FOOD, DRUG, COSMETIC LAW JOURNAL. V. 5- No. 1 (Mar. 1950)-. 0015-6361. Periodical. US. English. qt. $67.00. Commerce Clearing House, 4025 West Peterson Avenue, Chicago IL 60646. Tel (305)345-4100. Ind/Abst Leg. Resour. Index, Life Sci. Collect., Energy Inf. Abstr., Environ. Abstr., Index Leg. Period., Soc. Sci. Citation Index, Curr. Law Index. LC Microfilm. *Food, Drug, Cosmetic Law Quarterly.*

FOOD DRUG COSMETIC LAW QUARTERLY. V. 1-4. Periodical. US. English. qt.

FOOD DRUG COSMETIC LAW REPORTS. Main/Corp Commerce Clearing House. 0162-1122. Periodical. US. English. wk. $865.00. Commerce Clearing House Inc, 4025 West Peterson Avenue, Chicago IL 60646. Tel (312)583-8500. NLM WA 697 C734F. Reflects OFCCP policies and procedures, tells how its staff investigates and enforces contractor adherence to pledges made to comply with affirmative action rules to increase job opportunities for women, racial minorities, handicapped persons, disabled and Vietnam veterans.

FOR THE DEFENSE. 0091-1011. Periodical. US. English. qt. National Association Criminal Defense Lawyers, PO Box 12964, Austin TX 78711. LC K6. DD 345.7307505.

FORDHAM LAW REVIEW. Vol. 1, No. 1 (Nov. 1914)-. 0015-704X. Periodical. US. English. ir. $27.00. Fordham University, School of Law, 140 West 42nd Street, Lincoln Center/Room 214, New York NY 10023. Tel (212)841-5243. Ind/Abst Leg. Resour. Index, Sociol. Abstr., Index Leg. Period., Curr. Law Index, Lang. Lang. Behav. Abstr., Soc. Sci. Citation Index, Contents Curr. Leg. Period. bk rev. adv acc. Circ 1,300. (ctrl). Collection of articles written by experts and students on wide-ranging legal topics.

THE FORDHAM URBAN LAW JOURNAL. V. 1- Summer 1972-. 0199-4646. Periodical. US. English. qt. $15.00. Fordham University School of Law, 140 West 62nd Street, New York NY 10023. Tel (212)841-5247. Ed Dorothy E Cumby. Ind/Abst Leg. Resour. Index, Public Aff. Inf. Serv. Bull., Index Leg. Period., Curr. Law Index, Contents Curr. Leg. Period. LC K6. DD 340.05. Circ 1,500. (ctrl). Articles relating to urban law.

FOREIGN COUNSEL DIRECTORY. See Yearbooks, Almanacs, Directories.

FOREIGN INVESTMENT REGULATIONS, LABOUR AND EMPLOYMENT CONDITIONS IN THE ARAB WORLD. 0160-2020. US. English. an. Arab World and Iran Business Guides Inc, Harvard Square, Box 92 Cambridge, Boston MA 02138. DD 346.0709174927.

FOREIGN TAX PLANNING. Series/Titl Tax law and Practice Course Handbook Series. 0734-9157. US. English. an. Practising Law Institute, 810 7th Avenue, New York NY 10019. LC KF6419.Z9. DD 343.7305248, 347.3035248.

FORENSIA. See Medicine - Forensic Medicine, Medical Jurisprudence.

THE FORENSIC QUARTERLY. 0196-304X. Monographic Series. US. English. bm. $12.00. University of Iowa, Publishers Order Department GSB, Iowa City IA 52242. Tel (319)353-3432.

FORENSIC SERVICES DIRECTORY. See Yearbooks, Almanacs, Directories.

Law

FORFATTNINGAR OM UPPBORD M.M.
Main/Corp Sweden. SW. Swedish. ir. Liber Forlag, Prenumerations Order, 516289 Stockholm Sweden. DD 343.485042.

FORMAL OPINIONS. See Ethics.

FORO AMMINISTRATIVO (ANNUAL). (IL FORO AMMINISTRATIVO). Italian. an. 120.000 Domestic, 180.000 Foreign. Casa Editore Giuffre, Via Statuto 2, 20121 Milano Italy. Tel (02)652.341. DD 342.450664, 344.502664. *Foro Amministrativo e Delle Acque Pubbliche (Annual).*

IL FORO ITALIANO. 1876. 0015-783X. Periodical. IT. Italian. mo. $121.19. Nicola Zanichelli Editore, Casella Postale 227, 40100 Bologna Italy. bk rev.

IL FORO ITALIANO. MASSIMARIO. Began in 1930. Periodical. Italian. ir. Societa Editrice des Foro Italiano, Via Pietro Cossa 41, Roma Italy. DD 348.45041.

FORT WORTH COMMERCIAL RECORDER. Established 1903. 0015-8097. Periodical. US. English. da. $150.00. Fort Worth Commercial Recorder, PO Box 11038-3032, South Jones Street, Ft Worth TX 76109. Tel (817)926-5351. Ed Genevieve Ratcliff. LC K6. DD 349.76405, 347.6405. adv acc. Circ 550. Court and commercial business newspaper.

FORTECKNING OVER ADVOKATER OCH ADVOKATBYRAER AR JAMIE STADGAR FOR SVERIGES ADVOKATSAMFUND. (FORTECKNING OVER ADVOKATER OCH ADVOKATBYRAER). 0300-2055. Swedish. ir. Sveriges Advokatsamfund, Avenida Portugal S/N Jardim Europa, Stockholm Sweden.

FORUM. (THE FORUM). Nov./Dec. 1975-. 0381-8314. Periodical. CN. English. qt. Alberta Solicitor General, 10310 Jasper Avenue, Edmonton Alberta Canada. LC KEA572.A13. DD 345.71230505.

THE FORUM. (FORUM). 0015-8305. Periodical. US. English. qt $1.50. DC Chapter of the Federal Bar Association, 1815 H Street Northwest, Washington DC 20006. Ind/Abst Energy Res. Abstr.

FORUM. 0164-6931. Periodical. US. English. bm. $18.00. California Attorneys for Criminal Justice, 6430 Sunset Boulevard/Suite 521, Los Angeles CA 90028. LC KFC1102.A15. DD 345.7940505.

FORUM. Issue No. 1- Jan./Feb. 1979-. 0709-2180. Periodical. CN. English. bm. The Forum, Court Services Headquarters/6th Floor, 850 Burdett Avenue, Victoria British Columbia V8W 1B4 Canada. LC KEB533.A13. DD 347.7110105. *Court's Reporter, 0382-1706.*

THE FORUM. (FORUM). V. 1- Oct. 1965-. Periodical. English. m. $10.00 Members, $20.00 Nonmembers. American Bar Association, Circulation Department, 1155 East 60th Street, Chicago IL 60637. *News-O-Gram.*

THE FORUM. (FORUM). Vol. 16, No. 1 (Special Issue 1980)-. Periodical. US. English. qt. 1155 East 60th Street, Chicago IL 60637. index in last issue of volume - attached.

FORUM (CHICAGO, IL). (THE FORUM). Vol. 1, No. 1 (Oct. 1965)-. 0015-8356. Periodical. US. English. qt. American Bar Association, 750 North Lake Shore Drive, Chicago IL 60611. Tel (314)988-5555. Ind/Abst Coal Abstr., Index Leg. Period., Energy Res. Abstr., Curr. Law Index, Leg. Contents, Soc. Sci. Citation Index, Contents Curr. Leg. Period. LC K6. DD 346.7308605, 347.3068605. (cum index). *News-O-Gram.*

FRANCHISE LAW JOURNAL. Vol. 4, No. 1 (Summer 1984)-. 8756-7962. Periodical. US. English. qt. American Bar Association, Forum Committee on Franchising, 750 North Lake Shore Drive, Chicago IL 60611. LC KF2023.A15. DD 343.7308405, 347.3038405. *Journal of the Forum Committee on Franchising, 0732-1910.*

FRANCHISE LEGAL DIGEST. 0739-8239. Periodical. US. English. mo. International Franchise Association, 1350 New York Avenue NW/Suite 900, Washington DC 20005. Tel (202)628-8000. Ed Neil A Simon and Herbert A Hedden. LC KF2023.A15. DD 343.730887, 347.303887. bk rev. Circ 1,000. (ctrl). Articles reviewing current domestic and international legal and legislative developments concerning franchising and the implications of these developments for franchisors and franchisees. *Current Legal Digest, 0361-8390.*

FRANKFURTER WISSENSCHAFTLICHE BEITRAGE. RECHTS- UND WIRTSCHAFTSWISSENSCHAFTLICHE REIHE. Monographic Series. GW. German. ir. Vittorio Klostermann, Postfach 900601/ Frauenlobstrasse 22, 6000 Frankfurt 90 West Germany. Tel 0611/77 40 11.

FRANKLIN COUNTY LEGAL JOURNAL. V. 1- 1977/78-. 0164-2820. US. English. Franklin County Legal Journal, 164 Lincoln Way East, Chambersburg PA 17201. LC KFP52.F7. DD 348.74844043.

FREEDOM OF INFORMATION CASE LIST. VFOAT FOIA Case List. 0163-9390. US. English. an. US Government Printing Office, Superintendent of Documents, Washington DC 20402. LC KF5753.A58. DD 342.730853.

FROM THE STATE CAPITALS. JUSTICE POLICIES. VFOAT Justice Policies. 0749-2790. Periodical. US. English. wk. $175.00. Wakeman/Walworth Inc, PO Box 1939, New Haven CT 06509. *From the State Capitals. Prison Administration, 0734-0885; From the State Capitals. Judicial Administration (New Haven, Conn.), 0734-1091.*

FROM THE STATE CAPITALS. WOMEN AND THE LAW. Jan. 1984-. 0741-3572. Periodical. US. English. mo. Wakeman/Walworth Inc, Box 1939, New Haven CT 06509.

FTC : WATCH. VAT Federal Trade Commission : Watch. July 5, 1976-. 0196-0016. Periodical. US. English. bw. $441.00. FTC Watch, Box 2220, Springfield VA 22152. Tel (703)451-4575. Ed Arthur Amolsch. LC KF1602. DD 343.730805. bk rev. Covers the policies, programs, and personnel of the US Federal Trade Commission. Emphasis on in-depth, investigative reporting.

FUDOSAN ROPPO. Main/Corp Japan. Japanese. ir. 2800. Kinensha, 9-6 Higashi Ueno 2, Taito-ku (110), Tokyo Japan.

FUNDAMENTAL CONCEPTS OF ESTATE ADMINISTRATION. Series/Titl Estate Planning and Administration Course Handbook Series. 1976-. 0164-1255. US. English. an. Practising Law Institute, 810 Seventh Avenue, New York NY 10019. LC KF6585. DD 343.73053.

FUNDAMENTAL CONCEPTS OF ESTATE PLANNING. 1976-. 0733-0057. US. English. an. Practising Law Institute, 810 7th Avenue, New York NY 10019. LC KF750.Z9. DD 343.73053, 347.30352.

FUNDAMENTALS OF BANKRUPTCY LAW : ALI-ABA COURSE OF STUDY, MATERIALS. VFOAT ALI-ABA Course of Study, Materials. US. English. ALI-ABA Committee on Continuing Professional Education, 4025 Chestnut Street, Philadelphia PA 19104. LC KF1524.3.

FUNDAMENTALS OF SECURED TRANSACTIONS. (FUNDAMENTALS OF SECURED TRANSACTIONS : ALI-ABA COURSE OF STUDY MATERIALS). VFOAT ALI-ABA Course of Study Materials. 0732-4561. US. English. ALI-ABA, 4025 Chestnut Street, Philadelphia PA 19104.

FUNDHEFT FUR STEUERRECHT. GW. German. an. CH Beck'sche Verlagsbchngly, Postfach 400340/Wilhemstrass 9, 8 Munich West Germany.

FUNDSTELLEN- UND INHALTSNACHWEIS ARBEITS- UND SOZIALRECHT. Periodical. English. ir. Verlag R S Shultz, Berger Strasse 8-10/Sehang 4, D-8136 Percha-Kempfenhausen West Germany. Ed F Luber. DD 340.0943.

FURANI'S DIGEST OF THE OFFICIAL GAZETTE AL KUWAIT AL YOUM. English. ir. 135.00 Outside Kuwait. Furani's Translation and Advertising Company, PO Box 950, Safat Kuwait. DD 349.536705, 345.367005.

GACETA DE MADRID. Periodical. US. Spanish.

GACETA JUDICIAL. V. 1- 1887-. Spanish. ir.

GACETA JUDICIAL (ASUNCION, PARAGUAY). (GACETA JUDICIAL). V. 1, No. 1, (Nov. 1983)-. Spanish. mo. LC KHP72. DD 348.89204405, 348.92084405.

GACETA OFICIAL - PROCURADURIA GENERAL DE JUSTICIA DEL DISTRITO FEDERAL. Main/Corp Mexico (Federal District). Procuraduria General de Justicia. V. 1- (No. 1-). Spanish. ir. DD 348.725305.

GACETA OFICIAL - REPUBLICA DOMINICANA. Main/Corp Dominican Republic. DR. Spanish. Direct General Rentas Internas, Consultoria Juridica Poder, Santo Domingo Dominican Republic. DD 340.097293. *Boletin Oficial.*

GAKUSEIYO KAIJI HOKI SHU. Main/Corp Japan. Japanese. ir. 1800. c/o Seizando Building, 4-51 Minami Motocho Shinjuku-ku 160, Tokyo Japan.

GAMING & WAGERING BUSINESS. VFOAT Gaming and Wagering Business. Vol. 5, No. 10 (Oct. 1984)-. 8750-8222. Periodical. US. English. mo. $65.00 Domestic, $122.00 Canada. BMT Publications, 254 West 31st Street, New York NY 10001. DD 363. *Gaming Business, 0736-0916.*

GAO WORK INVOLVING TITLE V OF THE ENERGY POLICY AND CONSERVATION ACT OF 1975. Main/Corp United States. General Accounting Office. VFOAT Energy Policy and Conservation Act of 1975. 1977/78-. US. English. an. US General Accounting Office, Distribution Section, 441 G Street NW/Room 1518, Washington DC 20548.

THE GARGOYLE. 0148-9623. Periodical. US. English. qt. $0.50. The Gargoyle, University of Wisconsin-Madison Law School, Madison WI 53706. LC KF292.W57. DD 340.071177584.

GAUHATI LAW REPORTS. Periodical. English. mo. 160.00. Ashok Publishing House, Sikaria Building/1st Floor, A T Road, Gauhati 781001 India.

GAVEL. (THE GAVEL). 0093-1845. US. English. mo. State Bar Association of North Dakota, NDU Office Building/Suite 314, Bismark ND 58505. LC KF332.N6. DD 340.062784.

THE GAVEL. 0363-5783. US. English. sm. California Jury Verdicts, 901 F Street/Suite 120, Sacramento CA 95825. LC KFC52.S8. DD 348.794044.

GAVEL; NEWSLETTER OF THE ILLINOIS JUDGES ASSOCIATION. V. 1- Spring 1977-. 0147-8273. Periodical. US. English. Illinois Judges Association, 4924 West Iowa Street, Chicago IL 60654. LC KF200. DD 347.773014062.

GAZETTE DES TRIBUNAUX IVOIRIENS. Jan. 1982-. Periodical. French. mo. 12000.00. Gazette des Tribunaux Ivoiriens Maison des Juristes, 41 Boulevard Clozel, Abidjan Ivory Coast.

GAZETTE - KADUNA STATE OF NIGERIA. Main/Corp Kaduna, Nigeria (State). V. 10, No. 7 (Feb. 12, 1976)-. Periodical. NR. English. ir. 12.00 Overseas. Government Printer, Private Mail Bag 2020, Kaduna Nigeria. DD 340.096695. *Gazette.*

GAZETTE - LAW SOCIETY OF UPPER CANADA. (GAZETTE - THE LAW SOCIETY OF UPPER CANADA). Main/Corp Law Society of Upper Canada. V. 2- March 1968-. 0023-9364. Periodical. CN. English. ty. 15.00. Law Society of Upper Canada, 85 Richmond Street/Room 501, Toronto Ontario M5H 2C9 Canada. Tel (416)366-3726. Ed John D Honsberger. Ind/Abst Leg. Resour. Index. DD 340.06271. Circ 21,000. *Law Society Gazette, 0315-5404.*

GAZETTE - NIGER STATE OF NIGERIA. Main/Corp Niger (Nigeria). English. ir. 12.00. Government Printer, Private Mail Bag 48 Minna, Niger Nigeria. DD 349.669505.

GAZETTE OFFICIELLE DU QUEBEC. LAWS AND REGULATIONS. (GAZETTE OFFICIELLE DU QUEBEC. PART 2, LAWS AND REGULATIONS MICROFORM). Main/Corp Quebec (Province). 0706-3598. Periodical. CN. English. Micromedia Limited, 144 Front Street West, Toronto Ontario M5J 1G2 Canada. DD 348.7140205.

GAZETTE OFFICIELLE DU QUEBEC. PARTIE 2. LOIS ET REGLEMENTS. (GAZETTE OFFICIELLE DU QUEBEC, PARTIE 2; LOIS ET REGLEMENTS). Main/Corp Quebec (Province). VFOAT Quebec Official Gazette, Part 2. VAT Quebec Official Gazette. Part 2. Laws and Regulations. V. 105- Jan. 6, 1973-. 0703-5721. Periodical. CN. English (text also in French V. 105-109, No. 56). sm. Tel (418)643-5150. *Gazette Officielle du Quebec.*

Law

GAZETTE YEARBOOK. See Yearbooks, Almanacs, Directories.

GELTENDE RECHT (GERMANY (EAST). MINISTERRAT. BURO). (DAS GELTENDE RECHT). Aug. 1963-. German. ir. DD 349.431, 344.31. Gesetzes-Generalregister.

GENERAL AND PRIVATE LAWS, MEMORIALS AND RESOLUTIONS, OF THE TERRITORY OF DAKOTA, PASSED AT THE SESSION OF THE LEGISLATIVE ASSEMBLY. Main/Corp Dakota. VFOAT Dakota, Terr., Laws. US. English. Bowen & Kingsbury, Public Printers, Yankton SD 57078. LC KFN8625. DD 348.783023.

GENERAL AND SPECIAL LAWS OF THE STATE OF TEXAS. Main/Corp Texas. 43d- Legislature. US. English. Secretary of State, PO Box 13824/Capitol Station, Austin TX 78711. LC KFT1225. DD 347.764023, 347.640723. General Laws of the State of Texas Special Laws of the State of Texas.

GENERAL APPROPRIATIONS ACT. Main/Corp Philippines. English. ir. DD 343.599034, 345.990334.

THE GENERAL BAR. 0739-7178. US. English. an. General Bar, 15 Prospect Street, Paramus NJ 07652. LC KF190. DD 349.73025, 397.30025.

GENERAL LAWS AND MEMORIALS AND RESOLUTIONS OF THE TERRITORY OF DAKOTA. Main/Corp Dakota. US. English. be. LC KFN8625.

GENERAL LAWS OF EDUCATION RELATING TO SCHOOL COMMITTEES AS OF JANUARY 1 . . . . Main/Corp Massachusetts. VFOAT Massachusetts School Law. 1976-. US. English. an. Masbo Cooperative Corporation, 99 School Street, Weston MA 02193. LC KFM2790.3.A29. DD 344.744071, 347.440471.

GENERAL LAWS OF RHODE ISLAND. Main/Corp Rhode Island. US. English. ir. Michie Company, c/o Jim Shroyer, PO Box 717, Pelham AL 35124. Tel (804)295-6171.

GENERAL PRACTICE SECTION DIRECTORY. See Yearbooks, Almanacs, Directories.

GENKO KAIJI HOREI SHU (JAPAN). JA. Japanese. ir. 11500. Kaibundo, 48 Kanda Jimbocho 2 Chiyoda-ku, Tokyo Japan.

GEORGE MASON UNIVERSITY LAW REVIEW. Vol. 4, No. 1 (Spring 1981)-. 0741-8736. Periodical. US. English. sa. $6.00. George Mason University School of Law, 3401 North Fairfax Drive, Arlington VA 22201. Tel (703)841-2655. Ed John Martin. Ind/Abst Leg. Resour. Index, Index Leg. Period. LC K12. DD 340.05. bk rev. adv acc. Circ 500. Analysis of legal issues of current interest in general and administrative law issues in particular. GMU Law Review, 0742-4752.

THE GEORGE WASHINGTON LAW REVIEW. V. 1- Nov. 1932-. 0016-8076. Periodical. US. English. ir. $18.00. George Washington Law Review, 716 20th Street NW/Suite 302, Washington DC 20052. Tel (202)676-6835. Ed Ronald S Gross. Ind/Abst Leg. Resour. Index, Int. Aerosp. Abstr., Public Aff. Inf. Serv. Bull., Index Leg. Period., Soc. Sci. Citation Index, Sociol. Abstr., Contents Curr. Leg. Period., Curr. Law Index, Lang. Lang. Behav. Abstr. LC K7. DD 347.05. bk rev adv acc. Circ 2,000. (ctrl) Current trends and new developments in national legal issues with special emphasis on administrative, general constitutional, patent, and corporate law.

THE GEORGETOWN IMMIGRATION LAW QUARTERLY. Vol. 1, No. 1 (1981). Periodical. US. English. an. Georgetown University, Law Center, 605 G Street NW, East Potomac Building 417, Washington DC 20001. Tel (202)624-8374.

THE GEORGETOWN LAW JOURNAL. V. 1- Nov. 1912-. US. English. bm. $27.00 Domestic, $30.00 Foreign. Georgetown University Law Center, 600 New Jersey Avenue NW, Washington DC 20001. Tel (202)624-8230. Ind/Abst Public Aff. Inf. Serv. Bull., Index Leg. Period. LC LL-098 K7. DD 349.7305. bk rev. adv acc. Circ 2,750. Articles, student notes, and book reviews on the study of practice of law.

GEORGETOWN UNIVERSITY LAW CENTER IMMIGRATION LAW REPORTER. VFOAT Immigration Law Reporter. Fall 1983-. Periodical. US. English. Centro de Immigracion, Georgetown University Law Center, 600 New Jersey Avenue NW, Washington DC 20001. Immigration Monitoring Report, 0740-5677.

GEORGIA ADVANCE SHEETS. Main/Corp Georgia. Court of Appeals. Vol. 1, No. 1 (July 5, 1984)-. 8750-0515. Periodical. US. English. wk. $115.00. Darby Printing Company, 715 West Whitehall Street SW, Atlanta GA 30310. Tel (414)755-4521. Ed Robert V Vaughn. adv acc. Circ 2,100. Full text of official opinions of the Georgia Supreme Court and Court of Appeals, including research features such as table of cases, index, etc.

GEORGIA COURT RULES AND PROCEDURE. (GEORGIA COURT RULES AND PROCEDURE : WITH AMENDMENTS RECEIVED TO . . .). 1983-. 0749-2669. US. English. West Publishing Company, 50 West Kellogg Boulevard, PO Box 3526, St Paul MN 55165. LC KFG529. DD 347.758051, 347.580751.

GEORGIA COURTS DIRECTORY. See Yearbooks, Almanacs, Directories.

GEORGIA COURTS JOURNAL. 0147-7161. Periodical. US. English. 55 Marietta Street/Suite 2000, Atlanta GA 30303. LC KFG508.A15. DD 347.7580105.

GEORGIA CRIMINAL TRIAL PRACTICE. VFOAT Criminal Trial Practice. 1984 Ed.-. 0884-1632. US. English. an. Harrison Company Publishers, 3110 Crossing Park, Box 7500, Norcross GA 30091-7500. LC KFG575. DD 345.75805, 347.58055. Index each issue contains an index to its own contents - no vol index - loose.

GEORGIA JOURNAL OF INTERNATIONAL AND COMPARATIVE LAW. See Law - International Law.

GEORGIA LAW REPORTER. Main/Corp Georgia. Supreme Court. 0091-6498. US. English. wk. Darby Printing Company, 715 West Whitehall Street SW, Atlanta GA 30310. Tel (404)522-7242. LC KFG47. DD 348.758043.

GEORGIA LAW REVIEW (ATHENS, GA.: 1966). (GEORGIA LAW REVIEW). Vol. 1, No. 1 (Fall 1966)-. 0016-8300. Periodical. US. English. qt. $15.00. University of Georgia, School of Law, Athens GA 30602. Tel (404)542-7286. Ed David Nutter. Ind/Abst Leg. Resour. Index, Index Leg. Period., Curr. Law Index, Public Aff. Inf. Serv. Bull., Contents Curr. Leg. Period. (cum index). bk rev

THE GEORGIA LEGAL DIRECTORY. See Yearbooks, Almanacs, Directories.

GEORGIA LEGISLATIVE REVIEW. 1974-. 0362-5931. US. English. Clark College, Southern Center for Studies in Public Policy, Atlanta GA 30314. LC KFG15. DD 344.758.

GEORGIA STATE BAR JOURNAL. Vol. 1, No. 1 (Aug. 1964)-. 0016-8416. Periodical. US. English. qt. $8.00. Georgia Justice Center, 84 Peachtree Street/11th Floor, Atlanta GA 30303. Tel (404)522-6255. Ed James Gaulden. Ind/Abst Leg. Resour. Index, Index Leg. Period., Curr. Law Index. LC KF200. adv acc. Circ 16,800. Articles on substantive law. Georgia Bar Journal.

GEORGIA STATE BAR NEWS. Main/Corp State Bar of Georgia. V. 1- Sept. 1975-. Periodical. US. English. bm. 1510 Fulton National Bank Building, Atlanta GA 30303. LC KF200. DD 340.09758.

GEORGIA STATE UNIVERSITY LAW REVIEW. Vol. 1, No. 1 (Fall 1984)-. 8755-6847. Periodical. US. English. sa. $10.00 Domestic, $12.00 Foreign. Georgia State University Law Review, PO Box 492, University Plaza, Atlanta GA 30303-3098. DD 340.

DIE GESETZLICHE RENTENVERSICHERUNG. Series/Titl Solidus Buro-Leitfaden. German. ir. 33.00. Leitfadenverlag Dieter Sunholt, Berg 3, Assenhausen West Germany. LC KK3387.A24. DD 344.4302, 344.3042.

GEVERS INTERNATIONAL CONSULTANTS. SZ. English. an. LC K68. DD 340.025.

GEWERBLICHER RECHTSSCHUTZ UND URHEBERRECHT. INTERNATIONALER TEIL. 0435-8600. Periodical. German. mo. VCH Publishers Inc, 303 NW 12th Avenue, Deerfield Beach FL 33442. Tel (305)428-5566.

GILBERT CRIMINAL LAW AND PROCEDURE. VFOAT Criminal Law and Procedure. 53rd- Ed. US. English. an. $74.50. Matthew Bender & Company Inc, 1275 Broadway, Albany NY 12201. Tel (800)833-9844. Index in last issue of volume - loose - separately paged. Clevenger-Gilbert Criminal Law and Practice of New York.

GILBERT LAW SUMMARIES. CIVIL PROCEDURE. (CIVIL PROCEDURE). 1st Ed.-. 0161-830X. US. English. an. $11.95. Law Distributors, 14415 South Main Street, Gardena CA 90248. LC KF8841. DD 347.735, 347.3075.

GILBERT LAW SUMMARIES. COMMUNITY PROPERTY. (COMMUNITY PROPERTY). 0192-561X. US. English. an. 14415 South Main Street, Gardena CA 90248. LC KFC125.C6. DD 346.794042, 347.940642.

GILBERT LAW SUMMARIES. CONFLICT OF LAWS. (CONFLICT OF LAWS). 12th- Ed. 0270-2908. US. English. $10.50. Law Distributors, 14415 South Main Street, Gardena CA 90248. LC KF412. DD 340.9. Gilbert Law Summaries. Conflict of Laws, 0270-2908.

GILBERT LAW SUMMARIES. CONSTITUTIONAL LAW. VFOAT Constitutional Law. 17th- Ed. US. English. Law Distributors, 14415 South Main Street, Gardena CA 90248.

GILBERT LAW SUMMARIES. CRIMINAL LAW. (CRIMINAL LAW). 11th- ed. 0193-7200. US. English. $9.95. Law Distributors, 14415 South Main Street, Gardena CA 90248. LC KF9219.3. DD 345.73, 347.305. Criminal Law.

GILBERT LAW SUMMARIES: CRIMINAL PROCEDURE. (CRIMINAL PROCEDURE). 9th- Ed. 0193-8010. US. English. $10.50 per issue. Law Distributors, 14415 South Main Street, Gardena CA 90248. LC KF9619.3. DD 345.7305. Criminal Procedure, 0193-922X.

GILBERT LAW SUMMARIES. TRUSTS. VFOAT Trusts. 9th Ed. (1981). US. English. Law Distributors, 14415 South Main Street, Gardena CA 90248. Trusts.

GINKO TORIHIKI SHOROPPO (JAPAN). JA. Japanese. ir. 2800. Kinyu Zaisei Jijo Kenkyukai, 19 Minami Notomachi, Shinjuku-ku, Tokyo-to Japan.

GIORNALE DI DIRITTO DEL LAVORO E DI RELAZIONI INDUSTRIALI. V. 1, No. 1, (1979)-. Periodical. IT. Italian. qt. $35.64. Franco Angeli Editore Riviste, Via le Monza 106, 20127 Milano Italy. Tel (02)28.27.651/2/3/. LC K7. DD 344.4501, 344.5041.

GIURISPRUDENZA COMMERCIALE. 1- Jan./Feb. 1974-. IT. Italian. bm. 100.000 Domestic, 150.000 Foreign. Casa Editrice Dr A Giuffre, Via Statuto 2 Periodical Department, 20121 Milano Italy. Tel 02/652341. Ed Gaetano Castellano. adv acc. Circ 5,300. This journal is mainly intended for practitioners. The first part contains articles on topical subjects. The second part publishes the latest and most important decision.

GIURISPRUDENZA COSTITUZIONALE. Vol. 1- 1956-. 0436-0222. Periodical. IT. Italian. mo. 110.000 Domestic, 165.000 Foreign. Casa Editrice Dr A Giuffre, Via Statuto 2, 20121 Milano Italy. Tel 02/651342. Ed Vezio Crisafulli. adv acc. Circ 2,400.

GIURISPRUDENZA DI MERITO. Periodical. IT. Italian. bm. 75.000 Domestic, 115.000 Foreign. Casa Editrice, Dr A Giuffre, Via Statuto 2, 20121 Milano Italy. Tel 02/652341. Ed Angelo Jammuzzi. adv acc. Circ 5,000.

GLENDALE LAW REVIEW. V. 1- 1976-. 0363-2423. Periodical. US. English. sa. $9.00. Glendale Law Review, 220 North, Glendale Avenue, Glendale CA 91206. Tel (818)247-0770. Ed Norman Taylor. Ind/Abst Leg. Resour. Index, Public Aff. Inf. Serv. Bull., Index Leg. Period., Curr. Law Index. LC K7. DD 340.0973. Circ 500. General; interdisciplinary periodical on current and controversial issues.

GLORIA JURIS : SUATU HIMPUNAN KARANGAN ILMIAH DOSEN-DOSEN FAKULTAS HUKUM. Edition 1 (Semester 2. 1980)-. Periodical. IO. Indonesian. sa. Universitas Katolik Indonesia Atma Jaya, Fakultas Hukum, Biro Bantuan Hukum dan Penelitian, Jl Jenderal Sudirman 49A, Jakarta Selatan Indonesia. LC K7. DD 349.59805, 345.98005.

GODISNIK NA PRAVNIOT FAKULTET VO SKOPJE. Serbo-Croatian -C (summaries in English or French). ir.

Law

GOING INTERNATIONAL, INTERNATIONAL TRADE FOR THE NONSPECIALIST : ALI-ABA COURSE OF STUDY, MATERIALS. VFOAT ALI-ABA Course of Study, Materials. US. English. American Law Institute-American Bar Association Committee on Continuing Professional Education, 4025 Chestnut Street, Philadelphia PA 19104. LC KF390.B8. DD 343.73087, 347.30387.

GOLDEN GATE UNIVERSITY LAW REVIEW. V. 6- Fall 1975-. Periodical. US. English. ty. $20.00. Golden Gate University School of Law, 536 Mission Street, San Francisco CA 94105. Tel (415)442-7000. Ed Robert Dalby. Ind/Abst Index Leg. Period., Manage. Contents, Leg. Resour. Index, Curr. Law Index, Contents Curr. Leg. Period. LC K7. DD 340.09794. bk rev. adv acc. Circ 650. Concentrates on ninth circuit, women's legal issues, and general law. Golden Gate Law Review, 0098-6631.

GONZAGA LAW REVIEW. Vol. 1, No. 1 (Mar. 1966)-. 0046-6115. Periodical. US. English. qt. $21.56. Gonzaga University, School of Law, Spokane WA 99202. Tel (509)328-4220. Ed Joe Harrington. Ind/Abst Leg. Resour. Index, Index Leg. Period., Curr. Law Index, Contents Curr. Leg. Period. LC K7. DD 340.05. (cum index). bk rev. adv acc. Circ 1,000. (ctrl). A timely publication of recent developments in the legal field- particularly designed for the legal practitioners in Washington.

GONZAGA SPECIAL REPORT. VFOAT Gonzaga Special Report. Public Sector Labor Law, Public Sector Labor Law. Vol. 1 (1980)-. 0885-9868. Periodical. US. English. $5.50. Gonzaga Public Sector Report, c/o Gonzaga Student Bar Association, Gonzaga University School of Law, Spokane WA 99202. Ind/Abst Leg. Resour. Index. LC K7. DD 344.730189041353, 347. 304189041353.

GOTTINGER RECHTSWISSENSCHAFTLICHE STUDIEN. Vol. 1-. Monographic Series. GW. German. ir. Verlag Otto Schwartz and Company, Annastrasse 7, D-3400 Gottingen West Germany.

GOVERNMENT CONTRACTS SECTION NEWSLETTER. Jan. 1984-. 0742-8901. Periodical. US. English. Federal Bar Association, 1815 H Street NW, Washington DC 20006. LC KF842. DD 346.7302305, 347.3062305. Government Contracts Council Newsletter, 0741-5311.

GOVERNMENT CONTRACTS SERVICE. 0145-6598. US. English. ir. $450.00. Procurement Associates, 733 North Dodsworth Avenue, Covina CA 91724. Tel (213)966-4576. Ed Paul R McDonald Sr. LC KF846.5. DD 346.73023. adv acc.

GOVERNMENT GAZETTE. Main/Corp NAURU. Periodical. US. English. LC KTF.

THE GOVERNMENT GAZETTE OF MAURITIUS. Main/Corp Mauritius. Periodical. US. English. LC Microfilm LL-02194 KRQ. Government Gazette of the Colony of Mauritius.

GOVERNMENT RELATIONS STATUS REPORT. Main/Corp American Bankers Association. 0199-9990. US. English. American Bankers Association, 1120 Connecticut Avenue NW, Washington DC 20036. LC KF967. DD 346.73082.

GOVERNMENT UNION REVIEW. See Economics - Labor.

GOWER FEDERAL SERVICE : MINING. See Engineering - Mining Engineering.

GRAEZISTISCHE ABHANDLUNGEN. V. 1- 1965-. 0436-2756. Monographic Series. German. ir.

GRAND AND PETIT JUROR SERVICE IN THE UNITED STATES DISTRICT COURTS. (GRAND AND PETIT JUROR SERVICE IN UNITED STATES DISTRICT COURTS). 1982-. 0737-3309. US. English. an. Statistical Analysis and Reports Division, Administrative Office of the United States Courts, Washington DC 20544. LC KF8971.A152. DD 347.73225, 347.3062305. Juror Utilization in United States District Courts, 0098-3950.

GRIEVANCE AND ADJUDICATION SECTION REPORTS. Main/Corp Public Service Alliance of Canada. Grievance and Adjudication Section. Ser. 2, No. 2-. 0822-7810. Periodical. CN. English. ir. Free. Public Service Alliance of Canada, Grievance and Adjudication Section, 233 Gilmour Street, Ottawa Ontario K2P 0P1 Canada. DD 342.71068. Report on Grievances Submitted to Adjudication, 0318-6296.

GRUNDLAGEN UND PRAXIS DES WIRTSCHAFTSRECHTS. Monographic Series. GW. German. ir. Erich Schmidt Verlag GMBH, PO 7330, Viktoriastr 44-A, D4800 Bielefeld 1 West Germany. Tel 0521/6 60 61. Foundations of business law.

GRUPO ANDINO : LEGISLACION ECONOMICA Y SOCIAL DE LOS PAISES MIEMBROS. Main/Corp Junta del Acuerdo de Cartagena. Spanish. ir. $13.00. Apartado 548, Lima 18 Peru. Tel 41 42 12. Circ 400. (ctrl). Abstracts of economic and social legislation from five member countries of the Andean group: Bolivia, Colombia, Ecuador, Peru, and Venezuela.

GUAM REPORTS : CONTAINING OPINIONS OF THE DISTRICT, SUPERIOR AND SUPREME COURTS. Vol. 1 (1955-1979)-. US. English. ir. Equity Publishing Corporation, Oxford NH 03777. Tel (603)353-4351.

GUARDIANSHIP NEWS. 0276-6272. Periodical. US. English. mo. $48.00. Christian & Robertson Publishers, 85 Pine Grove Road, PO Box 674, Amherst MA 01004. LC KF553.A15. DD 346.7301805, 347.3061805.

GUIA DE TRIBUNALES NACIONALES Y DE LA PROVINCIA DE BUENOS AIRES. Spanish. ir. $17.00. La Diligencia Judicial, Av Juan B Justo 225-7. Piso 14, Buenos Aires Argentina. DD 347.82014025.

GUIA JUDICIAL DE BALEARES. Spanish. ir. Ricardo Anckerman, 100, Palma de Mallorca Spain.

GUIA PRACTICA DEL EXPORTADOR E IMPORTADOR. SUPLEMENTO. FASCICULO DE RESOLUCIONES DE CLASIFICACION. VFOAT Fasciculo de Resoluciones de Clasificacion. No. 1-. Spanish. ir. Lavalle 1125, P 3 P0 S Of 8, 1048 Buenos Aires Argentina. DD 343.82056, 348.20356.

GUIA PRACTICA DEL EXPORTADOR E IMPORTADOR Y PARA TODO HOMBRE DE NEGOCIOS. VFOAT Guia Practica del Exportador e Importador. Spanish. ir. Lavalle LL25, P 3O Of 8, 1048 Buenos Aires Argentina. DD 343.8208705, 348.2038705. Guia Practica del Exportador e Importador.

GUIA PRACTICA DEL EXPORTADOR E IMPORTADOR Y PARA TODO HOMBRE DE NEGOCIOS. SUPLEMENTO. VFOAT Guia Practica del Exportador e Importador - Suplemento. Spanish. ir. $720.00. Guia Practica del Exportador e Importador, Lavalle LL25, P. 3 Of 8, 1048 Buenos Aires Argentina. DD 343.8208705, 348.2038705.

GUIA PRACTICA DEL EXPORTADOR E IMPORTADOR Y PARA TODO HOMBRE DE NEGOCIOS. SUPLEMENTO DE LA SECCION INFORMATIVA. Spanish. ir. Guia Practica del Exportador e Importadoe S.A.C.I., Lavalle LL25, P. 3 Of. 8, 1048 Buenos Aires Argentina. DD 343.82087, 348.20387.

GUIA PROFESIONAL Y JUDICIAL. Main/Corp Ilustre Colegio Provincial de Abogados (Salamanca, Spain (Province)). Spanish. ir. Ilustre Colegio Provinciae de Abogados, Palacio de Justicia Gran Via 7, Apdo de Correos 117, Salamanca Spain. DD 340.0254625.

GUIA SOCIAL DEL TRABAJADOR. 1982-. 0826-8673. CN. Spanish. an. Quebec Federation of Labour, 4th Floor 2100 Papineau Avenue, Montreal Quebec H2K 4J4 Canada. DD 344.71401.

GUIDA SOCIAL DO TRABALHADOR. 1982-. 0826-8681. CN. Portuguese. an. Quebec Federation of Labour, 4th Floor/2100 Papineau Avenue, Montreal Quebec H2K 4J4 Canada. DD 344.71401.

GUIDE FISCALO-COMPTABLE. 1981-. FR. French. ir. Lamy, 155 rue Legendre, 75850 Paris Cedex 17 France. DD 346.440650202, 344.406650202.

GUIDE SOCIAL DU TRAVAILLEUR. 1982-. 0826-8665. CN. French. an. Federation des Travailleurs du Quebec, 4E Etage 2100 Avenue Papineau, Montreal Quebec H2K 4J4 Canada. DD 344.71401.

GUIDE TO LEGISLATION ON RESTRICTIVE BUSINESS PRACTICES. Main/Corp Organization for Economic Cooperation and Development. VFOAT Legislation on Restrictive Business Practices. 1961-. Periodical. English. ir. OECD Publications Center, 1750 Pennsylvania Avenue Northwest, Washington DC 20006. Tel (202)724-1857. Guide to Legislation on Restrictive Business Practices: Europe and North America.

GUIDE TO LOCAL AUTHORITIES ELECTIONS. (A GUIDE TO LOCAL AUTHORITIES ELECTIONS). 0826-9491. CN. English. LC KEA478.5.E43. DD 342.712307, 347.123027.

GUIDE TO PRACTICE AND PROCEDURE, U.S. DEPARTMENT OF ENERGY, BOARD OF CONTRACT APPEALS, CONTRACT ADJUSTMENT BOARD, FINANCIAL ASSISTANCE APPEALS BOARD, INVENTION LICENSING APPEALS BOARD. See Energy.

GUIDE TO RECORD RETENTION REQUIREMENTS. VFOAT Record Retention Guide. Began in 1955. 0271-6461. US. English. an. Superintendent of Documents, US Government Printing Office, Washington DC 20403. LC KF70.

GUILD NOTES. 0148-0588. Periodical. US. English. qt. $15.00. National Lawyers Guild, 853 Broadway/Suite 1705, New York NY 10003. Tel (212)260-1360. Ed Barbara Dudley. Ind/Abst Altern. Press Index. LC KF200. DD 340.05. bk rev. Circ 8,000. Articles of interest to progressive lawyers, legal workers, law students: International affairs, Central America, Native America, civil rights, economic rights, gay and women's rights, immigration, etc.

THE GUILD PRACTITIONER. VFOAT National Lawyers Guild Practitioner. Vol. 24, No. 1 (Winter 1965)-. 0017-5390. Periodical. US. English. qt. $10.00. National Lawyers Guild, 1715 Francisco Street, Berkeley CA 94703. Tel (415)848-0599. Ed Ed Dawley. Ind/Abst Public Aff. Inf. Serv. Bull. LC KF200. DD 340.05. bk rev. Circ 670. (ctrl). Journal on law and social change from a practical and theoretical viewpoint. Law in Transition, 0734-158X.

GUJARAT LAW TIMES. V. 1- 1964-. 0017-5528. Periodical. English. sm. Index in last issue of volume - attached.

GUJARAT REVENUE TRIBUNAL LAW REPORTER. 0017-5536. Periodical. English. ir.

GUYANA LAW JOURNAL. V. 1-. Periodical. GY. English. ir. $6.00 Per Issue to Students of Institutions in the Caribbean, $10.00 Per Issue all Other Sales. Department of Political Science and Law, Box 841, Georgetown Guyana South Africa. LC K7. DD 349.88105, 348.81005.

GYOSEI KANKEI HANREI KAISETSU. JA. Japanese. ir. 4950. Gyosei, 4-12 Ginza 7 Chuo-ku, Tokyo-to 162 Japan.

HA-PERAKLIT. VFOAT Hapraklit. Periodical. IS. Hebrew. qt. $25.00. Lishkat Orkhe Ha Din, PO Box 14152, Tel Aviv Israel. LC K16.

HALSBURY'S LAWS OF ENGLAND ANNUAL ABRIDGMENT. VFOAT Laws of England Annual Abridgment. 1974-. 0308-4388. UK. English. an. Butterworths, Box 63 Westbury House/Westbury Street, Guilford GU1 5BH England. LC KD310. DD 340.0941.

HALSBURY'S LAWS OF ENGLAND : CUMULATIVE SUPPLEMENT. UK. English. an.

HALSBURY'S STATUTORY INSTRUMENTS : BEING A COMPANION WORK TO HALSBURY'S STATUTES OF ENGLAND. Main/Corp Great Britain. UK. English. mo. D & S Publishers, PO Box 5105, Clearwater FL 33518. Tel (800)237-9707.

HAMLINE JOURNAL OF PUBLIC LAW. Vol. 3, Issue 1 (Winter 1981)-. 0736-1033. Periodical. US. English. sa. $10.00. Hamline University, School of Law, 1536 Hewitt Avenue, St Paul MN 65014. Tel (612)641-2371. Ed Michael Sharpe. LC K8. DD 344.73005, 347.304005. adv acc. Circ 1,000. Addresses issues of public law and policy considered by the executive, legislative, and judicial branches and administrative agencies. Journal of Minnesota Public Law, 0748-769X.

HAMLINE LAW REVIEW. Vol. 1978, No. 1-. 0198-7364. Periodical. US. English. ir. $11.00. Hamline University-Law Review, 1536 Hewitt Avenue, St Paul MN 55104. **Tel** (612)641-2350. **Ed** Dave Theisen. **Ind/Abst** Leg. Resour. Index, Index Leg. Period. **LC** K8. **DD** 340.05. bk rev. adv acc. **Circ** 1,200. The Hamline law review is published twice a year and is comprised of articles, notes, comments, book reviews, and symposium projects focusing on particular fields of law.

THE HAMLYN LECTURES. 1st- Series. Monographic Series. UK. English. ir. Associated Book Publishers, North Way Andover, Hampshire SP10 5BE England. **Tel** (01)583-9855. A series of lectures delivered by eminent figures in the field of British law. The purpose is to further the knowledge among the general public of the British legal system.

HANDBOOK - ALABAMA LAW INSTITUTE. **Main/Corp** Alabama Law Institute. 0149-0842. US. English. University of Alabama, Alabama Law Institute, Farrah Hall/Room 432, PO Box 1425, Tuscaloosa AL 35486. **LC** KFA27.L38. **DD** 340.062761.

HANDBOOK - OKLAHOMA BAR ASSOCIATION. **Main/Corp** Oklahoma Bar Association (Founded 1939). 0271-2571. US. English. Journal-Record Publishing Company, 621 North Robinson, Oklahoma City OK 73102. **LC** KF332.O4. **DD** 340.060766.

HANDBOOK ON SPECIALIZATION. **Main/Corp** ABA Standing Committee on Specialization. Aug. 1983-. 8756-887X. US. English. **LC** KF297.A1. **DD** 349.7305, 347.3005.

HANDBOOK - SOCIETY FOR THE RIGHT TO DIE. (HANDBOOK). **Main/Corp** Society for the Right to Die. 0276-8305. US. English. Society for the Right to Die, 250 West 57th Street, New York NY 10107. **LC** KF3827.E87. **DD** 344.730419, 347.304419.

HANDBUCH DES BREMISCHEN SCHULRECHTS. **Main/Corp** Bremen (Germany). Senator fur Bildung, Wissenschaft und Kunst. GE. German. ir. Senator fur Bildung, Wissenschaft und Kunst, J H Schmalfeldt Und Co, Geeren 6-8, 2800 Bremen 1 West Germany. **LC** KKB3378.A24. **DD** 344.435207.

HANDY REFERENCE GUIDE TO THE FAIR LABOR STANDARDS ACT. See Economics - Labor.

HANREI MINJI ROPPO ZENSHO. **Main/Corp** Japan. **VFOAT** Minji Roppo Zensho. 1982-. JA. Japanese. an. 3800. Daiichi Hoki Shuppan Kabushiki Kaisha, 11-17 Minami Aoyama 2 Minato-ku, Tokyo-to 107 Japan.

HANREITSUKI ROPPO ZENSHO. **Main/Corp** Japan. **VFOAT** Roppo Zensho. JA. Japanese. ir. 800. Kinensha, 2-9-6 Higashiueno Taito-ku, Tokyo Japan.

HANSARD OFFICIAL REPORT. **Main/Corp** Cayman Islands. Legislative Assembly. English. ir. Cayman Islands Government, Information Officer Government Administration Building, Grand Cayman British West Indies. **LC** J137.5. **DD** 354.729210005.

HANSARD OFFICIAL REPORT OF DEBATES, LEGISLATIVE ASSEMBLY OF ONTARIO. **Main/Corp** Ontario. Legislative Assembly. Standing Committee on Resources Development. CN. English. tw. $15.00 Per Session. Sessional Subscription Service, Information Services Branch, Ministry of Government Services, 5th Floor/880 Bay Street, Toronto Ontario M7A 1N8 Canada. **LC** J108. **DD** 328.71302. Legislature of Ontario Debates, Official Report (Hansard).

HANSON'S MANUAL OF EXAMINATION AND INSURANCE LAW HANDBOOK. US. English. ir. Insurance License Bureau Inc, 414 East Monroe Street, PO Box 610, Springfield MD 62705. **Tel** (217)544-4833. **LC** KFI1385.Z9. **DD** 346.773086076. Manual of Examination and Insurance Reference Guide for Illinois Insurance Agents and Brokers.

HANZAIGAKU ZASSHI. See Medicine - Psychiatry, Psychopathology.

HARTMANS TIJDSCHRIFT VOOR STUDERENDEN OPENBAAR BESTUUR. NE. Dutch. mo. Samson Uitgeverij BV, Postbus 4, 2400M Alphen-Rijin Netherlands. Hartmans Tijdschrift Ter Beoefening Van Het Administratief Recht.

HARVARD JOURNAL OF LAW AND PUBLIC POLICY. **VFOAT** Law and Public Policy. V. 1- 1978-. 0193-4872. US. English. ty. $22.50. Harvard Law School, Cambridge MA 02138. **Tel** (617)495-3105. **Ed** Karl W Saur. **Ind/Abst** Leg. Resour. Index, Public Aff. Inf. Serv. Bull., Index Leg. Period. **LC** K8. **DD** 340.0973. bk rev. **Circ** 1,100. A law review devoted, although not exclusively, to the exposition of conservative and libertarian perspectives on law, jurisprudence, and public policy.

HARVARD JOURNAL ON LEGISLATION. V. 1- Jan. 1964-. Periodical. US. English. sa. $15.00. Harvard Law School, Cambridge MA 02138. **Tel** (617)495-4400. **Ed** F Paul Bland. **Ind/Abst** Manage. Contents, Leg. Resour. Index, ABC Pol Sci, Public Aff. Inf. Serv. Bull., Index Leg. Period. **LC** Microfilm LL-0254K8. bk rev. A student-edited journal on legislative reform, presents detailed statements of how the law should be changed and proposes model acts for adoption by legislatures.

HARVARD LAW RECORD. V. 1- 1947-. 0017-8101. Periodical. US. English. ir. Harvard Law Record Corporation, 23 Everett Street, Cambridge MA 02138. **Tel** (617)495-4418. **Ed** Greg Klima. bk rev. adv acc. **Circ** 11,000. (ctrl). Oldest and largest law school newspaper with Harvard Law School alumni subscribers who average over $150,000 annual income. General legal topics are covered.

HARVARD LAW REVIEW. V. 1- Apr. 1887-. 0017-811X. US. English. Harvard Law Review Association, Gannett House, Cambridge MA 02138. **Tel** (617)495-7888. **Ind/Abst** Manage. Contents, Leg. Resour. Index, Hospit. Lit. Index, Account. Index. Suppl., ABC Pol Sci, ABI/Inform, Book Rev. Index, Public Aff. Inf. Serv. Bull., Index Leg. Period., Curr. Law Index, Leg. Contents, Soc. Sci. Citation Index, Contents Curr. Leg. Period. **LC** K8. **NLM** W1 HA635R. **CODEN** HALRAF. (cum index).

HARVARD WOMEN'S LAW JOURNAL. V. 1- 1978-. 0270-1456. US. English. an. $7.00. Harvard Law School, Cambridge MA 02138. **Tel** (617)495-3726. **Ed** Ruth Borenstein. **Ind/Abst** Leg. Resour. Index, Altern. Press Index, Public Aff. Inf. Serv. Bull., Index Leg. Period. **LC** K8. **DD** 349.73088042. bk rev. A student-edited journal devoted to the development of a feminist jurisprudence. Explores the impact of women on the law and the impact of the law on women.

HASTINGS CONSTITUTIONAL LAW QUARTERLY. V. 1- Spring 1974-. 0094-5617. Periodical. US. English. qt. $15.00. Hastings School of Law, 198 McAllister Street/Room 205, San Francisco CA 94102. **Tel** (415)565-4726. **Ed** David Thill. **Ind/Abst** Leg. Resour. Index, Index Leg. Period., Contents Curr. Leg. Period., Curr. Law Index, Leg. Resour. Index. **LC** K8. **DD** 342.73005. bk rev adv acc. **Circ** 1,000. (ctrl). Articles dealing with constitutional law-state and federal.

HASTINGS LAW JOURNAL. 0017-8322. Periodical. US. English. ir. $20.00. Hastings College of Law, 198 McAllister Street/Room 205, San Francisco CA 94102. **Tel** (415)565-4600. **Ind/Abst** Leg. Resour. Index, Index Leg. Period., Soc. Sci. Citation Index, Curr. Law Index, Contents Curr. Leg. Period. Hastings Journal (San Francisco, Calif.).

HAWAII BAR JOURNAL MICROFORM. Vol. 1 (1963)-. Periodical. US. English. $12.00. Hawaii Bar Journal, PO Box 26, Honolulu HI 96810. **Tel** (808)524-0330. **Ed** Edward C Kemper III. **LC** Microfilm (O). adv acc. **Circ** 2,550. Scholarly articles related to law. Hawaii Bar News.

HAWAII LEGAL REPORTER. 0147-1392. US. English. Legal Pub Hawaii Inc, PO Box 27611, Honolulu HI 96827. **LC** KFH47. **DD** 348.969046.

HAWAII PROSECUTOR-PUBLIC DEFENDER NEWSLETTER. 0363-0463. Periodical. US. English. mo. 119 Merchant Street/Room 400, Honolulu HI 96813. **LC** KFH575.A15. **DD** 345.96905.

HAZARDOUS WASTE AND TOXIC TORTS. (HAZARDOUS WASTE AND TOXIC TORTS : LAW AND STRATEGY). **VFOAT** Hazardous Waste and Toxic Torts Law & Strategy. Vol. 1, No. 1 (June 1985)-. 0884-3775. Periodical. US. English. mo. $165.00. Leader Publications, 111 8th Avenue, New York NY 10011. **DD** 355.

HAZARDOUS WASTE LITIGATION. Series/Titl Litigation and Administrative Practice Series** Litigation Course Handbook Series. 8756-1573. US. English. an. Practising Law Institute, 810 Seventh Avenue, New York NY 10019. **LC** KF1299.H39. **DD** 346.73038, 347.30638.

HAZARDOUS WASTE LITIGATION REPORTER. 1980. 0275-0244. Periodical. US. English. sm. Andrews Publications Inc, PO Box 200, Edgemont PA 19028. **Tel** (215)353-2565. **Ed** Leonard E B Andrews. **LC** KF3946.A59. **DD** 344.7304622, 347.3044622. The national journal or record of hazardous waste litigation.

HEALTH CARE LABOR MANUAL. NEWSLETTER. V. 1, No. 5- Oct. 1977-. 0197-3738. Periodical. US. English. bm. $186.00. Aspen Systems Corporation, 20010 Century Boulevard, Germantown MD 20767. **LC** KF3580.H4. **DD** 344.7301, 347.3041. **NLM** W1 HE299LI. Health Care Labor Review.

THE HEALTH FACILITIES COURT DIGEST. V. 1- Jan. 1977-. 0148-5385. Periodical. US. English. mo. $20.00. Juridical Digests Institute, 1860 Broadway, New York NY 10023. **LC** KF3825.A59. **DD** 344.7303211. **NLM** W1 HE335N.

HEALTH LABOR RELATIONS REPORTS. **VFOAT** HLR Reports. V. 1- Oct. 26, 1976-. 0148-4761. Periodical. US. English. bw. $50.00. Health Labor Relations Reports, 3 Interwood Place, PO Box 20241, Cincinnati OH 45220. **Tel** (513)221-3715. **Ed** Frank J Bardack. **NLM** W1 HE4015. Employee and labor relations in health care. Legal decisions in: at-will employment, wrongful discharge, discrimination, NLRB decisions, arbitration awards, contract settlements, workers' compensation, union organizing.

HEALTH LAW IN CANADA. Vol. 1, No. 1 (Spring 1980)-. 0226-8841. Periodical. CN. English. qt. $25.00. Health and Law in Canada, c/o Canadian Institute of Law and Medicine, PO Box 361 Station A, Rexdale Ontario M9W 5L3 Canada. **Ind/Abst** Leg. Resour. Index, Hospit. Lit. Index. **LC** KE3646.A13. **DD** 344.71041, 347.10441. **NLM** W1 HE402T.

HEALTH LAW PROJECT. LIBRARY BULLETIN. (LIBRARY BULLETIN). **VFOAT** Health Law Project Library Bulletin. 0163-3996. Periodical. US. English. mo. Free to Active Participants of HSA's in Pennsylvania, Consumer Organizations, Individual Consumers on Restricted Budgets, Legislators, Students, Educational Institutions, State Governments, $9.00 all Others. Health Law Project of the University of Pennsylvania, 133 South 36th Street/Room 410, Philadelphia PA 19104. **LC** KF3821.A15. **DD** 344.7304105. **NLM** W1 HE403.

HEALTH LAW VIGIL. V. 1- June 23, 1978-. 0270-3343. Periodical. US. English. bw. $326.00. American Hospital Association, 850 North Lakeshore Drive, Chicago IL 60611. **Tel** (312)280-6679. **Ed** Azike A Ntephe. **Ind/Abst** Hospit. Lit. Index. **NLM** W1 HE403H. **Circ** 4,000. A biweekly analysis of law-related developments affecting hospitals and the health care field.

THE HEALTH LAWYER. Vol. 1, No. 1 (Summer 1982)-. 0736-3443. Periodical. US. English. American Hospital Association, 850 North Lakeshore Drive/#810, Chicago IL 60611. **Tel** (312)280-6679. **Ed** Azike A Ntephe. **LC** KF3821.A15. **DD** 344.7304105, 347.3044105. **Circ** 100. On-line bibliographic database devoted to recent developments in health law.

HEALTH LAWYERS NEWS REPORT. See Medicine.

HEALTH MATRIX. Vol. 1, No. 1 (Winter 1983)-. 0748-383X. Periodical. US. English. qt. $72.00. Rynd Communications, 99 Painter Mill Road, Owings Mills, MD 21117. **Tel** (301)363-6400. **Ed** Dr Duncan Newhauser. **Ind/Abst** Hospit. Lit. Index. **NLM** W1. bk rev. **Circ** 500. Provides the multidisciplinary coverage required to keep informed on important issues and current developments in health care from legal, managerial and political perspectives.

HEALTH SYSTEMS PLAN : PURSUANT TO THE NATIONAL HEALTH PLANNING AND RESOURCES DEVELOPMENT ACT OF 1974 (PUBLIC LAW 93-641). **Main/Corp** Houston-Galveston Area Council. Health Systems Agency. **VFOAT** Health Systems Plan. Began with 1977. US. English. an. 3701 West Alabama, PO Box 22777, Houston TX 77027. **NLM** W2.

HEALTH SYSTEMS REPORT ALMANAC ON FEDERAL HEALTH ISSUES, PROPOSALS, ADMINISTRATIVE ACTIONS, LEGISLATION, PUBLIC LAWS. See Yearbooks, Almanacs, Directories.

HEALTHSPAN. **VFOAT** Health Span. Vol. 2, No. 1 (Jan. 1985)-. 0883-0452. Periodical. US. English. ir. Law and Business Inc, 855 Valley Road, Clifton NJ

Law

07013. Tel (201)472-7400. Ed Cliff Stromber and Michele L Robinson. **Ind/Abst** Hospit. Lit. Index. **DD** 344. **NLM** W1. bk rev. **Circ** 1,100. The report of health and business law. *Healthscan, 8755-2205.*

HEARING PROCESS STATUS REPORT. VFOAT White Book. V. 1, No. 1 (May 1979)-V. 2, No. 3 (Jan. 1980). 0194-1860. Periodical. US. English. mo. US Government Printing Office, Superintendent of Documents, Washington DC 20402. Tel (202)783-3238. **LC** KF2120. **DD** 343.7309202646.

HEARINGS AND REPORTS OF COMMITTEES OF THE CALIFORNIA LEGISLATURE : A LISTING. Main/Corp California. Legislature. Assembly. Office of Research. 0362-9929. US. English. Sacramento Assembly Office of Research, 1116 Ninth Street, Sacramento CA 95814. **LC** KFC20. **DD** 016.3287940765. *Hearings and Reports of Committees of the California Legislature: A Summary and Listing.*

HEARSAY : LEGAL AID PRACTICE NOTES AND INFORMATION BULLETIN OF THE LEGAL AID COMMISSION OF WESTERN AUSTRALIA. Main/Corp Legal Aid Commission of Western Australia. Periodical. English. bm. Director of Legal Aid, 105 Saint George's Terrace, GPO Box L916, Perth Western Australia 6001 Australia. **DD** 347.94101705, 349.41071705.

HEBDO INFORMATIONS. Periodical. French. wk. 200 Single Issue. Hebdo Informations, Immeuble Branly 1ER Etage Avenue du Colonel Parant, BP 2240, Libreville Gabon. **LC** K8. **DD** 349.672105, 346.721005.

HEIN ... ANNUAL CHECKLIST OF STATUTES (STATE AND TERRITORIAL). 1st (1973)-. US. English. an. William S Hein and Company Inc, Hein Building/1285 Main Street, Buffalo NY 114209.

HELR. THE HARVARD ENVIRONMENTAL LAW REVIEW. (THE HARVARD ENVIRONMENTAL LAW REVIEW). VFOAT HELR, H.E.L.R. Vol.4, No.1 (1980)-. Periodical. US. English. ir. $14.00. Harvard Law School, Cambridge MA 02138. Tel (617)495-3110. Ed Michael Proett. **Ind/Abst** Electron. Commun. Abstr. J., ISMEC Bull., Pollut. Abstr. Indexes, Saf. Sci. Abstr. J., Leg. Resour. Index, Sel. Water Resour. Abstr., Coal Abstr., Energy Inf. Abstr., Environ. Abstr., Public Aff. Inf. Serv. Bull., Energy Res. Abstr., Index Leg. Period. **LC** K5. **DD** 344.73046. bk rev. Scholarly articles on current topics in environmental law. *HELR. Harvard Environmental Law Review.*

THE HENNEPIN LAWYER. 1931. US. English. bm. $12.00. Hennepin County Bar Association, 430 Marquette Avenue, Minneapolis MN 55401. Tel (612)340-0022. Ed Nancy Klossner. adv acc. **Circ** 5,300. Articles to assist and educate lawyers about current issues and events relating to the changes in the laws and lawyers.

HENRY B. ZIMMER'S PROBLEMS & QUESTIONS IN CANADIAN TAXATION. VFOAT Problems & Questions in Canadian Taxation. VAT Problems & Questions in Canadian Taxation (Calgary), Problems and Questions in Canadian Taxation (Calgary). 1984-. 0824-6378. CN. English. an. $12.50 Per Vol. Henry B Zimmer's Problems & Questions in Canadian Taxation, c/o Cantax Seminars, 475-15055 5th Street SW, Calgary Alberta T2R 1K3 Canada. **DD** 343.71052. *Problems & Questions in Canadian Taxation, 0824-6386.*

HERRI-ARDURALARITZAZKO EUSKAL ALDIZKARIA. VFOAT Revista Vasca de Administracion Publica. 1 (Iraila-Abendua 1981)-. 0211-9560. Periodical. Basque (Spanish). ty. $24.00. Instiuto Vasco de Administracion Publica, Onati Guipuzcoa Spain. **LC** K8. **DD** 342.46606, 344.66026.

THE HIGH COURT MONTHLY BULLETIN. Main/Corp Uganda. High Court. Periodical. English. mo. Law Development Center, PO Box 7117/Makerere Hill, Kampula Uganda. **DD** 348.6761041. *Monthly Bulletin of Judgments and Orders.*

HIGHER EDUCATION LAW REPORT. 0742-0803. US. English. mo. Law Offices of J Andrew Usera, 4801 Massachusetts Avenue Northwest/Suite 400, Washington DC 20016. **LC** KF4225.A15. **DD** 344.7307405, 347.3047405.

HIGHLIGHTS OF STATE UNEMPLOYMENT COMPENSATION LAWS. Jan. 1982-. 0730-7624. US. English. an. National Foundation for Unemployment Compensation and Workers' Compensation, 600 Maryland Avenue SW, Washington DC 20024. **LC** KF3675.Z95. **DD** 344.73024, 347.30424.

HIKAKU HOSEI. VFOAT Journal of the Kinki University Comparative Law and Politics Institute. Edition- 1972-. Periodical. JA. Japanese. ir. Kinki Daigaku Hikakuho Seiji Kenkyujo, 4-1 Kowakae 3-chome, Higashi Osaka Japan. **LC** K8.

HIKKEI GAKKO SHOROPPO. Main/Corp Japan. VFOAT Gakko Shoroppo. JA. Japanese. ir. 1200. Kyodo Shuppan 5 Kanda Nishiki-Cho 2 Chiyoda-ku, Tokyo-to 101 Japan. Ed Sagara Iichi.

HIMPUNAN PERATURAN NEGARA. 0126-3730. English (Indonesian). qt. **DD** 349.59805, 345.98005.

HIMPUNAN PERATURAN-PERATURAN MENTERI PERTANIAN. Main/Corp Indonesia. Departement Pertanian. VFOAT Peraturan M.E.N.T.A.N. Began with 1969 Vol. Indonesian. an.

HIMPUNAN PERATURAN PERUNDANG-UNDANGAN PRODUK DEPARTEMEN AGAMA R. I. Main/Corp Indonesia. Departemen Agama. Indonesian. ir.

HINE'S INSURANCE COUNSEL. *See* Insurance.

HITOTSUBASHI JOURNAL OF LAW & POLITICS. *See* Political Science.

HOFSTRA ENVIRONMENTAL LAW DIGEST. VFOAT Environmental Law Digest. Vol. 1, No. 2 (Fall 1984)-. 0882-6765. Periodical. US. English. sa. $4.00. Hofstra Environmental Law Society, Hofstra University, School of Law, Hempstead NY 11550. Tel (516)560-5007. Ed Fran Cohen. **DD** 344. **Circ** 150. (ctrl). Digest provides reviews and analyses of significant developments in the field of environmental law and litigation. *Environmental Law Digest.*

HOFSTRA LABOR LAW JOURNAL. Vol. 2, No. 1 (Spring-Fall 1984)-. Periodical. US. English. sa. $12.00. Business Manager, Hofstra Labor Law Journal, Hofstra University/School of Law, Hempstead NY 11550. *Hofstra Labor Law Forum, 0739-8220.*

HOFSTRA LAW REVIEW. V. 1- 1973-. 0091-4029. Periodical. US. English. qt. $20.00. Hofstra University Law School, 1000 Fulton Avenue, Hempstead NY 11550. Tel (516)560-5910. Ed Linda Keenan. **Ind/Abst** Leg. Resour. Index, Index Leg. Period., Curr. Law Index, Contents Curr. Leg. Period. **LC** K8. **DD** 340.05. bk rev. adv acc. **Circ** 900. Scholarly articles on legal and social issues.

HOGAKU NO TOMO. JA. English. mo. Japan Publishing Trading Company Ltd, PO Box 5030, Tokyo International Tokyo 100-31 Japan.

HOKEI RON SHU : KENKYU KIYO. Main/Corp Shizuoka Daigaku. Hokei Tanki Daigakubu. JA. Japanese. ir. Shizuoka Daigaku, 836 Oya, Shizuoka Japan. **LC** K23.

HOKEN ROPPO. Main/Corp Japan. JA. Japanese. ir. 4500. Sansei Shobo, 39-4 Minamidai 4, Nakano-ku 164, Tokyo-to-Japan.

HOKENGAKU ZASSHI. VFOAT Journal of Insurance Science. Periodical. JA. Japanese. ir. Nihon Hoken Gakkai 6-5, Kanda Surugadai 3-chome, Chiyoda-ku Tokyo. **LC** K1241.A13.

HOKKAI GAKUEN DAIGAKU HOGAKKAI HOGAKU KENKYU. (HOGAKU KENKYU). VFOAT Hokkaigakuen Law Journal. V. 1- (1-). JA. Japanese. mo. Japan Publishers Trading Company Ltd, PO Box 5030, Tokyo International Tokyo 100-31 Japan. **Ind/Abst** Am. Hist. Life, Hist. Abstr., Part A, Mod. Hist. Abstr., Hist. Abst., Part B, Twent. Century Abstr., Hist. Abstr. **LC** K8.

HOLDSWORTH LAW REVIEW. Vol. 4, No. 2-. 0260-5864. Periodical. UK. English. sa. $12.26. University of Birmingham, PO Box 363, Faculty of Law, Birmingham England. Tel 021 472 1301. Ed Jeremy McBride. **LC** K8. **DD** 349.4205, 344.2005. bk rev. adv acc. **Circ** 300. A general law journal aimed at academics, students and practitioners dealing with issues of English comparative and international law. *Holdsworth.*

HOLMESTED AND GALE ONTARIO PRACTICE YEAR BOOK. *See* Yearbooks, Almanacs, Directories.

THE HONG KONG GOVERNMENT GAZETTE. *See* Public Administration.

HONG KONG LAW JOURNAL. Began in Jan. 1971. 0378-0600. Periodical. HK. English. ir. Hong Kong Law Journal, 1030 Princes Building, Hong Kong. Tel 5-260318. **LC** K8.

HOSPITAL CONTRACTS MANUAL. Vol. 1-. 0734-0028. US. English. ir. $235.00. Aspen Systems Corporation, PO Box 6018, Gaithersburg MD 20760. Tel (301)251-5000. (ctrl). Sample contract clauses, negotiating tips, a glossary of legal terms, alternative language, executive staff and trustee compensation guidelines, updated semi-annually.

HOSPITAL LAW. V. 1- 1968-. 0193-9246. Periodical. US. English. mo. American Hospital Association, 840 North Lake Shore Drive, Chicago IL 60611. **NLM** W1 HO8121.

HOSPITAL LAW MANUAL. ADMINISTRATORS VOLUME. 1959-. Periodical. US. English. qt. $410.00. Aspen Systems Corporation, Box 6018, Gaithersburg MD 20760. Tel (301)251-5000. (ctrl). Includes tabbed sections and 600 subject references that information you need quickly and easily. Thorough and authoritative in every detail, is subscribed by over half the hospitals in the US.

HOUSE AND SENATE REPORTS ON PUBLIC BILLS (NUMBERED, UNBOUND. Main/Corp United States. Congress. Periodical. US. English.

HOUSING LAW BULLETIN. Vol. 8, Issue 6 (Dec. 1978- Jan. 1979)-. 0277-8491. Periodical. US. English. National Housing Law Project, 1950 Addison Street, Berkeley CA 94704. Tel (415)548-9400. **LC** KF5722. **DD** 344.73063635, 347.30463635. *Law Project Bulletin (National Housing Law Project).*

HOUSTON BAR BULLETIN. Began in 1942. 0279-3997. Periodical. US. English. mo. $6.00. Houston Bar Association, 1300 Texas Commerce Bank Building/707 Travis Road, Houstin TX 77002. **LC** KF200. **DD** 340.060764.

HOUSTON LAW REVIEW. Vol. 1, No. 1 (Spring 1963)-. 0018-6694. Periodical. US. English. ir. $25.00. Houston Law Review, University of Houston Law Center, University Park, Houston TX 77004. Tel (713)749-3195. Ed Phyllis Schrader. **Ind/Abst** Leg. Resour. Index, Soc. Work Res. Abstr., Index Leg. Period., Curr. Law Index, Contents Curr. Leg. Period. (cum index). adv acc. **Circ** 1,100. Publishes articles and commentaries that discuss legal issues of current interest.

HOUSTON LAWYER. V. 1- Nov. 1963-. 0439-660X. Periodical. US. English. qt. $19.10. Houston Bar Association of Texas, Commerce Building/707 Travia/Suite 1300, Houston TX 77002.

HOW TO MANAGE YOUR LAW OFFICE. US. English. an. Matthew Bender & Company Inc, 1275 Broadway, Albany NY 12201. Tel (800)833-9844. (cum index).

HOW TO TRY A FEDERAL CRIMINAL CASE. INCLUDING FORMS AND FEDERAL RULES OF CRIMINAL PROCEDURE. US. English. ir. Dennis & Company Inc, 251 Main Street, Buffalo NY 14203.

HOWARD LAW JOURNAL. V. 1-. 0018-6813. Periodical. US. English. qt. Editorial and General Offices, Howard University, School of Law, 2900 Van Ness Street, Washington DC 20008. Tel (202)686-6570. **Ind/Abst** Leg. Resour. Index, Sociol. Abstr., Public Aff. Inf. Serv. Bull., Index Leg. Period., Lang. Lang. Behav. Abstr., Curr. Law Index, Index Leg. Period., Contents Curr. Leg. Period.

HUGHES ESTATE, SUMMARY OF PROBATE PROCEEDINGS. V. 1- Apr. 1976-. 0145-6083. US. English. Armadillo Publishing Company, PO Drawer 1415, La Porte TX 77571. **LC** KF759.H83. **DD** 346.73056.

HUKUM. Vol. 1 1974-. Indonesian. ir. Yayasan Penelitian dan Pengembangan Hukum, Jln Kartanegara 51 Kebayoran Baru, Jakarta Indonesia.

HUKUM DAN PEMBANGUNAN. Vol. 7, No. 2- Mar. 1977-. Periodical. IO. Indonesian. ir. $13.50. Fakultas Hukum Universitas, JL Cirebon 5, Jakarta Indonesia. **LC** K25. *Majalah Fakultas Hukum Universitas Indonesia.*

Law

HUKUM NASIONAL. V. 1- 1975-. Indonesian. ir. BPHN, Medan Merdeka Utara No 9, Jakarta Indonesia. **LC** K8. *Hukum Nasional.*

HUMAN RIGHTS. See Political Science - Civil Rights.

HUNGARIAN LAW REVIEW. 1961-. Periodical. HU. English (Hungarian). sa. Akademiai Kiado, POB 24, 1363 Budapest Hungary.

I.A.C.P. LAW ENFORCEMENT LEGISLATION AND LITIGATION REPORT. See Law Enforcement.

ICC REGISTER. (ICC REGISTER : A DAILY SUMMARY OF MOTOR CARRIER APPLICATIONS AND DECISIONS AND NOTES ISSUED BY THE INTERSTATE COMMERCE COMMISSION). **VFOAT** I.C.C. Register. **VAT** Interstate Commerce Commission Register. Sept. 30, 1983-. 0749-0534. Periodical. US. English. da. Superintendent of Documents, US Government Printing Office, Washington DC 20402. **LC** KF2250. **DD** 343.7309302646, 347. 3039302646.

I.C.C. SUPPLEMENTAL REPORTS. **Main/Corp** United States. Interstate Commerce Commission. V. 1- Jan./Feb. 1974-. 0094-4270. US. English. mo. $395.00. Commerce Law Services Inc, 1747 Penn Avenue NW, Washington DC 20006. **LC** KF2172.A2. **DD** 343.73088.

ICE. INSIDE CODE ENFORCEMENT. (ICE, INSIDE CODE ENFORCEMENT). **VFOAT** Inside Code Enforcemnet. 0161-3367. Periodical. US. English. $20.00. R L Sanderson, 327 South LaSalle Street, Chicago IL 60604. **LC** KF5701.A15. **DD** 343.73078.

IDAHO LAW REVIEW. V. 1- 1964-. 0019-1205. Periodical. US. English. ty. $15.00. University of Idaho, College of Law, Moscow ID 83843. **Tel** (208)885-7241. Ed Jacque Palmer. **Ind/Abst** Leg. Resour. Index, Sel. Water Resour. Abstr., Index Leg. Period., Curr. Law Index, Contents Curr. Leg. Period. **LC** K9. **DD** 340.0973. adv acc. **Circ** 1,000. General areas in the field of law with one issue devoted entirely to a yearly symposium with the topic varying each year.

THE IDC HOLLYWOOD LABOR GUIDE. See Economics - Labor.

IGD, INITIATION GENERALE AU DROIT. **Main/Corp** Centre de Formation Professionnelle et de Perfectionnemnet (France). **VFOAT** Initiation Generale au Droit, Formation Continue. FR. French. ir. Centre de Formation Professionnelle et de Perfectionnement, 8 rue des Bons-Enfants, 75056 Paris RP France. **DD** 349.440202, 344.400202.

I.J.A. REPORT. (IJA REPORT). **Main/Corp** Institute of Judicial Administration. Began with Oct. 1968 issue. 0018-991X. Periodical. US. English. qt. 40 Washington Square South, New York NY 10012. **LC** KF8732.A16. **DD** 347.7313.

ILLINOIS APPELLATE REPORTS. (ILLINOIS APPELLATE REPORTS : OFFICIAL REPORTS OF THE ILLINOIS APPELLATE COURT). **Main/Corp** Illinois. Appellate Court. **VFOAT** Illinois Appellate Court Reports. 3rd Ser. Vol. 24- 1975-. US. English. $17.85. Legal Division/Pantagraph Printers, PO Box 3366, Bloomington IL 61701. *Official Illinois Appellate Court Reports.*

ILLINOIS BAR JOURNAL. Began in 1931. 0019-1876. Periodical. US. English. mo. $20.00. Illinois State Bar Association, Illinois Bar Center, Springfield IL 62701. **Tel** (217)525-1760. **Ed** Isolde A Davidson. **Ind/Abst** Leg. Resour. Index, Energy Inf. Abstr., Environ. Abstr., Index Leg. Period. **LC** K9. **DD** 340.05. Index published separately - free - automatically sent. adv acc. **Circ** 27,000. Practical and analytical articles about Illinois law. *Quarterly Bulletin (Illinois State Bar Association).*

ILLINOIS CODE OF CIVIL PROCEDURE AND COURT RULES. 1983-. 8756-8969. US. English. an. West Publishing Company, 50 West Kellogg Boulevard, PO Box 43526, St Paul MN 55102. *Illinois Practice Act and Rules.*

ILLINOIS CONSTRUCTION LAW. 8755-691X. US. English. Professional Education Systems Inc, PO Box 1428, Eau Claire WI 54702. **Tel** (715)836-9700. **Ed** Karen A Welch. adv acc. **Circ** 200. (ctrl). A manual which provides a summary of topics which are of concern to members of the construction industry and an introduction to mechanics' lien law.

ILLINOIS CRIMINAL DEFENSE NEWSLETTER. Vol. 1 Sept. 1978-. Periodical. US. English. mo. Illinois Criminal Defense Newsletter, 130 North Wells, Chicago IL 60606. *Illinois Defender Project Newsletter.*

ILLINOIS FAIR EMPLOYMENT PRACTICE REPORTS. Vol. 1 1974-. US. English. Fair Employment Practices Commission, 179 West Washington, Chicago IL 60602. **LC** KFI1534.5.D5. **DD** 344.430113302642.

ILLINOIS JOURNAL OF FAMILY LAW. Vol. 1, No. 1 (Jan./Feb. 1984-). 0738-677X. Periodical. US. English. bm. $75.00. Mason Publishing Company, 366 Wacouta Street, St Paul MN 55109-1989. **LC** KFI1294.A15. **DD** 346.77301505, 347.76061505.

ILLINOIS LAW FINDER. 1982 Ed.-. 0883-2684. US. English. an. West Publishing Company, Box 64526, St Paul MN 55164-9979.

ILLINOIS REGISTER. V. 1, No. 15- Oct. 1977-. Periodical. US. English. wk. Secretary of State, Administration Code Unit, 201 West Monroe Street, Springfield IL 62756. **Tel** (217)782-9786. **LC** KFI1234.A2. **DD** 348.773025. **Circ** 1,000. Rules promulgated by state agencies and all action taken on existing rules. *Illinois Bulletin, 0148-8112.*

ILLINOIS REPORTS. **Main/Corp** Illinois. Supreme Court. 2nd Ser. Vol. 57 Mar. 1974- Jan. 1975. 0160-1199. US. English. ir. Legal Division, Pantagraph Printing, PO Box 1406, Bloomington IL 61701. **LC** KFI1245. **DD** 348.773043. *Cases Argued and Determined in the Supreme Court of Illinois, 0160-1180.*

ILLINOIS STUDENT LAWYER. (THE ILLINOIS STUDENT LAWYER). V. 1- Feb. 1974-. 0094-2235. US. English. ir. $7.00. Illinois Bar Association, Illinois Bar Center, Springfield IL 62701. **Tel** (217)525-1760. **LC** KF287. **DD** 340.071177356.

IMMIGRATION LAW AND PROCEDURE. US. English. ir. Matthew Bender & Company Inc, 1275 Broadway, Albany NY 12201. **Tel** (800)833-9844.

IMMIGRATION LAW BULLETIN. Vol. 1, No. 1, (Sept. 1979)-. Periodical. US. English. ir. NCIR, 1544 West 8th Street, Los Angeles CA 90017.

IMMIGRATION LAW REPORT. Vol. 1, No. 1 (May 1981)-. 0731-5767. Periodical. US. English. mo. $95.00. Clark Boardman Company Ltd, 435 Hudson Street, New York NY 10014. **LC** KF4802. **DD** 342.73082, 347.30282.

IMPACT. (IMPACT : A JOURNAL OF SAFETY LITIGATION NEWS FROM THE CENTER FOR AUTO SAFETY). 0162-4989. Periodical. US. English. bm. $45.00. Center for Auto Safety, 2001 South Street NW/Suite 410, Washington DC 20009. **Tel** (202)328-7700. **LC** KF1297.A8. **DD** 346.73038.

IMPOSTO DE RENDA. JURISPRUDENCIA. 1.2-1-. Portuguese. ir. Editora Resenha Tributaria, Rua Quatinga 12, 04140 Sao Paulo SP Brazil. **LC** KHD4626.4. **DD** 343.8105202648, 348. 1035202648.

IMPOSTO DE RENDA NA FONTE : TABELAS PRATICAS. **Main/Corp** Brazil. BL. Portuguese. ir. Rua Quatinga, 12 04140 Sao Paulo. **DD** 343.8105242.

IMPRESSIONS. **Main/Corp** France. Parlement (1946-). Assemblee Nationale. 1.- Legislature. French. ir. 4 rue Louvois, Paris France. **LC** J341 K8.

IMPUESTOS. **Main/Corp** La Ley, Sociedad Anonima Editora E Impresora. AG. Spanish. mo. $200.00. La Ley Sa, Sociedad Anonima Editoria e Impresora, Tucuman 1471, Buenos Aires Argentina. **LC** K12.

IMPUESTOS SUCESORIALES; REGIMEN LEGAL TRIBUTARIO. **Main/Corp** Colombia. **VFOAT** Regimen Legal Tributario. Periodical. CK. Spanish. ir. Editores y Distribuidores Asociados Ltda, Apartado Aereo 14965, Bogota Colombia. Ed on Cover of 1 Ed.: Alejandro Restrepo Correa.

IN IURE PRAESENTIA. Vol. 1-. Periodical. Italian. ir. 11000. Italia Edizioni Parallelo, Via 3 Settembre 7, Reggio Calabria Italy.

IN THE PUBLIC INTEREST. **Main/Corp** New Mexico. Attorney General's Office. Sept. 1984-. Periodical. US. English. ty. Office of the Attorney General, PO Drawer 1508, Santa Fe NM 87504. **LC** KFN4027.5.A8. **DD** 349.78905, 347.89005. *Quarterly Report.*

INA PROFESSIONAL LIABILITY BULLETIN, ATTORNEYS. **VFOAT** I.N.A. Professional Liability Bulletin, Attorneys. Vol. 1, No. 1 (Winter 1982)-. 0736-8399. Periodical. US. English. INA Loss Control Services Inc, 1600 Arch Street/PO Box 7728, Philadelphia PA 19101. **LC** KF313.A15. **DD** 346.73033, 347.30633.

INA PROFESSIONAL LIABILITY BULLETIN. SCHOOLS. (INA PROFESSIONAL LIABILITY BULLETIN, SCHOOLS). **VFOAT** I.N.A. Professional Liability Bulletin, Schools. 0736-8380. Periodical. US. English. INA Loss Control Services Inc, 1600 Arch Street/PO Box 7728, Philadelphia PA 19101. **LC** KF1309.A15. **DD** 344.73075, 347.30475.

INCL BRIEF *CEASED.* **VFOAT** I.N.C.L. Brief. **VAT** Insurance, Negligence, and Compensation Law Brief. Began with: Vol. 1, No. 3 (Jan. 1972). Periodical. US. English. qt. **LC** KF1164.A1. **DD** 346.7308605, 347.3068605.

INCL JOURNAL. **Main/Corp** New York State Bar Association. Insurance, Negligence and Compensation Law Section. **VAT** Insurance, Negligence and Compensation Law Section Journal. 0270-2061. Periodical. US. English. New York Bar Association, One Elk Street, Albany NY 12207. **LC** K14. **DD** 346.747086. *Journal of the Insurance, Negligence and Compensation Law Section, 0361-8471.*

INCOLA, ANUARIO DE JURISPRUDENCIA. See Yearbooks, Almanacs, Directories.

INCOME TAX ACT ANNOTATED. (INCOME TAX ACT . . . ANNOTATED). **Main/Corp** Canada. 1949-. 0527-7884. Periodical. CN. English. an. Richard de Boo Ltd, 70 Richmond Street East, Toronto Ontario N5C 1M8 Canada. **Ed** H H Stikeman. **DD** 343.7105202638. *Income War Tax and Excess Profits Tax Act, 0316-8360.*

INCOME TAX HIGHLIGHTS. (INCOME TAX HIGHLIGHTS OF . . .). 0276-6299. US. English. **LC** KF6369.3. **DD** 343.73052, 347.30352.

INCOME TAXES OUTSIDE THE UNITED KINGDOM. **Main/Corp** Great Britain. Board of Inland Revenue. US. English. Commerce Clearing House, 4025 West Peterson Avenue, Chicago IL 60646. **LC** K4504.2. **DD** 343.052.

INDEPENDENT ADVOCATE JOURNAL. 0744-0324. Periodical. US. English. wk. Independent Publications, 865 The Alameda, San Jose CA 95126. **LC** K9. **DD** 349.79405, 347.94005. *Advocate Journal, 0199-6479.*

INDEX COMMERCIAL JUDICIAIRE FINANCIER. (L'INDEX COMMERCIAL, JUDICIAIRE, FINANCIER). V. 1- Aug. 16, 1973-. 0317-6150. Periodical. CN. French. ir. $49. Information Judiciaire Commerciale et Financiere Inc, Bureau 305, 508 Est Av Grande, Quebec Quebec G1R 2K2 Canada. **DD** 348.714048.

INDEX DE LA LEGISLATION OUVRIERE. See Indexes/Abstracts.

INDEX-DIGEST OF DECISIONS AND OPINIONS OF THE UNITED STATES DEPARTMENT OF THE INTERIOR. See Indexes/Abstracts.

INDEX-DIGEST - UNITED STATES DEPARTMENT OF THE INTERIOR, OFFICE OF HEARINGS AND APPEALS. See Indexes/Abstracts.

INDEX OF CURRENT B.C. REGULATIONS. See Indexes/Abstracts.

INDEX OF LEGISLATION. See Indexes/Abstracts.

INDEX OF LOCAL LAWS OF THE COUNTIES, CITIES, TOWNS AND VILLAGES BY SUBJECT. See Indexes/Abstracts.

INDEX TO BILLS INTRODUCED IN UTAH LEGISLATIVE SESSION. See Indexes/Abstracts.

INDEX TO CANADIAN LEGAL PERIODICAL LITERATURE. See Indexes/Abstracts.

INDEX TO CANADIAN SECURITIES CASES. 1949-1974 . SUPPLEMENT. See Indexes/Abstracts.

Law

INDEX TO COMMONWEALTH LEGAL PERIODICALS. See Indexes/Abstracts.

INDEX TO COURSE HANDBOOKS. See Indexes/Abstracts.

INDEX TO CURRENT LEGAL RESEARCH IN CANADA. See Indexes/Abstracts.

INDEX TO FOREIGN LEGAL PERIODICALS AND COLLECTIONS OF ESSAYS. See Indexes/Abstracts.

INDEX TO GOVERNMENT REGULATION. See Indexes/Abstracts.

INDEX TO INDIAN LEGAL PERIODICALS. See Indexes/Abstracts.

INDEX TO LAWS OF FLORIDA. SPECIAL AND LOCAL LAWS. US. English. an. LC KFF40. DD 348.759028, 347.590828.

INDEX TO LEGAL PERIODICALS. See Indexes/Abstracts.

INDEX TO MINNESOTA LEGAL PERIODICALS. See Indexes/Abstracts.

INDEX TO NEW JERSEY LEGAL DECISIONS. See Indexes/Abstracts.

INDEX TO PERIODICAL ARTICLES RELATED TO LAW. See Indexes/Abstracts.

INDEX TO PERIODICAL CASE REPORTS. See Indexes/Abstracts.

INDEX TO RECENT NEW HAMPSHIRE CASES. See Indexes/Abstracts.

INDEX TO THE CODE OF FEDERAL REGULATIONS. See Indexes/Abstracts.

INDEX TO TITLE 40 OF THE CODE OF FEDERAL REGULATIONS : PROTECTION OF ENVIRONMENT. See Indexes/Abstracts.

INDEXES TO ONTARIO MUNICIPAL BOARD APPLICATIONS DISPOSED OF AND TO LAND COMPENSATION BOARD APPLICATIONS DISPOSED OF. See Indexes/Abstracts.

INDIAN ADVOCATE. V. 1- April/June 1961-. 0019-4301. Il. English. qt. Bar Association of India, Chamber #93/Supreme Court Building, New Delhi India 1100011.

INDIAN BAR REVIEW. Vol. 10 (1) (Jan.-Mar. 1983)-. Periodical. Il. English. qt. $25.00. M/S Universal Book Traders, 80 Gokhale Market Opposite Tis Hazari New Courts, Delhi 110 054 India. *Journal of the Bar Council of India.*

THE INDIAN EDUCATION ACT OF 1972; REPORT OF PROGRESS. Main/Corp United States. Office of Indian Education. VAT The Indian Education Act of Nineteen Hundred and Seventy-Two. 2nd 1975-. 0361-1590. US. English. an. US Department of Health Education and Welfare, Washington DC 20202. LC E97. DD 344.730791797.

INDIAN FEDERAL LEGISLATIVE DIGEST. Main/Corp Arizona Commission of Indian Affairs. Periodical. US. English. sa. Commission of Indian Affairs, 1645 West Jefferson, Phoenix AZ 85007. LC KF8208.8.A73. DD 346.73013.

INDIAN JOURNAL OF COMPARITIVE LAW. Periodical. English. LC K9. DD 340.2, 342.

INDIAN JUDGMENT REPORTER : IJR. VFOAT IJR. Periodical. English. mo. 195. Indian Judgmenet Reporter, Hig-C-1613 Rajaji Puram, Lucknow-226107 India. Tel 53421. Ed Rajesh Kumar Upadhyay. DD 348.5404405, 345.4084405. bk rev. adv acc. Circ 10,000. Publish judgements of supreme court of India.

INDIAN LAW REPORTER. Began with Jan. 1974 issue. Periodical. US. English. mo. $325.00. American Indian Laywer Training Program, 319 McArthur Boulevard, Oakland CA 94610. Tel (415)834-9333. Ed Patricia M Zell. Circ 625. (ctrl). Information service summarizing and reporting current developments in Indian law from federal, tribal and state courts and administrative agencies.

INDIAN LAW REPORTS. Il. English. mo. $43.20. Registrar, Delhi High Court of India, New Delhi India.

THE INDIAN LAW REPORTS. English. ir. Government of Karnataka, Director of Printing Stationery and Publications, Bangalore India. DD 348.5487043. *Indian Law Reports.*

INDIAN LAW REPORTS; KERALA SERIES. Periodical. Il. English. ir. Index published separately - free - automatically sent.

INDIAN SOCIO-LEGAL JOURNAL. Periodical. Il. English. sa. $15.00. Indian Institute of Comparative Law, Nr Ajai Clinic Sodala, Ajmer Road Jaipur 302006 India. Tel 65734. Ed K B Agrawal. LC K9. DD 340.1150954. bk rev. adv acc. Circ 1,200. A multidisciplinary publication dealing with the problems of law and society; it contains research papers from eminent jurists and sociologists of the world.

INDIANA CASES REPORTED IN NORTH EASTERN REPORTER, SECOND SERIES. VFOAT West's Indiana Cases. Began with 1-4 N.E. 2D issue. 0744-9046. Periodical. US. English. wk. West Publishing Company, 50 West Kellogg Boulevard, PO Box 3526, St Paul MN 55164. DD 340.

INDIANA CODE. SUPPLEMENT. 1978-. US. English. an. Indiana Legislative Service Agency, 302 State House, Indianapolis IN 46204. Tel (317)269-3550.

INDIANA CRIMINAL LAW REVIEW. V. 1- Oct. 1978-. Periodical. US. English. bm. Indiana Criminal Law Review, 200 Franklin Street, Porter IN 46304. Ed Richard Lee Owen II. bk rev. adv acc. Circ 350. (ctrl). Review of criminal law and procedure and articles pertaining to the same subject.

INDIANA DECISIONS AND LAW REPORTER. 0445-8664. Periodical. US. English. wk. Bobbs Merrill Company Inc, 4300 West 62nd Street, Indianapolis IN 46268.

INDIANA FAMILY LAW. Began in 1982. 0747-6981. Periodical. US. English. an. Michie Company, 609 East Market Street, Charlottesville VA 22906-7587.

INDIANA LAW JOURNAL. Periodical. US. English. qt $13.50. Indiana University School of Law, Law Building, Bloomington IN 47405. Tel (312)335-5175. Ind/Abst Soc. Sci. Citation Index, Curr. Law Index, Leg. Resour. Index, Index Leg. Period., Account. Index. Suppl. LC Microfilm LL-0113 K9. bk rev. adv acc. Circ 1,060. (ctrl). Articles and student notes on legal topics as well as business articles, political science works, sociological studies and scientific pieces with legal overtones.

INDIANA LAW REVIEW. V. 6- 1972-. 0090-4198. Periodical. US. English. qt. $15.00. Indianapolis Law School, 735 West New York Street, Indianapolis IN 46202. Tel (317)264-4039. Ed Eric J Graninger. Ind/Abst Leg. Resour. Index, Index Leg. Period., Curr. Law Index, Contents Curr. Leg. Period. LC K9. DD 340.09772. adv acc. Circ 1,600. Review and analysis of current developments in the law. *Indiana Legal Forum.*

THE INDIANA PUBLIC ACCOUNTANCY LAW, RULES AND REGULATIONS AND REGISTER OF CERTIFIED PUBLIC ACCOUNTANTS, PUBLIC ACCOUNTANTS, ACCOUNTING PRACTITIONERS, ACCOUNTANCY CORPORATIONS, ACCOUNTING PARTNERSHIPS. Main/Corp Indiana. State Board of Public Accountancy. VFOAT Public Accountancy Law, Rules and Regulations and Register of Certified Public Accountants, Public Accountants, Accounting Practitioners, Accountancy Corporations, Accounting Partnerships. US. English. LC HF5616.U5. DD 657.025772.

INDIANA REGISTER. V. 1- July 1, 1978-. 0193-1520. US. English. mo. $175.00. Legislative Services Agency, 302 State House, Indianapolis IN 46204. Tel (317)269-3550. Ed Linda Miller. Circ 900. Lists proposed and final rules of Indiana state agencies; also includes documents such as executive orders, opinions of the state attorney general, etc.

INDICE DA LEGISLACAO DO DISTRITO FEDERAL. See Indexes/Abstracts.

L'INDICE PENALE. See Indexes/Abstracts.

INDILEX. Jan./March 1974-. Spanish. ir. $3.30. Polo Ltd, Avenida Garibaldi 2579, Montevideo Uruguay.

INDUSTRIAL ACCIDENT LAW BULLETIN. VFOAT I.A.L.B., IALB. Began with issue for July 1984?. 8755-8270. Periodical. US. English. mo. $41.95. Quinlan Publishing Company, 131 Beverly Street, Boston MA 02331. LC KF3568.36. DD 346.7303.

INDUSTRIAL ARBITRATION SERVICE INDUSTRIAL REPORTS. VFOAT Industrial Reports. Vol. 1, Pt. 1 (June 1982)-. 0728-8417. Periodical. AT. English. mo. Law Book Company Ltd, 31 Market Street, Sydney Australia. *Industrial Arbitration Service Current Review, 0312-4029.*

INDUSTRIAL CASES REPORTS. 0306-2163. UK. English. mo. Incorporated Council Law Report, 3 Stone Buildings, Lincolns Inn, London WC2A 3XN England. LC KD3040.A38. DD 344.410102646. *Industrial Court Reports, 0306-9311.*

INDUSTRIAL INFORMATION BULLETIN. 0045-012X. AT. English. ir. Australian Government Publications Service, PO Box 84, Canberra 2600 Australia. Tel 062-95 4411. DD 344.91018914. *Industrial Information Bulletin, 0045-012X.*

INDUSTRIAL LAW JOURNAL, INCLUDING THE INDUSTRIAL LAW REPORTS. V. 1- May 1980-. Periodical. SA. English. ir. 50.00. Juta & Company Ltd, PO Box 123, Kenywn 7790 South Africa. Tel 711181. Ed Halton Cheadle, Martin Brassby and Edwin Cameron. bk rev. Circ 1,000. Comments on and explains and evaluates new legislation also comments and explains recent decisions of the industrial courts.

INDUSTRIAL LAW REPORTS (KUALA LUMPUR, MALAYSIA). (INDUSTRIAL LAW REPORTS). VFOAT I.L.R. Jan. 1983-. Periodical. English. mo. 150.00. Malaysian Current Law Journal, Sdn Bhd No 18 Lorong Bunus Enam, Off Jln Masjid India, Kuala Kumpur Malayasia. Tel (03)2740605/06. Ed Hamid Bin Ibrahim. adv acc. Circ 900. Our company has been appointed exclusively to publish Industrial Law Report as from 1983. There are no such journals in the country.

INDUSTRIAL LAWS OF SOUTH AFRICA. Main/Corp South Africa. Laws, Statutes, etc. SA. English. ir. 100.00. Juta & Company Ltd, PO Box 123, Kenywn 7790 South Africa. Tel 711181. Ed A DeKock. Circ 2,674. (ctrl). Leading textbook on the complex body of laws which regulate conditions of employment and the employer-employee relationship in South Africa kept up to date by regular revision services.

INDUSTRIAL RELATIONS LAW JOURNAL. Began with Spring 1976 issue. 0145-188X. Periodical. US. English. qt. $30.00. U C Press, 2120 Berkeley Way, Berkeley CA 94720. Tel (415)642-4191. Ed Doug Stone. Ind/Abst Manage. Contents, Leg. Resour. Index, ABI/Inform, Index Leg. Period., Contents Curr. Leg. Period., Curr. Law Index. LC K9. DD 344.73018905. bk rev. adv acc. Circ 1,100. Articles concerning industrial and labor relations law.

INDUSTRIAL RELATIONS LAW REPORTS. Began with Sept. 1972 issue. Periodical. UK. English. mo. $176.23. Industrial Relations Services, 67 Maygrove Road, London NW6 2EJ England. LC KD3005.A2. DD 344.410102642. (cum index).

INDUSTRIAL RELATIONS LEGAL INFORMATION BULLETIN. VFOAT Legal Information Bulletin. Periodical. UK. English. bw. 32.00. Industrial Relations Services, 67 Maygrove Road, London NW6 2EJ England. LC KD3002. DD 344.410105.

INDUSTRIAL TRIBUNAL REPORTS. UK. English. ir. Her Majesty Stationery Office, PO Box 276, London SW8 5DT England. Tel 01-622 3316. LC KD3095. DD 344.410102648, 344.104102648.

INEQUALITY IN EDUCATION. No. 1 (Oct. 10, 1969)-No. 23 (Sept. 1978). 0579-3475. Periodical. US. English. qt. Harvard Center for Law and Education, 79 Garden Street, Cambridge MA 02138. LC K9. DD 344.730798, 347.304798.

INFOLIOS. Main/Corp Colombia. Superintendencia de Notariado y Registro. Periodical. CK. Spanish. ir. $10.00. Superintendencia de Notariado y Registro Biblioteca, Calle 26 No 13-49 Interior 201 Piso A Bogota Colombia. LC K14. DD 347.861016. *SNR, Superintendencia de Notariado y Registro.*

Law

INFORMATICA E DIRITTO. Vol. 1- Jan./March 1975-. 0390-0975. IT. English, Italian or Spanish with summaries in English, French and Italian. ty. $40.00. Casa Edit Felice le Monnier, Post Box 202, 50100 Firenze Italy. **Ind/Abst** Comput. Control Abstr., Electr. Electron. Abstr., Sci. Abstr. Sect. A. Phys. Abstr., Comput. Rev. **LC** K9. **DD** 029.934005.

INFORMATION AGE. Vol. 4, No. 1 (Jan. 1982)-. 0261-4103. Periodical. UK. English. qt. Butterworth Scientific Limited, PO Box 63/Westbury House, Bury Street, Guilford GU2 5BH England. **Tel** 0483 31261. Ed Angela Jamieson. **Ind/Abst** Electron. Commun. Abstr. J., ISMEC Bull., Pollut. Abstr. Indexes, Saf. Sci. Abstr. J., Comput. Control Abstr., Electr. Electron. Abstr., Sci. Abstr. Sect. A. Phys. Abstr., Electron. Pub. Abstr. **LC** K3263.A13. **DD** 343.0780016405, 342. 3780016405. **CODEN** IAGEDX. bk rev. adv acc. (ctrl). Journal reports or advances in information technology and developments in national and international legislation. *Information Privacy,* 0141-3406.

INFORMATION BULLETIN - AMERICAN BAR ASSOCIATION. STANDING COMMITTEE ON SPECIALIZATION. (INFORMATION BULLETIN). 0736-2765. Periodical. US. English. American Bar Association, Standing Committee on Specialization, 1155 East 60th Street, Chicago IL 60637. **Tel** (312)988-5762. **LC** KF297.A1. **DD** 340.02373. adv acc. State by state information on lawyer specialization.

INFORMATION BULLETIN ON LEGAL ACTIVITIES WITHIN THE COUNCIL OF EUROPE AND IN MEMBER STATES. Main/Corp Council of Europe. Directorate of Legal Affairs. No. 1- June 1978-. Periodical. English. ir. 52.00. Book Sales Department of Morgan Grampian Ltd, Calderwood Street, GB-London SE18 6QH England. **DD** 341.242. *Exchange of Information Between the Member States on their Legislative Activity and Regulations, Newsletter on Legislative Activities; Legal Cooperation in Europe.*

INFORMATION BULLETIN - RAILROAD COMMISSION OF TEXAS, GAS UTILITIES DIVISION. Main/Corp Texas. Railroad Commission. Gas Utilities Division. US. English. $12.00. **LC** KFT1488. **DD** 343.764092.

INFORMATION LEGISLATIVE SERVICES. Vol. 7, No. 37 (Sept. 19, 1969)-. 0020-0115. Periodical. US. English. wk. $25.00. Pennsylvania School Board Association, 412 North 2nd Street/Box 1724, Harrisburg PA 171071. **Tel** (717)233-1642. *Information Legislative Service Report.*

INFORMATION PAMPHLET. Main/Corp California. Dept. of Justice. US. English. California Department of Justice/Information System, Room 600/State Building, 217 West First Street, Los Angeles CA 90012. **LC** KFC1100.A73. **DD** 345.794.

INFORMATION REPORT ON STATE LEGISLATION. Periodical. US. English. mo. Superintendent of Documents, US Government Printing Office, Washington DC 20402.

INFORMATIQUE ET SCIENCES JURIDIQUES. See Computers and Computer Science.

INFORMATIVO - ASSOCIACAO CATARINENSE DO MINISTERIO PUBLICO. Main/Corp Santa Catarina, Brazil. Ministerio Publico. Associacao Catarinense do Ministerio Publico. Portuguese. ir. Rua General Bittencourt N 83, Santa Catarina Brazil.

INFORMATIVO LEGAL RODRIGO. Began with March 1961 issue. PE. Spanish. mo. Asesores Financieros, Av Garcilaso de la Vega 810 Casilla 3218, Lima 100 Peru.

INFORMATIVO MAI DE ENSINO DO ESTADO DE MINAS GERAIS. See Education (General).

INFORMATOR (ANNUAL). (INFORMATOR). 0381-131X. CN. English (French). an. $88.00. Informator, Suite 703/59 Saint Jacques Street, Montreal Quebec H2Y 1K9 Canada. **DD** 347.714013.

L'INFORMATORE LEGISLATIVO (ITALY). Main/Corp Italy. Servizi Della Informazioni e Della Proprieta Letteraria, Artistica e Scientifica. Periodical. Italian. ir. Via PO 14, Roma Italy. **DD** 348.4501.

INFORME ANUAL DEL DIRECTOR ADMINISTRATIVO DE LOS TRIBUNALES. Main/Corp Puerto Rico. Office of Court Administration. Spanish. ir.

INFORME DE LABORES, SELECCION DE JURISPRUDENCIA, ESTADISTICAS. Main/Corp Bolivia. Corte Suprema de Justica. BO. Spanish. ir. Corte Suprema de Justicia de la Nacion, Casilla 211, Sucre Boliva.

INFORME DE LABORES . . . Y APERTURA DEL ANO JUDICIAL. Main/Corp Bolivia. Corte Superior (Distrito Judicial de Chuquisaca). Spanish. an. **LC** KHC2539.C48. **DD** 348.842404405, 348.424084405.

INSIDE. (INSIDE : NEWSLETTER OF THE CORPORATE COUNSEL SECTION OF THE NEW YORK STATE BAR ASSOCIATION). **VFOAT** Inside Newsletter. Vol. 1, No. 1 (Mar. 1982)-. 0736-0150. Periodical. US. English. New York State Bar Association, One Elk Street, Albany NY 12207. **Tel** (518)463-3200. Ed Terrence J Gallagher. **LC** KFN5345.A15. **DD** 346.74706605, 34747066605. **Circ** 1,000. (ctrl).

INSIDE DRUG LAW. Vol. 1, No. 1 (Aug. 1984)-. 0747-6213. Periodical. US. English. mo. $175.00. Vanguard Information Publications, PO Box 667, Chapel Hill NC 27514. **DD** 345.

INSTITUTE OF JUDICAL ADMINISTRATION. (INSTITUTE OF JUDICIAL ADMINISTRATION REPORT). 0146-7816. US. English. Institute of Judical Administration, Washington Square Village, New York 10012. **LC** KF8732.A16. **DD** 347.7313.

INSTITUTE ON ESTATE PLANNING. 1st-. US. English. ir. Matthew Bender & Company Inc, 1275 Broadway, Albany NY 12201. **Tel** (800)833-9844. **Ind/Abst** Curr. Law Index, Leg. Resour. Index, Index Leg. Period.

INSURANCE COUNSEL JOURNAL. See Insurance.

INSURANCE LAW. Main/Corp New York (State). 0148-2688. US. English. an. Matthew Bender & Company Inc, 1275 Broadway, Albany NY 12201. **Tel** (800)833-9844. **LC** KFN5290.A29. **DD** 346.747086.

INSURANCE LAW BULLETIN. VFOAT I.L.B. Began in 1980?. 8755-8254. Periodical. US. English. mo. $36.50. Quinlan Publishing Company Inc, 131 Beverly Street, Boston MA 02114. **DD** 346.

INSURANCE LAW JOURNAL (CHICAGO, ILL.) CEASED. (THE INSURANCE LAW JOURNAL). **VFOAT** Weekly Advance Digest of Current Insurance Decisions. No. 1 (Jan. 3, 1939)-No. 695 (Dec. 1980). 0020-4722. Periodical. US. English. mo. **LC** K9. *Insurance Law Journal (Saint Louis, MO.).*

INSURANCE LITIGATION REPORTER. Vol. 1, No. 1 (Sept. 1979)-. 0744-1045. Periodical. US. English. ir. PO Box 77903, San Francisco CA 94107. **Tel** (415)543-5433. Ed John K Dimugno. **Ind/Abst** Manage. Contents. **LC** KF1159. **DD** 346.7308602638, 347. 3068602638. **Circ** 1,750. Summaries and analyses of recent appellate decisions, trends and development of interest to the insurance lawyer and claims/risk manager. *Insurance Liability Reporter,* 0195-1858.

INTELLECTUAL PROPERTY JOURNAL. Vol. 1, No. 1 (July 1984)-. 0824-7064. Periodical. CN. English. ty. $56.00. Carswell Company Ltd, 2330 Midland Avenue, Agincourt Ontario M1S 1P7 Canada. **LC** K9. **DD** 346.04805.

INTELLIGENCE REPORT (CHICAGO, ILL.). (INTELLIGENCE REPORT). Began with issue for Mar. 1979. 0736-2773. Periodical. US. English. mo. A.B.A. Standing Committee on Law and National Security, 1155 East 60th Street, Chicago IL 60637. **LC** KF4850.A15. **DD** 344.73052, 347.30452.

INTER ALIA. V. 38, No. 2- Apr. 1973-. 0092-6086. Periodical. US. English. ir. $9.00. State Bar of Nevada, 834 Willow Street, Reno NV 89502. **Tel** (702)329-4100. Ed Ann Bersi. **Ind/Abst** Curr. Law Index, Leg. Resour. Index. **LC** K14. **DD** 34005. adv acc. **Circ** 2,500. Current information of the activities of the State Bar of Nevada, CLE programs, conventions and latest legal news, pictures and articles from the state. *Nevada State Bar Journal,* 0028-4092.

INTER-AMERICAN ARBITRATION. **VFOAT** I.A.C.A.C. Newsletter. **VAT** Inter-American Commercial Arbitration Commission Newsletter. No. 1 (1981)-. 0715-4771. Periodical. CN. English (Spanish). 10.00. Canadian Arbitration Conciliation and Amicable Composition Centre, c/o Institute for International Cooperation, University of Ottawa, Ottawa K1N 6N5 Canada. **Tel** (613)232-1476. Ed L Kos-Rabcewicz-Zubkowski. **DD** 341.522. **Circ** 350. (ctrl). International, commercial arbitration and conciliation.

INTER-PARLIAMENTARY BULLETIN. 6th- Year. Periodical. English French. qt. 14. Inter-Parliamentary Union, Place du Petit Saconex, 1211 Geneva 28 Switzerland. **Tel** (022)34 41 50. **Ind/Abst** Public Aff. Inf. Serv. Bull. Contains information on the work of the union and the activities of the organizaton, as well as articles on topical subjects. *Bulletin Interparlementaire.*

INTERIM DECISION. Main/Corp United States. Board of Immigration Appeals. US. English. ir. Superintendent of Documents, US Government Printing Office, Washington DC 20402.

INTERIM REPORT TO THE . . . LEGISLATURE. Main/Corp South Dakota. Legislature. State Legislative Research Council. US. English. an. State Legislature Research Council, State Capitol, Pierre SD 57501. **LC** KFS3020. **DD** 348.78301, 347.83081.

INTERIM STUDY COMMITTEE REFERENCE BULLETIN. VFOAT Reference Bulletin. No. 1 (Jan. 1980)-. US. English. an. **LC** KFU20. **DD** 340.309792.

INTERNAL REVENUE CODE. Main/Corp United States. **VFOAT** U.S. Code Congressional and Administrative News. 1954-. 0163-7177. US. English. an. West Publishing Company, 50 West Kellogg Boulevard, St Paul MN 55102. **LC** KF6276.526.A19. **DD** 343.730402632.

INTERNATIONAL BAR NEWS (LONDON , ENGLAND). See Law - International Law.

INTERNATIONAL BULLETIN FOR RESEARCH ON LAW IN EASTERN EUROPE. VFOAT Bulletin International de Recherches sur le Droit en Europe de l'est. V. 5- Dec. 1972-. Periodical. English, French, or German. sa. Deutsche Verlags-Anstalt GMBH, 7 1 Neckarstr 121, Stuttgart West Germany. **LC** K9. **DD** 340.0947. *Bulletin zur Ostrechtsforschung in den Landern des Europarates.*

INTERNATIONAL BUSINESS LAWYER. See Law - International Law.

INTERNATIONAL DIGEST OF HEALTH LEGISLATION. See Public Health and Safety.

INTERNATIONAL JOURNAL OF LAW AND PSYCHIATRY. V. 1- Feb. 1978-. 0160-2527. Periodical. US. English. qt. Pergamon Press, 395 Sawmill River Road, Elmsford NY 10523. **Ind/Abst** Leg. Resour. Index, Excerpta Med., Index Med., Psychol. Abstr., Index Leg. Period. **LC** K9. **DD** 614.19. **NLM** W1 IN769L. Available in microform.

INTERNATIONAL JOURNAL OF LAW LIBRARIES. See Library and Information Science.

INTERNATIONAL JOURNAL OF LEGAL INFORMATION. See Library and Information Science.

INTERNATIONAL JOURNAL OF THE SOCIOLOGY OF LAW. Vol. 7, No. 1 (Feb. 1979)-. 0194-6595. Periodical. UK. English. qt. $77.00. Academic Press, 4805 Sand Lake Road, Orlando FL 32819. **Tel** (305)345-4100. **Ind/Abst** Leg. Resour. Index, Sociol. Abstr., Soc. Welf. Soc. Plan./Policy Soc. Dev., Soc. Sci. Citation Index, Psychol. Abstr., Soc. Sci. Index, Curr. Law Index, Recent Publ. Artic. **LC** K9. **DD** 340.11505. *International Journal of Criminology and Penology,* 0306-3208.

INTERNATIONAL MONETARY AGREEMENTS ACTS. ANNUAL REPORT. (INTERNATIONAL MONETARY AGREEMENTS ACTS; ANNUAL REPORT). **Main/Corp** Australia. Dept. of the Treasury. 0314-2582. AT. English. an. $1.66. Australian Government Publishing Service, PO Box 84, Canberra Australian Capital Territory 2604 Australia. **LC** J905. **DD** 328.9401 S, 332.450994.

INTERNATIONAL PROCUREMENT COMMITTEE REPORT. VFOAT IPC Report. 8756-0135. Periodical. US. English. qt. Section of Public Contract Law, American Bar Association, 1155 East 60th Street, Chicago IL 60637. **LC** K884.A13. **DD** 346.02305, 342.62305.

Law

INTERNATIONAL REVIEW OF CONTEMPORARY LAW. 1982, 1-. Periodical. English. sa. Aijd, 49 Avenue Jupier, B1190 Bruxelles Belgium. LC JX3. DD 341.05. *Review of Contemporary Law.*

INTERNATIONAL TAX SUMMARIES. Began in 1982?. 8755-1551. US. English. an. John Wiley & Sons, 605 3rd Avenue, New York NY 10158. LC K4505.4. DD 343.04, 342.3.

THE INTERNATIONAL TRADE LAW JOURNAL CEASED. V. 1-7, No. 2. 0360-5833. US. English. sa. $8.00. University of Maryland, School of Law, 500 West Baltimore Street, Baltimore MD 21201. Ind/Abst Index Leg. Period. LC K9. DD 342.38705.

INTERPRETATION BULLETIN - ALBERTA TREASURY. CORPORATE TAX ADMINISTRATION. (INTERPRETATION BULLETIN). Main/Corp Alberta. Corporate Tax Administration. 0826-9505. CN. English. Alberta Treasury/Corporate Tax Administration, 9811-109 Street, Edmonton Alberta T5K 2L5 Canada. LC KEA513.A72. DD 343.712306705, 347.123076705.

INTERPRETATIONS OF EDUCATION LAWS : SUMMARY. *See* Education (General).

INTERPRETER RELEASES. Main/Corp American Council for Nationalities Service. V. 36, No. 21- June 1959-. Periodical. US. English. ir. $250.00. Interpreter Releases, 10 West 40th Street, New York NY 10018. Tel (615)377-3322. Ed Maurice Roberts. Circ 2,100. A publication on immigration, naturalization and related matters. Indispensable for immigration lawyers and practitioners in the field. *Interpreter Releases.*

INTERSTATE INFORMATION REPORT. *See* Transportation.

INTERSTATE TAX REPORT. (INTERSTATE TAX REPORT : ITR). VFOAT ITR. Vol. 1, No. 1 (Apr. 1981)-. 0731-5651. Periodical. US. English. mo. $175.00 New, $155.00 Renewal. Interstate Tax Report, 26 Veasey Street/Suite 401, New York NY 10007. LC KF6763.A15. DD 343.730526705, 347.303526705.

INTERTAX. Periodical. English, French, or German. ir. $135.00. Kluwer Law and Taxation Publishers, Staverenstraat 15, Deuenter Netherlands. Ed A J Radler. DD 343.404. bk rev. adv acc. Circ 1,500. Journal covering latest developments in international taxation with special emphasis on European taxation.

INTRODUCTION TO QUALIFIED PENSION AND PROFIT-SHARING PLANS. Series/Titl Tax Law and Estate Planning Series. Tax Law and Practice Course Handbook Series. Tax Law and Practice Course Handbook Series. 8756-9396. US. English. an. Practising Law Institute, 810 7th Avenue, New York NY 10019. LC KF3512.Z9. DD 344.7301252, 347.3041252.

INVESTMENT COMPANIES. *See* Business - Investments.

INVESTMENT COMPANIES REREGULATION AND THE CHANGING ROLE OF OUTSIDE DIRECTORS. (INVESTMENT COMPANIES REREGULATION AND THE CHANGING ROLE OF OUTSIDE DIRECTORS : ALI-ABA COURSE OF STUDY MATERIALS). Dec. 11-12, 1980. 0731-8278. US. English. American Law Institute, 4025 Chestnut Street, Philadelphia PA 19104. LC KF1078. DD 346.730666, 347.306666. *Investment Companies, the Changing Role of Outside Directors, 0190-5880.*

IOWA ADMINISTRATIVE BULLETIN. V. 1- June 14, 1978-. US. English. bw. $122.00. Iowa State Printing Division, Grimes Building, Des Moines IA 50319. Tel (515)281-8789. LC KFI4236. DD 342.777066.

IOWA ADVOCATE. 0578-6533. US. English. sa. University of Iowa, College of Law, Iowa City IA 52240. Tel (319)353-2121. LC KF292.I614. DD 340.05.

IOWA CIVIL RIGHTS COMMISSION, CASE REPORTS. *See* Political Science - Civil Rights.

IOWA CRIMINAL LAW BULLETIN. Periodical. US. English. mo. Iowa Department of Justice, Hoover State Office Building, Des Moines IA 50319. LC KFI4761.A59. DD 345.777002648.

IOWA ELECTION HANDBOOK WITH ELECTION LAWS OF IOWA. *See* Political Science.

IOWA INDUSTRIAL COMMISSIONER REPORT. VFOAT Industrial Commissioner Report. US. English. an. LC KFI4542. DD 344.777012102642, 347. 770412102642.

IOWA LAW REVIEW. Vol. 11, No. 1 (Dec. 1925)-. 0021-0552. Periodical. US. English. ir. $25.00 Domestic, $27.00 Foreign. State University of Iowa, College of Law, Iowa City IA 52240. Tel (319)353-4453. Ind/Abst Leg. Resour. Index, Account. Index. Suppl., Public Aff. Inf. Serv. Bull., Index Leg. Period., Curr. Law Index, Soc. Sci. Citation Index, Contents Curr. Leg. Period. LC K9. DD 349.77705. (cum index). adv acc. Circ 2,200. *Iowa Law Bulletin.*

IOWA LAWYERS DIARY AND MANUAL. US. English. Lawyers Diary and Manual, 240 Mulberry Street, Newark NJ 07101. LC KF192.I55. DD 340.025777.

IOWA LEGISLATIVE SERVICE. 0730-2479. US. English. West Publishing Company, 50 West Kellogg Boulevard, Box 3526, St Paul MN 55165. LC KFI4231. DD 348.77702205, 347.77082205.

IOWA RULES OF COURT. 1978-. 0742-9967. US. English. an. West Publishing Company, 50 West Kellogg Boulevard, PO Box 3526, St Paul MN 55165. LC KFI4729. DD 347.777051, 347.770751.

THE IRISH JURIST. N.S. V. 1- 1966-. Periodical. IE. English. an. 30.65. Irish Jurist, University College, Dublin 2 Ireland. Ed W N Osborough. Ind/Abst Index Leg. Period. bk rev. adv acc. Circ 800. Modern Irish law explained and analysed by academic writers, laws of other countries similarly examined where relevant, legal history including Roman Law and Common Law but with a special emphasis on the history of law in Ireland. *Irish Jurist, Together with Irish Jurist Reports.*

IRISH LAW REPORTS MONTHLY. Vol. 1, No. 1-. 0332-3293. IE. English. mo. $175.00. The Round Hall Press, Kill Lane, Blackrock County, Dublin Ireland. Tel 850922. Ed Bart D Daly. LC KDK63 1867.A2. DD 348.415041, 344.150841. adv acc. Circ 800. (crtl). Gives full text (with additional captions and headnotes) of the majority of judgements emanating from the high and superior courts in Ireland. *Irish Law Times and Solicitor's Journal, 0021-1281.*

IRISH LAW TIMES. June 1983-. Periodical. English. ir. $85.00. The Round Hall Press, Kill Lane, Blackrock County Dublin Ireland. Tel 850922. Ed Bart D Daly. LC KDK63 1867 .A2. DD 349.41505, 344.15005. bk rev. adv acc. Circ 650. (crtl). Current information service with regular features on legislation, family, labour and EEC law; news reports and occasional special supplements. *Irish Law Reports Monthly, 0332-3293.*

THE IRISH LAW TIMES AND SOLICITORS' JOURNAL. VFOAT Irish Law Times. V. 1- Feb. 2, 1867-. 0021-1281. Periodical. IE. English. wk. $85.00. Irish Law Times and Solicitors Journal, PO No 138, Botanic Road, Dublin 9 Ireland. DD 349.41505 344.15005.

IRISH REPORTS. IE. English. sa. Incorporated Council of Law Reports, Law Library/Four Courts, Dublin 7 Ireland.

IRS LETTER RULINGS. *See* Business - Public Finance.

ISAAC PITBLADO LECTURES ON CONTINUING LEGAL EDUCATION CEASED. 1960/61-1981. 0578-7726. Periodical. CN. English. an. Law Society of Manitoba, Law Courts, Winnipeg Manitoba R3G 0V7 Canada. DD 340.0971.

THE ISBA BLUE BOOK. VFOAT Directory of Official Personnel. VAT Illinois State Bar Association Blue Book. 1979/80-. US. English. an. Illinois State Bar Association, Illinois Bar Center, Springfield IL 62701. Tel (217)525-1760.

ISRAEL LAW REVIEW. V. 1- Jan. 1966-. 0021-2237. Periodical. IS. English. qt. $36.00. Hebrew University of Jerusalem, Mt Scopus POB 24100, Jerusalem Israel. Tel (02)88250. Ed Ruth Lapidoth. Ind/Abst Sociol. Abstr., Lang. Lang. Behav. Abstr., Contents Curr. Leg. Period. bk rev. adv acc. Circ 1,200. Contains articles on Jewish, international, comparative law, translations of case decisions, new-enacted laws.

ISSUES IN BANK REGULATION. *See* Business - Banking & Finance.

ISSUES IN LAW & MEDICINE. VFOAT Issues in Law and Medicine. 8756-8160. Periodical. US. English. bm. $24.00. Issues in Law and Medicine, PO Box 1586, Terre Haute IN 47808-1586. Tel (812)232-0103. Ed James Bopp Jr. adv acc. Circ 5,000. Focuses on medical and legal issues pertaining to medical treatment for the handicapped and disabled.

IT'S YOUR BUSINESS. 0198-7232. Periodical. US. English. Farnsworth Publishing Company, 78 Randall Avenue, Rockville Centre NY 11570. LC KF6296.A15. DD 343.730405.

IUDAU. Main/Corp Instituto Uruguayo de Derecho de Arrendamientos Urbanos. VFOAT Revista del Iudau. Began in 1975. Periodical. Spanish. ir. Ediciones Juridicas Amalio, M Fernandez, 25 De Mayo 477, Planta Baja Oficina 11, Montevideo Uruguay. LC K9. DD 346.89504342.

IUS CANONICUM. V. 1- Jan./June 1961-. 0021-325X. Periodical. SP. Spanish. sa. $30.00. Ediciones Universidad de Navar, Apartado 396, 31080 Pamplona Spain. Tel (48)25 68 50. Ed Tomas Rincon. LC K10. bk rev. Circ 400. It offers studies of the legal issues that have most recently arisen in the field of Canon Law.

IUS COMMUNE. GW. German. ir. 100.-. Vittorio Klostermann, Postfach 900601 Frauenlobstrabe 22, 6000 Frankfurt am Main 90 West Germany. Tel (0611)77 4011.

IUS COMMUNE. SONDERHEFTE. TEXTE UND MONOGRAPHIEN. 1- 1971-. Monographic Series. GW. German. ir. Vittorio Klostermann, Postfach 900601 Frauenlobstrabe 22, 6000 Frankfurt am Main 90 West Germany. Tel (0611)77 4011.

IVRA; RIVISTA INTERNAZIONALE DI DIRITTO ROMANO E ANTICO. 1- 1950-. 0021-3241. Periodical. IT. Italian. ir. Casa Editrice Dott Eugenio Jov Via Mezzocannone 109, 80134 Napoli Italy. Ed A Guarino and C Sanfilippo.

JAARVERSLAG VAN DIE SUID-AFRIKAANSE REGSKOMMISSIE. Main/Corp South Africa. Law Commission. VFOAT Annual Report of the South African Law Commission. 1974-. Afrikaans and English. ir. 1.40. The Government Printer, Private Bag X85, 0001 Pretoria South Africa. DD 340.30968.

JABALPUR LEGAL QUARTERLY. VFOAT JLQ. Vol. 1, No. 1 (Oct.-Dec. 1980-). Periodical. English. qt. N C Beohar, 24 Bharat Society, Nagpur Road, Jabalput-1 India. LC K10. DD 349.5405, 345.4005.

THE JAG JOURNAL. VAT Judge Advocate General Journal. Began with V. 1, No. 1, Aug. 1947. 0021-3519. Periodical. US. English. sa. Office of the Judge Advocate, General Department of the Navy, 200 Stovall Street, Alexandria VA 22332. Ind/Abst Public Aff. Inf. Serv. Bull., Index Leg. Period. DD 359.133.

JAHRBUCH DES SOZIALRECHTS DER GEGENWART. *See* Yearbooks, Almanacs, Directories.

JAHRBUCH FUR AFRIKANISCHES RECHT. *See* Yearbooks, Almanacs, Directories.

JAHRESFACHKATALOG : RECHT, WIRTSCHAFT, STEUERN. 0075-2886. GW. German. an. Elwert und Meuer, Hauptstrabe 101, D-1000 Berlin West Germany.

JAIL & PRISON LAW BULLETIN. VAT Jail and Prison Law Bulletin. V. 78, No. 9- Sept. 1978-. 0194-1372. Periodical. US. English. mo. $79.00. Americans Effective Law Enforcement, 501 Grandview Drive/#209, South San Francisco CA 94080. Tel (415)877-0731. LC KF9730.A15. DD 344.73035. *Jail Administration Law Bulletin, 0194-1054.*

JD. 1978-. 0272-0922. Periodical. US. English. an. Office of General Counsel, General Confernece of Seventh- Day Adventists, 6940 Carroll Avenue, Takoma Park MD 20012. LC KF200. DD 347.30285205.

JD/MBA QUARTERLY. VFOAT J.D./M.B.A. Quarterly. Vol. 1, No. 1 (Winter 1984)-. 0747-9093. Periodical. US. English. qt. JD/MBA Quarterly, 2415 South 9th Street, Arlington VA 22204. LC KF299.J35. DD 340.02373.

JEALOUS MISTRESS. (THE JEALOUS MISTRESS). V. 1- July 1973-. 0092-170X. US. English. $20.00. PO Box 487, Chapel Hill NC 27514. LC KF133. DD 348.73405.

JERNAL UNDANG-UNDANG. VFOAT Journal of Malaysian and Comparative Law. V. 1- May 1974-. Periodical. MY. English (Malay). sa. $15.00. University of Malaya, Department of Law, PO Box 1127, Kuala Lumpur Malaysia. **Tel** 565000/ 565425. **LC** K10. **DD** 340.09595.

JEWISH JURISPRUDENCE. Vol. 1-. 0276-1432. Monographic Series. US. English. ir. Harwood Academic Publishers, PO Box 786/Cooper Station, New York NY 10276. **Tel** (212)689-0360.

THE JEWISH LAW ANNUAL. V. 1- 1978-. English. an. E J Brill, PO Box 9000, 2300 PA Leiden The Netherlands. **Ind/Abst** Old Testam. Abstr. **LC** K10. **DD** 296.18. Reflects the place of Jewish law among the legal systems of the world. Includes historical, comparative and jursprudential analyses, and conflict of law problems involving Jewish law.

JOB SAFETY & HEALTH REPORT. *See* Business - Personnel Management.

JOGTUDOMANYI KOZLONY. Began in 1860. Periodical. HU. Hungarian. mo. Akademiai Kiado, POB 24, 1363 Budapest Hungary.

JOHN MARSHALL LAW JOURNAL. Spring 1977-. 0147-3689. US. English. John Marshall Law School, 105 Forest Avenue NE, Atlanta GA 30308. **LC** K10. **DD** 340.05.

THE JOHN MARSHALL LAW REVIEW. V. 13- Fall 1979-. 0270-854X. Periodical. US. English. qt. $12.00. John Marshall Law School, 315 South Plymouth Court, Chicago IL 60604. **Tel** (312)987-1415. **Ed** Mark D Krauskoph. **Ind/Abst** Index Leg. Period., Contents Curr. Leg. Period. **LC** K10. **DD** 340.05. bk rev. **Circ** 2,500. Articles, comments and casenotes on topics on the cutting edge of the law. *John Marshall Journal of Practice and Procedure.*

JOURNAL - CALIFORNIA TRIAL LAWYERS ASSOCIATION. (JOURNAL). **VFOAT** CTLA Journal. 0730-4919. Periodical. US. English. California Trial Lawyers Association, 1020 12th Street/3rd Floor, Sacramento CA 95814. **LC** K3. **DD** 347.7940705, 347.9407705. *California Trial Lawyers Journal, 0575-6316.*

JOURNAL - CORPORATION, FINANCE & BUSINESS LAW SECTION. **Main/Corp** State Bar of Michigan Corporation, Finance and Business Law Section. **VFOAT** Corporation Finance and Business Law Journal. **VAT** Journal - Corporation, Finance and Business Law Section. V. 1-. 0274-7812. Periodical. US. English. qt. $10.00. State Bar of Michigan, Cross Wrock Miller and Vieson, 400 Renaissance Center, Detroit MI 48243. *Newsletter.*

JOURNAL DE DROIT FISCAL. Periodical. BE. French. bm. 2.800. Etablissements Emile Bruylant, 67 rue de la Regence, 1000 Brussels Belgium. **Tel** 02/512 98 45. **LC** K10. **DD** 343.4930405. bk rev. **Circ** 1,000. Doctrine and jurisprudence.

JOURNAL DES DEBATS. INDEX. *See* Indexes/Abstracts.

JOURNAL DES TRIBUNAUX. 0021-812X. Periodical. BE. French. wk. $168.78. Maison F Larcier SA, 39 rue des Minimes, B-1000 Brussels Belgium. **Tel** 02/512 47 12 /512 96 79.

JOURNAL - INTEGRATED BAR OF THE PHILIPPINES. **Main/Corp** Integrated Bar of the Philippines. V. 1- June 1973-. Periodical. English. ir. $6.00. Integrated Bar of the Philippines, 955 Quezon Boulevard Extension, Quezon City Philippines. **LC** K9. **DD** 340.09599.

JOURNAL OF AFRICAN LAW. Began with Spring 1957. 0021-8553. Periodical. UK. English. sa. 12.00. School of Oriental and African Studies, University of London, Malet Street, London WC1E 7HP England. **Tel** 01-637-2388. **Ed** P E Slinn, S Coldham, and S A Poberts. **Ind/Abst** Leg. Resour. Index, Public Aff. Inf. Serv. Bull., Curr. Law Index. bk rev. adv acc. **Circ** 700. Articles and book reviews on all aspects of law relating to Africa.

JOURNAL OF AGRICULTURAL TAXATION & LAW. **VFOAT** Journal of Agricultural Taxation and Law. Vol. 5, No. 1 (Spring 1983)-. 0745-9181. Periodical. US. English. qt. $64.00. Warren Gorham & Lamont Inc, 210 South Street, Boston MA 02111. **Ind/Abst** Manage. Contents, Leg. Resour. Index. **LC** K1. **DD** 343.73076, 347.30376. *Agricultural Law Journal, 0193-6190.*

THE JOURNAL OF AIR LAW AND COMMERCE. *See* Aeronautics, Astronautics.

THE JOURNAL OF ARTS MANAGEMENT AND LAW. *See* The Arts (General).

JOURNAL OF BUSINESS LAW. (THE JOURNAL OF BUSINESS LAW). **VFOAT** Business Law. Began in 1957. 0021-9460. UK. English. an. $24.52. Sweet & Maxwell Ltd, North Way Andover, Hampshire SP10 5BE England. **Tel** 01-583-9855. **Ed** Alan Wells. **Ind/Abst** Manage. Contents, Leg. Resour. Index, Index Leg. Period., Curr. Law Index. **LC** K10. **DD** 346.0705. (cum index). bk rev. adv acc. **Circ** 2,500. Indicates trends in the development of business law as well as making a major contribution to the knowledge and understanding of foreign law required for international trade.

JOURNAL OF CHRISTIAN JURISPRUDENCE. (JOURNAL OF CHRISTIAN JURISPRUDENCE : A PUBLICATION OF THE O.W. COBURN SCHOOL OF LAW OF ORAL ROBERTS UNIVERSITY). 1980-. 0741-6075. Periodical. US. English. an. $8.95. Oral Roberts University of Cobourn, School of Law, 7777 South Lewis, Tulsa OK 74171. **Tel** (918)495-6042. **Ed** Florian Frederick Chess. **Ind/Abst** Leg. Resour. Index. **LC** K10. **DD** 261.5. bk rev. adv acc. **Circ** 1,500. (ctrl). Law journal concerned with legal issues confronting the Christian community and first amendment right of religious freedom.

JOURNAL OF COLLEGE AND UNIVERSITY LAW. (THE JOURNAL OF COLLEGE AND UNIVERSITY LAW). V. 1- Fall 1973-. 0093-8688. Periodical. US. English. ir. $35.00. Fred B Rotham & Company, 10368 West Centennial Road, Littleton CO 80127. **Tel** (303)979-5657. **Ed** Laura F Rothstein. **Ind/Abst** Leg. Resour. Index, Curr. Law Index, Index Leg. Period., Contents Curr. Leg. Period., Curr. Index J. Educ. **LC** K10. **DD** 344.7307405. bk rev. adv acc. The only law review entirely devoted to the concerns of higher education in the United States. *College Counsel.*

JOURNAL OF COMPARATIVE BUSINESS AND CAPITAL MARKET LAW. Vol. 5, No. 1 (Mar. 1983)-. 0167-9333. Periodical. English. qt. $244.00 Domestic, $90.50 Foreign. Elsevier Science Publishers, PO Box 211, 1000 AE Amsterdam Netherlands. **Tel** (020)5803911. **Ed** Robert Mundheimand Noyes Leech. **Ind/Abst** Leg. Resour. Index, Manage. Contents. **LC** K10. **DD** 346.06605, 342.66605. bk rev. adv acc. Permits the exchange of ideas and Information about legal developments relating to business operations and to the capital markets throughout the world. *Journal of Comparative Corporate Law and Securities Regulation, 0165-0165.*

JOURNAL OF CONSTITUTIONAL AND PARLIAMENTARY STUDIES. V. 1- Jan./Mar. 1967-. 0022-0043. Periodical. II. English. qt. $14.00. Institute of Constitutional and Parliamentary Studies, 18-21 Vithalbhai Patel House 8675438rg, New Delhi 1 India. **Ind/Abst** ABC Pol Sci. **LC** JQ201. **DD** 320.05.

THE JOURNAL OF CONTEMPORARY HEALTH LAW AND POLICY. 0882-1046. Periodical. US. English. an. $10.00. Catholic University of America, Law School/Leahey Hall, Washington DC 20064. **Tel** (202)635-5140. **Ed** George P Smith II. **DD** 344. bk rev. adv acc. **Circ** 450. (ctrl). Journal which discusses the relevant and timely issues confronting the legal, medical, and ethics profession.

JOURNAL OF CONTEMPORARY LAW. V. 1- Winter 1974-. 0097-9937. Periodical. US. English. sa. $10.00. University of Utah, College of Law, Salt Lake City UT 84112. **Tel** (801)581-3583. **Ind/Abst** Leg. Resour. Index, Index Leg. Period., Curr. Law Index, Leg. Contents, Contents Curr. Leg. Period. **LC** K10. **DD** 340.05. bk rev. adv acc. **Circ** 350. Legal journal focusing on current and controversial legal issues.

JOURNAL OF COPYRIGHT, ENTERTAINMENT, AND SPORTS LAW. Vol. 1, No. 1 (Summer 1982)-. 0740-8099. Periodical. US. English. ty. Tennessee Bar Association, 3622 West End Avenue, Nashville TN 37205. **Tel** (615)383-7421. **Ed** William L Warren. **Ind/Abst** Leg. Resour. Index. **DD** 346. **Circ** 300. Substantial law journal of interest to entertainment, sports and copyright lawyers.

THE JOURNAL OF CORPORATION LAW. V. 1- Fall 1975-. 0360-795X. Periodical. US. English. qt. $25.00 Domestic, $27.00 Foreign. University of Iowa, College of Law, Iowa City IA 52242. **Tel** (319)353-7078. **Ed** Mark K Harder. **Ind/Abst** Manage. Contents, Leg. Resour. Index, Account. Index. Suppl., Public Aff. Inf. Serv. Bull., Index Leg. Period., Curr. Law Index, Leg. Contents. **LC** K10. **DD** 346.7306605. bk rev. adv acc. **Circ** 900. (ctrl). We publish scholarly articles in the fields of corporations law, securities law, tax law, commercial and banking law, and labor law.

JOURNAL OF CRIMINAL JUSTICE. Began with Mar. 1973 issue. 0047-2352. Periodical. US. English. bm. Pergamon Press, 395 Sawmill River Road, Elmsford NY 10523. **Tel** (914)592-7700. **Ind/Abst** Leg. Resour. Index, Public Aff. Inf. Serv. Bull., Psychol. Abstr., Soc. Sci. Citation Index, Curr. Law Index. **LC** HV7231. **DD** 364.05. **CODEN** JCJUDJ.

JOURNAL OF CRIMINAL LAW. (THE JOURNAL OF CRIMINAL LAW). Vol. 1, No. 1 (Jan. 1937)-. 0022-0183. Periodical. UK. English. qt. $54.00. Tieto Ltd, Bank House/8-A Hill Road, Clevedon Avon BS21 7HH England. **Ind/Abst** Leg. Resour. Index, Curr. Law Index. Index published separately - free - automatically sent. Also available in microform edition from Kraus Microform.

JOURNAL OF CRIMINAL LAW & CRIMINOLOGY. (THE JOURNAL OF CRIMINAL LAW & CRIMINOLOGY). **VFOAT** Journal of Criminal Law and Criminology. V. 64- March 1973-. 0091-4169. Periodical. US. English. qt. $25.00. Williams & Wilkins, 428 East Preston Street, Baltimore MD 21202. **Ind/Abst** Excerpta Med., Public Aff. Inf. Serv. Bull., Curr. Contents Behav. Soc. Educ. Sci., Crim. Justice Period. Index, Chem. Abstr., Index Leg. Period., Soc. Sci. Index, Soc. Sci. Citation Index. **LC** K10. **DD** 364.05. **NLM** W1 JO611N. **CODEN** JCRLA. Each issue contains an index to its own contents - no vol index - loose. *Journal of Criminal Law, Criminology and Police Science, 0022-0205.*

THE JOURNAL OF CRIMINAL LAW AND CRIMINOLOGY (NORTHWESTERN UNIVERSITY (EVANSTON, ILL.). SCHOOL OF LAW : 1981). (THE JOURNAL OF CRIMINAL LAW AND CRIMINOLOGY). **VFOAT** Journal of Criminal Law & Criminology. Vol. 72, No. 1 (Spring 1981)-. 0091-4169. Periodical. US. English. qt. $25.00 Domestic, $28.00 Foreign. Northwestern University School of Law, 357 East Chicago Avenue, Chicago IL 60611. **Tel** (312)908-8467. **Ind/Abst** ABC Pol Sci, Psychol. Abstr., Index Leg. Period., Soc. Sci. Index. bk rev. **Circ** 2,800. Fccuses on criminal law and criminology. *Journal of Criminal Law & Criminology, 0019-4169.*

THE JOURNAL OF ENERGY LAW & POLICY. *See* Energy.

JOURNAL OF FAMILY LAW. Began publication with: Vol. 1, No. 1, published in 1961. 0022-1066. Periodical. US. English. qt. University of Louisville, 2301 South 3rd Street, Louisville KY 40208. **Ind/Abst** Leg. Resour. Index, Sociol. Abstr., Soc. Welf. Soc. Plan./Policy Soc. Dev., Energy Inf. Abstr., Environ. Abstr., Women Stud. Abstr., Index Leg. Period. **LC** K10. **DD** 346.7301505. (cum index).

JOURNAL OF HEALTH POLITICS, POLICY AND LAW. *See* Medicine.

THE JOURNAL OF JURISTIC PAPYROLOGY. **VFOAT** Rocznik Papirologii Prawniczej. V. 1- 1946-. 0075-4277. English (Vols. for 1962- in French or German). ARS Polona, Krakowskie Przedmiescie 7, 00-068 Warsaw Poland.

JOURNAL OF JUVENILE LAW. V. 1- June 1977-. 0160-2098. Periodical. US. English. an. Laverne College Law Center, 1950 3rd Street, Laverne CA 91750. **Tel** (818)593-3511. **Ind/Abst** Leg. Resour. Index, Index Leg. Period. **LC** K10. **DD** 345.7308. bk rev. adv acc. A law review limited to discussions of how various laws impact juveniles.

THE JOURNAL OF LAW AND COMMERCE. Vol. 1-. 0733-2491. Periodical. US. English. ir. $14.00. University of Pittsburgh, School of Law, Pittsburgh PA 15260. **Tel** (412)648-1359. **Ed** William Stubblefield. **Ind/Abst** Leg. Resour. Index, Index Leg. Period. **LC** K10. **DD** 346.730705, 347.306705. bk rev. adv acc. **Circ** 400. (ctrl). The journal provides a central forum for scholarship elaborating and clarifying commercial law as it exists and as it is likely to develop.

THE JOURNAL OF LAW & ECONOMICS. **VAT** Journal of Law and Economics. V. 1- Oct. 1958-. 0022-2186. Periodical. US. English. sa. $57.60. University of Chicago Press, PO Box 37005, Chicago IL 60637. **Ind/Abst** ABI/Inform, Index Leg. Period., Leg. Resour. Index, Manage. Contents, Soc. Sci. Index, Coal Abstr., Am. Hist. Life, Energy Res. Abstr., Excerpta Med., Hist. Abstr., Part A, Mod. Hist. Abstr., Hist. Abst., Part B, Twent. Century Abstr., Index Econ. Artic. J. Collect. Vol., Int. Labour Doc., Public Aff. Inf. Serv. Bull., Soc.

Sci. Citation Index, ABC Pol Sci, Contents Curr. Leg. Period., Curr. Law Index, Hist. Abstr. **LC** Law. **DD** 330.5. **CODEN** JLLEA7.

JOURNAL OF LAW & EDUCATION. VAT Journal of Law and Education. V. 1- Jan. 1972-. 0275-6072. Periodical. US. English. qt. $35.00 Domestic, $40.00 Foreign. Journal of Law & Education, PO Box 1936, Cincinnati OH 45201. **Tel** (513)421-4142. **Ind/Abst** Leg. Resour. Index, Educ. Index, Curr. Index J. Educ., Index Leg. Period. **LC** K10. **DD** 344.730705. bk rev. adv acc. **Circ** 1,300. (ctrl). Covers school law.

JOURNAL OF LAW AND INFORMATION SCIENCE. Vol. 1, No. 1-. Periodical. US. English. be. Gaunt and Sons, 301 Gulf Drive, Holmes Beach FL 33510. **Tel** (813)778-5211.

JOURNAL OF LAW AND POLITICS. V. 1, No. 1 (1983 Fall)-. Periodical. US. English. sa. $32.00. University of Virginia, School of Law, Charlottesville VA 22901. **Tel** (804)924-3743. **Ed** Michael M Fay. bk rev. adv acc. **Circ** 800. Devoted to analyzing the interaction between law, and politics, including the regulation of political parties and campaign finance, judicial selection, and the federalist system.

THE JOURNAL OF LAW AND RELIGION. **VFOAT** Journal of Law & Religion. Vol. 1, No. 1 (Summer 1983)-. 0748-0814. Periodical. US. English. sa. $12.00. Hamline University School of Law, 1536 Hewitt Avneue, St Paul MN 55104. **Tel** (612)641-2356. **Ed** Michael Scherschligt. **Ind/Abst** Relig. Index One, Period. adv acc. **Circ** 600. Interdisciplinary journal, published in law review format, presents articles which probe historical, theoretical, and practical ways in which religion, broadly defined, interacts with law.

JOURNAL OF LAW AND SOCIETY. Vol. 9, No. 1 (Summer 1982)-. 0263-323X. Periodical. UK. English. ty. $78.00 US. Basil Blackwell, 108 Cowley Road, Oxford OX4 1JF England. **Tel** 0865-722146. **Ed** P A Thomas. **Ind/Abst** Am. Hist. Life, Hist. Abstr., Sociol. Abstr. **LC** K2. **DD** 340.11505. bk rev. adv acc. Devoted to the study of the interaction of law with other social forces. *British Journal of Law and Society, 0306-3704.*

JOURNAL OF LEGAL EDUCATION. **VFOAT** Legal Education. V. 1- Autumn 1948-. 0022-2208. Periodical. US. English. qt. $20.00 Domestic, $24.00 Foreign. Cornell Law School, Myron Taylor Hall, Ithaca NY 14853. **Tel** (607)256-3379. **Ed** Roger C Cramton. **Ind/Abst** Leg. Resour. Index, Curr. Index J. Educ., Index Leg. Period., Curr. Law Index, Soc. Sci. Citation Index. **LC** UNC. (cum index). bk rev. **Circ** 5,000. (ctrl). The purpose is to foster a rich interchange of ideas and information about legal education and related matters.

JOURNAL OF LEGAL HISTORY. (THE JOURNAL OF LEGAL HISTORY). Vol. 1, No. 1 (May 1980)-. 0144-0365. Periodical. UK. English. ty. Frank Cass & Company Ltd, 11 Gainsborough Road, London E11 1RS England. **Ind/Abst** Leg. Resour. Index, Sociol. Abstr., Recent Publ. Artic. **LC** K10. **DD** 340.09.

JOURNAL OF LEGAL PLURALISM AND UNOFFICIAL LAW. **VFOAT** Journal of Legal Pluralism. No. 19 (1981)-. 0732-9113. Periodical. US. English. sa. F B Rothman & Company, 10368 Centennial Road, Littleton CO 80127. **Ind/Abst** Sociol. Abstr. **LC** K1. **DD** 340.05. *African Law Studies, 0002-0060.*

THE JOURNAL OF LEGAL STUDIES. V. 1- Jan. 1972-. 0047-2530. Periodical. US. English. sa. $20.00. Editor, Journal of Legal Studies, University of Chicago Law School, 1111 East 60th Street, Chicago IL 60637. **Ind/Abst** Leg. Resour. Index, Sociol. Abstr., ABC Pol Sci, Women Stud. Abstr., Index Leg. Period., Lang. Lang. Behav. Abstr., Curr. Law Index, Contents Curr. Leg. Period. **LC** K10. **DD** 340.05.

JOURNAL OF LEGAL THOUGHTS. Vol. 1, No. 1 (Jan. 1980)-. Periodical. English. ir. 5.00. Journal of Legal Thoughts, c/o Department of Law, University of Dacca, Dacca 2 Bangladesh. **LC** K10. **DD** 349.549205, 345.492005.

JOURNAL OF LEGISLATION. V. 3- 1976-. 0146-9584. US. English. an. $12.00. Notre Dame Law School, Notre Dame IN 46556. **Tel** (219)239-5918. **Ed** Wayne F Malecha. **Ind/Abst** Leg. Resour. Index, Coal Abstr., Energy Inf. Abstr., Environ. Abstr., ABC Pol Sci, Public Aff. Inf. Serv. Bull., Index Leg. Period., Energy Res. Abstr., Contents Curr. Leg. Period., Curr. Law Index. **LC** K14. **DD** 340.0973. bk rev. adv acc. **Circ** 1,800. (ctrl). Available on microform from University Microfilms. A student edited and published law review specializing in legislation, public policy, and regulatory affairs. *N.D. Journal of Legislation, 0360-4209.*

JOURNAL OF MARITIME LAW AND COMMERCE. Periodical. US. English. qt. $50.00. Jefferson Law Book Company, PO Box 1936, Cincinnati OH 45201. **Tel** (513)421-4142. **Ind/Abst** Soc. Sci. Citation Index, Leg. Resour. Index, Curr. Law Index, Leg. Contents, Index Leg. Period., Ocean. Abstr., Public Aff. Inf. Serv. Bull. Maritime law and commerce, related articles, recent judicial developements, book reviews, annotated bibliography texts and documents.

JOURNAL OF MARITIME LAW AND COMMERCE. Began in 1969. 0022-2410. Periodical. US. English. qt. $39.50. Jefferson Law Book Company, Division of Anderson Publishing Company, PO Box 1936, Cincinnati OH 45201. **Ind/Abst** Leg. Resour. Index, Sel. Water Resour. Abstr., Ship Abstr., Public Aff. Inf. Serv. Bull., Index Leg. Period. **LC** K10. **DD** 347.7505.

JOURNAL OF MEDIA LAW AND PRACTICE. Vol. 1, No. 1 (May 1980)-. 0144-0373. Periodical. UK. English. ty. 45.00. Frank Cass & Company Ltd, Gainsborough House/11 Gainsborough Road, London E11 1RS England. **Tel** (01)530-4226. **Ed** David Goldberg. **Ind/Abst** Sociol. Abstr., Soc. Welf. Soc. Plan./Policy Soc. Dev. **LC** K10. **DD** 343.09905, 342.39905. bk rev. adv acc. Focuses upon media studies - rules, regulations and decisions which report to govern the various media and which create the legal and normative framework within which they function.

JOURNAL OF MINNESOTA PUBLIC LAW. Vol. 1, Issue 1 (Spring 1980)-. 0748-769X. Periodical. US. English. sa. $6.00. Hamline University, School of Law, 1536 Hewitt Avenue, St Paul MN 55104.

JOURNAL OF PARALEGAL EDUCATION. 8755-7649. Periodical. US. English. sa. $15.00. Lea Nordicht Shedd, Legal Studies Department/Quinnipiac College, Mt Carmel Avenue, Hamden CT 06518. **Tel** (913)381-4458. **Ed** Lea Nordlicht Shedd. **LC** KF320.L4. **DD** 340.02373. adv acc. **Circ** 500. Articles concerning paralegal education and the paralegal profession.

JOURNAL OF PARTNERSHIP TAXATION. Vol. 1, No. 1 (Spring 1984)-. 0749-4513. Periodical. US. English. qt. $64.00 US, US Possessions, and Canada. Warren Gorham & Lamont Inc, 210 South Street, Boston MA 02111. **LC** K10. **DD** 343.73066205, 347.30366205.

JOURNAL OF PENSION PLANNING AND COMPLIANCE. **VFOAT** Journal of Pension Planning & Compliance. V. 3, No. 3 (May 1977)-. 0148-2181. Periodical. US. English. qt. $90.00. Panel Publishers, 14 Plaza Road, Greenvale NY 11548. **Tel** (516)484-0006. **Ed** Michael Fishbein. **Ind/Abst** Manage. Contents, Leg. Resour. Index, Trade Ind. Index, Account. Index. Suppl., ABI/Inform, Public Aff. Inf. Serv. Bull. **LC** K16. **DD** 344.730125205. **Circ** 2,500. (ctrl). A source for in-depth analyses of the latest rulings and legislation in pension planning a must for anyone designing, administering, or consulting on pension plans. *Pension and Profit-Sharing Tax Journal, 0145-3882.*

JOURNAL OF PLANNING AND ENVIRONMENT LAW. Jan. 1973-. 0307-4870. Periodical. UK. English. mo. 6.50. Sweet & Maxwell, 11 New Fetter Lane, London EC4P 4EE England. **Ind/Abst** Leg. Resour. Index, Archit. Period. Index, Coal Abstr., Public Aff. Inf. Serv. Bull., Energy Res. Abstr. **LC** K10. **DD** 346.42045. *Journal of Planning and Property Law, 0022-376X.*

JOURNAL OF PROCEEDINGS UPON APPLICATIONS TO THE SECRETARY OF STATE FOR PROVISIONAL ORDERS UNDER THE PRIVATE LEGISLATION PROCEDURE SCOTLAND ACT 1936. (PRIVATE LEGISLATION (SCOTLAND) PROCEDURE, JOURNAL OF PROCEEDINGS UPON APPLICATIONS TO THE SECRETARY OF STATE FOR PROVISIONAL ORDERS UNDER THE PRIVATE LEGISLATION PROCEDURE (SCOTLAND) ACT, 1936). **Main/Corp** Great Britain. Scottish Office. 0302-4113. UK. English. 0.21. Her Majestys Stationery Office, Scottish Office, 49 High Holburn, WC1V 6HB England. **LC** KDC768. **DD** 348.4101.

JOURNAL OF PRODUCTS LAW. Vol. 1, No. 1 (Mar. 1982)-. 0731-1249. Periodical. US. English. qt. $48.00. Symposia Press, PO Box 418, Morristown NJ 08057. **Tel** (609)235-8439. **Ind/Abst** Leg. Resour. Index. **LC** K10. **DD** 346.73038205, 347.30638205.

JOURNAL OF PRODUCTS LIABILITY. V. 1-. 0363-0404. Periodical. US. English. qt. Pergamon Press, 395 Sawmill River Road, Elmsford NY 10523. **Ind/Abst** Electron. Commun. Abstr. J., ISMEC Bull., Pollut. Abstr. Indexes, Saf. Sci. Abstr. J., Manage. Contents, Trade Ind. Index, Leg. Resour. Index, Eng. Index, Int. Aerosp. Abstr., ABI/Inform, Curr. Law Index, Sci. Cit. Index, Abr. Ed., Consum. Index Prod. Eval. Inf. Source, Eng. Index Annu., Eng. Index Mon., Eng. Index Energy Abstr., Eng. Index Bioeng. Abstr. **LC** K10. **DD** 346.73038. **NLM** W1 JO8443. **CODEN** JPLIDG. Available in microfiche and microfilm from Microforms International Marketing Corp.

THE JOURNAL OF PROFESSIONAL LEGAL EDUCATION. Vol. 1, No. 1 (June 1983)-. 0810-9729. Periodical. English. sa. $15.00. William W Gaunt & Sons Inc, Law Book Dealers/ Gaunt Building, 3011 Gulf Drive, Holmes Beach FL 33510. **LC** K10. **DD** 340.071194.

JOURNAL OF PSYCHIATRY & LAW. (THE JOURNAL OF PSYCHIATRY & LAW). **VFOAT** Psychiatry & Law. **VAT** Journal of Psychiatry and Law. V. 1- Spring 1973-. 0093-1853. Periodical. US. English. qt. $20.00. Federal Legal Publications, 95 Morton Street, New York NY 10014. **Ind/Abst** Leg. Resour. Index, Excerpta Med., Psychol. Abstr., Index Leg. Period. **LC** K10. **DD** 614.19. **NLM** W1 JO856H. **CODEN** JPSLAN.

JOURNAL OF PUBLIC LAW. V. 1- Spring 1952-. Periodical. English. ir. **LC** Microfilm (O).

JOURNAL OF REPRINTS FOR ANTITRUST LAW AND ECONOMICS. (THE JOURNAL OF REPRINTS FOR ANTITRUST LAW AND ECONOMICS). V. 1- Summer 1969-. 0022-4243. US. English. sa. $55.00. Federal Legal Publications Inc, 157 Chambers Street, New York NY 10007. **Tel** (212)619-4949. **Ed** Gerald N Epstein and Howard Nashel. **LC** K10. **DD** 340. (cum index). Articles on the subject of antitrust law and economics reprinted from major law reviews and economic journals.

JOURNAL OF REPRINTS OF DOCUMENTS AFFECTING WOMEN. V. 1, No. 1- July 1976-. 0362-062X. Periodical. US. English. qt. $60.00. Today Publication and News Services, National Press Building, Washington DC 20045. **Tel** (202)628-6663. **LC** KF478.A45. **DD** 342.73087.

JOURNAL OF SHIPPING, CUSTOMS & TRANSPORT LAWS. 0377-0494. Periodical. English. ir. 45.00. Milan Law Publishers, PO Box 4591, 15/2 Navjivan 8, Bombay India. **DD** 343.5409605.

THE JOURNAL OF SOCIAL WELFARE LAW. Nov. 1978-. 0141-8033. Periodical. UK. English. bm. $35.25. Sweet & Maxwell Ltd, North Way Andover, Hants SP10 5BE England. **Tel** 01-583-9855. **Ed** Jane Cramp. **Ind/Abst** Leg. Resour. Index, Curr. Law Index, Contents Curr. Leg. Period. **LC** K10. **DD** 344.410305. **NLM** W1 JO889C. bk rev. adv acc. **Circ** 1,000. Ideas and information about social welfare law for practising lawyers, welfare workers and all those involved in social administration.

JOURNAL OF SPACE LAW. V. 1- Spring 1973-. 0095-7577. US. English. sa. $42.00 Domestic, $47.00 Foreign. Journal of Space Law, University of Mississippi School of Law, University MS 38677. **Tel** (601)232-7361. **Ed** S Gorove. **Ind/Abst** Leg. Resour. Index, Int. Aerosp. Abstr., Index Leg. Period., Contents Curr. Leg. Period., Curr. Law Index. **LC** JX1. **DD** 341.47. bk rev. adv acc. **Circ** 2,000. A journal devoted to the legal problems arising out of man's activities in outer space with due attention to international and political aspects.

JOURNAL OF TAXATION OF INVESTMENTS. Vol. 1, No. 1 (Autumn 1983)-. 0747-9115. Periodical. US. English. qt. $64.00. Warren Gorham & Lamont Inc, 210 South Street, Boston MA 02111. **Ind/Abst** ABI/Inform. **LC** K10. **DD** 343.730524605, 347.303524605.

THE JOURNAL OF THE AMERICAN ACADEMY OF MATRIMONIAL LAWYERS. Vol. 1, No. 1 (Spring 1985)-. 0882-6714. Periodical. US. English. sa. American Academy of Matrimonial Lawyers, 53 West Jackson Boulevard/Suite 1301, Chicago IL 60604. **DD** 346.

Law

JOURNAL OF THE BAR COUNCIL OF INDIA CEASED. **Main/Corp** Bar Council of India. Periodical. II. English. qt. Managing Editor, AB/21 Mathura Road, New Delhi India. **LC** K2. **DD** 340.0954.

JOURNAL OF THE DENNING LAW SOCIETY. **Main/Corp** Denning Law Society. V. 1- Dec. 1963-. TZ. English. an. University of Dardes Sallam/Faculty of Law, PO Box 35034, Dares Sallam Tanzania.

JOURNAL OF THE FORUM COMMITTEE ON FRANCHISING. Vol. 1, No. 4 (Fall 1981)-. 0732-1910. Periodical. US. English. qt. $20.00. American Bar Association, 750 North Lake Shore Drive, Chicago IL 60611. **Tel** (312)621-9200. **LC** KF2023.A15. **DD** 343.7308405, 347.3038405. *Newsletter of the Forum Committee on Franchising.*

JOURNAL OF THE INDIAN LAW INSTITUTE. V. 1- Oct. 1958-. 0019-5731. Periodical. II. English. qt. 150.00. Indian Law Institute Opposite of Supreme Court of India, Bhagwandas Road, New Delhi India. **Tel** 389429. **Ed** Justice V S Desmpande. Index published separately - free - automatically sent. bk rev. adv acc. **Circ** 2,000. (ctrl) Legal research articles, notes, comments, and book reviews.

JOURNAL OF THE IRISH SOCIETY FOR LABOUR LAW. Vol. 2 (1983)-. 0790-0473. English. an. **Ind/Abst** Leg. Resour. Index. **LC** K10. **DD** 344.41501, 344.15041. *Journal (Irish Society for Labour Law), 0790-0473.*

THE JOURNAL OF THE KANSAS BAR ASSOCIATION. **Main/Corp** Kansas Bar Association. V. 36, No. 2- Summer 1967-. 0022-8486. Periodical. US. English. qt. $30.00. Kansas Bar Association, PO Box 1037, Topeka KS 66601. **Tel** (913)234-5696. **Ed** Patti Slider. **Ind/Abst** Leg. Resour. Index, Index Leg. Period., Curr. Law Index. **LC** K2. **DD** 340.09781. adv acc. **Circ** 4,600. (ctrl). Contains articles, reports, and practice aids of interest to the legal profession. *Journal of the Kansas Bar Association.*

JOURNAL OF THE LAW SOCIETY OF SCOTLAND. (JOURNAL OF THE LAW SOCIETY OF SCOTLAND). V. 23-11-. Periodical. English. mo. $50.00. Law Society of Scotland, Law Society Hall, 26 Drumsheugh Garden, Edinburgh EH3 7YR Scotland. **Tel** (031)226-7411. **Ed** William M Miller. **Ind/Abst** Curr. Law Index, Leg. Resour. Index. bk rev. adv acc. **Circ** 8,000. (ctrl). News and articles regarding Scots law.

THE JOURNAL OF THE LEGAL PROFESSION. Began with spring 1976 issue. 0196-7487. US. English. an. $7.00. University of Alabama, School of Law, Box 1435, University AL 35486. **Ind/Abst** Index Leg. Period., Curr. Law Index, Leg. Resour. Index. **DD** 340.

JOURNAL OF THE MISSOURI BAR. Vol. 1, No. 1 (Jan. 1945)-. 0026-6485. Periodical. US. English. ir. $8.00. The Missouri Bar, PO Box 119, Jefferson City MO 65102. **Tel** (314)635-4128. **Ed** E A Richter. **Ind/Abst** Leg. Resour. Index, Index Leg. Period., Curr. Law Index. **DD** 349. adv acc. **Circ** 15,000. (ctrl). Articles legal in nature. Mostly bread and butter articles for use by the lawyer in his everyday practice. *Missouri Bar Journal.*

JOURNAL OF THE NATIONAL ASSOCIATION OF ADMINISTRATIVE LAW JUDGES. Vol. 1, No.1 (Spring 1981)-. Periodical. US. English. sa. $15.00. National Association of Administrative Law Judges, 521 C12/Two World Circle, New York NY 10047. **Tel** (212)488-7391. **Ed** David J Agatstein. bk rev. adv acc. **Circ** 1,500. (ctrl). A scholarly review of developments in administrative law, from the point of view of administrative law judges.

JOURNAL OF THE SENATE, STATE OF FLORIDA. **Main/Corp** Florida. Legislature. Senate. 22nd Regular Session (1929)-. US. English. Secretary of the State of Florida, The Capitol/Suite 404, Tallahassee FL 32301. *Journal of the State Senate of Florida of the Session of . . . .*

JOURNAL OF THE SOCIETY OF PUBLIC TEACHERS OF LAW CEASED. 1924-1938. 0038-0016. UK. English. ir. Index in last issue of volume - attached. (cum index).

JOURNAL OF THE SUFFOLK ACADEMY OF LAW. Vol. 1, No. 1 (Winter 1980)-. Periodical. US. English. sa. Suffold Academy of Law, Suite 406/4175 Veteran Memorial Highway, Ronkonkama NY 11779. **Ind/Abst** Leg. Resour. Index. **LC** K10. **DD** 349.74705, 347.47005.

JOURNAL OFFICIEL. **Main/Corp** Zaire. French. ir. 28.40. Polais de Justice, Service du Journal Officiel, Kinshasa Zaire. **DD** 340.096751.

JOURNAL OFFICIEL DE LA REPUBLIQUE DE HAUTE VOLTA. **Main/Corp** Upper Volta. French. ir. 9.100. Chef du Sercice des Liaisons Interministerielles, BP 7030 Compte Cheque, Postal No 400, Ouagadougou Upper Volta. *Journal Officiel.*

JOURNAL OFFICIEL DE LA REPUBLIQUE ET CANTON DU JURA. **Main/Corp** Jura (Switzerland). French. wk. Journal Officiel de la Republique et Canton du Jura, rue des Moulins 21, 2800 Delemont Switzerland. **DD** 348.4943026, 344.9430826.

JOURNAL OFFICIEL DE LA REPUBLIQUE FRANCAISE. EDITION DES LOIS ET DECRETS : NUMERO COMPLEMENTAIRE. **Main/Corp** France. FR. French. ir. Direction des Journaux Off, 26 rue Des Aix, F 75727 Paris Cedex France. **DD** 340.0944.

JOURNAL OFFICIEL DE LA REPUBLIQUE TOGOLAISE. **Main/Corp** Togo. No. 1- Oct. 16, 1956-. US. French. **LC** Microfilm LL-02120 KFG. *Journal Officiel du Territoire du Togo.*

JOURNAL OFFICIEL. LOIS ET DECRETS. **Main/Corp** France. Periodical. FR. French. da. Direction Journax Officiels, 26 rue Dessaix, 75732 Paris Cedex 15 France.

JOURNAL - PAKISTAN BAR COUNCIL COUNCIL. **Main/Corp** Pakistan Bar Council. V. 1- Jan. 1978-. Periodical. English (Urdu). ir. 60.00, $12.00 US. Pakistan Bar Council, 1 Begum Road, Lahore Pakistan. **LC** K16. **DD** 349.549105.

THE JOURNAL RECORD. 0737-5468. Periodical. US. English. da. $60.00. Journal Record Publishers Company, 621 North Robinson, Oklahoma City OK 73102. **LC** K10. **DD** 349.76605, 347.66005.

JOURNAL - SUPREME COURT OF THE UNITED STATES. (JOURNAL). **Main/Corp** United States. Supreme Court. Began with 1889. 0270-9805. US. English. da. Supreme Court of the United States, Washington DC 20402. **DD** 347.732605.

JOURNEES DE LA SOCIETE DE LEGISLATION COMPAREE. Series/Titl Revue Internationale de Droit Compare. Yearly 1979-. FR. French. an. 90.00. Societe de Legislation Comparee, 28 rue Saint-Guillaume, 75007 Paris France. *Journees Juridiques.*

THE J.P. WEEKLY LAW DIGEST. VAT Justice of the Peace Weekly Law Digest. UK. English. wk. Justice of the Peace Ltd, Little London Chichester, Sussex England P019 1PG. **LC** KD296. **DD** 348.41046.

JTS INFORMA. VFOAT J.T.S. Informa. Vol. 1, No. 1 (June 30, 1980)-. Periodical. Spanish. ir. Publicaciones JTS Inc, PO Box 4509, Old San Juan Puerto Rico 00905. **LC** KGV70. **DD** 348.7295041, 347.2950841.

THE JUDGE. Periodical. US. English. ir. Syracuse University, College of Law, Syracuse NY 13210.

THE JUDGES' JOURNAL. V. 10, No, 2- Apr. 1971-. 0047-2972. Periodical. US. English. qt $17.00. American Bar Center, 750 North Lake Shore Drive, Chicago IL 60611. **Tel** (312)988-5555. **Ind/Abst** Leg. Resour. Index, Index Leg. Period., Contents Curr. Leg. Period., Curr. Law Index. **LC** K10. **DD** 347.73105. *Trial Judges' Journal, 0564-2116.*

JUDGES' RETIREMENT SYSTEM : ANNUAL FINANCIAL REPORT AND REPORT OF OPERATIONS FOR THE FISCAL YEAR ENDED JUNE 30 . . . . **Main/Corp** California. Public Employees' Retirement System. Board of Administration. 1st (1980)-. US. English. an. Public Employees' Retirement System, PO Box 1953, Sacramento CA 95809. **LC** KFC980. **DD** 347.794014, 347.940714.

JUDGMENTS OF THE ADMINISTRATIVE TRIBUNAL OF THE INTERNATIONAL LABOUR ORGANIZATION. VFOAT Judgements of the ILO Administrative Tribunal. Began in 1978. 0378-7362. English. sa. $28.50. ILO Publications, International Labour Office, CH-1211 Geneva 22 Switzerland. **LC** K1704.23. **DD** 341.7630268. *Official Bulletin. Series C.*

JUDICATURE. V. 1- June 1917-. 0022-5800. Periodical. US. English. bm. $18.00. American Judicature Society, 25 E Washington/Suite 1600, Chicago IL 60602. **Tel** (312)558-6900. **Ed** David Richart. **Ind/Abst** Public Aff. Inf. Serv. Bull., Contents Curr. Leg. Period., Curr. Law Index, Leg. Resour. Index, Index Leg. Period., Am. Hist. Life, Hist. Abstr., Soc. Sci. Citation Index. **LC** KF200. bk rev. adv acc. **Circ** 30,000. The administration of justice and its improvement, including consideration of court organization operation and personnel. *Journal of the American Judicature Society.*

JUDICIAL & LEGAL DIRECTORY. See Yearbooks, Almanacs, Directories.

JUDICIAL CONDUCT REPORTER. V. 1- Spring 1979-. 0193-7367. Periodical. US. English. qt. American Judicature Society, 200 West Montor Street/Suite 1606, Chichago IL 60606. **LC** KF8779.A15. **DD** 347.7313.

JUDICIAL CONFERENCE OF THE STATE OF OREGON. (JUDICIAL CONFERENCE OF THE STATE OF OREGON ANNUAL REPORT). **Main/Corp** Oregon. Judicial Conference. 0096-1434. US. English. an. Judicial Conference of the State of Oregon, Salem OR 97310. **LC** KFO2910. **DD** 347.79501.

JUDICIAL EDUCATION NEWS. V. 1- Mar. 1974-. 0094-5420. Periodical. US. English. bm. American Academy of Judicial Education, 737 Woodward Building/1426 H Street NW, Washington DC 20005. **LC** KF275. **DD** 340.071173.

THE JUDICIAL FELLOWS PROGRAM. **Main/Corp** United States. Supreme Court. 0270-0654. US. English. an. The Supreme Court of the United States, Washington DC 20543. **LC** KF277.C65. **DD** 347.73130711, 347.307130711.

JUDICIAL FUNCTION OUTLINE. 1977-. 0148-4982. US. English. an. College of the State Judiciary, Judicial College Building, University of Nevada, Reno NV 89557. **LC** KF8700.A59. **DD** 347.731.

JUDICIAL HIGHLIGHTS BULLETIN. V. 1- Mar. 1970-. 0449-5519. US. English. Pennsylvania Bar Association, PO Box 186, Harrisburg PA 17108. **LC** KFP81. **DD** 348.748046.

JUDICIAL NEWSLETTER. V. 1- Nov. 1974-. 0163-2078. Periodical. US. English. qt. 1505 West Cumberland Avenue, Knoxville TN 37916. **LC** KFT562.A15. **DD** 345.7680505.

JUDICIAL NOTICE. No. 1- May 1980-. 0279-859X. Periodical. US. English. mo. Ohio Judicial Conference, 30 East Broad Street, Columbus OH 43215.

JUDICIAL STATISTICS, ENGLAND AND WALES, FOR THE YEAR/CHANCELLOR'S DEPARTMENT. See Statistics.

THE JUDICIARY, STATE OF DELAWARE, ANNUAL REPORT. (THE JUDICIARY, STATE OF DELAWARE : ANNUAL REPORT). **Main/Corp** Delaware. Administrative Office of the Courts. 0098-0927. US. English. an. Administrative Office of the Courts, 1112 King Street, Wilmington DE 19801. **LC** KFD510.5.A3. **DD** 347.751013.

JULGADOS DO TRIBUNAL DE ALCADA CRIMINAL DE SAO PAULO. **Main/Corp** Sao Paulo, Brazil (State) Tribunal de Alcada Criminal. Portuguese. ir. 1160.00. Lex, Caixa Postal 12.888, Sao Paulo Brazil. **Tel** 549-0122. **Circ** 1,500. (ctrl). *Julgados.*

JURA: JURISTISCHE AUSBILDUNG. VFOAT Juristische Ausbildung. V. 1-. 0170-1452. Periodical. German. mo. Walter de Gruyter, 200 Saw Mill River Road, Hawthorn NY 10532. **Tel** (914)747-0110. **LC** K10. **DD** 349.4305.

JURIDICA. Spanish. ir. Av Cerro de las Torres 395 21 DF, Mexico City Mexico. **DD** 340.098.

JURIMETRICS JOURNAL. (JURIMETRICS JOURNAL : QUARTERLY JOURNAL OF THE AMERICAN BAR ASSOCIATION SPECIAL COMMITTEE ON ELECTRONIC DATA RETRIEVAL IN COOPERATION WITH THE LAW SCHOOL AND THE MENTAL HEALTH RESEARCH INSTITUTE, UNIVERSITY OF MICHIGAN). Vol. 8, No. 1 (Sept. 1966)-. 0022-6793. Periodical. US. English. qt. American Bar Association, 750 North Lake Shore Drive, Chicago IL 60611. **Tel** (312)988-5555. **Ed** Edward Gerjuoy. **Ind/Abst** Leg. Resour. Index, Comput. Control Abstr., Electr. Electron. Abstr., Sci. Abstr. Sect. A. Phys. Abstr., Comput. Rev., Sociol. Abstr., Phys. Abstr., Curr. Law Index, Lang. Lang. Behav. Abstr., Contents Curr. Leg. Period. **CODEN**

Law

JURJAD. (ctrl). Covers a range of topics on legal issues in science and technology. *M.U.L.L. Modern Uses of Logic In Law.*

JURIS. Began with Sept. 1967 issue. 0022-6807. US. English. qt. Free. Duquesne University School of Law, 900 Locust Street, Pittsburgh PA 15282. **Tel** (412)434-6305. Ed Matthew M Polka. **LC** K10. **DD** 340.0973. bk rev. adv acc. **Circ** 6,000. (ctrl). Legal newsmagazine covering topics of current legal interest on local, statewide and national level.

JURIS-CLASSEUR DE DROIT COMPARE. FR. French. sa. Editions Techniques, 123 rue d'Alesia, 75678 Paris Cedex 14 France.

JURIS NEWSLETTER. Main/Corp United States. Dept. of Justice. VAT Justice Retrieval and Inquiry System Newsletter. V. 1- Feb. 7, 1977-. US. English. US Department of Justice, Room 5348/10th and Constitution Avenue NW, Washington DC 20537. **LC** KF242.A1. **DD** 340.0285.

JURIS QUAESITOR. V. 1- Fall 1976-. 0146-2709. US. English. University of New Hampshire, UNH Student Press, Durham NH 03824. **LC** K10. **DD** 340.05.

JURISCIVEL DO S.T.F. VFOAT Revista Jurischvel DO S.T.F. V. 1- June 1972-. Portuguese. ir. Cultural Distribuidora de Livros, Rua Sergipe No 1 466, Sao Joaquim da Barra Brazil.

JURISPRUDENCE DU CONSEIL D'ETAT. Main/Corp France. Conseil d'Etat. 1973/74-. FR. French. ir. 20.00. La Documentation Francaise, 39 31 Quai Voltaire, 75340 Paris Cedex 07 France. **DD** 342.44066.

JURISPRUDENCE DU PORT D'ANVERS. *See* Transportation - Ships & Shipping.

JURISPRUDENCE EN DROIT DU TRAVAIL. DECISIONS DES COMMISSAIRES DU TRAVAIL. (JURISPRUDENCE EN DROIT DU TRAVAIL : DECISIONS DES COMMISSAIRES DU TRAVAIL). **Main/Corp** Quebec (Province). Centre de Recherche et de Statistiques sur le Marche du Travail. VAT Decisions des Commissarres du Travail. V. 11, No. 3 (July./Aug./Sept. 1979)-. 0707-2775. Periodical. CN. French. qt. Government du Quebec, 600 St Amable 4, Etage Quebec GIR 4Z1 Canada. **DD** 344.7140102646. *Jurisprudence en Droit du Travail (Decisions des Commissaires du Travail), 0707-2775.*

JURISPRUDENCE EN DROIT DU TRAVAIL. TRIBUNAL DU TRAVAIL. (JURISPRUDENCE EN DROIT DU TRAVAIL : TRIBUNAL DU TRAVAIL). **Main/Corp** Quebec (Province). Centre de Recherche et Statistiques Sur le Marche du Travail. No. 1 (Mar.1980)-. 0700-1681. Periodical. CN. French. qt. Gouvernement du Quebec, 600 St Amable 4E Etage, Quebec G1R 4Z1 Canada. **DD** 344.7140102643. *Jurisprudence en Droit du Travail.*

JURISPRUDENCE EXPRESS. Oct. 14, 1977-. 0705-3061. Periodical. CN. French. wk. 115.00. Societe Quebecoise d'Information Juridique, 276 rue Jacques/Suite 310, Montreal Quebec H2Y 1N3 Canada. **Tel** (514)842-8741. bk rev. **Circ** 12,000. *Journal of jurisprudence in Quebec.*

JURISPRUDENCE LOGEMENT. 0830-0380. CN. French. bm. Publications du Quebec, CP1005, Quebec Quebec G1K 7B5 Canada. **LC** KEQ426.A49. **DD** 346.714043405, 347.140643405. *Decisions de la Regie du Logement, 0226-885X.*

JURISPRUDENCIA ARAGONESA. Main/Corp Colegio de Abogados de Zaragoza. 1972-. Spanish. ir. **DD** 348.4655043.

JURISPRUDENCIA BRASILEIRA. 1-. Monographic Series. BL. Portuguese. ir. Jurua Editora, Av Visconde de Guarupauva, 2435-10 Andar, CEP 80 000, Curitiba Parana Brazil. **LC** KHD387.A48. **DD** 349.8105, 348.1005.

JURISPRUDENCIA BRASILEIRA CRIMINAL. Vol. 1-. Periodical. Portuguese. ir. $2940. Jurua Editora Av Visconde de Guarupauva, 2435 1 Andar, CEP 80.000 Curitiba Parana Brazil. **LC** KHD5402.A48. **DD** 345.81002648, 348.105002648.

JURISPRUDENCIA CATARINENSE. Main/Corp Santa Catarina, Brazil. Tribunal de Justica. V. 1- 3rd Quarter 1973-. Portuguese. ir. Santa Catarina Brazil Tribunal de Justica, Rua Duarte Schutel No 11, Caixa Postal 427 88.000 Florianapolis Brazil.

JURISPRUDENCIA DE SEGURIDAD SOCIAL Y SANIDAD. Periodical. SP. Spanish. ir. $28.00. Servicio de Publicaciones Secretaria General Technica, Ministerio de Sanidad y Seguridad Social Paseo Del Prado 18, Madrid 14 Spain. **DD** 344.460.

JURISPRUDENCIA DEL TRIBUNAL SUPREMO DE PUERTO RICO. Main/Corp Puerto Rico. Supreme Court. PR. Spanish. ir. $240.00. Jurisprudenica Tribun Sup Inc, PO Box 4509, Old San Juan Puerto Rico 00905. **DD** 348.7295041, 347.2950841.

JURISPRUDENCIA LABORAL Y DE SEGURIDAD SOCIAL. 0210-8836. SP. Spanish. ir. 6.000. Calle Lope de Vega 38, Madrid 14 Spain. **DD** 344.4602 344.6042. *Jurisprudencia Laboral, de Seguridad Social y Sanidad.*

JURIST (WASHINGTON, D.C.). *See* Religion, Mythology, Rationalism - Roman Catholic Church.

JURISTEN (DANMARKS JURIST- OG KONOMFORBUND). (JURISTEN). 0107-699X. Periodical. DK. Danish. ir. Danmarks Jurist-Og Konomforbund, Gothersgade 133, 1123 Kbenhavn K Denmark. **LC** K10. *Juristen & Konomen.*

JURISTENZEITUNG. V. 6-. 0022-6882. Periodical. GW. German. sm. $80.59. JCB Mohr/Paul Siebeck, Postfach 2040, 7400 Tuebingen West Germany. **Tel** 0 70 71/2 60 64. **Ind/Abst** Energy Res. Abstr. *Deutsche Rechts-Zeitschrift, Suddeutsche Juristen-Zeitung.*

JURISTISCHE ABHANDLUNGEN. Monographic Series. GW. German. ir. Vittorio Klostermann, Postfach 900601 Frauenlobstrasse 22, 6000 Frankfurt 90 West Germany. **Tel** 0611/ 77 40 11.

JURISTISCHE RUNDSCHAU. Vol. 1-. 0022-6920. Periodical. German. mo. Walter de Gruyter Inc, 200 Saw Mill River Road, Hawthorne NY 10532. **Tel** (914)747-0110.

JURISTISCHE STUDIEN. Main/Corp Tubingen. Universitat Rechts - und Wirtschaftswissenschaftliche Fakultat. Rechtswissenschaftliche Abteilung. Monographic Series. GW. German. ir. JCB Mohr-Paul Siebeck, Postfach 2040, 7400 Tuebingen West Germany. **Tel** 0 70 71/2 60 64.

JURY VERDICTS WEEKLY. JUDICIAL ARBITRATIONS. (JURY VERDICTS WEEKLY, JUDICIAL ARBITRATIONS). 0199-705X. Periodical. US. English. wk. $160.00. Jury Verdicts Weekly Inc, 738 Montecito Center/Suite A, Santa Rosa CA 95405. **Tel** (707)539-5454. Ed K W Raymond. adv acc. **Circ** 1,500. Reporting California arbitration hearings listing attorneys, expert witnesses and arbitrators plus awards.

JUS. V. 1- May 1974-. Periodical. Spanish. ir. Editorial Jus, Paseo Colon 270 of 202, Lima Peru. **LC** K10.

JUS GENTIUM. Vol. 1- 1949-. 0022-6963. IT. Italian. sa. 80.000. Jus Gentium, Casella Postale 410, 1-00100 Rome Centro Italy. **Tel** 6569012. Ed Giovanni Scazangella Arpino. bk rev.

JUS. JURISTISCHE SCHULUNG. (JURISTISCHE SCHULUNG). VFOAT JUS. Vol 1-. 0022-6939. Periodical. GW. German. ir. $48.21. C H Beck'Sche Verlagsbchhndlg, Wilhelmstrasse 9, Postfach 400340, 8 Muenchen 40 West Germany. **Tel** 089/3 81 89-1. **Ind/Abst** Coal Abstr., Energy Res. Abstr.

JUST CAUSE. Vol. 1, No. 1 (Winter 1983)-. 0824-281X. Periodical. CN. English. qt. 20.00. Canadian Legal Advocacy Information and Research Association of the Disabled, PO Box 3553/Station C, Ottawa Ontario K1Y 4J7 Canada. **Tel** (613)23-8515. Ed H Wierenga. **DD** 346.71013. bk rev. **Circ** 1,500. A journal of law and people with disabilities.

JUST COMPENSATION; A MONTHLY REPORT ON CONDEMNATION CASES. 19 -. 0738-6494. US. English. mo. $80.00. Just Compensation Inc, PO Box 5133, Sherman Oaks CA 91403. **Tel** (818)848-6765. Ed G Kanner. bk rev. Reports on developments in the law of eminent domain and inverse condemnation.

JUST IN TIME. V. 1-5, No. 5, Sept. 1976-Nov. 1981. 0383-8072. Periodical. CN. English. ir. $2.50. Carlton University, Department of Law, Colonel By Drive, Ottawa Ontario K1S 5B6 Canada. **DD** 340.05.

JUST IN TIME. TEACHER'S GUIDE. V. 4- Sept. 1979-. 0225-4778. Periodical. CN. English. qt. IPI Publishing Ltd, 44 Charles Street West/Suite 4410, Toronto Ontario M4Y 1R7 Canada. **Tel** (416)964-6662. Ed Daniel J Baum. **DD** 340.05. **Circ** 3,000. (ctrl). Easy to read magazine/newsletter with teacher's guide. Provides topical information for the layperson on major areas of Canadian law.

JUSTICE ASSISTANCE NEWS. Vol. 1, No. 1 (Feb. 1980)-. 0749-8195. Periodical. US. English. mo. Superintendent of Documents, US Government Printing Office, Washington DC 20402. **Ind/Abst** Index U.S. Gov. Period. **DD** 353. *LEAA Newsletter.*

JUSTICE FOR CHILDREN NEWSLETTER. 0711-2327. Periodical. CN. English. qt. Free to Members. Justice for Children, 455 Spadina Avenue, Toronto Ontario M5S 2G8 Canada. **DD** 346.710135.

JUSTICE MAGAZINE. V. 1- Feb. 1972-. Periodical. US. English. mo. Justice Publishers, PO Box 2141, Arlington VA 22202. **LC** K10. **DD** 345.73005.

JUSTICE MUNICIPALE. March/April 1981-. 0227-0811. Periodical. CN. French. ir. $25.15. Wilson E Lafleur Limited, 39 Quest rue Notre Dame, Montreal Quebec H2Y 1S5 Canada. **DD** 342.7140902643.

JUSTICE OF THE PEACE. V. 135, No. 47- Nov. 20, 1971-. Periodical. UK. English. wk. $76.63. Justice of the Peace Ltd, Little London Chichester, Sussex England PO19 1PG England. **LC** K10. **DD** 347.42016. *Justice of the Peace and Local Government Review.*

JUSTICE OF THE PEACE AND LOCAL GOVERNMENT REVIEW REPORTS CEASED. Vol. 91-V. 146. Periodical. UK. English. wk. *Justice of the Peace Reports (London, England).*

JUSTICE OF THE PEACE REPORTS (CHICHESTER, WEST SUSSEX). (JUSTICE OF THE PEACE REPORTS). Vol. 147 (Jan. 1983)-. 0264-3731. Periodical. UK. English. wk. $98.08. Justice of the Peace Ltd, Little London Chichester, Sussex England. *Justice of the Peace and Local Government Review Reports.*

JUSTICE (QUEBEC). (JUSTICE : LE MAGAZINE DU MINISTERE DE LA JUSTICE DU QUEBEC). Began with Mar.-Apr. 1979 issue. 0707-8501. Periodical. CN. French. bm. Direction des Communications, 1200 Route de L'Eglise, 9E Etage, Sainte-Foy Quebec G1V 4M1 Canada. **LC** KEQ1170.A72. **DD** 345.7140505, 347.1405505.

THE JUSTICE REPORTER. Series/Titl Law & Society Series. Vol. 1, No. 1 (Fall 1980)-. 0730-5087. Periodical. US. English. bm. $18.00. The Justice Reporter, Clark Boardman Company, 435 Hudson Street, New York NY 10014. **LC** KF9223.A15. **DD** 364.973.

JUSTICE WATCH. Vol. 5, No. 1 (Feb. 1982)-. Periodical. US. English. Justice Watch, 132 West 43 Street, New York NY 10036.

JUSTITIA. Periodical. US. English. qt. Capitol Complex, Carson City NV 89710. **LC** KFN1110.A15. **DD** 347.79301.

JUSTITIELE STATISTIEK. *See* Statistics.

JUSTITIELE VERKENNINGEN. Dutch. ir. Wetenschcappelijk Oderzoek- En Documentatiencentrum, Plein 2B, 'S-Gravenhage Netherlands. **LC** K10. **DD** 345.492005.

JUVENILE & FAMILY COURT JOURNAL. VAT Juvenile and Family Court Journal. V. 29, No. 2- May 1978-. 0161-7109. Periodical. US. English. qt. $24.00. National Council of Juvenile and Family Court, PO Box 8978, Renov NV 89507. **Tel** (702)784-6012. **Ind/Abst** Leg. Resour. Index. **LC** K10. **Circ** 3,000. (ctrl). The journal is a forum of articles centering on juvenile justice issues, usually in the form of several topics per issue. Occasionally, the journal will explore a single topic of current interest to juvenile justice professionals. *Journal of Juvenile & Family Courts, 0162-0525.*

JUVENILE AND FAMILY COURT NEWSLETTER. V. 8- Feb. 1978-. 0162-9859. Periodical. US. English. ir. $16.00. National Council of Juvenile Family, PO Box 8978, Reno NV 09507. **Tel** (702)784-6012. **LC** KF9772. **DD** 347.7308. *Juvenile Court Newsletter.*

Law

JUVENILE AND FAMILY LAW DIGEST. Vol. 13, No. 1 (July 1981)-. 0279-2257. Periodical. US. English. mo. $60.00. National Council Juvenile & Family, PO Box 8970, Reno NV 89507. **Tel** (702)784-6012. **Ed** Toni Hutcherson. **LC** KF9776.3. **DD** 346.730135, 347.306135. **Circ** 2,500. (ctrl). A law digest presenting the most recent and precedent setting cases in the juvenile and family courts across the nation. *Juvenile Law Digest, 0162-5055.*

JUVENILE COURT AND STATE YOUTH AUTHORITY. **Main/Corp** North Dakota. Social Service Board. **VFOAT** Delinquency, Dependency & Neglect, Special Proceedings. 1975-. US. English. an. Administrator of Research and Statistics, Management Services, Bismarck ND 58505. **LC** KFN8671.55. **DD** 345.78408. *Statistics, Juvenile Court and State Youth Authority, 0098-8782.*

JUVENILE COURT REPORT. See Sociology: General Works, Theory - Social Pathology, Welfare, Criminology.

JUVENILE COURT STATISTICS. See Statistics.

JUVENILE LAW NEWSLETTER. July 1972-. 0095-697X. Periodical. US. English. mo. National Juvenile Law Center, 3642 Lindell Boulevard, St Louis MO 63108. **LC** KF479.A73. **DD** 345.7308.

KAIJI ROPPO. **Main/Corp** Japan. Japanese. ir. Kaibundo, 48 Kanda Jimbocho 2 Chiyida-ku (101-91), Tokyo Japan.

KAISETSU KYOIKU ROPPO. **Main/Corp** Japan. JA. Japanese. ir. 2000. Sanseido, 1 Kanda Jinbocho 1, Chiyoda-ku 101, Tokyo Japan.

KANON : YEARBOOK OF THE SOCIETY OF THE LAW OF THE ORIENTAL CHURCHES. See Yearbooks, Almanacs, Directories.

KANSAI UNIVERSITY REVIEW OF LAW AND POLITICS. **VFOAT** Review of Law and Politics. No. 1 (Mar. 1980)-. 0388-886X. Periodical. English (German and Italian). an. Exchange Department (LP), Kansai University Library, PO Box 50, Suita Osaka 564 Japan. **LC** K11. **DD** 340.05.

KANSAS BARLETTER. Began with: Vol. 1 (1951). Periodical. US. English. mo. $25.00. Kansas Bar Association, PO Box 1037, Topeka KS 66601. **Tel** (913)234-5696. **Ed** Marcia Poell. adv acc. **Circ** 4,300. News of interest to lawyers, especially KBA happenings and digested legal opinions.

KANSAS COURT RULES AND PROCEDURE. (KANSAS COURT RULES AND PROCEDURE : WITH AMENDMENTS RECEIVED TO . . .). 0748-5255. US. English. $18.50. West Publishing Company, 50 West Kellogg Boulevard/PO Box 3526, St Paul MN 55165. **LC** KFK529. **DD** 347.781051, 347.810751.

KARLSRUHER JURISTISCHE BIBLIOGRAPHIE. See Bibliographies.

THE KARNATAKA LAW JOURNAL. Jan. 1974-. Periodical. English. ir. Mysore Law Journal, Sri Ram No 4, Fourth Cross Shankarapura, Bangalore-4 India. **DD** 340.095487. *Mysore Law Journal.*

THE KARNATAKA LAW JOURNAL. SUPPLEMENT. Jan. 1974-. Periodical. English. ir. Kamataka Law Journal etc, Sri Bam No 4, Fourth Cross, Shankarapura Bangalore-4 India. **DD** 340.095487.

KATALOG PERATURAN PERUNDANG-UNDANGAN REPUBLIK INDONESIA. Indonesian. ir. Pusat Dokumentasi Hukum, Fakultas Hukum, Universitas Indonesia, Jl Teuku Umar No 46, Jakarta Pusat Indonesia.

KATALOG VON LANDESGESETZEN UBER DEN UMWELTSCHUTZ CEASED. **Main/Corp** Verbindungsstelle der Bundeslander Beim Amt der Niederosterreichischen Landesregierung. 1973-. German. ir. Verbindungsstelle der Bundeslander, Minoritenplatz 8, 1014 Wien Austria.

KEADILAN. Periodical. Indonesian. ir. 100 Single Issue. Senat Mahasiswa, Jalan Sagan 1/3, Yokyakarta Indonesia. **LC** K11.

KENDELSER OM FAST EJENDOM. **Main/Corp** Dansk Ingenirforening Voldgiftsret. **VFOAT** Voldfigtskendelser Efter Almindelige Betingelser. 1- 1975-. Danish. ir. Juristforbundets Forlag, Gothergade 133 1045 K, Kbenhavn Denmark.

THE KENTUCKY AND TENNESSEE LEGAL DIRECTORY. See Yearbooks, Almanacs, Directories.

KENTUCKY BENCH & BAR. **VFOAT** Kentucky Bench and Bar. **VAT** Kentucky Bench and Bar. Began in Jan. 1975. 0164-9345. Periodical. US. English. qt. $8.00. Kentucky Bar Association, Kentucky Bar Center, West Main at Kentucky River, Frankfort KY 40601. **Tel** (502)564-3795. **Ind/Abst** Leg. Resour. Index, Curr. Law Index. *Kentucky Bar Journal, 0362-6113.*

KENTUCKY LAW JOURNAL. Began in 1913. 0023-026X. Periodical. US. English. qt. $20.00. Kentucky Law Journal, University of Kentucky, Lexington KY 40506. **Tel** (606)257-4747. **Ed** Mark Snell. **Ind/Abst** Leg. Resour. Index, Sociol. Abstr., Soc. Welf. Soc. Plan./Policy Soc. Dev., Public Aff. Inf. Serv. Bull., Index Leg. Period., Curr. Law Index, Lang. Lang. Behav. Abstr., Contents Curr. Leg. Period. (cum index). bk rev. **Circ** 1,300. (ctrl). Articles, notes, comments, and book reviews analyzing legal issues.

THE KENTUCKY LEGAL DIRECTORY. See Yearbooks, Almanacs, Directories.

KENTUCKY SCHOOL LAWS, ANNOTATED. **Main/Corp** Kentucky. Complete to Jan. 1, 1981-. US. English. be. **LC** KFK1590.A29. **DD** 344.76907102632, 347 69047102632. *School Laws of Kentucky, Annotated.*

THE KENYA GAZETTE. Periodical. US. English. wk. 1200. Government Printer Kenya, Office of President, Box 30128, Nairobi Kenya. **Tel** 334075. **LC** J8. **DD** 354.67620005. bk rev. adv acc. **Circ** 8,000.

KENYA HIGH COURT DIGEST. English. ir. PO Box 30197, Nairobi Kenya. **DD** 348.6762046.

THE KERALA HIGH COURT NOTES. English. ir. 15.00. A K Avirah, c/o Law Times Press, Arnakulam India. **DD** 348.5483041.

KERTHA PATRIKA. Periodical. IO. English (Indonesian). ir. Universitas Udayana Kantor Pusat, Fakultas Hukum dan Pengetahuan Masyarakat, Jalan Panglima Besar Sudirman, Denpasar Indonesia. **LC** K11. **DD** 349.59805.

KEY PERSONNEL DIRECTORY. See Yearbooks, Almanacs, Directories.

KEYES ENCYCLOPEDIC DICTIONARY OF PROCUREMENT LAW. See Encyclopedias & General Reference Books.

KHARTOUM LAW REVIEW. Vol. 1 (1979)-. Periodical. English. an. University of Khartoum, PO Box 321, Khartoum Sudan. **LC** K11. **DD** 349.62405, 346.24005.

KHOZIAISTVO I PRAVO. Began in 1977. Periodical. UR. Russian. mo. $38.00. Victor Kamkin Inc (71066), 12224 Parklawn Drive, Rockville MD 20852. **Tel** (301)881-5973. **LC** K11.

KHRONIKA ZASHCHITY PRAV V SSSR. V. 1.- No. 1- Nov. 1972/March 1973-. Periodical. US. Russian. IZD-Vo Khronika, 505 8th Avenue, New York NY 10018. **LC** K11.

KINDEX. See Indexes/Abstracts.

KING'S COUNSEL. Mar. 1936-. Periodical. UK. English. an. University of London, Kings College, Strand Street, WC 2R 1LS London England. **Ed** Blackburn. adv acc. **Circ** 500. Law journal of Kings College of London.

THE KINGSTON LAW REVIEW. V. 1- Nov. 1968-. 0453-8854. Periodical. UK. English. ir. William W Guant & Sons Limited, 3011 Gulf Drive, Holmes Beach FL 33510. **Tel** (813)778-5211. **Ind/Abst** Leg. Resour. Index, Curr. Law Index. **LC** K11. **DD** 340.0942.

KITAKYUSHU DAIGAKU HOSEI RONSHU. **VFOAT** Hosei Ronshu. Edition- (1-). Periodical. JA. English (Japanese). ir. Kitakyushu Daigaku Hogakubu Kitakata, Kokura Minami-ku Japan. **LC** K11.

KODIKAS EPITHEORESEOS ERGATIKOU DIKAIOU. **VFOAT** Kodix Epitheoreseos Ergatikou Dikaiou. GR. Greek, Modern. sm. Aristeidou 9, Athena 105 59 Greece. *Kodix Epitheoreseos Ergatikou Dikaiou.*

KOINONIKES ODEGOS TOU ERGAZOMENOU. 0826-8703. CN. Greek, Modern. an. Quebec Federation of Labour, 4th Floor/ 2100 Papineau Avenue, Montreal Quebec H2K 4J4 Canada. **DD** 344.71401.

KOLNER SCHRIFTEN ZUM EUROPARECHT. **VFOAT** Publications de Droit Europeen. V. 1-. Monographic Series. German (French). ir. Carl Heymanns Verlag KG, Gereonstrasse 18-32, 5000 Koeln 1 West Germany.

KOMMENTAR ZUM SCHWEIZERISCHEN ZIVILGESETZBUCH. SZ. German. ir. Schulthess Polygraph Verlag, Zwingliplatz 2, CH 8022 Zurich Switzerland.

KOMMENTARII SUDEBNOI PRAKTIKI. UR. Russian. an. 0.60. K64 Ul Chkalova 38-40.

KONKURS-, TREUHAND- UND SCHIEDSGERICHTSWESEN. Periodical. US. German. qt. $65.30. Carl Heymanns Verlag KG, Gereonstrasse 18-32, 5000 Koln 1 West Germany. **LC** K11. *Konkurs- und Treuhandwesen.*

KONSUMENTVERKETS FORFATTNINGSSAMLING. **Main/Corp** Sweden. Swedish. ir. Konsumentverket Fact, 162 10 Vallingby Sweden. **DD** 343.485075.

KOREAN JOURNAL OF COMPARATIVE LAW. V. 1- 1973-. 0377-0729. US. English. an. University of Washington Law School, Professor John O Haley, Seattle WA 98195. **Tel** (206)543-6543. **LC** K11. **DD** 340.205.

KOSCIO I PRAWO. 1-. 0208-7928. Periodical. Polish. ir. 70.00.

KRITISCHE JUSTIZ. Vol. 1- 1968-. 0023-4834. Periodical. GW. German. qt. 26.00. Europaische Verlagsanstalt, Metzlerstrasse 25, 6 Frankfurt 70 West Germany. **Ind/Abst** Energy Res. Abstr. **LC** K11. **DD** 340.0943.

KURASHI NO TAME NO HORITSU. Began in 1973. JA. Japanese. an. 1800. Daiichi Hoki Shuppan, 11-17 Minami Aoyama 2 Minato-ku, Tokyo-to Japan. **Ed** Wagatsuma Sakae Nakagawa Zennosuke, and Endo Hiroshi.

LA REVUE ADMINISTRATIVE. See Public Administration.

LABEO; RASSEGNA DI DIRETTO ROMANO. V. 1- 1955-). 0023-6462. Periodical. IT. Italian (English). ir. Casa Editrice Dott Eugenio Jov, Via Mezzocannone 109, 80134 Napoli Italy.

LABOR & EMPLOYMENT LAW. **VAT** Labor and Employment Law. V. 9, No. 3- Apr. 1979-. 0193-5739. Periodical. US. English. an. $6.00. American Bar Association, 750 North Lake Shore Drive, Chicago IL 60611. **Tel** (312)988-5555. **Ind/Abst** Leg. Resour. Index, Curr. Law Index. **LC** KF325.15. **DD** 344.730105. *Labor Relations & Employment, 0163-5077.*

LABOR CASES. **VFOAT** CCH Labor Cases. **VAT** Commerce Clearing House Labor Cases. Vol. 1 (1937-1939)-. US. English. ir. Commerce Clearing House, 4025 West Peterson Avenue, Chicago IL 60646. **Tel** (312)583-8500. **LC** KF3310.A2. Publishes federal and state decisions on labor issues, wage-hour issues in bound volumes.

LABOR CONTRACT LAW BULLETIN. **VFOAT** LCB. Apr. 1984-. 8755-7886. Periodical. US. English. mo. $36.80. Quinlan Publishing Company, 131 Beverly Street, Boston MA 02114. **DD** 344. *Collective Bargaining Law Bulletin.*

LABOR LAW. 1972-. US. English. ir. $315.00. Matthew Bender & Company Inc, 1275 Broadway, Albany NY 12201. **Tel** (800)833-9844.

LABOR LAW DEVELOPMENTS; PROCEEDINGS. **Main/Conf** Institute on Labor Law, Southwestern Legal Foundation. 10th- 1964-. US. English. an. Matthew Bender & Company Inc, 1275 Broadway, Albany NY 12201. **Tel** (800)833-9844. *Proceedings - Institute on Labor Law.*

LABOR LAW GUIDE CEASED. **Main/Corp** Commerce Clearing House. No. -1164. 0162-1645. US. English. wk.

LABOR LAW JOURNAL. V. 1- Oct. 1949-. 0023-6586. Periodical. US. English. mo. $65.00. Commerce Clearing House Inc, 4025 West Peterson Avenue, Chicago IL 60646. **Tel** (312)583-8500. **Ind/Abst** Manage. Abstr., Trade Ind. Index, Leg. Resour. Index, Int. Labour Doc., Hospit. Lit. Index, Women Stud. Abstr., Public Aff. Inf. Serv. Bull., Bus. Period. Index, Index Leg. Period., Curr. Law Index, Soc. Sci. Citation Index, Bus. Period. Index, Contents Curr. Leg. Period. **LC** K12. Presents significant articles union, management, law and government.

Law

LABOR LAW REPORT. 0193-1628. Periodical. US. English. mo. Matthew Bender & Company Inc, 235 45th Street, New York NY 10017. LC KF3365.K47 SUPPL. DD 344.730105.

LABOR LAW REPORTER. 1965-. Periodical. US. English. ir. CCH Australia Ltd, PO Box 230, North Ryde New South Wales 2113 Australia. Tel 02 888 2555.

LABOR LAW REPORTS : EMPLOYMENT PRACTICES. Main/Corp Commerce Clearing House. VFOAT Employment Practices. US. English.

LABOR LAW SECTION NEWSLETTER. Main/Corp New York State Bar Association. Labor Law Section. 0160-5186. Periodical. US. English. New York State Bar Association, One Elk Street, Albany NY 12207. Tel (518)463-3200. Ed Jack Sissman. LC KFN5556.A16. DD 344.7470105. Circ 1,550. (ctrl). Section newsletter/law journal dealing with property law and current issues.

LABOR LAWS OF INDIANA. Main/Corp Indiana. US. English. ir. $12.00. Indiana State Chamber Commerce, 1 North Capital/Suite 200, Indianapolis IN 46204.

LABOR LAWS OF MAINE. Main/Corp Maine. US. English. be. Department of Manpower Affairs, Bureau of Labor, Augusta ME 04330. LC KFM331.A29. DD 331.

THE LABOR LAWYER. Vol. 1, No. 1 (Winter 1985)-. 8756-2995. Periodical. US. English. qt. $22.00 Domestic, $27.00 Foreign. American Bar Association, Section on Labor and Employment Law, 750 North Lake Shore Drive, Chicago IL 60611. DD 344.

LABORATORY REGULATION MANUAL. 0272-3778. US. English. $750.00. Aspen Systems Corporation, PO Box 6018, Gaithersburg MD 20760. Tel (301)251-5000. Ed H Robert Halper and Hope S Foster. (ctrl). Covers existing or proposed state and federal laws and regulations affecting the operation of clinical laboratories.

LABOUR ARBITRATION CASES. V. 1-24, 1948/50-1972. 0023-690X. Periodical. CN. English. ir. 400.00. Canada Law Book Ltd, 240 Edward Street, Aurora Ontario L3Y 1B4 Canada. Tel (416)773-6300. Ed C G Simmons. adv acc. Series of labor reports devoted solely to the reporting of Grievance Awards from all Canadian Provinces and jurisdictions.

LABOUR ARBITRATION (VANCOUVER, B.C.). (LABOUR ARBITRATION). 1981-. 0821-2635. CN. English. an. $45.00 Per Vol. Continuing Legal Education Society of British Columbia, 203-1148 Hornby Street, Vancouver British Columbia V6Z 2C3 Canada. DD 344.7110189143. *Current Problems in Labour Arbitration, 0821-2627.*

LABOUR LAW JOURNAL. Began Apr. 1949. 0023-6977. Periodical. II. English. Current Book House, Maruti La Raghunath Dadaju Street, Bombay 1 India. Ind/Abst Bus. Period. Index, Hospit. Lit. Index.

LABOUR LAW NEWS. Vol. 1- No. 1-. 0380-2787. Periodical. CN. English. mo. Labour Law News, 85 Richmond Street West, Toronto Ontario M5H 2E5 Canada. DD 344.7101.

LACKAWANNA JURIST. V. 1- Dec. 14, 1888-. 0023-7078. Periodical. US. English. wk. Lackawanna Bar Association, Box 1216, Law Library Courthouse, Scranton PA 18501. Tel (717)342-8089. Ed F J Fitzsimmons and M E McDonald.

LAG & I.E. OCH AVTAL. VFOAT Arbetsrattslig Tidskrift Lag & Avtal. Periodical. SW. Swedish. ir. Stiftelsen Arbetsrattslig Tidskrift, Nybrogatan 30, Box 5167, 102 44 Stockholm Sweden. LC K12.

LAGEN OM ALLMAN FORSAKRING OCH ANDRA FORFATTNINGAR OM SOCIALFORSAKRING M.M. Main/Corp Sweden. SW. Swedish. ir. Riksforsakringsverket Forsakringskasseforbundet, Box 1751, 111 87 Stockholm Sweden.

LAMY COMMERCIAL. FR. French. ir. 155 rue Legendre, 75850 Paris Cedex 17 France. DD 343.4407202632, 344. 4037202632.

LAMY TRANSPORT (SOCIETE LAMY). (LAMY TRANSPORT). FR. French. ir. Societe Lamy, 155 rue Legendre, 75017 Paris France. DD 343.44093, 344.40393. *Lamy Transport (Services Lamy).*

LAND AND WATER LAW REVIEW. V. 1- 1966-. 0023-7612. Periodical. US. English. sa. $10.00. Land and Water Law Review, University of Wyoming, College of Law, University Station, Box 3035, Laramie WY 82071. Tel (307)766-3359. Ind/Abst Electron. Commun. Abstr. J., ISMEC Bull., Pollut. Abstr. Indexes, Saf. Sci. Abstr. J., Leg. Resour. Index, Life Sci. Collect., Sel. Water Resour. Abstr. LC K12. DD 344.7870636361. (cum index). bk rev. adv acc. Development of land, water, and natural resources law. Surveys important developments in Wyoming case law and statutory law. *Wyoming Law Journal.*

LAND COMPENSATION BOARD INDEX TO APPLICATIONS DISPOSED OF . . . . See Indexes/Abstracts.

LAND COMPENSATION REPORTS. V. 1- Nov. 1971-. 0380-4208. Periodical. CN. English. ir. 213.00. Canada Law Book Ltd, 240 Edward Street, Aurora Ontario L4G 3S9 Canada. Tel (416)773-6300. Ed A S Weinrib. LC KE5175.A45. DD 343.710252. adv acc. A series designed for those concerned with the expropriation process in Canada whether at the local, regional, provincial or federal level.

LAND LETTER. See Conservation & Natural Resources.

LAND USE & ENVIRONMENT LAW REVIEW. See Conservation & Natural Resources.

LAND USE LAW & ZONING DIGEST. See Economics - Economics: Land.

LANDINSPEKTREN; TIDSSKRIFT FOR OPMALINGSOG MATRIKELVAESEN. See Engineering.

LANDLORD TENANT LAW BULLETIN. VFOAT LTLTB. 0271-5228. Periodical. US. English. mo. $32.99. Quinlan Publishing Company Inc, 131 Beverly Street, Boston MA 02114. LC KF587.8. DD 346.730434, 347.306434.

LANDLORD VS. TENANT/NYC. VFOAT Landlord vs. Tenant NYC. 0883-0746. Periodical. US. English. mo. $112.00. Brownstone Publishing Inc, 304 Park Avenue South, New York NY 10010.

LANDMARK BRIEFS AND ARGUMENTS OF THE SUPREME COURT OF THE UNITED STATES : CONSTITUTIONAL LAW. Main/Corp United States. Supreme Court. V. 1-. 0194-4010. US. English. University Publications of America, Washington DC. Ed P B Kurland and G Casper. LC KF101.8. DD 342.7300264.

LARMAC CONSOLIDATED INDEX TO THE CONSTITUTION AND LAWS OF CALIFORNIA. VFOAT Larmac Consolidated Index to the Constitution and Laws of California. 1935-. US. English. an. $54.95. Recorder Printing & Publishing Co, 125 12th Street, San Francisco CA 94103. Tel (415)621-5400. Ed Francis Franzin Verducci. Circ 3,000. One-volume index to all California codes, general laws and the State Constitution, with full text of California Rules of Court.

LAVORO E PREVIDENZA OGGI. See Business - Personnel Management.

LAW ALMANAC. See Yearbooks, Almanacs, Directories.

THE LAW ALUMNI JOURNAL. Began with Fall 1965 issue. 0458-8428. Periodical. US. English. Law Alumni Journal, University of Pennsylvania, Law School, 3400 Chestnut Street, Philadelphia PA 19174.

LAW & BEHAVIOR CEASED. VAT Law and Behavior. V. 1-5, No. 2. 0147-7218. Periodical. US. English. qt. $15.00. Research Press, 2612 North Mattis Avenue, Champaign IL 61820. LC KF3828.A15. DD 344.73044.

LAW AND COMPUTER TECHNOLOGY CEASED. V. 1-13, No. 1/2. 0023-9178. US. English (French, German and Spanish). qt. Ind/Abst Leg. Resour. Index. LC K87. DD 029. CODEN LACTAK.

LAW AND CONTEMPORARY PROBLEMS. Vol. 1, No. 1 (Dec. 1933)-. 0023-9186. Periodical. US. English. qt. $32.50. Duke University, Law School, Durham NC 27706. Tel (919)684-3119. Ed Joyce S Rutledge. Ind/Abst Leg. Resour. Index, Hospit. Lit. Index, Sociol. Abstr., Soc. Welf. Soc. Plan./Policy Soc. Dev., Coal Abstr., Index Econ. Artic. J. Collect. Vol., ABC Pol Sci, Account. Index. Suppl., Writ. Am. Hist., Public Aff. Inf. Serv. Bull., Index Leg. Period., Soc. Sci. Index. LC K12. DD 340.05. adv acc. Circ 2,100. Available on microfilm from University Microfilms. Each issue is a symposium on a particular inter-disciplinary topic, with contributions by lawyers, academics in many disciplines, public officials, and law students.

LAW AND HISTORY REVIEW. Vol. 1, No. 1 (Spring 1983)-. 0738-2480. Periodical. US. English. sa. $30.00 Domestic, $40.00 Foreign. Cornell University, Myron Taylor Hall, Ithaca NY 14853. LC K12. DD 340.05.

LAW & HOUSING JOURNAL. VAT Law and Housing Journal. V. 5, No. 2- Fall 1977-. 0193-8290. US. English. an. Case Westen Reserve Law Student Service Association, 11075 East Boulevard, Cleveland OH 44106. Tel (216)851-6932. Ind/Abst Leg. Resour. Index. *Law and Housing Newsletter, 0197-4793.*

LAW AND HUMAN BEHAVIOR. V. 1-. 0147-7307. Periodical. US. English. qt. $105.00 Domestic, $118.00 Foreign. Plenum Publishing Corporation, 233 Spring Street, New York NY 10013. Tel (212)620-8000. Ed Bruce D Sales. Ind/Abst Leg. Resour. Index, Sociol. Abstr., Soc. Welf. Soc. Plan./Policy Soc. Dev., Excerpta Med., Biol. Abstr., Psychol. Abstr. LC K12. DD 340.05. NLM W1 LA942. CODEN LHBEDM. bk rev. adv acc. This journal is a multidisciplinary forum for articles and discussions of issues arising out of the relationship between human behavior and the law legal system and legal process.

LAW & INEQUALITY. VFOAT Law and Inequality. Vol. 1, No. 1 (June 1983)-. 0737-089X. Periodical. US. English. sa. $6.00. Minnesota Law School, 299 19th Avenue South, Minneapolis MN 55455. Tel (612)373-9075. Ed Suzanne Brandon. DD 340.05. bk rev. adv acc. Circ 750. Law and inequality. People's experiences of systematic oppression and how law contributes to lack of power. Plus, how law might remedy group-based oppression.

LAW & JUSTICE. VAT Law and Justice. No. 42- Hilary 1974-. Periodical. UK. English. qt. $20.69. Edmund Plowden Trust, 36 Westcar Lane, Walton on Thames Surrey KT12 5ES England. Ind/Abst Leg. Resour. Index, Curr. Law Index. LC K17. DD 340.05. *Quis Custodiet?.*

LAW AND LEGAL INFORMATION DIRECTORY. See Yearbooks, Almanacs, Directories.

LAW AND LEGISLATION IN THE GERMAN DEMOCRATIC REPUBLIC. Sept. 1959-. 0458-8460. Periodical. SZ. German. ir. $9.99. Kunst & Wissen Erich Bieber, Dufourstrasse 51, CH-8008 Zurich Switzerland. Tel 011-41-1-69 44 20. LC UNC.

LAW & LIBERTY CEASED. VAT Law and Liberty. V. 1- 1974?-. 0094-0615. Periodical. US. English. 1134 Crane Street, Menlo Park CA 94025. LC KF384.A1. DD 340.11505.

LAW AND PHILOSOPHY. Vol. 1, No. 1 (Apr. 1982)-. 0167-5249. Periodical. NE. English. ty. 62. Kluwer Academic Publishers Group, PO Box 322, 3300 AH Dordrecht Netherlands. Tel (31)78-334911. Ed Alan Mabe. Ind/Abst Leg. Resour. Index, Sociol. Abstr., Philos. Index. LC K12. DD 340.1. bk rev. adv acc. Circ 750. Philosophical reflection on the law informed by a knowledge of the law, and legal analysis informed by philosophical methods and principles.

LAW AND POPULATION BOOK SERIES. Monographic Series. US. English. ir. Sijthoff & Noordhoff International Publications, 20010 Century Boulevard, Germantown MD 20767.

LAW AND POPULATION PROGRAMME NEWSLETTER. Began with Apr. 1972 issue. 0148-6136. Periodical. US. English. Tufts University, Fletcher School of Law and Diplomacy, Medford MA 02155. LC K2000.A13. DD 344.048.

LAW & PSYCHOLOGY REVIEW. VAT Law and Psychology Review. Spring 1975-. 0098-5961. US. English. an. Law & Psychology Review, c/o University of Alabama, Box 1435, University AL 35486. Ind/Abst Leg. Resour. Index, Psychol. Abstr., Contents Curr. Leg. Period., Curr. Law Index. LC K12. DD 340.19.

LAW & SOCIETY NEWSLETTER. VFOAT Law and Society Newsletter. 8755-7088. US. English. LC KF200. DD 340.06.

LAW AND SOCIETY QUARTERLY. 0377-0869. Periodical. English. ir. $10.50. Centre for the Study of Law and Society, 20 Vithalbhai Patel House Rafi Marg, New Delhi India. LC K12. DD 340.11505. *Law and Society Newsletter.*

Law

LAW & SOCIETY REVIEW. VFOAT Law and Society Review. VAT Law and Society Review. V. 1- Nov. 1966-. 0023-9216. Periodical. US. English. qt. $65.00 Domestic, $67.00 Foreign. Law and Society Association, University of Denver, College of Law, 200 West 14th Avenue, Denver CO 80204. Tel (303)871-6306. Ed Robert Kidder. Ind/Abst Leg. Resour. Index, Soc. Sci. Index, Sociol. Abstr., Soc. Sci. Citation Index, Hist. Abst., Part B, Twent. Century Abstr., Contents Curr. Leg. Period., Lang. Lang. Behav. Abstr., Writ. Am. Hist., ABC Pol Sci, Am. Hist. Life, Public Aff. Inf. Serv. Bull., Abstr. Criminol. Penol., Hist. Abstr., Index Leg. Period., Int. Bibliogr. Soc. Sci., Polit. Sci. Gov. Public Policy Ser., Curr. Law Index, Soc. Welf. Soc. Plan./Policy Soc. Dev., Recent Publ. Artic. LC UNC. bk rev. adv acc. Circ 2,000. Accepts articles concerning political, social and economic aspects of law.

LAW AND STATE. Began with V. 1 in 1970. 0341-6151. Periodical. GW. English (translation of German works). sa. Institut fur Wissenschaftliche Zusammenarbeit, Landhausstr 18, D-7400 Tubingen Federal Republic of Germany. LC K12. DD 349.4305, 344.3005.

LAW AND THE WORKPLACE. 0747-6469. Periodical. US. English. bm. Proskauer Rose Goetz & Mendelsohn, 300 Park Avenue, New York NY 10022. LC KF3314. DD 344.7301, 347.3041.

LAW BOOKS IN PRINT. Began in 1957. US. English. ir. Glanville Publishers Inc, 75 Main Street, Dobbs Ferry NY 10522. Tel (914)693-1320.

LAW BOOKS PUBLISHED. V. 1- Jan./Apr. 1969-. 0023-9240. Periodical. US. English. qt. $106.00. Glanville Publishers Inc, 75 Main Street, Dobbs Ferry NY 10522. Tel (914)693-1320. LC KF1. DD 016.34.

LAW CALENDAR. Main/Corp Victoria, Australia. Law Dept. AT. English. ir. Law Department, 221 Queen Street, Melbourne Victoria 3001 Australia. DD 347.945013. *Law Calendar.*

LAW CENTER BULLETIN. Main/Corp New York University. School of Law. VFOAT Bulletin of the New York University Law Center. V. 1-21, No. 2. 0548-9245. Periodical. US. English. sa. New York University, Office of Development, 40 Washington Square 50, New York NY 10012. *Bulletin of the New York University Law Center.*

LAW DAY U.S.A. PLANNING GUIDE AND PROGRAM MANUAL. Main/Corp American Bar Association. VFOAT May 1, Law Day U.S.A. 1968-. US. English. an. Law Day USA Observance, American Bar Association, 1155 East 10th Street, Chicago IL 60637. *Law Day U.S.A. Program Manual, Law Day U.S.A. Planning Guide for Bar Associations.*

LAW FILE. Periodical. UK. English. mo. Free. Information and Public Relations, IPPF Central Office, 18-20 Lower Regent Street, London SW1Y 4PW England. Tel 01.839.2911. Ed Sunetra Puri. LC K2000.A13. DD 344.04805. Circ 1,200. (ctrl). Bulletin presents summaries from press, journals, documents and correspondence received at IPPF on all aspects including legal of family planning, population and development.

LAW FORUM SERIES. Monographic Series. US. English. ir. Ohio State University Press, 164 West 19 Avenue, Columbus OH 43201.

LAW IN AMERICAN SOCIETY. V. 1- May 1972-. 0197-3886. Periodical. US. English. qt. $10.00. Law in American Society Foundation, 33 North LaSalle Street/Suite 1700, Chicago IL 60602. LC K12. DD 340.071073.

LAW IN CONTEXT. Vol. 1 (1983)-. 0811-5796. Periodical. English. an. 9.95. La Trobe University Bookshop, La Trobe University, Bundoora Victoria 3083 Australia. Tel (03)479-2962. Ed P O'Malley. bk rev. adv acc. Circ 450. (ctrl).

LAW IN EASTERN EUROPE. No. 1-. 0075-823X. Monographic Series. English. bm. Sijthoff & Noordhoff International Publishing, 20010 Century Boulevard, Germantown MD 20767. DD 349.47.

LAW IN JAPAN : AN ANNUAL. Vol. 1 (1967)-. 0458-8584. US. English (Japanese). an. University of Washington, School of Law, Japanese American Society of Legal Studies, Seattle WA 98105.

LAW INFORMATION UPDATE CEASED. Vol. 1, No. 1 (Jan. 1983)-V. 2, No. 1 (Jan. 1984). 0000-0728. Periodical. US. English. ir. $175.00. R R Bowker, PO Box 1807, Ann Arbor MI 48106. Tel (212)916-1600. LC KF1. DD 016.34005. Update of Bowkers law books and serials in print with complete bibliographic data on new and forthcoming law books and serials.

LAW INSTITUTE JOURNAL : THE OFFICIAL ORGAN OF THE LAW INSTITUTE OF VICTORIA. Vol. 1, No. 1 (July 1st, 1927). 0023-9267. Periodical. AT. English. $40.58. Law Institute of Victoria, 470 Bourke Street, Melbourne Australia. Tel (03)6023922. Ed Maxwellyn Webberley. Ind/Abst Leg. Resour. Index, Index Leg. Period., Curr. Law Index. DD 347.05. Index published separately - free - automatically sent. (cum index). bk rev. adv acc. Circ 9,000. (ctrl). Articles on all aspects of law, reviews of judgements, book reviews, etc.

LAW JOURNAL. (CALCUTTA). Il. English. sm. $39.50. M/S Law Publishers, PO Box 77, Sardar Patel Marg, Allahabad-211 001 India.

LAW JOURNAL OF GURU NANAK DEV UNIVERSITY. VFOAT Law Journal. Periodical. Il. English. ir. Lakha Singh Sandhu Registrar, Guru Nanak Dev University, Amritsar 143005 India.

LAW JOURNAL OF MARUT BUNNAG INTERNATIONAL LAW OFFICE. Main/Corp Marut Bunnag International Law Office. English. ir. Marut Bunnag International Law Office, Bangkok Insurance Building/2nd Floor, 302 Silom Road, Bangkok Thailand. LC K12. DD 340.09593. *Law Journal.*

LAW LETTER & JOURNAL. VFOAT Law Letter and Journal. Vol. 1, No. 1 (Jan. 1984)-. 0883-0959. Periodical. US. English. bm. Virginia Trial Lawyers Association, PO Box 5127, Charlottesville VA 22905.

THE LAW LIBRARIAN. See Library and Information Science.

THE LAW LIBRARIAN'S PROFESSIONAL DESK REFERENCE AND DIARY. See Library and Information Science.

LAW LIBRARY BULLETIN. See Library and Information Science.

LAW LIBRARY LIGHTS. See Library and Information Science.

LAW LIBRARY NEWSLETTER. See Library and Information Science.

LAW, MEDICINE & HEALTH CARE. (LAW, MEDICINE & HEALTH CARE : A PUBLICATION OF THE AMERICAN SOCIETY OF LAW & MEDICINE). VFOAT Law, Medicine and Health Care. Vol. 9, No. 4 (Sept. 1981)-. 0277-8459. Periodical. US. English. bm. $40.00. American Society of Law and Medicine, 765 Commonwealth Avenue/16th Floor, Boston MA 02215. Tel (617)262-4990. Ed Barry Furrow. Ind/Abst Leg. Resour. Index, Hospit. Lit. Index, Sociol. Abstr., Cumul. Index Nurs. Allied Health Lit., Int. Nurs. Index. LC KF3821.A15. DD 344.7304105, 347.3044105. NLM W1 LA946. bk rev. adv acc. Circ 9,000. Publication providing the reader with practical reference information on topics of current concern in the medicolegal field. *Medicolegal News,* 0097-0085; *Nursing Law & Ethics,* 0270-6636.

LAW NOTES FOR THE GENERAL PRACTITIONER. Main/Corp American Bar Association. Section of General Practice. VFOAT Law Notes. Began publication in 1964. 0023-9305. Periodical. US. English. ir. American Bar Association, 750 North Lake Shore Drive, Chicago IL 60611. Tel (312)988-5555. *News for the General Practitioner.*

LAW NOTES (LONDON, ENGLAND). (LAW NOTES). V. 4, Pt. 1 (Jan. 1885)-. Periodical. UK. English. mo. DD 340.05. (cum index). *Gibson's Law Notes.*

LAW OF LIABILITY INSURANCE, BY ROWLAND H. LONG. See Insurance.

LAW OF OIL AND GAS LEASES. See Petroleum and Natural Gas.

THE LAW OF THE HANDICAPPED : REPORTER AND COMMENTATOR. Vol. 1, Issue 1-. 0733-6233. Periodical. US. English. bm. $18.00. RM Weiner, 142 Leahy Street, Jericho NY 11753. Tel (516)222-1744. Ed Richard M Weiner and Tapper Bragg. LC KF480.A15. DD 346.73013, 347.30613. bk rev. Circ 1,000. Current legal materials, articles, and cases concerning the law of the handicapped.

LAW OF THE LAND. Main/Corp Legal Assistance of North Dakota, Inc. VAT Law of the Legal Assistance of North Dakota. 0271-2032. US. English. Free. Legal Assistance of North Dakota Inc, 222 West Bowen Avenue, Bismarck ND 58501. LC KFN8684.5.P6. DD 344.78403258.

LAW OF WORKMEN'S COMPENSATION. US. English. ir. Matthew Bender and Company Inc, 1275 Broadway, Albany NY 12201. Tel (800)833-9844.

LAW OFFICE ECONOMICS AND MANAGEMENT. See Economics.

LAW OFFICE GUIDE IN COMPUTERS. (LAW OFFICE GUIDE IN COMPUTERS : LOGIC). VFOAT L.O.G.I.C. Vol. 1, No. 1 (Oct. 1983)-. 0739-5132. Periodical. US. English. mo. $65.00. 3315 Sacramento/Suite 407, San Francisco CA 94118. Tel (415)923-1747. Ed Rey Montez. LC KF320.A9. DD 651.84024344. bk rev. Circ 4,000. Lawyer's consumer publication reviewing and rating computer hardware and software designed for law firms.

LAW OFFICE INFORMATION SERVICE. See Bibliographies.

LAW OFFICE MANAGEMENT. See Business - Personnel Management.

LAW OFFICE MANAGEMENT & ADMINISTRATION REPORT. See Business - General Management.

THE LAW REFERENCER. Periodical. English. ir. $10.00. 35 Lawyer's Chambers, Supreme Court, New Delhi 110001 India. (cum index).

LAW RELATED TO THE DEPARTMENT OF SOCIAL SERVICES PASSED DURING THE LEGISLATIVE SESSION. (LAWS RELATED TO THE DEPARTMENT OF SOCIAL SERVICES, PASSED DURING THE LEGISLATIVE SESSION). Main/Corp Michigan. Series/Titl DSS Publication. 0148-4494. US. English. Michigan Department of Social Services, 200 South Capital Avenue, Lansing MI 48026. LC HV86 B .M536 SUBSER, KFM4549. DD 361.9774 S, 344.77403.

LAW RELATING TO PUBLIC SCHOOLS AND COMMUNITY COLLEGES. See Education (General).

THE LAW REPORTS. INDEX. See Indexes/Abstracts.

THE LAW REPORTS OF NIGERIA. Vol. 1 (1978)-. English. ir. Butterworth & Company Ltd, Palmgrove House/No 1 Shagamu Avenue, Ilupeju Lagos State Nigeria. DD 348.669041, 346.690841.

LAW REVIEW DIGEST. V. 1- (No. 1-). Periodical. US. English. bm. $39.00. Callaghan and Company, 3201 Old Glenview Road, Wilmette IL 60091. Tel (800)323-1336. Ed Larry A Bakken. LC UNC. Circ 1,300. Summarizes and indexes articles appearing in law reviews, bar journals, and legal periodicals.

LAW REVIEW JOURNAL. Began in 1978. 0734-1938. Periodical. US. English. $9.75. Legal Institute, 281 East Colorado Boulevard, Box 219, Pasadena CA 91102. Tel (818)405-1476. Ed Herman B Lancaster. LC KF250. DD 340.05. bk rev. Circ 200. Focuses on the production and management of law reviews.

LAW SCHOOL ADMINISTRATOR'S JOURNAL. (LAW SCHOOL ADMINISTRATOR'S JOURNAL : A LEGAL INSTITUTE PROJECT). Vol. 1, Issue 1-. 0741-1170. Periodical. US. English. ty. $9.75. Legal Institute, 281 East Colorado Boulevard, Box 219, Pasadena CA 91102. Tel (818)405-1476. Ed Herman B Lancaster. LC KF273. DD 340.071173. bk rev. Circ 200. Covers information useful in legal education administration.

LAW SCHOOL JOURNAL. Vol. 1, issue 1-. 0737-2590. Periodical. US. English. ty. $9.75. Legal Institute, 281 East Colorado Boulevard/Box 219, Pasadena CA 91102. Tel (818)405-1476. Ed Herman B Lancaster. LC KF283. DD 340.071173. bk rev. Circ 200. Provides information about succeeding in law school, about bar exams, and law careers.

LAW SCHOOL RECORD. Main/Corp University of Chicago. Law School. VFOAT University of Chicago Law School Record. 1- Autumn 1951-. 0529-097X. US. English. 1285 Main Street, Buffalo NY 14209.

Law

THE LAW SCHOOL TRANSCRIPT.
Began in 1977. 0737-1152. Periodical. US. English. University of Missouri, Tate Hall, Columbia Law School, Columbia MO 65201. **LC** KF292.M5914. **DD** 340.071177829.

LAW SOCIETY JOURNAL CEASED. V. 1-19, No. 1. 0023-9372. Periodical. AT. English.

LAW SOCIETY JOURNAL (SYDNEY, N.S.W. : 1982). (LAW SOCIETY JOURNAL : THE OFFICIAL JOURNAL OF THE LAW SOCIETY OF NEW SOUTH WALES). Vol. 20, No. 8 (Sept. 1982)-. Periodical. AT. English. mo. Law Society of New South Wales, 170 Phillip Street, Sydney New South Wales 2000 Australia. **Tel** 02 232 2511. **Ed** T S Dare. bk rev. adv acc. **Circ** 8,000. (ctrl). Legal journal primarily to inform members of the profession. *Journal of the Law Society of N.S.W.*

LAW TEACHER. (THE LAW TEACHER). 0306-9400. Periodical. UK. English. ty. 3.00. Sweet & Maxwell, 11 New Fetter Lane, London EC4P 4EE England. **Ind/Abst** Leg. Resour. Index. **LC** K12. **DD** 340.05. *Journal of the Association of Law Teachers, 0044-9628.*

LAW TEACHER'S JOURNAL. (LAW TEACHER'S JOURNAL : A LEGAL INSTITUTE PROJECT). Vol. 1, Issue 1-. 0741-1197. Periodical. US. English. ty. $9.75. Legal Institute, 281 East Colorado Boulevard, Box 219, Pasadena CA 91102. **Tel** (818)405-1476. **Ed** Herman B Lancaster. **LC** KF273. **DD** 340.07073. bk rev. **Circ** 200. Provides information about teaching law.

THE LAW TIMES. Began with July 1966. SI. English. ir. $12.00. University of Singapore, Law Club, Kentridge, Singapore 5 Republic of Singapore. **Tel** 7756666. **Ed** Tan Loke Khoon. **LC** K12. **DD** 349.595705. adv acc. **Circ** 700. Articles from Singapore judges, lawyers, and students on aspects of our legal system. Also foreign contributions concerning topical issues in law today.

LAW UNION NEWS. (THE LAW UNION NEWS). 0824-4421. Periodical. CN. English. ir. $10.00. Law Union of Ontario, Suite 100-203/2 Bloor Street West, Toronto Ontario M4W 3F2 Canada. **DD** 349.71305.

LAWASIA. **Main/Corp** Law Association for Asia and the Western Pacific. V. 1-5, Dec. 1969-Dec. 1974. Periodical. AT. English. sa. Butterworth, c/o Bennett EBSCO, 25 Mitchell, North Sydney 2060 New South Wales Australia. **LC** K12. **DD** 340.05.

LAWMARK. VFOAT Law Mark. Vol. 1, No. 1-. 0737-8971. Periodical. US. English. mo. Howard M Markman, 1201 Connecticut Avenue NW/12th Floor, Washington DC 20036.

LAWS AND RESOLUTIONS OF THE STATE OF MONTANA. **Main/Corp** Montana. VFOAT Laws of Montana. 1965-. US. English. ir. Montana Legislative Council, Room 138/State Capitol, Helena MT 59601. **LC** KFM9025. **DD** 348.786022. *Laws, etc. (Laws, Resolutions, and Memorials of the State of Montana).*

LAWS, MEMORIALS, AND RESOLUTIONS OF THE TERRITORY OF DAKOTA, PASSED AT THE SESSION OF THE LEGISLATIVE ASSEMBLY. **Main/Corp** Dakota. VFOAT Dakota Laws, Ter. US. English. Bowen & Kingsbury, Public Printers, Yankton SD 57078. **LC** KFN8625. **DD** 348.783023.

LAWS OF ANGUILLA. **Main/Corp** Anguilla. 1971-1973-. English. ir. **LC** KGJ7008. **DD** 348.72973, 347.2973.

LAWS OF ANTIGUA AND BARBUDA. **Main/Corp** Antigua and Barbuda. English. an. **LC** KGK8. **DD** 348.72974022, 347.29740822. *Laws, etc. Laws of Antigua.*

LAWS OF PUERTO RICO ANNOTATED. **Main/Corp** Puerto Rico. US. English. an. Equity Publication Corporation, Orford NH 03777. **Tel** (603)353-4351.

LAWS OF ST. CHRISTOPHER, NEVIS & ANGUILLA. **Main/Corp** Saint Kitts-Nevis-Anguilla. VFOAT Laws of Saint Christopher, Nevis & Anguilla. English. ir. **LC** KGW2008. **DD** 348.72973022, 347.29730822.

LAWS OF THE GAME AND UNIVERSAL GUIDE FOR REFEREES. **Main/Corp** Football Association International Federation. English. ir. Hitzigweg 11, 8032 Zurich Switzerland. **LC** GV943.4. **DD** 796.33402022.

LAWS OF THE REGENTS, UNIVERSITY OF COLORADO. **Main/Corp** University of Colorado, Boulder. Board of Regents. US. English. an. Secretary of the University and of the Board of Regents, Regent Hall, 201 University of Colorado, Boulder CO 80309.

LAWS OF THE STATE OF NEBRASKA PERTAINING TO THE GAME AND PARKS COMMISSION. **Main/Corp** Nebraska. VFOAT Nebraska Game Laws. US. English. an. Game and Parks Commission, 2200 North 33rd Street, Box 30370, Lincoln NE 68503. **LC** KFN453.A29. **DD** 344.782099. *Laws of the Game, Forestation and Parks Commission of State of Nebraska.*

LAWS RELATING TO FIRES AND FIREMEN, STATE OF CALIFORNIA. *See* Fire Prevention.

LAWS RELATING TO JUVENILES IN ONTARIO. **Main/Corp** United States. 0192-6926. US. English. Law Distributors, 11415 South Main Street, Gardena CA 90248.

LAWS RELATING TO STATE BANKS AND TRUST COMPANIES, SAVINGS BANKS, INDUSTRIAL BANKS, SAVINGS BANK LIFE INSURANCE, BUILDING OR SAVINGS AND LOAN ASSOCIATIONS. **Main/Corp** Connecticut. US. English. be. Connecticut State Office Building, Hartford CT 06103. **DD** 332.109746. Index in last issue of volume - attached.

LAWS RELATING TO THE PRACTICE OF MEDICINE AND SURGERY, PODIATRY, DISPENSING OPTICIANS, SPEECH PATHOLOGY, AUDIOLOGY, PHYSICAL THERAPY, PSYCHOLOGY, HEARING AID DISPENSERS, PHYSICIANS' ASSISTANTS, ACUPUNCTURE, RESPIRATORY THERAPY, RESEARCH PSYCHOANALYSTS AND MEDICAL MEDICAL ASSISTANTS /. **Main/Corp** California. VFOAT BMQA-Laws. 1978-. 8756-9329. US. English. Board of Medical Quality Assurance, 1430 Howe Avenue, Sacramento CA 95825. *Laws Relating to the Practice of Medicine and Surgery, Podiatry, Dispensing Opticians, Speech Pathology, Audiology, Physical Therapy, Psychology, Hearing Aid Dispensers, Physicians' Assistants and Acupuncture.*

LAWS RELATING TO THE PRACTICE OF OPTOMETRY, WITH RULES AND REGULATIONS. **Main/Corp** California. 0160-1326. US. English. California Department of Consumer Affairs, 1020 N Street, Sacramento CA 95814. **LC** KFC546.5.O6. **DD** 346.794041.

LAW/TECHNOLOGY. VFOAT Law Technology. 1980, 3rd Quarter- – Vol. 13, No. 3-. 0278-3916. Periodical. US. English (French, German, and Spanish). qt. $50.00. World Association of Lawyers, 1000 Connecticut Avenue NW, Washington DC 20036. **Ind/Abst** Leg. Resour. Index, Comput. Control Abstr., Electr. Electron. Abstr., Sci. Abstr. Sect. A. Phys. Abstr. **LC** K87. **DD** 344.095, 342.495. **CODEN** LATEDT. *Law and Computer Technology, 0023-9178.*

THE LAWYER. VFOAT Digest of Cases with Editorial Notes. V. 1- Oct./Dec. 1977-. Periodical. English. ir. $40.00. Trinidad and Tobago Bar Association, Treasurer, Sydney R R Martineau, Chambers, 13A Pembroke Street, Port of Spain Trinidad and Tobago. **DD** 349.7298305.

LAWYER DIRECTORY (BAR ASSOCIATION OF MONTGOMERY COUNTY, MARYLAND). *See* Yearbooks, Almanacs, Directories.

LAWYER GUIDE & DIRECTORY, LOS ANGELES COUNTY. *See* Yearbooks, Almanacs, Directories.

LAWYER HIRING & TRAINING REPORT. VFOAT Lawyer Hiring and Training Report. Vol. 4, No. 1 (June 1983)-. 0739-1706. Periodical. US. English. mo. $225.00. Lawyer Hiring and Training Report, 332 South Michigan Avenue/Suite 1460, Chicago IL 60604. **Tel** (312)922-0722. **Ed** Grace W Henning. **LC** KF276.5.A15. **DD** 340.07073. bk rev. Lawyer training and recruitment information. *Henning CLE Reporter, 0276-5004.*

LAWYER OF THE AMERICAS CEASED. V. 1-15. 0023-9445. Periodical. US. English. ty. $12.00 Domestic, $14.00 Foreign. School of Law, University of Miami, PO Box 248087, Coral Gables FL 33124. **Ind/Abst** Index Leg. Period. **LC** K12. **DD** 340.091812.

LAWYER-TO-LAWYER CONSULTATION PANEL. 1st- Ed. 0091-0430. US. English. an. 800 Caxton Building, Cleveland OH 44115. **LC** KF190. **DD** 340.02573.

LAWYERING SKILLS NEWS. Vol. 1, No. 1 (Mar. 1982)-. 0736-4938. Periodical. US. English. American Bar Association, Division of Professional Education, 10 West 35th Street, Chicago IL 60616. **LC** KF275.A15. **DD** 340.0715.

LAWYERS ALERT. (LAWYER'S ALERT). Vol. 1, No. 1 (Oct. 19, 1981)-. 0278-9817. Periodical. US. English. bw. $79.00. Lawyers Weekly Publications, 30 Court Square, Boston MA 02108. **Tel** (617)227-6034. **Ed** J Edward Pawlick. **LC** K12. **DD** 349.7305, 347.3005. adv acc. **Circ** 8,439. A concise, useful guide to new cases and trends in all areas of the law with profitable advice and ideas from the country's leading legal experts.

THE LAWYER'S ALMANAC. *See* Yearbooks, Almanacs, Directories.

LAWYERS' ARBITRATION LETTER. V. 1-. Periodical. US. English. qt. American Arbitration Association, 140 West 51st Street, New York NY 10020. **Tel** (212)484-4014. **Ed** Margaret Gibbins. For attorneys. Analysis of when arbitration is used, what federal and state statutes apply, how are attorneys fees assessed, and what procedural rules apply. *Lawyers' Arbitration Letter, Arbitration Law, 0518-2611.*

LAWYERS' DESKBOOK AND DIRECTORY. *See* Yearbooks, Almanacs, Directories.

LAWYERS DIARY AND MANUAL INCLUDING BAR DIRECTORY OF MASSACHUSETTS. *See* Yearbooks, Almanacs, Directories.

LAWYERS DIARY AND MANUAL INCLUDING BAR DIRECTORY OF NEW JERSEY. *See* Yearbooks, Almanacs, Directories.

LAWYERS' GUIDE TO MEDICAL PROOF. 1966-. US. English. an. Matthew Bender & Company Inc, 1275 Broadway, Albany NY 12201. **Tel** (800)833-9844. Index published separately - free - automatically sent.

LAWYERS' MEDICAL DIGEST. (LAWYER'S MEDICAL DIGEST). VFOAT LMD. Vol. 1, No. 1 (July 1984)-. 8755-5891. Periodical. US. English. mo. $129.00. Callaghan & Company, 3201 Old Glenview Road, Wilmette IL 60091. **Tel** (800)323-1336. **Ed** Steven Babitsky. **DD** 610. Each issue contains an index to its own contents - no vol index - loose. **Circ** 700. Summarizes and indexes articles appearing in medical journals.

LAWYER'S MEDICAL JOURNAL CEASED. V. 1-7, May 1965-1972. 0023-947X. Periodical. US. English. qt. **Ind/Abst** Leg. Resour. Index. **LC** K12. **NLM** W1 LA98.

LAWYER'S NEWSLETTER CEASED. (THE LAWYER'S NEWSLETTER). Began with: Aug. 1971. 0094-0224. Periodical. US. English. bm.

THE LAWYER'S PC. VFOAT Lawyer's P.C. VAT Lawyer's Personal Computer. Vol. 1, No. 1 (Sept. 1, 1983)-. 0740-0942. Periodical. US. English. sm. $46.40 Domestic, $58.40 Canada, $82.40 all Other Countries. R P W Publishing Corporation, PO Box 1108, Lexington SC 29072. **Tel** (803)359-9941. **Ed** Robert P Wilkins. **LC** KF320.A9. **DD** 340.0285416. bk rev. adv acc. **Circ** 4,000. (ctrl). Newsletter written for lawyers by lawyers using personal computers.

LAWYER'S PHONE BOOK. (THE LAWYER'S PHONE BOOK). 1968-. 0317-8668. Periodical. CN. English. an. Canada Law Book, 240 Edward Street, Aurora Ontario L4G 3S9 Canada. **DD** 340.025713.

LAWYERS' PROFESSIONAL LIABILITY UPDATE. 0883-1025. US. English. sa. ABA Standing Committee on Lawyers' Professional Liability, 1155 East 60th Street, Chicago IL 60637.

LAWYER'S REGISTER BY SPECIALTIES AND FIELDS OF LAW. 1st Ed. 0163-3147. US. English. an. $95.09. Lawyer to Lawyer Consultation Panel, 5325 Naiman Parkway, Cleveland OH 44139. **Tel** (216)248-0135. **Ed** Gail Grafchik. **LC** KF190. **DD** 340.02573. Each issue contains an index to its own contents - no vol index -

Law

loose. Circ 5,000. A list of lawyers from around the US and foreign countries by specialties, including a corporate counsel section.

LAWYER'S REGISTER BY SPECIALTIES AND FIELDS OF LAW INCLUDING A DIRECTORY OF CORPORATE COUNSEL. 5th Ed. (1983)-. 0883-2412. US. English. an. Lawyers Register Publishing Company, 5323 Naiman Parkway, Solon OH 44139. DD 340. Each issue contains an index to its own contents - no vol index - loose. *Lawyer's Register by Specialties and Fields of Law, 0163-3147.*

LAWYERS TITLE NEWS. Began in Aug. 1937. 0272-7161. Periodical. US. English. bm. Lawyers Title Insurance Company, PO Box 27567, Richmond VA 23261. Tel (804)355-8011. LC UNC.

LAWYERS WEEKLY GUIDEBOOK. Began with 1979 Vol. 0732-4901. US. English. an. Massachusetts Lawyers Weekly, 30 Court Square, Boston MA 02108. LC KFM2477. DD 349.74405, 347.44005. *Lawyers Weekly Guide to Massachusetts Courts and Lawyers.*

LDRC BULLETIN. VFOAT L.D.R.C. Bulletin. VAT Libel Defense Resource Center Bulletin. 0737-8130. Periodical. US. English. qt. $25.00. Libel Defense Resource Center, 708 Third Avenue/32nd Floor, New York NY 10017. LC KF1266.A15. DD 346.7303402648, 347. 3063402648.

LEADER'S EQUIPMENT LEASING NEWSLETTER. See Business.

LEADER'S LEGAL TECH NEWSLETTER. VFOAT Legal Tech Newsletter. Vol. 1, No. 1 (Apr. 1983)-. 0738-0186. Periodical. US. English. mo. $95.00. Leader Publications, 111 8th Avenue/Suite 900, New York NY 10011. Tel (800)221-8195. LC KF320.A9. DD 340.068. Reports on automating corporate or firm law office; includes product reviews, new technology applications, analyses of firm uses of computers and evaluations.

LEADER'S PRODUCT LIABILITY NEWSLETTER. VFOAT Product Liability Newsletter. Vol. 1, No. 1 (July 1982)-. 0733-513X. Periodical. US. English. mo. $97.00. Leader Publications, 111 Eighth Avenue/9th Floor, New York NY 10011. Tel (800)221-8195. Ed Cynthia Cooper. LC KF1296.A15. DD 346.73038205, 347.30638205. Reports on judicial, legislative, and regulatory developments in product liability law; includes verdicts, settlements, decisions, and advice on legal strategy by eminent practitioners.

LECOURT. V. 1- Spring 1976-. 0147-3190. Periodical. US. English. qt. $24.00. World Information Systems Exchange, PO Box 349, Phoenix AZ 85001. LC K87. DD 029.934.

LECTURE FAITE. (LECTURE FAITE : BULLETIN DE LA FEDERATION DES NOTAIRES DU QUEBEC). V. 1, No. 1, Aug. 15, 1980)-. 0714-8216. Periodical. CN. French. mo. Free. Federation des Notaires du Quebec, 8328 rue St-Denis, Montreal Quebec H2P 2G8 Canada. DD 347.714016. (ctrl).

LEGAL ACTION. (LEGAL ACTION : THE BULLETIN OF THE LEGAL ACTION GROUP). Jan. 1984-. 0266-3953. Periodical. UK. English. mo. Legal Action Group, 28A Highgate Road, London NW5 1NS England. Ind/Abst Leg. Resour. Index. *LAG Bulletin, 0306-7963.*

LEGAL ACTION IN NEW SOUTH WALES. Main/Corp SIB Publishing Company. AT. English. ir. SIB Publishing Company, 11/44 Bridge Street, Sydney Australia. DD 9440770269.

LEGAL ADMINISTRATOR (GLENVIEW, ILL. : 1982). (LEGAL ADMINISTRATOR). Vol. 1, No. 1 (Jan. 1982)-. 0745-0532. Periodical. US. English. qt. Association of Legal Administrators, 1800 Pickwick Avenue, Glenview IL 60025. Tel (312)724-7700. Ed Sheila Wertz. LC KF318.A1. DD 651.934. bk rev. adv acc. Circ 17,000. (ctrl). Directed to those in legal community with an interest in financial management, personnel management, systems and technology, and other law practice management issues.

THE LEGAL ADVISOR. VFOAT Advisor. Vol. 1, No. 1 (July 1984)-. 8756-7768. Periodical. US. English. mo. $138.00. Learning Associates International, 145 East Center Street, PO Box 3000, Provo UT 84603-3000. Ed Richard J Allen. DD 340.

LEGAL AID. Main/Corp Law Society (Great Britain). 25th- 1974/75-. UK. English. an. 49 High Holborn, London WC1V 6HB England. LC KD512.A13. DD 362.58. *Legal Aid and Advice.*

THE LEGAL AID NEWS. (LEGAL AID NEWS). V. 1- May 1975-. 0147-9458. Periodical. US. English. bm. Legal Aid Society, 15 Park Row, New York NY 10030. LC KF337.N45. DD 347.74701.

LEGAL ALERT. VFOAT Canadian Senior Executives' Legal Alert. Vol. 1, No. 1-. 0712-841X. Periodical. CN. English. mo. $175.00. Oyez, Suite 2210/65 Queen Street West, Toronto Ontario M5H 2M8 Canada. DD 346.71066024658.

LEGAL AND BUSINESS ASPECTS OF THE ADVERTISING INDUSTRY. Series/Titl Patents, Copyrights, Trademarks, and Literary Property Course Handbook Series. 1982-. 0882-0058. US. English. Practising Law Institute, 810 Seventh Avenue, New York NY 10019. DD 343. *Legal and Business Problems of the Advertising Industry.*

LEGAL ASPECTS OF MEDICAL PRACTICE. V. 5, No. 9- Sept. 1977-. 0190-2350. Periodical. US. English. mo. $48.00. Pharmaceutical Communications Inc, 42-15 Crescent Street, Long Island City NY 11101. Tel (212)937-4283. Ind/Abst Leg. Resour. Index, Energy Res. Abstr., Excerpta Med. LC KF3821.A15. DD 344.73041. NLM W1 LE448J. Index in last issue of volume - attached. *Journal of Legal Medicine, 0093-1748.*

LEGAL ASPECTS OF PHARMACY PRACTICE. V. 1- Sept. 1978-. 0191-8516. Periodical. US. English. bm. Professional Communications Associates, 625 North Michigan Avenue, Chicago IL 60611. LC KF2915.P4. DD 344.73042.

LEGAL ASPECTS OF PSYCHIATRIC PRACTICE. Vol. 1, No. 1 (Aug. 1984)-. 0883-0924. Periodical. US. English. bm. $30.00. Executive Editor, The Publishing Division, Sieber & McIntyre Inc, 625 North Michigan Avenue/Suite 800, Chicago IL 60611.

LEGAL ASSISTANCE NEWSLETTER. No. 15 (Dec. 1981)-. 0736-7309. Periodical. US. English. American Bar Association, Standing Committee on Legal Assistance for Military Personnel, 1155 East 60th Street, Chicago IL 60637. *Occasional Newsletter (American Bar Association. Standing Committee on Legal Assistance for Military Personnel), 0163-1373.*

LEGAL ASSISTANT TODAY. No. 1 (Fall 1983)-. 0741-7772. Periodical. US. English. qt. $17.97. Legal Assistant Today Inc, 6060 North Central Expressway/Suite 560, Dallas TX 75206. LC KF320.L4. DD 340.02373.

LEGAL ASSISTANTS. Series/Titl Commercial Law and Practice Course Handbook Series. 0730-3068. US. English. an. Practising Law Institute, 810 Seventh Avenue, New York NY 10019. LC KF319. DD 340.02373.

LEGAL ASSISTANTS UPDATE. (LEGAL ASSISTANTS : UPDATE). Vol. 1-. 0272-1961. Periodical. US. English. ir. $6.00. American Bar Association, 750 North Lake Shore Drive, Chicago IL 60611. Tel (312)988-5516. Ed Roger A Larson. LC KF320.L4. DD 340.02373. Circ 5,000. (ctrl). Reports on current trends and activities within the legal assistant profession. Series is directed to legal assistants, legal assistant educators, prospective students, lawyers, and generally those working in a legal environment.

LEGAL BIBLIOGRAPHIC DATA SERVICE. WEEKLY LISTING. See Bibliographies.

LEGAL BIBLIOGRAPHIC DATA SERVICE. WEEKLY SUBJECT LISTING. See Bibliographies.

LEGAL BIBLIOGRAPHY INDEX. See Indexes/Abstracts.

LEGAL BIBLIOGRAPHY JOURNAL. See Bibliographies.

LEGAL BRIEFS FOR EDITORS, PUBLISHERS, AND WRITERS. See Publishing.

LEGAL BRIEFS FOR THE CONSTRUCTION INDUSTRY. See Building and Construction.

LEGAL BULLETIN. (LEGAL BULLETIN - NATIONAL SAVINGS AND LOAN LEAGUE). Main/Corp National Savings and Loan League. 0547-7794. US. English. National Savings and Loan League, 1200 17th Avenue NW, Washington DC 20036. LC KF1009.A73. DD 346.73082. *Legal Bulletin.*

LEGAL BULLETIN. See Building and Construction.

THE LEGAL CIRCLE. 0145-2851. US. English. Chicago Constitutional Rights Foundation, 25 East Jackson/Room 1612, Chicago IL 60604. LC KF9223.A15. DD 345.77305.

LEGAL COMPILATION. (LEGAL COMPILATION : STATUTES AND LEGISLATIVE HISTORY, EXECUTIVE ORDERS, REGULATIONS, GUIDELINES AND REPORTS). Began with: Jan. 1973. US. English. ir. US Environmental Protection Agency, 41 M Street SW, Washington DC 20460. LC KF3775. DD 344.73046.

THE LEGAL CONNECTION. CORPORATIONS & LAW FIRMS. (THE LEGAL CONNECTION; CORPORATIONS & LAW FIRMS). VAT Legal Connection. Corporations and Law Firms. 1st- Ed. 0270-3424. US. English. ir. The Data Financial Press, PO Box 801, Menlo Park CA 94025. Tel (415)321-4553. Ed S P Harris. LC KF195.C6. DD 346.73066025.

LEGAL CONSIDERATIONS IN DENTISTRY. See Dentistry.

LEGAL CONTENTS. (LEGAL CONTENTS : LC). VFOAT LC. 0279-5787. Periodical. US. English. bw. Information Access Company, 11 Davis Drive, Belmont CA 94002. Tel (800)227-8431. *CCLP, Contents of Current Legal Periodicals, 0147-0493.*

LEGAL DIRECTORY FOR SOUTHERN NEVADA (THREE TIMES A YEAR). See Yearbooks, Almanacs, Directories.

LEGAL DIRECTORY OF WASHINGTON STATE. See Yearbooks, Almanacs, Directories.

THE LEGAL EAGLE. Apr. 1972-. Periodical. US. English. mo. New Jersey State Bar Association, 172 West State Street, Trenton NJ 08608. LC KF200. DD 340.062749.

LE'GAL-EASE. (LE'GAL-EASE : PUBLIC LEGAL EDUCATION SOCIETY LAW LETTER FOR SCHOOLS). Vol. 1, No. 1 (Spring 1983)-. 0824-3905. Periodical. CN. English. ty. Public Legal Education Society of Nova Scotia, 4th Floor/5162 Duke Street, Halifax Nova Scotia B3J 1N7 Canada. DD 349.7107.

LEGAL ECONOMICS. See Economics.

LEGAL EDUCATION NEWSLETTER. See Education (General).

THE LEGAL EXECUTIVE. V. 1- Jan. 1963-. 0024-0362. Periodical. UK. English. bm. $22.98. Institute of Legal Executives, Kempston Manor, Kempston Bedford MK42 7AB England. Tel 0234 857711. Ed Charles Blake. bk rev. adv acc. Circ 13,000. (ctrl). Articles on law reform; educational information for students of the Institute; general institute news and views, book reviews, classified and display advertising.

LEGAL HISTORY. V. 1- Jan. 1975-. 0377-0907. Periodical. II. English. ir. $50.00. K K Roy Private Ltd, PO Box 10210/55 Gariahat Road, Calcutta 700019 India. Tel (91)33-474872. Ed K K Roy. Ind/Abst Am. Hist. Life, Hist. Abstr., Part A, Mod. Hist. Abstr., Hist. Abst., Part B, Twent. Century Abstr., Hist. Abstr. LC K12. DD 340.09. bk rev. adv acc. Circ 2,000. Covers all facets of the history of law and institutions and antecedents in law of all countries.

LEGAL INFORMATION MANAGEMENT INDEX. See Indexes/Abstracts.

LEGAL INFORMATION SERVICE - NATIVE LAW CENTRE. (LEGAL INFORMATION SERVICE). No. 1- May 1979 -. 0225-2287. Periodical. CN. English. ir. Native Law Centre, University of Saskatchewan, Diefenbaker Center, Saskatoon Saskatchewan S7N 0W0 Canada. Tel (306)966-6189. Ed Zandra MacEachern. DD 346.71013. Circ 200. Reports dealing with various native law topics and issues of particular interest to native people and practitioners in the field of native law.

LEGAL INFORMATION SERVICE (TEHRAN, IRAN). (LEGAL INFORMATION SERVICE). Periodical. English. wk. PARS Associates Attorneys-at-Law, PO Box 2519, Tehran Iran. LC K12. DD 340.05.

THE LEGAL INTELLIGENCER. V. 1- Dec. 2, 1843-. Periodical. US. English. ir. $155.00. Legal Intelligencer, 10th and Spring Garden Street, Philadelphia PA 19123. Tel (215)236-2000. bk rev. adv acc. Circ 10,000. Trial lists, court verdicts, views of interest to the bar. Paper of record for the Philadelphia legal community.

THE LEGAL INVESTIGATOR. (THE LEGAL INVESTIGATOR : THE OFFICIAL JOURNAL OF THE NATIONAL ASSOCIATION OF LEGAL

Law

INVESTIGATORS, INC). 0741-417X. US. English. qt. $35.00. Julius Bombet, PO Box 3158, Baton Rouge LA 70821. Tel (504)383-8851. Ed Julius Bombet. LC KF8936. DD 363.250973. bk rev. adv acc. Circ 500. (ctrl). Devoted to articles about legal investigations, legal photography and other subjects of interest to legal investigators, detectives and private investigators.

THE LEGAL JOURNAL. 0195-1491. Periodical. US. English. wk $25.00. Legal Journal, PO Box 3035, Seminole FL 33542. Tel (813)541-3130. *Seminole Courier.*

LEGAL-LEGISLATIVE REPORTER NEWS BULLETIN. V. 1- Jan. 1967-. 0458-9599. Periodical. US. English. mo. Free to Members. International Foundation of Employee Benefit Plans, PO Box 69, Brookfield WI 53005. LC KF3512.A16. DD 340.

LEGAL LOOSELEAFS IN PRINT. 1981-. 0275-4088. US. English. an. $50.00. Info Sources Publications, 118 West 79th Street, New York NY 10024. Tel (212)595-3161. Ed Arlene L Eis. LC KF1. DD 016.34973, 016.3473. adv acc. Circ 1,000. The only bibliography of loose leafs, listing and indexing by subject over 2600 titles by 250 publishers, giving detailed bibliographic information on each title.

LEGAL MALPRACTICE REPORTER. 0363-2490. Periodical. US. English. mo. $25.00. Michie Company, PO Box 7587, Charlottesville VA 22906. LC KF1289.A59. DD 346.73033.

LEGAL MALPRACTICE REVIEW. June/July 1977-. 0148-2750. Periodical. US. English. bm. St Paul Fire and Marine Insurance Company, Professional Liability Risk Management Department, 385 Washington Street, St Paul MN 55102. LC KF313.A15. DD 346.73033.

LEGAL MEDICAL QUARTERLY. V. 1- Mar. 1977-. 0703-1211. Periodical. CN. English. qt. $30.00. Legal Medical Quarterly, 46 Park Hill Road, Toronto Ontario M6C 3N1 Canada. Ind/Abst Leg. Resour. Index, Hospit. Lit. Index. DD 614.190971. NLM W1 LE448Q.

LEGAL MEDICINE. 1980-. 0197-9981. US. English. be. W B Saunders Company, West Washington Square, Philadelphia PA 19105. Ed C H Wecht. Ind/Abst Leg. Resour. Index, Excerpta Med., Index Med., Energy Res. Abstr. LC RA1001. DD 614.1. NLM W1 LE448R. *Legal Medicine Annual, 0075-8590.*

LEGAL MEDICINE ANNUAL CEASED. 1969-. 0075-8590. US. English. be. $45.00. Holt Rinehart & Winston, 383 Madison Avenue, New York NY 10017. Tel (215)574-4808. Ed C H Wecht. Ind/Abst Chem. Abstr., Index Med., Curr. Law Index, Leg. Resour. Index. LC RA1011. DD 340.605. NLM W1 LE448T. CODEN LGMAAL.

A LEGAL MEMORANDUM. Main/Corp National Association of Secondary School Principals. 0192-6152. US. English. $65.00. National Association of Secondary School Principals, 1904 Association Drive, Reston VA 22091. LC KF4102. DD 344.7307, 347.3047.

LEGAL NEWSLETTER. June 1980-. 0732-4537. US. English. mo. Illinois Department of Personnel, Stratton Building/5th Floor, Springfield IL 62706. LC KFl1635. DD 342.773068, 347.730268.

LEGAL NEWSLETTER (WASHINGTON, D.C.). (LEGAL NEWSLETTER). Nos. 1 and 2 (Jan./Aug. 1982)-. 0739-5183. US. English. Free. Organization of American States, Department of Treaties Information and Publications, c/o General Secretariat, Washington DC 20006. LC KDZ1103. DD 340.05.

LEGAL NEWSLETTERS IN PRINT. 1985-. 8755-416X. US. English. an. $50.00. Information Sources Publishing 118 West 79th Street, New York NY 10024. Tel (212)595-3761. Ed Arlene L Eis. DD 340. adv acc. Circ 1,000. Lists 1,250 newsletters and newsletter-reporters that are law-related. Publisher and subject indexes included.

LEGAL NOTES. Main/Corp National Savings and Loan League. 0147-9490. US. English. National Savings and Loan League, 1101 15th Street NW, Washington DC 20005. LC KF1009.A15. DD 346.73073.

LEGAL NOTES. US. English. 4719 Brooklyn Avenue NE, Seattle WA 98105. LC JS303.W2. DD 352.

LEGAL NOTES & VIEWPOINTS QUARTERLY. VFOAT Legal Notes and Viewpoints Quarterly. Vol. 1, No. 1 (Nov. 1980)-. 0278-6745. Periodical. US. English. qt. $35.00.

Practising Law Institute, Department QKC, 810 7th Avenue, New York NY 10019. Tel (212)765-5700. LC K12. DD 349.7305, 347.3005. Makes available the best articles, outlines, and checklists from a cross section of Practicing Law Institute's most popular course handbooks.

LEGAL NOTES FOR EDUCATION. 1973. 0093-397X. Periodical. US. English. mo. $44.95. Information Research Systems, PO Box 409, Rosemount MN 55068. Tel (612)452-8267. LC KF4119.A1. DD 344.730705. School law.

LEGAL NOTES FOR INSURANCE. V. 1- July 1973-. 0094-0623. Periodical. US. English. mo. $39.95. Informational Research Systems, PO Box 409, Rosemount MN 55068. LC KF1164.A1. DD 346.7308605.

LEGAL OPINIONS OF THE OFFICE OF GENERAL COUNSEL. Main/Corp United States. Dept. of Housing and Urban Development. Office of General Counsel. 1977-. 0272-7129. US. English. an. US Department of Housing and Urban Development, 451 7th Street SW, Washington DC 20410. LC KF5726.A2. DD 346.73045, 347.30645.

LEGAL OPINIONS OF THE OFFICE OF GENERAL COUNSEL OF THE LAW ENFORCEMENT ASSISTANCE ADMINISTRATION, UNITED STATES DEPARTMENT OF JUSTICE. (LEGAL OPINIONS OF THE OFFICE OF GENERAL COUNSEL OF THE LAW ENFORCEMENT ASSISTANCE ADMINISTRATION). Main/Corp United States. Law Enforcement Assistance Administration. Office of General Counsel. 0098-3926. US. English. Office of General Counsel, Law Enforcement Assistance Administration, 633 Indiana Avenue NW, Washington DC 20530. LC KF9223.A554. DD 345.7305.

LEGAL PERIODICAL DIGEST CEASED. Periodical. US. English. ir. Tel (312)583-8500.

LEGAL PROBLEMS OF MUSEUM ADMINISTRATION: MATERIALS. (ALI-ABA COURSE OF STUDY : LEGAL PROBLEMS OF MUSEUM ADMINISTRATION : MATERIALS). VAT American Law Institute-American Bar Association Course of Study. Legal Problems of Museum Administration: Materials. 0191-3069. US. English. ALIABA Committee on Continuing Professional Education, 4025 Chestnut Street, Philadelphia PA 19104. LC KF4305.Z9. DD 344.73093.

LEGAL REFERENCE SERVICES QUARTERLY. Vol. 1, No. 1 (Spring 1981)-. 0270-319X. Periodical. US. English. qt. $60.00. Haworth Press, 28 East 22nd Street, New York NY 10010. Tel (212)228-2800. Ed Robert C Berring. Ind/Abst Comput. Control Abstr., Electr. Electron. Abstr., Sci. Abstr. Sect. A. Phys. Abstr., Libr. Inf. Sci. Abstr., Libr. Lit. LC K12. DD 340.072073. CODEN LRSQD9. bk rev. adv acc. Circ 830. This journal, practical and informative, enhances the knowledge of all law librarians about the continuously expanding volume of legal materials and their utility in legal research.

LEGAL RESEARCH AND LAW LIBRARY MANAGEMENT. SUPPLEMENT. VFOAT Supplement to Legal Research and Law Library Management. 1985-. US. English. be. Law Journal Seminars-Press Inc, 111 Eighth Avenue/Suite 900, New York NY 10011. *Supplement to Legal Research and Law Library Management.*

LEGAL RESEARCH JOURNAL. V. 1-. 0146-0382. US. English. bm. $9.75. Legal Institute, 281 East Colorado Boulevard, Box 219, Pasadena CA 91102. Tel (818)405-1476. Ed Herman B Lancaster. Ind/Abst Leg. Resour. Index, Curr. Law Index. LC KF240. DD 340.072073. bk rev. Circ 200. Focuses on the art and issues of legal research.

LEGAL RESPONSE : CHILD ADVOCACY AND PROTECTION. VFOAT Child Advocacy and Protection. Vol. 1, No. 1 (Apr./May 1979)-. Periodical. US. English. bm. American Bar Association, National Legal Resource Center, 1800 M Street NW, Washington DC 20036.

LEGAL SECRETARY'S NEWSLETTER CEASED. (THE LEGAL SECRETARY'S NEWSLETTER). V. 1-7, No. 6. 0318-8396. Periodical. CN. English. mo. $35.00. Moore/Parry Ltd, 3390 West 41st Avenue, Vancouver British Columbia V6N 3E2 Canada.

LEGAL SERIES. Main/Corp International Atomic Energy Agency. 1-. 0074-1868. Monographic Series. US. English. ir. UNIPUB, PO Box 1222, Ann Arbor MI 48106. Tel (800)521-8110.

LEGAL SERVICES COMMISSION REPORT. Main/Corp British Columbia. Legal Services Commission. 1st- 1975/76-. CN. English. an. Legal Services Commission, 1100 -675 West Hastings Street, Vancouver British Columbia V6B 1N2 Canada. LC KEB160.A72. DD 354.711008458.

LEGAL SHOCK. See Religion, Mythology, Rationalism - Theology.

THE LEGAL SIDE OF MEDICINE REPORT. Issue No. 101- Aug. 1978-. 0164-9272. Periodical. US. English. mo. $48.00. Institute for Management, 171 Saybrook Industrial Park, Old Saybrook CT 06475. NLM W1 LE449D.

LEGAL SUPPORT STAFF NEWSLETTER. VAT Legal Secretary's Newsletter (1980). Vol. 7, No. 6 (Oct. 1980)-. 0229-5393. Periodical. CN. English. Moore/Parry Ltd, 3390 West 41st Avenue, Vancouver British Columbia V6N 3E4 Canada. DD 651.934. *Legal Secretary's Newsletter, 0318-8396.*

LEGAL SYSTEMS LETTER. Vol. 1, No. 1 (July 1981)-. 0278-4149. Periodical. US. English. mo. Professional Publications Inc, PO Box 80280, Atlanta GA 30366. Tel (212)889-5666. LC KF320.A9. DD 349.730285, 347.300285.

LEGAL TIMES. Vol. 4, No. 38 (Mar. 1, 1982)-. 0732-7536. Periodical. US. English. wk. $135.00. Legal Times of Washington, 1601 Connecticut Avenue NW, Washington DC 20009. Ind/Abst Leg. Resour. Index, Nexis. LC K12. DD 340.05. *Legal Times of Washington (1978), 0162-7295.*

LEGAL TIMES OF NEW YORK. Apr. 25, 1983-. 0748-3368. Periodical. US. English. mo. Legal Times, 757 Third Avenue, New York NY 10017. LC K12. DD 349.74705, 347.47005.

LEGAL TIMES OF WASHINGTON (1982). (LEGAL TIMES OF WASHINGTON). Vol. 1, No. 1 (Mar. 1982)-. 0732-7544. Periodical. US. English. mo. Legal Times, 1601 Connecticut Avenue NW, Washington DC 20009.

LEGAL WRITING JOURNAL. Vol. 1, Issue 1-. 0732-4529. Periodical. US. English. ty. $9.75. Legal Institute, 281 East Colorado Boulevard, Box 219, Pasadena CA 91102. Tel (818)405-1476. Ed Herman B Lancaster. LC KF250. DD 808.06634. bk rev. Circ 200. Covers information about the art and techniques of legal communication.

LEGALIDAD SOCIALISTA : BOLETIN DE INFORMACION JURIDICA EDITADO POR LA FISCALIA GENERAL DE LA REPUBLICA. Periodical. Spanish. ir. $2.50. Fiscalia General de la Republica, San Parael No 3, Habana 2 Cuba. LC K12. DD 349.729105, 347.291005.

LEGALITY : A JOURNAL OF THE UNIVERSITY OF ZAMBIA LAW ASSOCIATION. Periodical. English. ir. University of Zambia, PO Box 2379, Lusaka Zambia. LC K12. DD 349.689405, 346.894005. *Law Bulletin (University of Zambia. Law Association).*

LEGI SOCIAL. 0223-4726. Periodical. FR. French. mo. 135. 54 rue de Chabrol, 75010 Paris France. DD 344.44005, 344.404005.

LEGIS BANCOS INFORMATIVO CVM. VFOAT Legisbancos. BL. Portuguese. ir. Legis Bancos Editora l.tda, Santa Luzia 799 GR 1902 ZC39, 20.000 Rio de Janeiro Brazil. DD 346.810666, 348.106666.

LEGIS BANCOS INFORMATIVO. IMPOSTO DE RENDA : IR. Main/Corp Brazil. VFOAT IR. Periodical. Portuguese. sa. Legis Bancos Editora Ltda, rue Santa Luzia 799 190, Andar Grupo 1902 CEP 20.030, 23666 Palm BR Rio de Janeiro RJ Brazil. LC KHD4582. DD 343.8105205, 348.1035205.

LEGISLACAO. Main/Corp Sao Paulo, Brazil (State). Collection No. 1- 1971-. Portuguese. ir. Coordenacao do Administracao Financeiro, Avenida Rangel Pestana No 300 - 170 Andar, Sal Paulo Brazil. DD 343.81603.

LEGISLACAO DE ENSINO DE 1O. E 2O. GRAUS. FEDERAL. Main/Corp Brazil. VFOAT Legislacao de Ensino de Primeiro e Segundo Graus. Portuguese. an. LC KHD3572.A27. DD 344.810705, 348.104705.

LEGISLACAO DO DISTRITO FEDERAL. Main/Corp Distrito Federal, Brazil. V. 1- 1960/62-. Portuguese. ir. Senado Federal Centro Grafico, Procuradoria-Geral do Distrito Federal,

Law

Edificio Brasilia 8 Andar Sector Bancario Sur, Brasilia Brazil.

LEGISLACAO DO ESTADO DE MATO GROSSO DO SUL. Main/Corp Mato Grosso do Sul (Brazil). Vol. 1 (1979)-. Portuguese. ir. Secreatria de Administracao, Av 31 de Marco 559 Ed Erpe, 2O Andar, 79.100 Campo Grande MS Brazil. **DD** 348.8172026, 348.1720826.

LEGISLACAO DO ESTADO DO RIO DE JANEIRO. Main/Corp Rio de Janeiro (State). BL. Portuguese. ir. Secretaria de Estado de Justica, Departamento Geral de Documentacao, Divisao de Divulgacao, Av Mal Floriano 227 ZC-05, Rio de Janeiro Brazil. (cum index).

LEGISLACAO DO ESTADO DO RIO DE JANEIRO. Main/Corp Rio de Janeiro (Brasil : State). Vol. 1 (1975)-. 0100-378X. BL. Portuguese. an. Avenida Erasmo Braga, 118 - 9O Andar, Rio de Janeiro ZC-P Brazil. **LC** KHD8103.7. **DD** 348.81026, 348.10826.

LEGISLACAO DO MUNICIPIO DO RIO DE JANEIRO. Main/Corp Rio de Janeiro. Portuguese. ir. **DD** 348.815023.

LEGISLACAO FEDERAL E MARGINALIA. Main/Corp Brazil. Series/Titl Lex Coletanea de Legislacao e Jurisprudencia. BL. Portuguese. ir. 202.00. Lex S A Editora, rua Machado de Assis 57, 01406 Sao Paulo Brazil. **Tel** (011)549-0122. **DD** 348.81024, 348.10824. **Circ** 13,000.

LEGISLACION VENEZOLANA. Main/Corp Venezuela. Spanish. an. Ed A R Brewer-Carias and G Burgueno Alvarez. **LC** KHW35. **DD** 348.870205.

LEGISLATIEF. IO. Indonesian. mo. 1000. Biro DPRD Propinsi Jawa Timur, Km 1 Jl Pahlawan No 18, Surabaya Indonesia. **LC** Law.

LEGISLATION CHECK LIST. 0095-8220. US. English. an. Illinois State Bar Association, Illinois Bar Center, Springfield IL 62701. **LC** KFI1215. **DD** 348.77301.

LEGISLATION ON DISPUTE RESOLUTION. 0742-261X. US. English. qt. American Bar Association, 1800 M Street NW, South Lobby, Washington DC 20036. *State Legislation on Dispute Resolution.*

LEGISLATION ON FOREIGN ARTICLES. (LEGISLATION ON FOREIGN RELATIONS THROUGH . . .). Main/Corp United States. Began with 1977. 0736-5985. US. English. an. US Government Printing Office, Superintendent of Documents, Washington DC 20402. **LC** KF4650.A29. **DD** 342.730412, 347.302412. Vols. for 1983- distributed to some depository libraries in microfiche. *Legislation on Foreign Relations, with Explanatory Notes.*

LEGISLATION PROVINCIALE. (LA LEGISLATION PROVINCIALE). **VAT** Legislation Provinciale. Bulletin Regulier. First issue Dec. 1972?. 0319-4892. Periodical. CN. French. Chambre de Commerce de la Province de Quebec, 500 rue St Francois-Xavier, Montreal Quebec H2Y 2T6 Canada. *Bulletin sur la Legislation Provinciale, 0319-4884.*

LEGISLATIVE ACTIONS AFFECTING HIGHER EDUCATION, WASHINGTON STATE LEGISLATURE. See Education (General) - Higher Education.

LEGISLATIVE ACTIVITIES REPORT OF THE COMMITTEE ON FOREIGN RELATIONS, UNITED STATES SENATE. See Political Science - International Relations.

LEGISLATIVE APPROPRIATIONS REPORT. Main/Corp Nevada. Legislative Counsel Bureau. Division of Fiscal Analysis. 0160-1245. US. English. be. Legislative Counsel Bureau, Legislative Building, Capitol Complex, Carson City NV 89710. **LC** HJ11. **DD** 353.979300722.

THE LEGISLATIVE BULLETIN. V. 1-. Periodical. US. English.

LEGISLATIVE BULLETIN - ASSOCIATION OF WASHINGTON CITIES. (LEGISLATIVE BULLETIN). 0740-4204. Periodical. US. English. ir. $15.00. Association of Washington Cities, 1076 South Franklin Street, Olympia WA 98501. **Tel** (206)753-4137. **LC** KFW431.A15. **DD** 348.797026, 347.970826. *Legislative Digest (Association of Washington Cities).*

LEGISLATIVE CALENDAR - UNITED STATES HOUSE OF REPRESENTATIVES, COMMITTEE ON RULES. See Public Administration.

LEGISLATIVE DIGEST : BILLS OF LABOR INTEREST PASSED BY THE NEW YORK STATE LEGISLATURE. Main/Corp New York (State). Dept. of Labor. US. English. wk. State Document Room or the Assembly Document Room, Capitol Building, Albany NY 12224. **LC** KFN5556. **DD** 344.747010262, 347.470410262. *Legislative Digest of Labor and Related Bills Introduced in the New York State Legislature.*

LEGISLATIVE FISCAL REPORT. Main/Corp Nevada. Legislative Counsel Bureau. 0363-2121. US. English. Legislative Counsel Bureau, Legislative Building, Carson City NV 89701. **LC** HJ11. **DD** 353.979300722.

LEGISLATIVE HISTORY MICROFORM. 61st Congress, 1st Session (March 15, 1909)-. US. English.

LEGISLATIVE HISTORY OF CAB REGULATIONS. Main/Corp United States. Civil Aeronautics Board. **VAT** Legislative History of Civil Aeronautics Board Regulations. Periodical. US. English. ir. Civil Aeronautics Board, Washington DC 20402.

LEGISLATIVE HISTORY OF TITLES I-XX OF THE SOCIAL SECURITY ACT. **VFOAT** Legislative History, Titles I-XX of the Social Security Act. Vol. 18 (1977-1978)- – 95th Congress-. 0732-6394. US. English. Technical Documents Branch, Division of Technical Documents and Privacy, Office of Regulations, Office of Operational Policy and Procedures, Social Security Administration, 6401 Security Boulevard, Baltimore MD 21235. **LC** KF3644.522.A14. **DD** 344.730230262 347.304230262. *Legislative History of Titles II, XVI, and XVIII of the Social Security Act.*

LEGISLATIVE MANUAL (NORTH CAROLINA. GENERAL ASSEMBLY. LEGISLATIVE SERVICES OFFICE). (LEGISLATIVE MANUAL). US. English. be. Legislative Services Office, 2129 State Legislative Building, Raleigh NC 27611. **LC** JK4130. **DD** 328.7560025.

THE LEGISLATIVE MANUAL OF THE STATE OF MINNESOTA. -1966. US. English. ir. Secretary of State Erdahl, State of Minnesota, St Paul MN 55101.

LEGISLATIVE MANUAL, STATE OF NEVADA. Series/Titl Bulletin (Nevada. Legislature. Legislative Counsel Bureau). US. English. be. *Legislative Manual of the Nevada Legislature.*

LEGISLATIVE MEMORANDUM. Main/Corp New York Civil Liberties Union. **VFOAT** NYCLU. No. 1-. Periodical. US. English. ir. New York Civil Liberties Union, 84 Fifth Avenue, New York NY 10011.

LEGISLATIVE MONITOR. 0279-8743. Periodical. US. English. mo. Michigan Association of Professions, 1407 South Harrison Road/Suite 350, East Lansing MI 48823. **Tel** (517)337-1725.

LEGISLATIVE NETWORK FOR NURSES. Began with issue for Sept. 19, 1984. 8756-0054. Periodical. US. English. bw. $125.00. LNN Inc, PO Box 44071, l'Enfant Plaza SW, Washington DC 20024.

LEGISLATIVE REPORT. V. 1- Oct. 23, 1978-. 0709-5333. Periodical. CN. English. ir. $65.00. Alberta Chamber of Commerce, 212 10201-104 Street, Edmonton Alberta T5J 1B2 Canada. **DD** 328.7123077.

LEGISLATIVE REPORT. Main/Corp Michigan Council for the Arts. US. English. an. Michigan Council for the Arts, 1200 16th Avenue, Detroit MI 48226. **LC** NX24.M5. **DD** 353.977400854.

LEGISLATIVE REPORT. Main/Corp Florida. Dept. of Legal Affairs. US. English. **LC** KFF79. **DD** 340.3.

LEGISLATIVE REPORT. Main/Corp Council on Black Minnesotans. 1981-. US. English. be. Council on Black Minnesotans, 504 Rice Street, St Paul MN 55103.

LEGISLATIVE REPORTER. 0092-1505. Periodical. US. English. wk. Commission on Law Enforcement and Criminal Justice, State Capitol Building, Lincoln NE 68509. **LC** KFN562.A73. **DD** 345.7820505.

LEGISLATIVE REVIEW. Main/Corp Montana Legislative Council. 0145-8604. US. English. be. Legislative Council, State Capital, Helena MT 59620. **LC** KFM9015. **DD** 348.78601.

LEGISLATIVE REVIEW. 1981-. US. English. an. *Comptroller's Legislative Review.*

LEGISLATIVE REVIEW ACTIVITY. (LEGISLATIVE REVIEW ACTIVITY : REPORT OF THE COMMITTEE ON FINANCE, UNITED STATES SENATE PURSUANT TO PARAGRAPH 8 OF RULE XXVI OF THE STANDING RULES OF THE SENATE). Main/Corp United States. Congress. Senate. Committee on Finance. 0099-1309. US. English. be. Superintendent of Documents, US Government Printing Office, Washington DC 20402. **LC** KF30.8. **DD** 328.730765.

LEGISLATIVE REVIEW ACTIVITY, REPORT OF THE COMMITTEE ON LABOR AND PUBLIC WELFARE, UNITED STATES SENATE. (LEGISLATIVE REVIEW ACTIVITY). Main/Corp United States. Congress. Senate. Committee on Labor and Public Welfare. 0361-0381. US. English. Superintendent of Documents, US Government Printing Office, Washington DC 20402. **LC** KF30.8. **DD** 344.73.

LEGISLATIVE REVIEW ACTIVITY - UNITED STATES. CONGRESS. SENATE. COMMITTEE ON LABOR AND HUMAN RESOURCES. (LEGISLATIVE REVIEW ACTIVITY : REPORT OF THE COMMITTEE ON LABOR AND HUMAN RESOURCES, UNITED STATES SENATE, DURING THE CONGRESS PURSUANT TO SECTION 136 OF THE LEGISLATIVE REORGANIZATION ACT OF 1946, AS AMENDED BY THE LEGISLATIVE REORGANIZATION ACT OF 1970). Main/Corp United States. Congress. Senate. Committee on Labor and Human Resources. 0730-2649. US. English. **LC** KF30.8. **DD** 344.73, 347.304. Vols. for (96th Congress, 1979-80-) distributed to some depository libraries in microfiche. *Legislative Review Activity.*

LEGISLATIVE REVIEW (NEW YORK (STATE). DEPT. OF AUDIT AND CONTROL). (LEGISLATIVE REVIEW). 1981-. US. English. an. **LC** KFN5750. **DD** 342.747, 347.4702. *Comptroller's Legislative Review.*

LEGISLATIVE ROUNDUP. 0024-0494. US. English. wk. Council on Legislation, American Medical Association, 535 North Dearborn Street, Chicago IL 60610. **NLM** W1 LE458.

LEGISLATIVE SERIES. 1919-. Periodical. English. ir. **LC** HD7809. (cum index). Includes the most important laws and regulations enacted throughout the world on labour and social security.

LEGISLATIVE STATUS REPORT - NATIONAL ASSOCIATION OF COMMUNITY HEALTH CENTERS. (LEGISLATIVE STATUS REPORT : A PUBLICATION OF THE NATIONAL ASSOCIATION OF COMMUNITY HEALTH CENTERS, INC). 0739-7690. US. English. **NLM** W1 LE459.

LEGISLATIVE STATUS REPORT - UNITED STATES. VETERANS ADMINISTRATION. (LEGISLATIVE STATUS REPORT). Main/Corp United States. 8755-4410. Periodical. US. English. mo. Veterans Administration, Office of the General Counsel, Legislative Reference and Research Section, 810 Vermont Avenue NW, Washington DC 20420.

LEGISLATIVE STUDIES QUARTERLY. V.1- Feb. 1976-. 0362-9805. Periodical. US. English. qt. $42.00 Domestic, $46.00 Foreign. Comparative Legislative Research, University of Iowa, 304 Schaeffer Hall, Iowa City IA 52242. **Tel** (319)353-5040. Ed Gerhard Loewenberg, Malcolm E Jewell, and Charles O Jones. **Ind/Abst** ABC Pol Sci, Writ. Am. Hist., Soc. Sci. Citation Index. **LC** JF501. **DD** 328.305. bk rev. adv acc. **Circ** 1,000. (ctrl). International journal devoted to publication of research on representative assemblies.

LEGISLATIVE SUMMARY. Main/Corp Connecticut. Dept. on Aging. US. English. an. Department on Aging, 80 Washington Street, Hartford CT 06115. **LC** KFC3950.A35. **DD** 344.74603263.

LEGISLATIVE SUMMARY - DEPARTMENT OF COMMUNITY AND REGIONAL AFFAIRS, DIVISION OF COMMUNITY AND RURAL DEVELOPMENT. (LEGISLATIVE SUMMARY). Main/Corp Alaska. Division of Community and Rural Development. V. 1- Jan. 24, 1977-. 0147-9644. Periodical. US. English. bw. Department of Community and Regional Affairs, Pouch B, Juneau AK 99811. **LC** KFA1207. **DD** 348.798026.

LEGISLATIVE TAX HANDBOOK, THE TEXAS LEGISLATURE. (LEGISLATIVE TAX HANDBOOK, THE . . . TEXAS LEGISLATURE). **VFOAT** Legislative Tax Handbook. 0730-8744. US. English. an. **LC** HJ2435. **DD** 343.7640405, 347.6403405.

Law

LEGISLATIVE TRENDS. CUMULATION. (LEGISLATIVE TRENDS). 0098-5791. US. English. University of the State of New York, State Education Department, Albany NY 12224. LC KFN5001. DD 016.348731.

LEGISLATURE OF ONTARIO DEBATES; OFFICIAL REPORT (HANSARD). Main/Corp Ontario. Legislative Assembly. Standing Procedural Affairs Committee. No. P-1- Apr. 27, 1978-. 0704-349X. Periodical. CN. English. da. $12.38. Treasury of Ontario, Clerk of Legislative Assembly, 9th Floor/Ferguson Block, Toronto Ontario M7A 1N3 Canada. Tel (416)965-2238.

LEGISLATURE OF ONTARIO DEBATES. OFFICIAL REPORT (HANSARD). STANDING COMMITTEE ON REGULATIONS AND OTHER STATUTORY INSTRUMENTS. (LEGISLATURE OF ONTARIO DEBATES). Main/Corp Ontario. Legislative Assembly. Standing Committee on Regulations and Other Statutory Instruments. No. I-1, 1st Session, 32nd Parliament (Nov. 9, 1981)-. 0711-9682. CN. English. $15.00 Per Session. Sessional Subscription Service, Central Purchasing Service, Print Procurement Section, Ministry of Government Services, 8th Floor/Ferguson Block, Parliament Buildings, Toronto Ontario M7A 1N3 Canada. DD 328.71302.

LEGISLAZIONE E GIURISPRUDENZA TRIBUTARIA. 1- June 1973-. 0304-0321. IT. Italian. mo. Casa Editrice Dr A Giuffre SNC, Via Statuto 2 Periodical Department, 20121 Milano Italy. Tel (02)652.341/2/3.

LEGISLAZIONE ECONOMICA. Series/Titl Diritto e Problemi Contemporanei. Began with Vol. for Sept. 1976-Aug. 1977. Italian. an. 26.000. DD 346.450705, 344.506705.

LEGISLETTER. VFOAT TBA Legisletter. Dec. 19, 1983-. 8756-5587. Periodical. US. English. Tennessee Bar Association, 3622 West End Avenue, Nashville TN 37205. LC KFT31. DD 349.76805, 347.68005.

LEIS. Main/Corp Sao Paulo, Brazil (State). Portuguese. ir. DD 349.8161.

THE LENDING LAW FORUM. V. 1- June 1975-. 0098-891X. US. English. bm. $43.20. Lending Law Forum, PO Box 208, Massapequa Park NY 11762. Tel (516)799-4003. Ed William M Aukamp. Ind/Abst Leg. Resour. Index. LC K12. DD 346.7307305. This newsletter covers legal developments in the field of commercial and consumer lending.

LENDING TRANSACTIONS AND THE BANKRUPTCY REFORM ACT. Series/Titl Corporate Law and Practice Course Handbook Series. Began with Vol. for 1978. 0733-0049. US. English. Practising Law Institute, 810 Seventh Avenue, New York NY 10019. LC KF1524.3. DD 346.73078, 347.30678.

LESBIAN/GAY LAW NOTES. (LESBIAN-GAY LAW NOTES). 8755-9021. Periodical. US. English. mo. $12.00. Bar Association for Human Rights of Greater New York, PO Box 1899 Grand Central Station, New York NY 10163. Tel (212)628-8532. Ed Arthur S Leonard. DD 342. Circ 500. Comprehensive report on legal issues affecting the rights of gay people. Law Group Notes.

LEVERAGED LEASING. Series/Titl Commercial Law and Practice Course Handbook Series. 0882-9950. US. English. Practising Law Institute, 810 Seventh Avenue, New York NY 10019.

LEX : COLETANEA DE LEGISLACAO E JURISPRUDENCIA. Portuguese. ir. 3.340,00. Lex Editora, Caixa Postal 12.888, Sao Paulo Brazil. Tel 549-0122. (cum index). Circ 8,418. (ctrl).

LEX COLLEGII; A LEGAL NEWSLETTER FOR INDEPENDENT HIGHER EDUCATION. VFOAT Collegii. 0749-9078. Periodical. US. English. qt. $24.00. Independent College Legal Information, PO Box 15541, Nashville TN 37215. LC KF4225.A15. DD 344.73074. Amicus (Nashville, Tenn.).

LEX (COLOMBO, SRI LANKA). (LEX). 1983-. CE. English (Sinhalese). an. Law Students' Union, Sri Lanka Law College, Sri Lanka Colombo. DD 349.549305 345.493005.

LEX-INTERDOC. VFOAT Lex Interdoc. Vol. 1, No. 1 (1st Quarter 1984)-. 0771-5102. Periodical. English (French). qt. $35.00. Lex-Interdoc, rue de la Montagne 34 Bte 11, B-1000 Brussels Belgium.

LEX, JURISPRUDENCIA DO SUPREMO TRIBUNAL FEDERAL. Main/Corp Brazil. Supremo Tribunal Federal. BL. Portuguese. mo. 344.00. Lex Editora, Caixa Postal 12.888, Cep 04106 Sao Paulo Brazil. Tel 549-0122. DD 348.81041. Circ 3,500. (ctrl).

LEX (PANAMA, PANAMA). (LEX : REVISTA DEL COLEGIO NACIONAL DE ABOGADOS DE PANAMA). Periodical. PN. Spanish. ir. El Colegio, Apartado Postal 4792, Panama 5 Republic de Panama. LC K12. DD 340.05.

LEY DE PRESUPUESTOS DEL SECTOR PUBLICO. Main/Corp Chile. Direccion de Presupuestos. Spanish. an. LC KHF4560.A27. DD 343.83034, 348.30334. Ley de Presupuestos.

LA LEY, REVISTA JURIDICA PARAGUAYA. VFOAT Revista Juridica Paraguaya: La Ley. V. 1, Jan./March 1978-. Periodical. Spanish. qt. La Ley SA, Tucuman 1471, 1050 Buenos Aires Argentina. LC K12. DD 349.89205.

LEYES PROMULGADAS. DECRETOS DE PODER EJECUTIVO. Main/Corp Uruguay. VFOAT Decretos del Poder Ejectivo. Spanish. ir. Presidencia de la Republica Centro de Difusion e Informacion, Plaza Independencia 776, Montevideo Uruguay. DD 348.895026.

LGA BILL OF PARTICULARS. Main/Corp Local Government Attorneys of Virginia. VAT Local Government Attorneys of Virginia Bill of Particulars. V. 1- June 1975-. 0360-3156. US. English. mo. 207 Minor Hall, University of Virginia, Charlottesville VA 22903. LC KFV2830.A59. DD 342.75509.

LIABILITY LEDGER. 0193-3388. Periodical. US. English. mo. $135.00. Federal-State Reports Inc, 2201 Wilson Boulevard, Arlington VA 22201. LC KF1296.A15. DD 346.73038.

LIAISON. V. 1- Jan. 1975-. 0703-9700. Periodical. CN. English (text in French). mo. Receiver General for Canada, Supply & Services, Ottawa Ontario K1A 0S9 Canada. DD 345.710505.

LIAS NEWSLETTER. VFOAT Law in American Society Newsletter. V. 1- Mar. 1977-. 0147-8729. Periodical. US. English. qt. $10.00. Law in American Society Foundation, 33 North LaSalle Street/Suite 1700, Chicago IL 60602. LC KF200. DD 340.071073.

LIBERACION Y DERECHO. V. 1- Jan./April 1974-. Periodical. Spanish. ir. $12.00 Single Issue. Universidad Nacional y Popular de Buenos Aires, Avda Figueroa Alcorta 2263, Buenos Aires Argentina. LC K12.

LIBERIAN CODE OF LAWS OF . . . : ADOPTED BY THE LEGISLATURE OF THE REPUBLIC OF LIBERIA . . . . Main/Corp Liberia. Vol. 1 (1956)-. US. English. ir. Cornell University Press, 124 Roberts Place, Ithaca NY 14853.

LIBERIAN LAW JOURNAL. V. 1- June 1965-. 0024-1970. Periodical. LB. English. ir. $6.00 Domestic, $10.00 Foreign. Louis Arthur Grimes School of Law, University of Liberia, Monrovia Liberia.

LIBRARY BULLETIN - UNITED STATES. DEPT. OF JUSTICE. OFFICE OF INFORMATION TECHNOLOGY. (LIBRARY BULLETIN). Main/Corp United States. Dept. of Justice. Office of Information Technology. 8756-0771. US. English. LC KF4. DD 016.34973, 016.3473. Library Bulletin.

LICENSED ATTORNEYS OF NORTH DAKOTA. VFOAT Directory : Licenses Attorneys of North Dakota. 0091-9055. US. English. Bismark State Bar Board, State Capitol, Bismark ND 58501. LC KF192.N69. DD 340.025784.

LICENSING, COUNTERSIGNING, AND SURPLUS LINE LAWS FOR THE 50 STATES, DISTRICT OF COLUMBIA, PUERTO RICO, AND THE VIRGIN ISLANDS. 0742-5120. US. English. an. $7.00. National Underwriter Company, 420 East Fourth Street, Cincinnati OH 45202.

LICENSING LAW AND BUSINESS REPORT. V. 1- May 1978-. 0162-5764. Periodical. US. English. bm. Clark Boardman Company Ltd, 435 Hudson Street, New York NY 10014. Tel (212)929-7500. Ind/Abst Leg. Resour. Index. LC KF3145.A15. DD 343.7307.

LIFE COMPANY TAX NEWSLETTER. See Insurance.

LIGNINGSVEJLEDNINGEN. Main/Corp Denmark. Statsskattedirektoratet. 0106-293X. DK. Danish. ir. Statsskattedirektoratet Ligningsafdelingen, Meldahlsgade 5, 1613 Kbenhavn V Denmark. DD 343.489040202, 344.890440202.

LIMITED OFFERING EXEMPTIONS: REGULATION D. (LIMITED OFFERING EXEMPTIONS, REGULATION D). Series/Titl Securities Law Series. 1983-. 0739-1889. US. English. an. Clark Boardman Company, 435 Hudson Street, New York NY 10014. LC KF1659.A152. DD 346.730652, 347.306652.

LIMITED PARTNERS LETTER. 0163-0652. Periodical. US. English. mo. $36.00. Prologue Press Inc, PO Box 315, Menlo Park CA 94025. LC KF6452.A15. DD 346.73066205.

LINCOLN LAW REVIEW (SAN FRANCISCO, CALIF.). (LINCOLN LAW REVIEW). Vol. 1, No. 1 (Dec. 1965)-. 0024-368X. Periodical. US. English. sa. $15.00. Lincoln University Law School, 281 Masonic Avenue, San Francisco CA 94118. Tel (415)221-1212. Ed Kammy Au. Ind/Abst Leg. Resour. Index, Index Leg. Period., Curr. Law Index, Contents Curr. Leg. Period. DD 340.05. (cum index). bk rev. adv acc. Circ 450. Concerns the discipline of law.

LIST OF BANK-RECOMMENDED ATTORNEYS. VAT List of Bank Recommended Attorneys. 1983-. 0738-4246. US. English. an. $30.00 Single Issue, $25.00 Standing Order. Rand McNally & Company, Financial Publishing Division, PO Box 7600, Chicago IL 60680. LC KF195.B3. DD 340.02573. Rand McNally List of Bank-Recommended Attorneys, 0361-7114.

LIST OF OFFICIAL COMMITTEES, COMMISSIONS AND OTHER BODIES CONCERNED WITH THE REFORM OF THE LAW. 0459-732X. UK. English. ir. Institute of Advanced Legal Studies, 25 Russell Square, London WC1B 5DR England. DD 340.3025.

LIST OF STATUTORY INSTRUMENTS. 1948-. Periodical. UK. English. mo. $35.25. Her Majestys Stationery Office, PO Box 276, London SW8 5DT England. Tel 01-622 3316. List of Statutory Rules and Orders.

LISTA DE LOS COLEGIOS DE ABOGADOS, NOTARIOS, PROCURADORES Y SECRETARIOS JUDICIALES DE MADRID Y GUIA JUDICIAL. Spanish. ir. Listas de Los Ilustres Colegios de Abogados, Notarios, Procuradores y Secretarios Judiciales de Madrid y Guia Judicial.

LISTA DE LOS SENORES QUE FORMAN LOS EXPRESADOS COLEGIOS. Main/Corp Colegio de Abogados de Zaragoza. VFOAT Guia Judicial de Aragon. Spanish. ir. DD 340.0254655.

LISTA DE SENORES COLEGIADOS. Main/Corp Ilustre Colegio de Abogados de Oviedo. Spanish. ir. Palacio de Justicia, Plaza Porlier No 5, Oviedo Spain.

LISTA DE SENORES COLEGIADOS, GUIA JUDICIAL Y ADMINISTRATIVA. Main/Corp Illustre Colegio Provincial de Abogados de Lerida. Spanish. ir. Illustre Colegio Provincial de Abogados de Lerida, Avenida Caudillo 11 10, Lerida Spain. DD 340.0254674.

LISTA NACIONAL DE BOLIVIA. Main/Corp Asociacion Latinoamericana de Libre Comercio. UY. Spanish. ir. Asociacion Latinoamericana de Libre Comercio, Casilla de Correo 577, Montevideo Uruguay. DD 343.876056.

LISTA NACIONAL DEL PARAGUAY. Main/Corp Asociacion Latinoamericana de Libre Comercio. 0571-4028. UY. Spanish. ir. Asociacion Latinoamericana de Libre Comercio, Casilla de Correo 577, Montevideo Uruguay. DD 343.892056.

LISTA NACIONAL DEL PERU. Main/Corp Asociacion Latinoamericana de Libre Comercio. 0571-4036. UY. Spanish. ir. Asociacion Latinoamericana de Libre Comercio, Cebollati 1461, Casilla de Correo 577, Montevideo Uruguay. DD 343.85056.

LITIGATING AN ANTITRUST CASE. 0196-3317. US. English. Practising Law Institute, 810 7th Avenue, New York NY 10019. LC KF9066.A5. DD 343.730720269.

Law

LITIGATION. V. 1- Winter 1975-. 0097-9813. Periodical. US. English. qt. $22.00. American Bar Association, 750 North Lake Shore Drive, Chicago IL 60611. **Tel** (312)988-5555. **Ed** William Pannill. **Ind/Abst** Index Leg. Period., Leg. Resour. Index, Contents Curr. Leg. Period., Curr. Law Index. **LC** K12. **DD** 347.73705. (ctrl). Journal for lawyers who try cases and judges who decide them. Provokes serious thought about how justice may be reached through advocacy.

LITIGATION. **VFOAT** Litigation Handbook. Periodical. US. English. ir. US Department of Housing and Urban Development, 451-7th Street SW, Washington DC 20410.

LITIGATION, ACTIONS, AND PROCEEDINGS BULLETIN. 0198-1498. Periodical. US. English. qt. Superintendent of Documents, US Government Printing Office, Washington DC 20402. **LC** KF9369.A59. **DD** 345.730263. Securities Violations Bulletin, 0270-742X.

LITIGATION AND ADMINISTRATIVE PRACTICE SERIES. 8756-4548. Monographic Series. US. English. ir. Practising Law Institute, 810 Seventh Avenue, New York NY 10019. **DD** 347.

LITIGATION COURSE HANDBOOK SERIES. **Main/Corp** Practising Law Institute. No. 1-. 8756-4491. US. English. ir. Practising Law Institute, 810 Seventh Avenue, New York NY 10019. **DD** 347.

LITIGATION NEWS. V. 1- Oct. 1975-. 0147-9970. Periodical. US. English. qt. $15.00 Membership. American Bar Association, 1155 East 60th Street, Chicago IL 60637. **Ind/Abst** Leg. Resour. Index. **LC** KF200. **DD** 345.73075.

LITIGATION NEWSLETTER TABLE OF CASES. June 1980-June 1982-. Periodical. US. English. sa.

LITIGATION UNDER THE FEDERAL FREEDOM OF INFORMATION ACT AND PRIVACY ACT. 5th Ed. (1980)-. 0748-8270. US. English. an. $35.00. FOIA Litigation Book Cnss, 122 MD Avenue SE, Washington DC 20002. **Tel** (202)544-5380. **Ed** Allan Adler. **LC** KF5753. **DD** 342.730853, 347.302853. **Circ** 2,000. Technical manual for attorneys covering all aspects of Freedom of Information Act and Privacy Act. Litigation under the Amended Federal Freedom of Information Act, 0748-8262.

LITIS. Yearly V. 1- Oct. 1974-. Periodical. Portuguese. ir. Rua Sao Salvador 31, Apt C-01 ZC-01, Rio de Janeiro Brazil. **LC** K12.

LITUANISTIKA V SSSR : PRAVO. **VFOAT** Pravo. No. 1-. Periodical. UR. Russian. 0.45 Single Issue. Akademiia Nauk Litevskoi SSR, Lietuvos Tsr Mokslu Akademija Visuomenes Mokslu, Informacijos Sektorius Vilnius Lithuanian SSR, 232600, Lenin Avenue 3, Vilnius Lithuanian SSR.

LIVERPOOL LAW REVIEW. (THE LIVERPOOL LAW REVIEW). Vol. 1, 1 (Autumn 1979)-. 0144-932X. Periodical. UK. English. sa. 3.00. Law Department of Liverpool Polytechnic, Hamilton House 24 Pall Mall, Liverpool L3 6HR England. **Ind/Abst** Leg. Resour. Index, Index Leg. Period. **LC** K12. **DD** 349.4105, 344.1005.

LIVLEX TRABALHISTA. Portuguese. ir. Editorial Dimensao, rua da Quitada 45, 30. Andar GB, Rio de Janeiro Brazil.

LLOYD'S LAW REPORTS. 0024-5488. UK. English. mo. $320.00. LLP Maritime and Business Publishers, 87 Terminal Drive, Plainview New York 11803. Lloyd's List Law Reports.

LOAN OFFICER'S LEGAL ALERT. (LOAN OFFICERS LEGAL ALERT). Vol. 1, No. 1 (Feb. 1985)-. 8756-1522. Periodical. US. English. mo. $72.00. Bryant McGrath, 33 West 60th Street, New York NY 10023. **DD** 346.

LOCAL AND PRIVATE LAWS OF THE STATE OF MISSISSIPPI. **Main/Corp** Mississippi. US. English.

LOCAL BAR OFFICERS' ADVANCE SHEET. 0093-0156. US. English. ir. $7.00. Illinois State Bar Association, 424 South Second, Springfield IL 62701. **Tel** (217)525-1760. **LC** KF332.I4. **DD** 340.09773.

THE LOCAL GOVERNMENT APPEALS TRIBUNAL REPORTS OF NEW SOUTH WALES. **Main/Corp** New South Wales. Local Government Appeals Tribunal. V. 1- 1972/73-. AT. English. ir. Methuen Law Book Company Ltd, c/o Bennett EBSCO, 35 Mitchell Street, North Sydney New South Wales 2060 Australia. **DD** 346.944045.

LOCAL GOVERNMENT LAW BULLETIN. 0362-5729. US. English. University of North Carolina at Chapel Hill, Chapel Hill Institute of Government, Chapel Hill NC 27514. **LC** KFN7830.A15. **DD** 342.75609.

LOIS DU QUEBEC. (STATUTES OF QUEBEC). **Main/Corp** Quebec (Province). 1969-. 0318-4447. Periodical. CN. English (text in French). ir. 990. Les Publications du Quebec, 1283 West Boulevard Charest, Quebec Quebec G1N 2C9 Canada. **Tel** (418)643-5195. **DD** 348.714022. bk rev. (ctrl). The English edition of the title 'Lois du Quebec' - Laws of Quebec, contains basic collection and yearly updates can be ordered on subscription basis. Statuts de la Province de Quebec, 0318-4455.

LONG RANGE JUDICIAL FACILITY PLAN. **VFOAT** Colorado Judicial Facilities. 0734-0524. US. English. an. Office of the State Court Administrator, Two East Fourteenth Avenue, Denver CO 80203. **LC** NA4472.C6. **DD** 725.15.

THE LOS ANGELES BAR JOURNAL. V. 51- Sept. 1975-. Periodical. US. English. Los Angeles County Bar Association, Suite 1212/606 South Olive Street, Los Angeles CA 90014. **LC** Microfilm O. Los Angeles Bar Bulletin.

THE LOS ANGELES DAILY JOURNAL. Began in 1888. 0362-5575. Periodical. US. English. da. $105.00. Daily Journal Company, 210 South Spring Street, PO Box 54026, Los Angeles CA 90054. **Tel** (213)625-2141. **Ind/Abst** Leg. Resour. Index, Curr. Law Index.

LOS ANGELES LAWYER. V. 1- Mar. 1978-. 0162-2900. Periodical. US. English. $20.00. Los Angeles County Bar Association, PO Box 55020, Los Angeles CA 90055. **Tel** (213)627-2727. **Ed** Susan Pettit. **Ind/Abst** Leg. Resour. Index. **LC** KF200. **DD** 340.06279493. bk rev. adv acc. **Circ** 18,000. (ctrl). Official magazine of Los Angeles County Bar Association. Features, consumer opinion and scholarly legal articles. Profiles of Association programs and projects, tax tips, practice tips and calendar included. Los Angeles Bar Journal, 0362-837X.

LOUISIANA BAR JOURNAL. V. 1- July 1953-. 0459-8881. Periodical. US. English. bm. Louisiana State Bar Association, 225 Baronne Street/Suite 210, New Orleans LA 70112. **Ind/Abst** Index Leg. Period. **LC** UNC. Louisiana Bar.

LOUISIANA CASES REPORTED IN SOUTHERN REPORTER, SECOND SERIES. **Main/Corp** Louisiana. Supreme Court. **VFOAT** West's Louisiana Cases. 182 So. 2nd- 1966-. 0745-4589. US. English. wk. $65.00. West Publishing Company, 1413-K Street NW, St Paul MN 55165. **LC** KFL47. **DD** 345.42.

LOUISIANA CIVIL CODE. Began in 1980. US. English. an. $18.00. West Publishing Company, PO Box 3526, St Paul MN 55165.

LOUISIANA CIVIL LAW AND PROCEDURE NEWSLETTER. Periodical. US. English. bw. $75.00. LA Civil Law & Procedure Newsletter, 330 Sunset Boulevard, Baton Rouge LA 70808.

LOUISIANA COASTAL LAW. **VFOAT** LCL Report. No. 1- Sept. 1971-. Periodical. US. English. ir. Louisiana State University, Sea Grant Legal Program, 56 Law Center/LSU, Baton Rouge LA 70803.

LOUISIANA CORPORATE NEWSLETTER. V. 1- Apr. 1972-. Periodical. US. English. sa. Louisiana State Bar Association, 212 O'Keefe Avenue/Suite 600, New Orleans LA 70112. **LC** KFL213.A73. **DD** 346.73066.

LOUISIANA LAW REVIEW. V. 1- Nov. 1938-. Periodical. US. English. bm. $37.06. LSU Law Center, Baton Rouge LA 70803. **Tel** (504)388-1681. **Ed** Mark Dodart. **LC** Microfilm UL-074 K12. bk rev. adv acc. **Circ** 1,600. Law in general.

THE LOUISIANA LEGAL DIRECTORY. See Yearbooks, Almanacs, Directories.

LOUISIANA REGISTER. V. 1- Jan. 1975-. 0098-8545. US. English. mo. $50.00. Louisiana Office of the State Register, PO Box 94095, Baton Rouge LA 70804-9095. **Tel** (504)342-5015. **Ed** Nancy Midkiff. **LC** KFL34.A2. **DD** 348.76301. **Circ** 1,300. State Government rules and regulations.

LOV OG RETT. INNHOLDSREGISTER. 0024-6980. NO. Norwegian. ir. $52.00. Universitetsforlaget, PO Box 2959-Toyen, Oslo 6 Norway. **Tel** 02 27 60 60. **Ed** Anders Bratholm. bk rev. adv acc. **Circ** 5,300. The main professional journal for legal matters in Norway.

LOYOLA ENTERTAINMENT LAW JOURNAL. **VFOAT** Loyola of Los Angeles Entertainment Law Journal. Vol. 2 (1982)-. 0740-9370. Periodical. US. English. $15.00. Business Manager, Loyola of Los Angeles Entertainment Law Journal, 1441 West Olympic Boulevard, Los Angeles CA 90015. **Tel** (213)736-1114. **Ed** Russell Clampit. **Ind/Abst** Leg. Resour. Index. **LC** K5. **DD** 344.73099, 347.30499. bk rev. **Circ** 350. Current review of recent developments in entertainment law. Entertainment Law Journal (Loyola of Los Angeles School of Law), 0273-4249.

LOYOLA LAW REVIEW. Vol. 1, No. 1 (May 1941)-. 0192-9720. Periodical. US. English. qt. $16.00 Domestic, $17.00 Foreign. Loyola University, Box 17, 6363 St Charles Avenue, School of Law, New Orleans LA 70118. **Tel** (504)865-2253. **Ed** Willard H Henson. **Ind/Abst** Leg. Resour. Index, Index Contents Leg. Period., Curr. Law Index, Contents Curr. Leg. Period. bk rev. **Circ** 1,200. Provides the advancement of legal education and scholarship. Analization of noteworthy cases.

LOYOLA OF LOS ANGELES LAW REVIEW. Began with Jan. 1972 issue. 0147-9857. Periodical. US. English. qt. Loyola University/Los Angeles School of Law, 1441 West Olympic Boulevard, Los Angeles CA 90015. **Tel** (213)736-1125. **Ind/Abst** Leg. Resour. Index, Index Leg. Period. **LC** K12. **DD** 340.05. Loyola University of Los Angeles Law Review.

LOYOLA UNIVERSITY OF CHICAGO LAW JOURNAL. **VFOAT** Loyola University Law Journal. V. 1- Winter 1970-. 0024-7081. Periodical. US. English. qt. $15.00. Loyola University of Chicago, 1 East Pearson Street, Chicago IL 60611. **Tel** (312)670-2945. **Ind/Abst** Leg. Resour. Index, Index Leg. Period. **LC** K12. **DD** 340.05. Index in last issue of volume - attached.

LPBA JOURNAL. **Main/Corp** Lawyer-Pilots Bar Association. **VAT** Lawyer Pilots Bar Association Journal. V. 1- Msr./Apr. 1980-. 0274-9319. Periodical. US. English. mo. $45.00. Lawyer Pilot Bar Association, John Yodice, 7315 Wisconsin Avenue, Bethesda MD 20014. **LC** KF2400.A15. **DD** 343.7309705, 347.3039705. Legal Eagles News, 0024-0354.

LRB SUMMARIES. (LRB SUMMARIES : SUMMARIES OF EVERY IMMIGRATION AND NATURALIZATION OPINION OF FEDERAL COURTS). **VFOAT** L.R.B. Summaries. 0740-2554. Periodical. US. English. mo. $30.00. Legal Research Bureau, PO Box 374, Kew Gardens NY 11415. **LC** KF4814. **DD** 342.7308202648, 347. 3028202648.

LRE PROJECT EXCHANGE. **VFOAT** L.R.E. Project Exchange. **VAT** Law-Related Education Project Exchange. Vol. 1, No. 1 (Spring 1981)-. 0734-0990. Periodical. US. English. ty. Free. YEFC American Bar Association, 1155 East Sixteenth Street, Chicago IL 60637. **LC** KF4208.5.L3. **DD** 340.071273.

LRE REPORT. **VFOAT** L.R.E. Report. **VAT** Law-Related Education Report. Vol. 1, No. 1 (Winter 1980)-. 0731-9711. Periodical. US. English. ty. American Bar Association, 750 North Lake Shore Drive, Chicago IL 60611. **Tel** (312)988-5725.

LUCKNOW LAW TIMES. Began with Jan. 1960 issue. Periodical. English. ir. Eastern Book Co, 34 Lalbagh, Lucknow 226 001 India. **Tel** 43171. **LC** Law. bk rev. adv acc. **Circ** 6,000. Contains acts, ordinances, rules and notifications of the central and U.P. governments, notifications of the Allahabad High Court, Supreme Court of India, Central and U.P. Board of Revenue and Allahabad Bar Council.

LUZERNE LEGAL REGISTER REPORTS. **VFOAT** Kulp's Luzerne Legal Register Reports. V. 1- 1882-. Periodical. US. English. ir. **Ed** G B Kulp.

L A M NEWS. **Main/Corp** Legal Aid Services Society of Manitoba. No. 1- Nov. 1974-. 0319-5740. Periodical. CN. English. ir. Legal Aid Services, Society of Manitoba, 325 Portage Avenue, Winnipeg Manitoba R3B 2B9 Canada.

MAANDSTATISTIEK POLITIE EN JUSTITIE. See Statistics.

MCKINNEY'S NEW YORK RULES OF COURT. (MCKINNEY'S NEW YORK RULES OF COURT : STATE AND FEDERAL). **VFOAT** New York Rules of Court. 1982-. 0747-7872. US. English. an. $16.00. West Publishing Company Inc, 170 Old

Law

Country Road, Mineola NY 11501. **LC** KFN5992. **DD** 347.747051, 347.470751. *New York Court Rules, 0747-8429.*

MCKINNEY'S SESSION LAWS OF NEW YORK. **Main/Corp** New York (State). 1951-. US. English. an. West Publishing Company, 170 Old Country Road, Mineola NY 11501. **LC** KFN5025. **DD** 345.12.

MADHYA PRADESH WEEKLY NOTES. **VFOAT** M.P. Weekly Notes. English. ir. .40. Law Journal Publications, Jayendraganj, Gwalior - 1 India. **DD** 348.543046, 345.430846.

MADHYAPRADSESA RAJAPATRA. **Main/Corp** Madhya Pradesh (India). English (Hindi). wk. **LC** Law.

MAGISTRATE (KAMPALA, UGANDA). (THE MAGISTRATE : JOURNAL OF THE UGANDA MAGISTRATES' ASSOCIATION). Vol. 1, No. 1 (Mar. 1972)-. Periodical. English. ir.

A MAGYAR ALLAM- ES JOGTUDOMANYI IRODALOM BIBLIOGRAFIAJA. 0209-8792. Hungarian. ir.

MAGYAR JOG (MAGYAR JOGASZ SZOVETSEG : 1982). (MAGYAR JOG : MJ). **VFOAT** MJ. 0025-0147. Periodical. Hungarian. mo. Magyar Jogasz Szovetseg, Szalay Utca 16, Budapest V Hungary. **LC** K13. *Magyar Jog Es Kulfoldi Jogi Szemle.*

MAHARASHTRA BAR COUNCIL JOURNAL. **Main/Corp** Bar Council of Maharashtra. Periodical. English. ir. 12.00. Bar Council of Maharashtra, High Court Extension 32, Bombay India. **DD** 340.0954792.

MAINE LAW REVIEW. Began with Apr. 1908 issue. 0566-2338. Periodical. US. English. sa. $14.00. University of Maine, School of Law, 246 Deering Avenue, Portland ME 04102. **Tel** (207)780-4357. **Ind/Abst** Index Leg. Period., Leg. Resour. Index, Curr. Law Index, Contents Curr. Leg. Period. **LC** K13. **Circ** 1,200. (ctrl). Scholarly analysis of current legal issues written by legal professionals, both teaching and practising, and by students of the University of Maine School of Law. *Maine Law Review, Portland University Law Review.*

MAINE LAW REVIEW (PORTLAND, ME. : 1963). (MAINE LAW REVIEW). Vol. 15 (1963)-. 0886-1854. Periodical. US. English. sa. University of Maine School of Law, 246 Deering Avenue, Portland ME 04102. **Ind/Abst** Index Leg. Period. **LC** K13. **DD** 340.05. Each issue contains an index to its own contents - no vol index - loose. Available on microfilm. *University of Maine Law Review.*

THE MAINE PROSECUTOR. BAIL MANUAL. (THE MAINE PROSECUTOR : BAIL MANUAL). **Main/Corp** Maine. Dept. of Attorney General. **VFOAT** Bail Manual. Jan. 1975-. 0148-5571. US. English. Department of Attorney General, State House, Augusta ME 04330. **LC** KFM576.6. **DD** 345.741072.

MAINE PROSECUTOR BULLETIN. (THE MAINE PROSECUTOR BULLETIN). Nov. 1973-. 0094-5439. US. English. mo. Law Enforcement Education Section, Criminal Division, Augusta ME 04330. **LC** KFM575.A73. **DD** 345.7410505.

THE MAINE PROSECUTOR. CRIMINAL LEGISLATION MANUAL. (THE MAINE PROSECUTOR, CRIMINAL LEGISLATION MANUAL). **VFOAT** Criminal Legislation Manual. 0098-079X. US. English. Law Enforcement Education Section, Department of the Attorney General, State House, August ME 04330. **LC** KFM562.A29. **DD** 345.74105.

MAINE REGISTER, STATE YEAR-BOOK AND LEGISLATIVE MANUAL. See Yearbooks, Almanacs, Directories.

MAINE REPORTER. **Main/Corp** Maine. Supreme Judicial Court. V. 215- 1966-. 0273-0944. US. English. an. West Publishing Company, 50 Kellogg Boulevard, St Paul MN 55102. **LC** KFM45. **DD** 345.52.

MAINE RULES OF COURT, WITH AMENDMENTS. **Main/Corp** Maine. Courts. US. English. an. West Publishing Company, 1413 K Street NW, St Paul MN 55165. **LC** KFM529. **DD** 347.741051.

MAJALAH FAKULTAS HUKUM UNIVERSITAS AIRLANGGA. V. 1, No. 1, (Apr./June 1980)-. Periodical. English (Indonesian). qt. Sedretariat, JLN Airlanggo No 4, Surabaya Indonesia. **LC** K13. **DD** 349.59805, 345.98005.

MAJALAH FAKULTAS HUKUM UNIVERSITAS INDONESIA. **Main/Corp** Universitas Indonesia. Fakultas Hukum. Began with Aug. 1971 issue. Periodical. IO. Indonesian. ir. Universitas Indonesia, Fakultas Hukum, J1 Teuku Umar 46, Jakarta Indonesia. **LC** K25.

MAJALLAT KULLIYAT AL-SHARIAH. **Main/Corp** Jamiat Al-Qarawiyin. Kulliyat Al-Shariah. Periodical. Arabic. ir. Jamiat Al-Qarawiyin Kulliyat Al-Shariah, PO Box 1728, Al-Atlas Fas, Al-Maghrib United Arab Republic (Egypt). **DD** 340.5905.

MAJOR LABOR-LAW PRINCIPLES ESTABLISHED BY THE N.L.R.B. AND THE COURTS. (MAJOR LABOR-LAW PRINCIPLES ESTABLISHED BY THE NLRB AND THE COURTS). **Main/Corp** Bureau of National Affairs, (Washington, D.C.). 0094-0313. US. English. $15.00 Per Copy. Bureau of National Affairs, 1231 25th Street Northwest, Washington DC 20037. **LC** KF3314. **DD** 344.7301.

MAJOR LEGISLATION OF THE CONGRESS. **VFOAT** MLC. 0277-2183. US. English. ir. US Government Printing Office, Superintendent of Documents, Washington DC 20402. **Tel** (202)783-3238. **LC** KF42. **DD** 348.7326, 347.30826. **NLM** W 33 AA1 M2. *Legislative Status Report.*

MAJOR RECOMMENDATIONS OF THE REGENTS FOR LEGISLATIVE ACTION. **Main/Corp** New York (State). University. Dec. 1966-. 0093-9935. US. English. an. The University of the State of New York, The State Education Department, Albany NY 12234. **LC** L182.G5. **DD** 379.747. *Major Proposals of the State Board of Regents for Legislative Action.*

MAL DE BLOCS. (LE MAL DE BLOCS : BULLETIN DE L'ASSOCIATION DES LOCATAIRES DE LONGUEUIL). No. 1 (Oct./Nov. 79)-. 0228-7838. Periodical. CN. French. bm. Free. L'Association, Le Mal de Blocs, Suite 102/832 Chemin Chambly, Longueuil Quebec J4H 3M1 Canada. **DD** 346.7140434.

MALAWI GOVERNMENT GAZETTE. Periodical. US. English. **LC** Microfilm LL-02195KRK.

MALAYA LAW REVIEW. Vol. 1, July 1959. 0542-335X. Periodical. Sl. English. sa. $22.50. Secretary Malaya Law Review, Faculty of Law, National University of Singapore, Kent Ridge, Singapore 0511 Singapore. **Tel** 7756666. Ed Lim Lin Heng. **Ind/Abst** Public Aff. Inf. Serv. Bull. (cum index). bk rev. adv acc. Legal journal of law articles, casenotes, legislation, comments, etc. on law in Singapore, Malaysian and Asian Countries. *University of Malaya Law Review.*

THE MALAYAN LAW JOURNAL. V. 1- July 1932-. 0025-1283. Periodical. Sl. English. mo. $123.48. Malayan Law Journal, 3 Shenton Way #1403, Singapore 0106 Republic of Singapore. **Tel** 2203684. Ed Al-Mansor Adabi. **DD** 349.595, 347.05. bk rev. adv acc. Publisher of the monthly journal, the Malayan Law Journal, sole law of court cases for Singapore, Malaysia and Brunei.

MALAYSIAN ACTS OF PARLIAMENT. **Main/Corp** Malaysia. **VFOAT** Acts of Parliament. 1980-. English. an. Malaysian Law Publishers, Room 201/2nd Floor Lee Yan Lian Building, Jalan Tun Perak Kuala Lumpur. **DD** 348.595023, 345.950823. *Acts Passed.*

MALAYSIAN CURRENT LAW JOURNAL. **VFOAT** Current Law Journal. Sept. 1981-. 0127-0699. Periodical. English. mo. $96.00. Malaysian Current Law Journal Sdn Bhd, Room 201/2nd Floor, Lee Yan Lian Building, Jln Tun Perak, Kuala Lumpur Malaysia. **LC** K13. **DD** 340.05.

MALPRACTICE DIGEST. 0094-6133. US. English. bm. St Paul Fire & Marine Insurance Company, Professional Liability Risk Management Department, 385 Washington Street, St Paul MN 55102. **LC** KF1289.A73. **DD** 346.7303305.

MALPRACTICE PREVENTION FOR HOSPITALS. V. 1- Jan. 1979-. 0193-6166. Periodical. US. English. David Karp Associates, 24 Fremont Road, San Rafael CA 94902. **LC** KFC6173.A15. **DD** 346.794033.

MALPRACTICE PREVENTION FOR PHYSICIANS. 0276-0495. Periodical. US. English. **LC** KF2905.3.A15. **DD** 346.730332, 347.306332.

MALPRACTICE PREVENTION REPORTER. Vol. 1, No. 1-. 0739-6031. Periodical. US. English. qt. $40.00 US and Canada, $55.00 Others. Duke Nordlinger Stern & Associates Incorporated, 1336 54th Avenue NE, St Petersburg FL 33703. **Tel** (813)527-1212. Ed Duke Nordlinger Stern. **LC** KF318. **DD** 346.73033, 347.30633. bk rev. **Circ** 5,000. Systems, procedures and techniques for preventing legal malpractice. Includes forms, annotated claims digests, reviews and bibliographies.

THE MALPRACTICE REPORTER. (THE MALPRACTICE REPORTER : MPR). **VFOAT** MPR. 0738-1026. Periodical. US. English. bm. $78.00. Public Reporting Services Inc, 496 Hudson Street #424, New York City NY 10014. **Tel** (212)989-8303. **LC** KF2905.3.A15. **DD** 346.73033205, 347.30633205. **Circ** 2,500. Comprehensive reporting for the medical, legal and health service communities on medical malpractice, drugs and devices.

THE MALPRACTICE REPORTER. ANESTHESIOLOGY. (THE MALPRACTICE REPORTER. ANESTHESIOLOGY : MPR). **VFOAT** Anesthesiology. 0738-1018. Periodical. US. English. bm. $78.00. Public Reporting Services Inc, 496 Hudson Street Suite 424, New York City NY 10014. **Tel** (212)989-8303. Ed Neil Fabricant. **LC** KF2910.A53. **DD** 346.730332, 347.306332. **Circ** 2,500. Comprehensive reporting for the medical, legal, health services and insurance communities on medical malpractice, drugs and devices.

THE MALPRACTICE REPORTER. HOSPITALS. (THE MALPRACTICE REPORTER. HOSPITALS : MPR). **VFOAT** Hospitals. 0738-1956. Periodical. US. English. bm. $78.00. Public Reporting Services Inc, 496 Hudson Street Suite 424, New York City NY 10014. **Tel** (212)989-8303. Ed Neil Fabricant. **LC** KF3825.3.A59. **DD** 346.73031, 347.30631. **Circ** 2,500. Comprehensive reporting for the medical, legal and health service community on medical malpractice, drugs and devices.

THE MALPRACTICE REPORTER. OB/GYN. (THE MALPRACTICE REPORTER. OB/GYN : MPR). **VFOAT** OB/GYN. 0738-1948. Periodical. US. English. bm. $128.00. Public Reporting Services Inc, 424 Hudson Street/Suite 424, New York NY 10014. **LC** KF2910.G943. **DD** 346.730332, 347.306332.

THE MALPRACTICE REPORTER. PODIATRY. (THE MALPRACTICE REPORTER. PODIATRY : MPR). **VFOAT** MPR. Vol. 1, No. 1 (July-Aug. 1984)-. 0749-3495. Periodical. US. English. bm. $78.00. Public Reporting Services Inc, 496 Hudson Street Suite 424, New York City NY 10014. **Tel** (212)989-8303. Ed Neil Fabricant. **DD** 346. **Circ** 2,500. Comprehensive reporting for the medical, legal and health service communities on medical malpractice, drugs, and devices.

THE MALPRACTICE REPORTER. SURGEON'S. (THE MALPRACTICE REPORTER. SURGEON'S : MPR). **VFOAT** Surgeon's. 0738-1964. Periodical. US. English. bm. $128.00. Public Reporting Services Inc, 424 Hudson Street/Suite 424, New York NY 10014. **LC** KF2905.3.A59. **DD** 346.73033205, 347.30633205.

MANAGING LEGALLY. **VFOAT** M.L. Aug. 1982-. 0747-5268. Periodical. US. English. mo. $39.44. Quinlan Publishing Company Inc, 131 Beverly Street, Boston MA 02114. **LC** KF3464.A59. **DD** 344.7301133, 347.3041133. (cum index). *Employee Discrimination Reporter.*

MANITOBA AND SASKATCHEWAN SUCCESSION DUTY AND GIFT TAX LEGISLATION. **Main/Corp** Manitoba. 2d- Ed. 0317-0306. Periodical. CN. English. CCH Canadian Ltd, 6 Garamond Court, Don Mills Ontario M3C 1Z5 Canada. **DD** 343.712705302632. *Manitoba and Saskatchewan Succession Duty and Gift Tax Acts, 0317-0314.*

MANITOBA DECISIONS. CIVIL AND CRIMINAL CASES. (MANITOBA DECISIONS, CIVIL AND CRIMINAL CASES). 1975-. 0380-0008. CN. English. mo. 190. Western Legal Publications, 301 - 1 Alexander Street, Vancouver British Columbia V6A 1B2 Canada. **Tel** (604)687-5671. **DD** 348.7127048. Digests of all available civil and criminal decisions from the Manitoba Court of Appeal, Court of Queen's Bench and County Courts filed by subjects.

MANITOBA LAW JOURNAL. V. 2- 1966-. 0076-3861. Periodical. CN. English. ty. 25.00. University of Manitoba, Robson Hall, Winnipeg 19 Manitoba R3T 2N2 Canada. **Tel** (204)474-9773. Ed Jill Duncan. **Ind/Abst** Curr. Law Index, Contents Curr. Leg. Period., Leg. Resour. Index, Index Leg. Period. **LC** K13. **DD** 349.712705. bk rev. adv acc. **Circ** 700. Scholarly publication of comments, analysis and criticism of judicial decisions, legislation and legal developments at the federal and provincial level.

Law

Manitoba Law School Journal, 0381-5587; Manitoba Bar News News.

MANITOBA REPORTS (FREDERICTON, N.B. : BOUND CUMULATION). (MANITOBA REPORTS). 2nd Ser., V. 1 (1979)-. 0713-7109. Periodical. CN. English. ir. $65.00 Each Volume. Maritime Law Book Ltd, PO Box 302, Fredericton New Brunswick E3B 4Y9 Canada. DD 348.7127043. Manitoba Reports, 0713-7109.

MANITOBA STATUTES AND RULES OF COURT JUDICIALLY CONSIDERED. VFOAT Western Weekly Reports. 1954/56-. CN. English. LC KEM60. DD 348.7127026, 347.1270826.

MANUAL DE CONSULTAS TRIBUTARIAS. CL. Spanish. mo. Ediciones Tecnicas Tributarias Ltda, Casilla 3571, Santiago de Chile. DD 343.8305205, 348.3035205.

MANUAL FOR COMPLEX AND MULTIDISTRICT LITIGATION. Main/Corp Federal Judicial Center. US. English. ir. Matthew Bender & Company Inc, 1275 Broadway, Albany NY 12201. Tel (800)833-9844.

MANUAL FOR THE USE OF THE LEGISLATURE OF THE STATE OF NEW YORK. Main/Corp New York (State). Dept. of State. 1840-. US. English. an. Department of State, 162 Washington Avenue, Albany NY 12231. LC JK3430. DD 320.9747.

MANUAL. NEW YORK BUILDING LAWS. Main/Corp New York Society of Architects. 1st Ed- 1911-. US. English. ir. $16.24. New York Society of Architects, 275 Seventh Avenue 15 Floor, New York NY 10001. Tel (212)675-6646. Ed Robert Friedlander. bk rev. adv acc. Circ 3,000. Nycadmincode buildings, housing maintanance code/multiple dwelling law plus updating service.

MANUAL - SOCIETY FOR THE RIGHT TO DIE. Main/Corp Society for the Right to Die. 1979/80-. 0198-8786. US. English. an. Society for the Right to Die, 250 West 57th Street, New York NY 10019. Tel (212)246-6973. Ed Peg Cameron. LC KF3827.E87. DD 344.730419. Circ 15,000. Comprehensive guide to recent developments in the right to die movement. Includes text and analysis of living will laws and checklist comparison chart of key provisions. Legislative Manual (New York. 1975), 0193-550X.

MANUEL FISCAL CANADIEN. VFOAT Renseignements Fiscaux Canada. First issue in 1975?. 0709-8057. CN. French. an. Free. DD 343.71052.

MARINE AFFAIRS BIBLIOGRAPHY. See Indexes/Abstracts.

MARINE FISHERIES MANAGEMENT REPORTER. No. 1 (Aug. 1982)-. 0730-3394. Periodical. US. English. ir. $375.00. Jonathan Publishing Company, 1152 Ingleside, Baton Rouge LA 70806. Tel (504)387-6098. Ed Gary Knight. Circ 150. Five-volume, loose-leaf service covering all documents related to marine fisheries management - statutes, treaties, regulations, legal opinions.

THE MARITIME ADVISOR. Vol. 1, No. 1 (Feb. 18, 1981)-. 0731-1486. Periodical. US. English. mo. $440.00. Maritime Advisory Services Inc, Suite 3147/One World Trade Center, New York NY 10048. LC KF1101.3. DD 343.7309602648, 347. 3039602648.

THE MARITIME LAWYER. V. 1- Mar. 1975-. 0099-0620. US. English. sa. $15.00. Tulane Maritime Law Society, Tulane University School of Law, New Orleans LA 70118. Tel (504)865-5959. Ed Andrew Bushspaum. Ind/Abst Leg. Resour. Index, Index Leg. Period., Curr. Law Index. LC K13. DD 343.7309605. bk rev. adv acc. Circ 1,000. A law review devoted exclusively to the law of admiralty, with particular emphasis on areas of current interest to the practicing admiralty bar.

MARQUETTE LAW REVIEW. V. 1- Dec. 1916-. 0025-3987. Periodical. US. English. qt. $15.00. Marquette University Law School, 1103 West Wisconsin Avenue, Milwaukee WI 53233. Tel (414)278-8696. Ed David Sarnacki. Ind/Abst Leg. Resour. Index, Public Aff. Inf. Serv. Bull., Index Leg. Period., Curr. Law Index, Contents Curr. Leg. Period. (cum period). bk rev. adv acc. Circ 1,300. (ctrl). Critical Analysis of developing areas of the law.

MARTINDALE-HUBBELL LAW DIRECTORY. See Yearbooks, Almanacs, Directories.

MARTIN'S ANNUAL CRIMINAL CODE. Main/Corp Canada. 1957-. 0527-7892. Periodical. CN. English. an. Canada Law Book Ltd, 80 Cowdray Court, Agincourt Ontario M1S 1S5 Canada. Ed J C Martin. DD 345.71. The Criminal Code of Canada.

MARTIN'S RELATED CRIMINAL STATUTES . . . . Main/Corp Canada. 1980-. 0710-1805. CN. English. an. Canada Law Book, 240 Edward Street, Aurora Ontario L4G 3S9 Canada. DD 345.71.

MARYLAND ADVANCE REPORTS. Main/Corp Maryland. Court of Appeals. VFOAT Cases Adjudged in the Court of Appeals of Maryland. 0199-0926. US. English. wk. West Publishing Company, PO Box 43526, St Paul MN 55164. DD 340. Advance Reports, Maryland Reports, Maryland Appellate Reports.

MARYLAND APPELLATE REPORTS, CASES ADJUDGED IN THE COURT OF SPECIAL APPEALS OF MARYLAND. Main/Corp Maryland. Court of Special Appeals. V. 1- 1967-. Periodical. US. English. ir. Michie Company, Box 7587, Charlottesville VA 22902. LC KFM1761. DD 343.09752.

THE MARYLAND BAR JOURNAL. V. 1- Oct. 1968-. 0025-4177. Periodical. US. English. mo. $15.00. Maryland Bar Journal, Suite 905/207 East Redwood Street, Baltimore MD 21202. Tel (301)685-7878. Ed N Polvinale. Ind/Abst Index Leg. Period. LC K13. DD 340.062752. adv acc. Circ 11,000. (ctrl). Evolves around law and law related ideas. Includes new legislation and current events relating to law.

MARYLAND LAW REVIEW. V. 1- Dec. 1936-. 0025-4282. US. English. ir. $20.00. University of Maryland School of Law, 500 West Baltimore Street, Baltimore MD 21201. Tel (301)528-7414. Ed Will Kaulbach. Ind/Abst Leg. Resour. Index, Public Aff. Inf. Serv. Bull., Index Leg. Period., Curr. Law Index, Contents Curr. Leg. Period. (cum index). bk rev. adv acc. Circ 2,200. Deals with all law topics. Publishes articles on specific topics, case analyses of critical cases and a general survey of developments in Maryland law.

MARYLAND LAWYERS' MANUAL. US. English. an. $50.00. Maryland State Bar Association, 905 Keyser Building, Calvert and Redwood Streets, Baltimore MD 21202. Tel (301)685-7878. Ed Michael Ruby. LC KF192.M36. DD 340.025752. adv acc. Circ 15,500. (ctrl). Directory of Maryland attorneys.

THE MARYLAND PROSECUTOR. 0748-2957. Periodical. US. English. D H Hugel State's Attorneys' Coordinator, 500 West Baltimore Street, Baltimore MD 21201. LC KFM1777.A15. DD 345.752005, 347.5205005.

MARYLAND REGISTER. V. 1- Oct. 17, 1974-. 0360-2834. US. English. bw. $75.00. Maryland Division of State Documents, PO Box 802, Annapolis MD 21404. Tel (301)269-2486. Ed Robert J Colborn Jr. LC KFM1234.A2. DD 348.752025. Circ 2,500. (ctrl). State rules and regulations, state contracts bids and awards executive orders. Legislative information, legislative bills, administrative rules from courts and procedures.

THE MARYLAND RESEARCHER. Began with July 1970 issue. 0047-6099. Periodical. US. English. mo. National Legal Research Group Inc, PO Box 7187, Charlottesville VA 22906. LC KFM1257. DD 348.752026.

MASSACHUSETTS ATTORNEY DISCIPLINE REPORTS : DECISIONS OF THE SUPREME JUDICIAL COURT OF MASSACHUSETTS. Main/Corp Massachusetts. Supreme Judicial Court. Vol. 1 (Sept. 1974-Dec. 1979)-. US. English. an. Butterworth Legal Publishers, 381 Elliot Street, Newton Upper Falls MA 02164. LC KFM2476.5.A2. DD 347.7440504, 347.40447504.

MASSACHUSETTS DECISIONS REPORTED IN NORTH EASTERN REPORTER, SECOND SERIES. 0744-818X. Periodical. US. English. wk. West Publishing Company, 50 West Kellogg Boulevard, St Paul MN 55165. DD 348.

MASSACHUSETTS DISCRIMINATION LAW REPORTER. (MDLR/MASSACHUSETTS DISCRIMINATION LAW REPORTER). V. 1- 1979-. 0199-5235. Periodical. US. English. mo. $185.00. New England Legal Publishers, PO Box 48, Boston MA 02101. Tel (617)891-6200. Ed Joseph Ambash. Each issue contains an index to its own contents - no vol index - loose. Circ 100.

THE MASSACHUSETTS FAMILY LAW JOURNAL. Vol. 1, No. 1 (Apr. 1983)-. Periodical. US. English. bm. $65.00. Butterworth Legal Publishers, 381 Elliot Street, Newton Upper Falls MA 02164. LC KFM2494.A15. DD 346.74401505, 347.44061505.

MASSACHUSETTS LAW REVIEW. V. 63- Jan./Feb. 1978-. 0163-1411. Periodical. US. English. qt. Massachusetts Bar Association, 20 West Street, Boston MA 02111. Tel (617)542-3602. Ed Philip M Cronin. Ind/Abst Leg. Resour. Index, Index Leg. Period. LC K13. DD 349.74405, 347.44005. adv acc. Circ 14,300. (ctrl). Scholarly legal publication. Massachusetts Law Quarterly.

MASSACHUSETTS LAWYERS DIARY AND MANUAL INCLUDING BAR DIRECTORY. (MASSACHUSETTS LAWYERS DIARY AND MANUAL : INCLUDING BAR DIRECTORY). VFOAT Lawyers Diary and Manual. 0738-369X. US. English. an. Massachusetts Lawyers Diary & Manual, PO Box 1232, Newark NJ 07101. LC KF192.M38. DD 340.025744. Lawyers Diary and Manual.

MASSACHUSETTS LAWYERS WEEKLY. VFOAT Lawyers Weekly. Began in 1972. 0196-7509. US. English. wk. $125.00. Massachusetts Lawyers Weekly, 30 Court Square, Boston MA 02128. Tel (617)227-6034. Ed Jane C Avery. LC K13. DD 349.74405. bk rev. adv acc. Circ 7,800. Court opinions summaries, bar association news, judges, courtroom assignments, front page news on the legal profession, seminar listings, court announcements on new rules, advertisements, etc.

MASSACHUSETTS LEGAL DIRECTORY, WITH RHODE ISLAND SECTION. See Yearbooks, Almanacs, Directories.

MASSACHUSETTS LEGISLATIVE DIRECTORY. See Yearbooks, Almanacs, Directories.

THE MASSACHUSETTS PROBATE COURTS ANNUAL REPORT. VFOAT Statistics and Report of the Probate Courts of the Commonwealth of Massachusetts as Reported by the Registers of Said Courts Under Chapter 819 of the Acts 1963 and as Compiled by the Chief Judge of the Probate Courts. 0148-7612. US. English. an. LC KFM2544. DD 346.744050269.

MASSACHUSETTS REGISTER. Periodical. US. English. wk. $125.00. Commonwealth of Massachusetts State House, St Bookstore/Room 102, Boston MA 02133. Tel (617)727-2834. LC KFM2436. DD 348.744025.

THE MASSACHUSETTS RESEARCHER. Began with July 1970 issue. 0047-6153. Periodical. US. English. mo. National Legal Research Group Inc, PO Box 7187, Charlottesville VA 22906. Tel (800)446-1870. LC KFM2457. DD 348.744046.

MASSCITIZEN. VFOAT Mass Citizen. VAT Massachusetts Citizen. Began with issue for Winter 1981. 8750-8516. Periodical. US. English. qt. Masspring/Publications Department, 37 Temple Place, Boston MA 02111. DD 328.

IL MASSIMARIO DEL FORO ITALIANO. IT. Italian. mo. $49.90. Nicola Zanichelli Editore, Casella Postale 227, 401000 Bologna Italy.

MASSIMARIO DI GIURISPRUDENZA DEL LAVORO. See Economics - Labor.

M.A.T.A. NEWSLETTER. (MATA NEWSLETTER). Main/Corp Missouri Association of Trial Attorneys. V. 1- Sept./Oct. 1973-. 0094-2995. US. English. 823 Walnut Street, Kansas City MO 64106. LC KF200. DD 347.77807062.

MATERIALI PER UNA STORIA DELLA CULTURA GIURIDICA. Main/Corp Genoa. Universita. Istituto di Filosofia del Diritto. 1- 1971-. IT. Italian. sm. 100.000 Domestic. 120.000 Foreign. Societa Editrice Il Mulino Spa, Via Santa Stefano 6, 40125 Bologna Italy. Tel 051/ 23 34 15. Ed G Tarello.

THE MATRIMONIAL LAW REPORTER. II. English. ir. 40.00. Matrimonial Law Reporter, 33/34 Gohale Mkt, Delhi 110006 India. DD 346.5401602642.

MAURITIUS LAW REVIEW. VFOAT Revue de Droit, de Doctrine, et de Jurisprudence Mauricienne. V. 1, No. 1, (Aug. 1977)-. Periodical. MF. English (French). ir. Mauritius Law Review, rue Jules Koenig, Port Louis Ile Maurice. LC K13. DD 340.05.

MD/PC. (MD/PC : MEDICAL LAW AND PRACTICE MANAGEMENT). VFOAT Medical Law and Practice Management. Vol. 1, No. 1-. 0735-4436. Periodical.

Law

US. English. Biomedical Information Corporation, 800 2nd Avenue, New York NY 10017. LC KF3821.A15. DD 344.73041, 347.30441.

MEALEY'S LITIGATION REPORT. NATIONAL TORT REFORM. VFOAT National Tort Reform. 0888-3114. Periodical. US. English. sm. $550.00. Mealey Publications, PO Box 446, Wayne PA 19087.

MEALEY'S LITIGATION REPORTS. ASBESTOS. VFOAT Asbestos. Feb. 10, 1984-. 0742-4647. Periodical. US. English. sm. $650.00. Mealey Publications, Box 446, Wayne PA 19087. Tel (215)688-6566. Ed Michael P Mealey. LC KF3964.A73. DD 344.73021, 347.30421. bk rev. Complete coverage of health and property damage claims involving asbestos.

MEALEY'S LITIGATION REPORTS. INSURANCE. VFOAT Insurance. Nov. 1984-. 8755-9005. Periodical. US. English. sm. $350.00. Mealey Publications, PO Box 446, Wayne PA 19087. Tel (215)688-6566. LC KF1147. DD 346.7308605, 347.3068605. bk rev. Document and editorial coverage of declaratory judgment actions involving insurance coverage for latent disease and property damage.

MEDDELELSER FRA STATSSKATTEDIREKTORATET OG LIGNINGSRADET. Main/Corp Denmark. Statsskattedirektoratet. Danish. ir. Meldahlsgade 5, 1613 Kbenhavn Denmark.

MEDIA LAW NOTES. (MEDIA LAW NOTES : NEWSLETTER FOR THE LAW DIVISION OF AEJ & THE MASS COMMUNICATIONS LAW SECTION OF AALS). 0736-1750. Periodical. US. English. qt. Free to Members, $10.00 to Non Members. Communications Media Center, New York Law School, 57 Worth Street, New York NY 10013. Ind/Abst Leg. Resour. Index. LC KF2750.A15. DD 343.7309905, 347.3039905. *Tortfeasor.*

MEDIA LAW REPORTER. Main/Corp Bureau of National Affairs (Washington, D.C.). VFOAT Media Law Reporter. 1-. US. English. wk. $452.00. Bureau of National Affairs Inc, 1231 25th Street NW, Washington DC 20037. Tel (202)452-4580. Ed Cynthia J Bolbach. bk rev. Circ 1,200. Reports on court decisions and other developments affecting the media.

MEDIATION QUARTERLY. (MEDIATION QUARTERLY : JOURNAL OF THE ACADEMY OF FAMILY MEDIATORS). VFOAT Mediation Quarterly Series. No. 1 (Sept. 1983)-. 0739-4098. Periodical. US. English. qt $40.00. Jossey-Bass Inc, 433 California Street, San Francisco CA 94104. Tel (415)433-1767. Ed John Allen Lemmon. LC KF9084.A15. DD 347.73905, 347.307905. Circ 1,200. Discusses techniques, applications, research, and theory of mediation as an alternative to litigation and a tool for resolving family-related conflicts.

THE MEDICAL LAW LETTER FOR PHYSICIANS, SURGEONS & HEALTH PROFESSIONALS. 0098-4833. Periodical. US. English. mo. $60.00. Medical Law Publications, 663 Fifth Avenue, New York NY 10022. LC KF1289.A15. DD 346.73033.

MEDICAL LIABILITY ADVISORY SERVICE. 0199-1272. Periodical. US. English. mo. Capitol Publications Inc, 1300 North 17th Street, Arlington VA 22209. Tel (703)528-5400. LC KF2905.3.A15. DD 346.730332, 347.306332. NLM W1 ME366H.

MEDICAL LIABILITY REPORTER. V. 1- Sept. 1979-. 0199-1833. US. English. mo. Litigation Research Group, PO Box 77903, San Francisco CA 94101. Tel (415)543-5433. Ed Kevin Bushnell. Ind/Abst Contents Curr. Leg. Period. LC KF2905.3.A59. DD 346.73033202648. (cum index). Circ 825. Summaries and analyses of recent appellate decisions, trends and developments of interest to people in the medical field.

MEDICAL MALPRACTICE LAW & STRATEGY. VFOAT Medical Malpractice Law and Strategy. Began in 1983. 0747-8925. Periodical. US. English. mo. $95.00. Leader Publications, 111 8th Avenue, New York NY 10011. Tel (800)221-8195. Ed Cynthia Cooper. DD 346. Reports on judicial and legislative developments in medical malpractice law; includes verdicts, settlements, articles on negotiation and litigation strategy by practitioners.

MEDICAL MALPRACTICE LAW & STRATEGY. VFOAT Medical Malpractice Law and Strategy. 0748-5026. Periodical. US. English. mo. $135.00. Leader Publications Inc, 111 8th Avenue, New York NY 10011. LC KF2905.3.A15. DD 346.73033205, 347.30633205.

MEDICAL MALPRACTICE LITIGATION. Series/Titl Litigation Course Handbook Series. 0277-7266. US. English. Practising Law Institute, 810 Seventh Avenue, New York NY 10019. LC KF2905.3.Z9. DD 346.730332, 347.306332.

MEDICAL MALPRACTICE LITIGATION REPORTER. Apr. 2, 1985-. 0882-8555. Periodical. US. English. sm. $600.00. Andrews Publications Inc, PO Box 200, 5123 West Chester Pike, Edgemont PA 19028. Tel (215)353-2565. Ed Leonard E B Andrews. DD 346. The national journal of record for medical malpractice litigation in the United States.

MEDICAL TRIAL TECHNIQUE QUARTERLY. ANNUAL. (MEDICAL TRIAL TECHNIQUE QUARTERLY ANNUAL). 1954/55-. 0161-3251. US. English. an. Callaghan & Company, 6141 North Cicero Avenue, Chicago IL 60643. NLM W1 ME5279. (cum index).

MEDICINE AND LAW. Vol. 1, No. 1 (June 1982)-. 0723-1393. Periodical. US. English. bm. $68.00. Springer Verlag-New York Inc, 175 5th Avenue, New York NY 10010. Tel (212)460-1500. Ed Amnon Carmi. Ind/Abst Excerpta Med., Index Med. LC K13. DD 344.04105, 342.4105. NLM W1 ME649F. An international publication dealing with medico-legal issues. Contains articles, court-decisions, and legislation on medical law, forensic medicine, medicine and law, psychiatry and law, psychology and law, and more.

MEDICOLEGAL NEWS CEASED. V. 1-9, No. 3. 0097-0085. Periodical. US. English. qt. Free to Members, $10.00 Nonmembers. American Society of Law and Medicine, 454 Brookline Avenue, Boston MA 02215. LC KF3821.A15. DD 344.7304105. NLM W1 ME768V.

MEDIZINRECHT : MEDR. VFOAT MEDR. V. 1, 1 (Jan./Feb. 1983)-. 0723-8886. Periodical. German. bm. $53.50. LC KK6206.A13. DD 344.4304105, 344.3044105. NLM W1 ME856.

MEIJI DAIGAKU KEIJI HAKUBUTSUKAN MOKUROKU. No. 1-. JA. Japanese. ir. Meiji Daigaku Keiji Hakubutsukan Iinkai, 1 Kanda Surugakai 1, Chiyoda-ku, Tokyo Japan. LC Z3306, DS803.

MEIJI DAIGAKU KEIJI HAKUBUTSUKAN NEMPO. 1-. JA. Japanese. ir. 1 Kanda Surugadai Chiyoda-ku, Tokyo Japan. LC DS803.

MELANESIAN LAW JOURNAL. Vol. 1, No. 1 (Dec. 1970)-. 0254-0657. English. sa. Ind/Abst Leg. Resour. Index. LC K13. DD 340.05.

MELDINGER OM JORDLOV OG KONSESJONSLOV. V. 1, No. 1, (June 1978)-. 0333-0818. Norwegian. ir.

MEMBERSHIP DIRECTORY - AMERICAN ACADEMY OF FORENSIC SCIENCES. See Yearbooks, Almanacs, Directories.

MEMBERSHIP DIRECTORY - AMERICAN PREPAID LEGAL SERVICES INSTITUTE. See Yearbooks, Almanacs, Directories.

MEMBERSHIP ROSTER OF THE AMERICAN SOCIETY OF HOSPITAL ATTORNEYS. Main/Corp American Society of Hospital Attorneys. VFOAT Roster of Membership - American Society of Hospital Attorneys. 0148-6330. US. English. American Hospital Association, 840 North Lake Shore Drive, Chicago IL 60611. LC KF195.H67. DD 340.02573.

MEMENTO PRATIQUE FRANCIS LEFEBVRE : AGRICULTURE. FR. French. ir. 15 rue Viete, 75017 Paris France. DD 343.4407605, 344.4037605.

MEMENTO PRATIQUE FRANCIS LEFEBVRE. COMPTABLE. FR. French. ir. 5 rue Jacques Bingen, 75017 Paris France. DD 346.44063, 344.40663.

MEMENTO PRATIQUE FRANCIS LEFEBVRE : FISCAL. 1976-. FR. French. an. $23.41. Editions Francis Lefebvre, 5 rue Jacques Bingen, 75854 Paris Cedex 17 France. DD 343.4404. *Memento Pratique du Contribuable.*

MEMENTO PRATIQUE FRANCIS LEFEBVRE : SOCIAL. FR. French. ir. Editions Francis Lefebvre, 15 rue Viete, 75017 Paris France. DD 344.4402.

MEMENTO PRATIQUE FRANCIS LEFEBVRE : SOCIETES COMMERCIALES. FR. French. an. Editions Lefebvre, 15 rue Viete, 17 Paris France. DD 346.44066, 344.40666. *Memento Pratique des Societes Commerciales.*

MEMOIRES DE LA SOCIETE POUR L'HISTOIRE DU DROIT ET DES INSTITUTIONS DES ANCIENS PAYS BOURGUIGNONS, COMTOIS ET ROMANDS. Main/Corp Societe pour l'Histoire du Droit et des Institutions des Anciens Pays Bourguignons, Comtois et Romands, Dijon. No. 1-. French. ir. (cum index).

MEMORIA DEL . . . FORO NACIONAL DE NOTARIADO Y REGISTRO. Main/Conf Foro Nacional de Notariado y Registro. Spanish. ir. LC KHH250.A15. DD 347.861016, 348.610716.

MEMORIE VAN VRAGEN EN ANTWOORDEN - COMMISSIE VOOR ALGEMENE EN JURIDISCHE ZAKEN. Main/Corp North Holland (Netherlands). Commissie voor Algemene en Juridische Zaken. Dutch. ir.

MEMPHIS STATE UNIVERSITY LAW REVIEW. VFOAT Memphis State Law Review. V. 1, No. 1 (Fall 1970)-. 0047-6714. Periodical. US. English. qt. $14.00. Memphis State University, School of Law, Memphis TN 38152. Ed Carol Chumney. Ind/Abst Leg. Resour. Index, Index Leg. Period., Curr. Law Index, Contents Curr. Leg. Period. LC K24. DD 340.05. (cum index). bk rev. Circ 700. Available on microfilm from University Microfilms International. Scholarly legal journal including works by students, faculty, and legal professionals. Concentrating primarily on Tennessee law. *Memphis State University Law Commentary,* 0543-4467.

MENSCH + RECHT : QUARTALSZEITSCHRIFT DER SCHWEIZERISCHEN GESELLSCHAFT FUR DIE EUROPAISCHE MENSCHENRECHTSKONVENTION (SGEMKO). VFOAT Mensch und Recht. Nr. 1 (May 1981)-. Periodical. German. qt. 12.50. SGEMKO, Postfach 10, 8127 Forch Germany. Tel (01)980-0454. Ed Ludwig A Minelli. LC K13. DD 342.4085, 344.0285. adv acc. Circ 13,000. Covers European Convention of Human Rights and Switzerland, Swiss courts and human rights; human rights policy of Switzerland.

MENTAL AND PHYSICAL DISABILITY LAW REPORTER. VFOAT MPDLR. Vol. 8, No. 1 (Jan.-Feb. 1984)-. 0883-7902. Periodical. US. English. bm. American Bar Association, 1800 M Street NW, Washington DC 20036. Ind/Abst Leg. Resour. Index. LC KF480.A15. DD 344.73044, 347.30444. NLM W1. *Mental Disability Law Reporter,* 0147-3700.

MENTAL DISABILITY LAW REPORTER CEASED. V. 1-7, No. 6. 0147-3700. Periodical. US. English. bm. $35.00. American Bar Association, Committee on the Mentally Disabled, 1800 M Street NW, Washington DC 20036. Ind/Abst Psychol. Abstr. LC KF480.A15. DD 344.7304405. NLM W1 ME9229M.

MENTAL HEALTH AND DEVELOPMENTAL DISABILITIES CODE, WITH ANNOTATIONS OF REQUIRED FORMS. Main/Corp Illinois. US. English. LC KFI1565.A333. DD 344.773044, 347.730444.

MENTAL HEALTH LAW REPORTER. Vol. 1, No. 1 (May 1983)-. 0741-5141. Periodical. US. English. mo. $87.00. Capitol Publications Inc, 1300 North 17th Street, Arlington VA 22209. LC KF480.A15. DD 345.7304, 347.3054.

MENTAL HYGIENE LAW. Main/Corp New York (State). Laws, Statutes, etc. 0164-2650. US. English. an. Matthew Bender & Company Inc, 1275 Broadway, Albany NY 12201. Tel (800)833-9844. LC KFN5620.A29. DD 344.747044.

MENTAL RETARDATION AND THE LAW. 0098-8111. US. English. President's Committee on Mental Retardation, 330 Independence Avenue Southwest, Washington DC 20201. LC KF480.A59. DD 344.730323. NLM W1 ME936JF.

MERCANTILE GAZETTE. Periodical. English. bw. $27.00. D N Adams Ltd, 8 Sheffield Crescent, Christchurch 5 New Zealand. LC HF4030.5. DD 658.8009931. *New Zealand Mercantile Gazette.*

MERCER LAW REVIEW. Vol. 1, No. 1 (Fall 1949)-. 0025-987X. Periodical. US. English. qt. $24.00. Mercer University School of Law, Macon GA 31207.

Law

Tel (912)744-2622. Ed Catharine Cox. Ind/Abst Leg. Resour. Index, Index Leg. Period., Curr. Law Index, Contents Curr. Leg. Period. DD 340.05. (cum index). bk rev. adv acc. Circ 1,800. (ctrl) Legal Periodical.

MEREDITH MEMORIAL LECTURES. 1975-. 0821-3690. Periodical. CN. French (English). an. DD 346.71066. *W. C. J. Meredith Memorial Lectures, 0509-5166.*

METADATA'S LEGALGRAM FOR THE COMMUNICATONS INDUSTRY. VFOAT Metadata's Legalgram. Vol. 1, No. 1 (Apr. 8, 1980)-. 0197-7458. Periodical. US. English. sm. $137.00. Metadata Inc, 441 Lexington Avenue, New York NY 10017. LC KF2750.A15. DD 343.7309905, 347.3039905.

MICHIE'S TEXAS TORT REPORTER. VFOAT Texas Tort Reporter. Began in 1984. 0742-3780. Periodical. US. English. mo. $130.00. The Michie Company, PO Box 7587, Charlottesville VA 22906. Tel (804)295-6171. LC KFT1395.A59. DD 346.7640302648, 347.6406302648. Service analyzing current tort cases in Texas.

MICHIGAN APPELLATE DIGEST. 0196-7649. Periodical. US. English. mo $90.00. Michigan Appellate Digest, 600 Washington Square Building, Lansing MI 48933. Tel (517)373-3869. LC KFM4248.1. DD 348.774046.

MICHIGAN BAR JOURNAL. (THE MICHIGAN BAR JOURNAL). V. 58- Jan. 1979-. 0164-3576. Periodical. US. English. mo. $25.00. State Bar of Michigan, 306 Townsend Street, Lansing MI 48933. Tel (517)372-9030. Ed Nancy F Brown. Ind/Abst Leg. Resour. Index, Index Leg. Period., Curr. Law Index. LC KF200. DD 349.7305. bk rev. adv acc. Circ 25,000. Journal of the State Bar of Michigan; includes substantial law articles as well as organization business. *Journal (State Bar of Michigan), 0162-5101.*

MICHIGAN DIGEST. US. English. ir.

MICHIGAN LAW REVIEW. Vol. 1, No. 1 (June 1902)-. 0026-2234. Periodical. US. English. ir. $32.00. University of Michigan, School of Law, 621 South State Street, Ann Arbor MI 48109-1215. Tel (313)763-5870. Ind/Abst Manage. Contents, Leg. Resour. Index, Index Leg. Period., Hospit. Lit. Index, Index Econ. Artic. J. Collect. Vol., Account. Index. Suppl., ABI/Inform, Writ. Am. Hist., Public Aff. Inf. Serv. Bull., Curr. Law Index, Soc. Sci. Citation Index, Contents Curr. Leg. Period. LC K13. DD 340.05. NLM W1 MI216. (cum index). bk rev. adv acc. Circ 3,000. A scholarly legal publication.

MICHIGAN LEGISLATIVE HANDBOOK. US. English. be. Secretary Senate W C Kandler, PO Box 30036, Michigan Senate, Lansing MI 48909. *Michigan Legislative Directory.*

THE MICHIGAN RESEARCHER. Began with June 1970 issue. 0047-7133. Periodical. US. English. mo. $99.00. National Legal Research Group Inc, PO Box 7187, Charlottesville VA 22906. Tel (800)446-1870. LC KFM4257. DD 348.744026.

MICHIGAN RULES OF COURT. 1984-. 8756-3568. Periodical. US. English. an. $17.50. West Publishing Company, 50 West Kellogg Boulevard, PO 64526, St Paul MN 55164. LC KFM4729. DD 347.774051, 347.740751. *Michigan Court Rules.*

MICHIGAN WORKERS' COMP DIGEST. Vol. 1, No. 1 (Dec. 1982)-. 0746-1461. Periodical. US. English. mo. $52.00. Pathfinder Associates Incorporated, 208 California Avenue, North Muskegon MI 49445. LC KFM4542.A59. DD 344.77402105, 347.74042105.

MIDWEST AGRICULTURAL LAW JOURNAL. Vol. 1, No. 1 (Oct./Nov. 1983)-. 0738-6753. Periodical. US. English. bm. $75.00. Mason Publishing Company, 366 Waucota Street, St Paul MN 55109-1989. LC KF1681.A15. DD 343.7707605, 347.7037605.

MIDWEST LABOR & EMPLOYMENT LAW JOURNAL. VFOAT Midwest Labor and Employment Law Journal. Vol. 1, No. 1 (Oct./Nov 1983)-. 0738-6761. Periodical. US. English. bm. $75.00. Mason Publishing Company, 366 California Street, St Paul MN 55109-1989. LC KF3302. DD 344.7701, 347.7041.

MIDWESTERN ADVOCATE. 0360-5094. Periodical. US. English. mo. Midwestern Advocate, 1536 Hewitt Avenue, St Paul MN 55104. LC KF292.M56414. DD 340.05.

MIFFLIN COUNTY LEGAL JOURNAL. V. 1-. US. English. ir. William Gaunt and Sons, 3011 Gulf Drive, Holmes Beach FL 33510. LC KFP52.M5.

MILITARY LAW REPORTER. 1973. 0193-3906. Periodical. US. English. bm. $270.00. Public Law Education Institute, 1346 Conn Avenue NW/Suite 610, Dupont Circle Building, Washington DC 20036. Tel (202)296-7590. Ed Lawrence M Baskir. Circ 550. Covers Judicial and administrative developments relating to the Armed Forces, National Guard, Vets benefits, civilian employees of military and all aspects of selective service law.

MILITARY LAW REVIEW. 1-. 0026-4040. Periodical. US. English. qt. US Government Printing Office, Superintendent of Documents, Washington DC 20402. Tel (202)783-3238. Ind/Abst Leg. Resour. Index, Index Leg. Period., ABC Pol Sci, Public Aff. Inf. Serv. Bull., Index U.S. Gov. Period., Curr. Law Index, Soc. Sci. Citation Index, Contents Curr. Leg. Period. LC K13. DD 343.7301. (cum index).

THE MILWAUKEE LAWYER. V. 1- Fall 1976-. 0148-3242. Periodical. US. English. qt. $12.00. Milwaukee Bar Association, 610 East Wisconsin Avenue, Milwaukee WI 53202-4604. Tel (414)274-6760. Ed Arthur J Harrington and Alyson K Sloan. LC KF200. DD 340.06277595. adv acc. Circ 5,000. All articles are law related and most written by attorneys or judges. *MBA Gavel.*

MINI-RECUEIL DE RENSEIGNEMENTS FISCAUX. 0821-0799. CN. French. an. Free. Mini-Recueil de Renseignements Fiscaux/Coopers & Lybrand, 630 Ouest Boul Dorchester, Montreal Quebec H3B 1W5 Canada. DD 343.7105205. (ctrl).

DE MINIMIS. Began with May 1966 issue. 0418-4432. US. English. McGeorge School of Law University of the Pacific, 3200 Fifth Avenue, Sacramento CA 95817. LC KF292.M314. DD 340.071179454.

MINNESOTA BUSINESS & COMMERCIAL LAW JOURNAL. VFOAT Minnesota Business and Commercial Law Journal. Vol. 1, No. 1 (May 1982)-. 0732-3425. Periodical. US. English. bm $75.00. Mason Publishing Company, 366 Wacouta Street, St Paul MN 55101-1989. LC KFM5552.A15. DD 346.7760705, 347.7606705.

MINNESOTA FAMILY LAW JOURNAL. Vol. 1, No. 1 (Nov. 1981)-. 0278-761X. Periodical. US. English. bm. $65.00. Mason Publishing Company, 366 Wacouta Street, St Paul MN 55101-1989. LC KFM5494.A15. DD 346.77601505.

MINNESOTA JOURNAL OF TRIAL ADVOCACY. Vol. 1, No. 1 (June 1982)-. 0732-3433. Periodical. US. English. bm. $75.00. Mason Publishing Company, 366 Wacouta Street, St Paul MN 55101-1989. LC KFM5938.A1. DD 347.7760705, 347.7607705.

MINNESOTA LAW ALUMNI NEWS. VFOAT Minnesota Law School News. V. 20, No. 2- Spring 1970-. 0540-2239. Periodical. US. English. bm. University of Minnesota, 285 Law Building/229 19th Avenue South, Minneapolis MN 55455. LC KF292.M57. DD 340.0711776579. *Law School News.*

MINNESOTA LAW REPORTS. Vol. 1, No. 1 (Oct. 15, 1982)-. 0734-7693. Periodical. US. English. sm. $155.00. Mason Publishing Company, 366. Wacouta Street, St Paul MN 55101-1989. LC KFM5445. DD 348.776043, 347.760843.

MINNESOTA LAW REVIEW. Vol. 1, No. 1 (Jan. 1917)-. 0026-5535. Periodical. US. English. ir. $12.50. Law School University of Minnesota, 229 19th Avenue South, Minneapolis MN 55455. Ind/Abst Leg. Resour. Index, Index Leg. Period., ABC Pol Sci. LC K13.

MINNESOTA LAW REVIEW; JOURNAL OF THE STATE BAR ASSOCIATION. V. 7-. Periodical. US. English. bm. $17.50. Minnesota Law Review Foundation, 285 Law Building, 229 19th Avenue South, Minneapolis MN 55455. Ind/Abst Public Aff. Inf. Serv. Bull., Soc. Sci. Citation Index, Index Leg. Period., Curr. Law Index, Leg. Resour. Index, ABC Pol Sci, Contents Curr. Leg. Period.

THE MINNESOTA LEGAL DIRECTORY. *See* Yearbooks, Almanacs, Directories.

MINNESOTA LEGAL REGISTER. V. 1- Jan. 17, 1968-. 0026-5543. Periodical. US. English. mo. $33.00. Register-Mirror, 1414 Soo Line Building, Minneapolis MN 55402.

MINNESOTA MOTOR VEHICLE LAW. US. English. ir. Mason Publishing Company, 366 Wacouta Street, 802 Finch Building, St Paul MI 55101.

MINNESOTA REAL ESTATE LAW JOURNAL. Vol. 1, No. 1 (Nov./Dec. 1981)-. 0278-7628. Periodical. US. English. bm. $65.00. Mason Publishing Company, 366 Wacouta Street, St Paul MN 55101-1983. LC KFM5512.A15. DD 346.7304305, 347.3064305.

MINSHARIM, TSAVIM VE-HODAOT SHEL MIFKEDET EZOR RETSUAT AZAH. Main/Corp Israel. Tseva Haganah Le-Yisrael. Mifkedet Ezor Retsuat Azah. Vol. 32- 1972-. Arabic and Hebrew. ir. *Minsharim, Tsavim Ve-Hodaot.*

MINUTES OF CONVOCATION CEASED. Main/Corp Law Society of Upper Canada. Began with: Vol. 1, in 1976. CN. English. Law Society of Upper Canada, Osgoode Hall, Toronto Ontario M5H 2N6 Canada.

MINUTES OF PROCEEDINGS AND EVIDENCE OF THE SPECIAL COMMITTEE ON REGULATORY REFORM. Main/Corp Canada. Parlement. Chambre des Communes. Comite Special sur la Reforme de la Reglementation. VFOAT Proces-Verbaux et Temoignages du Comite Special sur la Reforme de la Reglementation. Issue No. 1 (Sept. 16, 1980)-. 0710-6327. Periodical. CN. text in English and French in parallel columns. ir. Queen's Printer for Canada, Receiver General for Canada, Ottawa Ontario K1A 0S9 Canada. DD 348.71025.

MINUTES OF PROCEEDINGS AND EVIDENCE OF THE SPECIAL COMMITTEE ON STANDING ORDERS AND PROCEDURE. Main/Corp Canada. Parliament. House of Commons. Special Committee on Standing Orders and Procedure. Vol. No. 1 (June 22/29, 1982)-. 0715-8386. Periodical. CN. English (French). Canadian Government Publishing Centre, Supply and Services Canada, Hull Quebec K1A 0S9 Canada. LC KE4658.A23. DD 328.710505.

MINUTES OF PROCEEDINGS AND EVIDENCE OF THE STANDING COMMITTEE ON MANAGEMENT AND MEMBERS' SERVICES. Main/Corp Canada. Parlement. Chambre des Communes. Comite Permanent de la Gestion et des Services aux Deputes. VFOAT Proces-Verbaux et Temoignages du Comite Permanent de la Gestion et des Services aux Deputes. No. 1- Oct. 24, 1979-. 0228-0825. Periodical. CN. French (text also in English with French in parallel columns). Imprimeur de la Reine pour le Canada, c/o Receiver General for Canada, Ottawa Ontario K1A 0S9 Canada. DD 328.710731.

MINUTES OF PROCEEDINGS AND EVIDENCE OF THE SUB-COMMITTEE OF THE STANDING COMMITTEE ON AGRICULTURE ON FARM CREDIT ARRANGEMENTS. RELATIFS AU CREDIT AGRICOLE. Main/Corp Canada. Parliament. House of Commons. Sub-Committee of the Standing Committee on Agriculture on Farm Credit Arrangements. VFOAT Proces-Verbaux et Temoignages du Sous-Comite du Comite Permanent de l'Agriculture Charge d'Etudier les Accords Relatifs au Credit Agricole. Relatifs au Credit Agricole. No. 1 (Mar. 24/29, 1983)-. 0825-0146. CN. English (French). Canadian Government Publishing Centre, Supply & Services Canada, Hull Quebec K1A 0S9 Canada. LC KE1700.A23. DD 343.710760262, 347.103760262.

MINUTES OF PROCEEDINGS AND EVIDENCE OF THE SUB-COMMITTEE ON INDIAN WOMEN AND THE INDIAN ACT OF THE STANDING COMMITTEE ON INDIAN AFFAIRS AND NORTHERN DEVELOPMENT. Main/Corp Canada. Parliament. House of Commons. Sub-Committee on Indian Women and the Indian Act. VFOAT Indian Women and the Indian Act. Issue No. 1 (Sept. 1/8, 1982)-. 0825-012X. CN. English (French in parallel columns). Canadian Government Publishing Centre, Supply & Services Canada, Hull Quebec K1A 0S9 Canada. LC KE7722.W6. DD 342.710872, 347.102872.

MINUTES OF PROCEEDINGS OF THE ANNUAL CONFERENCE - ASSOCIATION OF SUPERINTENDENTS OF INSURANCE OF THE PROVINCES OF CANADA. Main/Corp Association of Superintendents of Insurance of the Provinces of Canada. Began with 1927 issue. 0315-7253. Periodical. CN. English. an. $19.35. Association of Superintendents of Insurance of the Provinces of Canada, 555 Yonge Street/6th Floor, Toronto Ontario M4Y 1Y7 Canada. DD 346.7108606171.

MISSISSIPPI CASES REPORTED IN THE SOUTHERN REPORTER, SECOND SERIES. Main/Corp Mississippi. Supreme Court. 182 So. 2d- 1966-. US. English. ir. LC KFM6645.

Law

MISSISSIPPI CODE 1972, ANNOTATED : ADOPTED AS THE OFFICIAL CODE OF THE STATE OF MISSISSIPPI BY THE 1972 SESSION OF THE LEGISLATURE. Main/Corp Mississippi. US. English. ir. $350.00. Harrison Company Publishing, 3110 Crossing Park, Norcross GA 30091. (cum index).

MISSISSIPPI COLLEGE LAW REVIEW. V. 1- June 1978-. 0277-1152. Periodical. US. English. sa. $8.00. Mississippi College Law Review, 151 East Griffith Street, Jackson MS 39201. Tel (601)944-1950. Ed Irene Howard. Ind/Abst Leg. Resour. Index, Index Leg. Period. LC K13. DD 340.09762. bk rev. adv acc. A student publication dealing with timely subjects in the law. Primarily Mississippi and Fifth-Circuit Oriented.

MISSISSIPPI LAW JOURNAL. V. 1- July 1928-. 0026-6280. Periodical. US. English. qt. $18.00. Mississippi Law Journal, PO Box 146, University MS 38677. Tel (601)232-7361. Ed Ralph C Brashier. Ind/Abst Leg. Resour. Index, Index Leg. Period. LC K13. DD 349.76205. (cum index). bk rev. adv acc. Circ 1,500. Publishes articles, comments, recent decisions, and book reviews in all areas of law. Contributors include academicians, attorneys, and law students.

MISSISSIPPI LAW JOURNAL. CUMULATIVE TEN-YEAR INDEX FOR VOLUMES 41-50. See Indexes/Abstracts.

THE MISSISSIPPI LEGAL DIRECTORY. See Yearbooks, Almanacs, Directories.

MISSOURI CASES REPORTED IN SOUTH WESTERN REPORTER, SECOND SERIES. Main/Corp Missouri. Supreme Court. VFOAT West's Missouri Cases. 0745-7642. US. English. wk. $65.00. West Publishing Company, 50 West Kellogg Boulevard, PO Box 3526, St Paul MN 55165. DD 340. *Missouri Decisions Reported in South Western Reporter, Second Series.*

MISSOURI JOURNAL OF DISPUTE RESOLUTION. Vol. 1984-. 0748-0768. Periodical. US. English. an. $7.00. Associate Editor/Missouri Law Review, 107 Tate Hall University of Missouri, Columbia MO 65211. DD 347.

MISSOURI JUDICIAL REPORT. Main/Corp Missouri. Office of State Courts Administrator. FY 1981/1982-. US. English. an. Office of State Courts Administrator, 1105 Rear Southwest Boulevard, Jefferson City MO 65101. LC KFM7871. DD 347.77801305, 347.78071305. *Annual Statistical Report, 0731-4000.*

MISSOURI JUVENILE COURT STATISTICS. See Statistics.

MISSOURI LAW FINDER. 1983 Ed.-. US. English. an. West Publishing Company, 50 West Kellogg Boulevard, PO Box 3526, St Paul MN 55165.

MISSOURI LAW REVIEW. V. 1- Jan. 1936-. 0026-6604. US. English. qt. $17.00. University of Missouri-Columbia Tate Hall School of Law, Columbia MO 65211. Tel (314)882-7055. Ed Ed Reeves. Ind/Abst Leg. Resour. Index, Public Aff. Inf. Serv. Bull., Index Leg. Period., Curr. Law Index, Contents Curr. Leg. Period. LC K13. (cum index). bk rev. adv acc. Circ 1,200. Publish articles, case notes and comments concerning all areas of law for use by legal practitioners, law students and law professors. *Law Series.*

THE MISSOURI LEGAL DIRECTORY. See Yearbooks, Almanacs, Directories.

MISSOURI REGISTER. Main/Corp Missouri. Office of the Secretary of State. V. 1- May 3, 1976-. 0149-2942. Periodical. US. English. mo. $56.00. Missouri Register, Secretary of State Administrative Rules Division, PO Box 778, Jefferson City MO 65102. Tel (314)751-3367. Ed Carolan Underwood. LC KFM7834.A2. DD 348.778025. Circ 850. Rules on agriculture, medicine, business, environment, education, conservation, housing, professional registration, mental health, medicare, aging, drugs, and law enforcement, affecting Missouri citizens.

MISSOURI RULES OF COURT, STATE AND FEDERAL. VFOAT Missouri Rules of Court. 1st. Ed. (1968)-. 0732-6556. US. English. an. West Publishing Company, 50 West Kellogg Boulevard, PO Box 3526, St Paul MN 55165. LC KFM8329. DD 347.778051, 347.780751.

MISSOURI'S PUBLIC DEFENDER AND APPOINTED COUNSEL PROGRAMS. 1978/79-. US. English. an. Public Defender Commission, 1105 Rear Southwest Boulevard, Jefferson City MO 65101. LC KFM8377. DD 345.77801. *Public Defender & Appointed Counsel Programs.*

MITTEILUNGEN - ARBEITSGEMEINSCHAFT FUR JURISTISCHES BIBLIOTHEKS- (GERMANY). Main/Corp Arbeitsgemeinschaft fur Juristisches Bibliotheks- und Dokumentationswesen (Germany). GW. German. ir. Mittelweg 187, 2 Hamburg 13 West Germany. LC Law.

THE MLA REPORT. VFOAT M.L.A. Report. VAT Maritime Law Association Report. Feb. 25, 1983-. 0742-762X. Periodical. US. English. sa. Maritime Law Association of the United States, One State Street Plaza, New York NY 10004. LC KF1097. DD 343.7309605, 347.3039605.

THE MOBAR BULLETIN. VFOAT Bulletin. Began with issue for Aug. 1974. 0732-1392. Periodical. US. English. qt. $2.00. Missouri Bar Association, 326 Monroe Street, Jefferson MO 65101. LC KF200. DD 340.060778.

MODERN CONSTITUTIONAL LAW. 1969-. US. English. ir. Lawyers Co-Operative Publishing Company, Aqueduct Building Broad Street, Rochester NY 14603. Index in last issue of volume - attached.

MODERN LAW AND SOCIETY. V. 1- 1968-. 0026-7953. GW. English. sa. 35,00. German Studies, Landhausstrasse 18, D7400 Tuebingen West Germany. Tel 07071/21882. Ind/Abst Sociol. Abstr., Soc. Welf. Soc. Plan./Policy Soc. Dev. DD 016.3. bk rev. Circ 2,000. (ctrl). Review of German language research contributions on law, political science, and sociology (with bibliographies).

MODERN LAW REPOTS, EMBODYING CASES DECIDED BY THE SUPREME COURT OF THE REPUBLIC OF SRI LANKA. Main/Corp Sri Lanka. Sresthadhikaranaya. V. 1- July 1975-. English or Sinhalese. ir. 2.50. C L Perera, 29/12 Visaka Road 4, Colombo Sri Lanka. DD 348.5493041.

MODERN LAW REVIEW. (THE MODERN LAW REVIEW). V. 1- June 1937-. 0026-7961. Periodical. UK. English. bm. Modern Law Review Ltd, 11 New Fetter Lane, London EC4 England. Ed R S T Chorley. Ind/Abst Leg. Resour. Index, Index Leg. Period. LC K13. Index published separately - free - automatically sent. (cum index)

MODERNE BESIGHEIDSREG : MB. VFOAT MB. Vol. 1, No. 1(Mar. 1979)-. Periodical. SA. Afrikaans (English). ty. 9.95. Butterworth & Company, 152-154 Gale Street, Durban 4001 South Africa. DD 346.680705, 346.806705.

MOHAN ROPPO. Main/Corp Japan. Japanese. ir. Sanseido, 1 Kanda Jimbocho 1, Chiyoda-ku 101 Tokyo Japan. *Mohan Roppo Zensho.*

MONASH UNIVERSITY LAW REVIEW. V. 1- Aug. 1974-. 0311-3140. Periodical. English. sa. 14.00. Monash University, Faculty of Law, Clayton Victoria 3168 Australia. Tel (03)541-0811. Ed Debra Mortimer and Stuart Brown. Ind/Abst APAIS, Aust. Public Aff. Inf. Serv., Leg. Resour. Index, Index Leg. Period., Curr. Law Index. LC K13. DD 340.0994. bk rev. adv acc. Microform.

MONATSSCHRIFT FUR DEUTSCHES RECHT. Vol. 1- Apr. 1947-. Periodical. GW. German. mo. $70.57. Dr Otto Schmidt KG, Postfach 511026, Ulmenallee 96-98, D5000 Koeln 51 West Germany. Tel 02 21/ 37 30 21. Ed K Mittelstein.

MONDE JURIDIQUE. (LE MONDE JURIDIQUE). Vol. 1, No 1 (Autumn 1984)-. 0828-4989. Periodical. CN. French. qt. 26.00. Le Monde Juridique, 381 Boul Richelieu, Saint-Basile-Le-Grand Quebec J0L 1S0 Canada. Tel (514)286-9283. Ed Andre Gagnon. DD 349.714. bk rev acc. adv acc. Circ 16,000. (ctrl). The legal profession with news about the law, how it is practiced, trends and features concerning major firms, small firms and lawyers and notaries and judges in Quebec, Canada and the world and court management.

MONEXICO : REVISTA DEL CONSEJO DE ESTADO. Series 2, No. 1, (Nov. 1982)-. Periodical. Spanish. ir. LC J183. DD 354.72850005.

MONITEUR BELGE. Main/Corp Belgium. VFOAT Belgisch Staatsblad. Began publication in 1831. Periodical. US. Dutch and French. da. Moniteur Belge, Rue Louvain 40-42, B-1000 Bruxelles Belgium. LC Microfilm LL-02131KJM.

LE MONITEUR, JOURNAL OFFICIEL DE LA REPUBLIQUE D'HAITI. Main/Corp Haiti (Republic). US. French.

MONITOR POLSKI. Main/Corp Poland. Began publication in 1918. US. Polish. LC Law.

MONOGRAPH : LEGAL AND ADMINISTRATIVE SERIES. Main/Corp European Broadcasting Union. VFOAT EBU Monograph. No. 4?-. Monographic Series. English. ir. European Broadcasting Union, Ancienne Rt 17A/Case Postale 193, CH 1211 Geneva 20 Switzerland. Tel 98 77 66. Series of monographs on administrative and legal aspects of radio and television broadcasting. *Legal Monograph, 0531-2841.*

MONOGRAPH SERIES - AMERICAN BAR ASSOCIATION. SECTION OF LITIGATION. Main/Corp American Bar Association. Section of Litigation. No. 1- 1976-). Monographic Series. US. English. ir. American Bar Association, 750 North Lake Shore Drive, Chicago IL 60611. Tel (312)988-5555.

MONOGRAPH SERIES - CRIMINAL LAW EDUCATION AND RESEARCH CENTER. Main/Corp New York University. Criminal Law Education and Research Center. 0590-0875. Monographic Series. US. English. ir. New York University, School of Law, Criminal Law Education and Research Center, New York NY 10003. CODEN CLEMA.

MONROE LEGAL REPORTER. V. 1- 1938/39-. 0275-0791. US. English. ir. William W Gaunt and Sons Inc, 3011 Gulf Drive, Homes Beach FL 33510. Ed C E De Puy. DD 348.74788044.

MONTANA CODE ANNOTATED : ADOPTED BY CHAPTER 1, LAWS OF 1979. Main/Corp Montana. Periodical. US. English. $150.00. Montana Legislative Council, Room 138 Capitol Station, Helena MT 59620. Tel (406)444-3064. Ed Legislative Council. Circ 3,200. Annotations to titles 1-90 of the MCA statute text-supplemental materials used in interpreting what has happened to the statutes i.e. case notes, attorney general opinions, supreme court decisions.

MONTANA LAW REVIEW. Vol. 1, No. 1 (Spring 1940)-. 0026-9972. Periodical. US. English. sa. University of Montana, Law School Association, Missoula MT 59801. Tel (406)243-2023. Ed Jacqueline Terrell. Ind/Abst Leg. Resour. Index, Index Leg. Period., Curr. Law Index, Contents Curr. Leg. Period. Index published separately - free - automatically sent. (cum index). adv acc. Circ 2,600. Legal publication with primary emphasis on issues of Montana law. *Proceedings of the Montana Bar Association, 0272-8281.*

THE MONTANA LAWYER. 0276-3788. Periodical. US. English. mo. $10.00. State Bar of Montana, PO Box 4669, 2030 11th Avenue, Helena MT 59604. Tel (406)442-7660.

MONTGOMERY COUNTY LAW REPORTER. V. 1- 1885-. US. English. wk. Montgomery Bar Association, 100 West Airy Street, Norristown PA 19401. Tel (215)279-9660. LC Microfilm LL0165 KFP52.M65.

MONTHLY BUSINESS & TAX BULLETIN. VAT Monthly Business and Tax Bulletin. 0115-1657. Periodical. English. ir. 45.00. The Tax Quarterly of the Philippines, Shurdut Building/Suite 506, Intramuros, PO Box 100 P A, Manila Philippines. DD 343.5990405.

THE MONTHLY LAW DIGEST. English. mo. 30.00 Each Issue. Monthly Law Digest Office, Katchery Road, Lahore Pakistan.

MONTHLY REPORT - ONTARIO LABOUR RELATIONS BOARD. See Economics - Labor.

MONTHLY ROLL CALL. Main/Corp Conservative Caucus Research, Analysis & Education Foundation. 0162-7678. Periodical. US. English. mo. Conservative Caucus Research Analysis and Education Foundation, 7777 Leesburg Pike/Suite 315, Falls Church VA 22043. LC JK1319. DD 328.730775.

MOORE'S FEDERAL PRACTICE. RULES PAMPHLET. VFOAT Moore's Federal Practice with Comments. 1975-. US. English. an. Matthew Bender & Company Inc, 1275 Broadway, Albany NY 12201. Tel (800)833-9844. *Moore's Federal Practice. Rules and Official Forms as Amended.*

Law

MOT. (LE MOT). No 1 (16 Nov. 1981)-. 0821-655X. Periodical. CN. French. ir. Centre de Traduction et de Terminologie Juridiques, Ecole de Droit, Universite de Moncton, Moncton New Brunswick E1A 3E9 Canada. **DD** 349.71014. *Bulletin d'Information (Universite de Moncton. Centre de Traduction et de Terminologie Juridiques).*

MOTOR VEHICLE REPORTS. V. 1-. 0709-5341. CN. English. an. $42.50. Carswell Company Ltd, 2330 Midland Avenue, Agincourt Ontario M1S 1P7 Canada. **LC** KE2112.A45. **DD** 343.71094605, 347.10394605. (cum index).

MOVING FORCE. V. 1- May 10, 1979-. 0195-7511. US. English. $48.00 for 5 Issues, $78.00 for 10 Issues. Communications Law Publishers, 1901 L Street North West, Washington DC 20036. **LC** KF2265 .A15. **DD** 343.7309483.

MP. Main/Corp Parana, Brazil (State). Ministerio Publico. Yearly V. 1- 1972-. Portuguese. ir. Ministerio Publico, Palacio da Justica 60 Andar (Centro Civico), 80000 Parama Brazil.

MPS IN THE NEWS. VAT Members of Parliament in the News. Vol. 1, No. 1 (Sept. 18, 1977)-. 0704-0377. Periodical. CN. English. bw. Free to all MPS, $6.25 Others. Tuk-Metaphor Clipping Division, PO Box 1267 Station A, Toronto Ontario M5W 1G7 Canada. **DD** 328.71073.

MSBA IN BRIEF. VAT Minnesota State Bar Association in Brief. Vol. 1, No. 1 (Oct. 1985)-. 0884-1667. Periodical. US. English. mo. Minnesota State Bar Association, 430 Marquette Avenue/Suite 403, Minneapolis MN 55401. **DD** 340.

MSRB REPORTS. VFOAT M.S.R.B. Reports. VAT Municipal Securities Rulemaking Board Reports. Began in 1981. 0277-0911. Periodical. US. English. mo. Municipal Securities Rulemaking Board, 1150 Connecticut Avenue NW/Suite 507, Washington DC 20036. **LC** KF6775.A15. **DD** 346.730922, 347.306922.

THE MULTINATIONAL CORPORATION REGULATORY GUIDEBOOK. VFOAT International Organizations Monitoring Service. 0273-0057. US. English. an. $264.00 Domestic, $274.00 Foreign. International Business-Government Counsellors Inc, 1625 Eye Street NW, Washington DC 20006. **LC** K1322. **DD** 346.07, 342.67.

MULTISTATE BAR REVIEW MANUAL. 1972-. 0098-4671. US. English. Multi-State Media, 8 Cottage Place, White Plains NY 10601. **LC** KF388. **DD** 340.0973.

MULTISTATE BAR REVIEW SERIES. Main/Corp Multistate Legal Studies, Inc. V. 1-. 0160-1334. US. English. $6.50 Single Issue. Multistate Legal Studies Inc, PO Box 9330, Wilmington DE 19809. **LC** KF388. **DD** 340.076.

MUNICIPAL AND PLANNING LAW REPORTS. V.1- Dec. 1976-. 0702-7206. Periodical. CN. English. mo. $70.00. The Carswell Company Ltd, 2330 Midland Avenue, Agincourt Ontario M1S 1P7 Canada. **DD** 346.7104502642.

THE MUNICIPAL ATTORNEY. V. 1- Oct. 1959-. 0027-3449. Periodical. US. English. bm. $25.00. National Institute of Municipal Law Officers, 1000 Connecticut Avenue NW/Suite 800, Washington DC 20036. Ind/Abst Leg. Resour. Index. **LC** K13. **DD** 340.05.

MUNICIPAL ATTORNEYS' OPINIONS. V. 1-. 0277-6294. US. English. ir. National Institute of Municipal Law Officers, 1000 Connecticut Avenue NW/Suite 800, Washington DC 20036.

MUNICIPAL BONDS. Series/Titl Real Estate Law and Practice Course Handbook Series. 0278-9043. US. English. an. Practising Law Institute, 810 Seventh Avenue, New York NY 10019. **LC** KF6775.Z9. **DD** 346.730922, 347.306922.

MUNICIPAL CODE OF CHICAGO. Main/Corp Chicago. Ordinances, etc. US. English. an. $137.50. Index Publishing Corporation, 323 West Randolph Street/2nd Floor, Chicago IL 60606. **Tel** (312)726-1477.

MUNICIPAL LAW COURT DECISIONS. Main/Corp National Institute of Municipal Law Officers, Washington, D.C. VFOAT NIMLO Municipal Law Court Decisions. V. 1- 1942-. 0027-3503. Periodical. US. English. bm. National Institute of Municipal Law Officers, 1000 Connecticut Avenue NW/Suite 800, Washington DC 20036.

MUNICIPAL LAW DOCKET. V. 1, No. 1- Jan. 1977-. 0148-3366. Periodical. US. English. National Institute of Municipal Law Officers, 839 17th Street NW, Washington DC 20006. **LC** KF5304. **DD** 342.7309.

MUNICIPAL LAW SECTION NEWSLETTER. Main/Corp New York State Bar Association. Municipal Law Section. V. 1- Jan. 1978-. 0196-5778. Periodical. US. English. Free. New York State Bar Association, One Elk Street, Albany NY 12207. **Tel** (518)463-3200. Ed Hanley Mandelkern. **LC** KFN5752.A15. **DD** 342.74709. **Circ** 1,200. (ctrl). Section newsletter. Current legal issues dealing with municipal law matters.

MUNICIPAL LITIGATION REPORTER. Vol. 1, Issue 1 (June 1981)-. 0278-1301. Periodical. US. English. mo. $150.00. Municipal Litigation Reporter, 810 Idylberry Road, San Rafael CA 94903. **LC** KF5304.A75. **DD** 342.730902638, 347.302902638.

MUNICIPALITIES AND CORPORATION CASES. 0377-757X. II. English. mo. 80.00. International Law Book Company, Nijhawan Building, 1562 Church Road, Kashmere Gate, New Delhi India. **DD** 342.5409.

MUNICIPIO PAULISTA : ASPECTOS JURIDICOS. Main/Corp Sao Paulo, Brazil (State). Procuradoria de Assistencia Juridica Aos Municipios. 1-. Portuguese. ir. Procuradoria de Assistencia Juridica Aos Municipios, 272- 4 E 5 Andares, Sao Paulo Brazil (State). (cum index).

NACHRICHTEN DER NIEDERSACHSISCHEN VERMESSUNGS- UND KATASTERVERWALTUNG. German. ir. 1.00 Single Issue. Nieders Landesvermessungsamt, Landesvermessung Warmbudkenkamp 2 3, Hannover West Germany. **DD** 346.43590432.

NACHSCHLAGEWERK DES BUNDESARBEITSGERICHTS. Periodical. GW. German. ir. Verlag C H Beck, Postfach 400340 Wilhelmstrasse 9, D8000 Munchen 40 West Germany. Ed Alfred Hueck.

N.A.D.A. TITLE AND REGISTRATION BOOK. VAT National Automobile Dealers Association Title and Registration Book. US. English. ir. $49.00. National Automobile Dealers Association, PO Box 7800, Costa Mesa CA 92628. **Tel** (800)622-6232. Ed Don Christy Jr. Summary of laws and regulations of the 50 states.

NARCOTICS LAW BULLETIN. 8755-8289. Periodical. US. English. mo. $35.90. Quinlan Publishing Company, 131 Beverly Street, Boston MA 02114. **LC** KF3890.A59. **DD** 344.730545.

NASBA DIGEST OF STATE ACCOUNTANCY LAWS AND STATE BOARD REGULATIONS. Main/Corp National Association of State Boards of Accountancy. VAT National Association of State Boards of Accountancy Digest of State Accountancy Laws and State Board Regulations. 0161-4290. US. English. 1211 Avenue of the Americas, New York NY 10036. **LC** KF2920.Z95. **DD** 344.7301761657.

NASSAU COUNTY BAR ASSOCIATION ANNUAL DIRECTORY. See Yearbooks, Almanacs, Directories.

NASSAU LAWYER. V. 1-29, No. 9. 0047-8695. Periodical. US. English. ir. $7.00. Bar Association of Nassau County, 15th and West Streets, Mineola NY 11501. **Tel** (516)288-5400. Ed Lester Forest Jr. **LC** K14. **DD** 340.09747. bk rev. adv acc. **Circ** 4,600. (ctrl). Covers bar association news, court decisions, substantive articles on contemporary legal issues.

NATAL UNIVERSITY LAW REVIEW : NULR : A PUBLICATION OF THE LAW STUDENTS OF THE UNIVERSITY OF NATAL. VFOAT NULR. Vol. 1, No. 1 (1972)-. SA. English. ir. University of Natal, King George 5th Avenue, Durban South Africa. **LC** K14. **DD** 340.05.

NATIONAL. V. 1- Jan. 1974-. 0315-2286. CN. English (includes some text in French). mo. Canadian Bar Association, 36 Bessemer Court Unit 3, Concord Ontario L4K 2T1 Canada. **Tel** (416)669-5373. **DD** 340.06271. *Journal, 0591-0919; Canadian Bar Bulletin, 0045-4443; Ontario Bar News.*

THE NATIONAL AND FEDERAL LEGAL EMPLOYMENT REPORT. Vol. 3, No. 2 (Aug. 1982)-. 0733-3285. Periodical. US. English. mo. $120.00. Federal Reports, PO Box 3709, Georgetown Station, Washington DC 20007. **Tel** (202)393-3311. Ed Hermann and Sutherland. **Circ** 5,000. (ctrl). Listing of attorney and law-related job opportunities with the US Government and other public/private employees in the US and abroad. *Federal Legal Employment Report, 0198-036X.*

NATIONAL ASSOCIATION FOR LAW PLACEMENT MEMBERSHIP DIRECTORY. See Yearbooks, Almanacs, Directories.

NATIONAL BANKING LAW REVIEW. Sept. 1982-. 0822-1081. Periodical. CN. English. ir. 110.00. Jewel Publications, 316 Dufferin Road, Montreal Quebec H3X 2Y5 Canada. **Tel** (514)486-9662. Ed Lazar Sarna. **DD** 346.7108205. bk rev. adv acc. Legal comments on recent judicial decisions and law.

NATIONAL BAR ASSOCIATION LAW JOURNAL. Vol. 11, No. 1-Vol. 12, No. 1. 0737-1594. Periodical. US. English. sa. National Bar Association Commercial Law Project, 1773 T Street NW, Washington DC 20009. **LC** K14. **DD** 346.730705 347.306705. *National Bar Journal.*

NATIONAL BAR ASSOCIATION MAGAZINE. Vol. 1, No. 1 (Summer 1983)-. 0741-0115. Periodical. US. English. qt. $10.00. National Bar Association, 1773 T Street Northwest, Washington DC 20009. **LC** KF200. **DD** 349.7305,347.3005.

THE NATIONAL BAR BULLETIN. Periodical. US. English. National Bar Association, 1773 T Street, Washington DC 20009. **LC** KF200. **DD** 340.06273.

NATIONAL BAR EXAMINATION DIGEST. Spring 1975-. 0098-2857. US. English. BRI Bar Review Institute Inc, 1909 K Street Northwest, Washington DC 20006. **LC** KF303. **DD** 340.0973.

NATIONAL BAR JOURNAL. V. 1-10. Periodical. US. English. ir.

NATIONAL COLLEGE OF THE STATE JUDICIARY. 0095-2028. US. English. an. University of Nevada, Judicial College Building, Reno NV 89507. **LC** KF270. **DD** 347.731407152.

NATIONAL CONSULTOR. 0271-9150. Periodical. US. English. qt. $35.00. National Association of Tax Consultants, 454 North 13th Street, San Jose CA 95112.

NATIONAL DIRECTORY OF PROGRESSIVE AND RANK & FILE LABOR LAWYERS. See Yearbooks, Almanacs, Directories.

NATIONAL HOOKUP. 0194-4754. Periodical. US. English. bm. $6.00. Indoor Sports Club Inc, 32 Margaret Drive, Loudenville NY 12211. **Tel** (518)459-8563. Ed Ruth B Meyetto. adv acc. **Circ** 1,300. (ctrl). The paper consists of news from chapters and districts, articles pertaining to the problems of the disabled, national and states laws for the disabled and poetry.

NATIONAL INSOLVENCY REVIEW. Vol. 1, No. 1 (Nov./Dec. 1983)-. 0822-2584. Periodical. CN. English. bm. 110.00. National Insolvency Review c/o Jewel Publications, 316 Dufferin Road, Montreal Quebec H3X 2Y5 Canada. **Tel** (514)486-9662. Ed Barbarn Winters. **DD** 346.7107805. bk rev. adv acc. Law comments on solvency and bankruptcy matters.

NATIONAL INSURANCE LAW REVIEW. Winter 1984 ed.-. 0743-7927. Periodical. US. English. qt. $125.00. NILS, 20675 Bahama Street, Chatsworth CA 91311. **LC** K14. **DD** 346.7308605,347.3068605. *National Insurance Law Review Service, 0147-8532.*

NATIONAL INSURANCE LAW REVIEW SERVICE. 0147-8532. Periodical. US. English. an. National Insurance Law Service, 20675 Bahama Street, Chatsworth CA 91311. **LC** K14. **DD** 346.73086.

THE NATIONAL LAW JOURNAL. V. 1- Aug. 7, 1978-. 0162-7325. Periodical. US. English. wk. $55.00. National Law Journal, 111 8th Avenue, New York NY 11102. **Tel** (212)741-8300. Ed Timothy S Robinson. Ind/Abst Energy Inf. Abstr., Environ. Abstr. **LC** K14. **DD** 340.0973. **Circ** 40,000. Largest-selling publication for lawyers in the US.

THE NATIONAL LAW JOURNAL : ANNUAL INDEX. See Indexes/Abstracts.

NATIONAL LAW REVIEW (NEW DELHI, INDIA). (NATIONAL LAW REVIEW). Began with Vol. 1, No. 1, Jan. 12-18, 1981. Periodical. English. wk. 20. **LC** K14. **DD** 349.5405,345.4005.

NATIONAL LAW REVIEW REPORTER. Began with Oct./Nov. 1979 issue. 0276-7546. Periodical. US. English. bm. $100.00. National Law

Law

Review Reporter Inc, 67 Park Avenue, New York NY 10016. LC K14. DD 349.7305,347.3005.

THE NATIONAL LAWYERS GUILD PRACTITIONER. VFOAT Guild Practitioner. 1937. 0730-532X. Periodical. US. English. qt. $10.00. National Lawyers Guild, Box 673, Berkeley CA 94701. Ed E A Dawley. bk rev. **Circ** 800. (ctrl). Incisive, timely informative quarterly on law and social change from a practical and theoretical viewpoint. Guild Practitioner, 0017-5390.

NATIONAL LEGAL BIBLIOGRAPHY. RECENT ACQUISITIONS OF MAJOR LEGAL LIBRARIES. See Bibliographies.

NATIONAL LEGAL BIBLIOGRAPHY. SUBJECT AREA LIST. AGRICULTURE, ANIMAL, AND FOOD LAW. See Bibliographies.

NATIONAL LEGAL BIBLIOGRAPHY. SUBJECT AREA LIST. CONSTITUTIONAL LAW, HUMAN RIGHTS AND CITIZENSHIP. See Bibliographies.

NATIONAL LEGAL BIBLIOGRAPHY. SUBJECT AREA LIST. CONSTITUTIONAL LAW, HUMAN RIGHTS, AND CITIZENSHIP. See Bibliographies.

NATIONAL LEGAL BIBLIOGRAPHY. SUBJECT AREA LIST. CONTRACT, LEASE AND SALES LAW. See Bibliographies.

NATIONAL LEGAL BIBLIOGRAPHY. SUBJECT AREA LIST. COPYRIGHT AND ENTERTAINMENT LAW. See Bibliographies.

NATIONAL LEGAL BIBLIOGRAPHY. SUBJECT AREA LIST. CRIMINAL LAW, PROCEDURE AND CRIMINOLOGY. See Bibliographies.

NATIONAL LEGAL BIBLIOGRAPHY. SUBJECT AREA LIST. EDUCATIONAL LAW. See Bibliographies.

NATIONAL LEGAL BIBLIOGRAPHY. SUBJECT AREA LIST. ENTERPRISE ORGANIZATION. See Bibliographies.

NATIONAL LEGAL BIBLIOGRAPHY. SUBJECT AREA LIST. EVIDENCE, PRACTICE AND PROCEDURE. See Bibliographies.

NATIONAL LEGAL BIBLIOGRAPHY. SUBJECT AREA LIST. FAMILY LAW AND SOCIAL WELFARE. See Bibliographies.

NATIONAL LEGAL BIBLIOGRAPHY. SUBJECT AREA LIST. LABOR AND EMPLOYMENT. See Bibliographies.

NATIONAL LEGAL BIBLIOGRAPHY. SUBJECT AREA LIST. LAW PRACTICE AND OFFICE MANAGEMENT. See Bibliographies.

NATIONAL LEGAL BIBLIOGRAPHY. SUBJECT AREA LIST. MEDICINE AND HEALTH LAW. See Bibliographies.

NATIONAL LEGAL BIBLIOGRAPHY. SUBJECT AREA LIST. MILITARY AND SECURITY LAW. See Bibliographies.

NATIONAL LEGAL BIBLIOGRAPHY. SUBJECT AREA LIST. MUNICIPAL AND ADMINISTRATIVE LAW AND POLITICS. See Bibliographies.

NATIONAL LEGAL BIBLIOGRAPHY. SUBJECT AREA LIST. TRANSPORTATION AND MARITIME LAW. See Bibliographies.

NATIONAL LEGAL CENTER NEWS. 0275-9233. Periodical. US. English. qt. Free. National Legal Center for the Public Interest, 1101 17th Street NW, Washington DC 20036. LC KF299.P8. DD 349.7305,347.3005.

NATIONAL PARALEGAL REPORTER : OFFICIAL PUBLICATION OF NATIONAL FEDERATION OF PARALEGAL ASSOCIATIONS. US. English. bm. $15.00. The National Paralegal, PO Box 40158, Overland Park KS 66204. **Tel** (913)381-4458. bk rev. adv acc. **Circ** 8,200. (ctrl). Articles pertaining to current issues in the paralegal profession.

NATIONAL PROPERTY LAW DIGESTS. 0363-8340. US. English. mo. National Property Law Digest, 7900 Wisconsin Avenue/Suite 200, Bethesda MD 20814. **Tel** (301)654-8004. LC KF567.8. DD 346.7304302648. (cum index).

NATIONAL PUBLIC EMPLOYMENT REPORTER. Began with Vol. 1, 1979. 0194-889X. Periodical. US. English. mo. $295.00. Labor Relations Press, PO Box 579, Fort Washington PA 19034. **Tel** (215)628-3113. Ed Jim Gasper. LC KF3580.G6. DD 344.7301890413530002648. (cum index). **Circ** 315. Abstracts of nationwide state labor board decisions, complete indexing, many access points, table of cases, citation tracker, microfiche option, parallel database, off-line searches.

NATIONAL REPORTER (FREDERICTON, N.B. : BOUND CUMULATION). (NATIONAL REPORTER). Vol. 1 (1974)-. 0317-641X. Periodical. CN. English. ir. $64.00 Per Vol. Maritime Law Book Ltd, Box 302, Fredericton New Brunswick E3B 4Y9 Canada. DD 348.71041.

NATIONAL TAX TRAINING PROGRAM. TAX PRACTICE FUNDAMENTALS FOR NONTAX PROFESSIONALS. (NATIONAL TAX TRAINING PROGRAM : TAX PRACTICE FUNDAMENTALS FOR NONTAX PROFESSIONALS). **Main/Corp** Ernst & Ernst. VFOAT Tax Practice Fundamentals for Nontax Professionals. 0149-323X. US. English. an. 1300 Union Commerce Building, 925 Euclid Avenue, Cleveland OH 44115. LC KF6450. DD 343.73067.

NATIONAL TORT LAW DIGESTS. Vol. 1 No. 1-. 0742-4388. US. English. mo. $96.00. National Tort Law Digests Inc, Suite 308/1301 20th Street Northwest, Washington DC 20036. LC KF1247.8. DD 346.730302648, 347.306302648.

THE NATIONAL TRAFFIC LAW NEWS. VFOAT NTLN. V. 1- Feb. 1974-. 0094-1875. US. English. mo. $79.00. National Traffic Law News, PO Box 278, Warrensburg MO 64093. **Tel** (402)464-3432. Ed Donald H Wallace. LC KF2231.A59. DD 347.730247. **Circ** 500. Publication providing synopses of appellate court cases from across the country concerning motor vehicle laws including drunk driving, speeding, license suspension.

NATIONAL WETLANDS NEWSLETTER. See Conservation & Natural Resources.

NATUR + I.E. UND RECHT. See Conservation & Natural Resources.

NATURAL RESOURCES & ENVIRONMENT. See Conservation & Natural Resources.

NATURAL RESOURCES JOURNAL. V. 1- Mar. 1961-. 0028-0739. Periodical. US. English. qt. $20.00. University of New Mexico, School of Law, 1117 Stanford NE, Albuquerque NM 87131. **Tel** (505)277-4820. Ed Albert E Utton. **Ind/Abst** Leg. Resour. Index, Index Leg. Period., Can. Environ., Life Sci. Collect., Excerpta Med., Sel. Water Resour. Abstr., Coal Abstr., Energy Inf. Abstr., Environ. Abstr., Index Econ. Artic. J. Collect. Vol., ABC Pol Sci, GeoRef, Curr. Law Index, Book Rev. Index, Energy Res. Abstr., Bibliogr. Agric., Public Aff. Inf. Serv. Bull., Soc. Sci. Citation Index, Leg. Contents, Recent Publ. Artic., Bibliogr. Index Geol., Contents Curr. Leg. Period. LC K14. CODEN NRJOAB. (cum index). bk rev. adv acc. **Circ** 1,700. An international, interdisciplinary forum devoted to the study of natural and environmental resources. The emphasis is on research directly related to public policy.

NATURAL RESOURCES LAW NEWSLETTER. Vol. 1, No. 1 (Nov. 1967)-. 0077-6084. Periodical. US. English. qt. $2.00. American Bar Association, 1155 East 60th Street, Chicago IL 60637. **Ind/Abst** Leg. Resour. Index. LC UNC. Mineral and Natural Resources Newsletter.

NATURAL RESOURCES LAWYER CEASED. (NATURAL RESOURCES LAWYER : JOURNAL OF THE SECTION OF NATURAL RESOURCES LAW, AMERICAN BAR ASSOCIATION). Vol. 1, No. 1 (Jan. 1968) - V. 17, No. 4 (Apr. 1985). 0028-0747. Periodical. US. English. qt. $20.00. **Ind/Abst** Leg. Resour. Index, Index Leg. Period., Life Sci. Collect., Sel. Water Resour. Abstr., Coal Abstr., Energy Inf. Abstr., Environ. Abstr., Energy Res. Abstr., GeoRef. LC K14. DD 346.73044, 347.3064.

NCBL NOTES. VFOAT N.C.B.L. Notes. VAT National Conference of Black Lawyers Notes. 0733-1851. Periodical. US. English. qt. $35.00. National Conference of Black Lawyers, 126 West 119th Street, New York NY 10026. **Tel** (212)864-4000.

NEBRASKA JUDICIAL NEWSLETTER. 0364-233X. US. English. State Court Administrator, Room 2412 State Capital, Lincoln NE 68509. LC KFN525.A15. DD 347.78201405.

NEBRASKA LAW REVIEW. V. 20- Mar. 1941-. 0047-9209. Periodical. US. English. qt. $18.00. University of Nebraska, College of Law, Lincoln NE 68503. **Tel** (402)472-1267. Ed Mark R Killenbuck. **Ind/Abst** Leg. Resour. Index, Sel. Water Resour. Abstr., Index Leg. Period., Curr. Law Index, Contents Curr. Leg. Period. LC K14. Index published separately - free - automatically sent. (cum index). adv acc. **Circ** 1,500. Topics in law of general interest to both practising attorneys and law school faculty. Nebraska Law Bulletin, 0196-4089.

THE NEBRASKA LEGAL DIRECTORY. See Yearbooks, Almanacs, Directories.

NEBRASKA REAL ESTATE LAW JOURNAL. Vol. 1, No. 1 (Sept./Oct. 1982)-. 0734-0818. Periodical. US. English. bm. $75.00. Mason Publishing Company, 366 Wacouta Street, St Paul MN 55101. LC KFN112.A15. DD 346.78204305, 347.82064305.

NEDERLANDS JURISTENBLAD : TEVENS ORGAAN DER NED. JURISTEN VEREENIGING. Vol. 23 No 1 (3 Jan. 1948). Periodical. NE. Dutch. wk. Libresso BV, Postbus 878, 7400 AW Deventer Netherlands. Nederlandsch Juristenblad.

NEDERLANDSE JURISPRUDENTIE. ONTEIGENING. NE. Dutch. qt. Libresso BV, Postbus 878, 7400 AW Deventer Netherlands. DD 348.492041.

NEGARIT GAZETA. Main/Corp Ethiopia. V. 1- Mar. 10, 1942-. Periodical. US. English (Amharic).

NEGLIGENCE AND COMPENSATION CASES ANNOTATED. V. 1-39. US. English. LC KF1280.A2. DD 347.5. (cum index). American Negligence Reports.

NEGOTIATIONS NEWS & SCHOOL LAW REPORTER. See Education (General) - Special Aspects of Education.

NEPAL MISCELLANEOUS SERIES. Vol. 1/77 (Jan. 25, 1977)-. English. ir. Nepal Press Digest Pvt Ltd, Lazimpat, Kathmandu Nepal.

NETWORK NEWS - CANADIAN LAW INFORMATION COUNCIL. (NETWORKS NEWS). Vol. 1, No. 1 (Mar. 1982)-. 0712-2985. Periodical. CN. English. ty. Free. Canadian Law Information Council, 2409 Yonge Street, Toronto Ontario M4P ZE7 Canada. DD 349.7105. (ctrl).

NEUE JURISTISCHE WOCHENSCHRIFT. VFOAT NJW, Neue Juristischw Wochenschrift. Began publication in 1949. 0341-1907. Periodical. GW. German. wk. $88.95. W E Saarbach GMBH, Postfach 101610, D-5000 Koeln 1 West Germany. **Tel** 02 21-23 46 31. **Ind/Abst** Coal Abstr., Energy Res. Abstr. Neue Juristische.

NEUE JUSTIZ. Vol. 1-. 0028-3231. Periodical. German. mo. $32.25. Kunst & Wissen Erich Bieber, Dufourstrasse 51, CH-8008 Zurich Switzerland. **Tel** 011-41-1-69 44 20. (cum index).

NEUE ZEITSCHRIFT FUR WEHRRECHT. 1.-. Periodical. GW. German. bm. $50.11. J Schweitzer Verlag, Geibelstr 8, D-8000 Muenchen West Germany.

NEVADA LEGAL NEWS. 0744-8902. Newspaper. US. English. da. $200.00. Nevada Legal News, PO Box 7407, Las Vegas NV 89125. **Tel** (702)382-2747.

NEW BRUNSWICK REPORTS (FREDERICTON, N.B.). (NEW BRUNSWICK REPORTS). 0713-8989. Periodical. CN. English. mo. Maritime Law Book Ltd, Box 302, Fredericton New Brunswick E3B 4Y9 Canada. DD 348.715043.

NEW BRUNSWICK REPORTS (FREDERICTON, N.B. : BOUND CUMULATION). (NEW BRUNSWICK REPORTS). 2nd Ser., V. 1 (1969)-. 0713-8989. Periodical. CN. English. ir. Maritime Law Book Ltd, Box 302, Fredericton New Brunswick E3B 4Y9 Canada. DD 348.715043.

NEW DIMENSIONS IN SECURITIES AND COMMODITIES LITIGATION : ALI-ABA COURSE OF STUDY MATERIALS. VFOAT Securities and Commodities Litigation. Apr. 26-27, 1984-. US. English. an. LC KF1440. DD 346.730666, 347.306666. *New Dimensions in Securities Litigation, Planning and Strategies.*

NEW DIRECTIONS ACTION LINE. VFOAT Action Line. V. 1- Jan. 1977-. 0197-8799. Periodical. US. English. bm. Action Line, 1302 18th Street NW, Washington DC 20036. *Group Legal Review, 0197-8802.*

NEW DIRECTIONS IN LEGAL SERVICES. Apr./May 1976-. 0145-8582. US. English. bm. $25.00. National Resource Center for Consumers of Legal Services, 1302 18th Street Northwest, Washington DC 20036. **Ind/Abst** Public Aff. Inf. Serv. Bull. LC KF310.G7. DD 362.

NEW ENGLAND JOURNAL ON CRIMINAL AND CIVIL CONFINEMENT. Vol. 9, No. 1 (Winter 1983)-. 0740-8994. Periodical. US. English. sa. $15.00. New England School of Law, 154 Stuart Street, Boston MA 02116. **Tel** (617)451-0010. **Ind/Abst** Leg. Resour. Index, Index Leg. Period. LC K14. *New England Journal on Prison Law, 0095-7364.*

NEW ENGLAND LAW LIBRARY CONSORTIUM NEWSLETTER. See Library and Information Science.

NEW ENGLAND LAW REVIEW. V. 4, No. 2- Spring 1969-. 0028-4823. US. English. qt. $15.00. New England Law Review, 154 Stuart Street, Boston MA 02116. **Tel** (617)451-0010. **Ed** Tory Weigand. **Ind/Abst** Leg. Resour. Index, Index Leg. Period., Curr. Law Index, Contents Curr. Leg. Period. (cum index). bk rev. adv acc. **Circ** 2,000. (ctrl). Available on microfilm from University Microfilms. Legal articles written by legal scholars on matters of current importance in the legal community. *Portia Law Journal, 0196-5646.*

NEW HAMPSHIRE BAR JOURNAL. V. 1- 1958-. 0548-4928. Periodical. US. English. qt. New Hampshire Bar Journal, 18 Centre Street, Concord NH 03301. **Tel** (603)224-6942. **Ed** Victor Somma. **Ind/Abst** Leg. Resour. Index, Index Leg. Period., Curr. Law Index. LC UNC. adv acc. **Circ** 2,700. Articles on current legal issues, commentaries, new statutes, case law, etc.

NEW HAMPSHIRE COURT SYSTEM. Main/Corp New Hampshire. Supreme Court. Judicial Planning Committee. 1st- 1978-. US. English. an. LC KFN1708. DD 347.74201.

NEW HAMPSHIRE LAW DIRECTORY & DAYBOOK. See Yearbooks, Almanacs, Directories.

NEW HAMPSHIRE LAW WEEKLY. 0362-1073. US. English. wk. $40.00. New Hampshire Law, 18 Centre Street, Concord NH 03301. **Tel** (603)224-6942. **Ed** Victor Somma. LC KF200. DD 340.09742. adv acc. **Circ** 2,700. Current New Hampshire Bar Association events, Supreme Court opinions, and legal articles.

NEW HAMPSHIRE REGISTER AND LEGISLATIVE MANUAL. VFOAT Annual Register of New Hampshire. No. 182- 1979/80-. US. English. an. Tower Publishing Company, 163 Middle Street, Portland ME 04101. *New Hampshire Register, State Year-Book and Legislative Manual.*

THE NEW HAMPSHIRE REPORTS. CURRENT CASES. Main/Corp New Hampshire. Supreme Court. Periodical. US. English. ir. Equity Publishing Corporation, Main Street, Orford NH 03777. **Tel** (603)353-4351. Index received separately bound from publisher.

NEW HAMPSHIRE REVISED STATUTES ANNOTATED. US. English. bm. $59.50. Equity Publ Corporation, Oxford NH 03777. **Tel** (603)353-4351.

NEW HAMPSHIRE RULEMAKING REGISTER. VFOAT Rulemaking Register. US. English. mo. $30.00. Office of Legislative Services, Administrative Procedures Division, Room 113 State House, Concord NH 03301. LC KFN1236. DD 348.742025, 347.420825.

THE NEW JERSEY EDUCATION LAW REPORT. See Education (General).

THE NEW JERSEY LAW JOURNAL. V. 1- Jan. 1878-. 0028-5803. Periodical. US. English. wk. $130.00. New Jersey Law Journal, PO Box 50, Newark NJ 07101. **Tel** (201)642-0075. **Ed** Joan Honig. **Ind/Abst** Curr. Law Index, Leg. Resour. Index. bk rev. adv acc. **Circ** 8,900. Newspaper for New Jersey lawyers. Read by all practising attorneys and judges in the state.

NEW JERSEY LAWYER. No. 88- Aug. 1979-. 0195-0983. Periodical. US. English. qt. New Jersey State Bar Association, 172 West State Street, Trenton NJ 08608. **Ind/Abst** Leg. Resour. Index, Index Leg. Period. LC KF200. DD 349.74905. *Bar Journal.*

NEW JERSEY LEGISLATIVE INDEX. See Indexes/Abstracts.

NEW JERSEY MUNICIPAL LAW NEWS. VFOAT Municipal Law News. Vol. 1, No. 1 (Jan. 1982)-. 0735-4010. Periodical. US. English. sa. $20.00. G & W Legal Publications Inc, PO Box 7701, Trenton NJ 08628. **Tel** (609)394-1910. **Ed** Lewis Goldshore and Marsha Wolf. LC KFN2231.A15. DD 342.74909, 347.49029. **Circ** 300.

NEW JERSEY REPORTS AND NEW JERSEY SUPERIOR COURT REPORTS. 8750-2658. Periodical. US. English. wk. $70.00. West Publishing Company, 50 W Kellogg Boulevard, St Paul MN 55102. DD 348.

NEW JERSEY SCHOOL LAW DECISIONS. 0146-7603. US. English. New Jersey Education Association, 180 West State Street, Trenton NJ 08608. LC KFN2190.A59. DD 344.7490702646.

NEW JERSEY SESSION LAW SERVICE. US. English. ir. Mr Don M Blauth, State House Annex/Room 112, Trenton NJ 08625.

NEW LAW JOURNAL. V. 116- Oct. 28, 1965-. 0306-6479. Periodical. UK. English. wk. D & S Publishers, PO Box 5105, Clearwater FL 33518. **Tel** (800)237-9707. **Ind/Abst** Leg. Resour. Index, Sociol. Abstr., Index Leg. Period., Lang. Lang. Behav. Abstr. *Law Times, Law Journal.*

NEW LEGISLATION OF THE AUSTRALIAN PARLIAMENT. No. 1- May 1973-. 0310-3668. English. ir. $12.00. Reporter Newspaper Company, Box 2757, GPO Sydney Australia. DD 348.9402.

NEW MEXICO CIVIL TRIAL REPORTER. V. 1- Jan./Feb. 1980-. 0276-8127. Periodical. US. English. bm. New Mexico Civil Trial Reporter, PO Box 826, Albuquerque NM 87103.

NEW MEXICO LAW REVIEW. Vol. 1, No. 1 (Jan. 1971)-. 0028-6214. Periodical. US. English. ty. $20.00. University of New Mexico, School of Law, 1117 Stanford, Albuquerque NM 87131. **Tel** (505)277-4820. **Ed** Pat Taylor. **Ind/Abst** Leg. Resour. Index, Index Leg. Period., Curr. Law Index, Contents Curr. Leg. Period. LC K14. DD 340.05. (cum index). adv acc. **Circ** 700. A survey of general law and New Mexico law.

NEW SOUTH WALES DISTRICT COURT REPORTS. Began with vol. for 1965. AT. English. ir. $8.75. Butterworths Ltd, 271-273 Lane Cove Road/North Ryde, Sydney New South Wales 2113 Australia. DD 348.944043.

NEW SOUTH WALES INDUSTRIAL GAZETTE. See Economics - Labor.

NEW SOUTH WALES LAW REPORTS. 1971-. 0312-1674. AT. English. ir. Methuen Law Book Company Ltd, 35 Mitchell Street, c/o Bennett-EBSCO, North Sydney New South Wales 2060 Australia. DD 348.944041. *State Reports, New South Wales, Land and Valuation Court Reports of New South Wales.*

NEW STATUTES AFFECTING THE CRIMINAL LAW. Main/Corp California. Legislature. Assembly. Committee on Criminal Justice. US. English. $5.20. Assembly Publications Office, Box 90 State Capitol, Sacramento CA 95814. LC KFC10.8. DD 345.794002632.

NEW YORK CITY CHARTER AND ADMINISTRATIVE CODE, ANNOTATED. Periodical. US. English. an. Williams Press Inc, PO Box 4025, Albany NY 12204. **Tel** (518)434-1141. Includes recodified New York City charter, building, housing maintenance, electrical and plumbing codes, real property assesment, social services, street and highways and city employees.

NEW YORK CIVIL PRACTICE. Main/Corp New York (State). US. English. ir. Matthew Bender & Company Inc, 1275 Broadway, Albany NY 12201. **Tel** (800)833-9844.

NEW YORK COURT OF APPEALS RECORDS AND BRIEFS ON MICROFILM. Main/Corp New York (State). Court of Appeals. V. 36- 1975-. US. English. ir. Hein Building, 1285 Main Street, Buffalo NY 14209.

NEW YORK . . . CPLR REDBOOK. Main/Corp New York (State). VFOAT New York . . . C.P.L.R. Redbook. US. English. an. Matthew Bender & Company Inc, 1275 Broadway, Albany NY 12201. **Tel** (800)833-9844. LC KFN5990. DD 347.74705, 347.47075. *CPLR, as amended by the Legislature and by the Judicial Conference, including tables and CPLR Amendments CPA & RCP-CPLR Cross Reference Tables Index.*

THE NEW YORK JURY VERDICT REPORTER. VFOAT Jury Verdict Reporter. Began in 1981. 0738-1697. Periodical. US. English. mo. $125.00. New York Jury Verdict Reporter, 15 Bayview Avenue, East Islip NY 11730. Each issue contains an index to its own contents - no vol index - loose.

NEW YORK LAND REPORT : A PROJECT OF THE NEW YORK LAND INSTITUTE. Vol. 1, (March 1980)-. Periodical. US. English. mo. $200.00. New York Land Institute, PO Box 365, Albany NY 12201. **Tel** (518)465-7412.

NEW YORK LAW FINDER. 1979-. 0277-0512. US. English. an. West Publishing Company, 50 West Kellogg Boulevard, PO Box 3526, St Paul MN 55165. LC KFN5061. DD 348.747028, 347.470828.

NEW YORK LAW JOURNAL. Began with Mar. 26, 1888 issue. 0028-7326. Periodical. US. English. da. New York Law Publishing Company, 111 Eighth Avenue, New York NY 10011. **Tel** (212)741-8300. **Ed** Charles Kiley. **Ind/Abst** New York Law J. Dig. Annot., Curr. Law Index, Leg. Resour. Index. bk rev. adv acc. **Circ** 14,000. Available on microfilm from Bell & Howell, Micro Photo Division. Available on microfiche. Legal publication.

NEW YORK LAW JOURNAL DIGEST-ANNOTATOR. (NEW YORK LAW JOURNAL DIGEST-ANNOTATOR : . . . . YEAR COVERING THE LOWER COURT OPINIONS OF THE FIRST AND SECOND JUDICIAL DEPARTMENTS AS PUBLISHED IN THE NEW YORK LAW JOURNAL). VAT New York Law Journal Digest Annotator. Vol. 46, No. 11 (Nov. 1982)-. 0745-4406. US. English. mo. $155.00. Law Journal Seminars-Press, 111 Eighth Avenue, New York NY 10011. *Clark's Digest-Annotator.*

NEW YORK LAW SCHOOL LAW REVIEW. V. 22-. 0145-448X. Periodical. US. English. **Ind/Abst** Public Aff. Inf. Serv. Bull., Index Leg. Period. *New York Law Forum, 0028-7318.*

NEW YORK LAWYER'S LETTER. 1950. 0275-7346. Periodical. US. English. ir. $66.00. Doran Publications, Northway 10 Users Road Executive Park, Ballston Lake NY 12019. **Tel** (518)877-7492. **Ed** John A Emmett. DD 340. **Circ** 1,300. Report of court cases and legislation of interest to New York attorneys.

NEW YORK NO-FAULT ARBITRATION REPORTS. VFOAT No-Fault Arbitration Reports. VAT New York No Fault Arbitration Reports. V. 1- Jan. 1977-. 0193-7693. US. English. mo. $60.00. American Arbitration Association, 140 West 51st Street, New York NY 10020. **Tel** (212)484-4004. **Ed** Colleen J McCann. **Circ** 650. Summaries of actual no-fault arbitration awards including master cases.

THE NEW YORK SCHOOL DISTRICT LAW LETTER. VFOAT School District Law Letter. Began with V. 1 In 1957. 0545-6339. Periodical. US. English. bm. $46.00. Doran Publications Inc, Northway 10 Executive Park, Ballston Lake NY 12019. **Tel** (518)877-7492. **Ed** Patricia A Fitzpatrick. DD 344. **Circ** 1,000. A publication reporting cases and legislation affecting education in New York State.

NEW YORK SEA GRANT LAW AND POLICY JOURNAL. VFOAT New York Sea Grant Law & Policy Journal. Vol. 3-. 0735-2409. Periodical. US. English. New York Sea Grant Institute, State University of New York and Cornell University, 411 State Street, Albany NY 12246. **Ind/Abst** Leg. Resour. Index. LC K23. DD 346.73046917,

Law

347.30646917. *Sea Grant Law and Policy Journal*, 0197-9906.

NEW YORK STATE BAR JOURNAL. V. 1- Mar. 1928-. 0028-7547. US. English. ir. $16.00. New York State Bar, One Elk Street, Albany NY 12207. **Tel** (607)723-9511. **Ed** Eugene C Gerhart. **Ind/Abst** Index Leg. Period., Curr. Law Index, Leg. Resour. Index, Public Aff. Inf. Serv. Bull. bk rev. adv acc. **Circ** 43,000. (ctrl). Articles and other material of general interest to the legal (and related) profession.

NEW YORK STATE CRIMINAL LAW REVIEW. VFOAT Criminal Law Review. 0271-6283. Periodical. US. English. mo. New York Bureau of Prosecution and Defense Services, 80 Centre Street, New York NY 10013. **LC** KFN6155.A59. **DD** 345.7470505, 347.4705505.

NEW YORK STATE JURY VERDICT REVIEW AND ANALYSIS. Vol. 1, No. 1 (Oct. 1983)-. 8750-8044. Periodical. US. English. mo. $150.00. Jury Verdict Review, 24 Commerce Street/Suite 1722, Newark NJ 07102.

NEW YORK STATE LAW DIGEST. No. 1- Mar. 1965-. 0028-7636. US. English. mo $16.00. New York State Bar Association, 1 Elk Street, Albany NY 12207. **Tel** (518)463-3200. **Ed** David D Siegel. **LC** UNC. **Circ** 44,000. (ctrl). A digest summarizing and analyzing recent New York and federal court cases and legislation of importance to New York practising attorneys. *Lawyer Service Letter*.

NEW YORK STATE TAX MONITOR. VFOAT Tax Monitor. Vol. 1, No. 1 (Sept. issue, 1983)-. 0737-5891. Periodical. US. English. mo. $195.00. Law Planning Reports Ltd, 19 West 36th Street, New York NY 10018. **DD** 343.

NEW YORK SUPPLEMENT. SECOND SERIES. V. 1- N.Y.S. 2D. 8750-264X. Periodical. US. English. wk. West Publishing Company, 50 West Kellogg Boulevard, St Paul MN 55102. **LC** KFN5045. **DD** 348.747043. *New York Supplement*.

NEW YORK TAX LAW. Main/Corp New York (State). VFOAT Tax Law & Regulations. 1977-. US. English. an. Matthew Bender & Company Inc, 1275 Broadway, Albany NY 12201. **Tel** (800)833-9844.

NEW YORK UNIVERSITY JOURNAL OF INTERNATIONAL LAW & POLITICS. Main/Corp New York University International Law Society. VFOAT Journal of International Law and Politics. **VAT** New York University Journal of International Law and Politics. V. 1- Apr. 1968-. 0028-7873. Periodical. US. English. qt. $15.00 Domestic, $17.00 Foreign. New York University School of Law, Journal of International Law and Politics, 249 Sullivan Street, New York NY 10012. **Ind/Abst** Am. Hist. Life, Hist. Abstr., Part A, Mod. Hist. Abstr., Hist. Abstr., Part B, Twent. Century Abstr., Leg. Resour. Index, ABC Pol Sci, Contents Curr. Leg. Period., Public Aff. Inf. Serv. Bull., Index Leg. Period. **LC** JX1. **DD** 341.05.

NEW YORK UNIVERSITY LAW REVIEW (1950). (NEW YORK UNIVERSITY LAW REVIEW). Vol. 25, No. 1 (Jan. 1950)-. 0028-7881. Periodical. US. English. bm. $20.00. New York University Law Review, 719 Broadway 5th Floor, New York NY 10003. **Tel** (212)777-7560. **Ind/Abst** Account. Index. Suppl., Index Leg. Period., Soc. Sci. Citation Index, Curr. Law Index, Leg. Resour. Index, Contents Curr. Leg. Period. Index in last issue of volume - attached. bk rev. adv acc. **Circ** 3,000. (ctrl). *New York University Law Quarterly Review*.

NEW YORK UNIVERSITY REVIEW OF LAW AND SOCIAL CHANGE. (REVIEW OF LAW AND SOCIAL CHANGE). V. 1- 1971-. 0048-7481. US. English. ty. $12.00 Domestic, $15.00 Foreign. New York University, School of Law, 719 Broadway/5th Floor, New York NY 10003. **Tel** (212)598-3919. **Ed** Rhinold Ponder and Amir Rosenthal. **Ind/Abst** Leg. Resour. Index, Index Leg. Period., Curr. Law Index, Contents Curr. Leg. Period. **LC** K14.E97. **DD** 301.115. bk rev. **Circ** 1,000. Publishes works that deal with issues of law and social policy which reflect a particular interest in the under-represented or under-privileged.

NEW YORK WORKERS COMPENSATION COMMENTS. See Economics - Labor.

NEW ZEALAND ADMINISTRATIVE REPORTS : NZAR. VFOAT NZAR. 1976-. 0110-1277. English. ir. **DD** 342.93106.

NEW ZEALAND DISTRICT COURT REPORTS. Vol. 1, Pt. 1-. English. ir. Butterworths of New Zealand Ltd, 33-35 Cumberland Place, Wellington New Zealand. **Ed** Tony Black. **DD** 348.931042, 349.310842. *Magistrates' Courts Decisions*.

THE NEW ZEALAND LAW JOURNAL. (THE NEW ZEALAND LAW JOURNAL : NZLJ). VFOAT NZLJ. Began with: Vol. 4, No. 1 (March 6, 1928). 0028-8373. Periodical. US. English. mo. D & S Publishers, PO Box 5105, Clearwater FL 33518. **Tel** (800)237-9707. **Ind/Abst** Leg. Resour. Index, Public Aff. Inf. Serv. Bull., Index Leg. Period., Curr. Law Index. Index published separately - free - automatically sent. (cum index). *Butterworths Fortnightly Notes*.

THE NEW ZEALAND LAW SOCIETY'S NEWS SHEET. English. ir. New Zealand Law Society, Box 5041, 26 Waring Taylor Street, Wellington 1 New Zealand. **DD** 340.09931.

NEW ZEALAND RECENT LAW. Vol. 1, No. 1 (Feb. 1975)-. Periodical. NZ. English. mo. $33.79. New Zealand Recent Law, PO Box 8695, Symonds Street, Auckland 1 New Zealand. **Circ** 1,200. (ctrl). Comment on decisions of the high court, court of appeal and family court; commercial notes and conveyancing; comment on statutes, bills and law reform. *Recent Law*.

NEWBERG ON CLASS ACTIONS. V. 1- 1977-. US. English. ir. $350.00. Shepards McGraw Hill, PO Box 1235, Colorado Springs CO 80901. **Tel** (800)525-2474. Index in last issue of volume - attached. Since its 1977 publication it has been the leading authority for class action law and litigation consulted by lawyers and judges nationwide.

NEWFOUNDLAND & PRINCE EDWARD ISLAND REPORTS. 0715-4755. Periodical. CN. English. ir. Maritime Law Book Ltd, Box 302, Fredericton New Brunswick E3B 4Y9 Canada. **DD** 348.717043.

NEWFOUNDLAND & PRINCE EDWARD ISLAND REPORTS (BOUND CUMULATION). (NEWFOUNDLAND & PRINCE EDWARD ISLAND REPORTS). Vol. 1 (1971)-. 0715-4755. CN. English. ir. $75.00 Per Vol. Maritime Law Book Ltd, Box 302, Fredericton New Brunswick E3B 4Y9 Canada. **DD** 348.717043.

NEWFOUNDLAND GAZETTE. (THE NEWFOUNDLAND GAZETTE). 0028-8888. Periodical. CN. English. wk. $45.00. Newfoundland Gazette, Confederation Building, St John Newfoundland A1C 5T7 Canada. **Tel** (709)576-3649. **Ed** David C B Dawe. **Circ** 1,300. (ctrl). Also available on microfilm from: Toronto, Micromedia and from New York Public Library. Includes legal notices, subordinate legislation, and statutory notices.

NEWS AND VIEWS - STATE BAR OF NEW MEXICO. (NEWS AND VIEWS). Began with Sept. 17, 1981 issue. 3749-375X. Periodical. US. English. wk. State Bar of New Mexico, 1117 Stanford NE, Albuquerque NM 87131. **LC** KF200. **DD** 340.06072. *State Bar of New Mexico Bulletin and Advance Opinions*, 0039-0038.

NEWS AND VIEWS (WASHINGTON, D.C.). (NEWS AND VIEWS). Periodical. US. English. bw. Administrative Office of the United States Courts, Probation Division, Washington DC 20544.

NEWS BRIEFS : A PUBLICATION OF THE LOUISIANA STATE BAR ASSOCIATION. Main/Corp Louisiana State Bar Association. Vol. 22, No. 1 (Apr.-May 1979)-. Periodical. US. English. Louisiana State Bar Association, 225 Baronne Street/Suite 210, New Orleans LA 70112. *LSBA News*.

NEWS BULLETIN - ARKANSAS BAR ASSOCIATION. Main/Corp Arkansas Bar Association. 0198-702X. Periodical. US. English. mo. Publications Assistant, Arkansas Bar Association, 400 West Markham Street, Little Rock AR 72201. **LC** KF200. **DD** 340.060767.

NEWS FROM DRAFTING WILLS AND TRUST AGREEMENTS : A SYSTEM APPROACH. Vol. 1, No. 2 (June 1982)-. Periodical. US. English. PO Box 729, Lexington SC 29072.

NEWS FROM THE HILL. 0270-0662. Periodical. US. English. mo. $48.00. Legislative Research International, PO Box 1511, Washington DC 20013. **Ed** Alice Cherian. Specifically designed to report new federal legislative developments (selected) relating to international business including export, import and foreign investment.

NEWS LETTER - BAR ASSOCIATION OF SRI LANKA. Main/Corp Bar Association of Sri Lanka. No. 1- Aug. 1975-. Periodical. English. ir. Bar Association of Sri Lanka, Law Library, Colombo 12 Sri Lanka. **DD** 340.0625493.

THE NEWS MEDIA & THE LAW. VAT News Media and the Law. V. 1- Oct. 1977-. 0149-0737. Periodical. US. English. mo. $20.00. News Media & The Law, 800 18th Street NW, Washington DC 20006. **Tel** (202)466-6313. **Ind/Abst** Leg. Resour. Index. **LC** KF2750.A15. **DD** 343.730998. *Press Censorship Newsletter*.

NEWS RELEASE. Main/Corp California. Administrative Office of the Courts. Periodical. US. English. ir.

NEWSLETTER - ABA CONSORTIUM FOR PROFESSIONAL EDUCATION. Main/Corp ABA Consortium for Professional Education. No. 1- Summer 1976-. 0149-3531. Periodical. US. English. American Bar Center, 1155 East 60th Street, Chicago IL 60637. **LC** KF200. **DD** 340.0715.

NEWSLETTER (AMERICAN ACADEMY OF PSYCHIATRY AND THE LAW). See Medicine - Psychiatry, Psychopathology.

NEWSLETTER - AMERICAN ASSOCIATION OF LAW LIBRARIES. See Library and Information Science.

NEWSLETTER - AMERICAN BAR ASSOCIATION. SECTION OF ECONOMICS OF LAW PRACTICE. (NEWSLETTER). 0742-7360. Periodical. US. English. American Bar Association, Economics Section, 1155 East 60th Street, Chicago IL 60637. **LC** KF318.A1. **DD** 340.06073.

NEWSLETTER & DIGEST OF SELECTED OPINIONS OF STATE ATTORNEYS GENERAL. 0094-226X. US. English. qt. Iron Works Pike, Lexington KY 40505. **LC** KF294.N24. **DD** 348.735.

NEWSLETTER- ASSOCIATION OF AMERICAN LAW SCHOOLS SECTION ON WOMEN IN LEGAL EDUCATION. Main/Corp Association of American Law Schools. Section on Women in Legal Education. Periodical. US. English. ir. Suite 370/One Dupont Circle, Washington DC 20036.

NEWSLETTER - BRITISH INSTITUTE OF INTERNATIONAL AND COMPARATIVE LAW. Main/Corp British Institute of International and Comparative Law. No. 2- Oct. 1973-. 0308-2482. Periodical. UK. English. qt. 32 Furnival Street, London EC4A 1JN England. **LC** JX31. **DD** 340.05. *Quarterly Newsletter*.

NEWSLETTER - CANADIAN ASSOCIATION OF LAW LIBRARIES. See Library and Information Science.

NEWSLETTER - COURT PRACTICE INSTITUTE. Main/Corp Court Practice Institute. 0098-9843. US. English. Court Practice Institute, 127 North Dearborn Street, Chicago IL 60602. **LC** KF8911.A3. **DD** 347.737.

NEWSLETTER - CRIMINAL LAWYERS' ASSOCIATION. (NEWSLETTER). 0715-5980. Periodical. CN. English. ir. $45.00. Criminal Lawyers Association, 3 Sultan Street, Toronto Ontario M5S 1L6 Canada. **DD** 345.00971.

NEWSLETTER - ENVIRONMENTAL LAW CENTRE. (NEWSLETTER). Vol. 1, No. 1 (Fall 1983)-. 0826-581X. Periodical. CN. English. qt. $10.00. Environmental Law Centre, 102-104th Street, Edmonton Alberta T5J 1B2 Canada. **DD** 344.712304605.

NEWSLETTER - LAW SOCIETY OF ALBERTA. (NEWSLETTER). **Main/Corp** Law Society of Alberta. VAT Newsletter - Canadian Bar Association, Alberta BR. 0715-3465. CN. English. ir. Free. Canadian Bar Association, Alberta Branch 640, 610-8th Avenue South West, Calgary Alberta T2P 1H1 Canada. **LC** KE361.A43. **DD** 340.0627123.

NEWSLETTER - MISSOURI COUNCIL ON CRIMINAL JUSTICE. Main/Corp Missouri. Council on Criminal Justice. V. 1- March 1978-. 0270-3262. Periodical. US. English. bm. **LC** HV7275. **DD** 364.977805. *MCCJ MEMO*.

Law

NEWSLETTER OF THE FOOD, DRUG, AND COSMETIC LAW SECTION. Vol. 1, No. 1 (July 1983)-. 0742-4051. Periodical. US. English. sa. New York State Bar Association, One Elk Street, Albany NY 12207. **Tel** (518)463-3200. **Ed** Charles J Raubicheck. **LC** KFN5630.A15. **DD** 344.74704205, 347.47044205. **Circ** 700. (ctrl). Section newsletter on current legal issues related to food, and drug topics.

NEWSLETTER - STATE BAR OF ARIZONA. V. 1- Aug. 1972-. 0099-1058. US. English. bm. State Bar of Arizona, 363 North First Avenue, Phoenix AZ 85004. **Tel** (602)252-4804. **LC** KF200. **DD** 340.062791. *Newsletter - State Bar of Arizona, 0099-1058.*

NEWSLETTER - VIRGINIA STATE BAR. YOUNGER MEMBERS CONFERENCE. (NEWSLETTER). **Main/Corp** Virginia State Bar. Younger Members Conference. V. 1- Oct. 1973-. 0094-2251. US. English. Virginia State Bar, Younger Members Conference, Fifth and Franklin Street, Richmond VA 23219. **LC** KF200. **DD** 340.05.

NEWSLETTER - WEST COAST ENVIRONMENTAL LAW RESEARCH FOUNDATION. (NEWSLETTER). **VFOAT** WCELRF Newsletter. **VAT** West Coast Environmental Law Research Foundation Newsletter. 0715-4275. Periodical. CN. English. bm. 30.00. West Coast Environmental Law Research Foundation, 1012-207 West Hastings Street, Vancouver British Columbia V6B 1H7 Canada. **Tel** (604)684-7378. **Ed** Christine Lundberg. **DD** 344.71046. bk rev. **Circ** 250. Environmental legal issues including newsbriefs, case comments and book reviews.

NEWSNOTES - CENTER FOR LAW AND EDUCATION (U.S.). (NEWSNOTES). Began with No. 1 (July 1979). 0276-203X. Periodical. US. English. Free. Center for Law and Education Inc, 6 Appian Way, Cambridge MA 02138. **LC** KF4102. **DD** 344.7307.

NIGERIAN BAR JOURNAL. Periodical. English. ir. $6.50. Nigerian Bar Association, c/o Nigerian Law School, Lagos Nigeria.

NIGERIAN CONSTITUTIONAL LAW REPORTS. **VFOAT** NCLR. Vol. 1 (1981)-. English. an. Nigerian Law Publications, 28 Sabiu-Ajose Crescent, Suru-Lere Lagos State Nigeria. **DD** 342.66900264, 346.690200264.

NIGERIAN CURRENT LAW REVIEW : THE JOURNAL OF THE NIGERIAN INSTITUTE OF ADVANCED LEGAL STUDIES. Jan. 1982-. 0189-207X. Periodical. English. qt. 16 per issue. Editor-in-Chief, Nigerian Institute of Advanced Legal Studies, University of Lagos, Lagos Nigeria. **LC** K14. **DD** 349.66905, 346.69005.

NIHON KYOIKUHO GAKKAI NEMPO. **VFOAT** Educational Law Review. No. 1-. JA. Japanese. ir. 1000. Nihon Kyoikuho Gakkai, 2-17 Kanda Jimbocho Chiyoda-ku, Tokyo Japan. **LC** K14.

N.J. STATE BAR ASSOCIATION. **Main/Corp** New Jersey State Bar Association. **VFOAT** State Bar Advocate. **VAT** New Jersey State Bar Association Advocate. V. 1- June 1976-. 0145-5044. US. English. New Jersey State Bar Association, 172 West State Street, Trenton NJ 08608. **LC** KF200. **DD** 340.062749.

NJCM-BULLETIN. **VFOAT** N.J.C.M.-Bulletin. Periodical. NE. Dutch. bm. 35.00. Nederlands Juristen Comite voor de Mensenrechten, Hugo de Grootstraat 27, 2311 XK Leiden Netherlands. **LC** K14.

NLADA BRIEFCASE CEASED. **VFOAT** Briefcase. **VAT** National Legal Aid and Defender Association Briefcase. Vol. 30, No. 2 (Nov. 1971)-V. 39, No. 1 (Fall 1982). 0362-5885. Periodical. US. English. qt. $15.00. 2100 M Street NW/Suite 601, Washington DC 20037. **Ind/Abst** Leg. Resour. Index, Index Leg. Period. *Briefcase (Chicago, III.).*

NLADA DEFENDER BRIEFBANK CATALOGUE. **VFOAT** N.L.A.D.A. Defender Briefbank Catalgue. 0732-3441. US. English. $5.00 NLDA Individual and Program Members, $10.00 to all Others. National Legal Aid and Defender Association, 1625 K Street NW, Washington DC 20006. **LC** KF9602. **DD** 345.730504405, 347.305504405.

NLADA WASHINGTON MEMO CEASED. **Main/Corp** National Legal Aid and Defender Association. **VFOAT** Washington Memo. **VAT** National Legal Aid and Defender Association Washington Memo. Apr. 1972-. 0196-1624. Periodical. US. English. mo. National Legal Aid and Defender Association, Suite 601/2100 M Street NW, Washington DC 20037. **LC** KF336.A3. **DD** 347.731.

NLP HEALTH LABOR RELATIONS ALERT. **VFOAT** N.L.P. Health Labor Relations Alert. **VAT** National Law Publishing Health Labor Relations Alert. No. 101 (Feb. 1981)-. 0272-636X. Periodical. US. English. mo. $89.00. Rynd Communications, 99 Painters Mill Road, Owings Mill MD 21117. **Tel** (301)363-6400. **LC** KF3580.H4. **DD** 344.73.041, 347.30441. **Circ** 250. A newsletter for health care administrators which summarizes the latest court decisions affecting health care facilities. Contains a wealth of information on labor and employment problems.

NOGYO ROPPO. **Main/Corp** Japan. 1976-. JA. Japanese. ir. 2800. Gakuyoshobo, 7-5 Fujimi 1-chome, Chiyoda-ku 102 Tokyo Japan. *Nogyo Shoroppo.*

NOISE REGULATION REPORTER. (BNA NOISE REGULATION REPORTER). **Main/Corp** Bureau of National Affairs (Washington, D.C.). **VFOAT** Noise Regulation Reporter. No. 1- May 27, 1974-. 0148-7957. Periodical. US. English. bw. $296.00. Bureau of National Affairs Inc, 1231 25th Street NW, Washington DC 20037. **Tel** (301)258-1033. **LC** KF3813.A73. **DD** 344.73046305.

NOLPE SCHOOL LAW JOURNAL CEASED. **Main/Corp** National Organization on Legal Problems of Education. **VFOAT** School Law Journal. **VAT** National Organization on Legal Problems of Education School Law Journal. V. 1-11. 0047-8989. Periodical. US. English. sa. $2.50 Single Issue. National Organization on Legal Problems of Education, 825 Western Avenue, Topeka KS 66606. **Ind/Abst** Educ. Index. **LC** K14. **DD** 344.730705.

NOLPE SCHOOL LAW REPORTER. **Main/Corp** National Organization on Legal Problems of Education. **VAT** National Organization on Legal Problems of Education School Law Report. 0364-9547. US. English. mo. 3601 Southwest 29th/Suite 223, Topeka KS 66614. **LC** KF4114. **DD** 344.7307.

NOLSLETTER. **Main/Corp** Northeast Ohio Legal Services. **VAT** Northeast Ohio Legal Services Letter, NOLS Letter. 0270-8884. US. English. Nolsletter, 804 Metropolitan Tower, Youngstown OH 44503. **LC** KFO84.5.P6. **DD** 344.77103258, 347.71043258.

NOMIKO VEMA. GR. Greek, Modern. mo. Akademias-Mavromichale 2, Athena Greece. **LC** K14. *Nomikon Vema.*

NOMIKON PERIODIKON DIKAIOSYNE. Periodical. Greek, Modern. ir. 200.00. Hodos Euolpidos 10 T T 111, Athens Greece. **LC** K14.

NOMOS (FORTALEZA, BRAZIL). (NOMOS). 1978-. Periodical. BL. Portuguese. ir. Universidade Federal do Ceara, Departamento de Direito Publico, 60000 Fortaleza Ceara Brazil. **LC** K14. **DD** 349.8105, 348.1005.

NON-PROFIT ORGANIZATION TAX LETTER. 0550-8401. Periodical. US. English. ir. $137.00. Organization Management Inc, Box 944, West Bethesda MD 20817-0944. **Tel** (702)968-7039. **Ed** George D Webster. **LC** KF6449.A73. **DD** 343.73052. Complete reporting of non-profit development. Written for non-profit organizations, their management and professional advisors. *Non-Profit Tax Letter.*

NONMUNJIP (CHUNGNAM TAEKAHHYO. POMNYUL HAENGJONG YONGUSO). (NONMUNJIP). **VFOAT** Journal of Law and Public Administration. Periodical. Korean (English). ir. **LC** K14.

NORMAS LEGALES. V. 1- June 1942-. Periodical. PE. Spanish. bm. Normas Legales, Calle Ayacucho 348 Y 350, Trujillo Peru. **Tel** 245803.

NORTH CAROLINA ATTORNEY GENERAL REPORTS. **Main/Corp** North Carolina. Dept. of Justice. 0364-362X. Periodical. US. English. sa. PO Box 629, Raleigh NC 27602. **LC** KFN7840. **DD** 348.75605. *Biennial Report of the Attorney General.*

THE NORTH CAROLINA BAR NEWSLETTER. 0193-6646. Periodical. US. English. North Carolina State Bar, Box 25850, Raleigh NC 27611.

NORTH CAROLINA CENTRAL LAW JOURNAL. Vol. 2, No. 1 (Spring 1970)-. 0549-7434. Periodical. US. English. ir. $10.00. NC Central University, School of Law, Durham NC 27707. **Tel** (919)683-6382. **Ed** J Keith Tart. **Ind/Abst** Leg. Resour. Index, Contents Curr. Leg. Period., Index Leg. Period., Curr. Law Index, Contents Curr. Leg. Period. **LC** UNC. **DD** 340.05. bk rev. adv acc. **Circ** 700. An open forum for the publication of any appropriately documented legal writing concerning new or evolving areas of the law and problems facing our nation's minorities. *North Carolina College Law Journal.*

NORTH CAROLINA COURT OF APPEALS REPORTS. V. 1- Spring session 1968-. 0549-7450. US. English. ir. State of North Carolina Judicial Department, PO Box 2448, Raleigh NC 27602. **LC** KFN7448. **DD** 348.756043.

THE NORTH CAROLINA LAW MONITOR. **VFOAT** Law Monitor. Vol. 1, No. 1 (Mar. 8, 1985)-. 0883-7783. Periodical. US. English. sm. $345.00. North Carolina Law Monitor, State Capital Services Inc, 3201 Glenwood Avenue, Raleigh NC 27611. **DD** 347. *North Carolina Case Reporter.*

NORTH CAROLINA LAW REVIEW. V. 1- June 1922-. 0029-2524. Periodical. US. English. ir. University of North Carolina, Chapel Hill School of Law, Chapel Hill NC 27514. **Tel** (919)862-3926. **Ed** Teresa Wynn Roseborough. **Ind/Abst** Leg. Resour. Index, Public Aff. Inf. Serv. Bull., Index Leg. Period., Ocean. Abstr., Curr. Law Index, Contents Curr. Leg. Period. **LC** K14. **DD** 345.32. (cum index). bk rev. adv acc. **Circ** 2,000. Articles, comments, and notes analyzing current legal problems and significant new developments in the law.

THE NORTH CAROLINA RESEARCHER. Began May 1970. 0048-0665. Periodical. US. English. mo. $95.00. The Research Group Inc, PO Box 7187, Charlottesville VA 22906. **LC** KFN7457. **DD** 348.756048.

NORTH CAROLINA RULES OF COURT, WITH AMMENDMENTS RECEIVED. (NORTH CAROLINA RULES OF COURT, WITH AMENDMENTS RECEIVED TO . . .). **VFOAT** North Carolina Rules of Court, Desk Copy. Began in 1973. 0732-281X. US. English. **LC** KFN7929. **DD** 347.756051, 347.560751.

NORTH CAROLINA STATE BAR QUARTERLY. (NORTH CAROLINA STATE BAR QUARTERLY : OFFICIAL PUBLICATION OF THE NORTH CAROLINA STATE BAR). Vol. 25, No. 1-. 0164-6850. Periodical. US. English. qt. $6.00. North Carolina State Bar, PO Box 25908, Raleigh NC 27611. **Tel** (919)828-4620. **Ed** Jennifer White. bk rev. adv acc. **Circ** 11,000. (ctrl). Contains material relating to the practice of law. *North Carolina Bar, 0048-0657.*

THE NORTH DAKOTA AND SOUTH DAKOTA LEGAL DIRECTORY. See Yearbooks, Almanacs, Directories.

NORTH DAKOTA DEPARTMENT OF PUBLIC INSTRUCTION. EVALUATION REPORT, TITLE I, ESEA. (EVALUATION REPORT : TITLE I, ESEA). **Main/Corp** North Dakota. Dept. of Public Instruction. **VFOAT** North Dakota Title I ESEA Evaluation Report. 0149-2187. US. English. an. North Dakota Department of Public Instruction, State Capitol, Bismark ND 58505. **Tel** (701)224-2292. **LC** LB2826.N9. **DD** 371.909784. **Circ** 1,000. (ctrl). This publication describes the state of the art for North Dakota Chapter 1 for 1983-84. *Annual Evaluation Report. Elementary and Secondary Education Act of 1965. Title 1. Public Law 89-10, 0092-7848.*

THE NORTH DAKOTA JUDICIAL MASTER PROGRAM. 1977/79-. 0148-9445. Periodical. US. English. be. Judicial Planning Committee, State Capitol, Bismark ND 58505. **LC** KFN9108. **DD** 347.78401.

NORTH DAKOTA JUDICIAL NEWS. 0362-1812. US. English. Bismark Supreme Court, State Capitol, Bismark ND 58505. **LC** KFN9108.A15. **DD** 347.784005.

NORTH DAKOTA LAW REPORTS. Vol. 1, No. 1 (Jan. 23, 1981)-. 0275-2557. US. English. bw. $199.50. Mason Publishing Company, 366 Wacouta Street, St Paul MN 55101. **LC** KFN8647. **DD** 348.784044, 347.840844.

NORTH DAKOTA LAW REVIEW. V. 27, No. 1- Jan. 1951-. 0029-2745. Periodical. US. English. qt. $18.00. University of North Dakota School of Law,

Office of Business Management, Grand Forks ND 58202. **Tel** (701)777-2941. **Ed** Colleen Reinke. **Ind/Abst** Leg. Resour. Index, Sel. Water Resour. Abstr., Index Leg. Period., Curr. Law Index, Contents Curr. Leg. Period. bk rev. adv acc. **Circ** 1,825. Compilation of legal articles and reviews of recent court cases. *North Dakota Bar Briefs.*

NORTH WESTERN REPORTER. SECOND SERIES. VFOAT Northwestern Reporter. V. 1- No. 2D. 8750-2704. Periodical. US. English. wk. $97.50. West Publishing Company, 50 West Kellogg Boulevard/PO Box 43526, St Paul MN 55164. **DD** 348.

THE NORTHAMPTON COUNTY REPORTER. VFOAT Northampton County Reports. V. 1-. US. English. ir. **Ed** H D Maxwell. Each issue contains an index to its own contents - no vol index - loose.

NORTHERN DECISIONS. Vol. 1, No. 1 (15 Apr. 1983)-. 0715-7983. CN. English. bw. $150.00. Canadian Arctic Resources Committee, 46 Elgin Street/Room 11, Ottawa Ontario K1P 5K6 Canada. **LC** KE5110.A13. **DD** 354.7100823.

NORTHERN DISTRICT OF CALIFORNIA DIGEST. V. 1- Winter 1979-. US. English. qt. 220 Bush Street, 21st Floor, San Francisco CA 94104.

NORTHERN ILLINOIS UNIVERSITY LAW REVIEW. Vol. 1, No. 1 (Winter 1980)-. 0734-1490. Periodical. US. English. sa. $8.00. Illinois University Law Review, Northern Illinois University, Dekalb IL 60115. **Tel** (815)753-0619. **Ed** Jacqueline M Gerber. **Ind/Abst** Leg. Resour. Index, Index Leg. Period. **LC** K14. **DD** 349.77305, 347.73005. adv acc. **Circ** 300. Review of current federal, state, and agency law, focusing on impact and analysis of recent court decisions. *Lewis University Law Review.*

THE NORTHERN IRELAND LAW REPORTS. Jan. 1925-. Periodical. UK. English. qt. 25. Inc Council Law Reporting, Royal Courts of Justice, Belfast Northern Ireland BT1 3JX. **Tel** Belfast 665086. **Ed** W D Trimblo. Index in last issue of volume - attached. bk rev. **Circ** 650. (ctrl). Selected judgements delivered by the Supreme Court of Judicare for Northern Ireland.

THE NORTHERN IRELAND LEGAL QUARTERLY. V. 1- Nov. 1936-. 0029-3105. Periodical. UK. English. qt. 28.00. Queens University of Belfast, SLS Legal Publications, Belfast BT7 Northern Ireland. **Tel** 243133. **Ed** Brian A Childs. **Ind/Abst** Leg. Resour. Index, Index Leg. Period., Curr. Law Index, Contents Curr. Leg. Period. **LC** K14. Index in last issue of volume - attached. bk rev. adv acc. **Circ** 700. A general journal on topics of journal, with special attention paid to the law of Northern Ireland.

NORTHERN KENTUCKY LAW REVIEW. V. 3, No. 2-. 0198-8549. Periodical. US. English. ir. $12.00. Northern Kentucky University, Law School, Nunn Hall, Highland KY 41076. **Ind/Abst** Leg. Resour. Index, Soc. Work Res. Abstr., Index Leg. Period., Public Aff. Inf. Serv. Bull. **LC** K14. **DD** 340.05. *Northern Kentucky State Law Forum, 0198-8530.*

THE NORTHERN NEW ENGLAND LEGAL DIRECTORY, MAINE, NEW HAMPSHIRE, AND VERMONT. *See* Yearbooks, Almanacs, Directories.

NORTHERNTIER LEGAL JOURNAL. Vol. 1, No. 1 (Jan. 9, 1982)-. 0735-5505. Periodical. US. English. wk. $10.00. Tioga County Bar Association, c/o George C Williams, 33 Pearl Street, Wellboro PA 16901. **LC** K14. **DD** 349.7485605, 347.4856005.

NORTHROP UNIVERSITY LAW JOURNAL OF AEROSPACE, ENERGY AND THE ENVIRONMENT. **Main/Corp** Northrop University. School of Law. V. 1- Winter 1979-. 0196-1489. Periodical. US. English. an. $6.00. Northrop University School of Law, 1155 West Arbor Vitae Street, Inglewood CA 90306. **Tel** (213)641-3470. **Ind/Abst** Leg. Resour. Index, Index Leg. Period., Int. Aerosp. Abstr., Curr. Law Index, Index Leg. Period. **LC** K14. **DD** 346.7304692. bk rev. adv acc.

NORTHWEST SUBURBAN BAR ASSOCIATION JOURNAL. US. English. mo. Northwest Suburban Bar Association, 1350 Northwest Highway, Mt Prospect IL 60056. **LC** KF200. **DD** 349.77305, 347.73005.

NORTHWEST TERRITORIES REPORTS. VFOAT N.W.T.R. **VAT** Northwest Territories Law Reports. Pt. 1 (Sept. 1983)-. 0824-3433. Periodical. CN. English. bm. $88.00. Northwest Territories Reports, 2330 Midland Avenue, Agincourt Ontario M1S 1P7 Canada. **DD** 348.7192042.

NORTHWESTERN UNIVERSITY LAW REVIEW. Vol. 47, No. 1 (Mar.-Apr. 1952)-. 0029-3571. Periodical. US. English. bm. $25.00 Domestic, $27.00 Foreign. Northwestern University, School of Law, 357 East Chicago Avenue, Chicago IL 60611. **Tel** (312)980-8467. **Ind/Abst** Manage. Contents, Leg. Resour. Index, Index Leg. Period., Sociol. Abstr., Soc. Welf. Soc. Plan./Policy Soc. Dev., ABC Pol Sci, Writ. Am. Hist., Public Aff. Inf. Serv. Bull., Curr. Law Index, Soc. Sci. Citation Index, Contents Curr. Leg. Period., Index Leg. Period. **LC** K14. **DD** 340.0. bk rev. adv acc. **Circ** 1,300. *Illinois Law Review (1939).*

NOSA MUNJE SARYE YONGUJIP. V. 1- Series. Korean. ir. 2500. Hanguk Nosa Munje Yongu Hyophoe, 241-1 3-Ka Ulchiro Chung-ku, Seoul Korea. **LC** K14.

NOTES FROM THE TARLTON LAW LIBRARY. **Main/Corp** Tarlton Law Library. Began with Vol. for 1966. 0029-4040. US. English. bm. $75.00. University of Texas, Law Library Publications Coordinator, 727 East 26th Street, Austin TX 78705-5799. **Tel** (512)471-7726. **Ed** Mary Menke. **LC** KF4. **DD** 016.3400973. **Circ** 115. Brief bibliographies, finding aids, recent library acquisitions.

NOTES OF RECENT DECISIONS RENDERED BY THE IMMIGRATION APPEAL BOARD. *See* Emigration and Immigration.

NOTICES OF JUDGEMENT UNDER THE FEDERAL FOOD, DRUG, AND COSMETIC ACT. FOODS. (NOTICES OF JUDGEMENT UNDER THE FEDERAL FOOD, DRUG, AND COSMETIC ACT : FOODS). **Main/Corp** United States. Food and Drug Administration. 1- March 1940-. Periodical. English. ir. **LC** HD9000.9.U5. *Notices of Judgement under the Food and Drugs Act: Food.*

NOTICIAS ADV. VFOAT Noticias A.D.V. Yearly Vol. 1, No. 1-. Periodical. Portuguese. ir. **LC** KHD211.A15. **DD** 349.8105, 348.1005.

NOTIZIARIO DEL CONSIGLIO REGIONALE DELLA LIGURIA. **Main/Corp** Liguria (Italy). Consiglio Regionale. Yearly V. 1- July 1973-. Italian. ir. Consiglio Regionale Della Liguria, Mura Santa Chiara 3 16128, Genova Italy.

NOTIZIARIO GIURIDICO REGIONALE. **Main/Corp** Unione Degli Industriali Della Provincia di Torino. 1- Sept/Oct. 1971-. Periodical. Italian. ir. V Fanti 17, Ferino Itlay. **LC** K25. **DD** 342.450905.

NOTRE DAME INTERNATIONAL LAW JOURNAL. Vol. 1 (1983)-. 0738-2057. Periodical. US. English. an. $5.00. Notre Dame International Law Journal, Notre Dame Law School, Notre Dame IN 46556. **LC** JX1. **DD** 341.05.

NOTRE DAME JOURNAL OF LAW, ETHICS & PUBLIC POLICY. VFOAT Journal of Law, Ethics, and Public Policy, Journal of Law, Ethics & Public Policy. **VAT** Notre Dame Journal of Law, Ethics, and Public Policy. Vol. 1, Inaugural Issue-. 0883-3648. Periodical. US. English. sa. $24.00. Notre Dame Law School, Thomas J White Center on Law & Government, Notre Dame IN 46556. **LC** K14. **DD** 340.11205.

THE NOTRE DAME LAW REVIEW. Vol. 58, No. 1 (Oct. 1982)-. 0745-3515. Periodical. US. English. ir. $18.00. Notre Dame Law School, PO Box 988, Notre Dame IN 46556. **Tel** (219)239-7097. **Ed** John D Goetz. **Ind/Abst** Leg. Resour. Index, Cathol. Period. Lit. Index, Index Leg. Period., Public Aff. Inf. Serv. Bull. **LC** K14. **DD** 340.05. bk rev. adv acc. **Circ** 1,800. (ctrl). Articles and book reviews by judges, lawyers, law professors and students analyzing current and emerging legal issues and developments. *Notre Dame Lawyer, 0029-4535.*

NOTRE DAME LAWYER *CEASED.* (THE NOTRE DAME LAWYER). Vol. 1-57. 0029-4535. Periodical. US. English. qt. **Ind/Abst** Int. Aerosp. Abstr., Cathol. Period. Lit. Index, Index Leg. Period., Public Aff. Inf. Serv. Bull.

NOUVEAU CODE DE PROCEDURE CIVILE ET CODE DE PROCEDURE CIVILE. **Main/Corp** France. **Series/Titl** Petits Codes Dalloz. **VFOAT** Code de Procedure Civile, Nouveau Code de Procedure Civile. Began with 1976 Vol. FR. French. an. 11 rue Soufflot, 75240 Paris Cedex 05 Dalloz. **DD** 347.4402632, 344.407502632. *Code de Procedure Civile. Code de Procedure Civile Annote d'Apres la Doctrine et la Jurisprudence, avec Renvois aux Publications Dalloz.*

LE NOUVEAU POUVOIR JUDICIAIRE. No. 271- May 1975-. Periodical. French. ir. 50.00. Union Sydicale des Magiotrats, 33 rue du Four, Paris France 75006. **DD** 347.44014. *Pouvoir Judiciaire.*

NOUVELLES DU RESEU - COUNSEIL CANADIEN DE LA DOCUMENTATION JURIDIQUE. (NOUVELLES DU RESEAU). Vol. 1, No 1 (Mar. 1982)-. 0713-4827. Periodical. CN. French. ty. Conseil Canadien de la Documentation Juridique, 2409 rue Yonge, Toronto Ontario M4P 2E7 Canada. **DD** 349.7105.

NOVA LAW JOURNAL. V. 1- Spring 1977-. 0149-6204. US. English. ty. $15.00. Nova University Law Center, 3100 SW 9th Avenue, Ft Lauderdale FL 33315. **Tel** (305)467-0309. **Ed** Robert C Levine. **Ind/Abst** Leg. Resour. Index, Index Leg. Period. **LC** K14. **DD** 340.09759. bk rev. adv acc. All topical issues of current legal problems explored in intellectual, stimulating analysis.

NOVA SCOTIA LAW NEWS. V. 1- June 1974-. 0316-6325. Periodical. CN. English. bm. 35.00. Nova Scotia Barristers Society, 1815 Upper Watter Street, Halifax Nova Scotia B3J 1S7 Canada. **Tel** (902)422-8335. **Ed** Mary Helleinev. **LC** KE361.N6. **DD** 340.09716. **Circ** 1,600. (ctrl). Digests of decisions of Nova Scotia courts, articles of interest to lawyers' digests of new Nova Scotia legislation.

NOVA SCOTIA REPORTS (FREDERICTON, N.B.). (NOVA SCOTIA REPORTS). 0048-0983. CN. English. ir. Maritime Law Book Ltd, Box 302, Fredericton New Brunswick E3B 4Y9 Canada. **DD** 348.716044.

NOVA SCOTIA REPORTS (FREDERICTON, N.B. : BOUND CUMULATION). (NOVA SCOTIA REPORTS). Vol. 1 1965/69)-V. 5 (1965/69. 0048-0983. Periodical. CN. English. ir. $75.00 Per Vol. Maritime Law Book Ltd, Box 302, Fredericton New Brunswick E3B 4Y9 Canada. **DD** 348.716043.

NOVAIA INOSTRANNAIA LITERATURA PO OBSHCHESTVENNYM NAUKAM : GOSUDARSTVO I PRAVO. 1976-. Periodical. UR. Multilingual (Russian). mo. 0.50 Single Issue. Ul Krasikova 28/45, Moskva Russian SFSR. **LC** K38. *Novaia Literatura po Gosudarstvu I Pravu za Rubezhom.*

NOVAIA SOVETSKAIA LITERATURA PO OBSHCHESTVENNYM NAUKAM : GOSUDARSTVO I PRAVO. 1976-. Periodical. UR. Russian. mo. 0.50 Single Issue. Ul Krasikova 28/45, Moskva Russian SFSR. **LC** K38. *Novaia Sovetskaia Literatura po Gosudarstvu I Pravu.*

NOVAS TABELAS DO IMPOSTO DE RENDA PARA . . . ASSALARIADOS E NAO-ASSALARIADOS. Portuguese. an. **LC** KHD4630. **DD** 343.810520212, 348.103520212.

NOVINKY LITERATURY : STAT A PRAVO. 1973-. CS. Multilingual (chiefly in Czech). qt. 48.00. Statini Knihovna CSR, Liliova 5, Praha Czechoslovakia. *Novinky Literatury. Spolecenske Vedy. Rada III: Stat A Pravo.*

NOW AND THEN. (NOW AND THEN : A NEWSLETTER FOR THOSE INTERESTED IN HISTORY AND LAW). Oct. 1979-. 0229-690X. Periodical. CN. English. ir. $15.48. Society of History & Law in Canada, York Univerity/Osgoode Hall Law School, Downsview Ontario Canada. **Tel** (416)667-2100. **DD** 349.7105.

NRC REGULATORY AGENDA. **Main/Corp** U.S. Nuclear Regulatory Commission. Division of Rules and Records. **VFOAT** N.R.C. Regulatory Agenda. **VAT** Nuclear Regulatory Commission Regulatory Agenda. Vol. 1, No. 1 (Jan. 31-Apr. 9, 1982)-. 0742-2652. US. English. qt. Superintendent of Documents, Government Printing Office, Washington DC 20402. **LC** KF2138. **DD** 343.73092505, 347.30392505. Issued also in microfiche.

NRECA-APPA LEGAL REPORTING SERVICE. (NRECA—APPA LEGAL REPORTING SERVICE). **Main/Corp** National Rural Electric Cooperative Association. **VAT** National Rural Electric Cooperative—American Public Power Association Legal Reporting Service. 0362-8833. Periodical. US. English. mo. $125.00. National Rural Electric Cooperative Association, 1800 Massachusetts Avenue NW, Washington DC 20036. **Tel** (202)857-9644. **Ed** William T Crisp. **LC** KF2125.A15. **DD** 343.73092. **Circ** 1,500. Editorial, electric utility legal cases, and annoucements of electric utility legal seminars. *NRECA Legal Reporting Service.*

Law

NSCLC WASHINGTON WEEKLY. Main/Corp National Senior Citizens Law Center. VAT National Senior Citizens Law Center Washington Weekly. 1974. 0277-7460. Periodical. US. English. ir. National Senior Citizens Law Center, 1302-18th Street NW/Suite 701, Washington DC 20036. Tel (202)887-5280. Ed Carla J Reimann. adv acc. Circ 1,800. (ctrl).

NSR. NATIONAL SHORTHAND REPORTER. VFOAT National Shorthand Reporter. 0274-5860. Periodical. US. English. mo. $25.00. National Shorthand Reporters Association, 118 Park Street SE, Vienna VA 22180. Tel (703)281-4677. Ed Mary Louise Gilman. bk rev. adv acc. Circ 19,000. News, features, technological updates on matters of concern to the court reporting profession. *National Shorthand Reporter, 0163-2450.*

NUCLEAR LAW BULLETIN. Main/Corp Organisation for Economic Co-Operation and Development. Nuclear Energy Agency. No. - 1972-. 0304-341x. Periodical. English. sa. $24.00. OECD Publications Center, 1750 Pennsylvania Avenue NW/Suite 1207, Washington DC 20006. Tel (202)724-1857. (cum index). Available on microfiche. Reports legislative and regulatory work on nuclear law and administrative decisions in most of the countries of the world and concerned with the development and exploitation of nuclear energy.

NUCLEAR REGULATION REPORTS. *See Energy.*

NUCLEAR REGULATORY LEGISLATION. (NUCLEAR REGULATORY LEGISLATION THROUGH THE . . .). Main/Corp United States. Began with 95th Congress, 2nd Session, 1978. 0736-5993. US. English. Superintendent of Documents, US Government Printing Office, Washington DC 20402. LC KF2138.A29. DD 346.730467924, 347.306467924. *Atomic Energy Legislation Through . . . .*

NUDIS VERBIS. V. 1- Winter 1976-. 0147-3573. Periodical. US. English. qt. PO Box 2448, Raleigh NC 27602. LC KFN7908.A15. DD 347.7560105.

THE NURSE, THE PATIENT & THE LAW. *See Medicine - Nursing.*

NUTRITION LEGISLATION NEWS. 8756-6060. Periodical. US. English. bm. $290.00 Per Congress, $150.00 Per Congressional Session. Nutrition Legislation Services, PO Box 75035, Washington DC 20013.

N.Y. COUNTY LAWYER. VFOAT NY County Lawyer. VAT New York County Lawyer. Sept. 1981-. Periodical. US. English. mo. Nork County Lawyers' Association, 14 Vesey Street, New York NY 10007. *Vesey Street Letter.*

NYS BOARD OF ELECTIONS FORMAL OPINION. Main/Corp New York (State). State Board of Elections. VFOAT N.Y.S. Board of Elections Formal Opinion. US. English. State of New York, State Board of Elections, 99 Washington Avenue, Albany NY 12210. LC KFN5710. DD 342.74707, 347.47027. *Formal Opinion, 0271-4736.*

OB/GYN LITIGATION REPORTER. VFOAT OB GYN Litigation Reporter. VAT OB GYN Litigation Reporter. 0735-9551. Periodical. US. English. sm. $600.00. Andrews Publications, PO Box 200, 5123 West Chester Pike, Edgemont PA 19028. Tel (215)353-2565. Ed Leonard Andrews. National journal of obstetrics and gynecology related litigation.

OBITER DICTA. 0029-7585. Periodical. CN. English. bw. $1.93. York University, Osgoode Law School, 4700 Keele Street, Downsview Ontario M3J 2R5 Canada. Tel (416)667-3141. Ind/Abst Curr. Law Index, Leg. Resour. Index. *Osgoode Hall Obiter Dicta.*

OBJECTION. No. 1 (Feb. 1982)-. 0711-7639. Periodical. CN. French. qt $10.00. Objection, CP 301 Succursale N, Montreal Quebec H2Y 3M4 Canada. DD 349.71405.

THE OBJECTOR. *See Military Science.*

OBSCENITY LAW BULLETIN. Vol. 1, No. 1 (Jan. 1977)-. 0195-1696. Periodical. US. English. bm. $10.00. National Obscenity Law Center, 475 Riverside Drive/Suite 239, New York NY 10115. Tel (212)870-3232. Ed Paul J McGeady. LC KF9444.A15. DD 344.73054705, 347.30454705. Circ 800. (ctrl). Current information on obscenity law and obscenity law decisions for use of prosecutors and other interested parties and libraries.

OBSHCHESTVENNYE NAUKI V SSSR. SERIIA 4 : GOSUDARSTVO I PRAVO. VFOAT Gosudarstvo I Pravo. VAT Obshchestvennye Nauki V SSSR. Seriia Chetyre : Gosudarstvo I Pravo. Began in 1974. 0202-2060. Periodical. UR. Russian. bm. Akademiia Nauk SSSR, Ul Krasikova D 28/45, Moskva USSR. LC K15.

OBSHCHESTVENNYE NAUKI ZA RUBEZHOM. SERIIA 4 : GOSUDARSTVO I PRAVO. VFOAT Gosudarstvo I Pravo. VAT Obshchestvennye Nauki za Rubezhom. Seriia Chetyre : Gosudarstvo I Pravo. Began in 1973. UR. Russian. qt. 1.00 Each Issue. Akademiia Nauk SSR, G-19 Ul Krasikova 28/45, Moskva USSR. LC K15.

OBSHTESTVO I PRAVO. Oct. 1979-. Periodical. BU. Bulgarian. ir. Suiuz Na Iuristite v Bulgariia, 1000 Sofiia, Ul Zhdanov No, Sofiia Bulgaria. LC K15.

OCBA BULLETIN. Main/Corp Orange County Bar Association. VAT Orange County Bar Association Bulletin. 0473-1212. US. English. 17291 Irvine Boulevard, Tustin CA 92680. LC KF200.

OCCASIONAL PAPERS / REPRINTS SERIES IN CONTEMPORARY ASIAN STUDIES. VFOAT Contemporary Asian Studies Series. No. 1-. 0730-0107. Monographic Series. US. English. bm. $15.00 Domestic, $20.00 Foreign. University of Maryland School of Law, 500 West Baltimore Street, Baltimore MD 21201. Tel (301)528-3870. Ed Jaw-ling Joanne Chang. Circ 800. Scholarly publication on East Asia, with emphasis on Chinese law, politics and international relations.

OCCASIONAL PAPERS - UNIVERSITY OF CHICAGO. LAW SCHOOL. Main/Corp University of Chicago. Law School. Vol. 1 1971-. Monographic Series. US. English. University of Chicago, Law School, Chicago IL 60637.

OCCASIONAL REPORT - LAW SOCIETY OF UPPER CANADA. Main/Corp Law Society of Upper Canada. No. 1- Jan. 30, 1976-. 0383-9656. Periodical. CN. English. ir. Law Society of Upper Canada, York University, Osgoode Hall, Downsview Ontario M3J 1P3 Canada. DD 340.09713.

OCCUPATIONAL HEALTH AND SAFETY LAW. V. 1- Apr. 1977-. 0706-5019. Periodical. CN. English. bm. $154.77. Corpus Information Service Ltd, 1450 Don Mills Road, Don Mills Ontario Canada M3B 2X7. Tel (416)445-6641. Ed Mark R Sabourin. DD 344.71046502632. Full text looseleaf service containing all Canadian occupational safety and health legislation. Includes a monthly newsletter and bi-monthly replacement page updates.

OCCUPATIONAL SAFETY & HEALTH CASES. *See Industrial Health & Safety.*

OCCUPATIONAL SAFETY AND HEALTH LAW. Series/Titl Litigation and Administrative Practice Series. Litigation Course Handbook Series. Began with 1978. 0737-1268. US. English. an. Practising Law Institute, 810 Seventh Avenue, New York NY 10019. NLM WA 33 AA1 O16.

OCEAN LAW MEMO. 0361-2473. Periodical. US. English. University of Oregon Law School, Ocean and Coastal Law Center, Eugene OR 97403. Tel (503)686-3845. Ed Jon L Jacobson. LC JX4419. DD 341.44805. Circ 1,500. Provides single-topic, substantive analysis of current issues in ocean law to all members of the ocean-oriented community and the interested public at large.

OF COUNSEL (NEW YORK, N.Y.). (OF COUNSEL). Vol. 1, No. 1 (Jan. 1982)-. 0730-3815. Periodical. US. English. mo. $195.00. Law & Business Inc, 855 Valley Road, Clifton NJ 07013. Tel (201)472-7400. Ed Larry Smith. LC KF300.A1. DD 340.02373. bk rev. adv acc. Circ 1,000. A management report for larger law firms and corporate law departments.

DIE OFFENTLICHE VERWALTUNG. V. 1-. 0029-859X. Periodical. GW. German. sm. W Kohlhammer Verlag GMBH, Hessbruhlstrasse 69, PF 800430, 7000 Stuttgart 80 West Germany. Ind/Abst Coal Abstr., Energy Res. Abstr.

OFFICE OF THE PRESIDENT DECISIONS ON LABOR ISSUES, WITH DOCTRINAL SUMMARIES AND NOTES. V. 1-. PH. English. ir. Philippine Law Gazette, 13 Mapayapa Street UP Village, Diliman Quezon City 3004 Philippines.

OFFICE OF WATER OPERATING GUIDANCE AND ACCOUNTABILITY SYSTEM. APPENDIX. Main/Corp United States. Environmental Protection Agency. Office of Water. VFOAT Operating Guidance and Accountability System. 0749-3568. US. English. US Environmental Protection Agency Office of Water, Washington DC 20460. DD 343.

OFFICERS, COUNCIL, COMMITTEES, AND SECTION MEMBERS. Main/Corp American Bar Association. Tort and Insurance Practice Section. 1980-1981-. 0731-9061. US. English. an. American Bar Association, 1155 East 60th Street, Chicago IL 60637. LC KF195.I5. DD 340.02573. *Directory of Officers, Council, Committees and Members, 0098-1249.*

OFFICERS, COUNCIL, COMMITTEES, AND SECTION MEMBERS. Main/Corp American Bar Association. Section of Public Utility Law. 0731-907X. US. English. American Bar Association, 1155 East 60th Street, Chicago IL 60637. LC KF195.P85. DD 343.7309025, 347.3039025.

OFFICES SHOPS AND RAILWAY PREMISES ACT 1963. REPORT BY THE SECRETARY OF STATE FOR EMPLOYMENT. (THE OFFICES, SHOPS, AND RAILWAY PREMISES ACT, 1963). Main/Corp Great Britain. Dept. of Employment. 0307-7071. UK. English. an. 0.26 1/2 Single Issue. Her Majestys Stationery Office, 49 High Holborn, London WC1V 6HB England. LC HD7695. DD 344.42012. *Offices, Shops, and Railway Premises Act, 1963.*

OFFICIAL BRAND LAWS. (OFFICIAL BRAND LAWS GOVERNING REGISTRATION, INVESTIGATION, INSPECTION AND RULES AND REGULATIONS OF THE NEBRASKA BRAND COMMITTEE). Main/Corp Nebraska. 0093-0229. US. English. Secretary of State, State Capitol/Suite 2300, Lincoln NE 68509. LC KFN246.A29. DD 343.782076.

OFFICIAL COMPILATION OF THE CODES, RULES AND REGULATIONS OF THE STATE OF NEW YORK. Main/Corp New York (State). Vol. 1 (Apr. 30, 1945)-. US. English. qt. Shepards McGraw Hill, PO Box 1235, Colorado Springs CO 80901.

OFFICIAL DECISIONS, OPINIONS AND RELATED MATTERS OF THE PUBLIC EMPLOYMENT RELATIONS BOARD OF THE STATE OF NEW YORK. 0279-1005. US. English. ir. $385.00. Labor Relations Press, PO Box 579, Fort Washington PA 19034. Tel (215)628-3113. Ed Al Celmer. Abstracts and full-text of GAO decisions. Complete indexing, cite tracker, statute tracker, citator, articles and parallel database.

OFFICIAL DIRECTORY - NEW JERSEY STATE BAR ASSOCIATION. *See Yearbooks, Almanacs, Directories.*

OFFICIAL EXPORT GUIDE. 0278-6389. US. English. an. $55.00. Budd Publications Inc, PO Box 7, New York NY 10004. LC KF1987.A15. DD 343.730878, 347.303878.

OFFICIAL GAME & FISH COMMISSION FISHING CODE OF REGULATIONS. Main/Corp Arkansas Game and Fish Commission. VFOAT Official Game and Fish Commission Fishing Code of Regulations. US. English. an. Arkansas Game and Fish Commission, Game & Fish Building, No 2 Natural Resources Drive, Little Rock AR 72205. LC KFA3854.A39. DD 346.76704695602636, 347. 67064695602636. *Guide to Hunting & Fishing Regulations. Fishing Edition.*

OFFICIAL GAZETTE - EAST CENTRAL STATE OF NIGERIA. Main/Corp East Central State (Nigeria). English. ir. $15.00. DD 340.096694.

OFFICIAL GAZETTE OF THE EAST AFRICAN COMMUNITY. Main/Corp East African Community. VFOAT E.A.C. Gazette. V. 1- Dec.1967-. US. English. mo. LC Microfilm LL-02191 KRD.

THE OFFICIAL GUIDE TO U.S. LAW SCHOOLS. (THE OFFICIAL GUIDE TO US LAW SCHOOLS). VAT Official Guide to United States Law Schools. 1986-87-. 0886-3342. US. English. an. $14.00. Publications, LSAC/LSAS Department 0-6/PO Box 63, Newtown PA 18940. DD 340. *Prelaw Handbook, 0146-9142.*

OFFICIAL JOURNAL OF THE EUROPEAN COMMUNITIES : DEBATES OF THE EUROPEAN PARLIAMENT. *See Public Administration.*

OFFICIAL JOURNAL OF THE EUROPEAN COMMUNITIES. L, LEGISLATION. (OFFICIAL JOURNAL OF THE EUROPEAN COMMUNITIES : LEGISLATION). V. 16- Jan. 1, 1973-. 0378-6978. LU. English. ir. $173.00.

Law

European Community Information Service, 2100 M Street NW/Suite 707, Washington DC 20037. **Ind/Abst** Coal Abstr. **DD** 340.094.

OFFICIAL OPINIONS FROM THE SUPREME JUDICIAL COURT OF MASSACHUSETTS. Main/Corp Massachusetts Supreme Judicial Court. 392 Mass. (May 25, 1984)-. US. English. wk. Bateman & Slade Inc, 45 Broad Street, Boston MA 02109. Each issue contains an index to its own contents - no vol index - loose. *Advance Sheet Opinions. Section 1.*

OFFICIAL REPORTS OF THE SUPREME COURT. Main/Corp United States. Supreme Court. VFOAT United States Reports. 0364-0973. US. English. ir. Superintendent of Documents, U S GPO, Washington DC 20402.

OGDEN'S REVISED CALIFORNIA REAL PROPERTY LAW. English. ir. (cum index).

OHA DIGEST. VAT Office of Hearings and Appeals Digest. 0271-2180. US. English. wk. Energy Focus, 2906 Upton Street Northwest, Washington DC 20008. **LC** KF2120.A59. **DD** 346.730467902636, 347.306467902636.

THE OHA LAW REPORTER. Main/Corp United States. Social Security Administration. Office of Hearings and Appeals. Began with Vol. 3, Jan. 1979. US. English. qt. Department of Health and Human Services, Social Security Administration, Office of Hearings and Appeals, Room 503/BCT-II, PO Box 2518, Washington DC 20013. *BHA Law Reporter.*

OHIO APPELLATE DECISIONS INDEX. CRIMINAL CASES. *See* Indexes/Abstracts.

OHIO BAR REPORTS. (OHIO BAR REPORTS : REPORTS OF CASES ARGUED AND DETERMINED IN ALL COURTS IN OHIO : ALSO CONTAINING THE SUMMARIES OF CIVIL AND CRIMINAL CASES FROM OHIO'S COURTS OF APPEALS AS APPEARED IN THE JULY-SEPTEMBER ISSUES OF THE OHIO STATE BAR ASSOCIATION REPORT MAGAZINE). 1st Series, V. 1 (July/Sept. 1982)-. 0742-9266. US. English. Ed William C Moore. **LC** KFO47.A33. **DD** 348.77104405, 347.71084405.

OHIO CIVIL PRACTICE, PROCEDURE, AND FORMS. Main/Corp Ohio. US. English. ir. Anderson Publishing Company, PO Box 1576, 646 Main Street, Cincinnati OH 45202. **Tel** (513)421-4142.

OHIO COURTS. Main/Corp Ohio. Supreme Court. Office of the Administrative Assistant. US. English. Supreme Court of Ohio, Office Administrative Director, Columbus OH 43215. **Tel** (614)466-3456.

OHIO COURTS SUMMARY. 1969-. US. English. an. Ohio Supreme Court, Office of the Administrative Director, Columbus OH 43215. **LC** KFO71. **DD** 347.77101.

OHIO CRIMINAL SUMMARIES. 0274-7634. Periodical. US. English. sm. $35.00 Members, $50.00 Nonmembers. Ohio Public Defenders Association, Room 421/8 East Long Street, Columbus OH 43215.

OHIO DISTRICT COURT REVIEW. V. 1- 1980-. 0274-7294. Periodical. US. English. mo. $175.00. Advocate Research Inc, 3620 North High Street, Columbus OH 43214. **Tel** (614)262-2539. Ed Gustav V Olsen. Summaries of Ohio Federal District Court opinions which are otherwise unreported.

OHIO JUVENILE COURT STATISTICS. *See* Statistics.

OHIO MONTHLY RECORD. V. 1- Feb. 1977-. 0163-0008. US. English. mo. $225.00. Banks Baldwin Law Publishing Company, PO Box 1974 University Center, Cleveland OH 04410. **Tel** (216)721-7373. An easy-to-use companion service updating the Ohio Administrative code. Following each month, subscribers receive all administrative agency rules adopted, amended, or rescinded.

OHIO MOTOR VEHICLE LAWS. Main/Corp Ohio. US. English. Ohio Department of Highway Safety, 240 Parsons Avenue, Columbus OH 43205. **LC** KFO297.A29. **DD** 343.7710946.

OHIO NORTHERN UNIVERSITY LAW REVIEW. V. 1- 1973-. 0094-534X. US. English. qt. $17.50. Ohio Northern University Law School, PO Box 153, Ada OH 45810. **Tel** (419)772-2248. Ed Kenneth E Fleisehmann. **Ind/Abst** Leg. Resour. Index, Index Leg. Period., Contents Curr. Leg. Period., Curr. Law Index. **LC** K15. **DD** 340.05. adv acc. Circ 1,250. (ctrl)

Law review containing articles on recent supreme court decision and lead articles on current legal issues. One issue per volume is Ohio Review. *Ohio Northern University Intramural Law Review.*

OHIO OFFICIAL REPORTS. Main/Corp Ohio. Courts. US. English. ir. Law Abstract Publishing Company, 71 East Elm Street, PO Box 564, Norwalk OH 44857.

OHIO OFFICIAL REPORTS. ADVANCE SHEETS. (OHIO OFFICIAL REPORTS : NEW SERIES : CASES ARGUED AND DETERMINED IN THE COURTS OF AND IN OHIO). Vol. 1, No. 1, New Series (July 12, 1982)-. 0744-9607. US. English. ir. $115.00. Anderson Publishing Company, 646 Main Street, Cincinnati OH 45201. **Tel** (513)421-4142. adv acc.

OHIO PROBATE CODE, ANNOTATED. Main/Corp Ohio. US. English. Banks-Baldwin Law Publishing Company, Cleveland OH 44106. **LC** KFO144.A29. **DD** 346.77105202632. *Ohio Revised Probate Code Annotated, Amended.*

OHIO PUBLIC EMPLOYEE REPORTER. VFOAT Public Employee Reporter (Ohio Edition). Vol. 1-. Periodical. US. English. Labor Relations Press, One Labor Relations Plaza, PO Box 579, Fort Washington PA 19034. **Tel** (215)628-3115. Abstracts and full-text of Ohio State Labor Board decisions. Complete indexing, many access points, table of cases, citation tracker, rules and regulations of boards, articles, database and off-line searches.

OHIO STATE BAR ASSOCIATION REPORT (1981). (OHIO STATE BAR ASSOCIATION REPORT). Vol. 54, No. 44 (Nov. 16, 1981. 0744-8376. Periodical. US. English. wk. $110.00. OSBA Report, 33 West 11th Avenue, Columbus OH 432011. **Tel** (614)421-2121. Ed William C Moore. **Ind/Abst** Leg. Resour. Index. **LC** KF200. **DD** 340.060771. adv acc. Circ 18,000. (ctrl). Full text opinions and summaries of opinions from all courts serving Ohio, articles on Ohio law, and specialized features on Ohio legislation and rules for attorneys, classified and display ads. *Ohio State Bar Association (Series), 0199-0322.*

OHIO STATE LAW JOURNAL. V. 9- Winter 1948-. 0048-1572. Periodical. US. English. $18.00. College of Law, 1659 North High Street, Columbus OH 43221. **Tel** (614)422-6892. Ed Robert L Hust. **Ind/Abst** Public Aff. Inf. Serv. Bull., Index Leg. Period. **LC** Microfilm (O). **DD** 340.05. (cum index). bk rev. adv acc. Circ 2,000. *Law Journal (Columbus, Ohio).*

OIL AND GAS LAW. US. English. an. $700.00. Matthew Bender & Company Inc, 1275 Broadway, Albany NY 12201. **Tel** (800)833-9844.

OIL & GAS (OXFORD, OXFORDSHIRE). (OIL & GAS : LAW AND TAXATION REVIEW). VFOAT O.G.L.T.R. No. 1 (July 1982)-. 0263-5070. Periodical. UK. English. mo. 155. ESC Publishing Ltd, 25 Beaumont Street, Oxford OX 2NP England. **Tel** (0865)512281. Ed Karen Troy. **LC** K3911.2. **DD** 343.0772, 342.3772. bk rev. adv acc. Circ 400. Publication for legal and tax experts, containing in-depth articles and a news section covering new legislation, fiscal matters and important legal cases.

OKINAWA HOGAKU. VFOAT Journal of the Association of Law, the Okinawa Kokusai University. Ed. 1973-. JA. Japanese. ir. Okinawa Kokusai Daigaku Hogakai, 276-2 Ginowan Japan. **LC** K15. **DD** 340.0952.

OKLAHOMA CITY UNIVERSITY LAW REVIEW. V. 1- Spring 1976-. 0364-9458. US. English. ty. $18.00. Oklahoma City University, 2501 North Blackwelder, Oklahoma City OK 73106. **Tel** (405)521-5280. Ed Edward Hasbrook. **Ind/Abst** Leg. Resour. Index, Index Leg. Period., Curr. Law Index. **LC** K15. **DD** 340.05. bk rev. adv acc. Circ 700.

OKLAHOMA DECISIONS REPORTED IN PACIFIC REPORTER, SECOND SERIES. VFOAT Oklahoma Decisions. 0747-2986. US. English. wk. $75.00. West Publishing Company, Box Box 43526, St Paul MN 55164. **DD** 348.

OKLAHOMA LAW REVIEW. V. 1- May 1948-. 0030-1752. Periodical. US. English. qt. $20.00. Oklahoma Law Review, 300 Timberdell Road, Norman OK 73019. **Tel** (405)325-5191. Ed Philip Hart. **Ind/Abst** Leg. Resour. Index, Account. Index. Suppl., Index Leg. Period., Curr. Law Index, Contents Curr. Leg. Period. **DD** 347.05. Index available. bk rev adv acc. Circ 1,250. Microform. A scholarly legal journal

with articles and student-written articles covering a wide range of national and state legal issues.

THE OKLAHOMA LEGAL DIRECTORY. *See* Yearbooks, Almanacs, Directories.

THE OKLAHOMA REGISTER. Vol. 1, No.1 (Nov. 1983)-. 0741-8612. Periodical. US. English. mo. $120.00. Oklahoma Department of Libraries, 200 Northeast 18th Street, Oklahoma City OK 73105. **Tel** (405)251-2502. Ed Susan Gilley. **LC** KFO1236. **DD** 348.76602505, 347.66082505. Oklahoma administrative rules and regulations. *Oklahoma Gazette, 0030-1728.*

OKLAHOMA SESSION LAWS. Main/Corp Oklahoma. 1936/37-. 0149-1105. US. English. **LC** KFO1225. **DD** 348.766022.

OLLON CHUNGJAE. VFOAT Press Arbitration Quarterly. Periodical. KO. Korean. qt. Ollon Chungjae Wiwonhoe, 1 L-ka Uijo-ro, Chung-ku, Seoul South Korea.

OLR SELECTED REPORT. Main/Corp Connecticut. General Assembly. Office of Legislative Research. VAT Office of Legislative Research Selected Report. 0360-1951. US. English. **LC** KFC3620. **DD** 340.09746.

OMBUDSMAN OFFICE PROFILES. 0714-6132. CN. English. an. Ombudsman Office Profiles, International Ombudsman Institute Faculty of Law/University of Alberta, Edmonton Alberta T6G 2H5 Canada. **DD** 342.0667025.

ON WATCH. 0149-6557. Periodical. US. English. mo. $10.00 Institutions, $6.00 Guild Members and Students, $7.50 Others. National Lawyers Guild, Military Law Task Force, Antioch School of Law, 1624 Crescent Place Northwest, Washington DC 20009. **LC** KF7202. **DD** 343.730105.

ONE ON ONE. (ONE ON ONE : NEWSLETTER OF THE GENERAL PRACTICE SECTION OF THE NEW YORK STATE BAR ASSOCIATION). 0733-639X. Periodical. US. English. qt. Free. New York State Bar Association, One Elk Street, Albany NY 12207. **Tel** (818)463-3200. Ed Vincent Alexander and Alan Scheinkman. **LC** KF200. **DD** 349.74705, 347.47005. Circ 4,000. (ctrl). We publish articles of interest to the general legal practitioners in New York.

ONE YEAR OF UNIFIED TAX PLANNING. Main/Corp R&R Newkirk. 1977-. 0162-072X. US. English. an. PO Box 1727, Indianapolis IN 46206. **LC** KF6571.A15. **DD** 343.73053.

ONTARIO ANNOTATED FAMILY LAW SERVICE (BOUND EDITION). (ONTARIO ANNOTATED FAMILY LAW SERVICE). 0824-4669. CN. English. an. Butterworth & Company, 2265 Midland Avenue, Scarborough Ontario M1P 4S1 Canada. **DD** 346.71301502638.

ONTARIO ANNUAL PRACTICE. (THE ONTARIO ANNUAL PRACTICE). 1973-. 0318-3556. Periodical. CN. English. an. 38.00. Canada Law Book, 240 Edward Street, Aurora Ontario L4G 3S9 Canada. **Tel** 773-6300. Ed James J Carthy. **DD** 347.71305. Includes changes in the rules of practice and all significant cases for the past 30 years. Updated annually with supplements covering amendments to the current rules, forms and tariffs made within the year. *Chitty's Ontario Annual Practice, 0084-8751.*

ONTARIO APPEAL CASES. Pt. 1 (Feb. 15, 1984)-. 0827-3308. CN. English. Maritime Law Book Ltd, PO Box 302, Fredericton New Brunswick E3B 4Y9 Canada. **DD** 348.713043.

ONTARIO APPEAL CASES (BOUND CUMULATION). (ONTARIO APPEAL CASES). Vol. 1 (1984)-. 0827-3308. Periodical. CN. English. ir. Maritime Law Book Ltd, PO Box 302, Fredericton New Brunswick E3B 4Y9 Canada. **DD** 348.713043.

ONTARIO BUSINESS CORPORATIONS ACT WITH REGULATIONS. Main/Corp Ontario. 1st- Ed. 0316-6481. Periodical. CN. English. an. CCH Canadian Ltd, 6 Garamond Court, Don Mills Ontario M3C 1Z5 Canada. **DD** 346.71306602633.

ONTARIO GAZETTE. (ONTARIO GAZETTE. PART II, REGULATION MICROFORM). VFOAT Ontario Gazette. Vol. 114, No. 1/52 (1981)-. 0030-2937. Periodical. CN. English. Micromedia Limited, 144 Front Street West, Toronto Ontario M5J 1G2 Canada. **DD** 348.71302505. *Ontario Gazette (Regulations), 0030-2937.*

ONTARIO LAWYER'S HANDBOOK WITH DIARY. VAT Ontario Lawyer's Handbook. 1980-. 0225-5936. CN. English. an. Butterworth & Company, 6 Thorncliff Park Drive, CANEBSCO,

Law

Toronto Ontario M4H 1H3 Canada. Ed B Sack. **DD** 340.09713. *Ontario Lawyer's Vade Mecum with Diary, 0709-2644.*

ONTARIO LAWYERS WEEKLY. Vol. 1, No. 1 (May 6, 1983)-. 0822-5745. Periodical. CN. English. wk. 45.00. Ontario Lawyers Weekly, 2265 Midland Avenue, Scarborough Ontario M1P 4S1 Canada. **Tel** (416)292-1421. **Ed** D M Fitz-James. **DD** 349.71305. bk rev. adv acc. **Circ** 10,000. A newspaper of legal affairs, jurisprudence and features of interest to lawyers and the legal community, published 48 times a year.

ONTARIO LEGAL AID PLAN, ANNUAL REPORT. **Main/Corp** Law Society of Upper Canada. 1967/68-. CN. English. an. Law Society of Upper Canada, Osgoode Hall, 130 Queen's Street North West, Toronto Ontario M5H 2N6 Canada. **LC** KEO173.A13. **DD** 344.71303258, 347.13043258.

ONTARIO MUNICIPAL BOARD REPORTS. V. 1- 1973-. 0318-7527. CN. English. ir. 142.00. Canada Law Book Ltd, 240 Edward Street, Aurora Ontario L4G 3S9 Canada. **Tel** (416)773-6300. **Ed** R T Beaman. **LC** KEO866.4. **DD** 342.713090264 342.7130902646. adv acc. Reports leading Ontario Municipal Board decisions as well as relevant cabinet decisions and court judgements.

ONTARIO SECURITIES ACT AND REGULATIONS WITH POLICY STATEMENTS. **Main/Corp** Ontario. 3rd- Ed. 0225-9613. CN. English. an. Richard de Boo Ltd, 70 Richmond Street East, Toronto Ontario N5C 1M8 Canada. **DD** 346.713066602633. *Securities Act and Regulations, 0225-9605.*

THE OPEN COURT EDUCATOR. 0730-5133. Periodical. US. English. ir. Open Court Publishing Company, Box 599, La Salle IL 61301. **Tel** (800)435-6850.

OPINION. Newspaper. US. English. bw. $10.00. University of New York at Buffalo Law School, 724 O'Brian Hall, Amherst NY 14260. **Tel** (716)636-2147. **Ed** Victor Siclari and Harry Bronson. bk rev. adv acc. **Circ** 2,000. (ctrl). Contains news and features articles concerning UB Law School, its students, the legal community and profession.

OPINION. **Main/Corp** New Mexico. Attorney General's Office. US. English. PO Drawn 1508, Santa Fe NM 87504-1508. **LC** KFN4040. **DD** 348.735, 347.3085.

OPINION DIGEST. **Main/Corp** Pennsylvania. State Ethics Commission. No. 2 (Nov. 29, 1979)-. US. English. **LC** KFP406.A59. **DD** 342.748088, 347.480288. *Advisory Opinion Digest.*

OPINION - STATE OF NEVADA, OFFICE OF THE ATTORNEY GENERAL. **Main/Corp** Nevada. Attorney General's Office. US. English. Office of the Attorney General, Capitol Complex, Carson City NV 89710. **LC** KFN1040. **DD** 348.79305, 347.93085.

OPINIONS OF COUNSEL AND REPORTS TO THE STATE BOARD OF EQUALIZATION AND ASSESSMENT. **Main/Corp** New York (State). State Board of Equalization and Assessment. **VFOAT** Opinions of Counsel and Reports. Vol. 6 (1977-80)-. US. English. **LC** KFN5881. **DD** 343.74705402646, 347.47035402646. *Opinions of Counsel.*

OPINIONS OF THE ATTORNEY GENERAL. **Main/Corp** North Dakota. Office of Attorney General. 0148-4524. Periodical. US. English. North Dakota Office of Attorney General, Bismarck ND 58505. **LC** KFN9040. **DD** 348.78405.

OPINIONS OF THE ATTORNEY GENERAL OF CALIFORNIA. **Main/Corp** California. Attorney General's Office. Vol. 1 1943-. Periodical. US. English. ir. Matthew Bender & Company Inc, 1275 Broadway, Albany NY 12201. **Tel** (800)833-9844.

OPINIONS OF THE ATTORNEY GENERAL OF KENTUCKY FOR THE PERIOD JANUARY 1, 1968- JOHN B. BRECKINRIDGE, ATTORNEY GENERAL, 1968-1972. **Main/Corp** Kentucky. Attorney General's Office. Periodical. US. English. qt. Bands Baldwin Law Publishing Company, PO Box 1974, University Center, Cleveland OH 44106. **Tel** (216)721-7373.

OPINIONS OF THE ATTORNEY GENERAL OF NEW JERSEY. **Main/Corp** New Jersey. Dept. of Law and Public Safety. Division of Law. 1949/50-. US. English. **LC** KFN2240. **DD** 348.74905.

OPINIONS OF THE ATTORNEY GENERAL OF OHIO. **Main/Corp** Ohio. Attorney General's Office. Ohio Attorney General Opinions. 1915/16-. 0748-6170. US. English. qt. $60.00. Banks Baldwin Law Publishing Company, PO Box 1974 University Center, Cleveland OH 44106. **Tel** (216)721-7373. (cum index). Published in cooperation with the office of the attorney general, the issues comprise all official opinions released during the period. *Annual Report of the Attorney General to the Governor of the State of Ohio.*

OPINIONS OF THE ATTORNEY GENERAL OF THE STATE OF OREGON. **Main/Corp** Oregon. Dept. of Justice. Vol. 34, No. 1 (July 1/Sept. 30, 1968)-. Periodical. US. English. ir. $60.00. Department of Justice, Attn Librarian, 100 State Office Building, Salem OR 97310. **LC** KFO2840. **DD** 348.79505, 347.95085. *Biennial Report and Opinions of the Attorney General of the State of Oregon.*

OPINIONS OF THE ATTORNEY GENERAL OF THE STATE OF WISCONSIN. **Main/Corp** Wisconsin. Attorney General's Office. V. 1- 1912/13-. US. English. ir. Wisconsin Department of Administration, Document Sales, 202 South Thornton Avenue, Madison WI 53702. **Tel** (608)266-3358. (cum index). *Biennial Report of the Attorney General of the State of Wisconsin.*

OPINIONS OF THE CORPORATION COUNSEL. **Main/Corp** District of Columbia. Corporation Counsel. V. 1- 1976/77-. US. English. an. Office of the Corporation Counsel, Washington DC 20004. **LC** KFD1640. **DD** 348.75305.

OPINIONS OF THE NEW YORK STATE COMPTROLLER. **Main/Corp** New York (State). Comptroller's Office. 0743-7668. US. English. mo. Lenz & Riecker Inc, Legal Publishing Division, 1 Columbia Place, Albany NY 10020. **LC** KFN5752. **DD** 342.74709026, 347.47029026. *Opinions of the Comptroller Relating to Municipal Government.*

OPINIONS ON REVIEW FOR THE YEAR . . . . **Main/Corp** Michigan. Workers' Compensation Appeal Board. US. English. an. Opinions Press, Box 1095, Big Rapids MI 49307. **LC** KFM4542. **DD** 344.774021, 347.740421.

ORANGE COUNTY BAR JOURNAL. Spring 1973-. 0096-3143. Periodical. US. English. qt. Orange County Bar Association, 17291 Irvine Boulevard/Suite 309, Tustine CA 92680. **LC** K15. **DD** 340.09794.

ORCAMENTO ANUAL - COORDENADORIA DE ORCAMENTO E PROGRAMACAO. **Main/Corp** Parana (Brazil : State). Coordenadoria de Orcamento e Programaco. **VFOAT** Lei Orcamentaria Anual - Coordenadoria de Orcamento e Programacao. Portuguese. ir. **DD** 345.81600722.

ORDERS IN COUNCIL. V. 1- Mar. 21, 1980-. 0227-3268. Periodical. CN. English. wk. $212.81. Richard de Boo Publishers, 81 Curlee Drive, Don Mill Ontario M3A 3P7 Canada. **Tel** (416)445-49400. **Ed** Kathryn Blackett. **DD** 348.71028. **Circ** 300. (ctrl). Provides all weekly descriptive listings of privy council orders when Federal Cabinet meets. Includes regulations, appointments, FIRA decisions, ministerial orders and proclamations.

ORDINANCES. **Main/Corp** Seychelles. Laws, Statutes, etc. JA. English. qt. $46.50. Japan Publishing Trading Company Ltd, PO Box 5030 Tokyo International, Tokyo 100-31 Japan.

OREGON BARS. (OREGON BARS : BUTTERWORTH ADVANCE REPORT SERIES). **VFOAT** Oregon B.A.R.S. **VAT** Oregon Butterworth Advance Report Series. Vol. 8, No. 12 (June 11, 1982)-. 0733-2475. Periodical. US. English. bw. $90.00. Butterworth Legal Publishers, 15014 Northeast 40th/Suite 205, Redmond WA 98052. **Tel** (206)881-3900. **Ed** Ray Krontz. **Circ** 300. (ctrl). Summarizes judicial opinions handed down by the Oregon Supreme Court, Court of Appeals, and Tax Court. *Oregon Appellate Reporter Service, 0273-9666.*

OREGON CASES REPORTED IN PACIFIC REPORTER, SECOND SERIES. **VFOAT** Oregon Cases. 0747-2994. US. English. wk. $75.00. West Publishing Company, PO Box 43526, St Paul MN 55164. **DD** 348.

OREGON LAND USE BOARD OF APPEALS DECISIONS. **VFOAT** Decisions. Vol. 1 (1980)-. US. English. Butterworth (Legal Publishers), 160 Roy Street/Suite 300, Seattle WA 98109. **LC** KFO2858. **DD** 346.795045 347.950645. (cum index).

OREGON LAW REVIEW. V. 1- April 1921-. 0196-2043. Periodical. US. English. 16.00. University of Oregon, 201 Law Center, Eugene OR 97403. **Tel** (503)686-3844. **Ed** Glenn Hovemann. **Ind/Abst** Leg. Resour. Index, Index Leg. Period., Curr. Law Index, Contents Curr. Leg. Period. **LC** K15. **DD** 349.79505. (cum index). bk rev. adv acc. **Circ** 1,000. (ctrl). Available on microfilm from Fred B Rothman & Co. Articles and comments on current legal issues of national interest as well as issues specific to Oregon and the Pacific Northwest.

OREGON LEGISLATION. **Main/Corp** Oregon State Bar. Committee on Continuing Legal Education. 0148-379X. US. English. Oregon State Bar, 1776 SW Madison Street, Portland OR 97205. **LC** KFO2415. **DD** 348.79501.

THE OREGON LITIGATION JOURNAL. Vol. 1, No. 1 (Oct. 1980)-. 0748-9064. US. English. Oregon State Bar, Section on Litigation, 1776 SW Madison Street, Portland OR 97205. **LC** KFO2938.A1. **DD** 347.79507505, 347.5077505.

OREGON REVISED STATUTES RELATING TO MENTAL HEALTH. **Main/Corp** Oregon. 0145-2614. US. English. Mental Health Division, 2575 Bittern Street NE, Salem OR 97310. **LC** KFO2765.A29. **DD** 344.795044.

OREGON RULES OF COURT. 1980-. 8756-3614. US. English. West Publishing Company, 50 West Kellogg Boulevard, PO Box 43526, St Paul MN 55164. **DD** 347.

OREGON STATE BAR BULLETIN (1941). (OREGON STATE BAR BULLETIN). **VFOAT** Bulletin. Vol. 1, No. 1 (July 1941)-. 0030-4816. Periodical. US. English. ir. $18.00. Oregon State Bar Bulletin, 1776 SW Madison Street, Portland OR 97205. **Tel** (503)224-4280. **Ed** Michelle McKenna. **LC** KF200. **DD** 340.025795. bk rev. adv acc. **Circ** 9,000. (ctrl). Articles and features of interest to the legal profession in Oregon. *Oregon State Bar Bulletin (1935).*

THE OREGON STATE BAR ECONOMIC SURVEY. *See* Economics.

OREKH HA-DIN. Periodical. IS. Hebrew. ir. Lishkat Orkhe Ha-Din, Be-Yisrael Ibn Gabirol 95, Tel-Aviv Israel.

ORGANIZACION LABOR. Spanish. ir. Organizacion Labor, El Paraguayo Independiente No 741, Asuncion Paraguay.

OSAR/OSALL. *See* Library and Information Science.

OSGOODE HALL LAW JOURNAL. V. 1- June 1958-. Periodical. CN. English. 40. Osgoode Hall Law School, York University 4700 Keele Street, Downsview Ontario M3J 2R5 Canada. **Tel** (416)667-3980. **Ed** Neil Brooks. **LC** K15. bk rev. adv acc. **Circ** 1,000. (ctrl). The journal is a forum for the exchange and expression of ideas about law, both practical and theoretical. The criterion of publication is quality and originality.

DER OSTERREICHISCHE AMTSVORMUND. Periodical. AU. German. ir. 50.-. Verein der Amtsvormunder Osterreichs, Alserbachstrasse 41, Postfach 144, 1091 Wien Austria. **Tel** (0222)343600. **LC** K15. bk rev. adv acc. **Circ** 10,000. (ctrl). The one and only journal for youth, family, marriage and official guardians affairs and the positions of the dedicated law.

OSTERREICHISCHE JURISTEN-ZEITUNG. Began in 1946. 0029-9251. Periodical. AU. German. da. 1,360.-. Manzsche Verlagsbuchhandlung, Kohlmarkt 16, 1014 Wien Austria. **Tel** (0222)63 17 81 0. bk rev. adv acc. **Circ** 3,600. (ctrl). Articles treating actual judicial themes, decisions of (Austrian) appeal courts and high (supreme) courts on private law, criminal law, constitutional law, and administrative law, book reviews included.

OSTERREICHISCHE LANDESBERICHTE ZUM INTERNATIONALEN KONGRESS FUR DAS RECHT DER ARBEIT UND DER SOZIALEN SICHERHEIT. *See* Economics - Labor.

OSTERREICHISCHES ANWALTSBLATT. Periodical. German. ir. 400.00. Osterreichischer Rechtsanwal Tskammertag, Rotenturmstrasse 13, 1010 Wien Austria. **LC** K15.

Law

OSTERREICHISCHES RECHT DER WIRTSCHAFT. V. 1, No. 1, (Sept. 1983)-. Periodical. German. mo. 480.00. Verlag Norbert Orac, Graben 17, 1010 Wien Austria. **LC** K15. **DD** 343.4360805, 344.3603805.

OSTERREICHISCHES VERWALTUNGSARCHIV CEASED. Periodical. AT. German. ir. Hollinek, Gallgasse 40 A, A 1130 Wien XIII Austria. **DD** 342.43606.

OSTEUROPA-RECHT. VAT Osteuropa Recht. 1- Yearly. 0030-6444. Periodical. GW. German. qt. Zenit Pressevertrieb GMBH, Postfach 810640, 7000 Stuttgart 80 W Germany.

OTTAWA LAW REVIEW. V. 1- 1966-. 0048-2331. Periodical. CN. English (includes some text in French). ty. $25.00. Ottawa Law Review for Canada, University of Ottawa Faculty of Law, Ottawa Ontario K1N 6N5 Canada. **Tel** (613)564-2919. Ed S Rodgers. **Ind/Abst** Leg. Resour. Index, Public Aff. Inf. Serv. Bull., Index Leg. Period., Curr. Law Index, Index Leg. Period., Contents Curr. Leg. Period. (cum index). bk rev. adv acc. **Circ** 900. Legal articles, comments, recent developments, book reviews, of current interest to academics and practising lawyers.

OTTAWA UPDATE. Vol. 1, No. 1 (Jan. 1984)-. 0824-670X. Periodical. CN. English. mo. Free. Canadian Chamber of Commerce, Suite 301/200 Elgin Street, Ottawa Ontario K2P 2J7 Canada. **DD** 971.064605. (ctrl).

AN OVERVIEW OF LEGISLATION IN THE SESSION OF THE ILLNOIS GENERAL ASSEMBLY. Main/Corp Illinois. Legislative Council. US. English. Illinois Legislative Council, Springfield IL 62706. **LC** KFI1215. **DD** 348.77301.

OXFORD JOURNAL OF LEGAL STUDIES. Vol. 1, No. 1 (Spring 1981)-. 0143-6503. Periodical. UK. English. ty. 15.00 Domestic, $38.00 US. Oxford Journals Press, Road Neadsen, London NW10 0DD England. **Ind/Abst** Leg. Resour. Index, Index Leg. Period. **LC** K15. **DD** 340.05.

OYO STATE OF NIGERIA GAZETTE. V. 1- April 1, 1976-. NR. English. ir. 12. Oyo State of Nigeria, Government Printer, Ibadan Nigeria. **DD** 340.096692.

OZW, OSTERREICHISCHE ZEITSCHRIFT FUR WIRTSCHAFTSRECHT. Periodical. AU. German. ir. 200.00. Verein fur Sozial- und Wirtschaftsforschung, Renngasse 12, 1010 Wien Austria. **LC** K15. **DD** 346.0705.

P-H FEDERAL TAXES. PRIVATE LETTER RULINGS. (P-H FEDERAL TAXES : PRIVATE LETTER RULINGS). Main/Corp Prentice-Hall, Inc. VFOAT Private Letter Rulings. VAT Prentice-Hall Federal Taxes. Private Letter Rulings. 1977-. 0192-1339. US. English. an. Prentice-Hall Inc, Englewood Cliffs NJ 07632. **LC** KF6289. **DD** 343.7304.

P-H FEDERAL TAXES. PRIVATE LETTER RULINGS. (P-H FEDERAL TAXES : PRIVATE LETTER RULINGS). VFOAT Private Letter Rulings. 0145-6768. Periodical. US. English. wk. $279.00. Prentice-Hall, Sylvan Avenue, Englewood Cliffs NJ 07632.

PACE ENVIRONMENTAL LAW REVIEW. Vol. 1, No. 1-. 0738-6206. Periodical. US. English. sa. $15.00 Domestic, $17.50 Foreign. Associated Faculty Press Inc, 90 South Bayles Avenue, Port Washington NY 11050. **LC** K16. **DD** 344.7304605, 347.3044605.

PACE LAW REVIEW. Vol. 1, No. 1 (1980)-. 0272-2410. Periodical. US. English. ty. $15.00. Pace University, 78 North Broadway, School of Law, White Plains NY 10603. **Tel** (914)681-4113. Ed Mary Keenan Harrington. **Ind/Abst** Leg. Resour. Index, Index Leg. Period. **LC** K16. **DD** 349.74705, 347.47005. bk rev. adv acc. **Circ** 500. A publication, comprised of both professional and student articles, addressing current legal issues. All articles are appropriately footnoted to provide easy access to information.

DE PACHT. Began with Jan. 1940 issue. Periodical. Dutch. ir. **Ind/Abst** Excerpta Med. **LC** K16.

PACIFIC LAW JOURNAL. VFOAT Review of Selected Nevada Legislation. V. 1 (1981)-. Periodical. US. English. an. $18.00. 3201 Donner Way, Sacramento CA 95817. **Tel** (916)739-7171. Ed Pamela Griffin. **Ind/Abst** Leg. Resour. Index, Index Leg. Period., Curr. Law Index, Contents Curr. Leg. Period. adv acc. **Circ** 3,300. (ctrl). Professional periodical devoted to scholarly legal analysis and commentary as well as in-depth reporting of California legislation.

PACIFIC REPORTER. SECOND SERIES. V. 1- (2D). 8750-2666. Periodical. US. English. wk. West Publishing Company, 50 West Kellogg Boulevard, PO Box 64526, St Paul MN 55164. **LC** KF135. **DD** 348. Pacific Reporter.

PACIFIC REPORTER. SECOND SERIES. CASES ARGUED AND DETERMINED IN THE SUPREME COURTS OF CALIFORNIA, KANSAS, OREGON, WASHINGTON, COLORADO, MONTANA, ARIZONA, NEVADA, IDAHO, WYOMING, UTAH, NEW MEXICO, OKLAHOMA. V.1- (2D) Aug. 28, 1931-. US. English. **LC** KF135.

PAGE ON THE LAW OF WILLS, INCLUDING PROBATE, WILL CONTESTS, EVIDENCE, TAXATION, CONFLICTS, ESTATE PLANNING, FORMS, AND STATUTES RELATING TO WILLS. US. English. an. Anderson Publishing Company, PO Box 1576, 646 Main Street, Cincinnati OH 45202.

PAGE'S OHIO REVISED CODE, ANNOTATED, CONTAINING THE TEXT OF THE OFFICIAL OHIO REVISED CODE, EFFECTIVE OCT. 1, 1953 CURRENT MATERIAL. Main/Corp Ohio. US. English. an. Anderson Publishing Company, PO Box 1576, 646 Main Street, Cincinnati OH 45202. **Tel** (513)421-4142.

PAKISTAN LAW JOURNAL. Periodical. English. ir. Punjab Council, 3-Turner Road, Lahore Pakistan. **DD** 340.095491.

PAKISTAN SUPREME COURT CASES. English. ir. $20.00. Pakistan Supreme Court Cases, 1 Turner Road (Near High Court), Lahore Pakistan. **DD** 348.5491044, 345.4910844.

THE PAKISTAN SUPREME COURT REPORTS. English. ir.

PAKISTAN TAX & CORPORATE LAWS. VFOAT Pakistan Tax and Corporate Laws. V. 1, No. 1 (Mar. 1983)-. English. mo. .300. T N Choudhry, 18-Temple Road, Lahore Pakistan. Ed N A Choudhry. **DD** 343.54910405, 345.49103405.

PALLYE YONGU. V. 1-Series. Periodical. Korean. ir. **LC** K16.

PANDEKTAI NEON NOMON KAI KIATAGMATON. Main/Corp Greece. Greek, Modern. mo. 250.00. T T 501 Euphorionos LLA, Athens Greece. Ed K Siphnaios.

PANEL DISCUSSION SERIES. Began with: Topic 1, issued in 1982. 0739-1978. Monographic Series. US. English. ir. $7.50. Special Committee on Dispute Resolution, American Bar Association, 1800 M Street NW/Suite 200, Washington DC 20036. **DD** 347.

PANTA-RHEI. VFOAT Edisi Pertama. Vol. 1 Juni 1975-. Periodical. Indonesian. ir. Senat Mahasiswa Fak Hakum and Peng Masyarajat, Universitas Sumatera Utara, Jalan Universitas 4, Medan Indonesia. **LC** K16. **DD** 340.09598.

THE PAPER BOOK OF THE DELTA THETA PHI LAW FRATERNITY. 0011-8060. Periodical. US. English. qt. Delta Theta Phi Law Fraternity, 666 High Street, Worthington OH 43085.

PAPERS AND PROCEEDINGS - WESTERN TRANSPORTATION LAW SEMINAR. See Transportation.

PAPERS PRESENTED AT THE MID-WINTER MEETING OF THE ALBERTA BRANCH OF THE CANADIAN BAR ASSOCIATION. (PAPERS PRESENTED AT THE . . . ANNUAL MID-WINTER MEETING OF THE ALBERTA BRANCH OF THE CANADIAN BAR ASSOCIATION). Main/Corp Canadian Bar Association. Alberta Branch. Mid-Winter Meeting. VAT Mid-Winter Meeting - Canadian Bar Association, Alberta Branch. 1981-. 0715-4534. CN. English. an. $100.00 Per Year. Canadian Bar Association, 4th Floor/680 8th Avenue SW, Calgary Alberta T2P 1G7 Canada. **DD** 349.7123. Selected Papers Presented at the Mid-Winter Meeting of the Alberta Branch, Canadian Bar Association, 0711-2025.

PAPERS USED AT THE ANNUAL EXAMINATIONS IN LAW HELD AT HARVARD UNIVERSITY. Main/Corp Harvard Law School. US. English. an. $10.25. Harvard Law School, Langdell Hall, Cambridge MA 02138. **Tel** (617)495-3100.

PAPUA NEW GUINEA LAW REPORTS. 1971/72-. 0085-4689. English. ir. Methuen Law Book Company Ltd, 35 Mitchell Street, c/o Bennett EBSCO, North Sydney New South Wales 2060 Australia. Papua and New Guinea Law Reports.

PARA FISCAL : ORGAO OFICIAL DA ASSOCIACAO DOS FISCAIS DE TRIBUTOS ESTADUAIS DO PARA. Periodical. Portuguese. mo. Ed Para-Fiscal, Rua Dom Pedro I No 273, Dro I No. 273 CEP 66.00 Belem Para Brazil. **LC** KHD7677.A15. **DD** 343.81150405, 348.11503405.

PARA-LEGAL UPDATE. Main/Corp National Legal Assistant Conference Center. VAT Para Legal Update. V. 1- Oct. 1976-. 0146-2954. US. English. qt. $15.00. National Legal Assistant Conference, 244 Wilshire Boulevard/Suite 301, Santa Monica CA 90403. **Tel** (213)453-1941. Ed Joseph E Deering Jr. **LC** KF320.L4. **DD** 340.023. bk rev. adv acc. **Circ** 2,000. Ideas for improvement and increased job satisfaction for legal assistants. Also updates law and procedures for legal assistants (paralegals).

THE PARALEGAL. Vol. 1, No. 1 (Jan./Feb. 1983). 0739-3601. Periodical. US. English. bm. $30.00. National Paralegal Association, 10 South Pine Street/PO Box 629, Doylestown PA 18901. **Tel** (215)348-5575. Ed William Cameron. **LC** KF320.L4. **DD** 340.02373. bk rev. adv acc. **Circ** 5,000. Circulated among the members of the Association who are practising paralegals, attorneys, paralegal educators, paralegal associations, law librarians, court personnel and the like.

PARASCOPE. (PARASCOPE : THE QUARTERLY PUBLICATION OF THE NATIONAL COMMITTEE OF APPELLATE COURT STAFF COUNSEL). Vol. 1-. 0738-1247. Periodical. US. English. qt. American Bar Association, National Committee of Appellate Court Staff Counsel, 155 East 60th Street, Chicago IL 60637. **LC** KF8750.A15. **DD** 347.732405.

PARECERES DA CONSULTORIA JURIDICA. Main/Corp Brazil. Congresso. Senado. Consultoria Jurdica. V. 1- 1973/75-. Periodical. Portuguese. ir. **DD** 328.81071.

PARECERES NORMATIVOS DA COORDENACAO DO SISTEMA DE TRIBUTACAO. Main/Corp Brazil. Coordenacao do Sistema de Tributacao. BL. Portuguese. ir. Mapa Fiscal Editora Ltda, rua Miguel Telles Junior 394, Sao Paulo SP Brazil.

PARKER DIRECTORY OF CALIFORNIA ATTORNEYS. See Yearbooks, Almanacs, Directories.

PARKER'S BUSINESS STATUTES AND SECURITIES RULES OF TEXAS. Main/Corp Texas. VFOAT Business Statutes and Securities Rules of Texas. 0749-0607. US. English. an. Parker & Son Publications Inc, Box 60001, Los Angeles CA 90060. **LC** KFT1405.A29. **DD** 346.764065, 347.640665.

THE PARTNERSHIP STRATEGIST. Vol. 1, No. 1 (Aug. 1982)-. 0734-2799. Periodical. US. English. mo. The Partnership Strategist, 10076 Boca Entrada Boulevard, Boca Raton FL 33433. **LC** KF1372.8. **DD** 346.73068205, 347.30668205.

PASICRISIE BELGE. RECUEIL GENERAL DE LA JURISPRUDENCE DES COURS ET TRIBUNAUX. 0031-2614. Periodical. BE. French. ir. 12.950. Etablissements Emile Bruylant, 67 rue de la Regence, 1000 Brussels Belgium. **Tel** 512/.98.45. **Circ** 1,100. Jurisprudence.

PASINOMIE. Main/Corp Belgium. Periodical. French. ir. Etablissements Emile Bruylant, 67 rue de la Regence, 1000 Brussels Belgium. **Tel** 2/512-9845. **Circ** 475. Collection of laws of Belgium with preparation and discussion of texts.

PASSPORT TO LEGAL UNDERSTANDING. (PASSPORT TO LEGAL UNDERSTANDING : THE NEWSLETTER ON PUBLIC EDUCATION PROGRAMS AND MATERIALS). Vol. 1, No. 1 (Winter 1983)-. 0737-7630. Periodical. US. English. sa. Free. American Bar Association, Commission on Public Understanding about the Law, 750 North Lake Shore Drive, Chicago IL 60611. **Tel**

Law

(312)988-5736. **Ed** Mary C Manemann. **LC** KF298. **DD** 349.7307, 347.3007. bk rev. adv acc. **Circ** 6,000. News about programs and materials that explain aspects of law to the general public; emphasis of late is on constitutional law and history.

PATENT LAW ANNUAL. See Copyright, Intellectual Property.

PATENT OFFICE EXAMINATION REVIEW COURSE. Main/Corp New York (City). Practising Law Institute. 0147-6173. Periodical. US. English. an. 1133 Avenue of the Americas, New York NY 10036. **LC** KF3120.Z9. **DD** 346.730486.

PATENT OFFICE RULES AND PRACTICES. See Copyright, Intellectual Property.

PATIENT CARE LAW. 0730-5524. Periodical. US. English. bm. $200.00. Action Kit for Hospital Law, 4614 5th Avenue c/o J Horty, Pittsburgh PA 15213. **Tel** (800)245-1205. **Ed** John Horty. **LC** KF3821.A15. **DD** 344.7304105, 347.3044105. **Circ** 500. (ctrl). A legal reference for nurses that discusses recent court cases, statutes and regulations and includes a reference manual and bi-monthly newsletters.

PATIENT RIGHTS DIGEST. V. 1- Nov. 1977-. 0147-7269. Periodical. US. English. bm. $18.00. Patient Rights Digest, PO Box 633, Randallstown MD 21133. **Tel** (301)655-2137. **LC** KF3823.A15. **DD** 344.730321.

PAYROLL TAXES. (PAYROLL TAXES : WITHHOLDING, DEPOSIT & REPORTING REQUIREMENTS). **Series/Titl** Tax Saving Opportunities Series. 1981-. 0734-8339. US. English. an. **LC** KF6436.Z95. **DD** 343.7305242, 347.3035242.

PBA BRIEF. Main/Corp Pennsylvania Bar Association. V. 23, No. 2- March 1978-. Periodical. US. English. mo. 100 South Street, PO Box 186, Harrisburg PA 17108.

PENANT. **VFOAT** Revue de Droit des Pays d'Afrique. Began with V. 72 (No. 692), June/Aug. 1962. 0336-1551. Periodical. FR. French. ty. Ediena, 17 rue Thiers, 78110 Le Vesinet France. **Ind/Abst** Int. Labour Doc., Recent Publ. Artic. **LC** K18. Recueil Penant.

PENNSYLVANIA BAR ASSOCIATION QUARTERLY. V. 1- June 1929-. 0196-2051. Periodical. US. English. qt. $10.00. Pennsylvania Bar Association, PO Box 186, Harrisburg PA 17108. **Tel** (717)238-6715. **Ed** S Lewis. **Ind/Abst** Leg. Resour. Index, Index Leg. Period., Curr. Law Index. **LC** K16. **DD** 340.060748.

PENNSYLVANIA BULLETIN. 1970. 0162-2137. Periodical. US. English. wk. $45.00. Commonwealth of Pennsylvania, Box 1365 State Book Store, Harrisburg PA 17125. **Tel** (717)783-1530. **Ed** M J Butchar. **LC** J1. **Circ** 12,000. Official rules and regulations of state agencies; analogous to federal register.

PENNSYLVANIA JUVENILE COURT DISPOSITIONS. 0092-3605. US. English. an. Juvenile Court Judges' Commission, Juvenile Statistics Division, PO Box 1234, Federal Square Station, Harrisburg PA 17108. **LC** KFP71.55. **DD** 345.74808, 347.48058.

PENNSYLVANIA LAW FINDER. 1983 Ed.-. 0741-5540. US. English. West Publishing Company, 50 West Kellogg Boulevard, PO Box 3526, St Paul MN 55165. **LC** KFP61. **DD** 348.748028, 347.480828.

PENNSYLVANIA LAW JOURNAL-REPORTER. **VFOAT** Pennsylvania Law Journal Reporter. 0279-8166. Periodical. US. English. wk. $235.00. Packard Press Corporation, 10th and Spring Garden Street, Philadelphia PA 19123. **Tel** (215)236-2000. **Ed** Sheryl Stern Chernoff. **LC** K16. bk rev. adv acc. **Circ** 10,000. Recent developments in Pennsylvania law and the practice of law in Pennsylvania. Pennsylvania Law Journal (Philadelphia, Pa. : 1977), 0160-8495.

THE PENNSYLVANIA LAWYER. V. 1- Feb. 1979-. 0193-4821. Periodical. US. English. bm. Pennsylvania Bar Association, 100 South Street Box 186, Harrisburg PA 17108. **LC** KF200. **DD** 340.09748.

THE PENNSYLVANIA POLICE CRIMINAL LAW BULLETIN. See Law Enforcement.

PENNSYLVANIA REPORTER. (PENNSYLVANIA REPORTER, COVERING CASES REPORTED IN ATLANTIC REPORTER, SECOND SERIES). **VFOAT** West's Pennsylvania Reporter. 1A. 2D-2A. 2D-. 0745-8037. US. English. wk. $65.00. West Publishing Company, 50 West Kellogg Boulevard, PO Box 3526, St Paul MN 55166. **DD** 345.42.

THE PENNSYLVANIA RESEARCHER. 0048-3249. Periodical. US. English. mo. $99.00. National Legal Research Group Inc, PO Box 7187, Charlottesville VA 22906. **Tel** (800)446-1870. **LC** KFP57. **DD** 348.748026.

PENNSYLVANIA TAX HANDBOOK. **VFOAT** Prentice-Hall Pennsylvania Tax Handbook. US. English. an. Prentice Hall Inc, Englewood Cliffs NJ 07632. **LC** KFP470. **DD** 343.74804, 347.48034.

PENNSYLVANIA WOMEN ANNUAL REPORT. See Women.

PENSION REVIEW BOARD REPORTS. Main/Corp Canada. Pension Review Board. **VFOAT** Recueil des Arrets du Conseil de Revision des Pensions. V. 1- 1972-. 0382-1587. Periodical. CN. English (French). qt. Receiver General for Canada, Statistics Canada Publications, Ottawa Ontario K1A 0T6 Canada. **DD** 343.71011.

PEPPERDINE LAW REVIEW. V. 1- 1973-. 0092-430X. Periodical. US. English. $15.00. Pepperdine University, School of Law, Malibu CA 90265. **Ed** Linda Koller. **Ind/Abst** Leg. Contents, Index Leg. Period., Leg. Resour. Index, Curr. Law Index, Contents Curr. Leg. Period. **LC** K16. **DD** 340.05. adv acc. **Circ** 621. (ctrl). microform. Current legal issues and analysis of cases.

PERATURAN DAERAH DAERAH ISTIMEWA YOGYAKARTA. Main/Corp Yogyakarta, Indonesia (Daerah Istimews). Indonesian. ir.

PERIODICAL SUBSCRIPTION PLAN. (INCLUDES REPORT, STATE COURT JOURNAL, SURVEY OF JUDICIAL SALARIES, AND ANNUAL REPORT). English. ir. 300 Newport Avenue, Williamsburg VA 23185.

PERIODIEK WOORDENBOEK VAN ADMINISTRATIEVE EN GERECHTELIJKE BESLISSINGEN. Dutch. qt. 60.65. Uitgeverij Fed BV, Postbus 23, 7400 Ga Denventer Netherlands. **LC** K16.

PERISCOPE. 0191-0302. US. English. $175.00. Peris, Box 573, Oxford NY 13830. **LC** KFN5562.P8. **DD** 344.74701890413539.

PERRY'S BROADCASTING AND THE LAW. **VFOAT** Broadcasting and the Law. 1970. 0161-5823. US. English. sm. $75.00. L & S Publishing Inc, Law Offices of Leibowitz/PA, 3050 Biscayne Boulevard/Suite 501, Miami FL 33137. **Tel** (305)576-4743. **Ed** John M Spencer. **LC** KF2801.A3. **DD** 343.7309945, 347.3039945. Reports on laws and regulations affecting radio/tv stations; explains FCC, FEC, EEOC, OSHA, FTC and court decisions; answers questions about all departments.

PERSONAL FINANCE LAW QUARTERLY REPORT CEASED. **VFOAT** Quarterly Report. Vol. 9, No. 2 (Spring 1955)-V. 38, No. 2 (Spring 1984). 0362-6342. Periodical. US. English. qt. $5.00. Attn Editor, 115 Broadway, New York NY 10006. **DD** 346. Quarterly Report (Conference on Personal Finance Law (U.S.)), 0883-4563.

PERSONAL INJURY ANNUAL. 1961-1981. US. English. an. Matthew Bender & Company Inc, 1275 Broadway, Albany NY 12201. **Tel** (800)833-9844. **Ind/Abst** Curr. Law Index, Leg. Resour. Index. **LC** KF8925.P4. **NLM** W1 PE844. (cum index).

PERSONAL INJURY DESKBOOK. 1982-. 0736-640X. US. English. an. M Bender, 235 East 45th Street, New York NY 10017. **Tel** (212)661-5050. **Ed** Gordon Ohlsson. **Ind/Abst** Leg. Resour. Index. **LC** KF8925.P4. **DD** 346.7303230269, 347. 3063230269. Selected legal and medical articles, including some original pieces, from the field of personal injury law. Prepared by leading specialists in the area. Personal Injury Annual.

PERSONAL INJURY NEWSLETTER. V. 1- 1958-. Periodical. US. English. bw. Matthew Bender & Company Inc, 1275 Broadway, Albany NY 12201. **Tel** (800)833-9844. **LC** KF8925.P4.

THE PERSONAL INJURY RESEARCHER. 0048-3435. Periodical. US. English. mo. $42.00. The Research Group Inc, PO Box 7187, Charlottesville VA 22906. **LC** KF1256.A75. **DD** 346.73032.

PERSONAL INJURY VERDICT REVIEWS. FOOD, LODGING, SPORTS & ENTERTAINMENT FACILITIES. **VFOAT** Food, Lodging, Sports & Entertainment Facilities. Began Publication Oct. 1983. 8755-5255. Periodical. US. English. qt. $60.00. Jury Verdict Research, 5325 Naiman Parkway/Suite B, Solon OH 44139. Verdict Reports, 0092-2293.

PERSONAL INJURY VERDICT REVIEWS. MEDIA AND GOVERNMENT. **VFOAT** Media and Government. Began in 1983. 0749-6567. Periodical. US. English. qt. $36.00. Jury Verdict Research, 5325 Naiman Parkway/Suite B, Solon OH 44139. **LC** KF1256.A75. **DD** 346.73032305, 347.30632305. Verdict Reports, 0092-2293.

PERSONAL INJURY VERDICT REVIEWS. RETAILING, BANKING, AND OTHER SERVICE ESTABLISHMENTS. **VFOAT** Retailing, Banking, and Other Service Establishments. Began in 1983. 0749-6583. Periodical. US. English. qt. $36.00. Jury Verdict Research, 5325 Naiman Parkway/Suite B, Solon OH 44139. **LC** KF1256.A75. **DD** 346.73032305, 347.30632305. Verdict Reports, 0092-2293.

PERSONAL INJURY VERDICT REVIEWS. TRUCKING, RAILROAD & MARINE LINES. **VFOAT** Trucking, Railroad & Marine Lines. Began in 1983. 0749-6591. Periodical. US. English. qt. $36.00. Jury Verdict Research, 5325 Naiman Parkway/Suite B, Solon OH 44139. **LC** KF1256.A75. **DD** 346.73032305, 347.30632305. Verdict Reports, 0092-2293.

PERSONAL INJURY VERDICT SURVEY. NEVADA EDITION. **VFOAT** Nevada Edition. 8755-6588. US. English. Jury Verdict Research, 5325 Naiman Parkway/Suite B, Solon OH 44139. **DD** 346.

PERSONAL LIABILITY DIGEST. V. 1- Feb. 1978-. 0149-6131. Periodical. US. English. qt. $18.00. Center for the Study of Civil Liberties and Civil Rights, PO Box 4361, Montgomery AL 36101. **LC** KF1306.A2. **DD** 342.73068.

HET PERSONEEL STATUUT : ORGAN VAN DE NEDERLANDSE VERENIGING VAN AMBTENAREN VAN DE BURGERLIJKE STAND (NEVABS). Periodical. Dutch. bm. Nederlandse Vereniging Van Ambtenaren Van de Burgerlijke Stand, Herrengracht 531-537, 1017 BV Amsterdam Netherlands.

PERSONNEL MANAGER'S LEGAL REPORTER. See Business - Personnel Management.

PERSONNELIST. MERIT SYSTEMS PROTECTION BOARD AND FEDERAL LABOR RELATIONS AUTHORITY CASE DECISIONS. See Economics - Labor.

PERSONNES C.L.E.F. **VAT** Personnes Common Law en Francais. 1984-. 0824-1902. CN. French. an. 10.00. Centre de Reference de la Documentation Juridique de Langue Francaise en Matiere de Common Law, 5E Etage 161 Ouest Ave Laurier, Ottawa Ontario K1P 5J2 Canada. **Tel** (613)236-9766. **DD** 340.5702571. adv acc. **Circ** 1,000. French language directory of Canada. Common Law: names and addresses.

PERSPECTIVE. (PERSPECTIVE : THE NEWSLETTER OF THE YOUNG LAWYERS SECTION). **Main/Corp** New York State Bar Association. Young Lawyers Section. 0743-6475. Periodical. US. English. qt. New York State Bar Association, One Elk Street, Albany NY 12207. **Tel** (518)463-3200. **Ed** Richard Dollinger. **LC** KF200. **DD** 349.74705, 347.47005. **Circ** 3,000. (ctrl). Young Lawyers Section Newsletter, 0733-8066.

PERSPECTIVES IN LAW & PSYCHOLOGY. **VFOAT** Law & Psychology. **VAT** Perspectives in Law and Psychology. V. 1-. 0160-4422. Monographic Series. US. English. ir. Plenum Press, c/o H Feldman, 233 Spring Street, New York NY 10013. **Tel** (212)620-8000. **LC** UNC. **NLM** W1 PE871AS.

PHARMACY LAW DIGEST. 1965. 0149-1717. US. English. an. $41.95. Harwal Publishing Company, PO Box 96, Media PA 19063. **Tel** (215)565-0747. **Ed** Joseph L Fink III. **LC** KF2915.P4. **DD** 344.73041. **NLM** QV 32 AA1 K2P. Covers all

Law

pharmaceutical jurisprudence for students and practitioners. In looseleaf with yearly supplements updating seven main sections.

PHILIPPINE CASE LAW. Main/Corp Philippines. Supreme Court. PH. English. mo. Rex Book Store, 856 Nicanor Reyes Sr St, Manila Philippines. DD 348.599041, 345.990841.

PHILIPPINE LAW AND JURISPRUDENCE. VFOAT Philjur. V. 1- Nov./Dec. 1977-. Periodical. PH. English. ir. $240.00. Current Events Digest Inc, 1223 Vergara & Pax, Quiapo Manila Philippine Islands. Tel 46-16-56. Ed Arturo M de Castro. DD 348.599046. Circ 2,000. (ctrl). Complete Philippine Supreme Court decisions, selected appellate courts cases digests, laws of general applications, and annotations, syllabi of Supreme Court cases.

PHILIPPINE LAW GAZETTE. V. 1- Jan. 1972-. Periodical. PH. English. ir. 100 Domestic, $28.00 US. Philippine Law Gazette, 13 Mapayapa Street, UP Village, Dilman Quezon City 3004 Philippines. DD 016.34009599.

PHILIPPINE LAW JOURNAL. V. 1- Aug. 1914-. 0031-7721. Periodical. PH. English. qt. $20.00 US. University of Philippines, College of Law, Quezon City D55 Philippines. Tel 98-32-01/02. Ed Dan Albert de Padua. Ind/Abst Sociol. Abstr., Lang. Lang. Behav. Abstr. Index published separately - free - automatically sent. bk rev. adv acc. Circ 4. (ctrl)

THE PHILIPPINE LAW REPORT. Periodical. PH. English. mo. $5.60. University of the Philippines Law Center, Diliman Quezon City Philippines. DD 348.599041.

PHILIPPINE PRESIDENTIAL DECREES AND OTHER VITAL LEGAL DOCUMENTS. Main/Corp Philippines. English. ir. Central Book Supply Inc, Alemar's Building 769 Rizal Avenue, Manila Philippines. DD 348.599025, 345.990825.

PHOROLOGIKE ENEMEROSIS. Main/Corp Greece. GR. Greek, Modern. mo. 3 Es Septembriou 22 Orophos, 5 Graph 6, Athenai Greece.

PHOROLOGIKE EPITHEORESIS. Periodical. Greek, Modern. ir. 500.00. Ekdosis Panelleniou Henoseos Ephoriakon Hypallelou, Akadimias 76, Athenai Greece. LC K16.

THE PHYSICIAN'S LEGAL ALERT. Vol. 1, No. 1 (June 1985)-. 0882-133X. Periodical. US. English. mo. $35.00. PSG Publishing Company Inc, 545 Great Road, Littleton MA 01460. Tel (617)486-8971. DD 346. Provides legal information affecting patient-physician relationships.

PIKE & FISCHER RADIO REGULATION. See Communication - Telecommunications.

PITTSBURGH LEGAL JOURNAL. Vol. 1-. 0032-0331. Periodical. US. English. mo. $90.00. Allegheny Bar Association, 920 City-County Building, Pittsburgh PA 15219. Tel (412)261-0518. Ed Robert L Byer. Each issue contains an index to its own contents - no vol index - loose. adv acc. Circ 6,100. (ctrl). Timely legal articles, court opinions, announcement of forthcoming educational programs and other events and other general information of interest to lawyers and judges.

PLACEMENT BULLETIN - ASSOCIATION OF AMERICAN LAW SCHOOLS. Main/Corp Association of American Law Schools. US. English. bm. $6.00. One Dupont Circle, Washington DC 20036.

PLADOYER. 1. Vol. No 1 (Feb. 1983)-. Periodical. German. ir. 50.-. Pladoyer, Engelstr 64, 8004 Zurich Switzerland. Tel 01 241 77 17. Ed H J Mosimann. LC K16. DD 349.49405, 344.94005. bk rev. adv acc. Circ 2,500. Magazine covering law making and application and related political issues in Switzerland.

PLANNING LEGISLATION IN NEW YORK STATE. See Housing and Urban Development.

PLANNING, ZONING, AND DEVELOPMENT LAWS. Main/Corp California. VFOAT State of California Planning, Zoning, and Development Laws. US. English. an. Office of Planning and Research, 1400 Tenth Street, Sacramento CA 95814. State of California Planning, Zoning, and Development Laws.

PLANO DA SAFRA ACUCAR E ALCOOL. Main/Corp Instituto do Acucar e do Alcool (Brazil). BL. Portuguese. ir. Instituto do Acucar E do Alcool, Praca Quinze de Novembro 42, Rio de Janeiro Brazil. LC Law.

PLATT'S ENERGY LITIGATION REPORT. VFOAT Energy Litigation Report. Vol. 2, No. 42 (Aug. 17, 1981)-. 0278-226X. Periodical. US. English. wk. $397.00. McGraw-Hill Inc, 1120 Vermont Avenue NW, Washington DC 20005. Ind/Abst Nexis. LC KF2120.A59. DD 346.73046790269, 347. Platt's OHA Digest, 0196-1454.

PLEA. PUBLIC LEGAL EDUCATION ASSOCIATION OF SASKATCHEWAN. (THE PLEA). VAT Public Legal Education Association of Saskatchewan. 0715-4224. Periodical. CN. English. Free to Members. Public Legal Education Association of Saskatchewan, Room 311/23rd Street, East Saskatoon Saskatchewan S7K 0J6 Canada. DD 349.712407.

THE PLEADER. 0196-6782. Periodical. US. English. North Dakota Trial Lawyers Association, PO Box 2359, Bismarck ND 58501. LC KF200. DD 347.7840705.

POINIKE EPITHEORESIS. Year 1- Ian. 1970-. Periodical. Greek, Modern. ir. 300.00. Oikas I Zacharopoulos, Arsaki 6 T T 131, Athens Greece. LC K16.

POINT OF VIEW. Periodical. US. English. bm. Alameda County District Attorneys Office, 1225 Fallon Street, Oakland CA 94612. LC KFC1100.A15. DD 345.794005.

POLICE MISCONDUCT AND CIVIL RIGHTS LAW REPORT. Vol. 1, No. 1 (Apr. 1983)-. 0738-0623. Periodical. US. English. qt. $45.00. Clark Boardman Company Ltd, 435 Hudson Street, New York NY 10014. LC KF4742. DD 342.73085, 347.30285.

POLICY AND PROCEDURES HANDBOOK. Main/Corp American Bar Association. VFOAT ABA Policy and Procedures Handbook. 0197-2596. US. English. American Bar Association, 1155 East 60th Street, Chicago IL 60637. LC KF325. DD 340.06073.

THE POLISH SOCIOLOGY OF LAW NEWSLETTER. Periodical. English. ir. Polish Sociological Association, Section on the Sociology of Law, UL Nowy Swait 72, 00-330 Warszawa Poland. LC K16. DD 340.11505.

POLY LAW REVIEW. V. 1- Summer 1975-. 0306-8706. UK. English. sa. 2.00. PCL School of Law, 235 High Holborn, London WC1 England. Ind/Abst Leg. Resour. Index. LC K16. DD 340.0941.

POLYGRAPH LAW REPORTER. See Law Enforcement.

POMMU YONGU. KO. Korean. an. Pommu Yonsuwon, 164 Uman-dong, Suwon-si Korea.

PONTIAC-OAKLAND COUNTY LEGAL NEWS. (PONTIAC-OAKLAND COUNTY LEGAL NEWS : OFFICIAL NEWSPAPER OF THE OAKLAND COUNTY COURTS). VFOAT Legal News. 0739-0203. Periodical. US. English. wk. 35.00. Pontiac-Oakland County Legal News Publishing Company, 185 Elizabeth Lake Road, PO Box 238, Pontiac MI 48056. Tel (313)338-4567. Ed Sheila R Ashcraft. bk rev. adv acc. Circ 1,550. Credit data, court dockets, legal notices, vital statistics, new businesses, all published weekly with timely features of interest to the legal, business and financial readership.

POPCHO. VFOAT Bup Jo. Periodical. KO. Korean. mo. Popcho Hyophoe, 77 Sejong-ro, Jongro-ku, Seoul South Korea.

POPSAHAK YON'GU. V. 1- 1974-. Periodical. Korean. ir.

POST MORTEM ESTATE PLANNING. 0734-4406. US. English. an. Practising Law Instutute, 810 7th Avenue, New York NY 10019. LC KF6585. DD 343.73053, 347.30353.

POSTAL LAWS AND REGULATIONS OF THE UNITED STATES OF AMERICA. VFOAT Postal Laws & Regulations of the USA. US. English. T Wierenga, PO Box 2007, Holland MI 49423. LC KF2661.9. DD 343.7309920263, 347. 3039920263.

POTOMAC LAW REVIEW. V. 1- Fall 1978-. 0192-9801. Periodical. US. English. sa. $6.00. Potomac School of Law, 2600 Virginia Avenue NW, Washington DC 20037. Ind/Abst Leg. Resour. Index. LC K16. DD 340.05.

POVERTY LAW REPORT. V. 1- Mar. 1973-. Periodical. US. English. ir. $15.00. Southern Poverty Law Center, 1001 South Hull Street, Montgomery AL 36104. Tel (205)264-0286. Ed H Randall Williams. Circ 90,000. (ctrl). To defend rights of poor and to educate public as to their rights. No charge to clients.

POVERTY LAW REPORTER. Main/Corp Commerce Clearing House. 1969-. US. English. Commerce Clearing House, 4025 West Peterson Avenue, Chicago IL 60646. LC KF390.5.P6. DD 340.

PRACTICAL LABOR LAW. COURSE MANUAL. (PRACTICAL LABOR LAW : COURSE MANUAL). 0195-3656. US. English. an. Federal Publications Inc, 1725 K Street NW, Washington DC 20006. LC KF3319.3. DD 344.7301.

PRACTICAL LAW BOOKS REVIEW. V. 1- Jan. 1978-. 0160-8177. Periodical. US. English. qt. $28.00. Library Management & Services, 5914 Highland Hills Drive, Austin TX 78731. LC KF1. DD 016.34. A quick reference to reviews of new legal publications by field of specialization.

THE PRACTICAL LAWYER. 1954. 0032-6429. Periodical. US. English. ir. $20.00. American Law Institute, 4025 Chestnut Street, Philadelphia PA 19104. Tel (215)243-1620. Ed Paul A Wolkin. Ind/Abst Leg. Resour. Index, Account. Index. Suppl., Index Leg. Period., Curr. Law Index, Comput. Rev., Contents Curr. Leg. Period. (cum index). adv acc. Circ 17,000. (ctrl). Contains articles on current legal issues, legal practice, and law office management.

PRACTICAL LAWYER'S LAW OFFICE MANAGEMENT MANUAL. (THE PRACTICAL LAWYER'S LAW OFFICE MANAGEMENT MANUAL). No. 3- 1972-. 0092-248X. US. English. ALI-ABA, 4025 Chestnut Street, Philadelphia PA 19104. LC KF318.A1. DD 340.068. Practical Lawyer. Law Office Manual.

THE PRACTICAL REAL ESTATE LAWYER. Vol. 1, No. 1 (Jan. 1985)-. 8756-0372. Periodical. US. English. bm. $22.00. ALI-ABA Committee on Continuing Professional Education, 4025 Chestnut Street, Philadelphia PA 19104. Tel (215)243-1656. Ed Mark T Carroll. LC KF566.A3. DD 346.7304305, 347.3064305. adv acc. Circ 5,000. Articles for lawyers on real property law issues, with practical, how-to-do-it orientation.

PRACTICAL SKILLS COURSE. Main/Corp Oregon State Bar. Committee on Continuing Legal Education. Periodical. US. English. Oregon State Bar, Continuing Legal Education, 1776 SW Madison Street, Portland OR 97205. LC KFO2481. DD 349.795.

PRACTICAL WILL DRAFTING. 1971-. 0192-3889. US. English. an. Practising Law Institute, 810 Seventh Avenue, New York NY 10019. LC KF755.Z9. DD 346.73054.

THE PRACTICING FAMILY LAWYER. V. 1- Spring 1977-. 0148-9763. Periodical. US. English. qt. $37.00. The Practising Family Lawyer Inc, 3711 Long Beach Boulevard PO Box 7888, Long Beach CA 90807.

PRAVNA MISAO. V. 1- Jan./Feb. 1969-. YU. Serbo-Croatian -R. bm. Jugoslovenska Knjica, PO Box 36, Beograd Yuguslavia. LC K16. Narodna Uprava.

PRAVNA MISUL. V. 1- 1957-. Periodical. BU. Bulgarian (tables of contents also in Russian and French). ir. Hemus, 6 Boulevard Rusky, Sofia Bulgaria. Scientific-Theoretical articles on top problems of all branches of the legal science and socialist law. Includes discussions, notes and information which spreads legal knowledge.

PRAVNICKE STUDIE. Vol. 1- 1953-. CS. Slovak (summaries in Russian, French or German). ir. Kubon and Sagner, Postfach 34 01 08, D-8000 Munchen 34 West Germany. Tel (089)52 20 27. Theoretical juridical journal which publishes comprehensive studies from all disciplines of valid law and on the theory of state and law.

PRAVNIK (PRAGUE, CZECHOSLOVAKIA). (PRAVNIK). Began in 1861. Periodical. Czech. mo. Kubon & Sagner, Postfach 34 01 08, Hess-Strasse 39/41, D-8 Munchen 34 West Germany. A theoretical scientific journal dealing with all aspects of the science of the state and law.

Law

PRAVNY OBZOR : CASOPIS USTAVU STATU A PRAVA SLOVENKEJ AKADEMIE VIED. Periodical. Slovak. Kubon & Sagner, Postfach 38 01 08, Hess-Strasse 39/41, D-8 Munchen 34 West Germany. **Tel** (089)52 20 27. **LC** UNC. An important tool in all legal matters. In wide use with lawyers, national committees and organisations.

PRAWO I ZYCIE. Periodical. PL. Polish. wk. ARS Polona, Krakowskie Przedmiescie 7, 00-068 Warsaw Poland. **LC** UNC.

PRE-LAW JOURNAL. (PRE-LAW JOURNAL : A LEGAL INSTITUTE PROJECT). **VFOAT** Pre Law Journal. Began in 1982. 0741-1162. Periodical. US. English. ty. $9.75. Legal Institute, 281 East Colorado Boulevard Box 219, Pasadena CA 91102. **Tel** (818)405-1476. Ed Herman B Lancaster. **LC** KF287. **DD** 340.071173. bk rev. **Circ** 200. Provides information of assistance in deciding to attend law school and in doing well in law school.

PRECEDENTS FOR THE CONVEYANCER. UK. English. bm. $68.96. Sweet & Maxwell Ltd, North Way Andover, Hampshire SP10 5BE England. **Tel** 01-583 9855. Ed Carol Tullo. **Circ** 3,000. (ctrl). New precedents with practical emphasis issued for the conveyancer.

PREGLED SUDSKE PRAKSE. 1- 1972-. Serbo-Croatian(R). ir. Narodne Novine, Ratkajev Prolaz BR 4, Zagreb Yugoslavia.

PRELAW ADVISER'S KIT. 0747-878X. US. English. **LC** KF285. **DD** 340.071173.

PRELAW HANDBOOK. Main/Corp Association of American Law Schools. 1971/72-. 0146-9142. US. English. an. Association of American Law Schools, Suite 370/1 Dupont Cirle, Washington DC 20036. **Tel** (215)968-1088. **LC** KF273. **DD** 340.071173. *Law Study and Practice in the United States, 0075-8264.*

PRENTICE-HALL 1040 HANDBOOK; HOW TO PREPARE INCOME TAX RETURNS. Main/Corp Prentice-Hall, Inc. **VAT** Prentice-Hall Ten Forty Handbook. 1979-. 0191-233X. US. English. an. $16.50 Each Issue. Prentice-Hall Inc, Department S103, Englewood Cliffs NJ 07632. **LC** KF6369.6. **DD** 343.73052.

PRENTICE-HALL FEDERAL REGULATORY WEEK. Main/Corp Prentice-Hall, Inc. **VFOAT** Federal Regulatory Week. V. 1- Oct. 1, 1979-. 0195-329X. US. English. wk. $297.00. Prentice Hall Inc, Sylvan Avenue, Englewood Cliffs NJ 07632. **LC** KF70. **DD** 348.7325.

PREPARATION OF ANNUAL DISCLOSURE DOCUMENTS. Series/Titl Corporate Law and Practice Course Handbook Series. 0276-6094. US. English. an. Practising Law Institute, 810 Seventh Avenue, New York NY 10019. **LC** KF1449. **DD** 346.730666, 347.306666.

PREPARING PERSONAL INJURY CASES FOR TRIAL. Series/Titl Litigation and Administrative Practice Series. Litigation Course Handbook Series. 0882-9748. US. English. Practising Law Institute, 810 Seventh Avenue, New York NY 10019.

PRESERVATION LAW REPORTER. Vol. 1, No. 1 (Jan. 1982)-. Periodical. US. English. bm. $155.00. National Trust for Historic Preservation, 1785 Massachusetts Avenue, Washington DC 20036. **Tel** (202)673-4033. Ed Harrison B Wetherill Jr. (cum index). bk rev. **Circ** 500. (ctrl). Looseleaf reporting service. Law of historic preservation and rehabilitation. Tax incentives, easements, financing, litigation, zoning and land use. Reference volume and bimonthly updates.

PRESIDENTIAL DECREES. Main/Corp Philippines. V. 1- 1972-. PH. English. ir. Allied Printing & Binding Company, 91-95 Panay Avenue, Quezon City Philippines. **DD** 348.59901.

PRESUPUESTOS GENERALES DEL ESTADO. Main/Corp Spain. Cortes Generales., Servicio de Estudios. Spanish. ir. **DD** 343.46034, 344.60334.

PRETRIAL ISSUES. V. 1- Dec. 1979-. 0270-2126. Periodical. US. English. Pretrial Services Resource Center, 918 F Street NW/Suite 500, Washington DC 20004. **LC** KF9645.A15. **DD** 347.737205.

PRETRIAL JUSTICE QUARTERLY. Began in Mar. 1972. 0093-111X. Periodical. US. English. qt. $5.00. Pennsylvania Pretrial Justice Federation, 1300 Fifth Avenue, Pittsburgh PA 15219. **LC** K16. **DD** 347.74807205. *Pretrial Justice Federation Newsletter.*

THE PRETRIAL REPORTER. See Sociology: General Works, Theory - Social Pathology, Welfare, Criminology.

PRETRIAL SERVICES ANNUAL JOURNAL. VFOAT Annual Journal. 1978-. Periodical. US. English. an. 1010 Vermont Avenue Northwest/Suite 200, Washington DC 20005. Ed D Alan Henry.

PREVENTIVE LAW REPORTER. Vol. 1, No. 1 (July 1982)-. Periodical. US. English. bm. PL Publishers, 15728 NE 144th Place, Woodinville MA 98072. **Tel** (206)483-5877. Ed David A Winn. **Ind/Abst** Leg. Resour. Index. bk rev. Techniques and ideas for avoiding disputes and minimizing liability exposure through appropriate planning and counseling. *Preventive Law Newsletter.*

PREVIEW OF UNITED STATES SUPREME COURT CASES. Dec. 7, 1973-. 0363-0048. US. English. $72.00. American Bar Association, 750 North Lake Shore, Chicago IL 60611. **Tel** (617)452-1701. Ed Barbara Kate Repa. **LC** KF4547.8. **DD** 348.73413. **Circ** 4,000. The only publication providing detailed advance analysis of every case orally argued before the Court.

PRIMEIRA INSTANCIA. No. 1- 1973-. Portuguese. ir. Associacao dos Magistrados de Primeira Instancia, Esplanada dos Ministerios, Bloco 6 - 7. Andar, Brasilia Brazil.

PRINCIPLES OF CIVIL SERVICE LAW. US. English. ir. Matthew Bender & Company Inc, 1275 Broadway, Albany NY 12201. **Tel** (800)833-9844. (cum index).

PRISON DECISIONS. V. 1- 1974-. 0270-2703. Periodical. US. English. mo. University of Toledo, College of Law, Toledo OH 43606. **LC** KF9728.A59. **DD** 344.7303502643.

PRISON LAW & ADVOCACY. VFOAT Prison Law and Advocacy. Vol. 1 (Jan./Feb. 1980)-. 0739-7577. Periodical. US. English. bm. $5.00 Institutionalized Persons, $35.00 Others. Prison Law & Advocacy, 343 South Dearborn #706, Chicago IL 60604. **Tel** KFI1788.A59. **DD** 344.77303505, 347.73043505.

PRISON LAW MONITOR. V. 1- June 1978-. 0161-9632. Periodical. US. English. mo. $20.00 Non-Profit Public Interest Organizations, $25.00 Other Institutions and Individuals, $6.00 State and Federal Prisoners. Prison Law Monitor, 1806 T Street NW, Washington DC 20009. **LC** KF9728.A15. **DD** 344.7303505.

PRIVACY ACT ISSUANCES. COMPILATION. (PRIVACY ACT ISSUANCES . . . COMPILATION). Began with 1976. 0190-8146. US. English. an. Office of the Federal Register, National Archives and Records Service, Washington DC 20408. **LC** KF5753.A329. **DD** 342.73085.

PRIVACY JOURNAL. Began with Nov. 1974 issue. 0145-7659. Periodical. US. English. mo. $89.00. Privacy Journal, PO Box 15300, Washington DC 20003. **Tel** (202)547-2865. Ed Robert Ellis Smith. **LC** JC599.U5. **DD** 323.44. bk rev. **Circ** 5,000. Newsletter on new technology, legislation and court cases affecting personal privacy, including medical, credit, government and financial records, plus wiretaps and lie detectors.

PRIVATE SECURITY CASE LAW REPORTER. 0738-6958. Periodical. US. English. mo. $168.00. Strafford Publications, 1375 Peachtree Street NE/Suite 260, Atlanta GA 30309. **LC** KF5399.5.P7. **DD** 345.73052, 347.30552.

PRO SE. 0093-8858. Periodical. US. English. sm. Pro, 400 Huntington Avenue, Boston MA 02115. **LC** KF4758.A73. **DD** 346.73013.

PRO SE. See Library and Information Science.

THE PROBATE COUNSEL. 1st- ed. US. English. an. Royal Publishing Company Inc, PO Box 2241, Palm Beach FL 33480. **Tel** (305)588-9773. Ed R A Sfraga. **Circ** 1,500. (ctrl). Listings by state, of law firms dealing in probate law. Also contains digest of probate laws, abstract and title company and real estate appraisal firms.

PROBATE LAW JOURNAL. Vol. 4, No. 3-. 0737-3112. Periodical. US. English. ty. $18.00. National College of Probate Judges Probate Law Journal, 765 Commonwealth Avenue, Boston MA 02215. **Tel** (617)353-4797. Ed Faye G Yoffa Stone. **LC** K16. **DD** 346.7305205, 347.3065205. bk rev. adv acc. **Circ** 1,000. Probate and family law tax, matters pertaining to trusts and estates, property settlements in divorce, constitutional rights in commitments, rights, and refusals of treatment. *National College of Probate Judges Probate Journal.*

PROBATE LAWYER. (THE PROBATE LAWYER). V. 1- Summer 1974-. 0094-999X. US. English. ir. American College of Probate, 10964 West Pico Boulevard, Los Angeles CA 90064. **Ind/Abst** Leg. Resour. Index, Curr. Law Index. **LC** KF765.A73. **DD** 346.7305205, 347.3065205.

PROBATE NOTES. VFOAT ACPC Probate Notes. Winter 1974/75-. 0098-2229. US. English. qt. $24.00. American College of Probate Counsel, 10964 West Pico Boulevard, Los Angeles CA 90064. **Tel** (213)475-1200. **LC** KF765.A15. **DD** 346.730505. *Newsletter - American College of Probate Counsel.*

PROBATE REPORTER. 0362-4773. Periodical. US. English. qt. Connecticut Probate Assembly, City Hall PO Box 388, Meriden CT 06450. **LC** KFC3744.A15. **DD** 346.7460505.

PROBLEMY PRAVOVEDENIIA. Vol. 33-. 0136-4936. Periodical. UR. Russian. ir. *Problemy Pravoznavstva, 0555-2931.*

PROBLEMY PRAWA KARNEGO. Series/Titl Prace Naukowe Uniwersytetu Slaskiego w Katowicach. 1-. Polish. ir. 40.00. Uniwersytet Slaski, Ul Bankowa 14, Katowice Poland. **LC** K16.

PROBLEMY PRAWA PRZEWOZOWEGO. Series/Titl Prace Naukowe Uniwersytetu Slaskiego w Ktaowicach. 1-. Periodical. Polish (summaries in English and Russian, (V. 3-)). ir. Uniwersytet Slaski, Ul Bankowa 14, 40-007 Katowice Poland. **LC** K16.

PROBLEMY SOTSIALISTICHESKOI ZAKONNOSTI. Vol. 1- 1976-. UR. Russian. an. Vyshcha Shkola, 310003 Kharkov-3 Ul Universitetskaia 16, Kharkov Ukrainian SSR.

PROCEEDINGS - AMERICAN BAR ASSOCIATION. SECTION OF LABOR RELATIONS LAW. Main/Corp American Bar Association. Section of Labor Relations Law. Periodical. US. English. an.

PROCEEDINGS - AMERICAN LAW INSTITUTE. Main/Corp American Law Institute. V. 1- February 23, 1923-. US. English. an. $38.00. American Law Institute, 4025 Chestnut Street, Philadelphia PA 19104. **Tel** (215)243-1626. Ed Michael Greenwald. **Circ** 300. Yearly volume containing transcript of American Law Institute (ALI) annual meeting, ALI annual report, and other information about the Institute's activities.

PROCEEDINGS - BAR ASSOCIATION OF THE STATE OF NEW HAMPSHIRE. Main/Corp Bar Association of the State of New Hampshire. (N.S.)V.1- 1899-. Periodical. US. English.

PROCEEDINGS IN THE MUNICIPAL COURTS. Main/Corp New Jersey. Administrative Office of the Courts. 0550-6387. US. English. an. State House Annex, Trenton NJ 08625. **LC** KFN1871. **DD** 345.7490247.

PROCEEDINGS OF NEW YORK UNIVERSITY ANNUAL NATIONAL CONFERENCE ON LABOR. Main/Conf New York University National Conference on Labor. 30th- 1977-. 0193-3418. US. English. an. Matthew Bender & Company Inc, 1275 Broadway, Albany NY 12201. **Tel** (800)833-9844. **LC** KF3319.A2. **DD** 344.7301. *Proceedings of New York University Annual Conference on Labor, 0069-8563.*

PROCEEDINGS OF SAN FERNANDO VALLEY COLLEGE OF LAW SYMPOSIUM ON LABOR LAW AND INDUSTRIAL RELATIONS. Main/Conf Symposium on Labor Law and Industrial Relations. 1st- 1978-. US. English. an. San Fernando Valley Law Review, 8353 Sepulveda Boulevard, Sepulveda CA 91343.

PROCEEDINGS OF THE ANNUAL INSTITUTE - EASTERN MINERAL LAW FOUNDATION (U.S.). ANNUAL INSTITUTE. (PROCEEDINGS OF THE . . . ANNUAL INSTITUTE). Main/Corp Eastern Mineral Law Foundation (U.S.). Annual Institute. 1st (Mar. 6 &

Law

7, 1980)-. 0733-6098. US. English. an. M Bender, 235 East 45th Street, New York NY 10017. **Ind/Abst** Index Leg. Period., GeoRef. **LC** KF1819.A2. **DD** 343.73077, 347.30377.

PROCEEDINGS OF THE . . . ANNUAL INSTITUTE OF OIL AND GAS LAW AND TAXATION. Main/Conf Institute on Oil and Gas Law and Taxation. 11th-. US. English. an. M Bender, 235 East 45th Street, New York NY 10017. (cum index). *Proceedings of the . . . Annual Institute on Oil and Gas Law and Taxation as it Affects the Oil and Gas Industry.*

PROCEEDINGS OF THE ANNUAL INSTITUTE ON MINERAL LAW. -3d. 0076-1087. US. English. Mineral Law Institute at LSU, P M Hebert Law Center/Room 275, Baton Rouge LA 70803. **Tel** (504)388-5837. Ed Thomas A Harrell. **LC** KF1849.A2. **DD** 346.73046823, 347.30646823. **Circ** 500. (ctrl). Contains papers presented at the annual Mineral Law Institute on the latest trends and developments in the oil, gas and mineral industry.

PROCEEDINGS OF THE . . . ANNUAL INSTITUTE ON OIL AND GAS LAW AND TAXATION AS IT AFFECTS THE OIL AND GAS INDUSTRY. *See* Petroleum and Natural Gas.

PROCEEDINGS OF THE ANNUAL INSTITUTE ON SECURITIES LAWS AND REGULATIONS. Main/Corp Institute on Securities Laws and Regulations. 1st- 1977-. 0161-4002. US. English. an. Matthew Bender, 235 East 45th Street, New York NY 10017. **LC** KF1439.A2. **DD** 346.730666.

PROCEEDINGS OF THE . . . ANNUAL MEETING, NATIONAL ACADEMY OF ARBITRATORS. Main/Corp National Academy of Arbitrators. Meeting. 8th (1955)-. US. English. an. Bureau of National Affairs, 9435 Key West Avenue, Rockville MD 20850. (cum index).

PROCEEDINGS OF THE ANNUAL MEETING OF THE LEGAL SECTION OF THE AMERICAN COUNCIL OF LIFE INSURANCE. *See* Insurance.

PROCEEDINGS OF THE . . . ANNUAL MEETING - UNIFORM LAW CONFERENCE OF CANADA. Main/Corp Uniform Law Conference of Canada. 59th (1977)-. English. ir. Free. Executive Director, PO Box 6000, Fredericton New Brunswick E3B 5H1 Canada. **Tel** (506)453-2226. **Circ** 400. (ctrl). Law reform. *Proceedings of the . . . Annual Meeting of the Uniform Law Conference of Canada.*

PROCEEDINGS OF THE . . . COLLOQUIUM ON THE LAW OF OUTER SPACE. Main/Conf Colloquium on the Law of Outer Space. 1st- 1958-. 0069-5831. US. English. ir. $50.00. American Institute of Aeronautics and Astronautics, PO Box 6416, Church Street Station, New York NY 10249. **Tel** (212)581-4300. **DD** 341.520631. Proceedings of International Institute of Space Law and the International Astronautical Federation annual colloquiums. Original papers on domestic and space law, property, nuclear power sources and more.

PROCEEDINGS OF THE COURT OF JUSTICE OF THE EUROPEAN COMMUNITIES. Main/Corp Court of Justice of the European Communities. VFOAT Activities de la Cour de Justice des Communautes Europeennes. Began in 1973. English (French, or German, 1973-). wk. Information Office of the Court of Justice of the European Communities, PO Box 1406, Luxembourg. **DD** 341.55.

PROCEEDINGS OF THE INSTITUTE ON PLANNING, ZONING AND EMINENT DOMAIN. (PROCEEDINGS OF THE INSTITUTE ON PLANNING, ZONING, AND EMINENT DOMAIN). **Main/Conf** Institute on Planning, Zoning, and Eminent Domain. Dec. 7-9, 1970-. 0730-3009. US. English. an. Matthew Bender, 235 East 45th Street, New York NY 10017. **Ind/Abst** Leg. Resour. Index. **LC** KF5692.A5. **DD** 346.73045, 347.30645. *Proceedings of the Institute on Planning and Zoning, 0537-9814; Proceedings of the . . . Institute on Eminent Domain (1966).*

PROCEEDINGS OF THE INSTITUTE ON PLANNING, ZONING, AND EMINENT DOMAIN : THE SOUTHWESTERN LEGAL FOUNDATION, MUNICIPAL LEGAL STUDIES CENTER, DALLAS, TEXAS, NOVEMBER 13-15, 1979. Main/Conf Southwestern Legal Foundation. Institute on Planning, Zoning, and Eminent Domain (1979

:*Dallas, Texas. US. English. an. Matthew Bender & Company Inc, 1275 Broadway, Albany NY 12201. **Tel** (800)833-9844. (cum index).

PROCEEDINGS OF THE NATIONAL HEALTH LAWYERS ASSOCIATION'S ANNUAL PROGRAM ON LONG TERM CARE AND THE LAW. Main/Corp National Health Lawyers Association. 0271-2865. US. English. Panel Publishers, 14 Plaza Road, Greenvale NY 11548. **LC** KF3826.N8. **DD** 344.7303216.

PROCEEDINGS OF THE NATIONAL HEALTH LAWYERS ASSOCIATION'S HEALTH LAW UPDATE. Main/Corp National Health Lawyers Association. VFOAT Health Law Update. US. English. an. Panel Publishers, 14 Plaza Road, Greenvale NY 11548. **LC** KF3821.A75. **DD** 344.73041. **NLM** W3 PR945SF.

PROCEEDINGS OF THE SENATE STANDING COMMITTEE ON LEGAL AND CONSTITUTIONAL AFFAIRS. Main/Corp Canada. Parliament. Senate. Standing Committee on Legal and Constitutional Affairs. VFOAT Deliberations du Comite Senatorial Permanent des Affaires Juridiques et Constitutionelles. CN. English (French). **LC** KE4213.2. **DD** 349.7105, 347.1005.

PROCEEDINGS OF THE SOUTH DAKOTA STATE BOARD OF EQUALIZATION. Main/Corp South Dakota State Board of Equalization. US. English. **LC** KFS3491.R4. **DD** 343.783054, 347.830354.

PROCEEDINGS OF THE STANDING COMMITTEE ON LEGAL AND CONSTITUTIONAL AFFAIRS. Main/Corp Canada. Parliament. Senate. Standing Committee on Legal and Constitutional Affairs. VFOAT Deliberations du Comite Senatorial Permanent des Affaires Juridiques et Constitutionnelles. Feb. 13, 1969-. 0576-3835. Periodical. CN. English (text in French, June 7, 1977-). Canada Parliament, Senate Standing Committtee on Legal Constitutional Affairs, Ottawa Ontario Canada. *Deliberations du Comite Senatorial Permanent des Affaires Juridiques et Constitutionnelles, 0576-3827.*

PROCEEDINGS - PUBLIC LAW SECTION OF THE STATE BAR OF CALIFORNIA. Main/Corp State Bar of California. Public Law Section. US. English. an. State Bar of California Public Law Section, 555 Franklin Street, San Francisco CA 94102. **LC** KFC678.A75. **DD** 342.794005, 347.940205.

PROCESS. V. 1- Jan. 1975-. Periodical. CN. English. mo. Justice Development Commission, United Kingdom Building, 409 Granville Street/Room 1019, Vancouver British Columbia V6C 1T8 Canada.

PROCURADORES. Spanish. ir. Junta Nacional de los Ilustres Colegios de Procuradores de Espana, Barbara de Braganza, Madrid 6 Spain. **DD** 340.0946.

PRODUCT LIABILITY INTERNATIONAL. V. 1- Jan. 1979-. Periodical. UK. English. mo. $220.00. LLP Maritime & Bus Publishing Inc, 87 Terminal Drive, Plainsview New York 11803. **LC** K16. **DD** 341.754.

PRODUCT LIABILITY TRENDS. V. 1- Aug. 1977-. 0164-9574. Periodical. US. English. mo. $115.00. National Legal Research Group Inc, PO Box 7187, Charlottsville VA 22906. **Tel** (800)446-1870. **LC** K953.A13. **DD** 346.038.

PRODUCT LIABILITY UPDATE. Series/ **Titl** Litigation and Administrative Practice Series. Litigation Course Handbook Series. 0192-5075. US. English. Practising Law Institute, 810 Seventh Avenue, New York NY 10019. Ed R J Phelan. **LC** KF1296.Z9. **DD** 346.73038.

PRODUCT SAFETY & THE LAW. 0094-5463. Periodical. US. English. mo. $30.00. Man & Manager Inc/Subscription Department, 87 Terminal Drive, Plainview NY 11803. **LC** KF3945.A73. **DD** 344.7304205.

PRODUCTS LIABILITY AND TRANSPORTATION LEGAL DIRECTORY. *See* Yearbooks, Almanacs, Directories.

PROFESSIONAL LIABILITY. Issue No. 1 (Jan. 1981)-. 0275-0503. Periodical. US. English. mo. $120.00. Professional Liability, 1852 Columbia Road Northwest/Suite 504, Washington DC 20009. **LC** KF1289.A15. **DD** 346.73033205, 347.30633205.

PROFESSIONAL LIABILITY REPORTER. 1976. 0145-3505. Periodical. US. English. mo. Litigation Research Group, PO Box 77903, San Francisco CA 94107. **Tel** (415)543-5433.

Ed William Jordan. **Ind/Abst** Contents Curr. Leg. Period. **LC** KF1289.A59. **DD** 346.73033. **Circ** 850. Reporting and analysis of legal developments in professional liability law.

THE PROFESSIONAL MONITOR. Vol. 16, No. 18 Apr./May 1982. 0744-7817. Periodical. US. English. mo. Michigan Association of the Professions, 230 North Washington Square/Suite H, Lansing MI 48933. *Legislative Monitor, 0279-8743.*

PROFESSIONAL PRACTICE OF PSYCHOLOGY. VFOAT Journal of Professional Practice in Psychology. Began with June 1980 issue. 0733-1568. Periodical. US. English. sa. $15.00. AASPB Central Office, PO Box 4389, Montgomery AL 36103. **Tel** (205)832-4580. Ed S Joseph Waver. **Ind/Abst** Psychol. Abstr. **LC** KF2910.P75. **DD** 344.73017611505, 347. 30417611505. bk rev. **Circ** 700. (ctrl). Regulating psychology.

PROFESSIONAL REGULATION NEWS. Began with Aug. 1981 issue. 0741-4749. Periodical. US. English. mo. $65.00 Members, $95.00 Nonmembers. Professional Regulation News, National Commission for Health Certifying Agencies, 1101 30th Street NW/Suite 108, Washington DC 20007. **LC** KF2905.1 .A15. **DD** 344.73041, 347.30441.

PROFESSIONAL RESPONSIBILITY. Main/Corp Bay Area Review Course, Inc. 1976-. 0362-8531. US. English. Bay Area Review Course Inc, 5900 Wilshire Boulevard/Suite 610, Los Angeles CA 90036. **LC** KF306.Z9. **DD** 174.30973. *Legal Ethics.*

THE PROFITABLE LAWYER. Vol. 1, No. L (July/Aug. 1984)-. 0743-5401. Periodical. US. English. mo. $85.00. The Profitable Lawyer, 855 Valley Road, Clifton NJ 07013. **Tel** (201)472-7400. Ed Larry Smith. bk rev. **Circ** 800. A new indispensable resource packed with highly specific information and ideas on how to run your firm efficiently and profitably.

PROGRAM MATERIALS. Main/Corp Estate Planning Institute, University of Georgia. US. English. an. University of Georgia, School of Law, Estate Planning Institute, Athens GA 30601. **LC** KFG140.A73. **DD** 346.758056.

PROGRAM MATERIALS FOR SEMINAR FOR GEORGIA DISTRICT ATTORNEYS. (PROGRAM MATERIALS). **Main/ Conf** Seminar for Georgia District Attorneys. 0092-5977. US. English. Institute of Continuing Education in Georgia, University of Georgian School of Law, Law Building, Athens GA 30601. **LC** KFG561.A73. **DD** 345.75805.

PROGRAMME OF CONSOLIDATION AND STATUTE LAW REVISION. Main/ Corp Scottish Law Commission. UK. English. ir. Her Majesty's Stationery Office, 13A Castle Street, Edinburgh EH2 3AR Scotland.

PROPERTY LAW BULLETIN. Periodical. UK. English. mo. 29.50. Oyez Publications Ltd, Norwich House 11/13 Norwich Street, London EC4A 1AB England. **LC** KD822. **DD** 346.41043, 344.10643.

PROPOSED LEGISLATIVE PROGRAM - DEPARTMENT OF THE INTERIOR. Main/Corp United States. Department of the Interior. VFOAT Department of the Interior Proposed Legislative Program. 1960-. Periodical. English. ir. *Preliminary Legislative Program - Department of the Interior.*

PROPOSTE SOCIALI. Yearly V. 1- Jan./March 1973-. 0303-5174. Periodical. Italian. ir. 10.000. Istituto di Patronato per l'Assistenza Sociale, Via Colossi 50, Roma 00146 Italy. **Ind/Abst** Foreign Lang. Index. **LC** K16.

THE PROSECUTOR : JOURNAL OF THE NATIONAL DISTRICT ATTORNEYS ASSOCIATION. Vol. 3, No. 4 (Jul.-Aug. 67)-. 0027-6383. Periodical. US. English. qt. NDAA Editor, 708 Pendleton Street, Alexandria VA 22314. **LC** K16. **DD** 345.7301. NDAA (Series).

THE PROSECUTORS' BULLETIN. Main/ Corp Wisconsin. Dept. of Justice. 0098-8774. US. English. Department of Justice, 819 North 6th Street/ Room 520, Milwaukee WI 53203. **LC** KFW2961. **DD** 345.77501.

PROSECUTORS' NOTES. English. ir. The Chief Legal Adviser Attention: Senior Legal Adviser/P J Mears, Police National Headquarter, Private Bag, Wellington New Zealand. **Tel** 749-499. Ed Paul Mears. **DD** 345.93101, 349.31051. **Circ** 200. Recent law and practical guidance on prosecuting in criminal courts.

Law

PROTECTING THE CORPORATE OFFICER AND DIRECTOR FROM LIABILITY. 0192-5547. US. English. an. Practising Law Institute, 810 Seventh Avenue, New York NY 10019. Ed J F Johnston. **LC** KF1423.Z9. **DD** 346.730664.

PROVINCE AND COURT RECORDS OF MAINE CEASED. Vol. 1-. US. English. ir. Maine Historical Society, 485 Congress Street, Portland ME 04111.

PROVINCIAL JUDGES JOURNAL. VFOAT Journal des Juges Provinciaux. V. 3, No. 1- Mar. 1979-. 0709-5139. Periodical. CN. English. qt. Free. Canadian Association of Provincial Court Judges, PO Box 246, Saint Stephen New Brunswick E3L 2X2 Canada. **DD** 347.7101405. (ctrl). *Canadian Provincial Judges Journal, 0701-1806.*

PROVINCIAL LEGISLATION. VAT Provincial Legislation. Regular Bulletin. Began publication in 1972. 0319-4906. Periodical. CN. English. Province of Quebec, Chamber of Commerce, 500 St Francois Xavier Street, Montreal Quebec H2Y 2T6 Canada. *Bulletin on Provincial Legislation, 0384-6067.*

PROYECTO DE PRESUPUESTO, SECTOR CENTRAL. Main/Corp Colombia. Direccion General del Presupuesto. 1978-. Periodical. Spanish. an. **LC** KHH4560.A22. **DD** 343.86103405, 348.61033405. *Colombia, Proyecto de Presupuesto.*

PROZESSRECHTLICHE ABHANDLUNGEN. Monographic Series. German. ir. Carl Heymanns Verlag KG, Gereonstrasse 18-32, 5000 Koln 1 West Germany.

THE PUBLIC ADMINISTRATOR AND THE COURTS. *See* Public Administration.

PUBLIC AND LOCAL ACTS OF THE LEGISLATURE OF THE STATE OF MICHIGAN. Main/Corp Michigan. 1933-. US. English. an. State of Michigan, Department of Management and Budget, General Services Section, Box 30026, Lansing MI 48909. **Tel** (517)322-1898. **LC** KFM4225. **DD** 348.774022. (ctrl). Laws enacted by the Michigan Legislature for a particular year. *Local Acts of the Legislature of the State of Michigan Passed at the Regular Session.*

PUBLIC AND SPECIAL ACTS. Main/Corp Connecticut. V. 36- Feb. Sess. 1972-. 0360-7704. US. English. 30 Trenety Street, Hartford CT 06115. **LC** KFC3625. **DD** 348.746022. *Public Acts Passed by the General Assembly, Special Acts and Resolutions of the State of Connecticut.*

PUBLIC CONTRACT LAW JOURNAL. Vol. 1, No. 1 (July 1967)-. 0033-3441. Periodical. US. English. sa. $8.00. American Bar Association, 750 North Lake Shore Drive, Chicago IL 60611. **Tel** (312)988-5555. Ed Matthew S Sinchak. **Ind/Abst** Leg. Resour. Index, Index Leg. Period., Curr. Law Index. **LC** K16. **DD** 346.7302305, 347.3062305. adv acc. (ctrl). Articles on all phases of state, local procurement and grant law by leading authorities.

PUBLIC CONTRACT NEWSLETTER. Began in 1965. 0569-3314. Periodical. US. English. ir. American Bar Association, 750 North Lake Shore Drive, Chicago IL 60611. **Tel** (312)988-5555. **Ind/Abst** Leg. Resour. Index, Curr. Law Index. **LC** KF849.A1. **DD** 346.73023.

PUBLIC EMPLOYEE LAW BULLETIN. 0739-9294. Periodical. US. English. mo. $36.85. Puinlan Publishing Company, 131 Beverly Street, Boston MA 02114. **DD** 342.

PUBLIC JUSTICE. Main/Corp Australian Bureau of Statistics. Tasmanian Office. **Series/Titl** Statistics of Tasmania. 1973/74-. AT. English. ir. Australian Bureau of Statistics, GPO Box 796, Sydney New South Wales 2001 Australia. **LC** HV7395. **DD** 364.9946.

THE PUBLIC LAND AND RESOURCES LAW DIGEST. V. 8- Fall 1979-. 0148-6489. Periodical. US. English. sa. $29.50. Rocky Mountain Mineral Law Foundation, University of Colorado, Fleming Law Building B-405, Boulder CO 80309. **Tel** (303)492-6545. Ed Mark Holland. **Ind/Abst** Coal Abstr., Energy Inf. Abstr., Environ. Abstr., GeoRef, Energy Res. Abstr. **LC** K16. **DD** 343.7302505. **Circ** 600. Reprints and references, natural resources, and law articles. *Rocky Mountain Mineral Law Review.*

THE PUBLIC LAND LAW REVIEW. Vol. 1, No. 1 (Spring 1980)-. 0732-0264. US. English. an. $8.00. University of Montana, School of Law, Missoula MT 59812. **Tel** (406)243-6568. Ed Jody Miller and Tamzin Brown. **LC** K16. **DD** 333.105. bk rev. adv acc. **Circ** 550. Publishes articles, notes and comments involving legal issues surrounding public lands, natural resources and Indian law.

PUBLIC LAW FORUM. VFOAT Saint Louis University Public Law Forum. Vol. 1 (1981)-. 0738-5390. US. English. an. $10.00. Saint Louis University Public Law Forum, 3700 Lindell Boulevard, Saint Louis MO 63108. **Tel** (314)658-3067. **Ind/Abst** Leg. Resour. Index, Public Aff. Inf. Serv. Bull. **LC** K16. **DD** 342.73, 347.302. **Circ** 150. Covers public law issues including: housing, ethics, medical technology and its legal impacts, international, economic, and industrial law issues, constitutional and criminal law.

PUBLIC LAWS OF THE STATE OF RHODE ISLAND AND PROVIDENCE PLANTATIONS PASSED AT THE GENERAL ASSEMBLY. Main/Corp Rhode Island. US. English. an. $61.75. Documents Distribution, Room 38 State House, Providence RI 02903. **Tel** (401)277-3614. Ed Stephen Cicilline. Each issue contains an index to its own contents - no vol index - loose. **Circ** 310. Contains the public laws, private acts and resolutions passed by the General Assembly that year. Published at the end of the year.

PUBLIC SECTOR ARBITRATION AWARDS CEASED. Began with V. 1- Feb. 1974-. Ceased with Dec. 1983 issue. 0093-9161. US. English. mo. $125.00. Labor Relations Press, Highland Office Center, 550 Pinetown Road, Fort Washington PA 19034. **LC** KF3450.P8. **DD** 344.730189041353.

PUBLIC SECTOR LABOR RELATIONS. *See* Economics - Labor.

PUBLIC SERVICE STAFF RELATIONS BOARD DECISIONS. Main/Corp Canada. Public Service Staff Relations Board. **VFOAT** PSSRB Decisions. VAT Recueil de Decisions de la CRTFP. Jan. 1, 1982/June 30, 1982-. 0822-1790. CN. English (with French text on inverted pages). sa. **LC** KE3240.F4. **DD** 344.7101890413540002648, 347.1041890413540002648.

PUBLIC UTILITIES LAW ANTHOLOGY. V. 1- 1974-. 0095-5086. US. English. International Library Inc, 2425 Wilson Boulevard, Arlington VA 22201. **LC** KF2094.A1. **DD** 343.730905.

PUBLICACIONES. Main/Corp Chile. Universidad, Santiago. Seminario de Derecho Publico. 1- 1959-). 0577-8573. Periodical. CL. Spanish. ir. Universidad de Chile, Casilla 10220, Santiago Chile.

PUBLICACIONES - QUITO. UNIVERSIDAD CENTRAL DEL ECUADOR. Main/Corp Quito. Universidad Central del Ecuador. Vol. 1 1951-. EC. Spanish. ir. Universidad de Central del Ecuador, Quito Ecuador. **DD** 340.09866.

PUBLICATIONS OF THE CONSORTIUM FOR COMPARATIVE LEGISLATIVE STUDIES. Main/Corp Consortium for Comparative Legislative Studies. **VFOAT** Comparative Legislative Studies Series. Monographic Series. US. English. ir. Duke University Press, College Station PO Box 6697, Durham NC 27708. **Tel** (919)684-6837.

PUBLICO. Periodical. chiefly Indonesian. ir. Bagian Penerbitan Universitas Brawijaya, Jl Laks Martadinata 80, Malang Indonesia. **LC** K16.

PUBLIKASI (YAYASAN LKB (INDONESIA)). (PUBLIKASI). 1-. Indonesian. an. Yayasan Lembaga Kesadaran Berkonstitusi, Jl Teuju Umar # 66, Jakarte Pusat Indonesia. **LC** K16.

PUBLISHING, ENTERTAINMENT, ADVERTISING AND ALLIED FIELDS LAW QUARTERLY. VFOAT Peal Quarterly. V.1- June 1961-. Periodical. US. English. qt. PEAL, Box 4134, Pittsburgh PA 15202. Ed A D Choka. **Ind/Abst** Curr. Law Index.

QUADERNI COSTITUZIONALI. Periodical. IT. Italian. ty. 80.000 Domestic, 110.000 Foreign. Societa Editrice Il Mulino Spa, Via Santo Stefano 6, 40125 Bologna Italy. **Tel** 051/ 23 34 15. **DD** 342.45, 344.502.

QUADERNI FIORENTINI PER LA STORIA DEL PENSIERO GIURIDICO MODERNO. N. 1- 1972-. French, German, Italian or Spanish. ir. 6000 Single Issue. Via Francesco Puccinotti 83, Firenze, 50129 Milano Italy.

QUAERE. Began with Oct. 1974 issue. 0362-3564. Periodical. US. English. bm. $5.00. Quaere Inc, Fraser Hall, University of Minnesota, Minneapolis MN 55455. **LC** KF292.M5714. **DD** 340.09776.

QUARTERLY - CHRISTIAN LEGAL SOCIETY. (QUARTERLY). **VFOAT** Christian Legal Society Quarterly. Vol. 2, No. 2 (Spring 1981)-. 0736-0142. Periodical. US. English. ir. $15.00. Christian Legal Society, PO Box 2069, Oak Park IL 60303. **Tel** (312)848-7735. Ed Lynn Robert Buzzard. **LC** KF200. **DD** 344.09, 342.49. bk rev. adv acc. **Circ** 4,000. Professional journal containing articles of interest to Christian lawyers, judges and law students. *Christian Legal Society Quarterly, 0275-6765.*

QUARTERLY DIGEST OF THE UNPUBLISHED DECISIONS OF THE COMPTROLLER GENERAL OF THE UNITED STATES. PERSONNEL LAW, MILITARY PERSONNEL CEASED. (QUARTERLY DIGEST OF UNPUBLISHED DECISIONS OF THE COMPTROLLER GENERAL OF THE UNITED STATES. PERSONNEL LAW, MILITARY PERSONNEL). Main/Corp United States. General Accounting Office. Index-Digest Section. **VFOAT** Personnel Law, Military Personnel. -V. 26, Nos. 1 & 2 (Oct. 1982-March 1983). 0092-8747. Periodical. US. English. qt. US General Accounting Office, Office of Administrative Services, Distribution Section Room 4522, 441 G Street NW, Washington DC 20548. **LC** KF7274.A57. **DD** 343.73013.

QUARTERLY DIGESTS OF UNPUBLISHED DECISIONS OF THE COMPTROLLER GENERAL OF THE UNITED STATES. PERSONNEL LAW, CIVILIAN PERSONNEL CEASED. Main/Corp United States. General Accounting Office. Index-Digest Section. **VFOAT** Personnel Law, Civilian Personnel. -V. 26, No. 2 (Jan.-March 1983). 0360-2281. Periodical. US. English. qt. US General Accounting Office, Office of the General Counsel, Index-Digest Section/Room 4522, 441 G Street NW, Washington DC 20548. **LC** KF5336.A75. **DD** 342.7306802646, 347.3026802646. *Quarterly Digest of Unpublished Decisions of the Comptroller General of the United States. Civilian Personnel.*

QUARTERLY DIGESTS OF UNPUBLISHED DECISIONS OF THE COMPTROLLER GENERAL OF THE UNITED STATES. PERSONNEL LAW, CIVILIAN PERSONNEL & MILITARY PERSONNEL. Main/Corp United States. General Accounting Office. Index-Digest Section. **VFOAT** Personnel Law, Civilian Personnel & Military Personnel, Personnel Law, Civilian Personnel and Military Personnel. Vol. 26, No. 3 (Apr.-June 1983)-. 0748-0555. Periodical. US. English. qt. US General Accounting Office, Office of the General Counsel, Index-Digest Section, 441 G Street NW/Room 4522, Washington DC 20548. **LC** KF5336.A75. **DD** 342.7306802646 347.3026802646. *Quarterly Digest of Unpublished Decisions of the Comptroller General of the United States. Personnel Law, Civilian Personnel, 0360-2281; Quarterly Digest Unpublished Decisions of the Comptroller General of the United States. Personnel Law, Military Personnel, 0092-8747.*

QUARTERLY DIGESTS OF UNPUBLISHED DECISIONS OF THE COMPTROLLER GENERAL OF THE UNITED STATES. PROCUREMENT LAW. Main/Corp United States. General Accounting Office. Index-Digest Section. **VFOAT** Procurement Law. 0092-8550. Periodical. US. English. qt. US General Accounting Office, Office of Administrative Services, Distribution Section/Room 4522, 441 G Street NW, Washington DC 20548. **LC** KF846.2. **DD** 346.7302302646. *Quarterly Digests of Unpublished Decisions of the Comptroller General of the United States. Transportation.*

QUARTERLY - INTERNATIONAL SOCIETY OF BARRISTERS. (QUARTERLY). **VFOAT** International Society of Barristers Quarterly. V. 1- 1966-. 0020-8752. Periodical. US. English. qt. $10.00. International Society of Barristers, 2200 First National Bank Building, Denver CO 80202. **Tel** (313)764-0540. Ed John W Reed. **LC** K9. **Circ** 700. Concerns litigation and trial advocacy. Includes topics of the courts, the jury, trial lawyers, and the adversary system. One issue is a pictorial membership roster.

QUARTERLY LAW NOTES AND ALUMNI NEWS. Main/Corp University of San Diego. School of Law. Fall 1975-. Periodical. US. English. qt. University of San Diego, School of Law,

Law

More Hall, Alcala Park, San Diego CA 92110. *Alumni Newsletter.*

QUARTERLY NEWSLETTER - STANDING COMMITTEE ON ENVIRONMENTAL LAW. Main/Corp American Bar Association. Standing Committee on Environmental Law. Fall 1975-. Periodical. US. English. qt. $12.00. American Bar Association/ Standard Committee on Environmental Law, 1800 M Street NW, Washington DC 20036. **Tel** (202)331-2276. Ed Elissa C Lichtenstein. **LC** KF200. **DD** 344.7304605. bk rev. **Circ** 2,400. Articles on current environmental law topics; book and conference notices; updates on American Bar Association environmental law activities.

QUARTERLY REPORT OF THE ATTORNEY GENERAL OF ALABAMA. Main/Corp Alabama. Attorney General's Office. V.1- Oct./Dec. 1935-. US. English. qt. $5.00. Skinner Printing Company, PO Box 1787, Montgomery AL 36108. *Biennial Report of the Attorney General to the Governor of the State of Alabama, 0093-5441.*

QUARTERLY SUPPLEMENT TO THE OKLAHOMA BAR JOURNAL. (THE OKLAHOMA BAR JOURNAL QUARTERLY). 0094-0070. US. English. qt. $25.00. Oklahoma Bar Association, PO Box 53036, State Capitol Station, Oklahoma City OK 73105. **Tel** (405)524-2365. Ed Martha M Snow. **LC** K15. **DD** 340.05. bk rev. adv acc. **Circ** 11,800. (ctrl). Contains scholarly articles on various areas of the law and publishes appellate court decisions and Bar Association news.

QUEENS BAR BULLETIN. Began with Oct. 1950 Issue. 0048-6302. Periodical. US. English. mo. Queens County Bar Association, 90-35-148th Street, Jamaica NY 11435. **LC** KF200. **DD** 340.060747243. *Queens County Bar Association Bulletin.*

QUEENS COLLEGE LAW JOURNAL. 0730-9724. Periodical. US. English. an. $3.50. Queens College, Political Science Department, 65-30 Kissena Boulevard, Flushing NY 11367. **Tel** (212)520-7000.

QUEEN'S LAW JOURNAL. V. 1- Mar. 1971-. 0316-778X. CN. English. sa. $19.35. Faculty of Law, Queen's University, Kingston Ontario K7L 3N6 Canada. **Tel** (613)547-5803. Ed D Wingfield. **Ind/Abst** Leg. Resour. Index, Index Leg. Period., Curr. Law Index, Contents Curr. Leg. Period. **LC** K17. **DD** 340.05. bk rev. adv acc. **Circ** 800. An academic journal publishing articles and book reviews of legal interest. *Queen's Intramural Law Journal, 0048-6310.*

QUEENSLAND LAND COURT REPORTS. Began with vol. for 1974. AT. English. an. Land Administration Commission, PO Box 168, Brisbane North Queensland 4000 Australia. **Tel** (07)224-0515. **DD** 343.9430250269. *Crown Lands Law Reports.*

QUEENSLAND LAW SOCIETY JOURNAL. (THE QUEENSLAND LAW SOCIETY JOURNAL). V. 1- July 1971-. 0313-4253. Periodical. AT. English. bm. 30.00. Queensland Law Society Inc, 96 Albert Street, GPO Box 1785, Brisbane Queensland 4001 Australia. **Tel** (07)2293911. Ed C MacDonald. **Ind/Abst** Leg. Resour. Index, Curr. Law Index. **LC** K17. **DD** 349.94305. bk rev. adv acc. **Circ** 3,50. (ctrl). Articles of general interest to lawyers in practise.

THE QUEENSLAND LAWYER. VFOAT Queensland Lawyer, Reports, Queensland Lawyer and Reports. V. 1- Feb. 1973-. 0312-1658. Periodical. AT. English. bm. Methuen Law Book Company Ltd, 35 Mitchell Street, c/o Bennett-EBSCO, North Sydney New South Wales 2060 Australia. **LC** Law. **DD** 348.943044. *Queensland Justice of the Peace and Report.*

QUEENSLAND REPORTS. VFOAT Queensland Law Journal. 1902-. AT. English. bm. Methuen Law Book Company, 35 Mitchell Street, c/o Bennet-EBSCO, North Sydney New South Wales 2060 Australia. *Queensland Law Journal Reports.*

QUESTIONE GIUSTIZIA. Yearly V. 1, No. 1-. Periodical. Italian. qt. 40.000. Franco Angelie Editore Riviste, V 1E Monza 106, 20127 Milano Italy.

THE QUINLAN PRIVATE TRUCK LAW REPORT. VFOAT Private Truck Law Report. Vol. 1, No. 1 Jan.-Mar. 1982. 0736-2846. US. English. qt. William A Quinlan, 3045 Riva Road, Riva MD 21140. **LC** KF2265.A15. **DD** 343.730948305, 347.303948305.

RABELS ZEITSCHRIFT FUR AUSLANDISCHES UND INTERNATIONALES PRIVATRECHT. V. 26-. 0033-7250. Periodical. GW. German. qt. Max Planck Institut, Mittelweg 187, 2000 Hamburg 13 West Germany. **LC** K1. (cum index). *Zeitschrift fur Auslandisches und Internationales Privatrecht.*

RACCOLTA SISTEMATICA DI GIURISPRUDENZA COMMENTATA. Monographic Series. IT. Italian. ir. Raccolta Sistematica di Cedam, Via Jappelli 5, Padova 1 Italy.

RACCOLTA UFFICIALE DELLE SENTENZE E ORDINANZE. Main/Corp Italy. Corte Costituzionale. 1956-. IT. Italian. ir. Corte Constituzionale Ufficio, Piazza del Quirinale, Roma Italy.

RACHT DER JUGEND UND DES BILDUNGSWESEN. 0034-1312. Periodical. GW. German. bm. 96.00. Hermann Luchterhand Verlag GMBH & Company KG, Heddesdorfer Str 31, Postfach 1780, 5450 Neuwied 1 West Germany. **Tel** 02631/80 10. Ed Sabine Saynisch. **LC** K18. **DD** 344.430705, 344.304705. bk rev. adv acc. Scholarly journal covering West German law and administration in the field of education. A forum for interaction between jurists, teachers, social scientists and administrators. *Recht der Jugend.*

RADIANSKE PRAVO. 0485-8573. Periodical. UR. Ukrainian. mo. $40.50. Victor Kamkin Inc (74424), 12224 Parklawn Drive, Rockville MD 20852. **Tel** (301)881-5973.

RAJASTHAN LAW WEEKLY. (THE RAJASTHAN LAW WEEKLY). 0377-7723. II. English. ir. K V Kalia, Man Bhawan 1st FL Ratanada Road, Jodhpur 342 001 India. **DD** 348.544043.

RAJASTHAN STATE CURRENT STATUTES. Periodical. English. mo. 45.00. Rajasthan State Current Statutes, High Court Road, Jodhpur (Raj) India. **DD** 348.54402205, 345.44082205.

RAJSHAHI UNIVERSITY LAW REVIEW. English. ir. **LC** K18. **DD** a49.549205, 345.492005.

RAPAT KERJA MAHKAMAH AGUNG- DEPARTEMEN KEHAKIMAN DENGAN PARA KETUA PENGADILAN TINGGI SELURUH INDONESIA. VFOAT Rapat Kerja. IO. Indonesian. an. **DD** 347.598005, 345.980705.

RAPPORT ANNUEL - COMMISSION DES SERVICES JURIDIQUES. (RAPPORT ANNUEL). Main/Corp Commission des Services Juridiques. Began in 1975. 0703-0762. CN. French. an. 2 Complexe Desjardins, Tour de l'Est Bureau 1400, Montreal Quebec H5B 1B3 Canada. **LC** KEQ180.A13. **DD** 354.71400845. *Rapport Annuel, 0703-0762.*

RAPPORT ANNUEL - CONSEIL DU STATUT DE LA FEMME. See Women.

RAPPORT ANNUEL - MINISTERE DE LA JUSTICE. Main/Corp Quebec (Province). Dept. of Justice. 1967-. CN. French. ir. Editeur Officiel du Quebec, 1283 Boul Charest Quest, Quebec Quebec G1N 2C9 Canada. **LC** KEQ787.A72. **DD** 354.714065.

RAPPORTS DE LA SECTION DES GRIEFS ET DE L'ARBITRAGE. Main/ Corp Alliance de la Fonction Publique du Canada. Section des Griefs et de l'Arbitrage. Ser. 2, No. 2-. 0822-7829. Periodical. CN. French. ir. Free. Alliance de la Fonction Publique du Canada, Section des Griefs et de l'Arbitrage, 233 rue Gilmour, Ottawa Ontario K2P 0P1 Canada. **DD** 342.71068. *Disposition d'Un Grief Soumis A Un Conseil d'Arbitrage, 0318-630X.*

RAPPORTS DE PRATIQUE DE QUEBEC CEASED. VFOAT Quebec Practice Reports. V. 1 - R.P. Nos. 9/10. 0384-6970. CN. French (text also in English).

RASSEGNA DI DIRITTO PUBBLICO. 0033-9512. Periodical. IT. Italian. qt. Libreria Scientifica Editrice, Corso Umberto 34, Napoli Italia.

RASSEGNA PARLAMENTARE. Year 1-4, Mar. 1959-Dec. 1962. 0486-0373. Periodical. IT. Italian. qt. 25.000 Domestic, 50.000 Foreign. Istituto Doc Legislativa Palazzo de Ginnasi, Via Dell Arco de Ginnasi Roma Italy. **Tel** (06)6793449. adv acc. **Circ** 2,000.

RASSEGNA TRIBUTARIA : RT. VFOAT RT. Periodical. Italian. ir. 110.000. Via Dello Statuto 2, 20121 Milano CCP N. 721209 Italy. **DD** 343.450402648, 344.503402648.

RATING AND VALUATION REPORTER. Periodical. UK. English. **Tel** 0483-233571. bk rev. adv acc. Law reports, articles, etc. on rating, land compensation and related subjects on land taxation. *Rating and Income Tax.*

RATING APPEALS. UK. English. an. Rating Publishers, 2 Paper Buildings, Temple EC4 England. Ed F A Amies. **LC** KD5534.A38. **DD** 343.4205402648.

LA RAZA LAW JOURNAL. VFOAT Raza Law Journal. Vol. 1, No. 1 (Spring 1983)-. 8755-8815. US. English. an. $10.00. La Raza Law Journal, Boalt Hall/Room 37, U C Berkeley, Berkeley CA 94720. **Tel** (415)642-5391. Ed Jose Varela. **LC** K18. **DD** 349.730896873, 347.30089686. bk rev. (ctrl). Investigates Hispanic social and legal issues.

READINGS IN LAW AND THE EXCEPTIONAL CHILD : DUE PROCESS. VFOAT Law and the Exceptional Child. 1980-. US. English. an. Special Learning Corporation, 42 Boston Post Road, Guilford CT 06437.

REAL ESTATE & THE LAW. See Real Estate.

REAL ESTATE FINANCE LAW JOURNAL. Vol. 1, No. 1 (Spring 1985)-. 0882-3413. Periodical. US. English. qt. $64.00. Federal Research Press, 65 Franklin Street, Boston MA 02110. **LC** K18. **DD** 346.7304364 347.3064364.

REAL ESTATE LAW AND PRACTICE COURSE HANDBOOK SERIES. Main/ Corp Practising Law Institute. No. 1- 1968-. 0548-7366. US. English. ir. $350.00. Practising Law Institute, 810 7th Avenue, New York NY 10019. **Tel** (212)765-5700. Offers the busy practitioner a quick and economical way to keep up with the current trends, developments, and problems in real estate law and practice.

REAL ESTATE LAW JOURNAL. V. 1- 1972-. 0048-6868. Periodical. US. English. qt. $75.60. Warren Gorham & Lamont Inc, 210 South Street, Boston MA 02111. **Tel** (800)225-2363. **Ind/Abst** Manage. Contents, Leg. Resour. Index, Energy Inf. Abstr., Environ. Abstr., ABI/Inform, Index Leg. Period., Soc. Sci. Citation Index, Contents Curr. Leg. Period., Curr. Law Index. **LC** K18. **DD** 346.7304305. Available on microform.

REAL ESTATE LAW REPORT. V. 1- June 1971-. 0162-752X. Periodical. US. English. mo. $81.90. Warren Gorham & Lamont, 210 South Street, Boston MA 02111. **Tel** (800)225-2363 Outside Massachusetts. **LC** KF570. **DD** 346.7304305. also available in microform from University Microfilms.

REAL ESTATE LICENSE LAW AND RULES AND REGULATIONS. US. English. $5.00. Detroit Board of Realtors, 1980 City National Bank Building, Detroit MI 48226. **LC** KFM4482.R4. **DD** 346.7740437.

THE REAL ESTATE TAX DIGEST. See Real Estate.

REAL PROPERTY. Main/Corp Bay Area Review Course, Inc. US. English. an. Bay Area Review Course Inc, 5900 Wilshire Boulevard, Los Angeles CA 90036. **LC** KF570.Z9. **DD** 346.73043.

REAL PROPERTY. 10th- Ed. 0198-893X. US. English. ir. Little Brown & Company, Law Division, 34 Beacon Street, Boston MA 02106. **LC** KF570.Z9. **DD** 346.73043. *Real Property.*

REAL PROPERTY LAW, REAL PROPERTY ACTIONS AND PROCEEDINGS LAW, AND RELATED MISCELLANEOUS STATUTES, AS AMENDED. Main/Corp New York (State). VFOAT Warren's Weed RPL-RPAPL. 1968-. US. English. an. Matthew Bender, 235 East 45th Street, New York NY 10017. **LC** KFN5140.A29. **DD** 346.7304302632.

REAL PROPERTY LAW REPORTER. VFOAT CEB Real Property Law Reporter. 1977-. Periodical. US. English. ir. $96.00. CEB Publication Sales, 2300 Shattuck Avenue, Berkeley CA 94704. **Tel** (415)642-5340. Ed Roger Bernhardt. Index published separately - free - automatically sent. Keeps current with important developments in real property practice. Features current published California cases, US Supreme Court cases and

Law

federal cases from courts in the ninth circuit, practice-oriented articles, and more.

REAL PROPERTY LAW SECTION NEWSLETTER. Main/Corp New York State Bar Association. Real Property Law Section. 0147-135X. US. English. Free. New York State Bar Association, One Elk Street, Albany NY 12207. **Tel** (518)463-3200. **Ed** Bernard Goldstein. **LC** KFN5140.A15. **DD** 346.74704305. **Circ** 5,000. (ctrl). Newsletter of real property law section. Section notes and current issues are discussed.

REAL PROPERTY, PROBATE AND TRUST JOURNAL. V. 1- Spring 1966-. 0034-0855. Periodical. US. English. qt. $22.00. American Bar Association, 750 North Lake Shore Drive, Chicago IL 60611. **Tel** (312)988-5555. **Ed** Jean A Mortland. **Ind/Abst** Manage. Contents, Leg. Resour. Index, Account. Index, Suppl., Index Leg. Period., Soc. Sci. Citation Index, Curr. Law Index, Contents Curr. Leg. Period. **LC** K18. (ctrl). Scholarly articles in the fields of estate planning, trust law and real property law. Newsletter of the Section of Real Property, Probate and Trust Law, Proceedings.

REAL PROPERTY REPORTS. V. 1- Mar. 1977-. 0703-4687. Periodical. CN. English. mo. $35.00 Each Volume. Carswell Company, 2330 Midland Aveneu, Agincourt Ontario M1S 1P7 Canada. **DD** 346.7104302642. (cum index).

REAL PROPERTY SECTION NEWS. Main/Corp Utah State Bar. Real Property Section. V. 1- May 1974-. Periodical. US. English. bm. 293 Kearns Building, Salt Lake City UT 84101. **LC** KFU112.A73. **DD** 346.79204305.

REAL PROPERTY TAX PLANNING. Main/Corp Tax Institute on Advanced Tax Planning for Real Property Transaction. 1st (1982)-. US. English. California Continuing Education of the Bar, Berkeley CA 94701. **LC** KF6540.A75. **DD** 343.73054, 347.30354. Each issue contains an index to its own contents - no vol index - loose.

DE REBUS. 0250-0329. Periodical. SA. Afrikaans (English). mo. 2.50 Single Issue. Association of Law Societies of The Republic of South Africa, 615 Volkskas Centre, Cor Pretonius and Van Der Walts Streets, Pretoria 0002 South Africa. **LC** K18. **DD** 349.6805, 346.8005. DR, De Rebus.

DE REBUS PROCURATORIIS. VFOAT South African Attorney's Journal. No. 1-. Periodical. SA. English (Afrikaans). ir. Association of Law Societies of the Republic of South Africa, 615 Volkskas Main Building, CNR Pretorius and van der Walts Streets, Pretoria 0002 South Africa. **LC** K18. **DD** 349.6805.

RECENT DECISIONS AFFECTING WILLS, TRUSTS AND TAXATION. Main/Corp American National Bank, St. Joseph, Mo. Trust Dept. 0161-2301. US. English. Kennedy Sinclaire Inc, Sixth and Francais Streets, St Joseph MO. **LC** KF755.A59. **DD** 346.73054.

RECENT DECISIONS, UNITED STATES SUPREME COURT. (RECENT DECISIONS, UNITED STATES SUPREME COURT). VFOAT Recent Decisions of the United States Supreme Court. 0732-4294. US. English. an. American Academy of Judicial Education, 510 Park Lane Building, 2025 Eye Street NW, Washington DC 20006. **LC** KF9614. **DD** 348.73413, 347.30844.

RECENT DEVELOPMENTS IN MARYLAND LAW. 0363-8006. Periodical. US. English. bw. $12.00. Lawsearch Inc, PO Box 5508, Derwood MD 20855. **LC** KFM1257. **DD** 340.09752.

RECHERCHES SUR L'HISTOIRE DES INSTITUTIONS ET DU DROIT. Main/Corp Association d'Histoire Comparative des Institutions et du Droit de la Republique Socialiste de Roumaine. 1-. Periodical. French. ir. Calea Victoriei Nr 125, Bucarest Romania. **LC** K1. **DD** 340.205.

RECHT. Periodical. German. ir. **LC** KK3665.A13. **DD** 347.43005, 344.307005.

RECHT (BERN, SWITZERLAND). (RECHT). V. 1, No. 1-. Periodical. German. ir. 72.00. Verlag Stampfli & Cie Ag, Postfach 2728, 3001 Bern Switzerland. **DD** 349.49405, 344.94005.

RECHT DER ELEKTRIZITATSWIRTSCHAFT. Began with Jan. 1939 issue. 0171-712X. Periodical. GW. German. mo. 85.00. Vereinigung Deutscher Elekrtizitatswerke, Stresemannallee 23, 6000 Frankfurt 70 West Germany. **Ind/Abst** Coal Abstr., Energy Res. Abstr. **LC** KK6852.A13. **DD** 343.430929, 344.303929.

RECHT DER INTERNATIONALEN WIRTSCHAFT. VFOAT RIW/AWD-Recht der Internationalen Wirtschaft. Began with issue for Jan. 1975. 0340-7926. Periodical. German. mo. 91.50 Quarterly. Verlagsgesellschaft Recht und Wirtschaft GMBH, Postfach 105 960, 6900 Heidelburg 1 West Germany. **Ind/Abst** Index Foreign Leg. Per. Collect. Essays. **LC** K1. **DD** 343.4308705, 344.3038705. Index published separately - free - automatically sent. Aussenwirtschaftsdienst des Betriebs-Beraters.

RECHT DER SCHULE. Periodical. AU. German. qt. 180.00. Manzsche Verlags- Und Universitatsbuchhandlung, Kohlmarkt 16, A-1014 Wien Austria. **LC** K18. **DD** 344.4360705, 344.304705.

DAS RECHT DER WIRTSCHAFT. GW. German. ir. Erich Schmidt Verlag GMBH, POB 7330-40/Viktoriastr 44-A, D4800 Bielefeld 1 West Germany. **Tel** 0521/66061. Business Law. Rechtsarchiv der Wirtschaft.

RECHT DER WOHNUNGSWIRTSCHAFT. V. 1, No. 1-. Periodical. German. mo. 84.00. J Schweitzer Verlag KG, Geibelstrasse 8, D-8000 Munchen 80 West Germany.

RECHT EN KRITIEK. 1975-. Dutch. ir. 20.00. Utigave Sun, Biileveldsingel 9, Nijmegen Netherlands. **LC** K18.

DAS RECHT IM AMT. V. 1-. Periodical. GW. German. mo. Hermann Luchterhand Verlag, Postfach 1780, 5450 Neuwied West Germany.

RECHT IN OST UND WEST. Vol. 1-. 0486-1485. Periodical. GW. German. bm. $16.67. Verlag A W Hayns Erben, Sonnenalle 63, D-1000 Berlin 44 West Germany. **Ind/Abst** Am. Hist. Life, Hist. Abstr., Part A, Mod. Hist. Abstr., Hist. Abst., Part B, Twent. Century Abstr. **LC** K18. **DD** 349.4305, 344.305. Index in first issue of next volume - attached.

RECHT UND GESELLSCHAFT. Vol. 1-. 0341-7050. German. ir. 10.80. C H Beck, Wilhelmstrasse 9, 8 Munchen 40 West Germany. **LC** K18.

RECHT UND SCHADEN. VFOAT R und S. 0343-9771. Periodical. GW. German. ir. $47.97. Information Verlag, Postfach 208, 7634 Kippenheim West Germany. **Tel** 07825/7114. **LC** K18. **DD** 346.4303, 344.3063. bk rev. adv acc. **Circ** 2,300. Includes insurance against damage, rules and regulations, compensation, identification and laws concerning insurance.

RECHTSBIBLIOGRAPHIE. See Bibliographies.

RECHTSGELEERD MAGAZIN THEMIS. Periodical. NE. Dutch. im. Libresso B V, PO Box 878, 7400 Aw Deventer Netherlands.

RECHTSPFLEGE. REIHE 2.1 : ZIVILGERICHTE. Main/Corp Germany (West). Statistisches Bundesamt. 1976-. Periodical. GW. German. ir. 6.40. W Kohlhammer, Hessbruhlstrasse 69, PF 800430, 7000 Stuttgart 80 West Germany. **DD** 347.4301. Bevolkerung und Kultur. Reihe 9: Rechtspflege. I. Organixation, Personal, Geschaftsanfall und -Erledigung der Ordentlichern Gerichte: Zivilgerichtsbarkeit.

RECHTSPFLEGE. REIHE 2.2 : STRAFGERICHTE. Main/Corp Germany (West). Statistisches Bundesamt. 1976-. GW. German. ir. 6.40. W Kohlhammer, Hessbruhlstrasse 69, PF 800430, 7000 Stuttgart 80 West Germany. **DD** 345.4300212. Bevolkerung und Kultur. Reihe 9: Rechtspflege. I. Organisation, Personal, Geschaftsanfall und -Erledigung der Ordentlichern Gerichte: Strafgerichtsbarkeit.

RECHTSPRAAK VREEMDELINGENRECHT. Dutch. an. **DD** 342.492083, 344.920283.

RECHTSPRECHUNG IN STRAFSACHEN. VFOAT Bulletin de Jurisprudence Penale. SZ. French and German. qt. $18.31. Staempfli & Cie Sa, Hallerstrasse 7-9 Postfach 2728 CH-3012 Berne Switzerland. **Tel** 4131/232323. **Ed** F Clerc. **DD** 345.494002084. **Circ** 1,800.

RECHTSPRECHUNG ZUM WIEDERGUTMACHUNGSRECHT. Began publication in Nov. 1949. Periodical. GW. German. qt. $27.60. C H Beckshe Verlagsbchhndlg, Wilhelmstrasse 9, Postfach 400430, 8000 Munchen 40 West Germany. Index in last issue of volume - attached.

RECHTSTHEORIE. Vol. 1-. 0034-1398. Periodical. GW. German. qt. Duncker & Humblot Verlag, Dietrich-Schaefer-Weg 9, 1000 Berlin 41 West Germany. **Tel** (030)7912026. **Ed** W Krawietz. **Ind/Abst** Philos. Index. **LC** K18. **DD** 340.105. Index in last issue of volume - attached. bk rev. adv acc. **Circ** 600. Theory of law, journal of logic, methodology, and sociology of the law.

RECOMMENDATIONS AND RESOLUTIONS. Main/Corp Council of Europe. Committee of Ministers. 1979-. English. an. Resolutions.

RECOMMENDATIONS FOR LEGISLATIVE CONSIDERATION ON PUBLIC EDUCATION IN TEXAS. Main/Corp Texas. Education Agency. US. English. be. Texas Education Agency, 201 East Eleventh Street, Austin TX 78701. **LC** KFT1590. **DD** 344.764071, 347.640471.

RECOMMENDATIONS OF THE WEST VIRGINIA BOARD OF EDUCATION FOR LEGISLATIVE ACTION. Main/Corp West Virginia. State Board of Education. US. English. an. West Virginia Board of Education, Executive Offices, Charleston West VA 25305. **LC** KFW1590. **DD** 344.754073, 347.540473.

RECOPILACION SOCIAL DE TEXTOS DE EXPOSICION OBLIGATORIA EN TODOS LOS CENTROS DE TRABAJO. Main/Corp Spain. Spanish. ir. 700.

RECORD - FEDERAL ELECTION COMMISSION. (RECORD). Publication began with Sept. 1975. 0145-8566. Periodical. US. English. mo. Federal Election Commission, 1325 K Street NW, Washington DC 20463. **Tel** (800)424-9530. **Ind/Abst** Index U.S. Gov. Period. **LC** KF4885.A15. **DD** 342.7307.

THE RECORD OF THE ASSOCIATION OF THE BAR OF THE CITY OF NEW YORK. Main/Corp Association of the Bar of the City of New York. V. 1- Feb. 1946-. 0004-5837. US. English. $30.00. Association of the Bar of the City of New York, 42 West 44th Street, New York NY 10036. **Tel** (212)382-6600. **Ed** Gene F Waters. **Ind/Abst** Index Leg. Period., Curr. Law Index, Leg. Resour. Index. adv acc. **Circ** 15,500. (ctrl). Legal reports, legal lectures, and legal bibliographies.

THE RECORDER. VFOAT San Francisco Law Journal. Periodical. US. English. da. $76.00. Recorder Printing & Publishing Company, 125 12th Streets, San Francisco CA 94103. **LC** K18.

RECREATION AND PARKS LAW REPORTER. (RECREATION AND PARKS LAW REPORTER : RPLR). VFOAT RPLR. Vol. 1, No. 1 (1st Quarter 1984)-. 0743-5649. Periodical. US. English. qt. $45.00 Members, $90.00 Nonmembers. NRPA Membership Department, 3101 Park Center Drive, Alexandria VA 22302. **LC** KF5638.A59. **DD** 346.73046783, 347.30646783.

RECUEIL DALLOZ SIREY. 6 Jan. 1965-. Periodical. FR. French. wk. $109.30. Dalloz, 11 rue Soufflot, 75240 Paris Cedex 05 France. Recueil Dalloz, Recueil Sirey.

RECUEIL DE DROIT FISCAL QUEBECOIS. 1977-. 0704-2035. Periodical. CN. French. an. Service des Publications SOQUIJ, 276 rue St Jacques Ste 310, Montreal Quebec H2Y 1N3 Canada. **DD** 343.7140402643.

RECUEIL DE FISCALITE. No. 1-. 0713-3618. Periodical. CN. French. qt. $8.00. Recueil de Fiscalite, c/o L'Association Quebecoise de Planification Successorale, Suite 24/1455 rue Peel, Montreal Quebec H3A 1T5 Canada. **DD** 343.71404.

RECUEIL DES ACTES ADMINISTRATIFS. Main/Corp Meurthe-et-Moselle, France (Dept.). Prefecture. French. tm.

RECUEIL DES ACTES ADMINISTRATIFS DE LA PREFECTURE DE LA REUNION. Main/Corp Reunion (Region). Prefecture. VFOAT Recueil des Actes Administratifs. FR. French. mo. 20. Imprimerie Departementale Cour du Secretariat General, 2 EME Bureau Avenue de la Victoire, 97-488 Saint-Denis Reunion. **DD** 348.698104505, 346.981084505. Recueil des Actes Admnistratifs.

Law

RECUEIL DES ACTES ADMINISTRATIFS DU DEPARTEMENT DE LA REUNION. Main/Corp Reunion. VFOAT Recueil des Actes Administratifs. French. ir. 40. DD 342.066, 342.266.

RECUEIL DES SENTENCES DE L'EDUCATION. Main/Corp Quebec (Province). Greffe des Tribunaux d'Arbitrage du Secteur de l'Education. 0001/0100-. 0704-7630. CN. French. wk. $96.73. Ministere des Communications, PO Box 1005, Quebec Quebec G1K 7B5 Canada. Tel (418)643-5150. LC KEQ696.T4. DD 344.71407, 347.14047.

RECUEIL PERIODIQUE DES JURIS-CLASSEURS : DROIT CIVIL. French. ir. 850.00. Editions Techniques, 123 rue d'Alesia, Paris France 75014. *Juris-Classeurs. Droit Civil.*

REDBOOK - TEXAS APARTMENT ASSOCIATION. (REDBOOK). Main/Corp Texas Apartment Association. 0731-0153. US. English. Texas Apartment Association Inc, 6225 Highway 290 E/ #204, Austin TX 78723. LC KFT1317. DD 346.7640434, 3476406434.

THE REFFKIN REPORT. Began in 1983. 0742-2660. Periodical. US. English. mo. The Reffkin Report, Circulation Department, 10076 Boca Entrada Boulevard, Boca Raton FL 33433. Ed Alan D Reffkin. LC KF2042.C6. DD 346.73077, 347.30677. *Reffkin Compliance Report, 0737-8165.*

REFORM. Began with issue for Jan. 1976. Periodical. AT. English. qt. $7.38. Australian Law Reform Commission, GPO Box 3708, Sydney New South Wales 2001 Australia. Tel (02) 2311733. DD 340.30994. adv acc. Circ 3,000. (ctrl) A regular bulletin of law reform news, views and information.

THE REGAN REPORT ON HOSPITAL LAW. V. 8, No. 3- June 1967-. 0034-317X. Periodical. US. English. mo. $36.00. Medica Press Inc, 1231 Fleet Bank Building, Providence RI 02903. Tel (401)421-4747. Ed A David Tammelleo. NLM W1 RE172CR. (ctrl). For over 25 years reporting the leading court cases on hospital law with legal lessons from actual court decisions, authoritative, educational and informative. *Regan Report.*

REGAN REPORT ON MEDICAL LAW. V. 1- 1968-). 0034-3188. Periodical. US. English. mo. $36.00. Medica Press, 1231 Industrial Bank Building, Providence RI 02903. Tel (401)421-4747. Ed A David Tammelleo. (ctrl). For over 25 years reporting the latest and leading court cases on medical law and medical malpractice from actual court decisions. Authoritative, educational, and informative.

REGAN REPORT ON NURSING LAW. (THE REGAN REPORT ON NURSING LAW). V. 1- June 1960-. 0034-3196. Periodical. US. English. mo. $36.00. Medica Press, 1231 Industrial Bank Building, Providence RI 02903. Tel (401)421-4747. Ed A David Tammelleo. Ind/Abst Cumul. Index Nurs. Allied Health Lit., Int. Nurs. Index. NLM W1 RE172D. (ctrl). For over 25 years reporting the leading court cases on nursing law with legal lessons from actual court decisions authoritative, educational and informative.

REGIMEN DE LA ADMINISTRACION PUBLICA. Periodical. AG. Spanish. mo. Talachuano 638 8P0S, of B, 1013 Buenos Aires Argentina. DD 342.820605, 348.202605.

REGISTER OF CURRENT COMMUNITY LEGAL INSTRUMENTS. V. 1- (July 1, 1979). US. English (also issued in Danish, Dutch, French, German, and Italian). ir. $46.00. European Community Information Service, 2100 M Street NW/Suite 707, Washington DC 20037. Tel (202)937-3519. DD 341.2422.

REGLAMENTACION LABORAL, INDUSTRIA Y COMERCIO. Main/Corp Spain. Laws, Statutes, etc. Spanish. ir. 300. Ediciones Alvarez, Paseo de Gracia 23, Barcelona Spain.

REGULATION. V. 1- July/Aug. 1977-. 0147-0590. Periodical. US. English. bm. $24.00. American Enterprise Institute, 1150 17th Street NW, Washington DC 20036. Tel (202)862-5931. Ind/Abst Manage. Contents, Hospit. Lit. Index, Coal Abstr., ABI/Inform, Energy Res. Abstr., Public Aff. Inf. Serv. Bull. LC K18. DD 342.730605. NLM W1 RE173I. CODEN REGUD4.

REGULATIONS, CODES AND PROTOCOLS. REPORT EPS 1-AP CEASED. (REGULATIONS, CODES AND PROTOCOLS - AIR POLLUTION CONTROL DIRECTORATE). VFOAT Reglements, Codes et Accords - Direction General de l'Assainissement de l'Air. VAT Reglements, Codes et Accords. Rapport EPS 1-AP, Rapport EPS 1-AP, Report EPS 1-AP. Began publication in 1972. Ceased in 1981?. 0713-9691. Monographic Series. CN. English (French).

REGULATORY ALERT. Main/Corp Research Institute of America, Inc. 0147-9091. Periodical. US. English. wk. Research Institute of America, 589 Fifth Avenue, New York NY 10017. LC KF1600.A15. DD 343.7307.

REGULATORY REPORTER (WASHINGTON, D.C.). *See* Sanitation, Environmental Technology.

RELATORIO DA GESTAO DA DIRETORIA DO INSTITUTO DOS ADVOGADOS DO RIO GRANDE DO SUL. Main/Corp Instituto dos Advogados do Rio Grande do sul. Diretoria. Portuguese. ir. Travessa Engenheiro Acilino de Carvalho 21, Edificio el Cairo 60 Andar, Porto Alegre Brazil.

RELAZIONE DELLA CORTE DEI CONTI AL PARLAMENTO SULLA GESTIONE FINANZIARIA DEGLI ENTI SOTTOPOSTI A CONTROLLO IN APPLICAZIONE DELLA LEGGE 21 MARZO 1958, N. 259. Italian. ir. DD 342.450664, 344.502664.

RELIGIOUS FREEDOM REPORTER. (RELIGIOUS FREEDOM REPORTER : A SERVICE OF THE CENTER FOR LAW AND RELIGIOUS FREEDOM). Vol. 1, No. 1 (Jan. 1981)-. 0275-3529. Periodical. US. English. mo. $105.00. Christian Legal Society, PO Box 2069, Oak Park IL 60303. Tel (312)848-7735. Ed James Parker. LC KF4783.A59. DD 342.73085202648, 347. 30285202648. Circ 300. A digest of cases dealing with religious freedom issues.

REMEDIES. Main/Corp Bay Area Review Course, Inc. 0098-7999. US. English. Bay Area Review Course Inc, 5900 Wilshire Boulevard, Los Angeles CA 90036. LC KF9010.Z9. DD 347.7377.

REPERTOIRE ANALYTIQUE DU BULLETIN JURIDIQUE. FR. French. ir. Tour Maine-Montparnasse, 33 Avenue du Maine Boites 45 et 46, 75755 Paris Cedex 15 France. DD 344.440202648, 344.404202648.

REPERTOIRE DE DROIT COMMERCIAL. FR. French. ir. Dalloz, 11 rue Soufflot, 75240 Paris Cedex 05 France.

REPERTOIRE DU NOTARIAT DEFRENOIS. Periodical. FR. French. ir. $76.50. Repertoire Notariat Defrenois, 83 Ave Denfert Rochereau, 75014 Paris France. DD 347.44016.

REPERTOIRE LEGISLATIF DE L'ASSEMBLEE DU QUEBEC. (REPERTOIRE LEGISLATIF DE L'ASSEMBLEE NATIONALE DU QUEBEC). Main/Corp Quebec (Province). Assemblee Nationale. 1977-. 0704-9730. CN. French. an. Editeur Officiel du Quebec, 1283 Boul Charest Quest, Quebec Quebec G1N 2C9 Canada. LC KEQ72. DD 348.714026, 347.140826.

REPERTORIO DE LEGISLACION DE NAVARRA. Main/Corp Navarre (Spain). 1979-. SP. Spanish. ir. DD 349.465205 344.652005.

REPERTORIO DE SENTENCIAS DEL TRIBUNAL CENTRAL DE TRABAJO. Main/Corp Spain. Tribunal Central de Trabajo. 1973-. Spanish. ir. DD 344.4601.

REPERTORIO LABORAL (ASUNCION, PARAGUAY). (REPERTORIO LABORAL). Periodical. Spanish. ir. 3.000. Calle Azara, 180 Casi Ind. Nacional, Oficina 110, Asuncion Paraguay. DD 344.8920105, 348.9204105.

REPORT - ADMINISTRATIVE OFFICE OF PENNSYLVANIA COURTS. Main/Corp Administrative Office of Pennsylvania Courts. 0148-9925. US. English. an. Administrative Office of Pennsylvania Courts, Room 1414/Three Pennsylvania Center Plaza, Philadelphia PA 19102. LC KFP71. DD 347.748013.

REPORT AND RECOMMENDATIONS TO THE GOVERNOR AND THE GENERAL ASSEMBLY. Main/Corp Illinois. Commission on Labor Laws. 1971-. 0148-3633. US. English. Commission on Labor Laws, Room 202/State Office Building, Springfield IL 62706. LC KFI1531. DD 344.77301.

REPORT - CENTER FOR CONSTITUTIONAL RIGHTS. Main/Corp Center for Constitutional Rights. Periodical. US. English. an. Center for Constitutional Rights, 853 Broadway, New York NY 10003.

REPORT - CINCINNATI BAR ASSOCIATION. (REPORT). 0732-0736. Periodical. US. English. Cincinnati Bar Association, 26E Sixth Street, Cincinnati OH 45202. LC KF200. DD 340.06077178. *CBA Report, 0091-5475.*

REPORT - COMMITTEE ON SUBORDINATE LEGISLATION. Main/Corp West Bengal. Legislature. Legislative Assembly. Committee on Subordinate Legislation. English. ir. DD 348.541401.

REPORT - CONNECTICUT. JUDICIAL REVIEW COUNCIL. Main/Corp Connecticut. Judicial Review Council. 1st (1978/80)-. US. English. ir. Judicial Review Council, PO Box 308, Manchester CT 06040. LC KFC4125.5.D5. DD 347.746014, 347.460714.

REPORT - CONNECTICUT. OFFICE OF COMMISSIONER OF CLAIMS. Main/Corp Connecticut. Office of Commissioner of Claims. US. English. Office of Commissioner of Claims, 54 Retreat Avenue, Hartford CT 06106. LC KFC3799.G6. DD 353.97460091.

REPORT - COUNCIL ON LEGAL EDUCATION FOR PROFESSIONAL RESPONSIBILITY. Main/Corp Council on Legal Education for Professional Responsibility. Vol. 1- 9/68-12/70-. Periodical. US. English. be. Council on Legal Education for Professional Responsibility, 280 Park Avenue, New York NY 10017.

REPORT - FEDERAL BAR ASSOCIATION. SECTION OF TAXATION. (REPORT). Winter 1984-. 0742-5317. Periodical. US. English. qt. $23.00 Domestic, $25.00 Foreign. Federal Bar Association, 1815 H Street Northwest, Washington DC 20006. Tel (202)638-0252. Ed Lynn P Weidberg. LC KF6272. DD 343.730405, 347.303405. bk rev. adv acc. Circ 15,500. Each issue focuses on a given topic or concern to those who practice or who have interest in federal law and adjudication. *Council on Taxation Report.*

REPORT FROM ATTORNEY GENERAL. OHIO. Main/Corp Ohio. Attorney General's Office. 0098-8820. US. English. Attorney General's Office, State House Annex, Columbus OH 43215. LC KFO427.5.A8. DD 353.97715.

REPORT FROM THE SELECT COMMITTEE ON EUROPEAN LEGISLATION, &C. Main/Corp Great Britain. Parliament. House of Commons. Select Committee on European Legislation, &C. UK. English. Her Majesty's Stationery Office, PO Box 276, London SW8 5DT England. DD 349.405.

REPORT - ILLINOIS. SUPREME COURT. Main/Corp Illinois. Supreme Court. US. English. an. 111 East Jefferson Street, Ottawa IL 61350. LC KFI1708. DD 347.773, 347.7307.

REPORT - INSTITUTE OF LAW RESEARCH AND REFORM. UNIVERSITY OF ALBERTA. (REPORT - INSTITUTE OF LAW RESEARCH AND REFORM, UNIVERSITY OF ALBERTA). No. 1-. 0317-1604. Monographic Series. CN. English. University of Alberta, Institute of Law Research and Reform, Edmonton Alberta T6G 2H5 Canada. DD 340.097123.

REPORT - JUDICIAL INQUIRY BOARD. (REPORT). Main/Corp Illinois. Judicial Inquiry Board. 1st- 1971/73-. 0093-8939. US. English. Judicial Inquiry Board, 205 West Wacker Drive/Suite 1515, Chicago IL 60606. LC KFI1725.5.A6. DD 347.773014.

REPORT - KERALA, INDIA (STATE). LEGISLATIVE ASSEMBLY. BUSINESS ADVISORY COMMITTEE. Main/Corp Kerala, India (State). Legislative Assembly. Business Advisory Committee. II. English. ir. India Legislative Assembly Kerala/Business Advisory Committee, Trivandrum India. DD 348.548301.

REPORT - LOS ANGELES DAILY JOURNAL. (REPORT). 0742-423X. Periodical. US. English. sm. The Daily Journal, PO Box 54026, Los Angeles CA 90054. LC K12. DD 349.79405, 347.94005.

REPORT - MINNESOTA. JUDICIAL COUNCIL. Main/Corp Minnesota. Judicial Council. 1st- 1937/39-. US. English.

REPORT - NATIONAL CENTER FOR STATE COURTS. Main/Corp National Center for State Courts. V. 1- 1974-. 0195-5241. US. English. mo. National Center for State Courts, 300 Newport

Law

Avenue, Williamsburg VA 23185. LC KF8736.A15. DD 347.7333, 347.3013.

REPORT - NEW ZEALAND. PUBLIC AND ADMINISTRATIVE LAW REFORM COMMITTEE. Main/Corp New Zealand. Public and Administrative Law Reform Committee. English. an. DD 342.93103, 349.31023. *Report of the Public and Administrative Law Reform Committee.*

REPORT OF ANNUAL SEMINAR ON ESTATE PLANNING. Main/Conf Seminar on Estate Planning. 0145-5079. US. English. an. LC KFK1340.A75. DD 343.769053.

REPORT OF ATTORNEY GENERAL TO THE GOVERNOR AND THE LEGISLATURE. Main/Corp Florida. Dept. of Legal Affairs. US. English. Department of Legal Affairs, The Capitol, Tallahassee FL 32304. LC KFF427.5.A8. DD 340.09759. *Report.*

REPORT OF CASE DECISIONS. UNITED STATES. FEDERAL LABOR RELATIONS AUTHORITY. Main/Corp United States. Federal Labor Relations Authority. VFOAT FLRA Report of Case Decisions. VAT Federal Labor Relations Authority Report of Case Decisions. Began with Apr. 19, 1979. 0147-3611. US. English. ir. Superintendent of Documents, US Government Printing Office, Washington DC 20402. *Report of Case Decisions, 0147-3611.*

REPORT OF CASES DETERMINED IN THE SUPREME COURT AND COURT OF APPEALS OF THE STATE OF NEW MEXICO. Main/Corp New Mexico. Supreme Court. VFOAT New Mexico Reports. V. 78-1967/68-. 0094-7148. US. English. West Publishing Company, Box 3526, 50 West Kellog Boulevard, St Paul MN 55166. LC KFN3645. DD 348.789043. *Report of Cases Determined in the Supreme Court of the State of New Mexico.*

REPORT OF FINDINGS AND RECOMMENDATIONS - COLORADO. GENERAL ASSEMBLY. STATUTORY REVISION COMMITTEE. Main/Corp Colorado. General Assembly. Statutory Revision Committee. Began with 1978 V. available. US. English. an. LC KFC1827.S73. DD 340.309788. on microfiche at Colorado State Depositories.

REPORT OF THE AGRICULTURE STUDY COMMITTEE OF SOUTH CAROLINA. Main/Corp South Carolina. General Assembly. Agriculture Study Committee. 0362-4226. US. English. PO Box 11753, Columbia SC 29211. LC KFS2039. DD 343.757076.

REPORT OF THE ATTORNEY GENERAL. Main/Corp Michigan. Attorney General's Department. US. English. be. Attorney General Department, Records and Opinions Section, 525 West Ottawa, Lansing MI 48913.

REPORT OF THE ATTORNEY GENERAL OF NEW MEXICO. Main/Corp New Mexico. Attorney General's Office. 1931/32-. 0749-2065. US. English. an. New Mexico Compilation Committee, PO Box 848, Santa FE NM 87501. Index published separately - free - upon request. (cum index). *Opinions of the Attorney General of New Mexico.*

REPORT OF THE ATTORNEY GENERAL TO THE CONGRESS OF THE UNITED STATES ON THE ADMINISTRATION OF THE FOREIGN AGENTS REGISTRATION ACT, AS AMENDED, FOR THE CALENDAR YEAR . . . . Began with 1942/45. US. English. an. US Department of Justice, Washington DC 20530. LC JX1896. DD 351.74. Vols. for (1981-) distributed to depository libraries in microfiche.

REPORT OF THE ATTORNEY GENERAL TO THE CONGRESS OF THE UNITED STATES ON THE ADMINISTRATION OF THE FOREIGN AGENTS REGISTRATION ACT OF 1938, AS AMENDED. Main/Corp United States. Attorney General. VFOAT Administration of the Foreign Agents Registration Act. US. English. an. US Department of Justice, Attorney General, Washington DC 20530.

REPORT OF THE BUILDING PERMIT ACTIVITY IN THE CITIES AND COUNTIES OF CALIFORNIA. See Building and Construction.

REPORT OF THE CHAIRMAN - IMMIGRATION APPEAL BOARD. See Emigration and Immigration.

REPORT OF THE COMMITTEE ON RULES. Main/Corp West Bengal. Legislature. Legislative Assembly. Committee on Rules. 1st- Mar. 1974-. English. ir. DD 328.541405.

REPORT OF THE COMMITTEE ON SUBORDINATE LEGISLATION. Main/Corp Punjab, India (State). Legislature. Legislative Assembly. Committee on Subordinate Legislation. Periodical. English. ir.

REPORT OF THE COMMONWEALTH MAGISTRATES' CONFERENCE. Main/Conf Commonwealth Magistrates' Conference. UK. English. Commonwealth Magistrates Association, 28 Fitzroy Square, London W1P 6DD England. DD 347.01.

REPORT OF THE FISCAL COMMITTEES ON THE EXECUTIVE BUDGET. See Public Administration.

REPORT OF THE IDAHO COMMISSION ON WOMEN'S PROGRAMS. (REPORT). Main/Corp Idaho. Commission on Women's Programs. 0097-9287. US. English. an. LC KFI91.W6. DD 346.796013.

REPORT OF THE ILLINOIS JUDICIAL CONFERENCE. Main/Conf Illinois Judicial Conference. US. English. an. LC KFI1708.A73. DD 347.77305. *Annual Report of the Illinois Judicial Conference.*

REPORT OF THE JOINT LEGISLATIVE COMMITTEE TO STUDY AND RECODIFY THE VILLAGE LAW. Main/Corp New York (State). Legislature. Joint Legislative Committee to Study and Recodify the Village Law. 5th- 1967-. US. English. an. New York State Legislature, R D Box 196 E, Albany NY 12203. LC KFN5758.5. DD 342.74709. *Report of the Joint Legislative Committee on Villages.*

REPORT OF THE JUDICIAL COUNCIL OF THE STATE OF NEW HAMPSHIRE. Main/Corp New Hampshire. Judicial Council. 1st-5th. US. English. be. State of New Hampshire, Judicial Council, Manchester NH 03105. LC JK2981. DD 347.9.

REPORT OF THE JUDICIAL DEPARTMENT, STATE OF CONNECTICUT. Main/Corp Connecticut. Judicial Dept. 1974/76-. 0098-8138. US. English. Judicial Department, PO Box 1350, Hartford CT 06811. LC KFC4108. DD 353.97465. *Report of the Judicial Council of Connecticut, 0190-7823.*

REPORT OF THE LAW REVISION COMMISSION. Main/Corp New York (State). Law Revision Commission. VFOAT Report, Recommendations, and Studies. 1935-. 0270-8612. US. English. an. New York State Law Revision Commission, Albany NY 12208. DD 347.09747. (cum index).

REPORT OF THE LAW SOCIETY OF SCOTLAND ON THE LEGAL AID SCHEME. Main/Corp Law Society of Scotland. VFOAT Annual Report on the Scottish Legal Aid Scheme. UK. English. an. LC KDC260.A13. DD 347.411012. *Report on the Legal Aid Scheme.*

REPORT OF THE LEGAL AID REVIEW COMMITTEE. Main/Corp Australia. Parliament. Legal Aid Review Committee. 1974-. English. ir. $2.00. LC J905.

REPORT OF THE MUNICIPAL COURT (SAN FRANCISCO). Main/Corp San Francisco. Municipal Court. 1978-. US. English. an. Municipal Court, San Francisco CA 94102. LC KFX2353.3.M8. DD 347.7946102, 347.9461072. *Annual Report of the Municipal Court.*

REPORT OF THE NORTH DAKOTA LEGISLATIVE AUDIT AND FISCAL REVIEW COMMITTEE. Main/Corp North Dakota. Legislative Assembly. Legislative Audit and Fiscal Review Committee. 0095-6341. US. English. be. North Dakota Legislative Assembly/Legislative Audit & Fiscal Review Committee, State Capital, Bismarck ND 58707. LC KFN9067. DD 343.784034.

REPORT OF THE OFFICE OF THE PUBLIC DEFENDER FOR THE STATE OF MARYLAND. (REPORT). Main/Corp Maryland. Office of the Public Defender. 1st-1972-. 0093-2159. US. English. Office of the Public Defender, Central Offices, 800 Equitable Building, Baltimore MD 21202. LC KFM1778.A73. DD 345.75201.

REPORT OF THE PROCEEDINGS OF THE ANNUAL MEETING OF THE . . . MISSOURI BAR ASSOCIATION. Main/Corp Missouri Bar Association. 1st- 1881-. Periodical. US. English.

REPORT OF THE PROCEEDINGS OF THE JUDICIAL CONFERENCE OF THE UNITED STATES. Main/Corp Judicial Conference of the United States. Sept. 1965-. US. English. sa. Administrative Office of the United States Courts, Washington DC 20544. Vols. for Mar. 1982- Distributed to depository libraries in microfiche. *Report of the Judicial Conference of the United States.*

REPORT OF THE SELECT COMMITTEE ON INSURANCE RATES, REGULATION AND RECODIFICATION OF THE INSURANCE LAW. Main/Corp New York (State). Legislature. Select Committee on Insurance Rates, Regulation and Recodification of the Insurance Law. 1974-. US. English. State of New York Legislature, Albany NY 12236. LC KFN5010.6. DD 346.747086. *Report of the Joint Legislative Committee on Insurance Rates, Regulation and Recodification of the Insurance Law.*

REPORT OF THE SESSION OF THE JOINT ECE/CODEX ALIMENTARIUS GROUP OF EXPERTS ON STANDARDIZATION OF QUICK FROZEN FOODS. Main/Corp Joint ECE/Codex Alimentarius Group of Experts on Standardization of Quick Frozen Foods. VAT Report of the Session of the Joint Economic Commission For Europe/Codex Alimentarius Group of Experts on Standardization of Quick Frozen Foods. English. ir. Joint ECE/Codex Alimentarius Group of Experts on Standardization of Quick Frozen Foods, Via Delle Terme di Caracalla, Rome 00100 Italy. LC TP372.3. DD 341.754756640285.

REPORT OF THE SPECIAL COMMITTEE ON THE RULES AND PROCEDURES OF THE LEGISLATIVE ASSEMBLY. Main/Corp Saskatchewan. Legislative Assembly. Special Committee on the Rules and Procedures of the Legislative Assembly. CN. English. Legislative Assembly of Saskatchewan, Legislative Building, Regina Saskatchewan Canada. LC KES470.A23. DD 328.712405.

REPORT OF THE STANDING JOINT COMMITTEE OF THE SENATE AND OF THE HOUSE OF COMMONS ON REGULATIONS AND OTHER STATUTORY INSTRUMENTS. Main/Corp Canada. Parliament. Standing Joint Committee on Regulations and Other Statutory Instruments. VFOAT Rapport du Comite Mixte Permanent du Senat et de la Chambre des Communes des Reglements et Autres Textes Reglementaires. 2d- 2d Session, 30th Parliament 1976/77-. Periodical. CN. English (French). $1.50 Domestic, $1.80 Foreign. Statistics Canada, Publication Distribution, Ottawa Ontario K1A 0T6 Canada. LC KE5024.A2. DD 348.7101. *Minutes of Proceedings and Evidence of the Standing Joint Committee on Regulations and Other Statutory Instruments.*

REPORT OF THE STATE CLAIMS COMMISSION. See Business - Public Finance.

REPORT OF THE STATE COMMISSION ON EMINENT DOMAIN CEASED. Main/Corp New York (State). State Commission on Eminent Domain. -1973. 0092-1076. US. English. State Commission on Eminent Domain, 835 State Office Building, 33 East Washington Street, Syracuse NY 13202. LC KFN5800. DD 343.747025.

REPORT ON ACTIVITIES - UNITED STATES. CONGRESS. HOUSE. COMMITTEE ON AGRICULTURE. (REPORT ON ACTIVITIES DURING THE . . . CONGRESS). Main/Corp United States. Congress. House. Committee on Agriculture. 0739-9995. US. English. be. US Government Printing Office, Superintendent of Documents, Washington DC 20402. LC KF31.8.A3. DD 343.73076, 347.30376. *Report of the Committee on Agriculture on Activities.*

REPORT ON ADMINISTRATIVE ADJUDICATION OF TRAFFIC INFRACTIONS. (REPORT ON ADMINISTRATIVE ADJUDICATION OF TRAFFIC INFRACTIONS : HIGHWAY SAFETY ACT OF 1973 (SECTION 222)). Began with 1975. 0363-0692. US.

Law

English. an. US Department of Transportation, National Highway Traffic Safety Administration, Washington DC 20590. **LC** KF2232. **DD** 343.7309460269.

A REPORT ON AN ACT TO REFORM THE STATUTES RELATING TO DRIVING UNDER THE INFLUENCE OF INTOXICATING LIQUOR OR DRUGS. March 1, 1983-. US. English. an. 221 State Street, Augusta ME 04333. **LC** HE5620.D7. **DD** 364.147.

REPORT ON APPLICATIONS FOR ORDERS AUTHORIZING OR APPROVING THE INTERCEPTION OF WIRE OR ORAL COMMUNICATION. (REPORT ON APPLICATIONS FOR ORDERS AUTHORIZING OR APPROVING THE INTERCEPTION OF WIRE OR ORAL COMMUNICATIONS FOR THE PERIOD . . .). **VFOAT** Wiretap Report. Began with 1968. 0097-7977. US. English. an. Statistical Analysis and Reports Division, Administrative Office of the United States Courts, Washington DC 20544. **LC** KF9670. **DD** 347.7364.

REPORT ON CASE HANDLING DEVELOPMENTS OF THE OFFICE OF THE GENERAL COUNSEL. Main/Corp United States. Federal Labor Relations Authority. Office of the General Counsel. Series/Titl FLRA Doc. Oct. 1, 1980 through Dec. 31, 1980-. 0278-3460. US. English. qt. Superintendent of Documents, US Government Printing Office, Washington DC 20402. **LC** KF5365.A59. **DD** 344.7301890413530002648, 347. 3041890413530002648. Report on Case Handling Developments of the Office of the General Counsel, Federal Labor Relations Authority.

REPORT ON KANSAS LEGISLATIVE INTERIM STUDIES TO THE LEGISLATURE. Main/Corp Kansas. Legislature. Legislative Coordinating Council. 0270-4331. US. English. Legislative Research Department, Statehouse/Room 545-N, Topeka KS 66612. **LC** KFK20. **DD** 347.81081.

REPORT ON LEGISLATIVE AND REVIEW ACTIVITIES OF THE COMMITTEE ON POST OFFICE AND CIVIL SERVICE. Main/Corp United States. Congress. Senate. Committee on Post Office and Civil Service. 0099-1317. US. English. Superintendent of Documents, Government Printing Office, Washington DC 20402. **LC** KF30.8. **DD** 328.730765.

REPORT ON REVIEWS AND HEARINGS ARISING FROM COMPLAINTS OF UNFAIR TRADE PRACTICES BY FOREIGN GOVERNMENTS PURSUANT TO SECTION 301, D, 2, OF THE TRADE ACT OF 1974. See Business - Commerce.

REPORT ON THE ACTIVITIES OF THE COMMITTEE ON ARMED SERVICES, UNITED STATES SENATE. Main/Corp United States. Congress. Senate. Committee on Armed Services. 0363-0706. US. English. be. US Government Printers Office, Washington DC 20402. **LC** KF30.8. **DD** 343.7301. Vols. for 98th Congress, 1st and 2nd session. Distributed to some depository libraries in microfiche.

REPORT ON THE ACTIVITIES OF THE COMMITTEE ON COMMERCE, SCIENCE, AND TRANSPORTATION. Main/Corp United States. Congress. Senate. Committee on Commerce, Science, and Transportation. Began with 95th Congress, 1977/78. 0273-4915. US. English. be. Superintendent of Documents, US Government Printing Office, Washington DC 20402. **LC** KF30.8. **DD** 328.7307658. Vols. for (Mar. 6, 1985-) distributed to some depository libraries in microfiche. Report of Activities, 0099-1775; Activity Report of the Committee on Commerce.

REPORT ON THE ACTIVITIES OF THE COMMITTEE ON THE JUDICIARY OF THE UNITED STATES SENATE DURING THE CONGRESS. (REPORT ON THE ACTIVITIES OF THE COMMITTEE ON THE JUDICIARY OF THE UNITED STATES SENATE DURING THE . . . CONGRESS : PURSUANT TO RULE XXVI OF THE STANDING RULES OF THE UNITED STATES SENATE). Main/Corp United States. Congress. Senate. Committee on the Judiciary. 0742-4078. US. English. **LC** KF30.8. **DD** 342.73052, 347.30252.

REPORT ON THE ADMINISTRATION OF CIVIL AND CRIMINAL JUSTICE IN THE STATE OF MAHARASHTRA. Main/Corp Maharashtra, India (State). 1960-. English. ir.

REPORT - STANDING STATUTORY INSTRUMENTS COMMITTEE CEASED. Main/Corp Ontario. Legislative Assembly. Standing Statutory Instruments Committee. Began with 1st issue for 2nd Session, 31st Parliament (June 1978)-2nd, 3rd Session, 31st parliament (Nov. 1979). 0226-0417. Periodical. CN. English. ir. Standing Statutory Instruments Committee, Legislative Assembly, Toronto Ontario M7A 1N3 Canada. **DD** 342.713066.

REPORT, SURVEY OF METROPOLITAN JUVENILE COURTS. Main/Corp National Center for State Courts. Vol. 1, No. 1 (Apr. 1980)-. US. English. National Center for State Courts, 300 Newport Avenue, Williamsburg VA 23185. **LC** KF9787. **DD** 345.7308105, 347.3058105.

REPORT TO THE GENERAL ASSEMBLY OF NORTH CAROLINA. PROGRESS REPORTS. Main/Corp North Carolina. General Assembly. Legislative Research Commission. US. English. State Legislative Building, Raleigh NC 27611. **LC** KFN7420. **DD** 328.7560773.

REPORT TO THE . . . GENERAL ASSEMBLY OF THE STATE OF ILLINOIS. Main/Corp Illinois. General Assembly. Law Revision Commission. June 1977-. US. English. Illinois Law Revision Commission, 5940 North Neva Avenue, Chicago IL 60631. **LC** KF1227.L38. **DD** 340.309773.

REPORT TO THE . . . LEGISLATURE IN RELATION TO THE CIVIL PRACTICE LAW AND RULES CEASED. Main/Corp New York (State). Judicial Conference. **VFOAT** Annual Report of the Judicial Conference to the Legislature on the Civil Practice Law and Rules. Began in 1963. Ceased in 1979. US. English. an.

REPORT - UNITED STATES. ATTORNEY (ILLINOIS : NORTHERN DISTRICT). (REPORT - UNITED STATES. ATTORNEY (ILLINOIS : NORTHERN DISTRICT)). Main/Corp United States. Attorney (Illinois : Northern District). 0731-1168. US. English. an. US Department of Justice, Office of the US Attorney, Northern District of Illinois, Chicago IL 60604. **LC** KF8700. **DD** 353.0088.

REPORT - UNITED STATES. TAX COURT. (REPORTS). Main/Corp United States. Tax Court. 0040-0017. Periodical. US. English. mo. Superintendent of Documents, US Government Printing Office, Washington DC 20402. **Tel** (202)783-3238. **DD** 343.

REPORTED DECISIONS OF THE SOCIAL SECURITY COMMISSIONER. SOCIAL SECURITY, CHILD BENEFIT, FAMILY INCOME SUPPLEMENTS, AND SUPPLEMENTARY BENEFIT ACTS. Main/Corp Great Britain. Dept. of Health and Social Security. **VFOAT** Social Security and Child Benefit Acts, Commissioner's Decisions. Vol. 9 (1980 to 1982)-. UK. English. **LC** KD3196.A2. **DD** 344.410202646, 344.104202646. Reported Decisions of the Commissioner under the Social Security and Child Benefit Acts.

THE REPORTER. 0484-4610. Periodical. US. English. mo. **LC** KF200. **DD** 340.09749.

REPORTER ON HUMAN REPRODUCTION AND THE LAW. 8756-2057. US. English. ir. $55.00. Legal-Medical Studies Inc, Box 8219 John F Kennedy Station, Boston MA 02114. **Tel** (617)723-9040. Ed T Carey. **DD** 346. Index published separately - free - upon request. bk rev. (ctrl). Survey and reports on legal developments affecting abortion, birth control, and other aspects of human reproduction.

REPORTER ON THE LEGAL PROFESSION. 1979-. 8755-7509. US. English. ir. $120.00. Legal Medical Studies Inc, PO Box 8219 JF Kennedy Station, Boston MA 02114. **Tel** (617)723-9040. Ed C Kindregan. **DD** 340. Index available. (cum index). bk rev. (ctrl). Legal profession, professional responsibility, lawyer discipline, fees, lawyer advertising, conflict of interest, regulation of professions. Indexed; table of cases.

REPORTER (WASHINGTON, D.C. : 1977). (THE REPORTER). Began with Aug. 1977. 0193-8134. Periodical. US. English. qt. Superintendent of Documents, US Government Printing Office, Washington DC 20402. **Tel** (202)783-3238. **Ind/Abst** Index U.S. Gov. Period., Curr. Law Index, Leg. Resour. Index, Am. Hist. Life, Hist. Abstr. **DD** 343.7301.

REPORTS - GREAT BRITAIN. VALUE ADDED TAX TRIBUNALS. Main/Corp Great Britain. Value Added Tax Tribunals. UK. English. 0.26 Single Issue. Her Majestys Stationery Office, PO Box 276, London SW8 5DT England. **LC** KD5586.A44. **DD** 343.42055.

REPORTS OF CASES ARGUED AND DETERMINED IN THE SUPERIOR COURT, APPELLATE DIVISION, CHANCERY DIVISION, LAW DIVISION, AND IN THE COUNTY COURTS OF THE STATE OF NEW JERSEY. Main/Corp New Jersey. Superior Court. V. 1- 1948-. US. English. West Publishing Company, Box 3526 50 Kellogg Boulevard, St Paul MN 55166. **DD** 345.42.

REPORTS OF CASES ARGUED AND DETERMINED IN THE TAX COURT OF NEW JERSEY. **VFOAT** New Jersey Tax Court Reports. Vol. 1-. 0731-2954. US. English. ir. West Publishing Company, 50 West Kellogg Boulevard, Box 3526, St Paul MN 55165. **LC** KFN2270. **DD** 343.7490402642, 347. 4903402642.

REPORTS OF CASES DECIDED IN THE APPELLATE DIVISION OF THE SUPREME COURT, STATE OF NEW YORK. Main/Corp New York (State). Supreme Court. Appellate Division. **VFOAT** Appellate Division Reports, Supreme Court, New York. V. 1-286, 1896-1955. 0276-9581. US. English. The Lawyers Co-Operative Publishing Company, Aqueduct Building, Rochester NY 14603. **LC** KFN5048. **DD** 345.42, 345.412. Index in last issue of volume - attached.

REPORTS OF CASES DETERMINED IN THE COURTS OF APPEAL OF THE STATE OF CALIFORNIA. **VFOAT** California Appellate Reports. 2d Ser., V. 246-276, Oct. 28, 1966/Dec. 6, 1966. US. English. **LC** KFC48. **DD** 348.794044. Reports of Cases Determined in the District Courts of Appeal of the State of California.

REPORTS OF FAMILY LAW. V. 1- 1971-. 0317-4859. Periodical. CN. English. ir. Caswell Company Ltd, 2330 Midland Avenue, Agincourt Toronto M2S 1P7 Canada. **Ind/Abst** Leg. Resour. Index. **DD** 346.7101502642. (cum index).

REPORTS OF IMPORTANT DECISIONS BY THE EMPLOYMENT APPEALS TRIBUNAL UNDER THE UNFAIR DISMISSALS ACT, 1977. Main/Corp Ireland. Employment Appeals Tribunal. Years 1977 and 1978-. IE. English. an. 2.47. Government Publications Sale Office, Sun Alliance House, Molesworth Street, Dublin 2 Ireland. **LC** KDK820. **DD** 344.415012596, 344.150412596.

REPORTS OF INTERNATIONAL ARBITRAL AWARDS. Main/Corp United Nations. Office of Legal Affairs. **VFOAT** Recueil des Sentences Arbituales. V. 1- 1948-. US. English (French). an. $33.00. United Nations Publications, Standing Orders Section, New York NY 10017. **Tel** (212)754-8302. A systematic collection of international arbitral awards.

REPORTS OF MASSACHUSETTS APPELLATE DIVISION (MONTHLY). (REPORTS OF MASSACHUSETTS APPELLATE DIVISION). Began in 1980. 0279-9413. Periodical. US. English. mo. Lawyers Weekly Publications, 30 Court Square, Boston MA 02108. Official Opinions from the Supreme Judicial Court of Massachusetts and the Appeals Court, Official Opinions from the Appellate Divisions of the District Court Department and the Boston Municipal Court.

REPORTS OF THE UNITED STATES TAX COURT. Main/Corp United States. Tax Court. **VFOAT** United States Tax Court Reports. Vol. 54 (Jan. 1, 1970 to Sept. 30, 1970)-. 8755-6294. US. English. ir. Claitors Law Books, 3165 South Acadian, PO Box 3333, Baton Rouge LA 70821. **Tel** (800)535-8141. Ed Mary T Pittman. **DD** 343. Reports of the Tax Court of the United States . . ., 8755-6111.

REPORTS ON PUBLIC BILLS (BOUND). Main/Corp United States. Congress. Periodical. US. English. ir. $1103.00. Superintendent of Documents, Government Printing Office, Washington DC 20402. **Tel** (202)783-3238.

REPORTS; OPINIONS, ORDERS, RULES, AND REGULATIONS - NEW YORK (STATE). PUBLIC SERVICE COMMISSION. See Public Administration.

REPRESENTING PROFESSIONAL ATHLETES AND TEAMS. Series/Titl Patents, Copyrights, Trademarks, and Literary Property Course Handbook Series. 0276-7627. US. English. an. Practising Law Institute, 810 7th Avenue, New York NY 10019. LC KF3989.Z9. DD 344.73099, 347.30499.

REPRESENTING PUBLICLY TRADED CORPORATIONS. Series/Titl Corporate Law and Practice Course Handbook Series. 0276-6639. US. English. an. Practising Law Institute, 810 7th Avenue, New York NY 10019. LC KF1440. DD 346.73066, 347.30666.

REPRINTED ACTS OF THE PARLIAMENT OF WESTERN AUSTRALIA. Main/Corp Western Australia. Laws, Statutes, etc. AT. English. ir. $498.04. Government Printer of New South Wales, PO Box 35, Pyrmont New South Wales 2009 Australia. Tel 692 1692.

RES GESTAE. Periodical. US. English. mo. Ind/Abst Leg. Resour. Index, Index Leg. Period. LC KF332.I5. DD 340.062772.

RES PUBLICA. No. 1- Feb. 1975-. Afrikaans. ir. Departement Staatsreg dn Regsfilosofie, Universiteit Van Die Ovx, Postbus 339, Bloemfontein South Africa. LC K18.

RESEARCH CONTRIBUTIONS OF THE AMERICAN BAR FOUNDATION. US. English. ir. American Bar Foundation, 1155 E 60th Street, Chicago IL 60637. Tel (312)988-6500. Ed Bette Sikes. Circ 500. Reprints of articles published in professional journals written by American Bar Foundation staff members or affiliated scholars.

RESEARCH IN LAW AND ECONOMICS. See Economics.

THE RESEARCH INSTITUTE LAWYERS TAX ALERT. VFOAT Lawyers Tax Alert. 0163-9994. Periodical. US. English. mo. $48.00. Research Institute of America, 589 Fifth Avenue, New York NY 10017. LC KF6352. DD 343.730405.

RESEARCH PUBLICATION (COLORADO. GENERAL ASSEMBLY. LEGISLATIVE COUNCIL). (RESEARCH PUBLICATION). Began publication in 1951. 0413-768X. Periodical. US. English. ir. Colorado General Assembly, 30 State Capital Building, Denver CO 80203. LC KFC1820.

RESOURCE MATERIALS. ESTATE PLANNING IN DEPTH. (RESOURCE MATERIALS : ESTATE PLANNING IN DEPTH). Main/Conf Ali-Aba Course of Study: Estate Planning in Depth. VFOAT Estate Planning in Depth, Resource Materials. 1st Ed.- 1972-. 0272-264X. US. English. LC KF750.Z9. DD 343.73053, 347.30353.

RESOURCE NEWS. V. 1- 197 -. Periodical. CN. English. mo. $12.50. University of Alberta/Legal Resource Center, Trade Centre South/10047-81 Avenue, Edmonton T6E 1W7 Canada. Tel (403)432-5732. Ed Shirley Serviss. bk rev. adv acc. Circ 3,100. A magazine designed to provide information to Albertans about the law and law-related activities and resources.

RESOURCE NEWS. (RESOURCE NEWS : A SERVICE OF THE LEGAL RESOURCE CENTRE). 0228-0779. Periodical. CN. English. ir. Free. Legal Resource Centre, Trade Centre South, University of Alberta, Extension 10047-81st Avenue, Edmonton Alberta T6E 1W7 Canada. DD 340.0607123. (ctrl).

RESOURCES - CANADIAN INSTITUTE OF RESOURCES LAW. (RESOURCES : THE NEWSLETTER OF THE CANADIAN INSTITUTE OF RESOURCES LAW). No. 1 (May 1982)-. 0714-5918. Periodical. CN. English. ir. Free. Resources, c/o Canadian Institute of Resource, Faculty of Law, University of Calgary, Calgary Alberta T2N 1N4 Canada. Tel (403)220-3200. Ed Theresa Goulet. DD 346.71046705. Circ 4,400. (ctrl). Resources offers timely comments on current resources law issues along with information about the Canadian Institute of Resources Law, its publications, and programs.

RESPONSA MERIDIANA. Began with Aug. 1964 issue. 0486-5588. Periodical. SA. Afrikaans or English. an. $5.00. Responsa Meridiana-Pro Leeman, University of Cape Town, Faculty of Law, Private Bag Randebosch, Capetown 7700 South Africa. Tel 69 8531. Ind/Abst Index Foreign Leg. Per. Collect. Essays. LC K18. DD 340.0968. adv acc. Circ 600. (ctrl). Essays on legal topics, written by law students.

RESPONSABILITA CIVILE E PREVIDENZA. Periodical. IT. Italian. bm. 50.000 Domestic, 75.000 Foreign. Casa Editrice Dr A Giuffre, Via Statuto 2 Periodical Department, 20121 Milano Italy. Tel 02/652341. Ed Gianguido Scalfi. bk rev. adv acc. Circ 5,500. This review publishes a well-coordinated and complete collection of juridical views concerning civil liability, state insurance and other forms of insurance.

RESUME. Main/Corp Louisiana. Legislature. US. English. an. LC KFL15. DD 348.76301, 347.63081. Resume.

RESUME, ACTS, RESOLUTIONS, AND VOTED BILLS. Main/Corp Louisiana. Legislature. US. English. LC KFL15. DD 348.76301, 347.63081.

RESUMES DE JURISPRUDENCE PENALE DU QUEBEC. Vol. 1, No. 1 (1983)-. 0822-7616. Periodical. CN. French. sm. $65.00. Resumes de Jurisprudence Penale du Quebec a/s Editions Yvon Blais, 430 rue St-Pierre, Montreal Quebec H2Y 2M5 Canada. DD 345.714002643.

RESUMES DES CAUSES EN INSTANCE A LA COUR SUPREME DU CANADA. Main/Corp Canadian Law Information Council. No. 18- 23 Jan. 1979-. 0709-6984. Periodical. CN. English. ty. $27.09. Cons Canadien Docu Juridique, 161 Ouest Ave Laurier, Ottawa Ontario K1P 5J2 Canada. Tel (613)236-9766. DD 347.710353. Resumes des Causes a Etre Entendues par la Cour Supreme du Canada, 0701-8614.

RESUMES DES DECISIONS RECENTES RENDUES PAR LA COMMISSION D'APPEL DE L'IMMIGRATION. See Emigration and Immigration.

RETAIL SECURITY DIGEST. Vol. 1, No. 1 (Jan. 1981)-. 0735-8520. US. English. Suite 2220/393 7th Avenue, New York NY 10001. LC KF2005.A15. DD 345.730268, 347.305268.

THE RETAINER. V. 1, No. 5- Feb. 1, 1972-. 0145-3491. Periodical. US. English. bw. Philadelphia Bar Association, 1339 Chestnut Street, Philadelphia PA 19103. LC KF200. DD 340.09748. New Philadelphia Lawyer.

RETFRD. 1-. Danish. ir. Modtryk Socialistisk Forlag, Anholtgade 4 Dk-8000 C, Aarhus Denmark. LC K18.

RETTENS GANG. Main/Corp Norske Advokatforening. Norwegian. ir. Norske Advokatforening, Kirkegaten 26 1, Oslo Norway.

REVIEW - AUSTRALIA. REMUNERATION TRIBUNAL. Main/Corp Australia. Remuneration Tribunal. AT. English. an. Australian Government Publishing Service, PO Box 84, Canberra Australian Capital Territory 2600 Australia. Tel 062-95 4411. DD 342.9406860264, 349.4026860264.

THE REVIEW - INTERNATIONAL COMMISSION OF JURISTS. (THE REVIEW). No. 1 (March 1969)-. 0020-6393. Periodical. SZ. English. sa. International Commission of Jurists, 109 Route de Chene, 1224 Chene-Boug Geneva Switzerland. Tel 49 35 45. Ed Niall Macdermot. Ind/Abst Public Aff. Inf. Serv. Bull., Curr. Law Index. LC K9. DD 340.05. Concerns human rights and the rule of law worldwide. Bulletin of the International Commission of Jurists, Journal of the International Commission of Jurists.

REVIEW OF CONTEMPORARY LAW CEASED. 5th Year, No. 1 (June 1958)-1981, 2. 0048-7473. Periodical. English (French). ir. Law in the Service of Peace.

REVIEW OF GHANA LAW. V. 1- May 1969-. 0034-6578. Periodical. English. ir. Council for Law Reporting, PO Box M 165, Accra Ghana. Ind/Abst Public Aff. Inf. Serv. Bull. LC K18. DD 340.05.

A REVIEW OF LEGAL EDUCATION IN THE UNITED STATES. See Education (General) - Higher Education.

THE REVIEW OF LITIGATION. Vol. 1, No. 1 (Winter 1980)-. 0734-4015. Periodical. US. English. ty. $18.00. Review of Litigation, University of Texas Law School, 727 East 26th Street, Austin TX 78705. Tel (512)471-4386. Ed Royal B Lea III. Ind/Abst Leg. Resour. Index, Index Leg. Period. LC K18. DD 347.7305, 347.30705. bk rev. adv acc. Circ 1,000. A national law journal reviewing issues of interest to the practising litigator.

THE REVIEW OF SECURITIES REGULATION CEASED. Vol. 1-17, No. 21. 0034-6756. Periodical. US. English. sm. Standard and Poors Corporation, 25 Broadway, New York NY 10004. Tel (212)208-8772. Ind/Abst Leg. Resour. Index. LC KF1432. DD 346.73066605.

REVIEW OF SOCIALIST LAW. V. 1- Mar. 1975-. 0165-0300. Periodical. NE. English. qt. 64.00. Kluwer Academic Publishing Group Distribution Center, PO Box 322, 3300 AH Dordrecht Netherlands. Tel 078-334248. Ed F J M Feldbrugge. LC K18. DD 340.091717. bk rev. adv acc. The review covers all areas of the legal systems in Eastern Europe, China and other socialist states.

REVIEW : SESSION OF THE CONGRESS. Main/Corp American Enterprise Institute for Public Policy Research. 1978-. 0197-5102. US. English. ir. American Enterprise Institute, 1150 17th Street NW, Washington DC 20036. LC KF42. DD 348.7326. Review. Session of the Congress, and Index of AEI Publications, 0360-165X.

REVISED CODE OF AMERICAN SAMOA. CUMULATIVE SUPPLEMENT. Main/Corp American Samoa. Laws, Statues, etc. US. English. ir. Equity Publishing, Oxford NH 03777. Tel (603)353-4351.

REVISED STATUTES OF NEBRASKA, 1943. Main/Corp Nebraska. V. 1- 1944-. US. English. ir. State Library of Nebraska, 3rd Floor/S-Statehouse, Lincoln NE 68509.

REVISTA ARGENTINA DE CIENCIAS PENALES. No. 1- Sept./Dec. 1975-. AG. Spanish. ir. Viamonte 1755, Buenos Aires Argentina. LC K19.

REVISTA BRASILEIRA DE DIREITO PROCESSUAL. V. 1- 1st Quarter 1975-. Portuguese. ir. Editora Vitoria Artes Graficas, Livraria e Editoria Universitaria de Direito, Rua Benjamin Constant, 117-10 Andar Salas 1A 5 01005, Sao Paulo Brazil. LC K19. DD 347.81005.

REVISTA - CARACAS. UNIVERSIDAD CATOLICA ANDRES BELLO. FACULTAD DE DERECHO. Main/Corp Caracas. Universidad Catolica Andres Bello. Facultad de Derecho. No. 1- 1965?-. Periodical. Spanish. ir.

REVISTA CHILENA DE DERECHO. V. 1-3, No. 1/3. Periodical. Spanish. ir. $30.00. Facultad de Derecho, Universidad Catolica de Chile, Biblioteca de Derecho, Casilla 114D, Santiago Chile. Tel 2294927. Ed Jose Luis. LC K19. DD 340.0983. bk rev. Circ 1,000. First hand theoretical and empirical legal studies on Chilean and comparative judicial systems, with judicial and administrative decisions, reports of legal experts and transportation of statutes.

REVISTA CHILENA DE HISTORIA DEL DERECHO. Periodical. CL. Spanish. ir. Editorial Andres Bello, Avendia Ricardo Lyon, 946 Providencia, Santiago Chile. Tel 225-36-00. Ind/Abst Am. Hist. Life, Hist. Abstr., Hist. Abstr., Part A, Mod. Hist. Abstr., Hist. Abst., Part B, Twent. Century Abstr.

REVISTA CUBANA DE DERECHO. Periodical. Spanish (summaries in English, French and Russian). ir. Instituto Cubana del Libro, Unidad Productora 04, Havana Cuba. LC K19.

REVISTA DA ACADEMIA PAULISTA DE DIREITO. Main/Corp Academia Paulista de Direito. Year 1- 1972-. Portuguese. ir. Sede Faculdade de Direito da Universidade de Sao Paulo, Largo de Sao Francisco 95, Sao Paulo Brazil. Tel 239.3083. LC K1. DD 340.0981. bk rev. adv acc. Circ 1,000. Readings about the faculty, articles of doctors of law and students of this school. The curriculum of the new professors and new courses of law.

REVISTA DA ASSOCIACAO DOS MAGISTRADOS, PARANA. Main/Corp Associacao dos Magistrados do Parana. Portuguese. ir. rua Alferes Poli 1658, Curitiba Brazil. LC K1. DD 340.0981.

REVISTA DA FACULDADE DE DIREITO DE PORTO ALEGRE. Main/Corp Rio Grande do Sul, Brazil (State). Universidade Federal. Faculdade de Direito. Yearly V. 5- 1971-. Portuguese. ir. Universidade Federal do Rio Grande do Sul, Av Joao Pessoa S/N, Porto Alegre 90.000

Law

Brazil. **LC** K16. *Revista da Faculdade de Direito de Porto Alegre.*

REVISTA DA PROCURADORIA GERAL DO ESTADO. Main/Corp Ceara (Brazil : State). Procuradoria Geral do Estado. Portuguese. ir. Procuradoria Geral do Estado Centro de Estudos e Treinamento, rua Silva Paulet 324 E 334, Fortaleza Brazil. **DD** 349.813105, 348.131005.

REVISTA DA PROCURADORIA GERAL DO ESTADO DE SAO PAULO. Main/Corp Sao Paulo, Brazil (State). Procuradoria Geral. 1-1971-. BL. Portuguese. ir. Rua Boa Vista 103, Sao Paulo Brazil. **LC** K23.

REVISTA DA PROCURADORIA GERAL DO ESTADO (MATO GROSSO DO SUL (BRAZIL). PROCURADORIA GERAL DO ESTADO). (REVISTA DA PROCURADORIA GERAL DO ESTADO). No. 1 (1979)-. Periodical. Portuguese. ir. Avenue Afonso Pena 2968, Mato Grosso do Sul Cep 79.100, Campo Grande Brazil. **LC** K19. **DD** 349.817205, 348.172005.

REVISTA DA PROCURADORIA-GERAL DO ESTADO (RIO GRANDE DO SUL (BRAZIL)). (REVISTA DA PROCURADORIA-GERAL DO ESTADO). **VFOAT** R.P.G.E. Began in 1979 with No. 24. Periodical. BL. Portuguese. ty. Instituto de Informatica Juridica da Procuradoria, Geral do Estado, Avenida Borges de Medeiros No 417, 110 Andar Porto Algere Brazil. **LC** K22. **DD** 342.810605, 348.102605. *Revista (Rio Grando do Sul (Brazil). Consultoria-Geral).*

REVISTA DE CIENCIAS SOCIALES (UNIVERSIDAD DE VALPARAISO. FACULTAD DE CIENCIAS JURIDICAS, ECONOMICAS Y SOCIALES). *See* Social Sciences (General).

REVISTA DE DERECHO. Spanish. ir. Corporacion de Estudios y Publicaciones, Apartado de Correos 1287, Quito Ecuador. **LC** K19.

REVISTA DE DERECHO COMERCIAL Y DE LA EMPRESA. V. 1-. Periodical. UY. Spanish. ir. $20.00. 25 de Mayo 555, ESC 303-304, Montevideo Uruguay. **LC** K19. **DD** 346.0705. *Revista de Derecho Comercial.*

REVISTA DE DERECHO FINANCIERO. 1-. Periodical. Spanish. ir. 70.00. **LC** K19. **DD** 343.0305, 342.3305.

REVISTA DE DERECHO FINANCIERO Y DE HACIENDA PUBLICA. V. 1- June 1951-. Periodical. Spanish. ir. **LC** K19.

REVISTA DE DERECHO PENAL (FUNDACION DE CULTURA UNIVERSITARIA). (REVISTA DE DERECHO PENAL). No. 1 (July 1980)-. Periodical. SP. Spanish. ty. $35.00. Fundacion de Cultura Universitaria, 25 de Mayo 537, Montevideo Uruguay. **LC** K19. **DD** 345.895005, 348.9505005.

REVISTA DE DERECHO POLITICO. 0210-7562. Periodical. SP. Spanish. qt. 1500. Departamento de Derecho, Politico Universidad Nacional de Educacion a Distancia, Ciudad Universitaria, Madrid 3 Spain. **LC** K19. **DD** 342.46005, 344.602005. (cum index).

REVISTA DE DERECHO PRIVADO. V. 1- Oct 15 1913-. Periodical. SP. Spanish. mo. $50.00. Editoriales Derecho Reunidas, Caracas 21, Apartado 4032, Madrid 4 Spain. **Ed** Felipe Clemente de Diego, J M Navarro de Palencia.

REVISTA DE DERECHO PRIVADO (CARACAS, VENEZUELA). (REVISTA DE DERECHO PRIVADO). **VFOAT** Derecho Privado. Yearly V. 1, No. 1, (Jan./Mar. 1983)-. Periodical. VE. Spanish. qt. $45.00. Apartado de Correos No 60379, Caracas 106 Venezuela. **LC** K19. **DD** 346.87005, 348.706005.

REVISTA DE DERECHO PROCESAL. Began in 1971. Spanish. ir. Editorial Juridica de Chile, Casilla 4256, Santiago Chile. **LC** K19.

REVISTA DE DERECHO PUBLICO. 1- Jan. 1963-. Periodical. SP. Spanish. qt. Editoriales de Derecho Reunida, Caracas 21, Apartado 4032, Madrid 4 Spain.

REVISTA DE DERECHO PUERTORRIQUENO. No. 1 (Sept. 1961)- No. 1-. Periodical. PR. Spanish (English). qt. Escuela de Derecho, Universidad Catolica, Ponce Puerto Rico 00731. **Ind/Abst** Leg. Resour. Index, Index Leg. Period., Curr. Law Index.

REVISTA DE DERECHO Y JURISPRUDENCIA. No. 1- Oct. 1970-. Spanish. mo. 1800. Calle Azara 180 c/o Independencia Nacional, Oficina 110, Asuncion Paraguay. **DD** 349.892, 348.92.

REVISTA DE DIREITO ADMINISTRATIVO. V. 1- Jan. 1945-. Periodical. BL. Portuguese. qt. 23.80 U.S. Fundacao Getulio Vargas, Caxia Postfach 9052, 188 ZC02 Rio de Janeiro Brazil. **Ed** Caio Tacito. **LC** K19. (cum index). **Circ** 3,000.

REVISTA DE DIREITO AGRARIO. Yearly V. 1- 2nd Quarter 1973-. Periodical. BL. Portuguese. ir. 35.00. Incra, Setor Bamcario Sul-Ed Bnde-14 Andar, Brasilia Brazil. **LC** K19.

REVISTA DE DIREITO COMPARADO LUSO-BRASILEIRO : PUBLICACAO SEMESTRAL DO INSTITUTO DE DIREITO COMPARADO LUSO-BRASILEIRO. Yearly V. 1, No. 1, (July 1982)-. Periodical. BL. Portuguese. sa. Companhia Editora Forense, Av Erasmo Braga 299 1O. E 2O. Andares, 20020 Rio de Janeiro Brazil. **LC** K19. **DD** 340.205, 342.005.

REVISTA DE DIREITO DA PROCURADORIA-GERAL DA JUSTICA DO ESTADO DO RIO DE JANEIRO. Main/Corp Rio de Janeiro (State). Procuradoria-Geral da Justica. Vol. 1- Mar./July 1975-. Periodical. BL. Portuguese. ty. Procuradoria-Geral da Justica, Av Nilo Pecanha 12 30 Andar Sala 308 ZC-P 20.000 Rio de Janeiro Brazil. **LC** K22.

REVISTA DE DIREITO DO TRABALHO. Yearly V. 1- 1973-. Portuguese. ir. Industrias Graficas Centrograf Ltd, rua Alencar Lima 35 Grupo 903/7, Petropolis Brazil. **LC** K19.

REVISTA DE DIREITO DO TRABALHO. Year 1- Jan./March 1976-. Portuguese. ir. $40.00. Editora Revista dos Tribunais, rua Conde do Pinhal 78, 01501 Sao Paulo Brazil. **Tel** 37 2433. **Ed** Alvaro Malheiros. **Ind/Abst** Int. Labour Doc. **LC** K19. **DD** 344.8101. bk rev. adv acc. **Circ** 5,000. Commentaries, leading articles and jurisprudence of labor law.

REVISTA DE DIREITO ECONOMICO. Yearly v. 1- (No. 1-). BL. Portuguese. ty. Cade, Av Nilo Pecanha, 50-90 Andar CEP 20.044, Rio de Janeiro Brazil. **LC** K19. **DD** 343.81087.

REVISTA DE DIREITO MILITAR. VFOAT Direito Militar. Periodical. Portuguese. ir. Ministero Publico Uniao, Pracado Tribunais Superiores, Brasilia Brazil. **LC** K19.

REVISTA DE DIREITO MUNICIPAL. Periodical. Portuguese. ir. Revista Juridica, Rua dos Andradas 1270, 7O Andar, Porto Alegre Brazil. **LC** K19. **DD** 342.8109.

REVISTA DE DIREITO PENAL E CRIMINOLOGIA. Periodical. Portuguese. sa. Companhia Editora Forense, Av Erasmo Braga 299 1O. E 2O. Andares, 20020 Rio de Janeiro Brazil. **LC** K19. **DD** 345.005, 342.5005. *Revista de Direito Penal (Faculdade de Direito Candido Mendes. Instituto de Ciencias Penais).*

REVISTA DE DIREITO TRIBUTARIO. Year 1- July/Sept. 1977-. Periodical. BL. Portuguese. ir. $45.00. Editora Revista dos Tribunais, rua Conde do Pinhal, 78 Sao Paulo Brazil. **Tel** 37 2433. **Ed** Alvaro Malheiros. **LC** K19. **DD** 343.8104. bk rev adv acc. **Circ** 5,000. Jurisprudence, commentaries and leading articles for tributary law.

REVISTA DE ESTUDIOS HISTORICO-JURIDICOS. 1- 1976-. CL. Spanish. an. $16.00 US, $18.00 Europe. Ediciones Universitarias de Valparaiso, Casilla 1415, Valparaiso Chile. **Tel** 252900. **Ind/Abst** Am. Hist. Life, Hist. Abstr., Part A, Mod. Hist. Abstr., Hist. Abst., Part B, Twent. Century Abstr. **Circ** 500. Academic magazine of essays and studies over history and law from the point of view of researching.

REVISTA DE HISTORIA DEL DERECHO. 1- 1973-. Spanish. ir. Instituto de Investigaciones de Historia del Derecho, Moreno 431 1 Piso Casilla de Correo 5227 C C, Buenos Aires Argentina. **LC** K19. **DD** 340.0982.

REVISTA DE INFORMATICA JURIDICA. Portuguese. ir. **LC** K19.

REVISTA DE INVESTIGACIONES JURIDICAS. Yearly V. 1- (No. 1-). Periodical. MX. Spanish. ir. Excuela Libre de Derecho Inst de Investigaciones Juridicas, Dr Vertiz No 12, Mexico 7 D F Mexico. **LC** K19. **DD** 349.7205. *Revista Juridica de la Escuela Libre de Derecho.*

REVISTA DE JURISPRUDENCIA DO TRIBUNAL DE JUSTICA DE MATO GROSSO DO SUL. Main/Corp Mato Grosso do sul (Brazil). Tribunal de Justica. Year 1, No. 1 (1st Quarterly 1979)-. BL. Portuguese. ir. Grafica e Papelaria Brasilia Ltda, rua 14 de Julho No 2536, Campo Grande Brazil. **DD** 348.8172043, 348.1720843.

REVISTA DE JURISPRUDENCIA DO TRIBUNAL DE JUSTICA DO ESTADO DE SAO PAULO. Main/Corp Sao Paulo, Brazil (State). Tribunal de Justica. Portuguese. ir. Tribunal de Justica, Praca Clovis Bevilacqua 351 - 60 - Conj 601, Sao Paulo 01018 Brazil.

REVISTA DE JURISPRUDENCIA FISCAL. VFOAT Jurisprudencia Fiscal. Vol. 75 (July 1975)-. PE. Spanish. sa. 4,000.00. Editorial de Derecho Tributario, Bolognesi 508 - Barranco, Lima Peru. **DD** 343.850405, 348.503405. *Revista Mensual de Jurisprudencia Fiscal.*

REVISTA DE JURISPRUDENCIA PERUANA. Yearly V. 1- Oct. 1943-. Periodical. Spanish. ir. **LC** K19.

REVISTA DE JURISPRUDENCIA Y DOCTRINA. Vol. 1, No. 1 Y 2-. Periodical. Spanish. qt. Secretaria de Publicaciones del Ministerio de Justicia, Av. 18 de Julio 1865, Montevideo Republica Oriental del Uruguay. **LC** K19. **DD** 349.89505, 348.95005.

REVISTA DE LA ASOCIACION NACIONAL DE ABOGADOS. Periodical. Spanish. ir. **LC** K19. **DD** 349.7205, 347.2005.

REVISTA DE LA ESCUELA DE DERECHO. Vol. 1, No. 1-. Periodical. MX. Spanish. ir. Escuela de Derecho de la Universidad Autonoma de San Luis Potosi, Av Cuahutemoc y Tomasa Estevez, San Luis Potosi SLP Mexico. **LC** K19. **DD** 349.7205, 347.2005.

REVISTA DE LA ESCUELA DE DERECHO Y CIENCIAS SOCIALES. Main/Corp Hermosillo, Mexico. Universidad de Sonora. Escuela de Derecho y Ciencias Sociales. **VFOAT** Revista de la Escuela de Derecho de la Universidad de Sonora. V. 1- July/Dec. 1975-. MX. Spanish. ir. Universidad de Sonora, Hermosillo Senora Mexico. **LC** K8. **DD** 340.0972.

REVISTA DE LA FACULTAD DE CIENCIAS JURIDICAS Y POLITICAS. No. 58 (1976)-. Periodical. Spanish. an. 45. Universidad de Central Venezuela, Caracas Venezuela. **LC** K19. **DD** 349.8705, 348.7005. *Revista de la Facultad de Derecho (Caracas, Venezuela).*

REVISTA DE LA FACULTAD DE DERECHO. Main/Corp Caracas. Universidad Santa Maria. Facultad de Derecho. No. 1- Jan./March 1972-. Periodical. VE. Spanish. an. $5.00. Departament de Publicaciones, Apartado 29068, Caracas Venezuela. **LC** K3.

REVISTA DE LA FACULTAD DE DERECHO DE LA UNIVERSIDAD COMPLUTENSE. Periodical. SP. Spanish. ir. 500. Facultad de Derecho, Ciudad Universitaria, Madrid 3 Spain. **LC** K25. **DD** 340.0946. *Revista de la Facultad de Derecho de Madrid.*

REVISTA DE LA FACULTAD DE DERECHO DE MEXICO. Main/Corp Universidad Nacional Autonoma de Mexico. Facultad de Derecho. Periodical. MX. Spanish. ir. 20.00. Facultad de Derecho, Ciudad Universitaria, Mexico 20 DF Mexico. **Tel** 548-81-80. **Ind/Abst** Am. Hist. Life, Hist. Abstr., Part A, Mod. Hist. Abstr., Hist. Abst., Part B, Twent. Century Abstr. bk rev. adv acc. **Circ** 2,000. (ctrl). Contains information on doctrinal essays, traditional law documents, book reviews, and general information of law events. *Revista de la Escuela Nacional de Jurisprudencia.*

REVISTA DE LA FACULTAD DE DERECHO : PUBLICACION DE LA FACULTAD DE DERECHO DE LA UNIVERSIDAD NACIONAL DE ROSARIO. V. 1, No. 1, (June 1981)-. 0325-9471. Periodical. Spanish. ir. Cordoba 2020 Rosario, COD Postal 20000, Republica Argentina. **LC** K19. **DD** 340.05.

REVISTA DE LA FACULTAD DE DERECHO Y CIENCIAS SOCIALES. Periodical. MX. Spanish. ir. Facultad de Derecho y Ciencias Sociales, Ciudad Universitaria, San Nicholas de los Garza, NL Mexico. **LC** K19. **DD** 340.05.

Law

REVISTA DE LEGISLACAO E DE JURISPRUDENCIA. Yearly V. 1- (No. 1-). PO. Portuguese. ir. Coimbra Editora R Ferreira, Borges 79, 3002 Coimbra Portugal. LC K19. (cum index).

REVISTA DE PROCESSO. Year 1- Jan./March 1976-. Portuguese. ir. $55.00. Editora Revista dos Tribunais, rua Conde do Pinhal 78, 01501 Sao Paulo Brazil. Tel 37 2433. Ed Alvaro Malheiros. LC K19. DD 347.8105. bk rev. adv acc. Circ 5,000. Jurisprudence commentaries and leading articles for lawsuit (civil, penal, and labor).

REVISTA DE SEGURIDAD SOCIAL. *See* Economics - Labor.

REVISTA DEL COLEGIO DE ABOGADOS DE GUATEMALA. Main/Corp Colegio de Abogados de Guatemala. Periodical. Spanish. ir.

REVISTA DEL COLEGIO DE ABOGADOS DE PUERTO RICO. Vol. 15, No. 1 (Nov. 1954)-. 0010-0579. Periodical. PR. Spanish (English). ty. Presidente Comision de la Revista Colegio de Abogados, Apartado 1900, San Juan Puerto Rico. Ind/Abst Leg. Resour. Index, Index Leg. Period. DD 349.7295, 347.295. *Revista de Derecho, Legislacion y Jurisprudence del Colegio de Abogados de Puerto Rico.*

REVISTA DEL DERECHO INDUSTRIAL. Yearly V. 1, No. 1, (January/April 1979)-. Periodical. AG. Spanish. ty. $44.00. Depalma S R L, Talcahuano 494, 1013 Buenos Aires Republic Argentina. LC K19. DD 346.048, 342.648.

REVISTA DEL INSTITUTO COLOMBIANO DE DERECHO PROCESAL. Vol. 1, No. 1-. Periodical. Spanish. ty. LC K19. DD 347.86105, 348.61075.

REVISTA DEL INSTITUTO DE DERECHO COMPARADO. Main/Corp Barcelona. Instituto de Derecho Comparado. No. 1-27. Periodical. Spanish. ir. Consejo Super Invest Cientifico, Vitruvio 8/Apartado 14 458, 28006 Madrid Spain.

REVISTA DEL INSTITUTO PERUANO DE DERECHO BANCARIO. Main/Corp Instituto Peruano de Derecho Bancario. V. 1- August 1978-. Periodical. Spanish. ir. LC K9. DD 346.85082.

REVISTA DEL INSTITUTO URUGUAYO DE DERECHO PENAL. V. 1, No. 1, (Jan./July1980)-. UY. Spanish. ir. Editorial Amalio M Fernandez, 25 De Mayo 477 P Baja Ofic 11, Montevideo Uruguay. LC K19. DD 345.895005, 348.9505005.

REVISTA DEL MINISTERIO DE JUSTICIA. Main/Corp Venezuela. Ministerio de Justicia. Yearly V. 1- April/June 1952-. Periodical. Spanish. ir. Free. Ministerio de Justicia, Piso ao Torre Sur Edificio Lincoln, Sabana Grande Apartado Postal 2084, Caracas Venezuela. Ind/Abst Foreign Lang. Index.

REVISTA DEL MINISTERIO PUBLICO : ORGANO DE DIVULGACION DEL MINISTERIO PUBLICO DE LA REPUBLICA DE VENEZUELA. VFOAT Ministerio Publico. Periodical. Spanish. ty. LC K26. DD 349.8705, 348.705. *Ministerio Publico (Venezuela. Ministerio Publico).*

REVISTA DEL PODER JUDICIAL DEL ESTADO DE TLAXCALA. No. 1- Jan./Mar. 1978-. Periodical. MX. Spanish. ir. Palacio de Justica, Plaza de la Constitucion No 23, Tlaxcala Tlax Mexico. LC K19. DD 340.09724.

REVISTA DEL TRIBUNAL FISCAL DEL ESTADO DE MEXICO. Main/Corp Mexico (State). Tribunal Fiscal. Periodical. MX. Spanish. ty. Segunda Sala del Tribunal Fiscal del Estado, Circuito Ingenieros No 39, Apartado Postal No 413, CD Satelite Naucalpan Mexico. LC K13. DD 343.725204, 347.252034.

REVISTA DO CURSO DE DIREITO. Periodical. BL. Portuguese. ir. Free. Universidade de Uberlandia, Faculdade de Direito, BI E S/25-C, 38400 Uberlandia Brazil. Tel 232.2000. LC K19. DD 349.8105, 348.1005. Circ 4,000. (ctrl) Doctrine: papers on laws and law theory. Notes and informations: papers on law related subjects.

REVISTA DO INSTITUTO DE DIREITO DA ENERGIA. Main/Corp Minas Gerais, Brazil. Universidade Catolica. Instituto de Diretito da Energia. Portuguese. ir. Instituto de Diretito da Energia, Avenida Dom Jose Gaspar 500, Belo Horizonte Brazil. LC K13. DD 343.81092.

REVISTA DO INSTITUTO DOS ADVOGADOS BRASILEIROS. Main/Corp Instituto dos Advogados Brasileiros. Yearly V. 1- (No. 1-). 0100-1752. BL. Portuguese. ir. Av Marechal Camara 210/5 Andar, Rio de Janeiro Brazil. LC K9.

REVISTA DO MINISTERIO PUBLICO DE PERNAMBUCO. Began in 1972. Portuguese. ir. Associacao do Ministerio Publico de Pernambuco, Rua Diario de Pernambuco 28-2 Andar, Recife Brazil. LC K19.

REVISTA DO TRIBUNAL DE CONTAS DO DISTRITO FEDERAL. Main/Corp Distrito Federal (Brazil). Tribunal de Contas. BL. Portuguese. ir. Praca Do Buriti 70000, Brasilia Brazil. LC K4.

REVISTA DO TRIBUNAL DE CONTAS DO MUNICIPIO DE SAO PAULO. Periodical. BL. Portuguese. ty. LC KHD9856. DD 343.816103, 348.16103305. *Revista.*

REVISTA DO TRIBUNAL DE CONTAS DO MUNICIPIO DO RIO DE JANEIRO. Periodical. Portuguese. ir. Tribunal de Contas do Municipio do Rio de Janeiro, Avenida Presidente Wilson 210/7O, Andar Castelo RJ Brazil. LC KHD9816. DD 343.81530305, 348.103305.

REVISTA DO TRIBUNAL DE JUSTICA. Main/Corp Sergipe, Brazil (State). Tribunal de Justica. Jan. 1975-. Periodical. Portuguese. ir. Tribunal de Justica, Praca Olimpio Campos 736, Aracaju Brazil. DD 340.09814.

REVISTA DO TRIBUNAL REGIONAL DO TRABALHO, 3A. REGIAO. Main/Corp Brazil. Tribunal Regional do Trabalho (3A. Regiao). Portuguese. ir. LC KHD1785.8. DD 344.810105, 348.104105.

REVISTA ESPANOLA DE DERECHO CONSTITUCIONAL. V. 1, No. 1, (Jan./April 1981)-. 0211-5743. Periodical. SP. Spanish. ir. $25.00. Centro de Estudios Constitucionales, Plaza de la Marina Espanola 9, Madrid 13 Spain. LC K19. DD 342.46005, 344.602005.

REVISTA - FEDERACION ARGENTINA DE COLEGIOS DE ABOGADOS. Main/Corp Federacion Argentina de Colegios de Abogados. V. 1- 1968-. 0430-1420. AG. Spanish. ir. Suazez 2030, Buenos Aires Argentina.

REVISTA FISCAL E DE LEGISLACAO DE FAZENDA. Began in 1930. Periodical. BL. Portuguese. ir. Apec Editora S A, rua Sorocaba 316 Botafogo, ZX 02 22.271, Rio de Janeiro Brazil. DD 343.810705, 348.103705.

REVISTA - INSTITUTO NACIONAL DE PREVIDENCIA SOCIAL. PROCURADORIA-GERAL. Main/Corp Instituto Nacional de Previdencia Social. Procuradoria-Geral. V. 1- Jan./Feb. 1970-. BL. Portuguese. ir. Rua Sao Jose 90, 14O. Andar Sala 1.411-E, Guanabara Brazil.

REVISTA INTERAMERICANA DE DIREITO PROCESSUAL PENAL. BL. Portuguese (Spanish). ir. Monetary Authority of Singapore, SIA Building, 77 Robinson Road, Singapore 1 Singapore. LC K19. DD 345.810505.

REVISTA JUDICIAL DE BUCARAMANGA; ORGANO DEL PODER JUDICIAL. Periodical. Spanish. ir.

REVISTA JURIDICA. Main/Corp Cuba. Fiscalia General de la Republica. CU. Spanish. ir. Fiscalia General de la Republic, San Rafael No 3, Havana 2 Cuba. DD 347.7291005, 347.29107005. *Revista de Informacion Juridica.*

REVISTA JURIDICA (CURITIBA, BRAZIL). (REVISTA JURIDICA). Yearly V. 1, No. 1, (Nov. 1981)-. Periodical. Portuguese. ir. DD 340.05.

REVISTA JURIDICA DA SUAM. Main/Corp Sociedade Unificada de Ensino Superior Augusto Motta. Yearly V. 2- 1978-. Portuguese. an. LC K19. DD 349.8105, 348.1005. *Revista Juridica.*

REVISTA JURIDICA DE LA UNIVERSIDAD INTERAMERICANA DE PUERTO RICO. Vol. 1, No. 1 (Jan./March of 1964)-. 0041-851X. Periodical. PR. Spanish (English). ty. $10.00. Interamerican University, GPO 3255, San Juan Puerto Rico 00936. Ind/Abst Leg. Resour. Index, Curr. Law Index. DD 340.05. (cum index)

REVISTA JURIDICA DEL PERU. Periodical. PE. Spanish. qt. $70.00. Julio Ayasta Gonzalez, Lampa 1115 of 905, Lima Peru. Tel 27-7854 246698. Ed Julio Ayasta Gonzalez. bk rev. adv acc.

REVISTA JURIDICA DO MINISTERIO PUBLICO CATARINENSE. Periodical. Portuguese. an. Ministerio Publico Catarinense, Praca XV de Novembro No 6, 88.000 Florianopolis SC Brazil. LC K19.

REVISTA JURIDICA LEMI. EDICAO NACIONAL. Periodical. Portuguese. ir. Editoria Lemi, rua Pecanha 402, Caixa Postal, Belo Horizonte Brazil. DD 349.8105. *Legislacao Mineira, Revista Juridica Lemi. Edicao Mensal: Sao Paulo.*

REVISTA JURIDICA LEMI. LEGISLACAO ESTADUAL. MINAS GERAIS. Main/Corp Minas Gerais (Brazil). VFOAT Revista Juridica L.E.M.I. Periodical. Portuguese. sm. Editora Lemi S A, Caixa Postal 1890, Belo Horizonte 30.000 Brazil. LC KHD7503.25.

REVISTA LTR. VFOAT LTR. Periodical. BL. Portuguese. mo. 19,840. LTR Editora Sao Paulo, rua Xavier de Toledo 114, 10 Andar CEP 01, Sao Paulo Brazil. Ind/Abst Int. Labour Doc. DD 344.810102648, 348.104102648. *Legislacao do Trabalho.*

REVISTA MEXICANA DE DERECHO PENAL. No. 1-25, 1961-1963. 0034-9992. Periodical. MX. Spanish. ir. Procuraduria General de Justicia del Distrito Federal, Avenida Ninos Heroes y Dr, Liceaga Mexico 7 D F Mexico.

REVISTA MEXICANA DE JUSTICIA. Periodical. MX. Spanish. bm. Consejo Editorial, San Juan de Letran, 9 Piso, 13 Mexico DF Mexico. LC K19. DD 349.7205, 347.2005.

REVISTA PERUANA DE DERECHO DE LA EMPRESA. Periodical. PE. Spanish. bm. Asesorandina S R Ltda, Av Salaverry 674 OF 403, Lima Peru. LC K19. DD 346.85065, 348.50665.

REVISTA - PROCURADORIA GERAL DO ESTADO. Main/Corp Bahia, Brazil (State). Procuradoria Geral do Estado. V. 1- 1976-. Portuguese. ir. Procuradoria Geral do Estado, Travessa da Ajuda No 2 -20 Andar, Salvador Brazil. LC K2. DD 340.09814.

REVISTA TRIBUTARIA. V. 1- July/August 1974-. Spanish. ir. Libreria - Editorial Amalio M Fernandez, 25 de Mayo 477 P Baja Of 11, Montevideo Uruguay. DD 343.8950405.

REVISTA - UNIVERSIDADE DE UBERLANDIA FACULDADE DE DIREITO. Main/Corp Universidade de Uberlandia Faculdade de Direito. V. 1- 1st Semester 1972-. Portuguese. ir. 25.00 Single Issue. Universidade de Uberlandia, Faculdade de Direito, Av Joao Pinheiro 556, 38400 Uberlandia Brazil. LC K25.

REVISTA URUGUAYA DE DERECHO CONSTITUCIONAL Y POLITICO. V. 1, No. 1 (June/July 1984)-. 0256-0151. UY. Spanish. bm. Reconquista, 338 Piso 7 Apartado 705, Montevideo Uruguay. LC K19. DD 342.895005 348.950205.

REVISTA URUGUAYA DE DERECHO PROCESAL. Began in 1975. Periodical. Spanish. ir. $10.00. Fundacion de Cultura Universitaria, 25 de Mayo 537, Montevideo Uruguay. LC K19. DD 347.89505.

REVISTA URUGUAYA DE ESTUDIOS ADMINISTRATIVOS. Yearly V. 1- Jan./June 1977-. Periodical. Spanish. ir. ACALI Editorial Ltda, Montevideo Uruguay. LC K19. DD 342.89506.

REVUE AUTOCHTONE. VFOAT Native Review. V. 1- July 1979-. 0226-7284. Periodical. CN. French (English). J Lagarde, Rural Route 2, Ile du Grand Calumet Quebec J0X 1J0 Canada. DD 342.7140872.

REVUE BENINOISE DE SCIENCES JURIDIQUES ET ADMINISTRATIVES. Periodical. French. ir. Universite Nationale du Benin, B P No 526, Cotonou Republique Populaire du Benin. LC K21. DD 349.668305, 346.683005.

REVUE CAMEROUNAISE DE DROIT. VFOAT Cameroon Law Review. Periodical. French (some summaries in English). ir. 1600. Editions CLE, BP 4048, Yvounde Cameroon. LC K21. DD 340.05.

REVUE CANADIENNE DU DROIT D'AUTEUR. (LA REVUE CANADIENNE DU DROIT D'AUTEUR : LA PROPRIETE LITTERAIRE ET ARTISTIQUE). Vol. 1, No. 1 (1980)-. 0227-2180. Periodical. CN. French. qt. $9.00. Revue Canadienne du Droit d'Auteur, McGill College, 1200 Avenue/Bureau 1710, Montreal Quebec H3B 4G7 Canada. Ind/Abst Point Repere. DD 346.710482.

Law

REVUE CRITIQUE DE JURISPRUDENCE BELGE. Vol. 1-. 0035-0966. Periodical. BE. French. ir. 4.400. Etablissements Emile Bruylant, 67 rue de la Regence, 1000 Brussels Belgium. **Tel** 2/512-9845. **Ind/Abst** Index Foreign Leg. Per. Collect. Essays. **Circ** 1,675. Commentary on Belgian law.

REVUE DE DROIT COMMERCIAL BELGE. **VFOAT** Tijdschrift Voor Belgisch Handelsrecht. Vol. 16- (Jan. 1983)-. Periodical. Dutch (French). mo. 2250.00. E Story - Scientia, de Jawblunne de Mexuflew 34-35, 1040 Brussels Belgium. **Tel** 02/736.7910. Ed I Verougstraete. bk rev. (ctrl). A working tool for trade-all during the year. It keeps you up-to-date of the latest state of business law with an index at the end of each year. *Jurisprudence Commerciale de Belgique.*

REVUE DE DROIT FRANCAIS COMMERCIAL, MARITIME ET FISCAL. 1.- Year. Periodical. French. qt. 60. 28 Boulevard Paul-Peytral, 13006 Marseille France.

REVUE DE DROIT JUDICIAIRE. **VFOAT** RDJ, R.D.J. Vol. 1, No 1-. 0822-5117. CN. English (French). 85.00. 39 rue Notre-Dame Ouest, Montreal Quebec N2Y 1S5 Canada. **Tel** 288-7153. Ed Hubert Reid. **LC** KEQ110. **DD** 348.71404305, 347.14084305. bk rev. **Circ** 1,000. (ctrl). Reports of jurisprudence on application of the civil procedure code of Quebec. *Rapports de Pratique de Quebec, 0384-6970.*

REVUE DE DROIT PENAL. (REVUE DE DROIT PENAL : PUBLICATION GENERALE DE DROIT ET DE JURISPRUDENCE DU BUREAU DES SUBSTITUTS DU PROCUREUR GENERAL DU QUEBEC). 0710-0906. Periodical. CN. French (English). wk. Free. Gouvernement du Quebec, 600 St Amable 4E Etage, Quebec G1R 4Z1 Canada. **DD** 345.714002643.

REVUE DE DROIT PENAL ET DE CRIMINOLOGIE. See Sociology: General Works, Theory - Social Pathology, Welfare, Criminology.

REVUE DE DROIT PENAL MILITAIRE ET DE DROIT DE LA GUERRE. **VFOAT** The Military Law and Law of War Review. 0556-7394. Periodical. BE. Multilingual (French, English, Dutch, German, Italian, and Spanish). ir. Auditorat General, Palais de Justice, B-1000 Brussels Belgium. **Ind/Abst** Index Foreign Leg. Per. Collect. Essays.

REVUE DE DROIT (SHERBROOKE). (REVUE DE DROIT). V. 1- 1970-. 0317-9656. CN. French (text also in English). sa. Universite de Sherbrooke, Faculte de Law, Sherbrooke Quebec J1K 2R1 Canada. **Tel** (819)821-7510. **Ind/Abst** Leg. Resour. Index, Point Repere, Index Leg. Period., Curr. Law Index. **LC** K21. **DD** 340.05. bk rev. adv acc. **Circ** 1,300. Also available on microform. General review of law: public law, commercial law, civil law and criminal law.

REVUE DE DROIT SOCIAL. **VFOAT** Tijdschrift Voor Sociaal Recht. 1962-. Periodical. BE. French (Flemish). ir. $58.08. Maison F Larcier SA, 39 rue des Minimes, B-1000 Bruxelles Belgium. **Ind/Abst** Foreign Lang. Index.

REVUE DE DROIT UNIFORME. **VFOAT** Uniform Law Review. 1973-. Periodical. US. English and French. ir. International Institute for the Unification of Private Law, 75 Main Street, Dobbs Ferry NY 10522. **DD** 340.9. *Jurisprudence de Droit Uniforme, Unification du Droit.*

REVUE DE JURISPRUDENCE DE LA COUR D'APPEL DE SAINT-DENIS/REUNION. No. 1 (Oct. 1980)-. FR. French. sa. Services des Publications, 12 Avenue de la Victoire, 97489 St-Denis Reunion. **DD** 348.44041, 344.40841.

REVUE DE LA RECHERCHE JURIDIQUE, DROIT PROSPECTIF. **VFOAT** Revue de la Recherche Juridique. Periodical. French. ty. 240. U E R Recherches Juridiques, 3 Avenue Robert Schuman, 13628 Aix-en-Provence Cedex France. **LC** K21. **DD** 349.4405, 344.4005. *Revue de Droit Prospectif.*

REVUE DE L'ARBITRAGE. 1955-. 0556-7440. Periodical. FR. French. qt. Librairies Techniques, 27 Place Dauphine, 75001 Paris France. **LC** K21.

REVUE DE PLANIFICATION FISCALE ET SUCCESSORALE. V. 1- Mar. 1979-. 0708-5079. Periodical. CN. French. qt. $5. Per No. Association Quebecoise de Planification Successorale, Bureau X-24, 1145 rue Peel, Montreal Quebec H3A 1T5 Canada. **DD** 343.71404.

REVUE DE SCIENCE CRIMINELLE ET DE DROIT PENAL COMPARE. Vol. 1-. 0035-1733. Periodical. FR. French. ir. 150. Librairie Sirey, 22 rue Soufflot, 75005 Paris France. **Ind/Abst** Index Foreign Leg. Per. Collect. Essays. **LC** K21. **DD** 345.44005. Index in last issue of volume - attached.

REVUE DU BARREAU. (LA REVUE DU BARREAU). V. 29, No 7- Sept. 1969-. 0383-669X. Periodical. CN. French. sm. $24.00. Barreau du Quebec, 445 St Lawrence Boulevard, Montreal Quebec H2Y 3T8 Canada. **Tel** (514)866-3901. **Ind/Abst** Leg. Resour. Index, Point Repere. **DD** 340.09714. adv acc. **Circ** 12,000. Covers civil law, criminal law, commercial law, comments on jurisprudence, civil rights, and administrative law. *Revue du Barreau du Quebec, 0005-6065.*

REVUE DU DROIT PUBLIC ET DE LA SCIENCE POLITIQUE EN FRANCE ET A L'ETRANGER. V. 1- 1894-. 0035-2578. Periodical. FR. French. bm. $45.23. Librairie Gen de Droit Jurispr, 20 rue Soufflot, 75005 Paris France. **Ed** F Larnaude. **Ind/Abst** Foreign Lang. Index, PAIS Foreign Lang. Index. **LC** JA11. (cum index).

REVUE DU NOTARIAT. (LA REVUE DU NOTARIAT). Began with: Vol 1 (Aug. 15th 1898). 0035-2632. Periodical. CN. French. qt. $20.00. CP 130 Outremont, Montreal Quebec H2V 4M8 Canada. **Ed** Roger Comtois. **Ind/Abst** Point Repere, Curr. Law Index, Leg. Resour. Index. (cum index). bk rev adv acc. **Circ** 3,727.

REVUE FIDUCIAIRE. INFORMATION HEBDOMADAIRES. **VFOAT** Informations Hebdomaires. FR. French. ir. 170.00. 54 rue de Chabrol, 75480 CCP 193-49 Paris France. **LC** K21. **DD** 343.440405.

REVUE FRANCAISE DE DROIT AERIEN. Vol. 1- 1946/47-. 0035-287X. Periodical. FR. French. qt. $41.82. Dalloz, 11 rue Soufflot, 75240 Paris Cedex 05 France. **Ind/Abst** Int. Aerosp. Abstr., Index Foreign Leg. Per. Collect. Essays. Index in last issue of volume - attached.

REVUE GENERALE DE DROIT. V. 1- 1970-. 0035-3086. CN. French. ty. $33.27. University of Ottawa Press, 603 Cumberland Avenue, Ottawa Ontario K1N 6N5 Canada. **Tel** (613)231-2270. **Ind/Abst** Leg. Resour. Index, Index Leg. Period., Curr. Law Index. *Justinien, 0449-4504.*

REVUE GENERALE DE FISCALITE. **VFOAT** R.G.F. Periodical. French. ir. C E D Samsom, Avenue Louise 485, 1050 Bruxelles Belgium. **Tel** (02)7207180. Ed Wolters Samsom Belgie NV. **DD** 343.4920405, 344.9303405. General financial, fiscal and revenue taxes information according to Belgian legislation.

REVUE GENERALE DE L'AIR ET DE L'ESPACE. V. 27, No. 1- 1964-. French. ir. 75.00. Editions Internationales, Cheque Postal Editions Internationales 1568-87, Paris France. **LC** K21. **DD** 343.09705. *Revue Generale de l'Air.*

REVUE HISTORIQUE DE DROIT FRANCAIS ET ETRANGER. Series 4, Yearly V. 1-. 0035-3280. Periodical. FR. French. ir. $56.27. Dalloz, 11 rue Soufflot, 75240 Paris Cedex 05 France. **Ind/Abst** Am. Hist. Life, Hist. Abstr., Part A, Mod. Hist. Abstr., Hist. Abst., Part B, Twent. Century Abstr., Recent Publ. Artic., Hist. Abstr. *Nouvelle Revue Historique de Droit Francais et Etranger.*

REVUE INTERDISCIPLINAIRE D'ETUDES JURIDIQUES. Began in 1978. Periodical. French. sa. Establissements Emile Bruylant, 67 rue de la Regence, 100 Brussels Belgium. **Tel** 02/512-9845.

REVUE INTERNATIONALE DE DROIT PENAL. 1st. Yearly V. No. 1, (1924)-. Periodical. FR. French (in or English). ir. $32.59. Editions ERES, 19 rue Gustave-Courbet, 31400 Toulouse France. **Tel** 00-33-61-528004 OR 538855.

REVUE INTERNATIONALE DE LA CONCURRENCE. **VFOAT** International Review of Competition Law. Periodical. FR. English (French). ir. 2 rue Fabert, 75007 Paris France. **LC** K21. **DD** 343.07205, 342.37205. *Communication (Ligue Internationale Contre la Concurrence d'Eloyale).*

REVUE INTERNATIONALE DE LA CROIX-ROUGE. 1. Vol. No. 1 (15 Jan. 1919)-. Periodical. SZ. French. bm. 30.00. Revue Internationale de la Croix-Rouge, 17 Avenue de la Paix, 1211 Geneve Switzerland. **Tel** 34.60.01. **Ed** Michel Testuz. bk rev. **Circ** 2,300. (ctrl). Articles on international humanitarian law, summary of Red Cross activities and happenings in the Red Cross world.

REVUE INTERNATIONALE DES DROITS DE L'ANTIQUITE. 3E SERIE. V. 1- 1954-. French. an. $21.64. Office Internationale des Periodiques, Avenue Louise 485, 1050 Bruxelles Belgium. **Tel** 02/513 66 75. *Archives d'Histoire du Droit Oriental, Revue International des Droits de l'Antiquite.*

REVUE INTERNATIONALE DU DROIT D'AUTEUR. 1-. 0035-3515. FR. French (text in English, Spanish, and German). qt $47.90. Revue Internationale du Droit d'Auteur, 225 Charles de Gaulle, 92200 Neuillys-Seine France. **Ind/Abst** Index Foreign Leg. Per. Collect. Essays. **LC** UNC. Index in first issue of next volume - attached. (cum index).

REVUE JURIDIQUE DE L'ENVIRONNEMENT. **VFOAT** RJE. 1977/1-. Periodical. FR. French. qt. $47.90. Revue Juridique de l'Environnement, 32 rue Turgot, F-87000 Limoges France. **LC** K21. **DD** 344.04605, 342.44605.

REVUE JURIDIQUE DU BURUNDI. V. 1, No. 1, (March 1980)-. Periodical. French. qt. 800.00 US and Canada. Societe d'Etudes Juridiques du Burundi A S B L, BP 1010, Bujumbura Burundi. **LC** K21. **DD** 340.05.

REVUE JURIDIQUE DU RWANDA. **VFOAT** Igazeti Isobanura Amategeko mu Rwanda. French (Kinyarwanda). ir. Universite National du Rwanda, Faculte de Droit, BP 117, Butare Rwanda Africa. **LC** K21. **DD** 340.0967511.

REVUE JURIDIQUE DU ZAIRE. Periodical. CG. French. ir. $10.00. Boite Postale 5, Lubumbashi Republic of Zaire. **LC** K21. **DD** 340.096751. *Revue Juridique du Congo.*

REVUE JURIDIQUE DU ZAIRE: DROIT ECRIT ET DROIT COUTUMIER. Periodical. French. ty. $46.00. Soc d'Etudes Juriduq d'Zaire, Secretariat General, BP 5502, Kinshasa Gombe Zaire. Ed Dibunda Kabuinji. bk rev. adv acc. **Circ** 1,000. (ctrl). Includes written law and customary law, studies of judicial doctrine, notes and comments of Zaire, Central Africa.

REVUE JURIDIQUE ET POLITIQUE, INDEPENDANCE ET COOPERATION. Vol. 18-. 0035-3574. FR. French. qt. $53.88. Editions d'Iena, 17 rue Thiers, 78110 le Vesinet France. **Ind/Abst** Int. Labour Doc., Foreign Lang. Index, Index Foreign Leg. Per. Collect. Essays. **LC** K21. Index in last issue of volume - attached. *Revue Juridique et Politique d'Outre-Mer.*

LA REVUE JURIDIQUE : ORGANE OFFICIEL DE L'ORDRE DES AVOCATS DU BARREAU DE PORT-AU-PRINCE. Vol. 1 (Nov. 1981)-. Periodical. French. qt. **LC** KGS239.P67. **DD** 340.06072945.

REVUE JURIDIQUE THEMIS. **VFOAT** Themis. 1970-. 0556-7963. Periodical. CN. French (text also in English). ty. Les Editions Themis Inc, Case Postale 6201 Succursale A, Montreal Quebec H3C 3T1 Canada. **Tel** (514)739-9945. **Ind/Abst** Index Leg. Period., Leg. Resour. Index, Point Repere, Curr. Law Index. **LC** K21. **DD** 349.71405, 347.14005. *Revue Juridique Themis de l'Universite de Montreal, 0380-8327.*

REVUE LEGALE. V. 1- 1869-. 0035-3604. Periodical. CN. French. bm. $44.88. Wilson E Lafleur Limited, 39 Quest rue Notre Dame, Montreal Quebec H2Y 1S5 Canada. **Tel** (514)288-7153.

REVUE PENITENTIAIRE ET DE DROIT PENAL (1940). (REVUE PENITENTIAIRE ET DE DROIT PENAL : BULLETIN DE LA SOCIETE GENERALE DES PRISONS). **VFOAT** Bulletin de la Societe Generale des Prisons. 64. Yearly Volume. Periodical. FR. French. qt. 200. Societe General des Prisons, Legis Criminel Secy, 27 rue de Fleurus, 75006 Paris France. bk rev. Journal for criminal law dealing with conditions in the prisons. *Revue Penitentiaire et de Droit Penal et Etudes Criminologiques.*

REVUE PRACTIQUE DE DROIT SOCIAL. Periodical. FR. French. mo. $49.89. Editions de la Vie Ouvriere, 33 rue Bouret, 75940 Paris Cedex 19 France.

REVUE TRIMESTRIELLE DE DROIT CIVIL (PARIS, FRANCE : 1980). (REVUE TRIMESTRIELLE DE DROIT CIVIL). 79E Year, No. 2 (April-June 1980)-. 0397-9873. Periodical.

Law

FR. French. ir. $47.46. Dalloz, 11 rue Soufflot, 75240 Paris Cedex 05 France. **Ind/Abst** Index Foreign Leg. Per. Collect. Essays. **LC** K21. **DD** 346.44, 344.406. (cum index). *Revue de Droit Civil.*

REVUE TRIMESTRIELLE DE DROIT COMMERCIAL ET DE DROIT ECONOMIQUE. Began with Jan./Mar. 1980 issue. 0244-9358. Periodical. FR. French. ir. $53.34. Dalloz, 11 rue Soufflot, 75240 Paris Cedex 05 France. **LC** K21. **DD** 346.440705, 344.406705. *Revue Trimestrielle de Droit Commercial.*

REVUE TRIMESTRIELLE DE DROIT EUROPEEN (COURT OF JUSTICE OF THE EUROPEAN COMMUNITIES). (REVUE TRIMESTRIELLE DE DROIT EUROPEEN). Yearly V. 16, No. 2, (April/June 1980)-. Periodical. FR. French. qt $47.28. Dalloz, 11 rue Soufflot, 75240 Paris Cedex 05 France. **Ind/Abst** Foreign Lang. Index. *Revue de Droit Europeen.*

REVUE TUNISIENNE DE DROIT. Tl. French. mo. $18.72. Faculte de Droit, Ctr Etude et de Rech et de Publ, Campus University, 1060 Tunis Tunisie.

RHODE ISLAND BAR JOURNAL. Vol. 1, No. 1 (Oct. 1952)-. Periodical. US. English. mo. Rhode Island Bar Association, 91 Friendship Street, Providence RI 02903. **Tel** (401)421-5740. **Ed** Helen Desmond McDonald. **Ind/Abst** Leg. Resour. Index, Curr. Law Index. **DD** 340.05. Index in last issue of volume - attached. bk rev. adv acc. **Circ** 3,100.

RIC SUPPLEMENT. *See* Religion, Mythology, Rationalism.

RIGHTS OF JUVENILES : THE JUVENILE JUSTICE SYSTEM. 1st Ed. (1974)-. US. English. ir. Clark Boardman Company, 435 Hudson Street, New York NY 10014. **Tel** (212)929-7500. **Ed** S M Davis.

RIVISTA CRITICA DEL DIRITTO PRIVATO CEASED. Vol. 1, No. 1 (Mar. 1983)-. Periodical. IT. Italian. qt. Societa Editrice Il Mulino, Via Santo Stefano 6, 40125 Bologna Italy.

RIVISTA DELLE SOCIETA. 0035-6018. Periodical. IT. Italian. bm. 80.000 Domestic, 120.000 Foreign. Casa Editrice, Dr A Giuffre, Via Statuto 2 Periodical Department, 20121 Milano Italy. **Tel** 02/652341. **Ed** Giuseppe Auletta. bk rev. adv acc. **Circ** 5,300. This magazine deals with problems of joint stock companies.

RIVISTA DI DIRITTO CIVILE. Vol. 1- 1955-. 0035-6093. Periodical. IT. Italian. bm. $44.55. Cedam Casa Editrice, Via Japelli 5, 35100 Padova Italy. **Ind/Abst** Index Foreign Leg. Per. Collect. Essays. **LC** K22. **DD** 346.005. Index published separately - bound from publisher - free - automatically sent. (cum index).

RIVISTA DI DIRITTO ED ECONOMIA VALUTARIA. Yearly Vol. 1979 - Issue 1. Periodical. IT. Italian. qt. 100.000. Societa Editrice Edizioni Giuridico-Scientifiche, Via Donizetti 37, 20122 Milano Italy. **LC** K22. **DD** 343.4503205, 344.5033205.

RIVISTA DI DIRITTO EUROPEO. 0035-6123. Periodical. IT. Italian. qt. $41.58. Rivista di Diritto Europeo, Via Degli Spagnoli 29, 00186 Rome Italy. **Tel** 06/6543832.

RIVISTA DI DIRITTO INTERNAZIONALE E COMPARATO DEL LAVORO. Yearly V. 1- 1953-. 0035-6166. Periodical. IT. Italian. sa. $23.76. Cedam Casa Editrice, Via Jappelli 5, 35100 Padova Italy.

RIVISTA DI DIRITTO PROCESSUALE. Periodical. IT. Italian. qt. $36.83. Cedam Casa Editrice, Via Jappelli 5, 35100 Padova Italy.

RIVISTA DI STORIA DEL DIRITTO ITALIANO. Yearly V. 1- (V. 1-). IT. Italian. ir. c/o Biblioteca Patetta Facolta, University of Torina, Via S Ottavio, 10124 Torina Italy.

RIVISTA GIURIDICA DEL LAVORO E DELLA PREVIDENZA SOCIALE : DOTTRINA. IT. Italian. ir. Via Dei Giordani 22, Roma Italy. **LC** K22. **DD** 344.4501. *Rivista Giuridica del Lavoro.*

RIVISTA GIURIDICA DEL LAVORO E DELLA PREVIDENZA SOCIALE. DOTTRINA, GIURISPRUDENZA. Periodical. IT. Italian. ir. 6000 Single Issue. Via dei Giordani 22, 00199 Roma Italy. **LC** K22. **DD** 344.450105, 344.504105. *Rivista Giuridica del Lavoro e della Previdenza Sociale. Dottrina.*

RIVISTA GIURIDICA DEL LAVORO E DELLA PREVIDENZA SOCIALE : GIURISPRUDENZA. Yearly V. 26- Jan./April 1975-. Italian. ir. Societa Edizioni Giuridiche del Lavoro, Via del Giordani 22, Rome Italy. **LC** K22. **DD** 344.450105. *Rivista Giuridica del Lavoro.*

RIVISTA INTERNAZIONALE DI FILOSOFIA DEL DIRITTO. Vol. 1- Jan./March 1921-. 0035-6727. Periodical. IT. Italian. ir. 50.000 Domestic, 75.000 Foreign. Casa Editrice, Dr A Giuffre, Via Statuto, 2 Periodical Department, 20121 Milano Italy. **Tel** 02/652341. **Ed** Sergio Cotta. **Ind/Abst** Philos. Index. **LC** K22. (cum index). adv acc. **Circ** 800. This is the only Italian journal and one of the oldest and internationally best known, dealing with philosophy of law.

RIVISTA ITALIANA DI DIRITTO E PROCEDURA PENALE. New Series, Year 1- 1958-. Periodical. IT. Italian. ir. 80.000 Domestic, 120.000 Foreign. Casa Editrice, Dr A Giuffre, Via Statuto 2, Periodical Department, 20121 Milano Italy. **Tel** 02/652341. **Ed** Cesare Pedrazzi. **LC** K22. bk rev. adv acc. **Circ** 3,100. *Rivista Italiana di Dritto Penale, Rivista di Diritto Processuale Penale.*

RIVISTA TRIMESTRALE DI DIRITTO E PROCEDURA CIVILE. Vol. 1- 1947-. Periodical. IT. Italian. ir. 70.000 Domestic, 105.000 Foreign. Casa Editrice Dr A Giuffre, Via Statuto 2, Periodical Department, 20121 Milano Italy. **Tel** 02/652341. **Ed** Federico Carpi and Umberto Romagnoli. **Ind/Abst** Index Foreign Leg. Per. Collect. Essays. Index published separately - free - automatically sent. (cum index). bk rev. adv acc. **Circ** 3,000. The continuously widening scope of this journal towards branches of law not strictly of a private nature, merely reflects the evolution of Italian juridical culture.

RIVISTA TRIMESTRALE DI DIRITTO PUBBLICO. Year 1- 1951-. 0557-1464. Periodical. IT. Italian. ir. 90.000 Domestic, 135.000 Foreign. Casa Editrice, c/o Dr A Giuffre, Via Statuto 2 Periodical Department, 20121 Milano Italy. **Tel** 01/652341. **Ed** Giovanni Miele and Massimo Serero Giammimi. bk rev. adv acc. **Circ** 2,100. The magazine publishes the most signification contribution from all the branches of public law and administrative science.

ROCKY MOUNTAIN MINERAL LAW INSTITUTE. PAPERS. V. 1- 1955-. Periodical. US. English. an. **Ind/Abst** Index Leg. Period.

ROCKY MOUNTAIN MINERAL LAW NEWSLETTER. 0557-8051. Periodical. US. English. mo. Rocky Mountain Mineral Law, Foundation Fleming Law Building, B405 University of Colorado, Boulder CO 80309. **Ind/Abst** Coal Abstr., GeoRef. **LC** KF5505.A15. **DD** 346.7304685, 347.3064685. *Newsletter (Rocky Mountain Mineral Law Foundation).*

ROCKY MOUNTAIN MINERAL LAW NEWSLETTER. WATER LAW. VFOAT Water Law. -V. 8, No. 12 (Dec. 1975). 0737-0431. Periodical. US. English. mo. $20.00. Rocky Mountain Mineral Law Foundation/Water Law Newsletter, Fleming Law Building Campus, Box 405, University of Colorado, Boulder CO 80309-0405. **Tel** (303)492-6545. **Ed** George A Gould. **LC** KF5552. **DD** 346.7304691, 347.3064691. **Circ** 575. Recent water law developments in courts, state legislatures, and state and federal regulatory agencies. *Water Law Newsletter (Boulder, Colo. : 1966).*

ROSENBERG'S RAG. *See* Political Science.

ROSTER. TERMS OF THE ACT. Main/Corp Tennessee. Board for Examiners in Landscape Architecture. US. English. Capitol Hill Building, 301 7th Avenue North, Nashville TN 37219. **LC** KFT329.L3528. **DD** 344.76801761712025.

THE ROSTRUM. V. 1- Sept. 1926-. Periodical. US. English. mo. $3.00. National Forensic League, PO Box 38, Ripon WI 54971-0038.

ROYAL GAZETTE. *See* Public Administration.

RULES ADOPTED BY THE COMMITTEES OF CONGRESS. Main/Corp United States. Congress. Joint Committee on Congressional Operations. 0360-3423. US. English. US Government Printers Office, Washington DC 20402. **LC** KF4946.A329. **DD** 328.7305.

RULES AND REGULATIONS - BOARD OF COSMETOLOGY. (RULES AND REGULATIONS). Main/Corp California. State Board of Cosmetology. 0094-4327. US. English. California State Board of Cosmetology, 1020 N Street, Sacramento CA 95808. **LC** KFC446.B4. **DD** 343.794078.

RULES AND REGULATIONS FOR OVERSEAS INDIANS. *See* Business - Investments.

RULES AND REGULATIONS OF THE NEW YORK STATE THRUWAY AUTHORITY. Main/Corp New York State Thruway Authority. 1974-. 0362-1103. US. English. New York State Thruway Authority, 200 Southern Boulevard, PO Box 189, Albany NY 12201. **LC** KFN5788.A39. **DD** 343.7470946. *Rules and Regulations for the Use and Occupancy of the Thruway System.*

RULES AND REGULATIONS - SOUTH CAROLINA. RESIDENTIAL HOME BUILDERS COMMISSION. Main/Corp South Carolina. Residential Home Builders Commission. 1976-. US. English. ir. 2221 Devine Street/Suite 312, Columbia SC 29205.

RULES AND REGULATIONS - UNITED STATES. FEDERAL COMMUNICATIONS COMMISSION. Main/Corp United States. Federal Communications Commission. US. English. ir. Rules Service Company, 7658 Standish Place/Suite 106, Rockville MD 20855. **Tel** (301)424-9402.

RULES AND REGULATIONS - UNITED STATES. NUCLEAR REGULATORY COMMISSION. Main/Corp United States. Nuclear Regulatory Commission. VFOAT United States Nuclear Regulatory Commission Rules and Regulations. Periodical. US. English. ir. Superintendent of Documents, United States Printing Office, Washington DC 20402. **Tel** (202)783-3238. *Rules and Regulations.*

RULES COMPENDIUM UNDER CENTRAL ACTS. Main/Corp Rajasthan, India. 1- 1963-. 0485-9383. Periodical. English. ir.

RULES GOVERNING THE COURTS OF THE STATE OF NEW JERSEY, 1969 REVISION, AS AMENDED. Main/Corp New Jersey. 0193-967X. US. English. West Publishing Company, 1413 K Street NW, St Paul MN 55165. **LC** KFN2329. **DD** 347.74905.

RULES OF CRIMINAL PROCEDURE FOR THE UNITED STATES DISTRICT COURTS. Main/Corp United States. US. English. an. US Government Printing Office, Superintendent of Documents, Washington DC 20402. Vols. for Aug. 1983- distributed to some depository libraries in microfiche.

RULES OF THE SUPREME COURT OF LOUISIANA, ADOPTED AUGUST 31, 1973, EFFECTIVE JANUARY 1, 1974 AS AMENDED . . . . Main/Corp Louisiana. Supreme Court. Periodical. US. English.

RUNDSCHAU FUR UMSATZSTEUER (COLOGNE, GERMANY : 1983). (RUNDSCHAU FUR UMSATZSTEUER). 0341-2733. Periodical. German. mo. 57.50 Half-Yearly. Verlag Dr Otto Schmidt KG, Ulmenallee 96-98, 5000 Koln 51 Marienb West Germany. **LC** K22. **DD** 343.4305505, 344.3045505. *Umsatzsteuer-Rundschau (Cologne, Germany : 1982).*

RUTGERS CAMDEN LAW JOURNAL CEASED. V. 1-11. 0036-0449. Periodical. US. English. qt. $12.50. Rutgers School of Law, 5th and Penn Streets, Camden NJ 08102. **Ind/Abst** Leg. Contents, Index Leg. Period. **LC** K22. **DD** 340.0973. (cum index).

RUTGERS COMPUTER & TECHNOLOGY LAW JOURNAL. VFOAT Rutgers Computer and Technology Law Journal. Vol. 8, No. 2-. 0735-8938. Periodical. US. English. sa. $28.00. Rutgers Law School, 15 Washington Street, Newark NJ NJ 07102. **Tel** (201)648-5549. **Ind/Abst** Leg. Resour. Index, Comput. Control Abstr., Electr. Electron. Abstr., Sci. Abstr. Sect. A. Phys. Abstr., Index Leg. Period. **CODEN** RCTJDM. bk rev. adv acc. **Circ** 1,500. Articles, in a law review format, which explore legal technology progresses. Includes computers, biotechnology, intellectual property, telecommunications. *Rutgers Journal—Computers, Technology and the Law, 0278-5633.*

RUTGERS LAW JOURNAL. Vol. 12, No. 1 (Fall 1980)-. 0277-318X. Periodical. US. English. qt. $17.50. Rutgers University, School of Law, 5th and Penn Streets, Camden NJ 08102. **Tel** (609)757-6177.

Ed Rebecca Borden. **Ind/Abst** Leg. Resour. Index, Leg. Contents, Index Leg. Period. **LC** K22. **DD** 349.7305, 347.3005. (cum index). bk rev. adv acc. **Circ** 1,200. (ctrl). Professional and student legal scholarship and book reviews. *Rutgers Camden Law Journal, 0036-0449.*

RUTGERS LAW REVIEW. V. 3- Feb. 1949-. 0036-0465. Periodical. US. English. qt. Rutgers Law School, 15 Washington Street, Newark NJ 07102. **Tel** (201)648-5391. **Ind/Abst** Leg. Resour. Index, Index Leg. Period., Leg. Contents, Curr. Law Index, Soc. Sci. Citation Index, Contents Curr. Leg. Period. *Rutgers University Law Review.*

DER SACHVERSTANDIGE. V. 1-. Periodical. GW. German. mo. $31.65. Verlag Neuer Merkur OMBH, PF 460805/Ingolstadterstr 63A, 8000 Munchen 46 West Germany. **Tel** 089/ 3 11 10 03. **LC** K23.

THE SACRAMENTO NEWSLETTER. 1947. 0486-8161. Periodical. US. English. wk. $35.00. The Sacramento Newsletter, 3333 Watt Avenue/Suite 112, Sacramento CA 95821. **Tel** (916)489-1552. **Ed** Gary L Queale. **Circ** 2,000. (ctrl). Comprehensive 4-page weekly report on California legislation, state local government. Reports and provides insight into current and proposed legislation.

SAE, SAMMLUNG ARBEITSRECHTLICHER ENTSCHEIDUNGEN. **Main/Corp** Bundesvereinigung der Deutschen Arbeitgeberverbande. **VFOAT** Sammlung Arbeitsrechtlicher Entscheidungen. German. ir. 48.00. Bundesvereinigung der Deutschen Arbeitgeberverbande, Postfach 51 01 08, Oberlander Ufer 72, 5000 Koln 51 West Germany. **LC** K2. *Sammlung Arbeitsrechtlicher Entscheidungen.*

ST. JOHN'S LAW REVIEW. **VFOAT** Saint John's Law Review. Vol. 1, No. 1 (Dec. 1926)-. 0036-2905. Periodical. US. English. qt. $12.00. St. John's Law Review, Fromkes Hall Grand Central and Utopia Parkways, Jamaica NY 11439. **Tel** (718)990-6654. **Ed** Tonianne Florentino. **Ind/Abst** Leg. Resour. Index, Account. Index. Suppl., Index Leg. Period. **LC** K23. **DD** 340.05. (cum index). **Circ** 3,000. A journal devoted to timely legal problems and survey of New York practice.

ST. LOUIS BAR JOURNAL. V. 1- May 1950-. 0581-3344. Periodical. US. English. qt. St Louis Bar Association, 806 St Charles Street, St Louis MO 63101.

THE ST. LOUIS COUNTIAN. **VAT** Saint Louis Countian. 0036-2948. Newspaper. US. English. da. $70.00. St Louis Countian, 8029 Forsyth, St Louis MO 63105. **Tel** (314)371-1161. **Ed** Jay Sewell. adv acc. **Circ** 1,800. New suits filed, bankruptcies, mechanic's liens, forclosures, transfers of property, marriages, bid notices, etc. Legal newspaper for credit information, business leads and more.

ST. LOUIS DAILY RECORD. Periodical. US. English. da. $125.00. St Louis Daily Record & St Louis Countian, 4356 Duncan Avenue, St Louis MO 63110. **Tel** (314)371-1161. **Ed** Jay Sewell. **LC** Microfilm LL-011 K23. adv acc. **Circ** 3,200. New suits filed, bankruptcies, mechanic's liens, foreclosures, transfers of property, marriages, bid notices, etc. Legal newspaper for credit information, business leads and more.

SAINT LOUIS UNIVERSITY LAW JOURNAL. V. 1, No. 4- Winter 1951-. 0036-3030. Periodical. US. English. qt. St Louis University Law Journal, c/o Ken J Mallin, 3700 Lindell Boulevard, St Louis MO 63108. **Tel** (314)658-2795. **Ind/Abst** Index Leg. Period., Curr. Law Index, Leg. Resour. Index, Contents Curr. Leg. Period. Index in last issue of volume - attached. (cum index). *Intramural Law Review (Saint Louis, MO.).*

ST. MARY'S LAW JOURNAL. **VAT** Saint Mary's Law Journal. V. 1- Spring 1969-. 0581-3441. Periodical. US. English. qt. $25.00. St Marys University School of Law, One Camino Santa Maria, San Antonio TX 78284. **Tel** (512)436-3439. **Ed** Fred Streck. **Ind/Abst** Leg. Resour. Index, Index Leg. Period., Curr. Law Index, Contents Curr. Leg. Period. **LC** K23. **DD** 340.05. Index in last issue of volume - attached. (cum index). adv acc. **Circ** 1,800. Devoted to the study and publication of scholarly material of practical value to students and members of the legal community.

SAINT PAUL LEGAL LEDGER. 1927. Newspaper. US. English. da. $50.00. Saint Paul Legal Ledger, 640 Minnesota Building, St Paul MN 55101. **Tel** (612)222-0059. **Ed** Samuel E Lewis Jr. adv acc. **Circ** 700. Daily business and legal newspaper.

SAISHIN TOKI ROPPO. **Main/Corp** Japan. JA. Japanese. ir. 3000. Akatsuki Shuppan Kabushiki Kaisha, 20 Kanda Jinbo-cho 2, Chiyoda-ku, Tokyo-to-Japan.

SALES TAX AFFAIRS. Periodical. English. ir. 45.00. Kamla Kuj, D-74 Anand Niketan, New Delhi 110021 India. **DD** 343.54055.

SAMMLUNG DER EIDGENOSSISCHEN GESETZE. **Main/Corp** Switzerland. 1848/50-. Periodical. SZ. German. wk. Staempfli & CIE SA, Hallerstrasse 7-9 Postfach 2728, CH-3001 Berne Switzerland. (cum index).

SAMMLUNG GELTENDER STAATSANGEHARIGKEITSGESETZE. 0080-5823. Monographic Series. GW. German. ir. Alfred Metzner Verlag, Postfach 970148, D-6000 Frankfurt West Germany.

THE SAMOAN PACIFIC LAW JOURNAL. V. 1- Jan./July 1973-. English and Samoan (Jan./July 1973, English only). ty. $10.00. American Samoa Bar Association, Court House, Pago Pago American Samoa 96799. **LC** K23. **DD** 340.099613.

SAN DIEGO LAW REVIEW. (THE SAN DIEGO LAW REVIEW). V. 1- Jan. 1964. 0036-4037. Periodical. US. English. qt. $20.00. University San Diego School of Law, Alcala Park, San Diego CA 92110. **Tel** (619)260-4531. **Ed** Richard J Doren. **Ind/Abst** Manage. Contents, Leg. Resour. Index, Sel. Water Resour. Abstr., Energy Inf. Abstr., Environ. Abstr., ABI/Inform, Index Leg. Period., Public Aff. Inf. Serv. Bull., Curr. Law Index, Ocean. Abstr., Contents Curr. Leg. Period. **DD** 349.79405, 347.94005. Index in last issue of volume - attached. (cum index). adv acc. **Circ** 1,000. (ctrl). Immigration, tax law, law of the sea, open topics.

SAN FERNANDO VALLEY LAW REVIEW. V. 6- Fall 1977-. 0193-9572. Periodical. US. English. an. San Fernando Valley Law Review, 8353 Sepulveda Boulevard, Sepulveda CA 91343. **Tel** (818)705-1885. **Ind/Abst** Leg. Resour. Index, Index Leg. Period. **LC** K25. **DD** 340.05. *University of San Fernando Valley Law Review, 0042-000X.*

THE SAN FRANCISCO ATTORNEY. Vol. 8, No. 3 (Apr. 1982)-. 0744-9348. US. English. mo. $10.00. Bar Association of San Francisco, 220 Bush Street, San Francisco CA 94104. **LC** KF200. **DD** 340.060794. *Brief Case (San Francisco, Calif.), 0520-9633.*

SAN FRANCISCO BARRISTER. Vol. 1, No. 1 (Jan./Feb. 1982)-. 0744-3072. Periodical. US. English. mo. San Francisco Barrister, 220 Bush Street/21st Floor, San Francisco CA 94104. **LC** KF200. **DD** 34006079461. *Barristers' Bailiwick, 0279-4314.*

SANGKAKALA PERADILAN. Indonesian. ir. 450. Ikatan Hakim Indonesia, Djl Siliwangi 151, Semaraney Indonesia. **LC** K23.

SANTA CLARA COMPUTER AND HIGH-TECHNOLOGY LAW JOURNAL. **VFOAT** Santa Clara Computer and High Technology Law Journal. Vol. 1, No. 1 (Jan. 1985)-. 0882-3383. Periodical. US. English. sa. $30.00. University of Santa Clara, School of Law, Santa Clara CA 95053. **DD** 340 #2 11.

SANTA CLARA LAW REVIEW. V. 16- 1975-. 0146-0315. Periodical. US. English. qt. $20.00. University of Santa Clara, School of Law, Santa Clara CA 95053. **Tel** (408)554-4074. **Ed** David W Miller. **Ind/Abst** Leg. Resour. Index, Sel. Water Resour. Abstr., Index Leg. Period., Curr. Law Index, Contents Curr. Leg. Period. **LC** K23. **DD** 340.09794. bk rev. adv acc. **Circ** 20,000. (ctrl). Articles, comments, case notes and book reviews on subjects of interest to the legal community. *Santa Clara Lawyer.*

SASKATCHEWAN DECISIONS. CIVIL AND CRIMINAL CASES. (SASKATCHEWAN DECISIONS, CIVIL AND CRIMINAL CASES). 1975-. 0319-7999. CN. English. mo. Western Legal Publications Ltd, 301 One Alexander Street, Vancouver British Columbia V6A 1B2 Canada. **Tel** (604)687-5671. **DD** 348.7124048.

SASKATCHEWAN LAW REVIEW. V. 32- Apr. 1967-. 0036-4916. Periodical. CN. English. sa. 18.00. University of Saskatchewan, College of Law, Saskatoon Saskatchewan S7N 0W0 Canada. **Ed** Ian Savage. **Ind/Abst** Leg. Resour. Index, Energy Res. Abstr., Index Leg. Period., Curr. Law Index, Contents Curr. Leg. Period. bk rev. **Circ** 1,700. (ctrl). Prints articles, case comments and book reviews of interest to Saskatchewan and Canadian practitioners and academics. *Saskatchewan Bar Review, 0380-8564.*

SASKATCHEWAN REPORTS. Began with issue 1 (Dec. 15, 1979)?. 0713-7095. CN. English. ir. $65.00 Per Vol. Maritime Law Book Ltd, Box 302, Fredericton New Brunswick E3B 4Y9 Canada. **DD** 348.7124043.

SASKATCHEWAN REPORTS (BOUND CUMULATION). (SASKATCHEWAN REPORTS). Vol. 1-. 0713-7095. CN. English. ir. $65.00 Per Vol. Maritime Law Book Ltd, Box 302, Fredericton New Brunswick E3B 4Y9 Canada. **LC** KES104. **DD** 348.7124041, 347.1240841.

SBAND NOTE PAD. **Main/Corp** State Bar Association of North Dakota. **VAT** State Bar Association of North Dakota Note Pad. V. 1- Oct. 29, 1976-. 0277-4763. US. English. State Bar Association of North Dakota, PO Box 2136, Bismarck ND 58501.

SBIRKA ZAKONU, CESKOSLOVENSKA SOCIALISTICKA REPUBLIKA. **Main/Corp** Czechoslovakia. Began in July, 1960. Czech. ir. 68.00. Federalni Statisticky Urad, Trziste 8, Praha 1 Mala Stran, Praha Czechoslovakia. *Sbirka Zakonu Republiky Ceskoslovenske.*

SCANDINAVIAN STUDIES IN LAW. V. 1- 1957-. 0085-5944. Periodical. SW. English. ir. $16.64. Almqvist and Wiksel, 108 Drottninggatan, PO Box 45150, S-104 30 Stockholm Sweden. **Tel** 85413160. **Ed** F Schmidt. **Ind/Abst** Index Foreign Leg. Per. Collect. Essays. Each issue contains an index to its own contents - no vol index - loose.

DER SCHOFFE. Vol. 1-. 0036-6250. Periodical. SZ. German. mo. Kunst & Wissen Erich Bieber, Dufourstrasse 51, CH-8008 Zurich Switzerland. **DD** 347.4310752, 344.3107752. Index in last issue of volume - attached.

SCHOOL LAW BULLETIN. **VFOAT** SLB. Nov. 1974-. 8755-8297. Periodical. US. English. mo. $37.10. School Law Bulletin, 131 Beverly Street, Boston MA 02114. **Tel** (617)542-0048. **Ed** E Michael Quinlan. **DD** 344. **Circ** 1,000. Brief synopses of actual court cases dealing with the education profession in an 8 page newsletter.

SCHOOL LAW BULLETIN (CHAPEL HILL, N.C.). (SCHOOL LAW BULLETIN). Began in Oct. 1970. Periodical. US. English. qt. $10.00. University of North Carolina, Institute of Government, Chapel Hill NC 27514. **Tel** (919)966-4119. **Ed** Robert E Phay. **Ind/Abst** Public Aff. Inf. Serv. Bull., Curr. Index J. Educ. (cum index). **Circ** 1,225. Written by school attorneys for school administrators and board members. One or two articles on subjects that directly affect the operation of schools.

SCHOOL LAW NEWS. V. 1- Dec. 12, 1973-. 0194-2271. Periodical. US. English. bw. $165.00. Capitol Publications Inc, 1300 North 17th Street, Arlington VA 22209. **Tel** (703)528-5400.

SCHOOL LAW REGISTER. 0275-0414. US. English. mo. $415.00. Capitol Publications Inc, 1300 North 17th Street, Arlington VA 22209. **Tel** (703)528-1100. **Ed** Leslie A Ratzlaff. (ctrl). Federal laws, regulations, proposed regulations and grant and policy notices affecting education.

SCHOOL LAWS OF KENTUCKY; ANNOTATED. **Main/Corp** Kentucky. 0091-1194. US. English. Kentucky Department of Education, 1923 Capital Plaza Tower, Frankfort KY 40601. **LC** KFK1590.A29. **DD** 344.76907.

THE SCHOOL LAWYER. V. 1- Feb. 4, 1980-. 0197-3541. Periodical. US. English. bw. $75.00. Education Information Services, Box 1231, Alexandria VA 22313. **LC** KF4114. **DD** 344.730702648.

THE SCHOOLS AND THE COURTS. V. 5- Feb. 1979-. 0164-3851. Periodical. US. English. qt. College Administration Publications, PO Box 8492, Asheville NC 28814. **Tel** (704)252-0883. **Ed** Beckham, Gehring and Young. **LC** KF4150.A59. **DD** 344.730702646. **Circ** 700. A review of selected higher court decisions in elementary and secondary education law and comprehensive reference for daily use. *School Student and the Courts, 0098-8952.*

SCHOOLS PROGRAM NEWSLETTER. 0706-1927. Periodical. CN. English. ir. Free. Schools Program, Legal Services Society, PO Box 12120, 555

Law

West Hastings Street, Vancouver British Columbia V6B 4N6 Canada. **LC** KEB445.7.L37. **DD** 340.0712711.

SCHRIFTEN ZUM BURGERLICHEN RECHT. GW. German. ir. Duncker & Humblot Verlag, Dietrich-Schaefer-Weg 9, 1000 Berlin 41 West Germany. **Tel** (030)7912026. Contributions to civil law.

SCHRIFTEN ZUM DEUTSCHEN UND EUROPAISCHEN ZIVIL, -HANDELS- UND PROZESSRECHT. Monographic Series. GW. German. ir. Verlag E & W Gieseking, Postfach 130120 Deckerstrasse 30, 48 Bielefeld 13 West Germany.

SCHRIFTEN ZUM OFFENTLICHEN RECHT. Monographic Series. GW. German. ir. Duncker und Humblot Verlag, Dietrich-Schaefer-Weg 9, 1000 Berlin 41 West Germany.

SCHRIFTEN ZUM PROZESSRECHT. Monographic Series. GW. German. ir. Duncker und Humblot Verlag, Dietrich-Schaefer-Weg 9, 1000 Berlin 41 West Germany.

SCHRIFTEN ZUM STRAFRECHT. Monographic Series. German. ir. Duncker und Humblot Verlag, Dietrich-Schaefer-Weg 9, 1000 Berlin 41 West Germany. **Tel** (030)7912026. Contributions to criminal law.

SCHRIFTEN ZUM WIRTSCHAFTSRECHT. *See* Economics.

SCHRIFTEN ZUR RECHTSGESCHICHTE. No. 1- 1970-. Periodical. GW. German. ir. Duncker und Humblot Verlag, Dietrich-Schaefer-Weg 9, 1000 Berlin 41 West Germany.

SCHRIFTEN ZUR RECHTSTHEORIE. Monographic Series. GW. German. ir. Duncker und Humblot Verlag, Dietrich-Schaefer-Weg 9, 1000 Berlin 41 West Germany. **Tel** (030)7912026. Contributions to theories of law, morals and ethics.

SCHRIFTENREIHE. Main/Corp Berlin. Freie Universitat. Institut fur Rechtssoziologie und Rechtstatsachenforschung. German. ir. Duncker und Humblot Verlag, Dietrich-Schaefer-Weg 9, 1000 Berlin 41 West Germany.

SCHWERPUNKTE DES KARTELLRECHTS. Main/Corp Forschungsinstitut fur Wirtschaftsverfassung und Wettbewerb (Cologne, Germany). Series/Titl Fiw-Schriftenreihe. German. ir. **LC** HB41.

THE SCOTS LAW TIMES; THE LANDS TRIBUNAL FOR SCOTLAND REPORTS. VFOAT Lands Tribunal for Scotland Reports. 1971-. 0036-908X. UK. English. wk. $199.22. WH Green & Son Limited, 2 & 4 St Gilis Street, Edinburgh EH1 1PU Scotland.

SCOTS MERCANTILE LAW STATUTES. Main/Corp Great Britain. 0308-1176. UK. English. an. **LC** KDC495.A29. **DD** 346.41107.

THE SCOTT REPORT. Vol. 1, No. 1 (Oct. 1981)-. 0730-1022. Periodical. US. English. mo. $187.00. Law and Technology Press, PO Box 3280, Manhattan Beach CA 90266. **Tel** (213)372-1678. Ed Michael D Scott. **Ind/Abst** Comput. Control Abstr., Electr. Electron. Abstr., Sci. Abstr. Sect. A. Phys. Abstr. **LC** K564.C6. **DD** 346.0705, 342.6705. **CODEN** SCREE9. bk rev. Reports on the legal problems of the computer industry.

SCOTTISH PLANNING LAW & PRACTICE. VFOAT Scottish Planning Law and Practice. No. 1 (Sept. 1980)-. 0144-8196. Periodical. UK. English. ty. 5.00. Planning Exchange, 186 Bath Street, Glasgow G2 4HG Scotland. **LC** KDC446.A13. **DD** 346.411045, 344.110645. (cum index).

SEA REPORTER. Main/Corp School Employers Association. VAT School Employers Association Reporter. V. 1- Oct. 1978-. 0193-1644. Periodical. US. English. mo. School Employers Association, 9300 East Imperial Highway, Downey CA 90204. **LC** KFC562.T4. **DD** 344.79401890413705.

SEARCH AND SEIZURE LAW REPORT. V. 1- Nov. 1973-. 0095-1005. US. English. mo. $75.00. Clark Boardman Company Ltd, 435 Hudson Street, New York NY 10014. **Ind/Abst** Leg. Resour. Index, Curr. Law Index. **LC** KF9630.A73. **DD** 345.73052. (cum index).

SEATTLE-KING COUNTY BAR BULLETIN (1979). (SEATTLE-KING COUNTY BAR BULLETIN). VFOAT Bar Bulletin. Sept. 1979-. 0745-3337. Periodical. US. English. mo. $10.00. Seattle-King County Bar Association, 320 Central Building, Seattle WA 98104. **LC** KF200. **DD** 340.06079777. *Bar Bulletin, 0196-2639*.

SEC DOCKET. Main/Corp United States. Securities and Exchange Commission. VFOAT S.E.C. Docket. Vol. 1, No. 1 (Feb. 13, 1973)-. 0091-4061. Periodical. US. English. wk. $110.00. Commerce Clearing House Inc, 4025 West Peterson Avenue, Chicago IL 60646. **Tel** (312)583-8500. **LC** KF1436.A2. **DD** 346.73066602648. Issues reproduce text of SEC rulings, opinions and other official actions as prepared by the agency.

THE SEC QUARTERLY BULLETIN. Main/Corp Philippines (Republic). Securities and Exchange Commission. Periodical. English. ir. 20.00. Securities & Exchange Commission, Box 104, Greenhills Metro Manila Philippines. **DD** 346.599066605.

THE SEC SPEAKS. (THE SEC SPEAKS IN . . .). VFOAT S.E.C. Speaks in . . . . VAT Securities and Exchange Commission Speaks. 0145-8744. US. English. Practising Law Institute, 810 7th Avenue, New York NY 10019. **LC** KF1440. **DD** 346.73092, 347.30692. *SEC Speaks, 0145-8744*.

SECOND CIRCUIT DIGEST. 0746-5254. US. English. mo. $7.50. Federal Bar Council, 370 Lexington Avenue, New York NY 10017.

SECOND CIRCUIT REDBOOK. Main/Corp Federal Bar Council. 1975/76-. 0146-163X. US. English. an. Free to Members of Federal Bar Council as part of dues, $35.00 Non-Members. Little Brown & Company, 41 Mt Vernon Street, Boston MA 02106. **LC** KF8840. **DD** 347.7322.

SECTION 8 HUD-SUBSIDIZED HOUSING, NEW TAX-EXEMPT FINANCING TECHNIQUES: MATERIALS. (ALI-ABA COURSE OF STUDY : SECTION 8 HUD-SUBSIDIZED HOUSING, NEW TAX-EXEMPT FINANCING TECHNIQUES : MATERIALS). 0191-2240. US. English. American Law Institute-American Bar Association Committee on Continuing Professional Education, 4025 Chestnut Street, Philadelphia PA 19104. **LC** KF695.Z9. **DD** 346.730436.

SECTION OF ADMINISTRATIVE LAW DIRECTORY. *See* Yearbooks, Almanacs, Directories.

SECTION OF TAXATION NEWSLETTER. VFOAT Newsletter. Vol. 1, No. 1 (Fall 1981)-. 0277-2361. Periodical. US. English. qt. Free to Members. American Bar Association's Section of Taxation, 1800 M Street Northwest, Washington DC 20036. **LC** KF6272. **DD** 343.730405, 347.303405.

SECURED CREDITORS AND LESSORS UNDER THE BANKRUPTCY REFORM ACT. Series/Titl Commercial Law and Practice Course Handbook Series. US. English. an. Practising Law Institute, 810 7th Avenue, New York NY 10019. **LC** KF1526. **DD** 346.73078, 347.30678.

SECURITIES AND FEDERAL CORPORATE LAW REPORT. Series/Titl Securities Law Series. Vol. 1, No. 1 (Jan. 1979)-. 0273-0685. US. English. mo. Clark Boardman Company Ltd, 435 Hudson Street, New York NY 10014. **Tel** (212)929 7500. **Ind/Abst** Leg. Resour. Index, Curr. Law Index. **LC** KF1432. **DD** 346.730666, 347.306666.

SECURITIES LAW HANDBOOK. Series/Titl Securities Law Series. 1978-. 0731-5805. US. English. an. Clark Boardman Company Ltd, 435 Hudson Street, New York NY 10014. **LC** KF1439. **DD** 346.730666, 347.306666.

SECURITIES LAW REVIEW. 1 (1969)-. 0080-8474. US. English. an. $65.00. Clark Boardman Company, 435 Hudson Street, New York NY 10014. **Tel** (212)929-7500. **Ind/Abst** Leg. Resour. Index, Curr. Law Index. **LC** KF1066.A32. **DD** 346.

SECURITIES REGULATION. 1st- Ed. US. English. Law Distributors, 14415 South Main Street, Gardena CA 90248.

SECURITIES REGULATION & LAW REPORT. VAT Securities Regulation and Law Report. Began with June 1, 1969 issue. 0037-0665. US. English. wk. Bureau of National Affairs Inc, 1231 25th Street NW, Washington DC 20037. **Tel** (301)258-1033. **LC** KF1439.A1. **DD** 346.730205.

SECURITIES REGULATION LAW ALERT. Vol. 17, No. 10 (July 1, 1984)-. 8756-209X. Periodical. US. English. sm. $96.00. Warren Gorham & Lamont Inc, 210 South Street, Boston MA 02111. **DD** 346. *Securities Regulation and Transfer Report, 0037-0673*.

SECURITIES REGULATION LAW JOURNAL. V. 1- Spring 1973-. 0097-9554. US. English. qt. Warren Gorham & Lamont, 210 South Street, Boston MA 02111. **Tel** (800)225-2363. **Ind/Abst** Manage. Contents, Leg. Resour. Index, Account. Index. Suppl., ABI/Inform, Index Leg. Period., Contents Curr. Leg. Period., Soc. Sci. Citation Index, Curr. Law Index. **LC** K23. **DD** 346.7309205. (cum index).

SECURITIES REGULATION SOURCEBOOK. Series/Titl Corporate Law and Practice Sourcebook Series. 0586-7789. US. English. Practising Law Institute, 1133 Avenue of the Americas, New York NY 10036. **LC** KF1439.A1. **DD** 346.73092.

SEFER ASYA. VFOAT Assia. V. 1-. Periodical. Hebrew. ir. Ed A Steinberg.

SEISETSU HOJINZEIHO. VFOAT Hojinzeiho. 54- Vol. 1979-. Japanese. ir. *Hojinzeiho*.

SELECAO DE PARECERES E ESTUDOS DA COORDENACAO DE LEGISLACAO E NORMAS DE ENSINO. Main/Corp Brazil. Coordenacao de Legislacao e Normas de Ensino. BL. Portuguese. ir. Departamento de Documentacao e Divulgacao, Brasilia Brazil. **DD** 344.81079167.

SELECTED JUDGEMENTS - HIGH COURT OF LAGOS STATE *CEASED*. (SELECTED JUDGEMENTS). Main/Corp Lagos State, Nigeria. High Court. 0331-0418. NR. English. mo. -/20/-. High Court Law Library, High Court of Lagos State, Tefawa Balewa Square, Lagos Nigeria. **LC** Law. **DD** 348.6691044.

SELECTED JUDGEMENTS OF THE OGUN STATE HIGH COURT. Main/Corp Ogun State (Nigeria). High Court. English. an. 5.00. Chief Registrar's Office, High Court of Justice, Abeokuta Nigeria. **DD** 348.6692043, 346.6920848.

SELECTED LIST OF ACQUISITIONS CATALOGED. (SELECTED LIST OF ACQUISITIONS CATALOGED - INSTITUTE OF JUDICIAL ADMINISTRATION, LIBRARY). Main/Corp Institute of Judicial Administration. Library. 0537-9342. US. English. Institute of Judicial Administration, 1 Washington Square, New York NY 10012. **LC** KF4. **DD** 016.3400973.

SELECTED LIST OF FEDERAL LAWS AND TREATIES RELATING TO SPORT FISH AND WILDLIFE. Main/Corp United States. Bureau of Sport Fisheries and Wildlife. 0093-4631. US. English. $0.20. Bureau of Sport Fisheries & Wildlife, Washington DC 20240. **LC** KF5640. **DD** 346.7304695.

SELECTED STATISTICS ON THE OFFICE OF ATTORNEY GENERAL. *See* Statistics.

LA SEMAINE JURIDIQUE. Began in 1924. Periodical. FR. French. wk. $85.00. Editions Techniques, 123 rue d'Alesia, 75678 Paris Cedex 14 France.

SEMANA DE ESTUDIOS DE DERECHO FINANCIERO. *See* Business - Public Finance.

SEMIANNUAL SURVEY OF MUNICIPAL LAW. VFOAT Survey of Municipal Law. Began with July 1978 issue. US. English. sa. County and Municipal Government Study Commission, 115 West State Street, Trenton NJ 08625. **LC** KFN2231.A152. **DD** 342.74909, 347.49029.

SEMPAKU ROPPO. Main/Corp Japan. Japanese. ir. 8000. Seizando Shoten, c/o Senzando Building, 4-15 Minami Motocho, Shinjuku-ku 160 Tokyo Japan.

SENATE ELECTION LAW GUIDEBOOK. 1980-. 0740-9834. US. English. be. **LC** KF4913. **DD** 342.73055, 347.30255. Vols. for (1980-) distributed to some depository libraries in microfiche. *Election Law Guidebook, Senate Campaign Information, 0162-590X*.

SENTENCIAS EN APELACION DE LAS AUDIENCIAS PROVINCIALES EN MATERIA CIVIL Y PENAL. Main/Corp Spain. Tribunal Supremo. Secretaria Tecnica. SP. Spanish. ir. Ministerio de Justicia, Centro de Publicaciones, Calle de San Bernardo, 662B Madrid 8 Spain. **DD** 347.46.

LE SENTENZE DELLA CORTE COSTITUZIONALE NEL . . . . Main/Corp Italy. Coret Costituzionale. 1979-. Italian. an. 5.000.

Law

SEQUENCIA (FLORIANOPOLIS, BRAZIL). (SEQUENCIA). Periodical. Portuguese. sa. LC K23. DD 340.05.

SERIES OF PROMINENT JUDGEMENTS OF THE SUPREME COURT UPON QUESTIONS OF CONSTITUTIONALITY. Main/Corp Japan. Saiko Saibansho. No. 1-. JA. Japanese (English). ir. Supreme Court of Japan, 4 2 Hayabusa Cho, Chiyada-ku Tokyo 102 Japan. DD 342.52002643.

SERVICES LAW CASES. Jan. 1974-. 0304-100X. II. English. ir. 30.00. International Law Book Company, 1562 Church Road, Kashmere Gate, New Delhi India. DD 342.54068.

SERVICES LAW REPORTER. Pt. 1- Jan. 1967-. Periodical. English. ir. Jagjit Singh Chawla, Kothi No 108-B Sector 27-A, Chandigarh India. DD 349.5404.

SESSION LAWS AND DIGEST. Main/Corp American Samoa. English (Samoan). ir. American Samoa Legislature, Legislative Reference Bureau, Fagatogo American Samoa. DD 348.9613022.

SESSION LAWS OF SOUTH DAKOTA. Main/Corp South Dakota. VFOAT Laws of South Dakota. 1979-. US. English. an. State Publications Company, Box 100, 303 East Sioux Avenue, Pierre SD 57501. LC KFS3025. DD 348.783022, 347.830822. *Session Laws of the State of South Dakota.*

SESSION LAWS OF THE VIRGIN ISLANDS. Main/Corp Virgin Islands of the United States. 1955-. US. English. ir. Equity Publ Corporation, Orford NH 03777. Tel (603)353-4351.

SESSION REVIEW. 0739-9979. Periodical. US. English. LC KFM5415. DD 328.7770765.

SETON HALL LAW REVIEW. V. 1- Spring 1970-. 0586-5964. Periodical. US. English. qt. $15.00. Seton Hall Law Review, 1095 Raymond Boulevard, Newark NJ 07102. Tel (201)622-4938. Ed James Clark. Ind/Abst Leg. Resour. Index, Index Leg. Period., Curr. Law Index, Contents Curr. Leg. Period. LC K23. DD 340.05. Index in last issue of volume - loose - separately paged. (cum index). bk rev. adv acc. Ideas in all aspects of the law with an emphasis on New Jersey. *Seton Hall Law Journal, 0742-6127.*

SETON HALL LEGISLATIVE JOURNAL. V. 1- 1975-. 0361-8951. US. English. sa. $10.00. Seton Hall Legislative Journal, 1095 Raymond Boulevard, Newark NJ 07102. Tel (201)643-4080. Ed Greg Battista. Ind/Abst Leg. Resour. Index, Index Leg. Period., Curr. Law Index, Contents Curr. Leg. Period. LC K23. DD 340.09749. Circ 1,200. (ctrl). Detailed analysis of current legislation written by legislators and experts in the field of law.

SEVENTH CIRCUIT DIGEST. Began in 1976. 0747-9387. US. English. ir. Bar Association of the Seventh Federal Circuit, Sidley & Austin, One First National Plaza, Chicago IL 60603. Ed H Helsinger.

THE SEX PROBLEMS COURT DIGEST. V. 1- Jan. 1970-. Periodical. US. English. mo. LC KF9325.A53. DD 345.73025302648. NLM W1 SE985.

SHAKAI HOKEN ROMU HANDOBUKKU. JA. Japanese. ir. Chuo Keizaisha, 31-2 Kanda Jinbocho 1, Chiyoda-ku 101, Tokyo Japan.

SHAKAI HOKEN ROMU ROPPO. Main/Corp Japan. Japanese. ir. 4000. Chuo Keizisha, 31-2 Kanda Jinbocho 1, Chiyoda-ku 101 Tokyo Japan.

SHAW'S DIRECTORY OF COURTS IN ENGLAND AND WALES. See Yearbooks, Almanacs, Directories.

SHAW'S DIRECTORY OF COURTS IN THE UNITED KINGDOM. See Yearbooks, Almanacs, Directories.

SHEPARD'S ACTS AND CASES BY POPULAR NAMES, FEDERAL AND STATE. Began in 1968. 0080-9233. US. English. an. $115.00. Shepards McGraw Hill, PO Box 1235, Colorado Springs CO 80901. Tel (800)525-2474. Acts are listed alphabetically by their popular names and followed by references to the United States Code and United States Statutes at large or to the specific state codes or session laws. *Table of Federal and State Cases by Popular Names.*

SHEPARD'S ARKANSAS CITATIONS. CASES AND STATUTES. VFOAT Arkansas Citations. 0730-3637. US. English. ir. $200.00. Shepards McGraw Hill, PO Box 1235, Colorado Springs CO 80901. Tel (800)525-2474. Gives you every citing reference to the statute in question ever made by your appellate courts.

SHEPARD'S ATLANTIC REPORTER CITATIONS (ADVANCE SHEET EDITION). (SHEPARD'S ATLANTIC REPORTER CITATIONS). V. 1- Mar. 1956-. 0488-6100. Periodical. US. English. ir. $340.00. Shepards McGraw Hill, PO Box 1235, Colorado Springs CO 80901. Tel (800)525-2474. Gives you every state and federal citation to every reporter case as cited anywhere throughout the entire National Reporter System.

SHEPARD'S CALIFORNIA CITATIONS. CASES. (SHEPARD'S CALIFORNIA CITATIONS : CASES). VFOAT California Citations. 5th- Ed. 0730-367X. US. English. ir. $630.00. Shepards McGraw Hill, PO Box 1235, Colorado Springs CO 80901. Tel (800)525-2474. Gives you every citing reference to the statute in question ever made by your appellate courts. *Shepard's California Citations and Annotations.*

SHEPARD'S CODE OF FEDERAL REGULATIONS CITATIONS. VFOAT Code of Federal Regulations Citations. V. 1- Mar. 1979-. 0730-465X. US. English. qt. $165.00. Shepards McGraw Hill, PO Box 1235, Colorado Springs CO 80901. Tel (800)525-2474. This comprehensive research system shows citations to the Code of Federal Regulations to presidential proclamations, presidential executive orders and reorganization plans.

SHEPARD'S COLORADO CITATIONS. CASES AND STATUTES. VFOAT Colorado Citations. 0730-2096. US. English. ir. Shepards McGraw Hill, PO Box 1235, Colorado Springs CO 80901. Tel (800)525-2474. Circ $245.00. Gives you every citing reference to the statute in question ever made by your appellate courts.

SHEPARD'S COLORADO CITATIONS. STATUTES. (SHEPARD'S COLORADO CITATIONS : STATUTES). VFOAT Colorado Citations. Statutes. 4th- Ed. 0730-2088. US. English. ir. Available only with cases. Shepards McGraw Hill, PO Box 1235, Colorado Springs CO 80901. Tel (800)525-2474. Gives you every citing reference to the statute in question ever made by your appellate courts. *Shepard's Colorado Citations.*

SHEPARD'S CORPORATION LAW CITATIONS. Vol. 1, No. 1 (Mar. 1984)-. 8750-1104. Periodical. US. English. qt. $250.00. Shepards McGraw Hill, 420 North Cascade Avenue, Colorado Springs CO 80903. Tel (800)525-2474. DD 346. An up-to-date timesaving comprehensive citation system. Provides coverage of federal court corporation cases reported in the United States Supreme Court.

SHEPARD'S FEDERAL ENERGY LAW CITATIONS (QUARTERLY). (SHEPARD'S FEDERAL ENERGY LAW CITATIONS). VFOAT Federal Energy Law Citations. Vol. 1, No. 1 (Apr. 1983)-. 0746-312X. Periodical. US. English. qt. $125.00. Shepards McGraw Hill, PO Box 1235, Colorado Springs CO 80901. Tel (800)525-2474. Gives you a valuable new reference source to case and statutory energy laws.

SHEPARD'S FEDERAL LABOR LAW CITATIONS. CASES, STATUTES, AND CROSS REFERENCES. VFOAT Federal Labor Law Citations. Cases, Statutes, and Cross References. 0559-779X. US. English. ir. $590.00. Shepards McGraw Hill, PO Box 1235, Colorado Springs CO 80901. Tel (800)525-2474.

SHEPARD'S FEDERAL LABOR LAW CITATIONS. CASES. (SHEPARD'S FEDERAL LABOR LAW CITATIONS: CASES). VFOAT Federal Labor Law Citations. 1st- Ed. 0730-4676. US. English. ir. $590.00. McGraw-Hill, PO Box 1235, Colorado Springs CO 80901. Tel (800)525-2474. Devoted to decisions and orders of the National Labor Relations Board and decisions of the federal courts on labor matters.

SHEPARD'S FEDERAL LAW CITATIONS IN SELECTED LAW REVIEWS. VFOAT Federal Law Citations in Selected Law Reviews. V. 1- Mar. 1974-. 0094-9531. US. English. ir. $135.00. Shepards McGraw Hill, PO Box 1235, Colorado Springs CO 80901. Tel (800)525-2474. LC KF105.2. DD 348.7347. A citation system showing citations in articles in selected leading reviews to the opinions of the United States Supreme Court reports.

SHEPARD'S FEDERAL OCCUPATIONAL SAFETY AND HEALTH CITATIONS. Vol. 1, No. 1 (Nov. 1981)-. 0732-7722. Periodical. US. English. qt. $130.00. Shepards McGraw Hill, PO Box 1235, Colorado Springs CO 80901. Tel (800)525-2474. LC KF3568.15. DD 344.73046502646 347. 30446502646. Provides citations to federal cases, administrative decisions and statutes dealing with occupational safety and health.

SHEPARD'S FEDERAL TAX CITATIONS. VFOAT Federal Tax Citations. 1st Ed. (1980)-. 0732-7714. US. English. qt. $320.00. Shepards McGraw Hill, PO Box 1235, Colorado Springs CO 80901. Tel (800)525-2474. Includes these outstanding features, cross-references, citations to statutory laws, citations to treasury regulations, citations to all federal tax cases including US Tax Court regular and memorandum decisions.

SHEPARD'S FEDERAL TAX LOCATOR. VFOAT Federal Tax Locator. V. 1- 1974-. 0730-4714. US. English. ir. $330.00. Shepards McGraw Hill, PO Box 1235, Colorado Springs CO 80901. Tel (800)525-2474. Complete index to all the current sources of law relating to federal taxation.

SHEPARD'S FLORIDA CITATIONS. CASES. (SHEPARD'S FLORIDA CITATIONS : CASES). VFOAT Florida Citations. 3rd- Ed. 0730-3726. US. English. ir. $74.00. PO Box 1235, Colorado Springs CO 80901. *Shepard's Florida Citations.*

SHEPARD'S FLORIDA CITATIONS. CASES AND STATUTES. (SHEPARD'S FLORIDA CITATIONS : CASES AND STATUTES). VFOAT Florida Citations. 0730-3718. US. English. ir. $265.00. Shepards McGraw Hill, PO Box 1235, Colorado Springs CO 80901. Tel (800)525-2474. Gives you every citing reference to the statute in question ever made by your appellate courts.

SHEPARD'S GEORGIA CASE NAME CITATOR. 8750-1074. Periodical. US. English. qt. $35.00. McGraw-Hill Inc, 420 North Cascade Avenue, Colorado Springs CO 80903. DD 348.

SHEPARD'S HAWAII CITATIONS. 1st- Ed. 0730-5885. US. English. ty. $170.00. Shepards McGraw Hill, PO Box 1235, Colorado Springs CO 80901. Tel (800)525-2474. Gives you every citing reference to the statute in question ever made by your appellate courts.

SHEPARD'S IDAHO CITATIONS. CASES AND STATUTES. VFOAT Idaho Citations. 0730-5893. US. English. ir. $200.00. Shepards McGraw Hill, PO Box 1235, Colorado Springs CO 80901. Tel (800)525-2474. Gives you every citing reference to the statute in question ever made by your appellate courts.

SHEPARD'S ILLINOIS CITATIONS. CASES AND STATUTES. VFOAT Illinois Citations. Cases and Statutes. 0730-3904. US. English. ir. $400.00. Shepards McGraw Hill, PO Box 1235, Colorado Springs CO 80901. Tel (800)525-2474. Gives you every citing reference to the statute in question ever made by your appellate courts.

SHEPARD'S IMMIGRATION AND NATURALIZATION CITATIONS. VFOAT Immigration and Naturalization Citations. 1st Ed. (1982)-. 0746-3138. US. English. qt. $135.00. Shepards McGraw Hill, PO Box 1235, Colorado Springs CO 80901. Tel (800)525-2474. Brings together important citations from all the sources you need to consider.

SHEPARD'S INDIANA CITATIONS. CASES AND STATUTES. VFOAT Indiana Citations. 0730-3831. US. English. ir. $325.00. Shepards McGraw Hill, PO Box 1235, Colorado Springs CO 80901. Tel (800)525-2474. Gives your every citing reference to the statute in question ever made by your appellate courts.

SHEPARD'S KENTUCKY CITATIONS. CASES AND STATUTES. VFOAT Kentucky Citations. 0730-3971. US. English. ir. $200.00. Shepards McGraw Hill, PO Box 1235, Colorado Springs CO 80901. Tel (800)525-2474. Gives you every citing reference to the statute in question ever made by your appellate courts.

Law

SHEPARD'S KENTUCKY CITATIONS. STATUTES. (SHEPARD'S KENTUCKY CITATIONS : STATUTES). **VFOAT** Kentucky Citations. 2d- Ed. 0730-3998. US. English. ir. Available only with Cases. Shepards McGraw Hill, PO Box 1235, Colorado Springs CO 80901. **Tel** (800)525-2474. Gives you every citing reference to the statute in question ever made by your appellate courts. *Shepard's Kentucky Citations.*

SHEPARD'S LAW REVIEW CITATIONS. **VFOAT** Law Review Citations. 1st- Ed. 0582-9887. US. English. ir. $75.00. Shepards McGraw Hill, PO Box 1235, Colorado Springs CO 80901. **Tel** (800)525-2474. **LC** KF105.2. Law review articles which often treat developing areas of law, are a good source of 'in-point' cases. To locate such authorities and to expand research in this area, this citator is an ideal tool.

SHEPARD'S MAINE CITATIONS. (SHEPARD'S MAINE CITATIONS: CASES AND STATUTES). **VFOAT** Maine Citations. 0730-5923. US. English. ir. $160.00. Shepards McGraw Hill, PO Box 1235, Colorado Springs CO 80901. **Tel** (800)525-2474. Gives you every citing reference to the statute in question ever made by your appellate courts.

SHEPARD'S MANUAL OF FEDERAL PRACTICE. US. English. an. $80.00. Shepards McGraw Hill, PO Box 1235, Colorado Springs CO 80901. **Tel** (800)525-2474. Completely revised and updated guide to litigation on the federal level.

SHEPARD'S MICHIGAN CITATIONS. CASES AND STATUTES. **VFOAT** Michigan Citations. 0730-4102. US. English. ir. $275.00. Shepards McGraw Hill, PO Box 1235, Colorado Springs CO 80901. **Tel** (800)525-2474. Gives you every citing reference to the statute in question ever made by your appellate courts.

SHEPARD'S MILITARY JUSTICE CITATIONS. **VFOAT** Military Justice Citations. V. 1- Mar. 1978-. 0163-1101. Periodical. US. English. ir. $115.00. Shepards McGraw Hill, PO Box 1235, Colorado Springs CO 80901. **Tel** (800)525-2474. A compilation of citations that gives you a comprehensive research tool to current decisions of military courts and official military codes, orders and more.

SHEPARD'S MINNESOTA CITATIONS. CASES AND STATUTES. **VFOAT** Minnesota Citations. 0730-4145. US. English. ir. $200.00. Shepards McGraw Hill, PO Box 1235, Colorado Springs CO 80901. **Tel** (800)525-2474. Gives you every citing reference to the statute in question ever made by your appellate courts.

SHEPARD'S MISSISSIPPI CITATION. CASES AND STATUTES. Vol. 25, No. 3 (Feb. 1982)-. 0734-0443. US. English. ir. $220.00. Shepards McGraw Hill, PO Box 1235, Colorado Springs CO 80901. **Tel** (800)525-2474. Gives you every citing reference to the statute in question ever made by your appellate courts. *Shepard's Mississippi Citations,* 0488-6119.

SHEPARD'S MONTANA CITATIONS. (SHEPARD'S MONTANA CITATIONS, CASES AND STATUTES). **VFOAT** Montana Citations. 2nd Ed 0730-5931. US. English. ir. $150.00. Shepards McGraw Hill, PO Box 1235, Colorado Springs CO 80901. **Tel** (800)525-2474. Gives you every citing reference to the statute in question ever made by your appellate courts. *Shepard's Montana Citations and Annotations.*

SHEPARD'S NEBRASKA CITATIONS. CASES AND STATUTES. **VFOAT** Nebraska Citations. 0730-594X. US. English. ir. $220.00. Shepards McGraw Hill, PO Box 1235, Colorado Springs CO 80901. **Tel** (800)525-2474. Gives you every citing reference to the statute in question ever made by your appellate courts.

SHEPARD'S NEBRASKA CITATIONS. STATUTES. (SHEPARD'S NEBRASKA CITATIONS : STATUTES). **VFOAT** Nebraska Citations. 5th- Ed. 0730-5966. US. English. ir. Available only with Cases. Shepards McGraw Hill, PO Box 1235, Colorado Springs CO 80901. **Tel** (800)525-2474. Gives you every citing reference to the statute in question ever made by your appellate courts. *Shepard's Nebraska Citations.*

SHEPARD'S NEW JERSEY CITATIONS. CASES. (SHEPARD'S NEW JERSEY CITATIONS : CASES). **VFOAT** New Jersey Citations. 5th- Ed. 0730-4218. US. English. ir. Available only with Cases. Shepards McGraw Hill, PO Box 1235, Colorado Springs CO 80901. **Tel** (800)525-2474. Gives you every citing reference to the statute in question ever made by your appellate courts. *Shepard's New Jersey Citations.*

SHEPARD'S NEW YORK COURT OF APPEALS CITATIONS, COMMON LAW AND CHANCERY. **VFOAT** New York Court of Appeals Citations, Common Law and Chancery. Vol. 1- 1941-. 0730-4277. US. English. ir. $275.00. Shepards McGraw Hill, PO Box 1235, Colorado Springs CO 80901. **Tel** (800)525-2474. Gives you every citing reference to the statute in question ever made by your appellate courts.

SHEPARD'S NEW YORK MISCELLANEOUS CITATIONS. **VFOAT** New York Miscellaneous Citations. 1st- Ed. 0730-4269. US. English. ir. $190.00. Shepards McGraw Hill, PO Box 1235, Colorado Springs CO 80901. **Tel** (800)525-2474. Gives you every citing reference to the statute in question ever made by your appellate courts.

SHEPARD'S NEW YORK STATUTE CITATIONS. **VFOAT** New York Statute Citations. V. 1- 1940-. 0730-4242. US. English. ir. $275.00. Shepards McGraw Hill, PO Box 1235, Colorado Springs CO 80901. **Tel** (800)525-2474. Gives you every citing reference to the statute in question ever made by your appellate courts.

SHEPARD'S NEW YORK SUPPLEMENT CITATIONS. **VFOAT** New York Supplement Citations. 2d- Ed. 0730-4234. US. English. ir. $450.00. Shepards McGraw Hill, PO Box 1235, Colorado Springs CO 80901. **Tel** (800)525-2474. Gives you every citing reference to the statute in question ever made by your appellate courts. *Shepard's New York Supplement Analyzed Citations and Annotations.*

SHEPARD'S NEW YORK SUPREME COURT CITATIONS. **VFOAT** New York Supreme Court Citations. Vol. 1- 1942-. 0730-4285. US. English. ir. $275.00. Shepards McGraw Hill, PO Box 1235, Colorado Springs CO 80901. **Tel** (800)525-2474. Gives you every citing reference to the statute in question ever made by your appellate courts.

SHEPARD'S NORTH CAROLINA CITATIONS. CASES AND STATUTES. **VFOAT** North Carolina Citations. 0730-2126. US. English. ir. $240.00. Shepards McGraw Hill, PO Box 1235, Colorado Springs CO 80901. **Tel** (800)525-2474. Gives you every citing reference to the statute in question ever made by your appellate courts.

SHEPARD'S NORTHWESTERN REPORTER CITATIONS. **VFOAT** Northwestern Reporter Citations. 2nd Ed. 0730-4706. US. English. ir. $400.00. Shepards McGraw Hill, PO Box 1235, Colorado Springs CO 80901. **Tel** (800)525-2474. Gives you every state and federal citation to every reporter case as cited anywhere throughout the entire National Reporter System.

SHEPARD'S OHIO CITATIONS. STATUTES. (SHEPARD'S OHIO CITATIONS : STATUTES). **VFOAT** Ohio Citations. 5th- Ed. 0730-4315. US. English. ir. Available only with Cases. Shepards McGraw Hill, PO Box 1235, Colorado Springs CO 80901. **Tel** (800)525-2474. Gives you every citing reference to the statute in question ever made by your appellate courts. *Shepard's Ohio Citations.*

SHEPARD'S OKLAHOMA CITATIONS. CASES AND STATUTES. **VFOAT** Oklahoma Citations. 0730-4323. US. English. ir. $200.00. Shepards McGraw Hill, PO Box 1235, Colorado Springs CO 80901. **Tel** (800)525-2474. Gives you every citing reference to the statute in question ever made by your appellate courts.

SHEPARD'S PARTNERSHIP LAW CITATIONS. 8750-1112. Periodical. US. English. qt. $125.00. Shepards McGraw Hill Inc, 420 North Cascade Avenue, Colorado Springs CO 80903. **Tel** (800)525-2474. **DD** 346. The only source available in this specialized field with in-depth coverage from formation to dissolution of a partnership.

SHEPARD'S PRODUCTS LIABILITY CITATIONS. 8750-1139. Periodical. US. English. qt. $115.00. Shepards McGraw Hill Inc, 420 North Cascade Avenue, Colorado Springs CO 80903. **Tel** (800)525-2474. **DD** 348. Easy-to-find, clear listing of case names and dates on every page. Plus a case name table listing cases alphabetically with both the plaintiff's and defendant's name.

SHEPARD'S PROFESSIONAL AND JUDICIAL CONDUCT CITATIONS. **VFOAT** Professional and Judicial Conduct Citations. Vol. 1, No. 1 (Nov. 1980)-. 0730-6229. US. English. Shepards McGraw Hill, PO Box 1235, Colorado Springs CO 80901. **Tel** (800)525-2474. **LC** KF308.A535. **DD** 174.30973. Attention is being given toward how lawyers and judges police their own professions.

SHEPARD'S RESTATEMENT OF THE LAW CITATIONS. **VFOAT** Restatement of the Law Citations. 1st- Ed. 0730-4641. US. English. ir. $170.00. Shepards McGraw Hill, PO Box 1235, Colorado Springs CO 80901. **Tel** (800)525-2474. Covering citations to the American Law Institute's Restatement of the Law, this research tool is of the utmost importance for attorneys throughout the nation.

SHEPARD'S SOUTHEASTERN REPORTER CITATIONS. **VFOAT** Southeastern Reporter Citations. 1st- Ed. 0730-4692. US. English. ir. $340.00. Shepards McGraw Hill, PO Box 1235, Colorado Springs CO 80901. **Tel** (800)525-2474. Gives you every state and federal citation to every reporter case as cited anywhere throughout the entire National Reporter System.

SHEPARD'S TENNESSEE CITATIONS. CASES. (SHEPARD'S TENNESSEE CITATIONS : CASES). **VFOAT** Tennessee Citations. 3rd- Ed. 0730-4447. US. English. ir. Available only with Statutes. Shepards McGraw Hill, PO Box 1235, Colorado Springs CO 80901. **Tel** (800)525-2474. Gives you every citing reference to the statute in question ever made by your appellate courts. *Shepard's Tennessee Citations.*

SHEPARD'S TENNESSEE CITATIONS. CASES AND STATUTES. **VFOAT** Tennessee Citations. 0730-4439. US. English. ir. $220.00. Shepards McGraw Hill, PO Box 1235, Colorado Springs CO 80901. **Tel** (800)525-2474. Gives you every citing reference to the statute in question ever made by your appellate courts.

SHEPARD'S TEXAS CITATIONS. STATUTES. (SHEPARD'S TEXAS CITATIONS : STATUTES). **VFOAT** Texas Citations. 4th- Ed. 0730-448X. US. English. ir. Available only with Cases. Shepards McGraw Hill, PO Box 1235, Colorado Springs CO 80901. **Tel** (800)525-2474. Gives you every citing reference to the statute in question ever made by your appellate courts. *Shepard's Texas Citations.*

SHEPARD'S UNITED STATES ADMINISTRATIVE CITATIONS. **VFOAT** United States Administrative Citations. 1st- Ed. 0582-9909. US. English. ir. $300.00. Shepards McGraw Hill, PO Box 1235, Colorado Springs CO 80901. **Tel** (800)525-2474. A comprehensive system showing citations to decisions and orders of federal administrative departments, courts, boards and commissions.

SHEPARD'S UNITED STATES CITATIONS. 5th- Ed. English. ir. $680.00. Shepards McGraw Hill, PO Box 1235, Colorado Springs CO 80901. **Tel** (800)525-2474. Provides a comprehensive system of legal research covering decisions of the US Supreme Court and statutes enacted by Congress. *Shepard's United States Citations and Annotations.*

SHEPARD'S UNITED STATES CITATIONS: CASES. A COMPILATION OF CITATIONS TO UNITED STATES SUPREME COURT CASES. 1st- Ed. US. English. ir. $680.00. Shepards McGraw Hill, PO Box 1235, Colorado Springs CO 80901. **Tel** (800)525-2474. **LC** KF101.2. Devoted to decisions and orders of the National Labor Relations Board and decisions of the federal courts on labor matters.

SHEPARD'S UNITED STATES PATENTS AND TRADEMARKS CITATIONS. **VFOAT** Shepards United States Citations: Patents, Patent Appeals, Copyrights, Cross Reference Tables. 1st- Ed. 0582-9917. US. English. ir. $345.00. Shepards McGraw Hill, PO Box 1235, Colorado Springs CO 80901. **Tel** (800)525-2474. Shows citations to the United States patents, trademarks and copyrights as well as to court decisions, administrative decisions and rules and

Law

regulations relating to patents, trademarks and copyrights.

SHEPARD'S WASHINGTON CITATIONS. CASES AND STATUTES. VFOAT Washington Citations. Cases and Statutes. 0730-4528. US. English. ir. $225.00. Shepards McGraw Hill, PO Box 1235, Colorado Springs CO 80901. Tel (800)525-2474. Gives you every citing reference to the statute in question ever made by your appellate courts.

THE SHINGLE. V. 1- Jan. 1938-. 0037-377X. Periodical. US. English. ir. $10.00. Philadelphia Bar Association, 1339 Chestnut Street/2nd Floor, Philadelphia PA 19107. Tel (215)686-5686. Ed Nancy L Hebble. LC K23. bk rev. adv acc. Circ 10,000. (ctrl). Law-related articles, news features, profiles, opinion pieces, humor, travel, and interviews. Directed to membership of Philadelphia Bar Association.

SHOROPPO. Main/Corp Japan. Began with Vol. for 1949. Japanese. ir. 16.00. Yuhikaku, 17 Kanda Jimbcho 2, Chiyoda-ku 101 Tokyo Japan.

SHUSHO NEMPO - HOMUSHO HOMU TOSHOKAN. Main/Corp Japan. Homusho. Homu Toshokan. Japanese, English, French or German. ir. c/o Homu Daijin Kambo Shiho Hosei Chosabu, 1-1 Kasumigaseki 1, Chiyoda-ku Tokyo 100 Japan. LC K40.

SIGNIFICANT DECISIONS OF THE SUPREME COURT. 1969/70- Term. 0162-0444. Periodical. US. English. an. $6.25. American Enterprise Institute Public Policy, 1150-17th Street NW, Washington DC 20036. Tel (202)862-5800. Ed B E Fein. LC KF4547.8. DD 348.7344.

SIGNIFICANT PROVISIONS OF STATE UNEMPLOYMENT INSURANCE LAWS. US. English. sa. US Department of Labor, Employment and Training Administration, Washington DC 20213.

SIGNIFICANT SEC FILINGS REPORTER. VAT Significant Securities and Exchange Commission Filings Reporter. 0199-6177. US. English. mo. $435.00. Washington Service Bureau Inc, 655 15th Street NW, Washington DC 20005. Tel (202)833-9200. Circ 300. (ctrl). Indexes and abstracts, significant and unusual proxy statements, registration statements and Williams Act filings from the Securities and Exchange Commission.

SIGNIFICANT STATE APPELLATE DECISIONS OUTLINE. Main/Corp National College of the State Judiciary. 1976-. 0145-8590. US. English. an. College of the State Judiciary, Judicial College Building, University of Nevada, Reno NV 89557. LC KF148. DD 348.7346.

SIMON'S TAX CASES. Jan. 12, 1973-. UK. English. an. 19 Cummings Park, Woburn MA 01801. LC KD5355.A2. DD 343.41040264.

SINGAPORE'S JUDICIAL & LEGAL DIRECTORY. See Yearbooks, Almanacs, Directories.

SKATTERETT. VFOAT Skatte Rett. 82-1-. 0333-2810. Periodical. NO. Norwegian. ir. 100.00 Students, 200.00 Others. Universitetsforlaget, Abonnementseksjonen Boks 2959 Tyen, Oslo 6 Norway. LC K23. DD 343.4810405, 344.8103405.

SLIP OPINION. Main/Corp United States. Supreme Court. Periodical. US. English. ir. US Government Printing Office, Superintendent of Documents, Washington DC 20402. Tel (202)783-3238.

AN SMU LAW SCHOOL STUDY. Main/Corp Dallas. Southern Methodist University. School of Law. US. English. ir. Southern Methodist University, Department of English, c/o Theresa Enos, Dallas TX 75275.

SNR, SUPERINTENDENCIA DE NOTARIADO Y REGISTRO. Main/Corp Colombia. Superintendencia de Notariado y Registro. Spanish. ir. LC K14. NR.

SOCIAL ACTION & THE LAW. See Social Sciences (General).

SOCIALISTICKA ZAKONNOST. Vol. 1-. Periodical. UR. Czech. mo. $18.00. Victor Kamkin Inc (70871), 12224 Parklawn Drive, Rockville MD 20852. Tel (301)881-5973.

SOCIEDAD Y DERECHO. Nov. 1973-Jan. 1974—. Spanish. ir. Jiron Huancavelica No 470-Of 308, Lima Peru. LC K23.

SOCIEDADES POR ACOES. Study 5-. Periodical. Portuguese. ir. Editora Resenha Universitaria, Rua Quatinga 12-3 Andar, 04140 Sao Paulo Brazil. LC K23. DD 346.8106605.

LE SOCIETA. Yearly V. 1, No. 1, Jan. 31, 1982)-. Periodical. Italian. mo. 200.000. IPSOA S.P.A.L., Go Augusto 8, 20122 Milano Italy.

SOCIOLOGIA DEL DIRITTO. 1-. 0390-0851. IT. Italian. ty. $29.70. Franco Angeli Editore Riviste, Via le Monza 106, 20127 Milano Italy. Tel (02)28.27.651/2/3. Ind/Abst Sociol. Abstr., Soc. Welf. Soc. Plan./Policy Soc. Dev. LC K23.

SOFTWARE PROTECTION. Vol. 1, No. 1-. 0733-1274. Periodical. US. English. mo. $127.00. Law and Technology Press, PO Box 3280, Manhattan Beach CA 90266. Tel (213)372-1678. Ed Michael D Scott. LC KF3024.C6. DD 346.730482, 347.306482. bk rev. A report on the legal, technical, and practical aspects of protecting computer software. Worldwide.

SOLAR LAW : PRESENT AND FUTURE : WITH PROPOSED FORMS. CUMULATIVE SUPPLEMENT. VFOAT Solar Law Cumulative Supplement. Began with 1980. US. English. an. $75.00. Shepards McGraw Hill, PO Box 1235, Colorado Springs CO 80901. Tel (800)525-2474. Tailored for attorneys who represent local government, builders, developers, and consumers. This updated reference book with forms has become the classic work in this controversial area of law.

THE SOLICITORS' DIARY CEASED. VFOAT Solicitor's Diary and Directory, Solicitor's Diary & Directory. UK. English. an. Waterlow Publishers Ltd, Maxwell House 74 Worship Street, London EC2A England. LC KD336. DD 340.02541.

THE SOLICITOR'S JOURNAL AND REPORTER. Vol. 1, No. 1 (Jan. 3, 1857)-V 50, No. 52 (Oct. 27, 1906). 0038-1047. Periodical. UK. English. ir. $80.00. Longman Group Ltd Journals Department, 21-27 Lamb's Conduit Street, London WC1N 3NJ England. Ind/Abst Index Leg. Period., Curr. Law Index, Leg. Resour. Index. (cum index). Legal Observer, and, Solicitors' Journal.

SOLICITORS' JOURNAL (LONDON, ENGLAND : 1928). (THE SOLICITOR'S JOURNAL). Vol. 72, No. 1 (Jan. 7, 1928)-. Periodical. UK. English. wk. $80.00. Solicitors' Journal, 21-27 Lamb's Conduit Street, London WC1N 3NJ England. Tel 01-242 2548. bk rev. adv acc. Circ 6,000. Magazine on UK and international law. Solicitors' Journal and Weekly Reporter.

SOLICITORS' LIABILITY INDEX. See Indexes/Abstracts.

SOMMAIRES DE DROIT DU TRAVAIL. 0223-7164. French. ir. 430. 18 Avenue de la Marne, 92600 Asnieres la France. DD 344.440105, 344.404105.

SOUNDS ABOUT SUNDAY (1981). (SOUNDS ABOUT SUNDAY). 0712-5836. Periodical. CN. English. Lord's Day Alliance Of Canada, Box 457, Islington Ontario M9A 4X4 Canada. DD 344.71012574. Sunday Update News, 0711-219X.

THE SOURCE BOOK OF AMERICAN STATE LEGISLATION. 1980-. 0730-1154. US. English. be. $7.00. ALEC, 418 C Street Northeast of the Capitol, Washington DC 20002. LC KF165. DD 348.73205, 347.320805. Suggested State Legislation (Washington, D.C.).

SOURCES OF COMPILED LEGISLATIVE HISTORIES. See Bibliographies.

THE SOUTH AFRICAN COMPANY LAW JOURNAL. 1977-. SA. English. qt. 20. Hyfam Promotions, PO Box 92296, Norwood 2117 South Africa. DD 346.6806605.

THE SOUTH AFRICAN LAW REPORTS. 1947. SA. English. qt. $85.91. Juta and Company Ltd, Box 123, Kenwyn 7790 South Africa. Tel 021/711181. Ed D S Fisher. Circ 5,570. (ctrl). Official reports of the South African law courts from 1947 including index table of cases overruled considered, discussed, etc.

SOUTH AFRICAN TAX CASES, INCLUDING DECISIONS OF THE SUPREME COURT OF SOUTH AFRICA, THE HIGH COURT OF RHODESIA AND THE SPECIAL COURTS FOR HEARING INCOME TAX APPEALS. Main/Corp South Africa. Supreme Court. Vol. 1, Pt. I- 1925-. 0038-2752. SA. English. ir. Juta and Company, Box 123, Kenwyn 7790 South Africa. Ind/Abst Index Foreign Leg. Per. Collect. Essays. (cum index).

THE SOUTH AUSTRALIAN STATE REPORTS. Main/Corp South Australia. Supreme Court. V. 1- 1971-. 0049-1470. AT. English. qt. Methuen Law Book Company Ltd, 35 Mitchell Street, c/o Bennett-EBSCO, North Sydney 2060 Australia. Index in last issue of volume - attached. State Reports, South Australia.

SOUTH CAROLINA LAW REVIEW. Vol. 15, No. 1-. 0038-3104. Periodical. US. English. qt. University of South Carolina, School of Law, Columbia SC 29208. Tel (803)777-5874. Ind/Abst Leg. Resour. Index, Index Leg. Period., Contents Curr. Leg. Period., Curr. Law Index. DD 340.05. (cum index). South Carolina Law Quarterly, 0276-9441.

SOUTH CAROLINA STATE REGISTER. V. 1- Mar. 18, 1977-. US. English. mo $75.00. South Carolina State Register, PO Box 11417, Columbia SC 29211. Tel (803)758-2306. LC KFS1836. DD 348.75701.

SOUTH DAKOTA LAW REVIEW. V. 1- Spring 1956-. 0038-3325. Periodical. US. English. ty. $15.00. University of South Dakota, School of Law, Vermillion SD 57069. Tel (605)677-5646. Ed C Frank Carbiener. Ind/Abst Leg. Resour. Index, Sel. Water Resour. Abstr., Index Leg. Period., Curr. Law Index, Contents Curr. Leg. Period. LC K23. DD 340.09783. (cum index). bk rev. adv acc. Circ 1,200. (ctrl). A scholarly legal journal. It publishes articles of both national and state interest and specializes in agricultural law.

SOUTH DAKOTA LEGISLATIVE MANUAL. VFOAT South Dakota Manual. 0362-2738. US. English. be. State Publishing Company, Pierre SD 57501. LC JK6531.

SOUTH DAKOTA REGISTER. 0191-1104. Periodical. US. English. wk. $20.00. Assistant Code Counsel of the Legislative Research Council, State Capitol Building, Pierre SD 57501. Tel (605)773-3251. Ed Thomas R Vickermann. LC KFS3036. DD 348.783028. Circ 330. Contains synopses of proposed rules filed with code counsel and adopted rules, executive orders and appointments, and Supreme Court rules filed with Secretary of State.

SOUTH DAKOTA UNIFIED COURTS. 0146-3241. US. English. State Capitol, Pierre SD 57501. LC KFS3510.A15. DD 347.78301.

SOUTH DAKOTA UNIFIED JUDICIAL SYSTEM. US. English. South Dakota Supreme Court, Office of Court Administration, Pierre SD 57501. LC KFS3510.A15. DD 347.7830105. South Dakota Unified Courts, 0146-3241.

SOUTH EASTERN REPORTER. SECOND SERIES. (SOUTH EASTERN REPORTER. SECOND SERIES. CASES ARGUED AND DETERMINED IN THE COURTS OF GEORGIA, NORTH CAROLINA, SOUTH CAROLINA, VIRGINIA, WEST VIRGINIA). VFOAT Southeastern Reporter. V. 1- S.E. 2D. 0584-4215. Periodical. US. English. wk. $97.50. West Publishing Company, 50 West Kellogg Boulevard, St Paul MN 55165. LC KF135.S6. DD 348.

SOUTH TEXAS LAW JOURNAL CEASED. Vol. 1, No. 1 (Apr. 1954)-. 0038-3546. Periodical. US. English. ir. $25.44. South Texas Law Journal Inc, 1303 San Jacinto Street, Houston TX 77002. Tel (713)659-8040. Ed R S Marsel. Ind/Abst Leg. Resour. Index, Index Leg. Period., Curr. Law Index, Contents Curr. Leg. Period. LC UNC. DD 340. (cum index). bk rev. adv acc. Circ 3,000. Articles on the American legal system by distinguished judges, lawyers and academics.

SOUTH TEXAS LAW REVIEW. Vol. 27, No. 1 (Spring 1986)-. Periodical. US. English. ty. $31.84. South Texas Law Review Inc, 1303 San Jacinto, Houston TX 77002. South Texas Law Journal, 0038-3546.

SOUTH WESTERN REPORTER. SECOND SERIES. VFOAT Southwestern Reporter. Vol. 1, 2D (Feb. 15-Mar. 7, 1928)-. 8750-2682. US. English. wk. West Publishing Company, 50 West Kellogg Boulevard, St Paul MN 55102. DD 348. South Western Reporter.

SOUTHERN CALIFORNIA GROUP LEGAL SERVICES DIRECTORY. See Yearbooks, Almanacs, Directories.

SOUTHERN CALIFORNIA LAW REVIEW. Vol. 1, No. 1 (Nov. 1927)-. 0038-3910. Periodical. US. English. bm. University of Southern California, 314 Law Center University Park, Los

Angeles CA 90007. **Tel** (213)743-6366. **Ind/Abst** Manage. Contents, Leg. Resour. Index, Index Leg. Period., Soc. Sci. Citation Index, Curr. Law Index, Contents Curr. Leg. Period. **LC** K23. **DD** 340.05. Index published separately - free - automatically sent. (cum index).

SOUTHERN ILLINOIS UNIVERSITY LAW JOURNAL. May 1976-. 0145-3432. Periodical. US. English. $15.00. Southern Illinois University, School of Law, Carbondale IL 62901. **Tel** (618)536-7711. **Ind/Abst** Index Leg. Period., Leg. Resour. Index, Curr. Law Index, Contents Curr. Leg. Period. **LC** K23. **DD** 340.05. adv acc. **Circ** 525. Publishes lead articles, casenotes, and comments on legal topics of general interest.

SOUTHERN METHODIST UNIVERSITY SYMPOSIA ON FEDERAL TAXATION. **Main/Corp** Southern Methodist University. School of Law. 0193-1083. Periodical. US. English. an. $49.50. Tax Research Institute of America, 589 5th Avenue, New York NY 10017.

SOUTHERN REPORTER. SECOND SERIES. (SOUTHERN REPORTER. SECOND SERIES. CASES ARGUED AND DETERMINED IN THE COURTS OF ALABAMA, FLORIDA, LOUISIANA, MISSISSIPPI). V. 1- SO. 2d. 8750-2690. Periodical. US. English. wk. West Publishing Company, 50 West Kellogg Boulevard, St Paul MN 55102. **LC** KF135.S8. **DD** 348. *Southern Reporter.*

SOUTHERN SCHOOL LAW DIGEST. 0361-0861. US. English. mo. 520 First Federal Building, Tuscaloosa AL 35401. **LC** KF4114. **DD** 344.750702648.

SOUTHERN UNIVERSITY LAW REVIEW. V. 1- Fall 1974-. 0099-1465. Periodical. US. English. sa. $10.00. Southern University, School of Law, Southern Branch PO, Baton Rouge LA 70813. **Tel** (504)771-2223. **Ind/Abst** Leg. Resour. Index, Index Leg. Period., Curr. Law Index, Contents Curr. Leg. Period. **LC** K12. **DD** 340.09763. bk rev. adv acc. Ideas in the areas of law- criminal and civil.

SOUTHWESTERN LAW JOURNAL. Vol. 2, No. 1 (Spring 1948)-. 0038-4836. Periodical. US. English. ir. $27.00. Southern Methodist University, School of Law, Dallas TX 75275. **Tel** (214)692-2594. **Ind/Abst** Leg. Resour. Index, Index Leg. Period., Curr. Law Index, Contents Curr. Leg. Period. **LC** K23. **DD** 340.05. (cum index). adv acc. **Circ** 1,200. Leading articles and student notes and comments covering timely subjects in Texas, national and international law. *Texas Law and Legislation.*

SOUTHWESTERN UNIVERSITY LAW REVIEW. **VFOAT** Southwestern Nevada Law Review. Vol. 3, No. 1 (Spring 1971)-. Periodical. US. English. qt. $10.00. SW University School of Law, 675 South Westmoreland Avenue, Los Angeles CA 90005. **Ind/Abst** Leg. Resour. Index, Index Leg. Period. **LC** K12. **DD** 340.05. (cum index). *Southwestern Law Review.*

SOVETSKOE GOSUDARSTVO I PRAVO. Began publication in 1939. 0132-0769. Periodical. UR. Russian (table of contents also in English). mo. $49.00. Victor Kamkin Inc (70866), 12224 Parklawn Drive, Rockville MD 20852. **Tel** (301)881-5973. **Ind/Abst** Sociol. Abstr., Soc. Welf. Soc. Plan./Policy Soc. Dev. **DD** 349.4709, 344.7009. *Sovetskoe Gosudarstvo.*

SOVIET JEWRY LAW REVIEW. V. 1- Jan. 1980-. 0272-2453. Periodical. US. English. Soviet Jewry Law Review, Suite 920/870 Market Street, San Francisco CA 94102. **LC** K23. **DD** 342.470873.

SOVIET LAW AND GOVERNMENT. V. 1- Summer 1962-. 0038-5530. Periodical. US. English (selected articles from Soviet Scholarly Journals in Translation (varies slightly)). qt. $178.50. M E Sharpe Inc, 80 Business Park Drive, Armonk NY 10504. **Tel** (914)273-1800. **Ed** Nils H Wessell. **Ind/Abst** Public Aff. Inf. Serv. Bull., Soc. Sci. Citation Index. **DD** 348.47. adv acc. **Circ** 350. Studies from a wide variety of Soviet sources on the interactions of law, government, and society in the USSR.

SOVIET STATUTES & DECISIONS. **VAT** Soviet Statutes and Decisions. V. 1- Fall 1964-. 0038-5840. Periodical. US. English. qt. $178.50. M E Sharpe Inc, 80 Business Park Drive, Armonk NY 10504. **Tel** (914)273-1800. **Ed** Peter B Maggs. **Ind/Abst** Public Aff. Inf. Serv. Bull. **LC** K23. **DD** 347.47. adv acc. **Circ** 200. Each volume is devoted to a specific area of legislation or administrative regulation.

SOZEIHO KENKYU. **VFOAT** Japan Tax Law Review. Vol. 1-. JA. Japanese. ir. Yuhikaku, 2-17 Kanda Jimbocho, Chiyoda-ku (101) Tokyo Japan. **LC** K23.

SOZIALPOLITIK UND ARBEITSRECHT. German. ir. Signum Verlag, 1010 Wien Bosendorferstrasse 2, Wien Austria. **DD** 344.43601.

SPEAKERS' OUTLINES, FEDERAL PRACTICE AND PROCEDURE. **VFOAT** Federal Practice and Procedure. 1981-. US. English. Missouri Bar, 326 Monroe Street, Jefferson City MO 65101. **LC** KF8841. **DD** 347.735, 347.3075.

SPECIAL COURT NEWS. Began with April 1980-. 0275-2913. Periodical. US. English. American Bar Association, National Conference of Special Court Judges, 1155 East 80th Street, Chicago IL 80837. **LC** KF8759.A15. **DD** 347.732805, 347.307405.

THE SPECIAL LAWS ENACTED BY THE REGULAR SESSION OF THE LEGISLATIVE ASSEMBLY. **Main/Corp** Oregon. **VFOAT** Oregon Special Laws. US. English. Legislative Council Comm, 5101 State Capitol, Salem OR 97310. **LC** KFO2425. **DD** 348.795024, 347.950824.

SPECIAL LECTURES OF THE LAW SOCIETY OF UPPER CANADA. **Main/Corp** Law Society of Upper Canada. 1950-. 0316-5310. CN. English. an. **DD** 340.09713.

SPECIALTY LAW DIGEST. EDUCATION. **VFOAT** Education. Began in 1981. 0275-2107. Periodical. US. English. ir. $206.00. Bureau of National Affairs Inc, 1231 25th Street NW, Washington DC 20037. **Tel** (301)258-1033. **LC** KF4114. **DD** 344.730702638, 347.304702638.

SPEER'S DIGEST OF TOXIC SUBSTANCES STATE LAW. (SPEER'S DIGEST OF TOXIC SUBSTANCES STATE LAW : . . . TRENDS, SUMMARIES & FORECASTS). **VFOAT** Toxic Substances State Law. 1983/84- Ed. 8756-7059. US. English. Strategic Assessments Inc, 5000 Butte Street, Suite 132, Boulder CO 80301. **LC** KF3958.Z95. **DD** 344.73046, 347.30446.

S.P.E.L.D - INFORMATION : DROIT ECONOMIE POLITIQUE SCIENCES SOCIALES ET HUMAINES ERUDITION. Periodical. FR. French. qt. SPELD Information, 6 rue Victor-Cousin, 75005 Paris France. **Tel** 46.33.69.10. **Ind/Abst** Foreign Lang. Index. **Circ** 6,000. Books to come and new publications in law, economics, political and social sciences.

THE SPERRY LAWYER. V. 1- Spring 1977-. 0148-0901. Periodical. US. English. ty. Sperry Rand Corporation, 1290 Avenue of the Americans, New York NY 10016. **LC** K23. **DD** 340.05.

SPIDELL'S CALIFORNIA TAXLETTER. **Main/Corp** Spidell Publishing Inc. **VFOAT** California Taxletter. 0194-8237. Periodical. US. English. mo. $47.00. Spidell Publishing Inc, 239 South Magnolia Avenue, Anaheim CA 92804. **Tel** (714)821-6950. **Ed** Robert A Spidell. **Circ** 6,000. (ctrl). Provides a review and analysis of new California tax laws and tax law changes and interpretations.

SPOKESWOMAN FOR ABORTION LAW REPEAL. Began publication in 1972?. 0700-8279. Periodical. CN. English. 0.15 Each Number. Spokeswoman, PO Box 5673 Station A, Toronto Ontario M5W 1P1 Canada.

SPORTS AND THE COURTS. Began with winter 1980 issue. 0733-0669. Periodical. US. English. qt. $30.00. Sports and the Courts, PO Box 2836, Winston Salem NC 27102. **Tel** (919)725-0583. **Ed** Herb Apparzeller and Tom Ross. **LC** KF4166.A59. **DD** 344.73075, 347.30475. **Circ** 2,000. (ctrl). Reports current legal cases in sports, physical education, and recreation with editorial comment for administrators, coaches, and physical educators.

SPORTS LAW REPORTER. V. 1- May 1978-. 0195-8623. Periodical. US. English. mo. $45.00 Students, $75.00 Others. Sports Law Reporter, PO Box 695, Bronxville NY 10708. **LC** KF3989.A59. **DD** 344.73099.

SPRAVNI PRAVO. Began in 1968. Periodical. Czech. ir. **Ind/Abst** Energy Res. Abstr. **LC** K23. **DD** 342.43706, 344.37026.

THE SRI LANKA ATTORNEY-AT-LAW. V. 1- Aug. 1974-. English. ir. 2.50 Each Issue. Institute of Legal Executives of Sri Lanka, 54 3/2 Australia Building 1, Colombo Sri Lanka (Ceylon). **DD** 340.095493.

SRINAGAR LAW JOURNAL. V. 1- July 1979-. English. mo. 80.000. SLJ Publications, Court Road, Srinagar India 190001. **LC** K23. **DD** 349.5405.

SSU FA YUAN KUNG PAO. V. 1- 1959-. 0561-7642. Periodical. Chinese. ir.

DER STAAT. Vol. 1-. 0038-884X. Periodical. German. ir. Duncker and Humbolt, Dietrich-Schafer-Weg 9, 1 Berlin 41 West Germany. **Ind/Abst** Energy Res. Abstr., Foreign Lang. Index. Index published separately - free - automatically sent.

THE STANDARD CALIFORNIA CODES. **Main/Corp** California. Began with: 10th Ed., published in 1949. Periodical. US. English. an. Matthew Bender & Company Inc, 1275 Broadway, Albany NY 12201. **Tel** (800)833-9844. **Ed** Warren L Hanna. **LC** KFC30.5.S7. **DD** 347.794005, 347.9407005. *Laws, etc. Chase California Codes.*

THE STANDARD PENAL CODE AND SELECTED PENAL PROVISIONS OF THE STATE OF CALIFORNIA. **Main/Corp** California. Began in 1981. 0747-8690. US. English. an. **LC** KFC30.5.S7. **DD** 345.794002632, 347.9405002632. *Laws, etc. Standard California Codes.*

STANDING COMMITTEE ON AGRICULTURE. *See* Agriculture.

STANFORD ENVIRONMENTAL LAW ANNUAL. V. 1- 1978-. 0197-7873. US. English. an. $10.00. Stanford University, Environmental Law Annual, Stanford CA 94305. **Tel** (415)497-4421. **Ed** Mark Matthews, David Sadwick and Thomas Waldo. **Ind/Abst** Index Leg. Period., Curr. Law Index, Leg. Resour. Index. **LC** K23. **DD** 344.7304605. **Circ** 250. A publication concerning a particular subject of concern for the field of environmental law.

STANFORD LAW REVIEW. V. 1- Nov. 1948-. Periodical. US. English. bm. Stanford Law Review, Crown Quadransle 42, Stanford CA 94305. **Tel** (415)497-2474. (cum index).

STANFORD LAWYER. Began with: 1966. 0585-0576. Periodical. US. English. sa. Stanford Law School, Crown Quadrangle, Stanford CA 94305. **Ind/Abst** Leg. Resour. Index. **DD** 340.

STATE AND LAW. **VFOAT** (Panstwo I Prawo). 0031-0980. Periodical. PL. Polish. mo. ARS Polona, Krakowskie Przedmiescie 7, 00-068 Warsaw Poland. **Ind/Abst** Am. Hist. Life, Hist. Abstr.

THE STATE BAR OF NEW MEXICO BULLETIN AND ADVANCE OPINIONS. (THE STATE BAR OF NEW MEXICO BULLETIN & ADVANCE OPINIONS). **VFOAT** Bulletin and Advance Opinions. V. 1-20, No. 36. 0039-0038. Periodical. US. English. wk.

STATE BAR SECTION REPORT. GENERAL PRACTICE. **Main/Corp** State Bar of Texas. US. English. State Bar of Texas, Box 12487 Capitol Station, Austin TX 78711. **LC** KF200. **DD** 347.764050405.

STATE COURT CASELOAD STATISTICS, ADVANCE REPORT. *See* Statistics.

STATE COURT CASELOAD STATISTICS, ANNUAL REPORT. *See* Statistics.

STATE COURT JOURNAL. V. 1- Winter 1977-. 0145-3076. Periodical. US. English. qt. $24.00. National Center for State Courts, 300 Newport Avenue, Williamsburg VA 23185. **Tel** (804)253-2000. **Ed** Madelyn McRae. **Ind/Abst** Leg. Resour. Index, Curr. Law Index, Contents Curr. Leg. Period. **LC** KF8732.A15. **DD** 347.733. **Circ** 2,000. (ctrl). Articles based on reports of projects carried out by NCSC staff. Column Washington perspective.

STATE DIRECTORY OF KENTUCKY. *See* Yearbooks, Almanacs, Directories.

STATE JUDICIARY NEWS. V. 1- May 1975-. 0363-1362. Periodical. US. English. Council of State Governments, PO Box 11910, Lexington KY 40511. **LC** KF8736.A15. **DD** 347.73105.

STATE LAW INDEX. *See* Indexes/Abstracts.

STATE LAWS AND PUBLISHED ORDINANCES, FIREARMS. 1980-. 0276-7651. US. English. an. Department of the Treasury, Bureau of Alcohol Tobacco and Firearms, ATF Distribution Center, 3800 Four Mile Run Drive, Arlington VA 22206. *Firearms, State Laws and Published Ordinances.*

STATE LAWS & REGULATIONS. **VAT** State Laws and Regulations. 0163-2914. US. English. an. Environment Information Center, 292 Madison Avenue, New York NY 10017. **LC** KF3775.Z95. **DD** 344.7304602648.

STATE LAWS GOVERNING BOXING AND WRESTLING IN CALIFORNIA WITH RULES AND REGULATIONS. (STATE LAWS GOVERNING BOXING AND WRESTLING IN CALIFORNIA, WITH RULES AND

Law

REGULATIONS). **Main/Corp** California. 0362-4579. US. English. State Athletic Commission, 1021 O Street/Room A-153, Sacramento CA 95814. **LC** KFC645.A29. **DD** 344.794099. *Rules, Regulations and Law Regulating Boxing and Wrestling Matches in California.*

STATE LEGISLATION IMPACTING MUNICIPALITIES. 0736-5640. US. English. an. **LC** KFC4031. **DD** 342.7460902648, 347.4602902648.

STATE NURSING LEGISLATION QUARTERLY. Vol. 3, No. 4 (Winter 1985)-. Periodical. US. English. qt. $30.00. American Nurse's Association, 2420 Pershing Road, Kansas City MO 64108. *State Legislative Report (Kansas City, MO.).*

STATE OF LOUISIANA, ACTS OF THE LEGISLATURE. *See* Public Administration.

THE STATE OF THE COLORADO JUDICIARY. Main/Corp Colorado. Supreme Court. 1969-. 0193-7081. US. English. an. Supreme Court of the State of Colorado, 323 State Capital, Denver CO 80203. **LC** KFC2310. **DD** 347.78803.

STATE OF THE JUDICIARY REPORT. Main/Corp Virginia. Supreme Court. US. English. an. Supreme Court of Virginia, Office of the Executive Secretary, 100 North Ninth Street/Third Floor, Richmond VA 23219. **LC** KFV2471. **DD** 347.75501021, 347.55071021. *State of the Judiciary Report.*

STATE REGISTER. STATE OF MINNESOTA. (STATE REGISTER). Vol. 1, No. 1 (July 13, 1976)-. 0146-7751. Periodical. US. English. wk. $130.00. Minnesota State Register and Public Documents Division, 117 University Avenue, St Paul MN 55155. **LC** KFM5436. **DD** 348.776025, 347.760825.

STATE WORKERS' COMPENSATION LAWS. US. English. sa. US Department of Labor, Employment Standards Administration, Office of State Liaison and Legislative Analysis, Division of State Workers' Compensation Programs, 200 Constitution Avenue NW, Washington DC 20210. *State Workmen's Compensation LAWS.*

STATISTICAL COMPILATION - ADMINISTRATIVE OFFICE OF THE COURTS. *See* Statistics.

STATISTICAL REPORT - EXECUTIVE OFFICE FOR U.S. ATTORNEYS. *See* Statistics.

STATISTICAL REPORT - STATE OF NEW YORK, OFFICE OF COURT ADMINISTRATION. *See* Statistics.

STATISTICAL SUMMARY OF THE COLORADO JUDICIARY. *See* Statistics.

STATISTICAL SUPPLEMENT TO THE ANNUAL REPORT OF THE ADMINISTRATIVE DIRECTOR OF THE COURTS. *See* Statistics.

STATISTICS OF CIVIL COURTS IN THE STATE OF TAMIL NADU FOR THE YEAR . . . . *See* Statistics.

STATISTICS ON JUDICIAL ADMINISTRATION. *See* Statistics.

STATISTIK UBER NS-PROZESSE. *See* Statistics.

STATISTIQUE CRIMINELLE DE LA BELGIQUE. *See* Statistics.

STATISTIQUES DE LA JUSTICE. CONTINENT ET ILES ADJACENTES. *See* Statistics.

STATISTIQUES DIVERSES. *See* Statistics.

STATISTIQUES JUDICIAIRES. *See* Statistics.

STATUS OF BILLS REPORT. Main/Corp Canada. Parliament. **VFOAT** Rapport sur le Statut des Bills. 30th Parliament, 2nd Session-. 0704-609X. CN. English (French). mo. $38.69. Status of Bills Report, 112 Kent Street, Suite 2010/Tower V, Ottawa Ontario K1P 5PS Canada. **Tel** (613)236-9766. **DD** 348.7101.

THE STATUTE LAW OF TASMANIA. Main/Corp Tasmania. **VFOAT** Tasmanian Statutes. 1981-. English. an. **DD** 348.946022, 349.460822. *Laws, etc. Acts of the Parliament of Tasmania.*

STATUTE LAW REVIEW. Spring 1980-. 0144-3593. Periodical. UK. English. ir. 39.00. Sweet & Maxwell, North Way Andover, Hampsire SP105BE England. **Tel** (01)583-9855. **Ed** A G Donaldson. **Ind/**Abst Leg. Resour. Index. **LC** K23. **DD** 348.4102205, 344.10822005. bk rev. adv acc. **Circ** 400. Covers matters relating to legislation and statute law reform.

STATUTES GOVERNING MUNICIPAL PLANNING AND ZONING. Main/Corp Connecticut. 1976-. US. English. 1179 Main Street, Hartford CT 06101. **LC** KFC4058.A29. **DD** 346.746045. *Selected Compilation of Connecticut Laws Concerning Planning and Zoning.*

STATUTES OF NEW BRUNSWICK. Main/Corp New Brunswick. **VFOAT** Lois du Nouveau-Brunswick. 0226-1219. Periodical. CN. English (French). an. 290. Queens Printer, PO Box 6000, Fredericton New Brunswick E3B 5H1 Canada. **Tel** (506)453-2520. **Circ** 1,000. Statutes of New Brunswick in looseleaf format. Updates mailed to subscribers twice yearly.

THE STATUTES OF NEW ZEALAND. Main/Corp New Zealand. **VFOAT** New Zealand Statutes. 1947-. NZ. English. an. $12.84. Government Printer New Zealand, Private Bag, Wellington New Zealand. *Statutes of the Dominion of New Zealand.*

STATUTES OF SASKATCHEWAN JUDICIALLY CONSIDERED. Main/Corp Saskatchewan. Laws, Statutes, Etc. 1965/77-. 0707-0748. CN. English. an. **DD** 348'.7124'026. *Saskatchewan Statutes and Rules of Court Judicially Considered, 0508-5845.*

STATUTES OF THE PROVINCE OF ALBERTA. Main/Corp Alberta. Mar. 15, 1906-Mar. 20/May 22, 1980. 0709-146X. Periodical. CN. English. an. Alberta Government, 11510 Kingsway, Edmonton Alberta T5G 2Y5 Canada.

STATUTES OF THE PROVINCE OF MANITOBA. Main/Corp Manitoba. Laws, Statutes, etc. CN. English. an. 25.00. Queens Printer, 200 Vaughn Street, Winnipeg Manitoba R3C 1T5 Canada. **Tel** (204)945-3103. **Circ** 1,500. (ctrl).

STATUTES OF THE PROVINCE OF NEWFOUNDLAND. Main/Corp Newfoundland. **VFOAT** Statutes of Newfoundland. Began with 1975/76. CN. English. an. 30.00. Queens Printer, Water Street West, St Johns Newfoundland Canada. **Tel** (709)576-3649. **Ed** David C B Dawe. **Circ** 1,000. Contains all acts as passed by the Legislature of the province. *Statutes of Newfoundland.*

STATUTORY REGULATIONS. Main/Corp New Zealand. Laws, Statutes, etc. English. wk. Government Printing Office of New Zealand, Private Bag, Wellington New Zealand.

STATUTORY RULES. Periodical. AT. English. ir. $70.10. Victorian Government Printer, PO Box 203, North Melbourne Victoria 3051 Australia.

STETSON LAW REVIEW. Vol. 8, No. 1 (Fall 1978)-. 0739-9731. Periodical. US. English. ir. $10.00. Stetson Law Review, 1401 61st Street South, St Petersburg FL 33707. **Tel** (813)343-1344. **Ind/**Abst Leg. Resour. Index, Index Leg. Period., Curr. Law Index. *Stetson Intermural Law Review, 0145-5842.*

STORRS LECTURES ON JURISPRUDENCE. Monographic Series. US. English. ir. Yale University Press, 92A Yale Station, New Haven CT 06520. **Tel** (203)436-7583.

STRAFRECHTLICHE ABHANDLUNGEN, NEUE FOLGE. Monographic Series. GW. German. ir. Duncker und Humblot Verlag, Dietrich-Schafer-Weg 9, 1 Berlin 41 West Germany.

STRAFVERTEIDIGER. Vol. 1, No. 1 (Feb. 1981)-. 0720-1605. Periodical. GW. German. mo. 178.00. Europaische Verlagsanstalt, Savignystrasse 61-63, 6000 Frankfurt/MA West Germany. **LC** K23. **DD** 345.430504405, 344.305504405.

STRIKES, STOPPAGES, AND BOYCOTTS. 0272-6548. US. English. an. Practising Law Institute, 810 7th Avenue, New York NY 10019. **LC** KF3431.Z9. **DD** 344.7301892, 347.3041892.

STUDENT GUIDE TO: GRADUATE LAW STUDY PROGRAMS. (STUDENT GUIDE TO GRADUATE LAW STUDY PROGRAMS). **VFOAT** Graduate Law Study Programs. 12th Ed. (1980)-. 0196-9773. US. English. an. New England School of Law, 126 Newbury Street, Boston MA 02116. **LC** K100.A4. **DD** 340.0711. *Directory of Graduate Law Programs, 0070-5608.*

STUDENT GUIDE TO : SUMMER LAW STUDY PROGRAMS. VFOAT Summer Law Study Programs. 7th- Ed. 0197-6656. US. English. be. $10.00. New England School of Law, 154 Stuart Street c/o Ellen Wayne, Boston MA 02116. **Tel** (617)451-0010. **Ed** Ellen Wayne and Betsy McCombs. **LC** KF266. **DD** 340.071173. (ctrl). Listing of law summer programs available throughout the world including program and curriculum information. *Directory of Summer Law Programs.*

STUDENT LAWYER (CHICAGO, ILL. : 1972). (STUDENT LAWYER). V. 1- Sept. 1972-. 0039-274X. Periodical. US. English. $17.00. American Bar Association, 750 North Lake Shore Drive, Chicago IL 60611. **Tel** (312)988-6048. **Ed** Lizanne Poppens. **Ind/**Abst Leg. Resour. Index, Curr. Law Index, Contents Curr. Leg. Period. **LC** K23. **DD** 340.05. adv acc. **Circ** 40,000. (ctrl). A features magazine for law students, covering sociolegal issues and practical, professional topics. *Student Lawyer Journal (Chicago, ILL. : 1967).*

STUDENT LAWYER LETTER. Periodical. US. English. mo. **LC** KF200. **DD** 340.05.

STUDENT PRESS LAW CENTER REPORT. (REPORT - STUDENT PRESS LAW CENTER). 0160-3825. Periodical. US. English. ty. $10.00. Student Press Law Center, 800 18th Street NW/Suite 300, Washington DC 20006. **Tel** (202)466-5242. **LC** KF4165.A15. **DD** 344.730793. **Circ** 3,900. Summarizes current controversies involving First Amendment rights of high school and college journalists.

STUDENTS LAW JOURNAL. Periodical. English. ir. Chancellor College, PO Box 280, Zomba Malawi. **LC** K23. **DD** 349.689705, 346.897005.

STUDIA ET DOCUMENTA AD IURA ORIENTIS ANTIQUI PERTINENTIA. V. 1- 1936-. Monographic Series. German (English). ir. E J Brill, PO Box 9000, 2300 PA Leiden the Netherlands.

STUDIA IURIDICA SILESIANA. Series/ Titl Prace Naukowe Uniwersytetu Slaskiego w Katowicach. 1(1976)-. Periodical. English (French, German, Polish, and Russian). ir. Uniwersytet Slaski Ul, Bankowa 14, 40-007 Katowice Poland. **LC** K23. **DD** 340.05.

STUDIA PRAWNICZE. Vol. 2-. 0039-3312. Periodical. PL. Polish. ir. 180.00. ARS Polona, Krakowskie Przedmiescie 7, 00-068 Warsaw Poland. **DD** 349.43805, 344.3805. *Zeszyty Prawnicze.*

STUDIES OF LAW IN SOCIAL CHANGE AND DEVELOPMENT. 1-. 0348-1964. Monographic Series. US. English. ir. Holmes & Meier Publishers Inc, 30 Irving Place, New York NY 10003.

STUDII SI CERCETARI JURIDICE. Year 1- 1956. Periodical. RM. Romany. qt. $56.00. Rompresfilatelia, PO Box 1362137, Bucharest Romania.

STUDY GUIDE FOR FEDERAL TAX COURSE. (STUDY GUIDE FOR . . . FEDERAL TAX COURSE). **VFOAT** Federal Tax Course Study Guide. 0730-6881. US. English. an. Commerce Clearing House Inc, 4025 West Peterson Avenue, Chicago IL 60646. **LC** KF6289.3. **DD** 343.7304076, 347.3034076.

THE STUDY OF FEDERAL TAX LAW. ESTATE AND GIFT TAXES. VFOAT Estate and Gift Taxes. 0741-7020. US. English. an. $44.50. CCH, 4025 West Peterson Avenue, Chicago IL 60646. **Tel** (312)583-8500. **LC** KF6572.A4. **DD** 343.73053, 347.30353. Reflects chapters 11, 12, and 13 of the Internal Revenue code. *Study of Federal Tax Law. Estate and Gift Tax Volume.*

THE STUDY OF FEDERAL TAX LAW. INCOME TAX, BUSINESS ENTERPRISES. (THE STUDY OF FEDERAL TAX LAW. INCOME TAX. BUSINESS ENTERPRISES). **VFOAT** Income Tax. 1981-1982-. 0738-1352. US. English. $44.50. CCH, 4025 West Peterson Avenue, Chicago IL 60646. **Tel** (312)583-8500. **LC** KF6450.A7. **DD** 343.7305268, 347.3035268. Combines authoritative explanations and problems with carefully selected cases to illustrate the rules on the taxation of corporations and their shareholders and the tax treatment of partnerships and partners. *Study of Federal Tax Law. Income Tax Materials, Business Enterprises, 0272-281X.*

Law

THE STUDY OF FEDERAL TAX LAW. INCOME TAX VOLUME. VFOAT Income Tax Volume. 1972-. US. English. an. Commerce Clearing House, 112 Avenue of the Americas, New York NY 10020. **LC** KF6368. **DD** 343.730520264.

THE STUDY OF FEDERAL TAX LAW. TRANSNATIONAL TRANSACTIONS. VFOAT Transnational Transactions. 1981-1982-. 0748-1454. US. English. an. $48.50. Commerce Clearing House, 4025 West Peterson Avenue, Chicago IL 60646. **Tel** (312)583-8500. **LC** KF6463. **DD** 343.73068, 347.30368. Covers the United States taxation of foreign entities that have income from sources outside the country.

STUDY OF MSPB APPEALS DECISIONS. (STUDY OF MSPB APPEALS DECISIONS FOR FY . . .). VFOAT Study of M.S.P.B. Appeals Decisions for FY . . . . VAT Study of Merit Systems Protection Board Appeals Decisions. 0743-5770. US. English. an. US Merit Systems Protection Board, 1120 Vermont Avenue, Washington DC 20419. **LC** KF5337. **DD** 342.730684, 347.302684.

SUBCONTRACTING; COURSE MANUAL. 0192-673X. US. English. an. Federal Publications Inc, 1725 K Street Northwest, Washington DC 20006. **LC** KF869.3. **DD** 346.73023.

SUBJECT INDEX TO THE ACTS OF THE AUSTRALIAN PARLIAMENT. See Indexes/Abstracts.

SUBJECT INDEX TO THE ILLINOIS REGISTER, WITH TABLES. See Indexes/Abstracts.

SUBJECT INDEX TO THE TASMANIAN STATUTES. See Indexes/Abstracts.

SUBJECT-MATTER INDEX AND TABLE OF CASES. See Indexes/Abstracts.

SUBJECT MATTER INDEX TO PUBLIC AND PRIVATE STATUTES OF NEW BRUNSWICK. See Indexes/Abstracts.

SUBJECT MATTER INDEXES. See Indexes/Abstracts.

SUFFOLK UNIVERSITY LAW REVIEW. V. 1- Spring 1967-. 0039-4696. Periodical. US. English. qt. $14.00. Suffolk University, 41 Temple Street, Boston MA 02114. **Tel** (617)723-4700. **Ed** Robert Pace. **Ind/Abst** Leg. Resour. Index, Index Leg. Period., Curr. Law Index, Contents Curr. Leg. Period. **LC** UNC. (cum index). bk rev. **Circ** 1,200. Reviews of cases and legal principles which are of interest to the practitioner.

SUFFOLK UNIVERSITY LAW SCHOOL ALUMNI DIRECTORY. See Yearbooks, Almanacs, Directories.

SUGGESTED STATE LEGISLATION (CHICAGO, ILL. : 1965). (SUGGESTED STATE LEGISLATION). Began in 1965. 0070-1157. US. English. an. $15.00. Council of State Governments, Iron Works Pike PO Box 11910, Lexington KY 40578. **Tel** (606)252-2291. **LC** KF165. **DD** 349.73, 347.309. **Circ** 5,000. Source of legislative ideas and drafting assistance. Program of Suggested State Legislation.

SULUH HUKUM YUSTITIA. Periodical. Indonesian (summaries in English). ir. Jln Diponegoro 86, Jakarta Indonesia. **LC** K10. Justitia.

SUMMARIES OF CASES TO BE HEARD BY THE SUPREME COURT OF CANADA. Main/Corp Canadian Law Information Council. VAT Summ. Cases Heard Supreme Court Can. No. 18- Jan. 23, 1979-. 0709-6968. Periodical. CN. English. $27.09. Canadian Law Information Council, 161 Laurier Avenue West/ 5th Floor, Ottawa Ontario K1P 5J2 Canada. **Tel** (613)236-9766. **DD** 347.710353. Supreme Court of Canada, Summaries of Cases to be Heard, 0701-8363.

SUMMARIES OF IMPORTANT LABOUR JUDGEMENTS. V. 1- 1964/70-. English. ir. 15.00. Punjab Haryana & Delhi Chamber of Commerce and Industry, Phelphs Building 9-A Connaught Place, New Delhi 110001 India. **DD** 344.540102646.

SUMMARY - ALBERTA SECURITIES COMMISSION. Main/Corp Alberta. Securities Commission. April 1975-. 0319-3667. CN. English. wk. Alberta Securities Commission, 10065 Jaspen Avenue, Edmonton Alberta T5J 3B1 Canada. **DD** 346.71230666.

SUMMARY JUDGEMENT. (SUMMARY JUDGMENT : A PUBLICATION FOR MEMBERS OF THE OHIO STATE BAR ASSOCIATION). Vol. 1, No. 1 (Nov. 1982)-. 0738-1972. Periodical. US. English. bm. Ohio State Bar Association, Ohio Legal Center, 33 West Eleventh Avenue, Columbus OH 43201. **LC** KF200. **DD** 340.060771. 2 Minute News.

SUMMARY OF ACTION. Main/Corp American Bar Association. House of Delegates. US. English. an. American Bar Association, 750 North Lake Shore Drive, Chicago IL 60611. **LC** KF325.135. **DD** 340.06273.

SUMMARY OF ACTION TAKEN BY THE HOUSE OF DELEGATES OF THE AMERICAN BAR ASSOCIATION. Main/Corp American Bar Association. House of Delegates. VFOAT Summary of Action of the House of Delegates. Feb. 1975-. Periodical. US. English. sa. American Bar Association, 1155 East 60th Street, Chicago IL 60637. Index in last issue of volume - attached. Summary of Action and Reports to the House of Delegates, 0092-0797.

SUMMARY OF ACTIVITIES - MENTAL HEALTH LAW PROJECT. Main/Corp Mental Health Law Project. 0363-2687. Periodical. US. English. qt. Mental Health Law Project, Suite 300/ 1220 19th Street Northwest, Washington DC 20036. **LC** KF480.A15. **DD** 344.73044.

SUMMARY OF ALASKA LEGISLATION. Main/Corp Alaska. Legislature. Legislative Affairs Agency. US. English. an. Legislative Affairs Agency, Pouch Y, State Capitol, Juneau AK 99811. **LC** KFA1215. **DD** 348.79801, 347.98081. Summary of Alaska Legislation.

SUMMARY OF CALIFORNIA LAW. Periodical. US. English. ir. Bancroft-Whitney Company, 301 Brannan Street, San Francisco CA 94107.

SUMMARY OF DECISIONS. Main/Corp Washington (State) Personnel Appeals Board. VFOAT Summaries for Personnel Appeals Board. Vol. 1 (July 1, 1981-June 30, 1982)-. US. English. **LC** KFW435.A59. **DD** 342.7970686, 347.9702686.

SUMMARY OF ELECTION LAWS ENACTED BY THE LEGISLATIVE ASSEMBLY. Main/Corp Oregon. 0095-2796. US. English. Elections Division Room 122, State Capitol, Salem MA 97310. **LC** KFO2820. **DD** 342.7950702638.

SUMMARY OF ENACTMENTS. Main/Corp Ohio. Legislative Service Commission. 0098-759X. US. English. an. Ohio Legislative Service Commission, PO Box 301, Columbus OH 43216. **LC** KFO15. **DD** 348.77101. Legislation.

SUMMARY OF ENACTMENTS. Main/Corp Texas. Legislature. Legislative Council. US. English. Texas Legislative Council, PO Box 12128, Austin TX 78767. **LC** KFT1215. **DD** 348.764023.

SUMMARY OF GENERAL LEGISLATION. Main/Corp Florida. Legislature., Joint Legislative Management Committee. 0090-1520. US. English. Florida Legislature/Joint Legislative Management Committee, Capital Building, Tallahassee FL 32304. **LC** KFF15. **DD** 348.731.

SUMMARY OF LEGISLATION. Main/Corp Nevada. Legislative Counsel Bureau. Research Division. US. English. Legislative Counsel Bureau, Legislative Building Capitol Complex, Carson City NV 89710. **LC** KFN615. **DD** 348.793026, 347.930826.

SUMMARY OF LEGISLATION APPROVED BY THE . . . SESSION OF THE . . . IOWA GENERAL ASSEMBLY, MEETING IN THE YEAR . . . . 1969-. US. English. an. Full Depository, Copies Available Free from Issuing Agency.

SUMMARY OF LEGISLATION (TOPEKA, KAN.). (SUMMARY OF LEGISLATION). US. English. an. Legislative Research Department, Statehouse Room 545-N, Topeka KS 66612. **LC** KFK15. **DD** 348.781026, 347.810826.

SUMMARY OF LEGISLATIVE ACTIVITIES - UNITED STATES. CONGRESS. HOUSE. COMMITTEE ON PUBLIC WORKS AND TRANSPORTATION. (SUMMARY OF LEGISLATIVE ACTIVITIES). Main/Corp United States. Congress. House. Committee on Public Works and Transportation. 0740-9427. US. English. be. **LC** KF4997.P8. **DD** 328.730765.

SUMMARY OF LEGISLATIVE APPROPRIATIONS. See Business - Public Finance.

SUMMARY OF PROCEEDINGS. MANAGEMENT INSTITUTE. (SUMMARY OF PROCEEDINGS . . . MANAGEMENT INSTITUTE). Main/Conf Management Institute. Began with 1971. 0276-5616. US. English. ir. William S Hein & Company, 1285 Main Street, Buffalo NY 14209. **Tel** (919)781-5060. **Ed** Patton G Wheeler. **LC** KF5107.Z9. **DD** 353.9388.

SUMMARY OF PUBLIC ACTS. Main/Corp Connecticut. General Assembly. Office of Legislative Research. 0093-9226. US. English. Connecticut General Assembly, Office of Legislative Research, State Capital, Hartford CT 06115. **LC** KFC3615. **DD** 348.746026.

SUMMARY OF PUBLIC ACTS OF INTEREST TO MUNICIPAL OFFICIALS. US. English. an. Municipal Technical Advisory Service of the University of Tennessee Headquarters, The University of Tennessee, Knoxville TN 37916. **LC** KFT38. **DD** 348.768023.

SUMMARY OF PUBLIC SECTOR LABOR RELATION POLICIES. Began with 1976. 0163-139X. US. English. an. US Department of Labor, Labor-Management Services Administration, Washington DC 20210. **LC** KF5365. **DD** 344.730189041353. Summary of State Policy Regulations for Public Sector Labor Relation.

A SUMMARY OF SELECTED LEGISLATION RELATED TO THE HANDICAPPED. Main/Corp United States. Dept. of Health, Education and Welfare. 1963/67-. 0148-625X. Periodical. US. English. US Department of Health Education & Welfare, US Government Printers Office, Washington DC 20202. **LC** KF3738. **DD** 344.730324.

SUMMARY OF THE PROCEEDINGS OF THE RHODE ISLAND GENERAL ASSEMBLY. Main/Corp Rhode Island. Legislative Council. US. English. an. **LC** KFR15. **DD** 328.74501.

SUMMER LEGAL EMPLOYMENT GUIDE. See Economics - Labor.

SUMULA TRIBUTARIA TRABALHISTA (SEMIMONTHLY). See Economics - Labor.

SUPLEMENTO TRABALHISTA LTR. Periodical. Portuguese. ir. Ltr Editora Ltda, Rua Apa 165, CEP 01201 Sao Paulo SP Brazil. **LC** KHD1782. **DD** 344.810102648, 348104102648.

SUPPLEMENT TO ATTORNEY'S GUIDE TO TRADE SECRETS. VFOAT Trade Secrets. US. English. ir. $9.00. Cal Continuing Education of The Bar Department CEB-S/2150 Shattuck Avenue, Berkeley CA 94704. **Tel** (415)642-5897.

SUPPLEMENT TO CAMPAIGN FINANCE LAW. Main/Corp Library of Congress. Congressional Research Service. American Law Division. VFOAT Campaign Finance Law. 1979-. US. English. be. Federal Election Commission, National Clearinghouse of Election Administration, Washington DC 20402.

SUPPLEMENTAL DIGEST AND INDEX OF PUBLISHED DECISIONS OF THE ASSISTANT SECRETARY OF LABOR FOR LABOR-MANAGEMENT RELATIONS PURSUANT TO EXECUTIVE ORDER 11491, AS AMENDED. Main/Corp United States. Federal Labor Relations Authority. July/Dec. 1978-. 0272-3883. US. English. Superintendent of Documents, US Government Printing Office, Washington DC 20402. **LC** KF5365.A57. **DD** 344.7301890413530002648, 347. 3041890413530002648. Supplemental Digest and Index of Published Decisions of the Assistant Secretary of Labor for Labor-Management Relations Pursuant to Executive Order 11491, as Amended, 0272-3883.

SUPREME COURT BULLETIN. 0199-5030. Periodical. US. English. ir. $21.00. Gillmore Group Publications, PO Box 410, Goffstown NH 03045. **Tel** (603)497-8154. **Ed** Robert Gillmore. adv acc. **Circ**

Law

7,000. Weekly summaries of every US Supreme Court opinion when opinions are handed down.

SUPREME COURT DECISIONS : SUBJECT INDEX AND DIGESTS. See Indexes/Abstracts.

SUPREME COURT DOCTRINES. 1975-. English. ir. Rex Printing Company, 84 P Florentine Street, Quezon City Philippines. DD 348.599041.

SUPREME COURT ECONOMIC REVIEW. Vol. 1 (1980 Term)-. 0736-9921. US. English. an. MacMillan Publishers Inc, 866 Third Avenue, New York NY 10022. LC K23. DD 343.7307, 347.3037.

THE SUPREME COURT JOURNAL. V. 1- 1937-. Periodical. English. bw. 76.00. Post Box 604, Madras-600004 India. Index published separately - free - automatically sent.

SUPREME COURT LAW REVIEW. (THE SUPREME COURT LAW REVIEW). VFOAT New Constitution and the Charter of Rights. V. 1- 1980-. 0228-0108. Periodical. CN. English (French). an. Butterworth & Company Ltd, 2265 Midland Avenue, Scarborough M1P 4S1 Canada. Ed E P Belobaba and E Gertner. Ind/Abst Leg. Resour. Index, Index Leg. Period. LC K23. DD 347.7103505, 347.1073505.

THE SUPREME COURT MONTHLY REVIEW. V. 1- Jan. 1968-. Periodical. English. mo. 36.00. 1/5 Edward Road, Lahore Pakistan. DD 349.54904.

SUPREME COURT OF CANADA DECISIONS. CIVIL AND CRIMINAL CASES. Main/Corp Canada. Supreme Court. Began with 1978 issue?. 0709-5600. CN. English. ir. Western Legal Publications Ltd, 301 One Alexander Street, Vancouver British Columbia V6A 1B2 Canada. Tel (604)687-5671. DD 348.71041.

THE SUPREME COURT PRACTICE. Main/Corp Great Britain. Supreme Court of Judicature. 1st- Ed. 0039-5978. UK. English. Sweet and Maxwell, 11 New Fetter Lane, London EC4 PEE England. DD 347.9942.

SUPREME COURT REPORTS. Main/Corp India. Supreme Court. II. English. mo. Editor Supreme Court Report, Supreme Court of India, New Delhi 110054 India.

SUPREME COURT REPORTS, ANNOTATED. English. ir. (cum index).

THE SUPREME COURT RESEARCHER. Began with Oct. 1970 issue. 0049-2612. Periodical. US. English. ir. $85.00. National Legal Research Group Inc, PO Box 7187, Charlottesville VA 22906. Tel (800)446-1870. LC KF101.1. DD 348.7346.

THE SUPREME COURT REVIEW. 1960-. 0081-9557. US. English. an. $35.00. University of Chicago Press, 5801 South Ellis Avenue, Chicago IL 60637. Ed Philip B Kurland, Gerhard Casper and Dennis J Hutchinson. Ind/Abst Leg. Resour. Index, ABC Pol Sci, Index Leg. Period., Curr. Law Index, Soc. Sci. Citation Index. LC KF4546. DD 347.9973. Circ 2,500. Provides a sustained and authoritative survey of the quality and implications of the court's most significant decisions, both past and present.

SURAT KEPUTUSAN DPRD PROPINSI KALIMANTAN SELATAN, KP. Main/Corp Kalimantan Selatan. Dewan Perwakilan Rakyat Daerah. VAT Surat Keputusan Dewan Perwakilan Rakyat Daerah Propinsi Kalimantan Selatan, KP. Indonesian. ir. DD 348.598301.

SURAT KEPUTUSAN KOMISI D DPRD PROPINSI JAWA TENGAH. Main/Corp Jawa Tengah, Indonesia. Dewan Perwakilan Rakyat Daerah. Komisi D. VAT Surat Keputusan Komisi D Dewan Perwakilan Rakyat Daerah Propinsi Jawa Tengah. Indonesian. ir. Surat Keputusan D.P.R.D. Propinsi Djawa Tengah, Komisi D.

SURVEY OF JUDICIAL SALARIES. See Economics - Labor.

SURVEY OF LAW. 1979-. 0271-2792. Periodical. US. English. an. American Bar Association, 1155 East 60th Street, Chicago IL 60637. LC KF178. DD 349.7305.

SURVEY OF LAW REVIEWS. V. 1- Summer 1974-. 0360-7372. US. English. qt. $20.00. Legal Information Services, Data Solutions Corporation, 6849 Old Dominion Drive, McLean VA 22101. LC KF8. DD 340.05.

SURVEY OF MALAYSIAN LAW. 1977-. 0217-3239. Sl. English. an. Malaysian Law Journal Ptd Ltd, 3 Shenton Way #14-03, Shenton House, Singapore 0106. Tel 2203684. Ed Visu Sinnadurai. DD 349.595, 345.95. Contains various aspects of Malaysian laws by law academicians on criminal justice, administrative, commerical, company, constitutional, contract, equity, trusts, evidence, family and Islamic law, etc.

SURVEY OF PHARMACY LAW. 1942-. 0098-714X. Periodical. US. English. NLM QV 32 AA1 S9.

THE SYDNEY LAW REVIEW. Vol. 1, No. 1 (April 1953)-. 0082-0512. AT. English. ir. Methuen Law Book Company Ltd, 35 Mitchell Street, c/o Bennett-EBSCO, North Sydney Wales 2060 Australia. Ind/Abst Leg. Resour. Index, APAIS, Aust. Public Aff. Inf. Serv., Index Leg. Period., Curr. Law Index, Contents Curr. Leg. Period. LC UNC. Index published separately - free - automatically sent.

SYLLABUS. (SYLLABUS). Vol. 12, No. 4 (Nov. 1981)-. Periodical. US. English. qt. $17.00. American Bar Association, 750 North Lake Shore Drive, Chicago IL 60611. Tel (312)988-5555. LC KF200. DD 340.071173. Legal Education Newsletter.

SYLVIA PORTER'S INCOME TAX GUIDE CEASED. 0491-8738. US. English. an. Avon Books, 1790 Broadway, New York NY 10019. Tel (212)399-9457. LC KF6369.6. DD 343.73052.

SYNOPSIS OF LAWS ENACTED BY THE STATE OF MARYLAND. Main/Corp Maryland. State Dept. of Legislative Reference. 0093-0520. US. English. an. $15.00. State Department of Legislative Reverence, 90 State Circle, Annapolis MD 21401. Tel (301)841-3810. LC KFM1238. DD 348.7527326. Circ 600. Synopsis of bills passed and vetoed each session and table of sections of code affected.

SYRACUSE LAW REVIEW. V. 1- Spring 1949-. 0039-7938. Periodical. US. English. qt. $18.00. Syracuse University College of Law, Ernest 1 White Hall, Syracuse NY 13210. Tel (315)423-3680. Ed Joe Saltarelli. Ind/Abst Leg. Resour. Index, Women Stud. Abstr., Index Leg. Period., Leg. Contents, Curr. Law Index, Soc. Sci. Citation Index, Contents Curr. Leg. Period. LC K23. DD 340.09747. adv acc. Circ 2,000. (ctrl). Brings you up-to-date with New York law and many scholarly aspects of the legal profession; great help in practice, research, and conversation.

TABLE OF ALBERTA LEGISLATION. Main/Corp Alberta. Public Affairs Bureau. VFOAT Table of Legislation. 0710-8958. CN. English. Alberta Public Affairs Bureau, 11510 Kingsway Avenue, Edmonton Alberta T5G 2Y5 Canada. LC KEA1. DD 348.712300294, 347.1230800294.

TABLE OF ALBERTA LEGISLATION. SUPPLEMENT. CN. English. Alberta Government Services Publications and Statutes, 11510 Kingsway Avenue, Edmonton Alberta Canada.

TABLE OF ALBERTA STATUTES. Main/Corp Alberta. Public Affairs Division. May 1976-. 0228-5371. CN. English. ir. $27.09. Alberta Statutes Province, Office of Queens Printer, Edmonton Alberta Canada. Tel (403)427-4952. LC KEA62. DD 348.7123028.

TAEHAN PYONHOSA HYOPHOE CHI. VFOAT Korean Federal Bar Association Journal. Periodical. KO. Korean. mo. Taehan Pyonhosa Hyophoe, 37 Sosomun-dong, Chung-ku, Seoul South Korea.

TANACSOK KOZLONYE. Main/Corp Hungary. Minisztertanacs. Hungarian. ir. 144.00. Minisztertnacs, Lapkiado Vallalat Budapest VII, Lenin Korut 9-11, Budapest Hungary.

TAR. TENNESSEE ADMINISTRATIVE REGISTER. NOTICE SECTION. (TAR, TENNESSEE ADMINISTRATIVE REGISTER. NOTICE SECTION). Main/Corp Tennessee. State Dept. Administrative Procedure Division. VFOAT Tennessee Administrative Register. VAT Tennessee Administrative Register. Notice Section. 0149-9718. Periodical. US. English. mo. $10.00. 580 Capitol Hill Building, Nashville TN 37219. LC KFT36.

TARIF DES DOUANES. Main/Corp France. Direction Generale des Douanes et Droits Indirects. 0767-4538. FR. French. ir. 80.00. Imprimerie des Journaux Officiels, 26 rue Desaix, 75727 Paris Cedex 15 France. Tel 45 78 61 39. DD 343.44056.

TARLTON LAW LIBRARY LEGAL BIBLIOGRAPHY SERIES. See Bibliographies.

TASB LEGISLATIVE NEWS. Main/Corp Texas Association of School Boards. VFOAT Legislative News. June 13, 1978-Feb. 23, 1979. Periodical. US. English. ir. Texas Association of School Boards, PO Box 400, Austin TX 78767. Tel (512)476-9116. Ed Tamara Thompson. Circ 10,000. (ctrl). Provides a concise report of proposed legislation while the Texas legislature is in session. Education Scene from Capitol Hill.

TAX AFFAIRS. Began in 1960. 0039-9965. Periodical. II. English. ir. Practical Tax Publishers, D-75 Anand Niketan, New Delhi 110021 India. LC K24. DD 343.540405.

TAX DIGEST (CORAL GABLES, FLA.). (TAX DIGEST). VFOAT Tax Savings Digest. Periodical. US. English. $124.00. HMD Inc, 159 Madeira Avenue, Coral Gables FL 33134. LC KF6296.A15. DD 343.730405.

TAX DIGEST (LONDON, ENGLAND). (TAX DIGEST). Periodical. UK. English. Institute of Chartered Accountants in England and Wales, PO Box 433, London EC2P2BJ England. LC KD5352. DD 343.410405, 344.103405.

TAX EXEMPT NEWS. See Business - Public Finance.

TAX EXEMPTIONS (OLYMPIA, WASH.). (TAX EXEMPTIONS). US. English. Washington State Department of Revenue, Research and Information Division, General Administration Building, Olympia WA 98504. LC KFW472. DD 343.7970523, 347.9703523.

TAX FACTS ON INVESTMENTS. VFOAT Tax Facts Two, Investments. 0739-6619. US. English. an. Nulaw Services, National Underwriter Company, 420 East Fourth Street, Cincinnati OH 45202. LC KF6415.A15. DD 343.7305246, 347.3035246.

TAX FACTS ON LIFE INSURANCE. 0145-1847. US. English. an. National Underwriter Company, 420 East 4th Street, Cincinnati OH 45202. LC KF6428.L5. DD 343.73052.

TAX GUIDE FOR ENGINEERS. 1977-. 0146-8235. US. English. an. Academic Information Service, PO Box 31391, Washington DC 20031. LC KF6369.8.E54. DD 343.73052.

TAX GUIDE FOR SALES REPRESENTATIVES. Main/Corp Commerce Clearing House. Series/Titl CCH Editorial Staff Publication. 0272-3719. US. English. $5.00. C C H, 4025 West Peterson Avenue, Chicago IL 60646. LC KF6369.8.S2. DD 343.73052024658.

TAX INFORMATION ON DEPRECIATION. Main/Corp United States. Internal Revenue Service. 0098-6992. US. English. US Department of the Treasury, Superintendent of Documents, US Government Printing Office, Washington DC 20402. LC KF6386. DD 343.73052.

TAX LAW REVIEW. V. 1- Oct./Nov. 1945-. 0040-0041. Periodical. US. English. qt. Warren Gorham & Lamont Inc, 210 South Street, Boston MA 02111. Tel (800)225-2363. Ind/Abst Manage. Contents, Leg. Resour. Index, Account. Index. Suppl., ABI/Inform, Public Aff. Inf. Serv. Bull., Index Leg. Period., Curr. Law Index, Contents Curr. Leg. Period. (cum index).

THE TAX LAWYER. (THE TAX LAWYER : BULLETIN OF THE SECTION OF TAXATION, AMERICAN BAR ASSOCIATION). Vol. 21, No. 1 (Fall 1967)-. 0040-005X. Periodical. US. English. qt. $35.00. American Bar Association, 750 North Lake Shore Drive, Chicago IL 60611. Tel (312)988-5555. Ed Albert C O'Neil. Ind/Abst Manage. Contents, Leg. Resour. Index, Account. Index. Suppl., ABI/Inform, Index Leg. Period., Curr. Law Index, Contents Curr. Leg. Period. LC K24. DD 343.730405, 347.303405. (cum index). adv acc. (ctrl). Articles and student notes and comments pertaining to taxation. Bulletin of the Section of Taxation, American Bar Association.

TAX LITERATURE REPORT. No. 1 (Jan. 13, 1984)-. 8755-0369. US. English. wk. Symposia Press Inc, PO Box 418, Moorestown NY 08057. DD 343.

TAX MANAGEMENT COMPENSATION PLANNING JOURNAL. Vol. 12, No. 1 (Jan. 1984)-. 0747-8607. Periodical. US. English. mo. $170.00. 1231 25th Street NW, Washington DC 20037. Ind/Abst Manage. Contents, Leg. Resour. Index. LC

Law

KF6289.8.E9. **DD** 343.730523, 347.303523. *Compensation Planning Journal, 0148-690X.*

TAX MANAGEMENT ESTATES, GIFTS, AND TRUSTS JOURNAL. Periodical. US. English. bm. $95.00. Tax Management Inc, 1231 25th Street NW, Washington DC 20037. **LC** KF6571.A15. **DD** 343.7305305, 347.305305. *Estates, Gifts and Trusts Journal, 0364-9253.*

THE TAX MANAGEMENT INTERNATIONAL FORUM. Vol. 1, No. 1 (1980)-. 0143-7941. Periodical. UK. English. qt. Tax Management International, 17 Dartmouth Street, London SW1H 9BL England. **LC** K4456.2. **DD** 343.0405, 342.3405.

TAX MANAGEMENT — PRIMARY SOURCES. SERIES II. Main/Corp Bureau of National Affairs (Washington, D.C.). Periodical. US. English. mo. Bureau of National Affairs Inc, 1231 25th Street NW, Washington DC 20037. **Tel** (301)258-1033. **LC** KF6365.

TAX MANAGEMENT REAL ESTATE JOURNAL. VFOAT Real Estate Journal. Vol. 1, No. 1 (Nov./Dec 1984)-. 8755-0628. Periodical. US. English. bm. $180.00 Initial Subscription, $160.00 Renewal. Bureau of National Affairs, 9435 Key West Avenue, Rockville MD 20850. **LC** KF6535.A15. **DD** 343.

TAX MONTHLY. (THE TAX MONTHLY). V. 1- Feb. 1974-. 0377-600X. Periodical. English. mo. 2.50 Each Issue. Income Tax Payers Association of Ceylon, 54 3/2 Australia Building 1, Colombo Ceylon (Sri Lanka). **DD** 343.54930405.

TAX PLANNING CHECKLIST. 0821-0764. CN. English. an. Free. Tax Planning Checklist, Coopers and Lybrand, 630 Dorchester Boulevard West, Montreal Quebec H3B 1W5 Canada. **DD** 343.710523. (ctrl).

TAX PLANNING IDEAS FOR INDIVIDUALS. CANADA. (TAX PLANNING IDEAS FOR INDIVIDUALS : CANADA). 0824-6343. CN. English. an. Free. Touche Ross Company, Suite 500/111 Richmond Street West, Toronto Ontario M5H 2G4 Canada. **DD** 343.71052. (ctrl).

TAX PLANNING INTERNATIONAL. V. 3, No. 6- June 1976-. Periodical. UK. English. mo. $175.00. Subscription Department, Tax Planning International, Watling Street Bletchley, Milton Keynes London MK2 2BW England. **LC** K4464.A13. **DD** 343.0405. *Tax Haven Review.*

TAX PLANNING INTERNATIONAL REVIEW. Vol. 8 No. 1 (Jan. 1981)-. Periodical. UK. English. mo. **LC** K4464.A13. **DD** 343.0405, 342.3405. *Tax Planning International, 0309-7900.*

TAX REPORTS, NEW ZEALAND. VFOAT Butterworths Taxation Service. V. 1- 1975-. 0110-0246. NZ. English. ir. Butterworths of New Zealand, 26-28 Waring Taylor Street, Box 472, Wellington New Zealand. **DD** 343.9310402642. *Decisions - New Zealand Taxation Board of Review, Australasian Tax Reports.*

TAX, SEC, AND ACCOUNTING ASPECTS OF CORPORATE ACQUISITIONS. VAT Tax, Securities and Exchange Commission, and Accounting Aspects of Corporate Acquisitions. 8756-5412. US. English. Practising Law Institute, 810 Seventh Avenue, New York NY 10019. **DD** 343. *Tax and Accounting Aspects of Corporate Reorganizations, 0883-4474.*

TAX SHELTER ANALYST. Vol. 1, No. 1 (Jan. 1984)-. 0742-888X. Periodical. US. English. mo. $144.00. Tax Shelter Analyst, 10076 Boca Entrada Boulevard, Boca Raton FL 33433-5897. **LC** KF6415.A15. **DD** 343.730523, 347.303523.

TAX SHELTERED INVESTMENTS HANDBOOK. Series/Titl Securities Law Series. Began in 1979. 0731-5821. US. English. an. Clark Boardman Company, 435 Hudson Street, New York NY 10014. Ed Robert J Haft and Peter M Fass. **LC** KF6415.A152. **DD** 343.730523, 347.303523.

TAX SHELTERED INVESTMENTS LAW REPORT. Vol. 1, No. 1 (May 1981)-. 0731-5759. Periodical. US. English. mo. $150.00. Clark Boardman Company Ltd, 435 Hudson Street, New York NY 10014. **Tel** (212)929-7500. **LC** KF6415.A15. **DD** 343.730523, 347.303523.

TAX TIPS FOR INDIVIDUALS. VAT C.G.A. Tax Tips for Individuals, Certified General Accountants Association Tax Tips for Individuals. 0823-9819. CN. English. an. Free. Certified General Accountants of Ontario, 4th Floor/480 University Avenue, Toronto Ontario M5G 1V2 Canada. **DD** 343.71052.

TAXATION AND BUSINESS DECISIONS. 1984 Ed.-. 0824-6661. CN. English. an. Taxation And Business Decisions c/o Clarence Byrd Inc, PO Box 10, Stittsville Ontario K0A 3G0 Canada. **DD** 343.7105205.

TAXATION FOR LAWYERS. V. 1- July/Aug. 1972-. 0161-178X. Periodical. US. English. bm. Warren Gorham & Lamont Inc, 210 South Street, Boston MA 02111. **Tel** (800)225-2363. **Ind/Abst** Manage. Contents, Leg. Resour. Index, Account. Index. Suppl., Contents Curr. Leg. Period., Curr. Law Index. **LC** K24. **DD** 343.730405.

THE TAXES ACTS. Main/Corp Great Britain. UK. English. Her Majestys Stationery Office, PO Box 276, London SW8 5DT England. **LC** KD5353.99. **DD** 343.420402632.

TAXES INTERPRETED. Began with July 16, 1962. 0040-0203. Periodical. US. English. bw. $197.00. Phillips Publishing Company, 7315 Wisconsin Avenue/Suite 1200N, Bethesda MD 20814. **Tel** (301)986-0666. **LC** UNC. **DD** 343.730405, 347.303405. Index published separately - free - automatically sent. *Tax Barometer, 0039-9981.*

TAYA YEI YA SA SAUNG. Burmese. ir. Taya Yon-Chok, Chief Court, Yankonmyo Burma.

TECHNICAL SERVICES LAW LIBRARIAN. See Library and Information Science.

TECHNOLOGY MANAGEMENT HANDBOOK. Series/Titl Licensing Law Library. 1979-. 0731-5856. US. English. an. $47.50. Clark Boardman, 435 Hudson Street, New York NY 10014. **Tel** (800)221-9428. **LC** K1528.A53. **DD** 344.095, 342.495.

TEL AVIV UNIVERSITY STUDIES IN LAW. V. 1- 1975-. IS. English. an. Tel Aviv University, Faculty of Law, Ramat-Aviv, Tel Aviv Israel. **LC** K24. **DD** 340.095694.

TELE-C.L.E.F. No 1 (Jan. 1983)-. 0822-451X. Periodical. CN. French. qt. $20.00. Centre de Reference de la Documentation Juridique de Langue Francaise en Matiere de Common Law, Place de Ville 161 Laurier Avenue West, 5th Floor, Ottawa Ontario K1P 5J2 Canada. **Tel** (613)236-9766. **DD** 340.570971. bk rev. adv acc. **Circ** 1,000. A French Language publication (4 times a year) on common law in Canada.

TEMPLE INTERNATIONAL AND COMPARATIVE LAW JOURNAL. VFOAT International and Comparative Law Journal. Vol. 1, No. 1 (Fall 1985)-. Periodical. US. English. sa. $12.00. Temple University School of Law, 1719 North Broad Street, Philadelphia PA 19122. **LC** PAR.

TEMPLE LAW QUARTERLY (PHILADELPHIA, PA. : 1945). (TEMPLE LAW QUARTERLY). Began with: Vol. 19, No. 2 (June 1945). 0040-2974. Periodical. US. English. qt. $15.00. Temple Law Quarterly, c/o Business Editor, 1719 North Broad Street, Philadelphia PA 19122. **Tel** (215)787-7868. Ed Timothy Rice. **Ind/Abst** Leg. Resour. Index, Index Leg. Period. **LC** K24. (cum index). bk rev. adv acc. **Circ** 2,000. Practitioner and student written scholarly articles on important, current cases and legal issues with a focus on conflicts between circuits and Pennsylvania law. *Temple University Law Quarterly, 0271-8316.*

TENNESSEE ATTORNEYS DIRECTORY. See Yearbooks, Almanacs, Directories.

TENNESSEE BAR JOURNAL. V. 1- Feb. 1965-. 0497-2325. Periodical. US. English. ir. $25.00. Tennessee Bar Association, 3622 West End Avenue, Nashville TN 37205. **Tel** (615)383-7421. Ed Gary N Hunt. **Ind/Abst** Leg. Resour. Index, Index Leg. Period., Curr. Law Index. **LC** UNC. bk rev. adv acc. **Circ** 5,600. (ctrl). Substantive law articles on Tennessee law, association news.

TENNESSEE CODE ANNOTATED ADVANCE ANNOTATION SERVICE. VFOAT Advance Annotation Service. Vol. 1, No. 1 (Dec. 1981)-. 0747-7074. Periodical. US. English. mo. $45.00. The Michie Company, PO Box 7587, Charlottesville VA 22906-7587. **Tel** (809)295-6171. Annotations to Tennessee and federal cases.

TENNESSEE COURT RULES ANNOTATED. Main/Corp Tennessee. Supreme Court. Began in 1981. 0747-7066. US. English. an. Michie Company, 609 East Market Street, Charlottesville VA 22906-7587. **Tel** (804)295-6171. **LC** KFT529. **DD** 347.768051, 347.680751.

THE TENNESSEE EMPLOYMENT LAW UPDATE. Vol. 1, No. 1 (Mar. 1986)-. 0886-8557. Periodical. US. English. mo. $50.00. John Carroll Enterprise Inc, PO Box 428, Chattanooga TN 37401. **DD** 344.

TENNESSEE LAW REVIEW. V. 1- Nov. 1922-. 0040-3288. Periodical. US. English. qt. $16.00 Domestic, $18.00 Foreign. College of Law, University of Tennessee, 1505 West Cumberland Avenue, Knoxville TN 37916. **Tel** (615)974-4464. Ed Nora Cannon. **Ind/Abst** Leg. Resour. Index, Index Leg. Period., Curr. Law Index, Contents Curr. Leg. Period. **LC** K24. **DD** 349.768. (cum index). bk rev. adv acc. **Circ** 1,500. Scholarly journal analyzing decisions and statutes of interest to the region and the nation.

TENNESSEE LAWYER. V. 1- Sept. 1952-. 0495-1328. Periodical. US. English. ir. Tennessee Bar Association, 3622 West End Avenue, Nashville TN 37205.

TENNESSEE LEGISLATIVE RECORD. Weekly, during the legislative session. Periodical. US. English. ir. $190.00. Tennessee Legislative Record, G-3 State Capitol, Nashville TN 37219. **Tel** (615)741-3511.

TENNESSEE LEGISLATIVE RESEARCHER. Began with Mar. 1974. 0164-4130. Periodical. US. English. sm. $58.00. The Research Group, PO Box 7187, Charlottesville VA 22906. **LC** KFT7. **DD** 348.768046.

THE TENNESSEE RESEARCHER. 0163-2604. Periodical. US. English. mo. $66.00. Research Group Inc, PO Box 7187, Charlottesville VA 22906. **LC** KFT57. **DD** 348.768046, 347.680846.

TERMINATION OF EMPLOYMENT. See Economics - Labor.

TEXAS ANTITRUST BULLETIN. Main/Corp State Bar of Texas. Antitrust and Trade Regulation Section. VFOAT State Bar Section Report. V. 1- Jan. 1977-. 0271-1923. US. English. qt. Federal Legal Publications Inc, 157 Chambers Street, New York NY 10007. **Tel** (212)243-5775. **LC** KFT1431.A15. **DD** 343.76407205.

TEXAS BAR JOURNAL. (TEXAS BAR JOURNAL MICROFORM). Vol. 1 (Jan. 1938)-. 0040-4187. Periodical. US. English. mo. $11.00 Domestic, $12.00 Foreign. Texas Bar Journal, Box 12487 Capitol Station, Austin TX 78711. **Tel** (512)475-2463. **Ind/Abst** Leg. Resour. Index, Index Leg. Period., Curr. Law Index. **LC** K24. **DD** 340.09764. (cum index).

TEXAS BRIEFCASE SHEPARD'S. VFOAT Shepard's Texas Briefcase Citations. 0270-529X. Periodical. US. English. qt. $34.00. Shepard's McGraw Hill, PO Box 1235, Colorado Springs CO 80901. **Tel** (800)525-2474. **LC** KFT1259. **DD** 348.764047 347.640847. Gives you the citing reference to the statute in question ever made by your appellate courts.

TEXAS ELECTION LAW, INCLUDING POLITICAL CALENDER, CONSTITUTIONAL PROVISIONS, ELECTION CODE, AND STATUTES. Main/Corp Texas. US. English. Hart Graphics Inc, PO Box 968, Austin TX 78767. **LC** KFT1620.A29. **DD** 342.74607.

TEXAS FAMILY LAW DIGEST. 1984-. 8755-7576. Periodical. US. English. an. $125.00. Michie Company, PO Box 7587, Charlottesville VA 22906. **Tel** (804)295-6171. **DD** 346.

TEXAS FAMILY LAW REPORTER. Vol. 1, No. 1 (Aug. 1983)-. 0743-9342. Periodical. US. English. mo. $120.00. Matthew Bender & Company Inc, 1275 Broadway, Albany NY 12201.

TEXAS HEALTH LAW REPORTER. Vol. 1, No. 1 (Apr. 1984)-. 0266-0806. Periodical. US. English. bm. Butterworth Legal Publishers, 11004 Metric Boulevard, Austin TX 78754. **LC** KFT1560.A15. **DD** 344.76404105, 347.64044105.

TEXAS INSURANCE LAW REPORTER. Vol. 1, No. 1 (June 1983)-. 0264-6307. Periodical. US. English. bm. $72.00. Butterworth Legal Publishers, 1321 Rutherford Lane/Suite 180, Austin TX 78753. **Tel** (512)835-7921. Ed David B Irons, Michael R Knox,

Law

and Robert O Lamb. LC KFT1385.A15. DD 346.76408605, 347.64068605. Circ 400. Feature articles and digests of Texas appellate court cases on insurance issues.

TEXAS JUDICIAL SYSTEM ANNUAL REPORT OF STATISTICAL AND OTHER DATA. See Statistics.

TEXAS JUVENILE PROBATION REPORT. Main/Corp Texas. Office of Court Administration. VFOAT Juvenile Probation Report. 1977-. 0197-291X. US. English. an. Texas Law Center, Office of Court Administration, 1414 Colorado Street, PO Box 12066, Austin TX 78711. Statistical and other Data on the State Juvenile Justice System.

TEXAS LAWYERS' CIVIL DIGEST. Vol. 19, No. 1 (Jan. 4, 1982)-. 0731-9088. Periodical. US. English. wk. State Bar of Texas, PO Box 12487, Capitol Station, Austin TX 78711. LC KFT1257. DD 348.764074, 347.640846. Texas Lawyers' Weekly Digest, 0098-8987.

TEXAS LEGAL DIRECTORY. See Yearbooks, Almanacs, Directories.

TEXAS OFFICIAL FEES. US. English. Hart Graphics, PO Box 968, Austin TX 78767. LC KFT1745.Z9. DD 347.764077.

TEXAS PERSONAL INJURY LAW REPORTER. Vol. 1, No. 1 (May 1983)-. 0264-4770. Periodical. US. English. bm. $72.00. Butterworth Legal Publishers, 1321 Rutherford Lane/Suite 180, Austin TX 78753. Tel (512)835-7921. Ed Frank R Southers. LC KFT1397.P3. DD 346.76640323, 347.6406323. Circ 400. Feature articles and digests of Texas appellate court decisions on personal injury issues.

TEXAS SCHOOL LAW BULLETIN. Main/Corp Texas. VFOAT Texas Public School Law Bulletin. 1976-. 0362-6334. Monographic Series. US. English. be. Texas Education Agency, 201 East Eleventh Street, Austin TX 78701. DD 344.764071. Each issue contains an index to its own contents - no vol index - loose.

TEXAS SCHOOL LAW NEWS (AUSTIN, TEX. : 1980). (TEXAS SCHOOL LAW NEWS). Vol. 1, No. 1 (Mar. 16, 1980)-. Periodical. US. English. ir. $88.00. Texas School Law News, PO Box 1406, Austin TX 78767. Tel (512)476-7229. Ed Eric Schulze. Circ 850. (ctrl). Latest developments on legal issues and public education in Texas. Texas School Law News.

TEXAS SOUTHERN UNIVERSITY LAW REVIEW CEASED. VFOAT Texas Southern Law Review. Vol. 2, No. 1 (Fall 1971)-V. 6, No. 2 (1981). 0092-3559. US. English. sa. $9.00. Law School, Texas Southern University, 3201 Wheeler Street, Houston TX 77004. Ind/Abst Index Leg. Period. LC K24. DD 340.05. Texas Southern Intramural Law Review, 0737-4623.

THE TEXAS SUPREME COURT JOURNAL. Main/Corp Texas. Supreme Court. V. 1- Sept. 14, 1957-. US. English. $54.86. Box 12132 Capitol Station, Austin TX 78711. LC KFT1245. DD 348.764044. Texas Supreme Court Reporter.

TEXAS TECH LAW REVIEW. VFOAT Law Review. Vol. 1, No. 1 (Fall 1969)-. 0564-6197. Periodical. US. English. ir. $25.00. Texas Tech Law Review, PO Box 4030, Lubbock TX 79409. Tel (806)742-3789. Ed Darren Woody. Ind/Abst Leg. Resour. Index, Index Leg. Period. LC K24. DD 340.05. Index Contents Curr. Leg. Period. LC K24. DD 340.05. Index in last issue of volume - attached. (cum index). bk rev. adv acc. Circ 1,273.

TEXTES D'INTERET GENERAL. Main/Corp France. FR. French. sw. Direction Journax Officiels, 26 rue Dessaix, 75732 Paris Cedex 15 France. DD 340.0944.

TEXTS ADOPTED CEASED. Main/Conf Conference of Local and Regional Authorities of Europe. VFOAT Textes Adoptes. Began with 11th session in 1976. Ceased 17th session (19-21 Oct. 1982). English (French). ir. DD 341.242. Texts Adopted.

THE THIRD BRANCH. Vol. 1, No. 1 (Dec. 1968)- 1968). 0040-6120. Periodical. US. English. mo. Federal Judicial Center, 1520 H Street NW-Dolley Madison HS, Washington DC 20005. Tel (202)633-6347. LC KF8700.A16. DD 347.9973.

THIRD WORLD LEGAL STUDIES. 1982-. US. English. an. Intworlsa, c/o International Center for Law in Development, 777 United Nations Plaza, New York NY 10017.

THREE-YEAR REPORT TO THE MEMBERSHIP OF THE NATIONAL COUNCIL OF JUVENILE COURT JUDGES. Main/Corp National Council of Juvenile Court Judges. 0147-5517. Periodical. US. English. ir. National Council Juvenile Family, PO Box 8978, Reno NY 89507. Tel (702)784-6012. LC KF9787. DD 345.7308.

THURGOOD MARSHALL LAW REVIEW. VFOAT Law Review. Vol. 7, No. 1 (Fall 1981)-. 0749-1646. Periodical. US. English. ir. $9.00. Thurgood Marshall Law Review, Business Manager, 3100 Cleburne Avenue, Box 45, Houston TX 77004. Tel (713)527-7011. Ind/Abst Index Leg. Period. bk rev. adv acc. Texas Southern University Law Review, 0092-3559.

TIDSKRIFT FOR RATTSSOCIOLOGI. VFOAT Rattssociologi. Vol 1 1983/84 No 1-. Periodical. English (Swedish). ir. 140.00. Tidskrift for Rattssociologi, Bredgatan 4, S-222 21 Lund Sweden. LC K24. DD 340.11505.

TIDSSKRIFT FOR RETTSVIDENSKAP. 0040-7143. Periodical. NO. Norwegian. ir. $45.00. Universitetsforlaget, PO Box 2959-Toyen, Oslo 6 Norway. Tel (02)276060. Ed Birger Stuevold Lassen and Magnus Aarbahhe. Ind/Abst Am. Hist. Life, Hist. Abstr. LC K24. bk rev. adv acc. Circ 2,500. Scientific journal of law and legal matters.

TIJDSCHRIFT RECHTSDOCUMENTATIE. 1980. Periodical. BE. Dutch. ir. $57.30. Uitgeverij Kluwer, Santvoorbeeklaan 21-23, 2100 Deurne Antwerpen Belgium. Tel 03 324-78-90. Ed R De Corte. bk rev. adv acc. Circ 2,200. Reference review: Informs every important change in law last month. Periodicals.

TIJDSCHRIFT VOOR ANTILLIAANS RECHT. Periodical. NE. Dutch. qt. Stichting Tijdschrift Voor Antilliaans Recht, Jan Noorduynweg 111, Curacao Netherlands Antilles. LC K24.

TIJDSCHRIFT VOOR CRIMINOLOGIE. See Sociology: General Works, Theory - Social Pathology, Welfare, Criminology.

TIJDSCHRIFT VOOR FAMILIE- EN JEUGDRECHT. VFOAT Familie- en Jeugdrecht. Vol. 1. Periodical. Dutch. bm. 50.00. W E J Tjeenk Willink BV, Postbus 25, 8000 AA Zwolle Netherlands. LC K24.

TIJDSCHRIFT VOOR MILIEU EN RECHT. VFOAT Milieu en Recht. 0165-1137. Periodical. NE. Dutch. bm. Libresso BV, Postbus 878, 7400 AW Deventer Netherlands. Ind/Abst Excerpta Med. LC K24. DD 344.49204605.

TIJDSCHRIFT VOOR PRIVAATRECHT. Vol. 1- Jan. Periodical. BE. Dutch (summaries in English, French, and German). qt. $69.16. E Story Scientia, Eekhout 2, 9000 Ghent Belgium. Tel 91/259413. Ed M Storme. LC K24. bk rev. Circ 1,800. Law.

TIJDSCHRIFT VOOR RECHTSGESCHIEDENIS. VFOAT Revue d'Histoire du Droit, The Legal History Review. Vol. 1-1918-. 0040-7585. Periodical. Dutch (Beginning with V. 3, No. 2, contributions are in French, and English, etc). qt. Kluwer Academic Publishing Group, PO Box 322, 3300 AH Dordrecht The Netherlands. Ind/Abst Am. Hist. Life, Hist. Abstr., Part A, Mod. Hist. Abstr., Hist. Abst., Part B, Twent. Century Abstr., Recent Publ. Artic. LC K24. DD 340.05. (cum index).

TITLE HANDBOOK. 0743-9768. US. English. Title Insurance And Trust, 6300 Wilshire Boulevard, Los Angeles CA 90048. LC KFC300. DD 346.79408688, 347.94068688.

TML LEGISLATIVE REPORT. Main/Corp Texas Municipal League. VAT Texas Municipal League Legislative Report. Periodical. US. English. ir. $25.00. Municipal Advisory Council of Texas, State Bank Building/Suite C, Austin TX 78701.

HO TO CHITSUJO. Periodical. JA. Japanese. ir. 1200. c/o Sen'I Boeki Kaikan. LC K8.

LA TOGA. Spanish. ir. Colegio de Abogados de Puerto Rico, Apartado 1900, San Juan Puerto Rico. DD 340.0627295.

TOIMINTAKERTOMUS. Main/Corp Finland. Korkein Hallinto-Oikeus. VFOAT Verksamhetsberattelse. 0357-9190. Fl. Finnish. ir. Korkein Hallinto-Oikeus, Pohjoisesplanadi 3, 00170 Helsinki 17 Finland.

TOKYO-TO KYOIKU REIKI SHU. Began with 1962 Ed. JA. Japanese. ir. 3000. 52 Nishi Gokencho, Shinjuku-ku 162 Tokyo Japan.

TOLLEY'S CAPITAL GAINS TAX. 1978-79-. UK. English. an. 7.75. Tolley Publishing Company Ltd, 102/104 High Street, Croydon CRO IND England. LC KD5550. DD 343.410524505, 344.103524505.

TOLLEY'S CAPITAL TRANSFER TAX. 1979-80-. UK. English. an. $16.78. Tolley Publishing Company, 17 Scarbrook Road, Croyden Surrey CRO 1SQ England. Tel (01)686-9141. Ed Jane Scollen. LC KD5560. DD 343.4105305, 344.1035305. A comprehensive guide to capital transfer tax since its introduction in 1974. The book covers relevant legislation, statements by the revenue and other official bodies in the United Kingdom.

TOLLEY'S INCOME TAX. See Business - Public Finance.

TOLLEY'S TAX CASES. Began with Vol. for 1976. UK. English. an. Tolley Publishing Company, 102/104 High Street, Croydon CRO IND England. Tel (01)686-9141. Ed Victor Grout. LC KD5356.3. DD 343.410402648, 344.103402648. This book contains summaries of almost 2,300 UK and Irish tax cases reported up to January 1986. All are relevant to current UK tax legislation.

TOLLEY'S TAXATION IN THE REPUBLIC OF IRELAND. UK. English. an. $16.78. Tolley Publishing Company, 17 Scarbrook Road, Croyden Surrey CRO 1SQ England. Tel (01)686-9141. Ed Glyn Saunders and Eric L Harvey. LC KDK1443. DD 343.4170405, 344.1703405. This book sets out the current Irish tax position as it relates to the 1984 finance act and other major legislative provision.

IL TOMMASO NATALE. Vol. 1- Jan./April 1973-. Italian. ir. Via Maqueda 172, Palermo Italy 90100. LC K24. DD 345.450505.

TOPICAL LAW. 1974-. 0265-9735. Periodical. UK. English. sa. 140. Department of Law, Polytechcic of North London Ladbroke House, 62/66 Highbury Grove, London N5 2AD England. Ed C Champness. bk rev. Circ 140. A general law review, articles frequently explain the role of various law. Related offices, public and private.

TORONTO LEGAL DIRECTORY. See Yearbooks, Almanacs, Directories.

TORT & INSURANCE LAW JOURNAL. VFOAT Tort and Insurance Law Journal. Vol. 21, No. 1 (Fall 1985)-. 0885-856X. Periodical. US. English. qt. $22.00 Domestic, $27.00 Foreign. American Bar Association, 750 North Lake Shore Drive, Chicago IL 60611. DD 346. Forum, 0015-8356.

TORT LAW LETTER. (THE TORT LAW LETTER). No. 1- Sept. 1973-. 0094-7849. US. English. mo. $10.00. Benchmark Publications, Box 487, Chapel Hill NC 27514. LC KF1287.8. DD 346.730305.

TORTS. Main/Corp Bay Area Review Course, Inc. 0098-7611. US. English. an. Bay Area Review Course Inc, 5900 Wilshire Boulevard, Los Angeles CA 90036. LC KF1250.Z9. DD 346.7303.

TORTS. 0149-5410. US. English. $9.95. Gilbert Law Summaries, 14415 South Main Street, Gardena CA 90248. LC KF1250.Z9. DD 346.7303.

TOURO LAW REVIEW. Vol. 1, No. 1 (Spring 1985)-. 8756-7326. Periodical. US. English. sa. $5.00. Touro Law Review, 300 Nassau Road, Huntington NY 11743. DD 340.

EN TOUTE JUSTICE (OTTAWA, ONT.). (EN TOUTE JUSTICE). Vol. 1, No 1 (Winter 1983)-. 0824-2801. Periodical. CN. French. qt. 20.00. Association Canadienne d'Assistance Juridique d'Information et de Recherche des Handicapes, C P 3553 Succursale C, Ottawa Ontario K1Y 4J7 Canada. Tel (613)230-8515. Ed H Wierenga. DD 346.71013. bk rev. Circ 500. A journal of law and people with disabilities.

THE TOWN-PLANNING AND LOCAL GOVERNMENT GUIDE. See Housing and Urban Development.

TOXIC CHEMICALS LITIGATION REPORTER. May 16, 1983-. 0737-8513. Periodical. US. English. sm. $600.00. Andrews Publications Inc, PO Box 200, 5123 West Chester Pike, Edgemont PA 19028. Tel (215)353-2565. Ed Leonard E B Andrews. LC KF3958.A59. DD 344.73042402638, 347. 30442402638. The national journal of record reporting toxic chemicals litigation.

TOXIC SUBSTANCES CONTROL ACT. (TOXIC SUBSTANCES CONTROL ACT (TSCA) : REPORT TO CONGRESS FOR FISCAL YEAR . . .).

Law

Main/Corp United States. Environmental Protection Agency. **VFOAT** Toxic Substances Control Act (T.S.C.A). Began with 1981. 0883-0576. US. English. an. US Environmental Protection Agency, Washington DC 20460. **LC** KF3958. **DD** 344.730424. *Administration of the Toxic Substances Control Act.*

TOXICS LAW REPORTER. 0887-7394. Periodical. US. English. wk. $860.00. The Bureau of National Affairs, 9435 Key West Avenue, Rockville MD 20850.

TRADE SECRETS LAW HANDBOOK. 1982-. 0732-0884. US. English. an. $52.50. Clark Boardman Company Ltd, 435 Hudson Street, New York NY 10014. **Tel** (212)929-7500. **LC** KF3197.A152. **DD** 346.73048, 347.30648.

TRADE UNION LAW. No. 1 (Dec. 1980)-. 0715-3309. Periodical. CN. English. bm. $50.00 Six Issues. Trade Union Law c/o Labour Studies Programme Capilano College, 2055 Russell Way, North Vancouver British Columbia V7J 3H5 Canada. **DD** 344.71018.

TRADEMARK LAW HANDBOOK. 1980-81-. 0731-5813. US. English. an. Clark Boradman & Company, 435 Hudson Street, New York NY 10014. **LC** KF3176.A32. **DD** 346.730488, 347.306488.

TRAITEMENTS, SOLDES ET INDEMNITES DES FONCTIONNAIRES A COMPTER DU . . . . **VFOAT** Traitements des Fonctionnaires. FR. French. ir. 48. Direction des Journaux Officels, 26 rue Desaix, 75732 Paris Cedex 15 France. **DD** 342.440686, 344.402686.

TRANSCRIPTS OF DEVELOPMENTS TAPES. **Main/Corp** California Continuing Education of the Bar. 0149-211X. US. English. an. California Continuing Education of the Bar, Department CEB-S 2150 Shattuck Avenue, Berkeley CA 94704. **LC** K3. **DD** 340.09794.

TRANSIT LAW REVIEW. V. 1- Spring/Summer 1977-. 0149-0656. Periodical. US. English. American Public Transit Association, 1100 17th Street Northwest, Washington DC 20036. **LC** K24. **DD** 343.7309805.

TRANSPORTATION LAW JOURNAL. (THE TRANSPORTATION LAW JOURNAL). V. 1- Feb. 1969-. 0049-450X. Periodical. US. English. ir. $15.00. University of Denver College of Law, 7039 East 18th Avenue, Denver CO 80220. **Tel** (303)871-6162. Ed Paul S Dempsey. **Ind/Abst** Manage. Contents, Leg. Resour. Index, Index Leg. Period., Curr. Law Index, Contents Curr. Leg. Period. **LC** K24. **DD** 343.73093. bk rev. adv acc. **Circ** 1,500. Publishes articles on national and international regulatory issues for the legal scholar, practising lawyers and other transportation practitioners.

TRANSPORTRECHT. 0170-5636. Periodical. German. bm. 89.00. Alfred Metzner Verlag, Zeppelinallee 43, 6000 Frankfurt AM Main 97 West Germany. **LC** K24. **DD** 343.4309305, 344.3039305. *Transport + Speditionsrecht.*

TRANSPR. Periodical. GW. German. qt. 10.50 Each Issue. Verlag Transportrecht GMBH, Heinrich-Bocking-Str 1A, 6600 Saarbrucken West Germany. **LC** KK6868.A13. **DD** 343.43093205, 344.30393205.

TRAVAUX DU COLLOQUE INTERNATIONAL DE DROIT COMPARE. **Main/Conf** Colloque International de Droit Compare. **VFOAT** Proceeding of the International Symposium on Comparative Law. 1er - 1963-. 0588-3172. CN. French (English). an. Editions de l'Universite d'Ottawa, Ottawa Ontario K1N 6NS Canada. **DD** 340.2.

TRAVEL AND ENTERTAINMENT, BUSINESS OR PLEASURE. (TRAVEL AND ENTERTAINMENT, BUSINESS OR PLEASURE). Series/Titl Tax Angles and Tax Savings Series. 0733-0030. US. English. an. $2.00. Commerce Clearing House, 4025 West Peterson Avenue, Chicago IL 60646. **LC** KF6395.T7. **DD** 343.730523, 347.303523.

TRAWICK'S FLORIDA PRACTICE AND PROCEDURE. **VFOAT** Florida Practice and Procedure. 1978-. 0191-7684. US. English. Harrison Company Publishers, 3110 Crossing Park, Norcross GA 30071. **LC** KFF530. **DD** 347.75905. *Florida Practice and Procedure, 0191-7676.*

TREATISE ON ENVIRONMENTAL LAW. US. English. ir. Matthew Bender & Company Inc, 1275, Broadway, Albany NY 12201. **Tel** (800)833-9844. Index published separately - free - automatically sent.

TREMEEAR'S CRIMINAL CODE AND MISCELLANEOUS STATUTES. **Main/Corp** Canada. Began publication in 1976?. 0226-1987. CN. English. an. **DD** 345.71002632.

TRENDS IN LEGAL SERVICES. 0098-8995. US. English. mo. Editorial Services, 1523 L Street Northwest, Washington DC 20005. **LC** KF300.A1. **DD** 340.0973.

TRENT LAW JOURNAL. (THE TRENT LAW JOURNAL). V. 1- 1977-. 0309-8990. UK. English. ir. Gaunt & Sons, 3011 Gulf Drive, Holmes FL 33510. **Tel** (813)778-5211. **Ind/Abst** Leg. Resour. Index. **LC** K24. **DD** 349.4105.

TRIAL. V. 1- Dec. 1964-. 0041-2538. Periodical. US. English. mo. $24.00. Association of Trial Lawyers of America, 1050 31st Street NW, Washington DC 20007. **Tel** (202)965-3500. Ed Anne R Grant. **Ind/Abst** Energy Inf. Abstr., Environ. Abstr., Index Leg. Period., Soc. Sci. Index, Curr. Law Index, Leg. Resour. Index, Soc. Sci. Citation Index, Hospit. Lit. Index. bk rev. adv acc. **Circ** 73,000. Educational information on lawyers, policy and trial techniques for plaintiff's lawyers. *Pl & E Bulletin.*

TRIAL ADVOCATE QUARTERLY. Vol. 1, No. 1 (Dec. 1981)-. 0743-412X. Periodical. US. English. qt. $20.00. Trial Advocate Quarterly Nova University Center for the Study of Law, 3100 SW 9th Avenue, Fort Lauderdale FL 33315. **Tel** (305)522-2300. Ed Michael L Richmond. **Ind/Abst** Leg. Resour. Index. **LC** KFF538.A1. **DD** 347.7590705, 347.5907705. **Circ** 1,500. (ctrl). Scholarly articles and recent cases on interest to attorneys representing defendants in civil litigation, to judges, and to all concerned with the development of tort law.

TRIAL AND TORT TRENDS. **VFOAT** Belli Seminar. 0564-2108. US. English. an. Ed M M Belli. **DD** 347.5. *Annual Convention.*

TRIAL BAR NEWS. **VFOAT** S.D.T.L.A. Trial Bar News. 0732-5959. Periodical. US. English. San Diego Trial Lawyers Association, 4420 Hotel Circle Court/Suite 155, San Diego CA 92108. **LC** KFC1025.A15. **DD** 347.79407, 347.94077.

THE TRIAL COURT REPORTER. US. English. Office of the Chief, Administrative Justice, The Trial Court, 300 New Court, Boston MA 02108. **LC** KFM2915. **DD** 347.7440105, 347.4407105.

TRIAL DIPLOMACY JOURNAL. V. 1- Spring 1978-. 0160-7308. Periodical. US. English. qt. $28.00. Trial Diplomacy Journal, 601 Skokie Boulevard L-7, Northbrook IL 60062. **Tel** (312)498-0040. Ed Janine Warsaw. **Ind/Abst** Leg. Resour. Index. **LC** KF8911.A3. **DD** 347.73705. bk rev. adv acc. **Circ** 4,000. Articles on trial techniques for trial lawyers and judges.

THE TRIAL LAWYER'S GUIDE. 0041-2546. Periodical. US. English. qt. The Trial Lawyer's Guide, 3201 Old Glenview Road, Wilmette IL 60091. Ed I Goldstein. **Ind/Abst** Index Leg. Period. **DD** 347.9.

TRIAL LAWYER'S GUIDE (ANNUAL). (THE TRIAL LAWYER'S GUIDE). 1957 Annual-. 0041-2546. US. English. an. Callaghan & Company, 3201 Old Glenview Road, Wilmette IL 60091. **Ind/Abst** Curr. Law Index. **DD** 347.9. (cum index).

TRIAL LAWYERS SECTION NEWSLETTER. Vol. 1, No. 1 (Dec. 1980)-. 0276-1009. Periodical. US. English. New York State Bar Association, 1 Elk Street, Albany NY 12207. **LC** KFN6015.A59. **DD** 347.7470705, 347.4707705.

TRIAL OF ACCIDENT CASES. US. English. sa. Matthew Bender & Company Inc, 1275 Broadway, Albany NY 12201. **Tel** (800)833-9844.

TRIAL TALK. **Main/Corp** Colorado Trial Lawyers Association. 0747-1378. Periodical. US. English. mo. $24.00. Colorado Trial Lawyers Association, 600 Grant Street #700, Denver CO 80203.

TRIBAL COURT REPORTER. V. 1- Mar. 1979-. 0271-4272. US. English. qt. $65.00. American Indian Lawyer Training Program Inc, 319 MacArthur Boulevard, Oakland CA 94610. **Tel** (415)834-9333. **LC** KF8220.A15. **DD** 347.73008997. Incorporated into Indian Law Reporter in 1983.

TRIBUNA DA JUSTICA. Periodical. BL. Portuguese. wk. 18000. Hemeron Editora S A, Avenida Aclimacao No 226, CEP 01531 Sal Paulo Brazil. **LC** KHD2501.A15.

TRIBUNA DA JUSTICA. SUPLEMENTO DE JURISPRUDENCIA. Periodical. BL. Portuguese. wk. Hemeron Editora S A, Av Aclimacao 225, CEP 01531 Sao Paulo Brazil. **LC** KHD72. **DD** 348.8104105, 348.1084105.

TRIBUNA DO ADVOGADO. Periodical. BL. Portuguese. ir. Conselho Seccional do Estado do rio de Janeiro da Ordem dos Advogados do Brasil, Avenida Marechal Camara 201-4 Andar, Rio de Janeiro Brazil. **DD** 340.062815.

I TRIBUNALI AMMINISTRATIVI REGIONALI. Yearly V. 1- Jan. 1975-. Periodical. IT. Italian. mo. $139.60. Casa Editrice Italedi, Piazza Cavour 19, 00193 Roma Italy.

TRIBUNAUX CORRECTIONNELS, COURS D'APPEL, CONSEILS DE GUERRE ET COUR MILITAIRE. See Statistics.

TRIBUTACION. Periodical. Spanish. ir. Departamento de Ingresos y Deuda Publica, Oficina Nacional de Presupuesto, Av Mexico Esq Leopoldo, Navarro 4To Piso, Santo Domingo Dominican Republic. **LC** K24. **DD** 343.80405.

TRISAKTI. Vol. 1- Jan. 1976-. Periodical. Indonesian. ir. Kampus Kompleks Barat, Jalan Kiai Tapa Jakarta-Barat, Jakarta Indonesia. **LC** K24.

TRUE BILL : THE NEWSLETTER OF THE PROSECUTOR COUNCIL. **Main/Corp** Texas. Prosecutor Council. Periodical. US. English. bm. **LC** KFT1777. **DD** 345.76401, 347.64051.

TRUST INDENTURE ACT OF 1939 RELEASE. **Main/Corp** United States. Securities and Exchange Commission. No. 1- Jan. 23, 1940-. US. English. ir. Securities and Exchange Commission, 500 North Capitol Street, Washington DC 20549.

TRUSTS. **Main/Corp** Bay Area Review Course, Inc. US. English. an. Bay Area Review Course Inc, 5900 Wilshire Boulevard, Los Angeles CA 90036. **LC** KF730.Z9. **DD** 346.73059.

TUBINGER RECHTSWISSENSCHAFTLICHE ABHANDLUNGEN. 0082-6731. GW. German. ir. JCB Mohr, Paul Siebeck, Postfach 2040, 7400 Tuebingen West Germany.

TULANE LAW REVIEW. V. 4- Dec. 1929-. Periodical. US. English. bm. Tulane Law Review Association, Tulane University Station, New Orleans LA 70118. (cum index). *Southern Law Quarterly.*

TULANE LAW REVIEW. TEN YEAR INDEX VOLUMES 46-55. See Indexes/Abstracts.

TULANE LAWYER. V. 1- Spring 1979-. Periodical. US. English. $20.00. Tulane University School of Law, Publication Center/Office University Relations, New Orleans LA 70118. **Tel** (504)865-5939. Ed Susan L Krinsky. bk rev. adv acc. **Circ** 5,000. (ctrl). Magazine for alumni and friends of Tulane Law School with occasional articles of general interest.

TUNG WU FA LU HSUEH PAO. **VFOAT** Soochow Law Review. V. 1- Periodical. CH. Chinese (English). sa. 200.00 Domestic, $8.00 US. Tung Wu Ta Hsueh, 1 Lane 129 Yen Ping South Road, Taipei Taiwan 100 Republic of China. **LC** K24.

TYDSKRIF VIR DIE SUID-AFRIKAANSE REG. **VFOAT** Journal of South African Law. Mar. 1976-. Periodical. SA. Afrikaans (English). tm. 33.00. Faculty of Law, Rand Afrikaans University, Box 123, Kenwyn 7790 South Africa. **Tel** 711181. Ed J C Sonnekus. **LC** K24. bk rev. **Circ** 1,100. Journal containing articles on all subjects pertaining to South African law with the emphasis on articles regarding law practice in South Africa.

TYDSKRIF VIR REGSWETENSKAP. Periodical. Afrikaans (abstracts in English). ir. 20.00. Fakulteit van Regsgeleerdheid, Universiteit van die Oranje-Vrystaat, Postbus 339, Bloemfontein South Africa. **Tel** (051)70711. Ed D C du Tort. **LC** K24. **DD** 340.0968. bk rev. adv acc. **Circ** 2,000. Devoted to original research in law, general juridical articles on law and practice, critical reviews, discussion of case law and legislation of South Africa.

U. S. TAX CASES. **VFOAT** CCH U.S. Tax Cases. Vol. 1 (1913-29)-. 0277-402X. US. English. sa. Commerce Clearing House Inc, 4025 West Peterson Avenue, Chicago IL 60646.

THE U-T LAWYER. V. 1- Fall 1962-. 0041-560X. Periodical. US. English. sa. University of Tennessee, College of Law, 1505 West Cumberland Avenue, Knoxville TN 37916.

U.C. DAVIS LAW REVIEW. **Main/Corp** University of California, Davis. School of Law. **VFOAT** University of California, Davis, Law Review. V. 13- Winter 1979/80-. 0197-4564. Periodical. US. English. qt. $20.00. University of California at Davis, School of

Law

Law, Davis CA 95616. Tel (916)752-2551. Ed Jon Sands and Michael Laurence. Ind/Abst Index Leg. Period., Curr. Law Index, Leg. Resour. Index, Contents Curr. Leg. Period. LC K3. DD 349.79405. bk rev. Circ 700. General articles on topical developments in the law. *UCD Law Review*.

UCLA-ALASKA LAW REVIEW. VFOAT UCLA Alaska Law Review. Vol. 1, No. 1 (Fall 1971)-Vol. 12, No. 1 & 2 (Fall 1982-Spring 1983). Periodical. US. English. sa. Ind/Abst Public Aff. Inf. Serv. Bull., Index Leg. Period. LC K3. DD 340.05. *Alaska Law Journal*.

UCLA JOURNAL OF ENVIRONMENTAL LAW & POLICY. See Sanitation, Environmental Technology.

UCLA LAW REVIEW. Main/Corp University of California, Los Angeles. School of Law. VFOAT University of California Los Angeles Law Review. VAT University of California at Los Angeles Law Review. V. 1- Dec. 1953-. 0041-5650. US. English. bm. $24.00 Domestic, $27.00 Foreign. UCLA Law Review, 405 Hilgard Avenue, Los Angeles CA 90024. Tel (213)825-4929. Ed Federico Cheever. Ind/Abst Women Stud. Abstr., ABI/Inform, Public Aff. Inf. Serv. Bull., Index Leg. Period., Soc. Sci. Citation Index, Leg. Resour. Index, Curr. Law Index, Leg. Contents, Contents Curr. Leg. Period. LC K25. DD 340.05. (cum index). bk rev. adv acc. Circ 1,600. A scholarly journal publishing work by law students, law faculty, and lawyers regarding issues of general interest in the law. *UCLA Intramural Law Review*.

THE UGANDA LAW FOCUS. V. 1- Oct. 1972-. UG. English. ir. 7.50 Per Copy. Law Den Center, PO Box 7117, Kampala Uganda. LC K25. DD 340.05.

UGYVEDI ERTESITO. 0230-8398. Periodical. HU. Hungarian. mo. 96.00. Orszagos Ugyvedi Tanacs, 1055 Budapest, Szemere U.8 Hungary. *Ugyvedi Kozlony*.

UMKC LAW REVIEW. VFOAT U.M.K.C. Law Review. VAT University of Missouri, Kansas City, Law Review. Began with Spring 1970. 0047-7575. Periodical. US. English. qt. $16.00. University of Missouri at Kansas City, 5100 Rockhill Road, Kansas City MO 64110. Tel (816)276-1656. Ind/Abst Leg. Resour. Index, Index Leg. Period., Contents Curr. Leg. Period., Curr. Law Index. LC K11. DD 349.77805, 347.78005. *University of Missouri at Kansas City Law Review, 0737-0636*.

UMWELTSCHUTZDELIKTE. German. an. LC KK6256.7. DD 345.430242, 344.305242.

UNE A L'AUTRE. See Medicine - Gynecology & Obstetrics.

UNIFORM COMMERCIAL CODE LAW JOURNAL. V. 1, No. 1 (Summer 1968)-. 0041-672X. Periodical. US. English. qt. Warren Gorham & Lamont, 210 South Street, Boston MA 02111. Tel (800)225-2363. Ind/Abst Manage. Contents, Trade Ind. Index, Leg. Resour. Index, ABI/Inform, Index Leg. Period., Curr. Law Index, Soc. Sci. Citation Index, Contents Curr. Leg. Period. LC K25. DD 347.7. CODEN UCCLA7.

THE UNIFORM COMMERCIAL CODE LAW LETTER. V. 1- Mar. 1967-. 0503-1966. Periodical. US. English. mo. $131.25. Warren Gorham Lamont Inc, 210 South Street, Boston MA 02111. Tel (800)225-2363 Outside Massachusetts.

UNIFORM COMMERCIAL CODE REPORTING SERVICE. VFOAT U.C.C. Reporting Service. Vol. 1-. US. English. ir. Callaghan, 3201 Old Glenview Road, Wilmette IL 60019. LC KF885. DD 347.70973.

A UNIFORM SYSTEM OF CITATION. US. English. ir. Harvard Law Review Association, Gannett House, Cambridge MA 02138. Tel (617)495-7888.

UNION DEMOCRACY REVIEW. See Economics - Labor.

UNION LABOR REPORT. See Economics - Labor.

UNION LIST OF LEGAL PERIODICALS, DISTRICT OF COLUMBIA AREA. Main/Corp Law Librarians' Society of Washington, D. C. US. English. ir. $115.00. Hogan and Hartson Law Firm, 815 Connecticut Avenue NW, Washington DC 20006. Tel (202)331-5799.

UNION LIST OF LEGISLATIVE HISTORIES. 1st- Ed. US. English. ir. $50.00. Fred B Rothman and Company, 10368 West Centennial Road, Littleton CO 80127. Tel (303)979-5657. This publication provides the user with a listing of the holdings of the libraries in Washington, DC area that have compiled in-house legislative histories on various legislative matters.

UNITED STATES ATTORNEYS BULLETIN. 0566-0785. Periodical. US. English. bw. LC KF127. DD 348.7326.

UNITED STATES ATTORNEYS' MANUAL. Title 1-. US. English. ir. Superintendent of Documents, Government Printing Office, Washington DC 20006. Tel (202)783-3238.

UNITED STATES CLAIMS COURT DIGEST. No. 1 (Aug. 1983)-. 8755-5980. US. English. mo. West Publishing Company, 50 West Kellogg Boulevard, PO Box 3526, St Paul MN 55165. LC KF125.C51. DD 348.7341505, 347.3084105.

UNITED STATES CLAIMS COURT REPORTER. Vol. 1-. 0740-8080. US. English. LC KF125.C5. DD 348.7344, 347.30844.

UNITED STATES CODE ANNOTATED. 1927-. Periodical. US. English. West Publishing Company, 950 University Avenue, Bronx NY 10452. DD 345.21. Index received separately bound from publisher. (cum index).

UNITED STATES CODE. SUPPLEMENT. Main/Corp United States. Began with 1940 Ed. US. English. an. US Government Printing Office, Superintendent of Documents, Washington DC 20402. *Laws, etc. Code of the Laws of the United States of America of a General and Permanent Character. Supplement*.

UNITED STATES COURT DIRECTORY (UNITED STATES. ADMINISTRATIVE OFFICE OF THE UNITED STATES COURTS). See Yearbooks, Almanacs, Directories.

UNITED STATES COURT OF INTERNATIONAL TRADE REPORTS. (UNITED STATES COURT OF INTERNATIONAL TRADE REPORTS : CASES ADJUDGED IN THE UNITED STATES COURT OF INTERNATIONAL TRADE). Vol. 1 (Nov. 1980-June 1981)-. 0740-9540. US. English. sa. Superintendent of Documents, US Government Printing Office, Washington DC 20402. LC KF6655.A2. DD 347.7328, 347.30728. *United States Customs Court Reports*.

UNITED STATES COURTS (WASHINGTON, D.C.). (THE UNITED STATES COURTS). 0149-9777. US. English. an. Administrative Office of the United States Courts, Washington DC 20544.

UNITED STATES COURTS (WASHINGTON, D.C. : 1980). (THE UNITED STATES COURTS). VFOAT Report of the Director of the Administrative Office of the United States Courts Workload for the Year Ended June 30. 0732-7900. US. English. an. LC KF180. DD 347.7313, 347.30713.

UNITED STATES CUSTOMS COURT REPORTS CEASED. (UNITED STATES CUSTOMS COURT REPORTS : CASES ADJUDGED IN THE UNITED STATES CUSTOMS COURT). VFOAT Customs Court Reports. Vol. 1 (July/Dec. 1938)-Vol. 85 (July/Oct. 1980). US. English. sa. US Government Printing Office, Superintendent of Documents, Washington DC 20402. DD 333.260973.

U.S. DISTRICT COURT FEDERAL FILINGS ALERT. VFOAT Federal Filings Alert. VAT United States District Court Federal Filings Alert. V. 6, No. 1- Jan. 14, 1980-. 0742-1087. Periodical. US. English. wk. $178.00. Want Publishing Company, 1511 K Street NW, Washington DC 20005. Tel (202)783-1887. Ed Robert S Want. Circ 1,200. Reports on new cases in selected areas of the law filed in federal courts around the country. *U.S. District Court Current Filings Alert*.

UNITED STATES DISTRICT COURTS SENTENCES IMPOSED CHART. Began with 1976/77. 0161-2093. US. English. an. Superintendent of Documents, US Government Printing Office, Washington DC 20402. LC KF183. DD 345.73077.

THE UNITED STATES GENERALIZED SYSTEM OF PREFERENCES. 8755-7843. US. English. an. $5.00. General Secretariat, Organization of American States, Washington DC 20006. LC KF6708.P7. DD 343.7305602636, 347. 3035602636.

UNITED STATES JUDICIAL REPORTER. 0094-2553. US. English. ir. $45.00. US Judicial Reporter, PO Box 541, Harrisburg PA 17018. LC KF105.1. DD 348.7344.

THE UNITED STATES LAW WEEK. V. 1- Sept. 5, 1933-. 0148-8139. Periodical. US. English. ir. Bureau of National Affairs Inc, 1231 15th Street NW, Washington DC 20037. Tel (301)258-1033. Ind/Abst Funk Scott Index Corp. Ind. *United States Weekly Law Journal*.

UNITED STATES LAWYERS REFERENCE DIRECTORY. See Yearbooks, Almanacs, Directories.

UNITED STATES REPORTS . . ., CASES ADJUDGED IN THE SUPREME COURT AT . . . . Main/Corp United States. Supreme Court. VFOAT Cases Adjudged in the Supreme Court at . . . . VAT United States Reports. Began with: Vol. 108, in 1882. US. English. ir. Superintendent of Documents, US Government Printing Office, Washington DC 20402. LC KF101. *United States Reports, Supreme Court*.

UNITED STATES SUPREME COURT RECORDS AND BRIEFS INDEX. See Indexes/Abstracts.

U.S. TAX CASES. (U.S. TAX CASES : CONSOLIDATED VOLUMES). V. 1 (1913/29)- – Cited 1 USTC. 0277-402X. US. English. sa. LC KF6280.A2.

UNIVERSITY OF ARKANSAS AT LITTLE ROCK LAW JOURNAL. VFOAT UALR Law Journal. V. 1-. 0162-8372. Periodical. US. English. qt $12.00. U A L R School of Law, 400 West Markham Street, Little Rock AR 72201. Ed Scott J Lancaster. Ind/Abst Leg. Resour. Index, Index Leg. Period. LC K25. DD 340.09767. adv acc. Circ 3,500. (ctrl). Scholarly law publication with particular emphasis on areas of interest to Arkansas lawyers.

UNIVERSITY OF BALTIMORE LAW REVIEW. V. 1- Winter 1971-. 0091-5440. US. English. ty. $10.00 Members, $15.00 Nonmember. University of Baltimore Law, 1420 North Charles Street, Baltimore MD 21201. Tel (301)625-3440. Ed Elizabeth Susan Vanlaningham Miller. Ind/Abst Leg. Resour. Index, Index Leg. Period., Curr. Law Index, Contents Curr. Leg. Period. LC K2. DD 340.05. bk rev. adv acc. Circ 1,500. Law review focusing on both, national and Maryland issues and trends.

UNIVERSITY OF BRIDGEPORT LAW REVIEW. V.1- 1980-. 0735-2832. Periodical. US. English. sa. $10.00. University of Bridgeport, 303 University Avenue, Bridgeport CT 06602. Tel (203)576-4068. Ed Jonathan Marks. Ind/Abst Leg. Resour. Index. LC K25. DD 340.05. bk rev. adv acc. Circ 500. Scholarly commentary on recent cases and significant trends in the law.

UNIVERSITY OF BRITISH COLUMBIA LAW REVIEW. VFOAT U. B. C. Law Review. V. 1- Mar. 1959-. 0068-1849. Periodical. CN. English. sa. Ind/Abst Leg. Resour. Index, Public Aff. Inf. Serv. Bull., Index Leg. Period. *University of British Columbia Legal Notes, 0497-2910*.

THE UNIVERSITY OF CHICAGO LAW REVIEW. V. 1- May 1933-. 0041-9494. Periodical. US. English. qt. $24.00. University of Chicago Law, 1111 East 60th Street, Chicago IL 60637. Tel (312)962-9593. Ed Richard Cordray. Ind/Abst Manage. Contents, Leg. Resour. Index, ABC Pol Sci, ABI/Inform, Index Leg. Period., Soc. Sci. Citation Index, Sociol. Abstr., Contents Curr. Leg. Period., Curr. Law Index, Lang. Lang. Behav. Abstr. DD 347.05. CODEN UCLRA2. bk rev. adv acc. Circ 2,100. Contains articles and book reviews by eminent legal authorities as well as comments by students on current legal problems.

UNIVERSITY OF CINCINNATI LAW REVIEW. VFOAT Cincinnati Law Review. V. 1- Jan. 1927-. 0009-6881. Periodical. US. English. qt. $16.00 Domestic, $19.00 Foreign. University of Cincinnati Law Review, College of Law, Cincinnati OH 45221. Tel (513)475-5081. Ed Lynn Marmer. Ind/Abst Leg. Resour. Index, Energy Inf. Abstr., Environ. Abstr., Index Leg. Period. LC K25. (cum index). bk rev. adv acc. Circ 1,100. (ctrl). Lead articles, comments and case notes all relating to law.

UNIVERSITY OF COLORADO LAW REVIEW. V. 35- Fall 1962-. 0041-9516. Periodical. US. English. qt. $20.00. University of Colorado Law Review, 290 Fleming Hall, Boulder CO 80309. Tel (303)492-6145. Ed David Brennan. Ind/Abst Leg.

Resour. Index, Sel. Water Resour. Abstr., Index Leg. Period. **LC** K25. **DD** 347.05. (cum index). bk rev. adv acc. **Circ** 900. (ctrl). As well as general law topics, at least one issue of the four each year is devoted to natural resources topic. *Rocky Mountain Law Review.*

UNIVERSITY OF DAYTON LAW REVIEW. V. 1, No. 2- May 1976-. 0162-9174. Periodical. US. English. ty. $11.75. University of Dayton Law, 300 College Park, Dayton OH 45469. **Tel** (513)229-3642. **Ed** Richard D Anglin. **Ind/Abst** Leg. Resour. Index, Index Leg. Period. **LC** K4. **DD** 340.05. adv acc. **Circ** 550. (ctrl). General coverage of all areas of law, with special emphasis on Ohio legislation and judicial decisions. *University of Dayton Intramural Law Review, 0363-2148.*

UNIVERSITY OF DETROIT JOURNAL OF URBAN LAW. **VFOAT** Journal of Urban Law. Vol. 54, Issue 1 (Fall 1976)-. 0161-7095. US. English. qt. $10.00. Editorial and Business Offices, 651 East Jefferson Avenue, Detroit MI 48226. **Ind/Abst** Leg. Resour. Index, Index Leg. Period. (cum index). *Journal of Urban Law.*

THE UNIVERSITY OF FLORIDA LAW CENTER NEWS. V. 1- Mar. 1964-. 0502-6679. US. English. ir. University of Florida Law, Center Association, Gainesville FL 32601.

UNIVERSITY OF FLORIDA LAW REVIEW. V. 1- Spring 1948-. 0041-9583. Periodical. US. English. ir. $20.00. University of Florida Law Review, College of Law, Gainesville FL 32611. **Tel** (904)392-2148. **Ed** Blan Teagle. **Ind/Abst** Leg. Resour. Index, Sel. Water Resour. Abstr., Index Leg. Period., Curr. Law Index, Contents Curr. Leg. Period. **LC** K25. (cum index). bk rev. adv acc. **Circ** 1,500. A legal periodical composed of articles written by educators, practitioners and students on topics of current interest to the legal community.

UNIVERSITY OF GHANA LAW JOURNAL. Vol. 1, No. 1-. 0041-9605. Periodical. GH. English. sa. $15.00. University of Ghana Law Journal, C E K Kumado, Legon NR Accra Ghana. **Tel** 775381. **Ed** F S Tsikata. bk rev. adv acc. **Circ** 1,000. Articles range from discussion of Ghanaian law, through discussion of African and third world legal issues to contributions on general legal theory. *Legon Law Journal.*

UNIVERSITY OF HAWAII LAW REVIEW. Vol. 1- Fall 1979-. 0271-9835. Periodical. US. English. sa. $16.00. University Hawaii, Research Corporation/2515 Dole Street, Honolulu HI 96822. **Tel** (808)948-6334. **Ed** Joyce McCarty. **Ind/Abst** Leg. Resour. Index, Index Leg. Period., Curr. Law Index, Contents Curr. Leg. Period. **LC** K25. **DD** 349.96905. bk rev. adv acc. **Circ** 500. Focus on Pacific Asian affairs, water use, and land use.

THE UNIVERSITY OF IFE (NIGERIA) LAW REPORTS. **Main/Corp** Ife. University. 1971-. English. ir. University of IFE, Periodicals Department, Ile-Ife Nigeria. **DD** 348.669046.

UNIVERSITY OF ILLINOIS LAW REVIEW. **VFOAT** Law Review. Vol. 1981, No. 1-. 0276-9948. Periodical. US. English. qt. $20.00. University of Illinois, 74 Law Building, 506 East Pennsylvania Avenue, Champaign IL 61820. **Tel** (217)333-3156. **Ind/Abst** Leg. Resour. Index, Index Leg. Period. **LC** K25. **DD** 349.7305, 347.3005. bk rev. adv acc. **Circ** 2,000. Scholarly legal periodical with national and international focus but mindful of Illinois practitioner needs. *University of Illinois Law Forum, 0041-963X.*

UNIVERSITY OF KANSAS LAW REVIEW. **Main/Corp** University of Kansas. School of Law. **VFOAT** Kansas Law Review. V. 1- Nov. 1952-. 0083-4025. Periodical. US. English. qt. $18.00. University of Kansas Law Review, Green Hall, Lawrence KS 66045. **Tel** (913)864-3463. **Ed** Sue Ann Bradford. **Ind/Abst** Leg. Resour. Index, Index Leg. Period. **LC** K25. (cum index). adv acc. **Circ** 1,300. Articles on recent developments in the law.

UNIVERSITY OF MIAMI LAW REVIEW. V. 12- Fall 1957-. 0041-9818. Periodical. US. English. ir. $18.00. University of Miami, School of Law, Coral Gables FL 33124. **Tel** (305)284-2464. **Ed** Thane Rosenbaur. **Ind/Abst** Sociol. Abstr., Contents Curr. Leg. Period., Index Leg. Period., Curr. Law Index, Leg. Resour. Index, Account. Index. Suppl., Lang. Lang. Behav. Abstr., Sel. Water Resour. Abstr., Public Aff. Inf. Serv. Bull. (cum index). bk rev. adv acc. **Circ** 3,000. (ctrl). *Miami Law Quarterly.*

UNIVERSITY OF MICHIGAN JOURNAL OF LAW REFORM. **Main/Corp** University of Michigan. Law School. V. 6- Fall 1972-. 0363-602X. Periodical. US. English. ty. $16.00. University of Michigan Law School, S-324 Legal Research, Ann Arbor MI 48109. **Tel** (313)763-2195. **Ed** John P Barker. **Ind/Abst** Leg. Resour. Index, Public Aff. Inf. Serv. Bull., Index Leg. Period., Curr. Law Index, Contents Curr. Leg. Period. **LC** K16. **DD** 340.05. bk rev. adv acc. **Circ** 1,000. (ctrl). Legal periodical focusing on law reform, drafting model statutes, constitutional reform and empirical research. *Journal of Law Reform, 0033-1546.*

UNIVERSITY OF MINNESOTA LAW SCHOOL NEWS. V. 1- 1951-. Periodical. US. English. ir. University of Minnesota Law School, 229 19th Avenue South, Minneapolis MN 55455.

UNIVERSITY OF NEW BRUNSWICK LAW JOURNAL. **VFOAT** Revue de Droit de l'Universite du Nouveau-Brunswick. V. 5- Jan. 1952-. 0077-8141. CN. English. an. 12.00. University of New Brunswick, Bag Service 44999, Fredericton New Brunswick E3B 2X1 Canada. **Tel** (506)453-4669. **Ed** Howard A Baker. **Ind/Abst** Leg. Resour. Index, Index Leg. Period. bk rev. adv acc. **Circ** 1,650. (ctrl). Publication devoted to consideration of certain legal issues, problems and philosophies through the preservation of articles, comments and case notes in widely ranging areas of law. *University of New Brunswick Law School Journal, 0315-520X.*

UNIVERSITY OF NEW SOUTH WALES LAW JOURNAL. (THE UNIVERSITY OF NEW SOUTH WALES LAW JOURNAL). **VFOAT** New South Wales Law Journal. Began with June 1975. Periodical. AT. English. ir. 14.75. University of New South Wales Law Journal, Faculty of Law, PO Box 1, Kinsington New South Wales 2033 Australia. **Tel** 662 3347. **Ed** Pat Fell, Ann Cormach and Christoper Taubman. **Ind/Abst** Leg. Resour. Index, APAIS, Aust. Public Aff. Inf. Serv., Index Leg. Period. Index in last issue of volume - loose - unpaged. bk rev. adv acc. **Circ** 600. One thematic issue centering around a topic of current legal interest - this year family law and one general issue each year.

UNIVERSITY OF PENNSYLVANIA LAW REVIEW. V. 93- 1944/45-. 0041-9907. US. English. bm. $28.00 Domestic, $32.00 Foreign. University of Pennsylvania, 3400 Chestnut Street/14, Philadelphia PA 19174. **Tel** (215)898-7060. **Ed** Michael Doss. **Ind/Abst** Leg. Resour. Index, ABC Pol Sci, Index Leg. Period., Soc. Sci. Citation Index, Contents Curr. Leg. Period., Curr. Law Index. **LC** K25. **DD** 340.09748. bk rev. adv acc. **Circ** 2,000. Publishes unsolicited articles that in any way relate to the law. We assume our readership will include students, academics, and practitioners. *University of Pennsylvania Law Review and American Law Register, 0749-9833.*

UNIVERSITY OF PITTSBURGH LAW REVIEW. **VFOAT** Law Review. V. 1, No. 1 (Mar. 1935)-. 0041-9915. Periodical. US. English. qt. $18.00. University of Pittsburgh Law Review, 3900 Forbes Avenue, Pittsburgh PA 15260. **Tel** (412)624-3912. **Ed** Kurt M Saunders and Andrew Ruymann. **Ind/Abst** Leg. Resour. Index, Women Stud. Abstr., Index Leg. Period. **LC** K25. (cum index). bk rev. adv acc. **Circ** 600. (ctrl). Publication of articles of current general interest to the legal community.

UNIVERSITY OF PUGET SOUND LAW REVIEW. V. 1- Fall 1977-. 0161-0708. Periodical. US. English. ty. $12.00. University of Puget Sound, 950 Broadway Plaza, Tacoma WA 98402. **Tel** (206)756-3200. **Ed** Alice Leiner. **Ind/Abst** Leg. Resour. Index, Index Leg. Period. **LC** K24. **DD** 340.05. **Circ** 1,000. Law review.

THE UNIVERSITY OF QUEENSLAND LAW JOURNAL. **VFOAT** Law Journal. Vol. 1, No. 1 (Dec. 1948)-. 0083-4041. AT. English. an. University of Queensland Press, PO Box 42, St Lucia Queensland 4067 Australia. **Tel** 377-2459. **Ind/Abst** Leg. Resour. Index, Index Leg. Period., APAIS, Aust. Public Aff. Inf. Serv., Curr. Law Index.

UNIVERSITY OF RICHMOND LAW REVIEW. V. 3- 1968-. 0566-2389. Periodical. US. English. qt. TC Williams School of Law, University of Richmond, Richmond VA 23173. **Ind/Abst** Leg. Resour. Index, Index Leg. Period., Curr. Law Index, Contents Curr. Leg. Period. **LC** K25. **DD** 340.0973. *University of Richmond Law Notes.*

UNIVERSITY OF SAN FRANCISCO LAW REVIEW. Began in Oct. 1966. 0042-0018. Periodical. US. English. qt. $16.00. University of San Francisco, 2130 Fulton Street, San Francisco CA 94117. **Tel** (415)666-6154. **Ind/Abst** Leg. Resour. Index, Index Leg. Period., Contents Curr. Leg. Period., Curr. Law Index. **DD** 340.05. (cum index). bk rev. adv acc. **Circ** 1,000. Nonprofit corporation symposium issue.

UNIVERSITY OF TASMANIA LAW REVIEW. Vol. 2, No. 1 (Nov. 1964)-. 0082-2108. Periodical. AT. English. an. 8.00. University of Tasmania, Box 252C, Hobart Tasmania, Australia. **Tel** (002)20-2628. **Ed** Frank Bates. **Ind/Abst** Leg. Resour. Index, Index Leg. Period., APAIS, Aust. Public Aff. Inf. Serv. **LC** K25. **DD** 340.05. bk rev. adv acc. **Circ** 500. Publishes articles on a wide range of legal subjects. *Tasmanian University Law Review.*

THE UNIVERSITY OF TOLEDO LAW REVIEW. (UNIVERSITY OF TOLEDO LAW REVIEW). **VFOAT** Toledo Law Review. V. 1- Winter 1969-. 0042-0190. Periodical. US. English. qt. $16.00. University of Toledo, 2801 West Bancroft Street, Toledo OH 43606. **Tel** (419)537-2962. **Ind/Abst** Leg. Resour. Index, Energy Inf. Abstr., Environ. Abstr., Index Leg. Period., Curr. Law Index. **LC** K24. **DD** 340.09771. Index in last issue of volume - attached. **Circ** 700. Scholarly discussion of current legal problems. Articles by legal scholars, professionals and students. *Student Law Journal, 0585-458X.*

UNIVERSITY OF TORONTO FACULTY OF LAW REVIEW. Vol. 31 (Aug. 1973)-. 0381-1638. CN. English. sa. **Ind/Abst** Leg. Resour. Index, Index Leg. Period. **DD** 340'.05. *Faculty of Law Review, 0381-162X.*

UNIVERSITY OF TORONTO LAW JOURNAL. (THE UNIVERSITY OF TORONTO LAW JOURNAL). V. 1- 1935-. 0042-0220. Periodical. CN. English. qt. 37.00 Domestic, 40.00 Foreign. University Toronto Press, Journals Department, 4201 Dufferin Street, Toronto Ontario M3H 5T8 Canada. **Tel** (416)667-7781. **Ed** R C B Risk. **Ind/Abst** Public Aff. Inf. Serv. Bull., Sociol. Abstr., Contents Curr. Leg. Period., Index Leg. Period., Curr. Law Index, Leg. Resour. Index, Lang. Lang. Behav. Abstr. bk rev. adv acc. **Circ** 600. (ctrl). General interest articles in all aspects of legal scholarship. Emphasis is on Canadian law.

THE UNIVERSITY OF VIRGINIA LAW SCHOOL FOUNDATION ANNUAL REPORT. (ANNUAL REPORT - UNIVERSITY OF VIRGINIA LAW SCHOOL FOUNDATION). 0504-3972. US. English. an. University of Virginia Law School Foundation, PO Box 3668, Charlottesville VA 22903. **LC** KF292.V572. **DD** 340.0711755481.

UNIVERSITY OF WEST LOS ANGELES LAW REVIEW. **VFOAT** Law Review. V. 1- June 1969-. 0083-4068. US. English. an. University of West Los Angeles School of Law, 12201 Washington Place, Los Angeles CA 90066. **Tel** (213)204-0000. **Ind/Abst** Leg. Resour. Index, Index Leg. Period., Curr. Law Index, Contents Curr. Leg. Period. **LC** K25. **DD** 340.05. Each issue contains an index to its own contents - no vol index - loose.

UNIVERSITY OF WESTERN AUSTRALIA LAW REVIEW. **VFOAT** Western Australia Law Review. Began with: Vol. 5 in 1960. 0042-0328. Periodical. AT. English. sa. Methuen Law Book Company Ltd, 35 Mitchell Street, c/o Bennett-EBSCO, North Sydney New South Wales 2060 Australia. **Ind/Abst** APAIS, Aust. Public Aff. Inf. Serv., Index Leg. Period., Public Aff. Inf. Serv. Bull., Contents Curr. Leg. Period., Curr. Law Index, Leg. Resour. Index. Each issue contains an index to its own contents - no vol index - loose. *Annual Law Review.*

UNIVERSITY OF WESTERN ONTARIO LAW REVIEW. **VFOAT** U. W. O. L. REV. **VAT** U.W.O.L. L.Rev. V. 15- 1976-. 0703-900X. Periodical. CN. English. sa. 24.00. University of Western Ontario, Faculty of Law, London Ontario N6A 3K7 Canada. **Tel** (519)679-3350. **Ed** J Samuels. **Ind/Abst** Leg. Resour. Index, Index Leg. Period. **LC** K27. **DD** 349.71305. bk rev. adv acc. **Circ** 500. (ctrl). Articles on current issues in Canadian and international law. Case commentaries and book reviews. *Western Ontario Law Review, 0083-8950.*

THE UNREPORTED JUDGEMENTS. **Main/Corp** India. Supreme Court. English. ir. 35.00. 861 Chopasani Road, Sardarpura Jodhpur India. **DD** 348.54044.

UNREVISED SYNOPTIC REPORT OF THE PROCEEDINGS OF THE LEGISLATIVE ASSEMBLY, PROVINCE OF NEW BRUNSWICK *CEASED.* **Main/Corp** New Brunswick. Legislative Assembly. **VFOAT** Compte Rendu Non Revise des Debats de l'Assemblee Legislative du Nouveau-Brunswick. Began in 1967 or 1968. 0825-6098. Periodical. CN. English (text also in French, -July, 18, 1981). ir. *Unrevised Synoptic Report of the Legislative Assembly of the Province of New Brunswick, 0825-6136.*

Law

UP AGAINST THE LAW. UK. English. Up Against the Law Collective, 66 York Way, London NL England. **LC** KD654.A13. **DD** 347.41.

U.P. LAW ALUMNI YEARBOOK. *See* Yearbooks, Almanacs, Directories.

UPDATE (ANNAPOLIS, MD.). (UPDATE). US. English. Department of Legislative Reference, 90 State Circle, Annapolis MD 21401. **LC** KFM1220. **DD** 349.75205, 347.52005.

UPDATE ON LAW-RELATED EDUCATION. V. 1- Spring 1977-. 0147-8648. Periodical. US. English. ty. $7.50. American Bar Association, 750 North Lake Shore Drive, Chicago IL 60611. **Tel** (312)988-5732. **Ed** Charles J White. **Ind/Abst** Curr. Index J. Educ. **LC** KF4208.5.L3. **DD** 340.071073. bk rev. adv acc. **Circ** 3,000. The award-winning magazine that is low on legal jargon and high on innovative ideas for teaching youngsters about law.

UPDATE ON STATE LEGISLATION. 0739-4004. Periodical. US. English. sm. $70.00. Ed Silverbrand Update on State Legislation Services, 1100 N Street 1-D, Sacramento CA 95814. **LC** KFC20. **DD** 348.79404305, 347.94084305.

URBAN LAW AND POLICY. V. 1- Jan. 1978-. 0165-0068. Periodical. English. ir. 244.00 Domestic, $90.50. Elsevier Science Publishers, PO Box 211, 1000 AE Amsterdam Netherlands. **Tel** (020)5803911. **Ed** Patrick McAuslan and Otto Hetzel. **Ind/Abst** Leg. Resour. Index, Energy Inf. Abstr., Environ. Abstr., Avery Index Archit. Period., Energy Res. Abstr. **LC** K25. **DD** 346.04505. bk rev. adv acc. Examines the ways particular laws operate in an urban environment or the way the interests of particular groups in towns and cities are catered for or not, or how laws influence the development of particular regulatory systems; articles will discuss the merits of different policies and various legal techniques and administrative systems.

URBAN LAW ANNUAL CEASED. 1968-82. 0566-3377. Periodical. US. English. sa. $15.00. Washington University, St Louis MO 63130. **Ind/Abst** Public Aff. Inf. Serv. Bull. **LC** KF5691.A152. **DD** 340.

THE URBAN LAW REVIEW. V. 1- Summer 1975-. 0363-244X. Periodical. US. English. ty. $10.00. University of Texas School of Law, 2500 Red River, Austin TX 78750. **LC** K25. **DD** 346.764045.

THE URBAN LAWYER. V. 1- Spring 1969-. 0042-0905. Periodical. US. English. qt. $24.50. American Bar Association, 750 North Lake Shore Drive, Chicago IL 60611. **Tel** (312)988-5555. **Ind/Abst** Leg. Resour. Index, Energy Inf. Abstr., Environ. Abstr., Index Leg. Period., Curr. Law Index, Contents Curr. Leg. Period., Soc. Sci. Citation Index. **LC** K25. **DD** 342.730905.

URBAN, STATE AND LOCAL LAW NEWSLETTER. V. 2- Winter 1979-. 0195-7686. Periodical. US. English. American Bar Association, 750 North Lake Shore Drive, Chicago IL 60611. **Tel** (312)988-5555. **Ind/Abst** Leg. Resour. Index, Curr. Law Index. **LC** KF5300. **DD** 342.730905. *State, Local, and Urban Law Newsletter, 0163-2922.*

USTREDNI VESTNIK CESKE SOCIALISTICKE REPUBLIKY. Main/Corp Czech Socialist Republic, (Czechoslovakia). CS. Czech. ir. 16.00. Ministerstvo Spravedlnosti CSR, Vysehradska 16 Praha 2, Upraze Czechoslovakia.

USTREDNY VESTNIK SLOVENSKEJ SOCIALISTICKEJ REPUBLIKY. Main/Corp Slovak Socialist Republic, Czechoslovakia. Slovak. ir. In. 00. Ministerstvo Spravodlivosti Slovenskej Socialistickej Republiky, Suvorovova Ul 16, Bratislava Czechoslovakia.

USURY LAWS AND MODERN BUSINESS TRANSACTIONS. Main/Corp New York (City). Practising Law Institute. **Series/Titl** Commercial Law and Practice Course Handbook Series. US. English. **LC** KF1036.Z9. **DD** 346.73073.

UTAH BAR JOURNAL. (THE UTAH BAR JOURNAL). Main/Corp Utah State Bar. V. 1- May/June 1973-. 0091-9691. Periodical. US. English. bm. Utah State Bar, 564 Kennecott Building, Salt Lake City UT 84111. **Ind/Abst** Leg. Resour. Index. **LC** K25. **DD** 340.05.

UTAH BAR LETTER. ANNUAL ROSTER OF ACTIVE RESIDENT UTAH ATTORNEYS. VFOAT Annual Roster of Active Resident Utah Attorneys. 0145-8558. US. English. an. Utah State Bar, 520 Continental Bank Building, Salt Lake City UT 84101. **LC** KF192.U8. **DD** 340.25792.

UTAH COURT RULES. Main/Corp Utah. 1984 Ed.-. 0747-7120. US. English. an. Michie Company, 609 East Market Street, Charlottesville VA 22906-7587. **Tel** (804)295-6171.

UTAH JUDICIAL BRIEFS. Main/Corp Utah. Office of the State Court Administrator. V. 1- July 1975-. 0147-3581. Periodical. US. English. qt. Office of the State Court, 250 East Broadway/Suite 240, Salt Lake City UT 84111. **LC** KFU510.5.A3. **DD** 347.79201305.

UTAH LAW REVIEW. Vol. 1, No. 1 (1949)-V. 9, No. 4 (Winter 1965). 0042-1448. Periodical. US. English. qt. $20.00. University of Utah, College of Law, Salt Lake City UT 84112. **Tel** (801)581-7337. **Ed** Carol Clawson. **Ind/Abst** Leg. Resour. Index, Sel. Water Resour. Abstr., Index Leg. Period., Curr. Law Index, Contents Curr. Leg. Period. **LC** K25. **DD** 340.05. (cum index). bk rev. adv acc. **Circ** 1,000. Legal related articles.

UTAH PROSECUTOR. (THE UTAH PROSECUTOR). 0093-7932. US. English. Statewide Association of Prosecutors of Utah, 530 East Fifth South/Suite 202, Salt Lake City UT 84102. **LC** KFU577.A73. **DD** 345.79201.

UTAH STATE BAR DIRECTORY. *See* Yearbooks, Almanacs, Directories.

UTAH STATE BULLETIN. Began with No. 85-9 (May 1, 1985). 0882-4738. US. English. sm. $125.00. CODE-CO Law Publishers, PO Box 1471, Provo UT 84603. **DD** 348. *State of Utah Bulletin.*

UTILITY SECTION NEWSLETTER. (UTILITY SECTION NEWSLETTER : A PERIODIC REPORT TO THE MEMBERS OF THE SECTION OF PUBLIC UTILITY LAW OF THE AMERICAN BAR ASSOCIATION). Vol. 1, No. 1 (Dec. 1, 1960)-. 0569-3349. Periodical. US. English. qt. American Bar Association, 1155 East 60th Street, Chicago IL 60637. **Ind/Abst** Leg. Resour. Index. **LC** KF2077. **DD** 343.7309, 347.3039.

UWI STUDENT'S LAW REVIEW. Main/Corp University of the West Indies, Cave Hill, Barbados. Law Faculty. VAT University of the West Indies Student's Law Review. V. 1- May 1976-. BB. English. ir. $4.00. University of the West Indies, Cave Hill Barbados. **LC** K25. **DD** 340.09729.

VALPARAISO UNIVERSITY LAW REVIEW. V. 1- Fall 1966-. 0042-2363. Periodical. US. English. qt. $16.00. Valparaiso University, School of Law, Valparaiso IN 46383. **Tel** (219)464-5034. **Ed** Laura Sever. **Ind/Abst** Leg. Resour. Index, Public Aff. Inf. Serv. Bull., Index Leg. Period., Contents Curr. Leg. Period., Curr. Law Index. **LC** K26. **DD** 340.0977298. bk rev. adv acc. **Circ** 600. We are a general law review accepting most types of articles. However, we enjoy a reputation for specializing in jurisprudential topics.

VANDERBILT LAW REVIEW. V. 1- Dec. 1947-. 0042-2533. Periodical. US. English. bm. $24.00. Vanderbilt Law Review, Vanderbilt University School of Law, Nashville TN 37240. **Tel** (615)322-4766. **Ed** Eric Fenichel. **Ind/Abst** Manage. Contents, Leg. Resour. Index, Account. Index. Suppl., Index Leg. Period., Curr. Law Index, Contents Curr. Leg. Period., Soc. Sci. Citation Index. **LC** K26. **DD** 340.5. bk rev. adv acc. **Circ** 1,400. The Review follows the customary law review format, containing articles and book reviews by eminent writers and scholars.

VEBA REPORT. VFOAT V.E.B.A. Report. Began with Vol. 1, No. 1 (Aug. 1983) Issue. 0747-8380. Periodical. US. English. bm. B C Eaton, PO Box 44294, Phoenix AZ 85064. **Ed** Berrien C Eaton and William L Raby. **LC** KF3517.A15. **DD** 344.7301255, 347.3041255.

VERDICT REPORTS CEASED. Main/Corp Jury Verdict Research, Inc. 0092-2293. US. English. wk. $90.00. Caxton Building, Cleveland OH 44115. **LC** KF1325.P3. **DD** 346.73032.

VERDICTS & SETTLEMENTS. VFOAT Verdicts and Settlements. Vol. 1, No. 1 (July 1981)-. 0744-5733. Periodical. US. English. mo. Litigation Research Group, PO Box 77903, San Francisco CA 94107. **Tel** (415)543-5433. **Ed** Anthony Hicks. **LC** KF446. **DD** 346.730302648, 347.306302648. **Circ** 875. Summaries of trial and pre-trial results of personal injury law cases.

VERDICTUM JURIS. 0279-2389. Periodical. US. English. sm. $145.00. Verdictum Juris, 121 North Harvard Avenue, Claremont CA 91711. **Tel** (714)621-3345. **Ed** Eldon S O'Brien. **Circ** 1,500. All civil jury verdicts from California courts. Indexed annually.

VERFASSUNG UND RECHT IN UBERSEE. Vol. 1-. 0506-7286. Periodical. GW. German. qt. Rothenbaumchaussee 19, 2 Hamburg 13 West Germany. **Ind/Abst** Foreign Lang. Index, Public Aff. Inf. Serv. Bull., Recent Publ. Artic. **DD** 342.005.

THE VERMONT BAR JOURNAL & LAW DIGEST. VFOAT Vermont Bar Journal and Law Digest. Vol. 9, No. 3 (June 1983)- 47-. 0748-4925. Periodical. US. English. bm. $20.00. Vermont Bar Association, PO Box 100, Montpelier VT 05602. **Tel** (802)223-2020. **Ed** Susan M Dole. bk rev. adv acc. **Circ** 1,500. Journal featuring law articles and case digests of interest to Vermont legal community. *Vermont Bar, 0193-7073.*

VERMONT LAW REVIEW. V. 1- 1976-. 0145-2908. US. English. sa. $15.00. Vermont Law Review, Vermont Law School, South Royalton Vermont 05068. **Tel** (802)763-8303. **Ed** Peter Racehe. **Ind/Abst** Leg. Resour. Index, Index Leg. Period., Curr. Law Index, Contents Curr. Leg. Period. **LC** K26. **DD** 340.09743. **Circ** 1,000. General law school publication with emphasis on current legal developments nationwide.

VERMONT STATUTES ANNOTATED. US. English. an. Equity Publishing Company, Orford NH 03777. **Tel** (603)353-4351.

VEROFFENTLICHUNGEN DER SCHWEIZERISCHEN KARTELLKOMMISSION. Main/Corp Switzerland. Schweizerische Kartellkommission. VFOAT Publications de la Commission Suisse des Cartels. V. 1-. SZ. Multilingual (German and French). qt. Orell Fuessli Zeitschriften, Dietzingerstrasse 3, 8036 Zuerich Switzerland.

VERSLAE VAN DIE GEKOSE KOMITEE OOR DIE BOSWETSONTWERP. Main/Corp South Africa. Parliament. House of Assembly. Select Committee on the Forest Bill. VFOAT Reports of the Select Committee on the Forest Bill. SA. Afrikaans (English). ir. Government Printer, Private Bag X85, Pretoria 0001 South Africa. **DD** 346.6804675.

VERSLAE VAN DIE GEKOSE KOMITEE OOR DIE MORATORIUMWYSIGINGSWETSONTWERP. Main/Corp South Africa. Parliament. House of Assembly. Select Committee on the Moratorium Amendment Bill. VFOAT Reports of the Select Committee on the Moratorium Amendment Bill. SA. Afrikaans (English). ir. 1.35. Government Printer, Private Bag X85, Pretoria 0001 South Africa. **DD** 346.68077.

VERSLAG - COMMISSIE WET OP HET CONSUMPTIEF GELDKREDIET. Main/Corp Netherlands (Kingdon, 1815-). Commissie Wet op het Consumptief Geldkrediet. 1973/75-. Dutch. ir. Commissie Wet Ophet Consumptief Geldkrediet, Staatsuitgeverij, S-Gravenhage Netherlands. **DD** 346.492073.

VERWALTUNG UND FORTBILDUNG. Vol. 1-. Periodical. GW. German. qt. 49.60. Carl Heymanns Verlag KG, Gereonstrasse 18-32, 5000 Koln 1 West Germany. **Tel** (0221)134022. **LC** JF1338.A2. **DD** 350.0007. bk rev. adv acc. **Circ** 1,500. (ctrl). Treatises on problems within the administrative complexity and the professional advanced training within it.

VERWALTUNGSARCHIV. V. 1- Oct. 1892-. 0042-4501. Periodical. German. ir. $37.85. Carl Heymanns Verlag KG, Gereonstrasse 18-32, 5000 Koln 1 West Germany. **Tel** (303)979-5657.

VERWALTUNGSPRAXIS DER BUNDESBEHORDEN. JURISPRUDENCE DES AUTORITES ADMINISTRATIVES DE LA CONFEDERATION. GIURISPRUDENZA DELLE AUTORITA AMMINISTRATIVE DELLA CONFEDERAZIONE. Main/Corp Switzerland. Justiz- und Polizeidepartement. VFOAT Jurisprudence des Autorites Administratives de la Confederation. French or German. ir. *Verwaltungsentscheide der Bundesbehorden.*

VERWALTUNGSRECHTSPRECHUNG IN DEUTSCHLAND. Periodical. GW. German. ir. $106.65. C H Beckscke Verlagsbchhndlg, Wilhelmstrasse 9, Postfach 400340, 8000 Muenchen 40 West Germany.

VERWALTUNGSRUNDSCHAU. Periodical. GW. German. mo. W Kohlhammer Verlag, Hessbruhlstrasse 69 Postfach 800430, 7000 Stuttgart, 80 West Germany. **LC** KK5571.2. **DD** 342.430605. *Staats- und Kommunalverwaltung.*

VERZEICHNIS RHEINLAND-PFALZISCHER RECHTS- UND VERWALTUNGSVORSCHRIFTEN. GW. German. an. 15.00. Ministerium der Justiz, Ernst-Ludwig-Strasse 3, 6500 Mainz West Germany. **LC** KKC616.A24. **DD** 342.434306, 344.343026.

VESEY STREET LETTER *CEASED.* Began with Dec. 1970- Ceased in 1981. Periodical. US. English. mo. **LC** KF200. **DD** 349.74705, 347.47005. *Bar Bulletin.*

VESTNIK MOSKOVSKOGO UNIVERSITETA. SERIIA XI : PRAVO. **Main/Corp** Moscow. Universitet. **VFOAT** Pravo. 1977-. Periodical. UR. Russian. bm. Victor Kamkin Inc, 12224 Parklawn Drive, Rockville MD 20852. **Tel** (301)881-5973. **LC** K13. *Vestnik. Seriia XII: Pravo.*

VICTORIA UNIVERSITY OF WELLINGTON LAW REVIEW. **VFOAT** Law Review. Vol. 2, No. 3 (Oct. 1957)-. 0083-6044. Periodical. US. English. ir. $30.00. Gaunt and Sons, 3011 Gulf Drive, Holmes Beach FL 33510. **Tel** (813)778-5211. **Ind/Abst** Leg. Resour. Index, Curr. Law Index, Index Leg. Period. **LC** K26. **DD** 340.05. (cum index). *Victoria University College Law Review.*

VIDEO LAW MONTHLY. 0741-5125. Periodical. US. English. mo. $48.00. Business Office, Video Law Monthly, 903 Sheffield Road, Auburn Hills MI 48057. **LC** KF2840.A15. **DD** 343.730994605, 347.303994605.

VIERTELJAHRESSCHRIFT FUR SOZIALRECHT. V. 1- 1973-. German (summaries in English). ir. 152.00. J Schweitzer Verlag, Genthiner Strasse 13, 1 30 Berlin W Germany. **LC** K26.

VIEW FROM SPRINGFIELD. *See* Public Administration.

VILLAGE LAW. **Main/Corp** New York (State). 0148-8015. US. English. ir. Matthew Bender & Company Inc, 1275 Broadway, Albany NY 12201. **Tel** (800)833-9844. **LC** KFN5758.5.A29.

VILLANOVA LAW REVIEW. V. 1- 1956-. 0042-6229. Periodical. US. English. ir. $17.50. Villanova University, School of Law, Villanova PA 19085. **Tel** (215)645-7050. **Ed** David R Moffitt. **Ind/Abst** Sociol. Abstr., Soc. Welf. Soc. Plan./Policy Soc. Dev., Index Leg. Period., Lang. Lang. Behav. Abstr., Leg. Resour. Index, Curr. Law Index, Contents Curr. Leg. Period. **LC** K26. bk rev. adv acc. **Circ** 1,600. (ctrl). Articles, essays and book reviews addressing significant recent developments in American law with emphasis on law in Pennsylvania and the third circuit court of appeals.

VIRGIN ISLANDS REPORTS. Vol. 1-. US. English. ir. Equity Publishing Corporation, Orford NH 03777. **Tel** (603)353-4351.

VIRGIN ISLANDS RULES AND REGULATIONS. VIRGIN ISLANDS REGISTER. **Main/Corp** Virgin Islands of the United States. Laws, Statutes, etc. US. English. ir. $30.00. Equity Publishing Corporation, Oxford NH 03777. **Tel** (603)353-4351.

THE VIRGINIA BAR ASSOCIATION JOURNAL. V. 1- Jan. 1975-. 0360-3857. Periodical. US. English. qt. $10.00. Bess C Wendell, 3849 West Weyburn Road, Richmond VA 23235. **Tel** (804)644-0041. **Ed** Charles E Friend. **Ind/Abst** Curr. Law Index, Leg. Resour. Index. **LC** KF200. **DD** 340.09755. bk rev. **Circ** 4,500. (ctrl). Practical 'How-to' articles for the practicing attorney on varied subjects with case histories.

VIRGINIA BAR NEWS. **VFOAT** VSB Virginia Bar News. Vol. 1, No. 1 (Jan. 1953)-. Periodical. US. English. mo. $12.00. Virginia State Bar, 700 East Main, 700 Building, Richmond VA 23219. **Tel** (804)786-2061. **Ed** Richard G Johnstone Jr. **LC** KF200. **DD** 340.062755. bk rev. adv acc. **Circ** 19,000. (ctrl). Topical features on federal and Virginia laws affecting practice of law. Includes features on law office management, computers and law books.

VIRGINIA CONTINUING LEGAL EDUCATION BULLETIN. 0196-5174. Periodical. US. English. mo. School of Law, University of Virginia, Charlottesville VA 22901. **LC** KF275.A15. **DD** 349.75505, 347.5505. *Virginia Continuing Legal Education, 0193-6654.*

VIRGINIA JOURNAL OF NATURAL RESOURCES LAW. Vol. 1, No. 1 (Spring 1981)-. 0748-8122. Periodical. US. English. sa. $15.00. University of Virginia, School of Law, Charlottesville VA 22901. **Tel** (804)924-3683. **Ind/Abst** Coal Abstr., Energy Inf. Abstr. **LC** K26. **DD** 346.73044, 347.30644.

VIRGINIA LAW REPORTS. **Main/Corp** Virginia. 1 VLR-. 8750-3247. US. English. ir. $175.00. Virginia Reports Reprings, 700 Building/Suite 1304, 700 East Main Street, Richmond VA 23219-2689. **DD** 349. *0745-0060.*

VIRGINIA LAW REVIEW. V. 1- Oct. 1913-. 0042-6601. Periodical. US. English. ir. $32.00. University of Virginia Law School, Charlottesville VA 22901. **Tel** (804)924-3079. **Ind/Abst** ABC Pol Sci, Account. Index. Suppl., ABI/Inform, Public Aff. Inf. Serv. Bull., Index Leg. Period., Sociol. Abstr., Curr. Law Index, Leg. Resour. Index, Am. Hist. Life, Hist. Abstr., Part A, Mod. Hist. Abstr., Hist. Abst., Part B, Twent. Century Abstr., Lang. Lang. Behav. Abstr., Contents Curr. Leg. Period., Hist. Abstr., Soc. Sci. Citation Index. **LC** K26. **DD** 349.75505. **CODEN** VLIBAD. (cum index). bk rev. adv acc. **Circ** 2,200. Published by students of the University of Virginia School of Law, covering all areas of legal scholarship.

VIRGINIA LAW WEEKLY. Began with: Vol. 1, Published May 27, 1948. 0042-661X. Periodical. US. English. sm. $12.00. University of Virginia, School of Law, Virginia Law Weekly, Charlottesville VA 22901. **Tel** (804)924-3070. **Ed** P F Hofer. **LC** UNC. adv acc. **Circ** 1,600. (ctrl). Student weekly devoted to coverage of school issues in current legal developments, law and education, etc.

VIRGINIA LAWS RELATING TO MINORS. 0193-5496. US. English. an. Harcourt Brace Jovanovich, 1 East First Street, Duluth MN 55802. **LC** KFV2491.M5. **DD** 346.755013.

VIRGINIA LAWYERS DESKBOOK. 0739-6678. US. English. an. Michie Company, POB 7587, Charlottesville VA 13951. **LC** KFV2477. **DD** 349.755, 347.55.

VIRGINIA LEGAL STUDIES. US. English. ir. University Press of Virginia, Box 3608, University Station, Charlottesville VA 22903. **Tel** (804)924-3468. **Ed** R Lillich. Various topics of importance in legal studies, international as well as American, dealt with in monographs. Most have more than one contributor.

THE VIRGINIA MAGISTRATE. **Main/Corp** Virginia. Attorney General's Office. US. English. Office of the Attorney General, Criminal Division, 900 Fidelity Building, 830 East Main Street, Richmond VA 23219. **LC** KFV2975.A59. **DD** 345.75505.

THE VIRGINIA PEACE OFFICER. **Main/Corp** Virginia. Attorney General's Office. 0147-6181. US. English. Office of the Attorney General, 900 Fidelity Building, Richmond VA 23219. **LC** KFV2975. **DD** 345.7550505.

THE VIRGINIA PROSECUTOR. **Main/Corp** Virginia. Attorney General's Office. US. English. J E Kulp, DY Attorney General Criminal Division, 900 Fidelity Building, 830 East Main Street, Richmond VA 23219. **LC** KFV2840. **DD** 348.75505.

THE VIRGINIA RESEARCHER. 0049-6499. Periodical. US. English. mo. National Legal Research Group Inc, PO Box 7187, Charlottesville VA 22906.

VIRGINIA TAX REVIEW. Vol. 1, No. 1 (Spring 1981)-. 0735-9004. Periodical. US. English. sa. $20.00. University of Virginia, School of Law, Charlottesville VA 22901. **Tel** (804)924-4726. **Ed** James P Holden Jr. **Ind/Abst** ABI/Inform. **LC** K26. **DD** 343.730505, 347.303505. adv acc. **Circ** 1,000. Publishes articles by distinguished academics and tax law practitioners, as well as student authors, on a variety of current tax topics of interest to the profession.

THE VIRGINIAS, MARYLAND, DELAWARE AND DISTRICT OF COLUMBIA LEGAL DIRECTORY. *See* Yearbooks, Almanacs, Directories.

VOICE FOR THE DEFENSE. 0364-2232. Periodical. US. English. mo. $10.00. Texas Criminal Defense Lawyers Association, 314 West 11th Street/ Suite 211, Austin TX 78701. **LC** KF9602. **DD** 345.730505.

VOLK + RECHT : ORGAN DER DEMOKRATISCHEN JURISTEN DER SCHWEIZ. **VFOAT** Volk und Recht. Periodical. SZ. German. ir. 12.00. DJS Volk + Recht, Postfach 1308, 4001 Basel Switzerland. **DD** 349.49405, 344.94005.

VOX JURIS TRABALHISTA. Periodical. Portuguese. ir. Sugestoes Literarias, Caixa Postal 3.422, Sao Paulo Brazil. **LC** K26.

WAGE-PRICE LAW & ECONOMICS REVIEW. *See* Economics.

WAKE FOREST LAW REVIEW. V. 7- 1970-. 0043-003X. Periodical. US. English. bm. $19.00. Wake Forest University, School of Law, Winston-Salem NC 27109. **Tel** (919)761-5439. **Ed** David Eldridge. **Ind/Abst** Index Leg. Period., Curr. Law Index, Leg. Resour. Index, Contents Curr. Leg. Period. **LC** K27. **DD** 340.05. (cum index). bk rev. adv acc. **Circ** 1,900. (ctrl). A comprehensive, updating publication which addresses and explains topics of current interest in the legal profession. *Intramural Law Review (Winston-Salem, N.C.).*

WARRANTY WATCH. 0363-9517. US. English. Federal State Reports Inc, PO Box 986, Arlington VA 22216. **LC** KF919.C6. **DD** 343.7308.

WASEDA BULLETIN OF COMPARATIVE LAW. Vol. 1 (1981)-. 0285-9211. Periodical. JA. English. an. Institute of Comparative Law, Waseda University, 6-1-1-chome Nishi Waseda Shinjuku Tokyo 160 Japan. **LC** K27. **DD** 340.205.

WASHBURN LAW JOURNAL. V. 1- Winter 1960-. 0043-0420. Periodical. US. English. ty. Washburn University of Topeka, School of Law, Topeka KS 66621. **Ed** Marta Linenberger. **Ind/Abst** Curr. Law Index, Contents Curr. Leg. Period., Leg. Resour. Index. **LC** K27. (cum index). **Circ** 2,000. A publication on current legal issues.

WASHBURN UNIVERSITY SCHOOL OF LAW ALUMNI DIRECTORY. *See* Yearbooks, Almanacs, Directories.

WASHINGTON AND LEE LAW REVIEW. V. 1- Fall 1939-. 0043-0463. US. English. qt. $17.00. Washington & Lee University, School of Law Lewis Hall, Lexington VA 24450. **Tel** (703)463-8566. **Ed** Dan Shaver. **Ind/Abst** Account. Index. Suppl., Index Leg. Period., Leg. Resour. Index, Curr. Law Index, Contents Curr. Leg. Period. **LC** K27. (cum index). adv acc. **Circ** 2,000. (ctrl). Scholarly publication of notes and comments on various areas of the law and the implications of new decisions and areas of law that affect the legal profession.

WASHINGTON BUSINESS LAW REPORTER. **VFOAT** Business Law Reporter. Vol. 1, No. 1 Nov.-Dec. 1982. 0735-8350. Periodical. US. English. bm. $42.60. Butterworth Legal Publishers, 15014 NE 40th/Suite 205, Redmond WA 98052. **LC** KFW152.A15. **DD** 346.79707, 347.97067.

WASHINGTON COUNTY REPORTS. V. 1- 1922-. US. English. an.

WASHINGTON COURT RULES; WITH AMENDMENTS. **Main/Corp** Washington (State). Courts. 1960-. US. English. an. West Publishing Company, 50 Kellogg Boulevard/PO Box 3526, St Paul MN 55164. **LC** KFW529. **DD** 347.79705.

WASHINGTON CREDIT LETTER DIGEST. **Main/Corp** Capitol Reports, Inc. 0195-959X. Periodical. US. English. mo. $96.00. Capitol Reports Inc, 1750 Pennsylvania Avenue NW, Washington DC 20006. **LC** KF1039.A15. **DD** 346.73073.

WASHINGTON CREDIT LETTER PRIVACY REPORT. **Main/Corp** Capitol Reports, Inc. 0195-9581. Periodical. US. English. mo. $120.00. Capitol Reports Inc, 1750 Pennsylvania Avenue NW, Washington DC 20006. **LC** KF1039.A15. **DD** 346.73073.

WASHINGTON DRUG LETTER (1979). (WASHINGTON DRUG LETTER). Began with Oct. 22, 1979 Issue. 0194-1291. Periodical. US. English. wk. $427.00. Washington Business Information Inc, 1117 North 19th Street/Suite 200, Arlington VA 22209. **Tel** (703)247-3426. **Ed** John Reichard. **LC** KF3885.A15. **DD** 344.730423305, 347.304423305. **NLM** W1 WA598B. Focuses on regulation and legislation affecting prescription and proprietary drugs. Offers news about FDA actions on new drug applications, manufacturing procedures, advertising and labeling, compliance cases, research and testing rules. *Washington Drug & Device Letter, 0162-2994.*

WASHINGTON LAW REVIEW. V. 43- 1967-. 0043-0617. US. English. qt. $20.00. Washington Law Review Association, University of Washington/ 226 Condon Hall, Seattle WA 98150. **Tel** (206)543-7293. **Ed** Cathy Parker. **Ind/Abst** Account. Index. Suppl., Index Leg. Period., Writ. Am. Hist., Sel.

Law

Water Resour. Abstr., Leg. Resour. Index, Curr. Law Index, Contents Curr. Leg. Period., Soc. Sci. Citation Index, Ocean. Abstr., Pollut. Abstr. Indexes. (cum index). adv acc. **Circ** 2,000. A scholarly journal published by the law students of the University of Washington School of Law. *University of Washington Law Review, 0190-6186.*

WASHINGTON LETTER. 0516-9968. Periodical. US. English. mo. $25.00. American Bar Association, 750 North Lake Shore Drive, Chicago IL 60611. **Tel** (202)331-2200. **Ed** Rhonda J McMillion. **LC** KF200. **DD** 348.7346. **Circ** 5,000. (ctrl). An update on legislation in Congress of interest to the legal profession.

THE WASHINGTON LOBBYISTS & LAWYERS DIRECTORY. *See* Yearbooks, Almanacs, Directories.

WASHINGTON LOBBYISTS/ LAWYERS DIRECTORY. *See* Yearbooks, Almanacs, Directories.

WASHINGTON NEWSLETTER - AMERICAN LIBRARY ASSOCIATION. WASHINGTON OFFICE. *See* Library and Information Science.

WASHINGTON REPORT ON HEALTH LEGISLATION & REGULATION. **VFOAT** Health Legislation and Regulation, Health Legislation & Regulation. 0740-7793. Periodical. US. English. wk. $367.00. McGraw-Hill Inc, 1120 Vermont Avenue NW/ Suite 1200, Washington DC 20005. *Washington Report on Health Legislation, 0098-2512.*

WASHINGTON REPORTS. 2D SERIES. **Main/Corp** Washington (State). Supreme Court. **VFOAT** Cases Determined in the Supreme Court of Washington. V. 1- Oct. 19, 1939-. US. English. bw. *Cases Determined in the Supreme Court of Washington.*

WASHINGTON STATE BAR NEWS. V. 1- Mar. 1947-. US. English. mo. $24.00. Washington State Bar Association, 505 Madison Street, Seattle, WA 98104. **Tel** (206)622-6054. **Ed** Carole A Grayson. **Ind/Abst** Index Leg. Period. adv acc. **Circ** 13,000. (ctrl). Legal articles and notices of interest to Washington lawyers.

WASHINGTON TARIFF & TRADE LETTER. *See* Business - Commerce.

WASHINGTON UNIVERSITY JOURNAL OF URBAN AND CONTEMPORARY LAW. **VFOAT** Journal of Urban and Contemporary Law. Vol. 24-. 8756-0801. Periodical. US. English. sa. $17.00. Washington University Journal of Urban and Contemporary Law, Washington University School of Law, St Louis MO 63130. **Tel** (314)889-6436. **Ind/Abst** Public Aff. Inf. Serv. Bull., Index Leg. Period. **LC** K25. **DD** 346.7304505, 347.3064505. adv acc. **Circ** 600. Law review that publishes articles discussing recent legal developments in topics affecting the urban community. For example: zoning, housing, environment, energy, transportation, and education. *Urban Law Annual, 0566-3377.*

WASHINGTON UNIVERSITY LAW QUARTERLY. **Main/Corp** Washington University (Saint Louis, MO.). School of Law. V. 22- 1936/37-. 0043-0862. Periodical. US. English. qt. $16.00. Washington University, PO Box 1120, St Louis MO 63130. **Tel** (314)889-6498. **Ed** JoAnne Levy. **Ind/ Abst** Index Leg. Period., Contents Curr. Leg. Period., Curr. Law Index, Leg. Resour. Index. **LC** K23. **DD** 349.7305. bk rev. adv acc. **Circ** 1,100. We print student and professional-written articles on current legal issues in a wide range of subject areas. *St. Louis Law Review, 0271-2849.*

WATER LAW NEWSLETTER (BOULDER, COLO. : 1976). (WATER LAW NEWSLETTER). Vol. 9, No. 1 (Spring 1976)-. 0737-044X. Periodical. US. English. ir. $20.00. Rocky Mountain Mineral Law Foundation, University of Colorado, Boulder CO 80309. **Tel** (303)442-6545. **Ed** George A Gould. **Ind/Abst** GeoRef, Energy Res. Abstr. **LC** KF5552. **DD** 346.7304691, 347.3064691. **Circ** 700. Summarizes cases and developments in water law. *Rocky Mountain Mineral Law Newsletter. Water Law, 0737-0431.*

WAYNE LAW REVIEW. Vol. 1, No. 1 (Winter 1954)-. 0043-1621. Periodical. US. English. qt. $23.00. 468 West Ferry Street, Detroit MI 48202. **Ind/Abst** Index Leg. Period. (cum index).

WBA NEWSLETTER. **Main/Corp** Women's Bar Association of Massachusetts. **VAT** Women's Bar Association Newsletter. V. 1, No. 2- Feb. 1980-. 0272-1201. Periodical. US. English. qt. $4.00. Women's Bar Association, 11 Beacon Street/ #605, Boston MA 02108. **LC** KF200. **DD** 340.060744. *Women's Bar Association Newsletter, 0272-121X.*

WEEKLY CALIFORNIA CITATOR. 0092-2560. US. English. wk. $100.00. Marshall F Johnson, 2528 5th Avenue, Sacramento CA 95818. **LC** KFC59. **DD** 348.794047.

WEEKLY CRIMINAL BULLETIN. V. 1-. 0703-1319. Periodical. CN. English. an. 221.00. Canada Law Book, 80 Cowdrey Court, Agincourt Ontario M1S 1S5 Canada. **Tel** (416)773-6300. **Ed** M Rosenberg and C Buhr. **DD** 345.7100264. A comprehensive summary, on a weekly basis, of all available criminal judgements handed down by Canadian courts.

WEEKLY DIGEST OF FAMILY LAW. Issue No. 1 (Jan. 4, 1982)-. 0713-7907. Periodical. CN. English. wk. $145.00. Weekly Digest of Family Law, Carswell Legal Publications, 2330 Midland Avenue, Agincourt Ontario M1S 1P7 Canada. **DD** 346.7101502648.

WEEKLY LAW DIGEST. Began in 1936. 0744-3145. Periodical. US. English. wk. $84.00. Daily Journal Company, 210 South Spring Street PO Box 54026, Los Angeles CA 90054. **Tel** (213)625-2141.

WEEKLY LAW REPORTS. Jan. 2, 1953-. UK. English. ir. Incorp Council Law Reporting, 3 Stone Building Lincolns Inn, London WC2A 3XN England. *Weekly Notes.*

WEEKLY LEGISLATIVE SUMMARY. Periodical. US. English. wk. Empire State Chamber of Commerce Inc, 150 State Street, Albany NY 12204.

THE WEEKLY REGULATORY MONITOR. **Main/Corp** Washington Monitor. 0161-2972. Periodical. US. English. wk. $300.00. The Washington Monitor Inc, 499 National Press Building, Washington DC 20045. **LC** KF5406.A15. **DD** 342.730605.

WEEKLY SUMMARY OF NLRB CASES. **Main/Corp** United States. National Labor Relations Board. Division of Information. **VAT** Weekly Summary of National Labor Relations Board Cases. W-1685 (Dec. 31, 1979-Jan. 4, 1980)-. 0364-8109. Periodical. US. English. wk. National Labor Relations Board, Washington DC 20570. **LC** KF3364. **DD** 344.730102648, 347.304102648. *Weekly Summary of N.L.R.B. Cases, 0364-8109.*

WEEKLY WRAP-UP. **Main/Corp** Minnesota. Legislature. House of Representatives. **VFOAT** Minnesota House of Representatives Weekly Wrap-up. Periodical. US. English. wk. Minnesota House of Representatives Information Office/Room 9, State Capitol, St Paul MN 55155. **LC** KFM5415. **DD** 342.77600262, 347.76020262.

WELDON TIMES. (THE WELDON TIMES). V. 1- April 1976-. 0702-8989. Periodical. CN. English. ir. Free. Dalhousie Law School, Dalhousie Law Society, Halifax Nova Scotia Canada. **DD** 340.071171622. (ctrl).

WERTPAPIER-MITTEILUNGEN. TEIL 4. ZEITSCHRIFT FUR WIRTSCHAFTS- UND BANKRECHT. (ZEITSCHRIFT FUR WIRTSCHAFTS- UND BANKRECHT). **Series/Titl** Wertpapier-Mitteilungen. Teil IV. Began in 1977. 0342-6971. Periodical. German. ir. 70.00 Each Month. Dusseldorfer Strasse 16, Postfach 31 46, 6000 Frankfurt AM 1 West Germany. **DD** 346.4307. *Wertpapier-Mitteilungen. Teil 4. Wirtschafts-, Wertpapier-, und Bankrecht, 0342-698X.*

WEST BENGAL LABOUR GAZETTE. Began with July 1957. Periodical. II. English. mo. Government of West Bengal, Department of Labour, Calcutta India. **DD** 344.54140105, 345. 41404105.

WEST INDIAN LAW JOURNAL. Oct. 1977-. 0253-7370. Periodical. JM. English. sa. $20.00. Council of Legal Education, PO Box 231, Kingston 7 Jamaica West Indies. **Tel** (809)9278112. **Ed** William A Roper, JP. **Ind/Abst** Index Leg. Period. **LC** K27. **DD** 340.09729. bk rev. adv acc. **Circ** 700. Legal and quasi-legal articles primarily related to the Commonwealth Caribbean and secondarily to countries with a common law tradition. *Jamaica Law Journal.*

WEST VIRGINIA LAW REVIEW. V. 52- Dec. 1949-. 0043-3268. Periodical. US. English. qt. $24.00. College of Law, West Virginia University, Morgantown WV 26506. **Tel** (304)293-2301. **Ed** Michele Grinberg. **Ind/Abst** Index Leg. Period., Contents Curr. Leg. Period., Curr. Law Index, Leg. Resour. Index. **LC** K27. **DD** 340.060754. (cum index). bk rev. adv acc. **Circ** 1,200. Legal issues relevant to West Virginia and the nation with one issue dedicated to coal related topics. *West Virginia Law Quarterly and the Bar.*

WEST VIRGINIA STATE BAR CONTINUING LEGAL EDUCATION BULLETIN. 0161-1909. Periodical. US. English. sm. $10.00. West Virginia State Bar, E-400 State Capitol, Charleston WV 25305. **LC** KF200. **DD** 340.9754.

WEST VIRGINIA STATE BAR JOURNAL. V. 1- Oct. 1975-. 0364-3425. US. English. qt $10.00. West Virginia State Bar Association, E-400 State Capitol, Charleston WV 25305. **Tel** (304)346-8414. **LC** KF200 B .W47. **DD** 340.09754. *West Virginia State Bar News.*

WESTCHESTER BAR JOURNAL. Vol. 10, No. 3 (Summer 1983)-. 0746-1844. Periodical. US. English. qt. $8.00. Westchester County Bar Association, 199 Main Street, White Plains NY 10601. **Tel** (914)761-3707. **Ed** Frank D Arcuri. bk rev. adv acc. **Circ** 2,500. (ctrl). The official publication of the Westchester County Bar Association and is issued for the purpose of presenting scholarly articles to its members. *Westchester Bar Topics (1976).*

WESTCHESTER LAW JOURNAL. 0049-7274. Periodical. US. English. wk. $35.00. Westchester Law Journal Inc, 175 Main Street, White Plains NY 10601. **LC** K27. **DD** 349.74727705, 347.47277005.

WESTERN LABOUR ARBITRATION CASES. 0317-6924. CN. English. ir. 70.00. The Continuing Legal Education Society of British Columbia, #200-1148 Hornby Street, Vancouver British Columbia V6Z 2C3 Canada. **Tel** (604)669-3544. **Ed** M A Hickling. **DD** 344.71101890264. The only comprehensive collection of grievance arbitration decisions in Western Canada. Includes extensive subject index, tables of cases cited, and indexes by arbitrator and ministry number.

WESTERN NATURAL RESOURCE LITIGATION DIGEST. **VFOAT** W.N.R.L. Fall 1981-. 0736-9972. Periodical. US. English. qt. Editor WNRL, 720 Sacramento Street, San Francisco CA 94108. **LC** KF5505.A59. **DD** 346.73046702648, 347. 30646702648.

WESTERN NEW ENGLAND LAW REVIEW. V. 1- Apr. 1978-. 0190-6593. Periodical. US. English. qt. Western New England College School of Law, Springfield MA 01119. **Tel** (413)782-3111. **Ind/Abst** Index Leg. Period. **LC** K27. **DD** 340.09744. **Circ** 2,000. Professional journal published by law students covering timely topics.

WESTERN SCHOOL LAW DIGEST CEASED. **VFOAT** Western Digest. Began with V. 1- Mar. 1976-. Ceased with Dec. 1981. 0363-4833. Periodical. US. English. mo. $45.00. School Law Digest Corporation, S56W23674 Maplewood Terrace, Waukesha WI 53187. **LC** KF4114. **DD** 344.780705.

WESTERN STATE UNIVERSITY LAW REVIEW. V. 2, No. 2- Spring 1975-. 0362-8892. Periodical. US. English. sa. $16.00. Western State University College of Law, 2121 San Diego Avenue, San Diego CA 92110. **Tel** (619)298-3111. **Ind/Abst** Index Leg. Period. **LC** K12. **DD** 340.05. *Western State Law Review.*

WESTERN TAX. Vol. 1, No. 1 (Sept. 1982)-. 0734-9904. Periodical. US. English. mo. $100.00. Butterworth Legal Publishers, 15014 NE 40th Street/ Suite 205, Redmond WA 98052. **LC** KF6750.A15. **DD** 343.730405, 347.303405.

WESTERN TAX REVIEW. Vol. 1, No. 1 (June 1979)-. 8755-0083. Periodical. US. English. sa. Washington State University, Department of Economics, c/o R R Hansen, Pullman WA 99164. **Tel** (509)335-4471. **Ed** Reed Hansen. **DD** 343. bk rev. adv acc. **Circ** 100. Government taxes, budgets, deficits, fiscal policy and efficiency.

WESTERN WEEKLY REPORTS. (WESTERN WEEKLY REPORTS : CURRENT SERIES). Vol. 1, No. 1 (1971)-. 0049-7525. Periodical. CN. English. ir. Carswell Legal Publications, 2330 Midland Avenue, Agincourt Ontario M1S 1P7 Canada. **Tel** (416)291-8421. **Ed** Laura M Wright. adv acc. Complete, accurate and up-to-date coverage of decisions of the courts of Western Canada and appeals to the Supreme Court of Canada. *0049-7525.*

Law

WEST'S ANNOTATED CALIFORNIA CODES. Main/Corp California. 1954-. US. English. West Publishing Company, 1413 K Street, NW, St Paul MN 55165. LC KFC30.5. DD 345.22.

WEST'S ATLANTIC DIGEST 2D. VFOAT Atlantic Digest 2D. V. 1- 1968-. Periodical. US. English. ir. West Publishing Company, 1413 K Street NW, St Paul MN 55165. LC KF135.A7. DD 345.52.

WEST'S BANKRUPTCY REPORTER. VFOAT Bankruptcy Reporter. V. 1- Jan. 1980-. 0199-5782. US. English. sm. $75.00. West Publishing Company, 50 West Kellogg Boulevard, PO Box 3526, St Paul MN 55165. LC KF1515.A2. DD 346.7307802642.

WEST'S CALIFORNIA DIGEST, 1850 TO DATE,. VFOAT California Digest. V. 1- 1951-. US. English. ir. DD 345.52. (cum index).

WEST'S CALIFORNIA REPORTER. VFOAT California Reporter. Began in 1977. 8750-2623. Periodical. US. English. wk. $97.50. West Publishing Company, 50 Kellogg Boulevard, St Paul MN 55102. LC KFC47. DD 348.794043. *California Reporter.*

WEST'S CALIFORNIA RULES OF COURT. STATE AND FEDERAL. (WEST'S CALIFORNIA RULES OF COURT : STATE AND FEDERAL). VFOAT California Rules of Court. 0147-1317. US. English. an. West Publishing Company, Box 3526, 50 West Kellogg Boulevard, St Paul MN 55102. LC KFC992. DD 347.79405.

WEST'S CRIMINAL LAW NEWS. VFOAT Criminal Law News. Vol. 1, No. 1 (May 2, 1984)-. 8750-2607. Periodical. US. English. wk. $157.50. West Publishing Company, 50 West Kellogg Boulevard, PO Box 64526, St Paul MN 55165-0526. DD 345.

WEST'S EDUCATION LAW DIGEST. VFOAT Education Law Digest. Mar. 1983-. 0741-5346. Periodical. US. English. West Publishing Company, 50 West Kellogg Boulevard, PO Box 3526, St Paul MN 55165. LC KF4110.3. DD 344.730702648, 347.304702648.

WEST'S EDUCATION LAW REPORTER. VFOAT Education Law Reporter. Vol. 1, No. 1 (Jan. 14, 1982)-. 0744-8716. US. English. bw. West Publishing Company, 50 West Kellogg Boulevard, PO Box 3526, St Paul MN 55165. LC KF4110.A2. DD 344.730702648, 347.304702648.

WEST'S FEDERAL CASE NEWS. V. 1- Jan. 1978-. 0162-2005. US. English. wk. $65.00. West Publishing Company, 50 West Kellogg Boulevard, PO Box 3526, St Paul MN 55165. LC KF127. DD 348.7346.

WEST'S FEDERAL FORMS. 1952-. US. English. ir. West Publishing Company, 1413 K Street NW, St Paul MN 55165. DD 347.93.

WEST'S FEDERAL TAX MANUAL WITH WESTLAW. VFOAT Federal Tax Manual with Westlaw. 1985 Ed.-. 0749-1034. US. English. an. West Publishing Company, 50 West Kellogg Boulevard, PO Box 3526, St Paul MN 55165. DD 343. *West's Federal Tax Guide with Westlaw, 0749-095X.*

WEST'S FEDERAL TAX SYSTEM. VFOAT Federal Tax System. 1981-1, No. 1 (Jan. 15, 1981)-. 0277-5158. US. English. wk. $150.00. West Publishing Company, 50 West Kellogg Boulevard, PO Box 3526, St Paul MN 55102. LC KF6272. DD 343.730405, 347.303405.

WEST'S FLORIDA DIGEST 2D. VFOAT Florida Digest 2D. 1984-. Periodical. US. English.

WEST'S ILLINOIS DECISIONS. VFOAT Illinois Decisions. 1 IL Dec.- Nov. 30, 1976-. 8750-2615. US. English. wk. $97.50. West Publishing Company, 50 Kellogg Boulevard, St Paul MN 55102. LC KFI1247. DD 348.773044.

WEST'S LOUISIANA SESSION LAW SERVICE. Main/Corp Louisiana. VFOAT Louisiana Session Law Service. 0148-1991. US. English. West Publishing Company, 1413 K Street NW, St Paul MN 55165. LC KFL25. DD 348.763022.

WEST'S LOUISIANA STATUTES ANNOTATED. Main/Corp Louisiana. V. 1- 1951-. Periodical. US. English. West Publishing Company, Box 3526, 50 West Kellogg Boulevard, St Paul MN 55166. DD 345.22.

WEST'S MCKINNEY'S FORMS. 1964-. US. English. bm. DD 347.93. Each issue contains an index to its own contents - no vol index - loose.

WEST'S MICHIGAN LEGISLATIVE SERVICE. Main/Corp Michigan. 1967, No. 1-. US. English. West Publishing Company, PO Box 3526, St Paul MN 55165.

WEST'S MILITARY JUSTICE DIGEST. No. 1- July 1980-. 0272-9334. US. English. West Publishing Company, 1413 K Street NW, St Paul MN 55165. LC KF7605.3. DD 343.730143, 347.303143.

WEST'S MILITARY JUSTICE REPORTER. VFOAT Military Justice Reporter. V. 1- 1975/76-. 0147-7315. Periodical. US. English. bw. $50.00. West Publishing Company, PO Box 3526/50 West Kellogg Boulevard, St Paul MN 55165. LC KF7605.A2. DD 343.730143. *Court-Martial Reports : Holdings and Decisions of the Courts of Military Review and United States Court of Military Appeals.*

WEST'S NEBRASKA DIGEST. 0147-717X. US. English. West Publishing Company, 1413 K Street NW, St Paul MN 55165. LC KFN57. DD 348.782046.

WEST'S NEW HAMPSHIRE DIGEST, 1760 TO DATE, COVERING CASES FROM STATE AND FEDERAL COURTS. VFOAT New Hampshire Digest. V. 1- 1951-. US. English. ir. West Publishing Company, Box 352, West Kellogg Boulevard, St Paul MN 55166. DD 345.32. (cum index).

WEST'S NEW JERSEY DIGEST. VFOAT New Jersey Digest. 1954-. US. English. ir. West Publishing Company, 1413 K Street NW, St Paul MN 55165. DD 345.32. (cum index).

WEST'S RHODE ISLAND DIGEST, 1783 TO DATE. VFOAT Rhode Island Digest. 1952-. US. English. ir. West Publishing Company, 1413 K Street NW, St Paul MN 55165. DD 345.32. (cum index).

WEST'S WYOMING DIGEST, A DIGEST OF WYOMING LEGAL AUTHORITIES, STATE AND FEDERAL. VFOAT Wyoming Digest. V. 1- 1956-. US. English. ir. West Publishing Company, 1413 K Street NW, St Paul MN 55165. DD 345.42, 345.412. (cum index).

WGO MONATSHEFTE FUR OSTEUROPAISCHES RECHT. Periodical. GW. German. ir. 58.00. Hansischer Gildenverlag J Heitmann, Theodorstrasse 41 C, Hamburg 50 West Germany. LC K27. WGO.

WHITE, NEW YORK CORPORATIONS : BCL, N-PCL AND RELATED STATUTES. Main/Corp New York (State). US. English. an. Matthew Bender & Company Inc, 1275 Broadway, Albany NY 12201. Tel (8000833-9844. LC KFN5340.A29. DD 346.747066.

WHITTIER LAW REVIEW. V. 1- 1978-. 0195-7643. Periodical. US. English. qt. $15.00. Whittier College School of Law, 5353 West Third Street, Los Angeles CA 90020. Tel (213)938-3621. Ed Lowell Rector Gates. Ind/Abst Index Leg. Period., Leg. Resour. Index, Curr. Law Index. LC K27. DD 349.79405. bk rev. Circ 500. (ctrl). We publish articles dealing with contemporary issues in the legal field. A wide variety of topics are discussed ranging from American constitutional law to copyright and business law.

DER WIENER RICHTER. No. 1 (Oct. 1981)-. Periodical. German. qt. Vereinigung der Osterreichischer Richter, Sektion Wien Justizpalast, 1016 Wien Austria. DD 349.4361305, 344.3613005.

WILLAMETTE LAW REVIEW. V. 15- Winter 1978-. 0191-9822. Periodical. US. English. qt $16.00. Willamette University, College of Law 250 Winter Street, Salem OR 97301. Tel (503)370-6300. Ed Rod Zeeb. Ind/Abst Index Leg. Period., Curr. Law Index, Leg. Resour. Index, Contents Curr. Leg. Period. LC K27. DD 340.05. adv acc. Circ 1,000. A scholarly publication which provides a timely forum for the discussion of legal issues and related legal problems. *Willamette Law Journal.*

WILLIAM AND MARY LAW REVIEW. V. 1- 1957-. 0043-5589. Periodical. US. English. qt. $20.00. Marshall Wythe School of Law, Williamsburg VA 23185. Ind/Abst Public Aff. Inf. Serv. Bull., Index Leg. Period., Leg. Resour. Index, Curr. Law Index, Contents Curr. Leg. Period. LC K27. DD 349.75505. (cum index). bk rev. adv acc. Circ 800. *William and Mary Review of Virginia Law (Williamsburg, VA. : 1949).*

WILLIAM MITCHELL ENVIRONMENTAL LAW JOURNAL. Vol. 1, No. 1 (May 1983)-. 0737-2795. US. English. an. $6.00. William Mitchell Environmental Law Society, 875 Summit Avenue, St Paul MN 55105. LC K27. DD 344.04605, 342.44605.

WILLIAM MITCHELL LAW REVIEW. V. 1- 1974-. 0270-272X. Periodical. US. English. qt. $16.00. Wm Mitchell College of Law, 875 Summit, St Paul MN 55105. Tel (612)227-9171. Ed John MacArthur. Ind/Abst Index Leg. Period., Leg. Resour. Index, Curr. Law Index, Contents Curr. Leg. Period. LC K27. DD 340.5. bk rev. adv acc. Circ 1,900. (ctrl). Articles by known authors regarding current legal issues.

WILLIAM MITCHELL OPINION. VFOAT Opinion. Began with: May 1959. 0511-9774. Periodical. US. English. ir. 875 Summit Avenue, St Paul MN 55105.

WILLS. Main/Corp Bay Area Review Course, Inc. US. English. an. Bay Area Review Course Inc, 5900 Wilshire Boulevard, Los Angeles CA 90036. LC KFC201.Z9. DD 346.794054.

WILLS FOR ALBERTA. 2nd Ed. (Aug. 1977)-. 0824-1406. CN. English. an. $5.95 Each Volume. International Self-Counsel Press, Head and Editorial Office, 306 West 25th Street, North Vancouver British Columbia Canada. DD 346.7123054. *Wills and Probate Procedure, 0824-1392.*

WINDSOR YEARBOOK OF ACCESS TO JUSTICE. See Yearbooks, Almanacs, Directories.

WIRTSCHAFTSRECHT. Vol. 1-. 5802-6320. Periodical. SZ. German (table of contents also in English and Russian). qt. Kunst & Wissen Erich Bieber, Dufourstrasse 51, CH-8008 Zurich Switzerland. LC UNC.

WIRTSCHAFTSTREUHANDERJAHRBUCH. 1978-. German. ir. Ed L Waldmann and P Schilling. DD 346.43607.

WIRTSCHAFTSWISSENSCHAFTLICHE UND WIRTSCHAFTSRECHTLICHE UNTERSUCHUNGEN. See Economics.

THE WISCONSIN ADMINISTRATIVE LAW DIGEST. US. English. an. Law Reporter Company, 625 East Saint Paul Avenue, Milwaukee WI 53202.

WISCONSIN ADMINISTRATIVE REGISTER. No. 1- Jan. 1956-. US. English. mo. Revisor of Statutes, 411 West State Capitol, Madison WI 53702.

THE WISCONSIN BAR BULLETIN. Vol. 22, No. 1 (Feb. 1949)-. 0043-6380. Periodical. US. English. mo. $18.00. State Bar of Wisconsin, 402 West Wilson Street, Madison WI 53703. Tel (608)257-3838. Ed Joyce R Hastings. Ind/Abst Index Leg. Period., Curr. Law Index, Leg. Resour. Index. (cum index). adv acc. Circ 14,500. (ctrl). Recent law changes and legal articles of interest to Wisconsin Bar Association members. *Bulletin of the Wisconsin Bar Association.*

WISCONSIN COURT RULES AND PROCEDURE, STATE AND FEDERAL. (WISCONSIN COURT RULES AND PROCEDURE ..., STATE AND FEDERAL). Began with Vol. for 1979. 0731-1907. US. English. an. West Publishing Company, PO Box 3526 50 Kellogg Boulevard, St Paul MN 55165. LC KFW2929. DD 347.775051, 347.750751.

WISCONSIN LAW REVIEW. Oct. 1920-. 0043-650X. Periodical. US. English. ir. $24.00. University of Wisconsin Law School, 975 Bascom Hall, Madison WI 53706. Tel (608)262-2109. Ed Ken Kraus. Ind/Abst Sociol. Abstr., Writ. Am. Hist., Public Aff. Inf. Serv. Bull., Index Leg. Period. Lang. Lang. Behav. Abstr., Soc. Sci. Citation Index, Contents Curr. Leg. Period., Curr. Law Index, Leg. Resour. Index. LC K27. DD 349.77505. (cum index). bk rev. Circ 1,800. (ctrl). Scholarly law journal perhaps with historical or sociological interest.

THE WISCONSIN LEGAL DIRECTORY. See Yearbooks, Almanacs, Directories.

WISCONSIN REPORTER. (WISCONSIN REPORTER : COVERING CASES REPORTED IN NORTH WESTERN REPORTER, SECOND SERIES). VFOAT West's Wisconsin Reporter. 0746-150X. US. English. wk. $80.00. West Publishing Company, 50 West Kellogg Boulevard, PO Box 64526, Saint Paul MN 55164-0526. DD 348.

WISCONSIN SECURITIES BULLETIN. See Business - Investments.

WISCONSIN SESSION LAWS. Main/Corp Wisconsin. VFOAT Laws of Wisconsin. 1911-. 0145-6628. US. English. be. LC KFW2425. DD 348.775022. *Laws of Wisconsin.*

Law

WISCONSIN STATUTES. Main/Corp
Wisconsin. US. English. ir. Wisconsin Department of Administration, Document Sales, 202 South Thornton Avenue, Madison WI 53702. **Tel** (608)266-3358.

WISSENSCHAFT UND GEGENWART.
VFOAT Juristische Reihe. Issue 1- 1969-. Periodical. GW. German. ir. Vittorio Klostermann, Postfach 900601, Frauenlobstrasse 22, 6000 Frankfurt 90 West Germany. **Tel** (0611)774011.

WISSENSCHAFTSRECHT, WISSENSCHAFTSVERWALTUNG, WISSENSCHAFTSFORDERUNG. Vol.1- Feb. 1968-. 0443-6976. Periodical. GW. German. ir. 130.-. JCB Mohr and Paul Siebeck, Postfach 2040, 7400 Tuebingen West Germany. **Tel** (07071)26064. bk rev. adv acc. The journal endeavours to help university administrators, lawyers, judges, legislators, scholars and the interested public in understanding the legal and administrative problems of modern research and teaching on the university level.

WISTRA. VFOAT W.I.S.T.R.A. Vol. 1, 82/1 (15. Jan. 1982)-. 0721-6890. Periodical. GW. German. bm. 20.00 Each Issue. Dr Peter Deubner Verlag GMBH, Durener Strasse 320 Postfach 41 02 68, 5000 Koln 41 West Germany. LC K27. DD 349.4305, 344.3005.

WOMEN & THE LAW REPORT. VFOAT Women and the Law Report. Vol. 1, No. 1 (Mar. 1983)-. 0741-4102. Periodical. US. English. mo. Newsletter Services Inc, 1545 New York Avenue NE, Washington DC 20002. LC KF477.A15. DD 342.73087805, 347.30287805.

WOMEN LAW REPORTER. Sept. 1, 1974-. 0095-1188. Periodical. US. English. sm. $275.00. Women Law Reporter Inc, 5141 Massachusetts Avenue, Washington DC 20016. LC KF4758.A15. DD 346.73013.

WOMEN LAWYERS' JOURNAL. Vol. 1, No. 1 (May 1911)-. 0043-7468. Periodical. US. English. qt. $12.00. National Association of Women Lawyers, 750 North Lake Shore Drive, Chicago IL 60611. **Tel** (312)988-6186. Ed Ann W Lake. Ind/Abst Curr. Law Index, Leg. Resour. Index. DD 340. bk rev. adv acc. Circ 1,600. Women in Law, Education and Promotion.

WOMEN'S LAW FORUM. 1st- 1979-. US. English. an. Golden Gate University, School of Law, 536 Mission Street, San Francisco CA 94105. **Tel** (415)442-7000. Ind/Abst Contents Curr. Leg. Period.

THE WOMEN'S LEGAL DEFENSE FUND NEWSLETTER. VFOAT W.L.D.F. Newsletter. 0736-9433. Periodical. US. English. qt. Women's Legal Defense Fund, 2000 P Street Northwest/Suite 400, Washington DC 20036. LC KF477.A15. DD 346.7301340269, 347. 3061340269.

WOMEN'S RIGHTS LAW REPORTER. V. 1- 0085-8269. Periodical. US. English. qt. $32.00. Women's Rights Law Reporter Inc, 15 Washington Street, Newark NJ 07102. **Tel** (201)648-5320. Ed Cindy Cappell and Lauren Firestone. Ind/Abst Sociol. Abstr., Soc. Welf. Soc. Plan./Policy Soc. Dev., Altern. Press Index, Contents Curr. Leg. Period., Public Aff. Inf. Serv. Bull., Women Stud. Abstr. LC KF478.A45. DD 346.73013. bk rev. adv acc. Circ 1,200. Available on microfilm from University Microfilms. Oldest specialized legal journal in US dealing with laws and cases affecting women. Designed as a forum for ideas, criticism, debate and analysis for the feminist and legal communities.

WOODROW WILSON JOURNAL OF LAW. 0161-0368. Periodical. US. English. ir. $13.50. Woodrow Wilson Journal of Law, 830 West Peachtree Street NW, Atlanta GA 30308. **Tel** (404)872-0198. LC K27. DD 340.05.

WORKERS' COMPENSATION LAW BULLETIN. 0748-7878. US. English. mo. $36.75. Quinlan Publishing Company, 131 Beverley Street, Boston MA 02114. DD 344. *Workmen's Compensation Law Bulletin.*

WORKERS' COMPENSATION LAW OF THE STATE OF ARKANSAS. Main/Corp Arkansas. US. English. American Insurance Association, 85 John Street, New York NY 10038. LC KFA3942.A29. DD 344.767021. *Workmen's Compensation Law of the State of Arkansas.*

WORKERS' COMPENSATION LAW OF THE STATE OF CONNECTICUT. Main/Corp Connecticut. US. English. American Insurance Association, 85 John Street, New York NY 10038. LC KFC3942.A29. DD 344.74602102632, 347. 46042102632. *Workmen's Compensation Law of the State of Connecticut.*

WORKERS' COMPENSATION LAW OF THE STATE OF GEORGIA. Main/Corp Georgia. US. English. American Insurance Association, New York NY 10038. LC KFG342.A29. DD 344.7802102632. *Workmen's Compensation Law of the State of Georgia.*

WORKERS' COMPENSATION LAW OF THE STATE OF HAWAII. Main/Corp Hawaii. US. English. American Insurance Association, 85 John Street, New York NY 10038. LC KFH342.A29. DD 344.96902102632.

WORKERS' COMPENSATION LAW OF THE STATE OF WISCONSIN. Main/Corp Wisconsin. US. English. American Insurance Association, 85 John Street, New York NY 10038. LC KFW2742.A29. DD 344.77502102632, 347. 75042102632. *Workmen's Compensation Law of the State of Wisconsin.*

THE WORKERS' COMPENSATION LAWS OF CALIFORNIA. Main/Corp California. 1975-. 0748-4135. US. English. an. M Bender, 235 East 45th Street, New York NY 10017. Ed W L Hanna. LC KFC592.A29. *Workmen's Compensation Laws of California.*

WORKERS' COMPENSATION LEGISLATION IN AUSTRALIA. 1980-. AT. English. an. Department of Social Security, PO Box 1, Woden Act 2606, Canberra Australia. DD 344.94021, 349.40421. *Conspectus of Workers Compensation Legislation in Australia.*

WORKERS' COMPENSATION MANUAL FOR UNION REPRESENTATIVES. Main/Corp Ohio AFL-CIO. 7th- Ed. 0195-671X. US. English. $60.00. Ohio AFL-CIO, 271 East State Street, Columbus OH 43215. LC KFO342. DD 344.771021. *Workmen's Compensation Manual for Union Representatives, 0195-6973.*

WORKERS' COMPENSATION REPORTER CEASED. V. 1, Pt. 12-V. 5, Pt. 6. 0706-9561. Periodical. CN. English. *Workmen's Compensation Reporter, 0706-9553.*

WORKERS' COMPENSATION REPORTS. Main/Corp New South Wales. Workers' Compensation Commission. V. 1- 1926-27-. AT. English. ir. Government Printing Office of New South Wales, PO Box 75, Pyrmont New South Wales 2009 Australia. LC HD7816.A82.

WORKING DOCUMENT - WISCONSIN LEGISLATIVE COUNCIL. Main/Corp Wisconsin. Legislative Council. No. 1-. Monographic Series. US. English. LC KFW2420. DD 347.77501.

WORKING PAPER - INSTITUTE OF LAW RESEARCH AND REFORM. UNIVERSITY OF ALBERTA. (WORKING PAPER - UNIVERSITY OF ALBERTA, INSTITUTE OF LAW RESEARCH AND REFORM). Began publication in 1971. 0317-1612. Monographic Series. CN. English. Free. University of Alberta, Institute of Law Research and Reform, Edmonton Alberta T6G 2H5 Canada. DD 340.097123.

WORKING PAPER - LAW REFORM COMMISSION OF CANADA. (WORKING PAPER - LAW REFORM COMMISSION OF CANADA). VFOAT Document de Travail. No. 1-. 0708-2827. Monographic Series. CN. English (French, each with special title page and separate paging French text on inverted pages). Law Reform Commission of Canada, 130 Albert Street/7th Floor, Ottawa Ontario K1A 0L9 Canada. DD 340.30971.

WORKMEN'S COMPENSATION LAW OF THE STATE OF COLORADO. Main/Corp Colorado. US. English. American Insurance Association, 85 John Street, New York NY 10038. LC KFC2142.A29. DD 344.788021, 347.880421.

WORKMEN'S COMPENSATION LAW OF THE STATE OF KENTUCKY. US. English. LC HD7816.U7.

WORKMEN'S COMPENSATION LAW OF THE STATE OF NEW HAMPSHIRE. US. English. LC HD7816.U7.

WORKMEN'S COMPENSATION LAW OF THE STATE OF PENNSYLVANIA. June 1915-. US. English. LC KFP342.A29. DD 331.825.

WORKMEN'S COMPENSATION LAW REVIEW. V. 1- 1974-. 0094-3436. US. English. an. $42.50. Wm S Hein, 1285 Main Street, Buffalo NY 14209. **Tel** (716)882-2600. Ed David Lloyd. LC K27. DD 344.73021. Circ 400. Although a variety of articles are presented, primary emphasis is on specific timely areas in each volume.

THE WORKMEN'S COMPENSATION LAWS OF CALIFORNIA. Main/Corp California. 1913-1973/74. US. English. an. Matthew Bender & Company Inc, 1275 Broadway, Albany NY 12201. **Tel** (800)833-9844. Ed W L Hanna.

WORLD LEGAL DIRECTORY. *See* Yearbooks, Almanacs, Directories.

WPNR, WEEKBLAD VOOR PRIVAATRECHT, NOTARIAAT EN REGISTRATIE. VFOAT Weekblad voor Privaatrecht, Notariaat en Registratie. Periodical. NE. Dutch. ir. 110.00. T Hoenstraat 5, S-Gravenhage Netherlands. DD 348.492046. *Weekblad voor Privaatrecht, Notaris-Ambt en Registratie.*

THE WRIT. Periodical. US. English. ir. Ohio Northern University, College of Law, Ada OH 45810.

WRIT (WASHINGTON, D.C.). (THE WRIT). Vol. 1, No. 1 (Winter 1980)-. 0198-8107. Periodical. US. English. qt. $6.00. The Writ, 640 14th Place Northeast, Washington DC 20002. LC K27. DD 349.7305, 347.3005.

WRONGFUL DISCHARGE LITIGATION REPORTER. May 6, 1986-. 0888-1197. Periodical. US. English. sm. $600.00. Andrews Publications Inc, PO Box 200, Edgemont PA 19028. DD 344.

WYOMING COURTS; NEWSLETTER OF THE WYOMING COURT SYSTEM. Main/Corp Wyoming. Judicial Planning Committee. US. English. bm. Judicial Planning Committee of Wyoming Supreme Court Building, Cheyenne WY 82002. LC KFW4710. DD 347.7870105.

THE WYOMING LAWYER. (THE WYOMING LAWYER : OFFICIAL PUBLICATION OF WYOMING STATE BAR). 8755-125X. Periodical. US. English. qt. PO Box 3388, Cheyenne WY 82001. DD 342.

WYOMING REPORTER. 344 P. 2D/356 P. 2D-. 0733-8325. US. English. an. West Publishing Company, 50 Kellogg Boulevard, Saint Paul MN 55102. DD 348.73428, 347.30841. *Wyoming Reports.*

YALE JOURNAL ON REGULATION. Vol. 1, No. 1-. 0741-9457. Periodical. US. English. sa. $19.00 institutions. Yale Journal on Regulation, 401A Yale Station, New Haven CT 06520. **Tel** (203)436-7679. Ed Douglas Smith and David Huebner. LC K29. DD 343.730705, 347.303705. bk rev. adv acc. Circ 800. A forum for the scholarly discussion and debate of regulatory issues and administrative law.

YALE LAW & POLICY REVIEW. VFOAT Yale Law and Policy Review. Vol. 1, No. 1 (Fall 1982)-. 0740-8048. Periodical. US. English. sa. $14.00 Domestic, $16.00 Foreign. Subscription Editor, Yale Law and Policy Review, Yale Law School, 401A Yale Station, New Haven CT 06520. LC K29. DD 340.05.

THE YALE LAW JOURNAL. V. 1- Oct. 1891-. 0044-0094. Periodical. US. English. ir. $32.00. Yale Law Journal, 401 A Yale Station, New Haven CT 06520. **Tel** (203)436-8244. Ind/Abst ABC Pol Sci, Index Econ. Artic. J. Collect. Vol., Account. Index. Suppl., ABI/Inform, Book Rev. Index, Public Aff. Inf. Serv. Bull., Index Leg. Period., Contents Curr. Leg. Period., Soc. Sci. Citation Index, Curr. Law Index, Leg. Resour. Index. LC K29. DD 340.05. bk rev. adv acc. Circ 4,500. (ctrl). Articles, student notes, and book reviews dealing with current legal topics.

YALE LAW REPORT. V. 1- 1954-. 0513-1391. Periodical. US. English. ir. Yale Law School Association, Box 410 A, Yale Station, New Haven CT 06520. **Tel** (203)436-3015. Ed Catherine lino. LC KF292.Y3. DD 340.097468. bk rev. Circ 9,000. (ctrl). Includes news about faculty, students, and alumni. *Alumni Newsletter (Yale Law School Association).*

THE YEAR-BOOK AND DIGEST. *See* Yearbooks, Almanacs, Directories.

YEARBOOK - NEW YORK COUNTY LAWYERS' ASSOCIATION. *See* Yearbooks, Almanacs, Directories.

YEARBOOK OF EUROPEAN LAW. *See* Yearbooks, Almanacs, Directories.

YEARBOOK OF PROCUREMENT ARTICLES. *See* Yearbooks, Almanacs, Directories.

THE YEARBOOK OF SCHOOL LAW. *See* Yearbooks, Almanacs, Directories.

Law—International Law

YEARBOOK OF THE CANADIAN BAR ASSOCIATION AND THE MINUTES OF PROCEEDINGS OF ITS ANNUAL MEETING. See Yearbooks, Almanacs, Directories.

YEARBOOK - SUPREME COURT HISTORICAL SOCIETY. See Yearbooks, Almanacs, Directories.

YEARLY ALL INDIA CRIMINAL DIGEST. 1971-. 0377-6719. II. English. ir. 17.50. Law Book Company, Sardar Patel Marg, Allahabad-1 India. DD 345.54002648.

YEARLY REVIEW - LAW REFORM COMMISSION OF SASKATCHEWAN. (YEARLY REVIEW . . .). Main/Corp Law Reform Commission of Saskatchewan. 1980-. 0711-0111. CN. English. an. Sturdy-Stone Centre, 122 Third Avenue North, Saskatoon Saskatchewan S7K 2H6 Canada. LC KES168.A72. DD 340.3097124.

THE YEARLY SUPREME COURT DIGEST. VFOAT Supreme Court Digest. 1966-. II. English. ir. Law Book Company, Sardar Patel Marg, Allahabad 1 India. DD 349.54051. *Supreme Court Digest.*

YLEISISSA ALIOIKEUKSISSA SYYTETYT JA TUOMITUT. See Statistics.

YOU & THE LAW. VFOAT You and the Law. Jan. 9, 1978-. 0731-1109. Periodical. US. English. bw. $39.72. Research Institute of America, 111 Radio Circle, Mt Kisco NY 10549. *Your Business and the Law, 0093-3503.*

YOUNG LAWYER (JEFFERSON, CITY, MO.). (THE YOUNG LAWYER). Began in Fall 1976. 0742-0234. Periodical. US. English. qt. Young Lawyers, PO Box 119, Jefferson City MO 65101. LC KF200. DD 340.060778. *YLS Newsletter.*

YOUNG LAWYERS NEWSLETTER. 0147-6777. Periodical. US. English. Illinois State Bar Association, Illinois Bar Center, Springfield IL 62701. LC KF200. DD 340.062773.

YOUR BUSINESS & THE LAW. (YOUR BUSINESS AND THE LAW). 0093-3503. Periodical. US. English. bw. Research Institute of America Inc, Research Institute Building, 589 Fifth Avenue, New York NY 10017. LC KF889.A1. DD 346.7306605.

YOUR PRODUCT AND THE LAW. Issue 501 (Jan. 1, 1983)-. 0741-4730. Periodical. US. English. sm. $78.00. Business Research Publications Inc, 817 Broadway, New York NY 10003. LC KF912.8. DD 346.730705, 347.306705. *Marketing In Action, Manufacturing and the Law.*

YOUR SCHOOL AND THE LAW. See Education (General).

YOUTH COURT REPORT. Periodical. US. English. an. Mississippi Department of Youth Services, 407 Woolfolk Building, Jackson MS 39201. *Mississippi Youth Court Statistics.*

YOUTH LAW NEWS. 0882-8520. Periodical. US. English. bm. $25.00. National Center for Youth Law, 1663 Mission Street/5th Floor, San Francisco CA 94103. Tel (415)543-3307. Ed Marcia Henry. DD 344. bk rev. Circ 4,000. Journal of the national center for youth law, providing by-monthly coverage of significant legal developments affecting poor children throughout the country.

YUGOSLAV LAW. VFOAT Droit Yougoslave. Jan./Apr. 1975-. 0350-2252. Periodical. YU. English (French). ir. $27.00. Mladost Export Import, POB 1028 Ilica 30, 41000 Zagreb Yugoslavia. LC K29. DD 340.09497. *New Yugoslav Law.*

YUKSEK SECIM KURULU KARARLAR. Main/Corp Turkey. Yuksek Secim Kurulu. 1972-. Turkish. ir. *Yuksek Secim Kurulu Ilke Karaplar.*

Z PROBLEMATYKI PRAWA PRACY I POLITYKI SOCJALNEJ. Series/Titl Prace Naukowe Uniwersytetu Slaskiego W Katowicach. Vol. 1-. Periodical. Polish (summaries in French and Russian). ir. 43.00. Uniwersytet Slaski Ul, Bankowa 14, 40-007 Katowice Poland. LC K16.

ZAGADNIENIA USTROJU PRAWNEGO ROLNICTWA. Vol. 1-. Periodical. Polish (summaries in French and Russian). ir. 40.00.

ZAMBIA LAW JOURNAL. Vol. 1, No. 1-. English. an. $6.00. University of Zambia, Box 2379, Lusaka Zambia. LC K30. DD 340.05.

ZAMBIA LAW REPORTS. ZA. English. ir. Council of Law Reporting, General Editor, Zambia Law Reports, PO Box RW67, Lusaka Zambia. DD 348.6894041.

ZEITSCHRIFT DER SAVIGNY, STIFTUNG FUR RECHTSGESCHICHTE . . . . AU. German. an. Germanistische Abteilung, Dr Karl Lueger-Ring 12, A-1014 Wein I Austria. Tel 0222-63 87 35-25. Ed Adolf Laufs and Werner Orgis. bk rev. adv acc. Well known German-speaking journal for the history of German law, covering research work from the very roots up to modern legacy.

ZEITSCHRIFT DER SAVIGNY-STIFTUNG FUR RECHTSGESCHICHTE. KANONISTISCHE ABTEILUNG. See History (General).

ZEITSCHRIFT DER SAVIGNY-STIFTUNG FUR RECHTSGESCHICHTE. ROMANISTISCHE ABTEILUNG. See History (General).

ZEITSCHRIFT FUR ARBEITSRECHT UND SOZIALRECHT. VFOAT ZAS. Vol. 1- Jan./Feb. 1966-. 0044-2321. Periodical. AU. German. bm. Manzsche Verlagsbuchhandlung, Kohlmarkt 16, 1014 Wien Austria. LC K30.

ZEITSCHRIFT FUR AUSLANDERRECHT UND AUSLANDERPOLITIK : ZAR. VFOAT ZAR. 1/1981-. Periodical. German. qt. 36.00. Nomos Verlagsgesellschaft, 7570 Baden-Baden, Postfach 610, Waldseestr 305, Baden-Baden West Germany. LC K30. DD 342.43083, 344.30283.

ZEITSCHRIFT FUR BERGRECHT. See Engineering - Mining Engineering.

ZEITSCHRIFT FUR DAS GESAMTE FAMILIENRECHT. 9.- Year. 0044-2410. Periodical. GW. German. mo. $76.29. Verlag E & W Gieseking GMBH, Postfach 130120 Deckersttrasse 30, 4800 Bielefeld 13 West Germany. Tel (0521/14674. *EHE und Familie in Privaten und Offentlichen Recht.*

ZEITSCHRIFT FUR DAS GESAMTE HANDELSRECHT UND WIRTSCHATSRECHT BEIHEFTE. V. 124- 1961/62-. 0044-2437. Periodical. German. *Zeitschrift fur das Gesamte Handelsrecht und Konkursrecht.*

ZEITSCHRIFT FUR DIE GESAMTE STRAFRECHTSWISSENSCHAFT. VFOAT Mitteilungsblatt der Fachgruppe Strafrecht in der Gesellschaft fur Rechtsvergleichung. Vol. 1-. 0084-5310. Periodical. German. qt. Walter de Gruyter & Company, 200 Sawmill River Road, Hawthorne NY 10532. Tel (914)747-0110. LC K30. DD 345.005 342.5005. (cum index).

ZEITSCHRIFT FUR GESETZGEBUNG UND RECHTSPRECHUNG IN GRAUBUNDEN. 82/1 (March 1982)-. Periodical. German. qt. 38.00 Students, 48.00 Others. Arcas Verlag, Werkstrasse 2, 7000 Chur Switzerland.

ZEITSCHRIFT FUR LUFT- UND WELTRAUMRECHT. VFOAT German Journal of Air and Space Law. Vo. 24, No. 2- June 1975-. 0340-8329. Periodical. US. German (English and French). qt. 158.-. Carl Heymanns Verlag Kg, Gereonstrasse 18-32, 5000 Koln 1 West Germany. Tel (0221)134022. Ind/Abst Int. Aerosp. Abstr., Energy Res. Abstr. LC K30. DD 343.09705. bk rev acc. Circ 600. (ctrl). Treatises statements and sentences to the legal problems of aviation security, space activities and emerging international law. Recent publications on the air and space law. *Zeitschrift fur Luftrecht und Weltraumrechtsfragen.*

ZEITSCHRIFT FUR RECHTSVERGLEICHUNG. 1.- Yearly Volume. Periodical. German. ir. Manzsche Verlags- und Universitatsbuchhandlung, Kohlmarkt 16, A-1014 Wien Austria. Tel (0222)4300. Ed H C Mult, Fritz Schwind, and Hans Hoyer. bk rev. Circ 720. (ctrl). Covers family law, torts, contracts, trusts, property, penal law, civil procedure, legal methods, European law, conventions, arbitration, continental law, Islamic law, common law, etc. *Osterreichische Heft fur die Praxis des Internationale und Auslandischen Rechts.*

ZEITSCHRIFT FUR SCHADENSRECHT : ZFS. VFOAT ZFS. No. 1, Issue 1 (Jan. 1980)-. 0173-0568. Periodical. German. mo. 35.40 Half Yearly. Juristischer Fachbuchverlag GMBH, Essen West Germany. LC KK1610.A13. DD 346.430305, 344.306305.

ZEITSCHRIFT FUR UNTERNEHMENS- UND GESELLSCHAFTSRECHT. V. 1- Jan. 1972-. Periodical. US. German. qt. Walter de Gruyter Inc, 200 Saw Mill River Road, Hawthorne NY 10532. Tel (914)747-0110. LC K30. DD 346.4306605.

ZEITSCHRIFT FUR VERWALTUNG. Periodical. German. ir. 960.00. Wirtschaftsverlag Dr A Orac, Graben 17, Wien 1010 Austria. DD 342.4360605.

ZEITSCHRIFT FUR WIRTSCHAFTSRECHT. VFOAT Z.I.P. Vol. 4, No. 1 (Jan. 20 1983)-. 0723-9416. Periodical. GW. German. mo. 36.50 Each issue. Kommunikationsforum Recht Wirtschaft Steuern Tagungs Und Verlagsgesellschaft MBH, Hohenstaufenring 43-45, D 5000 Koln 1 West Germany. LC KK2042. DD 346.4307805, 344.3067805. *Zeitschrift fur Wirtschaftsrecht und Insolvenzpraxis.*

ZEITSCHRIFT FUR ZIVILPROZESS. V. 1- 1879-. 0342-3468. Periodical. German. qt 180.-. Carl Heymanns Verlag KG, Gereonstrasse 18-32, 5000 Koln 1 West Germany. Tel (0221)134022. Ed M C Fritz Baur and Dieter Leipold. bk rev. adv acc. Circ 1,000. (ctrl). Treatises and decisions on the civil action.

ZESZYTY NAUKOWE INSTYTUTU BADANIA PRAWA SADOWEGO. Main/Corp Instytut Badania Prawa Sadowego. German (Polish and Russian). sa. ARS Polona, Krakowskie Przedmiescie 7, 00-068 Warsaw Poland.

ZFA, ZEITSCHRIFT FUR ARBEITSRECHT. VFOAT Zeitschrift Fur Arbeitsrecht. German. qt. 120.-. Carl Heymanns Verlag KG, Gereonstrasse 18-32, 5000 Koln 1 West Germany. Tel (0221)134022. Ed Gerhardt Bold and Wolfgang Zollue. LC K30. DD 344.7301. bk rev adv acc. Circ 1,200. Treatises, statements and sentences on the workers' right.

ZFBR, ZEITSCHRIFT FUR DEUTSCHES UND INTERNATIONALES BAURECHT. VFOAT Zeitschrift fur Deutsches und Internationales Baurecht. Vol. 1-. Periodical. GW. German. bm. 174.00. Bauverlag GMBH, Wittlesbacherstrasse 10, D-62 Wiesbaden West Germany. Tel (06121)791-0. Ed G Watzke and W Sofker. DD 343.4307869. bk rev. adv acc. Circ 2,000. Gives detailed information and authoritative analysis on the current state and latest developments in public, private and international building law including the relevant jurisdiction.

THE ZIMBABWE LAW JOURNAL. Vol. 19, Pt. 1 (Apr. 1979)-. Periodical. English. sa. Editor, Department of Law, University of Zimbabwe, PO Box MP 167 Mount Pleasant, Salisbury Zimbabwe. LC K22. DD 349.689105, 346.891005. (cum index). *Rhodesian Law Journal, 0035-483X.*

ZLR, ZEITSCHRIFT FUR DAS GESAMTE LEBENSMITTELRECHT. VFOAT Zeitschrift fur das Gesamte Lebensmittelrecht. Periodical. GW. German. qt. Deutscher Fachverlag GMBH PFCH 100606/Schumannstr 27 6000 Frankfurt 1 West Germany. Ind/Abst Int. Packag. Abstr. LC K30.

ZOLLDIENST. Main/Corp Bundesstelle fur Aussenhandelsinformation (Germany). Series/Titl Zoll Information. German. ir. Bundesstelle fur Aussenhandelsinformation, Postfach 108007, 5 Koln 1 West Germany. LC K4600.

ZONING AND PLANNING LAW HANDBOOK. Series/Titl Zoning and Land Use Law Library. 1981-. 0731-5791. US. English. an. Clark Boardman Company, 435 Hudson Street, New York NY 10014. LC KF5697.A152. DD 346.73045, 347.30645.

ZONING LAW AND PRACTICE. US. English. ir. Michie Company, PO Box 7587, Charlottesville VA 22906.

INTERNATIONAL LAW

LA ABOGADA INTERNACIONAL. THE INTERNATIONAL WOMAN LAWYER. VFOAT International Woman Lawyer. First issued in 1953?. 0567-5111. Periodical. US. Spanish. an. $1.00. International Federation of Women Lawyers, 150 Nassau Street, New York NY 10038.

Law—International Law

ACTA JURIDICA. V. 1- 1959-. 0001-592X. Periodical. HU. English (contributions in French, German or Russian). qt. $44.00 US. Akademiai Kiado, POB 24, 1363 Budapest Hungary. Tel 111-010. Ed Gy Eorsi. **Ind/Abst** Leg. Index, Public Aff. Inf. Serv. Bull., PAIS Foreign Lang. Index. bk rev. adv acc. **Circ** 600. Covers articles on socialist jurisprudence in Hungary as well as studies on the theoretical aspects of law and jurisprudence in western states.

AMERICAN JOURNAL OF INTERNATIONAL LAW. (THE AMERICAN JOURNAL OF INTERNATIONAL LAW). V. 1- Jan. 1907-. 0002-9300. Periodical. US. English. qt $36.00 Non-Members. American Journal of International Law, 2223 Massachusetts Avenue, Washington DC 20008. Ed J B Scott and Others. **Ind/Abst** Leg. Resour. Index, Int. Labour Doc., Sel. Water Resour. Abstr., ABC Pol Sci, Writ. Am. Hist., Ref. Source, Public Aff. Inf. Serv. Bull., Index Leg. Period., Soc. Sci. Index, Am. Hist. Life, Hist. Abstr., Part A, Mod. Hist. Abstr., Hist. Abstr., Part B, Twent. Century Abstr. LC JX1. DD 341.05. (cum index). Proceedings of the American Society of International Law at its Annual Meeting, 0272-5045.

AMNESTY INTERNATIONAL NEWSLETTER. V. 1- 1971-. 0308-6887. Periodical. UK. English. mo. $12.50. Amnesty International, 1 Easton Street, London WC1X 8DJ England. Tel 01-833 1771. **Circ** 50,000. (ctrl) A report of major initiatives and exposes in the human rights field, covering the latest reports and appeals by Amnesty International.

AN ANALYTICAL INDEX TO THE AMERICAN JOURNAL OF INTERNATIONAL LAW AND SUPPLEMENTS . . . AND THE PROCEEDINGS OF THE AMERICAN SOCIETY OF INTERNATIONAL LAW. See Indexes/Abstracts.

ANNUAIRE DE L'A.A.A. See Yearbooks, Almanacs, Directories.

ANNUAIRE DE LEGISLATION FRANCAISE ET ETRANGERE. See Yearbooks, Almanacs, Directories.

ANNUAIRE DE L'INSTITUT DE DROIT INTERNATIONAL. See Yearbooks, Almanacs, Directories.

ANNUAIRE EUROPEEN. See Yearbooks, Almanacs, Directories.

ANNUAIRE FRANCAIS DE DROIT INTERNATIONAL. See Yearbooks, Almanacs, Directories.

ANNUAL REPORT - ADVISORY COMMITTEE ON THE LAW OF THE SEA. Main/Corp United States. Advisory Committee on the Law of the Sea. 0360-0750. US. English. an. United States Department of State, 2201 C Street NW, Washington DC 20520. LC JX4422.U5. DD 353.008232.

ANNUAL REPORT - DEPARTMENT OF STATE, ADVISORY PANEL ON INTERNATIONAL LAW. (ANNUAL REPORT - ADVISORY PANEL ON INTERNATIONAL LAW). Main/Corp United States. Advisory Panel on International Law. 0147-4200. US. English. Advisory Panel on International Law, 2223 Mass Avenue NW, Washington DC 20008. LC JX234. DD 341.05.

ANNUAL REPORT - EAST AFRICAN COMMUNITY. Main/Corp East African Community. 1968-. English. ir. Information Division of East African Community, PO Box 1001, Arusha Tanzania. DD 341.249. Report.

ANNUAL REPORT - GOVERNOR'S COMMISSION ON THE UNITED NATIONS (WISCONSIN). Main/Corp Wisconsin. Governor's Commission on the United Nations. 12th- 1971-. US. English. an. Office of the Governor, Madison WI 53702. LC JX1977.A1. DD 341.23. Annual Report - Governor's Committee on the United Nations.

ANNUAL REPORT - INTERNATIONAL CENTRE FOR SETTLEMENT OF INVESTMENT DISPUTES. (ANNUAL REPORT). Main/Corp International Centre for Settlement of Investment Disputes. 1st- 1966/67-. 0074-2163. US. English. an. International Center for Settlement of Investment Disputes, 1818 H Street NW, Washington DC 20433. LC Law. DD 341.752.

ANNUAL REPORT - INTERNATIONAL FUD FOR AGRICULTURAL DEVELOPMENT. Main/Corp International Fund for Agricultural Development. 1978-. English. an. International Fund for Agricultural Development, Rome Italy. LC HD1431. DD 341.759.

ANNUAL REPORT OF THE EXECUTIVE DIRECTOR - UNITED NATIONS ENVIRONMENT PROGRAMME. Main/Corp United Nations Environment Programme. 1982-. English. an. LC HC79.E5. DD 341.762. Annual Review.

ANNUAL REPORT OF THE SECRETARY GENERAL TO THE GENERAL ASSEMBLY. (ANNUAL REPORT). Main/Corp Organization of American States. Secretary General. VFOAT Annual Report of the Secretary General - Organization of American States. 0078-6403. US. English. an. Organization of American States, General Secretariat, 1889 F Street NW, Washington DC 20006. LC F1402.A4. DD 341.187. NLM W1 OR663FH.

ANNUAL REPORT ON EXCHANGE ARRANGEMENTS AND EXCHANGE RESTRICTIONS - INTERNATIONAL MONETARY FUND. (ANNUAL REPORT ON EXCHANGE ARRANGEMENTS AND EXCHANGE RESTRICTIONS). Main/Corp International Monetary Fund. 1979-. 0250-7366. US. English. an. International Monetary Fund, 19th & G Street, External Relations, Washington DC 20431. LC K4440.A13. DD 341.751. Annual Report on Exchange Restrictions, 0085-2163.

ANNUAL REPORT - PHILIPPINE SOCIETY OF INTERNATIONAL LAW. Main/Corp Philippine Society of International Law. Began publication with 1962 issue. Periodical. PH. English. ir. Ateneo de Manila, Padre Faura, Manila Philippines.

ANNUAL REPORT - UNICEF. Main/Corp UNICEF. US. English. an. UNICEF Headquarters, United Nations, New York NY 10017. LC HV1. DD 341.766.

ANNUAL REPORT - UNITED NATIONS ASSOCIATION. Main/Corp United Nations Association of Great Britain and Northern Ireland. UK. English. an. United Nations Association, 93 Albert Embankment, London SE1 7TX England. LC JX1977.2.G7. DD 341.2341.

ANNUAL REVIEW OF THE CHEMICAL INDUSTRY. Main/Corp United Nations. Economic Commission For Europe. US. English. an. $18.00. LC JX1977, HD9650.1. DD 300, 338.4766002123.

ANNUAL SUMMARY OF LAWS AND REGULATIONS RELATING TO THE CONTROL OF NARCOTIC DRUGS. Main/Corp United Nations. Commission on Narcotic Drugs. Series Corp United Nations. Document. 1947-. English. ir. United Nations Commission on Narcotic Drugs, United Nations Publications, Sales Section/ Room A-3315, New York NY 10017. Tel (212)754-8302. LC JX1977. DD 614.3, 178.8.

ANUARIO DE DERECHO INTERNACIONAL. See Yearbooks, Almanacs, Directories.

ARCHIV DES VOLKERRECHTS. See Genealogy and Heraldry - Archives.

ARIZONA JOURNAL OF INTERNATIONAL AND COMPARATIVE LAW. VFOAT Revista de Derecho Internacional y Comparado de Arizona. Vol. 1, No. 1-. 0743-6963. Periodical. US. English (Spanish, or Portuguese with abstracts in English and Spanish). ir. $8.00 Domestic, $13.00 Foreign. University of Arizona, College of Law, Tucson AZ 85721. Tel (602)621-5593. Ed Kenneth Love. LC K1. DD 340.05. bk rev. adv acc. **Circ** 250. Articles authored by legal scholars, lawyers, and law students that provide practical and comparative information on legal matters pertaining to the United States and Latin America.

ASIL NEWSLETTER. Main/Corp American Society of International Law. Periodical. US. English. bm. Free. American Society International Law, 2223 Massachusetts Avenue NW, Washington DC 20008. Tel (202)265-4313. Ed Judith R Hall. **Circ** 5,200. (ctrl) Contains information of interest to society members including notices of meetings, conferences and publications.

ASILS INTERNATIONAL LAW JOURNAL. Main/Corp Association of Student International Law Societies. VAT Association of Student International Law Societies International Law Journal. V. 1- 1977-. 0161-1402. US. English. an. $10.00. Association of Students of International Law Society, 2224 Massachusetts Avenue NW, Washington DC 20008. Tel (202)387-8467. Ed Heidi V Jimenez. **Ind/Abst** Leg. Resour. Index, Index Leg. Period. LC JX1. DD 341.05. bk rev. adv acc. **Circ** 500. A scholarly publication soliciting solely student writing in the areas of international and comparative law.

AT THE COURT OF ST. JAMES'S. 1954-. 0067-0065. UK. English. an. Diplomatist Publishers Limited, Shooters Lodge, Windsor Forest Berks England. LC JX1783.

AUSSENPOLITISCHER BERICHT DES BUNDESMINISTERS FUR AUSWARTIGE ANGELEGENHEITEN. Main/Corp Austria. Bundesministerium Fur Auswartige Angelegenheiten. German. ir. LC JX1547.

BASIC FACTS ABOUT THE UNITED NATIONS. Main/Corp United Nations. Office of Public Information. May 15, 1947-. US. English. United Nations/Public Information, Sales Section/ Room A3315, New York NY 10017. LC JX1977.A37. DD 341.3.

BEITRAGE ZUM AUSLANDISCHEN UND INTERNATIONALEN PRIVATRECHT. Monographic Series. German. ir. Walter de Gruyter, 200 Saw Mill River Road, Hawthorne NY 10532. Tel (914)747-0110.

BEITRAGE ZUM INTERNATIONALEN WIRTSCHAFTSRECHT UND ATOMENERGIERECHT. See Economics - International Economics.

BILATERAL STUDIES IN PRIVATE INTERNATIONAL LAW. No. 1-. 0067-8562. Monographic Series. US. English. ir. Oceana Publications, 75 Main Street, Dobbs Ferry NY 10522.

BOSTON COLLEGE INTERNATIONAL AND COMPARATIVE LAW REVIEW. Vol. 2, No. 2-. 0277-5778. Periodical. US. English. sa. $12.00. Boston College Law School, 885 Centre Street, Newton MA 02159. Tel (617)552-8569. Ed Edward G McAnoney. **Ind/Abst** Leg. Resour. Index, ABC Pol Sci, Index Leg. Period., Curr. Law Index, Public Aff. Inf. Serv. Bull., Contents Curr. Leg. Period. LC K2. DD 340.05. bk rev adv acc. **Circ** 500. All areas of international and comparative law are dealt with. Boston College International and Comparative Law Journal, 0161-2832.

BOSTON COLLEGE THIRD WORLD LAW JOURNAL. VFOAT Third World Law Journal. Vol. 1, No. 1 (Spring 1980)-. 0276-3583. Periodical. US. English. sa. $10.00. Boston College Law School, 885 Centre Street, Newton Centre MA 02159. Tel (617)552-4316. Ed An-Ping Hsieh. **Ind/Abst** Leg. Resour. Index. LC K2. DD 340.091724. bk rev. **Circ** 300. A forum for scholarly legal works comparing and analyzing the legal systems in developing countries and the position of those countries in the global community.

BOSTON UNIVERSITY INTERNATIONAL LAW JOURNAL. VFOAT International Law Journal. Vol. 1, Issue 1 (Spring 1982)-. 0737-8947. Periodical. US. English. sa. $20.00. Boston University International Law Journal, 765 Commonwealth Avenue, Boston MA 02155. **Ind/Abst** Index Leg. Period. LC K2. DD 340.05.

BRITISH YEAR BOOK OF INTERNATIONAL LAW. See Yearbooks, Almanacs, Directories.

BROOKLYN JOURNAL OF INTERNATIONAL LAW. V. 1- Spring 1975-. 0740-4824. US. English. sa. $15.00 Domestic, $18.00 Foreign. Brooklyn Law School, 250 Joralemon Street, Brooklyn NY 11201. Tel (718)780-7971. Ed Cynthia Dachowitz, Barry Silberzweig. **Ind/Abst** Leg. Resour. Index, Index Leg. Period., Curr. Law Index, Contents Curr. Leg. Period. LC JX1. DD 341.05. bk rev. **Circ** 350. Covers international law, international trade, international relations.

BULLETIN - EUROPEAN PARLIAMENT. (BULLETIN). Main/Corp European Parliament. 0423-7846. English. ir. European Parliament, PO Box 1601, Luxembourg Luxembourg. LC JN32. DD 341.242.

Law—International Law

BULLETIN - UNITED NATIONS ASSOCIATION IN CANADA. Main/Corp United Nations Association in Canada. V. 1- May 1975-. 0317-6460. Periodical. CN. English (French). ir. United Nations Association in Canada, 63 Sparks Street/Room 808, Ottawa Ontario K1P 5A6 Canada. **DD** 341.2306271.

BUSINESS LAW BRIEF. Jan. 1984-. Periodical. UK. English. mo. 175 UK/Ireland, 190 Foreign. Financial Times Business Information, Tower House, Southampton Street, London WC2E 7HA England. **Tel** (01)240-9391. Ed A Hermann. **DD** 346.40705, 344.06705. bk rev. A survey of law in the. *European Law Letter, Eurolaw Commercial Intelligence; Commercial Law Reports.*

CALIFORNIA WESTERN INTERNATIONAL LAW JOURNAL. V. 1- Fall 1970-. Periodical. US. English. ty. $11.00 Domestic, $13.00 Foreign. California Western School of Law, 350 Cedar Street, San Diego CA 92101. **Tel** (619)232-1883. Ed David L Donnan. **Ind/Abst** Leg. Resour. Index, Writ. Am. Hist., Index Leg. Period., Contents Curr. Leg. Period., Curr. Law Index. **LC** JX1. **DD** 341.05. bk rev. adv acc. **Circ** 1,300. Microform. Concentrates on public and private international law, with a wide score of issues within these broad categorizations.

CAMBRIDGE STUDIES IN INTERNATIONAL AND COMPARATIVE LAW. Vol. 1 1946-. Monographic Series. UK. English. ir. Cambridge University Press, 510 North Avenue, New Rochelle NY 10801. **Tel** (914)235-0300.

CANADA-UNITED STATES LAW JOURNAL. **VAT** Canada United States Law Journal. V. 1- 1978-. 0163-6391. Periodical. US. English (French). an. $5.00. Case Western Reserve University, 11075 East Boulevard, Cleveland OH 44106. **Tel** (216)368-3291. Ed David Meany. **Ind/Abst** Leg. Resour. Index, Public Aff. Inf. Serv. Bull., Index Leg. Period. **LC** K3. **DD** 349.7105. (cum index). bk rev. adv acc. **Circ** 525. Articles on comparative aspects of United States and Canadian law, and international law affecting both nations.

CANADIAN BAR REVIEW. (THE CANADIAN BAR REVIEW). **VFOAT** Revue du Barreau Canadien. V. 1- Jan. 1923-. 0008-3003. Periodical. CN. French (text in English, 1923-19). qt. 40.00 Domestic, 50.00 Foreign. Canadian Bar Association, 130 Albert Street/Suite 1700, Ottawa Ontario K1P 5G4 Canada. **Tel** (613)237-2925. Ed A J McClean. **Ind/Abst** Leg. Resour. Index, Index Leg. Period., Curr. Law Index, Soc. Sci. Citation Index. (cum index). adv acc. **Circ** 34,000. (ctrl). This highly respected journal contains articles by eminent Canadian legal scholars on a broad range of legal issues.

CANADIAN WORLD FEDERALIST. V. 1- May 1975-. 0382-8662. Periodical. CN. English. bm. 8.00. World Federalists of Canada, 42 Elgin Street/Suite 32, Ottawa Ontario K1P 5K6 Canada. **Tel** (613)232-0647. Ed Fergus Watt. **DD** 341.2. bk rev. **Circ** 2,000. (ctrl). Examination, reports of latest developments leading to stronger international law, federalism (global and regional) and stronger UN. News of local, national, international people's movernents for world federalism.

CANADIAN YEARBOOK OF INTERNATIONAL LAW. See Yearbooks, Almanacs, Directories.

CARRIER CASE REPORTS. Oct. 1975-. 0362-2916. US. English. mo. $36.00. Traffic Analysis Service, PO Box 942, Duncan OK 73533. **LC** KF1091. **DD** 343.73093.

CARTA SEMANAL DE NOTICIAS - MINISTERIO DE RELACIONES EXTERIORES. Main/Corp Ecuador. Ministerio de Relaciones Exteriores. EC. Spanish. ir. Dpto de Informacion Y Prensa, 10 de Agosto y Carrion, Quito Ecuador. **LC** JX562.

CASE WESTERN RESERVE JOURNAL OF INTERNATIONAL LAW. **VFOAT** Journal of International Law. Vol. 1, No. 1 (Fall 1968)-. 0008-7254. Periodical. US. English. ty. $16.00. Case Western Reserve University, Grund Hall/11075 East Boulevard, Cleveland OH 44106. **Tel** (216)368-3291. Ed Ellin Rosenthal. **Ind/Abst** Leg. Resour. Index, Sel. Water Resour. Abstr., Index Leg. Period., Soc. Sci. Citation Index, Contents Curr. Leg. Collect. Essays, Int. Labour Doc. **LC** JX1. **DD** 341.05. **NLM** W1 CA901S. bk rev. **Circ** 600. Available also on microfilm. A scholarly journal of international law composed of articles by experts, student notes, recent developments, book reviews and conferences.

CHINESE YEARBOOK OF INTERNATIONAL LAW AND AFFAIRS. See Yearbooks, Almanacs, Directories.

LA CHRONIQUE JUDICIAIRE D'HAITI. Began with Oct. 1980 issue. Periodical. French. mo. 24.00. La Chronique Judiciaire d'Haiti, 217 rue de Centre, PO Box 1453, Port-au-Prince Haiti. **Tel** 2-9203. **LC** K3. **DD** 349.729405, 347.294005. bk rev. adv acc. **Circ** 10,000. (ctrl). Articles from Haitian scholars on laws in the country, current problems and book review analysis.

CHUNG-KUO KUO CHI FA NIEN KAN. **VFOAT** Chinese Yearbook of International Law. 1982-. CH. Chinese. an. 3.00. Chung-Kuo Tui Wai Fan I Chu, Pan Kung SSU, Pei-Ching China. **LC** JX18. **DD** 341.05.

CHUNG-KUO TAI PIAO TUAN CHU HSI LIEN HO KUO YU KUAN HUI I WEN CHIEN CHI. CC. Chinese. sa. 1.50. Hsin Hua Shu Tien, Pei-Ching Fa Hsing So, Peking China. **LC** JX1977.2.C5. **DD** 341.2351. *Wo Kuo Tai Piao Tuan Chu Hsi Lien Ho Kuo Yu Kuan Hui i Wen Chien Chi.*

COLLECTION OF THE AGREEMENTS CONCLUDED BY THE EUROPEAN COMMUNITIES. Vol. 6 (1976)-. US. English. European Community Information Inc, 2100 M Street NW/Suite 707, Washington DC 20037. **Tel** (202)862-9500.

COLUMBIA JOURNAL OF TRANSNATIONAL LAW. V. 3- Fall 1964-. 0010-1931. Periodical. US. English. ty. $24.00 Domestic, $25.50 Foreign. Columbia Journal of Transnational Law Association, 435 West 116th Street, New York NY 10027. **Tel** (212)280-3742. Ed Douglas Doetsch. **Ind/Abst** Leg. Resour. Index, ABC Pol Sci, Sociol Abstr., Index Leg. Period., Am. Hist. Life, Hist. Abstr., Part A, Mod. Hist. Abstr., Hist. Abst., Part B, Twent. Century Abstr. **DD** 341.05. (cum index). bk rev. adv acc. **Circ** 1,000. Dedicated to the concept of transnational law including both civil and criminal aspects, what we know as public and private international law, and which involves individual states, corporations or other groups. *International Law Bulletin, 0734-3272.*

THE COMPARATIVE AND INTERNATIONAL LAW JOURNAL OF SOUTHERN AFRICA. **VFOAT** Tydskrif vir Regsvergelyking en Internasionale Reg van Suidelik Afrika, Jornal de Direito Comparativo e Internacional Para os Paises do Sul da Africa, Journal de Droit Compare et International des Pays de l'Afrique Australe, Zeitschrift fur Rechtsvergleichung und Internationales Recht des Sudlichen Afrika. Vol. 1 March 1968-. 0010-4051. Periodical. SA. English. ty. 30.00. Institute of Foreign and Comparative Law, University of South Africa, PO Box 392, Pretoria 0001 South Africa. **Tel** (012)325-4450. Ed J Joubert. **Ind/Abst** Recent Publ. Artic. **LC** K3. **DD** 340.068. bk rev. adv acc. **Circ** 500. (ctrl). Contributions and facts on foreign laws, in particular African; comparative law; private and public international law; constitutional law; recent legal developments Southern Africa.

CORNELL INTERNATIONAL LAW JOURNAL. V. 1- Spring 1968-. 0010-8812. US. English. sa. $11.50. Cornell International Law, Cornell Law School/Myron Taylor Hall, Ithaca NY 14853. **Tel** (607)256-6403. Ed Barbara L Krause. **Ind/Abst** Soc. Sci. Citation Index, Public Aff. Inf. Serv. Bull., Curr. Law Index, Leg. Resour. Index, Index Leg. Period., Contents Curr. Leg. Period. **LC** JX1. **DD** 341.05. (cum index). bk rev. **Circ** 1,000. Student-edited publication dealing with legal problems of international dimensions. Includes student comments on recent developments in international law and notes on unresolved problems facing international legal community.

CORPS DIPLOMATIQUE ACCREDITE A HELSINKI. Main/Corp Finland. Ulkoasiainministerio. French. ir. **LC** JX1808.3. **DD** 351.1892.

CURRENT RESEARCH ON PEACE AND VIOLENCE. V. 1- 1978-. 0356-7893. Periodical. Fl. English. qt $14.00. Tampere Peace Research Institute, PO Box 447, Hameenkatu 13, BA SF 33101 Tampere 10 Finland. **Tel** 31/32535. Ed Tapio Varis. **Ind/Abst** Sociol. Abstr., Soc. Welf. Soc. Plan./Policy Soc. Dev. **LC** JX1901. **DD** 327.17205. bk rev. adv acc. **Circ** 500. Questions of peace research, armament-disarmament, international relations, and conflict studies. *Instant Research on Peace and Violence, 0046-967X.*

CURSO DE DERECHO INTERNACIONAL : CONFERENCIAS. Series/Titl Ediciones Juridicas de las Americas. **VFOAT** Conferencias. August 1982-. US. English (French, Portuguese, and Spanish). an. **LC** JX54. **DD** 341. *Conferencias e Informes.*

DENVER JOURNAL OF INTERNATIONAL LAW AND POLICY. **VFOAT** Journal of International Law and Policy. V. 1- Fall 1971-. 0196-2035. US. English. sa. University of Denver, College of Law, Porter AD Building/7039 East 18th Avenue, Denver CO 80220. **Tel** (303)871-6000. **Ind/Abst** Leg. Resour. Index, Sel. Water Resour. Abstr., Coal Abstr., Energy Inf. Abstr., Environ. Abstr., Public Aff. Inf. Serv. Bull., Index Leg. Period., Curr. Law Index, Contents Curr. Leg. Period. **LC** JX1. **DD** 341.05.

THE DEPARTMENT OF STATE BULLETIN. (DEPARTMENT OF STATE BULLETIN). Publication began with July 1, 1939. 0041-7610. Periodical. US. English. mo. Superintendent of Documents, US Government Printing Office, Washington DC 20402. **Ind/Abst** Pop. Mag. Rev., Writ. Am. Hist., Index U.S. Gov. Period., Chem. Abstr., Public Aff. Inf. Serv. Bull., Read. Guide Period. Lit., Predicasts, Energy Inf. Abstr., Environ. Abstr. **LC** JX232. **DD** 353.1. **CODEN** DSBUAM. *Press Releases, Treaty Information Bulletin.*

DEPOTS VOLONTAIRES, SAISIES (1980). (DEPOTS VOLONTAIRES, SAISIES). **VFOAT** Depots Volontaires et Saisies. **VAT** Semaine Commerciale. Depots Volontaires, Saisies (1980), Index Annuel des Depots Volontaires et Saisies (1980). Ed. 1980-. 0711-3579. CN. French. an. $50,00. Depots Volontaires Saisies, CP 310 Succursale B, Quebec Quebec G1K 7B1 Canada. **DD** 346.714077. *Depots Volontaires, Saisies (Edition Provinciale), 0711-3595; Depots Volontaires, Saisies (Edition de Montreal), 0711-3587.*

DETROIT COLLEGE OF LAW REVIEW. No. 1- 1975-. 0099-135X. Periodical. US. English. qt. $14.00. Detroit College of Law, 136 East Elizabeth Street, Detroit MI 48201. **Tel** (313)965-0150. **Ind/Abst** Leg. Resour. Index, Index Leg. Period., Curr. Law Index. **LC** K4. **DD** 340.05. bk rev. **Circ** 930. *Detroit Law Review.*

DIE DEUTSCHE RECHTSPRECHUNG AUF DEM GEBIETE DES INTERNATIONALEN PRIVATRECHTS. Periodical. German. ir. Walter de Gruyter, 200 Sawmill River Road, Hawthorne NY 10532. **Tel** (914)747-0110.

DGFK-INFORMATIONEN. Main/Corp Deutsche Gesellschaft fur Friedens- und Konfliktforschung. Periodical. GW. German. ir. Theaterplatz 28, 53 Bonn-Bad Godesberg West Germany. **LC** JX1903.

DIGEST OF UNITED STATES PRACTICE IN INTERNATIONAL LAW. 1978-. Periodical. US. English. ir. *Digest of United States Practice in International Law.*

DIKAIO KAI POLITIKE (THESSALONIKE, GREECE : 1982). (DIKAIO KAI POLITIKE). **VFOAT** Law and Politics. 1 (Jan.-Apr. 1982)-. Periodical. GR. Greek, Modern. ty. $70.00 Europe, $90.00 US. Paratiritis Publishing House, 15 Al Stavrou Str, Thessaloniki Greece. **Tel** I Manoledakie. Ed A Manesis and D Tsatsos. bk rev. adv acc. **Circ** 3,000. (ctrl). Law problems including international law, and their relationship with the social and politic conditions.

DIPLOMATIC AND CONSULAR CORPS : REPUBLIC OF GUYANA. English. ir. Ministry of Foreign Affairs, 95 Carmichael Street, Georgetown Guyana. **LC** JX1772. **DD** 341.33.

DIPLOMATIC AND CONSULAR DIRECTORY (LILONGWE, MALAWI). See Yearbooks, Almanacs, Directories.

DIPLOMATIC AND CONSULAR REPRESENTATION IN MALTA. Main/Corp Malta. Ministry of Foreign Affairs. Jan. 1979-. MM. English. ir. Ministry of Foreign Affairs, Palazzo Parisio, Merchants Street, Valletta Malta. **LC** JX1802.7. **DD** 351.892094585. *Diplomatic and Consular Representation in Malta.*

Law—International Law

DIPLOMATIC, CONSULAR AND OTHER REPRESENTATION IN THE DEMOCRATIC SOCIALIST REPUBLIC OF SRI LANKA. Main/Corp Sri Lanka. Rajya Araksake Ha Videsa Katayutu Amatyamsaya. VFOAT Sri Lanka Prajatantrika Samajavadi Janarajaye Rajya Tantrika, Konsal Ha Sesu Niyojama. 1979-. CE. English. ir. 7.75. Government Publications Bureau, PO Box 500, Secretariat, Colombo 1 Sri Lanka. LC JX1859.S75. DD 351.892095493. *Diplomatic, Consular and Other Representation in the Republic of Sri Lanka.*

DIPLOMATIC LIST, CONSULAR LIST. Main/Corp Malaysia. Ministry of Foreign Affairs. English. ir. LC JX1859.M32. DD 351.84209595. *Diplomatic List, Consular List, Foreign Affairs Staff List.*

DIPLOMATIC LIST (WASHINGTON, D.C.). (DIPLOMATIC LIST). Series/Titl Department of State Publication. 0012-3099. Periodical. US. English. qt. Superintendent of Documents, US Government Printing Office, Washington DC 20402. LC JX1705.

DIPLOMATIC REGISTER AND DESK REFERENCE. 0736-0959. Periodical. US. English. sa. $299.95. Spex International Ltd, 51 East 42nd Street, New York NY 10017. LC JX1705. DD 351.8920973.

DIRECTORY OF DIPLOMATIC MISSIONS. See Yearbooks, Almanacs, Directories.

DIRECTORY OF MEMBERS - INTERNATIONAL BAR ASSOCIATION, SECTION ON BUSINESS LAW. See Yearbooks, Almanacs, Directories.

DIRECTORY OF OPPORTUNITIES IN INTERNATIONAL LAW. See Yearbooks, Almanacs, Directories.

DIRECTORY OF THE COMMISSION OF THE EUROPEAN COMMUNITIES. See Yearbooks, Almanacs, Directories.

DIRECTORY OF THE UNITED NATIONS ORGANIZATION AND SPECIALIZED AGENCIES IN IRAQ. See Yearbooks, Almanacs, Directories.

DOC. - COUNCIL OF EUROPE, PARLIAMENTARY ASSEMBLY. Main/Corp Council of Europe. Parliamentary Assembly. FR. English and French. ir. Council of Europe, Avenue d'l Europe, 67 Strasbourg France. LC JN22. DD 341.242. *Doc.*

DOCUMENTS JURIDIQUES INTERNATIONAUX. Vol. 1 (Sept. 1982)-. 0714-931X. Periodical. CN. French. ir. Documents Juridiques Internationaux c/o Editions Yvon Blais, C P 180, Cowansville Quebec J2K 3H6 Canada. DD 341.05.

DOCUMENTS, WORKING PAPERS - COUNCIL OF EUROPE, PARLIAMENTARY ASSEMBLY. Main/Corp Council of Europe. Parliamentary Assembly. VFOAT Documents de Seance - Conseil de l'Europe, Assemblee Parlementaire. Sess. 26- Pt. 2- V. 3- 24/30 Sept. 1974-. US. English (French). ir. Manhatten Publ Co, 80 Brook Street, Croton-On-Hudson NY 10520. LC JN22. DD 341.242. *Documents.*

DOKUMENTE - INSTITUT FUR INTERNATIONALE ANGELEGENHEITEN DER UNIVERSITAT HAMBURG. Main/Corp Hamburg. Universitat. Institut fur Internationale Angelegenheiten. GW. English, French, German or Spanish. ir. Alfred Metzner Verlag, Postfach 970148, D-6000 Frankfurt West Germany. LC JX77.

EUROPEAN COMPETITION LAW REVIEW : ECLR. VFOAT ECLR. Vol. 1, No. 1 (1980)-. 0144-3054. Periodical. UK. English. qt. 50.00. ESC Publishing Ltd, 25 Beaumont Street, Oxford OX1 2NP England. Tel (0865)512281. Ed Julian Maitland-Walker. DD 343.4072, 344.0372. bk rev. adv acc. Update of developments in national jurisdictions in the European community.

EVERYONE'S UNITED NATIONS. 9th- Ed. 1979-. US. English. ir. $9.95. United Nations, Sales Section Room A 3315, New York NY 10017. Tel (212)754-8302. LC JX1977.A37. DD 341.23. Each issue contains an index to its own contents - no vol index - loose. Basic history book describing the structure and activities of the United Nations since its founding in 1945. Specialized agencies related to the United Nations are also covered. *Everyman's United Nations, 0071-3244.*

FLORIDA INTERNATIONAL LAW JOURNAL. Vol. 1, No. 1 (Fall 1984)-. 0882-6420. Periodical. US. English. sa. $12.00. Florida International Law Journal, Holland Law Center, University of Florida, Gainesville FL 32611. Tel (904)392-4980. Ed Juan Rodriguez. DD 341. Circ 300. The journal is a semiannual publication convering various issues of international law. Topics include business, trade, human rights, and international relations.

FORDHAM INTERNATIONAL LAW FORUM. Vol. 1, No. 1 (Fall 1977)-V. 3, No. 2 (1979-1980). 0741-1944. Periodical. US. English. ty. $12.00. Fordham University School of Law, 140 West 62nd Street, New York NY 10023. Ind/Abst Index Leg. Period. LC JX1. DD 341.05.

FORDHAM INTERNATIONAL LAW JOURNAL. Vol. 4, No. 1-. 0747-9395. Periodical. US. English. sa. $8.00. Lincoln Center, 140 West 62nd Street, New York NY 10023. Ind/Abst Leg. Resour. Index, Index Leg. Period. LC JX1. DD 341.05. *Fordham International Law Forum, 0741-1944.*

FOREIGN TAX LAW BI-WEEKLY BULLETIN. 0095-7291. Periodical. US. English. ir. $100.00. PO Box 2187, Ormond Beach FL 32074. Tel (904)258-7035. Ed Donald O Wallace. DD 343.0405. bk rev. Circ 5,000. (ctrl). Covers comparative tax and commercial law, synopses of foreign laws, conducting business abroad, new and proposed laws, investment, labor and social security laws (all foreign).

THE GEORGE WASHINGTON JOURNAL OF INTERNATIONAL LAW AND ECONOMICS. Vol. 16, No. 1 (1981)-. Periodical. US. English. ty. $15.00. The George Washington Journal of International Law and Economics, National Law Center, 720 20th Street NW/B-302, Washington DC 20052. Tel (202)676-7164. Ed Katherine Garrett. bk rev. Circ 1,200. (ctrl). Articles and student-written notes on areas of interest in international law and comparative law. *Journal of International Law and Economics.*

GEORGETOWN INTERNATIONAL REVIEW. V. 1- 1975-. 0360-6082. US. English. Georgetown International Relations Association, 1800 K Street NW/Suite 520, Washington DC 20006. LC JX1. DD 327.05.

GEORGIA JOURNAL OF INTERNATIONAL AND COMPARATIVE LAW. (THE GEORGIA JOURNAL OF INTERNATIONAL AND COMPARATIVE LAW). V. 1- Fall 1970-. Periodical. US. English. ty. $8.00 Domestic, $9.00 Foreign. University of Georgia, School of Law, Athens GA 30601. Ind/Abst Leg. Contents, Index Foreign Leg. Per. Collect. Essays, Index Leg. Period., Leg. Resour. Index, Public Aff. Inf. Serv. Bull. LC K7. DD 341.05. Available in microform from University Microfilms.

GERMAN YEARBOOK OF INTERNATIONAL LAW. See Yearbooks, Almanacs, Directories.

GROTIANA (1980). (GROTIANA). Vol. 1 (1980)-. NE. English (French and German). an. 60. Van Gorcum & Company BV, PO Box 43, 9400 AA Assen Netherlands. Tel 05980-46846. Ed A C Eyffinger. LC JX18. DD 341.05. bk rev. adv acc. Circ 400. (ctrl). The journal intends to be a forum for exchanges concerning the philosophical, ethical and legal fundamentals of the search for an international order.

A GUIDE TO THE UNITED STATES TREATIES IN FORCE. 1982 Ed-. 0736-5713. US. English. an. $50.00. William S Hein & Company, 1285 Main Street, Buffalo NY 14209. Ed I I Kavass and A Sprudza. LC JX236.5. DD 341.026473.

HARVARD INTERNATIONAL LAW JOURNAL. V. 8- Winter 1967-. 0017-8063. US. English. sa. $15.00. Harvard Law School, Austin Hall, Cambridge MA 02138. Tel (617)495-3146. Ed John Barquin. Ind/Abst Leg. Resour. Index, ABC Pol Sci, Public Aff. Inf. Serv. Bull., Index Leg. Period., Contents Curr. Leg. Period., Curr. Law Index. LC JX1. DD 341.05. bk rev. Student-edited journal of international law; publishes articles and notes on matters of current interest to lawyers practicing international law. *Harvard International Law Club Journal.*

HASTINGS INTERNATIONAL AND COMPARATIVE LAW REVIEW. V. 1- Winter 1977-. 0149-9246. Periodical. US. English. sa. $15.00. Hastings College of Law, 198 McAllister Street/Room 205, San Francisco CA 94102. Tel (415)565-4750. Ed Tom Ruby. Ind/Abst Leg. Resour. Index, ABC Pol Sci, Index Leg. Period. LC K8. DD 341.05. bk rev. adv acc. Public/private international law; comparative law, international business/taxation; articles by academicians, judges, practitioners and students written notes.

HOUSTON JOURNAL OF INTERNATIONAL LAW. V. 1- Spring 1978-. 0194-1879. Periodical. US. English. sa. $15.00 Domestic, $18.00 Foreign. Houston Journal of International Law, 4800 Calhoun, Houston TX 77004. Tel (713)749-3774. Ed Russell Rains. Ind/Abst Leg. Resour. Index, Index Leg. Period. LC JX1. DD 341.05. bk rev. adv acc. Circ 500. (ctrl). Timely, scholarly discussions of recent developments in international law including international tax, trade, business, and oil and gas. Quality submissions welcome.

HUMAN RIGHTS LAW JOURNAL : HRLJ. VFOAT HRLJ. Vol. 1 (1980)-. 0174-4704. Periodical. US. English. qt. $60.76. N P Engel, 3608 South 12th Street/I Patton, Arlington VA 22204. Tel (703)920-0874. LC K8. DD 341.48105. *Human Rights Review.*

IIC. VFOAT International Review of Industrial Property and Copyright Law. 0018-9855. Periodical. English. ir. 290.-. VCH Verlagsgesellschaft MBH, Pappelallee 3, D-6940 Weinheim West Germany. Tel (305)438-5566. Ed F K Beier and G Schricker. LC K9. DD 341.75805. bk rev. adv acc. Circ 1,360. Articles, decisions and other materials of international importance in the fields of patents, copyrights, designs, trademarks, unfair competition, and related antitrust problems.

INDEX : CANADA TREATY SERIES. See Indexes/Abstracts.

INDEX TO RESOLUTIONS OF THE GENERAL ASSEMBLY. See Indexes/Abstracts.

THE INDIAN JOURNAL OF INTERNATIONAL LAW. V. 1- 1960-. 0019-5294. Periodical. II. English. qt. $35.00. Indian Society of International Law, 7-8 Scindia H/Kasturba Gandhi M, New Delhi 110001 India. Ind/Abst Contents Curr. Leg. Period.

INDUSTRIAL PLANNING AND PROGRAMMING SERIES. Series Corp United Nations. Document ST/CID. 1-. Monographic Series. US. English. LC JX1977.

INFORMATIVO JURIDICO (WASHINGTON, D.C.). (INFORMATIVO JURIDICO). Nos. 1 & 2 (Jan.-Aug. 1982)-. 0747-6574. US. Spanish. ty. $12.00. General Secretariat, Organization of American States, Washington DC 20006. Tel (202)789-6284. Ed Christian Garcia-Godoy. LC KDZ1103. DD 341.24505. Circ 600. International law and legal developments within the interamerican system (Latin America, the Caribbean and the United States).

INPUT-OUTPUT BIBLIOGRAPHY. See Bibliographies.

THE INTERNATIONAL AND COMPARATIVE LAW QUARTERLY. V. 1- Jan. 1952-. 0020-5893. Periodical. UK. English. qt. British Institute of International and Comparative Law, Charles Clore HS-17 Russell Square, London WC1B 5DR England. Tel 01-636 5802-3-4. Ed Kenneth R Simmonds. Ind/Abst ABC Pol Sci, Index Leg. Period., Public Aff. Inf. Serv. Bull., Curr. Law Index, Leg. Resour. Index, Soc. Sci. Citation Index. DD 340.05. adv acc. Circ 2,200. Public and private international law, comparative law, European law and Commonwealth law. *International Law Quarterly, Journal of Comparative Legislation and International Law; Transactions for the Year (Grotius Society).*

INTERNATIONAL BAR NEWS (LONDON , ENGLAND). (INTERNATIONAL BAR NEWS). Began with May 1980 issue. 0143-7453. Periodical. UK. English. International Bar Association, 2 Harewood Place, Hanover Square, London W1R 9HB England. Tel 01-629-1206. Ed Ruth Elden. LC K110.I47. DD 340.06. bk rev. adv acc. Circ 9,000. Membership news and conference proceedings. *International Bar Journal, 0047-0589.*

INTERNATIONAL BUSINESS LAWYER. Jan. 1973-. 0309-7676. UK. English. mo. 70.00. International Bar Association, 2 Harewood Place, Hanover Square, London W1R 9HB England.

Tel (01)629-1206. **Ed** Ruth Elden. **Ind/Abst** Leg. Resour. Index, Coal Abstr., Curr. Law Index. **LC** K9. **DD** 346.0705. bk rev. adv acc. **Circ** 6,300. International law and practice relating to business, commercial and corporate law.

INTERNATIONAL COURT OF JUSTICE. **Main/Corp** United Nations. Office of Public Information. US. English. ir. $2.00. United Nations Publications, Sales Section/Room A-3315, New York NY 10017. **Tel** (212)754-8302. Contains a brief explanation of the aims, functions and organization of the World Court.

INTERNATIONAL FINANCIAL LAW REVIEW. May 1982-. 0262-6969. Periodical. UK. English. mo. $285.00. Beverley Matthews, Euromoney Publications Ltd, Nestor House, Playhouse Yard, London EC4V 5EX England. **Ind/Abst** ABI/Inform. **LC** K9. **DD** 346.07, 342.67. *International Contract.*

INTERNATIONAL LAW NEWS. (THE INTERNATIONAL LAW NEWS). V. 1- Jan. 1972-. 0047-0813. US. English. qt. American Bar Association, Section of International Law, 1155 East 60th Street, Chicago IL 60637. **Tel** (202)331-2239. **Ed** Gerold W Libby. **Ind/Abst** Leg. Resour. Index. **LC** JX1. **DD** 341.05. adv acc. **Circ** 12,000. (ctrl). Current items of interest for members of the Section of International Law and Practice, ABA, including law notes, committee activity reports, meetings/conference information and new publications.

INTERNATIONAL LAW PERSPECTIVE. V. 1- Jan. 1975-. 0098-7719. Periodical. US. English. mo. $80.00. International Law Perspective, 1523 L Street Northwest/Suite 606, Washington DC 20005. **Tel** (202)638-1855. **LC** JX1. **DD** 341.05. Reports on current and significant developments in international law and trade, covering the congress, courts, and publications.

THE INTERNATIONAL LAW REPORTER. Periodical. English. ir. $8.00. Kishan Lal Chopra, 590 Sector 7-B Urban Estate, Faridabad India. **LC** JX18. **DD** 341.05.

INTERNATIONAL LAW REPORTS. 0309-0671. UK. English. ir. Grotius Publications Ltd, PO Box 115, Cambridge CB3 9BP England. **Tel** (0223)311032. **Ed** E Lauterpacht. (cum index). adv acc. Full reports of decisions of international and national tribunals, relating to public international law.

INTERNATIONAL LAW REPORTS. Year 1950-. UK. English. an. **LC** JX68. *Annual Digest and Reports of Public International Law Cases.*

THE INTERNATIONAL LAWYER. V. 1- Oct. 1966-. 0020-7810. US. English. qt. $22.00. American Bar Association, 750 North Lake Shore Drive, Chicago IL 60611. **Tel** (312)988-5555. **Ind/Abst** Leg. Resour. Index, Sel. Water Resour. Abstr., Recent Publ. Artic., Index Leg. Period., Contents Curr. Leg. Period., Curr. Law Index. **LC** JX1. **DD** 341.05. bk rev. adv acc. (ctrl).

INTERNATIONAL LAWYER'S NEWSLETTER. Vol. 1- Fall 1979-. Periodical. US. English. bm. $61.62. International Lawyers, 4801 Massachusetts Avenue NW/Suite 400, Washington DC 20016. **Tel** (612)823-9007.

INTERNATIONAL LEGAL MATERIALS. Vol. 1, No. 1 (Aug. 1962)-. 0020-7829. US. English. bm. American Society of International Law, 2223 Massachusetts Avenue NW, Washington DC 20008. **Tel** (202)265-4313. **Ind/Abst** Leg. Resour. Index, ABC Pol Sci, Public Aff. Inf. Serv. Bull., Curr. Law Index. **LC** JX68. **DD** 341.1.

INTERNATIONAL LEGAL PRACTITIONER. Began with Vol. 4(III) Nov. 1979 issue. 0309-7684. Periodical. UK. English. ir. 50.00. International Bar Association, 2, Harewood Place Hanover Square, London W1R 9HB England. **Tel** 01-629-1206. **Ed** Ruth Elden. **LC** K110.I47. **DD** 340.05. bk rev. adv acc. **Circ** 2,500. General legal practice. *International Bar Journal.*

INTERNATIONAL MEDIA LAW : A MONTHLY BULLETIN ON RIGHTS, CLEARANCES AND LEGAL PRACTICE. **VFOAT** IML. Vol. 1, No. 1 (Oct. 1982)-. Periodical. UK. English. mo. 21/27 Lamb's Conduit Street, London WCIN 3NJ England. **LC** K4240.A13. **DD** 341.757.

INTERNATIONAL PRACTITIONER'S NOTEBOOK. Began with: No. 8 (Nov. 1979). Periodical. US. English. qt. American Branch of the International Law Association, 14 Wall Street, New York NY 10005. *Practitioner's Notebook.*

INTERNATIONAL PROTECTION OF INDUSTRIAL PROPERTY. V. 1-. Periodical. English. ir. 50.00. ARS-Polona-Ruch, Centrala Handlu Zagranicznego, Ul Krakowskie Przediescie 7, 00-068 Warszawa Poland. **LC** K9. **DD** 341.75809438.

INTERNATIONAL REVIEW OF LAW AND ECONOMICS. Vol. 1, No. 1 (June 1981)-. 0144-8188. Periodical. UK. English. sa. $65.00. Butterworth Scientific Limited, PO Box 63, Westbury House/Bury Street, Guildford GU2 5BH England. **Tel** 0444 459188. **Ed** A I Ogus and C K Rowley. **Ind/Abst** Leg. Resour. Index, Index Econ. Artic. J. Collect. Vol., Index Leg. Period. **LC** K9. **DD** 343.410705, 344.103705. Designed to close a gap in the available journal facilities for publishing the growing volume of research on the important interface between economics and law.

INTERNATIONAL STUDIES. V. 1- July 1959-. 0020-8817. Periodical. II. English. qt. $40.00. Asia Books and Periodicals Company, 11 Darya Ganj, New Delhi 110002 India. **Tel** 268645. **Ind/Abst** ABC Pol Sci, Am. Hist. Life, Public Aff. Inf. Serv. Bull., Hist. Abstr., Part A, Mod. Hist. Abstr., Hist. Abstr., Recent Publ. Artic., Hist. Abst., Part B, Twent. Century Abstr. **LC** JX18.

INTERNATIONAL TAX AGREEMENTS. *See* Business - Public Finance.

INTERNATIONAL TAX AGREEMENTS. **VFOAT** World Guide to International Tax Agreements. Vol. 1-. Periodical. US. English. ir. $9.50. United Nations Publications, Sales Section/Room A-3315, New York NY 10017. **Tel** (212)754-8302. Looseleaf series covering all types of international taxation agreements on income and fortune, moveable capital, commercial, industrial, and agricultural enterprises, or maritime and air transport enterprises. *Double Taxation and Fiscal Evasion.*

INTERNATIONAL TAX & BUSINESS LAWYER. **VAT** International Tax and Business Lawyer. Began with Spring 1983. Periodical. US. English. sa. $20.00. University of California, 33 Boalt Hall/School of Law, Berkeley CA 94720. **Tel** (415)642-9759. bk rev. adv acc. **Circ** 500. (ctrl). Legal periodical covering law and policy related issues of transnational business and taxation, including dispute resolution and the work of international organizations.

IPRAX : PRAXIS DES INTERNATIONALEN PRIVAT- UND VERFAHRENSRECHTS. **VFOAT** I.PRAX. 1981, Vol. 1-. Periodical. GW. German. bm. 57.00. Ernst und Werner Giesking Deckerstrasse 30, Postfach 130 120, 4800 Biefield 13 West Germany. **LC** K9. **DD** 340.905.

IRAN-UNITED STATES CLAIMS TRIBUNAL REPORTS. **VFOAT** Iran-U.S. Claims Tribunal Reports. Vol. 1 (1981-82)-. UK. English. Grotius Publications Ltd, PO Box 115, Cambridge CB3 9BP England. **Tel** (0223)311032. **Ed** S R Pirrie. adv acc. The only complete and fully indexed report of this unique and important tribunal. Decide claims between Itan and the United States.

IRANIAN ASSETS LITIGATION REPORTER. 1980. 0277-2922. Periodical. US. English. sm. $2000.00. Andrews Publications Inc, PO Box 200, Edgemont PA 19028. **Tel** (215)353-2565. **Ed** Leonard E B Andrews. **LC** JX238.I7. **DD** 341.55. The national journal or record of Iranian assets ligigation.

THE ITALIAN YEARBOOK OF INTERNATIONAL LAW. *See* Yearbooks, Almanacs, Directories.

JAHRBUCH FUR INTERNATIONALES RECHT. *See* Yearbooks, Almanacs, Directories.

JAHRBUCH FUR OSTRECHT. *See* Yearbooks, Almanacs, Directories.

JOURNAL DU DROIT INTERNATIONAL. 0021-8170. Periodical. FR. French. mo. Editions Techniques, 123 rue d'Alesia, 75678 Paris Cedex 14 France. **Tel** 46 29 21 30. **Ed** B Goldman and P Kahn. **Ind/Abst** Int. Labour Doc., Foreign Lang. Index. bk rev. *Journal du Droit International Prive.*

THE JOURNAL OF CONFLICT RESOLUTION. Vol. 1, No. 4 (Dec. 1957)-. 0022-0027. Periodical. US. English. qt. Sage Publications Inc, 275 South Beverly Drive, Beverly Hills CA 90212. **Tel** (213)274-8003. **Ind/Abst** Am. Hist. Life, Hist. Abstr., Part A, Mod. Hist. Abstr., Hist. Abst., Part B, Twent. Century Abstr., Predicasts, ABC Pol Sci, Soc. Sci. Index, Public Aff. Inf. Serv. Bull., Psychol. Abstr., Humanit. Index, Funk Scott Index Corp. Ind., Soc. Sci. Citation Index, Sociol. Abstr., Abstr. Engl. Stud., Hist. Abstr. **LC** JX1901. **NLM** W1 JO595M. **CODEN** JCFRAL. (cum index). Available on microfilm from University Microfilms. *0731-4086.*

JOURNAL OF INTERNATIONAL ARBITRATION. Vol. 1, No. 1 (Apr. 1984)-. 0255-8106. Periodical. English. qt. 175. Journal of International Arbitration, PO Box 93, 1211 Geneva 11 Switzerland. **LC** K10. **DD** 341.522.

THE JOURNAL OF INTERNATIONAL LAW AND ECONOMICS *CEASED.* V. 5, No. 2-V. 15, No. 3. 0022-2003. Periodical. US. English. ty. **Ind/Abst** ABI/Inform, Energy Inf. Abstr., Environ. Abstr., Contents Curr. Leg. Period., Index Leg. Period., Public Aff. Inf. Serv. Bull. **LC** K10. **DD** 341.7505. *Journal of Law and Economic Development.*

JOURNAL OF PEACE SCIENCE *CEASED.* V. 1-4. 0094-3738. Periodical. US. English. sa. $12.00. Peace Science Society, International Department of Peace Science, 3718 Locust Street, University of Pennslyvania, Philadelphia PA 19174. **Ind/Abst** Index Econ. Artic. J. Collect. Vol. **LC** JX1291.

JOURNAL OF WORLD TRADE LAW. *See* Economics - International Economics.

JUDGMENTS OF THE UNITED NATIONS ADMINISTRATIVE TRIBUNAL. **Main/Corp** United Nations. Administrative Tribunal. **Series Corp** United Nations. Document. No. 1/70- 1950-57-. US. English. ir. $42.00. United Nations, Sales Section/Room A 3315, New York NY 10017. **Tel** (212)754-8302. **LC** JX1977. **DD** 341.137. Claims and appeals by individuals against the Secretary General of the United Nations and the United Nations Joint Staff Pension Board and subsequent judgements of the United Nations Administrative Tribunal.

KEY OFFICERS OF FOREIGN SERVICE POSTS. **Series/Titl** Department of State Publication. 0023-0790. Periodical. US. English. ty. Superintendent of Documents, US Government Printing Office, Washington DC 20402. **Tel** (202)783-3238. **LC** JX1705.

KIME'S INTERNATIONAL LAW DIRECTORY. *See* Yearbooks, Almanacs, Directories.

KOKUSAI JOYAKUSHU. Began in 1950. JA. Japanese. ir. 2200. Yuhikaku, 17 Kanda Jinbo-Cho 2 Chiyoda-Ku, Tokyo-To 101 Japan. **Ed** Yokota Kisaburo and Takano Yuichi. **LC** JX178.

KONSULARISCHE VERTRETUNGEN UND ANDERE VERTRETUNGEN IN DER BUNDESREPUBLIK DEUTSCHLAND UND BERLIN (WEST). **Main/Corp** Germany (West). Auswartiges Amt. German. ir. VWV Verlag fur Wirtschaft und Verwaltung Gmbh, Korberstrasse 15, Frankfurt Am Main 50 West Germany. **LC** JX1795. *Konsularischen Vertretungen in der Bundesrepublik Deutschland und im Land Berlin.*

LAW AND INTERNATIONAL AFFAIRS. V. 1- Jan. 1975-. Periodical. BG. English. sa. $6.00. Bangladesh Institute of Law and International Affairs, 501 Ehanmondi Residential Area Road No 7, Dacca 5 Bangladesh. **LC** K12. **DD** 340.095492.

LAW AND POLICY IN INTERNATIONAL BUSINESS. V. 1- Winter 1969-. 0023-9208. Periodical. English. qt. $20.00 Domestic, $22.00 Foreign. **Tel** (202)624-8283. **Ed** Terrence G Berg. **Ind/Abst** Manage. Contents, Leg. Resour. Index, Public Aff. Inf. Serv. Bull., Index Leg. Period. **LC** K12. **DD** 343.73087. bk rev. adv acc. **Circ** 1,900. Analyzes laws and policies of government and international organizations affecting transnational business and economics. The foremost journal in its field.

LEGAL ISSUES OF EUROPEAN INTEGRATION. 1974-. 0377-0915. Periodical. NE. English. sa. 118.00. Kluwer Academic Publishing Group, PO Box 322, 3300 AH Dordrecht Netherlands. **Tel** 05700-91126. **Ed** Albert J Rodler. **LC** K12. **DD** 341.242. bk rev. adv acc. **Circ** 1,500. Designed to provide information on international aspects of taxation. It covers direct/indirect taxation in European countries and gives topical reviews of EEC taxation developments.

LEGAL REVIEW. (THE LEGAL REVIEW). 0712-516X. Periodical. CN. English. mo. Free. Calgary Legal Guidance, 100 A 315-10 Avenue Southeast, Calgary Alberta T2G 0W2 Canada. **DD** 349.712305.

LIST OF DIPLOMATIC AND CONSULAR MISSIONS, TRADE AND INTERNATIONAL ORGANIZATIONS. **VFOAT** List of Diplomatic Missions, Consular Missions, Trade and International Organizations.

Law—International Law

English. sa. 40. Ministry of Foreign Affairs, Protocol Division, PO Box 9000, Dar Es Salaam Tanzania. **LC** JX1873.T3. **DD** 351.892097678. *Diplomatic Missions, Consular Missions, Trade and International Organizations, 0376-8392.*

LIST OF DIPLOMATIC CORPS. Main/Corp Qatar. Protocol Dept. English. ir. Qatar Protocol Department, PO Box 250, Doha Qatar. **LC** JX1859.Q3. **DD** 351.892.

LIST OF MEMBERS - WORLD PEACE COUNCIL. Main/Corp World Council of Peace. English. ir. Information Centre of the World Peace Council, Lonnrotinkatu 25 A 5 KRS, PO Box 1811, 00180 Helsinki 18 Finland. **LC** JX1907. **DD** 327.1720601.

LISTA DEL CUERPO DIPLOMATICO. Main/Corp Spain. Ministerio de Asuntos Exteriores. Spanish. ir. **LC** JX1819.

LISTE DE MESSIEURS LES MEMBRES DU CORPS DIPLOMATIQUE ET CONSULAIRE. French. an. **LC** JX1859.L4. **DD** 351.892095692. *Liste des Messieurs les Membres du Corps Diplomatique.*

LISTE DE MM. LES MEMBRES DU CORPS DIPLOMATIQUE (FRANCE. MINISTERE DES RELATIONS EXTERIEURES). (LISTE DE MM. LES MEMBRES DU CORPS DIPLOMATIQUE). VFOAT Liste de M.M. les Membres du Corps Diplomatique. French. ir. **LC** JX1793. **DD** 354.4400892. *Liste de MM. les Membres du Corps Diplomatique (France. Ministere des Affaires Etrangeres).*

LISTE DES MEMBRES DU CORPS DIPLOMATIQUE. Main/Corp Switzerland. Eidgenossisches Politisches Departement. English. ir. **LC** JX1823. **DD** 351.592.

LISTE DIPLOMATIQUE - DEPARTEMENT DU PROTOCOLE. Main/Corp Egypt. Departement du Protocole. French. ir. **LC** JX1863. **DD** 351.892.

LISTE DU CORPS DIPLOMATIQUE AU CAIRE. English. ir. Office National d'Edition de Presse et d'Imprimrie. **LC** JX1863.

LISTE DU CORPS DIPLOMATIQUE - REPUBLIQUE DU SENEGAL. Main/Corp Senegal. FR. French. ir. Impr Nationale, B P 637, 59506 Douai Cedex France. **LC** JX1873.S4. **DD** 351.892. *Liste Diplomatique et Consulaire.*

LLOYD'S MARITIME AND COMMERCIAL LAW QUARTERLY. Main/Corp Lloyd's (Firm). May 1974-. 0306-2945. Periodical. UK. English. qt. $130.00. LLP Maritime and Business Publishers, 87 Terminal Drive, Plainview NY 11803. **Ind/Abst** Leg. Resour. Index, Index Leg. Period., Ship Abstr., Curr. Law Index. **LC** K12. **DD** 343.09605.

LOYOLA OF LOS ANGELES INTERNATIONAL AND COMPARATIVE LAW JOURNAL. VFOAT International and Comparative Law Journal. Vol. 4 (1981)-. 0277-5417. Periodical. US. English. ty. $25.00. Joe Chrisensen Inc, 1441 West Olympic Boulevard, Los Angeles CA 90015. **Tel** (213)736-1112. Ed Ed Kania. bk rev. adv acc. **Circ** 300. The journal addresses legal international issues which are relevent and timely in the international world of business and politics. *Loyola of Los Angeles International and Comparative Law Annual, 0277-5409.*

MCGILL LAW JOURNAL. VFOAT Revue de Droit de McGill. V. 1- Autumn 1952-. 0024-9041. Periodical. CN. English (includes some text in French). qt. 30.00 Domestic, 34.00 Foreign. McGill University, 3644 Pell Street, Montreal Quebec H3A 1W9 Canada. **Tel** (514)845-8824. Ed Raj Pande and Henry Sehultz. **Ind/Abst** Leg. Resour. Index, Index Leg. Period., Curr. Law Index, Contents Curr. Leg. Period. (cum index). bk rev. adv acc. **Circ** 2,000. (ctrl). Articles concerning Canadian and international law, legal issues, legal history, and the development of law.

MAURITIUS DIRECTORY OF THE DIPLOMATIC CORPS. *See* Yearbooks, Almanacs, Directories.

MEALEY'S LITIGATION REPORTS. IRANIAN CLAIMS. VFOAT Iranian Claims. Feb. 3, 1984-. 0742-4655. Periodical. US. English. sm. $1,200.00. Mealey Publications, PO Box 446, Wayne PA 19087. **Tel** (215)688-6566. Ed Michael P Mealey.

LC JX238.I7. **DD** 341.67026873055. bk rev. Coverage and texts of litigation and arbitration between United States and Iranian companies and entities.

MEDEDELINGEN VAN DE NEDERLANDSE VERENIGING VOOR INTERNATIONAAL RECHT. Main/Corp Nederlandse Vereniging Voor Internationaal Recht. No. 1- 1910-. NE. Dutch (English). ir. Kluwer BV, Box 23, Deventer Netherlands.

MICHIGAN YEARBOOK OF INTERNATIONAL LEGAL STUDIES. *See* Yearbooks, Almanacs, Directories.

MONOGRAPHS ON APPROPRIATE INDUSTRIAL TECHNOLOGY. No. 1-. Monographic Series. US. English. United Nations, Sales Section/Room A 3315, New York NY 10017. **LC** JX1977. **DD** 300 S, 338.9.

MULTILATERAL TREATIES DEPOSITED WITH THE SECRETARY-GENERAL. 1981-. US. English. an. $60.00. United Nations Publications, Sales Section/Room A-3315, New York NY 10017. **Tel** (212)754-8302. **LC** JX171. **DD** 341.0262. Lists country ratifications of treaties and other international instruments. *Multilateral Treaties in Respect of Which the Secretary General Performs Depository Functions. Lists of Signatures, Ratifications, Accessions, etc.*

MULTILATERAL TREATIES IN RESPECT OF WHICH THE SECRETARY-GENERAL PERFORMS DEPOSITARY FUNCTIONS. LISTS OF SIGNATURES, RATIFICATIONS, ACCESSIONS, ETC CEASED. Main/Corp United Nations. **Series Corp** United Nations. Document. US. English. an. United Nations Publications, Sales Section/Room A3315, New York NY 10017. **LC** JX1977. **DD** 341.0262.

NAMIBIA BULLETIN. 1973-. 0377-7588. Periodical. US. English. qt. United Nations, Sales Section/Room A 3315, New York Ny 10017. **LC** JX1977.2.A45. **DD** 341.23688.

NATO HANDBOOK. Main/Corp North Atlantic Treaty Organization. VFOAT NATO Handbook. **VAT** North Atlantic Treaty Organization Handbook. Jan. 1971-. BE. English. an. NATO Handbook, Department of State, Washington DC 20520. **LC** JX1393. **DD** 341.243. *North Atlantic Treaty Organization.*

NETHERLANDS INTERNATIONAL LAW REVIEW. VFOAT N.I.L.R. Began with Vol. 22 in 1975. 0165-070X. Periodical. NE. English (French). qt. 92.00. Kluwer Academic Publishing Group Distribution Center, PO Box 322, 3300 AH Dordrecht Netherlands. **Tel** 078-334248. Ed P Morris. **Ind/Abst** Contents Curr. Leg. Period. **LC** JX18. **DD** 341.05. bk rev. adv acc. Review of international law published in cooperation with the TMC Asser Institute. *Nederlands Tijdschrift Voor Internationaal Recht, 0028-2138.*

NETHERLANDS YEARBOOK OF INTERNATIONAL LAW. *See* Yearbooks, Almanacs, Directories.

NEW PERSPECTIVES. V. 1- May 1971-. Periodical. English. bm. $5.00. World Peace Council, Loennrotinkatu 25A, Box 181, 14 Helsinki 18 Finland. **Tel** 64 90 04. **LC** JX1901.

NEWSLETTER - AMERICAN ASSOCIATION FOR THE INTERNATIONAL COMMISSION OF JURISTS. (NEWSLETTER - AMERICAN ASSOCIATION FOR THE INTERNATIONAL COMMISSION OF JURISTS, INC) Main/Corp American Association for the International Commission of Jurists. Began in 1977. 0731-5295. Periodical. US. English. $2.25. American Association for the International Commission of Jurists, 777 United Nations Plaza, New York NY 10017. **Tel** (212)972-0883. Ed Meg Henry. **LC** K3236.2. **DD** 341.48105. **Circ** 1,000. Activities reports of International Commission of Jurists and its US section. General articles on human rights conditions, international law and foreign policy regarding human rights.

NEWSLETTER - DEPARTMENT OF STATE. (DEPARTMENT OF STATE NEWS LETTER). Main/Corp United States. Dept. of State. VFOAT Department of State Newsletter. No. 1 (May 1961)-No. 229 (Dec. 1980). 0041-7629. Periodical. US. English. mo. Superintendent of Documents, US Government Printing Office, Washington DC 20402.

Tel (202)783-3238. **Ind/Abst** Index U.S. Gov. Period., Public Aff. Inf. Serv. Bull. **LC** JX1. **DD** 353.0089205.

NIGERIAN ANNUAL OF INTERNATIONAL LAW. V. 1- 1976-. English. ir. Oxford University Press, 1600 Pollitt Drive, Fairlawn NJ 07410. **LC** JX18. **DD** 341.05.

NIHON NO KAIYO SEISAKU. No. 1-. Japanese. ir. **LC** JX4131.

NORDISK TIDSSKRIFT FOR INTERNATIONAL RET. VFOAT Acta Scandinavica Juris Gentium. Vol. 1-. 0029-151X. Periodical. DK. Danish (articles in English, Norwegian or Swedish). ir. Krohns Boatrykkeri, Sct Peders Strae de 45, 1453 Copenhagen K Denmark. Ed E Bruel. **LC** JX18. **DD** 341.05.

NORDISK TIDSSKRIFT FOR INTERNATIONAL RET. VFOAT Acta Scandinavica Juris Gentium. Publikationsserie. No. 1-. Monographic Series. DK. Danish. ir. 320.-. Krohns Bogtrykkeri, Sct Peders Strae de 45, 1453 Copenhagen K Denmark. **Tel** (1)152166. Ed Isi Foighel, Allan Philip, and Bengt Broms. bk rev. adv acc. **Circ** 1,000. Publishes qualified articles of both dogmatic and critical character of importance to the Nordic countries.

NORTH CAROLINA JOURNAL OF INTERNATIONAL LAW AND COMMERCIAL REGULATION. VFOAT NC J. Int'l L. & Comm. Reg. Vol. 2. No. 1 (Winter 1977)-. 0743-1759. Periodical. US. English. ir. $16.00. University of North Carolina, School of Law, Chapel Hill NC 27514. **Tel** (919)962-4402. Ed Barbara Rand Morgenstern. **Ind/Abst** Leg. Resour. Index, Index Leg. Period., Curr. Law Index. **LC** K10. **DD** 341.75405. bk rev. adv acc. **Circ** 750. (ctrl). Journal dedicated to coverage of current legal problems in areas of international trade, banking, taxation, and investment. *Journal of International Law and Commercial Regulation, 0160-113X.*

NORTHWESTERN JOURNAL OF INTERNATIONAL LAW & BUSINESS. VAT Northwestern Journal of International Law and Business. V. 1- Spring 1979-. 0196-3228. Periodical. US. English. qt. $25.00 Domestic, $27.00 Foreign. Northwestern University School Law, 357 East Chicago Avenue, Chicago IL 60611. **Tel** (312)908-8467. **Ind/Abst** Leg. Resour. Index, Index Leg. Period., Public Aff. Inf. Serv. Bull., Curr. Law Index. **LC** K14. bk rev. adv acc. **Circ** 900. Focuses on private international law and business.

NSTZ : NEUE ZEITSCHRIFT FUR STRAFRECHT. VFOAT N.ST.Z. Periodical. German. mo. 14.50 Single Issue. C H Becksche Verlagsbuchhandlung, Wilhelmstrasse 9, 8000 Munchen West Germany. **LC** KK7972. **DD** 345.43005, 344.305005.

NVWZ : NEUE ZEITSCHRIFT FUR VERWALTUNGSRECHT. VFOAT N.VW.Z. V. 1, 1 (15 Feb. 1982)-. 0721-880X. Periodical. GW. German. mo. 240.00. C H Beckscke Verlagsbuchhandlung, Wilhelmstrasse 9, 8000 Munchen West Germany. **LC** KK5571.2. **DD** 342.4306, 344.3026. *Verwaltungsrechtsprechung in Deutschland.*

OCEAN DEVELOPMENT AND INTERNATIONAL LAW. *See* Earth Sciences - Oceanography.

OCEANS POLICY STUDY SERIES. 8755-0474. Periodical. US. English. Oceana Publications, 75 Main Street, Dobbs Ferry NY 10522. **DD** 333. *Oceans Policy Study, 0275-3006.*

OFFICIAL JOURNAL OF THE EUROPEAN COMMUNITIES. C, INFORMATION AND NOTICES. (OFFICIAL JOURNAL OF THE EUROPEAN COMMUNITIES : INFORMATION AND NOTICES). V. 16- Jan. 15, 1973-. 0378-6986. Periodical. LU. English. ir. Office for the Official Publications of the European Communities, Case Postal 1003, Luxembourg Luxembourg. **Ind/Abst** Coal Abstr. **LC** JN15. **DD** 341.242.

OSTERREICHISCHE ZEITSCHRIFT FUR OFFENTLICHES RECHT UND VOLKERRECHT. Began in 1977. 0378-3073. Periodical. German (English and French). qt. Springer Verlag-New York Inc, 175 5th Avenue, New York NY 10010. **Tel** (212)460-1500. Ed F Koja, I Seidl-Hohenveldern, K Stern, E Suy, L Wildhaber and K Zemanek. **LC** K15. **DD** 340.05. **CODEN** OZORAA. Austrian journal of public and international law,

Law—International Law

including articles on practical and theoretical questions of public law in different countries, administrative, constitutional law and social studies. *Osterreichische Zeitschrift fur Oeffentliches Recht*, 0029-9634.

PEACE AND THE SCIENCES. July/Sept. 1964-. Periodical. English. qt. $15.96. Gazzetta Zeitschriften, Muellwaldplatz 5, A-1040 Vienna Austria. **Tel** 656437. **LC** JX1901. *Nuclear Energy*.

PHILIPPINE SEAS. 1 (1/1982)-. 0115-9003. Periodical. English. sa. **LC** JX18. **DD** 341.4509599.

THE PHILIPPINE YEARBOOK OF INTERNATIONAL LAW. See Yearbooks, Almanacs, Directories.

POLISH YEARBOOK OF INTERNATIONAL LAW. See Yearbooks, Almanacs, Directories.

PROCEEDINGS OF THE ANNUAL CONFERENCE - CANADIAN COUNCIL ON INTERNATIONAL LAW. **Main/Corp** Canadian Council on International Law. VFOAT Travaux du Congres Annuel - Conseil Canadien de Droit International. 1st- 1972-. 0317-9087. Periodical. CN. English (includes some text in French). an. 12.00. Canadian Council on International Law, 236 Metcalfe Street, Ottawa Ontario K2P 1R3 Canada. **Tel** (613)235-0442. **DD** 341. **Circ** 300.

PROCEEDINGS OF THE ANNUAL MEETING - AMERICAN SOCIETY OF INTERNATIONAL LAW. **Main/Corp** American Society of International Law. 68th- 1974-. 0272-5037. US. English. an. $15.00. American Society of International Law, 2223 Massachusetts Avenue NW, Washington DC 20008. **Tel** (202)265-4313. **Ind/Abst** Index Leg. Period., Curr. Law Index. bk rev. adv acc. (ctrl). *American Journal of International Law*, 0002-9300.

PRONTUARIO DE LA LEGISLACION EDUCATIVA DE AMERICA. **Main/Corp** Organization of American States. Dept. of Educational Affairs. US. English or Spanish. qt. Departamento de Asuntos Educativos, Union Panamericana, Washington DC 20006. **DD** 341.767.

PROSPECTUS WITH REPORT OF ACTIVITIES - STOCKHOLM INTERNATIONAL PEACE RESEARCH INSTITUTE. **Main/Corp** Stockholm International Peace Research Institute. English. ir. SIPRI, Pipers Vag 28, S-171 73 Solna Sweden. **LC** JX1907. **DD** 327.1720711487.

PUBLIC INTERNATIONAL LAW. V. 1-. 0340-7349. English (Multilingual). sa. $34.00. Springer Verlag-New York Inc, 175 5th Avenue, New York NY 10010. **Tel** (212)460-1500. Ed R Bernhardt, K Doehring and J A Frowein. **LC** Z6461, JX3091. **DD** 016.341. bk rev. Systematic bibliography of public international law.

PUBLICACIONES Y CONFERENCIAS : INFORME TRIMESTRAL - DEPARTAMENTO DE PUBLICACIONES Y CONFERENCIAS. **Main/Corp** Organization of American States. Dept. of Publications and Conferences. VFOAT Publications and Conferences. US. English and Spanish. qt. Organization of American States, 1889 F Street Northwest, Washington DC 20006. **LC** F1402. **DD** 341.245 S, 341.245.

PUBLICATIONS OF THE INTERNATIONAL BUREAU OF FISCAL DOCUMENTATION. See Business - Accounting.

RAZORUZHENIE, VELENIE VREMENI. Periodical. UR. Russian. 0.45 Single Issue. **LC** JX1974.7.

RECUEIL DES LOIS, DECRETS, ET ARRETES. **Main/Corp** Belgium. VFOAT Verzameling der Wetten, Decreten, en Besluiten. BE. Dutch (French). wk. Moniteur Belge, rue de Louvain 40-42, 1000 Bruxelles Belgium. *Recueil des Lois et Arretes Royaux de Belgique*.

RELAZIONE PROVVISORIA DEL CONSIGLIO DIRETTIVO PER L'ANNO. **Main/Corp** Societa Italiana per l'Organizzazione Internazionale. Consiglio Direttivo. IT. Italian. ir. Palazzetto di Venezia, Via S. Marco 3, Roma Italy. **LC** JX1908.I8. **DD** 341.206045.

REPERTOIRE OF THE PRACTICE OF THE SECURITY COUNCIL. **Main/Corp** United Nations. Dept of Political and Security Council Affairs. **Series Corp** United Nations. Document. 1946-51-. US. English. ir. United Nations Publications, Sales Section/Room A3315, New York NY 10017. **LC** JX1977. **DD** 341.135.

REPORT - GREAT BRITAIN. PARLIAMENT. HOUSE OF COMMONS. SELECT COMMITTEE ON EUROPEAN COMMUNITY SECONDARY LEGISLATION. **Main/Corp** Great Britain. Parliament. House of Commons. Select Committee on European Community Secondary Legislation. 1st- 1972/73-. UK. English. 29. Her Majestys Stationery Office, PO Box 276, London SW8 5DT England. **DD** 341.242.

REPORT OF THE CONFERENCE - INTERNATIONAL LAW ASSOCIATION. **Main/Corp** International Law Association. 1873. 0074-6738. UK. English. be. $25.66. International Law Association, 3 Paper Buildings/The Temple, London EC4Y 7EU England. **Tel** 01-353 2904. (ctrl). Contains reports of the international committees submitted to the Conference; a record of discussions at Conference working sessions, and substantive resolutions passed. *Report of the Conference*.

REPORT OF THE SECRETARY-GENERAL OF THE CARIBBEAN COMMUNITY. **Main/Corp** Caribbean Community. VFOAT Secretary-General's Report. English. ir. Caribbean Community Secretariat, Bank of Guyana Building, PO Box 10827, Georgetown Guyana. **LC** HC151.A1. **DD** 341.245.

REPORT OF THE UNITED NATIONS VISITING MISSION TO THE TRUST TERRITORY OF THE PACIFIC ISLANDS. **Main/Corp** United Nations. Trusteeship Council. **Series Corp** United Nations. Document T. Periodical. English. ir. United Nations Publications, Sales Section, Room A-3315, New York NY 10017. **LC** JX4021. *Report on the Trust Territory of the Pacific Islands, Collected Works*.

REPORT ON COMPETITION POLICY. **Main/Corp** Commission of the European Communities. English. an. $11.00. European Community Information Service, 2100 M Street NW/Suite 707, Washington DC 20037. **Tel** (202)862-9547. **LC** HF1532.92. **DD** 341.754. Gives general view of the anti-trust policy followed during the past year. Includes general competition policy, policy toward enterprises, state aids, and the development on concentration, competition, and competitiveness.

REPORT ON THE WORK OF ITS SESSIONS. **Main/Corp** United Nations. Commission on International Trade Law. **Series Corp** United Nations. General Assembly. Official Records. Supplement. US. English. United Nations Commission on International Trade Law, Sales Section Room A3315, New York NY 10017. **Tel** (212)754-8302. **LC** JX1977. **DD** 341.754.

REPORT - UNITED NATIONS. COMMITTEE ON ECONOMIC CO-OPERATION IN CENTRAL AMERICA. **Main/Corp** United Nations. Committee on Economic Co-Operation in Central America. **Series Corp** United Nations. Document. 1952/53-. 0497-9087. US. English. an. **LC** JX1977.

REPORT - UNITED NATIONS' COUNCIL FOR NAMIBIA. **Main/Corp** United Nations. Council for Namibia. **Series Corp** United Nations. General Assembly. Official Records. US. English. an. $3.00. United Nations for Namibia, Sales Section/Room A 3315, New York NY 10017. **LC** JX1977. **DD** 341.23688.

REPORTS OF CASES BEFORE THE COURT. **Main/Corp** Court of Justice of the European Communities. 1959-. 0378-7591. US. English. ir. European Community Information Service, 2100 M Street NW/Suite 707, Washington DC 20037. **DD** 341.2420268. *Reports of Cases before the Court*.

RESOLUTIONS AND DECISIONS ADOPTED BY THE GENERAL ASSEMBLY. **Main/Corp** United Nations. General Assembly. US. English. $12.00. United Nations, Sales Section, New York NY 10017. **LC** JX1977, JX1977. **DD** 300.8S, 341.2322026.

RESOLUTIONS AND DECISIONS, ANNEXES, SUMMARY RECORDS. **Main/Corp** World Health Organization. Executive Board. English. ir. **LC** RA 8.A4. **DD** 341.765. *Summary Records*.

REVIEW OF THE COUNCIL'S WORK. **Main/Corp** Council of the European Communities. 20th- 1972-. US. English. ir. European Community Information Service, 2100 M Street/Suite 707, Washington DC 20037. **Tel** (202)862-9500. **LC** HC241.2. **DD** 341.75.

REVISTA DE DOUTRINA E JURISPRUDENCIA. 0101-8868. Periodical. Portuguese. ty. 50.00. Tribunal de Justica do Distrito Federal e dos Territorios, Palacio da Justica Praca do Buriti Sala 249, Brasilia DF Brazil. **Tel** (061)226-1009. **LC** KHD6706. **DD** 348.81041, 348.10841. **Circ** 3,000. (ctrl). Appelate court decisions and sentences by judges of the first degree and judicial studies.

REVISTA DIPLOMATICA E INTERNACIONAL. Began in 1966. Spanish. ir. Casilla 1598, la Paz Bolivia. **LC** JX9. **DD** 327.205.

REVISTA ESPANOLA DE DERECHO INTERNACIONAL. V. 1- 1948-. 0034-9380. Periodical. SP. Spanish. ty. Consejo Super Invest Cientific, Vitruvio 8, Apartado 14 458, 28006 Madrid Spain. **Ind/Abst** Index Foreign Leg. Per. Collect. Essays. **LC** JX9.

REVUE BELGE DE DROIT INTERNATIONAL. LOUVAIN = BELGIAN REVIEW OF INTERNATIONAL LAW. VFOAT Belgian Review of International Law. Louvain, Belgian Review of International Law. 1965, 1-. 0035-0788. Periodical. BE. Multilingual (French, English, and Dutch). sa. 2.383. Establissements Emile Bruylant, 67 rue de la Regence, 1000 Brussels Belgium. **Tel** 02/512-9845. **Ind/Abst** Index Foreign Leg. Per. Collect. Essays, Public Aff. Inf. Serv. Bull., Foreign Lang. Index, PAIS Foreign Lang. Index. **LC** JX3. **DD** 341.05. Index in last issue of volume - attached. bk rev. adv acc. **Circ** 1,000. Belgian journal of international law; doctrine and legislation.

REVUE CRITIQUE DE DROIT INTERNATIONAL PRIVE. Vol. 1- Jan./Feb. 1905-. 0035-0958. Periodical. FR. French. qt. $47.50. Dalloz, 11 rue Soufflot, 75240 Paris Cedex 05 France. **Ind/Abst** Index Foreign Leg. Per. Collect. Essays. **LC** JX6002. Index in last issue of volume - attached. (cum index).

REVUE DE DROIT INTERNATIONAL, DE SCIENCES DIPLOMATIQUES ET POLITIQUES (THE INTERNATIONAL LAW REVIEW). VFOAT International Law Review. Yearly Vol. 1-. 0035-1091. Periodical. SZ. French (English, German and Italian). qt. 160.-. Revue de Droit International, Case Postale 138, CH-1211 Geneve 12 Switzerland. Ed C L Heinbach. Articles of law, international law and political science in French, English, German and/or Italian.

REVUE DE DROIT INTERNATIONAL ET DE DROIT COMPARE. Vol. 1- 1908-. 0035-1105. Periodical. BE. French. qt. 2.760. Establissements Emile Bruylant, 67 rue de la Regence, 1000 Brussels Belgium. **Tel** 2/512-9845. **Ind/Abst** Index Foreign Leg. Per. Collect. Essays. **LC** K21. bk rev. adv acc. **Circ** 750. Journal of international law and comparative law; doctrine and legislation.

REVUE EGYPTIENNE DE DROIT INTERNATIONAL. VFOAT Majallah Al-Misriyah Lil-Qanun Al-Dawli. V. 1- 1945-. 0080-259X. UA. Arabic (English and French). ir. 25. Egyptian Society of International Law, 16 Avenue Ramses, Lecaire Cairo Egypt. **Tel** 743162. Ed Waheed Raafat. **Ind/Abst** ABC Pol Sci. **LC** JX3. (cum index). bk rev. International law and international relations.

REVUE GENERALE DE DROIT INTERNATIONAL PUBLIC. V. 1- 1894-. 0035-3086. Periodical. FR. French. qt. Editions a Pedone, 13 rue Soufflot, 75005 Paris France. **Ind/Abst** Index Foreign Leg. Per. Collect. Essays. **LC** JX3.

REVUE IRANIENNE DES RELATIONS INTERNATIONALES. VFOAT Iranian Review of International Relations. No. 3- Summer 1975-. 0378-990X. French (English). ir. 2.00. Centre des Hautes Etudes Internationales, Universite de Teheran, 43 Av Anatole France, Teheran Iran. **Ind/Abst** Public Aff. Inf. Serv. Bull., Foreign Lang. Index. **LC** JX18. **DD** 327.05. *International Relations*.

RIVISTA DI DIRITTO INTERNAZIONALE. Vol. 1- 1906-. 0035-6158. Periodical. IT. Italian. qt. 55.000 Domestic, 85.000 Foreign. Casa Editrice Dr A Giuffre, Via Statuto 2 Periodical Department, 20121 Milano Italy. **Tel** 02/652341. Ed Gaetano Morelli. **Ind/Abst** Index Foreign Leg. Per. Collect. Essays. Index in last issue of volume - attached. (cum index). bk rev. adv acc. **Circ**

Law—International Law

800. This journal deals with public as well as private international law.

RIVISTA DI DIRITTO INTERNAZIONALE PRIVATO E PROCESSUALE. Vol. 1- 1965-. 0035-6174. Periodical. IT. Multilingual (Italian and French). qt. $41.58. Cedam Casa Editrice, Via Japelli 5, 35100 Padova Italy. **Ind/Abst** Index Foreign Leg. Per. Collect. Essays. Index in last issue of volume - attached.

SCHWEIZERISCHES JAHRBUCH FUR INTERNATIONALES RECHT. See Yearbooks, Almanacs, Directories.

SEMIANNUAL REPORT TO THE COMMISSION ON SECURITY AND COOPERATION IN EUROPE. **Main/Corp** United States. Dept. of State. 0148-1924. US. English. sa. US Department of State, Washington DC 20520. LC JX1393.C65. DD 327.17094.

SEW. **VAT** Sociaal-Economische Wetgeving. Periodical. Dutch. ir. 146. Tjeenk Willink, Postbus 25, 8000 AA Zwolle Netherlands. **Tel** (038)211444. **Ed** J Bourgeios. bk rev. adv acc. **Circ** 1,000. Specialized in law and economics according to the relations between member states of the European accent on the Netherlands and Belgium. Sociaal-Economische Wetgeving. Europa/Benelux/Nederland.

SOUTH AFRICAN YEARBOOK OF INTERNATIONAL LAW. See Yearbooks, Almanacs, Directories.

SOVETSKII EZHEGODNIK MEZHDUNARODNOGO PRAVA. **VFOAT** Soviet Year-Book of International Law. 1958-. 0584-5335. UR. Russian (summaries in English, tables of contents in Chinese, French, English and German). ir. Victor Kamkin Inc, 12224 Parklawn Drive, Rockville MD 20852. **Tel** (301)881-5973. LC JX21.

STANFORD JOURNAL OF INTERNATIONAL LAW. Vol. 16 (Summer 1980)-. 0731-5082. Periodical. US. English. sa. $18.00. Stanford University, School of Law, Stanford CA 94305. **Tel** (415)497-2654. **Ed** Laura Hills. **Ind/Abst** Leg. Resour. Index, ABC Pol Sci, Soc. Sci. Citation Index, Int. Polit. Sci. Abstr., Public Aff. Inf. Serv. Bull., Index Leg. Period., Index Foreign Leg. Per. Collect. Essays, Index Period. Artic. Relat. Law. LC JX1. DD 341.05. bk rev. adv acc. **Circ** 500. International law. Stanford Journal of International Studies, 0081-4326.

STATISTICAL PAPERS - UNITED NATIONS. STATISTICAL OFFICE. See Statistics.

STUDIES IN TRANSNATIONAL LEGAL POLICY. US. English. ir. American Society of International Law, 2223 Mass Avenue NW, Washington DC 20008. **Tel** (202)265-4313. The serial deals with various topics of international law varying from international investment, trade, monetary reform to international telecommunications, terrorism, and UN systems.

SUMMARY OF PASSPORT STATISTICS. See Statistics.

SUMMARY OF THE DECISIONS TAKEN AT THE MEETINGS AND TEXTS OF THE RESOLUTIONS APPROVED. **Main/Corp** Organization of American States. Permanent Council. Began in 1971. 0250-6319. US. English. an. Organization of American States, 1889 F Street Northwest, Washington DC 20006. LC KDZ1171.A4. DD 341.245. Summary of the Decisions Taken at the Meetings and Texts of Resolutions Approved.

SYRACUSE JOURNAL OF INTERNATIONAL LAW AND COMMERCE. V. 1- OCT. 1972-. 0093-0709. Periodical. US. English. sa. $5.00. Syracuse University, College of Law, Syracuse NY 13210. **Ind/Abst** Manage. Contents, Leg. Resour. Index, Sel. Water Resour. Abstr., ABI/Inform, Index Leg. Period. LC JX1. DD 341.05.

TAX NEWS SERVICE. **Main/Corp** International Bureau of Fiscal Documentation. Began with Jan. 15, 1965 issue. English. ir. 225 Domestic, 250 Foreign. International Bureau of Fiscal Documentation, PO Box 20237, 1000 HE Amsterdam Netherlands. **Tel** (0)20-26.77.26. LC K4456.2. DD 343.0405. Concise newssheet reporting by air twice per month latest tax changes/developments worldwide.

TEXAS INTERNATIONAL LAW JOURNAL. Vol. 7, No. 1 (Summer 1971)-. 0163-7479. Periodical. US. English. ir. $20.00. Texas International Law Journal, 727 East 26th Street, Austin TX 78705. **Tel** (512)471-5453. **Ed** Ruth Rickard. **Ind/Abst** Leg. Resour. Index, Index Leg. Period., Curr. Law Index, Contents Curr. Leg. Period. LC JX1. DD 341.05. Index in last issue of volume - loose - separately paged. (cum index). bk rev. adv acc. **Circ** 650. Journal of articles, student works, and book reviews in the various fields of transnational law. Also includes coverage of domestic law with international implications. Texas International Law Forum.

TRADING LAW. Vol. 1, No. 1-. Periodical. UK. English. ir. $55.17. Barry Rose Law Periodicals Ltd, Little London Chichester, West Sussex PO19 1PG England. **Tel** 0243/ 783637. LC KD2200.A13. DD 343.4108 344.1038.

TRANSNATIONAL PERSPECTIVES. 0376-6403. SZ. English. qt. $7.00. Transnational Perspectives, Case Postale 161, 1211 Geneva 16 Switzerland. **Ind/Abst** Public Aff. Inf. Serv. Bull. LC JX1901. DD 341.205. World Federalist, Contact.

TRAVAUX DE JURIDICTION INTERNATIONALE. 0082-6030. Monographic Series. SZ. French. ir. Librarie Droz SA, 11 rue Massot, 1211 Geneva Switzerland.

TRAVAUX DU COMITE FRANCAIS DE DROIT INTERNATIONAL PRIVE. **Main/Corp** Comite Francais de Droit International Prive. Vol. 1. FR. French. ir. $7.32. Editions du CNRS, 295 rue St Jacques, 75005 Paris France. **Tel** 43-26-56-11. LC JX6012. DD 341.506244.

TREATIES IN FORCE. **Main/Corp** United States. Dept. of State. Office of the Legal Adviser. **Series Corp** United States. Dept. of State. Publication. Began publication with 1929 issue. US. English. an. Superintendent of Documents, US Government Printing Office, Washington DC 20402. LC JX236. DD 341.273.

TREATY ROLLS PRESERVED IN THE PUBLIC RECORD OFFICE. **Main/Corp** Great Britain. Public Record Office. UK. English. H M Stationery Office, PO Box 276, London SW8 5DT England. LC JX636 1955. DD 327.42.

TREATY SERIES. **Main/Corp** United Nations. **VFOAT** Recueil des Traites. V. 1- 1946/47-. 0379-8267. US. English (French). ir. United Nations Publications, Sales Section Room A-3315, New York NY 10017. **Tel** (212)754-8302. LC JX170. DD 341.2. (cum index). The text of every treaty and international agreement entered into by any member state of the United Nations. Treaty Series, 0379-8267.

TREATY SERIES. **Main/Corp** South Africa. **VFOAT** Verdragreeks. Monographic Series. SA. Issued in Afrikaans and English. ir. Pretoria Government Printer, Private Bag X85, Pretoria 0001 South Africa. LC JX1040.A58. DD 341.268.

TUAIRISC OIFIGIUIL - AN COMHCHOISTE AR REACHTAIOCHT TANAISTEACH NA GCOMHPHOBAL EORPACH. **Main/Corp** Ireland (EIRE). Parliament. Joint Committee on the Secondary Legislation of the European Communities. **VFOAT** Official Report - Joint Committee on the Secondary Legislation of the European Communities. English. ir. -/-/2 1/2 Each Issue. Stationery Office, Government Publications Sale Office, G P O Arcade 1, Dublin- Ireland. LC HC241.25.I7. DD 341.75.

TURKISH FOREIGN POLICY REPORT. **Main/Corp** Turkey. Dsisleri Bakanlg. Arastrma Dairesi. No. 1- Feb. 7, 1975-. English. ir. Ministry of Foreign Affairs, 56 Karnanfil Sokak Yenischir Ankara Turkey. LC JX1002. DD 327.561.

TURKS AND CAICOS ISLANDS CONSOLIDATED INDEX OF STATUTES AND SUBSIDIARY LEGISLATION TO . . . . See Indexes/ Abstracts.

UCLA PACIFIC BASIN LAW JOURNAL. Vol. 1, No. 1 (Winter 1982)-. Periodical. US. English. sa. $15.00. UCLA Pacific Basin Law Journal, UCLA School of Law, 405 Hilgard Avenue, Los Angeles CA 90024. **Tel** (213)206-6286. **Ed** Constance C Arvie. **Ind/Abst** Leg. Resour. Index, Public Aff. Inf. Serv. Bull. bk rev. adv acc. Scholarly articles and commentaries on various legal issues effecting the nations which constitute the Pacific Basin Rim.

UNESCO BULLETIN. **Main/Corp** Nepal. National Commission for UNESCO. NP. English and Nepali. ir. United Nations, Sales Section Room A 3315, New York NY 10017. LC AS4.U825. DD 341.767.

UNESCO YEARBOOK ON PEACE AND CONFLICT STUDIES. See Yearbooks, Almanacs, Directories.

UNHCR CEASED. **Main/Corp** Office of the United Nations High Commissioner for Refugees. **VAT** United Nations High Commissioner for Refugees. July 1972-Mar./Apr. 1981. 0503-3918. Periodical. English. LC JX4292.R4. DD 341.486. UNHCR Bulletin.

UNITED NATIONS JURIDICAL YEARBOOK. See Yearbooks, Almanacs, Directories.

UNITED NATIONS LAW REPORTS. V. 1- Sept. 1966-. Periodical. US. English. mo. $75.00 Domestic $90.00 Foreign. Walker and Company, 720 5th Avenue, New York NY 10019. **Tel** (212)265-3632. **Ed** John Carey. (cum index). Extracts from a wide range of United Nation documents of legal significance.

UNITED NATIONS LEGISLATIVE SERIES. 0082-8300. Monographic Series. US. English. ir. $32.00. United Nations Publications, Sales Section/Room A-3315, New York NY 10017. **Tel** (212)754-8302. DD 341.268. Includes compilations of legal texts submitted by governments on selected topics.

U.N. OBSERVER & INTERNATIONAL REPORT. **VAT** United Nations Observer and International Report. V. 1-. Newspaper. US. English. mo. $15.00 US and US Possessions, $35.00 Elsewhere. Suite 2001/200 Park Avenue, New York NY 10017.

UNITED NATIONS RESOLUTIONS ON PALESTINE AND ARAB-ISRAELI CONFLICT. 1975-. English. ir. **Tel** 814174. LC JX1977.2.P34. DD 341.235694. **Circ** 3,000. Includes all pertinent resolutions on the Palestine question passed by the United Nations and its subsidiary organs during the year.

UNITED NATIONS RESOLUTIONS ON PALESTINE AND THE ARAB-ISRAELI CONFLICT. (QARARAT AL-UMAM AL-MUTTAHIDAH BI-SHAN FILASTIN WA-AL-SIRA AL-ARABI-AL-ISRAILI). Began with Vol. for 1975. Arabic. an. 15.00. Shari Anis Al-Nusuli Mutafarri Min Shari Firdan, Bayrut Lubnan. LC JX1977.2.P34.

UNITED NATIONS RESOLUTIONS. SERIES 1. RESOLUTIONS ADOPTED BY THE GENERAL ASSEMBLY. **VFOAT** Resolutions Adopted by the General Assembly. Vol. 1 (1946-1948)-. 0886-6686. US. English. ir. Oceana Publications, 75 Main Street, Dobbs Ferry NY 10522. DD 341.

UNITED NATIONS SYSTEM OF ORGANIZATIONS. **VFOAT** United Nations System of Organizations and Directory of Senior Officials. US. English. an. LC JX1977.8.O35. DD 354.12.

UNITED STATES TREATIES AND OTHER INTERNATIONAL AGREEMENTS. **Main/Corp** United States. Publication Began with 1950. 0083-3487. US. English. an. Superintendent of Documents, US Government Printing Office, Washington DC 20402. LC JX231. DD 341.273.

THE UNIVERSITY OF MIAMI INTER-AMERICAN LAW REVIEW. **VFOAT** Inter-American Law Review. Vol. 16, No. 1 (Spring 1984)-. Periodical. US. English. ty. $14.00. School of Law, University of Miami, PO BOx 248087, Coral Gables FL 33124. **Tel** (305)284-5562. **Ed** Alfred Scope. **Ind/Abst** Leg. Resour. Index. bk rev. adv acc. **Circ** 1,000. A valuable source of information regarding recent legal developments in the Western Hemisphere and around the globe. Lawyer of the Americas, 0023-9445.

VANDERBILT JOURNAL OF TRANSNATIONAL LAW. V. 5- Winter 1971-. 0090-2594. Periodical. US. English. qt. $14.00. Vanderbilt University, School of Law, Nashville TN 37240. **Tel** (615)322-2284. **Ind/Abst** Leg. Resour. Index, Public Aff. Inf. Serv. Bull., Index Leg. Period., Curr. Law Index, Contents Curr. Leg. Period. LC JX1. DD 341.05. Vanderbilt International, 0042-2525.

VERTEGENWOORDIGINGEN VAN HET KONINKRIJK DER NEDERLANDEN IN HET BUITENLAND. NE. Dutch. sa. Staatsuitgeverij, Christoffel Plantijnstraat 1, S- Gravenhage Netherlands. LC JX1806.

Vertegenwoordigingen van Nederland in het Buitenlang.

VIEWS AND ESTIMATES OF THE COMMITTEE ON FOREIGN AFFAIRS ON THE BUDGET. (VIEWS AND ESTIMATES OF THE COMMITTEE ON FOREIGN AFFAIRS ON THE BUDGET FOR FISCAL YEAR). **Main/Corp** United States. Congress. House. Committee on Foreign Affairs. Began with issue for 1979/80. 0278-4939. US. English. an. Superintendent of Documents, Government Printing Office, Washington DC 20402. **LC** JX1706.A2. **DD** 353.0072. *Views and Estimates of the Committee on International Relations on the Budget.*

VIRGINIA JOURNAL OF INTERNATIONAL LAW. V. 3- 1963-. 0042-6571. Periodical. US. English. qt. $25.00. Virginia Journal of International Law, University of Virginia School of Law, Charlottesville VA 22901. **Tel** (804)924-3415. **Ind/Abst** Sel. Water Resour. Abstr., ABC Pol Sci, Index Leg. Period., Soc. Sci. Citation Index, Leg. Resour. Index, Curr. Law Index, Contents Curr. Leg. Period. **LC** JX1. **DD** 341.05. (cum index). bk rev. adv acc. **Circ** 900. Devoted to all fields to public and private international law-arbitration, litigation, act of state doctrine, human rights, law of the sea, and others. *Journal of the John Bassett Moore Society of International Law.*

VOLUNTARY FUNDS ADMINISTERED BY THE UNITED NATIONS HIGH COMMISSIONER FOR REFUGEES ACCOUNTS, AND REPORT OF THE BOARD OF AUDITORS. **Main/Corp** United Nations. Office of the United Nations High Commissioner for Refugees. US. English. United Nations Publications, Sales Section/Room A3315, New York NY 10017. **LC** TX1977. **DD** 341.232 S, 341.486.

WEST INTERNATIONAL LAW BULLETIN. **VFOAT** Law Bulletin. 0748-9056. Periodical. US. English. qt. $60.00 Domestic, $80.00 Foreign. International Law Bulletin, West Publishing Company, 170 Old Country Road, Mineola NY 11501. **LC** K1001.2. **DD** 346.0705, 342.76005.

WISCONSIN INTERNATIONAL LAW JOURNAL. Vol. 1 (1982)-. 0743-7951. Periodical. US. English. an. $8.00. University of Wisconsin, Law School, Madison WI 53706. **Tel** (608)262-2126. **Ed** Christopher Jaekels. **DD** 341. **Circ** 200. Scholarly review of international law issues prepared by student and professional writers in the field.

WORK ACCOMPLISHED BY THE INTER-AMERICAN JURIDICAL COMMITTEE DURING ITS REGULAR MEETING. **Main/Corp** Inter-American Juridical Committee. US. English. Organization of American States, 17th Constitution Avenue NW, Washington DC 20006. **LC** F1405.5 1959, JX1261. **DD** 341245 S, 341.05. *Report of the Inter-American Juridical Committee on the Work Accomplished during its Meeting.*

WORLD FEDERALIST NEWSLETTER. **VFOAT** Newsletter. V. 1-6, Issue 2. 0196-2574. Periodical. US. English. qt. $5.00. World Federalist Association, PO Box 15250, Washington DC 20003-0250. **Tel** (202)546-3950. **Ed** Lawrence Abbott. **Circ** 9,500. (ctrl). World peace through world law.

WORLD MILITARY EXPENDITURES AND ARMS TRANSFERS. Began with 1974. US. English. an. Superintendent of Documents, US Government Printing Office, Washington DC 20402. **Tel** (202)783-3238. **LC** JX1974.A1. **DD** 338.47355005. *World Military Expenditures and Arms Trade.*

WORLD TAX REPORT. Periodical. UK. English. mo. 175 UK & Eire, 190 Foreign. Financial Times Business Information, Tower House, Southampton Street, London WC2E 7HA England. **Tel** (01)240-9391. **Ed** Clive Wolman. **LC** K4456.2. **DD** 343.0405, 342.3405. bk rev. A survey of world developments in taxation.

WORLDLAW. **VFOAT** World Law. July-Aug. 1984-. 0748-9692. Periodical. US. English. bm. $115.00. Worldlaw, 12021 Wilshire Boulevard/Suite 428, Los Angeles CA 90025. **DD** 341.

THE YALE JOURNAL OF WORLD PUBLIC ORDER CEASED. Vol. 7, No. 1 (Fall 1980)-Vol. 9, No. 2 (Spring 1983). 0734-0494. Periodical. US. English. sa. $10.00. Yale Law School, Box 410 A Yale Station, New Haven CT 06520. **Ind/Abst** Index Leg. Period. **LC** JX1. **DD** 341.05. *Yale Studies in World Public Order, 0363-1397.*

YEARBOOK : COMMERCIAL ARBITRATION. See Yearbooks, Almanacs, Directories.

YEARBOOK OF THE INTERNATIONAL LAW COMMISSION. See Yearbooks, Almanacs, Directories.

YEARBOOK - UNITED NATIONS. COMMISSION ON INTERNATIONAL TRADE LAW. See Yearbooks, Almanacs, Directories.

ZEITSCHRIFT FUR AUSLANDISCHES OFFENTLICHES RECHT UND VOLKERRECHT. 0044-2348. Periodical. GW. German. qt. 228.-. W Kohlhammer GMBH Verlag, Hessbruhlstrasse 69, Postfach 800430, 7000 Stuttgart 80 West Germany. **Tel** 0711-7863-1. **Ind/Abst** ABC Pol Sci, Foreign Lang. Index, Energy Res. Abstr., PAIS Foreign Lang. Index. **LC** K30. **DD** 341.05. (cum index). bk rev. adv acc. (ctrl). Contains discussions of foreign civil law and international law as well as opinions and book reviews.

LAW ENFORCEMENT

AAMVA BULLETIN. **VAT** American Association of Motor Vehicle Administrators Bulletin. 1936. 0001-0154. Periodical. US. English. mo. $12.50. American Association of Motor Vehicle Administration, 1201 Connecticut Avenue NW/Suite 910, Washington DC 20036. **Tel** (202)296-1955. **Ed** Robert S Brown Jr. **Circ** 3,000. (ctrl). An association of state and provincial officials responsible for the administration and enforcement of motor vehicle and traffic laws in the United States and Canada. *Bulletin (American Association of Motor Vehicle Administrators).*

A.E.L.E. LAW ENFORCEMENT LEGAL DEFENSE MANUAL. (AELE LAW ENFORCEMENT LEGAL DEFENSE MANUAL). **Main/Corp** Americans For Effective Law Enforcement. **VFOAT** Law Enforcement Legal Defense Manual. 0092-2552. US. English. qt. $60.00. Law Enforcement Legal Defense Manual, 421 Ridgewood Avenue c/o J Manak, Glen Ellyn IL 60137. **Tel** (312)858-6092. **LC** KF1307.A73. **DD** 346.7303.

AL-AMN. Periodical. Arabic. mo. Shurtat Dubayy, Far Al-Alaqat Al-Ammah, SB 1493, Dubayy Al-Imarat Al-Arabiyah Al-Muttahidah, Dubayy Trucial States. **LC** HV7551.

AL-SHURTAH. Periodical. Arabic. ir. 100. S B 253. **LC** HV7551.

ALABAMA POLICE JOURNAL. 0274-7448. Periodical. US. English. qt. Alabama Police Journal, Route 3 Box 800, Vernon AL 35592.

ALMANAK KEPOLISIAN REPUBLIK INDONESIA. See Yearbooks, Almanacs, Directories.

AMERICAN JOURNAL OF POLICE. (AMERICAN JOURNAL OF POLICE : AN INTERDISCIPLINARY JOURNAL OF THEORY AND RESEARCH). Vol. 1, No. 1-. 0735-8547. Periodical. US. English. sa. $22.00. Editor Pilgrimage Inc, Rt 11 B ox 553, Jonesboro TN 37659. **LC** HV7551. **DD** 363.205.

ANNUAL LAW ENFORCEMENT SERVICES REPORT (U.S.). **Main/Corp** United States. Bureau of Indian Affairs. Division of Law Enforcement Services. **VFOAT** Combined Tribal and Bureau Law Enforcement Services Annual Report. 0363-9258. US. English. an. US Department of the Interior, Bureau of Indian Affairs Division of Law Enforcement Services, Washington DC 20245. **LC** E98.C87. **DD** 364.

ANNUAL PERSONNEL AND BUDGET STUDY OF OREGON LAW ENFORCEMENT AGENCIES. **Main/Corp** Oregon. Board on Police Standards and Training. Research and Management Services. US. English. an. Oregon Board on Police Standard and Training, Suite 404/Executive House, 325 13th Street NE, Salem OR 97310. **LC** HV7571.O7. **DD** 363.2209795.

ANNUAL REPORT - ARKANSAS. COMMISSION ON LAW ENFORCEMENT STANDARDS AND TRAINING. **Main/Corp** Arkansas. Commission on Law Enforcement Standards and Training. US. English. an. **LC** HV7571.A7. **DD** 363.20715.

Law Enforcement

ANNUAL REPORT - AUSTRALIAN CAPITAL TERRITORY. POLICE. **Main/Corp** Australian Capital Territory. Police. AT. English. ir. $0.52. Commonwealth Government Printing Office, PO Box 84, Canberra ACT 2600 Australia. **LC** J905, HV7862. **DD** 328.9401 S, 363.20994.

ANNUAL REPORT - BOARD OF PAROLE. **Main/Corp** United States. Board of Parole. Periodical. US. English. an. US Department of Justice Board of Parole, 9th Street and Pennsylvania Avenue, Washington DC 20537.

ANNUAL REPORT - COMMONWEALTH OF VIRGINIA, CRIMINAL JUSTICE SERVICES COMMISSION. **Main/Corp** Virginia. Criminal Justice Services Commission. 1976-. US. English. an. Criminal Justice Services Commission, 9 No. 12th Street, Richmond VA 23219. **LC** HV7571.V83. **DD** 353.9755007407. *Biennial Report - Criminal Justice Officers Training and Standards Commission, 0146-2504.*

ANNUAL REPORT - FEDERAL ENFORCEMENT TRAINING CENTER. (ANNUAL REPORT). **Main/Corp** Federal Law Enforcement Training Center. 1978-. 0740-3038. US. English. an. Federal Law Enforcement Training Center, Glynco GA 31520. **LC** HV8143. **DD** 363.20715. Vols. for 1981/1982- distributed to depository libraries in microfiche.

ANNUAL REPORT - IOWA DEPARTMENT OF PUBLIC SAFETY. **Main/Corp** Iowa. Dept. of Public Safety. 1978-. US. English. Iowa Department of Public Safety, Wallace State Office Building, Des Moines IA 50319. **LC** HV7571.I8.

ANNUAL REPORT - KENTUCKY LAW ENFORCEMENT COUNCIL. **Main/Corp** Kentucky Law Enforcement Council. 0095-6384. US. English. an. Kentucky Law Enforcement Council, Box 608, Eastern Kentucky University, Richmond VA 40475. **LC** HV8145.K4. **DD** 353.97690074.

ANNUAL REPORT - LOS ANGELES (CALIF.) POLICE DEPT. (ANNUAL REPORT). **Main/Corp** Los Angeles (Calif.). Police Dept. 1950-. 0275-0872. US. English. an. **LC** HV7595.L7. **DD** 352.20979494. *Annual Report of the Police Department, City of Los Angeles, California.*

ANNUAL REPORT - LOUISIANA. DEPT. OF PUBLIC SAFETY. **Main/Corp** Louisiana. Dept. of Public Safety. 194 -. US. English. an. Louisiana Department of Public Safety, POB 66614, Baton Rouge LA 70896. **LC** HV7571.L8. **DD** 351.74.

ANNUAL REPORT - MANITOBA. POLICE COMMISSION. **Main/Corp** Manitoba. Police Commission. 1st- 1972-. CN. English. an. Manitoba Police Commission, 219 Kennedy Street, Winnipeg Manitoba Canada. **LC** HV7642.M3. **DD** 363.2097127.

ANNUAL REPORT - MICHIGAN. DEPT. OF STATE POLICE. **Main/Corp** Michigan. Dept. of State Police. 1965-. US. English. an. Michigan Department of State Police, 714 South Harrison Road, East Lansing MI 48823. **LC** HV7571.M5. **DD** 353.97740074. *Annual Report.*

ANNUAL REPORT - NEBRASKA COMMISSION ON LAW ENFORCEMENT AND CRIMINAL JUSTICE. **Main/Corp** Nebraska Commission on Law Enforcement and Criminal Justice. 0360-0483. US. English. an. Nebraska Commission on Law Enforcement and Criminal Justice, State Capitol, Lincoln NB 68509. **LC** HV7277. **DD** 353.97820075. *Annual Report for Nebraska Law Enforcement Training Center.*

ANNUAL REPORT - NEBRASKA STATE PATROL. **Main/Corp** Nebraska. State Patrol. 0094-1247. US. English. an. Nebraska State Patrol, PO Box 94637 State House, Lincoln NE 68509. **LC** HV7571.N25. **DD** 353.97820074.

ANNUAL REPORT - NEW MEXICO. STATE POLICE. **Main/Corp** New Mexico. State Police. 1st- 1939-. US. English. an. New Mexico State Police, PO Box 1628, Sante Fe NM 87501. **LC** HV7571.N6. **DD** 351.7409789.

ANNUAL REPORT OF THE LAW ENFORCEMENT ACADEMY BUREAU, STATE OF MONTANA, DEPARTMENT OF JUSTICE. **Main/Corp** Montana. Law Enforcement Academy Bureau. US. English. an. Montana State University, Room 5/Colter

Law Enforcement

Hall, Bozeman MT 59715. LC HV7571.M9. DD 364.0711786. *Annual Report of the Montana Law Enforcement Academy, 0093-9048.*

ANNUAL REPORT OF THE MAURITIUS POLICE FORCE. Main/Corp Mauritius. Police Force. English. ir. L C Achille, Government Printer, Place d'Armes, Port Louis Mauritius. LC HV7848.M3. DD 354.69820074.

ANNUAL REPORT OF THE NEW JERSEY ELECTION LAW ENFORCEMENT COMMISSION. Main/Corp New Jersey. Election Law Enforcement Commission. 0098-5775. US. English. an. New Jersey Law Enforcement Commission, 28 West State Street, Trenton NJ 08608. LC JK1991.5.N5. DD 329.02509749.

ANNUAL REPORT OF THE ROYAL VIRGIN ISLANDS POLICE FORCE. Main/Corp British Virgin Islands. Police Force. 0304-792X. English. ir. LC HV7685.B7. DD 354.7297250074.

ANNUAL REPORT ON THE ORGANIZATION AND ADMINISTRATION OF THE ROYAL POLICE FORCE OF ANTIGUA. (ANNUAL REPORT ON THE ORGANIZATION AND ADMINISTRATION). Main/Corp Antigua. Royal Police Force. 0304-8071. English. ir. LC HV7685.A55. DD 354.729740074.

ANNUAL REPORT - STATE OF MICHIGAN, DEPARTMENT OF STATE POLICE, LAW ENFORCEMENT OFFICERS TRAINING COUNCIL. (ANNUAL REPORT - STATE OF MICHIGAN, LAW ENFORCEMENT OFFICERS TRAINING COUNCIL). Main/Corp Michigan. Law Enforcement Officers Training Council. 0363-9215. US. English. an. 7426 North Canal Road, Lansing MI 48913. LC HV7571.M53. DD 353.97740074.

ANNUAL REPORT - STATE OF NEVADA, DEPARTMENT OF MOTOR VEHICLES, HIGHWAY PATROL DIVISION. Main/Corp Nevada. Dept. of Motor Vehicles. Highway Patrol Division. 1971-. Periodical. US. English. an. Department of Motor Vehicles, 555 Wright Way, Carson City NV 89701. *Annual Report - State of Nevada, Department of Motor Vehicles, Law Enforcement Division.*

ANNUAL REPORT - STATE OF NEW HAMPSHIRE, DEPARTMENT OF SAFETY, DIVISION OF STATE POLICE. (ANNUAL REPORT - STATE OF NEW HAMPSHIRE, DIVISION OF STATE POLICE). Main/Corp New Hampshire. Division of State Police. 0364-0647. US. English. an. Department of Safety, Concord NH 03301. LC HV7571.N4. DD 353.97420074.

ANNUAL REPORT - STATE OF NEW MEXICO, GOVERNOR'S ORGANIZED CRIME PREVENTION COMMISSION. See Sociology: General Works, Theory - Social Pathology, Welfare, Criminology.

ANNUAL REPORT TO THE GOVERNOR AND MEMBERS OF THE ALASKA STATE LEGISLATURE. Main/Corp Alaska Police Standards Council. VFOAT Annual Activities Report - Alaska Police Standards Council. 0149-5461. US. English. an. Alaska Police Standards Council, Pouch AS/450 Whitter Street, Juneau AK 99811. LC HV8145.A4. DD 363.209798.

ANNUAL REPORT TO THE LEGISLATURE - CORRECTIONAL ASSOCIATION OF NEW YORK. Main/Corp Correctional Association of New York. US. English. an. 135 East 15th Street, New York NY 10003.

ANNUAL REPORT - UNITED STATES PARK POLICE. Main/Corp United States Park Police. US. English. an. United States Park Police, 1100 Ohio Drive Southwest, Washington DC 20242. LC HV7561. DD 353.0074.

ANNUAL REPORT - UTAH LAW ENFORCEMENT PLANNING AGENCY. Main/Corp Utah. Law Enforcement Planning Agency. 1973-. 0098-0439. US. English. an. Utah Law Enforcement Planning Agency, Room 304 State Office Building, Salt Lake City UT 84114. LC HV7294. DD 353.97920074.

ANNUAL REPORT - WASHINGTON STATE PATROL. Main/Corp Washington State Patrol. 1981-. US. English. an. Washington State Patrol, General Administration Building AX-12, Olympia WA 98504. Tel (206)753-4453. LC HV8145.W2. DD 353.9797007406. Circ 1,500. (ctrl). A descriptive report of the Washington State Patrol's activities by narrative and charts.

ANNUAL REVIEW - ALBERTA HIGHWAY PATROL DIVISION. Main/Corp Alberta. Highway Patrol Division. 1977-. CN. English. LC HV7642.A4. DD 354.71230074.

ARIZONA POLICE LAW BULLETIN. 0148-0049. Periodical. US. English. qt. LC KFA2975.A15. DD 345.79105.

ARREST LAW BULLETIN. VFOAT A.L.B. Began in 1976. 8755-8300. Periodical. US. English. mo. $35.95. Quinlan Publishing Co, Boston MA 02114. DD 345. Index published separately - free - automatically sent.

ARSON ANALYSIS NEWSLETTER. See Chemistry - Analytical Chemistry.

ASSAULTS ON FEDERAL OFFICERS CEASED. 1976-1981. 0148-4257. US. English. United State Department of Justice, Federal Bureau of Investigation, Washington DC 20535. LC HV8143. DD 364.155. *Analysis of Assaults on Federal Officers.*

ATF CURIOS AND RELICS LIST. Main/Corp United States. Bureau of Alcohol, Tobacco, and Firearms. VFOAT Curios and Relics List. VAT Alcohol, Tobacco and Firearms Curios and Relics List. 0196-3686. US. English. US Government Printing Office, Superintendent of Documents, Washington DC 20402. LC TS532.4. DD 683.400750973. *Curios and Relics List and Operations by Federally Licensed Firearms Collectors, 0160-6581.*

AUSTRALIAN POLICE JOURNAL. V. 1- Oct. 1946-. 0005-0024. Periodical. AT. English. qt. Government Printing Office, Box 45, Sydney 2001 Australia. Tel 02 339 0277. Ed Phil Peters. Ind/Abst Excerpta Med. LC HV7551. bk rev. Circ 17,000. (ctrl). To advance the education of police in work related subjects.

BHAYANGKARA. 1 (June 1982)-. 0216-2563. Periodical. English (and Indonesian). qt. Lembaga Perguruan Tinggi Ilmu Kepolisian, Jl Tirtayasa Raya 6, Jakarta Indonesia. LC HV7551.

BIENNIAL REPORT - ILLINOIS LOCAL GOVERNMENTAL LAW ENFORCEMENT OFFICERS TRAINING BOARD. Main/Corp Illinois Local Governmental Law Enforcement Officers Training Board. 1979-1980-. US. English. be. Illinois Local Governmental Law Enforcement Officers Training Board, Lincoln Tower, Plaza Suite 400/524 South Second Street, Springfield IL 62706. Tel (217)782-4540. LC HV8145.I3. DD 352.209773. Circ 1,500. (ctrl). Report of local governmental grants-in-aid by state of Illinois for law enforcement training. *Annual Report.*

BIENNIAL REPORT OF EXAMINING AND LICENSING BOARDS - MINNESOTA BOARD OF PEACE OFFICER STANDARDS AND TRAINING. Main/Corp Minnesota Board of Peace Officer Standards and Training. 1976-8-. US. English. be. Minnesota Board of Peace/ Officer Standards and Training, 500 Metro Square Building, St Paul MN 55101. LC HV8145.M6. DD 353.97760074.

BIENNIUM REPORT OF THE LAW ENFORCEMENT ACADEMY BUREAU, STATE OF MONTANA, DEPARTMENT OF JUSTICE FOR THE FISCAL YEARS ENDING . . . . Main/Corp Montana. Law Enforcement Academy Bureau. US. English. be. Montana Department of Justice, 620 South Sixteenth Avenue, Bozeman MT 59715. LC HV7571.M9. DD 363.20711786.

BREATH TESTS IN NEW ZEALAND. Main/Corp New Zealand. Ministry of Transport. Economics Division. Statistics Branch. English. ir. LC HE5620.D7.

BRITISH COLUMBIA POLICE JOURNAL. VFOAT Police Journal. VAT Police Journal (Vancouver). Vol. 1, No. 1 (Autumn 1978)-. 0706-2893. Periodical. CN. English. qt. 8.00. British Columbia Police Journal, 1550-409 Granville Street, Vancouver BC V6C 1T2 Canada. LC HV8159.B7. DD 363.209711.

BULLETIN - NATIONAL EMPLOYMENT LISTING SERVICE FOR THE CRIMINAL JUSTICE SYSTEM. See Economics - Labor.

THE CALIFORNIA HIGHWAY PATROLMAN. 0008-1140. Periodical. US. English. mo. California Association of Highway Patrolmen, PO Box 161209, Sacramento CA 95816. Tel (916)452-6751. Ed Carol Perri. adv acc. Circ 18,000. We are a general interest publication with an emphasis on traffic safety, early California history and consumer interest pieces.

THE CALIFORNIA PEACE OFFICER. Jan./Feb. 1980-. 0199-7025. Periodical. US. English. bm. $15.00. California Peace Officers Association, 2012 H Street/Suite 102, Sacramento CA 95814. Tel (916)446-7847. Ed Leslie McGill. bk rev. adv acc. Circ 5,400. (ctrl). Magazine for members of California Peace Officers Association providing information on association happenings, legislation, and articles of interest in the field of professional law enforcement. *California Peace Officers' Association Newsletter.*

CAMPUS LAW ENFORCEMENT JOURNAL. Began with Vol. for 1971. 0739-0394. Periodical. US. English. bm. $24.00. International Association of Campus Law Enforcement Administration, 638 Prospect Avenue, Hartford CT 06105. Tel (203)233-4531. LC HV8290. DD 363.2.

CANADA GUNSPORT. See Recreation, Leisure - Sports.

CANADIAN PEACE OFFICER. V. 1- April 1975-. 0318-806X. Periodical. CN. English. qt. $2. Canadian Peace Officer, 8612 151 Avenue, Edmonton Alberta T5E 5Y2 Canada. DD 363.205.

CANADIAN POLICE CHIEF CEASED. V. 55-70, No. 4. 0315-2464. Periodical. CN. English (includes some text in French). qt. Canadian Police Chief, 116 Albert Street/Suite 1002, Toronto Ontario K1P 5G3 Canada. *Canadian Police Bulletin, 0315-2448.*

CANADIAN POLICE CHIEF. NEWSLETTER. (CANADIAN POLICE CHIEF NEWSLETTER). Vol. 1, No. 1 (Jan. 1982)-. 0713-4517. Periodical. CN. English. mo. $20.00. Canadian Police Chief Newsletter, c/o CACP, Suite 1002/116 Albert Street, Ottawa Ont K1P 5G3 Canada. DD 363.230971. *Canadian Police Chief.*

CENSUS OF LOCAL LAW ENFORCEMENT PERSONNEL. Jan. 1983-. US. English. be. Illinois Local Governmental Law Enforcement Officers Training Board, Lincoln Tower Plaza, Suite 400, 524 South Second Street, Springfield IL 62706. LC HV8145.I3. DD 331.12513632209773. *Local Law Enforcement Officers Census, State of Illinois.*

CHIAN MUNJE. Periodical. KO. Korean. mo. Chian Munje, Yonguso 163-3 2-Ka Ulchiro Chung-Ku, Seoul Korea. LC HV8258.A2.

CHIAO TUNG HSUEH KAN. First published in June 1978-. CH. Chinese. ir. Chung Yang Ching Kuan Hsueh Hsiao, Chiao Tung Hsi Hsueh Hui, Taipei Taiwan. LC HV8079.5.

CHING CHENG HSUEH PAO. VFOAT Journal of Police Science. First published in 1982. Periodical. CH. Chinese. sa. $100.00. Chung Yang Ching Kuan Ksueh, Hsiao Ching Chuen Yen Chiu So, Taipei Taiwan. LC HV7551. DD 363.205.

CHING HSUEH TSUNG KAN. VFOAT Police Science Quarterly. Periodical. Chinese. ir. LC HV7551. *Ching Cha Hsueh Shu Shi Kan.*

CLO NEWS. Main/Corp Citizens for Law and Order. VAT Citizens for Law and Order News. 0164-4815. Periodical. US. English. bm. $10.00. Citizens for Law & Order, Box 13089, Oakland CA 94661. Tel (415)531-4664.

COMPARATIVE DATA REPORT. 0271-6704. US. English. US Department of Justice, Bureau of Justice Statistics, Washington DC 20531. LC HV7965. DD 363.20973.

COMPREHENSIVE ANNUAL FINANCIAL REPORT OF THE HIGHWAY PATROLMENS RETIREMENT FUND FOR THE FISCAL YEAR ENDING JUNE 30 . . . - (MINNESOTA). See Economics - Labor.

Law Enforcement

COMPREHENSIVE LAW ENFORCEMENT AND CRIMINAL JUSTICE PLAN AND ACTION GRANT APPLICATION. Main/Corp Hawaii. State Law Enforcement Planning Agency. US. English. an. State Law Enforcement Planning Agency, Room 412, Kamamaku Building, 1010 Richards Street, Honolulu HI 96813. LC HV8330.5. DD 364.9969.

COMPREHENSIVE PLAN - GOVERNOR'S COMMISSION ON LAW ENFORCEMENT AND THE ADMINISTRATION OF JUSTICE - (MARYLAND). Main/Corp Maryland. Governor's Commission on Law Enforcement and the Administration of Justice. US. English. an. Suite 302, Executive Plaza One, Cockeysville MD 21030. LC HV7270. DD 364.

CONSTABLE. (THE CONSTABLE). V. 1- March 1967-. 0414-6883. Periodical. English. mo. Philippine Constabulary, Camp Crame, Quezon City Philippine. LC HV8255.A2. DD 363.209599.

CORRECTIONS DIGEST. 1969. Periodical. US. English. bw. $99.00. Washington Crime News Services, 7043 Wimsatt Road, Springfield VA 22151. Tel (703)941-6600. Ed Betty B Bosarge. bk rev. Circ 2,000. A newsletter for the administrator, policy maker and legislator. Covers significant developments in the corrections field.

CRIMINAL JUSTICE. VFOAT Annual Editions: Criminal Justice. 0272-3816. Periodical. US. English. an. $8.95. Dushkin Publishing Group, Sluice Dock, Guilford CT 06437. Tel (203)453-4351. Ed John Sullivan and Joseph Victor. LC HV8138. DD 364.97305. An updated collection of public press articles covering current issues in criminal justice. Includes topic guide and complete index. *Annual Editions: Readings in Criminal Justice.*

CRIMINAL JUSTICE ACTION PLAN. Main/Corp Nebraska Commission on Law Enforcement and Criminal Justice. 0091-9195. US. English. Natural Resources Commission, PO Box 94725 State Capitol Building, Lincoln NE 68509. LC HV7277. DD 363.2.

CRIMINAL JUSTICE IN SOUTH DAKOTA. Main/Corp South Dakota. Division of Law Enforcement Assistance. 0361-7378. US. English. an. Division of Law Enforcement Assistance, 118 West Capitol, Pierre SD 57501. LC HV7291. DD 364.

CRIMINAL JUSTICE REVIEW. See Sociology: General Works, Theory - Social Pathology, Welfare, Criminology.

CSIS FORUM. (CSIS FORUM : NEWS FOR AND ABOUT THE CANADIAN SECURITY COMMUNITY). Main/Corp Canadian Society for Industrial Security. VAT Canadian Society for Industrial Security Forum. July 1976-Summer 1982. Periodical. CN. English (includes some text in French). bm. $13.93. CSIS Incorporated, 55 York Street/Suite 512, Toronto K2C 3M1 Canada. Tel (416)363-3374. Ed Michael Chevacilit. DD 363.289. bk rev. adv acc. Circ 1,000. (ctrl). Education and communications vehicle for professional security managers.

DEFENSE MANUAL. VFOAT Law Enforcement Legal Defense Manual. 78-1 (Sept. 1978). 0191-877X. Periodical. US. English. qt. $65.00. Law Enforce Legal Defence Manual, 421 Ridgewood Avenue, Glen Ellyn IL 60137. Tel (312)858-6092. Ed James P Manak. LC KF1307.A73. DD 347.735, 347.3075. adv acc. Circ 750. A publication for law enforcement officers and attorneys dealing with civil liability issues. *AELE Law Enforcement Legal Defence Manual, 0092-2552.*

DEUTSCHE POLIZEI. Began publication with Jan. 1950 issue. 0012-057X. Periodical. GW. German. mo. Veriagsanstalt Deutsche Polizei, GMBH Frosttr 3A, 01 Hilden West Germany. LC HV7551.

DEVELOPMENT OF STATEWIDE CRIMINAL JUSTICE STANDARDS AND TRAINING SYSTEM. (DEVELOPMENT OF STATEWIDE CRIMINAL JUSTICE STANDARDS AND TRAINING SYSTEM ANNUAL REPORT). Main/Corp New Hampshire Police Standards and Training Council. 0363-9134. US. English. an. New Hampshire Technical Institute, Fan Road, Concord NH 03301. LC HV8143. DD 363.2071.

DIRECTORY OF COUNTY OFFICERS OF KANSAS. See Yearbooks, Almanacs, Directories.

DIRECTORY OF LAW ENFORCEMENT AND CRIMINAL JUSTICE EDUCATION. See Yearbooks, Almanacs, Directories.

DIRECTORY OF LAW ENFORCEMENT PROFESSORS. See Yearbooks, Almanacs, Directories.

DIRECTORY OF UNITED STATES PROBATION OFFICERS. See Yearbooks, Almanacs, Directories.

ENFORCEMENT JOURNAL. V. 10, No. 4- Aug./Sept. 1971-. 0042-2347. Periodical. US. English. qt. $5.00. National Police Officers Association America, 1316 Gardiner Lane/Suite 204, Louisville KY 40213. Tel (502)451-7550. Ed John W Lewis. bk rev. adv acc. Circ 4,000. (ctrl). Professional updating on new ideas in the police profession. Contains new police products, awards program, etc. *Valor, 0504-9881.*

ESTIMATES. PART III, ROYAL CANADIAN MOUNTED POLICE. VFOAT Budget des Depenses. CN. English (French). $9.00 Domestic, $10.80 Foreign. Canadian Government Publishing Centre, Supply and Services Canada, Ottawa Ontario K1A 0S9 Canada. LC HV7641. DD 354.710074.

EXPENDITURE AND EMPLOYMENT DATA FOR THE CRIMINAL JUSTICE SYSTEM. Main/Corp United States. Bureau of Justice Statistics. 1978-. Periodical. US. English. an. US Department of Justice, Bureau of Justice Statistics, Washington DC 20531. *Expenditure and Employment Data for the Criminal Justice System.*

FBI LAW ENFORCEMENT BULLETIN. VFOAT Law Enforcement Bulletin. VAT Federal Bureau of Investigation Law Enforcement Bulletin. Began with V. 4, No. 10 (Oct. 1935). 0014-5688. Periodical. US. English. mo. Director of Federal Bureau of Investigation, Washington DC 20535. Ind/Abst Index U.S. Gov. Period., Soc. Sci. Index. *Fugitives Wanted by Police.*

FEDERAL PROBATION. See Sociology: General Works, Theory - Social Pathology, Welfare, Criminology.

FLORIDA POLICE JOURNAL. 0015-4229. Periodical. US. English. qt. $3.00. Florida Peace Officers Association, PO Box 60516, Jacksonville FL 32236.

FLORIDA SECURITY & INVESTIGATORS JOURNAL. (FLORIDA SECURITY & INVESTIGATORS JOURNAL : OFFICIAL PUBLICATION OF THE FLORIDA SECURITY AND INVESTIGATORS ASSOCIATION, INC). VFOAT Florida Security and Investigators Journal. 0747-3117. Periodical. US. English. qt. Florida Security & Investigators Association, PO Box 40, Bryceville FL 32009.

THE GDG REPORT. Began with issue for Jan. 1985. 0883-3087. Periodical. US. English. qt. $35.00. The GDG Report, PO Box 632, Trumbull CT 06611. Tel (203)371-0136. Ed Glenn D Gawkowski. DD 623. bk rev. Circ 1,000. (ctrl). Detailed reports on unusual or covert weapons, reports on weapons based books to law enforcement or related agencies.

GEO-DRUG ENFORCEMENT PROGRAM. Main/Corp United States. Drug Enforcement Administration. 0361-7394. US. English. US Department of Justice, Drug Enforcement Administration, 1405 Eye Street NW, Washington DC 20537. LC HV5825. DD 363.2.

GUARDMOUNT. VFOAT Guardmount Newsletter. Jan./Feb. 1985-. 0883-0843. Periodical. US. English. bm. $20.00. Guardmount Inc, PO Box 37891, Omaha NE 68137. Tel (402)895-5601. Ed Patricia Ewing-Grimes. DD 363. adv acc. Circ 2,000. Newsletter for the Armed Forces Police. Also contains security related information, and employment opportunities in the security industry.

HADSHOT HA-MISHTARAH. Periodical. Hebrew. ir. 55.00. Hadshot Ha-Mishtarah BM, POB 14011, Tel-Aviv Israel. LC HV7838.P3.

HEBDO POLICE. 0229-6470. Periodical. CN. French. ir. $0,75 le No. Hebdo Police, 4270 rue Papineau, Montreal Quebec H2H 1S9. DD 364.9714.

HIGHWAY TOPICS. Periodical. US. English. mo. Town and County Officiers, Training School of the State of New York, 90 State Street, Albany NY 12207.

IACP LAW ENFORCEMENT LEGAL REVIEW. Main/Corp International Association of Chiefs of Police. VAT International Association of Chiefs of Police Law Enforcement Legal Review. No. 1- July 1972-. Periodical. US. English. mo. $40.00. International Association of Chiefs of Police, 13 Firstfield Road, Gaithersburg MD 20878. Tel (301)948-0922. LC KF9614. DD 345.7305.

I.A.C.P. LAW ENFORCEMENT LEGISLATION AND LITIGATION REPORT. (IACP LAW ENFORCEMENT LEGISLATION AND LITIGATION REPORT). Main/Corp International Association of Chiefs of Police. Legislative Research Unit. 0047-0554. Periodical. US. English. mo. $21.00. International Association of Chiefs of Police, 11 Firstfield Road, Gaithersburg MD 20760. LC K9. DD 345.73005.

IDENTIFICATION NEWS. 0019-1450. Periodical. US. English. mo. $25.00. International Association for Identification, PO Box 92059, Columbia SC 29290. Tel (803)776-2001. Ed Walter Thomas. bk rev. Circ 2,500. (ctrl). Technical information and procedures used by persons actively engaged in the forensic science.

ILLINOIS POLICE & LAW ENFORCEMENT DIRECTORY. See Yearbooks, Almanacs, Directories.

THE INDIAN POLICE JOURNAL. Began publication with July 1954 Issue. 0537-2429. Periodical. II. English. qt. Indian Police Journal, Curzon Road, Barrack 1688/Gandhi Marg, New Delhi 110001 India. LC HV7551.

INFORMANT. Began in 1975. US. English. Criminal Justice Division of the Attorney Generals Office, Justice Building, Little Rock AR 72201. LC KFA4175.A15. DD 345.7670505.

INFORMATIVO. Main/Corp Brazil. Departamento de Policia Federal.Divisao de Communicacao Social. Periodical. Portuguese. ir. Departamento de Policia Federal, Ed Bnde 6 Andar, Brazil. LC HV7239.

INFORME ANUAL - ESTADO LIBRE ASOCIADO DE PUERTO RICO, POLICIA DE PUERTO RICO. (INFORME ANUAL - POLICIA DE PUERTO RICO). Main/Corp Puerto Rico. Insular Police. 0095-0483. PR. Spanish. ir. Superintendente, Apartado 938 Hato Rey, San Juan Puerto Rico. LC HV7680. DD 363.2097295.

INTERNATIONAL CRIMINAL POLICE REVIEW. No. 1- Sept. 1946-. 0367-729X. Periodical. English. ir. Senor Director General de Seguridad, Oficillia Mayor Puerta de Sol, Madrid Spain. Ind/Abst Excerpta Med. LC HV7551. DD 351.7405.

INTERNATIONAL DRUG REPORT. Main/Corp International Narcotic Enforcement Officers Association. V. 15- Jan. 1974-. 0148-4648. Periodical. US. English. mo. $25.00. International Narcotic Enforcement Officers, 112 State Street/Suite 1310, Albany NY 12207. Tel (518)463-6232. Ed Celeste Morga. LC HV5800. DD 362.293. bk rev. Circ 10,000. (ctrl). Drug abuse enforcement- law- research- education-training- statistics-legal implications. *International Narcotic Report, 0020-806X.*

INTERSERVICE JOURNAL OF MILITARY & POLICE SCIENCE AND THE INTELLIGENCE PROFESSION. See Military Science.

JOURNAL DE LA FEDERATION DES POLICIERS DU QUEBEC. Vol. 6, No. 3 (Sept. 1982)-. 0821-1183. Periodical. CN. French. qt. Free to Members. Federation des Policiers du Quebec, 480 rue Gilford, Montreal Quebec H2J 1N3 Canada. DD 363.209714. *Revue Officielle, 0705-1344.*

JOURNAL OF CALIFORNIA LAW ENFORCEMENT. V. 1- 1966-. 0449-5063. Periodical. US. English. qt. $20.00. California Peace Officers Association, 2012 H Street/Suite 102, Sacramento CA 98514. Tel (916)446-7847. Ed Leslie Johnson. Circ 2,000. (ctrl). Professional journal containing scholarly articles on current issues in the law enforcement and criminal justice field.

JOURNAL OF POLICE SCIENCE AND ADMINISTRATION. V. 1- Mar. 1973-. 0090-9084. Periodical. US. English. qt. $10.00. International Association of Chiefs Police, 13 Firstfield Road, Gaithersburg MD 20878. Tel (301)948-0922. Ind/Abst Psychol. Abstr., Soc. Sci. Citation Index, Soc. Sci. Index, Sociol. Abstr., Curr. Law Index, Leg. Resour. Index, Lang. Lang. Behav. Abstr., Excerpta Med. LC HV7551. DD 363.205. CODEN JPSADR.

1611

Law Enforcement

Journal of Criminal Law, Criminology and Police Science, 0022-0205.

JOURNAL OF SECURITY ADMINISTRATION. Vol. 1, No. 2 (Fall 1978)-. 0195-9425. Periodical. US. English. sa. $30.00. JSA/Editorial Office, 10501 SW 99 Street, Miami FL 33176. **Tel** (305)279-9437. Ed Norman R Bottom Jr. **LC** HV8290. **DD** 363.28905. bk rev. adv acc. **Circ** 5,000. Only academic, refereed journal in its field. Security and loss control is the focus. *Journal of Security Administration and Private Police,* 0195-9433.

JUSTICE QUARTERLY. (JUSTICE QUARTERLY : JQ). **VFOAT** JQ. Vol. 1, No. 1 (Mar. 1984)-. 0741-8825. Periodical. US. English. qt. $50.00. University of Nebraska at Omaha, 1313 Farnam on the Mall, Omaha NE 68182-0115. **Tel** (402)554-3580. Ed Rita Simon. bk rev. adv acc. **Circ** 2,000. (ctrl). Development of knowledge in criminal justice. Solicit scholarship and research in other justice related areas.

THE JUSTICE SYSTEM JOURNAL. V. 1- Winter 1974-. 0098-261X. Periodical. US. English. ir. $54.00. Institute for Court Management, 1331 17th Street, Denver CO 80202. **Tel** (303)293-3063. Ed Roger A Hanson. **Ind/Abst** Leg. Resour. Index, Index Leg. Period., Soc. Sci. Citation Index, Curr. Law Index. **LC** K10. **DD** 347.7313. bk rev. adv acc. **Circ** 900. Articles that discuss research experience and ideas concerning the operation of courts and related agencies.

JUVENILE JUSTICE DIGEST. 1972. 0094-2413. Periodical. US. English. sm. $99.00. Washington Crime News Service, 7043 Wimsatt Road, Springfield VA 22151. **Tel** (703)941-6600. Ed Betty B Bosarge. bk rev. **Circ** 2,000. The latest legislative and policy developments, trends, court decisions and resource materials for the administrator and policy maker.

JUVENILE JUSTICE PLAN FOR NEW JERSEY, APPLICANTS GUIDE. Main/Corp New Jersey. State Law Enforcement Planning Agency. **Series/Titl** Dissemination Document. 1982-84-. US. English. an. State Law Enforcement Planning Agency, CN 083, Trenton NJ 08625. **LC** HV7280. **DD** 364.3609749. *Criminal/Juvenile Justice Plan for New Jersey, Applicants Guide.*

JUVENILE LAW REPORTS. V. 1- July 1979-. 0276-9603. Periodical. US. English. mo. $67.00. Knehans Miller Publications, PO Box 88, Warrensburg PA 64093. **Tel** (816)429-1102. Ed Dane C Miller. **Circ** 300. A quick and easy reference to juvenile cases decided in the federal and state courts.

KAGAKU KEISATSU KENKYUJO NEMPO. Japanese. ir. Kagaku Keisatsu Kenkyujo, 6 Sanancho Khiyoda-Ku, Tokyo 102 Japan. **LC** HV7826.

KRIMINOLOGISCHE FORSCHUNGEN. Monographic Series. GW. German. ir. Duncker und Humblot Verlag, Dietrich-Schaefer-Weg 9, 1000 Berlin 41 West Germany. **Tel** (030)7912026. Ed H Mayert and J Hellmer. Research in Criminology.

LAW AND ORDER. Began with Jan. 1953 issue. 0023-9194. Periodical. US. English. mo. $31.25. Law and Order, 1000 Skokie Boulevard, Wilmette IL 60091. **Tel** (312)256-8555. Ed Bruce Cameron. **LC** HV7551. bk rev. adv acc. **Circ** 25,000. (ctrl). Designed to reach the chief executives in policing agencies with the latest information relating to their profession.

LAW ENFORCEMENT AGENCIES OF TEXAS, A SURVEY. SUMMARY. (LAW ENFORCEMENT AGENCIES OF TEXAS : A SURVEY. SUMMARY). Main/Corp Texas. Commission on Law Enforcement Officer Standards and Education. 1976-. 0149-3159. US. English. an. Texas Commission of Law Enforcement, 503 East Sam Houston Office Building, Austin TX 78781. **LC** HV8145.T4. **DD** 347.764016.

LAW ENFORCEMENT AND CRIMINAL JUSTICE EDUCATION DIRECTORY. See Yearbooks, Almanacs, Directories.

LAW ENFORCEMENT BULLETIN. Main/Corp Wisconsin. Crime Information Bureau. Periodical. US. English. bw. Crime Information Bureau, PO Box 2718, Madison WI 53701.

LAW ENFORCEMENT COMMUNICATIONS. - Jan./Feb. 1985. 0193-0540. Periodical. US. English. mo. $15.00. Media Horizons Inc, 50 West 23rd Street, New York NY 10010. **Tel** (212)645-1000. Ed Douglas Neiss. bk rev. adv acc. **Circ** 24,000. (ctrl).

LAW ENFORCEMENT DEGREE PROGRAMS ENROLLMENT DATA. Main/Corp Texas. Commission on Law Enforcement Officer Standards and Education. Education Section. Spring Semester 1973-. US. English. **LC** HV8145.T4. **DD** 363.2.

THE LAW ENFORCEMENT LEGAL REPORTER INCORPORATED. 1978. 0195-0290. Periodical. US. English. mo. $21.00. Law Enforcement, PO Box 1356, Torrance CA 90505. **Tel** (213)375-7284. Ed Elliott E Alhadeff. **Circ** 2,800. (ctrl). Review of recent case decisions affecting California law enforcement in criminal area and application analysis.

LAW ENFORCEMENT LEGAL SUMMARIES. US. English. State of California, Department of Justice, PO Box 13427, Sacramento CA 95813. **LC** KFC1155.A73. **DD** 345.79405.

LAW ENFORCEMENT LEGISLATIVE BUY-FUND : BIENNIUM REPORT. US. English. be. Bureau of Criminal Apprehension, 1246 University Avenue, St Paul MN 55104. **LC** HV8073. **DD** 353.97760074.

LAW ENFORCEMENT MISCONDUCT BULLETIN. VFOAT L.E.M. Began with issue for Jan. 1983?. 8755-8238. Periodical. US. English. qt. $43.75. Quinlan Publishing Co, 131 Beverly Street, Boston MA 02114. **DD** 345.

LAW ENFORCEMENT NEWS. 1975-. 0364-1724. Periodical. US. English. sm. $50.00. Law Enforcement News, 444 West 56th Street, New York NY 10102. **Tel** (212)489-3592.

LAW ENFORCEMENT OFFICERS KILLED AND ASSAULTED. 1982-. 0747-7961. US. English. an. US Department of Justice, Federal Bureau of Investigation, Washington DC 20535. **LC** HV8143. **DD** 363.232. *Law Enforcement Officers Killed,* 0191-2712; *Assaults on Federal Officers,* 0148-4257.

LAW ENFORCEMENT REPORT. 0094-8438. Periodical. US. English. bm. US Postal Service, Communications & Public Affairs, Washington DC 20260. **LC** HE6094. **DD** 343.73099202643. *Law Enforcement Report,* 0094-8438.

THE LAW OFFICER'S BULLETIN. 0145-6571. Periodical. US. English. bw. $75.00. Bureau of National Affairs Inc, 1231 25th Street NW, Washington DC 20037. **Tel** (301)258-1033. **LC** KF9202. **DD** 345.73005.

THE LAW OFFICER'S POCKET MANUAL. 0271-7182. US. English. an. Bureau of National Affairs Inc, 1231 25th Street NW, Washington DC 20037. **Tel** (301)258-1033.

LEAA NEWSLETTER. Main/Corp United States. Law Enforcement Assistance Administration. VAT Law Enforcement Assistance Administration Newsletter. V. 1-9, No. 1. Periodical. US. English. mo.

THE LEGAL INVESTIGATOR. See Law.

LIABILITY REPORTER. Main/Corp Americans for Effective Law Enforcement. 0271-5481. US. English. mo. $79.00. American Effective Law Enforcement, 501 Grandview Drive/#209, South San Francisco CA 94080. **Tel** (415)877-0731. **LC** KF1307.A73. **DD** 346.73033. *A.E.L.E. Law Enforcement Legal Liability Reporter,* 0092-0940.

LIBRARY BOOK CATALOG; AUTHOR CATALOG. SUPPLEMENT. See Library and Information Science.

LIBRARY BOOK CATALOG; SUBJECT CATALOG. SUPPLEMENT. See Library and Information Science.

LIBRARY BOOK CATALOG; TITLE CATALOG. SUPPLEMENT. See Library and Information Science.

LOUISIANA PEACE OFFICER. V. 1- 1943-. Periodical. US. English. mo. I D Anderpont, PO Box 64537, Baton Rouge LA 70806. **Tel** (504)926-7020. *Louisiana Policeman.*

MADHYAPRADESA PULISA PATRIKA. M. P. POLICE JOURNAL. VFOAT M.P. Police Journal. Began publication in 1958. Periodical. Hindi (English). ir. **LC** HV7551.

THE MAGISTRATE. Began in 1921. Periodical. UK. English. mo. $20.69. Magistrates Association, 28 Fitzroy Square, London W1P 6DD England. **Tel** 01 387 2302. Ed E R Horsman Esq OBE. **LC** KD7302. **DD** 347.41016. bk rev. adv acc. **Circ** 26,000. (ctrl). Short articles relating to law and practice of British magistrates' courts.

MAJALLAT AL-SHURTAH. Arabic. ir. 0.10. PO Box 288, Al-Khartoum 8715 Sudan. **LC** HV8276.S8.

MAJALLAT AL-SHURTAH. VFOAT Revue de Police. Periodical. Arabic and French. bm. 1.50. PO Box 437, Al-Rabat Morocco. **LC** HV8276.M6.

MARYLAND POLICE AND CORRECTIONAL TRAINING COMMISSIONS REPORT TO THE GOVERNOR, THE SECRETARY OF PUBLIC SAFETY AND CORRECTIONAL SERVICES, AND MEMBERS OF THE GENERAL ASSEMBLY. Main/Corp Maryland. Police Training Commission. Began with Vol. for 1974/75. 0148-2602. US. English. an. Pikesville Professional Building/Suite 14, 7 Church Lane, Pikesville MD 21208. **LC** HV7270. **DD** 363.20715. *Annual Report to the Governor and Members of the General Assembly - Maryland Police Training Commission,* 0148-2610; *Annual Report to the Governor, the Secretary of Public Safety and Correctional Services and Members of the General Assembly,* 0090-9963.

THE MAURITIUS POLICE MAGAZINE. English (French). an. Managing Editor c/o Police Headquarters, Line Barracks, Port Louis Mauritius. **LC** HV7861.A2. **DD** 363.2096982.

MICHIGAN STAR. 8750-636X. Periodical. US. English. bm. $.75 Members. Dale Corporation, 2722 Trowbridge, Hantramck MI 48212. **Tel** (502)451-2700.

MINNESOTA POLICE JOURNAL. Began publication with 1928 issue. 0026-5624. Periodical. US. English. bm. Police Press Inc, 6857 Oxford Street, Minneapolis MN 55426. **Tel** (612)920-3367. Ed Michael R Hoffman. bk rev. adv acc. **Circ** 7,000. News and technical information for law enforcement officers of all ranks.

MISSISSIPPI'S BLUE & GRAY. VFOAT Mississippi's Blue and Gray. Vol. 1, No. 1 (Apr. 1980)-. Periodical. US. English. mo. *Magnolia Trooper.*

MONATSSCHRIFT FUR KRIMINOLOGIE UND STRAFRECHTSREFORM. [026-9301. Periodical. German. bm. 128.-. Carl Heymanns Verlag KG, Gereonstrasse 18-32, 5000 Koln 1 West Germany. **Tel** (0221)134022. Ed H Schuler-Springorium. **Ind/Abst** Foreign Lang. Index. bk rev. adv acc. **Circ** 1,000. (ctrl). Science on criminology and its reform of the penal law. *Monatsschrift fur Kriminalbiologie und Strafrechtsreform.*

MORALITY IN MEDIA INC. NEWSLETTER. VFOAT MM Newsletter. 1962. 0027-1004. Periodical. US. English. ir. $5.00. Morality in Media Newsletter, 474 Riverside Drive, New York NY 10115. **Tel** (212)870-3222. Ed Evelyn Dukovic. bk rev. **Circ** 50,000. Reports on the traffic in pornography getting to children, on obscenity law and its enforcement, on cases, decisions, community anti-porn activity.

MUNDO POLICIAL. Portuguese. ir. 180.00. Editorial Policial, rua Santana 1256, Buenos Aires Argentina. **LC** HV7551.

THE NATIONAL CENTURION. 1983. 0735-6323. Periodical. US. English. mo. National Centurion, PO Box 27957, San Diego CA 92128. **Tel** (619)282-6295. Ed Diane Ingalls and Walter Arm. bk rev. adv acc. **Circ** 30,000. A police lifestyle magazine covering all segments of the law enforcement field. News, corrections, labor, history, interviews and reference articles.

NATIONAL DIRECTORY OF LAW ENFORCEMENT ADMINISTRATORS AND CORRECTIONAL INSTITUTIONS. See Yearbooks, Almanacs, Directories.

THE NATIONAL FIRE & ARSON REPORT. VAT National Fire and Arson Report. Vol. 1, No. 1 (May/June 1982)-. Periodical. US. English. bm. $50.00. National Fire and Arson Report, PO Box 476, Lilburn GA 30247. **Tel** (404)921-3074. Ed R L Kennedy. bk rev. adv acc. **Circ** 1,200. (ctrl). Fire and arson investigation. Latest investigative techniques, current legal issues, resource materials and seminars.

Law Enforcement

THE NATIONAL SHERIFF. Began in 1948. 0028-016X. Periodical. US. English. bm. National Sheriffs' Association, 1250 Connecticut Avenue, Washington DC 20036. LC HV7551. DD 352.23. Sheriffs' Newsletter.

NEW HAMPSHIRE COMPREHENSIVE LAW ENFORCEMENT PLAN. Main/Corp New Hampshire. Governor's Commission on Crime and Delinquency. 0094-7628. US. English. Commission on Crime & Delinquency, 18 Centre Street, Concord NH 03301. LC KFN1762. DD 364.

NEW JERSEY'S FINEST CEASED. 0028-5994. Periodical. US. English. mo. $12.00. Finest Publishing Company, PO Box 434, Arlington VT 05250. Tel (800)451-6000.

NIHON TANTEI MEIKAN. 1978-. JA. Japanese. ir. 5000. Esu Ai Esu, 16 Minatocho 4, Naka-Ku, Yokohama Japan. LC HV8099.J3.

NIMLO RESEARCH REPORT. No. 155-. Monographic Series. US. English. ir. National Institute of Municipal Law Officers, 1000 Connecticut Avenue NW/Suite 800, Washington DC 20036. LC KF5305. DD 342'.73'09. Report (National Institute of Municipal Law Officers).

NORTH DAKOTA PEACE OFFICER. 0744-5148. Periodical. US. English. qt. Executive Secretary John H Keating, PO Box 2763, Bismarck ND 58505.

OFFICE OF RESEARCH PROGRAMS LIST OF SELECTED PUBLICATIONS & RESEARCH PROJECTS IN PROGRESS. Main/Corp National Institute of Law Enforcement and Criminal Justice. Office of Research Programs. 0148-7213. US. English. US Department of Justice, Law Enforcement Assistance Administration, Washington DC 20531. LC Z5703.5.U5, HV8138. DD 016.364973.

OFFICIAL JOURNAL - ILLINOIS POLICE ASSOCIATION. Main/Corp Illinois Police Association. 1947. 0019-2171. Periodical. US. English. bm. $12.00. Police Press Inc, 6857 Oxford Street, Minneapolis MN 55426. Tel (612)920-3367. Ed Michael R Hoffman. LC HV7551. DD 363.209773. bk rev. adv acc. Circ 20,000. News and technical information for law enforcement officers of all ranks.

OHIO LAW ENFORCEMENT TRAINING BULLETIN. Vol. 1, No. 1 (Apr./May 1959)-. Periodical. US. English. bm. $10.00. Case Western Research University, Gund Hal 11075 East Boulevard, Cleveland OH 44106. Tel (216)368-3308.

OREGON'S COMPREHENSIVE CRIMINAL JUSTICE PLAN. Main/Corp Oregon. Law Enforcement Council. VFOAT Application for Action Grant. 0361-7254. US. English. Law Enforcement Council, 2001 Front Street NE, Salem OR 97310. LC HV7287. DD 364.

P.A.L. PREVENT, AVOID LOSSES. (P. A. L., PREVENT, AVOID LOSSES). VFOAT P.E.P., Prevenir, Eviter Pertes. V. 1- June 1977-. 0707-2228. Periodical. CN. English (French). qt. Free. Loss Prevention Committee, Room 339 Fauteux Hall University of Ottawa, Ottawa Ontario K1N 6N5 Canada. DD 364.40971384. (ctrl).

PEACE OFFICER. 0031-3556. Periodical. US. English. bm. $15.00. Fraternal Order of Police, 30500 Van Dyke, Room 600, Warren MI 48093.

PEACE OFFICER LAW REPORT. Main/Corp California. Dept. of Justice. 1971?-. 0198-6791. Periodical. US. English. mo. Department of Justice, Legal Projects, 3580 Wilshire Boulevard, Los Angeles CA 90010.

PENNSYLVANIA LAW ENFORCEMENT JOURNAL. V. 1- Dec. 1975-. 0161-9136. Periodical. US. English. bm. Police Law Enforcement Journal, 500 Barnett Place, Hohokus NJ 07423. LC HV8145.P4. DD 363.209748.

THE PENNSYLVANIA POLICE CRIMINAL LAW BULLETIN. Began in 1972. 0098-7174. US. English. mo. $14.00. The Pennsylvania Police, 2579 Warren Road, Indiana PA 15701. Tel (412)465-5165. Ed Stanley Colten. LC KFP575.A59. DD 345.74805. Circ 1,200. The major objective of the publication is to keep Pennsylvania police abreast of developments in criminal law that affect police practices in the state of Pennsylvania.

PERSPECTIVES - AMERICAN PROBATION AND PAROLE ASSOCIATION. (PERSPECTIVES). 0821-1507. Periodical. US. English (issue for V. 7, No. 1, Text in French). ir. Free to Members. American Probation and Parole Association, 2104 Otis Street, Durham NC 27707. DD 364.630971.

POLICE. (POLICE : A REPORT ON MINNESOTA'S PEACE OFFICER TRAINING). Main/Corp Minnesota. Peace Officer Training Board. 0160-578X. US. English. be. LC HV8145.M6. DD 363.2071.

POLICE AND LAW ENFORCEMENT. 1972-. 0092-8933. US. English. ir. $47.50. AMS Press Inc, 56 East 13th Street, New York NY 10003. Tel (212)777-4700. Ed Daniel J Homart and Daniel B Kennedy. LC HV8138. DD 363.20973. Articles covering the major facets of police work in America, theoretical and applied, as part of the criminal justice system.

POLICE & SECURITY BULLETIN. VAT Police and Security Bulletin. V. 12, No. 7- Nov. 1980-. 0271-7565. Periodical. US. English. mo. $48.00. Lomond Systems Inc, PO Box 88, Mt Airy MD 21771. Tel (301)829-1496. Ed Lowell H Hattery. bk rev. New methods, research findings, experience reports, computers and other technology; criminal justice, crime prevention, security and safety; as interrelated systems; literature of merit. Systems, Technology & Science for Law Enforcement & Security, 0039-8055.

THE POLICE BADGE. 0147-8877. Periodical. US. English. bm. $8.50. The Police Badge, 746 Chapel Street, New Haven CT 06510.

THE POLICE CAREER INFORMATION DIGEST. Vol. 1, Issue 1, (July/Aug. 1984)-. 8756-355X. Periodical. US. English. bm. $16.95. Police Career Information Digest, Department LEC, PO Box 1672, Eaton Park FL 33840. Tel (813)666-3184. Ed Michael D'Alto. LC HV8143. DD 363.202373. adv acc. Circ 1,500. (ctrl). Includes a list of current criminal justice job openings, feature articles, classified advertisements, limited display ads, and newsbriefs.

THE POLICE CHIEF. 1934. 0032-2571. Periodical. US. English. mo. $15.00. International Association of Chiefs of Police, 13 Firstfield Road, Gaithersburg MD 20878. Tel (301)948-0922. Ed Charles E Higginbotham. Ind/Abst Public Aff. Inf. Serv. Bull., Soc. Sci. Index, Soc. Sci. Citation Index. bk rev. adv acc. Circ 22,000. (ctrl). The official publication of the International Association of Chiefs of Police. Reports the major advances in the administration of law enforcement agencies. Police Chiefs News.

THE POLICE CHRONICLE. 0747-2579. Periodical. US. English. mo. $7.20. Police Chronicle, 285 Dorchester Avenue, Boston MA 02127. Tel (617)268-5180.

THE POLICE EMPLOYMENT GUIDE. 1980. 0194-0813. US. English. an. $10.60. Sam Houston University, NELS Criminal Justice Center, Huntsville TX 77341. Tel (409)294-1692. Ed Laure Pegoda. Circ 10,000. A resource tool for those interested in state and city police departments. List of qualifications, hearing procedures and general information concerning these law enforcement agencies.

POLICE FORCE STATISTICS. See Statistics.

POLICE JOURNAL. (THE POLICE JOURNAL). V. 1- Jan. 1928-. 0032-258X. Periodical. UK. English. qt. $38.31. Barry Rose Law Periodicals Ltd, E Row Little London, Chichester W Sussex PO19 1PG England. Ind/Abst Excerpta Med. LC HV7551. DD 363.209171241. (cum index).

POLICE LABOR MONTHLY. Vol. 1, No. 1 (June 1982)-. 0749-5595. Periodical. US. English. mo. $85.00. Justex Systems, PO Box 6224, Huntsville TX 77340. Tel (409)291-7981. Ed Jerry L Dowling. DD 363. Circ 500. Labor relations issues pertaining to law enforcement including new court rulings, legislation, economic analysis, union development, settlements, and trends.

POLICE LABOR REVIEW. No. 1- July 1974-. Periodical. US. English. mo. $50.00. International Association of Chiefs of Police, 12 Firstfield Road, Gaithersburg MD 20878. Tel (301)948-0922. Ed International Assn of Chiefs of Police. LC HV7551. DD 363.20973. Circ 400. Synopses of latest developments in police labor relations.

POLICE LIFE (ANNUAL). (POLICE LIFE). English. an. $4.00. LC HV8253.A2. DD 363.2095957. Police Life Annual.

THE POLICE MARKSMAN. 0164-8365. Periodical. US. English. bm. $12.00. Police Marksman, PO Box 17690, Montgomery AL 36117. Tel (205)271-2010. Ed Charles L Dees. bk rev. adv acc. Circ 18,000. Police training magazine dedicated to police firearms training and officer survival.

POLICE OFFICER MINIMUM STANDARD OF TRAINING. US. English. LC HV8145.N6. DD 363.20715.

POLICE OFFICER/EMPLOYEE RIGHTS LAW BULLETIN. VFOAT Police Officer, Employee Rights Law Bulletin. Began with issue for July 1984?. 8755-8246. US. English. mo. $38.50. Quinlan Publishing Company, 131 Beverly Street, Boston MA 02114. DD 344.

POLICE-POLICE. V. 1- June 1977-. 0704-6987. Periodical. CN. French. mo. $1.00 Per No. Les Ecrits du Palais, CP 700 Succursale C, Montreal Quebec H2L 4L5 Canada. DD 364.1509714.

POLICE PRODUCT NEWS. VFOAT Police. 1976. 0164-5196. Periodical. US. English. mo. $17.95. Police Product News, PO Box 847, Carlsbad CA 92008. Tel (619)483-2511. Ed Kim Pallas. LC HV7936.E7. DD 363.23028. bk rev. adv acc. Circ 36,000. Keeping law enforcement officers up-to-date on the law enforcement profession through new product development and examining trends in the field.

POLICE REVIEW. (REVUE DE LA POLICE). VFOAT Police Review. V. 1- Apr. 1977-. 0703-9239. Periodical. CN. English (French). ty. Free. Police Review, 91 McComber Street, Chateauguay Quebec J6J 3G2 Canada. DD 363.205. (ctrl).

POLICE REVIEW. Began in 1893. Periodical. UK. English. wk. Police Review Publishing Company, 14 St Cross Street, London EC1N 8FE England. Tel 01/242-1432. Ed Miss Doreen May. LC HV7551. DD 351.74. bk rev. adv acc. Circ 30,000 Weekly. Police related law and features.

POLICE SCIENCE ABSTRACTS. See Indexes/Abstracts.

POLICE STATISTICS ACTUALS. See Statistics.

POLICE STATISTICS (CHARTERED INSTITUTE OF PUBLIC FINANCE AND ACCOUNTANCY. STATISTICAL INFORMATION SERVICE. See Statistics.

POLICE STATISTICS, TASMANIA. See Statistics.

POLICE-STUDIES. Vol. 1, No. 1 (Mar. 1978)-. 0141-2949. Periodical. US. English. qt. $25.00. Anderson Publishing Company, PO Box 1576, 646 Main Street, Cincinatti OH 45202. Tel (513)421-4142. Ed Dorothy Bracey. Ind/Abst Sociol. Abstr., Soc. Welf. Soc. Plan./Policy Soc. Dev., Public Aff. Inf. Serv. Bull. LC HV7551. DD 363.205. bk rev. adv acc. Circ 451. (ctrl). Comprehensive source of information for practitioners and scholars interested in learning about the latest international developments in police management, education, science, and technology.

POLICE WORLD. UK. English. qt. $9.20. Police World c/o Dennis Bailey, 24 Oslars Way, Fulbourn Camb CR1 5DS England. LC HV7551. DD 363.205.

THE POLICE YEARBOOK. See Yearbooks, Almanacs, Directories.

POLITIE-ALMANAK. See Yearbooks, Almanacs, Directories.

POLIZEI, TECHNIK, VERKEHR. Began in 1956. Periodical. GW. German. mo. $14.81. Verlagsgesellschaft MBH & Company, Juliusstrabe 2, 62 Wiesbaden West Germany. LC HV8079.5.

POLIZEI, VERKEHR + TECHNIK. VFOAT Polizei, Verkehr und Technik. Periodical. German. mo. 64.-. Schmidt-Romhild, Postfach 2151, 2400 Lubeck 1 West Germany. Tel (0451)16005-0. Ed Scheiber. LC HV8079.5. DD 363.23320943. adv acc. (ctrl). Manual for the German police. Main parts are: traffic, automobile and dallistic. Polizei, Technik, Verkehr.

POLYGRAPH LAW REPORTER. V. 1- Sept. 1978-. 0196-1179. Periodical. US. English. qt. $36.00. American Polygraph Association, PO Box 1061, Severna Park MD 21146. Tel (301)647-0936. Ed Norman Ansley. LC KF9666.A15. DD 345.73052. bk rev. Circ 3,200. Reporting service on current cases, regulations and statutes. It also updates reference: The Law and the Polygraph: A Compilation of Polygraph Case Law and Statutory Law.

PORAC LAW ENFORCEMENT NEWS. (PORAC LAW ENFORCEMENT NEWS : OFFICIAL PUBLICATION OF THE PEACE OFFICERS'

Law Enforcement

RESEARCH AND EDUCATION FOUNDATION). **VFOAT** Porac News. **VAT** Peace Officers Research Association of California News. 0744-1983. Periodical. US. English. mo. Porac, Suite Senator Hotel, 12th and L Street, Sacramento CA 95814.

POST ALLOCATION OF FUNDS AND TRAINING ACTIVITY SUMMARY. **Main/Corp** California. Commission on Peace Officer Standards and Training. **VAT** Peace Officer Standards and Training Allocation of Funds and Training Activity Summary. 0147-8060. US. English. Commission on Peace Officer Standards and Training, 7100 Bowling Drive/Suite 250, Sacramento CA 95823. **LC** HV7254.

PP; POLICIA PORTUGUESA. No. 193- May/June 1969-. Portuguese. ir. 4.50 Single Issue. Comando-Geral da PSP, Avenida Antonio Augusto de Aguiar 18, Lisboa Portugal. **LC** HV7551. *Policia Portuguesa.*

PROBATION AND PAROLE LAW REPORTS. Vol. 2, No. 1 (Jan. 1980)-. 0276-6965. Periodical. US. English. mo. $67.00. Knehans Miller Publications, PO Box 88, Warrensburg MO 64093. **Tel** (816)429-1102. **Ed** Dane C Miller. **LC** KF9750.A59. **DD** 345.73077, 347.30577. **Circ** 500. A quick and easy reference to probation and parole cases decided in the federal and state courts. *Probation and Parole Law Summaries, 0194-1801.*

PROGRESS REPORT - MAINE LAW ENFORCEMENT PLANNING AND ASSISTANCE AGENCY. (PROGRESS REPORT). **Main/Corp** Maine. Law Enforcement Planning & Assistance Agency. 1972-. 0090-6107. US. English. an. 295 Water Street, Augusta ME 04330. **LC** HV7269. **DD** 353.97410074.

PROTECTION OFFICER MAGAZINE. (THE PROTECTION OFFICER MAGAZINE). Vol. 1, No. 1 (Apr. 1984)-. 0823-9304. Periodical. CN. English. qt. $32.00. Protection Officer Magazine, PO Box 6004 Station A, Calgary Alberta T2H 2L3 Canada. **DD** 363.2890971. *PPM (Professional Protection Magazine), 0823-9290.*

PROTECTION OFFICER TRAINING BULLETIN. (THE PROTECTION OFFICER TRAINING BULLETIN). Vol. 1, No. 1 (Mar. 1984)-. 0823-9649. Periodical. CN. English. qt. Protection Officer Publications, PO Box 6005 Station A, Calgary Alberta T2H 1L3 Canada. **DD** 363.289.

PRZSTEPCZOSC NA SWIECIE. Periodical. Polish. ir. 24.00. Panstwowe Wydawnictwo Naukowe, Instytut Problematyki Przestepcxosci, A1 Swlerczewskiego 127, Skrytka Pocztowa 275, 00-958 Warszawa Poland. **Tel** 20.18.03. **Ed** Brunon Holyst. **LC** HV6005. adv acc. **Circ** 780. (ctrl). Problems of criminality and social pathology in the world; methods of the prevention and struggle against it in different countries.

QUARTERLY - ROYAL CANADIAN MOUNTED POLICE. (THE QUARTERLY). **Main/Corp** Royal Canadian Mounted Police. **VFOAT** RCMP Quarterly. Vol. 44, No. 2 (Spring 1979)-. 0824-9415. Periodical. CN. English. qt. $5.00. The Editor RCMP Quarterly, RCMP HQ Ottawa, Ottawa Ontario K1A 0R2 Canada. **LC** HV7551. **DD** 363.20971. *R C M P Quarterly, 0033-6858.*

R C M P QUARTERLY. **Main/Corp** Royal Canadian Mounted Police. **VFOAT** Revue Trimestrielle de la G R C. V. 32, No. 2-V. 44, No. 1. 0033-6858. Periodical. English (French, July 1971-). qt. $3.86. Royal Canadian Mounted Police, RCMP Headquarters, Ottawa Ontario K1A 0R2 Canada. **Ed** C S Murdoch. **bk rev. Circ** 20,000. Socio-historic articles on matters related to the traditions, history and present-day activities of the Royal Canadian Mounted Police. *Royal Canadian Mounted Police Quarterly, 0317-8260.*

REPORT OF HER MAJESTY'S CHIEF INSPECTOR OF CONSTABULARY. **Main/Corp** Great Britain. Inspectors of Constabulary. UK. English. 0.70. Her Majestys Stationery Office, 49 High Holborn, London WC1V 6HB England. **LC** HV7725.

REPORT OF THE COMMISSIONER OF THE SOUTH AFRICAN POLICE. **Main/Corp** South African Police. 1911-. English. an. **LC** HV7848.S7.

REPORT OF THE NATIONAL POLICE COMMISSION. **Main/Corp** India. National Police Commission. 1st-. II. English. an. 4.00. Jain Book Agency, Connaught Place, New Delhi 1 India. **LC** HV7808. **DD** 354.54007406.

REPORT ON FRINGE BENEFITS AND RELATED PRACTICES AFFECTING POLICEMEN. **Main/Corp** New York (State). Public Employment Relations Board. 0147-5355. US. English. Public Employment Relations Board, 50 Wolf Road, Albany NY 12205. **LC** HV8145.N7. **DD** 331.255.

REPORT ON THE ESTABLISHMENT AND WORK OF THE STATES POLICE FORCE. **Main/Corp** Jersey. UK. English. 0.25. **LC** HV7726.J4. **DD** 352.2094234.

REPORTED OFFENSES AND ARRESTS. NEW YORK STATE. (REPORTED OFFENSES AND ARRESTS). **Main/Corp** New York (State). Dept. of Correctional Services. Division of Research. 0090-2160. US. English. Alfred E Smith, State Office Building, PO Box 7033, Albany NY 12225. **LC** HV7282. **DD** 364.9747.

RETAIL SECURITY MANAGEMENT LETTER. **VFOAT** Retail Security Management. 0883-2234. Periodical. US. English. mo. $127.00. Strafford Publications Inc, 1375 Peachtree Street NE/Suite 260, Atlanta GA 30367. **Tel** (404)881-1141. **DD** 381. bk rev. A news and information monthly edited exclusively for the executive with security and loss prevention responsibility in the retail and shopping center environments.

RETRAITE. (LE RETRAITE). First issue in July 1973?. 0317-9222. CN. French. Association de Bienfaisance et de Retraite de la Police de Montreal, 480 rue Gilford, Montreal Quebec H2J 1N3 Canada. **DD** 301.435.

REVISTA DE DIREITO CIVIL. Year 1- July/Sept. 1977-. Periodical. BL. Portuguese. ir. $42.00. Editora Refista dos Tribunals, rua Conde do Pinhal, 78-01501, Sao Paulo Brazil. **Tel** 37 2433. **Ed** Alvaro Malheiros. **LC** K19. **DD** 346.81. bk rev. adv acc. **Circ** 5,000. Jurisprudence commentarys and leading articles for civil jurisdiction.

REVISTA POLICIA NACIONAL DE COLOMBIA. **Main/Corp** Colombia. Policia Nacional. Periodical. CK. Spanish. ir. Carrera 7A No 13-58 Oficina 801, Apartado Aereo 21356, Bogota Columbia. **LC** HV7551. *Revista.*

REVUE DE LA SURETE DU QUEBEC CEASED. (LA REVUE DE LA SURETE DU QUEBEC). **Main/Corp** Surete du Quebec. V. 1-12 Issue No. 3-. 0381-2758. Periodical. CN. French (text also in English). mo. Edifice du Ministere de la Justice, 1701 rue Parthemais, Bureau 749/CP 1400 Succursale C, Montreal Quebec H2L 4K7 Canada. **Ind/Abst** Point Repere.

REVUE DE L'ASSOCIATION DES POLICIERS RETRAITES DE LA C. U. M. **Main/Corp** Associations des Policiers Retraites de la C. U. M. V. 1- Sept. 1976-. 0701-0672. Periodical. CN. French. qt. $6.00 Membership Per Year. Association de Bienfaisance et de Retraite de la Police de Montreal, 480 Gilford, Montreal Quebec H2J 1N3 Canada. **DD** 363.206271428.

REVUE INTERNATIONALE DE CRIMINOLOGIE ET DE POLICE TECHNIQUE. See Sociology: General Works, Theory - Social Pathology, Welfare, Criminology.

RIVISTA ITALIANA DI DIRITTO DEL LAVORO. Vol. 1, N. 1 (Jan.-Mar. 1982)-. Periodical. IT. Italian (summaries in English, French, German and Spanish). qt. 60.000 Domestic, 90.000 Foreign. Casa Editrice, Dr A Giuffre, Via Statuto 2, 20121 Milano Italy. **Tel** 02/652341. **Ed** Giuseppe Pera. **Ind/Abst** Foreign Lang. Index. **LC** K22. **DD** 344.450105 344.504105. bk rev. adv acc. **Circ** 3,500. This journal publishes articles by the most well-known students of labour law. *Rivista di Diritto del Lavoro.*

THE ROLE OF BEHAVIORAL SCIENCE IN PHYSICAL SECURITY. **Series/Titl** NBS Special Publication. Law Enforcement Equipment Technology. 1st- 1976-. 0271-3144. US. English. an. Superintendent of Documents, US Government Printing Office, Washington DC 20402. **Ed** J J Kramer. **LC** QC100, HV7431. **DD** 602.18 S, 364.4. **CODEN** XNBSAV.

SAGE CRIMINAL JUSTICE SYSTEMS ANNUAL. V.1- 1972-. US. English. sa. Sage Publishing Inc, 275 South Beverly Drive, Berverly Hills CA 90212.

SCARLET & GOLD. 1st- Ed. 0316-4209. Periodical. CN. English. an. $6.00. Scarlet & Gold, 813-675 West Hastings Street, Vancouver British Columbia V6B 1N2 Canada. **Tel** (604)253-3767. **Ed** E A MacDonald. **DD** 354.710074. bk rev adv acc. **Circ** 2,000. Features true stories written by veterans and articles relating to veteran activities.

SCLEOA UPDATE. **VFOAT** S.C.L.E.O.A. Update. **VAT** South Carolina Law Enforcement Officers Association Update. 8750-3808. Periodical. US. English. bm. SCLEOA, 421 Zimalcrest Drive, Columbia SC 29210.

SCROGGINS NATIONAL LAW ENFORCEMENT DIRECTORY. See Yearbooks, Almanacs, Directories.

SEARCH AND SEIZURE BULLETIN. Began with Apr. 1964 issue. 0037-0193. Periodical. US. English. mo. $36.00. Quinlan Publishing Company, 131 Beverly Street, Boston MA 02114. **DD** 345. Index published separately - free - automatically sent.

SEARCHLIGHT. Began in 1973. US. English. bm. Chicago Crime Commission, 79 West Monroe Street, Chicago IL 60603.

SECURITY AND SPECIAL POLICE LEGAL UPDATE. **VFOAT** Security Legal Update. 0741-482X. Periodical. US. English. bm. $36.00. Americans for Effective Law Enforcement Inc, 501 Grandview Drive/Suite 209, South San Francisco CA 94080. **LC** KF5399.5.P7. **DD** 344.730522, 347.304522.

SECURITY LETTER. See Business - General Management.

SECURITY SYSTEMS ADMINISTRATION. Vol. 11, No. 10 (Oct. 1982)-. 0745-6751. Periodical. US. English. mo. PTN Publishing Corporation, 101 Crossways Park West, Woodbury NY 11797. *Security Industry & Product News, 0745-3329.*

SECURITY WORLD. V. 1- July 1964-. 0037-0703. Periodical. US. English. mo. Cahners Publishing Company, 270 St Paul Street, Denver CO 80206. **Tel** (303)388-4511. **Ind/Abst** Predicants, Funk Scott Index Corp. Ind. **LC** HV8290.

SERVAMUS. Periodical. SA. Afrikaans (English). ir. 9.00. Sarp-Uitgevers, Wachthuis 255 Schoenanstraat 230, Pretoria 0001 South Africa. **Tel** (012)21-6703. **Ed** C P de Wel Crafford. **LC** HV8271.A5. **DD** 363.20968. bk rev. adv acc. **Circ** 49,300. (ctrl). Caters for the educational and social needs of the South African police force. *SAP.*

THE SHERIFF'S STAR. (SHERIFF'S STAR). Began with Issue for Mar. 1957?. 0488-6186. Periodical. US. English. mo. $5.00. Florida Sheriffs Association, PO Box 1487, Tallahassee FL 32302. **Tel** (904)877-2165.

SHURTAH (SHURTAT JUMHURIYAT AL-SUDAN AL-DIMUQRATIYAH. QISM AL-ALAQAT AL-AMMAH). (AL-SHURTAH : MAJALLAT SHURTAT JUMHURIIYAT AL-SUDAN AL-DIMUQRATIYAH). Periodical. Arabic. qt. 2.50 Single Issue. Al-Khartum S B 288 Sudan. **LC** HV7551.

SICHERHEITSBEAUFTRAGTER. 0300-3337. Periodical. GW. German. ir. Dr Curt Haefner Verlag, Bachstrasse 14, 6900 Heidelberg West Germany.

SINGAPORE POLICE JOURNAL. Periodical. SI. English. ir. $1.00 Each Issue. Thomson Road, Singapore 11 Singapore. **LC** HV7551. **DD** 363.2095952.

SPRING 3100. **VAT** Spring Thirty-One Hundred. Began in Mar. 1930?. 0038-8572. Periodical. US. English. mo. **LC** HV7551. **DD** 352.2.

SRI LANKA POLICE JOURNAL. Periodical. English. ir. 2.00 Each Issue. The Editorial Board, PO Box 1517, 15 Longdon Place 7, Colombo Sri Lanka (Ceylon). **LC** HV7804.8.A2. **DD** 363.2095493.

STATE OF NEVADA COMPREHENSIVE CRIMINAL JUSTICE PROGRESS REPORT. **Main/Corp** Nevada. Commission on Crime, Delinquency, and Corrections. **VFOAT** Nevada Comprehensive Criminal Justice Progress Report. US. English. an. State of Nevada, Commission on Crime Delinquency & Corrections, Carson City NV 89701. **LC** HV7278. **DD** 364.9793.

STATE OF NEW YORK COMPREHENSIVE CRIME CONTROL PLAN. **Main/Corp** New York (State). Division of Criminal Justice Services. 0360-0629. US. English. Division of Criminal Justice Services, 270 Broadway, New York NY 10007. **LC** HV7282. **DD** 364.

STATE PEACE OFFICERS JOURNAL. VFOAT Journal. 0192-4222. Periodical. US. English. bm. State Peace Officers Journal, PO Box 13155, Editorial Department, Houston TX 77019.

STATISTICAL DATA. See Statistics.

STATISTICAL INFORMATION SERVICE : POLICE FORCE AND REGIONAL CRIME SQUAD STATISTICS, ACTUALS. See Statistics.

THE SUPREME COURT CASES. Main/Corp India (Republic). Supreme Court. II. English. ir. 43.00 Pounds. Eastern Book Company, 34 Lalbagh, Lucknow - 226 001 India. Tel 43171,44328,46517. Ed Surendra Malik and P L Malik. DD 348.54046. bk rev. adv acc. Circ 6,000. Contains reports of both reportable and non-reportable cases of the Supreme Court of India.

SYSTEMS, TECHNOLOGY & SCIENCE FOR LAW ENFORCEMENT & SECURITY. VFOAT STS Newsletter. VAT Systems, Technology and Science for Law Enforcement and Security. 0039-8055. Periodical. US. English. mo. $24.00 Domestic, $30.00 Foreign. 21771.

TENNESSEE LAW ENFORCEMENT JOURNAL. 0040-327X. Periodical. US. English. qt. Callan Publishing Inc, 3033 Excelsior Boulevard, Minneapolis MN 55416.

THE TEXAS LAWMAN. 0040-442X. Periodical. US. English. mo. $25.00. Sheriffs Association of Texas, Box 4488 North Austin Station, Austin TX 78765. Tel (512)458-9114. Ed Dolores Shirley. adv acc. Circ 2,000.

TEXAS POLICE JOURNAL. V. 1- 1953-. 0040-4594. Periodical. US. English. mo. $15.00. Texas Police Association, Box 4247, Austin TX 78751. Ed Ayres Compton. bk rev. Circ 3,000. (ctrl). Articles on law enforcement with subjects of interest to officers from all jurisdictions: prosecutors, judges and persons engaged in law enforcement training.

TOP SECURITY. Periodical. UK. English. sm. Tieto Ltd, 293 Kingston Road, Surrey England. LC HV7551. DD 364.12.

TRIBAL AND BUREAU LAW ENFORCEMENT SERVICES AUTOMATED DATA REPORT. B08. ZUNI AGENCY-LES. Main/Corp United States. Bureau of Indian Affairs. Division of Law Enforcement Services. Jan. 1, 1983-Dec. 31, 1983-. US. English. an. *Tribal and Bureau Law Enforcement Services Automated Data Report. Zuni Agency and Reservation.*

TRIBAL AND BUREAU LAW ENFORCEMENT SERVICES AUTOMATED DATA REPORT : BILLINGS AREA. Main/Corp U.S. Indian Police Training Center. US. English. an. LC E78.M9. DD 364.108997.

TRIBAL AND BUREAU LAW ENFORCEMENT SERVICES AUTOMATED DATA REPORT. NAVAJO AREA. (TRIBAL AND BUREAU LAW ENFORCEMENT SERVICES AUTOMATED DATA REPORT : NAVAJO AREA). Main/Corp U.S. Indian Police Training Center. 0198-8891. US. English. an. US Department of Interior, Bureau of Indian Affairs, Washington DC 20240. LC E99.N3. DD 364.108997.

TRIBAL AND BUREAU LAW ENFORCEMENT SERVICES AUTOMATED DATA REPORT. PHOENIX AREA. (TRIBAL AND BUREAU LAW ENFORCEMENT SERVICES AUTOMATED DATA REPORT : PHOENIX AREA). Main/Corp U.S. Indian Police Training Center. V. 1- 1978-. 0270-2290. US. English. an. LC E78.A7. DD 364.089970791.

TRIBAL AND BUREAU LAW ENFORCEMENT SERVICES AUTOMATED DATA REPORT. TOTAL ALL AREAS. (TRIBAL AND BUREAU LAW ENFORCEMENT SERVICES AUTOMATED DATA REPORT : TOTAL ALL AREAS). Main/Corp U.S. Indian Police Training Center. 0198-8905. US. English. an. US Department of Interior, Bureau of Indian Affairs, Washington DC 20240. LC E98.C87. DD 364.108997.

UNIFORM CRIME REPORT FOR THE STATE OF MICHIGAN. Main/Corp Michigan. Dept. of State Police. 15th Ed.- 1973-. 0360-9146. US. English. an. Michigan Department of State Police, 714 South Harrison Road, East Lansing MI 48823. LC HV6793.M5. DD 364.9774. *Uniform Crime Report.*

UNIFORM CRIME REPORTS, STATE OF FLORIDA. VFOAT Crime in Florida. 1971-. US. English. an. Florida Department of Law Enforcement, PO Box 1489, Tallahassee FL 32302. LC HV7259. DD 364.109759.

UNIFORM CRIME REPORTS, STATE OF NEW JERSEY. VFOAT Crime in New Jersey. 1967-. 0548-5851. US. English. an. State of New Jersey, Division of State Police, Uniform Crime Reporting Unit, Box 7068, West Trenton NJ 08625. LC HV9475.N5. DD 364.9749.

WASHINGTON CRIME NEWS SERVICES' NARCOTICS CONTROL DIGEST. VFOAT Narcotics Control Digest. V.1- Jan. 6, 1971-. 0027-786X. Periodical. US. English. bw. $99.00. Washington Crime News Services, 7043 Wimsatt Road, Springfield VA 22151. Tel (703)941-6600. Ed Betty B Bosarge. Ind/Abst Crim. Justice Period. Index. bk rev. Circ 1,000. Information for supervisors, investigators, legislators and policy makers. Includes the latest news of federal, state and local activities, court decisions, etc. *Bulletin du Groupement Europeen Pour la Recherche Scientifique en Stomatologie & Odontologie, 0303-7479.*

WETTBEWERB IN RECHT UND PRAXIS : WRP. VFOAT WRP. 0172-049X. Periodical. GW. German. mo. 414.14 Domestic, 420.00 Foreign. Deutscher Fachverlag GMBH, Postfach 100606 Schumannstr 27, 6000 Frankfurt 1 West Germany. Tel (069)17433212. Ed Jabine Klamroth. LC KK6456.A13. DD 343.4307205, 344.3037205. bk rev. adv acc. Circ 1,800. (ctrl). Competition, premium and discount law, trade mark law and their significance for competition, antitrust law, advertising law and international competition law. *Wettbewerb in Recht und Praxis mit Kartellrecht.*

LEATHER AND FUR INDUSTRY

AMERICAN SHOEMAKING. 0003-1038. Periodical. US. English. wk. $29.00. Shoe Trades Publishing Company P O Box 198, Cambridge MA 02140. Tel (617)492-2387. Ed James Sutton. bk rev. adv acc. Circ 3,000. Footwear Manufacturing.

ANNUAL REPORT - RAJASTHAN STATE TANNERIES LIMITED. Main/Corp Rajasthan State Tanneries Limited. 1st- 1972/73-. 0302-4881. English. ir. Rajasthan State Tanneries Ltd, P-6 Tilak Marg C Scheme, Jaipur India. LC TS959.I4. DD 338.76675209544.

ARPEL. Periodical. IT. English (Italian, French, German and Spanish). qt. ARS Arpel, Via Ippolito Nievo 33, 20145 Milano Italy. Tel 02/315 951. International magazine on leathergoods, luggage and leather garments.

BEDRIJFSGEGEVENS VOOR DE DETAILHANDEL IN KOFFERS EN LEDERWAREN. Main/Corp Economisch Instituut Voor Het Midden- en Kleinbedrijf. Dutch. ir. Neuhuyskade 94 - Postbus 2818, S'Gravenhage The Netherlands. LC HD9780.N2.

CANADIAN FOOTWEAR JOURNAL. See Clothing and Fashion.

CUOIO, PELLI, MATERIE CONCIANTI. 0011-3034. Italian. bm. Stazione Sperimentale Pelli, Via Pogioreale 39, 80143 Naples Italy. Ind/Abst CIS Abstr., Chem. Abstr., Bibliogr. Agric. CODEN CPMAAJ. *Bollettino della Regia Stazione Sperimentale per l'Industria delle Pelli e delle materie Concianti, Napoli, 0366-2209.*

CURRENT LEATHER LITERATURE. V. 1- 19687-. 0011-3638. Periodical. English. ir. LC TS940. DD 685.2208.

DANSK PELSDYRAVL. Began in 1944. 0011-6424. Periodical. Danish. mo. *Dansk Pelsdyrblad.*

DEALER'S AND TRAPPER'S LISTING BOOK. 0276-2803. US. English. Stroudsburg Fur Dressing Corporation, 1031 King Street, Stroudsburg PA 18360. LC HD9944.U44. DD 380.143675302573.

EMPRESS CHINCHILLA BREEDER. V. 30- Jan. 1974-. 0094-3282. Periodical. US. English. mo. $15.00. Empress Chinchilla Breeders Co, PO Box 402, Morrison CO 80465. Tel (303)697-4421. Ind/Abst Bibliogr. Agric. *Empress Chinchilla, 0013-6905.*

EUROPEAN LEATHER GUIDE CEASED. UK. English. an. $75.09. Benn Business Information Services, PO Box 20 Sovereign Way, Tonbridge Kent TN9 1RQ England. Tel (0732) 362666. Ed John Hedges. LC TS945. DD 338.476850254. adv acc. Circ 1,800. Fully international in coverage, this directory includes the following sections: tanners and merchants, hide and skin suppliers, chemical suppliers, machinery manufacturers, trade organizations, and buyer's guide.

FOOTWEAR FOCUS. 0162-6345. Periodical. US. English. qt. $25.00. Footwear Focus Magazine, 1414 Avenue of the Americas/7th Floor, New York NY 10019. Tel (212)752-2555. Ed Anisa Mycak. LC HD9787.U4. DD 338.4768530973. bk rev. adv acc. Circ 20,000. (ctrl). Magazine for shoe retailers, buyers and store managers, featuring new shoe fashions, profiles of retailers and manufacturers, industry news, how-to articles for improving business.

FUR AGE WEEKLY. 0016-2884. Periodical. US. English. wk. $36.00. Fur Age Weekly, 127 West 30th Street, New York NY 10001. Tel (212)239-4983. Ed E R Harrowe. bk rev. adv acc. Circ 5,000. Vertical publication of the world fur trade.

FUR CHIC. Began publication in Mar. 1978. 0225-6452. Periodical. CN. English. ir. 27.00 US/Canada, 35.00 Others. Publicon Publishing, Fur Chic Fourrure 4626 St Catherine Street, West Montreal Quebec H3Z 1S3 Canada. DD 685.2405.

FUR PRODUCTION. Main/Corp Canada. Statistique Canada. Section du Betail et des Produits Animaux. VFOAT Production de Fourrure. 1970/71-. 0318-787X. Periodical. CN. Multilingual (text in English and French). an. Receiver General for Canada, Statistics Canada Publications, Ottawa Ontario K1A 0T6 Canada. *Fur Production.*

FUR RANCHER. V. 58- Jan. 1978-. 0744-7701. Periodical. US. English. mo. Communications Marketing Inc, 7535 Office Ridge Circle, Eden Prairie MN 55344. *U.S. Fur Rancher.*

FUR TRADE JOURNAL. V. 49, No. 3- Mar. 1971-. 0381-8535. Periodical. CN. English. mo. $10.83. Clay Publishing Company, Bewdley Ontario K0L 1E0 Canada. Tel (416)797-2281. Ed Charlotte Clay. bk rev. adv acc. Circ 1,000. (ctrl). Animal husbandry and care for mink and fox. *Fur Trade Journal of Canada, 0016-2973.*

HIDES AND SKINS. 0142-1891. Periodical. UK. English. sa. $42.56. Commonwealth Secretariat, Marlborough House/Pall Mall, London SW1Y 5HX England. Tel 01 839 2411. Ed Economics Affairs Division. LC HD9778.A1. DD 382.4567520212. Reviews world hides and skins situation. Contains up-to-date statistics on livestock slaughterings, utilisation, prices and trade in hides and skins and production of leather. *Hides and Skins Quarterly.*

INDIA LEATHER & LEATHER PRODUCTS DIRECTORY. See Yearbooks, Almanacs, Directories.

INDUSTRIA USOARA. PIELARIE, CONFECTII DIN PIELE, PRELUCRAREA CAUCIUCULUI SI A MASELOR PLASTICE, STICLA, CERAMICA FINA, ARTICOLE CASNICE SI JUCARII, UTILAJE PENTRU INDUSTRIA USOARA. VFOAT Pielaire, Confectii Din Piele, Prelucrarea Cauciucului Si A Maselor Plastice, Sticla, Ceramica Fina, Articole Casnice Si Jucarii, Utilaje Pentru Industria Usoara. Began in 1974. Periodical. Romanian (abstracts in English, French, German, and Russian). mo. B N R S R, Sectorul 3, Bucuresti Romania. Ind/Abst Coal Abstr. *Industria Usoara. Seria B.*

L'INDUSTRIE DE LA CHAUSSURE ET DES CUIRS ET PEAUX BRUTS ET TANNES DANS LES PAYS DE L'OCDE. Main/Corp Organisation for Economic Co-Operation and Development. VFOAT Footwear, Raw Hides and Skins and Leather Industry in OECD Countries. 1973/74-. French (English). ir. $4.50. Organisation for Economic Co-Operation and Development, 2 rue Andre-Pascal, 75775 Paris Cedex 16 France. LC HD9778.A2. DD 338.47675. *Industrie des Cuirs et Peaux et de la Chaussure dans les Pays de l'OCDE.*

INDUSTRY WAGE SURVEY : LEATHER TANNING AND FINISHING. See Economics - Labor.

INTERNATIONAL FUR FASHION REVIEW. 0823-6976. Periodical. CN. English. ir. $50.00. International Fur Fashion Review, 1470 Peel Street/Suite 328, Montreal PQ H3A 1T1 Canada. Tel

(514)844-9326. Ed Marsha Ross. DD 391. adv acc. Circ 3,000. (ctrl). Complete world-wide coverage of fur industry news, fashion, feature articles, etc.

JOURNAL. V. 57, No. 1- Jan./Feb. 1973. Periodical. English. bm. 25.00. Society of Leather Technologists and Chemists, 3 Branch Lane Huddersfield, West Yorks HD2 2ED England. Tel 0422-72592. Ed R G H Elliott. bk rev. adv acc. Circ 900. Scientific and technical articles on every subject relating to manufacture of leather. *Journal of the Society of Leather Trades' Chemists.*

JOURNAL & REPORT. Main/Corp National Union of the Footwear, Leather & Allied Trades. VAT Journal and Report. Aug./Sept. 1977-. Periodical. UK. English. bm. $4.60. National Union Footwear, Leather Trades/Grange Earl Barton, Northampton NN6 OJH England. *Monthly Journal and Report.*

THE JOURNAL OF THE AMERICAN LEATHER CHEMISTS ASSOCIATION. Main/Corp American Leather Chemists Association. V. 1- 1906-. 0002-9726. Periodical. US. English. mo. American Leather Chemists Association, c/o Campus Station 14, Cincinnati OH 45221. Ind/Abst Eng. Index Annu., Eng. Index Mon., Eng. Index Bioeng. Abstr., Eng. Index Energy Abstr., Sel. Water Resour. Abstr., Energy Inf. Abstr., Environ. Abstr., Biol. Abstr., Chem. Abstr., Sci. Cit. Index, Abr. Ed., Eng. Index. LC TS940. DD 675.205. CODEN JALCAQ.

KAWA TO HAKIMONO. VFOAT Leather & Footwears. Japanese. ir. Tokyo-to Sangyo Rodo Kaikan, 106 Hashiba 1, Taito-ku Tokyo Japan. LC HD9780.A1.

KOZARSTVI. 0023-4338. Periodical. CS. Czech (tables of contents also in Russian, English, and German). mo. Artia, PO Box 790, Praha 1 Czechoslovakia. Ind/Abst CIS Abstr., Chem. Abstr., Bibliogr. Agric. LC TS940. CODEN KOZAAT.

KOZHEVENNO-OBUVNAIA PROMYSHLENNOST. Began with: 1959, No. 1. 0023-4354. Periodical. UR. Russian. mo. $31.50. Victor Kamkin Inc (70436), 12224 Parklawn Drive, Rockville MD 20852. Tel (301)881-5973. Ind/Abst Art Archaeol. Tech. Abstr., CIS Abstr., Chem. Abstr. CODEN KOOPAJ. Index in last issue of volume - attached.

LEATHER AND SHOES. (LEATHER & SHOES). Vol. 115, No. 1 (Jan. 3, 1948)-. 0023-9747. Periodical. US. English. mo. $16.00. Rumpf Publishing Company, 1800 Oakton Street, Des Plaines IL 60018. Tel (312)298-6210. DD 338. adv acc. Circ 4,000. Serving the footware tanning and leather goods industry. *Hide and Leather and Shoes.*

LEATHER BUYERS GUIDE. 0075-8345. US. English. an. Rumpf Publishing Company, 300 West Adam Street, Chicago IL 60606. LC HD9780.U5. DD 338.4768502573. *L & S Leather Buyers Guide and Leather Trade Marks for Shoe and Accessory Leathers.*

LEATHER INDUSTRIES. VFOAT Industrie du Cuir. 1981-. 0319-8898. CN. English (French). an. $6.65 Domestic, $7.95 Foreign. Publication Sales and Services, Statistics Canada, Ottawa Ontario K1A 0T6 Canada. DD 338.476850971.

THE LEATHER MANUFACTURER. See Manufacturing.

LEATHER SCIENCE. Began publication with Jan. 1963 issue. 0023-9771. Periodical. English. mo. $25.00. Central Leather Research Institution, Adyar Madras 20 India. Tel 412616. Ed G Thiyagarajan. Ind/Abst Art Archaeol. Tech. Abstr. LC TS940. CODEN LESCA. bk rev. adv acc. Circ 150. Contains original research articles, short communications, process papers, notes and news items. *Bulletin of the Central Leather Research Institute.*

LEATHER TANNERIES (FINAL) CEASED. (LEATHER TANNERIES). Series/Titl Annual Census of Manufactures. VAT Tanneries. 1960-1980. 0384-3270. CN. English (French). an. Receiver General for Canada, Statistics Canada Publications, Ottawa Ontario K1A 0T6 Canada. DD 338.476850971. *Leather Tanning Industry, 0384-3289.*

DAS LEDER. Began publication in 1950. 0024-0176. Periodical. GW. German. mo. 79.60. E Roether Verlag, P O Box 4101 Berliner Allee 56, D-6100 Darmstadt West Germany. Tel 06151/33 2 55. Ind/Abst Art Archaeol. Tech. Abstr., Chem. Abstr. LC TS940. CODEN LEDEA8. bk rev. adv acc. Circ 2,200. Trade periodical for leather chemistry and technology, exclusively read by the experts and key personnel in the leather producing and converting industry.

LEDERINDUSTRIE. Series/Titl Produktiestatistieken Industrie. VFOAT Tanneries and Leather Finishing. 0168-471X. NE. Dutch (summaries in English). an. 9.50. Centraal Bureau Voor de Statistiek, Prinses Beatrixlaan 428, Postbus 959, 2270 AZ Voorburg Netherlands.

LEDERWARENINDUSTRIE, EXCL. KLEDING. Series/Titl Produktiestatistieken Industrie. VFOAT Lederwarenindustrie, Exclusief Kleding. 1982-. 0168-5139. NE. Dutch (summaries in English). an. 9.50. Centraal Bureau Voor de Statistik, Prinses Beatrixlaan 428, Postbus 959, 2270 AZ Voorburg Netherlands. *Produktiestatistieken: Lederwarenindustrie, Excl. Kleding.*

LEXPORT. Main/Corp Export Promotion Council for Finished Leather & Leather Manufactures. English. ir. Export Promotion Council for Finished Leather & Leather Manufactures, 15/46 Civil Libes, PO Box No 198, Kanpur 208001 India. LC HD9780.162.

LLOYD'S CANADIAN FOOTWEAR AND LEATHER DIRECTORY. See Yearbooks, Almanacs, Directories.

LOCAL 1-FLM TEMPO. VFOAT Local 1 FLM Tempo. VAT Local One Fur, Leather and Machine Tempo. Vol. 18, No. 2 (June 1984)-. 8750-8311. Periodical. US. English. bm. United Food & Commercial Workers International Union, 815-16th Street Northwest, Washington DC 20006. *FLM Joint Board Tempo, 0162-5969.*

LSL: LEDER, SCHUKE, LEDERWAREN. VFOAT Leder, Schuhe, Lederwaren. V. 1-. 0024-0192. Periodical. SZ. German. mo. Kunst & Wissen Erich Bieber, Dufourstrasse 51, CH-8008 Zurich Switzerland. Ind/Abst Chem. Abstr. LC TS940. DD 685.05. CODEN LSLEBB.

MAKE IT WITH LEATHER. VFOAT Leather. Began with Vol. 16, No. 6 (Oct./Nov. 1972). 0738-4718. Periodical. US. English. bm. Leather Craftsman Inc, PO Box 1396, Fort Worth TX 76101. Tel (817)595-1933. Available on microfilm from University Microfilms International. *Craftsman (Fort Worth, Tex.).*

MISCELLANEOUS LEATHER GOODS, LEATHER BELTING, BOOT & SHOE FINDINGS. Main/Corp Canada. Bureau of Statistics. 1933-. Periodical. CN. English. an. Statistics Canada Publications Distributions, Ottawa Ontario K1A 0T6 Canada. LC HD9780.C2. DD 338.47685.

MONTHLY BULLETIN - NATIONAL CHINCHILLA BREEDERS OF CANADA. Main/Corp National Chinchilla Breeders of Canada. VFOAT Bulletin Mensuel - Eleveurs Nationaux de Chinchilla du Canada. Began with Jan. 1955 issue. 0027-8963. Periodical. CN. English (includes some text in French). mo. $15.48. National Chinchilla Breeders Canada, RR 10, Brampton Ontario L6V 3N2 Canada. Tel (613)257-3898. Ed Jocelyn E Morley. adv acc. (ctrl). On all areas of chinchilla, illness, disease, animal husbandry, ranch management, show results, pelt marketing.

NORTH AMERICAN RETAIL FURRIERS DIRECTORY. See Yearbooks, Almanacs, Directories.

PRZEGLAD SKORZANY. Began in 1946. 0370-1743. Periodical. PL. Polish. mo. ARS Polona, Krakowskie Przedmiescie 7, 00-068 Warsaw Poland. Ind/Abst Chem. Abstr. LC TS940. CODEN PRZKAX.

REPORT ON FUR FARMS. Main/Corp Canada. Bureau of Statistics. Livestock and Animal Products Section. VFOAT Rapport sur les Fermes a Fourrure. 0318-7888. CN. English. an. 30.00 Domestic, 31.00 Foreign. Receiver General for Canada, Statistics Canada Publications, Ottawa Ontario K1A 0T6 Canada. Tel (800)268-1151. Number of fur farms and fur animals, number and value of pelts taken, by province and kinds; exports and imports. *Fur Farms of Canada.*

REVISTA DE LA FEDERACION MEXICANA DE QUIMICOS Y TECNICOS DEL CUERO. Periodical. MX. Spanish. bm. Tehuantepec 255 Primer Piso, Mexico 7 DF Mexico.

REVUE TECHNIQUE DES INDUSTRIES DU CUIR. V. 15- May 15, 1942-. 0035-4236. Periodical. FR. French. mo. Societe de Publicatns le Cuir, 54 rue Rene Boulanger, Paris 10E France. Ind/Abst Excerpta Med., CIS Abstr., Art Archaeol. Tech. Abstr., Chem. Abstr. CODEN RTICAS.

SCIENTIFUR. V. 1. No. 1- Feb. 1977-. 0105-2403. Periodical. English. qt. $38.67. NJF's Fur Animal Division, 48 H Roskildevej, DK 3400 Hilleroed Denmark. Tel 02-261410. Ed Gunnar Joergensen. bk rev. adv acc. Circ 500. Original scientific reports and abstracts regarding all aspects in production of farmed fur-bearing animals.

SHOE FACTORIES AND BOOT AND SHOE FINDINGS MANUFACTURERS CEASED. Series/Titl Annual Census of Manufactures. VFOAT Fabriques de Chaussures et Fabricants de Crepins pour Chaussures, Fabriques de Chaussures et Manufacturiers de Crepins en Cuir. 1960-1980. 0384-4986. CN. English. an. 0.70. DD 338.4768530971. *The Leather Footwear and Leather Boot and Shoe Findings Industries, 0384-4994.*

SHOE FACTORY BUYER' GUIDE. US. English. ir. Tel (617)492-2387. adv acc. Circ 2,500. Buyers' guide for footwear manufacturing industry.

SHOES ON PARADE. 0037-4083. Periodical. US. English. wk. $198.00. Retail Reporting Bureau, 101 Fifth Avenue, New York NY 10003. Tel (212)255-9595.

SHOWCASE. V. 1- Fall 1975-. 0361-3232. Periodical. US. English. bm. $35.00. Luggage & Leather Goods, 350 Fifth Avenue, New York NY 10118. Tel (212)695-2340. LC HD9999.L83. DD 338.47685510973.

SISTEMA DE INFORMACAO ESTATISTICA PARA A INDUSTRIA NACIONAL DE COUROS : BOLETIM DE INFORMACOES. Main/Corp Instituto Brasileiro do Couro, Calcados e Afins. Portuguese. ir. Instituto Brasileiro do Couro, Calcados E Afins, Caixa Postal 48 93.600, Estancia Velha Brazil. LC HD9778.B7.

STATISTICAL REVIEW OF THE FUR SEASON IN NORTHERN FUR CONSERVATION AREAS. See Statistics.

THE TANNER. Began in 1946?. Periodical. II. English. mo. $25.00. Asia Books & Periodicals Company, 11 Darya Ganj, New Delhi 110002 India. Tel 268645,271378-275542. LC TS940. DD 675.

TECHNICUIR. V. 1- 1967-. Periodical. FR. French. ir. SETIC, 54 rue Rene Boulanger, Paris 10E France.

THE TRAPPER AND PREDATOR CALLER. VFOAT Trapper & Predator Caller. Began with Aug. 1984 issue. 8750-233X. Periodical. US. English. mo. $10.00. The Trapper & Predator Caller, PO Box 550, Sutton NE 68979. Tel (402)773-4343. Ed Rich Faler. DD 799. bk rev. adv acc. Circ 50,000. (ctrl). Covers the rural fur trade; taking and marketing of animal skins to be manufactured into garments, harvesting a renewable resource when managed biologically by state agencies. *Trapper, 0739-0599.*

VOGUE PELLE. No. 2 (Feb. L981)-. Periodical. IT. Italian. qt. Edizioni Conde Nast S.P.A., Piazza Castello 27, 20121 Milano Italy. LC TT524. DD 391.2. *Vogue Italia. Pelle.*

WEEKLY BULLETIN - WEEKLY BULLETIN LEATHER SHOE NEWS CO. Main/Corp Weekly Bulletin Leather Shoe News Co. Periodical. US. English. wk. $22.00. Weekly Bulletin of Leather & Shoe News, 46 Summer Street, Boston MA 02110. Tel (617)542-2436. Ed Louis C Schwaab. LC TS940. DD 338.4768505. adv acc. Circ 3,100. Weekly news, markets, trade information for tanning and footwear manufacturing leather garment fields. *Weekly Bulletin of Leather & Shoe News.*

LIBRARY AND INFORMATION SCIENCE

16 MM FILMS AVAILABLE FROM THE NORTHWESTERN REGIONAL LIBRARY. Main/Corp Northwestern Regional Library System (Ont). Began publication in 1975?. 0225-2937. CN. English. an. Northwestern Regional

Library and Information Science

Library System, 910 Victoria Avenue, Thunder Bay Ont P7C 1B4 Canada. **DD** 011.37.

AALT TECHNICIAN. (THE A A L T TECHNICIAN). **Main/Corp** Alberta Association of Library Technicians. **VAT** Alberta Association of Library Technicians Technician. V. 1- Sept. 1975-. 0703-5276. Periodical. CN. English. qt. $7.00. Alberta Association of Library Technicians, Technician 6-4408, 4th Street North West, Calagary Alberta T2K 1A2 Canada. **DD** 023.5.

AALT TECHNICIAN BULLETIN. Main/Corp Alberta Association of Library Technicians. **VAT** Alberta Association of Library Technicians Technician Bulletin. No. 1-. 0228-9490. Periodical. CN. English. ir. Free to members. Alberta Association of Library Technicians, PO Box 700, Edmonton Alberta T5J 2L4 Canada. **DD** 023.3.

ABCD, RESUMOS E SUMARIOS. Vol. 1-. Portuguese. ir. **LC** Z666. **DD** 016.02.

ABHA. ANNUAL BIBLIOGRAPHY OF THE HISTORY OF THE PRINTED BOOK AND LIBRARIES. See Bibliographies.

ABI-TECHNIK. VFOAT A.B.I.-Technik. 0720-6763. Periodical. German. qt. 70.00. Verlag Karlheinz Holz, Friedrichstrasse 55 Postfach 33 29, 6200 Wiesbaden 1 West Germany. **Ind/Abst** Libr. Inf. Sci. Abstr. **LC** Z678.9.A1. **DD** 025.302854.

ABSTRACTS, STRENGTHENING RESEARCH LIBRARY RESOURCES PROGRAM. See Indexes/Abstracts.

ACCADEMIE E BIBLIOTECHE D'ITALIA. Yearly V. 1- July/Aug 1927-. 0001-4451. Periodical. IT. Italian. bm. $19.00. Organizzazione Rab S R L, Via Crocifisso 51/Iscrizione A, Rome Italy. **Ind/Abst** MLA Int. Bibliogr. Books Artic. Mod. Lang. Lit., Libr. Inf. Sci. Abstr. *Rivista Delle Biblioteche E Degli Archivi.*

ACCES (INFORMATECH FRANCE-QUEBEC). (ACCES). No. 1 (Jan. 1981)-. 0226-9309. Periodical. CN. French. qt. Free. Informatech France-Quebec, C P 160, Montreal Quebec H5A 1A7 Canada. **DD** 025.06505. *Info-I F Q, 0706-1943.*

ACCESS. No. 1- July 1974-. 0317-039X. Periodical. CN. English. Free. Greater Vancouver Library Council, 3622 East 1st Avenue, Vancouver BC V5M 1C3 Canada. **DD** 027.406271133.

ACCESS. (ACCESS : A NEWSLETTER OF THE LONDON PUBLIC LIBRARIES, GALLERIES, MUSEUMS). 0710-0132. Periodical. CN. English. mo. Free. London Public Libraries, 305 Queens Avenue, London Ontario N6B 3L7 Canada. **DD** 027.471326. *Calendar of Events (London, Ont.).*

ACCESS: MICROCOMPUTERS IN LIBRARIES. (ACCESS, MICROCOMPUTERS IN LIBRARIES). **VFOAT** Access. Vol. 1, No. 1 (July 1981)-. 0277-0784. Periodical. US. English. qt. $11.00. DAC Publications, 47438 Westoak Road, Westfir OR 97463. **Ind/Abst** Libr. Inf. Sci. Abstr. **LC** Z678.9.A1. **DD** 025.0405.

ACCESSIONS LIST, BANGLADESH. See Bibliographies.

ACCESSIONS LIST. BRAZIL. See Bibliographies.

ACCESSIONS LIST, BRAZIL. CUMULATIVE LIST OF SERIALS. See Bibliographies.

ACCESSIONS LIST. INDIA. See Bibliographies.

ACCESSIONS LIST. INDIA. QUINQUENNIAL SERIALS CUMULATION. ANNUAL SUPPLEMENT. See Bibliographies.

ACCESSIONS LIST, MIDDLE EAST. See Bibliographies.

ACCESSIONS LIST. NEPAL. See Bibliographies.

ACCESSIONS LIST. SOUTH ASIA. See Bibliographies.

ACCESSIONS LIST. SOUTH ASIA. SERIALS SUPPLEMENT. See Bibliographies.

ACCESSIONS LIST, SOUTHEAST ASIA. See Bibliographies.

ACCESSIONS LIST. SOUTHEAST ASIA. CUMULATIVE LIST OF INDONESIAN SERIALS. See Bibliographies.

ACCESSIONS LIST. SOUTHEAST ASIA. CUMULATIVE LIST OF MALAYSIA, SINGAPORE AND BRUNEI SERIALS. See Bibliographies.

ACCESSIONS LIST. SOUTHEAST ASIA. CUMULATIVE LIST OF SERIALS, BURMA, THAILAND, AND LAOS. See Bibliographies.

ACCESSIONS LIST. SRI LANKA. See Bibliographies.

ACCESSIONS OF NORTH AMERICAN AND LATIN AMERICAN INTEREST ADDED TO THE LIBRARY. UK. English. an. The Library, 183 Euston Road, London NW1 2BP England.

ACCESSIONSKATALOG - DENMARK. RIGSBIBLIOTEKAREMBEDET. Main/Corp Denmark. Rigsbibliotekarembedet. **VFOAT** Flleskatalog Over Danske Videnskabelige Og Faglige Bibliotekers Erhvervelser AF Udenlandsk Litteratur. V. 1- 1953-. 0084-9715. DK. Danish. an. 1205.37. Bibliotekscentralen, Telegrafvej 5, DK 2750 Ballerup Denmark. **Tel** (02)974000. **LC** Z941. Available in microfiche. Union catalogue of the acquisitions of foreign literature in Danish academic libraries. *Katalog Over Erhvervelser Af Nyere Udenlandsk Litteratur Ved Statens Offentlige Biblioteker.*

ACCESSIONSKATALOG FOR DRAMATISK BIBLIOTEK. Main/Corp Copenhagen. Universitet. Dramatisk Bibliotek. DK. Danish. an. 40.16. Bibliotekscentralen, Telegrafvej 5, DK 2750 Ballerup Denmark. **Tel** (02)974000. **Circ** 400. (ctrl). Available in microform. Union catalogue of the acquisitions of foreign literature in Danish academic libraries.

A.C.C.L. UNION LIST OF SERIALS. (A. C. C. L. UNION LIST OF SERIALS). **Main/Corp** Alberta Council of College Librarians. **VAT** Alberta Council of College Librarians Union List of Serials. Began publication in 1973?. 0226-7195. CN. English. ir. $30. Alberta Council of College Librarians, c/o Learning Resources Centre, Southern Alberta Institute of Technology, 1301-16th Avenue North West, Calgary Alta T2M 0L4 Canada. **DD** 018.134.

ACQUISITION, BIBLIOGRAPHY, CATALOGUING NEWS. No. 1 (June 1981). 0725-0037. AT. English. ir. Free. National Library of Australia, Sales & Subscription Unit, Canberra ACT 2600 Australia. **Tel** (062)621646. **LC** Z870.A1. **DD** 027.594. News of recent acquisitions and developments in bibliography and cataloguing. *Rod News.*

ACQUISITIONS DE LA BIBLIOTHEQUE. SELECTION. See Bibliographies.

ACQUISITIONS LIST - CENTRE OF CRIMINOLOGY LIBRARY. UNIVERSITY OF TORONTO. (ACQUISITIONS LIST - CENTRE OF CRIMINOLOGY LIBRARY, UNIVERSITY OF TORONTO). **Main/Corp** University of Toronto. Centre of Criminology. Library. 0701-0524. Periodical. CN. English. ty. 10.00. University of Toronto, Centre of Criminology, 130 St. George Street 8th Floor, Toronto M5S 1A5 Canada. **Tel** (416)978-7124. **Ed** Jane Gladstone. **DD** 016.364. **Circ** 200. List catalogued books and reports plus newly acquired uncataloged materials added to the criminology library collection.

ACQUISITIONS - METROPOLITAN TORONTO LIBRARY. CANADIAN HISTORY DEPARTMENT. (ACQUISITIONS). **Main/Corp** Metropolitan Toronto Library. Canadian History Dept. Vol. 1, No. 1 (Sept. 1982)-V. 1, No. 4 (Dec. 1982). 0226-2487. Periodical. CN. English. mo. Free. Metropolitan Toronto Library Board, 789 Yonge Street, Toronto Onario M4W 2G8 Canada. **DD** 016.971.

ACQUISITIONS - METROPOLITAN TORONTO LIBRARY. GENERAL REFERENCE DEPARTMENT. (ACQUISITIONS - METROPOLITAN TORONTO LIBRARY. GENERAL REFERENCE DEPT). **Main/Corp** Metropolitan Toronto Library. General Reference Dept. Vol. 1, No. 1 (Mar. 1980)-. 0226-2509. Periodical. CN. English. mo. Free. Metropolitan Toronto Library Board, 789 Yonge Street, Toronto Ontario M4W 2G8 Canada. **DD** 016.02. *Selected List of New Titles, 0227-7476.*

ACQUISITIONS NEWSLETTER - CANBERRA, AUSTRALIA. NATIONAL LIBRARY. Main/Corp Canberra, Australia. National Library. Began with Aug. 1970 issue. AT. English. ir. National Library of Australia, ACT 2600, Canberra Australia. **LC** Z975.C3. **DD** 027.5944.

ACRL PUBLICATIONS IN LIBRARIANSHIP. Main/Corp Association of College and Research Libraries. **VAT** Association of College and Research Libraries. Publications in Librarianship. No. 34-. 0193-1784. Monographic Series. US. English. American Library Association, 50 East Huron Street, Chicago IL 60611. **LC** Z674. **DD** 658.8090705730941. *ACRL Monograph.*

ACSI-ON. Vol. 1, No. 1 (Feb. 1983)-. 0821-5049. Periodical. CN. French. ir. Free. Association Canadienne des Sciences de l'Information Section de Montreal, C P 159 Succursale Cote-des-Neiges, Montreal Quebec H3S 2S5 Canada. **DD** 025.00971. (ctrl).

ACTA UNIVERSITATIS SZEGEDIENSIS. ACTA BIBLIOTHECARIA. Main/Corp Szeged, Hungary. Tudomanyegyetem (Founded 1940). **VFOAT** Acta Bibliothecaria. V.1- 1955-. Periodical. HU. Hungarian. ir. Akademiai Kiado, POB 24, 1363 Budapest Hungary.

ACTION FOR LIBRARIES. V. 1- Oct. 1975-. 0363-0250. Periodical. US. English. mo. Bibliographical Center of Research, Rock Mountain Region, 1777 Bellaire/Suite 425, Denver CO 80222. **Tel** (303)691-0550. **Ed** Joyce Coyne. **Ind/Abst** Libr. Inf. Sci. Abstr. bk rev. **Circ** 2,500. Newsletter for members of library services network in the Rocky Mountain region.

ACTIVITIES OF THE LUSAKA CITY LIBRARIES. Main/Corp Lusaka, Zambia. City Libraries Section. ZA. English. ir. Lusaka City Libraries, Lusaka Zambia. **LC** Z858.L87. **DD** 027.46894. *Activities of City Library Section.*

ADDITIONS AND ACCESSIONS - REFERENCE SECTION. EDUCATION CENTRE LIBRARY. TORONTO BOARD OF EDUCATION. (ADDITIONS AND ACCESSIONS - REFERENCE SECTION, EDUCATION CENTRE LIBRARY, TORONTO BOARD OF EDUCATION). **Main/Corp** Toronto Board of Education. Education Centre. Library. Reference Section. 0227-2431. Periodical. CN. English. mo. Library Education Centre, Toronto Board of Education, 155 College Street, Toronto Ontario M5T 1P6 Canada. **DD** 017.567.

ADDRESS LIST, REGIONAL AND SUBREGIONAL LIBRARIES FOR THE BLIND AND PHYSICALLY HANDICAPPED. VFOAT Regional and Subregional Libraries for the Blind and Physically Handicapped. Began with Apr. 1976. 0163-3805. US. English. sa. National Library Service for the Blind and Physically Handicapped, 1291 Taylor Street NW, Washington DC 20542. **LC** Z675.B6. **DD** 027.66302573. **NLM** Z 675.B6 A227.

ADLIB UPDATE. No. 1 (June 23, 1984)-. 8755-9846. US. English. sa. Free. Advanced Lib. Concepts, 9343 Tech Center Drive Suite 175, Sacramento CA 95826. **DD** 025.

ADMINISTRATIVE NOTES (UNITED STATES.) INFORMATION DISSEMINATION/ SUPERINTENDENT OF DOCUMENTS. LIBRARY PROGRAMS SERVICE). (ADMINISTRATIVE NOTES (UNITED STATES). INFORMATION). Vol. 4, No. 1 (Jan. 1983)-. Periodical. US. English. ir. US Government Printing Office, Library Programs Service, Washington DC 20402. **LC** Z675.D4. **DD** 025.26. *Administrative Notes (United States. Superintendent of Documents. Library and Statutory Distribution Service).*

ADMINISTRATOR'S DIGEST (ORINDA, CALIF.) CEASED. (ADMINISTRATOR'S DIGEST). Vol. 1, No. 1 Dec. 1965- Vol. 17, No. 10 Dec. 1982. 0001-8422. Periodical. US. English. mo.

ADVANCED TECHNOLOGY LIBRARIES. VFOAT AT/L. V. 1- Jan. 1972-. 0044-636X. Periodical. US. English. mo. $63.00. Knowlgdge Industry Publishing Inc, 701 Westchester Avenue, White Plains NY 10604. **Tel** (914)328-9157. **Ed** Judy Duke. **Ind/Abst** Predicasts, Funk Scott Index Corp. Ind. **LC** Z671. **DD** 020.5. **NLM** Z699.A1 A244. **CODEN** ATLBA. bk rev. adv acc. Newsletter of automation news and issues affecting libraries. *Advanced Technology Libraries, 0044-636X.*

ADVANCES IN INFORMATION SYSTEMS SCIENCE. V. 1-. 0065-2784. US. English. ir. Plenum Press, Attn H Feldman, 233 Spring Street, New York NY 10013. **Tel** (212)620-8000. **Ed** J

1617

Library and Information Science

T Tou. **Ind/Abst** Comput. Control Abstr., Electr. Electron. Abstr., Sci. Abstr. Sect. A. Phys. Abstr., Phys. Abstr. **LC** Z699.A1. **DD** 029.7. **CODEN** AISYBH.

ADVANCES IN LIBRARIANSHIP. V. 1- 1970-. 0065-2830. US. English. ir. Academic Press, 4805 Sand Lake Road, Orlando FL 32887. **Tel** (305)345-4100. Ed Melvin J Voigt. **LC** Z674. **DD** 020.5. **NLM** Z 671 A244. **CODEN** AVLSA.

ADVANCES IN LIBRARY ADMINISTRATION AND ORGANIZATION. Vol. 1 (1982)-. 0732-0671. US. English. an. Jai Press Inc, 36 Sherwood Place, Greenwich CT 06836. **LC** Z678. **DD** 025.105.

ADVENT. V. 1- Mar. 1980-. 0226-174X. Periodical. CN. English. mo. Free. Advent, Carleton University Library, Ottawa Ont K1S 5B6 Canada. **DD** 027.771384.

ADVERTISEMENT DIGEST : LIBRARY AND INFORMATION SERVICES. VFOAT AD:LIS. V. 1- July/Dec. 1978-. 0194-0392. Periodical. US. English. ir. Information Digest, PO Box 165, Morton Grove IL 60053. **Tel** (312)965-1456. Ed Chung I Park. **LC** Z684. **DD** 022.90294. Abstracts of advertisements of computers, library technologies, and information services.

AFRICAN JOURNAL OF ACADEMIC LIBRARIANSHIP. Vol. 1, No. 1 (June 1983)-. Periodical. English. sa.

AGRICULTURAL LIBRARIES INFORMATION NOTES. Publication began with Vol. 1, No. 1 (Jan. 1975). 0095-2699. Periodical. US. English. mo. Free. National Agriculture Library, 10301 Baltimore Boulevard, Beltsville MD 20705. **Tel** (301)344-3937. Ed Maria G Pisa. **Ind/Abst** Libr. Inf. Sci. Abstr., Bibliogr. Agric. **LC** Z675.A8. **DD** 026.630973. bk rev. **Circ** 3,000. Channel of communication to libraries, technical information specialists, extension workers, and scientists on agricultural information activities.

AGRICULTURAL LIBRARIES INFORMATION NOTES. SUPPLEMENT. No. 1- Feb. 1978-. Periodical. US. English. National Agriculture Library, 10301 Baltimore Boulevard, Beltsville MD 20705.

AISPLAYBACK. VAT Association of Information Systems Professionals Playback. 0824-6505. Periodical. CN. English. mo. Free to members. Association of Information Systems Professionals, Ottawa Chapter, PO Box 652, Ottawa Ontario K1P 5P7 Canada. **DD** 020.62471384. Iwplayback.

AJL BULLETIN CEASED. VFOAT A.J.L. Bulletin. Began in Jan. 1967. Ceased V. 17, No. 2, Winter 1983. 0734-0516. Periodical. US. English. sa. **Ind/Abst** Libr. Inf. Sci. Abstr. **LC** Z675.J4. **DD** 027.6308992405. Drop Box.

AJL NEWSLETTER. Main/Corp Association of Jewish Libraries. VAT Association of Jewish Libraries Newsletter. 0747-6175. Periodical. US. English. qt. $25.00 Members. AJL Newsletter, c/o Irene S Levin/ 48 Georgia Street, Valley Stream NY 11580. **Tel** (516)285-6099. Ed Irene S Levin. **DD** 027. bk rev. adv acc. **Circ** 750. News and book reviews for Synagogue School and Center, and Judaic studies programs.

AKTUALNYE VOPROSY BIBLIOTECHNOI RABOTY. 1982-. 0203-4972. Periodical. UR. Russian. an. 0.45. Izdatelstvo Kniga, 103009 Moskva, Ul Nezhdanovoi 8/ 10, Moskva Russian SFSR. **LC** Z819.A1. **DD** 027.04705.

AL-TAWTHIQ AL-ILAMI. VFOAT Informational Documentation. Periodical. Arabic. qt. 5.00 Domestic, 10.00 Foreign. Markaz Al Tawthiq Al Ilami Li Duwal Al Khalik Al Arabi, S B 5063, Baghdad Iraq. Tel 5564171. bk rev. **Circ** 2,500. (ctrl). Studies and articles and reports; documentation of major anniversaries and conferences and seminars.

ALA HANDBOOK OF ORGANIZATION. Main/Corp American Library Association. VAT American Library Association Handbook of Organization. 1971/72-. 0084-6406. US. English. an. Free to Members. American Library Association, 50 East Huron Street, Chicago IL 60611. **LC** Z673.A5. **DD** 020.62173. **NLM** Z 673.A5A3. ALA Organizational Information.

ALA HANDBOOK OF ORGANIZATION AND MEMBERSHIP DIRECTORY. See Yearbooks, Almanacs, Directories.

ALA MEMBERSHIP DIRECTORY. See Yearbooks, Almanacs, Directories.

ALA PUBLICATIONS CHECKLIST. Main/Corp American Library Association. Headquarters Library. VAT American Library Association Publications checklist. 1979-. 0193-810X. US. English. an. American Library Association, 50 East Huron Street, Chicago IL 60611. Ed J M Lee. **LC** Z666. **DD** 016.02.

ALA SURVEY OF LIBRARIAN SALARIES. See Economics - Labor.

ALA WASHINGTON NEWSLETTER (WASHINGTON, D C : 1984). (ALA WASHINGTON NEWSLETTER). VFOAT A.L.A. Washington Newsletter. VAT American Library Association Washington Newsletter. Vol. 36, No. 2 (Mar. 2, 1984)-. Periodical. US. English. ir. $15.00. Washington Newsletter, Box 54, 110 Maryland Avenue NE, Washington DC 20002. **Tel** (202)547-4440. **Ind/ Abst** Libr. Lit. Washington Newsletter (American Library Association. Washington Office), 0001-1746.

THE ALA YEARBOOK. See Yearbooks, Almanacs, Directories.

THE ALA YEARBOOK OF LIBRARY AND INFORMATION SERVICES. See Yearbooks, Almanacs, Directories.

ALABAMA LIBRARIAN. (THE ALABAMA LIBRARIAN). V. 1- Dec. 1949-. 0002-4295. Periodical. US. English. mo. $5.00. Alabama Library Association, Post Office Box BY, University AL 35486. **Tel** (205)752-6681. Ed Beebe McKinley. **LC** Z671. **DD** 020.623. (cum index). bk rev. adv acc. **Circ** 2,000. (ctrl). Information about libraries, librarians and support groups in Alabama or of interest in the Alabama area.

ALABAMA PUBLIC LIBRARY SERVICE ANNUAL REPORT. 1976/77-. US. English. an. 6030 Monticello Drive, Montgomery AL 36130. **Tel** (205)277-7330. Ed Anthony W Miele. **LC** Z678.4.A3. **DD** 027.4761. **Circ** 1,700. A report of the programs and projects of the State Library for the fiscal year, includes a directory of public libraries and statistical information pertinent to Alabama's public libraries. Alabama Public Libraries, Statistics of Public Libraries in Alabama.

ALASKA LIBRARY DIRECTORY. See Yearbooks, Almanacs, Directories.

ALBERTA LIBRARY BOARD REPORT. VAT Annual Report - Alberta Library Board. 1978/79-. 0715-1640. CN. English. an. Alberta Library Board, 12th Floor CN Tower 10004-104 Avenue, Edmonton Alberta T5J 0K5 Canada. **LC** Z883.A12. **DD** 021.82097123.

ALBERTA LIBRARY DIRECTORY . . . . See Yearbooks, Almanacs, Directories.

ALBERTA PUBLIC LIBRARY STATISTICS. See Statistics.

ALKI. (ALKI : THE WASHINGTON LIBRARY ASSOCIATION JOURNAL). 8756-4173. Periodical. US. English. ty. $14.00. c/o V Louise Saylor, The Library of Eastern Washington University, Cheney WA 99004. **Tel** (509)359-7893. Ed V Louise Saylor. bk rev. adv acc. **Circ** 1,200. Contains philosophical and substantive analyses of current and enduring issues for and about Washington libraries, personnel and advocates as well as exchanges of opinion and information.

ALLOCATION OF FEDERAL FUNDS. US. English. an. Missouri State Library, 308 East High Street, PO Box 387, Jefferson City MO 65102. **LC** Z683. **DD** 021.8309778.

ALTERNATIVE LIBRARY LITERATURE. (ALTERNATIVE LIBRARY LITERATURE : A BIENNIAL ANTHOLOGY). 1982/ 1983-. 0749-6885. Periodical. US. English. be. $37.50. Oryx Press, 2214 North Central at Encanto, Phoenix AZ 85004-1483. **Tel** (602)254-6156. Ed Sanford Berman and James P Danky. **LC** Z716.4. **DD** 020.5. **Circ** 600. Articles selected represent major out-of-the-mainstream concerns and viewpoints of 1982/1983, with sources ranging from established periodicals to genuinely "alternative" publications.

AMERICAN DOCUMENTATION. V. 1-20. Periodical. US. English. Journal of Documentary Reproduction, 0097-4250.

AMERICAN INDIAN LIBRARIES NEWSLETTER. Vol. 1, No. 1 (Fall 1976)-. 0193-8207. Periodical. US. English. ty. $7.00. American Library Association, 50 East Huron, Chicago IL 60611. **LC** Z711.8. **DD** 025.5276308997.

AMERICAN LIBRARIES. V. 1- Jan. 1970-. 0002-9769. Periodical. US. English. mo. $40.00. American Library Association, 50 East Huron Street, Chicago IL 60611. **Tel** (312)944-6780. Ed Arthur Plotnik. **Ind/Abst** Mag. Index, Predicasts, Hospit. Lit. Index, Pop. Mag. Rev., Educ. Index, Biogr. Index, Libr. Lit., Public Aff. Inf. Serv. Bull., Read. Guide Period. Lit., Educ. Index, Libr. Inf. Sci. Abstr., Book Rev. Index, Curr. Index J. Educ., Media Rev. Dig., Access, Funk Scott Index Corp. Ind. **LC** Z673.A5. **DD** 020.973. **NLM** Z 673 A508. bk rev. adv acc. **Circ** 45,000. (ctrl). Available on microfilm from University Microfilms International. News, feature articles, commentary on issues, product information, practical advice, monthly calendar of events, and job listings in library and information science. ALA Bulletin, 0364-4006.

AMERICAN LIBRARY DIRECTORY. See Yearbooks, Almanacs, Directories.

AMERICAN LIBRARY DIRECTORY UPDATING SERVICE. See Yearbooks, Almanacs, Directories.

AMERICAN LIBRARY LAWS. 1st- 1930-. US. English. American Library Association, 50 East Huron Street, Chicago IL 60611. **Tel** (312)944-6780.

THE AMERICAN MARITIME LIBRARY. V. 1- 1970-. 0065-9207. Monographic Series. US. English. ir. Harper and Row, Keystone Industrial Park, Scranton PA 18512. **Tel** (717)343-4761.

ANALYSES OF NEW JERSEY PUBLIC LIBRARY STATISTICS FOR . . . . See Statistics.

ANALYSES OF THE ILLINOIS PUBLIC LIBRARY STATISTICS. See Statistics.

ANNALS OF LIBRARY SCIENCE AND DOCUMENTATION. V. 1- March 1954-. 0003-4835. Periodical. English. qt. $20.00. INSDOC, 14 Satsang Vihar Marg, New Delhi 110067 India. **Tel** 26 86 45. **Ind/Abst** Libr. Inf. Sci. Abstr. **LC** Z671. **DD** 020.5. Annals of Library Science.

ANNUAIRE DES BIBLIOTHECAIRES-CONSEILS DU QUEBEC. See Yearbooks, Almanacs, Directories.

ANNUAIRE DES MEMBRES - ASSOCIATION DES BIBLIOTHEQUES DE LA SANTE DU CANADA. See Yearbooks, Almanacs, Directories.

ANNUAIRE DES MEMBRES DE L'ASSOCIATION DES BIBLIOTHECAIRES FRANCAIS. See Yearbooks, Almanacs, Directories.

ANNUAL BRIEF - SASKATCHEWAN LIBRARY ASSOCIATION. (ANNUAL BRIEF). Main/Corp Saskatchewan Library Association. 1980-. 0710-9962. CN. English. an. Saskatchewan Library Association, Box 3388, Regina Saskatchewan S4P 3H1 Canada. **DD** 021.0097124. Annual Brief to the Minister-in-Charge of Libraries, 0705-7806.

ANNUAL CHECKLIST OF PUBLICATIONS OF THE STATE OF ARIZONA. (ANNUAL CHECKLIST OF PUBLICATIONS OF THE STATE OF ARIZONA RECEIVED BY THE LIBRARY, ARCHIVES, AND PUBLIC RECORDS DIVISION DURING THE FISCAL YEAR). Main/Corp Arizona. Division of Library, Archives, and Public Records. VFOAT Checklist of Publications of the State of Arizona. 1972/73-. 0570-9326. US. English. an. Library Archives and Public Records Division, Phoenix AZ 85007. **LC** Z1223.5.A75, J87.A6. **DD** 015.791. Annual Checklist of Publications of the State of Arizona, 0570-9326.

ANNUAL CONFERENCE MINUTES - R.T.S.D. BOARD OF DIRECTORS. (ANNUAL CONFERENCE MINUTES). Main/Corp American Library Association. Resources and Technical Services Division. Board of Directors. 0095-2877. US. English. an. American Library Association, 50 East Huron Street, Chicago IL 60611. **LC** Z673.A526. **DD** 025.0206273.

ANNUAL PROGRAM; LIBRARY SERVICES AND CONSTRUCTION ACT - SOUTH CAROLINA. STATE LIBRARY, COLUMBIA. Main/Corp South Carolina. State Library, Columbia. 1972/73-. 0364-7803. US. English. an. South Carolina State Library, 1500 Senate Street, PO Box 11469, Columbia SC 29201. **LC** Z732.S72. **DD** 021.009757. South

Library and Information Science

Carolina State Plan for the Use of Library Services and Construction Funds.

ANNUAL REPORT. Main/Corp Kansas Library Network. Board. 1981-. US. English. an. State Library of Kansas, 535 Kansas Avenue, Topeka KS 66603. LC Z674.82.K37. DD 021.6509781.

ANNUAL REPORT & DIRECTORY OF OKLAHOMA LIBRARIES. See Yearbooks, Almanacs, Directories.

ANNUAL REPORT - ARIZONA. DEPT. OF LIBRARY, ARCHIVES, AND PUBLIC RECORDS. Main/Corp Arizona. Dept. of Library, Archives & Public Records. US. English. an. LC Z733. DD 353.979100852.

ANNUAL REPORT - BENIN UNIVERSITY. LIBRARY. Main/Corp Benin University. Library. 1970/71-. English. ir. Benin City University Library, Benin City Nigeria. LC Z858.B45. DD 027.76693.

ANNUAL REPORT - BIBLIOGRAPHICAL CENTER FOR RESEARCH. See Bibliographies.

ANNUAL REPORT - BINGHAMTON PUBLIC LIBRARY. Main/Corp Binghamton Public Library. 0270-7225. US. English. an. Binghamton Public Library, 78 Exchange Street, Binghamton NY 13901. LC Z733. DD 027.474776.

ANNUAL REPORT - BIOMEDICAL LIBRARY REVIEW COMMITTEE, NATIONAL LIBRARY OF MEDICINE, NATIONAL INSTITUTES OF HEALTH. Main/Corp United States. National Library of Medicine. Biomedical Library Review Committee. US. English. an. National Library of Medicine, National Institutes of Health, 9000 Rockville Pike, Bethesda MD 20014.

ANNUAL REPORT - BRITISH LIBRARY. Main/Corp British Library. Board. 1st- 1973/74-. UK. English. an. Free to libraries. British Library Board, 2 Sheraton Street, London W1V 4BM England. Tel (01)636-1544. LC Z792. DD 027.542142. Circ 4,000. (ctrl). Facts and figures, new services, chief events, policies of UK National Library.

ANNUAL REPORT - DOCUMENTS EXPEDITING PROJECT. (ANNUAL REPORT). Main/Corp Documents Expediting Project. 0094-6060. US. English. an. Documents Expediting Project, Library of Congress, 10 First Street SE, Washington DC 20540. LC Z689. DD 025.2.

ANNUAL REPORT FOR FISCAL YEAR - VIRGIN ISLANDS BUREAU OF LIBRARIES, MUSEUMS, AND ARCHAEOLOGICAL SERVICES. Main/Corp Virgin Islands Bureau of Libraries, Museums, and Archaeological Services. VI. English. an. Bureau of Libraries Museums and Archaeological Services, PO Box 390, Charlotte Amalie St US Virgin Islands. LC Z753.V57. DD 027.0729722.

ANNUAL REPORT FOR THE YEAR ENDED - MALAWI NATIONAL LIBRARY SERVICE. BOARD. Main/Corp Malawi National Library Service. Board. Periodical. English. an. LC Z858. DD 027.56897. Annual Report.

ANNUAL REPORT - GENERAL LIBRARY BUREAU, STATE LIBRARY OF PENNSYLVANIA. Main/Corp State Library of Pennsylvania. General Library Bureau. 0097-9856. US. English. an. Pennsylvania State Library, General Library Bureau, Harrisburg PA 17126. LC Z733.P3992. DD 027.5748.

ANNUAL REPORT - GHANA LIBRARY BOARD. Main/Corp Ghana. Library Board. 1956/ 57-. 0433-9401. English. ir. LC Z858.G6.

ANNUAL REPORT - GRADUATE DEPARTMENT OF LIBRARY AND INFORMATION SCIENCE, THE CATHOLIC UNIVERSITY OF AMERICA. (ANNUAL REPORT - GRADUATE DEPT. OF LIBRARY AND INFORMATION SCIENCE, THE CATHOLIC UNIVERSITY OF AMERICA). Main/ Corp Catholic University of America. Graduate Dept. of Library and Information Science. 0272-9385. US. English. an. Graduate Department of Library & Information Science, Catholic University of America, Washington DC 20064. LC Z669.C37. DD 020.711753.

ANNUAL REPORT - INDIAN NATIONAL SCIENTIFIC DOCUMENTATION CENTRE. Main/Corp Indian National Scientific Documentation Centre. II. English. an. Free. Indian National Scientific Documentation Centre, Hillside Road, New Delhi 110012 India. LC Z674.5.I52. DD 025.00954.

ANNUAL REPORT - INGLEWOOD PUBLIC LIBRARY. Main/Corp Inglewood Public Library. US. English. an. City of Inglewood Public Library, 101 West Manchester Boulevard, Inglewood CA 90301.

ANNUAL REPORT - JAMAICA LIBRARY ASSOCIATION. Main/Corp Jamaica Library Association. JM. English. an. Jamaica Library Association, PO Box 58, Kingston 5 Jamaica. LC Z673.J18. DD 020.62347292.

ANNUAL REPORT - JOHN CRERAR LIBRARY. Main/Corp John Crerar Library, Chicago. 1976/77-. US. English. an. The John Crerar Library, 35 West 33rd Street, Chicago IL 60616. LC Z733.C52. DD 026.000977311. Crerar, 0091-5890.

ANNUAL REPORT - KANO STATE LIBRARY. Main/Corp Kano State Library. 1971/ 72-. English. ir. Kano State Library, PMB 3094, Kano Nigeria. LC Z858. DD 027.56695.

ANNUAL REPORT - MARYLAND. STATE PUBLICATIONS DEPOSITORY AND DISTRIBUTION PROGRAM. Main/Corp Maryland. State Publications Depository and Distribution Program. 1st (Jan. 1, 1983-June 30, 1983)-. US. English. an. LC Z1223.5.M3, J87.M3. DD 021.6509752.

ANNUAL REPORT - MIDWEST REGION LIBRARY NETWORK. Main/ Corp Midwest Region Library Network. VFOAT MidInet Annual Report. 1976/77-. US. English. an. Midwest Region Library Network, 2420 Nicolet Drive, Green Bay WI 54302.

ANNUAL REPORT - MISSISSIPPI LIBRARY COMMISSION. Main/Corp Mississippi. State Library Commission. 0146-4361. US. English. an. PO Box 10700, Jackson MS 39209-0700. Tel (601)359-1036. Ed Tricia Hollis. LC Z732. DD 021.009762. (ctrl). A report of the Mississippi Library Commission's activities and progress for the fiscal year. Biennial Report.

ANNUAL REPORT - NATAL PROVINCIAL LIBRARY SERVICE AND MUSEUM SERVICES. Main/Corp Natal Provincial Library Service. VFOAT Jaarverslag - Natalse Provinciale Biblioteek en Museumdienste. SA. Afrikaans and English. ir. Natal Provincial Library Services, Pietermaritzburg South Africa. LC Z857.N3. DD 021.009684.

ANNUAL REPORT - NATIONAL LIBRARY OF AUSTRALIA. Main/Corp National Library of Australia. 8th- 1967/68-. AT. English. an. 10.00. National Library of Australia, Canberra Australian Capital Territory 2600 Australia. LC Z871. DD 027.5944. Overview of the range of the library's operations. Annual Report of the Council.

ANNUAL REPORT - NATIONAL MEDICAL LIBRARIES ASSISTANCE ADVISORY BOARD, NATIONAL INSTITUTES OF HEALTH. Main/Corp National Medical Libraries Assistance Advisory Board. US. English. an. National Medical Libraries Assistance Advisory Board, National Institutes of Health 9000 Rockville Pike, Bethesda MD 20014.

ANNUAL REPORT - NEBRASKA LIBRARY COMMISSION. Main/Corp Nebraska Library Commission. 0099-0299. US. English. an. Nebraska Library Commission, 1420 P Street, Lincoln NE 68508. LC Z732.N37. DD 021.009782.

ANNUAL REPORT - NOVA SCOTIA COMMUNICATIONS AND INFORMATION CENTRE. Main/Corp Nova Scotia. Communications and Information Centre. 1972/73-. 0318-5575. Periodical. CN. English. an. Nova Scotia Communications and Information Centre, Hollis Building, Halifax B3J 3C4 Canada. LC P87. DD 026.354716008.

ANNUAL REPORT - OCLC. (ANNUAL REPORT). Main/Corp OCLC. 1977/1978-. 0730-5125. US. English. an. OCLC Inc, 1125 Kinnear Road, Columbus OH 43212. LC Z732.O5. DD 021.650973. Annual Report, 0090-8673.

ANNUAL REPORT OF OHIONET. Main/ Corp Ohionet. 1977/1979-. 0270-0107. US. English. an. Free. Ohionet, 1500 West Lane Avenue, Columbus OH 43221. Tel (614)486-2966. Ed Ronald E Diener. LC Z674.82.O38. DD 021.65. Circ 250. (ctrl). Summary of the previous fiscal year of Ohionet. Includes annual audit, program statement, list of member libraries, advisory council members and copy of the articles of incorporation.

ANNUAL REPORT OF THE BOARD OF THE NATIONAL FREE LIBRARY OF ZIMBABWE FOR THE YEAR ENDED . . . . Main/Corp National Free Library of Zimbabwe. Board. 0068-3612. English. an. Dugald Niven Library, 12th Avenue, Bulawayo Zimbabwe. LC Z858.N347. DD 027.46891.

ANNUAL REPORT OF THE CATALOG DEPARTMENT TO THE UNIVERSITY LIBRARIAN, UNIVERSITY OF CALIFORNIA, BERKELEY. (ANNUAL REPORT OF THE CATALOG DEPARTMENT TO THE UNIVERSITY LIBRARIAN). Main/Corp California. University. Library. Catalog Dept. 0098-7204. US. English. an. University of California/ Catalog Department, 2120 Berkeley Way, Berkeley CA 94720. LC Z733. DD 025.30979467.

ANNUAL REPORT OF THE CENTER FOR RESEARCH LIBRARIES. Main/ Corp Center for Research Libraries. 1st- 1949/50-. 0577-6929. US. English. an. Center for Research Libraries, 6050 South Kenwood Avenue, Chicago IL 60637. Tel (312)955-4545. Ed Sally Brickman. Circ 150.

ANNUAL REPORT OF THE CONNECTICUT STATE LIBRARY. Main/Corp Connecticut State Library. US. English. an. Connecticut State Library, 231 Capitol Avenue, Hartford CT 06115.

ANNUAL REPORT OF THE DEPARTMENT OF PUBLIC LIBRARIES (KARNATAKA, INDIA). Main/Corp Karnataka, India. Dept. of Public Libraries. 1972/73-. 0304-7563. English. ir. LC Z846. DD 354.548700852.

ANNUAL REPORT OF THE GOVERNMENT DOCUMENTS DEPARTMENT - NEW MEXICO STATE LIBRARY. Main/Corp New Mexico State Library. Government Documents Dept. US. English. an. New Mexico State Library, Santa Fe NM 87503. LC Z733.N508. DD 027.578956.

ANNUAL REPORT OF THE LIBRARIAN OF CONGRESS. Main/Corp Library of Congress. 1865/66-. 0083-1565. US. English. an. Superintendent of Documents, US Government Printing Office, Washington DC 20402. LC Z733. DD 027.5753.

ANNUAL REPORT OF THE LIBRARY. MALAWI NATIONAL LIBRARY. (ANNUAL REPORT). Main/Corp Malawi National Library. 1968/69-. 0581-0906. English. ir. Blantyre Government Printer, PO Box 893, Blantyre Malawi. LC Z858. DD 027.56897.

ANNUAL REPORT OF THE LIBRARY SERVICE, MINISTRY OF INFORMATION (NIGERIA). Main/Corp North Central State, Nigeria. Ministry of Information. Library Service. 1974/75-. English. ir. LC Z678.8.N5. DD 021.009669.

ANNUAL REPORT OF THE MALDEN (MASS.) PUBLIC LIBRARY. Main/Corp Malden, Mass. Public Library. VFOAT Annual Reports of the Trustees and Librarian. 0194-116X. US. English. an. Malden Public Library, 36 Salem Street, Malden MA 02148. LC Z733. DD 027.474461.

ANNUAL REPORT OF THE NATIONAL LIBRARIAN (OTTAWA). (ANNUAL REPORT OF THE NATIONAL LIBRARIAN). Main/Corp National Library of Canada. VFOAT Rapport Annuel du Directeur General de la Bibliotheque Nationale. 1971/ 72-. 0315-9949. CN. English (text in French, 1975/76). an. Free. National Library of Canada, Ottawa Ontario K1A 0N4 Canada. Tel (613)996-7400. Ed Wendy Neumann. LC Z736.N37. DD 027.571384. Circ 4,000. Bilingual report of a Canadian federal government department: National Library of Canada. Report of the National Librarian, 0315-9957; Rapport Annuel du Directeur General de la Bibliotheque Nationale, 0315-9965.

ANNUAL REPORT OF THE OHIO LIBRARY ASSOCIATION. Main/Corp Ohio Library Association. US. English. an. Ohio Library Association, 40 South Third Street, Columbus OH 43215. LC Z673.O353. DD 020.6234771.

ANNUAL REPORT OF THE PARLIAMENTARY LIBRARIAN (CANADA). Main/Corp Canada. Library of Parliament. VFOAT Rapport Annuel du Bibliothecaire Parlementaire. Periodical. CN. English (French). an.

Library and Information Science

Library of Parliament, Ottawa Ontario Canada. **DD** 027.65.

ANNUAL REPORT OF THE UNIVERSITY LIBRARIAN FOR VICTORIA UNIVERSITY OF WELLINGTON. Main/Corp Victoria University of Wellington. Library. English. an. **LC** Z871.V53. **DD** 027.793127.

ANNUAL REPORT OF THE UNIVERSITY LIBRARIAN (UNIVERSITY OF QUEENSLAND). Main/Corp University of Queensland. Libraries. English. an. **LC** Z871.Q44. **DD** 027.7943.

ANNUAL REPORT OF THE UNIVERSITY LIBRARIES (STANDFORD UNIVERSITY). Main/Corp Stanford University. Libraries. US. English. an. Stanford University Library, Stanford CA 94305. **LC** Z733. **DD** 027.779473.

ANNUAL REPORT - ONONDAGA COUNTY PUBLIC LIBRARY. (ANNUAL REPORT). Main/Corp Onondaga County Public Library. 0883-3508. US. English. an. Onondaga County Public Library, 335 Montgomery Street, Syracuse NY 12304.

ANNUAL REPORT - PUBLIC LIBRARIES BOARD (UGANDA). Main/Corp Uganda. Public Libraries Board. English. ir. Public Libraries Board, PO Box 7117/38 William Street, Kampala Uganda. **LC** Z678.8.U38. **DD** 027.46761.

ANNUAL REPORT - REGIONAL LIBRARY BUREAU (NORTHERN). Main/Corp Regional Library Bureau (Northern). UK. English. an. **LC** Z791. **DD** 027.042.

ANNUAL REPORT - SOUTH DAKOTA STATE LIBRARY. Main/Corp South Dakota State Library. US. English. an. **LC** Z733.S7293. **DD** 027.5783.

ANNUAL REPORT - SOUTH WESTERN REGIONAL LIBRARY SYSTEM (ENGLAND). Main/Corp South Western Regional Library System (England). 26th (1962-63)-. UK. English. an. South Western Regional Library System, Central Library College, Green Bristol BS1 5TL England. **LC** Z791.S63. **DD** 020.6232423. *Annual Report for the Year Ended 31st March . . . .*

ANNUAL REPORT - SOUTHEASTERN LIBRARY NETWORK. Main/Corp Southeastern Library Network. 0099-085X. US. English. an. 615 Peachtree Street NE/Suite 820, Atlanta GA 30308. **LC** Z732.A13. **DD** 021.650975.

ANNUAL REPORT - SPECIAL LIBRARIES ASSOCIATION. Main/Corp Special Libraries Association. 0191-2593. US. English. an. Special Libraries Association, 1700 18th Street Northwest, Washington DC 20009. **Tel** (202)234-4700. Ed David Malinak. **LC** Z673. **DD** 026.06234747. **Circ** 2,000. (ctrl). Review of Association activity in the past year. Report contains updated membership statistics and reports from SLA leadership, executive director, committees and representatives.

ANNUAL REPORT - TEXAS STATE LIBRARY AND ARCHIVES COMMISSION. Main/Corp Texas State Library and Archives Commission. Began with vol. for 1978/79. US. English. an. **LC** Z675.S7. **DD** 027.5764. *Annual Report.*

ANNUAL REPORT TO THE PRESIDENT - UNIVERSITY OF MINNESOTA LIBRARIES. Main/Corp Minnesota. University. Libraries. Periodical. US. English. an. University of Minnesota, University Libraries, Wilson Library, Minneapolis MN 55455. **LC** Z733. *Report of the University Librarian and Division of Library Instruction.*

ANNUAL REPORT - UNITED STATES. NATIONAL COMMISSION ON LIBRARIES AND INFORMATION SCIENCE. Main/Corp United States. National Commission on Libraries and Information Science. **VFOAT** Library and Information Services in a Learning Society. 1980-81-. 0091-2972. US. English. an. Superintendent of Documents, US Government Printing Office, Washington DC 20204. *Annual Report to the President and the Congress.*

ANNUAL REPORT - WAYNE STATE UNIVERSITY, UNIVERSITY LIBRARIES. Main/Corp Wayne State University, Detroit. University Libraries. US. English. an. Wayne State University, University Libraries, Detroit MI 48202. **LC** Z733.D5. **DD** 027.777434. *Report.*

ANNUAL REPORT - WEST VIRGINIA LIBRARY COMMISSION. Main/Corp West Virginia Library Commission. US. English. an. *Report.*

ANNUAL REPORT - WESTERN AUSTRALIA. SUPREME COURT. LAW LIBRARY. Main/Corp Western Australia. Supreme Court. Law Library. English. an. **LC** Z871.W53. **DD** 026.349941.

ANNUAL REPORT - WESTERN STATE LIBRARY. Main/Corp Western State Library. 0302-4873. English. an. PMB 5082, Ibadan Nigeria. **LC** Z858.W47. **DD** 027.56692.

ANNUAL REVIEW OF INFORMATION SCIENCE AND TECHNOLOGY. V. 1- 1966-. 0066-4200. US. English. an. Knowledge Industry Publishing Company, 701 Westchester Avenue, Plains NY 10604. **Tel** (914)328-9157. **Ind/Abst** Comput. Control Abstr., Electr. Electron. Abstr., Sci. Abstr. Sect. A. Phys. Abstr., Chem. Abstr., Soc. Sci. Citation Index, Phys. Abstr. **LC** Z699.A1. **DD** 029.708. **NLM** Z 699.A1 A625. **CODEN** ARISBC. Each issue contains an index to its own contents - no volume index-loose. (cum index).

ANNUAL STATISTICAL BULLETIN - WASHINGTON STATE LIBRARY. *See* Statistics.

ANNUAL STATISTICS OF MEDICAL SCHOOL LIBRARIES IN THE UNITED STATES AND CANADA. *See* Statistics.

ANUARIO DE BIBLIOTECOLOGIA, ARCHIVOLOGIA E INFORMATICA. *See* Yearbooks, Almanacs, Directories.

APLA BULLETIN. Main/Corp Atlantic Provinces Library Association. **VAT** Atlantic Provinces Library Association Bulletin. V. 1- June 1936-. 0001-2203. Periodical. CN. English. bm. $15.00. Atlantic Provinces Library Association, Dalhousie University, Halifax Nova Scotia Canada. **Tel** (709)772-2468. Ed Joy Tillotson. **LC** Z673.A877. **DD** 020.623. (cum index). bk rev. adv acc. **Circ** 500. Articles and news of interest to Atlantic region library workers and trustees.

APLIC BULLETIN. VFOAT Bulletin ABPAC. **VAT** Association of Parliamentary Librarians in Canada Bulletin, Bulletin Association des Bibliothecaires Parlementaires au Canada. No. 1 (Sept. 1983)-. 0825-186X. Periodical. CN. English (French). sa. Free to member and other libraries on request. Association of Parliamentary Librarians in Canada, c/o President of Ontario Legislative Library, Legislative Building, Queen's Park, Toronto Ontario M7A 1A2 Canada. **DD** 027.506071.

APLIC SPECIAL PUBLICATION. (A.P.L.I.C. SPECIAL PUBLICATION). Main/Corp Association for Population/Family Planning Libraries and Information Centers, International. No. 1-. 0883-7376. Monographic Series. US. English. Association for Population/Family Planning, Libraries and Information Centers International, 165 South Second Street, Clarion PA. **Ind/Abst** Popul. Index. **DD** 026.

ARBEITEN AUS DEN BIBLIOTHEKEN DER BERGAKADEMIE FREIBERG/DDR UND DER TECHNISCHEN UNIVERSITAT MISKOLC/VR UNGARN. Main/Corp Freiberg, Ger. Bergakademie. Bibliothek. V. 1- 1976-. German. ir. **LC** Z671.

ARBEITSBERICHT - ARBEITSSTELLE FUR DAS BIBLIOTHEKSWESEN. Main/Corp Deutscher Bibliotheksverband (German : West). Arbeitsstelle fur das Bibliothekswesen. Series/Titl Bibliotheksdienst. Beiheft. GW. German. ir. Deutscher Bibliotheksverband, Arbeitsstelle fur das Bibliothekswesen Fehrbelliner Platz 3, 1 Berlin 31 West Germany. **LC** Z674, Z673.A1. **DD** 020.5 S, 020.5.

ARBEITSBERICHT - ZENTRALSTELLE FUR MASCHINELLE DOKUMENTATION. Main/Corp Zentralstelle fur Maschinelle Dokumentation. GW. German. ir. Zentralstelle fur Maschinelle Dokumentation, D-6000 Frankfurt, Am Main 71 Herriotstrasse 5, Postfach 71 03 70, Frankfurt West Germany. **LC** Z699.A1.

ARBOK - LANDSBOKASAFN ISLANDS. *See* Yearbooks, Almanacs, Directories.

ARCHIVES ET BIBLIOTHEQUES DE BELGIQUE. *See* Genealogy and Heraldry - Archives.

ARCHIVO DE ABIESI. *See* Genealogy and Heraldry - Archives.

ARGUS JOURNAL. First issue in August 1975. 0317-6452. Periodical. CN. French (text also in English). ir. Free. Corporation des Bibliothecaires/Professionels du Quebec, 360 rue le Moyne, Montreal Quebec H2Y 1Y3 Canada. **DD** 020.6234714.

ARGUS (MONTREAL, QUEBEC : 1971). (ARGUS). Began with Nov.-Dec. 1971 issue. 0315-9930. Periodical. CN. in French. bm. $20.00. Secretariat de la Corporation des Bibliothecaires Professionnels du Quebec, 360 rue la Moyne, Montreal Quebec H2Y 1Y3 Canada. **Ind/Abst** Libr. Inf. Sci. Abstr., Libr. Lit. **LC** Z673.C9533. **DD** 020.971. *Bulletin de Nouvelles.*

ARKANSAS DOCUMENTS. *See* Bibliographies.

ARKANSAS LIBRARIES. Ser. 2, V. 1- June 1944-. 0004-184X. Periodical. US. English. qt. Arkansas Library Association, PO Box 2275, Little Rock AR 72203. **Tel** (501)372-1424. Ed Bob Razer. **Ind/Abst** Libr. Lit., Writ. Am. Hist. **LC** Z732. **DD** 027.0767. bk rev. adv acc. Any aspect of libraries or librarianship in Arkansas and other articles and material of interest to Arkansas librarians. *Arkansas Libraries.*

ARL STATISTICS. *See* Statistics.

ARQUIVO COIMBRAO (BOLETIM DA BIBLIOTECA MUNICIPAL). Main/Corp Coimbra. Biblioteca Municipal. V. 1- July 1923-. Periodical. Portuguese. ir. **LC** Z946. **DD** 027.44698.

ART DOCUMENTATION. (ART DOCUMENTATION : BULLETIN OF THE ART LIBRARIES SOCIETY OF NORTH AMERICA). Vol. 1, No. 1 (Feb. 1982)-. 0730-7187. Periodical. US. English. qt. $35.00. Arlis/Na, 3775 Bear Creek Circle, Tuscon AZ 85749. **Tel** (602)749-9112. **Ind/Abst** Libr. Inf. Sci. Abstr. **LC** Z5937, Z674.2. **DD** 026.7. bk rev. adv acc. **Circ** 1,200. Includes articles and information relevant to art librarianship and visual resources curatorship, and art libraries society news. *Arlis/Na Newsletter, 0090-3515.*

ART LIBRARIES JOURNAL. V. 1- Spring 1976-. 0307-4722. Periodical. UK. English. qt. $15.33. ARLIS/Art Libraries Society, Trent Polytechnic Library, Dryden Street, Nottingham NG1 4FZ England. **Tel** (01)882-0910. Ed Beth Houghton. **Ind/Abst** Avery Index Archit. Period. Second Ed. Revis. Enlarged Suppl., Libr. Inf. Sci. Abstr., Libr. Lit., Repert. Int. Litt. Art. **LC** Z675.A85. **DD** 026.7. bk rev. adv acc. **Circ** 600. Concerned with the documentation, bibliography and librarianship of art and design throughout the world. *ARLIS Newsletter.*

ARTISTS IN CANADA, FILES IN THE NATIONAL GALLERY LIBRARY. VFOAT Artistes au Canada, Dossiers a la Bibliotheque de la Galerie Nationale. Began with the Vol. for 1975. 0705-7342. CN. English (text in French). an. **LC** Z699.5.A75. **DD** 025.0670922. *Check List of Canadian Artists' Files in the Library, 0706-8263.*

ASGL NEWSLETTER. VAT Association of Saskatchewan Government Libraries Newsletter. Vol. 1, No. 1 (Mar. 1978)-. 0228-930X. Periodical. CN. English. ir. Free. Association of Saskatchewan Government Libraries, 352 Winnipeg Street, Regina Saskatchewan S4P 3V7 Canada. **DD** 027.57124. *ASGL News, 0228-9318.*

ASIA SELECT RECENT ACQUISITIONS. Main/Corp Michigan State University. 0147-0620. US. Multilingual. qt. Free. Michigan State University Libraries, International Library, East Lansing MI 48824.

ASIS HANDBOOK & DIRECTORY. *See* Yearbooks, Almanacs, Directories.

ASLIB BOOK-LIST. V. 1- Oct. 1935-. 0001-2521. Periodical. UK. English. mo. 25.-. ASLIB The Association for Information Management, Information House/26-27 Boswell Street, London WC1N 3J2 England. **Tel** (01)430-2671. Ed Ann Kerridge. **Ind/Abst** Ref. Source. **LC** Z7403. **DD** 016.5. (cum index). bk rev. adv acc. **Circ** 2,500. (ctrl). News of events in the library and information fields, including details of ASLIB's activities (conferences, courses, publications and 12 special interest groups).

ASSISTANT LIBRARIAN. V. 68- Jan. 1975-. 0004-5152. Periodical. UK. English. mo. $25.00. Association of Assistant Librarians, Tim Phillips/The Library, Kiddermirster F E College, Hoo Road, Kiddermirster DY1D 1LX England. **Tel** 0562 66311. Ed Debbie Shorley. **Ind/Abst** Libr. Inf. Sci. Abstr., Ref. Source, Libr. Lit. bk rev. adv acc. **Circ** 1,300. (ctrl). Librarianship, information science and literary subjects of interest to go-ahead professionals. A.A.L.

Library and Information Science

is the 'Ginger' group of the library association (British). AL.

ASTIS CURRENT AWARENESS BULLETIN. See Indexes/Abstracts.

AT A GLANCE. V. 1- Aug. 1978-. 0708-0263. Periodical. CN. English. bm. Free. Vice-Chairperson Edmonton Chapter CASLIS, 82 Fairway Drive, Edmonton Alberta T6J 2C5 Canada. **DD** 026.000971233. (ctrl)

AT THE LIBRARY. V. 1- Mar. 1977-. 0702-7559. Periodical. CN. English. mo. Free. Regina Public Library, 2311 Twelfth Avenue, Regina Saskatchewan S4P 0N3 Canada. **Tel** (306)569-7595. Ed Anne Campbell. **DD** 027.471244. bk rev. **Circ** 10,000. (ctrl) Lists library programs and services available throughout a system of eight branch libraries and two booktrailers.

ATLA BIBLIOGRAPHY SERIES. See Bibliographies.

ATLA MONOGRAPH SERIES. Main/Corp American Theological Library Association. No. 1- 1972-). Monographic Series. US. English. ir. Scarecrow Press Inc, PO Box 656, Metuchen NJ 08840.

ATLANTIC PROVINCES CHECKLIST. V. 1- 1957-. 0571-7817. CN. English. an. $10.00. Atlantic Provinces Library Association, Ralph Pickard Bell Library, Sackville New Brunswick E0A 3C0 Canada. **DD** 016.9715.

ATULU. (L'ATULU). V. 1- Feb. 1979-. 0226-3688. Periodical. CN. French. mo. Free. Bibliotheque de Quebec, 37 rue Ste-Angele, Quebec G1R 4G5 Canada. **DD** 028.105. (ctrl)

AUDIO-FILE. VFOAT Fichier Central. CN. English (June 1983)-. 0823-7859. Periodical. CN. English (French with French text on inverted pages). ir. Limited Free Distribution. Audio-File, Canadian Independent Record Production Association, 144 Front Street West/Suite 330, Toronto Ontario M5J 2L7 Canada. **DD** 025.067899120971.

AUDIOVISUAL LIBRARIAN. (THE AUDIOVISUAL LIBRARIAN). 0302-3451. UK. English. qt. $49.00. Library Association Publishing Ltd, 17 Summerhouse Road, London N16 0NA England. Ed Helen Harrison. **Ind/Abst** Cumul. Index Nurs. Allied Health Lit., Libr. Inf. Sci. Abstr., Ref. Source, Libr. Lit. LC Z717. **DD** 025.17705. bk rev. adv acc. **Circ** 4,000. This official journal of the ASLIB and (UK) Library Association. Covers news, issues and events in the AV world.

AURORA. (THE AURORA : NORTHERN LIGHTS LIBRARY CO-OPERATIVE NEWSLETTER). Vol. 1, No. 1 (Aug. 1982)-. 0714-7058. Periodical. CN. English. bm. Northern Lights Library Co-Operative, Box 2070, Grand Centre Alta T0A 1T0 Canada. **DD** 027.471233.

AUSTRALASIAN COLLEGE LIBRARIES. Vol. 1, No. 1 (May 1983)-. 0811-112X. Periodical. English. qt. 28.00. Australasian College Librarians, Sacae Library Holbrooks Road, Underdale SA 5032 Australia. **Tel** (08)352-0011. Ed A L Bundy. **Ind/Abst** Libr. Inf. Sci. Abstr. bk rev. adv acc. **Circ** 450. (ctrl). Articles, reviews, current awareness on developments in libraries and library schools in post secondary colleges in Australia, New Zealand and southwest Pacific.

AUSTRALIAN ACADEMIC AND RESEARCH LIBRARIES. VFOAT AARL. V. 1- Autumn 1970-. 0004-8623. Periodical. AT. English. qt. 20.00. La Trobe University Library, Bundoora Victoria 3083 Australia. **Tel** 478 3122. Ed J I Horacek. **Ind/Abst** Ref. Source, Inf. Sci. Abstr., Libr. Inf. Sci. Abstr., Libr. Lit., APAIS, Aust. Public Aff. Inf. Serv. LC Z675.U5. **DD** 027.70994. bk rev. adv acc. **Circ** 1,050. Articles dealing with librarianship in academic (mainly university and tertiary college) libraries in Australia. Comprehensive statistic information is published in a supplement.

AUSTRALIAN LIBRARY JOURNAL. (THE AUSTRALIAN LIBRARY JOURNAL). V. 1-. 0004-9670. Periodical. AT. English. ir. Library Association of Australia, 376 Jones Street, Ultimo New South Wales 2007 Australia. **Ind/Abst** Libr. Inf. Sci. Abstr., Ref. Source, APAIS, Aust. Public Aff. Inf. Serv., Libr. Lit. LC Z671. **DD** 020.5. (cum index). Available on microfilm from University Microfilms International.

AUSTRALIAN SCHOOL LIBRARIAN. 1964. 0005-0199. Periodical. AT. English. qt. $23.61. Box 280, East Melbourne 3002 Australia. **Tel** 03 725 2492. Ed Berres Colville. School Library Journal.

AUSTRALIAN SPECIAL LIBRARIES NEWS. Began with July 1967 issue. 0005-027X. Periodical. AT. English. ir. $10.00. Special Libraries Section, Library Association of Australia, PO Box 90 2121, Epping Australia. **Ind/Abst** APAIS, Aust. Public Aff. Inf. Serv., Libr. Inf. Sci. Abstr. LC Z675.A2. **DD** 026.000994.

AUTOMATIC DOCUMENTATION AND MATHEMATICAL LINGUISTICS. V. 1- Spring 1967-. 0005-1055. Periodical. US. English (Russian). bm. Allerton Press Inc., 150 Fifth Avenue, New York, NY 10011. **Tel** (212)924-3950. **Ind/Abst** Math. Rev., MLA Int. Bibliogr. Books Artic. Mod. Lang. Lit., Comput. Rev. LC Z699.A1. **DD** 025. **NLM** Z 699.A1 A939. **CODEN** ADMLAE.

AUTOMATION IN LIBRARIES. Main/Corp C.A.C.U.L Workshop On Library Automation. V. 1- 1967-. CN. English. an. Canadian Library Association, 151 Sparks Street, Ottawa Ont K1P 5E3 Canada.

AXIS. Mar. 1974-. 0381-6796. Periodical. CN. English. ir. Waterloo Regional Library, Marsland Centre 7th Floor 20 Erb Street West, Waterloo Ontario N2L 1T2 Canada. **DD** 027.471344.

AXIS. V. 1- Aug. 1976-. 0192-8007. Periodical. US. English. ir. $15.00. Metropolitan Washington Council of Government, 1875 Eye Street NW/Suite 200, Washington DC 20006. **Tel** (212)223-6800.

B P L BEEP. (THE B P L BEEP). Main/Corp Barrie Public Library. V. 1, No. 3- June/July 1974-. 0701-094X. Periodical. CN. English. bm. Barrie Public Library, Barrie Ontario Canada. **DD** 027.471317. Take One, 0701-0958.

BACA. VFOAT Read. V. 1- 1974-. 0125-9008. Periodical. IO. English or Indonesian. bm. $5.00. Pusat Dokumentaso Olmial Natl, PO Box 3065/JKT, Djakarta Indonesia. **Ind/Abst** Libr. Inf. Sci. Abstr. LC Z671.

BARN OCH KULTUR. V. 16- 1970-. 0037-6477. Periodical. SW. Swedish. bm. Bibliotekstjanst AB, Box 1706, S-221 01 Lund Sweden. **Ind/Abst** Libr. Inf. Sci. Abstr. Skolbiblioteket.

BASIC STATE PLAN AND ANNUAL PROGRAM. Main/Corp Alabama Public Library Service. 0095-361X. US. English. an. 155 Administrative Building, Montgomery AL 36104. LC Z732.A2. **DD** 027.4761.

BASIS NEWS. No. 2 (Mar./Apr. 1983)-. 0715-9765. Periodical. CN. English. bm. Information Management Group Infomart, 164 Merton Street, Toronto Ontario M4S 3A8 Canada. **DD** 025.04. Basisnews, 0715-9765.

BAY STATE LIBRARIAN. Began with Vol. 46 (Jan. 1956). 0005-6944. Periodical. US. English. ty. $15.00. Massachusetts Library Association, 432 Great Road, Acton MA 01720. **Tel** (617)263-5144. **Ind/Abst** Libr. Lit. LC Z673.M4. **DD** 020.623. Available on microfilm from University Microfilms, V. 59-. Massachusetts Library Association Bulletin, 0275-8784.

BBA LIBRARY BIOCHIMICA ET BIOPHYSICA ACTA LIBRARY. VFOAT Biochimica et Biophysica Acta Library. V. 1- 1963-. Periodical. US. English. ir. Elsevier Science Publ Co Inc, PO Box 1663 Grand Central Station, New York NY 10163.

BBL, BIBLIOTEKSBLADET. VFOAT Biblioteksbladet. V. 55-. 0006-1867. Periodical. SW. Swedish. mo. $34.60. Swedish Library Association, Box 1706, 221 01 Lund Sweden. **Tel** 046 140480. Ed Barbro Blomberg. **Ind/Abst** Libr. Inf. Sci. Abstr., Libr. Lit. bk rev. adv acc. **Circ** 5,400. (ctrl) Reflects the Swedish library world. BBL.

BCSLA BIBLIOGRAPHIES. (B C S L A BIBLIOGRAPHIES). Main/Corp British Columbia School Librarians' Association. VAT British Columbia School Librarians' Association Bibliographies. No. 1- May 1978-. 0709-4442. Periodical. CN. English. British Columbia School Librarians' Association, 105-2235 Burrard Street, Vancouver BC V6J 3H9 Canada. **DD** 028.52.

BEHAVIORAL & SOCIAL SCIENCES LIBRARIAN. VAT Behavioral and Social Sciences Librarian. V. 1- Fall 1979-. 0163-9269. Periodical. US. English. qt. $60.00. Haworth Press, 28 East 22nd Street, New York NY 10010. **Tel** (212)228-2800. Ed Ellen Gilbert. **Ind/Abst** Excerpta Med., Cumul. Index Nurs. Allied Health Lit., Libr. Inf. Sci. Abstr., Ref. Source, Public Aff. Inf. Serv. Bull., Curr. Index J. Educ., Libr. Lit., Soc. Sci. Citation Index, Electr. Electron. Abstr., Phys. Abstr., Comput. Control Abstr., Cumul. Index Nurs. Allied Health Lit., Sci. Abstr. Sect. A. Phys. Abstr. LC Z675.S6. **DD** 026.3005. **NLM** Z 675.S6 B419. **CODEN** BSSLDR. bk rev. adv acc. **Circ** 628. The journal proudly presents the latest research - from retrospective examinations to contemporary innovations - by leading librarians in this field.

BENDEL LIBRARY JOURNAL. Vol. 1, No. 1 (June 1978)-. 0331-555X. Periodical. English. sa. 2.65 US & Canada. Bendel State Library, PMB 1127, Benin City Nigeria. **Ind/Abst** Libr. Inf. Sci. Abstr. LC Z857.N5. **DD** 027.0669.

THE BENTLEY LIBRARY ANNUAL. Main/Corp Bentley Historical Library. VFOAT Annual Report of the Bentley Historical Library, Michigan Historical Collections. 0362-6881. US. English. an. University of Michigan, 115 Johnston Hall, Ann Arbor MI 48109. LC Z733.B476. **DD** 026.77435.

BERETNING - BIBLIOTEKSTILSYNET. Main/Corp Denmark. Bibliotekstilsynet. 1973/74-. Danish. ir. Bibliotekstilsynet, Neils Jeuls Gade 5, 1059 Kbenhavn K Denmark. LC Z823.A1.

BERETNING FOR UNDERVISNINGSARET . . . . Main/Corp Danmarks Biblioteksskole. 0107-9700. DK. Danish. an. Danmarks Biblioteksskole, Birketinget 6, 2300 Kbenhavn S Denmark. LC Z669.5.D4.

BERITA PERPUSTAKAAN. Periodical. IO. Indonesian. ir. Jalan Medan Merdeka Selatan 11, Jakarta Indonesia. LC Z671.

BERITA PUSTAKAWAN. V. 1- Oct. 1973-. IO. Indonesian. ir. Ikatan Pustakawan Indonesia, Merdeka Selatan No 11, Jakarta Indonesia. LC Z673.I28.

BERLINER SIGELVERZEICHNIS MIT SYSTEMATISCHEM VERZEICHNIS DER SAMMELGEBIETE WISSENSCHAFTLICHER LITERATUR IN BERLIN (WEST). GW. German. ir. Garystr 39, 1000 Berlin 33 West Germany. LC Z81.B4. Berliner Sigelverzeichnis.

BETRIEBSSTATISTIK - VEREIN DEUTSCHER BIBLIOTHEKARE. Main/Corp Verein Deutscher Bibliothekare. German. ir. Verlag und Vertrieb: Deutscher Bibliotheksverband Publikationsabteilung, 1 Berlin 31, Fehrbelliner Platz 3, Berlin West Berlin Germany. LC Z801.A1. **DD** 021.00943.

BIBLIA. JA. English. sa. Tenri Central Library, Tenri University, Tenri Nara Japan.

BIBLIO. See Bibliographies.

BIBLIOGRAFI OVER EUROPISKE KUNSTNERES EXLIBRIS. See Bibliographies.

BIBLIOGRAPHIC GUIDE - UNIVERSITY OF LANCASTER LIBRARY. See Bibliographies.

BIBLIOGRAPHIE SPECIALE ANALYTIQUE. See Bibliographies.

BIBLIOTECA DEGLI HISTORIAE MUSICAE CULTORES. 1- 1952-. 0073-2516. Periodical. IT. Italian. ir. Casa Editrice Leo S Olschki, Casella Postale PO Box 66, Firenze Italy.

BIBLIOTECA DI ANTICHITA CIPRIOTE. 1-. Monographic Series. IT. French and Italian. ir. Edizioni Dell Ateno, Casella Postal 7216, 00100 Rome Italy.

BIBLIOTECA DI CULTURA ORGANARIA E ORGANISTICA. V. 1- 1968-). Periodical. IT. Italian. ir. Patron Liberaia Internazionale, 24 V Zamboni, Bologna Italy.

BIBLIOTECA DI STORIA TOSCANA MODERNA E CONTEMPORANEA. STUDI E DOCUMENTI. 1-. Monographic Series. IT. Italian. ir. Casa Editrice Leo S Olschki, Casella Postale PO Box 66, 50100 Firenze Italy.

BIBLIOTECA DI STUDI AMERICANI. 1- 1954-. 0519-6396. Monographic Series. IT. Italian. ir. Edizioni di Storia e Letteratura, Via Lancellotti 18, Rome Italy.

BIBLIOTECA NAPOLETANA. Periodical. IT. Italian. ir. Libreria Scientifica Editrice, Corso Umberto 1 38 40, Naples Italy.

BIBLIOTECA PUBLICA INFORMATIVO. VFOAT BP Informativo. V. 1- (No. 1-). Periodical. BL. Portuguese. ir. Avenida Sao Luis 281, Sao Paulo SP Brazil.

Library and Information Science

BIBLIOTECA STORICA TOSCANA : SEZIONE DI STORIA DEL RISORGIMENTO. 1-. Monographic Series. IT. Italian. ir. Casa Editrice Leo S Olschki, Casella Postale PO Box 66, 50100 Firenze Italy.

BIBLIOTECAS Y ARCHIVOS. No. 1- 1967-. 0006-1743. MX. Spanish. ir. Escuela Nacional Biblioteconia, Viaducto Miguel Aleman 155, Mexico 13 DF Mexico. LC Z739.A1.

BIBLIOTECHNOE DELO I BIBLIOGRAFIA V SSSR : BIBLIOGRAFICHESKAIA INFORMATSIIA. 1984, Vol. 1-. 0208-1997. Periodical. UR. Russian. mo. LC Z666. *Bibliotekovedenie I Bibliografovedenie V SSSR.*

BIBLIOTECOLOGIA Y DOCUMENTACION (ASOCIACION DE BIBLIOTECARIOS GRADUADOS DE LA REPUBLICA ARGENTINA). (BIBLIOTECOLOGIA Y DOCUMENTACION). V. 1, No. 1 (Jan.-June 1979)-. 0325-6251. Periodical. AG. Spanish. sa. Casilla de Correo 68, Sucursal 1, Buenos Aires Argentina. Ind/Abst Libr. Inf. Sci. Abstr. LC Z671. DD 020.5.

BIBLIOTEKA KOMSOMOLSKOI PRAVDY. 1957-. Periodical. UR. Russian. mo. $10.00. Victor Kamkin Inc (70051), 12224 Parklawn Drive, Rockville MD 20852. Tel (301)881-5973. Ed T Kurella.

BIBLIOTEKA UZBEKISTANA. Began in 1976. Periodical. UR. Russian (Uzbek). 0.25. LC Z819.U93.

BIBLIOTEKAR. V. 1- 1954-. Periodical. Bulgarian. ir. Ind/Abst Libr. Inf. Sci. Abstr. LC Z671.

BIBLIOTEKAR. V.1- 1948/49-. 0006-1816. Periodical. YU. Serbo-Croatian -R. bm. Narodna Biblioteka, Knes Michailova 56, Belgrade Yugoslavia. Ind/Abst Libr. Inf. Sci. Abstr. LC Z671. (cum index).

BIBLIOTEKAR. 0006-1808. Periodical. Russian. mo. $15.50. Victor Kamkin Inc (70080), 12224 Parklawn Drive, Rockville MD 20852. Tel (301)881-5973. Ind/Abst Libr. Inf. Sci. Abstr., Libr. Lit. *Krasnyi Bibliotekar.*

BIBLIOTEKARZ. 0208-4333. Periodical. PL. Polish. bm. ARS Polona, Krakowskie Przedmiescie 7, 00-068 Warsaw Poland. Ind/Abst Libr. Inf. Sci. Abstr., Libr. Lit. LC Z671.

BIBLIOTEKETS FORTEGNELSE OVER NYERHVERVELSER. Main/Corp Commission of the European Communities. Library (Brussels, Belgium). VFOAT Verzeichnis der Neuerwerbungen der Bibliothek, List of Additions to the Library. V. 23, 1 (Jan. 1981)-. Danish (Multilingual). mo. European Community Information Service, 2100 M Street NW/Suite 707, Washington DC 20037. LC Z935.B94. DD 017.509493.

BIBLIOTEKOVEDENIE I BIBLIOGRAFIJA ZA RUBEZOM. (BIBLIOTEKOVEDENIE I BIBLIOGRAFIIA ZA RUBEZHOM). Vol. 1- 1958-. 0320-7838. Periodical. UR. Russian. mo $18.60. Victor Kamkin Inc, 12224 Parklawn Drive, Rockville MD 20852. Tel (301)881-5973. Ind/Abst Libr. Inf. Sci. Abstr. LC Z671. NLM Z 671 B581. (cum index).

BIBLIOTEKOVEDENIE I BIBLIOGRAFOVEDENIE : INOSTRANNAIA LITERATURA. VFOAT Inostrannaia Literatura. 1978-. Periodical. UR. Russian (Multilingual). mo. 0.25 Per Issue. Informatsionnyi Tsentr Po Problemam Kultury I Iskisstva, 101000 Moskva Tsentr, Prospekt Kalinina 3 Gosudarstvennaia, Biblioteka SSSR Imeni V I Lenina, Moskva Russian SFSR. LC Z666.

BIBLIOTEKOVEDENIE I BIBLIOGRAFOVEDENIE V SSSR. See Bibliographies.

BIBLIOTEKOZNAWSTWO. Main/Corp Breslau. Uniwersytet. 1- 1955-. 0524-4471. Periodical. Polish (summaries in French or Russian). ir. LC Z671.

BIBLIOTEKSVEJVISER. 1970-. Danish. ir. Bibliotekscentralen, Trekronegade 15 2500 Valby, Kbenhavn Denmark. LC Z823.A1.

BIBLIOTEKU ZINATNES ASPEKTI. See Bibliographies.

BIBLIOTHECA AEGYPTIA. Vol. 1- 0732-6467. Monographic Series. US. English. ir. Undena Publications, POB 97, Malibu CA 90265.

BIBLIOTHECA AMERICANA (CORAL GABLES, FLA.). (BIBLIOTHECA AMERICANA). Vol. 1, No. 1 (Sept. 1982)-. 0734-1865. Periodical. US. English (Spanish). ir. $60.00. Bibliotheca Americana, PO Box 24-1048, University of Miami State, Coral Gables FL 33124. Tel (305)442-0364. LC E11. DD 970.005.

BIBLIOTHECA GERMANICA. 0067-7477. Monographic Series. SZ. German. ir. Francke Verlag, Neuengasse 43, Postfach 1445, CH-3001 Bern Switzerland. Tel 031/22 17 15.

BIBLIOTHECA HUMANISTICA ET REFORMATORICA. 1- 1971-. Monographic Series. NE. Multilingual. ir. De Graff Publishers, POB 6 Zuideinde 40, Nieuwkoop Netherlands.

BIBLIOTHECA MEDICA CANADIANA. V. 1- Jan. 1979-. 0707-3674. Periodical. CN. English (text also in French). bm. P J Fawcett Medical Library, University of Manitoba, 770 Bannatyne Avenue, Winnipeg Manitoba R3E 0W3 Canada. Ind/Abst Libr. Inf. Sci. Abstr. DD 026.61. *CHLA/ABSC Newsletter,* 0700-5474.

BIBLIOTHECA ROMANICA (BERNE), SERIES PRIMA : MANUALIA ET COMMENTATIONES. Monographic Series. SZ. Multilingual (French, German, and Italian). ir. Francke Verlag, Neuengasse 43 Postfach 1445, CH-3001 Bern Switzerland. Tel 031/22 17 15.

BIBLIOTHEEK EN SAMENLEVING. Yearly V. 1- Feb. 1973-. Periodical. NE. Dutch. 47.40. Nederlands Bibliotheek en Lektuurcentrum, Postbus 2054, 'S-Gravenhage The Netherlands. Tel 070-264351. Ed Frans J Stein. Ind/Abst Libr. Inf. Sci. Abstr. LC Z671. bk rev. adv acc. Circ 5,200. (ctrl). Informative, speculative and critical articles on public library work and its role in society. *Mens en Boek, Openbare Bibliotheek.*

BIBLIOTHEEKGIDS. (DE BIBLIOTHEEKGIDS). Volume 1-. 0006-1956. Periodical. BE. Dutch. qt. Bibliotheek Van Limburg, Begijnhof Zuivelmarket, 3500 Hasselt Belgium. Ind/Abst Libr. Inf. Sci. Abstr., Libr. Lit. LC Z671. DD 020.5.

BIBLIOTHEK. (BIBLIOTHEK FORSCHUNG UND PRAXIS). Began in 1977. 0341-4183. Periodical. GW. German. ty. K G Saur Verlag, Postfach 711009/ Possenbacherst 2B, D8000 Muenchen 71 West Germany. Tel (089) 798901. Ind/Abst Libr. Inf. Sci. Abstr., Libr. Lit. LC Z671. DD 020.5.

BIBLIOTHEK DES BUCHWESENS. V. 1- 1972-. Periodical. GW. German. ir. $50.00. Anton Hiersemann Verlag, Rosenbergstrasse 113 PF 723, D-7000 Stuttgart 1 West Germany. Tel (711)658264. adv acc. Circ 1,000.

BIBLIOTHEKAR. (DER BIBLIOTHEKAR). Began with: 4. Yearly Vol. 1 (Jan. 1950). 0006-1964. Periodical. GE. German. mo. 51.-. Deutscher Buch Export-Import, Leninstrasse 16, DDR-701 Leipzig East Germany. Tel Leipzig 7801. Ind/Abst Libr. Inf. Sci. Abstr., Libr. Lit. LC Z671. bk rev. adv acc. Circ 12,000. Deals with current questions and problems in theory and practice of library and information science. Also contains literary contributions, short biographies of authors, bibliography and events. *Volksbibliothekar, Buchbesprechung.*

BIBLIOTHEKS-FORUM BAYERN. (BIBLIOTHEKSFORUM BAYERN). Yearly V. 1- 1973-. 0340-000X. GW. German. ir. K G Saur Verlag, Postfach 711009, Possenbacherstr 2B, D8000 Muenchen 71 West Germany. Tel (089)79-89-01. Ind/Abst Libr. Inf. Sci. Abstr. LC Z801.B3. DD 021.009433.

BIBLIOTHEKSDIENST. Began with: Apr. 1967. 0006-1972. Periodical. WB. German. mo. 42.00. Deutsches Bibliotheksinstitut, Bundesalle 184/185, D1 Berlin 31 West Germany. Tel (030)85050. Ed Helmut Rosner, Peter Borchardt and Werner Beck. Ind/Abst Libr. Inf. Sci. Abstr. LC Z801.A1. bk rev. adv acc. Circ 2,200. Articles and short information on German librarianship. *Buchereidienst,* 0340-2231.

BIBLIOTHEQUE DE LA PLEIADE. No. 1-. Monographic Series. French. ir.

BIBLIOTHEQUE DES ARCHIVES DE PHILOSOPHIE. 0523-5057. Monographic Series. FR. French. ir. Beauchesne Editeur, 72 rue des Saints Peres, 75007 Paris France.

BIBLIOTHEQUE DES ECOLES FRANCAISES D'ATHENES ET DE ROME. Issue 1-. Newspaper. French. ir. Diffusion de Boccard, 11 rue de Medicis, 75006 Paris France.

BIBLIOTHEQUE DES LETTRES MODERNES. 1- 1959-. Periodical. SZ. French. ir. Librarie Droz SA, 11 rue Massot, 1211 Geneva 12 Switzerland.

BIBLOS. V. 1- 1925-. PO. Portuguese. an. 1500. Biblioteca de Faculdade, Universidade de Coimbra, Coimbra Portugal. Tel 25551/2. (cum index). bk rev. Circ 750. Archaeology, visual arts, classical studies, music, literature, numismatics, philosophy, sociology, religion and geography.

BIBURIO : RYUKYU DAGAKU FUZOKU TOSHOKAN HO. VFOAT Ryukyu Dagaku Fuzoku Toshokan Ho, The University of the Ryukyus Library Bulletin. in Japanese. ir. 1 Tonokuracho 3-Chome, Naha Japan. LC Z846.

BIBUROSU. VFOAT Biblos, Monthly Report of Special Libraries. V. 1- April, 1950-. 0006-2030. Periodical. Japanese. ir. LC Z675.A2. NLM Z 671 B599.

BIENNIAL REPORT OF THE TEXAS LIBRARY AND HISTORICAL COMMISSION. Main/Corp Texas. Library and Historical Commission. 1909/1910-. 0146-5635. US. English. be. Free. Texas State Library, Capitol Station, Austin TX 78711. LC Z732. DD 027.50976431.

BIENNIAL REPORT OF THE TEXAS STATE LIBRARY AND ARCHIVES COMMISSION. Main/Corp Texas State Library and Archives Commission. 1978/79-79/80 -. US. English. be. Texas State Library and Archives Commission, Box 12927 Capital Station, Austin TX 78711. LC Z732. DD 027.5764.

BIOLOGIE VEGETALE, SCIENCES AGRICOLES. LEXIQUE. See Agriculture.

BIOSCENE. VFOAT Bio Scene. 1-. 0090-3337. Periodical. US. English. bm. Free. Biosciences Information Service, 2100 Arch Street, Philadelphia PA 19103. Tel (215)587-4800. Ed Ann Marie Stefany. Circ 10,000. A newsletter reporting items of interest to users of Biological Abstracts and the BIOSIS Previews Database.

BIULETYN-BIBLIOTEKI JAGIELLONSKIEJ. Began publication in 1948. Periodical. Polish. ir. LC Z818.K89.

BLACK CAUCUS NEWSLETTER. Main/Corp ALA Black Caucus. 8755-9277. Periodical. US. English. bm. $6.00. George C Grant, PO Box 3403 Stockton State College, Pomona NJ 08240. Tel (609)652-6860. Ed George C Grant. DD 020. bk rev. adv acc. Circ 900. (ctrl). Official publication of the Black Caucus of the American Library Association. Contains news, reviews, vacancy announcements and advertisements of interest to and about black librarians.

BLIBAD : BULLETIN DE LIAISON A L'INTENTION DES BIBLIOTHECAIRES, ARCHIVISTES ET DOCUMENTALISTES AFRICAINS. VFOAT Bulletin de Liaison a l'Intention des Bibliothecaires, Archivistes et Documentalistes Africains. No. 1 (Jan. 1976)-. French. ir. Ecole des Bibliothecaires Archivistes et Documentalistes de l'Universite de Dakar, B P 3252, Dakar Senegal.

THE BLISS CLASSIFICATION BULLETIN. V. 1- Aug. 1954-. Periodical. US. English. Ed H E Bliss. LC Z696.B59.

BLLD ANNOUNCEMENT BULLETIN. Main/Corp British Library. Lending Division. VAT British Library Lending Division Announcement Bulletin. 75/1- Jan. 1975-. 0308-4094. UK. English. mo. British Library Document Supply Center, Boston Spa, Wetherby West Yorkshire LS23 7BQ England. LC Z7403 Q158.5. DD 016.5. NLM Z 7405.R4 N112. *BLL Announcement Bulletin,* 0301-2085.

B.N.B. MARC DOCUMENTATION SERVICE PUBLICATIONS. VFOAT Marc Documentation Service Publications. No. 1-. UK. English. Council of the British National Bibliography, British Mueseum 7th and 9th Rathbone Streets, London W1P 2AL England. LC Z699.4.M2. DD 025.30285 S.

THE BODLEIAN LIBRARY RECORD. See Bibliographies.

BOGENS VERDEN. (BV, BOGENS VERDEN : TIDSSKRIFT FOR DANSK BIBLIOTEKSVSEN). V. 50, No. 1, (Feb. 1968)-. Periodical. DK. Danish. ir.

Library and Information Science

Denmarks Bibliotelsforeningen, Trekronergade 15, Copenhagen Valby Denmark. **Ind/Abst** Libr. Lit. *Bogens Verden.*

BOK OG BIBLIOTEK. (BOK OG BIBLIOTEK : TIDSSKRIFT FOR BIBLIOTEKER OG BOGVENNER). Vol. 1, No. 1 (Feb. 1934)-. 0006-5811. Periodical. NO. Norwegian. bm. Statens Bibliotektilsyn, Postboks 8145, Oslo 1 Norway. **Tel** (02)33 61 55. **Ind/Abst** MLA Int. Bibliogr. Books Artic. Mod. Lang. Lit., Libr. Inf. Sci. Abstr., Libr. Lit. **LC** Z671. **DD** 020.5. (cum index). *For Folkeoplysning.*

BOLETIM ABDF. VFOAT Boletim A.B.D.F. New Series, V. 1, No. 1 (March/May 1978)-. 0101-7268. Periodical. Portuguese. qt. Associacao dos Bibliotecarios do Distrito Federal, CRN 702/703 Bl G Sobreloja, 70.000 Brasilia DF Brazil. **LC** Z769.A1. **DD** 027.081. *Boletim DA ABDF.*

BOLETIM DE BIBLIOGRAFIA PORTUGUESA. DOCUMENTOS NAO TEXTUAIS. VFOAT Documentos Nao Textuais. Jan./Dec. 1981-. Portuguese. an. Biblioteca Nacional de Lisboa, Campo Grande 83, 1752 Lisboa Codex Portugal. *Boletim de Bibliografia Portuguesa.*

BOLETIM INFORMATIVO - FUNDACAO CALOUSTE GULBENKIAN, SERVICOS DE BIBLIOTECAS. **Main/Corp** Fundacao Calouste Gulbenkian. Servicos de Bibliotecas. Portuguese. ir. Fundacao Calouste Gulbenkian, Servicos de Bibliotecas, Avenida de Berna, Lisboa Portugal. **LC** Z946.

BOLETIN. **Main/Corp** Asociacion de Bibliotecas Universitarias y Especializadas de Nicaragua. Periodical. Spanish. ir. Apartado 68, Leon Nicaraqua. **LC** Z675.U5.

BOLETIN BIBLIOGRAFICO - BIBLIOTECA NACIONAL DE ANTROPOLOGIA E HISTORIA. *See* Bibliographies.

BOLETIN BIBLIOGRAFICO (CENTRO CATALOGRAFICO CENTROAMERICANO). (BOLETIN BIBLIOGRAFICO). No. 1 (June 1978)-. 0378-4800. Spanish. mo. **LC** Z693.5.C35. **DD** 025.3505.

BOLETIN BIBLIOTECA NACIONAL INFORMA. No. 3 (August/Oct. 1976)-. Spanish. ir. Biblioteca Nacional de Venezuela, Apartado 6525, Caracas 101 Venezuela. *Biblioteca Nacional Informa.*

BOLETIN DE INFORMACION (MADRID, SPAIN). (BOLETIN DE INFORMACION). No. 1 (Sept./Oct. 1982)-. Periodical. SP. Spanish. bm. Secretaria General Tecnica Servicio de Publicaciones, Agustin de Bethancourt 25, Madrid 3 Spain.

BOLETIN DE LA BIBLIOTECA DE LOS TRIBUNALES DEL DISTRITO FEDERAL FUNDACION ROJAS ASTUDILLO. **Main/Corp** Caracas. Biblioteca de los Tribunales del Distrito Federal Fundacion Rojas Astudillo. No. 1-. 0528-0761. Periodical. Spanish. ir. Biblioteca de los Tribunales del Distrito Federal Fundacion Rojas Astudillo, Edificio Gradillas B 40 Piso, Caracus Venezuela.

BOLETIN DE LA SOCIEDAD DE BIBLIOTECARIOS DE PUERTO RICO. **Main/Corp** Sociedad de Bibliotecarios de Puerto Rico. VFOAT SBPR Boletin. English (Spanish). ir. **LC** Z753.P9. **DD** 027.07295.

BOLETIN - GUATEMALA (CITY) BIBLIOTECA NACIONAL. **Main/Corp** Guatemala (City). Biblioteca Nacional. Vol. 1 May 1932-. Periodical. Spanish. ir. **LC** Z887.G91. **DD** 027.57281.

BOLETIN INFORMATIVO DE LA ASOCIACION DE BIBLIOTECARIOS GRADUADOS DE LA REPUBLICA ARGENTINA. **Main/Corp** Asociacion de Bibliotecarios Graduados de la Republica Argentina. Periodical. AG. Spanish. ir. Asociacion de la Republica Argentina, Cordoba 1558 C de Correo 68 Suc 1, Buenos Aires Argentina. **LC** Z765.A1.

BOLETIN PARA LAS BIBLIOTECAS ESCOLARES. Periodical. Spanish. ir. Departamento de Bibliotecas Escolares y Servicos Audiovisuales, Ministerio de Education, Calle 76 Y Avenida 29-E, Marianao 14, Le Habanna Cuba. **LC** Z675.S3.

BOLETIN - UNIVERSIDAD DE LA REPUBLICA, ESCUELA UNIVERSITARIA DE BIBLIOTECOLOGIA Y CIENCIAS AFINES ING. FEDERICO E. CAPURRO, BIBLIOTECA. **Main/Corp** Montevideo. Universidad. Escuela Universitaria de Bibliotecologia y Ciencias Afines Ing Federico E. Capurro. Biblioteca. UY. Spanish. ir. Tristan Narvaja 1427, Montevideo Uruguay. **LC** Z783.A1. *Boletin Informativo.*

BOLLETTINO DELL'ISTITUTO CENTRALE PER LA PATOLOGIA DEL LIBRO ALFONSO GALLO. **Main/Corp** Istituto Centrale per la Patologia del Libro Alfonso Gallo. V. 32- 1973/74-. 0391-5972. Periodical. IT. Italian (summaries in English). an. $11.88. Inst Central Patologia Libro, Via Milano 76, 00184 Rome Italy. **Ind/Abst** Abstr. Bull. Inst. Paper Chem., Chem. Abstr. **LC** Z701. **NLM** Z 700 R763B. **CODEN** BICGDW. *Bollettino Dell'Istituto di Patologia del Libro Alfonso Gallo.*

BOLLETTINO D'INFORMAZIONI - ASSOCIAZIONE ITALIANA BIBLIOTECHE. **Main/Corp** Associazione Italiana Biblioteche. VFOAT Biblioteche Speciali e Servizi d'Informazione. N.S., Year 1- Jan./Feb. 1961-. 0004-5934. Periodical. IT. Italian. qt. 50.000. Associazione Italiana Bibliote, Via Milano 76, 00184 Roma Italy. **Tel** (06)493532. **Ind/Abst** Libr. Inf. Sci. Abstr., Libr. Lit. **LC** Z671. bk rev. adv acc. **Circ** 3,000. Librarianship, professional education, national and local policies, public university and national libraries, special libraries.

BOOK CATALOGUE OF THE NIAGARA REGIONAL LIBRARY SYSTEM CEASED. (BOOK CATALOGUE OF THE NIAGARA REGIONAL LIBRARY SYSTEM. SUBJECT SECTION). **Main/Corp** Niagara Regional Library System. 1976-Jan./June 1979. 0702-827X. Periodical. CN. English. an. $200.00. Niagara Regional Library System, 15 Lloyd Street, Sainte-Catherines Ontario L2S 2N7 Canada. **DD** 017.5.

BOOK CATALOGUE OF THE NIAGARA REGIONAL LIBRARY SYSTEM. **Main/Corp** Niagara Regional Library System. Jan. 1977-July/Sept. 1978. Periodical. CN. English. mo. Niagara Regional Library System, 15 Lloyd Street, Sainte Catherines Ontario L2S 2N7 Canada. **DD** 018.1.

BOOK REPORT (COLUMBUS, OHIO). (THE BOOK REPORT). Vol. 1, No. 1 (May/June 1982)-. 0731-4388. Periodical. US. English. ir. $30.00. Linworth Publishing Co, 2950 North High Street, PO Box 14466, Columbus OH 43214. **Tel** (614)261-6584. Ed Carolyn Hamilton. **Ind/Abst** Book Rev. Index. **LC** Z675.S3. **DD** 027.82230973. bk rev. adv acc. **Circ** 8,000. Information features for middle school, junior high, and high school librarians and reviews of books, film, and software.

BOOKLEGGER MAGAZINE. V. 1- Nov./Dec. 1973-. 0092-7686. Periodical. US. English. bm. $8.00. Booklegger Magazine, 72 Ord Street, San Francisco CA 94114. **LC** Z671. **DD** 020.5.

BOOKLIST CEASED. (THE BOOKLIST). Began with V. 66, published in Sept. 1969. 0006-7385. Periodical. US. English. sm. American Library Association, 50 East Huron Street, Chicago IL 60611. **Tel** (312)944-6780. **Ind/Abst** Book Rev. Index, Media Rev. Dig., Libr. Lit., Ref. Source. **LC** Z1035.A1. **DD** 028.105. *Booklist and Subscription Books Bulletin, 0730-8957.*

THE BOOKMARK. V. 1- Sept. 1948-. 0735-0295. Periodical. US. English. ty. $5.00. The Bookmark, University of Idaho Library, Moscow ID 83843. **Tel** (208)882-6841. Ed Richard J Beck and Gail J Eckwright. **Ind/Abst** Libr. Lit., Libr. Inf. Sci. Abstr. bk rev. **Circ** 1,000. (ctrl). A newsletter for the academic community of the University of Idaho. Contains articles, statistics and news items about the library and libraries in general.

BOOKS AT IOWA. No. 1- Oct. 1964-. 0006-7474. Periodical. US. English. sa. $10.00. Friends of University of Iowa Library, University of Iowa Library, Iowa City IA 52240. **Tel** (319)353-4564. Ed Frank Paluka. **Ind/Abst** Abstr. Engl. Stud., MLA Int. Bibliogr. Books Artic. Mod. Lang. Lit., Annu. Bibliogr. Engl. Lang. Lit., Years Work Eng. Stud. **LC** Z881 .I644. **DD** 027.7777655. (cum index). **Circ** 500. Brief description of special collections in the University of Iowa libraries, with special emphasis on literature and the arts.

BOOKS IN LIBRARY AND INFORMATION SCIENCE. V. 1-. Monographic Series. US. English. ir. Marcel Dekker/ Continuation Department, 270 Madison Avenue, New York NY 10016. **Tel** (212)696-9000. Ed A Kent. **Ind/ Abst** Math. Rev. This is an ongoing series. Each title in the seris has a different subject.

BOOKS ON LIBRARY SCIENCE ADDED TO THE ELIZABETH DAFOE LIBRARY. **Main/Corp** University of Manitoba., Library. Pt. 1- Apr. 12, 1973-. 0318-4811. CN. English. ir. Verification Department, Elizabeth Dafor Library, University of Manitoba, Winnipeg Manitoba R3T 2N2 Canada. **DD** 016.02.

BOOKS PURCHASED FOR DISPLAY PURPOSES. *See* Bibliographies.

BOSTON UNIVERSITY AFRICANA LIBRARIES NEWSLETTER. No. 17- June 1978-. Periodical. US. English. ir. Free. Library University or Illinois, Room 328/1408 West Gregory Drive, Urban IL 61801. **Tel** (217)333-6335. Ed Yvette Scheven. **Circ** 475. News of new publications, especially those not in the book trade, reports of acquisition trip, minutes of relevant meetings. *Africana Libraries Newsletter, 0148-7868.*

THE BOWKER ANNUAL OF LIBRARY & BOOK TRADE INFORMATION. VFOAT Bowker Annual Library and Book Trade Information. 17th Ed. (1972)-. 0068-0540. US. English. an. $69.95. R R Bowker Company, PO Box 1807, Ann Arbor MI 48106. **Tel** (212)916-1600. **LC** Z731. **DD** 020.5. **NLM** Z 671 A512. (ctrl). This standard in library and book trade information is more efficient and more useful than ever, with more business and statistical information. *Bowker Annual of Library and Book Trade Information, 0068-0540.*

BREEZE. (THE BREEZE). V. 1- March 1976-. 0700-3641. Periodical. CN. English. ty. Free. Chinook Regional Library, 1240 Chaplin Street West, Swift Current Saskatchewan S9H 0G7 Canada. **DD** 027.471243. (ctrl).

BRIO. *See* Music.

BRITISH COLUMBIA GOVERNMENT PUBLICATIONS MONTHLY CHECKLIST. *See* Bibliographies.

BRITISH LIBRARIANSHIP AND INFORMATION SCIENCE. 1966/1970-1971/1975. Periodical. UK. English. ir. British Library Association, 7 Ridgmount Street/Store Street, London WC1E 7AE England. **LC** Z666. **DD** 020.941. *Five Years' Work in Librarianship.*

BRITISH LIBRARIANSHIP AND INFORMATION WORK. 1976-1980-. UK. English. Library Association Pub Ltd, 7 Ridgmount Street, London WC1E 7AE England. **LC** Z666. **DD** 020.941. *British Librarianship and Information Science.*

BRITISH LIBRARY JOURNAL. (THE BRITISH LIBRARY JOURNAL). V. 1- Spring 1975-. 0305-5167. UK. English. sa. $28.00. Publications Sales Unit, The British Library, Boston Spa, Wetherby, West Yorkshire LS23 7BQ England. **Tel** (01)636-1544. Ed A Searle. **Ind/Abst** Am. Hist. Life, Hist. Abstr., Part A, Mod. Hist. Abstr., Hist. Abst., Part B, Twent. Century Abstr., MLA Int. Bibliogr. Books Artic. Mod. Lang. Lit., Repert. Int. Litt. Art, Years Work Eng. Stud., Hist. Abstr. **LC** Z921.B854. **DD** 027.542142. **Circ** 900. Articles deal with aspects of the British Library's Bibliography, lists of acquisitions, and often illustrated.

BRITISH LIBRARY RESEARCH & DEVELOPMENT NEWSLETTER. (THE BRITISH LIBRARY RESEARCH & DEVELOPMENT NEWSLETTER). No. 1- Sept. 1974-. 0305-1714. UK. English. ir. Free. British Library Research & Development Department, 2 Sheraton Street, London W1V 4BH England. **Tel** (01)636-1544. Ed A P Warshaw. **Ind/Abst** Electron. Pub. Abstr., Manage. Market. Abstr. **LC** Z671. **Circ** 4,000. Details on new research grants, seminars etc. Funded by the British Library Department. News and abstracts of our new publications. *OSTI Newsletter.*

BRITISH REPORTS, TRANSLATIONS AND THESES RECEIVED BY THE BRITISH LIBRARY LENDING DIVISION, INCLUDING MATERIAL FROM THE REPUBLIC OF IRELAND. *See* Bibliographies.

Library and Information Science

BRN & BGER. VFOAT Brn Og Bger. 0006-7792. Periodical. Danish. ir. 200.00. Danmarks Skolebiblioteksforenings Sekretariat, Frankrigsgade 4, 2300 Kbenhavn S Denmark. **Ind/Abst** Libr. Inf. Sci. Abstr. **LC** Z671. **DD** 027.809489. *Brn Og Boger.*

BUCH UND BIBLIOTHEK. VFOAT BUB. Vol. 23- 1971-. 0340-0301. Periodical. German. ir. Bock & Herchen Verlag, Postfach 327, 7410 Reutlingen West Germany. **Ind/Abst** Libr. Lit., Libr. Inf. Sci. Abstr. *Bucherei und Bildung.*

BULLETIN ABQ. (BULLETIN A B Q). **Main/Corp** Quebec Library Association. **VFOAT** Q L A Bulletin. V. 13, No. 2- Nov. 1971-. 0380-7150. Periodical. CN. English (French). ir. c/o Dawson College Library, 1001 Sherbrooke Street East, Montreal Quebec H2L 1L3 Canada. **Ind/Abst** Libr. Inf. Sci. Abstr. *Bulletin de Nouvelles*, 0380-7134.

BULLETIN - ASSOCIATION INTERNATIONALE POUR LES SERVICES ET TECHNIQUES D'INFORMATION EN SCIENCES SOCIALES. **Main/Corp** Association Internationale pour les Services et Techniques d'Information en Sciences Sociales. V. 1- Nov. 1976-. 0384-9546. Periodical. CN. French. qt. Association Internationale pour d'Information en Sciences Sociales, Secretariat Canadien Diassist, c/o Centre d'Echange de Donnees en Sciences Sociales, 151 rue Slater, Ottawa Ontario K1P 5N1 Canada. **DD** 029.93005.

BULLETIN - BIBLIOTHEQUE CENTRALE DE PRET DE L'OUTAOUAIS. (THE BULLETIN : THE NEWS FROM THE BCPO). **Main/Corp** Bibliotheque Centrale de Pret de l'Outaouais. **VFOAT** News from the BCPO. No. 1 (Sept. 1983)-. 0824-7153. Periodical. CN. English. ir. Free to Members. BCPO, 221 Freeman Road, Hull Quebec J8Z 1V7 Canada. **DD** 027.471422.

BULLETIN - CANADIAN TALENT LIBRARY. **Main/Corp** Canadian Talent Library. Began in 1962. 0319-664X. Periodical. CN. English. ir. Canadian Talent Library, 38 Yorkville Avenue, Toronto Ont Canada M4W 1L5. **Tel** (416)924-1411.

BULLETIN DE LA BIBLIOTHEQUE CENTRALE DE PRET DE LA COTE-NORD. (BULLETIN). V. 1, No. 1, (Dec. 1981)-. 0711-706X. Periodical. CN. French. ir. Free to Members, $2.50 for Nonmembers. Bibliotheque Centrale de Pret de la Cote-Nord, 405 Avenue Bronchu, Sept-Iles Quebec G4R 2W 9 Canada. **DD** 027.471417.

BULLETIN DE LA BIBLIOTHEQUE NATIONALE DU QUEBEC CEASED. **Main/Corp** Bibliotheque Nationale du Quebec. Vol. 1, No 3-V. 16, No 5, Sept. 1967-Dec. 1982. 0045-1967. Periodical. CN. French. qt. **Ind/Abst** Libr. Inf. Sci. Abstr. *Bulletin de la Bibliotheque Saint-Sulpice*, 0523-5111.

BULLETIN DE LA BIBLIOTHEQUE NATIONALE (FRANCE) CEASED. **Main/Corp** France. Bibliotheque Nationale. Vol. 1-6, No. 2. 0338-4446. Periodical. FR. French. qt. 48.00. 58 rue Richelieu, 75084 Paris Cedex 02 France. **Ind/Abst** Libr. Inf. Sci. Abstr. **LC** Z927.P22. **DD** 027.54436.

BULLETIN DES ACQUISITIONS DE LA BIBLIOTHEQUE (COMMISSION OF THE EUROPEAN COMMUNITIES) CEASED. **Main/Corp** Commission of the European Communities. Library Luxembourg. **VFOAT** List of Additions to the Library. US. French (Multilingual). ir. European Community Information Service, 2100 M Street NW/ Suite 707, Washington DC 20037. **Tel** (202)862-9500. **LC** Z7161, H61. **DD** 016.3. *Neuerwerbungen der Bibliothek.*

BULLETIN DES BIBLIOTHEQUES DE FRANCE. Vol. 1- Jan. 1956-. 0006-2006. Periodical. FR. French. bm. Bulletin des Bibliotheques de France, 3/5 Boulevard Pasteur, 75015 Paris France. **Tel** (33)-1-45-39-25-75. **Ind/Abst** Libr. Inf. Sci. Abstr., Libr. Lit. **LC** Z671. The main professional journal in France. Deals with publishing, reading, databases, computer and technical and scientific information. *Bulletin d'Informations, Bulletin de Documentation Bibliographique.*

BULLETIN D'INFORMATIONS - ASSOCIATION DES BIBLIOTHECAIRES FRANCAIS. (BULLETIN D'INFORMATIONS DE L'ASSOCIATION DES BIBLIOTHECAIRES FRANCAIS). **VFOAT** Bulletin d'Informations. 0004-5365. Periodical. FR. French. qt. $35.26. Association des Bibliothecaires Francais, 65 rue de Richelieu, 75002 Paris France. **Ind/Abst** Libr. Inf. Sci. Abstr.

BULLETIN - GEORGIAN BAY REGIONAL LIBRARY SYSTEM. **Main/Corp** Georgian Bay Regional Library System. Began publication April 1967. 0380-8076. Periodical. CN. English. qt. Georgian Bay Regional Library System, 30 Morrow Road, Barrie Ontario L4N 3V8 Canada. **DD** 027.471315.

BULLETIN (INDIAN LIBRARY ASSOCIATION). (BULLETIN). **VFOAT** ILA Bulletin. Vol. 1, No. 1 (Jan./Mar. 1965). 0019-5782. Periodical. II. English. qt. $20.00. Indian Library Association, A/40-41 FL 201 Ansal Buliding Dr Mukerjee, Nagar 110009 New Delhi India. **Tel** 7117743. Ed Krishan Kumar. **Ind/Abst** Libr. Inf. Sci. Abstr. bk rev. adv acc. **Circ** 2,000. (ctrl). Library and information science.

BULLETIN - INTERNATIONAL ASSOCIATION OF ORIENTALIST LIBRARIANS. **Main/Corp** International Association of Orientalist Librarians. Began with Spring 1976 issue. 0161-7397. Periodical. US. English. sa. $12.00. Secretariat International Association of Orientalist Librarians, c/o Asian Studies Program, University of Hawaii, 1890 East-West Road, Honolulu HI 96822. **Ind/Abst** Libr. Inf. Sci. Abstr. **LC** Z688.A75. **DD** 026.00095. *Newsletter - International Association of Orientalist Librarians*, 0146-6992.

BULLETIN - JEWISH PUBLIC LIBRARY CEASED. **Main/Corp** Jewish Public Library (Montreal, Quebec). **VFOAT** Buletin Aydishe Felks Biblietek. Began publication 1971. Ceased with issue for June 1980. 0381-9884. Periodical. CN. text in English, French and Yiddish. bm. $5.00 Each No. Jewish Public Library, 5151 Cote St Catherine Road, Montreal Quebec H3W 1M6 Canada. **DD** 027.6309714281. *News Bulletin.*

THE BULLETIN - LOUISIANA LIBRARY ASSOCIATION. (THE BULLETIN). **Main/Corp** Louisiana Library Association. V. 1-28, No. 3. 0024-6867. Periodical. US. English. qt.

BULLETIN (MALAWI NATIONAL LIBRARY SERVICE BOARD). (BULLETIN). No. 30 (Nov. 1981)-. MW. English. ir. **LC** Z857.M3. **DD** 017.5096897. *Bulletin (Malawi National Library Service).*

BULLETIN OF OUTSTANDING ACQUISITIONS OF THE METROPOLITAN TORONTO CENTRAL LIBRARY. **Main/Corp** Metropolitan Toronto Central Library. V. 1- June 1975-. 0383-2791. Periodical. CN. English. Metropolitan Toronto Library Board, 789 Yonge Street, Toronto Ontario M4W 2G8 Canada. **DD** 018.1. *Quarterly Bulletin of Outstanding Achievements of the Metropolitan Toronto Central Library*, 0383-2783.

BULLETIN OF THE AMERICAN SOCIETY FOR INFORMATION SCIENCE. **Main/Corp** American Society for Information Science. V. 1- June/July 1974-. 0095-4403. Periodical. US. English. bm. American Society Information Science, 1010 16th Street NW/ 2nd Floor, Washington DC 20036. **Tel** (202)659-3644. Ed Thomas Lennox. **Ind/Abst** Mag. Index, Hospit. Lit. Index, Predicasts, Coal Abstr., ABI/Inform, GeoRef, Libr. Inf. Sci. Abstr., Public Aff. Inf. Serv. Bull., Curr. Index J. Educ., Libr. Lit., Comput. Control Abstr., Electr. Electron. Abstr., Sci. Abstr. Sect. A. Phys. Abstr., Funk Scott Index Corp. Ind., Phys. Abstr. **LC** Z699.A1. **DD** 020.5. **CODEN** BASICR. adv acc. *ASIS Newsletter*, 0001-2513.

BULLETIN OF THE ASSOCIATION OF BRITISH THEOLOGICAL AND PHILOSOPHICAL LIBRARIES. **Main/Corp** Association of British Theological and Philosophical Libraries. No. 1- Nov. 1956-. 0305-781X. Periodical. UK. English. ty. 10.00. ABTAPL, Honorary Treasurer, Heythrop College, 11-13 Cavendish Square, London W1M 0AN England. **Tel** (01)580-6941. Ed John V Howard. **Ind/Abst** Libr. Inf. Sci. Abstr. **LC** Z675.T4. **DD** 026.200941. (cum index). bk rev. adv acc. **Circ** 170. Carries news and information on the bibliography of theology and philosophy in the United Kingdom.

BULLETIN OF THE CONGREGATIONAL LIBRARY. **Main/Corp** American Congregational Association, Boston. Library. V. 1- Oct. 1949-. 0010-5821. Periodical. US. English. ty. $5.00. Congregational Library, 14 Beacon Street, Boston MA 02108. **Tel** (617)523-0470. Ed Harold F Worthley. **LC** Z881. **DD** 026.258. bk rev. **Circ** 1,000. (ctrl). One article per issue on Congregational Christian history plus reviews of all new books purchased during preceding four months. *Quarterly Bulletin - Congregational Library*, 0364-7250; *Report of the Directors.*

BULLETIN OF THE FRIENDS OF THE OWEN D. YOUNG LIBRARY. 0734-2012. Periodical. US. English. Friends of the Owen D Young Library, St Lawrence University, Canton NY 13617. **LC** Z733.O943. **DD** 021.7.

BULLETIN OF THE GENERAL THEOLOGICAL LIBRARY. **Main/Corp** Boston. General Theological Library. V. 1- 1908-. 0361-0837. Periodical. US. English. qt. $1.00. General Theological Library, 14 Beacon Street, Boston MA 02108. **LC** Z7755.

BULLETIN OF THE JOHN RYLANDS UNIVERSITY LIBRARY OF MANCHESTER. V. 55- Autumn 1972-. 0301-102X. Periodical. UK. English. sa. John Rylands University Library, Deansgate, Manchester M-3 3EH England. **Tel** 061-834-5343. Ed F Taylor. **Ind/Abst** Abstr. Engl. Stud., Annu. Bibliogr. Engl. Lang. Lit., Am. Hist. Life, Hist. Abstr., Part A, Mod. Hist. Abstr., Hist. Abst., Part B, Twent. Century Abstr., MLA Int. Bibliogr. Books Artic. Mod. Lang. Lit., Old Testam. Abstr., New Testam. Abstr., Relig. Index One, Period., Repert. Int. Litt. Art, Hist. Abstr., Years Work Eng. Stud., Recent Publ. Artic. Articles on the library's collections of early printed books and manuscripts, palaeographical and bibliographical studies and the humanities. *Bulletin of the John Rylands Library*, 0021-7239.

BULLETIN OF THE MEDICAL LIBRARY ASSOCIATION. **Main/Corp** Medical Library Association. V. 1- July 1911-. 0025-7338. Periodical. US. English. qt. $75.00. Medical Library Association Inc, 919 North Michigan Avenue/Suite 3208, Chicago IL 60611. **Tel** (312)266-2456. Ed Susan Crawford. **Ind/Abst** Life Sci. Collect., Hospit. Lit. Index, Excerpta Med., Index Med., Cumul. Index Nurs. Allied Health Lit., Biol. Abstr., Libr. Inf. Sci. Abstr., Ref. Source, Public Aff. Inf. Serv. Bull., Libr. Lit., Comput. Control Abstr., Electr. Electron. Abstr., Sci. Abstr. Sect. A. Phys. Abstr., Phys. Abstr., Sci. Cit. Index, Abr. Ed., Soc. Sci. Citation Index. **NLM** Z 675.M4 M489B. **CODEN** BMLAAG. bk rev. adv acc. **Circ** 6,200. Covers developments on the technical, administrative and biomedical information, research issues of interest to health science librarians as well as articles on education of librarians.

BULLETIN - OHIO LIBRARY ASSOCIATION. (BULLETIN). Vol. 49, No. 3 (July 1979)-. 0276-6981. Periodical. US. English. ty. $9.00. Ohio Library Association, Suite 230/40 South 3rd Street, Columbus OH 43215. **Tel** (614)221-9057. Ed Martha Alt. **Ind/Abst** Libr. Lit. **LC** Z673. **DD** 027.0771. bk rev. adv acc. (ctrl). Professional journal in the field of library science and information services. *OLA Bulletin (Ohio Library Association : 1979)*, 0737-2027.

BULLETIN PERPUSTAKAAN DAN DOKUMENTASI. 0304-5773. Periodical. Indonesian. ir. 200 Single Issue. Asosiasi Perpustakaan, Perpustakaan SPS Jalan Merdeka Selatan II, Jakarta Indonesia. **LC** Z671.

BULLETIN SIGNALETIQUE. 101 : SCIENCE DE L'INFORMATION, DOCUMENTATION. French. ir. Centre De Documentation, 26 Rue Boyer, Paris France 75971. **LC** Z699.2. **DD** 020.5. **NLM** ZQ 1 B936Q. *Bulletin Signaletique. 101: Information Scientifique et Technique.*

BULLETIN - SOCIETE DES DIPLOMES DE L'ECOLE DE BIBLIOTHECONOMIE DE L'UNIVERSITE DE MONTREAL. **Main/Corp** Universite de Montreal. Ecole de Biblioteconomie. Societe des Diplomes. Discontinued in 196-?. 0700-5431. Periodical. CN. French. Societe des Diplomes de l'Ecole de Biblioteconomie, Universite de Montreal, CP 6128, Montreal Quebec H3C 3J7 Canada. **DD** 020.6234714.

BULLETIN - SPECIAL LIBRARIES ASSOCIATION. FLORIDA CHAPTER. (BULLETIN). **VFOAT** Bulletin of the Florida Chapter, SLA. 0740-9753. Periodical. US. English. qt. $15.00. Florida Chapter of the Special Libraries Association, c/o Municipal Reference Library, City Hall, 400 South

Library and Information Science

Orange Avenue, Orlando FL 32801. LC Z732.F6. *Bulletin of the Florida Chapter, SLA.*

BULLETIN - SPECIAL LIBRARIES ASSOCIATION. GEOGRAPHY AND MAP DIVISION. (BULLETIN). **Main/Corp** Special Libraries Association. Geography and Map Division. No. 8 (June 1951)-. 0036-1607. Periodical. US. English. qt. $17.00. Geography and Map Division, Special Libraries Association, 9927 Edwar Avenue, Bethesda MD 20814-2111. **Tel** (301)530-0628. Ed Mary Murphy. **Ind/Abst** GeoRef, Ref. Source, Libr. Inf. Sci. Abstr., Libr. Lit., Inf. Hotline. **LC** Z673. **CODEN** SGBUB2. (cum index). bk rev. **Circ** 900. Medium of exchange of information, news, and research in the field of geographic and cartographic bibliography, literature and libraries.

BULLETIN - SPECIAL LIBRARIES ASSOCIATION, NORTH CAROLINA CHAPTER. **Main/Corp** Special Libraries Association. North Carolina Chapter. VFOAT NC SLA Bulletin. 0195-9077. Periodical. US. English. qt. $5.00. North Carolina Chapter, Special Libraries Association, 201 West Rice Street, Landis NC 28088.

BULLETIN - SPECIAL LIBRARIES ASSOCIATION. SAN FRANCISCO BAY REGION CHAPTER. (BULLETIN). **Main/Corp** Special Libraries Association. San Francisco Bay Region Chapter. VFOAT Bulletin - San Francisco Bay Region Chapter, Special Libraries Association. 0277-2124. Periodical. US. English. bm. Special Libraries Association, c/o 2333 Market Street 19th Floor, San Francisco CA 94105.

BULLETIN - WESTCHESTER LIBRARY ASSOCIATION CEASED. **Main/Corp** Westchester Library Association. VFOAT WLA Bulletin. Ceased publication with V. 41, No. 6 in June 1980. Periodical. US. English. qt. **LC** Z673.

BUSINESS LIBRARY NEWSLETTER. See Business.

BUTLLETI DE L'ASSOCIACIO DE BIBLIOTECARIS DE CATALUNYA. 0212-0135. Periodical. Catalan. sa. 300. **LC** Z673.A745. **DD** 027.0467.

BUYING FOR LIBRARIES. Autumn 1984-. Periodical. UK. English. sa. Free. Alan Armstrong & Associates Ltd, 76 Park Road, London NW1 4SH England. **Tel** (01)258-3740. Ed Nigel Oxbrown. **LC** Z689. **DD** 025.2. bk rev. adv acc. **Circ** 15,000. (ctrl). News and reviews of products and services for the library and information world.

C. V. L. G. SERIALS LIST. (C V L G SERIALS LIST). **Main/Corp** Central Vancouver Librarians Group. VAT Central Vancouver Librarians Group Serials List. Began with 1973 issue. 0703-5799. CN. English. an. $25.00 Per Number. Central Vancouver Librarians Group, Library, Swan Wooster Engineering Company Ltd, 1525 Robson Street, Vancouver British Columbia V6G 1C3 Canada. **DD** 016.05.

CABLE LIBRARIES. V. 1- May 1973-. 0161-7605. Periodical. US. English. mo. $15.00. Box 565, Ridgefield CT 06877. **LC** Z716.8. **DD** 021.28.

CAHIERS DE LA DOCUMENTATION. (LES CAHIERS DE LA DOCUMENTATION). VFOAT Bladen voor de Documentatie. V. 1- 1947-. 0007-9804. Periodical. BE. French. qt. $41.50. Association Belge de Documention, rue Sainte Gertrude 10, 1400 Nivelles Be 056 Belgium. **Ind/Abst** Libr. Inf. Sci. Abstr. **LC** Z1008. **DD** 025.05.

THE CALENDAR - CHILDREN'S BOOK COUNCIL (NEW YORK, N.Y.). (THE CALENDAR). Began in 1945?. 0008-0721. Periodical. US. English. Children's Book Council Inc, 67 Irving Place, New York NY 10003. **DD** 028.

CALIFORNIA ACADEMIC LIBRARIES LIST OF SERIALS MICROFORM. 1980 ED.-. 0198-8433. US. English. University of California, Division of Library Automation, Berkeley CA. *University of California Union List of Serials, 0146-1923.*

CALIFORNIA LIBRARY DIRECTORY. See Yearbooks, Almanacs, Directories.

CALIFORNIA LIBRARY DIRECTORY. See Yearbooks, Almanacs, Directories.

CALIFORNIA LIBRARY LAWS. See Law.

CALIFORNIA LIBRARY STATISTICS. See Statistics.

CALIFORNIA LIBRARY STATISTICS AND DIRECTORY. See Statistics.

CALIFORNIA LIBRARY TRUSTEES DIRECTORY. See Yearbooks, Almanacs, Directories.

CALIFORNIA PUBLIC LIBRARY OUTLET DIRECTORY. See Yearbooks, Almanacs, Directories.

CALIFORNIA PUBLIC LIBRARY SALARY SURVEY. 1983-. 0740-7491. US. English. an. California State Library, Library Development Services Bureau, PO Box 2037, Sacramento CA 95809. **LC** Z682. **DD** 331.2810209794. *California Library Statistics and Directory, 0148-4583.*

CALS NEWSLETTER. VAT Canadian Association of Library Schools Newsletter. No. 4 (Dec. 1978)-. 0229-7566. Periodical. CN. English. Free. Sinikka Koskiala, School of Library and Information Science, University of Western Ontario, London Ontario N6A 5B9 Canada. **DD** 020.71171. *Newsletter (Canadian Association of Library Schools), 0315-0763.*

CAMLS NEWS. **Main/Corp** Cleveland Area Metropolitan Library System. VFOAT C.A.M.L.S. News. VAT Cleveland Area Metropolitan Library System News. V. 3- 1977-. 0730-093X. Periodical. US. English. ir. Cleveland Area Metropolitan Library System, 11000 Euclid Avenue #309, Cleveland OH 44106. *Newsletter, 0730-3548.*

CANADIAN INFORMATION INDUSTRY ASSOCIATION. (CANADIAN INFORMATION INDUSTRY ASSOCIATION : NEWSLETTER). Vol. 1, No. 1 (Sept. 1980)-. 0227-8804. Periodical. CN. English. ir. Free. Canadian Information Industry Association, Suite 900A/77 Metcalfe Street, Ottawa Ont K1P 5L6 Canada. **DD** 338.47025. (ctrl).

CANADIAN JOURNAL OF INFORMATION SCIENCE. (THE CANADIAN JOURNAL OF INFORMATION SCIENCE). VFOAT Revue Canadienne des Sciences de l'Information. V. 1- May 1976-. 0380-9218. CN. English (French). an. Free to Members of CAIS, $10.00 All Others. Canadian Association for Information Science, PO Box 158 Station A, Ottawa Ontario K1N 8V2 Canada. **Ind/Abst** Libr. Inf. Sci. Abstr., Comput. Control Abstr., Electr. Electron. Abstr., Foreign Lang. Index, Sci. Abstr. Sect. A. Phys. Abstr., Public Aff. Inf. Serv. Bull., Libr. Lit. **LC** Z1007. **DD** 020.5. **CODEN** CJISDE.

CANADIAN LIBRARY HANDBOOK CEASED. VFOAT Guide des Bibliotheques Canadiennes. 1979/80-. 0707-9680. CN. English (text also in French). an. Micromedia Limited, 144 Front Street West 5th Floor, Toronto Ont M5J 2L7 Canada. **Tel** (416)593-5211. **LC** Z735.A1. **DD** 021.02571.

CANADIAN LIBRARY JOURNAL. V. 26- Jan./Feb. 1969-. 0008-4352. Periodical. CN. English. bm. $19.35Members, $35.00 Others. Canadian Library Association, 151 Sparks Street, Ottawa Ontario K1P 5E3 Canada. **Tel** (613)232-9625. Ed Shelia Nelson. **Ind/Abst** Electron. Commun. Abstr. J., ISMEC Bull., Pollut. Abstr. Indexes, Saf. Sci. Abstr. J., Am. Hist. Life, Hist. Abstr., Part A, Mod. Hist. Abstr., Hist. Abst., Part B, Twent. Century Abstr., Can. Period. Index, Libr. Inf. Sci. Abstr., Comput. Control Abstr., Electr. Electron. Abstr., Sci. Abstr. Sect. A. Phys. Abstr., Ref. Source, Can. Educ. Index, Curr. Index J. Educ., Libr. Lit., Soc. Sci. Citation Index, Phys. Abstr., Hist. Abstr. **CODEN** CLIJBX. bk rev. adv acc. **Circ** 6,000. (ctrl). A forum for discussion, analysis and evaluation of issues in librarianship. *Canadian Library, 0316-604X.*

CANADIAN VIEWPOINT (WILLOW GROVE, PA.). (CANADIAN VIEWPOINT). Series/Titl Information Management Portfolio. Began in 1981. 0277-9285. Periodical. US. English. bm. $50.00 Includes Membership. International Information/Word Processing Association, 1015 North York Road, Willow Grove PA 19090. **DD** 020.62471.

CANADIANA AUTHORITIES. (CANADIANA AUTHORITIES MICROFORM). VFOAT Canadiana, Vedettes d'Autorite. 26/12/79-. 0225-1574. CN. English (French). qt. **DD** 025.322. *C A N/M A R C: Authorities, 0701-810X.*

CAPE LIBRARIAN. (THE CAPE LIBRARIAN : OFFICIAL MONTHLY JOURNAL OF THE CAPE PROVINCIAL LIBRARY SERVICE). VFOAT Kaapse Bibliotekaris : Amptelike Maandblad van die Kaapse Provinsiale Biblioteckdiens. Began in Nov. 1957. 0008-5790. Periodical. SA. Afrikaans (and English). The Administration, PO Box 2108, Cape Town South Africa. **Ind/Abst** Libr. Inf. Sci. Abstr. **LC** Z671. **DD** 021.

CARD NUMBER INDEX TO LIBRARY OF CONGRESS CATALOGING ENTRIES. See Indexes/Abstracts.

THE CARIBBEAN LAW LIBRARIAN : BULLETIN OF THE CARIBBEAN ASSOCIATION OF LAW LIBRARIES. Vol. 1, No. 1 (Nov. 1984)-. 0255-7118. Periodical. English. $15.00. Caribbean Law Librarian, c/o Norman Manley Law School, Mona Campus, PO Box 231, Jamaica West Indies. Ed Leslie P Fenty.

CARIBOO-THOMPSON NICOLA TATTLER. 0700-5377. Periodical. CN. English. Cariboo-Thompson Nicola Tattler, 749 Notre Dame Drive, Kamloops British Columbia V2C 5N8 Canada. **DD** 027.47114.

CARTA INFORMATIVA. NEWSLETTER. **Main/Corp** Association of Caribbean University and Research Libraries. V.1- (No. 1-). Periodical. Spanish (English). ir.

CATALOG OF PUBLICATIONS - AMERICAN LIBRARY ASSOCIATION. See Bibliographies.

CATALOGING & CLASSIFICATION QUARTERLY. VFOAT Cataloging and Classification Quarterly. Vol. 1, No. 1 (Fall 1980)-. 0163-9374. Periodical. US. English. qt. $72.00. Haworth Press, 28 East 22nd Street, New York NY 10010. **Tel** (212)228-2800. Ed Ruth C Carter. **Ind/Abst** Electron. Commun. Abstr. J., ISMEC Bull., Pollut. Abstr. Indexes, Saf. Sci. Abstr. J., Libr. Inf. Sci. Abstr., Comput. Control Abstr., Electr. Electron. Abstr., Sci. Abstr. Sect. A. Phys. Abstr., Libr. Lit., Phys. Abstr. **LC** Z693.A15. **DD** 025.305. **CODEN** CCQUDB. bk rev. adv acc. **Circ** 1,139. It has the latest advances in principles and techniques of cataloging, subject analysis, cataloging administration, networking, and a host of other bibliographic functions.

CATALOGING SERVICE BULLETIN. **Main/Corp** Library of Congress. Processing Services. No. 1 (Summer 1978)-. 0160-8029. Periodical. US. English. qt. $18.00. Library of Congress, Cataloging Distribution Service, Washington DC 20541. **Tel** (202)287-6100. **LC** Z693.A15. **DD** 025.0205. (cum index). Contains the most current information relating to the Library of Congress cataloging and classification practices. *Cataloging Service, 0041-7890.*

CATALOGING SERVICE BULLETIN INDEX. See Indexes/Abstracts.

CATALOGO - CENTRO DE DOCUMENTACION Y BIBLIOTECA, CASA DE CHILE EN MEXICO. **Main/Corp** Casa de Chile en Mexico. Centro de Documentation y Biblioteac. Spanish. ir. Casa de Chile en Mexico, Centro de Documentacion y Biblioteca, Av Universidad 1134, Colonia del Valle, Mexico 12 DF Mexico.

CATALOGS AND TECHNICAL PUBLICATIONS - LIBRARY OF CONGRESS. CATALOGING DISTRIBUTION SERVICE. (CATALOGS AND TECHNICAL PUBLICATIONS). **Main/Corp** Library of Congress. Cataloging Distribution Service. 0743-6181. US. English. an. Free. CDS Library of Congress, Washington DC 20541. **Tel** (202)287-6100. **LC** Z733.U58. **DD** 016.025313. A catalog listing Cataloging Distribution Service publications.

CATALOGUE & INDEX. No. 1- 1966-. 0008-7629. Periodical. UK. English. qt. $9.20. The Library Association, 7 Ridgmount Street, London WC1E 7AE England. **Tel** 0232 245133. Ed Rodney Brunt. **Ind/Abst** Libr. Inf. Sci. Abstr., Libr. Lit. **LC** Z695. NLM Z 695.7 C357. bk rev. **Circ** 3,500. (ctrl). Articles on cataloging and indexing and other related matters including the planning production or maintenance of library catalogues.

CATALOGUE DES MICROEDITIONS. **Main/Corp** Bibliotheque Nationale du Quebec. Service de Microphotographie. 1974-. 0384-9724. CN. French. Bibliotheque National du Quebec, Ministere des Affaires Culturelles, 1700 rue Saint-Denis, Montreal Quebec H2X 3K6 Canada. **DD** 015.714.

CATALOGUE DES PUBLICATIONS ET DES DOCUMENTS DES COMMUNAUTES EUROPEENES RECUS A LA BIBLIOTHEQUE DE LA COMMISSION. **Main/Corp** Commission of the European Communities. Library Luxembourg. VFOAT Catalogue of European Community Publications and

Received at the Commission Library. French (Multilingual). qt. European Community Information Inc, 2100 M Street NW/Suite 707, Washington DC 20037. **Tel** (202)862-9500. **LC** Z7161, H61. **DD** 016.3. *Bulletin des Acquisitions.*

CATALOGUE GENERAL DES LIVRES IMPRIMES DE LA BIBLIOTHEQUE NATIONALE. AUTEURS . . . *CEASED.* **Main/Corp** France. Bibliotheque Nationale. Departement des Imprimes. V. 1-231. French. ir. **LC** Z927.

CATALOGUE OF DEPARTMENTALLY-OWNED FILMS HOUSED WITH FILM LIBRARY. **Main/Corp** University of Texas at Austin. Film Library. US. English. The University of Texas at Austin, PO Box W, Austin TX 78712.

CATALYST (DES MOINES, IOWA : 1971). (THE CATALYST). Vol. 25, No. 2 (Mar. 1971)-. 0730-711X. Periodical. US. English. bm. Free to members, $6.00 Non-members. Iowa Library Association, 921 Insurance Exchange Building, Des Moines IA 50309. **LC** Z673. **DD** 020.6234777. *ILA Catalyst.*

CATHOLIC LIBRARY WORLD. (THE CATHOLIC LIBRARY WORLD). V. 1- Nov./Dec. 1929-. 0008-820X. Periodical. US. English. bm. $35.00. Catholic Library Association, 461 West Lancaster Avenue, Haverford PA 19041. **Tel** (215)649-5251. **Ed** John T Corrigan. **Ind/Abst** Energy Inf. Abstr., Environ. Abstr., Libr. Inf. Sci. Abstr., Ref. Source, Cathol. Period. Lit. Index, Libr. Lit., Libr. Sci. Abstr., Book Rev. Index, Ref. Book Rev. Index, Curr. Index J. Educ. **LC** Z671. **DD** 020.5. (cum index). bk rev. adv acc. **Circ** 3,000. (ctrl). Provides current information on library and information science topics, media reviews, new product news and advertising. *CLA Booklist.*

CB (MEXICO CITY, MEXICO : 1980). (CB). Vol. 3, No. 4 (June 1980)-. MX. Spanish. ir. $14.00. Ciencia Bibliotecaria, Apdo Postal 76-065, Mexico 21 DF Mexico. **LC** Z671. **DD** 020.5. *Ciencia Bibliotecaria, 0185-0105.*

CDC LIBRARY SERIAL HOLDINGS. (CDC LIBRARY SERIAL HOLDINGS). **Main/Corp** CDC Library (U.S.). **VFOAT** C.D.C. Library Serial Holdings. **VAT** Center for Disease Control Library Serial Holdings, Centers for Disease Control Library Serial Holdings. 0748-853X. US. English. US Public Health Service, Center for Disease Control, Atlanta GA 30333. **LC** Z6660, R5. **DD** 016.6105.

CENSUS OF LIBRARIES (NEW ZEALAND). **Main/Corp** New Zealand. Dept. of Statistics. **Series/Titl** Department of Statistics Publication. English. Department of Statistics, Private Bag, Wellington New Zealand. *Census of Libraries.*

THE CENTER FOR RESEARCH LIBRARIES CATALOGUE. MONOGRAPHS. SUPPLEMENT. (THE CENTER FOR RESEARCH LIBRARIES CATALOGUE : MONOGRAPHS. SUPPLEMENT). **Main/Corp** Center for Research Libraries (U.S.). 1st-. 0098-7662. US. English (Multilingual). Center for Research Libraries, 6050 South Kenwood Avenue, Chicago IL 60637. **LC** Z733. **DD** 018.10977311.

CENTRO NACIONAL DE RESTAURACION DE LIBROS Y DOCUMENTOS : ACTIVIDADES. SP. Spanish. ir. El Centro, Serrano 115, Madrid 6 Spain. **LC** Z701. **DD** 025.7.

CENTROMIDICA. **Main/Corp** Centro Taller Regional de Restauracion y Microfilmacion de Documentos Para el Caribe y Centroamerica. Yearly Vol. 1- Oct. 1977-. Spanish. ir. **LC** Z701.

CHAIRMAN'S ANNUAL REPORT - KENY LIBRARY ASSOCIATION. **Main/Corp** Kenya Library Association. KE. English. ir. Kenya Library Association, PO Box 46031, Nairobi Kenya. **LC** Z673. **DD** 020.62346762.

CHAIRMAN'S ANNUAL REPORT - TANZANIA LIBRARY ASSOCIATION. **Main/Corp** Tanzania Library Association. English. ir. Tanzania Library Association, PO Box 2645, Dar es Salaam Tanzania. **LC** Z673.T22. **DD** 020.622678.

CHAIRMAN'S REPORT - EAST AFRICAN LIBRARY ASSOCIATION. KENYA BRANCH. **Main/Corp** East African Library Association. Kenya Branch. English. ir. Kenya Library Association, PO Box 46031, Nairobi Kenya. **LC** Z673. **DD** 020.6226762.

CHALLENGE TO CHANGE. LIBRARY APPLICATIONS OF CONCEPTS. (CHALLENGE TO CHANGE : LIBRARY APPLICATIONS OF CONCEPTS). No. 1-. 0276-0525. Monographic Series. US. English. ir. Libraries Unlimited, PO Box 263, Littleton CO 80160. **LC** UNC.

CHANNEL. (CHANNEL : THE NEWSLETTER OF THE NEW ENGLAND LIBRARY INFORMATION NETWORK). V. 1- 1971-. 0045-6330. Periodical. US. English. New England Board of Higher Education, 40 Grove Street, Wellesley MA 02181. **Tel** (617)235-8071.

CHATTERBOX. V. 1- Nov. 1976-. 0701-0893. Periodical. CN. English. bm. Free. Cariboo-Thompson Nicola Library System, 749 Notre Dame Drive, Kamloops British Columbia V2C 5N8 Canada. **DD** 027.471141. (ctrl).

CHECK-LIST OF VIRGINIA STATE PUBLICATIONS. 1926-. 0364-7293. US. English. an. $2.00. Virginia State Library, 11th and Capitol Streets, Richmond VA 23219. **LC** Z881.V81.

CHECKLIST OF AVAILABLE VERMONT STATE PUBLICATIONS. **Main/Corp** Vermont. Dept. of Libraries. 0190-2091. US. English. an. Vermont Department of Libraries, Montepelier VT 05602.

CHIAO YU TZU LIAO KO HSUEH. **VFOAT** Journal of Educational Media Science. Vol. 18, No. 1 (Autumn 1980)-. 0377-9890. Periodical. CH. English (Chinese). qt. 4.00. Journal of Educational Media, Tamkang University Tamsui, Taipei Taiwan 251 Republic of China. **Tel** (02)621-5656. **Ed** Shih-Hsion Huang, Hwa-Wei Lee and Chang C Lee. **Ind/Abst** Libr. Inf. Sci. Abstr., Public Aff. Inf. Serv. Bull. adv acc. **Circ** 1,500. Library science, information science, audiovisual and educational technology. *Chiao Yu Tzu Liao Ko Hsueh Yueh Kan.*

CHICAGO LIBRARY SYSTEM COMMUNICATOR *CEASED.* V. 1- (Jan./Feb. 1976)-V. 6, No. 4 (July/Aug. 1981). 0147-4707. Periodical. US. English. bm. Free. Chicago Library System, 425 North Michigan Avenue, Chicago IL 60611.

CHIMIE PURE ET CHIMIE APPLIQUEE. LEXIQUE. 0154-0327. FR. French. an. Informascience, Centre de Documentation Scientifique et Technique Service des Abonnements, 26 rue Boyer, 75971 Paris Cedex 20 France. **LC** Z695.1.C5. **DD** 025.4966.

CHING PAO HSUEH KAN. **VFOAT** Qingbao Xuekan. Periodical. CC. Chinese. qt. 0.50. Post Office Cheng-Tu Shih, Cheng-Tu Shih China. **LC** Z671. **DD** 020.5.

CHING PAO KO HSUEH. **VFOAT** Information Science. No. 1 (Jan. 1980)-. Periodical. CC. Chinese. bm. 0.50. Chung-Kuo Kuo Chi Shu Tien, PO Box 2820, Peking China. **LC** Z671. **DD** 020.5.

CHINOOK REGIONAL LIBRARY DIRECTORY. *See* Yearbooks, Almanacs, Directories.

CHLA. ABSC NEWSLETTER. (C H L A/A B S C NEWSLETTER). **Main/Corp** Association des Bibliotheques de la Sante du Canada. **VAT** Canadian Health Library Association Newsletter, Association des Bibliotheques de la Sante du Canada. Newsletter. No. 1- Winter 1977-. 0700-5474. Periodical. CN. French (text in English). ir. Free to Members. Memorial University of Newfoundland, Health Sciences Centre, c/o R B Fredericksen, St John's Newfoundland A1B 3W6 Canada. **Ind/Abst** Libr. Inf. Sci. Abstr. **DD** 020.62271. *Can Group News, 0703-8615.*

THE CHRISTIAN LIBRARIAN : THE JOURNAL OF THE ASSOCIATION OF CHRISTIAN LIBRARIANS. Began in 1957. 0412-3131. Periodical. US. English. qt. $15.00. Association of Christian Librarians, PO Box 4, Cedarville OH 45314. **Tel** (513)766-2211. **Ed** Ron Jordahl. **Ind/Abst** Libr. Inf. Sci. Abstr., Comput. Control Abstr., Electr. Electron. Abstr., Sci. Abstr. Sect. A. Phys. Abstr., Christ. Period. Index, Phys. Abstr. **CODEN** CHLIDJ. bk rev. adv acc. **Circ** 425. Includes professional articles, book reviews of library science, reference and religious books, and a review of current library literature.

CHUNG-HUA MIN KUO TU SHU KUAN NIEN CHIEN. Chinese. an. **LC** Z845.T3. **DD** 027.0951249.

CHURCH & SYNAGOGUE LIBRARIES. **VAT** Church and Synagogue Libraries. 1967. 0009-6342. Periodical. US. English. bm. $15.00. Church & Synagogue Library, PO Box 1130, Bryn Mawr PA 19010. **Tel** (215)853-2870. **Ed** William H Gentz. **Ind/Abst** Christ. Period. Index. **LC** Z675.C5. **DD** 027.670973. bk rev. adv acc. **Circ** 3,200. (ctrl). Articles, news, book and media reviews for the church or synagogue librarian.

CIENCIA DA INFORMACAO. V. 1- 1972-. 0100-1965. Periodical. BL. Portuguese (summaries in English). sa. $24.00. IBICT, SCN-Quadra 2 Blocok, 70710 Brasilia DF Brazil. **Tel** (061)2266599. **Ed** IBICT. **Ind/Abst** Libr. Inf. Sci. Abstr., Foreign Lang. Index. **LC** Z1007. bk rev. adv acc. **Circ** 1,000. (ctrl). Original papers about specific problems on information science and technology in Brazil; translations of relevant papers, reviews, communications, news, letters to editor, editorials, etc.

CIRCULAR OF INFORMATION. **Main/Corp** New York State Library. School. 1910/1911-. US. English. ir. **LC** Z669.N5. *Circular of Information Concerning the Library School.*

CLA HANDBOOK AND MEMBERSHIP DIRECTORY. *See* Yearbooks, Almanacs, Directories.

CLA MEMBERSHIP LIST. (C L A MEMBERSHIP LIST). **Main/Corp** Canadian Library Association. 1974/75-. 0702-908X. CN. English. Canadian Library Association, 151 Sparks Street, Ottawa Ontario K1P 5E3 Canada. **DD** 020.62271. *C L A Organization Handbook.*

CLEAR PURPOSE, COMPLETE COMMITMENT. Vol. 1 (1973-1977)-. US. English. an. Louisiana State Library, PO Box 131, Baton Rouge LA 70821. **LC** Z732.L88. **DD** 027.0763.

CLENEXCHANGE. **Main/Corp** Continuing Library Education Network and Exchange. **VFOAT** Clenexchange Newsletter. V. 1- Sept. 1975-. 0360-0688. Periodical. US. English. qt. $20.00. Nancy Bolt, 1088 Fox Run Road, Milford OH 15150. **Tel** (513)248-0083. **LC** Z668. **DD** 020.710973.

CLIC QUARTERLY. (CLIC QUARTERLY : A JOURNAL OF OPINION, RESEARCH AND ADVOCACY IN THE FIELD OF LIBRARY AND INFORMATION RESOURCES MANAGEMENT). **VAT** Citizens' Library Council of New York State Quarterly. Vol. 1, No. 1 (March 1982)-. 0736-0045. Periodical. US. English. qt. $54.00. Citizens Library Council of New York State, 135 West Avenue, Draper Hall 113, Albany NY 12222. **Tel** (518)455-6288. **Ed** Richard S Halsey. **Ind/Abst** Libr. Inf. Sci. Abstr., Libr. Lit. adv acc. **Circ** 400. Deals with advocacy, opinion, and research in library, cultural, and information fields. Different types of library allied institution highlighted in each issue. *CLIC Newsletter (Citizens' Library Council of New York State).*

CLR RECENT DEVELOPMENTS. **Main/Corp** Council on Library Resources. **VFOAT** Recent Developments. **VAT** Council on Library Resources Recent Developments. V. 1- Dec. 1972-. 0034-1169. Periodical. US. English. ir. Council on Library Resources, One Dupont Circle NW, Suite 620, Washington DC 20036. *Recent Developments.*

CLSI NEWSLETTER. **Main/Corp** CL Systems, Inc. **VAT** CL Systems, Inc. Newsletter. No. 1- Summer 1976-. 0363-9479. Periodical. US. English. sa. CL Systems Inc, 81 Norwood Avenue, Newtonville MA 02160. **Tel** (617)965-6310.

CMLEA JOURNAL. **Main/Corp** CMLEA. **VAT** California Media and Library Educators Association Journal. V. 1- Fall 1977-. 0196-3309. Periodical. US. English. sa. $15.00. California School Libraries Journal of Media and Technology, Burlingame CA 94010. **Tel** (415)692-2350. **LC** Z675.S3. **DD** 027.809794. *California School Libraries, Journal of Media and Technology.*

THE COINT REPORTS. **VAT** Communication and Information Technology Reports. Vol. 1, No. 1-. 0198-8840. Periodical. US. English. ir. $14.00. The Advertisement Digest, Box 165, Morton Grove IL 60053. **Tel** (312)965-1456. **Ed** C I Park. bk rev. Syntheses-digest of new developments of information technologies that affect information services, with a single topic every issue.

COLLECTION BUILDING. V. 1-. 0160-4953. Periodical. US. English. qt. $55.00. Neal-Schuman Publishers Inc, 23 Cornelia Street, New York NY 10014. **Tel** (212)620-5990. **Ed** Arthur Curley. **Ind/Abst** Libr. Inf. Sci. Abstr., Libr. Lit. **LC** Z689. **DD** 025.21. Collection Building seeks to address issues problems and concerns encountered by librarians working in the field of collection development.

COLLECTION MANAGEMENT. V. 1, No. 3/4- Fall/Winter 1976/77-. 0146-2679. Periodical. US. English. qt. $75.00. Haworth Press, 23 East 22nd

Street, New York NY 10010. **Tel** (212 228-2800. **Ed** Brenda Hamilton White. **Ind/Abst** Libr. Lit., Cumul. Index Nurs. Allied Health Lit., Libr. Inf. Sci. Abstr. **LC** Z703.6. **DD** 020.5. **CODEN** COMADF. bk rev. adv acc. **Circ** 1,287. An indispensable reference on effective collection development in elementary and secondary schools. *De-Acquisitions Librarian, 0098-2121.*

COLLECTION UPDATE. No. 1- 1979-. 0226-3300. Periodical. CN. English. ir. Collection Update Library, University of Guelph, Guelph Ontario N1G 2W1 Canada. **DD** 027.771343.

COLLECTIONS DE RECHERCHE DES BIBLIOTHEQUES CANADIENNES. **VFOAT** Research Collections in Canadian Libraries. 0316-0327. Monographic Series. CN. French (English). Statistics Canada, Publications Distribution, Ottawa Ontario K1A 0T6 Canada. **DD** 021.00971.

COLLECTIONS OF THE ILLINOIS STATE HISTORICAL LIBRARY. Vol. 1-34. US. English. ir. Illinois State Historical Library, Old State Capitol, Springfield IL 62706. **LC** F536. (cum index).

COLLECTIONS - UNIVERSITY OF DELAWARE. LIBRARY. **Main/Corp** University of Delaware. Library. Vol. 1-. 8755-3473. Periodical. US. English. ir. Free. University of Delaware Library Associates, University of Delaware Library, Newark DE 19717-5267. **DD** 027.

COLLEGE & RESEARCH LIBRARIES. **VAT** College and Research Libraries. V. 1- Dec. 1939-. 0010-0870. Periodical. US. Englihs. bm. **Tel** (916)454-6230. **Ind/Abst** Educ. Index, Libr. Lit., Electron. Commun. Abstr. J., ISMEC Bull., Pollut. Abstr. Indexes, Saf. Sci. Abstr. J., Am. Hist. Life, Hist. Abstr., Part A, Mod. Hist. Abstr., Int. Labour Doc., Annu. Bibliogr. Engl. Lang. Lit., Libr. Inf. Sci. Abstr., Book Rev. Index, Public Aff. Inf. Serv. Bull., Curr. Index J. Educ., Ref. Source. **LC** Z671. **NLM** Z 671 C697. (cum index). bk rev. adv acc. **Circ** 10,000. Articles in all fields of interest and concern to academic and research librarians-scholarly and research oriented. Major scholarly serial in field of academic librarianship.

COLLEGE & RESEARCH LIBRARIES NEWS. **VAT** College and Research Libraries News. Jan. 1967, No. 1 Dec. 1979, No. 11. 0099-0086. Periodical. US. English. $10.00. American Library Association, 50 East Huron Street, Chicago IL 60611. **Tel** (312)944-6780. **Ind/Abst** Electron. Commun. Abstr. J., ISMEC Bull., Pollut. Abstr. Indexes, Saf. Sci. Abstr. J., Libr. Inf. Sci. Abstr., Public Aff. Inf. Serv. Bull., Libr. Lit. **DD** 020. **NLM** Z 671 C697A. *ACRL News.*

COLORADO LIBRARIES. 1974. 0147-9733. Periodical. US. English. qt. $25.00 Domestic, $35.00 Foreign. Colorado Library Association, PO Box 7507, Colorado Springs CO 80933. **Tel** (303)593-3291. **Ed** Ingrid Schierling. **Ind/Abst** Libr. Inf. Sci. Abstr., Libr. Lit. bk rev. adv acc. **Circ** 1,000. (ctrl). Contains articles describing activities of libraries in Colorado, as well as current innovations in library science. *CL, Colorado Libraries.*

COLUMBIA LIBRARY COLUMNS. Vol. 1 Fall 1951-. 0010-1966. Periodical. US. English. ir. $12.00. Friends of Columbia Libraries, 535 West 114th Street, New York NY 10027. **Ind/Abst** Abstr. Engl. Stud., MLA Int. Bibliogr. Books Artic. Mod. Lang. Lit., Annu. Bibliogr. Engl. Lang. Lit., Libr. Lit., Years Work Eng. Stud. **LC** Z671. **DD** 020.5. (cum index).

COLUMBIA UNIVERSITY STUDIES IN LIBRARY SERVICE. Vol. 1 1934-. 0069-6374. Monographic Series. US. English. ir. Columbia University Press, 136 South Broadway, Irvington-on-Hudson NY 10533.

COM-O-LIB. **Main/Corp** Colleges of Applied Arts and Technology. Committee of Librarians. Began publication in 197-. 0383-9842. Periodical. CN. English. ir. $5. Editor J Feeley, Algonquin College, 1385 Woodroffe Avenue, Ottawa Ontario K2G 1V8 Canada. **DD** 027.7062713.

COMIC RESEARCH LIBRARY NEWSLETTER. 0710-1074. Periodical. CN. English. ir. Free. Comic Research Library, Cassidy British Columbia V0R 1H0 Canada. **DD** 741.505.

COMLA NEWSLETTER. Periodical. English. qt. 17 Domestic, $30.00 Others. Commonwealth Library Association, c/o Executive Secretary, PO Box 14 Mandeville, Manchester Jamaica West Indies. **Tel** (809)962-0703. **Ed** Paul Xuereb. **Ind/Abst** Libr. Inf. Sci. Abstr. bk rev. adv acc. **Circ** 500. (ctrl). Articles of special interest to librarians with emphasis on commonwealth countries, including small island nations together with Australia, Britain, Canada, India and Nigeria; also news items culled from COMLA members library association newsletters.

COMLINE. Vol. 1, No. 1 (Nov. 1984)-. 8755-4143. Periodical. US. English. ty. Free. Blackwell Library Systems Inc, 310 East Shore Road, Great Neck NY 11023. **DD** 025.

COMMENT - CENTRAL ONTARIO REGIONAL LIBRARY SYSTEM. (COMMENT). Vol. 6, No. 6 (June 1976)-. 0225-6150. Periodical. CN. English. mo. Central Ontario Regional Library System, 129 Church Street South, Richmond Hill Ontario L4C 1W4 Canada. **DD** 027.471354. *C.O.R.L. Comment, 0319-2954.*

COMMITTEE ON EAST ASIAN LIBRARIES BULLETIN. (BULLETIN - ASSOCIATION FOR ASIAN STUDIES, INC., COMMITTEE ON EAST ASIAN LIBRARIES). **Main/Corp** Association for Asian Studies. Committee on East Asia Libraries. No. 53- July 1977-. 0148-6225. Periodical. US. English. ty. $25.00. Committee on East Asian Libraries, c/o East Asia Library University of Washington, Seattle WA 98195. **Tel** (609)452-3182. **Ed** Diane Perushek. **LC** Z688.E25. **DD** 026.95. bk rev. adv acc. **Circ** 350. (ctrl). *Newsletter - Association for Asian Studies.*

COMMONWEALTH OF MASSACHUSETTS PUBLICATIONS RECEIVED BY THE MASSACHUSETTS STATE LIBRARY. (COMMONWEALTH OF MASSACHUSETTS PUBLICATIONS RECEIVED BY THE MASSACHUSETTS STATE LIBRARY. BULLETIN). **Main/Corp** Massachusetts. State Library, Boston. **VFOAT** Bulletin - Massachusetts State Library. March 1962-. 0465-1898. US. English. mo. Massachusetts State Library Publications Department, 341 State House, Boston MA 02133. **LC** Z1223.5.M35. Available on microfilm.

COMMUNICATIONS AND INFORMATION HANDLING EQUIPMENT AND SERVICES. V. 1, No. 2- Jan./June 1979-. 0195-6612. Periodical. US. English. sa. Advertisement Digest, PO Box 165, Morgantown Grove IL 60053. **Tel** (312)965-1456. **Ed** Chung I Park. **LC** Z684. **DD** 659.1902. Abstracts of advertisements and evaluations of computers, library technologies, and information services. *Advertisement Digest: Library and Information Services, 0194-0392.*

COMMUNICATIONS FOR BETTER LIVING. Began in 1984?. 8755-9579. Periodical. US. English. mo. Interfaith Publications, 1433 17th Street, Denver CO 80202. **DD** 028.

THE COMMUNICATOR. Vol. 1, No. 1 (Oct. 1981)-. 0277-8955. Periodical. US. English. mo. Free. The Communicator, 425 North Michigan Avenue, Chicago IL 60611. *Chicago Library System Communicator, 0147-4707; Chicago Public Library Newsletter.*

COMMUNITY & JUNIOR COLLEGE LIBRARIES. **VFOAT** Community and Junior College Libraries. Vol. 1, No. 1 (Fall 1982)-. 0276-3915. US. English. qt. $45.00. Haworth Press, 28 East 22nd Street, New York NY 10010. **Tel** (212)228-2800. **Ed** Peggy Holleman and Joseph Borowski. **Ind/Abst** Libr. Inf. Sci. Abstr., Comput. Control Abstr., Electr. Electron. Abstr., Sci. Abstr. Sect. A. Phys. Abstr. **LC** Z675.J8. **DD** 027.705. **CODEN** CJCLDV. adv acc. **Circ** 399. Many of the most innovative techniques in librarianship are coming from the community and junior college library setting. Read about them first in this journal.

COMPTE RENDU ET DOCUMENTS. **Main/Corp** Association of Parliamentary Librarians in Canada. Conference. **VFOAT** Report and Documents. CN. English (French). be. **LC** Z675.G7. **DD** 027.50601.

COMPUTER USE IN MASSACHUSETTS LIBRARIES. Dec. 1982-. 0742-9886. US. English. an. Massachusetts Board of Library Commissioners, 648 Beacon Street, Boston MA 02215. **LC** Z768.9.A3. **DD** 027.0744.

CONFERENCE SERIES - INTERNATIONAL ASSOCIATION OF MARINE SCIENCE LIBRARIES AND INFORMATION CENTERS. (CONFERENCE SERIES). **Main/Conf** International Association of Marine Science Libraries and Information Centers. 8755-6332. Periodical. US. English. an. $10.00. University of Texas, Marine Science Institute, Port Arkansas TX 78373-1267.

CONNECTICARD ANNUAL STATISTICAL REPORT. *See* Statistics.

CONNECTICUT LIBRARIES (1954-). 1955. 0010-616X. Periodical. US. English. mo. $25.00 Domestic, $30.00 Foreign. Connecticut Library Association, 231 Capitol Avenue, State Library, Hartford CT 06106. **Tel** (203)278-6685. **Ed** David L Kapp. **Ind/Abst** Libr. Lit. adv acc. **Circ** 850. Short articles (2500 words) and news items relating to library activities in Connecticut and to activities of the Connecticut Library Association.

CONNECTION. April 1973-. 0319-2156. Periodical. CN. English. mo. Free. Edmonton Public Library, #7 Winston Churchill Square, Edmonton Alberta T5J 2V4 Canada. **DD** 027.471233.

CONSER MICROFICHE. **VFOAT** NLC/BNC Conser Microfiche. 1975/78-. 0707-3747. CN. English (French). Library of Congress, Cataloging Distribution Service, Washington DC 20541. **Tel** (202)287-6100. **DD** 018.134. **NLM** Z 6945 C753. (cum index). Includes all serial records in the CONSER (Conversion of Serials) data base.

CONSER TABLES. Began with Feb. 1979. 0190-3608. US. English. ir. Library of Congress, Cataloging Distribution Service, Washington DC 20541. **Tel** (202)287-6100. **LC** Z699.4.C25. **DD** 025.343. A brief reference tool for those using the records in the CONSER data base.

CONSERVATION ADMINISTRATION NEWS. **VFOAT** CAN. No. 1 (June 1979)-. 0192-2912. Periodical. US. English. qt. $18.00. University of Tulsa, McFarlin Library, 600 South College Avenue, Tulsa OK 74104. **Tel** (918)592-6000. **Ed** Robert H Patterson. **Ind/Abst** Libr. Inf. Sci. Abstr. bk rev. adv acc. **Circ** 500. Publication of library and archival preservation.

CONTACT *CEASED.* V. 1- Mar. 1976- Ceased with issue for Summer 1982?. 0381-6818. Periodical. CN. English. Ontario Library Association, 239A Bloor Street West, Toronto Ontario M6S 1P6 Canada. **DD** 027.4713.

CONTRIBUTIONS IN LIBRARIANSHIP AND INFORMATION SCIENCE. No. 1-. 0084-9243. Monographic Series. US. English. ir. Greenwood Press, 88 Post Road West, Box 5007, Westport CT 06881. **Tel** (203)226-3571. **Ed** Paul Wasserman. **LC** UNC.

CONTRIBUTIONS TO LIBRARIANSHIP. No. 1-. 0145-8485. Monographic Series. US. English. ir. University of Texas at Austin, Perry Castaneda Library 3.200, Austin TX 78713-7330. **Tel** (512)471-3811. **Ed** Mary Pound. Monographs based on work programs of the general libraries, University of Texas at Austin.

CONTRIBUTIONS TO LIBRARY SCIENCE. BIBLIOTEEKUNDIGE HYDRAES. **Main/Corp** South Africa. State Library. No. 1- 1961-. Monographic Series. SA. English. ir. The State Library, PO Box 397, Pretoria 0001 South Africa. **LC** Z674.

CORE COLLECTION. **Main/Corp** Baker Library. Began with: 1970-71. 0730-6121. US. English. an. $17.50 $15.00. Harvard Business School, Baker Library, Soldiers Field Road, Boston MA 02163. **Tel** (617)495-6405. **LC** Z7164.C81, HF5351. **DD** 016.33. **Circ** 600. Index to Baker library's reading room collection of over 3,000 books with best and most recent titles. Subject index contains entries relevant to a wide variety of research, from accounting and executive ability to venture capital and women employment.

CORPORATE AUTHOR AUTHORITY LIST. 0741-3270. US. English. an. National Technical Information Service, US Department of Commerce, 5285 Port Royal Road, Springfield VA 22161. **LC** Z695.8. **DD** 025.49.

THE COUNTY LINE. **Main/Corp** Toledo-Lucas County Public Library. Periodical. US. English. mo. Toledo-Lucas County Public Library, 325 Michigan Street, Toledo OH 43624.

CRAB. (THE CRAB). V. 1- Aug. 1971-. 0300-7561. Periodical. US. English. bm. $15.00. Maryland Library Association, 115 West Franklin Street, Baltimore MD 21201. **Tel** (301)685-5760. **Ed** Howard Hubbard and Steven Wooldridge. **LC** Z673.M393. **DD** 027.0752. bk rev. adv acc. **Circ** 1,100. (ctrl). Available on microfilm from Xerox University Microfilms. Aimed at supplying information of interest to members of the Maryland Library Association- personnel, workshops, etc. *Maryland Libraries (1955).*

CRANE LIBRARY NEWS. Vol. 1, No. 1 (Oct. 30, 1970)-. 0316-7372. Periodical. CN. English. ir. Charles Crane Memorial Library University of British

Library and Information Science

Columbia, 1874 East Mall, Vancouver British Columbia V6T 1W5 Canada. **DD** 027.663.

CRANE LIBRARY NEWS SUBSTITUTE. 0827-3766. Periodical. CN. English. ir. Free. Charles Crane Memorial Library, University of British Columbia, 1874 East Mall, Vancouver British Columbia V6T 1W5 Canada. **DD** 027.663.

CRANE LIBRARY UPDATE. 0228-9571. Periodical. CN. English. Crane Library, 2075 Westbrook Mall, Vancouver British Columbia V6T 1W5 Canada. **DD** 018.138. *Crane Library Update Circular, 0228-9563.*

CRANE LIBRARY W.I.P. (CRANE LIBRARY W.I.P. : WORKS IN PROGRESS AT CRANE LIBRARY U.B.C). **VAT** Crane Library Works in Progress, Works in Progress at Crane Library U.B.C. Mar. 13, 1979-. 0228-9555. Periodical. CN. English. Crane Library, 2075 Wesbrook Mall, Vancouver British Columbia V6T 1W5 Canada. **DD** 018.138.

CUADERNOS - VENEZUELA. UNIVERSIDAD CENTRAL, CARACAS. ESCUELA DE PERIODISMO. **Main/Corp** Venezuela. Universidad Central, Caracas. Escuela de Periodismo. V. 1- 1959-. 0506-6131. VE. Spanish. ir. Universidad Central Caracas, Escuela de Periodismo, Caracas Venezuela.

CULTURE STATISTICS : CENTRALIZED SCHOOL LIBRARIES IN CANADA. *See* Statistics.

CULTURE STATISTICS. PUBLIC LIBRARIES IN CANADA. *See* Statistics.

CUM NOTIS VARIORUM. *See* Music.

CUMULATIVE MICROFORM REVIEWS. 1972/76-. 0162-0940. US. English. ir. $75.00. Microform Review Inc, 520 Riverside Avenue Box 405, Westport CT 06880. **Tel** (203)226-6967. Reviews hundreds of micropublications that have been published in microform review.

CURRENT AWARENESS LIBRARY LITERATURE *CEASED*. (CALL; CURRENT AWARENESS — LIBRARY LITERATURE). **VFOAT** Call (Current Awareness—Library Literature). V. 1, No. 1 (Jan./Feb. 1972)-. 0091-5270. Periodical. US. English. bm. Goldstein Associates, 35 Whittemore Road, Framingham MA 01701. **Ind/Abst** Libr. Lit. **LC** Z666. **DD** 016.02.

CURRENT AWARENESS SERVICE (CAMBRIDGE, MASS.). (CURRENT AWARENESS SERVICE). Began in Sept. 1981. 0882-3677. Periodical. US. English. mo. $12.50. Gutman Library, 6 Appian Way, Cambridge MA 02138.

CURRENT BOOK REVIEW CITATIONS *CEASED*. 1976-82. 0360-1250. US. English. an. **LC** Z1035.A1. **DD** 028.1.

CURRENT CATALOG PROOF SHEETS, SEMIWEEKLY PROOF. **Main/Corp** National Library of Medicine (U.S.). Periodical. US. English. wk. $96.00. Medical Library Association Inc, 919 North Michigan Avenue/Suite 3208, Chicago IL 60611. **Tel** (312)266-2456. **Circ** 450. Timely printed version of the National Library of Medicine cataloging; contains cataloging records of English language, materials, including CIP packets, with index every fourth issue.

CURRENT ISSUES IN LIBRARIANSHIP. No. 1-. Monographic Series. US. English. The Pierian Press, PO Box 1808, Ann Arbor MI 48106.

CURRENT RESEARCH IN LIBRARY & INFORMATION SCIENCE (LIBRARY ASSOCIATION. (CURRENT RESEARCH IN LIBRARY & INFORMATION SCIENCE). **VFOAT** Current Research in Library and Information Science. Vol. 1, No. 1 (March 1983)-. 0263-9254. Periodical. UK. English. qt. 79 Domestic, $171.00 US, 95 Others. Library Association Publishing, 7 Ridgemount Street, London WC1E 7AE England. **Tel** (01)636-7543. Ed P T Biggs. **Ind/Abst** Electron. Pub. Abstr. **LC** Z669.7. **DD** 020.72. adv acc. **Circ** 400. Details of current research projects worldwide in librarianship, information work and archives. Covers all aspects. Doctoral theses included. Sub-doctoral disertations listed. Contextual subjects covered. *Radials Bulletin.*

CURRENT SERIALS RECEIVED - BRITISH LIBRARY LENDING DIVISION. (CURRENT SERIALS RECEIVED). **Main/Corp** British Library. Lending Division. Began in Sept. 1975. 0309-0655. Periodical. UK. English. an. $44.45. British Library, Bibliographic Service Division, 2 Sheraton Street, London W1V 4BH England. **Tel** 01-636 1544. **LC** Current Issues Only. **NLM** ZQ 1 C974. *Current Serials Received by the BLL.*

CURRENT STUDIES IN LIBRARIANSHIP. **VFOAT** CSIL. V. 1- Spring 1977-. 0742-8227. Periodical. US. English. an. $8.00. University of Rhode Island, Graduate School of Library & Information Science, Kingston RI 02881. **Tel** (401)792-2947. Ed L B Woods. **Ind/Abst** Libr. Inf. Sci. Abstr. Articles published of general interest to all types of librarians.

CYLCHGRAWN LLYFRGELL GENEDLAETHOL CYMRU. **Main/Corp** National Library of Wales. **VFOAT** The National Library of Wales Journal. V. 1- 1939-. 0011-4421. Periodical. UK. English. sa. $10.73. National Library of Wales, Aberystwyth, Dyfed SY23 3BU Wales. **Tel** 9970 3816. **Ind/Abst** Abstr. Engl. Stud., MLA Int. Bibliogr. Books Artic. Mod. Lang. Lit., Am. Hist. Life, Hist. Abstr., Repert. Int. Litt. Art, Years Work Eng. Stud. **Circ** 400. (ctrl)

THE DAEDALUS LIBRARY. V. 1- 1965-. 0070-2536. Monographic Series. US. English. ir. Beacon Press, 25 Beacon Street, Boston MA 02108.

DAIGAKU TOSHOKAN KYORYOKU NYUSU. 0388-5623. Periodical. JA. Japanese. ir. 3000 Institution. Gakujutsu Bunken Fukyukai, c/o Tokyo Kodai Ookayama 2, Meguro-Ku 152, Tokyo-To-Japan. **LC** Z675.U5.

DATABASE. **VFOAT** Database Magazine. V. 1- Sept. 1978-. 0162-4105. Periodical. US. English. qt. $78.00. Online Inc, 11 Tannery Lane, Weston CT 06883. **Tel** (203)227-8466. **Ed** Helen Gordon. **Ind/Abst** Comput. Control Abstr., Electr. Electron. Abstr., Libr. Lit., Cumul. Index Nurs. Allied Health Lit., Curr. Index J. Educ., Libr. Inf. Sci. Abstr., Microcomput. Index. **LC** Z699.A1. **DD** 029.705. **CODEN** DTBSDQ. bk rev. adv acc. **Circ** 3,000. Has lengthy in-depth articles on database usage, and comparisons and evaluations.

DATABASES ONLINE. (DATABASES ONLINE IN . . .). 1981-. 0275-9152. US. English. an. $15.00 Members, $18.00 Nonmembers. American Society for Information Science, 1010 16th Street NW, Washington DC 20036. **LC** Z699.A1. **DD** 025.302854.

DBPH NEWSLETTER. **VFOAT** D.B.P.H. Newsletter. **VAT** Division for the Blind and Physically Handicapped Newsletter. Spring 1976-. 0737-6235. Periodical. US. English. qt. Free. Texas State Library DBPH, Austin TX 78711. **Tel** (512)463-5458. **Ed** Patsy Castro. **Circ** 18,000. Library related information, new services available, services provided by other agencies, newly acquired large print and recorded casette books for the blind and physically handicapped.

DEPARTMENTAL LIBRARY ACQUISITIONS - DEPARTMENT OF PUBLIC WORKS. (DEPARTMENTAL LIBRARY ACQUISITIONS). **Main/Corp** Canada. Dept. of Public Works. Library. **VFOAT** Acquisitions de la Bibliotheque Centrale. 0709-3829. Periodical. CN. English (French). Departmental Library, Department of Public Works, Sir Charles Tupper Building, Ottawa Ontario K1A 0M2 Canada. *Acquisitions, 0701-8509.*

DETAILED STATISTICAL DATA FOR OHIO PUBLIC LIBRARIES. *See* Statistics.

DEUTSCHES BIBLIOTHEKSADRESSBUCH. August 1, 1974-. GW. German. ir. Verlag Dokumentation, Postfach 71 10 09, 8000 Munchen 71 West Berlin East Germany. **LC** Z801.A1.

DEVELOPMENT NEWS. (DEVELOPMENT NEWS FOR LIBRARIES : A PUBLICATION OF THE MICHIGAN LIBRARY CONSORTIUM). Vol. 1, No. 1 (Jan./Feb. 1983)-. 0736-8534. Periodical. US. English. bm. $20.00 Members, $25.00 Non-Members. Michigan Library Consortium, 6810 South Cedar Street/Suite 88, Lansing MI 48910.

DEWEY DECIMAL CLASSIFICATION ADDITIONS, NOTES, AND DECISIONS. **VFOAT** D.C. AND. Vol. 2, No. 2 (Spring 1971)-. 0191-3646. US. English. **LC** Z696.D5. **DD** 025.431. *Decimal Classification Additions, Notes, and Decisions, 0083-1573.*

DFW, DOKUMENTATION, INFORMATION. **VFOAT** Dokumentation, Information. V. 20- Oct./Nov. 1971-. 0373-8825. Periodical. GW. German. bm. $63.35. Nordwest Verlag, Gunterstrasse 21, 3000 Hannover 81 West Germany. **Ind/Abst** Libr. Inf. Sci. Abstr. **LC** Z699.A1. *Dokumentation, Fachbibliothek, Werksbucherei.*

DIALOGUE. Nov. 1973-. 0700-3048. Periodical. CN. English. ir. Free. Eastern Ontario Library System, 200 Cooper Street/Suite 6, Ottawa Ontario K2P 0G1 Canada. **Ind/Abst** Index Book Rev. Humanit. **DD** 027.4097138. (ctrl).

DICTIONARY CATALOG OF THE COLUMBIA UNIVERSITY LAW LIBRARY. SUPPLEMENT. **Main/Corp** Columbia University. Libraries. Law Library. 1st- 1973-. 0098-7395. US. Multilingual (English). G K Hall, 70 Lincoln Street, Boston MA 02111. **Tel** (617)423-3990. Ed G K Hall. **DD** 016.34. One of the largest, this library contains about 465,000 volumes, rich in legal literature of the U.S. and the British Commonwealth, and excellent coverage of Roman and medieval law.

DICTIONARY CATALOG OF THE RESEARCH LIBRARIES. **Main/Corp** New York (City). Public Library. Research Libraries. Jan. 1972-Dec. 1980. 0094-9728. US. English. mo. New York City Public Library, 5th Avenue at 42nd Street, New York NY 10018. **LC** Z881.N588. **DD** 019.1.

DICTIONARY CATALOG. SUPPLEMENT. **Main/Corp** New York (City) Public Library. Schomburg Collection of Negro Literature and History. 1st- 1967-. US. English. **LC** Z881.N592.

DIKTA. V. 1- Spring 1976-. 0363-5414. Periodical. US. English. qt. $8.00. Southern Conference of Librarians for the Blind & Physically Handicapped, PO Box 12927, Austin TX 78711. **Tel** (512)475-4758. **Ed** Bonnie Peele. **Ind/Abst** Libr. Inf. Sci. Abstr. **LC** Z711.92.P5. **DD** 027.66505. bk rev. **Circ** 140. News and information concerning library services to the blind and physically handicapped.

DIRECTIONS. V. 1- Aug. 1975-. 0360-473X. Periodical. US. English. mo. $1.00. Baker & Taylor Co, 50 Kirby Avenue, Somerville NJ 08876. **Ind/Abst** GeoRef. **LC** Z671. **DD** 020.5.

DIRECTORIES AND ASSOCIATIONS OF THE BOOK TRADE AND LIBRARIANSHIP. ADRESSBUCHER UND VERBANDE DES BUCH- UND BIBLIOTHEKSWESENS. *See* Yearbooks, Almanacs, Directories.

DIRECTORIO COLOMBIANO DE UNIDADES DE INFORMACION. *See* Yearbooks, Almanacs, Directories.

DIRECTORIO DE SERVICIOS DE INFORMACION Y DOCUMENTACION EN EL URUGUAY. *See* Yearbooks, Almanacs, Directories.

DIRECTORY AND STATISTICS OF OREGON LIBRARIES. *See* Yearbooks, Almanacs, Directories.

DIRECTORY - CASLIS, CALGARY CHAPTER. *See* Yearbooks, Almanacs, Directories.

DIRECTORY - CENTRAL ONTARIO REGIONAL LIBRARY SYSTEM. *See* Yearbooks, Almanacs, Directories.

DIRECTORY - EASTERN ONTARIO LIBRARY SYSTEM. ANNUAIRE - FEDERATION DES BIBLIOTHEQUES DE L'EST DE L'ONTARIO. *See* Yearbooks, Almanacs, Directories.

DIRECTORY INFORMATION SERVICE. *See* Yearbooks, Almanacs, Directories.

DIRECTORY - INTERNATIONAL ASSOCIATION OF LAW LIBRARIES. *See* Yearbooks, Almanacs, Directories.

DIRECTORY - LAKE ONTARIO REGIONAL LIBRARY SYSTEM. *See* Yearbooks, Almanacs, Directories.

DIRECTORY - LIBRARY OF CONGRESS. *See* Yearbooks, Almanacs, Directories.

DIRECTORY - MEDICAL LIBRARY ASSOCIATION. *See* Yearbooks, Almanacs, Directories.

DIRECTORY, MEMBER LIBRARIES, GEORGIAN BAY REGIONAL LIBRARY SYSTEM. *See* Yearbooks, Almanacs, Directories.

DIRECTORY - NIAGARA REGIONAL LIBRARY SYSTEM. *See* Yearbooks, Almanacs, Directories.

DIRECTORY, NON-OPERATING LIBRARY BOARDS - GEORGIAN BAY REGIONAL LIBRARY SYSTEM. *See* Yearbooks, Almanacs, Directories.

Library and Information Science

DIRECTORY - NORTH CENTRAL REGIONAL LIBRARY SYSTEM. See Yearbooks, Almanacs, Directories.

DIRECTORY - NORTH CENTRAL REGIONAL LIBRARY SYSTEM. See Yearbooks, Almanacs, Directories.

DIRECTORY - NORTHEASTERN REGIONAL LIBRARY SYSTEM. See Yearbooks, Almanacs, Directories.

DIRECTORY OF ALBERTA GOVERNMENT LIBRARIES. See Yearbooks, Almanacs, Directories.

DIRECTORY OF ARTS LIBRARIES AND RESOURCE COLLECTIONS IN AUSTRALIA. See Yearbooks, Almanacs, Directories.

DIRECTORY OF AUSTRALIAN ACADEMIC LIBRARIES. See Yearbooks, Almanacs, Directories.

DIRECTORY OF COLORADO LIBRARIES . . . & LIBRARY STATISTICS. See Yearbooks, Almanacs, Directories.

DIRECTORY OF CONTINUING EDUCATION OPPORTUNITIES FOR LIBRARY, INFORMATION, MEDIA PERSONNEL. See Yearbooks, Almanacs, Directories.

A DIRECTORY OF DELAWARE LIBRARIES. See Yearbooks, Almanacs, Directories.

DIRECTORY OF EAST ASIAN COLLECTIONS IN AMERICAN LIBRARIES. See Yearbooks, Almanacs, Directories.

THE DIRECTORY OF FEE-BASED INFORMATION SERVICES. See Yearbooks, Almanacs, Directories.

DIRECTORY OF HEALTH SCIENCES LIBRARIES IN THE UNITED STATES. See Yearbooks, Almanacs, Directories.

DIRECTORY OF INDUSTRIAL RELATIONS LIBRARIES IN CANADA. See Yearbooks, Almanacs, Directories.

DIRECTORY OF LAW LIBRARIES. See Yearbooks, Almanacs, Directories.

DIRECTORY OF LIBRARIES AND ARCHIVAL INSTITUTIONS IN PRINCE EDWARD ISLAND. See Yearbooks, Almanacs, Directories.

DIRECTORY OF LIBRARIES AND INFORMATION SERVICES IN THE PHILADELPHIA AREA. See Yearbooks, Almanacs, Directories.

DIRECTORY OF LIBRARIES IN MANITOBA. See Yearbooks, Almanacs, Directories.

DIRECTORY OF LIBRARIES IN NEWFOUNDLAND AND LABRADOR. See Yearbooks, Almanacs, Directories.

DIRECTORY OF LIBRARIES IN NORTHWESTERN ONTARIO. See Yearbooks, Almanacs, Directories.

DIRECTORY OF LIBRARY AND INFORMATION CONSULTANTS IN METROPOLITAN WASHINGTON. See Yearbooks, Almanacs, Directories.

DIRECTORY OF LIBRARY ASSOCIATIONS IN CANADA. See Yearbooks, Almanacs, Directories.

DIRECTORY OF LIBRARY RELATED ORGANIZATIONS IN THE ATLANTIC PROVINCES. See Yearbooks, Almanacs, Directories.

DIRECTORY OF LIBRARY REPROGRAPHIC SERVICES; A WORLD GUIDE. See Yearbooks, Almanacs, Directories.

A DIRECTORY OF LIBRARY SYSTEMS IN NEW YORK STATE. See Yearbooks, Almanacs, Directories.

DIRECTORY OF LONDON PUBLIC LIBRARIES. See Yearbooks, Almanacs, Directories.

DIRECTORY OF MEMBERS AND LIBRARIES - INDIAN LIBRARY ASSOCIATION. See Yearbooks, Almanacs, Directories.

DIRECTORY OF MEMBERS - MANUSCRIPT SOCIETY (U.S.). See Yearbooks, Almanacs, Directories.

DIRECTORY OF MISSOURI LIBRARIES. See Yearbooks, Almanacs, Directories.

DIRECTORY OF NEW BRUNSWICK LIBRARIES. See Yearbooks, Almanacs, Directories.

DIRECTORY OF O.C.U.L. LIBRARIES. See Yearbooks, Almanacs, Directories.

DIRECTORY OF OHIO LIBRARIES (COLUMBUS, OHIO : 1980). See Yearbooks, Almanacs, Directories.

DIRECTORY OF OPERATING LIBRARIES - GEORGIAN BAY REGIONAL LIBRARY SYSTEM. See Yearbooks, Almanacs, Directories.

DIRECTORY OF PENNSYLVANIA ACADEMIC AND RESEARCH LIBRARIES. See Yearbooks, Almanacs, Directories.

DIRECTORY OF PUBLIC LIBRARY SERVICES IN VICTORIA. See Yearbooks, Almanacs, Directories.

DIRECTORY OF PUBLIC LIBRARY SERVICES, WESTERN AUSTRALIA. See Yearbooks, Almanacs, Directories.

DIRECTORY OF SASKATCHEWAN LIBRARIES. See Yearbooks, Almanacs, Directories.

DIRECTORY OF SCHOOLS OFFERING LIBRARY SCIENCE. See Yearbooks, Almanacs, Directories.

DIRECTORY OF SPECIAL LIBRARIES AND INFORMATION CENTERS. See Yearbooks, Almanacs, Directories.

DIRECTORY OF SPECIAL LIBRARIES AND INFORMATION CENTERS IN TEXAS. See Yearbooks, Almanacs, Directories.

DIRECTORY OF SPECIAL LIBRARIES IN AUSTRALIA. See Yearbooks, Almanacs, Directories.

DIRECTORY OF SPECIAL LIBRARIES IN THE MONTREAL AREA. See Yearbooks, Almanacs, Directories.

DIRECTORY OF SPECIAL LIBRARIES (SEMMON TOSHOKAN KYOGIKAI). See Yearbooks, Almanacs, Directories.

DIRECTORY OF THE NEW YORK METROPOLITAN REFERENCE AND RESEARCH LIBRARY AGENCY, METRO AND METROPOLITAN NEW YORK REGIONAL INTERSYSTEM COOPERATIVE LIBRARY NETWORK, INTERSHARE. See Yearbooks, Almanacs, Directories.

DIRECTORY OF WESTCHESTER LIBRARIES AND MEDIA CENTERS AND BUYERS GUIDE. See Yearbooks, Almanacs, Directories.

DIRECTORY - OHIO EDUCATIONAL LIBRARY/MEDIA ASSOCIATION. See Yearbooks, Almanacs, Directories.

DIRECTORY - SOUTH CENTRAL REGIONAL LIBRARY SYSTEM. See Yearbooks, Almanacs, Directories.

DIRECTORY - TEXAS LIBRARY ASSOCIATION. See Yearbooks, Almanacs, Directories.

DJURNAL PERPUSTAKAAN. Periodical. Indonesian or English. ir. Perpustakaan Umum Makassar, JL. Kajaolailidjo 16, PO Box 16, Ujung Pandang Indonesia. **LC** Z671.

DLA BULLETIN. VFOAT University of California Division of Library Automation Bulletin. Vol. 1, No. 1 (Feb. 1981)-. 0272-037X. Periodical. US. English. ir. DLA Bulletin, University of California Division of Library Automation, 186 University Hall, Berkeley CA 94720. **Ind/Abst** Libr. Inf. Sci. Abstr.

DOCUMENTACION BIBLIOTECOLOGICA. No. 1- 1970-. Periodical. BL. Spanish. ir. Centro de Documentacion Bibliotecologica, Universidad Nacional del Sur, Bahia Blanca Brazil. **LC** Z671.

DOCUMENTALISTE. 1964-. 0012-4508. Periodical. FR. French. bm. 315 Domestic, and 360 Foreign. ADBS, 5 Avenue Franco Russe, 75007 Paris France. **Tel** (1)4551 05 04. Ed A Chonez. **Ind/Abst** Libr. Lit. bk rev. adv acc. **Circ** 4,000.

DOCUMENTATION ABSTRACTS. See Indexes/Abstracts.

DOCUMENTATION ET BIBLIOTHEQUES. V. 19- March 1973-. 0315-2340. Periodical. CN. French. qt. $23.21. ASTED, 7243 rue Saint-Denis, Montreal H2R 2E3 Quebec Canada. **Tel** (514)271-3349. **Ind/Abst** Point Repere, Can. Period. Index, Libr. Inf. Sci. Abstr., Comput. Control Abstr., Electr. Electron. Abstr., Sci. Abstr. Sect. A. Phys. Abstr., Libr. Lit., Phys. Abstr. **LC** Z735.A1. **DD** 020.5. **CODEN** DCBBBO.

DOCUMENTATION, LIBRARIES AND ARCHIVES : STUDIES AND RESEARCH. Began with No. 1, 1972. Periodical. English. ir. UNESCO, 7 Place de Fontenoy, 75700 Paris France.

DOCUMENTS TO THE PEOPLE. (DTTP. DOCUMENTS TO THE PEOPLE). VFOAT DTTP. V. 3- Sept. 1974-. 0270-5095. Periodical. US. English. qt. $15.00. ALA Government Documents Round Table, 8304 Tomlinson Avenue, L Decker, Bethesda MD 20817. **Tel** (202)287-7491. **Ind/Abst** Libr. Inf. Sci. Abstr. **DD** 025. Documents to the People, 0270-5095.

DORLS TECHNICAL SERVICES COMMITTEE'S INFORMATION EXCHANGE. (D O R L S TECHNICAL SERVICES COMMITTEE'S INFORMATION EXCHANGE). VFOAT Information Exchange. **VAT** Directors of Ontario Regional Library Systems Technical Services Committee's Information Exchange. V. 1- Oct. 1976-. 0703-1688. Periodical. CN. English. mo. Free. Provincial Library Service, 14th Floor/Mowat Block, Queens Park, Toronto Ontario M7A 2R9 Canada. **DD** 025.0205. (ctrl).

DOWNEAST LIBRARIES. VFOAT Down East Libraries. Began with: Vol. 1, No. 1 in 1973. 0738-5684. Periodical. US. English. qt. Free to Members, $6.00 Others. Maine Library Association, Local Government Center Community Drive, Augusta ME 04330. **DD** 025. Downeast Newsletter.

DREXEL LIBRARY QUARTERLY. V. 1- Jan. 1965-. 0012-6160. Periodical. US. English. qt. $30.00 Domestic, $35.00 Foreign. College of Information Studies, Drexel University, Ann Tanner, Philadelphia, PA 19104. **Tel** (215)895-2483. Ed Anne B Tanner. **Ind/Abst** Curr. Index J. Educ., Inf. Sci. Abstr., Libr. Lit., Libr. Inf. Sci. Abstr., Public Aff. Inf. Serv. Bull., Curr. Contents, Soc. Sci. Citation Index. **LC** Z671. **DD** 020.5. **NLM** Z 671 D777. **CODEN** DRLQB. **Circ** 1,000. Each issue contains six to eight articles devoted to a single topic of current interest to library and information professionals.

DUNDURN JOURNAL. No. 1- Jan. 1978!-. 0707-2309. Periodical. CN. ir. Free. Dundurn Press, Box 245 Station F, Toronto Ontario M4Y 2L5 Canada. **DD** 028.105. (ctrl).

DYNIX DATALINE. Began in 1984. 8756-2294. Periodical. US. English. bm. Dynix Inc, 1455 West 820 North, Provo UT 84601. **DD** 025.

EALING OCCASIONAL PAPERS IN THE HISTORY OF LIBRARIES. No. 1- 1972-. UK. English. School of Librarianship/Ealing Technical College, St Mary's Road W, 5 London England. **LC** Z791.A1. **DD** 027.042.

ECHANGE. (L'ECHANGE). V. 1- Jan. 1978-. 0706-5205. Periodical. CN. French. ir. $15.00. Bibliotheque Centrale de Pret de l'Abitibi-Temiscamingue, C P 266, Noranda Quebec J9X 2A9 Canada. **DD** 027.471413.

ECRILU. (L'ECRILU). Vol. 1, No. 2 Sept. 1981-. 0711-1169. Periodical. CN. French. qt. $3.86. Federation Quebecoise Loisir Litteraire, 1415 East rue Jarry, Montreal Quebec H2E 2Z7 Canada. **Tel** (514)374-4700. **DD** 028.805. Bulletin d'Information (Federation Quebecoise du Loisir Litteraire), 0228-9814.

EDICIONES. Main/Corp Universidad Central de Venezuela. Biblioteca Central. V. 1- 1961-. 0506-5992. VE. Spanish. ir. Universidad Central, Biblioteca, Caracas Venezuela.

EDICIONES BIBLIOTECA JOSE AGUSTIN ARANGO CH. BOLETIN CULTURAL. Monographic Series. PN. Spanish. ir. Banco Nacional de Panama, Casilla Postal 5220, Panama 5 Panama.

EDUCATION & CURRICULUM SERIES. No. 1- 1973-. US. English. ir. Syracuse University Printing Services, 125 College Place, Syracuse NY 13210. **Tel** (315)423-2911. **LC** Z668. **DD** 020.7.

Library and Information Science

EDUCATION AND LIBRARY BOARDS, GRANT AIDED SCHOOLS, INSTITUTIONS OF FURTHER EDUCATION, AND LIBRARIES. See Education (General).

EDUCATION LIBRARIES. 1975. 0148-1061. Periodical. US. English. ty. $15.00. Special Library Association, Education Division, Rider College Library, c/o Hope Tillman, 2083 Lawrenceville Road, Lawrenceville NJ 08648. **Tel** (609)896-5115. Ed Hope Tillman. **Ind/Abst** Libr. Inf. Sci. Abstr., Curr. Index J. Educ. **LC** Z675.P3. **DD** 027.7. bk rev. adv acc. **Circ** 400. Practical journal for librarians in the field of education and library science. *Bulletin (Special Libraries Association. Education Division), 0360-098X*

EDUCATION LIBRARIES BULLETIN. No. 1 (Spring 1958)-. 0013-1407. Periodical. UK. English. ty. $7.66. University of London, Institute for Education Library, 11-13 Ridgemount Street, London WC1E 7AH England. **Tel** 01-637 0846. Ed Norman W Beswick. **Ind/Abst** Libr. Inf. Sci. Abstr. bk rev. adv acc. **Circ** 700. All aspects of bibliography and librarianship in the field of education and its related social sciences. *Library Bulletin (University of London. Institute of Education), Newsletter (International Society of Training College Librarians).*

EFLA EVALUATIONS. **Main/Corp** Educational Film Library Association. **VFOAT** E.F.L.A. Evaluation. **VAT** Educational Film Library Association Evaluations. 0146-3152. US. English. qt. $140.00. Educational Film Library Association, 45 John Street/Suite 301, New York NY 10038. **Tel** (212)227-5599. Ed Judith Trojan. **Ind/Abst** Media Rev. Dig. **Circ** 1,000. (ctrl). Capsule reviews of films and video appearing as finalists and winners in EFLA's annual American Film Festival.

EINFUHRUNG IN DIE INFORMATION UND DOKUMENTATION. 0070-9522. Monographic Series. German. ir. Deutscher Buch Export-Import, Leninstrasse 16, DDR-701 Leipzig East Germany. **Tel** 7 13 70.

ELECTRONIC LIBRARY. (THE ELECTRONIC LIBRARY : THE INTERNATIONAL JOURNAL FOR MINICOMPUTER, MICROCOMPUTER, AND SOFTWARE APPLICATIONS IN LIBRARIES). Vol. 1, No. 1 (Jan. 1983)-. 0264-0473. Periodical. UK. English. qt. $65.00. Learned Information Inc, 143 Old Marlton Pike, Medford NJ 08055. **Tel** (609)654-6266. **Ind/Abst** Cumul. Index Nurs. Allied Health Lit., Libr. Inf. Sci. Abstr., Print. Abstr. **LC** Z678.9. **DD** 025.0202854.

THE ELEMENTARY SCHOOL LIBRARY COLLECTION. 1st- Ed. US. English. be. $79.95. Elementary School Library Collection, 1807 Pembroke Road, Greensboro NC 27408. **Tel** (919)275-7336. Ed Lois Winkel. bk rev. **Circ** 6,000. Classified catalog of visual materials for libraries serving preschool-6th grade children that implement the curricular and are of interest to young people.

EMC. EDUCATIONAL MEDIA SPECIAL INTEREST COUNCIL. (EMC : NEWSLETTER). **VFOAT** Educational Media Council. **VAT** Educational Media Special Interest Council. Vol. 10, No. 3 (Apr. 1981)-. 0824-782X. Periodical. CN. English. ir. 3.00. Newfoundland Teachers' Association Educational Media Council, 3 Kenmount Road, St John's Newfoundland A1B 1W1 Canada. **Tel** (709)229-6559. Ed K Bruce Lane. **DD** 027.8060718. **Circ** 500. (ctrl). Forum for teachers interested in educational media and resourced-based teaching. *Media Newfoundland, 0824-183X.*

EMERGENCY LIBRARIAN. V. 1- 1973-. 0315-8888. Periodical. CN. English. ir. $35.00. Dyad Services, Box 1563, Buffalo NY 14240. **Tel** (416)365-1148. Ed Ken Havcock. **Ind/Abst** Women Stud. Abstr., Libr. Inf. Sci. Abstr., Book Rev. Index, Ref. Source, Can. Educ. Index, Libr. Lit., New Period. Index, Libr. Lit. bk rev. adv acc. **Circ** 5,400. Also available in microfiche format. Essential reading for school and public librarians. Provocative and stimulating.

ENCORE. V. 1- Mar. 1978-. 0709-2660. Periodical. CN. English. qt. Free to Members. Midwestern Library System, 637 Victoria Street North, Kitchener Ontario N2H 5G4 Canada. **DD** 021.409713.

ENCYCLOPEDIA OF INFORMATION SYSTEMS AND SERVICES. 1st Ed.-. 0734-9068. US. English. ir. Gale Research, Book Tower, Detroit MI 48226. **Tel** (800)521-0707. Ed John Schmidttroth. **LC** Z674.3. **DD** 025.0403. **NLM** Z 674.5.A2 E56. Provides detailed descriptions of more than 3,500 organizations in the US and other countries that produce and/or provide access to computerized information in all subject areas.

ENCYCLOPEDIA OF LIBRARY AND INFORMATION SCIENCE. See Encyclopedias & General Reference Books.

ENCYCLOPEDIA OF LIBRARY AND INFORMATION SCIENCE. SUPPLEMENT. See Encyclopedias & General Reference Books.

ENERGIE. LEXIQUE. See Energy.

LES ENSEIGNEMENTS PROFESSIONNELS. **Main/Corp** Ecole National Superieure des Bibliotheques (France). FR. French. ir. Ecole Nationale Superieures des Bibliotheques, 2 rue de Louvois, Paris 2E France. **LC** Z669.5.F7. **DD** 020.71144.

DIE ENTWICKLUNG DES BIBLIOTHEKSWESENS IN DER DEUTSCHEN DEMOKRATISCHEN REPUBLIK. German. ir. Hermann-Matern-Strasse 57 104, Berlin East Germany. **LC** Z803.A1.

ENVIRONMENT CANADA LIBRARIES BIBLIOGRAPHY SERIES. See Bibliographies.

ERIC DESCRIPTOR AND IDENTIFIER USAGE REPORT. US. English. an. 1200 Chambers Road/3rd Floor, Columbus OH 43212.

ESPIAL DATA BASE DIRECTORY. See Yearbooks, Almanacs, Directories.

ESTIMATES. PART III, NATIONAL LIBRARY OF CANADA. CN. English (French). $6.00 Domestic, $7.20 Foreign. Canadian Government Publishing Centre, Supply and Services Canada, Ottawa Ontario K1A 0S9 Canada. **LC** Z736.N37. **DD** 027.571.

ESTUDIOS BIBLIOTECARIOS. **Main/Corp** Columbus Memorial Library. No. 1- 1960-. Periodical. US. Spanish. ir.

ESTUDOS AVANCADOS EM BIBLIOTECONOMIA E CIENCIA DA INFORMACAO. Vol. 1 (1982)-. Periodical. Portuguese. an. **LC** Z665. **DD** 020.

ETHNIKE BIBLIOTHEKE. **Main/Corp** Hetaireia Makedonikon Spoudon. GR. Greek, Modern. ir. Society of Macedonian Studies, 4 Vas Sophias Street, Thessaloniki Greece.

EX LIBRIS. **Main/Corp** International Development Research Centre (Canada). Library. V. 10, No. 1 (Jan. 1981)-. 0226-9791. Periodical. CN. English (French and Spanish). mo. International Development Research Center, PO Box 8500, Ottawa Ontario K1G 3H9 Canada. **Ind/Abst** Popul. Index. **DD** 016.33091724. *Library I D R C Library Bulletin, 0380-1411.*

EXPLORATIONS IN MUSIC LIBRARIANSHIP. No. 1- June 1966-. Periodical. US. English. **LC** ML111.

EXPRESSION CEASED. V. 1-4, No. 1. 0380-0482. Periodical. CN. English. sa. Free to Members, $5. to others. Ontario Library Association, 2397A Bloor Street West, Toronto Ontario M6S 1P6 Canada. **Ind/Abst** Libr. Inf. Sci. Abstr. **DD** 020.5.

FACHBIBLIOGRAPHISCHER DIENST: BIBLIOTHEKSWESEN CEASED. Vol. 2- 1966-. GW. German. ir. Deutsches Bibliotheksinstitut, Bundesallee 184/185, D-1000 Berlin 31 West Germany. **LC** Z666. *Fachbibliographischer Dienst.*

FAO-LIB CATALOGUE OF MONOGRAPHS MICROFORM. **Main/Corp** David Lubin Memorial Library. **VFOAT** Catalogue of Monographs. **VAT** Food and Agriculture Organization Library Catalogue of Monographs. Began with 1976-77?. English. ir. *Cumulative Catalogue of Monographs.*

IL FAUT LIRE. No. 1- May 1978-. 0709-6488. Periodical. CN. French. ir. Free to Libraries, $50.00 Others. DMR Inc, 317 rue Benjamin Hudon, Ville Saint-Laurent Quebec H4N Canada. **DD** 028.105.

FAXON LIBRARIANS' GUIDE CEASED. (FAXON . . . LIBRARIANS' GUIDE). **VFOAT** Librarians' Guide. 1976-1980. 0146-2660. US. English. an. $10.00. FW Faxon Company Incorporated, 15 Southwest Park, Westwood MA 02090. **LC** Z6941, PN4832. **DD** 011.34. *Faxon Librarians' Guide to Periodicals.*

FAXON LIBRARIANS' GUIDE TO CONTINUATIONS. (FAXON . . . LIBRARIANS' GUIDE TO CONTINUATIONS). **VFOAT** Librarians' Guide to Continuations. 1981-. 0272-4537. US. English. ir. Free, Faxon Customers, $5.00 Others. FW Faxon Company Incorporated, Faxon Building, 15 Southwest Park, Westwood Mass 02090. **LC** Z692.S5. **DD** 025.2832.

FAXON LIBRARIANS' GUIDE TO SERIALS. (FAXON . . . LIBRARIANS' GUIDE TO SERIALS). **VFOAT** Librarians' Guide to Serials. 1981-. 0275-8466. US. English. an. $15.00, Free to Faxon Customers. FW Faxon Company Incorporated, 15 Southwest Park, Westwood MA 02090. **LC** Z6941. **DD** 025.2832. *Faxon Librarians' Guide, 0146-2660.*

FBR AKTUELLT. **Main/Corp** Forskningsbiblioteksradet. V. 1- May 1973-. Swedish (summaries in English). ir. Box 6404 113 82 6, Stockholm Sweden. **LC** Z675.R45.

FEDERATION OF CHILDREN'S BOOK GROUPS YEARBOOK. See Yearbooks, Almanacs, Directories.

FEDLINK TECHNICAL NOTES. VFOAT F.E.D.L.I.N.K. Technical Notes. **VAT** Federal Library and Information Network Technical Notes. Vol. 1, No. 1 (Feb. 1983)-. 0737-4178. Periodical. US. English. mo.

FELICITER. V. 1- Jan. 1956-. 0014-9802. Periodical. CN. English. mo. Free to Members. Canadian Library Association, 151 Sparks Street, Ottawa Ontario K1P 5E3 Canada.

FID DIRECTORY . . . . See Yearbooks, Almanacs, Directories.

FID NEWS BULLETIN. (F.I.D. NEWS BULLETIN). Year 1-. 0014-5874. Periodical. NE. English. mo. 65.00. International Federation Documentation, PO Box 90402, 2509 LK The Hague Netherlands. Ed S Keenan. bk rev. adv acc. **Circ** 1,500. A section featuring news from national members, starting in this issue, news from national members will become a regular feature of the bulletin.

FID/CR NEWSLETTER. **Main/Corp** International Federation for Documentation. Committee on Classification Research. Periodical. II. English. ir. FID/CR Newsletter, 112 Cross Road 11/Maleswaram, Bangalore 560003 India.

FIJI LIBRARY ASSOCIATION NEWSLETTER. Began with Nov. 1973 issue. Periodical. FJ. English. mo. Fiji Library Association, PO Box 2292, Government Buildings, Suva Fiji. Ed Marieta Inta. **LC** Z845.F5. **DD** 027.09611. bk rev. adv acc. **Circ** 120. A newsletter containing news and activities of libraries and librarians in Fiji.

FILM INFORMATION. V. 1- 1970-. 0015-1297. Periodical. US. English. mo. $7.00. Film Information, Box 500, Manhattanville Station, New York NY 10027. Available on microfilm from Xerox University Microfilm.

FILM LIBRARY CATALOGUE - NATIONAL HEALTH AND WELFARE. (FILM LIBRARY CATALOGUE). **Main/Corp** Canada. Health and Welfare Canada. **VFOAT** Catalogue de la Cinematheque. **VAT** Catalogue de la Cinematheque - Ministere de la Sante Nationale et du Bien-Etre Social. 0713-6099. CN. English (French). Health and Welfare of Canada, Information Directorate, Ottawa Ontario K1A 0K9 Canada. **DD** 018.137.

FILMS 16 MM - EASTERN ONTARIO REGIONAL LIBRARY SYSTEM. (FILMS 16 MM). **Main/Corp** Eastern Ontario Library System. **VFOAT** 16 MM Film Catalogue. **VAT** 16MM Film Catalogue Available from the Public Libraries of Eastern Ontario. 1st Ed. (1980/81)-. 0714-5055. CN. English (French). an. $3.00 Each Number. Eastern Ontario Regional Library System, Suite 6/200 Cooper Street, Ottawa Ontario K2P 0G1 Canada. **DD** 018.137.

FINANCIAL ASSISTANCE FOR LIBRARY EDUCATION. 1969-1970-. 0569-6275. US. English. an. $1.00. American Library Association, 50 East Huron, Chicago IL 60611. **Tel** (312)944-6780. **LC** Z668. **DD** 020.711. **Circ** 3,000. Directory of scholarships, assistantships for library education, primarily at masters level. Includes listings from a variety of sources such as schools, associations, etc. *Fellowships, Scholarships, Grants-in-Aid, Loan Funds, and other Financial Assistance for Library Education.*

Library and Information Science

FINANCIAL STATEMENT FOR THE PERIOD COVERING FROM 1ST JANUARY TO 31ST DECEMBER ... - TANZANIA LIBRARY ASSOCIATION. Main/Corp Tanzania Library Association. English. an. Tanzania Library Association, PO Box 2645, Dar es Salaam Tanzania. LC Z673.T22. DD 020.6234678.

FLAG. FOOTHILLS LIBRARY ASSOCIATION GAZETTE. (THE FLAG : THE FOOTHILLS LIBRARY ASSOCIATION GAZETTE). VAT Foothills Library Association Gazette. Vol. 1, No. 1 (Sept. 1979)-. 0228-7137. Periodical. CN. English. Free. J Paine, Department of Communications Media, University of Calgary, Calgary Alberta T2N 1N4 Canada. DD 020.62271233. (ctrl).

FLC NEWSLETTER CEASED. VFOAT Federal Libraries. VAT Federal Library Committee Newsletter. Began with No. 1 (Oct. 20, 1965). Ceased with No. 131 (Aug. 1984). 0014-5939. Periodical. US. English. ir. Federal Library Committee, Navy Yard Annex/ Room 400, Library of Congress, Washington DC 20540. Ind/Abst Libr. Inf. Sci. Abstr. LC UNC. NLM Z 675.G7 F106.

FLICC NEWSLETTER. VAT Federal Library and Information Center Committee Newsletter. No. 132 (Jan. 1985)-. 0882-908X. Periodical. US. English. ir. Federal Library and Information Center Committee, Library of Congress, Washington DC 20540. Tel (202)287-1372. Ed Christiana C Zirps. Ind/Abst Libr. Inf. Sci. Abstr. LC Z675.G7. DD 027.50973. Circ 2,600. Reports on the activities of the Federal Library and Information Center community, disseminating news about and of interest to the federal information community and information concerns of the nation at large. *FLC Newsletter, 0014-5939.*

FLICKERTALE NEWSLETTER. Periodical. US. English. mo. $10.00. North Dakota State Library Commission, Bismark North Dakota 58505.

FLORIDA INTERCOM. V. 1- Dec. 1969-. Periodical. English. ir. Florida State Library, R A Gray Building, Tallahassee FL 32301.

FLORIDA LIBRARIES. V. 1- July 1949-. 0046-4147. Periodical. US. English. qt. Florida Library Association, 2020 West Fairbanks Avenue, Winter Park FL 32789. LC Z732.F6. DD 027.0759.

FLORIDA LIBRARY DIRECTORY. See Yearbooks, Almanacs, Directories.

FOCAL POINT. Apr. 1977-. 0708-9090. Periodical. CN. English. ir. Free. Toronto Public Libraries, 40 Orchard View Boulevard, Toronto Ontario M4R 1B9 Canada. DD 027.4713541.

FOCUS. V. 1- May 1975-. 0318-0247. Periodical. CN. English. mo. $8.00. Ontario Library Association, 2397A Bloor Street West, Toronto Ontario M6S 1P6 Canada. LC Z673. DD 020.6234713. *OLA Newsletter, 0318-0239.*

FOCUS. Sept. 1974-. 0319-4566. CN. English. Kingston Public Library, Kingston Ont Canada. DD 027.471372.

FOCUS, LIBRARY SERVICE TO OLDER ADULTS, PEOPLE WITH DISABILITIES. VFOAT Focus. Began with 1983, No. 1. 0740-4956. Periodical. US. English. mo. $6.00 Domestic, $8.40 Foreign. Eunice Lovejoy, 172 W Main Street, Westerville OH 43081. Tel (614)882-4791. Ed Eunice G Lovejoy. bk rev. Circ 500. Discusses library programs and resources for older adults and people with disabilities.

FOCUS ON INDIANA LIBRARIES. Began publication with July 1947 issue. 0015-5152. Periodical. US. English. mo. $12.00. Indiana Library Association, 310 North Alabama/Suite A, Indianapolis IN 46204. Tel (317)636-6059. Ed Beth K Steele. LC Z732.I4. DD 020.623. bk rev. adv acc. Circ 3,500. Monthly newspaper with current Indiana news for libraries, job openings, calendar, features. Official publication of Association, State Library. Occasional special inserts on one topic.

FOCUS ON INTERNATIONAL & COMPARATIVE LIBRARIANSHIP. V.1- 1967-. 0305-8468. Periodical. English. ir. $15.00. International & Comparative Library Group, 25 Bromford Gardens/2 Westfield Road, Edgbaston Birmingham B15 3XD United Kingdom. Ind/Abst Libr. Inf. Sci. Abstr. DD 020.

FOCUS ON THE CENTER FOR RESEARCH LIBRARIES. Main/Corp Center for Research Libraries (U.S.). VFOAT Focus. V. 1, Issue 1 (Jan-Feb 1981)-. 0275-4924. Periodical. US. English. bm. $10.00 Non-members, Free to members. Center for Research Libraries, 5721 South Cottage Grove Avenue, Chicago Il 60637. Tel (312)955-4545. Ed Sally Brickman. LC Z675.R45. DD 027.70973. Circ 4,000. News of programs, policies, collections and new acquisitions for CRL members and staff. *Newsletter, 0008-9087.*

FOCUS (REGINA, SASK.). (FOCUS). 0015-5179. Periodical. CN. English. free. Saskatchewan Library, 1352 Winnipeg Street, Regina Saskatchewan S4P 3V7 Canada. Tel (306)787-2977. Ed Jim Oxman. LC Z735.S26. DD 027.47124. bk rev. Circ 5,000. (ctrl). Information related to the operation and management of libraries in Saskatchewan. *Focus on Saskatchewan Libraries, 0015-5179.*

THE FOLGER FACSIMILES. US. English. ir. Folger Library, East Capitol Street, Washington DC 20003.

FOLGER LIBRARY NEWSLETTER. Main/Corp Folger Shakespeare Library. Began with Oct. 1969 issue. 0015-5438. US. English. bm. $5.00. Folger Library, East Capital Street, Washington DC 20003. Tel (202)544-7077. Ed Janet Alexander Griffin. LC Z733.W3. DD 026.82233. Circ 2,6000. (ctrl). The newsletter contains articles on departmental activities and a calendar of events which may be attended by the public.

THE FOOTLOOSE LIBRARIAN. See Travel.

FOR REFERENCE. VFOAT Newsletter - New York Metropolitan Reference and Research Library Agency. No. 1- Oct. 1966-. 0015-685X. Periodical. US. English. ir. Metro, 11 West 40th Street, New York NY 10018.

FORTHCOMING MEETINGS - LIBRARY, FACULTY OF LIBRARY SCIENCE, UNIVERSITY OF TORONTO. (FORTHCOMING MEETINGS). 0713-5874. Periodical. CN. English. mo. 16.00 Domestic, 21.00 US, 25.00 all other countries. Faculty of Library Science, University of Toronto, 140 ST George Street/Room 408, Toronto Ontario M5S 1A1 Canada. Tel (416)978-7064. Ed Ellen James. DD 020. Circ 200. A listing of conferences, seminars, workshops, meetings, etc. of interest to professional librarians and library workers.

FOUNDATIONS IN LIBRARY AND INFORMATION SCIENCE. V. 1-. Monographic Series. US. English. ir. $47.50. JAI Press, PO Box 1678, Greenwich CT 06836. Tel (203)661-7602. Ed Robert D Stueart.

FREE AND INEXPENSIVE LEARNING MATERIALS CEASED. VFOAT F & I Learning Materials. Began with issue for 1941. 0733-1886. US. English. be. LC AG600. DD 016.3713.

FRIENDSCRIPT. V. 1- Spring 1979-. 0192-5539. Periodical. US. English. qt. University of Illinois Library Friends, 230 University Library, Urbana IL 61801.

FROM THE ACIR LIBRARY, PERIODICAL INDEX. See Indexes/Abstracts.

FROM THE STATE LIBRARIAN'S DESK. No. 1-34. US. English. ir. California State Library, Library and Courts Building PO Box 2037, Sacramento CA 95809. LC Z732.C2. DD 027.0794.

FULL BIBLIOGRAPHIC RECORD - CARLETON UNIVERSITY. See Bibliographies.

FUND OG FORSKNING I DET KONGELIGE BIBLIOTEKS SAMLINGER. Main/Corp Copenhagen. Kongelige Bibliotek. Vol. 1- 1954-. 0069-9896. DK. Danish (summaries in English, French, or German). an. 100.00. Det Konglige Bibliotek, Christians Bruygge 8, DK-1219 Kobenhavn K Denmark. Tel 01150111. Ind/Abst Art Archaeol. Tech. Abstr. LC Z941. (cum index). Circ 500.

GARLAND REFERENCE LIBRARY OF SOCIAL SCIENCE. DEVELOPMENTAL DISABILITIES. Series/Titl Garland Reference Library of Social Science. VFOAT Developmental Disabilities. Vol. 1-. Monographic Series. US. English. Ed Manny Sternlicht. NLM W1.

GENEALOGICAL LIBRARY JOURNAL. Vol. 2, No. 4, (1982), Issue 8-. Periodical. US. English. qt. Tel (213)320-7766. bk rev. Circ 500. (ctrl). Lists new books in the field of genealogy, with secondary emphasis on new listings for heraldry, and closely related areas. *Genealogical Library Quarterly, 0883-0584.*

GEODEX RETRIEVAL SYSTEM FOR GEOTECHNICAL ABSTRACTS. See Indexes/Abstracts.

GEODEX SYSTEM-S. (GEODEX SYSTEM/S). Main/Corp Geodex International. 0161-1550. Periodical. US. English. ir. Geodex International, 669 Broadway, PO Box 279, Sonoma CA 95476. Tel (707)938-0001. *Geodex Structural Information Service.*

THE GEORGIA LIBRARIAN. Began with issue for Mar. 1964. 0016-8319. Periodical. US. English. qt $10.00. Georgia Library Association, PO Box 833, Tucker GA 30084. Tel (404)329-6846. Ed James Dorsey. Ind/Abst Libr. Lit. LC Z732.G4. DD 020.9758. bk rev. adv acc. Circ 1,250. Available on microfilm from University Microfilms International. News of Georgia libraries. Articles on all aspects of librarianship.

THE GET READY SHEET. 0148-7566. Periodical. US. English. bw. $19.00. Mid-York Library System, 1600 Lincoln Ave, Utica NY 13502. Tel (315)735-8328. Ed Debra J Holland. adv acc. Circ 1,000. Provide advance information about: author interviews on TV and radio talk shows; movie and TV tie-ins; and interesting news on the world of books.

GHANA LIBRARY JOURNAL. 1- Oct. 1963-. 0016-9552. Periodical. GH. English. sa. $3.00. Ghana Library Journal, PO Box 4105, Accra Ghana.

GLABC DIRECTORY. See Yearbooks, Almanacs, Directories.

GODISNJAK - NARODNA BIBLIOTEKA SRBIJE. Main/Corp Narodna Biblioteka sr Srbije. YU. Serbo-Croatian -C (summaries in English, French, or Russian). ir. Narodna Biblioteka Srbije, Skerliceva 1, Beograd Yugoslavia. LC Z841. *Godisnjak.*

GOOD LIBRARIES. Periodical. US. English. ir. Free. Headway Publications, 1700 Port Manleigh Circle, Newport Beach CA 92660.

GOVERNMENT INFORMATION QUARTERLY. V. 1, No. 1-. 0740-624X. Periodical. US. English. qt. $45.00. JAI Press, 36 Sherwood PLace PO Box 1678, Greenwich CT 06836-1678. LC Z688.G6. DD 011.53. NLM Z 688.G6.

GRADUATE SCHOOL OF LIBRARY SCIENCE NEWSLETTER. Main/Corp McGill University. Graduate School of Library Science. Oct. 1981-. 0715-481X. CN. English. an. Free. McGill University, Graduate School of Library Science, 3459 McTavish Street, Montreal Quebec H3A 1Y1 Canada. DD 020.711714281. (ctrl). *Alumni Newsletter (McGill University). Graduate School of Library Science), 0226-0123.*

GUIA DAS BIBLIOTECAS DO ESTADO DE MINAS GERAIS. 1977-. Portuguese. ir. LC Z769.M56.

GUIA DE BIBLIOTECAS UNIVERSITARIAS BRASILEIRAS. 1979-. BL. Portuguese. ir. LC Z675.U5. DD 027.002581.

GUIDE DE LA BIBLIOTHEQUE DU CENTRE AUDIO-VISUEL - COLLEGE JEAN-DE-BREBEUF. (GUIDE DE LA BIBLIOTHEQUE DU CENTRE AUDIO-VISUEL). Main/Corp College Jean-de-Brebeuf. Bibliotheque du Pavillon Lalemant. 81/82-. 0712-8533. CN. French. an. Free. Guide de la Bibliotheque du Centre Audio-Visuel, c/o College Jean-de-Brebeuf, Bilbiotheque du Pavillon Lalemant, 5625 Avenue Decelles, Montreal Quebec H3T 1W4 Canada. DD 025.567714281. (ctrl). *Guide de la Bibliotheque, Politiques du Centre Audio-Visuel, 0227-6542.*

GUIDE DE L'USAGER - UNIVERSITE DU QUEBEC A TROIS-RIVIERES. SERVICE DE LA BIBLIOTHEQUE. (LE GUIDE DE L'USAGER). Main/Corp Universite du Quebec A Trois-Rivieres. Service de la Bibliotheque. No. 1-. 0823-5686. CN. French. an. Bibliotheque Universite du Quebec a Trois-Rivieres, C P 500, Trois-Rivieres Quebec G9A 5H7 Canada. DD 025.567711445. *Guide de l'Usager, 0225-5200.*

GUIDE DES USAGERS - UNIVERSITE DE SHERBROOKE. BIBLIOTHEQUE GENERALE. (GUIDE DES USAGERS). Main/Corp Universite de Sherbrooke. Bibliotheque Generale. 0824-8095. CN. French. an. Free. Universite de Sherbrooke, Services des Bibliotheques, Sherbrooke Quebec J1K 2RI Canada. DD

025.56771466. (ctrl). *Guide de la Bibliotheque Generale, 0824-8087.*

GUIDE GENERAL DES COMITES - ASTED. (GUIDE GENERAL DES COMITES). **Main/Corp** ASTED. 1983-. 0824-8613. CN. French. an. Free. Association pour l'Avancement des Sciences et des Techniques de la Documentation, 7243 rue St-Denis, Montreal Quebec H2R 2E3 Canada. **DD** 020.6234714. *Annuaire des Comites et Delegation, 0229-7418.*

GUIDE TO MICROFORMS IN PRINT. SUPPLEMENT. *See* Yearbooks, Almanacs, Directories.

GUIDE TO PERIODICALS AND AND NEWSPAPERS IN THE EASTERN ONTARIO LIBRARY SYSTEM. (PERIODICALS - EASTERN ONTARIO LIBRARY SYSTEM). **Main/Corp** Federation des Bibliotheques de l'Est de l'Ontario. **VFOAT** Periodique - Federation des Bibliotheques de l'Est d'Ontario. 1977-. 0705-1263. Newspaper. CN. French (English). Bibliotheque Publique d'Ottawa, 120 rue Metcalfe, Ottawa Ontario K1P 5M2 Canada. **DD** 016.05. *Alphabetical List of the Periodicals Received by the Ottawa Public Library, 0705-1255.*

GUIDE TO PROVINCIAL LIBRARY AGENCIES IN CANADA. **VFOAT** Guide des Organismes Provinciaux Charges des Bibliotheques au Canada. 1981-. 0319-9908. CN. English (and French with French text on inverted pages). ir. **LC** Z735.A1. **DD** 354.7100852.

GUIDE TO THE VOCABULARY OF BIOLOGICAL LITERATURE. (A GUIDE TO THE VOCABULARY OF BIOLOGICAL LITERATURE). 1970-. 0090-5941. US. English. an. Biosciences Information Service, 2100 Arch Street, Philadelphia PA 19103. **LC** Z695.1.B5. **DD** 025.33574. **NLM** Z 5321 B615B.

GUIDES TO THE HARVARD LIBRARIES. Began in 1947. Monographic Series. US. English. ir. Harvard University Library, Wadsworth House, Cambridge MA 02138. **LC** Z733. **DD** 027.7744.

GUYANA LIBRARY ASSOCIATION BULLETIN. Vol. 1, No. 1 (July 1970)-. Periodical. GY. English. ir. Guyana Library Association, PO Box 10240, Georgetown Guyana. **Ind/Abst** Libr. Inf. Sci. Abstr. **DD** 020.62.881.

HANDBOOK AND DIRECTORY - AMERICAN SOCIETY FOR INFORMATION SCIENCE. *See* Yearbooks, Almanacs, Directories.

HANDBOOK FOR STUDENTS - DALHOUSIE UNIVERSITY. SCHOOL OF LIBRARY SERVICE. (HANDBOOK FOR STUDENTS - DALHOUSIE UNIVERSITY, SCHOOL OF LIBRARY SERVICE). **Main/Corp** Dalhousie University. School of Library Service. Began with 1973 issue. 0317-865X. Periodical. CN. English. an. Dalhousie University, School of Library Service, Halifax Nova Scotia B4H 4H8 Canada. **DD** 020.71171622.

HANDBUCH DER OFFENTLICHEN BIBLIOTHEKEN. 1972-. 0301-9225. German. ir. Deutscher Bibliotheksberband, Fehrbelliner Platz 3, 1000 31 Berlin West Germany. **LC** Z801. *Handbuch der Offentlichen Buchereien.*

HANGUG NUIHAG DOSEGWAN. (HANGUK UIHAK TOSOGWAN). **VFOAT** Bulletin of Korean Medical Library Association. 0250-9083. Periodical. KO. Korean. ir. Yonsei University, 134 Shinchon Dong, Seoul 120 Korea. **Ind/Abst** Chem. Abstr. **NLM** Z 675.74 H239.

HANGUK CHONGBO KWAHAKHOE CHI. **VFOAT** Journal of the Korea Information Science Society. Periodical. English (Korean). ir. Hanguk Chongbo Kwahakhoe, c/o Kwangun Kongkwa Taehak, Chonja Kyesanso Wolgye-dong, Tobong-ku, Seoul South Korea. **Ind/Abst** Comput. Control Abstr., Electr. Electron. Abstr., Sci. Abstr. Sect. A. Phys. Abstr. **LC** Z699.A1. **CODEN** HJKHDC.

THE HARVARD LIBRARIAN. V. 1- Dec. 1957-. 0073-0564. US. English. ir. Free. Harvard University Library, Wadsworth House, Cambridge MA 02138. **Tel** (617)495-3650. **Ed** Pamela Matz. **Ind/Abst** Libr. Inf. Sci. Abstr. **LC** Z881. **DD** 027.77444. **Circ** 3,500. (ctrl). News of Harvard libraries, major exhibits, publications, and personnel, with occasional essays on collections and librarianship.

HARVARD LIBRARY BULLETIN. **Main/Corp** Harvard University. Library. **VFOAT** HLB. V. 1- Winter 1947-. 0017-8136. Periodical. US. English. qt. Harvard University Library, Wadsworth House, Cambridge MA 02138. **Tel** (617)495-3650. **Ed** Kenneth E Carpenter. **Ind/Abst** Am. Hist. Life, Hist. Abstr., Part A, Mod. Hist. Abstr., Hist. Abst., Part B, Twent. Century Abstr., Abstr. Engl. Stud., MLA Int. Bibliogr. Books Artic. Mod. Lang. Lit., Hist. Abstr., Writ. Am. Hist., Libr. Inf. Sci. Abstr., Years Work Eng. Stud., Recent Publ. Artic. **LC** Z881. **DD** 027.7744. **NLM** Z 881 H339H. (cum index). adv acc. **Circ** 5,000. Diverse scholarly essays on bibliography and the history holdings and exhibitions of Harvard libraries. *Harvard University Library Notes.*

HCL CATALOGING BULLETIN. **Main/Corp** Hennepin County Library. Technical Services Division. **VFOAT** H.C.L. Cataloging Bulletin. **VAT** Hennepin County Library Cataloging Bulletin. 1973. 0732-894X. US. English. bm. $12.00. Hennepin County Library, 12601 Ridgedale Drive, Minnetonka MN 55343. **Tel** (612)541-8561. **LC** Z693.A15. **DD** 025.305. **Circ** 200. Reports on subject headings innovated or reformed at Hennepin County Library, together with new notes and cross-references. *Cataloging Bulletin, 0093-528X.*

HEALTH LIBRARIES REVIEW. **VFOAT** Libraries Review. V. 1, No. 1 (Mar. 1984)-. 0265-6647. Periodical. UK. English. qt. **LC** Z675.M4. **DD** 026.610941.

HEALTH SCIENCES INFORMATION IN CANADA. LIBRARIES. (HEALTH SCIENCES INFORMATION IN CANADA). **VFOAT** Information en Sciences de la Sante au Canada. 1979-. 0708-9465. Periodical. CN. English (French). an. $11.61. National Research Council, Canada Institute of Scientific and Technical Information, Ottawa Ontario K1A 0S2 Canada. **DD** 026.610971. **NLM** Z 675.M4 H4305.

HEALTH SCIENCES SERIALS. *See* Medicine.

HELLIS NEWSLETTER. (HELLIS NEWSLETTER : HEALTH LITERATURE LIBRARY & INFORMATION SERVICES). **VFOAT** H.E.L.L.I.S. Newsletter. **VAT** Health Literature Library & Information Services Newsletter. Vol. 1, No. 1 (Mar. 1982)-. 0254-2595. Periodical. English. sa. Library, World Health Organiation Regional Office for South East Asia/World Health House, New Delhi-110002 India. **NLM** Z 675.M4 H477.

HERALD OF LIBRARY SCIENCE. V. 1- Jan. 1962-. 0018-0521. Periodical. II. English. qt. $44.00. Lucknow University, c/o P Kaula, C-193 Indira Nagar, Lucknow-226 016 India. **Tel** 75791. **Ed** P N Kaula. **Ind/Abst** Comput. Control Abstr., Electr. Electron. Abstr., Sci. Abstr. Sect. A. Phys. Abstr., Libr. Inf. Sci. Abstr., Libr. Lit., Phys. Abstr. **LC** Z671. **CODEN** HLBSAB. Index published separately - free - automatically sent. Special numbers have been brought out on specific aspects of library and information science. The features includes book reviews and comprehensive "Notes and News" from several countries.

THE HERITAGE OF LIBRARIANSHIP SERIES. No. 1-. 0278-7792. Monographic Series. US. English. ir. Libraries Unlimited, PO Box 263, Littleton CO 80160. **Tel** (303)770-1220. **Ed** M Harris. **LC** UNC.

HIGH ROLLER. **VFOAT** Highroller. V. 14, No. 5- May/June 1977-. 0197-6044. Periodical. US. English. qt. $20.00. Nevada Library Association, c/o Eldo County Library, Elko NV 89801. **Tel** (702)738-3066. **Ed** Hailie Gunn. **LC** Z732.N38. **DD** 027.0793. bk rev. adv. acc. **Circ** 300. (ctrl). Publication of state library organization with items and articles of interest to those working in libraries and pertaining to the state organization. *Nevada Libraries High Roller, 0148-5946.*

HLA JOURNAL. US. English. an. Hawaii Library Association, 1514 Makalampa Drive, Honolulu HI 96818. *Hawaiian Library Association Journal.*

HLABC FORUM. *See* Medicine.

HOKUSHINETSU CHIKU KOKURITSU DAIGAKU TOSHOKAN KYOGIKAI NEMPO. No. 21-. JA. Japanese. ir. c/o Fukio Daigaku Fazoku, Toshokan 9-1 Bunkyo 3-Chome, Fukui Japan. **LC** Z675.U5. *Hokushin Chiku Kokuritsu Daigaku Toshokan Kyogikai Nempo.*

HOSPITAL LIBRARIES. V. 1- July 1, 1976-. 0145-8930. Periodical. US. English. bw. Hospital Libraries, PO Box 624, Oak Park IL 60303. **Ind/Abst** Libr. Inf. Sci. Abstr. **NLM** W1 HO812T.

HSL NEWSLETTER. (H S L NEWSLETTER). **Main/Corp** Memorial University of Newfoundland. Health Sciences Library. **VAT** Health Sciences Library Newsletter. No. 26- May 1978-. 0709-0730. Periodical. CN. English. Free. Health Sciences Library, Memorial University of Newfoundland, St John's Newfoundland A1C 5S7 Canada. **DD** 016.61. (ctrl). *Medical Library Newsletter & Recent Acquisitions List, 0701-3205.*

THE HUNTINGTON LIBRARY QUARTERLY. **Main/Corp** Henry E. Huntington Library and Art Gallery, San Marino, California. V. 1- Oct. 1937-. 0018-7895. Periodical. US. English. qt. $20.00. Henry E Huntington Library and Art Gallery, 1151 Oxford Road, San Marino CA 91108. **Tel** (818)405-2171. **Ed** Guilland Sutherland. **Ind/Abst** Am. Hist. Life, Hist. Abstr., Part A, Mod. Hist. Abstr., Hist. Abst., Part B, Twent. Century Abstr., Abstr. Engl. Stud., MLA Int. Bibliogr. Books Artic. Mod. Lang. Lit., Annu. Bibliogr. Engl. Lang. Lit., Artbibliogr. Mod., Writ. Am. Hist., Index Book Rev. Humanit., Humanit. Index, Recent Publ. Artic. **LC** Z733.S24. **DD** 027.479493. bk rev. **Circ** 1,200. A journal for the study of European and American civilisation, its literature, history and art. *Huntington Library Bulletin.*

HUSH. Jan. 1976-. 0382-5922. Periodical. CN. English. qt. Oxford County Library, Woodstock Ontario N4S 6J8 Canada. **DD** 027.471346.

HYOGO KENRITSU TOSHOKAN ZOSHO MOKUROKU. 1973-. Japanese. ir. Hyogo Kenritsu Toshokan, 1-27 Akashi Koen, Akashi Japan. **LC** Z955.H9.

IASLIC BULLETIN. **Main/Corp** Indian Association of Special Libraries and Information Centres. V. 1- April 1956-. 0018-8441. Periodical. II. English. qt. Indian Association of Special Libraries Information Center, P291 Cit Scheme No 6M Kankurga Calcutta 700054 India. **Ind/Abst** Libr. Inf. Sci. Abstr. **LC** Z671.

IATUL PROCEEDINGS. **Main/Corp** International Association of Technological University Libraries. English. ir. Chalmers University of Technological Library, c/o N Fjallbrant, S-41296 5 Sweden. **Tel** 31-810100. **Ed** Nancy Fjallbrant. **Ind/Abst** Electr. Electron. Abstr., Comput. Control Abstr., Phys. Abstr., Libr. Lit., Eng. Index. adv acc. **Circ** 750. Theme issues on various aspects of library and information work including interlending user education, online services. Regional issues include Australia. *IATUL Newsletter.*

ICARBS. V. 1- Fall/Winter 1973-. 0360-8409. US. English. ir. $5.00. Morris Library, c/o David Koch, Carbondale IL 62901. **Tel** (618)453-2516. **Ed** David Koch and Alan Cohn. **Ind/Abst** Abstr. Engl. Stud., MLA Int. Bibliogr. Books Artic. Mod. Lang. Lit. **LC** Z881.C25. **DD** 051. **Circ** 600. Publishes research emanating from Morris Library's special research collections. Funded by friends of Morris Library Group (Southern Illinois University).

IDRC LIBRARY BULLETIN *CEASED.* (I D R C LIBRARY BULLETIN). **Main/Corp** International Development Research Centre. Library. **VFOAT** Bulletin de la Bibliotheque du C R D I. **VAT** International Development Research Centre Library Bulletin, Bulletin de la Bibliotheque du Centre de Recherches pour le Developpement International. V. 4-9, No. 9. 0380-1411. Periodical. CN. English (includes French publications). mo. Free. *New Library Acquisitions, 0380-142X.*

IFLA ANNUAL. **Main/Corp** International Federation of Library Associations and Institutions. 1976-. English (French and German). an. $28.50. K G Saur Verlag, 175 Fifth Avenue, New York NY 10010. **Tel** (212)932-1302. **LC** Z673. **DD** 030.621. **NLM** Z 673 I12. Proceedings of annual International Federation of Library Associations (IFLA) conference and official annual reports on IFLA activities of the year. *IFLA Annual.*

IFLA DIRECTORY. *See* Yearbooks, Almanacs, Directories.

IFLA JOURNAL. **Main/Corp** International Federation of Library Associations and Institutions. V. 3-. 0340-0352. Periodical. English (summaries in French and German). qt. $39.77. IFLA, PO Box 95312, 2509 CH Hague Netherlands. **Tel** (70)140884. **Ind/Abst** Libr. Lit. bk rev. adv acc. **Circ** 2,000. Contains articles on activities in IFLA context; articles with international relevance only; IFLA news. *IFLA Journal, 0340-0352.*

ILLINOIS HEALTH SCIENCES LIBRARIES SERIAL HOLDINGS LIST. (ILLINOIS HEALTH AND SCIENCE LIBRARIES SERIAL HOLDINGS LIST). **VFOAT** Illinois Serial

Library and Information Science

Holdings List. 9th Ed. (1982)-. 0148-0650. US. English. be. University of Illinois at the Medical Center, Library of the Health Sciences, PO Box 7509, Chicago IL 60680. **LC** Z6660, R129. **DD** 016.6105. Available in microform. *Illinois Health Sciences Libraries Serial Holdings List, 0148-0650.*

ILLINOIS LIBRARIES. Vol. 1- Jan.1919-. 0019-2104. Periodical. US. English. mo. Free. Illinois State Library, Centennial Building, Springfield IL 62756. **Tel** (217)782-5870. **Ed** Irma R Bostian. **Ind/Abst** Libr. Inf. Sci. Abstr., Libr. Lit. **LC** Z732.I2. **DD** 020.6234773. **Circ** 9,000. (ctrl). A reference magazine for librarians, library schools, trustees, etc. Information for all types of libraries.

MC JOURNAL (INTERNATIONAL INFORMATION MANAGEMENT CONGRESS). (IMC JOURNAL). **VAT** International Information Management Congress Journal. Vol. 19, No. 1 (First Quarter 1983)-. Periodical. US. English. qt. $40.00. International Information Management Congress, PO Box 34404, Bethesda MD 20817. **Tel** (301)983-0604. **Ed** Nancy Boyer. bk rev. adv acc. **Circ** 25,000. Application and technical articles on document-based information systems. *IMC Journal (International Micrographic Congress : 1978), 0019-0012.*

THE IMPRINT. (THE IMPRINT). Vol. 1- 1977-. 0046-8746. Periodical. US. English. mo. Onondaga County Public Library, 335 Montgomery Street, Syracuse NY 13202.

THE IMPRINT OF THE STANFORD LIBRARIES ASSOCIATES. Main/Corp Stanford University. Libraries. Associates. Vol. 1 Apr 1975-. 0149-421X. US. English. sa. Association of Standard University Libraries, Stanford University Libraries, Stanford CA 94305. **Tel** (415)497-9078. **Ed** Shannon Moffat. **Ind/Abst** Libr. Inf. Sci. Abstr. **LC** Z881.S797. **DD** 027.779473. **Circ** 750. Articles about books, literature, art, music, collecting and libraries for friends of the Stanford University Libraries.

IMPRINT OREGON. (IMPRINT : OREGON). Vol. 1- Spring 1974-. 0094-0232. Periodical. US. English. sa. $1.00 Single Issue. Library of the University of Oregon, Eugene OR 97403. **LC** Z881. **DD** 051. *Call Number.*

IMPROMPTU. *See* Music.

IN THE GROOVE. 0737-5972. Periodical. US. English. mo. $18.00. In the Groove, 1448 West Rosecrans Avenue, Gardena CA 90249. **Tel** (213)532-9024. **Ed** Sherri Honer. A catalog of recordings for Librarians dealing with audio and video from billboards.

INDEX - BRITISH COLUMBIA SCHOOL LIBRARIANS' ASSOCIATION. *See* Indexes/Abstracts.

INDEX FRANCAIS-ANGLAIS DES VEDETTES-MATIERE. *See* Indexes/Abstracts.

INDEX OF CONFERENCE PROCEEDINGS RECEIVED. *See* Indexes/Abstracts.

INDEX OF NLM SERIAL TITLES. *See* Indexes/Abstracts.

INDEX TO FREE PERIODICALS. *See* Indexes/Abstracts.

INDEX TO RESEARCH FRONTS IN ISI/BIOMED. *See* Indexes/Abstracts.

INDEX TO THE CATALOGING SERVICE BULLETIN. *See* Indexes/Abstracts.

INDIAN LIBRARIAN. V. 1- June 1946-. 0019-5774. Periodical. II. English. qt. Taru Books and Journals, G-159 Pashchim Vihar, New Delhi 110063 India. **Ind/Abst** Curr. Contents, Libr. Inf. Sci. Abstr., Libr. Lit. **LC** Z671. **DD** 020.5. (cum index). Available on microfilm from University Microfilms International.

INDIAN LIBRARY MOVEMENT. V. 1- Mar. 1974-. 0377-7367. Periodical. English. ir. $10.00. Editor, 148 Allenby Lines, Ambala Cantt India. **LC** Z845.I4. **DD** 021.00954.

INDIAN LIBRARY SCIENCE ABSTRACTS. *See* Indexes/Abstracts.

INDIANA LIBRARIES. Vol. 1, No. 1 (Spring 1981)-. 0275-777X. Periodical. US. English. qt. $10.00. Indiana Library Association, 310 North Alabama/Suite A, Indianapolis IN 46204. **Tel** (317)636-6059. **Ed** Ray Tevis. adv acc. **Circ** 1,700. Four issues yearly, four articles on theme with one potpourri issue of general interest. *Library Occurrent, 0024-2454.*

INDIANA MEDIA JOURNAL. V. 1- Fall 1978-. 0164-7660. Periodical. US. English. ir. Indiana Media Journal, c/o Dr Reck, School of Education, 1204 Indiana State University, Terre Haute IN 47809. **Tel** (812)237-2926. **Ed** Robert Little. **Ind/Abst** Libr. Lit. adv acc. **Circ** 1,000. (ctrl). Contains library and media information and articles. *Hoosier School Libraries, 0018-4802.*

INFORMATICS ABSTRACTS. *See* Indexes/Abstracts.

INFORMATION AND LIBRARY MANAGER. Vol. 1, No. 1 (June 1981)-. 0260-6879. Periodical. UK. English. qt. $27.58. E L M Publications, Seaton House Kings Ripton, Cambs PE17 2NJ United Kingdom. **Tel** 04873 238. **Ed** Stephen Roberts. **Ind/Abst** Libr. Inf. Sci. Abstr. **LC** Z678. **DD** 025.1. bk rev. adv acc. **Circ** 450. Library and information work plus some information technology.

INFORMATION AND LIBRARY SERVICES DIRECTORY. *See* Yearbooks, Almanacs, Directories.

INFORMATION AND REFERRAL. (INFORMATION AND REFERRAL : THE JOURNAL OF THE ALLIANCE OF INFORMATION AND REFERRAL SYSTEMS). Vol. 1, No. 1 (Spring 1979)-. 0278-2383. Periodical. US. English. sa. $30.00. Alliance of Information, 1100 West 42nd Street Suite 310, Indianapolis IN 46208. **Tel** (317)923-8727. **Ed** Micheal Speciale. **Ind/Abst** Sociol. Abstr., Soc. Welf. Soc. Plan./Policy Soc. Dev., Comput. Control Abstr., Electr. Electron. Abstr., Sci. Abstr. Sect. A. Phys. Abstr., Libr. Inf. Sci. Abstr., Public Aff. Inf. Serv. Bull. **LC** HV85. **DD** 361.97307. **CODEN** IREFD9. bk rev. adv acc. **Circ** 500. Concerned with practical and theoretical issues related to the impact of information and referral systems on the design and delivery of human services.

INFORMATION BULLETIN - WESTERN ASSOCIATION OF MAP LIBRARIES. Main/Corp Western Association of Map Libraries. 1969. 0049-7282. Periodical. US. English. ty. $20.00 Domestic, $23.00 Foreign and Canada. Western Association of Map Libraries, c/o University of California/SD Stevens, Santa Cruz CA 95064. **Tel** (408)429-2364. **Ed** Larry Cruse. **Ind/Abst** Libr. Inf. Sci. Abstr., GeoRef, Libr. Lit. bk rev. adv acc. **Circ** 425. (ctrl). Origianally intended as a journal for West Coast map librarians, now of interest to map librarians everywhere; articles and bibliographies; list of new maps; atlas and book reviews. *Newsletter - Western Association of Map Libraries.*

INFORMATION C.B. Main/Corp Quebec (Province). Centrale des Bibliotheques. **VAT** Information Centrale des Bibliotheques. No. 11- June 1977-. Periodical. CN. French. ty. Governement du Quebec, Ministere de l'Education, 1685 East rue Fluery, Quebec Quebec H2C 1T1 Canada. **LC** Z735.Q4. **DD** 027.4714. *C.B. Information.*

INFORMATION DEVELOPMENT. Vol. 1, No. 1 (Jan. 1985)-. 0266-6669. Periodical. UK. English. qt. 36.00 Domestic, $58.00 US. Mansell Publishers Ltd, 6 All Saints Street, London N1 9RL England. **Tel** (01)837-6676. **Ed** J Stephen Parker. bk rev. adv acc. **Circ** 550. Provides authoritative coverage of developments in information work throughout the world, with particular emphasis on the information needs and problems of developing countries.

INFORMATION FOR DECISION-MAKING, ANNUAL PROGRAM FOR LIBRARY DEVELOPMENT IN ARKANSAS. Main/Corp Arkansas State Library. US. English. an. One Capitol Mall, Little Rock AK 72201. **LC** Z732.A7. **DD** 0270767.

INFORMATION FOR MEMBERS - NOVA SCOTIA LIBRARY ASSOCIATION. (INFORMATION FOR MEMBERS). Main/Corp Nova Scotia Library Association. 1983/1984-. 0826-1946. CN. English. an. Free to Members. Nova Scotia Library Association, c/o Heather MacKenzie, Halifax City Regional Library, 5381 Spring Garden Road, Halifax Nova Scotia B3J 1E9 Canada. **DD** 020.6234716. *Members Handbook.*

INFORMATION HOTLINE. V. 8- Jan. 1976-. 0360-5817. Periodical. US. English. mo. $115.00. Science Associates International Inc, 1841 Broadway, New York NY 10023. **Tel** (212)265-4995. **Ind/Abst** Predicasts, Int. Packag. Abstr., Libr. Inf. Sci. Abstr., Electron. Pub. Abstr., Funk Scott Index Corp. Ind. **LC** Q223. **DD** 029.9505. **CODEN** INHODN. bk rev. *Information News and Sources, 0360-3148.*

INFORMATION INTELLIGENCE, ONLINE LIBRARIES, AND MICROCOMPUTERS. VFOAT Libraries and Microcomputers, Online Libraries and Microcomputers, Information Intelligence. Vol. 1, No. 1 (Sept. 1983)-. 0737-7770. Periodical. US. English. $35.00. Information Intelligence Inc, PO Box 31098, Phoeniz AZ 05046. **Ind/Abst** Libr. Inf. Sci. Abstr.

INFORMATION INTERCHANGE. V. 1- Jan. 1974-. 0197-2847. Periodical. US. English. ty. William Pullen Library, Georgia State University, 33 Gilmer South East, Atlanta GA 30303.

INFORMATION MARKET PLACE. 1978-79. 0162-878X. US. English. ir. R R Bowker, PO Box 1807, Ann Arbor MI 48106. **LC** Z674.3. **DD** 025.3025. **NLM** Z 674.3 I43.

INFORMATION MEDIA & TECHNOLOGY : THE JOURNAL OF NRCD. VFOAT Information Media and Technology. Periodical. UK. English. qt. 27 Domestic, 30.00 Foreign. PO Box 109, College Lane, Hatfield Herts AL10 9AB England. **Tel** 07072 79691. **Ed** B J S Williams. **LC** Z48. **DD** 686.405. bk rev. **Circ** 1,000. Covers the applications and technology of micrographic, reprographic and other new media for documentation including optical disks, CD-ROM and car systems. *Reprographics Quarterly, 0306-2880.*

INFORMATION PROCESSING & MANAGEMENT. VAT Information Processing and Management. V. 11- June 1975-. 0306-4573. Periodical. UK. English. bm. Pergamon Press, 395 Sawmill River Road, Elmsford NY 10523. **Tel** (914)592-7700. **Ind/Abst** Manage. Contents, ABI/Inform, Comput. Control Abstr., Electr. Electron. Abstr., Sci. Abstr. Sect. A. Phys. Abstr., Libr. Lit., Eng. Index Annu., Eng. Index Mon., Eng. Index Bioeng. Abstr., Eng. Index Energy Abstr., Biol. Abstr., Libr. Inf. Sci. Abstr., Chem. Abstr., Electron. Pub. Abstr., Curr. Index J. Educ., Comput. Rev., Soc. Sci. Citation Index, Eng. Index, Phys. Abstr. **LC** Z699.A1. **DD** 029.05. **CODEN** IPMADK. Available on microfilm from Microforms International Marketing Corp. (MIMC). *Information Storage and Retrieval, 0020-0271.*

INFORMATION REPORTS AND BIBLIOGRAPHIES. *See* Bibliographies.

INFORMATION RETRIEVAL & LIBRARY AUTOMATION. VFOAT Information Retrieval & Library Automation Newsletter. **VAT** Information Retrieval and Library Automation. V. 9, No. 2- July 1973-. 0020-0220. Periodical. US. English. mo. $48.00 Domestic, $58.00 Foreign. Lomond Systems Inc, PO Box 88, Mt Airy MD 21771. **Tel** ((301)829-1496. **Ed** Mary Tonne Schaefer. **Ind/Abst** Electron. Commun. Abstr. J., ISMEC Bull., Pollut. Abstr. Indexes, Saf. Sci. Abstr. J., Book Rev. Index. bk rev. A monthly summary of research, events and literature of scientific and technical information systems. *Information Retrieval & Library Automation Letter.*

INFORMATION SCIENCES. V. 1-. 0020-0255. Periodical. US. English. ir. Elsevier Science Publishers, PO Box 1663, Grand Central Station, New York NY 10163. **Ind/Abst** Math. Rev., Comput. Control Abstr., Electr. Electron. Abstr., Sci. Abstr. Sect. A. Phys. Abstr., Electron. Commun. Abstr. J., ISMEC Bull., Pollut. Abstr. Indexes, Saf. Sci. Abstr. J., Eng. Index Annu., Eng. Index Mon., Eng. Index Bioeng. Abstr., Eng. Index Energy Abstr., MLA Int. Bibliogr. Books Artic. Mod. Lang. Lit., Sci. Cit. Index, Abr. Ed., Sociol. Abstr., Int. Aerosp. Abstr., Phys. Abstr., Comput. Rev., Eng. Index. **LC** Z699.A1. **DD** 029.7. **CODEN** ISIJBC.

INFORMATION SERVICES & USE. VFOAT Information Services and Use. Vol. 1, No. 1 (Mar. 1981)-. 0167-5265. Periodical. English. bm. Elsevier Science Publishers, PO Box 211, 1000 AE Amsterdam Netherlands. **Tel** (020)5803.911. **Ind/Abst** Electron. Commun. Abstr. J., ISMEC Bull., Pollut. Abstr. Indexes, Saf. Sci. Abstr. J., Manage. Contents, Fluidex, Comput. Control Abstr., Electr. Electron. Abstr., Sci. Abstr. Sect. A. Phys. Abstr., Libr. Inf. Sci. Abstr., Electron. Pub. Abstr. **LC** Z699.A1. **DD** 025.0405. **CODEN** ISUDX8.

THE INFORMATION SOCIETY. Vol. 1, No. 1 (1981)-. 0197-2243. Periodical. US. English. ir. $60.00. Crane Russak and Company, 3 East 44th Street, New York NY 10017. **Tel** (212)867-1490. **Ed** Joseph Becker. **Ind/Abst** ABI/Inform, Comput. Control Abstr., Electr. Electron. Abstr., Sci. Abstr. Sect. A. Phys. Abstr., Electron. Pub. Abstr., Phys. Abstr., Comput. Rev. **LC** Z668. **DD** 020.5. **CODEN** INSCD8. bk rev. adv acc. **Circ** 600. Focuses on the social, economic, and political implications of the information age.

Library and Information Science

INFORMATION SOURCES. See Yearbooks, Almanacs, Directories.

INFORMATION TECHNOLOGY AND LIBRARIES. Vol. 1, No. 1 (Mar. 1982)-. 0730-9295. Periodical. US. English. qt. $10.00 Members, $20.00 Others. American Library Association, 50 East Huron Street, Chicago IL 60611. **Ind/Abst** ABI/Inform, Comput. Control Abstr., Electr. Electron. Abstr., Sci. Abstr. Sect. A. Phys. Abstr., Comput. Inf. Syst. Abstr. J., Comput. Rev., Curr. Contents, Curr. Index J. Educ., Inf. Sci. Abstr., Libr. Inf. Sci. Abstr., Libr. Lit., Mag. Index, Newsearch, Q. Bibliogr. Comput. Data Process., Sci. Abstr. **LC** Z678.9.A1. **DD** 025.302854. **NLM** Z 699.A1 J86. **CODEN** ITLBDC. Available on microfilm from University Microfilms. Journal of Library Automation, 0022-2240.

INFORMATION UND DOKUMENTATION : ANNOTIERTE TITELLISTE. **Main/Corp** Germany (Democratic Republic, 1949-). Zentralinstitut fur Information und Dokumentation. Multilingual (German). ir. 3.00 Single Issue. 117 Berlin, Kopernicker Str 325, Berlin West Germany. **LC** Z699.2. **DD** 016.029.

INFORMATOR BIBLIOTEKA - UKRAINSKE TOVARYSTVO VZAIMNOI POMOCHI V KANADI. (INFORMATOR BIBLIOTEKA). **Main/Corp** Ukrainske Tovarystio Vzaimnoi Pomochi V Kanadi Branch No. 20 (Vancouver, B. C.).Biblioteka. 1980-. 0821-767X. CN. Ukrainian. an. Library Ukrainian Orthodox Church, 154 10th Avenue East, Vancouver British Columbia Canada. **DD** 027.63. Library Bulletin, 0821-7661.

INFORMATSIINYI BIULETEN - UKRAINSKA BIBLIOTEKA IMENY S. PETLIURY V PARYZHI. **Main/Corp** Ukrainska Biblioteka Imeny S. Petliury V Paryzhi. V. 1- (No. 1-35). Ukrainian. ir. 6 rue de Palestine, Paris France 75019. **LC** Z927.

INFORMATSIONNYE MATERIALY. **Main/Corp** Akademiia Nauk SSSR. Nauchnyi Sovet Po Kompleksnoi Problema Kibernetika. Began in 1967. UR. Russian. 0.24 Single Issue. Sovetskoe Radio, Ul Vavilova 40, Moskva Russia. **LC** Q300.

INFORMATYKA. **Series/Titl** Zeszyty Naukowe Politechniki Slaskiej. No. 1-. 0434-0760. Periodical. Polish (summaries in English and Russian). mo. ARS Polona, Krakowskie Przedmiescie 7, 00-068 Warsaw Poland. **LC** Z699.A1. **DD** 001.605.

INFORME BIENAL - BANCO DEL LIBRO. **Main/Corp** Banco Del Libro. Spanish. ir. Banco del Libro, Apartado 10 914, Caracas Venezuela. **LC** Z786.

THE INFORMER. V. 1- 1975-. 0195-4318. Periodical. US. English. qt. $10.00. Iesmp Inc, PO Box 668, Fort Valley GA 31030. **Tel** (912)825-7645. Ed Dorothy M Haith. bk rev. adv acc. **Circ** 3,000. Subjects related to black librarianship.

INNER BARK. (THE INNER BARK). V. 1- July 1973-. 0700-3196. Periodical. CN. English. mo. Free. Public Services Main Library, University of Saskatchewan, Saskatoon Saskatchewan S7N 0W0 Canada. **DD** 027.771242. (ctrl).

INPUT. Jan. 1977-. 0706-151X. CN. English. ir. $15.00. Editor Input, Government Publications Department, Library University of Waterloo, Waterloo Ontario N2L 3G1 Canada. **DD** 025.173.

INTER-EXLIBRIS. **Main/Corp** Frederikshavn Kunstmuseum. 1978-. DK. Danish (English and German). an. Frederikshavn Kunstmuseum, Kallsvej 2, DK 9900 Frederikshavn Denmark. **LC** Z995. **DD** 769.5.

INTER FOLIA. No. 1- Oct. 1953-. Periodical. MX. Spanish. ir. Apartado 1625, Monterrey N L Mexico. **LC** Z885.N83.

INTERCOM. V. 1- July 1971-. 0047-0414. Periodical. US. English. mo. $15.00. D C Library Association, Box 14177/Benjamin Franklin Square, Washington DC 20044. **LC** Z732.D62. **DD** 020.5. D.C. Libraries.

INTERFACE. V. 1- Fall 1978-. 0270-6717. Periodical. US. English. qt. $10.00. ASCLA/ALA, 50 East Huron Street, Chicago IL 60611. **Tel** (312)944-6780. Ed Sue Medina. bk rev. adv acc. **Circ** 1,500. Microform. Covers latest developments and news about state libraries, library networks and cooperatives, and libraries serving special populations. ASLA President's Newsletter, 0044-9660; HRLSD Journal, 0196-7371.

INTERLENDING & DOCUMENT SUPPLY. (INTERLENDING & DOCUMENT SUPPLY : THE JOURNAL OF THE BRITISH LIBRARY LENDING DIVISION). **VFOAT** Interlending and Document Supply. Vol. 11, No. 1 (Jan. 1983)-. 0264-1615. Periodical. UK. English. qt. 22.00. British Library, Lending Division, Boston Spa, Wetherby West Yorkshire LS23 7BQ England. **Tel** 0937 8434 34. Ed David N Wood. **Ind/Abst** Comput. Control Abstr., Electr. Electron. Abstr., Sci. Abstr. Sect. A. Phys. Abstr., Libr. Inf. Sci. Abstr., Libr. Lit. **LC** Z921.B854. **DD** 027.542. **CODEN** IDSUDQ. adv acc. **Circ** 1,300. International in scope, it covers developments in individual countries and transactions between countries, also new methods of document delivery. Interlending Review, 0140-2773.

INTERNATIONAL BIBLIOGRAPHY, INFORMATION, DOCUMENTATION. See Bibliographies.

INTERNATIONAL CATALOGUING. V. 1- Jan./Mar. 1972-. 0047-0635. Periodical. UK. English. qt. $27.00. International Federation of Library Associations and Institutions, POB 95312, 2509 CH The Hague Netherlands. **Tel** (031)5567092. **Ind/Abst** Libr. Inf. Sci. Abstr., Libr. Lit. **LC** Z693.A15. **NLM** Z 695.7 I61. Index in first issue of next volume - loose - unpaged. Newsletter of the IFLA Committee on Cataloguing.

INTERNATIONAL CLASSIFICATION. V. 1- May 1974-. 0340-0050. Periodical. GW. English (German). ty. $35.91. Indeks-Verlag, Woogstrasse 36A, 6 Frankfurt 50 West Germany. **Tel** 069-52 36 90. Ed Ingetraut Dahlberg. **Ind/Abst** Comput. Control Abstr., Electr. Electron. Abstr., Sci. Abstr. Sect. A. Phys. Abstr., Libr. Inf. Sci. Abstr., Libr. Lit., Energy Res. Abstr., Soc. Sci. Citation Index, Phys. Abstr. **LC** Z696. **DD** 025.405. **CODEN** INCLDN. bk rev. adv acc. **Circ** 700. (ctrl). Covers classification, taxonomy, concept theory, indexing, terminology, organization of knowledge, theory of science-articles, reports, communications, bibliographies, news sections and letters.

INTERNATIONAL FORUM ON INFORMATION AND DOCUMENTATION. V. 1-. 0304-9701. Periodical. NE. English. qt. 100.-. International Federation for Documentation, PO Box 90402, 2509 LK The Hague Netherlands. Ed A Mikhailov. **Ind/Abst** Comput. Control Abstr., Electr. Electron. Abstr., Sci. Abstr. Sect. A. Phys. Abstr., Libr. Inf. Sci. Abstr., Libr. Lit., Soc. Sci. Citation Index, Phys. Abstr. **LC** Z1007. **DD** 020.5. **CODEN** IFIDD7. bk rev. adv acc. **Circ** 450. The journal is intended to cover the most important problems of information theory and practical activities which are of interest to information specialists all over the world.

INTERNATIONAL INDEX TO PERIODICALS (ANNUAL CUMULATION). See Indexes/Abstracts.

INTERNATIONAL INFORMATION, COMMUNICATION & EDUCATION. **VFOAT** I.N.I.C.A.E. Vol. 1, No. 1 (Mar. 1982)-. Periodical. English. sa. $34.00. The Manager of International Information Communication and Education, C-1 Banaras Hindu University, Varanasi 221005 India. **Ind/Abst** Libr. Inf. Sci. Abstr. **LC** Z671. **DD** 020.5.

INTERNATIONAL JOURNAL OF LAW LIBRARIES CEASED. V. 1-9. 0340-045X. Periodical. English. ir. $12.00. Klaus Menzinger Juristisches Seminar, Werthmannplatz, D-78 Freiburg West Germany. **Ind/Abst** Libr. Inf. Sci. Abstr. **LC** Z675.L2. **DD** 026.34005. Bulletin - International Association of Law Libraries, Newsletter - International Association of Law Libraries, 0196-8890.

INTERNATIONAL JOURNAL OF LEGAL INFORMATION. (INTERNATIONAL JOURNAL OF LEGAL INFORMATION : IJLI : THE OFFICIAL PUBLICATION OF THE INTERNATIONAL ASSOCIATION OF LAW LIBRARIES). **VFOAT** IJLI. Vol. 10, No. 1 (Feb. 1982)-. 0731-1265. Periodical. US. English. ir. $60.00. Biblthk Rechtswissenschft University, c/o K Menzinger Werthmannplatz 1, 7800 Freiburg West Germany. Ed Ivan Siphov. **Ind/Abst** Leg. Resour. Index, Libr. Inf. Sci. Abstr. **LC** Z675.L2. **DD** 026.34005. bk rev. adv acc. **Circ** 600. (ctrl). International Journal of Law Libraries.

THE INTERNATIONAL JOURNAL OF MICROGRAPHICS & VIDEO TECHNOLOGY. **VFOAT** International Journal of Micrographics and Video Technology. Vol. 1, No. 1-. 0743-9636. Periodical. UK. English. qt. Pergamon Press, 395 Sawmill River Road, Elmsford NY 10523. **Ind/Abst** Comput. Control Abstr., Electr. Electron. Abstr., Sci. Abstr. Sect. A. Phys. Abstr., Libr. Inf. Sci. Abstr., Print. Abstr., Electron. Pub. Abstr. **LC** Z265. **DD** 686.4305. **CODEN** IJMTDZ. Available in microform. Microdoc, 0026-2684 Micropublishing of Current Periodicals; 0364-3999.

INTERNATIONAL JOURNAL OF REVIEWS IN LIBRARY AND INFORMATION SCIENCE. 0740-5138. Periodical. US. English. ty. $15.00. Rosary College, Graduate School of Library and Information Science, River Forest IL 60305.

INTERNATIONAL LIBRARY MOVEMENT : ILM. **VFOAT** ILM. Began in 1979. Periodical. US. English. qt. $110.00. International Library Movement, Model Town, Ambala City 134 003 India. **Ind/Abst** Libr. Inf. Sci. Abstr. **LC** Z671. **DD** 020.5.

INTERNATIONAL LIBRARY REVIEW. V. 1- Jan. 1969-. 0020-7837. Periodical. UK. English. qt. $118.80. Academic Press, 4805 Sand Lake Road, Orlando FL 32819. **Tel** (305)345-4100. **Ind/Abst** Am. Hist. Life, Hist. Abstr., Part A, Mod. Hist. Abstr., Hist. Abst., Part B, Twent. Century Abstr., Recent Publ. Artic., Libr. Inf. Sci. Abstr., Curr. Index J. Educ., Soc. Sci. Citation Index. **LC** Z671. **NLM** Z 671 I61.

INTERNATIONAL SERIES OF MONOGRAPHS IN LIBRARY AND INFORMATION SCIENCES. Monographic Series. US. English. ir. Pergamon Press, c/o Cashier, 395 Sawmill Road, Elmsford NY 10523.

INTERNATIONALES BIBLIOTHEKS- HANDBUCH. **Series/Titl** Handbuch der Technischen Dokumentation und Bibliographie, Bd. 8. **VFOAT** World Guide to Libraries. Vol. 2-. 0000-0221. GW. English (German). ir. **LC** Z721. **DD** 027.0025. Internationales Bibliotheksadressbuch.

INVENTARI DEI MANOSCRITTI DELLE BIBLIOTECHE D'ITALIA. Vol. 1- 1890-. 0075-0026. IT. Italian. ir. Casa Edtrice, Viale Europa, CP 66 1-50126 Florence Italy. Ed G Mazzatinti. Inventari dei Manoscritte Delle Biblioteche d'Italia.

IOWA PUBLIC LIBRARY STATISTICS. See Statistics.

IOWA REGIONAL LIBRARY SYSTEM STATISTICS. See Statistics.

IOWA STATE UNIVERSITY LIBRARY INSTRUCTION MANUAL. **VFOAT** Library Instruction Manual. US. English. ir. Waveland Press Inc, PO Box 400, Prospect Heights IL 60070. **LC** Z670. **DD** 025.5677. Library Instruction Manual.

IREBI. INDICES DE REVISTA DE BIBLIOTECOLOGIA. **VFOAT** Indices de Revistas de Bibliotecologia. No. 1- Apr. 1973-. Periodical. Spanish. ir. **LC** Z666. **DD** 020.5.

IRISH LIBRARY BULLETIN. V. 1- Jan. 1940-. Periodical. English. bm. **LC** Z1035.

ISBN REVIEW. **Main/Corp** International ISBN Agency. **VAT** International Standard Book Number Review. V. 1- 1977-. 0342-4634. English. ir. 24.00. K G Saur Verlag, POB 7110 09 Possenbacherstr 2B, D-8000 Munchen 71 West Germany.

ISHIDATAMI. **Main/Corp** Nagasaki Kenritsu Nagasaki Toshokan. No. 1- May 1973-. Periodical. Japanese. ir. Nagasaki Kenritsu Nagasaki Toshokan, 1 Kami Nishiyamacho (850), Nagasaki Japan. **LC** Z845.J4.

ISI ONLINE. **VFOAT** I.S.I. Online. **VAT** Institute for Scientific Information Online. Vol. 1, No. 1 (July 1984)-. 0748-9722. Periodical. US. English. qt. ISI, 3501 Market Street, Philadelphia PA 19104. **DD** 025.

ISTORIIA BIBLIOTECHNOGO DELA V SSSR. 1- 1975-. Periodical. UR. Russian. an. 0.62. Gos Biblioteka SSSR, Prospekt Kalinina 3, Moskva Russian SFSR. **LC** Z819A1.

JAARBOEK OPENBARE BIBLIOTHEKEN. See Yearbooks, Almanacs, Directories.

JAARVERSLAG - BIBLIOTHEEKRAAD. **Main/Corp** Netherlands (Kingdom, 1815-). Bibliotheekraad. German. ir. Bibliotheekraad, Postbus 230 Burg Elsenlaan 241, 2280 Ae Rijswijk Netherlands. **LC** Z678.8.N4.

Library and Information Science

JAARVERSLAG - PROVINCIALE BIBLIOTHEEKCENTRALE GELDERLAND. Main/Corp Provinciale Bibliotheekcentrale Gelderland. Dutch. an. LC Z815.G44.

JAGGER JOURNAL. Main/Corp University of Cape Town Libraries. No. 1 (Dec. 1980)-. SA. English. an. 5.00. J W Jagger Library, University of Cape Town Private Bag, Rondesbosch 7700 Cape Province South Africa. Tel (021)69-8531. Ed B H Watts. Ind/Abst Libr. Inf. Sci. Abstr. LC Z858.U417. DD 027.7687. Circ 200. (ctrl). Making known the contents of the special collections at University of Cape Town libraries, and reporting on the professional concerns of the libraries' staff.

JAHRESBERICHT - GESE::SCJAFT FUR INFORMATION UND DOKUMENTATION. Main/Corp Gesellschaft fur Information und Dokumentation. 0174-3287. German. an. Gesellschaft fur Information und Dokumentation MBH, Lyoner Strasse 44-48 Araballa-Center, D-6000 Frankfurt 71 West Germany. LC Z699.A1. DD 025.0405.

JIGYO NEMPO - TOKYO TORITSU CHUO TOSHOKAN. Main/Corp Tokyo Toritsu Chuo Toshokan. JA. Japanese. ir. 7-13 Minami Azabu 5, Minato-Ku (106) Tokyo Japan. LC Z846.T6754.

JOINT SERIALS CATALOGUE OF WESTERN AUSTRALIAN ACADEMIC LIBRARIES. 0726-9587. English. ir. LC Z6945, PN4832. DD 011.34. Joint Serials Catalogue of Murdoch University, University of Western Australia, Western Australian Institute of Technology Libraries.

JOURNAL - HAWAII LIBRARY ASSOCIATION. (JOURNAL). Main/Corp Hawaii Library Association. VFOAT HLA Journal. 0017-8586. Periodical. US. English. an. Hawaii Library Association, 1514 Makalampa Drive, Honolulu HI 96818. Ind/Abst Libr. Lit. LC Z673. DD 020.624.

JOURNAL HOLDINGS FOR NASA LIBRARIES. 1974-. Periodical. US. English.

THE JOURNAL OF ACADEMIC LIBRARIANSHIP. (JOURNAL OF ACADEMIC LIBRARIANSHIP). V. 1- Mar. 1975-. 0099-1333. Periodical. US. English. bm. $38.00 Domestic, $42.00 Foreign. Post Office Box 8330, Ann Arbor MI 48107. Tel (313)662-3925. Ed Richard Dougherty. Ind/Abst Libr. Inf. Sci. Abstr., Book Rev. Index, Educ. Index, Ref. Source, Curr. Index J. Educ., Libr. Lit., Soc. Sci. Citation Index. LC Z671. DD 020.5. bk rev. adv acc. Circ 3,000. (ctrl). Articles, features, and book reviews for the academic library professional.

JOURNAL OF EDUCATION FOR LIBRARIANSHIP CEASED. V. 1-24. 0022-0604. Periodical. US. English. qt. $18.00. Journal of Education for Librarianship, 471 Park Lane, State College PA 16801. Ind/Abst Comput. Control Abstr., Electr. Electron. Abstr., Sci. Abstr. Sect. A. Phys. Abstr., Libr. Inf. Sci. Abstr., Educ. Index, Curr. Index J. Educ., Libr. Lit. LC Z671. DD 020. NLM Z 671 J86. CODEN JLELA. Directory of Association of American Library Schools, 0197-579X; Newsletter (Association of American Library Schools); Report of Meeting.

JOURNAL OF EDUCATION FOR LIBRARY AND INFORMATION SCIENCE. Vol. 25, No. 1 (Summer 1984)-. 0748-5786. Periodical. US. English. qt. $30.00. Association for Library and Information Science Education, 471 Park Lane, State College PA 16803-3208. Tel (814)238-0254. Ed Charles D Patterson. Ind/Abst Curr. Index J. Educ., Educ. Index, Inf. Sci. Abstr., Libr. Inf. Sci. Abstr., Libr. Lit., Soc. Sci. Citation Index. LC Z671. DD 020.5. bk rev. Circ 2,000. Scholarly journal in the field of library and information science education; presents research, teaching methods and issues; international scope; association news. Journal of Education for Librarianship, 0022-0604.

JOURNAL OF INFORMATION SCIENCE. V. 1- Apr. 1979-. 0165-5515. Periodical. English. bm. Elsevier Science Publishers, PO Box 211, 1000 AE Amsterdam Netherlands. Tel (020)5803.911. Ind/Abst Manage. Contents, Eng. Index Annu., Eng. Index Mon., Eng. Index, Eng. Index Bioeng. Abstr., Eng. Index Energy Abstr., Excerpta Med., Fluidex, World Text Abstr., Ship Abstr., ABI/Inform, Comput. Control Abstr., Electr. Electron. Abstr., Sci. Abstr. Sect. A. Phys. Abstr., Libr. Inf. Sci. Abstr., Ref. Source, Libr. Lit., Comput. Rev., Soc. Sci. Citation Index. LC Z1007. DD 020.5. CODEN JISCDI. Information Scientist.

JOURNAL OF LAW AND INFORMATION SCIENCE. See Law.

JOURNAL OF LIBRARIANSHIP. Periodical. UK. English. qt. $65.00. Library Association, 7 Ridgemount and Store Streets, London WC1E 7AE England. Tel 01-636-7543. Ed Frances Moore. Ind/Abst Soc. Sci. Citation Index, Phys. Abstr., Libr. Lit., Comput. Control Abstr., Electr. Electron. Abstr. bk rev. adv acc. Contains published articles reporting and reflecting significant work and developments in all fields of library and information work, particularly the results of research and investigation.

JOURNAL OF LIBRARY ADMINISTRATION. V. 1- Spring 1980-. 0193-0826. Periodical. US. English. qt. $82.00. Haworth Press, 28 East 22nd Street, New York NY 10010. Tel (212)228-2800. Ed John R Rizzo. Ind/Abst Manage. Contents, Libr. Inf. Sci. Abstr., Public Aff. Inf. Serv. Bull. LC Z678. DD 025.105. Index in last issue of volume - attached. bk rev. adv acc. Circ 1,440. The journal actively seeks out the modern advances being made in the professional management field and applies them to the library setting.

JOURNAL OF LIBRARY AND INFORMATION SCIENCE. V. 1- June 1976-. Periodical. II. English. sa. $10.00. University of Delhi, c/o Department of Library Science/Art Faculty Building, New Delhi 110007 India. Ind/Abst Libr. Inf. Sci. Abstr., Libr. Lit. LC Z671. DD 020.5.

JOURNAL OF LIBRARY AUTOMATION CEASED. V. 1-14. 0022-2240. Periodical. US. English. qt. Ind/Abst Libr. Inf. Sci. Abstr., Ref. Source, Public Aff. Inf. Serv. Bull. LC Z678.9.A1. DD 025.0018. NLM Z 699.A1 J86. CODEN JLAUAY. JOLA Technical Communications, 0021-3748.

THE JOURNAL OF LIBRARY HISTORY. (THE JOURNAL OF LIBRARY HISTORY : JLH). VFOAT JLH, J.L.H. Vol. 9, No. 1 (Jan. 1974)-. 0275-3650. Periodical. US. English. qt. $26.00. University of Texas Press, Box 7819, Austin TX 78712. Tel (512)471-4531. Ed Donald G Davis Jr. Ind/Abst Libr. Lit., MLA Int. Bibliogr., Books Artic. Mod. Lang. Lit., Writ. Am. Hist., Book Rev. Index, Am. Hist. Life, Hist. Abstr., Bull. Bibl. Fr., Libr. Inf. Sci. Abstr., Soc. Sci. Citation Index, Curr. Awareness Libr. Lit. LC Z671. DD 027.009. bk rev. adv acc. Circ 800. (ctrl). Explores collections of graphic records and their creators and users in the context of cultural history. Journal of Library History, Philosophy, and Comparative Librarianship, 0090-8894.

JOURNAL OF LIBRARY SERVICE. V. 1- Aug. 1971-. Periodical. II. English. ir. 22.00. 1760 Gandhi Road, Ahmedabad 1 India. LC Z845.I4. DD 020.954.

JOURNAL OF NAL ASSOCIATES. VAT Journal of the National Agricultural Library Associates. New Series, V. 4, No. 1/2 (Jan./June 1979)-. 0277-2841. Periodical. US. English. ir. Association of National Agriculture Libraries, 10301 Baltimore Boulevard, Beltsville MD 20705. Tel (301)344-3937. Ind/Abst Am. Hist. Life, Hist. Abstr., Agricola, Bibliogr. Agric. LC Z733. DD 026.630973. Associates NAL Today, 0364-9431.

JOURNAL OF ORGANOMETALLIC CHEMISTRY LIBRARY. 1-. 0378-5203. Monographic Series. NE. English. ir. Elsevier Science Publishing Company Inc, PO Box 1663, Grand Central Station, New York NY 10163. Ind/Abst Chem. Abstr. LC UNC. NLM W1 JO804MB. CODEN JOCLD7.

JOURNAL OF PHILIPPINE LIBRARIANSHIP. Vol. 1, No. 1 (Mar. 1968)-. 0022-359X. Periodical. PH. English. sa. 15.00. Institute of Library Science, University of The Philippines, 3rd Floor/Gonzales Hall, Diliman Quezon City 3004 Philippines. Ed Rosa M Vallejo. Ind/Abst Libr. Inf. Sci. Abstr., Libr. Lit. adv acc. Circ 500. (ctrl). Deals with all aspects of library and information work in the Philippines.

JOURNAL OF THE AMERICAN SOCIETY FOR INFORMATION SCIENCE. Main/Corp American Society for Information Science. V. 21- Jan./Feb. 1970-. 0002-8231. Periodical. US. English. bm. John Wiley & Sons, 605 Third Avenue, New York NY 10158. Tel (800)526-5368. Ind/Abst Predicasts, Sociol. Abstr., Excerpta Med., Coal Abstr., Cumul. Index Nurs. Allied Health Lit., Abstr. Bull. Inst. Paper Chem., Int. Aerosp. Abstr., ABI/Inform, GeoRef, Ref. Source, Eng. Index, Eng. Index Annu., Eng. Index Mon., Public Aff. Inf. Serv. Bull., Curr. Index J. Educ., Libr. Lit., Comput. Control Abstr., Electr. Electron. Abstr., Sci. Abstr. Sect. A. Phys. Abstr., Hospit. Lit. Index, Comput. Rev., Soc. Sci. Citation Index, Phys. Abstr., Am. Hist. Life, Hist. Abstr. LC Z1007. DD 020.5. NLM Z 1007 A51. CODEN AISJB6. American Documentation, 0096-946X.

JOURNAL OF THE CANADIAN LIBRARY SCIENCE SOCIETY. (THE JOURNAL OF THE CANADIAN LIBRARY SCIENCE SOCIETY). Main/Corp Canadian Library Science Society. VFOAT La Revue de la Societe de Bibliotheconomie Canadienne. No. 1-5. 0708-2274. Periodical. CN. English (includes some text in French). an. $11.61. Societe Bibliotheconomie Canada, 123 Cambie Street, Vancouver British Columbia V6B 4RB Canada. Tel (604)682-7228. Ind/Abst Libr. Inf. Sci. Abstr. LC Z671. DD 020.5. Canadian Library Progress, 0315-2693.

JOURNAL OF THE KERALA UNIVERSITY ORIENTAL RESEARCH INSTITUTE AND MANUSCRIPTS LIBRARY CEASED. Main/Corp University of Kerala Oriental Research Institute & MSS Library. Periodical. Sanskrit or English. ir.

THE JOURNAL OF THE RUTGERS UNIVERSITY LIBRARIES. Main/Corp Rutgers University. Library. V. 38- June 1976-. Periodical. US. English. sa. $15.00. Rutgers University Library, New Brunswick NJ 08903. Tel (201)932-7601. Ed Pamela Spence Richards. Ind/Abst Am. Hist. Life, Hist. Abstr., Part A, Mod. Hist. Abstr., Hist. Abstr., Part B, Twent. Century Abstr. Circ 750. (ctrl). Articles on the history of libraries, New Jersey history and the history of publishing as well as on bibliographical topics. Journal of the Rutgers University Library, 0036-0473.

JOURNAL OF UGANDAN LIBRARIES. Periodical. UG. English. sa. Editor of Journal of Ugandan Libraries, East African School of Librarianship, Makerere University, PO Box 7062, Kampala Uganda. LC Z857.U3. DD 027.06761. Uganda Libraries.

JOURNAL - ZAMBIA LIBRARY ASSOCIATION. Main/Corp Zambia Library Association. VFOAT Zambia Library Association Journal. V. 1- Mar. 1969-. 0049-853X. Periodical. English. sa. $27.40. Zambia Library Association, PO Box 2839, Lusaka Zambia. Ind/Abst Libr. Inf. Sci. Abstr. LC Z857.Z3.

JOURNALINK. VAT Journal Link. 0192-1010. US. English. Sigma Data Computing Corporation, 12730 Twinbrook Parkway, Rockville MD 20852. LC Z675.G7. DD 027.502573.

JOURNALS AVAILABLE IN THE ERDA LIBRARY. Main/Corp United States. Energy Research and Development Administration. Library. US. English. sa. Energy Research and Development Administration, Division of Administrative Services, 20 Massachusetts Avenue NW, Washington DC 20545.

J.P.L. NEWS. Vol. 11, No. 1 Jan./Feb. 1982. 0713-7443. Periodical. CN. English (text includes English, French, and Yiddish). bm. Free. J P L News, c/o Jewish Public Library, 5151 Cote Street Catherine Road, Montreal Quebec H3W 1M6 Canada. DD 027.63. (ctrl). Bulletin, 0381-9884.

JUDAICA LIBRARIANSHIP. Vol. 1, No. 1 (Fall 1983)-. 0739-5086. Periodical. US. English. sa. $25.00. Judaica Librarianship, c/o S Friedman, 26 Pitney Street, West Orange NJ 07025. Ind/Abst Index Jew. Period. LC Z675.J4. AJL Bulletin, 0734-0516.

JUST B'TWX US. V. 1- 1970-. 0075-4587. Periodical. US. English. ir. $5.00 for 2 years. University of Colorado Libraries Interlibrary Loan Service, Box 184, Boulder CO 80309. Tel (303)492-6176. Ed Allison Cowgill and Virginia Boucher. bk rev. Circ 400. Deals with interlibrary loan matters.

KAMPO - OSAKA GAIKOKUGO DAIGAKU FUZOKU TOSHOKAN. Main/Corp Osaka Gaikokugo Daigaku Fuzoku Toshokan. No. 1- 1974-Yearly Issue. Japanese. ir. Fuzoku Toshokan, Uehonmachi 8-chome, Osaka Japan. LC Z955.

KANE : HITOTSUBASHI DAIGAKU FUZOKU TOSHOKAN HO. VFOAT Hitotsubashi Daigaku Fuzoku Toshokan Ho, The Hitotsubashi University Library Bulletin. 0387-8783. Periodical. JA. Japanese. ir. Hitotsubashi Daigaku

Library and Information Science

Fuzoku Toshokan, 1 Naka 2, Kunitachi-shi Japan. LC Z955.K814.

KARACHI UNIVERSITY LIBRARY: AN ANNUAL REPORT. Main/Corp University of Karachi Library. PK. English. ir. Karachi University Library, Karachi 32 Pakistan. LC Z846. DD 027.7549183.

KAZE DAYORI. Japanese. ir. 1 Minami Josanjimamachi 2 Chome, Tokushima 770 Japan. LC Z955.

KENTUCKY LIBRARIES. Vol. 45, No. 1 (Winter 1980)-. 0732-5452. Periodical. US. English. qt. $12.00. Paducah Public Libraries, c/o Tom Sutherland, 555 Washington Street, Paducah KY 42001. Tel (502)443-2664. Ed Bob Smith. Ind/Abst Libr. Lit. LC Z732.K37. DD 027.0769. bk rev. adv acc. Circ 1,200. (ctrl). Library articles. Kentucky Library Association Bulletin, 0022-734X.

KENTUCKY LIBRARY ASSOCIATION BULLETIN CEASED. V. 1-44. 0022-734X. Periodical. US. English. qt.

KEYSTONE (FLORIDA STATE LIBRARY) CEASED. (THE KEYSTONE). Vol. 1, No. 1 (Fall 1968)-V. 11, No. 3 (June/July 1982). Periodical. US. English. bm.

KIRJASTOLEHTI. Vol. 1 1908-. 0023-1843. Periodical. FI. Finnish. mo. 170.-. Akakeeminen-Kirjakuppa, PO Box 128, 00101 Helsinki Finland. Tel (90)651 122. Ind/Abst Libr. Inf. Sci. Abstr., Libr. Lit. (cum index).

KLA MEMBERSHIP DIRECTORY. See Yearbooks, Almanacs, Directories.

KLEINE SCHRIFTEN. Main/Corp Bonn. Universitat. Forschungsstelle fur Buchwissenschaft. 1- 1964-. 0524-0379. Periodical. GW. German. ir. J B Metzler, Postfach 529, 7000 Stuttgart 1 West Germany. Ind/Abst MLA Int. Bibliogr. Books Artic. Mod. Lang. Lit.

KNIHOVNICTVI A BIBLIOGRAFIE. Periodical. CS. Czech. bm. Artia, PO Box 790, Praha 1 Czechoslovakia. LC Z671.

KODAE TOSOGWAN PO = THE KOREA UNIVERSITY LIBRARY BULLETIN. Main/Corp Koryo Taehakkyo. Chungang Tosogwan. VFOAT Korea University Library Bulletin. Periodical. KO. Korean. ir. 1 Anam-Dong, Songbuk-Ku Seoul South Korea. LC Z955.K6634.

KOKURITSU KOKKAI TOSHOKAN GEPPO. VFOAT National Diet Library Monthly Bulletin. Edition- April 1961-. 0027-9153. Periodical. JA. Japanese. ir. 170.00. Yurindo Insatsu, 47 Shiba Nishikubo Tomecho Minato-Ku, Tokyo 105 Japan. LC Z955.T585. NLM Z 955 K77G.

KOKURITSU KOKKAI TOSHOKAN SHOKUIN MEIBO. JA. Japanese. ir. Kokuritsu Kokkai Toshokan, 10-1 Nagatacho Chiyoda-Ku, 100 Tokyo Japan. LC Z846.

KOKURITSU KOKKAI TOSHOKAN TO KOKYO TOSHOKAN TO NO KYORYOKU GYOMU NI KANSURU TOKEI. Japanese. ir. LC Z845.J4.

KOMPLEKTOVANIE I ISPOLZOVANIE KNIZKNYKH FONDOV MASSOVYKH BIBLIOTEK. Periodical. UR. Russian. LC Z819.A1.

KONYVTARI FIGYELO. V. 1- 1955-. 0023-3773. Periodical. HU. Hungarian. bm. Akademiai Kiado, POB 24, 1363 Budapest Hungary. Tel 160-100/517. Ed Gero Zsoltne. bk rev. adv acc. Circ 1,000. A multi-purpose journal which contains all aspects of the librarianship in Hungary and in foreign countries.

KONYVTAROS. V. 6-. 0450-7886. Periodical. Hungarian. m. LC Z674. Konyv.

KRAUS CURRICULUM DEVELOPMENT LIBRARY. CUMULATIVE SUBJECT INDEX. See Indexes/Abstracts.

KURZDARSTELLUNG DER DOKUMENTATIONS-LEITSTELLE MODERNER ORIENT UND TATIGKEITSBERICHT. Main/Corp Hamburg. Deutsches Orient-Institut Dokumentations-Leitstelle Moderner Orient. German. ir. Neuer Jungfernstieg 26, D-2000 Hamburg 36 West Germany. LC Z802.H176.

KYUSHU GEIJUTSU KOKA DAIGAKU ZOKA TOSHO NOKUROKU. Japanese, English, French, German or Italian. ir. 226 Siobara Minami-Ku (815), Fukuoka Japan. LC Z955.F824. DD 025.43.

LAMA NEWSLETTER. Main/Corp Library Administration and Management Association. VAT Library Administration and Management Association Newsletter. V. 5- Jan. 1979-. 0193-0451. Periodical. US. English. qt. Library Administration and Management Association, 50 East Huron Street, Chicago IL 60611. Tel (312)944-6780. Ed Edward Garteu. Ind/Abst Libr. Inf. Sci. Abstr. LC Z678. DD 025.105. bk rev. adv acc. Circ 4,500. (ctrl). The newsletter seeks to bring members substantive articles, reviews and news in the library management field, applicable to all types of libraries. LAD Newsletter, 0098-7972.

THE LAMP. (THE LAMP : URBAN LIBRARIES COUNCIL NEWSLETTER). 8755-075X. Periodical. US. English. qt. Urban Libraries Council, 425 North Michigan Avenue, Chicago IL 60611. DD 021. Newsletter (Urban Library Trustees Council).

LARC SERIES ON AUTOMATED ACTIVITIES IN HEALTH SCIENCES LIBRARIES. VFOAT Automated Activities in Health Science Libraries. V. 1- 1975-. 0095-0181. Monographic Series. US. English. NLM Z 678.A1 L105.

LASIE. (LASIE : INFORMATION BULLETIN OF THE LIBRARY AUTOMATED SYSTEMS INFORMATION EXCHANGE). Vol. 1, No. 1 (June, 1970). 0047-3774. Periodical. AT. English. bm. LASIE Australia Company Ltd, PO Box 602, Lane Cove New South Wales 2066 Australia. Ind/Abst Comput. Control Abstr., Electr. Electron. Abstr., Sci. Abstr. Sect. A. Phys. Abstr., Libr. Inf. Sci. Abstr., Libr. Lit., APAIS, Aust. Public Aff. Inf. Serv., Phys. Abstr. CODEN IBLEAS. (cum index).

LATIN AMERICAN SERIALS LIST. VFOAT Benson Latin American Collection Serials List. Began with May 1982. Periodical. US. English. $20.00. Publications of the General Libraries, University of Texas at Austin, PO Box P, Austin TX 78713-7330. Tel (512)471-3811. Ed Mary Pound. Lists serial titles and their bound holdings in the Benson Collection with OCLC records as of May 29, 1982.

THE LAW LIBRARIAN. V. 1- Apr. 1970-. 0023-9275. Periodical. UK. English. ty. $16.48. Sweet & Maxwell Limited, North Way, Andover Hants SP10 5BE England. Tel 9-387-7050. Ed B M Wells. Ind/Abst Leg. Resour. Index, Libr. Inf. Sci. Abstr., Libr. Lit., Curr. Law Index, Contents Curr. Leg. Period. LC Z675.L2. DD 026.3400942. bk rev. adv acc. Circ 750. Law librarianship, legal bibliography, legal databases, aspects of librarianship, publishing, computer-assisted information retrieval and information work as they affect law libraries.

THE LAW LIBRARIAN'S PROFESSIONAL DESK REFERENCE AND DIARY. 1982-. 0278-3908. US. English. an. $20.00. Infosources Publishing, 118 West 79th Street, New York NY 10024. LC Z675.L2. DD 026.3400973.

LAW LIBRARY BULLETIN. 0145-8612. US. English. State Library of Pennsylvania, Box 1601, Harrisburg PA 17126. LC KF4. DD 016.3400973.

LAW LIBRARY LIGHTS. Periodical. US. English.

LAW LIBRARY NEWSLETTER. 0147-1376. Periodical. US. English. mo. Ms Judith Goater, 15 Inverness Way East, Englewood CO 80110. LC Z675.L2. DD 026.3405.

LC ACQUISITION TRENDS CEASED. Main/Corp Library of Congress. VFOAT L.C. Acquisition Trends, Acquisition Trends. VAT Library of Congress Acquisition Trends. Began with No. 1, July 1977. Ceased with No. 11 (Apr. 1982). 0146-8936. Periodical. US. English. sa. Library of Congress, Washington DC 20540. LC Z733. DD 025.2. National Program for Acquisitions and Cataloging Progress Report, 0190-8170; LC Special Foreign Acquisitions Program Newsletter, 0191-0906.

L.C. CLASSIFICATION. ADDITIONS AND CHANGES. (L.C. CLASSIFICATION : ADDITIONS AND CHANGES). Main/Corp United States. Library of Congress. Subject Cataloging Division. VAT Library of Congress Classification. Additions and Changes. List 1- March/May 1928-. 0041-7912. US. English. qt. $55.00. Library of Congress, Cataloging Distribution Service, Washington DC 20541. Tel (202)287-6100. LC Z696. DD 025.4. Contains the additions and changes made in the course of daily application of the classification schedules at the Library of Congress.

L.C. SUBJECT HEADINGS WEEKLY LISTS. Main/Corp Library of Congress. Subject Cataloging Division. VFOAT LC Subject Headings Weekly Lists. VAT Library of Congress Subject Headings Weekly Lists (Washington, D.C.). 1984, Lists 1 through 4-. 8755-6146. Periodical. US. English. mo. LC Z695. DD 025.49.

L.C. SUBJECT HEADINGS WEEKLY LISTS. Main/Corp Library of Congress. Subject Cataloging Division. VFOAT LC Subject Headings Weekly Lists. VAT Library of Congress Subject Headings Weekly Lists. 1984, Lists 1-19 (Oct. 1984)-. 8755-366X. US. English. bm. Gale Research Company, Penobscot Building, Detroit MI 48226. DD 025.

LCOMM NEWS. Vol. 1, No. 1 (Oct. 1973)-. Periodical. US. English. mo. $8.00. Library Council of Metro Milwaukee, 814 West Wisconsin Avenue, Milwaukee WI 53233. Tel (414)271-8470. Ed Janis Trebby. adv acc. Circ 420. (ctrl). Newsletter of council and member activities with news of the library community in the Milwaukee metropolitan area, Wisconsin, and beyond.

LCPA BROADSIDE. VFOAT L.C.P.A. Broadside. VAT Library of Congress Professional Association Broadside. Vol. 1, No. 1 (Jan. 3, 1983)-. 0736-296X. Periodical. US. English. ir. Free. Library of Congress, Professional Association of Library of Congress, Washington DC 20540. LC Z733.U6. DD 027.573088092.

LCPA NEWSLETTER. Main/Corp Library of Congress. Professional Association. VAT Library of Congress Professional Association Newsletter. V. 2, No. 5- May 1971-. 0098-1648. Periodical. US. English. bm. Free. Library of Congress Professional Association, c/o Staff Relations Office, LJ G112 Library of Congress, Washington DC 20540. LC Z733. DD 027.5753. (ctrl).

LCPA'S INDEX TO LIBRARY OF CONGRESS INFORMATION BULLETIN. See Indexes/Abstracts.

AN LEABHARLANN. VFOAT Irish Library. N. Ser. V. 1-29. 0023-9542. Periodical. UK. English. qt. 14.80. Leabharlann an the Irish Library, 53-54 Upper Mount Street, Dublin 2 Ireland. Ed Peter Fox and Andrew Morrow. Ind/Abst Libr. Inf. Sci. Abstr. bk rev. adv acc. Northern Ireland Libraries.

LEADS. Main/Corp American Library Association. US. English. qt. $12.00. American Library Association, 50 East Huron Street, Chicago IL 60611. Ind/Abst Libr. Lit.

LEAFLET. (LEAFLET : THE NEWSLETTER FOR THE BRANCHES OF LAMBTON COUNTY LIBRARY). Vol. 1, #1 (Jan. 1980)-. 0710-8095. Periodical. CN. English. bm. Free. Leaflet, Box 100, Wyoming Ontario N0N 1T0 Canada. DD 027.471327.

LECTURE NOTES IN CONTROL AND INFORMATION SCIENCES. V. 1- 1978-. 0170-8643. English. ir. Springer Verlag-New York Inc, 175 5th Avenue, New York NY 10010. Tel (212)460-1584. Ind/Abst Comput. Control Abstr., Electr. Electron. Abstr., Sci. Abstr. Sect. A. Phys. Abstr. Contains topics on analysis and optimization of systems, performance evaluation, methodology, and theory of networks and information.

LEGISLATURE LIBRARY ANNUAL REPORT. (ANNUAL REPORT - LEGISLATURE LIBRARY). Main/Corp Alberta. Legislative Assembly. Legislature Library. VAT Annual Report - Legislature Library. Edmonton Alberta. 1974-. 0383-3712. CN. English. an. Free. Legislature Library, 216 Legislature Building, Edmonton Alberta T5K 2B6 Canada. Tel (403)422-5085. LC Z736. DD 027.571233. Circ 250.

LETTER OF THE LAA. (THE LETTER OF THE LAA). Main/Corp Library Association of Alberta. Issue No. 1- Nov. 1977-. 0705-4890. Periodical. CN. English. ir. Library Association of Alberta, Box 5739 Station L, Edmonton Alberta T6C 4G2 Canada. DD 020.62347123. LAA-LAA-LAA, 0318-8566.

LETTER TO LIBRARIES (SALEM, OR. : 1983). (LETTER TO LIBRARIES). Oct. 1984-. 0747-5608. Periodical. US. English. mo. Oregon State Library, State Library Building, Salem OR 97310-0640. LC Z732.O8. DD 027.5795. Watermark (Salem, Or.), 0194-2999.

LETTRE DU PRESIDENT - CORPORATION DES BIBLIOTHECAIRES PROFESSIONNELS DU QUEBEC. (LETTRE DU PRESIDENT). **Main/Corp** Corporation des Bibliothecaires Professionnels du Quebec. 0709-1354. Periodical. CN. French. ir. Corporation des Bibliothecaires, Professionnels du Quebec, 360 rue le Moyne, Montreal Quebec H2Y 1Y3 Canada. **DD** 020.6234714.

LHRT. **VFOAT** Library History Round Table Newsletter. Fall 1979-. 0737-4984. Periodical. US. English. sa. Free to members. American Library Association, Library History Round Table, 50 East Huron Street, Chicago IL 60611. **Tel** (312)944-6780. **Ed** Ronald H Fritze. **Circ** 350. (ctrl). Newsletter of the American Library Association's Library History Round Table. News of LHRT, library history and related fields. *ALHRT: American Library History Round Table Newsletter.*

LIAISON 2. (LIAISON II). Began publication in summer 1977?. 0702-3839. Periodical. CN. English. Niagara Regional Library System, 15 Lloyd Street, Sainte Catherines Ontario L2S 2N7 Canada. **DD** 027.471351. *Liaison, 0700-3390.*

LIBRA DATABASE MONTHLY INDEX. *See* Indexes/Abstracts.

LIBRARIAN'S ANNUAL REPORT. **Main/Corp** Kenyatta University College. Library. 1981/82-. English. an. **LC** Z858.K43. **DD** 027.767625. *Annual Report.*

LIBRARIANS' BROWSER *CEASED.* **VFOAT** Home Grown Books Librarians' Browser. Vol. 1, No. 1-2 (Spring-Summer 1981)-. 0276-0010. Periodical. US. English. qt. Home Grown Books, 300 Barclay Road, Chapel Hill NC 27514. **Ind/Abst** Book Rev. Index.

LIBRARIANS' HANDBOOK. 0093-1888. US. English. an. Free to qualified customers. EBSCO Industries, c/o J K Weed, PO Box 1943, Birmingham AL 35201. **Tel** (205)991-6600. **Ed** Sandra Gipson. adv acc. **Circ** 20,000. A listing of thousands of serials complete with ordering information.

LIBRARIANS' NEWSLETTER. **VFOAT** John Wiley & Sons Librarians' Newsletter. 0194-0112. Periodical. US. English. ir. John Wiley and Sons, 605 Third Avenue, New York NY 10158. **Tel** (212)850-6000.

LIBRARIANS PHONE BOOK. (THE LIBRARIANS PHONE BOOK). 1980-. 0195-332X. US. English. ir. RR Bowker, PO Box 1807, Ann Arbor MI 48106. **LC** Z720.A4. **DD** 020.922, 020.2573. **NLM** Z 720.A4 L697.

LIBRARIAN'S WORLD. 0739-0297. Periodical. US. English. qt. $10.00 Domestic, $13.00 Foreign. Evangelical Church Library Association, PO Box 353, Glen Ellyn IL 60138. **Tel** (312)668-0519. **Ed** Nancy Dick. bk rev. adv acc. **Circ** 800. (ctrl). Reviews of current Christian books and media promotional tips technical and other helps geared to church librarians.

LIBRARIES FOR COLLEGE STUDENTS WITH HANDICAPS. 1976-. 0149-547X. US. English. 65 South Front Street, Columbus OH 43215. **LC** Z711.92P2. **DD** 027.6.

LIBRARIES IN MAINE. US. English. an. Department of Educational and Cultural Services, Maine State Library, State House Station 64, Augusta MD 04333. **LC** Z732.M2. **DD** 027.0025741. *Libraries of Maine.*

LIBRARIES IN THE NEWS. V. 2, No. 9-Sept. 4, 1971-. Periodical. US. English. mo. Office of Public Libraries and Interlibrary Cooperation, 300 Hanover Building, 480 Cedar Street, St Paul MN 55101.

LIBRARIES IN THE UNITED KINGDOM AND THE REPUBLIC OF IRELAND. UK. English. ir. $26.50. Oryx Press, 2214 North Central at Encanto/Suite 103, Phoenix AZ 85004. **Tel** (602)254-6156. **Ed** Marion Colthorpe. **LC** Z791.A1. **DD** 027.002541. A unique directory of central libraries; polytechnic libraries; selected national, government, and special libraries; and schools of librarianship. Addresses and telephone numbers are provided.

LIBRARIES, INFORMATION CENTERS AND DATABASES IN SCIENCE AND TECHNOLOGY : A WORLD GUIDE. **VFOAT** Bibliotheken, Informationszentren und Datenbasen fur Wissenschaft und Technik : EIN Internationales Verzeichnis. 1st Ed.-. 0176-7593. English (German). be. **LC** Z675.T3. **DD** 026.6025.

LIBRARIES (TULSA, OKLA.). (LIBRARIES). **VFOAT** Libraries Newsletter. No. 1 (Fall 1983)-. 0748-2035. Periodical. US. English. bm. Libraries, Director of Libraries, PL203 McFarlin Library, The University of Tulsa, Tulsa OK 74119. **DD** 027.

LIBRARY ACQUISITIONS. PRACTICE AND THEORY. (LIBRARY ACQUISITIONS : PRACTICE AND THEORY). **VFOAT** Library Acquisitions, LAPT. V. 1- Jan. 1977-. 0364-6408. Periodical. US. English. qt. Pergamon Press, 395 Sawmill River Road, Elmsford NY 10523. **Tel** (914)592-7700. **Ind/Abst** Electron. Commun. Abstr. J., ISMEC Bull., Pollut. Abstr. Indexes, Saf. Sci. Abstr. J., Comput. Control Abstr., Electr. Electron. Abstr., Sci. Abstr. Sect. A. Phys. Abstr., Libr. Inf. Sci. Abstr., Libr. Lit. **LC** Z689. **DD** 025.21. **CODEN** LAPTDK. Available in microform from Pergamon and/or Microforms International Marketing Co.

LIBRARY AIDS. No. 1-. 0147-9326. Monographic Series. US. English. Scholars Press, University of Montana, Missoula MT 59801. **LC** UNC.

LIBRARY & ARCHIVAL SECURITY. **VFOAT** Library and Archival Security. Began with Vol. 2, No. 3/4. 0196-0075. Periodical. US. English. qt. $72.00. Haworth Press, 28 East 22nd Street, New York NY 10010. **Tel** (212)228-2800. **Ed** Peter Gellatly. **Ind/Abst** Libr. Inf. Sci. Abstr., Libr. Lit. **LC** Z679.6. **DD** 025.82. bk rev. adv acc. **Circ** 661. The vital areas of security planning, policies, procedures, and strategies for both libraries and archives are the focus of this highly praised and important journal. *Library Security Newsletter, 0094-0216.*

LIBRARY AND INFORMATION NEWS. **VFOAT** Library & Information News. Periodical. UK. English. mo. 39.90. Library and Information News Ltd, 2 Arkwright Road, Reading RG2 0SQ England. **Tel** (0734)751855. **Ind/Abst** Electron. Pub. Abstr. bk rev. adv acc. **Circ** 1,000. Concise paragraphs of news, services, people, computer technology, books, courses, conferences, etc., all geared towards the library and information professional.

LIBRARY AND INFORMATION SCIENCE. Began with: No. 6 (1968). 0373-4447. JA. English (Japanese). an. 17.00. Mita Society Library of Information Science, Keio University Mita Minato-Ku, Tokyo 108 Japan. **Tel** 03-453-3920. **Ed** Yoshinari Tsuda. **Ind/Abst** Comput. Control Abstr., Electr. Electron. Abstr., Sci. Abstr. Sect. A. Phys. Abstr., Libr. Inf. Sci. Abstr., Libr. Lit., Phys. Abstr., Soc. Sci. Citation Index. **LC** Z671. **CODEN** LIFSBL. **Circ** 1,750. Thoughts and findings in the fields of library and information science. *Library Science.*

LIBRARY & INFORMATION SCIENCE ABSTRACTS. *See* Indexes/Abstracts.

LIBRARY AND INFORMATION SCIENCE EDUCATION STATISTICAL REPORT. *See* Statistics.

LIBRARY & INFORMATION SCIENCE RESEARCH. **VFOAT** Library and Information Science Research. Vol. 5, No. 1 (Spring 1983)-. 0740-8188. Periodical. US. English. qt. $52.00. Ablex Publishing Corp, 355 Chestnut Street, Norwood NJ 07648. **Tel** (201)767-8450. **Ed** Jane Robbins-Carter. **Ind/Abst** Sociol. Abstr., Libr. Inf. Sci. Abstr., Libr. Lit. **LC** Z671. **DD** 020.5. bk rev. adv acc. **Circ** 500. Reports results of library research to practicing librarians emphasizing application of research in planning, management, and operation of libraries. *Library Research, 0164-0763.*

LIBRARY AND INFORMATION SCIENCE UPDATE. No. 74 (May 1982)-. 0820-0521. Periodical. CN. English. mo. Free. Library and Information Science Update, 140 St George Street, Toronto Ontario M5S 1A1 Canada. **DD** 016.02. (ctrl). *Library Science Update, 0383-9087.*

LIBRARY & INFORMATION SCIENCES. **VAT** Library and Information Sciences. 0364-6467. US. English. wk. $65.00. National Technical Information Service, 5285 Port Royal Road, Springfield VA 22161. **Tel** (703)487-4650. **Ind/Abst** Libr. Lit. **CODEN** LBISBL.

LIBRARY AND INFORMATION TECHNOLOGY SERIES. No. 1-. 0743-7900. Monographic Series. US. English. ir. $25.00. American Library Association, Publishing Services, 50 East Huron Street, Chicago IL 60611. **Tel** (602)965-5889. **Ed** William G Potter. **DD** 025. bk rev. adv acc. **Circ** 6,000. Material related to all aspects of library and information technology. Major topics of interest are automation,telecommunications, video/cable and audiovisual techniques and equipment.

THE LIBRARY & LIBRARIAN. V. 1-. Periodical. English. ir. 20. Ravishanker Shukla Chowk, Nayapar Raipur (MP), Raipur India. **LC** Z845.I4. **DD** 020.954.

LIBRARY AND REFERENCE FACILITIES IN THE AREA OF THE DISTRICT OF COLUMBIA. Began in 1943. 0191-2798. US. English. ir. Knowledge Industry, 701 Westchester Avenue, White Plains NY 10604. **Tel** (914)328-9157. **Ed** Margaret Jennings. **NLM** Z 732.D6 U58L. A directory of research facilities in and around Washington.

THE LIBRARY ASSOCIATION OF ALBERTA OCCASIONAL PAPER. **VFOAT** Occasional Paper. No. 1-. 0075-904X. CN. English. ir. Southern Alberta Institute of Technology, 1301 16 Avenue NW, Calgary Alberta Canada. **Tel** (403)934-5334. **Ed** Marg Gamble. adv acc. **Circ** 530. (ctrl). Covers president's message; executive reports; financial statement; news from libraries around the province; across Canada news; and forthcoming events.

LIBRARY ASSOCIATION RECORD. V. 1-24, Jan. 1899-Dec. 1922. 0024-2195. Periodical. UK. English. mo. 46 Domestic, 56 Foreign. Library Association, 7 Ridgemont Street, London WC1E 7AE England. **Tel** (01)636-7543. **Ed** Jane Jenkins. **Ind/Abst** Ref. Source, Libr. Inf. Sci. Abstr., Libr. Lit., Curr. Index J. Educ. **LC** Z671. **NLM** Z 671 L695. bk rev. adv acc. **Circ** 26,000. (ctrl). Covers news, letters, professional interest articles, obituaries and calendars. *Library.*

LIBRARY AUTOMATION NEWSLETTER. Vol. 1, No. 1 (Nov. 3, 1980)-. 0823-759X. Periodical. CN. English. ir. Free. Library Automation Newsletter, c/o Associate Librarian, Douglas Library, Queen's University, Kingston Ontario K7L 5C4 Canada. **Tel** (613)547-5950. **Ed** Lin Good. **DD** 027.771372. (ctrl). An in-house journal, telling staff and users what is happening in the Queens University library automated systems.

LIBRARY BINDINGS. Vol. 1, No. 1 (Dec. 1970)-. 0228-541X. Periodical. CN. English. qt. Free. Southeast Regional Library, Box 550, Weyburn Saskatchewan S4H 2K7 Canada. **DD** 027.471244.

LIBRARY BOOK CATALOG. AUTHOR CATALOG. **Main/Corp** National Institute of Law Enforcement and Criminal Justice. Office of Technology Transfer. **VFOAT** Author Catalog. V. - 1972-. US. English. be. US Department of Justice, Law Enforcement Administration, Office of Technology Transfer, Washington DC 20402.

LIBRARY BOOK CATALOG; AUTHOR CATALOG. SUPPLEMENT. **Main/Corp** United States. Law Enforcement Assistance Administration. Library. **VFOAT** Author Catalog. 1973-. US. English. an. US Department of Justice, Law Enforcement Assistance Administration, National Institute of Law Enforcement and Criminal Justice, Office of Technology Transfer, Washington DC 20531.

LIBRARY BOOK CATALOG. PERIODICALS CATALOG. **Main/Corp** National Institute of Law Enforcement and Criminal Justice. Office of Technology Transfer. **VFOAT** Periodicals Catalog. 1972-. US. English. US Department of Justice, Law Enforcement Administration, Office of Technology Transfer, Washington DC 20402.

LIBRARY BOOK CATALOG; SUBJECT CATALOG. **Main/Corp** National Institute of Law Enforcement and Criminal Justice. Office of Technology Transfer. **VFOAT** Subject Catalog. V. 1-1972-. US. English. be. US Department of Justice, Law Enforcement Administration, Office of Technology Transfer, Washington DC 20402.

LIBRARY BOOK CATALOG; SUBJECT CATALOG. SUPPLEMENT. **Main/Corp** United States. Law Enforcement Assistance Administration. Library. **VFOAT** Subject Catalog. 1973-. US. English. an. US Department of Justice, Law Enforcement Assistance Administration, National Institute of Law Enforcement and Criminal Justice, Office of Technology Transfer, Washington DC 20531.

LIBRARY BOOK CATALOG. TITLE CATALOG. **Main/Corp** National Institute of Law Enforcement and Criminal Justice. Office of Technology Transfer. **VFOAT** Title Catalog. V. 1-

Library and Information Science

1972-. US. English. be. US Department of Justice, Law Enforcement Administration, Office of Technology Transfer, Washington DC 20402.

LIBRARY BOOK CATALOG; TITLE CATALOG. SUPPLEMENT. Main/Corp United States. Law Enforcement Assistance Administration. Library. VFOAT Title Catalog. 1973-. US. English. an. US Department of Justice, Law Enforcement Assistance Administration, National Institute of Law Enforcement and Criminal Justice, Office of Technology Transfer, Washington DC 20531.

THE LIBRARY BOOKSELLER : BOOKS WANTED BY COLLEGE AND UNIVERSITY LIBRARIES. Vol. 1-. 0024-2217. Periodical. US. English. bw. $75.00. Albert Saifer Publisher, Box 51, Town Center, West Orange NJ 07052. Tel (201)731-5701. Ed Albert Saifer. Books wanted by university and college libraries. There is no charge for listings.

LIBRARY BULLETIN. Main/Corp Great Britain. Dept. of the Environment. Library. No. 1- 1972-. Periodical. UK. English. ir. $79.68. Department of the Environment and Transportation Library, 2 Marsham Street/Room C3/01, London SW1P 3EB England. Tel 01 212 4847. Circ 2,000. Abstracts of current literature on social and environmental planning, roads, traffic, transport, countryside, recreation, housing and local government, water supply, waste disposal, pollution and conservation. Index to Periodical Articles, Classified Accessions List.

LIBRARY BULLETIN. No. 1- Feb. 1971-). 0073-9723. Monographic Series. SI. English. ir. Institute of Southeast Asian Studies, Heng Mui Keng TR, Pasir Panjang, Singapore 0511 Republic of Singapore. Tel 7780955. Circ 1,000. A series on Southeast Asian librarianship and bibliography, each number on a different topic.

LIBRARY BULLETIN. Main/Corp Australia Music Centre. Periodical. AT. English. ir. Australia Music Centre, PO Box 9, Grosvenor Street, Sydney New South Wales 2000 Australia.

LIBRARY BULLETIN - BOREAL INSTITUTE FOR NORTHERN STUDIES. (LIBRARY BULLETIN - BOREAL INSTITUTE FOR NORTHERN STUDIES LIBRARY). Main/Corp Boreal Institute for Northern Studies. Library. V. 1- Jan. 1980-. 0225-4484. Periodical. CN. English. mo. Boreal Institute for Northern Studies, Library, University of Alberta, Edmonton Alberta T6G 2E9 Canada. DD 016.998. Library Accessions List, 0315-601X.

LIBRARY BULLETIN - CENTER ON SOCIAL WELFARE POLICY AND LAW. Main/Corp Center on Social Welfare Policy and Law. US. English. bw. Center on Social Welfare Policy & Law, 95 Madison Avenue, New York NY 10016.

LIBRARY BULLETIN - DARTMOUTH COLLEGE. Main/Corp Dartmouth College. Library. V. 1-5. Apr. 1931-1953. 0011-6750. Periodical. US. English. sa. Dartmouth College, Room 115/Baker Library, Hanover NH 03755. Tel (603)646-2235. Ed Virginia L Close and Lois A Krieger. (cum index). Circ 925. Articles describe features of speicial interest and research value of the library's collections.

LIBRARY BULLETIN - TEXAS DEPARTMENT OF WATER RESOURCES. See Water Resources.

LIBRARY CATALOG OF THE METROPOLITAN MUSEUM OF ART. SUPPLEMENT CEASED. Main/Corp Metropolitan Museum of Art (New York, N.Y.). Library. VFOAT Supplement. 1st-. US. English. ir. G K Hall, 70 Lincoln Street, Boston MA 02111. Tel (617)423-3990. LC Z881.

LIBRARY COMPENSATION REVIEW. Vol. 1, No. 1 (Winter 1982)-. 0730-3785. Periodical. US. English. qt. $25.00. Graduate Library School, University of Arizona, 1515 East First Street, Tucson AZ 85721. Ind/Abst Libr. Inf. Sci. Abstr. LC Z682.3. DD 331.281020922.

LIBRARY CURRENTS. Vol. 1, No. 1 (Jan. 1984)-. 0741-4188. Periodical. US. English. mo. $36.00. Practical Perspectives, PO Box 1796, Grass Valley CA 95945. Tel (916)272-5212. Ed Joan Frye Williams. bk rev. Circ 925. Summaries of key books, articles and reports in the library, management, and technical literature.

LIBRARY DEVELOPMENTS (AUSTIN, TEX.). (LIBRARY DEVELOPMENTS). Vol. 1, No. 1 (Jan.-Feb. 1974)-. 0145-5397. Periodical. US. English. bm. Free. Texas State Library Library Development Division, Box 12927 Capitol Station, Austin TX 78711. Tel (512)463-5465. Ed Barbara S Crosby. bk rev. Circ 700. (ctrl). A publication of the Library Development Division, this publication announces workshops and seminars, use of state and federal funds, reports of boards and commissions, and use of LSC.

LIBRARY DIRECTORY. See Yearbooks, Almanacs, Directories.

LIBRARY GRANT PROGRAMS. 0090-4880. US. English. New Jersey State Library, PO Box 1898, Trenton NJ 08625. LC Z732.N6. DD 025.1109749.

LIBRARY HANDBOOK - WILFRID LAURIER UNIVERSITY. (LIBRARY HANDBOOK). Main/Corp Wilfrid Laurier University. Library. 0713-7818. CN. English. an. Office of the Librarian, Wilfrid Laurier University, Waterloo Ontario N2L 3C5 Canada. DD 027.771344.

LIBRARY HERALD. V. 1-. Periodical. US. English. qt. $25.00. Delhi Library Association, PO Box 1270 Queens Garden, Delhi 6 India. Tel 7112721. Ed C P Vashishth. Includes original contributions, reviews in library information science, documentation and computer application in library operations.

LIBRARY HI TECH. VFOAT Library Hitech. Vol. 1, No. 1 (Summer 1983)-. 0737-8831. Periodical. US. English. qt. $45.00. Pierian Press, PO Box 1808, Ann Arbor MI 48106. Tel (313)434-5530. Ed C Edward Wall. Ind/Abst Electron. Commun. Abstr. J., ISMEC Bull., Libr. Inf. Sci. Abstr., Microcomput. Index, Libr. Lit. LC Z671. DD 020.5. bk rev. adv acc. Circ 10,200. Covers state-of-the-art library and information systems, hardware, software, and services, written in understandable terms.

LIBRARY HI TECH NEWS. VFOAT Library High Tech News. Vol. 1, No. 1 (Jan. 1984)-. 0741-9058. Periodical. US. English. mo. $65.00. Pierian Press, PO Box 1808, Ann Arbor MI 48106. Tel (313)434-5530. Ed C Edward Wall. LC Z678.9.A1. DD 025.0202854. bk rev. adv acc. Circ 10,200. News, reviews, and current bibliography of state-of-the-art library and hardware, software, and services.

LIBRARY HISTORY. V. 1-Spring 1967-. 0024-2306. Periodical. UK. English. sa. 6.50. Library Historical Group, c/o Mrs Johnston, 15 Drummond Road, Leeds LS16 5LB West Yorks England. Tel 01-636-1544. Ed P H Morrish. Ind/Abst Am. Hist. Life, Hist. Abstr., Part A, Mod. Hist. Abstr., Hist. Abst., Part B, Twent. Century Abstr., Libr. Inf. Sci. Abstr., Libr. Lit., Hist. Abstr. LC Z721. bk rev. adv acc. Circ 1,500. (ctrl). History of various types of libraries. Libraries and book collections. Newsletter - Library History Group.

LIBRARY HOTLINE. Vol. 12, No. 27 (Sept. 5, 1983)-. 0740-736X. Periodical. US. English. wk. RR Bowker Company, 205 East 42nd Street, New York NY 10017, (subscription address: Bowker Subscription Service PO Box 1429 Riverton NJ 08077). Tel (800)257-7894. LC Z671. DD 020.5. LJ/SLJ Hotline, 0000-0078.

THE LIBRARY IMAGINATION PAPER. V. 1 Winter 1979-. 0197-5587. Periodical. US. English. qt. $16.00. Library Imagination Paper, 1000 Byus Drive, Charleston WV 25311. Tel (304)345-2378. Ed Carol Bryan. Circ 2,000. Award-winning, reproducible library clip art and ideas for use on library promotional materials. In-depth articles on library PR topics by field experts.

LIBRARY INDUSTRY. No. 1- Aug. 1971-. Periodical. English. ir. $0.50 Single Issue. M Jayathissa, No 19 Road 22/7, Kampong Tunku, Petaling Jaya Malaysia. LC Z671. DD 020.5.

LIBRARY INFO. No. 7- Apr. 1974-. 0316-523X. Periodical. CN. English. mo. Lake Erie Regional Library System, 305 Queen's Avenue, London Ontario N6B 1X2 Canada. DD 027.47133. For Your Info, 0316-5221.

LIBRARY INFORMATION BULLETIN. Main/Corp Markaz Al-Tawthiq Al-Qawmi. English. ir. National Documentation Centre, PO Box 2404, Khartoum Sudan. LC Z965.K46. DD 018.

LIBRARY ISSUES. (LIBRARY ISSUES : BRIEFINGS FOR ACADEMIC OFFICERS). Vol. 1, No. 1 (Sept. 1980)-. 0734-3035. Periodical. US. English. bm. $25.00. Library Issues, PO Box 8330, Ann Arbor MI 48107. Tel (313)662-3925. Ed Richard M Dougherty. LC Z675.U5. DD 027.70973. Circ 600. Briefings for faculty and administrators addressing topics most crucial to academic libraries.

LIBRARY ISSUES : BRIEFINGS FOR FACULTY AND ADMINISTRATORS. Vol. 2, No. 1 (Sept. 1981)-. Periodical. US. English. bm. $25.00. Mountainside Publishing Co, PO Box 8330, Ann Arbor MI 48107. Tel (313)662-3925. Ed Richard Dougherty. (ctrl). Briefings for faculty and administrators of academic libraries. Library Issues: Briefings for Academic Officers.

LIBRARY JOTTINGS. V. 1- Sept. 1977-. 0227-2571. Periodical. CN. English. ir. Free. Library Jottings, 405 Main Street, Yarmouth Nova Scotia B5A 1G3 Canada. DD 021.82060716.

LIBRARY JOURNAL. 0363-0277. Periodical. US. English. R R Bowker, PO Box 1427, Riverton NJ 08077. Ind/Abst Educ. Index, Libr. Lit., Annu. Bibliogr. Engl. Lang. Lit., Art Archaeol. Tech. Abstr., Book Rev. Index, Cumul. Index Nurs. Allied Health Lit., Curr. Index J. Educ., Hospit. Lit. Index, Int. Labour Doc., Libr. Inf. Sci. Abstr., Media Rev. Dig., Pop. Mag. Rev., Predicasts, Ref. Source. LC Z671. DD 020.5. NLM Z 671 L6963. LJ, Library Journal, 0360-3113.

LIBRARY LECTURES. No. 1- Mar. 1965/May 1966-. 0085-2759. US. English. Louisiana State University Library, Baton Rouge LA 70803. LC Z671. DD 020.

LIBRARY LECTURES. (LIBRARY LECTURES, THE UNIVERSITY OF TENNESSEE, KNOXVILLE). Main/Corp University of Tennessee, Knoxville. Library. VFOAT University of Tennessee Library Lectures. No. 28/30- 1976/78-. 0270-059X. US. English. te. University of Tennessee, College Library, Knoxville TN 37916. LC Z674. DD 016.02. University of Tennessee Library Lectures.

LIBRARY LETTER - SIR GEORGE WILLIAMS UNIVERSITY. (LIBRARY LETTER). Main/Corp Sir George Williams University. Library. Vol. 1, No. 1 (Feb. 18, 1974)-. 0712-3140. Periodical. CN. English. ir. Sir George Williams University, 1455 de Maisonneuve Boulevard West, Montreal 107 Quebec Canada. DD 027.7714281.

LIBRARY LIFE : NEW ZEALAND LIBRARY ASSOCIATION NEWSLETTER. No. 1 (Feb. 1978)-. 0110-4373. Periodical. English. mo. $8.44. New Zealand Library Association Inc, PO Box 12-212, Wellington New Zealand. Tel 735-834. Ed D Morns. LC Z673.N683. DD 020.6234931. adv acc. Circ 2,200. Newsletter. New Zealand Library Association Newsletter.

LIBRARY LIST. Main/Corp National Agricultural Library (U.S.). No. 1- 1942-. US. English. National Agricultural Library, 10301 Baltimore Boulevard, Beltsville MD 20705. LC Z881.U4. DD 016.63.

LIBRARY LIT. . . . THE BEST . . . . VAT Library Literature. 1- 1970-. 0085-2767. US. English. an. Scarecrow Press, PO Box 656, 52 Liberty Street, Metuchen NJ 08840. Tel (201)548-8600. Ed B Katz and J J Schwartz. LC Z671. DD 020.5.

LIBRARY LITERATURE. See Indexes/Abstracts.

LIBRARY MANAGEMENT BULLETIN. Began with issue for Fall 1977. 0271-3306. Periodical. US. English. qt. $25.00 Domestic, $27.00 Foreign. Irene Gilbride, Litton Systems Library, Guidance & Control Systems Division, 5500 Conoga Avenue, Woodland Hills CA 91365. Ind/Abst Libr. Inf. Sci. Abstr. LC Z675.A2. DD 025.19605.

LIBRARY MANAGEMENT (MCB PUBLICATIONS (FIRM)). (LIBRARY MANAGEMENT). 0143-5124. Periodical. UK. English. bm. $299.95. MCB Publications, 198/200 Keighley Road, Bradford West Yorkshire BD9 4JQ England. Tel (0274)499821. Ed Janet Shuter. Ind/Abst Libr. Inf. Sci. Abstr. LC Z678. DD 025.105. adv acc. Circ 300. The series aims to provide the librarians with practical help and guidance in meeting the demands of the managerial role.

LIBRARY MANAGEMENT NEWS. 0140-4903. Periodical. UK. English. qt. Information Officer for Library Management, Department of Library and Information Studies, Loughborough University, Loughborough Leichestershire LE11 3TU England. Ind/Abst Libr. Inf. Sci. Abstr. LC Z678. DD 025.105.

LIBRARY MICROMATION NEWS. VFOAT LMN. 0262-7841. Periodical. UK. English. qt. Information Technology Centre, 309 Regent Street, London W1R 8AL England.

LIBRARY NETWORKS. 1975-. 0145-9627. US. English. be. $25.50. Knowledge Industry Publications, 2 Corporate Park Drive, White Plains NY 10604.

LIBRARY NEWS BULLETIN. ANNUAL STATISTICAL ISSUE. *See* Statistics.

LIBRARY NEWS - DEPARTMENT OF SCHOOL LIBRARIES. (LIBRARY NEWS). Dec. 1980-. 0229-0162. Periodical. CN. English. mo. Free. Library News, 2790 Oxford Street, Halifax Nova Scotia V5M 1Y8 Canada. **DD** 352.9452. *Newsletter, 0318-546X.*

LIBRARY OCCURRENT *CEASED.* V. 1-26, No. 12. 0024-2454. Periodical. US. English. qt.

THE LIBRARY OF CONGRESS. Began with 1975/76. 0162-6426. US. English. an. Library of Congress, Central Services Division, Washington DC 20540. **LC** Z663. **DD** 027.5753.

LIBRARY OF CONGRESS ACQUISITIONS. MANUSCRIPT DIVISION. **Main/Corp** Library of Congress. Manuscript Division. 1979-. 0275-9616. US. English. an. Free. Library of Congress, Washington DC 20540. **LC** Z733.L735. **DD** 027.573.

LIBRARY OF CONGRESS ACQUISITIONS. RARE BOOK AND SPECIAL COLLECTIONS DIVISION. **Main/Corp** Library of Congress. Rare Book and Special Collections Division. 1980-. 0739-7526. US. English. Library of Congress, Rare Book and Special Collections Division, Washington DC 20540. **LC** Z733.U6. **DD** 027.573. **NLM** Z 733.U4.

LIBRARY OF CONGRESS CALENDAR OF EVENTS. **Main/Corp** United States. Library of Congress. Information Office. **VFOAT** Calendar of Events in the Library of Congress. Jan. 1978-. 0160-9653. Periodical. US. English. mo. Printing and Processing Section, Central Services Division, Library of Congress, Washington DC 20540. **LC** Z881.U49. **DD** 027.575.3. *Calendar of Events in the Library of Congress, 0008-0748.*

LIBRARY OF CONGRESS INFORMATION BULLETIN. **VFOAT** L.C. Information Bulletin, LC Information Bulletin. Vol. 31, No. 1 (Jan. 6, 1972)-. 0041-7904. Periodical. US. English. wk. Free. Information Office, Library of Congress, Washington DC 20540. **Tel** (202)287-5108. **Ed** Bruce Tapper. **Ind/Abst** Art Archaeol. Tech. Abstr., Index U.S. Gov. Period., Public Aff. Inf. Serv. Bull., Libr. Lit. **LC** Z733.U57. **DD** 027.573. **NLM** Z 733 L697. bk rev. **Circ** 10,000. News of Library of Congress: exhibitions, literary/music events, symposia, cataloging/online networking publications, copyright office, federal libraries, library conference reports. *Information Bulletin (Library of Congress), 0364-3980.*

LIBRARY OF CONGRESS NAME HEADINGS WITH REFERENCES *CEASED.* **Main/Corp** United States. Library of Congress. Began with Jan./Mar. 1974-. No longer available in book format after the 1980 annual. 0093-0563. Periodical. US. English (Multilingual). ir. Catalog Distribution Service, Library of Congress, Building No 159/Navy Yard Annex, Washington DC 20541. **LC** Z695.1.P4. **DD** 025.32.

LIBRARY OF CONGRESS SELECTED PUBLICATIONS. 1981-. 0734-7286. US. English. an. Library of Congress, 10 First Street SE, Publications Office, Washington DC 20540. **LC** Z733.U6. **DD** 027.573.

LIBRARY OF CONGRESS SUBJECT HEADINGS. 8th- Ed. US. English. ir. Library of Congress, Cataloging Distribution Serive, Washington DC 20541. **Tel** (202)287-6100. Contains headings established and applied by the Library of Congress through December 1978, including a full cumulation of subject headings for children's literature.

LIBRARY OF MICHIGAN NEWSLETTER. **VFOAT** Newsletter. Vol. 1, No. 1 (July 1983)-. 0739-8379. Periodical. US. English. bm. Free. Library of Michigan, Public Relations Committee, PO Box 30007, Lansing MI 48909. *State Library Newsletter (Michigan. State Library Services).*

LIBRARY OWNER'S MANUAL. **Main/Corp** Concordia University. Libraries. 1979/80-. 0225-8307. CN. English. an. Library Owner's Manual, Concordia University Libraries, 1455 de Maisonneuve Boulevard West, Montreal Quebec H3B 1M8 Canada. **DD** 027.7714281. *Owner's Manual, 0709-6712.*

LIBRARY POCKETFUL. (A LIBRARY POCKETFUL). 0713-5386. CN. English. an. A Library Pocketful, c/o D Pilkey, Learning Resources Libraries, Roywood Public School, 11 Roywood Drive, Don Mills Ontario M3A 2C7 Canada. **DD** 027.8222.

LIBRARY PR NEWS. **VAT** Library Public Relations News. Vol. 1, No. 1 & 2 (Jan./Feb. 1978)-. 0164-9566. Periodical. US. English. bm. $24.95. Library Educational Institute Inc, R D #1 Box 219, New Albany PA 18833. **Tel** (717)746-1842. **Ed** Phil Bradbury. bk rev. **Circ** 3,000. Devoted to library public relations, display and promotion. Innovative publicity and programming ideas, book and product reviews, exhibit and display techniques. *Tips from Clip, Evil John's Almanac.*

LIBRARY PROGRESS INTERNATIONAL. **VFOAT** Library Progesss. Periodical. English. sa. $24.00. A K Sharma Library Progress, PO Box 38, Modinagar GZB-201204, Delhi India. **Ind/Abst** Libr. Inf. Sci. Abstr. **LC** Z730. **DD** 027.01724.

THE LIBRARY QUARTERLY. V. 1- Jan. 1931-. 0024-2519. Periodical. US. English. qt. $16.00. The University of Chicago Press, 11030 South Langley Avenue, Chicago IL 60628. **Ed** W M Randall. **Ind/Abst** Mag. Index, Am. Hist. Life, Hist. Abstr., Part A, Mod. Hist. Abstr., Hist. Abst., Part B, Twent. Century Abstr., Annu. Bibliogr. Engl. Lang. Lit., Comput. Control Abstr., Electr. Electron. Abstr., Sci. Abstr. Sect. A. Phys. Abstr., Ref. Source, Libr. Inf. Sci. Abstr., Book Rev. Index, Libr. Lit., Public Aff. Inf. Serv. Bull., Curr. Index J. Educ., Recent Publ. Artic. **LC** Z671. **DD** 020.5. **NLM** Z 671 L6964I. **CODEN** LIBQAS. (cum index). Available on microfilm from University Microfilms.

LIBRARY RESEARCH NEWS. V. 1- Winter 1968/69-. 0024-9270. Periodical. CN. English. sa. $5.42. McMaster University Press, Mills Memorial Library, Hamilton Ontario L8S 4L6 Canada. **Tel** (416)525-9140. **Circ** 130. Description of archives and collections held at McMaster University.

LIBRARY RESOURCES & TECHNICAL SERVICES. **VAT** Library Resources and Technical Services. V. 1- Winter 1957-. 0024-2527. Periodical. US. English. qt. $20.00. American Library Association, 50 East Huron Street, Chicago IL 60611. **Tel** (312)944-6780. **Ind/Abst** Hospit. Lit. Index, Comput. Control Abstr., Electr. Electron. Abstr., Sci. Abstr. Sect. A. Phys. Abstr., Art Archaeol. Tech. Abstr., Book Rev. Index, Libr. Lit., Libr. Inf. Sci. Abstr., Curr. Index J. Educ., Sci. Cit. Index, Abr. Ed., Public Aff. Inf. Serv. Bull., Book Rev. Digest, Soc. Sci. Citation Index, Phys. Abstr. **LC** Z671. **DD** 025.06273. **NLM** Z 695.7 L697. **CODEN** LRTSAH. *Serial Slants, 0559-5258; Journal of Cataloging and Classification.*

LIBRARY RESOURCES FOR THE BLIND & PHYSICALLY HANDICAPPED. **VAT** Library Resources for the Blind and Physically Handicapped. 0364-1236. US. English. an. Free to eligible recipients. National Library Service for the Blind and Physically Handicapped, Library of Congress, Washington DC 20542. **LC** Z675.B6. **DD** 027.66302573. **NLM** Z 675.B6 L697. (ctrl). *Directory of Library Resources for the Blind and Physically Handicapped, 0278-7857.*

LIBRARY RESOURCES NOTES. **Main/Corp** United States. Library of Congress. Reference Dept. No. 1- Mar. 1974-. 0095-4098. US. English. Library of Congress, Reference Department, Washington DC 20520. **LC** Z733.U63. **DD** 025.0209753.

LIBRARY REVIEW. V. 1- Spring 1927-. 0024-2535. Periodical. UK. English. qt. 30.65. Holmes McDougall Bookselling, 30 Clydeholm Road, Clydeside Industry, Estat/Glasgow G14 OBJ Scotland. **Tel** (041)954-2271. **Ed** Graham Jones. **Ind/Abst** Abstr. Engl. Stud., Book Rev. Index, Libr. Inf. Sci. Abstr., Libr. Lit., Ref. Source. **LC** Z671. **DD** 020.5. bk rev. adv acc. **Circ** 1,000. A state of the art journal constituting a forum for research findings.

LIBRARY REVIEW (LOUISVILLE, KY.). (LIBRARY REVIEW). 0041-9788. US. English. an. $7.50. University of Louisville, Belknap Campus, Louisville KY 40292. **Tel** (502)588-6762. **Ed** George T McWhorter. **LC** Z881 .L898. **DD** 027.776944. **Circ** 300. (ctrl). Articles researched in the Special Collections of the University of Louisville libraries and news of the library associates, a friends of the library group.

THE LIBRARY SCENE *CEASED.* V, 1-11, No. 1. 0090-8746. Periodical. US. English. qt. $5.00 Domestic, $6.00 Canada. Library Binding Institute, 322 Stuart Street, Boston MA 02116. **Ind/Abst** Libr. Inf. Sci. Abstr., Libr. Lit. **LC** Z671. **DD** 020.5. **NLM** Z 671 L6967. *Library Binder.*

LIBRARY SCIENCE *CEASED.* No. 1 (1963)-No. 5 (1967). JA. chiefly Japanese with some English. an. Japan Publishing Trading Company Ltd, PO Box 5030, Tokyo International, Tokyo 100-31 Japan. **LC** Z671.

LIBRARY SCIENCE ABSTRACTS. *See* Indexes/Abstracts.

LIBRARY SCIENCE UPDATE *CEASED.* No. 1-73. 0383-9087. Periodical. CN. English. mo. $10.00. Library Science Update, Faculty of Library Science, University of Toronto, 140 St George Street, Toronto Ontario M5B 2T4 Canada. **DD** 016.02.

LIBRARY SCIENCE WITH A SLANT TO DOCUMENTATION. V. 1- Mar. 1964-. 0024-2543. Periodical. II. English. qt. $20.00. Sarada Ranganathan Endowment for Library Science, DRTC 112 Cross Road 11 Malleswaram, Bangalore India. **Ind/Abst** Libr. Inf. Sci. Abstr., Libr. Lit. **NLM** Z 671 L697H. Index published separately - free - automatically sent.

LIBRARY SERIES. No. 1 (1935)-. 0075-5001. Monographic Series. US. English. ir. University of Kansas, Libraries Exchange and Gift Department, Lawrence KS 60074.

LIBRARY SERVICE TO THE PEOPLE OF NEW YORK STATE. (Oct. 1, 1978-Sept. 30, 1983)-. US. English. an. The New York State Library, Cultural Education Center, Albany NY 12230. **LC** Z678.5.N7. **DD** 027.0747. *Long-Range Plan for Library Service to the People of New York State, Utilizing Local, State, and Federal Resources.*

LIBRARY SERVICES AND CONSTRUCTION ACT. **Main/Corp** Alaska State Library. US. English. an. Alaska State Library, State Office Building, Pouch G, Juneau AK 99801. **LC** Z733.A324. **DD** 027.5798.

LIBRARY SERVICES AND CONSTRUCTION ACT ANNUAL PROGRAM. **Main/Corp** Connecticut State Library. Dept. of Planning and Research. **VFOAT** L.S.C.A. Connecticut. US. English. Connecticut State Library, 231 Capital Avenue, Hartford CT 06115. **LC** Z732.C8. **DD** 027.0746.

LIBRARY SERVICES AND CONSTRUCTION ACT, ANNUAL REPORT. **Main/Corp** Texas. State Library, Austin. US. English. an. **LC** Z732.T25. **DD** 025.1109764.

LIBRARY SERVICES FOR AUSTRALIA *CEASED.* **Main/Corp** Australian Advisory Council on Bibliographical Services. 1956/70-. AT. English. an. Sales and Subscriptions Section, National Library of Australia, Canberra Australian Capital Territory 2600 Australia. **LC** Z870.A1. **DD** 021.00994.

LIBRARY SOFTWARE REVIEW. (LIBRARY SOFTWARE REVIEW : SR). **VFOAT** SR. Vol. 3, No. 1 (Mar. 1984)-. 0742-5759. Periodical. US. English. bm. $58.00 Domestic, $63.00 Foreign. Meckler Publishing, 520 Riverside Avenue, Westport CT 06880. **Ind/Abst** Fluidex, Microcomput. Index, Consum. Index Prod. Eval. Inf. Source. **LC** QA76.6. **DD** 001.6425. *Software Review, 0278-2634.*

LIBRARY STATISTICS OF COLLEGES AND UNIVERSITIES IN THE PACIFIC NORTHWEST. **VFOAT** Library Statistics of Colleges & Universities in the Pacific Northwest. 8755-4267. US. English. **LC** Z675.U5. **DD** 027.70979.

LIBRARY STATISTICS OF COLLEGES AND UNIVERSITIES. INSTITUTIONAL DATA. *See* Statistics.

LIBRARY STATISTICS OF ILLINOIS COLLEGES AND UNIVERSITIES. *See* Statistics.

LIBRARY TECHNOLOGY REPORTS. V. 12- Jan. 1976-. 0024-2586. Periodical. US. English. bm. $145.00. American Library Association, 50 East Huron Street, Chicago IL 60611. **Tel** (312)944-6780. **Ind/Abst** Libr. Lit., Mag. Index, Consum. Index Prod. Eval. Inf. Source, Libr. Inf. Sci. Abstr., Microcomput. Index, Hospit. Lit. Index. **LC** Z684. **DD** 022.9. **NLM** Z 671 L697M.

LIBRARY TRENDS. Vol. 1, No. 1 (July 1952)-. 0024-2594. Periodical. US. English. qt. $30.00 Domestic, $32.50 Foreign. University of Illinois Press, 54 East Gregory Drive, Champaign IL 61820. **Tel** (217)333-0950. **Ed** Charles H Davis. **Ind/Abst** Mag. Index, Pop. Mag. Rev., Annu. Bibliogr. Engl. Lang. Lit., Comput. Control Abstr., Electr. Electron. Abstr., Sci. Abstr. Sect. A. Phys. Abstr., Libr. Inf. Sci. Abstr., Public Aff. Inf. Serv. Bull., Curr. Index J. Educ., Libr. Lit., Soc. Sci. Citation Index, Phys. Abstr. **LC** Z671. **DD** 020.5. **NLM** Z 671 L698. **CODEN** LIBTA3. **Circ** 3,900. Focuses on library and information science

Library and Information Science

topics of interest to practicing librarians and information scientists and also to educators and students.

LIBRARY TRUSTEE NEWSLETTER : SERVING THE SPECIALIZED INFORMATION NEEDS OF THE PUBLIC LIBRARY TRUSTEE. V. 1, Nos. 1 & 2- Jan./Feb. 1978-. Periodical. US. English. bm.

LIBRARY WORKER. See Economics - Labor.

LIBREEZE. VFOAT Li Breeze. V. 1- Sept./Oct. 1978-. 0226-711X. Periodical. CN. English. bm. Free. Calgary Public Library, 616 Macleod Trail South East, Calgary Alberta T2G 2M2 Canada. DD 027.471233.

LIBRI. Vol. 1- 1950-. 0024-2667. Periodical. DK. English. qt. $62.97. Munksgaard Ltd, 35 Norre Sogade, DK-1370 Copenhagen K Denmark. Tel 1.12.70.30. Ed Palle Birkelund. Ind/Abst MLA Int. Bibliogr. Books Artic. Mod. Lang. Lit., Foreign Lang. Index, Libr. Inf. Sci. Abstr., Libr. Lit., Public Aff. Inf. Serv. Bull., Soc. Sci. Citation Index. LC Z671. DD 020.5. NLM Z 671 L699. bk rev. Circ 1,200. Original papers on all aspects of librarianship including the history of books and publishing.

LIBSAT. Vol. 1, No. 1 (Apr. 1982)-. 0712-6115. Periodical. CN. English. ir. $1.00 Per No. Libsat, c/o Ganaoque Public Library, 100 Park Street, Ganaoque Ontario K7G 2Y5 Canada. DD 027.40207.

LIJST VAN AANWINSTEN. Main/Corp Universiteit van Amsterdam. Bibliotheek. VFOAT Lijst van Aanwinsten der Universiteitsbibliotheek van Amsterdam. NE. Dutch. mo. Bibliotheek Technische Hogesch, Postbus 98, Delft The Netherlands. Aanwinsten.

LINCOLN LIBRARY OF ESSENTIAL INFORMATION (COLUMBUS, OHIO : 1982). (THE LINCOLN LIBRARY OF ESSENTIAL INFORMATION). 42nd Ed. (1982)-. 0735-0813. US. English. an. LC AG105. DD 031. New Lincoln Library Encyclopedia, 0192-1177.

LINDA HALL LIBRARY MISCELLANY. VFOAT Miscellany. No. 1- Autumn 1980-. 0273-0227. Periodical. US. English. ir. Free. Paul Peterson Editor, Miscellany Linda Hall Library 5109 Cherry Street, Kansas City MO 64110. Tel (816)363-5020. Ed Paul Peterson. bk rev. Circ 3,500. Information on activities, services and collections of Linda Hall Library of Science and Technology, for its friends and users.

LINK. V. 1- Dec. 1975-. 0383-0535. Periodical. CN. English. ir. Greater Victoria Public Library, 794 Yates Street, Victoria British Columbia V8W 1L4 Canada. DD 027.471134.

LINK. V. 5, No. 1- Jan. 1977-. 0703-7007. Periodical. CN. English. mo. Free. Mississauga Library System, 110 Dundas Street West, Mississauga Ontario L5B 1H3 Canada. DD 027.4713535. Mississauga Library Link, 0380-4704.

LINK UP (HALIFAX N.S.). See Computers and Computer Science.

LINXLETTER. VFOAT Linx Letter. V. 1, Issue 1 (Jan./Feb. 1982)-V. 3, Issue 6 (Nov./Dec. 1984). 0733-4281. Periodical. US. English. bm. Faxon, 15 Southwest Park, Westwood MA 02090. DD 025.

LISTE D'ACQUISITIONS - UNIVERSITE DE MONTREAL. BIBLIOTHEQUE DE BIBLIOTHECONOMIE. (LISTE D'ACQUISITIONS : BIBLIOTHECONOMIE). Main/Corp Universite de Montreal. Bibliotheque de Bibliotheconomie. No. 1-. 0823-0889. CN. French (summaries in English). Bibliotheque de Bibliotheconomie Universite de Montreal, C P 6128, Montreal Quebec H3C 3J7 Canada. DD 016.02. Acquisitions, 0384-5664.

LISTE DE NOUVEAUTES - COLLEGE DE L'ASSOMPTION. BIBLIOTHEQUE DU SECONDAIRE. (BIBLIOTHEQUE DU SECONDAIRE, LISTE DE NOUVEAUTES). Main/Corp College de l'Assomption. Bibliotheque. 0826-1342. Periodical. CN. French. ir. College de l'Assomption Bibliotheque, 270 Boulevard l'Ange-Gardien, l'Assomption Quebec J0K 1G0 Canada. DD 017.1.

LISTE DES NOUVEAUTES - COLLEGE DE L'ASSOMPTION. BIBLIOTHEQUE DU COLLEGIAL. (BIBLIOTHEQUE DU COLLEGIAL, LISTE DES NOUVEAUTES). Main/Corp College de l'Assomption. Bibliotheque. 0826-1334. Periodical. CN. French. ir. College de l'Assomption Bibliotheque, 270 Boulevard l'Ange-Gardien, l'Assomption Quebec J0K 1G0 Canada. DD 017.1.

LISTE OFFICIELLE DES MEMBRES - ASSOCIATION DES BIBLIOTHECAIRES DU QUEBEC. Main/Corp Quebec Library Association. VFOAT Official Membership List - Quebec Library Association. 1971-. 0383-0160. CN. English (French). an. Quebec Library Association, c/o Dawson College Library, 1001 Sherbrooke Street East, Montreal Quebec H2L 1L3 Canada. DD 020.6534714.

LITA NEWSLETTER. Main/Corp Library and Information Technology Association (U.S.). VFOAT L.I.T.A. Newsletter. VAT Library and Information Technology Association Newsletter. No. 1 (Winter 1980)-. 0196-1799. Periodical. US. English. qt. Free to Members. ALA Library and Information Technology Association, 50 East Huron Street, Chicago IL 60611. LC Z678.9.A1. DD 020.2854.

LITTLE BUZZ. Vol. 1 (Jan. 1981)-. 0824-5339. CN. English. an. Free. Northwestern Regional Library System, 910 Victoria Avenue, Thunder Bay Ontario P7C 1B4 Canada. DD 027.6250971312. (ctrl).

LJ SPECIAL REPORT. VAT Library Journal Special Report. No. 1-. 0362-448X. Monographic Series. US. English. Library Journal, R R Bowker Co, Xerox Publishing Division, 1180 Avenue of the Americas, New York NY 10036. Ind/Abst Bibliogr. Agric. LC UNC.

LJ/SLJ HOTLINE CEASED. VFOAT Hotline. VAT Library Journal, School Library Journal Hotline. V. 1-12, No. 26. 0000-0078. Periodical. US. English. $27.00. R R Bowker Company, 1180 Avenue of the Americas, New York NY 10036. LC Z671. DD 020.5.

LLA BULLETIN. Main/Corp Louisiana Library Association. VAT Louisiana Library Association Bulletin. V. 28, No. 4- Winter 1965-. 0196-3023. Periodical. US. English. bm. $10.00. Louisiana Library Association, c/o Chris Thomas, PO Box 131, Baton Rouge LA 70821. Tel (504)342-4928. Ed Bob Heriard. Ind/Abst Libr. Lit. bk rev. adv acc. Circ 1,750. (ctrl). Reports of Louisiana activities, articles of interest to Louisiana readers, annual conference report, membership directory, financial and budgetary statements, book reviews. Bulletin - Louisiana Library Association, 0024-6867.

LMG REPORT ON DATA AND WORD PROCESSING FOR LIBRARIES. (THE L M G REPORT ON DATA AND WORD PROCESSING FOR LIBRARIES). Main/Corp Library Management Group. VFOAT L M G Report. V. 1- Feb. 1980-. 0227-2636. Periodical. CN. English. ir. 45.00. LMG The Library Management Group, PO Box 251, New Westminster British Columbia V3L 4Y6 Canada. Ind/Abst Comput. Control Abstr., Electr. Electron. Abstr., Sci. Abstr. Sect. A. Phys. Abstr., Libr. Inf. Sci. Abstr. DD 025.0202854. CODEN LRDLDL.

L.M.R.U. REPORT. Main/Corp Library Management Research Unit (Great Britain). VFOAT LMRU Report. 0309-4804. Monographic Series. UK. English. ir. Loughborough University in Technology, Library Management Research Unit, Leicestershire LE11 3TU England. LC UNC. DD 025.10941.

LOEX NEWS. VAT LIBRARY ORIENTATION-INSTRUCTION EXCHANGE NEWS. V. 1- 1974-. 0739-0386. Periodical. US. English. qt. $45.00. Eastern Michigan University, University Library, Ypsilanti MI 48197. Tel (313)487-0168. Ed Carolyn Kirkendall. Circ 1,000. (ctrl). Informal reports and notices of current news in the field of library instruction in school, special, public and academic libraries.

LONG RANGE PROGRAM FOR LIBRARY DEVELOPMENT IN ALASKA. US. English. Department of Education, Alaska State Library, Pouch G, Juneau AK 99811. LC Z732.A3. DD 027.0798. Long Range Program. Library Development in Alaska, 0094-8829.

LONG-RANGE PROGRAM FOR LIBRARY DEVELOPMENT IN MISSISSIPPI. SUPPLEMENT. Main/Corp Mississippi. State Library Commission. US. English. PO Box 10700, Jackson MS 39209 -0700. LC Z678.4.M7. DD 027.0762.

LONG-RANGE PROGRAM... UPDATE & EXTENSION AND ANNUAL PROGRAM. Main/Corp Oklahoma. Dept. of Libraries. VFOAT Long-Range Program . . . Update and Extension and Annual Program. Periodical. US. English. an. LC Z678.4.O5. DD 021.8309766. LSCA Annual Program.

LONG ROOM. VFOAT Longroom. No. 1- Spring 1970-. 0024-631X. Periodical. English. ir. LC Z921.D86. DD 021.7094183.

LRIS NEWSLETTER. (L R I S NEWSLETTER). Main/Corp Alberta. Land-Related Information Systems Co-Ordination Project. VAT Land Related Information Systems Newsletter. V. 1- Nov. 1979-. 0709-4590. Periodical. CN. English. bm. Free. Land-Related Information Systems/Co-Ordination Project, 10th Floor/Petroleum Plaza Plaza/North Tower, 9945 - 108 Street, Edmonton Alberta T5K 2G6 Canada. DD 025.063337.

LRL CHECKLIST OF PUBLICATIONS DEPOSITED WITH THE LEGISLATIVE REFERENCE LIBRARY. SUBJECT INDEX. See Indexes/Abstracts.

LRMP. . . : LIBRARY RESOURCES MARKET PLACE. 1981-. Periodical. US. English. ir. $43.50. R R Bowker, PO Box 1807, Ann Arbor MI 48106.

LS/2000 COMMUNIQUE. VFOAT LS Two Thousand Communique. VAT Local Systems Two Thousand Communique. No. 1 (Fall 1984)-. 0749-4165. Periodical. US. English. qt. Free. OCLC Local Systems, 6565 Frantz Road, Dublin OH 43017. Tel (614)764-6000. Ed Patrick J Mullin. DD 025. Circ 4,000. (ctrl). Newsletter on OCLC's local library systems LSY2000 which features news, developments, and new publications.

LTBC, LIBRARY TECHNICIANS ASSOCIATIONOF BRITISH COLUMBIA. (LTBC : LIBRARY TECHNICIANS ASSOCIATION OF BRITISH COLUMBIA). VAT Library Technicians Association of British Columbia. Vol. 8, No. 5 (July 1982)-. 0715-7533. Periodical. CN. English. ir. Library Technicians Association of British Columbia, PO Box 67515, Vancouver British Columbia V5W 3T9 Canada. DD 020.6234711. BCALT, 0822-6725.

LUSOLT TALK. Main/Corp Lakehead University. School of Library Technology. VFOAT L U S O L T Talk. VAT Lakehead University School of Library Technology Talk. V. 1- Dec. 1979-. 0226-0115. Periodical. CN. English. ir. Free. School of Library Technology, Lakehead University, Thunder Bay Ontario P7B 5E1 Canada. DD 020.71171312. (ctrl).

LUTHERAN LIBRARIES. V. 1- 1958-. 0024-7472. Periodical. US. English. qt. $10.00. Lutheran Church Library Association, 122 West Franklin Avenue, Minneapolis MN 55404. Tel (612)870-3623. Ed Ron Klug. (cum index). bk rev. adv acc. Circ 6,000. Articles of interest to church librarians including library techniques and promotion; reviews of current books for church libraries; news of LCLA Chapter activities.

M S L A V A NEWSLETTER. See Education (General) - Theory, Practice of Education.

M300 AND PC REPORT. VFOAT M 300 and PC Report. Vol. 1, No. 1 (Sept. 1984)-. 0743-7633. Periodical. US. English. mo. $37.00. Meckler Publishing, 11 Ferry Lane West, Westport CT 06680. Tel (203)226-6967. Ed Nancy J Melin. Ind/Abst Microcomput. Index. DD 001. bk rev. adv acc. Circ 1,300. Information on developments and uses of the IBM PC for libraries; reviews programs (new and existing).

MADE IN CANADA. ARTISTS IN BOOKS. (MADE IN CANADA). Main/Corp National Library of Canada. VFOAT Artists in Books. 1-. 0228-7749. CN. English (text in French). an. National Library of Canada, 395 Wellington, Ottawa Ontario K1A 0N4 Canada. DD 016.70971.

MAGAZINE - HALIFAX CITY REGIONAL LIBRARY. (MAGAZINES). Main/Corp Halifax City Regional Library. 1983-. 0822-6512. CN. English. an. Halifax City Regional Library, 5381 Spring Garden Road, Halifax Nova Scotia B3J 1E9 Canada. DD 018.134. Periodical Holdings, 0822-6504.

MAJALAH HIMPUNAN PUSTAKAWAN CHUSUS INDONESIA. Main/Corp Himpunan Pustakawan Chusus Indonesia. Periodical. English or Indonesian. ir. $5.00. Luwarsih Pringgoadisurjo D/A Pusat Dokumentasi Inmiah Nasional, Jalan Raden Saleh 43, Jakarta Indonesia. LC Z675.A2.

MAJALAH ILMU PERPUSTAKAAN DAN INFORMATIKA. V. 1, No. 1 (Jan./Apr. 1981)-. 0216-7506. Periodical. IO. Indonesian. ty. 2250. d/a Jurusan Ilmu Perpustakaan FSUI,

Library and Information Science

Kompleks UI Rawamangun, Jakarta Timur Indonesia. LC Z669.5.I6.

MAJALAH IPI. **Main/Corp** Ikatan Pustakawan Indonesia. **VAT** Majalah Ikatan Pustakawan Indonesia. Periodical. Indonesian (English). ir. $7.00. Ikatan Pustakawan Indonesia, c/o Bagian Penebitan, Departemen Kesehatan, Jalan Prapatan 10, Jakarta Indonesia. LC Z671. DD 020.5.

MAJALAH PERPUSTAKAAN. Dec. 1978-. Periodical. Indonesian. ir. Badan Pengembangan Perpustakaan Daerah Tk I Sum. Utara, Jalan Iskandar Muda No 270, Lantai II-Atlas, Medan Indonesia. LC Z845.S85.

MAJALLAH PERPUSTAKAAN MALAYSIA. (MAJALAH PERPUSTAKAAN MALAYSIA). Periodical. MY. English (Malay). an. $5.64. University Malaya/Co-Oper Bookshop, Kuala Lumpur 22-11, Lembah Pantai Malaysia. **Ind/Abst** Libr. Inf. Sci. Abstr. LC Z845.M3. DD 027.0595. *Majallah Perpustakaan Malaysia.*

MAKTABAH AL-ARABIYAH (BEIRUT, LEBANON). (AL-MAKTABAH AL-ARABIYAH). **VFOAT** Almaktabah Al-Arabiah. No. 1, (Haziran 1983)-. Periodical. LE. Arabic. mo. 10.00 Single Issue. Binayat Samiramis, Al-Hamra Al-Tabiq Al-Thalith, Shaqqah 33 SB 13/5416, Beirut Lebanon. LC Z464.A65.

MALT NEWSLETTER. Vol. 3, No. 1 (Jan. 1979)-. 0710-3417. Periodical. CN. English. ir. Manitoba Association of Library Technicians, Box 1872, Winnipeg Manitoba R3C 3R1 Canada. DD Q20.62347127. *Newsletter (Manitoba Association of Library Technicians), 0826-6816.*

THE MANAGEMENT OF CHANGE : STUDIES IN THE EVOLUTION OF LIBRARY SYSTEMS. Periodical. US. English. ir. Shoestring Press, Linnet Books, Hamden CT 06501.

MANAGING INFORMATION. V. 1-. Monographic Series. US. English. Sage Publications Inc, 275 S Beverly Drive, Beverly Hills CA 90212.

MANNUS-BIBLIOTHEK. N. F. V. 1- 1970-. Monographic Series. German. ir. *Mannus-Bucherei.*

MANUAL & DIRECTORY - ONTARIO JOINT FICTION RESERVE. See Yearbooks, Almanacs, Directories.

MARCHEMOS (EL PASO, TEX.). (MARCHEMOS). 0731-2741. US. Spanish. mo. $100.00. Library of Congress, Cataloging Distribution Service, Washington DC 20541. **Tel** (202)287-6100. Includes information about all the data elements in the MARC serials communications format, as well as local data elements which are used in association with the CONSER project.

MARIGOLD LIBRARY SYSTEM DIRECTORY. See Yearbooks, Almanacs, Directories.

MARIGOLD REPORT. No. 1- Nov. 1979-. 0226-5737. Periodical. CN. English. mo. Free. Marigold Library System, c/o South Alberta Library Services, 616 Mcleod Trail South East, Calgary Alberta T2G 2M2 Canada. DD 027.471233.

MASSACHUSETTS STATE PUBLICATIONS. **Main/Corp** State Library of Massachusetts. 1978-. US. English. an. $2.12. Massachusetts State Library, Boston MA 02133. LC Z1223.5.M35, J87.M4. DD 015.744. Each issue contains an index to its own contents - no vol index - loose. *Massachusetts Executive Department Publications, 0362-9546.*

MATERIALIEN DER TAGUNG DES INTERNATIONALEN VERBANDES DER BIBLIOTHEKAR-VEREINE. **Main/Corp** International Federation of Library Associations. German. ir. LC Z673.

MAUL : MIYAGI-KEN DAIGAKU TOSHOKAN KYOKAI KAIHO. **Main/Corp** Miyagi-Ken Daigaku Toshokan Kyokai. JA. Japanese. ir. Miyagi-Ken Daigaku Toshokan Kyokai Maul Henshu Iinkai, c/o Tohoku Daigaku Fuzoku, Toshokan Sendai Japan. LC Z845.M59.

MEDDELELSER FRA RIGSBIBLIOTEKAREN. **VFOAT** Arsstatistik, Arsberetninger. 0461-5298. DK. Danish. qt. Free. Det Kongelige Bibliotek, Christians Brygge 8, 1219 Copenhagen Denmark.

MEDIA: LIBRARY SERVICES JOURNAL. Began in 1970?. 0009-6423. Periodical. US. English. qt. $11.00. Materials Services Department, 127 9th Avenue North, Nashville TN 37203. **Tel** (615)251-2000. DD 027.

MEDIA SPECTRUM. Vol. 1, No. 1 (Spring 1974)-. 0731-3675. Periodical. US. English. qt. $10.00. Michigan Association for Media in Education, 39886 Shoreline Drive, Mt Clemens MI 48045. **Tel** (313)764-8240. **Ed** Margaret Grazier and Marilyn Matecum. adv acc. **Circ** 1,200. (ctrl) Information about trends, materials, programs, and research in education, technology, and library science relevant to the school library media profession.

MEDICAL LIBRARY NEWS - MCGILL UNIVERSITY. (MEDICAL LIBRARY NEWS). **Main/Corp** McGill University. Medical Library. No 1 (Dec. 1979)-. 0715-5557. Periodical. CN. English. ir. Free. Medical Library News, 3655 Drummond Street, Montreal Quebec H3G 1Y6 Canada. DD 026.6109714281. *Medical Library Bulletin.*

MEDICAL REFERENCE SERVICES QUARTERLY. Vol. 1, No. 1 (Spring 1982)-. 0276-3869. Periodical. US. English. qt. $62.00. Haworth Press, 28 East 22nd Street, New York NY 10010. **Tel** (212)228-2800. **Ed** Sandra M Wood. **Ind/Abst** Hospit. Lit. Index, Excerpta Med., Cumul. Index Nurs. Allied Health Lit., Comput. Control Abstr., Electr. Electron. Abstr., Sci. Abstr. Sect. A. Phys. Abstr., Biol. Abstr., Libr. Inf. Sci. Abstr., Libr. Lit. LC R118.2. DD 025.52766105. NLM Z 699.5 M39 M489. CODEN MRSQDK. bk rev. adv acc. **Circ** 906. It deals with topics of current interest and practical value for those who provide reference services to health sciences personnel in clinical, educational, or research settings.

MEDICAL SUBJECT HEADINGS. **Main/Corp** National Library of Medicine (U.S.). 1st- Ed. 0565-811X. US. English. ir. Superintendent of Documents, GPO Washington DC 20402. **Tel** (202)783-3238. LC Z695.1.M48. DD 025.3361. NLM Z 695.1 M4 M489.

MEDICAL SUBJECT HEADINGS. ANNOTATED ALPHABETIC LIST. 0147-5711. US. English. ir. $23.00. National Technical Information Service, 5285 Port Royal Road, Springfield VA 22161. LC Z695.1.M48. DD 025.4961. NLM Z 695.1 M4 M4894.

MEDICAL SUBJECT HEADINGS. TREE STRUCTURES. (MEDICAL SUBJECT HEADINGS : TREE STRUCTURES). **Main/Corp** United States. National Library of Medicine. Medical Subject Heading Section. 1980-. 0147-099X. Periodical. US. English. ir. $31.00. National Technical Information Service, 5285 Port Royal Road, Springfield VA 22161. LC Z695.1.M48. DD 025.3361. NLM Z 695.1 M4 M492.

MEETINGS (LIBRARY JOURNAL). (MEETINGS). **Series/Titl** LJ Special Report. 1980-. 8755-1810. US. English. an. $64.00. Library Journal, 1180 Avenue of the Americas, New York NY 10036. **Tel** (212)916-1921. **Ed** John N Berry III. DD 020. bk rev. adv acc. **Circ** 26,000. Full service publication addressed to the needs and interests of those who buy book and nonbook materials and equipment in public, academic, special, and business libraries.

MEKHANIZATSIIA I AVTOMATIZATSIIA. UR. Multilingual (Russian). 0.23. Biblioteka Akademii Nauk SSSR Birzhevaia Linia D 7, 199164 Leningrad Russia. LC Z678.9.A2.

MELA NOTES. **Main/Corp** Middle East Librarians Association. **VAT** Middle East Librarians Association Notes. No. 1- Fall 1973-. 0364-2410. Periodical. US. English. ir. $10.00. Middle East Librarians Association, Room 308 Main Library at OSU 1858 Neil Avenue Mall, Columbus OH 43210. **Tel** (614)422-3362. **Ed** Basima Bezirgan. **Ind/Abst** Libr. Inf. Sci. Abstr. bk rev. adv acc. **Circ** 175. Articles and reviews on Middle East librarianship and area studies.

MELANGES DE LA BIBLIOTHEQUE DE LA SORBONNE. Vol. 1 (1980)-. Periodical. FR. French. an. LC Z798.B53. DD 027.74436.

MEMBERSHIP DIRECTORY - ALBERTA ASSOCIATION OF LIBRARY TECHNICIANS. See Yearbooks, Almanacs, Directories.

MEMBERSHIP DIRECTORY - ATLANTIC PROVINCES LIBRARY. See Yearbooks, Almanacs, Directories.

MEMBERSHIP DIRECTORY - CANADIAN ASSOCIATION FOR INFORMATION SCIENCE. See Yearbooks, Almanacs, Directories.

MEMBERSHIP DIRECTORY - FLA. See Yearbooks, Almanacs, Directories.

MEMBERSHIP DIRECTORY - FLORIDA LIBRARY ASSOCIATION. See Yearbooks, Almanacs, Directories.

MEMBERSHIP DIRECTORY - INTERNATIONAL ASSOCIATION OF MARINE SCIENCE LIBRARIES AND INFORMATION CENTERS. See Yearbooks, Almanacs, Directories.

MEMBERSHIP DIRECTORY - LIBRARY ASSOCIATION OF ALBERTA. See Yearbooks, Almanacs, Directories.

MEMBERSHIP DIRECTORY - MINNESOTA LIBRARY ASSOCIATION. See Yearbooks, Almanacs, Directories.

MEMBERSHIP DIRECTORY. NEWFOUNDLAND AND LABRADOR. See Yearbooks, Almanacs, Directories.

MEMBERSHIP LIST - ASLIB. **Main/Corp** ASLIB. 1964-. 0066-8524. UK. English. ir. ASLIB, 26 27 Boswell Street, Information House, London WC1N 3FZ England. LC Z673.A627133. DD 020.62242. *Year Book - ASLIB.*

MEMBERSHIP LIST - CANADIAN ASSOCIATION OF MUSIC LIBRARIES. (MEMBERSHIP LIST). **Main/Corp** Canadian Association of Music Libraries. **VFOAT** Liste des Membres. 1984-. 0828-7007. CN. English (text in French). an. Canadian Association of Music Libraries, c/o Music Division, National Library of Canada, 395 Wellington Street, Ottawa Ontario K1A 0N4 Canada. DD 026.7802571. *Official Membership List, 0820-7631.*

MEMO FROM MUNICIPAL. No. 1-. 0712-2586. Periodical. CN. English. bm. Free. Memo From Municipal, Municipal Reference Library City Hall, Toronto Ontario M5H 2N1 Canada. DD 027.571354105. (ctrl).

MEMORANDUM - AMERICAN LIBRARY ASSOCIATION. OFFICE FOR INTELLECTUAL FREEDOM. (MEMORANDUM). **Main/Corp** American Library Association. Office for Intellectual Freedom. 0734-3086. Periodical. US. English. mo. $10.00. American Library Association, Office for Intellectual Freedom, 50 East Huron Street, Chicago IL 60611. **Tel** (312)944-6780. **Ed** Judith F Krug. **Circ** 725. A brief information communication designed for chairpersons and members of American Library Association Chapter Library Associations giving news about legislation and Supreme Court decisions.

MERLIN CEASED. V. 1-10, No. 5. 0383-9265. Periodical. CN. English. mo. Free. Midwestern Regional Library System, 637 Victoria Street North, Kitchener Ontario N2H 5G4 Canada. DD 027.471344.

METRO MISCELLANEOUS PUBLICATION. 0732-801X. Monographic Series. US. English. ir. $10.00 Domestic, $14.00 Foreign. New York Metropolitan Reference and Research Library, Agency 55 Willoughby Street, Brooklyn NY 11201. **Tel** (718)852-8700. **Ed** Christine Stenstrom. DD 011. **Circ** 1,600. Carries news about metro-sponsored services, programs and policies of interest to metro members and the library community in general. *Metro Miscellaneous.*

METROPOLITAN TORONTO LIBRARY. SCIENCE & TECHNOLOGY DEPT. ACQUISITIONS. (ACQUISITIONS - METROPOLITAN TORONTO LIBRARY. SCIENCE & TECHNOLOGY DEPT). **Main/Corp** Metropolitan Toronto Library. Science & Technology Dept. V. 1- March 1980-. 0226-255X. Periodical. CN. English. mo. Metropolitan Toronto Library Board, 789 Yonge Street, Toronto Ontario M4W 2G8 Canada. DD 016.5.

MEZHDUNARODNYI FORUM PO INFORMATSII I DOKUMENTATSII. Periodical. UR. Russian. qt. $7.50. Victor Kamkin Inc, 12224 Parklawn Drive, Rockville MD 20852. **Tel** (301)881-5973.

MICHIGAN LIBRARIAN CEASED. **VFOAT** Michigan Librarian Newsletter. V. 3-46. 0026-2242. Periodical. US. English. sa. LC Z673. DD 020.623. *Michigan School Librarian.*

Library and Information Science

MICHIGAN LIBRARIAN NEWSLETTER CEASED. Vol. 47, No. 1 (Feb. 1981)-V. 50, No. 7 (Nov./Dec. 1984). 0149-435X. Periodical. US. English. $15.00. Michigan Librarian Newsletter, 415 West Kalamazoo, Lansing MI 48933. **Tel** (517)487-6868. Ed Marianne Gessner. **LC** Z673. **DD** 020.6234774. bk rev. adv acc. **Circ** 2,200. (ctrl). Professional journal of the Michigan Library Association. *Michigan Librarian, 0026-2242.*

MICHIGAN LIBRARY AUTOMATION DIRECTORY. See Yearbooks, Almanacs, Directories.

MICHIGAN LIBRARY DIRECTORY. See Yearbooks, Almanacs, Directories.

MICHIGAN LIBRARY STATISTICS (MICHIGAN. STATE BOARD OF EDUCATION). See Statistics.

MICRO SOFTWARE REPORT. See Computers and Computer Science.

MICROEDITIONS DE LA BIBLIOTHEQUE. CATALOGUE. (MICROEDITIONS DE LA BIBLIOTHEQUE). **Main/Corp** Bibliotheque Nationale du Quebec. Service de Microphotographie. 1979-. 0707-848X. CN. French. an. Free. Bibliotheque Nationale du Quebec, 1700 rue Saint Denis, Montreal Quebec H2X 3K6 Canada. **DD** 018.136. **Circ** 1,000. Titles, descriptions and prices of the microphotographies of old and rare books, periodicals or retrospective newspapers available to libraries and other documentation centers. *Catalogue des Microeditions, 0384-9724.*

MICROFORM REVIEW. INDEX. See Indexes/Abstracts.

MICROLOG. MICROFICHE COLLECTIONS. (MICROLOG. MICROFICHE COLLECTIONS). **VFOAT** Microlog, Collections de Microfiche. **VAT** Microfiche Collections, Colections de Microfiche. Jan. 1983-. 0823-2113. Periodical. CN. English (French). mo. Free with Subscription of Microlog Index. Micromedia Ltd, 144 Front Street West, Toronto Ontario M5J 1G2 Canada. **DD** 015.71053.

MIDWINTER MEETING MINUTES - AMERICAN LIBRARY ASSOCIATION. CATALOGING AND CLASSIFICATION SECTION. EXECUTIVE COMMITTEE. (MIDWINTER MEETING MINUTES). **Main/Corp** American Library Association. Cataloging and Classification Section. Executive Committee. 0731-3853. US. English. an. American Library Association, 50 East Huron Street, Chicago IL 60611. **LC** Z673.A5227. **DD** 020.62273.

MINNA NO TOSHOKAN. Vol. 1-. Periodical. JA. Japanese. ir. Toshokan Mondai Kenkyukai, c/o Nerima Kuritsu Shakujii, Toshokan 16-31, Shakujiidai 1, Nerima-Ku 177, Tokyo Japan. **LC** Z845.J4.

MINUTES OF THE ... MEETING. **Main/Corp** Association of Research Libraries. 1st- 1932-. Periodical. US. English. sa. $25.00. Association of Research Libraries, 1527 New Hampshire Avenue NW, Washington DC 20009. **Tel** (202)232-2466. Ed Nicola Davis. Edited proceedings of the semiannual membership meetings of the association, including both program and business sessions.

MINUTES OF THE MEETING. **Main/Corp** Council of National Library Associations. US. English. **LC** Z673. **DD** 020.622.

MINUTES OF THE MEETING - ASSOCIATION OF RESEARCH LIBRARIES. **Main/Corp** Association of Research Libraries. 1st- Dec. 1932-. 0044-9652. US. English. sa. $25.00. Association of Research, 1527 New Hampshire Avenue NW, Washington DC 20009. **Tel** (202)232-2466. Ed Nicola Daval. **LC** Z673. **DD** 020.6. **NLM** Z 673 A849M. (cum index). **Circ** 500. Edited proceedings of the semiannual membership meetings of the association, including both program and business sessions.

MISSISSIPPI LIBRARIES. V. 43- Spring 1979-. 0194-388X. Periodical. US. English. qt. $16.00. Mississippi Libraries, Box 470, Attn Rachel Smith, Clinton MS 39056. **Tel** (601)924-9102. Ed Ruth Ann Grant. **Ind/Abst** Libr. Lit. **LC** Z671. **DD** 021.009762. bk rev. adv acc. **Circ** 1,200. Publishes significant articles, news and other data of interest to Mississippi librarians and library users. *Mississippi Library News, 0026-6302.*

MITTEILUNGSBLATT - VERBAND DER BIBLIOTHEKEN DES LANDES NORDRHEIN WESTFALEN. **Main/Corp** Verband der Bibliotheken des Landes Nordrhein-Westfalen. N.F. 1.- Vol.-. 0042-3629. Periodical. GW. German. qt. K G Saur Verlag, Postfach 711009/Possenbacherstrasse 2B, D8000 Muenchen 71 West Germany. **Tel** (089) 798901. **Ind/Abst** Libr. Inf. Sci. Abstr. **LC** Z671. **DD** 020. (cum index).

MLA NEWS LETTER - MINNESOTA LIBRARY ASSOCIATION. (MLA NEWSLETTER). **VFOAT** M.L.A. Newsletter. **VAT** Minnesota Library Association Newsletter. Vol. 1, No. 1 (July 5, 1974)-. 0748-9285. Periodical. US. English. ir. $12.00. Minnesota Library Association, 1315 Lowry Avenue North, c/o Regional Library, Minneapolis MN 55411-1398. **Tel** (612)521-1735. Ed David Barton and Marge Barton. adv acc. **Circ** 1,000. (ctrl). News and announcements of Minnesota library issues, continuing education events and job listings. *North Country Librarian.*

THE MLC PACKET/MISSISSIPPI LIBRARY COMMISSION. **VFOAT** Packet. Periodical. US. English. mo. *Packet.*

MLC UPDATE. (MLC UPDATE : THE NEWSLETTER OF THE MICHIGAN LIBRARY CONSORTIUM). **VAT** Michigan Library Consortium Update. Vol. 1, No. 1 (Sept./Oct. 1980)-. 0275-7583. Periodical. US. English. bm. Michigan Library Consortium, 720 Science Library, Wayne State University, Detroit MI 48202.

MO INFO. (MO INFO). **VFOAT** Newsletter. 0884-2205. Periodical. US. English. bm. Missouri Library Association, Executive Office, Parkade Plaza/Suite 9, Columbia MO 65203. **Tel** (314)449-4627. adv acc. **Circ** 1,400. News and information about activities and members of Missouri Library Association; other items of state or national interest related to libraries. *Newsletter - Missouri Library Association, 0581-0205.*

MODERN AVIATION LIBRARY. V. 1-. 0196-1527. Monographic Series. US. English. Modern Aviation Library, Blue Ridge Summit PA 17214. **LC** TL501. **DD** 629.13.

MOMBUSHO TOSHOKAN YORAN. **Main/Corp** Japan. Mombusho. Toshokan. Japanese. ir. Mombusho Toshokan, 2-2 Kasumigaseki 3 Chiyoda-Ku, Tokyo Japan. **LC** Z846.

MONOGRAPHIC SERIES - LIBRARY OF CONGRESS CEASED. (MONOGRAPHIC SERIES). **Main/Corp** Library of Congress. **Series/Titl** Library of Congress Catalogs. Began with Jan./March 1974. Ceased 1982. 0093-0571. Periodical. US. English. qt. Cataloging Distribution, Service Library of Congress Washington DC 20541. **LC** Z881.U49. **NLM** Z 881 L698.

MONTANA LIBRARY DIRECTORY, WITH STATISTICS OF MONTANA PUBLIC LIBRARIES. See Statistics.

MONTHLY MEMO - MAINE LIBRARY ASSOCIATION AND MAINE STATE LIBRARY. **Main/Corp** Maine Library Association. V. 1- May 1979-. Periodical. US. English. mo. Maine Municipal Association, Community Drive, Augusta ME 04330. *Downeast Libraries, 0738-5684.*

MONTHLY PERIODICAL INDEX. See Indexes/Abstracts.

MOUSAION. No. 1-. 0027-2639. Monographic Series. SA. text in English, French, German, Italian or Spanish. sa. $2.07. University of South Africa, Box 392, Department of Publ Services, Pretoria 0001 South Africa. **Tel** (012)429-3111.

MOUSAION II CEASED. **VFOAT** Mousaion Two. No. 1-12. Monographic Series. SA. English (Afrikaans). ir. **Ind/Abst** Libr. Inf. Sci. Abstr. *Mousaion.*

MPLA NEWSLETTER. **Main/Corp** Mountain Plains Library Association. **VAT** Mountain Plains Library Association Newsletter. V. 20- 1975/76-. 0145-6180. Periodical. US. English. bm. $36.00. Mountain Plains Library Association, ID Weeks Library, University South, Dakota, Vermillion SD 57069. **Tel** (605)677-6082. Ed Jim Dertien. **LC** Z671. **DD** 021.00978. adv acc. **Circ** 1,250. (ctrl). Happenings in and of interest to librarians in the Mountain Plains Library Association. *Mountain/Plains Library Association Quarterly.*

MRL BULLETIN. **Main/Corp** Detroit. Public Library. Municipal Reference Library. **VAT** Municipal Reference Library Bulletin. 0415-505X. Periodical. US. English. Detroit Public Library, 5201 Woodward Avenue, Detroit MI 48207.

MUG'M NEWSLETTER. **Main/Corp** Medline Users Group of the Midwest. Periodical. US. English. Midwest Health Science Library Network Library of the Health Sciences, University of Illinois at the Medical Center, Box 7509, Chicago IL 60680.

MULTITYPE LIBRARY COOPERATIVE NEWS. V. 2- July 1973-. 0094-0364. Periodical. US. English. mo. Illinois Regional Library Council, 125 Tower Drive, Burr Ridge IL 60521. *Intertype Library Cooperative News.*

MUNHON CHONGBOHAK PO. **VFOAT** Journal of the Library and Information Science Society. V. 1- (1984)-. Periodical. Korean. ir. Chonnam Taehakkyo Munhon Chongbohak Yonguhoe, 300 Yongbong-Dong Puk-Ku, Kwangju-Si Korea. **Tel** 55-0011. Ed Sang Wan Han. **LC** Z671. **Circ** 1,000. (ctrl). To study the trends in the library and information science field.

MUNICIPAL REFERENCE LIBRARY ACQUISITIONS. **Main/Corp** Metropolitan Toronto Library Board. Municipal Reference Library. V. 1- Mar. 1980-. 0226-2533. Periodical. CN. English. Free. Municipal Reference Library, 79 Yonge Street, Toronto Ontario M4W 2G8 Canada. **DD** 016.3077. (ctrl). *Selected List of New Titles, 0381-033X.*

MUSZAKI EGYETEMI KONYVTAROS. Periodical. HU. Hungarian. sa. XI Budafoki UT 4-6, Budapest Hungary. **LC** Z675.U5.

NAGOYA KOGYO DAIGAKU FUZOKU TOSHOKAN GAIYO. JA. Japanese. ir. Nagoya Kogyo Daigaku Fuzoku Toshokan, Gokishocho Showaku, Nagoya 466 Japan. **LC** Z846.N334.

NAME AUTHORITIES. CUMULATIVE MICROFORM EDITION. (NAME AUTHORITIES MICROFORM). **Main/Corp** Library of Congress. Catalog Publication Division. Began with 1977/Sept. 1979. 0195-9093. Periodical. US. English (Multilingual). bm. $225.00. Advanced Library Systems, 93 Main Street, Andover MA 01810. **Tel** (617)470-0610. **LC** Microfiche Z695.1. *Library of Congress Name Headings with References, 0093-0563.*

NATIONAL AGRICULTURAL LIBRARY CATALOG. **Main/Corp** United States. National Agricultural Library. 1966/70-. 0027-8505. US. English. mo. Rowman & Littlefield, 81 Adams Drive, Totowa NJ 07512. **LC** Z5076. **DD** 016.63. **NLM** Z 675.A8 N277. (cum index). Reference work.

NATIONAL CENTRAL LIBRARY NEWSLETTER. **Main/Corp** Kuo Li Chung Yang Tu Shu Kuan (China). **VFOAT** Kuo Li Chung Yang Tu Shu Kuan Tung Hsun. Began in Apr. 1969. 0034-5016. Periodical. CC. English. qt. National Central Library, Taipei Taiwan. **LC** Z846.K864. **DD** 027.551249.

NATIONAL LIBRARIAN. (NATIONAL LIBRARIAN : THE NLA NEWSLETTER). **VFOAT** NLA Newsletter. V. 2, No. 4- Nov. 1977-. 0191-359X. Periodical. US. English. qt. $15.00. National Librarians Association, D Hanson, Drawer B College Station, Pullman WA 99165. **Tel** (517)463-7227. Ed Peter Dollard. **Ind/Abst** Libr. Inf. Sci. Abstr. Professional concerns of librarians: certification, standards of performance, quality of education, ethics, and professional welfare. *NLA Newlsetter.*

NATIONAL LIBRARY NEWS. **VFOAT** Nouvelles de la Bibliotheque Nationale. V. 1- Jan./Mar. 1969-. 0027-9633. Periodical. CN. English (French separate paging, French text on inverted pages). ir. Free. National Library of Canada, 395 Wellington Street, Ottawa Ontario K1A 0N4 Canada. **Tel** (613)995-7969. Ed Wendy Newmann. **Ind/Abst** Libr. Inf. Sci. Abstr. **LC** Z883.076. **DD** 027.571384. **Circ** 4,000. (ctrl). Information on programs and services of the National Library of Canada of interest to the library community. *Accessible, 0315-0003.*

NATIONAL LIBRARY OF MEDICINE AUDIOVISUALS CATALOG. **VFOAT** Audiovisuals Catalog, NLM Audiovisuals Catalog. Began with 1977. 0149-9939. Periodical. US. English. qt. US Government Printing Office, Superintendent of Documents, Washington DC 20402. **LC** R835. **DD** 016.61. **NLM** W 18 N28015.

NATIONAL LIBRARY OF MEDICINE AVLINE CATALOG. **Main/Corp** United States. National Library of Medicine. **VFOAT** NLM Avline Catalog. **VAT** National Library of Medicine Audiovisual On-Line Catalog. 0146-3063. US. English. 8600 Rockville Pike, Bethesda MD 20014. **LC** R835. **DD** 016.61. **NLM** W 18 N2802.

NATIONAL LIBRARY OF MEDICINE CURRENT CATALOG. ANNUAL CUMULATION. **VFOAT** Current Catalog. Annual Cumulation, N.L.M. Current Catalog, Current Catalog. Began with 1966. 0090-3132. US. English.

Library and Information Science

an. US Government Printing Office, Superintendent of Documents, Washington DC 20402. **LC** Z675.M4. **DD** 610,016. **NLM** Z 675.M4 U578NC. *National Library of Medicine Catalog.*

NATIONAL LIBRARY OF MEDICINE CURRENT CATALOG. CUMULATIVE LISTING. VFOAT Current Catalog. Began with Jan.-Mar. 1966 issue. 0090-3132. Periodical. US. English. qt. Superintendent of Documents, US Government Printing Office, Washington DC 20402. **NLM** Z 675.M4 U578NC. *National Library of Medicine Catalog.*

NATIONAL LIBRARY OF MEDICINE PROGRAMS AND SERVICES. 1977-. 0163-4569. US. English. an. National Library of Medicine, National Institutes of Health, Bethesda MD 20205. **NLM** Z 675.M4 U56AN. *Programs and Services, 0093-0393.*

NATIONAL LIBRARY TECHNICAL NEWS. Main/Corp National Library of Canada. 1983/1 (Jan. 1983)-. 0820-8093. Periodical. CN. English (French). ir. **DD** 025.020971. *National Library News, 0027-9633.*

NATIONAL PRESERVATION NEWS. No. 1 (July 1985)-. 0882-4339. Periodical. US. English. qt. Free to Institutions. Library of Congress, National Preservation Program, Office LM G07, Washington DC 20540. **LC** Z701. **DD** 025.7.

THE NATIONAL UNION CATALOG. LC CARD NUMBER INDEX. See Indexes/Abstracts.

NATIONAL UNION CATALOG. REGISTER OF ADDITIONAL LOCATIONS. See Bibliographies.

NEBRASKA LIBRARY ASSOCIATION QUARTERLY. Vol. 1, No. 1 (Spring 1970)-. 0028-1883. Periodical. US. English. qt. $8.00. Creighton University, 2500 California Street/Ray Means, Omaha NE 68178. Ed John Felton. bk rev. adv acc. **Circ** 960. (ctrl). News and events about Nebraska, official organization of the Nebraska Library Association and library information in general.

NELA NEWSLETTER. Main/Corp New England Library Association. **VAT** New England Library Association Newsletter. V. 1- Jan. 1969-. 0027-6448. Periodical. US. English. qt. $25.00. New England Library Association, 436 Grant Road, Acton MA 01720. **Tel** (617)263-5144. **LC** Z673. **DD** 020.623274.

NELB LINK. Main/Corp New England Library Board. **VAT** New England Library Board Link. V. 1- Mar. 1976-. 0362-1618. Periodical. US. English. bm. Free Domestic, $3.00 Others. NELB, 231 Capitol Avenue, Hartford CT 06115.

NENPO. Main/Corp Hyogo Kenritsu Toshokan. VFOAT Hyogo Kenritsu Toshokan Nenpo. Japanese. an. Hyogo Kenritsu Toshokan, 1-Ban 27-Go Akashi Koen, Akashi-Shi 673 Japan. **LC** Z846.H9.

NETWORK. V. 1- Jan. 1974-. 0093-3341. Periodical. US. English. qt. $24.00. Wise, PO Box 2-J, Tempe AZ 85282. **LC** Z678.9.A1. **DD** 025.0202854. *LARC Newsletter.*

NETWORK PLANNING PAPER. No. 1-. 0160-9742. Monographic Series. US. English. ir. Library of Congress, Cataloging Distribution Services, Washington DC 20541. **Tel** (202)287-6100. **LC** UNC. **DD** 025.0405. **NLM** Z 674.7 N476.

NETWORKING IN KENTUCKY. Began in 1984. US. English. ir.

DIE NEUE BUCHEREI. 1964-. 0028-3126. Periodical. German. ir. **LC** Z801.

NEVADA LIBRARY DIRECTORY AND STATISTICS. See Statistics.

NEW ACQUISITIONS IN THE IAEA AND UNIDO LIBRARIES. Main/Corp International Atomic Energy Agency. Library. **VAT** New Acquisitions in the International Atomic Energy Agency and United Nations Industrial Development Organization Libraries. V. 13, No. 9- Sept. 1971-. 0377-1733. English. ir. International Atomic Energy Agency, Karntner Ring 11, PO Box 590, A-1011 Vienna Austria. **LC** Z5160. **DD** 016.539705. *IAEA Library, New Acquisitions.*

NEW BOOKS IN THE COMMUNICATIONS LIBRARY. Main/Corp University of Illinois at Urbana-Champaign. Communications Library. 0734-8142. Periodical. US. English. qt. University of Illinois Urbana-Champaign, 119 Gregory Hall, Urbana IL 61801. **Tel** (217)333-2350.

NEW BOOKS - LIBRARY, MINISTRY OF FORESTS. Main/Corp British Columbia. Ministry of Forests. Library. V. 1- Sept. 1978-. 0707-0446. Periodical. CN. English. bm. Library Ministry of Forests, 1450 Government Street, Victoria British Columbia V8W 3E7 Canada.

NEW DIRECTIONS IN LIBRARIANSHIP. No. 1-. 0147-1090. Monographic Series. US. English. ir. Greenwood Press, 88 Post Road W, Box 5007, Westport CT 06881. **Tel** (203)226-3571. **LC** UNC. This series provides a focus for new and sometimes controversial ideas under discussion in the library world.

NEW ENGLAND LAW LIBRARY CONSORTIUM NEWSLETTER. Vol. 1, No. 1 (Nov. 1983)-. 0749-3169. Periodical. US. English. mo. Free. New England Law Library Consortium, Harvard Law School Library/Langdell Hall, Cambridge MA 02138. **Tel** (617)495-3176. Ed Joan Duckett. **DD** 026. **Circ** 75. News items concerning acquisitions, collections and the personnel of the New England Law Library Consortium, Inc.

NEW HAMPSHIRE LIBRARY STATISTICS. See Statistics.

NEW INFORMATION SYSTEMS & SERVICES. VFOAT New Information Systems and Services. Issue 1 (Mar. 1979)-. Periodical. US. English. ir. Gale Research, Book Tower, Detroit MI 48226. Ed John Schmidttroth. **NLM** Z 674.5.A2 E56A. Periodical supplements to EISS. Furnish articles on new systems and services and on major changes affecting those already listed.

NEW JERSEY AREA LIBRARY DIRECTORY. See Yearbooks, Almanacs, Directories.

NEW JERSEY LIBRARIES. -1967. 0028-5811. Periodical. US. English. qt. New Jersey Library Association, 116 West State Street, Trenton NJ 08608. **Tel** (609)394-8032. Ed Joyce Smothers. **LC** Z732.N6. **DD** 021.009749. adv acc.

NEW JERSEY PUBLIC LIBRARIES. See Statistics.

NEW JERSEY PUBLIC LIBRARY DIRECTORY. See Yearbooks, Almanacs, Directories.

THE NEW LIBRARY SCENE. Vol. 1, No. 1 (Sept./Oct. 1982)-. 0735-8571. Periodical. US. English. bm. $18.00. Library Binding Institute, 1421 East Wayzata Boulevard/Suite 51, Wayzata MN 55391. **Tel** (612)475-2241. Ed Sally Grauer. **Ind/Abst** Libr. Lit., Inf. Sci. Abstr. **LC** Z671. **DD** 025.705. bk rev. adv acc. **Circ** 3,000. Semi-specialized publication for librarians. Focus on conservation preservation, collection management, user services, and binding operations. *Library Scene, 0090-8746.*

NEW LIBRARY WORLD. V. 73-. 0307-4803. Periodical. UK. English. mo. 22.00. NLW Journals Ltd, 16 Pembridge Road, London W11 England. **Tel** 048373 238. Ed Edward Dudley. **Ind/Abst** Libr. Inf. Sci. Abstr., Libr. Lit. **LC** Z671. Index published separately - free - automatically sent. bk rev. adv acc. **Circ** 1,100. Topical and professional issues in library and information work and the book trade. *Library World.*

NEW MEXICO LIBRARIES NEWSLETTER. V. 1-3, No. 4. Periodical. US. English. ir. New Mexico Libraries, PO Box 25084, Albuquerque NM 87125. **Tel** (505)344-3705. Ed Kintree Van. adv acc. **Circ** 700. Articles on libraries and librarians in New Mexico, also New Mexico Library Association News. *New Mexico Libraries.*

NEW MEXICO LIBRARY DIRECTORY. See Yearbooks, Almanacs, Directories.

NEW MEXICO LIBRARY STATISTICS. See Statistics.

NEW NOTES (DOWNSVIEW, ONT.). (NEW NOTES). Vol. 1, No. 1 (Sept./Oct. 1981)-. 0821-476X. Periodical. CN. English. ir. Free. North York Public Library, 120 Martin Ross Avenue, Downsview Ontario M3J 2R5 Canada. **DD** 027.4713541. (ctrl).

NEW PUBLICATIONS FOR PLANNING LIBRARIES. LIST NO. 6. URBAN AND REGIONAL PLANNING. Main/Corp Council of Planning Librarians. **Series Corp** Council of Planning Librarians. Exchange Bibliography. **VAT** New Publications for Planning Libraries. List Number Six. Urban and Regional Planning. 0360-1544. Periodical. US. English. Council of Planning Libraries Exchange Bibliographies, PO Box 229, Monticello IL 61856. Ed Mary Vance.

NEW PUBLICATIONS FOR PLANNING LIBRARIES. LIST NO. 9. LAND USE. Main/Corp Council of Planning Librarians. **Series Corp** Council of Planning Librarians. Exchange Bibliography. **VAT** New Publications for Planning Libraries. List Number Nine. Land Use. 0360-1552. Periodical. US. English. Council of Planning Libraries Exchange Bibliographies, PO Box 229, Monticello IL 61856.

NEW PUBLICATIONS LIST - UTLAS. (NEW PUBLICATIONS AWARENESS LIST - UNIVERSITY OF TORONTO LIBRARY AUTOMATION SYSTEMS). **Main/Corp** University of Toronto. Library Automation Systems. **VAT** UTLAS. New Publications Awareness List, University of Toronto Library Automation Systems. New Publications Awareness List. Dec. 7, 1979-. 0709-8987. Periodical. CN. English. wk. University of Toronto Library Automation Systems, 130 Saint George Street, Toronto Ontario M5S 1A5 Canada. **DD** 011.

NEW SERIAL TITLES. Began with Jan. 1953. 0028-6680. US. English. mo. $350.00. Library of Congress, Cataloging Distribution Service, Washington DC 20541. **Tel** (202)287-6100. **LC** Z6945.U5, PN4832. **DD** 016.05. **NLM** Z 6945 N532. (cum index). Includes reports of all serials contributed to the CONSER file. Each CONSER record lists NUC location symbols for reporting libraries. *Serial Titles Newly Received, 0090-0060.*

NEW SOUTH WALES GOVERNMENT DEPARTMENT LIBRARIES. AT. English. ir. Government Departments Unit, State Library of New South Wales, Level 8 CAGA Centre, 8-18 Bent Street, Sydney 2000 Australia. **LC** Z870.N43. **DD** 027.509944.

NEW SPECIAL LIBRARIES : A PERIODIC SUPPLEMENT TO THE SEVENTH EDITION OF DIRECTORY OF SPECIAL LIBRARIES AND INFORMATION CENTERS. See Yearbooks, Almanacs, Directories.

NEW YORK AND NEW JERSEY REGIONAL MEDICAL LIBRARY NEWS. V.1-. Periodical. US. English. bm. New York Academy of Medicine, 2 East 103rd Street, New York NY 10029.

THE NEW YORK PUBLIC LIBRARY DIRECTORY OF COMMUNITY SERVICES. See Yearbooks, Almanacs, Directories.

NEW YORK STATE ANNUAL PROGRAM STATEMENT. Main/Corp New York (State). State Library, Albany. US. English. an. University of the State of New York, State Education Department, Albany NY 12234. **LC** Z678.4.N7. **DD** 027.0747.

NEW ZEALAND LIBRARIES. V. 1- Aug. 1937-. 0028-8381. Periodical. NZ. English. qt. 32.00. New Zealand Library Association Inc, PO Box 12-212, Wellington 1 New Zealand. **Tel** 735-834. Ed V Elliott. **Ind/Abst** Libr. Lit., Index New Z. Period., Libr. Inf. Sci. Abstr. **LC** Z671. **DD** 020.5. Index published separately - free - automatically sent. bk rev. adv acc. **Circ** 2,000. Aims to record significant developments in New Zealand librarianship, promote discussion on matters of library interest, contribute to continuing education and publish results of library research.

A NEWBERRY NEWSLETTER. No. 1- Sept. 1973-. Periodical. US. English. qt. Free. Newberry Library, 60 West Walton Street, Chicago IL 60610. **Tel** (312)943-9090. Ed Terry Sullivan. **Circ** 5,500. Matters pertaining to the Newberry Library and its various activities: acquisitions, development, research and education, and library services, conservation, etc.

THE NEWCASTLE FORGOTTEN FANTASY LIBRARY. 0163-6251. Monographic Series. US. English. ir. Borgo Press, PO Box 2845, San Bernardino CA 92406. **Tel** (714)884-5813. Ed Robert Reginald. **Circ** 2,000.

NEWS. Main/Corp Freedom to Read Foundation. 0046-5038. US. English. Freedom to Read Foundation, 50 East Huron Street, Chicago IL 60611. **Tel** (312)944-6780. Ed Judith F Krug. **LC** KF4774.A16. **DD** 342.73085. bk rev. **Circ** 1,700. (ctrl). Covers activities of the Freedom to Read Foundation in defending freedom of speech and of the press.

NEWS - ALBERT-WETMORLAND-KENT REGIONAL LIBRARY. EXTENSION DEPARTMENT. (NEWS - ALBERT-WESTMORLAND-KENT REGIONAL LIBRARY). **Main/Corp** Bibliotheque Regionale Albert-

Library and Information Science

Westmorland-Kent. Dep. de l'Extension. **VFOAT** Nouvelles - Bibliotheque Regionale Albert-Westmorland-Kent. V. 1- Oct. 1971-. 0315-355X. Periodical. CN. French (English). Bibliotheque Regionale Albert-Westmorland-Kent, CP 708, Moncton New Brunswick E1C 8M9 Canada.

NEWS & CLUES : NEWSLETTER OF THE SAN JOAQUIN VALLEY LIBRARY SYSTEM AND THE AREA WIDE LIBRARY NETWORK. 0730-1618. Periodical. US. English. mo $25.00. San Joaquin Valley Library System, 2420 Mariposa, Fresno CA 93721. **Tel** (209)488-3229. **Ed** Sharon Vandercook. bk rev. **Circ** 500. (ctrl). Announcement and news of interest to libraries in the San Joaquin Valley.

NEWS AND NOTES OF THE MARYLAND HISTORICAL SOCIETY. See Museums.

NEWS AND VIEWS OF THE SOUTH CAROLINA LIBRARY ASSOCIATION. V. 1, No.1- Feb. 1979-. Periodical. US. English. ir. Route 3, 169 Irwin Road, Lexington SC 29072.

NEWS BULLETIN. Main/Corp Ohio Library Association. V. 1-19. Periodical. English. ir.

NEWS BULLETIN. Main/Corp Special Libraries Association. Boston Chapter. Began with Sept. 1934 issue. Periodical. US. English. bm. $5.00. Special Libraries Association, 675 Massachusetts Avenue/Reppucci, Cambridge MA 02139. **Tel** (617)426-3000. **LC** Z671.

NEWS FOR SOUTH CAROLINA LIBRARIES. Main/Corp South Carolina. State Library, Columbia. 0146-1842. Periodical. US. English. mo. Free. South Carolina State Library, 1500 Senate Street, PO Box 11469, Columbia SC 29211. **LC** Z732.S72. **DD** 021.009757. (ctrl). News for South Carolina Libraries, 0146-1842.

NEWS FROM C.U.N.Y. LIBRARIES. (NEWS FROM C.U.N.Y. LIBRARIES : A PUBLICATION OF THE LIBRARY ASSOCIATION OF THE CITY UNIVERSITY OF NEW YORK). **VFOAT** News from CUNY Libraries. 0747-6035. Periodical. US. English. bm. News from C.U.N.Y. Libraries, c/o Hunter College Libraries, 695 Park Avenue, New York NY 10021.

NEWS FROM THE LIBRARY OF CONGRESS. See Bibliographies.

NEWS - MANITOBA HEALTH LIBRARIES ASSOCIATION. See Medicine.

NEWS - NATIONAL LIBRARY OF MEDICINE. See Medicine.

NEWS - NOVA SCOTIA LIBRARY ASSOCIATION CEASED. **Main/Corp** Nova Scotia Library Association. **VFOAT** NSLA Newsletter. V. 1-8, No. 2. 0229-897X. Periodical. English. ir.

NEWSLETTER - ALBERTA COUNCIL OF COLLEGE LIBRARIANS. Main/Corp Alberta Council of College Librarians. V. 1- Jan 1978-. 0707-7327. Periodical. CN. English. sa. $7.74. Alberta Council of College Librarians, 332 6th Avenue SE, Calgary Alberta T2G 4S6 Canada. **DD** 027.7097123.

NEWSLETTER - AMERICAN ASSOCIATION OF LAW LIBRARIES. Main/Corp American Association of Law Libraries. V. 8- Sept. 1976-. 0572-4953. US. English. mo. A.A.L.L., 53 West Jackson Boulevard, Chicago IL 60637. **LC** Z675.L2. **DD** 026.34006273. American Association of Law Libraries Newsletter.

NEWSLETTER - AMERICAN THEOLOGICAL LIBRARY ASSOCIATION. Main/Corp American Theological Library Association. **VFOAT** ATLA Newsletter. **VAT** American Theological Library Association Newsletter. V. 1- Nov. 1953-. 0003-1399. Periodical. US. English. qt. American Theological Library Association, Duke University, Durham NC 27701. **LC** Z675.T4.

NEWSLETTER - ARLIS-NA CEASED. (ARLIS/NA NEWSLETTER). **Main/Corp** Arlis/North America. V. 1-9, No. 6. 0090-3515. Periodical. US. English. bm. $25.00. Brand Library, 1601 West Mountain Street, Glendale CA 91201. **Ind/Abst** Libr. Inf. Sci. Abstr. **LC** Z5937. **DD** 026.7. Available on microfiche from University Microfilms International.

NEWSLETTER - ASSOCIATION OF RESEARCH LIBRARIES. Main/Corp Association of Research Libraries. **VFOAT** A.R.L. Newsletter, Libraries Newsletter. No. 33 (Mar. 12, 1969)-. 0066-9652. Periodical. US. English. ir. $15.00. Association of Research Libraries, 1527 New Hampshire Avenue NW, Washington DC 20009. **Tel** (202)232-2466. **Ed** Nicola Daval. **LC** Z671. **DD** 021. **NLM** Z 673 A849N. **Circ** 1,300. Current information on the association and its programs and activities as well as other issues of interest to research libraries. ARL Newsletter.

NEWSLETTER - BRITISH LIBRARY. Main/Corp British Library. Bibliographic Services Division. **VFOAT** BSD Newsletter. No. 1 (May 1976)-. 0308-230X. Periodical. UK. English. qt. Free. British Library, Bibliographic Service Division, 2 Sheraton Street, London W1V 4BH England. **Tel** (01)636-1544. **Ed** Andy Stephens. **Circ** 4,000. Journal of the British Library Bibliographic Services Division. Contains articles of interest to all users of the division's products and services and future plans and policies.

NEWSLETTER - CANADIAN ASSOCIATION OF LAW LIBRARIES. Main/Corp Canadian Association of Law Libraries. **VFOAT** Bulletin - Association Canadienne des Bibliotheques de Droit. No. 1- June 1970-. 0319-5376. Periodical. CN. English (includes some text in French). ir. $34.83. University of Manitoba, Law Library, c/o Debbie Benson, Winnipeg Manitoba R3T 2N2 Canada. **Ind/Abst** Libr. Inf. Sci. Abstr. **DD** 016.34'00971. C A L L News, 0319-5384; CALL News, 0319-5384.

NEWSLETTER - CANADIAN ASSOCIATION OF MUSIC LIBRARIES. See Music.

NEWSLETTER - CANADIAN ASSOCIATION OF TOY LIBRARIES. Main/Corp Canadian Association of Toy Libraries. Began with Winter 1978 issue. 0709-5619. Periodical. CN. English. sa. 25.00. Canadian Association of Toy Libraries, Suite 1207/50 Quebec Avenue, Toronto Ontario M6P 4B4 Canada. **Tel** (416)766-1452. **Ed** J von Levetzow. **DD** 026.688720971. bk rev. adv acc. **Circ** 500. (ctrl). Play and toy libraries, parenting and childhood. Newsletter, 0703-2099.

NEWSLETTER - CANADIAN LIBRARY TRUSTEES' ASSOCIATION. Main/Corp Canadian Library Trustees' Association. Dec. 1967-. 0068-9149. Periodical. CN. English. c/o Canadian Library Association, 151 Sparks Street, Ottawa K1L 5E3 Canada.

NEWSLETTER - CANADIAN TOY LIBRARY ASSOCIATION. Main/Corp Canadian Toy Library Association. No. 6- Summer 1977-. 0703-2099. Periodical. CN. English. sa. Free to Members with membership $5.00. Canadian Toy Library Association, c/o White Oaks Toy Library, 70 McCraney Street East, Oakville Ontario L6A 1H4 Canada. **DD** 026.688720971. Toy Lending Centres Newsletter, 0703-2080.

NEWSLETTER - CASSETTE INFORMATION SERVICES. See Education (General) - Theory, Practice of Education.

NEWSLETTER - CENTENNIAL COLLEGE. COLLEGE BIBLIOCENTRE DIVISION. (NEWSLETTER - CENTENNIAL COLLEGE, COLLEGE BIBLIOCENTRE DIVISION). **Main/Corp** Centennial College of Applied Arts and Technology. College Bibliocentre Division. **VFOAT** C B Newsletter. No. 16- July 1975-. 0380-5379. Periodical. CN. English. qt. Free. Centennial College, College Bibliocentre Division, 20 Railside Road, Don Mills Ontario M3A 1A4 Canada. **DD** 027.7713541. Newsletter, 0315-4254.

NEWSLETTER - CENTRE FOR RESEARCH IN LIBRARIANSHIP. FACULTY OF LIBRARY SCIENCE. UNIVERSITY OF TORONTO. (NEWSLETTER - CENTRE FOR RESEARCH IN LIBRARIANSHIP, FACULTY OF LIBRARY SCIENCE, UNIVERSITY OF TORONTO). **Main/Corp** University of Toronto. Centre for Research in Librarianship. No. 1- 1976-. 0383-9079. Periodical. CN. English. ir. Free. Centre for Research in Librarianship, Faculty of Library Science, University of Toronto, 140 St George Street, Toronto Ontario M5S 2T4 Canada. **DD** 020.720713541.

NEWSLETTER - CHANGE. (NEWSLETTER). July 1982-. 0821-6657. CN. English. an. Free. Newsletter c/o Shirley Sefton Saskatchewan Provincial Library, 1352 Winnipeg Street, Regina Saskatchewan S4P 3V7 Canada. **DD** 025.0409713541. (ctrl).

NEWSLETTER - CHINESE AMERICAN LIBRARIANS ASSOCIATION. (NEWSLETTER). No. 13 (Aug. 1978)-. 0736-8887. Periodical. US. English. ty. $15.00. c/o Chiou-Sen Chen, Acquisitions Department, Alexander Library, Rutgers University, New Brunswick NJ 08903. **Tel** (614)422-2704. **Ed** Daphne C Hsueh. bk rev. **Circ** 500. (ctrl). Containing news items promoting Sino-American librarianship, CALA activities and members' activities. Newsletter to Members and Friends.

NEWSLETTER - CONSORTIUM OF RHODE ISLAND ACADEMIC AND RESEARCH LIBRARIES. (NEWSLETTER). **Main/Corp** Consortium of Rhode Island Academic and Research Libraries. Vol. 1, No. 1 (March 1982)-. 0882-6846. Periodical. US. English. ty.

NEWSLETTER - COOPERATIVE ON INFORMATION TECHNOLOGY. (NEWSLETTER). No. 1 (Apr. 26, 1982)-. 0712-6859. Periodical. CN. English. ir. Free. Cooperative on Information Technology, Room 622, 140 St George Street, Toronto Ontario M5S 1A1 Canada. **DD** 025.04060713. (ctrl).

NEWSLETTER - DEPARTMENT OF SCHOOL LIBRARIES. HALIFAX, N.S CEASED. (NEWSLETTER - DEPARTMENT OF SCHOOL LIBRARIES, HALIFAX, N. S). **Main/Corp** Halifax (N.S.). Dept. of School Libraries. Nov. 1974-Oct./Nov. 1980. 0318-546X. Periodical. CN. English. ir. Department of School Libraries, Board of School Commissioner Commissioners, City of Halifax, 2790 Oxford Street, Halifax Nova Scotia B3L 2V5 Canada. **DD** 027.806171622. Halifax City School Library System Newsletter, 0318-5451.

NEWSLETTER - FINGER LAKES LIBRARY SYSTEM. Main/Corp Finger Lakes Library System. V. 1- Sept. 1979-. 0195-4016. Periodical. US. English. Finger Lakes Library System, PO Box 219, 314 North Cayuga Street, Ithaca NY 14850.

NEWSLETTER - FLOWER VETERINARY LIBRARY. Main/Corp Flower Veterinary Library. Vol. 24, No. 4 (July/Sept. 1982)-. Periodical. US. English. qt. Cornell University Libraries Veterinary Library Newsletter.

A NEWSLETTER FOR COPAR. See Architecture.

NEWSLETTER - FRIENDS OF THE OTTAWA PUBLIC LIBRARY. (NEWSLETTER). **VFOAT** Bulletin. **VAT** Bulletin - Amis de la Bibliotheque Publique d'Ottawa. Vol. 1, No. 2 (Nov. 1983)-. 0822-658X. Periodical. CN. English (French text on inverted pages). ir. Free to members. Friends of the Ottawa Public Library, 120 Metcalfe Street, Ottawa Ontario K1P 5M2 Canada. **DD** 027.406071384. Friends (Ottawa, Ont.), 0820-9901.

NEWSLETTER - GEAC LIBRARY INFORMATION SYSTEM. (NEWSLETTER). Vol. 1, No. 1 (Winter 1981)-. 0226-9295. Periodical. CN. English. sa. Free. GEAC Newsletter, 350 Steelcase Road West, Markham Ontario L3R 1B3 Canada. **DD** 025.0405.

NEWSLETTER - IFLA. SECTION OF BIOLOGICAL AND MEDICAL SCIENCES LIBRARIES. Main/Corp International Federation of Library Associations and Institutions. Section of Biological and Medical Sciences Libraries. **VAT** Newsletter - International Federation of Library Associations and Institutions. Section of Biological and Medical Libraries. 0250-4294. Periodical. US. English. qt. $10.00. University of Illinois, PO Box 7509, Library of Chic Health, Chicago IL 60680. **Tel** (312)996-7000.

NEWSLETTER - INDIA OFFICE LIBRARY AND RECORDS CEASED. **Main/Corp** India Office Library and Records. -No. 25. Periodical. UK. English. ir.

NEWSLETTER - MANITOBA LIBRARY TRUSTEES ASSOCIATION. (NEWSLETTER). Winter 1979-. 0823-1184. Periodical. CN. English. ir. Free. Manitoba Library Trustees Association, c/o Pat Downey, Coulter Manitoba R0M 0G0 Canada. **DD** 027.47127. (ctrl). Manitoba Library Trustees Association (Newsletter), 0823-1176.

NEWSLETTER - MAP ONLINE USERS GROUP. (NEWSLETTER). **Main/Corp** Map Online Users Group. No. 5 (Oct. 1980)-. 0749-338X. Periodical. US. English. ir. $10.00. University of South Carolina, Map Library, Columbia SC 29208. **Tel** (803)777-2802. **Ed** Linda D Cottrell. **DD** 025. **Circ** 100. News and information for map catalogers and reference librarians using map online data bases. Newsletter, 0749-3398.

NEWSLETTER - MARIGOLD LIBRARY SYSTEM. (NEWSLETTER). Vol. 1, No. 1 (Apr. 1982)-. 0713-2727. Periodical. CN. English. qt. Free. Marigold Library System Newsletter, Box 1830, Strathmore Alberta T0J 3H0 Canada. **DD** 027.471233.

Library and Information Science

NEWSLETTER - MIDWEST REGION LIBRARY NETWORK. Main/Corp Midwest Region Library Network. VFOAT MidNet Newsletter. No. 1-18. 0278-6753. Periodical. US. English. qt. Midwest Region Library Network, University of Chicago, 1225 East 60th Street, Chicago IL 60637. Tel (414)465-2750.

NEWSLETTER - MISSOURI LIBRARY ASSOCIATION CEASED. Main/Corp Missouri Library Association. VFOAT MLA Newsletter. Vol. 1- Feb. 1970-. 0581-0205. Periodical. US. English. bm. $6.00 Domestic, $10.00 Foreign. Missouri Library Association, Parkdale Plaza #9, Columbia MO 65203. Tel (314)449-4627. Ed Marilyn McLeod. LC Z673. adv acc. Circ 1,400. News and information about activities and members of the Missouri Library Association, plus other items of state or national interest related to libraries.

NEWSLETTER - MUSIC OCLC USERS GROUP. See Music.

NEWSLETTER OF THE YELLOWHEAD REGIONAL LIBRARY. Main/Corp Yellowhead Regional Library. V. 4, No. 4- Oct. 1978-. 0708-1979. Periodical. CN. English. ir. Yellowhead Regional Library, PO Box 400, Spruce Grove Alberta T0E 2C0 Canada. Tel (403)962-2003. Ed Louise Frolek. DD 027.471233. Circ 300. (ctrl). Newsletter for library personnel in the region. Contains reviews and other news relevant to the region. Nexus, 0383-0748.

NEWSLETTER ON INTELLECTUAL FREEDOM. VFOAT Intellectual Freedom. Began with June 1952 issue. 0028-9485. Periodical. US. English. bm $25.00. American Library Association, 50 East Huron Street, Chicago IL 60611. Tel (312)944-6780. Ed Judith F Krug. Ind/Abst Libr. Lit. LC Z671. (cum index). bk rev. Circ 3,000. Available on microfilm from University Microfilms International. Coverage of censorship incidents affecting libraries, schools, the press, etc. Reports in court decisions and legislation affecting 1st Amendment rights; includes review and bibliography.

NEWSLETTER - ONTARIO ASSOCIATION OF LIBRARY TECHNICIANS. (NEWSLETTER). VFOAT Nouvelles. Vol. 1, No. 1 (Apr. 10, 1976)-. 0229-2645. Periodical. CN. English (French). ty. $5.00. Ontario Association of Library Technicians, PO Box 682, Oakville Ont L6J 5C1 Canada. DD 023.3.

NEWSLETTER (ROUND TABLE OF NATIONAL CENTRES FOR LIBRARY SERVICES). See Bibliographies.

NEWSLETTER - SOCIAL RESPONSIBILITIES ROUND TABLE CEASED. Main/Corp American Library Association. Social Responsibilities Roundtable. VFOAT SRRT Newsletter. No. 73. 0065-9096. Periodical. US. English. qt. $5.00 Members. American Library Association, 50 East Huron Street, Chicago IL 60611.

NEWSLETTER - SOUTHEAST ASIAN RESEARCH MATERIALS GROUP. See General Interest - General Interest-Asia.

NEWSLETTER - UNIVERSITY OF ILLINOIS AT URBANA-CHAMPAIGN. GRADUATE SCHOOL OF LIBRARY SCIENCE. (NEWSLETTER - UNIVERSITY OF ILLINOIS AT URBANA-CHAMPAIGN, GRADUATE SCHOOL OF LIBRARY SCIENCE). Main/Corp University of Illinois at Urbana-Champaign. Graduate School of Library Science. 1- Spring 1980-. 0277-528X. Periodical. US. English. sa. Free. Graduate School of Library Science, 410 David Kinley Hall, University of Illinois, Urbana IL 61801.

NEWSLETTER - UNIVERSITY OF TORONTO. FACULTY OF LIBRARY SCIENCE CEASED. (NEWSLETTER - UNIVERSITY OF TORONTO, FACULTY OF LIBRARY SCIENCE). Main/Corp University of Toronto. Faculty of Library Science. No. 5-22. 0318-4110. CN. English. Free to Alumni. University of Toronto, Faculty of Library Science, 140 St George Street, Toronto Ontario M5S 2T4 Canada. DD 020.711713541. Newsletter, 0318-4102.

NEWSLINE - MANITOBA LIBRARY ASSOCIATION. (NEWSLINE : NEWSLETTER OF THE MANITOBA LIBRARY ASSOCIATION). Main/Corp Manitoba Library Association. 0227-6569. Periodical. CN. English. bm. Free to Members. Newsline, 6 Farmer Avenue West, Winnipeg Manitoba R2M 0Y2 Canada. DD 027.07127. MLA Newsline, 0700-3684.

NEXUS. V. 4, No. 3- Sept. 1977-. Periodical. US. English. ir. Central Colorado Library System, 11111 East Mississippi Avenue, Aurora CO 80012.

NFAIS NEWSLETTER. VFOAT N.F.A.I.S. Newsletter. VAT National Federation of Abstracting and Indexing Services Newsletter. V. 15- Feb. 1973-. 0090-0893. Periodical. US. English. bm $85.00. N F A I S, 112 South 16th Street, Philadelphia PA 19102. Tel (215)563-2406. Ed M Lynne Neufeld. Ind/Abst Predicasts, Funk Scott Index Corp. Ind. NLM Z 1007 N558. CODEN NFNLA6. bk rev. Circ 600. Indexing, database, and information industry news, plus book reviews, calendar, and opinion columns. Federation Newsletter, News from Science Abstracting and Indexing Services, 0028-9124.

NGOMA. 0712-2829. Periodical. CN. English. qt. $10.00. NGOMA, c/o Overseas Book Centre, 321 Chapel Street, Ottawa Ontario K1N 7Z Canada. DD 021.8.

NGOMA. 0712-2837. Periodical. CN. French. qt. $10.00. NGOMA, c/o Centre du Livre Pour Outre-Mer, 321 rue Chapel, Ottawa Ontario K1N 7Z2 Canada. DD 021.8.

NIGERBIBLIOS. 0331-0000. Periodical. English. ir. National Library of Nigeria, 4 Wesley Street PM 12626, Lagos Nigeria. Ind/Abst Libr. Inf. Sci. Abstr. LC Z965.L24. DD 027.5669.

NIGERIAN LIBRARIES. V. 1- Feb. 1964-. 0029-0122. Periodical. NR. English. ty. Ibadan University Libraries, Department of Library Studies, Ibadan Nigeria. Ind/Abst Libr. Inf. Sci. Abstr. LC Z673.N698. Wala News.

NIHON NOGAKU TOSHOKAN KYOGIKAI KAIHO. VFOAT Bulletin of the Japan Association of Agricultural Librarians and Documentalists. JA. Japanese. ir. c/o Seio Building, 29-31 Sakuragaoka Shibuya-Ku, Tokyo Japan. LC Z674.5.J32.

NILITE NEWS. Began in Dec. 1971. 0319-2792. Periodical. CN. English. Niagara College of Applied Arts and Technology, Woodlawn Road, Welland Ontario L3B 5S2 Canada. DD 023.5.

NIMH LIBRARY ACQUISITION LIST. Main/Corp National Institute of Mental Health (U.S.). Library. VFOAT N.I.M.H. Library Acquisitions List. US. English. mo. National Institute of Mental Health, 5600 Fishers Lane, Rockville MD 20857.

NLC OVERTONES CEASED. Main/Corp Nebraska Library Commission. VFOAT Overtones. VAT Nebraska Library Commission Overtones. Ceased with V. 9, No. 10-11 (Oct./Nov. 1982). 0149-5011. Periodical. US. English. bm $25.00. Nebraska Library Commission, 1420 P Street, Lincoln NE 68508. Tel (513)223-5065. DD 021. Overtones from the Underground, 0084-9218.

N.L.R. NATIONAL LIBRARY REPORTER. (NLR : NATIONAL LIBRARY REPORTER). VFOAT National Library Reporter. V. 1- Oct. 7, 1974-. 0095-053X. Periodical. US. English. sm. $35.00. 9482 Kilimanjaro Road, Columbia MD 21045. LC Z731. DD 021.00973.

NNRLIS NOTES. Main/Corp National Natural Resources Library and Information System. VAT National Natural Resources Library and Information System Notes. No. 1- July 1979-. Periodical. US. English. ir. US Department of the Interior, Office of Library and Information Services, Washington DC 20240. Natural Resources Library Newsletter, 0193-5704.

NOMINAL LIST OF PRACTISING LIBRARIANS IN NIGERIA. 1974-. NR. English. an. National Library of Nigeria, 4 Wesley Street, PMB 12626, Lagos Nigeria. LC Z965, Z720.A46N5. DD 016.9669, 020.922.

NON SOLUS. No. 1- 1974-. 0094-8977. US. English. an. $10.00. Publication Office of the University of Illinois, Graduate School of Library Science, 249 Armory, Urbana-Champaign IL 61820. LC Z733. DD 027.777366.

NORDISK TIDSKRIFT FOR BOK-OCH BIBLIOTEKSVASEN. Vol. 1- 1914-. 0029-148X. Periodical. SW. Swedish. qt. $25.00. Almqvist & Wiksell, 108 Drottninggatan, PO Box 45150, S-104 30 Stockholm Sweden. Tel 85413160. Ed I Collijn. Ind/Abst MLA Int. Bibliogr. Books Artic. Mod. Lang. Lit., Libr. Inf. Sci. Abstr., Libr. Lit., Recent Publ. Artic. LC Z671. Index in last issue of volume - attached. (cum index).

NORTH AMERICAN LIBRARY EDUCATION DIRECTORY AND STATISTICS. See Yearbooks, Almanacs, Directories.

NORTH CAROLINA LIBRARIES. V. 1- 1942-. 0029-2540. Periodical. US. English. qt. North Carolina Library Association, Appalachian State University, PO Box 212, Boone NC 28607. Ed Robert Burgin. Ind/Abst Libr. Lit. LC Z671. DD 020.623. bk rev. adv acc. Circ 2,200. All aspects of librarianship, especially in North Carolina.

NORTH DAKOTA ACADEMIC LIBRARY STATISTICS. See Statistics.

NORTH DAKOTA STATE PLAN FOR LIBRARY DEVELOPMENT. Main/Corp North Dakota. State Library Commission. 0160-0095. US. English. ND State Library Commission, State Capitol, Bismarck ND 58505. LC Z678.4.N9. DD 021.009784.

NORTH-HOLLAND MATHEMATICAL LIBRARY. V. 1-. Monographic Series. English. ir. Elsevier Science Publishing, PO Box 1663 Grand Central Station, New York NY 10163. Ind/Abst Comput. Control Abstr., Electr. Electron. Abstr., Sci. Abstr. Sect. A. Phys. Abstr., Phys. Abstr., Math. Rev.

NORTHERN AIR. V. 1- Feb. 1969-. 0048-0754. CN. English. ir. Free. Wapiti Regional Library, 145-12 Street East, Prince Albert Saskatchewan S6V 1B7 Canada. Tel (306)764-0712. Ed Karen Labuik. DD 027.471242. bk rev. Circ 250. (ctrl). House organ: library events, procedures, problems, news, and ideas, etc.

NORTHERN LIBRARIES BULLETIN. 0048-0789. Periodical. US. English. ir. Alaska Division of State Libraries, Pouch G, Juneau AK 99801. Tel (907)465-2926. Newsletter of the Northern Libraries Colloquy sharing information on the North.

NOTABLE WORKS AND COLLECTIONS. Main/Corp University of Saskatchewan. Library. Oct. 1975-. 0380-9676. Periodical. CN. English. sa. Collection Development Department, Main Library, University of Saskatchewan, Saskatoon Saskatchewan C7N 0W0 Canada. DD 017.1.

NOTE D'INFORMATION (ASSOCIATION DES BIBLIOTHECAIRES FRANCAIS). (NOTE D'INFORMATION). 0180-4278. FR. French. ir. Association des Bibliothecaires Francais, 65 rue de Richelieu, 75002 Paris France. DD 020.

NOTES FOR MEDICAL CATALOGERS. Began with V. 1, No. 1, March 1965. 2078-2025. US. English. an. National Technical Information Service, US Department of Commerce, Springfield VA 22161. NLM Z 695.1 M4 N911.

NOTES FROM THE TARLTON LAW LIBRARY. See Law.

NOTES ON SELECTED ACQUISITIONS. Main/Corp Columbia University. Libraries. 0572-8312. Periodical. US. English. Columbia University Libraries, 345 East 47th Street Engineering Society Library, New York NY 10017.

NOTES ON SPECIAL DEVELOPMENTS IN THE PROGRAM. Main/Corp National Serials Data Program. No. 1- Aug. 1972-. 0090-001X. Periodical. US. English. National Serials Data Program, Washington DC 20540. LC Z695.7. DD 025.34302854.

NOTICIERO DE LA AMBAC. Main/Corp Asociacion Mexicana de Bibliotecarios. Periodical. MX. Spanish. ir. Asociacion Mex Bibliotecarios, Apartado Postal 127-132, Mexico 7 DF Mexico. Tel 548 73 64. adv acc. Circ 1,000. (ctrl). The serial contains information about conferences scholarships courses and others in Mexico and foreign.

NOUVELLES - ASSOCIATION DES BIBLIOTHEQUES DE L'ONTARIO. GUILDE DES SERVICES EN FRANCAIS. (NOUVELLES : BULLETIN D'INFORMATION SUR LES BIBLIOTHEQUES PUBLIQUES). VFOAT Bulletin d'Information sur les Bibliotheques Publiques de l'Ontario. Oct. 1980-. 0822-7527. Periodical. CN. French. ir. Association des Bibliotheques de l'Ontario, Guilde des Services en Francais c/o Federation des Bibliotheques du Centre-Nord, 334 Sud rue Regent, Sudbury Ontario P3C 4E2 Canada. DD 020.6234713.

NOUVELLES DE LA BIBLIOTHEQUE CENTRALE DE PRET. REGION DU SAGUENAY-LAC-SAINT-JEAN. (LES NOUVELLES DE LA BIBLIOTHEQUE CENTRALE DE PRET). Main/Corp Bibliotheque Centrale de Pret du Saguenay-Lac-Saint-Jean. V. 1, No. 2- May 1974-. 0316-0432. CN. French. Bibliotheque Centrale de Pret du Saguenay-Lac-Saint-Jean, 100 Ouest rue Price, Alma Quebec G8B 4S1 Canada. DD 027.471416. Bulletin de Nouvelles, 0318-1448.

Library and Information Science

NOVAIA SOVETSKAIA I INOSTRANNAIA LITERATURA PO BIBLIOTEKOVEDENIIU I BIBLIOGRAFII. UR. Multilingual (Russian). mo. 0.16. Tsentr Prospekt Kalinina 3, Moskva 101000 Russia. LC Z666.

NOVEDADES BAC. VAT Novedades Biblioteca Agropecuaria de Colombia. Spanish (text in English). ir. *Novedades Snica.*

NOVINKY KNIHOVNICKE LITERATURY. Vol. 1-. Periodical. CS. Czech. ir. Artia, PO Box 790, Praha 1 Czechoslovakia. LC Z671.

NSLA NEWS. (NSLA NEWS : NOVA SCOTIA LIBRARY ASSOCIATION NEWSLETTER). VFOAT Nova Scotia Library Association Newsletter. **VAT** Nova Scotia Library Association News. Vol. 8, No. 3 (Mar. 1981)-. 0319-8545. Periodical. CN. English. Free to Members, Membership, $5.00. D C Rankin, NSLA Membership Committee, c/o Dalhousie School of Library Science, Dalhousie University, Halifax Nova Scotia B3H 4H8 Canada. **DD** 020.6234716. *News, 0319-8545.*

NSUKKA LIBRARY NOTES. 0331-1481. Periodical. English. ir. University of Nigeria, Nsukka Nigeria. **Tel** 771939. **Circ** 400. (ctrl). Articles in library and information science. News about staff and development in library services.

NUC. U.S. BOOKS. Series/Titl Library of Congress Catalogs. VFOAT N.U.C. Jan. 1983-. 0734-7642. US. English. mo. $245.00 Domestic, $260.00 Foreign. Customer Services Nuc Desk, Cataloging Distribution Service, Library of Congress, Washington DC 20541. **Tel** (202)287-6100. Contains bibliographic or catalog entries prepared by the Library of Congress or by one of the libraries which contributes reports to the UUC.

NURSING SUBJECT HEADINGS. Periodical. US. English. Seventh Day Adventist Hospital Association, PO Box 871, Glendale CA 91209. LC Z695.1.N8. **DD** 610.73014.

NUWSLETTER : NEWS OF THE UNIVERSITY OF WISCONSIN SYSTEM LIBRARIES. VFOAT N.U.W.S. Letter Nuwsletter. **VAT** News of the University of Wisconsin System Libraries. No. 1 (May 1983)-. 0739-215X. Periodical. US. English. ir. Free. University of Wisconsin c/o Steve Marquardt/McIntyre Library, Eau Claire WI 54701.

NYLA BULLETIN. Main/Corp New York Library Association. **VAT** New York Library Association Bulletin. V. 1- Feb. 15, 1953-. 0027-7134. Periodical. US. English. New York Library Association, 15 Park Row/Suite 434, New York NY 10038. **Tel** (212)227-8032. Ed Gerald R Shields. LC Z671. **DD** 020.5. adv acc. **Circ** 3,000. (ctrl). Reports news, concerns and issues involving librarians and librarianship in New York State and beyond.

OBZORNAIA INFORMATSIIA : BIBLIOTEKOVEDENIE I BIBLIOGRAFOVEDENIE. VFOAT Bibliotekovedenie I Bibliografovedenie. Periodical. UR. Russian. sa. $4.80. Victor Kamkin Inc, 12224 Parklawn Drive, Rockville MD 20852. **Tel** (301)881-5973.

OCCASIONAL ACQUISITIONS - LIBRARY & INFO SERVICES. NATIONAL INDIAN BROTHERHOOD CEASED. (OCCASIONAL ACQUISITIONS - LIBRARY & INFO SERVICES, NATIONAL INDIAN BROTHERHOOD). Main/Corp National Indian Brotherhood. Information Services. 1-25. 0383-7211. Periodical. CN. English. National Indian Brotherhood of Canada, 1st Floor/102 Bank Street, Ottawa Ontario K1P 5N4 Canada. **DD** 016.97100497. *Weekly Acquisitions List, 0317-7858.*

OCCASIONAL PAPER - WESTERN ASSOCIATION OF MAP LIBRARIES. (OCCASIONAL PAPER). Main/Corp Western Association of Map Libraries. No. 1-. 0278-3835. Monographic Series. US. English. ir. Western Association of Map Libraries, c/o S Stevens University of California, Santa Cruz CA 95064. **Tel** (408)429-2364. Ed Stanley D Stevens. **Ind/Abst** GeoRef. Occasional papers relate to map collections in libraries and archives. They include bibliographies of related material.

OCCASIONAL PAPERS - FOUNDATION CENTER. Main/Corp Foundation Center. No. 1- 1968-. 0548-7250. US. English. Foundation Center Library, 888 7th Avenue, New York NY 10019.

OCCASIONAL PAPERS IN MIDDLE EASTERN LIBRARIANSHIP. No. 1 1979-. 0278-4882. English. an. LC Z673.M64. **DD** 020.956.

OCCASIONAL PAPERS - UNIVERSITY OF ILLINOIS GRADUATE SCHOOL OF LIBRARY SCIENCE CEASED. Main/Corp University of Illinois at Urbana-Champaign. Graduate School of Library Science. Began in 1966. Ceased with No. 147, Dec. 1980. 0073-5310. Monographic Series. US. English. *Occasional Papers - University of Illinois Graduate School of Library Science, 0073-5310.*

OCCASIONAL PAPERS - UNIVERSITY OF ILLINOIS (URBANA-CHAMPAIGN CAMPUS). GRADUATE SCHOOL OF LIBRARY AND INFORMATION SCIENCE. (OCCASIONAL PAPERS). No. 148 (June 1981)-. 0276-1769. Monographic Series. US. English. ir. $12.00. University of Illinois, Publishing Office, Graduate School of Library and Information Science, 505 R Armory Street/#249, Champaign IL 61820. **Tel** (217)333-1359. Ed James S Dowling. **Circ** 5. Deals with some aspect of librarianship and consists of manuscripts which, because of length, detail, specialization or temporary interest would not be published in a library periodical. *Occasional Papers - University of Illinois Graduate School of Library Science, 0073-5310.*

OCCASIONAL PAPERS - VIRGINIA LIBRARY ASSOCIATION. Main/Corp Virginia Library Association. 0195-6329. Periodical. US. English. ir. William Prince, Virginia Library Association, Virginia Polytechnic Institute, Blacksburg VA 24061.

OCCASIONAL PUBLICATION. Main/Corp Tennessee. University. Libraries. No. 1- 1970-. Monographic Series. US. English. ir. University of Tennessee, Main Library, Knoxville TN 37916.

OCCASIONAL RESEARCH PAPER (BRIGHAM YOUNG UNIVERSITY. SCHOOL OF LIBRARY AND INFORMATION SCIENCES). (OCCASIONAL RESEARCH PAPER - SCHOOL OF LIBRARY AND INFORMATION SCIENCES, BRIGHAM YOUNG UNIVERSITY). No. 1-. 0148-2068. Monographic Series. US. English. ir. Brigham Young University, 5042 Hbll, Dr Nathan Smith, Provo UT 84602. LC UNC.

OCLC MICRO. See Computers and Computer Science.

OCLC NEWSLETTER. Main/Corp OCLC. No. 135 (April 1981)-. Periodical. US. English. ir. OCLC Inc, 6565 Frantz Road, Dublin OH 43017. **Tel** (614)486-3661. **Ind/Abst** Libr. Inf. Sci. Abstr. *OCLC Newsletter.*

OCULA COUNCIL NEWSLETTER. (O C U L A COUNCIL NEWSLETTER). Main/Corp Ontario College & University Library Association. V. 2, No. 1-V. 6, No. 1. 0709-5589. Periodical. CN. English. qt. Free to Members. OCULA, Ontario Library Association, 2397 Bloor Street West, Toronto Ontario M6S 1P6 Canada. **DD** 027.7062713. *Council Newsletter, 0702-0708.*

ODL SOURCE. Main/Corp Oklahoma. Dept. of Libraries. **VAT** Oklahoma Department of Libraries Source. V. 1- Nov. 1976-. 0193-3086. Periodical. US. English. mo. Oklahoma Department of Libraries, 200 NE 18th Street, Oklahoma City OK 73105. *ODL Newsletter.*

OFFENTLICHE BIBLIOTHEKEN IN BADEN-WURTTEMBERG. German. ir. Staatliche Fachstelle fur das Offentliche Bibliothekswesen Freiburg, Lorracher Strasse 5A, 7800 Freiburg West Germany. LC Z801.B25. **DD** 027.44346.

OFFICIAL DIRECTORY OF NEW JERSEY LIBRARIES AND MEDIA CENTERS. VFOAT Official Directory of New Jersey Libraries and Media Centers, and Buyers Guide. 1984-. 0748-2469. Periodical. US. English. an. $29.95. LDA Publishing, 4236 209 Street, Bayside NY 11361. **Tel** (718)224-0485. Ed Paul V Ippolito. LC Z732.N6. **DD** 027.0025749. adv acc. **Circ** 900. Over 1,500 libraries, public, academic, special, public and private schools are listed. A single source of information including: special collection, computers, software, etc. All heavily indexed. *Directory of New Jersey Libraries and Media Centers, and Buyers Guide, 0749-3525.*

OHIO LIBRARIES. Main/Corp Ohio. Auditor of State. 1972-. 0360-8069. US. English. an. Ohio Libraries, c/o Thomas E Furguson, Columbus OH 43216. LC Z732.O5. **DD** 025.1109771. *Ohio Public Libraries.*

OHIO LIBRARY TRUSTEE. Began publication in 1939?. 0030-0977. Periodical. US. English. qt $9.00. Ohio Library Trustees Association, Suite 230/40 South 3rd Street, Columbus OH 43215. **Tel** (614)221-9057. Ed A Chapman Parsons. **Circ** 2,000. (ctrl). A bulletin providing articles and news about public library operations in Ohio and Ohio trustee members of OLTA.

OHIO MEDIA SPECTRUM. V. 29- Jan. 1977-. 0192-6942. Periodical. US. English. qt. $25.00. Ohio Educational Library Media, 40 South Third Street, Columbus OH 43215. **Tel** (513)253-6177. Ed Connie E Ark. **Ind/Abst** Libr. Inf. Sci. Abstr., Libr. Lit. LC Z675.S3. **DD** 027.8. bk rev. adv acc. **Circ** 2,000. (ctrl). A publication of Ohio Educational Library Media Association. Provides information applicable to the daily jobs of library/media specialists everywhere. *Bulletin - Ohio Association of School Librarians, 0030-0799; Educational Media in Ohio.*

OKINAWA TOSHOKAN KYOKAI SHI. JA. Japanese. ir. c/o Okinawa Kenritsu Toshokan, 312 Aza Yorimaya, Naha Japan. LC Z671.

OKLAHOMA LIBRARIAN. 1- Spring 1950-. 0030-1760. Periodical. US. English. bm. Oklahoma Librarian, 300 Hardy Drive, Edmond OK 73034. **Ind/Abst** Libr. Inf. Sci. Abstr., Libr. Lit. LC Z732. **DD** 020.6234766.

OMS ANNUAL REPORT. Main/Corp Association of Research Libraries. Office of Management Studies. **VAT** Office of Management Studies Annual Report. 1978-. 0278-7946. US. English. an. Association of Research Libraries, 1527 New Hampshire Avenue NW, Washington DC 20009. LC Z675.U5. **DD** 027.7. *Annual Report - Association of Research Libraries, Office of University Library Management Studies, 0271-0064.*

ON LINE. VFOAT CSLA on Line. Began with V. 1- Sept. 1974. Ceased with Oct. 1975 issue (V. 2, No. 1)?. 0315-9558. Periodical. CN. English. Miss Karen Smith Editor, 57 Hampton Crescent, London Ontario N6H 2N7 Canada. **DD** 027.806271.

ON-LINE REVIEW. See Computers and Computer Science.

THE ONE-PERSON LIBRARY. VFOAT 1 Person Library. Vol. 1, No. 1 (May 1984)-. 0748-8831. Periodical. US. English. mo. $45.00. OPL Resources Ltd, PO Box 948 Murray Hill Station, New York NY 10156.

ONLINE. V. 1- Jan. 1977-. 0146-5422. Periodical. US. English. bm. $78.00. Online Inc, 11 Tannery Lane, Department 1B, Weston CT 06883. **Tel** (203)227-8466. Ed J Pemberton. **Ind/Abst** Bus. Period. Index, Libr. Lit., Mag. Index, Trade Ind. Index, Chem. Abstr., Comput. Control Abstr., Cumul. Index Nurs. Allied Health Lit., Curr. Index J. Educ., Electr. Electron. Abstr., Eng. Index, Libr. Inf. Sci. Abstr., Microcomput. Index, Phys. Abstr., Soc. Sci. Citation Index, Sci. Cit. Index, Abr. Ed., Sci. Abstr. Sect. A. Phys. Abstr., Eng. Index Annu., Eng. Index Mon., Eng. Index Energy Abstr., Eng. Index Bioeng. Abstr. LC Z699.A1. **DD** 001.64404. **CODEN** ONLIDN. bk rev. adv acc. **Circ** 5,000. Covers the whole spectrum of functions in the online world.

ONTARIO LIBRARY REVIEW CEASED. V. 32. No. 1-V. 66, No. 2. 0030-2996. Periodical. CN. English. qt. Free to Secondary Schools, Colleges and Universities. 14th Floor Mowat Block, Queens Park, Toronto Ontario M7A 1C5 Canada. **Ind/Abst** Libr. Inf. Sci. Abstr. *Ontario Library Review and Canadian Periodical Index.*

OPEN DOOR. (THE OPEN DOOR). 0709-8634. Periodical. CN. English. ir. Free to Members. Vancouver Island Regional Library, 10 Strickland Street, Nanaimo British Columbia Canada. **DD** 027.4711.

OPEN LETTER TO LIBRARY WORKERS IN THE C.O.R.L. REGION. **VAT** Open Letter to Library Workers in the Central Ontario Regional Library System Region, OLA RPLD Open Letter to Library Workers in the C.O.R.L. Region, Ontario Library Association Regional and Public Libraries Division. Open. Dec. 1976-. 0709-5961. Periodical. CN. English. ir. Free. D McFadyen Town of Markham Public Libraries, Thornhill Community Centre Branch, 7755 Bayview Avenue, Thornhill Ontario L3T 4T1 Canada. **DD** 020.6234713. (ctrl).

OPENERS. Vol. 1, No. 1 (Spring 1981)-. 0734-6794. Periodical. US. English. qt. American Library Association, 50 East Huron Street, Subscription Department, Chicago IL 60611.

OPERATING PLAN - STATE LIBRARY OF OHIO. (OPERATING PLAN). **Main/Corp** Ohio. State Library, Columbus. 0097-823X. Periodical. US. English. Columbus State Library, 65 South Front Street, Columbus OH 43215. **LC** Z733.S83. **DD** 027.577157.

OPTICAL INFORMATION SYSTEMS IN LIBRARIES. 0886-019X. Periodical. US. English. bm. Meckler Publishing, 11 Ferry Lane West, Westport CT 06880.

OPUSCULUM. Vol. 1, No. 1-. 0358-5581. Periodical. Finnish (Swedish, with abstracts in English). qt. 120. Helsinkin Yliopiston Kirjasto, PL312, 00171 Helsinki 17 Finland. **LC** Z829.A1.

ORBIS ACADEMICUS. **VFOAT** Problemgeschichten der Wissenschaft in Dokumenten und Darstellungen. V. 1- 1951-. 0474-330X. Monographic Series. GW. German. ir. Verlag Karl Alber, Hermann-Herder-Strasse 4, D-7800 Freiburg West Germany.

OREGON COUNTRY LIBRARY. Vol. 1-. Monographic Series. US. English. Rainy Day Press, PO Box 3035, Eugene OR 97403.

ORGANIZATSIIA SISTEMATICHESKIKH I PREDMETNYKH KATALOGOV NAUCHNYKH BIBLIOTEK. Vol. 1-. Periodical. UR. Russian. 0.74. 101000 Prospekt Kalinina 3, Moskva Russian SFSR. **LC** Z693.A15.

AZ ORVOSI KONYVTAROS. 0030-6010. HU. Hungarian. qt. Akademiai Kiado, POB 24, 1363 Budapest Hungary. **Ind/Abst** Libr. Inf. Sci. Abstr. **LC** Z675.M4. **NLM** Z 675.M4 O79.

OSAKA FURITSU NAKANOSHIMA TOSHOKAN KIYO. **Main/Corp** Osaka Furitsu Nakanoshima Toshokan. No. 11-. JA. Japanese. ir. Osaka Furitsu Nakanoshima Toshokan, 27 Nakanoshima 1-chome Kita-ku, Osaka Japan. **LC** Z955. *Osaka Furitsu Toshokan Kiyo.*

OSAKA FURITSU NAKANOSHIMA TOSHOKAN ZOKA TOSHO MOKUROKU. **Main/Corp** Osaka Furitsu Nakanoshima Toshokan. 1973-. JA. Multilingual (English, German, Japanese). ir. Osaka Furitsu Nakanoshima Toshokan, 27 Nakanoshima 1-chome Kita-ku, Osaka Japan. **LC** Z955. *Osaka Furitsu Toshokan Zoka Tosho Mokuro.*

OSAKA FURITSU YUHIGAOKA TOSHOKAN ZOKA TOSHO MOKUROKU. **Main/Corp** Osaka Furitsu Yuhigaoka Toshokan. 1973-. JA. Japanese. ir. Osaka Furitsu Yuhigaoka Toshokan, 21-1 Reijincho Tennoji-ku, Osaka Japan. **LC** Z955. *Osaka Furitsu Toshokan Zoka Tosho Mokuro.*

OSAR/OSALL. SA. English. ir. 5.00. Organisasie van Suid-Afrikaanse Regsbiblioteke, L Davis, PO Box 2439, Johannesburg 2000 South Africa. **LC** Z675.L2. **DD** 026.34000968.

OTTAWA BULLETIN. (BULLETIN D'OTTAWA - CANADIAN ASSOCIATION FOR INFORMATION SCIENCE). **Main/Corp** Canadian Association for Information Science. Ottawa Chapter. **VAT** Bulletin d'Ottawa. No. 3- Mar. 1977-. 0703-2137. Periodical. CN. English (includes some text in French). qt. Free to Members, Membership $15.00 Per Year. Canadian Association for Information Science, PO Box 2323 Station D, Ottawa Ontario K1P 5W5 Canada. **DD** 020.62271. *Ottawa Chapter Bulletin, 0384-742X.*

OUR LIBRARY PRESENTS . . . . **Main/Corp** United States International Trade Commission. Library. US. English. mo. The Library, United States International Trade Commission, Washington DC 20436. *Library News & Acquisitions.*

OUTLOOK ON RESEARCH LIBRARIES. Vol. 1, No. 1 (Oct. 1978)-. 0165-2818. Periodical. English. mo. $135.00. Elsevier Science Publishers, PO Box 211, 1000 AE Amsterdam Netherlands. **Tel** (212)867-9040. **Ind/Abst** Libr. Inf. Sci. Abstr. **LC** Z675.R45.

THE OUTRIDER. 0030-7319. Periodical. US. English. mo. Wyoming State Library, Supreme Court & State Library Building, Cheyenne WY 82001. **Tel** (307)777-5915. **Ed** Linn Rounds. **Circ** 1,550. News about the state library, other Wyoming libraries and the field in general.

THE OWLET. Began publication in 1960. 0030-7602. Periodical. US. English. bm. $2.00. Adron Summit County Public Library, 55 South Main Street, Akron OH 44326. **Tel** (216)762-7621. **Ed** Patricia H Latshaw. **Circ** 2,000. A newsletter published for the friends of the Akron-Summit County Public Library, governmental officials and the general public. It tells about library activities, new staff, and gives a complete calendar of library events.

P C L A NEWSLETTER. **Main/Corp** Polish Canadian Librarians Association. **VAT** Polish Canadian Librarians Association Newsletter. V. 1- July/Aug. 1977-. 0703-5527. Periodical. CN. English (Polish). bm. Free. Polish Canadian Librarians Association, c/o H Bednarska and R Clancy Cameron Library, University of Alberta, Edmonton Alberta T6G 2E1 Canada. **DD** 020.62271. (ctrl).

I P L O NEWS. **Main/Corp** Institute of Professional Librarians of Ontario. Began with Dec. 1971 issue. 0319-4442. Periodical. CN. English. Free. Institute of Professional Librarians of Ontario, 36B Prince Arthur Avenue, Toronto Ontario M5R 1A9 Canada. **DD** 020.6234713. (ctrl).

P-NOTES. 0378-7656. English. ir. 40.00. International Federation Documentation, PO Box 90402, 2509 LK The Hague Netherlands. **LC** Z696. **DD** 025.432. Proposals for revision and extension of the Universal Decimal System. *PE.*

PAGINAS DE CONTENIDO. **VFOAT** Ciencias de la Informacion. Periodical. CR. Spanish. ir. Aibda Apartado 74, Turrialba Costa Rica.

PAKISTAN LIBRARY BULLETIN. V. 1- Sept. 1968-. 0030-9966. Periodical. PK. English (Urdu). qt. 60.00. Library Promotion Bureau, University Karachi/PO Box 8421, Karachi 32 Pakistan. **Ed** M Adil Usmani. **Ind/Abst** Am. Hist. Life, Hist. Abstr., Part A, Mod. Hist. Abstr., Hist. Abst., Part B, Twent. Century Abstr., Libr. Inf. Sci. Abstr., Libr. Lit., Hist. Abstr. (cum index). bk rev. adv acc. **Circ** 1,500. (ctrl). Pakistan library bulletin, university library number school and childrens library number. *Pakistan Library Bulletin.*

PALLISER PAGES. V. 1, No. 1-. 0824-152X. Periodical. CN. English. ir. Free. Palliser Regional Library, PO Box 2500, Moose Jaw Saskatchewan S6H 6Y2 Canada. **DD** 027.471244. (ctrl).

PAMPHLETS. **Main/Corp** Library Association. No. 1- 1950-. Monographic Series. UK. English. ir.

PANDUAN PUSTAKAWAN. English or Malay. ir. Perpustakaan Negara Malaysia, Tingkat 7 Bangunan UMBC, Kuala Lumpur Malaysia. **LC** Z857.M35. **DD** 020.255951.

PAPER CONSERVATION NEWS. **VFOAT** PC News. V. 1- May 1973-. 0092-5497. Periodical. US. English. bm. $5.00. H Wayne Eley Associates, 15 Broadway, New Haven CT 06511. **LC** Z701. **DD** 025.84.

PAPERS OF THE . . . ANNUAL MEETING OF THE SEMINAR ON THE ACQUISITION OF LATIN AMERICAN LIBRARY MATERIALS. **Main/Conf** Seminar on the Acquisition of Latin American Library Materials. 26th (1981)-. US. English. an. *Final Report and Working Papers of the . . . Seminar on the Acquisition of Latin American Library Materials.*

PAPERS PRESENTED AT THE ALLERTON PARK INSTITUTE. (PAPERS). **Main/Corp** Allerton Park Institute. 1- 1956-. 0536-4604. US. English. an. University of Illinois, School of Library Science, Graduate School, 249 Armory Building, 505 East Armory Street, Champaign IL 61820. **Tel** (217)333-1359. **Ed** James S Dowling. Includes the collected papers presented at the annual Allerton Park Institute on various aspects of librarianship. Each volume is indexed.

LA PAROLA E IL LIBRO. Began in 1918. IT. Italian. mo. Societa Grafica Romana, Via Ignazio Pettinengo 39, 00159 Rome Italy. **LC** Z1035.4.

PAST AND LIKELY FUTURE OF 58 RESEARCH LIBRARIES, 1951-1980. (THE PAST AND LIKELY FUTURE OF 58 RESEARCH LIBRARIES, 1951-1980 : A STATISTICAL STUDY OF GROWTH AND CHANGE). **Main/Corp** Purdue University, Lafayette, Ind. Instructional Media Research Unit. 0092-7724. US. English. an. **LC** Z675.R45. **DD** 027.70973. **NLM** Z 675.R45 P291. *Past and Likely Future of 58 Research Libraries, 1951-1980: A Statistical Study of Growth and Change.*

PERFORMANCE BUDGET - DEPARTMENT OF PUBLIC LIBRARIES. **Main/Corp** Andhra Pradesh (India). Dept. of Public Libraries. English. ir. **LC** Z845.A5. **DD** 027.45484.

PERIODICAL HOLDINGS IN THE LIBRARIES OF THE ANCHORAGE AREA AND IN SOUTHEAST ALASKA LIBRARIES. 1972-. US. English. **LC** Z6945. **DD** 016.05.

PERIODICAL NOTES. 0882-4118. Periodical. US. English. mo. $5.00. Dallas Theological Seminary, Mosher Library, 3909 Swiss Avenue, Dallas TX 75204.

PERIODICALS CURRENTLY RECEIVED. **Main/Corp** Engineering Societies Library. **VFOAT** E.S.L. Periodicals Currently Received. 1978-. US. English. be. Engineering Societies Library, 345 East 47th Street, New York NY 10017. **Tel** (212)644-7611.

PERIODICALS NEWS - SCIENCE REFERENCE LIBRARY. **Main/Corp** British Library. Science Reference Library. UK. English. mo. Science Reference Library, 10 Porchester Gardens, London W2 4DE England. **LC** Z7403, Q158.5. **DD** 016.505.

PERMUTED MEDICAL SUBJECT HEADINGS. US. English. an. $17.00. National Technical Information Service, 5285 Port Royal Road, Springfield VA 22161. **Tel** (703)487-4650. **LC** Z695.1.M48. **DD** 025.4961. **NLM** Z 695.1 M4 M12.

PHARMACOCHEMISTRY LIBRARY. V. 1-. 0165-7208. Monographic Series. English. ir. Elsevier/North-Holland Inc, 52 Vanderbilt Avenue, New York NY 10017. **Ind/Abst** Chem. Abstr. **LC** UNC. **NLM** W1 PH272L. **CODEN** PHLIDQ.

PHILSOM/S: PERIODICAL HOLDINGS IN THE LIBRARY OF THE SCHOOL OF MEDICINE BY SUBJECT. **Main/Corp** Washington University, St. Louis, Mo. Libraries. Library of the School of Medicine. **VFOAT** Philsom/Philsoms. **VAT** Periodical Holdings in the Library of the School of Medicine by Subject. US. English. $6.00 Per Copy. Washington University, School of Medicine, Box 8132, 4580 Scott Avenue, St Louis MO 63110. **LC** Z6660, R129. **DD** 016.6105. **NLM** ZW 1 P573. *Library Publication Number One: Philsom, Periodical Holdings in the Library of the School of Medicine, Library Publication Number Two: Philsoms, Periodical Holdings in the Library of the School of Medicine by Subject.*

PHYSIQUE, CHIMIE. LEXIQUE. *See* Chemistry - Physical and Theoretical Chemistry.

PICTURESCOPE. V. 1- Feb. 1953-. 0031-9694. Periodical. US. English. qt. Free to members. L Cowan, Room 73 New York Public Library 5th Avenue & 42nd Street, New York NY 10018. **Ind/Abst** Art Archaeol. Tech. Abstr., Libr. Inf. Sci. Abstr. **LC** Z692.P5. **DD** 026.0005. (cum index).

PILS. **VFOAT** Pacific Information and Library Services Newsletter. V. 1- Spring 1977-. 0161-4517. Periodical. US. English. qt. Pacific Information and Library Services Newsletter, University of Hawaii at Manoa, School of Library Studies, Honolulu HI 96822. **Tel** (808)948-7321. **Ed** Miles M Jackson. bk rev. **Circ** 400. (ctrl). Newsletter of interest to practitioners in the Pacific Islands area.

PLA BULLETIN. **Main/Corp** Pennsylvania Library Association. **VAT** Pennsylvania Library Association Bulletin. V. 24- Jan. 1969-. 0197-9299. Periodical. US. English. ir. $12.00. Pennsylvania Library Association, 126 Locust Street, Harrisburg PA 17101. **Tel** (717)233-3113. **Ed** Tony Arms. **Ind/Abst** Libr. Lit. adv acc. **Circ** 2,000. (ctrl). Association news, current happenings in library and information science and events in libraries in Pennsylvania. *Bulletin-Pennsylvania Library Association.*

PLAFSEP. PROCESSING, LIBRARIES. ANECDOTES, FACETIAE, SATIRE, ETC. PERIODICALS. (PLAFSEP. PROCESSING (LIBRARIES)—ANECDOTES, FACETIAE, SATIRE, ETC.—PERIODICALS). **VFOAT** Processing (Libraries)—Anecdotes, Facetiae, Satire, etc.—Periodicals. V. 1- Nov. 1977-. 0149-6417. Periodical. US. English. Wellesley Free Library, Box 308, Wellesley MA 02181.

PLAIN TALK. **Main/Corp** Piedmont Libraries Acquisitions Information Network. **VAT** Piedmont Libraries Acquisitions Information Network Talk. V. 1-. 0148-4141. Periodical. US. English. qt. Free. The Editors, Plain Talk, Acquisitions Department, Duke University Library, Durham NC 27706.

PLANNING GUIDE. ESEA IV. PART B. LIBRARIES AND LEARNING RESOURCES. (PLANNING GUIDE ESEA IV, PART B : LIBRARIES AND LEARNING RESOURCES). **Main/Corp** New York (State). Bureau of School Libraries. **VAT** Planning Guide Elementary and Secondary Education Act Four, Part B: Libraries and Learning Resources. 0148-0413. US. English. University of the State of New York, State Education Department, Albany NY 12224. **LC** LB2825. **DD** 379.1510973.

Library and Information Science

PLUG IN. V. 1- Oct. 13, 1977-. 0704-0628. CN. English. Free. Midwestern Regional Library System, 637 Victoria Street North, Kitchener Ont N2H 5G4 Canada. **DD** 025.020971344. (ctrl).

PNLA QUARTERLY. Main/Corp Pacific Northwest Library Association. **VAT** Pacific Northwest Library Association Quarterly. V. 1- Oct. 1936-. 0030-8188. Periodical. US. English. qt. $15.00. Pacific Northwest Library Association, PO Box 5098, L M Carter and R Carter, Bellingham WA 98227. **Tel** (604)980-3254. **Ed** L M Carter and R Carter. **Ind/Abst** Ref. Source, Libr. Lit., Libr. Inf. Sci. Abstr. **LC** Z673.P11. **DD** 020.623. (cum index). bk rev. adv acc. **Circ** 1,200. Professional library journal serving all types of provinces in the Pacific Northwest.

POOLE'S INDEX TO PERIODICAL LITERATURE. *See* Indexes/Abstracts.

PORADNIK BIBLIOTEKARZA. Began publication with Oct. 1949 issue. 0032-4752. Periodical. PL. Polish. mo. ARS Polona, Krakowskie Przedmiescie 7, 00-068 Warsaw Poland. **Ind/Abst** Libr. Inf. Sci. Abstr. **LC** Z671.

POSITIVE. (POSITIVE : A NEWSLETTER FOR SLIDE AND PHOTOGRAPH CURATORS OF VISUAL ARTS IN CANADA). Vol. 1, No. 1 (Feb. 1977)-. 0229-9712. Periodical. CN. English. ir. $2.00. Positive, c/o B Messer, Visual Arts Department, University of Western Ontario, London Ontario N6A 5B7 Canada. **DD** 025.1773.

PRAPFALLS. (PRAPFALLS : NEWSLETTER OF THE PROVINCIAL/REGIONAL LIBRARY ASSOCIATION PRESIDENTS). Issue No. 1 (Jan. 1982)-. 0712-9726. Periodical. CN. English. ir. $10.00. Prapfalls, c/o Frances Morrison Library, 311 23rd Street, Saskatoon Saskatchewan S7K 0J6 Canada. **DD** 026.6230971.

PREVIEWS CEASED. V. 2, No. 4-V. 9, No. 4. 0000-0051. Periodical. US. English. mo. $17.00 Domestic, $19.00 Foreign. 1180 Avenue of the Americas, New York NY 10036. **Ind/Abst** Media Rev. Dig. **LC** Z689. **DD** 028.1. *Library Journal/School Library Journal Previews: News and Reviews of Non-Print Media.*

THE PRINCETON UNIVERSITY LIBRARY CHRONICLE. V. 1- Nov. 1939-. 0032-8456. Periodical. US. English. ir. $15.00. Rare Books Division, Princeton University, Library Chronicle, Princeton NJ 08544. **Ed** Patricia H Marks. **Ind/Abst** Am. Hist. Life, Hist. Abstr., Part A, Mod. Hist. Abstr., Hist. Abst., Part B, Twent. Century Abstr., Abstr. Engl. Stud., MLA Int. Bibliogr. Books Artic. Mod. Lang. Lit., Annu. Bibliogr. Engl. Lang. Lit., Writ. Am. Hist., Abstr. Engl. Stud., Hist. Abstr., Years Work Eng. Stud., Recent Publ. Artic. **LC** Z733.P93. **DD** 027.774967. (cum index). **Circ** 2,500. A scholarly journal publishing articles based upon research conducted in Firestone Library's Department of Rare Books and Special Collections. *Biblia.*

PRIVATE LIBRARY. (THE PRIVATE LIBRARY). V. 2-8, 1958-Winter 1967. 0032-8898. Periodical. UK. English. qt. $30.00. Private Library Association, 3 Hazelwood House, New River Crst, Palmers Green London N13 5RE England. **Ind/Abst** Abstr. Engl. Stud., Index Book Rev. Humanit., Libr. Lit. **LC** Z990. (cum index). *PLA Quarterly.*

PRO SE. Vol. 1, No. 1 (Apr. 12, 1984)-. Periodical. US. English.

PROBLEME DE INFORMARE SI DOCUMENTARE. VFOAT Information and Documentation Problems. 0032-924X. Periodical. RM. English and Romanian, with summaries in French and Russian. qt. Ilexim Press Department, PO Box 1-136-1-137, Bucharest Romania. **Ind/Abst** Comput. Control Abstr., Electr. Electron. Abstr., Sci. Abstr. Sect. A. Phys. Abstr., Libr. Inf. Sci. Abstr. **LC** Z1007. **DD** 029.7. **CODEN** PIDCA6.

PROCEEDINGS - CONFERENCE OF AUSTRALIAN PARLIMENTARY LIBRARIANS. Main/Conf Conference of Australian Parliamentary Librarians. English. ir. Australian Government Pub Service, PO Box 84, Canberra Australian Capital Territory 2600 Australia. **LC** Z675.G7. **DD** 027.594.

PROCEEDINGS - CONFERENCE ON FEDERAL INFORMATION RESOURCES. Main/Conf Conference on Federal Information Resources. **VFOAT** Federal Information Resources: Conference Proceedings. 1st- 1970-. US. English. an. Federal City College Press, Media Services Division, Washington DC 20001. **LC** Z675.G7. **DD** 027.50973.

PROCEEDINGS - EXECUTIVE CONFERENCE ON ORGANIZING AND MANAGING INFORMATION. Main/Conf Executive Conference on Organizing and Managing Information. 1957-. US. English. an. **Ed** S F Harper. **LC** Z675.B8. **DD** 026.65.

PROCEEDINGS OF THE ANNUAL CONFERENCE. Main/Corp Scottish Library Association. 0582-303X. UK. English. an. 4.00. Scottish Library Association, Motherwell Business Centre, Coursington Road, Motherwell ML1 1PW Scotland. **Tel** (0698) 52526. **Ed** Alan F Taylor. **LC** Z673. adv acc. **Circ** 500. The publication contains the papers given at the Annual Conference of the Annual Conference of the Scottish Library Association.

PROCEEDINGS OF THE ANNUAL CONFERENCE - ASSOCIATION OF CANADIAN MAP LIBRARIES. *See* Geography.

PROCEEDINGS OF THE ASIS ANNUAL MEETING. Main/Corp American Society for Information Science. **VAT** Proceedings of the American Society for Information Science Annual Meeting. V. 11- 1974-. 0044-7870. US. English. an. Knowledge Industry Publishing Inc, 701 Westchester Avenue, White Plains NY 10604. **Tel** (914)328-9157. **Ed** Carol Parkhurst. **Ind/Abst** Eng. Index Annu., Eng. Index Mon., Eng. Index Bioeng. Abstr., Eng. Index Energy Abstr., Chem. Abstr. **NLM** Z 699.A1 A508P. **CODEN** PAISDQ. Papers and abstracts from the annual meeting, American Society for Information Science, 1985. *Proceedings of the American Society for Information Science, 0160-0044.*

PROCEEDINGS OF THE CLINIC ON LIBRARY APPLICATIONS OF DATA PROCESSING. Main/Conf Clinic on Library Applications of Data Processing. **VFOAT** Library Applications of Data Processing. 1st- 1963-. 0069-4789. US. English. an. University of Illinois at Urbana-Champaign, Graduate School of Library Science, Urbana-Champaign IL 61801. **Ed** H Goldhor. **LC** Z678.9.A1. **NLM** Z 678.9.A1 C641P. Each issue contains an index to its own contents - no vol index - loose.

PROCEEDINGS OF THE NORTHERN LIBRARIES COLLOQUY. Main/Conf Northern Libraries Colloquy. 0702-0147. CN. English. Arctic Institute of North America, 1020 Pine Avenue West, Montreal Quebec H3A 1A2 Canada. **LC** Z6005.P7, G606. **DD** 016.9198.

PROCEEDINGS OF THE PUBLIC LIBRARIES BOARD STAFF CONFERENCE AND SEMINAR. Main/Corp Uganda. Public Libraries. Board. English. ir. Public Libraries Board, PO Box 4262, Kampala Uganda. **LC** Z857. **DD** 027.46761.

PROCEEDINGS, PAPERS AND SUMMARIES OF DISCUSSIONS AT THE . . . CONFERENCE. Main/Corp Library Association. **VFOAT** Proceedings of the Annual Conference. UK. English. an. Library Association, 7 Ridgmount St, London WC1E 7AE England. **LC** Z673.L7. **DD** 020.622.

PROFESSIONAL DOCUMENT RETRIEVAL. 8755-0253. Periodical. US. English. qt. $15.00. The Information Store Inc, 5th Floor Publishing Division 140 Second Street, San Francisco CA 94105. **Tel** (415)543-4636. **Ed** Michael R Kennedy. bk rev. **Circ** 250. Newsletter reporting on the state of the art of document retrieval, including sources and services, technology, management, and legal issues.

PROGNOZIROVANIE RAZVITIIA BIBLIOTECHNOGO DELA V SSSR. Main/Corp Moscow. Publichnaia Biblioteka. Nauchno-Issledovatelskii Otdel Bibliotekovedeniia i Teorii Bibliografii. Vol. 1- 1972-. UR. Russian. 0.53 Each Issue. **LC** Z819.A1.

PROGRAM. V. 13- 1979-. Periodical. UK. English. qt. ASLIB Publications, Information House, 26/27 Boswell Street, London WC1N 3JZ England. **Tel** 430 2671. **Ed** Lucy Tedd. bk rev. adv acc. **Circ** 1,600. Devoted to all aspects of the use of computers in libraries, including networks information systems, databases, data structures, file compaction hardware and software developments. *Program.*

PROGRAM - CANADIAN LIBRARY ASSOCIATION CONFERENCE. (PROGRAM - CANADIAN LIBRARY ASSOCIATION, CONFERENCE). **Main/Corp** Canadian Library Association. Began publication 1946?. 0381-1476. CN. English. an. Free. Canadian Library Association, 151 Sparks Street, Ottawa Ontario K1P 5E3 Canada. **DD** 020.62271.

PROGRESS REPORT - COUNCIL OF FEDERAL LIBRARIES. COMMITTEE ON CLASSIFICATION. (PROGRESS REPORT). **Main/Corp** Council of Federal Libraries (Canada). Committee on Classification. **VFOAT** Rapport d'Etape. **VAT** Rapport d'Etape - Conseil des Bibliotheques du Gouvernement Federal Comite de la Classification. 0826-1911. CN. English (with French on inverted pages). **DD** 023.700971.

PROGRESS REPORT - F.I.A.B. (PROGRESS REPORT). **Main/Corp** International Federation of Library Associations. **VAT** Progress Report - Federation Internationale de Associations de Bibliothecaires. 0377-7693. English. ir. Netherlands Congress Building Tower, 3rd Floor, POB 9128, Hague the Netherlands. **LC** Z672. **DD** 020.621.

PROGRESS REPORT - STATE UNIVERSITY OF NEW YORK AT BUFFALO. HEALTH SCIENCES LIBRARY. Main/Corp State University of New York at Buffalo. Health Sciences Library. US. English. State University of New York at Buffalo, Buffalo NY 14214. **LC** Z733.S837. **DD** 026.610974797.

PROJECT. PROGRESS NEWSLETTER. (PROJECT : PROGRESS NEWSLETTER). 1- 1976-. 0702-8032. Periodical. CN. English. ir. Free. Canadian Library Association, 151 Sparks Street, Ottawa Ontario K1P 5E3 Canada. **DD** 027.471.

PRZEGLAD BIBLIOTECZNY. Vol. 1- 1927-. 0033-202X. PL. Polish. qt. ARS Polona, Krakowskie Przedmiescie 7, 00-068 Warsaw Poland. **Ind/Abst** Libr. Inf. Sci. Abstr. **LC** Z671. *Przeglad Biblioteczny.*

PRZEGLAD PISMIENNICTWA ZAGADNIEN INFORMACJI. PL. Polish. bm. ARS Polona, Krakowskie Prezediescie 7, 00-068 Warsaw Poland.

PUBLIC LIBRARIES. V. 17- Spring 1978-. 0163-5506. Periodical. US. English. qt. $18.00. PLA, 50 East Huron Street, Chicago IL 60611. **Tel** (312)944-6780. **Ind/Abst** Libr. Inf. Sci. Abstr., Libr. Lit. **LC** Z731. **DD** 027.473. bk rev. adv acc. **Circ** Yes. Articles and regular features on public library services. Includes book review column. *PLA Newsletter, 0022-6998.*

PUBLIC LIBRARIES IN QUEENSLAND, STATISTICAL BULLETIN. *See* Statistics.

PUBLIC LIBRARY ABSTRACTS. *See* Indexes/Abstracts.

PUBLIC LIBRARY EXPENDITURE IN SCOTLAND. UK. English. an. Scottish Library Association, Motherwell Business Centre, Coursington Road, Motherwell ML1 1PW Scotland. **Tel** (0698)52526. **Ed** EN Drummond. **LC** Z791.S35. **DD** 025.1109411. **Circ** 80. (ctrl). A summary and analysis of forthcoming expenditure by the 41 local authorities in Scotland with responsibility for library services.

PUBLIC LIBRARY PROGRAM GUIDELINES. Main/Corp National Endowment for the Humanities. Division of Public Programs. 1978/79-. 0195-6922. US. English. an. National Endowment for the Humanities, Division of Public Programs, Public Library Program, 806 15th Street NW, Mail Stop 406, Washington DC 20506. **LC** Z731. **DD** 021.83.

PUBLIC LIBRARY QUARTERLY. V. 1- Spring 1979-. 0161-6846. Periodical. US. English. qt. $24.00 Domestic, $29.00 Canada. Haworth Press, 149 Fifth Avenue, New York NY 10010. **Ind/Abst** Libr. Inf. Sci. Abstr., Libr. Lit.

PUBLIC LIBRARY STATISTICS. *See* Statistics.

PUBLIC LIBRARY STATISTICS . . . ESTIMATES. *See* Statistics.

PUBLICATIONS CLEARING HOUSE BULLETIN. Began with V. 1 (1978) issue. 0734-9106. Periodical. US. English. ty. $5.00. M Miller Sears Law Library, SUNY Amherst Campus, Buffalo NY 14260. **LC** Z675.L2. **DD** 025.218634973.

PUBLICATIONS IN LIBRARIANSHIP. Main/Corp University of California, Berkeley. V. 1-. Monographic Series. US. English. ir. University of California Press, 2120 Berkeley Way, Berkeley CA 94720. **Tel** (415)642-4191.

PUBLICATIONS RESOURCE MANUAL. Main/Corp Illinois. Office of the Superintendent of Public Instruction. Publications and Library

Library and Information Science

Resources Section. 0094-2987. US. English. Publications Section, 325 South 5th Street, Springfield IL 62706. **LC** Z5819. **DD** 016.37.

QUARTERLY BULLETIN OF RECENT ACCESSIONS. Main/Corp Kern County Free Library, Bakersfield, Calif. V. 1- Jan. 1920-. Periodical. US. English. qt. Kern County Free Library, 1315 Truxtum Street, Bakersfield CA 93301. **LC** Z881.B14. **DD** 017.1.

QUARTERLY BULLETIN OF THE SOUTH AFRICAN LIBRARY. Main/Corp South African Library. **VFOAT** Kwartaalblad van die Suid-Afrikaanse Biblioteek. V. 1- Sept. 1946-. 0038-2418. Periodical. SA. English (Afrikaans). qt. 15. South African Public Library, PO Box 496, Cape Town 8000 South Africa. **Tel** 1,000. **Ed** P E Westra. **Ind/Abst** Am. Hist. Life, Hist. Abstr., Part A, Mod. Hist. Abstr., Hist. Abst., Part B, Twent. Century Abstr., Libr. Inf. Sci. Abstr., Recent Publ. Artic., Hist. Abstr. **LC** Z965. **DD** 027.468. (cum index). adv acc. (ctrl). Africana (biography and bibliography) cape, and social history collections of the South African library.

QUARTERLY JOURNAL OF RLA. Main/Corp Rejasthan Library Association. **VFOAT** Rajasthana Pustakalaya Sangha Patrika. **VAT** Quarterly Journal of Rajasthan Library Association. V. 1- Mar. 1974-. Periodical. English or Hindi. ir. 191 Motimarg Bupunagar, Jaipur 302004 India. **LC** Z845.R34.

QUARTERLY JOURNAL OF THE LIBRARY OF CONGRESS CEASED. (THE QUARTERLY JOURNAL OF THE LIBRARY OF CONGRESS). Began with V. 21, 1964. Ceased with V. 40, No. 4 (Fall 1983). 0041-7939. Periodical. US. English. qt. Library of Congress, 10 First Street Southeast, Washington DC 20540. **Ind/Abst** Abstr. Engl. Stud., Libr. Inf. Sci. Abstr., Index U.S. Gov. Period., Public Aff. Inf. Serv. Bull., Writ. Am. Hist., Recent Publ. Artic. **NLM** Z 881 U582Q. *Quarterly Journal of Current Acquisitions, 0090-0095.*

QUARTERLY JOURNAL OF THE LIBRARY OF CONGRESS. Main/Corp United States. Library of Congress. V. 1- July/Sept. 1943-. 0041-7939. Periodical. US. English. qt. $6.45. Superintendent of Documents, US Government Printing Office, Washington DC 20402. **LC** Z881.U49. **DD** 051.

QUEBEC/AMERIQUE. Vol. 1, No. 1-. 0708-3130. CN. French. sa. $1.00 Each Number. Quebec/Amerique, Bureau 801, 450 East rue Sherbrooke, Montreal Quebec H2L 1J8 Canada. **DD** 028.105.

QUEENS COLLEGE STUDIES IN LIBRARIANSHIP. No. 1-. 0146-8677. Monographic Series. US. English. Queens College Press, G-101 Queens College, Flushing NY 11367.

QUICK SILVER MESSENGER SERVICE. (QUICK SILVER MESSENGER SERVICE : NEWSLETTER OF THE YOUNG ADULT CAUCUS OF THE SASKATCHEWAN LIBRARY ASSOCIATION). Vol. 1, No. 1 (Spring 1981)-. 0711-1460. Periodical. CN. English. ty. 5.00. Young Adult Caucus of the Saskatchewan Library Association, PO Box 3388, Regina Saskatchewan S4P 3H1 Canada. **Tel** 569-7774. **Ed** Ken Vaughan. **DD** 027.62605. bk rev. **Circ** 50. (ctrl). Issues affecting young adult library service, reviews of Canadian materials for young adults, information of conferences, workshops, people who work with youth.

QUILL, QUEENSLAND INTER-LIBRARY LIAISON. VFOAT Queensland Inter-Library Liaison, QUILL. V. 1- June 1960-. Periodical. AT. English. qt. $0.15 Single Issue. Queensland Branch of the Library Association of Australia, William Street, Brisbane 4000 Australia. **LC** Z870.Q44. **DD** 021.009943.

R & D PROJECTS IN DOCUMENTATION AND LIBRARIANSHIP. Main/Corp International Federation for Documentation. **VFOAT** R & D Projects. **VAT** R and D Projects in Documentation and Librarianship. V.1- 1971-. 0301-4436. Periodical. English. bm. 85.00. International Federation Documentation, PO Box 90402, 2509 LK The Hague Netherlands. **Ed** E de Regt. **Circ** 425. Includes information on publications which are devoted inpart or totally to publishing data on research and development projects in librarianship, documentation information science, archivalship records management as well as related fields.

RADIALS BULLETIN CEASED. **VAT** Research and Development - Information and Library Science Bulletin. 1974-1982, No. 2. 0302-2706. UK. English. sa. Library Association, 7 Ridgmount and Store Street, London WC1E 7AE England. **LC** Z699.7. **DD** 020.72.

RAIBURARIANZU FORAMU. VFOAT Librarians Forum. Vol. 1, No. 1 (Spring 1984)-. 0289-5420. Periodical. JA. Japanese. qt. 2520. Nihon Fakuson Kabushiki Kaisha, 8-ban 1-go Shinjuku 7-chome, Tokyo-to 106 Japan.

RAPPORT ANNUAL - CORPORATION DES BIBLIOTHECAIRES PROFESSIONNELS DU QUEBEC. (RAPPORT ANNUEL). **Main/Corp** Corporation des Bibliothecaires Professionnels du Quebec. **VFOAT** Annual Report. 8E(1977)- . -. 0226-8019. CN. French (English). an. Corporation des Bibliothecaires, Professionnels du Quebec, 360 rue Lemoyne, Montreal Quebec H2Y 1Y3 Canada. **DD** 020.6234714. *Rapports Annuels, 0228-6505.*

RAPPORT ANNUEL - SOCIETE QUEBECOISE D'INFORMATION JURIDIQUE. (RAPPORT ANNUEL). **Main/Corp** Societe Quebecoise d'Information Juridique. **VAT** SOQUIJ Rapport Annuel, Rapport Annuel - SOQUIJ. 1976/77-. 0710-6394. CN. French. an. Societe Quebecoise d'Information Juridique, 276 rue St Jacques/Suite 310, Montreal Quebec H2Y 1N3. **DD** 026.349714.

RAPPORT D'ACTIVITE - CENTRE D'ETUDES DES SYSTEMES D'INFORMACION DES ADMINISTRATIONS (FRANCE). Main/Corp Centre d'Etudes des Systemes d'Information des Administrations (France). FR. French. ir. Centre d'Etudes des Systemes d'Information des Administrations/Zac de Bonneveine, 122 Av de Hambourg, 13008 Marseille France.

RAPPORT D'ACTIVITES - BIBLIOTHEQUE ADMINISTRATIVE. MINISTERE DES COMMUNICATIONS. (LA BIBLIOTHEQUE ADMINISTRATIVE : RAPPORT D'ACTIVITES POUR . . .). **Main/Corp** Quebec (Province). Ministere des Communications. Bibliotheque Administrative. 0710-0582. CN. French. an. Gouvernement du Quebec, 600 St Amable 4E Etage, Quebec G1R 4Z1 Canada. **DD** 027.5714. *Rapport d'Activites, 0710-0582.*

RAPPORT D'ACTIVITES - LA BIBLIOTHEQUE ADMINISTRATIVE. Main/Corp Quebec (Province). Direction Generale de l'Edition Gouvernementale. Bibliotheque Administrative. CN. French. l'Editeur Officiel du Quebec, 1283 West Boul Charest, Quebec Quebec G1N 2C9 Canada. **LC** Z736. **DD** 027.5714.

RAPPORT DU SERVICE DE LA BIBLIOTHEQUE DE L'UNIVERSITE DU QUEBEC A CHICOUTIMI. (RAPPORT DU SERVICE DE LA BIBLIOTHEQUE DE L'UNIVERSITE DU QUEBEC A CHICOUTIMI POUR L'ANNEE . . .). **Main/Corp** Universite du Quebec a Chicoutimi. Bibliotheque. 1980/81-. 0822-4986. CN. French. an. Bibliotheque de l'Universite du Quebec a Chicoutimi, 555 Boul de l'Universite, Chicoutimi Quebec G7H 2B1 Canada. **DD** 027.771416.

RAPPORT - NORTH CENTRAL REGIONAL LIBRARY SYSTEM. (RAPPORT). **Main/Corp** North Central Regional Library System (Ont.). 0715-5867. Periodical. CN. English. bw. Free. North Central Regional Library System, 334 Regent Street South, Sudbury Ont P3C 4E2 Canada. **DD** 027.4713. (ctrl).

RARE BIRD. V. 1, No. 3- Mar. 1972-. 0380-2566. Periodical. CN. English. ir. c/o M Brown, 101-7201 Granville Street, Vancouver British Columbia V5W 1V8 Canada. *Congregational Libraries Newsletter, 0380-2574.*

RASD UPDATE. Main/Corp American Library Association. Reference and Adult Services Division. **VAT** Reference and Adult Services Division Update. V. 1- May/June 1980-. 0198-8344. Periodical. US. English. bm. $6.00. American Library Association, 50 East Huron Street, Chicago IL 60611. **Tel** (312)944-6780. **Ed** Steven Atkinson. **Circ** 4,800. Official newsletter of the American Library Association Reference and Adult Services Division. News of the division and about related activities. *Messages from Mars, 0163-0237.*

RAYON. (LE RAYON). V. 1, No. 2, (Dec. 1981)-. 0715-8912. Periodical. CN. French. ir. Free to Residents. Bibliotheque Centrale de Pret des Laurentides, C P 239, Ste Agathe des Monts Quebec J8C 3A3 Canada. **DD** 027.471422. *Qui Suis-Je? (Sainte-Agathe-des-Monts, Quebec), 0822-0565.*

RECENT ADDITIONS - MUNICIPAL REFERENCE LIBRARY. (RECENT ADDITIONS). **Main/Corp** Chicago (Ill.). Municipal Reference Library. Began with April 1958 issue. 0300-7081. US. English. mo. Municipal Reference Library, Room 1004/City Hall, Chicago IL 60602. **LC** Z881.C53. **DD** 011.34. *Selected List of New Books in the Municipal Reference Library.*

RED TAPE (DETROIT, MICH.). (RED TAPE). **VFOAT** Redtape. No. 1 (Jan.-Feb. 1979)-. 0735-7427. Periodical. US. English. ir. Godort-Michigan, c/o Detroit Public Library, 5201 Woodward Avenue, Detroit MI 48202. **LC** Z688.G6. **DD** 015.77453.

REFER. (REFER : JOURNAL OF THE RSIS). Vol. 1, No. 1 (Spring 1980)-. 0144-2384. Periodical. UK. English. sa. 3.00 Nonmembers Foreign. Mrs F V Winkworth, RSIS Sales Agent, 16 Springfield Ovington, Northumberland NE42 6EH England. **Ind/Abst** Libr. Inf. Sci. Abstr. **LC** Z711. **DD** 025.520941.

REFERENCE BOOKS BULLETIN. 8755-0962. Periodical. US. English. an. American Library Association, 50 East Huron Street, Chicago IL 60611. **DD** 028. *Reference and Subscription Book Reviews, 0080-0430.*

THE REFERENCE LIBRARIAN. No. 1/2 (Fall/Winter 1981)-. 0276-3877. Periodical. US. English. sa. $75.00. Haworth Press, 28 East 22nd Street, New York NY 10010. **Tel** (212)228-2800. **Ed** Bill Katz, Gordon Stevenson and Ruth Fraley. **Ind/Abst** Electron. Commun. Abstr. J., ISMEC Bull., Pollut. Abstr. Indexes, Saf. Sci. Abstr. J., Comput. Control Abstr., Electr. Electron. Abstr., Sci. Abstr. Sect. A. Phys. Abstr., Libr. Inf. Sci. Abstr. **LC** Z711. **DD** 025.52. **CODEN** RELBD6. adv acc. **Circ** 847. Each issue deals with a particular topic that is of current concern, interest, and practical value for the practicing reference librarian.

REFERENCE SERIES. Main/Corp University of Toronto. Library. Reference Dept. Monographic Series. CN. English. ir. University Toronto Library, Toronto Ontario Canada.

REFLECTIONS. V. 4, No. 1- 1976-. 0384-0697. Periodical. CN. English. Lakeland Library Region, 1791 110th Street, PO Box 813, North Battleford Saskatchewan S9A 2Y2 Canada. **DD** 027.471242. *0384-0689.*

REGARD SUR LA BIBLIOTHEQUE DU COLLEGE DE L'ASSOMPTION. Main/Corp College de l'Assomption. Bibliotheque. No. 1 (Sept. 1983)-. 0822-2983. Periodical. CN. French. mo. Free. Bibliotheque College de l'Assomption, 270 Boulevard, l'Ange-Gardien l'Assomption Quebec J0K 1G0 Canada. **DD** 027.7714416.

REGISTER OF INDEXERS. *See* Indexes/Abstracts.

REGISTER OVER GALLANDE SFS-FORFATTNINGAR. Swedish. ir. Allmana Forlaget, Fack 103, 10 2 Stockholm Sweden. **DD** 016.34009485.

REGLEMENTS - A S T E D. Main/Corp Asted. 1973-. 0384-5095. CN. French. Free to Members. ASTED, 360 rue Lemoyne, Montreal Quebec H2Y 1Y3 Canada. **DD** 020.6234714. *Reglements et Reglements Administratifs de l'Association Canadienne des Bibliothecaires de Langue Francaise, 0228-6424.*

REGLES DE CATALOGAGE ANGLO-AMERICAINE. VERSION FRANCAISE. BULLETIN. (REGLES DE CATALOGAGE ANGLO-AMERICAINE, VERSION FRANCAISE). No. 1- June 1974-. 0318-8000. Periodical. CN. French. Association pour l'Avancement des Sciences et des Techniques de la Documentation, 360 rue le Moyne, Montreal Quebec H2Y 1Y3 Canada. **DD** 025.3205.

REMARC DATABASE NEWS. VFOAT R.E.M.A.R.C. Database News. Vol. 1, No. 1 (Mar. 1981)-. 0732-4812. Periodical. US. English. Carrollton Press Inc, 1611 North Kent Street/Suite 910, Arlington VA 22209. **Tel** (703)525-5940. **Ind/Abst** Libr. Inf. Sci. Abstr.

REPORT - DELHI. PUBLIC LIBRARY. Main/Corp Delhi. Public Library. 1951/52-. 0418-5749. II. English. ir. New Delhi Public Library/Delhi Library Board, New Delhi India.

REPORT - DIVISION OF LIBRARY DEVELOPMENT AND SERVICES, MARYLAND STATE DEPARTMENT OF EDUCATION. (REPORT - DIVISION OF LIBRARY DEVELOPMENT AND SERVICES). **Main/Corp** Maryland. Division of Library Development and

Library and Information Science

Services. 0147-5703. US. English. Maryland Department of Education, PO Box 8717, Friendship International, Baltimore MD 21240. **LC** Z678.4.M3. **DD** 021.09752.

REPORT - DUBLIN. NATIONAL LIBRARY OF IRELAND. COUNCIL OF TRUSTEES. **Main/Corp** Dublin. National Library of Ireland. Council of Trustees. English. ir. -/-/7 1/2. Stationery Office, Government Publications Sales Office, GPO Arcade 1, Dublin Ireland. **LC** Z792. **DD** 027.5415.

REPORT FROM THE LIBRARIES. NIGERIA. UNIVERSITY, NSUKKA. **Main/Corp** Nigeria. University, Nsukka. English. ir. University of Nigeria, Lusaka Zambia. **LC** Z858.N67. **DD** 027.7669.

REPORT - GREATER LONDON RECORD OFFICE AND LIBRARY. See Genealogy and Heraldry - Archives.

REPORT - MELBOURNE. UNIVERSITY. LIBRARY. **Main/Corp** Melbourne. University. Library. AT. English. ir. Melbourne University Press, PO Box 278, Carlton South Victoria 3053 Australia. **LC** Z871. **DD** 027.794.

REPORT OF ACCESSIONS. **Main/Corp** Houghton Library. US. English. Harvard College Library, Wadsworth House, Cambridge MA 02138. **LC** Z733.H341. **DD** 016.09.

REPORT OF THE ANNUAL CONFERENCE - SASKATCHEWAN LIBRARY ASSOCIATION. (REORT OF THE ANNUAL CONFERENCE). **Main/Corp** Saskatchewan Library Association. May 1983-. 0828-5578. CN. English. an. Saskatchewan Library Association, c/o Saskatoon Public Library, 311 23rd Street East, Saskatoon Saskatchewan S7K 0J6 Canada. **DD** 020.62347124. Proceedings of the Annual Conference, 0703-8313.

REPORT OF THE DIRECTOR OF LIBRARIES (OREGON). **Main/Corp** Oregon. State Board of Higher Education. 1944/46-. US. English. be. **LC** Z732.O8.

REPORT OF THE DIRECTOR OF UNIVERSITY LIBRARIES TO THE VICE PRESIDENT OF UNIVERSITY SERVICES. (REPORT OF THE DIRECTOR OF UNIVERSITY LIBRARIES TO THE VICE PRESIDENT OF UNIVERSITY SERVICES - STATE UNIVERSITY OF NEW YORK AT BUFFALO). **Main/Corp** State University of New York at Buffalo. University Libraries. 8756-2782. US. English. an. **LC** Z733.S837. **DD** 027.774797.

REPORT OF THE DIVISION OF LIBRARY, ARCHIVES AND PUBLIC RECORDS - ARIZONA. **Main/Corp** Arizona. Division of Library, Archives and Public Records. 62d-1973/74-. 0360-0211. US. English. an. **LC** Z733. **DD** 353.979100852.

REPORT OF THE LIBRARIAN. **Main/Corp** Louisville Presbyterian Theological Seminary (1901-) Library. US. English. an. Louisville Presbyterian Theological Seminary, 1044 Alta Vista Road, Louisville KY 40205. **LC** Z733. **DD** 026.2.

REPORT OF THE LIBRARIAN. **Main/Corp** Gregg-Graniteville Library. **VFOAT** USC Aiken Library Report. US. English. an. Library, University of South Carolina at Aiken, 171 University Parkway, Aiken SC 29801. **Tel** (803)648-6821. **Ed** Frankie H Cubbedge. **LC** Z733.G84. **DD** 027.775775. (ctrl). Report of the library's activities for the fiscal year. Includes narrative and statistical sections.

REPORT OF THE LIBRARIAN TO THE PRESIDENT. **Main/Corp** Allegheny College, Meadville, Pa. Library. US. English. an. Allegheny College, Library, Meadville PA 16335. **LC** Z733. **DD** 027.7748.

REPORT OF THE LIBRARY SCIENCE DEPARTMENT. **Main/Corp** Karachi. University. Dept. of Library Science. PK. English. ir. Univ of Karachi, Department of Library Science, Karachi 32 Pakistan. **LC** Z669.5.P3. **DD** 027.7549183.

REPORT OF THE STATE LIBRARY OF TASMANIA. **Main/Corp** Tasmanian Library Board. 1st- Jan./June 1944-. AT. English. an. Tasmanian Government Printer, GPO Box 307C, Hobart Tasmania 7000 Australia. **LC** Z871. **DD** 027.5946.

REPORT OF THE TRUSTEES OF THE NATIONAL LIBRARY OF NEW ZEALAND AND OF THE NATIONAL LIBRARIAN. **Main/Corp** National Library of New Zealand. English. ir. Natl Library of New Zealand, Private Bag 44 The Terrace, Wellington 1 New Zealand. **LC** Z871.N36. **DD** 027.593127.

REPORT ON THE LIBRARY. **Main/Corp** University of Western Australia. Library. 1960-. AT. English. an. 15.00. University of Western Australia, PO Box 6075 Hay Street East, Perth Western Australia 6009 Australia. **Tel** (09)325-7686. **Ed** Adrian Kenyon. **LC** Z871. **DD** 027.7941. bk rev. adv acc. **Circ** 5,000. (ctrl). General interest music magazine, about all aspects of music in Western Australia.

REPORT ON THE NATIONAL LIBRARY SERVICE. **Main/Corp** Botswana National Library Service. English. ir. Botswana National Library Service, Private Bag 36, Gaberones Botswana Africa. **LC** Z857.B68. **DD** 021.009681.

REPORT - SIERRA LEONE. LIBRARY BOARD. **Main/Corp** Sierra Leone. Library Board. English. ir. **LC** Z858.

REPORT - SWARTHMORE COLLEGE, SWARTHMORE, PENNSYLVANIA. **Main/Corp** Swarthmore College, Swarthmore, Pennsylvania Library. US. English. an. Swarthmore College, Swarthmore PA 19081. **LC** Z733. **DD** 027.7748.

REPORT TO SENATE - UNIVERSITY OF MALAWI. LIBRARIES. **Main/Corp** University of Malawi. Libraries. English. ir. University of Malawi Libraries, PO Box 280, Zomba Malawi. **LC** Z858.U46. **DD** 027.76897. Report to the Senate on the University Libraries.

A REPORT TO THE COMMUNITY. **Main/Corp** John Crerar Library, Chicago. 0272-8613. US. English. Natl Trans Center, 35 West 33rd Street, Chicago IL 60616. **LC** Z881.C52. **DD** 026.000977311.

REPORT TO THE PUBLIC PRINTER. **Main/Corp** Depository Library Council to the Public Printer (U.S.). Began with 1st, 1972/76. 0191-3824. US. English. an. US Government Printing Office, Superintendent of Documents, Washington DC 20402. **LC** Z675.D4. **DD** 027.50973.

REPORT - UNIVERSITY OF COLORADO. LIBRARIES. **Main/Corp** University of Colorado. Libraries. 0069-6161. Periodical. US. English. an. University of Colorado, Campus Box 450, Boulder CO 80309.

REPORT - WASHINGTON UNIVERSITY (ST. LOUIS, MO.). **Main/Corp** Washington Unviersity (St. Louis, Mo.). Libraries. US. English. an. Washington University, St Louis MO 63130. **LC** Z733. **DD** 027.7778.

REPORTER. 0277-6537. Periodical. US. English. ir. Mid-York Library System, 16 Lincoln Avenue, Utica NY 13502.

RESEARCH COLLECTIONS IN CANADIAN LIBRARIES. **VFOAT** Collection de Recherche des Bibliotheques Canadiennes. 0316-0319. Monographic Series. CN. English. Ottawa Resources Survey Division, Supply & Services, Ottawa Ontario K1A 0S9 Canada. **DD** 021.00971.

THE RESEARCH LIBRARIES GROUP NEWS. **VFOAT** RLG News. Issue No. 1- July 1980-. 0196-173X. Periodical. US. English. ty. The Research Libraries Group Inc, Jordon Quadrangle, Stanford CA 94305. RLIN Newsletter, 0163-2388.

RESEARCH LIBRARIES IN OCLC. **VFOAT** Research Libraries in O.C.L.C. No. 1 (Jan. 1981)-. 0273-2351. Periodical. US. English. qt. OCLC, 6565 Frantz Road, Dublin OH 43017. **Ind/Abst** Libr. Inf. Sci. Abstr. **LC** Z674.82.O15. **DD** 027.70973.

RESEARCH LIBRARY, RECENT ACQUISITIONS CEASED. **Main/Corp** Board of Governors of the Federal Reserve System (U.S.). No. -455. 0145-0301. Periodical. US. English. sm.

RESEARCH STRATEGIES. (RESEARCH STRATEGIES : RS). **VFOAT** RS. Vol. 1, No. 1 (Winter 1983)-. 0734-3310. Periodical. US. English. qt $32.00. Mountainside Publishing Company, PO Box 8330, Ann Arbor MI 48107. **Tel** (313)662-3925. **Ed** Sharon Hogan. **Ind/Abst** Libr. Inf. Sci. Abstr., Libr. Lit. **LC** Z675.U5. **DD** 025.5677. bk rev. adv acc. (ctrl). A journal of library concepts and instruction.

RESEARCH STUDIES IN LIBRARY SCIENCE. No. 1-. 0080-1739. Monographic Series. US. English. ir. Libraries Unlimited, Box 263, Littleton CO 80160. **Tel** (303)770-1220. **LC** Z674. Monographic series.

RESOURCE CATALOGUE. **Main/Corp** Alberta. Provincial Film Library. 0823-3306. CN. English. Provincial Film Library, Audio Visual Services Branch, Public Affairs Bureau, 11510 Kingsway Avenue, Edmonton Alberta T5G 2Y5 Canada.

RESOURCE SHARING & INFORMATION NETWORKS. **VFOAT** Resource Sharing and Information Networks. Vol. 1, No. 1/2 (Fall/Winter 1983)-. 0737-7797. Periodical. US. English. qt. $75.00. Haworth Press Inc, 28 East 22nd Street, New York NY 10010. **Tel** (212)228-2800. **Ed** Wilson Luguire. **Ind/Abst** Electron. Commun. Abstr. J., ISMEC Bull., Pollut. Abstr. Indexes, Saf. Sci. Abstr. J., Comput. Inf. Syst. Abstr. J., Excerpta Med., Libr. Inf. Sci. Abstr., Resour. Educ. **LC** Z672. **DD** 021.6505. adv acc. **Circ** 592. Provides a forum for ideas on the basic theoretical and practical problems faced by planners, practitioners, and users of network services. Resource Sharing & Library Networks, 0270-3173.

RESOURCES IN LIBRARY AND INFORMATION SCIENCE. No. 1- Mar. 1978-. 0197-4742. Periodical. US. English. mo. Office of Public Libraries and Interlibrary Cooperation, 301 Hanover Building, 480 Cedar Street, St Paul MN 55101. Professional Resources for Librarians, 0193-7731.

RESUMEN DE ACTIVIDADES - COMISION NACIONAL PARA LA ORGANIZACION DEL SISTEMA NACIONAL DE SERVICIOS DE BIBLIOTECAS E INFORMATION HUMANISTICA, CIENTIFICA Y TECNOLOGICA. **Main/Corp** Venezuela. Comision Nacional para la Organizacion del Sistema Nacional de Servicios de Bibliotecas e Informacion Humanistica, Cientifica y Tecnologica. 1977-. Spanish. ir. **LC** Z678.8.V4.

RETRIEVAL CODE INDEX - DATA RESOURCES OF CANADA. See Indexes/Abstracts.

REUNIONES BIBLIOTECOLOGICAS. US. English. Organization of American States, 1889 F Street NW, Washington DC 20006. **DD** 020.8.

REVIEW - SCHOOL LIBRARIES BRANCH, SOUTH AUSTRALIA EDUCATION DEPARTMENT. See Literature.

REVIEWING LIBRARIAN. (THE REVIEWING LIBRARIAN). Began with V. 1, Nov. 1974. 0318-0948. Periodical. CN. English. qt. $15.48. Ontario Library Association, 73 Richmond Street West/Suite 402, Toronto Ontario M5H 1Z4 Canada. **Tel** (416)363-3388. **Ed** Fay Blostein. **LC** Z675.S3. **DD** 028.1. bk rev. adv acc. **Circ** 1,200. (ctrl). Reviewing medium includes books, magazines, government publications, aural and visual media, feature article, an awareness column directed at curriculum and general interest needs of young people.

REVISITA DE ARCHIVOS BIBLIOTECAS Y MUSEOS (MADRID, SPAIN : 1897). See Genealogy and Heraldry - Archives.

REVISTA AIBDA. (REVISTA AIBDA : REVISTA DE LA ASOCIACION INTERAMERICANA DE BIBLIOTECARIOS Y DOCUMENTALISTAS AGRICOLAS). **VFOAT** Revista A.I.B.D.A. **VAT** Revista Asociacion Interamericana de Bibliotecarios y Documentalistas Agricolas. V. 1, No. 1 (Jan./June 1980)-. 0250-3190. Periodical. Spanish (English, Portuguese, or French). sa. **Ind/Abst** Libr. Inf. Sci. Abstr. **CODEN** REVADJ.

REVISTA CHILENA DE BIBLIOTECOLOGIA Y DOCUMENTACION. V. 1- June./Dec. 1975-. Periodical. CL. Spanish. be. Departamento de Bibliotecologia, University de Chile Casilla, 147 Santiago Chile. **LC** Z771.A1.

REVISTA DA ESCOLA DE BIBLIOTECONOMIA DA UFMG. (REVISTA DA ESCOLA DE BIBLIOTECONOMIA DA UNIVERSIDADE FEDERAL DE MINAS GERAIS). **Main/Corp** Minas Gerais, Brazil. Universidade Federal. Escola de Biblioteconomia. V. 1- March/Sept. 1972-. 0100-0829. Periodical. BL. Portuguese (summaries in English). sa. $15.00 US. Caixa Postal 1906-Ciudade University, Pampulha Brazil. **Tel** (031)441.11.31. **Ind/Abst** Libr. Inf. Sci. Abstr., Libr. Lit. **LC** Z671. **DD** 020.5. bk rev. adv acc. **Circ** 1,200. Covers bibliographies, education, information, and books.

REVISTA DE BIBLIOTECONOMIA DE BRASILIA. 0100-7157. Periodical. BL. Portuguese or Spanish, with summaries in English. ir. Caixa Postal 15-2833, Brazil. **Ind/Abst** Libr. Inf. Sci. Abstr., Libr. Lit. **LC** Z769.A1.

REVISTA DE LA BIBLIOTECA, ARCHIVO Y MUSEO DEL AYUNTAMIENTO DE MADRID. **Main/Corp** Madrid (Spain). Ayuntamiento. No. 1/2- 1977-. SP. Spanish. sa. Delegacion de Cultura del Ayuntamiento de Madrid, Plaza de la Villa 4, Madrid 12 Spain. **LC** Z671. *Revista de la Biblioteca, Archivo y Museo de Madrid.*

REVISTA DE LA BIBLIOTECA NACIONAL JOSE MARTI. **Main/Corp** Havana. Biblioteca Nacional Jose Marti. Vol. 1-4 (V. 1-6), Jan. 1909- Dec. 1912. Periodical. CU. Spanish. ir. Empresa Ediciones Cubanas, Obispo 461, Apartado 605, Ciudad Havana Cuba. **LC** Z897. **DD** 015.7291. (cum index).

REVISTA DE LLIBRERIA ANTIQUARIA. Periodical. SP. Catalan (Spanish). sa. 450. Revista de Llibreria Antiquaria, Paletes 4, Barcelona 34 Spain. **LC** Z990. **DD** 070.5094672.

REVISTA DEL SINASBI. **Main/Corp** Comision Coordinadora del Sistema Nacional de Servicios de Bibliotecas e Informacion Humanistica. **VAT** Revista del Sistema Nacional de Servicios de Bibliotecas e Informacion Humanistica, Cientifica y Tecnologica. No. 1-. Periodical. VE. Spanish. ir. Comision Coordinadora Sinasbi, Apartado Postal 68350, Altamira Caracas 106 Venezuela.

REVISTA ESPANOLA DE DOCUMENTACION CIENTIFICA. **Series/Titl** Publicacion del Consejo Superior de Investigaciones Cientificas. Vol. 1, No. 1 (1977)-. 0210-0614. Periodical. SP. Spanish. qt. $25.70. Jaquin Costa 22, Madrid 6 Spain. **Ind/Abst** Libr. Inf. Sci. Abstr. **LC** Z695.1.S3. **DD** 025.65.

REVISTA INTERAMERICANA DE BIBLIOTECOLOGIA. Began with Jan./Apr. 1978 issue. 0120-0976. Periodical. Spanish. ty. $10.00. Escuela Interamericana de Bibliotecologia, Universidad de Antioquia, Medellin Colombia. **Ind/Abst** Libr. Inf. Sci. Abstr. **LC** Z738.A1. **DD** 027.08.

REVISTA LATINOAMERICANA DE DOCUMENTACION. 0101-3394. Periodical. Portuguese (Spanish, some summaries in English). sa. Avenida W 3 Norte Quadra, 511 Bloco A, 70 750 Brasilia Distrito Federal Brazil. **Ind/Abst** Libr. Inf. Sci. Abstr. **LC** Z738.A1. **DD** 020.5.

REVISTA UNIVERSIDAD PONTIFICIA BOLIVARIANA. *See* Education (General) - Higher Education.

REVOLTING LIBRARIAN *CEASED.* (THE REVOLTING LIBRARIAN). Began with Oct. 1973. Ceased with V. 9, No. 4 (Winter 1982/83). 0316-8840. Periodical. CN. English. qt. Free to Members. Ontario Library Association, 73 Richmond Street West/Suite 402, Toronto Ontario M5H 1Z4 Canada. **LC** Z675.S3. **DD** 027.809713.

RILA BULLETIN. **Main/Corp** Rhode Island Library Association. **VAT** Rhode Island Library Association Bulletin. 1927. 0146-8685. Periodical. US. English. mo. $12.50. Rhode Island Library Association, 150 Empire Street, Providence RI 02903. **Ed** Linda Walton. adv acc. **Circ** 710. (ctrl). Newsletter with brief articles of interest to librarians with emphasis on Rhode Island libraries. *Bulletin of the Rhode Island Library Association.*

RIO GRANDE CHAPTER BULLETIN. **Main/Corp** Special Libraries Association. Rio Grande Chapter. 0272-9644. Periodical. US. English. qt. Rio Grande Chapter, 3312 Black Hills Road NE, Albuquerque NM 87111. **Tel** (505)299-3527.

RISALAT AL-MAKTABAH. **VFOAT** Majallat Risalat Al-Maktabah. V. 1- Oct. 1965-. Arabic (English). ir. 20.00. Jamiyat Al-Maktabat, Al-Urduniyah, PO Box 6289, Amman Jordan. **Tel** 629412. **Ed** Hani Al-Amad. **Ind/Abst** Libr. Inf. Sci. Abstr. bk rev. **Circ** 1,000. Covers articles in library book reviews, bibliography of recently published books, and library news.

ROD NEWS. **Main/Corp** Canberra, Australia. National Library. Resources Organization and Development Branch. No. 1- June 1979-. AT. English. ir. Research and Organization and Development Board, Editor, National Library of Australia, Canberra ACT 26 Australia. **LC** Z871. **DD** 027.594.

ROUND TABLE. Began publication in 197-. 0384-0123. Periodical. CN. English. Georgian Bay Regional Library System, 30 Morrow Road, Barrie Ontario L4N 3V8 Canada. **DD** 027.471315.

RQ. V. 1- Nov. 1960-. 0033-7072. Periodical. US. English. qt. American Library Association, 50 East Huron Street, Chicago IL 60611. **Tel** (312)944-6780. **Ind/Abst** Am. Hist. Life, Hist. Abstr., Part A, Mod. Hist. Abstr., Hist. Abst., Part B, Twent. Century Abstr., Pop. Mag. Rev., Libr. Inf. Sci. Abstr., Book Rev. Index, Public Aff. Inf. Serv. Bull., Ref. Source, Curr. Index J. Educ., Libr. Lit., Mag. Index, Soc. Sci. Citation Index, Bibliogr. Index, Hist. Abstr. **LC** Z671. **DD** 025.520973. **NLM** Z 671 R115.

RTSD NEWSLETTER. **Main/Corp** American Library Association. Resources and Technical Services Division. **VAT** Resources and Technical Services Division Newsletter. V. 1- Jan. 1976-. 0360-5906. Periodical. US. English. $12.00. American Library Association, 50 East Huron Street, Chicago IL 60611. **Ind/Abst** Libr. Lit. **LC** Z731. **DD** 020.62273.

RURAL LIBRARIES. Vol. 1, No. 1 (Winter 1980)-. 0276-2048. Periodical. US. English. sa. $6.00. Clarion University Pennsylvania, Foundation Center of Library Science, Clarion PA 16214. **Tel** (814)226-2386. **Ed** Bernard Vaurek. **Ind/Abst** Libr. Inf. Sci. Abstr., Libr. Lit. (ctrl).

S. A. L. T. NEWSLETTER. **Main/Corp** Saskatchewan Association of Library Technicians. Mar. 1973-. 0702-7745. Periodical. CN. English. qt. Free to Members. SALT, 2233 MacKinnon Avenue, Saskatoon Saskatchewan S7J 1N5 Canada. **DD** 023.5.

S. L. I. S NEWSLETTER. (S L I S NEWSLETTER). **Main/Corp** University of Western Ontario. School of Library and Information Science. V. 1- Oct. 1975-. 0380-8041. Periodical. CN. English. ir. School of Library and Information Science, University of Western Ontario, London Ontario N6A 5B9 Canada. **DD** 020.71171326.

N S S L A BULLETIN. **Main/Corp** Nova Scotia School Library Association. **VAT** Nova Scotia School Library Association Bulletin. Began publication in 1977 (V. 5, No. 1). 0707-2457. Periodical. CN. English. Nova Scotia Teachers Union, 106 Dutch Village Road, Halifax Nova Scotia B3L 4G1 Canada. **DD** 027.809716. *S L A Bulletin, 0380-2035.*

SABINE/MAGAZINE. No. 1- Jan. 1980-. 0227-2261. Periodical. CN. French. ir. Informatech France-Quebec, 20 Edison Place Bonaventure, Montreal Quebec H5A 1A7 Canada. **DD** 025.04.

SAHIFAT AL-MAKTABAH. **VFOAT** Egyptian Library Journal. Journal 1, March 1969-. Periodical. Arabic. ty. 35 Al-Galaa Street, Al-Qahirah United Arab Republic Egypt. **LC** Z671.

SALALM NEWSLETTER. **Main/Corp** Seminar on the Acquisition of Latin American Library Materials. **VAT** Seminar on the Acquisition of Latin American Library Materials Newsletter. V. 1- Jan. 1973-. 0098-6275. Periodical. US. English. qt. $5.00. University of Wisconsin in Madison, Memorial Library SALALM Secretariat, Madison WI 53706. **Tel** (608)262-3240. **Ed** Marian Goslinga. **LC** Z689. **DD** 025.2. **Circ** 500. (ctrl). Organ of the seminar on the acquisition of Latin American library materials deals with all aspects of Latin American librarianship.

SALARY STATISTICS FOR LARGE PUBLIC LIBRARIES. *See* Statistics.

SALE CATALOGUES OF LIBRARIES OF EMINENT PERSONS. UK. English. ir. H W Wilson, 950 University Avenue, Bronx NY 10452. **Tel** (215)588-8400.

SALG NEWSLETTER. **VFOAT** S.A.L.G. Newsletter. No. 1 (Jan. 1973)-. 0307-1456. Periodical. UK. English. sa. South Asia Library Group, c/o Institute of Commonwealth Studies, 27 Russell Square, London WC1B 5DS England. **Ind/Abst** Libr. Inf. Sci. Abstr.

SASKATCHEWAN LIBRARY. V. 19, No. 2- May 1966-. 0036-4924. Periodical. CN. English. sa. Saskatchewan Library Association, Box 3388, Regina Saskatchewan S4P 3H1 Canada.

SASKATCHEWAN LIBRARY FORUM. No. 1- Nov. 1977-. 0703-8321. Periodical. CN. English. ir. $25.00. Saskatchewan Library Association, Box 3388, Regina Saskatchewan S4P 3H1 Canada. **Ed** Susan M Clark. **DD** 020.62347124. bk rev. adv acc. **Circ** 300. (ctrl). For individuals interested in library service particularly on prairies and Northern Canada.

SASKATCHEWAN NATIVE LIBRARY SERVICES NEWSLETTER. Vol. 1, No. 1 (Feb. 1981)-. 0229-9496. Periodical. CN. English. ir. $7.74. Saskatchewan Native Library Services, 220 28th Street West, Saskatoon Saskatchewan S7N 1M6 Canada. **Tel** (306)652-9447. **Ed** L Fritz, H Grimson, J Murray. **DD** 026.97000497. bk rev. **Circ** 40. Articles, bibliographies, book reviews in the areas of native library services and native education.

SCHNELLSTATISTIK ALLGEMEINER OFFENTLICHER BIBLIOTHEKEN. **Main/Corp** Deutscher Bibliotheksverbank (Germany : West). Arbeitsstelle fur das Bibliothekswesen. German. ir. Deutscher Bibliotheksverband Publikationsabteilung, Fehrbelliner Platz 3 1000 31, Berlin West Germany. **LC** Z801.A1.

SCHOOL LIBRARIAN. (THE SCHOOL LIBRARIAN). V. 17- March 1969-. 0036-6595. Periodical. UK. English. qt. $30.65. School Library Association, Victoria House, 29-31 George Street, Oxford OX1 2AY England. **Tel** 0865-722746. **Ed** Joan Murphy. **Ind/Abst** Libr. Inf. Sci. Abstr., Book Rev. Index, Libr. Lit. **LC** Z675.S3. **DD** 027.80942. bk rev. adv acc. **Circ** 4,500. Articles on library skills, library management, children's writers. Substantial review section covering books for all ages. *School Librarian and School Library Review.*

THE SCHOOL LIBRARIAN'S WORKSHOP. V. 1- Sept. 1980-. 0271-3667. Periodical. US. English. mo. $39.00. Library Learning Resources Inc, 61 Greenbriar Drive, Berkeley Heights NJ 07922. **Tel** (201)499-3406. **Ed** Ruth Toor and Hilda K Weisburg. **Circ** 5,500. Current trends, teaching library skills, bibliographies, bulletin boards, pencil games and reference questions, all in 16 pages, ten times a year. For grades K-12.

SCHOOL LIBRARIES IN CANADA. Vol. 1, No. 1 (Autumn 1980)-. 0227-3780. Periodical. CN. English. qt. $27.09. Canadian Library Association, 151 Sparks Street, Ottawa Ontario K1P 5E3 Canada. **Tel** (613)232-9625. **Ind/Abst** Can. Educ. Index, Libr. Lit. **DD** 027.80971. *Moccasin Telegraph (Canadian School Library Association), 0076-9878.*

SCHOOL LIBRARY MEDIA ANNUAL. **VFOAT** School Library Media. Vol. 1 (1983)-. 0739-7712. US. English. an. $35.00. Libraries Unlimited Inc, PO Box 263, Littleton CO 80160. **Tel** 770-1220. **Ed** Shirley Aaron. **LC** Z675.S3. **DD** 027.805. Essential reference tool for district and regional media centers and is highly recommended for purchase and use by individual building level media personnel.

SCHOOL LIBRARY MEDIA QUARTERLY. (SCHOOL LIBRARY MEDIA QUARTERLY : JOURNAL OF THE AMERICAN ASSOCIATION OF SCHOOL LIBRARIANS). Vol. 10, No. 1 (Fall 1981)-. 0278-4823. Periodical. US. English. qt. $30.00. American Library Association, 50 East Huron Street, Chicago IL 60611. **Tel** (312)944-6780. **Ed** Marilyn W Greenberg. **Ind/Abst** Libr. Inf. Sci. Abstr., Educ. Index, Except. Child Educ. Resour., Book Rev. Index, Curr. Contents, Soc. Behav. Sci., Curr. Index J. Educ., Except. Child Educ. Abstr., Inf. Sci. Abstr., Libr. Lit., Media Rev. Dig., Ref. Serv. Rev. **LC** Z675.S3. **DD** 027.805. bk rev. adv acc. **Circ** 7,500. (ctrl). Read by building level library media specialists, district supervisors, and library educators. It covers the selection of print and nonprint media and the development of programs and services for K-12 libraries. *School Media Quarterly, 0361-1647.*

SCHOOL LIBRARY SERVICE RECORD. **Main/Corp** Wisconsin. Division for Library Services. **VFOAT** Wisconsin School Library Service Record. 1970-. US. English. Division for Library Services, 126 Langdon Street, Madison WI 53702. **LC** Z732.W8. **DD** 027.809775.

SCHOOL MEDIA QUARTERLY *CEASED.* V. 1-9. 0361-1647. Periodical. US. English. qt. $7.50 Members, $15.00 Non-Members. American Library Association, 50 East Huron Street, Chicago IL 60611. **Ind/Abst** Ref. Source, Libr. Lit., Book Rev. Index, Curr. Contents, Soc. Behav. Sci., Curr. Index J. Educ., Except. Child Educ. Abstr., Inf. Sci. Abstr., Media Rev. Dig. **LC** Z675.S3. **DD** 627.805. *School Libraries.*

Library and Information Science

SCHOOL MEDIA STATISTICS. See Statistics.

SCHWEIZERISCHE BIBLIOTHEKEN. BIBLIOTHEQUES SUISSES. See Statistics.

SCI-TECH NEWS. Began in 1949. 0036-8059. Periodical. US. English. qt. $13.00. Sci-Tech News, PO Box 1414, Canoga Park CA 91304. **Tel** (818)702-1155. Ed R M Ballard. **Ind/Abst** Comput. Control Abstr., Electr. Electron. Abstr., Sci. Abstr. Sect. A. Phys. Abstr., Libr. Inf. Sci. Abstr. **DD** 020. NLM Z 671 S416. **CODEN** STNWAM. bk rev. adv acc. **Circ** 3,750. By and for librarians and information specialists in the fields of science and technology. *Alchemical Libraries Almanack.*

SCIENCE AND TECHNOLOGY : A PURCHASE GUIDE FOR BRANCH AND PUBLIC LIBRARY. **Main/Corp** Pittsburgh. Carnegie Library. Science and Technology Dept. 1963-1954, 1973-. Periodical. English. ir.

SCIENCE & TECHNOLOGY LIBRARIES. VFOAT Science and Technology Libraries. Vol. 1, No. 1 (Fall 1980)-. 0194-262X. Periodical. US. English. qt. $72.00. Haworth Press, 28 East 22nd Street, New York NY 10010. **Tel** (212)228-2800. Ed Ellis Mount. **Ind/Abst** Comput. Control Abstr., Electr. Electron. Abstr., Sci. Abstr. Sect. A. Phys. Abstr., Public Aff. Inf. Serv. Bull., Libr. Lit. **LC** Z675.T3. **DD** 026.0005. **CODEN** STELDF. adv acc. **Circ** 1,013. This journal provides scientifically prepared material that represents the viewpoints, concerns, and perspectives of the sci-tech librarianship community.

SCOTTISH LIBRARIES. 0080-8091. UK. English. te. Scottish Library Association Publications, Coursington Road, Motherwell ML1 1PW Scotland. **Tel** (0698)52526. Ed P B Freshwater. **LC** Z791.S35. **DD** 027.0411. adv acc. **Circ** 400. (ctrl) A review of developments in all types of library and information services in Scotland over a 5 year period.

SEIRI GIJUTSU ZENKOKU KAIGI GIJUROKU. First conference held in 1970. JA. Japanese. ir. 600. c/o Nihon Toshokan Kyokai, 1251 Ueno Koen Taito-ku, Tokyo 110 Japan. **LC** Z688.5.

SELECTED ACCESSIONS - LEGISLATIVE LIBRARY CEASED. **Main/Corp** Manitoba. Legislative Assembly. Library. Ceased with issue for Mar. 1981. 0381-4645. CN. English. mo.

SELECTED FEDERAL AND STATE BOOK PROGRAM INFORMATION. 1976 Ed-. 0278-0518. US. English. an. Association of American Publishers, 1 Park Avenue, New York NY 10016. **LC** Z731. **DD** 021.830973.

SELECTED LIBRARY ACQUISITIONS. **Main/Corp** United States. Dept. of Transportation. Library Services Division. 0145-9309. US. English. mo. Department of Transportation, Office of the Secretary Office of Administrative Operations, Library Services Division, Washington DC 20590.

SELECTED LIST OF ACCESSIONS CEASED. **Main/Corp** Canada. Atmospheric Environment Service. Library. VFOAT Liste d'Acquisitions Choisies. Ceased with issue for Nov./Dec. 1980. 0708-3505. Periodical. CN. English (French). ir. Atmospheric Environment Service, 4905 Dufferin Street, Toronto Ontario M3H 5T4 Canada. *Selected List of Additions to Head Office Library.*

SELECTED SERIAL RESOURCES FOR QUEENSLAND PUBLIC LIBRARIES. VFOAT Selected Serial Resources. English. ir. **LC** Z6945, PN4832. **DD** 016.05.

SEMI-ANNUAL REPORT - STATE OF CONNECTICUT, CONNECTICUT STATE LIBRARY. (SEMI-ANNUAL REPORT - CONNECTICUT STATE LIBRARY). **Main/Corp** Connecticut State Library, Hartford. 0148-1088. Periodical. US. English. sa. Connecticut State Library, 231 Capitol Avenue, Hartford CT 06115. **LC** Z713.5.U. **DD** 024.609746.

SEMMON TOSHOKAN. VFOAT Semmon Toshokan Kyogikai Kaiho. No. 40- 1969-. Periodical. JA. Japanese. qt. 2000. c/o Kokuritsu Kokkai Toshokan, 10-1 Nagatacho-1 Chiyoda-Ku, Tokyo 100 Japan. **LC** Z671. *Semmon Toshokan Kyogikai Kaiho.*

SENARAI AHLI - PERSATUAN PERPUSTAKAAN MALAYSIA. **Main/Corp** Persatuan Perpustakaan Malaysia. MY. Malay. ir. **LC** Z673.

SERIAL HOLDINGS. **Main/Corp** South Carolina. University. Library. 1976-. US. English. sm. South Carolina University, Library, Columbia SC 29208.

SERIAL HOLDINGS - B. C. MEDICAL LIBRARY SERVICE. **Main/Corp** British Columbia Medical Library Service. June 1976-. 0383-8684. CN. English. British Columbia Medical Library Service, 1807 West 10th Avenue, Vancouver British Columbia V6T 2A9 Canada. **DD** 016.605. *Journal Holdings, 0383-8676.*

SERIAL HOLDINGS IN NEWFOUNDLAND LIBRARIES. **Main/Corp** Memorial University of Newfoundland. Library. 10th- Ed. 0709-0536. CN. English. an. Memorial University of Newfoundland, Library, St Johns Newfoundland A1B 3Y1 Canada. **DD** 016.05. *Serial Holdings in the Libraries of Memorial University of Newfoundland, St. John's Public Library and College of Trades and Technology, 0316-6597.*

SERIAL HOLDINGS IN THE PENNSYLVANIA STATE UNIVERSITY LIBRARIES AT UNIVERSITY PARK. **Main/Corp** Pennsylvania. State University. Libraries. 1969-. US. English. an. Pennsylvania State University, Pattie Library/Room E 506, University Park PA 16802. **Tel** (814)863-0404.

SERIAL PUBLICATIONS CURRENTLY RECEIVED AND ON ORDER. **Main/Corp** Eastern Virginia Medical School, Norfolk, VA. Moorman Memorial Library. 19-. US. English. ir. Eastern Virginia Medical School, PO Box 1980, Norfolk VA 23501.

SERIAL PUBLICATIONS IN GEOGRAPHY. **Main/Corp** Carol M. Newman Library. No. 1- 1975-. 0163-7711. US. English. an. Department of Geography, 243 Henderson Hall, Virginia Polytechnic Institute and State University, Blacksburg VA. **LC** Z6003, G116. **DD** 016.9105.

SERIALS AND JOURNALS IN THE M.I.T. LIBRARIES. **Main/Corp** Massachusetts Institute of Technology. Libraries. VAT Serials and Journals in the Massachusetts Institute of Technology Libraries. 12th- Ed. 0542-9560. US. English. sa. $10.00. Massachusetts Institute of Technology Libraries, Room 14S-310, Cambridge MA 02139. **LC** Z6945. **DD** 016.05. *Current Serials and Journals in the M.I.T. Libraries.*

SERIALS CURRENTLY RECEIVED BY THE NATIONAL AGRICULTURAL LIBRARY. **Main/Corp** National Agricultural Library (U.S.). 1974-. US. English.

THE SERIALS DIRECTORY. See Yearbooks, Almanacs, Directories.

SERIALS HOLDINGS CATALOGUE - LIBRARY. UNIVERSITY OF VICTORIA. (SERIALS HOLDINGS CATALOGUE - UNIVERSITY OF VICTORIA, LIBRARY). **Main/Corp** University of Victoria (B.C.). Library. Interim 10th- Ed. 0318-174X. Periodical. CN. English. University of Victoria Library, PO Box 1700, Victoria British Columbia V8W 2Y2 Canada. **DD** 016.05. *List of Serials, 0318-1820.*

SERIALS HOLDINGS CATALOGUE - SERIALS DIVISION. UNIVERSITY OF VICTORIA LIBRARY. (SERIALS HOLDINGS CATALOGUE - SERIALS DIVISION, UNIVERSITY OF VICTORIA LIBRARY). **Main/Corp** University of Victoria (B.C.). Library. Nov. 1978-. 0702-0740. Periodical. CN. English. ir. University of Victoria, McPherson Library, Serials Division, PO Box 1800, Victoria British Columbia V8W 2Y3 Canada. **DD** 016.05.

SERIALS HOLDINGS LIST. **Main/Corp** Georgia. Institute of Technology, Atlanta. Library. Monographic Series. US. English. ir.

SERIALS HOLDINGS - WILFRID LAURIER UNIVERSITY. (SERIALS HOLDINGS MICROFORM). **Main/Corp** Wilfrid Laurier Univeristy. Library. Feb. 15, 1983-. 0823-5406. CN. English. an. Serials Department, The Library, Wilfrid Laurier University, Waterloo Ontario N2L 3C5 Canada. **DD** 018.134. *Journals, Series, Annuals List, 0229-1851.*

SERTEK. **Main/Corp** Universite de Montreal. Service des Bibliotheques. Direction des Services Techniques. No. 1- Mar. 1975-. 0317-0322. CN. French. ir. Free. Universite de Montreal Service des Bibliotheques, Direction des Services Techniques C P 6128, Montreal Quebec H3C 3J7 Canada. **DD** 027.7714281.

SHAN-HSI CHIAO YU (TAI-YUAN SHIH, CHINA). (SHAN-HSI CHIAO YU). VFOAT Shanxi Jiaoyu. Periodical. CH. Chinese. mo. 0.25. Post Office, Tai-Yuan Shih China.

SHARE (BERKELEY, CALIF.). (SHARE). VFOAT Sisters Have Resources Everywhere. VAT Sisters Have Resources Everywhere (Berkeley, Calif.). 0273-2343. US. English. ir. Women Library Workers, 2027 Parker Street, Berkeley CA 94704. **Tel** (415)843-0533. **LC** Z720.A4. **DD** 020.922.

SHOSHI SAKUIN TEMBO. V. 1-. Japanese. ir. 4200. Nichigai Asoshietsu, 23-8 Omori Kita 1-Chome, Ota-ku 143 Tokyo Japan. **LC** Z695.9.

SHOW-ME LIBRARIES. V. 1- Oct. 1949-. 0037-4326. Periodical. US. English. qt. $10.00. Missouri State Library, PO Box 387, Truman Street Office Building, Jefferson City MO 65102. **Tel** (314)751-2680. Ed Madeline Matson. **Ind/Abst** Libr. Inf. Sci. Abstr., Libr. Lit. **LC** Z671. **DD** 027.0778. bk rev. **Circ** 2,500. (ctrl). News features and editorials about Missouri libraries and librarians.

THE SIERRA LEONE LIBRARY JOURNAL. V. 1- Jan. 1974-. Periodical. SL. English. sa. Editor: J S T Thompson, PO Box 94, Fourah Bay College University of Sierra Leone, Freetown Sierra Leone. **Ind/Abst** Libr. Inf. Sci. Abstr. **LC** Z857.A2. **DD** 021.009664.

SIG NEWSLETTER. **Main/Corp** American Society for Information Science. Special Interest Group on Behavioral and Social Sciences (SIG/BSS). BSS-1— Mar. 1975-. Periodical. US. English. ir. $3.00. American Society for Information Science, 1010 16th Street NW 2nd Floor, Washington DC 20036. *ASIS Special Interest Group in the Behavioral and Social Sciences Newsletter.*

SINGAPORE LIBRARIES. V. 1- 1971-. 0085-6118. SI. English. an. $15.00. Library Association of Singapore, c/o National Library, Stamford Road, Singapore 6. **Ind/Abst** Libr. Inf. Sci. Abstr., Libr. Lit. **LC** Z845.S5. **DD** 020.5.

SKOLEBIBLIOTEKSARBOG. Began with Vol. for 1967/68. Danish. ir. Danmarks Skolebiblioteksforening, Stationsvej 3, 4070 Kirke Hyllinge Denmark. **LC** Z675.S3.

SLA NEWS. **Main/Corp** Scottish Library Association. VAT Scottish Library Association News. Began publication with No. 1 in 1955. 0048-9786. Periodical. UK. English. bm. $9.96. Scottish Library Association, Motherwell Business Centre, Coursington Road, Motherwell ML1 1PW Scotland. Ed Dennis M Groark. **Ind/Abst** Libr. Inf. Sci. Abstr., Libr. Lit. bk rev. adv acc. **Circ** 2,500. (ctrl). Articles of interest to those engaged in library and information spheres, news of Association work, membership, book reviews and etc. *News Sheet.*

SLE. SCHOOL LIBRARY EVENTS. (SLE : SCHOOL LIBRARY EVENTS). VFOAT School Library Events. Sept. 81/82-. 0713-0295. Periodical. CN. English. mo. Free. School Library Events, c/o Mslava, Manitoba Teachers' Society, 191 Harcourt Street, Winnipeg Manitoba R3J 3H2 Canada. **DD** 027.805.

SLJ, SCHOOL LIBRARY JOURNAL. VFOAT School Library Journal. V. 21, No. 5- Jan. 1975-. 0362-8930. Periodical. US. English. mo. RR Bowker Company, 1180 Avenue of the Americas, New York NY 10036, (subscription address: Bowker Subscription Service PO Box 1426 Riverton NJ 08077). **Tel** (800)257-7894. **Ind/Abst** Book Rev. Index, Child. Mag. Guide, Educ. Index, Libr. Inf. Sci. Abstr., Libr. Lit., Pop. Mag. Rev., Subj. Index Child. Mag., Curr. Index J. Educ., Libr. Inf. Sci. Abstr., Book Rev. Digest, Access. **LC** Z675.S3. **DD** 0127.805. *School Library Journal, 0000-0035.*

SMALL COMPUTERS IN LIBRARIES. See Computers and Computer Science.

SMALL LIBRARIES PUBLICATIONS. No. 1-. US. English. ir.

SMITHSONIAN INSTITUTION LIBRARIES RESEARCH GUIDE. 0732-7447. Monographic Series. US. English. G K Hall & Company, 70 Lincoln Street, Boston MA 02111.

SNOWSHOE. (SNOWSHOE : NEWSLETTER OF THE N.W.T. LIBRARY ASSOCIATION). Vol. 1, No. 1 (Spring 1984)-. 0825-4753. Periodical. CN. English. qt. $5.00 Members, $15.00 Nonmembers. Northwest Territories Library Association, PO Box 694, Yellowknife Northwest Territories X1A 2N5 Canada.

Library and Information Science

DD 027.0719205. Newsletter (Northwest Territories Library Association), 0825-4974.

SOMENI. V. 1- Apr. 1971-. Periodical. English. ir. LC Z857.T3.

SOMETHING ABOUT THE AUTHOR. AUTOBIOGRAPHY SERIES. VFOAT Autobiography Series. Vol. 1-. 0885-6842. US. English. sa. $50.00. Gale Research Company, Book Tower, Detroit MI 48226. DD 028.

SOUNDINGS. V. 1- May 1969-. 0038-1853. US. English. an. $3.00. University of California at Santa Barbara, 129 Library, Santa Barbara CA 93106. Tel (805)961-3474. Ed Donald E Fitch. Ind/Abst Am. Hist. Life, Hist. Abstr., Part A, Mod. Hist. Abstr., Hist. Abst., Part B, Twent. Century Abstr., MLA Int. Bibliogr. Books Artic. Mod. Lang. Lit. LC Z881.C1579. DD 081. Circ 850. (ctrl). Articles on library collections and recent acquisitions, plus campus lectures on library related topics, occasional poems, and translations.

THE SOURCEBOOK OF LIBRARY TECHNOLOGY. 1965/75-. 0275-6811. US. English. be. $50.00. American Library Association, 50 East Huron Street, Chicago IL 60611. Tel (312)944-6780. NLM Z 671 S724.

SOURCES. Main/Corp New Mexico. University. General Library. No. 1- Apr. 1973-. 0094-9981. Monographic Series. US. English. ir. University of New Mexico, Bookstore, Albuquerque NM 87131.

SOURCES & RESOURCES. ADDITIONS & DELETIONS. (SOURCES & RESOURCES : ADDITIONS & DELETIONS). Vol. 1, No. 1 (Nov. 1978)-. 0229-4605. Periodical. CN. English. ir. British Columbia School Librarians' Association, c/o A Thacker, 2561 Western Avenue, North Vancouver British Columbia V7N 3L2 Canada. DD 027.809711.

SOUTH AFRICAN JOURNAL FOR LIBRARIANSHIP AND INFORMATION SCIENCE. VAT Suid-Afrikaanse Tydskrif vir Biblioteek- en Inligtingwese. Vol. 49, No. 1 (July 1981)-. 0038-240X. Periodical. SA. Afrikaans (English). qt. 20.00. Bureau for Scientific Publications, PO Box 1758, Pretoria 0001 South Africa. Tel (012)260207. Ed H de Bruin. Ind/Abst Comput. Control Abstr., Electr. Electron. Abstr., Sci. Abstr. Sect. A. Phys. Abstr., Libr. Inf. Sci. Abstr., Libr. Lit. LC Z671. CODEN SATIDG. bk rev. Circ 2,700. Descriptive and research articles in library and information science. South African Libraries.

SOUTH AFRICAN LIBRARIES CEASED. VFOAT Suid-Afrikaanse Biblioteke. V. 1-48. 0038-240X. Periodical. SA. Afrikaans (English). qt. Ind/Abst Libr. Lit. LC Z671. DD 020.5. (cum index). Available on microfilm from University Microfilms International.

SOUTH ASIA LIBRARY NOTES & QUERIES. VAT South Asia Library Notes and Queries. No. 1- Mar. 1978-. 0197-5366. Periodical. US. English. ir $8.00. Association for Asian Studies, University of Chicago, 1100 East 57th Street, Room 560, Chicago IL 60637. Tel (312)962-8429. LC Z3185, DS335. DD 026.954.

THE SOUTH CAROLINA LIBRARIAN. V. 1- 1956-. 0038-3112. Periodical. US. English. sa. $3.00. South Carolina Library Association, c/o L Mitlin Dacas Library Winthrop, Rock Hill SC 29733. Tel (803)323-2131. Ed Laurance R Mitlin. Ind/Abst Libr. Lit. LC Z732.S72. bk rev. adv acc. Circ 1,000. Articles about librarianship in South Carolina. South Carolina Library Bulletin.

SOUTH CAROLINA PUBLIC LIBRARY ANNUAL STATISTICAL SUMMARY. See Statistics.

SOUTH DAKOTA LIBRARY DIRECTORY. See Yearbooks, Almanacs, Directories.

THE SOUTHEASTERN LIBRARIAN. V. 1- Spring 1951-. 0038-3686. Periodical. US. English. qt. $35.00. The Southeastern Librarian, c/o Claudia Medori PO Box 987, Tucker GA 30085. Tel (404)939-5080. Ed Linda Lucas. Ind/Abst Libr. Lit. LC Z673. DD 020.623 (cum index). adv acc. Circ 1,800. (ctrl). Subjects and information of interest to professional librarians.

SPEC FLYER. Main/Corp Association of Research Libraries. Systems and Procedures Exchange Center. VAT Systems and Procedures Exchange Center Flyer. No. 1- Sept. 1973-. 0160-3574. Periodical. US. English. ir. ARL Office of Management Studies, 1527 New Hampshire Avenue NW, Washington DC 20036. Tel (202)232-8656. Ed Maxine K Sitts. Collections of selected documents from major research libraries. Two-page management overview. Each issue on specific topic. Results of surveys. Trends, issues.

SPEC KIT. Main/Corp Association of Research Libraries. Systems and Procedures Exchange Center. 1- 1973-. Periodical. US. English. mo. $150.00 Domestic, $210.00 Foreign. ARL Office of Management Studies, 1527 New Hampshire Avenue Northwest, Washington DC 20036. Tel (202)232-8656. Ed Maxine K Sitts. Circ 400. Collections of selected documents from major research libraries. Two-page management overview. Each issue on specific topic. Results of surveys, trends, and issue.

SPECIAL COLLECTIONS. Vol. 1, No. 1 (Fall 1981)-. 0270-3157. Periodical. US. English. qt. $95.00. Haworth Press, 149 Fifth Avenue, New York NY 10010. Tel (212)228-2800. Ed Lee Ash. Ind/Abst Libr. Inf. Sci. Abstr. LC Z688.A2. DD 026.332105. adv acc. Circ 252. Survey of subject collections in libraries, with reviews of the reference literature in library and private collections of the United States and Canada.

SPECIAL LIBRARIES. V. 1- Jan. 1910-. 0038-6723. Periodical. US. English. qt. $53.00. Special Libraries Association, 1700 18th Street NW, Washington DC 20009. Tel (202)234-4700. Ed Lori E Balsam. Ind/Abst Mag. Index, Hist. Abstr., Phys. Abstr., Electr. Electron. Abstr., Sci. Abstr. Sect. A. Phys. Abstr., Art Archaeol. Tech. Abstr., Libr. Inf. Sci. Abstr., Book Rev. Index, Bus. Period. Index, Ind. Arts Index, Libr. Lit., Public Aff. Inf. Serv. Bull., Curr. Index J. Educ., Hospit. Lit. Index, Book Rev. Digest, Soc. Sci. Citation Index, Cumul. Index Nurs. Allied Health Lit., Am. Hist. Life, ABI/Inform, Int. Aerosp. Abstr., Comput. Control Abstr. LC Z671. DD 026. NLM Z 671 S741. CODEN SPLBAN. (cum index). bk rev. adv acc. Circ 14,000. (ctrl).

SPECIAL LIBRARIES IN THE EDMONTON AREA. Main/Corp Canadian Association of Special Libraries and Information Services., Edmonton Chapter. 0711-1770. CN. English. an. CASLIS Edmonton Chapter, 10436 8th Avenue, Edmonton Alberta T6E 1X6 Canada. DD 026.0002571233. Special Libraries in the Edmonton Metropolitan Area, 0228-8214.

SPEL, SELECTED PUBLICATIONS IN EUROPEAN LANGUAGES. VFOAT Selected Publications in European Languages. No. 1- Feb. 1973-. 0307-5354. UK. English. qt. $3.83. College of Librarianship, Wales LLanbadarn Fawr, Aberystwyth Dyfed SY223AS Wales. LC Z666. DD 020.5.

SPRINGFIELD CITY LIBRARY BULLETIN. Main/Corp Springfield, Mass. City Library. Jan. 1970-. 0038-8599. Periodical. US. English. bm. Springfield Library and Museums Association, Springfield MA 01103. City Library Bulletin.

SRI LANKA LIBRARY REVIEW. V.4, No.2- 1972/73-. Periodical. English or Sinhalese. ir. $1.00. University of Sri Lanka, Colombo Campus PO Box 1698, Colombo Sri Lanka. LC Z845.C4. Ceylon Library Review, 0009-0867.

SSU-CHUAN TU SHU KUAN HSUEH PAO. VFOAT Sichuan Tushuguan Xuebao. Began with Mar. 1979 issue. Periodical. CC. Chinese (English (1980, No. 4)). qt. Ssu-Chuan Sheng Tu Shu Kuan Hsueh Hui Cheng-Tu China. LC Z671. DD 020.5.

STAFF NEWS BULLETIN. Main/Corp Evansville, Indiana. Public Library. 0014-3669. US. English. sm. Evansville Public Library, 22 Southeast Fifth Street, Evansville IN 47708.

STAFF NEWS - CHICAGO PUBLIC LIBRARY CEASED. Main/Corp Chicago Public Library. Vol. 1, No. 1 (Sept. 1922)-. Periodical. US. English. mo. Chicago Public Library, 425 North Michigan Avenue/12th Floor, Chicago IL 60611. Tel (312)269-2900. LC Z733. DD 027.477311.

STAFF NOTES. See Music.

STAFF REPORTER - ENOCH PRATT FREE LIBRARY, BALTIMORE. Main/Corp Enoch Pratt Free Library, Baltimore. 1933. 0013-8495. Periodical. US. English. ir. $2.50. Enoch Pratt Library, 400 Cathedral Street, Baltimore MD 21201. Tel (301)396-5494. Ed Averil J Kadis. Circ 500. (ctrl). Newsletter with information on innovative and traditional library services; meeting, conference, and workshop reports; announcements of budgetary decisions and policy changes; discussions of personnel problems, etc.

STAINLESS STEELS DIGEST. See Metals & Metallurgy.

START OF MESSAGE. No. 1- Aug. 1975-. 0361-0241. Periodical. US. English. ir. Catalog Department, Cleveland Health Sciences Library, 2119 Abington Road, Cleveland OH 44106. NLM W1 ST797.

STATE LIBRARIAN. (STATE LIBRARIAN : JOURNAL OF THE CIRCLE OF STATE LIBRARIANS). Vol. 23. No. 1 (Mar. 1975)-. 0305-9189. Periodical. UK. English. ty. 15 Domestic, 5.50 Foreign. State Librarian c/o C Murphy, Rm 1020 Thames House South & Millbank London SW1P 4QJ England. Ed Christopher Murphy. Ind/Abst Libr. Inf. Sci. Abstr., Libr. Lit. LC Z675.G7. DD 027.541. bk rev. adv acc. Circ 700. Journal of the circle of state librarians describes development within, or that affect, national and government libraries. Bulletin of The Circle of State Librarians.

THE STATE LIBRARY AGENCIES, A SURVEY PROJECT REPORT. 1st- Ed. Periodical. US. English. American Library Association, 50 East Huron Street, Chicago IL 60611.

STATE LIBRARY NEWSLETTER CEASED. Main/Corp Michigan. State Library Services. Periodical. US. English.

STATISTICAL REPORT OF THE JAMAICA LIBRARY SERVICE. See Statistics.

STATISTICAL SUMMARY. See Statistics.

STATISTICS OF OHIO LIBRARIES FOR . . . . See Statistics.

STATISTICS OF PUBLIC LIBRARIES. See Statistics.

STATISTICS OF PUBLIC SCHOOL LIBRARIES/MEDIA CENTERS. See Statistics.

STATISTICS OF SOUTH DAKOTA PUBLIC LIBRARIES. See Statistics.

STATISTICS OF VIRGINIA PUBLIC LIBRARIES AND INSTITUTIONAL LIBRARIES. See Statistics.

STATISTIEK VAN DE OPENBARE BIBLIOTHEKEN. VFOAT Statistics on Public Libraries. 0168-3462. NE. Dutch. an. 13.50. Centraal Bureau Voor de Statistiek, Staatsuitgeverij, 'S-Gravenhage Netherlands. LC Z815.A1.

STATISTIK DER KOMMUNALEN OFFENTLICHEN BIBLIOTHEKEN DER BUNDESREPUBLIK, REGIONALSTATISTIK. Main/Corp Deutscher Bibliotheksverband (Germany : West). Arbeitsstelle fur das Bibliothekswesen. VFOAT Gesamtstatistik. German. ir. Deutscher Bibliotheksverband Publikationsabteilung, Berlin West Germany. LC Z801.A1.

STATISTIK FRAN ENSKILDA LANDER. See Statistics.

DIE STATISTISCH ERFASSTEN ARBEITSERGEBNISSE DER STAATLICHEN ALLGEMEINBIBLIOTHEKEN UND GEWERKSCHAFTSBIBLIOTHEKEN DER HAUPTSTADT DER DDR BERLIN. See Statistics.

STATISTISCHE UBERSICHTEN FUR DAS JAHR (UNIVERSITAT KIEL. INSTITUTS FUR WELTWIRTSCHAFT. BIBLIOTHEK). See Statistics.

STATISZTIKAI TAJEKOZTATO. SZAKKONYVTARAK. See Statistics.

STATNI VEDECKE KNIHOVNY CSR. Czech. ir. LC Z795.A1.

STEP UP YOUR AWARENESS. VFOAT Research Library. Step Up Your Awareness. 0145-4684. Periodical. US. English. mo. Free to Qualified Subscribers. G D Searle & Company, PO Box 5110, Chicago IL 60680.

STRATEGY (LIBRARIES & LEARNING, INC.). (STRATEGY). Vol. 2, No. 1-. 0227-4760. Periodical. CN. English. $36.00. Libraries & Learning Inc, 284 Avenue Road, Toronto Ontario M4V 2G7

Library and Information Science

Canada. **DD** 027.805. *Strategy (Moore & Moore Design), 0227-4760.*

STUDENT CONTRIBUTION SERIES. **Main/Corp** University of Maryland. School of Library and Information Services. No. 1- 1967-. Periodical. US. English. ir. University of Maryland, School of Library, Attn Mrs Herman, College Park MD 20742. **Tel** (301)454-2590. Various subjects relating to courses in the graduate school of library and information services.

STUDIEHANDBOG. **Main/Corp** Danmarks Biblioteksskole. 1972/73-. Danish. ir. Danmarks Biblioteksskole, Birketinget 6 2300 S, Kbenhavn Denmark. **LC** Z669.5.D4. *Studievejledning.*

STUDIES IN LIBRARIANSHIP. **Main/Corp** Denver. University. Graduate School of Librarianship. Periodical. US. English. ir. University of Denver Libraries, University Park, Denver CO 80210. **Tel** (303)753-2557. *Studies in Librarianship.*

SUBJECT CATALOG OF THE LIBRARY. SUPPLEMENT. See Bibliographies.

SUBJECT COLLECTIONS. 1st- Ed. 0000-0140. US. English. ir. R R Bowker, 1180 Avenue of the Americas, New York NY 10036.

SUBJECT DIRECTORY OF SPECIAL LIBRARIES AND INFORMATION CENTERS. See Yearbooks, Almanacs, Directories.

SUBJECT GUIDE TO BOOK REVIEWS. 8756-002X. Periodical. US. English. mo. $60.00. Daniel Hill Popular Information Press, PO Box 646, Salem OR 97308. **DD** 028.

SUBJECT HEADINGS IN MICROFORM. **Main/Corp** Library of Congress. Subject Cataloging Division. **VFOAT** Library of Congress Subject Headings in Microform. Began with Jan./Mar. 1976. 0361-5242. Periodical. US. English. qt. Library of Congress, Cataloging Distribution, Service Building 159 Navy Yard Annex, Washington DC 20541. **LC** Z663.78. Also available in 16-millimeter microfilm.

THE SUBJECT INDEX TO PERIODICALS. See Indexes/Abstracts.

SUMMARY OF PROCEEDINGS. ANNUAL CONFERENCE - AMERICAN THEOLOGICAL LIBRARY ASSOCIATION. **Main/Corp** American Theological Library Association. **VFOAT** ATLA Proceedings. **VAT** American Theological Library Association Proceedings. 1st- 1947-. 0066-0868. US. English. an. $20.00. American Theological Library Association, St Memorial School of Theology Archabbey Library, St Meinrad IN 47577. **Tel** (812)357-6718. Ed Betty O'Brien. **LC** Z673. **DD** 026.2. **Circ** 700. Papers presented at the annual conference and reports of committees. Minutes of the ATLA board.

SUPPLEMENT TO LC SUBJECT HEADINGS. **Main/Corp** Library of Congress. Subject Cataloging Division. Began with Jan. 1974. Periodical. US. English. qt. Cataloging Distribution Service, Library of Congress, Washington DC 20541. **Tel** (202)287-6100.

SURVEY OF LIBRARY MATERIAL EXPENDITURES AT STANFORD UNIVERSITY LIBRARIES. **Main/Corp** Stanford University. Libraries. 0360-2435. US. English. an. Stanford University Libraries, Stanford CA 94305. **LC** Z733.S813. **DD** 025.197779473.

SYMBOLS OF AMERICAN LIBRARIES. 0095-0874. US. English. $6.50. Library of Congress, Cataloging Distribution, Washington DC 20541. **Tel** (202)287-6100. **LC** Z881.U49. **DD** 018.1. A directory of identification symbols for libraries in the United States and Canada. *Symbols Used in the National Union Catalog of the Library of Congress.*

SYNERGY. 0164-8993. Periodical. US. English. mo. Talon Staff of The University of Texas, 5323 Harry Hines Boulevard, Dallas TX 75235. **Tel** (214)688-2085. Ed Melanie Feduska. **Circ** 2,000. (ctrl).

SYNOPSIS. 0332-656X. Periodical. NO. Norwegian (summaries in English). ir. Free. Riksbibliotektjenesten, Postboks 2439 Solli, Oslo 2 Norway. **Tel** 47 2 55 85 10. Ed Elisabeth Colbiornsen. **Ind/Abst** Libr. Inf. Sci. Abstr. **LC** Z671. **DD** 020.5. bk rev. **Circ** 1,630. News of interest to professional librarians, taken from various journals in Scandinavia, Europe and USA. Reports and articles by Norwegians.

SYNTHESE HISTORICAL LIBRARY. Vol. 1-. 0082-111X. Monographic Series. NE. English. ir. Kluwer Boston Inc, 190 Old Derby Street, Hingham MA 02043. **Ind/Abst** Math. Rev.

SYSTEMS RESEARCH AND INFORMATION SCIENCE. (INTERNATIONAL JOURNAL OF SYSTEMS RESEARCH). Began in 1985. 0882-3014. Periodical. US. English. qt. STBS Ltd, 1 Bedford Street, London WC2E 9PP England. Ed Frank George. **DD** 003. **CODEN** ISISE8. bk rev. adv acc.

TALON ANNUAL REPORT. SOUTH CENTRAL REGIONAL MEDICAL LIBRARY PROGRAM. (TALON ANNUAL REPORT). **Main/Corp** Talon Regional Medical Library Program. **VFOAT** Annual Report - Talon Regional Medical Library Program. **VAT** Texas, Arkansas, Louisiana, Oklahoma, New Mexico Annual Report. South Central Regional Medical Library Program. 1970-. 0190-7565. US. English. an. **NLM** Z 675.M4 T152T.

TASCHENBUCH INFORMATION & DOKUMENTATION. **VFOAT** Taschenbuch Information und Dokumentation. 1983-. 0723-4074. GW. German. ir. 19.80. IDD Verlag fur Internationale Dokumentation/Werner Flach KG, Altkonigstrasse 10, 6000 Frankfurt 1 West Germany. **LC** Z674.3. **DD** 020.202.

TAX FOUNDATION'S LIBRARY BULLETIN. **VFOAT** Library Bulletin. Sept./Oct. 1978-. 0736-6469. US. English. Tax Foundation, 1875 Connecticut Avenue NW, Washington DC 20009. **LC** Z7164.T23, HJ9. **DD** 016.336200973. *Library Bulletin, 0362-8426.*

TECHNICAL SERVICES LAW LIBRARIAN. V. 5- Sept. 1979-. 0195-4857. Periodical. US. English. qt. $4.00. American Association of Law Library, 53 West Jackson Boulevard, Chicago IL 60604. **Tel** (816)276-1650. Ed Michele M Finerty. adv acc. **Circ** 280. Covers all aspects of law library technical services, including cataloging, acquisitions, preservation, online systems, and networking. *Law Cataloger.*

TECHNICAL SERVICES NEWSLETTER CEASED. **Main/Corp** Inter-University Library Council (Ohio). **VFOAT** IULC Technical Services Newsletter. V. 1-8, No. 4. 0198-795X. Periodical. US. English. qt. $5.00. Brian Alley, Miami University Libraries, Oxford OH 45056.

TECHNICALITIES. Vol. 1, No. 1 (Dec. 1980)-. 0272-0884. Periodical. US. English. mo. $36.00. Oryx Press, 2214 North Central at Encanto, Phoenix AZ 85004. **Tel** (602)254-6156. Ed Jennifer Cargill and Brian Alley. **Ind/Abst** Libr. Inf. Sci. Abstr., Libr. Lit. **LC** Z671. **DD** 020.5. bk rev adv acc. **Circ** 700. News, feature articles, reviews, columns, letters and interviews provide readers a wide array of thought provoking material within a refreshing informal newsletter.

TECHNICKA KNIHOVNA. V. 1- 1957-. 0049-3171. CS. Czech. mo. Artia, PO Box 790, Praha 1 Czechoslovakia. **Ind/Abst** Comput. Control Abstr., Electr. Electron. Abstr., Sci. Abstr. Sect. A. Phys. Abstr., Libr. Inf. Sci. Abstr., Phys. Abstr. **LC** Z675.T3. **CODEN** TEKNAM.

TELEDOC. **Main/Corp** Universite du Quebec Vice-Presidence aux Communications. Vol. 1, No. 1 (Feb. 1978)-. 0227-6208. Periodical. CN. French. ir. Free. Vice-Presidence aux Communications, Universite du Quebec, 2875 Boul Laurier, Ste-Foy Quebec G1V 2M3 Canada. **DD** 025.0409714.

TEXAS LIBRARIES. V. 1- Nov. 1909-. 0040-4438. Periodical. US. English. qt. Free. Texas Libraries, Texas State Library Box 12927 Capitol Station, Austin TX 78711. **Tel** (512)463-5493. Ed Susan Hildebrand. **Ind/Abst** Am. Hist. Life, Hist. Abstr., Part A, Mod. Hist. Abstr., Hist. Abst., Part B, Twent. Century Abstr., Writ. Am. Hist., Libr. Lit. **LC** Z671. **DD** 027.0764. bk rev. **Circ** 2,000. Library technology; library techniques; general library news (statewide); feature items on books, reading, history, genealogy, research, persons involved with literature research, libraries.

TEXAS LIBRARY JOURNAL. V. 26, No. 1- Mar. 1950-. 0040-4446. Periodical. US. English. qt. $12.00. Texas Library Association, 3355 Bee Cave Road/Suite 603, Austin TX 78746. **Tel** (512)328-1518. Ed Gloriana St Clair. **Ind/Abst** Libr. Lit. **DD** 020. adv acc. **Circ** 4,000. Contains regular columns on reference, automation, user education oral. History grants intellectual freedom, etc. *News Notes.*

TEXAS PUBLIC LIBRARY STATISTICS FOR . . . . See Statistics.

THE THEATRE LIBRARY ASSOCIATION. (THE THEATRE LIBRARY ASSOCIATION. MEMBERSHIP LIST). 0148-3056. US. English. an. Theatre Library Association, 111 Amsterdam Avenue, New York NY 10023. **LC** Z675.T36. **DD** 026.7920621.

THEORY AND DECISION LIBRARY. Monographic Series. US. English. ir. Kluwer Boston Inc, 190 Old Derby Street, Hingham MA 02043. **Ind/Abst** Psychol. Abstr.

THESAURUS - AMERICAN PETROLEUM INSTITUTE. (THESAURUS). **Main/Corp** American Petroleum Institute. Central Abstracting and Indexing Service. 1st- Ed. 0193-5151. US. English. an. American Petroleum Institute, Central Abstracting and Indexing Service, 275 Madison Avenue, New York NY 10016. **LC** Z695.1.P43. **DD** 025.336655. *Information Retrieval System, Subject Authority List.*

THESAURUS, MANUFACTURING ENGINEERING TERMS. See Manufacturing.

TIENS. (LE TIENS : DES NOUVELLES DE LA B.C.P.O.L). Feb. 1979-. 0316-8441. Periodical. CN. French. bm. Bibliotheque Centrale de Pret de l'Outaouais et des Laurentides, 3000 221 Chemin Freeman, Hull Quebec J8Z 1V7 Canada. **DD** 027.471422. *Nouvelles de la Bibliotheque Centrale de Pret, 0710-104X.*

TITLE INDEX - CARLETON UNIVERSITY. See Indexes/Abstracts.

TITLE VARIES. V. 1- Dec. 1973-. 0092-6108. Periodical. US. English. bm. $3.00. Title Varies, PO Box 704, Chapel Hill NC 27514. **LC** Z692.S5. **DD** 025.343. **CODEN** TIVRA. Index published separately - free - automatically sent.

TL. TENNESSEE LIBRARIAN. (TL, TENNESSEE LIBRARIAN). **VFOAT** Tennessee Librarian. V. 29, No. 2- Spring 1977-. 0162-1564. Periodical. US. English. qt. $10.00. Tennessee Library Association, PO Box 120095, Nashville TN 37212. **Tel** (615)523-0786. Ed Barbara Dyer. **Ind/Abst** Libr. Lit. **LC** Z671. **DD** 020.6234768. bk rev. adv acc. **Circ** 1,400. (ctrl). News and information about Tennessee libraries and articles which inform and foster the profession of librarianship and which promote adequate library service for the people of Tennessee. *Tennessee Librarian, 0040-3296.*

TLA NEWSLETTER (1983). (TLA NEWSLETTER). 0378-3375. Periodical. TZ. English. ir. Tanzania Library Association, PO Box 2645, Dar es Salaam Tanzania. **LC** Z857.T3. **DD** 027.0678. *Newsletter (Tanzania Library Association).*

TOHYOP HOEBO. **VFOAT** K.L.A. Bulletin. V. 23, No. 1 (Jan./Feb. 1982)-. Periodical. KO. Korean. bm. Hanguk Tosogwan Hyophoe, 100 177 1 Ka Hoehyon Dong Chung Ku, Seoul 100 Korea. **LC** Z673. *Tosogwan Yongu.*

TOKYO CHIKU KOKURITSU DAIGAKU TOSHOKAN NETTOWAKU KENKYUKAI KENKYU HOKOKU. 1981-1986-. JA. Japanese. ir. 980. Gakukjutsu Bunken Fukyukai c/o Tokodai 12 Ookayama 2, Meguro-Ku Tokyo-To 152 Japan. **LC** Z674.83.J3.

TOP OF THE NEWS. V. 1, No. 1- Oct. 1942-. 0040-9286. Periodical. US. English. qt. American Library Association, 50 East Huron Street, Chicago IL 60611. **Tel** (312)944-6780. **Ind/Abst** Libr. Inf. Sci. Abstr., Book Rev. Index, Ref. Source, Libr. Lit., Media Rev. Dig., Curr. Index J. Educ. **LC** Z718.1.A1. **DD** 027.6205. Available on microfilm from University Microfilms.

TOPICAL INDEX FOR THE ANNUAL EDITIONS BASIC REFERENCE LIBRARY. See Indexes/Abstracts.

TORRENS. See Museums.

TOSHOKAN HAKUSHO. Began with 1972 issue. Japanese. ir. Nihon Toshokan Kyokai, 1-10 Taishido 1 Setagaya-Ku, Tokyo Japan. **LC** Z845.J4.

TOSHOKAN JANARU. JA. Japanese. ir. Tokyo Geijutsu Daigaku Fuzoku Toshokan, Ueno Koen Taito-ku, Tokyo Japan. **LC** Z955.T687.

Library and Information Science

TOSHOKAN JOHO DAIGAKU KENKYU HOKOKU. VFOAT Research Report of University of Library and Information Science. V. 1, No. 1, (1982.6)-. 0287-0010. Periodical. English (Japanese). sa. Toshokan Joho Daigaku Kasuga 1-2 Yatabe-Machi, Tsukuba-Gun Ibaraki-Ken 305 Japan.

TOSHOKAN NENKAN. 1982-. JA. Japanese. an. 9800. Nihon Toshokan Kyokai, 1-10 Taishido 1, Setagaya-Ku, Tokyo-To Japan. LC Z845.J4.

TOSHOKAN TANKI DAIGAKU KIYO. VFOAT Memoirs of the Toshokan Tanki Daigaku. No. 1- 1966-. 0385-4493. Periodical. Japanese (summaries in English). ir. LC Z671.

TOSHOKANGAKU KYOIKU TANTOSHA MEIBO. Japanese. ni. LC Z669.5.J3.

TOSHOKANGAKU NEMPO. VFOAT Doshisha Daigaku Toshokangaku Nempo. Began in 1975. JA. Japanese. an. Doshisha Daigaku Toshokan Shisho Katei, Higashi-Iru Imadegawadori Karasumaru Kamigyo-ku, Kyoto-shi Japan. LC Z671.

TOSHOKANHO. THE TOTTORI UNIVERSITY LIBRARY INFORMATION. Main/Corp Tottori Daigaku. Toshokan. VFOAT Tottori University Library Information. JA. Japanese. ir. 1-1 Koyamacho, 680 Tottori Japan. LC Z955.T822.

TOSHOKANKAI. VFOAT The Library World. Began in May 1947. 0040-9669. Periodical. JA. Japanese. bm. Japan Institute of Library Science, Toshokangaku Kenkyuswitsu, Tenri Nara 632 Japan.

TOSOGWAN. VFOAT Bulletin of the Central National Library. Periodical. KO. Korean. ir. Kungnip Chungang Tosogwan, 100-177 Hoehyeon-Dong 1-Ka, Jung-Gu Seoul Korea. LC Z671.

TOSOGWAN. VFOAT Bulletin of Central National Library. Periodical. Korean. ir.

TOSOGWAN HWICHONG. Main/Corp Kungnip Chungang Tosogwan (Seoul, Korea). VFOAT The Information Book of the Central National Library. English (Korean). an. Kungnip Chungang Tosogwan, 100-177 1-ka Hoehyon-dong Chung-ku, Seoul Korea. LC Z846.K85.

TOYAMA KENRITSU TOSHOKAN NENKAN ZOKA TOSHO MOKUROKU. Began with 1970 issue. Japanese. ir. Toyama Kenritsu Toshokan, 206-3 Chayamachi, Toyama 930-01 Japan. LC Z955.

TRAINING AND EDUCATION. (TRAINING AND EDUCATION : A JOURNAL FOR LIBRARY AND INFORMATION WORKERS). Vol. 1, No. 1-. 0264-8466. Periodical. UK. English. ty. 25. College of Librarianship Wales Llanbadarn Fawr, IM Johnson, Aberystwyth Dyfed England. Tel (970)3181. Ed R J Prytherch. Ind/Abst Libr. Inf. Sci. Abstr. bk rev. adv acc. Circ 1,100. (ctrl). Authoritative articles on all aspects of the education and training of professional and other workers in libraries and information centers. International in coverage, but British emphasis. Leg News.

TRAIT D'UNION - BIBLIOTHEQUE CENTRALE DE PRET DE L'ESTRIE. (LE TRAIT D'UNION). V. 1, No. 2, (April 1983)-. 0822-0344. Periodical. CN. French. qt. Free. Bibliotheque Centrale de Pret de l'Estrie, 4155 rue Brodeur, Sherbrooke Quebec J1L 1K4 Canada. DD 027.4714605. (ctrl). Anonyme, 0715-7487.

TRAVAUX ET RECHERCHES GRIC. VFOAT Travaux et Recherches du Gric. VAT Travaux et Recherches Groupe de Recherche en Information et Communication. 1-. 0703-1297. Monographic Series. CN. French. ir. Edi-Gric, Dep d'Information et de Communication Pavillon, Casault Universite Laval, Quebec Quebec G1K 7P4 Canada. LC UNC. DD 001.5105.

LA TROBE LIBRARY JOURNAL. V. 1- Apr. 1968-. 0041-3151. AT. English. sa. $7.89. State Library Association of Victoria, Swanston Street, Melbourne Victoria 3000 Australia. Ind/Abst APAIS, Aust. Public Aff. Inf. Serv. LC Z975. DD 027.4945.

TU SHU CHING PAO KUNG TSO. VFOAT Library and Information Service. Began with Feb. 1980 issue. 0252-3116. Periodical. Chinese. bm. Guozi Shudian, Edificio Sidan, Apartado Postal 399, Peking China Mainland. Ind/Abst Libr. Inf. Sci. Abstr. LC Z671. DD 020.5. Tu Shu Kuan Kung Tso.

TU SHU KUAN HSUEH YU TZU HSUN KO HSUEH. VFOAT Journal of Library & Information Science. V. 1- Apr. 1975-. 0363-3640. Periodical. US. Chinese (English). ir. $10.00. Chinese Culture Service, PO Box 444, Oak Park IL 60303. Ind/Abst Libr. Inf. Sci. Abstr., Public Aff. Inf. Serv. Bull. LC Z671.

TU SHU KUAN TSA CHIH. VFOAT Tushuguan Zazhi. 1982, 1-. Periodical. CH. Chinese. qt. 0.46. Shang-Hai Shih Pao Kan Fa Hsing Chu Shanghai China. LC Z671. DD 020.5.

TU SHU YU TU SHU KUAN. V. 1-. Periodical. Chinese. ir. $2.50 Each Issue. LC Z845.T3.

TUDOMANYOS ES MUSZAKI TAJEKOZTATAS. 0041-3917. Periodical. HU. Hungarian (table of contents and summaries in English, Russian and German). mo. 840.-. Akademiai Kiado, POB 24, 1363 Budapest Hungary. Tel 136-471. Ed Peter Szanto. Ind/Abst Libr. Inf. Sci. Abstr., Electr. Electron. Abstr., Phys. Abstr., Comput. Control Abstr., Sci. Abstr. Sect. A. Phys. Abstr. LC Q4. CODEN TMTAAG. bk rev. Circ 1,300. Studies, reports, reviews, news, etc. on library and information science. Contributions from Hungarian and foreign authors. Muszaki Konyvtarosok Tajekoztatoja.

THE TURNBULL LIBRARY RECORD. No. 1- Jan. 1940-Nov. 1962. 0110-1625. Periodical. NZ. English. sa. $8.44. Alexander Turnbull Library Endowment Trust, Box 12-349, Wellington New Zealand. Tel 04-722 101. Ed J E Traue and Penelope Griffith. LC Z975. Circ 1,100. (ctrl). Articles reflect the library's major collecting and research interests: New Zealand, Australia, and Pacific; Milton and early modern English studies; rare books; fine printing.

UBC DATA LIBRARY CATALOGUE. (UBC DATA LIBRARY CATALOGUE. MICROFORM). Main/Corp University of British Columbia. Data Library. VFOAT Catalogue. VAT Catalogue - University of British Columbia. Data Library (Microform). 0713-8172. CN. English. an. Free. UBC Data Library Catalogue, c/o University of British Columbia, Data Library/Room 206, 6356 Agricultural Road, Vancouver British Columbia V6T 1W5 Canada. DD 016.303380971. (ctrl). Catalogue, 0319-5201.

UBC LIBRARY BULLETIN. Main/Corp University of British Columbia. Library. VAT University of British Columbia Library Bulletin (1973). 0229-5954. Periodical. CN. English. ir. Free. University of British Columbia Library, 2075 Wesbrook Place, Vancouver British Columbia V6T 1W5 Canada. DD 027.7871133. (ctrl). University of British Columbia Library Bulletin.

UCLA LIBRARIAN. Main/Corp University of California, Los Angeles. Library. VAT University of California at Los Angeles Librarian. V. 1- Oct. 16, 1947-. US. English. mo. Friends of UCLA Library, University of California, 405 Hildard Avenue, Los Angeles CA 90024. Tel (213)825-1201. LC Z881. DD 027.7794.

ULRICH'S INTERNATIONAL PERIODICALS DIRECTORY. See Yearbooks, Almanacs, Directories.

UMBRAL 2000 I.E. DOS MIL. Vol. 1- Jan./July 1972-. AG. Spanish. ir. Direccion de Ensenanza Superior, Avda 44 No 790, La Plata Argentina. LC Z765.A1. DD 020.5.

THE UNABASHED LIBRARIAN. No. 1- Fall 1971-. 0049-514X. Periodical. US. English. qt. $20.00. Unabashed Librarian, US Government Printing Office, Box 2631, New York NY 10116. Ind/Abst Public Lit. LC Z671. DD 020.5. The "How I Run My Library Good" letter. Contains practical ideas, forms, procedures, library life, library humor, library poetry booklists, etc.

UNION CATALOG OF SERIALS CURRENTLY RECEIVED IN THE LIBRARIES OF THE UNIVERSITY OF WISCONSIN, MADISON. (UNION CATALOG OF SERIALS CURRENTLY RECEIVED IN THE LIBRARIES OF THE UNIVERSITY OF WISCONSIN—MADISON). Main/Corp Wisconsin. University—Madison. Library. 1974-. 0145-8507. US. Multilingual (English). an. University of Wisconsin, Memorial, Library, Madison WI 53706. LC Z6945, PN4832. DD 016.05.

UNION LIST OF PERIODICALS - CASLIS. CALGARY CHAPTER. (UNION LIST OF PERIODICALS). Main/Corp Canadian Association of Special Libraries and Information Services., Calgary Chapter. 1983-. 0822-1685. CN. English. an. $150.00. Union List of Periodicals, c/o Susan Tyrrell, Panarctic Oils Ltd, 11th Floor/815-8th Avenue SW, PO Box 190, Calgary Alberta T2P 2H6 Canada. DD 018.134. Union List of Serials, 0712-6972.

UNION LIST OF PERIODICALS IN THE DEPARTMENT OF COMMUNICATIONS LIBRARIES AND DOCUMENTATION CENTRES. Main/Corp Canada. Dept. of Communications. VFOAT Repertoire Collectif des Periodiques dans les Bibliotheques et les Centres de Documentation du Ministere des Communications. 1979-. 0226-0506. CN. English (French). Department of Communications, 171 Slater Street, Ottawa Ontario K1A 0S9 Canada. DD 018.134. Periodicals in C. R. C. Library, 0381-2499.

UNION LIST OF SCIENTIFIC SERIALS IN CANADIAN LIBRARIES. See Bibliographies.

UNION LIST OF SERIALS - LAKE ONTARIO REGIONAL LIBRARY SYSTEM. Main/Corp Lake Ontario Regional Library System. 4th- Ed. 0709-5317. CN. English. an. Lake Ontario Regional Library System, 88 Wright Crescent, Kingston Ontario K7L 4T9 Canada. DD 016.05. Periodical Holdings of Resource Libraries, 0709-5309.

U.S. ENVIRONMENTAL PROTECTION AGENCY LIBRARY SYSTEM BOOK CATALOG. Main/Corp United States. Environmental Protection Agency. Library Systems Branch. VFOAT EPA Book Catalog. VAT United States Environmental Protection Agency Library System Book Catalog, Environmental Protection Agency Book Catalog. 1973-. 0161-5645. Periodical. US. English. an. Environmental Protection Agency, Office of Planning and Management, Office of Administration Management and Organization Division, Library Systems Branch, Springfield VA 22161. Available on microfiche from the National Technical Information Service.

UNIVERSITY AND COLLEGE LIBRARIES; STATISTICS OF NORTH CAROLINA. See Statistics.

UNIVERSITY OF ALBERTA DATA LIBRARY CATALOGUE. VFOAT Data Library Catalogue. 0713-7591. CN. English. $9.90 Each Volume. University of Alberta Bookstore, Students' Union Building, Edmonton Alberta T6G 2J7 Canada. DD 018.1.

UNIVERSITY OF FLORIDA LIBRARIES. Main/Corp Florida. University, Gainesville. Libraries. No. 1-2. US. English. ir. University of Florida Press, 15 NW 15th Street, Gainesville FL 32601.

UNIVERSITY OF WATERLOO LIBRARY SERIALS LIST. (SERIALS LIST). 1966-. 0316-5949. Periodical. CN. English. an. University of Waterloo Library, Waterloo Ontario N26 EG1 Canada. DD 016.05. Serial Holdings.

UNIVERSITY PRESS BOOKS FOR PUBLIC LIBRARIES. VFOAT Books for Public Libraries. Began with 1st Ed., 1979. 0731-2857. US. English. an. LC Z731. DD 025.2187473.

UNRAVEL. V. 1- Nov. 1976-. 0700-382X. Periodical. CN. English. mo. Georgian Bay Regional Library System, 30 Morrow Road, Barrie Ontario L4N 3V8 Canada. DD 028.7.

UPDATE - CHINOOK REGIONAL LIBRARY. (UPDATE). Vol. 1, No. 1 (Fall 1984)-. 0828-7694. Periodical. CN. English. sa. Free. Chinook Regional Library, 1240 Chaplin Street West, Swift Current Saskatchewan S9H 0G8 Canada. DD 027.47243.

UPDATE: GCLC. (UPDATE, GCLC). VFOAT Update, G.C.L.C. VAT Update: Greater Cincinnati Library Consortium. 0743-9652. Periodical. US. English. qt. Free. The Greater Cincinnati Library Consortium, 3333 Vine Street/Suite 45220, Cincinnati OH 45220. Tel (513)751-4422. Ed Pat Yannarella. Circ 365. Newsletter of the Greater Cincinnati Library Consortium.

UPDATE (LIBRARY OF CONGRESS. NATIONAL LIBRARY SERVICE FOR THE BLIND AND PHYSICALLY HANDICAPPED). (UPDATE). Began with V. 1, No. 6, May-June 1978. Periodical. US. English. mo. $10.00. Libertarian Review Foundation, 1320 G Street SE, Washington DC 20003. Tel (2020547-2770. Update, 0160-9203.

Library and Information Science

URBAN ACADEMIC LIBRARIAN. Vol. 1, No. 1 (Spring 1981)-. 0276-9298. Periodical. US. English. ir. $8.00. Hunter College Library, 695 Park Avenue, New York NY 10021. **LC** Z668. **DD** 020.715. *Lacuny Journal, 0094-615X.*

URISA NEWS. (URISA NEWS : COMMUNICATIONS OF THE URBAN & REGIONAL INFORMATION SYSTEMS ASSOCIATION). **VFOAT** U.R.I.S.A. News. **VAT** Urban and Regional Information Systems Association News. Issue 65 (Fall 1982)-. 0749-9531. Periodical. US. English. qt. URISA Secretariat, 4720 Montgomery Lane/Suite 506, Bethesda MD 20814. **DD** 025. *URISA.*

USBE NEWS. Main/Corp Universal Serials and Book Exchange. **VFOAT** USBE/News. **VAT** Universal Serials and Book Exchange News. V. 28- Jan. 1976-. 0364-5215. US. English. USBE/News, 3335 V Street Northeast, Washington DC 20018. **LC** Z690. **DD** 025.26. *Newsletter - United States Book Exchange, 0041-753X.*

UTAH PUBLIC LIBRARY SERVICE. Main/Corp Utah. State Library Commission. 1967-. US. English. an. State Library Commission of Utah, 2150 52nd West/Suite 16, Salt Lake City UT 84115. **LC** Z732.U8. **DD** 027.4792. *Annual Report for Utah Public Library Service.*

UTLAS NEWSLETTER. (U T L A S NEWSLETTER). **Main/Corp** University of Toronto. Library Automation Systems. V. 4, No. 10- Oct. 1979-. 0225-1760. Periodical. CN. English. mo. Free. Newsletter Editor, University of Toronto, Library Automation Systems, 130 Saint George Street, Toronto Ontario M5G 1A5 Canada. **DD** 025.54. *Newsletter, 0700-4397.*

V MIRE KNIG; KRITIKO-BIBLIOGRAFICHESKII ZHURNAL. See Bibliographies.

V POMOSHCH MASSOVYM BIBLIOTEKAM. 1973-. UR. Russian. 0.11. Kniga, Tsentr, Prospekt Kalinina 3, Moskva Russian SFSR. **LC** Z819.A1.

VASLA. Main/Corp Special Libraries Association. Virginia Chapter. 0042-1723. Periodical. US. English. qt. Special Libraries Association, 1700 18th Street NW, Washington DC 20009. **Tel** (202)234-4700. **LC** Z675.A2. **DD** 026.00060755.

VEHICLE. (LE VEHICULE : BULLETIN D'INFORMATION DU SERVICE DES BIBLIOTHEQUES D'ENSEIGNEMENT A L'INTENTION DES BIBLIOTHEQUES DU RESEAU COLLEGIAL). No. 1 (Jun. 1979)-. 0225-5480. Periodical. CN. French. Gouvernement du Quebec, 600 St Amable 4E Etage, Quebec G1R 4Z1 Canada. **DD** 027.709714.

VERMONT LIBRARY DIRECTORY. See Yearbooks, Almanacs, Directories.

VIDEODISC AND OPTICAL DISK. See Computers and Computer Science.

VIJNANA SARASVATI. VFOAT Vijnana Saraswati : A Quarterly Oriental Research Journal of the Andhra Pradesh Government Oriental Manuscripts Library & Research Institute. Vol. 1, No. 1 (Jan. 1984)-. Periodical. II. English (Telugu). qt. 25.00. Andhra Pradesh Government Oriental Research, Institute Tarnaka, Hyderabad 500007 India.

VINE; A VERY INFORMAL NEWSLETTER FOR LIBRARY AUTOMATION. VFOAT V.I.N.E. No. 1-Oct. 1971-. 0305-5728. Periodical. UK. English. ir. $41.38. Polytechnic of Central London, 309 Regent Street, London WIR 8AL England. **Tel** (01)580-4562. **Ed** Patricia Manson. **Circ** 650. (ctrl). Very informal newsletter for libraries and librarians.

VIRGINIA LIBRARIAN NEWSLETTER. V. 23- Spring 1977-. 0273-3951. Periodical. US. English. qt. Virginia Librarian, PO Box 12445, Richmond VA 23241. **LC** Z673.V82. **DD** 020.6234755.

VITAL NOTES ON MEDICAL PERIODICALS : A PUBLICATION OF THE MEDICAL LIBRARY ASSOCIATION. See Medicine.

VIVLIOGRAPHIKA. Year 1- (No. 1-). Greek, Modern. ir. 3 Vamva Street, T T 138 Athenai Greece. **LC** Z671.

VOICE OF YOUTH ADVOCATES. (VOYA. VOICE OF YOUTH ADVOCATES). **VFOAT** Voice of Youth Advocates. V. 1- April 1978-. 0160-4201. Periodical. US. English. bm. $27.00. Voice of Youth Advocates, 3936 West Colonial Parkway, Virginia Beach VA 23452. **Tel** (804)498-3693. **Ed** Dorothy M Broderick. **Ind/Abst** Libr. Inf. Sci. Abstr., Book Rev. Index, Ref. Source, Libr. Lit. bk rev. adv acc. **Circ** 3,000. Articles, bibliographies on library information services to adolescents, reviews of materials for, about, and by adolescents.

VOICE OF Z 39. No. 1- Jan. 1979-. 0163-626X. Periodical. US. English. ty. $100.00. National Information Standards Organization, Building 101/Room E-106, Gaithersburg MD 20899. **Tel** (301)921-3241. **Ed** Patricia R Harris. **LC** Z672. **DD** 025. bk rev. **Circ** 1,000. News on standards development in library science, information services and publishing. *ANSI News about Z39, 0028-8942.*

WAPITI. (THE WAPITI). Vol. 1, No. 1 (Nov. 1981)-. 0713-0546. Periodical. CN. English. sa. The Wapiti, Wapiti Regional Library, 145-12th Street East, Prince Albert Saskatchewan S6V 1B7 Canada. **DD** 027.471242.

WAR LIBRARY BULLETIN. Vol. 1, No. 1 (Aug. 1917)-No. 9 (May 1919). Periodical. US. English. ir. **LC** Z675.W2.

WASHINGTON NEWSLETTER. VFOAT ALA Washington Newsletter. V. 1- Jan. 27, 1949-. 0001-1746. Periodical. US. English. ir. **LC** Z671. *Federal Relations News.*

WASHINGTON NEWSLETTER - AMERICAN LIBRARY ASSOCIATION. WASHINGTON OFFICE. (WASHINGTON NEWSLETTER). -V. 36, No. 1 (Feb. 3, 1984). 0001-1746. Periodical. US. English. ir. $15.00. ALA Washington Newsletter Office, 110 Maryland Avenue NE Suite 101, Washington DC 20002. **Tel** (202)547-4440. **Ed** Eileen D Cooke and Carol C Henderson. **Ind/Abst** Libr. Lit. **LC** Z671. **DD** 020.5. **NLM** Z 671 W318. Legislation affecting libraries. *ALA Washington Newsletter.*

WASHINGTON UNIVERSITY LIBRARY STUDIES. Main/Corp Washington University, St. Louis. Libraries. **VFOAT** Library Studies. 1- 1950-. 0508-1165. Monographic Series. US. English. Washington University, PO Box 1120, St Louis MO 63130.

WATERMARK (SALEM, OR.) CEASED. (WATERMARK). Began with issue for Jan. 1977. Ceased with issue for Jan./May 1982. 0194-2999. US. English. mo. Watermark, State Library Building, Salem OR 97310. **Tel** (503)3784245. **LC** Z732.O8. **DD** 027.5795. *Letter to Libraries.*

WEEKLY LIBRARY BULLETIN. VFOAT Library Bulletin. Arabic (English). wk. **LC** Z6958.S33. **DD** 011.34.

WEEKLY LIST OF ACCESSIONS TO THE LIBRARY. See Bibliographies.

WES-CAN A S I S NEWSLETTER. (THE WES-CAN A S I S NEWSLETTER). **Main/Corp** American Society for Information Science. Western Canada Chapter. No. 23- Dec. 1976-. 0702-8725. Periodical. CN. English. Free. Western Canada Chapter of ASIS, c/o 8734-119 Street, Edmonton Alberta T6G 1W8 Canada. **DD** 029.70627123. (ctrl). *A.I.R.A. - Wes-Can A.S.I.S. Newsletter, 0382-4969.*

WEST BENGAL INFORMATION DIRECTORY. See Yearbooks, Almanacs, Directories.

WEST VAN BOOKMAN. V. 1- July 1973-. 0317-0446. Periodical. CN. English. ir. Free. West Vancouver Memorial Library, 1950 Marine Drive West, Vancouver British Columbia V7V 1J8 Canada. **DD** 027.471133.

WEST VIRGINIA LIBRARIES. V. 1- 1947-. 0043-3276. Periodical. US. English. qt. $15.00. West Virginia Library Association, West Virginia University, Main Library, PO Box 6069, Morgantown WV 26506. **Tel** (304)293-5395. **Ed** Mildred Moyers. **Ind/Abst** Libr. Inf. Sci. Abstr., Libr. Lit. **LC** Z673. **DD** 027.0754. bk rev. adv acc. **Circ** 1,000. (ctrl). Articles, news, events concerning libraries as well as the association.

WHSTC LIBRARY CATALOG. VAT Western Hemisphere Short Title Catalog Project Library Catalog. No. 1-. 0712-9297. Monographic Series. CN. English. WHSTC Project, School of Library and Information Science, University of Western Ontario, London Ontario N6G 1H1 Canada. **LC** UNC. **DD** 010.

WIDENER LIBRARY SHELFLIST. Main/Corp Harvard University. Library. No. 1 - 1965-. 0083-9892. Monographic Series. US. English. ir. Harvard University Press, 79 Garden Street, Cambridge MA 02138. **Tel** (617)661-3761.

THE WIENER LIBRARY BULLETIN. V. 1-. 0043-5333. Periodical. UK. English. an. Wiener Library, 4 Devonshire Street, London W1N 2BH England. **Ind/Abst** Am. Hist. Life, Hist. Abstr., Part A, Mod. Hist. Abstr., Hist. Abst., Part B, Twent. Century Abstr. **LC** Z921.W6. **DD** 909.82.

WILLIAM ANDREWS CLARK MEMORIAL LIBRARY SEMINAR PAPERS. PAPERS DELIVERED AT THE CLARK LIBRARY SEMINAR. 1952-. 0575-4909. Monographic Series. US. English. ir. $15.00. Regents of the University California, 2520 Cimarron Street, Los Angeles CA 90018. **Tel** (213)731/8529. **Ed** Nancy M Shea. **Circ** 200. (ctrl).

WILLIAM L. CLEMENTS LIBRARY ANNUAL REPORT. Main/Corp Michigan. University. William L. Clements Library. 2nd- 1924/25-. US. English. an. University of Michigan, 115 Johnston Hall, Ann Arbor MI 48109. **LC** Z733. **DD** 026.973.

WILSON LIBRARY BULLETIN. V. 1- Nov. 1914-. 0043-5651. Periodical. US. English. mo. $30.00. H W Wilson Company, 950 University Avenue, Bronx NY 10452. **Tel** (212)588-8400. **Ed** Milo Nelson. **Ind/Abst** Educ. Index, Libr. Lit., Public Aff. Inf. Serv. Bull., Read. Guide Period. Lit., Libr. Inf. Sci. Abstr., Hist. Abstr., Am. Hist. Life. **LC** Z1217. **DD** 020.5. (cum index). bk rev. adv acc. (ctrl). Devoted to libraries and librarianship, information science, books and publishing, plus technological communications.

WIP FUN. (WIP FUN : WORKS IN PROGRESS OF FUN-STUFF). **Main/Corp** Crane Library. **VAT** Works in Progress Fun. Vol. 1, No. 1 (Nov. 1982)-. 0824-4782. Periodical. CN. English. ir. Free. Crane Library, 1874 East Mall, Vancouver B C V6T 1W5 Canada. **DD** 011.38. (ctrl).

WISCONSIN LIBRARY BULLETIN. V. 1- Jan. 1905-. 0043-6526. Periodical. US. English. qt. Free to Wisconsin public and school libraries, $5.00 Others. Division of Library Services, Department of Public Instruction, 126 Langdon Street, Madison WI 53702. **Ind/Abst** Libr. Lit. **LC** Z732.W8. **DD** 020.5. (cum index).

WISCONSIN LIBRARY SERVICE RECORD. Main/Corp Wisconsin. Division for Library Services. 1973-. 0361-2848. US. English. an. Division for Library Services, 126 Langdon Street, Madison WI 53702. **LC** L216, Z732.W8. **DD** 025.509775.

THE WLN PARTICIPANT. (WLN PARTICIPANT). **VFOAT** Participant. **VAT** Washington Library Network Participant. 0278-6303. Periodical. US. English. qt. Western Library Network, Mail Stop AJ-11, Olympia WA 98504. **Tel** (206)459-6706. **Ed** David Wasser. **DD** 025. **Circ** 1,000. (ctrl). Publication detailing activities of the Western Library Network, an agency of the state of Washington.

WLW JOURNAL. Main/Corp Women Library Workers (U.S.). **VAT** Women Library Workers Journal. V. 5- Jan./Feb. 1980-. 0272-1996. Periodical. US. English. qt $39.00. Women Library Workers, 2027 Parker Street, Berkeley CA 94704. **Tel** (415)540-5322. **Ed** Carol Starr. **Ind/Abst** Libr. Inf. Sci. Abstr., Ref. Source, Libr. Lit. bk rev. adv acc. **Circ** 500. (ctrl). Works to end discrimination against women in libraries and librarianship. *Women Library Workers, 0738-629X.*

WOLFENBUTTELER BEITRAGE. No. 1- 1972-. 0300-2012. GW. German. ir. 58.-. Vittorio Klostermann, Postfach 900601 Frauenlobstrabe 22, 6000 Frankfurt am Main 90 West Germany. **Tel** (0611)77 4011. **Ind/Abst** MLA Int. Bibliogr. Books Artic. Mod. Lang. Lit., Recent Publ. Artic., Years Work Eng. Stud.

THE WORK OF ASLIB. Main/Corp ASLIB. **VFOAT** Annual Report and Accounts. UK. English. an. ASLIB, 3 Belgrave Square, London SW1X 8PL England. **LC** Z673. **DD** 020.622. **NLM** Z 673 A835W.

WORLD GUIDE TO LIBRARIES. VFOAT Internationales Bibliotheks-Handbuch. No. 6- 0000-0221. US. English (German). ir. $158.00. Gale Research, Book Tower, Detroit MI 48226. **Ed** H Lengenfelder. Provides details on 43,000 libraries worldwide, the new edition adds over 2,000 libraries while deleting 1,000 defunct libraries. *Internationales Bibliotheks-Handbuch, 0000-0221.*

WORLD GUIDE TO SPECIAL LIBRARIES. VFOAT Internationales Handbuch der Spezialbibliotheken. 1st Ed.-. 0724-8717. US. English. ir. $124.00. Gale Research, Book Tower, Detroit MI 48226. Tel (313)961-2242. Ed H Lengenfelder. A detailed subject index provides access by 27 specific subject terms.

WORLDWIDE ART & LIBRARY NEWSLETTER. See The Arts (General).

WVLC NEWSLETTER. Main/Corp West Virginia. Library Commission. Science & Cultural Center. VAT West Virginia Library Commission Newsletter. 0149-0567. Periodical. US. English. qt. West Virginia Library Commission, Science and Culture Center, Charleston WV 25305. LC Z732.W5. DD 021.009754.

WYOMING LIBRARY ROUNDUP. 0043-9738. Periodical. US. English. ty. $10.00. Wyoming Library Association, 2800 Central Avenue, Cheyenne WY 82001. Tel (307)777-5915. Ed Linn Rounds. Ind/Abst Libr. Lit. LC Z671. DD 020.623. bk rev. Circ 750. (ctrl). Articles about Wyoming libraries and what they are doing. Book reviews and information on activities of the Wyoming Library Association.

YAKUGAKU TOSHOKAN. VFOAT Pharmaceutical Library Bulletin. Began with 1931 Vol. 1 Jan. 1956 Issue. 0386-2062. Periodical. Japanese. ir. Faculty of Pharmaceutical Sciences, 3-1 Hongo 7 Minato-Ku, Tokyo Japan. Ind/Abst Chem. Abstr. LC Z675.P48. NLM Z 675.P5 Y15. CODEN YATODW.

THE YALE UNIVERSITY LIBRARY GAZETTE. V. 1- June 1926-. 0044-0175. Periodical. US. English. sa. $20.00. Yale University Library, Publications Office, Box 1603A, Yale Station, New Haven CT 06520. Tel (203)436-1049. Ed Stephen Parks. Ind/Abst Abstr. Engl. Stud., Am. Hist. Life, Annu. Bibliogr. Engl. Lang. Lit., Artbibliogr. Mod., Hist. Abstr., Part A, Mod. Hist. Abstr., Hist. Abstr., Part B, Twent. Century Abstr., MLA Int. Bibliogr. Books Artic. Mod. Lang. Lit., Writ. Am. Hist., Hist. Abstr., Years Work Eng. Stud. LC Z733. DD 027.77468. (cum index). Circ 1,200. (ctrl). Articles based on collections in various divisions of Yale Library and news of recent acquisitions. Occasionally catalogues of current exhibitions.

YAYA. Issue # 1 (July 1984)-. 0824-1457. Periodical. CN. English. ir. 6.50 Domestic, 8.50 Foreign. Yaya, c/o L Amey School of Library Service Dalhousie University, Halifax NS B3H 4H8 Canada. Tel (902)424-3656. Ed L J Amey. DD 027.62606071. bk rev. Circ 150. National newsletter of young adult special interest group of Canadian Library Association. News for librarians serving teenagers.

YEAR BOOK. See Yearbooks, Almanacs, Directories.

YELLOWBACK LIBRARY. VFOAT Yellow Back Library. Periodical. US. English. bm. $8.00. Gil O'Gara, 2019 Southeast Street, Des Moines IA 50315.

YOUR NEWSLETTER. Vol. 1, No. 1 (Sept. 1976)-. 0229-7914. Periodical. CN. English. mo. Library Services, Vancouver School Board, 2530-43rd Avenue East, Vancouver British Columbia V5R 2Y7 Canada. DD 027.809711.

YUL SERIALS LIST. (Y U L SERIALS LIST). Main/Corp York University, Toronto, Ont. Libraries. VAT York University Libraries Serials List. Began publication in 1978. 0225-5081. Periodical. CN. English. qt. $24.00. Microcatalogues, Room 310, Scott Library York University, 4700 Keele Street, Downsview Ont M3J 2R2 Canada. DD 016.05.

ZEITSCHRIFT FUR BIBLIOTHEKSWESEN UND BIBLIOGRAPHIE. See Bibliographies.

ZEITSCHRIFT FUR BIBLIOTHEKSWESEN UND BIBLIOGRAPHIE. SONDERHEFT. 1- 1963-. 0514-6364. Periodical. GW. German. ir. 100.-. Vittorio Klostermann, Postfach 900601 Frauenlobstrabe 22, 6000 Frankfurt am Main 90 West Germany. Tel (0611)77 4011.

ZENTRALBLATT FUR BIBLIOTEKSWESEN. 21.- Volume 1904-. 0044-4081. Periodical. SZ. German. mo. $50.56. Kunst & Wissen Erich Bieber, Dufourstrasse 51, CH-8008 Zurich Switzerland. Tel 011-41-1-69 44 20. Ind/Abst Libr. Inf. Sci. Abstr., Libr. Lit., Soc. Sci. Citation Index. LC Z671. NLM Z 671 Z56. (cum index). Centralblatt fur Bibliothekswesen.

THE ZIMBABWE LIBRARIAN. Vol. 11, Nos. 1 and 2 (Jan. -June 1979)-. 0035-4848. Periodical. English. sa. $10.00. Zimbabwe Librarian, PO Box 3133, Harare Zimbabwe. Ed Roger Stringer. adv acc. Circ 350. Journal of the Zimbabwe Library Association. Articles on library and information services in Zimbabwe. Rhodesian Librarian.

LINGUISTICS

AAA, ARBEITEN AUS ANGLISTIK UND AMERIKANISTIK. VFOAT Arbeiten aus Anglistik und Amerikanistik. No. 1- 1976-. 0171-5410. German. sa. 64,-. Gunter Narr Verlag, Postfach 2567, 7400 Tuebingen 5 West Germany. Tel (07071)78091. Ed Gunter Narr. Ind/Abst MLA Int. Bibliogr. Books Artic. Mod. Lang. Lit. LC PE3. adv acc. (ctrl). English and American studies (includes language, literature and civilization).

AATSEEL'S NEWSLETTER. See Education (General).

ABHANDLUNGEN FUR DIE KUNDE DES MORGENLANDES. Main/Corp Deutsche Morgenlandische Gesellschaft. 1. Vol. No. 1-. GW. German. ir. Franz Steiner Verlag GMBH, Postfach 347, D7000 Stuttgart 1 West Germany. Tel (0711) 2582229. Ed E Wagner. Monographs dedicated to Oriental and African languages and literatures.

ABHINAYA. Periodical. II. in Bengali. ir. 15.00. Dilipa Bandyopadhyaya, 131 Harish Mukherjee Road, Calcutta 70002 India. LC PK1712.5.

ACLALS BULLETIN. See Literature.

ACOPEL. See Literature.

ACRONYMS, INITIALISMS & ABBREVIATIONS DICTIONARY. See Encyclopedias & General Reference Books.

ACTA LINGUISTICA ACADEMIAE SCIENTIARUM HUNGARICAE. Vol. 1- 1951-. 0001-5946. Periodical. HU. English (French, German, and Russian). qt. $44.00. Akademiai Kiado, POB 24, 1363 Budapest Hungary. Tel 111-010. Ed J Herman and F Kiefer. Ind/Abst MLA Int. Bibliogr. Books Artic. Mod. Lang. Lit., Lang. Lang. Behav. Abstr., Annu. Bibliogr. Engl. Lang. Lit., Lang. Teach., Sociol. Abstr. LC P25. Index in last issue of volume - attached. bk rev. adv acc. Circ 900. Finno-Ugric, Slavonic, Germanic, Oriental and Romance linguistics and general linguistics.

ACTA LINGUISTICA HAFNIENSIA. Vol. 9, No. 1-. 0374-0463. Periodical. DK. English (articles in French and German). ir. $40.43. C A Reitzel Forlag AS, Norregade 20, DK-1165 Copenhagen K Denmark. Tel 01/ 12 24 00. Ind/Abst MLA Int. Bibliogr. Books Artic. Mod. Lang. Lit., Lang. Lang. Behav. Abstr., Lang. Teach., Sociol. Abstr. Acta Linguistics, 0105-001X.

ACTA ORIENTALIA. V. 1- 1922-. 0001-6438. English (contributions in various languages). an. 330.00 Domestic, 362.00 Foreign. Munksgaard International Publishers Limited, 35 Norre Sogade, DK-1370 Copenhagen K Denmark. Tel 45 12 70 30. Ed Soren Egerod. Ind/Abst MLA Int. Bibliogr. Books Artic. Mod. Lang. Lit., Recent Publ. Artic. LC PJ1. Circ 500. Oriental culture and languages. Monde Oriental.

ACTA UNIVERSITATIS CAROLINAE. PHILOLOGICA. 1958-. 0567-8269. CS. German and English. ir. Artia, Ve-Smeckach 30, Praha 1 Czechoslovakia. Ind/Abst Sociol. Abstr., Lang. Lang. Behav. Abstr. LC P9. Acta Universitatis Carolinae.

ACTAS DEL CONGRESO INTERNACIONAL DE HISPANISTAS. Main/Corp International Congress of Hispanists. 1.- 1962-. Spanish (English). ir. LC PC4021.

ACTES - CANADIAN ASSOCIATION OF APPLIED LINGUISTICS. MEETING. Main/Corp Canadian Association of Applied Linguistics. Meeting. VFOAT Actes. CN. English (English, French, and German). ir. 16.00. Universite Montreal, Sec de Lacla CP 6128, Montreal Quebec H3C 357 Canada. Tel (418)656-3232. LC P51. DD 418.007. bk rev. adv acc. Circ 600. (ctrl). Text on applied linguistics, teaching of English and French as second languages and translations.

Linguistics

THE ACTFL FOREIGN LANGUAGE EDUCATION SERIES. See Education (General).

A.C.T.F.L. REVIEW OF FOREIGN LANGUAGE EDUCATION. See Education (General).

ACTUALITE TERMINOLOGIQUE. (L'ACTUALITE TERMINOLOGIQUE). V. 1- Jan. 1968-. 0001-7779. Periodical. CN. French (English). mo. Receiver General for Canada, Supply and Services, Ottawa Ontario K1A 0S9 Canada. Tel (819)997-2560.

ADAB (JAMIAT AL-KHARTUM. KULLIYAT AL-ADAB). (ADAB : MAJALLAT KULLIYAT AL-ADAB, JAMIAT AL-KHARTUM). 4- (1981)-. Periodical. Arabic. ir. Adab: Majallat Kulliyar Al-Adab, Jamiat Al-Khartum, Sudan. LC PJ6001. Majallat Kulliyat Al-Adab.

ADDRESSES AND DISCUSSIONS PRESENTED AT THE ... ANNUAL READING CONFERENCE. See Education (General).

ADFL BULLETIN. Main/Corp Association of Departments of Foreign Languages. VAT Association of Departments of Foreign Languages Bulletin. V. 8- Sept. 1976-. 0148-7639. Periodical. US. English. ty. $15.00. Association of Departments of Foreign Languages, 62 5th Avenue, New York NY 10011. Tel (212)741-5592. Ed Richard I Brod. Ind/Abst Curr. Index J. Educ. LC P57.U7. DD 405. (cum index). bk rev. adv acc. Circ 1,500. Concerned with professional and pedagogical matters relating to language teaching in colleges and universities. Bulletin of the Association of Departments of Foreign Languages, 0148-8066.

ADVANCES IN DISCOURSE PROCESSES. V.2-. 0164-0224. Monographic Series. US. English. ir. Ablex Publishing Corp, 355 Chestnut Street, Norwood NJ 07648. Tel (201)767-8450. Ed Roy O Freedle. Book series of monographs and edited volumes on all aspects of discourse analysis. Discourse Processes: Advances in Research and Theory.

ADVANCES IN READING/LANGUAGE RESEARCH. VAT Advances In Reading, Language Research. Vol. 1 (1982)-. 0735-0171. US. English. an. $49.50. Jai Press Inc, 36 Sherwood Place, PO Box 1678, Greenwich CT 06836. Tel (203)661-7602. Ed Barbara Hutson. Ind/Abst Psychol. Abstr. LC LB1049. DD 428.4.

ADVANCES IN THE TEACHING OF MODERN LANGUAGES. V.1- 1964-. Periodical. US. English. an. LC PB35. DD 407.

AEVUM. Began in 1927. 0001-9593. Periodical. IT. Italian. ty. Soc Edit Vita E Pensiero, Largo Agostino Gemelli 1, 20102 Milano Italy. Ind/Abst Am. Hist. Life, Hist. Abstr., Part A, Mod. Hist. Abstr., Hist. Abstr., Part B, Twent. Century Abstr., MLA Int. Bibliogr. Books Artic. Mod. Lang. Lit., Old Testam. Abstr., Sociol. Abstr., Lang. Lang. Behav. Abstr., Hist. Abstr. LC AP37.

AFRICA. V. 1- Jan. 1928-. 0001-9720. Periodical. UK. English (French and German). qt. St Dunstan's Chambers, 10-11 Fetter Lane, London E C 4 England. Ed D Westermann and D G Brackett. Ind/Abst Soc. Sci. Index, Hist. Abstr., Am. Hist. Life, Index Book Rev. Humanit., MLA Int. Bibliogr. Books Artic. Mod. Lang. Lit. LC PL8000. DD 496.05.

AFRICAN LANGUAGE REVIEW. V. 6- 1967-. UK. English. ir. Frank Cass & Company Ltd, 11 Gainsborough Road, London E11 1RS England. Tel 01-530-4226. LC PL8000. DD 496. Sierra Leone Language Review.

AFRICAN LANGUAGE STUDIES CEASED. Series/Titl Collected Papers in Oriental and African Studies. No. 1-17. 0065-3985. UK. English. an. LC PL8003. DD 496.05.

AFRICAN LANGUAGES. VFOAT Langues Africaines. V. 1-. UK. English (French). $13.00. International African Institute, 210 High Holborn, London WC1V 7BW England. LC PL8000. DD 496. Journal of African Languages, 0021-8545; African Language Review.

AFRICANA-SAMMLUNG UND AFRICANA-KATALOG IN DER STADTBIBLIOTHEK WINTERTHUR. Main/Corp Stadtbibliothek Winterthur. Series/Titl Mitteilungen der Basler Afrika Bibliographien. VFOAT Africana Sammlung und Africana Katalog in der Stadtbibliothek Winterthur. SZ. English (German). ir.

Linguistics

Basler Afrika Bibliographien, Postfach 2037, CH-4001 Basel Switzerland. **LC** Z7106, PL8000. **DD** 016.496.

AFRIKA UND UBERSEE. V. 36- Mar. 1952-. 0002-0427. Periodical. GW. German, English and French. ir. 115.00. Dietrich Reimer, Unter Den Eichen 57, D1000 Berlin 45 West Germany. **Tel** 030/ 831 40 81/82. **Ind/Abst** MLA Int. Bibliogr. Books Artic. Mod. Lang. Lit., Recent Publ. Artic. **LC** PL8000. **DD** 496.05. *Zeitschrift fur Eingeborenen-Sprachen.*

AFRIQUE ET LANGAGE. 0337-2634. Periodical. FR. French. sa. 70. Librairie-Editions l'Harmattan, 18 rue des Quatre-Vents, 75006 Paris France. **LC** PL8000. **DD** 409.6.

AFRO-HISPANIC REVIEW. (AFRO-HISPANIC REVIEW : PUBLICATION OF THE AFRO-HISPANIC INSTITUTE). **VFOAT** Afro Hispanic Review. Vol. 1, No. 1 (Jan. 1982)-. 0278-8969. Periodical. US. English (Spanish). ir. $15.00. Afro Hispanic Institute, 3306 Ross Place NW, Washington DC 20008. **Tel** (202)966-7783. Ed Stanley Cyrus. **Ind/Abst** MLA Int. Bibliogr. Books Artic. Mod. Lang. Lit. **LC** PQ7081.A1. **DD** 860.80896073. bk rev. adv acc. **Circ** 1,500. Bi-lingual journal of Afro-Hispanic literature and culture to promote incorporation of this rich heritage into scholarly world.

AFROASIATIC DIALECTS. V. 1-. 0732-6416. Monographic Series. US. English. ir. Undena Publications, PO Box 97, Malibu CA 90265. **Tel** (818)366-1744. Ed T Penchoen. **LC** UNC. **Circ** 300. Descriptions of Afroasiatic languages and data oriented.

AFROASIATIC LINGUISTICS. Series/Titl Monographic Journals of the Near East. **VFOAT** AAL. Began in 1974. 0362-3637. Monographic Series. US. English. ir. Undena Publications, PO Box 97, Malibu CA 90265. **Tel** (818)366-1744. Ed R Schuh. **Ind/Abst** MLA Int. Bibliogr. Books Artic. Mod. Lang. Lit., Lang. Lang. Behav. Abstr., Old Testam. Abstr., Sociol. Abstr. bk rev. **Circ** 300. Linguistic contributions from Afroasiatic language group.

I AIN'T LYING. Vol. 1, No. 1 (Spring 1981)-. 0885-7970. Periodical. US. English. ir. $4.20. Mississippi Cultural Crossroads, Box 89 ASU, Lorman MS 39096.

AJALT. Main/Corp Kokusai Nihongo Fukyu Kyokai (Japan). **VFOAT** Ajaruto. 1978-. Periodical. JA. English (Japanese). ir. Kokusai Nihongo Fukyu Kyokai, c/o Takahashi Building 38, Asabu Miyashitacho, Minato-ku 106, Tokyo Japan. **LC** PL519.

AKADEMIAJ STUDOJ. 1983-. 0824-3050. CN. Esperanto. an. 18.00. Akademiaj Studoj c/o Esperanto Press, Bailieboro Ont K0L 1B0 Canada. **Tel** (705)939-6088. Ed R Eichholz. **DD** 499.99205. bk rev. **Circ** 200. Linguistic discussion about details of Esperanto, the inter-ethnic language.

AKTUALNYE PROBLEMY LEKSIKOLOGII I SLOVOOBRAZOVANIIA. V. 1- 1972-. UR. Russian. .70 Per Issue. **LC** PG2025.

AL-ARABIYAH : JOURNAL OF THE AMERICAN ASSOCIATION OF TEACHERS OF ARABIC. VFOAT Al-Arabiyah : Majallat Rabitat Asatidhat Al-Lughah Al-Arabiyah. Began with Spring/Autumn 1975 Issue. Periodical. US. Arabic (English). sa. $20.00. Journal of the American Association of Teachers of Arabic, 256 Dieter Cunz Hall, 1841 Millikin Road, Columbus OH 43210. **Tel** (614)422-9255. Ed Frederic J Cadora. **LC** PJ6001. **DD** 492.705. bk rev. adv acc. **Circ** 250. (ctrl). Published by the American Association of Teachers of Arabic, Al-Carabiyya features scholarly pedagogical articles and reviews in the fields of Arabic language, literature and linguistics. *NASHRA.*

AL-MADINAH. V. 1-. Periodical. Arabic. ir. Al-Maghrib, PO Box 6595 Al-Dar, Al-Bayda, Morocco. **LC** PJ6001.

AL-MAJALLAH AL-ARABIYAH LIL-DIRASAT AL-LUGHAWIYAH. VFOAT Arab Journal of Language Studies. V. 1, No. 1, (August 1982)-. Periodical. Arabic. sa. P O Box 26, Khartoum Sudan. **LC** PJ6001.

AL-QISSAH. V. 1- Sept. 1974-. Periodical. UA. Arabic. qt. 0.15 Per Copy. Nadi Al-Qissah, 68 Qasr el Inee Street, United Arab Republic Egypt. **LC** PJ7677.

ALBERTA MODERN LANGUAGE JOURNAL. V. 13, No. 1- Fall 1974-. 0318-5176. CN. English (includes some text in French). ty. Alberta Teachers Association, 11010-142 St Barnett House, Edmonton Alberta T5N 2R1 Canada. **Tel** (403)453-2411. **Ind/Abst** Can. Educ. Index. **DD** 407. bk rev. (ctrl). *Modern Language Journal, 0318-5168.*

ALGONQUIAN AND IROQUOIAN LINGUISTICS. 6:1 (1981)-. 0711-382X. Periodical. CN. English. ir. $3.09. University of Manitoba, c/o OJ Nichols, Department of Native Studies, Winnipeg Manitoba R3T 2N2 Canada. **Tel** (204)474-9676. Ed John D Nichols. **DD** 497.305. bk rev. **Circ** 200. American Indian languages and literatures, especially Algonquian and Iroquoian: news, running bibliography by language, technical articles, and research notes. *Algonquian Linguistics, 0703-4768.*

THE ALIGARH JOURNAL OF ENGLISH STUDIES. *See* Literature.

ALLC BULLETIN. VFOAT A.L.L.C. Bulletin. Began in 1981. 0305-9855. Periodical. English. qt. **Ind/Abst** MLA Int. Bibliogr. Books Artic. Mod. Lang. Lit., Sci. Abstr., Lang. Lang. Behav. Abstr., Lang. Teach., Comput. Control Abstr., Electr. Electron. Abstr. **LC** P98. **DD** 410.2854. **CODEN** ALLCB5. *Bulletin.*

ALLC JOURNAL. *See* Literature.

ALOCANA. Began publication in 1951. 0569-1176. Periodical. in Hindi. ir. **LC** PK1931.

ALPHABETICAL LIST OF ENGLISH LANGUAGE BOOK TITLES AVAILABLE FROM CANADIAN SOURCES. (ALPHABETICAL LIST OF ENGLISH LANGUAGE BOOK TITLES AVAILABLE FROM CANADIAN SOURCES MICROFORM). June 83-. 0824-3352. Periodical. CN. English. Canadian Telebook Agency, Suite 209 31 Wellesley Street East, Toronto Ontario M4Y 1G7 Canada. **DD** 011.221.

ALT- UND NEU-INDISCHE STUDIEN. *See* Literature.

DER ALTSPRACHLICHE UNTERRICHT. Series 1- 1951-. 0002-6670. Periodical. German. bm $25.77. W E Saarbach GMBH, Postfach 101610, D5000 Koeln 1 West Germany. (cum index).

ALUMETO. (ALUMETO : INFORMBULTENO DE KANADA ESPERANTO-ASOCIO). **VFOAT** Informbulteno de Kanada Esperanto-Asocio. No. 1 (Jan. 1983)-. 0823-2539. Periodical. CN. Esperanto. bm. Free. Kanada Esperanto-Asocio, P O Box 518 Station B, Montreal Quebec H3B 3K3 Canada. **DD** 499.99205.

AMERICAN JOURNAL OF COMPUTATIONAL LINGUISTICS. VFOAT AJCL. Vol. 1- 1974-. Periodical. US. English. qt. $30.00. Dr Donald E Walker, ACL SRI International, Menlo Park CA 94025. **LC** MICROFICHE P98.

THE AMERICAN LANGUAGE JOURNAL. Vol. 1, No. 1 (Fall 1982)-. 0734-7545. Periodical. US. English. an. $5.00. Ken Stratton Managing Editor, CESL Building 100/University of Arizona, Tucson AZ 85721. **Tel** (316)231-7000. Ed Collen Gray. **LC** PE1128.A2. **DD** 428.007. adv acc. **Circ** 1,000. Papers applicable to intensive English programs: curriculum, evaluation, administration, teacher-training, theory, and practice.

AMERICAN SPEECH. V. 1- Oct. 1925-. 0003-1283. Periodical. US. English. qt. $18.00. University of Alabama Press, PO Box 2877, University AL 35486. **Tel** (919)684-6561. Ed Ronald R Butters. **Ind/Abst** Abstr. Engl. Stud., Am. Hist. Life, Hist. Abstr., Part A, Mod. Hist. Abstr., Hist. Abst., Part B, Twent. Century Abstr., MLA Int. Bibliogr. Books Artic. Mod. Lang. Lit., Lang. Lang. Teach., Ref. Source, Index Book Rev. Humanit., Humanit. Index, Sociol. Abstr., Years Work Eng. Stud., Hist. Abstr. **LC** PE2801. **DD** 420.97. Index in last issue of volume - attached. bk rev. adv acc. **Circ** 1,070. Concerned principally with the English language in the western hemisphere, the journal welcomes articles dealing with current usage, dialectology, the history and structure of English.

AMERICAN UNIVERSITY STUDIES. SERIES I, GERMANIC LANGUAGES AND LITERATURE. VFOAT American University Studies. 0721-1392. Monographic Series. US. English (German). ir. P Lang Publishing Inc, 34 East 39th Street, New York NY 10016. **LC** UNC. *American University Studies. Series 1, Germanic Languages and Literatures, 0721-1392.*

AMERICAN UNIVERSITY STUDIES. SERIES IV, ENGLISH LANGUAGE AND LITERATURE. VFOAT American University Studies. Began in 1984. 0741-0700. Monographic Series. US. English. ir. Peter Lang Publishing, 34 East 39th Street, New York NY 10016. **LC** UNC. *American University Studies. Series IV, Anglo-Saxon Language and Literature, 0724-1453.*

AMERICAN UNIVERSITY STUDIES. SERIES VI, FOREIGN LANGUAGE INSTRUCTION. VFOAT Foreign Language Instruction. Vol. 1-. 0739-6406. US. English. ir. Peter Lang Publishing, 34 East 39th Street, New York NY 10016.

AMERINDIA. 1-. Periodical. FR. French or Spanish. an. $7.05. Assn Ethnolinguistique Amerind, B P 431, 75233 Paris Cedex 05 France. Ed Sybille Toumi. **Ind/Abst** MLA Int. Bibliogr. Books Artic. Mod. Lang. Lit. **LC** PM101. **DD** 497. bk rev. **Circ** 200. American Indian linguistics and ethnolinguistics.

AMPITOUFE. Main/Corp Association Manitobaine des Professeurs de Francais. No. 1-. 0709-387X. Periodical. CN. French (text in English). Association Manitobaine des Professeurs de Francaise, 244 rue Ruby, Winnipeg Manitoba R3C 2E2 Canada. **Ind/Abst** Can. Educ. Index. **DD** 440.7107127.

AMSTERDAM STUDIES IN THE THEORY AND HISTORY OF LINGUISTIC SCIENCE. SERIES 4, CURRENT ISSUES IN LINGUISTIC THEORY. (AMSTERDAM STUDIES IN THE THEORY AND HISTORY OF LINGUISTIC SCIENCE. SERIES 4 : CURRENT ISSUES IN LINGUISTIC THEORY). **VFOAT** Current Issues in Linguistic Theory. V. 1- 1975-. 0304-0763. Monographic Series. NE. English. ir. John Benjamins North America, One Buttonwood Square/202, Philadelphia PA 19130. **Tel** (215)564-6379. Ed E F Konrad Koerner. **Ind/Abst** MLA Int. Bibliogr. Books Artic. Mod. Lang. Lit. A theory-oriented series which offers an alternative outlet for meaningful contributions to current linguistics in order to foster a diversity of opinion in the discipline.

AMSTERDAM STUDIES IN THE THEORY AND HISTORY OF LINGUISTIC SCIENCE. SERIES I, AMSTERDAM CLASSICS IN LINGUISTICS, 1800-1925. VFOAT Amsterdam Classics in Linguistics, 1800-1925. Monographic Series. US. English. ir. John Benjamins North America, One Buttonwood Square, Philadelphia, PA 19130. **Tel** (215)564-6379. Ed E F Konrad Koerner. New editions of important 19th and 20th century works with context-setting introductions by current specialists in linguistics.

AMSTERDAMER BEITRAGE ZUR ALTEREN GERMANISTIK. Vol. 1- 1972-. NE. English or German. ir. Editions Rodopi N V, Keizersgracht 302-304, Amsterdam The Netherlands. **Ind/Abst** MLA Int. Bibliogr. Books Artic. Mod. Lang. Lit.

ANALECTA LINGUISTICA. Began with Vol. for 1971. 0044-8176. Periodical. HU. Latin (Multilingual). sa. $58.00. John Benjamins BV, PO Box 52519, Amsteldijk 41, 1007 HA Amsterdam Netherlands. **Tel** (020)738156. Ed A Rona-Tas. **Ind/Abst** MLA Int. Bibliogr. Books Artic. Mod. Lang. Lit. **LC** Z7003, P121. **DD** 016.41. Aims to promote orientation in the ever increasing literature on linguistics. Offers a selected and classified bibliography of linguistic monographs, with special emphasis on East-European publications.

ANALECTA MALACITANA : REVISTA DE LA SECCION DE FILOLOGIA DE LA FACULTAD DE FILOSOFIA Y LETRAS. VFOAT Anmal. Vol. 1, -. Periodical. Spanish. sa. $12.00. Universidad de Malaga, Facultad de Filosofia y Letras, Malaga Spain. **LC** P9. **DD** 410.5.

ANALELE STIINTIFICE. SERIE NOUA. SECTIUNEA III E, LINGVISTICA-LITERATURA. V. 21 (1975)-. RM. Romanian (French and English). an. Ilexim Press, PO Box 1-136-1-137, Bucharest Romania. **Ind/Abst** MLA Int. Bibliogr. Books Artic. Mod. Lang. Lit. *Analele Stiinfifice ale Universitatii al I. Cuza din Iasi. Serie Noua. Sectiunea III E, Lingvistica, Analele Stiintifice ale Universitatii Al. I. Cuza din Iasi. Serie Noua. Sectiunea III, F, Literatura.*

ANALELE UNIVERSITATII BUCURESTI : LIMBI GERMANICE. Main/Corp Universitatea Din Bucuresti. Romanian (English, or German with summaries in the other

Linguistics

languages). ir. Universitatea din Bucuresti, Soseaua Panduri Nr 90, Bucuresti Romania. LC PD10.

ANALELE UNIVERSITATII BUCURESTI : LIMBI SI LITERATURI STRAINE. VFOAT Limbi Si Literaturi Straine. Vol. 26, 1- 1977-. Periodical. English (French, German, Romanian, Russian, and Serbo-Croatian). an. Universitatea Bucuresti, Ilexim Department, Export-Import Presa, PO Box 136-137, Bucuresti Romania. LC P1.A1. DD 410.5. *Analele Universitatii Bucurest I. Filologie.*

ANALELE UNIVERSITATII BUCURESTI. LIMBI SLAVE. (ANALELE UNIVERSITATII BUCURESTI: LIMBI SLAVE). Main/Corp Universitatea Din Bucuresti. 0068-3248. RM. Romanian (Russian with summaries in Russian). ir. Universitetea din Bucuresti, Soseaua Panduri Nr 90, Bucuresti Romania. Ind/Abst MLA Int. Bibliogr. Books Artic. Mod. Lang. Lit. LC PG1. *Analele. Seria Stiinte Sociale. Filologie.*

ANALELE UNIVERSITATII DIN CRAIOVA: STIINTE FILOLOGICE. Main/Corp Universitatea Din Craiova. VFOAT Analele Universitatii Din Craiova. Seria: Stiinte Filologice. Periodical. RM. Romanian (summaries in English, French, German, or Italian). ir. Universitatii din Craiova, A1 I Cuza St No 31, Craiova The Socialist Republic of Romania. LC P9.

ANALISA. 1970/71-. Malay. ir. LC PL5101.

ANALIZ STILEI ZARUBEZHNOI KHUDOZHESTVENNOI I NAUCHNOI LITERATURY. Vol. 1-. UR. Russian. 0.68 Single Issue. IZD-VO Leningradskogo Universiteta, 199164 L V-164 Universitetskaia Nab 7/9, Leningrad Russian SFSR. LC PE1001.

ANATOLICA. See Archaeology.

ANGLIA. See Literature.

ANGLIA (TUBINGEN). BUCHREIHE. See Literature.

ANGLICA GERMANICA CEASED. VFOAT British Studies in Germanic Languages and Literatures. V. 1-13. 0066-1791. Monographic Series. English (German). ir. Walter de Gruyter Inc, 200 Sawmill River Road, Hawthorne NY 10532. Tel (914)747-0110. Ed L Forster, A T Hatto and E C Stahl.

ANGLISTICA. V. 1-. 0066-1805. Monographic Series. DK. English. ir. Rosenkilde and Bagger Publ Department, 3 Kron-Prinsens- Gade, Coppenhagen Denmark. LC UNC. DD 820.9.

ANGLISTISCHE FORSCHUNGEN. Vol. 1 1901. Monographic Series. GW. German. ir. Carl Winter Universitatsverlag, Postfach 1866, Lutherstrasse 59, D6900 Heidelberg West Germany. Tel 6221-49111. Ind/Abst MLA Int. Bibliogr. Books Artic. Mod. Lang. Lit. English linguistics and literature.

ANISHINAABE GIIGIDOWIN. V. 1- Jan. 1976-. 0195-3400. Periodical. US. English (Algonquian). ir. Free. John Nichols Native Teacher Education Program, Faculty of Education Lakehead University, Thunder Bay Ontario P7B 5E1 Canada. Ed J Nichols and E Nyholm. DD 497'.3.

ANNALAS DA LA SOCIETA RETORUMANTSCHA. See History (General) - History of Europe.

ANNALES DE L'UNIVERSITE D'ABIDJAN. SERIE D : LETTRES. See Literature.

ANNALES UNIVERSITATIS SCIENTIARUM BUDAPENTINENSIS DE ROLANDO EOTVOS NOMINATAE. SECTIO PHILOLOGICA MODERNA. Main/Corp Eotvos Lorand Tudomanyegyetem. V. 1- 1969/70-. English (French, German, Italian, Romanian or Russian). ir. PO Box 149, HI 389 Budapest Hungary. LC P10. *Annales Universitatis Scientiarum Budapestinensis de Rolando Eotvos Nominatae. Section Philologica.*

ANNALES UNIVERSITATIS SCIENTIARUM BUDAPESTINENSIS DE ROLANDO EOTVOS NOMINATAE. SECTIO LINGUISTICA. Main/Corp Eotvos Lorand Tudomanyegyetem. 1- 1970-. 0572-7251. Periodical. English, French, German or Russian. ir. LC P25.

ANNALI - INSTITUTO UNIVERSITARIO ORIENTALE, SEZIONE GERMANICA. ANGLISTICA. (ANNALI. ANGLISTICA). VFOAT Anglistica, Aion Anglistica. Vol. 17, N. 1-. 0391-5956. Periodical. IT. English (Italian). ty. La Sezione, International Book Center - Herder, Piazza Montecitorio/117-13 Roma, Napoli Italy. Ind/Abst MLA Int. Bibliogr. Books Artic. Mod. Lang. Lit. LC PE9. DD 420.5. *Annali (Istituto Universitario Orientale (Naples, Italy). Sezione Germanica).*

ANNALI - INSTITUTO UNIVERSITARIO ORIENTALE, SEZIONE GERMANICA. FILOLOGIA GERMANICA. (ANNALI. FILOLOGIA GERMANICA). VFOAT Filologia Germanica, Aion Filologia Germanica. 17 (1974)-. 0392-6540. Periodical. English (German and Italian). an. La Sezione, International Book Center - Herder, Piazza Montecitorio/117-13 Roma, Napoli Italy. Ind/Abst MLA Int. Bibliogr. Books Artic. Mod. Lang. Lit. LC PD9. DD 430.5. *Annali (Istituto Universitario Orientale (Naples, Italy). Sezione Germanica).*

ANNALI - INSTITUTO UNIVERSITARIO ORIENTALE, SEZIONE GERMANICA. STUDI TEDESCHI. See Literature.

ANNALI (ISTITUTO UNIVERSITARIO ORIENTALE (NAPLES, ITALY)). (ANNALI - ISTITUTO ORIENTALE DI NAPOLI). V. 1-10, No.1-2, 1929-Dec. 1937/Mar. 1938. Periodical. IT. Italian (English and French). qt. 80.000. Herder Editrice E Liberia, International Book Center, Piazza Montecitorio 120, 00186 Rome Italy. Ed R Rubinacci and L Cagni. Ind/Abst Old Testam. Abstr., Art Archaeol. Tech. Abstr., Sociol. Abstr., Lang. Lang. Behav. Abstr. LC PJ6. DD 490.5. bk rev. *Annali (Instituto Orientale di Napoli).*

ANNALI - SEZIONE ROMANZA. Main/Corp Istituto Orientale di Napoli. Sezione Romanza. V. 1- 1959-. 0547-2121. Periodical. IT. Italian (English, French, German, Portuguese or Spanish with some summaries in Italian). sa. $11.88. Licosa Libreria Comm Sansoni, Pa Via Lamarmora 45, 50121 Firenze Italy. Ind/Abst MLA Int. Bibliogr. Books Artic. Mod. Lang. Lit. LC PC4. (cum index). *Annali - Istituto Orientale di Napoli.*

ANNALS OF THE BHANDARKAR ORIENTAL RESEARCH INSTITUTE. See Literature.

ANNEE LEXICOGRAPHIQUE. V. 1 (1977)-. French. an. LC PJ1430. DD 493.1.

L'ANNEE PHILOLOGIQUE. Vol. 1. FR. French. an. Societe Edition Belles Lettres, 95 Boulevard Raspail, 75006 Paris France. LC Z7016.

ANNUAIRE DE L'INSTITUT DE PHILOLOGIE ET D'HISTOIRE ORIENTALES ET SLAVES. See Yearbooks, Almanacs, Directories.

ANNUAIRE DES SERVICES FRANCAIS AU MANITOBA. See Yearbooks, Almanacs, Directories.

ANNUAL BIBLIOGRAPHY OF ENGLISH LANGUAGE AND LITERATURE. See Bibliographies.

ANNUAL OF ARMENIAN LINGUISTICS. V. 1- 1980-. 0271-9800. US. English (French or German). an. $22.00. Cleveland State University, c/o J A Greppin, Cleveland OH 44115. Tel (216)687-3967. Ed J A C Greppin. Ind/Abst MLA Int. Bibliogr. Books Artic. Mod. Lang. Lit. LC PK8001. DD 491.99205. bk rev. adv acc. Circ 200. A scholarly journal dealing with Armenian linguistics.

ANNUAL REPORT - COMMISSIONER OF OFFICIAL LANGUAGES. Main/Corp Canada. Office of the Commissioner of Official Languages. VFOAT Rapport Annuel. 1st- 1970/71-. 0382-1161. CN. English (French, with special title page and separate paging. French text on inverted pages). an. Free. Commissioner of Official Languages, 66 Slater Street/Room 2019, Ottawa Ontario K1A 0T8 Canada. Tel (613)995-0768. LC JL25. DD 409.71. Circ 10,000. (ctrl). Provides Senators and members of Parliament as well as the general public with a yearly assessment of developments in language reform across Canada.

ANNUAL REPORT - INSTITUTE OF LINGUISTICS. Main/Corp Institute of Linguistics. English. ir. Institute of Linguistics, PO Box 489, North Central State Zaria Nigeria. LC PL8021.N5. DD 410.5.

ANNUAL REPORT OF THE INSTITUTE OF PHONETICS, UNIVERSITY OF COPENHAGEN. (ANNUAL REPORT OF THE INSTITUTE OF PHONETICS OF THE UNIVERSITY OF COPENHAGEN). Began publication with V. 1 for 1966. 0589-6681. English. ir. Kobenhavns Universitet Offset AFD, 96 Njalsgade, DK Copenhagen Denmark. Ind/Abst MLA Int. Bibliogr. Books Artic. Mod. Lang. Lit. LC P215.

ANNUAL REPORT - STATE INSTITUTE OF LANGUAGES, KERALA. Main/Corp State Institute of Languages, Kerala. II. English. ir. State Institute of Languages, Kerala Trivandrum India. LC PK1501.S73. DD 354.54830085.

ANNUAL REVIEW OF APPLIED LINGUISTICS. VFOAT ARAL. 1980-. 8756-5625. US. English. an. Newbury House Publishers Inc, Rowley MA 01969. Ind/Abst MLA Int. Bibliogr. Books Artic. Mod. Lang. Lit. LC P129. DD 410.5.

ANNUAL REVIEW OF THE ROYAL INSCRIPTIONS OF MESOPOTAMIA PROJECT. VFOAT Annual Review of the RIM Project. Vol. 1 (1983)-. 0822-2525. CN. English. an. $20.00. RIM Project, University Of Toronto 280 Huron Street, Toronto Ont M5S 1A1 Canada. DD 492.1.

ANTENNE. (L'ANTENNE). V. 1- Dec. 1969-. 0701-1865. Periodical. CN. French. mo. Societe des Traducteurs du Quebec, 203 Ouest Boulevard Saint-Joseph, Montreal Quebec H2T 2P9 Canada. DD 418.02062714.

ANTHROPOLOGICAL LINGUISTICS. V. 1- 1959-. 0003-5483. Periodical. US. English. qt. $15.00. Indiana University, Department of Anthropology, Rawles Hall 108, Bloomington IN 47405. Tel (812)335-1472. Ed Florence M Voegelin and Martha B Kendall. Ind/Abst MLA Int. Bibliogr. Books Artic. Mod. Lang. Lit., Sociol. Abstr., Soc. Welf. Soc. Plan./Policy Soc. Dev., Lang. Lang. Behav. Abstr., Annu. Bibliogr. Engl. Lang. Lit., Lang. Teach., Soc. Sci. Citation Index, Bibliogr. Index, Years Work Eng. Stud. bk rev. adv acc. Circ 1,000. Languages spoken but not usually written. Problems in synchronic and diachronic linguistics. Social uses of language in western and non-western societies, kinship systems, speech styles and registers, conversational analysis, metaphor and sematic anthropology, as well as theoretical and methodological considerations of language and speech.

ANUARIO DE ESTUDIOS FILOLOGICOS. See Yearbooks, Almanacs, Directories.

ANUARIO DE FILOLOGIA. See Yearbooks, Almanacs, Directories.

ANUARIO (UNIVERSIDAD CENTRAL DE VENEZUELA. ESCUELA DE LETRAS). See Yearbooks, Almanacs, Directories.

ANZEIGER FUR SLAVISCHE PHILOLOGIE. V. 1- 1966-. 0066-5285. Periodical. AU. German. ir. Akademische Druck U Verlag, Neufeldweg 75 POB 598, A-8011 Graz Austria. Tel 0316/41 1 53. LC PG1. DD 491.805. bk rev. adv acc. Critical reports, announcements and discussions of new important publications, detailed reviews, essays and scientific research.

APPLIED LINGUISTICS. Vol. 1, No. 1 (Spring 1980)-. 0142-6001. Periodical. UK. English. ty. $46.00. Oxford University Press, Journals Department, Walton Street, Oxford 0X2 6DP England. Tel 0865-56767. Ed Alan Davies. Ind/Abst Lang. Lang. Behav. Abstr., Lang. Teach. LC P129. DD 418.005. bk rev. adv acc. Concerned with the relationship between theory and practice, covers work applying theoretical studies to practical problems. Promotes a principled approach to language learning.

APPLIED PSYCHOLINGUISTICS. V. 1- Feb. 1980-. 0142-7164. Periodical. UK. English. qt. $60.00. Cambridge University Press, 510 North Avenue, New Rochelle NY 10801. Tel (914)235-0300. Ed Catherine E Snow and John L Locke. Ind/Abst MLA Int. Bibliogr. Books Artic. Mod. Lang. Lit., Lang. Lang. Behav. Abstr., Excerpta Med., Biol. Abstr., Lang. Teach., Except. Child Educ. Resour., Psychol. Abstr., Curr. Index J. Educ. LC P37. DD 401.9. NLM W1 AP528M. CODEN APPSDZ. bk rev. Articles address the nature, acquisition, and impairments of language expression and comprehension, including writing and reading.

APPRENEZ L'ANGLAIS AU CANADA, APPRENEZ LE FRANCAIS AU CANADA. See Education (General).

APPROACHES TO SEMIOTICS. PAPERBACK SERIES. 0066-5576. Monographic Series. English or French. ir. Walter de Gruyter Inc, 200 Sawmill River Road, Hawthorne NY 10532. Tel (914)747-0110.

ARAPAHO LANGUAGE AND CULTURE INSTRUCTIONAL MATERIALS SERIES. No. 1-. Monographic Series. US. English. Arapaho Language and Culture Commission, PO Box 771, Ethete WY 82520.

Linguistics

ARCHIV FUR ORIENTFORSCHUNG. See Genealogy and Heraldry - Archives.

ARCHIV FUR PAPYRUSFORSCHUNG UND VERWANDTE GEBIETE. See Genealogy and Heraldry - Archives.

ARCHIVIO GLOTTOLOGICO ITALIANO. See Genealogy and Heraldry - Archives.

ARCHIVUM LINGUISTICUM. See Genealogy and Heraldry - Archives.

ARCTOS. V. 1-2, 1930-31. 0066-6998. Fl. Multilingual. ir. Akakeeminen-Kirjakuppa, PO Box 128, 00101 Helsinki Finland.

ARGOS. Yearly V. 1- 1977-. Periodical. AG. Spanish. an. Asociacion Argentina de Estudios Clasicos, Laprida L7L8-LO/A, L425 Buenos Aires Argentina. LC PA9.

ARIZONA ENGLISH BULLETIN. Vol. 1 (Oct. 1958)-. 0004-1483. Periodical. US. English. ir. $20.00. Arizona English Teachers Association, Mesa Community College, Mesa AZ 85202. **Tel** (602)833-1261. Ed Margaret B Fleming. bk rev. **Circ** 500. Concerns the teaching of English language arts.

ARKIV FOR NORDISK FILOLOGI. See Genealogy and Heraldry - Archives.

ART-LANGUAGE. V. 1- May 1969-. 0587-3584. UK. English. qt. Arts Bibliographie, 37 Great Russell Street, London WC1 England. LC P1. DD 408.

ASHA MONOGRAPHS. VAT American Speech-Language-Hearing Association Monograph. No. 12-. 0066-071X. Monographic Series. US. English. ir. American Speech-Language-Hearing Association, 10801 Rockville Pike, Rockville MD 20352. **Tel** (301)897-5700. Ed Robin Chapman. **Ind/Abst** Index Med. NLM W1 A152B. **Circ** 5,000. Reports of integrated series of experiments or of complex and extensive projects in speech, hearing, and language sciences. *Journal of Speech and Hearing Disorders. Monograph Supplement.*

THE ASIAN MESSENGER CEASED. V. 1-6, No. 1. Periodical. English. ir. $4.50. LC P92.A7. DD 301.16095.

ASSYRIOLOGICAL MISCELLANIES. Vol. 1 (1980)-. 0106-4800. Periodical. English. an. 20,00. Institute of Assyriology, University of Copenhagen, Kejsergade 2 DK-1155 Denmark. LC PJ3102. DD 492.1.

ASSYRIOLOGICAL STUDIES. 0066-9903. Monographic Series. US. English. ir. Oriental Institute, 1155 East 58th Street, Publications Office, Chicago IL 60637. **Tel** (312)952-1240. Ed Tom Holland. LC UNC. **Circ** 750. Specialized studies dealing with ancient Near Eastern languages that include Amorite, Akkadian, Aramaic, Sumerian and Hittite.

ATAQ JOURNAL. (A T A Q JOURNAL). **Main/Corp** Association des Traducteurs Anglophones du Quebec. **VAT** Association des Traducteurs Anglophones du Quebec Journal. V. 1- June 1978-. 0706-9987. Periodical. CN. English. bm. Free. Association des Traducteurs Anglophones du Quebec, Room 602/751 Victoria Square, Montreal Quebec H2Y 2J3 Canada. DD 448.02. (ctrl).

ATIMARSA. Periodical. Hindi. ir. 5.00. Yugantara Presa, S-362 Greater Kailash-I, New Delhi 110048 India. LC PK2047.

A.U.M.L.A. (A.U.M.L.A. : JOURNAL OF THE AUSTRALASIAN UNIVERSITIES MODERN LANGUAGE ASSOCIATION). **VFOAT** AUMLA. No. 1 (Aug. 1953)-. 0001-2793. Periodical. AT. English. sa. $11.80. AUMLA Australia, 25 Dorset Street, c/o L Campbell, Epping New South Wales Australia 2121. **Tel** 866534. Ed J Hay. **Ind/Abst** Abstr. Engl. Stud., MLA Int. Bibliogr. Books Artic. Mod. Lang. Lit., APAIS, Aust. Public Aff. Inf. Serv., Annu. Bibliogr. Engl. Lang. Lit., Index Book Rev. Humanit. LC PB1. DD 410.5. (cum index). bk rev. adv acc. **Circ** 1,300. (ctrl). A journal of literary criticism, philology and linguistics.

AUSTRALIAN JOURNAL OF LINGUISTICS. (AUSTRALIAN JOURNAL OF LINGUISTICS : JOURNAL OF THE AUSTRALIAN LINGUISTIC SOCIETY). Vol. 1, No. 1 (June 1981)-. 0726-8602. Periodical. AT. English. sa. 25.00. University of Queensland, Department of English, St Lucia QLD 4067 Australia. **Tel** (07)377-3527. Ed R D Huddleston. **Ind/Abst** Lang. Behav. Abstr., APAIS, Aust. Public Aff. Inf. Serv. LC P1. DD 410.5.

bk rev. adv acc. **Circ** 400. Concerned with all branches of general linguistics.

B : STUDIES. Main/Corp Yugoslav Serbo-Croatian—English Contrastive Project. 1- 1969-. English. ir. LC PG1229.

BA SHIRU. V. 1- Spring 1970-. 0883-7996. Periodical. US. English. sa. University of Wisconsin, Department of African Languages & Literature, 866 Van Hise Hall, Madison WI 53706. **Ind/Abst** MLA Int. Bibliogr. Books Artic. Mod. Lang. Lit. LC PL8000. DD 496.

BABEL. No. 1-27, Apr. 1956-Oct. 1964. 0005-3503. Periodical. AT. English. ty. 35.00. Dr A L Chamberlain, School of French, PO Box 1, Kensington 2033 Australia. **Tel** (02)6972314. Ed A L Chamberlain. **Ind/Abst** Sociol. Abstr., APAIS, Aust. Public Aff. Inf. Serv., Soc. Welf. Soc. Plan./Policy Soc. Dev., Lang. Lang. Behav. Abstr., Lang. Teach., Curr. Index J. Educ., MLA Int. Bibliogr. Books Artic. Mod. Lang. Lit. bk rev. adv acc. **Circ** 2,500. Articles of interest to teachers of all foreign and second languages, to applied linguists and sociolinguists section on practical classroom techniques.

BAHANA. Began with June 1966 issue. 0005-3988. Periodical. MY. Malay. qt. Dewan Bahasa Dan Pustaka, Peti Surat 803, Kuala Lumpur Malaysia. LC PL5101.

BAHASA DAN SASTRA. 1-. Indonesian. ir. Jalan Diponegoro 82 Kotak Pos 2625, Jakarta Indonesia. LC PL5071. *Bahasa Dan Kesusastraan, 0522-0238.*

BALKAN-ARCHIV. 1. V. (1925)-4. V. (1928). 0170-8007. German (Italian, and Romanian). an. Helmut Buske Verlag, Schluterstr 14, D-2000 Hamburg 13 West Germany. LC P3. DD 409.496. *Jahresbericht des Instituts fur Rumanische Sprache (Rumanisches Seminar) zu Leipzig.*

BALKANSKO EZIKOZNANIE. VFOAT Linguistique Balkanique. Vol. 1-. 0075-9678. Periodical. BU. French (German, English, and Russian). qt. Hemus, 6 Boulevard Rusky, Sofia Bulgaria. **Ind/Abst** MLA Int. Bibliogr. Books Artic. Mod. Lang. Lit. LC P381.B3.

BALSHANUT 'IVRIT HOFSHIT BULETIN LEVALSHANUT 'IVRIT, HISHUVIT, FORMALIT VE-SHIMUSHIT (HEBREW COMPUTATIONAL LINGUISTICS). VFOAT Hebrew Computational Linguistics. 1- 1969-. Periodical. IS. Hebrew or English. an. Bar-Ilan University, Ramai-Gan Israel. **Ind/Abst** Lang. Lang. Behav. Abstr., MLA Int. Bibliogr. Books Artic. Mod. Lang. Lit., Sociol. Abstr. LC PJ4503.

BALSHANUT SHIMUSHIT. Nov. 1-. Periodical. IS. English (French, or Hebrew). ir. E Rubinstein, 1 King David Street, Jerusalem Israel. LC P9. DD 410.

BALTO-SLAVIANSKIE ISSLEDOVANIIA. 1980-. UR. Russian. an. 4.20. LC PG8001. DD 491.905.

LA BANQUE DES MOTS. 1- 1971-. 0067-3951. Periodical. FR. French. sa. 175.-. Conseil Internationale de Langue Francaise, 103 rue de Lille, 75007 Paris France. **Tel** (1)47050793. **Ind/Abst** Point Repere. LC PC2689. bk rev. adv acc. **Circ** 2,000. Maintain the unity of the French language in the world. A service review devoted to science, technology and business subjects completing existing dictionaries.

BARRON'S REGENTS EXAMS AND ANSWERS. FRENCH LEVEL 3, COMPREHENSIVE FRENCH. (BARRON'S REGENTS EXAMS AND ANSWERS : FRENCH LEVEL 3, COMPREHENSIVE FRENCH). **Main/Corp** Barron's Educational Series, Inc. **VAT** Barron's Regents Exams and Answers: French Level Three, Comprehensive French. 0146-6895. US. English. $2.50. Barrons Educational Series, 113 Crossways Park Drive, Woodbury NY 11797. LC PC2119. DD 440.76.

BASLER STUDIEN ZUR DEUTSCHEN SPRACHE UND LITERATUR. No. 1- 1942 -. 0067-4508. Monographic Series. SZ. German. ir. Francke Verlag, Neuengesse 43, Postfach 1445, CH-3001 Bern Switzerland. **Tel** (031)22 17 15. **Ind/Abst** MLA Int. Bibliogr. Books Artic. Mod. Lang. Lit.

BCATML NEWSLETTER. (THE BCATML NEWSLETTER). 0229-0235. Periodical. CN. English (includes some text in French). mo. British Columbia Teacher's Federation, 105-2235 Burrard Street, Vancouver British Columbia V6J 3H9 Canada. DD 407. (ctrl).

BEITRAGE ZUR DEUTSCHEN PHILOLOGIE. Vol. 1-. 0522-6341. Monographic Series. GW. German. ir. Wilhelm Schmitz Verlag, Postfach 21108, Pestalozstr 1-3, D-6300 Giessen West Germany. **Ind/Abst** MLA Int. Bibliogr. Books Artic. Mod. Lang. Lit. *Giessener Beitrage zur Deutschen Philologie. Neue Folge.*

BEITRAGE ZUR ERFORSCHUNG DER DEUTSCHEN SPRACHE. 1. Vol. 0232-2714. German (English). ir. 56.00. Deutscher Buch Export-Import, Leninstrasse 16, DDR-701 Leipzig East Germany. **Tel** Leipzig 7801. **Ind/Abst** MLA Int. Bibliogr. Books Artic. Mod. Lang. Lit. LC PF3003. DD 430.5. **Circ** 1,050. (ctrl). Contributions to the research of the German language. The annual volumes contain the latest research findings in the German language. *Beitrage zur Geschichte der Deutschen Sprache und Literature (Halle an der Saale, Germany).*

BEITRAGE ZUR GESCHICHTE DER DEUTSCHEN SPRACHE UND LITERATUR. V. 77-. 0005-8076. Periodical. GW. German. ty. $59.41. Max Niemeyer Verlag, Postfach 21 40, 7400 Tuebingen 1 West Germany. **Tel** (0 70 71) 81104. Ed Hans Fromm. **Ind/Abst** MLA Int. Bibliogr. Books Artic. Mod. Lang. Lit., Years Work Eng. Stud. LC PF3003. bk rev. adv acc. Contributions on Germanic languages and literatures (from the beginning to early new high German).

BEITRAGE ZUR KLASSISCHEN PHILOLOGIE. Vol. 1-. 0522-6821. Monographic Series. GW. German. ir. Verlag Anton Hain/Athenaeum, Postfach 1220, 6240 Koenigstein West Germany. **Tel** (06174)3021. Ed Ernst Heitsch, Reinhold Merkelbach, and Clemens Zintzen. bk rev. adv acc. Classical philology.

BEITRAGE ZUR ROMANISCHEN PHILOLOGIE. Vol. 1, 1961-. 0005-8181. Periodical. WB. German (Multilingual). sa. Kunst & Wissen Eirch Bieber, Dufourstrasse 51, CH-8008 Zurich Switzerland. **Tel** 01/69 44 20. Ed W Krauss and R Schober. **Ind/Abst** MLA Int. Bibliogr. Books Artic. Mod. Lang. Lit., Lang. Lang. Behav. Abstr., Sociol. Abstr. LC PC3.

BEITRAGE ZUR SCHWEIZERDEUTSCHEN MUNDARTFORSCHUNG. V. 1- 1949-. Monographic Series. SZ. German. ir. Huber & Co Verlag, CH 8500 Frauenfeld Switzerland. *Beitrage zur Schweizerdeutschen Grammatik.*

BELARUSKAIA MOVA. Vol. 5-. Periodical. UR. Belorussian. 1.50. VYD-VA BDU, Maskouskaia 15, Minsk USSR. **Ind/Abst** MLA Int. Bibliogr. Books Artic. Mod. Lang. Lit. LC PG2831. *Belaruskaia Mova I Movaznaustva.*

BERLINER BEITRAGE ZUR NAMENFORSCHUNG. V. 1- 1967-. 0572-6263. Monographic Series. GE. German. ir. Deutscher Buch Export-Import, Leninstrasse 16, DDR-701 Leipzig East Germany. **Tel** 2917911. Ed H H Bielfeldt and T Witkowski. **Ind/Abst** MLA Int. Bibliogr. Books Artic. Mod. Lang. Lit. The names of settlements in the former province of Brandenburg are illustrated documentarily with regard to their history and explained linguistically with a view to make the knowledge obtained usable for the history of Germanic and Slav languages.

BHARATIYA NEPALI VANMAYA. VFOAT Vanmaya. 1 (1980)-. Periodical. Nepali. an. 8.00. Nepali Sahitya Sancayika Prakasana, C-14 Super Market, Darjiling India. LC PK2598.Z9.

BHASHA. 1- 1962-. 0523-1418. Periodical. II. Hindi. qt. 10 Domestic, 1.17 Pounds, $3.80. Ministry of Education, Government of India, New Delhi India. **Tel** 605211. Ed Jagdish Chatorvedi. LC PK2030. bk rev. **Circ** 1,000. Selected stories, poems, and articles of all modern Indian languages are published in Hindi in this journal.

BHASHA ANI JIVANA : MARATHI-ABHYASA-PARISHAD-PATRIKA. V. 1, No. 1 (July 1983)-. Periodical. Marathi. qt. 40.00. Marathi Abhyas Parishad, A/2 Parimal Apte Road, Pune 411001 India. **Tel** 59258. Ed Ashok R Kelkar. bk rev. adv acc. **Circ** 250. (ctrl). Popular articles, stories, etc. bearing on language communication, media, education, literature, etc. with special reference to Marathi language India.

Linguistics

BIBLIOGRAPHIC ANNUAL IN SPEECH COMMUNICATION. See Bibliographies.

BIBLIOGRAPHIE AMERICANISTE. LINGUISTIQUE AMERINDIENNE. See Bibliographies.

BIBLIOGRAPHIE FREMDSPRACHIGER GERMANICA. See Bibliographies.

BIBLIOGRAPHIE LINGUISTISCHER LITERATUR. VFOAT BLL. No. 4- 1978-. GW. German. an. 434.-. Vittorio Klostermann, Postfach 900601, Frauenlobstobe 22, 6000 Frankfurt Am Main 90 West Germany. Tel (0611)77 4011. Ed Lehmann. Bibliographie Unselbstandiger Literatur. Linguistik.

BIBLIOGRAPHY OF ENGLISH LANGUAGE AND LITERATURE. See Bibliographies.

BIBLIOGRAPHY OF THE SUMMER INSTITUTE OF LINGUISTICS, AUSTRALIAN ABORIGINES BRANCH UP TO . . . . See Bibliographies.

BIBLIOTHECA ORIENTALIS. See History (General) - History of Asia.

BIBLIOTHEQUE RUSSE. Main/Corp Paris. Universite. Institut d'Etudes Slaves. V. 1- 1912-. Monographic Series. FR. French. ir. Institut d'Etudes Slaves, 9 rue Michelet, 75006 Paris France. Tel (1)43 26 50 89. Circ 500. Series dedicated to Russian linguistics, literature, history of ideas and art.

BIJDRAGEN EN MEDEDELINGEN. Main/Corp Akademie Van Wetenschappen, Amsterdam. Dialecten-Commissie. Began publication in 1934. Monographic Series. Dutch, English, German. ir. LC PF703.

BIJDRAGEN TOT DE TAAL-, LAND- EN VOLKENKUNDE. See Anthropology.

BIKORET U-FARSHANUT. See Literature.

BILINGUAL RESOURCES. V. 1- Fall 1977-. 0197-6737. Periodical. US. English. ty. $7.00. California State University Los Angeles, 5151 State University Drive, Los Angeles CA 90032. LC LC3731. DD 371.970973.

BILINGUAL REVIEW. (THE BILINGUAL REVIEW). VFOAT Revista Bilingue, La Revista Bilingue. V. 1- Jan./April 1974-. 0094-5366. Periodical. US. English (Spanish). ty. $24.00. Bilingual Review Press, Box M Campus Post Office, Suny-Binghamton NY 13901. Tel (607)724-9495. Ed Gary D Keller. Ind/Abst Lang. Lang. Behav. Abstr., MLA Int. Bibliogr. Books Artic. Mod. Lang. Lit., Sociol. Abstr., Educ. Index, Curr. Index J. Educ. LC P115. DD 401. bk rev. adv acc. Circ 2,000. Available on microfilm from University Microfilms International. A scholarly journal devoted to the linguistics and literature of bilingualism and bilingual education in the United States.

BIULETYN ZWIAZKU NAUCZUCIELSTWA POLSKIEGO W KANADZIE. (BIULETYN ZWIAAZKU NAUCZYCIELSTWA POLSKIEGO W KANADZIE). VFOAT Biuletyn. 0821-3917. Periodical. CN. Polish. qt. Free to Members. Polish Teacher's Association in Canada, 288 Roncesvalles Avenue, Toronto Ont M6R 2M4 Canada. DD 491.8507071.

THE BLUE GUITAR. See Literature.

BOLA BIBLIOGRAPHIC REPORTS FOR TRANSLATORS & INTERPRETERS OF SPANISH. See Bibliographies.

BOLETIM DE LINGUISTICA. Yearly V. 1- March 1974-. Portuguese. ir. Circulo de Estudos Linguisticos, Centro de Ciencias Humanes, Universidade Estudual de Londrina, Caixa Postal 2003, Londrina Brazil. LC P9.

BOLETIN - ACADEMIA NORTEAMERICANA DE LA LENGUA ESPANOLA. Main/Corp Academia Norteamericana de la Lengua Espanola. VFOAT Boletin de la Academia Norteamericana de la Lengua Espanola. No. 1-. 0884-0091. US. Spanish. ir. $8.00. D Juan Aviles, GPO, Box 349, New York NY 10016. Ind/Abst MLA Int. Bibliogr. Books Artic. Mod. Lang. Lit. LC PC4826. DD 460.

BOLETIN - COMISION PERMANENTE DE LA ASOCIACION DE ACADEMIAS DE LA LENGUA ESPANOLA. (BOLETIN). Main/Corp Asociacion de Academias de la Lengua Espanola. Comision Permanente. Began with April/June 1965 issue.

0301-6560. SP. Spanish. Real Academica Espanola, Filipe IV No 4, Madrid 14 Spain. LC PC4008.

BOLETIN DE LA ACADEMIA CHILENA CORRESPONDIENTE DE LA REAL ACADEMIA ESPANOLA. Main/Corp Academia Chilena, Santiago de Chile. V. 1- 1915-. Periodical. Spanish. ir. Ind/Abst Am. Hist. Life, Hist. Abstr., Part A, Mod. Hist. Abstr., Hist. Abst., Part B, Twent. Century Abstr. LC AS81.

BOLETIN DE LA ACADEMIA COLOMBIANA. Main/Corp Academia Colombiana. V. 1- June 1936-. 0001-3773. Periodical. CK. Spanish. qt. $20.00. Academia Colombiana, Apartado 13-922, Bogota 1 Colombia. Ind/Abst MLA Int. Bibliogr. Books Artic. Mod. Lang. Lit., Sociol. Abstr., Soc. Welf. Soc. Plan./Policy Soc. Dev., Lang. Lang. Behav. Abstr., Hist. Abstr., Part A, Mod. Hist. Abstr., Hist. Abst., Part B, Twent. Century Abstr. LC AS82. DD 056.1.

BOLETIN DE LA ACADEMIA HONDURENA DE LA LENGUA. Main/Corp Academic Hondurena de la Lengua. Yearly V. 1- (No. 1-). 0065-0471. Periodical. HO. Spanish. ir. 10.00. Academia Hondurena de Lengua, Apartado Postal 38, Tegucigalpa Honduras. Tel 22-08-66. Ed Jorge Fidel Duron. LC AS64.A3. DD 056.1. adv acc. Circ 1,000. To enhance and improve the Spanish language.

BOLETIN DE LA ACADEMIA PERUANA DE LA LENGUA NUEVA EPOCA. (BOLETIN DE LA ACADEMIA PERUANA DE LA LENGUA). Main/Corp Academia Peruana de la Lengua. No. 1- 1967-. 0567-6002. PE. Spanish. an. $4.00. Academi Peruana de la Lengua, Ancash 769, Lima 1 Peru.

BOLETIN DE LA REAL ACADEMIA ESPANOLA. Main/Corp Real Academia Espanola. Vol. 1 (Issue 1-). 0210-4822. Periodical. SP. Spanish. ty. 27. Real Academia Espanola, Felipe IV, 4 Madrid Spain. Tel 91-2394605. Ind/Abst Am. Hist. Life, Hist. Abstr., Part A, Mod. Hist. Abstr., Hist. Abst., Part B, Twent. Century Abstr., MLA Int. Bibliogr. Books Artic. Mod. Lang. Lit. LC AS302. DD 056.1. (cum index). Circ 2,000. List of new words into Spanish dictionary and studies above Spanish language.

BOLETIN INFORMATIVO - INSTITUTO MIGUEL DE CERVANTES. Main/Corp Instituto Miguel de Cervantes. 1979-. SP. Spanish. ir. Inst Miguel Cervantes Filo Hi, Duque de Medinaceli 4, Madrid 14 Spain. LC PC4019. DD 860.9.

BOLLETINO - CENTRO DI STUDI FILOLOGICI E LINGUISTICI SICILIANI. Main/Corp Centro di Studi Filologici e Linguistici Siciliani. Yearly V. 1- 1953-. 0577-277X. Periodical. IT. Italian. ir. Licosa Libreria Comm Sansani, Via Lamarmora 45, 50121 Firenze Italy. Ind/Abst MLA Int. Bibliogr. Books Artic. Mod. Lang. Lit.

BOLLETTINO DELL'ATLANTE LINGUISTICO MEDITERRANEO. VFOAT Bulletin de l'Atlas Linguistique Mediterraneen. 1- 1959-. 0067-9879. IT. Italian. ir. Casa Editrice Leo S Olschki, Casella Postale PO Box 66, Firenze Italy. Ind/Abst MLA Int. Bibliogr. Books Artic. Mod. Lang. Lit.

BOLLETTINO DI STUDI LATINI. Vol. 1- 1971-. 0006-6583. Periodical. IT. Italian. sa. $35.64. Societa Editrice Napoletana, Corso Umberto 34, 80138 Naples Italy.

BRITISH JOURNAL OF LANGUAGE TEACHING. (THE BRITISH JOURNAL OF LANGUAGE TEACHING : ORGAN OF THE BRITISH ASSOCIATION FOR LANGUAGE TEACHING). Began with Spring 1980 issue. 0144-0888. Periodical. UK. English. ty. 15. Mrs E A Dyson-Business Mgr, 21 The Green, The Paddocks, Charlbury Oxon OX7 3QA England. Tel (0608)810386. Ed A P Dyson. Ind/Abst Lang. Lang. Behav. Abstr., Lang. Teach. LC P51. DD 418.007. bk rev. adv acc. Circ 2,000. All aspects of foreign language, teaching and learning. Audio-Visual Language Journal, 0004-7589.

BRNO STUDIES IN ENGLISH. Series/Titl Spisy University J. E. Purkyne V Brne, Filosofica Fakulta. V. 1- 1959-. English. ir. Universita J E Purkyne, Janac Kovo Nam 2A, Brno Czechoslovakia. Ind/Abst Abstr. Engl. Stud., MLA Int. Bibliogr. Books Artic. Mod. Lang. Lit., Lang. Lang. Behav. Abstr., Lang. Teach. LC AS142. DD 420.05.

BUDGET D'EQUIPEMENT ET DE RECHERCHE. Main/Corp University of Yaounde. Departement des Langues Africaines et Linguistique. CM. French. ir. Universite de Yaounde, Dept des Langues Africaines et Linguistics, Yaounde Cameron. LC P59.U545. DD 410.72.

BULETINUL UNIVERSITATII DIN GALATI. FASCICULA I, STIINTE SOCIALE SI UMANISTE. Periodical. English (French and Romanian). an. Redactia Buletinului, 6200 Galati Str, Republicii Nr 47 Romania. LC P1.A1.

BULLETIN ANALYTIQUE DE LINGUISTIQUE FRANCAISE. V. 1- 1969-. 0007-408X. Periodical. French. qt. Masson Publishing USA Inc, 211 East 43rd Street/Room 1306, New York NY 10017. Tel (212)370-1937. Bulletin Analytique de Lexicologie.

BULLETIN - ASSOCIATION CANADIENNE DE LINGUISTIQUE. (BULLETIN). Main/Corp Canadian Linguistic Association. 1 (Spring 1984)-. 0825-2823. CN. English (French). an. Free. Canadian Linguistic Association, c/o G Harmer Room 501 Administration Building Carleton University, Ottawa Ontario K1S 5E6 Canada. DD 410.6071. (ctrl).

BULLETIN - ASSOCIATION FOR LITERARY AND LINGUISTIC COMPUTING CEASED. Main/Corp Association for Literary and Linguistic Computing. VFOAT ALLC Bulletin. Began in 1973. 0305-9855. UK. English. qt. $15.00. 6 Sevenauks Avenue, Henter Moor, Stockport SK4 4AW England. Ind/Abst MLA Int. Bibliogr. Books Artic. Mod. Lang. Lit. LC P98. DD 410.2854. CODEN ALLCB5.

BULLETIN CILA. Main/Corp Commission Interuniversitaire Suisse de Linguistique Appliquee. VAT Bulletin Commission Interuniversitaire Suisse de Linguistique Appliquee. 8-. 0251-7256. Periodical. SZ. French (English or German). sa. 40.-. University Neuchatel, Center of Linguistiques Appliquee, Avenue 1st Mars 26, CH-2000 Neuchatel Switzerland. Tel (038) 24 71 61. Ind/Abst Lang. Lang. Behav. Abstr., Lang. Teach. LC P51. DD 418.007. bk rev. adv acc. Publication of the language department of the University of Neuchatel. Articles on the study of foreign languages, methodology, applied linguistics, theory, and application in the classroom. Bulletin de la Commission Interuniversitaire Suisse de Linguistique Appliquee.

BULLETIN DE LA CORPORATION DES TRADUCTEURS ET INTERPRETES DU NOUVEAU-BRUNSWICK. Main/Corp Corporation des Traducteurs et Interpretes du Nouveau-Brunswick. VFOAT Bulletin of the Corporation of Translations and Interpreters of New Brunswick. Vol. 1, No. 1 (June 1980)-. 0228-6564. Periodical. CN. French (English). ir. Free. Bulletin de la CTINB, CP 427, Fredericton New Brunswick E3B 5A4 Canada. DD 418.0205.

BULLETIN DE LA SOCIETE DE LINGUISTIQUE DE PARIS. Main/Corp Societe de Linguistique de Paris. Vol. 1- 1869-. 0037-9069. Periodical. FR. French. sa. $160.00. M L S, 42048 rue de la Colonie, 75013 Paris 13 France. Ind/Abst MLA Int. Bibliogr. Books Artic. Mod. Lang. Lit., Sociol. Abstr., Lang. Lang. Behav. Abstr., Years Work Eng. Stud.

BULLETIN DE L'ACLA. (BULLETIN DE L'A C L A). Main/Corp Canadian Association of Applied Linguistics. VFOAT Bulletin of the C A A L. May 1980-. 0709-9207. Periodical. CN. English (French). Canadian Association of Applied Linguistics Secretariat, Universite de Montreal, PO Box 6128 Station A, Montreal Quebec H3C 3J7 Canada. Ind/Abst MLA Int. Bibliogr. Books Artic. Mod. Lang. Lit., Lang. Teach. DD 418.007.

BULLETIN DE L'ALCAM. Main/Corp Institut des Sciences Humaines, Yaounde, Cameroon. Unite de Recherche Linguistique et Phonetique. VAT Bulletin de l'Atlas Linguistique du Cameroun. 1-. French. ir. institut des Sciences Humaines, BP 73, Yaounde Cameroon. Ind/Abst MLA Int. Bibliogr. Books Artic. Mod. Lang. Lit. LC P381.C34.

BULLETIN DE L'ASSOCIATION GUILLAUME BUDE. Main/Corp Association Guillaume Bude. No. 1 (Oct. 1923)-. 0004-5527. Periodical. FR. French. qt. Societe Edition Belles Lettres, 95 Boulevard Raspail, 75006 Paris France. Ind/Abst MLA Int. Bibliogr. Books Artic. Mod. Lang. Lit. LC PA12. (cum index).

BULLETIN DE LIAISON - CENTRE DE LINGUISTIQUE THEORIQUE ET APPLIQUEE, UNIVERSITE NATIONALE DU ZAIRE. Main/Corp Universite Nationale du Zaire. Campus de Lubumbashi. Centre de Linguistique Theorique et

Linguistics

Appliquee. Periodical. CG. French. ir. 100. Universite Nationale du Zaire, Faculte des Lettres, B P 1607, Lubumbashi Congo (Zaire). LC PC3680.Z3. DD 440.7.

BULLETIN DES ETUDES AFRICAINES. See History (General) - History of Africa.

BULLETIN D'INFORMATIONS PROUSTIENNES. See Literature.

BULLETIN DU CERCLE JUIF. VFOAT Bulletin du Cercle Juif de Langue Francaise. No. 1- Nov. 1954-. 0577-3415. Periodical. CN. French. mo. Congres Juif Canadien, 1590 Avenue McGregor, Montreal Quebec H3G 1C5 Canada.

BULLETIN - GREAT BRITAIN. SCOTTISH EDUCATION DEPARTMENT. CENTRAL COMMITTEE ON ENGLISH. See Education (General) - Theory, Practice of Education.

BULLETIN LINGUISTIQUE, ETHNOLOGIQUE ET TOPONYMIQUE. French or German. ir. Institut Grand-Ducal Section de Linguistic de Folklore et de Toponymie, 5 rue Large Compte Cheques Postaux, Luxembourg 8776 Luxembourg. LC P1.A1. DD 410.5. Bulletin Linguistique et Ethnologique.

BULLETIN OF HISPANIC STUDIES. V. 26-Jan./Mar. 1949-. 0007-490X. Periodical. UK. English (Spanish, Portuguese, Catalan or French). qt. 66.00. Liverpool University Press, PO Box 147, Liverpool L69 3BX England. Tel (051)709-6022. Ed Dorothy Sherman Severin. Ind/Abst MLA Int. Bibliogr. Books Artic. Mod. Lang. Lit., Annu. Bibliogr. Engl. Lang. Lit., Index Book Rev. Humanit., Recent Publ. Artic. LC PC4008. DD 860.5. (cum index). bk rev. adv acc. The only learned journal published in Britain devoted exclusively to the languages and literature of Spain, Portugal and Latin America. Bulletin of Spanish Studies.

BULLETIN OF THE MIDWEST MODERN LANGUAGE ASSOCIATION CEASED. (BULLETIN). Main/Corp Midwest Modern Language Association. Began in 1968. Ceased with V. 16, No. 2. 0026-3419. Periodical. US. English. sa. $10.00. Midwest Modern Language Association, English and Philosophy, University of Iowa, 423 EPB, Iowa City IA 52242. Tel (319)353-3291. Ed Maria A Duarte. Ind/Abst Abstr. Engl. Stud., MLA Int. Bibliogr. Books Artic. Mod. Lang. Lit. LC P1.A1. bk rev. adv acc. Circ 2,200. (ctrl). Essays on the study and teaching of literature and language, particularly in relation to theoretical, political, historical, and cultural issues.

THE BULLETIN OF THE ZAMBIA LANGUAGE GROUP. Main/Corp Zambia Language Group. English. ir. Zambia Language Group, PO Box 2379, Lusaka Zambia. LC PL8021.Z3. DD 301.21.

BULLETIN SIGNALETIQUE - CENTRE NATIONAL DE LA RECHERCHE SCIENTIGIQUE. 524. SCIENCES DU LANGAGE. (BULLETIN SIGNALETIQUE. 524, SCIENCES DU LANGAGE). VFOAT Sciences du Langage. Began with Vol. 23 (1969). 0007-5590. Periodical. FR. French. qt. $45.23. Service des Abonnements du CDSH, 54 du Raspail, 75270 Paris Cedex 06 France. Tel 544-3849. LC P2. DD 016.41. NLM ZQ 1 B936SMR. bk rev. adv acc. Circ 650. (ctrl). Linguistic theory, philosophy of language, epistemology, descriptive, comparative, historical linguistics, history of linguistics, discourse studies, sociolinguistics, ethnolinguistics and applied linguistics. Bulletin Signaletique. 24, Sciences du Langage, Bulletin Signaletique. C (19-24): Sciences Humaines.

BULLETIN - SOCIETE ROMAINE DE LINGUISTIQUE ROMANE. Main/Corp Societe Roumaine de Linguistique Romane. VFOAT Bulletin de la Societe Roumaine de Linguistique Romane. 1- 1964-. Periodical. RM. Romanian. an. Ilexim Press Department, PO Box 1-136-1-137, Bucharest Romania.

BURRELLE'S BLACK MEDIA DIRECTORY. See Yearbooks, Almanacs, Directories.

BURRELLE'S HISPANIC MEDIA DIRECTORY. See Yearbooks, Almanacs, Directories.

BWLETIN Y BWRDD GWYBODAU CELTAIDD. (THE BULLETIN OF THE BOARD OF CELTIC STUDIES). Main/Corp University of Wales. Board of Celtic Studies. VFOAT Bwletin y Bwrdd Gwybodau Celtaidd. V. 1- Oct. 1921-. 0142-3363. Periodical. UK. English. qt. $13.49. University of Wales Press, 6 Gwennyth Street Cathays, Cardiff CF2 4YD Wales. Tel 31919. Ed D Ellis Evans, J Beverley Smith, and Robin G Livens. Ind/Abst Abstr. Engl. Stud., Am. Hist. Life, Hist. Abstr., Part A, Mod. Hist. Abstr., Hist. Abst., Part B, Twent. Century Abstr., MLA Int. Bibliogr. Books Artic. Mod. Lang. Lit., Art Archaeol. Tech. Abstr., Years Work Eng. Stud. LC PB2101. DD 491.66. adv acc. Circ 300. The senior journal of the Board of Celtic Studies has three sections: language and literature, archaeology and art, history and law.

C. A. U. T. G. NEWSLETTER. Main/Corp Canadian Association of University Teachers of German. V. 1, No. 2- Mar. 1973-. 0384-5311. Periodical. CN. English. sa. Canadian Association of University Teachers of German, Box 102/Station R, Toronto Ontario M4G 3T2 Canada. DD 438.007. Newsletter.

C C D FOREIGN LANGUAGE NEWSLETTER. 1- 1962-. 0529-2654. Periodical. US. English. 401 Walnut Street, Philadelphia PA 19106.

C-L/CLL. COUNSELING-LEARNING COMMUNITY LANGUAGE LEARNING NEWSLETTER. VFOAT Counseling-Learning Community Language Learning Newsletter. 0197-6893. Periodical. US. English. qt. $6.00. C-L/CLL Newsletters, PO Box 383, East Dubuque IL 61025. Tel (815)747-3071.

CA VA. See Education (General) - Theory, Practice of Education.

CAHIER DE LINGUISTIQUE. No. 1- 1971-. 0315-4025. Periodical. CN. French. Les Presses de l'Universite du Quebec, C P 250 Succursale N, Montreal Quebec H2X 3M4 Canada. Ind/Abst MLA Int. Bibliogr. Books Artic. Mod. Lang. Lit., Lang. Teach. LC P2. DD 410.5.

CAHIERS D'ALLEMAND. 1- 1970-. Periodical. FR. French. sa. Societe Nouvelle Didier Erudition, 6 rue de la Sorbonne, 75005 Paris France.

CAHIERS DE LEXICOLOGIE. Vol. 1- 1959-. 0007-9871. FR. French. ir. 140.00. Society Nouvelle Didier Erudition, 6 rue de la Sorbonne 75005 Paris France. Tel 4354 47 57. Ed B Quemada. Ind/Abst MLA Int. Bibliogr. Books Artic. Mod. Lang. Lit., Lang. Lang. Behav. Abstr., Lang. Teach., Sociol. Abstr. Circ 2,000. Journals of lexicology publishing the inquiries in lexicology of the National Institute of French Languages.

CAHIERS DE LINGUISTIQUE. ASIE ORIENTALE. VFOAT Asie Orientale. No. 1- March 1977-. 0153-3320. Periodical. FR. French (English). sa. 150.00. Center de Recherches Linguistics sur l'Asie Orientale, 54 Boulevard Raspail, 75270 Paris Cedex 06 France. Tel 544.39.79. bk rev. adv acc. Lingustics-languages of Eastern Asia.

CAHIERS DE LINGUISTIQUE HISPANIQUE MEDIEVALE. No. 1- 1976-. FR. French or Spanish. ir. Librairie Klincksieck, 11 rue de Lille, Paris France. LC PC4001. DD 460.

CAHIERS DE LINGUISTIQUE THEORIQUE ET APPLIQUEE. 1-. 0007-988X. Periodical. RM. English (French, German, Italian, Russian, and Spanish). sa. Ilexim Press Department, PO Box 1-136-1-137, Bucharest Romania. Ind/Abst MLA Int. Bibliogr. Books Artic. Mod. Lang. Lit., Sociol. Abstr., Lang. Lang. Behav. Abstr. LC P1.A1.

CAHIERS DE L'INSTITUT DE LINGUISTIQUE. Main/Corp Institut de Linguistique de Louvain. V. 1-. 0303-3880. BE. French. ir. 1200. Editions Peeters, Bondgenotenlaan 153 PB 41, B 3000 Leuven Belgium. Ind/Abst MLA Int. Bibliogr. Books Artic. Mod. Lang. Lit., Sociol. Abstr., Lang. Lang. Behav. Abstr., Lang. Teach. LC P2. DD 410.5. adv acc. (ctrl.)

CAHIERS DE L'INSTITUT DU MOYEN-AGE GREC ET LATIN. Main/Corp Kbenhavns Universitet. Institut for Grsk og Latinsk Middelalderfilologi. 1-. 0591-0358. Monographic Series. DK. English (German or Latin). ir. Erik Paludan/Intl Boghandel, Fiolstraede 10, DK 1171 Copenhagen K Denmark. Tel 01/15 06 75. LC PA1009.

CAHIERS DU CENTRE UNIVERSITAIRE DE LA REUNION. Main/Corp Centre Universitaire de la Reunion. French. ir. Universitaire de la Reunion, rue de la Victoire, Saint-Denis Reunion. LC P381.R46. DD 440.96981.

CAHIERS IVOIRIENS DE RECHERCHE LINGUISTIQUE. VFOAT CIRL. No. 1 (April 1977)-. Periodical. IV. French. sa. $10.60. Institute Linguistique Appliquee, 08 BP.887, Abidjan 08 Ivory Coast. LC P381.I9. DD 409.6668.

CAHIERS LINGUISTIQUES D'OTTAWA. Began with V. for Sept. 1971. 0315-3967. CN. English (French). ir. 5.00. University of Ottawa, Department of Linguistics, 78 Laurier E, Ottawa Ontario K1N 6N5 Canada. Tel (613)231-2943. Ind/Abst MLA Int. Bibliogr. Books Artic. Mod. Lang. Lit., Lang. Lang. Behav. Abstr., Lang. Teach., Sociol. Abstr. LC P1.A1. DD 410.5. bk rev. Circ 250. Papers on applied and theoretical linguistics written in French or English representing original contributions to the field.

CAIET DE SEMIOTICA. 1-. Romanian (English and French, with summaries in Russian). ir. 17.00. LC P99. DD 808.00141.

CALCULI. Jan. 1967-. 0008-0632. Periodical. US. English. bm. Free. Dartmouth College, Department of Classics, c/o Stephen V F Waite, Hanover NH 03755. LC PA50. DD 480.

CALGARY WORKING PAPERS IN LINGUISTICS. VFOAT CWP in Linguistics. 0823-0579. CN. English. an. $4.00. University of Calgary, Logos Department of Linguistics, 2920-24th Avenue NW, Calgary Alberta T2N 1N4 Canada. DD 410.5.

CALL NEWS AND REVIEWS. VFOAT Call News & Reviews. VAT Computer-Assisted Language Learning News and Reviews. Vol. 1, No. 1-. 8755-7134. Periodical. US. English. bm. $20.00. Call Publications, PO Box 18708, Los Angeles CA 90007. DD 407.

CAMBRIDGE STUDIES IN LINGUISTICS. Vol. 1 1969-. 0068-676X. Monographic Series. UK. English. ir. Cambridge University Press, The Edinburgh Building, Shaftesbury Road, Cambridge CB2 2RU England. Tel 0223 312393. Ed Penny Carter. Ind/Abst MLA Int. Bibliogr. Books Artic. Mod. Lang. Lit. Monographs on all aspects of theoretical linguistics.

CANADIAN JOURNAL OF LINGUISTICS. VFOAT Revue Canadienne de Linguistique. V. 6, No. 2 I.E.V. 7, No. 1- Fall 1961-. 0008-4131. Periodical. CN. English (text also in French). sa. 30. Canadian Linguistic Association, Queen's University, c/o D Wilson, Kingston Ontario K7L 3N6 Canada. Tel (613)231-5573. Ed William Cowan. Ind/Abst MLA Int. Bibliogr. Books Artic. Mod. Lang. Lit., Sociol. Abstr., Soc. Welf. Soc. Plan./Policy Soc. Dev., Lang. Lang. Behav. Abstr., Annu. Bibliogr. Engl. Lang. Lit., Lang. Teach., Index Book Rev. Humanit., Soc. Sci. Citation Index, Years Work Eng. Stud. bk rev. Circ 700. Also available in microfiche format. Articles and book reviews on linguistics. Journal of the Canadian Linguistic Association, 0319-5732.

CANADIAN JOURNAL OF RESEARCH IN SEMIOTICS CEASED. (THE CANADIAN JOURNAL OF RESEARCH IN SEMIOTICS). VFOAT Le Journal Canadien de Recherche Semiotique. V. 1-8. 0316-7917. Periodical. CN. English (text also in French). ty. $6.00. Madeleine Monod, Secretary-Treasurer of the C.S.R.A., Secondary Education Department, University of Alberta, Edmonton Alberta Canada. LC P99. DD 001.5601.

CANADIAN MODERN LANGUAGE REVIEW. (THE CANADIAN MODERN LANGUAGE REVIEW). VFOAT Revue Canadienne des Langues Vivantes, La Revue Canadienne des Langues Vivantes. Began with issue for Sept. 1944. 0008-4506. Periodical. CN. English (includes some text in French, German, Italian, Polish, Russian, Spanish and Ukrainian). qt. Canadian Modern Language Review, 34 Butternut Street, Toronto Ontario M4K 1T7 Canada. Ind/Abst MLA Int. Bibliogr. Books Artic. Mod. Lang. Lit., Sociol. Abstr., Lang. Lang. Behav. Abstr., Lang. Teach., Educ. Index, Can. Educ. Index, Curr. Index J. Educ. LC PB5. DD 410.7. Also available on microfilm from University Microfilms.

CANADIAN QUILL. Vol. 11, No. 2 (Nov. 1981)-. 0714-5721. Periodical. CN. English. ir. Canadian Quill, c/o New Brunswick Teachers Association, PO Box 752, Fredericton New Brunswick E3B 5R6 Canada. Ind/Abst Can. Educ. Index. DD 420.712715. Chautauqua, 0710-7757.

CARLETON PAPERS IN APPLIED LANGUAGE STUDIES. Vol. 1 (1984)-. 0824-7714. CN. English. an. $7.00 Per Vol. Centre for Applied Language Studies, Carleton University, Ottawa Ontario K1S 5B6 Canada. DD 418.007.

Linguistics

CEA FORUM. Main/Corp College English Association. VAT College English Association Forum. V. 1- Oct. 1970-. 0007-8034. Periodical. US. English. qt. Department of English, Texas A & M University, College Station TX 77843. Ind/Abst Index Am. Period. Verse, Curr. Index J. Educ. LC PE11. DD 820.71173. *CEA Critic.*

CELESTINESCA. V. 1- May 1977-. 0147-3085. Periodical. US. English (French or Spanish). sa. $6.00 Domestic, $8.00 Foreign. University of Georgia, Department of Romance Languages, c/o J T Snow, Athens GA 30602. Tel (404)542-8997. Ed Joseph T Snow. Ind/Abst MLA Int. Bibliogr. Books Artic. Mod. Lang. Lit. LC PQ6428. DD 862.2. bk rev. Circ 350. (ctrl). Treats Rojas' Spanish masterpiece Celestina and its derivatives and analogs, translations and stage adaptions, editions and illustrations. Includes news and bibliography sections.

CENTRAL ASIATIC JOURNAL. *See* History (General) - History of Asia.

CERCETARI DE LINGVISTICA. V. 1- 1956-. 0373-1545. Periodical. RM. Romanian (summaries in French, German, or Russian). sa. Ilexim Press Department, PO Box 1-136/1-137, Bucharest Romania. Ind/Abst Lang. Lang. Behav. Abstr., MLA Int. Bibliogr. Books Artic. Mod. Lang. Lit., Sociol. Abstr. *Studii Si Cercetari Stiintifice.*

CESKOSLOVENSKA RUSISTIKA. VFOAT Casopis Pro Slovanske Jazyky, Literaturu A Dejiny SSSR. Vol. 1- 1956-. 0009-0638. Periodical. CS. Czech (tables of contents and summaries in Russian). $34.00. John Benjamins BV, Amsteldijk 44, PO Box 52591, 1007 HA Amsterdam Holland. Tel (020)738156. Ed R V Hrabe. Ind/Abst MLA Int. Bibliogr. Books Artic. Mod. Lang. Lit., Sociol. Abstr., Lang. Lang. Behav. Abstr. LC PG1.

C'EST-A-DIRE. V. 1- 1 Nov. 1960-. 0577-4179. Periodical. CN. French. ir. Canadian Broadcasting Corp, CP 6000, Montreal Quebec Canada. DD 448.105.

CHILD LANGUAGE TEACHING AND THERAPY. Vol. 1, No. 1 (Feb. 1985)-. 0265-6590. Periodical. UK. English. ty. $50.00. Edward Arnold Publishers Ltd, Woodlands Park Avenue, Maidenhead Berks England.

CHILDREN'S LANGUAGE. V. 1-. 0163-2809. US. English. Gardner Press Inc, 19 Union Square West, New York NY 10003. LC P118. DD 401.9. NLM W1 CH696H.

CHOSONO YONGU. First issue 1949-. Periodical. US. Korean. Amerasian Data Research Services, PO Box 564, Hyattsville MD 20782. LC PL901.

CHUNG HSUEH YU WEN. VFOAT Zhongxueyuwen. Periodical. Chinese. ir. 0.34. LC PL1065. DD 495.1071251.

CHUNG-KUO HSUEH SHU NIEN KAN. VFOAT Annual Journal of Chinese Studies. No. 1- 1976-. Chinese. ir. Alumni Association of Research, Institute of the Chinese Literature, Taiwan Normal University, Taipei Taiwan. LC PL1071.

CHUNG-KUO WEN TZU (CHUNG-KUO WEN TZU PIEN CHI WEI YUAN HUI). (CHUNG-KUO WEN TZU). Periodical. US. Chinese. ir. $8.00. Mei-Kuo I Wen Yin Shu Kuan, 21 Vista Court South, San Francisco CA 94080. LC PL1004. DD 495.109.

CHUNG-KUO YU WEN (TAIPEI, TAIWAN). (CHUNG-KUO YU WEN). Began in 1952. 0578-1930. Periodical. CH. Chinese. mo. $230.00. Chung-Kuo Yu Wen Yueh Kan She, PO Box 7-89, Tai-Pei Taiwan. LC PL1004. DD 495.105.

CHUNG-KUO YU YEN HSUEH PAO (PEKING, CHINA : 1983). (CHUNG-KUO YU YEN HSUEH PAO). VFOAT Chinese Linguistics. April 1983-. Periodical. Chinese (table of contents also in English). an. 2.00. Hsin Hua Shu Tien, Pei-Ching Fa Hsing So, Peking China. LC PL1004. DD 495.105.

CHUNG WEN HSUEH HSI. *See* Literature.

CHUNGGUGO SEGYE. First issue 1984-. Periodical. KO. Chinese (Korean). mo. 33,600. Chunggugo Segyesa, 58-14 1-Ka Sinmunno Chongno-Ku, Seoul 110 Korea. LC PL1121.K6.

CHUNGMUN HAKPO. First Issue-. Periodical. Chinese (Korean). ir. LC PL1007.

CHUTETSUBUN GAKKAI HO. Main/Corp Todai Chutetsubun Gakkai. VFOAT Bulletin of the Sinologicao Society, University of Tokyo. No. 1-. JA. Japanese. ir. c/o Chutetsu Kenkyushitsu Tokyo Daigaku, Hongo Bunkyo-ku, Tokyo Japan. LC PL1006.

CHUVASHSKII IAZYK, LITERATURA I FOLKLOR. Began in 1972. UR. chiefly in Russian. 1.31 Single Issue. Nauchno-Issl IN-T, Moskovskii Prospekt 29 Korpus 1, Cheboksary Russia. LC PL381.

CIRCUIT (MONTREAL, QUEBEC). (CIRCUIT). No. 1 (June 1983)-. 0821-1876. Periodical. CN. French. qt. $20,00. Societe des Traducteurs du Quebec, Bureau 340, 1010 Ouest rue Ste-Catherine, Montreal Quebec H3B 1G1 Canada. DD 418.0205.

CIVILTA CLASSICA E CRISTIANA. 1st Year. No. 1 (April 1980)-. 0392-8632. Periodical. IT. Italian. ty. Piazza Manin 3/3, 16122 Genova Switzerland. Ind/Abst MLA Int. Bibliogr. Books Artic. Mod. Lang. Lit., Recent Publ. Artic. LC PA9. DD 880.09. *Rivista di Studi Classici.*

CLA JOURNAL. Main/Corp College Language Association (U.S.). VAT College Language Association Journal. V. 1- Nov. 1957-. 0007-8549. Periodical. US. English. qt. $30.00. College Language Association, Morehouse College, Box 728, Atlanta GA 30314. Tel (404)681-2800. Ed Cason L Hill. Ind/Abst Abstr. Engl. Stud., MLA Int. Bibliogr. Books Artic. Mod. Lang. Lit., Women Stud. Abstr., Annu. Bibliogr. Engl. Lang. Lit., Index Book Rev. Humanit., Humanit. Index. LC P1.A1. bk rev. adv acc. Circ 1,400. (ctrl). Literary criticism and book reviews.

COLECCION FILOLOGICA. Vol. 1 1952-. 0436-2888. SP. Spanish. ir. Universidad de Granada, Facultad de Farmica, Granada Spain.

COLLECTION DE GRAMMAIRES. Main/Corp Paris. Universite. Institut d'Etudes Slaves. 1- 1921-. Monographic Series. FR. French. ir. Institut d'Etudes Slaves, 9 rue Michelet, 75006 Paris France. Tel (1)43 26 50 89. Russian, Polish, Slovak and Bulgarian grammars.

COLLEGE COMPOSITION AND COMMUNICATION. VFOAT Composition and Communication. V. 1- March 1950-. 0010-096X. Periodical. US. English. qt. National Council of Teachers of English, 1111 Kenyon Road, Urbana IL 61801. Tel (212)960-8759. Ed Richard L Larson. Ind/Abst Annu. Bibliogr. Engl. Lang. Lit., MLA Int. Bibliogr. Books Artic. Mod. Lang. Lit., Lang. Lang. Behav. Abstr., Curr. Index J. Educ., Sociol. Abstr. LC PE1001. DD 808.0420711. (cum index). bk rev. adv acc. Circ 9,923. (ctrl). Articles of interest to college level teachers of composition and communication.

COLLEGE ENGLISH. V. 1- Oct. 1939-. 0010-0994. Periodical. US. English. mo. $35.00. National Council of Teachers of Education, 1111 Kenyon Road, Urbana IL 61801. Tel (205)348-6488. Ed James Raymond and W W Hatfield. Ind/Abst MLA Int. Bibliogr. Books Artic. Mod. Lang. Lit., Sociol. Abstr., Lang. Lang. Behav. Abstr., Women Stud. Abstr., Annu. Bibliogr. Engl. Lang. Lit., Lang. Teach., Ref. Source, Index Am. Period. Verse, Index Book Rev. Humanit., Educ. Index, Curr. Index J. Educ., Sociol. Abstr., Years Work Eng. Stud. LC PE1. DD 820.71173. bk rev. adv acc. Circ 15,326. (ctrl). Articles and issues of interest to English and language arts teachers at the college level.

COLLOQUIA GERMANICA. Vol. 1 1967-. 0010-1338. Periodical. English (German). qt. Francke Verlag, Neuengasse 43, Postfach 1445, CH-3001 Bern Switzerland. Tel 031/22 17 15. Ind/Abst MLA Int. Bibliogr. Books Artic. Mod. Lang. Lit., Index Book Rev. Humanit., Years Work Eng. Stud.

COLUMBIA UNIVERSITY WORKING PAPERS IN LINGUISTICS. VFOAT Working Papers in Linguistics. No. 1- Feb. 1975-. Periodical. US. English. ir. $4.00. Columbia University, Department of Linguistics, Attn: Managing Editor, New York NY 10027. Ed William Diver. Ind/Abst MLA Int. Bibliogr. Books Artic. Mod. Lang. Lit. (ctrl). Linguistics journal.

COMMENTATIONES HUMANARUM LITTERARUM. Main/Corp Suomen Tiedeseura. 0069-6587. Monographic Series. Fl. English (French, German or Swedish). ir. Academic Bookstore, Box 128, SF-00101 Helsinki 10 Finland. Ind/Abst MLA Int. Bibliogr. Books Artic. Mod. Lang. Lit., Sociol. Abstr., Lang. Lang. Behav. Abstr. LC P9. *Oversigt af Finska Vetenskaps-Societetens Forhandlingar.*

COMMENTS ON ETYMOLOGY. Began publication with Vol. 1 in Oct. 1971?. 0740-0330. Periodical. US. English. ir. $10.00. University of Missouri, Department of Applied Arts & Cultural Studies c/o Professor Cohen, Rolla MO 65401. Tel (314)341-4185. Ed Gerald Cohen. Circ 70. Etymology and indo-European norphology.

COMMUNICATION AND CYBERNETICS CEASED. 8-. 0340-0034. Monographic Series. English. ir. Springer Verlag-New York Inc, 175 5th Avenue, New York NY 10010. Tel (212)460-1500. Ind/Abst Math. Rev. LC UNC. NLM W1 CO427X. Topics include speech analysis, theory of language, linguistics, and syntactic pattern recognition. *Kommunikation und Kybernetik in Einzeldarstellungen, 0075-6601.*

COMMUNICATION QUARTERLY. *See* Communication - Broadcasting.

COMMUNICATION - SERVICE DE L'EDUCATION DES ADULTES DE LA C. E. C. M. Main/Corp Commission des Ecoles Catholiques de Montreal. Service de l'Education des Adultes. V. 1- June 1975-. 0380-3848. Periodical. CN. French. Commission des Ecoles Catholiques de Montreal, 3737 Est rue Sherbrooke, Montreal Quebec H1X 3B3 Canada. DD 448.00710714281.

COMPARATIVE ROMANCE LINGUISTICS NEWSLETTER. VFOAT CRLN. Began with issue for June 1951. 0010-4167. Periodical. US. English. sa. $8.00. Southern Illinois University, c/o Lee Hartman, Department of Foreign Languages, Carbondale IL 62901. Tel (618)536-5571. Ed Lee Hartman. Ind/Abst MLA Int. Bibliogr. Books Artic. Mod. Lang. Lit. LC PC1. DD 440.05. bk rev. Circ 100. Romance linguistics: personalia and bibliography.

CONTACT. V. 2 I.E. 3- Jan. 1976-. 0227-2938. Periodical. CN. English. qt. Free to members. Teachers of English as a Second Language Association of Ontario, PO Box 7014 Station A, Toronto Ontario M5W 1X7 Canada. DD 420.7. *TESL Association of Ontario, 0227-292X.*

CONVERGENCES (SAINTE-FOY, QUEBEC). (CONVERGENCES). V. 1, No. 1 (Summer 84)-. 0825-6632. Periodical. CN. French. qt. Free. Alliance Champlain, 3831 Pelissier, Sainte-Foy Quebec G1X 3Y9 Canada. DD 440.60714. (ctrl).

LA CORONICA. V. 1- Fall 1972-. 0193-3892. Periodical. US. English. sa. $25.00. Muskingum College, Department of Modern Languages, Russel V Brown, New Concord OH 43762. Ind/Abst MLA Int. Bibliogr. Books Artic. Mod. Lang. Lit. LC PC4001. DD 860.5.

COURRIER DE L'ENSEIGNEMENT INDIVIDUALISE A TOUTES LES ANIMATRICES ET A TOUS LES ANIMATEURS DE 2E CYCLE DE L'ELEMENT. (LE COURRIER DE L'ENSEIGNEMENT INDIVIDUALISE A TOUTES LES ANIMATRICES ET A TOUS LES ANIMATEURS DU 2E CYCLE DE L'ELEMENTAIRE). V. 1- Sept. 1970-. 0380-9757. Periodical. CN. French. Le Courrier du Francais-Cadre, 2673 Avenue de Ronde, Quebec Quebec G1J 4G5 Canada. DD 448.3421.

COURRIER PEDAGOGIQUE A TOUTES LES ANIMATRICES ET A TOUS LES ANIMATEURS DU COURS ELEMENTAIRE. (LE COURRIER PEDAGOGIQUE A TOUTES LES ANIMATRICES ET A TOUS LES ANIMATEURS DU COURS ELEMENTAIRE). V. 8, No. 1- Oct. 1977-. 0225-6479. Periodical. CN. French (English). mo. Longpre-Dessureault, Le Courrier Pedagogique, 2673 rue de la Ronde, Quebec Quebec G1J 4G5 Canada. DD 448.34. *Courrier du Francais-Cadre a Toutes les Animatrices du 1er Cycle de l'Elementaire, 0380-9722; 0380-9730.*

COURSES FOR FOREIGNERS IN SPAIN. Main/Corp Spain. Ministerio de Educacion Y Ciencia. Secretaria General Tecnica. VFOAT Courses for Foreign Students in Spain. English. ir. Ministerio de Educacion Y Ciencia, Madrid Spain. LC PC4068.S8. DD 460.7046.

CRITICA HISPANICA. *See* Literature.

CRONACHE ERCOLANESI. 1- 1971-. IT. Italian. an. Gaetano Macchiaroli Editor, Via Carducci 59, 80121 Naples Italy 4NZ Romanzo.

CROSS CURRENTS (ANN ARBOR, MICH.). (CROSS CURRENTS). Series/Titl Michigan Slavic Materials. (1982)-. 0748-0164. US. English. an. Department of Slavic Languages and Literatures, University of Michigan, Ann Arbor MI 48109. LC PG13, D1055. DD 491.8, 001.10943.

CRUX. V. 1- 1967-. 0250-0035. Periodical. SA. English. qt. $2.11 4.50. Foundation for Education Science and Technology, PO Box 1758, Pretoria

Linguistics

South Africa. Tel 26-0035. Ed M M Hacksley. **Ind/Abst** MLA Int. Bibliogr. Books Artic. Mod. Lang. Lit., Lang. Teach. bk rev. **Circ** 3117. Journal for the teaching of English as a first, second or foreign language. It is intended for practising teachers in schools.

CUADERNOS DE FILOLOGIA CLASICA. 1- 1971-. Periodical. SP. Spanish. sa. Universidad de Madrid, Facultad de Filosofia Y Letras, Madrid 3 Spain. **LC** PA9.

CUADERNOS DE FILOLOGIA. II, STUDIA LINGUISTICA HISPANICA. VFOAT Studia Linguistica Hispanica. 1- Periodical. Catalan (German or Spanish). ir. **Ind/Abst** MLA Int. Bibliogr. Books Artic. Mod. Lang. Lit. **LC** PC4008. **DD** 460.05. *Cuadernos de Filologia (Universidad de Valencia. Seccion de Filologia Moderna).*

CUADERNOS DE INVESTIGACION FILOLOGICA. VFOAT C.I.F. V. 1- May 1975-. Periodical. French (Spanish). ir. 800. Secretaria de Publicaciones, Colegio Universitario de Logrono Espana, Logrono Spain. **Tel** 34/41/23-16-99. **LC** P1.A1. (cum index). **Circ** 400. (ctrl). Includes articles about classical, French, English, and Spanish literature and linguistics.

CUADERNOS DE TRADUCCION E INTERPRETACION. VFOAT Quaderns de Traduccio I Interpretacio. 1-. Periodical. Catalan (English and Spanish). sa. $7.00. Servei de Publications, Universitat Autonoma de Barcelona, Edifici Rectorat Belaterra, Barcelona Spain. **LC** P306.A1.

CUDZIE JAZYKY. Main/Corp Pedagogicka Fakulta V Banskej Bystrici. **Series/Titl** Acta Facultatis Paedagogicae Banska Bystrica. VFOAT Seria Spolocenskovedna. Cudzie Jazyky. 1- 1972-. German or Slovak. ir. 6.00. **LC** P25.

CUNYFORUM. Began with Fall 1976 issue. Periodical. US. English. an. $5.00. Cunyforum, City University of New York, Graduate School, 33 West 42nd Street, New York NY 10036. **Tel** (212)790-4602. **Ind/Abst** MLA Int. Bibliogr. Books Artic. Mod. Lang. Lit. **LC** P1. **DD** 410.5.

CURRENT INQUIRY INTO LANGUAGE AND LINGUISTICS. 1-. Monographic Series. CN. English. ir. Linguistic Research Inc, Box 5677 Postal Station L, Edmonton Alberta T6C4G1 Canada. **Tel** (403)922-2252. **Ind/Abst** MLA Int. Bibliogr. Books Artic. Mod. Lang. Lit.

CURRENT RESEARCH IN FRENCH STUDIES AT UNIVERSITIES AND POLYTECHNICS IN THE UNITED KINGDOM. Vol. 14 (1981-82)-. Periodical. UK. English. an. $9.71. K H Francis Westbury, Bossington Lane, Porlock Somerset TA24 8HD England. **Tel** 0643-862264. Ed K H Francis. **Circ** 350. Catalogue of postgraduate research in French studies (languages, literature, civilization) at United Kingdom universities and polytechnics. *Current Research in French Studies at Universities and University Colleges in the United Kingdom.*

CURRENT RESEARCH IN FRENCH STUDIES AT UNIVERSITIES AND UNIVERSITY COLLEGES IN THE UNITED KINGDOM CEASED. V. 13. UK. English. an. Dr Marjorie Shaw, Department of French, The University, Sheffield S10 2TN England. **LC** Z2175.A2, PC2071. **DD** 016.8409.

DAIYAMONDO GENDAI EIGO NO KISO CHISHIKI. VFOAT Essentials of Present-Day English. 0303-0512. JA. English (Japanese). ir. 750. Daiyamondo Sha, 4-2 Kasumigaseki 1-Chome Chiyoda-Ku, Tokyo 100 Japan. **LC** PE1130.J3.

DALJE. V. 1, No. 1 (Spring 1982)-. Periodical. Serbo-Croatian -R. qt. 600.00. Nisro Osloboenje, 71000 Sarajevo Pavla, Goranina 13 Yugoslavia. **LC** PB5.

DEGRES. V. 1-. 0376-8163. Periodical. BE. Multilingual (English, French, German, Italian or Spanish). qt. $17.00. De la Banque de Bruxelles, Place de Jamblinne de Meux 1, B-1040 Bruxelles Belgium. **Ind/Abst** MLA Int. Bibliogr. Books Artic. Mod. Lang. Lit., Sociol. Abstr., Lang. Behav. Abstr. **LC** P99. **DD** 405.

DELO; MESECNI KNJIZEVNI CASOPIS. See Literature.

DESCRIPTION AND ANALYSIS OF CONTEMPORARY STANDARD RUSSIAN. 1- 1959-. 0070-3826. US. English. ir. Walter de Gruyter Inc, 200 Sawmill River Road, Hawthorne NY 10532. **Tel** (914)747-0110.

DEUTSCH ALS FREMDSPRACHE. Vol. 1-. 0011-9741. Periodical. German. bm. $17.62. Kunst & Wissen Erich Bieber, Dufourstrasse 51, CH-8008 Zurich Switzerland. **Tel** 01/69 44 20. **Ind/Abst** MLA Int. Bibliogr. Books Artic. Mod. Lang. Lit., Lang. Lang. Behav. Abstr., Lang. Teach., Sociol. Abstr. **DD** 430.

DEUTSCH-SLAWISCHE FORSCHUNGEN ZUR NAMENKUNDE UND SIEDLUNGSGESCHICHTE. No. 1- 1956-. 0070-3893. Periodical. German. ir. Deutscher Buch Export-Import, Leninstrasse 16, DDR-701 Leipzig East Germany. **Ind/Abst** MLA Int. Bibliogr. Books Artic. Mod. Lang. Lit.

DEUTSCHE LEHRER IM AUSLAND. Began with 1, 1954?. 0418-8802. Periodical. GW. German. ir. $18.26. Hermann Schroedel Verlag KG, Postfach 810760, 3 Hannover 81 West Germany. **Tel** 0511/83 88-1.

DEUTSCHE REIHE FUR AUSLANDER. REIHE C: ERGANZUNGSHEFTE ZU GRAMMATISCHEN FRAGEN. VFOAT Erganzungshefte zu Grammatischen Fragen. 1- 1961-. 0418-8993. Monographic Series. GW. German. ir. Huber, Max-Hueber-Strasse 4, D-8045 Ismaning Bei Munich West Germany.

DIE DEUTSCHE SCHRIFT. German. ir. 24.00. Bund fur Deutsche Schrift, PO Box 1110, D-2908 Ahlhorn West Germany. **Tel** 04435/1313. **LC** PF3153. bk rev. adv acc. Promotion of German lettering.

DEUTSCHE SPRACHE. Began in 1973. 0340-9341. Periodical. German. ir. 48.00. Bei Munchen, M Heuber, Krausstr 30, 8045 Ismaning West Germany. **Ind/Abst** Lang. Lang. Behav. Abstr., MLA Int. Bibliogr. Books Artic. Mod. Lang. Lit., Lang. Teach. **LC** PF3003.

DEUTSCHE SPRACHE IN EUROPA UND UBERSEE. Vol. 1- 1977-. 0170-3153. Monographic Series. GW. German. ir. Franz Steiner Verlag, Postfach 347, D7000 Stuttgart 1 West Germany. **Tel** (0711)2582229. Ed J Gerighausen and J Jakob. **Ind/Abst** Lang. Lang. Behav. Abstr. Monographs dedicated to the German language as spoken by minorities all over the world.

DEUTSCHUNTERRICHT. See Literature.

DEWAN BAHASA. Began Sept. 1957. MY. Malay. mo. Dewan Bahasa Dan Pustaka, Peti Surat 803, Kuala Lumpur Malaysia. **LC** PL5101. Malay language and linguistics.

DIALOGUE - COUNCIL OF MINISTERS OF EDUCATION. (DIALOGUE). Vol. 1, No. 1 (June 1982)-. 0715-7037. Periodical. CN. English (French text on inverted pages). qt. Free. Council of Ministers of Education Canada, Suite 5-200, 252 Bloor Street West, Toronto Ontario M5S 1V5 Canada. **DD** 407.0971.

DIALOGUE IMMERSION. VFOAT Revue Dialogue Immersion. V. 3. No 2 (Feb. 1984)-. 0824-4189. Periodical. CN. French. Free. Dialogue d'Immersion, c/o Conseil d'Immersion Association des Instituteurs du Nouveau-Brunswick, C P 752, Fredericton New Brunswick E3B 5R6 Canada. **DD** 440.7. (ctrl). *Je Porte, Tu Portes, 0712-9653.*

DIALOGUES ET CULTURES. No. 21 (Mar. 1981)-. 0226-6881. Periodical. CN. French. sa. $7.99. World Congress of Teachers of French, 1 Avenue Leon Journault, 92310 Sevres France. **Tel** 46 26 53 16. **DD** 440.7. adv acc. **Circ** 1,500. (ctrl). Proceedings of the World Congress of Teachers of French. *Dialogues (Quebec, Quebec), 0253-0007.*

DINE BIZAAD NANILIIH. VFOAT Navajo Language Review. V. 1- Winter 1974-. 0094-5870. Periodical. US. English or Navajo. sa. $8.00. Center for Applied Linguistics, Paul R Platero Editor, c/o Department of Linguistics/Room 20E, 225 Massachusetts Institute of Technology, Cambridge MA 02139. **Ind/Abst** MLA Int. Bibliogr. Books Artic. Mod. Lang. Lit. **LC** PM2006. **DD** 497.2.

DIRECTORY - INTERNATIONAL READING ASSOCIATION. See Yearbooks, Almanacs, Directories.

DIRECTORY OF BILINGUAL SPEECH-LANGUAGE PATHOLOGISTS AND AUDIOLOGISTS. See Yearbooks, Almanacs, Directories.

DIRECTORY OF MEMBERS - AMERICAN PHILOLOGICAL ASSOCIATION. See Yearbooks, Almanacs, Directories.

DIRECTORY OF PROGRAMS IN LINGUISTICS IN THE UNITED STATES & CANADA. See Yearbooks, Almanacs, Directories.

DISCOURSE. (DISCOURSE : BERKELEY JOURNAL FOR THEORETICAL STUDIES IN MEDIA AND CULTURE). No. 1 (Fall 1979)-. 0730-1081. Periodical. US. English. ir. $20.00. Discourse, PO Box 4667, Berkeley CA 94704. **Tel** (415)843-3545. **LC** P87. **DD** 302.23405. Theoretical studies in media and culture.

DISCOURSE PROCESSES. V. 1- Jan./Mar. 1978-. 0163-853X. Periodical. US. English. qt. $69.50. Ablex Publishing Corp, 355 Chestnut Street, Norwood NJ 07648. **Tel** (201)767-8450. Ed Roy O Freedle. **Ind/Abst** MLA Int. Bibliogr. Books Artic. Mod. Lang. Lit., Lang. Lang. Behav. Abstr., Lang. Teach., Curr. Index J. Educ. **LC** P302. **DD** 410.5. adv acc. **Circ** 650. Forum for articles exchanging ideas from diverse disciplines which share a common interest in discourse.

DISKUSSION DEUTSCH. 1-. Volume (Issue 1-). 0342-1589. Periodical. GW. German. bm. 16.23. Moritz Diesterweg, Postfach 110651, D-6 Frankfurt 11 West Germany. **Tel** (0611)13010. Ed Hubert Ivo, Valentin Merkelbach, Rosemarie Rigol, and Hansthiel. (cum index). adv acc. Directed at all those teaching German. It includes articles on didactic and methodological questions regarding German language and literature.

DISORDERS OF HUMAN COMMUNICATION. 1-. 0173-170X. Monographic Series. US. English. ir. Springer Verlag-New York Inc, 175-5th Avenue, New York NY 10010. **Tel** (212)460-1584. **LC** UNC. **NLM** W1 DI762. Communication disorders-articulation and surgical care of voice disorders.

DISPOSITIO. See Literature.

DISPUTATIONES RHENO-TRAJECTINAE. Main/Corp Utrecht. Rijksuniversiteit. Instituut Voor Oosterse en Slavische Talen. Vol. 1 1957-. 0083-4998. Dutch. ir. Walter de Gruyter Inc, 200 Sawmill River Road, Hawthorne NY 10532. **Tel** (914)747-0110.

DOCUMENTI DI FILOLOGIA. 1- 1957-. 0419-5434. Italian. ir.

DOCUMENTS DE LINGUISTIQUE QUANTITATIVE. 1-. 0085-4786. Monographic Series. FR. French. ir. Dunod, 92 rue Bonaparte, Paris 6EME France.

DOCUMENTS PEDAGOGIQUES. Main/Corp Paris. Universite. Institut d'Etudes Slaves. Monographic Series. FR. French. ir. Institut d'Etudes Slaves, 9 rue Michelet, 75006 Paris France. **Tel** (1)43 26 50 89. **Circ** 800. Language teaching handbooks (Russian and Slavic).

DOGU DILLERI. VFOAT Eastern Languages. Vol. 1- 1964-. 0419-5795. Periodical. Turkish (French, Arabic, Persian, or Urdu). ir. **LC** DS1.

DQR. DUTCH QUARTERLY REVIEW OF ANGLO-AMERICAN LETTERS. See Literature.

DRIEMAANDELIJKSE BLADEN. Year 1- 1949-. NE. Dutch. qt. Stichting Sasland, Postbus 1127, Groningen Netherlands. **Tel** 050-115309. Ed J van der Kooi. bk rev. **Circ** 400. Dialectology, regional history, literature and folklore; regional culture. *Driemaandelijksche Bladen.*

DRLAV : DOCUMENTATION ET RECHERCHE EN LINGUISTIQUE ALLEMANDE CONTEMPORAINE, VINCENNES. VFOAT Documentation et Recherche en Linguistique Allemande Contemporaine, Vincennes. Began in 1972. 0754-9296. Periodical. French (English and German). ir. 68. DRLAV, 26 rue Mousset-Robert F, 75012 Paris France.

DRUM (AMHERST, MASS.). See Literature.

DUQUESNE STUDIES. PHILOLOGICAL SERIES. Vol. 1 1960-. 0070-7694. US. English. Duquesne Studies Philological, Duquesne University Press, Pittsburgh PA 15219.

DUTCH STUDIES. See History (General) - History of Europe.

EACROTANAL INFORMATION. See Anthropology.

ECHOS. (LES ECHOS). Vol. 2, No. 1 (Oct./Nov. 1983)-. 0826-5097. Periodical. CN. English (French). bm. Free. Societe de la Maison Francaise de Calgary, 44-16 16 Street Southwest, Calgary Alberta T2T 4H9 Canada. **DD** 440.6071233. *Echos du Centre. English & French, 0826-5070.*

L'ECRIT DU TEMPS. 1 (Spring 1982)-. 0293-9320. Periodical. FR. French. sa. 170.00. Les Editions de Minuit, 7 rue Bernard-Palissy, 75006 Paris France. **Tel** 222.37.94. **LC** P211. **DD** 001.54305.

THE EFL GAZETTE. VFOAT E.F.L. Gazette. **VAT** English as a Foreign Language Gazette. 0732-5819. Periodical. UK. English. ir. Pergamon Press, 395 Sawmill River Road, Elmsford NY 10523. **Ind/Abst** Lang. Teach.

EIGAKUSHI KENKYU. English (Japanese). ir. Nihon Eigakushi Gakkai, c/o Keio Gijuku Daigaku Shin, Kenkyushitsu 1-1 Hiyoshi 4 Kohoku-Ku, Yokohama-Shi Japan. **LC** DA4.

EIGO EIBUNGAKU KENKYU. (STUDIES IN ENGLISH LANGUAGE AND LITERATURE). **VFOAT** English Language and Literature. No. 25 (Mar. 1975)-. Japanese or English. an. **Ind/Abst** MLA Int. Bibliogr. Books Artic. Mod. Lang. Lit.

EIGO EIBUNGAKU RONSO. First issue No. 4-. Japanese or English. ir. Ryukoku Daigaku Eigo Eibungaku Kenkyukai, Shichijo Omiya Shimokyo-Ku, Kyoto Japan. **LC** PE9. *Ryukoku Daigaku Eigo Eibungaku Ronso.*

EIGO KENKYU. (THE STUDY OF ENGLISH). English. mo. Kinokuniya Bookstores of America, 1581 Webster Street, San Francisco CA 94115. **Tel** (415)567-7625.

EIGSE. Began with: Vol. 1, Part 1 in 1939. 0013-2608. Periodical. IE. English (Gaelic). an. $9.20. National University of Ireland, 49 Merrion Square, Dublin 2 Ireland. **Tel** 01/767246. **Ed** Tomas O Concheanainn. **Ind/Abst** MLA Int. Bibliogr. Books Artic. Mod. Lang. Lit. bk rev. **Circ** 500. Irish language and literary studies.

EKLITRA. 1- 1967-). 0424-7175. FR. French. qt. 70,00. Eklitra/Association Culturelle Picarde, Chez M Pauchet 7 rue Naurile Garet Appru 3, 80000 Amiens France. **Tel** (22) 43 23 60. **Ed** Eklitra. bk rev. adv acc. Folklore, linguistics, literature, history and traditions.

ELNA NEWSLETTER. **Main/Corp** Esperanto League for North America. **VAT** Esperanto League for North America Newsletter. Began in 1973. 0030-5065. Periodical. US. English (Esperanto). bm. $7.50. Esperanto League North America, Box 1129, El Cerrito CA 94530. **Tel** (415)653-0998. **Ed** Cathy Schulze. bk rev. adv acc. **Circ** 1,000. Articles discussing the language problem around the world and the potential use of Esperanto as a solution.

ELOS. No. 1-. Periodical. BL. French (Portuguese). ir. $70.00 Single Issue. Associacao Brasileira dos Professores Universitarios de Frances, Avenida Presidente Antonio Carlos 58 40, 20020 Rio de Janeiro Brazil. **LC** PC2068.B7. **DD** 440.7081.

ELT DOCUMENTS. **VFOAT** English Language Teaching Documents. Began in 1971. 0736-2048. Periodical. UK. English. ir. $30.00. Pergamon Press, 395 Sawmill River Road, Elmsford NY 10523. **Ind/Abst** Lang. Lang. Behav. Abstr., Lang. Teach., Sociol. Abstr.

ELT FORUM JOURNAL OF ENGLISH STUDIES. V. 1- Mar. 1978-. Periodical. II. English. ir. $6.00. Elt Forum India, c/o Department of English, University Centre Tellicherry, Kerala 670101 India. **Ind/Abst** Lang. Teach. **LC** PE1128.A2. **DD** 820.5.

ENGLISCH. Vol. 1-. 0013-8185. Periodical. German (English). ir. **Ind/Abst** Lang. Lang. Behav. Abstr.

ENGLISH AND AMERICAN STUDIES IN GERMAN. 1968-. GW. German. an. Max Niemeyer Verlag, Postfach 21 40, 7400 Tuebingen 1 West Germany. **Ed** Horst Weinstock. **LC** PE3. **DD** 420.5. Summaries of these and monographs on English and American languages and literatures. Published in German.

ENGLISH EDUCATION. **VFOAT** EE, English Education. V. 1- Fall 1969-. 0007-8204. Periodical. US. English. qt. National Council of Teachers of English, 1111 Kenyon Road, Urbana IL 61801. **Tel** (412)624-6187. **Ed** Allen Berger. **Ind/Abst** Educ. Index, Curr. Index J. Educ., Soc. Sci. Citation Index. **LC** LA632. **DD** 370.942. bk rev. **Circ** 3,000. (ctrl). Articles of interest to educators teaching future English teachers. *Selected Addresses Delivered at the Conference on English Education, 0573-3561.*

ENGLISH JOURNAL. V. 1- Jan. 1912-. 0013-8274. Periodical. US. English. mo. $40.00. National Council of Teachers of English, 111 Kenyon Road, Urbana IL 61801. **Tel** (217)328-3870. **Ed** Alleen Nilsen and Ken Donelson. **Ind/Abst** Abstr. Engl. Stud., Educ. Index, Curr. Index J. Educ., MLA Int. Bibliogr. Books Artic. Mod. Lang. Lit., Lang. Lang. Behav. Abstr., Annu. Bibliogr. Engl. Lang. Lit., Lang. Teach., Film Lit. Index, Book Rev. Index, Index Am. Period. Verse, Media Rev. Dig., Read. Guide Period. Lit., Mag. Index, Sociol. Abstr., Years Work Eng. Stud. **LC** PE1. **DD** 420.5. (cum index). bk rev. adv acc. **Circ** 47,000. (ctrl). Articles on any phase of English teaching or any topic concerning English teachers in middle, junior, or senior high school. Often themed.

ENGLISH LANGUAGE TEACHING JOURNAL *CEASED.* (ENGLISH LANGUAGE TEACHING JOURNAL : ELT). **VFOAT** ELT. Began with V. 28, No. 1 Nov. 1973. Ceased with V. 35, No. 4 July 1981. 0013-8290. Periodical. UK. English. qt. $6.00. **LC** PE1128.A2. **DD** 420.7. Available on microfilm. *English Language Teaching.*

ENGLISH LANGUAGE TEACHING JOURNAL. (ELT JOURNAL). Vol. 36/1 (Oct. 1981)-. 0307-8337. Periodical. UK. English. qt. $45.00. Oxford University Press, Journals Department, Walton Street, Oxford OX2 6DP England. **Tel** (0865)56767. **Ed** Richard Rossner. **Ind/Abst** Curr. Index J. Educ., Educ. Index, Lang. Teach., Lang. Lang. Behav. Abstr. **LC** PE1128.A2. **DD** 428.007. bk rev. **Circ** 5,000. (ctrl). An international journal for teachers of English as a foreign language. It contains survey articles, reviews, correspondence and an announcement section. *English Language Teaching Journal.*

ENGLISH PHILOLOGICAL STUDIES. V. 8- 1963-. 0308-0129. UK. English. ir. **Ind/Abst** MLA Int. Bibliogr. Books Artic. Mod. Lang. Lit. *English and Germanic Studies.*

ENGLISH STUDIES IN AFRICA. V. 1- Mar. 1958-. 0013-8398. Periodical. SA. English. sa. $7.23. University of Witwatersrand Press, PO Box 1176, Johannesburg 2000 South Africa. **Ind/Abst** Abstr. Engl. Stud., MLA Int. Bibliogr. Books Artic. Mod. Lang. Lit., Annu. Bibliogr. Engl. Lang. Lit., Index Book Rev. Humanit., Lang. Lang. Behav. Abstr., Sociol. Abstr., Years Work Eng. Stud.

ENGLISH STUDIES IN CANADA. V. 1- Spring 1975-. 0317-0802. Periodical. CN. English. qt. $11.61. English Studies in Canada, University of Alberta, Department of English, Edmonton Alberta T6G 2E5 Canada. **Ed** Rowland McMaster. **Ind/Abst** Abstr. Engl. Stud., MLA Int. Bibliogr. Books Artic. Mod. Lang. Lit., Index Book Rev. Humanit., Years Work Eng. Stud. bk rev. (ctrl).

ENGLISH STUDIES SERIES. No. 1-. Monographic Series. UK. English. ir. Oxford University Press, 16-00 Pollitt Drive, Fairlawn NJ 07410.

ENGLISH STUDIES. TRANSLATION SUPPLEMENT. V.7- 1925-. Periodical. English. ir. **Ind/Abst** Index Book Rev. Humanit.

ENGLISH USAGE IN SOUTHERN AFRICA. V. 1- 1970-. 0046-2098. English. ir. **LC** PE3452 .S64. **DD** 427.968.

ENGLISH WORLD-WIDE. **VFOAT** English World Wide. **VAT** English World Wide. 1:1 (1980)-. 0172-8865. Periodical. English. sa. $57.14. Heinle & Heinle Enterprises, 29 Lexington Road, Concord MA 01741. **Ind/Abst** Lang. Lang. Behav. Abstr., Lang. Teach. *Retail Sales by Standard Industrial Classification, 0091-4789.*

ENSAIOS DE LITERATURA E FILOLOGIA. Vol. 1-. Periodical. Portuguese. ir. **LC** PA25. **DD** 480.05.

L'ENSEIGNEMENT DU RUSSE. 0300-2608. Periodical. FR. French (Russian). an. 60. Institut d'Etudes Slaves, 9 rue Michelet, 75006 Paris France. **Tel** (1)4236-5089. bk rev. adv acc. **Circ** 700. Pedagogical journal devoted to the teaching of Russian.

EOS. V. 1- 1894-. 0012-7825. Periodical. PL. Latin (Polish and other languages). sa. **Ind/Abst** MLA Int. Bibliogr. Books Artic. Mod. Lang. Lit. **LC** P1.A1.

ERIC FOCUS REPORTS ON THE TEACHING OF FOREIGN LANGUAGES. 0085-0101. Periodical. US. English. ir. Modern Language Association of America, 62-5th Avenue, New York NY 10011.

THE ESP JOURNAL. **VAT** English for Specific Purposes Journal. Vol. 1, No. 1 (Fall 1980)-. 0272-2380. Periodical. US. English. sa. Pergamon Press, Attn Cashier 395 Sawmill River Road, Elmsford NY 10523. **Ind/Abst** Lang. Teach. **LC** PE1128.A2. **DD** 828.007.

ESPANOL ACTUAL. No. 1- Nov. 10, 1963-. 0425-2772. Periodical. SP. Spanish. sa. $12.00. Arco Libros SA, Juan Bautista de Toledo 28, 28002 Madrid Spain. **Tel** (91)4-16-13-70. **Ind/Abst** MLA Int. Bibliogr. Books Artic. Mod. Lang. Lit., Lang. Teach.

ESTIMATES. PART III, OFFICE OF THE COMMISSIONER OF OFFICIAL LANGUAGES (CANADA). **VFOAT** Budget des Depenses. CN. English (French). $3.00 Domestic, $3.60 Foreign. Canadian Government Publishing Centre, Supply and Services Canada, Ottawa Ontario K1A 0S9 Canada. **LC** P119.32.C3. **DD** 354.7100854.

ESTIMATES. PART III, SECRETARY OF STATE, OFFICIAL LANGUAGES PROGRAM (CANADA). **VFOAT** Budget des Depenses. CN. English (French). $6.00 Domestic, $7.20 Foreign. Canadian Government Publishing Centre, Supply and Services Canada, Ottawa Ontario K1A 0S9 Canada. **LC** P119.32.C3. **DD** 354.710085.

ESTUDIOS FILOLOGICOS. No. 1-. 0071-1713. CL. Spanish. an. $8.00. Universidad Austral de Chile, Instituto de Filologia, Valdivia Chile. **Ind/Abst** MLA Int. Bibliogr. Books Artic. Mod. Lang. Lit., Am. Hist. Life, Hist. Abstr., Hist. Abstr., Part A, Mod. Hist. Abstr., Hist. Abst., Part B, Twent. Century Abstr. **LC** P25. bk rev. adv acc. **Circ** 700. Publishes studies specializing in linguistics and literature.

ESTUDIOS ROMANICOS. V. 1-. Periodical. SP. Spanish. ir. Universidad de Murcia, Departamento de Filologia Romanica, Murcia Spain. **LC** PC13. **DD** 440.05.

ESTUDOS LINGUISTICOS. Began in 1978. Periodical. BL. Portuguese. ir. Instituto de Idiomas, Yazigi SC AV 9 Julo 3166, Sao Paulo Brazil. **LC** P9. **DD** 410.5.

ETC. **VFOAT** Et Cetera. V. 1- Aug. 1943-. 0014-164X. Periodical. US. English. qt. $6.00. International Society for General Semantics, Box 2469, San Francisco CA 94126. **Ind/Abst** MLA Int. Bibliogr. Books Artic. Mod. Lang. Lit., Annu. Bibliogr. Engl. Lang. Lit., Psychol. Abstr., Humanit. Index, Index Book Rev. Humanit. **LC** B840. **DD** 149.9. **NLM** W1 ET423. Available on microfilm from University Microfilms.

ETHNOLOGUE. 0364-9288. US. English. Wycliffe Bible Translators, Box 1960, Santa Ana CA 92702. **LC** P371. **DD** 410.

ETUDES BAUDELAIRIENNES. *See* Literature.

ETUDES CELTIQUES. *See* Literature.

ETUDES DE LINGUISTIQUE APPLIQUEE. V. 1- 1962-. 0071-190X. Periodical. FR. French. qt. 341.00. Societe Nouvelle Didier Erudition, 6 rue de la Sorbonne, 75005 Paris France. **Tel** (1)43544757. **Ed** G Galissori. **Ind/Abst** MLA Int. Bibliogr. Books Artic. Mod. Lang. Lit., Sociol. Abstr., Lang. Lang. Behav. Abstr., Lang. Teach. **LC** P1.A1. **DD** 418.005. adv acc. **Circ** 1,500. Most important magazine of linguistics and didactics in languages.

ETUDES FINNO-OUGRIENNES. V. 1- 1964-. English (French, German or Russian). ir. Librairie Klincksiek, 11 rue de Lille, Paris France. **LC** PH1. **DD** 494.505.

ETUDES GERMANIQUES. Vol. 1 (No. 1-). 0014-2115. Periodical. FR. French (German). qt. 380.-. Soc Nouvelle Didier Erudition, 6 rue de la Sorbonne, 75005 Paris France. **Tel** 4354 47 57. **Ed** Grappin. **Ind/Abst** MLA Int. Bibliogr. Books Artic. Mod. Lang. Lit., Sociol. Abstr., Lang. Lang. Behav. Abstr. **LC** DD1. (cum index). bk rev. adv acc. **Circ** 2,000. Publishes the investigations of the Germanic and Scandinavian worlds throughout the world.

ETUDES LINGUISTIQUES. 1- 1962-. 0071-2124. Monographic Series. French. ir.

EUPHORION (HEIDELBERG, GERMANY). (EUPHORION). 45. Vol., 1. No. 0014-2328. Periodical. GW. German. qt. Carl Winter Universitatsverlag, Postfach 1866, Lutherstrasse 59, D6900 Heidelberg West Germany. **Tel** (06221)69111. **Ed** Rainer Grunter and Arthur Henkel. **Ind/Abst** MLA Int. Bibliogr. Books Artic. Mod. Lang. Lit. **LC** PN4. **DD** 809. bk rev. adv acc. **Circ** 1,600. (ctrl). Germanic linguistics and literature. *Dichtung und Volkstum.*

FAN I TUNG HSUN. **VFOAT** Translators' Notes. No. 1 (Feb. 1980)-. Periodical. CC. Chinese. bm. 0.33. Chung-Kuo Kuo Chi Shu Tien, PO Box 2820, Peking China. **LC** PN241.A1. **DD** 418.0205.

FANG YEN. **VFOAT** Fangyan. Periodical. CC. Chinese. bm. $10,80. China Publication Centre, PO Box 2820, Beijing China. **Tel** 5007744. **Ed** Li Rong. **LC** PL1501. **DD** 495.17. bk rev. **Circ** 8,000. All aspects of dialectology. Description, (phonology, lexicon and

Linguistics

grammar), distribution, grouping and development of Chinese dialects.

FENIX. V. 1- Winter 1978-. Periodical. US. Spanish (Portuguese). sa. 3.00. Department of Spanish and Portuguese, University of California at Irvine, Irvine CA 92717.

FILOLOGIA E CRITICA (SALERNO EDITRICE). (FILOLOGIA E CRITICA). Year 1, issue 1 (Jan./April 1976)-. 0391-2493. Periodical. Italian. ty. 55.000. Salerno Editrice, Via Di Donna Olimpia 186, 00152 Rome Italy. **Tel** (06) 5315684/8. Ed Enrico Malato. bk rev. adv acc. **Circ** 600. Research on history of Italian literature and Italian romance philology.

FILOLOGIA MODERNA. No. 1- Oct. 1960-. 0046-3841. Periodical. SP. Spanish (English, French, German, Italian). Seccion de Filologia Moderna Facultad Filologia, Cuidad Univ, Madrid-3 Spain. **Ind/Abst** MLA Int. Bibliogr. Books Artic. Mod. Lang. Lit., Annu. Bibliogr. Engl. Lang. Lit.

FILOLOGIAI KOZLONY. Vol. 1-. 0015-1785. Periodical. HU. Hungarian (summaries in Russian and various other languages). qt. $21.00 US. Akademiai Kiado, POB 24, 1363 Budapest Hungary. **Tel** 111-010. Ed M Horanyi. **Ind/Abst** MLA Int. Bibliogr. Books Artic. Mod. Lang. Lit., Bibliogr. Engl. Lit. bk rev. **Circ** 500. Covers the whole of modern European philology. Research results in various national literatures, comparative studies, literary theory, poetics, literary translation, analytical reviews. *Egyetemes Philologiai Kozlony.*

FILOLOGICHESKIE ZAPISKI. No. 1- 1971-. UR. Russian. LC PG2025.

FILOLOGIE. Periodical. French (Romanian). ir. LC PL601. DD 410.5.

FILOLOGISKT ARKIV. 1- 1955-. 0083-6745. Swedish. an. Almqvist & Wiksell, 108 Drottninggatan, PO Box 45150, S104 30 Stockholm Sweden. LC P17. DD 410.5. *Antikvariska, Historiska Studier.*

FILOLOHICHNI NAUKY NA UKRAINI: POKAZHCHYK LITERATURY ZA . . . RIK. 1978-. UR. Ukrainian (Russian). an. LC Z7003, P121.

FILOLOHIIA. Main/Corp Kharkov. Universytet. UR. Ukrainian. 1.40 single issue. LC AS262. *Seriia Filolohichna.*

FINNO-UGRISTIKA. Began in 1978. 0135-6569. Periodical. UR. Russian. 1.20. Mordovskii Gosudarstvennyi Universitet Imeni NP Ogareva, 430000 Saransk, Ul Bolshevistskaia 68, Saransk Russian SFSR. LC PH1.

FIRST LANGUAGE. V. 1, Pt. 1, No. 1 (Feb. 1980)-. 0142-7237. Periodical. UK. English. ty. Alpha Academic, Halfpenny Furze, Mill Lane, Chalfont St Giles Buckinghamshire HP8 4NR England. **Ind/Abst** Lang. Teach.

THE FLORIDA ENGLISH JOURNAL. Periodical. US. English. ir.

FLORIDA SPEECH COMMUNICATION JOURNAL. *See* Communication.

FM CEASED. VFOAT Annali Dell'Istituto di Filologia Moderna Dell'Universita di Roma. 1977-. IT. Italian. ir.

FOCUS. TEACHING ENGLISH LANGUAGE ARTS. (FOCUS : TEACHING ENGLISH LANGUAGE ARTS). VFOAT Teaching English Language Arts. 0163-5425. Periodical. US. English. ty. Ohio University, Department of English Language and Literature, Ellis Hall 353, Athens OH 45701. LC LB1576. DD 420.7.

FOLIA LINGUISTICA. V. 1- 1967-. 0165-4004. Periodical. English (articles in German, French, and Spanish). ir. Walter de Gruyter Inc, 200 Sawmill River Road, Hawthorne NY 10532. **Tel** (914)747-0110. **Ind/Abst** Am. Hist. Life, Hist. Abstr., MLA Int. Bibliogr. Books Artic. Mod. Lang. Lit., Lang. Lang. Behav. Abstr., Lang. Teach. Linguist. Abstr., Sociol. Abstr., Hist. Abstr., Part A, Mod. Hist. Abstr., Hist. Abstr., Part B, Twent. Century Abstr.

FOLIA SLAVICA. V. 1-. 0160-9394. Periodical. US. English. ty. $30.00. Slavica Publishers Inc, PO Box 14388, Columbus OH 43214. **Tel** (614)268-4002. Ed Charles E Gribble. **Ind/Abst** MLA Int. Bibliogr. Books Artic. Mod. Lang. Lit. LC PG1. DD 491.8. bk rev. **Circ** 500. Linguistics and philology relating to languages of Eastern Europe and the Soviet Union.

FOLIO. *See* Literature.

FOREIGN LANGUAGE ANNALS. V. 1, Oct. 1967-. Periodical. US. English. bm. $76.00. American Council on Foreign Languages, 579 Broadway, Hastings-on-Hudson NY 10706. **Tel** (914)478-2011. Ed Vick Galloway. **Ind/Abst** Lang. Lang. Behav. Abstr., Lang. Teach., Educ. Index, Curr. Index J. Educ. LC PB1. adv acc. **Circ** 8,000. (ctrl) Articles that describe innovative and successful teaching methods. Report educational research or experimentation or are relevant to the concerns and problems of the profession. *Foreign Language Annals, 0015-718X; Accent on ACTFL, 0271-7492.*

FORNERI. (IL FORNERI). V. 1, No. 1, (Jan. 1981)-. 0713-0627. Periodical. CN. English (text in French and Italian). qt. Free to Members, $5.00 Others. Il Forneri, Canadian Society for Italian Linguistics and Language Teaching, 756 Ossington Avenue, Toronto Ontario M6G 3T9 Canada. DD 450.7071.

FORO LITERARIO. *See* Literature.

FORUM. V. 1- (No. 1-). Periodical. US. English. mo. National Clearinghouse for Bilingual Education, 1500 Wilson Boulevard/Suite 802, Rosslyn VA 22209. **Ind/Abst** Lang. Teach.

FORUM DER LETTEREN. *See* Literature.

FORUM FOR MODERN LANGUAGE STUDIES. Periodical. UK. English. qt. 62.50. Scottish Academic Press Limited, 33 Montgomery Street, Edinburgh EH7 5JX Scotland. **Tel** (031)556-2796. Ed J R Ashcroft and D D R Owen. **Ind/Abst** MLA Int. Bibliogr. Books Artic. Mod. Lang. Lit., Years Work Eng. Stud. bk rev. adv acc. **Circ** 450. Studies in the field of European language and literature, including English and American, from the Middle Ages to the present.

THE FORUM OF PHI SIGMA IOTA. VFOAT Forum. 0883-5640. Periodical. US. English. $2.00. Phi Sigma Iota, Portland State University, c/o Professor Frank Vecchio, Portland OR 97207. **Tel** (203)773-8550. Ed Sharon Magnokelli. DD 406. adv acc. **Circ** 20,000.

FOUNDATIONS OF LINGUISTICS. US. English. ir. Elsevier Science Publishing Company Inc, PO Box 1663, Grand Central Station, New York NY 10163.

LE FRANCAIS DANS LE MONDE. Vol. 1-. 0015-9395. Periodical. FR. French. bm. Dawson-France SA, BP 40-91, Palaiseau France. **Ind/Abst** MLA Int. Bibliogr. Books Artic. Mod. Lang. Lit., Sociol. Abstr., Lang. Lang. Behav. Abstr., Lang. Teach., Curr. Index J. Educ., MLA Int. Bibliogr. Books Artic. Mod. Lang. Lit., Lang. Lang. Behav. Abstr. LC PC2065. (cum index).

FRANCAIS MODERNE. (LE FRANCAIS MODERNE). V. 1 (June 1933)-. 0015-9409. Periodical. FR. French. qt. $18.62. Librairie Pedagogique Centre, 70 Avenue Victor Hugo, 86500 Montmorillon France. **Tel** 49/910199. **Ind/Abst** MLA Int. Bibliogr. Books Artic. Mod. Lang. Lit., Lang. Teach., Index Book Rev. Humanit., Sociol. Abstr., MLA Int. Bibliogr. Books Artic. Mod. Lang. Lit., Lang. Lang. Behav. Abstr. (cum index).

FRANKFURTER BEITRAGE ZUR GERMANISTIK. Vol. 1 1967-. 0071-9226. Monographic Series. GW. German. ir. Verlag Gehlen, Daimlerstr 12 Postfach 2201, Bad Homburg West Germany. **Ind/Abst** MLA Int. Bibliogr. Books Artic. Mod. Lang. Lit.

FRANKFURTER PHONETISCHE BEITRAGE. V. 1-. Periodical. German. ir. LC P214. DD 414.

FREMDSPRACHEN. Began in Fall 1957. 0016-0970. Periodical. German. qt. $15.04. Kunst & Wissen Erich Bieber, Dufourstrasse 51, CH-8008 Zurich Switzerland. **Tel** 011-41-1-69 44 20. **Ind/Abst** MLA Int. Bibliogr. Books Artic. Mod. Lang. Lang. Behav. Abstr., Sociol. Abstr.

DER FREMDSPRACHLICHE UNTERRICHT. 0340-2207. Periodical. GW. German. ir. 22.00. Verlag E Klett, Rotebuhlstrasse 77, 7000 Stuttgart 1 West Germany. **Ind/Abst** Lang. Teach. LC PB35.

FRENCH-ENGLISH TRANSLATORS EXCHANGE. (FRENCH-ENGLISH TRANSLATORS EXCHANGE : FETX). VFOAT FETX. VAT French English Translators Exchange. 1 (Jan.-Feb. 1981)- – Vov. 1, No. 1-. 0275-4436. Periodical. US. English. bm. $20.00. Translation Research Institute, 5914 Pulaski Avenue, Philadelphia PA 19144.

FSL. FRENCH SECOND LANGUAGE DIRECTORY FOR CANADA. *See* Yearbooks, Almanacs, Directories.

FU JEN STUDIES : LITERATURE & LINGUISTICS. No. 6- 1973-. English. ir. $2.00. Sr Heliena Krenn Science & Language Library, Fu Jen University, Hsinchuang China. **Ind/Abst** MLA Int. Bibliogr. Books Artic. Mod. Lang. Lit. LC P1. DD 410.5. *Fu Jen Studies: Natural Sciences & Foreign Languages.*

GACETA LITERARIA. No. 1- May 1973-. Periodical. Spanish. ir. Apartado 40.001, Madrid Spain. LC P9.

GAIKOKU BUNGAKU. Japanese or English. ir. c/o Utsunomiya Daigaku Gaikoku Bungaku Kenkyushitsu, Minemachi 350, Utsunomiya 320 Japan. LC PN9.

GAIKOKUGAKU KENKYU. 1- 1974-. Japanese. ir. Tsuchiyamacho Nada-ku, Kobe Japan. LC AS552.K5.

GAKKAI NYUSU. Main/Corp Society for the Teaching of Japanese as a Foreign Language. JA. Japanese. ir. Nihongo Kyoiku Gakkai c/o Dai 4 Mori Building, 19-12 Toranomon 1 Minato-Ku, Tokyo-To 105 Japan. LC PL539.3.

GAKUJUTSU KENKYU : GAIKOKUGO GAIKOKU BUNGAKU HEN. VFOAT Scientific Researches. 24- 1975-. Japanese or English. ir. Waseda Daigaku Kyoikugakubu, 6-1 Nishi Waseda 1, Shinjuku-Ku, Tokyo Japan. LC P9. *Gakujutsu Kenkyu: Sogohen.*

GAKUJUTSU KENKYU : KOKUGO KOKUBUNGAKU HEN. VFOAT Scientific Researches. No. 24-. Japanese. ir. LC PL501. *Gakujutsu Kenkyu: Sogohen.*

GALPAGUCCHA. Periodical. Bengali. qt. 15.00. Hiralal Chakravarti, 64 Sitaram Ghosh Street, Calcutta 700009 India. LC PK1712.

GAZETTE DE L'ANNEE DU FRANCAIS. (LA GAZETTE DE L'ANNEE DU FRANCAIS). No. 1- Feb. 1978-. 0705-1735. Periodical. CN. French. ir. Free. Le Comite de Soutien, l'Annee du Francais Tele-Universite, 3108 Chemin Ste-Foy, Ste-Foy Quebec G1X 1P8 Canada. DD 440.9714.

GEKKAN KOTOBA. VFOAT Kotoba. 1st Ed. Nov. 1977-. Periodical. JA. Japanese. ir. Eichosha 3-3, Iidabashi 3, Chiyoda-Ku (102), Tokyo Japan. LC PL501.

GENDAI YOGO NO KISO CHISHIKI. VFOAT Jijy Kokumin: Jitenban. Began in 1948. 0431-1213. Japanese. ir. Jiyu Kokumin Sha, Kyobashi 2-8, Chuo-Ku Daiichi Biru Tokyo Japan. LC PL684.

GENERAL LINGUISTICS. V. 1- Winter 1955-. 0016-6553. Periodical. US. English. qt. $63.50. Pennsylvania State University Press, 215 Wagner Building, General Linguistics, University Park PA 16802. **Tel** (814)865-1327. **Ind/Abst** MLA Int. Bibliogr. Books Artic. Mod. Lang. Lit., Lang. Lang. Behav. Abstr., Annu. Bibliogr. Engl. Lang. Lit., Lang. Teach., Index Book Rev. Humanit., Sociol. Abstr., Soc. Sci. Citation Index, Years Work Eng. Stud. (cum index).

GENERAL SEMANTICS BULLETIN. No. 1/2- Autumn/Winter 1949/1950-. 0072-0771. US. English. an. Institute of General Semantics, 3029 Eastern Avenue, Baltimore MD 21224. **Tel** (301)276-7033. **Ind/Abst** Sociol. Abstr., Lang. Lang. Behav. Abstr. LC B820. DD 149.9, 190. (cum index).

GENGO BUNKA KENKYU. VFOAT Studies in Language and Culture. 1- 1975-. Japanese or English with summaries in English, German, or Russian. ir. Osaka Baigaku Gengo Bunkabu, 1-1 Machikaneyama (560), Toyonaka Japan. LC P9.

GENGO BUNKA KENKYU (MATSUYAMA-SHI, JAPAN). (GENGO BUNKA KENKYU). VFOAT Studies in Language and Literature. 0286-2093. Periodical. English (Japanese). sa. Matsuyama Shoka Daigaku Shokei Kenkyukai, 4-Banch 2 Bunkyo-Cho, Matsuyama-Shi Japan. LC P9.

GENGO BUNKA RONSHU. VFOAT Gengobunka Ronshu. No. 1-. JA. English (German or Japanese). ir. Tsukuba Daigaku, 1-1 Tennodai 1 Sakuramura Niihari-Gun, Ibaraki-Ken 305 Japan. LC PB5. DD 405.

GENGO BUNKA SENTA KIYO. No. 1 (1980)-. 0285-0400. Japanese. ir. LC P57.J3.

Linguistics

GENGO BUNKABU KIYO. VFOAT Language and Culture. Vol. 1-. 0286-3855. Periodical. English (French, Japanese and Russian). ir. **Ind/Abst** MLA Int. Bibliogr. Books Artic. Mod. Lang. Lit. LC P9. DD 410.5. *Gaikokugo Gaikugo Bungaku Kenkyu.*

GENGO NO KAGAKU. VFOAT Sciences of Language: The Journal of the Tokyo Institute for Advanced Studies of Language. No. 1-. Japanese or English. ir. Tokyo Gengo Kenkyujo, c/o Rebo Senta Building 4-5, Nishi Shijuku 8, Shijuku-Ku 160, Tokyo Japan. LC P9.

GENGOGAKU ENSHU. English (Japanese). ir. Tokyo Daigaku Bungakubu Gengogaku, Kankyushitsu 3-1 Hongo 7 Bunkyo-Ku, Tokyo 113 Japan. LC P9. DD 410.5.

GENJI MONOGATARI NO TANKYU. No. 1-. JA. Japanese. ir. Kazama Shobo Showa, 1-34 Kanda Jimbocho Chiyoda-Ku, Tokyo Japan. LC PL788.4.Z5.

GEOLINGUISTICS. Began with Vol. for 1974. 0190-4671. US. English. an. $15.00. Dr William C Woofloson, Bronx Community College, Bronx NY 10453. **Ind/Abst** MLA Int. Bibliogr. Books Artic. Mod. Lang. Lit., Lang. Lang. Behav. Abstr. LC P130. DD 409.

GEORGETOWN UNIVERSITY PAPERS ON LANGUAGES AND LINGUISTICS. No. 12-. 0160-2853. Periodical. US. English. sa. $6.00. Georgetown University Press, School of Languages and Linguistics, Washington DC 20057. **Ind/Abst** Lang. Teach. LC P1. DD 405. *Georgetown University Working Papers on Languages and Linguistics, 0149-0087.*

GEORGETOWN UNIVERSITY ROUND TABLE ON LANGUAGES AND LINGUISTICS. VFOAT G.U.R.T., Georgetown University Round Table on Languages and Linguistics, GURT, Georgetown University Round Table on Languages and Linguistics. 1973-. 0196-7207. US. English. an. Georgetown University, School of Languages and Linguistics, Washington DC 20057. **Tel** (202)625-4824. **Ind/Abst** Lang. Lang. Behav. Abstr., MLA Int. Bibliogr. Books Artic. Mod. Lang. Lit. LC P53. DD 410.5. *Report of the Annual Round Table Meeting on Linguistics and Language Studies.*

GERMANIC NOTES. See Literature.

GERMANISCH-ROMANISCHE MONATSSCHRIFT. Vol. 1- Jan. 1909-. 0016-8904. Periodical. GW. German. qt. 100.00. Carl Winter Universitatsverlag, Postfach 1866, Lutherstrasse 59, D6900 Heidelberg West Germany. **Tel** 6221-49111. Ed Heinrich Schroder. **Ind/Abst** MLA Int. Bibliogr. Books Artic. Mod. Lang. Lit., Sociol. Abstr., Annu. Bibliogr. Engl. Lang. Lit., Index Book Rev. Humanit., Lang. Lang. Behav. Abstr., Years Work Eng. Stud. LC PB3. (cum index). bk rev. Germanic and Romanic linguistics.

GERMANISTIK. See Literature.

GERMANISTIK (BERLIN, GERMANY). (GERMANISTIK). 0524-8414. GW. German. sa. 48.00. Werbegemeinschaft Elwert und Meurer GMBH, Berlin 62 West Germany. LC Z7037, PF3071. DD 016.43.

GERMANISTISCHE ABHANDLUNGEN. Vol. 1-. 0435-5903. Monographic Series. GW. German. ir. J B Metzlersche Verlagsbuchhan, Kernerstrasse 43, 7000 Stuttgart 1 West Germany. **Ind/Abst** MLA Int. Bibliogr. Books Artic. Mod. Lang. Lit.

GERMANISTISCHE ARBEITSHEFTE. Vol. 1 1970-. Monographic Series. GW. German. ir. Max Niemeyer Verlag, Postfach 21 40, 7400 Tuebingen 1 West Germany. Ed Otmar Werner. Textbooks in Germanic linguistics for students of German.

GERMANISTISCHE LINGUISTIK. 1- 1969-. 0072-1492. Monographic Series. GW. German. ir. Georg Olms Verlag GMBH, Hagentorwall 7, D-3200 Hildesheim West Germany. **Ind/Abst** Lang. Teach. LC PF3025.

GERMANISTISCHE MITTEILUNGEN. 0771-3703. Periodical. GW. German. sa. 48.00. Duemmler-Verlag, POB 1480, 5300 Bonn 1 West Germany. **Tel** (02)427-9960. Ed Peter Nelde. **Ind/Abst** MLA Int. Bibliogr. Books Artic. Mod. Lang. Lit. LC PF3068.B4. bk rev adv acc. **Circ** 1,000. German language and literature.

GERMANISTISCHE SCHRIFTENREIHE DER NORWEGISCHEN UNIVERSITATEN UND HOCHSCHULEN. No. 1- 1963-. 0435-5911. Monographic Series. NO. German. ir. Universitetsforlaget, PO Box 2959, Toyen Oslo 6 Norway.

GERTSENOVSKIE CHTENIIA : INOSTRANNYE IAZYKI. Main/Corp Leningrad. Gosudarstvennyi Pedagogicheskii Institut Imeni A.I. Gertsena. Periodical. UR. Russian. LC P9.

GIORNALE ITALIANO DI FILOLOGIA. V. 1- Feb. 1948-. 0017-0461. Periodical. IT. Italian. qt. $24.95. Libreria Gia Nardecchia, Piazza Cavour 25, 00193 Rome Italy. Ed Nino Scivoletto. **Ind/Abst** MLA Int. Bibliogr. Books Artic. Mod. Lang. Lit. LC P9. **Circ** 1,000. (ctrl). Serious contribution to scientific research in textual criticism, literary exegesis, historical reconstruction and cultural investigation.

GIORNALINO (NEW YORK, N.Y.). See Education (General) - Special Aspects of Education.

GLAS KANADSKIH SRBA. VFOAT Voice of Canadian Serbs. Began with Dec. 27, 1934 issue. Periodical. US. Serbo-Croatian -C. wk. $23.21. Avala Printing Publishing Company, 1297 Drovillard Road, Windsor Ontario N8Y 2R6 Canada. LC F1035.S47.

GLOSSA. V. 1- 1967-. 0017-1271. Periodical. CN. English (includes articles written in any language using Latin or Cyrillic alphabets. sa. $12.38. Simon Fraser University, Department of Modern Languages, Burnaby British Columbia V5A 1S6 Canada. **Ind/Abst** MLA Int. Bibliogr. Books Artic. Mod. Lang. Lit., Lang. Lang. Behav. Abstr., Lang. Teach., Sociol. Abstr., Abstr. Anthropol., Years Work Eng. Stud.

GLOSSARIA INTERPRETUM. Vol. 1 1957-. 0072-4750. English. ir. Elsevier Science Publ Company Inc, PO Box 1663, Grand Central Station, New York NY 10163.

GLOTTA; ZEITSCHRIFT FUR GREICHISCHE UND LATEINISCHE SPRACHE. Vol. 1-. 0017-1298. Periodical. GW. Multilingual. qt. $34.98. Vandenhoeck and Ruprecht, Postfach 3753, Theaterstr 13, D 3400 Goettingen West Germany. **Tel** 0551/65061. Ed P Kretschmer and Wilhelm Kroll. **Ind/Abst** MLA Int. Bibliogr. Books Artic. Mod. Lang. Lit. LC PA3.

GLOTTODIDACTICA. V. 1- 1966-. 0072-4769. PL. text in English, German or Russian. ir. Ars Polona, Krakowskie Przedmiescie 7, 00-068 Warsaw Poland. **Ind/Abst** MLA Int. Bibliogr. Books Artic. Mod. Lang. Lit., Lang. Lang. Behav. Abstr., Lang. Teach., Sociol. Abstr.

GOPPINGER ARBEITEN ZUR GERMANISTIK. No. 1-. Monographic Series. GW. German. ir. Alfred Kummerle, Schillerstr 8, D-7230 Goppingen East Germany. **Ind/Abst** MLA Int. Bibliogr. Books Artic. Mod. Lang. Lit.

GOTEBORGER GERMANISTISCHE FORSCHUNGEN. Vol. 1 1955-. 0072-4793. Monographic Series. German. ir. Almqvist & Wiksell, 108 Drottninggatan, PO Box 45150, S 104 30 Stockholm Sweden.

GOTHENBURG STUDIES IN ENGLISH. See Literature.

GRAMMATICA (TOULOUSE, FRANCE). (GRAMMATICA). Series Corp Universite de Toulouse-le Mirail. Annales. 1- 1972-. FR. French. ir. 15.00 Single Issue. Universite de Toulouse-Le Miral, Services des Publications, 4 rue Albert-Lautman, 31070 Toulouse France. LC PC2002.

GRAMMATICA UNIVERSALIS. Vol. 1 1966-. 0436-2829. German. ir. Friedrich Frommann Verlag, Postfach 500460, 7000 Stuttgart 50 West Germany.

GRANDE DIZIONARIO DELLA LINGUA ITALIANA. Italian. ir. LC PC1625.

GRAZER BEITRAGE. Vol. 1- 1973-. 0376-5253. NE. English (German, Italian, or French). ir. Rodopi, Keizersgracht 302-304, Amsterdam Netherlands. **Ind/Abst** MLA Int. Bibliogr. Books Artic. Mod. Lang. Lit. LC PA1.A1.

GRAZER LINGUISTISCHE STUDIEN. VFOAT GLS. V. 1- Feb. 1975-. Monographic Series. German (English or French). ir. LC P1.A1. DD 410.5.

GRUNDRISS DER SLAVISCHEN PHILOLOGIE UND KULTURGESCHICHTE. JA. German. ir. Walter de Gruyter, 200 Sawmill River Road, Hawthorne NY 10532. **Tel** (914)747-0110.

GUIDE TO PROGRAMS IN LINGUISTICS. 8th- Ed. 0363-2210. US. English. *University Resources in the United States and Canada for the Study of Linguistics, 0362-482X.*

HAMBURGER BEITRAGE FUR RUSSISCHLEHRER. 0072-9515. Monographic Series. German (Russian). ir. Ed Irene Nowikowa.

HAMBURGER PHILOLOGISCHE STUDIEN. 1- 1962-. 0072-9582. Monographic Series. GW. German. ir. Helmut Buske Verlag, Schluestr 14, 2 Hamburg 13 West Germany. **Tel** (040)452522. **Ind/Abst** MLA Int. Bibliogr. Books Artic. Mod. Lang. Lit. **Circ** 400.

HAMBURGER PHONETISCHE BEITRAGE. V. 1- 1972-. Monographic Series. US. German. ir. John Benjamins North America, One Buttonwood Square, Philadelphia PA 19130. **Tel** (215)564-6379. Studies in phonetics and linguistics.

HANDBOOK - UNIVERSITY OF ZAMBIA. DEPT. OF LITERATURE & LANGUAGES. Main/Corp University of Zambia. Dept. of Literature & Languages. English. ir. 0.50. University of Zambia, Department of Literature & Languages, POB 32379, Lusaka Zambia. LC PC59.U55. DD 407.116894.

HANDES AMSORYA. Vol. 1-. Periodical. AU. Armenian. qt. Mechitharisten Congregation in Wein, Mechitharistengasse 4, 1070 Vienna Austria. **Ind/Abst** MLA Int. Bibliogr. Books Artic. Mod. Lang. Lit.

HANNAM OMUNHAK. VFOAT Hannam Language and Literature. V. 7, 8 Happyong-Ho-. Periodical. Korean. ir. LC PL901. *Sungjon Omunhak.*

HARVARD STUDIES IN SYNTAX AND SEMANTICS. V. 1- Nov. 1975-. 0148-1134. US. English. ir. Harvard University, Linguistics Department/Science Center, Cambridge MA 02138. **Tel** (617)495-4054.

HARVARD UKRAINIAN STUDIES. See History (General) - History of Europe.

HARVEST (DACCA, BANGLADESH). (HARVEST : AN ANNUAL OF THE DEPARTMENT OF ENGLISH, JAHANGIRNAGAR UNIVERSITY). Vol. 3 (1978-79)-. English. an. LC PE9. DD 410.5. *Bulletin of the Department of English, Jahangirnagar University.*

HAWLIYAT FAR AL-ADAB AL-ARABIYAH. VFOAT Annales du Departement des Lettres Arabes. Journal 1, (1981)-. 0250-9970. Periodical. LE. Arabic. an. Jamiat Al-Qiddis Yusuf, SB 293, Bayrut Lebanon. LC DS36.

HEBREW ANNUAL REVIEW. V. 1- 1977-. 0193-7162. US. English. an. $20.00. Ohio State University Department of Judaic and Near Eastern Languages and Literatures, 1841 Milliken Road, Columbus OH 43210. **Tel** (614)422-9255. Ed Reuben Ahroni. **Ind/Abst** Lang. Lang. Behav. Abstr., Relig. Index One, Period. LC PJ4501. DD 892.409. **Circ** 750. Studies in the areas of Hebrew language, Hebrew literature, and methodology of teaching Hebrew.

HEBREW STUDIES. See Religion, Mythology, Rationalism - Judaism.

HEUTIGES DEUTSCH. REIHE 1: LINGUISTISCHE GRUNDLAGEN. VFOAT Linguistische Grundlagen. V. 1- 1970-. 0073-201X. Monographic Series. US. German. ir. Adlers Foreign Books Inc, 162 Fifth Avenue, New York NY 10010.

HIGHWAY ONE. V. 1- Winter 1978-. 0705-386X. Periodical. CN. English. ty. Free to Members. Highway One, University of Calgary, Department of Curriculum and Instruction, Faculty of Education, Calgary Alberta T2N 1N4 Canada. **Ind/Abst** Can. Educ. Index. DD 428.00712.

HIMALANGUE. V. 1- Nov. 1973-. English. ir. $0.50 Single Issue. Basudev Sharma, 1/11 Bhotebahal, Kathmandu Nepal. LC P1. DD 410.8.

HISPANIA. V. 1- Feb. 1918-. 0018-2133. Periodical. US. English (Portuguese, Spanish). qt. $25.00. American Association of Teachers of Spanish and Portuguese, Mississippi State University, PO Box 6349, University MS 39762-6349. **Tel** (601)325-2041. Ed Theodore Sackett, James R Chatham. **Ind/Abst** MLA Int. Bibliogr. Books Artic. Mod. Lang. Lit., Lang. Lang. Behav. Abstr., Book Rev. Index, Index Book Rev. Humanit., Educ. Index, Curr. Index J. Educ., Lang. Teach., Bibliogr. Index. LC PC4001. DD 460.5. (cum index). bk rev adv acc **Circ** 12,000. A scholarly journal devoted to the interests of the teaching of Spanish and Portuguese.

HISPANIC LINGUISTICS. VFOAT HL. Vol. 1, No. 1 (Spring 1984)-. 0742-5287. Periodical. US. English (Spanish). sa. $35.00. Hispanic Linguistics, 1317 Cathedral of Learning, University of Pittsburgh, Pittsburgh PA 15260. LC PC4001. DD 460.5.

HISPANIC REVIEW. V. 1- Jan. 1933-. 0018-2176. Periodical. US. English. qt. $27.50. Hispanic Review, University of Pennsylvania/Williams

Linguistics

Hall, Philadelphia PA 19104. **Tel** (215)898-7420. Ed Russell P Sebold. **Ind/Abst** Am. Hist. Life, Hist. Abstr., Part A, Mod. Hist. Abstr., Hist. Abst., Part B, Twent. Century Abstr., MLA Int. Bibliogr. Books Artic. Mod. Lang. Lit., Sociol. Abstr., Ref. Source, Index Book Rev. Humanit., Soc. Sci. Index, Humanit. Index, Lang. Behav. Abstr., Hist. Abstr., Recent Publ. Artic. **LC** PQ6001. **DD** 460.5. (cum index). bk rev. adv acc. **Circ** 1,500. Journal devoted to research in the Hispanic languages and literatures.

HISPANO-ITALIC STUDIES. VAT HISPANO ITALIC STUDIES. No. 1-. 0160-3493. US. English (text in French, German. Italian, Portuguese, or Spanish). ir. Hispano-Italic Studies, Georgetown University Press, School of Languages and Linguistics/ Georgetown University, Washington DC 20057. **LC** PQ6042.I5. **DD** 809.

HISPANOFILA. See Literature.

HISTORIOGRAPHIA LINGUISTICA. V. 1- 1974-. 0302-5160. Periodical. NE. English, French, or German. ir. $70.00. John Benjamins BV, PO Box 52519, Amsteldijk 44, 1007 HA Amsterdam Netherlands. **Tel** (020)738156. Ed E F Konrad Koerner and Hans-Josef Niederehe. **Ind/Abst** MLA Int. Bibliogr. Books Artic. Mod. Lang. Lit., Lang. Lang. Behav. Abstr., Lang. Teach., Sociol. Abstr., Bibliogr. Index. **LC** P61. **DD** 410.9. Intended to serve the ever growing scholarly interest of linguists, psycholinguists, and philosophers of language of divergent persuasions in the history of linguistic thought.

HOJA INFORMATIVA DE LITERATURA Y FILOLOGIA. See Literature.

HONYAKU NO SEKAI. Periodical. JA. Japanese. ir. 6480. c/o Daini Dempa Building, 14-10 Soto Kanda 2, Chiyoda-Ku Tokyo Japan. **LC** P306.A1.

HSIU TZU HSUEH HSI. VFOAT Xiucixuexi. 1982/1-. Periodical. CH. Chinese. qt. 0.43. Post Office Nan-Chang, China. **LC** PL1271. **DD** 808.04951.

HUMAN COMMUNICATION CANADA. Vol. 7, No. 1 (Jan./Feb. 1983)-. 0822-5486. Periodical. CN. English (includes some text in French). bm. Administrative Secretary Department of Speech Pathology, Children's Hospital, 401 Smyth Road, Ottawa Ontario K1H 8L1 Canada. **Tel** (613)737-2373. Ed Elaine Pressman. **DD** 618.92855055. bk rev adv acc. **Circ** 1,500. (ctrl) Covers speech language pathology and audiology, communications, use of technology for the disabled. *Hear Here, Human Communication, 0319-1419.*

HUMANITAS. V. 1-. PO. Portuguese. be. Instituto Estudos Classicos, Faculdade Letras, Coimba Portugal. **LC** PA9.

HWASUL. Periodical. Korean. bm. Hanguk Hwasul Kyoyukhoe, 462-2 Pyongchang-Dong Chongno-Ku, Seoul 110 Korea. **LC** PN4003.

IAZYK I OBSHCHESTVO. Vol. 1-. Periodical. UR. Russian. 1.5. Saratov, Izdatelstvo Saratovskogo Universiteta, Universiteetskaia 42, Saratov Russian SFSR. **LC** P40.

IAZYKI I TOPONIMIIA. Vol. 1-. Periodical. UR. Russian. 0.96 Single Issue. IZD-VO Tomskogo Universiteta, Ul Nikitina 19/1, Tomsk Russian SFSR. **LC** P25.

IBERO-ROMANIA. (IBEROROMANIA). 1.-3. Year., Feb. 1969-1971. 0019-0993. Periodical. German (Catalan, English, French, Portuguese, or Spanish). ir. **Ind/Abst** MLA Int. Bibliogr. Books Artic. Mod. Lang. Lit. **LC** PC4001.

IDIOMATICA. V. 1- 1973-. Monographic Series. GW. German. ir. Max Niemeyer Verlag, Postfach 2140, 7400 Tuebingen 1 West Germany. Ed Arno Ruoff. Monographs on German language as spoken in the Southwestern area of West Germany, in Austria (Vorarlberg), and Liechtenstein.

IJAL-NATS MONOGRAPH. No. 1-. 0271-373X. Monographic Series. US. English. University Microfilms International, 300 North Zeeb Road, Ann Arbor MI 48106. **LC** UNC.

ILLINOIS ENGLISH BULLETIN. Began on Mar. 1, 1909. 0019-2023. Periodical. US. English. mo. Illinois Association of Teachers of English, 608 South Wright Street, Urbana IL 61801. **LC** PE11. **DD** 808.

ILLINOIS STUDIES IN LANGUAGE AND LITERATURE. V. 17, No. 1-2 (1934)-. 0073-5175. Monographic Series. US. English. ir. **LC** P25. *University of Illinois Studies in Language and Literature.*

THE INCORPORATED LINGUIST. (THE INCORPORATED LINGUIST : THE JOURNAL OF THE INSTITUTE OF LINGUISTS). Vol. 1, No. 1 (Jan. 1962). 0019-3534. Periodical. UK. English. qt. $15.33. Institute of Linguists, 24A Highbury Grove, London N5 2EA England. Ed John Sykes. **Ind/Abst** MLA Int. Bibliogr. Books Artic. Mod. Lang. Lit., Sociol. Abstr., Lang. Lang. Behav. Abstr., Ship Abstr., Lang. Teach. **LC** P1. **DD** 410.5. bk rev. adv acc. **Circ** 6,000. Contains articles of interest to professional and leisure linguists on all aspects of language, its use and application. *Linguists' Review.*

INDIA-WEST. VFOAT India West. V. 1- Nov. 1975-. Periodical. US. English. wk. $20.00. India West Publications, 5901 Christie Avenue #301, Emeryville CA 94608-1934. **Tel** (415) 652-3552. Ed Bina Murarka. bk rev. adv acc. **Circ** 8,000. Newspaper for Indian community settled in US. Covers news from India and about indians in US.

INDIAN JOURNAL OF APPLIED LINGUISTICS. V. 1- Jan./June 1975-. 0379-0037. Periodical. II. English or Hindi. be. $35.00. Asia Books and Periodicals, 11 Darya Ganj, New Delhi 110002 India. **Tel** 268645. **Ind/Abst** Lang. Teach. **LC** PK101. adv acc.

INDIANA ENGLISH. VFOAT Indiana Folklore. V. 1- 1977-. Monographic Series. US. English. ir. $6.00. Indiana Council of Teachers, Indiana State University, Terre Haute IN 47809. **Tel** (812)232-6311. **LC** PE65. **DD** 420. *Indiana English Journal, 0019-6584.*

INDIRECTIONS. V. 1- Fall 1975-. 0227-2547. Periodical. CN. English. ty. Free to Members. Ontario Council of Teachers of English, Indirections, 750 Kingston Road, Toronto Ontario M4E 1R7 Canada. **Ind/Abst** Can. Educ. Index. **DD** 420.70713.

INDO-IRANIAN JOURNAL. See Philosophy.

INDOGERMANISCHE FORSCHUNGEN. V. 1-. 0341-1850. GW. German. an. Walter de Gruyter and Company, 200 Sawmill River Road, Hawthorne NY 10532. **Tel** (914)747-0110. **Ind/Abst** Annu. Bibliogr. Engl. Lang. Lit., Index Book Rev. Humanit., MLA Int. Bibliogr. Books Artic. Mod. Lang. Lit., Sociol. Abstr., Lang. Lang. Behav. Abstr. **LC** P501. (cum index).

INDOLOGIA BEROLINENSIS. Monographic Series. German. ir.

INFORMATIONEN ZUR DEUTSCHDIDAKTIK. 1-. Periodical. GW. German. ir. $21.11. Neuer Verlag BTW Herausgeber, Arbeitsgemeinschaft fur Deutschdidaktik, Universitat Klagenfurt, Universitatsstrabe 67, A-9010 Klagenfurt Austria. **Tel** 0511/ 83 88 1. **LC** PF3065.

INFORMATSYE BYULETIN FUN NATSYONALN KOMITET FAR YIDISH BAYM KANADER YIDISHN KONGRES. Merz 1973-. 0821-3933. Periodical. CN. Yiddish (text in Hebrew script). qt. Free. Canadian Jewish Congress, 1590 Doctor Penfield Avenue, Montreal Quebec H3G 1C5 Canada. **DD** 437.947. (ctrl).

ININCO. VFOAT I.N.I.N.C.O. Periodical. Spanish. qt. **LC** P87. **DD** 001.5105.

INITIALES. (INITIALES : TRAVAUX DES ETUDIANTS, DEPARTEMENT DE FRANCAIS, UNIVERSITE DALHOUSIE). VFOAT Initials : Students' Writings, Department of French, Dalhousie University. Vol. 1 (1981)-. 0710-4278. CN. French (text in English). an. $2.00. Dalhousie University, c/o H R Runte, Department of French, Halifax Nova Scotia B3H 3J5 Canada. **DD** 440.

INNOVATIONS IN LINGUISTICS EDUCATION. Vol. 1, No. 1-. 0733-270X. Periodical. US. English. sa. $5.35. Indiana University Linguistics Club, 310 Lindley Hall, Bloomington IN 47401. **Tel** (812)335-8673. Ed Daniel Dinnsen. bk rev. adv acc. **Circ** 400. For faculty and graduate students. Data-based problems, teaching approaches, and critical discussions.

INOSTRANNYE IAZYKI V VUZAKH UZBEKISTANA. UR. Russian. 1.60 Single Issue. Tashkenskii Gos Ped IN-T, Ul Pedagogicheskaia, Tashkent 103 Russia. **LC** PB38.R8.

INOSTRANNYE JAZYKI V SKOLE. (INOSTRANNYE IAZYKI V SHKOLE). 1941-. 0130-6073. UR. Russian. bm. $15.50. Victor Kamkin Inc (73181), 12224 Parklawn Drive, Rockville MD 20852. **Tel** (301)881-5973. **Ind/Abst** Lang. Lang. Behav. Abstr., MLA Int. Bibliogr. Books Artic. Mod. Lang. Lit., Sociol. Abstr. **LC** PB5.

INTERCHANGE - NEWCOMER SERVICES BRANCH. (INTERCHANGE). No. 9 (Oct. 1980)-. 0712-5267. Periodical. CN. English. ir. Free. **DD** 428.0070713541. (ctrl). *Interchanges, 0712-5259.*

INTERCOM. Oct. 1974-. 0700-9429. Periodical. CN. English. ir. Business Linguistic Center, 110 Sherbrooke Street West/Suite 2403, Montreal Quebec H3A 1G8 Canada. **DD** 410.62714.

INTERCOM. Oct. 1974-. 0700-9437. Periodical. CN. French. ir. Centre de Linguistique de l'Enterprise, 1110 Ouest rue Sherbrooke/Bureau 2503, Montreal Quebec H3A 1G8 Canada. **DD** 410.62714.

INTERDISCIPLINAIR TIJDSCHRIFT VOOR TAAL- & TEKSTWETENSCHAP. See Literature.

INTERLANGUAGE STUDIES BULLETIN - UTRECHT CEASED. VFOAT ISB-Utrecht. V. 1- Jan. 1976-. Periodical. English. sa. 25.00. ISB-Utrecht Insttitute Engelse Taal, Utrecht 2506 Netherlands. **Tel** (030)334114. Ed J N Pankhurst and M A Sharwood Smith. **Ind/Abst** Lang. Lang. Behav. Abstr. bk rev. adv acc. **Circ** 1,000. (ctrl). Interdisciplinary research into second language acquisition exploring potential contribution of generative grammar, neurolinguistics, and psycholinguistics.

INTERNATIONAL DIALOGUE. VFOAT Dialogo Internazionale. 0263-6514. Periodical. UK. English (French and Italian). Odnowa Ltd, Hamilton Road, London W4 1AL England.

INTERNATIONAL JOURNAL OF PSYCHOLINGUISTICS CEASED. V. 1-8. 0165-4055. Periodical. English. qt. Walter de Gruyter Inc, 200 Saw Mill River Road, Hawthorne NY 10532. **Ind/Abst** Lang. Lang. Behav. Abstr., Lang. Teach. NLM W1 IN777I.

INTERNATIONAL JOURNAL OF SLAVIC LINGUISTICS AND POETICS. VFOAT IJSLP. Began publication with: 1/2 in 1959?. 0166-1094. Periodical. English (French, German, Polish or Russian). sa. Slavica Publications Inc, PO Box 14388, Columbus OH 43214. **Tel** (614)268-4002. bk rev. **Circ** 500.

INTERNATIONAL JOURNAL OF THE SOCIOLOGY OF LANGUAGE. VFOAT I.J.S.L., IJSL. 0165-2516. Monographic Series. NE. English. qt. $98.25. Walter de Gruyter Inc, 200 Sawmill River Road, Hawthorne NY 10532. **Tel** (914)747-0110. Ed J A Fishman. **Ind/Abst** MLA Int. Bibliogr. Books Artic. Mod. Lang. Lit., Sociol. Abstr., Lang. Lang. Behav. Abstr., Psychol. Abstr., Lang. Teach., Soc. Sci. Citation Index, Bibliogr. Index, Years Work Eng. Stud. **LC** P40. **DD** 401.9. CODEN ISLGAH. bk rev. adv acc. **Circ** 800. (ctrl). Dedicated to the development of the sociology of language in its broadest sense, as a truly international and interdisciplinary field.

INTERNATIONAL REVIEW OF SLAVIC LINGUISTICS. V. 1-. 0703-5330. Periodical. CN. English (includes some text in French and Slavic Languages). $20.00 Institutions. Linguistic Research, PO Box 5677/Station L, Edmonton Alberta Canada. **Ind/Abst** MLA Int. Bibliogr. Books Artic. Mod. Lang. Lit., Lang. Lang. Behav. Abstr., Lang. Teach. **LC** PG1. **DD** 491.8.

INTERNATIONALE BIBLIOTHEK FUR ALLGEMEINE LINGUISTIK. INTERNATIONAL LIBRARY OF GENERAL LINGUISTICS. VFOAT International Library of General Linguistics. V. 1- 1971-. GW. German (English). ir. Wilhelm Fink Verlag, Ohmstrasse 5, 8 Munchen 40 West Germany. **Tel** 89/ 348017-18. Ed Eugenio Coseriu.

L'INTERPRETE. Periodical. SZ. French or German. qt. 15,-. Association of Intrepretes Traducteurs, Case Stand 388, 1211 Geneve 11 Switzerland. **Tel** (022)28.80.25. Ed Marianne Wanstall-Sayty. **LC** P306.A1. **DD** 418.02. bk rev. adv acc. **Circ** 1,000. Professional magazine on linguistics and translations.

INUKTITUT. See Ethnic.

IRAL, INTERNATIONAL REVIEW OF APPLIED LINGUISTICS IN LANGUAGE TEACHING. VFOAT International Review of Applied Linguistics in Language Teaching, Revue Internationale de Linguistique Appliquee Enseignement des Langues, Internationale Zeitschrift fur Angewandte Linguistik in der Spracherziehung. V. 1- Feb. 1963-. 0019-042X. Periodical. UK. English (French, or German, with

Linguistics

summaries in the languages other than that of the article). qt. Oxford University Press, Journals Department, Walton Street, Oxford OX2 6DP England. Tel 0865/ 56767. Ind/Abst MLA Int. Bibliogr. Books Artic. Mod. Lang. Lit., Lang. Lang. Behav. Abstr., Educ. Index, Index Book Rev. Humanit., Curr. Index J. Educ., Psychol. Abstr., Lang. Teach. CODEN IRALA4.

IRANSKOE IAZYKOZNANIE. 1980-. Periodical. UR. Russian. an. 2.60. Nauka, Moskva K-45, Ul Zhdanova 12/1, Moskva Russian SFSR. LC PK6001. DD 491.505.

IRIAN. See Anthropology.

ISURI : DO. HARISIMHA GAURA VISVAVIDYALAYA, SAGARA KE HINDI-VIBHAGA KE ANTARGATA KRIYASILA BUNDELI-PITHA KA AYOJANA. 1 (83-84)-. Periodical. II. Hindi (Bundeli). ir. 25.00. Department of Hindi, Dr Hari Singh Gaur Univ, Sagar India. Tel 2475/20. Ed Kantikumar Jain. bk rev. Circ 1,500. (ctrl). Concentrates on dialect, literature, and culture of Bundelkhand.

L'ITALIA DIALETTALE; RIVISTA DI DIALETTOLOGIA ITALIANA. V.1- 1924-. Periodical. IT. Italian. an. Arti Grafiche Pacini Mariotti, Via S Maria 36, 56100 Pisa Italy. Ed Clemente Merlo. Ind/Abst MLA Int. Bibliogr. Books Artic. Mod. Lang. Lit. LC PC1701. DD 457.

ITALIA MEDIOEVALE E UMANISTICA. 1- 1958-. 0579-0409. IT. Italian. an. Editrice Antenore, Via G Rusca 15, 35100 Padova Italy. Ind/Abst MLA Int. Bibliogr. Books Artic. Mod. Lang. Lit., Repert. Int. Litt. Art.

ITALICA. V. 1- Apr. 1924-. 0021-3020. Periodical. US. English (Italian). qt. $8.00. American Association of Teachers of Italian, 601 Casa Italiana, Columbia University, New York NY 10017. Ind/Abst MLA Int. Bibliogr. Books Artic. Mod. Lang. Lit., Curr. Index J. Educ. LC PC1068.U6. DD 450.5. (cum index).

ITALICA : BULLETIN OF THE AMERICAN ASSOCIATION OF TEACHERS OF ITALIAN. Vol. 3, No. 1 (Feb. 1926)-. Periodical. US. English. qt. Italica, 601 Casa Italiana Columbia University, New York NY 10027. LC PC1068.U6. DD 450.7. Also available on microfilm. Bulletin of the American Association of Teachers of Italian.

ITALIENISCH. See Literature.

ITL. INSTITUUT VOOR TOEGEPASTE LINGUISTIK. (ITL). Main/Corp Katholieke Universiteit te Leuven. Institut voor Toegepaste Linguistik. V. 1- 1968-. 0019-0829. Periodical. BE. Dutch (English and German). qt. $19.00. Institut voor Toegepaste Linguistik, Blijde Inkomststr 21, B-3000 Leuven Belgium. Tel 016/238851. Ed N Delbecque. Ind/Abst MLA Int. Bibliogr. Books Artic. Mod. Lang. Lit., Index Book Rev. Humanit., Lang. Lang. Behav. Abstr., Sociol. Abstr. LC P123. bk rev. Circ 400. Contains articles and book reviews in the field of applied linguistics, i.e. lanaguage teaching and foreign language teaching.

IZKUSTVOTO NA PREVODA. 1-. BU. Bulgarian (summaries in English, French, German, and Russian). ir. 1.381. Ul G Gensv 4, Sofiia Bulgaria. LC PN241.A1.

IZVESTIIA NA INSTITUTA ZA BULGARSKI EZIK. Main/Corp Bulgarska Akademiia Na Naukite, Sofia. Institut Za Bulgarski Ezik. Vol. 1 1952-. 0068-3787. Periodical. BU. Bulgarian. an. Hemus, 6 Boulevard Rusky, Sofia Bulgaria. Ind/Abst MLA Int. Bibliogr. Books Artic. Mod. Lang. Lit. LC PG801.

JAARBOEK. See Yearbooks, Almanacs, Directories.

JAHRBUCH . . . DES INSTITUTS FUR DEUTSCHE SPRACHE. See Yearbooks, Almanacs, Directories.

JAHRBUCH DEUTSCH ALS FREMDSPRACHE. See Yearbooks, Almanacs, Directories.

JAHRBUCH FUR INTERNATIONALE GERMANISTIK. See Yearbooks, Almanacs, Directories.

JAHRBUCH FUR INTERNATIONALE GERMANISTIK. REIHE B, GERMANISTISCHE DISSERTATIONEN IN KURZFASSUNG. See Yearbooks, Almanacs, Directories.

JALT JOURNAL. Vol. 1, No. 1-2 (Nov. 1979)-. Periodical. English. sa. Ind/Abst Lang. Teach.

JAZYKOVEDNE STUDIE. 0448-9241. CS. Slovak (some articles in Russsian). ir. Kubon & Sagner, Postfach 34 01 08, D-8000 Munchen 34 West Germany. Tel 020-738156. LC PG5201.

JAZYKOVEDNY CASOPIS. Began in 1946. 0021-5597. Periodical. GW. Slovak. sa. Kubon & Sagner, Postfach 34 01 08, 8 Munchen 34 West Germany. Tel (089)52 20 27. LC P9. Strictly devoted to linguistics, the journal prints articles about the contemporary written and spoken Slovak with consideration of the various dialects.

JEGP, JOURNAL OF ENGLISH AND GERMANIC PHILOLOGY. (JEGP. JOURNAL OF ENGLISH AND GERMANIC PHILOLOGY). VFOAT Journal of English and Germanic Philology. V. 58- Jan. 1959-. 0363-6941. US. English. qt. $35.00 Domestic, $37.50 Foreign. University of Illinois Press, 54 East Gregory Drive, Champaign IL 61820. Tel (217)333-0950. Ed Dale Kramer. Ind/Abst Abstr. Engl. Stud., MLA Int. Bibliogr. Books Artic. Mod. Lang. Lit., Annu. Bibliogr. Engl. Lang. Lit., Book Rev. Index, Humanit. Index, Index Book Rev. Humanit., Recent Publ. Artic., Years Work Eng. Stud. bk rev. adv acc. Circ 1,600. Available on microfilm from University Microfilms. Scholarly articles and book reviews in English literature and language, American literature, German and Scandinavian languages and literatures. Journal of English and Germanic Philology, 0022-0868.

JEWISH LANGUAGE REVIEW. VFOAT JLR. 1 (1981)-. 0333-8347. Periodical. English. an. Ind/Abst MLA Int. Bibliogr. Sociol. Abstr. LC PJ5061. DD 408.9924.

JEZIK IN SLOVSTVO. Began publication with Oct. 1955 issue. 0021-6933. Periodical. Slovenian. ir. Ind/Abst MLA Int. Bibliogr. Books Artic. Mod. Lang. Lit., Lang. Lang. Behav. Abstr. LC PG1801.

JEZYK POLSKI. Vol. 1- 1913-. 0021-6941. Periodical. PL. Polish. bm. ARS Polona, Krakowskie Przedmiescie 7 Warsaw 00-068 Poland. Ind/Abst MLA Int. Bibliogr. Books Artic. Mod. Lang. Lit. LC PG6001. DD 491.8505. (cum index).

JEZYKOZNAWSTWO. 1-. Polish. ir. 36.00. LC PG6004.

JIJI EIGO KENKYU = THE STUDY OF CURRENT ENGLISH. VFOAT Study of Current English. Periodical. Japanese (English). mo. Kinokuniya Bookstores, 1581 Webster Street, San Francisco CA 94115. Tel (415)567-7625.

JISTA. Main/Corp Indian Scientific Translators Association. V. 1- Mar. 1972-. Periodical. English. ir. $3.50. c/o Insdoc, Hillside Road 12, New Delhi India. LC P306.A1. DD 418.02.

THE JORDAN ACADEMY OF ARABIC : ANNUAL REPORT. Main/Corp Majma Al-Lughan AL-Arabiyah Al-Urduni. Oct. 1, 1972-Sept. 30, 1977-. English. an. Jordan Academy of Arabic, Box 13268, Amman Jordan. LC PJ6011. DD 492.706056958.

JOURNAL ASIATIQUE. Ser. 3, V. 1-14, Jan. 1836-Dec. 1842. Periodical. FR. French. ir. Libraries Paul Geuthner, 12 rue Vanin, Paris 6E France. LC PJ4. Nouveau Journal Asiatique.

JOURNAL DE LA LANGUE FRANCAISE SOIT EXACTE, SOIT ORNEE. Ser. 1- Sept. 1784-. ir. Slatkine Reprints, PO Box 765, 1211 Geneva 3 Switzerland. LC PC2002. DD 440.5.

JOURNAL OF AFRICAN LANGUAGES AND LINGUISTICS. V. 1- Apr. 1979-. 0167-6164. Periodical. English. sa. $27.50. Foris Publications, PO Box 509, 3300 AM Dordrecht Netherlands. Tel (78)510454. Ed Thilo C Schadeberg. Ind/Abst MLA Int. Bibliogr. Books Artic. Mod. Lang. Lit., Lang. Lang. Behav. Abstr. LC PL8000. DD 409.6. bk rev. adv acc. Circ 400. A broad-based, international journal of wide academic scope, which offers articles on all aspects of African language studies.

JOURNAL OF CHILD LANGUAGE. V. 1- May 1974-. 0305-0009. Periodical. UK. English. ty. Cambridge University Press, 510 North Avenue, New Rochelle NY 10801. Tel (914)235-0300. Ind/Abst MLA Int. Bibliogr. Books Artic. Mod. Lang. Lit., Sociol. Abstr., Lang. Lang. Behav. Abstr., Educ. Index, Curr. Index J. Educ., Psychol. Abstr., Lang. Teach., Soc. Sci. Citation Index, Years Work Eng. Stud. LC P118. DD 401.9. NLM W1 JO583L.

JOURNAL OF CHINESE LINGUISTICS. VFOAT Chung-Kuo Yu Yen Hsueh Pao. V. 1- Jan. 1973-. 0091-3723. Periodical. US. English. sa. $25.00.

Project on Linguistic Analysis, 2222 Piedmont, Berkeley CA 94720. Tel (415)642-5937. Ed William S-Y Wang. Ind/Abst MLA Int. Bibliogr. Books Artic. Mod. Lang. Lit., Lang. Lang. Behav. Abstr., Ref. Source, Curr. Index J. Educ., Sociol. Abstr. LC PL1001. DD 495.1. bk rev. adv acc. Circ 500. The journal publishes works on all aspects of the Chinese language: historical and descriptive, theoretical and applied, social, psychological, literary, etc.

THE JOURNAL OF ENGLISH LANGUAGE AND LITERATURE. Vol. 27, No. 1 (Spring 1981)-. Periodical. KO. English (title also in Korean). qt. English Language and Literature Association of Korea, 89-2 Shinmoon-Ro 2-Ka Chongro-Ku Seoul 110 Republic of Korea. English Language and Literature.

THE JOURNAL OF ENGLISH LANGUAGE TEACHING (INDIA). V. 1- June 1965-. 0022-0876. Periodical. II. English. bm. English Language Teachers Association, 169 R K Mutt Road, Madras 28 India. Ind/Abst Lang. Teach. Linguist. Abstr. LC PE1068.I4.

JOURNAL OF ENGLISH LINGUISTICS. 1967. 0075-4242. Periodical. US. English. sa. $15.00. University of Wisconsin, English Department, West Kretzschmar, Whitewater WI 53190. Tel (414)472-1979. Ed William A Kretzschmar Jr. Ind/Abst Sociol. Abstr., Lang. Lang. Behav. Abstr., MLA Int. Bibliogr. Books Artic. Mod. Lang. Lit., Years Work Eng. Stud., Lang. Teach., Ref. Source, Index Book Rev. Humanit. LC PE1001. DD 420.05. bk rev. adv acc. Circ 600. (ctrl). An international journal devoted to articles and reviews of books on the modern and historical periods of the English language.

THE JOURNAL OF ENGLISH STUDIES. Periodical. II. English. sa. $10.00. Journal of English Studies, Regional Engineering College, Warangal 506004 AP India. Ind/Abst Abstr. Engl. Stud. LC PE1. DD 420.5.

JOURNAL OF HISPANIC PHILOLOGY. VFOAT JHP. V. 1- Autumn 1976-. 0147-5460. Periodical. US. English (Spanish). ty. $40.00. Journal of Hispanic Philology, Florida State University, Department of Modern Language, Tallahassee FL 32306. Tel (904)385-4148. Ed Daniel Eisenberg. Ind/Abst Ref. Source, Index Book Rev. Humanit., MLA Int. Bibliogr. Books Artic. Mod. Lang. Lit., Int. Bibliogr. Zeitschriftenliteratur Allen Gebieten Wissens. LC PC4001. DD 460.5. bk rev. adv acc. Circ 500. Literature and historical linguistics of the Iberian peninsula through 1700.

JOURNAL OF INDO-EUROPEAN STUDIES. (THE JOURNAL OF INDO-EUROPEAN STUDIES). V. 1- Spring 1973-. 0092-2323. Periodical. US. English. qt. Journal of Indo-European Studies, 1133 13th Street NW/Suite C2, Washington DC 20005. Tel (202)789-0231. Ed Roger Pearson. Ind/Abst MLA Int. Bibliogr. Books Artic. Mod. Lang. Lit., Lang. Lang. Behav. Abstr., Abstr. Anthropol., Sociol. Abstr. LC CB201. DD 910.03. adv acc. Linguistics, archaeology, and mythology of Indo-European peoples.

JOURNAL OF ITALIAN LINGUISTICS. VFOAT Italian Linguistics. V. 3- 1978-. Periodical. NE. English. sa $32.50. Foris Publications, PO Box 509, 3300 AM Dordrecht The Netherlands. Tel (078)510454. Ed V Lo Cascio. Ind/Abst MLA Int. Bibliogr. Books Artic. Mod. Lang. Lit., Lang. Lang. Behav. Abstr., Lang. Teach. bk rev. adv acc. Circ 500. Promotes and co-ordinates studies in Italian language and linguistics, and supplied useful comparative material for linguists not directly concerned with Italian studies. Italian Linguistics.

JOURNAL OF LANGUAGE ARTS AND COMMUNICATION (J.L.A.C.). VFOAT J.L.A.C. Vol. 1, No. 1 (Mar. 1980)-. Periodical. English. ir. $12.00. The Business Manager of J L A C Department of Language Arts, University of Ibadan, Ibadan Nigeria.

THE JOURNAL OF LANGUAGE FOR INTERNATIONAL BUSINESS. VFOAT JOLIB, J.O.L.I.B. Vol. 1, No. 1 (Spring 1984)-. 8755-0504. Periodical. US. English (Multilingual). sa. $25.00 Domestic, $35.00 Foreign. American Graduate School of International Management, Thunderbird Campus, Department of Modern Languages, Glendale AZ 85306. Tel (602)978-7259. Ed Jorge H Valdivieso. DD 418. bk rev. adv acc. Circ 300. The only periodical devoted to the teaching and study of foreign languages and English for international business.

JOURNAL OF LINGUISTICS. Began with: Vol. 1 (Apr. 1965)-. 0022-2267. Periodical. UK. English. sa. $60.00. Cambridge University Press, 510

North Avenue, New Rochelle NY 10801. **Tel** (914)235-0300. **Ed** Nigel Vincent. **Ind/Abst** MLA Int. Bibliogr. Books Artic. Mod. Lang. Lit., Lang. Lang. Behav. Abstr., Lang. Teach., Index Book Rev. Humanit., Curr. Index J. Educ., Humanit. Index, Sociol. Abstr., Soc. Sci. Citation Index, Abstr. Anthropol., Years Work Eng. Stud. **LC** P1. **DD** 410.5. bk rev. Available in microfilm. Covers the whole field of linguistics from phonetics and phonology, through syntax and semantics to pragmatics and the intersection of linguistics with related disciplines.

JOURNAL OF LITERARY SEMANTICS. 1- Apr. 1972-. 0341-7638. Periodical. GW. English. ty. 66.-. Julius Groos Verlag, Postfach 102423 Hertzstrasse 6, 6900 Heidelberg 1 West Germany. **Tel** 06221/303621. **Ed** Trevor Eaton. **Ind/Abst** MLA Int. Bibliogr. Books Artic. Mod. Lang. Lit., Lang. Lang. Behav. Abstr., Index Book Rev. Humanit., Sociol. Abstr., Lang. Teach. **LC** PN54. **DD** 809. bk rev. adv acc. **Circ** 600. Theoretical linguistic, applied lingustics; articles on all aspects of literary semantics and such of a philosophical nature attempting to relate the study of literature ot other disciplines.

JOURNAL OF MALTESE STUDIES. *See* Literature.

JOURNAL OF MAYAN LINGUISTICS. V. 1- Spring 1978-. 0195-475X. Periodical. US. English. ir. $20.00. Geology Science Publishers, Louisiana State University, Department of Geology, Baton Rouge LA 70803. **Tel** (504)388-6245. **Ed** Jill Brody and William Hanks. **Ind/Abst** MLA Int. Bibliogr. Books Artic. Mod. Lang. Lit. **LC** PM3961. **DD** 497.4. bk rev. **Circ** 125. Mayan linguistics, Mayan languages, and linguistic treatment of Mayan hieroglyphics and Mayan culture.

JOURNAL OF MULTILINGUAL AND MULTICULTURAL DEVELOPMENT. Vol. 1, No. 1-. 0143-4632. Periodical. UK. English. bm. $86.00. Multilingual Matters Ltd, Bank House 8-A Hill Road, Clevedon Avon BS21 7HH England. **Ind/Abst** Sociol. Abstr., Lang. Lang. Behav. Abstr., Lang. Teach., Curr. Index J. Educ. **LC** P115. **DD** 404.205.

JOURNAL OF NEAR EASTERN STUDIES. V. 1- Jan. 1942-. 0022-2968. Periodical. US. English. qt. $16.00 Domestic, $17.00 Foreign. University of Chicago Press, 5801 Ellis Avenue, Chicago IL 60637. **Ind/Abst** MLA Int. Bibliogr. Books Artic. Mod. Lang. Lit., Sociol. Abstr., Old Testam. Abstr., New Testam. Abstr., Art Archaeol. Tech. Abstr., Ref. Source, Soc. Sci. Index, Chem. Abstr., Relig. Index One, Period., Humanit. Index, Recent Publ. Artic. **LC** DS41. **DD** 492.05. **CODEN** JNESBT. Available in microfilm from University Microfilms. *American Journal of Semitic Languages and Literatures, 0017-9495.*

JOURNAL OF NORTHWEST ATLANTIC FISHERY SCIENCE. Vol. 1 (1980)-. 0250-6408. Periodical. CN. English. sa. $24.00. Department of Semitic Languages, University of Stellenbosch, 7600 Stellenbosch South Africa. **Tel** (02231) 73156. **Ed** F C Fensham. **Ind/Abst** Biol. Abstr., Life Sci. Collect. **LC** SH1. **DD** 639.2091631. **CODEN** JNFSD2. **Circ** 450. North-West semitic languages-literature, theology, history and linguistics. *Research Bulletin, 0074-2651.*

JOURNAL OF PHONETICS. V. 1- Jan. 1973-. 0095-4470. Periodical. UK. English. qt. $151.50. Academic Press, 4805 Sand Lake Road, Orlando FL 32819. **Tel** (305)345-4100. **Ind/Abst** MLA Int. Bibliogr. Books Artic. Mod. Lang. Lit., Lang. Lang. Behav. Abstr., Lang. Teach., Psychol. Abstr., Soc. Sci. Citation Index. **LC** P221. **DD** 414.05. **CODEN** JPHNB9.

JOURNAL OF PRAGMATICS. V. 1- Apr. 1977-. 0378-2166. Periodical. English. bm. Elsevier Science Publishers, PO Box 211, 1000 AE Amsterdam The Netherlands. **Tel** (020)5803.911. **Ind/Abst** Sociol. Abstr., Lang. Lang. Behav. Abstr., Philos. Index, Lang. Teach. **LC** P99.4.P72. **DD** 410.5.

JOURNAL OF PSYCHOLINGUISTIC RESEARCH. **VFOAT** Psycholinguistic Research. V. 1- 1971-. 0090-6905. Periodical. US. English. bm. $195.00 Domestic, $218.00 Foreign. Plenum Press, 233 Spring Street, New York NY 10013. **Tel** (212)620-8000. **Ed** R W Richer. **Ind/Abst** MLA Int. Bibliogr. Books Artic. Mod. Lang. Lit., Sociol. Abstr., Index Med., Lang. Lang. Behav. Abstr., Lang. Teach., Biol. Abstr., Psychol. Abstr., Curr. Contents, Soc. Sci. Citation Index, Abstr. Anthropol. **LC** P106. **DD** 001.51. **NLM** W1 JO857J. **CODEN** JPLRB7. bk rev. adv acc. This international journal publishes carefully selected papers from the several disciplines engaged in psycholinguistic research.

JOURNAL OF SPEECH AND HEARING DISORDERS. V. 1- 1936-. 0022-4677. Periodical. US. English. qt. $68.00. American Speech Language and Hearing Association, 10801 Rockville Pike, Rockville MD 20852. **Tel** (301)897-5700. **Ed** Janis M Costello. **Ind/Abst** Educ. Index, Index Med., Soc. Sci. Citation Index, Sociol. Abstr., Sci. Cit. Index, Abr. Ed., MLA Int. Bibliogr. Books Artic. Mod. Lang. Lit., Lang. Lang. Behav. Abstr., Psychol. Abstr., Curr. Index J. Educ. (cum index). adv acc. **Circ** 52,700. Nature and treatment of disordered speech, hearing and language.

JOURNAL OF SPEECH AND HEARING RESEARCH. (JOURNAL OF SPEECH AND HEARING RESEARCH : A PUBLICATION OF THE AMERICAN SPEECH AND HEARING ASSOCIATION). V. 1- March 1958-. 0022-4685. Periodical. US. English. qt. $68.00. American Speech-Language-Hearing Association, 10801 Rockville Pike, Rockville MD 20852. **Tel** (301)897-5700. **Ed** Theodore J Glattke and Tanya M Gallagher. **Ind/Abst** Lang. Lang. Behav. Abstr., MLA Int. Bibliogr. Books Artic. Mod. Lang. Lit., Excerpta Med., Annu. Bibliogr. Engl. Lang. Lit., Comput. Control Abstr., Electr. Electron. Abstr., Sci. Abstr. Sect. A. Phys. Abstr., Except. Child Educ. Resour., Educ. Index, Biol. Abstr., Chem. Abstr., Index Med., Curr. Index J. Educ., Psychol. Abstr., Energy Res. Abstr., Bibliogr. Index, Soc. Sci. Citation Index, Sociol. Abstr., Phys. Abstr., Hospit. Lit. Index. **LC** RC423. **NLM** W1 JO902N. **CODEN** JSPHAH. adv acc. **Circ** 51,700. Studies of the processes and disorders of speech, hearing and language.

JOURNAL OF TAMIL STUDIES. V. 1-2, Apr. 1969-70. 0022-4855. Periodical. II. English. sa. $10.00. International Institute of Tamil Studies, CPT Campus T T T I PO, Madras 600113 India. **Ed** S V Subramanian and R Vijayalakshmi. **Ind/Abst** MLA Int. Bibliogr. Books Artic. Mod. Lang. Lit. **LC** PL4758.A2. bk rev. adv acc. Areas of language and literature, linguistics, drama, folk arts, music, dance, costumes, grammar comparative literature, palm leaf manuscripts. *Tamil Culture.*

JOURNAL OF THE AMERICAN ORIENTAL SOCIETY. **Main/Corp** American Oriental Society. V. 1- 1843/49-. 0003-0279. Periodical. US. English. qt. $53.00. American Oriental Society, 329 Sterling Memorial Library, New Haven CT 06520. **Tel** (203)436-1040. **Ed** Ernest Bender. **Ind/Abst** MLA Int. Bibliogr. Books Artic. Mod. Lang. Lit., Old Testam. Abstr., New Testam. Abstr., Index Book Rev. Humanit., Humanit. Index, Relig. Index One, Period. **LC** PJ2. (cum index). bk rev. adv acc.

JOURNAL OF THE ATLANTIC PROVINCES LINGUISTIC ASSOCIATION. **Main/Corp** Atlantic Provinces Linguistic Association. **VFOAT** JAPLA/RALPA, J.A.P.L.A./R.A.L.P.A., Revue de l'Association de Linguistique des Provinces Atlantiques. V. 1- 1978-. 0706-6910. Periodical. CN. English (French). an. $11.61. Memorial University, Linguistics Department, St John's Newfoundland A1B SX9 Canada. **Tel** (709)737-8134. **Ed** Sandra Clarke. **Ind/Abst** MLA Int. Bibliogr. Books Artic. Mod. Lang. Lit. **LC** P1. **DD** 410.5. bk rev. adv acc. **Circ** 150. Articles on descriptive and theoretical linguistics.

JOURNAL OF THE CHINESE LANGUAGE TEACHERS ASSOCIATION. **VFOAT** Chung-Kuo Yu Wen Chiao Shih Hsueh Hui Hsueh Pao. Began in Feb. 1966. 0009-4595. Periodical. US. English (Chinese). ty. $30.00. Chinese Language Teachers Association, Seton Hall University, Asian Studies, South Orange NJ 07079. **Tel** (201)761-9447. **Ed** Hsueh Fen-Sheng. **Ind/Abst** MLA Int. Bibliogr. Books Artic. Mod. Lang. Lit., Lang. Lang. Behav. Abstr., Curr. Index J. Educ., Sociol. Abstr. **Circ** 550. Available on microform. Study and research of Chinese language teaching, linguistics and literature in the west. *Newsletter (Chinese Language Teachers Association).*

JOURNAL OF THE INTERNATIONAL PHONETIC ASSOCIATION. **Main/Corp** International Phonetic Association. Vol. 1, No. 1 (June 1971)-. 0025-1003. Periodical. UK. English (French). sa. International Phonetic Association, University College Gower Street, London WC1E 6BT England. **Ind/Abst** MLA Int. Bibliogr. Books Artic. Mod. Lang. Lit., Lang. Lang. Behav. Abstr., Lang. Teach., Sociol. Abstr. **LC** P215. *Maitre Phonetique.*

JOURNAL OF THE LANGUAGE ASSOCIATION OF EASTERN AFRICA. **Main/Corp** Language Association of Eastern Africa. V. 1- 1970-. 0023-8325. Periodical. English. sa. East African Literature Buerau, PO Box 30022, Nairobi Kenya. **Ind/Abst** MLA Int. Bibliogr. Books Artic. Mod. Lang. Lit., Sociol. Abstr., Lang. Lang. Behav. Abstr. **LC** PL8016. **DD** 496.

THE JOURNAL OF THE POLYNESIAN SOCIETY. *See* Anthropology.

JOURNAL OF VISUAL, VERBAL LANGUAGING. **VFOAT** J.L. Vol. 1, No. 1 (Fall 1981)-. 0748-7525. Periodical. US. English. sa. $25.00 US and Canada with Membership Fee. Ron Sutton/ Ivla Treasurer, American University, 50C-MGC-300, Washington DC 20016.

THE JOURNAL OF WEST AFRICAN LANGUAGES. 0022-5401. Periodical. UK. English. sa. $30.00. Summer Institute of Linguistics, 7500 West Camp Wisdom Road, Dallas TX 75236. **Tel** (214)298-3331. **Ed** John Bendor-Samuel. **Ind/Abst** Sociol. Abstr., Lang. Lang. Behav. Abstr., MLA Int. Bibliogr. Books Artic. Mod. Lang. Lit. bk rev. adv acc. **Circ** 250. (ctrl). Publishes articles on West African languages including descriptive, comparative and sociolinguistic aspects.

JSL, JOURNAL OF THE SCHOOL OF LANGUAGES. (JOURNAL OF THE SCHOOL OF LANGUAGES). **Main/Corp** Jawaharlal Nehru University. School of Languages. 0377-0648. Periodical. English. sa. 24.00. Wiley Eastern Private Ltd, J 43A South Extension 1, 110 049 New Delhi India. **Ind/Abst** MLA Int. Bibliogr. Books Artic. Mod. Lang. Lit. **LC** P1. **DD** 405.

JURNAL BAHASA MODEN : JURNAL PUSAT BAHASA, UNIVERSITI MALAYA. V. 1 (July 1983)-. 0127-3957. Periodical. MY. Malay (text in English). sa. Pusat Bahasa Universiti Malaya, Lembah Pantai, Kuala Lumpur 22-11 Malaysia.

JURNAL BUDAYA MELAYA. **Main/Corp** Universiti Kebangsaan. Institut Bahasa, Kesusastraan Dan Kebudayaan Melayu. V. 1-. MY. Malay (English). ir. Jurnal Budaya Melaya, Institut Bahasa, Kesusasteraan Dan Kebudayaan, Melayu Universiti Kebangsaan, Kuala Lumpur Malaysia. **LC** PL5101. **DD** 959.004992.

KAIGAI GENGOGAKU JOHO. **Series/Titl** Sophia Linguistica Special Publications. **VFOAT** Current Trends in Overseas Linguistics. No. 1- (1978-1980)-. JA. Japanese. ir. 2600. Taishukan Shoten, 3-24 Kanda Nishiki-Cho, Chiyoda-Ku, Tokyo-To Japan. **LC** P9.

KANAZAWA DAIGAKU BUNGAKUBU RONSHU. BUNGAKUKA HEN. **VFOAT** Studies and Essays. Edition (1980)-. Periodical. JA. Japanese. ir. Kanazawa Daigaku Bungakubu, 1-1 Marunouchi, Kanazawa-Shi 920 Japan. **LC** PB5.

KEEPING UP WITH AMERICAN ENGLISH TODAY. **VFOAT** American English Today. Vol. 1, No. 1-. 0272-1392. Periodical. US. English. mo. $59.00. American English Press Inc, PO Box 401865, Dallas TX 75240. **LC** PE2801. **DD** 427.973.

KENKYU HOKOKU SHU - KOKURITSU KOKUGO KENKYUJO. **Main/Corp** Kokuritsi Kokugo Kenkyujo. **Series/Titl** Kokuritsu Konkgo Kenkyujo Hokoku. **VFOAT** Occasional Papers. 1- 1978-. JA. Japanese. ir. Kokuritsu Kokugo Kenkyujo, 9-14 Nishigaoka 3, Kita-Ku 115, Tokyo Japan. **LC** PL501.

KENKYU NENKAN. **Main/Corp** Kokugo Kyoiky Kenkyujo. No. 1-. 0302-8801. JA. Japanese. ir. **LC** PL519.

KISWAHILI. V. 40, No. 2- Sept. 1970-. Periodical. TZ. English (Swahili). sa. $15.00. Institute of Swahili Research, PO Box 35110, Dar es Salaam Tanzania. **Tel** 49162/49143. **Ed** D P B Massamba and M M Mulokozi. **Ind/Abst** MLA Int. Bibliogr. Books Artic. Mod. Lang. Lit. **LC** PL8701. bk rev. **Circ** 5,000. Academic articles and research papers on various aspects of Kiswahili and Bantu literature linguistics, and vocabulary and book reviews. *Swahili.*

KLAGENFURTER BEITRAGE ZUR SPRACHWISSENSCHAFT. V. 1-. Periodical. German. ir. Klagenfurter Sprachwissenschaftliche Gesellschaft etc, Fischlstr 43/37, 9020 Klagenfurt Austria. **LC** P3.

KLASGIDS. Periodical. SA. Afrikaans. ty. 3.50. Klasgids, Posbus 1758, Pretoria 0001 South Africa. **Ind/Abst** MLA Int. Bibliogr. Books Artic. Mod. Lang. Lit. **LC** PF861.

Linguistics

KLEINE TEXTE FUR VORLESUNGEN UND UBUNGEN. No. 1- 1903-. Periodical. GW. German. ir. Walter de gruyter, Postfach 110240, D-1000 Berlin 30 West Germany. Tel 030/26005-0. Small texts for recitals and language exercises.

KNJIZEVNOST I JEZIK. 0454-0689. Periodical. YU. Serbo-Croatian -R. qt. Ind/Abst MLA Int. Bibliogr. Books Artic. Mod. Lang. Lit. LC PG1201.

KODAI ROSHIA KENKYU. VFOAT Studia Philologica Palaeorussica. Japanese (Polish and Russian). ir. Nihon Kodai Roshia Kenkyukai, c/o Kyoto Daigaku Kyoyobu Roshiago Kenkyushitsu, Yoshida Nihonmatsu Chosakyo Ku, Kyoto-Shi 606 Japan. LC PG2739.

KODIKAS/CODE, ARS SEMEIOTICA. VFOAT ARS Semeiotica. Vol. 4/5, No. 1 (Jan. 1982)-. 0147-5045. Periodical. English (text in French or German). sa. $40.00. John Benjamins BV, PO Box 52519, Amsteldijk 44, 1007 HA Amsterdam Netherlands. Tel (020)738156. Ed Achim Eschbach, Ernest W B Hess-Luttich, Mihai Nadin and Jurgen Trabant. Ind/Abst MLA Int. Bibliogr. Books Artic. Mod. Lang. Lit. LC P99. DD 401.41. Publishes articles, reviews, discussions, informations and reports in semiotics. *Kodikas/Code, 0171-0834; ARS Semeiotica, 0147-5045.*

KOKUGOGAKU. VFOAT Studies in the Japanese Language. Began with Oct. 1948 issue. Periodical. JA. Japanese (added table of contents in English). qt. $37.00. Japan Publishing Trading Company Ltd, PO Box 5030, Tokyo International, Tokyo 10031 Japan.

KOKUGOGAKU NO SEKAI. Main/Corp Kokugogaku Zeminaru, Onomichi Tanki Daigaku. JA. Japanese. ir. LC PL501.

KOMMUNIKATION UND KYBERNETIK IN EINZELDARSTELLUNGEN. See Communication.

KOMUNIKA. 0126-2491. Periodical. IO. Indonesian. ir. 1800 1500 Students. Biro Hubungan Masyarakat Lembaga Ilmu Pengetahuan Indonesia, Jl Teuku Tjhik Ditiro 43, Jakarta Indonesia. LC P87.

KOPENHAGENER BEITRAGE ZUR GERMANISTISCHEN LINGUISTIK. 1- 1972-. 0105-0257. German. ir. Ind/Abst MLA Int. Bibliogr. Books Artic. Mod. Lang. Lit. LC PD3.

KPA BULLETIN. Main/Corp Kentucky Philological Association. Meeting. VFOAT Kentucky Philological Association Bulletin. Began in 1974. 0277-3384. US. English. an. Murray State University, Print Services, Murray KY 42071. Ind/Abst MLA Int. Bibliogr. Books Artic. Mod. Lang. Lit. LC PN31. DD 809.

KRITIKON LITTERARUM. V. 1-. Periodical. GW. French, German, Russian or Spanish. qt. $50.32. Thesen Verlag Vowinckel & Company, Kittlerstrasse 34, 6100 Darmstadt West Germany. LC P1.A1.

KUGO KUNGMUNHAK YONGAM. 1977- Year. KO. Korean. ir. 9.000. Iu Chulpansa, 19-8 5-Ro Chungmu-Ro, Chung-Ku, Seoul South Korea. LC PL901.

KUKCHE OMUN. VFOAT Kookje Language and Literature. Began in 1979. Periodical. KO. Korean. ir. Kukche Taehak Kugo Kungmun Hakkwa, 2-3 Chungjong-No 2-Ka Sodaemun-Ku, Seoul Korea. LC PL901.

KULA, KARTEI UNVEROFFENTLICHTER LINGUISTISCHER ARBEITEN ZUR DEUTSCHEN SPRACHE DER GEGENWART. VFOAT Kartei Unveroffentlichter Linguistischer Arbeiten zur Deutschen Sprache der Gegenwart. 1- 1973-. German. ir. Institut fur Deutsche Sprache, Deutschen Sprache der Friedrichsplatz 12 68, Mannheim West Germany. LC Z7036, PF3073.

KULTURA SLOVA. Vol. 1- 1967-. 0023-5202. Periodical. Slovak. Kubon & Sagner, Postfach 34 01 08, Hess-Strasse 39/41, D-8 Munchen 34 West Germany. Tel (089)52 20 27. LC PG5201. Contains studies of leading Slovak philologists. Marked attention is paid to the problem of special terminology, its normalization and application in practice.

KULTURA SLOVA. Vol. 10- 1976-. UR. Russian. 0.36. Nauk Dumka, Riepina 3, Kyiv Russia. LC PG3814. *Ridne Slovo.*

KWARTALNIK NEOFILOLOGICZNY. Vol. 1- 1954-. 0023-5911. Periodical. PL. Polish (table of contents also in French and Russian). qt. ARS Polona, Krakowskie Przedmiescie 7, 00-068 Warsaw Poland. Ind/Abst Abstr. Engl. Stud., MLA Int. Bibliogr. Books Artic. Mod. Lang. Lit., Lang. Lang. Behav. Abstr., Annu. Bibliogr. Engl. Lang. Lit., Sociol. Abstr. LC PB5.

LA-MATHIL. VFOAT Lamatchil. Periodical. US. Hebrew. wk. $5.00. 515 Park Avenue, New York NY 10016. LC PJ4569.

THE LACUS FORUM. (LACUS FORUM). Main/Corp Linguistic Association of Canada and the United States. VFOAT Linguistic Association of Canada and the United States Forum. 1st- 1974-. 0195-377X. US. English. an. Hornbeam Press Inc, 6520 Courtwood Drive, Columbia SC 29206. LC P21. DD 410.5.

LADDER (WASHINGTON, D.C.). (THE LADDER). 0882-1828. Periodical. US. English. bm. $10.00. The Ladder, c/o Plan, 2311 18th Street NW, Washington DC 20009. DD 418.

LALIES : ACTES DES SESSIONES DE LINGUISTIQUE ET DE LITTERATURE. VFOAT Actes des Sessions de Linguistique et de Litterature. 1 (3-7 Sept. 1979)-. Periodical. FR. French. an. 45 rue d'Ulm, Paris France. LC P21. DD 405. *Actes des Sessions de Linguistique.*

LAMPAS. Volume 1- July 1968-. Periodical. NE. Dutch. ir. 50.50. Dick Coutinho BV, Badlaan 2, Muiderberg Netherlands. Tel 02942-1888. Ed Dick Coutinho. Ind/Abst Recent Publ. Artic. (cum index). bk rev. adv acc. Circ 1,100. Magazine for Dutch classical linguistics.

LE LANGAGE ET L'HOMME. No.1- May 1966-. 0458-7251. Periodical. BE. French (German or Flemish). ir. $10.00. Institut Marie Haps, rue d'Arlon 11, B-1040 Bruxelles Belgium. Tel 02-513 00 69. Ind/Abst Lang. Teach., Lang. Lang. Behav. Abstr., Sociol. Abstr. bk rev. Circ 500. Psycholinguistics, neurolinguistics, socio-linguistics, translation and terminology.

LANGAGE ET SOCIETE. VFOAT LS, Langage et Societe. Began in 1977. 0181-4095. Periodical. French. qt. $21.00. Maison des Sciences de l'Homme, Langage et Societe, 54 Bd Raspail, 75270 Paris Cedex 06 France. LC P40. DD 401.9.

LANGAGES. 1- March 1966-. 0458-726X. Periodical. FR. French. qt. $17.65. Larouses & Company, 572 5th Avenue, New York NY 10036. Ind/Abst MLA Int. Bibliogr. Books Artic. Mod. Lang. Lit., Lang. Lang. Behav. Abstr., Lang. Teach., Sociol. Abstr. International linguistic review published in French by Larouses. Each issue is devoted to a specific topic.

LANGENSCHEIDTS' SPRACH-ILLUSTRIERTE. 0023-8252. Periodical. GW. German. qt. Langenscheidt KG, Crellestra 29/30, 1 Berlin 62 Germany.

LANGUAGE. V. 1- Mar. 1925-. 0097-8507. Periodical. US. English. qt. $40.00. Linguistic Society of America, 428 East Preston Street, Baltimore MD 21202. Ind/Abst Annu. Bibliogr. Engl. Lang. Lit., MLA Int. Bibliogr. Books Artic. Mod. Lang. Lit., Sociol. Abstr., Lang. Lang. Behav. Abstr., Lang. Teach., Index Book Rev. Humanit., Curr. Index J. Educ., Ref. Source, Humanit. Index. LC P1. DD 405. (cum index).

LANGUAGE. VFOAT Yu Wen Lun Chi. First published in 1972-. Chinese or English. ir. $3.12. Singapore Linguistic Society, 177-A Outram Park, 3 Singapore. LC P121.

LANGUAGE AND AUTOMATION. No. 1- Spring 1970-. 0023-8287. Periodical. US. English. qt. Tel (202)298-9292. LC Z7004.L3. DD 016.02994.

LANGUAGE & COMMUNICATION. VFOAT Language and Communication. Vol. 1, No. 1 (1981)-. 0271-5309. Periodical. UK. English. qt. Pergamon Press, 395 Sawmill River Road, Elmsford NY 10523. Tel (914)592-7700. Ind/Abst MLA Int. Bibliogr. Books Artic. Mod. Lang. Lit., Sociol. Abstr., Lang. Lang. Behav. Abstr., Comput. Control Abstr., Electr. Electron. Abstr., Sci. Abstr., Lang. Teach., Psychol. Abstr. LC P87. DD 001.5105. CODEN LACOD8.

LANGUAGE AND LANGUAGE LEARNING. No. 1-. 0458-7294. English. ir. Oxford University Press, 16-00 Pollitt Drive, Fair Lawn NJ 07410.

LANGUAGE AND LITERATURE (SAN ANTONIO, TEX.). (LANGUAGE AND LITERATURE). VFOAT LNL. Vol. 7, 1-3-. Periodical. US. English. an. Trinity University, Bates Hoffer, Box 306, San Antonio TX 78284. Tel (512)736-7519. Ed Bates L Hoffer. bk rev. adv acc. Circ 200. Language-oriented analyses of major works of fiction, reviews of books in the field and experimental literary criticism. *Linguistics in Literature, 0147-0906.*

LANGUAGE AND SOCIETY. VFOAT Langue et Societe. No. 1 (Autumn 1979)-. 0709-7751. Periodical. CN. English (French). qt. Free. Commissioner Official Language, 66 Slater Street, Ottawa Ontario K1A 0T8 Canada. Tel (613)995-0629. Ed Christine Sirois. DD 404.20971. Circ 6,500. (ctrl). A bilingual magazine for those interested in language issues in Canada and other countries.

LANGUAGE AND SPEECH. V. 1- Jan./Mar. 1958-. 0023-8309. Periodical. UK. English. qt. $140.00. Kingston Press Services Ltd, 28 High Street, Teddington Middlesex England. Ind/Abst MLA Int. Bibliogr. Books Artic. Mod. Lang. Lit., Sociol. Abstr., Lang. Lang. Behav. Abstr., Index Med., Int. Aerosp. Abstr., Lang. Teach., Curr. Index J. Educ., Psychol. Abstr., Soc. Sci. Citation Index, Years Work Eng. Stud. LC P1. DD 414.05. NLM W1 LA615.

LANGUAGE AND STYLE. V. 1- Winter 1968-. 0023-8317. Periodical. US. English. qt. Queens College, Editorial Services, Flushing NY 11367. Tel (212)520-7208. Ed E L Epstein. Ind/Abst MLA Int. Bibliogr. Books Artic. Mod. Lang. Lit., Index Book Rev. Humanit., Sociol. Abstr., Years Work Eng. Stud. LC PN203. DD 808.005. bk rev. Circ 600. Articles on style in all of its manifestations, in all of the arts, and in all of its social and cultural contexts.

LANGUAGE CENSUS REPORT. US. English. an. California State Department of Education, 721 Capitol Mall, Sacramento CA 95814. LC P115.5.C27. DD 312.9.

LANGUAGE FOR LEARNING. Vol. 1, No. 1 (Feb. 1979)-. 0142-4645. UK. English. ty. Language in Education Center, University of Exeter, School of Education, St Luke's Exeter EX1 2LU England. Ind/Abst Lang. Teach. LC LC201.5. DD 420.71141.

LANGUAGE FORUM. Periodical. II. English or Hindi. qt. $10.00. Asia Books & Periodicals Company, 11 Darya Ganj, New Delhi 110002 India. Tel 268645,271378,275542. LC P1.A1. DD 405.

LANGUAGE IN FOCUS (MISSISSAUGA, ONT.). (LANGUAGE IN FOCUS). VAT Ecco. Language in Focus, Association of English Co-Ordinators and Consultants of Ontario. Language in Focus. No. 1-. 0823-4159. Periodical. CN. English. ir. Free to members. Ecco Monographs Peel Board of Education, 73 King Street West, Mississauga Ontario L5B 1H5 Canada. DD 420.7.

LANGUAGE IN SOCIETY. V. 1- Apr. 1972-. 0047-4045. Periodical. UK. English. qt. $70.00. Cambridge University Press, 510 North Avenue, New Rochelle NY 10801. Tel (914)235-0300. Ed Dell Hymes, Allen Grimshaw and William Labov. Ind/Abst Abstr. Engl. Stud., MLA Int. Bibliogr. Books Artic. Mod. Lang. Lit., Sociol. Abstr., Lang. Behav. Abstr., Lang. Teach., Index Book Rev. Humanit., Curr. Index J. Educ., Ref. Source, Psychol. Abstr., Bibliogr. Index, Soc. Sci. Citation Index. LC P41. DD 301.21. CODEN LGSCBO. bk rev. International journal of sociolinguistics concerned with all branches of the study of speech and language as aspects of social life.

LANGUAGE INTERVENTION SERIES. V. 1-. 0190-0382. Monographic Series. US. English. ir. University Park Press, 233 East Redwood Street, Baltimore MD 21202. Ed R L Schiefelbusch. LC UNC. NLM W1 LA616S.

LANGUAGE LEARNING. V. 1- Jan. 1948-. 0023-8333. Periodical. US. English. qt. $42.00. Language Learning, 1076 Frieze Building, University of Michigan, Ann Arbor MI 48109. Tel (313)763-9216. Ed John A Upsheer. Ind/Abst MLA Int. Bibliogr. Books Artic. Mod. Lang. Lit., Lang. Lang. Behav. Abstr., Annu. Bibliogr. Engl. Lang. Lit., Lang. Teach., Index Book Rev. Humanit., Educ. Index, Curr. Index J. Educ., Soc. Sci. Citation Index, Sociol. Abstr., Bibliogr. Index, Abstr. Anthropol. LC P1. DD 407. NLM W1 LA617. (cum index). bk rev. Circ 2,500. Research articles in applied linguistics, the application of linguistic method and philosophical perspective to problem areas usually viewed as lying outside the traditional concerns of linguistics.

Linguistics

LANGUAGE LEARNING AND COMMUNICATION. VFOAT Chung Ying yu wen Chiao Hsueh. Vol. 1, No. 1 (Spring 1982)-. 0278-3894. Periodical. US. English (Chinese). ty. $40.00. John Wiley & Sons, 605 Third Avenue, New York NY 10158. **Ind/Abst** MLA Int. Bibliogr. Books Artic. Mod. Lang. Lit.

LANGUAGE MONTHLY. No. 1 (Oct. 1983)-. 0265-2137. Periodical. UK. English (French or German). mo. 17.00 Domestic, 19.00 Foreign. Praetorius Limited, 5 East Circus Street, Nottingham NG1 5AH England. **Tel** (602)411087. **Ed** Geoffrey Kingscott. **LC** P1. **DD** 405. bk rev. adv acc. **Circ** 1,000. International news magazine for the language professions covering all developments in translation and language teaching.

LANGUAGE PROBLEMS & LANGUAGE PLANNING. VFOAT Language Problems and Language Planning. V. 4- Spring 1980-. 0272-2690. Periodical. US. English (Multilingual). ty. $15.00. University of Texas Press, Box 7819, Austin TX 78712. **Tel** (512)471-4531. **Ed** Humphrey Tonkin. **Ind/Abst** MLA Int. Bibliogr. Books Artic. Mod. Lang. Lit., Curr. Index J. Educ., Lang. Teach. **LC** P40.5.L35. **DD** 409. bk rev. adv acc. **Circ** 700. (ctrl). An international journal that examines the practical issues raised by efforts to find political solutions to language problems within and among nations. *Lingvaj Problemoj Kaj Lingvo-Planado, 0165-2672.*

LANGUAGE SCIENCES. Vol. 1- Mar. 1979-. Periodical. JA. English. sa. 65.00. International Christian University, 10-2 3 Chome Osawa Mitaka, Tokyo 181 Japan. **Tel** 0422-33-3205. **Ed** Fred C C Peng. **Ind/Abst** MLA Int. Bibliogr. Books Artic. Mod. Lang. Lit., Sociol. Abstr., Lang. Lang. Behav. Abstr., Lang. Teach., Curr. Index J. Educ. **LC** P1. **DD** 410.5. bk rev. **Circ** 550. (ctrl). Interdisciplinary forum for free exchange of scholastic ideas on the study of language. It includes social linguistics, psycholinguistics, neurolinguistics, child language and general linguistics. *Language Sciences, 0023-8341.*

LANGUAGE, SPEECH & HEARING SERVICES IN SCHOOLS. VFOAT Language, Speech, and Hearing Services in Schools, L.S. & H.S.S., LS and HSS, LS & HSS, L.S.H.S.S., LSHSS. Began in 1971. 0161-1461. Periodical. US. English. qt. $30.00. American Speech-Language-Hearing Association, 10801 Rockville Pike, Rockville MD 20852. **Tel** (301)897-5700. **Ed** Patricia A Broen. **Ind/Abst** Educ. Index, Except. Child Educ. Resour., Curr. Index J. Educ., Psychol. Abstr., Sociol. Abstr., Lang. Lang. Behav. Abstr. **NLM** W1 LA617R. **CODEN** LGSHA4. adv acc. **Circ** 51,000. Speech hearing and language services for children in schools. *Speech & Hearing Services in Schools.*

LANGUAGE TEACHING. Vol. 15, No. 1 (Jan. 1982)-. 0261-4448. Periodical. UK. English. qt. $65.00. Cambridge University Press, 510 North Avenue, New Rochelle NY 10801. **Tel** (212)688-8888. **Ed** Valerie Kinsella. **LC** PB35. **DD** 407. bk rev. adv acc. Aims to help people concerned with the teaching and learning of languages kept up-to-date with the latest findings in research, language studies and applied linguistics. *Language Teaching & Linguistics. Abstracts, 0306-6304.*

LANGUAGE TEACHING & LINGUISTICS. ABSTRACTS. *See* Indexes/Abstracts.

LANGUAGES OF ASIA AND AFRICA. 0261-0116. Monographic Series. UK. English. ir. Routledge & Kegan Paul, 9 Park Street, Boston MA 02108.

LANGUAGES OF SOUTH INDIA. **Main/Corp** Metropolitan Toronto Library Board. Languages Co-Ordinator. 0316-7429. Periodical. CN. English. Languages Co-Ordinator, Metropolitan Toronto Library Board, 229 College Street, Toronto Ontario M5T 1R4 Canada. **DD** 018.12948.

LANGUE ET LITTERATURE FRANCAISES AU CANADA. 6- 1970-. 0384-5710. Periodical. CN. French. ir. Presses de l'Universite Laval, CP 2447, Ave de la Medecine, Ste Foy Quebec G1K 7R4 Canada. *Bibliotheque Francaise et Romane. Serie E: Langue et Litterature Francaises au Canada, 0067-8384.*

LANGUE FRANCAISE. Began with: 1 (Feb. 1969). 0023-8368. Periodical. FR. French. qt. Inter Presse Service, 12 rue Paul LeLong, 75095 Paris Cedex 02 France. **Ind/Abst** MLA Int. Bibliogr. Books Artic. Mod. Lang. Lit., Lang. Lang. Behav. Abstr., Lang. Teach. **LC** PC2002.

LANGUES ET LINGUISTIQUE. VFOAT Travaux du Departement de Langues et Linguistique. **VAT** Langues et Linguistiques. No 1 (1975)-. 0226-7144. Periodical. CN. English (French and Spanish). an. 7.00. Departement de Langues et Linguistique, Faculte des Lettres, Universite Laval, Quebec G1K 7P4 Canada. **Tel** (418)656-3642. **Ind/Abst** MLA Int. Bibliogr. Books Artic. Mod. Lang. Lit., Sociol. Abstr. **LC** P1.A1. **DD** 410.5. bk rev. adv acc. **Circ** 450. Publishes articles and reviews on linguistic theories and their application to various disciplines of linguistics, to specific languages to other fields.

LES LANGUES MODERNES. Began with May 1903 issue. 0023-8376. Periodical. FR. French. ir. 225. Association des Prof de Langue, 19 rue de la Glaciere, 75013 Paris France. **Tel** (1)47 07 94 82. **Ed** Daniel Thomieres. **Ind/Abst** MLA Int. Bibliogr. Books Artic. Mod. Lang. Lit., Lang. Lang. Behav. Abstr., Annu. Bibliogr. Engl. Lang. Lit., Lang. Teach., Sociol. Abstr. **LC** PB2. bk rev. adv acc. **Circ** 5,000. The main French journal devoted to foreign language learning and teaching.

LATINITAS. Began with issue for Jan. 1953. 0023-883X. Periodical. IT. Latin. ir. $13.00. 1-00120 Citta del Vaticano, Vatican City. **Tel** 0039-6-6384648. **Ind/Abst** MLA Int. Bibliogr. Books Artic. Mod. Lang. Lit. **LC** PA2009. (cum index). bk rev. adv acc. **Circ** 1,500. A review of various subjects: linguistics, literature, philology, history, sciences, and diarium Latinum (Latin diary).

LEBENDE SPRACHEN. 1.- Yearly volume. 0023-9909. Periodical. GW. German. qt. $19.63. Langenscheidt KG, Crellestr 29, Berlin 62 West Germany. **Ed** S F Krollmann and G Haensch. **Ind/Abst** MLA Int. Bibliogr. Books Artic. Mod. Lang. Lit., Lang. Lang. Behav. Abstr., Lang. Teach. **LC** PB5. bk rev. adv acc. **Circ** 4,000. Multilingual glossaries of specialized terminology from all areas/articles on the theory/practice of translation and the training of analyses of translations.

LEEDS STUDIES IN ENGLISH. V. 1- 1967-. 0075-8566. UK. English. an. University of Leeds, School of English, Leeds LS2 9JT England. **Ind/Abst** Abstr. Engl. Stud., MLA Int. Bibliogr. Books Artic. Mod. Lang. Lit., Years Work Eng. Stud. **LC** PE10. **DD** 805. *Leeds Studies in English and Kindred Languages.*

LEEDS TEXTS AND MONOGRAPHS: NEW SERIES. *See* Education (General) - Higher Education.

LEIDSE GERMANISTISCHE EN ANGLISTISCHE REEKS. *See* Literature.

LEIDSE ROMANTISCHE REEKS. *See* Literature.

LEKTOS. V. 1- Apr. 1975-. 0360-9790. Periodical. US. English. sa. $6.00. University of Louisville, c/o Program in Linguistics, Room 214/Humanities Building, Louisville KY 40208. **LC** P1. **DD** 410.5.

LEMBAGA. Vol. 1- Oct. 1970-. Indonesian. ir. **LC** PL5071.

LENGAS. Vol. 1-. Periodical. FR. French (Occitan). sa. 60.00. Universite Paul Valery, Centre d'Etudes Occitanes, B P 5043, 34032 Montpellier Cedex France. **LC** PC3371. **DD** 301.21.

LENGUAJES. Yearly V. 1- April 1974-. Periodical. Spanish. ir. Ediciones Nueva Vision, Tucuman 3748, Buenos Aires Argentina. **LC** P9.

LENGUAS MODERNAS. **Main/Corp** Venezuela. Universidad Central, Caracas. Instituto de Lenguas Modernas. Vol. 1 1954. 0503-8448. VE. Spanish. ir. Universidad Central, Institute de Lenguas Modernas, Caracas Venezuela.

LESHONENU. VFOAT Lesonenu. No. 1, April 1928-. 0024-1091. Periodical. IS. Hebrew (English). qt. $20.00. Academy of Hebrew Language, PO Box 3449, Jerusalem Israel. **Tel** 02-632242. **Ed** J Blan. **Ind/Abst** Old Testam. Abstr., MLA Int. Bibliogr. Books Artic. Mod. Lang. Lit., Lang. Lang. Behav. Abstr. **LC** PJ4503. bk rev. (ctrl). A journal for the study of the Hebrew language and cognate subjects.

LESHONENU LA-AM. 1945. IS. Hebrew. ir. $15.00. Academy of Hebrew Language, PO Box 3449, Jerusalem Israel. **Tel** 02/632242. **Ed** Eli Eytan. **Ind/Abst** MLA Int. Bibliogr. Books Artic. Mod. Lang. Lit. **LC** PJ4513. bk rev. (ctrl). A popular journal of the Hebrew language. *Leshonenu La-Am.*

LETOPIS INSTITUTA ZA SERBSKI LUDOSPYT. **Main/Corp** Bautzen, Ger. Institut za Serbski Ludospyt. **VFOAT** Jahresschrift des Instituts fur Sorbische Volksforschung, Rjad A : Rec a Literatura. V. 1- 1952-. 0522-506X. Periodical. SZ. Czech (text in Wendic, German, Polish). sa. $11.97. Kunst & Wissen Erich Bieber, Dufourstrasse 51, CH-8008 Zurich Switzerland. **Tel** 011-41-1-69 44 20. **LC** PG5631.

LETRA (RIO DE JANEIRO, BRAZIL). *See* Literature.

LETRAS DE HOJE. No. 1- Oct. 1967-. 0047-4428. Periodical. BL. Portuguese. qt. $105.00. Pontificia Univ Catolica, AV Ipirange 6681 Porto Alegre, Rio Grande Do Sul Brazil. **Tel** (0512)369400. **Ed** Bro Elvo Clemente. **LC** P25. **Circ** 1,000. Covers linguistics, literature, criticism, bilingualism, phrasalgrammar, language contact, phonetical literary theory, comparative literature, sociolinguistics, second language reading, poetry, drama.

LEVENDE TALEN. Began with issue for 1930. Periodical. NE. Dutch. mo. $39.52. Ver Van Leraren-Levende Talen, Postbus 104, 7740 AC Coevorden Netherlands. **Tel** 05240-2732. **Ind/Abst** MLA Int. Bibliogr. Books Artic. Mod. Lang. Lit., Sociol. Abstr., Lang. Teach., Lang. Lang. Behav. Abstr., Annu. Bibliogr. Engl. Lang. Lit. **LC** PB5. **DD** 405. (cum index). *Berichten en Mededeelingen.*

LEXIA (PONTIFICIA UNIVERSIDAD CATOLICA DEL PERU. DEPARTAMENTO DE HUMANIDADES). (LEXIS). Began in 1977. 0254-9239. Periodical. PE. Spanish. sa. $21.00. Pontif Universidad Catolica del Peru Fondo Editorial, Apartado 1761, Lima 100 Peru. **Ind/Abst** MLA Int. Bibliogr. Books Artic. Mod. Lang. Lit. **LC** P9. **DD** 405.

LEXICON. Periodical. JA. English (German, Japanese and Spanish). ir. Iwasaki Linguistic Circle, Tokyo Japan. **LC** P1.A1. **DD** 410.5.

LILI, ZEITSCHRIFT FUR LITERATURWISSENSCHAFT UND LINGUISTIK. VFOAT Zeitschrift fur Literaturwissenschaft und Lingusitik. **VAT** Literaturwissenschaft und Linguistik, Zeitschrift fur Literaturwissenschaft und Linguisitk. Vol. 3- (No. 11-). 0049-8653. GW. German. qt. $29.22. Vandenhoeck & Ruprecht, Postfach 3753 Theaterstr 13, D 3400 Goettingen West Germany. **Tel** (0551)65061. **Ind/Abst** MLA Int. Bibliogr. Books Artic. Mod. Lang. Lit., Lang. Lang. Behav. Abstr., Lang. Teach. **LC** P3. *Zeitschrift fur Literaturwissenschaft und Linguistik.*

LIMBA SI LITERATURA. *See* Literature.

LIMBA SI LITERATURA ROMANA. **Main/Corp** Societatea de Stiinte Filologice din Republica Socialista Romania. Periodical. RM. Romanian. qt. Ilexim Press Department, PO Box 1-136-1-137, Bucharest Romania.

LINGUA. V. 1- Dec. 1947-. 0024-3841. Periodical. English (French). mo. Elsevier Science Publishers, PO Box 211, 1000 AE Amsterdam Netherlands. **Tel** (020)5803.911. **Ind/Abst** MLA Int. Bibliogr. Books Artic. Mod. Lang. Lit., Sociol. Abstr., Lang. Lang. Behav. Abstr., Lang. Teach., Index Book Rev. Humanit., Soc. Sci. Citation Index. **LC** P9. **DD** 405. **NLM** W1 LI633. (cum index).

LINGUA E LITERATURA. Vol. 1- 1972-. 0101-4862. BL. French (Portuguese or Spanish). an. **Ind/Abst** MLA Int. Bibliogr. Books Artic. Mod. Lang. Lit. **LC** P1.A1.

LINGUA E STILE. Vol. 1 (Jan./Apr. 1966)-. 0024-385X. Periodical. IT. Italian (summaries in English and Russian). ty. 100.000 Domestic, 130.000 Foreign. Societa Editrice Il Mulino Spa, Via Santo Stefano 6, 40125 Bologna Italy. **Tel** (051)233415. **Ind/Abst** MLA Int. Bibliogr. Books Artic. Mod. Lang. Lit., Lang. Lang. Behav. Abstr., Lang. Teach., Sociol. Abstr. **LC** P9. *Quaderni.*

LINGUA NOSTRA. Began with Feb. 1939 issue. 0024-3868. Periodical. IT. Italian. qt. $40.00. Licosa Libreria Comm Sansoni, Via Lamarmora 45, 50121 Firenze Italy. **Tel** 055/59751/2/3. **Ind/Abst** MLA Int. Bibliogr. Books Artic. Mod. Lang. Lit., Sociol. Abstr., Lang. Lang. Behav. Abstr., Lang. Teach. **LC** PC1001. (cum index).

LINGUA POSNANIENSIS. 1-. 0079-4740. PL. English (Polish, French, and other languages). an. ARS Polona, Krakowskie and Przedmiescie, 00-068 Warsaw Poland. **Ind/Abst** MLA Int. Bibliogr. Books Artic. Mod. Lang. Lit., Lang. Lang. Behav. Abstr.,

Index Book Rev. Humanit., Sociol. Abstr. **LC** P25. **DD** 410.5.

LINGUAGEM (RIO DE JANEIRO, BRAZIL). (LINGUAGEM). Yearly V. 1, No. 1-. Periodical. BL. Portuguese. sa. $20.00. Presenca Edicoes, rua do Cadete 204, Grupo 302 22.220, Rio de Janeiro Brasil. **LC** P9. **DD** 410.5.

LINGUE DEL MONDO. Yearly V. 1- Jan.? 1934-. Periodical. IT. Italian. bm. $40.00. Ed Valmartina, Viale Gramsci 42, 50132 Firenze Italy. **Tel** 055/24 29 57-8. **Ed** Matilde Dandolo. bk rev. adv acc. Concerns language teaching, translations, new books in general and current happenings in the language field.

LINGUISTIC ANALYSIS. V. 1- 1975-. 0098-9053. Periodical. US. English. ir. $79.00. Linguistic Analysis, M K Brame, 5706 30th Avenue NE, Seattle WA 98105. **Tel** (206)522-6853. **Ind/Abst** MLA Int. Bibliogr. Books Artic. Mod. Lang. Lit., Lang. Teach., Soc. Sci. Citation Index, Comput. Rev., Years Work Eng. Stud. **LC** P123. **DD** 410.

LINGUISTIC BIBLIOGRAPHY FOR THE YEARS . . . . *See* Bibliographies.

LINGUISTIC INQUIRY. Began with Jan. 1970 issue. 0024-3892. Periodical. US. English. qt. $70.00. MIT Press Journals, 28 Carleton Street, Cambridge MA 02142. **Tel** (617)253-1916. **Ed** Samuel Jay Keyser. **Ind/Abst** MLA Int. Bibliogr. Books Artic. Mod. Lang. Lit., Lang. Lang. Behav. Abstr., Lang. Teach., Sociol. Abstr., Soc. Sci. Citation Index, Years Work Eng. Stud. **LC** P1. **DD** 410.5. adv acc. **Circ** 2,700. Rigorous research on current topics in linguistic theory.

THE LINGUISTIC REPORTER *CEASED.* Vol. 1 (Apr. 1959)-V. 25, No. 4 (Dec. 1982/Jan. 1983). 0024-3906. Periodical. US. English. mo. **Ind/Abst** Lang. Lang. Behav. Abstr., Annu. Bibliogr. Engl. Lang. Lit., Lang. Teach. **LC** P1. **DD** 410.

LINGUISTIC REVIEW. (THE LINGUISTIC REVIEW). Vol. 1, No. 1 (Jan. 1981)-. 0167-6318. Periodical. English. qt. $55.00. Foris Publications, PO Box 509, 3300 AM Dordrecht Holland. **Tel** 078-510454. **Ed** Riny Huybregts, Jan Koster and Henk van Riemsdyk. **Ind/Abst** Lang. Lang. Behav. Abstr. adv acc. **Circ** 800. High quality papers in syntax, semantics, phonology and morphology.

LINGUISTICA ANTVERPIENSIA. 1- 1967-. 0304-2294. Periodical. BE. Dutch. an. 600. RUCA, Schildersstraat 41, 2000 Antwerpen Belgium. **Ed** J van Haver. **Ind/Abst** MLA Int. Bibliogr. Books Artic. Mod. Lang. Lit., Lang. Lang. Behav. Abstr., Lang. Teach., Sociol. Abstr. bk rev. **Circ** 250. Linguistics, applied linguistics, translations.

LINGUISTICA ESPANOLA ACTUAL. **VFOAT** LEA. I/1-. Periodical. SP. Spanish. sa. $19.00. Arco Libros S A, Juan Bautista de Toledo 28, 28002 Madrid Spain. **LC** PC4008. **DD** 460.5.

LINGUISTICA Y LITERATURA : REVISTA DEL DEPARTAMENTO DE ESPANOL. Periodical. Spanish. ir. Departamento de Espanol, Facultad de Ciencias y Humanidades, Universidad de Antioquia, Apartado Aereo 1226, Medellin Colombia. **LC** P9. **DD** 409.8.

LINGUISTICS. 1- Oct. 1963-. 0024-3949. Periodical. NE. English (French and German). mo. $180.00. Walter de Gruyter Inc, 200 Saw Mill River Road, Hawthorne NY 10532. **Tel** (914)747-0110. **Ed** Wolfgang Klein. **Ind/Abst** MLA Int. Bibliogr. Books Artic. Mod. Lang. Lit., Lang. Lang. Behav. Abstr., Index Book Rev. Humanit., Lang. Teach., Soc. Sci. Citation Index. **LC** P1.A1. **DD** 410.5. **NLM** W1 LI634. (cum index). bk rev. adv acc. **Circ** 1,200. Provides an international forum for research in the language sciences.

LINGUISTICS AND LANGUAGE BEHAVIOR ABSTRACTS : LLBA. *See* Indexes/Abstracts.

LINGUISTICS AND PHILOSOPHY. V. 1- Jan. 1977-. 0165-0157. Periodical. NE. English. ty. 63 Domestic. Kluwer Academic Publishers Group, PO Box 322, 3300 AH Dordrecht Netherlands. **Tel** (31)78-334911. **Ed** R Cooper and R E Grandy. **Ind/Abst** MLA Int. Bibliogr. Books Artic. Mod. Lang. Lit., Lang. Lang. Behav. Abstr., Philos. Index, Lang. Teach. **LC** P1.A1. **DD** 410.1. bk rev. adv acc. **Circ** 1,250. Studies focused on natural language: philosophy of language, linguistics, artificial intelligence, logic, questions and problems raised by linguistics as a science.

LINGUISTICS IN DOCUMENTATION. V. 1-. 0075-9651. US. English. ty. Committee on Linguistics in Documentation, 1717 Massachusetts Avenue NW, Washington DC 20036. **LC** Z7001. **DD** 029.941. **NLM** Z 699.2 L755.

LINGUISTICS IN LITERATURE *CEASED.* **VFOAT** LNL. V. 1-6. 0147-0906. US. English. ty. $12.00. Linguistics in Literature, Trinity University, PO Box 306, San Antonio TX 78284. **LC** PB1. **DD** 410.5.

LINGUISTICS OF THE TIBETO-BURMAN AREA. Began with Fall 1974 issue. 0731-3500. Periodical. US. English. sa. Graham Thurgood Editor, California State University, Department of Linguistics, Fresno CA 93740. **Ind/Abst** MLA Int. Bibliogr. Books Artic. Mod. Lang. Lit. **LC** PL3551. **DD** 495.4005.

LINGUISTIK UND DIDAKTIK *CEASED.* Yearly Vols. 1-13 (1-50). 0047-472X. Periodical. German. qt. **Ind/Abst** MLA Int. Bibliogr. Books Artic. Mod. Lang. Lit., Lang. Lang. Behav. Abstr., Lang. Teach. **LC** P51. **DD** 407.

LA LINGUISTIQUE. Began in 1965. Periodical. FR. French (English). sa. 250 Domestic, $27.78. Presses Universitaires France, 12 rue Jean-de-Beauvais, 75005 Paris France. **Tel** (1)326-2216. **Ed** F Bentolila. **Ind/Abst** MLA Int. Bibliogr. Books Artic. Mod. Lang. Lit., Lang. Lang. Behav. Abstr., Sociol. Abstr., Lang. Teach. **LC** P2. Both pure and applied linguistics are considered in this publication, as instruments of communication and expression. Structure of language is examined as a function of its use.

LINGUISTISCHE ARBEITEN UND BERICHTE. (LINGUISTISCHE ARBEITEN). Periodical. German. ir. Germanistik der Freien Universitat Berlin, Habelschwerdter Allee 45, 1000 Berlin 33 West Germany. **Ind/Abst** MLA Int. Bibliogr. Books Artic. Mod. Lang. Lit. **LC** P3.

LINGUISTISCHE BERICHTE. 1- 1969-. 0024-3930. Periodical. GW. German (with contribution in English or French). bm. $49.42. Westdeutscher Verlag GMBH, Postfach 5829, D6200 Wiesbaden 1 West Germany. **Ind/Abst** MLA Int. Bibliogr. Books Artic. Mod. Lang. Lit., Lang. Lang. Behav. Abstr., Lang. Teach., Sociol. Abstr., Years Work Eng. Stud. **LC** P1.A1.

LINGUISTISCHE REIHE. V. 1- 1970-. Periodical. German (text and summaries in English and French). ir. Adlers Foreign Books Inc, 162 Fifth Avenue, New York NY 10010.

LINGUISTISCHE STUDIEN. **Series/Titl** Sprache der Gegenwart. 1- 1972-. Periodical. GE. German. ir. Veb Max Niemeyer Verlag, Postfach 130, 701 Leipzig East Germany.

LINGVISTICAE INVESTIGATIONES. V. 1-. 0378-4169. Periodical. NE. French (English). sa. $70.00. John Benjamins BV, PO Box 52519, Amsteldijk 44, 1007 HA Amsterdam Netherlands. **Tel** (020)738156. **Ed** M Gross, J C Chevalier and C Leclere. **Ind/Abst** MLA Int. Bibliogr. Books Artic. Mod. Lang. Lit., Lang. Lang. Behav. Abstr., Lang. Teach. **LC** P1.A1. **DD** 410.5. Devoted to general linguistics, it publishes articles in and bearing on all languages, but it intends to emphasize the study of French.

LINGVISTICAE INVESTIGATIONES. SUPPLEMENTA. **VFOAT** LIS. V. 1-. Periodical. English. ir. John Benjamins, Amsteldijk 44, PO Box 52519, 1007 Amsterdam The Netherlands. **Tel** 020-738156. **Ed** Chevalier, Gross, Lecterc. **Ind/Abst** MLA Int. Bibliogr. Books Artic. Mod. Lang. Lit. French and general linguistics, modern linguistic theory and fundamental descriptive studies.

LINGVISTIKA I PROBLEMY STILIA. No. 1-. Periodical. UR. Russian. 0.85 Single Issue. **LC** P9.

LISTE DES ACQUISITIONS - INFORMATHEQUE DE LINGUISTIQUE. UNIVERSITE D'OTTAWA. (LISTE DES ACQUISITIONS - UNIVERSITE D'OTTAWA, INFORMATHEQUE DE LINGUISTIQUE). **Main/Corp** Universite d'Ottawa. Informatheque de Linguistique. **VFOAT** List of Accessions - University of Ottawa, Linguistic Documentation Centre. June 1974-. 0317-1981. CN. English (French). Linguistics Documentation Centre, University of Ottawa, Ottawa Ontario K1N 6N5 Canada. **DD** 016.41.

LIVRET DU DEPARTEMENT DES LANGUES AFRICAINES ET LINGUISTIQUE. **Main/Corp** University of Yaounde. Department des Langues Africaines et Linguistique. CM. English (French). ir. Universite de Yaounde, Faculte des Lettres et Sciences Humaines, Yaounde Cameron. **LC** P59.U545. **DD** 410.

LLBA, LANGUAGE AND LANGUAGE BEHAVIOR ABSTRACTS. *See* Indexes/ Abstracts.

LLEN CYMRU. *See* Literature.

LORE AND LANGUAGE. *See* Folklore.

LOU PROUVENCAU A L'ESCOLO. Periodical. French. ir. 15 Single Issue. C C P 1394-90 Marseille, 84 rue des Trois-Freres Carasso, 13004 Marseille France. **LC** PC3201. **DD** 449.05.

LTA CONFERENCE. (ANNUAL REPORT, LTA CONFERENCE . . .). **Main/Corp** Nova Scotia Teachers Union. Language Teachers Association. Conference. **VAT** Nova Scotia Teachers Union. Annual Report. LTA Conference. 1977-. 0707-2147. CN. English (includes some text in French). an. Nova Scotia Teachers Union, 106 Dutchvillage Road, Halifax Nova Scotia Canada. **DD** 406.0716.

LUMO. 0024-7367. Periodical. CN. Esperanto. qt. 20.00. Kanada Esperanto-Association, Box 126 Stn Beaubien, Montreal QC Canada H2G 3C8. **Tel** (514)495-8442. **Ed** Brian Kaneen. **Circ** 400. Activities of national and international Esperanto movement. Esperanto literature.

LUMO. (LUMO : LA KANADA ESPERANTO-REVUO). **VFOAT** Kanada Esperanto-Revuo. Vintro 1983/1984-. 0827-3154. Periodical. CN. Esperanto. qt. Free to Members. Kanada Esperanto-Asocio, PO Box 126, St Beaubien Montreal Quebec H2G 3C8 Canada. **DD** 499.99205. *Alumeto, 0823-2539.*

LUND STUDIES IN ENGLISH. 1-. 0076-1451. Monographic Series. SW. English. ir. CWK Gleerup Publisher-Liber, PO Box 1205, 22105 Lund Sweden. **Tel** 46-40-70650. **Ind/Abst** Abstr. Engl. Stud., MLA Int. Bibliogr. Books Artic. Mod. Lang. Lit. Discussion on the subjects of English language and literature.

LUNDER GERMANISTISCHE FORSCHUNGEN. 1.- 1934-. SW. Swedish. ir. Liber International, S-205 10 Malmo Sweden. **Ind/Abst** MLA Int. Bibliogr. Books Artic. Mod. Lang. Lit.

LA LUZ. 0886-179X. Periodical. US. English. ir. The Alan Company, Box 16250, Clayton MO 63105. **Tel** (314)531-1668.

MAAL OG MINNE. Began publication in 1909. 0024-855X. Periodical. NO. Norwegian. qt. 95,-. Forlagssentralens Tidsskrif, Postboks 6079 Etterstad, N-0601 Oslo 6 Norway. **Tel** (02)687600. **Ed** Einar Lundeby and Bjarne Fidjestol. **Ind/Abst** MLA Int. Bibliogr. Books Artic. Mod. Lang. Lit. **LC** PD1503. (cum index). bk rev. **Circ** 500. Scholarly articles and papers on Norwegian language past and present medieval literature, place names and folklore. *Norvegia.*

MAARAV. V. 1- Autumn 1978-. 0149-5712. Periodical. US. English (Hebrew). sa. $10.00 Domestic, $12.00 Foreign. Maarav, 2444 Wilshire Boulevard/Suite 510, Santa Monica CA 90403. **Ind/Abst** New Testam. Abstr., Old Testam. Abstr., Elenchus Bibliogr. Bibicus, Int. Zeitschriftenschan Bibelwissenschaft Grenzgeb. **LC** PJ3001. **DD** 492.

MCGILL WORKING PAPERS IN LINGUISTICS. **VFOAT** Cahiers Linguistiques de McGill. Vol. 1, No. 1 (Dec. 1983)-. 0824-5282. Periodical. CN. English. sa. 12.00. McGill Working Papers in Linguistics, McGill University, 1001 Sherbrooke Street West, Montreal Quebec H3A 1G5 Canada. **Tel** (514)392-4433. **Ed** E Guilfoyle. **DD** 410.5. **Circ** 200. Theoretical and applied linguistics including syntax, phonology, morphology, semantic, first and second language acquistion, neurolinguistics, sociologistics, and text linguistics.

MACHIKANEYAMA RONSO : BUNGAKUHEN. **VFOAT** Machikaneyama Ronso. No. 5-. JA. Japanese (some summaries in English, French, or German). ir. Osaka Daigaku Bungakubu, 1-1 Machikaneyamacho, Toyonaka Osaka Japan. **LC** P9. *Machikaneyama Ronso.*

MAGYAR NYELV. Vol. 1-. 0025-0228. Periodical. Hungarian. ir. **Ind/Abst** MLA Int. Bibliogr. Books Artic. Mod. Lang. Lit., Sociol. Abstr. **LC** PH2001. **DD** 494.51105. (cum index).

MAGYAR NYELVOR. V. 1- 1872-. 0025-0236. Periodical. HU. Hungarian. qt. Akademiai Kiado, Box 24, 1363 Budapest Hungary. **Tel** 161-053. **Ed** L Lorincze. **Ind/Abst** MLA Int. Bibliogr. Books Artic. Mod. Lang. Lit., Sociol. Abstr. (cum index). bk rev. **Circ** 3,300.

Linguistics

A MAGYAR TUDOMANYOS AKADEMIA NYELV- ES IRODALOMTUDOMANYOK OSZTALYANAK KOZLEMENYEI. Vol. 1-. 0025-0368. HU. Hungarian. qt. Akademiai Kiado, POB 24, 1363 Budapest Hungary. **Ind/Abst** MLA Int. Bibliogr. Books Artic. Mod. Lang. Lit., Lang. Lang. Behav. Abstr. **LC** PH2011. **DD** 494.511060439.

A MAGYARORSZAGI NYELVTUDOMANY BIBLIOGRAFIAJA. See Bibliographies.

MAHADIR AL-JALSAT. Main/Corp Majma Al-Lughah Al-Arabiyah (Cairo, Egypt). 1934-. Arabic. ir. **LC** PJ6011.

MAITHILI AKADAMI PATRIKA. VFOAT Methili Akadami Patrika. Periodical. Maithili. bm. 15.00. Maithili Academy Patna. **LC** PK1828.A2.

MAJALAH PEMBINAAN BAHASA INDONESIA. V. 1, No. 1 (March 1980)-. 0126-4737. Periodical. IO. Indonesian. qt $15.00. P T Bhratara Karya Aksara, Kotak Pos 39/JNG, Jakarta Timur Indonesia. **LC** PL5071.

MAJALLAT KULLIYAT AL-LUGHAT WA-AL-TARJAMAH. VFOAT Faculty of Languages & Translation Studies. No. 1-. Periodical. UA. Arabic (English, French, German, or Spanish). ir. **LC** P9. **DD** 405.

MAL SORI. VFOAT Journal of the Phonetic Society of Korea. Periodical. KO. Korean. ir. Taehan Umsong Hakhoe, San 56-1 Sillim-Dong, Kwanak-Ku, Seoul South Korea. **LC** P215.

MAL (YONSE TAEHAKKYO. HANGUGO HAKTANG). (MAL). VFOAT Journal of Korean Language Institute. Periodical. English (Korean). an. Yonse Taehakkyo Hangugo Haktang, 134 Sinchon-Dong Sodaemun-Ku, Seoul Korea. **LC** PL901.

MALEDICTA. V. 1- Summer 1977-. 0363-3659. Periodical. US. English. an. $25.00. Maledicta Press, 331 South Greenfield Avenue, Waukesha WI 53186. **Tel** (414)542-5853. Ed Reinhold A Aman. **Ind/Abst** MLA Int. Bibliogr. Books Artic. Mod. Lang. Lit., Sociol. Abstr., Lang. Lang. Behav. Abstr. **LC** P409. **DD** 418. bk rev. **Circ** 4,000. Essays and glossaries on offensive language (insults, curses, slurs) in all languages.

MALEDICTA PRESS PUBLICATIONS. 1-. 0363-9037. Monographic Series. US. English. ir. Maledicta Press, 331 S Greenfield Ave, Waukesha WI 53186. **Tel** (414)542-5853. Ed Reinhold A Aman. **Circ** 4,000. Dictionaries of ethnic, racial, sexual slurs. Originals and reprints.

MANITOBA MODERN LANGUAGE BULLETIN CEASED. Began with Fall 1967 issue. Ceased with V. 16, No. 2, Winter 1981/82. 0315-2111. Periodical. CN. English. ty. Manitoba Teachers' Society, 191 Harcourt Street, Winnipeg Manitoba R3J 3H2 Canada.

MANITOBA MODERN LANGUAGE JOURNAL. Vol. 16, No. 3 (Spring 1982)-. 0820-6066. Periodical. CN. English. ty. Free. Manitoba Modern Language Journal, c/o Manitoba Teachers Society, 191 Harcourt Street, Winnipeg Manitoba R3J 3B2 Canada. **Ind/Abst** Can. Educ. Index. **DD** 407. (ctrl). Manitoba Modern Language Bulletin, 0315-2111.

MANTATOPHOROS. Began with Nov. 1972 issue. 0306-0020. Periodical. English (Greek). sa. 17.50. ABN-Bank, Adam No 54.95.19.122, Amsterdam Netherlands. **LC** DF701.

MARBURGER BEITRAGE ZUR GERMANISTIK. Vol. 1- 1963-. 0542-6499. Monographic Series. GW. German. ir. N G Elwert Verlag, Postfach 1128, Reitgasse 7+9, D-3550 Marburg West Germany. **Ind/Abst** MLA Int. Bibliogr. Books Artic. Mod. Lang. Lit.

ELS MARGES. 1- May 1974-. Periodical. SP. Catalan. ty. $13.25. Curial Ediciones Catalaneo, Bruc 144, 37 Barcelona Spain. **Tel** 258 81 01/ 207 13 40. **LC** PC3801.

MASOROT. Series/Titl Pirsume Mifal Masorot Ha-Lashon Shel Edot Yisrael. VFOAT Studies in Language Traditions. V. 1-. 0334-1674. Periodical. Hebrew. ir. **LC** PJ4545.

MATERIALI E CONTRIBUTI PER LA STORIA DELLA NARRATIVA GRECO-LATINA. Main/Corp Perugia. Universita. Istituto di Filoligica Latina. 1-. IT. Italian. ir. Editrice Elia, Viale dell'Universita 21-23, 00185 Roma, Perugia Italy. **LC** PA3040.

MATERIALS FOR THE ASSYRIAN DICTIONARY. See Encyclopedias & General Reference Books.

MATERIALY - RESPUBLIKANSKA NARADA Z PYTAN ONOMASTYKY. Main/Corp Respublikanska Narada Z Pytan Onomastyky. VFOAT Pytannia Onomastyky. 2-. UR. Ukrainian (Russian). **LC** PG303.

MATERIAUX POUR L'ETUDE DE L'EXTREME-ORIENT MODERNE ET CONTEMPORAIN. ETUDES LINGUISTIQUES. Main/Corp Maison des Sciences de l'Homme (Paris, France). 1- 1966-). 0076-5252. Monographic Series. US. French. ir. Walter de Gruyter Inc, 200 Saw Mill River Road, Hawthorne NY 10532. **Tel** (914)747-0110.

MAYGAMV. VFOAT Maigaum, Periodical. Konkani (in (Kannada Script)). sm. 25.00. G D'Souza Kala Kuteer Mannagudda, Bangalore 3 India. **LC** PK2231.

MEDDELANDEN FRAN INSTITUTIONEN FOR NORDISKA SPRAK VID STOCKHOLMS UNIVERSITET. VFOAT MINS. No. 1-. 0348-3568. Monographic Series. SW. Swedish. ir. Inst for Nordiska Sprak, Stockholms Universitet, S-106 91 Stockholm Sweden. **Tel** (08)162543. Ed C H Platzack. adv acc. Papers and monographs about language, mainly Swedish.

MEDEDELINGEN VAN HET P.J. MEERTENS-INSTITUUT. See Folklore.

MEDIEN. Periodical. German. ir. 32.00. Verlag Volker Spiess, Postfach 147, 1000 Berlin 62 West Germany. **LC** P87.

MEDIOEVO ROMANZO. Vol. 1- 1974-. 0390-0711. Periodical. IT. Italian. ty. 90.000 Domestic, 120.000 Foreign. Societa Editrice Il Mulino Spa, Via Santo Stefano 6, 40125 Bologna Italy. **Ind/Abst** MLA Int. Bibliogr. Books Artic. Mod. Lang. Lit., Recent Publ. Artic. **LC** PC4.

MEDITERRANEAN LANGUAGE REVIEW. Vol. 1-. Periodical. English (French, German, Italian, and Spanish). ir. Otto Harrassowitz Verlag, D-6200 Wiesbaden, 1 Taunusstrasse 14, Postfach 2929 Federal Republic of Germany.

MEDIUM AEVUM. See Literature.

MELANGES - INSTITUT DOMINICAIN D'ETUDES ORIENTALES DU CAIRE. Main/Corp Institut Dominicain d'Etudes Orientales du Caire. VFOAT M.I.D.E.O. 1- 1954-. 0575-1330. Periodical. French. ir. Sirovic Bookshop, PO Box 615, Cairo Egypt. **LC** PJ9. **DD** 492.705.

MELBOURNE SLAVONIC STUDIES. V. 1- 1967-. AT. English (Russian). an. 10.00. University of Melbourne, Department of Russian Language and Literature, Parkville Victoria 3052 Australia. **Tel** 03 344 5193. Ed P V Cubberley and R Sussex. **Ind/Abst** MLA Int. Bibliogr. Books Artic. Mod. Lang. Lit. **LC** PG1. **DD** 491.8. **Circ** 150. Covers any Slavonic area, but especially language and literature.

MEMBERSHIP DIRECTORY - AATG. See Yearbooks, Almanacs, Directories.

MEMBERSHIP DIRECTORY - AMERICAN ASSOCIATION OF TEACHERS OF FRENCH. See Yearbooks, Almanacs, Directories.

MEMORIILE SECTIEI DE STIINTE FILOLOGICE, LITERATURA SI ARTE. VFOAT Memoirs of the Section of Philological Sciences, Literature and Arts of the Academy of the Socialist Republic of Romania. Periodical. RM. Romanian (English, French, and Russian). ir. LEI 9, 25. Calea Victoriei 125, R-79717 Bucuresti Romania. **LC** P1.A1. **DD** 405.

MENG YA. VFOAT Mengya. Began in 1956. Periodical. CH. Chinese. mo. $6.21. China Publication Centre, PO Box 2820, Beijing China. **LC** PL2250. Chun Chung Wen i (Shang-Hai, China), Chieh Tou Wen I; Kung Jen Hsi Tso.

MESTER. See Literature.

META. V. 11- Mar. 1966-. 0026-0452. Periodical. CN. French (English). qt. $17.02. Presses de l'Universite, University of Montreal, CP 6128, Montreal Quebec H3C 3J7 Canada. **Tel** (514)343-6321. Ed Andre Clas. **Ind/Abst** Lang. Lang. Behav. Abstr., MLA Int. Bibliogr. Books Artic. Mod. Lang. Lit., Point Repere, Sociol. Abstr. adv acc. **Circ** 3,000. (ctrl). Features wide-ranging articles on linguistics applied to translating and interpreting: translation theory, stylistics, comparative terminological studies, automatized translating, documentation, etc. Journal des Traducteurs, 0316-3024.

MICHIGAN GERMANIC STUDIES. V. 1- Spring 1975-. 0098-8030. Periodical. US. Multilingual (English or German). sa. $25.00 Domestic, $26.00 Foreign. University of Michigan, Department of Germanic Languages and Literatures, 3110 Modern Language Building, Ann Arbor MI 48109-1275. **Tel** (313)764-8018. Ed Valentine C Hubbs. **Ind/Abst** MLA Int. Bibliogr. Books Artic. Mod. Lang. Lit., Sociol. Abstr., Recent Publ. Artic. **LC** PD1. **DD** 430.05. bk rev. adv acc. **Circ** 300. Scholarly articles on Germanic literatures and linguistics.

MICHIGAN ROMANCE STUDIES. See Literature.

MICHIGAN SLAVIC CONTRIBUTIONS. 1- 1968-). 0076-8103. Monographic Series. US. English. ir. University of Michigan, Department of Slavic Languages & Literatures, Ann Arbor MI 48109.

MICHIGAN SLAVIC MATERIALS. No. 1-. 0543-9930. Monographic Series. US. Russian. ir. University of Michigan, Slavic Department, 3040 Modern Language Building, Ann Arbor MI 48109. **Tel** (313)763-4496. **LC** PG13.

MICHIGAN SLAVIC TRANSLATIONS. No. 1- 1972-. Monographic Series. US. English. ir. University of Michigan, Department of Slavic Languages & Literature, Ann Arbor MI 48109.

MID-HUDSON LANGUAGE STUDIES. V. 1- 1978-. 0272-717X. US. English. **Ind/Abst** MLA Int. Bibliogr. Books Artic. Mod. Lang. Lit. **LC** PN2. **DD** 809.

MIN TSU YU WEN. VFOAT Minzu Yuwen. Began in Feb. 1979. Periodical. Chinese. bm. $5.40. China Publication Centre, PO Box 2820, Beijing China. **Tel** 890771. Ed Fu Mao-Ji. **LC** PL1004. **DD** 495.105. **Circ** 4,000. (ctrl). Contains description of Chinese minority languages and general linguistics, and comparative studies of Sino-Tibetan, Kam-Tai and Miao-Yao languages.

MINNESOTA ENGLISH JOURNAL. Periodical. US. English. sa. $10.00. Minnesota Council Teachers English, Box 53 Mankato State University, Mankato MN 56001. **Tel** (218)755-2000.

MINORITY AND SECOND LANGUAGE EDUCATION. ELEMENTARY AND SECONDARY LEVELS. See Education (General).

MINOS. V. 1- 1951-. 0544-3733. Periodical. SP. Multilingual. ir. University of Salamanca, Apartado 325, Salamanca Spain. **Tel** 923 21 40 30. **Ind/Abst** MLA Int. Bibliogr. Books Artic. Mod. Lang. Lit. **LC** P1035.

MISCELANEA DE ESTUDIOS ARABES Y HEBRAICOS. V. 1- 1952-. 0544-408X. Periodical. Spanish. sa. **LC** PJ3001. **DD** 492.05.

MISZELLEN. Series/Titl Hamburger Phonetische Beitrage. Began with Vol. for 1973. 0341-3187. English (French and German). an. Helmut Buske Verlag, Schluterstrasse 14, POB 13 22 55, D-2000 Hamburg 13 West Germany. **LC** P1.A1. **DD** 414.05.

MITHILA-BHARATI. 1- 1969-. Periodical. Maithili. ir. **LC** PK1811.

MITTELLATEINISCHES JAHRBUCH. See Yearbooks, Almanacs, Directories.

MLA DIRECTORY OF PERIODICALS. See Yearbooks, Almanacs, Directories.

MLA JOB INFORMATION LIST. ENGLISH ED. See Occupations and Careers.

MLA NEWSLETTER. Main/Corp Modern Language Association of America. VAT Modern Language Association Newsletter. V. 1-. 0160-5720. Periodical. US. English. qt. $3.00. Modern Language Association of America, 62 5th Avenue, New York NY 10011. **Tel** (212)741-5588. adv acc. **Circ** 28,000. The newsletter contains articles of professional interest to members of the MLA.

MLBD SERIES IN LINGUISTICS. Vol. 1-. Monographic Series. English. ir. Motilal Banarsidass, 41 U A Bungalow Road, Delhi 110 007 India.

MLN. See Literature.

THE MODERN LANGUAGE JOURNAL. V. 1- Oct. 1916-. 0026-7902. Periodical. US. English. qt. $15.00 Domestic, $18.00 Foreign. MLJ Business Office, University of Wisconsin Press, 114 North Murray Street, Madison WI 53715. **Ind/Abst** Annu. Bibliogr. Engl. Lang. Lit., Educ. Index, Lang. Teach.,

Lang. Lang. Behav. Abstr., MLA Int. Bibliogr. Books Artic. Mod. Lang. Lit., Sociol. Abstr., Book Rev. Index, Index Book Rev. Humanit., Int. Index Multi Media Inf., Media Rev. Dig., Psychol. Abstr., Curr. Index J. Educ. **LC** PB1. **DD** 407. **CODEN** MOLJA8.

MODERN LANGUAGE QUARTERLY. **VFOAT** MLQ. V. 1- Mar. 1940-. 0026-7929. Periodical. US. English. qt. $15.00. University of Washington, 4045 Brooklyn Avenue NE JA 15, Seattle WA 98105. **Tel** (206)543-5900. **Ind/Abst** Annu. Bibliogr. Engl. Lang. Lit., Abstr. Engl. Stud., MLA Int. Bibliogr. Books Artic. Mod. Lang. Lit., Index Book Rev. Humanit., Soc. Sci. Index, Humanit. Index, Years Work Eng. Stud. **LC** PB1. **DD** 405.

MODERN LANGUAGE REVIEW. (THE MODERN LANGUAGE REVIEW). V. 1- Oct. 1905-. 0026-7937. Periodical. UK. English. qt. Modern Humanities Research Association, Downing College, Cambridge England. **Ind/Abst** Annu. Bibliogr. Engl. Lang. Lit., Abstr. Engl. Stud., MLA Int. Bibliogr. Books Artic. Mod. Lang. Lit., Book Rev. Index, Index Book Rev. Humanit., Ref. Source, Soc. Sci. Index, Humanit. Index. **LC** PB1. **DD** 405. Index in last issue of volume - attached. (cum index). *Modern Language Quarterly.*

MODERN LANGUAGES. *See* Education (General).

MODERN PHILOLOGY. Began with V. 1, June 1903. Periodical. US. English. qt. University of Chicago Press, PO Box 37005, Chicago IL 60637. **Tel** (312)753-3347. **Ind/Abst** Humanit. Index.

MODERNA SPRAK. V. 1- 1907. 0026-8577. Periodical. SW. Swedish. qt. 165.-. Modern Language Teachers Association, Storangens Standvag 2, 131 41 Nacka Sweden. **Tel** 08/7163257. **Ed** Gustav Korlen. **Ind/Abst** Abstr. Engl. Stud., MLA Int. Bibliogr. Books Artic. Mod. Lang. Lit., Lang. Lang. Behav. Abstr., Annu. Bibliogr. Engl. Lang. Lit., Lang. Teach., Sociol. Abstr., Years Work Eng. Stud. **LC** PB5. **DD** 410.5. (cum index). bk rev. adv acc. **Circ** 1,700. Articles on the English, German, and French languages; also has literature reviews.

MODERNE SPRACHEN. Vol. 1- 1956?. 0026-8666. Periodical. AU. German. sa. Verband der Osterreichischen Neuphilologen, Universitsstr 11, 1010 Wien 1 Austria. **Ind/Abst** MLA Int. Bibliogr. Books Artic. Mod. Lang. Lit., Lang. Teach.

MON-KHMER STUDIES. 0147-5207. US. English. an. $10.00. University of Hawaii Press, 2840 Kolowalu Street, Honolulu HI 96822. **Tel** (808)948-8697. **Ed** Stephen O'Harrow. **Ind/Abst** MLA Int. Bibliogr. Books Artic. Mod. Lang. Lit. **LC** PL4301. **DD** 495.93. **Circ** 200. Original contributions that advance knowledge of the structure and history of individual Mon-Khmer languages or contribute to the reconstruction of proto-Mon-Khmer and proto-Austroasiatic.

MONATSHEFTE. *See* Literature.

MONATSHEFTE (MADISON, WIS. : 1946). (MONATSHEFTE). **VFOAT** Monatshefte fur Deutschen Unterricht, Deutsche Sprache und Literatur. Vol. 38, No. 1 (Jan. 1946)-. 0026-9271. Periodical. US. German and English. qt. University of Wisconsin Press, 114 North Murray Street, Madison WI 53715. **Tel** (608)262-4952. **Ind/Abst** MLA Int. Bibliogr. Books Artic. Mod. Lang. Lit., Index Book Rev. Humanit. **LC** PF3003. **DD** 430.5. (cum index). *Monatshefte fur Deutschen Unterricht.*

LA MONDA LINGVO-PROBLEMO. V. 1-6. 0026-9344. Periodical. US. articles in various languages with summaries in Esperanto. ty. $39.00. Esperanto Language Service Company, 452 Aldine Apartment 501, Chicago IL 60657. **Ind/Abst** Sociol. Abstr.

MONT FOLLICK SERIES. V. 1- 1969-. Monographic Series. UK. English. ir. Manchester University Press, Journals Department, Oxford Road, Manchester M13 9PL England. **Tel** 061 273 5539. **Ed** W Haas. Series of volumes based on lectures devoted to the study of written language.

MONUMENTA GERMANIAE ACUSTICA. KATALOG. **Series/Titl** Phonai. Lautbibliothek der Europaischen Sprachen und Mundarten. Deutsche Reihe A. 1965-. 0544-9863. German. ir. **LC** PF5002.

MOVOZNAVSTVO; NAUKOVI ZAPYSKY. V. 1- 1941-. 0027-2833. UR. Ukrainian. bm. $14.50. Victor Kamkin Inc (74309), 12224 Parklawn Drive, Rockville MD 20852. **Tel** (301)881-5973. **Ind/Abst** Sociol. Abstr., Lang. Lang. Behav. Abstr., MLA Int. Bibliogr. Books Artic. Mod. Lang. Lit. **LC** PG3801.

THE MST ENGLISH QUARTERLY. V. 1- 1951-. 0047-5289. Periodical. PH. English. qt. Office of Supervisors of Secondary English, Manila Science HS Taft Avenue, Manila Philippines. **Ed** Thelma A Soriano. **Ind/Abst** Lang. Teach. bk rev. adv acc. **Circ** 700. Publishes articles on the teaching of language, reading, and literature at the secondary level including lesson plans found workable in teaching English as an alternative language.

MULIKA. *See* Literature.

MUNCHENER OSTASIATISCHE STUDIEN. *See* Literature.

MUNCHENER STUDIEN ZUR SPRACHWISSENSCHAFT. Vol. 1-. 0100-2910. Periodical. GW. German. ir. Kitzinger in Kommission, Schelling Str 25, 8 Muenchen 40 West Germany. **Tel** (089)283537. **Ind/Abst** MLA Int. Bibliogr. Books Artic. Mod. Lang. Lit., Lang. Lang. Behav. Abstr., Sociol. Abstr. **LC** P25. **Circ** 400. (ctrl). Linguistics for Indo-German, Indo-Arian and all the old languages in the Middle East area.

MUNCHNER GERMANISTISCHE BEITRAGE. **VFOAT** Munchener Germanistische Beitrage. 0077-1872. Monographic Series. GW. German. ir. Wilhelm Fink Verlag, Ohmstrasse 5, 8 Muenchen 40 West Germany. **Tel** -89/348017-18. **Ed** Wolfgang Harms, Renate von Heydebrand, and Theo Vennemann. **Ind/Abst** MLA Int. Bibliogr. Books Artic. Mod. Lang. Lit. *Munchener Germanistische Beitrage.*

MUNHWA OYON. Periodical. English (Korean). ir. Chusik Hoesa Munhwa Oyon, P O Box Sodaemun Ucheguk Sodaemun-Ku, Seoul 120 Korea. **LC** PE1131.

MUNHWAO HAKSUP. V. 1- June 1968-. Periodical. Korean. ir. **LC** PL901.

MUSEUM PHILOLOGUM LONDINIENSE. V. 1-. English, French or Italian. ir. A Hakkert, Calle Alfambra 26, Las Palmas G C Spain. **LC** PA1.A1. **DD** 880.05.

MUSU KALBA. **Main/Corp** LTSR Paminklu Apsaugos Ir Krastotyros Draugija. Kalbos Komisija. UR. Lithuanian. Traku 2, Vilnius Lithuanian SSR. **LC** PG8501.

MUTTERSPRACHE. 1949-. 0027-514X. Periodical. GW. German. ir. 96.-. Gesellschaft fuer Deutsche Sprache EV, Postfach 26 69, D6200 Wiesbaden 1 West Germany. **Tel** 06121/ 52 2779. **Ed** Otto Nuessler. **Ind/Abst** MLA Int. Bibliogr. Books Artic. Mod. Lang. Lit., Lang. Lang. Behav. Abstr., Sociol. Abstr. **LC** PF3003. **DD** 430.5. bk rev. adv acc. **Circ** 1,000. Journal for usage and research of the German language. Theoretical foundations of language research, semantics, etymology, technical language, current language of German in the world, also directed at non-linguists. *Muttersprache.*

NAAMKUNDE. Volume 1- 1969-. Periodical. NE. Dutch (Flemish with some English and German). qt. Naamkunde, Keizersgracht 569-571, Amsterdam Netherlands. **Ind/Abst** MLA Int. Bibliogr. Books Artic. Mod. Lang. Lit., Lang. Lang. Behav. Abstr. **LC** PF701. *Mededelingen.*

NACHRICHTEN DER AKADEMIE DER WISSENSCHAFTEN IN GOTTINGEN. 1, PHILOLOGISCH-HISTORISCHE KLASSE. (NACHRICHTEN DER AKADEMIE DER WISSENSCHAFTEN IN GOTTINGEN PHILOLOGISCH-HISTORISCHE KLASSE). **Main/Corp** Akademie der Wissenschaften, Gottingen. Philologisch-Historische Klasse. 1941-. 0065-5287. Periodical. GW. German. ir. Vandenhoeck & Ruprecht, Postfach 3753, Theaterstr 13, D 3400 Goettingen West Germany. **Tel** 0551/ 65061. **Ind/Abst** Energy Res. Abstr. adv acc.

NAFSA STUDIES AND PAPERS. ENGLISH LANGUAGE SERIES. **Main/Corp** National Association for Foreign Student Affairs. **VAT** National Association for Foreign Student Affairs Studies and Papers. English Language Series. No. 1/ 2-. US. English. an. **LC** PE1128.A2.

NALLD JOURNAL. (NALLD JOURNAL : NEWSLETTER OF THE NATIONAL ASSOCIATION OF LANGUAGE LABORATORY DIRECTORS). **VAT** National Association of Learning Laboratory Directors Journal. 0027-5905. Periodical. US. English. ty. $20.00. University of Louisville Academic Publishers, Administrative Building, Louisville KY 40292. **Tel** (502)588-5417. **Ind/Abst** Lang. Lang. Behav. Abstr., Curr. Index J. Educ., Lang. Teach., Sociol. Abstr. **LC** PB36. **DD** 418.007. *NALLD Newsletter.*

NAME GLEANER. (THE NAME GLEANER). **VFOAT** Glanure des Noms. V. 1- Sept. 1976-. 0700-9445. Periodical. CN. French (English). ir. 10.00. A Rayburn Secretariat Noms Geographiques, 580 rue Booth, Ottawa Ontario K1A 0E4 Canada. **DD** 412.05.

NAMES. V. 1- Mar. 1953-. 0027-7738. Periodical. US. English. qt. $30.00 Domestic, $35.00 Foreign. American Name Society, 7 East 14th Street, 17U W H Finke, New York NY 10003. **Tel** (212)929-8434. **Ed** Kelsie B Harder. **Ind/Abst** Hist. Abstr., Part A, Mod. Hist. Abstr., Hist. Abst., Part B, Twent. Century Abstr., MLA Int. Bibliogr. Books Artic. Mod. Lang. Lit., GeoRef, Ref. Source, Index Book Rev. Humanit., Bull. Signal., Onoma, Hist. Abstr., Am. Hist. Life, Geogr. Abstr., Bibliogr. Index Geol., Hist. Abstr., Recent Publ. Artic. **LC** P769. **DD** 929.405,910.3. (cum index). bk rev. **Circ** 1,200. Study of personal, place and literary names, as well as trade-names, slang, and nick-names.

NAOS, NOTES AND MATERIALS FOR THE LINGUISTIC STUDY OF THE SACRED. **VFOAT** Notes and Materials for the Linguistic Study of the Sacred. Vol. 1, No. 1 (Winter 1984-1985)-. Periodical. US. English (issued also in a Spanish translation). ty.

NASE REC. Vol. 1- 1917-. 0027-8203. Periodical. CS. Czech. bm. Kubon and Sagner, Postfach 34 01 08, 8 Munchen 34 West Germany. **Tel** (089)52 20 27. **LC** PG4004. Deals with problems of Czech and of language culture in general. Contains articles on the structure of Czech, on its stylistic variants, and on the norm and codification of the standard literary language.

NATIONAL NEWSLETTER - CANADIAN PARENTS FOR FRENCH. (NATIONAL NEWSLETTER). **VAT** CPF National Newsletter, Canadian Parents for French National Newsletter. Issue No. 10 (June 1980)-. 0715-8904. Periodical. CN. English. Canadian Parents for French, PO Box 8470 Terminal, Ottawa Ontario K1G 3H6 Canada. **DD** 440.7071. *Newsletter (Canadian Parents for French), 0229-7671.*

NATURAL LANGUAGE & LINGUISTIC THEORY. **VFOAT** Natural Language and Linguistic Theory. Vol. 1, No. 1-. 0167-806X. Periodical. English. qt. $58.00. D Reidel Publishing Company, PO Box 17, 3300 AA Dordrecht Netherlands. **Tel** (31)78-334911. **Ed** F Heny and J Maling. **LC** P1. **DD** 410.5. bk rev. adv acc. **Circ** 1,000. Discussion of theoretical research paying attention to natural language data, bridging descriptive work and highly theoretical, less empirical work.

NAVALAKATHA. *See* Literature.

NEOLOGIE EN MARCHE. No. 16 (1980)-. 0713-214X. Periodical. CN. French (certaines livraisons comprennent du texte en Anglais). Gouvernement du Quebec, 600 St Amable 4E Etage, Quebec G1R 4Z1 Canada. **DD** 448.105. *Neologie en Marche. Serie A. Langue Generale, 0380-9366; Neologie en Marche. Serie B. Langues de Specialties, 0701-7995.*

NEOLOGIE EN MARCHE. SERIE B. LANGUES DE SPECIALITES. **Main/Corp** Quebec (Province). Office de la Langue Francaise. CN. English (French). Editeur Officiel du Quebec, 1283 Boul Charest Quest, Quebec PQ G1N 2C9 Canada. **LC** PC3631. **DD** 447. *Neologie en Marche. Serie B. Langues de Specialites, 0701-7995.*

NEOPHILOLOGICA. **Series/Titl** Prace Naukowe Uniwersytety Slaskiego W Katowicach. V. 1-. 0208-5550. French (text in German). ir. 58.00. Uniwersytet Slaski, Ul Bankowa 14, 40-007 Katowice Poland. **LC** PB5. **DD** 410.5.

NEOPHILOLOGUS. V. 1- 1915-. 0028-2677. Periodical. NE. English (text in French, German, Italian and Spanish). qt. $70.97. Wolters-Noordhoff, Postbus 58, 9700 MB Groningen Netherlands. **Tel** 050/22 68 86. **Ind/Abst** Abstr. Engl. Stud., Lang. Lang. Behav. Abstr., Index Book Rev. Humanit., Sociol. Abstr., MLA Int. Bibliogr. Books Artic. Mod. Lang. Lit. **LC** PB5. **DD** 410.5. (cum index).

NEPALI AKADAMI PATRIKA. *See* Literature.

NEPOLNOZNACHNYE SLOVA. Began in 1974. Periodical. UR. Russian. 0.60. IZD-VO Stavropolskaia Pravda, Stavropol Ul Spartaka 10, Stavropol Russia SFSR USSR. **LC** PG2380.

NEUE GERMANISTIK. *See* Literature.

NEUINDISCHE STUDIEN. Vol. 1- 1970-. Monographic Series. German and English. ir. **LC** 1502.

NEUROLINGUISTICS. 1-. 0301-6412. Monographic Series. English. ir. **Ed** R Hoops and Y Lebrun. **Ind/Abst** Lang. Lang. Behav. Abstr., Biol. Abstr. **NLM** W1 NE328K. **CODEN** NEURDL.

Linguistics

NEW SPEAKERS AND LECTURERS. Issue No. 1 (Apr. 1982)-. 0731-2466. US. English. sa. $125.00. Gale Research Company, Book Tower, Detroit MI 48226. Ed Jacqueline O'Brien and Paul Wasserman. LC PN4007. DD 808.5102573. Two supplements will update speakers and lecturers: how to find them by providing information on new speakers and lecture bureaus.

NEWSLETTER - ALBERTA ENGLISH LANGUAGE ARTS COUNCIL OF THE ALBERTA TEACHERS' ASSOCIATION. Main/Corp Alberta English Language Arts Council. V. 17- July 1979-. 0708-8302. Periodical. CN. English. ir. Alberta English Language Arts Council, Alberta Teachers' Association, 11010 - 142 Street, Edmonton Alberta T5N 2R1 Canada. DD 428.007. Newsletter, 0382-5019.

NEWSLETTER - AMERICAN DIALECT SOCIETY. Main/Corp American Dialect Society. V. 1- Feb. 1969-. 0002-8193. Periodical. US. English. ty. American Dialect Society, MacMurray College/English Department, Jacksonville IL 62650. Ind/Abst MLA Int. Bibliogr. Books Artic. Mod. Lang. Lit. LC PE2801. DD 427.973.

NEWSLETTER - LANGUAGE TEACHERS ASSOCIATION CEASED. Main/Corp Nova Scotia Teachers Union. Language Teachers Association. V. 18, No. 2 (Apr. 1977)-V. 26, No. 2. 0703-1262. Periodical. CN. English. ty. Nova Scotia Teachers Union, PO Box 1060, Armdale Nova Scotia B3L 4L7 Canada. DD 407. Newsletter, 0384-0808.

NEWSLETTER OF THE GYPSY LORE SOCIETY, NORTH AMERICAN CHAPTER. See Anthropology.

NICHIJOGO SHINDAN. 1-. JA. Japanese. ir. 240 Single Issue. Asahi Shinbunsha 3-2, Tsukiji 5 Chuo-Ku, Tokyo-To 104 Japan. LC PL645.

NICHTKONVENTIONELLE LITERATUR LINGUISTIK : INHALTSVERZEICHNIS DER NEUERWERBUNGEN. Series/Titl Sondersammelgebiet Linguistik. German (English, French, or Spanish). ir. Stadt-Und Universitatsbibliothek Frankfurt Am Main, 6000 Frankfurt Am Main 1, Bockenheimer Landstrasse 134-138, Frankfurt West Germany. Tel (069)7907235. LC Z7003, P121. DD 016.4105. Covers speech, language, linguistics, neurolinguistics, psycholinguistics, sociolinguistics, syntax, semantics, phonoloy, and language teaching.

NIEDERDEUTSCHES WORT. Began in 1960. 0078-0545. GW. German. an. Aschendorffsche Verlagsbuchhndlung, Postfach 1124, 4400 Munster West Germany. Tel 251/6901. Ind/Abst MLA Int. Bibliogr. Books Artic. Mod. Lang. Lit. LC PF5601. Contributions to the philology of low-German.

NIEUWE TAALGIDS. (DE NIEUWE TAALGIDS). Vol. 1, 1907-. 0028-9922. Periodical. NE. Dutch. bm. $49.75. Wolters-Noordhoff BV, Postbus 58, 9700 MB Groningen Netherlands. Tel 050-16 2189. Ind/Abst Lang. Lang. Behav. Abstr., MLA Int. Bibliogr. Books Artic. Mod. Lang. Lit., Sociol. Abstr. LC PF4. DD 439.3105.

NIHONGO KYOIKU. VFOAT Journal of Japanese Language Teaching. 0389-4037. JA. English (Japanese). ir. 10000 Membership. Nihongo Kyoiku Gakkai, Society for the Teaching of Japanese as a Foreign Language, c/o 4th Mori Building, 19-12 Toranomon 1-Chome Minato-Ku, Tokyo 105 Japan. LC PL539.3.

NIHONGO TO NIHONGO KYOIKU. 3- 1974-. JA. Japanese. ir. Keito Gijuku Daigaku Kokusai Senta, 15-45 Mita 2-Chome Minato-Ku, Tokyo 108 Japan. LC PL501.

NIMLA. (JOURNAL OF THE MODERN LANGUAGE ASSOCIATION OF NORTHERN IRELAND). VFOAT N.I.M.L.A. Oct. 1978-. 0143-859X. Periodical. UK. English. sa. Secretary of the Editorial Board, Department of Modern Languages, New University of Ulster, Coleraine BT52 1SA Northern Ireland. Ind/Abst Lang. Teach. LC PB1. DD 405.

NM. NEUSPRACHLICHE MITTEILUNGEN AUS WISSENSCHAFT UND PRAXIS. (NEUSPRACHLICHE MITTEILUNGEN AUS WISSENSCHAFT UND PRAXIS : NM). VFOAT NM. 0028-3983. Periodical. German. qt. $19.24. Cornelsen-Velhagen & Klasing, Postfach 8729, D-4800 Bielefeld 1 Germany. Tel 05217872 211. Ind/Abst MLA Int. Bibliogr. Books Artic. Mod. Lang. Lit., Lang. Lang. Behav. Abstr. LC PB3. DD 808.5102573. bk rev. adv acc. Circ 4,750. Essays about educational matters concerning modern languages e.g. English, French, Dutch, Spanish and Italian.

NONMUNJIP CEASED. VFOAT Theses Collection, A Collection of Themes and Essays. V. 1 Series (1968)-. Periodical. KO. Multilingual. an. Hanguk Oegugo Taehak, 270 Imun-dong, Tongdaemun-ku Seoul Korea. LC P9. DD 405.

NORDIC JOURNAL OF LINGUISTICS. V. 1-. 0332-5865. Periodical. No. English. be. 33.-. Universitetsforlaget, PO Box 2959-Toyen, Oslo 6 Norway. Tel (45)-2-27 60 60. Ed Eva Ejerhed. Ind/Abst MLA Int. Bibliogr. Books Artic. Mod. Lang. Lit., Lang. Lang. Behav. Abstr., Psychol. Abstr. LC P1.A1. DD 410.5. Circ 400. Concerned with all branches of linguistics; publishes replies and comments on articles published in the journal and review articles or reviews on current books. Norwegian Journal of Linguistics. Norsk Tidsskrift for Sprogvidenska.

NORDISKT NAMNFORSKARREGISTER. Series/Titl Norna-Rapporter. 1973-. Swedish. ir. Nordiska Samarbetskommitten, for Namnforskning, St Johannesgatan 11 S-7522, Uppsala Sweden. LC P321.9.

NORDLYD. NR. 1-. Periodical. NO. English (German or Norwegian). ir. Free. School of Languages and Literature, PO Box 1090, 9001 Troms Norway. LC P1.A1. DD 410.5.

NOTES AND QUERIES. See Literature.

NOTES ON LINGUISTICS. No. 1 (Jan. 1977)-. 0736-0673. Periodical. US. English. qt. $9.40. Summer Institute of Linguistics, 7500 West Camp Wisdom Road, Dallas TX 75236. Tel (214)298-3331. Ed Eugene Loos. Ind/Abst MLA Int. Bibliogr. Books Artic. Mod. Lang. Lit. LC P1. DD 410.5. bk rev. Circ 850. (ctrl) Designed to provide linguistic fieldworkers with news, reviews, announcements and articles that will create a current interest in linguistics.

NOTES ON LITERACY. 0737-6707. Periodical. US. English. qt. $7.50 Domestic, $8.50 Foreign. Dallas Center Bookstore/Summer Institute of Linguistics, 7500 West Camp Wisdom Road, Dallas TX 75236. Tel (214)298-3331. Ed Joice Franklin and Peggy Wendell. DD 410. bk rev. Circ 600. Containing articles written by orthography and applied practical topics pertaining to literacy projects world-wide occasional paper.

NOTORU DAMU SEISHIN JOSJI DAIGAKU KIYO : GAIKOKUGO GAIKOKU BUNGAKU HEN. VFOAT Notre Dame Seishin University Kiyo: Foreign Language Studies, Foreign Literature. V. 1- (Tsukan No. 12)-. JA. Japanese. ir. Notoru Damu Seishin Joshi Daigaku, 16-9 Ifukucho 2, Okayama 700 Japan. LC P9. N68A. Kiyo.

NOTRE LANGUE ET NOTRE CULTURE. V. 1- Fall 1970-. 0380-5352. Periodical. CN. French. ir. ATA/Le Conseil Francais, 11010 142 St Barnett House, Edmonton Alberta T5N 2R1 Canada. Tel 403-453-2411. Ind/Abst Can. Educ. Index.

NOUVELLES - ASSOCIATION DES PROFESSEURS DE FRANCAIS DES UNIVERSITES ET COLLEGES CANADIENS. (NOUVELLES). 0821-4549. Periodical. CN. French. Association des Professeurs de Francais des Universites et Colleges Canadiens, c/o Y Lacroix, Dep d'Etudes Litteraires, Universite du Quebec A Montreal, C P 8888 Succursale A, Montreal Quebec H3C 3P8 Canada. DD 440.71171. Nouvelles, 0708-7500.

NOUVELLES DE LA REPUBLIQUE DES LETTRES (NAPLES, ITALY). (NOUVELLES DE LA REPUBLIQUE DES LETTRES). 1981-1-. 0392-2332. Periodical. English (French, German, Italian, and Spanish). sa. $47.00. Prismi Editrice Politechnica Napoli, Via F Caracciolo 17, 80122 Napoli Italy. Ind/Abst MLA Int. Bibliogr. Books Artic. Mod. Lang. Lit. LC AS222.N775. DD 050.

NOUVELLES DE L'ACPI. (LES NOUVELLES DE L'ACPI). VFOAT CAIT News. VAT Nouvelles de l'Association Canadienne des Professeurs d'Immersion Canadian Association of Immersion Teachers News. 0822-9333. Periodical. CN. English (French). ty. Free to Members, $15.00 Nonmembers, $20.00 Institutions. Canadian Association of Immersion Teachers, PO Box 8843 Alta Vista Terminal, Ottawa Ontario K1G 3H8 Canada. DD 448.2421.

LES NOUVELLES INSTRUCTIONS POUR L'ENSEIGNEMENT DES LETTRES DANS LE SECOND CYCLE DU SECOND DEGRE. French. ir. 37 rue Jacob, 75270 Paris Cedex 06 France. LC P57.F8. DD 410.712044.

NOVAIA INOSTRANNAIA LITERATURA PO OBSHCHESTVENNYM NAUKAM : IAZYKOZNANIE. 1976-. UR. Multilingual (Russian). mo. 0.30 Single Issue. Akademiia Nauk SSSR, Ul Krasikova 28/45, Moskva Russia. LC Z7003, P9. Novaia Inostrannaia Literatura Po Iazykoznaniiu.

NOVOE V RUSSKOI LEKSIKE : SLOVARNYE MATERIALY. 77-. UR. Russian. an. 1.40. Izdatelstvo Russkii Iazyk, 103009 Moskva, K-9 Pushkinskaia Ul, Moskva Russian SFSR. LC PG2680.

NOVOE V ZARUBEZHNOI LINGVISTIKE. Vol. 8-. Periodical. UR. Russian. 2.00. Zubovskii Bulvar 17, Moskva 119021 USSR. LC P25. Novoe V Lingvistike.

NUEVA REVISTA DE FILOLOGIA HISPANICA. Vol. 1- July/Sept. 1947-. 0185-0121. Periodical. MX. Spanish. sa. $71.00. Colegio de Mexico, Camino al Ajusco, 20 Pedregal Sta Teresa, 10740 Mexico DF Mexico. Tel 568-68-49. Ed Antonio Alatorre and Beatriz Garza Cuaron. Ind/Abst MLA Int. Bibliogr. Books Artic. Mod. Lang. Lit., Sociol. Abstr., Am. Hist. Life, Hist. Abstr., Hist. Abstr., Part A, Mod. Hist. Abstr., Hist. Abst., Part B, Twent. Century Abstr. LC PC4008. DD 460.5. bk rev. Circ 2,000. (ctrl). Prinicipal themes are on Hispanic and Hispanic American literature and Hispanic linguistics, theory and methodology on literature and linguistics, reviews, articles and a classified bibliography.

NYELVTUDOMANYI KOZLEMENYEK. 1-. 0029-6791. Periodical. HU. Hungarian. sa. Akademiai Kiado, PO Box 24, Budapest 1363 Hungary. Tel 161-053. Ed P Hajdu and K Redei. Ind/Abst MLA Int. Bibliogr. Books Artic. Mod. Lang. Lit., Lang. Lang. Behav. Abstr., Sociol. Abstr. LC AS142. bk rev. Circ 700.

NYSVENSKA STUDIER. Began in 1921. 0345-8768. Periodical. SW. Swedish. an. $11.51. Almqvist & Wiksell, 108 Drottninggatan, PO Box 45150, S-104 30 Stockholm Sweden. Ind/Abst MLA Int. Bibliogr. Books Artic. Mod. Lang. Lit. LC PD5004. Sprak Och Stil.

OBRABOTKA SIMVOLNOI INFORMATSII. Main/Corp Akademiia Nauk SSSR. Vychislitelnyi Tsentr. Vol. 1- 1973-. UR. Russian. 0.47 Each Issue. Akademiia Nauk SSSR, V-333 Ul Vavilova 40, Moskva Russia. LC P98.

OBSERVATIONS GRAMMATICALES ET TERMINOLOGIQUES. 1- 1972/74-. 0703-2005. CN. French. an. Free. Secretariat General, Universite de Montreal, CP 6128 Succursale A, Montreal Quebec H3C 3J7 Canada. DD 448.005. (ctrl).

OBSHCHESTVENNYE NAUKI V SSSR. SERIIA 6 : IAZYKOZNANIE. VFOAT Iazykoznanie. VAT Obshchestvennye Nauki V SSSR. Seriia Shest : Iazykoznanie. Began in 1973. Periodical. UR. Russian. bm. Akademiia Nauk SSSR, Ul Krasikova D 28/45, Moskva USSR. LC P9.

OBSHCHESTVENNYE NAUKI ZA RUBEZHOM. SERIIA 6 : IAZYKOZNANIE. VFOAT Iazykoznanie. VAT Obshchestvennye Nauki za Rubezhom. Seriia Shest: Iazykoznanie. Began in 1973. UR. Russian. qt. Akademiia Nauk SSSR, UL Krasikova D 28/45, Moskva USSR. LC P9.

OCCASIONAL PAPER - UNIVERSITY OF SYDNEY, AUSTRALIAN LANGUAGE RESEARCH CENTRE. Main/Corp Sydney. University. Australian Language Research Centre. No. 1-. 0042-0093. English. ir. Ind/Abst Lang. Lang. Behav. Abstr. LC PE3601.

OCCASIONAL PAPERS IN SLAVIC LANGUAGES AND LITERATURE. Vol. 1, No. 1 (Summer 1982)-. 0739-8972. Periodical. US. English (articles in French or Russian). be. Department of Slavic Language and Literature, University of Washington, Thomason Hall, Seattle WA 98155. Tel (206)543-6848. LC PG1. DD 491.7.

Linguistics

OCCASIONAL PUBLICATIONS - EPIGRAPHIC SOCIETY. (OCCASIONAL PUBLICATIONS - THE EPIGRAPHIC SOCIETY). **Main/Corp** Epigraphic Society. V. 1-. 0192-5148. US. English. ir. $25.00. The Epigraphic Society, 6625 Bamburgh Drive, San Diego CA 92117. **Tel** (619)571-1344. Ed Barry Fell. **LC** CN1. **DD** 905. bk rev. **Circ** 800. Discovery and decipherment of ancient rock-cut inscriptions. Relates epigraphs, especially in West Europe, Mediterranean and America.

OCCASIONAL PUBLICATIONS IN ANTHROPOLOGY. LINGUISTICS SERIES. **VFOAT** Linguistics Series. No. 1- 1970-. Monographic Series. US. English. ir. Univeristy of Northern Colorado, Museum of Anthropology, Greeley CO 80639. **LC** P25. **DD** 572.

OCEANIA LINGUISTIC MONOGRAPHS. No. 1-. Monographic Series. AT. English. ir. University of Sydney, Sydney New South Wales Australia 2006. **Tel** (02) 692-2666. Ed L R Hiatt. adv acc. **Circ** 300. Treatises or collections of essays on anthropological topics within the ethnographic region of Oceania. They are occasional publications.

OCEANIC LINGUISTICS. V. 1- Summer 1962-. 0029-8115. Periodical. US. English. sa. $13.00. University of Hawaii Press, 2840 Kolowalu Street, Honolulu HI 96822. **Tel** (808)948-8697. Ed George W Grace. **Ind/Abst** Lang. Lang. Behav. Abstr., MLA Int. Bibliogr. Books Artic. Mod. Lang. Lit., Sociol. Abstr., Recent Publ. Artic. **LC** PL5001. **DD** 499.2. bk rev. adv acc. **Circ** 375. Devoted exclusively to the study of the indigenous languages of the Oceanic area: the aboriginal languages of Australia, the Papuan languages spoken in New Guinea, and the languages of the Austronesian family.

OCEANIC LINGUISTICS SPECIAL PUBLICATION. No. 1-. 0078-3188. Monographic Series. US. English. ir. University of Hawaii Press, 2840 Kolowalu Street, Honolulu HI 96822. **Tel** (808)948-8697. **Ind/Abst** MLA Int. Bibliogr. Books Artic. Mod. Lang. Lit.

OCTE NEWSLETTER. 0828-4636. Periodical. CN. English. ir. $25.00. **DD** 420.70713.

ODENSE UNIVERSITY STUDIES IN ENGLISH. (STUDIES IN ENGLISH). **VFOAT** Odense University Studies in English. V. 1- 1969-. 0078-3293. Monographic Series. DK. English. ir. Odense University Press, 36 Pjentedamsgade, DK 5000 Odense Denmark. **Tel** (09)14 16 11. **Ind/Abst** MLA Int. Bibliogr. Books Artic. Mod. Lang. Lit. Language studies of English and American literature.

ODENSE UNIVERSITY STUDIES IN SCANDINAVIAN LANGUAGES AND LITERATURES. Vol. 3-. Monographic Series. DK. Danish. ir. Odense University Press, 36 Pjentedamsgade, DK 5000 Odense Denmark. **Tel** (09)14 16 11. **LC** PD1513. Studies in Scandinavian Languages.

OEGUK MUNHWA YONGU. **VFOAT** Foreign Cultural Research. Periodical. KO. English (Korean). ir. Choson Taehakkyo Oeguk Munhwa Yonguso 17 Pullo-dong, Tong-ku Kwangju-si Korea. **LC** P9.

OKAZOU. (OKAZOU : BANQUE D'IDEES ET DE RENSEIGNEMENTS EN ALS). Vol. 1, No. 1-. 0713-4274. Periodical. CN. English (French 1980-). qt. Free. Okazou, Centre Educatif et Culturel, 8101 Boulevard Metropolitain, Montreal Quebec H1J 1J9 Canada. **DD** 428.244107.

OKINAWA KOKUSAI DAIGAKU BUNGAKUBU KIYO: EIBUNGAKKA-HEN. **VFOAT** Bulletin of Department of English, Okinawa Kokusai University. JA. English (Japanese). ir. Okinawa Kokusai Daigaku Bungakubu, 276-2 Aza Ginowan, Okinawa-Ken, Ginowan Japan. **LC** PE9. **DD** 425.05.

OLD ENGLISH NEWSLETTER. See Literature.

OLD ENGLISH NEWSLETTER. SUBSIDIA. See Literature.

OLLON HAKPO. **VFOAT** Hanyang Communication Review. V. 1- (1980)-. Periodical. KO. Korean (with summaries in English). ir. Hanyang Taehakkyo Sinmun Pangsong Yonguso, 17 Haengdang-dong, Seongdong-gu 133, Seoul South Korea. **LC** P92.K6.

OMUN YONGU. V. 1- Oct. 1973-. Periodical. Korean. ir. 200 Each Issue. Ilchogak, 9 Kongpyong-Dong Chongno-Ku, Seoul Korea. **LC** PL901.

ONO (CHUNGNAM TAEHAKKYO. PUSOL ONO HULLYONWON). (ONO). **VFOAT** Language. Periodical. English (Korean). an. Chungnam Taehakkyo Pusol Ono Hullyonwon, 220 Kungdon-ri Yusong-Up, Chungnam Korea 300-31. **LC** P9.

ONOHAK. **VFOAT** Eoneohag. V. 1-. Periodical. KO. Korean (summaries in English or French). ir. Hanguk Ono Hakhoe, c/o Department of LInguistics, Seoul National Unviersity, Seoul 151 Korea. **LC** P9.

ONOMA. V. 1- 1950-. 0078-463X. Periodical. BE. French. ty. 1500. Editions Peeters SA, Bondgenotenlaan 153, Box 41, B 3000 Leuven Belgium. **Ind/Abst** MLA Int. Bibliogr. Books Artic. Mod. Lang. Lit. **LC** P323. (cum index). adv acc. (ctrl).

ONOMATOLOSKI PRILOZI. **VFOAT** Contributions Onomatologiques. 1-. Periodical. Serbo-Croatian -C (summaries in English, French, German, and Russian). ir. **LC** P323.4.Y8.

ONSEIGAKKAI KAIHO. THE BULLETIN. **Main/Corp** Nihon Onseigakkai. **VFOAT** Bulletin. 0911-0402. JA. English (Japanese). ir. 6,000.00. Nihon Onseigakkai, 13-12 Daita, 2 Setagaya-Ku (155) Tokyo Japan. **Tel** 03-414-5363. Ed Masao Onishi. **Ind/Abst** Lang. Lang. Behav. Abstr. **LC** PL541. **Circ** 1,300. Brief essays (about 2,000 words) on phonetics: speech theory, speech education, speech pathology and speech art.

ONTARIO NEWSLETTER - CANADIAN PARENTS FOR FRENCH. ONTARIO CHAPTER. (ONTARIO NEWSLETTER). Issue No. 12 (Fall 1982)-. 0826-1857. Periodical. CN. English. qt. $5.00. Canadian Parents for French, Ontario Chapter, PO Box 8470 Terminal, Ottawa Ontario K1G 3H6 Canada. **DD** 440.70713. Ontario Newsletter (Canadian Parents for French), 0826-1849.

ONZE TAAL (AMSTERDAM, NETHERLANDS). (ONZE TAAL : ORGAAN VAN HET GENOOTSCHAAP ONZE TAAL). Vol. 1, No. 1 (March 1932)-. Periodical. Dutch. mo. 20. Genootschap Onze Taal, Prinsessegracht 23, 2514 AP Den Haag Netherlands. **Tel** 070-609107. Ed J Renkema. bk rev. adv acc. **Circ** 15,000. Covers all aspects of the Dutch language including spelling, grammar, idioms, dialects, new words, etymology, new trends, etc. Helps the layman to use his own language as correctly as possible.

ORIENS. V. 1-. Periodical. NE. English (French or German). sa. E J Brill, POB 9000, 2300 PA Leiden The Netherlands. **Ind/Abst** Am. Hist. Life, Hist. Abstr., Part A, Mod. Hist. Abstr., Hist. Abstr., Part B, Twent. Century Abstr., Hist. Abstr. **LC** DS1. **DD** 950.05. (cum index).

ORIENTAL INSTITUTE COMMUNICATIONS. **Main/Corp** University of Chicago. Oriental Institute. No. 1-. 0146-678X. Monographic Series. US. English. ir. University of Chicago Press, PO Box 37005, Chicago IL 60637. **LC** PJ2. **DD** 956.005.

ORIENTALIA LOVANIENSIA PERIODICA. 1 (1970)-. 0085-4522. BE. English, French or German. ir. 1400. Editions Peeters, Boldgenotenlaan 153, BP 41, B 3000 Leuven Belgium. **Ind/Abst** MLA Int. Bibliogr. Books Artic. Mod. Lang. Lit., Old Testam. Abstr. **LC** DS1. adv acc. (ctrl).

ORIZONT. See Literature.

THE ORTESOL JOURNAL. **Main/Corp** Oregon Teachers of English to Speakers of Other Languages. V. 1-. 0192-401X. Periodical. US. English. ir. $8.95. Oregon Teacher of English to Speakers of Other Languages, 15203 SE River Forest Drive, Milwaukie OR 97222. **LC** PE1128.A2. **DD** 428.2407.

OSMANIA PAPERS IN LINGUISTICS. V. 1- Feb. 1975-. Periodical. IN. English. ir. $1.50 Single Issue. Osmania University, Department of Linguistics, Hyderabad India 500007. **Ind/Abst** Lang. Lang. Behav. Abstr. **LC** P1. **DD** 410.5.

OTIA. 1965-. Periodical. BE. French. an. Otia Bulletin de l'Associa-, 7 Place Vingt-Aout, Liege Belgium. **LC** PA2. **DD** 480.05. Bulletin Semestrial - Universite de Liege, Association des Classiques.

OUR HERITAGE. V. 1- 1953-. English (Bengali and Sanskrit). ir. **LC** PK101. (cum index).

OUTLOOK FOR THE MEDIA. **Main/Corp** Paine, Webber, Mitchell, Hutchins. Conference. 10th (1983)-. 0737-8858. US. English. an. $85.00. Knowledge Industry Publications Inc, 701 Winchester Avenue, White Plains NY 10604. **LC** P96.F672. **DD** 001.510973. Annual Conference on the Outlook for the Media.

PACIFIC COAST PHILOLOGY. V. 1- April 1966-. 0078-7469. US. Multilingual (English, French, German and Spanish). an. $5.00. Philological Association of Pacific Coast, English Department, University of Oregon, Eugene OR 97403. **Tel** (619)265-6219. **Ind/Abst** MLA Int. Bibliogr. Books Artic. Mod. Lang. Lit., Years Work Eng. Stud. **LC** P1.A1. adv acc. **Circ** 1,200. (ctrl). Scholarship in languages and literatures.

PACIFIC LINGUISTICS. SERIES A, OCCASIONAL PAPERS. No. 10 (1967)-. 0078-7531. English. ir. Australian National University, Box 4-School of Pacific Studies, Canberra Australian Capital Territory 2600 Australia. Publications. Series A, Occasional Papers.

PACIFIC LINGUISTICS. SERIES B : MONOGRAPHS. No. 7-. 0078-754X. Monographic Series. AT. English. ir. Australian National University, Box 4 School of Pacific Studies, Canberra Australian Capital Territory 2600 Australia. Linguistic Circle of Canberra Publications Series B: Monographs.

PACIFIC LINGUISTICS. SERIES C : BOOKS. No. 1- 1965-. 0078-7558. Monographic Series. AT. English. ir. Australian National University, Box 4, School of Pacific Studies, Canberra Australian Capital Territory 2600 Australia.

PACIFIC LINGUISTICS. SERIES D : SPECIAL PUBLICATIONS. No. 3-. 0078-7566. Monographic Series. AT. English. ir. Australian National University, Box 4 School of Pacific Studies, Canberra Australian Capital Territory 2600 Australia. **LC** UNC. (cum index). Bulletin - Linguistic Circle of Canberra.

PAIDEIA. Began publication with Jan./Feb. 1946 issue. 0030-9435. Periodical. IT. Italian. bm. 30.000. Paideia Editrice, Via Corsica 130, 25125 Brescia Italy. Ed Paideia Editrice. **Ind/Abst** MLA Int. Bibliogr. Books Artic. Mod. Lang. Lit. **LC** Z1007. (cum index). bk rev. **Circ** 1,000.

PAKS - ARBEITSBERICHT. **Main/Corp** Stuttgart. Universitat. Institut fur Linguistik. **VFOAT** Project on Applied Contrastive Linguistics. German. ir.

PALAESTRA . . . UNTERSUCHUNGEN UND TEXTE AUS DER DEUTSCHEN UND ENGLISCHEN PHILOLOGIE. 1- 1898-. Periodical. GW. German. ir. Vandenhoeck & Ruprecht, Postfach 3753/Theaterstr 13, D-3400 Goettingen West Germany. **Tel** 0551/65061.

PALLAS (TOULOUSE, FRANCE). (PALLAS). Began in 1953. FR. French (summaries in English). an. Regisseur d'Service, Publications l'Universite d'Toulouse-Mirail, 56 rue Taur, 31000 Toulouse France. **Tel** 23 07 50. **LC** PA2. **DD** 937.005.

PANGON. Series/Titl Pangon Chosa Yongu Pogoso. 1 (1979. 1.)-. Periodical. KO. Korean. sa. 1,300. Hanguk Chongsin Munhwa Yonguwon, 50 Unjung-Dong, Songnam-Si South Korea. **LC** PL941.

PAPERS AND STUDIES IN CONTRASTIVE LINGUISTICS. **VFOAT** Polish-English Contrastive Project. V. 1-. 0137-2459. English. ir. 20.00. Adam Mickiewicz University, 61 712 Poznan Poland. Ed Jacek Fisiak. **Ind/Abst** MLA Int. Bibliogr. Books Artic. Mod. Lang. Lit., Lang. Lang. Behav. Abstr. **LC** P134. **DD** 410.5. bk rev. adv acc. **Circ** 1,200. (ctrl). The journal is devoted to contrastive and comparative linguistics. It carries original contributions both theoretically oriented as well as applied concerning English and other languages.

PAPERS FROM THE REGIONAL MEETING OF THE CHICAGO LINGUISTIC SOCIETY. (PAPERS FROM THE REGIONAL MEETING, CHICAGO LINGUISTIC SOCIETY). **Main/Corp** Chicago Linguistic Society. 4th- 1968-. 0577-7240. US. English. an. $11.00. Chicago Linguistic Society, 1050 East 59th Street/314 A, Chicago IL 60637. **Tel** (312)962-8529. **Ind/Abst** Lang. Lang. Behav. Abstr., Sociol. Abstr., Years Work Eng. Stud. **LC** P21. **DD** 410. **Circ** 1,000. Current research in all branches of modern linguistics plus every year a special volume devoted to a particular topic of current or perennial interest in linguistic studies.

PAPERS IN EAST ASIAN LANGUAGES. Vol. 1 (1983)-. 0747-5519. Periodical. US. English. ir. $7.00. Department of East Asian Languages and Literatures, University of Hawaii

Linguistics

at Manoa, 1890 East West Road, Honolulu HI 96822. Tel (808)945-7272. Ed Gerald B Mathias, Robert Cheng and Ho-min Sohn. LC PJ9. DD 495. bk rev. adv acc. Circ 150. Scholarly discussion of any aspect of East Asian languages.

PAPERS IN JAPANESE LINGUISTICS. Series/Titl Linguistic Communications. 1-. Periodical. US. English. ir. $25.00. Pennsylvania State University, c/o Dr John Hinds Center for EFL 305 Sparks Building, University Park PA 16802. Tel (814)865-7365. Ed John Hinds. LC PL501. DD 491.605. bk rev. Circ 500. Current approaches to Japanese linguistics including sociolinguistics, theoretical linguistics, and discourse analysis.

PAPERS IN LINGUISTICS. Began publication in 1969. 0031-1251. CN. English. ir. Linguistic Research Inc, Box 5677, Postal Station L, Edmonton Alberta T6C 4G1 Canada. Tel (403)421-0145. Ind/Abst MLA Int. Bibliogr. Books Artic. Mod. Lang. Lit., Sociol. Abstr., Lang. Lang. Behav. Abstr., Index Book Rev. Humanit., Lang. Teach. Linguist. Abstr., Years Work Eng. Stud.

PAPERS IN ROMANCE. See Literature.

PAPERS IN SLAVIC PHILOLOGY. Series/Titl Michigan Slavic Publications. 1-. 0161-8822. Periodical. US. English. ir. University of Michigan, Department of Slavic Languages, 3040 Modern Language Building, Ann Arbor MI 48109. LC PG13. DD 491.805.

PAPERS ON LANGUAGE & LITERATURE. (PAPERS ON LANGUAGE & LITERATURE : PLL). VFOAT Papers on Language and Literature. Vol. 2, No. 1 (Winter 1966)-. 0031-1294. Periodical. US. English. qt. $22.00 Domestic, $24.00 Foreign. Business Manager PLL, Southern Illinois University at Edwardsville, Edwardsville IL 62026-1434. Tel (618)692-2119. Ed Alvin Sullivan. Ind/Abst Abstr. Engl. Stud., MLA Int. Bibliogr. Books Artic. Mod. Lang. Lit., Lang. Lang. Behav. Abstr., Index Book Rev. Humanit., Humanit. Index, Recent Publ. Artic. LC PR1. DD 820.9. (cum index). bk rev. adv acc. Circ 850. (ctrl). Literary history, theory, and interpretation. Publishes essays dealing with writings in English, American, French, German, Spanish, Russian and other languages, Brief notes and a review essay included. Papers on English Language & Literature.

PAPIERE ZUR LINGUISTIK. 1979. Periodical. GW. German. sa $26.62. Gunter Narr Verlag, Postfach 2567, 7400 Tuebingen 5 West Germany. Tel 07071-78091. Ed Johannes Bechert and Willi Mayerthaler. LC P3. bk rev. adv acc. Circ 800. Analyses theoretical linguistics and its connection with analytical philosophy of formal and normal language. Munchner Papiere Zur Linguistik.

PAPIERE ZUR TEXTLINGUISTIK. VFOAT Papers in Textlinguistics. V. 1- 1972-. Monographic Series. US. English, French or German. ir. John Benjamins North America, One Buttonwood Square, Philadelphia PA 19130. Tel (215)564-6379. Ind/Abst MLA Int. Bibliogr. Books Artic. Mod. Lang. Lit. Irregularly issued series of monographs on textlinguistics.

PARALLELES (UNIVERSITE DE GENEVE. ECOLE DE TRADUCTION ET D'INTERPRETATION). (PARALLELES : CAHIERS DE L'ECOLE DE TRADUCTION ET D'INTERPRETATION DE L'UNIVERSITE DE GENEVE). No. 1 (Feb. 1978)-. French (English, German, Italian and Spanish). an. $7.43. Ecole Traduction Interpretaria, University of Geneve, 19 Place Augustin CH-1211 Geneve 4 Switzerland.

PARLERS ET TRADITIONS POPULAIRES DE NORMANDIE. See Folklore.

PASAA. V. 3, No. 2- Oct. 1973-. 0125-2488. Periodical. English or Thai. sa. Chulalongkorn University, Language Institute, Pasaa Business Manager, Bangkok 10500 Thailand. Ind/Abst MLA Int. Bibliogr. Books Artic. Mod. Lang. Lit., Lang. Lang. Behav. Abstr., Lang. Teach. Bulletin of the English Language Center.

PATMA-BANASIRAKAN ANDES. (PATMA-BANASIRAKAN HANDES ISTORIKO-FILOLOGICHESKII ZHURNAL). 1958-. 0130-6812. Periodical. UR. Armenian (Russian). qt. Victor Kamkin Inc (77805), 12224 Parklawn Drive, Rockville MD 20852. Tel (301)881-5973. Ind/Abst Am. Hist. Life, Hist. Abstr., Part A, Mod. Hist. Abstr., Part B, Twent. Century Abstr., MLA Int. Bibliogr. Books Artic. Mod. Lang. Lit., Artbibliogr. Mod. (cum index).

PERFICIT. Periodical. Spanish. ir. $4.00. LC PA9.

PERSPECTIVES ON WRITING AND SPEECH : RESEARCH, INSTRUCTION, AND CURRICULUM DEVELOPMENT. 0192-2017. Periodical. US. English. Community College Press, New York City Community College, Brooklyn NY 11201. LC PE1001. DD 001.54071173.

PHASIS. V. 1- Sep. 1973-. Portuguese. ir. rua Carangola 288 - 7 Andar, Caixa Postal 905, Belo Horizonte Brazil. LC P9.

PHILIPPINE JOURNAL OF LINGUISTICS. Began in June 1970. 0048-3796. Periodical. PH. English. sa. 25.00. PSSC Central Subscription Service, Greenhills PO Box 655, San Juan Rizal D-738 Philippines. Tel 922-9621. Ed Andrew B Gonzalez. Ind/Abst MLA Int. Bibliogr. Books Artic. Mod. Lang. Lit., Lang. Lang. Behav. Abstr. LC P1. DD 410.5. bk rev. adv acc. Circ 1,000. Presents original studies in descriptive, comparative, historical and area linguistics as well as papers on the application of theory to language teaching.

PHILOLOGICA PRAGENSIA. 1- 1958-. 0048-3885. Periodical. CS. English (French, German, and Spanish). qt $40.00. John Benjamins BV, Amsteldijk 44, PO Box 52519, 1007 HA Amsterdam Holland. Tel (020)738156. Ed J O Fischer, I Poldauf and VI Horky. Ind/Abst Abstr. Engl. Stud., MLA Int. Bibliogr. Books Artic. Mod. Lang. Lit., Lang. Lang. Behav. Abstr., Annu. Bibliogr. Engl. Lang. Lit., Lang. Teach., Linguist. Abstr., Years Work Eng. Stud. LC P1.A1. DD 410.5. Deals with modern philology, linguistics and literature. Philologica.

PHILOLOGICAL PAPERS. V. 5-. 0363-3470. Monographic Series. US. English. West Virginia University, Morgantown WV 26506. Ind/Abst MLA Int. Bibliogr. Books Artic. Mod. Lang. Lit., Abstr. Engl. Stud., Annu. Bibliogr. Engl. Lang. Lit. Philological Studies, 0363-4124.

PHILOLOGICAL QUARTERLY. VFOAT PQ. V. 1- Jan. 1922-. 0031-7977. Periodical. US. English. qt. $54.00. University of Iowa, Publications Order Department GSB, Iowa City IA 52242. Tel (319)353-4171. Ed William Kupersmith. Ind/Abst Abstr. Engl. Stud., MLA Int. Bibliogr. Books Artic. Mod. Lang. Lit., Sociol. Abstr., Lang. Lang. Behav. Abstr., Annu. Bibliogr. Engl. Lang. Lit., Years Work Eng. Stud., Book Rev. Index, Index Book Rev. Humanit., Soc. Sci. Index, Humanit. Index, Recent Publ. Artic. LC P1. DD 410.5. (cum index). bk rev. adv acc. Circ 2,200. A journal of scholarship and criticism of classical and modern languages and literatures.

PHILOLOGISCHE STUDIEN UND QUELLEN. 1- 1956-. 0554-0674. Monographic Series. GW. German. ir. Erich Schmidt Verlag GMBH, POB 7330-40/Viktoriastr 44A, D4800 Bielefeld 1 West Germany. Tel 0521-66061. Ed Wolfgang Binder and Hugo Moser. Ind/Abst MLA Int. Bibliogr. Books Artic. Mod. Lang. Lit. Philological studies and sources.

PHOENIX. Korean. ir. Ind/Abst MLA Int. Bibliogr. Books Artic. Mod. Lang. Lit. LC PR1.

PHONAI. LAUTBIBLIOTHEK DER EUROPAISCHEN SPRACHEN UND MUNDARTEN. DEUTSCHE REIHE. Vol. 1- 1965-. 0554-0992. Monographic Series. GW. German. ir. Max Niemeyer Verlag, Postfach 2140, 7400 Tuebingen 1 West Germany. Tel 07071/81104. Ed Edeltraud Knetschke and Margret Sperlbaum. Circ 500. Covers text phonetic and normalized of tape recorded conversations in German dialects with linguistic analysis.

POLONISTYKA. Began in 1948. Periodical. PL. Polish. ir. ARS Polona, Krakowskie Przedmiescie 7, 00-068 Warsaw Poland. LC PG6001.

PORADNIK JEZYKOWY. Began publication in 1901. Periodical. PL. Polish. mo. ARS Polona, Krakowskie Przedmiescie 7, 00-068 Warsaw Poland. Ed R Zawilinski.

PRACE JEZYKOZNAWCZE. Series/Titl Prace Naukowe Uniwersytetu Slaskiego W Katowicach. Began in 1969. PL. Polish (summaries in English or French). ir. 15.00 Single Issue. UL Bankowa 14, Katowice Poland. LC PG6025.

PRACE JEZYKOZNAWCZE. Main/Corp Krakow. Wyzsza Skoa Pedagogiczna. VFOAT Travaux Linguistiques. Began in 1970. Polish. ir. 28.00 Each Issue. Naukowe Wyzszej Szkoy Pedagogicznej, Ksiegania Naukowa Dom Ksiazki, Ul Podwale 6, Krakow Poland. LC AS142.K66.

PRACI BHASAVIJNAN. VFOAT Indian Journal of Linguistics. V. 1- Jan./June 1974-. Periodical. II. English. sa. 30.00 Domestic, $15.00 Foreign. Bangiya Vijnan Parishad, P-23 Raja Rajkrishna Street, Calcutta 700006 India. Tel 55-0660. Ed Bhakti P Mallik. Ind/Abst MLA Int. Bibliogr. Books Artic. Mod. Lang. Lit. LC P1. DD 410.5. bk rev adv acc. Circ 525. (ctrl). Dedicated to the development of all branches of linguistics in general and Indian linguistics in particular. It invites papers on theoretical and experimental linguistics and interdisciplinary studies throughout the world.

PRAGUE BULLETIN OF MATHEMATICAL LINGUISTICS. (THE PRAGUE BULLETIN OF MATHEMATICAL LINGUISTICS). No.1 (1964)-. 0032-6585. Periodical. CS. English or Russian. sa. Charles University, Malostranske Nam 25, 11800 Praha 1 Czechoslovakia. Tel 532136. Ed Eva Hajicova. Ind/Abst Lang. Lang. Behav. Abstr., Comput. Control Abstr., Electr. Electron. Abstr., Sci. Abstr. Sect. A. Phys. Abstr., Phys. Abstr., Math. Rev., Sociol. Abstr., MLA Int. Bibliogr. Books Artic. Mod. Lang. Lit. CODEN PBMLAT. bk rev. Circ 800. Attention focussed on mathematical linguistics and its applications. Papers published in English, German, and French.

PREPODAVANIE INOSTRANNYKH IAZYKOV. Vol. 1- 1973-. Periodical. UR. Russian. qt. LC Z5818.L35.

PRESENCE FRANCOPHONE. See Literature.

PRE/TEXT. VFOAT Pretext. Vol. 1, No. 1/2 (Spring/Fall 1980)-. 0731-0714. Periodical. US. English. qt. $20.00. University of Texas at Arlington, English Department, c/o V J Vitanza, Box 19035, Arlington TX 76019. Tel (817)273-2692. Ed Victor J Vitanza. Ind/Abst Lang. Lang. Behav. Abstr., MLA Int. Bibliogr. Books Artic. Mod. Lang. Lit. LC P301. DD 808.005. bk rev. adv acc. Circ 500. Exploratory articles on the interdisciplinary nature of rhetorical theory and metatheory, including research on written communication.

PRILOZI I GRAA. Main/Corp Yugoslav Serbo-Croatian—English Contrastive Project. 1- 1969-. 0449-5527. English. ir. LC PG1229.

PRISMA. V. 4- Summer 1975-. 0380-8815. CN. English (includes some text in German). sa. Saskatchewan Teachers Federation, 2317 Arlington Avenue, Saskatoon Saskatchewan S7J 2H8 Canada. DD 438.007. Jetzt Wird Deutsch Gesprochen, 0380-8807.

PROBLEMY IZUCHENIIA INOSTRANNYKH IAZYKOV V ZAOCHNOI I VECHERNEI VYSSHEI SHKOLE. Began in 1976. Periodical. UR. Russian. 0.70. Izdatelstvo Lgu Im. A A Zhdanova, 199164 Leningrad B-164, Universitetskaia Nab. 7/9, Leningrad Russian SFSR. LC PB38.R8.

PROCEEDINGS - ALL INDIA CONFERENCE OF LINGUISTS. Main/Corp All India Conference of Linguists. 1st- 1970-. English. ir. LC PK1501.

PROCEEDINGS AND TRANSACTIONS OF THE ALL-INDIA ORIENTAL CONFERENCE. Main/Conf All-India Oriental Conference. 1st- 1919-. II. English. ir. 150.00. Bhandarkar Oriental Research Institute, Poona 411004 India. Tel 56936. Ed R N Dandekar. LC PJ21. DD 490.6354. (cum index). (ctrl).

PROCEEDINGS OF NELS. Main/Corp North Eastern Linguistic Society. VFOAT NELS. VAT Proceedings of North Eastern Linguistic Society. 0883-5500. US. English. an. Graduate Linguistic Student Association, Linguistics Department, University of Massachusetts, Amherst MA 01003. Tel (413)545-0885. Circ 500. This is the proceedings of annually held North Eastern Linguistics Society. Proceedings of the . . . Annual Meeting of the North Eastern Linguistic Society, 0742-3209.

PROCEEDINGS OF THE . . . ANNUAL MEETING OF THE ATLANTIC PROVINCES LINGUISTIC ASSOCIATION. Main/Corp Atlantic Provinces Linguistic Association, Meeting. 5th (Nov. 27/28, 1981)-. 0820-8204. CN. English (French). an. 15.00. Proceedings of the . . . Annual Meeting of the Atlantic Provinces Linguistic Association, c/o Linguistics Department, Memorial University, St Johns Newfoundland A1B 3X9 Canada. Tel (709)737-8134. DD 410.5. Circ 150. Descriptive and theoretical linguistics, languages dialects of Atlantic Canada.

Linguistics

Papers from the ... Annual Meeting of the Atlantic Provinces Linguistic Association (1980), 0228-8419.

PROCEEDINGS OF THE ANNUAL MEETING OF THE BERKELEY LINGUISTICS SOCIETY. Main/Corp Berkeley Linguistics Society. 1st- 1975-. 0363-2946. US. English. an. $16.25. Berkeley Linguistics Society, University of California, Berkeley CA 94720. Tel (415)642-2757. LC P21. DD 410.5. Circ 1,000. This volume contains the proceedings of the yearly conference held in Berkeley, California. The conference attracts linguists from across the country.

PROCEEDINGS OF THE CAMBRIDGE PHILOLOGICAL SOCIETY. Main/Corp Cambridge Philological Society. 1 (Lent term, 1882)/2 (Easter term, 1882)-. 0068-6735. UK. English. an. LC P11. DD 410.5.

PROCEEDINGS OF THE CLASSICAL ASSOCIATION. Main/Corp Classical Association. V.1- 1904-. UK. English. an. LC PA11.

PROCEEDINGS OF THE LINGUISTIC CIRCLE OF MANITOBA AND NORTH DAKOTA. Main/Corp Linguistic Circle of Manitoba and North Dakota. V. 1- May 1959-. 0075-9597. Periodical. CN. English. an. University of North Dakota, Prof Ben Collins, Department of English, Grand Forks ND 58202. Tel (701)777-3321. DD 410.5.

PROCEEDINGS. SUPPLEMENT. Main/Corp Cambridge Philological Society. No. 1- 1965-). 0068-6743. Periodical. UK. English. Basil Blackwell Publishers Journals Department, 108 Cowley Road, Oxford OX4 1JF England.

PROFESSION. 0740-6959. US. English. an. Modern Language Association, 62 Fifth Avenue, New York NY 10011. LC P57.U7. DD 405.

PROFESSIONAL SERVICES DIRECTORY OF THE AMERICAN TRANSLATORS ASSOCIATION. *See* Yearbooks, Almanacs, Directories.

PROFIL MIT ECCO. *See* Bibliographies.

PROGRESSIVE FORENSICS. VFOAT Forensics. Vol. 1, No. 1 (Nov. 1983)-. 0742-3837. Periodical. US. English. ty. $12.00. Stanley-Clark Publishers, Progressive Forensics, PO Box 1362, Starkville MS 39759. LC PN4071. DD 808.5105.

PROHEMIO. V. 1- April 1970-. Periodical. Spanish. ty. LC P9.

PROTEE. V. 1- Dec. 1970-. 0300-3523. Periodical. CN. French. ty. $15.48. University of Quebec Chicoutimi, Department of Arts and Lettres, 555 University Boulevard, Chicoutimi Quebec G7H 2B1 Canada. Tel (418)545-5375. Ed Pierre Ouellet. Ind/Abst Point Repere, Hist. Abstr., Am. Hist. Life, Hist. Abstr., Part A, Mod. Hist. Abstr., Hist. Abst., Part B, Twent. Century Abstr. bk rev. adv acc. Circ 500. (ctrl) Multidisciplinary journal in the field of semiotics: theoretical and applied to literature, arts, language, culture, etc.

PRZEGLAD RUSYCYSTYCZNY. Vol. 1-. Periodical. Polish (Russian). ir. Rsw Prasa-Ksiazka-Ruch Centrala Kolportazu Prasy I Wydawnictw, Ul Towarowa 28, 00-958 Warszawa Poland. LC PG2068.P6.

PSYCHO-LINGUA. V. 1- Jan. 1971-. 0377-3132. Periodical. English (Hindi). sa. $2.50. Psycholinguistic Association of India, c/o Ravishankar University MP, Raipur India. Ind/Abst Lang. Lang. Behav. Abstr., Psychol. Abstr. LC P1.A1. DD 410.

PUBBLICAZIONI. CONTRIBUTI, SERIE III. SCIENZE FILOLOGICHE E LETTERATURA. Main/Corp Universita Cattolica del Sacro Cuore. 1- 1960-. Monographic Series. Italian. ir. LC P25.

PUBLICACIONES. SERIES MINOR. Main/Corp Columbia. Instituto Caro Y Cuervo. Vol. 1 1950-. 0073-9928. Monographic Series. CK. Spanish. ir. Institute Caro y Cuervo, Apartado Aereo 51502, Bogota Colombia. Tel 2558289. Circ 2,000. (ctrl).

PUBLICATION B - CENTRE INTERNATIONAL DE RECHERCHES SUR LE BILINGUISME. (PUBLICATION B). 1-. 0704-7037. Periodical. CN. English (French). International Center for Research on Bilingualism, 6th Floor Pavillon Casault, Universite Laval, Quebec Quebec G1K 7P4 Canada. Tel (418)656-3232. DD 404.205. adv acc. Circ 150. (ctrl).

PUBLICATION G - CENTRE INTERNATIONAL DE RECHERCHE SUR LE BILINGUISME. (PUBLICATION G . . .). 1-. 0714-8682. Monographic Series. CN. English (French). International Center for Research on Bilingualism, 6th Floor/Pavillon Casault Universite Laval, Quebec G1K 7P4 Canada. DD 404.205.

PUBLICATIONS - DAKAR. UNIVERSITE. SECTION DE LANGUES ET LITTERATURES. Main/Corp Dakar. Universite. Section de Langues et Litteratures. VFOAT Dakar. Universite. Section de Langues et Litteratures. No. 1- 1957-. 0418-2960. Periodical. SG. French. ir. Dakar Universite, Section de Langues et Litteratur, Dakar Fann Senegal.

PUBLICATIONS IN CONDUCT AND COMMUNICATION. Main/Corp University of Pennsylvania. VFOAT Conduct and Communication. 1- 1969-. 0556-2678. US. English. ir. University of Penn Press, 3933 Walnut Street, Philadelphia PA 19104. Tel (215)243-6261.

PUBLICATIONS IN LINGUISTICS. Main/Corp University of California, Berkeley. US. English. University of California, Linguistics Department, Berkeley CA 94720. Ind/Abst MLA Int. Bibliogr. Books Artic. Mod. Lang. Lit.

PUBLICATIONS OF THE ARKANSAS PHILOLOGICAL ASSOCIATION. Main/Corp Arkansas Philological Association. V. 1- Fall 1974-. 0160-3124. Periodical. US. English. ty. $18.00. University of Central Arkansas, c/o R Lowrey, PO Box S, Conway AR 72032. Tel (501)450-3180. Ed Robert E Lowrey. Ind/Abst MLA Int. Bibliogr. Books Artic. Mod. Lang. Lit. LC PB1. DD 410.5. bk rev. adv acc. Circ 200. (ctrl). Literary criticism, scholarship, book reviews, and original poetry in English and modern languages.

PUBLICATIONS OF THE MISSOURI PHILOLOGICAL ASSOCIATION. Main/Corp Missouri Philological Association. V. 1- 1976-. 0194-035X. US. English. an. University of Missouri-Rolla, Rolla MO 65401. Ed F M Patterson. Ind/Abst MLA Int. Bibliogr. Books Artic. Mod. Lang. Lit. LC PB1. DD 809.

PUBLICATIONS OF THE MODERN LANGUAGE ASSOCIATION OF AMERICA. (PMLA : PUBLICATIONS OF THE MODERN LANGUAGE ASSOCIATION OF AMERICA). Vol. 44, No. 1 (March 1929)-. 0030-8129. Periodical. US. English. bm. $60.00. Modern Language Association of America, 62 5th Avenue, New York NY 10011. Tel (212)741-5588. Ed English Showalter. Ind/Abst Annu. Bibliogr. Engl. Lang. Lit., Abstr. Engl. Stud., MLA Int. Bibliogr. Books Artic. Mod. Lang. Lit., Lang. Lang. Behav. Abstr., Sociol. Abstr., Humanit. Index, Recent Publ. Artic. LC PB6. DD 809. (cum index). adv acc. Circ 26,000. Publishes articles of interest to those concerned with the study of language and literature. It is receptive to a variety of topics. *Publications of the Modern Language Association of America, 0030-8129.*

PUBLISISTIK. VFOAT Madjalah Ilmiah Bidang Komunikasi Massa Publisistik. Began with June 1964 issue. 0555-6406. Periodical. Indonesian. ir. LC P92.172.

PUNJAB JOURNAL OF ENGLISH STUDIES : PJES. VFOAT PJES. Vol. 1 (1982)-. English. an. 25.00. Department of English, Guru Nanak Dev University, Amritsar-143005 India. LC PE10. DD 820.9.

QUADERNI DELL'ATLANTE LESSICALE TOSCANO. VFOAT Quaderni. 1-. Periodical. Italian. ir. LC PC1001. DD 457.5.

QUADERNI DELL'ISTITUTO DI LINGUA E LETTERATURA LATINA. No. 1-. Periodical. IT. Italian. ir. 7000. Edizioni Dell'Ateneo & Bizzarri, Casella Postale 7216, 00100 Roma Italy. LC PA2004. DD 470.5.

QUADERNI DI FILOLOGIA GERMANICA DELLA FACOLTA DI LETTERE E FILOSOFIA DELL'UNIVERSITA DI BOLOGNA. Vol. 1 (1980)-. Periodical. English (German and Italian). ir. 10,000.00. Longo Editore, PO Box 431, Ravenna Cas Post, Bologna Italy. Ind/Abst MLA Int. Bibliogr. Books Artic. Mod. Lang. Lit. LC PD9. DD 430.05.

QUADERNI DI FILOLOGIA MODERNA. 1-. Periodical. IT. Italian. ir. LC PB4. DD 809 S 809.

QUADERNI DI FILOLOGIA ROMANZA. V. 1- 1959-. 0480-8614. Italian. ir.

QUADERNI DI LINGUE E LETTERATURE STRANIERE. Periodical. Italian. ir. Via Notarbartolo 5, 90141 Palermo Italy. LC PB4. DD 405.

QUADERNI DI SEMANTICA. 1st Yr, N. 1 (Jan.-June 1980)-. Periodical. IT. English (text in French and Italian). sa. 100.000 Domestic, 120.000 Foreign. Societa Editrice Il Mulino Spa, Via Santo Stefano 6, 40125 Bologna Italy. Tel 051/ 23 34 15. Ind/Abst MLA Int. Bibliogr. Books Artic. Mod. Lang. Lit. LC P325. DD 412.05.

QUADERNI PATAVINI DI LINGUISTICA. 1 (1979-80)-. Periodical. English (Italian). ir. 12.000. CLESP, Cooperativa Libraria Editoriale Studentesca Patavina, Riviera Tito Livio 33, 35100 Padova Italy. LC P1.A1. DD 410.5.

QUARTERLY BULLETIN OF THE AMERICAN ASSOCIATION OF TEACHERS OF ESPERANTO. Main/Corp American Association of Teachers of Esperanto. VFOAT Kvaronjara Bulteno de la Amerika Asocio de Instruistoj de Esperanto. 0002-7499. Periodical. US. English (Esperanto). qt. $5.00. American Association Teachers Esperanto, 4710 Dexter Drive #3, Santa Barbara CA 93110-1325. Tel (805)967-5241. Ed Dorothy Holland. bk rev. Circ 100. (ctrl). News of Esperanto classes in the US and abroad. Foreign language teaching methods. Information on Esperanto teaching materials and meetings.

THE QUARTERLY JOURNAL OF SPEECH. V. 53, No. 1 (Feb. 1967)-V. 53, No. 1-4 Index (Dec. 1967). Periodical. US. English. qt. Ind/Abst Educ. Index, Biogr. Index. *Quarterly Journal of Speech Education.*

QUELLEN UND FORSCHUNGEN ZUR SPRACH- UND KULTURGESCHICHTE DER GERMANISCHEN VOLKER. NEUE FOLGE. 1-. 0481-3596. Monographic Series. WB. German. ir. Walter de Gruyter & Company, 200 Sawmill River Road, Hawthorne NY 10532. Tel (914)747-0110. Ind/Abst MLA Int. Bibliogr. Books Artic. Mod. Lang. Lit.

QUICKBORN. Periodical. GW. German. qt. $24.00. Quickborn, Deichstr 48/50, 2000 Hamburg 11 West Germany. *Mitteilungen.*

QUINTO LINGO : THE MULTILINGUAL MAGAZINE. Vol.1, No.1 (August 1964)-. 0033-6602. Periodical. US. English. bm. Quinto Lingo, PO Box 9340, Alexandria VA 22304. Tel (703)370-3750. Ed Endel Peedo. LC UNC. DD 418.008. bk rev. adv acc. Circ 15,000.

R-C-L. READING CANADA LECTURE. (R-C-L : READING-CANADA-LECTURE). VFOAT Reading-Canada-Lecture. VAT Reading Canada, Canada Lecture. Vol. 1, No. 1 (Jan. 1981)-. 0710-6556. Periodical. CN. English (includes some text and summaries in French). qt. $25.00. A Forester Camosun College, 1950 Lansdowne Road, Victoria British Columbia V8P 5J2 Canada. Ind/Abst Can. Educ. Index. DD 418.007071.

R L S. REGIONAL LANGUAGE STUDIES. NEWFOUNDLAND. (R L S, REGIONAL LANGUAGE STUDIES . . . NEWFOUNDLAND). No. 1- Oct. 1968-. 0079-9335. Periodical. CN. English. ir. Memorial University of Newfoundland, Department of Folklore, St Johns Newfoundland A1C 5S7 Canada. Tel (709)753-1200. Ind/Abst MLA Int. Bibliogr. Books Artic. Mod. Lang. Lit., Lang. Lang. Behav. Abstr., Sociol. Abstr. DD 427.9718.

RADOVI STAROSLAVENSKOG INSTITUTA. Vol. 1-. Serbo-Croatian -R (summaries in French). ir. MLADOST Export Import, PO Box 1028 Ilica 30, 41000 Zagreb Yugoslavia. Ind/Abst Sociol. Abstr., Lang. Lang. Behav. Abstr.

RAJASTHAN JOURNAL OF ENGLISH STUDIES. (THE RAJASTHAN JOURNAL OF ENGLISH STUDIES). V. 1- July/Dec. 1974-. 0377-3310. Periodical. English. sa. $10.00. Km Manju Joshi Memorial Society, Mathur House, Behind Jain School, Sikar India. LC PE9. DD 820.9954.

RAJASTHANNI SABADA KOSA. 1962-. Rajasthani. ir. LC PK2707.

RAPPORT ANNUEL - CONSEIL DE LA LANGUE FRANCAISE. Main/Corp Quebec (Province). Conseil de la Langue Francaise. 1977/78-. 0229-9259. CN. French. an. Editeur Officiel du Quebec, 1283 Boul Charest Quest, Quebec Quebec G1N 2C9 Canada. LC PC3601. DD 440.60714.

Linguistics

RAPPORT D'ACTIVITE - OFFICE DE LA LANGUE FRANCAISE. Main/Corp Quebec (Province). Office de la Langue Francaise. 1977/78-. 0707-1795. CN. French. an. Editeur Officiel du Quebec, 1283 Boul Charest Quest, Quebec PQ G1N 2C9 Canada. LC PC3601. DD 354.7140085. *Regie de la Langue Francaise, 0708-2940.*

RAPPORT D'ACTIVITES DU . . . . Main/Corp Centre for Linguistic and Historical Studies by Oral Tradition. VFOAT Report on the Activities. English (French). ir. Oua-Celhto, BP 878, Niamey Nigeria Africa.

RAPPORTS HET FRANSE BOEK. See Literature.

RASHTRABHASHA SANDESA : HINDI SAHITYA SAMMELANA KA MUKHAPATRA. Periodical. Hindi. sm. LC PK1931.

RASSEGNA ITALIANA DI LINGUISTICA APPLICATA. Yearly V. 1- Jan./April 1969-. 0033-9725. Periodical. IT. some articles in English. ir $21.98. Bulzoni Editore S R L, 14 Via dei Liburni, 00185 Rome Italy. Ind/Abst MLA Int. Bibliogr. Books Artic. Mod. Lang. Lit., Lang. Lang. Behav. Abstr., Lang. Teach., Curr. Index J. Educ.

READ (UKARUMPA, PAPUA NEW GUINEA). (READ). Began with issue for Sept. 1966. Periodical. PP. English. sa. $2.95. Summer Institute of Linguistics, Box 233, Ukarumpa Via Lae Papua New Guinea Australia. Ed Dennis and Susan Malone. LC Z1003.5.P36. DD 028.909953. bk rev. Circ 500. Articles, reports and reviews in the general area of promoting literacy and literature, especially in Vernacular and in Third World areas.

READING IN A FOREIGN LANGUAGE : JOURNAL OF THE LANGUAGE STUDIES UNIT (MODERN LANGUAGES DEPARTMENT. See Education (General) - Theory, Practice of Education.

READING RESEARCH AND INSTRUCTION. See Education (General) - Special Aspects of Education.

READING RESEARCH QUARTERLY. V. 1- Fall 1965-. 0034-0553. Periodical. US. English (summaries in French and Spanish). qt. $30.00. International Reading Association, 800 Barksdale Road, PO Box 8139, Newark DE 19711. Tel (302)731-1600. Ind/Abst Lang. Lang. Behav. Abstr., Lang. Teach., Except. Child Educ. Resour., Educ. Index, Curr. Index J. Educ., Psychol. Abstr., Soc. Sci. Citation Index, Sociol. Abstr. LC LB1050. DD 428.4072. CODEN RRQUA6.

READINGS IN SPANISH-ENGLISH CONTRASTIVE LINGUISTICS. 1973-. PR. English. ir. $4.50. Inter American University Press, PO Box 1293, Hato Rey Puerto Rico. Ed R Nash. LC PC4099. DD 418.

RECHERCHES EN LINGUISTIQUE ETRANGERE. Series/Titl Annales Litteraires de l'Universite de Besancon. 1-. FR. French. ir. Les Belles Lettres, 95 Boulevard Raspail Vie, Paris France. LC AS161, P2. DD 084.1 S, 410.

RECHERCHES LINGUISTIQUES A MONTREAL CEASED. VFOAT Montreal Working Papers in Linguistics. V. 1-17. 0700-4907. CN. English (French). an. Dep de Linguistique, Universite de Montreal, Montreal Quebec Canada. DD 410.5.

RECUEIL LINGUISTIQUE DE BRATISLAVA. V. 1- 1948-. Czech (German, English, French, or Russian). ir. Kubon & Sagner, Postfach 34 01 08, D-8000 Munchen 34 West Germany. Tel 020-738156. LC P25.

REFERATI I SAOPSTENJA - NAUCNI SASTANAK SLAVISTA U VUKOVE DANE. Main/Conf Naucni Sastanak Slavista u Vukove Dane. 1- 1971-. Serbo-Croatian(R). ir. Meunarodni Slavisticki Centar, Studetski Trg 3/1, Beograd Yugoslavia. LC PG1207.

REFLECTOR (UNIVERSITY PARK, MD.). (THE REFLECTOR). Vol. 1 (Fall 1981)-. 0739-7356. Periodical. US. English. ty. $10.00. The Reflector, 4017 Tennyson Road, University Park MD 20782. LC HV2474. DD 419.05. NLM W1 RE1698P.

RELC JOURNAL. Main/Corp Regional Language Centre. VAT Regional English Language Centre Journal. V. 8- June 1977-. 0033-6882. Periodical. English. sa. $10.00. Oxford University Press, 875 Bukit Timah Road, Singapore 10 Malaya. Ind/Abst Lang. Lang. Behav. Abstr., Lang. Teach., MLA Int. Bibliogr. Books Artic. Mod. Lang. Lit. LC HC188.M29. DD 428.007059. *RELC Journal, 0033-6882.*

RENDEZ-VOUS CEC. VFOAT Rendez-Vous. VAT Rendez-Vous. Centre Educatif et Culturel. No. 1-. 0712-9505. Periodical. CN. English (French). ir. Free to Clients. Rendez-Vous Cec, c/o Centre Educatif et Culturel, 8101 Metropolitain Boulevard, Montreal Quebec H1J 1J9 Canada. DD 448.242107.

RENDEZVOUS. (RENDEZVOUS : FOR NEW BRUNSWICK'S FRENCH SECOND LANGUAGE TEACHERS). 0711-1177. Periodical. CN. English. ty. Free. New Brunswick Teachers' Association, PO Box 752, Fredericton New Brunswick E3B 5R6 Canada. Ind/Abst Can. Educ. Index. DD 448.007. (ctrl) *French III Times, 0711-4605.*

RENDICONTI (ACCADEMIA NAZIONALE DEI LINCEI. CLASSE DI SCIENZE MORALI, STORICHE E FILOLOGICHE). (ATTI DELLA ACCADEMIA NAZIONALE DEI LINCEI. RENDICONTI). Periodical. IT. Italian. mo. $83.16. Atti della Accademia Nazionale, Via della Lungara 10, Rome Italy. *Rendiconti della Classe di Scienze Morali, Storiche.*

REPERTOIRE - SOCIETE DES TRADUCTEURS DU QUEBEC. See Yearbooks, Almanacs, Directories.

REPORT OF THE PHONOLOGY LABORATORY. Main/Corp University of California, Berkeley. Phonology Laboratory. VFOAT RPL. No. 1 (July 1976)-. 0749-1654. US. English. ir. $5.00. Phonology Laboratory, Department of Linguistics, University of California, Berkeley CA 94720. Tel (415)642-4938. Ed John J Ohala. Ind/Abst Lang. Lang. Behav. Abstr. Circ 300. Examines speech production, perception, and the psychoacoustic bases of historical sound change, and exemplify frontline instrumental and psycholinguistic techniques.

RESEARCH PAPERS - DEPARTMENT OF TAMIL, UNIVERSITY OF KERALA. Main/Corp University of Kerala. Dept. of Tamil. V. 5- 1974-. Periodical. II. English. an. University of Kerala, Department of Tamil, Trivandrum India. LC PL4751. DD 494.81105. *Journal of the Department of Tamil.*

RESEARCH REPORT - NATIONAL COUNCIL OF TEACHERS OF ENGLISH. Main/Corp National Council of Teachers of English. VFOAT NCTE Research Report. No. 1-. 0085-3739. Monographic Series. US. English. ir. National Council of Teachers of English, 1111 Kenyon Road, Urbana IL 61801. LC PE1011. DD 428.007.

RESOURCE GUIDE TO READING & LANGUAGE ARTS PROGRAMS & MATERIALS. 1973/74-. 0092-4423. US. English. $1.50. MacMillan Professionals Magazines Inc, 22 West Putnam Avenue, Greenwich CT 06830. LC Z5814.R25. DD 016.428207.

REVISTA BRASILEIRA DE LINGUA E LITERATURA. 1- 1st Half 1979-. 0101-8248. Periodical. BL. Portuguese. ir. Livraria Padrao, rua Miguel Couto 40, Rio de Janeiro Brazil. Ind/Abst MLA Int. Bibliogr. Books Artic. Mod. Lang. Lit. LC PC5001. DD 469.05.

REVISTA BRASILEIRA DE LINGUISTICA CEASED. Vol. 1- 1974-. Periodical. BL. English and Portuguese. sa. Editora Vozes, rua Frei Luis 100, Caixa Postal 23, Petropolis Rio de Janeiro Brazil. Ind/Abst MLA Int. Bibliogr. Books Artic. Mod. Lang. Lit., Lang. Lang. Behav. Abstr. LC P1.A1.

REVISTA DE ESTUDIOS HISPANICOS. See Literature.

REVISTA DE ESTUDIOS HISPANICOS. Began with V. 1 (May 1967). 0034-818X. Periodical. US. Spanish (English). ty. $15.00. Revista de Estudios Hispanicos, Vassar College, Department of Spanish Studies, Poughkeepsie NY 12601. Tel (914)452-7000. Ind/Abst Index Book Rev. Humanit., MLA Int. Bibliogr. Books Artic. Mod. Lang. Lit. DD 460. Available on microfilm from University Microfilms International.

REVISTA DE FILOLOGIA DE LA UNIVERSIDAD DE LA LAGUNA. No. 1 (1982)-. Periodical. SP. Arabic (Spanish). an. Secretariado de Publicaciones, de la Universidad de la Laguna, Tenerife Spain.

REVISTA DE FILOLOGIA Y LINGUISTICA DE LA UNIVERSIDAD DE COSTA RICA. Main/Corp Universidad de Costa Rica. VFOAT Revista de Filologia y Linguistica. CR. Spanish. ir. $5.00. Universidad de Costa Rica, Oficina de Coordinacion Editorial, Ciudad Universitaria Rodrigo Facio, San Jose Costa Rica. LC P9.

REVISTA DE INTERLINGUA. Periodical. Interlingual. mo. 10. Editions Interlingua, Ric Berger Prof, 1110 Morges Switzerland. LC PM8400. DD 499.99305.

REVISTA DE LENGUAS EXTRANJERAS. No.1- 1970-. Periodical. Spanish (some articles in English). ir. LC P1.A1.

REVISTA ESPANOLA DE LINGUISTICA. Vol. 1, No. 1 (Jan./June 1971)-. 0210-1874. Periodical. SP. Spanish (summaries of articles in English). sa. Editorial Gredos SA, Sanchez Pacheos 81, Apt 2076, Madrid Spain. Ind/Abst MLA Int. Bibliogr. Books Artic. Mod. Lang. Lit., Lang. Teach. LC P9.

REVISTA LATINOAMERICANA DE ESTUDIOS ETNOLINGUISTICOS. V. 1, (Year 1981)-. Periodical. PE. Spanish. an. Ignacio Prado Pastor, Jiron Cuzco 484 Lima Peru. Ed I Prado Pastor. LC PM101. DD 498.05.

REVISTA LETRAS. VFOAT Letras. No. 21/22 (1973/1974)-. 0100-0888. BL. Portuguese (English, German and Spanish). ir. Curso de Letras do Setor e Ciencias Humanas, Letras e Artes da Universidade Federal do Parana, rua General Caneiro, 460 - 110 Andar, Caixa Portal 756, 80000 Curitiba Parana Brasil. Ind/Abst MLA Int. Bibliogr. Books Artic. Mod. Lang. Lit. LC PB5. DD 410.5.

REVISTA LETRAS T.A. Yearly V. 2- 1975-. Periodical. BL. Portuguese. ir. Suam, Av Paris 72 ZC 24, Cep 20.000 Bonsucesso Brazil. LC P9. DD 410.5. *Revista de Letras TA.*

REVISTA PORTUGUESA DE FILOLOGIA. V. 1- 1947-. 0484-8128. PO. Portuguese. ir. Casa do Castelo, rue da Sofia 47, Coimbra 3000 Portugal. Ind/Abst MLA Int. Bibliogr. Books Artic. Mod. Lang. Lit. LC PC5001. DD 469.05. (cum index).

REVISTA SINTAXIS. VFOAT Sintaxis. V. 1- Nov. 1975-. Spanish. ir. Casilla 1093, Montevideo Uruguay. LC AS89.A1.

REVISTA VALENCIANA DE FILOLOGIA. V. 1- Jan./April 1951-. 0556-705X. SP. Spanish. ir. Consejo Super Invest Cientific, Vitruvio 8, Apartado 14 458, 28006 Madrid Spain. LC P9.

REVUE BELGE DE PHILOLOGIE ET D'HISTOIRE. VFOAT Belgisch Tijdschrift voor Philologie en Geschiedenis. V. 1- Jan. 1922-. 0035-0818. Periodical. BE. French (some articles in English, German, and Flemish). qt. $36.56. Revue Belge de Philologie et d'Histoire, 4 Boulevard de l Empereur, B 1000 Brussels Belgium. Ind/Abst MLA Int. Bibliogr. Books Artic. Mod. Lang. Lit., Annu. Bibliogr. Engl. Lang. Lit., Sociol. Abstr., Am. Hist. Life, Hist. Abstr., Lang. Lang. Behav. Abstr., Hist. Abstr., Part A, Mod. Hist. Abstr., Hist. Abst., Part B, Twent. Century Abstr., Recent Publ. Artic. LC P2. DD 410.5. (cum index). bk rev. adv acc. Circ 1,000. Covers history, antiquity to contemporary Europe, plus philology: modern and classical and Belgian historical bibliography.

REVUE DE L'ASSOCIATION QUEBECOISE DE LINGUISTIQUE. Vol. 1, No 1/2 (1981-1982)-. 0714-5683. Periodical. CN. French. qt. $25.00. University of Sherbrooke, AQL Department d'Etudes Francaise, Sherbrooke QC J1K 2R1 Canada. Tel (819)378-8157. Ed Henri Wittmann. Ind/Abst MLA Int. Bibliogr. Books Artic. Mod. Lang. Lit., Lang. Lang. Behav. Abstr. DD 410.5. bk rev. adv acc. Circ 500. (ctrl). Original research in linguistics.

REVUE DE LINQUISTIQUE ROMANE. V. 1- Jan./June 1925-. 0035-1458. FR. French. sa. Societe de Linguistique Romane, 44 Avenue la Liberation, 54000 Nancy France. Ind/Abst MLA Int. Bibliogr. Books Artic. Mod. Lang. Lit., Lang. Teach., Index Book Rev. Humanit., Lang. Lang. Behav. Abstr., Sociol. Abstr. LC PC2. DD 440.05. (cum index). bk rev. Circ 1,200. Articles about romance languages and literatures, dialectology, lexicology, lexicography, and romance philology.

Linguistics

REVUE DE PHONETIQUE APPLIQUEE. VFOAT Phonetique Appliquee. Began in 1965. Periodical. BE. English (text in French, or German). qt. 220. Soc Nouvelle Didier Erudition, 6 rue de la Sorbonne, 75005 Paris France. **Tel** 4354 47 57. **Ed** R Renard. **Ind/Abst** MLA Int. Bibliogr. Books Artic. Mod. Lang. Lit., Lang. Lang. Behav. Abstr., Lang. Teach., Sociol. Abstr. LC P1. DD 418.005. **Circ** 1,500. Publishes the works of phonetiticans in Belgium, France and the entire world.

REVUE DE PRESSE ET D'INFORMATION - CONSEIL DE LA LANGUE FRANCAISE. (REVUE DE PRESSE ET D'INFORMATION). 0710-8125. Periodical. CN. French (English). Gouvernement du Quebec, 600 St Amable 4E Etage, Quebec G1R 4Z1 Canada. DD 440.9714.

REVUE DES ETUDES LATINES. 1- Yearly (Vol. 1-). 0373-5737. FR. French. an. Societe Edition Belles Lettres, 95 Boulevard Raspail, 75006 Paris France. **Ind/Abst** MLA Int. Bibliogr. Books Artic. Mod. Lang. Lit. LC PA2002. DD 470.5. (cum index).

REVUE DES LANGUES ROMANES. V. 1- 1870-. Periodical. FR. French. sa. 150.-. Regissuer Recettes de l'Universite, Universite Paul Valery, BP 1085, Montpellier France. **Tel** 16 67 63 91 10. **Ind/Abst** MLA Int. Bibliogr. Books Artic. Mod. Lang. Lit. (cum index). bk rev. adv acc.

REVUE DU MOYEN AGE LATIN. V. 1 (Jan./Mar. 1945)-. FR. French. an. LC PA2801.

REVUE QUEBECOISE DE LINGUISTIQUE. Vol. 11, No 1-. 0710-0167. Periodical. CN. French. ir. 25.00. Revue Quebecoise de Linguistique, CP 95, Trois-Rivieres Quebec G9A 5E3 Canada. **Tel** (819)378-8157. **Ed** Henri Wittman. **Ind/Abst** MLA Int. Bibliogr. Books Artic. Mod. Lang. Lit., Point Repere. DD 410.5. bk rev. adv acc. **Circ** 500. (ctrl). Diffusion of original research on linguistics, French language in North-America, artificial intelligence systems based on French, languages of Francophone countries. Cahier de Linguistique, 0315-4025.

REVUE ROMANE. See Literature.

REVUE ROUMAINE DE LINGUISTIQUE. V. 9, No 1-. 0035-3957. Periodical. English, French, German, and Russian. $60.00. Ilexim Press, PO Box 1-136-1-137, Bucharest Romania. **Ind/Abst** MLA Int. Bibliogr. Books Artic. Mod. Lang. Lit., Lang. Lang. Behav. Abstr., Lang. Teach. LC P1.A1. (cum index). Revue de Linguistique.

RHETORIC REVIEW. VFOAT R.R. Vol. 1, No 1 (Sept. 1982)-. 0735-0198. Periodical. US. English. sa. $8.00. Southern Methodist University, Department of English/Theresa Enos, Dallas TX 75275. **Tel** (214)692-2945. **Ed** Theresa Enos. **Ind/Abst** MLA Int. Bibliogr. Books Artic. Mod. Lang. Lit. DD 808.005. bk rev. adv acc. **Circ** 1,000. A general journal of rhetoric and composition offering essays on current movements in rhetoric and the teaching of writing.

RHETORICA. Vol. 1, No. 1 (Spring 83)-. 0734-8584. Periodical. US. English. sa. $30.00. University of California Press, 2120 Berkeley Way, Berkeley CA 94720. **Tel** (415)642-4191. **Ed** James J Murphy. **Ind/Abst** MLA Int. Bibliogr. Books Artic. Mod. Lang. Lit. DD 808. bk rev. adv acc. **Circ** 600. Articles on the theory and practice of rhetoric in all periods and in all languages.

RICERCHE SLAVISTICHE. V. 1- 1952-. 0391-4127. IT. Italian. an. Licosa Libreria Comm Sansani, Via Lamarmora 45, 50121 Firenze Italy. **Tel** 579751. **Ed** Sante Gracio Hi. **Ind/Abst** MLA Int. Bibliogr. Books Artic. Mod. Lang. Lit. LC DR25. Research in Slavic linguistics.

RIVISTA DEGLI STUDI ORIENTALI. V. 1- 1907-. 0392-4866. Periodical. IT. Italian (English, French or German). $17.82. Bardi Editore, Salita de Crescenzi 16, 00186 Roma Italy. **Ind/Abst** MLA Int. Bibliogr. Books Artic. Mod. Lang. Lit. LC PJ6.

RIVISTA DI CULTURA CLASSICA E MEDIOEVALE. See Literature.

RIVISTA DI FILOLOGIA E DI ISTRUZIONE CLASSICA. Yearly V. 1- 1873-. 0035-6220. Periodical. IT. Italian. qt. Casa Editrice Loescher, Via Vittorio-Amedeo 2-18, Turin Italy.

RIVISTA DI STUDI ITALIANI. See Literature.

RLA. VFOAT Revista de Linguistica Aplicada. V. 1- 1963-. 0033-698X. CL. Spanish (English and French). an. $6.00. Universite de Concepcion, Educacion Facultie Human y Arte, Casilla 2307, Concepcion Chile. **Tel** 34985-Anexo 2143. **Ed** Max S Echeverria. **Ind/Abst** Lang. Lang. Behav. Abstr., Lang. Teach., Sociol. Abstr. LC P9. bk rev. adv acc. **Circ** 700. Linguistics: theoretical and applied. Spanish psycho and socialinguistics. Araucanian linguistics, language and learning.

ROCENKA KATEDER RUSISTIKY NA FILOZOFICKE A PEDAGOGICKE FAKULTE UNIVERZITY PALECKEHO. Series/Titl Rossica Olomucensia. 1973-. Periodical. Czech (Russian, with summaries in the other language). an. Fakulte Univerzity Paleckeho, Vytisk Neprodejny, Olomouc Czechoslovakia. LC PG2010. DD 491.705. Rocenka Katedry i.e. Kateder Rusistiky na Filosoficke a Pedagogicke Fakulte University Palackeho.

ROCKY MOUNTAIN REVIEW OF LANGUAGE AND LITERATURE. See Literature.

ROMANCE MONOGRAPHS. See Literary and Political Reviews.

ROMANCE NOTES. V. 1- Nov. 1959-. 0035-7995. Periodical. US. English (French or Spanish). ir. $15.00. University of North Carolina, Department of Romance Languages, Chapel Hill NC 27514. **Ed** Carol Sherman. **Ind/Abst** MLA Int. Bibliogr. Books Artic. Mod. Lang. Lit., Annu. Bibliogr. Engl. Lang. Lit., Years Work Eng. Stud. LC PC1. (cum index). adv acc.

ROMANCE PHILOLOGY. V. 1- Aug. 1947-. 0035-8002. Periodical. US. English (Multilingual). qt. $45.00. University of California Press, 2120 Berkeley Way, Berkeley CA 94720. **Tel** (415)642-4191. **Ed** Joseph Duggan. **Ind/Abst** MLA Int. Bibliogr. Books Artic. Mod. Lang. Lit., Annu. Bibliogr. Engl. Lang. Lit., Index Book Rev. Humanit., Soc. Sci. Index, Abstr. Folk. Stud., Lang. Lang. Behav. Abstr., Humanit. Index, Sociol. Abstr. LC PC1. DD 479.05. (cum index). bk rev. adv acc. **Circ** 600. Available on microfilm from University Microfilms. Articles on areas of historical romance linguistics and medieval romance literatures.

ROMANIA. V. 1.- (No. 1-). 0035-8029. Periodical. French. qt. Societe des Amis de la Romania, 284 Boulevard Raspail, 75014 Paris France. **Ind/Abst** MLA Int. Bibliogr. Books Artic. Mod. Lang. Lit., Index Book Rev. Humanit. LC PC2. DD 440.05. (cum index).

ROMANIC REVIEW. See Literature.

ROMANICA HELVETICA. 1935-. 0080-3871. Periodical. English (French, German or Italian). ir. Francke Verlag, Neuengasse 43 Postfach 1445, CH-3001 Bern Switzerland. **Tel** 031/22 17 15.

ROMANISCHE BIBLIOGRAPHIE. See Bibliographies.

ROMANISCHE FORSCHUNGEN. 1- No. 0035-8126. Periodical. GW. German. qt. 208.-. Vittorio Klostermann, Postfach 900601, Frauenlobstrabe 22, 6000 Frankfurt Am Main 90 West Germany. **Tel** (0611)77 4011. **Ind/Abst** MLA Int. Bibliogr. Books Artic. Mod. Lang. Lit., Index Book Rev. Humanit. LC PC3.

ROMANISTISCHE ZEITSCHRIFT FUR LITERATURGESCHICHTE. VFOAT Cahiers d'Histoire des Litteratures Romanes. 1-. Yearly Vol. 0343-379X. Periodical. GW. German (French). qt. 100.00. Carl Winter Universitatsverlag, Postfach 1866 Lutherstrasse 59, D6900 Heidelberg West Germany. **Tel** (06221)69111. **Ed** Erich Kohler and Henning Krauss. bk rev. adv acc. **Circ** 660. (ctrl). Romanic linguistics and literature.

ROMANISTISCHES JAHRBUCH. See Yearbooks, Almanacs, Directories.

ROMANOSLAVICA. 1- 1958-. 0557-272X. RM. Romanian (with summaries in Russian). an. $45.00. Ilexim Press, PO Box 1-136-1-137, Bucharest Romania. **Ind/Abst** MLA Int. Bibliogr. Books Artic. Mod. Lang. Lit. LC PC601.

ROMANSKOE I GERMANSKOE IAZYKOZNANIE. No. 4- 1974-. UR. Russian. an. 1.00. Izdatelstvo Vysheishaia Shkola, 220048 Minsk Parkovaiaa Magistral, 11, Minsk Belorussian SSR. **Ind/Abst** MLA Int. Bibliogr. Books Artic. Mod. Lang. Lit. LC PC5. Voprosy Filologii.

RON SHU - KOMAZAWA DAIGAKU GAIKOKUGOBU. Main/Corp Komazawa Daigaku, Tokyo. Gaikokugobu. Began in 1972. Periodical. JA. Japanese. ir. Komazawa Daigaku Gaikokugobu, 23-1 Komazawa 1-chome, Setagaya-ku, Tokyo Japan. LC P9.

ROSSICA OLOMUCENSIA. Monographic Series. Czech. ir. Rocenka Kateder Rusistiky na Filozoficke a Pedagogicke, Fakulte Univerzity Palackeho, Olomouc 77180 Czechoslovakia. **Tel** 22441. bk rev. (ctrl). Brings papers dealing with the Russian language and literature including reviews of important works in Slavic linguistics and literature.

RSSI. RECHERCHES SEMIOTIQUES. SEMIOTIC INQUIRY. (RSSI : RECHERCHES SEMIOTIQUES.DELETE). VFOAT R.S.S.I., Recherches Semiotiques, Semiotic Inquiry, RSSI : Semiotic Inquiry. Vol. 1, No. 1-. 0229-8651. Periodical. CN. English (text also in French). qt. $30.95. Victoria College, University of Toronto, 73 Queens Park East/Room 305 NAB, Toronto Ontario M5S 2K7 Canada. **Tel** (416)978-3870. **Ed** Paul Bouissac. **Ind/Abst** MLA Int. Bibliogr. Books Artic. Mod. Lang. Lit. LC P99. DD 001.51. bk rev. adv acc. **Circ** 500. (ctrl). Research in semiotics in all humanistic fields including the arts, architecture, anthropology, biology and sociology. Canadian Journal of Research in Semiotics, 0316-7917.

RUSISTICKY SBORNIK OLOMOUCKO-LUBLINSKY. 1-. Periodical. Czech (Polish, or Russian, with summaries in one of the other languages). ir. Slavisticka Knihovna Filozoficke Fakulty, Univerzity Palackeho, Krizkovskeho 10, 771 80 Olomouc, Praha Czechoslovakia. LC P19, PG2900.A1. DD 491.705.

RUSSIAN LANGUAGE JOURNAL. VFOAT Russkii Iazyk, Etudes de Russe. V. 20- (No. 75/76-). 0036-0252. Periodical. US. English (Russian). ty. Michigan State University, Department of German and Russian, East Lansing MI 48824. **Tel** (517)353-2941. **Ed** N P Avtonomoff. **Ind/Abst** MLA Int. Bibliogr. Books Artic. Mod. Lang. Lit., Sociol. Abstr., Lang. Lang. Behav. Abstr., Lang. Teach., Index Book Rev. Humanit., Curr. Index J. Educ. (cum index). V Pomoshch Prepodavateliu Russkogo Iazyka V Amerike.

RUSSIAN LINGUISTICS. V. 1- July 1974-. 0304-3487. Periodical. NE. English or Russian. ty. 74. Kluwer Academic Publishers Group, PO Box 322, 3300 AH Dordrecht Netherlands. **Tel** (31)78-334911. **Ed** L Durovic, A G F Vanltolk and W Leufeldt. **Ind/Abst** MLA Int. Bibliogr. Books Artic. Mod. Lang. Lit., Lang. Lang. Behav. Abstr., Lang. Teach., Index Book Rev. Humanit., Sociol. Abstr. LC PG2001. bk rev. adv acc. **Circ** 400. Grammar, phonetics and phonology, morphology, syntax and semantics, philological problems, Russian grammar and discourse analysis.

RUSSKAIA RECH. Jan./Feb. 1967-. 0036-0368. Periodical. UR. Russian. bm. $12.00. Victor Kamkin Inc (70788), 12224 Parklawn Drive, Rockville MD 20852. **Tel** (301)881-5973. **Ind/Abst** MLA Int. Bibliogr. Books Artic. Mod. Lang. Lit. LC PG2003.

RUSSKII IAZYK I LITERATURA V UZBEKSKOI SHKOLE. 1958-. Periodical. UR. Russian. mo. $13.50. Victor Kamkin Inc, 12224 Parklawn Drive, Rockville MD 20852. **Tel** (301)881-5973. LC PG2068.U9.

RUSSKII IAZYK V ESTONSKII SHKOLE. Periodical. UR. Russian. bm. $6.50. Victor Kamkin Inc, 12224 Parklawn Drive, Rockville MD 20852. **Tel** (301)881-5973. LC AS262.T22, PG2129. E8.

RUSSKII IAZYK V MOLDAVSKOI SHKOLE : UCHEBNO-METODICHESKII ZHURNAL MINISTERSTVA PROSVESHCHENIIA MOLDAVSKOI SSR. 0202-5418. Periodical. UR. Russian. bm. 0.20 Single Issue. Ministerstvo, 277033 Kishinev, Pr Lenina 85, Ministerstvo Prosveshcheniia Mssr, Kishinev Moldavian SSR. LC PG2068.M6. DD 491.7800704981.

RUSSKII IAZYK V NATSIONALNOI SHKOLE. Vol. 1- Jan./Feb. 1957-. 0557-5435. Periodical. UR. Russian. bm. $10.00. Victor Kamkin Inc (70789), 12224 Parklawn Drive, Rockville MD 20852. **Tel** (301)881-5973. **Ind/Abst** Lang. Lang. Behav. Abstr., Sociol. Abstr. LC PG2065.

RUSSKII IAZYK V SREDNAM POVOLZHE. Periodical. UR. Russian. LC PG2750.V6.

RUSSKII VODEVIL. Periodical. UR. Russian. 0.22. Iskusstva, Tsvetnoi Bulvar 25, Moskva USSR. LC PG3253.

RUSSKIJ JAZYK ZA RUBEZOM. (RUSSKII IAZYK ZA RUBEZHOM). 1/1967-. 0036-0384. Periodical. UR. Russian. bm. $23.50.

Linguistics

Victor Kamkin Inc (70792), 12224 Parklawn Drive, Rockville MD 20852. **Tel** (301)881-5973. **Ind/Abst** MLA Int. Bibliogr. Books Artic. Mod. Lang. Lit., Sociol. Abstr., Lang. Lang. Behav. Abstr.

RUSSKIJ JAZYK ZA SKOLE. (RUSSKII IAZYK V SHKOLE). Began with: V. 1, in 1936. 0036-0376. Periodical. UR. Russian. bm. $12.00. Victor Kamkin Inc (73334), 12224 Parklawn Drive, Rockville MD 20852. **Tel** (301)881-5973. **Ind/Abst** MLA Int. Bibliogr. Books Artic. Mod. Lang. Lit., Lang. Lang. Behav. Abstr., Sociol. Abstr. LC L51. (cum index). *Russkii Iazyki Literatura V Srednei Shkole.*

SAGA BOOK OF THE VIKING SOCIETY FOR NORTHERN RESEARCH. *See* Literature.

SAGAMI KOKUBUN. **Main/Corp** Sagami Joshi Daigaku Kokubun Kenkyukai. No. 1-. JA. Japanese. ir. c/o Sagami Joshi Daigaku, Kokubunka Dai 1 Kenkyushitsu 1-1 Bunkyo 2-Chome, Sagamihara 228 Japan. LC PL501.

SAIS ARBEITSBERICHTE AUS DEM SEMINAR FUR ALLGEMEINE UND INDOGERMANISCHE SPRACHWISSENSCHAFT. VFOAT S.A.I.S. Arbeitsberichte aus dem Seminar fur Allgemeine und Indogermanische Sprachwissenschaft. 0720-4035. German. ir. LC P3. DD 410.5.

SAMSKRTA SAHITYA PARISHAT. Began publication in 1918. Periodical. Sanskrit. ir. LC PK401.

SAMSKRTAPRATIBHA. VFOAT Samskrita Pratibha. 1.- 1959-. 0558-3764. Periodical. Sanskrit. an. $2.00. Sahitya Akademi, National Academy of Letters, Rabindra Bhalan, New Delhi 110001 India. LC PK401.

SAMSKRTAVIMARSAH. V. 1- July 1973-. English (Sanskrit). ir. 15.00. Rashtriya Sanskrit Sansthan, 60, New Delhi India. LC PK401. *Vimarsa.*

SATARANGI CAMALA. Periodical. Hindi. ir. LC PK1921.

SBORNIK PEDAGOGICKE FAKULTY V PLZNI. CIZI JAZYKY. VFOAT Cizi Jazyky. Czech (German, or Russian, with summaries in the other languages). ir. 22.00 Single Issue. LC PB35.

SBORNIK PEDAGOGICKE FAKULTY V USTI NAD LABEM. RADA CIZICH JAZYKU. VFOAT Rada Cizich Jazyku. Began with vol. for 1974. Czech (English, German, or Russian, with summaries in the other languages). ir. 24.00. LC PB5.

SBORNIK STATEI PO FRANTSUZSKOI LINGVISTIKE I METODIKE PREPODAVANIIA INOSTRANNOGO IAZYKA V VUZE. V. 3- 1971-. UR. Russian. 0.35 Single Issue. Moskovskii Gos Pedagog In-T Inostrannykh Iazykov, Fakultet Frantsuzskogo Iazyka, B-14 Rosto Kinskii Proezd DBA, Moskva Russian SFSR. LC PC2073. *Doklady I Soobshcheniia.*

SCANDINAVIAN STUDIES. V. 1- June 1911-. 0036-5637. Periodical. US. English. qt. Scandinavian Studies, 3072 Foreign Language Building, 707 South Mathews Street, Urbana IL 61802. **Tel** (913)843-1235. **Ind/Abst** Humanit. Index, MLA Int. Bibliogr. Books Artic. Mod. Lang. Lit., Am. Hist. Life, Hist. Abstr. LC PD1505. DD 439.506273. (cum index).

SCANDO-SLAVICA. SUPPLEMENTUM. VFOAT Scando Slavica Supplementum. 1-. Monographic Series. English (French or German). ir. Munksgaard International Publishers Limited, 35 Norre Sogade, DK-1370 Copenhagen K Denmark. **Tel** 45 12 70 30. LC PG1.

SCHATZKAMMER DER DEUTSCHEN SPRACHE, DICHTUNG UND GESCHICHTE. *See* Literature.

SCHOLASTIC VOICE. V. 48, No. 2- Feb. 2, 1970-. 0032-6380. Periodical. US. English. ir. Scholastic Magazines, PO Box 644, Lyndhurst NJ 07071. **Tel** (800)631-1586. LC PE1001. DD 420.5. *Practical English, A Scholastic Magazine.*

SCHRIFTEN DER SCHWEIZERISCHEN GESELLSCHAFT FUR VOLKSKUNDE. *See* Folklore.

SCHRIFTEN ZUR PHONETIK, SPRACHWISSENSCHAFT UND KOMMUNIKATIONSFORSCHUNG CEASED. No. 1-. GE. German. ir. Deutscher Buch Export-Import, Leninstrasse 16, DDR-701 Leipzig 2102 East Germany.

SCHULZEITUNG. V. 4, No. 1- Oct. 1977-. 0705-8276. Periodical. CN. English (German). ir. Waterloo County Board of Education, PO Box 68, Kitchener Ontario N2H 3W5 Canada. **DD** 438.0071071345. *Schulzeitung Concordia Courier, 0705-8284.*

SCHWEIZER VOLKSKUNDE. *See* Folklore.

SCHWEIZERISCHES ARCHIV FUR VOLKSKUNDE. *See* Genealogy and Heraldry - Archives.

SCHWEIZERISCHES IDIOTIKON. WORTERBUCH DER SCHWEIZERDEUTSCHEN SPRACHE. *See* Yearbooks, Almanacs, Directories.

SCHWERPUNKTE ANGLISTIK CEASED. Monographic Series. GW. German. R Oldenbourg Verlag, Postfach 801360, D-8000 Munich 80 West Germany.

SCOTTISH GAELIC STUDIES. Vol. 1, Pt. 1 (Apr. 1926)-. 0080-8024. Periodical. UK. English. ir. **Ind/Abst** MLA Int. Bibliogr. Books Artic. Mod. Lang. Lit. LC PB1501. DD 491.63. (cum index).

SCOTTISH LANGUAGE. No. 1 (Autumn 1982)-. 0264-0198. UK. English. an. 15.75. University of Aberdeen, ALSS Department of English, Old Aberdeen AB9 2UB Scotland. **Tel** (031)677-1011. Ed Hans Speitel. **Ind/Abst** MLA Int. Bibliogr. Books Artic. Mod. Lang. Lit. LC PR8514. DD 427.94105. bk rev. adv acc. Circ 800. (ctrl). A scholarly journal that publishes articles on all aspects of the languages of Scotland.

SCRIPTA CLASSICA ISRAELICA. V. 1- 1974-. 0334-4509. IS. Multilingual (English, German or Latin). an. $10.00. Jerusalem Academic Press, PO Box 2390, Jerusalem Israel. **Ind/Abst** Recent Publ. Artic. LC PA1.

THE SECOL REVIEW. VFOAT S.E.C.O.L. Review. VAT Southeastern Conference on Linguistics Review. Vol. 6, No. 1 (Spring 1982)-. 0730-6245. Periodical. US. English. ty. $13.00. SECOL Review, Box 275, Murfreesboro TN 37132. **Tel** (615)898-2608. Ed Reza Ordoubadian. **Ind/Abst** MLA Int. Bibliogr. Books Artic. Mod. Lang. Lit. LC P1. DD 410.5. bk rev. adv acc. Circ 500. (ctrl). Covers all areas in linguistics, including phonology, morphology, syntax, socio-linguistics, psycho-linguistics, etc. *SECOL Bulletin, 0192-3277.*

SEINAN GAKUIN DAIGAKU EIGO EIBUNGAKU RON SHU. VFOAT Studies in English Language and Literature. Began with June 1960 issue. JA. Japanese or English. ir. 2-92 Nishishin, 6-chome Nishi-ku (814), Fukuoka Japan. LC PE9.

SELECTA (CORVALLIS, OR.). (SELECTA : JOURNAL OF THE PNCFL, PACIFIC NORTHWEST COUNCIL ON FOREIGN LANGUAGES). Vol. 1 (1980)-. 0277-0598. Periodical. US. English (French, German, Italian, or Spanish). an. Portland State University, Department of Foreign Languages and Literature, Portland OR 97207. **Ind/Abst** MLA Int. Bibliogr. Books Artic. Mod. Lang. Lit. LC PB11. DD 405. *Proceedings, 0363-8391.*

SELECTED ARTICLES FROM LANGUAGE LEARNING. No. 1-. 0559-3468. US. English. ir. University of Michigan, Language Learning, 1001 North University Building, Ann Arbor MI 48109.

SELECTED BIBLIOGRAPHIES IN LANGUAGE AND LITERATURE. *See* Bibliographies.

SEMASIA. Vol. 1-. NE. Multilingual (English, French or German). ir. Editions Rodopi, Keizersgaacht 302-304, Amsterdam The Netherlands. **Ind/Abst** MLA Int. Bibliogr. Books Artic. Mod. Lang. Lit., Lang. Lang. Behav. Abstr., Sociol. Abstr. LC PB3. DD 410.5.

SEMINAR. V. 1- Spring 1965-. 0037-1939. Periodical. CN. English (German, includes some text in French). qt. $20.00. University of Toronto Press, 5201 Dufferin Street, Downsview Ontario M3H 5T8 Canada. **Tel** (416)667-7781. Ed P O'Neill. **Ind/Abst** MLA Int. Bibliogr. Books Artic. Mod. Lang. Lit., Index Book Rev. Humanit. LC PF3001. DD 430.5. bk rev. adv acc. (ctrl). A journal of Germanic studies.

SEMIOSIS. 1- 1976, Issue 1-. 0170-219X. Periodical. GW. German (English or French). qt. $23.46. Agis Verlag, Postfach 3, 7570 Baden-Baden 19 West Germany. Ed Max Bense and Elisabeth Walther. **Ind/Abst** Lang. Lang. Behav. Abstr., MLA Int. Bibliogr. Books Artic. Mod. Lang. Lit. bk rev. adv acc. Semiotics and its applications.

SEMIOTIC SCENE CEASED. V. 1-4, No. 3. 0196-0865. Periodical. US. English. qt. $25.00 Institution, $15.00 Individual Member, $10.00 Student Member. Semiotic Society Secretariat, PO Box 1214, Bloomington IL 47401. **Ind/Abst** MLA Int. Bibliogr. Books Artic. Mod. Lang. Lit., Lang. Lang. Behav. Abstr. *Bulletin of Literary Semiotics, 0196-0385; Semiotic Scene, 0196-0865.*

SEMIOTICA. V. 1- 1969-. 0037-1998. English (French). mo. Walter de Gruyter Inc, 200 Saw Mill River Road, Hawthorne NY 10532. **Tel** (914)747-0110. Ed Thomas A Sebeok. **Ind/Abst** MLA Int. Bibliogr. Books Artic. Mod. Lang. Lit., Sociol. Abstr., Lang. Lang. Behav. Abstr., Film Lit. Index, Lang. Teach., Index Book Rev. Humanit., Repert. Int. Litt. Art. LC B820. bk rev. adv acc. Circ 850. Devoted to the study of signs and symbols in different societies and their cultural relevance. *Social Science Information.*

SEMIOTICS. 1980-. 0742-7611. US. English. an. LC P99. DD 001.51.

SERIE LINGUISTICA. No. 3- 1974-. Portuguese. ir. Summer Institute of Linguistics, Departamento de Estudos Tecnicos, Caixa Postal 14-2221, 7000 Brasilia Brazil. **Ind/Abst** MLA Int. Bibliogr. Books Artic. Mod. Lang. Lit. LC PM5151.

SERIE LINGUISTICA PERUANA. Monographic Series. US. English. ir. Summer Institute Linguistic Bookstore, 7500 West Camp Wisdom, Dallas TX 75236. **Tel** (214)298-3331. **Ind/Abst** MLA Int. Bibliogr. Books Artic. Mod. Lang. Lit.

SHAAR LA-MATHIL. Periodical. Hebrew. wk. LC PJ4569. *La-Mathil, Shaar La-Kore He-Hadash.*

SHINBUNGAKU HYORON. VFOAT Japanese Journalism Review. JA. Japanese. an. Nihon Shinbun Gakkai, 3-1 Hongo 7, Bunkyo-Ku, Tokyo-To Japan. LC P87.

SIGN LANGUAGE STUDIES. 1- 1972-. 0302-1475. Periodical. US. English. qt. $40.00. Linstok Press, 9306 Mintwood, Silver Spring MD 20901. **Tel** (301)585-1939. Ed William C Stokoe. **Ind/Abst** MLA Int. Bibliogr. Books Artic. Mod. Lang. Lit., Lang. Teach., Except. Child Educ. Resour., Curr. Index J. Educ., Sociol. Abstr., Lang. Lang. Behav. Abstr. LC HV2350. DD 001.56. NLM W1 SI388. bk rev. adv acc. Circ 450. Serves as a forum for reporting research into nonvocal communication, facial expression, gesticulation, face-to-face communication, kinesics, proxemics, and language networks.

SIGNIFICACAO. No. 1- August 1974-. French or Portuguese, with summaries in English. ir. Centro de Estudos Semioticos A J Greimas, rua Ramos de Azevedo 423, Jardim Paulista 14.100, Ribeirao Preto Brazil. LC P99.

SIJO MUNHAK. Periodical. KO. Korean. ir. 1,300. Sijo Munhak, 48-4 Puam-Dong, Congno-Ku, Seoul South Korea. LC PL975.6. *Sijo Munhak.*

SINMUN KWA PANGSONG. Periodical. Korean. ir. 5,000. Hanguk Sinmun Yonguso, 31 1-Ka Taepyongno, Chung-Ku, Seoul Korea. LC P87. *Sinmun Pyongnon (Hanguk Sinmun Yonguso).*

SINTAKSIS PREDLOZHENIIA I SVERKHFRAZOVOGO EDINSTVA V ANGLIISKOM IAZYKE. Periodical. UR. Russian. 0.90 Each Issue. Rostovskii-Na-Donu Gosudarstvennyi Pedagogicheskii Institut G Rostov-Na-Donu, Engelsa 33, Rostov-Na-Donu Russian SFSR. LC PE1361.

SISTEMNOE OPISANIE LEKSIKI GERMANSKIKH IAZYKOV. Vol. 1-. Periodical. UR. Russian. 0.70. Izdatelstvo Lgu im. A. A. Zhdanova, 199164 Leningrad, Universitetskaia Nab 7/9, Leningrad Russian SFSR. LC PE1585.

SITZUNGSBERICHTE DER SACHSISCHE AKADEMIE DER WISSENSCHAFTEN, LEIPZIG, PHILOLOGISCH-HISTORISCHE KLASSE. **Main/Corp** Sachsische Akademie der Wissenschaften, Leipzig. Philologisch-Historische Klasse. Vol. 1- 1849-. 0080-5300. Periodical. GW. German. ir. Akademie Verlag, Leipziger Strasse 3-4, DDR 108 Berlin West Germany. LC AS182. DD 410.5. *Berichte uber die Verhandlungen der Koniglich Sachsischen Gesellschaft der Wissenschaften du Leipzig.*

SKRIFTER - NORSK SPRAKRAD. **Main/Corp** Norsk Sprakrad. Norwegian. ir. LC PD2602.A3. DD 439.82. *Skrifter.*

SLAVIA. Began with: Vol. 1, in 1922. 0037-6736. Periodical. Czech. qt. Kubon & Sagner, Postfach 34 01 08, D-8 Muenchen 34 West Germany. **Tel** (089)52

20 27. **Ind/Abst** MLA Int. Bibliogr. Books Artic. Mod. Lang. Lit., Lang. Lang. Behav. Abstr., Sociol. Abstr. (cum index). The oldest review in the field of Slavistics from Czechoslovakia. Publishes articles, discussions, reviews, criticism, etc. all on comparative Slavonic linguistics and literature.

SLAVIA OCCIDENTALIS. Vol. 1- 1921-. 0081-0002. PL. Polish (summaries in English and French). ir. ARS Polona, Krakowskie Przedmiescie 7, 00-068 Warsaw Poland. **Ind/Abst** Sociol. Abstr., Lang. Lang. Behav. Abstr. **LC** D377.A1. (cum index).

SLAVIA ORIENTALIS. Vol. 6- Oct.. 1957-. 0037-6744. Periodical. PO. Polish (table of contents in Russian and English). qt. ARS Polona, Krakowskie Przedmiescie 7, 00-068 Warsaw Poland. **Ind/Abst** MLA Int. Bibliogr. Books Artic. Mod. Lang. Lit., Sociol. Abstr., Am. Hist. Life, Hist. Abstr., Lang. Lang. Behav. Abstr., Hist. Abstr., Part A, Mod. Hist. Abstr., Hist. Abst., Part B, Twent. Century Abstr. Available on microfilm. *Kwartalnik Instytutu Polsko-Radzieckiego.*

SLAVIC AND EAST EUROPEAN JOURNAL. **VFOAT** SEEJ. V. 1- 1957-. 0037-6752. Periodical. US. English. qt. $20.00. American Association of Teachers of Slavic-East European Languages, University of Arizona, Modern Language Building, Tuscon AZ 85287. **Tel** (602)621-7341. **Ed** Ernest Scatton. **Ind/Abst** MLA Int. Bibliogr. Books Artic. Mod. Lang. Lit., Lang. Lang. Behav. Abstr., Annu. Bibliogr. Engl. Lang. Lit., Lang. Teach., Ref. Source, Index Book Rev. Humanit., Curr. Index J. Educ., Humanit. Index. (cum index). bk rev. adv acc. **Circ** 1,500. (ctrl). Articles of scholarly nature on Slavic and East European languages, literatures, cultures, and pedagogy to advance language teaching. *AATSEEL Journal.*

SLAVIC SERIES. **Series/Titl** Current Inquiry into Language and Linguistics, 21 Etc. 6-. Monographic Series. US. English. ir. $96.00. Boreal Scholarly Publishers and Distributors Ltd, 9725-106 Street #105, Edmonton Alberta Canada T5K 1B5. **Tel** (403)421-0145. **Ed** A L Vanek. bk rev. adv acc. **Circ** 800. All aspects of human communication. *Slavic Linguistics.*

SLAVICA *CEASED.* **Series/Titl** Acta Universitatis Palackianae Olomucensis. Philologica. Began in 1971. Ceased with 3rd No. in 1972. Czech (Polish). an. **LC** P19, PG13. *Series Slavica.*

SLAVICA LUNDENSIA. 1-. German (Russian, Polish with summaries in English). ir. **LC** PG13. *Sprakliga Bidrag.*

SLAVICA OLOMUCENSIA. 4-. Periodical. Czech (with summaries in German and Russian). ir. 33.00. Ustredni Knihovna Filozoficke Fakulty, Univerzity Palackeho Krizkovskeho 10, 771 80 Olomouc Czechoslovakia. **LC** P19, PG1. *Slavica.*

SLAVICA PRAGENSIA. 1- 1959-. 0583-5380. CS. Czech (English, German, Russian, or other languages). ir. University Karlovy, 116 38 Praha 1 Nam Krasnoarmejcu 1 Ceskoslovensko.

SLAVICA SLOVACA. Vol. 1- 1966-. 0037-6787. Periodical. GW. Slovak. qt. Kubon and Sagner, Postfach 34 01 08, D-8 Munchen 34 West Germany. **Tel** (089)52 20 27. **Ind/Abst** Sociol. Abstr. **LC** PG1. Linguistics and literary criticism are its subjects with special devotion to comparative linguistics of Slovak and other Slavic languages.

SLAVISTICA : PROCEEDINGS OF THE INSTITUTE OF SLAVISTICS OF UKRANIAN FREE ACADEMY OF SCIENCES. No. 1-. Periodical. CN. English (Ukrainian). ir. **LC** PG1.

SLOVENSKA REC. Vol. 1- Sept. 1932-. 0037-6981. Periodical. GW. Slovak. bm. Kubon and Sagner, Postfach 34 01 08, D-8000 Munchen West Germany. **Tel** (089)52 20 27. **Ind/Abst** MLA Int. Bibliogr. Books Artic. Mod. Lang. Lit., Sociol. Abstr., Lang. Lang. Behav. Abstr. **LC** PG5201. Prints studies on the problems of Slovak orthography, pronunciation, and grammar. Special attention is devoted to theory of style and culture of the language.

SLOVO. 1- 1952-. 0583-6255. YU. Slovak (summaries in French). an. $30.00. Mladost Export Import, PO Box 1028, Ilica 30, 41000 Zagreb Yugoslavia. **Ind/Abst** MLA Int. Bibliogr. Books Artic. Mod. Lang. Lit., Lang. Lang. Behav. Abstr., Sociol. Abstr. **LC** PG1.

SLOVO NA STOROZHI. **VFOAT** Word on Guard, La Parole en Garde. No. 1- 1964-. 0583-6263. Periodical. CN. Ukrainian. ir. $5.00. Ukrainian Language Association, 911 Carling Avenue, Ottawa Ontario Canada. **Tel** 2254447. **Ed** J B Rudnyckyi. **Ind/Abst** MLA Int. Bibliogr. Books Artic. Mod. Lang. Lit. **DD** 491.7905. bk rev. adv acc. **Circ** 750. (ctrl). Yearbook devoted to cultivation and preservation of the Ukrainian language in Ukraine and in Ukrainian disapora.

SLOVO V SISTEMNYKH OTNOSHENIIAKH. UR. Russian. 0.70 Single Issue. Ministerstvo Prosvechsheniia RSFSR, Ul K Libknekhta 9, Sverdlovsk Russia. **LC** AS262.S86, PG2175.

SOCIOLINGUISTICS NEWSLETTER. *See* Sociology: General Works, Theory.

SOCJOLINGWISTYKA. **Series/Titl** Prace Naukowe Uniwersytetu Slaskiego W Katowicach. 1-. Periodical. Polish (table of contents in French and Russian). ir. **LC** P40.

SOGANG OMUN. Vol. 1-. Periodical. KO. Korean. ir. Toso Chulpan Taeram, 87-1 Konyji-Dong, Chongno-Ku Seoul Korea. **LC** PL901.

SOUTH CENTRAL REVIEW. Vol. 1, No. 1 & 2 (Spring/Summer 1984)-. 0743-6831. Periodical. US. English. qt. $8.00 Members, $10.00 Non-Members. South Central Modern Language Association, Texas A & M University, Department of English, College Station TX 77843. **Ind/Abst** Abstr. Engl. Stud., MLA Int. Bibliogr. Books Artic. Mod. Lang. Lit. **LC** PB1. **DD** 809. *South Central Bulletin, 0038-321X.*

SOUTHEAST ASIAN REVIEW OF ENGLISH. Vol. 1, No. 1 (Dec. 1980)-. 0127-046X. Periodical. English. sa. $4.50. University of Malaya, Co-op Bookshop, PO Box 1127, Jalan Pantai Baru, Kuala Lumpur Malaysia. **Ind/Abst** MLA Int. Bibliogr. Books Artic. Mod. Lang. Lit. **LC** PE9. **DD** 820.8.

SOUTHERN CALIFORNIA OCCASIONAL PAPERS IN LINGUISTICS. **VFOAT** Occasional Papers in Linguistics. No. 1- July 1973-. Monographic Series. US. English. S C O P I L, Los Angeles CA 90007.

SOUTHWEST JOURNAL OF LINGUISTICS. Vol. 6, No. 1 (Spring 1983)-. 0737-4143. Periodical. US. English. sa. $30.00. Lasso Secretary-Treasurer, University of Texas at El Paso, Department of Modern Languages, El Paso TX 79968. **Tel** (915)747-5801. **Ed** Jon Amastae. **Ind/Abst** MLA Int. Bibliogr. Books Artic. Mod. Lang. Lit. **LC** P1. **DD** 410.5. bk rev. adv acc. **Circ** 250. (ctrl). All aspects of theoretical, general, and descriptive linguistics. *Journal of the Linguistic Association of the Southwest, 0732-2615.*

SOVETSKOE FINNO-UGROVEDENIE. **VFOAT** Soviet Fenno-Ugric Studies. 1- 1965-. 0038-5182. Periodical. UR. Russian. qt. Victor Kamkin Inc (78210), 12224 Parklawn Drive, Rockville MD 20852. **Tel** (301)881-5973. **Ind/Abst** MLA Int. Bibliogr. Books Artic. Mod. Lang. Lit., Sociol. Abstr., Lang. Lang. Behav. Abstr.

SPEAKERS BUREAU INTERNATIONAL. *See* Yearbooks, Almanacs, Directories.

SPEAQ JOURNAL. (S P E A Q JOURNAL). **Main/Corp** Societe pour la Promotion de l'Enseignement de l'Anglais (Langue Seconde) au Quebec. Began publication in 1977 or 1978. 0225-3550. Periodical. CN. English (includes some text in French). qt. Limited to members- membership $15.00 per year. Societe pour la Promotion de l Enseignement de l'Anglais au Quebec, PO 278 Station la Cite, Montreal Quebec H2W 2N8 Canada. **Ind/Abst** Lang. Teach., Can. Educ. Index. **DD** 428.0070714. *S P E A Q Journal, 0225-3550.*

SPEAQ-OUT. (SPEAQ-OUT : BULLETIN DE LA SOCIETE POUR LA PROMOTION DE L'ENSEIGNEMENT DE L'ANGLAIS, LANGUE SECONDE, AU QUEBEC). 0229-6535. Periodical. CN. English (French). sa. Free to Members. SPEAQ, Suite 1903/2121 Saint Mathieu Street, Montreal Quebec H3H 2J3 Canada. **DD** 420.70714.

SPECIAL PUBLICATIONS - AMERICAN PHILOLOGICAL ASSOCIATION. (SPECIAL PUBLICATIONS). 0065-9703. Monographic Series. US. English. ir. Scholars Press, PO Box 2268, Chico CA 95927. **DD** 410.

SPEECH AND LANGUAGE: ADVANCES IN BASIC RESEARCH AND PRACTICE. *See* Physically Impaired.

SPEECH COMMUNICATION DIRECTORY. *See* Yearbooks, Almanacs, Directories.

SPEECH INDEX. *See* Indexes/Abstracts.

SPOKEN ENGLISH. *See* Education (General) - Special Aspects of Education.

SPOLECENSKE VEDY : PHILOLOGIA. **Main/Corp** Bratislava. Univerzita. Pedagogicka Fakulta. Slovak (summaries in Russian and German). ir. **LC** PG5207.

SPRAAKVAARD. 0038-8440. Periodical. SW. Swedish. qt. 37.50. Svenska Spraknamnden, Lundagatan 42 Uppg 5, 5 tr 117 27 Stockholm Sweden. **Tel** 08/680150. **Ind/Abst** MLA Int. Bibliogr. Books Artic. Mod. Lang. Lit. bk rev. Linguistics and language planning.

SPRACHE & KOGNITION. **VFOAT** Sprache und Kognition. Vol. 1, No. 1 (July 1982)-. 0253-4533. Periodical. German. qt. $45.00. Hogrefe International Inc, 14-14 Bruce Park Avenue, Toronto Ontario M4P 2S3 Canada. **Tel** (416)482-6339. **Ed** D Doerner, J Engelkamp and H Grimm. **Ind/Abst** Psychol. Abstr. **LC** P37. **DD** 401.9. **NLM** W1 SP6744. Publishes empirical and theoretical papers as well as critical overviews which deal with language and cognition and their interaction.

SPRACHE IM TECHNISCHEN ZEITALTER. 1- 1961-. 0038-8475. Periodical. GW. German. mo. Literarisches Colloquium, AM Sandweder 5, 1000 Berlin 39 West Germany. **Ind/Abst** Philos. Index. **LC** P3. **DD** 410.5.

SPRACHE UND DATENVERARBEITUNG. Vol. 1-. 0343-5202. Periodical. GW. German. sa. Saarbruecker Druck-Verlag GMBH, Postfach 442, Halbergstrasse 3, D660 Saarbruecken West Germany. **Tel** (0681)64941. **Ed** Harald Zimmermann, Winfried Lenders. **Ind/Abst** MLA Int. Bibliogr. Books Artic. Mod. Lang. Lit., Lang. Lang. Behav. Abstr., Comput. Control Abstr., Electr. Electron. Abstr., Sci. Abstr. Sect. A. Phys. Abstr., Energy Res. Abstr. **LC** P98. **CODEN** SPDADH. bk rev. adv acc. Draws from all fields pertaining to mechanized work with language as a medium of communication and information.

SPRACHE UND LITERATUR IN WISSENSCHAFT UND UNTERRICHT. **VFOAT** Sprache und Literatur. 14. Yearly, 1. Half yearly – 51-. 0724-9713. Periodical. GW. German. sa. $16.76. Wilhelm Fink Verlag, Ohmstrasse 5, 8 Muenchen 40 West Germany. **Tel** 089/348017. **Ed** Hans Jurgen Heringer, Gerhard Kurz and Gerhard Stotzel. **Ind/Abst** MLA Int. Bibliogr. Books Artic. Mod. Lang. Lit. bk rev. adv acc. **Circ** 3,000. (ctrl). Topical discussions and recent research findings in the fields of language and literature. *Linguistik und Didaktik.*

SPRACHKUNST. Vol. 1-. 0038-8483. Periodical. AU. German (English, French or Russian). sa. 420.-. Osterreichischen Akademie Wissenschaften, Dr Ignaz, Seipelpl 2, A-1010 Wien Austria. **Tel** 52-96-81. **Ed** V Herbert Foltinek, Heinz Kindermann and Gunther Wytrzens. **Ind/Abst** MLA Int. Bibliogr. Books Artic. Mod. Lang. Lit., Index Book Rev. Humanit. **LC** P3. bk rev. **Circ** 500. The different treatises are written in German, English, French and Russian. Mainly deals with Sprachkunst (art of language).

SPRACHSPIEGEL. Vol. 1-. 0038-8513. Periodical. German. ir. **Ind/Abst** MLA Int. Bibliogr. Books Artic. Mod. Lang. Lit. **LC** PF3003. **DD** 430.5.

SPRACHWISSENSCHAFT. Vol. 1- 1976-. Periodical. GW. German. qt. 76.00. Carl Winter Universitatsverlag, Postfach 1866, Lutherstrasse 59, D6900 Heidelberg West Germany. **Tel** (06221)69111. **Ed** Rudolf Schiiheichel. bk rev. adv acc. **Circ** 550. (ctrl). Linguistics.

SPRAK NYTT. **VFOAT** Spraknytt. 1. Vol.- 1973-. Periodical. NO. Norwegian. ir. Norsk Sprakrad, Postboks 8107 Dep, Oslo 1 Norway. **LC** PD2601.

SPRINGER SERIES IN LANGUAGE AND COMMUNICATION. *See* Communication.

SPROG OG KULTUR. Vol. 1-. 0038-8645. DK. Danish. qt. Universitetsforlaget, PO Box 2959-Toyen, Oslo 6 Norway. **Ind/Abst** MLA Int. Bibliogr. Books Artic. Mod. Lang. Lit. **LC** DL101.

STATEMENT (FORT COLLINS, CO). (STATEMENT : JOURNAL OF THE COLORADO LANGUAGE ARTS SOCIETY). 1965. US. English. ty. $10.00. Colorado State University, English Department, Attn Bill McBride, Fort Collins CO 80523. **Tel** (303)491-6428. **Ed** William G McBride. bk rev. **Circ** 1,200. (ctrl). Focus of journal is on all aspects of language, arts and education. Kindergarten through graduate level.

Linguistics

STATISTIKA RECHI I AVTOMATICHESKII ANALIZ TEKSTA. UR. Russian. 1.84. IZD-VO Nauka, B-164, Leningrad Russia. LC P98.

STATUS REPORT ON SPEECH RESEARCH. VFOAT Speech Research. Began with Feb. 1965. Periodical. US. English. ir. National Technical Information Service, 5285 Port Royal Road, Springfield VA 22161. Tel (703)487-4650. Ind/Abst Lang. Lang. Behav. Abstr., Sociol. Abstr. ERIC Version for July/Dec. 1981- distributed to depository libraries in microfiche.

STOCKHOLM STUDIES IN ENGLISH. 1- 1937-. Monographic Series. SW. English. ir. Almqvist & Wiksell, 108 Drottningatan, PO Box 45150, S-104 30 Stockholm Sweden. Ind/Abst MLA Int. Bibliogr. Books Artic. Mod. Lang. Lit.

STRUKTURNAIA I PRIKLADNAIA LINGVISTIKA. Periodical. UR. Russian. 1.07 Each Issue. IZD-VO Leningradskogo Universiteta, 199164 Leningrad, Unviersitetskaia Nab 7/9, Leningrad Russian SFSR. LC P9.

STUDI DI FILOLOGIA E LETTERATURA. 1-. Periodical. Italian (English or Spanish). ir. LC P1.A1.

STUDI DI LESSICOGRAFIA ITALIANA. Vol. 1-. Periodical. IT. Italian. an. Licosa Libreria Comm Sansani, Via Lamarmora 45, 50121 Firenze Italy. Tel 579151. Ed D'Arco Silvio Avalle. LC PC1600. DD 452.05. Italian lexicography.

STUDI E PROBLEMI DI CRITICA TESTUALE. V. 1- Oct. 1970-. 0049-2361. Periodical. IT. Italian. sa. $26.73. Studi e Problemi Critica Test, Via Castiglione 8, 40124 Bologna Italy. Ind/Abst MLA Int. Bibliogr. Books Artic. Mod. Lang. Lit. LC P47.

STUDI E SAGGI LINGUISTICI. 1- 1961-. 0085-6827. IT. Italian. an. $22.58. Professor Tristano Bolelli, Via S Maria 36, 56100 Pisa Italy. Ind/Abst MLA Int. Bibliogr. Books Artic. Mod. Lang. Lit.

STUDI FILOSOFICI. 1-. Periodical. IT. French (Italian, with English summaries). ir. 4000 Each Issue. Istituto Universitario Orientale, Via Nardones 113, 80132 Napoli Italy. LC B4. DD 105.

STUDI GERMANICI. See Literature.

STUDI LINGUISTICI SALENTINI. Began in 1965. Periodical. Italian. ir. Associazione Linguistica, Villa Sebaste Via Per Campi 73051, Novoli (Leese) Italy. LC PC1809.S24.

STUDIA ANGLICA POSNANIENSIA. V. 1- 1968-. 0081-6272. PL. English. an. ARS Polona, Krakowskie Przedmiescie 7, 00-068 Warsaw Poland. Ind/Abst MLA Int. Bibliogr. Books Artic. Mod. Lang. Lit., Lang. Lang. Behav. Abstr., Lang. Teach. LC PE1.

STUDIA CELTICA. V. 1- 1966-. 0081-6353. UK. English. an. $32.57. University of Wales Press, 6 Gwennyth Street Cathays, Cardiff CF2 4YD Wales. Tel 31919. Ed J E Caerwyn Williams. Ind/Abst MLA Int. Bibliogr. Books Artic. Mod. Lang. Lit. LC PB1001. DD 491.605. bk rev adv acc. Circ 300. Attracts contributions from scholars in Indo-European philology, continental and insular Celtic; an indispensable tool for specialists in Celtic.

STUDIA FENNICA. V. 1- 0085-6835. Fl. Finnish (English). ir. Finnish Literature Society, Hallituskatu 1, 00171 Helsinki 17 Finland. Tel (90)171-229. Ed Lauri Honko. Ind/Abst MLA Int. Bibliogr. Books Artic. Mod. Lang. Lit., Abstr. Anthropol. LC PH107. DD 494.54105. (ctrl). Recent Finnish research on folkloristics, folk life and linguistics in English or German.

STUDIA GERMANICA GANDENSIA. See Literature.

STUDIA GRAMATYCZNE. Series/Titl Prace Instytutu Jezyka Polskiego. 1-. 0208-4074. Periodical. English (Polish and Russian). ir. 60.00. LC P201. DD 415.

STUDIA GRAMMATICA. 1- 1962-. 0081-6469. GE. German. ir. Deutscher Buch Export-Import, Leninstrasse 16, DDR-701 Leipzig East Germany. Ind/Abst MLA Int. Bibliogr. Books Artic. Mod. Lang. Lit., Lang. Lang. Behav. Abstr., Sociol. Abstr.

STUDIA LINGUISTICA. Vol. 1-. 0039-3193. Periodical. SW. French (articles in English, German, and Swedish). ir. 100. Liber International, S-205 10, Malmo Sweden. Ind/Abst MLA Int. Bibliogr. Books Artic. Mod. Lang. Lit., Sociol. Abstr., Lang. Lang. Behav. Abstr., Lang. Teach., Index Book Rev.

Humanit., Years Work Eng. Stud. LC P9. DD 405. bk rev. Circ 800. (ctrl). General linguistics.

STUDIA LINGUISTICA. Series/Titl Acta Universitatis Wratislaviensis. 1- 1974-. PL. Polish (summaries in English, French or German). ir. 20.00 Single Issue. LC P25.

STUDIA LINGUISTICA ET PHILOLOGICA. Vol. 1-. 0886-0432. Monographic Series. US. English. ir. Anma Libri, PO Box 876, Saratoga CA 95070. Ind/Abst MLA Int. Bibliogr. Books Artic. Mod. Lang. Lit. DD 410.

STUDIA NEOPHILOLOGICA. Began with Vol. 1 (1928). 0039-3274. Periodical. SW. English (French or German). sa. 220. Studia Neophilologica, Tyska Institutionen, Box 513, S-751 20 Uppsala Sweden. Tel 46-18-155400. Ed Lars Hermodsson. Ind/Abst Abstr. Engl. Stud., MLA Int. Bibliogr. Books Artic. Mod. Lang. Lit., Lang. Lang. Behav. Abstr., Annu. Bibliogr. Engl. Lang. Lit., Index Book Rev. Humanit., Years Work Eng. Stud. LC PB5. DD 405. (cum index). bk rev. adv acc. Circ 700. Publishes articles on English, German and Romance languages and literatures, and reviews of books in these fields.

STUDIA PHILOLOGIAE SCANDINAVICAE UPSALIENSIA. 1- 1961-. 0081-6809. Monographic Series. SW. Swedish or English. ir. Almqvist & Wiksell, 108 Drottninggatan, PO Box 45150, S-104 30 Stockholm Sweden.

STUDIA PHILOLOGICA SALMANTICENSIA. No. 1- 1977-. Periodical. SP. Spanish. an. University of Salamanca, Apartado 325, Salamanca Spain. Tel 923 21 40 30.

STUDIA PHONETICA. 1- 1969-. 0829-2167. Monographic Series. CN. French. ir. Society Nouvelle Didier Erudition, 6 rue de la Sorbonne, 75005 Paris France. Tel (514)288-7191. Ind/Abst MLA Int. Bibliogr. Books Artic. Mod. Lang. Lit.

STUDIA POLONISTYCZNE. 1- 1973-. PL. Polish (summaries in English, French, German, or Russian). ir. LC PG6025.

STUDIA ROMANICA ET ANGLICA ZAGRABIENSIA. N. 1- 1956-. 0039-3339. YU. English (Italian or French). sa. 20. Filozofski Fakultet, D Salaja 3 41000 Zagreb Yugoslavia. Tel 513.177/302. Ed Vojmir Vinja. Ind/Abst MLA Int. Bibliogr. Books Artic. Mod. Sociol. Abstr., Annu. Bibliogr. Engl. Lang. Lit., Lang. Lang. Behav. Abstr., Lang. Teach. LC PC13. Circ 500. Romance linguistics and literatures, English linguistics and literature, articles published in all Romance languages and in English.

STUDIA ROMANICA. SERIES LINGUISTICA. Main/Corp Kossuth Lajos Tudomanyegyetem. No. 1.- 1964-. 0418-4564. Periodical. ir. Tankonyvkiado, Szalay u 10 14 Postfiok 20, H 1055 Budapest V Hungary.

STUDIA UNIVERSITATIS BABES-BOLYAI. PHILOLOGIA. Main/Corp Universitatea Babes-Bolyai. Periodical. English (French, Romanian, or Russian). an. Ilexim Press Department, PO Box 1-136-1-137, Bucharest Romania. LC P19. DD 405. Studia Universitatis Babes-Bolyai. Series Philologia.

STUDIE A PRACE LINGUISTICKE. 1-. 0585-5675. Monographic Series. Czech (summaries in English and Russian). ir. LC P9.

STUDIEN ZUM FRUHNEUHOCHDEUTSCHEN. 1-. Monographic Series. GW. German. ir. Carl Winter Universitatsverlag, Postfach 1866/Lutherstrasse 59, D6900 Heidelberg West Germany. Tel 6221-49111. Studies of early new high-German language translations of German Bible translations.

STUDIER I MODERN SPRAKVETENSKAP. VFOAT Stockholm Studies in Modern Philology. V. 1-16. 0585-3583. SW. Swedish (English, French, German, Spanish, or occasionally other languages). ir. Almqvist & Wiksell, 108 Drottninggatan, PO Box 45150, S-104 30 Stockholm Sweden. Tel Telex 85413160. Ind/Abst MLA Int. Bibliogr. Books Artic. Mod. Lang. Lit. LC PB18.

STUDIER I NORDISK FILOLOGI. Vol. 1- 1910-. 0356-0376. Fl. Swedish. Svenska Litteratursallskapet I Finland, Snellmansgatan 9-11, 00170 Helsinki 17 Finland. Ind/Abst MLA Int. Bibliogr. Books Artic. Mod. Lang. Lit. (cum index).

STUDIES IN AFRICAN LINGUISTICS. V. 1- Mar. 1970-. 0039-3533. Periodical. US. English. qt. African Studies Center, University of California, Los Angeles CA 90024. Tel (213)825-8703. Ed Russell G Schuh. Ind/Abst MLA Int. Bibliogr. Books Artic. Mod. Lang. Lit., Sociol. Abstr., Lang. Lang. Behav. Abstr. LC PL8000. DD 496. adv acc. Circ 300. Descriptive and theoretical linguistics using African languages as the primary data source.

STUDIES IN ENGLISH AND AMERICAN. V. 2-. 0134-1790. HU. English. ir. Ind/Abst MLA Int. Bibliogr. Books Artic. Mod. Lang. Lit. LC PE25. DD 420.5. Angol es Amerikai Folologiai Tanulmanyok. Studies in English and American Philology.

STUDIES IN ENGLISH LITERATURE & LINGUISTICS. Main/Corp Kuo Li Tai-Wan Shih Fan Ta Hsueh. Ying Yu Hsi. VFOAT Ying Yu Yen Chiu Chi Kan. VAT Studies in English Literature and Linguistics. Began with 1976 issue. English. ir. Department of English, National Taiwan Normal, University Taipei Taiwan. LC PE9. DD 420.5. Concentric.

STUDIES IN HAMITO-SEMITIC. Series/Titl Zeszyty Naukowe Uniwersytetu Jagiellonskiego. VFOAT Studia Hamito-Semitica. 1-. English. ir. 24.00 Each Issue. Krakow Ul Smolensk 14, Warszawa Poland. LC PG6014.

STUDIES IN LANGUAGE. Vol. 1, No. 1-. 0378-4177. Periodical. NE. English. ty. $82.00. John Benjamins BV, Amsteldijk 44, PO Box 52519, 1007 HA Amsterdam Netherlands. Ed John W M Verhaar. Ind/Abst Math. Rev., MLA Int. Bibliogr. Books Artic. Mod. Lang. Lit., Lang. Lang. Behav. Abstr., Lang. Teach., Index Book Rev. Humanit. Deals with subjects basic to contemporary linguistics and philosophy, in the sense that it focusses on the foundations of language. Foundations of Language, 0015-900X.

STUDIES IN LANGUAGE AND LINGUISTICS. 1969/70-. 0586-6928. US. English. ir. Texas Western Press, University of Texas at El Paso, El Paso TX 79968. LC P25. DD 410.

STUDIES IN LANGUAGE LEARNING. (STUDIES IN LANGUAGE LEARNING : PUBLICATION OF THE LANGUAGE LEARNING LABORATORY, UNIVERSITY OF ILLINOIS AT URBANA-CHAMPAIGN). Began in 1975. 0736-9867. Periodical. US. English. Language Learning Laboratory, University of Illinois at Urbana Champaign, G-70 Foreign Languages Building, 707 South Mathews, Urbana IL 61801. Tel (217)333-9776. Ed C C Cheng. Ind/Abst MLA Int. Bibliogr. Books Artic. Mod. Lang. Lit., Lang. Teach. LC P129. DD 418.005. bk rev. Circ 300. Primarily concerned with applied linguistics, and specifically with language acquisition, language pedagogy, stylistics, and language planning.

STUDIES IN LINGUISTICS. Main/Corp Odense Universitet. VFOAT Odense University Studies in Linguistics. V. 1-. 0078-3315. Monographic Series. DK. German (English). ir. Odense University Press, 36 Pjentedamsgade, DK 5000 Odense Denmark. Tel (09)14 16 11. No.

STUDIES IN PHILOLOGY. See Literature.

STUDIES IN ROMANCE LANGUAGES. V. 1- 1970-. 0085-6894. Monographic Series. US. English (French or Spanish). ir. University Press of Kentucky, University of Kentucky, Lexington KY 40506-0024. Ind/Abst MLA Int. Bibliogr. Books Artic. Mod. Lang. Lit. DD 440. Each issue contains an index to its own contents - no vol index - loose.

STUDIES IN SECOND LANGUAGE ACQUISITION. Began with Vol. 1, 1977. 0272-2631. Periodical. US. English (French, German, and Spanish). ty. $45.00. Cambridge University Press, 32 East 57th Street, New York NY 10022. Tel (212)688-8885. Ed Albert Valdman. Ind/Abst Lang. Teach., Curr. Index J. Educ. LC P118. DD 401.9. bk rev. adv acc. Circ 500. (ctrl). A journal of international scope, devoted to problems and issues in second language acquisition and foreign language learning.

STUDIES IN THE HISTORY AND THEORY OF LINGUISTICS. Main/Corp Indiana University. Monographic Series. US. English. ir. Indiana University Press, 10th & Morton Street, Bloomington IN 47401.

STUDIES IN THE LINGUISTIC SCIENCES. VFOAT SLS. V. 1- Spring 1971-. 0049-2388. Periodical. US. English. sa. $12.00. University of Illinois Department of Linguistics, 4088 Foreign Language Building 707 South Mathews, Urbana IL 61801. Tel (217)333-3563. Ed Charles W Kisseberth. Ind/Abst MLA Int. Bibliogr. Books Artic. Mod. Lang. Lit., Lang. Lang. Behav. Abstr., Lang.

Linguistics

Teach. LC P1. DD 410.5. bk rev. Circ 225. Latest original research by the faculty and especially students of the Department of Linguistics, University of Illinois.

STUDII DE LITERATURA ROMANA SI COMPARATA. 1-. Periodical. Romanian (summaries in English, French, German and Russian). ir. LC PN9. DD 809.

STUDII SI CERCETARI LINGVISTICE. Year 1- 1950-. 0039-405X. RM. Romanian. bm. Ilexim Press Department, PO Box 1-136-1-137, Bucharest Romania. Ind/Abst MLA Int. Bibliogr. Books Artic. Mod. Lang. Lit., Lang. Lang. Behav. Abstr., Sociol. Abstr.

STUDIME FILOLOGJIKE. V. 18(1)- 1964-. Periodical. AA. Albanian. qt. $4.15. Book Distribution Enterprise, rue Konferenca e Pezes, Tirana Albania. Ind/Abst Am. Hist. Life, Hist. Abstr., Part A, Mod. Hist. Abstr., Hist. Abstr., Part B, Twent. Century Abstr., MLA Int. Bibliogr. Books Artic. Mod. Lang. Lit., Hist. Abstr. LC PG9501. *Buletin. Seria Shkencat Shoqerore.*

STUTTGARTER ARBEITEN ZUR GERMANISTIK. See Literature.

STYLE. See Literature.

SUDASIATISCHE SPRACHWISSENSCHAFTLICHE STUDIEN. Series/Titl Linguistische Studien (Akademie der Wissenschaften der DDR. Zentralinstitut fur Sprachwissenschaft). Reihe A. Vol. 1 (1981)-. 0138-4694. German. ir. Zentralinstitut fur Sprachwissenschaft, 108 Berlin, Otto-Muschke-Str 22/23 East Germany.

SUGIA, SPRACHE UND GESCHICHTE IN AFRIKA. VFOAT Sprache und Geschichte in Afrika. Vol. 1- 1979-. 0170-5946. GW. German (English, French, with summaries in the other languages). ir. H Buske, Postfach 132255 Schluterstrabe 14, D 2000 Hamburg West Germany. Tel (040)452522. LC PL8000. DD 409.6. Language and linguistics and history of Africa.

SUMMARY OF INVESTIGATIONS RELATING TO READING. See Education (General) - Theory, Practice of Education.

SUMMER INSTITUTE OF LINGUISTICS PUBLICATIONS IN LINGUISTICS. VFOAT Publications in Linguistics. No. 53-. Monographic Series. US. English. $4.00. Dallas Center Book Store, Summer Institute of Linguistics, 7500 West Camp Wisdom Road, Dallas TX 75236. Tel (214)298-3331. Ed Eugene Loos. bk rev. Circ 900. (ctrl). Intended to provide linguistic field-workers with news, reviews, announcements, and articles that wil stimulate a current interest in linguistics. *Summer Institute of Linguistics Publications in Linguistics and Related Fields, 0079-7669.*

SUMMER INSTITUTE OF LINGUISTICS PUBLICATIONS IN LINGUISTICS AND RELATED FIELDS. VFOAT Publications in Linguistics and Related Fields. No. 8-21. 0079-7669. Monographic Series. US. English. ir. Summer Institute of Linguistics, 7500 West Camp Wisdom Road, Dallas TX 75436. Tel (214)291-7479. Ed Desmond C Derbyshire. Ind/Abst MLA Int. Bibliogr. Books Artic. Mod. Lang. Lit. Circ 250. Includes studies in phonology and grammar of indigenous languages spoken in various parts of the world. Various models are followed. Some comparative studies and textbooks. *Linguistic Series (Summer Institute of Linguistics).*

SUPOSTAVITELNO EZIKOZNANIE. Vol. 3-. Periodical. BU. Bulgarian (summaries in English and Russian). ir. Ruski No 15, Sofiiski Universitet Dliment Okhridski, 1000 Sofiia Bulgaria. Ind/Abst Lang. Lang. Behav. Abstr. LC PG831. DD 491.81505. *Biuletin za Supostavitelno Izsledvane na Bulgarskiia Ezik S Drugi Ezitsi.*

SURVIVANT. (LE SURVIVANT : ORGANE OFFICIEL DE L'ASSOCIATION DES CITOYENS DE CULTURE FRANCAISE D'AMERIQUE). V. 1, No. 1, (Aug. 1976)-. 0227-4582. Periodical. CN. French. ir. Free. Le Survivant, CP 155, La Sarre Quebec J9Z 2X5 Canada. DD 440.60714.

SVESKE ZADUZBINE IVE ANDRICA. 1982/1- – Vol. 1, No. 1-. Periodical. German (Serbo-Croatian). ir. Zaduzbina Ive Andrica, Brankova 23, 11000 Beograd Yugoslavia. LC PG1418.A6.

SWISS PAPERS IN ENGLISH LANGUAGE AND LITERATURE. VFOAT S.P.E.L.L. 0743-7226. Monographic Series. US. English. be. AMC Press Inc, 57 East 13th Street, New York NY 10003.

SYNTAX AND SEMANTICS. V. 1- 1972-. 0092-4563. US. English. an. Academic Press, 4805 Sand Lake Road, Orlando FL 32887. Tel (305)345-4100. Ed John P Kimball. Ind/Abst MLA Int. Bibliogr. Books Artic. Mod. Lang. Lit. LC P1. DD 410.5.

SYSTEM (LINKOPING, SWEDEN). (SYSTEM). Began with Vol. 1 (1973). 0346-251X. Periodical. UK. English. ty. $35.00. Pergamon Press Inc, Maxwell House Fairview Park, Elmsford NY 10523. Ind/Abst Curr. Index J. Educ., Lang. Lang. Behav. Abstr., Lang. Teach. LC P51. DD 418.007.

TAAL EN TONGVAL. 1-. Vol. 0039-8691. Periodical. BE. Dutch. sa. 500. Taal en Tongval, Visitatiestraat 187, B-9110 Gent Belgium. Tel (091)510507. Ed V F Vanacker. Ind/Abst MLA Int. Bibliogr. Books Artic. Mod. Lang. Lit. LC PF701. DD 439.31705. bk rev. adv acc. Circ 300. Studies on dialects, Netherlands and northern part of Belgium.

TALANYA. 1- 1972-. English. ir. $5.50. Mouton, PO Box 482-2076, The Hague Netherlands. LC P1. DD 427.994.

TAUNANG ULAT - SURIAN NG WIKANG PAMBANSA. Main/Corp Philippines (Republic). Institute of National Language. VFOAT Annual Report - Institute of National Language. English (Tagalog). an. LC PL6059. DD 499.21. *Annual Report.*

TE REO. V. 1- 1958-. 0494-8440. NZ. English. an. 28.00. Linguistic Society of New Zealand, c/o University of Auckland, Auckland New Zealand. Tel 737-999. Ed C Corne. Ind/Abst MLA Int. Bibliogr. Books Artic. Mod. Lang. Lit., Lang. Teach. adv acc. Circ 350. Scientific description and study of the evolution and structure of languages. With special attention to indigenous and European languages in the Pacific.

TEACHING ENGLISH IN THE TWO-YEAR COLLEGE. V. 1- Fall 1974-. 0098-6291. Periodical. US. English. qt. $15.00. National Council of Teachers of Education, 1111 Kenyon Road, Urbana IL 61801. Tel (919)757-6383. Ed Bertie Fearing and John Hutchens. Ind/Abst Educ. Index, Curr. Index J. Educ. LC PE1065. DD 807.1173. bk rev. adv acc. Circ 500. (ctrl). Articles of interest to English and language arts teachers in the two-year college system.

TEACHING LANGUAGE THROUGH LITERATURE. V. 12- Dec. 1972-. 0362-2746. Periodical. US. English. sa. $6.00 Domestic, $8.00 Foreign. Teaching Language Through Literature, Fordham University, Box 707, Bronx NY 10458. Tel (212)579-2000. Ed Maxine G Cutler. Ind/Abst MLA Int. Bibliogr. Books Artic. Mod. Lang. Lit., Lang. Teach., Educ. Index. DD 407. bk rev. Circ 1,000. Provides teaching models of literary texts in the foreign languages for classroom use and demonstrates teaching language through literature. *Newsletter - Modern Language Association Conference, 0544-6600.*

TEACHING OF ENGLISH. Main/Corp Florida. State University, Tallahassee. School of Education. 1956- Bulletin No. 1-. US. English. ir. Florida State University, School of Education, Tallahassee FL 32203. LC LB1631. DD 808.

TECH WRITING TIPS. No. 1-. 0887-5324. Periodical. US. English. mo. $100.00. J S Hanna House, 183 Gifford Way, Sacramento CA 95864. DD 808.

TELE-C.L.E.F. See Law.

TENNESSEE LINGUISTICS. Vol. 1, No. 1 (Winter 1981)-. 0740-8021. Periodical. US. English. sa. Alan Slotkin Editor, Tennessee Conference on Linguistics, Department of English, Box 5053, Tennessee Technological University, Cookeville TN 38501. LC P1. DD 410.5. *Bulletin (Tennessee Conference on Linguistics).*

TENNESSEE PHILOLOGICAL BULLETIN. Vol. 1, No. 1 (Apr. 1964)-. 0735-0783. US. English. an. Ind/Abst MLA Int. Bibliogr. Books Artic. Mod. Lang. Lit. LC PB1. DD 410.5.

TERMINOGRAMME. (TERMINOGRAMME : BULLETIN DE LA DIRECTION DE LA TERMINOLOGIE). No. 1 (Jan. 1980)-. 0225-3194. Periodical. CN. French. bm. $9.28. Les Publications du Quebec, Ministere des Comm CP 1005, Quebec Quebec G1K 7B5 Canada. Tel (418)643-5150. DD 440.9714.

TERMINOLOGIE. V. 9- (41E-). 0225-1981. Periodical. CN. French. ir. DD 448.105. *Bulletin, 0225-1973.*

TERMNET NEWS : JOURNAL OF THE INTERNATIONAL NETWORK FOR TERMINOLOGY (TERMNET). Began in 1980. 0251-5253. Periodical. English (French). ir. Free. Austrian Standards Institute, Infoterm Postfach 130, Heinestr 38, A-1021 Wien Austria. Tel (0222)267535. LC P305. DD 418.0205. bk rev. Circ 1,200. (ctrl). Gives an overview of all terminological activities in the world. Current awareness service to all Termnet partners. Future trends in terminology and other information-related fields.

TESL CANADA JOURNAL. VFOAT Revue TESL du Canada. VAT Teaching English as a Second Language Canada Journal, Revue Teaching English as a Second Language du Canada. Vol. 1, No. 1 (Jan. 1984)-. 0826-435X. Periodical. CN. English (includes some text in French). sa. $12.00. Faculty of Education, McGill University, 3700 McTavish Street, Montreal Quebec H3A 1Y2 Canada. DD 420.7.

TESL REPORTER. See Education (General) - Special Aspects of Education.

TESOL MEMBERSHIP DIRECTORY. See Yearbooks, Almanacs, Directories.

TEXAS LINGUISTIC FORUM. Began in 1975. 0741-2576. Monographic Series. US. English. ir. Texas Linguistics, University of Texas, Calhoun Hall 501, Austin TX 78712. Tel (512)471-1701. LC P1. DD 410.5. Circ 200. A collection of working papers in linguistics published by the Department of Linguistics at the University of Texas at Austin.

TEXAS STUDIES IN LITERATURE AND LANGUAGE. See Literature.

TEXT & KONTEXT. (TEXT & I.E., UND KONTEXT). VAT Text und Kontext. Vol. 1-. 0105-7014. Periodical. German. sa. 40.00. Anschrift der Redaktion: Kbenhavns Universitet, Institut for Germansk Filologi, Ster Voldgade 10, 1350 Kobenhavn Denmark. Ind/Abst MLA Int. Bibliogr. Books Artic. Mod. Lang. Lit. LC PD3.

TEXT (HAGUE, NETHERLANDS). (TEXT). Vol. 1-1-. 0165-4888. Periodical. US. English. ir. $53.50. Walter de Gruyter Inc, 200 Saw Mill River Road, Hawthorne NY 10532. Ind/Abst Lang. Lang. Behav. Abstr. LC P302. DD 001.51.

TEXTBOOK SERIES - AMERICAN PHILOLOGICAL ASSOCIATION. (TEXTBOOK SERIES). 0278-6400. Monographic Series. US. English. ir. Scholars Press, 101 Salem Street, PO Box 2268, Chico CA 95927.

TEXTES PUBLIES PAR L'INSTITUT D'ETUDES SLAVES. Main/Corp Institut d'Etudes Slaves. 1-. 0079-001X. Monographic Series. FR. French. ir. Institut d'Etudes Slaves, 9 rue Michelet, 75006 Paris France. Tel (1)42 26 50 89. Circ 300. Old Slavic and old Russian texts.

THEORETICAL LINGUISTICS. V. 1- 1974-. 0301-4428. Periodical. US. English. ir. $62.00. Walter de Gruyter Inc, 200 Saw Mill River Road, Hawthorne NY 10532. Tel (914)747-0110. Ed Helmut Schnelle. Ind/Abst Math. Rev., Lang. Lang. Behav. Abstr., Lang. Teach. LC P1. DD 410.5. bk rev. adv acc. Publishes natural and constructed languages. Linguistic methodology is included as well as the theory of meaning, syntax, phonology and phonetics.

THESAURUS. Vol. 7- 1951-. 0040-604X. Periodical. CK. Spanish. ty. $12.00. Instituto Caro Y Cuervo, Apartado Aereo 20002, Bogota Colombia. Ind/Abst MLA Int. Bibliogr. Books Artic. Mod. Lang. Lit., Sociol. Abstr., Lang. Lang. Behav. Abstr., Lang. Teach., Am. Hist. Life, Hist. Abstr. Index published separately - free - automatically sent. (cum index). bk rev. Essays on philology, linguistics, and literature; book reviews. *Boletin del Instituto Caro Y Cuervo.*

THESAURUS LINGUAE GRAECAE; NEWSLETTER. VFOAT TLG Newsletter. No. 1- Apr. 1973-. 0361-8641. US. English. ir. University of California, Irvine CA 92717.

TIJDSCHRIFT VOOR NEDERLANDS EN AFRIKAANS : T.N.A. VFOAT T.N.A. Vol. 1 (1/83 March)-. 0723-9890. Periodical. Afrikaans (text in Dutch, English, and German). ty. $17.85. Frans J Lukassen Verlag, Dr Josef-Fiegerstr 6, 5042 Erftstadt 12 West Germany. LC PF1.

TIJDSCHRIFT VOOR NEDERLANDSCHE TAAL-EN LETTERKUNDE. See Literature.

TINTA. Vol. 1, No. 1 (May 1981)-. US. Spanish. sa. Tinta, Department of Spanish And Portuguese UCSB, Santa Barbara CA 93106.

TINTA (SANTA BARBARA, CALIF.). See Literature.

Linguistics

TOGIL MUNHAK. VFOAT Koreanische Zeitschrift fur Germanistik. Periodical. KO. Korean (German). ir. Hanguk Togo Tongmun Hakhoe, c/o German Department Seoul National University, Seoul Korea. LC PT9. DD 830.9.

TOKAI DAIGAKU KIYO. GAIKOKUGO KYOIKU SENTA. VFOAT Bulletin of the Foreign Language Center, Tokai University. 0389-3081. Periodical. JA. English (Japanese). ir. Tokai Daigaku Shuppankai, c/o Tokai Bldg., 27-4 Shinjuku 3, Shinjuku-Ku 160, Tokyo-To Japan. LC PB5.

TONAM HAKPO. Series 1-. Periodical. KO. Korean. ir. Not For Sale. Tonham Hakhoe, 318-4 Tongson-Dong 4-Ka, Songbuk-Ku, Seoul South Korea. LC PL901.

TRACES; LINGUISTIQUE SEMIOTIQUE. VFOAT Revue Traces. Yearly V. 1- (1-). Periodical. MR. French. sa. 36.00. A Bounfour, Revue Traces, 18 rue Brihi, Rabat Morocco. LC P99. DD 405.

TRACTS - SOCIETY FOR PURE ENGLISH. Main/Corp Society for Pure English. No. 1-. Monographic Series. US. English. LC PE25. DD 420.5.

TRADUIRE. 0395-773X. Periodical. FR. French. qt. $24.61. Societe Francaise Traducteurs, 11 rue de Navarin, 75009 Paris France. Tel 48 78 43 32. Ed Denise Baccara. bk rev. adv acc. Circ 1,800. (ctrl). General and specific information on translation and translating problems and news. Glossaries on specialised subject matters. Reviews of books on translation and dictionaries.

TRANSACTIONS OF THE AMERICAN PHILOLOGICAL ASSOCIATION. Main/Corp American Philological Association. V. 104-1974-. 0360-5949. US. English. an. $40.00. Scholars Press, PO Box 1608, Decatur GA 30031. Tel (404)329-6950. Ind/Abst Recent Publ. Artic. LC P11. DD 480.05. Transactions and Proceedings of the American Philological Association, 0065-9711.

TRANSACTIONS OF THE YORKSHIRE DIALECT SOCIETY. Main/Corp Yorkshire Dialect Society. V. 1- (Pt. 1-). UK. English. an. 2.50. Mr S Ellis, Senior Lecturer in English, The University of Leeds, Bradford England. Ed K E Smith. Ind/Abst MLA Int. Bibliogr. Books Artic. Mod. Lang. Lit., Years Work Eng. Stud. bk rev. Circ 800. (ctrl). Yorkshire and other dialects of English folklife and language lore.

TRANSLATIO. V. 6- Feb. 1967-. 0381-9965. Periodical. CN. French (text in English). Association des Traducteurs et Interpretes de l'Ontario, 457A rue Sussex, Ottawa Ontario K1N 6Z4 Canada. Bulletin de l'ATIO, 0381-9957.

TRANSLATION REVIEW. No. 1- Spring 1978-. 0737-4836. Periodical. US. English. ty. $15.00. American Literary Translators Association, University of Texas, Box 830688, Richardson TX 75083-0688. Tel (214)690-2093. Ed Rainer Schulte. Ind/Abst MLA Int. Bibliogr. Books Artic. Mod. Lang. Lit. bk rev. adv acc. Circ 700. Provides a forum for the exchange of ideas on the art and craft of literary translation. Publishes essays, articles, and reviews.

TRANSLATIONS INDEX (AMERICAN SOCIETY FOR METALS). See Indexes/Abstracts.

TRANSLATOR REFERRAL, TRANSLATION SERVICES DIRECTORY. See Yearbooks, Almanacs, Directories.

TRANSMISSION. (TRANSMISSION : BULLETIN D'INFORMATION DE L'ASSOCIATION DES TRADUCTEURS LITTERAIRES). VFOAT Literary Translators' Association Newsletter. Vol. 1, No. 1 (July 1982)-. 0824-510X. Periodical. CN. English (French). sa. Free. Transmission, c/o Mrs Jane Brierley, 41 Chesterfield Avenue, Montreal Quebec H3Y 2M4 Canada. DD 418.0206071.

TRAVAUX DE LINGUISTIQUE ET DE LITTERATURE. 1.-. 0082-6057. Periodical. French (Italian or Spanish). ir. C.C.L.S., BP 22, 41350 Vineuil France. Tel 54/ 78 77 41. Ind/Abst MLA Int. Bibliogr. Books Artic. Mod. Lang. Lit., Sociol. Abstr., Lang. Lang. Behav. Abstr. LC PC2.

TRAVAUX DE L'INSTITUT DE LINGUISTIQUE DE LUND. Main/Corp Lund. Universitet. Fonetiska Institutionen. 1-8, 1959-70. 0459-9985. Monographic Series. SW. English, French, and German. ir. Liber International, S-205 10 Malmo Sweden. Tel 46-40-70650.

TRAVAUX DE L'INSTITUT DE PHONETIQUE D'AIX. Main/Corp Institut de Phonetique d'Aix-en-Provence. FR. English or French. ir. Universite Institut Phoenique, 29 Ave r Schumann, Aix-en-Provence France. LC P215. DD 414.

TSURUMI DAIGAKU KIYO. DAI 1-BU, KOKUGO KOKUBUNGAKU HEN. VFOAT Bulletin of Tsurumi College. 0389-8008. Japanese. ir. Tsurumi Daigaku, 1-3 Tsurumi 2 Turumi-Ku, Yokohama-Shi 230 Japan. LC PL501.

TSURUMI DAIGAKU KIYO. DAI 2-BU, GAIKOKUGO GAIKOKU BUNGAKU HEN. VFOAT Bulletin of Tsurumi College. 0389-8016. Periodical. Japanese. ir. Tsurumi Daigaku, 1-3 Tsurumi 2 Tsurumi-Ku, Yokohama-Shi 230 Japan. LC P9.

TUBINGER BEITRAGE ZUR LINGUISTIK. Began in 1969. 0564-7959. Monographic Series. GW. German (English and French). ir. Gunter Narr Verlag, Postfach 2567, 7400 Tuebingen 5 West Germany. Tel 07071-78091. Ed Gunter Narr. Publications dedicated to linguistic topics.

TVORCHESTVO A. P. CHEKHOVA. Vol. 1-. Periodical. UR. Russian. Ministerstvo Prosveshceniia RSFSR, Rostovskii-Na-Donu, Gosudarstvennyi, Pedagogicheskii Institut, Ul Engelsa 33, Rostov-Na-Donu Russian SFSR. LC PG3458.Z8.

TZU LIAO HUI PIEN. VFOAT Ziliaohuibian. Vol. 1-. CH. Chinese. ir. Shan-Hsi Shih Fan Hsueh Yuan, Tai-Yuan China. LC PL1071. DD 495.1.

TZU SHU YEN CHIU. VFOAT Cishu Yanjiu, Etude Lexicographique, Lexicographical Studies. April 1979-. CC. Chinese. bm. 0.50. Hsin Hua Shu Tien Shang-Hai Fa Hsing So, Shanghai China. LC PL1401. DD 495.1305.

TZU TIEN YEN CHIU TSUNG KAN. VFOAT Cidian Yanjiu Congkan. 1 (Feb. 1980)-. CH. Chinese. ir. 0.78. Ssu-Chuan Sheng Hsin Hua Shu Tien Cheng-Tu China. LC PL1411. DD 495.13028.

UKRAINS'KE MOVOZNAVSTVO. Vol. 1- 1973-. 0320-3077. UR. Ukrainian. an. Vydavnyche Obiednannia Vyshcha Shkola Tarasovskaia, Kyiv Russia. Ind/Abst MLA Int. Bibliogr. Books Artic. Mod. Lang. Lit. LC PG3801.

ULULA. No. 1 (1984)-. 0747-8011. Periodical. US. English (French, Portuguese, and Spanish). an. $3.00. University of Georgia, Department of Romance Languages, Athens GA 30602. DD 440.

UNILETRAS : REVISTA DO DEPARTAMENTO DE LETRAS DA UEPG. Periodical. BL. Portuguese. an. Free. Departamento de Letras Universidade Estadual de Ponta Grossa, Praca Santos Andrade S/No 84.100 Ponta Grossa PR Brazil. Tel 0422.243966. LC PN9. DD 805. Circ 800. (ctrl). Essays on language, linguistics, and literary sciences. Publishing short stories and poems.

UNISA ENGLISH STUDIES. Main/Corp University of South Africa. Dept. of English. VAT University of South Africa English Studies. V. 1- Mar. 1968-. 0041-5359. Periodical. SA. English. sa. $2.31. University of South Africa, PO Box 392, Pretoria 0001 South Africa. Tel (012)429-3111. Ed Shirley Kossick. Ind/Abst MLA Int. Bibliogr. Books Artic. Mod. Lang. Lit., Years Work Eng. Stud. LC PR1. DD 820.9. bk rev. Circ 2,000. (ctrl). Contains English literary articles and reviews.

UNIVERSITY OF CALIFORNIA PUBLICATIONS IN MODERN PHILOLOGY. VFOAT Publications in Modern Philology. Vol. 1, No. 1 (May 8, 1909)-. 0068-6492. Monographic Series. US. English. ir. University California Press, 1095 Essex Street, Richmond CA 94804-2112. Tel (415)642-0061. Ind/Abst MLA Int. Bibliogr. Books Artic. Mod. Lang. Lit. LC PB13. Circ 850.

UNIVERSITY OF MICHIGAN PAPERS IN LINGUISTICS. Main/Corp Michigan. University. Dept. of Linguistics. VFOAT Papers in Linguistics. Began with V. 1, No. 1 in 1973?. 0740-6193. Periodical. US. English. sa. $15.00. University of Michigan, 1076 Freize Building, Ann Arbor MI 48109.

UNIVERSITY OF NORTH CAROLINA STUDIES IN GERMANIC LANGUAGES AND LITERATURES STUDIES IN THE GERMANIC LANGUAGES AND LITERATURES. (STUDIES IN THE GERMANIC LANGUAGES AND LITERATURES). Main/Corp University of North Carolina (Chapel Hill Campus). No. 1-. 0081-8593. Monographic Series. US. English. ir. University of North Carolina Press, University of North Carolina, Chapel Hill NC 27514. Ind/Abst MLA Int. Bibliogr. Books Artic. Mod. Lang. Lit. LC PD25. DD 430.82.

UNIVERSITY OF TORONTO ROMANCE SERIES. See Literature.

DIE UNTERRICHTSPRAXIS. See Education (General) - Theory, Practice of Education.

UNTERSUCHUNGEN ZUR ROMANISCHEN PHILOLOGIE. V. 1- 1967-. 0566-2818. Monographic Series. GW. German. ir. Verlag Anton Hain Meisenheim, Postfach 180, D-6554 Meisenheim West Germany. Tel (067)53/24 88. Ind/Abst MLA Int. Bibliogr. Books Artic. Mod. Lang. Lit.

UNTERSUCHUNGEN ZUR SPRACH- UND LITERATURGESCHICHTE DER ROMANISCHEN VOLKER. See Literature.

URBAN LANGUAGE SERIES. 0566-8824. Monographic Series. US. English. ir. Center for Applied Linguistics, 3520 Prospect Street, NW Washington DC 20007.

US WURK. Vol. 1-. 0042-1235. Periodical. NE. Frisian. qt. Fries Institut der Rijksuniversiteit/Westersingel 28-30, Groningen Netherlands. Tel (050)635944. Ind/Abst MLA Int. Bibliogr. Books Artic. Mod. Lang. Lit., Sociol. Abstr. Circ 400. (ctrl). Covers Frisian linguistics, language history and literature.

THE USF LANGUAGE QUARTERLY. VFOAT U.S.F. Language Quarterly, Language Quarterly. VAT University of South Florida Language Quarterly. V. 15, No. 1-2 (Fall/Winter 1976)-. 0732-3042. Periodical. US. English. $6.00. USF Language Quarterly, University of South Florida, Fowlers Avenue, c/o A M Gessman, Tampa FL 33620. Tel (813)974-2221. Ed Albert M Gessman. Ind/Abst Lang. Lang. Behav. Abstr., Abstr. Engl. Stud., MLA Int. Bibliogr. Books Artic. Mod. Lang. Lit., Annu. Bibliogr. Engl. Lang. Lit. LC P1.A1. DD 809. (cum index). bk rev. Circ 500. (ctrl). Scholarly papers in the areas of literature, linguistics, and language education. Language Quarterly, 0458-7359.

UTAH STUDIES IN LITERATURE AND LINGUISTICS. See Literature.

V POMOSHCH PREPODAVATELIAM INOSTRANNYKH IAZYKOV. Vol. 1- 1964-. Russian. ir. LC P57.R9.

VAICARIKI. V. 1- July 1971-. Periodical. Hindi. ir. Bharativa Vidva Mandira Sodha Pratisshthana, Bikaner, Bikaner India. LC DS401.

VERBATIM. V. 1- 1974-. 0162-0932. Periodical. US. English. qt. $10.00. Verbatim, Box 668, Essex CT 06426. Tel (203)767-8248. Ed Laurence Urdang. Ind/Abst Abstr. Engl. Stud., Sociol. Abstr., MLA Int. Bibliogr. Books Artic. Mod. Lang. Lit. LC PE1001, P1. DD 420.05, 405. bk rev. adv acc. Circ 10,000. An informative, amusing, entertaining periodical, the largest circulation magazine of its kind in the world. Articles, reviews, correspondence and book club.

VERBUM (NANCY, FRANCE). (VERBUM : REVUE DE LINGUISTIQUE PUBLIEE PAR L'UNIVERSITE DE NANCY II). Vol.1, Issue 1 (1978)-. Periodical. FR. French. ty. 12.79. Presses Universitaires Nancy, 25 rue Baron Louis-B P 454, 54001 Nancy Cedex France. Tel (8)337-37-65. Ed R Hodot. bk rev. adv acc. Circ 500.

VEROFFENTLICHUNGEN DER KOMMISSION FUR LINGUISTIK UND KOMMUNIKATIONSFORSCHUNG. No. 1- 1973-. German. ir. Dr Ignaz-Seipel-Platz, 2, A-1010 Wien Austria. LC AS142.

VERSANTS. See Literature.

VERSLAGEN EN MEDEDELINGEN - KONINKLIJKE ACADEMIE VOOR NEDERLANDSE TAAL- EN LETTERKUNDE. Main/Corp Koninklijke Academie voor Nederlandse Taal- en Letterkunde. Periodical. Dutch. ir. Secretariaat Koningstraat 18, Gent Belgium. LC PF1001. Verslagen en Mededelingen - Koninklijke Academie voor Nederlandse Taal- en Letterkunde.

Linguistics

VESTNIK MOSKOVSKOGO UNIVERSITETA. SERIIA IX : FILOLOGIIA. Main/Corp Moskovskii Gosudarstvennyi Universitet Im. M. V. Lomonsova. 3-. Periodical. UR. Russian. bm. Victor Kamkin Inc, 12224 Parklawn Drive, Rockville MD 20852. Tel (301)881-5973. Ind/Abst MLA Int. Bibliogr. Books Artic. Mod. Lang. Lit., Chem. Abstr., Sociol. Abstr., Am. Hist. Life, Hist. Abstr., Lang. Lang. Behav. Abstr. LC P19. *Vestnik. Seriia X: Filologiia.*

VICUS CUADERNOS. LINGUISTICA *CEASED.* (VICUS CUADERNOS : LINGUISTICA). VFOAT Linguistica. V. 1-. 0165-7666. Periodical. English (Spanish). ir. John Benjamins BV, Amsteldijk 44, PO Box 52519, 1007 HA Amsterdam Holland. Ind/Abst MLA Int. Bibliogr. Books Artic. Mod. Lang. Lit. LC P1.A1. DD 498.

VILAG ES NYELV. Periodical. HU. Hungarian. ir. 33.60. Magyar Eszperanto Szovetseg, Kenyermezo U 6, 1081 Budapest VIII Hungary. LC P9.

VISHVESHVARANAND INDOLOGICAL JOURNAL. See Literature.

VISNYK. SERIIA FILOLOHICHNA. Main/Corp Lvov. Universytet. No. 1-. 0460-0452. UR. Russian (Ukrainian). LC PG3801.

VISVA HINDI DARSANA. No. 1- January 1979-. Periodical. II. Hindi. ir. 4.00. Visva Hindi Pratishthana, C-13 Press Enclave, New Delhi 110017 India. LC PK1931.

VITA LATINA. 0042-7306. French. qt. Aubanel, 7 Place Street Pierre, 84028 Avignon France.

VOPROSY ADYGEISKOGO IAZYKOZNANIIA. No. 1-. Periodical. UR. Russian. 1.00. LC PK9201.A4. DD 491.99.

VOPROSY FILOLOGII. Main/Corp Leningrad. Universitet. Filologicheskii Fakultet. Began in 1970. UR. Russian. 1.13. IZD-VO Leningradskogo Universitets, Universitetskaia Nab 7/9, Leningrad 199164 Russia. LC P19.

VOPROSY GERMANSKOI FILOLOGII. Periodical. UR. Russian. 0.95 Single Issue. Kaliniskii Gosudarstvennyi Universitet, 170013 Kalinin 13 Zheliabova 33, Kalinin Russian SFSR. LC PF3095.

VOPROSY IAPONSKOI FILOLOGII. No. 1-. UR. Russian. ir. LC PL523.

VOPROSY IAZYKOZNANIIA. Jan./Feb. 1952-. Periodical. UR. Russian. bm. $48.00. Victor Kamkin Inc (70158), 12224 Parklawn Drive, Rockville MD 20852. Tel (301)881-5973. Ind/Abst MLA Int. Bibliogr. Books Artic. Mod. Lang. Lit., Sociol. Abstr., Lang. Lang. Behav. Abstr. LC P9.

VOPROSY KLASSICHESKOI FILOLOGII. 1-. 0507-3529. UR. Russian. LC PA9.

VOPROSY RUSSKOGO IAZYKOZNANIIA. Vol. 1-. Periodical. UR. Russina. 1.21 Single Issue. K-9 Ul Gertsena 5/7, Moskva USSR. LC PG2003.

VOPROSY SLOVOOBRAZOVANIIA V INDOEVROPEISKIKH IAZYKAKH. Vol. 1-. UR. Russian. 1.50. Izdatelstvo TGU, Ul Nikitina 17, Tomsk 29 USSR. LC P615.

VOPROSY STRUKTURY GERMANSKIKH IAZYKOV. Periodical. UR. Russian. 1.00 Single Issue. LC PD95.

VORTICE. V. 1- Spring 1974-. US. Spanish. ty. $6.00. Department of Spanish and Portuguese, Stanford University, Stanford CA 94305. Ind/Abst MLA Int. Bibliogr. Books Artic. Mod. Lang. Lit. LC PC4008. DD 460.05.

VOX LATINA. Periodical. Latin. qt. Vox Latina, Fachbereich 6 der Universitat, D6600 Saarbrucken West Germany. Tel 302-2592. bk rev adv acc. Circ 1,500. Text on various topics in Latin.

VOX ROMANICA. Vol. 1-. 0042-899X. German (French or Italian). sa. Francke Verlag, Neuengasse 43 Postfach 1445, CH-3001 Bern Switzerland. Tel 031/22 17 15. Ind/Abst MLA Int. Bibliogr. Books Artic. Mod. Lang. Lit., Lang. Lang. Behav. Abstr., Sociol. Abstr. LC PC1.A1. DD 479.105.

WAI KUO YU. VFOAT Waiguoyu, Foreign Languages. Periodical. CH. Chinese (English). bm. 0.35. Shang-Hai Shih Pao Kan Fa Hsing Chu, Shang-Hai China. LC P9.

WARD-PHILLIPS LECTURES IN ENGLISH LANGUAGE AND LITERATURE. 1- 1967-. 0083-7210. US. English. ir. University of Notre Dame Press, Notre Dame IN 46556.

WATNO DUR. See Literature.

WEE GIANT. See Literature.

WELT DER SLAVEN. See Literature.

WEN TZU YU WEN HUA. VFOAT Character and Culture. 1981, 1-. CH. Chinese. ir. 0.45. Han Tzu Hsien Tai Hua Yen Chiu, Hui Pei-Ching China. LC PL1175. DD 495.105.

WEST AFRICAN JOURNAL OF MODERN LANGUAGES. VFOAT Revue Ouest Africaine des Langues Vivantes. No. 1- Jan. 1976-. 0331-0531. Periodical. NR. English (French). an. $25.00. University of Ibadan, Department of Languages & Linguistics, Ibadan Nigeria. Ind/Abst MLA Int. Bibliogr. Books Artic. Mod. Lang. Lit., Lang. Lang. Behav. Abstr., Lang. Teach.

WESTERN EUROPEAN SPECIALISTS SECTION NEWSLETTER. VFOAT WESS Newsletter, W.E.S.S. Newsletter. 0734-4503. Periodical. US. English. sa. Free. WESS Newsletter, University of California-Santa Cruz, Collection Planning Unit, Santa Cruz CA 95064. (ctrl). *Western European Language Specialists Newsletter.*

WHERE TO LEARN ENGLISH IN GREAT BRITAIN. See Education (General).

WIENER BEITRAGE ZUR ENGLISCHEN PHILOLOGIE. Began with Vol. 1, 1895. 0083-9914. Monographic Series. AU. German (English). an. Wilhelm Braumuller, Servitengasse 5, 1092 Wien Austria. Tel 02 22-34 81 24. Ed Wilhelm Braumuller. Ind/Abst MLA Int. Bibliogr. Books Artic. Mod. Lang. Lit. LC PR13. DD 420.5. Circ 600. Yearbooks of studies in English language and literature.

WIENER BEITRAGE ZUR KULTURGESCHICHTE UND LINGUISTIK. See Anthropology.

WIENER LINGUISTISCHE GAZETTE. Issue 1-. AU. English or German with summaries in the other language. ir. Institut fur Sprachwissenschaf, Liechtensteinstrasse 46A/1/9, A-1090 Wien Austria. Ind/Abst MLA Int. Bibliogr. Books Artic. Mod. Lang. Lit., Lang. Teach. LC PF3003.

WIENER SLAVISTISCHES JAHRBUCH. See Yearbooks, Almanacs, Directories.

WIENER STUDIEN. Vol. 1-. 0084-005X. AU. English (German). an. Graz Dr Karl Leugerring 12, A1014 Wien Austria. LC PA3. DD 480.05.

WISCONSIN ENGLISH JOURNAL. See Education (General) - Theory, Practice of Education.

WISCONSIN SPANISH TEACHER. See Education (General) - Theory, Practice of Education.

WOMEN AND LANGUAGE NEWS. VFOAT Women & Language News. V. 1- Jan. 1976-. 8755-4569. Periodical. US. English. ty. Women and Language News, Centenary College of Louisiana, 2911 Centenary Boulevard, Shreveport LA 71104. DD 401.

WOORDENBOEK DER NEDERLANDSCHE TAAL. Vol. 1-. Dutch. ir. Martinus Nijhoff Publishers, PO Box 163 Spulboulevard 50, 3300AD Dordrecht Netherlands. LC PF625.

WORD. V. 1- Apr. 1945-. 0043-7956. Periodical. US. English. ir. $55.00. International Linguistic Association, c/o C Cooper, 1975 Linden Boulevard, Elmont NY 11003. Tel (212)978-8080. Ind/Abst Lang. Lang. Behav. Abstr., Sociol. Abstr., MLA Int. Bibliogr. Books Artic. Mod. Lang. Lit., Lang. Teach., Index Book Rev. Humanit. LC P1. (cum index).

WORD WAYS. VFOAT Journal of Recreational Linguistics. V. 1- Feb. 1968-. 0043-7980. Periodical. US. English. qt. $14.00. Dr A Ross Eckler, Route 18 Spring Valley Road, Morristown NJ 07960. Tel (201)538-4584. Ed A Ross Eckler. Ind/Abst MLA Int. Bibliogr. Books Artic. Mod. Lang. Lit., Lang. Lang. Behav. Abstr., Sociol. Abstr. LC GV1507.W8. bk rev adv acc. Circ 500. Serious and light-hearted articles on playing with words. Exploring the sight and sound of language.

WORK PAPERS - SUMMER INSTITUTE OF LINGUISTICS, UNIVERSITY OF NORTH DAKOTA SESSION. (WORKPAPERS OF THE SUMMER INSTITUTE OF LINGUISTICS, UNIVERSITY OF NORTH DAKOTA). Main/Corp Summer Institute of Linguistics. V. 1- 1957-. 0361-4700. US. English. an. Summer Institute of Linguistic Inc, 7500 West Camp Wisdom Road, Dallas TX 75236. Tel (214)298-3331. LC P1. DD 410. Collections of a wide variety of linguistic papers.

WORKING PAPERS IN LANGUAGE & LINGUISTICS. July 1975-. Periodical. AT. English. sa. 5.00. Tasmanian State Institute of Technology, Division Teacher Education, PO Box 1214, Launceston 7250 Tasmania Australia. Tel 003-260245. Ed Thao Le and Mike McCausland. Circ 100. (ctrl). General linguistics and associated fields: sociolinguistics, psycholinguistics and applied linguistics.

WORKING PAPERS IN LINGUISTICS. No. 1-. Periodical. AT. English. ir. University of Melbourne, Department of English, Parkville Vict 3052 Australia. LC P1. DD 410.5.

WORKING PAPERS IN LINGUISTICS (SEATTLE, WASH.). (WORKING PAPERS IN LINGUISTICS). Periodical. US. English. sa. $3.50. University of Washington, Department of Linguistics, Washington DC 98195. Tel (206)543-2046. Circ 300. Research papers in linguistics.

WORKPAPERS IN PAPUA NEW GUINEA LANGUAGES. V. 1- 1973-. PP. English. ir. Summer Institute of Linguistics, PO Box 397 SIL Bookroom, Ukarumpa Lea Papua New Guinea. Ind/Abst MLA Int. Bibliogr. Books Artic. Mod. Lang. Lit. LC PL6601. DD 499.12.

WORLD LANGUAGE ENGLISH. Vol. 1, No. 1 (Oct. 1981)-. 0278-4335. Periodical. UK. English. qt. $40.00. Pergamon Press Inc, Fairview Park, Elmsford NY 10523. Ind/Abst Lang. Teach., Recent Publ. Artic. LC PE1128.A2. DD 428.007.

THE WRITING INSTRUCTOR. See Education (General) - Special Aspects of Education.

YALE STUDIES IN ENGLISH. No. 1- 1898-. 0084-3482. US. English. ir. Yale University Press, 92A Yale Station, New Haven CT 06520. Tel (203)436-7583. Ind/Abst Annu. Bibliogr. Engl. Lang. Lit., MLA Int. Bibliogr. Books Artic. Mod. Lang. Lit.

YEARBOOK OF ENGLISH STUDIES. See Yearbooks, Almanacs, Directories.

YEARBOOK OF ITALIAN STUDIES. See Yearbooks, Almanacs, Directories.

YEAR'S WORK IN ENGLISH STUDIES. See Literature.

YEAR'S WORK IN MODERN LANGUAGE STUDIES. (THE YEAR'S WORK IN MODERN LANGUAGE STUDIES). VFOAT Modern Language Studies, Year's Work in. V. 1- 1929/30-. 0084-4152. UK. English. an. The Modern Humanities Research Association, Kings College Strand, London WC2R 2LS England. Ind/Abst MLA Int. Bibliogr. Books Artic. Mod. Lang. Lit. LC PB1. DD 405.8.

YELMO. No. 1 (Aug/Sept. 1971)-. 0006-6966. Periodical. SP. Spanish. bm. $27.00. La Revista Professor de Espanol, Apartado 877, Madrid Spain. Ind/Abst Lang. Lang. Behav. Abstr., Curr. Index J. Educ., Sociol. Abstr., Lang. Teach. LC PC4065.

YIDISHE SHPRAKH. VFOAT Yiddish Language. Vol. 1 (Jan./Feb. 1941)-. 0044-0442. Periodical. US. Yiddish. ir. $5.00. Yivo Institute for Jewish Research, 1048 Fifth Avenue, New York NY 10028. Tel 506700. Ed Mordkhe Schaechter. Ind/Abst MLA Int. Bibliogr. Books Artic. Mod. Lang. Lit., Sociol. Abstr. LC PJ5111. Circ 1,000. Devoted to the problems of standard Yiddish.

YONGDAE YONGO YONGMUNHAK. VFOAT English Language and Literature, Yeungnam University. 1st Issue (1982)-. Periodical. Korean. ir. Yongnam Taehakkyo Yongo Yongmunhak Yongusil, 214 Tae-Dong Kyongsan-Up, Kyongbuk Korea. LC PE9. (ctrl).

YONGHAK NONJIP. VFOAT English Studies. Periodical. KO. English (Korean). ir. Soul Taehakkyo Yongo Yongmun Hakhoe, San 56 Sillim-dong, Kwanak-ku, Seoul South Korea. Tel 880-5193. Ed Song Nak-Heon. LC PE9. (ctrl). The contents included are as follows: phonology, semantics, syntax and English history in linguistics and criticism,

Literary and Political Reviews

novels, poetry and plays in American and English literature.

YONSE OMUNHAK. VFOAT Journal of the Yonsei Language and Literature. Periodical. KO. Korean. ir. Yonse Taehakkyo Kugo Kungman Hakkwa, 134 Sinchon-Dong, Sodaemun-Ku, Seoul South Korea. LC PL901.

YORK PAPERS IN LINGUISTICS. 0307-3238. Periodical. UK. English. an. $6.89. University of York, Department of Language Heslington, York Y0A 5DD England. Tel (0904)59861. Ind/Abst Lang. Teach., Years Work Eng. Stud.

YU WEN CHIAO HSUEH CHEN TI. VFOAT Yuwen Jiaoxue Zhendi. Periodical. CH. Chinese. ir. 0.32. Yu-Nan Jen Min Chu Pan She, Kun-Ming China. LC PL1068.C6. DD 495.107051.

YU WEN CHIAO HSUEH TUNG HSUN. VFOAT Yuwen Jiaoxue Tongxun. Periodical. CC. Chinese. ir. 0.34. Chung-Kuo Kuo Chi Shu Tien, PO Box 399, Pei-Ching China. LC PL1068.C6. DD 495.107.

YU WEN CHIAO YEN. VFOAT Yuwen Jiaoyan. Periodical. CH. Chinese. ir. 0.27. Post Office, Hang-Chou Shih China. LC PL2258. DD 495.107.

YU WEN CHIH SHIH TSUNG KAN. Periodical. CH. Chinese. ir. 0.50. Ti Chen Chu Pan She, 63 Fu Hsing Road, Peking China Mainland. LC PL1071. DD 495.1.

YU WEN LUN TSUNG. VFOAT Yuwen Luncong. Vol. 1- (June 1981)-. Periodical. CH. Chinese. ir. 1.10. Hsin Hua Shu Tien Shang-Hai Fa Hsing So, Shanghai China. LC PL1071. DD 495.1.

YU WEN YUEH KAN. VFOAT Yuwenyuekan. Periodical. CH. Chinese. mo. 4.80. Office of South China Normal University, Kuang-Chou Shih China. Tel 774911. Ed Tang Qi-Yun. LC PL1009. DD 495.105. bk rev. Circ 130,000. Concerns the common knowledge of the past and present language and literature to meet the need of the youth.

YU YEN HSUEH LUN TSUNG. Vol. 1- (Oct. 1957)-. Periodical. CH. Chinese. ir. 0.96. Hsin Hua Shu Tien Pei-Ching Fa Hsing So, Peking China. LC P9. DD 410.

YU YEN YEN CHIU. VFOAT Yuyan Yanjiu. First published in (July 1981)-. Periodical. CH. Chinese. ir. 1.00. Hua Chung Kung Hsueh Yuan Chu Pan She Fa Hsing Pu Wu-han Shih, Hu-pei China. LC PL1004. DD 495.1.

YU YEN YEN CHIU LUN TSUNG. VFOAT Linguistic Studies. Periodical. CC. Chinese. ir. 1.31. Tien-Chin Shih Hsin Hua Shu Tien, Tientsin China.

YUGNTRUF. No. 1- November 1964-. 0098-3640. US. Yiddish. ir. $5.00. Yugntruf Inc, 3328 Bainbridge Avenue, New York NY 10467. Tel (212)654-8540. Ed Paul Glasser. Ind/Abst MLA Int. Bibliogr. Books Artic. Mod. Lang. Lit. LC PJ5111. bk rev. adv acc. Circ 2,000. Young adult oriented articles, neons and fiction in Yiddish on various aspects of Yiddish-speaking Jewish life.

ZA BUKVITE, KIRILO METODIEVSKI VESTNIK. VFOAT Kirilo Metodievski Vestnik. Periodical. Bulgarian. sa. LC PG601.

ZBORNIK MATICE SRPSKE ZA SLAVISTIKU. VFOAT Review of Slavic Studies. 26-. 0350-0470. Periodical. Serbo-Croatian -C (summaries in English, German, and Russian). sa. LC PG13. Zbornik za Slavistiku.

ZDL: ZEITSCHRIFT FUR DIALEKTOLOGIE UND LINGUISTIK. Yearly Vol. 1-. 0044-1449. Periodical. GW. German. ir. 129. Franz Steiner Verlag GMBH, Postfach 347, D7000 Stuttgart 1 West Germany. Tel (0711)2582229. Ed J Goeschel. Ind/Abst MLA Int. Bibliogr. Books Artic. Mod. Lang. Lit., Sociol. Abstr., Lang. Lang. Behav. Abstr., Years Work Eng. Stud. bk rev. adv acc. Circ 700. Articles and reviews about German linguistics, especially dialects.

ZEITSCHRIFT FUR AGYPTISCHE SPRACHE UND ALTERTUMSKUNDE. Vol. 1- July 1863-. 0044-216X. Periodical. German. sa. Kunst & Wissen Erich Bieber, Dufourstrasse 51, CH-8008 Zurich Switzerland. Tel 011-41-1-69 44 20. LC PJ1004. (cum index).

ZEITSCHRIFT FUR CELTISCHE PHILOLOGIE. Began with: Vol. 24, No. 1/2, in 1953. 0084-5302. Periodical. GW. German. an. $39.77. Max Niemeyer Verlag, Postfach 21 40, 7400 Tuebingen 1 West Germany. Ind/Abst MLA Int. Bibliogr. Books Artic. Mod. Lang. Lit., Years Work Eng. Stud. bk rev. adv acc. Contributions on Celtic languages and literatures. Zeitschrift fur Keltische Philologie und Volkforschung.

ZEITSCHRIFT FUR DEUTSCHE PHILOLOGIE. Vol. 1-. 0044-2496. Periodical. GW. German. qt. Erich Schmidt Verlag GMBH, POB 7330-40/Viktoriastr 44-A, D4800 Bielefeld 1 West Germany. Tel 0521/66061. Ed Werner Besch, Hugo Moser, Harmut Steinecke, and Benno van Wiese. Ind/Abst MLA Int. Bibliogr. Books Artic. Mod. Lang. Lit., Lang. Lang. Behav. Abstr., Index Book Rev. Humanit. LC PF3003. bk rev. adv acc. German philology.

ZEITSCHRIFT FUR DEUTSCHE PHILOLOGIE. BEIHEFT. No. 1-. Monographic Series. GW. German. ir. Erich Schmidt Verlag GMBH, POB 7330-40/Viktoriastr 44-A, D4800 Bielefeld 1 West Germany. Tel 0521/66061. Ed Werner Besch, Hugo Moser, Hartmut Steinecke, and Benno von Wiese. bk rev. adv acc. German philology.

ZEITSCHRIFT FUR DIALEKTOLOGIE UND LINGUISTIK. (ZEITSCHRIFT FUR DIALEKTOLOGIE UND LINGUISTIK : ZDL). VFOAT Z.D.L. Began with annual Vol. 36 in 1969. 0044-1449. Periodical. GW. German. ty. Frank Steiner Verlag GMBH, Postfach 5529, Friedrichstrasse 24, D-6200 Wiesbaden West Germany. Ind/Abst MLA Int. Bibliogr. Books Artic. Mod. Lang. Lit., Sociol. Abstr., Lang. Lang. Behav. Abstr., Index Book Rev. Humanit. LC PF5001. DD 437.005. Zeitschrift fur Mundartforschung.

ZEITSCHRIFT FUR GERMANISTISCHE LINGUISTIK. VFOAT ZGL. 1- 1973-. 0301-3294. Periodical. German. ir. Walter de Gryuter Inc, 200 Saw Mill River Road, Hawthorne NY 10532. Tel (914)747-0110. Ind/Abst MLA Int. Bibliogr. Books Artic. Mod. Lang. Lit., Lang. Teach. LC PF3003. Zeitschrift fur Deutsche Sprache.

ZEITSCHRIFT FUR PHONETIK, SPRACHWISSENSCHAFT UND KOMMUNIKATIONSFORSCHUNG. Vol. 14- 1961-. 0044-331X. Periodical. SZ. German (articles in English, French, or Russian). bm. $80.95. Kunst & Wissen Erich Bieber, Dufourstrasse 51, CH-8008 Zurich Switzerland. Tel 011-41-1-69 44 20. Ind/Abst MLA Int. Bibliogr. Books Artic. Mod. Lang. Lit., Lang. Teach., Index Book Rev. Humanit., Sociol. Abstr., Lang. Lang. Behav. Abstr. Zeitschrift fur Phonetik und Allgemeine Sprachwissenschaft.

ZEITSCHRIFT FUR ROMANISCHE PHILOLOGIE. BEIHEFTE. See Literature.

ZEITSCHRIFT FUR SLAVISCHE LITERATUR, KUNST UND WISSENSCHAFT. Vol. 1-2. German. ir. Ed J E Schmaler. LC PG1. DD 491.8.

ZEITSCHRIFT FUR SLAVISCHE PHILOLOGIE. Began with: Vol. 1, in 1924. 0044-3492. Periodical. GW. German. sa. 132.00. Carl Winter Universitatsverlag, Postfach 1866, Lutherstrasse 59, D6900 Heidelberg West Germany. Tel 6221-49111. Ind/Abst MLA Int. Bibliogr. Books Artic. Mod. Lang. Lit., Sociol. Abstr., Lang. Lang. Behav. Abstr., Index Book Rev. Humanit. LC PG1. DD 491.805. (cum index). Slavic philology.

ZEITSCHRIFT FUR VERGLEICHENDE SPRACHFORSCHUNG. Vol. 82-. 0044-3646. Periodical. GW. German. ir. $39.04. Vandenhoeck and Ruprecht, Postfach 3753, Theaterstr 13, D 3400 Goettingen West Germany. Tel 0551/65061. Ind/Abst MLA Int. Bibliogr. Books Artic. Mod. Lang. Lit. Zeitschrift fur Vergleichende Sprachforschung auf dem Gegiete der Indogermanischen Sprachen.

ZENKOKU TANKI DAIGAKU KIYO RONBUN SAKUIN. GOGAKU BUNGAKU HEN. VFOAT Bulletin of Junior Colleges SIC Cumulative Index in Japan. 1950-1979-. Japanese. ir. 29000. Saitama Fukushikai, 7-31 Horinouchi 3 Niiza-Shi, Saitama-Ken 352 Japan. LC Z7003, P121.

ZIELSPRACHE DEUTSCH. March 1970-. 0012-1479. Periodical. German. qt. Adlers Foreign Books Inc, 28 West 25th Street, New York NY 10010. Deutschunterricht fur Auslander.

ZIELSPRACHE ENGLISCH. Jan. 1972-. 0342-6173. Periodical. German (English). ir. 16.50. Heuber, Krausstrasse 30, 8045 Ismaning Bei Munchen West Germany. Ind/Abst Lang. Lang. Behav. Abstr., Lang. Teach. LC PE1001. DD 420.

ZIELSPRACHE RUSSISCH. Began in 1980. 0173-9522. Periodical. German (Russian). qt. $29.85. Adlers Foreign Books Inc, 162 Fifth Avenue, New York NY 10010. Ind/Abst Lang. Lang. Behav. Abstr., Lang. Teach. Russisch.

LITERARY AND POLITICAL REVIEWS

ABHANDLUNGEN - MARBURGER GELEHRTEN GESELLSCHAFT. Main/Corp Marburger Gelehrten Gesellschaft. Monographic Series. GW. German. ir. Wilhelm Fink Verlag, Ohmstrasse 5, 8 Muenchen 40 West Germany. Tel -89/348017-18.

ABRAXAS. 0361-1663. US. English. qt. $8.00. Abraxas Press Inc, 2518 Gregory Street, Madison WI 53711. Tel (608)266-3259. Ed Ingrid Swanberg. (cum index). bk rev. adv acc. Circ 600. Contemporary poetry, prose, and criticism. Reviews of small press books, perspectives on the current literary and political scene. Graphics, photos, humor, lyric forms, and narrative poems included.

ADVOCATE. (THE ADVOCATE). Vol. 1, No. 1 (Fall 1981)-. 0730-3114. Periodical. US. English. ty. $20.00. 235 Aderhold Building, University of Georgia, Attn: S L Root Jr, Athens GA 30602. Tel (404)542-5674. Ed Shelton L Root Jr. LC Z1037. DD 028.5. bk rev adv acc. Circ 1,000. Addresses important issues, suggests and examines practices, reviews hardcovers and paperbacks. Contributions by critics, authors, illustrators, publishers, scholars, and practitioners.

AFKAR. Periodical. Arabic. ir. Al-Markaz Al-Arabi Lil-Funun Wa-Al-Lugnat, 7 B Shari Al-Diwan, Garden City, Cairo Egypt. LC AP95.A6.

THE AGNI REVIEW. No. 1-. 0191-3352. Periodical. US. English. sa. $15.00. The Agni Review, PO Box 229, Cambridge MA 02238. Tel (413)367-9500. Ed Sharon Dunn. Ind/Abst Index Am. Period. Verse. adv acc. Circ 1,200. (ctrl). Magazine of poetry and fiction. Contributors include Vorie Graham, Michael Benedikt, Joyce Carol Oates, Mary Morris, Denise Levertov, Scamus Heaney, Derek Walcott, and Desmond O'Grady.

AL-ARABI. VFOAT Alaraby. Began with: No. 1 (Dec. 1958). Periodical. KU. Arabic. mo. 6.00. Kuwait Ministry of Information, Box 193, Safat Kuwait. Tel 2427141. Ed Mohamed Al-Rumeihi. Ind/Abst Hist. Abstr., Am. Hist. Life, Hist. Abstr., Part A, Mod. Hist. Abstr., Hist. Abstr., Part B, Twent. Century Abstr. LC AP95.A6. (cum index). bk rev. adv acc. Circ 300,000. (ctrl). A cultural Arabic magazine.

THE ALTADENA REVIEW. V. 1- Summer 1978-. 0162-8208. Periodical. US. English. sa. $5.00. Altadena Review, PO Box 212, Altadena CA 91001. Ed Robin Shectman. bk review. Circ 200. Poetry, reviews of books of poetry, interviews with poets and articles of interest to poetry writers and readers.

ALTDEUTSCHE TEXTE IN KRITISCHEN AUSGABEN. Vol. 1-. Monographic Series. GW. German. ir. Wilhelm Fink Verlag, Ohmstrasse 5, 8 Muenchen 40 West Germany. Tel -89/348017-18. Ed Werner Schroder.

THE AMERICAN BOOK REVIEW. V. 1- Dec. 1977-. 0149-9408. US. English. bm. $18.00. American Book Review, PO Box 188 Cooper Union Street, New York NY 10003. Ed John Tytell and Rochelle Ratner. Ind/Abst Book Rev. Index. bk rev. adv acc. Circ 11,000. The only nationally distributed review medium, which treats with equal seriousness, the literary publications of the small, large, and university presses.

AMERICAN LITERARY REALISM, 1870-1910. VAT American Literary Realism, Eighteen Hundred and Seventy, Nineteen Hundred and Ten. No. 1- Fall 1967-. 0002-9823. Periodical. US. English. sa. $10.00 Domestic, $12.00 Foreign. University of Texas at Arlington, Department of English, Box 19035, Arlington TX 76019. Tel (817)273-2729. Ed James M Moffett. Ind/Abst Abstr. Engl. Stud., Am. Hist. Life, Hist. Abstr., Part A, Mod. Hist. Abstr., Hist. Abstr., Part B, Twent. Century Abstr., MLA Int. Bibliogr. Books Artic. Mod. Lang. Lit., Ref. Source, Index Book Rev. Humanit., Hist. Abstr., Years Work Eng. Stud. (cum index). bk rev. Circ 650.

Bibliographic and critical material dealing with American Realism 1870-1910.

THE AMERICAN POETRY REVIEW. V. 1- Nov./Dec. 1972-. 0360-3709. Periodical. US. English. bm. $9.50. Temple University of Center City, 1616 Walnut Street/Room 405, Philadelphia PA 19103. **Tel** (215)732-6770. **Ed** David Ronanno, Stephen Berg and Arthur Vogelsang. **Ind/Abst** Abstr. Engl. Stud., MLA Int. Bibliogr. Books Artic. Mod. Lang. Lit., Book Rev. Index, Index Am. Period. Verse, Index Book Rev. Humanit., New Period. Index. **LC** PS580. bk rev. adv acc. **Circ** 24,000. The best in contemporary poetry, criticism and reviews.

AMERICAN REVIEW. (AR : AMERICAN REVIEW). **VFOAT** American Review. No. 16-26. US. English. ty. $5.95. Bantam Books, 666 5th Avenue, New York NY 10019. **Ind/Abst** Abstr. Engl. Stud. **LC** PS1. **DD** 810.5. *New American Review, 0028-4211.*

THE AMERICAN SPECTATOR. V. 11- Nov. 1977-. 0148-8414. Periodical. US. English. $21.00. The American Spectator, PO Box 1969, Bloomington IN 47402. **Tel** (812)334-2715. **Ed** R Emmett Tyrrell Jr. **Ind/Abst** Book Rev. Index, Public Aff. Inf. Serv. Bull. **LC** AP2. **DD** 051. bk rev. adv acc. **Circ** 42,000. Available on microfilm from University Microfilms. A monthly compendium of wit and wisdom covering political and cultural topics, along with some of the best book reviews anywhere. *Alternative.*

AMERIKA KENKYU. **VFOAT** The American Review. 0387-2815. JA. Japanese (with summaries in English). ir. Tokyo Daigaku Kyoyobu, c/o Center for American Studies, 8-1 Komaba 3 Meguro-ku (153), Tokyo Japan. **Ind/Abst** Writ. Am. Hist., Recent Publ. Artic. **LC** E151.

ANALES DE LA LITERATURA ESPANOLA CONTEMPORANEA. *See* Yearbooks, Almanacs, Directories.

THE ANALYSIS OF LITERARY TEXTS : CURRENT TRENDS IN METHODOLOGY. **Series/Titl** Studies in Literary Analysis. **VFOAT** Current Trends in Methodology. No. 3/4- 1977/78-. US. English (Spanish). Department of Foreign Languages and Bilingual Studies, 106 Ford Hall, Eastern Michigan University, Ypsilanti MI 48197. *Analysis of Hispanic Texts: Current Trends in Methodology.*

THE ANGLO-WELSH REVIEW. V. 1- (No. 1-). 0003-3405. Periodical. English. ir. 7.50 Domestic, $15.00 Foreign. Five Arches Press, Tenby, Dyfed SA70 8EE England. **Tel** (0834) 3131. **Ed** Greg Hill. **Ind/Abst** MLA Int. Bibliogr. Books Artic. Mod. Lang. Lit., Years Work Eng. Stud. **LC** PR8901. bk rev. adv acc. **Circ** 1,000. Carries some or best contemporary writing from Wales in English (poetry and prose) with articles and a complete coverage of the Anglo-Welsh book scene.

ANTIGONISH REVIEW. (THE ANTIGONISH REVIEW). V. 1- Spring 1970. 0003-5661. Periodical. CN. English. qt. $7.74. St Francis Xavier University, Antigonish Nova Scotia B2G 1C0 Canada. **Tel** (902)867-3962. **Ed** George S Sanderson. **Ind/Abst** Abstr. Engl. Stud., MLA Int. Bibliogr. Books Artic. Mod. Lang. Lit., Years Work Eng. Stud. **LC** PN2. bk rev. adv acc. **Circ** 900. Publishes poetry, short fiction, light critical articles on modern and contemporary writers, and book reviews of both national and international authors, artists portfolios.

THE ANTIOCH REVIEW. V. 1- Spring 1941-. 0003-5769. Periodical. US. English. qt. $25.00. Antioch Review, PO Box 148, Yellow Springs OH 45387. **Tel** (513)767-7386. **Ed** Robert S Fogarty. **Ind/Abst** Am. Hist. Life, Hist. Abstr., Part A, Mod. Hist. Abstr., Hist. Abst., Part B, Twent. Century Abstr., Abstr. Engl. Stud., MLA Int. Bibliogr. Books Artic. Mod. Lang. Lit., Soc. Welf. Soc. Plan./Policy Soc. Dev., Philos. Index, Annu. Bibliogr. Engl. Lang. Lit., Index Am. Period. Verse, Index Book Rev. Humanit., Int. Index, Public Aff. Inf. Serv. Bull., Soc. Sci. Index, Humanit. Index, Film Lit. Index, Lang. Lang. Behav. Abstr., Book Rev. Index, Hist. Abstr. **LC** AP2. **DD** 051. bk rev. adv acc. **Circ** 4,500. Contemporary articles in humanities, social sciences, politics, economics, literature and all areas of broad intellectual concern. Lively, distinctive prose. *Monocle.*

ANTIQUARIAN BOOK MONTHLY REVIEW. **VFOAT** ABMR. V. 1- (No. 1-). 0306-7475. Periodical. UK. English. mo. 12 Domestic, 16 US/Canada, 19 Australia. ABMR Pub Ltd, 52 St Clements, Oxford OX4 1AG England. **Tel** (0865)721615. **Ed** John A Kinnane. **LC** Z990. **DD** 002.075. bk rev. adv acc. **Circ** 3,000. Articles, reports and reviews of interest to book collectors, booksellers and libraries, modern and antiquarian.

ARBITRIUM : ZEITSCHRIFT FUR REZENSIONEN ZUR GERMANISTISCHEN LITERATURWISSENSCHAFT. Vol. 1, Jan. Issue 1-. Periodical. German (English). ty. 98.-. C H Beckshe Verlagsbchhndlg, Wilhelmstrasse 9/Pstfch 400340, 8000 Munich 40 West Germany. **Tel** (089)3818689-331. **Ed** Wolfgang Fritswald and Wolfgand Harus. bk rev. adv acc. **Circ** 500. (ctrl). Reviews of scholarly books on German literature. Criticism.

L'ARC. No 1- 1958-. 0003-7974. Periodical. FR. French. qt. $32.59. L'Arc, le Revest Sanit Martin, 04230 St-Etienne-les Orgues France. **Tel** (92)75 17 16. **Ed** Le Jas. **Ind/Abst** MLA Int. Bibliogr. Books Artic. Mod. Lang. Lit. adv acc. This journal brings together outstanding figures in literatures, philosophy or artists for direct studies of the current principles of thoughts and art of today.

ATLANTIC PROVINCES BOOK REVIEW. (THE ATLANTIC PROVINCES BOOK REVIEW). Nov. 1974-. 0316-5981. Periodical. CN. English. Saint Mary's University, Halifax Nova Scotia B3H 3C3 Canada. **Tel** (902)429-9780. **Ed** Terry Wahlen. **Ind/Abst** Book Rev. Index. **DD** 028.105. bk rev. adv acc. **Circ** 32,000. (ctrl). Scholarly reviews of books and other publications that are Atlantic Canada-directed.

AU JOUR LE SIECLE. **Series/Titl** La Revue des Lettres Modernes. 1-. Monographic Series. FR. French. ir. 73 rue du Cardinal-Lemoine, 75005 Paris France.

AUSTRALIAN BOOK REVIEW. *See* Publishing - Books and Bookmaking.

AUSTRALIAN JOURNAL OF EARLY CHILDHOOD. 1976. 0312-5033. Periodical. AT. English. qt. $15. Australian Early Childhood Association, PO Box 105 Knox Street, Watson ACT 2602 Australia. **Tel** (062)416 900. **Ed** Margaret Clyde. **Ind/Abst** Curr. Index J. Educ. bk rev. adv acc. **Circ** 2,000. Each issue contains articles in the field of early childhood including research projects, book reviews, details of forthcoming conferences and other relevant articles.

AXIOS (LOS ANGELES, CALIF.). (AXIOS). **VFOAT** Axios Newsletter. Began with Sept. 1981. 0278-551X. Periodical. US. English. mo. $10.00. Axios Inc, 800 South Euclid Street, Fullerton CA 92632. **Tel** (714)526-2131. **Ed** Daniel John Gorham. bk rev. **Circ** 12,512. To challenge, provoke and startle.

AZERBAJDZANSKOR NEFTJANOE HOZJAJSTVO. (AZERBAIDZHANSKOE NEFTIANOE KHOZIAISTVO). **VFOAT** Azarbaijan Neft Tasarrufaty. Began Dec. 1921. 0365-8554. Periodical. UR. Russian (text in Azerbaijani). mo. $33.50. Victor Kamkin Inc (76307), 12224 Parklawn Drive, Rockville MD 20852. **Tel** (301)881-5973. **Ind/Abst** GeoRef, Chem. Abstr. **CODEN** AZNKAY. Index in last issue of volume - attached. *Narodnoe Khoziaistvo.*

BEITRAGE ZUR ROMANISCHEN PHILOLOGIE DES MITTELALTERS. V. 1-. 0067-5202. Monographic Series. GW. German. ir. Wilhelm Fink Verlag, Ohmstrasse 5, 8 Muenchen 40 West Germany. **Tel** 89/348017-18. **Ed** Hans-Wilhelm Klein and Ernstpeter Ruhe.

BELFAGOR. Vol. 1- Jan. 1946-. 0005-8351. Periodical. IT. Italian. bm. Casa Editrice Leo S Olschki, Casella Postale PO Box 66, Firenze Italy. **Ind/Abst** Am. Hist. Life, Hist. Abstr., Part A, Mod. Hist. Abstr., Hist. Abst., Part B, Twent. Century Abstr., MLA Int. Bibliogr. Books Artic. Mod. Lang. Lit., Hist. Abstr., Recent Publ. Artic. **LC** AP37. **DD** 055.1. Index published separately - free - automatically sent.

THE BELLINGHAM REVIEW. Vol. 1, No. 1 (Jan. 1977)-. 0734-2934. Periodical. US. English. sa. $4.50. The Signpost Press Inc, 412 North Statestreet, Bellingham WA 98225. **Tel** (206)734-9781. **Ed** Knute Skinner. **LC** PS501. **DD** 810.8. bk rev. **Circ** 700. We publish poetry, fiction, and drama of palpable quality; also reviews, drawings and photographs.

THE BERKELEY MONTHLY. 1969. 0191-7080. Periodical. US. English. mo. $10.00. Berkeley Monthly, 910 Parker Street, Berkeley CA 94710. **Tel** (415)848-7900. **Ed** Tracy Johnston. bk rev. adv acc. **Circ** 80,000. (ctrl). Emphasizes on good writing above all, and covers the arts, local personalities and politics. Of special concern is humor, fun, and off-beat personal stories.

THE BERKELEY POETRY REVIEW. Periodical. US. English. ir. University of California, 201 Sproul Hall, Berkeley CA 94720. **Tel** (415)524-8065.

BERKSHIRE REVIEW. V. 1- Spring 1965-. 0005-920X. Periodical. US. English. qt. Berkshire Review, PO Box 633, Williamstown MA 01267. **Ind/Abst** Index Am. Period. Verse. **LC** AP2. **DD** 051.

BILL-DALE MARCINKO'S AFTA. **VFOAT** Afta. 0193-7782. Periodical. US. English. qt. $8.00. Bill Dale Marcinko, Editor, 153 George Street/Apartment 2, New Brunswick NJ 08901. **Tel** (201)828-5467. **Ed** Bill Dale Marcinko. bk rev. adv acc. **Circ** 25,000. Reviews, books, comics, films, videotapes, record albums, new publications, and covers political and sexual issues, especially relating to homosexuality, lesbianism, and feminism.

BITSARON. **VFOAT** Bitzaron. V. 1- 1939-. 0006-3932. Periodical. US. Hebrew (summaries in English). qt. $15.00. Bitzaron, PO Box 623, Cooper Station, New York NY 10003. **Tel** (212)598-3987. **Ed** Hayin Leat. **Ind/Abst** MLA Int. Bibliogr. Books Artic. Mod. Lang. Lit., Hist. Abstr., Am. Hist. Life, Hist. Abstr., Part A, Mod. Hist. Abstr., Hist. Abst., Part B, Twent. Century Abstr. **DD** 059. bk rev. adv acc. (ctrl). Literary criticism: biblical, medieval, and modern studies of Jewish interest.

THE BLACK WARRIOR REVIEW. **VFOAT** BWR, Fall 1980, BWR, B.W.R. Vol. 1, No. 1 (Fall 1974)-. 0193-6301. Periodical. US. English. sa. $10.00. Black Warrior Review, Box 2936, University AL 35486. **Tel** (205)348-4518. **Ed** Lynn Domina. **Ind/Abst** MLA Int. Bibliogr. Books Artic. Mod. Lang. Lit., Book Rev. Index. **LC** PS1. **DD** 810.5. bk rev. adv acc. **Circ** 700. Publishes poetry, fiction, essays, and reviews by both established and developing writers to present and award-winning collection in each issue.

THE BLOOMSBURY REVIEW. 1980. 0276-1564. Periodical. US. English. mo. $10.00. Owaissa Communications Co Inc, PO Box 8928, Denver CO 80201. **Tel** (303)455-0593. **Ed** Thomas Auer. **DD** 028. bk rev. adv acc. **Circ** 8,000. (ctrl). Book reviews, interviews with authors, and essays about the book industry.

BOOK TALK. *See* Publishing - Books and Bookmaking.

BOOKS FOR YOUR CHILDREN. V. 1- 1966-. UK. English. ty. 3.50 Domestic, 5.00 Foreign. Attn Anne Wood, 90 Gillhurst Road, Harborne 17 Birmingham England. **Tel** 021-454-5453. **Ed** Barry and Anne Wood. **LC** Z1037.A1. **DD** 028.1. bk rev. adv acc. **Circ** 18,000. Review of children's books both newly published and those republished to enable parents to select suitable books for their children.

BORDERLINES (DOWNSVIEW, ONT.). (BORDERLINES). **VFOAT** Border Lines. No. 1 (Fall 1984)-. Periodical. CN. English. qt. 25.00. Bethune College of York University, 4700 Keele Street, Downsview Ontario M3J 1P3 Canada. **Tel** (416)667-6278. bk rev. adv acc. **Circ** 2,000. Covers social and political perspectives on art, literature, music, communications, social movements and the arts.

DER BOTE. Periodical. German. ir. 15.-. 8000 Munchen 2, Walterhstr 28, Munchen West Germany. **Tel** (089)533328. **Ed** Heinz Jacobi. **LC** PT1141.A2. bk rev. **Circ** 1,000. Works of Heinz Jacobi. *Martin-Greif-Bote.*

BROADSIDE CRITICS SERIES. Monographic Series. US. English. ir. Alexander Crummell Center, 74 Glendale Avenue, Highland Park MI 48203.

BROOKLYN LITERARY REVIEW. (BROOKLYN LITERARY REVIEW : THE BROOKLYN COLLEGE ALUMNI LITERARY REVIEW). **VFOAT** Brooklyn College Alumni Literary Review. No. 5-. 0883-2846. Periodical. US. English. sa. Brooklyn College Alumni Association, 2401 Glenwood Road, Brooklyn NY 11210. *Brooklyn College Alumni Literary Review, 0732-9709.*

BULLETIN BAKHTINE. (LE BULLETIN BAKHTINE). **VFOAT** The Bakhtin Newsletter. No. 1 (1983)-. 0821-6886. CN. English. an. 8.00. C Thomson, Department of French Studies, Queen's University, Kingston Ontario K7L 3N6 Canada. **Tel** (613)376-3016. **Ed** Clive Thomson. **DD** 060.8019505. bk rev. adv acc. Bibliographical and reviews on Mikhail Bakhtin and the Bakhtin circle.

BULLETIN DE LA CLASSE DES LETTRES ET DES SCIENCES MORALES ET POLITIQUES. Main/Corp Academie Royale des Sciences, des Lettres et des Beaux-Arts de Belgique, Brussels. Classe des Lettres et des Sciences Morales et Politiques. Periodical. BE. French. mo. 1.200 1.200. Academie Royale Med Belgique, rue Decale 1, 1000 Bruxelles Belgium. **Tel** 512 85 50. **Ind/Abst** Am. Hist. Life, Hist. Abstr., Part A, Mod. Hist. Abstr., Hist. Abst., Part B, Twent. Century Abstr. Index in last issue of volume - attached. **Circ** 500. (ctrl). Literary and political reviews. *Bulletins de la Classe des Lettres et des Sciences Morales.*

BYRON JOURNAL. (THE BYRON JOURNAL). No. 1- 1973-. 0301-7257. UK. English. an. $10.00. Bryon Society Journal Ltd, 259 New Jersey Avenue, Collingswood NJ 08108. **Tel** (609)838-0514. **Ed** J Drummond Bone and Ian Scott-Kilvert. **Ind/Abst** MLA Int. Bibliogr. Books Artic. Mod. Lang. Lit., Ref. Source, Years Work Eng. Stud. **LC** PR4379. **DD** 821.7. bk rev. adv acc. **Circ** 3,000. Scholarly articles, essays, and book reviews concerning the English Romantic poet, Lord Byron, and his circle.

EL CAIMAN BARBUDO. No. 1- Jan. 1966-. Periodical. CU. Spanish. mo. $15.77. Empresa Ediciones Cubanas, Obispo 461/Apartado 605, Ciudad de la Habana Cuba.

CANADIAN BOOK REVIEW ANNUAL. 1975-. 0383-770X. CN. English. an. $54.13. Simon & Pierre, POB 280 Adelaide Postal Station, Toronto Ont M5C 2J4 Canada. **Tel** (416)363-6767. **Ed** Dean Tudor and Ann Tudor. **LC** F1001. **DD** 028.1. Index in last issue of volume - attached. bk rev. **Circ** 2,000. Succinct interesting reviews of new Canadian books within five basic categories: reference materials, humanities and applied arts, literature, social sciences, science and technology.

CANADIAN FORUM. (THE CANADIAN FORUM). V. 1- Oct. 1920-. 0008-3631. Periodical. CN. English. mo. $44.88. Canadian Forum, 70 Bond Street, Ground Floor, Toronto Ontario M5B 2J3 Canada. **Tel** (416)365-1148. **Ed** John Hutchinson. **Ind/Abst** Mag. Index, Can. Period. Index, Book Rev. Index, Index Book Rev. Humanit., Book Rev. Digest. adv acc. **Circ** 6,500. Also available on microfilm from: Ann Arbor, Mich., University Microfilms. Available on microfilm from: Toronto, Micromedia. Political/literature and poems. *Rebel, Willison's Monthly.*

CANADIAN REVIEW OF STUDIES IN NATIONALISM. VFOAT Revue Canadienne des Etudes sur le Nationalisme. V. 1- Fall 1973-. 0317-7904. CN. English (includes some text in French). ir. $9.00. University of Prince Edward Island CRSN c/o Professor W Isenor, Charlottetown Prince Edward Island C1A 4P3 Canada. **Tel** (902)566-0527. **Ed** Thomas Spira. **Ind/Abst** Am. Hist. Life, Hist. Abstr., Part A, Mod. Hist. Abstr., Hist. Abst., Part B, Twent. Century Abstr., ABC Pol Sci, Sociol. Abstr., Public Aff. Inf. Serv. Bull., Foreign Lang. Index, Hist. Abstr. **LC** JC311. **DD** 320.5405. bk rev. adv acc. **Circ** 600. (ctrl). Articles, review essay, book reviews, and annotated bibliographies dealing with nationalism, ethnic issues and related topics.

CARIBBEAN REVIEW. V. 1- Spring 1969-. 0008-6525. Periodical. US. English. qt. $32.00. Caribbean Review Inc, Florida International University, Tamiami Trail, Miami FL 33199. **Tel** (305)554-2246. **Ed** Barry B Levine. **Ind/Abst** Am. Hist. Life, Hist. Abstr., Part A, Mod. Hist. Abstr., Hist. Abst., Part B, Twent. Century Abstr., Artbibliogr. Mod., Public Aff. Inf. Serv. Bull., Recent Publ. Artic., Hist. Abstr. **LC** AP6. **DD** 079.7295. bk rev. adv acc. **Circ** 5,000. Available on microfilm from University Microfilms. Dedicated to Latin America, the Caribbean and their emigrant groups. Fact-filled and fresh debate about the issues and personalities that concern this important region.

CATALOGUE OF GOVERNMENT AND TANU PUBLICATIONS. VFOAT Orodha ya Vitabu Vya Tanu na Serikali. English or Swahili. ir. Government Publications Agency, PO Box 1801, Dar es Salaam Tanzania. **LC** Z3753.T3, J801. **DD** 015.678. *Government and Tanu Publications List.*

CENOBIO. Vo. 1- 1952-. 0008-896X. Periodical. French and Italian. ir. **Ind/Abst** MLA Int. Bibliogr. Books Artic. Mod. Lang. Lit.

CENTURY (ALBUQUERQUE, N.M.). (CENTURY). Vol. No. 1 (Oct. 1, 1980)-. 0272-1082. Periodical. US. English. sm. $32.00 Domestic, $37.00 Foreign. Century, PO Box 709, Albuquerque NM 87103. **LC** AP2. **DD** 051.

THE CHAUCER REVIEW. V. 1- Summer 1966-. 0009-2002. Periodical. US. English. qt. $18.00. Pennsylvania State University Press, 215 Wagner Building, University Park PA 16802. **Tel** (814)865-1327. **Ind/Abst** Humanit. Index, MLA Int. Bibliogr. Books Artic. Mod. Lang. Lit., Abstr. Engl. Stud., Years Work Eng. Stud. **LC** PR1901.

CHENG CHIH PING LUN. VFOAT Political Review, The Political Review. Began with Sept. 10, 1958 issue. Periodical. CH. Chinese. mo. 480.00. Cheng Chih Ping Lun She, PO Box 1303, Taipei Taiwan China. **LC** D839. **DD** 951.2490505.

CHICAGO REVIEW. *See* Literature.

CHILDREN'S BOOK REVIEW INDEX. *See* Indexes/Abstracts.

CHILDREN'S BOOK REVIEW SERVICE. V. 1- Sept. 1972-. 0090-7987. US. English. ir. $35.00. Childrens Book Review Service, 220 Berkeley Place 1D, Brooklyn NY 11217. **Tel** (718)622-4036. **Ed** Ann L KalkhoffF. **Ind/Abst** Book Rev. Index. **LC** Z1037.A1. **DD** 028.1. bk rev. **Circ** 350. Reviews of children's trade books for ages pre-school through high school. Reviewers either work with children or young adults or have subject specialities.

CHILDREN'S LITERATURE ASSOCIATION QUARTERLY. Periodical. CN. English. qt. $35.00. University of Wisconsin-Stout, English Department, Virginia Wolf, Menomonie WI 54751. **Tel** (317)494-2355. **Ed** Perry Nodelman. **Ind/Abst** MLA Int. Bibliogr. Books Artic. Mod. Lang. Lit. **LC** PN1008.2. **DD** 809.89282. bk rev. adv acc. **Circ** 1,500. (ctrl). Articles critique a wide variety of works from children's literature. Ideas for teaching children's literature using literary criticism are also presented. *CHLA Newsletter.*

CHILDREN'S LITERATURE REVIEW. 1976-. 0362-4145. Periodical. US. English. sa. $78.00. Gale Research Company, Book Tower, Detroit MI 48226. **Ed** Gerard J Senick. **LC** PN1009.A1. **DD** 028.52. Continuing series provides excerpts from criticism on past and present authors of children's books.

THE CHOWDER REVIEW. No. 1- Winter 1973-. 0146-3225. Periodical. US. English. sa. Chowder Review, PO Box 33, Wollaston MA 02170. **Ind/Abst** Index Am. Period. Verse. **LC** PS580. **DD** 811.505.

CHRONICLES OF CULTURE. Began with issue for Sept. 1977. 0163-1187. Periodical. US. English. mo. $18.00. The Rockford Institute, 934 North Main, Rockford IL 61103. **Tel** (815)964-5811. **Ed** Thomas Fleming. **LC** PN80. **DD** 028.1. bk rev. **Circ** 7,500. Journal of conservative political thought aimed at the young American intelligensia. Book reviews, play reviews and editorial comment.

CINCINNATI POETRY REVIEW. VFOAT CPR, C.P.R. No. 1- Spring 1975-. Periodical. US. English. sa. University of Cincinnati, Department of English/069, Cincinnati OH 45221. **Tel** (513)475-4484. **Ed** Dallas Wiebe. **Circ** 1,100. Original contemporary poetry.

C.L.C. CONTEMPORARY LITERARY CRITICISM. (CONTEMPORARY LITERARY CRITICISM). No. 1- 1973-. 0091-3421. US. English. ir. $64.00. Gale Research Co, Book Tower, Detroit MI 48826. **Tel** (800)521-0707. **Ed** E Borkland. **LC** PN771. **DD** 809.04. Provides detailed biographical and bibliograpical entries on 125 influential Twentieth Century critics in the English language.

COLLEGE POETRY REVIEW. V. 39- Spring 1976-. Periodical. US. English. sa. $14.00. National Poetry Association, Box 218, Agoura CA 91301.

COLUMBIA REVIEW. 0010-1982. Periodical. US. English. sa. $4.00. Columbia Review, 304 Ferris Booth Hall, Columbia University, New York NY 10027. **LC** AP2.

COLUMBIA ROAD REVIEW. V. 1- Aug. 1980-. 0271-4299. Periodical. US. English. bm. King Publications, PO Box 19332, Washington DC 20036. **Tel** (202)332-7079. **Ed** Kathryn E King. bk rev. adv acc. **Circ** 300. Review magazine of books, periodicals, etc. from Southern presses.

COMMENTARY. 1- , 1972-74. 0084-8956. Periodical. SI. English. qt. 2.50. University of Singapore, Kent Ridge, Singapore 5 Republic of Singapore. **Tel** 7791811. **Ed** Zaibun Siraj. **LC** DS501. **DD** 915.9005. adv acc. **Circ** 5,000. (ctrl). The journal consists of articles on economic, social and cultural affairs, comments on current issues in Singapore and elsewhere and literary materials.

THE COMPARATIST. V. 1- 1977-. 0195-7678. US. English. an. $10.00. Eniko M Basa, 707 Snider Lane, Silver Spring MD 20904. **Tel** (301)384-4657. **Ed** Mechtild Cranston. **Ind/Abst** MLA Int. Bibliogr. Books Artic. Mod. Lang. Lit. **LC** PN855. **DD** 809. **Circ** 400. (ctrl). Articles on most aspects of comparative literary studies.

COMPARATIVE CRITICISM. 1-. 0144-7564. Periodical. UK. English. an. Cambridge University Press, Bently House, 200 Euston Road, London NW1 2DB England. **Ind/Abst** MLA Int. Bibliogr. Books Artic. Mod. Lang. Lit. **LC** PN863. **DD** 809.

CONCH REVIEW OF BOOKS. (THE CONCH REVIEW OF BOOKS). V. 1, No. 1- March 1973-. 0092-7708. Periodical. US. English. qt. $15.00 Domestic, $17.00 Foreign. Conch Magazine Ltd, 102 Normal Avenue, Symphony Circle, Buffalo NY 14213. **Tel** (716)885-3686. **Ed** S O Anozie. **Ind/Abst** MLA Int. Bibliogr. Books Artic. Mod. Lang. Lit. **LC** Z3501. **DD** 028.1096. bk rev. adv acc. **Circ** 1,000. In-depth and timely reviews of books and audiovisual materials about Africa, and comprehensive coverage of African book publishing and libraries.

CONJUNCTIONS. 1 (Winter 81-82)-. 0278-2324. Periodical. US. English. sa. $20.00. Conjunctions, 33 West Ninth Street, New York NY 10011. **Tel** (212)477-1136. **Ed** Bradford Morrow. **LC** PN6010.5. **DD** 805. bk rev. adv acc. **Circ** 5,500. Literary journal featuring contemporary poetry, fiction, essays, interviews, translations, reviews, artwork. "It is now apparent that 'Conjunctions" has developed into a major literary periodical. . .a first rate literary review.".

CONJUNTO. Yearly V. 1- (No. 1-). 0010-5937. Periodical. CU. Spanish. qt. $14.00. Empresa Edicines Cubanas, Sub-Direccion Exportacion, Oreilly 407 Ciudad Habana Cuba. **Circ** 20,000. (ctrl). A magazine of letters and ideas; it contains articles, essays, fiction, poetry, literary criticism, interviews, book reviews, art criticism and cultural news from Latin-American and Caribbean countries.

CONTREPOINT. No. 1- May 1970-. 0010-7964. Periodical. FR. French. qt. $46.57. SERC Contrepoint, 4 rue de Stockholm, 7500 Paris France. **Tel** 294 10 10.

CONVORBIRI LITERARE. V. 1- March 1, 1867-. RM. Romanian. mo. Ilexim Press Department, PO Box 1-136-1-137, Bucharest Romania. **LC** AP86.

COTTONWOOD REVIEW. 1965. 0147-149X. Periodical. US. English. ty. Cottonwood, University of Kansas, Union Box J, Lawrence KS 66045. **Ed** George F Wedge. bk rev. **Circ** 500. Publishes a wide variety of poetry and fiction styles but tends not to accept academic writing, workshop produce or rhymed couplets. Past issues include Stafford, Day, Merwin, and Elliott. *Cottonwood.*

CRAPOUILLOT. New Series, V. 1-72, 1948-66. Periodical. FR. French. qt. Dawson France, BP 40 F-91, Palaiseau France. **Tel** 009-0122. **LC** AP20.

THE CRESSET. *See* Religion, Mythology, Rationalism - Protestantism.

IL CRISTALLO. 1st Year, No. 1 (May 1959)-. 0011-1449. Periodical. IT. Italian. ty. 10.000. Centro de Cultura Dell'Alto Adige, Via Napoli 1, 39100 Bolzano Italy. **Tel** (0471)45057. **Ind/Abst** MLA Int. Bibliogr. Books Artic. Mod. Lang. Lit. bk rev. adv acc. **Circ** 1,000.

CRITERE. No.1- Feb. 1970-. 0384-0174. Periodical. CN. French. sa. $27.09. College Ahuntsic, 9155 St Hubert, Montreal Quebec H2M 1Y8 Canada. **Tel** (514)389-9068. **Ind/Abst** Point Repere. An interdisciplinary and topical journal, cultural and literary. A serious journal whose themes are always in direct line with the great questions debated in society.

CRITERIO. No. 1-. 0011-1473. Periodical. AG. Spanish. ir. $50.00. Editorial Criterio, Junin 627, 1026 Buenos Aires Argentina. **Tel** 46 7925. **LC** AP63.

CRITICAL TEXTS. Issue No. 1 (Summer 1982)-. 0730-2304. Periodical. US. English. ir. $10.00. Critical Texts/Columbia University, English Department 602 Philosophy Hall, New York NY 10027. **Tel** (212)864-0936. **Ed** Joseph Childers. bk rev. adv acc. **Circ** 450. A book review of recent works on literary, political and philosophical theories, containing essays and interviews with prominent scholars in these fields.

CRITICISM. V. 1- Winter 1959-. 0011-1589. Periodical. US. English. qt. $45.00. Wayne State University Press, 5959 Woodward Avenue, Detroit MI 48202. **Tel** (313)577-6602. **Ed** Arthur Marotti. **Ind/Abst** Humanit. Index, MLA Int. Bibliogr. Books Artic. Mod. Lang. Lit., Book Rev. Index, Abstr. Engl. Stud. bk rev. adv acc. **Circ** 1,200. Examines literature and arts of all periods and nations either individually or in their inter-relationships and also the critical theory regarding them.

CRITIQUE. Vol. 1 No.1-). 0011-1600. Periodical. FR. French. mo. 337.00 Domestic, 415.00 Foreign. Les Editions de Minuit, 7 rue Bernard-Palissy, Paris 75006 France. **Tel** 222.37.94. **Ed** Jean Piel. **Ind/Abst** Sociol. Abstr., MLA Int. Bibliogr. Books Artic. Mod. Lang. Lit., Index Book Rev. Humanit., Lang. Lang. Behav. Abstr., MLA Int. Bibliogr. Books Artic. Mod. Lang. Lit. **LC** Z1007. General review of French and other language publications on literature and philosophy.

CRITIQUE. V. 1-. 0011-1619. Periodical. US. English. qt. $25.00. Heldref Publications, 4000 Albemarle Street NW/Suite 302, Washington DC 20016. **Tel** (202)362-6445. **Ed** Gail Lowery. **Ind/Abst** Abstr. Engl. Stud., Book Rev. Index, MLA Int. Bibliogr. Books Artic. Mod. Lang. Lit., Annu. Bibliogr. Engl. Lang. Lit., Index Book Rev. Humanit., Soc. Sci. Index, Humanit. Index. **LC** PN3503. **DD** 809.3. (cum index). adv acc. **Circ** 1,361. Available on microfiche from Microcard Editions. Closely focused, critical essays on contemporary fiction and serious detailed discussions on the fiction of our time are presented in this journal. *Faulkner Studies.*

CROTON REVIEW. V. 1- Summer 1978-. 0741-6210. Periodical. US. English. an. $10.00 for 2 years. Croton Review, PO Box 277, Croton-on-Hudson NY 10520. **Tel** (914)271-3144. **Ed** Ruth Lisa Schechter. adv acc. **Circ** 2,000. Quality prose and poetry from known and unknown US writers. Art, essay and interviews from distinquished writers (non-solicited). Criteria for acceptance: language, substance, craft, originality. Guidelines sent to queries with SASE. Contemporary writers.

THE CULTURAL WATCHDOG NEWSLETTER. Periodical. US. English. mo. $15.00. Cultural Watchdog Newsletter, c/o Louis Ehrenkrantz/6 Winslow Road, White Plains NY 10606. **Tel** (212)986-0223.

CUMBERLAND POETRY REVIEW. Vol. 1, No. 1 (Winter 1981)-. 0731-7980. Periodical. US. English. sa. $12.00. Cumberland Poetry Review, PO Box 120128 Acklin Station, Nashville TN 37212. **Tel** (615)373-8948. **Ed** Donald Davie, Eva K Touster and Bob Darrell. **LC** PS580. **DD** 811.008. **Circ** 250. Devoted to fine poetry and criticism, present poets of diverse origins. Our obligation is to support the poet's effort to keep up the language.

DELTA; A LITERARY REVIEW *CEASED.* No. 1-62. 0011-7986. Periodical. UK. English. ty. **DD** 820.

THE DENVER QUARTERLY. (DENVER QUARTERLY). V. 11, No. 4- Winter 1977-. 0011-8869. Periodical. US. English. qt. $16.00. University of Denver, Department of English, Denver CO 80208. **Tel** (313)871-2892. **Ed** David Milofsky. **Ind/Abst** Annu. Bibliogr. Engl. Lang. Lit., MLA Int. Bibliogr. Books Artic. Mod. Lang. Lit., Index Am. Period. Verse, Index Book Rev. Humanit., MLA Int. Bibliogr. Books Artic. Mod. Lang. Lit., Years Work Eng. Stud. **LC** AP2. **DD** 051. bk rev. adv acc. Available on microfilm from University Microfilms, Ann Arbor, Mich. A journal of modern culture, including poetry, fiction, and essays and reviews. *University of Denver Quarterly, 0041-9540.*

DERIVES. No 1-. 0383-7521. Periodical. CN. French. qt. $12.38. Editions Derives, C P 398 Succ M, Montreal Quebec H1V 3M5 Canada. **Tel** (514)722-2742. **Ed** Jean Jonassaint. **Ind/Abst** Point Repere. **LC** PQ3912.5. **DD** 840.8. bk rev. adv acc. **Circ** 800. Interdisciplinary and intercultural review: arts, literature, social topics, music, movies, book reviews, etc. on/of Third World, Quebec and minorities.

DIACRITICS. V. 1- Fall 1971-. 0300-7162. Periodical. US. English. qt. Johns Hopkins University Press, 701 West 40th Street/Suite 275, Baltimore MD 21211. **Tel** (301)338-6987. **Ed** Philip Lewis. **Ind/Abst** Abstr. Engl. Stud., MLA Int. Bibliogr. Books Artic. Mod. Lang. Lit., Sociol. Abstr., Film Lit. Index, Index Book Rev. Humanit., Years Work Eng. Stud. **LC** PN80. **DD** 805. bk rev. adv acc. **Circ** 1,338. A forum for critics writing on criticism. Extensive reviews of important books and films considering the content and methodology.

DICKINSON STUDIES. No. 34- Dec. 1978-. 0164-1492. Periodical. US. English. sa. $60.00. Higginson Press, 4508-38th Street, Brentwood MD 20722. **Tel** (301)864-8527. **Ed** F L Morey. **Ind/Abst** MLA Int. Bibliogr. Books Artic. Mod. Lang. Lit. **LC** Z8230.5. **DD** 016.8114. bk rev. adv acc. **Circ** 250. (ctrl). Emily Dickinson criticism. *Emily Dickinson Bulletin, 0046-1881.*

DIDASCALIES : CAHIERS OCCASIONNELS DE L'ENSEMBLE THEATRAL MOBILE. *See* Theater.

DOG RIVER REVIEW. Vol. 1, No. 1 (Spring 1982)-. 0749-260X. Periodical. US. English. sa. $6.00. Dog River Review, PO Box 125, Parkdale OR 97041-0125. **Tel** (503)352-6494. **Ed** LAurence F Hawkins Jr. **DD** 810. adv acc. **Circ** 200. Mature poetry - all forms; fiction to 2,500 words. Black and white art. Reviews, satire and short plays.

DRUZHBA NARODOV. 1939-. 0012-6756. Periodical. UR. Russian. mo. $43.00. Victor Kamkin Inc (70250), 12224 Parklawn Drive, Rockville MD 20852. **Tel** (301)881-5973. **Ind/Abst** MLA Int. Bibliogr. Books Artic. Mod. Lang. Lit. **LC** PN6065.R9.

ELH. VFOAT Journal of Literary History. V. 1- Apr. 1934-. 0013-8304. Periodical. US. English. qt. $49.00. Johns Hopkins University Press, 701 West 40th Street/Suite 275, Baltimore MD 21211. **Tel** (301)338-6987. **Ed** Ronald Paulson. **Ind/Abst** Abstr. Engl. Stud., MLA Int. Bibliogr. Books Artic. Mod. Lang. Lit., Annu. Bibliogr. Engl. Lang. Lit., Years Work Eng. Stud., Humanit. Index, Recent Publ. Artic. **LC** PR1. **DD** 820.9. adv acc. **Circ** 2,000. Devoted to criticism and interpretation of English and American literature. Emphasis is placed on major works of poetry and prose from the 16th to the 20th Centuries.

ENCLITIC. V. 1- Spring 1977-. 0193-5798. Periodical. US. English. sa. $36.00. Enclitic, 200 Folwell 9 Pleasant Street SE, Minneapolis MN 55455. **Ed** John O'Kane. **Ind/Abst** MLA Int. Bibliogr. Books Artic. Mod. Lang. Lit., Film Lit. Index. bk rev. adv acc. **Circ** 1,500. A review of film, literary and cultural criticism that provides an engaging forum for practical and theoretical discussion of changing issues in the humanities and social sciences.

ESPRIT. No. 1-463, Oct. 1932-Dec. 1976. 0014-0759. Periodical. French. mo. $56.54. Revue Espirit, 19 rue Jacob, 75006 Paris France. **Tel** 633 25 45. **Ind/Abst** MLA Int. Bibliogr. Books Artic. Mod. Lang. Lit., Point Repere, Am. Hist. Life, Hist. Abstr., Book Rev. Index, Hist. Abstr., Part A, Mod. Hist. Abstr., Hist. Abst., Part B, Twent. Century Abstr. **LC** AP20. **DD** 054.

ESSAYS IN CRITICISM. V. 1- Jan. 1951. 0014-0856. Periodical. UK. English. qt. 38.00. Essays in Criticism, 6A Rawlinson Road, Oxford OX2 6UE England. **Tel** 0865 55062. **Ed** Stephen Wall. **Ind/Abst** Abstr. Engl. Stud., MLA Int. Bibliogr. Books Artic. Mod. Lang. Lit., Annu. Bibliogr. Engl. Lang. Lit., Index Book Rev. Humanit., Soc. Sci. Index, Humanit. Index, Years Work Eng. Stud. **LC** PR1. (cum index). bk rev. adv acc. **Circ** 2,500. Available on microfilm. A journal in academic criticism and book reviews in English literature.

L'ESTAMPILLE. Began publication in 1969. Periodical. FR. French. mo. 21121 Fontaine-les-Dijon, 21000 Dijon France.

ETUDES ANGLAISES. Vol. 1-. 0014-195X. Periodical. FR. French. qt. $36.45. Societe Nouvelle Didier Erudition, 6 rue de la Sorbonne, 75005 Paris France. **Tel** 4354.47.57. **Ed** Serge Sourel. **Ind/Abst** Abstr. Engl. Stud., MLA Int. Bibliogr. Books Artic. Mod. Lang. Lit., Annu. Bibliogr. Engl. Lang. Lit., Index Book Rev. Humanit., Sociol. Abstr., Lang. Lang. Behav. Abstr., Years Work Eng. Stud. **LC** PR1. **DD** 820.9. bk rev. adv acc. **Circ** 2,000. The best established review of English and American literature in France with a wide international circulation. We also publish articles on British and American civilization.

EUREKA REVIEW. Winter 1975/76-. 0363-1850. US. English. an. $5.25. University of Cincinnati, Department of English, Cincinnati OH 45221. **LC** PS1. **DD** 810.8005.

EUROPE; REVUE LITTERAIRE MENSUELLE. Began in 1923. 0014-2751. Periodical. FR. French. mo. 350.00 Domestic, 430.00 Foreign. Europe/Revue Litteraire, 146 rue Faubourg Poissonniere, 75010 Paris France. **Tel** 281 91 03. **Ed** Messidor. **Ind/Abst** MLA Int. Bibliogr. Books Artic. Mod. Lang. Lit., Coal Abstr. **LC** AP20. bk rev. adv acc. **Circ** 6,000. One of the most important French literary reviews, founded in 1923. Monthly publication with studies on literature but also poems and short stories of contemporary writers.

FIVE FINGERS REVIEW. No. 1-. US. English. Five Fingers Poetry, 100 Valencia Street/Suite 303, San Francisco CA 94103.

FLAMMES VIVES. Yearly V. 3-. 0015-3486. Periodical. FR. French. bm. Editions du Carmel, C C P 166 49 U Marseille, Vanasque 84210 Pernes France.

FLORIDA REVIEW (ORLANDO, FLA.). (THE FLORIDA REVIEW). Began with Vol. 1 in 1972. 0742-2466. Periodical. US. English. an. $6.00. Department of English, University of Central Florida, Orlando FL 32816. **Tel** (305)275-2038. **Ed** Pat Rushin. adv acc. **Circ** 1,000. High literary quality fiction that delights, instructs, and is not afraid to take risks. Clear, strong poems filled with real things, real people, real emotions that advance our knowledge of the human heart.

FOLIO (BINGHAMTON, N.Y.). (FOLIO). Vol. 1, No. 1 (May 1983)-. 0738-0445. Periodical. US. English. sa. SUNY at Binghamton, Box C LNG 79, Political Science Department, Binghamton NY 13901. **LC** JA1. **DD** 320.05.

FOLLIES. 0162-721X. Periodical. US. English. mo. Random House Publishers, 11-6 201 East 50th Street, New York NY 10022.

FORTNIGH. VFOAT Independent Review for Northern Ireland. Sept. 25, 1970-). 0046-4694. Periodical. UK. English. bm. $35.25. Fortnight Publications Ltd, 7 Lower Crescent, Belfast BT7-1NR Ireland. **Tel** 232353. **Ed** Andy Pollak. bk rev. adv acc. **Circ** 6,000. Northern Ireland independent review of current affairs, books and arts.

FORUM LITERARIO. Periodical. US. Spanish. mo. Dukardo Hinestrosa, PO Box 27645, Hollywood CA 90027. **Tel** (213)939-1915. *Cuervo International.*

THE FRENCH-AMERICAN REVIEW *CEASED.* (FAR, THE FRENCH-AMERICAN REVIEW). **VFOAT** French-American Review. V. 1-V. 5, No. 2. 0160-0419. Periodical. US. English (French). ty. $7.50. PO Box 30660A, TCU Station, Ft Worth TX 76129. **Ind/Abst** MLA Int. Bibliogr. Books Artic. Mod. Lang. Lit., Writ. Am. Hist. **LC** PQ1. **DD** 805.

FRENCH FORUM. V. 1- Jan. 1976-. 0098-9355. Periodical. US. Multilingual (English or French). ty. $20.00. French Forum, PO Box 5108, Lexington KY 40505. **Tel** (606)299-9530. **Ed** Raymond C and Virginia A La Charite. **Ind/Abst** MLA Int. Bibliogr. Books Artic. Mod. Lang. Lit., Index Book Rev. Humanit. **LC** PQ1. **DD** 840.9. bk rev. adv acc. **Circ** 500. (ctrl). A journal of literary criticism. It publishes articles in English and French on important subjects.

THE FRENCH REVIEW. V. 1- Nov. 1927-. 0016-111X. Periodical. US. English or French. bm. $20.00 US and Canada, $22.00 Foreign. American Association of French Teachers, University of Illinois, 57 East Armory Avenue, Champaign IL 61820. **Tel** (217)333-2842. **Ed** Stirling Haig. **Ind/Abst** MLA Int. Bibliogr. Books Artic. Mod. Lang. Lit., Sociol. Abstr., Lang. Lang. Behav. Abstr., Recent Publ. Artic., Lang. Teach., Book Rev. Index, Educ. Index, Index Book Rev. Humanit., Curr. Index J. Educ. **LC** PC2001. **DD** 440.5. (cum index). bk rev. adv acc. **Circ** 12,000. (ctrl). French language, literature, pedagogy at all levels of the profession. Reviews of French novels, poetry, textbooks, linguistics, civilization and films plus relevant ads and announcements.

GARCIA LORCA REVIEW. Began in 1973. 0162-0029. Periodical. US. English. sa. New York University, c/o Dr L Klibbe, 19 University Place/Room 600, New York NY 10003. **Tel** (716)395-2269. **Ed** Grace Alvarez-Altman. **Ind/Abst** MLA Int. Bibliogr. Books Artic. Mod. Lang. Lit. **LC** PQ6613.A763. **DD** 868.6209. bk rev. **Circ** 300. (ctrl). Bibliographies, reviews, poetry and interesting articles on the life and works of Federico Garcia Lorca.

GDR MONITOR. No. 1 (Summer 1979)-. Periodical. UK. English. sa. $10.00. Loughborough University of Technology, Department of European Studies, Leicestershire LE11 3TU England. **Tel** 0509 263171. **Ed** Ian Wallace. **LC** DD261. **DD** 943.108705. bk rev. **Circ** 200. Provides an independent forum for discussion of all aspects of the life of the GDR.

GENRE (UNIVERSITY OF ILLINOIS AT CHICAGO CIRCLE). (GENRE). Vol. 1, No. 1 (Jan. 1968)-. 0016-6928. Periodical. US. English. qt. $18.00 Domestic, $20.00 Foreign. University of Oklahoma, Department of English, 760 Van Fleet Oval, Norman OK 73019. **Tel** (405)325-4661. **Ed** R Schleifer. **Ind/Abst** Abstr. Engl. Stud., MLA Int. Bibliogr. Books Artic. Mod. Lang. Lit. **LC** PN80. **DD** 801.95. bk rev. adv acc. **Circ** 800. (ctrl). A publication devoted to criticism of genre. Questions of genre in relation to interpretation of major literary texts, historical development of specific genres and theoretical discussion.

THE GEORGIA REVIEW. V. 1- Spring 1947-. 0016-8386. Periodical. US. English. qt. $9.00 Domestic, $12.00 Foreign. Georgia Review, University of Georgia, Athens GA 30602. **Tel** (404)542-3481. **Ed** Stanley W Lindberg. **Ind/Abst** Abstr. Engl. Stud., MLA Int. Bibliogr. Books Artic. Mod. Lang. Lit., Annu. Bibliogr. Engl. Lang. Lit., Film Lit. Index, Book Rev. Index, Index Am. Period. Verse, Index Book Rev. Humanit., Humanit. Index, Lang. Lang. Behav. Abstr., Hist. Abstr., Sociol. Abstr., Writ. Am. Hist., Am. Hist. Life, Hist. Abstr., Part A, Mod. Hist. Abstr., Hist. Abst., Part B, Twent. Century Abstr., Years Work Eng. Stud., Recent Publ. Artic. **LC** AP2. **DD** 051. bk rev. adv acc. **Circ** 4,400. The best in American thought/literature. Essays, poetry, fiction, graphics, book reviews for an interdisciplinary audience.

THE GERMANIC REVIEW. V. 1- Jan. 1926-. 0016-8890. Periodical. US. English (contributions in German). qt. $30.00. Heldref Publications, 4000 Albemarle Street NW/Suite 302, Washington DC 20016. **Tel** (202)362-6445. **Ed** John Cronin. **Ind/Abst** MLA Int. Bibliogr. Books Artic. Mod. Lang. Lit., Sociol. Abstr., Recent Publ. Artic., Index Book Rev. Humanit., Lang. Lang. Behav. Abstr., Years Work Eng. Stud. **LC** PD1. **DD** 430.05. bk rev. adv acc. **Circ** 1,031. Devoted to studies dealing with the Germanic languages and literature, each issue contains written analyses of prose and poetry from German literature.

GIORNALE ITALIANO DI FILOLOGIA. *See* Linguistics.

GOETHE YEARBOOK. *See* Yearbooks, Almanacs, Directories.

GRADIVA. V. 1- Summer 1976-. 0363-8057. Periodical. US. Multilingual (English or Italian). qt. $12.00. University of New York Stonybrook, Department of French & Italian, Stonybrook NY 11794. **Tel** (516)246-7739. **Ed** G Carpetto and L Fontanella. **Ind/Abst** MLA Int. Bibliogr. Books Artic. Mod. Lang. Lit. **LC** PN80. **DD** 809. bk rev. adv acc. **Circ** 300. Literary criticism with focus on psychoanalysis, semiotics, structuralism, Marxist, historcist and methodologies.

GRAHAM HOUSE REVIEW. V. 1- Summer 1976-. 0145-7780. Periodical. US. English. sa. $2.50. Graham House Press, PO Box 489, Englewood NJ 07631. **LC** PS580. **DD** 811.5408.

THE GRAMERCY REVIEW. (GRAMERCY REVIEW; A JOURNAL OF CONTEMPORARY POETRY AND FICTION). V. 1- 1977-. 0194-4029. Periodical. US. English. qt. Gramercy Review, 5536 Bryant Street, Pittsburgh PA 15206. **Tel** (213)741-5872.

GREAT RIVER REVIEW. V. 1-. 0160-2144. Periodical. US. English. sa. $7.00. Great River Review, 211 West 7th Street, Winona MN 55987. **Tel** (507)454-6564. **Ed** Orval Lund. **LC** PS273. **DD** 810.80054. bk rev. adv acc. **Circ** 750. Dedicated to publishing the best in fiction, creative poetry, and pays particular attention to midwestern writers.

THE GREENFIELD REVIEW. V. 1-. 0017-4041. Periodical. US. English. sa. $10.00. Greenfield Review, c/o Joseph Bruchac, RDI Box 80, Greenfield Center NY 12833. **Tel** (518)584-1728. **Ed** Joseph and Carol Brucher. **Ind/Abst** Index Am. Period. Verse. **LC** PN6010.5. **DD** 809. bk rev. adv acc. **Circ** 1,000. (ctrl). A multicultural literary magazine with a focus on contemporary poetry.

GREENHOUSE REVIEW. 0162-0304. Periodical. US. English. ty. Greenhouse Review, 126 Escalona Drive, Santa Cruz CA 95060. **LC** PS580. **DD** 811.5408.

GRONK. Ser. 1, No. 1- Jan. 1967-). 0017-453X. Periodical. CN. English. ir. Ganglia Press, 239 Queen Street West, Toronto Ontario Canada.

HARD CRABS. 0198-1099. Periodical. US. English. mo. $4.00. Maryland Writers Council, 16 West Franklin Street, Baltimore MD 21201. **Tel** (301)685-5239.

HARPER'S MAGAZINE. (HARPER'S). Began with Sept. 1976 issue. 0017-789X. Periodical. US. English. mo. $18.00. Harpers Magazine, PO Box 1937, Marion OH 43305. **Tel** (212)481-5220. **Ed** Lewis H Lapham. **Ind/Abst** Mag. Index, Energy Inf. Abstr., Environ. Abstr., Film Lit. Index, Pop. Mag. Rev., Read. Guide Period. Lit., Biogr. Index, Infobank, Index Book Rev. Humanit., Index Am. Period. Verse, Media Rev. Dig., Abr. Read. Guide, Book Rev. Index, Book Rev. Digest. **LC** AP2. **DD** 051. bk rev. adv acc. **Circ** 150,137. Thoughtful, social and political dialogue made accessible and uniquely entertaining, for today's busy reader. Regular features include annotation, readings, forum, and the popular Harper's index. *Harper's Magazine, 0017-789X.*

THE HEMINGWAY REVIEW. Vol. 1, No. 1 (Fall 1981)-. 0276-3362. Periodical. US. English. sa. $15.00. Northeastern University, c/o Jas Nigel, Department of English, Boston MA 02115. **Tel** (419)634-4518. **Ed** Charles M Oliver. **Ind/Abst** Abstr. Engl. Stud., MLA Int. Bibliogr. Books Artic. Mod. Lang. Lit., Index Book Rev. Humanit. **LC** PS3515.E37. **DD** 813.52. bk rev. **Circ** 700. Criticism of the works of Hemingway. *Hemingway Notes, 0046-7243.*

THE HENRY JAMES REVIEW. V. 1- Nov. 1979-. 0273-0340. Periodical. US. English. ir. $17.00 Domestic, $19.00 Canada, $22.00 all other countries. Henry James Review, Louisiana State University, Department of English, Baton Rouge LA 70803-5001. **Tel** (504)388-2865. **Ed** Daniel Mark Fogel. **Ind/Abst** Abstr. Engl. Stud., MLA Int. Bibliogr. Books Artic. Mod. Lang. Lit., Index Book Rev. Humanit. **LC** PS2124. **DD** 813.4. bk rev. adv acc. **Circ** 500. (ctrl). Devoted to essays, notes, and reviews about the American novelist Henry James (1843-1916) and includes an annual review of James studies.

THE HIRAM POETRY REVIEW. No. 1- Fall/Winter 1966-. 0018-2036. Periodical. US. English. sa. $4.00. Hiram Poetry Review, PO Box 162, Hiram OH 44234. **Tel** (216)569-3211. **Ed** Hale Chatfield and Carol Donley. **Ind/Abst** Index Am. Period. Verse, Index Book Rev. Humanit. **LC** PS580. **DD** 811.505. bk rev. **Circ** 300. (ctrl). Poetry and reviews of poetry books and magazines.

HISPANIC JOURNAL. V. 1- Fall 1979-. 0271-0986. Periodical. US. English. sa. $12.00. Indiana University of Pennsylvania, Department of Foreign Languages, 433 Sutton Hall, Indiana PA 15705. **Tel** (412)357-2327. **Ed** Joseph B Spieker. **Ind/Abst** MLA Int. Bibliogr. Books Artic. Mod. Lang. Lit. **LC** PC4001. bk rev. **Circ** 600. (ctrl). Articles of literary criticism of Spanish and Latin American literature, language and culture. Book reviews and summaries are included.

HOFMANNSTHALBLATTER. (HOFMANNSTHAL BLATTER). Issue 1-. 0441-6813. Periodical. GW. German. sa. Hugo Von Hofmannsthal, Postfach 900 511, D-6 Frankfurt 90 West Germany. **Ind/Abst** MLA Int. Bibliogr. Books Artic. Mod. Lang. Lit. **LC** PT2617.O47.

THE HOLLINS CRITIC. V. 1- Feb. 1964-. 0018-3644. Periodical. US. English. ir. $5.00 Domestic, $6.50 Foreign. The Hollins Critic, Box 9538, Hollins College VA 24020. **Tel** (703)362-6316. **Ed** John Rees Moore. **Ind/Abst** Abstr. Engl. Stud., MLA Int. Bibliogr. Books Artic. Mod. Lang. Lit., Annu. Bibliogr. Engl. Lang. Lit., Index Am. Period. Verse, Years Work Eng. Stud. **LC** PS1. bk rev. **Circ** 550. Available on microfilm from University Microfilms. Single essay on contemporary author's entire work; brief sketch and checklist of author's work and artist's sketch of subject. Poems and brief book reviews.

HOLLOW SPRING REVIEW OF POETRY. V. 1-. 0147-2631. Periodical. US. English. sa. $6.00. Hollow Spring Review, PO Box 76, Berkshire MA 01224.

HOPKINS QUARTERLY. (THE HOPKINS QUARTERLY). V. 1- April 1974-. 0094-9086. Periodical. US. English. qt. 8.00. Department of Language Studies, Mohawk College, PO Box 2034, Hamilton Ontario L8N 3T2 Canada. **Tel** (416)575-1212. **Ed** Richard F Giles. **Ind/Abst** MLA Int. Bibliogr. Books Artic. Mod. Lang. Lit., Abstr. Engl. Stud. **LC** PR4803.H44. **DD** 821.8. bk rev. adv acc. **Circ** 375. Articles, notes, reviews on G.M. Hopkins and his circle: Bridges, Dixon, and Patmore. Literary and biographical works-critical, appreciative, and scholarly-published.

HORIZON. V. 1- Sept. 1958-. 0018-4977. Periodical. US. English. mo. Horizon Magazine, PO Box 37104, Washington DC 20013. **Ind/Abst** Pop. Mag. Rev., Read. Guide Period. Lit., Abr. Read. Guide, Am. Hist. Life, Hist. Abstr., Part A, Mod. Hist. Abstr., Hist. Abst., Part B, Twent. Century Abstr. **LC** AP2. **DD** 051. (cum index).

THE HORN BOOK MAGAZINE. V. 21, No. 3- May/June 1945-. 0018-5078. Periodical. US. English. bm. $30.00. Horn Book, Park Square Building, 31 St James Avenue, Boston MA 02116. **Tel** (617)482-5198. **Ed** Anita Silbey. **Ind/Abst** Pop. Mag. Rev., Book Rev. Digest, Book Rev. Index, Curr. Index J. Educ., Libr. Lit., Media Rev. Dig., Child. Mag. Guide, Artbibliogr. Mod., Read. Guide Period. Lit., Subj. Index Child. Mag. **LC** Z1037.A1. bk rev. adv acc. **Circ** 22,000. Also available on microfilm from University Microfilms. All about books for children and young adults: book reviews, articles, columns, news and information. *Horn Book.*

HOY. V. 1- June 1-7 1977-. Periodical. Spanish. ir. $35.00 Single Issue. Araucaria LTDA, Eliodoro Yanez 890, Santiago Chile. **LC** AP63. **DD** 056.1.

THE HUDSON REVIEW. V. 1- Spring 1948-. 0018-702X. Periodical. US. English. qt. $8.00 Domestic, $9.00 Foreign. Hudson Review Inc, 65 East 55th Street, New York NY 10022. **Ind/Abst** Abstr. Engl. Stud., MLA Int. Bibliogr. Books Artic. Mod. Lang. Lit., Sociol. Abstr., Annu. Bibliogr. Engl. Lang. Lit., Film Lit. Index, Index Am. Period. Verse, Soc. Sci. Index, Index Book Rev. Humanit., Book Rev. Index, Humanit. Index. **LC** AP2. **DD** 805. Available on microfilm from University Microfilms.

HURON REVIEW. Periodical. US. English. sa. Huron Review, 423 South Franklin Avenue, Flint MI 48503.

HUSSERL STUDIES. Vol. 1, No. 1-. 0167-9848. Periodical. English (text in German). ty. Kluwer Academic Publishing Group, Box 322, 3300 AH Dordrecht Netherlands. **Tel** (617)749-5262.

IBSEN NEWS AND COMMENT : NEWSLETTER OF THE IBSEN SOCIETY OF AMERICA. No. 1 (Spring 1980)-. US. English. an. $6.00. Pratt Institute, Dekalb Hall 3, Brooklyn NY 11205. **Tel** (212)636-3794. **Ed** Rold Fjelde and Yvonne Shafer. bk rev. News items, articles, interviews, book and play reviews on text interpretation and productions of Ibsen's dramas annually in North America.

ILLINOIS WRITERS REVIEW. Vol. 1, No. 1 (Apr. 1981)-. 0733-9526. Periodical. US. English. sa. $10.00. Illinois Writers Inc, PO Box 562, Macomb IL 61455. **Tel** (217)398-8526. **Ed** Curtis White. bk rev. **Circ** 300. Reviews and essays concerning primarily Illinois writers and publishers. Includes information for writers. Focused on, but not limited to, Illinois concerns.

INDIAN SCHOLAR. *See* Literature.

INTERNATIONAL FICTION REVIEW. (THE INTERNATIONAL FICTION REVIEW). **VFOAT** I.F.R., IFR. Began with issue for Jan. 1974. 0315-4149. Periodical. CN. English. sa. $12.00. University of New Brunswick, Department of German and Russian, Fredericton New Brunswick E3B 5A3 Canada. **Tel** (506)453-4636. **Ed** Saad Elkhadem. **Ind/Abst** MLA Int. Bibliogr. Books Artic. Mod. Lang. Lit. **LC** PN3311. **DD** 809.3005. bk rev. **Circ** 500. (ctrl). Publishes scholarly articles that deal with world fiction.

INTERNATIONAL POETRY REVIEW. V. 1- Spring 1975-. 0145-0786. Periodical. US. French, German, Spanish, or English. sa. $7.00. International Poetry Review, c/o Evalyn Gill, PO Box 2047, Greensboro NC 27402. **Tel** (919)273-1711. **Ed** Evalyn P Gill. **LC** PN6099. **DD** 808.81. adv acc. **Circ** 250. (ctrl). Translation of contemporary poetry in bilingual format. Also poetry originally in English.

THE INTERNATIONAL PORTLAND REVIEW. 1980-. 0278-2952. US. English (multilingual, with translations). $5.95. The International Portland Review, PO Box 751, Portland OR 97207. **LC** PN6099. **DD** 808.81. *Portland Review, 0360-3091.*

INTERNATIONALE BIBLIOGRAPHIE DER REZENSIONEN WISSENSCHAFTLICHER LITERATUR. *See* Bibliographies.

THE IOWA REVIEW. V. 1- Winter 1970-. 0021-065X. Periodical. US. English. ty. $20.00. University of Iowa, Publishing Order Department GSB, Iowa IA 52242. **Tel** (319)353-4171. **Ed** David Hamilton. **Ind/Abst** Abstr. Engl. Stud., MLA Int. Bibliogr. Books Artic. Mod. Lang. Lit., Index Am. Period. Verse, Index Book Rev. Humanit., Years Work Eng. Stud. **LC**

PS501. **DD** 810.8. bk rev. adv acc. **Circ** 1,000. Available on microfilm from University Microfilms. A literary journal devoted to publishing quality fiction, poetry, essays, and criticism.

IRISH LITERARY SUPPLEMENT. Vol. 1, No. 1 (Spring 1982)-. 0733-3390. Periodical. US. English. sa. $6.00. Irish Studies, 114 Paula Boulevard, Selden NY 11784. **Tel** (516)698-8243. **Ed** Robert G Lowery. bk rev. adv acc. **Circ** 4,000. Reviews Irish interest books.

IRISH UNIVERSITY REVIEW. Vol. 1, No. 1 (Autumn 1970)-. 0021-1427. Periodical. IE. English. sa. $25.00. University College, c/o Dr Maurice Harmon, Department of English, Belfield Dublin 4 Ireland. **Tel** 693244. **Ed** Maurice Harmon. **Ind/Abst** Abstr. Engl. Stud., Index Book Rev. Humanit., MLA Int. Bibliogr. Books Artic. Mod. Lang. Lit., Years Work Eng. Stud. **LC** PR8700. **DD** 820.809415. bk rev. adv acc. **Circ** 1,000. (ctrl). Journal of Anglo-Irish literature and criticism. *University Review (Dublin, Ireland), 0566-2478.*

JAHRESRING; EIN SCHNITT DURCH LITERATUR UND KUNST DER GEGENWART. 0448-1631. GW. German. an. Zenit Pressevertrieb GMBH, Postfach 810640, 7000 Stuttgart 80 West Germany. **Tel** (0711)2631-0. **Ind/Abst** MLA Int. Bibliogr. Books Artic. Mod. Lang. Lit. **LC** PT1141. A description of literary, arts, and cultural reviews with every issue changing focal point-country.

JAMES JOYCE QUARTERLY. V. 1- Fall 1963-. 0021-4183. Periodical. US. English. qt. $13.00 Domestic, $15.00 Foreign. University of Tulsa, 600 South College, Tulsa OK 74104. **Tel** (918)592-6000. **Ed** Thomas F Staley. **Ind/Abst** Abstr. Engl. Stud., MLA Int. Bibliogr. Books Artic. Mod. Lang. Lit., Humanit. Index, Annu. Bibliogr. Engl. Lang. Lit., Ref. Source, Index Book Rev. Humanit., Years Work Eng. Stud. **LC** PR6019.O9. **DD** 823.912. (cum index). bk rev. adv acc. **Circ** 1,400. Critical studies on all aspects of James Joyce, including scholarly essays, notes, and book reviews.

JEWISH FRONTIER. V. 1- June 1933-. 0021-6453. Periodical. US. English. mo. $15.00 US, $17.50 Canada, $20.00 Foreign. Jewish Frontier, 15 East 26th Street/13th Floor, New York NY 10010. **Tel** (212)683-3530. **Ed** Jonathan J Goldberg. **Ind/Abst** Public Aff. Inf. Serv. Bull., Guide Soc. Sci. Relig. Period. Lit. **LC** DS19. **DD** 956.9. bk rev. adv acc. **Circ** 4,500. Political-cultural journal examining Jewish and Israeli affairs from a Labor Zionist perspective. Also, includes relevant fiction and poetry.

JEWISH SOCIALIST CRITIQUE. V. 1- (No. 1-). Periodical. US. English. qt. Jewish Socialist Critique, 2000 Center Street/Room 1366, Berkeley CA 94704.

JOHNSONIAN NEWS LETTER. 1940. 0021-728X. US. English. qt. $5.00. Johnsonian Newsletter, 610 Philosophy Hall/Columbia University, New York NY 10027. **Tel** (212)280-3918. **Ed** John Middendorf. bk rev. **Circ** 1,800. News of interest to 18th century scholars, particularly Johnsonians; lists of conferences, new books, recent articles.

THE JOURNAL OF COMMONWEALTH LITERATURE. Sept. 1965-. 0021-9894. Periodical. UK. English. sa. $36.00. Hans Zell Publishers, PO Box 56, Oxford OX1 3EL England. **Tel** (0865)512934. **Ed** Alastair Niven and Angus Calder. **Ind/Abst** MLA Int. Bibliogr. Books Artic. Mod. Lang. Lit., Annu. Bibliogr. Engl. Lang. Lit., Humanit. Index, Abstr. Engl. Stud., Years Work Eng. Stud. **LC** PR1. **DD** 820.05. adv acc. **Circ** 1,200. The first issue comprises of critical articles on aspects Commonwealth writing past and present; the second is a bibliographical review of the previous year's publications.

JOURNAL OF LITERARY CRITICISM. Vol. 1, No. 1 (June 1984)-. Periodical. II. English. sa. Doaba House, 1668 Nai Sarak, Delhi 110006 India.

KAIROS (OAKLAND, CALIF.). (KAIROS). Vol. 1, No. 1-. 0277-710X. Periodical. US. English. sa. $13.00. Hermes House Press, c/o A Mandell/127 West 15th Street, New York NY 10011. **Tel** (212)691-9773. **Ed** Alan Mandell and William Rasch. **LC** PN2. **DD** 805. bk rev. adv acc. **Circ** 350. Social and cultural criticism, poetry, reviews, contemporary issues and the arts.

KANAVA. Vol. 1, No. 2-. 0355-0303. Periodical. FI. Finnish. ir. Yhtynut Kunalehdet Oy, Hietalahdenranta 13, 00180 Helsinki 18 Finland. **Ind/Abst** MLA Int. Bibliogr. Books Artic. Mod. Lang. Lit. **LC** AP80. *Aika.*

KARAMU. 0022-8990. Periodical. US. English. be. $1.50. Eastern Illinois University, Karamu Association/English Department, Charleston IL 61920. **Tel** (217)581-5614. **Ed** John Z Guzlowski. bk rev. adv acc. **Circ** 500. (ctrl). We publish contemporary and experimental fiction and poetry for a college educated audience.

KENTUCKY POETRY REVIEW. VFOAT KPR. V. 12- Winter 1976-. Periodical. US. English. sa. $8.00. Kentucky Poetry Review, 1568 Cherokee Road/Wade Hall, Louisville KY 40205. **Tel** (502)451-5516. **Ed** Wade Hall. bk rev. **Circ** 400. Original poetry on any subject or form. *Approaches, 0003-7133.*

THE KENYON REVIEW. V. 1-32 (No. 1-128). 0163-075X. Periodical. US. English. qt. Kenyon Review, Box 1308-L, Fort Lee NJ 07024. **Tel** (614)427-3339. **Ind/Abst** Abstr. Engl. Stud., MLA Int. Bibliogr. Books Artic. Mod. Lang. Lit., Annu. Bibliogr. Engl. Lang. Lit., Index Book Rev. Humanit., Humanit. Index, Years Work Eng. Stud. **LC** AP2. **DD** 051. bk rev. adv acc. **Circ** 5,000. Poetry, fiction, essays, book reviews.

THE KEY REPORTER. V. 1- Winter 1936-. 0023-0804. Periodical. US. English. qt. $1.00. Phi Beta Kappa, 1811 Q Street NW, Washington DC 20009. **Tel** (202)265-3808. **Ed** Priscilla S Taylor. **LC** LJ85.P2. **DD** 371.852. bk rev. **Circ** 200,000. Scholarly newsletter containing one feature article and perhaps 50 brief book reviews of general interest. *Phi Beta Kappa Annals.*

KIRKUS REVIEWS. V. 37- 1969-. 0042-6598. Periodical. US. English. ir. Kirkus Reviews, 200 Park Avenue South, New York NY 10003. **Tel** (212)777-4554. **Ed** Ron de Paolo. **Ind/Abst** Book Rev. Index. **LC** Z477. **Circ** 5,000. (ctrl). Pre-publication book reviews usually two months prior to publication. All the new fiction, the significant non-fiction, bi-monthly 24 issues per year. *Kirkus Service.*

KLEINE DEUTSCHE PROSADENKMALER DES MITTELALTERS. Vol. 1- 1965-. 0075-6318. Monographic Series. GW. German. ir. Wilhelm Fink Verlag, Ohmstrasse 5, 8000 Muenchen 40 West Germany. **Tel** 89/348017-18.

KLIATT YOUNG ADULT PAPERBACK BOOK GUIDE. VFOAT Young Adult Paperback Book Guide. V. 12- Winter 1978-. 0199-2376. Periodical. US. English. 27.00 Domestic, 29.00 Canada. Kliatt Young Adult Paperback, 425 Watertown Street, Newton MA 02158. **Tel** 965-4666. **Ed** Doris Hiatt and Claire Rosser. **Ind/Abst** Book Rev. Index. bk rev. adv acc. **Circ** 2,000. Reviews on books recommended for young adults, their teachers and their librarians. *Kliatt Paperback Book Guide.*

THE KOBRIN LETTER. V. 1- Sept. 1980-. 0271-1990. Periodical. US. English. ir. $12.00. Dr Beverly Kobrin, 732 Greer Road, Palo Alto CA 94303. **Tel** (415)856-6658. **Ed** Beverly Kobrin. bk rev. Reviews best children's nonfiction books for teachers and librarians, provides practical ideas for using nonfiction in the classroom.

KOERS. Jan. 1- Aug. 1933-. 0023-270X. Periodical. SA. Afrikaans. qt. Die Koers Vereniging, Pothefstroom, 2520 South Africa. *Wagtoring, Watoring.*

KROKODIL. Began with: July 1, 1922 issue. 0130-2671. Periodical. UR. Russian. ir. $38.00. Victor Kamkin Inc (70448), 12224 Parklawn Drive, Rockville MD 20852. **Tel** (301)881-5973. **LC** AP115.

KULTURA. Began with July 1947 issue. 0023-5148. Periodical. Polish. mo. $58.00. Institut Litteraire, 91 Avenue de Poissy/Mesnil le Roi, 78600 Maisons Laffitte France. **Tel** 33-3/962 10 04. **Ind/Abst** MLA Int. Bibliogr. Books Artic. Mod. Lang. Lit. **LC** AP54.

THE LANGSTON HUGHES REVIEW. (THE LANGSTON HUGHES REVIEW : OFFICIAL PUBLICATION OF THE LANGSTON HUGHES SOCIETY). Vol. 1, No. 1 (Spring 1982)-. 0737-0555. Periodical. US. English. sa. $7.00. George H Bass, Executive Editor, The Langston Hughes Review, Brown University, Providence RI 02912. **Tel** (401)863-3137. **Ed** George Houston Bass. **LC** PS3515.U274. **DD** 818.5209. bk rev. adv acc. **Circ** 260. Publishes articles and notes on the life and work of Langston Hughes, and his contemporaries and the Hughesian tradition.

LATIN AMERICAN LITERARY REVIEW. V. 1- Fall 1972-. 0047-4134. Periodical. US. English. sa. $27.00. University of Pittsburgh, 1309 Cathedral of Learning, Pittsburgh PA 15260. **Tel** (412)351-3987. **Ed** Yvette E Miller. **Ind/Abst** MLA Int. Bibliogr. Books Artic. Mod. Lang. Lit. **LC** PQ7081.A1. **DD** 860.9. bk rev. adv acc. **Circ** 1,000. (ctrl). Literatures of Latin America and Latin American minorities in the United States. Contains feature articles, reviews of recent literary works, translations of poetry plays and prose fiction, and arts.

THE LATIN AMERICAN YEARLY REVIEW. V. 1- 1973-. Periodical. FR. English. an. $4.00. American College in Paris, 65 Quai d'Orsay, 75007 Paris France. **LC** F1414.2. **DD** 320.98003.

THE LAUREL REVIEW. (LAUREL REVIEW). V. 1- 1961-. 0023-9003. Periodical. US. English. sa. $8.00. Department of English, West Virginia Wesleyan College, Buckhannon WV 26201. **Tel** (304)472-8000. **Ed** Mark DeFoe. **Ind/Abst** Annu. Bibliogr. Engl. Lang. Lit. adv acc. **Circ** 500. Published poetry and fiction from Appalachian America and Canada and from all across the US and abroad.

LECTOR (BERKELEY, CALIF.). (LECTOR). Vol. 1, No. 1 (June 1982)-. 0732-8001. Periodical. US. English. bm. $40.00 US/Canada, $44.00 Others. California Spanish Language Data Base, PO Box 4273, Berkeley CA 94704. **Tel** (415)893-8702. **Ed** Roberto Cabello-Argandona. bk rev. adv acc. **Circ** 3,000. (ctrl). Hispanic cultural and book review journal.

LIBERAL AND FINE ARTS REVIEW. Vol. 1, No. 1 (Jan. 1981)-. 0731-8200. Periodical. US. English. sa. $8.00. Eastern New Mexico University, c/o Milton A Swenson, Portales NM 88130. **Tel** (505)562-2771. **Ed** Milton A Swenson. **Ind/Abst** MLA Int. Bibliogr. Books Artic. Mod. Lang. Lit. bk rev. adv acc. **Circ** 650. (ctrl). Devoted to scholarly and creative arts in the humanities: scholarly papers, poetry, short stories, pictorial art works, and music. Also includes book reviews. *Liberal Arts Review, 0731-8219.*

LINES REVIEW. Began with Jan. 1954 issue. 0459-4541. Periodical. UK. English. qt. 3.60. M McDonald, Edgefield Road Loanhead, Midlothian EH20 9SY England. **Tel** (031)440-0246. **Ed** Trevor Royle. bk rev. **Circ** 600. Poetry reviews. *Lines.*

THE LION AND THE UNICORN. V. 1-. 0147-2593. Periodical. US. English. an. $7.50. Lion and the Unicorn, Brooklyn College, Department of English, Brooklyn NY 11210. **Tel** (718)780-5195. **Ed** G DeLuca and R Natov. **Ind/Abst** Abstr. Engl. Stud., MLA Int. Bibliogr. Books Artic. Mod. Lang. Lit. **LC** PN1009.A1. **DD** 809.89282. bk rev. adv acc. **Circ** 1,000. (ctrl). International critical journal of books for children. Each issue explores one theme or genre, or one aspect of the field of children's literature. Issues include book reviews, critical pieces and interviews.

LITERARY MAGAZINE REVIEW. Vol. 1, No. 1 (Winter 1982)-. 0732-6637. Periodical. US. English. qt. $10.00. Kansas State Univ, Dept of English c/o Writers Soc, Manhattan KS 66506. **Tel** (913)532-6716. **Ed** G W Clift. **LC** PN4878.3. **DD** 810.9. **Circ** 350. Devoted to reviews of the current issues of literary magazines, here and abroad, and to commentary concerning the contemporary writing scene.

LITERARY REVIEW (LONDON, ENGLAND : 1979). (THE LITERARY REVIEW). No. 1 (Oct. 1979)-. 0144-4360. Periodical. UK. English. mo. 11.40. Literary Review and Quarto, 513 London Road, Thornton Heath, London Surrey CR46 6AR England. **Ed** Gillian Greenwood. **LC** NX645. **DD** 082. *Quarto (London, England : 1979).*

LITERATURE CRITICISM FROM 1400 TO 1800. VFOAT Literature Criticism from Fourteen Hundred to Eighteen Hundred. Vol. 1-. 0740-2880. US. English. Gale Research Co, Penobscot Building, Detroit MI 48226. **LC** PN86. **DD** 809.

LITERATURNAIA ARMENIIA. V. 1- 1958-. 0024-483X. Periodical. UR. Russian. mo. $39.50. Victor Kamkin Inc (77784), 12224 Parklawn Drive, Rockville MD 20852. **Tel** (301)881-5973. **Ind/Abst** MLA Int. Bibliogr. Books Artic. Mod. Lang. Lit.

LITERATURNAIA GAZETA. Newspaper. UR. Russian. wk. $43.00. Victor Kamkin Inc (50067), 12224 Parklawn Drive, Rockville MD 20852. **Tel** (301)881-5973. **Ind/Abst** MLA Int. Bibliogr. Books Artic. Mod. Lang. Lit., Sociol. Abstr., Lang. Lang. Behav. Abstr.

LITERATURNAIA ROSSIIA : EZHENEDEL'NIK PRAVLENIIA SOIUZA PISATELEI RSFSR I PRAVLENIIA MOSKOVSKOI PISATEL'SKOI ORGANIZATSII. Began publication in 1963. Periodical. UR. Russian. wk. $32.50. Victor Kamkin Inc (50232), 12224 Parklawn Drive, Rockville MD 20852. **Tel** (301)881-5973.

Literary and Political Reviews

LITERATURNYI KIRGIZSTAN. V. 1- 1955-. 0459-5637. Periodical. UR. Russian. bm. $23.50. Victor Kamkin Inc (77360), 12224 Parklawn Drive, Rockville MD 20852. **Tel** (301)881-5973. *Almanakh.*

LONDON MAGAZINE (LONDON, ONT.). (LONDON MAGAZINE). Vol. 1, No. 1 (Oct./Nov. 1980)-. 0711-6233. Periodical. CN. English. ir. $1.00 per No. London Magazine, 304 York Street, London Ontario N6B 1P8 Canada. **DD** 917.1326.

THE LONDON REVIEW OF BOOKS. **VFOAT** London Review. Vol. 1, No. 1 (25 Oct. 1979)-Oct. 25, 1979. 0260-9592. Periodical. US. English. ir. $41.38. London Review of Books, Tavistock House So, Tavestock Square, London WC1H 9JZ England. **Tel** 01 388 6751. **Ed** Karl Miller. **Ind/Abst** Book Rev. Index, Years Work Eng. Stud. bk rev. adv acc. **Circ** 15,000. Covers anthropology, the arts, history, literary and political reviews, poetry, short stories, sociology, philosophy, biography, etc.

LOOMING. 1- 1923-. Periodical. UR. Estonian. mo. $27.00. Victor Kamkin Inc (78174), 12224 Parklawn Drive, Rockville MD 20852. **Tel** (301)881-5973. **Ind/Abst** MLA Int. Bibliogr. Books Artic. Mod. Lang. Lit. **LC** AP95.E4.

THE LOUISVILLE REVIEW. No. 1- Fall 1976-. 0148-3250. Periodical. US. English. sa. University of Louisville, Department of English, Louisville KY 40298. **Tel** (502)636-3213. **LC** PS501. **DD** 810.80054.

LUTHERISCHE MONATSHEFTE. *See* Religion, Mythology, Rationalism.

LYNN RIVER REVIEW. Vol. 1-. 0821-1485. Periodical. CN. English. ir. Lynn River Review, 27 Ormond Crescent, Simcoe Ontario N3Y 1Y3 Canada. **DD** C810.80054. *Lynnwood Literary Review.*

THE MCNEESE REVIEW. V. 1- Spring 1948-. 0885-467X. US. English. an. $3.00. McNeese State University, Lake Charles LA 70609. **Ind/Abst** Abstr. Engl. Stud., MLA Int. Bibliogr. Books Artic. Mod. Lang. Lit., Years Work Eng. Stud. **LC** AS36. **DD** 051.

MADISON REVIEW. No. 1- Spring 1972-. Periodical. US. English. University of Wisconsin, Department of English/Helen C White, 600 North Park, Madison WI 53706.

THE MANHATTAN REVIEW. Vol. 1, No. 1 (Spring 1980)-. 0275-6889. Periodical. US. English. ir. $12.00. Philip Fried, 304 Third Avenue/Suite 4A, New York NY 10010. **Tel** (212)228-4336. **Ed** Philip Fried. **LC** PN1010. **DD** 811.008. adv acc. **Circ** 500. Poetry interviews with poets of international orientation mixture of American and foreign work relation of poetry to other fields.

MANY CORNERS. 1973. Periodical. US. English. ir. $8.50. Many Corners, 1503 Washington Avenue South, Minneapolis MN 55454. **Tel** (612)333-0031. **Ed** Barry Casselman. bk rev. adv acc. **Circ** 20,000. Independent monthly newspaper featuring political analysis, coverage of performing arts, restaurants travel, and book reviews.

MASSACHUSETTS STUDIES IN ENGLISH. (MSE. MASSACHUSETTS STUDIES IN ENGLISH). Began with Spring 1967 issue. 0047-6161. Periodical. US. English. sa. $10.00. University of Massachusetts, Bartlett Hall, Amherst MA 01003. **Ed** James M Dutcher. **Ind/Abst** Abstr. Engl. Stud., MLA Int. Bibliogr. Books Artic. Mod. Lang. Lit., Lang. Lang. Behav. Abstr., Sociol. Abstr., Years Work Eng. Stud. **LC** PR1. **DD** 820. adv acc. **Circ** 200. Critical essays on literature written in English.

MEDIUM AEVUM; PHILOLOGISCHE STUDIEN. V. 1- 1963-. 0543-3533. Monographic Series. GW. German. ir. Wilhelm Fink Verlag, Ohmstrasse 5, 8000 Muenchen 40 West Germany. **Tel** -89/348017-18. **Ed** Friedrich Ohly, Kurt Ruh and Werner Schroder. **Ind/Abst** Humanit. Index.

MEMPHIS STATE REVIEW. Vol. 1, No. 1 (Fall 1980)-. 0732-2968. Periodical. US. English. sa. $3.00. Memphis State Review, Department of English, Memphis State University, Memphis TN 38152. **Tel** (901)454-2668. **Ed** William Page. **LC** PS536.2. **DD** 810.8. bk rev. adv acc. **Circ** 500. Poetry, short stories, interviews, book reviews, parts-of-novels. Poetry to two pages. Fiction to 4,500 words. Energetic imagery, emotional honesty and a sense of style will please us. *Phoenix (Memphis, Tenn.).*

MERIDIAN (BUNDOORA, VIC.). (MERIDIAN : THE LA TROBE UNIVERSITY ENGLISH REVIEW). Vol. 1, No. 1 (May 1982)-. 0728-5914. Periodical. English. sa. 18.00. Subscription Department/La Trobe University Bookshop, La Trobe University, Bundoora Vic 3083 Australia. **Tel** 478-3122. **Ed** John Barnes. **LC** PN2. **DD** 809. bk rev. adv acc. **Circ** 500.

MERKUR. 0026-0096. Periodical. GW. German. mo. Ernst Klett Verlag, Postfach 809, 700 Stuttgart 1 West Germany. **Ed** J Moras and H Paeschke. **Ind/Abst** Abstr. Engl. Stud., MLA Int. Bibliogr. Books Artic. Mod. Lang. Lit., Philos. Index, Recent Publ. Artic., Writ. Am. Hist., Foreign Lang. Index, Hist. Abstr., Am. Hist. Life, Hist. Abstr., Part A, Mod. Hist. Abstr., Hist. Abst., Part B, Twent. Century Abstr. **LC** AP30. **DD** 053.

THE METAPHYSICAL REVIEW. No. 1 (July 1984)-. Periodical. AT. English. ir. $25.00. Bruce Gillespie, GPO Box 5195 AA, Melbourne Victoria 3001 Australia. **Tel** (03)419-4797. **Ed** Bruce Gillespie. bk rev. adv acc. **Circ** 200. (ctrl). Reviews and general articles about science fiction fantasy, films, music, the science fiction social world (fandom), and nostalgia.

MICHIGAN QUARTERLY REVIEW. V. 1- Jan. 1962-. 0026-2420. Periodical. US. English. qt. $15.00. University of Michigan, 3032 Rackham Building, Ann Arbor MI 48109. **Tel** (313)764-9265. **Ind/Abst** Am. Hist. Life, Hist. Abstr., Part A, Mod. Hist. Abstr., Hist. Abst., Part B, Twent. Century Abstr., MLA Int. Bibliogr. Books Artic. Mod. Lang. Lit., Annu. Bibliogr. Engl. Lang. Lit., Index Am. Period. Verse, Index Book Rev. Humanit., Book Rev. Index, Public Aff. Inf. Serv. Bull., Abstr. Engl. Stud., Humanit. Index, Years Work Eng. Stud., Hist. Abstr. **LC** AS30. **DD** 051. Available on microfilm from University Microfilms. *Michigan Alumnus Quarterly Review.*

MID-AMERICAN REVIEW. **VFOAT** Mid American Review. Vol. 1, No. 1 (Spring 1981)-. 0747-8895. Periodical. US. English. sa. $6.00. Department of English, Bowling Green State University, Bowling Green OH 43403. **Tel** (419)372-2725. **Ed** Robert Early. **LC** PS501. **DD** 810.8. bk rev. adv acc. **Circ** 500. A small press literary review which publishes fiction and poetry by contemporary authors. *Itinerary.*

MIDWEST POETRY REVIEW. 0745-8738. Periodical. US. English. qt. $10.00. River City Publishers, Box 776, Rock Island IL 61201.

THE MILFORD SERIES, POPULAR WRITERS OF TODAY. **VFOAT** Popular Writers of Today. 0163-2469. Monographic Series. US. English. ir. The Borgo Press, PO Box 2845, San Bernardino CA 92406. **Tel** (714)884-5813. **Ed** R Reginald. **Circ** 500. Critiques of popular authors and/or interviews with a group of authors or genre. It generally covers work of a writer as opposed to his life.

MILTON STUDIES. V. 1- 1969-. 0076-8820. US. English. ir. University of Pittsburgh Press, Pittsburgh PA 15260. **Tel** (412)624-4110. **Ind/Abst** Abstr. Engl. Stud., MLA Int. Bibliogr. Books Artic. Mod. Lang. Lit., Years Work Eng. Stud. **LC** PR3579. **DD** 821.4. (cum index). Criticism and analysis of the works of John Milton.

MINNESOTA REVIEW. (THE MINNESOTA REVIEW). No. 1-4. 0026-5667. Periodical. US. English. sa. $12.00. Minnesota Review, English Department at Suny-Stony Brook, Stony Brook NY 11794. **Tel** (516)246-5080. **Ed** Helen Cooper, Michael Sprinker and Susan Squier. **Ind/Abst** MLA Int. Bibliogr. Books Artic. Mod. Lang. Lit., Annu. Bibliogr. Engl. Lang. Lit., Film Lit. Index, Index Am. Period. Verse, Years Work Eng. Stud. bk rev. adv acc. **Circ** 1,000. Available on microfilm from University Microfilms. Publishes fiction, poetry, essays and reviews of a political and social orientation. Encourages non-sectarian, Marxist and feminist writings. *Minnesota Review.*

MODERN FICTION STUDIES. **VFOAT** MFS. Vol. 1- Feb. 1955-. 0026-7724. Periodical. US. English. qt. $15.00 Domestic, $18.00 Foreign. Purdue University, c/o Nellie Fink, English Department, Lafayette IN 47907. **Tel** (317)494-3758. **Ed** William T Stafford. **Ind/Abst** Abstr. Engl. Stud., MLA Int. Bibliogr. Books Artic. Mod. Lang. Lit., Annu. Bibliogr. Engl. Lang. Lit., Book Rev. Index, Index Book Rev. Humanit., Soc. Sci. Index, Humanit. Index, Years Work Eng. Stud. **LC** PS379. **DD** 809.3. bk rev. **Circ** 35. (ctrl). Criticism of modern fiction, 1880 to present.

MOLODAJA GVARDIJA. (MOLODAIA GVARDIIA). V. 1- Apr./May 1922-. 0131-2251. Periodical. UR. Russian. mo. $36.00. Victor Kamkin Inc (70544), 12224 Parklawn Drive, Rockville MD 20852. **Tel** (301)881-5973. **Ind/Abst** MLA Int. Bibliogr. Books Artic. Mod. Lang. Lit.

MONOGRAPH SERIES - UNIVERSITY OF TULSA. (MONOGRAPH SERIES). **Main/Corp** University of Tulsa. No. 9- 1970-. Monographic Series. US. English. ir. University of Tulsa, Academic Publications, Tulsa OK 74104. **Tel** (918)592-6000. **Ed** Mary O'Toole. **Ind/Abst** MLA Int. Bibliogr. Books Artic. Mod. Lang. Lit. **LC** PR13. **DD** 809. **Circ** 500. Various aspects of literature and criticism. *Monograph Series.*

MOTHER JONES. V. 1- Feb./Mar. 1976-. 0362-8841. Periodical. US. English. $18.00. Mother Jones, 1663 Mission Street, San Francisco CA 94103. **Tel** (415)558-8881. **Ed** Deirdre English. **Ind/Abst** Mag. Index, Energy Inf. Abstr., Environ. Abstr., Pop. Mag. Rev., Women Stud. Abstr., GeoRef, Altern. Press Index, Public Aff. Inf. Serv. Bull., Media Rev. Dig., Access, Altern. Press Index. **LC** AP2. **DD** 051. bk rev. adv acc. Offers a powerful mixture of award-winning investigative journalism combined with hefty doses of fiction, science, the arts and features on people out to make a difference.

IL MULINO. Vol. 1- (No. 1-). 0027-3120. Periodical. IT. Italian. bm. 90.000 Domestic, 120.000 Foreign. Societa Editrice Il Mulino Spa, Via Santo Stefano 6, 40125 Bologna Italy. **Tel** 051/ 23 34 15. **Ind/Abst** Sociol. Abstr., Lang. Lang. Behav. Abstr. **LC** AP37. **DD** 055.1.

MUNCHENER ROMANISTISCHE ARBEITEN. 1.- Issue. Monographic Series. GW. German. ir. Wilhelm Fink Verlag KG, Ohmstrasse 5, D8000 Muenchen 40 West Germany. **Tel** 89/ 348017-18. **Ed** Hans Sckommodau.

MUSKEG REVIEW. (THE MUSKEG REVIEW). V. 2-. 0316-9243. Periodical. CN. English. an. Art and Literary Society, Lakehead University Department of English, Thunder Bay Ontario P7B 5E1 Canada. **DD** C810.80054. *Art & Literary Review, 0316-9235.*

NAS SOVREMENNIK. (NASH SOVREMENNIK). 1956-. 0027-8238. Periodical. UR. Russian. mo. $29.50. Victor Kamkin Inc (73274), 12224 Parklawn Drive, Rockville MD 20852. **Tel** (301)881-5973. **Ind/Abst** MLA Int. Bibliogr. Books Artic. Mod. Lang. Lit. **LC** PG3227. *God Shesnadtsatyi-Dvadtsat Vtoroi.*

THE NASSAU LITERARY REVIEW. 0883-2374. Periodical. US. English. sa. Free on campus, $8.00 off campus. Princeton University, Room 401 University Place, Princeton NJ 08544. *Nassau Lit, 0360-2222.*

NATION (NEW YORK, N.Y. : 1865). (THE NATION). Began with issue for July 6, 1865. 0027-8378. Periodical. US. English. $40.00. The Nation, 72 Fifth Avenue, New York NY 10011. **Tel** (212)242-8400. **Ed** Victor Navasky. **Ind/Abst** Film Lit. Index, Altern. Press Index, Index Am. Period. Verse, Biogr. Index, Pooles Index Period. Lit., Read. Guide Period. Lit., Book Rev. Digest, Book Rev. Index, Infobank, Media Rev. Dig., Energy Inf. Abstr., Environ. Abstr., Pop. Mag. Rev., Soc. Sci. Citation Index, Mag. Index. **LC** AP2. **DD** 051. (cum index). bk rev. adv acc. **Circ** 60,000. Available in microfilm from Xerox University Microfilm. America's oldest weekly review of politics and the arts, liberal and feisty.

NEMAN. Began publication in 1945. Periodical. UR. Russian. mo. $27.00. Victor Kamkin Inc (74968), 12224 Parklawn Drive, Rockville MD 20852. **Tel** (301)881-5973. **Ind/Abst** MLA Int. Bibliogr. Books Artic. Mod. Lang. Lit.

NEUE LITERATUR. Periodical. German. mo. Ilexim Press Department, PO Box 1-136-1-137, Bucharest Romania. **LC** AP86.

NEVA. (NEVA : ORGAN SOIUZA SOVETSKIKH PISATELEI SSSR). 1955, 1 (Apr. 1955)-. 0028-4009. Periodical. UR. Russian. mo. $38.00. Victor Kamkin Inc (73276), 12224 Parklawn Drive, Rockville MD 20852. **Tel** (301)881-5973. **Ind/Abst** MLA Int. Bibliogr. Books Artic. Mod. Lang. Lit. **LC** AP50.

THE NEW HUNGARIAN QUARTERLY. V. 1-. 0028-5390. Periodical. English. qt. Akademiai Kiado, POB 24, 1363 Budapest Hungary. **Ed** I Boldizsar. **Ind/Abst** MLA Int. Bibliogr. Books Artic. Mod. Lang. Lit., Music Index, Am. Hist. Life, Hist. Abstr. **LC** DB901. *Hungarian Quarterly.*

NEW LITERARY HISTORY. V. 1- Oct. 1969-. 0028-6087. Periodical. US. English. ty. $44.00. Johns Hopkins University Press, 701 West 40th Street/Suite 275, Baltimore MD 21211. **Tel** (301)338-6987. **Ed** Ralph Cohen. **Ind/Abst** Am. Hist. Life, Hist. Abstr., Part A, Mod. Hist. Abstr., Hist. Abst., Part B, Twent. Century Abstr., Abstr. Engl. Stud., MLA Int. Bibliogr.

Books Artic. Mod. Lang. Lit., Sociol. Abstr., Recent Publ. Artic., Film Lit. Index, Humanit. Index, Lang. Lang. Behav. Abstr., Years Work Eng. Stud., Hist. Abstr. **LC** PR1. **DD** 820.1. bk rev. adv acc. **Circ** 1,575. Centers on literary theory and interpretation- the reason for literary change, the definition of periods, and the evolution of styles, conventions, and genres.

NEW LITERATURE REVIEW. Began in 1975. 0314-7495. Periodical. AT. English. sa. New Literature Review, Department of English ANU, PO Box 4, Canberra Australian Capital Territory Australia. **Ind/Abst** MLA Int. Bibliogr. Books Artic. Mod. Lang. Lit., Aust. Public Aff. Inf. Serv. **LC** PR9080. **DD** 820.99171241. *ARNA.*

THE NEW ORLEANS REVIEW. V. 1- Fall 1968-. 0028-6400. Periodical. US. English. qt. $30.00. New Orleans Review, Box 195, 6363 Saint Charles Avenue, Loyola University, New Orleans LA 70118. **Tel** (504)865-2152. **Ed** John Mosier. **Ind/Abst** Abstr. Engl. Stud., MLA Int. Bibliogr. Books Artic. Mod. Lang. Lit., Index Am. Period. Verse, Index Book Rev. Humanit. **LC** AP2. **DD** 051. **Circ** 1,500. A literary and arts magazine publishing the finest in contemporary fiction, poetry, and literary and film criticism.

NEW STATESMAN (LONDON, ENGLAND : 1957). (NEW STATESMAN). Vol. 54, No. 1373 (July 6, 1957)-. 0028-6842. Periodical. UK. English. wk. $67.00. Statesman & Nation Publ Co Ltd, 14-16 Farringdon Lane, London EC1R 3AU England. **Tel** (01)253 2001. **Ed** Hugh Stephenson. **Ind/Abst** Abstr. Engl. Stud., Annu. Bibliogr. Engl. Lang. Lit., Film Lit. Index, Book Rev. Index, Media Rev. Dig., Soc. Sci. Index. **LC** AP4. **DD** 052. Index published separately - free - automatically sent. bk rev. adv acc. **Circ** 30,000. An independent weekly magazine. Socialist is concerned with politics and the arts. *New Statesman and Nation.*

NEW TRADITIONS. *See* Religion, Mythology, Rationalism - Judaism.

NEW VIRGINIA REVIEW. V. 1- 1979-. 0163-2299. US. English. an. New Virginia Review Inc, PO Box 415, Norfolk VA 23510. **LC** PS558.V5. **DD** 810.809755.

THE NEW YORK REVIEW OF BOOKS. VFOAT New York Review. V. 1- Feb. 1963-. 0028-7504. Periodical. US. English. ir. $30.00 Domestic, $36.00 Canada, $38.00 all other countries. Subscriber Service Department, PO Box 940, Farmingdale NY 11737. **Tel** (212)757-8070. **Ed** Robert Silvers and Barbara Epstein. **Ind/Abst** Book Rev. Index, Book Rev. Digest, Mag. Index, Women Stud. Abstr., Index Am. Period. Verse, Read. Guide Period. Lit., Years Work Eng. Stud. bk rev. adv acc. **Circ** 125,000. (ctrl). Well developed essays concerning both history i.e. literary etc. and current political affairs and issues. Most recent issues contain essays concerning Byron, Charlie Chaplin, Poland, and Picasso.

THE NEW YORK TIMES BOOK REVIEW. VFOAT Book Review. Began: Sept. 9, 1923. 0028-7806. Periodical. US. English. wk. $26.00 Domestic, $30.00 Foreign. New York Times, 229 West 43rd Street, New York NY 10036. **Tel** (212) 556-7292. **Ed** George Woods. **Ind/Abst** Sociol. Abstr., Annu. Bibliogr. Engl. Lang. Lit., Book Rev. Index, Index Book Rev. Humanit., Abr. Read. Guide, Read. Guide Period. Lit. (cum index). bk rev. adv acc. **Circ** 78,000. Current literary trends are discussed in several special features-about books and authors, paperback talk, spring and fall review of new books, childrens and Christmas issues. *New York Times Book Review and Magazine.*

NEW ZEALAND SLAVONIC JOURNAL. 1974. 0028-8693. Periodical. NZ. English. an. $9.01. Victoria University of Wellington, Department of Russian, Private Bag, Wellington New Zealand. **Tel** 721000. **Ed** Patrick Waddington. **Ind/Abst** Am. Hist. Life, Hist. Abstr., MLA Int. Bibliogr. Books Artic. Mod. Lang. Lit. bk rev. **Circ** 150. Publishes articles and book reviews on Russian and other Slavonic literature, languages, history and general culture, including those of the Soviet Union and its Slavonic neighbors.

NEWEST REVIEW. (THE NEWEST REVIEW). V. 1- June 1975-. 0380-2817. Periodical. CN. English. ir. $11.61. Newest Press, Box 394 Sub PO 6, Saskatoon Saskatchewan S7N 0W0 Canada. **Tel** (306)934-1444. **Ed** Paul Denham. **DD** 028.105. bk rev. adv acc. **Circ** 750. Regional review of the Canadian prairies. Contains journalism and essays about the region, top western Canadian fiction, poetry and review of literature, theatre and art.

NINETEENTH-CENTURY LITERATURE CRITICISM. VFOAT 19th Century Literature Criticism. Vol. 1-. 0732-1864. US. English. ir. $88.00. Gale Research Company, Book Tower, Detroit MI 48226. **Ed** Harris and Tennyson. **LC** PN761. **DD** 809.034. Provides excerpts from criticism of about 25 authors of the nineteenth century as well as biographical information.

THE NORTH AMERICAN REVIEW. V. 1- May 1815-. 0029-2397. Periodical. US. English. qt. $4.00. University of Northern Iowa, 587 Fifth Avenue, Cedar Falls IA 52401. **Ed** J Sparks, E Everett, J R Lowell, and H C Lodge. **Ind/Abst** Int. Index, Read. Guide Period. Lit., Soc. Sci. Index, Humanit. Index. **LC** AP2. (cum index).

NORTH COUNTRY ANVIL. V. 1- June 1972-. Periodical. US. English. ir. $8.50. North Country Anvil, PO Box 37, Billville MN 55957. **Tel** (507)798-2366. **Ed** Jack Miller. bk rev. adv acc. **Circ** 1,000. A regional publication of the Upper Midwest encompassing social critique, decentralist philosophy, environmental concerns, literature, poetry and grassroots activism.

NORTHWEST REVIEW. V. 1- Spring 1957-. 0029-3423. Periodical. US. English. ir. $30.00. University of Oregon, 369 PLC, Department of English, Eugene OR 97403. **Tel** (503)686-3957. **Ed** John Witte. **Ind/Abst** Abstr. Engl. Stud., MLA Int. Bibliogr. Books Artic. Mod. Lang. Lit., Index Am. Period. Verse, Index Book Rev. Humanit., Years Work Eng. Stud. **LC** AP2. (cum index). bk rev. adv acc. **Circ** 1,500. Poetry, fiction, art, book reviews and essays. Frequent book issues on northwestern issues, writers and culture.

NOTES ON CONTEMPORARY LITERATURE. 1- Jan. 1971-. 0029-4047. Periodical. US. English. bm. $6.00 Domestic, $10.00 Foreign. English Department, West Georgia College, Carrollton GA 30118. **Tel** (404)854-1220. **Ed** W S Doxey. **Ind/Abst** Abstr. Engl. Stud., MLA Int. Bibliogr. Books Artic. Mod. Lang. Lit. bk rev. adv acc. **Circ** 200. Criticisms and explications of literature since 1940.

NOUVELLE ECOLE. 0048-0967. Periodical. FR. French. qt. $30.59. S E P P, 13 rue Charles Lecocq, 75737 Paris Cedex 15 France.

NOVYI MIR. Began in 1925. 0130-7673. Periodical. UR. Russian. mo. $47.50. Victor Kamkin Inc (70636), 12224 Parklawn Drive, Rockville MD 20852. **Tel** (301)881-5973. **Ind/Abst** Lang. Lang. Behav. Abstr., MLA Int. Bibliogr. Books Artic. Mod. Lang. Lit., Sociol. Abstr., Recent Publ. Artic. **LC** AP50.

NUOVA ANTOLOGIA. V. 1- Jan. 1866-. 0029-6147. Periodical. IT. Italian. ir. 45.00. Le Monnier, Casella Postale 202, 50100 Firenz Italy. **Tel** (055)6813801. **LC** AP37. **DD** 055. (cum index). adv acc.

NUOVA ANTOLOGIA. V. 325-. 0029-6147. Periodical. IT. Italian. qt. $32.67. Le Monnier, Casella Postale 202, 50100 Firenze Italy. **Tel** 055-6813801. **Ind/Abst** Abstr. Engl. Stud., MLA Int. Bibliogr. Books Artic. Mod. Lang. Lit., Annu. Bibliogr. Engl. Lang. Lit., Am. Hist. Life, Hist. Abstr., Abstr. Engl. Stud. Index in last issue of volume - attached. bk rev. adv acc. **Circ** 8,100. The new periodical tries to recover the tradition of the Antologia. The review is meant to be a new opening to foreign culture, ready to start a dialogue with the outside world, beyond the limits of a still lingering narrow-minded provincialism. *Nuova Antologia de Lettere, Scienze de Arti.*

ODYSSEY. V. 1- Dec. 1975-. 0362-3947. Periodical. US. English. sa. $6.00. Oakland University, 212 Varner, Rochester MI 48063. **Tel** (313)370-4450. **Ed** Brian F Murphy. **Ind/Abst** MLA Int. Bibliogr. Books Artic. Mod. Lang. Lit. **LC** AS36.O24. **DD** 051. bk rev. adv acc. **Circ** 350. Literary, art, and media criticism, creative endeavors, historical, philosophical and linguistic work.

OEUVRES ET CRITIQUES. V. 1-. 0338-1900. Periodical. English or French. sa. $21.75. Gunter Narr Verlag, Postfach 2567, D7400 Tuebingen 5 West Germany. **Tel** 07071-78091. **Ed** Wolfgang Leiner. **Ind/Abst** MLA Int. Bibliogr. Books Artic. Mod. Lang. Lit. **LC** PQ2. **DD** 840.9. (cum index). bk rev. adv acc. **Circ** 1,100. Each volume discusses a literary work, an author or a group of works belonging to a special epoch or genre.

OGONEK. 1- Apr. 1, 1923-. 0030-0721. Periodical. UR. Russian. wk. $81.00. Victor Kamkin Inc (70663), 12224 Parklawn Drive, Rockville MD 20852. **Tel** (301)881-5973. **Ind/Abst** Int. Aerosp. Abstr. **LC** AP50.

THE OHIO REVIEW. VFOAT OR. Vol. 13, No. 1 (Fall 1971)-. 0360-1013. Periodical. US. English. ty. $12.00. Ohio University, Ellis Hall, Athens OH 45701-2979. **Tel** (614)594-5889. **Ed** Wayne Dodd. **Ind/Abst** MLA Int. Bibliogr. Books Artic. Mod. Lang. Lit., Index Am. Period. Verse, Index Book Rev. Humanit., Years Work Eng. Stud. **LC** AS30. **DD** 081. bk rev. adv acc. **Circ** 2,000. (ctrl). Publishes the best of contemporary American poetry, fiction, essays, and book reviews. *Ohio University Review, 0078-4257.*

OXFORD LITERARY REVIEW. (THE OXFORD LITERARY REVIEW). 1974. 0305-1498. Periodical. UK. English. sa. 25.00. Oxford Literary Review, Department of English, The University, Southampton S09 5N United Kingdom. **Ed** Robert Young. **Ind/Abst** MLA Int. Bibliogr. Books Artic. Mod. Lang. Lit., Years Work Eng. Stud. **LC** AP4. **DD** 052. bk rev. adv acc. **Circ** 1,000. Critical analyses of literary, philosophical, political, psychoanalytical and feminist theory.

PARNASSUS. POETRY IN REVIEW. (PARNASSUS : POETRY IN REVIEW). V. 1- Fall/Winter 1972-. 0048-3028. Periodical. US. English. sa. $20.00. Poetry in Review Foundation, 205 West 89th Street/Apt 8F, New York NY 10024. **Tel** (212)787-3569. **Ed** Herbert Leibowitz. **Ind/Abst** Abstr. Engl. Stud., MLA Int. Bibliogr. Books Artic. Mod. Lang. Lit., Book Rev. Index, Index Book Rev. Humanit. **LC** PN6099.6. **DD** 809.1. bk rev. adv acc. Since 1972, Parnassus is the only poetry magazine devoted to reviewing. It discussed important international and domestic publications and is often used in writing workshops.

PARTISAN REVIEW. V. 3, No. 6- Oct. 1936-. 0031-2525. Periodical. US. English. qt. $7.50 Domestic, $8.10 Foreign. Boston University, 985 Commonwealth Avenue/Room 230, Boston MA 02215. **Tel** (617)353-4260. **Ind/Abst** Humanit. Index, MLA Int. Bibliogr. Books Artic. Mod. Lang. Lit., Sociol. Abstr., Lang. Lang. Behav. Abstr., Annu. Bibliogr. Engl. Lang. Lit., Artbibliogr. Mod., Film Lit. Index, Book Rev. Index, Index Am. Period. Verse, Index Book Rev. Humanit., Int. Index, Soc. Sci. Index, Am. Hist. Life, Hist. Abstr., Abstr. Engl. Stud., Years Work Eng. Stud., Hist. Abstr., Part A, Mod. Hist. Abstr., Hist. Abst., Part B, Twent. Century Abstr. **LC** HX1. **DD** 335.05. (cum index). *Partisan Review & Anvil.*

PASSAIC REVIEW. 0731-4663. Periodical. US. English. sa. $7.50. c/o Forstmann Library, 195 Gregory Avenue, Passaic NJ 07055. **Tel** (201)471-8077.

THE PAWLEYS ISLAND PERSPECTIVE. 0276-0851. Periodical. US. English. bm. $6.00. Pawleys Island Perspective Inc, PO Box 1260, Pawleys Island SC 29585.

PERETS. Began with June 1941 issue. Periodical. UR. Ukrainian. sm. $25.00. Victor Kamkin Inc (74393), 12224 Parklawn Drive, Rockville MD 20852. **Tel** (301)881-5973. **LC** AP115.

PERSPECTIVES. (PERSPECTIVES : A REVIEW JOURNAL OF THE COOPERATIVE SERVICES FOR CHILDREN'S LITERATURE, UNIVERSITY OF TOLEDO). Began in 1984. 0883-6086. Periodical. US. English. ty. $7.50. Editor of Perspectives Cooperative Services for Children's Literature College of Education and Allied Professions, 159 Snyder Building, University of Toledo, Toledo OH 43606. **Tel** (419)537-4300. **Ed** Hughes Moir. **DD** 028. bk rev. adv acc. **Circ** 1,000. (ctrl). Reviews of children's and young adult book with suggested activities for integrating literature in K-12 curricula.

THE PHOENIX. V. 1- Mar./May 1938-. 0031-8310. Periodical. US. English. ir. Morning Star Farm, West Whatley Via Rural Free Delivery, Haydenville MA 01039. **Ed** James Cooney. **LC** AP2. **DD** 051. bk rev. Regarding all governments as enemies of the people. It refuses to be collaborator with detention camps, torturers, and executioners in the anti-human states of society.

PIEDMONT LITERARY REVIEW. 0275-357X. Periodical. US. English. ir. $10.00. Piedmont Literary Society, PO Box 3656, Danville VA 24543. **Tel** (804)793-0956. **Ed** David Craig. bk rev. **Circ** 400. Poetry and short stories. A newsletter that contains contests, markets and tips for writers.

PN REVIEW (MANCHESTER, GREATER MANCHESTER : 1979). (PN REVIEW). VFOAT P.N. Review. No. 10 (1979)-. 0144-7076. Periodical. UK. English. bm. 29.00. Bailey Brothers and Swifen Ltd, Warner House, Folkestone Kent CT19 6PH England. **Tel** (061)834-8730. **Ed**

Michael Schmidt. **Ind/Abst** Abstr. Engl. Stud., MLA Int. Bibliogr. Books Artic. Mod. Lang. Lit. **LC** PN1010. **DD** 808.81. (cum index). bk rev. adv acc. **Circ** 2,000. Each issue includes editorial news and notes, reports, readers' letters and extensive reviews. The body of magazine consists of poems, translations, interviews, and informal pieces. *Poetry Nation Review.*

POETRY CANADA REVIEW. Vol. 1, No. 2 (Winter 1979/80)-. 0709-3373. Periodical. CN. English (includes some text in French). qt. 22.00 Domestic, $22.00 US. ECW Press, 307 Coxwell Avenue, Toronto Ontario M4L 3B5 Canada. **Tel** (416)694-3348. **Ed** Robert Billings. **DD** C811.5408. bk rev. adv acc. **Circ** 2,000. Canada's only magazine that concentrates on poetry. Reviews all current Canadian books of poetry, publishes memoirs, columns and contains over 100 poems in each issue. *Poetry Canada, 0708-496X.*

POETRY REVIEW. V. 1- Jan. 1912-. 0032-2156. Periodical. UK. English. qt. 11.00. Poetry Society Inc, 21 Earls Court Square, London SW 5 England. **Tel** 01-373-7861. **Ed** Mick Imlah. **Ind/Abst** Abstr. Engl. Stud., Index Book Rev. Humanit., MLA Int. Bibliogr. Books Artic. Mod. Lang. Lit. **LC** PN1010. **DD** 821.008. bk rev. adv acc. **Circ** 4,000. Covers new poems; reviews of books of and about contemporary and 20th Century poetry. Includes articles, memoirs and other prose by poets. Competitions etc. *Poetical Gazette.*

THE POISONED PEN. Periodical. US. English. qt. $12.00. Jeffrey Meyerson, 50 1st Place, Brooklyn NY 11231. **Tel** (212)596-7739.

IL PONTE. Vol. 1- Apr. 1945-. 0032-423X. Periodical. IT. Italian. bm. $20.79. Luciano Manzuoli Editore, Via G Modena 20-22, 50129 Firenze Italy. **Ed** P Calamandrei. **Ind/Abst** Am. Hist. Life, Hist. Abstr., Part A, Mod. Hist. Abstr., Hist. Abst., Part B, Twent. Century Abstr., MLA Int. Bibliogr. Books Artic. Mod. Lang. Lit., Hist. Abstr. **LC** AP37. **DD** 055.1. Index in last issue of volume - attached.

POPULAR TALISMAN BULLETIN. **VFOAT** Talisman Bulletin. Since 1960. 0032-4655. Periodical. US. English. bm. Talisman Company, Box 948, Chicago IL 60690.

POWYS REVIEW. (THE POWYS REVIEW). No. 1- Spring 1977-. 0309-1619. Periodical. UK. English. sa. 5. St Davids University College, Department of English, c/o The Editor, Lampeter Dyfed Great Britain. **Tel** 0570 422018. **Ed** Belinda Humfrey. **Ind/Abst** MLA Int. Bibliogr. Books Artic. Mod. Lang. Lit. **LC** PR6031.O867. bk rev. adv acc. **Circ** 1,000. Critical study of the works of John Cowper Powys, T F Powys and Llewelyn Powys and related literature from 1880 to the present.

PRAXIS. V. 1- Spring 1976-. 0161-0414. Periodical. US. English. ir. $10.00. Praxis, Box 20 North Campus Union Cornell University, Ithaca NY 14853. **LC** AS30. **DD** 051.

PRIVATE EYE. No. 1- 1961-. Periodical. UK. English. bw. $16.85. Private Eye, Mortimer House, 230-236 Lavender Hill, London SW11 1LE England. **Tel** (01)228-0425.

PROMENY. METAMORPHOSES. **VFOAT** Metamorphoses, Premeny. Vol. 1- 1964-. 0033-1058. Periodical. US. Czech (Slovak). qt. $14.00. Promeny, c/o George S Kouba, 701-20 Chesterton Drive, Ottawa Ontario K2E 6Z7 Canada. **Tel** (212)392-3104. **Ind/Abst** MLA Int. Bibliogr. Books Artic. Mod. Lang. Lit. bk rev. **Circ** 850.

PROSTOR. 1960, 1 (Jan. 1960)-. Periodical. UR. Russian. mo. $38.00. Victor Kamkin Inc (75796), 12224 Parklawn Drive, Rockville MD 20852. **Tel** (301)881-5973. *Sovetskii Kazakhstan.*

PROTEE. *See* Linguistics.

PUBLIC DOCUMENTS (BATON ROUGE, LA.). (PUBLIC DOCUMENTS). 0099-2410. US. English. sa. Louisiana State Library, PO Box 131, Baton Rouge LA 70821. **LC** Z1223.5.L7, J87.L8. **DD** 015.763. **NLM** W2 AL6 D85P. *Semi-Annual List of the Public Documents of Louisiana.*

PUERTO DEL SOL. 0738-517X. Periodical. US. English or Spanish. an. $7.50. Puerto Del Sol, Box 3 E New Mexico State University, Las Cruces NM 88003. **Tel** (505)646-3931. **Ed** Kevin McIlvoy. **LC** PS580. **DD** 810.80054. bk rev. adv acc. **Circ** 900. Includes book reviews, interviews with Western and Southwestern authors (such as Anaya, Waters, Siko, Hinojosa), poetry and fiction- both conventional and experimental.

PULPSMITH. Vol. 1, No. 1 (Spring 1981)-. 0276-0436. Periodical. US. English. qt. $8.00. The Smith, 5 Beekman Street, New York NY 10038. *Smith (New York, N.Y. : 1975).*

QUADERNI IBERO-AMERICANI. 1- Aug./Oct.1946-. 0033-4960. Periodical. IT. Italian (Spanish, French, or English). sa. $20.00. Assoc Relazioni Culrura Spagna, Palazzo Dell University Via PO 19, Torino Italy. **Tel** (011)83.27.43. **Ed** Giovanni Maria Bertini. **Ind/Abst** MLA Int. Bibliogr. Books Artic. Mod. Lang. Lit. **LC** F1401. **DD** 940. bk rev. adv acc. **Circ** 1,100. Articles about Spanish, Portuguese, and Latin-American literature, reviews of Spanish (Hispanic) books.

QUESTIONS LITURGIQUES. Vol. 51-. Periodical. French. qt. $11.86. Abbaye du Mont Cesar, 202 Mechelsestraat 202, 3000-Leuven Belgium. **Tel** 016/22 41 75. Index in last issue of volume - attached. *Questions Liturgiques et Paroissiales.*

QUILT. **VFOAT** Ishmael Reed & Al Young's Quilt. 1-. 0277-593X. Periodical. US. English. qt. $11.80. Harris Publ Company Inc, 1115 Broadway, New York NY 10010. **Tel** (212)807-7100.

QUIMERA (BARCELONA, SPAIN). (QUIMERA). No. 1 (Nov. 1980)-. 0211-3325. Periodical. SP. Spanish. mo. 5.000.-. Montesinos Editor SA, 11 6 R, c/o Ronda San Pedro, Barcelona 10 Spain. **Tel** 219 92 11. **Ind/Abst** MLA Int. Bibliogr. Books Artic. Mod. Lang. Lit. **LC** PN778. **DD** 809. bk rev. adv acc. **Circ** 22,000. (ctrl). Literature and reviews of books.

RAISE THE STAKES. (RAISE THE STAKES : THE PLANET DRUM REVIEW). 0278-7016. Periodical. US. English. ty. $10.00. Planet Drum Foundation, PO Box 31251, San Francisco CA 94131.

RAND RESEARCH REVIEW. **VFOAT** Research Review. Began in: 1977. 0740-9281. Periodical. US. English. ty. Rand Corporation, 1700 Main Street, Santa Monica CA 90406.

RARITAN. Vol. 1, No. 1 (Summer 1981)-. 0275-1607. Periodical. US. English. qt. $16.00. Raritan, 165 College Avenue, New Brunswick NJ 08903. **Tel** (201)932-7887. **Ed** Richard Poirier. **Ind/Abst** Abstr. Engl. Stud., MLA Int. Bibliogr. Books Artic. Mod. Lang. Lit. **LC** AS30. **DD** 051. bk rev. adv acc. **Circ** 3,500. Focuses on workings of cultural power, how movements help determine critical attitudes toward ideas in literature, media, social sciences and arts. Essays, essay reviews, some poetry and fiction.

RAZON Y FE; REVISTA HISPANO-AMERICANA DE CULTURA. V. 1- (V. 1-). 0034-0235. Periodical. SP. Spanish. mo. $45.00. Centro Loyola, Pablo Aranda 3, Madrid 6 Spain. **Tel** (91)262 49 30. **Ind/Abst** MLA Int. Bibliogr. Books Artic. Mod. Lang. Lit., New Testam. Abstr., Hist. Abstr., Am. Hist. Life, Recent Publ. Artic. **LC** AP60. (cum index). adv acc. **Circ** 7,000. Relation between religion and culture in wide sense: politics, economy, social and cultural questions.

RECOVERING LITERATURE. V. 1- Spring 1972-. 0300-6425. Periodical. US. English. an. $6.50. Recovering Literature, PO Box 805, Alpine CA 92001. **Tel** (619)445-4341. **Ed** Gerald Butler. **Ind/Abst** Abstr. Engl. Stud., MLA Int. Bibliogr. Books Artic. Mod. Lang. Lit. bk rev. adv acc. **Circ** 500. Literary criticism.

REFORMATIO. *See* Religion, Mythology, Rationalism - Protestantism.

RELIGIOUS BOOK REVIEW. *See* Religion, Mythology, Rationalism.

RENDICONTI. **Main/Corp** Accademia Nazionale dei Lincei, Rome. Classe di Scienze Morali, Storiche, Critiche e Filologiche. Ser. 5, V. 1-33, 1892-1924. 0001-4435. Periodical. IT. Italian. ir. Academia Nazionale del Lincei, Via Delle Lungara 10, 00165 Roma Italy. **LC** AS222. **DD** 508. *Rendiconti.*

REVIEW. V. 1- 1979-. 0190-3233. US. English. an. University Press of Virginia, Box 3608/University Station, Charlottesville VA 22903. **Tel** (804)924-3468. **Ed** J O Hoge and J L W West, III. **Ind/Abst** MLA Int. Bibliogr. Books Artic. Mod. Lang. Lit., Essay Gen. Lit. Index, Years Work Eng. Stud. **LC** PR1. **DD** 820.9. Publishes important review-essays and reviews of scholarly literature. Aiming to publish 'definitive' reviews of significant works of literary scholarship.

THE REVIEW OF CONTEMPORARY FICTION. (REVIEW OF CONTEMPORARY FICTION). Vol. 1, No. 1 (Spring 1981)-. 0276-0045. Periodical. US. English. ty. $22.00. Review of Contemporary Fiction, 1817 North 9th Avenue, Elmwood Park IL 60635. **Tel** (312)453-2024. **Ed** John O'Brien. **Ind/Abst** MLA Int. Bibliogr. Books Artic. Mod. Lang. Lit. **LC** PN3503. **DD** 809.3. bk rev. adv acc. **Circ** 1,500. Devoted to criticism of contemporary fiction. Includes essays, interviews, fiction and book reviews.

REVIEW OF NATIONAL LITERATURES. Vol. 1, No. 1 (Spring 1970)-. 0034-6640. Monographic Series. US. English. ir. Griffon House Publications, PO Box 81, Whitestone NY 11357. **Tel** (718)767-8380. **Ind/Abst** Abstr. Engl. Stud., MLA Int. Bibliogr. Books Artic. Mod. Lang. Lit. **LC** PN2. **DD** 809.

THE REVIEW OF POLITICS. V. 1- Jan. 1939-. 0034-6705. Periodical. US. English. qt. $20.00. Review of Politics, Box B, Notre Dame IN 46556. **Tel** (219)239-6623. **Ed** Donald P Kommers. **Ind/Abst** Am. Hist. Life, Hist. Abstr., Part A, Mod. Hist. Abstr., Hist. Abst., Part B, Twent. Century Abstr., ABC Pol Sci, Book Rev. Index, Cathol. Period. Lit. Index, Soc. Sci. Index, Humanit. Index, Public Aff. Inf. Serv. Bull., Soc. Sci. Citation Index, Hist. Abstr., Recent Publ. Artic. **LC** JA1. **DD** 320.5. bk rev. adv acc. **Circ** 1,300. Primarily interested in philosophical and historical approach to political realities.

REVIEWERS' CONSENSUS. (REVIEWERS' CONSENSUS : EVALUATIONS FROM REVIEWS OF BOOKS FOR CHILDREN AND ADOLESCENTS). V. 1- 1976-. 0164-341X. Periodical. US. English. qt. $15.00. Willow Tree Press, PO Box 3400, San Leandro CA 94578. **Ed** Ned Luzmoor.

REVISTA DE CRITICA LITERARIA LATINOAMERICANA. Vol. 1- 1st Semester 1975-. 0252-8843. PE. Spanish Portuguese. sa. 15.00. Latinoamericana Editores, Avenida Benavides 3074-la Castellana, Lima 18 Peru. **Tel** 011-51-14-456353. **Ind/Abst** MLA Int. Bibliogr. Books Artic. Mod. Lang. Lit. **LC** PQ7081.A1. **DD** 860. bk rev. adv acc. **Circ** 1,500. (ctrl). Criticism on Latin American literature, bibliographies, notes, studies (essays), book reviews, etc.

REVISTA DE LETRAS (FORTALEZA, BRAZIL). (REVISTA DE LETRAS : RL). **VFOAT** RL. Vol. 1, No. 1-. Periodical. BL. Portuguese. sa. Centro de Humanidades, Universidade Federal do Ceara, Caixa Postal 819, 60.000 Fortaleza Ceara Brasil. **LC** AS80.A1. **DD** 070.594098131.

REVISTA DE OCCIDENTE. No. 1- April/June 1980-. Periodical. SP. Spanish. mo. $35.32. Revista de Occidente, Genova 23, Madrid 4 Spain. **Ind/Abst** Abstr. Engl. Stud., Am. Hist. Life, Hist. Abstr., Part A, Mod. Hist. Abstr., Hist. Abst., Part B, Twent. Century Abstr. *Revista de Occidente, 0034-8635.*

LA REVUE D'EN FACE. No. 1 (May 1977)-. Periodical. FR. French. qt. La Revue d'En Face, Editions Savelli, 33 Building, Saint-Martin 75003 Paris France.

REVUE DES DEUX MONDES (PARIS, FRANCE : 1982). (REVUE DES DEUX MONDES). 0151-914X. Periodical. FR. French. mo. 280.50. Revue des Deux Mondes, 15 rue de l'Universite, 75007 Paris France. **Tel** (1) 42-61-21-49. **Ind/Abst** MLA Int. Bibliogr. Books Artic. Mod. Lang. Lit., Am. Hist. Life. **LC** AP20. **DD** 054.1. adv acc. Covers literature, politics, history, art, and sciences. *Nouvelle Revue des Deux Mondes, 0151-914X.*

LA REVUE DES LIVRES POUR ENFANTS. No. 56- Oct. 1977-. Periodical. FR. French. bm. $13.30. Ecole Natle Super Bibl, Joie par les Livres, 8 rue Saint-Bon, 75004 Paris 4 France. **Tel** 887-61-95. **LC** PN1009.A1. **DD** 028.52. bk rev. adv acc. **Circ** 4,000. (ctrl). Critical survey of new books for children from eight months up to fourteen years of age. General information and articles on children's literature and libraries. *Bulletin d'Analyse de Livres Pour Enfants.*

REVUE LITTERAIRE DU C.E.G.E.P. DE GRANBY. May 1979-. 0229-2297. Periodical. CN. French. C.E.G.E.P. de Granby, 50 rue St-Joseph, Granby Quebec J2G 6T6 Canada. **DD** C840.8092375. *Liber . . ., 0229-2289.*

RIMBAUD VIVANT. Periodical. FR. French. sa. $6.66. Amis de Rimbaud, 137 rue du Ranelagh, 75016 Paris France.

ROAD APPLE REVIEW. V. 1- Winter 1968/69-. 0035-7200. Periodical. US. English. qt. $4.00. Road Runner Press, 3263 Shorewood Drive, Oshkosh WI 54901.

ROMANCE MONOGRAPHS. No. 1- 1972-. Monographic Series. US. English or French. ir. Romance Monographs Inc, PO Box 7553, University MS 38677. **Tel** (601)234-0001. **Ed** Jack Davis Brown. Literary criticism in the area of romance languages.

ROMANIAN COMMUNION. VFOAT Comuniunea Romanessca, Communiunea Rom Aneasca. V. 1, No. 1 (Jan./March 1973)-. 0197-1441. Periodical. US. English (Romanian). qt. Comuniunea Romameasca, 19965 Piopelle, Detroit MI 48203. **Tel** (313)893-9237. **Ed** George Alexe. **LC** DR212. **DD** 909.0459. bk rev. **Circ** 500. Literary magazine of Romanian theology, culture and art promoting the heritage of Romanian-American ethnicity, spirituality and national friendship.

ROMANIAN REVIEW. V.19, No. 3- 1965-. Periodical. English. ir. Romanian Review, 1 Piata Scinteii, PO Box 33-28, Bucharest 71341 Romania. **Ind/Abst** MLA Int. Bibliogr. Books Artic. Mod. Lang. Lit. *Rumanian Review.*

RONDA LITERARIA. Periodical. AG. Spanish. ir. Distribuidora Torres, Charcas 3918, 1425 Buenos Aires Argentina.

RYUKYU DAIGAKU KOKUBUNGAKU TETSUGAKU RON SHU. VFOAT Ryudai Review of Japanese Literature & Philosophy. English or Japanese. ir. Ryukyu Daigaku Ho-Bungakubu, Shuri, Naha Japan. **LC** AS552.R8.

ST. ANDREWS REVIEW. VAT Saint Andrews Review. V. 1- Fall/Winter 1970-. 0036-2751. Periodical. US. English. sa. $12.00. St Andrews Presbyterian College, St Andrews Review, Laurinburg NC 28352. **Tel** (919)276-3652. **Ed** Bill Grim. **Ind/Abst** Abstr. Engl. Stud. **LC** PS1. **DD** 808.8004. bk rev. adv acc. **Circ** 620. Poetry, fiction, and essays addressed to cultural affairs.

SAMISDAT. V. A, No. 1-. 0883-3540. US. English. ir. Samisdat, Box 129, Richford VT 05476. **Ed** Merritt Clifton. **DD** 810.

SAMISDAT. Vol. 4, No. 1- (#8-). 0226-840X. US. English. ir. Samisdat, Box 129, Richford VT 05476. **Tel** (514)263-4439. **Ed** Merritt Clifton. **Ind/Abst** Index Am. Period. Verse. **DD** 810.80054. bk rev. adv acc. **Circ** 300. Literature and literary reviews from ecologically aware, socially responsible semi-libertarian viewpoint. *Berkeley Samisdat Review, 0883-3702.*

SAMTIDEN. Vol. 1-. 0036-3928. Periodical. NO. Norwegian. bm. $33.84. Forlagssentralens Tidsskrif, Postboks 6005 Etterstad, Oslo 6 Norway. **Ind/Abst** Am. Hist. Life, Hist. Abstr., Part A, Mod. Hist. Abstr., Hist. Abst., Part B, Twent. Century Abstr., MLA Int. Bibliogr. Books Artic. Mod. Lang. Lit., Artbibliogr. Mod., Hist. Abstr. **LC** AP45. (cum index).

SAN FRANCISCO REVIEW OF BOOKS. VFOAT San Francisco Review. V. 1- Apr. 1975-. 0194-0724. Periodical. US. English. bm. $9.00. c/o R E Nowicki, 1111 Kearny Street, San Francisco CA 94133. **Tel** (415)777-2923. **Ed** R E Nowicki. **Ind/Abst** Book Rev. Index. bk rev. adv acc. **Circ** 5,000. Contains book reviews, interviews with authors, profiles, reviews of films, theatre, dance, art, and news of Bay area publishing.

SCIENCE FICTION REVIEW. 1975. 0036-8377. Periodical. US. English. qt. $9.00. Science Fiction Review, PO Box 11408, c/o Richard E Geis, Portland OR 97211. **Tel** (503)282-0381. **Ed** Richard E Geis. **Ind/Abst** Book Rev. Index. bk rev. **Circ** 2,000. Available in microform from Oxford Microform Publications Ltd. Interviews, articles, reviews, letters, columns by science fiction and fantasy professionals and aficionados discussing the science fiction and fantasy field and craft of its writing. *Alien Critic.*

SCIENCE-FICTION STUDIES. VAT Science Fiction Studies. V. 1- Spring 1973-. 0091-7729. Periodical. CN. English. ty. 22.00 Domestic, $18.00 US, $21.50 Others. McGill University, SFS Department of English, 853 Sherbrooke Street West, Montreal Quebec H3A 2T6 Canada. **Tel** (514)392-8979. **Ed** R M Philmus. **Ind/Abst** Abstr. Engl. Stud., MLA Int. Bibliogr. Books Artic. Mod. Lang. Lit., Humanit. Index, Ref. Source, Index Book Rev. Humanit. **LC** PN3448.S45. **DD** 809.3876. bk rev. adv acc. **Circ** 1,050. (ctrl). An academic journal devoted to the critical appraisal of science fiction.

SCOLIES. 1- 1971-. French. ir.

SCREE. Began in 1974?. 0360-2672. Periodical. US. English. ir. $8.50. Duck Down Press, PO Box 1047, Fallon NV 89406. **Tel** (702)423-6643.

SCRUTINY. V. 1- Jan./June 1974-. Periodical. English. ir. $8.00. International Forum, Post Box No 1090, Islamabad Pakistan. **LC** DS376. **DD** 954.91005.

THE SECRETARY OF STATE'S BOOKSTORE CATALOG. Main/Corp Massachusetts. Office of the Secretary of State. US. English. Michael Joseph Connolly Secretary of State, State Bookstore/Room 116, State House, Boston MA 02133. **LC** Z1223.5.M35, J87.M4. **DD** 015.744053. *State Bookstore Catalogue.*

SERRA D'OR. Began in 1969. 0037-2501. Periodical. Catalan. mo. $30.00. Monestir de Montserrat, Apartat 121, Barcelona Spain. **Ind/Abst** Am. Hist. Life, Hist. Abstr., Part A, Mod. Hist. Abstr., Hist. Abst., Part B, Twent. Century Abstr., Recent Publ. Artic. **LC** DP302.C57. **DD** 946.7005.

THE SEWANEE REVIEW. *See* Literature.

SFBRI: SCIENCE FICTION BOOK REVIEW INDEX. VFOAT Science Fiction Book Review Index. 1970. 0085-5979. US. English. an. Science Fiction Book Review, 3608 Meadow Oaks Lane, Bryan TX 77801. **Tel** (409)845-2316. **Ed** H W Hall. **Circ** 600. Index to book reviews of science fiction and fantasy books.

SHAKESPEAREAN CRITICISM. (SHAKESPEAREAN CRITICISM : EXCERPTS FROM THE CRITICISM OF WILLIAM SHAKESPEARE'S PLAYS AND POETRY, FROM THE FIRST PUBLISHED APPRAISALS TO CURRENT EVALUATIONS). Vol. 1-. 0883-9123. US. English. an. Gale Research Company, Book Tower, Detroit MI 48226. **Ed** Laurie Lanzen Harris. **DD** 822 #2 11.

THE SHAW REVIEW *CEASED.* V. 1-23, No.3. 0037-3354. Periodical. US. English. ty. Shaw Review, S234 Burrowes Building South, University Park PA 16802. **LC** PR5366. **DD** 822.912.

SILVERFISH REVIEW. No. 1-. 0164-1085. Periodical. US. English. ty. $14.00. Silverfish Review, PO Box 3541, Eugene OR 97403. **Tel** (503)342-2344. **Ed** Rodger Moody. **LC** PS536.2. **DD** 810.8. bk rev. adv acc. **Circ** 500. Poetry, fiction, and reviews; translations are also showcased, and there is an annual chapbook contest for poetry.

SIMAN KERIAH. *See* Literature.

SIMCOE REVIEW. No. 1- Winter 1976-. 0226-3424. Periodical. CN. English. sa. $2.00. English Department, Governor Simcoe Secondary School, 15 Glenview Avenue, St Catharines Ontario L2N 2Z7 Canada. **DD** C810.08092375.

SIPAPU. V. 1- (No.1-) Jan. 1970-. Periodical. US. English. sa. $8.00. Noel Peattie, Route 1 Box 216, Winters CA 95694. **Tel** (916)752-1032. **Ed** Noel Peattie. **Ind/Abst** Altern. Press Index. (cum index). bk rev. **Circ** 450. Reviews, interviews and conference news of dissent literature, alternative and small presses, including Third World, feminist, peace, ecological, and poetry.

SLOBODA. VFOAT Liberty. 0037-6868. Periodical. US. Serbo-Croatian -R. wk. $25.00. Sloboda, 3909 West North Avenue, Chicago IL 60647. **LC** AP56.

SMALL PRESS REVIEW. V. 1- (No. 1-). 0037-7228. Periodical. US. English. mo. $22.00. Dustbooks, Box 100, Paradise CA 95969. **Tel** (916)877-6110. **Ed** Len Fulton. **Ind/Abst** Book Rev. Index, New Period. Index. **LC** WNC. (cum index). bk rev. adv acc. **Circ** 2,500. (ctrl). A running document containing news, reviews, features, and updates on the listing in the international directory.

SOCIAL ANARCHISM. Vol. 1, No. 1 (Winter 1980)-. 0196-4801. Periodical. US. English. sa. $10.00. Social Anarchism, 2743 Maryland Avenue, Baltimore MD 21218. **Tel** (301)243-6987. **Ed** H J Ehrlich. **Ind/Abst** Altern. Press Index. **LC** HX821. **DD** 335.8305. bk rev. adv acc. **Circ** 1,000. Articles, investigative reporting, essays, historical notes, practical proposals, poetry, short fiction and book reviews relating to social anarchism and anarchist-feminism.

SONNTAG. Vol. 1-. 0038-1411. Periodical. SZ. German. wk. Kunst & Wissen Erich Bieber, Dufourstrasse 51, CH-8008 Zurich Switzerland. **Tel** (011)411694420.

SONORA REVIEW. No. 1- Fall 1980-. 0275-5203. US. English. sa. $5.00. University Arizona/ Deparment of English, c/o Marvin Diogenes, Tucson AZ 85721. **Tel** (602)621-1387. **Ed** Antonya Nelson. **LC** PS1. **DD** 810.8. bk rev. adv acc. **Circ** 1,000. Literary fiction and poetry. Also book reviews, interviews, and special issues.

SOUTH ASIAN REVIEW - SOUTH ASIAN LITERARY ASSOCIATION. (SOUTH ASIAN REVIEW). VFOAT S.A.L.A. Journal. 0275-9527. Periodical. US. English. an. $10.00 US and Canada, $15.00 Foreign. University of North Florida, Department of Language and Literature, Jacksonville FL 32216. **Tel** (904)646-2818. **Ed** Satya S Pachori. **Ind/Abst** MLA Int. Bibliogr. Books Artic. Mod. Lang. Lit. **Circ** 150. (ctrl). Covers South Asian literature, culture, linguistics, east-west literary relations.

THE SOUTH ATLANTIC QUARTERLY. V. 1- Jan. 1902-. 0038-2876. Periodical. US. English. qt. $16.00. Duke University Press, College Station, Box 6697, Durham NC 27708. **Tel** (919)684-2173. **Ed** Oliver W Ferguson. **Ind/Abst** Am. Hist. Life, Hist. Abstr., Part A, Mod. Hist. Abstr., Hist. Abst., Part B, Twent. Century Abstr., Abstr. Engl. Stud., MLA Int. Bibliogr. Books Artic. Mod. Lang. Lit., Annu. Bibliogr. Engl. Lang. Lit., Women Stud. Abstr., Writ. Am. Hist., Recent Publ. Artic., Book Rev. Index, Index Book Rev. Humanit., Int. Index, Years Work Eng. Stud., Soc. Sci. Index, Humanit. Index, Hist. Abstr., Public Aff. Inf. Serv. Bull. **LC** AP2. **DD** 051. bk rev. adv acc. **Circ** 1,100. Founded in 1902, it is the oldest scholarly periodical in general humanities in the United States, publishing essays and reviews of current interest in literature, politics, history, and the arts.

SOUTH ATLANTIC REVIEW. (SOUTH ATLANTIC REVIEW : THE PUBLICATION OF THE SOUTH ATLANTIC MODERN LANGUAGE ASSOCIATION). Vol. 46, No. 1 (Jan. 1981)-. 0277-335X. Periodical. US. English. qt. $15.00. South Atlantic Modern Language Association, University of North Carolina, 120 Dey Hall 014A, Box 4, Chapel Hill NC 27514. **Tel** (919)962-7165. **Ed** Siegfried Mews. **Ind/Abst** Annu. Bibliogr. Engl. Lang. Lit., Abstr. Engl. Stud., MLA Int. Bibliogr. Books Artic. Mod. Lang. Lit. **LC** PB1. **DD** 809. bk rev. adv acc. **Circ** 4,400. (ctrl). Scholarly articles and book reviews. *SAB, South Atlantic Bulletin.*

SOUTH CAROLINA REVIEW. (THE SOUTH CAROLINA REVIEW). V. 1- Nov. 1968-. 0038-3163. Periodical. US. English. sa. $5.00. Clemson University, Department of English, Clemson SC 29631. **Tel** (803)656-3229. **Ed** Richard J Calhoun. **Ind/Abst** Abstr. Engl. Stud., MLA Int. Bibliogr. Books Artic. Mod. Lang. Lit., Book Rev. Index, Index Am. Period. Verse, Index Book Rev. Humanit., Am. Hist. Life, Hist. Abstr., Years Work Eng. Stud., Hist. Abstr., Part A, Mod. Hist. Abstr., Hist. Abst., Part B, Twent. Century Abstr. **LC** PS558.S6. **DD** 810.80054. bk rev. adv acc. **Circ** 600. Fiction, poetry, and criticism of the quality that has earned several Pushcart nominations and national awards.

SOUTHERLY. Began with Sept. 1939 issue. 0038-3732. Periodical. AT. English. qt. $18.45. English Association, PO Box 667, Chatswood New South Wales 2067 Australia. **Tel** 559 2223. **Ed** G A Wilkes. **Ind/Abst** Abstr. Engl. Stud., MLA Int. Bibliogr. Books Artic. Mod. Lang. Lit., APAIS, Aust. Public Aff. Inf. Serv., Index Book Rev. Humanit. **LC** AP7. **DD** 820.5. bk rev. **Circ** 1,000. A review of Australian literature comprising critical articles and reviews and creative writing both fiction and poetry.

SOUTHERN POETRY REVIEW. Vol. 5, No. 1 (Fall 1964)-. 0038-447X. Periodical. US. English. sa. $4.00. University of North Carolina, Department of English, Charlotte NC 28223. **Tel** (704)597-4225. **Ed** Robert Grey. **Ind/Abst** Index Am. Period. Verse. **LC** PS580. **DD** 811.008. bk rev. **Circ** 1,000. Not a regional magazine, though we function naturally as an outlet for new southern talent. We emphasize variety and intensity. No restrictions on style, content or length. *Impetus (De Land, Fla.).*

SOUTHERN REVIEW. V. 1- 1963-. 0038-4526. Periodical. AT. English. ty. 15.00. University of Adelaide, Business Editor, Department of English, Adelaide South Australia 5001 Australia. **Tel** (08)228-5623. **Ed** Robert Sellick. **Ind/Abst** Annu. Bibliogr. Engl. Lang. Lit., Abstr. Engl. Stud., MLA Int. Bibliogr. Books Artic. Mod. Lang. Lit., APAIS, Aust. Public Aff. Inf. Serv., Index Book Rev. Humanit., Years Work Eng. Stud. **LC** PR1. **DD** 820.9. adv acc. **Circ** 300. Literary and interdisciplinary essays both traditional and representative of newer and more radical styles of critical discourse.

SOUTHWEST REVIEW. V. 10- Oct. 1924-. 0038-4712. Periodical. US. English. qt. $10.00. Southwest Review, Southern Methodist University, Box 4374, Dallas TX 75275. **Tel** (214)692-3736. **Ed** Willard Spiegelman. **Ind/Abst** Abstr. Engl. Stud., MLA Int. Bibliogr. Books Artic. Mod. Lang. Lit., Annu. Bibliogr. Engl. Lang. Lit., Index Book Rev. Humanit.,

Abstr. Pop. Cult., Am. Hist. Life, Humanit. Index, Book Rev. Index, Guide Rev. Books Hisp. Am., Index Am. Period. Verse, Hist. Abstr., Part A, Mod. Hist. Abstr., Hist. Abst., Part B, Twent. Century Abstr., Hist. Abstr., Years Work Eng. Stud. (cum index). bk rev. adv acc. **Circ** 1,600. Fiction, poetry, essays and interviews by well-known and exciting new writers. Recent issues feature Amy Clampitt, Margaret Drabble, Gordon Lish, James Merrill, Nigel Nicolson. *Reviewer of Richmond, Reviewer, 0275-245X; Texas Review.*

THE SOUTHWESTERN REVIEW. Began with Vol. for Spring 1975. 0276-7155. US. English. an. Southwestern Review, Department of English, The University of Southwestern Louisiana, Lafayette LA 70504. **LC** PS501. **DD** 810.8.

THE SOVIET REVIEW. V. 1- Aug. 1960-. 0038-5794. Periodical. US. English. qt. $40.00. M E Sharpe Inc, 80 Business Park Drive, Armonk NY 10054. **Tel** (914)273-1800. **Ed** A Joseph Hollander. **Ind/Abst** MLA Int. Bibliogr. Books Artic. Mod. Lang. Lit., Sociol. Abstr., Lang. Lang. Behav. Abstr. **LC** AS261. **DD** 057.1. adv acc. **Circ** 700. A unique survey of current work in economics, archeology, law, education, government, anthropology, literature, history, psychology, philosophy, and sociology drawn from a broad range of Soviet publications. *Soviet Highlights.*

LE SPECTACLE DU MONDE. Began with Apr. 1962 issue. 0038-6944. Periodical. FR. French. mo. Compagnie Francaise Journaux, 41 rue d'Uzes, 75081 Paris Cedex 02 France. **Tel** 233 21 84. **LC** AP20. **DD** 054.1.

STANFORD FRENCH REVIEW. V. 1- Spring 1977-. 0163-657X. Periodical. US. English (French). ty. $35.00. Anma Libri, PO Box 876, Saratoga CA 95070. **Tel** (415)851-3375. **Ed** Katarina Kivel. **Ind/Abst** MLA Int. Bibliogr. Books Artic. Mod. Lang. Lit., Writ. Am. Hist., Recent Publ. Artic. **LC** PQ1. **DD** 840.9. bk rev. adv acc. Scholarly journal in French literature, history and culture.

STANFORD ITALIAN REVIEW. I, 1 (Spring 1979)-. 0730-6857. Periodical. US. English (Italian). sa. $25.00. Anma Library, PO Box 876, Saratoga CA 95070. **Tel** (415)851-3375. **Ed** John Freccero. **Ind/Abst** MLA Int. Bibliogr. Books Artic. Mod. Lang. Lit. **LC** PQ4001. adv acc. Scholarly journal in Italian literature, history and culture.

STANFORD LITERATURE REVIEW. Vol. 1, No. 1 (Spring 1984)-. Periodical. US. English. sa. $30.00. Anma Libri, PO Box 876, Saratoga CA 95070. **Tel** (415)851-3375. **Ed** D Wellbery. adv acc. University research journal in comparative literature and literary theory.

STARMONT STUDIES IN LITERARY CRITICISM (MERCER ISLAND, WASH.). (STARMONT STUDIES IN LITERARY CRITICISM). 1-. 0737-1306. Monographic Series. US. English. ir. Starmont House, Box 851, Mercer Valley WA 98040.

THE STATESMAN. 0039-0313. Periodical. PK. English. wk. The Statesman, 260-C Commercial Area Pechs, Karachi 29 Pakistan. **Tel** 435627. **Ed** Mohammad Owais. **LC** AP8. **DD** 052. bk rev. adv acc. **Circ** 5,000. Contains information about international-affairs, economic-affairs, book reviews, sports and films.

STONE LION REVIEW. VFOAT Stone Lion. No. 1-. 0747-6744. Periodical. US. English. sa. $3.50. Stone Lion Review, 2 Divinity Avenue, Cambridge MA 02138. **Tel** (607)547-1422. **Ed** Elise A DeVido. **LC** DS1. **DD** 950.05. bk rev. adv acc. **Circ** 500. The journal wishes to offer a forum for both academic and popular writings in an attempt to reflect the diverse thinking of the community. We carry poetry, prose, interviews, photos, art, etc.

STONY HILLS. V. 1-. 0146-2067. Periodical. US. English. ty. $5.00. D Kruchkow, Weeks Mills, New Sharon NE 04955. **Ind/Abst** Book Rev. Index.

STUDIEN UND QUELLEN ZUR VERSGESCHICHTE. 1- 1966-. 0585-5810. Monographic Series. GW. German. ir. Wilhelm Fink Verlag, Ohmstrasse 5, 8 Muenchen 40 West Germany. **Tel** -89/348017-18. **Ed** Karl Bertau and Werner Schroder.

SVENSK TIDSKRIFT. V. 1- 1911-. 0039-677X. Periodical. SW. Swedish. mo. $12.64. Svensk Tidskrift, Linnegatan 28-30 IV, 11447 Stockholm Sweden. **Tel** (08)675955. **Ind/Abst** Am. Hist. Life, Hist. Abstr., Part A, Mod. Hist. Abstr., Hist. Abst., Part B, Twent. Century Abstr., Hist. Abstr. **LC** AP48. **DD** 058.7. (cum index).

SWEDISH BOOK REVIEW. 1983: 1 (Oct. 1983)-. 0265-8119. Periodical. UK. English. sa. Valerie Gustaveson, 260 East San Jose Avenue, Claremont CA 91711. **LC** PT9368. **DD** 839.709. *Swedish Books.*

SYN OG SEGN. V. 1-. 0039-7717. Periodical. NO. Norwegian. qt. Forlagsentralens Tidskriftaved, Postboks 6079 Etterstad, N-0601 Oslo 6 Norway. **Ind/Abst** MLA Int. Bibliogr. Books Artic. Mod. Lang. Lit. **LC** AP45. **DD** 058.3982.

SYRACUSE SCHOLAR. Vol. 1, No. 1 (Winter 1979-1980)-. 0276-6345. Periodical. US. English. sa. $10.00. Syracuse Scholar, Syracuse University, 125 College Place, Syracuse NY 13210. **LC** AS30. **DD** 051.

SZPILKI. Began in 1935. 0039-8152. Periodical. PO. Polish. wk. ARS Polona, Krakowskie Przedmiescie 7, 00-068 Warsaw Poland. **LC** AP54.

TAMKANG REVIEW. VFOAT Tan Chiang Ping Lun. V. 1-Apr. 1970-. 0049-2949. Periodical. CH. English (Chinese). qt. 11.00. Tamkang Review, Graduate School of Language and Literature, Tawkang University, Tamsui Taipei. **Tel** (02)6215656-329. **Ed** Chiu-Lang Chi. **Ind/Abst** MLA Int. Bibliogr. Books Artic. Mod. Lang. Lit., Years Work Eng. Stud. **LC** PL2250. **DD** 895.109. bk rev. adv acc. **Circ** 1,000. Publishes comparative studies of Chinese and foreign literatures, including the classical and modern literatures of East Asia and the West.

TEMPS MODERNES. (LES TEMPS MODERNES). Vol. 1, (No. 1-). 0040-3075. Periodical. FR. French. mo. 460.00. Editions Gallimard, 49 rue de la Vanne, 92120 Montrouge France. **Tel** 656 89 00. **Ind/Abst** MLA Int. Bibliogr. Books Artic. Mod. Lang. Lit., Annu. Bibliogr. Engl. Lang. Lit., Foreign Lang. Index, Am. Hist. Life, Hist. Abstr., Sociol. Abstr., Lang. Lang. Behav. Abstr., Hist. Abstr., Part A, Mod. Hist. Abstr., Hist. Abst., Part B, Twent. Century Abstr., Recent Publ. Artic. **LC** AP20.

THE TENNESSEE WILLIAMS REVIEW. Vol. 3, No. 1 (Spring 1981)-. 0276-993X. Periodical. US. English. sa. $6.00. Tennessee Williams Review, University of Michigan, 1079 East Engineering Building, Ann Arbor MI 48109. **Ind/Abst** MLA Int. Bibliogr. Books Artic. Mod. Lang. Lit. **LC** PS3545.I5365. **DD** 812.54. *Tennessee Williams Newsletter, 0732-0639.*

THE TEXAS REVIEW. V. 1- Spring 1980-. Periodical. US. English. sa. $4.00. Sam Houston State University, English Department, Huntsville TX 77341. **Tel** (713)294-1429. **Ed** Paul Ruffin. bk rev. adv acc. **Circ** 750. (ctrl). Poetry, fiction, essays, reviews, and interviews. *Sam Houston Literary Review.*

TEXTE (TORONTO). (TEXTE). 1 (1982)-. 0715-8920. Periodical. CN. French. an. $18.00. Texte Trinity College, Toronto Ontario M5S 1H8 Canada. **Tel** (416)978-2652. **Ed** B T Fitch and Andew Oliver. **LC** PN3. **DD** 809. **Circ** 1,000. Available on microfiche. Theory-orineted in French and comparative literature exploring, by theme, contemporary literary preoccupations. Contains analytical bibliography, index, contributions from major critics in each issue.

THE VILLAGE VOICE. VFOAT Voice. V. 1- Oct. 26, 1955-. 0042-6180. Periodical. US. English. wk. $32.76. Village Voice FCA, 842 Broadway, New York NY 10003. **Tel** (212)475-3300. **Ed** David Schneiderman. **Ind/Abst** Energy Inf. Abstr., Environ. Abstr., Music Index, Film Lit. Index, Book Rev. Index, Infobank, Media Rev. Dig. **LC** AP2. **DD** 071.471. bk rev. adv acc. **Circ** 151,828. Covers NYC, national and social issues. In-depth feature articles and editorial columns. Reviews films, plays, book exhibits and TV. Movies, plays, galleries and cultural events listings.

THIRD WORLD BOOK REVIEW. Vol. 1, No. 1-. 0265-1432. Periodical. UK. English. bm. $30.65. Third World Communications, Kwame Nkrumah House 173 Old Street, London EC1 England. **Tel** 01-608 0447. **Ed** Kofi Buenor Hadjor. bk rev. adv acc. **Circ** 2,000. Topical and informed discussion of issues and people in the Third World and is also the most comprehensive available review of all literature and publications about and from the Third World.

THE THOMAS HARDY SOCIETY REVIEW. V. 1- 1975-. UK. English. an. 12 Domestic, 15 Foreign. Thomas Hardy Society, Kate N Fowler, Park Farm, Tolpuddle Dorchester, Corset DT2 7HG England. **Tel** 455775. **Ed** J C Gibson. **LC** PR4752. **DD** 823.8. bk rev. adv acc. **Circ** 800. (ctrl). Articles, reviews, letters and reports on events such as lectures and walks related to Thomas Hardy.

TITLE INDEX OF CURRENT REVIEWS. 0739-4616. Periodical. US. English. mo. $55.00. Maureen Fennie-Collura, PO Box 403, Lewistown NY 14092. **Tel** (716)837-9315. **Ed** Maureen Fennie-Collura. **Circ** 150. Indexes book reviews from library review media: Booklist, Kirkus, Library Journal, Publisher Weekly, New York Times Book Review also Time Magazine, McNaughton Selections and Booking Ahead.

THE TOTH-MAATIAN REVIEW. VFOAT Toth Maatian Review. Vol. 1, No. 1 (Apr. 1982)-. 0740-7564. Periodical. US. English (French, German, Italian, Spanish, Russian). qt. $16.00 Domestic, $20.00 Foreign. 3101 20th Street, Lubbock TX 79410. **Tel** (806)797-2788. **Ed** Harold W Milnes. bk rev. **Circ** 250. Criticism and dissident opinion in science. Also in arts, humanities, religion and philosophy. Contains original learned papers in same subject headings.

TRANSACTIONS OF THE SAMUEL JOHNSON SOCIETY OF THE NORTHWEST. **Main/Corp** Samuel Johnson Society of the Northwest. 0828-6515. CN. English. an. 50.00 Domestic, $40.00 US. Samuel Johnson Society of the Northwest, c/o R H Carnie, University of Calgary, 2500 University Drive North West, Calgary Alberta T2N 1N4 Canada. **Tel** (403)220-4680. **Ed** W Magee and R H Carnie. **Ind/Abst** Abstr. Engl. Stud. **DD** 828.609. **Circ** 1,360. (ctrl). Research tool abstracting articles concerning literature (including literary criticism); abstracts indicate the contents of an article as concisely as possible and without editorial bias-quick guide to utility of an article.

TRIVIA. Vol. 1 (Fall 1982)-. 0736-928X. Periodical. US. English. ty. $18.00. Trivia, PO Box 606, North Amherst MA 01059. **Ed** Lisa Weil. **Ind/Abst** Altern. Press Index. **LC** HQ1402. **DD** 305.420973. bk rev. adv acc. **Circ** 5,000. Feminist theory and scholarship, critical essays, reviews, translations, experimental forms. Necessary sustenance for the labrys-toting mind.

TURKISH STUDIES ASSOCIATION BULLETIN. No. 1- Oct. 1976-. 0275-6048. Periodical. US. English. sa. $25.00. Turkish Studies Association, 1421 North Day Road, c/o M Hoell, Tucson AZ 85715. **Tel** (602)885-8049. **Ed** Alan W Fisher. (cum index). bk rev. adv acc. **Circ** 350. (ctrl). Articles, news, and reviews of Turkish and Ottoman studies. *Newsletter (Turkish Studies Association), 0275-6056.*

TWENTIETH-CENTURY LITERARY CRITICISM. **Main/Corp** Gale Research Company. V. 1- 1978-. 0276-8178. US. English. ir. $88.00. Gale Research Company, Book Tower, Detroit MI 48226. **Tel** (800)521-0707. **Ed** D Poupard and J Person. **DD** 809.04. Excerpts from representative criticism on the great novelists, poets and playwrights of the period 1900-1960.

THE UKRAINIAN REVIEW. V. 1- Dec. 1954-. 0041-6029. Periodical. UK. English. qt. $24.52. Association Ukrainians in Great Britain Ltd, 49 Linden Grds Notting Hill Gt, London W2 4HG England. **Tel** (01)229-0140. **Ed** Slava Sbecsko. **Ind/Abst** Am. Hist. Life, Hist. Abstr., Part A, Mod. Hist. Abstr., Hist. Abst., Part B, Twent. Century Abstr., MLA Int. Bibliogr. Books Artic. Mod. Lang. Lit., Hist. Abstr. **LC** DK508.A2. **DD** 947.7. bk rev. adv acc. **Circ** 1,100. (ctrl). Political magazine devoted to the study of Ukraine, including the religion and history of Ukraine.

ULBANDUS REVIEW. V. 1- Fall 1977-. 0163-450X. Periodical. US. English (Russian). sa. $6.00. Columbia University, Department of Slavic Languages, New York NY 10027. **Tel** (212)280-3941. **Ed** Richard Borden. **Ind/Abst** MLA Int. Bibliogr. Books Artic. Mod. Lang. Lit. bk rev. adv acc. **Circ** 500. Literary criticism, book reviews, and translations of Russian and other Slavic literatures.

UNIVERSITY OF PORTLAND REVIEW. **Main/Corp** Portland, OR. University. V. 1- June 1948-. 0041-9923. Periodical. US. English. sa. $1.00. University of Portland, 5000 North Willamette Boulevard, Portland OR 97203. **Tel** (503)283-7144. **Ed** Thompson M Faller. **Ind/Abst** Abstr. Engl. Stud. **LC** AS36. **DD** 378.795. bk rev. **Circ** 1,000. All literature which comments on the human condition and presents information on expanding knowledge in different fields, with relevance to the contemporary scene.

UNIVERSITY OF TORONTO REVIEW. V. 1- 1977-. 0708-4382. CN. English. an. University of Toronto Review, University of Toronto, 12 Hart House

Circle, Toronto Ontario M5S 1A6 Canada. **DD** C810.8092379.

UNIVERSITY OF WINDSOR REVIEW. (THE UNIVERSITY OF WINDSOR REVIEW). Began with Spring 1965 issue. 0042-0352. Periodical. CN. English (includes some text in French). sa. 10.00. University of Windsor, English Department, Dr Eugene McNamara, Windsor Ontario N9B 3P4 Canada. **Tel** (519)253-4232. **Ind/Abst** Am. Hist. Life, Hist. Abstr., Part A, Mod. Hist. Abstr., Hist. Abst., Part B, Twent. Century Abstr., Abstr. Engl. Stud., MLA Int. Bibliogr. Books Artic. Mod. Lang. Lit., Annu. Bibliogr. Engl. Lang. Lit., Can. Period. Index, Index Book Rev. Humanit., Years Work Eng. Stud., Hist. Abstr. **LC** AS42.W5. bk rev. **Circ** 600. (ctrl). Covers short fiction, poetry, reviews, some literary criticism.

UOMINI E LIBRI. IT. Italian. bm. 55.000. Edizioni Effe Emme, Viale E Caldara 8, 20122 Milano Italy. **Tel** 5463685. **Ed** Mario Miccinesi. **Ind/Abst** MLA Int. Bibliogr. Books Artic. Mod. Lang. Lit. **LC** PQ4001. bk rev. adv acc. **Circ** 7,500. Literary review of criticism and literary information.

UT REVIEW; A CONTINUING ANTHOLOGY OF POETRY *CEASED.* V. 1 V. 7, No. 2. US. English. **Ed** D Locke.

UTOPIAN CLASSROOM. Vol. 9, Issue 2 (Summer 1981)-. Periodical. US. English. qt. $12.00. Performing Arts Social Society, Box 1174, San Francisco CA 94101. **Tel** (415)566-6502. *Utopian Eyes, Storefront Classroom.*

VANDERBILT POETRY REVIEW *CEASED.* V. 1- Spring/Summer 1972-. 0363-2040. Periodical. US. English. sa. $4.50. Vanderbilt University, Box 5405 Station B, Nashville TN 37235. **Tel** (615)322-2975. **Ed** Mike Cornwell, Anthony Lathrop and E Thomas Wood. **LC** PN6099.6. **DD** 808.81. adv acc. **Circ** 3,000. Compilation of fiction, poetry, photography and interviews produced by the Vanderbilt community. Its appearance was widely hailed by the Nashville Press as an extension of the University's literary tradition.

VANDERBILT STREET REVIEW. Vol. 4 (1983)-. 0275-7672. US. English. an. $5.65. Vanderbilt Street Review, 911 West Vanderbilt Street, Stephensville TX 76401. **Tel** (817)968-4267. **Ed** Natrelle Young. bk rev. adv acc. **Circ** 400. The best of contemporary literature. Short stories, poetry and essays. *Vanderbilt Review of Prose and Poetry.*

VATRA. Periodical. US. Romanian. mo. Ilexim Press Department, PO Box 1-136-1-137, Bucharest Romania. **LC** Microfilm 05640 PC, PC800.

VELTRO. (IL VELTRO). Vol. 1- Apr. 1957-. 0042-3254. Periodical. IT. Italian (Summaries in English, French, German, and Spanish). bm. Veltro Editrice, Via S Nicola de Cesarini 3, 00186 Rome Italy. **Tel** (06)6565410. **Ind/Abst** Am. Hist. Life, Hist. Abstr., Part A, Mod. Hist. Abstr., Hist. Abst., Part B, Twent. Century Abstr., MLA Int. Bibliogr. Books Artic. Mod. Lang. Lit., Recent Publ. Artic. **LC** AP37. **DD** 055.1. (cum index). bk rev. adv acc. **Circ** 6,000. Original research in the areas of past and current Italian values and problems, reactions between Italy and other countries, cultures and societies.

VERDE OLIVO. Yearly V. 1- 1960-. 0506-6913. Periodical. CU. Spanish. wk. $57.78. Empresa Ediciones Cubanas, Sub-Direccion Exportacion, Oreilly 407 Ciudad Habana Cuba. **LC** AP63.

VERIDIAN. Vol. 1, No. 1 (July 1981)-. 0731-938X. Periodical. US. English. mo. $10.00. Veridian, PO Box 2324, Bloomington IN 47402.

VERTICE. Began in 1943?. 0042-4447. Periodical. PO. Portuguese. mo. Vertice, rua das Fangas 55 A2 PO, Coimbra Portugal. **Ind/Abst** MLA Int. Bibliogr. Books Artic. Mod. Lang. Lit. **LC** AP66. **DD** 056.9.

VICTORIAN PERIODICALS REVIEW. VFOAT V.P.R. Vol. 12, No. 1 (Spring 1979)-. 0709-4698. Periodical. CN. English. qt. $17.00. Southern Illinois University at Edwardsville, English Department, Edwardsville IL 62026. **Tel** (314)692-2256. **Ed** Barbara Quinn Schmidt. **Ind/Abst** Am. Hist. Life, Hist. Abstr., MLA Int. Bibliogr. Books Artic. Mod. Lang. Lit., Ref. Source, Recent Publ. Artic., Years Work Eng. Stud., Hist. Abstr., Part A, Mod. Hist. Abstr., Hist. Abst., Part B, Twent. Century Abstr. **DD** 052. bk rev. **Circ** 603. Historical, critical, bibliographical articles on the editorial and publishing history of Victorian newspapers, magazines, and reviews. *Victorian Periodicals Newsletter, 0049-6189.*

VIEW. V. 1- 1978-. Periodical. US. English. ir. Crown Point Press, 1555 San Pablo Avenue, Oakland CA 94612. **Tel** (415)835-5104.

THE VIRGINIA QUARTERLY REVIEW. V. 1- Apr. 1925-. 0042-675X. Periodical. US. English. qt. $10.00. Virginia Quarterly Review, 1 West Range, Charlottesville VA 22903. **Tel** (804)924-3124. **Ed** Staige D Blackford. **Ind/Abst** Am. Hist. Life, Hist. Abstr., Part A, Mod. Hist. Abstr., Hist. Abst., Part B, Twent. Century Abstr., Abstr. Engl. Stud., MLA Int. Bibliogr. Books Artic. Mod. Lang. Lit., Annu. Bibliogr. Engl. Lang. Lit., Writ. Am. Hist., Book Rev. Index, Index Book Rev. Humanit., Int. Index, Public Aff. Inf. Serv. Bull., Soc. Sci. Index, Index Am. Period. Verse, Humanit. Index, Book Rev. Digest, Years Work Eng. Stud. **LC** AP2. **DD** 051. (cum index). bk rev. adv acc. **Circ** 4,000. A national journal of literature and discussion.

VIRGINIA WOOLF MISCELLANY. VFOAT V.W.M. Vol. 1, No. 1 (Fall 1973). 0736-251X. Periodical. US. English. ir. $5.00. California State College at Sonoma, 1801 East Cotati Avenue, Department of English, Rohnert CA 94928. **Tel** (707)664-2140. **Ed** J J Wilson. **Ind/Abst** Abstr. Engl. Stud., MLA Int. Bibliogr. Books Artic. Mod. Lang. Lit. **LC** PR6045.O72. **DD** 823.912. bk rev. **Circ** 1,500. A modest newsletter keeping the Virginia Woolf scholars and lay readers and fans in touch with one another, coming out twice a year.

VISION. V.1- Nov. 1950-. 0042-6911. Periodical. MX. Spanish. sm. $52.00. Vision Inc, Suc en Mexico, Hamburgo #20, Deleg Cuauhtemoc, Mexico 06600 DF Mexico. **Tel** 531-3144.

VITCHYZNA; LITERATURNO-KHUDOZHNII ZHURNAL. 0042-7470. Periodical. UR. Ukrainian. mo. $38.00. Victor Kamkin Inc (74087), 12224 Parklawn Drive, Rockville MD 20852. **Tel** (301)881-5973. **LC** AP58.U5.

VYZVOLNYI SHLIAKH. VFOAT Liberation Path. 0042-9422. Periodical. UK. Ukrainian. mo. $40.00. Ukrainian Publishers Ltd, 200 Liverpool Road, London N1 1LF England. **Tel** 01 607 6266. **Ed** Illia Dmytriw. **Ind/Abst** MLA Int. Bibliogr. Books Artic. Mod. Lang. Lit. **LC** AP58.U5. bk rev. **Circ** 2,500. Ukrainian political, social scientific and literary magazine in Ukrainian language.

WALT WHITMAN REVIEW *CEASED.* V. 1- Jan. 1955-. 0043-017X. Periodical. US. English. qt. $4.00 Domestic, $4.60 Foreign. Wayne State University Press, Detroit MI 48202. **LC** PS3229. **DD** 811.3. (cum index).

THE WASHINGTON BOOK REVIEW. Vol. 1, No. 1 (Aug./Sept. 1981)-. 0277-2132. Periodical. US. English. bm. $12.00. Washington Book Review, PO Box 1998, Washington DC 20013. **LC** Z1035.A1. **DD** 028.1.

WASHOUT REVIEW. V. 1- Oct. 1975-. 0149-6077. Periodical. US. English. qt. $5.00. Washout Publishing Company, PO Box 2752, Schenectady NY 12309. **LC** PS580. **DD** 811.5408.

WEBSTER REVIEW. Vol. 1, No. 1 (Spring 1974)-. 0363-1230. Periodical. US. English. sa. $5.00. Webster Review, Webster University, 470 East Lockwood, Webster Groves MO 63119. **Tel** (314)432-2657. **Ed** Nancy Schapiro. **Ind/Abst** Index Am. Period. Verse. **LC** PN6010.5. **DD** 808.8. **Circ** 1,000. Publishes contemporary international stories, poems, essays and interviews. Emphasizes translations of the above from all languages into English. We look for high quality.

WEN HSUEH P'ING LUN. VFOAT Wenxue Pinglun. Began in 1959. Periodical. CC. Chinese. bm. 6.00. China Publication Centre, PO Box 2820, Beijing China. **Tel** 5007744/2638. **Circ** 50,000. (ctrl).

WEST COAST REVIEW OF BOOKS. V. 1- Oct./Nov. 1974-. 0095-3555. Periodical. US. English. bm. $15.00. West Coast Review of Books, 1501 North Hobart Boulevard, Los Angeles CA 90027. **Tel** (213)464-2662. **Ed** D David Dreis. **Ind/Abst** Book Rev. Index. **LC** Z1035.A1. **DD** 028.1. bk rev. adv acc. **Circ** 70,000. More than 100 reviews of the latest books plus articles and features.

WEST HILLS REVIEW. V. 1- Fall 1979-. Periodical. US. English. an. $5.00. Walt Whitmans Birthplace, 246 Old Walt Whitman Road, Huntington Station NY 11746. **Tel** (516)427-5240. **Ed** William Fahey. bk rev. **Circ** 500. Poetry, prose, art and photography in the tradition of Walt Whitman.

WESTERN WORLD REVIEW. V. 1- Dec. 1965-. 0043-4299. Periodical. US. English. qt. Western World Press, PO Box 366, Sun City CA 92381.

THE WESTIGAN REVIEW OF POETRY. V. 1- (No. 1-) 1970-). Periodical. US. English. ir. University of Utah, English Department, c/o Don Stap, Salt Lake City UT 84112. **Tel** (801)335-5914.

WILLIAM CARLOS WILLIAMS REVIEW. V. 6- Spring 1980-. 0196-6286. Periodical. US. English. sa. $8.00. Swarthmore College, English Department, c/o Peter Schmidt, Swarthmore PA 19081. **Tel** (215)447-7156. **Ed** Peter Schmidt. **Ind/Abst** Abstr. Engl. Stud., MLA Int. Bibliogr. Books Artic. Mod. Lang. Lit. **LC** PS3545.I544. **DD** 811.52. bk rev. adv acc. **Circ** 400. (ctrl). A journal devoted to publishing articles, reviews, unpublished writings, and other material relating to the life and work of William Carlos Williams (1883-1963). *William Carlos Williams Newsletter, 0099-216X.*

WISCONSIN REVIEW. 0043-6631. Periodical. US. English. ir. $4.00. University of Wisconsin-Oshkosh, Box 276 Dempsey Hall, Oshkosh WI 54901. **Tel** (414)424-2267. **Ed** Particia Haebig and Debbie Guenther. **LC** AP2. **DD** 051. bk rev. **Circ** 2,000. (ctrl). We publish poetry in all forms, fiction to 5000 words, reviews, interviews, articles of literary interest and artwork that is suitable for offset printing.

WITTENBERG REVIEW OF LITERATURE & ART. VAT Wittenberg Review of Literature and Art. V. 1-. 0147-0868. US. English. Wittenberg Review of Literature & Art, Box 1 Recitation Hall/Whittenberg Univ, Springfield OH 45501. **LC** PS580. **DD** 811.5408.

THE WOMEN'S REVIEW OF BOOKS. Vol. 1, No. 1 (Oct. 1983)-. 0738-1433. Periodical. US. English. mo. $25.00. Wellesley College Center for Research on Women, Wellesley MA 02181. **Tel** (617)431-1453. **Ed** Linda Gardiner. **Ind/Abst** Book Rev. Index, Altern. Press Index. **LC** HQ1101. **DD** 028.1088042. bk rev. adv acc. **Circ** 9,000. We publish in-depth book reviews of books in all areas of women's studies and feminist writing, academic and general-interest, including reviews of poetry and fiction by women.

WORMWOOD REVIEW. (THE WORMWOOD REVIEW). V. 1- Winter 1960-. 0043-9401. Periodical. US. English. qt. Wormwood Review Press, PO Box 8840, Stockton CA 95208-0840. **Tel** (209)466-8231. **Ed** Marvin Malone. **Ind/Abst** Index Am. Period. Verse. **LC** PS580. **DD** 811.5408. (cum index). bk rev. **Circ** 700. Traditional to experimental poetry and prose-poems communicating the human situation in modern society. Includes small, press reviews.

WRITER'S DIGEST. V. 1, No. 4- Mar. 1921-. 0043-9525. Periodical. US. English. mo. $21.00. Writer's Digest, 9933 Alliance Road, Cincinnati OH 45242. **Tel** (513)984-0717. **Ed** Bill Brohaugh. **Ind/Abst** Read. Guide Period. Lit., Mag. Index, Access. **LC** PN101. bk rev. adv acc. **Circ** 187,277. Available on microfiche from Bell & Howell and on microfiche, microfilm and 16MM film from University Microfilms. Advice on how to become a published author. *Successful Writing.*

YALE REVIEW. V. 1-19, May 1892-Feb. 1911. Periodical. US. English. qt. $22.00. Yale University Press, 92A Yale Station, Journals Department, New Haven CT 06520. **Tel** (203)436-7583. **Ind/Abst** Humanit. Index.

YEARBOOK OF COMPARATIVE CRITICISM. *See* Yearbooks, Almanacs, Directories.

DIE ZEIT. Newspaper. German. wk. $39.00. Team Publications, 111 Merton Street/Suite 205, Toronto Ontario M4S 3A7 Canada. **Tel** (416)488-6100. **Ed** Haug V Kuenheim. adv acc. **Circ** 8,500. (ctrl).

ZEITSCHRIFT DER SAVIGNY-STIFTUNG FUR RECHTSGESCHICHTE. GERMANISTISCHE ABTEILUNG. Vol. 1 (1880)-. SZ. German. ir. Kunst & Wissen Erich Bieber, Dufourstrasse 51, CH-8008 Zurich Switzerland. **Ind/Abst** Recent Publ. Artic. Index in last issue of volume - attached. (cum index). *Zeitschrift fur Rechtsgeschichte.*

ZEITWENDE. VFOAT Zeitwende die Neue Furche. 39.- Yearly Vol. Periodical. GW. German. qt. $14.85. Barenreiter Verlag, Postfach 10 03 29, D-3500 Kassel West Germany. **Tel** 0567/30011-17. **Ed** Wolfgang Bohme. adv acc. **Circ** 700. (ctrl). Reviews with contributions of science, spirit and literature.

ZNAMJA. (ZNAMIA). Began with 1931 issue. 0044-4898. Periodical. UR. Russian. mo. $38.00. Victor Kamkin Inc (70331), 12224 Parklawn Drive, Rockville MD 20852. **Tel** (301)881-5973. **Ind/Abst** MLA Int. Bibliogr. Books Artic. Mod. Lang. Lit. **LC** AP50.

Literature

LITERATURE

3 SYMBOL FOR CENT PULP CEASED. VFOAT Pulp. Began with V. 1-5, No. 11. 0381-937X. Periodical. CN. English. bm. PO Box 48806 Station Bentall, British Columbia Canada.

5 GREAT ROMANCES. See Romance and Adventure.

13TH MOON. VAT Thirteenth Moon. V. 1- 1973-. 0094-3320. Periodical. US. English. sa. $13.00. 13th Moon, Box 309, New York NY 10025. Ed Marilyn Hacker. Ind/Abst MLA Int. Bibliogr. Books Artic. Mod. Lang. Lit., Index Am. Period. Verse. LC PS508.W7. DD 810.5405. bk rev. adv acc. Circ 1,500. A feminist literary magazine publishing work by women writers.

36 MANIERES. VAT TRENTE-SIX MANIERES. No. 1- Nov. 1978-. 0708-2495. Periodical. CN. French. $2.50 le no. Les Editions Trente-Six, CP 2114 Succursale B, Hull Que J8X 3Y3 Canada. DD 843.01.

A. 0147-7196. Periodical. US. English. sa. A Press Limited, Box 311, Laguna, NM 87026. Tel (505)988-1183.

A. (A : A JOURNAL OF CONTEMPORARY LITERATURE). Vol. 1, No. 1 (Fall 1976)-. 0732-4650. Periodical. US. English. an. $5.00. A /A Journal of Contemporary Literature, Box 42A510, York Station CA 90042.

AAA, ARBEITEN AUS ANGLISTIK UND AMERIKANISTIK. See Linguistics.

AATF NATIONAL BULLETIN. See Education (General).

AATSP PORTUGUESE NATIONAL NEWSLETTER. See Education (General).

ABBEY. V. 1, No. 1- Spring 1970-. Periodical. US. English. qt. David Greisman, 5011-2 Green Mountain Circle, Columbia MD 21044. Tel (301)730-4272.

ABHANDLUNGEN FUR DIE KUNDE DES MORGENLANDES. See Linguistics.

ABHINAYA. See Linguistics.

ABHIRUCI (NEW DELHI, INDIA). (ABHIRUCI). V. 1, No. 1 (Feb. 1981)-. Periodical. II. Hindi. qt. 15.00. Radhakrishna Prakashan, 2 Ansari Road Dariyagunj, New Delhi 110002 India. LC PK2030.

ABRATES. Main/Corp Associacao Brasileira de Tradutores. VAT Associacao Brasileira de Tradutores. Yearly V. 1- June 1976-. Periodical. Portuguese. ir. Assaciacao Brasileira de Tradutores, Av Almirante Barroso 97, 3 Andar, Rio de Janeiro Brazil. LC PN241.A1.

ABRIDGED READERS' GUIDE TO PERIODICAL LITERATURE (ANNUAL). See Indexes/Abstracts.

ABSTRACTS OF ENGLISH STUDIES. See Indexes/Abstracts.

ACLALS BULLETIN. VFOAT A.C.L.A.L.S. Bulletin. VAT Association for Commonwealth Literature and Language Studies Bulletin. Began publication in 1967. 0157-6283. Periodical. CN. English. ir. University of Guelph, Department of English, Professor G Douglas Killam, Guelph Ontario N1G 2W1 Canada. Ind/Abst Abstr. Engl. Stud., MLA Int. Bibliogr. Books Artic. Mod. Lang. Lit.

ACM GUIDE TO COMPUTING LITERATURE. Main/Corp Association for Computing Machinery. VAT Association for Computing Machinery Guide to Computing Literature. 1977-. 0149-1199. US. English. an. $10.00 Members, $25.00 Nonmembers. Association for Computing Machinery, PO Box 12105, New York NY 10249. LC QA75.5. DD 016.00164. Each edition indexes over 15,000 books, reports, theses, articles and papers from journals and proceedings from both ACM and other sources. Computing Reviews. Bibliography and Subject Index of Current Computing Literature, 0149-1202.

ACOPEL. Main/Corp Asociacion Colombiana de Profesores de Espanol Y Literatura a Nivel Superior. No. 1- Nov. 1971-. Spanish. ir. Calle 31 No 83B-150, Medellin Colombia. LC PC4018. DD 460.5.

ACTA LITERARIA. No. 1-. Periodical. CL. English and Spanish. an. $6.00 US. Universite de Conception, Educ Facul Human Y Arte, 2307 Concepcion Chile. Tel 34985 Anexo 2530. Ed Luis Munoz G. LC PN1. DD 809. bk rev. Circ 600. Theoretical Literary studies; critical, historical and bibliographical analyses, preferably related to Spanish literatures.

ACTA LITTERARIA ACADEMIAE SCIENTIARUM HUNGARICAE. V. 1 (1957)-. 0567-7661. Periodical. HU. English (French, Italian, German, or Russian). qt. Akademiai Kiado, POB 24, 1363 Budapest Hungary. Tel 111-010. Ed G Tolnai. Ind/Abst Annu. Bibliogr. Engl. Lang. Lit., MLA Int. Bibliogr. Books Artic. Mod. Lang. Lit. bk rev. adv acc. Circ 550. Emphasis is laid on the relation between Hungarian literature and the literatures of other European countries in the Middle Ages, during the epochs of the renaissance, the reformation, the enlightenment, etc.

ACTAS DEL CONGRESO INTERNACIONAL DE HISPANISTAS. See Linguistics.

ACTS (SAN FRANCISCO, CALIF.). (ACTS). 1 (June 1982)-. 0749-3908. Periodical. US. English. David L Strauss, 324 Bartlett Street #9, San Francisco CA 94110. DD 818.

ADAB WA-NAQD. Periodical. UA. Arabic. ir. .50 Single issue. Hizb Al-Tajammu Al-Watani Al-Taqaddumi Al-Wahdawi, 1 Shari Karim Al-Dawlah, Al-Qahirah Egypt. LC PJ7501.

ADRIFT. No. 1 (Spring 1983)-. 0736-4970. Periodical. US. English. sa. $5.00. Adrift, 239 East 5th Street Apartment 4D, New York NY 10003.

AEB. ANALYTICAL & ENUMERATIVE BIBLIOGRAPHY. See Bibliographies.

AESTHETE. (THE AESTHETE). V. 1 March 1973-. 0381-6656. Periodical. CN. English. qt. $.75 Per No. Aesthete, c/o #1 378 Lafontaine, Vanier Ontario K1L 6X8 Canada. DD C810.80054.

AFKAR. 0515-5649. Periodical. PK. Urdu. mo. $34.01. Afkar Monthly, Robson Road, Karachi Pakistan. LC AP95.U7.

AFRICA. V. 1- (No. 1-). Periodical. Portuguese. ir. 140.00. Rua da Alcantara 53, Lisboa Portugal. LC PQ9900.

AFRICAN LITERATURE TODAY. No. 1- 1968-. 0065-4000. Periodical. UK. English. an. Africana Publishing Company, 30 Irving Place, New York NY 10003. Tel (212)254-4100. Ed E D Jones. Ind/Abst Abstr. Engl. Stud., MLA Int. Bibliogr. Books Artic. Mod. Lang. Lit., Humanit. Index. LC PL8010. DD 896. Bulletin of the Association for African Literature in English.

L'AFRIQUE LITTERAIRE. No. 54-55 (4th Quarter 1979-1st Quarter 1980)-. 0245-8160. Periodical. FR. French. qt $19.96. L'Afrique Litteraire SA, 2 rue Cretet, 75009 Paris France. Ind/Abst MLA Int. Bibliogr. Books Artic. Mod. Lang. Lit., Recent Publ. Artic. Afrique Litteraire et Artistique.

AFRO-HISPANIC REVIEW. See Linguistics.

THE AGE OF JOHNSON. 0884-5816. Periodical. US. English. an. $50.00. AMS Press Inc, 56 East 13th Street, New York NY 10003. Tel (212)777-4700. bk rev. Studies Samuel Johnson and his circle in all aspects of the age: literature, history, the arts, etc.

AICHI KENRITSU DAIGAKU BUNGAKUBU RON SHU : EIBUNGAKUKA HEN. VFOAT Bulletin of the Faculty of Literature, Aichi Prefectural University. No. 21- May. JA. Japanese. ir. 3-8 Takadacho Mizuho-Ku, Nagoya Japan. LC PE9. Aichi Kenritsu Daigaku Bungakubu Ron Shu: Gogaku, Bungaku.

AICHI KENRITSU DAIGAKU BUNGAKUBU RON SHU : IPPAN KYOIKU HEN. VFOAT Bulletin of the Faculty of Literature, Aichi Prefectural University. No. 21- May. JA. Japanese. ir. Aicha Kenritsu Daigaku, 3-28 Takadacho Mizuho-Ku, Nagoya Japan. LC AS552.A34.

AICHI KENRITSU DAIGAKU BUNGAKUBU RON SHU : KOKUBUNGAKUKA HEN. VFOAT Bulletin of the Faculty of Literature, Aichi Prefectural University. No. 21- May. JA. Japanese. ir. 3-28 Takadacho Mizuho-Ku, Nagoya Japan. LC PL700.

Aichi Kenritsu Daigaku Bungakubu Ron Shu: Gogaku, Bungaku.

AKTUALNYE PROBLEMY LEKSIKOLOGII I SLOVOOBRAZOVANIIA. See Linguistics.

AKZENTE. Vol. 1-. 0002-3957. Periodical. GW. German. bm. $20.94. Carl Hanser Verlag, Postfach 860420, Kolbergerstr 22, 8 Muenchen 86 West Germany. Tel 089/9 26 94-0. Ed W Hollerer and H Bender. Ind/Abst MLA Int. Bibliogr. Books Artic. Mod. Lang. Lit. LC PT1141.A2. DD 830.8.

AL-ADAB AL-AJNABIYAH. V. 1- July 1974-. Periodical. Arabic. ir. Ittihad Al-Kuttab Al-Arab, Shari Murshid Al-Khatir, PO Box 323, Dimashq Syria. LC PN9.

AL-ADIB AL-MUASIR. Periodical. Arabic. ir. 2. Ittihad Al-Udaba Fi Al-Iraq, Andalus Sq PO Box 217, Baghdad Iraq. LC PJ7501.

AL-FAJR AL-ADABI. VFOAT Fajr Al Adabi. Periodical. IS. Arabic. mo. $60.00 US. Al I Al-Khalili, S B 20517, Al-Quds Israel. Tel (02)283336. Ed Ali Khalili. bk rev. Circ 5,000. Concerns Palestinian literature, folklore, culture, and the arts published from the occupied territories.

AL-HIKMAH. V. 1- (No. 1-). Periodical. Arabic. mo. 125. Ittihad Al-Udaba, PO Box 98, Adan Yemen. LC PJ8001.Y4. Hikmah Al-Yamaniyah.

AL-KATIB AL-ARABI. V. 1, No. 1, (Nov. 1981)-. Periodical. Arabic. qt. Al-Amanah Al-Ammah Lil-Ittihad Al-Amm Lil-Udaba Wa-Al-Kuttab, S B 4091, Al-Arab Baghdad Iraq. LC PJ7625.

AL-MADINAH. See Linguistics.

AL-MAWQIF AL-ADABI. VFOAT Maoukef Al Adabi. V. 1-. Periodical. Arabic. ir. 1.00. Irrihad Al-Kuttab Al-Arab, Shari Murshid Khatir, Dimashq Syria. LC PJ7501.

AL-SHARQ. HA-MIZRAH. VFOAT Mizrah, The East. V. 1- Huzayran 1970-. Periodical. Arabic. ir. $20.00. Sahifat Al-Anba, PO Box 428, Al-Quds Israel. LC PJ8190.I8.

AL-TALIAH AL-ADABIYAH. Arabic. ir. Cinema Al-Khayyan Street, Baghdad Iraq. LC PJ7501.

AL-THAQAFAH. V. 1- Jan. 1975-. Arabic. ir. 2.00 Per Copy. Midhat Akkash, PO Box 2570, Dimashq Syria. LC PJ7501.

AL-THAQAFAH AL-AJNABIYAH. VFOAT Ath-Thkafa al-Ajnebiah. Began in 1980. Periodical. IQ. Arabic. bm. $14.00. Al-Thaqafah Al-Ajnabiyah Dairat Al-Shuun Al-Thaqafiyah, Wa-Al-Nashr Shari Sl-Khulafa, Baghdad Iraq BAGHD'AD, IRAQ. LC PN9.

AL-THAQAFAH AL-USBUIYAH. Periodical. Arabic. ir. 0.50 Single Issue. Shari Al-Arjantin, PO Box 2570, Dimashq Syria.

AL-VIDYU AL-ARABI. VFOAT Videoarab. No. 0-. Periodical. UK. Arabic. mo. $2.50. Tip: Trytel International Publications Ltd, 26/28 Agnes Road, London W3 7YF England. LC PN1992.95.

ALA BULLETIN : A PUBLICATION OF THE AFRICAN LITERATURE ASSOCIATION. Main/Corp African Literature Association. VFOAT A.L.A. Bulletin. Vol. 8, No. 1 (Winter 1982)-. 0146-4965. Periodical. CN. English. qt. 25.00. African Literature Association, University of Alberta Department of Comparative Literature, Edmonton Alta T6G 2E6 Canada. Tel (403)432-5535. Ed S H Arnold. LC PL8009.5. DD 809.8896. bk rev. adv acc. Circ 500. (ctrl). News about all aspects of African literature. DIASPORA LITERATURES AND LIBERATION STRUGGLES. ALA Newsletter.

ALA NEWSLETTER CEASED. Main/Corp African Literature Association. VAT African Literature Association Newsletter. V. 1-7. 0146-4965. Periodical. English. qt.

ALAKANANDA. August 1973-. Periodical. in Hindi. ir. 12.00. Ramasarana Dhaundiyala, G-375 Srinivaspur, New Delhi 110024 India. LC PK2047.

ALALUZ. Yearly Vol. 1- 1969-. 0044-7064. Periodical. US. Spanish. sa. $30.00. Professor Ana Maria Fagundo, University of California Department of Literature & Language, Riverside CA 92502. Tel (714)787-3406. Ed Ana Maria Fagundo. bk rev. Circ 500. A journal of contemporary poetry and short stories (Spain and Spanish American countries) are included.

Literature

ALAM AL-QISSAH YUSDIRUHA NADI AL-QISSAH BI-AL-ISKANDARIYAH. V. 1, No. 1 (Aug./Sept. 1979)-. Periodical. UA. Arabic. qt. 0.20 Single Issue. 8 Shari Talatharb, Al-Attarin Al-Iskandariyah Egypt. LC PJ7677. DD 892.730108.

THE ALAN REVIEW. VFOAT A.L.A.N. Review. VAT Assembly On Literature for Adolescents Review. Vol. 6, No. 2 (Winter 1979)-. 0882-2840. Periodical. US. English. ty. $10.00. National Council Teachers of English, 1111 Kenyon Road, Urbana IL 61801. Tel (217)328-2870. DD 028. *ALAN Newsletter.*

ALASKA QUARTERLY REVIEW. Vol. 1, No. 1&2 (Fall 1982)-. 0737-268X. Periodical. US. English. qt. 10.00. Alaska Quarterly Review, Department of English, 3221 Providence Drive, Anchorage AK 99508. Tel (907)786-1327. Ed Ronald Spatz and James Liszka. LC PN2. DD 809.03. bk rev. Circ 1,000. We publish fiction, poetry, traditional and experimental and literary criticism and reviews with emphasis on the relation between contemporary philosophy and literature.

ALCHEMIST. (THE ALCHEMIST). Began with Jan. 1975 issue. 0384-8523. Periodical. CN. English. ir. $10.00. The Alchemist, Box 123, Lasalle H8R 3T7 Quebec Canada. Ed Marco Fraticelli. DD C810.80054. Circ 500. (ctrl). A magazine of prose, poetry, haiku and graphics. We are looking for material which explores the possibilities.

ALEPH (MANIZALES, COLOMBIA). (ALEPH). VFOAT Revista Aleph. Began in 1966. 0120-0216. Periodical. CK. Spanish. qt. $100.00. Revista Aleph, Apartado Aereo No 1080, Manizales Colombia South America. Tel 640-85. Ed Carlos-Enrique Ruiz. LC AP63. DD 056.1. adv acc. Circ 2,000. Essays about subjects of literature and philosophy. Also includes interviews, poems, stories, manuscripts of important writers and cultural notices, Each edition includes a musical composition in serial form.

THE ALEXANDER LECTURES. Main/Corp Toronto. University. Alexander Foundation. (1929/30-). 0065-616X. Monographic Series. US. English. ir. University of Toronto Press Journals Department, 33 East Tupper Street, Buffalo NY 14203.

ALFOLD. V. 1956-. Periodical. HU. Hungarian. mo. Akademiai Kiado, POB 24, 1363 Budapest Hungary. Ind/Abst MLA Int. Bibliogr. Books Artic. Mod. Lang. Lit. LC AP82.

ALIF (CAIRO, EGYPT). (ALIF : JOURNAL OF COMPARATIVE POETICS). VFOAT Journal of Comparative Poetics. No. 1 (Spring 1981)-. Periodical. UA. Arabic (and English). an. $10.00. ALIF Department of English and Comparative Literature, The American University In Cairo, P O Box 2511, Cairo Arab Republic of Egypt. LC PN1. DD 809.

THE ALIGARH JOURNAL OF ENGLISH STUDIES. V. 1- 1976-. Periodical. II. English. sa. $6.00. Aligarh Muslim University, Department of English, Alegarh 202001 India. Ind/Abst MLA Int. Bibliogr. Books Artic. Mod. Lang. Lit. LC PR1. DD 820.9.

L'ALIGHIERI. Vol. 1- Jan./July 1960-. 0516-6551. IT. Italian. ir. Alighieri, Piazza Sonnino 5, 00153 Roma Italy. Ind/Abst MLA Int. Bibliogr. Books Artic. Mod. Lang. Lit. LC PQ4331.

ALINEA. 1/81-. Periodical. German. ty. 20.00. Redaktion Alinea, Postfach 37, CH-1700, Freiburg 6 Switzerland. LC PT1141.A2. DD 830.8.

ALIVE (GUELPH. 1980). (ALIVE : ANTI-IMPERIALIST CULTURE WORK IN THE SPIRIT OF NORMAN BETHUNE & LU XUN). No. 167 (May 1980)-. 0229-0251. Periodical. CN. English. ir. $12.50. Alive, PO Box 1331, Guelph Ontario N1H 6N8 Canada. DD C810.80355. *Alive Weekly Magazine, 0705-7369; Alive Magazine (1980), 0827-2573.*

ALL RARE MAGAZINE OF FANTASY. VFOAT All Rare. No. 1 (Spring 1980)-. 0737-4909. Periodical. US. English. qt. $16.00. Comicade Enterprises, P O Box 12, Buffalo NY 14205. LC P96.F46. DD 809.3876.

ALLC JOURNAL. VFOAT A.L.L.C. Journal. VAT Association For Literary and Linguistic Computing Journal. Vol. 1, No. 1 (Summer 1980)-. 0143-3385. Periodical. UK. English. sa. University of Hull, c/o Rex Last, Department of German, Hull HU6 7RX England. Ind/Abst MLA Int. Bibliogr. Books Artic. Mod. Lang. Lit., Lang. Lang. Behav. Abstr., Lang. Teach., Comput. Control Abstr., Electr. Electron. Abstr., Sci. Abstr. LC P98. DD 410.2854. CODEN AJOUDS.

ALLEGORICA. V. 1- Spring 1976-. 0363-2377. Periodical. US. English. sa. $10.00 Domestic, $12.00 Foreign. University of Texas at Arlington, Department of English, Arlington TX 76019. Tel (817)860-8702. Ed R Zacha and S Turbeville. Ind/Abst MLA Int. Bibliogr. Books Artic. Mod. Lang. Lit. LC PN661. DD 808.8002. bk rev. adv acc. Circ 250. Literal translations of Medieval and Renaissance literary works and documents unavailable in English or only in outmoded or inadequate translations - also articles and reviews.

ALLMENDE. 1981/No. 1-. 0720-3098. Periodical. German. ty. 19.80 Single Issue. LC PT1141.A2. DD 830.8.

ALMANACH DU CRIME. See Yearbooks, Almanacs, Directories.

ALMANAKH. (ALMANAKH . . . KLUBA RUSSKIKH PISATELEI). 80-. Periodical. US. Russian. an. $7.95. 20-44 Crescent Street Apt 2A, New York NY 11105. LC PG3516.

ALPHA. VFOAT Alpha Literary Journal. V. 1- Oct. 1976-. 0701-0656. Periodical. CN. English. mo. Acadia University, Students Union Building, Wolfville Nova Scotia Canada. DD C810.80054.

ALT- UND NEU-INDISCHE STUDIEN CEASED. Main/Corp Hamburg. Universitat Seminar fur Kultur und Geschichte Indiens. 1- 1928-. GW. German. ir. Franz Steiner Verlag GMBH, Postfach 347, D7000 Stuttgart 1 West Germany. Tel (0711)2582229. Ed L Schmithausen and A Wezcer. Ind/Abst Math. Rev. Monographs about Indian literatures and languages both ancient and modern.

ALTRI TERMINI. N. 1- May. 1972-. Periodical. Italian. ir. 4500. Via Edificio Soolastico 33, Marano Di Napoli 33 Italy. LC PN5.

AMANUENSIS. V. 1- Spring 1971-. 0044-7412. Periodical. US. English. sa. $2.00. LC PS501. DD 700.973.

AMAZING. (AMAZING : SCIENCE FICTION STORIES). VFOAT Amazing/Fantastic. Vol. 27, No. 9 (Nov. 1980)-. 0279-1706. Periodical. US. English. bm. $9.00. TSR Hobbies, PO Box 110, Lake Geneva WI 53147. Tel (414)248-3625. Ed George H Scithers. bk rev. adv acc. Circ 8,000. (ctrl). Offers a diverse range of science-fiction and fantasy stories by leading authors. Poems, artwork, book and film reviews included. *Amazing Stories, Fantastic, 0014-7508.*

AMBIT. VFOAT Ambit Magazine. No. 1 (Summer 1959)-. 0002-6972. Periodical. UK. English. qt. $15.00. Ambit, 17 Priory Gardens, London N6 England. Tel 01 340 3566. Ed Martin Bax. LC PR1098. DD 820.8. bk rev. adv acc. Circ 2,000. Britain's leading avante garde magazine, includes poetry, stories, drawings, and criticism, all direct from the late 20th Century. Compulsive reading and viewing.

AMERICAN HUMOR. V. 1-10, No. 2. 0193-7146. Periodical. US. English. sa. $13.00. M Thomas Inge, Department of English/Virginia Commonwealth University, Richmond VA 23284. Ind/Abst MLA Int. Bibliogr. Books Artic. Mod. Lang. Lit. LC PS438. DD 817.009.

AMERICAN LITERARY SCHOLARSHIP. Began with 1963. 0065-9142. US. English. an. Duke University Press, PO Box 6697, College Station, Durham NC 27708. Tel (919)684-2173. Ind/Abst MLA Int. Bibliogr. Books Artic. Mod. Lang. Lit. LC PS3. DD 810.

AMERICAN LITERATURE. V. 1- Mar. 1929-. 0002-9831. Periodical. US. English. qt. $22.00. Duke University Press, College Station, Box 6697, Durham NC 27708. Tel (919)684-2173. Ed Edwin H Cady and Louis J Budd. Ind/Abst Abstr. Engl. Stud., Annu. Bibliogr. Engl. Lang. Lit., Book Rev. Index, MLA Int. Bibliogr. Books Artic. Mod. Lang. Lit., Humanit. Index, Index Book Rev. Humanit., Ref. Source, Women Stud. Abstr., Writ. Am. Hist., Am. Hist. Life, Hist. Abstr., Part A, Mod. Hist. Abstr., Hist. Abstr., Part B, Twent. Century Abstr., Soc. Sci. Index, Years Work Eng. Stud., Hist. Abstr. LC PS1. DD 810.5. (cum index). bk rev. adv acc. Circ 4,500. A journal of literary history, criticism, and bibliography, covering the works of American authors, past and present.

AMERICAN LITERATURE, ENGLISH LITERATURE, AND WORLD LITERATURES IN ENGLISH. Monographic Series. US. English. ir $62.00. Gale Research, Book Tower, Detroit MI 48226. Tel (800)521-0707. Ind/Abst MLA Int. Bibliogr. Books Artic. Mod. Lang. Lit. A series of annotated bibliographies listing English-language sources in the field of American, English and world literature.

AMERICAN MAN. See Sociology: General Works, Theory.

AMERICAN NOTES AND QUERIES. SUPPLEMENT. VFOAT Studies in English and American Literature. V. 1-. Monographic Series. US. English. ir. Whitston Publishing Company, PO Box 958, Troy NY 12181. Tel (518)283-4363. Ed John Cotler and Lawrence Thompson. Ind/Abst Abstr. Engl. Stud., Humanit. Index. Circ 200. Material relevant to the journal-American Notes and Queries.

THE AMERICAN PEN. V. 1- Summer 1969-. 0003-0376. Periodical. US. English. qt. American Center of PEN, 48 5th Avenue, New York NY 10003. LC PN22. DD 80601. Available on microfilm from University Microfilms International.

THE AMERICAN RAG. V. 1- Fall 1978-. 0163-8211. Periodical. US. English. qt. $11.00. The American Rag c/o Frederick Douglass, Creative Arts Center Inc, 1 East 104th Street Suite 370, New York NY 10029. LC PS501. DD 700.5.

AMERICAN STUDIES IN SCANDINAVIA. See History (General) - History of North, South, and Central America.

AMERICAN UNIVERSITY STUDIES. SERIES I, GERMANIC LANGUAGES AND LITERATURE. See Linguistics.

AMERICAN UNIVERSITY STUDIES. SERIES IV, ENGLISH LANGUAGE AND LITERATURE. See Linguistics.

AMERICAN UNIVERSITY STUDIES. SERIES XIX, GENERAL LITERATURE. VFOAT American University Studies. Vol. 1-. 0743-6645. Monographic Series. US. English. ir. Peter Lang Publishing, 34 East 39th Street, New York NY 10016. DD 800.

AMERICAN UNIVERSITY STUDIES. SERIES XVIII, AFRICAN LITERATURE. VFOAT African Literature. Vol. 1-. 0742-1923. Monographic Series. US. English. ir. Peter Lang Publishing Company, 34 East 39th Street, New York NY 10016. LC UNC. DD 820.

AMERICAN VOICE (LOUISVILLE, KY.). (THE AMERICAN VOICE). No. 1-. 0884-4356. Periodical. US. English. qt. $12.00. Kentucky Foundation for Women Inc, Heyburn Building/Suite 1215, Broadway at Fourth Avenue, Louisville KY 40202. LC PAR. DD 813.

AMON HEN. Periodical. UK. English. bm. Tolkien Society, 11 Regal Way, Harrow Middlesex HA3 0RZ England. LC PR6039.O32. DD 828.91209. bk rev. (ctrl). The Society is dedicated to promoting research into, and educating the public in, the life and works of Professor J R R Tolkien.

AMPITOUFE. See Linguistics.

AMRTAYANA. VFOAT Amrutayan. Periodical. II. in Oriya. qt. 3.00. QR No VII R-1 Unit-1, Bhubaneswar 751009 India. LC PK2574.5.

AMSTERDAMER BEITRAGE ZUR ALTEREN GERMANISTIK. See Linguistics.

AMSTERDAMER PUBLIKATIONEN ZUR SPRACHE UND LITERATUR. Vol. 1-. Monographic Series. NE. German. ir. Humanities Press, Atlantic Highlands NJ 07716. Ed Cola Minis. Ind/Abst MLA Int. Bibliogr. Books Artic. Mod. Lang. Lit. Monographs in literature, written mainly in German.

AN-HUI WEN HSUEH. VFOAT Anhui Wenxue. Periodical. CH. Chinese. mo. China Publication Centre, PO Box 2820, Beijing China.

ANAHUTA. Periodical. II. in Hindi. ir. 5.00. Anahuta Phorama, 100 Satya Niketana, Nayi Dilli 110021 India. LC PK2030.

ANAIS (LOS ANGELES, CALIF.). (ANAIS). Vol. 1 (1983)-. 8755-3910. US. English. an. $7.00 Domestic, $8.00 Foreign. Anais Nin Foundation, 2335 Hidalgo Avenue, Los Angeles CA 90039. DD 818.

ANALELE STIINTIFICE. SERIE NOUA. SECTIUNEA III E, LINGVISTICA-LITERATURA. See Linguistics.

Literature

ANALELE UNIVERSITATII BUCURESTI : LITERATURA UNIVERSALA SI COMPARATA. Main/Corp Universitatea Din Bucuresti. VFOAT Literatura Universala Si Comparata. V. 18- 1969-. Romanian (some articles in French or German). ir. Ind/Abst MLA Int. Bibliogr. Books Artic. Mod. Lang. Lit. LC PN9. *Analele. Seria Stiinte Sociale: Filologie.*

ANALES CERVANTINOS. See Yearbooks, Almanacs, Directories.

ANALES DE LITERATURA HISPANOAMERICANA. See Yearbooks, Almanacs, Directories.

ANALES GALDOSIANOS. See Yearbooks, Almanacs, Directories.

ANALIZ STILEI ZARUBEZHNOI KHUDOZHESTVENNOI I NAUCHNOI LITERATURY. See Linguistics.

ANALOG ANNUAL. 1975-. 0362-7403. US. English. an. $1.50. Pyramid Books, 757 Third Avenue, New York NY 10017. LC PS648.S3. DD 808.8387605.

ANALOG SCIENCE FACT/SCIENCE FICTION. V. 1- Jan. 1930-. Periodical. US. English. mo. Ed J W Campbell.

ANALOG SCIENCE FICTION SCIENCE FACT. (ANALOG SCIENCE FICTION/SCIENCE FACT). VFOAT Analog. 0161-2328. Periodical. US. English. mo. $19.50. Davis Publications, 380 Lexington Avenue, New York NY 10017, (subscription address: Fulfillment Corp of America Box 1936 Marion OH 43305). Tel (212)557-9100. Ed Stanley Schmidt. Ind/Abst MLA Int. Access, Book Rev. Index. LC PZ1.A1, PN6120.95.S33. DD 823.087605. bk rev. adv acc. Circ 100,000. Novelettes and short stories by masters of science fiction. Hard science articles on new and newsworthy topics. Regular columns about timely, controversial issues.

ANALOG YEARBOOK. See Yearbooks, Almanacs, Directories.

I & L. IDEOLOGIES & LITERATURE. (I & L, IDEOLOGIES & LITERATURE). VFOAT Ideologies & Literature. VAT Ideologies and Literature. V. 1- (No. 1-). 0161-9225. Periodical. US. English (Spanish, Portuguese or French). ty. Institute for the Study of Ideologies and Literature, 4 Folwell Hall, 9 Pleasant Street SE, Minneapolis MN 55455. Tel (612)373-7998. Ind/Abst MLA Int. Bibliogr. Books Artic. Mod. Lang. Lit. LC PN51. DD 860.9.

THE ANDREJ BELYJ SOCIETY NEWSLETTER. No. 1 (1982)-. 0743-2410. Periodical. US. English. an. $10.00. University of California, Department of Literature and Linguistics, Riverside CA 92506. Tel (714)787-5726. Ed Olga Muller Cooke. adv acc. Circ 100. Abstracts, letters, bibliographies.

ANDVARI. 1.-. Icelandic. ir. (cum index).

ANGLIA. (ANGLIA : ZEITSCHRIFT FUR ENGLISCHE PHILOLOGIE). Vol. 1- 1878-. 0340-5222. Periodical. GW. German. qt. 158.00. Max Niemeyer Verlag, Postfach 21 40, 7400 Tuebingen 1 West Germany. Ed Helmut Gneuss. Ind/Abst Index Book Rev. Humanit., MLA Int. Bibliogr. Books Artic. Mod. Lang. Lit., Amers. Engl. Stud., Lang. Lang. Behav. Abstr., Annu. Bibliogr. Engl. Lang. Lit. LC PE3. (cum index). bk rev adv acc. Contributions on English (especially old and middle English) and American languages and literatures.

ANGLIA (TUBINGEN). BUCHREIHE. Monographic Series. GW. German. ir. Max Niemeyer Verlag, Postfach 2140, 7400 Tuebingen 1 West Germany. Ed Helmut Gneuss. Ind/Abst Sociol. Abstr., Lang. Lang. Behav. Abstr. Monographs on English literature and language.

ANGLISTISCHE FORSCHUNGEN. See Linguistics.

ANNALES BENJAMIN CONSTANT. No. 1-. 0263-7383. French. ir. 30.00 Membership. Voltaire Foundation, Taylor Institution, Oxford OX1 3NA England. LC PQ2211.C24. DD 848.609. *Cahiers Benjamin Constant, Bulletin de l'Association Benjamin Constant.*

ANNALES DE BRETAGNE. Vol. 1-80. 0003-391X. Periodical. FR. French. qt. $23.95. Universite Haute Bretagne, Avenue Gaston, 35 Rennes France. Ind/Abst MLA Int. Bibliogr. Books Artic. Mod. Lang. Lit. LC DC611.B841. (cum index).

ANNALES DE L'UNIVERSITE D'ABIDJAN. SERIE D : LETTRES. Main/Corp Universite D'Abidjan. VFOAT Litterature. V. 2-. 0587-4114. Monographic Series. IV. French. an. Ind/Abst MLA Int. Bibliogr. Books Artic. Mod. Lang. Lit. LC P25. DD 410.5. *Annales de L'Ecole des Lettres et des Sciences Humaines.*

ANNALES DU CENTRE DE RECHERCHES SUR L'AMERIQUE ANGLOPHONE. See Ethnic.

ANNALES - FONDATION MAURICE MAETERLINCK. Main/Corp Fondation Maurice Maeterlinck. VFOAT Annales de la Fondation M. Maeterlinck. V. 1- 1955-. 0531-9773. BE. French. an. M Robert Van Noffel, 123 Avenue des Statuaires, Uccle Bruxelles Belgium. LC PQ2625.A6. DD 848.809.

ANNALI DELLA SCUOLA NORMALE SUPERIORE DI PISA, CLASSE DI LETTERE E FILOSOFIA. Began in 1971. 0392-095X. Periodical. French (Italian). qt. $20.00. Scuola Normale Superiore, Pubblicazioni della Classe di Lettere, 56100 Pisa Italy. Ind/Abst MLA Int. Bibliogr. Books Artic. Mod. Lang. Lit., Am. Hist. Life, Hist. Abstr., Repert. Int. Litt. Art. LC AS222. DD 065.55. *Annali . . . Lettere, Storia e Filosofia.*

ANNALI DI CA' FOSCARI. VFOAT Annali Della Facolta di Lingue E Letterature Straniere di Ca Foscari. Vol. 1 1962-. Periodical. IT. Italian. ir. $11.88. Paideia Editrice, Via Corsica 130, 25123 Brescia Italy.

ANNALI D'ITALIANISTICA. Vol. 1 (1983)-. 0741-7527. Periodical. US. English (and Italian). an. $16.00. Annali D'Italianistica, 304 O'Shaughnessy Hall, Notre Dame IN 46556. Tel (219)239-7319. Ed Dino S Cervigni. LC PQ4001. DD 850.9. bk rev. adv acc. Circ 450. Promotes the study of Italian literature in its cultural context, monographic in nature, the journal is receptive to a variety of topics and critical approaches.

ANNALI - INSTITUTO UNIVERSITARIO ORIENTALE, SEZIONE GERMANICA. STUDI TEDESCHI. (ANNALI. STUDI TEDESCHI). VFOAT Studi Tedeschi, Aion Studi Tedeschi. 17 (1974)-. 0392-6532. Periodical. IT. German (Italian). ty. 10.000. La Sezione, International Book Center - Herder, Piazza Montecitorio 117-13 - Roma, Napoli Italy. Ind/Abst MLA Int. Bibliogr. Books Artic. Mod. Lang. Lit. LC PT5. DD 430.5. *Annali (Istituto Universitario Orientale (Naples, Italy)). Sezione Germanica.*

ANNALS OF THE BHANDARKAR ORIENTAL RESEARCH INSTITUTE. V. 1- 1918/20-. 0378-1143. II. English. an. $31.00. Indian Books & Periodical, 3341 Christian Colong, Pyarey Lal Road, New Delhi 110005 India. Tel 26 86 45. Ed R N Dandekar and G B Pabule. Ind/Abst MLA Int. Bibliogr. Books Artic. Mod. Lang. Lit. LC PK101. (cum index). bk rev. Circ 1,250. Research papers on various aspects of oriental studies in general and indology in particular.

L'ANNEE BALZACIENNE. 1960-1979. 0084-6473. FR. French. ir. Edition Garnier, 19 rue des Plantes, 75014 Paris France. Ind/Abst MLA Int. Bibliogr. Books Artic. Mod. Lang. Lit. LC PQ2177.A2. *Etudes Balzaciennes.*

L'ANNEE . . . DE LA SCIENCE-FICTION ET DU FANTASTIQUE. 1977-1978-. 0183-9950. French. an. Julliard, 8 rue Garanciere, Paris France. LC P96.S34. DD 808.83876.

ANNOTATED SECONDARY BIBLIOGRAPHY SERIES ON ENGLISH LITERATURE IN TRANSITION. See Bibliographies.

ANNUAL BIBLIOGRAPHY OF COMPUTER-ORIENTED BOOKS. See Bibliographies.

ANNUAL BIBLIOGRAPHY OF ENGLISH LANGUAGE AND LITERATURE. See Bibliographies.

ANNUAL BIBLIOGRAPHY OF VICTORIAN STUDIES. See Bibliographies.

ANNUAL REPORT - MALONE SOCIETY. (ANNUAL REPORT - THE MALONE SOCIETY). Main/Corp Malone Society, London. 1907-. 0580-5228. UK. English. an. Malone Society, 2 Church Street, Beckley Oxford England. LC PR621. DD 822.009.

THE ANNUAL WORLD'S BEST SF. VFOAT Donald A. Wollheim Presents the Annual World's Best SF. 1972 -. US. English. an. Daw Books Inc, 1301 Avenue of The Americas, New York NY 10019. Ed D A Wollheim. *World's Best Science Fiction.*

ANNUALE MEDIAEVALE. Series/Titl Duquesne Studies. V. 1-. 0066-4456. US. English. an. Humanities Press, Atlantic Highlands NJ 07716. Tel (201)872-1441. Ed B Beranek. Ind/Abst MLA Int. Bibliogr. Books Artic. Mod. Lang. Lit., Annu. Bibliogr. Engl. Lang. Lit., Years Work Eng. Stud. LC D111. DD 940.105. Critical essays on medieval literature.

EL ANO CULTURAL ESPANOL. Series/Titl Literatura Y Sociedad. 1979-. Spanish. an. Editorial Castalia, Zurbano 39, Madrid 10 Spain. LC PQ6001. DD 946.08305. *Ano Literario Espanol.*

ANTOLOGIA. Yearly V. 1- (No. 1-). Periodical. Spanish. ir. Ediciones Figaro, Av Ceballos 274, Chivilcoy Argentina. LC PQ7083. DD 860.

ANTOLOGIA A KANADAI MAGYAR IROK KONYVE. Main/Corp Kanadai Magyar Irok Kore. VFOAT Anthology of the Canadian Hungarian Authors' Association. 1- 1969-. 0319-521X. CN. Hungarian. an. J Miska, c/o Canada Agriculture Research Station, Lethbridge Alberta Canada. DD C894.51108003.

ANUARIO (ACADEMIA DE LETRAS DO ESTADO DO RIO DE JANEIRO). See Yearbooks, Almanacs, Directories.

ANUARIO DA LITERATURA BRASILEIRA. See Yearbooks, Almanacs, Directories.

ANUARIO DE LETRAS. See Yearbooks, Almanacs, Directories.

THE APALACHEE QUARTERLY. Periodical. US. English. qt. $14.00. Apalachee Quarterly, PO Box 20106, Tallahassee FL 32304. Tel (904)385-6859. Ed Barbara Hamby & Allen Woodman. bk rev. adv acc. Circ 500. Publishes the best in fiction, poetry and essays.

APPALACHIAN HERITAGE. V. 1- Winter 1973-. 0363-2318. Periodical. US. English. qt. $12.00. Appalachian Heritage, Hutchins Library, Berea College, Berea KY 40404. Tel (606)986-9341. Ed Sidney Saylor Farr. LC PS553. DD 810.80975. bk rev. Circ 700. A publication containing fiction, poetry, essays, interviews, and articles about southern mountain people.

L'APPRODO LETTERARIO. Vol. 4- (New Series). Periodical. IT. Italian. qt. Edizioni Rai Radiotelevisione Itlaiana, Via Arsenale 41, Torino Roma Italy. LC PN5. Index published separately - free - automatically sent.

APROPOS. (L'APROPOS). Vol. 1, No 1 (1983)-. 0823-6550. Periodical. CN. French. ty. 11. Apropos, C P 592, Alymer Quebec J9H 6L1 Canada. Tel (819)771-1701. DD C840.8097142. bk rev. Circ 1,000. French language prose and poetry from local and other contributors; literary reviews; interviews; drawings and cartoons.

APUNGO. V. 1- Feb./March 2029- 1973-. in Nepali. ir. 0.50 Per Issue. Loka Mana Maske, 12/76 Mills Area, Koshi Anchal, Viratanagara India. Ed Loka Mana Maske. LC PK2598.A2.

APUNTES. Periodical. Spanish. ir. Pontificia Universidad Catolica de Chile, Escuela de Teatro, Diagonal Oriente 3300, Santiago Chile. LC PN508. DD 862.009.

ARAISA. 1975-. Spanish. ir. Centro de Estudios Latinamericanos, Romulo Gallegos, Apartado Postal 29076, Caracas Venezuela. LC F1401.

ARARAT. V. 1- (No.1-). 0003-7583. Periodical. US. English. qt. $10.00. AGBU of America, 585 Saddle River Road, Saddle Brook NJ 07662. Tel (201)797-7600. Ed Leo Hamalian. LC AP2. bk rev adv acc. Circ 2,200. (ctrl). A literary quarterly covering Armenian subject matter including fiction, history, poetry, art, film, theatre, religion, dance, cooking, costume, and past and present cultural traditions.

ARBA SICULA. Vol. 1-. 0271-0730. Periodical. US. English (Italian, and Sicilianitalian). an. $6.00. Saint Finbar, 138 Bay 20th Street, Brooklyn NY 11214. Tel (718)331-0613. Ed Alissandro Caldiero and Gaetano Giacchi. LC PQ5902.S5. DD 850.809458. Circ 1,500. (ctrl). Proverbs, poetry, anecdotes, historical commentary; both contemporary and classical Sicilian.

ARCADE (MONTREAL, QUEBEC). (ARCADE). No. 1-. 0714-5926. Periodical. CN. French. sa. $3,00. Arcade a/s C Bertrand, Bureau 2 5010 Rue

Literature

De Lanaudiere, Montreal Quebec H2J 3R1 Canada. DD C840.80054.

ARCADIA. V. 1-. 0003-7982. Periodical. English (French or German). ty. $47.00. Walter de Gruyter & Company, 200 Saw Mill River Road, Hawthorne NY 10532. Tel (914)747-0110. Ind/Abst MLA Int. Bibliogr. Books Artic. Mod. Lang. Lit., Index Book Rev. Humanit. LC PN851. DD 809. bk rev. adv acc. Circ 800. The journal publishes papers on studies of comparative literature.

ARCHIPELAG : A. See Political Science - Socialism, Communism, Anarchism, Utopianism.

ARCHIV FUR DAS STUDIUM DER NEUEREN SPRACHEN UND LITERATUREN (1961). See Genealogy and Heraldry - Archives.

ARCHIV FUR LITERATUR UND VOLKSDICHTUNG. See Genealogy and Heraldry - Archives.

ARCHIVES DES LETTRES MODERNES. See Genealogy and Heraldry - Archives.

ARCHIVES D'HISTOIRE DOCTRINALE ET LITTERAIRE DU MOYEN AGE. See Genealogy and Heraldry - Archives.

ARIEL. V. 1- Jan. 1970-. 0004-1327. Periodical. CN. English. qt $16.00. University of Calgary, Department of English, 2500 University Drive, Calgary T2N 1N4 Alberta Canada. Tel (403)220-4657. Ed Ian Adam. Ind/Abst Abstr. Engl. Stud., Humanit. Index, MLA Int. Bibliogr. Books Artic. Mod. Lang. Lit., Index Book Rev. Humanit., Years Work Eng. Stud. LC PR1. DD 820.9. bk rev. adv acc. Circ 900. A review of Interantional English Literature. *Review of English Literature.*

ARIRANG (YEN-CHI SHIH, CHINA). (ARIRANG). VFOAT Arirang. Periodical. Korean. ir. LC PL998.C62.

THE ARIZONA QUARTERLY. V. 1- Spring 1945-. 0004-1610. Periodical. US. English. qt. $5.00. University of Arizona, Arizona Quarterly, 541 B Main Library, Tucson AZ. Tel (602)621-6396. Ed Albert F Gegenheimer. Ind/Abst Am. Hist. Life, Hist. Abstr., Part A, Mod. Hist. Abstr., Hist. Abst., Part B, Twent. Century Abstr., Abstr. Engl. Stud., MLA Int. Bibliogr. Books Artic. Mod. Lang. Lit., Annu. Bibliogr. Engl. Lang. Lit., Index Am. Period. Verse, Index Book Rev. Humanit., Abstr. Engl. Stud., Hist. Abstr., Years Work Eng. Stud. LC AP2. DD 051. bk rev. Available on microfilm from University Microfilms. Literary magazine designed for general literary audience- articles, stories, poems, and book reviews.

THE ARK RIVER REVIEW. V. 1- Spring 1971-. 0044-8885. Periodical. US. English. ir. $5.00. c/o Anthony Sobin, English Department WSU, Wichita KS 67208. Ind/Abst Index Am. Period. Verse. LC PS501. DD 810.80054.

THE ARMCHAIR DETECTIVE. V. 1- 1967-. 0004-217X. Periodical. US. English. qt. $20.00. Armchair Detective, 129 West 56th Street, New York NY 10019. Tel (212)765-0902. Ed Michael Seidman. Ind/Abst MLA Int. Bibliogr. Books Artic. Mod. Lang. Lit., Film Lit. Index. LC PS374.D4. (cum index). bk rev. adv acc. Circ 3,500. Devoted to detective and mystery fiction. Interviews, reviews, and critical articles about mystery fiction. Won an award for excellence from the Edgar Allan Poe awards committee.

THE ARNOLDIAN. Began with V. 3, Fall 1975. 0160-4848. US. English. sa. US Naval Academy, Department of English, Annapolis MD 21402. Ind/ Abst Abstr. Engl. Stud., MLA Int. Bibliogr. Books Artic. Mod. Lang. Lit. LC PR4023. DD 821.8. *Arnold Newsletter, 0094-5897.*

ARTFUL DODGE. Began in 1979. 0196-691X. Periodical. US. Multilingual. ir. $16.00. Artful Dodge, PO Box 1473, Bloomington IN 47402. Tel (812)332-0310. Ed Daniel Bourne. bk rev. adv acc. Circ 500. Publishes new American literature plus translations from all over, especially Eastern Europe. Interviews with Borges, Laughlin, Merwin, Milosz, Sarraute, etc. Sophisticated graphics.

ARTHUR RIMBAUD. Series/Titl La Revue des Lettres Modernes. 1- 1972-. French. ir. 30. Lettres Modernes, CCP 10671-19, Paris France. LC PN3. DD 841.8.

ARTS & LETTRES DU QUEBEC. VFOAT Arts et Lettres du Quebec. VAT Arts et Lettres du Quebec. Vol. 4 (1983)-. 0820-7232. CN. French. an.

7,00 per no. Arts & Lettres du Quebec, 6383 Avenue Faribault, Montreal Quebec H1N 1G5 Canada. DD C840.80054. *Cahiers d'Arts et Lettres du Quebec.*

ARXIU DE TEXTOS CATALANS ANTICS. See Bibliographies.

ASCENT. V. 1- 1975-. 0098-9363. Periodical. US. English. ty. $4.00. University of Illinois, Department of English, 100 English Building, Urbana Champaign IL 61801. Ind/Abst Index Am. Period. Verse. LC PS501. DD 810.8005.

ASHITA: GEKKAN HAISHI. Japanese. ir. 1000. Nashi No Shin No Kai, 14-30-704 Kami Osaki 3, Shinagawa-Ku (141), Tokyo Japan. LC PL759.A1.

ASPECT. No. 1- 0004-4911. Periodical. US. English. qt. $2.75 Per Copy. Aspect Inc, 66 Rogers Avenue, Somerville MA 02144. Ind/Abst Index Am. Period. Verse. LC PS1. DD 810.8.

ASPEN GROVE. No. 1. 0316-9022. Periodical. CN. English. 75. Brandon University, Department of English, Brandon Manitoba R7A 6A9 Canada. DD C810.5.

ASSAYS : CRITICAL APPROACHES TO MEDIEVAL AND RENAISSANCE TEXTS. Vol. 1- 1981. 0275-0058. US. English. an. University of Pittsburgh Press, 127 North Bellefield Avenue, Pittsburgh, PA 15260. Tel (412)624-4110. LC PN661. DD 809.02. Critical approaches to medieval and renaissance texts.

ATENS CONFERENCE REPORT. (A T E N S CONFERENCE REPORT). Main/Corp Association of Teachers of English of Nova Scotia. VAT Association of Teachers of English of Nova Scotia Conference Report. 1977-. 0705-8586. CN. English. an. Association of Teachers of English of Nova Scotia, c/o Nova Scotia Teachers Union, PO Box 1060, Armdale Nova Scotia B3L 4L7 Canada. DD 820.7.

ATQ. THE AMERICAN TRANSCENDENTAL QUARTERLY. VFOAT American Transcendental Quarterly. No. 37- Winter 1978-. 0149-9017. Periodical. US. English. qt. $14.00 Domestic, $15.00 Foreign. American Transcendental, University of Rhode Island, English Department, Kingston RI 02881. Tel (401)792-5931. Ind/Abst Abstr. Engl. Stud., MLA Int. Bibliogr. Books Artic. Mod. Lang. Lit. *American Transcendental Quarterly, 0003-1410.*

ATROPOS. V. 1- Spring 1978-. 0708-5389. Periodical. CN. English (includes some text in French). sa. $5.00 Domestic, $6.00 Foreign. Atropos Publishing, 325 Prince Edward Avenue, Otterburn Heights Quebec J3H 1W Canada. DD C810.80054.

AUKYEAME. V. 1- 1960?-. English. ir.

A.U.M.L.A. See Linguistics.

AURA. V. 1, No. 1- Fall 1974-. Periodical. US. English. sa. Aura, PO Box 76 University Center, University Station Birmingham AL 35294. Tel (205)934-3216. Ed Andrea Mathews. Circ 500. Publishes quality poetry, prose, and art by both published and unpublished writers and artists.

AURORA-BUCHREIHE. 1-. Monographic Series. GW. German. ir. Eichendorff-Gesellschaft, Fau Thorbeckeverlag, Postfach 546, 7480 Sigwamugen West Germany. Tel 07571/3016. Circ 1,000. Monographies on life and work of Joseph von Eichendorff and the romantic period.

AUSGEWAHLTE NEUERE LITERATUR. See Bibliographies.

AUSLANDSDEUTSCHE LITERATUR DER GEGENWART. Vol. 1-. Monographic Series. GW. German. ir. Georg Olms Verlag AG, Hagentorwall 7, D-32 Hildesheim West Germany. Tel 05121/37007. Ed Alexander Ritter. The development of German literature in foreign countries, such as US, Romania, Belgium and Israel.

THE AUSTRALIAN AUTHOR. Began with issue for Jan. 1969. 0045-026X. Periodical. AT. English. qt. $12.00. Australian Society of Authors, 22 Alfred Street Milsons Point, NSW 2061 Australia. Tel (02)92-7235. Ed Rob Pullan. LC PN101. DD 808.020994. adv acc. Circ 2,000.

THE AUSTRALIAN DIGEST. 0067-1843. AT. English. Methuen Law Book Company Ltd, 35 Mitchell Street, c/o Bennett-EBSCO, North Sydney New South Wales 2060 Australia.

AUSTRALIAN JOURNAL OF FRENCH STUDIES. V. 1- Jan./Apr. 1964-. 0004-9468. Periodical. AT. English (French). ir. $20.00. Monash University, Department of French, Clayton Victoria 3168 Australia. Tel (03)541-2217. Ed Wallace Kirsop. Ind/Abst Am. Hist. Life, Hist. Abstr., Part A, Mod. Hist. Abstr., Hist. Abst., Part B, Twent. Century Abstr., MLA Int. Bibliogr. Books Artic. Mod. Lang. Lit., APAIS, Aust. Public Aff. Inf. Serv., Hist. Abstr. LC PQ1. DD 840.9. (cum index). bk rev. Circ 530. History and criticism of French literature, French history and bibliography.

AUSTRALIAN JOURNAL OF READING. V. 1- Aug. 1978-. 0156-0301. Periodical. AT. English. qt. 25. Australian Reading Association, School of Education Flinders University, Bedford Park SA 5042 Australia. Ed Joelie Hancock. Ind/Abst Curr. Index J. Educ. bk rev. adv acc. Circ 4,000. (ctrl). Articles and reviews on the teaching of reading and related language arts.

AUSTRALIAN LITERARY STUDIES. V. 1- June 1963-. 0004-9697. Periodical. AT. English. sa. 18.00 Domestic, 22.00 Foreign. Australian Literary Studies, PO Box 88, St Lucia Queensland 4067 Australia. Ed Laurie Hergenhan. Ind/Abst MLA Int. Bibliogr. Books Artic. Mod. Lang. Lit., Annu. Bibliogr. Engl. Lang. Lit., Index Book Rev. Humanit., APAIS, Aust. Public Aff. Inf. Serv. LC PR9400. DD 820.9994. bk rev. adv acc. Circ 1,200. A critical, historical and bibliographical journal devoted to the study of Australian literature.

AUTHOR (LONDON, ENGLAND : 1949). (THE AUTHOR). Publication began with: Vol. 59, No. 3 (Spring 1949). 0005-0628. Periodical. UK. English. qt. Society of Authors, 84 Drayton Gardens, London SW10 England. Tel (01)373-6642. Ed Derek Parker. Ind/Abst Libr. Inf. Sci. Abstr. LC PN101. DD 808.02505. bk rev. adv acc. Circ 4,000. Covers authorship and relative business. *Author, Playwright and Composer.*

AUTHORS GUILD BULLETIN. May 1956-. 0404-3030. Periodical. US. English. ir. LC PN121. *Author's League Bulletin.*

AUTHORS IN THE NEWS. V. 1-. 0145-1499. US. English. ir. $72.00. Gale Research, Book Tower, Detroit MI 48226. Tel (800)521-0707. Ed B Nykoruk. LC CT220. DD 920.073. Two volumes offer a compilation of news stories, feature articles, profiles, etc., of over 500 writers, journalists, media people, etc.

AUTOBUS. Periodical. IT. in Italian. qt. 6000. Edizioni Lerici, Via del Babuino 96, Rome Italy. LC PQ4001. DD 808.8.

AVRORA. 0587-5927. Periodical. US. Russian. mo. $22.50. Victor Kamkin Inc (70033), 12224 Parklawn Drive, Rockville MD 20852. Tel (301)881-5973.

AWARD STORIES. STUDENT WRITING CONTEST. (AWARD STORIES : STUDENT WRITING CONTEST). Main/Corp Canada Permanent Trust Company. VFOAT Compositions Couronnees : Concours Litteraire Etudiant. 1975-. 0703-8631. CN. English (cover and prefatory material in French). an. Canada Permanent Trust Co, The Permanent Executive Offices/Room 1502, 320 Bay Street, Toronto Ontario M5H 2P6 Canada. DD C813.01.

AWP NEWSLETTER. Main/Corp Associated Writing Programs. VAT Associated Writing Programs Newsletter. 1967. 0194-6498. Periodical. US. English. bm. $10.00. Associated Writing Programs, Old Dominion University, Norfolk VA 23508. Tel (804)440-3840. Ed Mari Lonano. adv acc. Circ 8,500. Aspects of creative writing, teaching, and publishing as it relates to our membership.

BACONIANA. V. 1, May-Oct. 1892. Periodical. UK. English. an. $3.07. Francis Bacon Society, 56 Westbury Road, New Malden Surrey KT3 5AX England. Tel 01 942 6147. Ed N B Fermor. LC PR2941. bk rev. Circ 250. Studies and comments on Francis Bacon's philosophy, the vindication of his character, and the Bacon-Shakespeare authorship controversy. *Journal of the Francis Bacon Society.*

BAGAINCA. Annual 1, No. 1 (Jeshtha 2038 May/ June 1981)-. Periodical. NP. in Nepali. qt. 2.00. Bagainca Traimasika Karyalaya, 16/2 Thamela Tola, Kathmandu Nepal. LC PK2598.A2.

BAIKA REVIEW. in Japanese. ir. Baika Joshi Daigaku Ei-Bei Bungakukai, 171 Shukunosho (567), Ibaraki Japan. LC PR1.

Literature

THE BAKER STREET JOURNAL. V. 1-4, No. 1, Jan. 1946-Jan. 1949. 0005-4070. Periodical. US. English. qt. $12.50. Fordham University Press, University Box L, Bronx NY 10458. **Tel** (212)579-2320. Ind/Abst Abstr. Engl. Stud., MLA Int. Bibliogr. Books Artic. Mod. Lang. Lit., Annu. Bibliogr. Engl. Lang. Lit. LC PR4623. DD 823.8. (cum index). adv acc. **Circ** 1,600. An irregular quarterly of Sherlockiana, it contains articles on Sherlock Holmes and the Sherlockian scene.

BAKKA MAGAZINE. No. 3- Fall/Winter 1975-. 0702-1437. Periodical. CN. English. an. $2. Per No. Bakka Book Stores Ltd, 282-286 Queen Street West, Toronto Ontario M5V 2A1 Canada. **DD** 808.83876. Bakka, 0702-1429.

BALTO-SLAVIANSKIE ISSLEDOVANIIA. See Linguistics.

BAMLA CHOTA GALPA. Periodical. II. in Bengali. ir. 2.50. Svadesaranjana Datta, 18 Padmapukur Road, Calcutta-20, Kalakata India. LC PK1716.

BANG. Periodical. Spanish. ir. $1.50. Apartado De Correos 9331, Barcelona Spain. LC PN6700.

BARBEQUE PLANET. 0364-2194. US. English. $0.50 Per Copy. 4414 Illinois Avenue, Nashville TN 37209. LC PS501. DD 810.5.

BAROQUE. Issue 1- 1965-. Periodical. FR. French. ir. Baroque, 30 rue la Banque, 82 Montaudan France. Ind/Abst MLA Int. Bibliogr. Books Artic. Mod. Lang. Lit. Journees Internationales d'Etude du Baroque Actes.

BASAR CEASED. 1975-. Periodical. Norwegian. ir. 15.00. J W Cappelens Forlag, Postboks 6005, Etterstad Norway. LC PT8301.

BASIS. See Philosophy.

BASLER STUDIEN ZUR DEUTSCHEN SPRACHE UND LITERATUR. See Linguistics.

THE BAUM BUGLE. 0005-6677. Periodical. US. English. ir. $10.00. International Wizard of Oz Club Inc, 220 North 11th Street, Escauba MI 49829. Ind/Abst MLA Int. Bibliogr. Books Artic. Mod. Lang. Lit., Ref. Source. LC PS3503.A923. DD 812.4.

BAY ZIK. (BAY ZIKH). VFOAT By Zich. No. 1- 1972-. 0302-8178. Yiddish. ir. Komitet Jar Yidisher Kultur in Yisroel, 228 Bnei Ephraim Street Maoz Aviv, Tel Aviv Israel. LC PJ5161.A1.

BCTLA REVIEWS. VAT British Columbia Teacher-Librarians Association Reviews. Vol. 9, No. 1 (Oct. 1983)-. 0826-5054. Periodical. CN. English. Free to members. BCTLA, 2235 Burrard Street, Vancouver British Columbia V6J 3H9 Canada. DD 028.105. B C S L A Reviews, 0700-5288.

BEACON REVIEW. 0730-5184. Periodical. US. English. qt. Le Beacon Presse, 2511 1/2 E Yeslar Way, Seattle WA 98122.

BEAU-COCOA. No. 1- Autumn 1968-. 0067-4737. Periodical. US. English. sa. c/o L Addison, PO Box 409, New York NY 10035. LC PS508.N3. DD 810.80896.

THE BECKETT CIRCLE. VFOAT Le Cercle de Beckett. V. 1- Spring 1978-. 0732-2224. Periodical. US. English. sa. Ohio State University, 4240 Campus Drive, Lima OH 45804. **Tel** (419)228-2641.

BEIHEFT ZUM BULLETIN JUGEND + LITERATUR. 13-. 0172-0910. Monographic Series. GW. German. ir. Eulenhof-Verlag Ehrhardt, Heinold Eulenhof, D-2351 Hardebek West Germany. Beihefte Zum Bulletin Jugend + Literatur.

BEITRAGE ZUR GESCHICHTE DER DEUTSCHEN SPRACHE UND LITERATUR. See Linguistics.

BEITRAGE ZUR LITERATUR DES XV. BIS XVIII. JAHRHUNDERTS. Vol. 1-. Monographic Series. GW. German or English. ir. Franz Steiner Verlag GMBH, Postfach 347, D7000 Stuttgart 1 West Germany.

BELOIT FICTION JOURNAL. Vol. 1, No. 1 (Fall 1985)-. 0883-9131. Periodical. US. English. sa. $9.00. Beloit Fiction Journal, Beloit College, PO Box 11, Beloit WI 53511. DD 813.

THE BENIN REVIEW. No. 1- June 1974-. Periodical. NR. English. sa. $12.00. Ethiope Publishing Corporation, PMB 1192, Benin City Nigeria. Ind/Abst MLA Int. Bibliogr. Books Artic. Mod. Lang. Lit. LC PR9344.5. DD 820.8096.

BERENICE. Yearly V. 1, 1 (Nov. 1980)-. IT. French (and Italian). ty. Lucaarini, Viale Mazzini 146, 00195 Roma Italy. LC PQ2. DD 840.9.

BERITA PENDIDIKAN SASTRA DAN SENI. Main/Corp Institut Keguruan Dan Ilmu Pendidikan, Manado, Indonesia. Fakultas Keguruan Sastra Seni. Indonesian (English). ir. Institut Keguruan Dan ILMU Pendidikan, Jalan Jusuf Hasiru, Manado Indonesia. LC PN9.

THE BERKLEY SHOWCASE. V. 1- 1980-. US. English. Berkley Publishing Co, 200 Madison Avenue, New York NY 10016. Ed V Schochet and J Silbersack.

BESSATSU BUNGEI SHUNJU. VFOAT Bungei Shunju Bessatsu. Jan. 1946. Periodical. JA. Japanese. qt. 650 Per Issue. Bungei Shunju, 23 Kioi-Cho 3, Chiyoda-Ku 102, Tokyo-To Japan. LC AP95.J2.

BEST AMERICAN SHORT STORIES (BOSTON, MASS. : 1978). (THE BEST AMERICAN SHORT STORIES). 1978-. 0067-6233. Periodical. US. English. an. $14.45. Houghton Mifflin Company, Wayside Road, Burlington MA 01803. **Tel** (225)800-3362. Ed Robie Macauley. The best American short stories of the year as chosen by a distinguished writer of fiction. Previous judges include Gail Godwin, John Updike, Anne Tyler and others. Best American Short Stories . . . and the Yearbook of the American Short Stories (Boston, Mass. : 1975), 0067-6233.

BEST CANADIAN STORIES. 1977-. 0703-9476. CN. English. an. $12.95. Oberon Press, 401A Inn of the Provinces, Ottawa Ontario K1R 7S8 CANADA. Ed David Helwig. LC PZ1, PR9197.3. DD C813.01. Circ 2,000. Best short stories published annually. New Canadian Stories, 0316-7518.

BEST DETECTIVE STORIES OF THE YEAR CEASED. 1945-1981. 0067-625X. US. English. an. E P Dutton, 2 Park Avenue, New York NY 10016. LC PZ1. DD 813.5082.

BEST SCIENCE FICTION. 0091-9217. US. English. Ace Books, 1120 Avenue of the Americas, New York NY 10036. LC PZ1.A1, PS648.S3. DD 813.0876.

BEST SCIENCE FICTION OF THE YEAR. (THE BEST SCIENCE FICTION OF THE YEAR). No. 1- 1972-. 0095-7119. US. English. an. $1.50 Per Issue. Ballantine Books, 201 East 50th Street, New York NY 10022. LC PZ1.A1, PS648.S3. DD 813.0876.

BEST SCIENCE FICTION STORIES OF THE YEAR. 1st- 1972-. 0092-8119. US. English. an. Clarke Irwin & Co Ltd, 791 St Claire Avenue West, Toronto Ont Canada. **Tel** (416)654-3211. LC PZ1, PS648.S3. DD 813.0876.

BEST SELLERS. V. 1- Apr. 3, 1941-. 0005-9625. Periodical. US. English. mo. $18.00. Best Sellers, University of Scranton, Scranton PA 18510. **Tel** (717)961-7530. Ed Edward Gannon. Ind/Abst Book Rev. Index, Ref. Source, Cathol. Period. Index, Cathol. Period. Lit. Index, Book Rev. Digest. LC Z1007. DD 028. (cum index). bk rev. Circ 1,200. All book reviews: 120 a month, approximately. Children's literature section.

BEST SF. 1967-. US. English. an. Putnam, 301 East Erie, Chicago IL 60611. Ed H Harrison and B W Aldiss. LC PZ1.A1, PS648.S3. DD 823.9108.

THE BEST SHORT PLAYS. 1937-. 0067-6284. US. English. an. Chilton Book Company, PO Box Riverton NJ 08077. **Tel** (215)964-4000. Ed Margaret Gardner Mayorga. LC PN6120.A4. DD 812.5082. (cum index).

BEST WORLD SHORT STORIES. 1947-. 0737-8580. US. English. an. Appleton Century Crofts, 292 Madison Avenue, New York NY 10017. Ed John Cournos and Sybil Norton. LC PZ1. DD 808.831.

BHARATIYA VIDYA. See Religion, Mythology, Rationalism.

BHASHA. See Linguistics.

BHOJAPURI SAMSARA. V. 1- August 1977-. Periodical. in Bhojpuri. mo. LC PK1828.A2.

BIBLIOFANTASIAC. (THE BIBLIOFANTASIAC). 0821-7572. Periodical. CN. English. bm. $1.25 Per No. 802 Pape Avenue, Toronto Ontario M4K 3S7 Canada. DD C813.087608.

BIBLIOGRAFIA ESPANOLA. 1958-. 0523-1760. Periodical. SP. Spanish. Editora Nacional, Torregalindo 10, Madrid 16 Spain. LC Z2685.

BIBLIOGRAFIA LITERARNEJ VEDY A UMELECKEJ LITERATURY. KNIHY. See Bibliographies.

BIBLIOGRAPHIE DE LA LITTERATURE FRANCAISE DU MOYEN AGE A NOS JOURS. See Bibliographies.

BIBLIOGRAPHIE DER DEUTSCHEN SPRACH- UND LITERATURWISSENSCHAFT. See Bibliographies.

BIBLIOGRAPHIE DER FRANZOSISCHEN LITERATURWISSENSCHAFT. See Bibliographies.

BIBLIOGRAPHIE DES AUTEURS MODERNES DE LANGUE FRANCAISE (1801-19). See Bibliographies.

BIBLIOGRAPHIE LINGUISTISCHER LITERATUR. See Linguistics.

BIBLIOGRAPHIEN ZUR DEUTSCHEN LITERATUR DES MITTELALTERS. See Bibliographies.

BIBLIOGRAPHIES AND INDEXES IN AMERICAN LITERATURE. See Indexes/Abstracts.

BIBLIOGRAPHIES AND INDEXES IN WORLD LITERATURE. See Indexes/Abstracts.

BIBLIOGRAPHIES OF MODERN AUTHORS (SAN BERNARDINO, CALIF.). See Bibliographies.

BIBLIOGRAPHY OF AMERICAN LITERATURE. See Bibliographies.

BIBLIOGRAPHY OF ENGLISH LANGUAGE AND LITERATURE. See Bibliographies.

BIBLIOGRAPHY OF MODERN HEBREW LITERATURE IN TRANSLATION. See Bibliographies.

BIBLIOTECA ROMANICA HISPANICA. I. TRATADOS Y MONOGRAFIAS. 1- 1952-. 0519-7198. Monographic Series. SP. Spanish. ir. Editorial Gredos SA, Sanchez Pacheco 81, Madrid 2 Spain.

BIBLIOTECA ROMANICA HISPANICA. II. ESTUDIOS Y ENSAYOS. 1- 1950-. 0519-7201. Monographic Series. SP. Spanish. ir. Editorial Gredos SA, Sanchez Pacheco 81, Madrid 2 Spain.

BIBLIOTECA ROMANICA HISPANICA. III. MANUALES. 1- 1950-. 0519-721X. Monographic Series. SP. Spanish. ir. Editorial Gredos SA, Sanchez Pacheco 81, Madrid 2 Spain.

BIBLIOTECA ROMANICA HISPANICA. IV. TEXTOS. 1- 1950-. 0519-7228. Monographic Series. SP. Spanish. ir. Editorial Gredos SA, Sanchez Pacheco 81, Madrid 2 Spain.

BIBLIOTECA ROMANICA HISPANICA. V. DICCIONARIOS. 1- 1954-. 0519-7236. Monographic Series. SP. Spanish. ir. Editorial Gredos SA, Sanchez Pacheco 81, Madrid 2 Spain.

BIBLIOTECA ROMANICA HISPANICA. VI. ANTOLOGIA HISPANICA. 1- 1956-. 0519-7244. Monographic Series. SP. Spanish. ir. Editorial Gredos SA, Sanchez Pacheco 81, Madrid 2 Spain.

BIBLIOTECA ROMANICA HISPANICA. VII. CAMPO ABIERTO. 1- 1961-. 0519-7252. Monographic Series. SP. Spanish. ir. Editorial Gredos SA, Sanchez Pacheco 81, Madrid 2 Spain.

BIBLIOTECA ROMANICA HISPANICA. VIII. DOCUMENTOS. 1- 1962-. 0519-7260. Monographic Series. SP. Spanish. ir. Editorial Gredos SA, Sanchez Pacheco 81, Madrid 2 Spain.

BIBLIOTEKA ESTRADA. VFOAT Estrada. Periodical. UR. Bulgarian. LC PG1020.7.

Literature

BIBLIOTEKA OGONEK. Periodical. UR. Russian. wk. $16.00. Victor Kamkin Inc (70668), 12224 Parklawn Drive, Rockville MD 20852. Tel (301)881-5973. LC PG3201.

THE BIBLIOTHECK. See Bibliographies.

BIBLIOTHEK. Main/Corp Literarischer Verein in Stuttgart. Periodical. German. ir. Tel (711)63 82 64. (cum index). adv acc. Circ 900. Editions of old German literary texts 800 to 1,600.

BIBLIOTHEQUE D'HUMANISME ET RENAISSANCE. TRAVAUX ET DOCUMENTS. See History (General) - History of Europe.

BIBLIOTHEQUE RUSSE. See Linguistics.

BIG DEAL. No. 1- Spring 1973-. 0146-7042. US. English. an. $21.00. Barbara Baracks Big Deal, PO Box 830, Peter Stuyvesant Station, New York NY 10009. LC PS501. DD 811.5405.

BIKHAMA. Vol. 1, No. 1-. Periodical. II. Nepali. qt. 2.00. Bikhama Parivara Rincheupong, W Sikkim India. Ed hari Shrestha Bandhu and Rincheupong, and W Sikkim. LC PK2598.A2. adv acc. Circ 500.

BIKORET U-FARSHANUT. VFOAT Criticism and Interpretation. 1- Mar. 1970-. Periodical. summaries in English. ir. Bar-Ilan University, Ramt Gan Israel. Tel (03)718619. Ed Avraham Shaanan. Ind/Abst MLA Int. Bibliogr. Books Artic. Mod. Lang. Lit. bk rev. Circ 500. (ctrl). Jewish studies in literature, linguistics, history and aesthetics.

BILINGUAL REVIEW. See Linguistics.

BINDU. Periodical. in Hindi. ir. 10.00. LC PK2047.

BIOGRAPHY. See Biographies.

BIRTHDAY BOOK. (THE BIRTHDAY BOOK). VFOAT Literary Storefront Birthday Book. No. 1-. 0228-3298. CN. English. an. $3.50 Per Issue. The Literary Storefront, #1-314 West Cordova Street, Vancouver BC V6B 1E8 Canada. DD C811.5408.

BISVARUPA. VFOAT Biswarupa. Periodical. in Oriya. mo. 4.50. Jagadish Rath 73, Kharabela Nagar Unit 3, Bhubaneswar 751001 India. LC PK2574.5.

BIULETYN POLONISTYCZNY. V. 1- (No. 1-). 0067-902X. Periodical. PL. Polish. qt. ARS Polona, Krakowskie Przedmiescie 7, 00-068 Warsaw Poland. LC PG7001.

BLACK AMERICAN LITERATURE FORUM. V. 10, No. 4- Winter 1976-. 0148-6179. Periodical. US. English. qt. Indiana State University, School of Education, c/o Joe Weixlmann, Terre Haute IN 47809. Tel (812)237-2970. Ed Joe Weixlmann. Ind/Abst Abstr. Engl. Stud., MLA Int. Bibliogr. Books Artic. Mod. Lang. Lit., Film Lit. Index, Ref. Source, Index Am. Period. Verse, Humanit. Index. LC E185.5. DD 810.9896078. bk rev. Circ 1,075. (ctrl). Critical and pedagogical essays on black american literature, bibliographies, interviews, book reviews, poetry, visual arts, etc. Negro American Literature Forum, 0028-2480.

BLACK BEAR. VFOAT Black Bear Review. 8756-0666. Periodical. US. English. sa. $5.00. Black Bear Publications, PO Box 373, Croydon PA 19020-0957. Tel (215)788-3543. Ed Ave Jeanne & Ron Zettlemoyer. bk rev. Circ 500. (ctrl). Literary magazine publishing well crafted contemporary poetry and artwork. Themes used are: war/peace, environmental, political and minorities.

BLACK MESSIAH. 0737-5522. Periodical. US. English. ty. $12.00. Vagabond Press, 1610 North Water Street, Ellensburg WA 98926. LC PS501. DD 810.8.

BLACK ORPHEUS. Vol. 1 Sept. 1957. 0067-9100. Periodical. NR. English. sa. Lagos University Press, Publishing Division, PO Box 132, Akoka-Yaba University Lagos, Lagos Nigeria. Ind/Abst MLA Int. Bibliogr. Books Artic. Mod. Lang. Lit. LC PL8000.

BLAKE. V. 11- (No. 41-). 0160-628X. Periodical. US. English. qt. $18.00 Foreign. University of New Mexico, Department of English, c/o Morris Eaves, Albuquerque NM 87131. Tel (505)277-3103. Ed Morris Eaves. Ind/Abst Abstr. Engl. Stud., MLA Int. Bibliogr. Books Artic. Mod. Lang. Lit., Index Book Rev. Humanit., Annu. Bibliogr. Engl. Lang. Lit., Int. Bibliogr., Annu. Romant. Bibliogr. LC PR4147. DD 760.0924. (cum index). bk rev. adv acc. Circ 800. Scholarly journal covering all material relevant to study of William Blake, 18th Century British poet, painter, and engraver. Blake Newsletter, 0006-453X.

BLAKE STUDIES CEASED. Began with V. 1-, Fall 1968-. Ceased V. 9, No. 1/2, 1980. 0006-4548. Periodical. US. English. sa. $7.50. Department of English, Memphis State University, Memphis TN 38152. Ind/Abst Abstr. Engl. Stud., MLA Int. Bibliogr. Books Artic. Mod. Lang. Lit. LC PR4147. DD 700.924. Available in reduced form or xerograph reprint from University Microfilm Library Services.

BLATTER + BILDER. See The Arts (General).

BLATTER DER CARL-ZUCKMAYER-GESELLSCHAFT. Began with issue for Nov. 1975. Periodical. German. ir. 36.00. Carl-Zuckmayer-Gesellschaft Hebbelstrasse 26, D-6500 Mainz 31 - Lerchenberg West Germany. LC PT2653.U33. DD 832.912.

BLM. BONNIERS LITTERARA MAGASIN. (BLM ; BONNIERS LITTERARA MAGASIN). VFOAT Bonniers Litterara Magasin. Vol. 10- 1941-. 0005-3198. Periodical. SW. Swedish. ir. 150. Ahlen & Akerlunds Forlags AB, Box 3263, Stockholm 3 S103-63 Sweden. Tel 08-229120. Ed Lennart Hagerfos & Ola Larsuro. Ind/Abst Annu. Bibliogr. Engl. Lang. Lit. bk rev. adv acc. Circ 6. (ctrl). Essays and reviews concerning modern as well as classical literatures, swedish as well as international. Bonniers Litterara Magasin.

BLOODROOT (GRAND FORKS, N.D.). (BLOODROOT). No. 1 (Fall 1976)-. 0161-2506. Periodical. US. English. ir. Bloodroot, Box 891, Grand Forks ND 58201. Tel (701)772-8106. Ed Linda L Ohlsen. LC PS508.W7. DD 810.809287. Circ 800. (ctrl). Contents include short fiction and poetry.

BLUE BUFFALO. Vol. 1, No. 1 (Oct. 1982)-. 0820-8352. Periodical. CN. English. ir. $1.00 Per No. Blue Buffalo, 922-9th Avenue SE, Calgary Alta T2G 0S4 Canada. DD C810.8097123.

THE BLUE GUITAR. V. 1- 1975-. Periodical. IT. English (Italian). an. 30.-. Herder Editrice E Liberia, Piazza Montecitorio 121, Rome Italy. Ed Angela Giannitrapani. LC PR1098. DD 820.800914. bk rev.

BLUE MOON. 1984 Ed.-. 0743-2917. Periodical. US. English. an. $5.00. Red Herring Press, 1209 West Oregon Street, Urbana IL 61801. DD 813.

BLUELINE. VAT Blue Line. V. 1- Summer/Fall 1979-. 0198-9901. Periodical. US. English. sa. $5.00. Blueline, Attention: Alice Gilborn, Blue Mountain Lake NY 12812. Tel (518)352-7365. Ed Alice Gilborn. bk rev. Circ 700. Features quality prose, fiction and poetry about the Adirondacks and other areas similar in geography and spirit.

BLUESTONE : THE LITERARY QUARTERLY. No. 1- 1964-. 0006-5188. Periodical. US. English. ir. Woodstock Creative Arts, Box 355, Wookdstock NY 12498.

BOGG. Began in 1968. Periodical. US. English. ty. $7.50. John Elsberg, 422 North Cleveland Street, Arlington VA 22201. Ed John Elsberg. DD 820.

BOGUS REVIEW. 8756-8500. Periodical. US. English. an. Bogusbooks, 120 West 9th Street #10A, New York NY 10025. DD 810.

BOKREVY. Began in 1970. 0005-2833. Periodical. SW. Swedish. qt. Bibliotekstjanst AB, Box 1706, S-221 01 Lund Sweden. LC Z1035.5.

BOLETIM DE BIBLIOGRAFIA PORTUGUESA. PUBLICACOES EM SERIE. See Bibliographies.

BOLETIN - ACADEMIA NORTEAMERICANA DE LA LENGUA ESPAÑOLA. See Linguistics.

BOLETIN DE LA ACADEMIA CHILENA CORRESPONDIENTE DE LA REAL ACADEMIA ESPANOLA. See Linguistics.

BOLETIN DE LA ACADEMIA COLOMBIANA. See Linguistics.

BOLETIN DEL INSTITUTO AMIGOS DEL LIBRO ARGENTINO. Main/Corp Instituto Amigos del Libro Argentino. No. 1-14. Periodical. AG. Spanish. ir.

BOLLETTINO DI STUDI LATINI. See Linguistics.

BOMBAY GIN. 0160-4694. Periodical. US. English. LC PS501. DD 810.80054.

BONANTE CEASED. (LA BONANTE). No. 1-V. 10, No. 1. 0380-4860. CN. French. an. $1.50 Per No. Module des Lettres, Universite du Quebec a Chicoutimi, 930 East rue Jacques-Cartier, Chicoutimi Quebec G7H 2B1 Canada. DD C840.8092379.

BOOK FORUM. V. 1- Summer 1974-. 0094-9426. Periodical. US. English. qt. $20.00. Hudson River Press, PO Box 126, Rhinecliff NY 12574. Tel (212)861-8328. Ed Marshall Hayes. Ind/Abst Abstr. Engl. Stud., MLA Int. Bibliogr. Books Artic. Mod. Lang. Lit., Book Rev. Index. LC AS30. DD 052. bk rev. adv acc. Circ 4,400. Discussion of current literary and social issues as reflected in current scholarly books.

BOOKS IN KOREAN. Main/Corp Metropolitan Toronto Library Board. Languages Co-Ordinator. 0316-7445. Periodical. CN. English. qt. Languages Co-Ordinator, Metropolitan Toronto Library Board, 229 College Street, Toronto Ontario M5T 1R4 Canada. DD 016.8957.

BOOKS NOW. V. 1- July 31, 1978-. 0707-6924. Periodical. CN. English. wk. Free. Our Books Atlantic, PO Box 968, Halifax NS B3L 4K9 Canada. DD C810.809715. (ctrl).

BOREALIS. V. 1, No. 1-2. 0706-9014. Periodical. CN. English. qt. 10.00. Northern Star Press, PO Box 3174 South, Halifax NS B3J 3H5 Canada. DD C813.0876.

BOSS. 1- Summer 1966-. 0006-792X. Periodical. US. English. ir. Reginald Gay, Box 370 Madison Square Station, New York NY 10159. LC PN6010.5. DD 808.8.

BOSTON REVIEW (CAMBRIDGE, MASS. : 1982). See The Arts (General).

BOULEVARD (NEW YORK, N.Y.). (BOULEVARD). Vol. 1, No. 1 & 2 (Winter 1986)-. 0885-9337. Periodical. US. English. sa. $7.00. Suite 9R/4 Washington Square Village, New York NY 10012. DD 810.

BOUNDARY 2. VAT Boundary Two. V. 1- Fall 1972-. 0190-3659. Periodical. US. English. ty. $25.00. Boundary 2, SUNY-Binghamton, Binghamton NY 13901. Tel (607)777-2743. Ed William V Spanos. Ind/Abst Abstr. Engl. Stud., MLA Int. Bibliogr. Books Artic. Mod. Lang. Lit., Index Am. Period. Verse, Years Work Eng. Stud. LC PN2. DD 808.8004. bk rev adv acc. Circ 1,500. Publishes essays on contemporary critical theory and postmodern literature and culture.

BOX 749. VAT Box Seven Forty Nine. V. 1- Fall 1972-. 0364-3344. Periodical. US. English. ir. $7.00. Seven Square Press of the Printable Arts Society, Box 749, Old Chelsea Station, New York NY 10011. LC PS501. DD 810.5.

BRECHT-JAHRBUCH CEASED. 1974-1980. 0341-9525. GW. German (English). an. LC PT2603.R397. DD 832.912. Brecht Heute.

THE BRECHT YEARBOOK. See Yearbooks, Almanacs, Directories.

BRIDGE (BELGRADE, SERBIA). (THE BRIDGE). VFOAT Brucke. 1-56/58. 0006-9833. Periodical. YU. Serbo-Croatian (French and English). sm. Association of Groat Writers, Zadruzna Stamps Zagreb, Dalmatinska ULica 12 Yugoslavia. LC PG560. DD 891.8208.

THE BRITISH JOURNAL FOR EIGHTEENTH-CENTURY STUDIES. VFOAT British Journal for 18th-Century Studies. V. 1- Spring 1978-. 0141-876X. Periodical. UK. English. sa. 30.00. Voltaire Foundation, Taylor Institution, St Giles Oxford OX1 3NA England. Tel 0865 512931. Ed Dennis Fletcher. Ind/Abst Index Book Rev. Humanit. bk rev. adv acc. Circ 500. Covers all aspects of eighteenth-century studies. Newsletter -British Society for Eighteenth-Century Studies.

BRONTE NEWSLETTER. No. 1 (1982)-. 0737-6340. US. English. an. Bronte Society, 335 Grove Street, Oradell NJ 07649. LC PR4168. DD 823.909.

BRONTE SOCIETY PUBLICATIONS. TRANSACTIONS. (BRONTE SOCIETY TRANSACTIONS). 0309-7765. UK. English. an. $10.00. Keighley Printers, Custodian, Bronte Parsonage Haworth, Keighley West Yorks England. Ind/Abst Abstr. Engl. Stud., Annu. Bibliogr. Engl. Lang. Lit. LC PR4168. DD 823.809. Transactions and Other Publications.

BROWNING INSTITUTE STUDIES. (STUDIES). V. 1- 1973-. 0092-4725. US. English. an. $23.50. Browning Institute, PO Box 2983, Grand Central Station, New York NY 10163. Ed Adrienne Munich. Ind/Abst MLA Int. Bibliogr. Books Artic. Mod. Lang. Lit., Years Work Eng. Stud. LC PR4229. DD 821.805. adv acc. Circ 700. All aspects of

Literature

Victorian literary and cultural history. Bibliography of the Brownings and articles about their lives and works are regular features.

BROWNING SOCIETY NOTES. VFOAT Notes. V. 1- June 1970-. Periodical. UK. English. ty. $18.00. Browning Society of London, c/o Great Comp The Barn, Platt Nr Seven-Oaks, Kent TN 158QS England. Ed Paul Kenny and Joseph Bristow. Ind/Abst Abstr. Engl. Stud., MLA Int. Bibliogr. Books Artic. Mod. Lang. Lit., Years Work Eng. Stud. bk rev. adv acc. Circ 250. Literary-The Brownings, their circle and contemporaries.

BRUNTON'S MISCELLANY. V. 1- Autumn 1977-. Periodical. UK. English. ty. 4.95. Brunton's Miscellany, 28 A Dundas Street, Edinburgh EH3 6JN Scotland. LC PR8629. DD 820.5.

BUDDHIPRAKASA. Began publication in 1848. Periodical. Gujarati. ir. LC AP95.G8.

BUFANDA DEL SOL. (LA BUFANDA DEL SOL). 0304-1417. Spanish. ir. Editorial Universitaria, AP 11-32, Quito Ecuador. LC PQ7081.A1.

BUKARESHTER SHRIFTN. VFOAT Scrieri Bucurestene. Combined Vol. 1-. Periodical. Yiddish. ir. LC PJ5120.

BUKKU ENDO TSUSHIN. No. 2-. Periodical. Japanese. ir. Aoyama Tsuyoshi, 21-6 Hongyotoku, Ichikawa Japan. LC PL700.

BUKKYO BUNGAKU KENKYU. No. 1-12-Week, 1930 38-48-1963-73. Japanese. ir. Hozokan, Karasumaru Higashi Shimokyo-Ku, Kyota Japan. LC PL721.B8.

BULGARSKI EZIK I LITERATURA. V. 1- 1958-. 0525-096X. Periodical. BU. Bulgarian. qt. Hemus, 6 Boulevard Rusky, Sofia Bulgaria. LC PG801.

BULLETIN BIBLIOGRAPHIQUE DE LA SOCIETE INTERNATIONALE ARTHURIENNE. See Bibliographies.

BULLETIN DE LA SOCIETE DES AMIS DE MARCEL PROUST ET DES AMIS DE COMBRAY. Began in 1950. 0583-8452. FR. French. ir. Boite Postal 25, 28120 Illiers Combray France. Ind/Abst MLA Int. Bibliogr. Books Artic. Mod. Lang. Lit. LC PQ2631.R63. DD 843.912.

BULLETIN DE LA SOCIETE PAUL CLAUDEL. See Biographies.

BULLETIN DES AMIS D'ANDRE GIDE. Yearly V. 1- (No. 1-). Periodical. FR. French. qt. Association des Amis d'Andre Gide, Universite de Lyon II, 69500 Bron France.

BULLETIN DES AMIS DE MARCEL PROUST ET DES AMIS DE COMBRAY. No. 32-. French. ir. Societe des Amis de Marcel Proust et des Amis de Combray, BP 25, 28120 Illiers-Combray France. LC PQ2631.R63. DD 843.914. Bulletin de la Societe des Amis de Marcel Proust et des Amis de Combray.

BULLETIN D'INFORMATIONS ET DE RECHERCHES. L'AMITE CHARLES PEGUY. (BULLETIN D'INFORMATIONS ET DE RECHERCHES). Began with Jan./Mar. 1978 issue. 0180-8567. Periodical. FR. French. qt. 4 rue Auguste Bartholdi, 75015 Paris France. Ind/Abst MLA Int. Bibliogr. Books Artic. Mod. Lang. Lit. LC PQ2631.E25. DD 848.91209. Feuillets (Amitie Charles Peguy).

BULLETIN D'INFORMATIONS PROUSTIENNES. No. 1- Spring 1975-. 0338-0548. Periodical. FR. French. sa. $9.32. Presses de l'Ecole Normale, 45 rue d'Ulm, 75230 Paris France. Tel 329 1225. Circ 300. Analysis of Marcel Proust's manuscripts. Bibliography of Proustian studies. The perfect companion for the Proustomaniac.

BULLETIN HISPANIQUE. V. 1- Jan./Mar. 1899-. 0007-4640. Periodical. French (English, Italian and Spanish). ir. Bulletin Hispanique, Ed Biere, 18-22 rue du Peugue, 33 Bordeaux France. Ind/Abst MLA Int. Bibliogr. Books Artic. Mod. Lang. Lit., Recent Publ. Artic., Am. Hist. Life, Hist. Abstr., Hist. Abstr., Part A, Mod. Hist. Abstr., Hist. Abst., Part B, Twent. Century Abstr. LC PQ6001. DD 860.9. (cum index).

BULLETIN OF HISPANIC STUDIES. See Linguistics.

BULLETIN OF THE COMEDIANTES. Main/Corp Comediantes (Association). V. 1- March 1949-. Periodical. US. English or Spanish. sa. $14.00. Auburn University, Department of Foreign Languages, Auburn AL 36849. Tel (205)826-4345. Ed James Parr. LC PQ6098.7. DD 862.309. bk rev. adv acc. A journal which strives to advance criticism and scholarship dealing with the Comedia. It contains book reviews and forum sections. It has a distinguished editorial board, while retaining the Mentidero Section.

BULLETIN OF THE MIDWEST MODERN LANGUAGE ASSOCIATION. See Linguistics.

THE BULLETIN OF THE NEW YORK C. S. LEWIS SOCIETY CEASED. Vol. 1, No. 11-Vol.2, No. 4 (Whole No. 11-16). 0883-9972. Periodical. US. English. mo. $7.00. New York C S Lewis Society, 419 Springfield Ave, Westfield NJ 07092. Tel (201)233-4032. Ed Jerry L Daniel. Ind/Abst MLA Int. Bibliogr. Books Artic. Mod. Lang. Lit. LC PR6023.E926. DD 828. bk rev. Circ 500. (ctrl). Essays, reviews, notes regarding the life and works of C. S. Lewis along with discussions of modern scholarship about Lewis.

BULLETIN OF THE SCIENCE FICTION WRITERS OF AMERICA. VFOAT S.F.W.A. Bulletin. 0192-2424. Periodical. US. English. qt. $10.00. Science Fiction Writers of America, Box H, Peter Pautz, Wharton NJ 07885. LC PS374.S35. DD 813.087609. 0036-1364.

BULLETIN SIGNALETIQUE. 523. HISTOIRE ET SCIENCES DE LA LITTERATURE. See History (General) - History of Europe.

BULLETIN - SOCIETE CHATEAUBRIAND. Main/Corp Societe Chateaubriand, Chatenay-Malabry, France. No. 1-6, 1930-37. 0081-0754. FR. French. an. Societe Chareaubriand, 122 Boulevard de Courcelles, 75017 Paris France. LC PQ2206.Z5. DD 843.65. Circ 600. Unedited scholarly letters and documents from the best specialists of the French literature of Romanticism. Always contains current bibliography and whole page illustrations.

BUNGA RAMPAI ILMU SASTRA. No. 2-. Periodical. IO. English (Indonesian). sa. Fakultas Sastra Universitas Padjadjaran, Dipati Ukur 35, Bandung Indonesia. LC PN9. DD 809. Bunga Rampai Ilmu-Ilmu Sastra.

BUNGAKU KUKAN. 1- March 1979-. Japanese. ir. 980. Nijisseiki Bungaku Kenkyukai, Issued by Kenkyukai, c/o Hosei Daigaku 62-Nenkan, Ichigaya Tamachi 162, Tokyo Japan. LC PN9.

BUNGEI GENGO KENKYU : BUNGEIHEN. VFOAT Studies in Language and Literature: Literature. 1- 1976-. Japanese. ir. Ibarkai-Ken Niihari-Gun, Sakura-Mura Tsukuba Daigaku, Bungi Gengogukukei, Oaza Tsumaki 30031 Japan. LC PN9.

BUNGEI KAGOSHIMA. Began with Vol. for 1972. JA. Japanese. ir. 1 Shiroyamacho 1, Kagoshima 892 Japan. LC PL886.K272.

BUNGEI KENKYU. No. 1-. Periodical. JA. Japanese. an. Meiji Daigaku Bungei Kenkyukai, c/o Daigakuin 8-Kai Kanda Surugadai Chiyoda-Ku, Tokyo Japan. LC PN9.

BUNGEI TECHO. No. 1- 1975-. Japanese. ir. 650. Mei Pen Kurabu, c/o Mr Asano 9-55 Minami Marunsuchi, Tou Japan. LC PL886.M542.

BUNGEI YOKOHAMA. April 1972 Edition-. JA. Japanese. ir. Yokohama-Shi Kyoiku Iinkai, 1-1 Minatocho, Naka-ku, Yokohama Japan. LC PL887.Y64.

BUNRIN. Periodical. Japanese. ir. Shoin Joshi Gakuin Shoin, Joshi Gakuin Tanki Daigaku Gakujutsu Kenkyukai Shinohara Obanoyama-cho, 1-Chome Nada-ku, Kobe-shi 657 Japan. LC PL700.

BURNS CHRONICLE AND CLUB DIRECTORY. See Yearbooks, Almanacs, Directories.

BYE CADMOS. 1975-. 0363-5236. Periodical. US. English. sa. American Institute for Writing Research, PO Box 2129, New York NY 10017.

IL CAFFE; SATIRICO DI LETTERATURA E ATTUALITA. Began publication in 1953. 0007-9553. Periodical. IT. Italian. qt. Officina Edizione, Passeggiata di Ripette 25, 00186 Rome Italy.

CAHIERS - ASSOCIATION INTERNATIONALE DES ETUDES FRANCAISES. Main/Corp Association Internationale des Etudes Francaises. 0571-5865. FR. French. an. Societe Edition Belles Lettres, 95 Boulevard Raspail, 75006 Paris France. Ind/Abst MLA Int. Bibliogr. Books Artic. Mod. Lang. Lit.

CAHIERS CRITIQUES DE LA LITTERATURE. No. 1-4, Sept., 1976-Fall 1978. Periodical. FR. French. qt $15.00. Eurographic, 32 rue des Annelets, 75019 Paris France.

CAHIERS D'ANALYSE TEXTUELLE. Vol. 1 1959-. 0575-0466. Periodical. FR. French. an. Societe Edition Belles Lettres, 95 Boulevard Raspail, 75006 Paris France. Ind/Abst MLA Int. Bibliogr. Books Artic. Mod. Lang. Lit., Lang. Lang. Behav. Abstr., Sociol. Abstr. LC PQ53. (cum index).

LES CAHIERS DE LA NOUVELLE. No. 1 (Mar.1983)-. Periodical. French (English). ir. $16.00. Presses del'Universite Angers, Bibliotheque, Universite Boulevard Lavoisier, 49045 Angers Cedex France.

CAHIERS DE L'AMITIE HENRI BOSCO. No. 2- 1973-. Periodical. FR. French. an. $11.97. L'Amitie Henri Bosco, 76 1 des Baumettes, 06200 Nice France. bk rev. Bosco (Henri). Bulletin Henri Bosco.

CAHIERS DE L'EST CEASED. Began with No. 1 (Jan. 1975). Ceased with Jan. 1980 issue. Periodical. French. qt. LC PN849.E9. DD 809.8947.

CAHIERS D'ETUDES GERMANIQUES. No 3 (1979)-. 0751-4239. Periodical. French. an. 55 (Single Issue). Marie-Helene Varnier, Bibliotheque de l'Uer d'Etudes Germaniques Universite de Provence, 29 Avenue Robert Schuman, 13621 Aix-en-Provence France. LC PT2. DD 830.9. Etudes Germaniques (Universite d'Aix-Marseille. Centre d'Etudes Germaniques).

CAHIERS ELIE FAURE. 1 (1981)-. Periodical. French. an. Mme Chatelain, Le Roches Le Perreon, 69830 St Georges de Reneins, Cognac France. LC PQ2611.A86. DD 844.912.

CAHIERS ELISABETHAINS. VFOAT Bulletin du Centre d'Etudes et de Recherches Elisabethaines de L'Universite Paul Valery, Montpellier. No. 1- Jan. 1972-. 0054-7678. Periodical. FR. English (French). sa. 35.00. Centre d'Etudes et de Recherches Elisabethains, L'Universite Paul Valery, BP 5043, 34032 Montpellier France. Ind/Abst MLA Int. Bibliogr. Books Artic. Mod. Lang. Lit. LC PR1. DD 820.9003.

CAHIERS HENRI BOSCO. 21-. French. an. bk rev. Circ 500. (ctrl). Life, works of Henri Bosco, French author, XX's. Critical articles on Henri Bosco and French literature. Cahiers de l'Amitie Henri Bosco.

CAHIERS JEAN COCTEAU. 1- 1969-. 0068-5178. Periodical. FR. French. ir. Sodis, 128 Avenue Mare Hal de Lattre de Tassigny, 77400 Lagny France. Ind/Abst MLA Int. Bibliogr. Books Artic. Mod. Lang. Lit.

CAHIERS JEAN GIRAUDOUX. 1-. 0150-6943. FR. French. ir. 200 Domestic, $25.00 Foreign. Societe des Amis de Jean Giraudoux, 1 Bis rue Louis Jouvet, 87300 Bellac France. Tel 55.67.12.79. Ind/Abst MLA Int. Bibliogr. Books Artic. Mod. Lang. Lit. LC PQ2613.I74. DD 848.91209. bk rev. Circ 2,000. Unknown texts of Jean Giraudoux; specialized articles about Giraudoux's books, and international activities of the Association.

CAHIERS MARCEL PROUST. 1- 1927-. 0068-5186. Monographic Series. FR. French. ir. Sodis, 128 Avenue Marechal Lattre Tassigny, 77400 Lagny France.

CAHIERS PAUL LEAUTAUD. No. 1-. 0713-4258. Periodical. CN. French. ir. $4.00 Per Number. Association des Amis de Paul l'Eautaud, CP 606 Succursale N, Montreal Quebec H2X 3M6 Canada. DD 848.91209.

CAHIERS PAUL-LOUIS COURIER. No. 1- Nov. 1968-. 0084-8239. FR. French. ir. $11.44. Ste des Amis de PL Courier, 17 rue Claude-Debussy 37 Tours, CCP Paris France. Tel (47)20 22 66. bk rev. adv acc. Circ 300. (ctrl). To have known the life and work of Paul Louis Courier in honoring his memory.

CAHIERS ROUMAINS D'ETUDES LITTERAIRES. 1973- No. 1-. Periodical. RM. English (French or German). an. $58.00. Rompresfilatelia, PO Box 1362137, Bucharest Romania. Tel 001631 Telex. Ind/Abst MLA Int. Bibliogr. Books Artic. Mod. Lang. Lit. LC PN1. DD 805.

CAHIERS SAINT-EXUPERY. 1- 1980-. FR. French. ir. Gallimard, 5 rue Sebastien Bottin, Paris Cedex 7E France. LC PQ2637.A274. DD 848.91209.

CAHIERS SAINT-JOHN PERSE. Began in 1978. Periodical. French. ir. **Ind/Abst** MLA Int. Bibliogr. Books Artic. Mod. Lang. Lit. **LC** PQ2623.E386. **DD** 848.91209.

CAHIERS STAELIENS. 1929-1939. 0575-1276. Periodical. FR. French. sa. $6.15. Societe des Etudes Staeliennes, 148 rue de Longchamp, 75016 Paris France. **Tel** 222 49 39. **Ed** Norman King. **Ind/Abst** MLA Int. Bibliogr. Books Artic. Mod. Lang. Lit. bk rev. adv acc. **Circ** 500. Articles, reviews and documents concerning Germaine de Stael, Benjamin Constant and the Coppet Group.

CAHIERS VICTORIENS & EDOUARDIENS. **VFOAT** Cahiers Victoriens et Edouardiens. No. 6 (Mar. 1978)-. 0220-5610. Periodical. English (French). sa. Universite Paul Valery, BP 5043, 34032 Montpellier Cedex France. **Ind/Abst** MLA Int. Bibliogr. Books Artic. Mod. Lang. Lit. **LC** PR463. **DD** 820.9008. *Cahiers d'Etudes et de Recherches Victoriennes et Edouardiennes.*

CALEDONIAN (PRINCE GEORGE, B.C.). (CALEDONIAN). 0381-856X. Periodical. CN. English. ir. Free. Caledonian, 3330 22nd Avenue, Prince George British Columbia V2N 1P8 Canada. **DD** C810.8092379.

CALIBAN (TOULOUSE, FRANCE). (CALIBAN). Began in 1964. 0575-2124. FR. Multilingual (English or French, with a summary in the other language). an. Universite de Toulouse le Miral, Service des Publications, 56 rue du Taur, Toulouse France. **Ind/Abst** Abstr. Engl. Stud., MLA Int. Bibliogr. Books Artic. Mod. Lang. Lit. **LC** PR1. **DD** 820.9.

CALIFORNIA QUARTERLY. Began with Summer 1971 issue. 0045-3978. Periodical. US. English. qt. $10.00. University of California at Davis, 100 Sproul Hall, Davis CA 95616. **Tel** (916)752-1990. **Ed** Elliot L Gilbert. **Ind/Abst** Index Am. Period. Verse. **LC** NX1. **DD** 700.5. bk rev. adv acc. **Circ** 350. Publishes poetry and short fiction of the highest literary quality, with emphasis on stylistic distinction.

CALLALOO. No. 1 (Dec. 1976)-. 0161-2492. Periodical. US. English. ty. $12.00. University of Kentucky, English Department, Charles H Rowell, Lexington KY 40506. **Tel** (606)257-6984. **Ed** Charles H Rowell. **Ind/Abst** Abstr. Engl. Stud., MLA Int. Bibliogr. Books Artic. Mod. Lang. Lit. **LC** NX506. **DD** 700.8996075. bk rev. adv acc. **Circ** 1,000. Gives special attention to black south arts and literature. Also publishes black writers nationwide, and writers in the Carribbean and Africa.

CALLISTO RISING. Vol. 1, No. 1-. 0714-8011. Periodical. CN. English. ir. $1.00 Per No. Callisto Rising, c/o E B Klassen, 1329 Balmoral Road, Victoria British Columbia V8R 1L6 Canada. **DD** 809.387605.

CALYX. June 1976-. 0147-1627. Periodical. US. English. ir. $22.50. Journal of Art & Literature By Women, PO Box B, Corvallis OR 97339. **Tel** (503)753-9384. **Ed** Margarita Donnelly. **LC** PS508.W7. **DD** 810.809287. bk rev. adv acc. **Circ** 5,000. One of the most innovative and provocative feminist literary journals. "A first rate journal of art and literature by women." Bill Katz, Magazines for Libraries.

CAMBRIDGE QUARTERLY. (THE CAMBRIDGE QUARTERLY). V. 1- Winter 1965-. 0008-199X. Periodical. UK. English. ty. $45.00. Oxford University Press, Journals Department, Walton Street, Oxford OX2 6DP England. **Tel** (0865)56767. **Ed** D Gervais, R D Gooder, J Harvey, H A Mason, A P Newton, and W W Robson. **Ind/Abst** Abstr. Engl. Stud., MLA Int. Bibliogr. Books Artic. Mod. Lang. Lit., Annu. Bibliogr. Engl. Lang. Lit., Index Book Rev. Humanit., Humanit. Index, Years Work Eng. Stud. Index published separately - free - automatically sent. bk rev. adv acc. **Circ** 650. Principally devoted to literary criticism. Also publishes articles on painting, sculpture, music and cinema.

CAMEO. V. 1- Dec. 1979-. 0197-3363. Periodical. US. English. mo. $12.00. Public Enterprises Inc, 50 Rockefeller Plaza, New York NY 10020. **LC** PZ1, PS648.L6. **DD** 823.0080354.

CAMOES (LISBON, PORTUGAL). (CAMOES). 1 (July/August 1980)-. Periodical. PO. Portuguese. ir. 50.00 Single Issue. Editorial Caminho Sarl, R Cidade Quelimane, 3-C Olivais Sul, 1800 Lisboa Portugal. **LC** PQ9212. **DD** 869.12.

CAMP DE L'ARPA. Yearly V. 1- May 1972-. in Spanish. ir. 30. Valencia 72, Barcelona Spain. **LC** PN6.

CAMROSE REVIEW. (THE CAMROSE REVIEW). 1-. 0823-6712. Periodical. CN. English. ty. $8.00. Camrose Review, 3908-65 St Camrose, Alta T4V 3R9 Canada. **DD** C810.80054.

CANADIAN AUTHOR & BOOKMAN *CEASED.* (THE CANADIAN AUTHOR AND BOOKMAN). V. 17- April 1940-. 0008-2937. Periodical. CN. English. qt. $6.97. Canadian Authors Association, 24 Ryerson Avenue, Toronto Ontario M5T 2P3 Canada. **Tel** (416)364-4203. **Ed** Anne Osborne. **LC** PN101. **DD** 029.605. bk rev. adv acc. **Circ** 2,500. (ctrl). Articles of interest to new and established authors. Markets, book reviews; accepts poetry and short fiction entries. Awards and scholarships are also included. *Canadian Author, 0319-1524; Canadian Bookman, 0319-1532.*

CANADIAN CHILDREN'S LITERATURE. No. 1-. 0319-0080. CN. English (includes some text in French). ir. $10.83. Canadian Childrens Literature, Box 335, Guelph Ontario N1H 6K5 Canada. **Tel** (519)824-4120. **Ed** Mary Rubio and Elizabeth Waterston. **Ind/Abst** Abstr. Engl. Stud., Can. Period. Index, Book Rev. Index. **LC** PN1009.A1. **DD** C810.9928205. bk rev. adv acc. **Circ** 1,000. Articles and book reviews focus on themes of interest to readers of Canadian children's books.

THE CANADIAN C.S. LEWIS JOURNAL. No. 1- Jan. 1979-. Periodical. CN. English (and French). qt. $7.00. Canadian CS Lewis Journal, Dunsfold Godalming, Surrey GU8 4PF England. **Tel** 048 649 390. **Ed** Stephen Schofield. bk rev. adv acc. **Circ** 220. Usually, articles/items concerning C S Lewis.

CANADIAN ESSAY AND LITERATURE INDEX. *See* Indexes/Abstracts.

CANADIAN FICTION MAGAZINE. No. 1- Winter 1971-. 0045-477X. Periodical. CN. English. qt. $36.00. Canadian Fiction Magazine, PO Box 946/ Station F, Toronto Ontario M4Y LN9 Canada. **Ed** Geoffrey Hancock. **Ind/Abst** Abstr. Engl. Stud., Can. Period. Index, Can. Essay Lit. Index, J. Can. Fict., Abstr. Pop. Cult., MLA Int. Bibliogr. Books Artic. Mod. Lang. Lit. adv acc. **Circ** 1,000. Canada's finest contemporary short story periodical.

CANADIAN INDIA STAR. (THE CANADIAN INDIA STAR). **VFOAT** India Star. 0319-8715. CN. English. mo. 15.00 Domestic, 20.00 Foreign. Asia Times, 1433 Bloor Street West, Toronto Ontario M6P 3L6 Canada. **Tel** (416)533-8243. **Ed** S Singh. **DD** 954.005. bk rev. adv acc. **Circ** 5,000. (ctrl). News and views of South Asia. *India Star, 0317-2090.*

CANADIAN JOURNAL OF ITALIAN STUDIES. Began with issue for Fall 1977. 0705-3002. Periodical. CN. Italian (text also in English, with some text in French). qt. $15.00. Canadian Journal of Italian Studies, McMaster University, PO Box 1012, Hamilton Ontario L8S 1C0 Canada. **Ind/Abst** Am. Hist. Life, Hist. Abstr., MLA Int. Bibliogr. Books Artic. Mod. Lang. Lit. **LC** PQ4001. **DD** 850.9.

CANADIAN LITERATURE. **VFOAT** Literature Canadienne. No. 1- Summer 1959-. 0008-4360. Periodical. CN. English (includes some text in French). qt. University of British Columbia, #223-2029 West Mall, Vancouver BC V6T 1W5 Canada. **Tel** (604)228-2780. **Ed** William H New. **Ind/Abst** Humanit. Index. adv acc. **Circ** 2,000. Quarterly of criticism and review devoted to Canadian writers and writing in English and French. Now in its 25th year.

CANADIAN WRITER'S JOURNAL. June 1984-. 0827-293X. Periodical. CN. English. bm. $10.00. Canadian Writer's Journal, c/o Ronald J Cooke, 58 Madsen Avenue, Beaconsfield Quebec H9W 4T7 Canada. **DD** 808.0205.

CANADIAN WRITING NEWS BULLETIN. (CANADIAN WRITING NEWSBULLETIN). Vol. 1, No. 1 (Spring 1982)-. 0712-7413. Periodical. CN. English. sa. Free. Writers Union of Canada, 24 Ryerson Avenue, Toronto Ontario M5T 2P3 Canada. **DD** C810.5. (ctrl).

CANCELLED LEAVES. V. 1- Nov. 1978-. 0706-6899. Periodical. CN. English. ir. University of Western Ontario, School of Library and Information Science, London Ontario N6A 3K7 Canada. **DD** C811.5408.

CANSCAIP NEWS. **Main/Corp** Canadian Society of Children's Authors, Illustrators and Performers. **VAT** Canadian Society of Children's Authors, Illustrators and Performers News. V. 1- Fall 1978-. 0708-594X. Periodical. CN. English. qt. $11.61. CANSCAIP, Box 280 Station L, Toronto Ontario M6E 4Z2 Canada. **Tel** (416)922-7736. **Ed** Barbara Greenwood. **DD** C810.9928205. adv acc. **Circ** 800. Market information, profiles, columns of interest to professional writers, illustrators, performers, teachers and librarians in children's culture.

CANTO *CEASED.* V. 1, Spring 1977. Ceased with V. 4, No. 1. 0146-8995. Periodical. US. English. qt. $12.50. Canto, 9 Bartlet Street, Andover MA 01810. **LC** PN2. **DD** 805.

CAPILANO REVIEW. (THE CAPILANO REVIEW). 1/1 (Spring 1972)-. 0315-3754. Periodical. CN. English. ir. 10.00 Domestic, 11.00 Foreign. The Capilano Review, 2055 Purcell Way, North Vancouver British Columbia V7J 3H5 Canada. **Tel** (604)986-1911. **Ed** Dorothy Jantzen. **Circ** 550. Avante garde and experimental poetry, short drama, fiction, and visual art. Previously unpublished only.

CARFAX (HULL, QUEBEC). (CARFAX). No. 1 (March/April/May 1984)-. 0825-5326. Periodical. CN. French. qt. $10,00. Carfax A/S P D LaCroix, 56-B Rue Garneau, Hull Quebec J8X 1R8 Canada. **DD** 808.83876.

CARIB. No. 1 (1979)-. JM. English. an. $2.00 Membership Fee. David Williams Secretary/ Wiaclals English Department, University of the West Indies, Kingston 7 Jamica. **LC** PE3301. **DD** 409.729.

CARIBE. V. 1- Spring 1976-. 0148-9968. Periodical. US. Spanish. sa. $10.00. Department of European Languages and Literature, 1890 East-West Road, University of Hawaii, Honolulu HI 96822. **LC** PQ7081.A1. **DD** 860.

CARLETON GERMANIC PAPERS. V. 1- 1973-. 0317-7254. Periodical. CN. English (includes some text in French and German). an. 3.00. Carleton University, Department of German, Ottawa Ontario K1S 5B6 Canada. **Tel** 231-2605. **Ind/Abst** MLA Int. Bibliogr. Books Artic. Mod. Lang. Lit. **LC** PT1. **DD** 830.9. **Circ** 180. (ctrl). Learned journal with emphasis on Germanic literature (past and present).

CARLYLE NEWSLETTER. No. 1- March 1979-. UK. English. an. $12.00. Royal Military College, Department of English, c/o A Skabarnicki, Kingston Ontario Canada. **Tel** (613)545-7335. **Ed** Anne Skabarnicki, K J Feilding and Ian Campbell. **Ind/Abst** MLA Int. Bibliogr. Books Artic. Mod. Lang. Lit. bk rev. **Circ** 200. The newsletter focuses on Thomas Carlyle and his circle and informs readers of conferences, new publications, and advances in Carlyle studies.

CAROLINA QUARTERLY. Vol. 1 Fall 1948-. 0008-6797. Periodical. US. English. ty. $10.00. Carolina Quarterly, Greenlaw Hall/University North, Chapel Hill NC 27514. **Tel** (919)962-0244. **Ed** Emily Stockard. **Ind/Abst** Book Rev. Index, Index Am. Period. Verse, Index Book Rev. Humanit. (cum index). bk rev. adv acc. **Circ** 800. (ctrl). Available on microfilm from University Microfilms. Original fiction and poetry. Emphasizing control over language. Some artwork and photography.

THE CARRELL. V. 1- June 1960-. 0008-6894. US. English. an. $5.00 Single Issue. Friends University of Miami Library, Box 248214, Coral Gables FL 33146. **Tel** (305)284-4585. **Ed** Ronald P Naylor and Lawrence Donovan. **Ind/Abst** MLA Int. Bibliogr. Books Artic. Mod. Lang. Lit., Annu. Bibliogr. Engl. Lang. Lit., Years Work Eng. Stud. **Circ** 500. Original poetry, literary reviews, and art by faculty and students at the University of Miami and other places.

CARTE ITALIANE. Vol. 1 (1979-80)-. 0737-9412. US. English. an. $8.00. University of California, Department of Italian, 340 Royce Hall, Los Angeles CA 90024. **Tel** (213)825-1940. bk rev. adv acc. **Circ** 400. (ctrl). Scholarly publication of graduate student articles in all areas of Italian culture, focusing on literature and language.

CASA DE LAS AMERICAS. Yearly V. 1- (No. 1-). 0008-7157. Periodical. CU. Spanish. bm. Empresa Ediciones Cubanos, Obispo 461 Apartado 605, Clubao de La Habana Cuba. **Ind/Abst** Am. Hist. Life, Hist. Abstr., Part A, Mod. Hist. Abstr., Hist. Abst., Part B, Twent. Century Abstr., MLA Int. Bibliogr. Books Artic. Mod. Lang. Lit., Artbibliogr. Mod. **LC** PN6. **DD** 860.8098. *America.*

CASCADE (GREELY, ONT.) *CEASED.* (CASCADE). V. 1, No. 1 (Winter 1982)-No. 3 (Sept. 1982). 0821-641X. Periodical. CN. English. ir. $10.00. Cascade, PO Box 70, Greely Ontario K0A 1Z0 Canada. **DD** C813.087608.

CASSIOPEIA (BRAMPTON, ONT.). (CASSIOPEIA). Issue 1 (Feb. 1980)-. 0227-6127. Periodical. CN. English. ir. Free. Brampton Writers' Workshop, 25 Mordon Court, Brampton Ontario L6V 2B5 Canada. **DD** C810.80054.

CATALOG OF COPYRIGHT ENTRIES. FOURTH SERIES. PART 1. NONDRAMATIC LITERARY WORKS. *See* Copyright, Intellectual Property.

Literature

CATALOGO DEI PERIODICI ITALIANI. See Bibliographies.

CATALOGUS TRANSLATIONUM ET COMMENTARIORUM: MEDIAEVAL AND RENAISSANCE LATIN TRANSLATIONS AND COMMENTARIES. V. 1-. 0528-2594. US. English (Latin). ir. Catholic University of America Press, PO Box 4852, Hampden Station, Baltimore MD 21211. Tel (202)635-5052. LC Z7016. DD 016.88.

CATALYST. V. 1- March 1975-. 0381-5005. Periodical. CN. English (includes some text in French). $5. Domestic, $6. Foreign. Prison Arts Foundation, 143 5th Avenue, Brantford Ontario N3S 1A3 Canada. DD C810.80920692.

CATHEDRA. Spanish. ir. Ciudad Universitaria, Facultad de Filosofia y Letras de la Universidad Autonome de Nuevo Leon, Monterrey Mexico. LC AS63.N77.

CCLM NEWSLETTER. Main/Corp Coordinating Council of Literary Magazines. VAT Coordinating Council of Literary Magazines Newsletter. 1967. 0273-3315. Periodical. US. English. qt $5.00. CCLM News, 2 Park Avenue, New York NY 10016. Tel (212)481-5245. Ed Kevin Duffy. bk rev. adv acc. Circ 1,500. Publication of news, views and information for literary magazines, publishers, and writers. *Newsletter - CCLM, 0192-9887.*

THE CENTENNIAL REVIEW. (CR. THE CENTENNIAL REVIEW). VFOAT Centennial Review. V. 19- 1975-. 0162-0177. Periodical. US. English. qt. $5.00. Michigan State University, 110 Morrill Hall, East Lansing MI 48824. Tel (517)355-1905. Ed Linda Wagner. Ind/Abst Abstr. Engl. Stud., Sociol. Abstr., Annu. Bibliogr. Engl. Lang. Lit., MLA Int. Bibliogr. Books Artic. Mod. Lang. Lit., Index Am. Period. Verse, Writ. Am. Hist., Am. Hist. Life, Hist. Abstr. bk rev Circ 1,000. Concerned with the interrelations among the disciplines. *Centennial Review, 0162-0177.*

CENTRAL APPALACHIAN REVIEW. Fall 1982-. 0733-8694. US. English. an. Central Appalachian Review, Davis and Elkins College, Elkins WV 26241. LC PS537. DD 810.80974.

CERVANTES. (CERVANTES : BULLETIN OF THE CERVANTES SOCIETY OF AMERICA). V. 1, No. 1 and 2 (Fall 1981)-. 0277-6995. Periodical. US. English (Spanish). sa. $15.00. Vassar College, Cervantes Society of America, c/o P R Kenworthy, Poughkeepsie NY 12601. Tel (914)452-7000. Ind/Abst MLA Int. Bibliogr. Books Artic. Mod. Lang. Lit. LC PQ6337. DD 863.3.

CESKA LITERARNI VEDA. BOHEMISTIKA. Series/Titl Literarnevedne Prace. VFOAT Bohemistika. Czech. ir. LC Z2138.L5, PG5000.

CESKA LITERARNI VEDA : NESLOVANSKE LITERATURY. 1974-. Multilingual (Czech). ir. Ustav Pro Ceskov A Svetovou Literaturu CSAV, Strahovske Nadvori 132, Praha Czechoslovakia. LC Z6519, PN695. *Bibliografie Literarnevednych Occidentalik V Ceskem Tisku.*

CESKA LITERATURA. Vol. 1- March 1953-. 0009-0468. Periodical. CS. Czech (tables of contents and summaries in English, French, German and Russian). bm. $45.00. John Benjamins BV, Amsteldijk 44, PO Box 52519, 1007 HA Amsterdam Holland. Tel (202)738156. Ed L Stoll. Ind/Abst Am. Hist. Life, Hist. Abstr., Part A, Mod. Hist. Abstr., Hist. Abstr., Part B, Twent. Century Abstr., MLA Int. Bibliogr. Books Artic. Mod. Lang. Lit. LC PG5000.

CESKOSLOVENSKA SLAVISTIKA. LITERATURA, FOLKLOR. VFOAT Literatura, Folklor. Periodical. Czech. ir. LC PG500.

CESKY JAZYK A LITERATURA. 1- 1951-. 0009-0786. Periodical. CS. Czech. ir. Artia, PO Box 790, Ve Smeckach 30, Praha 1 Czechoslovakia.

CHAMPS D'APPLICATION. 1- Winter 1974-. 0317-3399. CN. French. ir. $1.75 Per No. Champs d'Application, CP 771, Trois-Rivieres Quebec G9A 5J9 Canada. DD C840.5.

CHANDRABHAGA. No. 1- Summer 1979-. Periodical. English. ir. Chandrabhaga Society, Tinkonia Bagicha, Cuttack 753001 India. Ind/Abst MLA Int. Bibliogr. Books Artic. Mod. Lang. Lit. LC PN2. DD 805.

CHANG-CHIANG. VFOAT Changjiang Wenxuecongkan. Periodical. CC. Chinese. qt. Chung-Kuo Kuo Chi Shu Tien, PO Box 2820, Peking China. LC PL2250. DD 895.109.

CHANGE CEASED. 1-42. 0577-537X. Monographic Series. FR. French. ir. Seuil Etc, BP 80 27 rue Jacob, Paris Cedex 06 France. DD 808.8.

CHANGES MAGAZINE. VFOAT Changes. 0093-9064. US. English. $2.50 Single Issue. Box 92, Bisbee AZ 85603. LC PS501. DD 810.80054.

CHANGJAK KWA PIPYONG. Periodical. KO. Korean. ir. 1,000 Single Issue. Changjak Kwa Pipyong, 4 Naengchon-Dong, Sodaemun-Ku, Seoul South Korea. LC PL950.2.

CHAO HUA (PEKING, CHINA). (CHAO HUA). Series/Titl Erh Tung Wen Hsueh Tsung Kan. Periodical. Chinese. ir. 1.15. LC PZ10.82. DD 895.1089282.

CHAPBOOK - THE MAINE WRITERS' CONFERENCE. Main/Conf Maine Writers' Conference. No. 1-. 0075-2717. US. English. an. Pejepscot Press, 10 Mason Street, Brunswick ME 04011. LC PS548.M2. DD 810.82.

THE CHARIOTEER. No. 1- Summer 1960-. 0577-5574. US. English. an. $15.00. Parnassos Greek Culture Society of New York, Box 2928 Grand Central Station, New York NY 10163. LC PA5273. DD 889.3408.

THE CHARITON REVIEW. V. 1- Spring 1975-. 0098-9452. US. English. sa. $4.00. Chariton Review, Northeast Missouri State University, Kirksville MO 63501. Tel (816)785-4499. Ed Jim Barnes. Ind/Abst Am. Period. Verse. LC PS501. DD 810.8005. bk rev. adv acc. Circ 350. Contemporary fiction, poetry, translations, book reviews. Excellence only.

CHARLES LAMB BULLETIN. (THE CHARLES LAMB BULLETIN). New Series No. 1 (Jan. 1973)-. 0308-0951. Periodical. UK. English. qt. 12.00. Charles Lamb Society, 24 Ellsworthy, Flat 3, London NW3 3DL England. Tel 01-586-5112. Ed Mary Wedd. Ind/Abst Abstr. Engl. Stud., MLA Int. Bibliogr. Books Artic. Mod. Lang. Lit., Years Work Eng. Stud. LC PR4863. DD 824.7. bk rev. Circ 350. (ctrl) Devoted to the work of Charles Lamb and his contemporaries. Articles and book reviews. *C.L.S. Bulletin.*

CHASQUI (WILLIAMSBURG, VA.). (CHASQUI). Began with Jan./Feb. 1972 issue. 0145-8973. Periodical. US. English (Spanish, or Portuguese). ty. $12.00. Howard M Fraser, Department of Modern Languages, College of William and Mary, Williamsburg VA 23185. Tel (804)253-4362. Ed Thomas E Lyon. Ind/Abst MLA Int. Bibliogr. Books Artic. Mod. Lang. Lit. LC PQ7081.A1. DD 860.998. bk rev. adv acc. Circ 300. (ctrl) Criticism of literature from the Hispanic world, book reviews, critical articles, bibliographies, creative writing, cultural notes, graphic arts.

CHECK MATE. (CHECKMATE). Main/Corp Manitoba Association of Teachers of English. Began with March 1975? issue. 0382-8360. Periodical. CN. English. Manitoba Teachers' Society, 191 Harcourt Street, Winnipeg Manitoba R3J 3H2 Canada. DD 820.7107127.

CHELSEA. Began with No. 6, published winter 1960. 0009-2185. Periodical. US. English. an. $5.00. Chelsea Association Inc, Box 5880, Grand Central Station, New York NY 10163. Tel (212)988-2276. Ed Sonia Raiziss, A de Palchi, B Swann & R Foerster. Ind/Abst Index Am. Period. Verse. adv acc. Circ 1,300. Includes poetry, fiction, translations, essays, and artwork. *Chelsea Review.*

CHESTERTON REVIEW. (THE CHESTERTON REVIEW). V. 1- Fall/Winter 1974-. 0317-0500. Periodical. CN. English. sa. $20.00. St Thomas More College, c/o The Editor, 1438 College Drive, Saskatoon Saskatchewan Canada. Tel (306)966-8900. Ed Ian Boyd. Ind/Abst Am. Hist. Life, Hist. Abstr., Part A, Mod. Hist. Abstr., Hist. Abstr., Part B, Twent. Century Abstr., MLA Int. Bibliogr. Books Artic. Mod. Lang. Lit., Hist. Abstr., Years Work Eng. Stud. LC PR4453.C4. DD 828.91209. bk rev. adv acc. Deals with the life and work of G K Chesterton. The review also considers the thought of other important Twentieth-Century thinkers.

CHI TUNG WEN I. VFOAT Jidong Wenyi. Periodical. CC. Chinese. bm. 0.25. Post Office, Tang-Shan Shih China.

CHIANG NAN. VFOAT Jiangnan Literature. First published in 1981. Periodical. CC. Chinese. qt. 1.00. Chiang Nan Wen Hsueh She, 1 Sui An Lu, Hang-Chou Che-Chiang Mainland. LC PL2250. DD 895.108.

CHIANG-SU SAN WEN HSUAN. Periodical. CC. Chinese. an. 0.75. Hsin Hua Shu Tien, Chiang-Su Sheng China. LC PL3031.K552. DD 895.14508095113.

CHICAGO CREATIVE WRITERS. (CHICAGO CREATIVE WRITERS : THE CHICAGO CREATIVE WRITERS REGISTRY OF THE CHICAGO COUNCIL ON FINE ARTS). 0737-1837. Periodical. US. English. Chicago Council on Fine Arts, 78 East Washington Street, Chicago IL 60606. LC PS285.C47. DD 810.2577311.

CHICAGO REVIEW. V. 1- Winter 1946-. 0009-3696. Periodical. US. English. qt $18.00. Faculty Exchange, Box C University of Chicago, Chicago IL 60637. Tel (312)753-3571. Ed Robert Sitko. Ind/Abst Annu. Bibliogr. Engl. Lang. Lit., MLA Int. Bibliogr. Books Artic. Mod. Lang. Lit., Index Am. Period. Verse, Index Book Rev. Humanit., Humanit. Index. LC AP2. DD 051. (cum index). bk rev. adv acc. Circ 2,000. Available on microfilm from University Microfilms. Established in 1946, Chicago Review provides a continuing forum for contemporary poetry, essays, fiction, plays translations, reviews, and art.

CHICOREL INDEX TO SHORT STORIES IN ANTHOLOGIES AND COLLECTIONS. See Indexes/Abstracts.

CHIMERES. Began in 1969. 0276-7856. Periodical. US. English (French). sa. $10.00. University Kansas, Department French & Italian, 2056 Wescoe Hall, Lawrence KS 66045. Tel (913)864-4056. Ed Hope Christiansen, Hilda Doerry and Karen Pearson. Ind/Abst MLA Int. Bibliogr. Books Artic. Mod. Lang. Lit. LC PQ1. DD 840.08. bk rev. adv acc. Circ 130. A journal of French and Italian literature which serves as a forum of critical expression for young scholars.

CHIN CHAO. VFOAT Jinzhao. Chinese. ir. $0.68 Single Issue. LC PL2303.

CHINA'S SCREEN. 0577-893X. Periodical. English. qt. $19.00. China Books & Periodicals Inc, 2929 24th Street, San Francisco CA 94110. Ind/Abst Film Lit. Index. LC PN1993.5.C4. DD 791.4305.

CHINESE LITERATURE. Autumn 1951-. 0009-4617. Periodical. CH. English. qt. $25.00. China Books & Periodicals Inc, 2929 24th Street, San Francisco CA 94110. Tel (415)282-2994. Ind/Abst MLA Int. Bibliogr. Books Artic. Mod. Lang. Lit. LC DS777.55. DD 951.005.

CHINESE LITERATURE (CODA PRESS). (CHINESE LITERATURE). VFOAT Chung-Kuo Wen Hsueh. Vol. 1 No. 1 (Jan. 1979)-. 0161-9705. Periodical. US. English. sa. Coda Press, 700 West Badger Road, Suite 101, Madison WI 53713. LC PL2250. DD 895.109. Also issued on microfilm.

CHINESE LITERATURE, ESSAYS, ARTICLES, REVIEWS. VFOAT CLEAR. 0161-9705. Periodical. English (some Chinese). $20.00. University of Wisconsin, Department of East Asian Language and Literature, c/o Amy Margulies, Madison WI 53706. Tel (608)262-9688. Ind/Abst MLA Int. Bibliogr. Books Artic. Mod. Lang. Lit. bk rev adv acc. Circ 300. Issued also on microfilm by: University Microfilms Internationsl. A journal on Chinese literature, modern and traditional. *Chinese Literature (CODA Press), 0161-9705.*

CHINESE PEN. Autumn 1972-. Periodical. English. ir. $8.00. Chinese Center, 9th Floor, 277 Roosevelt Road, Section 3, Taipei Taiwan. LC PL2250. DD 895.108005.

CHING MING. VFOAT Ching Ming Wen Hsueh Chi Kan. Periodical. CC. Chinese. qt. 1.00. Chung-Kuo Chi Shu Tien, PO Box 399, Peking China. LC PL2513. DD 895.109005.

CHING NIEN WEN HSUEH. VFOAT Qingnian Wenxue. Periodical. Chinese. bm. 0.40. Post Office Peking, Peking China. LC PL2303. DD 895.109005.

CHINOPERL PAPERS. Main/Conf Conference on Chinese Oral and Performing Literature. VFOAT Chung-Kuo Yen Chang Wen I Yen Chiu Hui Lun Chi. VAT Chinese Oral and Performing Literature Papers. No. 6 (1976)-. 0193-7774. US. chiefly English with some Chinese. ir. $20.00. China-Japan Program, Cornell University, 140 Uris Hall, Ithaca NY 14853. Tel (607)256-6222. Ed Harold Shadick. LC PL2253. DD 782.810951. Circ 300. Contains articles dealing primarily with oral Chinese literature (popular story telling, opera, ceremonial chanting, folksong) and various genres of Chinese verse and prose. *Chinoperl News.*

CHONSON MUNHAK. Periodical. KO. Korean. ir. Hakyonsa, 28-3 2-Ka Taepyon-No, Chung-Ku Seoul Korea. **LC** PL969.8.

CHOSA KENKYU HOKOKU. No. 1-. JA. Japanese. ir. Kokubungaku Kenkyu Shiryokan Bunken Shiryobu, 16-10 Toyo-Machi 1-Chome Shinagawa-Ku, Tokyo-To 142 Japan. **LC** Z3308.L5, PL716. *Kokubungaku Bunken Shiryo Shozai Chosa Mokuroku.*

CHRISTIANITY & LITERATURE. VFOAT Christianity and Literature. V. 22, No. 2- Winter 1973-. 0148-3331. Periodical. US. English. qt. $10.00. Baylor University, English Department, Waco TX 76798. **Tel** (817)755-2122. **Ed** James Barcus. **Ind/Abst** Abstr. Engl. Stud., MLA Int. Bibliogr. Books Artic. Mod. Lang. Lit., Relig. Index One, Period. **LC** PN49. **DD** 810.80054. (cum index). bk rev. adv acc. **Circ** 2,000. (ctrl). The journal publishes essays, articles, book views, a quarterly bibliography, and creative writing which explore the relationship between Christianity and literature. *Newsletter of the Conference on Christianity and Literature.*

CHRONICA. Began 1967. 0009-5931. Periodical. US. English. sa. $10.00. Medieval Association of the Pacific, Rhetoric Department, University of California at Davis, Davis CA 95616. **Ed** Bradford Blaine. bk rev. **Circ** 325. (ctrl).

LA CHRONIQUE DES ECRITS EN COURS. No. 1 (May 81)-. Perioidcal. FR. French. ir. 35 Single Issue. Editions de L Equinoxe, 55 rue de Rivoli, 75001 Paris France. **LC** PQ1141. **DD** 840.8.

CHU FENG. Periodical. CH. Chinese. qt. 0.40. Chung-Kuo Kuo Chi Shu Tien, PO Box 2820, Peking China. **LC** PL2445. **DD** 398.20951.

CHU-HOKUO HIKAKU BUNKA KENKYU. 1 (1979)-. Danish (German, Japanese, Norwegian, and Swedish). an. Osaka Gaikokugo Daigaku, 2734 Aomatani, Minoo-shi 562 Japan.

CHU JEN. Vol. 1-, 1981-. Periodical. CC. Chinese. ir. 0.99. Hsin Hua Shu Tien Shang-Hai Fa, Hsing So Shanghai, Shanghai China. **LC** AP215.C5. **DD** 895.1089282.

CHU PEN. VFOAT Juben. Began in Jan. 1952. Periodical. CC. Chinese. mo. 0.40. Chung-kuo Kuo Chi Shu Tien, PO Box 2820, Pei-ching China Mainland. **LC** PL2603. **DD** 895.125.

CHU PEN YUAN TI. VFOAT Juben Yuandi. Periodical. CH. Chinese. bm. 0.48. Chung-Kuo Kuo Chi Shu Tien, Peking China. **LC** PN1609.C6. **DD** 809.2.

CHUGOKU BUNGAKU KENKYU (WASEDA DAIGAKU. CHUGOKU BUNGAKKAI). (CHUGOKU BUNGAKU KENKYU). 0385-0919. JA. Japanese. an. Waseda Daigaku Chugoku Bungakukai, c/o Waseda Daigaku Bungakubu Chugoku Bungaku Kenkyushitsu Nai 42 Toyamacho Shinjuku-Ku, Tokyo Japan. **LC** PL2250.

CHUGOKU BUNGAKUHO. VFOAT Journal of Chinese Literature. No. 1- (Oct. 1954)-. 0578-0934. JA. Japanese (summaries in English). an. Japan Publication Trading Company, PO Box 5030, Tokyo International, Tokyo 100-31 Japan. **Ind/Abst** MLA Int. Bibliogr. Books Artic. Mod. Lang. Lit. (cum index).

CHUN FENG (SHEN-YAND SHIH, CHINA). (CHUN FENG). VFOAT Chun Feng Hsiao Shuo Yueh Kan. Periodical. CC. Chinese. bm. 0.80. Chung-Kuo Chu Pan Tui Wai Mao I Tsung Kung SSU, PO Box 614, Pei-Ching China. **LC** PL2513. **DD** 895.109005. *Chun Feng Wen I Tsung Kan.*

CHUNG FU HSUAN CHI. Periodical. CH. Chinese. ir. $100.00. Chung Yang Jih Pao, 83 Chung Hsiao West Road, 1 Section, Taipei Taiwan. **LC** PL2513. **DD** 895.108951249.

CHUNG-KUO CHIN TAI WEN HSUEH YEN CHIU. VFOAT Modern Chinese Literature Studies. V. 1-. Chinese. ir. **LC** PL2303. **DD** 895.109005.

CHUNG-KUO HSIEN TAI WEN HSUEH YEN CHIU TSUNG KAN. VFOAT Zhongguo Xian Dai Wen Xue Yan Jiu Congkan. 1 (1979)-. Periodical. CC. Chinese. ir. Pei-Ching Chu Pan She, Pei-Chung China Mainland. **LC** PL2302.

CHUNG-KUO WEN HSUEH YEN CHIU NIEN CHIEN. 1981-. CH. Chinese. an. 6.00. Hsin Hua Shu Tien, Pei-Ching Fa Hsing So, Peking China. **LC** PL2251. **DD** 895.109.

CHUNG-KUO WEN I NIEN CHIEN. 1932-. Periodical. US. Chinese. Center for Chinese Research Materials, Association of Research Libraries, 1527 New Hampshire Avenue, Washington DC 20036. **LC** PL2303.

CHUNG PIEN HSIAO SHUO HSUAN. VFOAT Zhong Pien Xiao Shuo Xuan. Periodical. CH. Chinese. an. 1.45. Hsin Hua Shu Tien, Pei-Ching Fa Hsing So, Peking China. **LC** PL2653. **DD** 895.13508.

CHUNG PIEN HSIAO SHUO NIEN PIEN. 1980-. CH. Chinese. an. 1.69. Chiang-Su Sheng Hsin Hua Shu Tien Nan-Ching, Nan-Ching China. **LC** PL2653. **DD** 895.13508.

CHUNG WAI WEN HSUEH. VFOAT Chung-Wai Literary Monthly. No. 1- June 1, 1972-. CH. Chinese. mo. $25.00. Chung Wai, Department of Foreign Language and Literature National, Taiwan 107 Republic of China. **Tel** (02)3510231. **Ed** Chang Ching-Erh. **Ind/Abst** MLA Int. Bibliogr. Books Artic. Mod. Lang. Lit. **LC** PN9. adv acc. **Circ** 2,000. Introduces both Western and Chinese literatures, including theories, criticism, poetry, novels, and essays.

CHUNG WEN HSUEH HSI. VFOAT Chinese Learning. First published in Sept. 1975-. Periodical. Chinese. ir. $2.00 Single Issue. Shih Tai Chu Pan She, Time Press, 17/F Flat B7, Canal Road, Hsiang-Kang Hong Kong. **LC** PL1068.H6.

CHUNGGUK MUNHAK. VFOAT Journal of Chinese Literature. Periodical. Chinese (Korean). ir. Chungmunhakkwa Yongusil, Yonse University, Seoul Korea. **LC** PL2250.

CHUNGHAKSAENG CHANGMUN SON. Periodical. Korean. ir. **LC** PL998.C62.

CHYANKUTI. V. 1- Vaisakha 2030- 1973-. Nepali. ir. 1.00 Single Issue. Rashtravadi Svatantra Vidyarthi Mandala, Sankhuwasabha, Khandavari Nepal. **LC** PK2598.A2.

CIMARRON REVIEW. No. 1- Sept. 1967-. 0009-6849. Periodical. US. English. qt. $10.00. Oklahoma State University, 208 Life Sciences East, Arts Sciences Studies, Stillwater OK 74078. **Tel** (405)624-6573. **Ed** Neil J Hackett. **Ind/Abst** MLA Int. Bibliogr. Books Artic. Mod. Lang. Lit., Index Am. Period. Verse. **LC** AS36. (cum index). **Circ** 500. High-quality essays, stories and poems that mirror contemporary society in all its aspects.

CIRCULO - CIRCULO DE CULTURA PANAMERICANO. (CIRCULO). Began publication in 1970?. 0009-7349. Periodical. US. chiefly Spanish. **Ind/Abst** MLA Int. Bibliogr. Books Artic. Mod. Lang. Lit. **LC** F1408.3. **DD** 860.

CLA JOURNAL. *See* Linguistics.

CLASSICAL AND MODERN LITERATURE. Vol. 1, No. 1 (Fall 1980)-. 0197-2227. Periodical. US. English. qt. $23.00. Classical and Modern Literature, PO Box 629, Terre Haute IN 47808. **Tel** (812)237-2362. **Ed** James O Loyd and Virginia Leon de Vivero. **Ind/Abst** MLA Int. Bibliogr. Books Artic. Mod. Lang. Lit., Book Rev. Index. **LC** PN883. **DD** 809. bk rev. adv acc. **Circ** 350. Articles on the inter-relationships between classical and modern literatures and book reviews.

CLAUDEL STUDIES. V. 1- 1972-. 0090-1237. US. Multilingual. sa. $10.00. Department of French, University of Dallas, Irving TX 75061. **Tel** (214)721-5229. **Ed** Moses M Nagy. **Ind/Abst** MLA Int. Bibliogr. Books Artic. Mod. Lang. Lit., Recent Publ. Artic. **LC** PQ2605.L2. **DD** 848.91209. bk rev. **Circ** 400. (ctrl). Journal publishes research papers, articles, monographs, notes, and reviews on Claudel. It has also published translations and taped discussions. The journal assumes the endeavor to make Claudel's work known. *Claudel Newsletter, 0069-4568.*

CLAVE DE SOL. V. 1- Oct. 1972-. Periodical. Spanish. ir. $144.00. Luzal Publicidad, Palace 52-75 Oficina 205, Medelin Colombia. **LC** PN6.

CLEARWATER JOURNAL. Vol. 1, No. 1 (Winter 1982)-. 0733-6683. Periodical. US. English. sa. $6.00. Clearwater Press, 1115 V Avenue, Legrunde OR 97850.

CLIMATE. 28- Autumn 1978-. Periodical. NZ. English. ir. 4.00 2 issues, 6.00 3 issues. Climate, The Editor, PO Box 10153, The Terrace, Wellington New Zealand. **LC** PR9634. **DD** 820.8. *Mate.*

CLIO; TRIMESTRALE DE STUDI STORICI. 1- 1965-. 0578-5251. Periodical. IT. Italian. Marzorati Editore, Via Piero Martinetti 6, Milano 20147 Italy. **Ind/Abst** MLA Int. Bibliogr. Books Artic. Mod. Lang. Lit., Recent Publ. Artic.

CLUES. (CLUES : A JOURNAL OF DETECTION). Vol. 1, No. 1 (Spring 1980)-. 0742-4248. Periodical. US. English. ir. $12.50. Bowling Green University, Popular Cultural Building, Bowling Green OH 43403. **Tel** (419)372-7866. **Ed** Pat Browne. **Ind/Abst** MLA Int. Bibliogr. Books Artic. Mod. Lang. Lit. bk rev. adv acc. **Circ** 800. Discusses all aspects of mystery fiction including film and television.

COLBY LIBRARY QUARTERLY. (THE COLBY LIBRARY QUARTERLY). Series 1, No. 1-16, 1943-46. 0010-0552. Periodical. US. English. qt. $6.00. Colby Library Quarterly, Colby College Library, Waterville ME 04901. **Tel** (207)872-3297. **Ed** John H Sutherland. **Ind/Abst** Am. Hist. Life, Hist. Abstr., Part A, Mod. Hist. Abstr., Hist. Abst., Part B, Twent. Century Abstr., Abstr. Engl. Stud., MLA Int. Bibliogr. Books Artic. Mod. Lang. Lit., Annu. Bibliogr. Engl. Lang. Lit., Years Work Eng. Stud., Hist. Abstr. **LC** Z881. **DD** 027.7741. **Circ** 600. Articles on literature in English, special interests: Maine and regional literature and history, Irish Literature, art and literature.

COLECCION DE CLASICOS. Spanish. ir. **LC** PQ6171.

COLLECTION ENCRE. VFOAT Encre. Published since Feb. 1978?. 0228-0337. Periodical. CN. French. ir. Free. Revue Encre, Cegep de St-Laurent B-41, 625 Boulevard Ste Croix, St-Laurent Quebec H4L 3X7Canada. **DD** C840.809283.

COLLECTION STENDHALIENNE. 1-. 0530-9220. Monographic Series. SZ. French. ir. Editions du Grand-Chene, Chemin de Montagny, CH 1603 Aran Switzerland.

COLLECTIONS - MALONE SOCIETY, LONDON. **Main/Corp** Malone Society. V. 1-. Monographic Series. UK. English. ir. **LC** PR621.

COLLEGE LITERATURE. V. 1- Winter 1974-. 0093-3139. Periodical. US. English. ty. $6.00. West Chester State College, New Main Building, West Chester PA 19383. **Tel** (215)436-2901. **Ed** Bernard Oldsey. **Ind/Abst** Abstr. Engl. Stud., MLA Int. Bibliogr. Books Artic. Mod. Lang. Lit., Book Rev. Index, Years Work Eng. Stud. **LC** PR1. **DD** 809. bk rev. adv acc. **Circ** 1,000. (ctrl). Scholarly articles on major works and authors regularly taught in American Colleges and Universities.

COLOQUIO. LETRAS. (COLOQUIO : LETRAS). No. 1- March 1971-. Periodical. PO. Portuguese. bm. $30.00. Empresa Nacional de Publicade, Av da Liberdad 226, Apartado 2346, Lisbon Portugal. **Tel** 76 50 40/9. **Ed** David Mourao-Ferreira. **Ind/Abst** MLA Int. Bibliogr. Books Artic. Mod. Lang. Lit. **LC** NX7. **DD** 700.5. bk rev. **Circ** 4,000. (ctrl). Literary essays on Portuguese language, theory of literature and general literature. *Coloquio.*

COLORADO-NORTH REVIEW. 0194-0589. Periodical. US. English. qt. $6.00. University of Northern Colorado, University Center, Greeley CO 80639. **Tel** (303)351-4347. **Ed** Colette E Strassburg. **LC** PS1. **DD** 810.8. **Circ** 6,000. Submissions of poetry, short fiction, photography and artwork compiled in a magazine. *Nova.*

DE COLORES. Began with Winter 1973 issue. 0145-2681. Periodical. US. English and Spanish. ir. Pajarito Publications, PO Box 7264, Albuquerque NM 87194. **Tel** (505)242-8075. **LC** PS508.M4. **DD** 808.8986872073.

COLUMBIA ESSAYS ON MODERN WRITERS. Vol. 1 1964-. 0069-6315. US. English. ir. Columbia University Press, 136 South Broadway, Irvington-on-Hudson NY 10533.

COMITATUS. V. 1- Dec. 1970-. 0069-6412. Periodical. US. English. an. $9.00. University of California, Center of Medieval and Renaissance Studies, 405 Hilgard Avenue, Los Angeles CA 90024. **Tel** (213)825-1880. **Ed** Gary Remer. **Ind/Abst** MLA Int. Bibliogr. Books Artic. Mod. Lang. Lit. **LC** PR251. **DD** 820.9. bk rev. **Circ** 250. Contains articles in the field of medieval and renaissance studies by graduate students across the country.

COMMENTAIRE. No. 1- March 1978-. 0180-8214. Periodical. FR. French. qt. 150. Commentaire, Service Abonnements, 31 Cours des Juilliottes, 94704 Maisons-Alfort Cedex France. **LC** AP20.

COMMONWEALTH ESSAYS & STUDIES. **Series/Titl** Publications de la Societe Francaise d'Etudes du Commonwealth. VFOAT Commonwealth: Melanges. English (French). ir. **Tel** 35.74.36.37. **Ind/Abst** MLA Int. Bibliogr. Books Artic. Mod. Lang. Lit. bk rev. adv acc. **Circ** 500. (ctrl).

Literature, civilization, language of former commonwealth countries - advanced research. *Commonwealth: Miscellanies.*

COMMONWEALTH NOVEL IN ENGLISH. VFOAT C.N.I.E. Vol. 1, No. 1 (Jan. 1982)-. 0732-6734. Periodical. US. English. sa. $14.00. Commonwealth Publishing, c/o S R Jamkhand, Center for Asian Studies, Austin TX 78712. **Tel** (817)273-2692. **Ed** Sudhakar R Jamkhandi. **Ind/Abst** Abstr. Engl. Stud., MLA Int. Bibliogr. Books Artic. Mod. Lang. Lit. **LC** PR9080. **DD** 823.0099171241. bk rev. adv acc. **Circ** 300. Features broad-based analyses of narrative strategies and textual criticism of commonwealth English novels.

COMMONWEALTH QUARTERLY. V. 1- Dec. 1976-. Periodical. English. ir. $10.00. Vikramraj Urs, V V Mohalla 2823, VIII Gross Mysore 2 Karnataka State India. **Ind/Abst** MLA Int. Bibliogr. Books Artic. Mod. Lang. Lit. **LC** PK5461.A1. **DD** 805.

COMMUNICATIONS FROM THE INTERNATIONAL BRECHT SOCIETY. VFOAT Communications, Brecht Newsletter. Vol. 1, No. 1 (Dec. 1971)-. 0740-8943. Periodical. US. English (German). sa. Free to Members of IBA. University of Illinois, Department of Germanic Languages, c/o Karl-Heinz Schoeps, Urbana IL 61801. **LC** PT2603.R397. **DD** 832.912.

COMPARATIVE DRAMA. V. 1- Spring 1967-. 0010-4078. Periodical. US. English. qt. $20.00. Comparative Drama, Western Michigan University, Kalamazoo MI 49008. **Tel** (616)345-0985. **Ind/Abst** Abstr. Engl. Stud., MLA Int. Bibliogr. Books Artic. Mod. Lang. Lit., Humanit. Index, Book Rev. Index, Index Book Rev. Humanit., Recent Publ. Artic. **LC** PN1601. **DD** 809.2.

COMPARATIVE LITERATURE. V. 1- Winter 1949-. 0010-4124. Periodical. US. English. qt. $19.00. University of Oregon, 223 Friendly Hall, Eugene OR 97403. **Tel** (503)686-4013. **Ed** Chandler B Beall and Thomas Hart. **Ind/Abst** Abstr. Engl. Stud., MLA Int. Bibliogr. Books Artic. Mod. Lang. Lit., Annu. Bibliogr. Engl. Lang. Lit., Book Rev. Index, Index Book Rev. Humanit., Soc. Sci. Index, Humanit. Index, Years Work Eng. Stud. **LC** PN851. **DD** 805. (cum index). bk rev. **Circ** 3,500. Articles which explore important problems in literary theory and literary history. Not confined to a single national literature.

COMPARATIVE LITERATURE IN CANADA. VFOAT Litterature Comparee au Canada. V. 1- Spring 1969-. 0045-7795. Periodical. CN. English (French). sa. 4.00 Domestic, 5.00 Foreign. University of Alberta, Department of Comparative Literature, Edmonton Alberta T6G 2E6 Canada. **Tel** (403)432-4924. **Ed** P A Robberecht. **LC** PN855. **DD** 809.8971. adv acc. **Circ** 500. Includes association business, abstracts of learned papers, new publications by members, miscellaneous information about comparative literature.

COMPARATIVE LITERATURE STUDIES. VFOAT CLS. Comparative Literature Studies. V. 1- 1964-. 0010-4132. Periodical. US. chiefly in English. qt. $54.00. University of Illinois Press, 54 East Gregory Drive, Champaign IL 61820. **Tel** (217)333-0950. **Ed** A Owen Aldridge. **Ind/Abst** Annu. Bibliogr. Engl. Lang. Lit., MLA Int. Bibliogr. Books Artic. Mod. Lang. Lit., Book Rev. Index, Index Book Rev. Humanit., Humanit. Index, Abstr. Engl. Stud., Years Work Eng. Stud. **LC** PN851. **DD** 809. bk rev. adv acc. **Circ** 900. Articles on literary history and criticism, history of ideas, literary relations between East, West, North, and South America.

COMPLETE CATALOGUE FROM KENYA LITERATURE BUREAU. *See* Bibliographies.

COMPOUND FRACTURE. 1-. 0227-3195. Periodical. CN. English. Compound Fracture Frog Manor, 8833-92 Street, Edmonton Alberta T6C 3P9 Canada. **DD** 808.8387605.

CONCOURS LITTERAIRE. 1980-. 0822-546X. CN. French. an. Concours Litteraire, 415 rue des Ecoles, Drummondville Quebec J2B 1J3 Canada. **DD** C840.8092375.

CONCURSO NACIONAL DE CUENTO JORGE GAITAN DURAN. **Main/Corp** Instituto de Cultura y Belles Artes. **Series/Titl** Coleccion Casa de la Cultura. Spanish. ir. **LC** PQ8176.S5. **DD** 863.01.

CONDITIONS. 1-. 0147-8311. Periodical. US. English. ty. Conditions, PO Box 56 Van Brunt Station, Brooklyn NY 11215. **Tel** (718)788-8654. **Ed** Allison Clarke. **Ind/Abst** Index Am. Period. Verse, Altern. Press Index. **LC** PS508.W7. **DD** 810.80054. bk rev. adv acc. **Circ** 3,000. A feminist literary magazine with an emphasis on writings by lesbians.

CONFERENCE ON MODERN JEWISH STUDIES ANNUAL. VFOAT CMJS Annual. 0270-9392. Periodical. US. English. an. $2.50. Queens College Press, Kiely Hall 802, Flushing NY 11367. **Tel** (212)520-7208. **Ed** Joseph C Landis. **LC** PJ5120. **DD** 809.88924. bk rev. **Circ** 750. Research and criticism in Jewish literature in any language and in the historical and cultural context. English translations of literature and criticism accepted.

CONFRONTATION. No. 1- Spring 1968-. 0010-5716. Periodical. US. English. sa. $8.00. Confrontation, CW Post of Liu, English Department, Greenvale NY 11548. **Tel** (516)299-2391. **Ed** Martin Tucker. **Ind/Abst** Index Am. Period. Verse. **LC** PS501. bk rev. **Circ** 2,000. Available on microfilm from University Microfilms. Literate fiction, poems, essays open to all forms and styles. High quality is only criterion.

THE CONRAD NEWS. Periodical. English. an. Society of Friends of the Polish Maritime Museum in Gdansk, UL Szeroka 67/68, 80-835 Gdansk Poland. **LC** PR6005.O4. **DD** 823.912.

THE CONRADIAN : THE JOURNAL OF THE JOSEPH CONRAD SOCIETY (U.K.). VFOAT Journal of the Joseph Conrad Society (U.K.). Vol. 6, No. 1 (April 1980)-. Periodical. UK. English. sa. $8.43. Owen Knowles, University of Hull, English Department, Hull HU6 7XR England. **Tel** 01-0482-46311. **Ed** Owen Knowles. bk rev. adv acc. **Circ** 700. The life and works of Joseph Conrad. *Journal of the Joseph Conrad Society (U.K.).*

CONRADIANA. V. 1- Summer 1968-. 0010-6356. Periodical. US. English. ty. $10.00 Domestic, $12.00 Foreign. Texas Tech University, Box 4530, Lubbock TX 79409-4530. **Tel** (806)742-2527. **Ed** David Leon Higdon. **Ind/Abst** Abstr. Engl. Stud., Ref. Source, Index Book Rev. Humanit., Am. Humanit. Index, MLA Int. Bibliogr. Books Artic. Mod. Lang. Lit., Twent. Century Lit. **LC** PR6005.O4. **DD** 813. bk rev. adv acc. **Circ** 800. Studies of the life and works of Joseph Conrad and his period.

CONSENSO *CEASED.* Began with V. 1- (No. 1-). Ceased with No. 6, 1980?. 0193-7030. Periodical. US. Spanish. sa. **LC** PQ6170. **DD** 860.5.

CONSTRUCTIONS. 1984-. US. English (French). an. **LC** PQ1. **DD** 840.9.

CONSUMPTION. V. 1- Fall 1967-. Periodical. US. English. qt.

CONTACT II. V. 1- (No. 1-). 0197-6796. Periodical. US. English. bm. $14.00. Contact II, 50 Broadway, New York NY 10004. **Tel** (212)674-0911. **Ed** Maurice Kenney and J G Gosciak. bk rev. adv acc. **Circ** 2,500. Reviews of poetry, contemporary and small press and notes on poets, literary events and regional literary centers and includes anthologies of poets from different parts of America.

CONTEMPORARY AUTHORS. *See* Bibliographies.

CONTEMPORARY AUTHORS AUTOBIOGRAPHY SERIES. VFOAT Contemporary Authors. Vol. 1-. 0748-0636. US. English. ir. Gale Research Company, Book Tower, Detroit MI 48226. **Ed** Adele Savleission. **LC** PN453. **DD** 809. Fills the need for a single convenient source of first-person details on today's fiction and nonfiction writers in all genres.

CONTEMPORARY AUTHORS, CUMULATIVE INDEX, INCLUDING REFERENCES TO ALL ENTRIES IN CONTEMPORARY AUTHORS, CONTEMPORARY AUTHORS, PERMANENT SERIES AND CONTEMPORARY LITERARY CRITICISM, SOMETHING ABOUT THE AUTHOR. *See* Indexes/Abstracts.

CONTEMPORARY AUTHORS. NEW REVISION SERIES. *See* Bibliographies.

CONTEMPORARY DRAMATISTS. **Series/Titl** Contemporary Writers of the English Language. Began in 1972. US. English. ir. $65.00. St Martins Press Inc, 175 5th Avenue, New York NY 10010. **Tel** (212)674-5151. **Ed** James Vinson and Daniel Kirkpatrick. Guide to the most important living English-language dramatists, with biography, bibliography and criticism.

CONTEMPORARY LITERATURE. V. 1- Winter 1960-). 0010-7484. Periodical. US. English. qt. University of Wisconsin Press, 114 North Murray Street, Madison WI 53715. **Tel** (608)262-4952. **Ind/Abst** Humanit. Index, MLA Int. Bibliogr. Books Artic. Mod. Lang. Lit., Abstr. Engl. Stud., Years Work Eng. Stud.

CONTEMPORARY NOVELISTS. 1972-. UK. English. ir. $65.00. St Martins Press Inc, 175 5th Avenue, New York NY 10010. **Tel** (212)674-5151. **Ed** James Vinson and Daniel Kirkpatrick. Guide to the most important living English-language novelists, with biography, bibliography and criticism of each author listed.

IL CONTESTO. Vol. 1- Jan. 1977-. Periodical. Italian. ir. $15.00. Argalia Editore Urbino, Conto Corrent, Postale N 15/920, Urbino Italy. **LC** PQ4001.

CONTINENT. 1-. French. ir. **LC** PG3214.

CONTINENTAL DRIFTER. Vol. 1, No. 1 (1984)-. 0743-3107. Periodical. US. English. an. $3.00. Continental Drifter, Campus Box 226, Department of English, University of Colorado, Boulder CO 80309. *Continental Drift, 0743-3093.*

CONTRAST. V. 1- (1-). 0589-574X. Periodical. SA. English (Afrikaans). sa. $5.17. Contrast, PO Box 3841, Cape Town South Africa. **Tel** 72 42 54. **Ed** G L Haresnape. **Ind/Abst** MLA Int. Bibliogr. Books Artic. Mod. Lang. Lit. **LC** AP9. bk rev. adv acc. **Circ** 900. Publishes high quality, creative and critical work, short stories, poetry, reviews, of particular interest to students of Africa and Southern African literature.

CONTRIBUTI DELL'ISTITUTO DI FILOLOGIA MODERNA : SERIE INGLESE. **Main/Corp** Milan. Universita Cattolica del Sacro Cuore. Istituto di Filologia Moderna. **Series/Titl** Scienze Filologiche e Letteratura. V. 1- 1974-. IT. English (Italian). ir. 15.500. 110 Largo Gemelli, 1 Milan 20123 Italy. **LC** PR1.

CONTRIBUTIONS TO THE STUDY OF SCIENCE FICTION AND FANTASY. *See* Romance and Adventure.

CONTRIBUTIONS TO THE STUDY OF WORLD LITERATURE. 0738-9345. Monographic Series. US. English. ir. Greenwood Press, 88 Post Road West, Westport CT 06881. **LC** UNC.

COPPER TOADSTOOL. No. 1- Dec. 1976-. 0707-090X. Periodical. CN. English. sa. $1.50 Per Number. Soda Publications, 7500 Bridge Street, Richmond British Columbia V6Y 2S7 Canada. **DD** C813.0876.

CORNELL STUDIES IN ENGLISH. VFOAT Studies in English. Began with Vol. 1- 1916. 0070-0045. Monographic Series. US. English. ir. Cornell University Press, 124 Roberts Place, Ithaca NY 14853. **Ind/Abst** Abstr. Engl. Stud., MLA Int. Bibliogr. Books Artic. Mod. Lang. Lit. **DD** 810.

CORNELL UNIVERSITY EAST ASIA PAPERS. **Main/Corp** Cornell University. China-Japan Program. **VFOAT** Cornell East Asia Papers. No. 1-. 8756-5293. Monographic Series. US. English. ir. China-Japan Program, 140 C Uris Hall/Cornell University, Ithaca NY 14853. **Tel** (607)256-6222. **Ed** Charles Peterson. **DD** 950. **Circ** 700. Manuscripts of all types on scholarly topics pertaining to the general China-Japan region, which in the opinion of its editorial board, merit wide circulation.

CORONA (BOZEMAN, MONT.). (CORONA). Vol. 1-. 0270-6687. US. English. an. $8.50. Montana State University, Departments of History and Philosophy, Bozeman MT 59717. **Tel** (406)994-5200. **Ed** Lynda Sexon and Michael Sexon. **Ind/Abst** MLA Int. Bibliogr. Books Artic. Mod. Lang. Lit. bk rev. adv acc. **Circ** 1,500. Includes speculative essays, criticism, musical scores, artwork, photography, short stories and poetry. Intended for those who see boundaries as entrances and ends as beginnings.

CORPUS. (CORPUS : BULLETIN DU PROJET CORPUS D'EDITIONS CRITIQUES). 1 (Spring 1982)-. [713-3480. Periodical. CN. French. ir. Free. Projet Corpus d'Editions Critiques Faculte des Arts Universite d'Ottawa, 164 rue Waller, Ottawa Ontario K1N 6N5 Canada. **Tel** (613)564-4218. **Ed** Romeo Arbour. **DD** C840.9. **Circ** 1,200. (ctrl). Articles in relation with authors and literary works and the problems arising from the critical edition of texts.

CQ. CONNECTICUT QUARTERLY. (CONNECTICUT QUARTERLY : CQ). **VFOAT** CQ. Vol. 1, No. 1 (March 1979)-. 0270-5702. Periodical. US.

English. qt. $7.50 Domestic, $9.00 Foreign. Connecticut Quarterly, PO Box 68, Enfield CT 06082.

CRAZY HORSE. Began publication with first issue in 1969. 0011-0841. Periodical. US. English. sa. $8.00. University of Arkansas, Little Rock, 3rd and University, English Department, Little Rock AR 72204. **Tel** (501)569-3160. **Ed** Russell Murphy. **LC** PS580. **DD** 811.5408. adv acc. **Circ** 500. Publishes quality poetry, fiction, and criticism by new and established writers.

CRAZYHORSE. **VFOAT** Crazy Horse. No. 18- Spring 1979-. 0011-0841. Periodical. US. English. sa. $8.00. Crazyhorse Association, University of Arkansas at Little Rock, Little Rock AR 72204. **Tel** (501)569-3160. **Ed** Russell Murphy. adv acc. **Circ** 500. Publishes quality poetry, fiction, and criticism by new and established writers. *Crazy Horse.*

CREATIVE PERSON. Vol. 1, No. 1 (Fall 1984)-. 8755-7606. Periodical. US. English. qt. $12.00 Domestic, $15.00 Foreign. Carol Bryan Imagines, 1000 Byus Drive, Charleston WV 25311. **DD** 051.

CRIMINAL JUSTICE LITERATURE. 0363-1419. Periodical. US. English. mo. Criminal Justice Library Unit, 1735 Benson Avenue, Evanston IL 60201. **LC** Z5118.C9, HV8138. **DD** 016.364973.

CRITICA HISPANICA. Vol. 1, No. 1-. 0278-7261. Periodical. US. English (text in Spanish). sa. $14.00 Domestic, $15.00 Foreign. St Thomas of Villanova University, South Campus, 905 SW 1st Avenue, Miami FL 33130. **Tel** (305)545-9881. **Ed** Manuel Laurentino Suarez. **Ind/Abst** MLA Int. Bibliogr. Books Artic. Mod. Lang. Lit. **LC** PQ6001. **DD** 860.9. bk rev. adv acc. **Circ** 812. (ctrl). A journal devoted to scholarly articles and notes dealing with Hispanic literature and linguistics.

CRITICA LETTERARIA. Yearly V. 1- 1973-. Periodical. IT. Italian. qt. $17.82. Lofredo Editore Napoli Spa, Via Consalvo 99 H Parco San Lu, 80125 Napoli Italy. **LC** PQ4001. *Filologia E Letteratura.*

A CRITICAL BIBLIOGRAPHY OF FRENCH LITERATURE. *See* Bibliographies.

THE CRITICAL QUARTERLY. Vol. 1, No. 1 (Spring 1959)-. 0011-1562. Periodical. UK. English. qt. 17.75. Manchester University Press, Journals Department, Oxford Road, Manchester M13 9PL England. **Tel** (061)273-5539. **Ed** J R Banks, C B Cox, A E Dyson, W Hutchings, D J Palmer, and A Young. **Ind/Abst** Abstr. Engl. Stud., MLA Int. Bibliogr. Books Artic. Mod. Lang. Lit., Annu. Bibliogr. Engl. Lang. Lit., Index Book Rev. Humanit., Humanit. Index, Years Work Eng. Stud. **LC** AP4. **DD** 820.5. bk rev. adv acc. **Circ** 2,040. A forum for new writing on literature and the arts.

THE CRITICAL REVIEW. No. 8- 1965-. 0070-1548. AT. English. an. $5.61. University of Melbourne, Bookroom/PO Box 278 Carlton S, Victoria 3053 Australia. **Tel** (03) 344 6216. **Ed** S L Goldberg. **Ind/Abst** APAIS, Aust. Public Aff. Inf. Serv., Abstr. Engl. Stud., MLA Int. Bibliogr. Books Artic. Mod. Lang. Lit., Index Book Rev. Humanit., Years Work Eng. Stud. **Circ** 600. A journal of substantial and provocative criticism over a wide range of literature and literary topics. *Melbourne Critical Review.*

THE CRNLE REVIEWS JOURNAL. **VFOAT** RJ. **VAT** Centre for Research in the New Literatures in English Reviews Journal. No. 1 (1979)-. 0157-3705. Periodical. AT. English. sa. $8.85. Flinders University South Australia Crnle, Bedford Park, South Australia 5042 Australia. **Tel** 2752459. **Ed** Susan Hosking. bk rev. adv acc. **Circ** 250. (ctrl). Critical survey of English language literary publishing from the Post-Colonial Societies of the Commonwealth and beyond.

CROC. **VFOAT** C R O C. No 1- Oct. 1979-. 0226-6083. Periodical. CN. French. mo. 41.00. Ludcom Inc, 5800 Ave Monkland, Montreal Que H4A 1G1 Canada. **Tel** (514)483-6320. **Ed** Jacques Hurtubise. **DD** 741.59714. bk rev. adv acc. **Circ** 76,168. (ctrl). French humor magazine containing the best comedy writers and cartoonists of Eastern Canada contribute satire, parody, caricature and comic art.

CROSS-CANADA WRITERS' QUARTERLY. Vol. 2, No. 3 (Summer 1980). 0227-2652. Periodical. CN. English. qt. $10.06. Cross Canada Writers Quarterly, PO Box 277 Station F, Toronto Ontario M4Y 2L7 Canada. **Tel** (416)690-0917. **Ed** Ted Plantos. **DD** C810. bk rev. adv acc. **Circ** 2,500. The Canadian literary writer's magazine, examining the creative and working processes in Canadian literature through articles, interviews, profiles, plus new poems and short stories by Canada's best. *New Writers' News, 0229-2467.*

CROSS CURRENTS (ANN ARBOR, MICH.). *See* Linguistics.

CRSCL NEWSLETTER. (CRSCL NEWSLETTER : CANADIAN RESEARCH SOCIETY FOR CHILDREN'S LITERATURE NEWSLETTER). **VAT** Canadian Research Society for Children's Literature Newsletter. No. 1 (Jan. 1983)-. 0820-8247. Periodical. CN. English. ir. 2.00. School of Library and Information Science, University of Western Ontario, London Ontario N6G 1H1 Canada. **Tel** 679-3542. **Ed** Catherine Ross and Delilah Deane-Zairi. **DD** 809.89282072. **Circ** 125. Lists addresses, publications, and current research of Canadian researchers on children's literature. *Canadian Research Society for Children's Literature (Newsletter), 0710-1406.*

CTHULHU CALLS. V. 1- July 1973-. Periodical. US. English. qt. Northwest Community College, Powell WY 82435. **LC** PS374.S35. **DD** 810.80054.

CUADERNO LITERARIO AZOR. **VFOAT** Cuadernos Literarios Azor. Began in 1964. Spanish. ir. 50. Ediciones Rondas, C Peligro 8, Barcelona 12 Spain. **LC** PQ6170.

CUADERNOS DE COMUNICACION & INFORMACION. No. 1 (Jul.-Set. 1979)-. PE. Spanish. ir. $16.00. Prolongacion Arenales, 183 San Isidro, Lima 27 Peru. **LC** P87. **DD** 302.2.

CUADERNOS DE FILOLOGIA. III, LITERATURAS, ANALISIS. **VFOAT** Literaturas, Analisis. 1-2-. German (Spanish). ir. **Ind/Abst** MLA Int. Bibliogr. Books Artic. Mod. Lang. Lit. **LC** PQ6001. **DD** 860.9. *Cuadernos de Filologia (Universidad de Valencia. Seccion de Filologia Moderna).*

CUADERNOS DE INVESTIGACION FILOLOGICA. *See* Linguistics.

CUADERNOS DE LA CATEDRA MIGUEL DE UNAMUNO. *See* Philosophy.

CUADERNOS PARA INVESTIGACION DE LA LITERATURA HISPANICA. No. 1- 1978-. 0210-0061. Periodical. Spanish. qt. $20.00. Fundacion Libreria, Alcala 93, Madrid 9 Spain. **Tel** (91)4311122. bk rev. Spanish and Hispanoamerican literature (critic, history, etc.).

CUENTOS PARA OIR. 1.- 1976-. Periodical. UY. Spanish. ir. Radio Sarandi Enriqueta, Compte Y Rique 1281, Montevideo Uraguay. **LC** PQ8517.5.

LA CULTURA. *See* Philosophy.

CUMBERLANDS. V. 14- Fall 1977-. 0163-1209. Periodical. US. English. sa. $5.00. **LC** PS501. **DD** 810.80054. *Cumberlands, Twigs.*

CUNY ENGLISH FORUM. **VAT** City University of New York English Forum. Vol. 1-. 0736-3974. US. English. an. AMS Press, 56 East 13th Street, New York NY 10003. **Tel** (212)777-4700. **DD** 809. A wide-ranging collection from Old English to the present, both new interpretations of traditional approaches and cross-disciplinary explorations.

CURRENT RESEARCH IN FRENCH STUDIES AT UNIVERSITIES AND POLYTECHNICS IN THE UNITED KINGDOM. *See* Linguistics.

CURRICULUM RESOURCES. 1-. 0714-6124. Monographic Series. CN. English (includes French publications). Vancouver School Board, Education Services Group, 1595 West 10th Avenue, Vancouver British Columbia V6J 1Z8 Canada. **DD** 011.62.

THE CURWOOD COLLECTOR *CEASED.* V. 1-5. 0147-0965. US. English. The Curwood Collector, 1825 Osaukie Road, Owosso MI 48867. **LC** PS3505.U92. **DD** 813.52.

CUTBANK. **VFOAT** Cut Bank. **VAT** Cut Bank. 1 (Spring 1973)-. 0734-9963. Periodical. US. English. sa. $6.50. Cutbank, University of Montana, English Department #7410, Missoula MT 59812. **Ed** Pamela Uschuk. **Ind/Abst** Index Am. Period. Verse. **LC** PS501. **DD** 810.8. bk rev. adv acc. **Circ** 350. Microfiche. Poetry and fiction of high quality by known and unknown authors from across the US and abroad. Black and white art and photos when space available.

CYGNUS. 1979-. Periodical. II. English. ir. $15.00. Department of English & Modern European Language, Lucknow University, Lucknow-226 007 India. **LC** PR1.

THE D. H. LAWRENCE REVIEW. **VAT** David Herbert Lawrence Review. V. 1- Spring 1968-. 0011-4936. Periodical. US. English. ir. $12.00. DH Lawrence Review, c/o D Jackson 204 Memorial Hall University of Delaware, Newark DE 19716. **Tel** (302)454-1480. **Ed** Dennis Jackson. bk rev. **Circ** 600. The journal is a forum for criticism, scholarship, reviews, and bibliography of the work of D. H. Lawrence and his circle. Published 3 times yearly.

DADA SURREALISM. *See* The Arts (General) - Art.

DADZIS. Began in 1957. Periodical. UR. Latvian. sm. 0.20 Single Issue. Latvijas Kp Ck Izdevniecibа, 226908 Pdp Valnu Iela 2, Riga USSR. **LC** PN6211.L3.

DAINIKA BAMLA (ANNUAL). (DAINIKA BAMLA). **VFOAT** Dainika Bamla, Barshika Samkhya. 1981-. Periodical. Bengali. an. **LC** PK1712.5.

DALHOUSIE FRENCH STUDIES. Vol. 1 (Oct. 1979)-. 0711-8813. CN. English (includes some text in French). an. $12.00 US. University of Dalhousie, Department of French, Halifax Nova Scotia Canada B3H 3J5. **Tel** (904)424-2430. **Ed** Michael Bishop. **DD** 840.9. **Circ** 300. Articles and poems.

DAMANA. V. 1- 2030- 1973-. Nepali. ir. 5.00. Badri Pradsada Apadha, Suman Kunja 25/497 Tangal, Kathamadaum Nepal. **LC** PK2598.A2.

DAMASCUS ROAD. Vol. 1-. 0418-3142. Monographic Series. US. English. ir. Damascuc Road, 6271 Hill Drive, Wescosville PA 18106. **LC** PS613.

DANDELION. V. 1- Summer 1975-. 0383-9575. Periodical. CN. English. sa. $2.25 Per No. Distribution Limited to Calgary, Banff and Saskatoon. Dandelion, 806-9th Avenue Southeast, Calgary Alberta T2G 0S2 Canada. **DD** C810.80054. (cum index).

DANSKE STUDIER. Vol. 1-12 1904-15. 0106-4525. Periodical. DK. Danish. qt. 15. C A Reitzels Forlag, Noerregade 210, 1165 Koebenhavn K Denmark. **Ed** Iver Kjaer and Flemming Nielsen. **Ind/Abst** MLA Int. Bibliogr. Books Artic. Mod. Lang. Lit. **LC** PD3004. (cum index). bk rev. **Circ** 700. Studies in Danish literature, linguistics and folklore, inclusive of book reviews regarding reference literature covering these fields. *Dania.*

DAOYU JIKAN. (TAO YU CHI KAN). **VFOAT** Island Quarterly. V. 1-. 0303-0954. Periodical. Chinese. ir. $0.30 Each Issue. 7 Jalan Lateh, Singapore 13 Singapore. **LC** PL3097.S5.

DAPHNIS. Began in 1972. 0300-693X. Periodical. NE. German. ir. Editions Rodopi NV, Keizergracht 302-304, Amsterdam The Netherlands. **Ind/Abst** MLA Int. Bibliogr. Books Artic. Mod. Lang. Lit. **LC** PT177. **DD** 830.9. *Zeitschrift fur Mittlere Deutsche Literatur.*

DARK FANTASY (GANANOQUE, ONT.). (DARK FANTASY). 0710-2860. Periodical. CN. English. qt. $5.00 for 5 issues. Dark Fantasy, c/o Shadow Press, PO Box 207, Gananoque Ontario K7G 2T Canada. **DD** C813.087608.

DAUGAVA. July 1977-. Periodical. UR. Russian. mo. Daugava Riga, 226081 Gsp Ul Balasta Dambis, Riga Latvian SSR. **Ind/Abst** MLA Int. Bibliogr. Books Artic. Mod. Lang. Lit. **LC** PG9145.R1.

DDR-PERIODICA. **VAT** Deutsche Democratische Republik-Periodica. GE. German. ir. Democratische Republik-Periodica, Leninstrasse 16, Postfach 160, 701 Leipzig West Germany. **LC** Z6956.G3, PN5214.P4.

DEBACLE. V. 1- 1978-. 0706-5639. CN. French. an. $3.00 Per Number. R Plamondon, #9-71 rue Trudeau Duberger, Quebec G1P 3J9 Canada. **DD** C840.5.

DEDALE. 1-. French. ir. Marabout S A, 65 rue de Limbourg, Verviers B-4800 Belgium. **LC** PQ1276.S35. **DD** 843.0876.

DEGRE SECOND. No. 1- July 1977-. 0148-561X. Periodical. US. English and French. ir. $17.00 US. Virginia Polytechic Institute, Department of Language & Literature, 108 Holden, Blacksburg VA 24061. **Tel** (703)961-5233. **Ed** W Pierre Jacoebee. **Ind/Abst** MLA Int. Bibliogr. Books Artic. Mod. Lang. Lit. **LC** PQ1. bk rev. adv acc. **Circ** 225. Studies in French and, occasionally, francophone literatures.

DEKALB LITERARY ARTS JOURNAL. Began with 1, 1966. 0011-7714. Periodical. US. English. qt. $10.00. DeKalb Community College, 555 Indian Creek Drive, Clarkston GA 30021. **Tel** (404)299-4119. **Ed** Frances S Ellis. **Ind/Abst** Abstr. Engl. Stud. **Circ** 1,000. (ctrl). Previously unpublished poetry, fiction, drama, art, music accepted from general public and published fall, winter and spring.

DELAP'S F & SF REVIEW. **VFOAT** Delap's F and SF Review, F & SF Review. **VAT** Delap's Fantasy and Science Fiction Review. 0161-7931.

Literature

Periodical. US. English. mo. $20.00. PO Box 46572, West Hollywood CA 90046.

DELO; MESECNI KNJIZEVNI CASOPIS. 1- March 1955-. 0011-7935. Periodical. YU. Serbo-Croatian -R. mo. $20.00. Nolit, Terazije 31 Fah 133, Belgrade Yugoslavia. **Tel** 332-398. Ed Jovica Acin. **Ind/Abst** MLA Int. Bibliogr. Books Artic. Mod. Lang. Lit. **LC** AP56. bk rev. adv acc. **Circ** 2,000. (ctrl). Contains poetry and poetics texts from Yugoslavia essays and reviews of books.

DES LIVRES ET DES JEUNES. (DES LIVRES ET DES JEUNES : REVUE DE L'ASSOCIATION CANADIENNE POUR L'AVANCEMENT DE LA LITTERATURE DE JEUNESSE). Vol. 1, No. 1 (Nov. 1978)-. 0706-795X. Periodical. CN. French. ty. $7.50. Des Livres et des Jeunes, 2500 Boulevard Universite Cite, Universitaire, Sherbrooke Quebec J1K 2R1 Canada. **Ind/Abst** Point Repere. **LC** Z1037.2. **DD** 028.534089114.

DESCANT. No. 1- Nov. 1970-. 0382-909X. Periodical. CN. English. qt. $13.93. Descant/Canada, Station P Box 314, Toronto Ontario Canada M5S 2S8. Ed Karen Mulhallen. **Circ** 750. (ctrl). Quality stories, poems, interviews, graphics and prose.

DETSKAIA LITERATURA. Began in 1950. 0418-7946. Periodical. UR. Russian. an. Victor Kamkin, 12224 Parklawn Drive, Rockville MD 20852. **LC** PN1009.R8.

DEUS LOCI. (DEUS LOCI : THE LAWRENCE DURRELL NEWSLETTER). **VFOAT** Lawrence Durrell Newsletter. Vol. 1, No. 1 (Sept. 1977)-. 0707-9141. Periodical. CN. English. qt. $3.50. Okanagan College, Department of English, James A Brigham, 1000 Klo Road, Kelowna British Columbia V1Y 4X8 Canada. **Tel** (604)762-5445. **Ind/Abst** MLA Int. Bibliogr. Books Artic. Mod. Lang. Lit. **LC** PR6007.U76. **DD** 828.91209.

DEUTSCHE LITERATURZEITUNG. Vol. 1-. 0012-043X. Periodical. German. mo. $47.60. Kunst & Wissen Erich Bieber, Dufourstrasse 51, CH-8008 Zurich Switzerland. **Tel** 01/69 44 20.

DEUTSCHE NEUDRUCKE. REIHE : BAROCK. 1- 1966-. 0418-8926. Monographic Series. GW. English. ir. Walter de Gruyter, Postfach 110240, D-1000 Berlin 30 West Germany. **Tel** (914)747-0110.

DEUTSCHE VIERTELJAHRSSCHRIFT FUR LITERATURWISSENSCHAFT UND GEISTESGESCHICHTE. Vol. 1 (No. 1-)-. 0012-0936. Periodical. GW. German. qt. $51.29. J B Metzlersche Verlagsbuchhdl, Kernerstrasse 43, 7000 Stuttgart 1 West Germany. **Ind/Abst** MLA Int. Bibliogr. Books Artic. Mod. Lang. Lit., Annu. Bibliogr. Engl. Lang. Lit., Philos. Index, Years Work Eng. Stud. **LC** PN4. (cum index).

DEUTSCHUNTERRICHT. V. 1, July. 1948-. 0012-1460. German. mo. $20.78. Kunst & Wissen Erich Bieber, Dufourstrasse 51, CH-8008 Zurich Switzerland. **Tel** (011)1-41-69 44 20. **Ind/Abst** Sociol. Abstr., Lang. Lang. Behav. Abstr.

DIALOG. V. 1- May 1956-. 0012-2041. Periodical. PL. Polish. mo. ARS Polona, Krakowskie Przedmiescie 7, 00-068 Warsaw Poland. **Ind/Abst** MLA Int. Bibliogr. Books Artic. Mod. Lang. Lit. **LC** PN1607. (cum index).

DIALOGOS. **VFOAT** Artes/Letras/Ciencias Humanas/Di Alogos. V. 1- (No. 1-). 0012-2114. Periodical. Spanish. ir.

DIANA'S BIMONTHLY. **VFOAT** Diana's. Began with Feb. 1972 issue. 0046-0222. Periodical. US. English. sa. Diana's Bimonthly Press, 71 Elmgrove Avenue, Providence RI 02906. **LC** PS501. **DD** 810.8.

DICKENS QUARTERLY. Vol. 1, No. 1 (Mar. 1984)-. 0742-5473. Periodical. US. English. qt. $10.00. University of Louisville, Academic Publications, Administration Building, Louisville KY 40292. **Ind/Abst** Abstr. Engl. Stud., MLA Int. Bibliogr. Books Artic. Mod. Lang. Lit. **LC** PR4579. **DD** 823.8. *Dickens Studies Newsletter, 0012-2432.*

DICKENS STUDIES ANNUAL. V. 1- 1970-. 0084-9812. US. English. an. $39.50. AMS Press Inc, 56 East 13th Street, New York NY 10003. **Tel** (212)777-4700. Ed Michael Timko, Fred Kaplan and Edward Guiliano. **Ind/Abst** MLA Int. Bibliogr. Books Artic. Mod. Lang. Lit., Years Work Eng. Stud. **LC** PR4579. **DD** 823.8. bk rev. Essays and longer articles on Dickens as well as on other Victorian novelists, and on the history or aestetic of Victorian fiction. *Dickens Studies, 0419-1099.*

DICKENS STUDIES NEWSLETTER *CEASED.* V. 1-14. 0012-2432. Periodical. US. English. qt. **Ind/Abst** Abstr. Engl. Stud., MLA Int. Bibliogr. Books Artic. Mod. Lang. Lit. **LC** PR4579. **DD** 823.8.

DICTIONARY OF LITERARY BIOGRAPHY YEARBOOK. *See* Yearbooks, Almanacs, Directories.

DIDEROT STUDIES. 1- 1949-. 0070-4806. Periodical. SZ. English or French. ir. Librairie Droz, 11 rue Massot, 1211 Geneve Switzerland. Ed Guiragussian. **Ind/Abst** MLA Int. Bibliogr. Books Artic. Mod. Lang. Lit. **LC** PQ1979. **DD** 848508. bk rev. **Circ** 500. French literature: Diderot.

DIECIOCHO. V. 1- Spring 1978-. 0163-0415. Periodical. US. Spanish (English or Portuguese). sa. $12.00. Eva M Kahilouto Rudat, Diechicho, PO Box 252, Ithaca NY 14850. **Ind/Abst** MLA Int. Bibliogr. Books Artic. Mod. Lang. Lit. **LC** PQ6069. **DD** 860.05.

DIETSCHE WARANDE EN BELFORT. Vol. 1 Jan. 1900-. 0012-2645. Periodical. BE. Dutch. mo. 1200. Postbus 137, 3000 Leuven 3 Belgium. **Ind/Abst** MLA Int. Bibliogr. Books Artic. Mod. Lang. Lit., Annu. Bibliogr. Engl. Lang. Lit., Appl. Mech. Rev., Math. Rev., Comput. Rev., Bibliogr. Engl. Lit. bk rev adv acc. **Circ** 1,600. (ctrl). Publishing of creative work: poetry, prose of young and old, very severe selection. Reviews of books on literature and of novels. *Dietsche Warande, Belfort.*

DIME NOVEL ROUND-UP. **VFOAT** Round-Up. V. 21 No. 11- Nov. 1953-. 0012-2814. Periodical. US. English. bm. $5.00. Dime Novel Round-Up, 821 Vermont Street, Lawrence KS 66044. **LC** PS374.D5. **DD** 813.008. (cum index). *Reckless Ralph's Dime Novel Round-Up.*

DIMENSION; CONTEMPORARY GERMAN ARTS AND LETTERS. V. 1- 1968-. 0012-2882. Periodical. US. English (German). ty. $22.00. Dimension, PO Box 7032, Austin TX 78712. **Tel** (512)345-0622. Ed A Leslie Willson. **LC** AP2. **DD** 830.800914. (cum index). **Circ** 1,000. Contemporary German writing in a bilingual form with many first-time publications of German poetry, prose, and drama.

DIRECTION *CEASED.* No. 1, July 1975. Ceased with with 1978 issue. 0380-9056. Periodical. CN. English. sa. $1.50 Per No. Direction Founders College, York University, 4700 Keele Street, Downsview Ontario M3T 2R3 Canada. **DD** C810.0054.

DIRECTORY - EDITORIAL FREELANCERS ASSOCIATION (U.S.). *See* Yearbooks, Almanacs, Directories.

DIRECTORY OF EDITORIAL RESOURCES. *See* Yearbooks, Almanacs, Directories.

DIRECTORY OF FLORIDA MARKETS FOR WRITERS. *See* Yearbooks, Almanacs, Directories.

DISCURSO LITERARIO. **VFOAT** Revista de Temas Hispanicas. Vol. 1, No. 1 (Autumn 1983)-. 0737-8742. Periodical. US. English (Portuguese and Spanish). sa. $30.00. Juan Manuel Marcos, Department of Foreign Languages and Literatures, Oklahoma State University, Stillwater OK 74078. **Tel** (405)624-5825. Ed Juan Manuel Marcos. **LC** PQ7081.A1. **DD** 860.0998. bk rev acc. **Circ** 500. Literary criticism and creative writing on Hispanic and Luso-Brazilian to topics.

DISCUSSIONS IN DEVELOPMENTAL DRAMA. **VFOAT** Canadian Studies in Drama, Calgary Studies in Drama. DDD1-. 0318-7462. Periodical. CN. English. University of Calgary, Department of Drama, Calgary Alberta T2N 1N4Canada.

DISKUSSION DEUTSCH. *See* Linguistics.

DISPOSITIO. V. 1- (No. 1-). 0734-0591. Periodical. US. English (French, Portuguese, or Spanish). ty. $11.00. Department of Romanic Languages, University of Michigan, Ann Arbor MI 48109. **Ind/Abst** MLA Int. Bibliogr. Books Artic. Mod. Lang. Lit., Film Lit. Index. **LC** P99. **DD** 001.5105.

DISTINGUISHED LECTURERS SERIES. No. 1-. 0196-9684. Monographic Series. US. English. ir. Bureau of Business Research, University of Texas at Austin, c/o M Herndy, Austin TX 78712. **LC** UNC.

DIVERSIONS. V. 1- 1969-. 0382-8301. CN. English. an. Burnaby Creative Writers Society, 5512 Neville Street, Burnaby British Columbus V5J 2H7 Canada. **DD** C810.80054.

DIVYAJYOTIH. Sanskrit. ir. 12.00. Divyajyoti Office, Simala India. **LC** PK401.

DIXIONARIO ENCICLOPEDICO DELLA LETTERATURA ITALIANA. *See* Encyclopedias & General Reference Books.

DNEVNAIA ZVEZDA; VOSTOCHNYI ALMANAKH. UR. Russian. 1.54 Single Issue. Khudozh Lit-ra, B-78 Novo-Basmannaia 19, Moskva USSR. **LC** PJ486.

DOG'S BREATH. Vol. 1, No. 1 (Spring 1983)-. 0827-2905. Periodical. CN. English. sa. $1.50 per No. Dog's Breath, c/o English Department of Huron College, London Ontario N6G 1H3 Canada. **DD** C810.80054.

DOGSOLDIER. 0094-3118. US. English. $1.75. Dogsoldier/E 323 Boone, Spokane WA 99202. **LC** PS507. **DD** 810.80054.

DOLPHIN (ARHUS, DENMARK). (THE DOLPHIN : PUBLICATIONS OF THE ENGLISH DEPARTMENT, UNIVERSITY OF AARHUS). No. 1 (Feb. 1979)-. 0106-4487. Periodical. English (Danish). sa. **LC** UNC. **DD** 820.9.

DORIS LESSING NEWSLETTER. V. 1- Winter 1976-. 0882-486X. Periodical. US. English. sa. $10.00 Members. Doris Lessing Newsletter, c/o Pat C Hoy II, US Military Academy, Department of English, West Point NY 10996. **Ind/Abst** Abstr. Engl. Stud., MLA Int. Bibliogr. Books Artic. Mod. Lang. Lit. **DD** 823.

DOSHISHA GAIKOKU BUNGAKU KENKYU. **VFOAT** Doshisha Studies in Foreign Literature. Began in 1971. JA. Japanese, English, French or German. ir. 1000. Doshisha Gaikoku Bungaku, Kami-Kyo-Ku, Kyoto Japan. **LC** PN9.

DOSHISHA KOKUBUNGAKU. Began in 1961. Japanese. ir. Doshisha Daigaku Kokubun Gakkai, Higashi Iru, Imadegawadori Karasumaru, Kamigyo-Ku, Kyoto-Shi Japan. **LC** PL700.

DOSTOEVSKY STUDIES : JOURNAL OF THE INTERNATIONAL DOSTOEVSKY SOCIETY. Vol. 1 (1980)-. Periodical. US. English (French, German, or Russian). an. $12.00. International Dostoevsky Society, c/o Nadine Natov, 3707 Emily Street, Kensington MD 20895. **Tel** (202)676-7084. Ed Rudolf Neuhauser and Nadine Natov. **Ind/Abst** MLA Int. Bibliogr. Books Artic. Mod. Lang. Lit. **LC** PG3328.Z6. **DD** 891.733. *Bulletin (International Dostoevsky Society), 0047-0686.*

DQR. DUTCH QUARTERLY REVIEW OF ANGLO-AMERICAN LETTERS. (DUTCH QUARTERLY REVIEW OF ANGLO-AMERICAN LETTERS). **VFOAT** DQR, Dutch Quarterly Review. V. 1-. 0046-0842. Periodical. NE. English. qt. $15.00. Editions Rodopi NV, Keizersgracht 302-304, Amsterdam The Netherlands. **Ind/Abst** Abstr. Engl. Stud., MLA Int. Bibliogr. Books Artic. Mod. Lang. Lit., Sociol. Abstr. **LC** PE9. **DD** 810.

DRAGONFIELDS. (DRAGONFIELDS : TALES OF FANTASY). No. 3 (Summer '80)-. 0708-5508. Periodical. CN. English. ir. $5.00 Per Number. Triskell Press, PO Box 9480, Ottawa Ontario K1G 3V2 Canada. **DD** 820.8015. *Beyond the Fields We Know, 0708-9872; Dragonbane, 0229-2904.*

DRAGONFLY. V. 1- Jan. 1973-. 0364-359X. Periodical. US. English. qt. $12.00. Dragonfly-East/West Quarterly, c/o R Tice, 7372 Zana Lane, Magna UT 84044. **Tel** (503)253-0889. Ed Richard Tice and Jack Lyon. **LC** PS593.H3. **DD** 811.06. bk rev. **Circ** 400. Contemporary English and Japanese Haiku, historical and critical articles on Haiku, quarterly contests, oriental calligraphy and artwork. *Haiku Highlights.*

THE DREISER NEWSLETTER. V. 1- Spring 1970-. 0012-6098. Periodical. US. English. sa. $4.00. Indiana State Univ, Department of English, Terre Haute IN 47809. **Tel** (812)237-3164. Ed Richard W Dowell. **LC** PS3507.R55. **DD** 813.52. bk rev. **Circ** 240. It is dedicated to stimulating, coordinating and reporting Dreiser scholarship. Critical articles are welcome but priority given to bibliographical materials. Annual checklist of Dreiser scholarship.

DRIFTWOOD. 1973-. 0382-7984. CN. English. ir. J Millons Creative Writing, Continuing Education Division, Algonquin College, 1385 Woodroffe Avenue, Ottawa Ontario K2G 1V8 Canada 2749463. **DD** C810.8092379.

DRUM (AMHERST, MASS.). (DRUM). Began with 1969 issue. Periodical. US. English. ir. Drum, 325 New Africa House 115 U MA, Amherst MA 01003.

DRUZHBA. Began in 1977. Periodical. UR. Russian. bm. $19.00. Victor Kamkin Inc (70258), 12224 Parklawn Drive, Rockville MD 20852. **Tel** (301)881-5973. **LC** PG3227.

DRUZHBA (IOSHKAR-OLA, R.S.F.S.R.). (DRUZHBA). No. 1 (1975)-. 0135-7832. Periodical. UR. Russian. an. **LC** PG3504.M28.

DSH ABSTRACTS. *See* Indexes/Abstracts.

DUDHERI. Periodical. Nepali. ir. 3.00. **LC** PK2598.A2.

EARLY AMERICAN LITERATURE. V. 3- Spring 1968-. 0012-8163. Periodical. US. English. ty. $10.00. University of North Carolina Press, Box 2288, Chapel Hill NC 27514. **Tel** (919)962-4039. **Ed** Everett Emerson. **Ind/Abst** Am. Hist. Life, Hist. Abstr., Part A, Mod. Hist. Abstr., Hist. Abst., Part B, Twent. Century Abstr., Abstr. Engl. Stud., MLA Int. Bibliogr. Books Artic. Mod. Lang. Lit., Writ. Am. Hist., Index Book Rev. Humanit., Humanit. Index, Relig. Index One, Period., Recent Publ. Artic. **LC** PS501. (cum index). bk rev. adv acc. **Circ** 700. Publishes scholarship and criticism in the literature of the Seventeenth and Eighteenth Centuries and the early national period (to about 1820). *Early American Literature Newsletter, 0739-8301.*

EARLY DRAMA, ART, AND MUSIC MONOGRAPH SERIES. *See* The Arts (General).

ECRIRE. (ECRIRE : VADE-MECUM A L'USAGE DES ECRIVAINS, JOURNALISTES ET PIGISTES). 1982-. 0711-5474. CN. French. an. $14.95 Per Volume. Ecrire, Le March E de l Ecriture CP 148, Succursale Youville Montreal Quebec H2P 2V4 Canada. **DD** 808.02509714.

ECRITOIRE. (L'ECRITOIRE : REVUE ETUDIANTE DU MODULE ETUDES LITTERAIRES DE L'UQAM). Vol. 2, No. 1 Sept. 1979-. 0229-7043. Periodical. CN. French. sa. $1.00 Per No. Module Etudes Litteraires, Universite de Quebec A Montreal, CP 8888 Succursale A, Montreal Quebec H3C 3P8 Canada. **DD** C840.8092375. *Read Building, 0711-1045.*

ECRITS DU CANADA FRANCAIS. 1-. 0013-0729. Periodical. CN. French. ir. Ecrits du Canada Francais, 5754 Avenue Deom, Montreal Que H3S 2N4 Canada. **Tel** (514)738-9296. **Ind/Abst** Point Repere. **DD** C840.8.

ECRITURE FRANCAISE DANS LE MONDE. Vol. 2, Nos. 1/2 (1980)- – Nos. 3/4- -. 0228-7951. Periodical. CN. French. ir. $7.74. Editions Naaman, CP 697, Sherbrooke Quebec J1H 5K5 Canada. **Tel** (819)563-1117. **DD** 840.9. bk rev. adv acc. **Circ** 3,000. Independent, international and cultural journal of creative writing. Mouthpiece for French language authors and authors born in France but living outside their native country. *Ecriture Francaise, 0708-4838.*

EDDA. Vol. 1- 1914-. 0013-0818. Periodical. NO. Norwegian. bm. $35.00. Universitetsforlaget, PO Box 2959-Toyen, Oslo 6 Norway. **Tel** 02 27 60 60. **Ed** Ase Hiorth Lervik. **Ind/Abst** MLA Int. Bibliogr. Books Artic. Mod. Lang. Lit., Index Book Rev. Humanit. **LC** PN9. (cum index). bk rev. **Circ** 1,100. Scandinavian journal of literary research.

EDEBIYAT. V. 1-. 0364-6505. Periodical. US. English. sa. $10.00. Middle East Center of the University of Pennsylvania, 383 Williams Hall/CU 19174, Philadelphia PA 19174. **LC** PJ2. **DD** 809.8956.

EDO JIDAI BUNGAKUSHI. No. 1-. Periodical. Japanese. ir. c/o Inoue Toshiyuki, Edo Jidai Bungakushi Kankokai, 30-24 Kasumigaoka 2-Chome, Higashi-Ku 813, Fukuoka-Shi Japan. **LC** PL726.35.

EIBUNGAKU HYORON. **VFOAT** Review of English Literature. No. 1-. Japanese or English. ir. Yoshida Nihonmatsucho, Sakyoku 606, Kyoto Japan. **LC** PR1.

EIDOS (SUFFERN, N.Y.). (EIDOS (SUFFERN, N.Y.)). Vol. 1, No. 1 (Apr. 1984)-. 8755-3198. Periodical. US. English. qt. $5.00. EIDOS, c/o Sally M Gall, 29 Bayard Lane, Suffern NY 10901. **DD** 808.

EIGO EIBUNGAKU KENKYU. *See* Linguistics.

EIGSE. *See* Linguistics.

EIRE-IRELAND. *See* Ethnic.

EKHO; LITERATURNYI ZHURNAL. 1-. Periodical. Russian. ir. 60.00. RTL/Ardis Publishers, Carl R Proffer, 2901 Heatherway, Ann Arbor MI 48104. **LC** PG3516.

THE ELLEN GLASGOW NEWSLETTER. Vol. 1, No. 1 (Oct. 1974)-. 0160-7545. Periodical. US. English. sa. $2.00 Membership. Edgar E MacDonald, Box 565, Ashland VA 23005. **Ind/Abst** MLA Int. Bibliogr. Books Artic. Mod. Lang. Lit. **LC** PS3513.L34. **DD** 813.52.

ELLERY QUEEN. **VFOAT** Ellery Queen's Mystery Magazine. 0744-0022. Periodical. US. English. ir. Ellery Queen, Box 1930, Marion OH 43305. *Ellery Queen's Mystery Magazine, 0013-6328.*

ELLIPSE. 1-. 0046-1830. Periodical. CN. English (French). ir. C.P. 10 Faculte des Arts, Universite de Sherbrooke, Sherbrooke Quebec J1K 2R1 Canada. **Ind/Abst** Abstr. Engl. Stud., Point Repere. **LC** PR9194. **DD** 808.8.

ELLIPSE. (ELLIPSE MICROFORM). 1 (Fall 1969)-. 0046-1830. Periodical. CN. English (French). Micromedia Limited, 144 Front Street West, Toronto Ontario MJ5 1G2 Canada. **DD** 808.89971.

ELOIZES. (ELOIZES : REVUE DE L'ASSOCIATION DES ECRIVAINS ACADIENS). 1 (Spring 80)-. 0228-0124. Periodical. CN. French. sa. $7.74. Association des Ecrivains, Acadiens, 351 rue St Georges, Moncton New Brunswick E1C 1W8 Canada. **Tel** (506)854-3491. **DD** C840.809715. bk rev. **Circ** 300. Poetic and prosaic texts of varied lengths and authors, drama extracts, essays, chronicles, etc.

EMPIRE FOR THE SF WRITER. **VFOAT** Empire Science Fiction. **VAT** Empire for the Science Fiction Writer. 1974. 0279-8085. Periodical. US. English. qt. $9.00. Empire Science Fiction, c/o Unique Graphics, 1025-55th Street, Oakland CA 94608. **Tel** (415)655-3024. **Ed** Millea Kenin. bk rev. adv acc. **Circ** 1,800. Consists of articles, interviews, reviews, columns by and for science fiction/fantasy writers: how to write, research, market fiction in these genres.

ENCOMIA. V. 1- Spring 1975-. 0363-4841. US. English. an. $7.50. Goshen College, Judith M Davis Secretary Treasurer, Goshen IN 46526. **Tel** (219)533-3161. **Ind/Abst** MLA Int. Bibliogr. Books Artic. Mod. Lang. Lit. **LC** PN661. **DD** 809.02.

ENDANGERED FAECES. 0145-5494. US. English. $2.00. Strage Faeces Press, 122 New Wickham Drive, Penfield NY 14625. **LC** PS501. **DD** 810.80054.

ENDLICH WAS NEUES. German. ir. Suslieferung Durch den Chr Gauke Verlag, 3510 Hann Munden, Postfach 153, Giessen West Germany. **LC** PT1175.

ENGLISCH-AMERIKANISCHE STUDIEN. (ENGLISCH AMERIKANISCHE STUDIEN). **VFOAT** East. Vol. 1-. 0172-1992. Periodical. GW. German (English). ir. 44.-. East Postfach 2565, D-4400 Munster West Germany. **Tel** (251)22795. **Ed** Dieter M Keiner. **LC** PE3. **DD** 420.5. bk rev. adv acc. **Circ** 3,000. (ctrl). Journal for English and American studies in the fields of literature, language, history, politics and culture.

ENGLISH. V. 1- (No. 1-). 0013-8215. Periodical. UK. English. ty. $40.00. Oxford University Press, Journals Department, Walton Street, Oxford OX2 6DP England. **Tel** 0865-56767. **Ed** M Dodsworth and H Baron. **Ind/Abst** Abstr. Engl. Stud., Annu. Bibliogr. Engl. Lang. Lit., Index Book Rev. Humanit., Lang. Lang. Behav. Abstr., MLA Int. Bibliogr. Books Artic. Mod. Lang. Lit., Sociol. Abstr. **LC** PR5. **DD** 820.9. Index published separately - free - automatically sent. bk rev. adv acc. **Circ** 652. A journal of literary criticism publishing essays and reviews aimed at readers in higher education covering creative and critical scholarly work. *Bulletin (English Association), Pamphlet (English Association : 1913).*

ENGLISH AND AMERICAN STUDIES IN GERMAN. *See* Linguistics.

ENGLISH IN AFRICA. V. 1- Mar. 1974-. 0376-8902. SA. English. sa. $2.89. Institute for Study English in Africa, Rhodes University, Box 94, Grahamstown 6140 South Africa. **Ind/Abst** MLA Int. Bibliogr. Books Artic. Mod. Lang. Lit. **LC** PR9340. **DD** 820.8096.

ENGLISH IN AUSTRALIA. **VFOAT** Journal of the Australian Association for the Teaching of English. No. 1 (Nov. 1965)-. 0046-208X. Periodical. AT. English. qt. $12.00. Australian Association for the Teaching of English Inc, PO Box 203, Norwood SA 5067 Australia. **Tel** (08)427022. **Ed** Maunie O'Neill. **Ind/Abst** Curr. Index J. Educ. bk rev. adv acc. **Circ** 4,800. Articles of language arts for teachers and students. One issue consists only of book reviews.

ENGLISH LANGUAGE NOTES. V. 1- Sept. 1963-. 0013-8282. Periodical. US. English. qt. $30.00 Domestic, $35.00 Foreign. University of Colorado, Campus Box 226, Boulder CO 80540. **Tel** (303)492-7176. **Ed** J Wallace Donald. **Ind/Abst** Abstr. Engl. Stud., MLA Int. Bibliogr. Books Artic. Mod. Lang. Lit., Annu. Bibliogr. Engl. Lang. Lit., Recent Publ. Artic., Ref. Source, Index Books Rev. Humanit., Years Work Eng. Stud. **LC** PE1. **DD** 420.5. bk rev. adv acc. **Circ** 1,400. Short scholarly articles on literature in the English language, all countries and all periods from medieval through modern.

ENGLISH LITERARY RENAISSANCE. V. 1- Winter 1971-. 0013-8312. Periodical. US. English. ty. $17.50. Business Manager ELR, Department of English, University of Massachusetts, Amherst MA 02002. **Tel** (413)545-0372. **Ed** Arthur F Kinney. **Ind/Abst** Am. Hist. Life, Hist. Abstr., Part A, Mod. Hist. Abstr., Hist. Abst., Part B, Twent. Century Abstr., Abstr. Engl. Stud., MLA Int. Bibliogr. Books Artic. Mod. Lang. Lit., Recent Publ. Artic. **LC** PR1. **DD** 820.9002. adv acc. **Circ** 1,000. A publication of texts, studies, and bibliographies in the intellectual context and literary achievement of Tudor and Stuart England.

ENGLISH LITERARY STUDIES. ELS MONOGRAPH SERIES. **VFOAT** English Literature Studies. **VAT** English Literary Studies Monograph Series. No.1-. 0829-7681. Monographic Series. CN. English. ir. 12.00. University of Victoria, Department of English, PO Box 1700, Victoria British Columbia Canada. **Tel** 721-7236. **Ed** Samuel L Macey. **Ind/Abst** MLA Int. Bibliogr. Books Artic. Mod. Lang. Lit. **Circ** 400. Literary critical studies of major authors writing in English.

ENGLISH LITERATURE IN TRANSITION, 1880-1920. **VAT** English Literature in Transition, Eighteen Hundred and Eighty-Nineteen Hundred and Twenty. V. 6- 1963-. 0013-8339. Periodical. US. English. qt. $9.00 Domestic, $11.00 Foreign. Arizona State University, Department of English, Tempe AZ 85257. **Tel** (602)965-3168. **Ed** Robert Langenfeld. **Ind/Abst** MLA Int. Bibliogr. Books Artic. Mod. Lang. Lit., Annu. Bibliogr. Engl. Lang. Lit., Humanit. Index, Ref. Source, Index Book Rev. Humanit., MLA Int. Bibliogr. Books Artic. Mod. Lang. Lit., Years Work Eng. Stud., Abstr. Engl. Stud. bk rev. adv acc. **Circ** 800. Vols. 1-11 available from Kraus Reprint Corporation. A quarterly on British literature and culture (1880-1920). Publishes articles, bibliographies, and reviews. *English Fiction in Transition, 1880-1920, 0364-3549.*

ENGLISH MISCELLANY. Vol. 1 1950-. 0425-0575. English, French, German, Italian or Spanish. ir. **Ind/Abst** Abstr. Engl. Stud., MLA Int. Bibliogr. Books Artic. Mod. Lang. Lit., Annu. Bibliogr. Engl. Lang. Lit. **LC** PR13.

ENGLISH STUDIES. V. 1- Feb. 1919-. 0013-838X. Periodical. NE. English. bm. 86.-. Swets & Zeitlinger BV, 347 Heereweg, 2161 Ca Lisse The Netherlands. **Tel** 02521-19113. **Ed** T A Birrell. **Ind/Abst** Annu. Bibliogr. Engl. Lang. Lit., Lang. Teach., Humanit. Index, Lang. Lang. Behav. Abstr., MLA Int. Bibliogr. Books Artic. Mod. Lang. Lit., Sociol. Abstr., Women Stud. Abstr., Years Work Eng. Stud. **LC** PE1. **DD** 420.5. Index published separately - free - automatically sent. (cum index). bk rev. adv acc. **Circ** 2,000. The scope of English Studies ranges from diachronic and synchronic studies of the English language, to the literatures both past and present of the English speaking world. *Student's Monthly.*

ENGLISH STUDIES SERIES. *See* Linguistics.

ENSEMBLE. **VFOAT** Internationales Jahrbuch fur Literatur. Vol. 1-. GW. English (French, German, Italian or Spanish). ir. Deutscher Taschenbuch Verlag, Friedrichstrasse 1A, 8000 Muenchen 40 West Germany. **Tel** 0 89/38 17 06. **LC** PN6010.

ENVIOS; CUADERNOS DE LITERÁTURA. Began with Aug. 1971 issue. 0091-522X. Periodical. US. Spanish. qt. $4.00. PO Box M-228, Hoboken NJ 07030. **LC** PQ7370.

EPIEGRAM MATERIALS. (EPIEGRAM. MATERIALS). Vol. 6M, No. 1 (1 Oct. 1977)-. Periodical. US. English. mo. $40.00. Epie Institute, PO Box 839, Water Mill NY 11976. **Tel** (516)283-4922. **Ind/Abst** Educ. Index, Consum. Index Prod. Eval. Inf. Source. *Epigram.*

EPITAPH. Began in 1943?. 0340-0603. Periodical. German (English). ir. 8.20. F Weber, Kapuzinerstrasse 41 8000 5, Munchen West Germany. **LC** PT1141.A2.

ERASME. **VFOAT** Collection Erasme. 1- 1959-. 0425-1687. Monographic Series. French. ir.

E.R.B.IVORE. **VAT** Erbivore, Edgar Rice Burroughs-Ivore. #3 (July 1967)-. 0710-0388. Periodical. CN. English. ir. **DD** 809.387. *Fantastic Worlds of Burroughs & Kline, 0710-037X.*

ERH TUNG WEN HSUEH HSUAN KAN. **VFOAT** Er Tong Wen Xue Xuan Kan. 1981, 1-. Periodical. CH. Chinese. ir. 0.36. Hsin Hua Shu Tien Shang-Hai Fa, Hsing So Shanghai China. **LC** AP215.C5. **DD** 895.1099282.

ERH TUNG WEN HSUEH YEN CHIU. **VFOAT** Ertong Wenxue Yanjiu. Began in 1959. Periodical. CC. Chinese. ir. 0.40. Shao Nieh Erh Tung Chu Pan She, Shang-Hai Fa Hsing So, Shanghai China Mainland. **LC** PL2449. **DD** 895.1099282.

ERINDALE REVIEW. Vol. 1 (1982)-. 0828-7686. CN. English. an. $5.00. Erindale College Student Union, University of Toronto, Erindale College, Mississauga Ontario L5L 1C6 Canada. **DD** C810.80054.

ESCRITA. Year 1- 1975-. Periodical. BL. Portuguese. ir. Vertente Editura Ltda, rua dr Homera de Melo 446, 05007 Sao Paulo SP Brazil. **Ind/Abst** MLA Int. Bibliogr. Books Artic. Mod. Lang. Lit. **LC** PQ9500.

ESCRITURA. No. 1- Jan./June 1976-. Periodical. VE. Spanish. sa. $9.00. Escritura Escuela de Litras, Universidad Central de Venezuela, Caracas Venezuela. **Ind/Abst** MLA Int. Bibliogr. Books Artic. Mod. Lang. Lit.

ESELSOHR. Periodical. German. sa. G Pilz, Stifterstrasse 4A, 4320 Perg Austria. **LC** PT1141.A2.

ESPACES DE SAINT-JOHN PERSE. 1/2-. FR. French. ir. Diffusion Librairie H Champion, 7 Quai Malaquais, 75006 Paris France. **LC** PQ2623.E386. **DD** 848.91209.

ESPERIENZE LETTERARIE. Vol. 1- Jan./Mar. 1976-. 0392-3495. Periodical. IT. Italian. qt. $23.76. Societa Editrice Napoletana, Corso Umberto 348, 80138 Naples Italy. **Ind/Abst** MLA Int. Bibliogr. Books Artic. Mod. Lang. Lit. **LC** PQ4001.

ESPIRAL/ REVISTA. 1-. Periodical. Spanish. ir. 1,400. Editorial Fundamentos, Caracas 15, Madrid Spain. **LC** PQ6170. **DD** 860.9.

L'ESPRIT CREATEUR. V. 1- Spring 1961-. 0014-0767. Periodical. US. English or French. qt. $64.00. Louisiana State University, Department of French and Italian, Baton Rouge LA 70803. **Tel** (504)388-6713. **Ed** John D Erickson. **Ind/Abst** MLA Int. Bibliogr. Books Artic. Mod. Lang. Lit., Book Rev. Index, Index Book Rev. Humanit. bk rev. adv acc. **Circ** 800. Topical journal of French literature and literary theory and criticism.

ESQ. **VAT** Emerson Society Quarterly. No. 54- 1st Quarter 1969-. 0093-8297. Periodical. US. English. qt. $15.00. Washington State University Press, Pullman WA 99164-5910. **Tel** (509)335-3518. **Ed** Fred Bohm. **Ind/Abst** Abstr. Engl. Stud., Bibliogr. Engl. Lit., MLA Int. Bibliogr. Books Artic. Mod. Lang. Lit., Index Book Rev. Humanit., Years Work Eng. Stud. **LC** PS1629. **DD** 810.9003. bk rev. **Circ** 660. A journal of the American Renaissance, devoted to the study of 19th Century American Literature. *Emerson Society Quarterly, 0013-6670.*

ESSAY AND GENERAL LITERATURE INDEX. *See* Indexes/Abstracts.

ESSAYS AND STUDIES. **Main/Corp** English Association (Great Britain). V. 1-32, 1910-46. UK. English. an. John Murray Publ Ltd, 65 Clerkenwell Road, London Ec1 England. **Tel** (800)221-3845. **LC** PR13. **DD** 820.4. **Circ** 300. (ctrl). An anthology of essays usually on a wide range of subjects from medieval to modern. A new collector is appointed each year by the English Association.

ESSAYS AND STUDIES (ATLANTIC HIGHLANDS, N.J.). (ESSAYS AND STUDIES). US. English. an. **Ind/Abst** Abstr. Engl. Stud. A long established series of critical essays, presenting scholarship and critical insight spanning a broad range in time and genres from the fourteenth century to the present day.

ESSAYS BY DIVERS HANDS. (ESSAYS BY DIVERS HANDS, BEING THE TRANSACTIONS OF THE ROYAL SOCIETY OF LITERATURE). **Main/Corp** Royal Society of Literature of the United Kingdom, London. V. 1-3. 0080-4584. Monographic Series. UK. English. ir.

ESSAYS IN FRENCH LITERATURE. No. 1 (Nov. 1964)-. 0071-139X. AT. English. an. University Bookshop, University of Western Australia, Nedlands Western Australia 6009 Australia. **Ind/Abst** MLA Int. Bibliogr. Books Artic. Mod. Lang. Lit.

ESSAYS IN LITERATURE. Vol. 1- Spring 1974-. 0094-5404. Periodical. US. English. sa. $5.00. Western Illinois University, Department of English, 222 Simpkins Hall, Macomb IL 61455. **Tel** (309)298-2212. **Ed** Thomas P Joswick. **Ind/Abst** Abstr. Engl. Stud., MLA Int. Bibliogr. Books Artic. Mod. Lang. Lit. **LC** PN2. **DD** 805. **Circ** 500. Scholarly critical essays on British, American, and foreign-language literature.

ESSAYS IN POETICS. V. 1- Apr. 1976-. Periodical. UK. English. sa. Department of Russian Studies, Universtiy of Keele, Keele Staffs, Keele ST5 England. **LC** PN2. **DD** 805.

ESSAYS ON CANADIAN WRITING. No. 1- Winter 1974-. 0316-0300. CN. English. qt. $13.93. Essays on Canadian Writing, 307 Coxwell Avenue, Toronto Ontario M4L 3B5 Canada. **Tel** (416)694-3348. **Ed** Jack David and Robert Lecker. **Ind/Abst** Book Rev. Index, Abstr. Engl. Stud., MLA Int. Bibliogr. Books Artic. Mod. Lang. Lit. bk rev. adv acc. **Circ** 1,700. Each issue contains full-length scholarly essays on all periods and genres of Canadian literature. Review articles, bibliographies and interviews round out the foremost critical journal in its field.

ESTRENO. V. 1- Winter 1975-. 0097-8663. Periodical. US. Spanish (English). sa. $19.00. University of Cincinnati, Department of Romance Languages and Literature, Cincinnati OH 45221. **Tel** (513)475-6726. **Ed** Patricia W O'Connor. **Ind/Abst** MLA Int. Bibliogr. Books Artic. Mod. Lang. Lit. **DD** 862. (cum index). bk rev. adv acc. **Circ** 600. (ctrl). Unpublished Spanish plays, research articles, reviews of plays and books and material of interest to scholars or professionals of 20th Century Spanish theater.

ESTUDIOS DE LITERATURA ARGENTINA. 1-. Periodical. Spanish. ir. 25 de Mayo, 217 Buenos Aires Argentina. **LC** PQ7600. **DD** 860.9982.

ESTUDIOS FILOLOGICOS. *See* Linguistics.

ETHOS. 1- 1973-. FR. Romanian. an. Virgil Ierunca, Boite Postale 255, 19 Paris SN France. **LC** PC800.

ETHOS (TORONTO, ONT.). (ETHOS). Vol. 1, No. 1 (Summer 1983)-. 0714-0339. Periodical. CN. English. qt. Ethos c/o Ethos Cultural Development Foundation, 316 Dupont Street, Toronto Ontario M5R1V9 Canada. **Tel** (926)8157(416). **Ed** Janis Rapoport. **DD** C810.80054. adv acc. **Circ** 2,100. The leading edge of the new work of books established as well as emerging writers, leaders, and artistis from around the world.

ETUDES ANGLO-AMERICAINES. FR. English or French. ir. Etudes Anglo-Americaines, 2 rue Gay Lussac, 22 Saint-Brieuc, CCP 1027, 2 Rennes France. **LC** PR403. **DD** 820.9.

ETUDES BAUDELAIRIENNES. V. 1- 1969-. 0531-9455. Periodical. SZ. French. ir. Editions de la Baconniere SA, 19 Avenue du College, CH-2017 Boudry Switzerland. **Tel** (038) 42 10 04. **Ed** Marc Eifeldinger and Claude Pichois. **LC** PQ2191.Z5. **Circ** 1,000. Intended as a meeting point for critics. Publishes studies, comments and documents that contribute to deepen our knowledge of Baudelaire.

ETUDES CELTIQUES. No. 1- June 1936-. 0373-1928. FR. French. sa. $21.29. Etudes Celtiques, 6 CNRS 15 Quai A France, 75007 Paris France. **Ed** J Vendryes. **Ind/Abst** MLA Int. Bibliogr. Books Artic. Mod. Lang. Lit., Years Work Eng. Stud. (cum index). *Revue Celtique.*

ETUDES DE LETTRES. V. 1-27, 1934-57. 0014-2026. Periodical. SZ. French. qt. 40. Faculte des Lettres, l'University de Lausanne, Batiment Central Dorigny, 1015 Lausanne Switzerland. **Tel** 21/46.31.69. **Ind/Abst** Abstr. Engl. Stud., MLA Int. Bibliogr. Books Artic. Mod. Lang. Lit., Years Work Eng. Stud. bk rev. Research of the members of the faculty, contributions by authors invited by the faculty, study results, proceedings and monographic issues. Each issue deals with one specific subject.

ETUDES FRANCAISES. V. 1- Feb. 1965-. 0014-2085. Periodical. CN. French. ty. $20.12. Presses de l'Universite, Universite of Montreal, CP 6128, Montreal Quebec H3C 3J7 Canada. **Tel** (514)343-6321. **Ed** Laurent Mailhot. **Ind/Abst** Am. Hist. Life, Hist. Abstr., Part A, Mod. Hist. Abstr., Hist. Abst., Part B, Twent. Century Abstr., MLA Int. Bibliogr. Books Artic. Mod. Lang. Lit., Artbibliogr. Mod., Point Repere, Hist. Abstr. adv acc. **Circ** 700. Mainly literary, this thematic periodical deals with various questions that relate arts to human sciences, language to writings.

ETUDES GERMANIQUES. *See* Linguistics.

ETUDES IRLANDAISES. No. 1-. 0183-973X. Monographic Series. FR. English and French. ir. 75. Universite de Lille III, BP 149, 59653 Villeneuve Cedex France. **Tel** (20)91 92 02. **Ind/Abst** MLA Int. Bibliogr. Books Artic. Mod. Lang. Lit. **LC** DA925. **DD** 941.5082405. bk rev. adv acc. **Circ** 1,000. Contains Irish writings, literary studies, studies in history, civilization, bibliographies, book reviews and activities of Irish interest.

ETUDES LITTERAIRES (UNIVERSITE LAVAL). (ETUDES LITTERAIRES). V. 1- April 1968-. 0014-214X. Periodical. CN. French. ir. Defactement de Letterature, Universite Laval, Ste-Foy Quebec G1K 7P4 Canada. **Tel** (418)656-7844. **Ed** Louise Milot. **Ind/Abst** MLA Int. Bibliogr. Books Artic. Mod. Lang. Lit., Point Repere, Index Book Rev. Humanit. **LC** PQ2. **DD** 840.9. bk rev. adv acc. **Circ** 800. (ctrl). Theorical studies in literature, cinema, and theater.

ETUDES PROUSTIENNES. **Series/Titl** Cahiers Marcel Proust. Began in 1973. FR. French. ir. Gallimard, 5 rue Sebastien Bottin, Paris 7 France. **LC** PQ2631.R63. **DD** 843.912.

EUDORA WELTY NEWSLETTER. V. 1- Winter 1977-. 0146-7220. Periodical. US. English. sa. Eudora Welty Newsletter, University of Toledo, Department of English, Toledo OH 43603. **Tel** (419)537-2318. **Ed** W U McDonald. **Ind/Abst** MLA Int. Bibliogr. Books Artic. Mod. Lang. Lit. **Circ** 210. Primary and secondary bibliographies and bibliographic notes on Eudora and her works, news about Welty publications, conferences on her writing and library collections.

THE EUGENE O'NEILL NEWSLETTER. Vol. 1, No. 1 (May 1977)-. 0733-0456. Periodical. US. English. ty. Suffolk University, Frederick Wilkins, Boston MA 02114. **Tel** (617)723-4700. **Ed** Frederick C Wilkins. **Ind/Abst** MLA Int. Bibliogr. Books Artic. Mod. Lang. Lit., Abstr. Engl. Stud. bk rev. adv acc. **Circ** 350. Essays on O'Neill's life, work and times plus book and performance reviews, photos, news, notes and queries and records of the Eugene O'Neill society and activity around the world.

EUPHORION. BEIHEFTE. Vol. 1-. 0531-2167. Monographic Series. GW. German. ir. Carl Winter Universitatsverlag, Postfach 1866, Lutherstrasse 59, D6900 Heidelberg West Germany. **Tel** 6221-49111. Supplement to Euphorion, history of literature.

EVELYN WAUGH NEWSLETTER. V. 1- Spring 1967-. 0014-3693. Periodical. US. English. ty. $4.50. Nassau Community College, English Department, Garden City NY 11530. **Tel** (516)222-7186. **Ed** Paul A Doyle. **Ind/Abst** Abstr. Engl. Stud., MLA Int. Bibliogr. Books Artic. Mod. Lang. Lit., Years Work Eng. Stud. **DD** 823. bk rev. adv acc. **Circ** 219. Research, biographical and bibliographical articles and reviews relating to the life and writings of English satirist and novelist Evelyn Waugh.

EVENT. V. 1- Spring 1971-. 0315-3770. Periodical. CN. English. ty. $8.00. Sunday School Board/ Southern Baptist Convention, 127-9th Avenue North, Nashville TN 37234.

EXETASIS. V.1- 1974?-. 0163-7282. Periodical. US. English. ir. $5.00. California State University, F McMahon Ed, Northridge CA 91324. **Tel** (818)885-2853. **Ed** Fred McMahon. **Circ** 350. Scholarly essays about rhetoric used in major communications and events: speeches, campaigns, movies, music, etc.

EXIT. V. 2- Fall 1979-. 0195-3516. Periodical. US. English. ty. $7.00. Routes/Creative Arts Projects, Rd#1 Box 339, Glenmont NY 12077. *Entrance.*

THE EXPLICATOR. V. 1- Oct. 1942-. 0014-4940. Periodical. US. English. qt. $30.00. Heldref Publications, 4000 Albemarle Street NW/Suite 302, Washington DC 20016. **Tel** (202)362-6445. **Ed** Gail Lowery. **Ind/Abst** Abstr. Engl. Stud., MLA Int. Bibliogr. Books Artic. Mod. Lang. Lit., Annu. Bibliogr. Engl. Lang. Lit., Humanit. Index, Years Work Eng. Stud. **LC** PR1. (cum index). adv acc. **Circ** 2,235. An informative journal used as an academic guide to various interpretations of literary matter.

EXTRAPOLATION. V. 1- Dec. 1959-. 0014-5483. Periodical. US. English. qt. $25.00. Kent State University Press, Kent OH 44242. **Tel** (216)672-7913. **Ed** Thomas D Clareson. **Ind/Abst** Abstr. Engl. Stud.,

MLA Int. Bibliogr. Books Artic. Mod. Lang. Lit., Humanit. Index. **LC** PN3448.S45. **DD** 808.8387605. (cum index). bk rev. adv acc. **Circ** 1,000. Series scholarly study of science fiction and fantasy. Contains analytic articles, bibliographic studies and lively discussion for scholar, teacher and science fiction fan.

EZHEGODNIK KNIGI SSSR. 1930-. UR. Russian. an. *Ezhegodnik Gosudarstvennoi Tsentralnoi Knizhnoi Palaty RSFSR.*

EZIK I LITERATURA. 1946-. Periodical. Bulgarian (tables of contents also in English). ir. **Ind/Abst** MLA Int. Bibliogr. Books Artic. Mod. Lang. Lit., Lang. Lang. Behav. Abstr. **LC** PG801.

FABULA (LILLE, FRANCE). (FABULA). 1 (Mar. 1983)-. 0755-0960. Periodical. FR. French (English). sa. 100. Presses Universitaires de Lille, 9 rue Auguste Angellier, 59046 Lille France. **LC** PR823. **DD** 823.009.

FAIG. Periodical. Catalan. ty. Omnium Cultural, Apartat 255, Manresa Spain. **LC** PN9.

THE FALCON. No. 1- Summer 1970-. 0014-7079. Periodical. US. Englishs. sa. $2.00. Mansfield State College, Belknap Hall, Mansfield PA 16933. **Ind/Abst** Index Am. Period. Verse. **LC** PS501. **DD** 810.5. Available on microfilm from University Microfilms.

FAMILY ALBUM. (THE FAMILY ALBUM). 0094-5862. US. English. an. $6.95. **LC** PN6014. **DD** 808.8. *Gold Star Family Album.*

FAMOUS PULP CLASSICS. No. 1- 1975-. 0363-0560. US. English. $25.00. Fax Collector's Editions Inc, Box F, West Linn OR 97068. **LC** PS509.A3. **DD** 813.0876.

FANTARAMA. Began publication in 1971. 0704-7320. Periodical. CN. English. mo. Pubbug Press Publications, 11220 Bird Road, Richmond British Columbia V6X 1N8 Canada. **DD** 809.387605.

FANTASTIC. V. 1- Summer 1952-. 0014-7508. Periodical. US. English. qt. $4.00 Domestic, $4.50 Foreign. Ultimate Publishing Co, Box 7 Oakland Gardens, Flushing NY 11364. **LC** AP2. **DD** 808.8387605.

FANTASY BOOK. V. 1, No. 1 (Oct. 1981)-. 0277-0717. Periodical. US. English. qt. $12.00. Fantasy Book Enterprises, PO Box 60126, Pasadena CA 91106. **Tel** (213)428-4124. **Ed** Dennis Mallonee. adv acc. **Circ** 5,000. (ctrl). Features illustrated short fiction with an emphasis on fantasy and science fiction.

FAR-WESTERN FORUM. V. 1- Feb. 1974-. 0094-0887. US. English. ty. $10.00. Editor of Far-Western Forum, 20 Poppy Lane, Berkeley CA 94708. **Ind/Abst** Abstr. Engl. Stud., MLA Int. Bibliogr. Books Artic. Mod. Lang. Lit. **LC** PN2. **DD** 809.

THE FAULKNER NEWSLETTER & YOKNAPATAWPHA REVIEW. VFOAT Faulkner Newsletter. Vol. 1, No. 1 (Jan/Mar 1981). 0733-6357. Periodical. US. English. qt. $10.00. Yoknapatawpha Press, PO Box 248, Oxford MS 38655. **Tel** (601)234-0908. **Ed** William Boozer. **LC** PS3511.A86. **DD** 813.52. bk rev. adv acc. **Circ** 500. (ctrl). Publication in news format, illustrated, about the life and works of William Faulkner, including book reviews and bibliographical checklist.

FAUST-BLATTER *CEASED.* No. 1/2-38. 0532-9752. Periodical. German. ir. **Ind/Abst** MLA Int. Bibliogr. Books Artic. Mod. Lang. Lit. **DD** 830. *Blatter der Knittlinger Faust-Gedenkstatte und des Faust-Museums.*

FEASTS & SEASONS. VFOAT Feasts and Seasons. V. 1, No. 1 (Jan./Feb. 1980)-. 0197-5137. Periodical. US. English. bm. $20.00 Domestic, $25.00 Foreign. Cahill & Co, 145 Palisade Street, Dobbs Ferry NY 10522. **LC** PN6010.5. **DD** 808.8.

FENAISON. 1-. 0712-3566. Periodical. CN. French. ir. Fenaison, c/o Seminaire de Quebec, 1 Cote de la Fabrique, Quebec Quebec G1B 4R7 Canada. **DD** C840.8092375.

FETTFLECK. AU. German. ir. $12.00 Single issue. Antonio Fian, Auenweg 6, 9800 Spittal/Drau Austria. **LC** PT3827.C3.

FICTION. V. 1- 1972-. 0046-3736. Periodical. US. English. ir. $10.00. City College of New York, Department of English, Covenent Avenue and 138th Street, New York NY 10031. **Tel** (212)690-6694. **LC** PN6010.5. **DD** 808.831.

FICTION (EXILE PRESS). (FICTION). Began publication with 1983. 0883-7503. US. English. an. Exile Press, PO Box 1768, Novato CA 94948. **Ed** Guy Daniels and Leslie Woolf Hedley. **LC** PS648.S5. **DD** 813.0108.

FICTION INDEX. *See* Indexes/Abstracts.

FICTION INTERNATIONAL. No. 1- Fall 1973-. 0092-1912. Periodical. US. English. sa. $24.00. San Diego State University Press, 5402 College Avenue, San Diego CA 92115. **Tel** (619)265-6220. **Ind/Abst** Abstr. Engl. Stud., Book Rev. Index. **LC** PN3311. **DD** 805.

THE FICTION MAGAZINE. Vol. 1, No. 1 (Spring 1982)-. 0263-6565. Periodical. UK. English. qt. $22.22. Fiction Magazine, 12/13 Clerkenwell Green, London EC1 England. **Tel** 250 1504. **Ed** Judy Cooke. bk rev. adv acc. **Circ** 7,500. Short stories, articles, interviews and reviews.

FIDDLEHEAD. (THE FIDDLEHEAD). No. 1- Feb. 1945-. 0015-0630. Periodical. CN. English. qt. 14.00 Domestic, $15.00 US. University of New Brunswick, Observatory, PO Box 4400, Fredericton New Brunswick E3B 5A3 Canada. **Tel** (506)454-3591. **Ed** Michael Taylor. **Ind/Abst** Can. Period. Index, Index Book Rev. Humanit. **LC** PR9291.N4. **DD** C810.80054. bk rev. adv acc. **Circ** 800. Also available on microfilm: Toronto: Micromedia, 1978-. Short stories, poetry, literary reviews, and drawings. Canada's oldest literary magazine.

FIN DE SIGLO. No. 1 (June 1982)-. Periodical. Spanish. ir. 4400. Fin de Siglo, Apartado 1724, Jerez de la Frontera Bogota Colombia. **LC** PN6. **DD** 808.8.

FINDING THE RIGHT SPEAKER. US. English. $10.00 Members, $20.00 Nonmembers. American Society of Association Executives, 1575 Eye Street Northwest, Washington DC 20005. **LC** PN4007. **DD** 808.5102573.

FIREBIRD (HARMONDSWORTH, MIDDLESEX). (FIREBIRD). 1-. Periodical. UK. English. an. **LC** PR1307. **DD** 823.008.

FIREWEED. Issue 1- Autumn 1978-. 0706-3857. Periodical. CN. English. qt. $13.93. Fireweed Collective, PO Box 279 Station B, Toronto Ontario M5T 2W2 Canada. **DD** C810.809287.

FIRST ENCOUNTER. V. 1- 1969-. 0382-6201. Periodical. CN. English. ir. English Department, Mount Allison University, Sackville New Brunswick E0A 3C0 Canada. **DD** C810.8092379. *Trial.*

FLANNERY O'CONNOR BULLETIN. (THE FLANNERY O'CONNOR BULLETIN). V. 1- 1972-. 0091-4924. US. English. an. $4.00. Georgia College, PO Box 708, Milledgeville GA 31061. **Tel** (912)453-4047. **Ed** Sarah Gordon. **Ind/Abst** Abstr. Engl. Stud. **LC** PS3565.C57. **DD** 813.54. bk rev. adv acc. **Circ** 500. Critical studies of the writings of Flannery O'Connor.

FOCUS. US. English. **LC** PN2. **DD** 809.04.

FOCUS ON ROBERT GRAVES. No. 1- Jan. 1972-. 0190-650X. Periodical. US. English. University of Colorado Libraries, PO Box 184, Boulder CO 80309. **Ed** E Mason. **Ind/Abst** MLA Int. Bibliogr. Books Artic. Mod. Lang. Lit. **LC** PR6013.R35. **DD** 821.912.

FOLIA LITERARIA. No. 1-. Spanish. ir. Club de Caza y Pesca Entre Alcorte y Joly-1744-Moreno, Casilla de Correo No 123, Moreno Argentina.

FOLIO. Began in 1970. 0882-3030. Monographic Series. US. English (French, or Spanish). $8.00. Department of Foreign Languages, State University of New York, Brockport NY 14420. **Tel** (716)395-2269. **Ed** Martha O'Nan. **Ind/Abst** MLA Int. Bibliogr. Books Artic. Mod. Lang. Lit. **DD** 809. bk rev. adv acc. **Circ** 500. (ctrl). Contains articles on foreign languages and literatures.

FOLK LITERATURE OF THE SEPHARDIC JEWS. 1- 1971-. US. English. ir. University of California Press, 1095 Essex Street, Richmond CA 94804-2112. **Tel** (213)825-1911. **Ed** James Kubeck. Folk literature of the Sephardic Jews.

FONTANE BLATTER. V. 1- 1965-. 0015-6175. Periodical. GE. German. sa. 15,40. Deutscher Buch Export-Import, Leninstrasse 16, DDR-701 Leipzig East Germany. **Tel** Potsdam 4751. **Ind/Abst** MLA Int. Bibliogr. Books Artic. Mod. Lang. Lit. (cum index). bk rev. **Circ** 1,000. (ctrl). Unknown texts by Theodore Fontane. Secondary literature: interpretations, analyses, comparatives, literary-historicals. Personal bibliographies.

FONTES RERUM MEXICANARUM. V. 1/ 1-. Periodical. Spanish (summary in English, French, and German). ir. Akademische Druck U Verlag, Auerspergasse 12, A-8010 Graz Austria.

FOOM. No. 1- Spring 1973-. 0192-8090. Periodical. US. English. qt. $4.00. Marvel Comics Group, 575 Madison Avenue, New York NY 10022. **LC** PN6725. **DD** 741.5973.

FORGE. No. 1- 1970-. Periodical. UK. English. qt. Brockhouse Ltd, Victoria Works Hill Top, W Bromwich, Midlands England. **Ind/Abst** ISMEC Bull.

FORMATIONS (MADISON, WIS.). (FORMATIONS). Vol. 1, No. 1 (Spring 1984)-. 0741-5702. Periodical. US. English. ty. $30.00. University of Wisconsin Press, Journals Division, 114 North Murray Street, Madison WI 53715. **DD** 810.

FORO LITERARIO. VFOAT FL. Vol. 1, No. 1 (1st Half 1977)- – Vol. 1-. Periodical. UY. Spanish. an. 10.00. Foro Literario, Viejo Pancho 2585, Montevideo Uruguay. **Tel** 79 64 36. **Ed** Julio Ricci. **LC** PQ7081.A1. **DD** 860.8098. bk rev. adv acc. **Circ** 1,000. (ctrl). A serial which includes creative literature essays, reviews, linguistics, and notes on Latin American topics. The oldest such journal in Uruguay.

FORSCHUNGSPROBLEME DER VERGLEICHENDEN LITERATURGESCHICHTE. 1- 1951-. 0071-7703. GW. German. ir. Max Niemeyer Verlag, Postfach 2140, D7400 Tuebingen 1 West Germany. **Tel** (0 70 71)81104. **Ed** Kurt Wais. Monographs in comparative literature.

FORUM. VFOAT Forum at Iowa on Russian Literature. V. 1- Fall 1976-. 0164-288X. Periodical. US. English. $5.00 Single Issue. University of Maryland, Germanic and Slavic Department, c/o John Glad/ Director of Slavic Studies, Foreign Languages Building, College Park MD 20742. **LC** PG2901. **DD** 891.709.

FORUM DER LETTEREN. Vol. 1. 0015-8496. Periodical. NE. Dutch. qt. 66.00. Smits B V, Westeinde 135, 2512 GW Den Haag Netherlands. **Tel** 070/89 53 90. **Ind/Abst** MLA Int. Bibliogr. Books Artic. Mod. Lang. Lit., Index Book Rev. Humanit., Am. Hist. Life, Hist. Abstr., Am. Hist. Life, Hist. Abstr., Part A, Mod. Hist. Abstr., Hist. Abst., Part B, Twent. Century Abstr. **LC** PN9. bk rev. adv acc. **Circ** 800. (ctrl). Literature and linguistic articles and reviews. *Museum.*

FORUM ITALICUM. VFOAT FI. V. 12- Spring 1978-. 0014-5858. Periodical. US. English (French, Italian, Portuguese, or Spanish). sa. $20.00. Forum Italicum, Ohio State University, Department of Romance Languages, c/o A Mancini, Columbus OH 43210. **Tel** (614)422-2203. **Ed** M Ricciardelli and Albert N Mancini. **Ind/Abst** MLA Int. Bibliogr. Books Artic. Mod. Lang. Lit., Recent Publ. Artic. bk rev. adv acc. **Circ** 700. (ctrl). Literature, language and culture of Italy and other countries in relation to Italy. Includes poetry, fiction and translations. *FI. Forum Italicum, 0014-5858.*

FOUNDATION. No. 1- March 1972-. Periodical. US. English. ty. Gregg Press, Division of G K Hall & Co, 70 Lincoln Street, Boston MA 02111. **LC** PN3448.S45. **DD** 823.087609.

FOUR QUARTERS. Began publication in 1951. 0015-9107. Periodical. US. English. qt. La Salle College, 20th and Oleney Avenues, Philadelphia PA 19141. **Tel** (215)951-1171. **Ed** John Christopher Kleis. **Ind/Abst** Annu. Bibliogr. Engl. Lang. Lit., Index Am. Period. Verse. **LC** AP2. **DD** 051. (cum index). **Circ** 400. Available on microfilm from University Microfilms. Fiction, poetry and essays for college-educated audience with literary interests. Emphasis on technical mastery combined with genuine insight.

THE FOUR ZOAS. 0362-0247. Periodical. US. English. ir. $12.00. Four Zoas Night House Ltd, PO Box 111, Ashuelot Village, New Hampshire MA 03441.

FOUR ZOAS JOURNAL. Began publication with No. 1 in 1972. 0198-9928. Periodical. US. English. ir. $12.50 for 3 Numbers. Four Zoas, 7 Sherman St, Boston MA 02129.

FOXFIRE. V. 1- Spring 1967-. 0015-9220. Periodical. US. English. qt. $9.00. Foxfire Fund, Rabun Gap GA 30568. **Tel** (404)746-5318. **Ed** Margie Bennett and Eliot Wigginton. **Ind/Abst** MLA Int. Bibliogr. Books Artic. Mod. Lang. Lit. **LC** PS1. **DD** 917.5. **Circ** 3,500. (ctrl). The contents are drawn from the indigenous Appalachian culture from which the Rabun County High School students who edit it hale.

Literature

FRAGMENTOS DE BARRO. VFOAT Pieces of Clay. 1st (Spring 1976)-. Periodical. US. English (Spanish). an. San Diego Mesa College, 7250 Mesa College Drive, San Diego CA 92111. LC PS508.M4. DD 810.8086872.

FRANCOIS MAURIAC. Series/Titl La Revue des Lettres Modernes. 1- 1975-. French. ir. Lettres Moderns, 73 rue du Cardinal Lemoine, Paris France 75005. LC PN3. DD 848.91209.

FREE-FALL (BANFF, ALTA.). (FREE-FALL). 1975-. 0714-4172. CN. English. an. Free. Banff Centre, School of Fine Arts, Box 1020, Banff Alberta T0L 0C0 Canada. DD C810.80054. (ctrl). *Fellfield*, 0714-4164.

THE FREE LANCE. Began in 1953. 0016-0369. Periodical. US. English. an. Free Lance, 6005 Grand Avenue, Cleveland OH 44104. **Tel** (216)431-7116. LC PS501.

FREE MEDIA BULLETIN. No. 1- 1969-. 0702-8873. Periodical. CN. English. $6.00 Per Number. 212-5600 Dalhousie Road, Vancouver 8 British Columbia V6T 1W4 Canada. DD 805.

FREEFAN JOURNAL. (THE FREEFAN JOURNAL). 1 (Oct. 28, 1981)-. 0712-2152. Periodical. CN. English. Freefan Journal, c/o S Wagar, 861A Danforth Avenue, Toronto Ontario M4J 1L8 Canada. DD 809.387605.

FREELANCE. Began publication in 1969?. 0705-1379. Periodical. CN. English. ir. $23.21. Saskatchewan Writers Guild, PO Box 3986, Regina Saskatchewan S4P 3R9 Canada. **Tel** (306)522-0811. Ed Victor Jerrett Enns. DD C810.90054. bk rev. **Circ** 600. News on the writing scene in Saskatchewan and Canada. Columns on writing, market information: also poetry and short fiction.

FREIBORD. V. 1- (No. 1-). Periodical. AU. German. ir. 40.00 Single Issue. Freibord, Aegidig 6/19, 1060 Wien Austria. LC PT1141.A2. DD 830.800914.

FRENCH 17. See Bibliographies.

FRENCH 20 BIBLIOGRAPHY. See Bibliographies.

FRENCH LITERATURE SERIES. V. 1- 1973-. 0271-6607. Monographic Series. US. English. ir. University of South Carolina, Department of Foreign Languages, Columbia SC 29208. **Tel** (803)777-6088. Ed A M Hardee. **Ind/Abst** MLA Int. Bibliogr. Books Artic. Mod. Lang. Lit. **Circ** 300. Topical studies of French literature.

FRENCH STUDIES. V. 1- Jan. 1947-. 0016-1128. Periodical. UK. English (French). qt. 30 Domestic, $60.00 Foreign. M J Tilby, Selwyn College, Cambridge CB3 9DQ England. **Tel** (0223)62381. Ed Malcolm Bowie. **Ind/Abst** MLA Int. Bibliogr. Books Artic. Mod. Lang. Lit., Artbibliogr. Mod., Recent Publ. Artic., Index Book Rev. Humanit., Am. Hist. Life, Hist. Abstr., Part A, Mod. Hist. Abstr., Hist. Abst., Part B, Twent. Century Abstr. LC PQ1. DD 840.5. (cum index). bk rev. adv acc. **Circ** 2,000. Scholarly articles in the fields of French language and literature from the Middle Ages to the present day. Occasional articles on French history and painting.

FRENCH STUDIES IN SOUTHERN AFRICA. VFOAT Cahiers de l'AFSSA. No. 1- 1971/72-. French. ir. 6.00. Association for French Studies in Southern Africa, University of Cape Town, Department of Romance Studies, Private Bag Rondesbosch, Cape Town South Africa. **Ind/Abst** MLA Int. Bibliogr. Books Artic. Mod. Lang. Lit. LC PQ2. DD 840.9968.

FRONT. (THE FRONT). 3 (Aug. 1978)-. 0709-2830. Periodical. CN. English. ir. The Front, PO Box 1355, Kingston Ontario K7L 5C6 Canada. DD C810.80054. *It Needs to Be Said/The Front*, 0383-6622.

FRUITS. No. 1, (Dec. 1983)-. 0760-7237. Periodical. French. ir. LC PN3. DD 805.

F.T.A., PHOENIX. (F.T.A./PHOENIX). Vol. 3, No. 6 (Dec. 1982)-. 0821-7548. Periodical. CN. English. bm. $7.50. Science Fiction Association of Victoria, PO Box 1772, Victoria British Columbia V8W 2Y3 Canada. DD C813.087608. *Phoenix and F.T.A.*, 0821-753X.

FU-CHIEN WEN HSUEH. VFOAT Fujian Wenxue. Periodical. CH. Chinese. mo. $9.18. China Publication Centre, PO Box 2820, Beijing China.

FU JEN STUDIES : LITERATURE & LINGUISTICS. See Linguistics.

FUNNYWORLD. Began with No. 1, Oct. 1966. 0071-9943. US. English. $1.50 Single Issue. 1716 Barkston Court, Atlanta GA 30341. **Ind/Abst** Film Lit. Index. LC PN6725. DD 741.5973.

FYRSTI BOKAFLOKKUR MALS OG MENNIGAR. Vol. 1-. 0427-797X. Icelandic. ir. Mal OG Mennigar, Laugavegier 18, 101 Reysjavik Iceland. DD 839.6.

GACETA LITERARIA. See Linguistics.

GADFLY (EAST RETFORD, NOTTINGHAMSHIRE). (THE GADFLY). Vol. 5, No. 1 (Feb. 1982)-. Periodical. UK. English. qt. Brynmill Press, I5 Cobwell Road, Retford Notts DN22 7BN England. *Human World*, 0018-7313.

GAGANANCALA. Periodical. Hindi. qt. 12.00. LC PK2046.

GALAXY MAGAZINE. (GALAXY READER). 1st-. 0435-0464. Periodical. English. ir. Ed H L Gold. LC PZ1.G22.

GALILEO. No. 1- Sept. 1976-. Periodical. US. English. bm. $7.50. Galileo, 339 Newberry Street, Boston MA 02115. LC PS648.S3. DD 813.0876.

GALLERIA. 1-. 0016-4097. Periodical. IT. Italian. bm. $11.88. Casa Ed Salvatore Sciascia, Corso Unmerto 111, 93100 Caltanisetts Italy. **Ind/Abst** MLA Int. Bibliogr. Books Artic. Mod. Lang. Lit.

GALLIMAUFRY. V. 1- Summer. 0161-2549. Periodical. US. English. sa. $4.00 (4 issues). Gallimaufry, 359 Frederick, San Francisco CA 94117. Ed M MacArthur. LC PS501. DD 810.80054.

GARGOYLE. No. 1- Aug. 1976-. 0162-1149. Periodical. US. English. ty. $12.00. Paycock Press, PO Box 3567, Washington DC 20007. **Tel** (202)333-1544. Ed Richard Peabody and Gretchen Johnson. bk rev. adv acc. **Circ** 2,500. Writing for the eighties, we print the best work of the young and the neglected. Poetry, fiction, interviews, graphics and reviews.

GARIMA. Periodical. Nepali. ir. 5.00. LC PK2598.A2.

GASOLINE RAINBOW. V. 1- 1977-. 0706-5280. CN. English. an. $10.00 Per Number. U of A Literary Society, University of Alberta, Department of English, Edmonton Alberta T6G 2E1 Canada. DD C813.5408.

EL GATO TUERTO. 1 (Summer 1984)-. 8755-3651. Periodical. US. Spanish. ty. $8.00 Domestic, $10.00 Foreign. Ediciones El Gato Tuerto, PO Box 210277, San Francisco CA 94121. **Tel** (415)752-0473. Ed Carlota Caulfield and Servando Gonzalez. DD 705. bk rev. adv acc. **Circ** 2,500. Contains articles on: Hispanic America, poetry, short stories, essays, art, criticism, literature, book reviews, Cuba, and literary criticism.

GAVEA-BROWN. VAT Gavea, Brown. Vol. 1, No. 1 (Jan./June, 1980)-. 0276-7910. Periodical. US. English (Portuguese). sa. $10.00. Gavea-Brown Center, Brown University, Portuguese and Brazilian Studies, Box O, Providence RI 02912. **Tel** (401)863-3042. Ed Onesimo T Almeida. LC PQ9470. DD 810.808691. bk rev. **Circ** 1,500. A bilingual journal of Portuguese-American letters and studies.

THE GAYOSO STREET REVIEW. Vol. 1, No. 1-. 0270-0085. Periodical. US. English. ty. $6.00. The Gayoso Street Review, PO Box 11736, Memphis TN 38111. LC PS501. DD 810.8.

THE GAZETTE. V. 1- Winter 1979-. 0193-533X. Periodical. US. English. qt. $12.50 Individual Membership, $15.00 Joint Membership. The Wolfe Pack, PO Box 822, Ansonia Station, New York NY 10023. LC PS3537.T733. DD 813.52.

GEKKAN KOTOBA. See Linguistics.

GENDAI TANKA. Began with 1966 issue. Japanese. ir. 2300. c/o Yoshida, 2-16 Minami Ikebukuro 1 Toshima-Ku, Tokyo Japan. LC PL758.A1.

GENGO BUNKA KENKYU (MATSUYAMA-SHI, JAPAN). See Linguistics.

GENGO BUNKA RONSHU. See Linguistics.

GEORG BRANDES ARBOG. See Yearbooks, Almanacs, Directories.

GEORGE HERBERT JOURNAL. V. 1- Fall 1977-. 0161-7435. Periodical. US. English. sa. $12.00 Domestic, $15.00 Foreign. Sacred Heart University, English Department, Sidney Gottlieb, Bridgeport CT 06606. **Tel** (201)846-8487. Ed Sidney Gottlieb. **Ind/Abst** Abstr. Engl. Stud., MLA Int. Bibliogr. Books Artic. Mod. Lang. Lit. LC PR3508. DD 821.3. bk rev adv acc. **Circ** 450. Publishes essays, notes, and reviews on materials relevant to George Herbert in particular and 17th Century literature and thought in general.

THE GERMAN QUARTERLY. V. 1- Jan. 1928-. 0016-8831. Periodical. US. English. qt. $8.00. American Association of Teachers of German, 523 Building Route 38/Suite 201, Cherry Hill NJ 08034. **Tel** (609)663-5264. Ed Henry J Schmidt. **Ind/Abst** Educ. Index, MLA Int. Bibliogr. Books Artic. Mod. Lang. Lit., Sociol. Abstr., Lang. Teach., Ref. Source, Book Rev. Index, Index Book Rev. Humanit., Lang. Lang. Behav. Abstr. LC PF3001. DD 430.7. bk rev adv acc. **Circ** 7,700. (ctrl). Literature and literary scholarship from the outstanding authorities in the German speaking world with book reviews, special reports and announcements.

GERMANIC NOTES. V. 1- 1970-. 0016-8882. Periodical. US. English (German). qt. $8.00. Erasmus Press, 225 Culpepper, Lexington KY 40502. Ed Richard F Krummel. **Ind/Abst** MLA Int. Bibliogr. Books Artic. Mod. Lang. Lit. LC PD1. DD 430.05. bk rev. **Circ** 500. All aspects of literature, history, and folklore of German-speaking countries, Low Countries, and Scandinavia.

GERMANIC STUDIES IN AMERICA. No. 30-. 0721-3727. Monographic Series. English (German). ir. Verlag Peter Lang AG, Jupiterstrasse 15, PO Box 277, CH-3000 Berne 15 Switzerland. **Tel** 031/32 11 22. **Ind/Abst** MLA Int. Bibliogr. Books Artic. Mod. Lang. Lit. **Circ** 450. Reevaluates the Historia von D Johann Fausten as a work of formulaic fiction which inverts the structural pattern of the medieval saints' legends, subverting Catholic values in favor of Lutheran ones. *German Studies in America*.

GERMANICA. 1- 1960-. 0072-1484. Monographic Series. FR. French or German. ir. Societe Nouvelle Didier Erudition, 6 rue de la Sorbonne, 75005 Paris France. **Tel** 4354 47 57. Collection of doctorate thesis in the French universities-13 titles published.

GERMANISTIK. Vol. 1-. 0016-8912. Periodical. GW. German. qt. $48.86. Max Niemeyer Verlag, Postfach 21 40, 7400 Tuebingen 1 West Germany. **Tel** 07071/81104. Ed Tilman Kromer. **Ind/Abst** MLA Int. Bibliogr. Books Artic. Mod. Lang. Lit. LC Z2235.A2. bk rev. adv acc. Journal with reviews and bibliographical references of monographs and contributions on German literature and language.

GERMANISTISCHE MITTEILUNGEN. See Linguistics.

GERMANISTISCHE SCHRIFTENREIHE DER NORWEGISCHEN UNIVERSITATEN UND HOCHSCHULEN. See Linguistics.

GERMANO-SLAVICA. No. 1- Spring 1973-. 0317-4956. Periodical. CN. English (German). sa. $5.42. University of Waterloo, Department of German and Slavic Language and Literature, Waterloo Ontario N21 3G1 Canada. **Tel** (519)885-1211. Ed S Hoefert. **Ind/Abst** MLA Int. Bibliogr. Books Artic. Mod. Lang. Lit. LC PT123.S58. bk rev. adv acc. **Circ** 300. (ctrl). A Canadian journal of Germanic and Slavic comparative studies.

GHOST DANCE. Vol. 1. 0016-9633. Periodical. US. English. qt. Ghostdance Press, 526 Forest, East Lansing MI 48823. Ed H Fox. LC PS501. DD 810.80054.

GIRLS & BOYS TOGETHER. See Bibliographies.

GLYPH. No. 1-. 0364-1708. Periodical. US. English. ty. $5.00. c/o Richard Hoffman, 130 West 16th Street, New York NY 10011. LC PS501. DD 810.8005.

GLYPH. 1-. 0148-088X. Periodical. US. English. ir. University of Minnesota Press, 2037 University Avenue Southeast, Minneapolis MN 55455. **Tel** (612)376-3266. Ed Wlad Godzich, Henry Sussman and Samuel Weber. **Ind/Abst** Abstr. Engl. Stud. LC PN2. DD 808.8. Each volume in this issue will focus on a specific critical issue.

GOETHE-ALMANACH. See Yearbooks, Almanacs, Directories.

GOETHE-JAHRBUCH. See Yearbooks, Almanacs, Directories.

GOLDEN TAFFY CEASED. 1971/72-1981/82. 0319-6690. CN. English. an. $1.55. Saskatchewan Teachers Federation, 2317 Arlington Avenue, Saskatoon Saskatchewan S7J 2H8 Canada. DD C810.80928205.

Literature

DI GOLDENE KEYT. No. 1 (Winter 1949)-. Periodical. IS. Hebrew. qt. $30.00. Di Goldene Keyt, Rechow Weizmann 30, Tel Aviv Israel. Tel (3)21-81-91. Ed Abraham Sutzkewer. **Ind/Abst** MLA Int. Bibliogr. Books Artic. Mod. Lang. Lit. **LC** DS101. (cum index). bk rev. Periodical for literature and social problems.

GOTHENBURG STUDIES IN ENGLISH. 1- 1952-. 0072-503X. Monographic Series. SW. English. ir. Humanities Press, Atlantic Highlands NJ 07716-1289. Ed Alvar Ellegard and Erik Frykman. **Ind/Abst** Abstr. Engl. Stud., MLA Int. Bibliogr. Books Artic. Mod. Lang. Lit., Years Work Eng. Stud. The series includes these and other studies by members of the English Department, Gothenburg University.

GOTHIC. V. 1- June 1979-. 0193-0184. Periodical. US. English. sa. $3.00. Gothic Press, PO Box 80051, Baton Rouge LA 70898. **Tel** (504)766-2906. Ed Gary William Crawford. **Ind/Abst** MLA Int. Bibliogr. Books Artic. Mod. Lang. Lit. **LC** PR830.T3. **DD** 823.0872. bk rev. **Circ** 300. (ctrl) A journal devoted to the study of Gothic literature.

GRAHAM GREENE ANNUAL. 0738-0763. US. English. an. $15.00 Single Volume. Penkeville Publishing Company, Box 212, Greenwood FL 32443.

GRAIN. V. 1- June 1973-. 0315-7423. Periodical. CN. English. sa. $2.00. Box 1885, Saskatoon Saskatchewan Canada. **LC** PR9194. **DD** 810.80054.

GRAND STREET. Vol. 1, No. 1 (Autumn 1981)-. 0734-5496. Periodical. US. English. qt. $24.00. Grand Street, 50 Riverside Drive, New York NY 10024. **Tel** (212)496-6088. Ed Ben Sonnenberg. **LC** PN6010.5. **DD** 808.8. bk rev. adv acc. **Circ** 2,100. Stories, poems, articles and translations. "Our end-of-century." 'Dial Magazine'. Leon Edel, "Splendid." Norman Mailer.

GRANI. V. 1- (No. 1-). Periodical. GW. Russian. qt. $28.40. Possev Verlag V Gorachek KG, Flurscheideweg 15, D-6230, Frankfurt West Germany. **Tel** 069/34 1265. **Ind/Abst** MLA Int. Bibliogr. Books Artic. Mod. Lang. Lit. adv acc. (ctrl) Includes poetry, novels, short stories, book reviews.

GRANITSA; LENINGRADSKIE PISATELI O POGRANICHNIKAKH. Vol. 1- 1968-. UR. Russian. 0.87 Single Issue. Lenizdat, Fontanka 59, Leningrad Russia. **LC** PG3228.A72.

GRANTA. Began in 1889. Periodical. UK. English. qt. $33.71. Granta, 44A Hobson Street, Cambridge CB1 1NL England. **Tel** 315290. Ed Bill Buford. adv acc. **Circ** 30,000. Paperback magazine publishing fiction and cultural and political journalism: fiction (including novellas and works-in-progress), essays, political analysis, journalism, etc.

GRANTS AND AWARDS AVAILABLE TO AMERICAN WRITERS. See Bibliographies.

GRANTS AND AWARDS AVAILABLE TO FOREIGN WRITERS. 1973-. 0093-3163. US. English. an. $2.00. Pen American Center, 156 Fifth Avenue, New York NY 10010. **LC** PN171.P75. **DD** 807.9.

GRAVIDA (MONTREAL, QUEBEC). (GRAVIDA). No. 1, (Fall 1983)-. 0824-8974. Periodical. CN. French. qt. $10,00. Gravida, 920 Gilford, Montreal Quebec H2J 1P2 Canada. **DD** C840.80054.

THE GRAYWOLF ANNUAL. (THE GRAYWOLF ANNUAL : SHORT STORIES). 0743-7471. US. English. an. Graywolf Press, PO Box 142, Port Townsend WA 98368. **DD** 813.

THE GREAT LAKES REVIEW. V. 1- Summer 1974-. 0360-1846. US. English. sa. $10.00. Central Michigan University, c/o Ron Primeau, 122 Anspach Hall, Mt Pleasant MI 48859. **Tel** (312)583-4050. **Ind/Abst** Abstr. Engl. Stud., MLA Int. Bibliogr. Books Artic. Mod. Lang. Lit. **LC** PS273. **DD** 810.80977.

GREEN RIVER REVIEW. V. 1- Nov. 1968-. 0017-4009. Periodical. US. English. sa. $6.00. Green River Review, Box 56, University Center MI 48710. **Tel** (517)790-4000. **Ind/Abst** Index Am. Period. Verse. **LC** PS501. **DD** 810.80054.

GREEN'S MAGAZINE. V. 1- No. 1 (Fall 1972)-. 0824-2992. Periodical. US. English. qt. $3.00 Per No. Green's Magazine, PO Box 3236, Regina Saskatchewan S4P 3H1 Canada. **DD** 810.80054.

GREYFRIAR. V. 1- 1958-. 0533-2869. US. English. an. Department of English, Siena College, Loudonville NY 12211. **LC** PN2.

GRIMOIRE. V. 1, No. 4- April 7, 1978-. 0706-764X. Periodical. CN. French. ir. $5.00. Secretariat de l'Association des Auteurs des Cantons de l'Est, 143 rue des Mesanges, St-Elie d'Orford Quebec J0B 2S0 Canada. **DD** C840.627146. *Bulletin de l'Association des Auteurs des Cantons de l'Est, 0706-7631.*

GRUB STREET. 0149-4228. Periodical. US. English. $1.50 Single Issue. Alan Ball, 2839 Valentine Avenue, Bronx NY 10458. **LC** PS501. **DD** 810.5.

GRUNDLAGEN DER GERMANISTIK. V. 1- 1966. 0533-3350. Monographic Series. German. ir. Erich Schmidt Verlag GMBH, PO 7330-40, Viktoriastr 44 A, D-800 Bielefeld 1 West Germany. **Tel** 0521/66061. **Ind/Abst** MLA Int. Bibliogr. Books Artic. Mod. Lang. Lit. German philology.

GUARD THE NORTH. Began with Dec. 1972 issue. 0700-9917. Periodical. CN. English. ir. 0.50 Per No. Guard the North, PO Box 65583, Vancouver British Columbia V5N 5K5 Canada. **DD** 809.38760%.

GUEST AUTHOR. 1978-. 0160-6565. US. English. an. $7.45. Hermes Press, 51 Lenox Street, Brockton MA 02401. **LC** PN452. **DD** 802.5.

GUIDE DES PRIX LITTERAIRES. 1.- Ed. French. ir. **LC** PN171.P75.

GUION LITERARIO. Yearly V. 1, No. 1- Jan., 1956-. 0017-5447. Periodical. ES. Spanish. ir. Departamento Editorial, Del Ministerio de Cultura, San Salvador El Salvador.

GULLIVERIANA. 1970-. English. ir. Scholars Fascimiles & Reprints, PO Box 344, Delmar NY 12054. **Tel** (513)439-5978. **LC** PZ1.

GUNAKESARI. V. 1- Asvina/Marga 2029- Oct./Dec. 1972-. Nepali. ir. 1.00 Single Issue. 15/7 Kshetrapati, Kathamadaum Nepal. **LC** PK2598.A2.

THE G.W. REVIEW. VFOAT GW Review. Vol. 1, No. 1 (1980)-. 8756-8640. Periodical. US. English. ir. G W Review, Box 20 Marvin Center the George Washington University 800 21st Street Northwest, Washington DC 20052. **LC** PS501. **DD** 810.8.

THE GYPSY SCHOLAR. V. 1- Fall 1973-. Periodical. US. English. ty. $5.00. Michigan State University, Department of English, East Lansing MI 48824. **LC** PR1. **DD** 820.9.

HAEOE MUNHAK. V. 1- July, 1927 issue. Periodical. KO. Korean. ir. 6,000. Hyondaesa, 62-6 4-Ka Chungmu-Ro, Chung-Ku Seoul Korea. **LC** PN9.

HAIKU BUNGAKUKAN KIYO. VFOAT Haiku Bungakukan Kiyo. No. 1-. 0389-4274. JA. Japanese. ir. 1500 Single Issue. Haijin Kyokai 28-10, Huakunin-cho 3 Shinjuku-ku, Tokyo Japan. **LC** PL729.A1.

HAMBONE. V. 1- Spring 1974-. 0733-6616. Periodical. US. English. sa. $12.00. Mr Nathaniel Mackey, 132 Clinton Street, Santa Cruz CA 95062. **Tel** (408)426-3072. Ed Nate Mackey.

HAMLET STUDIES. V. 1- Apr. 1979-. Periodical. II. English. ir. $14.00. Vikas Publishing House Pvt Ltd, 5 Ansari Road, New Delhi 110002 India. **Ind/Abst** Abstr. Engl. Stud., MLA Int. Bibliogr. Books Artic. Mod. Lang. Lit. **LC** PR2807. **DD** 822.33.

HANDBUCH DER DEUTSCHEN LITERATURGESCHICHTE. SZ. German. ir. Francke Verlag, Neuengasse 43, Postfach 1445, CH-3001 Bern Switzerland. **Tel** 031/22 17 15.

HANGING LOOSE. 1 (Fall 1966)-. 0440-2316. Periodical. US. English. ty. $7.50. Hanging Loose, 231 Wyckoff Street, Brooklyn NY 11217. **Tel** (617)929-8302. Ed Ron Schreiber and Robert Hershon. **Ind/Abst** Index Am. Period. Verse. **LC** PS580. **DD** 811.008. **Circ** 1,500. A poetry and literature magazine published since 1966. Features a special section of poets of high school. Approximately 72-80 pages per issue. 20th anniversary double issue coming in Fall, 1986. *Things (New York, N.Y.), 0563-4660.*

HANGUK MUNHAK. V. 1- Nov. 1973-. Periodical. Korean. ir. 300 Single Issue. 269 Chongjin-Dong Chongno-Ku, Seoul Korea. **LC** PL950.2.

HANGUK MUNHAK NONCHONG. VFOAT Theses Sic on Korean Literature. Periodical. Korean. ir. **LC** PL951.

HANGUK MUNHAK PIPYONG SONJIP. V. 1-Series ('81)-. Periodical. KO. Korean. ir. 4.500. IU Chulp Ansa 19-8, 5-Ka Chungmu-Ro, Chung-Ku Seoul Korea. **LC** PL951.

HANGUK P. E. N. VFOAT The Korean P. E. N. Periodical. KO. English (Korean). ir. Kukche Pen Kullop Hanguk Ponbu, 163 Anguk-dong, Chongno-ku Seoul South Korea. **LC** PN121. **DD** 895.7408.

HANGUK UI MUNHAK. Series/Titl Hanguk Munhak Hyophoe Sahwajip. V. 1-Series. Periodical. KO. Korean. ir. 1,500. Hanguk Munhak Hyophoe, Samuguk 32, Tangju-Dong Seoul Korea. **LC** PL950.2.

HANNAM OMUNHAK. See Linguistics.

HARVARD ENGLISH STUDIES. 1- 1970-. 0073-0513. Periodical. US. English. ir. Harvard University Press, 79 Garden Street, Cambridge MA 02138. **Tel** (617)495-2606. **Ind/Abst** MLA Int. Bibliogr. Books Artic. Mod. Lang. Lit. **DD** 810.

HARVARD JOURNAL OF ASIATIC STUDIES. See History (General) - History of Asia.

HARVARD SLAVIC STUDIES. V. 1- 1953-. 0449-3495. US. English. ir. Harvard University Press, 79 Garden Street, Cambridge MA 02138. **Tel** (617)661-3761. **Ind/Abst** MLA Int. Bibliogr. Books Artic. Mod. Lang. Lit. **DD** 891.

HARVARD STUDIES IN COMPARATIVE LITERATURE. Began publication with Vol. 1 in 1910?. 0073-0696. Monographic Series. US. English. ir. Harvard University Press, 79 Garden Street, Cambridge MA 02138. **Tel** (617)495-2606. **Ind/Abst** MLA Int. Bibliogr. Books Artic. Mod. Lang. Lit. **DD** 805.

HARVEST. 1974-. 0362-7888. Periodical. US. English. Connecticut Writers League, PO Box 78, Farmington CT 06032.

HAWAII REVIEW. V. 1, No. 2- Spring 1973-. 0093-9625. Periodical. US. English. sa. $7.00. University of Hawaii, Department of English, 1733 Donaghho Road, Honolulu HI 96822. **Tel** (808)948-8548. Ed Rodney Morales. **LC** PS571.H3. **DD** 810.80054. bk rev. adv acc. **Circ** 4,000. Poetry, prose and reviews written by both local and non-local writers. Topics may deal with Hawaii and the Pacific Basin, but do not exclude subjects and ideas about other areas. *Hawaii Literary Review, 0090-8274.*

HEBBEL JAHRBUCH. See Yearbooks, Almanacs, Directories.

HEBREW UNIVERSITY STUDIES IN LITERATURE AND THE ARTS. VFOAT HSLA. Vol. 11, No. 1 (Spring 1983)-. 0333-5690. Periodical. IS. English (French). ty. $17.00. Magnes Press, Hebrew University, Jerusalem 91904 Israel. **Ind/Abst** Abstr. Engl. Stud., MLA Int. Bibliogr. Books Artic. Mod. Lang. Lit. **LC** PN1. **DD** 809. *Hebrew University Studies in Literature.*

HEI-LUNG-CHIANG HSI CHU. Periodical. CH. Chinese. qt. 0.30. Ha-Erh-Pin Shih Yu Chu, Harbin China. **LC** PL2603. **DD** 895.12009.

HEINE-JAHRBUCH. See Yearbooks, Almanacs, Directories.

HEIRS. V. 1- Mar. 1968-. 0017-9884. US. English, Spanish or Chinese. an. Heirs, 3562 18th Street, San Francisco CA 94110. **Tel** (415)824-8604.

HELICON. V. 1- 1938-. Periodical. NE. English (German, Spanish, French or Italian). ir. E J Brill, POB 9000, 2300 PA Leiden The Netherlands. **LC** PN1.

HELIKON. Began in 1964. 0017-999X. Periodical. Hungarian (table of contents in French, English, and Russian). qt. Akademiai Kiado, PO Box 24, 1363 Budapest Hungary. **Tel** 667-271. Ed B Kopeczi. **Ind/Abst** Am. Hist. Life, Hist. Abstr., MLA Int. Bibliogr. Books Artic. Mod. Lang. Lit. **LC** PN9. **DD** 809. bk rev. **Circ** 1,400. Comparative literature. *Vilagirodalmi Figyelo.*

HELO. No. 1- April/June 1974-. Periodical. Rajasthani. ir. 10.00. Srinarayana Sarma, Jana Jana Karyala, Kote Gate, Bikaner 334001 India. **LC** PK2708.45.

HEMINGWAY NOTES CEASED. Vol. 1, No. 1 (Spring 1971)-V. 6, No. 2 (Spring 1981). 0046-7243. Periodical. US. English. sa. **Ind/Abst** Abstr. Engl. Stud. **LC** PS3515.E37. **DD** 813.52. Also available on microfilm.

HERMAEA; GERMANISTISCHE FORSCHUNGEN. V. 1-35, 1905-40. 0440-7164. Monographic Series. GW. German. ir. Max Niemeyer Verlag, Postfach 21 40, 7400 Tuebingen 1 West Germany. **Tel** (07071)81104. Ed Hans Fromm, Hans-Joachim Mahl. **Ind/Abst** MLA Int. Bibliogr. Books

Literature

Artic. Mod. Lang. Lit. Monographs on German literature.

HIGHLIGHTS OF THE LITERATURE. Series/Titl Work in America Institute Studies in Productivity. 1-. 0149-8703. Monographic Series. US. English. ir. Pergamon Press Inc, Fairview Park, Elmsford NY 10523.

HIKAKU BUNGAKU. VFOAT Journal of Comparative Literature. 1st Vol. (1958)-. 0440-8047. Periodical. JA. Japanese (Some articles and summaries in English, French, or German). an. Japan Publishing Trading Company Inc, 5030 Tokyo International, Tokyo 100-31 Japan. Hikaku Bungaku Kenkyu.

HIKAKU BUNGAKU KENKYU (TODAI HIKAKU BUNGAKU-KAI). (HIKAKU BUNGAKU KENKYU). VFOAT Etudes de Litterature Comparee. Began in 1954. 0437-455X. Periodical. JA. Japanese (summaries in English, French and German). sa. $8.82. The Asahi Press, Kishikanda 3-3-5, Chiyoda-ku Tokyo 101 Japan. Tel 03-263-3321. LC PN851. bk rev. Circ 2,200. (ctrl). Monographs (with abstracts in English, etc.), essays and reviews in comparative literature and culture.

HIMALI SAUGATA. V. 1- 2028- 1971-. 0377-9661. Nepali. ir. 2.00. Sunsasari Hilla Humali Pustakalaya Sunsari Dist, Himali Pustakalaya, Mehendra Nagara Nepal. LC PK2598.A2.

HINDI SAHITYABDAKOSA. 1- 1967-. Hindi. ir. LC 2030.

HIRATRA. VFOAT Revio Hiratra. Periodical. Malagasy (French). ir. Departement de Langue Litterature et Civilisation Malgaches, B P 907 Postes 611 et 612, Antananarivo Malaysia.

HISPAMERICA. Vol. 1- (No. 1-). 0363-0471. Periodical. US. Spanish. ty. $30.00. Hispamerica, 5 Pueblo Court, Gaithersburg MD 20878. Tel (301)948-3494. Ed Saul Sosnowski. Ind/Abst MLA Int. Bibliogr. Books Artic. Mod. Lang. Lit. LC PQ7081.A1. DD 860.9. bk rev. adv acc. Circ 1,000. (ctrl). Spanish American literature: essays, fiction, poetry, interviews, reviews, drama by internationally known and by new authors.

HISPAMERICA. ANEJO. 1- 1975-. 0363-048X. US. Spanish. $15.00. 1402 Erskine Street, Takoma Park MD 20014. LC PQ7081.A1. DD 860.9.

HISPANIC REVIEW. See Linguistics.

HISPANOFILA. V. 1- (No. 1-). 0018-2206. Periodical. US. English or Spanish. ty. $13.50. University of North Carolina, 234 Dey Hall, Chapel Hill NC 25714. Tel (919)962-1069. Ed Fred Clark. Ind/Abst MLA Int. Bibliogr. Books Artic. Mod. Lang. Lit., Index Book Rev. Humanit., Recent Publ. Artic. LC PQ6001. DD 860.5. (cum index). bk rev. Circ 500.

HOJA INFORMATIVA DE LITERATURA Y FILOLOGIA. 1- 1973-. Periodical. SP. Spanish. bm. Hoja Informativa de Literatura Fundacion Juan March, Castello 77, Madrid 6 Spain. Index published separately - free - automatically sent.

HOOVER ESSAYS. 0748-4380. Periodical. US. English. Public Affairs Coordinator, Hoover Institution/Stanford University, Stanford CA 94305. LC AS30. DD 081.

DIE HOREN. Yearly V. 1- (1st Edition). 0018-4942. Periodical. GW. German. qt. $19.88. Wirtschaftsverlag NW GMBH, Postfach 101110, 2850 Bremerhaven West Germany. Tel (0471)46093. Ed Kurt Morawietz. bk rev. adv acc. Circ 5,500.

HORISONT (VASSA, FINLAND). (HORISONT). Began in 1954. 0018-4950. Periodical. Swedish. bm. 50.00. Kerstin Troberg, Bollgatan 12 C, 65230 Vasa 23 Finland. LC PT9958. (cum index).

HORIZONS SF. 0229-1215. Periodical. CN. English. mo. $0.50 Per Number. UBC Science Fiction Society, Box 75, Student Union Building, University of British Columbia, Vancouver British Columbia Canada. DD C813.087608. Horizons (Vancouver, B.C. : 1979), 0229-1207.

THE HORROR SHOW. Began Nov. 1982. 0748-2914. Periodical. US. English. qt. $14.00. Phantasm Press Star, Route 1 Box 151, T Oak Run CA 96069. Tel (916)472-3540. Ed David B Silva. bk rev. adv acc. Circ 2,200. Slanted toward the horror fan, it includes an equal presentation of fiction and non-fiction. Modern horror at its best.

HOUSMAN SOCIETY JOURNAL. See Biographies.

HSI CHU HSUEH HSI. VFOAT Xijuxuexi. Periodical. CH. Chinese. ir. 0.55. Chung-Kuo Kuo Chi Shu Tien, PO Box 2820, Pei-Ching China. LC PL2357. DD 895.12005.

HAI HSIA. VFOAT Hai Xia. V. 1 Jan. 1981. Periodical. CH. Chinese. qt. 1.00. Fu-Chien Sheng Hsin Hua Shu Tien, Fu-Chou China. LC PL12513. DD 895.109005.

HSIAO HSI TSUNG KAN. VFOAT Xiaoxi Congkan. Periodical. CC. Chinese. ir. 0.25. Hsing Hua Shu Tien Shang-Hai fa Shing so Shanghai China. LC PL2603. DD 895.12508.

HSIAO SHUO LIN (HARBIN, CHINA). (HSIAO SHUO LIN). VFOAT Xiaoshuolin. Periodical. CH. Chinese. mo. 0.35. Post Office, Harbin China. LC PL2443. DD 895.13508.

HSIAO SHUO YUEH PAO. VFOAT Xiaoshuo Yuebao. Began with Jan. 1980 issue. Periodical. CC. Chinese. mo. $10.26. China Publication Centre, PO Box 2820, Beijing China.

HSIEN TAI TSO CHIA. VFOAT Modern Writers. Periodical. CC. Chinese. mo. 0.42. Chung-kuo Chi Shu Tien, PO Box 2820, Pei-Ching China.

HSIN-CHIANG MIN CHIEN WEN HSUEH. V. 1, (Dec. 1981)-. Periodical. CH. Chinese. ir. 0.47. Hsin-Chiang Hsin Hua Shu Tien Wu-Lu-Mu-Chi China. LC PL2446. DD 398.209516.

HSIN-CHIANG WEN HSUEH. VFOAT Xinjiang Wenxue. Periodical. CH. Chinese. mo. 0.30. Chuan kuo Ko Yu Chu China.

HSIN KANG. VFOAT Xingane. Began with July 1956 issue. Periodical. CC. Chinese. mo. 0.35. Chung-Kuo Chu Pan Tui Wai Mao I Kung Ssu, Tien-Chin Fen Kung Ssu, Tien-Chin Shih China. LC PL2513. DD 895.109005.

HSIN WEN HSUEH SHIH LIAO. VFOAT Xinwenxue Shiliao. V. 1, 1978-. Periodical. CC. Chinese. qt. 1.00. Chung-Kuo Kuo Chi Chu Tien, PO Box 2820, Pei-Ching China Mainland. LC PL2303. DD 895.109005.

HSIN YA HSUEH SHU CHI KAN = NEW ASIA ACADEMIC BULLETIN. Main/Corp HongKong. Chinese University. New Asia College. VFOAT New Asia Academic Bulletin. V. 1- 1978-. Periodical. HK. English (Chinese): ir. $12.90. Chinese University of Hong Kong, New Asia College, Shatin New Territories Hong Kong. Tel 0-6352608. LC PL2274. DD 809. Circ 1,000. The bulletin is published at irregular intervals. It carries academic articles on a specific topic, such as East-West comparative literature, Confucianism, China's Management reforms, anthropology, etc.

HSPRWT. (HA-SIFRUT). VFOAT Hasifrut. Began with: V. 1, in 1968. 0017-8284. Periodical. IS. Hebrew (summaries in English). ir. $36.00. Zmora Bitan Publishers Ltd, PO Box 39085, Tel-Aviv Israel. Tel (03)420420. Ed Benjamin Hrushovsky. Ind/Abst Lang. Lang. Behav. Abstr., MLA Int. Bibliogr. Books Artic. Mod. Lang. Lit., Sociol. Abstr. LC PJ5001. bk rev. adv acc. Circ 700. Dedicated to theoretical problems of literary texts, comparative studies of world literature, and research of Hebrew and Yiddish literature, occasionally it includes semiotics and linguistics.

HU-PEI TUAN PIEN HSIAO SHUO NIEN KAN. See Yearbooks, Almanacs, Directories.

HVEDEKORN; TIDSSKRIFT FOR LITTERATUR OG GRAFIK. Began publication in 1927. 0018-8093. Periodical. English. mo. Borgens Forlag GL, Valbygardsvej 33, DK2500 Valby Denmark. Klinte.

HYONDAE MUNHAK. Periodical. KO. Korean. ir. 1.000 Single Issue. Hyondae Munhak SA, 136-46 Yonji-Dong Chongno-Ku, Seoul South Korea. LC PL950.2.

HYPERION. V. 1- Winter 1970-. 0018-8328. Periodical. US. English. sa. $5.00. Paul Foreman, 2311-C Woolsey Street, Berkeley CA 94705.

ICARUS. No. 1- May 1950-). 0019-1027. Periodical. IE. English. ir. University of Dublin, Trinity College, Regent House, Dublin 2 Ireland.

ICHOR. VFOAT Ichor. 1 (Winter 1980)-. 0229-1495. Periodical. CN. English. qt. $8.50. Crescent Publications, PO Box 419/Station A, Ottawa Ontario K1N 8V4 Canada. DD C838.540808.

ICLM INFORMATION - BULLETIN. VFOAT I.C.L.M. Information - Bulletin. English. an. LC PN34. DD 806.01.

ICONOMATRIX CEASED. V. 1, No. 1-. 0382-876X. Periodical. CN. English. qt $9.00. Iconomatrix, PO Box 2/Station A, Fredericton New Brunswick E3B 4Y2 Canada. DD C810.80054.

IDEALS. 0019-137X. Periodical. US. English. bm. Ideals Publishing Company, PO Box 141000, Nashville TN 37214. Tel (615)889-9000. DD 051.

IDYLLE MAGAZINE. No. 1 Sept. 1978-. 0702-0120. Periodical. CN. French. mo. $10.00. Les Editions Sfonda Ltee, 287 Ouest rue Principale, Magog Quebec J1X 2A8 Canada. DD 808.8385.

IGARA. VFOAT IGRA. 1 (745 1984)-. Periodical. Hebrew. an. LC PJ5001.

ILLINOIS ENGLISH BULLETIN OFFICIAL PUBLICATION OF THE ILLINOIS ASSOCIATION OF TEACHERS OF ENGLISH. See Education (General) - Theory, Practice of Education.

IMAGE (ST. LOUIS, MO.). (IMAGE). VFOAT Image Magazine. 0748-1780. Periodical. US. English. ty. $6.00. Image, PO Box 28048, St Louis MO 63119. Tel (314)296-9662. Ed Anthony J Summers. DD 810. bk rev. Circ 600. A collection of poetry, fiction, artwork, reviews, photographs and creative works.

IMAGES ABOUT MANITOBA CEASED. V. 1, No. 1, Nov. 1975. Ceased with V. 1, No. 4. 0383-6991. Periodical. CN. English. 1.00. Dyck, 11 Tahoe Bay, Winnipeg Manitoba R2J 2W3 Canada. DD C810.80054.

IMAGINE . . . . VFOAT Revue de Science-Fiction Quebecoise. Vol. 1- Sept./Nov. 1979-. 0709-8855. Periodical. CN. French. bm. $11.61. Imagine, 4923 Avenue Dorna 1, Montreal Quebec H3W 1W1 Canada. Tel (514)340-1617. Ed Catherine Saouter-Caya. DD 808.83876. bk rev. adv acc. Circ 1,000. Mainly concerned with science fiction, presents short stories, book reviews and essays on various topics.

L'IMMAGINE RIFLESSA. Yearly V. 1- Jan./April 1977-. Periodical. Italian. ty. 23.000 Domestic, $23.00 Foreign. Tilgher-Genova, Conto Corrente Postale 4/15564, Genova Italy. Tel (010)891140. Ed Nicolo Pasero. LC PN5. DD 805. bk rev. adv acc. Circ 1,000. A journal of sociology of the literature which pays attention to the literary text in connection with the social context in which it appears.

IMOTOTACHI NO KAGARIBI. Vol. 1-. JA. Japanese. ir. 600. Kodansha, 2-12-21 Otowa Bunkyo-Ku, Tokyo Japan. LC PL756.6.W3.

IMPULSE. 0304-1239. Periodical. German. ir. 80.00. E Schwarcz, Sensengasse 4 1090, Wien Austria. LC PT1141.A2.

IMPULSE. See Social Sciences (General).

IN FORMA DI PAROLE. Vol.10 (Mar. 1980)-. Czech (German and Italian). ty. 20.000. Coop Editoriale Elitropia, Via Benedetto Croce 19, 42100 Reggio Emilia Italy. LC PN5. DD 808.8.

INCIDENCES. New Series V. 1- Jan./Dec. 1977-. 0705-4165. Periodical. CN. French. ty. Universite d'Ottawa, 65 Hastey Avenue/Morisset Hall, Ottawa Ontario K1N 6N5 Canada. DD 840'.9. Co-Incidences, 0019-3402.

THE INDEPENDENT SHAVIAN. Began with Vol. 1, No. 1 (Oct. 1962). 0019-3763. Periodical. US. English. ty. $15.00. Bernard Shaw Society Inc, Box 1373, Grand Central Station, New York NY 10163. Tel (212)989-7833. Ed Richard Nickson, Daniel Leary and Douglas Laurie. Ind/Abst Abstr. Engl. Stud., MLA Int. Bibliogr. Books Artic. Mod. Lang. Lit., Years Work Eng. Stud. LC PR5366. DD 822.912. bk rev. adv acc. Circ 300. Available in microform from University Microfilms International. Articles by and about G B Shaw. Regional.

INDEX OF AMERICAN PERIODICAL VERSE. See Indexes/Abstracts.

INDEX ON CENSORSHIP. See Indexes/Abstracts.

INDEX TO BRITISH LITERARY BIBLIOGRAPHY. See Indexes/Abstracts.

AN INDEX TO LITERATURE IN THE NEW YORKER. See Indexes/Abstracts.

INDEX TO THE SCIENCE FICTION MAGAZINES (CAMBRIDGE, MASS. : 1979). See Indexes/Abstracts.

Literature

INDEX TO THE SEMI-PROFESSIONAL FANTASY MAGAZINES. See Indexes/Abstracts.

INDIAN AUTHOR. V. 1-. Periodical. English. ir. $3.00. Authors Guild of India, C 12 South Extension Park I, New Delhi 110049 India. LC PN109. DD 809.8954.

THE INDIAN JOURNAL OF ENGLISH STUDIES. Began publication in 1960. 0537-6554. Periodical. II. English. an. $4.84. Indian Association of English Studies, Dr KL Sharma/C-72, Sarejini Marg/Jaipur India. Ind/Abst Annu. Bibliogr. Engl. Lang. Lit., Years Work Eng. Stud. LC PR1.

INDIAN LITERATURE. V. 1- Oct. 1957-. 0019-5804. Periodical. II. English. bm. $6.00. Sahitya Akademi National Academy of Literatures, Rabindra Bhavan Ferozeshah Road, New Delhi 110001 India. Tel 38 86 67. Ind/Abst Abstr. Engl. Stud., MLA Int. Bibliogr. Books Artic. Mod. Lang. Lit., Annu. Bibliogr. Engl. Lang. Lit. LC AP8.

INDIAN SCHOLAR. Vol. 1, No. 1 (Jan. 1979)-. II. English. sa. $10.00. Dr J Srihari Rao Editor, Indian Scholar 3 Vivekanand, Nagar Raipur 492001 Madhya Pradesh India. Ed J Srihari Rao. LC PR9480. DD 809.8954. bk rev. adv acc. Circ 1,000.

INDIANA WRITES CEASED. V. 1-4. 0149-3361. Periodical. US. English. qt.

INFORMATION LITTERAIRE. (L'INFORMATION LITTERAIRE). Vol. 1 (Jan/Feb. 1949). 0020-0123. Periodical. French. ir. Ind/Abst MLA Int. Bibliogr. Books Artic. Mod. Lang. Lit. LC PN3.

INKLINGS. 1-. 0190-0234. Periodical. US. English (also in other languages). ir. Mudborn Press, 209 West de la Guerra, Santa Barbara CA 93101.

INNER CIRCLE. (THE INNER CIRCLE). No. 1-. 0823-6461. Periodical. CN. English. ty. Free. Kingston Psychiatric Hospital, PO Box 603, Kingston Ontario L7L 4X3 Canada. DD C810.80920824. (ctrl).

INOSTRANNYE JAZYKI V SKOLE. See Linguistics.

INS AND OUTS. 0167-3696. Periodical. English. ir. $15.00 Europe and England, $20.00 Others. Ins and Outs Press, PO Box 3759, Amsterdam Holland. LC PR9091. DD 820.8.

INSCAPE. V. 30- 1974-. 0094-2715. US. English. an. $1.50. Pasadena City College, English Department, 1570 East Colorado Boulevard, Pasadena CA 91106. Tel (213)578-7371. LC PS508.C6. DD 810.80054. *Pipes of Pan*.

INSIDE. No. 1- Feb. 1975-. 0380-2957. Periodical. CN. English. 25 Per No. E Kluge, #302 60 High Street, Nelson British Columbia V1K 3Z4 Canada. DD C810.80054.

INSIDE/OUT. VAT Inside Out (New York, N.Y. : 1980). Vol. 1, No.1 (Spring 1980)-. 0275-021X. Periodical. US. English. ir. Time Capsule Inc, Inside Out, GPO Box 1185, New York NY 10116. Tel (212)675-7197. Ed Matthew Hejna and Marc Crawford. adv acc. Circ 3,000. Fiction, poetry and artwork from America's prisons.

INTERDISCIPLINAIR TIJDSCHRIFT VOOR TAAL- & TEKSTWETENSCHAP. VFOAT Interdiscipliniar Tijdschrift Voor Taal- en Tekstwetenschap. Vol. 1, No. 1 (Sept. 1981)-. 0167-4773. Periodical. NE. Dutch. qt. 91.25. Foris Publications, Postbus 509, 3300 AM Dordrecht Netherlands. Tel (78)510454. Ed T A van Dijk. bk rev. adv acc. Circ 600. Interdisciplinary journal for the study of language and text.

INTERIM (NEW YORK, N.Y. 1982). (INTERIM). 0742-7409. Periodical. US. English. an. $8.95. Willis Locker and Owens Publishing, 71 Thompson Street, New York NY 10012. Tel (212)966-4629.

INTERIOR VOICE. VFOAT Interior Voice Regional Arts Magazine. No. 1 (Winter 1981/82)-. 0715-4011. Periodical. CN. English. qt. $1.50 Per No. Interior Voice, PO Box 117, Kelowna British Columbia V1Y 7N2 Canada. DD C810.80054.

INTERNATIONAL CHECKPOINT. Vol. 1, No. 1 (1983)-. 0715-7622. Periodical. CN. English. ir. $15.00. Canadian Book Publishers Council, 45 Charles Street East/7th Floor, Toronto Ontario M4Y 1S2 Canada. DD 011.62.

INTERNATIONAL DIRECTORY OF LITTLE MAGAZINES AND SMALL PRESSES. See Yearbooks, Almanacs, Directories.

INTERNATIONALES ARCHIV FUR SOZIALGESCHICHTE DER DEUTSCHEN LITERATUR. See Genealogy and Heraldry - Archives.

INTERPRETATIONS (MEMPHIS, TENN.). (INTERPRETATIONS). Began in 1968. 0196-903X. Periodical. US. English. sa. $5.00 Domestic, $7.50 Foreign. Interpretations, Memphis State University, Department of English, Memphis TN 38152. Ind/Abst MLA Int. Bibliogr. Books Artic. Mod. Lang. Lit. LC PR1. DD 820.9.

INTERSTATE. No. 1- Spring 1974-. 0363-9991. Periodical. US. English. qt. $5.00. Interstate, PO Box 7068, Austin TX 78722. Tel (512)451-8874. Ed Loris Essary. bk rev. Circ 500. (ctrl). Non-traditional writing and art; strong international emphasis.

INTI. Began in 1974. 0732-6750. Periodical. US. English (Spanish). sa. $20.00. Providence College, c/o Roger Carmosino, Department of Modern Languages, Providence RI 02918. Tel (401)865-2111. Ed Roger B Carmosino. Ind/Abst MLA Int. Bibliogr. Books Artic. Mod. Lang. Lit., Index Am. Period. Verse. LC PQ6001. DD 860.05. bk rev. adv acc. Circ 1,000. Hispanic literature, literary criticism, poetry, short stories, interviews, review of books, special issues on renown contemporary authors with a complete updated bibliography on each author.

INTREPID. No. 1- Mar. 1964-. 0020-9864. US. English. be. $6.00. Intrepid, PO Box 110/Central Park Station, Buffalo NY 14215. Tel (716)884-1891. Ed A de Loach. (cum index).

IO. No. 6- 1969-. 0021-0331. US. English. ir. $32.00. North Atlantic Books, 2320 Blake Street, Berkeley CA 94704. Tel (415)540-7934. Ed Richard Grossinger. LC PS536.2. DD 810.8005. Circ 2,000. A series of issues on geography, alchemy, dreams, baseball, history of science, internal martial arts, aesthetics of literature and film, native thought, anthropology, and psychology. *IO Magazine*.

IRISH LITERARY STUDIES. 1-. 0140-895X. Monographic Series. US. English. ir. Barnes and Noble Books, 81 Adams Drive, Totowa NJ 07512. Tel (201)256-8600. Ed Homer Dickens. (ctrl).

IRODALOMTORTENETI KOZLEMENYEK. VFOAT ITK. 1-. 0021-1486. Periodical. HU. Hungarian. bm. $20.00. Akademiai Kiado, POB 24, 1363 Budapest Hungary. Tel 667-271. Ed F Biro. Ind/Abst MLA Int. Bibliogr. Books Artic. Mod. Lang. Lit. bk rev. Circ 140. History of Hungarian literature.

IRON. VFOAT Iron Magazine. Periodical. UK. English. qt. $3.00. Iron Press, 5 Marden Terrace, Tyne and Wear NE 30, Cullercoats North Shields 4PD England. LC PN6010.5. DD 805.

ISAAC ASIMOV'S MARVELS OF SCIENCE FICTION. VFOAT Marvels of Science Fiction. Vol. 2 (Fall-Winter 1979)-. 0278-9590. Periodical. US. English. $2.25 Per Copy. Davis Publications Inc, 380 Lexington Avenue, New York NY 10017. Ed George Scithers. LC PN6120.95 .S33. DD 813.087608. *Isaac Asimov's Masters of Science Fiction*.

ISAAC ASIMOV'S SCIENCE FICTION ANTHOLOGY. VFOAT Science Fiction Anthology. Vol. 1 (1979)-. 0278-9604. Periodical. US. English. $2.50 Per Copy. Davis Publications Inc, 380 Lexington Avenue, New York NY 10017. LC PN6120.95.S33. DD 813.087608.

ISAAC ASIMOV'S SCIENCE FICTION MAGAZINE. VFOAT Science Fiction Magazine. 1st issue (Spring 1977)-. 0162-2188. Periodical. US. English. ir. $13.50. Issac Asimovs Science Fiction Magazine, 380 Lexington Avenue, New York NY 10017. Tel (212)527-9100. Ed Gardner Dozois. LC PN6120.95. DD 813.087608. bk rev. adv acc. Circ 125,000. Science fiction and fantasy stories.

ISKUSSTVO LEKTORA. Vol. 1- 1973-. UR. Russian. 0.16 Single Issue. Znanie, Tsentr Proezd Servoa D 4, Moskva Russia. LC PN4193.L4.

ISLANDICA. Vol. 1-. US. English. ir. Cornell University Press, 124 Roberts Place, Ithaca NY 14853. LC PT7102.

ISLANDS. Began with Spring 1972 issue. 0110-0858. Periodical. NZ. English. qt. $20.27. Mr Robin Rudding, 4 Sealy Road, Torbay Auckland 10 New Zealand. Tel 0011 64940 39007. Ind/Abst Abstr. Engl. Stud. LC PZ1, PR9637.3. DD 823.01.

ISTAHARA. VFOAT Istahar. Periodical. Oriya. qt. 5.00. Nityananda Satpathy, C-30 Utkal University Campus, Bhubaneswar 7510 India. LC PK2574.5.

ISURI : DO. HARISIMHA GAURA VISVAVIDYALAYA, SAGARA KE HINDI-VIBHAGA KE ANTARGATA KRIYASILA BUNDELI-PITHA KA AYOJANA. See Linguistics.

ITALIA CHE SCRIVE. (L'ITALIA CHE SCRIVE). Vol. 1- April, 1918-. 0021-2881. Periodical. IT. Italian. mo. Italia Che Scrive, Via Angelo Secchi 3, Rome Italy. Ind/Abst MLA Int. Bibliogr. Books Artic. Mod. Lang. Lit. LC Z2345. (cum index).

ITALIAN STUDIES. V. 1- July 1937-. 0075-1634. UK. English. an. $16.40. WM Dawson & Sons Limited, Cannon House/Folkestone, Kent CT19 5EE England. Tel 0303 57421. Ind/Abst MLA Int. Bibliogr. Books Artic. Mod. Lang. Lit., Ref. Source.

ITALIANISTICA. Vol. 1- Jan./Apr. 1972-. 0391-3368. Periodical. Italian. ir. 8.000. Marzorati, Via P Martinetti 6, Milano 20147 Italy. Ind/Abst MLA Int. Bibliogr. Books Artic. Mod. Lang. Lit. LC PQ4001.

ITALIENISCH. 1 (1 May 1979)-. 0171-4996. Periodical. GW. German. sa. 8.11. Moritz Diesterweg, Postfach 110651, D-6 Frankfurt 11 West Germany. Tel (069)13010. bk rev. adv acc. Journal for the Italian language and literature in science and education. Scientific journal directed at language teachers on all levels of education.

ITON 1977 LE-SIFRUT ULE-TARBUT. Vol. 1- Feb./Mar. 1977-. Periodical. Hebrew. ir. 40.00. PO Box 16452, Tel-Aviv Israel. LC PJ5001.

IUG : IZDANIE NA DRUZHESTVOTO NA PISATELITE—KHASKOVO. 1980-. Periodical. UR. Bulgarian. an. 1.51. LC PG1000. DD 891.8108.

JAARBOEK. See Yearbooks, Almanacs, Directories.

JABBERWOCKY. V. 1- 1969-. 0305-8182. Periodical. UK. English. qt. 8.00 Domestic, $13.00 Foreign. Lewis Carroll Society, 47 Summerville Gardens Cheam, Sutton Surrey Sn1 2BU England. Ed Selwyn Goodacre. Ind/Abst MLA Int. Bibliogr. Books Artic. Mod. Lang. Lit., Index Book Rev. Humanit. LC PR4612. DD 828.809. bk rev. Circ 300. (ctrl). Articles relating to the life and works of Lewis Carroll/Charles Dodgson.

JACK LONDON NEWSLETTER. Began with issue for July/Dec. 1967. 0021-3837. Periodical. US. English. ty. $10.00. H C Woodbridge, Department of Foreign Language and Literature, Southern Illinois University, Carbondale IL 62901. Ind/Abst Abstr. Engl. Stud., MLA Int. Bibliogr. Books Artic. Mod. Lang. Lit.

JAHRBUCH DER DEUTSCHEN SCHILLERGESELLSCHAFT. See Yearbooks, Almanacs, Directories.

JAHRBUCH DER JEAN-PAUL-GESELLSCHAFT. See Yearbooks, Almanacs, Directories.

JAHRBUCH DER KARL-MAY-GESELLSCHAFT. See Yearbooks, Almanacs, Directories.

JAHRBUCH DER KUNSTHISTORISCHEN SAMMLUNGEN IN WIEN. See Yearbooks, Almanacs, Directories.

JAHRBUCH DES FREIEN DEUTSCHEN HOCHSTIFTS. See Yearbooks, Almanacs, Directories.

JAHRBUCH DES WIENER GOETHE-VEREINS. See Yearbooks, Almanacs, Directories.

JAHRBUCH - DEUTSCHE AKADEMIE FUR SPRACHE UND DICHTUNG DARMSTADT. See Yearbooks, Almanacs, Directories.

JAHRBUCH - DEUTSCHE SHAKESPEARE-GESELLSCHAFT WEST. See Yearbooks, Almanacs, Directories.

JAHRBUCH DEUTSCHER DICHTUNG. See Yearbooks, Almanacs, Directories.

Literature

JAHRBUCH FUR FINNISCH-DEUTSCHE LITERATURBEZIEHUNGEN. See Yearbooks, Almanacs, Directories.

JAHRBUCH (THOMAS-MORUS-GESELLSCHAFT). See Yearbooks, Almanacs, Directories.

JAHRESGABE - KLAUS-GROTH-GESELLSCHAFT. Main/Corp Klaus-Groth-Gesellschaft (Germany). Began in 1955. 0453-9842. Periodical. German. ir. Klaus-Groth-Gesellschaft, Luttenheid 48, 2240 Heide in Holstein Germany. Ind/Abst MLA Int. Bibliogr. Books Artic. Mod. Lang. Lit. LC PT4848.G7. DD 831.7.

JAM TO-DAY. No. 1- 1973-. 0362-8302. Periodical. US. English. an. $4.50. Jam Today, PO Box 249, Northfield VT 05663. Ed Don Stanford and Judith Stanford. LC PS501. DD 810.90054. bk rev. adv acc. Circ 300. High quality poetry and fiction by unknown and little known writers.

JAPANESE LITERATURE TODAY. No. 1- Mar. 1976-. English. ir. Japanese P E N Club, 265 Shuwa Residential Hotel 9-1-7 Akasaka Minato-Ku, Tokyo Japan. LC PL700. DD 895.609. *Japan P.E.N. News.*

JAYANTI. Volume 1 Jan. 1973-. Periodical. Tamil. ir. 3.50. Ne Ci Campmurtti, 33 First Main Road New Colony Chromepet, Madras-44 India. LC PL4758.5.

JAZYKOVEDNE STUDIE. See Linguistics.

JE NE VEUX PAS MOURIR A L'ACADEMIE FRANCAISE. Vol. 1, No. 1-. 0820-6333. Periodical. CN. French. mo. $1.95 Per No. Charlie Val, C P 363 Succursale Verdun, Verdun Quebec H4G 3G1 Canada. DD C848.5407.

JEFFERSONIAN REVIEW. (THE JEFFERSONIAN REVIEW). 0094-1360. Periodical. US. English. bm. $5.00. F Conneen III Productions Ltd, PO Box 3864, Charlottesville VA 22903. LC PS559.C55. DD 810.80054.

JELENKOR. (JELENKOR : IRODALMI ES MUVESZETI FOLYOIRAT). Periodical. HU. Hungarian. mo. Akademiai Kiado, POB 24, 1363 Budapest Hungary. Tel 72-10673. Ind/Abst MLA Int. Bibliogr. Books Artic. Mod. Lang. Lit. bk rev. Circ 3,000. Deals mainly with the comtemporary Hungarian literature: poems, prose pieces, and chapters of novels. Book reviews and critical works are published regularly. Is considered to be the best Hungarian literary periodical.

JEN MIN WEN HSUEH. VFOAT Renmin Wenxue. Began with Oct. 1949 issue. Periodical. CH. Chinese. ir. 0.40. Chung-Kuo Kuo Chi Shu Tien, PO Box 2820, Pei-Ching China. LC PL2513. DD 895.108005.

JEOPARDY. 1966-. 0021-5880. Periodical. US. English. an. $2.00. Western Washington University, Department of Humanities, Belingham WA 98225. Tel (206)676-3118. Ed Susan E Hilton. Circ 4,000. Finest quality poetry, prose and artwork.

JEWISH ART QUARTERLY. V. 1- Fall 1974-. 0361-7173. Periodical. US. English. qt. $1.00 Single Issue. c/o Alan Kaufman, Jewish Community House, 475 West 140th Street, New York NY 10031. LC PS508.J4. DD 810.5.

JEWISH BOOK ANNUAL. 1943/44-. 0075-3726. US. English (Hebrew and Yiddish Sections, each with special T.-P). an. $17.50. Jewish Book Council of America, 15 East 26th Street, New York NY 10016. Ed S Grayzel. DD 016.296, 016.8924. *Jewish Book Week Annual.*

JEZIK : CASOPIS ZA KULTURU HRVATSKOGA KNJIZEVNOG JEZIKA. 0021-6925. Periodical. YU. Serbo-Croatian -R. ir. $16.00. Mladost Export Import, POB 1028, Ilica 30, 41000 Zagreb Yugoslavia. Ind/Abst MLA Int. Bibliogr. Books Artic. Mod. Lang. Lit. LC PG1201.

JEZYK ROSYJSKI. V. 1- (1-). Periodical. PO. Polish (Russian). bm. ARS Polona, Krakowskie Przedmiescie 7, 00-068 Warsaw Poland. LC PG2068.P6.

JEZYKOZNAWSTWO. See Linguistics.

JIDO BUNGAKU KENKYU. JA. Japanese. ir. 800 Single Issue. Nihon Jido Bungaku Gakkai, c/o Tokyo Kyoiku Kenkyujo 48-23 Sakae-Cho Kita-Ku, Tokyo-To 114 Japan. LC PL751.5.

JIVANA SAHITYA. Periodical. Hindi. ir. 6.00. Sasta Sahitya Mandal, New Delhi India. LC 2030.

JOCHI DAIGAKU DOITSU BUNGAKU RONSHU. VFOAT Beitrage zur Deutschen Literatur. 1- 1964-. Japanese or German. ir. Jochi Daigaku/Bungakubu, Dokubungaku Ken-Kyushitsu, 7 Kioicho Chiyoda-Ku Tokyo Japan. LC PT9.

THE JOHN COLET ARCHIVE OF AMERICAN LITERATURE, 1620-1920. See Genealogy and Heraldry - Archives.

JOHN DONNE JOURNAL. (JOHN DONNE JOURNAL : STUDIES IN THE AGE OF DONNE). Vol. 1, No. 1-2-. 0738-9655. Periodical. US. English. sa. $16.00 Domestic, $18.00 Foreign. John Donne Journal, Box 8105 NCSU, Raleigh NC 27695-8105. Tel (919)737-3870. Ed M Thomas Hester and R V Young. Ind/Abst MLA Int. Bibliogr. Books Artic. Mod. Lang. Lit. LC PR2248. DD 821.3. bk rev. adv acc. Circ 500. Features critical and textural studies (essays and notes on the poetry and prose of Donne and other 17th century authors) on any subject or text, Donne's birth and the Restoration.

JORNALIVRO. Periodical. BL. Portuguese. ir. 2.00 Single Issue. Arte & Communicacao Editora, rua Joao Adolfo 118 10 Andar, Sao Paulo Brazil. LC PN9.

JOSE (METROPOLITAN MANILA, PHILIPPINES). (JOSE). Vol. 1, No. 1 (Oct. 1982)-. Periodical. PH. English. qt. President's Center for Special Studies, Division of Journals and Publications, Eastchem Building, 14 Ilang-Ilang Street, Quezon City Philippines. LC PR9550.45. DD 820.809599.

JOSEPH CONRAD TODAY. V. 1- Oct. 1975-. 0162-413X. Periodical. US. English. qt. $6.50 Domestic, $8.00 Foreign. Joseph Conrad Today, School of Liberal Arts, Auburn University at Montgomery, Montgomery AL 36193. Tel (205)271-9406. Ed Susan Willis. LC PR6005.O4. DD 823.914. bk rev. adv acc. Circ 200. Programs, reports, abstracts of Conrad Society, reports and abstracts of other Conrad meetings, publications, research and issues related to Conrad and his works.

JOURNAL OF ARABIC LITERATURE. V. 1- 1970-. 0085-2376. English. ir. E J Brill, PO Box 9000, 2300 PA Leiden The Netherlands. Ind/Abst MLA Int. Bibliogr. Books Artic. Mod. Lang. Lit., Index Book Rev. Humanit., Relig. Index One, Period. LC PJ7501. DD 892.705. Deals with Arabic literature in the narrow sense of imaginative writing in verse and prose. Provides a forum for the discussion of Arabic literature, both classical and modern.

JOURNAL OF ARTS & IDEAS. See The Arts (General).

JOURNAL OF BECKETT STUDIES. No. 1 (Winter 1976)-. 0309-5207. Periodical. UK. English. sa. $10.50. Riverrun Press, c/o John Calder, 1170 Broadway/Suite 807, New York NY 10001. Tel (212)889-6850. Ed Stanley Gontarsky. Ind/Abst MLA Int. Bibliogr. Books Artic. Mod. Lang. Lit., Index Book Rev. Humanit. bk rev. adv acc. Circ 5,000. Scholarly analyses, reviews, and articles on the work of Samuel Beckett and related literature and drama.

JOURNAL OF CANADIAN FICTION. V. 1- Winter 1972-. Periodical. CN. English.

THE JOURNAL OF ENGLISH LANGUAGE AND LITERATURE. See Linguistics.

JOURNAL OF EVOLUTIONARY PSYCHOLOGY. 0737-4828. Periodical. US. English. qt. $12.00. Paul Neumarkt, Editor-in-Chief, 5117 Forbes Avenue, Pittsburgh PA 15213. Tel (412)621-7057. Ed Paul Neumarkt. Ind/Abst MLA Int. Bibliogr. Books Artic. Mod. Lang. Lit., Psychol. Abstr. LC PN56.P93. DD 801.92. bk rev. Circ 300. Articles on literature from psychological aspect either Freudian or Jungian or any other psychological aspect; also poetry.

JOURNAL OF HISPANIC PHILOLOGY. See Linguistics.

JOURNAL OF INDIAN WRITING IN ENGLISH. (THE JOURNAL OF INDIAN WRITING IN ENGLISH). V. 1- Jan. 1973-. 0302-1319. English. ir. $3.00. G S Balarama Gupta, c/o Department of English, Post-Graduate Centre 2, Gulbarga India. Ind/Abst MLA Int. Bibliogr. Books Artic. Mod. Lang. Lit. LC PR9480. DD 320.9954.

THE JOURNAL OF IRISH LITERATURE. Vol. 1, No. 1 (Jan. 1972)-. 0047-2514. Periodical. US. English. ir. Journal of Irish Literature, PO Box 361, Newark DE 19711. Ind/Abst Engl. Stud., MLA Int. Bibliogr. Books Artic. Mod. Lang. Lit., Index Book Rev. Humanit., Years Work Eng. Stud. LC PR8830. DD 820.809415. Also issued on microfilm by Xerox University Microfilms.

JOURNAL OF LITERARY SEMANTICS. See Linguistics.

JOURNAL OF LITERARY STUDIES. Periodical. English. sa. $30.00 US. LC PN2. DD 809.

JOURNAL OF LITERATURE AND AESTHETICS. VFOAT J.L.A. Periodical. English. qt. $9.00. Dr S Sreenivasan, Department of English/T K M M College, Nangiarkulangara Haripad Keraka-690 513 India. LC PN2. DD 808.8.

JOURNAL OF MALTESE STUDIES CEASED. No. 1- 1961-. 0075-4285. Periodical. MM. English or Italian. ir. University of Malta, Publications Office, Msida Malta. Tel 36451. Ed Oliver Friggieri. DD 492.77. bk rev. Circ 1,000. A scientific approach on Maltese and foreign scholars to the knowledge of Malta's cultural heritage in the fields of language and literature.

JOURNAL OF MODERN LITERATURE. 1970. 0022-281X. Periodical. US. English. ty. $16.00. Temple University, Journal of Modern Literature, c/o M Bebe, 921 Anderson Hall, Philadelphia PA 19122. Tel (215)787-8505. Ed Maurice Beebe. Ind/Abst Humanit. Index, MLA Int. Bibliogr. Books Artic. Mod. Lang. Lit., Abstr. Engl. Stud., Years Work Eng. Stud., Film Lit. Index, Index Book Rev. Humanit. LC PN2. DD 809.04. bk rev. Circ 1,800. (ctrl) Available on microfilm from University Microfilms. A scholarly journal devoted to modernist literature from a historical and research-based standpoint.

THE JOURNAL OF NARRATIVE TECHNIQUE. V. 1- Jan. 1971-. 0022-2925. Periodical. US. English. ty. $10.00. Eastern Michigan University, Ypsilanti MI 48197. Tel (313)487-0150. Ed George Perkins. Ind/Abst Abstr. Engl. Stud., MLA Int. Bibliogr. Books Artic. Mod. Lang. Lit., Years Work Eng. Stud. LC PE1425. DD 820.9. (cum index). bk rev. Circ 900. Narrative theory of literature in English. Academic journal.

THE JOURNAL OF PRE-RAPHAELITE STUDIES. See The Arts (General).

JOURNAL OF SOUTH ASIAN LITERATURE. V. 9- Spring 1973-. 0091-5637. Periodical. US. English. sa. $23.00 Domestic, $24.00 Foreign. Michigan State University, Asian Studies Center, 101 Center for International Progress, East Lansing MI 48824. Tel (517)353-1680. Ed Carlo Coppola. Ind/Abst MLA Int. Bibliogr. Books Artic. Mod. Lang. Lit., Index Book Rev. Humanit. LC PK1501. DD 891.1. bk rev. adv acc. Circ 450. Selections of South Asian literature, both critical writings and translations of original works. *Mahfil*, 0025-0503.

JOURNAL OF SPANISH STUDIES. TWENTIETH CENTURY CEASED. (JOURNAL OF SPANISH STUDIES : TWENTIETH CENTURY). V. 1-8. 0092-1807. Periodical. US. English. ty. $6.00. Kansas State University, Department of Modern Languages, Manhattan KS 66506. LC PQ6001. DD 860.9006.

JOURNAL OF TAMIL STUDIES. See Linguistics.

JOURNAL OF THE AMERICAN STUDIES ASSOCIATION OF TEXAS. Main/Corp American Studies Association of Texas. V. 1- 1970-. 0587-5064. US. English. an. $6.00. American Studies Association of Texas, c/o Dr Marvin Harris ETBC, Marshall TX 75670. Tel (214)935-7963. Ed Marvin Harris. LC E169.1. DD 917.30305. Circ 150. (ctrl). Scholarly articles on American life and literature, both applied and theoretical.

JOURNAL OF THE DEPARTMENT OF ENGLISH (UNIVERSITY OF CALCUTTA. DEPT. OF ENGLISH). (JOURNAL OF THE DEPARTMENT OF ENGLISH). Vol. 14, No. 1 (1978-79)-. Periodical. II. English. sa. 10.00. UCAC/Secretary, Calcutta University, Journal and Bulletin Section, Asutosh Building, Calcutta 700073 India. Ind/Abst MLA Int. Bibliogr. Books Artic. Mod. Lang. Lit. LC PR1. DD 820.9. *Bulletin of the Department of English.*

JOURNAL OF THE H. G. WELLS SOCIETY. (JOURNAL - H. G. WELLS SOCIETY). Main/Corp H.G. Wells Society. VAT Journal of the Herbert George Wells Society. No. 1- Spring 1972-. 0308-1397. Periodical. UK. English. qt. 1.00. H G Wells Society, 125 Markyate Road, Dagenham Essex RM8 2LB England. LC PR5776. DD 823.912. *Wellsian, H. G. Wells Society Bulletin*, 0440-0348.

Literature

JOURNAL OF THE ILLINOIS SPEECH & THEATRE ASSOCIATION. Main/Corp Illinois Speech & Theatre Association. VAT Journal of the Illinois Speech and Theatre Association. 0145-5516. US. English. Editor, Department of Communications Arts and Sciences, Western Illinois University, Macomb IL 61455. LC PN4073. DD 808.508.

JOURNAL OF THE KAFKA SOCIETY OF AMERICA. 7th Year, No. 2 (Dec. 1983)-. Periodical. US. English. sa. Temple University, Department of Germanic and Slavic Languages and Literatures, HB330/Zip 022-35, Philadelphia PA 19122. Tel (215)787-8270. bk rev. adv acc. Circ 300. Articles, bibliography and information on Kafka in English and German language. *Newsletter of the Kafka Society of America.*

JOURNAL OF THE ORIENTAL INSTITUTE. Main/Corp Baroda (City). Oriental Institute. V. 1- Sept. 1951-. 0030-5324. Periodical. II. English. qt. $15.00. Oriental Institute, University of Baroda, PO Box 75, Baroda India. Ed Mahamaho Padhraya and S G Kantawala. Ind/Abst MLA Int. Bibliogr. Books Artic. Mod. Lang. Lit. PJ25. bk rev. Circ 550. Includes indological articles of textual and cultural problems of epic studies, notices of MSS. Book reviews, publication of works, survey of oriental journals.

JOURNAL OF THE ROCKY MOUNTAIN MEDIEVAL AND RENAISSANCE ASSOCIATION. Main/Corp Rocky Mountain Medieval and Renaissance Association. V. 1- 1980-. 0195-8453. Periodical. US. English. an. $15.00. Northern Arizona University, Department of English, Box 6032, Flagstaff AZ 86011. Tel (602)523-4456. Ed James Fitzmaurice. Ind/Abst Am. Hist. Life, Hist. Abstr., MLA Int. Bibliogr. Books Artic. Mod. Lang. Lit., Hist. Abstr., Part A, Mod. Hist. Abstr., Hist. Abst., Part B, Twent. Century Abstr. LC CB351. DD 909.07. bk rev. adv acc. Circ 200. Medieval and Renaissance studies: history, literature, art, philosophy and music.

JOURNAL OF UKRAINIAN GRADUATE STUDIES. VFOAT Zhurnal Vyshchyky Ukrainoznaychykh Studii. V. 1- Fall 1976-. 0701-1792. Periodical. CN. English (includes some text in Ukrainian). sa. $4.00. c/o Department of Slavic Languages and Literatures, 21 Sussex Avenue, University of Toronto, Toronto Ontario M5S 1A1 Canada. DD 947.71005.

JOURNAL - POST-GRADUATE DEPARTMENT OF ENGLISH. GAUHATI UNIVERSITY. (JOURNAL). Main/Corp Gauhati, India. University Post-Graduate Dept. of English. 0302-9492. English. an. LC PR1. DD 820.9.

JUBILEE (GORRIE). (JUBILEE). No. 1- June 1974-. 0316-8417. Periodical. CN. English. ir. $3.00. Jubilee Press, Rural Route #2, Gorrie Ontario N0G 1X0 Canada. DD C810.80054.

JULES VERNE. 1-. FR. French. ir. 50.00. Lettres Modernes, 73 rue du Cardinal Lemoine CCP Paris 10671-19, 75005 Paris France. LC PN3.

JUNELI. Periodical. II. Nepali. ir. 0.75. Dayalakshmi Chapakhana, Bhojpur India. LC PK2598.A2.

JUNG SHU WEN HSUEH TSUNG KAN. No. 1 (Sept. 1979)-. Periodical. CC. Chinese. qt. 1.06. Fu-Chien Shen Hisn Hua Shu, Tien Fu-Chou China. LC PL2513. DD 895.109005.

JUNGE LITERATUR AUS OSTERREICH. '80-. German. an. LC PT3823. DD 830.809436.

JUNIOR BOOK AWARDS. Main/Corp Boys' Clubs of America. US. English. LC Z1037. DD 028.5.

JVALAMUKHI. No. 1, (September 1980)-. Periodical. KO. Hindi. an. 10.00. Yoshiaki Suzuki, 5-9 Matsuyama 4-chome Kiyose-shi, Tokyo Japan. LC PK2030.

JYOTSNA. Hindi. ir. 15.00. Jyotsna Karylana, Bandhu Kuti Path 8, Rajendranagar Patna 800016 India. LC PK2030.

KAHANI. Periodical. II. Hindi. ir. 8.00. Sarasvati Presa, 5 Sardar Patel Marg, Allahabad India. LC PK2077.

KAIE. CAHIERS DE LA NOUVELLE LITTERATURE. VFOAT Cahiers de la Nouvelle Litterature. July 1978 Edition-. Periodical. Japanese. ir. 680. Tojusha, 18 Kanda Jimbocho, Chiyoda-Ku, Tokyo Japan. LC PL726.8.

KAIKISEN. April 1983 Edition 1- Tachi-. Periodical. JA. Japanese. bm. 500 Single Issue. Kaikisen, No Kai 15-10 Higashi Kamata 1 Ota-Ku, Tokyo-to 144 Japan. LC PL755.8.

KAIROS. Volume 1- 1959-. 0022-7757. Periodical. AU. German. qt. 320.-. Otto Muller Verlag, Ernest Thun Strasse 11, A-6021 Salzburg Austria. Tel 0662/72152. Ed Kurt Klinger, Jeannie Ebner and Rudolf Henz. Ind/Abst New Testam. Abstr., Relig. Index One, Period. LC BL1. bk rev. adv acc. Circ 2,500. Literary texts with Austrian authors. Contributions to literary science of Austria.

KAKATIYA JOURNAL OF ENGLISH STUDIES. V. 1- Mar. 1976-. Periodical. English. ir. $1.00. Kakatiya University/Department of English, Vidyaratmapur Warangal Andhra Pradesh, 506001 India. LC PR9480. DD 820.9.

KAKU. Fall Edition 1977-. Periodical. JA. Japanese. ir. 580. Kaiho Shuppansho, 1247 Kuboyoshicho, Naniwa-Ku 556, Osaka Japan. LC PL755.8.

KALAMA. Periodical. Hindi. ir. LC PK2030.

THE KALEIDOSCOPE. (THE KALEIDOSCOPE). No. 1-. 0748-8742. Periodical. US. English. sa. $5.50. United Cerebral Palsy of Akron and Summit County, 318 Water Street, Akron OH 44308. LC PS153.P48. DD 810.803520816.

KALKI. V. 1-. 0022-7994. Periodical. US. English. ir. $18.00. East Texas State University, Hall Lang 213/JB Cabell Society, Commerce TX 75428. Tel (214)886-5264. Ed Paul Spencer. Ind/Abst MLA Int. Bibliogr. Books Artic. Mod. Lang. Lit. (cum index). bk rev. Circ 350. (ctrl). A scholarly journal which publishes critical essays on Cabell and his contemporaries, book reviews, and diverse information about the period from 1900 to 1950 or so.

KALULU. V. 1- June 1976-. Periodical. English. ir. 0.50 Single Issue. University of Malawi/English Department, Box 280, Zomba Malawi Central Africa. LC GR358.5. DD 398.2096897.

KANKAVATI. Periodical. Gujarati. ir. 10.00. Dahyabhai Jivanaji Nayaka, Nani Chipwad Ambaji Road 1, Surata India. Ed D J Nayaka. LC PK1855.

KANSAS QUARTERLY. V. 1- Winter 1968-. 0022-8745. Periodical. US. English. qt. $15.00 Domestic, $16.00 Foreign. Kansas State University, 122 Denison Hall/English Department, Manhattan KS 66506. Tel (913)532-6716. Ed Harold Schneider, Ben Nyberg, John Rees, and W R Moses. Ind/Abst Am. Hist. Life, Hist. Abstr., Part A, Mod. Hist. Abstr., Hist. Abst., Part B, Twent. Century Abstr., Abstr. Engl. Stud., MLA Int. Bibliogr. Books Artic. Mod. Lang. Lit., Writ. Am. Hist., Index Am. Period. Verse, Years Work Eng. Stud., Hist. Abstr. LC AP2. DD 051. adv acc. Circ 1,300. Focuses on the writing, history, art, and culture of Mid-America and the US at large, a literary and cultural arts journal. *Kansas Magazine.*

KANSAS WRITER'S MARKET. 1977-. 0146-3217. US. English. Golden Grain Press, Amorita OK 73719. LC PN101. DD 808.005.

KARLSRUHER ALMANACH FUR LITERATUR. See Yearbooks, Almanacs, Directories.

KARMAL (BEIRUT, LEBANON). (AL-KARMAL). VFOAT Alkarmel. No. 1, (Winter 1981)-. Periodical. Arabic. qt. Ittihad Al-Amm Lil-Kuttab Wa-Al-Sahaflyin Al-Filastiniyin, SB 14/5010, Beirut Lebanon. LC PN9.

KATATHESE. Greek, Modern. ir. Ekdoseis Boukoumane, Boukoumanis Publications, 57 Acadimias Street T T 143, Athenai Greece. LC PA5271.

KATHALAKSHMI. Periodical. Marathi. ir. LC PK2416.

KATHANA. Pravesanka (Julai-Agasta 1980)-. Periodical. II. Hindi. bm. 15.00. Kathan Sampadakiya Karyalaya, B-3/4 Ranapratap Bagh, Delhi 110007 India. LC PK2046.

KEEPSAKE SERIES. Main/Corp Book Club of California. 1933/34-. Periodical. US. English. an.

KEILSCHRIFTURKUNDEN AUS BOGHAZKOI. Began publication in 1921. GE. German. an. Deutscher Buch Export-Import, Leninstrasse 16, DDr-701 Leipiz East Germany. LC PJ3721.B6.

KENTUCKY ROMANCE QUARTERLY. (KENTUCKY ROMANCE QUARTERLY : KRQ). VFOAT KRQ, K.R.Q. Began with V. 14, 1967. 0364-8664. Periodical. US. English. qt. $21.00. University Press of Kentucky, 102 Lafferty Hall/University of Kentucky, Lexington KY 40506. Tel (606)257-8439. Ed John E Keller. Ind/Abst MLA Int. Bibliogr. Books Artic. Mod. Lang. Lit., Lang. Lang. Behav. Abstr., Index Book Rev. Humanit., Sociol. Abstr. LC P1. DD 840.09. (cum index). bk rev. adv acc. Topics in romance languages and literatures. *Kentucky Foreign Language Quarterly*, 0023-0332.

KESENIAN MASYARAKAT. VFOAT Social Culture. V. 1- Sept. 1971-. Periodical. English (Malay Sept. 1971, 1973, Malay only). ir. Commercial Malay Literary Service, PO Box 150, Geylang Singapore. LC PN2960.S5.

KHAVATIN DAIJIST. V. 1- May 1972-. Periodical. Urdu. ir. Hamidah Bano, Urdu Bazar, Karaci Pakistan. LC PK2151.

KIELER STUDIEN ZUR DEUTSCHEN LITERATURGESCHICHTE. Vol. 1- 1963-. 0453-8501. Monographic Series. GW. German. ir. K Wachholtz Verlag, Postfach 2769, D-2350 Neumunster West Germany. Tel 04321/567 28. Ed Erich Trunz. Ind/Abst MLA Int. Bibliogr. Books Artic. Mod. Lang. Lit. Circ 600. (ctrl). History of literature from Schleswig-Holstein.

KIKAN REKISHI TO BUNGAKU. VFOAT Rekishi to Bungaku. Periodical. JA. Japanese. ir. 720. Heibonsha 4, Yonbancho, Chiyods-Ku Tokyo Japan. LC PL740.65.H54.

KIKAN SOZO. VFOAT Sozo. Fall Edition 1976-. JA. Japanese. ir. 980. Seibunsha, 1 Ichigaya Sadoharacho 1, Shijuku-Ku Tokyo Japan. LC PL700.

KIPLING JOURNAL. (THE KIPLING JOURNAL; THE ORGAN OF THE KIPLING SOCIETY). No. 1- March 1927-. 0023-1738. Periodical. UK. English. qt. Kipling Society, Department of English/Rockford College, Rockford IL 61108. Ind/Abst MLA Int. Bibliogr. Engl. Stud., MLA Int. Bibliogr. Books Artic. Mod. Lang. Lit., Annu. Bibliogr. Engl. Lang. Lit. LC PR4856. DD 823.89.

KIRUTAYUKAM. 1 (Jan./Feb. 1981)-. Periodical. Tamil. ir. LC PL4758.45.

KISWAHILI. See Linguistics.

KITABNAMAH-I RAHAVARD. VFOAT Ketabnamen Rahavard. Began in 1983?. 0747-9034. Periodical. US. Persian, Modern. mo. $50.00. Rahavard Publications, 8306 Wilshire Boulevard/Suite 105, Beverly Hills CA 90211. DD 808.

KITABU CHA JUA. US. English. $6.00. PO Box 771, San Francisco CA 94101. LC AP2. DD 810.80896. *Journal of Black Poetry.*

KIWON. VFOAT Age. Periodical. KO. Korean. ir. 300 Single Issue. Kiwon, 129-15 Chung-Dong, Chungnim-Ku, Seoul South Korea. LC PL950.2.

KLEINE TEXTE FUR VORLESUNGEN UND UBUNGEN. See Linguistics.

KO ERH CHIN WEN HSUEH. VFOAT Keerqinwenxue. Periodical. CC. Chinese. bm. 0.25. Hsin Hua Shu Tien, Nei Meng-ku China. LC PL3031.M62. DD 895.10995177.

KO HUAN HAI YANG. VFOAT S F Ocean. 1981, 1-. Periodical. CC. Chinese. qt. 1.00. Hsin Hua Shu Tien Pei-Ching Fa Hsing So Peking China. LC PL2629.S34. DD 895.13087608.

KOJO. V. 1, No. 1, First Issue No. 2-. Periodical. JA. Japanese. ir. 300. Kojo Sha, c/o Kusakabe Kojo Sha, 143-9 Kita Akitsu, Tokorozawa 359 Japan. LC PL755.8.

KOKOTSUGAKU. VFOAT Journal for Oracle Bone Studies. Japanese. ir. 2500. c/o Toyo Bunka Kenkyujo, Tokyo Daigaku, Hongo 7-Chome (113), Tokyo Japan. LC PL2447.

KOKUBUNGAKU KENKYU SHIRYOKAN HO. Vol. 1 (1st Edition). JA. Japanese. ir. Free. Kokubungaku Kenkyu Shiryokan, 16-10 Yutakamachi 1-Chome, Shinagawa-Ku 142, Tokyo Japan. Tel (03)785-7131. LC Z7072, PL523. Circ 1,700. Newsletter of National Institute of Japanese Literature.

KOKUBUNGAKU KENKYU SHIRYOKAN KIYO. VFOAT Bulletin of the National Institute of Japanese Literature. No. 1-. Japanese. ir. Kokubungaku Kenkyu Shiryokan, 1-16-10 Yutaka-Cho Shinagawa-Ku, Tokyo 142 Japan. Tel (03)785-7131. LC PL700. adv acc. Circ 500. Collected papers written by the scholars of the National Institute of Japanese Literature. On the classic Japanese literature and philological problems.

KOKUBUNGAKU KENKYU SHIRYOKAN ZO CHIKUJI KANKOBUTSU MOKUROKU = CATALOG OF PERIODICALS ACQUIRED IN THE NATIONAL INSTITUTE OF JAPANESE LITERATURE. See Bibliographies.

Literature

KOKUBUNGAKU NENJIBETSU RONBUNSHU. CHUKO. 1980-. JA. Japanese. an. 23900 (Set). Hobun Shuppan, 10-29 Asama-Machi 2 Higashikurume-Shi, Tokyo-To 2 Japan. LC PL726.2.

KOKUBUNGAKU NENJIBETSU RONBUNSHU. CHUSEI. 1980-. JA. Japanese. an. 9500 Per Volume in 2 Parts. Hobun Shuppan, 10-29 Sengen-Cho 2 Higashikurume-Shi, Tokyo-To Japan. LC PL726.3.

KOKUBUNGAKU NENJIBETSU RONBUNSHU. JODAI. 1981-. Japanese. an. 9800 Per Volume. Hobun Shuppan, 10-29 Drnhrn-Cho Higashikurume-Shi, Tokyo-To 18 Japan. LC PL726.12.

KOKUBUNGAKU NENJIBETSU RONBUNSHU. KINDAI. 1 (1981)-. JA. Japanese. an. 7600. Hobun Shuppan, 10-29 Asama-Machi Higashikurume-Shi, Tokyo-To 20 Japan. LC PL726.55.

KOKUBUNGAKU NENJIBETSU RONBUNSHU. KINSEI. 1980-. JA. Japanese. an. 9800 Per Volume in 2 parts. Hobun Shuppan, 10-29 Sengen-Cho, 2 Higashikurume-Shi, Tokyo-To Japan. LC PL726.35.

KOKUBUNGAKU NENJIBETSU RONBUNSHU. KOKUBUNGAKU IPPAN. 1980-. JA. Japanese. an. 8800 Per Volume. Hobun Shuppan, 10-29 Sengen-Cho 2 Higashikurume-Shi, Tokyo-To Japan. LC PL700.

KOKUBUNGAKU NENKAN. See Bibliographies.

KOKUGO TO KOKUBUNGAKU. 1st Ed. (May 1924)-. Periodical. JA. Japanese. mo. 12,900. Oversea Courier Service Inc, No 9 Shibaura 2-Chrome Minato-Ku, Tokyo 108 Japan. Tel 03-208-2251. Ind/Abst MLA Int. Bibliogr. Books Artic. Mod. Lang. Lit. First line post-graduate research work and new research theses on Japanese literature.

KOKUGOGAKU NO SEKAI. See Linguistics.

KOKUSAI NIHON BUNGAKU KENKYU SHUKAI KAIGIROKU. Main/Conf International Conference on Japanese Literature in Japan. VFOAT Proceedings of the International Conference on Japanese Literature in Japan. No. 1-: 1977-. JA. Japanese (with abstracts in English). ir. Kokubungaku Kenkyu Shiryokan, 16-10 Yutakacho, Shinagawa-Ku Tokyo 142 Japan. Tel (03)785-7131. LC PL703. Circ 800. (ctrl). Proceedings of the International Conference on Japanese Literature in Japan.

KOLNER ROMANISTISCHE ARBEITEN. 0075-6520. Monographic Series. SZ. German. ir. Librarie Droz SA, 11 rue Massot, 1211 Geneva Switzerland. Ind/Abst MLA Int. Bibliogr. Books Artic. Mod. Lang. Lit. Literature of romance languages.

KOMABANO: KAMPO. See Bibliographies.

KOMMUNAL LITTERATUR. 0023-3056. Periodical. Swedish. ir. Bibliotekstjanst AB, Box 1706, 22101 Lund Sweden.

KOMMUNAL LITTERATURTJANST. Periodical. SW. Swedish. bm. $26.62. Bibliotekstjanst AB, Box 1706, S-221 01 Lund Sweden. LC Z7164.L8.

KONTEKST. 1972-. UR. Russian. an. 1.67. Nauka, 103717 GSP K-62 Podsosenskii Per 21, Moskva USSR Russia. Ind/Abst MLA Int. Bibliogr. Books Artic. Mod. Lang. Lit. LC PN9.

KORENI. 1-. Bulgarian. ir. LC PG1020.7.

KORTARS. 0023-415X. Periodical. HU. Hungarian. mo. Akademiai Kiado, POB 24, 1363 Budapest Hungary. Ind/Abst MLA Int. Bibliogr. Books Artic. Mod. Lang. Lit. LC PH3144.

KPA BULLETIN. See Linguistics.

KRAUS HEFTE. Vol. 1- Jan. 1977-. Periodical. GW. German. qt. $12.50. Text Kritik GMBH, Levelingstrasse 6A, 8000 Munchen 80 West Germany. LC PT2621.R27.

KREMIKOVSKO SIIANIE. 1976-. BU. Bulgarian. ir. LC PG1020.7.

KRITIK. Vol. 1- (No. 1-). 0454-5354. Periodical. DK. Danish. qt. Munksgaard Ltd, 35 Norre Sogade, DK-1370 Copenhagen K Denmark. Ind/Abst MLA Int. Bibliogr. Books Artic. Mod. Lang. Lit. LC PN9. (cum index).

KRITIKAS GADAGRAMATA. Began with Vol. for 1972. UR. Latvian. an. 1.30. Leisma, Padomju Bulv 24, Riga Latvian SFSR. Ind/Abst MLA Int. Bibliogr. Books Artic. Mod. Lang. Lit. LC PG9000.

KRITIKON LITTERARUM. See Linguistics.

KRITISCH AKKOORD. Series/Titl Maerlantpocket. Periodical. Dutch. an. LC PT5001.

KU SHIH HUI. VFOAT Gushihui. Began with July 1963 issue. Periodical. CC. Chinese. bm. 0.18. Chung-Kuo Kyo Chi Shu Tien, PO Box 2920, Peking China Mainland. LC PL2653. DD 895.130108.

KU SHIH TSUNG KAN. VFOAT Gu Shi Cong Kan. Periodical. CC. Chinese. ir. 0.29. Hsin Hua Shu Tien, Chung-ching Fa Hsing So, Chung-ching China.

KU TAI WEN HSUEH LI LUN YEN CHIU. V. 1-. CC. Chinese. ir. Shang-Hai Ku Chi Chu Pan She Shang-Hai China. LC PL2254. DD 801.950951.

KU TIEN WEN HSUEH. V. 1-. CH. Chinese. an. Taiwan Hsueh Sheng Shu Chu, 298 lo SSU Fu Lu ThirdSection, Taipei Taiwan China. LC PL2250. DD 895.109.

KU TIEN WEN HSUEH LUN TSUNG. 1 (May 1980)-. Periodical. CC. Chinese. ir. Shen-Hsi Sheng Hsin Hua Shu Tien Hsi-An China. LC PL2254.

KU TIEN WEN HSUEH LUN TSUNG (CHI LU SHU SHE). (KU TIEN WEN HSUEH LUN TSUNG). Periodical. CH. Chinese. ir. 1.90. Chi Lu Shu She, Shan Tung China. LC PL2254. DD 895.109.

KUANG-HSI WEN HSUEH. V. 7, (July 1980)-. Periodical. CH. Chinese. mo. 0.30. Post Office, China. LC PL3031.K883. DD 895.108005. *Kuang-Hsi Wen I.*

KUKCHE OMUN. See Linguistics.

KULTUR OG KLASS. VFOAT Kultur & Klasse. Began with Vol. 8, No. 29, published in 1977. Periodical. Danish. qt. Tel 2 42.40.00. Ind/Abst MLA Int. Bibliogr. Books Artic. Mod. Lang. Lit. LC AP30. bk rev. adv acc. Circ 1,000. Literature, cultural studies, mass communications, semiotics. *Tidsskriftet Poetik.*

KULTURA SLOVA. See Linguistics.

KUN LUN. V. 1, 1982-. Periodical. CH. Chinese. ir. 1.00. Hsin Hua Shu Tien Pei-Ching Fa Hsing So, Peking China. Tel 663-7604. Ed Cheng Bu-Tao. LC PL2303. DD 895.109005. bk rev. adv acc. A big sized military literature journal. Concerns mostly novels, biographies, book reviews, short stories, play writing, script writing, proses and poetry, etc.

KUNAPIPI. Vol. 1, No. 1-. 0106-5734. Periodical. DK. English. ir. $7.74. University of Aarhus, Department of English, Building 326, 8000 Aarhus C Denmark. Tel 06-136711. Ed Anna Rutherford. Ind/Abst MLA Int. Bibliogr. Books Artic. Mod. Lang. Lit. adv acc. Circ 800. Arts magazine with special emphasis on the new literatures written in English. Aims to introduce the work of new or little known writers of talent, to provide critical evaluation of the work of living authors both famous and unknown, and to be truly international. *Commonwealth Newsletter.*

KUO WAI WEN HSUEH. V. 1-. CH. Chinese. qt. 0.45. Pei-Ching Ta Hsuen Chu Pan She, Peking China. LC PN80. DD 809.

KYESONG MUNHAK. V. 1- (1981)-. Periodical. Korean. ir. 2.000. Kyesong Munhakhoe, 277 Taesin-Dong Chung-Ku, Taegu Korea. LC PL969.8.

KYOKA KENKYU. 1974 Edition-. Japanese. ir. Ishikawa Kindai Bungakukan, 2-13 Hirosaka 2 (920), Kanazama Japan. LC PL809.Z9.

KYONGHUI MUNHAK. V. 1-. Korean. an. LC PL969.8.

L.-F. CELINE. Series/Titl La Revue des Lettres Modernes. 1- 1974-. FR. French. ir. Lettres Modernes, 73 rue du Cardinal-Lemoine, 75005 CCP Paris 10671-19 France. LC PN3. DD 809.

LA REVUE DES LETTRES MODERNES. JEAN GIONO. (JEAN GIONO). Series/Titl La Revue des Lettres Modernes. 1-. 0180-9423. Periodical. FR. French. ir. Lettres Moderns, CCP 10671-19, 73 rue du Cardinal-Lemoine, Paris France 75005. LC PN3.

LAGNIAPPE. V. 1- Spring 1974-. 0193-7588. Periodical. US. English. qt. $1.00 Single Issue. Lagniappe Magazine, PO Box 1073, Oxford MS 38655. LC PS551. DD 810.8.

LANDFALL. V. 1- Mar. 1947-. 0023-7930. Periodical. English. qt. $16.90. The Caxton Press, PO Box 25-088, Christchurch New Zealand. Ed David Dowling. Ind/Abst Abstr. Engl. Stud., MLA Int. Bibliogr. Books Artic. Mod. Lang. Lit., Am. Hist. Life, Hist. Abstr., Abstr. Engl. Stud., Hist. Abstr., Part A, Mod. Hist. Abstr., Hist. Abst., Part B, Twent. Century Abstr. LC AP7. DD 052. (cum index). bk rev. adv acc. Circ 1,800. (ctrl). Short stories, poetry, reviews, interviews, commentary, criticism, art, etc.

LANGUAGE AND LITERATURE (SAN ANTONIO, TEX.). See Linguistics.

LAOMEDON REVIEW. V. 1- Dec. 1974/Jan. 1975-. 0382-8824. Periodical. CN. English. 5.00 Domestic, 2.30 Great Britain, Australia, New Zealand, 8.00 all other countries. Subscription Service, Department of Erindale College, University of Toronto, 3359 Mississauga Road, Mississauga Ontario L5L 1C6 Canada. DD C810.8092379.

LATIN AMERICAN INDIAN LITERATURES CEASED. Began with Vol. 1, Spring 1977. Ceased with Vol. 8. 0160-8045. Periodical. US. English. sa. $25.00. Geneva College, Mary Preuss, Department of Foreign Languages, Beaver Falls PA 15010. Tel (412)846-5100. Ed Mary H Preuss. Ind/Abst MLA Int. Bibliogr. Books Artic. Mod. Lang. Lit., Relig. Index One, Period. LC PM151. DD 897. bk rev. adv acc. Circ 300. (ctrl). Studies and texts of Latin American Indian literatures, book reviews, article abstracts, mayaglyphs, rock art report, and extensive bibliography.

LATIN AMERICAN LITERATURE AND ART REVIEW CEASED. VFOAT Review. No. 20 (Spring 1977)-23. 0748-2426. Periodical. US. English (Spanish). ty. $24.00. Center for Inter-American Relations, 680 Park Avenue, New York NY 10020. Tel (212)249-8950. Ed Lori Carlson. LC F1401. DD 700.5. bk rev. adv acc. Circ 3,000. Available on microfilm from University Microfilms. Latin American literature in English translation articles on the arts in Latin America. *Review (Center for Inter-American Relations : 1968), 0069-1445.*

LATIN AMERICAN LITERATURE AND ARTS REVIEW. (LATIN AMERICAN LITERATURE & ARTS REVIEW). 27-. 0748-2442. Periodical. US. English (Spanish). ty. $20.00. Center for Inter-American Relations, 680 Park Avenue, New York NY 10021. Tel (212)249-8950. Ed Lori M Carlson. Ind/Abst MLA Int. Bibliogr. Books Artic. Mod. Lang. Lit. LC F1401. DD 700.5. bk rev. adv acc. Circ 3,000. Latin American literature in translation. *Review (Center for Inter-American Relations : 1979), 0748-2434.*

LATINITAS. See Linguistics.

LAUREATY LENINSKOGO KOMSOMOLA. 1967-. UR. Russian. 1.63. Molodaia Gvardiia, A-30 Suschevskaia Ul 21, Moskva USSR. LC PG3199.

LAVORO CRITICO. 1- Jan./Mar. 1975-. Periodical. Italian. ir. 7.000. Edizioni di Giardini, Via Santa Bibbiana 28, 56100 Pisa Italy. LC PQ4001.

LEACOCK FESTIVAL OF HUMOR ANNUAL CEASED. (THE LEACOCK FESTIVAL OF HUMOUR ANNUAL). V. 1-2. 0319-311X. CN. English. an. Leacock Festival of Humour Foundation, Box 992, Orillia Ontario L3V 6K8 Canada. DD C817.5405.

THE LEAFLET. See Education (General).

LEBARON RUSSELL BRIGGS PRIZE HONORS ESSAYS IN ENGLISH. 0075-8396. Monographic Series. US. English. ir. Harvard University Press, 79 Garden Street, Cambridge MA 02138. Tel (617)661-3761.

LEGACY (AMHERST, MASS.). (LEGACY). Vol. 1, No. 1 (Spring 1984)-. 0748-4321. Periodical. US. English. sa. $18.00. Legacy, Department of English, Bartlett Hall, University of Massachusetts, Amherst MA 01003. Tel (413)545-4270. Ed Martha Ackmann, Karen Dandurand and Joanne Dobson. DD 810. bk rev. adv acc. Circ 500. A journal of nineteenth-century American women writers: literary, historical, cultural, biographical and bibliographical articles.

LEIDSE GERMANISTISCHE EN ANGLISTISCHE REEKS. 1- 1962-. 0458-9971. Monographic Series. NE. English, Dutch and German. ir. E J Brill Leiden, Plantijnstraat 2, 2321 JC Leiden Netherlands. Tel (071-31 26 24. This series comprises publications by members of Leiden University in the field of English language and literature and Germanic languages and literatures in the widest sense.

LEIDSE ROMANTISCHE REEKS. 0075-8647. Monographic Series. NE. Dutch. ir. E J Brill Leiden, Plantijnstraat 2, 2321 JC Leiden The Netherlands. **Tel** (0)71-31 26 24. This series comprises publications by members of the Leiden University in the field of Romanistic languages and literatures.

LENAU-FORUM. Year 1- 1969-. 0024-0788. Periodical. AU. German. ir. Internationale Lenau-Gesellschaft, Postfach 295, A-1031 Wien Austria. **Ind/Abst** MLA Int. Bibliogr. Books Artic. Mod. Lang. Lit. **LC** PT2393.Z4.

LESEBUCH DER DEUTSCHEN SCIENCE FICTION. Series/Titl Edition Futurum. 1984-. 0175-9272. German. an. **LC** PT747.S34. **DD** 833.087609.

LESSING YEARBOOK. *See* Yearbooks, Almanacs, Directories.

LETRA (RIO DE JANEIRO, BRAZIL). (LETRA). Year 1, No. 1 (Jan./July 1980)-. Periodical. BL. Portuguese. ir. Universidade Federal do Rio de Janeiro, Faculdade de Letras, Av Chile No 330, Rio de Janeiro Brazil. **LC** P9. **DD** 410.5.

LETRAS DE BUENOS AIRES. Yearly 1, No. 1, (Oct./Dec. 1980)-. Periodical. AG. Spanish. qt. Tagle, 2572 6 Piso D, 1425 Buenos Aires Argentina. **LC** PQ7600. **DD** 860.8.

LETRAS DE DEUSTO. V. 1- (No. 1-). 0210-3516. Periodical. SP. Spanish. ty. 10. Department de Publicaciones, University de Deusto, Apartado 1, Bilbao Spain. **Tel** 4453100. **Ind/Abst** Am. Hist. Life, Hist. Abstr., MLA Int. Bibliogr. Books Artic. Mod. Lang. Lit. bk rev. adv acc.

LETRAS DE GUATEMALA. 1 (Jun. de 1980)-. Periodical. Spanish. sa. **LC** PQ7490. **DD** 460.997281.

LETRAS DE HOJE. *See* Linguistics.

LETRAS FEMENINAS. Vol. 1, No. 1 (Spring 1975)-. 0277-4356. Periodical. US. English (Spanish). sa. $15.00. Texas A & M University, Modern Language Department, c/o Dr A Martinez, College Station TX 77843. **Tel** (409)845-2175. **Ed** Adelaida Lopez de Martinez. **Ind/Abst** Index Am. Period. Verse. **LC** PQ6055. **DD** 860.809287. bk rev. adv acc. **Circ** 500. Creative writings by Hispanic women and critical studies of Hispanic women writers.

THE LETTER EXCHANGE. 0882-3804. Periodical. US. English. ty. $10.00. The Readers League, Box 6218, Albany CA 94706. **Tel** (415)526-7412. **Ed** Stephen Sikora. **Circ** 2,000. A magazine for letter-writers, containing listing for correspondence on literature, movies, culture, daily life, etc. Devoted to the revival of personal correspondence. *Reader's League Catalogue of Correspondence.*

LETTERATURA ITALIANA CONTEMPORANEA. Yearly V. 1, No. 1 (Sept./Dec. 1980)-. Periodical. IT. Italian. ty. 27.000. Via Trionfale 8406, 00135 Roma Italy. **LC** PQ4087. **DD** 850.8.

LA LETTERATURA ITALIANA. STUDI E TESTI. VFOAT Studi e Testi. Vol. 1-. IT. Italian. ir. Riccardo Ricciardi Editore, Via G Morone 3, 20121 Milano Italy.

LETTERATURE D'AMERICA. Yearly V. 1, No. 1, (Winter 1980)-. Periodical. IT. Italian (summaries in English, Portuguese, and Spanish). qt. Editore Mario Bulzoni, Via Dei Liburni, 14 Conto Corente, Postale 31054000, 00185 Roma Italy. **LC** PN843. **DD** 809.891812.

LETTERATURE D'OLTRALPE E D'OLTREOCEANO. SAGGI E STUDI. 1- 1972-). Monographic Series. IT. Italian. ir. Casa Editrice Leo S Olschki, Casella Postale, PO Box 66, 50100 Firenze Italy.

LETTERE ITALIANE. Began publication with Vol. 1, Jan./Mar. 1949. 0024-1334. Periodical. IT. Italian. qt. Casa Editrice, Leo S Olschki, Casella Postale, PO Box 66, 50100 Firenze Italy. **Ed** G Searpat. **Ind/Abst** MLA Int. Bibliogr. Books Artic. Mod. Lang. Lit., Sociol. Abstr., Lang. Lang. Behav. Abstr. **LC** PQ4001.

LETTERS. V. 1- Summer 1974-. Periodical. US. English. an. Letters, PO Box 614, Saratoga Springs NY 12866. **LC** PN6069.W65. **DD** 810.809287.

LETTRES QUEBECOISES. No. 1- Mar. 1976-. 0382-084X. Periodical. CN. French. qt. $7.74. Les Editions Jumonville, CP 1840 Station B, Montreal Quebec H3B 3L4 Canada. **Tel** (514)525-9518. **Ed** Adrien Therio. **Ind/Abst** Point Repere. **DD** C840.9. bk rev. adv acc. **Circ** 5,000. (ctrl). This is a magazine of "l'actualite litteraire" for Quebec. We present all the best books published in the field of literature, (novels, poetry, theatre, essays).

LES LETTRES ROMANES. Vol. 1, No.1 (Feb. 1947)-. Periodical. BE. French. qt. 650. Les Lettres Romanes, Place Blaise Pascal 1, B 1348 Louvain L Neuve Belgium. **Tel** (010)434921. **Ind/Abst** MLA Int. Bibliogr. Books Artic. Mod. Lang. Lit., Index Book Rev. Humanit., Years Work Eng. Stud. **LC** PC2. bk rev. **Circ** 600. (ctrl). Publishes articles, critical reviews and bibliographical notes about history of the romance literatures and their authors.

LETTURE CLASSENSI. Began in 1966. 0459-1623. IT. Italian. ir. Cas Post, PO Box 431, Ravenna Italy. **LC** PQ4331. **DD** 851.1.

THE LIBRARY CHRONICLE OF THE UNIVERSITY OF TEXAS AT AUSTIN. New Ser., No. 1 (Mar. 1970)-. 0024-2241. Periodical. US. English. sa. $25.00. Humanities Research Center, PO Box 7219, Austin TX 78713. **Tel** (512)471-9113. **Ed** Dave Pliphant and Tom Zigal. **Ind/Abst** Abstr. Engl. Stud., Annu. Bibliogr. Engl. Lang. Lit., MLA Int. Bibliogr. Books Artic. Mod. Lang. Lit., Am. Hist. Life, Hist. Abstr., Part A, Mod. Hist. Abstr., Hist. Abst., Part B, Twent. Century Abstr., Artbibliogr. Mod., Years Work Eng. Stud., Hist. Abstr. **DD** 027. **Circ** 250. Literary and art criticism, correspondence of authors and artists, theatre and film history, research in bibliography and book arts, reproduction of photographs and artworks. *Library Chronicle of the University of Texas, 0885-4351.*

LIEN HO PAO . . . TUAN PIEN HSIAO SHUO CHIANG TSO PIN CHI. Series/Titl Lien Ho Pao Tsung Shu. CH. Chinese. an. 100.00. Lin Ching Chu Pan Shih Yeh Kung Ssu, 555 Chung Hsiao East Road, 4 Section, Taipei Taiwan. **LC** PL2653. **DD** 895.130108.

LIKHT SHTRALN. VFOAT Licht-Stralen. Periodical. US. Yiddish. 150 Hewes Street, Brooklyn NY 11211. **LC** PJ5120.

LILI, ZEITSCHRIFT FUR LITERATURWISSENSCHAFT UND LINGUISTIK. *See* Linguistics.

LIMBA ROMANA. (LIMBA ROMINA). Year 3-L3. 0024-3523. Periodical. RM. Romanian. bm. Ilexim Press Department, PO Box 1-136-1-137, Bucharest Romania. **Ind/Abst** MLA Int. Bibliogr. Books Artic. Mod. Lang. Lit., Sociol. Abstr., Lang. Lang. Behav. Abstr. **LC** PC601. *Limba Romana.*

LIMBA SI LITERATURA. Main/Corp Societatea de Stiinte Filologice din Republica Socialista Romania. RM. Romanian. qt. $42.00. Ilexim Press Department, PO Box 1-136-1-137, Bucharest Romania. **LC** PC601. *Limba si Literatura.*

LINDEN LANE MAGAZINE. Vol. 1, No. 1 (Jan./March 1982)-. 0736-1084. Periodical. US. Spanish. ir. $10.80. Linden Lane Magazine, PO Box 2384, Princeton NJ 08540-0384. **Tel** (609)921-3420. **Ed** Belkis Cuza Male. bk rev. adv acc. **Circ** 3,000. (ctrl). Work of writers and artists of our hemisphere; all submissions will appear in their original form (English or Spanish).

LINE (BURNABY, B.C.). (LINE). No. 1 (Spring 1983)-. 0820-9081. Periodical. CN. English. sa. 16.00. c/o English Department, Simon Fraser University, Burnaby British Columbia V5A 1S6 Canada. **Ed** Roy Miki. **DD** 820.9. bk rev. **Circ** 250. Archival items, essays, reviews, bibliographies related to the line of post 1945 Canadian, American and British writers whose work issues from that of Pound, W C Williams, H D Stein and Olson.

LINES REVIEW. No. 1- July 1952-. 0459-4541. Periodical. UK. English. qt.

LING NAN WEN SHIH. Began in 1983. Periodical. CC. Chinese. sa. 1.00. Kuang-Chou Ku Chi Shu Tien, 338 Pei-Ching Road, Kuang-Chou China. **LC** DS793.K7. **DD** 951.27005.

LINGUISTICA Y LITERATURA : REVISTA DEL DEPARTAMENTO DE ESPANOL. *See* Linguistics.

LININGTON LINEUP. Jan. 84-. 8756-5609. Periodical. US. English. qt. $12.00 Domestic, $15.00 Foreign. Rinehart S Potts, 1223 Glen Terrace, Glassboro NJ 08028. **Tel** (609)589-1571. **Ed** Rinehart S Potts. **LC** PS3562.I515. **DD** 813.54. bk rev. adv acc. **Circ** 400. (ctrl). Study works of Elizabeth Linington (pseudonyms Anne Blaisdell, Lesley Egan, Egan O'Neill, Dell Shannon); historical fiction and mysteries.

LINQ. VFOAT Literature in North Queensland. V. 1- Sept. 1971-. Periodical. AT. English (French or German). ty. $44.27. Editorial Committee, James Cook University, Department of Engineering, Townsville Queensland 4811 Australia. **Ind/Abst** MLA Int. Bibliogr. Books Artic. Mod. Lang. Lit.

LIRE. No. 1 1976-. 0338-5019. Periodical. FR. French. mo. Lire, 67 Avenue de Wagram, 75017 Paris France.

LITARATURA I MASTATSTVA. Periodical. UR. Belorussian. sw. $28.00. Victor Kamkin Inc (63856), 12224 Parklawn Drive, Rockville MD 20852. **Tel** (301)881-5973. **LC** UNC.

LITERA. V. 1-. 0459-5106. Periodical. English. ir. **LC** PN2. **DD** 405. *Ingiliz Filolojisi Dergisi.*

LITERARNI MESICNIK. 1972-. 0300-2446. Periodical. CS. Czech. ir. ARTIA, PO Box 790, Praha 1 Czechoslovakia. **Ind/Abst** MLA Int. Bibliogr. Books Artic. Mod. Lang. Lit. **LC** PG5000.

LITERARY AND JOURNALISTIC AWARDS IN CANADA. VFOAT Les Prix de Litterature et de Journalisme au Canada. 1923/73-. 0382-0343. Periodical. CN. English and French. be. $3.50. Statistics Canada, Publications Distribution, Ottawa Ontario K1A 0T6 Canada. **DD** C810.79.

LITERARY AND LIBRARY PRIZES. 4th Ed.-. 0075-9880. US. English. ir. R R Bowker Co, PO Box 1807, Ann Arbor MI 48106. **LC** PN171.P75. *Literary Prizes and Their Winners, 0730-5850.*

LITERARY CAVALCADE. V. 1- Oct. 1948-. 0024-4511. Periodical. US. English. mo. 22.95. Scholastic Tab Publications, 123 Newkirk Road, Richmond Hill Ontario Canada. **Tel** (416)883-5300. **LC** AP2. **DD** 051.

THE LITERARY CRITERION. Began in 1952?. Periodical. II. English. qt. $12.00. Bangalore University, CN Srinath Department of English, Jnanabharathi Bangalore 56 India. **Tel** 41977. **Ed** C D Narasimhaiah and C N Srinath. **Ind/Abst** Abstr. Engl. Stud., Annu. Bibliogr. Engl. Lang. Lit., MLA Int. Bibliogr. Books Artic. Mod. Lang. Lit. **LC** PR1. **DD** 820.9. (cum index). bk rev. adv acc. **Circ** 750. Focus is on Indian literature in English, Commonwealth and American literature. Textual and analytical criticism of most important and relevant contemporary writing is encouraged.

LITERARY CRITICISM REGISTER. (LITERARY CRITICISM REGISTER : LCR). VFOAT LCR. Vol. 1, No. 1 (Feb. 1983)-. 0733-2165. US. English. mo. $48.00. Literary Criticism Register, PO Drawer CC, Deland FL 32720. **Tel** (904)736-6029. **Ed** Sims D Kline. **LC** Z2011, PR83. **DD** 016.8209. adv acc. **Circ** 1,000. A listing of studies in English and American literature. A current contents reference tool with full bibliographic citations to articles, books, and dissertations in the field.

THE LITERARY HALF-YEARLY. V. 1- Jan 1960-. 0024-4554. II. English. ir. $14.00. H H A Gowda, University of Mysore, Mysore 9 India. **Ed** Anniah Gowda. **Ind/Abst** Abstr. Engl. Stud., MLA Int. Bibliogr. Books Artic. Mod. Lang. Lit., Annu. Bibliogr. Engl. Lang. Lit. **LC** AP8. **DD** 820.5. (cum index).

LITERARY MARKET PLACE WITH NAMES & NUMBERS. VFOAT LMP with Names and Numbers. VAT Literary Market Place with Names and Numbers. 32nd- Ed. 0161-2905. US. English. an. R R Bowker Company, PO Box 1807, Ann Arbor MI 48106. **Tel** (800)521-0600. **LC** PN161. **DD** 070.520973. *Literary Market Place, 0161-2891; Names and Numbers, 0075-9899.*

LITERARY MARKET REVIEW. No. 1- Mar. 1980-. 0198-151X. Periodical. US. English. qt. Kunnupampil P Andrews, 73-47 -225th Street, Glen Oaks NY 11004.

LITERARY MARKETS. No. 1 (Jan./Feb. 1982)-. 0712-4384. Periodical. CN. English. bm. $8.51. Literary Markets, Suite 104, Point Roberts WA 98281. **Tel** (604)277-4829. **Ed** Bill Marles. **DD** 070.502571. bk rev. **Circ** 1,600. Newsletter outlines publishing opportunities for poets and fiction writers.

LITERARY MONOGRAPHS. V. 1-. 0075-9902. Monographic Series. US. English. ir. University of Wisconsin Press, Box 1379, Madison WI 53701. **LC** PR13. **DD** 809.

Literature

LITERARY ONOMASTICS STUDIES.
Began with Vol. for 1974. 0160-8703. US. English. an. $10.00. State University College, Department of Foreign Language and Literature, Brockport NY 14420. Tel (716)395-5273. Ed Grace Alvarez-Altman. **Ind/Abst** MLA Int. Bibliogr. Books Artic. Mod. Lang. Lit. **LC** PN56.N16. **DD** 809. bk rev. **Circ** 200. Research in the use of names of authors, their significance and how they affect the interpretation of the work.

LITERARY READER. Main/Corp Writers Workshop, Calcutta. 1st- 1972-. II. Periodical. ir. 60.00. 169/92 Lake Gardens, Calcutta 45 India. **LC** PR9480. **DD** 828.

LITERARY RESEARCH NEWSLETTER.
V. 1- Jan. 1976-. 0362-1294. Periodical. US. English. qt. $8.00. Manhattan College, Department of English, c/o M A O'Donnell, Bronx NY 10471. **Tel** (212)920-0121. Ed Vincent Tollers. **Ind/Abst** MLA Int. Bibliogr. Books Artic. Mod. Lang. Lit., Ref. Source, Index Book Rev. Humanit. **LC** PN73. **DD** 809. bk rev. **Circ** 400. Covers all aspects of literary research including enumerative and descriptive bibliography, textual criticism, and pedagogy.

THE LITERARY REVIEW. V. 1- Autumn 1957-. 0024-4589. Periodical. US. English. qt. $12.00. Farleigh Dickinson University, 285 Madison Avenue, Madison NJ 07940. Tel (201)377-4050. Ed Walter Cummins. **Ind/Abst** MLA Int. Bibliogr. Books Artic. Mod. Lang. Lit., Annu. Bibliogr. Engl. Lang. Lit., Index Am. Period. Verse, Index Book Rev. Humanit., Soc. Sci. Index, Humanit. Index, Years Work Eng. Stud. **LC** AP2. **DD** 051. bk rev. **Circ** 1,100. Available on microfilm from University Microfilms. Fiction, poetry, and literary essays of high quality, both in original English and in translation.

LITERARY REVIEW. (THE LITERARY REVIEW). V. 1- Jan./March 1974-. 0304-1123. English. ir. 20.00. A-3/6 Nurakabagar, Lucknow 226007 India. **LC** Z1035.A1. **DD** 028.1.

LITERARY REVIEW CEASED. (THE LITERARY REVIEW). Vol. 1, No. 1 (1983)-. 0820-8999. Periodical. CN. English. sa. $4.00. Literary Review c/o Writers' Workshop, Room 173 University College/University of Western Ontario, London Ontario N6A 3K7 Canada. **DD** C810.80054.

LITERARY SKETCHES. 0024-4597. Periodical. US. English. mo. $3.00. Literary Sketches, Box 711, Williamsburg VA 23185. Tel (804)229-3603. Ed Mary Lewis Chapman. **Ind/Abst** Abstr. Engl. Stud. bk rev. adv acc. **Circ** 550. Literary biographies of well known writers, reviews, and interviews.

LITERARY VOICES. No. 1-. 0197-2146. Periodical. US. English. Borgo Press, PO Box 2845, San Bernardino CA 92406. Tel (714)884-5813. Ed R Reginald. **LC** PN137. **DD** 810.9. **Circ** 1,000. Usually a collection of interviews with writers of a particular area, era or genre.

DER LITERAT; ZEITSCHRIFT FUR LITERATUR UND KUNST. 1.-. 0024-4622. Periodical. German. ir. Postfach 102235, 6000 Frankfurt MN West Germany.

LITERATUR FUR LESER. 1978-. 0343-1657. Periodical. GW. German. qt. 49.80. R Oldenbourg Verlag, Postfach 801360, D8000 Munchen 80 West Germany. **Tel** (089)41120. bk rev. adv acc. **Circ** 1,500.

LITERATUR IN WISSENSCHAFT UND UNTERRICHT. (LITERATUR IN WISSENSCHAFT UND UNTERRICHT : LWU). Vol. 1-. 0024-4643. Periodical. GW. German. qt. 26.-. Englisches Seminar der Univers, Olhausenstrasse 40-60, 2300 Keil Germany. Tel 431-8803343. Ed P G Buchloh, D Joger, H Kause, and P Nicolaisen. **Ind/Abst** Abstr. Engl. Stud., MLA Int. Bibliogr. Books Artic. Mod. Lang. Lit. **LC** PN4. bk rev. adv acc. **Circ** 1,800. A journal of close reading in the English, French and German languages.

LITERATUR UND KRITIK. Volume 1- (issue 1-). 0024-466X. Periodical. AU. German. ir. $22.08. Otto Mueller, Ernest-Thun-Strasse 11, A-5020 Salzburg Austria. **Ind/Abst** MLA Int. Bibliogr. Books Artic. Mod. Lang. Lit. **LC** PN4. **DD** 809.

LITERATUR UND WIRKLICHKEIT. 1- 1967-. 0075-9937. Periodical. German. ir. Bouvier Verlag H Grundmann, AM Hof 32-Postfach 1268, 5300 Bonn 1 West Germany. **Ind/Abst** MLA Int. Bibliogr. Books Artic. Mod. Lang. Lit.

LITERATURA. Began in 1972. Periodical. PL. Polish. mo. ARS Polona, Krakowskie Przedmiescie 7, 00-068 Warsaw Poland. **Ind/Abst** MLA Int. Bibliogr. Books Artic. Mod. Lang. Lit. **LC** PG7001. Wspoczesnosc.

LITERATURA. 1.-. 0133-2368. Periodical. HU. Hungarian. qt. Akademiai Kiado, PO Box 24, 1363 Budapest Hungary. Tel 667-271. Ed M Beladi. **Ind/Abst** MLA Int. Bibliogr. Books Artic. Mod. Lang. Lit. **LC** PH3001. **Circ** 950.

LA LITERATURA ARGENTINA; REVISTA BIBLIOGRAFICA. See Bibliographies.

LITERATURA CHILENA, CREACION Y CRITICA. Yearly V. 5, No. 15 (Jan/March/Winter 1981)- V. 5, No. 1-. 0730-0220. Periodical. US. Spanish. qt. $18.00. Literatura Chilena Creacion y Critica, PO Box 3013, Hollywood CA 90028. **LC** PQ7900. **DD** 860.80983. Literatura Chilena en el Exilio, 0278-7288.

LITERATURA, DITY, CHAS. 1979-. Periodical. UR. Ukrainian. 0.90. Vydavnytstvo Veselka, Kyiv-4, Baseina 1/2, Kyiv Ukrainian SSR. **LC** PG3930.

LITERATURA I ISKUSSTVO NARODOV SSSR I ZARUBEZHNYKH STRAN. 1958-. Periodical. UR. Russian. bm. Victor Kamkin Inc, 12224 Parklawn Drive, Rockville MD 20852. Tel (301)881-5973. **LC** Z6519.

LITERATURA RADZIECKA. 0024-4716. Periodical. UR. Russian. mo. Victor Kamkin Inc, 12224 Parklawn Drive, Rockville MD 20852. **Tel** (301)881-5973.

LITERATURA V SHKOLE. 0024-4724. Periodical. UR. Russian. bm. $11.00. Victor Kamkin Inc (73227), 12224 Parklawn Drive, Rockville MD 20852. **Tel** (301)881-5973. Russkii Iazyk I Literatura V Srednei Shkole.

LITERATURE AND BELIEF. Vol. 1 (1981)-. 0732-1929. Periodical. US. English. an. $4.00. Literature and Belief, Brigham Young University, A-279 Jesse Knight Building, Provo UT 84602. **Tel** (801)378-2304. Ed Jay Fox. **Ind/Abst** Abstr. Engl. Stud., MLA Int. Bibliogr. Books Artic. Mod. Lang. Lit. **LC** PN49. **DD** 809.93382. bk rev. **Circ** 1,000. (ctrl). Publishes scholarly, interpretative articles that focus on moral/religious considerations, bibliographical articles, book reviews, short stories, interviews, personal essays or poems.

LITERATURE & HISTORY. Mar. 1975-. UK. English. sa. $9.20. Thames Polytechnic, Wellington Street, Department Humanities, London SEI8 EPT England. Ed P Widdowson, P Brooker, P Humm, P Stigant, F Duke, and H Can. **Ind/Abst** Am. Hist. Life, Hist. Abstr., Part A, Mod. Hist. Abstr., Hist. Abstr., Part B, Twent. Century Abstr., MLA Int. Bibliogr. Books Artic. Mod. Lang. Lit., Index Book Rev. Humanit., Years Work Eng. Stud., Hist. Abstr. **LC** AS122.T45. **DD** 052. bk rev. adv acc. **Circ** 700. Journal concerned to investigate the relations between writing history and ideology.

LITERATURE AND PSYCHOLOGY.
Began in 1951. 0024-4759. Periodical. US. English. qt. $8.00. Morton Caplan, Department of English, Fairleigh Dickinson University, Teaneck NJ 07666. **Ind/Abst** Abstr. Engl. Stud., MLA Int. Bibliogr. Books Artic. Mod. Lang. Lit., Annu. Bibliogr. Engl. Lang. Lit., Index Book Rev. Humanit., Humanit. Index. **LC** PN49. CODEN LIPSA. Vols. 1-6 available on microfilm from University Microfilms.

LITERATURE IN PERFORMANCE. Vol. 1, No. 1 (Nov. 1980)-. 0734-0796. Periodical. US. English. sa. $15.00. Managing Editor, University of Arizona, Department of Speech Communication, Tucson AZ 85721. **Ind/Abst** MLA Int. Bibliogr. Books Artic. Mod. Lang. Lit. **LC** PN2. **DD** 809.

LITERATURE, MUSIC, FINE ARTS. Began in 1968. 0024-4775. Periodical. GB. English. sa. 39.-. German Studies, Landhausstr 18, 74 Tuebingen West Germany. Tel 07071/26246. Ed Hohnholz. **Ind/Abst** Abstr. Engl. Stud. **LC** NX1. **DD** 700.5. bk rev. **Circ** 2,000. (ctrl). A review of German-language research contributions on literature, music, and fine arts. With bibliographies.

LITERATURE (WASHINGTON, D.C.).
(LITERATURE). VFOAT Literature Program. 0197-8829. US. English. an. National Endowment for the Arts, 1100 Pennsylvania Avenue, Washington DC 20506. **Tel** PN51. **DD** 810.79.

LITERATUREN ZBOR. Began publication in 1954. 0024-4971. Periodical. Macedonian. ir. **Ind/Abst** MLA Int. Bibliogr. Books Artic. Mod. Lang. Lit. **LC** PG1161.

LITERATURMAGAZIN. VFOAT Literatur Magazin. 1-. Monographic Series. US. German. ir. Adlers Foreign Books Inc, 162 Fifth Avenue/Rowohlt Verlag, New York NY 10010.

LITERATURNAIA CHECHENO-INGUSHETIIA. Periodical. UR. Russian. **LC** PG3505.G76.

LITERATURNAIA GRUZIIA. V. 1- 1957-. 0458-0311. Periodical. UR. Russian. mo. $35.00. Victor Kamkin Inc (76117), 12224 Parklawn Drive, Rockville MD 20852. Tel (301)881-5973.

LITERATURNAIA UCHEBA. 1978-. Periodical. UR. Russian. bm. $24.00. Victor Kamkin Inc (70499), 12224 Parklawn Drive, Rockville MD 20852. **Tel** (301)881-5973. **LC** PG3227.

LITERATURNOE OBOZRENIE. Jan. 1973-. 0321-2904. Periodical. UR. Russian. mo. $33.50. Victor Kamkin Inc (70498), 12224 Parklawn Drive, Rockville MD 20852. Tel (301)881-5973. **Ind/Abst** MLA Int. Bibliogr. Books Artic. Mod. Lang. Lit. **LC** PG2900.

LITERATURNYI AZERBAIDZHAN. V. 1-1931-. Periodical. UR. Russian. mo. $25.00. Victor Kamkin Inc (76424), 12224 Parklawn Drive, Rockville MD 20852. **Tel** (301)881-5973.

LITERATURNYI KURER. VFOAT Literary Courier. No. 1-. Periodical. US. Russian (English). mo. Lambs Club, c/o Literary Courier, 130 West 44 Street, New York NY 10036.

LITERATURWISSENSCHAFT UND SOZIALWISSENSCHAFTEN. 1- 1971-. Periodical. GW. German. ir. J B Metzler Verlag, Kernerstrasse 43 Postfach 529, 7000 Stuttgart 1 West Germany. Tel 711-223067(69). A monographic series on literature-art-culture under different German political systems; history of German literature.

LITERATURWISSENSCHAFTLICHES JAHRBUCH. See Yearbooks, Almanacs, Directories.

LITFASS. Vol. 1- Jan. 1976-. Periodical. German. ir. 16.00. Postfach 420464, D-1000 Berlin 42 East Germany. **LC** PT1141.A2.

LITIR NEWSLETTER OF VICTORIAN STUDIES. VFOAT Litir Newsletter. VAT Litir Newsletter. No. 1 (Spring 1983)-. 0821-4077. Periodical. CN. English. ty. Free. Litir Database c/o Department of English, University of Alberta, Edmonton Alberta T6G 2E5 Canada. **DD** 820.9008. (ctrl).

LITTERATUR, TEATER, FILM. 1- 1972. Monographic Series. Swedish. ir. Liber International, S-205 10 Malmo Sweden. Tel 46-40-70650. Dissertations on the subjects literature, theatre and motion pictures.

LITTERATURE AFRICAINE. 1- 1964-. 0459-5815. Monographic Series. French. ir.

LITTERATURE OF ART. (THE LITERATURE OF ART). VAT Lit. Art. V. 1-. 0141-335X. UK. English. mo. $12.00. Art Book Company, 136 East 65 Street, New York NY 10021.

LITTERATURES DE LANGUES EUROPEENNES AU TOURNANT DU SIECLE, LECTURES D'AUJOURD'HUI. SERIE D, PERSPECTIVE CRITIQUE. (LES LITTERATURES DE LANGUES EUROPEENNES AU TOURNANT DU SIECLE, LECTURES D'AUJOURD'HUI. SERIE D, LA PERSPECTIVE CRITIQUE SOVIETIQUE). Series/Titl Travaux du Groupe de Recherches International 1900. VFOAT Perspective Critique Sovietique. No. 1-. CN. English (French, and Russian). Groupe de Recherches International, 1900 Comparative Literature Carleton University, Ottawa Ontario Canada.

LES LITTERATURES POPULAIRES DE TOUTES LES NATIONS. V. 1-47, 1881-1903. Monographic Series. French. ir.

LITTERATURES (UNIVERSITE DE TOULOUSE-LE MIRAIL : 1980).
(LITTERATURES). No 1 (Spring 1980)-. 0563-9751. FR. French. L'Universite de Toulouse-Mirail, 56 rue Taur, 3100 Toulouse France. Tel 23 07 50. **Ind/Abst** MLA Int. Bibliogr. Books Artic. Mod. Lang. Lit. **LC** FN3. **DD** 809. Litteratures (Universite de Toulouse-Le Mirail : 1971).

Literature

THE LITTLE REVIEW. V. 1- Spring 1969-. 0024-5054. Periodical. US. English. sa. Marshall University, English Department, Huntington WV 25701. **Ind/Abst** Index Am. Period. Verse.

LIU CHUAN. **VFOAT** Liuquan. Periodical. CH. Chinese. qt. 1.00. Shan-Tung Sheng Hsin Hua Shu Tien Chi-Nan China. **LC** PL2513. **DD** 895.108005.

LIUBYSTOK *CEASED.* No. 1-16. 0382-4667. Periodical. CN. Ukrainian. qt. P Rojenko, 281 Garden Avenue, Toronto Ontario M6R 1J4 Canada. **DD** 891.7908003.

LIVING HAND. 1- Fall 1973-. English. ir. $2.50. Compton Press, c/o Paul Auster, 29 rue Descartes, Paris 5 France. **LC** PN6010.5. **DD** 808.8004.

LIVRES ET AUTEURS QUEBECOIS. 1969-. 0316-2621. Periodical. CN. French. an. Les Presses de l'Universite Laval, Cite Universitaire, Quebec Quebec G1K 7R4 Canada. **Ind/Abst** MLA Int. Bibliogr. Books Artic. Mod. Lang. Lit., Point Repere. **DD** C840.9005. *Livres et Auteurs Canadiens,* 0076-0153.

LLEN CYMRU. V. 1, No. 1 (Gorf. 1950)-. 0076-0188. Periodical. UK. Welsh. an. 3.50. University of Wales Press, 6 Gwennyth Street Cathays, Cardiff CF2 4YD Wales. **Tel** 31919. Ed A O H Jarman. **Ind/Abst** MLA Int. Bibliogr. Books Artic. Mod. Lang. Lit. bk rev. adv acc. **Circ** 300. Serves the needs of researchers in the field of Welsh literary history. Embraces all periods and publishes articles of literary and historical criticism.

LOCANA. **VFOAT** Lochana. Vol. 1, No. 1 (June 1983)-. Periodical. II. Kannada. sa. 6.00. B M SRI Memorial Foundation, 54-3rd Cross Gavipuram Extension, Bangalore 560019 India. **LC** PL4650.

LOCUS. Series/Titl The Gregg Press Science Fiction Series. 1- June 27, 1968-. US. English. Gregg Press, 70 Lincoln Street, Boston MA 02111. **LC** PN3448.S45. **DD** 813.0876.

LOCUS (CAMBRIDGE, MASS.). (LOCUS). Issue 1-182. 0047-4959. Periodical. US. English. mo. $26.00. Locus Publications, PO Box 13305, Oakland CA 94661. **Tel** (415)339-9196. Ed Charles N Brown. bk rev. **Circ** 8,000. A trade journal for science fiction professionals and interested readers. It covers the publishing industry as well as the literary side.

THE LONDON COLLECTOR. US. English. ir. $0.50. Wolf House Books, PO Box 290K, Cedar Springs MI 49319. **LC** PS3523.O46. **DD** 818.5209.

LONG POND REVIEW. 8756-5099. Periodical. US. English. be. $5.00. Russ Steinke, Sufford Community College/English Department, Selden Long Island NY 11784. **Tel** (516)451-4110. Ed Russ Steinke. bk rev. adv acc. **Circ** 500.

THE LONG STORY. No. 1 (Spring 1983)-. 0741-4242. US. English. an. The Long Story, 11 Kingston Street, North Andover MA 01845. **Tel** (617)686-7638. Ed R Peter Burnham. **LC** WMLC L 83/400. **Circ** 450. For serious literary people; publishes long stories (8-20,000 words) of various genres, eight themes, with a preference for committed fiction.

LOTUS. **VFOAT** Lutus. No. 6- Oct. 1970-. Periodical. UA. English (French, Arabic). qt. $8.00. Permanent Bureau Afro-Asia Writers, 104 Kasrel Aini Street, Cairo United Arab Republic. **Ind/Abst** MLA Int. Bibliogr. Books Artic. Mod. Lang. Lit. **LC** PN2. **DD** 808.8004. *Afro-Asian Writings.*

LOVE MAKES THE WORLD GO AWRY. No. 1-. 0227-5449. Periodical. CN. English. qt. $2.00. F Skene, 207 West 21st Avenue, Vancouver British Columbia V5Y 2E4 Canada. **LC** C813.5403.

LU HSUN YEN CHIU NIEN KAN. **VFOAT** Annual of Lu Xun Study. 1979-. CC. Chinese. an. 3.00. Chung Kuo Kuo Chi Shu Tien, PO Box 399, Pei-Ching China Mainland. **LC** PL2754.S5. **DD** 895.135.

LU HSUN YEN CHIU (PEKING, CHINA : 1980). (LU HSUN YEN CHIU). **VFOAT** Luxun Yanjiu. 1 (Dec. 1980)-. Periodical. CH. Chinese. ir. 1.30. Hsin Hua Shu Tien, Pei-Ching Fa Hsing So Peking China. **LC** PL2754.S5. **DD** 895.18509.

LU HSUN YEN CHIU TZU LIAO. **VFOAT** Luxun Yanjiu Ziliao. CC. Chinese. ir. 1.00. Hsin Hua Shu Tien, Tien-Chin Shih China. **LC** PL2754.S5. **DD** 895.135.

LU HSUN YEN CHIU WEN TSUNG. **VFOAT** Luxun Yanjiu Wencong. 1 (March 1980)-. Periodical. CC. Chinese. ir. 1.08. Hu-Nan Jen Min Chu Pan She 14, Chan Lan Kuan Lu, Chang-Sha China. **LC** PL2754.S5. **DD** 895.135.

LUCEAFARUL. Periodical. US. Romanian. wk. Ilexim Press Department, PO Box 1-136-1-137, Bucharest-Romania. **LC** Microfilm 03179 PC, PC800.

LUFTSKIBET. V. 1, No. 1-. 0107-3982. Periodical. DK. Danish. ir. 68.50 Single Issue. Rhodos, Strandgade 36, 1401 Kobenhavn K Denmark. **LC** PN9.

LULU REVU. No. 1- July 1978-. 0709-8030. Periodical. CN. English. ir. $4.00 per 6 issues. Pubbug Press Publications, 11220 Bird Road, Richmond British Columbia V6X 1N8 Canada. **DD** 813.0876.

LUMO. See Linguistics.

LUNA. V. 1- 1975-. Periodical. AT. English. sa. $6.64. Luna, PO Box 36, East Melbourne 3002 Australia. bk rev. **Circ** 300. Poetry, prose, short stories, reviews and articles.

LUVAH. No. 1, (Dec. 1982)-. Periodical. French. qt. 100. Luvah, Arcier Roche Lez Beaupre 25220 France. **LC** PQ1141. **DD** 840.8.

MAAL OG MINNE. See Linguistics.

MADHUMATI. Periodical. Hindi. ir. 10.00. Rajasthan Sahitya Akademi (Sangam), Udayapura India. **LC** PK2103.R3.

MAGAZINE LITTERAIRE. Began with Nov. 1966 issue. 0024-9807. Periodical. FR. French. mo. $34.59. Magazine Litteraire, 40 rue des Saints-Peres, Paris 7E France. **Ind/Abst** Point Repere. **LC** PN3. **DD** 809.

THE MAGAZINE OF FANTASY AND SCIENCE FICTION. V. 1- Fall 1949-. 0024-984X. Periodical. US. English. mo. $19.50. Mercury Press, PO Box 56, Cornwall CT 06753. **Tel** (203)672-6376. Ed Edward L Ferman. **Ind/Abst** Book Rev. Index, Mag. Index. **LC** AP2. **DD** 051. adv acc. **Circ** 60,000. Publishing fantasy and science fiction short stories, along with book and film reviews and a science column by Issac Asimov.

MAGOOK. No. 1- Oct. 29 1977-. 0702-6803. Periodical. CN. English. ir. $1.95 per no. Magook Publishers Ltd, 254 Bartley Drive, Toronto Ontario M4A 1G1 Canada. **DD** C810.809282.

MAGYAR NYELVJARASOK. V. 1- 1951-. 0541-9298. Hungarian (summaries in English, French, German or Russian). an. Ed G Barczi. **Ind/Abst** MLA Int. Bibliogr. Books Artic. Mod. Lang. Lit. **LC** PH2701. *Magyar Nepnyelv.*

THE MAHANADI REVIEW. Periodical. English. qt. Mahanadi Books, Mansingpatna Math Lane, Cuttack 753008 India. **LC** PR9494. **DD** 891.105.

MAITHILI AKADAMI PATRIKA. See Linguistics.

MAIZE (SAN DIEGO, CALIF.). (MAIZE). Vol. 1, No. 1 (Fall 1977)-. 0272-5967. Periodical. US. English (Spanish). qt. Centro Cultural de la Raza Publications, PO Box 8251, San Diego CA 92102. **Ind/Abst** MLA Int. Bibliogr. Books Artic. Mod. Lang. Lit., Index Am. Period. Verse. **LC** PS508.M4. **DD** 810.8086872073.

MAJALLAH. Main/Corp Majma Al-Lughah Al-Arabiyah Bi-Dimashq. **VFOAT** Revue. Magazine 41-Jan. 1966-. Periodical. SY. Arabic. qt. $4.00. Arab Academy of Damascus, PO Box 327, Damascus Syria. **Ind/Abst** MLA Int. Bibliogr. Books Artic. Mod. Lang. Lit. **LC** PJ6001. Index in last issue of volume - attached. *Majallah.*

MALAHAT REVIEW. (THE MALAKAT REVIEW). No. 1- Jan. 1967-. 0025-1216. Periodical. CN. English. qt. **Ind/Abst** Abstr. Engl. Stud., MLA Int. Bibliogr. Books Artic. Mod. Lang. Lit., Index Am. Period. Verse. **DD** 808.8'004.

MALAWIAN WRITERS SERIES. Began publication in 1974. Monographic Series. English. ir. Popular Publications, PO Box 5592, Limbe Malawi.

MALCOLM LOWRY NEWSLETTER *CEASED.* **VFOAT** Newsletter. No. 1 (Fall 1977)-. 0228-8427. Periodical. CN. English. sa. $4.00. Wilfrid Laurier University, Department of English, Waterloo Ontario N2L 3C5 Canada. **Tel** (519)884-1970. Ed Paul Tiessen. **Ind/Abst** MLA Int. Bibliogr. Books Artic. Mod. Lang. Lit. **LC** PR6023.O96. **DD** 813.54. bk rev. **Circ** 100. Includes short items and longer articles of interest to Lowry scholars around the world.

THE MALCOLM LOWRY REVIEW. No. 15 (Fall 1984)-. 0828-5020. Periodical. CN. English. sa. $20.00. Wilfrid Laurier University, Department of English, Waterloo Ontario N2L 3C5 Canada. **Tel** (519)884-1970. Ed Paul Tiessen. bk rev. **Circ** 125. Work related to the life and writing of Malcolm Lowry. *Malcolm Lowry Newsletter,* 0228-8427.

MALINI. See Ethnic.

MALTESE TALES. V. 1- Spring 1980-. 0274-7022. Periodical. US. English. bm. $18.00. Maltese Tales, PO Box 6501, Yuma AZ 85364. **Tel** (602)344-2371.

MAMASHEE. V. 1, Issue No. 2- June 1977-. 0702-7575. Periodical. CN. English. qt. Mamashee, R R #1, Inwood Ontario N0N 1K0 Canada. **DD** C810.80054. *Quest for a Common Denominator,* 0700-5482.

MANA. V. 2- Oct. 1977-. Periodical. English. sa. $3.63. South Pacific Creative Arts Society, PO Box 5083, Suva Fiji Islands. **Ind/Abst** MLA Int. Bibliogr. Books Artic. Mod. Lang. Lit. *Mana Review.*

MANASABHARATI : SRI RAMACARITAMANASA CATUSSATABDI SAMAROHA SAMITI, MADHYAPRADESA, BHOPALA KI MASIKA MUKHAPATRIKA. Periodical. Hindi. mo. 30.-. Gandhi Bhavan Shamala Hills, Bhopal 462002 India. **Tel** 73837. Ed Gorelal Shukla. **LC** PK1947.9.T83. bk rev. adv acc. **Circ** 2,300. Devoted to study and appreciation of the legend of Ramchandra as sung in Sanskrit and other languages against the backdrop of Indian culture. *Manasa Samacara.*

MANG CHUNG. **VFOAT** Mang Zhong. Periodical. CC. Chinese. mo. 0.35. Chung-Kuo Kuo Chi Shu Tien, PO Box 2820, Pei-Ching China. **LC** PL2303. **DD** 895.109005.

MANGALADIPA. Hindi. ir. 5.00. Mangaladipa Prakasana, 44 Khattar Ali Lane 4, Bambai India. **LC** PK2047.

MANJARI. 0304-1247. English. an. 3.00. A Sen, B-42 Panchshila Enclave, New Delhi 110017 India. **LC** PK2047. **DD** 891.4305.

MANTEIA. No. 1- 1967-. 0025-2492. Periodical. French. ir.

MANTHANA (KATHMANDU, NEPAL). (MANTHANA). Periodical. Nepali. bm. $6.00. Lajimpat, Post Box 1766, Kathmandu 711000 Nepal. **LC** PK2598.A2.

THE MANUSCRIPT. 1973-. US. English. Horace Mann School, 231 West 246th Street, Bronx NY 10471. **LC** PS536.2. **DD** 811.5408.

MANUSCRIPTUM : REVISTA TRIMESTRIALA EDITATA DE MUZEUL LITERATURII ROMANE. Began with Year 1, No. 1, 1970. Periodical. RM. Romanian. qt. Ilexim Press, PO Box 1-136-1-137, Bucharest Romania. **Ind/Abst** MLA Int. Bibliogr. Books Artic. Mod. Lang. Lit. **LC** PC800.

MANUSKRIPTE. 0025-2638. Periodical. AU. German. qt. 180,-. Forum Stadtpark, Stadtpark 1, A-8010 Graz Austria. **Tel** (0316)75608. **LC** PT1141.A2. **Circ** 3,200. (ctrl). Previously unpublished works in literature mostly of young authors.

MAPLE LEAF RAG. (THE MAPLE LEAF RAG). #1 (Nov. 1983)-. 0823-8626. Periodical. CN. English. ir. $0.50. Maple Leaf Rag, c/o Garth Spencer 1296 Richardson Street, Victoria British Columbia V8V 3E1 Canada. **DD** 809.387605.

MARCHE ROMANE. Vol. 1- June 1951-. 0542-6669. Periodical. BE. French. qt. $11.86. Association des Romanistes, Universit Place Cockeill 3, B-000 Liege Belgium. **Ind/Abst** MLA Int. Bibliogr. Books Artic. Mod. Lang. Lit. **LC** PC2.

MARGENES (PUEBLA, MEXICO). (MARGENES). Periodical. Spanish. qt. $6.00. Escuela de Filosofia Y Letras, 3 Ote 403, Puebla Mexico. **LC** PN6. **DD** 808.8.

MARIANNE MOORE NEWSLETTER. **VFOAT** MMN. V. 1- Spring 1977-. 0145-8779. Periodical. US. English. sa. $4.00. Rosenbach Museum & Library, 2010 Delancey Place, Philadelphia PA 19103. **Tel** (215)732-1600. Ed Patricia C Willis. **Ind/Abst** Abstr. Engl. Stud., MLA Int. Bibliogr. Books Artic. Mod. Lang. Lit., Ref. Source. **LC** PS3525.O5616. **DD** 811.52. bk rev. **Circ** 400. Contains unpublished work by Moore, facsimiles, sources, criticism, and bibliography.

MARK TWAIN JOURNAL. Began publication with V. 9, No. 4 (Summer, 1954). 0025-3499. Periodical. US. English. sa. $10.00. Mark Twain Journal, c/o Department of English, Charleston SC

29424. **Tel** (803)723-0487. **Ed** Thomas A Tenney. **Ind/Abst** Abstr. Engl. Stud., MLA Int. Bibliogr. Books Artic. Mod. Lang. Lit., Annu. Bibliogr. Engl. Lang. Lit. **LC** PS1329. **DD** 817.44. **Circ** 700. Emphasis is on factual treatment of Twain's life and works, drawing on contemporary sources such as letters, interviews, and photographs. *Mark Twain Quarterly.*

MARK TWAIN SOCIETY BULLETIN. V. 1- Feb. 1978-. 0272-6378. Periodical. US. English. sa. $4.00 Domestic, $5.00 Foreign. Mark Twain Society, PO Box 3225, Elmira NY 14905. **Tel** (607)734-6943. **Ed** Herbert Wisbey and Robert Jerome. bk rev. Mark Twain material.

THE MARKHAM REVIEW. V. 1-. 0025-3820. Periodical. US. English. sa. $6.00. Wagner College, Horrmann Library-Grymes Hill, Staten Island NY 10301. **Tel** (212)390-3001. **Ind/Abst** Abstr. Engl. Stud., MLA Int. Bibliogr. Books Artic. Mod. Lang. Lit., Years Work Eng. Stud.

MARSH & MAPLE. Began publication in 1974?. 0384-093X. Periodical. CN. English. Marsh & Maple, Scotian Pen Guild, Box 173, Dartmouth Nova Scotia B2Y 3Y3 Canada. **DD** C810.5.

MARZBLATT. German. ir. Literarisches Infozentrum, 4250 Bottrop Bahnhofstrasse 24, Bottrop West Germany. **LC** PT1141.A2.

MASTERPLOTS ANNUAL. *See* Bibliographies.

MASTERSKAIA. Vol. 1- 1975-. UR. Russian. 0.28. Molodaia Gvardiia, K-30 Sushchevskaia 21, Moskva USSR. **LC** PN145.

MATERIALI E CONTRIBUTI PER LA STORIA DELLA NARRATIVA GRECO-LATINA. *See* Linguistics.

MATIPANI. **VFOAT** Mati Pani. Periodical. Maithili. mo. 22.00. Bhavani Prakashan, Mudlidhar Press Musallapur, Patna 800006 India. **LC** PK1818.45.

MATRIX (LENNOXVILLE). (MATRIX). V. 1- Spring 1975-. 0318-3610. CN. English. sa. $7.74. Champlain College, Box 510, Lennoxville Quebec Canada. **Tel** (819)564-3653. **Ed** Philip Lanthier. **DD** C810.80054. bk rev. **Circ** 400. Fiction, poetry and reviews mainly by Canadian writers, with special emphasis on writing from Quebec.

MAYA MARATHI. **VFOAT** Mai Marathi. 0303-3066. Periodical. Marathi. mo. 20.00. Brhanmaharashtra Mandala, Pahad Ganj, Navi Dilli India. **LC** PK2400.

MEANJIN (MELBOURNE, VIC.). (MEANJIN). 1-. 0815-953X. Periodical. AT. qt. 20.00 Domestic, 24.00 Foreign. Meanjin/University of Melbourne, Parkville 3052, Victoria Australia. **Tel** (03)344-6950. **Ed** Judith Brett. **Ind/Abst** Abstr. Engl. Stud., MLA Int. Bibliogr. Books Artic. Mod. Lang. Lit., Index Book Rev. Humanit., Aust. Public Aff. Inf. Serv. bk rev. adv acc. **Circ** 3,000. Australian writing: fiction, poetry, reviews, essays on culture, history, politics, literature and the arts. A journal of writing and discussion of a broad range of Australian cultural concerns. *Meanjin Quarterly.*

MEDIEVAL & RENAISSANCE DRAMA IN ENGLAND. **VFOAT** Medieval and Renaissance Drama in England. 1-. 0731-3403. US. English. an. $42.50. AMS Press, 56 East 13th Street, New York NY 10003. **Tel** (212)777-4700. **Ed** C Harvington and M Barnett. **LC** PR621. **DD** 822.009. bk rev. Historical investigations and critical studies in English drama from the beginnings to 1642.

MEDIUM AEVUM. V. 1- May 1932-. 0025-8385. Periodical. UK. English. sa. $22.98. Society for the Study of Medieval Languages and Literatures, Dr D G Patterson, Magdalen College, Oxford OX1 4AU England. **Ed** A V C Schmidt, L Seiffert and N Mann. **Ind/Abst** Humanit. Index, Annu. Bibliogr. Engl. Lang. Lit., Abstr. Engl. Stud., MLA Int. Bibliogr. Books Artic. Mod. Lang. Lit., Ref. Source, Index Book Rev. Humanit., Years Work Eng. Stud. **LC** PB1. **DD** 405. Index published separately - free - automatically sent. (cum index). bk rev. adv acc. **Circ** 1,000. Available on microfilm from Oxford Microfilm Publications. Mediaeval European languages, literature and related subjects (e.g. history, art). *Arthuriana.*

MEDLEMSFORTECKNING. **Main/Corp** Sveriges Forfattarforbund. Swedish. ir. Box 5252 102 45 5, Stockholm Sweden. **LC** PT9205.S85.

MEGAFON. Issue 1- (NO. 1-) 1975-. Periodical. AG. Spanish. sa. Fernado Garcia Cambeiro, Cochabamba 244, 1150 Buenos Aires Argentina. **Tel** (54) (1)-361-0473. adv acc. **Circ** 1,000. Literary critique, poetry, accounts, studies, and philosophy.

MEHKERE YERUSHALAYIM BE-SIFRUT IVRIT. **VFOAT** Jerusalem Studies in Hebrew Literature. 1-. 0333-693X. Periodical. IS. Hebrew. ir. Magnes Press, The Hebrew University, Jerusalem 91904 Israel.

MELANGES MALRAUX MISCELLANY. (MELANGES MALRAUX). **VFOAT** Malraux Miscellany. V. 1- Spring 1969-. 0025-892X. Periodical. US. English and French. sa. $18.00. University of Alberta Department of Romance Languages, c/o Robert Thornberry, Edmonton Alberta Canada T6G 2E6. **Tel** (403)432-2003. **Ed** Robert S Thornberry. **Ind/Abst** MLA Int. Bibliogr. Books Artic. Mod. Lang. Lit. **LC** PQ2625.A716. **DD** 842.912. bk rev. Traditional and modern approaches to the works and biography of Andre Malraux: historical, political, theoretical, comparative, etc. Documents, inedits and bibliographies are also published.

MELBOURNE SLAVONIC STUDIES. *See* Linguistics.

MELIBEA. Yearly V. 1- Nov. 1975-. Spanish. ir. Casimiro Ulloa 125, Lima Peru. **LC** F3401. **DD** 056.1.

MELUS. **VAT** Multi-Ethnic Literature of the United States. Began with Sept. 1974 issue. 0163-755X. Periodical. US. English. qt. $15.00. University of Cincinnati, American Ethnic Studies, c/o W C Miller, Cincinnati OH 45221. **Ind/Abst** Abstr. Engl. Stud., MLA Int. Bibliogr. Books Artic. Mod. Lang. Lit., Humanit. Index. **LC** PN843. **DD** 808.89973.

MELVILLE SOCIETY EXTRACTS. No. 34- May 1978-. 0193-8991. Periodical. US. English. qt. $10.00. Glassboro State College, Department of English, Dr D Yanella, Glassboro NJ 08028. **Tel** (609)863-6001. **Ed** Donald Yannella. **Ind/Abst** Abstr. Engl. Stud., MLA Int. Bibliogr. Books Artic. Mod. Lang. Lit. bk rev. adv acc. **Circ** 700. (ctrl). Life, times, and writings of the American author Herman Melville (1819-1891). *Extracts - Melville Society, 0193-7626.*

MEMORIA DEL CONGRESO INTERNACIONAL DE LITERATURA IBEROAMERICANA. **Main/Corp** Congreso Internacional de Literatura Iberoamericana. 1.-. Monographic Series. Spanish. ir. $40.00. Instituto Internacional de CL, 1312 University of Pittsburgh, Pittsburgh PA 15260. **Ed** Alfredo A Roggiano. adv acc. **Circ** 2,000. Essays, notes, reviews, and bibliographies on Iberoamerican literature.

MEMORIILE SECTIEI DE STIINTE FILOLOGICE, LITERATURA SI ARTE. *See* Linguistics.

MENCKENIANA. No. 1- Spring 1962-. 0025-9233. Periodical. US. English. qt. $8.00. Enoch Pratt Free Library, 400 Cathedral Street, Baltimore MD 21201. **Tel** (301)396-5305. **Ind/Abst** Abstr. Engl. Stud., MLA Int. Bibliogr. Books Artic. Mod. Lang. Lit. **LC** PS3525.E43.

THE MENDOCINO REVIEW. 0278-1190. Periodical. US. English. an. $5.95. Mendocino Graphics, PO Box 888, Mendocino CA 95460. **Tel** (707)964-3831. **Ed** Camille Ranker. adv acc. **Circ** 5,000. An annual collection of previously unpublished short stories, poetry, art works and photographs from around the world. Approximately 200 pages.

MENG YA. *See* Linguistics.

MERIDIANO 70 I.E. SETENTA. No. 1- Autumn 1975-. Periodical. US. Spanish (English). sa. $3.00. Meridiano 70 Batts Hall 112, University of Texas, Austin TX 78712. **LC** PQ6001. **DD** 860.80064.

MERVYN PEAKE REVIEW. (THE MERVYN PEAKE REVIEW). No. 3- Autumn 1976-. 0309-1309. Periodical. SZ. English. sa. $22.00. Mervyn Peake Society, Les 3 Chasseurs, 1411 Orzens Vaud Switzerland. **Ind/Abst** Abstr. Engl. Stud., MLA Int. Bibliogr. Books Artic. Mod. Lang. Lit. **LC** PR6031.E183. **DD** 741.0924. *Newsletter - The Mervyn Peake Society.*

MESTER. V. 1- Apr. 1970-. 0160-2764. Periodical. US. Portuguese (Spanish). sa. $14.00. Mester, Department of Spanish, University of California, Los Angeles CA 90024. **Tel** (213)825-1430. **Ed** Kathleen O'Donnell. **Ind/Abst** MLA Int. Bibliogr. Books Artic. Mod. Lang. Lit., Index Am. Period. Verse. **LC** UNC. **DD** 860. bk rev. adv acc. **Circ** 400. Dedicated to the studies of Hispanic and Luso-Brazilian literatures and linguistics. Publishes articles by well-known scholars as well as by graduate students.

METAMORFOSIS. *See* The Arts (General).

METMENYS. No. 1- 1959-. 0543-615X. Periodical. US. Lithuanian. sa. $10.00. AM & M Publications, 3308 West 62nd Place, Chicago IL 60629. **Tel** (312)434-8836. **Ed** Vytautas Kavolis. **Ind/Abst** MLA Int. Bibliogr. Books Artic. Mod. Lang. Lit. **LC** AP95.L5. **DD** 059. (cum index). bk rev. **Circ** 850. (ctrl). Publishes contemporary writings of Lithuanian writers and poets, articles on philosophy, social sciences, linguistics, folklore literary essays and reviews and reproductions of contemporary Lithuanian artworks.

MICHIGAN ROMANCE STUDIES. Vol. 1-. 0270-3629. Periodical. US. English (French). ir. University of Michigan, Department of Romance Languages, Ann Arbor MI 48109. **Tel** (313)764-5373. **Ed** 500. **Ind/Abst** MLA Int. Bibliogr. Books Artic. Mod. Lang. Lit. **LC** PC1. **DD** 840.09. adv acc. Essays in English on language and literature in romance languages.

THE MICKLE STREET REVIEW. No. 1- 1979-. 0194-1313. Periodical. US. English. an. $8.00. Walt Whitman Association, 328 Mickle Street, Camden NJ 08103. **Tel** (609)964-5383. **Ed** Geoffrey Sill. **LC** PS3224. **DD** 811.3. bk rev. adv acc. **Circ** 500. (ctrl). Published by the Walt Whitman Association which maintains the Whitman house as a historic site. Includes poetry, essays, and reviews on Walt Whitman.

MID-AMERICAN REVIEW. *See* Literary and Political Reviews.

MIDDLE ENGLISH TEXTS. **VFOAT** MET. 1-. Monographic Series. English. ir. Carl Winter Universitatsverlag, Postfach 1822/Lutherstrasse 59, D6900 Heidelberg West Germany. **Ed** M Gorlach and O S Pickering. Designed to be complementary to the EETS programme. Verse and prose of all kinds are considered. Includes unprinted texts and new editions of texts inadequately edited in the past.

MIESIECZNIK LITERACKI. Vol 1-. 0026-3567. Periodical. PL. Polish. mo. ARS Polona, Krakowskie Przedmiescie 7, 00-068 Warsaw Poland. **Ind/Abst** MLA Int. Bibliogr. Books Artic. Mod. Lang. Lit. **LC** AP54.

MILTON QUARTERLY. V. 4- Mar. 1970-. 0026-4326. US. English. qt. $12.00. Ohio University, Department of English, Roy C Flannagan-Editor, Athens OH 45701. **Tel** (614)594-6422. **Ed** Roy Flannagan. **Ind/Abst** Abstr. Engl. Stud., MLA Int. Bibliogr. Books Artic. Mod. Lang. Lit., Index Book Rev. Humanit., Humanit. Index, Years Work Eng. Stud. **LC** PR3579. **DD** 821.4. bk rev. adv acc. **Circ** 1,000. Articles and news items relating to the writings and life of John Milton, seventeenth century English poet and prose writer. *Milton Newsletter, 0146-4922.*

MIMALAH. Lyah 1- Kachala/Silla 1094- 1973-. Periodical. Newari. ir. 3.00 Each Issue. Prema Ratna Tuladhar, 12/262 Nhyokha, PB 267 Kathmandu, Yem India. **LC** PL3801.N5.

MIN CHIEN WEN HSUEH LUN TAN. **VFOAT** Minjianwenxueluntan. Began in May 1982. Periodical. CC. Chinese. qt. 0.45. Hsin Hua Shu Tien, Pei-Ching fa Hsing so Peking China. **LC** PL2445. **DD** 398.20951.

MIN CHIEN WEN I CHI KAN. **VFOAT** Minjian Wenyi Jikan. V. 1, (Nov. 1981)-. Periodical. CH. Chinese. sa. 1.25. Hsin Hua Shu Tien Shang-Hai Fa Hsing So Shanghai China. **LC** PL2446. **DD** 398.20951.

MINNESOTA ENGLISH JOURNAL. *See* Linguistics.

MIR (PHILADELPHIA, PA.). (MIR). **VFOAT** Peace. 1-. Periodical. US. Russian. Publishing House of Peace Inc, PO Box 6162, Philadelphia PA 19115. **LC** PG3227. *Shalom.*

MIRIAD. No. 1 (July 1980)-. 0713-6722. Periodical. CN. English. qt. $1.50 Per No. Miriad, 61 Warren Avenue, Toronto Ontario M4A 1Z5 Canada. **DD** 809.387605.

THE MISCELLANY. 28- Aug. 1968-. Periodical. II. English. bm. $18.00. Professor P Lal, 162-92 Lake Gardens, Calcutta India 700045. **Tel** 46-8325. **Ed** P Lal. **LC** PR9494. **DD** 820.8. bk rev. **Circ** 500. Poetry, fiction, drama, criticism by Indians who use English as a medium of creative expression. Material must have relevance for Indian life and culture. *Writers Workshop.*

MISSISSIPPI REVIEW. **VFOAT** MR, Mississippi Review. V. 1- Jan. 1972-. 0047-7559. Periodical. US. English. ir. $10.00. Mississippi Review, Southern Station Box 1544, Hattiesburg MS 39406.

Literature

Tel (601)266-4321. Ed Frederick Barthelme. **Ind/Abst** Index Am. Period. Verse. **LC** PS501. **DD** 810.80054. bk rev. adv acc. **Circ** 2,000. (ctrl) Available on microfilm from University Microfilms. Contemporary, nonregional fiction and poetry, interviews and criticism.

THE MISSOURI REVIEW. V. 1- Spring 1978-. 0191-1961. Periodical. US. English. ty. University of Missouri, English Department, 231 A and S, Columbia MO 65211. **Tel** (314)882-6066. Ed Speer Morgan and Greg Michalson. **Ind/Abst** MLA Int. Bibliogr. Books Artic. Mod. Lang. Lit., Index Am. Period. Verse. **LC** PS1. **DD** 810.80054. bk rev. adv acc. **Circ** 2,000. Fiction, poetry, interviews, reviews, essays, and other literary features.

MITRE. (THE MITRE). 83/84-. 0822-9120. CN. English. an. Students' Representative Council, Bishop's University, PO Box 2133, Lennoxville Quebec J1M 1Z7 Canada. **DD** C810.80054. *New Mitre (1980), 0711-4532.*

MITTELLATEINISCHE STUDIEN UND TEXTE. V. 1- 1965-. 0076-9754. Monographic Series. NE. German or English. ir. EJ Brill, PO Box 9000, 2300 PA Leiden The Netherlands.

MIYAGI-KEN BUNGEI NENKAN. Began in 1970. JA. Japanese. ir. Miyagi-Ken Geijutsu Kyokai Bungeibu, c/o Shiratori Building 1, Kasugacho 6, Sendai 980 Japan. **LC** PL886.M582.

MLA DIRECTORY OF PERIODICALS. *See* Yearbooks, Almanacs, Directories.

MLADA KULTURA. V. 1- Sept. 1972-. chiefly in Serbo-Croatian. ir. 100.00. Knjizevna Omaldina Beogradee, Georgi Dimitrova BR 5, Beograd Yugoslavia. **LC** PG560.

MLN. VAT Modern Language Notes. V. 1- Jan. 1886-. 0026-7910. Periodical. US. English (with some articles in Italian, Spanish, German, and French). ir. $55.00. Johns Hopkins University Press, 701 West 40th Street/Suite 275, Baltimore MD 21211. **Tel** (301)338-6987. Ed Paul Olson. **Ind/Abst** Humanit. Index, Sociol. Abstr., MLA Int. Bibliogr. Books Artic. Mod. Lang. Lit., Years Work Eng. Stud. **LC** PB1. **DD** 809. (cum index). bk rev. adv acc. **Circ** 1,748. Publishes articles on the theory, interpretation and history of Romance and Germanic languages. It has pioneered the introduction of modern continental criticism into American scholarship. *Modern Language Notes, 0149-6611.*

MODERN AUSTRIAN LITERATURE. V. 1- Spring 1968-. 0026-7503. Periodical. US. English. qt. $15.00. Modern Austrian Literature, California State College, Department for Language, Riverside CA 92502. **Tel** (714)787-5603. Ed Donald G Daviau. **Ind/Abst** MLA Int. Bibliogr. Books Artic. Mod. Lang. Lit., Ref. Source. **LC** PT3810. **DD** 830.99436. bk rev. adv acc. **Circ** 650. (ctrl). A journal devoted to Austrian literature and culture of the 19th and 20th centuries. *Journal of the International Arthur Schnitzler Research Association.*

MODERN BRITISH LITERATURE *CEASED.* V. 1-5, No. 1/2. Periodical. US. English. sa. **Ind/Abst** Abstr. Engl. Stud.

MODERN CHINESE LITERATURE NEWSLETTER. V. 1- Feb. 1975-. 0190-2369. Periodical. US. English. sa. $8.00. University of California, Oriental Languages Department, PO Box 66221, Los Angeles CA 90066. **LC** PL2303. **DD** 895.108005.

MODERN DRAMA. *See* Theater.

MODERN HEBREW LITERATURE. Spring 1975-. 0334-4266. Periodical. IS. English. sa. 6.00. Institute of Translat Hebrew Literature, 66 Sheomo Hamepech Street, Tel Aviv Israel. **Tel** (03)244421. Ed Anat Feinberg. **Ind/Abst** MLA Int. Bibliogr. Books Artic. Mod. Lang. Lit. **LC** PJ5001. **DD** 892.409. bk rev. adv acc. **Circ** 400. Helps the English-speaking reader keep abreast of Israel's literary scene. Includes a great variety of literary topics and reviews of recent works. Just revamped into a new magazine format. *Hebrew Book Review.*

MODERN INDIAN SHORT STORIES. V. 1- 1975-. English. ir.

MODERN JEWISH STUDIES ANNUAL. VFOAT MJS Annual. 2- 1978-. 0270-9406. Periodical. US. English (Yiddish). an. $2.50. Queens College Press, Flushing NY 11367. **LC** PS153.J4. **DD** 810.98924. *Conference on Modern Jewish Studies Annual, 0270-9392.*

MODERN LANGUAGE STUDIES. Began with Feb. 1971 issue. 0047-7729. Periodical. US. English. qt. $26.00. Modern Language Studies, Department of English, Box 1852, Brown University, Providence RI 02912. **Tel** (401)863-3756. Ed David H Hirsch. **Ind/Abst** Abstr. Engl. Stud., MLA Int. Bibliogr. Books Artic. Mod. Lang. Lit. **LC** PB1. **DD** 410.5. bk rev. **Circ** 2,000. Publishes articles of interest to teachers and scholars in the area of English, American, and comparative literature and of the modern languages. *NEMLA Newsletter, 0550-7073.*

MODERNA SPRAK. *See* Linguistics.

MODERNIST STUDIES. LITERATURE & CULTURE 1920-1940 *CEASED.* (MODERNIST STUDIES : LITERATURE & CULTURE 1920-1940). V. 1-4. 0316-5973. Periodical. CN. English. ty. 6.00 Canada and US, 7.00 Other Countries. University of Alberta, Department of English Modernist Studies, Edmonton Alberta T6G 2E1 Canada. **DD** 809.042.

MONATSHEFTE. V.1- 1899-. 0026-9271. Periodical. US. Multilingual (English, German). qt.

MONDE A L'ENVERS. (LE MONDE A L'ENVERS). First issue in July 1979. 0225-302X. Periodical. CN. French. ir. $1.00 Per No. Editions Heritage Inc, CP 8, Saint-Lambert Quebec J4P 3N4 Canada. **DD** C847.5405.

MONMOUTH REVIEW. V. 1- Spring 1972-. 0085-3534. US. English. an. Monmouth College, Cedar Avenue, West Long Beach NJ 07764. **LC** PS1. **DD** 810.80054.

MONTEMORA. 1- Fall 1975-. Periodical. US. English, French, Japanese or Spanish. $3.50 Each Issue. Montemora Foundation, Box 336 Cooper Station, New York NY 10003. **LC** PN6010.5. **DD** 805.

MONTHLY NEWS BULLETIN. Main/Corp Sahitya Akademi. Began in 1964. 0581-300X. Periodical. II. English. ir. Sahitya Akademi, Rabindra Bhavan, 35 Ferozeshan Road, New Delhi India. **LC** PK101. **DD** 891.1.

MONTREAL WRITERS' FORUM. V. 1- Oct. 1978-. 0707-5316. Periodical. CN. English. ir. 5.50. Montreal Writers' Forum, Box 333, Morin Heights Quebec J0R 1H0 Canada. **DD** C810.80054.

MOODY STREET IRREGULARS. No. 1- Winter 1978-. 0196-2604. Periodical. US. English. ir. $9.00. Moody Street Irregulars, PO Box 157, Clarence Center NY 14023. **Tel** (716)741-3393. Ed Joy Walsh. **Ind/Abst** MLA Int. Bibliogr. Books Artic. Mod. Lang. Lit. bk rev. adv acc. **Circ** 1,000. A newsletter devoted to the life and work of the American author Jack Kerovac.

MOOSEHEAD REVIEW. (THE MOOSEHEAD REVIEW). Vol. 1, No. 1 (1977)-. 0228-7404. Periodical. CN. English. sa. $4.26. Moosehead Review, PO Box 169, Ayer's Cliff, Quebec Quebec J0B 1C0 Canada. **Tel** (416)361-0618. **DD** C810.80054.

MORAVSKA LIRA. Serbo-Croatian(R). ir. 6.00 Each Issue. **LC** PG1400.

MORE. 1980-. Bulgarian. an. 1.76. **LC** PG1044.B87.

MOREANA. VFOAT Bulletin Thomas More. Vol. 1, No. 1 (Sept. 1963)-. 0047-8105. Periodical. FR. English (text in French). qt. $50.00. Association Amici Thomae Mori, 29 rue Volney BP 808, 49 Angers France. **Tel** 41888398. Ed Germain Marchadour. **Ind/Abst** Abstr. Engl. Stud., MLA Int. Bibliogr. Books Artic. Mod. Lang. Lit., Am. Hist. Life, Hist. Abstr., Hist. Abst., Part B, Twent. Century Abstr., Hist. Abstr., Part A, Mod. Hist. Abstr. (cum index). bk rev. **Circ** 1,000. Provides news about the life, writings, and world of More. Discusses lives, translations, theses, plays, and other documents.

MOSAIC (WINNIPEG, MAN.). (MOSAIC). Began with: Vol. 1, in Oct. 1967. 0027-1276. Periodical. CN. English (includes some text in French). qt. $43.53. Mosaic, University of Manitoba, 208 Tier Building, Winnipeg Manitoba R3T 2N2 Canada. **Tel** (204)474-9763. **Ind/Abst** Abstr. Engl. Stud., MLA Int. Bibliogr. Books Artic. Mod. Lang. Lit., Can. Period. Index, Index Book Rev. Humanit., Access. **LC** PN2. **DD** 809.

MOST. Vol. 1- 1954-. 0027-1438. Periodical. US. Slovak. sa. $4.00. Slovak Institute, 2900 East Boulevard, Cleveland OH 44115. **LC** AP58.S53.

MOT (MONTREAL). (LE MOT). V. 1, No. 2- Mar./April 1974-. 0316-3105. Periodical. CN. French. sa. Centre Traduction Terminologie, Universite de Moncton Ecole Centre, Moncton New Brunswick E1A 3E9 Canada. **Tel** (506)858-4560. **DD** C840.5. *0316-3091.*

MOTIF (COLUMBUS, OHIO). *See* Folklore.

MOVING OUT. *See* Women.

MOYEN FRANCAIS (PALERMO, ITALY). (LE MOYEN FRANCAIS). 1-. 0226-0174. Monographic Series. CN. English (text in French, and Italian). sa. $38.50. Ed Ceres, CP 1386, Place Bonaventure, Montreal Quebec H5A 1H3 Canada. **Tel** (514)937-7138. Ed G Di Stefano and R M Bidler. **Ind/Abst** MLA Int. Bibliogr. Books Artic. Mod. Lang. Lit. **DD** 840.9022. bk rev. adv acc. **Circ** 500. Presents studies, unedited texts, bibliographies which illustrates the actual tendencies of research on the French language and literature of the 14th and 15th centuries.

MOZNAYIM. N. S., V. 1-. 0027-2892. Periodical. IS. Hebrew. mo. $25.00. Ludwig Mayer Ltd, POB 1174, 91000 Jerusalem Israel. **Tel** 03 223208. Ed H Pessah. bk rev. Official organ of the Israeli Writers Association.

MSS (BINGHAMTON, N.Y.). (MSS). VFOAT M.S.S. Vol. 1, No. 1 (Spring 1981)-. 0738-9469. Periodical. US. English. ir. $15.00. State University of New York at Binghamton, L M Rosenberg and Joanna Higgins, Binghamton NY 13901. **Tel** (607)798-2404. Ed L M Rosenberg and Joanna Higgins. **LC** PS501. **DD** 810.8. bk rev. adv acc. **Circ** 500. Regularly introduces important new writers to publishing and continues in John Gardner's commitment to excellence and new genius.

THE MST ENGLISH QUARTERLY. *See* Linguistics.

MULCH. V. 1- Apr. 1971-. 0027-3112. Periodical. US. English. qt. $10.00. Mulch Press, c/o King, 326A Fourth Street, Brooklyn NY 11215. **LC** PN6010.5. **DD** 808.8004.

MULIKA. No. 1- 1971-. Periodical. Swahili. ir. Secretary/Institute of Swahili Research/University of Dares Salaam, PO Box 35091, dar es Dalaam Tanzania. **LC** PL8701.

MUNCHENER OSTASIATISCHE STUDIEN. Vol. 1- 1970-. Monographic Series. GW. German. ir. Franz Steiner Verlag GMBH, Postfach 347, D7000 Stuttgart 1 West Germany. **Tel** (0711)2582229. Ed W Bauer. Monographs about Chinese, Japanese and Korean literature, history, philosophy, and language.

MUNDUS ARABICUS. VFOAT Alam Al-Arabi. Vol. 1 (1981)-. 8755-4925. US. English (Arabic). an. Dar Mahijar PO Box 56, Cambridge MA 02238. **DD** 892.

MUNHAK KWA CHISONG. Periodical. KO. Korean. ir. 1,000 Single Issue. Munhak Kwa Chisong SA, 35-84 Tongui-Dong Chongno-Ku, Seoul South Korea. **LC** PL950.2.

MUNHAK SASANG. Periodical. KO. Korean. ir. 1,000 Single Issue. Munhak Sasang SA, 101 Choson-Dong Chongno-Ku, Seoul South Korea. **LC** PL950.2.

MUNHAK UI SIDAE. V. 1- (1983)-. Periodical. KO. Korean. ir. 3,200. Pulpit Chulpansa, 2-39 Yokchon-Dong Unpyong-Ku, Seoul Korea. **LC** PL969.8.

MUNTAKHAB AFSANE. 1963-. Urdu. ir. Ed Ahraz Naqvi. **LC** PK2190.

MUNU. Periodical. Korean. ir. **LC** PL950.2.

MUSIL-FORUM. 1. Vol., 1 (1. Halbjahresheft 1975)-. English (French, German, and Italian). sa. 45.-. Internationale Robert-Musil-Gesellschaft Geschaftsstelle und Vertrieb, Universitat Bau 35 Z 417, D 6600 Saarbrucken 11 West Germany. **Tel** (0681)302-3334. **LC** PT2625.U8. **DD** 833.912. bk rev. **Circ** 700. (ctrl). Devoted to Robert Musil and the Austrian literature. Regular features, where readers, authors, and editors debate each other.

MUTTERSPRACHE. *See* Linguistics.

MVR. VFOAT Mississippi Valley Review of Creative Writing. 0270-3521. Periodical. US. English. sa. $6.00. Western Illinois University, Department of English, Macomb IL 61455. Ed Forrest Robinson. **Circ** 400. Covers stories and poems.

MYTHLORE. VFOAT Myth Lore. Began with Jan. 1969 issue. 0146-9339. Periodical. US. English. qt. Mythlore, PO Box 6707, Altadena CA 91001. **Tel** (818)284-0848. **Ind/Abst** Abstr. Engl. Stud., MLA Int. Bibliogr. Books Artic. Mod. Lang. Lit. **LC** PR478.F35. **DD** 809.3876. bk rev. adv acc. **Circ** 600. (ctrl). A

Literature

journal of studies relating to the works of J R R Tolkien, C S Lewis and Charles Williams in particular, fantasy and mythology in general. *Tolkien Journal.*

NADI AL-QISSAH (ALEXANDRIA, EGYPT). (NADI AL-QISSAH). V. 1, No. 1-. Periodical. Arabic. mo. 1 Tariq AL-Zaim Jamal Abd Al-Nasir Qasr Thaqafat Al-Hurriyah, Al-Iskandariyah Egypt. LC PJ8216.

NAMES. See Linguistics.

NAMI. Began publication in January 1967. Periodical. JA. Japanese. mo. 700.00. Shincho Sha, 71 Yaraicho Shinjuku-Ku, Tokyo-To 162 Japan. LC PL700.

NANCY DREW MYSTERY STORIES. 1-. Monographic Series. US. English. LC PZ7.K23.

NAPJAINK. Periodical. HU. Hungarian. mo. Akademiai Kiado, POB 24, 1363 Budapest Hungary. LC PH3001.

NAQSH. Periodical. Urdu. ir. LC PK2151.

NATUNA PRAWAHA. Periodical. Assamese. ir. 3.50. Renn Goswami, Jaya Press Gauhati - 3, Guwaha India. LC PK1560.

NATUNA PURUSHA. V. 1- October 1972-. Periodical. Assamese. ir. 1.00 Single Issue. Hema Cetiya, Amolapati Assam, Dibrugara India. LC PK1560.

NAULO MUKTI. Vol. 1, No 1 (Feb./March 1981)-. Periodical. II. Nepali. bm. 2.00. Janardan Thapa, 27/249 Kelgarh Colony, Varanasi 221002 India. LC PK2597.5.

NAVA-PATHA. Patha 1, Paila 1 July/August/September 2037 Oct./Nov. 1980-). Periodical. II. Nepali. qt. 3.00. Hem Bahadur Chetri Pharas Path Balibakhani, Gangtok 737101 India. LC PK2598.A2.

NAVALAKATHA. 0028-1492. Gujarati. mo. 26.00. Saha Sevantilala Cimanalala Evergreen Industrial State, Block No 47 Shakti Mill Lane Hans Road Mahalakshomi, Bombay -11 India. LC PK1858.

NAVARAGA. VFOAT Nava-Raga. Periodical. II. Nepali. qt. 12.00. Bikash Pustakalaya, Som Tea Garden, Darjeeling India. LC PK2597.5.

NAYA. 0376-6578. Hindi. qt. 8.00. Naya Office, 38/276 Rajendranagar-16, Patsna India. LC PK2030.

NAYA PRATIKA. Vol. 1- Jan. 1974-. Periodical. II. Hindi. mo. National Publishing House, 2125 Ansari Road, 23 Daryaganj Delhi 110 002 India. LC PK2039.

NEBRASKA NEWSPAPER. Began in 1948. 0028-1913. Periodical. US. English. mo. $5.00. Nebraska Press Association, 206 South 13th/Suite 723, Lincoln NE 68508. Tel (402)476-2851. LC PN4700. DD 071.82.

NEBULA. No. 1- Feb. 1975-. 0317-2104. CN. English. qt. $11.61. Nebula Press, 970 Copeland Street, North Bay Ontario Canada. Tel (705)472-5127. DD C810.80054.

THE NEBULA AWARDS. No. 18-. 0741-5567. US. English. an. Arbor House Publishing Company, 235 East 45th Street, New York NY 10017. LC PS648.S3. DD 813.087608. *Nebula Award Stories (New York, N.Y.: 1982), 0731-6690.*

NEDERLANDS INTERNATIONAAL PRIVATRECHT : REPERTORIUM OP VERDRAGENRECHT, WETGEVING, RECHTSPRAAK EN LITERATUUR. 0167-7594. Periodical. NE. Dutch. ty. 60.00. T.M.C. Asser Instituut, Postbus 30461, 2500 GL S-Gravenhage The Netherlands.

NEI MENG-KU TUAN PIEN HSIAO SHUO HSUAN. Periodical. CC. Chinese. ir. 1.25. Hsin Hua Shu Tien, Nei Meng-ku, China.

NEOHELICON. V. 1-. 0324-4652. Periodical. HU. English (French, German or Russian). sa. $48.00. John Benjamins BV, PO Box 52519, Amsteldijk 44, 1007 HA Amsterdam Netherlands. Tel (020)738156. Ed M Szavolcsi and G M Vajda. Ind/Abst MLA Int. Bibliogr. Books Artic. Mod. Lang. Lit. LC PN851. DD 809. An organ for studies in comparative and world literature. Focusses on studies which further a synthetic presentation of literary epochs, periods, trends and movements from a comparative point of view.

NEOLOGY. 0228-913X. Periodical. CN. English. ir. Free. Neology, PO Box 4071, Edmonton Alberta T6A 4S8 Canada. DD 823.087609. (ctrl). *Newsletter (Edmonton Science Fiction and Comic Arts Society), 0228-9121.*

NEPALI AKADAMI PATRIKA. VFOAT Akadami Patrika. Periodical. Nepali. ir. 2.00. LC PK2595.

THE NESFA INDEX. See Indexes/Abstracts.

NEUDRUCKE DEUTSCHER LITERATURWERKE. NEUE FOLGE. 1-. 0077-7668. Periodical. GW. German. ir. Max Niemeyer Verlag, Postfach 21 40, 7400 Tuebingen 1 West Germany. Ed Hans Heurik Krummacher. Ind/Abst MLA Int. Bibliogr. Books Artic. Mod. Lang. Lit. Critical editions of German literature, especially 16th-18th centuries.

NEUE BEITRAGE ZUR LITERATURWISSENSCHAFT. Vol. 1- 1955-. 0548-2712. Monographic Series. GW. German. ir. Deutscher Buchexport Import, Postfach 160, DDR-7010 Leipzig East Germany. Ind/Abst MLA Int. Bibliogr. Books Artic. Mod. Lang. Lit.

NEUE DEUTSCHE LITERATUR. VFOAT NDL. Neue Deutsche Literatur. 1.- Yr. Vol. 0028-3150. Periodical. SZ. German. mo. $27.31. Kunst & Wissen Erich Bieber, Dufourstrasse 51, CH-8008 Zurich Switzerland. Tel 011-41-1-69 44 20. LC PT3. DD 830.9.

NEUE GERMANISTIK. Vol. 1, No. 1 (Fall 1980)-. 0730-1359. Periodical. US. English (German). sa. University of Minnesota, Department of German, 201 Folwell Avenue, 9 Pleasant Street, Minneapolis MN 55455. Tel (612)373-4498. Ind/Abst MLA Int. Bibliogr. Books Artic. Mod. Lang. Lit. LC PF3001. DD 830.9. bk rev. Circ 200. Promotes interest in German language graduate studies by providing a publication-forum for graduate students.

NEW AMERICAN PLAYS. Vol. 1-. US. English. ir. Farrar Straus and Giroux Inc, 19 Union Square West, New York NY 10003. Ed Robert W Corrigan. LC PS634.

THE NEW BLACK MASK QUARTERLY. VFOAT Black Mask. No. 1-. 0883-4512. Periodical. US. English. qt. $27.80. Harcourt Brace Jovanovich Publishers, 1250 Sixth Avenue, San Diego CA 92101 (subscription address: 129 West 56th Street New York NY 10019). Tel (212)765-0902. Ed Matthew Bruccoli and Richard Layman. DD 813. Circ 150. Publication featuring the best from the modern masters of detective, intrigue, suspense, and mystery fiction. Includes short stories, excerpts and interviews.

NEW CANADIAN FANDOM. Vol. 1, No. 1, Whole No. 1 (Apr./May 1981)-. 0229-1932. Periodical. CN. English. ir. $2.00 for 4 issues. New Canadian Fandom, c/o R Runte, Box 4655, Southside PO, Edmonton Alberta T6E 5G5 Canada. DD 809.387605.

NEW CLASSIC CEASED. No. 1- 1975-. SA. Multilingual (Afrikaans or English). ir. 2.00. PO Box 78, Dube 1800, Johannesburg South Africa. Ind/Abst MLA Int. Bibliogr. Books Artic. Mod. Lang. Lit. LC PL8014.S62. DD 820. *Classic.*

NEW DIMENSIONS. 1st- Ed. 1971-. Monographic Series. US. English. ir. Harper & Row Publishing Co, Keystone Industrial Park, Scranton PA 18512. Tel (717)343-4761. LC PZ1. DD 823'.0876.

NEW DIMENSIONS SCIENCE FICTION. VFOAT New Dimensions. 0099-0906. US. English. an. Harper & Row, 10 East 53rd Street, New York NY 10022. LC PZ1.A1, PS648.S3. DD 813.0876. *New Dimensions.*

NEW ENGLAND REVIEW AND BREAD LOAF QUARTERLY. (NEW ENGLAND REVIEW AND BREAD LOAF QUARTERLY : NER/BLQ). VFOAT NER/BLQ. Vol. 5, No. 1-2 (Autumn-Winter 1982)-. 0736-2579. Periodical. US. English. qt. $33.00. NER/BLQ, Box 170, Hanover NH 03755. Tel (603)795-4027. Ed Jim Schley. Ind/Abst MLA Int. Bibliogr. Books Artic. Mod. Lang. Lit., Index Book Rev. Humanit. LC PN2. DD 808.8. bk rev. adv acc. Circ 2,000. (ctrl). *New England Review, 0164-3177.*

NEW ENGLISH DRAMATISTS. 1-. 0548-4510. Periodical. UK. English. Penguin Books, 7110 Ambassador Road, Baltimore MD 21207. LC PR1272. DD 822.91408.

NEW GENERATION. V. 1- 1979-. Periodical. US. English. an. Office of the President, Florida State University, Tallahassee FL 32306. LC PS558.F6. DD 810.809283.

NEW GERMAN CRITIQUE. V. 1- Winter 1973-. 0094-033X. Periodical. US. English. ty. $8.00. University of Wisconsin, German Department, Box 413, Milwaukee WI 53201. Ind/Abst MLA Int. Bibliogr. Books Artic. Mod. Lang. Lit., Sociol. Abstr., Altern. Press Index. LC PT1. DD 914.303.

NEW GERMAN STUDIES. VFOAT N.G.S., NGS. Vol. 1, No. 1 (Spring 1973)-. 0307-2770. Periodical. UK. English. ty. $11.49. University of Hull, Department of German, Hull HU6 7RX England. Tel 0482 49 7649. Ed Alan Best. Ind/Abst MLA Int. Bibliogr. Books Artic. Mod. Lang. Lit. LC PF3001. DD 830.8. (cum index). bk rev. adv acc. Circ 300. Articles dealing with German language, literature and institutions.

THE NEW INFINITY REVIEW. Publication began with: Vol. 1 (1974). Periodical. US. English. qt. James R Pack, PO Box 412, South Point OH 45680. Tel (614)377-4182.

THE NEW LAUREL REVIEW. V. 1- 1971/72-. 0145-8388. Periodical. US. English. sa. $10.00. Attn Lee Grue, 828 Lesseps Street, New Orleans LA 70117. Tel (504)947-6001. Ed Lee Meitzen Grue. Ind/Abst MLA Int. Bibliogr. Books Artic. Mod. Lang. Lit. bk rev. Circ 500. (ctrl). Contains poetry, short fiction, translation and visual art. Also, essays by artists on art, interviews critical articles and detachable art.

NEW LETTERS. V. 38- Fall 1971-. 0146-4930. Periodical. US. English. qt. $15.00. University of Missouri, Kansas City MO 64110. Tel (816)276-1168. Ed David Ray. Ind/Abst Abstr. Engl. Stud., MLA Int. Bibliogr. Books Artic. Mod. Lang. Lit., Index Am. Period. Verse, Index Book Rev. Humanit. LC PS501. DD 820.8. adv acc. Circ 2,000. A literary featuring fiction, poetry, art, photography, scholarship, satire, and special issues. *University Review.*

NEW LITERATURE & IDEOLOGY. VFOAT New Literature and Ideology, We Are The Heirs of Norman Bethune. No. 19- Feb. 1976-. 0702-7532. Periodical. CN. English. ir. National Publication Center, Box 727 Adelaide Station, Toronto M5C 2J8 Ontario Canada. Tel (416)252-3658. Ind/Abst Abstr. Engl. Stud. *Alive Magazine: Literature & Ideology, 0318-6512.*

NEW OBSERVATIONS. Began in 1981. 0737-5387. Periodical. US. English (text in French). bm. $22.00 Domestic, $24.00 Foreign. New Observations Publications Inc, 144 Greene Street, New York NY 10012. Tel (212)966-6071. Ed Ciri Johnson. adv acc. Circ 500. One of the prominent outlets for a great variety of intellectual and artistic forces. Every month a different guest-editor compiles an entire issue according to his/her preferences.

THE NEW RENAISSANCE. See The Arts (General).

NEW RIVER REVIEW. No. 1- Fall 1975-. 0360-1455. Periodical. US. English. sa. $4.00. Radford College Station, 5741 RC, Radford VA 24147. Tel (703)731-5289. LC PS501. DD 810.80054.

THE NEW SOUTHERN LITERARY MESSENGER. 0730-515X. Periodical. US. English. qt. $4.00. Charles M Lohmann, 302 South Laurel Street, Richmond VA 23220. Tel (804)780-1244. Ed Charles Lohmann. Circ 2,000. (ctrl). Stories and local poetry for lovers of fresh air, unfamiliar and unregulated, informed and formulated disfaculated and unfunktified good stuff-hot of cold.

NEW STORIES. 1- 1976-. UK. English. Arts Council of Great Britain, 105 Piccadilly W1V0AU, London England. LC PZ1, PR1309.S5. DD 823.01.

NEW VOICES. 0094-4645. US. English. $2.50 single issue. D Fried, 102 Butterville Road, New Paltz NY 12561. LC PS536.2. DD 810.8.

NEW WRITERS. V. 1- Fall 1973-. 0092-6698. US. English. $1.95 Per issue. Literary Workshop Publications, 507-5th Avenue, New York NY 10017. LC PZ1.A1, PS648.S5. DD 813.01.

NEW WRITING AND WRITERS. VFOAT NWW, New Writing and Writers. No. 13-. Periodical. UK. English. 4.95. John Calder Publishers Ltd, 18 Brewer Street, London WIR 4AS England. LC PN6019. DD 808.8004. *New Writers, 0548-7102.*

NEW YORK LITERARY FORUM. V. 1- Spring 1978-. 0149-1040. Monographic Series. US. English. sa. $25.00. New York Literary Forum, 21 East 79th Street, New York NY 10021. Tel (212)535-4329. Ed Jeanine P Plottel. Ind/Abst MLA Int. Bibliogr. Books Artic. Mod. Lang. Lit., Abstr. Engl. Stud. bk rev. Circ 3,000. Each volume deals with a topic of current interest to scholars and students of literature and the arts. Example: comedy, fragments, melodrama, and women's autobiographical writings.

Literature

NEW ZEALAND FICTION. 1- 1970-. 0077-9970. Monographic Series. US. English. ir. Oxford University Press, 16-00 Pollitt Drive, Fair Lawn NJ 07410.

THE NEWS-LETTER OF THE SOCIETY FOR THE STUDY OF SOUTHERN LITERATURE. Main/Corp Society for the Study of Southern Literature. V. 1- May 1968-. 0197-8071. US. English. sa. $4.00 Domestic. $4.50 Foreign. Society for the Study of Southern Literature, PO Box 2625 Mississippi State University, Mississippi State MS 39762. Tel (601)325-3644. Ed Susan Snell. LC PS261. DD 810.9975. Circ 400. Organized to promote the scholarly study of Southern literature, history and culture.

NEWSBANK : LITERATURE. Periodical. US. English. mo. Index received separately bound from publisher. (cum index).

NEWSBOY. See Biographies.

NEWSLETTER - ACADEMY OF CANADIAN WRITERS. (NEWSLETTER). Vol. 1, No. 1 (Sept. 1979)-. 0712-9955. Periodical. CN. English. qt. Free. Academy of Canadian Writers, 295 Fennell Avenue, Hamilton Ontario L9C 5R Canada. DD C810.5.

NEWSLETTER - AUGUST DERLETH SOCIETY. Main/Corp August Derleth Society. V. 1-. 0272-9911. Periodical. US. English. qt. George Marx, 20 East Deleware Place, Chicago IL 60611. LC PS3507.E69. DD 818.5209.

NEWSLETTER - CENTRE FOR EDITION EARLY CANADIAN TEXTS. (NEWSLETTER). No. 1 (1982)-. 0713-3960. CN. English. an. Newsletter, c/o Centre for Editing Early Canadian Texts, Room 1901/Arts Tower, Carleton University, Ottawa Ontario K1S 5B6 Canada. DD 808.02.

NEWSLETTER - FRIENDS OF GEORGE SAND. (NEWSLETTER). VFOAT George Sand Newsletter. Vol. 1, No. 1 (Winter 1977 & 1978)-. 0161-6544. Periodical. US. English (French). sa. $10.00. Hofstra University/UCCIS, 1000 Fulton Avenue, Hempstead NY 11550. Tel (516)560-5669. LC PQ2417. DD 843.7.

NEWSLETTER - NATHANIEL HAWTHORNE SOCIETY. Main/Corp Nathaniel Hawthorne Society. V. 1- Spring 1975-. 0162-9824. Periodical. US. English. sa. $4.00. Hawthorne Longfellow Library, Bowdoin College, Brunswick ME 04011. Tel (207)725-8731. Ed John Idol Jr. Ind/Abst MLA Int. Bibliogr. Books Artic. Mod. Lang. Lit. Circ 400. Nathaniel Hawthorne studies.

NEWSLETTER OF THE KAFKA SOCIETY OF AMERICA CEASED. Main/Corp Kafka Society of America. 1st-7th Year, No. 1. 0741-6202. Periodical. US. English (German). sa. $10.00 Members. Kafka Society of America, Temple University, Department of German and Slavic Languages and Literatures, Philadelphia PA 19122. Ind/Abst MLA Int. Bibliogr. Books Artic. Mod. Lang. Lit. LC WMLC L 83/618.

NEWSLETTER OF THE VICTORIAN STUDIES ASSOCIATION OF WESTERN CANADA. Main/Corp Victorian Studies Association of Western Canada. VAT Newsletter - Victorian Studies Association of Western Canada. V. 1- Fall 1972-. 0703-5500. Periodical. CN. English. sa. Free to Members, Membership $10.00. C Gordon-Craig, Department of English, University of Alberta, Edmonton Alberta T6G 2E1 England. DD 820.9008.

NEWSLETTER - SOCIETY OF THE SEVEN SAGES. (NEWSLETTER). 1 (Jan. 15, 1976)-. 0701-9890. CN. English. an. 5.00. Society of the Seven Sages, c/o Hans R Runte, Department of French/Dalhousie University, Halifax Nova Scotia B3H 3J5 Canada. Tel (902)424-2430. Ed Hans R Runte. DD 806. bk rev. adv acc. Circ 150. (ctrl). Reports on research activities in Sindbad and Seven Sages studies.

NEWSLETTER - WRITERS' GUILD OF ALBERTA. (NEWSLETTER). VFOAT WGA Newsletter. Vol. 1, No. 1 (Dec. 1980)-. 0821-4204. Periodical. CN. English. ir. 12.00. Writers' Guild of Alberta, #101-10022-103 Street, Edmonton Alberta T5J 0 Canada. Tel (403)426-5892. Ed M Riskin. DD 808.0205. adv acc. Circ 650. (ctrl). Newsletter for Alberta writers, lists markets, competitions, books out, reading, and contains articles of interest to writers.

NEWSLETTER-WRITERS GUILD OF AMERICA, WEST. Main/Corp Writers Guild of America, West. 0043-9533. Periodical. US. English. ni. $20.00. Writers Guide of America, 8955 Beverly Boulevard, Los Angeles CA 90048. Tel (213)550-1000. Ed Allen Rivkin. adv acc. Circ 7,500. (ctrl).

NEWSLETTER - WRITERS' UNION OF CANADA. Main/Corp Writers' Union of Canada. No. 1- June 1973-. 0382-831X. Periodical. CN. English. ir. Writers' Union of Canada, 5 Sultan Street, Toronto Ontario M5S 1L6 Canada. DD 806.

NGAM : CAHIERS DU DEPARTEMENT DE LITTERATURE AFRICAINE COMPAREE, UNIVERSITE DE YAOUNDE. No. 1/2 (Jan./June 1977)-. Periodical. CM. French (English). sa. B Fonlon, Department of Negro African Literature, University of Yaounde, PO Box 755, Yaounde Cameroun West Africa.

NIGHTWINDS. Vol. 1, No. 1 (Summer 1979)-. 0715-5549. Periodical. CN. English. ir. $5.00. Nightwinds, PO Box 1442, Guelph Ontario N1H 6N9 Canada. DD C813.087608.

NIHON BUNGAKU. VFOAT Japanese Literature. Began with No. 1, Nov. 1958. Periodical. JA. Japanese. ir. Nihon Bungaku Kyokai, 17-10 Minami Otsuka 2-Chome Toshima-Ku, Tokyo Japan. LC PL700. (cum index).

NIHON EIGA SHINARIO SENSHU. JA. Japanese. ir. 2200. Eijinsha 32-10 Higashi, Ikebukuro 5 Toshima-Ku, Tokyo-To 170 Japan. LC PN1997.A1.

NIHON HADI KYOKAI KAIHO = BULLETIN OF THE THOMAS HARDY SOCIETY OF JAPAN. JA. Japanese. ir. Nihon Hadi Kyokai, c/o Kanazawa Daigaku Hobungakubu Eibungaku, Kenkyushitsu Marunouchi, Kanazawa Japan 920. LC PR4752.

NIHONGO NIHON BUNGAKU. VFOAT Japanese & Japanese Literature. No. 1- Ki. Japanese. ir. Hojin Daigaku Tohogo Bungakkai, 510 Chung-Cheng Lu, Taiwan-Sho Shinshochin Chuseiro, Shinsho Taiwan. LC PL889.T282.

NIMBUS TWO. Vol. 2, No. 2 (Spring 1981)-. 0710-2658. Periodical. CN. English. qt. $6.00. Nimbus Press, 69 Chatworth Drive, Toronto Ontario M4R 1R8 Canada. DD C810.80054. Nimbus, 0708-5656.

NIMROD. Began in 1956. 0029-053X. Periodical. US. English. sa. $26.00. Arts/Humanities Council Tulsa, 2210 South Main, Tulsa OK 74114. Tel (918)584-3333. Ed Francine Ringold. Ind/Abst Index Am. Period. Verse. LC SK223.H9. adv acc. Circ 2,000. International journal of fiction and poetry, publishes vigorous new writing. Two yearly issues: The Awards Issue and the Thematic Issue.

NINETEENTH-CENTURY FICTION. VFOAT Journal of Victorian Fiction. V. 1- Summer 1945-. 0029-0564. US. English. qt. $20.00. University of California Press, 2120 Berkeley Way, Berkeley CA 94720. Tel (415)642-4191. Ed G B Tennyson and Thomas Wortham. Ind/Abst Soc. Sci. Index, Humanit. Index, Hist. Abstr., Am. Hist. Life, Women Stud. Abstr., Abstr. Engl. Stud., MLA Int. Bibliogr. Books Artic. Mod. Lang. Lit., Years Work Eng. Stud. LC PR873. DD 823.809. (cum index). bk rev. adv acc. Circ 2,600. Available on microfilm and Xerograph facsimile from University Microfilms. Articles on Austen, Scott, Dickens, Thackeray, the Brontes, Trollope, Meredith, and James are supplemented by others on lesser writers as well as on literary history and theory.

NINETEENTH-CENTURY FRENCH STUDIES. V. 1- Fall 1972-. 0146-7891. Periodical. US. English (French). qt. $24.00. Nineteenth-Century French, 6 Pine Drive, Fredonia NY 14063. Tel (716)673-3380. Ed Thomas H Goetz. Ind/Abst MLA Int. Bibliogr. Books Artic. Mod. Lang. Lit., Mod. Lang. Abstr., Index Book Rev. Humanit., Romant. Move. Sel. Crit. Bibliogr., Rev. Hist. Litt. Fr. LC PQ1. DD 840.9. bk rev. adv acc. Circ 700. Studies on all aspects of nineteenth-century French literature and criticism and related fields. Extensive book review section on a broad range of related topics.

NINETEENTH CENTURY STUDIES. No. 1- Jan. 1973-. Periodical. II. English. ir. $8.00. Biographical Research Centre, 1/3 Krishnaram Bose Street, Calcutta-4 India. LC PK101. DD 891.409004.

NIRANTARA. VFOAT Nirantar. 1. Samkhya (Srabana 1391 July 1984)-. Periodical. Bengali. ir. 10.00 per issue. 2/4 C Sahajahan Road, Mohammadpur Dhaka 7 Bengal. LC PK1712.5.

NISTRU : ORGAN AL UNIUNII SKRIITORILOR DIN RSS MOLDOVENIASKE. Periodical. UR. Moldavian. mo. 277612 Kishineu, Str Kievului 98, Kishineu Moldavian SSR. LC PC794.M66. DD 891.708. NISTRUL.

NMAL. NOTES ON MODERN AMERICAN LITERATURE. (NMAL, NOTES ON MODERN AMERICAN LITERATURE). V. 1, No. 2- Spring 1977-. 0163-8246. Periodical. US. English. ty. $5.00. St Johns University, English Department, Jamaica NY 11439. Tel (718)969-8000. Ed Edward Guerschi and Lee Richmond. Ind/Abst Abstr. Engl. Stud., MLA Int. Bibliogr. Books Artic. Mod. Lang. Lit. LC PS221. DD 810.9005. Circ 1,500. Publishes criticism on American literature 900 to the present, we welcome short and concise contributions of roughly 1,000 words. Notes on Modern American Literature, 0164-1360.

NMFG. NO MONEY FROM THE GOVERNMENT. (NMFG : NO MONEY FROM THE GOVERNMENT). VFOAT No Money from the Government. No. 1 (Feb. 1976)-. 0827-3979. Periodical. CN. English. DD C810.80054.

NORD CEASED. No. 1, Fall 1971. Ceased with No. 7. 0315-3789. Periodical. CN. French (includes some text in English). ty. $4.95 Per Number. Librairie Garneau Ltee, CP 7600 Charlesbourg, Quebec Quebec G1G 5W7 Canada. DD C840.5.

NORSK LITTERR ARBOK. See Yearbooks, Almanacs, Directories.

NORSKE NOVELLER. Norwegian. ir. LC PT8721.

THE NORTH AMERICAN MENTOR MAGAZINE. VFOAT North American Mentor. Began with: V. 1 (Spring 1964). 0549-7078. Periodical. US. English. qt. $12.00. John Westburg and Associates, Fennimore WI 53809. Tel (608)822-6237. Ed John and Mildred Westburg. bk rev. Circ 500. Often at odds with current contemporary literary and political trends, non-religious, non-partisan, concerned with minorities but not a "minority" publication.

NORTH CAROLINA STUDIES IN THE ROMANCE LANGUAGES AND LITERATURES. No. 132-. 0081-8666. Monographic Series. US. English (French, Italian or Spanish). ir. University of North Carolina Press, Box 2288, Chapel Hill NC 27514. Tel (919)966-3561. Ind/Abst MLA Int. Bibliogr. Books Artic. Mod. Lang. Lit. Studies in the Romance Languages and Literatures, 0081-8666.

THE NORTH STONE REVIEW. No. 1- Spring 1971-. Periodical. US. English. an. North Stone Review, Box 14098, University Station, Minneapolis MN 55414. Ind/Abst Index Am. Period. Verse. LC PS1. DD 810.80054. Available from Xerox University Microfilms.

NORTHERN NEW ENGLAND REVIEW. V. 1-. 0190-3012. Periodical. US. English. an. $3.50. Franklin Pierce College, PO Box 825, Rindge NH 03461. Tel (603)899-5111. bk rev. adv acc. Circ 600. (ctrl). The only currently published literary journal which prints exclusively the works of Northern New England residents. Publishes poetry, fiction, and articles which reflect the attitudes of the region.

NOTA BENE (PARIS, FRANCE). (NOTA BENE). No. 1 (Winter 1981)-. 0249-6275. Periodical. FR. French. qt. 140. 9 rue Ampere, Paris 75017 France. LC PN6023. DD 809.

NOTES & FURPHIES. VFOAT Notes and Furphies. Began with Oct. 1978 issue. Periodical. AT. English. sa. 12. Notes & Furphies c/o Dr J Wieland, University of Wollongong/Department of English, Wollongong New South Wales 2500 Australia. Tel (067)732604. Ed Julian Craft and Ken Stewart. adv acc. Circ 400. (ctrl). Bulletin of Association for the Study of Australian Literature specialising in news research reports and notes about Australian literature.

NOTES AND QUERIES. V. 1- Nov. 1849-. 0029-3970. Periodical. UK. English. qt. 26.00 Domestic/52.00 US & 32.00 Other. Oxford University Press, Journals Department Walton Street, Oxford OX2 6DP England. Ed E G Stanley, D Hewitt and G Black. Ind/Abst Abstr. Engl. Stud., Humanit. Index, Am. Hist. Life, Hist. Abstr., Part A, Mod. Hist. Abstr., Hist. Abstr., Part B, Twent. Century Abstr., MLA Int. Bibliogr. Books Artic. Mod. Lang. Lit., Annu. Bibliogr. Engl. Lang. Lit., Index Book Rev. Humanit., Recent

Literature

Publ. Artic., Years Work Eng. Stud., Hist. Abstr. LC AG305. DD 032. NLM AG 105 N911. (cum index). bk rev. adv acc. Circ 1,300. (ctrl). Some Vols. available on microfilm from University Microfilms, Ltd. Devoted principally to English language and literature, lexicography, history, and scholarly antiquarianism. Emphasis is on the factual rather than the speculative.

NOTES ON MISSISSIPPI WRITERS. V. 1- Spring 1968-. 0029-4071. Periodical. US. English. sa. $3.00. Notes on Mississippi Writers, Box 433 Southern Station, Hattiesburg MS 39401. Tel (601)266-4319. Ed Hilton Anderson. Ind/Abst Abstr. Engl. Stud., MLA Int. Bibliogr. Books Artic. Mod. Lang. Lit. LC PS266.M7. DD 810.99762. bk rev. Circ 300. Scholarly works about writers from Mississippi.

NOTRE DAME ENGLISH JOURNAL CEASED. VFOAT N.D.E.J., NDEJ. V. 1-4, 1961-1964. 0029-4500. Periodical. US. English. ty. $12.00. Notre Dame English Journal, University of Notre Dame, Notre Dame IN 46556. Ind/Abst Abstr. Engl. Stud., Cathol. Period. Lit. Index, Relig. Index One, Period.

NOTTINGHAM FRENCH STUDIES. V. 1- May 1962-. 0029-4586. Periodical. UK. English (French). sa. $7.66. University of Nottingham, University Park, Nottingham NG7 2RD England. Ed L Thorpe. Ind/Abst MLA Int. Bibliogr. Books Artic. Mod. Lang. Lit. LC PQ1. DD 840.9. French literature.

NOUAISON. Vol. 1, No. 1 (Spring 1984)-. 0825-5830. Periodical. CN. French. ir. $4.00 Per Number. Librairie Clement Morin et Fils, 4125 Boulevard des Forges, Trois Rivieres Quebec Canada. DD C840.9971445.

NOUS JOURNAL. V. 1- Spring 1975-. 0318-2835. CN. English. ir. $1.50. All About Us/Nous Autres Inc, PO Box 1985, Ottawa Ontario K1P 5R5 Canada. DD C810.80928205.

NOUVELLE BARRE DU JOUR. (LA NOUVELLE BARRE DU JOUR). No. 58- Sept. 1977-. 0704-1888. Periodical. CN. French. ir. 45.00 Domestic, 55.00 Foreign. La Nouvelle Barre du Jour, CP 131 Outremont, Outremont Quebec H2V 4M8 Canada. Tel (514)526-6653. Ed Michel Gay. Ind/Abst Point Repere. LC PQ3912.5. DD C840.5. adv acc. Circ 800. Modern fiction: poetry and prose, theory and practice, feminism: theory and fiction, frequent special issues. Barre du Jour, 0005-6057.

NOUVELLE LITTERATURE ET IDEOLOGIE. No. 21- Aug. 1977-. 0703-8011. Periodical. CN. French. ir. Institut Norman Bethune, Le Centre National de Publications, CP 727 Succursale Adelaide, Toronto Ontario M5C 2J8 Canada. DD 808.8004.

NOVAIA INOSTRANNAIA LITERATURA PO OBSHCHESTVENNYM NAUKAM : LITERATUROVEDENIE. 1976-. Periodical. UR. Russian (Multilingual). mo. 0.60 Single Issue. Akademiia Nauk SSSR, In-T Nauch Informatsii Po Obsnchestvennym Naukam, Ul Krasikova 28/45, Moskva USSR. LC Z6513, PN583. Novaia Inostrannaia Literatura po Literaturovedeniiu.

NOVAIA SOVETSKAIA LITERATURA PO OBSHCHESTVENNYM NAUKAM : EKONOMIKA. 1976-. UR. Russian. mo. 0.70. Akademiia Nauk SSSR, Ul Krasikova 28/45, Moskva USSR. LC Z7165.R9, HC335. Novaia Sovetskaia Ekonomicheskaia Literatura.

NOVAIA SOVETSKAIA LITERATURA PO OBSHCHESTVENNYM NAUKAM : LITERATUROVEDENIE. 1976-. UR. Russian. mo. 0.40 Single Issue. Akademiia Nauk SSSR, Ul Krasikova 28/45, Moskva Russia. LC Z6513, PN583. Novaia Sovetskaia Literatura po Literaturovedeniiu.

NOVE KNIHY. 5. RIJ. 1960-. Periodical. CS. Czech (Slovak). wk. Artia, PO Box 790, Praha 1 Czechoslovakia. LC Z2133. Nove Knihy V Jednote, Knizni Novinky.

NOVEL; A FORUM ON FICTION. V. 1- Fall 1967-. 0029-5132. Periodical. US. English. ty. $6.00. Editors of Novel, Box 1984, Brown University, Providence RI 02919. Ind/Abst Humanit. Index, Abstr. Engl. Stud., MLA Int. Bibliogr. Books Artic. Mod. Lang. Lit., Index Book Rev. Humanit. LC PN3311. (cum index).

NOVELLEREGISTER. See Bibliographies.

NOVINKY LITERATURY. SPOLECENSKE VEDY. RADA VI, JAZYKOVEDA-LITERARNI VEDA. VFOAT Spolecenske Vedy. Rada VI, Jazykoveda-Literarni Veda. Periodical. CS. Czech. qt. Artia, Ve Smechach 30, Prague 1 Czechoslavakia.

OS NOVOS POETAS DO CEARA; ANTOLOGIA. 1.- 1970-. Portuguese. ir. H Galeno, Casa de Juvenal Galeno, Fortaleza Brazil. LC PQ9691.C42.

NOVYJ ZURNAL. See Ethnic.

NOWY WYRAZ. Periodical. PL. Polish. ir. RSW Prasa-Ksiazka-Ruch Modziezowa Agencja Wydawnicza, Biuro Kolportazu Wydawnictw Zagranicznych Ruch, Ul Wronia 23, Warszawa Poland. LC PG7001.

NRL, NEUE RUSSISCHE LITERATUR. VFOAT Neue Russische Literatur. 1978-. Periodical. (Russian). ir. $14.00. Institut fur Slawistik, Akademiestrasse 24, A-5020 Salzburg Austria. LC PG3227. DD 891.708.

NUEVA REVISTA DE FILOLOGIA HISPANICA. See Linguistics.

NUIT BLANCHE (QUEBEC, QUEBEC). (NUIT BLANCHE). VFOAT Bulletin. No 6 (Spring/Summer 1982)-. 0823-2490. Periodical. CN. French. bm. 12,50 Domestic, 25,00 Foreign. Nuit Blanche, 1026 rue St-Jean/Bureau 303, Quebec Province of Quebec G1R 1R7 Canada. DD 809.0405. Presents book reviews, each issue a dossier about contemporary literature. Bulletin Pantoute.

NUNG MIN WEN HSUEH. Periodical. CC. Chinese. bm. 0.25. Post Office, Ho-Pei China.

OBERISUKU. VFOAT Obelisk. 1-. JA. Japanese. ir. 1800. Kase Teiko c/o Mr Kunihiro Soeda, 309 Owada Yachiyo-Shi Chiba-Ken 276, Tokyo Japan. LC PN9.

OBSHCHESTVENNYE NAUKI V SSSR. SERIIA 7 : LITERATUROVEDENIE. VFOAT Obshchestvenedia. VAT Obshchestvennye Nauki V SSSR. Seriia Sem : Literaturovedenie. Began in 1973. Periodical. UR. Russian. qt. Akademiia Nauk SSR, G-19 Ul Krasikova 28/45, Moskva USSR. LC PN9.

OBSHCHESTVENNYE NAUKI ZA RUBEZHOM. SERIIA 7 : LITERATUROVEDENIE. VFOAT Literaturovedenie. VAT Obshchestvennye Nauki za Rubezhom. Seriia Sem : Literaturovedenie. Began in 1973. UR. Russian. qt. 1.00 Each Issue. Akademiia Nauk SSR, Ul Krasikova D 28/45, Moskva USSR. LC PN9.

OBSIDIAN. V. 1- Spring 1975-. 0360-6724. Periodical. US. English. sa. $8.50. Wayne State University, c/o A Aubert, Department English, Detroit MI 48202. Tel (313)577-3213. Ind/Abst MLA Int. Bibliogr. Books Artic. Mod. Lang. Lit., Index Am. Period. Verse, Index Book Rev. Humanit. LC PR1110.B5. DD 820.80896.

OBSIDIANE. Began in 1978. Periodical. FR. French. bm. $10.64. Association Loi, 1901 50 rue des Abbesses, 75018 Paris France. LC PN6024. DD 808.8.

O'CASEY ANNUAL (ATLANTIC HIGHLANDS, N.J.). (O'CASEY ANNUAL). No. 1-. 0278-5641. Periodical. US. English. an. Humanities Press, 171 1st Avenue, Atlantic Highlands NJ 07716. Tel (201)872-1441. Ed Robert G Lowery. LC PR6029.C33. DD 822.912. bk rev. An established forum for scholarship and criticism on a wide variety of topics in O'Casey studies.

OCCASIONAL PAPERS IN MODERN LANGUAGES. Main/Corp University of Hull. No. 1- 1965-. Monographic Series. UK. English. ir. University of Hull, Publications Committee, Hull HU6 7RX England. Ind/Abst MLA Int. Bibliogr. Books Artic. Mod. Lang. Lit.

OCCASIONAL PAPERS IN SLAVIC LANGUAGES AND LITERATURE. See Linguistics.

OCCIDENT. Founded 1881. 0029-7879. Periodical. US. English. sa. LC PS508.C6. DD 810.8.

OCHERK. 79-. Periodical. UR. Russian. 0.80. Sovremennik, Iartsevskaia 4 Izdatelstvo Sovremennik, 121351 Moskva G-351 Russia. LC PG3263.

ODENSE UNIVERSITY STUDIES IN SCANDINAVIAN LANGUAGES AND LITERATURES. See Linguistics.

ODI. V. 1- July 1972-. 0302-3044. Periodical. English (Chichewa). sa. $5.00. Editor ODI, Chancellor College, PO Box 380, Zomba Malawi. Ind/Abst MLA Int. Bibliogr. Books Artic. Mod. Lang. Lit. LC PL8014.M32. DD 820.8.

OEGUK MUNHAK. VFOAT The Literature Today. V. 1- (1984-Summer)-. Periodical. KO. Korean. qt. 3,500. Oeguk Munhak, 569 Socho-dong Kangnam-ku, Seoul Korea. LC PN9.

THE OHIO JOURNAL. V. 1- May 1973-. 0740-2139. Periodical. US. English. sa. $5.00. Ohio Journal, Ohio State University, Department of English, Columbus OH 43210. Tel (614)422-2242.

OHIOANA QUARTERLY. VFOAT Ohioana, of Ohio and Ohioans. V. 9, No. 3- Autumn 1966-. 0030-1248. Periodical. US. English. qt. $6.00. Martha Kinney Cooper, Ohioana Library Association, Ohio Departments Building/Room 1105, 65 South Front Street, Columbus OH 43215. Tel (614)466-3831. Ed James P Barry. Ind/Abst Abstr. Engl. Stud. bk rev. Circ 2,000. Articles about Ohio writers, literature, arts. Articles by Ohioans on literature and the arts. Reviews of books by Ohians or on Ohio Ohians. Ohioana.

OKINAWA KOKUSAI DAIGAKU BUNGAKUBU KIYO: EIBUNGAKKA-HEN. See Linguistics.

OLD ENGLISH NEWSLETTER. V. 1- Apr. 1967-. 0030-1973. Periodical. US. English. sa. $6.00. Old English Newsletter, Cemers Suny-Binghamton, Binghamton NY 13901. Tel (607)777-2130. Ed P E Szarmach. Ind/Abst MLA Int. Bibliogr. Books Artic. Mod. Lang. Lit., Years Work Eng. Stud. LC UNC. bk rev. Circ 900. Bibliography, reviews, news and notes about research and teaching in Anglo-Saxon studies.

OLD ENGLISH NEWSLETTER. SUBSIDIA. VFOAT Subsidia. Vol. 1-. 0739-8549. Monographic Series. US. English. ir. $3.00. Old English Newsletter, Cemers Suny-Binghamton, Binghamton NY 13901. Tel (607)777-2130. Ed P E Szarmach. LC UNC. DD 829.09. Circ 100. Research and teaching aids in Anglo-Saxon studies.

OLSON. No. 1- Spring 1974-. 0149-5437. US. English. sa. $10.00. University of Connecticut Library, Special Collections Department, Storrs CT 06268. Ind/Abst MLA Int. Bibliogr. Books Artic. Mod. Lang. Lit. LC PS3529.L655. DD 811.54.

ONS ERFDEEL. 1- 1957-. Periodical. BE. Dutch (articles in French). ir. $26.68. Stichting ons Erfdeel VZW, Murissonstraat 260, B-8530 Rekkem Belgium. Tel 056/41 12 01. Ind/Abst MLA Int. Bibliogr. Books Artic. Mod. Lang. Lit. bk rev. adv acc. Circ 10,000. (ctrl). Contains considerations about literature, arts of design, music, theatre, film and cabaret.

ONTARIO REVIEW. (THE ONTARIO REVIEW). No. 1- Fall 1974-. 0316-4055. Periodical. CN. English. sa. $8.00. Ontario Review Press, 9 Honey Brook Drive, Princeton NJ 08540. Tel (609)737-9542. Ed Raymond J Smith. Ind/Abst MLA Int. Bibliogr. Books Artic. Mod. Lang. Lit., Index Am. Period. Verse, Index Book Rev. Humanit. LC NX1. DD 700.5. adv acc. Circ 900. Publishes fiction, poetry, interviews, essays, photographs, graphics and translations, mainly by North American writers and artists.

THE OPEN CELL. V. 1- 1969-. 0030-3380. US. English. $3.00 4 Issues. The Open Cell, PO Box 52, Berkeley CA 94701. LC PS501. DD 810.80054.

OPEN LETTER. No. 1-9. 0048-1939. Periodical. CN. English. ty. Open Letter, 104 Lyndhurst Avenue, Toronto Ontario M5R 2Z7 Canada. Tel (416)922-9912.

OPEN READING. Second Series No. 1- Mar. 1972-. Periodical. US. English. ir. Sonomas State College, c/o Divison of Humanities, Rohnert Park CA 94928.

OPINION; LITERARY QUARTERLY. V. 1- Winter 1974-. Periodical. II. English. qt. A D Gorwala, 40 C Ridge Road, Bombay India. LC PR9494. DD 820.80954.

OPOVIDANNIA. 1981-. Periodical. UR. Ukrainian. an. 1.40. LC PG3940.

ORBIS LITTERARUM. Began in 1943. 0105-7510. Periodical. DK. Danish (French, English and German). qt. Munksgaard Ltd, 35 Norre Sogade, DK-1370 Copenhagen K Denmark. Tel 1.12.70.30. Ed Morten Nojgaard. Ind/Abst MLA Int. Bibliogr. Books Artic. Mod. Lang. Lit., Abstr. Engl. Stud., Annu. Bibliogr. Engl. Lang. Lit., Index Book Rev. Humanit., Years Work Eng. Stud. LC PN1. DD 809. (cum index). bk rev. adv acc. Circ 550. Study of European and American literature, concentrating on literary theory and the principles of literary history and criticism.

ORBIT. 1- 1966-. 0474-3326. US. English. ir. Harper and Row, 10 East 53rd Street, New York NY 10022. LC PZ1.A1. DD 808.8387605.

ORBIT (GAYA, INDIA). (ORBIT). 1982, No. 1-. Periodical. English. sa. $6.00. Dr H M Prasad, 296 Anugrahpuri, Gaya 823001 India. LC PR1.

ORCRIST. No. 1-. 0474-3369. US. English. ir. University of Wisconsin c/o R C West 1922 Madison Street, Madison WI 53711. Tel (608)255-3067. Ind/

Abst MLA Int. Bibliogr. Books Artic. Mod. Lang. Lit. LC PR6039.O32. DD 828.91209.

ORGAN. (THE ORGAN). V. 1- Fall 1976-. 0703-1246. Periodical. CN. English. ir. $3. Per No. The Organ, c/o L Mundwiler, 269 Church Avenue, Winnipeg Manitoba R2W 1B9 Canada. DD C810.80054.

ORGAN. (THE ORGAN). V. 1- Jan. 1977-. 0703-1254. Periodical. CN. English. ir. The Organ, Fraser Valley College, 34194 Marshall Road, Abbotsford British Columbia V25 5E4 Canada. DD C810.8092379.

ORIENS. *See* Linguistics.

ORIENTALIA LOVANIENSIA PERIODICA. *See* Linguistics.

ORIJIN SHOSETSU JIDAI. 1977- Edition. Japanese. ir. 1000. Orijin Shobo, c/o Tanimoto Building, 1-22 Shimo Meguro, 3-Chome, Meguro-Ku, Tokyo Japan. LC PL770.A1.

ORIZONT. 1st Year- Jan. 1964-. Periodical. RM. Romanian. wk. Ilexim Press, PO Box 1-136-1-137, Bucharest Romania. Ind/Abst MLA Int. Bibliogr. Books Artic. Mod. Lang. Lit. LC PC601.

ORTE. Periodical. German and/or Romansch. ir. 35.- Domestic, 40.- Foreign. W Bucher, R Egger, Postfach 2028, 8033 Zurich Switzerland. Tel (01)363 02 34. Ed Werner Bucher. LC PN849.S9. bk rev. adv acc. Circ 2,000. Modern, actual literature.

OSIRIS. No. 1- 1972-. 0095-019X. Periodical. US. English (French, German). sa. $7.00. OSIRIS MA, Box 297, Deerfield MA 01342. Tel (413)774-4027. Ed Andrea Moorhead. Ind/Abst Index Am. Period. Verse. adv acc. Circ 750. An international multi-lingual journal publishing contemporary poetry, prose, and essays in English, French, Spanish and Italian, and other texts in a bilingual format.

OSTERREICH IN GESCHICHTE UND LITERATUR. *See* History (General) - History of Europe.

OSTERREICHISCH-UNGARISCHE REVUE. 1.-5. Year., 1863-67. Periodical. German. ir.

OTHER VOICES (HIGHLAND PARK, ILL.). (OTHER VOICES). 8756-4696. Periodical. US. English. sa. $9.00. Other Voices, 820 Ridge Road, Highland Park IL 60035. Tel (312)831-4684. Ed Delores Weinberg. Circ 1,500. An independent market for quality fiction. We are dedicated to original fresh diverse stories and novel-experts, and to publishing new and established writers.

OTROK IN KNJIGA. 1- 1972-. Slovenian (summaries in English and German). ir. LC PN1009.A1.

OUTERBRIDGE. Vol. 1, No. 1 (Spring 1977)-). Periodical. US. English. an. $4.00. The College of Staten Island, A 323, Staten Island NY 10301. Tel (718)390-7654. Ed Charlotte Alexander. Circ 700. Crafted poems, stories; special issues (see newsletters); interest in new voices; celebrating 10th anniversary.

OXFORD GERMAN STUDIES. Began in 1966. 0078-7191. UK. English. an. 4.75. W A Meeuws Publisher, Oxford OX1 5DR England. Ind/Abst MLA Int. Bibliogr. Books Artic. Mod. Lang. Lit., Recent Publ. Artic. LC PT1. DD 830.9.

OXFORD SLAVONIC PAPERS. *See* History (General) - History of Europe.

PACIFIC MOANA QUARTERLY *CEASED.* VFOAT Pacific Quarterly. Vol. 3, No. 1 (Jan. 1978)-. 0110-3970. Periodical. NZ. English. qt. $90.00. Outrigger Publishers, PO Box 13-049, Hamilton New Zealand. Tel 55910. Ed Norman Simms. LC PN1. DD 805. bk rev. adv acc. Circ 600. Multi-cultural, multi-lingual interaction of new and older traditions and creative activities in all parts of the world especially Asia-Pacific rim. *New Quarterly Cave.*

PACIFIC QUARTERLY MOANA. VFOAT PQM. Vol. 7, No. 1 (Jan. 1982)-. 0110-3970. Periodical. US. English. qt. $30.00. Outrigger Publishers, 814 Broadway, New York NY 10003. Ind/Abst Abstr. Engl. Stud., MLA Int. Bibliogr. Books Artic. Mod. Lang. Lit. LC PN1. DD 808.8. *Pacific Moana Quarterly.*

PACIFIC REVIEW (SAN DIEGO, CALIF.). (PACIFIC REVIEW). Began in 1982. 0739-8360. US. English. an. $5.00. Campanile Press, San Diego State University, San Diego CA 92182. LC PS536.2. DD 810.8. *Pacific Poetry and Fiction Review, 0743-8648.*

PAEKSU MUNHAK. Periodical. Korean. ir. LC PL972.7.

PAIDEUMA. V. 1- Spring/Summer 1972-. 0090-5674. Periodical. US. English. ty. $24.00 Domestic, $28.00 Foreign. 305 EM, University of Maine at Orono, Orono ME 04469. Tel (207)581-3831. Ed Carroll F Terrell. Ind/Abst Abstr. Engl. Stud., MLA Int. Bibliogr. Books Artic. Mod. Lang. Lit., Index Book Rev. Humanit. LC PS3531.O82. DD 811.52. bk rev. Circ 685. A journal devoted to Ezra Pound scholarship.

PAKISTANI ADAB. V. 1- November 1974-. Periodical. Urdu. ir. 20.00. 141-A Sindhi Muslim Housing Society, Saidah Gazdar. Ed Saidah Gazdar. LC PK2151.

PALABRA (PHOENIX, ARIZ.). (LA PALABRA). Vol. 1, No. 1 (Spring 1979)-. 0277-1535. Periodical. US. Spanish. sa. $15.00. La Palabra, 1616 East Westchester Drive, Tempe AZ 85282. Tel (602)838-7237. Ed Justo S Alarcon. Ind/Abst MLA Int. Bibliogr. Books Artic. Mod. Lang. Lit. LC PQ7070. DD 860.8. bk rev. Chicano literature and criticism, Mexican-American, literary.

PALANTE. VFOAT Palante y Palante. 1- 1961?-. 0552-9395. Periodical. CU. Spanish. wk. $72.00. Empresa Ediciones Cubanas, Sub-Direccion Exportacion, Oreilly 407, Cicudad Habana Cuba. Circ 40,000. (ctrl). A satirical humor magazine. This 16-page tabloid is printed in two colors in photogravure. Caricatures, photos and texts of a humorous nature on the current national and international political, economic, cultural and sports scenes.

PAMANA. Periodical. English. ir. 100. Cultural Center of the Philippines, Roxas Boulevard, Manila Philippines. Tel 8323876. Ed Alejandrino G Hufana. LC NX1. DD 700.9599. adv acc. Circ 1,000. (ctrl). Literary works on poetry, short stories, essays, and plays depending on available materials.

PAMIETNIK LITERACKI. Vol. 1-. 0031-0514. Periodical. PL. Polish. qt. ARS Polona, Krakowskie, Przedmiescie 7, 00-068, Warsaw Poland. Ind/Abst MLA Int. Bibliogr. Books Artic. Mod. Lang. Lit., Am. Hist. Life, Hist. Abstr., Hist. Abst., Part B, Twent. Century Abstr., Hist. Abstr., Part A, Mod. Hist. Abstr. LC PG7001. DD 891.8509. *Pamietnik Towarzystwa Literackiego Imienia Adama Mickiewicza.*

PAMIETNIK LITERACKI (ZWIAZEK PISARZY POLSKICH NA OBCZYZNIE). (PAMIETNIK LITERACKI). V. 1-. Periodical. UK. Polish. 5.00 Single Issue. Polska Fundacja Kulturalna, 9 Charleville Road, London W14 9JL England. LC PG7367.

PAMIETNIK TEATRALNY. V. 1-. 0031-0522. Periodical. PL. Polish (summaries in French). qt. ARS Polona, Krakowskie Przedmiescie 7, 00-068 Warsaw Poland. LC PN2859.P6.

PANACHE. No. 1- 1965-. 0031-062X. US. English. $1.25 Single Copy. Panache Inc, 17 West 8th Street, New York NY 10010. LC PS501. DD 810.80054.

PANDORA. V. 1, No. 3-. 0275-519X. Periodical. US. English. ir. $10.00. Empire Books, c/o Jean Lorrah, Box 625, Murray KY 42071. Ed Jean Lorrah and Lois Wickstrom. bk rev. adv acc. Circ 700. (ctrl). Covers science fiction and fantasy, artwork, poetry, articles, and reviews. *Pandora, a Femzine, 0162-0142.*

PANJANDRUM. 0092-5535. Periodical. US. English. ir. $14.00. Panjandrum Press, 11321 Iowa Avenue Suite 1, Los Angeles CA 90025. Tel (213)477-8771. LC PN6099.6. DD 810.80054.

PANORAMA OF CZECH LITERATURE. 1 (1980)-. CS. English. ir. Panorama of Czech Literature, Halkova Ulice 1, 120 72 Prague 2 Czechoslovakia. Tel 24 54 49. Ed Ivo Kral and Jiri Deji. LC PG5145.E1. DD 891.8608. Circ 5,000. (ctrl). Excerpts from contemporary novels and poems.

PAO KAO WEN HSUEH HSUAN KAN. First published in 1984. Periodical. CC. Chinese. bm. 0.55. Hsin Hua Shu Tien, Cheng-Tu China. LC PL2614. DD 895.14508.

THE PAPERBACK PRICE GUIDE. 1st Ed. (1980)-. 0730-2932. US. English. Overstreet Publications, 780 Hunt Cliff Drive NW, Cleveland TN 37311. Ed K B Hancer. LC Z1033.P3. DD 018.40973.

PAPERS IN ROMANCE. V. 1- Spring 1979-. 0195-7260. Periodical. US. English. ty. $28.00. University of Washington, Department of Romance and Literature, Seattle WA 98195. Tel (206)545-2084. Ind/Abst MLA Int. Bibliogr. Books Artic. Mod. Lang. Lit. LC PC1. DD 440.05.

PAPERS ON FRENCH SEVENTEENTH CENTURY LITERATURE. VFOAT P.F.S.C.L., PFSCL. No. 1 (1973)-. 0343-0758. Periodical. US. English (French). sa. $12.00. Editor of PFSCL, University of Washington, Department of Comparative Literature, GN-32, Seattle WA 98195. Ind/Abst MLA Int. Bibliogr. Books Artic. Mod. Lang. Lit., Index Book Rev. Humanit. LC PQ243. DD 840.9004.

PAPERS ON LANGUAGE & LITERATURE. *See* Linguistics.

PARADIGMA. 1- Jan. 1977-. Periodical. Italian. ir. LC PQ4001.

PARERGON. No. 1- Dec. 1971-. 0313-6221. Periodical. NZ. English. an. 22.13. A N Z A M R S, c/o Mrs S Jack, History Department/University of Sydney, Sydney New South Wales 2006 Australia. Tel 692-2166. Ed Elizabeth Jeffries. Ind/Abst MLA Int. Bibliogr. Books Artic. Mod. Lang. Lit. LC CB351. DD 914.03105. Circ 350. Scholarly research articles on a wide range of medieval and Renaissance subjects, principally literature, languages, music, visual arts and history and politics. *ANZAMRS Bulletin.*

THE PARIS REVIEW. Began with Feb. 1953 issue. 0031-2037. US. English. qt. $16.00. Paris Review, 45-39 171 Place, Flushing NY 11358. Tel (718)539-7085. Ed George Ames Plimpton. Ind/Abst Abstr. Engl. Stud., Annu. Bibliogr. Engl. Lang. Lit., Index Am. Period. Verse, Humanit. Index. LC AP4. DD 051. adv acc. Circ 9,000. Publishes fiction and poetry of superlative quality. The interview series includes the most important contemporary writers discussing their work and the craft of writing in general.

PARLONS RAISON. VFOAT Parlons Raison (Meditations). No. 14, (Aug./Sept. 1983)-. 0821-3003. Periodical. CN. French. bm. Parlons Raison, CP 241, St-Lambert Quebec J4P 3N8 Canada. DD C848.5408. *Meditations. Francais, 0826-0842.*

PARNASSO. Vol. 1-. 0031-2320. Periodical. FI. Finnish. ir. Valiolehdet OY, Heitalahdenranta 13, Helsinki 18 Finland. Ind/Abst MLA Int. Bibliogr. Books Artic. Mod. Lang. Lit. LC PN9. DD 809. *Ajan Kirja, Nakoala.*

LA PAROLA LETTERARIA. 1-. Monographic Series. IT. Italian. ir. N Zanichelli Editore S P A, Via Irnerio 34, 40126 Bologna Italy.

PAROUSIES. 1-. 0302-9719. Greek, Modern. mo. 15.00. Smyrnis 1, T T 624 Athenai Greece. LC PA5050.

PARVAZ. Periodical. Urdu. ir. 10.00. Parvaz Pres, Books Market, Ludhyana India. LC PK2151.

PASSAGES. No. 1, (Autumn 1983)-. 0824-4510. Periodical. CN. French. qt. 15.00. A A C E, 86 Wellington Road, Sherbrooke Quebec J1H 5B8 Canada. Tel (819)821-2221. DD C840.809714. Circ 250. Our magazine is literary, and presents a selection of short novels or of poetry, written in French. The director of publication is Jean Civil.

PASSAGES NORTH. 1979. 0278-0828. Periodical. US. English. sa. $2.00. William Bonifas Fine Arts Center, 7th Street & 1st Avenue South, Escanaba MI 49829. Tel (906)786-3833. Ed Elinor Benedict. adv acc. Circ 2,000. High quality fiction and poetry in tabloid size with graphic arts.

LA PASSERELLE. 1- Winter 1969/70-. 0031-2711. Periodical. FR. French. qt. Pierre Bearn, 60 rue Monsieur le Prince, Paris France. Tel 326 22 73. Ed Pierre Bearn. LC AP20. Journal is written by one single author. Strictly literary. Has been defending a literary style and a philosophy that is very humaine. Sponsored by the Academie Francaise.

PAUL VALERY. Series/Titl La Revue des Lettres Modernes. 1- 1974-. FR. French. ir. 40.00. Lettres Modernes, 73 rue du Cardinal-Lemoine, 75005 CCP Paris 10671-19 France. LC PN3, PQ2643.A26. DD 848.91209 S, 848.91209.

PAUNCH. Began in 1963. 0031-3262. Periodical. US. English. sa. Arthur Efron, 123 Woodward Avenue, Buffalo NY 14214. Tel (716)836-7332. Ed Arthur Efron. Ind/Abst Abstr. Engl. Stud., MLA Int. Bibliogr. Books Artic. Mod. Lang. Lit., Index Am. Period. Verse. LC PN2. DD 805.

THE PAWN REVIEW. V. 1- Jan. 1976-. 0162-0061. Periodical. US. English. ir. Pawn Review, 2903 Windsor Road, Austin TX 78703. Tel (512)471-9113. Ed Thomas Zigal. bk rev. Circ 500. Literary.

PEBBLE. No. 1- Autumn 1968-. 0031-3696. Periodical. US. English. qt. The Best Cellar Press, 118 South Boswell Avenue, Crete NE 68333. Ind/Abst Index Am. Period. Verse. LC PS580. DD 811.5408.

THE PEMBROKE MAGAZINE. No. 1- 1969-. 0097-496X. US. English. an. $3.00. Pembroke State University, Box 60, Pembroke NC 28372. Tel

Literature

(919)521-4214. Ed Shelby Stephenson. LC PS1. DD 810.8005. bk rev. adv acc. **Circ** 500. Pembroke Magazine is open to writing.

PEMENANG ANTOLOGI HADIAH KARYA SASTRA. Malay. an. $3.00. LC PL5135.

PENSEE FRANCAISE. 1946. 0031-479X. Periodical. US. English. bm. La Pensee Francaise, 35 rue Gayet, 4200 Saint Etienne France. Tel 77 33 27 29. Contains poems, stories, short stories of French authors; read and appreciated all over the world.

PEQUOD. V. 1- Spring 1974-. 0149-0516. Periodical. US. English. sa. $6.00 (2 Years). Pequod, Box 491, Forest Knolls CA 94933. **Ind/Abst** Index Am. Period. Verse. LC PN6010.5. DD 808.8004.

PERSEA. V. 1- 1977-. US. English. $3.95. Persea Books Inc, 225 Lafayette Street, New York NY 10012. LC PN6010.5. DD 808.8.

THE PERSONAL HISTORY, ADVENTURES, EXPERIENCES & OBSERVATIONS OF PETER LEROY. (THE PERSONAL HISTORY, ADVENTURES, EXPERIENCES & OBSERVATIONS OF PETER LEROY : A SERIAL NOVEL BY ERIC KRAFT). **VFOAT** Personal History, Adventures, Experiences and Observations of Peter Leroy. Vol. 1, No. 1-. 0743-6769. US. English. qt. $4.95 (Single Issue). Apple-Wood Books, Box 2870, Cambridge MA 02139. LC PS3561.R22. DD 813.54.

PERSONNEL LITERATURE. V. 1 1941-. 0031-5753. Periodical. US. English. mo. Superintendent of Documents, Government Printing Office, Washington DC 20402. Tel (202)783-3238. LC Z7164.C81, HF5549.A2. DD 016.3501. **NLM** Z 7164.C81 P467. Index in last issue of volume - attached.

PERSPECTIVES ON CONTEMPORARY LITERATURE. Began with issue for May 1975. 0098-7301. Periodical. US. English. an. $7.50. University Press of Kentucky, Lexington KY 40506-0024. **Ind/Abst** MLA Int. Bibliogr. Books Artic. Mod. Lang. Lit.

PERSUASIONS (VICTORIA, B.C.). (PERSUASIONS). Issue No. 2 (Dec. 16, 1980)-. 0821-0314. CN. English. an. $8.00. Jane Austen Society of North America, 1575 Rockland Avenue, Victoria British Columbia V8S 1W4 Canada. Tel (604)598-8458. Ed Joan Austen Keigh. **Ind/Abst** MLA Int. Bibliogr. Books Artic. Mod. Lang. Lit. DD 823.7. **Circ** 2,000. (ctrl) A journal devoted to Jane Austen, her life, literature and times.

PETIT ALMANACH DES LETTRES. See Yearbooks, Almanacs, Directories.

PHALGU : PHALGU SAHITYA SAMSADARA MUKHAPATRA. Periodical. II. Oriya. ir. 4.00. Phalgu Sahitya Sansad, Nehru Nagar Berhampur 3 India. LC PK2574.5.

PHILOMEL. Spring 1981-. Periodical. US. English. an. $2.00. Philomathean Society, University of Pennsylvania Box H College Hall, Philadelphia PA 19104. Tel (215)898-8907. **Circ** 4,000. (ctrl) A literary omnibus of fiction, poetry, essays of a general nature, and interviews. Era (Philomathean Society of The University of Pennsylvania).

PHILOSOPHICAL SPECULATIONS IN SCIENCE FICTION & FANTASY. **VFOAT** Philosophical Speculations. **VAT** Philosophical Speculations in Science Fiction and Fantasy. Vol. 1, No. 1 (Mar. 1981)-. 0276-0886. Periodical. US. English. qt. Burning Bush Publications, PO Box 7708, Newark DE 19711.

PHILOSOPHY AND LITERATURE. See Philosophy.

PHOENIX. See Linguistics.

PISATEL I ZHIZN. No. 1-. 0554-2065. UR. Russian. ir. LC PG2900. DD 891.709.

PLANET CEASED. No. 1-49/50. 0048-4288. Periodical. UK. English. bm. **Ind/Abst** Abstr. Engl. Stud.

PLAYS IN PROCESS. See Theater.

PLOUGHSHARES. Began with Sept. 1971 Issue. 0048-4474. Periodical. US. English. qt. $14.00. Ploughshares, PO Box 529, Cambridge MA 02139. Tel (617)926-9875. Ed Dewitt Henry and Susannah Lee. **Ind/Abst** MLA Int. Bibliogr. Books Artic. Mod. Lang. Lit., Index Am. Period. Verse. LC NX1. DD 700.904. bk rev. adv acc. **Circ** 4,000. New poetry, fiction essays edited on a revolving basis by professional writers to reflect different and contrasting points of view. Each issue is a quality paperback averaging 250 pages.

PLUCKED CHICKEN. 1- Nov. 1977-. Periodical. US. English. qt. $10.00. Editor/Will Peterson, PO Box 160, Morgantown WV 26505. LC PS501. DD 810.8.

PODIUM. 1- Apr. 1971-. Periodical. German. ir.

PODVIG (PERIODICAL). (PODVIG). Periodical. UR. Russian. LC PG3273.

POE STUDIES. V. 4- June 1971-. 0090-5224. US. English. sa. $12.00. Washington State University Press, Office of Comptroller, Pullman WA 99164. Tel (509)335-3518. Ed Fred Bohm. **Ind/Abst** Engl. Stud., MLA Int. Bibliogr. Books Artic. Mod. Lang. Lit., Index Book Rev. Humanit., Years Work Eng. Stud. LC PS2631. DD 818.309. bk rev. **Circ** 530. Devoted to the scholarly inquiry of the literature of and about Edgar Allan Poe. Poe Newsletter, 0032-1877.

POESIE UND WISSENSCHAFT. Vol. 1- 1967-. 0554-3762. Monographic Series. GW. German. ir. Lothar Stiehm Verlag, Postfach 105802/ Hausackerweg 16, 6900 Heidelberg West Germany. Tel 06221/21354. Ed Lothar Stiehm. **Ind/Abst** MLA Int. Bibliogr. Books Artic. Mod. Lang. Lit. Literature studies and comparative literature.

POETICA. Vol. 1- Jan. 1967-. 0303-4178. Periodical. NE. German. ir. $72.50. BR Gruner BV, Nieuwe Herengracht 31, 1011 RM Amsterdam Netherlands. Tel 20-264371. Ed Karl Maurer. **Ind/Abst** Abstr. Engl. Stud., MLA Int. Bibliogr. Books Artic. Mod. Lang. Lit., Index Book Rev. Humanit., Sociol. Abstr., Lang. Lang. Behav. Abstr. LC P3. bk rev. adv acc. **Circ** 750. (ctrl) Interdisciplinary studies in international literature including articles on general problems of theory, criticism and history plus original contributions from German, English, Romance, Slavonic and classical literature.

POETS AND AUTHORS. 0149-9831. Periodical. US. English. an. Harlo Press, 16721 Hamilton Avenue, Detroit MI 48203. Tel (313)864-1529. LC PS536.2. DD 810.80054. Harlo's Anthology of Modern-Day Poets and Authors, 0090-2632.

PORTICO. V. 1-5, No. 3/4. 0702-8512. Periodical. CN. English. qt. Peerless Publications Ltd, Manor House, Bank Square Chepstow, Gwent South Wales United Kingdom. DD C810.8092379.

PORTLAND REV. (PORTLAND REVIEW). Vol. 27, No. 1 (Fall/Winter Quarter 1981)-. Periodical. US. English (text in some selections in their original language). ty. Portland Review, PO Box 751, Portland OR 97207. **Ind/Abst** Index Am. Period. Verse. International Portland Review, 0278-2952.

POTBOILER. Vol. 1, No. 1 (July 1980)-. 0228-3344. Periodical. CN. English. ir. $2.25 Each Number. Potboiler Magazine, 8741 Bennett Road, Richmond British Columbia V6Y 1N6 Canada. DD C813.0876.

POTTERSFIELD PORTFOLIO. (THE POTTERSFIELD PORTFOLIO). No. 1- 1979/80-. 0226-0840. CN. English. an. $2.60 Each Number. Pottersfield Press, RR 2, Porters Lake Nova Scotia B0J 2S0 Canada. **Ind/Abst** Index Am. Period. Verse. DD C810.809715.

POUR TA BELLE GUEULE D'AHURI. (POUR TA BELLE GUEULE D'AHURI : SCIENCE-FICTION, FANTASTIQUE, BANDES DESSINEES). Vol. 1, No. 1-. 0227-4485. Periodical. CN. French. bm. $1.75 Each Number, $10.00 for Six Numbers. Pour ta Belle Gueule d'Ahuri, 411-4120 Chemin Ste-Foy, Ste-Foy Quebec G1V 1S5 Canada. DD 808.83876.

THE POWYS NEWSLETTER. 1- 1970-. US. English. ir. Colgate University Press, 303 Lawrence Colgate University, Hamilton NY 13346. **Ind/Abst** MLA Int. Bibliogr. Books Artic. Mod. Lang. Lit. LC PR6031.O867. DD 828.91209.

PRACE POLONISTYCZNE. Began in 1937. 0079-4791. PL. Polish. an. ARS Polona, Krakowskie Przedmiescie 7, 00-068 Warsaw Poland. **Ind/Abst** MLA Int. Bibliogr. Books Artic. Mod. Lang. Lit. LC PG7001. DD 891.8509. (cum index).

PRADALGE. **VFOAT** Literaturos Metrastis Pradalge. 1- 1964-. Periodical. UK. Lithuanian. **Ind/Abst** MLA Int. Bibliogr. Books Artic. Mod. Lang. Lit. LC PG8713.

PRAGUE STUDIES IN ENGLISH. English. ir. University Karlovy, 116 38 Praha 1 Nam, Krasnoarmejcu 1 Ceskoslovensko. Prispevky k Dejinam Reci a Literatury Anglicke.

PRAIRIE FIRE (WINNIPEG, MAN.). (PRAIRIE FIRE). Vol. 4, No. 3 (Jan./Feb 1983)- - Whole No. 23-. 0821-1124. Periodical. CN. English. 20.00 Domestic, 24.00 Foreign. Prairie Fire, 374 Donald Street/3rd Floor, Winnipeg Manitoba R3B 2J2 Canada. Tel (204)943-9066. Ed Andris Taskans. DD C810.80054. bk rev. adv acc. **Circ** 900. Publishes poetry, fiction, drama, essays, book reviews, interviews and artwork. It is concerned primarily with the contemporary writing of Canada's prairie provinces. Writers News Manitoba, 0707-3852.

PRAIRIE JOURNAL OF CANADIAN LITERATURE. (THE PRAIRIE JOURNAL OF CANADIAN LITERATURE). No. 1 (Fall 1983)-. 0827-2921. Periodical. CN. English. sa. 12.00. Prairie Journal of Canadian Literature, PO Box G997 Station G, Calgary Alberta T3A 3G2 Canada. Ed A Burke. DD C810.809712. bk rev. **Circ** 200. (ctrl) Poems, short fiction, one-act plays and critical work promoting Canadian literature, prairie writers and western presses, new and established authors welcome. Also interviews with authors.

PRAIRIE SCHOONER. V. 1- Jan. 1927-. 0032-6682. Periodical. US. English. qt. $15.00. Prairie Schooner, 201 Andrews, Department of English, Lincoln NE 68588. Tel (402)472-1800. Ed Hugh Luke and Hilda Raz. **Ind/Abst** MLA Int. Bibliogr. Books Artic. Mod. Lang. Lit., Annu. Bibliogr. Engl. Lang. Lit., Index Am. Period. Verse, Index Book Rev. Humanit., Book Rev. Index, Humanit. Index. LC AP2. DD 061. bk rev. adv acc. **Circ** 2,000. Fiction, poetry, essays, interviews, articles and reviews.

PRAKAMPANA. Jhokka 1- April 2030- 1973-. Periodical. Nepali. ir. 31.00 Each Issue. Premaprasada Ligala, Pulchok Butabal, Butavala Nepal. LC PK2598.A2.

PRAKASITA MANA. Periodical. Hindi. ir. 9.00. Karyalaya, 25 Dariba Kalan Delhi-6, Dili India. LC PK2030.

PRANGANA. V. 1- Vaisasha/Jeshtha 2030- 1973-. Periodical. Nepali. ir. 8.00. Ramesa Tivari, 17/350 Tangal Gairidhara, Kathamadaum India. Ed Ramesa Tivari, LC PK2598.A2.

PRANGANA (POKHARA, NEPAL). (PRANGANA). Periodical. NP. Nepali. qt. 3.00. 3/101 Tersapatti, Pokhara Nepal. LC PK2598.A2.

PRASADA (CALCUTTA, INDIA). (PRASADA). **VFOAT** Prashad. Periodical. Bengali. mo. 108.00. Prashad Press and Publications, 42 Indian Mirror Street, Calcutta 70001 India. Tel 24-3184. Ed Pronob Kumar Bose. bk rev. adv acc. **Circ** 4,200. (ctrl). Non political, socio-economic novels.

PRAYASA. V. 1- 2029- 1972-. Nepali. ir. 1.00 Each Issue. Tinpaini Biratnagar-2, Kathamadaum Nepal. LC PK2598.A2.

PRESENCE FRANCOPHONE CEASED. No. 1-25. 0048-5195. Periodical. CN. French. sa. 16.00. Universite de Sherbrooke, Sherbrooke Quebec J1K 2R1 Canada. Tel (819)821-7266. Ed Louis Painchaud. **Ind/Abst** MLA Int. Bibliogr. Books Artic. Mod. Lang. Lit. bk rev. adv acc. **Circ** 500. Literature and French language written throughout the world, sociological aspects, comparative literature, the different French language.

PRETEXTES (CEGEP DE TROIS-RIVIERES. SERVICES PEDAGOGIQUES). (PRETEXTES). April 1981-. 0711-4966. Periodical. CN. French. ir. Free to Members. Sevice d'Information du Cegep de Trois-Rivieres, 3500 rue de Courval, Trois-Rivieres Quebec G9A 5E6 Canada. DD C840.8092375.

PREVIEW. No. 1-23. 0381-0135. Periodical. US. English. Kraus Reprint, Route 100, Millwood NY 10546. LC PR9194. DD 810.8.

PRIAMURE MOE. UR. Russian. 1.05. Khabarocshoe Knizhnoe Izd-Vo, UL IM Lenina 181, Russia. LC PG3504.A48.

PRIMAVERA. 1975-. 0364-7609. US. English. ir. $5.00. Salsedo Press, c/o University Feminist Organization, Ida Noyes Hall, 1212 East 59th Street, Chicago IL 60637. **Ind/Abst** Index Am. Period. Verse. LC PS508.W7. DD 810.809287. adv acc. **Circ** 1,000. Poetry, fiction and graphics focussing on women's experiences.

Literature

PRISM INTERNATIONAL. V. 4- Summer 1964-. 0032-8790. Periodical. CN. English. qt. $14.00. Prism International, Department of Creative Writing, University of British Columbia, East 462 1866 Main Hall, Vancouver British Columbia V6T 1W5 Canada. Tel (604)228-2514. Ed Steve Noyes. Circ 850. Publishes contemporary poetry, fiction, and drama from around the world. *Prism*, 0380-2345.

PRISMAL/CABRAL. VFOAT Cabral. Began with No. 3/4 (Spring 1979) issue. 0738-8667. Periodical. US. Spanish (text in Portuguese or English). sa. $20.00. University of Maryland, Department of Spanish and Portuguese, N Levinson, College Park MD 20742. Tel (301)454-4305. Ed Emma Bvenocentora. Ind/Abst MLA Int. Bibliogr. Books Artic. Mod. Lang. Lit. LC PQ7082.5. DD 860.0998. bk rev. adv acc. Circ 150. Literary magazine published by the graduate students of the University of Maryland and that includes original prose, poetry and literary criticism. *Prismal*.

PRIZE ARTICLES : THE BENJAMIN FRANKLIN MAGAZINE AWARDS. 1954-. US. English. an. Ballantine Books, 101 5th Avenue, New York NY 10003. Ed Llewellyn Miller. LC PS659. DD 818.5082.

PRIZE COLLEGE STORIES. 1961-. 0079-5445. US. English. an. LC PZ1.

PRIZE STORIES. 1947-. 0079-5453. US. English. an. $16.95. Doubleday & Company Inc, Direct Mail Order Division, 501 Franklin Avenue, Garden City NY 11530. LC PZ1. DD 813.0108. *O. Henry Memorial Award Prize Stories*.

PROBLEMY ISTORII KRITIKI I POETIKI REALIZMA. Periodical. UR. Russian. 1.00. Kuibyshevskii, Gosudarstvennyi Universitet, G Kuibyshev, Ul Adad Pavlova 1, Kuibyshev Russian SFSR. LC PG2949.

PROBLEMY METODA I ZHANRA. Periodical. UR. Russian. 1.57 Each Issue. Izd-Vo Tomsogo Universiteta, 29 Ul Nikitina 17, Tomsk USSR. LC PG2900.

PROBLEMY SOVETSKOI LITERATURY, METOD, ZHANR, KHARAKTER. Vol. 1-. Periodical. UR. Russian. 1.00 Each Issue. LC PG3021.

PROCEEDINGS OF THE AMERICAN ACADEMY AND INSTITUTE OF ARTS AND LETTERS. See The Arts (General).

PROCEEDINGS OF THE COMPARATIVE LITERATURE SYMPOSIUM - TEXAS TECH UNIVERSITY. Main/Corp Texas Tech University. Interdepartmental Committee on Comparative Literature. V. 3- 1970-. 0084-9103. Monographic Series. US. English. ir. Texas Tech University Library, Tech Press Sales Office, Box 4240, Lubbock TX 79409. Tel (806)742-1569. Ed Wendell M Aycock. Ind/Abst MLA Int. Bibliogr. Books Artic. Mod. Lang. Lit., Abstr. Engl. Stud., Years Work Eng. Stud. Circ 1,000. Proceedings of the Comparative Literature Symposium, Texas Tech University, results from annual symposia organized by Texas Tech University's Interdepartmental Committee on Comparative Literature. *Proceedings of the Comparative Literature Symposium - Texas Technological College.*

PROCEEDINGS OF THE ... CONVENTION - DOROTHY L. SAYERS HISTORICAL AND LITERARY SOCIETY. Main/Corp Dorothy L. Sayers Historical and Literary Society. Convention. 1981-. 0143-0610. UK. English. Dorothy L Sayers, Historical and Literary Society, Roslyn House, Witham Essex England. LC PR6037.A95. DD 823.912. *Proceedings of the Seminar*.

PROCEEDINGS OF THE LEEDS PHILOSOPHICAL AND LITERARY SOCIETY, LITERARY AND HISTORICAL SECTION. See Philosophy.

PROCEEDINGS OF THE ROYAL IRISH ACADEMY. Main/Corp Royal Irish Academy. 3rd Ser. V. 1, No. 1 (Dec. 1888)-. IE. English. an. Proceedings of the Royal Irish Academy, 19 Dawson Street, Dublin 2 Ireland. *Proceedings of the Royal Irish Academy.* Science Literature and Antiquities.

PROFIL MIT ECCO. See Bibliographies.

PROOFTEXTS. VAT Proof Texts. Vol. 1, No. 1 (Jan. 1981)-. 0272-9601. Periodical. US. English. ty. $32.00. Johns Hopkins University Press, 701 West 40th Street/Suite 275, Baltimore MD 21211. Tel (301)338-6987. Ed Alan Mintz and David Roskies. Ind/Abst MLA Int. Bibliogr. Books Artic. Mod. Lang. Lit., Old Testam. Abstr. LC PJ5001. DD 892.409. bk rev. adv acc. Circ 1,045. Encompasses literary approaches to classical Jewish sources, the study of modern Hebrew and Yiddish literature, and Jewish writing in other languages.

DE PROPRIETATIBUS LITTERARUM. SERIES DIDACTICA. Began with 1, 1972. Periodical. English. ir. Walter de Gruyter, 200 Sawmill River Road, Hawthorne NY 10532. Tel (914)747-0110. Ind/Abst MLA Int. Bibliogr. Books Artic. Mod. Lang. Lit.

DE PROPRIETATIBUS LITTERARUM. SERIES MAIOR. 1- 1967-. 0070-3060. Monographic Series. NE. English (French and German). ir. Mouton, PO Box 482, Hague The Netherlands.

DE PROPRIETATIBUS LITTERARUM. SERIES PRACTICA. 1-. 0070-3087. Monographic Series. English and German. ir. Walter de Gruyter Inc, 200 Sawmill River Road, Hawthorne NY 10532. Tel (914)747-0110. Ind/Abst MLA Int. Bibliogr. Books Artic. Mod. Lang. Lit.

PROSE STUDIES. Vol. 3, No. 1 (May 1980)-. 0144-0357. Periodical. UK. English. ty. Ind/Abst MLA Int. Bibliogr. Books Artic. Mod. Lang. Lit., Index Book Rev. Humanit. LC PR750. DD 828.08. *Prose Studies, 1800-1900*.

PROSPICE. Vol. 1- 1973-. 0308-2776. Periodical. UK. English. sa. 6.00 Sterling, 10.00 US, 12.50 Canada. Johnston Green Distribution Ltd, PO Box 1 Portree, Isle of Skye 1V519BT Scotland. Tel (44)478252 257. Ed J C R Green and Roger Elkin. bk rev. adv acc. Circ 1,000. Scotland's international literary magazine.

PROUST RESEARCH ASSOCIATION NEWSLETTER. No. 1- Mar. 1969-. 0048-5659. US. English (French). ir. Free. University of Kansas Proust Research Association, Department of French and Italian, Lawrence KS 66045. Tel (913)864-3388. Ed J Theodore Johnson Jr. Ind/Abst MLA Int. Bibliogr. Books Artic. Mod. Lang. Lit. LC PQ2631.R63. DD 843.912. bk rev. Circ 300. Aims to provide a forum for the discussion of problems relating to current research on Marcel Proust.

PROZAH. Periodical. IS. Hebrew. ir. 180.00. Prozah, Box 6072, Tel Aviv Israel. LC PJ5038.

PUBLICACIONES. SERIES MINOR. See Linguistics.

PUBLICATIONS - DAKAR. UNIVERSITE. SECTION DE LANGUES ET LITTERATURES. See Linguistics.

PUBLICATIONS. EXTRA SERIES. Main/Corp Early English Text Society. No. 1-126. 1867-1920. Periodical. English. ir.

PUBLICATIONS IN LANGUAGE AND LITERATURE. Main/Corp Washington State University. V. 1-. Monographic Series. US. English. ir. University of Washington Press, Seattle WA 98105.

PUBLICATIONS OF THE ENGLISH GOETHE SOCIETY. V. 1-14, 1886-1912. Monographic Series. UK. English. an. $22.00. University College of London, English Goethe Society, Department of German/Gower Street, London WC1 England. Tel 01-387 7050. Ind/Abst MLA Int. Bibliogr. Books Artic. Mod. Lang. Lit. LC PT2046. (cum index).

PUBLICATIONS OF THE MODERN LANGUAGE ASSOCIATION OF AMERICA. See Linguistics.

PUBLICATIONS - POITIERS. UNIVERSITE. CENTRE DE RECHERCHES LATINO-AMERICAINES. Main/Corp Poitiers. Universite. Centre de Recherches Latino-Americaines. 1975-. Monographic Series. English (French or Portuguese). ir. LC PQ7081.A1. DD 860.

PUBLISHED. Began 1985?. 0882-7400. Periodical. US. English. mo. $7.50 Domestic, $10.00 Foreign. Platen Publishing Company, 14240 Beledsoe Street, Sylmar CA 91342. DD 810.

PUERTO DEL SOL. See Literary and Political Reviews.

PULP VOICES, OR, SCIENCE FICTION VOICES. Series/Titl The Milford Series. Popular Writers of Today. VFOAT Science Fiction Voices. 0747-7600. US. English. Borgo Press, PO Box 2845, San Bernardino CA 92406. Tel (714)884-5813. Ed R Reginald. LC PS374.S35. DD 813.087609. Circ 1,000. A collection of interviews with a group of writers or litterateurs, connected with a particular sub-genre or time period. *Science Fiction Voices*, 0164-1093.

PULS (LONDON, ENGLAND). (PULS). 0143-5531. Periodical. UK. Polish. qt. $15.00. Puls Publications, BCM Box 697, London WXIN 3XX United Kingdom. LC PG7001.

PUNCH. VFOAT London Charivari. V. 1- (No. 1-). 0033-4278. Periodical. UK. English. wk. 61.30. Punch Publishers Ltd, Watling Street Bletchley, Milton Keynes MK2 2BW England. Tel 0908-71981. Ed Alan Coren. Ind/Abst Book Rev. Index, Media Rev. Dig. LC AP101. DD 827.008. adv acc. Circ 78,000. An absorbing magazine full of English humour and full of fine literary comment by the best English writers.

PUNDIT. (THE PUNDIT). June 1981-. 0712-1318. Periodical. CN. English. mo. $18.00. International Save the Pun Foundation, PO Box 5040, Terminal A, Toronto Ontario M5W 1N4 Canada. DD C818.5407.

PURANAM. VFOAT Purana. Began publication with July 1959 issue. Periodical. II. English and Sanskrit. sa. $7.16. All-India Kashiraj Trust, Fort Ramnagar, Varanasi UP India. LC PK2918.P8.

PURO CUENTO (BOGOTA, COLOMBIA). (PURO CUENTO : REVISTA DE IRREALIDADES). No. 1 (1981)-. Periodical. Spanish. bm. Apartado Aereo, 666 Bogota Columbia. Ed D Sanchez Juliao.

THE PUSHCART PRIZE. (THE PUSHCART PRIZE. . . : BEST OF THE SMALL PRESSES). 1976/77-. US. English. an. $25.00. Pushcart Press, PO Box 380, Wainscott NY 11975. Tel (516)324-9300. Ed Bill Henderson. LC PS501. DD 810.80054. Circ 3,000. An anthology of the best from our small presses - annual.

PYNCHON NOTES. 1 (Oct. 1979)-. 0278-1891. Periodical. US. English. ty. $6.00. John M Krafft, Suffolk County Community College, Department of English, Brentwood NY 11717. Tel (516)434-6776. Ed John M Krafft and Khachig Tololyan. Ind/Abst Abstr. Engl. Stud., MLA Int. Bibliogr. Books Artic. Mod. Lang. Lit. LC PS3531.Y53. DD 813.54. bk rev. adv acc. Circ 250. Dedicated to all aspects of Pynchon's works, and their relations to the contexts of contemporary, American, and comparative literature.

QAUMI RAJ. V. 1- Jan. 26, 1974-. Periodical. Urdu. ir. 5.00. Dairiktoret Janral af Informeshan aind Pablik Rileshanz, Bombay 400032 India. LC PK2151.

QUADERNI DI CRITICA. Yearly V. 1- Jan. 1973-. Periodical. ir. 6000. V Cicerone 28, Roma 00193 Italy. LC PN5.

QUADERNI D'ITALIANISTICA. V. 1- Spring 1980-. 0226-8043. Periodical. CN. English (text also in Italian). ir. Free to members, 13.00 US/Canada, 25.00 all other countries. Canadian Society for Italian Studies, L G Sbrocchi, Department of Slavic Studies and Modern Languages, University of Ottawa, Ottawa Ontario K1N 6N5 Canada. Ind/Abst MLA Int. Bibliogr. Books Artic. Mod. Lang. Lit. DD 850.9.

QUADERNI PORTOGHESI. 1- Spring 1977-. 0391-3090. Periodical. Italian (summaries in English and Portuguese). ir. $12.00. Giardini, C C Postale N 22-11528, Piso Italy. Ind/Abst MLA Int. Bibliogr. Books Artic. Mod. Lang. Lit. LC PQ9009. DD 869.05.

QUADERNI (UNIVERSITA DEGLI STUDI DI LECCE. ISTITUTO DI LINGUE E LETTERATURE STRANIERE). (QUADERNI). N. 1 (1979)-. Periodical. English (French, German, and Italian). an. LC PN1. DD 809.

QUARRY. V. 1- Spring 1952-. 0033-5266. Periodical. CN. English (includes some text in French). qt. $12.38. Quarry Press, Box 1061, Kingston Ontario K7L 4Y5 Canada. Tel (613)544-5400. Ed Bob Hilderley. Ind/Abst Can. Period. Index, Index Book Rev. Humanit. bk rev. adv acc. Circ 900. New poetry, fiction, book reviews by established and emerging Canadian and American writers.

QUARRY CEASED. 1976-1980/82. English. ir. Craighall News, Jan Smuts Avenue, Craighall Park, Johannesburg 2196 South Africa. LC PR9364. DD 820.

QUARRY WEST. No. 5- 1976. 0736-4628. Periodical. US. English. sa. $6.00. Quarry West, Porter College, U C S X, Santa Cruz CA 95064. Tel (408)429-2155. Ed Ken Weisner. LC PS501. DD 810.8. bk rev. Circ 500. Poetry, short stories, articles,

Literature

reviews, and art. *Quarry (Santa Cruz, Calif.),* 0033-5266.

QUARTERLY CHECK-LIST OF LITERARY HISTORY. V. 1- Oct. 1958-. 0033-5398. Periodical. US. English. qt.

QUARTERLY WEST. No. 1 (Fall 1976)- (Fall 1976). 0194-4231. Periodical. US. English. sa. $6.50. University of Utah, 312 Olpin Union, Salt Lake City UT 84112. Tel (801)581-3938. Ed Wyn Cooper. **Ind/Abst** Index Am. Period. Verse. **LC** PS501. **DD** 810.8. bk rev. adv acc. **Circ** 1,000. We print the very best poetry and fiction we can find, we also print book reviews and interviews with writers, and essays.

QUEST FOR A COMMON DENOMINATOR. V. 1- Spring 1977-. 0700-5482. Periodical. CN. English. $1.25 Each Number. M Drage, RR 1, Inwood Ontario N0N 1K0 Canada. **DD** C810.80054.

QUEST STAR. VAT Quest/Star. Vol. 4, No. 1 (Oct. 1981)- - Issue No. 13-. 0277-5360. Periodical. US. English. mo. MW Communications, 247 Fort Pitt Boulevard, Pittsburgh PA 15222. **LC** P96.S34. **DD** 813.087609. *Questar, 0270-9252.*

LA QUINZAINE LITTERAIRE. VFOAT Quinzaine. No. 1- 15 Mar. 1966-. 0048-6493. Periodical. FR. French. sm. $44.70. La Quinzaine Litteraire, 43 rue du Temple, Paris 4E France. Tel (1) 887 48 58. **Ind/Abst** MLA Int. Bibliogr. Books Artic. Mod. Lang. Lit. **LC** AP20. **DD** 054.

QUOTE. Began in 1940. 0273-6705. Periodical. US. English. sm. $24.00 Domestic, $26.00 Canada. Quote Publications Company, 148 International Boulevard, 565 Sussex Place, Atlanta GA 30303. **LC** PN6081. **DD** 081. Index published separately - free - automatically sent.

RADDLE MOON. (THE RADDLE MOON). 1-. 0826-5909. Periodical. CN. English. sa. $10.00. The Raddle Moon, Box 3, Department of Creative Writing, University of Victoria, PO Box 1700, Victoria British Columbia V8W 2Y2 Canada. **DD** 808.8004. *From an Island, 0706-8093.*

RADICAL REVIEWER. (THE RADICAL REVIEWER). Vol. 1, No. 1 (June 1980)-. 0229-0340. Periodical. CN. English. ir. The Radical Reviewer, c/o Kinesis, 1090 West 7th Avenue, Vancouver British Columbia V6H 1B3 Canada. **DD** 809.89287.

RADIO FREE RAIN FOREST. No. 1- Dec. 1968-. 0319-373X. CN. English. **DD** C810.80054.

RADUGA. V. 1- 1951-. 0033-8591. Periodical. UR. Russian. mo. $38.00. Victor Kamkin Inc (74420), 12224 Parklawn Drive, Rockville MD 20852. Tel (301)881-5973. **Ind/Abst** MLA Int. Bibliogr. Books Artic. Mod. Lang. Lit.

RAIN FOREST (PORT ALBERNI, B.C.). (RAIN FOREST). Spring 1979-. 0712-7871. CN. English. an. $2.00 Each Volume. Rain Forest, c/o Dorothy Allen, Rain Forest Publishing Committee, Rural Route 1 Port Alberni, British Columbia V9Y 7L5 Canada. **DD** C810.80971134.

RAJASTHAN UNIVERSITY STUDIES IN ENGLISH. Main/Corp Jaipur, India (Rajasthan). University of Rajasthan. English. ir. **Ind/Abst** MLA Int. Bibliogr. Books Artic. Mod. Lang. Lit. **LC** PR1. **DD** 820.9.

HE RAMA. Periodical. Hindi. ir. 10.00. Valmiki Asrama, Kingsway Camp, Delhi 110009 India. **LC** PK2030.

RAMPIKE MAGAZINE. Vol. 1, Issue 1-. 0711-7647. Periodical. CN. English. ty. $9.28. Rampike Magazine, 95 Rivercrest Road, Toronto Ontario M6S 4H7 Canada. Tel (416)767-6713. Ed Karl Jirgens. **DD** C810.80054. adv acc. **Circ** 2,000. (ctrl). Contemporary art and writing by internationally renowned talents; featuring sophisticated media experimentation within a thematic format.

RAM'S HORN (HANOVER, N.H.). (THE RAM'S HORN). 0272-2747. Periodical. US. English. qt. $15.00. Language Outreach Education, Dartmouth College, Hanover NH 03755. **LC** PB35. **DD** 418.0071.

THE RANDOM REVIEW. 1982-. US. English. an. Random House, 201 East 50th Street, New York NY 10022. Ed Gary Fisketjon and Jonathan Galassi. **DD** 810.9005.

RAPPORTI. Periodical. Italian. ir. 5.000. Argileto, C.C. Postale N 1/28973, Intestato ad Argileto Editore, Rome Italy. **LC** PQ4001.

RAPPORTS HET FRANSE BOEK. VFOAT Franse Boek. 41.- Vol. Periodical. NE. Dutch (text in French). qt. 55.00. Vereniging Bevordering Studie Frans, c/o Dr J J Spa/Prns Hendrikkade 83, 1501 AG Zaandam Netherlands. Tel 075-160024. Ed S A Varga. bk rev. adv acc. **Circ** 1,000. Accent is laid on book reviews in the domain of French and on articles, that resume briefly, the state of the art of various French disciplines. *Franse Boek.*

RASSKAZ. 77-. Periodical. UR. Russian. an. 1.80. Sovremennik, Iartsevskaia 4 Izdatelstvo Sovremennik, 121351 Moskva G-351 Russia. **LC** PG3283.

RASTER. Began with 1- Apr. 1967-. 0033-9938. Periodical. NE. Dutch. qt. $26.95. De Bezige Bij, PO Box 5184, 1007 AD Amsterdam Netherlands.

RAW. Vol. 1, No. 1 (Fall 1980)-. 0742-4434. Periodical. US. English. sa. $15.00. Raw Books & Graphics Inc, 27 Greene Street, New York City NY 10013. Tel (212)226-0146. Ed Grancoise Mouly and Art Spiegelman. **LC** AP101. **DD** 817.5408. bk rev. adv acc. **Circ** 13,000.

READ. 0034-0359. Periodical. US. English. bw. $10.50. Xerox Educational Publications, PO Box 16626, Columbus OH 43216. Tel (203)638-2617. Ed Edwin A Hoey. **Circ** 400,000. High interest magazine for reading, English and language arts classroom. Provides reading experiences in many genres with associated skills activities. Published 18 times during school year.

THE READER'S ADVISER: AN ANNOTATED GUIDE TO THE BEST IN PRINT, IN LITERATURE, BIOGRAPHIES, DICTIONARIES, ENCYCLOPEDIA, BIBLES CLASSICS, DRAMA, POETRY, FICTION, SCIENCE, PHILOSOPHY, TRAVEL, HISTORY. 10th-. US. English. ir. R R Bowker Company, PO Box 1807, Ann Arbor MI 48106. Tel (313)761-4700. *Reader's Adviser and Bookman's Manual.*

READER'S CHOICE (TORONTO, ONT.). (READER'S CHOICE). VFOAT Readers Choice. VAT Readers Choice (Toronto). Vol. 1, No. 1 (Spring 1982)-. 0712-4376. Periodical. CN. English. ir. $3.00 Per No. Reader's Choice, PO Box 205, 205/Station S, Toronto Ontario M5M 4L7 Canada. **DD** C8130108.

READING PLUS. 0882-6196. US. English. an. Peter Lang Publishing Inc, 62 West 45th Street/4th Floor, New York NY 10036. Tel (212)302-6740. Ed Mary A Caws. Interdisciplinary series on thoughts to enhance classical and modern works.

REAL. See Yearbooks, Almanacs, Directories.

REALLEXIKON DER DEUTSCHEN LITERATURGESCHICHTE. *See* Encyclopedias & General Reference Books.

RECENT POLAR LITERATURE CEASED. Ceased with 1980. Periodical. UK. English. ty. **LC** Z6005.P7. **DD** 016.998.

RECHERCHES ANGLAISES ET AMERICAINES. VFOAT Ranam. No. 2- 1969-. 0557-6989. FR. French (English). an. Univ Sciences Humaines de Strasbourg, 22 rue Descartes, 67084 Strasbourg Cedex France. Tel 88613939. **Ind/Abst** Abstr. Engl. Stud., MLA Int. Bibliogr. Books Artic. Mod. Lang. Lit. **LC** E169.1. **DD** 084.1 S, 973. adv acc. **Circ** 500. Literature, art, leisure etc. in the Anglo-American world. *Etudes Anglaisas et Americaines.*

RECHERCHES GERMANIQUES. No 1- 1971-. 0399-1989. FR. Multilingual (French and German). an. $7.18. Universite des Sciences Humaines de Strasbourg, 22 rue Descartes, Strasbourg Cedex France. Tel (88) 61 39 39. **Ind/Abst** MLA Int. Bibliogr. Books Artic. Mod. Lang. Lit. **LC** DD61. adv acc. German literature and culture.

RECHERCHES SUR LE SURREALISME. 1- 1976-. French (English, German, or Italian). ir. $10.00. The Peter de Ridder Press, BP 168, 2160 Ad Lisse Pays-Bas Netherlands. **LC** PQ307.S95. **DD** 840.9091. Each issue contains an index to its own contents - no vol index - loose.

RECUEIL DE DROLERIES POUR LES SOIREES DU RIRE. V. 1- Sept. 1979-. 0226-5583. Periodical. CN. French. ir. $1.00 Each Number. Sos Desesperes, 618 rue Principale, la Perade Quebec G0X 2J0 Canada. **DD** C848.0708.

RED CEDAR REVIEW. V. 1- Spring 1963-. 0034-1967. Periodical. US. English. sa. $7.00. Michigan State University, 325 Morril Hall, East Lansing MI 48824. Tel (517)355-9659. Ed Judy A Hartje. **LC** PS501. bk rev. **Circ** 500. Innovative long-running literary magazine covering: short fiction, poetry, book reviews, graphic arts, and interviews.

RED FOX REVIEW. VFOAT Red Fox. V. 1- 1974-. 0742-454X. Periodical. US. English. an. Mohegan Community College, Mohegan Fine Arts Committee, Norwich CT 06360. Tel (203)886-1931. Ed James Coleman. **Circ** 750. A journal of fiction and poetry- graphics when we can locate some.

RELC JOURNAL. *See* Linguistics.

RENACIMIENTO (RIO PIEDRAS, P.R.). (RENACIMIENTO). V. 1, No. 1 (Jan./June 1981)-. Periodical. Spanish. sa. $8.00. Apartado 21487, UPR Station, Rio Piedras Puerto Rico 00931. **LC** PQ7081.A1. **DD** 808.8998.

RENAISSANCE CEASED. Began with June 1974 issue. 0319-6402. Periodical. CN. English. ir. Free to Senior Citizens of Scarbourgh. Renaissance, c/o Applied Arts Office, Centennial College, 651 Warden Avenue, Scarborough Ontario M1L 3Z6 Canada. **Ind/Abst** Humanit. Index. **DD** C810.80928505.

RENAISSANCE AND REFORMATION. VFOAT Renaissance et Reforme. V. 1-12, No 2, Oct. 1964-Winter 1976. 0034-429X. Periodical. CN. French (English). sa. 25.00. Victoria College, University of Toronto, Toronto Ontario M5S 1K7 Canada. Tel (416)978-4042. Ed Kenneth R Bartlett. **Ind/Abst** Am. Hist. Life, Abstr. Engl. Stud., MLA Int. Bibliogr. Books Artic. Mod. Lang. Lit., Book Rev. Index, Index Book Rev. Humanit. **LC** CB359. **DD** 940.2. bk rev. **Circ** 650. An interdisciplinary journal printing original substantial contributions to scholarship in all areas of Renaissance and Reformation studies in both English and French.

RENAISSANCE AND RENASCENCES IN WESTERN LITERATURE. Vol. 1, No. 1 (Summer 1979)-. 0193-9815. Periodical. US. English. qt. $7.00 Domestic, $9.00 Foreign. Allentown College, Department of English, c/o Wilson F Engel III Editor, Center Valley PA 18034. **Ind/Abst** MLA Int. Bibliogr. Books Artic. Mod. Lang. Lit. **LC** PN883. **DD** 809.

RENAISSANCE PAPERS. 1954-. US. English. an. $10.00. Duke University, Department of English, c/o Porter, Durham NC 27706. Tel (919)684-2741. Ed Dale B J Randall and Joseph A Porter. **Ind/Abst** Annu. Bibliogr. Engl. Lang. Lit., Abstr. Engl. Stud., MLA Int. Bibliogr. Books Artic. Mod. Lang. Lit. **Circ** 200. A selection of papers read at the annual meeting of the Southeastern Renaissance Conference.

RENASCENCE. V. 1- Autumn 1948-. 0034-4346. Periodical. US. English. qt. $15.00 Domestic $17.00 Foreign. Marquette University, 1212 West Wisconsin Avenue/Room 505, Milwaukee WI 53233. Tel (414) 224-7448. Ed Joseph Schwartz. **Ind/Abst** Abstr. Engl. Stud., MLA Int. Bibliogr. Books Artic. Mod. Lang. Lit., Annu. Bibliogr. Engl. Lang. Lit., Cathol. Period. Lit. Index, Cathol. Period. Index, Humanit. Index, Mod. Lang. Abstr. **LC** PN2. (cum index). **Circ** 700. (ctrl). Essays on values in literature from a Christian perspective.

RENDEZVOUS. (RENDEZVOUS : IDAHO STATE UNIVERSITY JOURNAL OF ARTS AND LETTERS). Vol. 1, No. 1 (Spring 1966)-. 0034-4400. Periodical. US. English. sa. $3.00. Idaho State University Campus, PO Box 8113, Pocatell ID 83209-0009. Tel (208)236-2845. **Ind/Abst** Abstr. Engl. Stud., MLA Int. Bibliogr. Books Artic. Mod. Lang. Lit. **LC** AS30. **DD** 051. bk rev. **Circ** 200. A journal encouraging innovative, speculative and creative work that will generate thoughtful consideration by non-specialists.

REPERTOIRE - CANADIAN SOCIETY FOR RENAISSANCE STUDIES. *See* Yearbooks, Almanacs, Directories.

REPERTOIRE DES PRIX LITTERAIRES. No. 1- 0715-1519. CN. French. **DD** 807.9. *Guide des Prix Litteraires Decernes au Quebec.*

REPERTORIEN ZUR DEUTSCHEN LITERATURGESCHICHTE. *See* Indexes/Abstracts.

REPERTORIO AMERICANO. Year 1- Oct./Dec. 1974-. Periodical. CR. Spanish. ir. $8.00. Administracion Y Canje: Instituto de Estudios Latinoamericanos, Apartado 86, Heredia Costa Rica. Tel 37-6478. **LC** F1401. **DD** 980.005. bk rev. **Circ** 1,000. (ctrl). Latin American and Spanish subjects related to literature, linguistics, social sciences, art, education, and philosophy.

REPORT FOR THE YEAR - JANE AUSTEN SOCIETY. **Main/Corp** Jane Austen Society. Began publication in 1944. UK. English. an. Jane Austen Society, 40 High Street, Alton Hampshire GU34 1BQ England. **Ind/Abst** Abstr. Engl. Stud. **LC** PR4036.A1.

REPORTS AND PROCEEDINGS - CENTRE FOR EDITING EARLY CANADIAN TEXTS. (REPORTS AND PROCEEDINGS). **Main/Corp** Centre for Editing Early Canadian Texts. 1982-. 0714-8860. CN. English. an. CEECT Reports and Proceedings, Room 1901/Arts Tower, Carleton University, Ottawa Ontario K1S 5B6 Canada. **DD** 808.02.

REPOSITORY *CEASED.* Began with No. 11- Summer 1974. Ceased in 1981. 0317-0845. Periodical. CN. English. qt. $2.00. Repository Press, Rural Route 7, Buckhorn Road, Prince George British Columbia V2N 2J5 Canada. **DD** C819.80054. *Seven Persons Repository, 0315-7415.*

REPRESENTATIVE AMERICAN SPEECHES. **Series/Titl** The Reference Shelf. 1937/38-. 0197-6923. US. English. an. H W Wilson Company, 950 University Avenue, Bronx NY 10452. **Ed** O Peterson. **LC** PS668. **DD** 815.5082. (cum index).

RESEARCH IN AFRICAN LITERATURES. V. 1- Spring 1970-. 0034-5210. Periodical. US. English. qt. $6.00. Editor Research in African Literatures, Box 7457, University of Texas, Austin TX 787712. **Ind/Abst** Abstr. Engl. Stud., MLA Int. Bibliogr. Books Artic. Mod. Lang. Lit., Sociol. Abstr., Humanit. Index. **LC** PL8010. **DD** 809.896.

RESEARCH OPPORTUNITIES IN RENAISSANCE DRAMA. **Main/Conf** Modern Language Association Conference on Research Opportunities in Renaissance Drama. 8- 1965-. 0098-647X. US. English. an. University of New Orleans, PO Box 1387, New Orleans LA 70148. **Ind/Abst** Abstr. Engl. Stud., MLA Int. Bibliogr. Books Artic. Mod. Lang. Lit., Annu. Bibliogr. Engl. Lang. Lit. **LC** PR621. **DD** 822.209. *Renaissance Drama, 0486-3739.*

RESEARCH PAPERS - DEPARTMENT OF TAMIL, UNIVERSITY OF KERALA. *See* Linguistics.

RESISTANCES. **VFOAT** Revue Resistances. No. 1 (Winter 1982)-. 0711-6403. Periodical. CN. French. ir. $7.00. Revue Resistances, CP 535, Succursale A, Jonquiere Quebec G7X 7W4 Canada. **DD** C840.80054.

RESONNANCES. No 1-. Periodical. FR. French. ir. 45. 18 rue Marlot, 51100 Reims, France. **LC** PQ1141. **DD** 840.8.

RESOURCE GUIDE TO READING & LANGUAGE ARTS PROGRAMS & MATERIALS. *See* Linguistics.

RESOURCES FOR AMERICAN LITERARY STUDY. V. 1- Spring 1971-. 0048-7384. US. English. sa. $12.00 Domestic and Canada, $15.00 Elsewhere. Resources of American Literary Study, University of Maryland, Department of English, College Park MD 20742. **Ed** Jackson R Bryer. **Ind/Abst** MLA Int. Bibliogr. Books Artic. Mod. Lang. Lit. **LC** Z1225. **DD** 016.81. bk rev. **Circ** 400. Evaluative bibliographical essays on major authors, works, genres, trends, and periods, Also informative accounts of significant collections of research materials of literary and cultural interest available in archives and libraries.

RESTORATION. (RESTORATION : STUDIES IN ENGLISH LITERARY CULTURE, 1660-1700). V. 1- Spring 1977-. 0162-9905. Periodical. US. English. sa. $8.00. University of Tennessee, Department of English, Knoxville TN 37996. **Tel** (615)974-5401. **Ed** J M Armistead. **Ind/Abst** MLA Int. Bibliogr. Books Artic. Mod. Lang. Lit. **LC** PR437. **DD** 820.9004. adv acc. **Circ** 450. British and British Colonial culture from 1660-1700, including literature, philosophy, theology, fine arts, theatre, science, and history; to enhance appreciation of Restoration literary culture.

REVIEW - CENTER FOR INTER-AMERICAN RELATIONS. (REVIEW : LATIN AMERICAN LITERATURE & ARTS). **VFOAT** Latin American Literature & Arts. 24-25/26. 0748-2434. Periodical. US. English (Spanish). ty. $22.00. Center of Inter-American Relations, 680 Park Avenue, New York NY 10021. **Tel** (212)249-8950. **Ed** Alfred Mac Adam. **Ind/Abst** MLA Int. Bibliogr. Books Artic. Mod. Lang. Lit. **LC** F1401. **DD** 700.5. bk rev. adv acc. **Circ** 3,000. Articles and reviews on Latin American literature and cultural interests. *Latin-American Literature and Art Review, 0748-2426.*

REVIEW OF ENGLISH STUDIES. (THE REVIEW OF ENGLISH STUDIES). V. 1-25 (No. 1-100). 0034-6551. Periodical. UK. English. qt. $39.85 US, 33 Others. Oxford University Press, Journals Department, Walton Street, Oxford OX2 6DP England. **Tel** 0865/56767. **Ed** R E Alton. **Ind/Abst** Abstr. Engl. Stud., MLA Int. Bibliogr. Books Artic. Mod. Lang. Lit., Lang. Lang. Behav. Abstr., Annu. Bibliogr. Engl. Lang. Lit., Book Rev. Index, Ref. Source, Index Book Rev. Humanit., Soc. Sci. Index, Humanit. Index, Sociol. Abstr., Years Work Eng. Stud., Recent Publ. Artic. **LC** PR1. **DD** 820.9. bk rev. adv acc. **Circ** 2,030. Academic journal concerned with English literature and English language from the earliest period up to the present day.

REVIEW - SCHOOL LIBRARIES BRANCH, SOUTH AUSTRALIA EDUCATION DEPARTMENT. (REVIEW). 0310-5202. Periodical. English. qt. School Libraries Branch, Box 1152 GPO, Adelaide 5001 Australia. **Ind/Abst** Libr. Inf. Sci. Abstr. **LC** Z1037.A1. **DD** 028.162.

REVISOR. (DE REVISOR). Vol. 1-. 0302-8852. Periodical. Dutch. ir. 45.00. Athenaeum, Keizergracht 608, Amsterdam Netherlands. **Ind/Abst** MLA Int. Bibliogr. Books Artic. Mod. Lang. Lit. **LC** PT5460.

REVISTA BRASILEIRA DE LINGUA E LITERATURA. *See* Linguistics.

REVISTA CANADIENSE DE ESTUDIOS HISPANICOS. V. 1- Autumn 1976-. 0384-8167. Periodical. CN. Spanish (includes some text in English and French). ty. $12.38. Carleton University, Department of Spanish, Ottawa Ontario K1S 5B6 Canada. **Tel** (613)231-4465. **Ind/Abst** MLA Int. Bibliogr. Books Artic. Mod. Lang. Lit. **LC** CB226. **DD** 860.9. *Reflexion, 0034-3005.*

REVISTA CHICANO-RIQUENA. Yearly Vol. 1 Spring 1973-. 0360-7860. Periodical. US. English (Spanish). qt. $20.00. University of Houston, 4800 Calhoun Road, Houston TX 77004. **Tel** (713)749-4768. **Ed** Julian Olivares, Jose Saldivar. **Ind/Abst** MLA Int. Bibliogr. Books Artic. Mod. Lang. Lit. **LC** PS508.M4. **DD** 810.80868. bk rev. adv acc. **Circ** 3,000. Hispanic literature in the US.

REVISTA DA ACADEMIA ALAGOANA DE LETRAS. **Main/Corp** Academia Alagoana de Letras. Yearly V. 1- 1975-. Periodical. Portuguese. ir. **LC** PQ9500. **DD** 869.08.

REVISTA DA ACADEMIA GOIANA DE LETRAS. **Main/Corp** Academia Goiana de Letras. Yearly V. 1- 1957-. Portuguese. ir. Academia Goiana de Letras, Avenida Goias 310 S/905, Goiania Brazil. **LC** PQ9502.

REVISTA DA ACADEMIA PERNAMBUCANA DE LETRAS. **Main/Corp** Academia Pernambucana de Letras. Began with Jan./Mar. 1901 issue. Portuguese. ir. Academie Pernambucana de Letras, Av rue Barbosa 1596, Recife Brazil. **LC** PQ9502.A59.

REVISTA DE ESTUDIOS HISPANICOS. Vol. 1- 1971-. 0378-7974. Periodical. PR. Spanish. sa. $5.00. University de Puerto Rico, Fac de Humanidades, Box 21787 UPR Station, Rio Piedras Puerto Rico 00931. **Tel** 764-000. **Ed** Jose Luis Vega. **Ind/Abst** MLA Int. Bibliogr. Books Artic. Mod. Lang. Lit. **LC** PC4001. **DD** 460. bk rev. adv acc. **Circ** 1,000. Articles and research studies on Hispanic literature, linguistics and folklore. *Revista de Estudios Hispanicos.*

REVISTA DE ESTUDIOS HISPANICOS. *See* Linguistics.

REVISTA DE ISTORIE SI TEORIE LITERARA. Vol. 1- 1952-. 0034-8392. Periodical. RM. Romanian (summaries and table of contents in French and Russian). qt. Ilexim Press Department, PO Box 1-136-1-137, Bucharest Romania. **Ind/Abst** MLA Int. Bibliogr. Books Artic. Mod. Lang. Lit. **LC** PN9.

REVISTA DE LITERATURA. Vol. 1- No. 1 (Jan./Mar. 1952)-. 0034-849X. Periodical. SP. Spanish. sa. Consejo Super Invest Cientific Vitruvio, 8/Apartado 14 458, 28006 Madrid Spain. **Tel** 262 96 34. **Ind/Abst** MLA Int. Bibliogr. Books Artic. Mod. Lang. Lit., Am. Hist. Life, Hist. Abstr., Hist. Abstr., Part A, Mod. Hist. Abstr., Hist. Abst., Part B, Twent. Century Abstr. **LC** PN6. *Cuadernos de Literatura, Revista Bibliografica y Documental.*

REVISTA DE LITERATURA CUBANA. V. 1, No. 0, (July 1982)-. Periodical. Spanish. sa. $12.61. Ediciones Cubanas, Obispo Number 461, Aptdo 605, Ciudad Havana Cuba.

REVISTA DE LITERATURA HISPANOAMERICANA. Vol. 1- (No. 1-). Periodical. VE. Spanish. sa. $6.57. Universidad del Zulia, Apartado 1490, Maracaibo Venezuela. **LC** PQ7081.A1.

REVISTA HISPANICA MODERNA. Vol. 1, No. 1 (Oct. 1934)-. 0034-9593. Periodical. US. Spanish. qt. Hispanic Institute, Columbia University, 612 West 116th Street, New York NY 10027. **Tel** (212)280-4940. **Ind/Abst** MLA Int. Bibliogr. Books Artic. Mod. Lang. Lit. **LC** PQ6001. **DD** 860.5. *Boletin del Instituto de las Espanas.*

REVISTA IBEROAMERICANA. V. 1- (No. 1-). 0034-9631. Periodical. US. Spanish. ir. $30.00. University of Pittsburgh, 1312 C L, Institute of International Literature Iberoamericana, Pittsburgh PA 15260. **Tel** (412)624-3359. **Ind/Abst** MLA Int. Bibliogr. Books Artic. Mod. Lang. Lit. **LC** PQ7081.A1. **DD** 860.5.

REVISTA OFICIAL DE LA ASOCIACION GENERAL DE AUTORES DEL URUGUAY. **Main/Corp** Asociacion General de Autores del Uruguay. UY. Spanish. ir. Associacion General de Autores del Uruguay, Canelones 1130, Montevideo Uruguay. **LC** PQ8510. *Boletin.*

REVISTA SCRIITORILOR ROMANI. 1- 1962-. 0080-2441. Romanian. ir.

REVISTAS ESPANOLAS CON ISSN. *See* Bibliographies.

REVUE CELFAN. **VFOAT** Celfan Review. Vol. 1, No. 1 (Nov. 1981)-. Periodical. US. French (English). ty. $20.00. Editor Celfan, Temple University, Department of French and Italian, Philadelphia PA 19122. **Tel** (215)787-8259. **Ed** Eric Sellin. **Ind/Abst** MLA Int. Bibliogr. Books Artic. Mod. Lang. Lit. bk rev. **Circ** 150. Short articles on the francophone. Literature of North Africa and literature by French writers from North Africa.

LA REVUE CELINIENNE. No. 1-. Periodical. French. ir. La Revue Celinienne, c/o M Laudelout Trolieberg 20, 3200 Kessel-Lo Belgique.

REVUE DE BELLES-LETTRES. 0035-1016. Periodical. SZ. French. ty. 60.00 Domestic, $30.00 Foreign. Editions Medecine & Hygiene, Case Postale 229, CH-1211 Geneve 4 Switzerland. **Tel** (022) 46 93 55.

REVUE DE LITTERATURE COMPAREE. 1. Yearly V. (1921-). 0035-1466. Periodical. FR. French. qt. 385. Societe Nouvelle Didier Erudition, 6 rue de la Sorbonne, 75005 Paris France. **Tel** 4354 47 521. **Ed** Voisirie. **Ind/Abst** Annu. Bibliogr. Engl. Lang. Lit., MLA Int. Bibliogr. Books Artic. Mod. Lang. Lit., Index Book Rev. Humanit., Years Work Eng. Stud. **LC** PN851. (cum index). bk rev. adv acc. **Circ** 2,500. The oldest magazine of comparative literature - publishes the comparatist throughout the entire world.

REVUE DES ETUDES ARMENIENNES. Vols. 1-11 (V. 1-). 0080-2549. FR. French. ir. $26.61. M Mahe, 7 rue Max Dornmoy, Paris 75018 France. **Ind/Abst** MLA Int. Bibliogr. Books Artic. Mod. Lang. Lit., Repert. Int. Litt. Art. **LC** PK8001.

REVUE DES ETUDES ITALIENNES. V. 1-3. Jan./Mar. 1936-1938. 0035-2047. Periodical. FR. French. qt. $23.95. Revue des Etudes Italiennes, Alexandre 3 Cours la Reine, 75 Paris 8E France. **Ind/Abst** Am. Hist. Life, Hist. Abstr., Part A, Mod. Hist. Abstr., Hist. Abst., Part B, Twent. Century Abstr., MLA Int. Bibliogr. Books Artic. Mod. Lang. Lit., Hist. Abstr. **LC** PQ4001. **DD** 850.5. adv acc. *Etudes Italiennes.*

REVUE DES ETUDES LATINES. *See* Linguistics.

REVUE DES ETUDES MAISTRIENNES. No. 3- 1977-. 0337-6702. FR. French. an. Societe Edition Belles Lettres, 95 Boulevard Raspail, 75006 Paris France. *Etudes Maistriennes.*

REVUE DES LETTRES MODERNES. (LA REVUE DES LETTRES MODERNES). Vol. 1, No. 1 (Feb. 1954)-. 0035-2136. Periodical. FR. French. ir. $106.43. Lettres Modernes Minard, 73 rue de Cardinal Lemoine, 75005 Paris France. **Ind/Abst** MLA Int. Bibliogr. Books Artic. Mod. Lang. Lit. **LC** PN3.

REVUE D'HISTOIRE LITTERAIRE DE LA FRANCE. Yearly Vol. 1-. 0035-2411. Periodical. FR. French. ir. Librairie Armand Colin, 103 Boulevard St Michel, 75005 Paris Cedex 5 France. **Tel** 543 32 11. **Ind/Abst** Am. Hist. Life, Hist. Abstr., Part A, Mod. Hist. Abstr., Hist. Abst., Part B, Twent.

Literature

Century Abstr., MLA Int. Bibliogr. Books Artic. Mod. Lang. Lit., Index Book Rev. Humanit., Recent Publ. Artic., Years Work Eng. Stud. LC PQ2. DD 840.9. (cum index).

REVUE D'HISTOIRE LITTERAIRE DU QUEBEC ET DU CANADA FRANCAIS. 2 (1980-1981)-. 0228-8796. Periodical. CN. French. $20.00. Les Editions Bellarmin, 8100 Boul Saint-Laurent, Montreal Quebec H2P 2L9 Canada. LC PQ3900. DD 840.99714. *Histoire Litteraire du Quebec.*

REVUE D'HISTOIRE LITTERAIRE DU QUEBEC ET DU CANADA FRANCAIS. Series/Titl Collection Histoire Litteraire du Quebec et du Canada Francaise. 2 (1980/1981)-. 0713-7958. Periodical. CN. French. sa. 30.95. University of Ottawa Press, c/o Rene Dionne, Ottawa Ontario K1N 6N5 Canada. DD C840.99714. Contains French-Canadian literature, Quebec and French-American history and bibliographies. *Histoire Litteraire du Quebec, 0228-8796.*

LA REVUE DU BAS-POITOU ET DES PROVINCES DE L'OUEST. V. 1- 1888-. 0556-767X. Periodical. French. ir. (cum index).

REVUE FRANCAISE D'HISTOIRE DU LIVRE. New Series, Yearly 1- 1971-. 0037-9212. FR. French. qt. French. 50.00 Domestic, 95.00 Foreign. Societe d'Edition et de Documentation Agricole, 25 rue du General-Foy, 75008 Paris France. **Tel** 293.33.43. LC Z119. DD 001.552. Reference book on French literature and history.

REVUE FRONTENAC. VFOAT Frontenac Review. No. 1 (1983)-. 0715-9994. CN. English (French). an. $5.00 Per Number; First Issue Free. Frontenac Review, Queen's University, Department of French Studies, Kingston Ontario K7L 3N6 Canada. DD 809.0305.

REVUE ROMANE. Began with: V. 1, 1966. 0035-3906. Periodical. DK. French. sa. $30.38. Munksgaard Ltd, 35 Norre Sogade, DK-1370 Copenhagen K Denmark. **Tel** 1.12.70.30. Ed Nils Soelberg. **Ind/Abst** MLA Int. Bibliogr. Books Artic. Mod. Lang. Lit., Lang. Lang. Behav. Abstr., Sociol. Abstr. bk rev acc. **Circ** 350. A journal devoted to Romance language and literature.

RHETORIC SOCIETY QUARTERLY. VFOAT RSQ, R.S.Q. Began with Winter 1976 issue. 0277-3945. Periodical. US. English. qt. $6.00 Members. Rhetoric Society of America, St Cloud State University, Department of Philosophy, St Cloud MN 56301. **Ind/Abst** MLA Int. Bibliogr. Books Artic. Mod. Lang. Lit. LC PN171.4. DD 808.005.

RHETORIK. V. 1 (1980)-. GW. German. an. Friedrich Frommann Verlag, Postfach 50 04 60, 7000 Stuttgart 50 West Germany.

RIVER CITY REVIEW (LOUISVILLE, KY.). (RIVER CITY REVIEW). No. 1 (Fall 1982)-. 0734-497X. Periodical. US. English. ir. River City Review, PO Box 34275, Louisville KY 40232. **Tel** (502)459-8040. Ed Richard L Neumayer and Alan Naslund. adv acc. **Circ** 600. Modern fiction, poetry, black and white, two-dimensional art and short drama with a strong story line.

RIVER STYX. 0149-8851. Periodical. US. English. sa. $36.00. Big River Association, 7420 Cornell Avenue, St Louis MO 63130. **Tel** (314)725-0602. Ed Jan Garden Castro. LC PS501. DD 810.8. adv acc. **Circ** 1,000. (ctrl). A biannual publication devoted to multicultural literature and art.

RIVERSEDGE. VAT Rivers Edge. Vol. 1, No.1 (Spring 1977)-. 0272-9598. Periodical. US. English. ty. Riversedge Press, PO Box 1547, Edinburg TX 78539. **Tel** (512)383-7266. LC PS558.T4. DD 810.8097644.

RIVERSIDE QUARTERLY. V. 1- (1-). 0035-5704. Periodical. CN. English. qt. Riverside Quarterly, PO Box 40/University Station, Regina Saskatchewan Canada. **Ind/Abst** Annu. Bibliogr. Engl. Lang. Lit. Also available in microfilm format. *Inside.*

RIVISTA DI CULTURA CLASSICA E MEDIOEVALE. Vol. 1- Jan./Apr. 1959-. 0035-6085. Periodical. IT. Italian (French, German, Latin or English). ty. 40.000. Edizioni dell A Teneo, Casella Postale 7216, 00100 Rome Italy. **Tel** 7578853. **Ind/Abst** MLA Int. Bibliogr. Books Artic. Mod. Lang. Lit. LC PA9.

RIVISTA DI LETTERATURA ITALIANA. V. 1, 1-. Periodical. Italian. ty. 65.000. Via Santa Bibbiana 28, 56100 Pisa Italy. LC PQ4001. DD 850.8.

RIVISTA DI LETTERATURE MODERNE E COMPARATE. Vol. 1- March 1946-. Periodical. IT. Italian. ir. Licosa Libreria Comm Samsani, Via Lamarmora 45, 50121 Firenze Italy. LC PN5. DD 805.

RIVISTA DI STUDI ITALIANI. VFOAT RSI. Year 1, No. 1 (June 1983)-. 0821-3216. Periodical. CN. Italian (English). sa. $23.21. University of Toronto, c/o Anthony Verna, Department of Italian Studies, Toronto Ontario M5S 1A1 Canada. **Tel** (416)236-1519. Ed Anthony Verna. DD 945.005. bk rev. adv acc. **Circ** 500. (ctrl). A scholarly interdisciplinary journal of Italian language and literature within the context of other European literatures and cultures.

ROBINSON JEFFERS NEWSLETTER. No. 1 (Nov. 19, 1962)-. 0300-7936. Periodical. US. English. ir $4.00. Occidental College Library, 1600 Campus Road, Los Angeles CA 90041. **Tel** (213)259-2671. Ed Robert J Brophy. **Ind/Abst** Abstr. Engl. Stud., MLA Int. Bibliogr. Books Artic. Mod. Lang. Lit. LC PS3519.E27. DD 811.52. (cum index). bk rev. **Circ** 230. News notes, book reviews, biographical information, and critical articles about Robinson Jeffers.

ROCKBOTTOM. No. 1- Summer 1976-. 0146-1419. Periodical. US. English. qt. $5.00. Mudborn Press, 209 West de la Guerra, Santa Barbara CA 93101. LC PS501. DD 810.

ROCKY MOUNTAIN REVIEW OF LANGUAGE AND LITERATURE. V. 29- Spring 1975-. 0361-1299. Periodical. US. English. qt. $16.00. Boise State University, Carol Martin/English Department, Boise ID 83725. **Tel** (208)385-1246. Ed Carol A Martin. **Ind/Abst** Abstr. Engl. Stud., Book Rev. Index, MLA Int. Bibliogr. Books Artic. Mod. Lang. Lit., Annu. Bibliogr. Engl. Lang. Lit., Lang. Lang. Behav. Abstr. LC PB1. DD 805. bk rev. adv acc. **Circ** 1,200. (ctrl). English and foreign language articles, linguistics, popular culture, feminist literary studies, original poetry and short fiction, translations. *0035-7626.*

ROCZNIK SLAWISTYCZNY. VFOAT Revue Slavistique. Vol. 1- 1908-. 0080-3588. Periodical. PL. Polish (Bulgarian, French and other languages). sa. ARS Polona, Krakowskie Przedmiescie 7, 00-068 Warsaw Poland. **Ind/Abst** MLA Int. Bibliogr. Books Artic. Mod. Lang. Lit. LC PG1.

ROD MCKUEN'S FOLIO. No. 1- Spring 1974-. Periodical. US. English. qt. $16.00. Rod McKuen, Montcalm Productions, 8440 Santa Monica Boulevard, Los Angeles CA 90069. LC PS3525.A264. DD 811.54.

ROD SERLING'S THE TWILIGHT ZONE MAGAZINE. VFOAT Twilight Zone Magazine. Vol. 1, No. 1 (Apr. 1981)-. 0279-6090. Periodical. US. English. mo. $22.00 Domestic, $27.00 Foreign. TZ Publications Inc, 800 Second Avenue, New York NY 10017. LC PS648.F3. DD 813.087608.

RODOSHA BUNGAKU. June 1979. Periodical. JA. Japanese. an. 600. Orijin Shuppan Senta, c/o Meja Kagurazaka, 16 Iwatocho, Shinjuku-ku Tokyo 162 Japan. LC PL756.L33.

THE ROHMER REVIEW. 0145-5753. Periodical. US. English. ir. Robert E Briney, 4 Forest Avenue, Salem MA 01970. LC PS3545.A653. DD 813.52.

ROMAN. No. 1, (Fall 1982)-. Periodical. FR. French. qt. $25.94. Presses de la Renaissance, 198 Boulevard Saint Germain, 75007 Paris France. **Tel** 548-59-82. LC PQ1271. DD 843.008. **Circ** 3,000.

ROMANCE. See *Romance and Adventure.*

ROMANCES CEASED. Periodical. CU. Spanish. mo. Empresa Ediciones Cubanas, Sub-Direccion Exportacion, Oreilly 407 Ciudad, Habana Cuba. LC AP63.

ROMANHA. No. 1-. Periodical. JA. Japanese. ir. 500. Izumo Shoten, c/o Nakabayashi Building, Kanda Tacho 2, Chiyoda-ku, Tokyo Japan. LC PL726.65.

ROMANIA LITERARA. Year 1- (No. 1-). Periodical. US. Romanian. wk. Ilexim Press Department, PO Box 1-136-1-137, Bucharest Romania. **Ind/Abst** MLA Int. Bibliogr. Books Artic. Mod. Lang. Lit.

ROMANIC REVIEW. V. 1- Jan. 1910-. 0035-8118. Periodical. US. English. qt. $27.00. Columbia University, Department of French and Romance Philology, 521 Philosophy Hall, New York NY 10027. **Tel** (212)280-2500. Ed Michael Riffaterre. **Ind/Abst** MLA Int. Bibliogr. Books Artic. Mod. Lang. Lit., Annu. Bibliogr. Engl. Lang. Lit., Index Book Rev. Humanit., Soc. Sci. Index, Humanit. Index. LC PC1. DD 840.09. bk rev. adv acc. Academic journal of romance languages and literature.

ROMANISCHE FORSCHUNGEN. See Linguistics.

ROMANISTISCHE ZEITSCHRIFT FUR LITERATURGESCHICHTE. See Linguistics.

THE ROMANTIC MOVEMENT. See Bibliographies.

ROMANTICISM PAST AND PRESENT. VFOAT R.P.P. Vol. 5, No. 1-. 0733-6519. Periodical. US. English. sa. $7.00. Northeastern University, Department of English, c/o S Peterfreund, Boston MA 02115. **Tel** (617)437-3967. Ed Stuart Peterfreund. **Ind/Abst** Am. Hist. Life, Hist. Abstr., MLA Int. Bibliogr. Books Artic. Mod. Lang. Lit., Artbibliogr. Mod. LC PR3579. DD 821.4. bk rev. adv acc. **Circ** 300. (ctrl). Explores the romantic sense of the past. Primarily English in orientation but does publish articles that are interdisciplinary and comparatist in orientation. *Milton and the Romantics, 0145-529X.*

ROMANTISME. 1/2- 1971-. 0048-8593. Periodical. FR. French. bm. Editions CDU & Sedes, 88 Boulevard Saint Germain, 75005 Paris France. **Ind/Abst** MLA Int. Bibliogr. Books Artic. Mod. Lang. Lit., Recent Publ. Artic. LC PN603.

THE ROMANTIST. No. 1- 1977-. 0161-682X. Periodical. US. English. an. $5.00. Saracinesca House, 3610 Meadowbrook Avenue, Nashville TN 37205. **Ind/Abst** MLA Int. Bibliogr. Books Artic. Mod. Lang. Lit. LC PS1462. DD 808.8014.

ROOM OF ONE'S OWN. V. 1- Spring 1975-. 0316-1609. CN. English. ir. $9.28. Growing Room Collective, PO Box 46160 Station G, Vancouver British Columbia V6R 4G5 Canada. **Tel** (604)736-0851. Ed Reid, Robertson, Schendlinger, Wachtel, Wilson and Wexler. DD C810.80928705. bk rev. adv acc. **Circ** 1,200. Publishes original prose and poetry as well as literary criticism and reviews of feminist interest.

ROSSICA OLOMUCENSIA. See Linguistics.

ROTHNIUM MAGAZINE. VAT Rothnium. V. 1- Apr. 1977-. 0702-7303. Periodical. CN. English. ir. $1.25 Per No. Cygolian Press, PO Box 471, Owen Sound Ontario N4K 5P7 Canada. DD 823.0876.

THE ROUNDUP. See History (General) - History of North, South, and Central America.

RUBICON (MONTREAL, QUEBEC). (RUBICON). No. 1 (Spring 1983)-. 0715-8610. Periodical. CN. English. be. 12.00. McGill University, 853 Sherbrooke Street West, Montreal Quebec H3A 2T6 Canada. **Tel** (514)286-0652. Ed Peter O'Brien. DD 805. bk rev. adv acc. **Circ** 750. Journal of contemporary writing and visual art. We publish poetry, fiction, book artwork, with an emphasis on Canadian work. *McGill Literary Journal, 0709-2393.*

RUCH LITERACKI. V. 1- (No. 1-) July/Oct. 1960-. 0035-9602. Periodical. PL. Polish. bm. ARS Polona, Krakowskie Przedmiescie 7, 00-068 Warsaw Poland. **Ind/Abst** MLA Int. Bibliogr. Books Artic. Mod. Lang. Lit. LC PG7001.

RUFANTHOLOGY. V. 1- Winter 1976-. 0381-1158. Periodical. CN. English (includes some text in French). Protestant School Board of Greater Montreal, 6000 Fielding Avenue, Montreal Quebec H3X 1T4 Canada. DD C810.809237505.

RUHRTANGENTE. German. ir. Argus-Verlag, 567 Opladen AM Monchshof 12, Opladen W Germany. LC PT3805.W4.

RUNE. V. 1- Spring 1974-. 0316-2192. Periodical. CN. English. bm. $1. Per No. Rune University of Toronto, St Michael's College, PO Box 299, Toronto Ontario M5S 1J4 Canada. DD C810.5.

RUPTURE (TORONTO, ONT.). (RUPTURE). Vol. 1, No. 1 (Summer 1983)-. 0822-9600. Periodical. CN. English. qt. $12.00 Per No., $30.00 Per Year. Rupture, PO Box No 732 Station A, Toronto Ontario M5W 1G2 Canada. DD 891.4209.

RUSISTICKY SBORNIK OLOMOUCKO-LUBLINSKY. See Linguistics.

RUSSIAN LITERATURE. 1-. 0304-3479. NE. English (text in French, German or Russian). ir. Elsevier Science Publishers, PO Box 211, 1000 AE

Literature

Amsterdam Netherlands. **Tel** (020)5803.911. Ed N A Nilsson and J van der Eng. **LC** PG2900.A1. **DD** 891.7005.

RUSSIAN LITERATURE TRIQUARTERLY. Began with Fall 1971 issue. 0048-881X. Periodical. US. English. ty. $40.00. Ardis, 2901 Heatherway, Ann Arbor MI 48105. **Tel** (313)971-2367. Ed E Proffer. **Ind/Abst** MLA Int. Bibliogr. Books Artic. Mod. Lang. Lit., Ref. Source, Index Am. Period. Verse. **LC** PG2901. **DD** 891.708. (cum index). bk rev. **Circ** 500. (ctrl). Clothbound. A journal devoted to Russian literature in translation. Criticism and book reviews included.

THE RUSSIAN REVIEW. See History (General) - History of Europe.

RUSSKAJA LITERATURA. (RUSSKAIA LITERATURA). 1 (1957)-. 0131-6095. Periodical. UR. Russian. qt. $26.00. Victor Kamkin Inc (70783), 12224 Parklawn Drive, Rockville MD 20852. **Tel** (301)881-5973. **Ind/Abst** MLA Int. Bibliogr. Books Artic. Mod. Lang. Lit. (cum index).

RUSSKII IAZYK I LITERATURA V UZBEKSKOI SHKOLE. See Linguistics.

RUSSKII IAZYK V SREDNAM POVOLZHE. See Linguistics.

RUSSKII VODEVIL. See Linguistics.

RUSSKOE VOZROZHDENIE. See Religion, Mythology, Rationalism - Eastern Christian Churches.

RUSYCYSTYCZNE STUDIA LITERATUROZNAWCZE. Series/Titl Prace Naukowe Uniwersytetu Slaskiego W Katowicach. Began in 1977. Periodical. Polish. ir. 92.00. Uniwersytet Slaski, Ul Bankowa 14, 40-007 Katowice Poland. Ed Gabriela Porebina. **LC** PG3015.

RYUKYU DAIGAKU HO-BUNGAKUBU KIYO : KOKUBUNGAKU RONSHU. **Main/Corp** Ryukyu Daigaku. Ho-Bungakubu. **VFOAT** Bulletin of the College of Law and Literature, University of the Ryukyus: Japanese Literature. JA. Japanese. ir. Ryukyu Daigaku Ho-Bungakubu, 1 Shuri Tonokuracho 3-chome, Naha Okinawa Japan 903. **LC** PL700.

S FP3S NEWSLETTER. Began publication in 1974?. 0384-0948. Periodical. CN. English. S FP3S Newsletter, PO Box 65583, Vancouver British Columbia V5N 5K5 Canada. **DD** 809.387605.

SACITRA ORIYA SAHITYA. Periodical. Hindi. ir. 12.00. A K de Hazra, Haripur Rd, Cuttak - 1, Kataka India. **LC** PK2570.

SAGA BOOK OF THE VIKING SOCIETY FOR NORTHERN RESEARCH. **Main/Corp** Viking Society for Northern Research, London. V. 1- 1892/96-. UK. English. ir. $11.49. Viking Society, University College, Gower Street, London WC 1 England. **Tel** 01 387 7050. Ed A R Faulkes. **Ind/Abst** MLA Int. Bibliogr. Books Artic. Mod. Lang. Lit. **LC** DA750. (cum index). bk rev. **Circ** 600. (ctrl). Covers Scandinavian literature, language, history, art, folklore, largely medieval.

SAHITYA. Periodical. II. Manipuri. ir. 5.60. **LC** PL4001.M315.

SAHITYA SANKETA. Periodical. II. Nepali. qt. 3.00. Nepali Sahitya Adhyayana, Samiti Town Hall, Kalimpong India. **LC** PK2597.5.

SAHITYA-SAURABHA. V. 1- Jan. 1972. Periodical. Hindi. ir. 20.00. Sahitya Saurabha, Bangalore India. **LC** PK2077.

SAHITYALOCANA. V. 1- Jan. 1973-. Periodical. Hindi. ir. 6.00. Sarasvati Presa Buka Dipo, 3788 Netaji Subhash Marg 6, Dilli India. **LC** PK2030.

SAHITYATIRTHA. Periodical. Bengali. an. 6.00. 67 Pathuriaghat Street, Calcutta 700006 India. **LC** PK1700.

SAJJANA. V. 1- November 2029- 1972-. Periodical. Nepali. ir. 1.00. Biratnagar-3, Viratanagura Nepal. **LC** PK2598.A2.

SAMADARSI. **VFOAT** Samadarshi. Periodical. Oriya. qt. 2.00. Nilachal Prakashani, Link Road, Cuttack 753009 India. **LC** PK2574.5.

SAMAKALINA BHARATIYA SAHITYA. **VFOAT** Samkaleen Bharateeya Sahitya. V. 1, No. 1 (July/September 1980)-. Periodical. II. Hindi. qt. 16.00. Sahitya Akademi, Ravidra Bhavan, New Delhi 110 001 India. **LC** PK2977.H5.

SAMAVETA SVARA. Vol. 1- May 1972-. Periodical. Hindi. ir. 5.00. 75 Jawaharlal Nehru Marg - 1, New Delhi India. **LC** PK2030.

SAMBODHANA. Periodical. Hindi. ir. 10.00. Gulfam Khan, Chand Pole, Kankroli Rjasthan India. **LC** PK2030.

SAMPLINGS. 1981-. 0711-1827. CN. English. an. Free. Samplings, c/o English Department, Peel Board of Education, 73 King Street West, Mississauga Ontario L5B 1H5 Canada. **DD** C810.809282.

SAMSKRTAPRATIBHA. See Linguistics.

THE SAMUEL BUTLER NEWSLETTER. Vol. 2, No. 1 (June 1979)-. 0278-7350. Periodical. US. English. qt. $8.00 Domestic, $10.00 Foreign. The Samuel Butler Society, c/o James A Donovan Jr, 4100 Cathedral Avenue NW, Washington DC 20016. **Ind/Abst** MLA Int. Bibliogr. Books Artic. Mod. Lang. Lit. **LC** PR4349.B7. **DD** 828.809. *Samuel Butler Society Newsletter, 0161-8806.*

SAN JOSE STUDIES. V. 1- Feb. 1975-. 0097-8051. US. English. ty. $18.00. San Jose Studies, San Jose State University, c/o O C Williams, San Jose CA 95192. **Tel** (408)277-2841. Ed Fauneil Joyce Rinn. **Ind/Abst** Am. Hist. Life, Hist. Abstr., Part A, Mod. Hist. Abstr., Hist. Abst., Part B, Twent. Century Abstr., Abstr. Engl. Stud., MLA Int. Bibliogr. Books Artic. Mod. Lang. Lit., Sociol. Abstr., Soc. Welf. Soc. Plan./Policy Soc. Dev., Women Stud. Abstr., Writ. Am. Hist., Lang. Lang. Behav. Abstr., Hist. Abstr. **LC** AS36.C17. **DD** 051. **Circ** 350. Journal of general and scholarly interest featuring critical, creative, and informative writing in the arts, business, humanities, social sciences, and science; uses poetry and fiction.

SAN WEN CHI KAN. 1-. Periodical. Chinese. qt. **LC** PL2623. **DD** 895.145080951249.

SAN WEN HSUAN. Periodical. CH. Chinese. an. 125.00. Chiu Ko Chu Pan She, PO Box 36-445, Tai-Pei Shih Taiwan. **LC** PL3031.T32. **DD** 895.145080951249.

SAND PATTERNS. V. 1-. 0316-5167. Periodical. CN. English. qt. $1.00 Per No. Sand Patterns Publications, PO Box 321, Charlottetown PEI C1A Canada. **DD** C810.80054.

SANDS AND CORAL. 1948-. PH. English. an. $7.00. Silliman University, Dumaguete City 6501 Philippines. **LC** PR9992.P4. **DD** 820.809599.

SARA INNUN ADONG MUNHAK. Periodical. KO. Korean. ir. 2,500. Ingansa, 68 Chungsin-dong Chongno-ku, Seoul Korea. **LC** PL969.5.

EL SARAPE. No. 1-. 0747-9425. Periodical. US. English (Spanish). an. $4.00. Night Jar Press, Box 3E New Mexico State University, Las Cruces NM 88003. **DD** 808.

SARASVATI-SUSHAMA. Periodical. English, Hindi, or Sanskrit. ir. **LC** PK401.

SATTARA DASAKA. Periodical. Bengali. ir. 6.00. Gita Ganguli, 78/2 Biren Roy Road West, 61 Kalakata India. **LC** RK1700.

SATURDAY REVIEW. (SATURDAY REVIEW READER). No. 1- 1951-. Periodical. US. English. **LC** PS536. **DD** 810.82.

SATURDAY REVIEW. V. 9, No. 7 (Mar./Apr. 1983)-. 2159-1655. Periodical. US. English. bm. $16.00 Domestic, $21.00 Canada. Saturday Review, 488 Madison Avenue, New York NY 10022, (susbscription address: Communication Data Services 112 Tenth Street Des Moines IA 50309). **Tel** (800)247-5470. **Ind/Abst** Read. Guide Period. Lit., Abr. Read. Guide, Annu. Bibliogr. Engl. Lang. Lit., Book Rev. Index, Film Lit. Index, GeoRef, Infobank, Media Rev. Dig., Predicasts, Energy Inf. Abstr., Environ. Abstr. **LC** AP2. **DD** 051. **CODEN** SAREAP. Available also in 35mm microfilm and microfiche. *Saturday Review (New York, 1975), 0351-1655.*

SAUL BELLOW JOURNAL. Vol. 1, No. 2 (Spring/Summer 1982)-. 0735-1550. Periodical. US. English. sa. $12.00. c/o Liela Goldman, 6533 Post Oak Drive, West Bloomfield MI 48033. **Tel** (313)855-4324. Ed Liela Goldman. **Ind/Abst** MLA Int. Bibliogr. Books Artic. Mod. Lang. Lit. **LC** PS3503.E4488. **DD** 813.52. bk rev. Critical and biographical articles on the works of Saul Bellow as well as book reviews. *Saul Bellow Newsletter.*

THE SAYERS REVIEW. 1976- V. 1, No. 1-. Periodical. US. English. ty. $7.00. Christie McMenomy, 3138 Sawtelle Boulevard #4, Los Angeles CA 90066.

Ind/Abst MLA Int. Bibliogr. Books Artic. Mod. Lang. Lit.

SBORNIK. RADA C: LITERARNI HISTORIE. **Main/Corp** Prague. Narodni Muuzeum. **VFOAT** Acta. Series C: Historia Litterarum. V. 1- 1956-. Periodical. Czech (tables of contents also in Russian, English, and other languages). ir. **LC** PG5000.

SCANDINAVIAN STUDIES. See Linguistics.

SCANDINAVICA. V. 1- May 1962-. 0036-5653. Periodical. UK. English. sa. $40.00. University of East Anglia, Norwich NR4 7TJ England. **Tel** (0603) 56161. Ed James McFarlane. **Ind/Abst** Am. Hist. Life, Hist. Abstr., Part A, Mod. Hist. Abstr., Hist. Abst., Part B, Twent. Century Abstr., MLA Int. Bibliogr. Books Artic. Mod. Lang. Lit., Index Book Rev. Humanit. **LC** PT7001. **DD** 839.505. (cum index). bk rev. adv acc. **Circ** 450. Scandinavian culture and literature of the modern age.

SCANDO-SLAVICA. V. 1-. 0080-6765. English (French, German, Italian, and Russian). an. Munksgaard Ltd, 35 Norre Sogade, DK-1370 Copenhagen K Denmark. **Tel** 1.12.70.30. Ed Gunnar Jacobsson. **Ind/Abst** MLA Int. Bibliogr. Books Artic. Mod. Lang. Lit., Recent Publ. Artic. **LC** PG1. **DD** 491.805. (cum index). **Circ** 700. Slavic and Baltic philology, literature, history, and archaeology.

SCANDO-SLAVICA. SUPPLEMENTUM. See Linguistics.

SCHATZKAMMER DER DEUTSCHEN SPRACHE, DICHTUNG UND GESCHICHTE. **VFOAT** Schatzkammer. 0740-1965. Periodical. US. German. sa. 5.00. University of South Dakota, Department of Modern Languages, c/o Werner Kitzler, Vermillion SD 57069. **Tel** (605)677-6061. Ed Werner Kitzler. **Ind/Abst** MLA Int. Bibliogr. Books Artic. Mod. Lang. Lit., Lang. Lang. Behav. Abstr. bk rev. **Circ** 1,000. Poems, short creative works, and translations by German-Americans, reference materials, and reviews of current books are included; for teachers of German at all levels. *Schatzkammer der Deutschen Sprachlehre, Dichtung und Geschichte.*

SCHOLAR CRITIC. Vol. 1, No. 1 (Jan. 1981)-. Periodical. II. English. ty. $10.00. Scholar Critic Faculty of English & Foreign Languages, Gandhigram Rural Institute, Gandhigram-624302 DT Madurai Tamilnadu India. **LC** PN2. **DD** 808.8.

SCHOLAR'S CHOICE : SIGNIFICANT CURRENT THEOLOGICAL LITERATURE FROM ABROAD. See Religion, Mythology, Rationalism - Theology.

SCHRIFTEN DER GOETHE-GESELLSCHAFT. **Main/Corp** Goethe-Gesellschaft (Weimar, Germany). Began publication with Vol. 1, 1885. German. ir. Deutscher Buch Export-Import, Leninstrasse 16, DDR-701 Leipzig East Germany. **Tel** 2071. **LC** PT2045. The contents are comprising texts by Goethe and on Goethe.

SCHRIFTEN DER THEODOR-STORM-GESELLSCHAFT. **Main/Corp** Theodor-Storm-Gesellschaft. Schrift 1- 1952-. 0082-3880. GW. German. an. Westholsteinische Verlagsanst, Postfach 1880, D-2240 Heide West Germany. **Tel** 0481/691-0. **Ind/Abst** MLA Int. Bibliogr. Books Artic. Mod. Lang. Lit. **Circ** 1,600.

SCHRIFTTUM ZUR DEUTSCHEN KUNST. See Bibliographies.

SCHWEIZER ANGLISTISCHE ARBEITEN. **VFOAT** Swiss Studies in English. 1- 1936-. Monographic Series. SZ. English (German). ir. Francke Verlag, Neuengasse 43, Postfach 1445, CH-3001 Bern Switzerland. **Tel** 031/22 17 15. **Ind/Abst** MLA Int. Bibliogr. Books Artic. Mod. Lang. Lit.

SCIENCE FICTION. V. 1- June 1977-. 0314-6677. Periodical. AT. English. ty. V Ikin, University of Western Australia, Department of English, Nedlands Western Australia 6009 Australia. **Tel** 09-448-5301. Ed V Ikin. **Ind/Abst** MLA Int. Bibliogr. Books Artic. Mod. Lang. Lit. bk rev. adv acc. **Circ** 1,500. Essays on science fiction books and writers, interviews, book reviews, regular columnists commenting on the science fiction field.

SCIENCE FICTION AND FANTASY BOOK REVIEW INDEX : SFFBRI. See Indexes/Abstracts.

SCIENCE FICTION CHRONICLE. 1979. 0195-5365. Periodical. US. English. mo. $30.00. Science Fiction Chronicle, PO Box 4175, New York

Literature

NY 10163. Tel (718)643-9011. Ed Andrew I Porter. Ind/Abst MLA Int. Bibliogr. Books Artic. Mod. Lang. Lit. bk rev. adv acc. Circ 3,700. Science fiction, fantasy news, reviews, letters, market reports, forthcoming book information, convention calendar, awards, columns, interviews, editorials, photos, for writers, editors, professionals, readers.

THE SCIENCE FICTION REVIEW MONTHLY. 0361-7009. Periodical. US. English. mo. $11.00 US & Canada, $16.00 Others. Bran Dougal, 56 8th Avenue, New York NY 10014.

SCINTILLA (TORONTO, ONT.). (SCINTILLA). Vol. 1 (1984)-. 0824-6009. CN. English (includes some text in French). an. $3.00 Per Vol. Centre for Medieval Studies, 39 Queen's Park Crescent East, Toronto Ontario M5S 1A1 Canada. DD 809.02.

SCOTTISH GAELIC STUDIES. See Linguistics.

SCOTTISH LITERARY JOURNAL. V. 1- July 1974-. 0305-0785. UK. English. 15.75. Association for Scottish Literary Studies, Taylor Building, Aberdeen AB9 2UB Scotland. Tel (041)339-8855. Ed Kenneth Buthlay. Ind/Abst Abstr. Engl. Stud., MLA Int. Bibliogr. Books Artic. Mod. Lang. Lit., Index Book Rev. Humanit. LC PR8514. DD 820.809411. bk rev. adv acc. Circ 800. (ctrl) A scholarly journal that publishes articles on Scottish literature and Scottish writers of all periods. *Scottish Literary News.*

SCOTTISH LITERARY JOURNAL. SUPPLEMENT. No. 1- Summer 1975-. 0305-0785. Periodical. UK. English. Ind/Abst Abstr. Engl. Stud. LC PR8514. DD 891.6309.

SCOTTISH SHORT STORIES. 1973-. UK. English. an. 3.50. Collin's, St James Place, London England. LC PZ1.A1, PR8676.

SCRIVENER. (SCRIVENER : JOURNAL OF CREATIVE WRITING). Vol. 1, No. 1 (Spring 1980)-. 0227-5090. Periodical. CN. English. sa. 3.86. McGill University/Scrivener, 853 Sherbrooke Street West, Montreal Quebec H3A 2T6 Canada. Tel (514)392-4483. Ed Antonia Cima. DD C810.80054. bk rev. adv acc. Circ 1,000. Creative journal for literary and visual arts.

SEACADEMY. V. 1- Sept. 1978-. 0226-1820. CN. English (Chinese). an. Free. Seacademy University of Alberta, Box 219 Sub 11, Edmonton Alberta T6G 2E0 Canada. DD C895.108005. (ctrl).

SEAHORSE. (SEAHORSE : THE ANAIS NIN/HENRY MILLER JOURNAL). VFOAT Anais Nin/Henry Miller Journal. Vol. 1, No. 1 (Feb. 21, 1982)-. 0731-5333. Periodical. US. English. qt. $5.00. Ohio State University Libraries, Richard R Centing, 1858 Neil Avenue, Columbus OH 43210. Ed Richard R Centing. Ind/Abst Abstr. Engl. Stud., MLA Int. Bibliogr. Books Artic. Mod. Lang. Lit. LC PS221. DD 810.90052.

THE SEATTLE REVIEW. Began with Spring 1978 issue. 0147-6629. US. English. sa. $3.50. Padelford Hall GN-30, University of Washington, Seattle WA 98195. LC PS536.2. DD 810.8.

SECOLUL 20. VAT Secolul Twenty. 1- Jan. 1961-. 0037-0517. Periodical. RM. Romanian. mo. Ilexim Press Departement, PO Box 1-136-1-137, Bucharest Romania. Ind/Abst MLA Int. Bibliogr. Books Artic. Mod. Lang. Lit. LC PN6065.R8. DD 809.04. (cum index).

SECOND COMING. V. 1- 1972-. 0048-9956. Periodical. US. English. sa. $8.50. Second Coming Press, PO Box 31249, San Francisco CA 94131. Tel (415)647-3679. Ed A D Winans. Ind/Abst Index Am. Period. Verse. adv acc. Circ 1,500. International literary journal praised by library journals: Bill Katz, Herb Gold Bukowski, Josephline Miles Ferlincletti, plus many others. Avant Garde at its best.

SEGYE MUNHAK. VFOAT Shi Jie Wenxue. Periodical. Korean. ir. LC PN6065.K6.

SELECAO DE LIVROS PARA A INFANCIA E JUVENTUDE. Portuguese. bm. Fundacao Nacional do Livro Infantil e Juvenil, rua da Imprensa 16 5O. Andar Salas 508-510, CEP 20030 Rio de Janeiro RJ Brazil. LC Z1037.7. DD 028.162.

SELECTED BIBLIOGRAPHIES IN LANGUAGE AND LITERATURE. See Bibliographies.

SELECTED PAPERS FROM THE WEST VIRGINIA SHAKESPEARE AND RENAISSANCE ASSOCIATION. Spring 1976-. Periodical. US. English. an. $5.00. Marshall University, Department of History, Huntington WV 25701. Tel (304)696-6781. Ed Michael J Galgano. Ind/Abst MLA Int. Bibliogr. Books Artic. Mod. Lang. Lit. LC PR2887. DD 822.33. Circ 200. Articles in the areas of Shakespeare and of the Renaissance.

SELECTIONS FROM THE CFUW WRITING PROJECT. 1977/78-. 0823-860X. CN. English. an. Canadian Federation of University Women Library and Creative Arts Committee, c/o J Sinclair, 1427 Beimer Avenue, Mississauga Ontario L5H 2A9 Canada. DD C810.809287.

SELECTIONS - MODERN LANGUAGES SERVICES BRANCH. (SELECTIONS). No. 1 (Mar. 1983)-. 0826-3310. Periodical. CN. English. ir. Limited free distribution. Province of British Columbia, Information Service, 1450 Government Street, Victoria British Columbia V8W 3E7 Canada. DD 011.62.

SEMIOSIS. See Linguistics.

THE SENECA REVIEW. Began with May 1970 issue. 0037-2145. Periodical. US. English. sa. $6.000. Hobart & William Smith College, Box 115, Geneva NY 14456. Tel (315)789-5500. Ind/Abst Index Am. Period. Verse. LC PN6010.5. DD 808.8. adv acc. Circ 500.

SENRYU NENKAN. 1972-. JA. Japanese. ir. 1500. Yuzankaku, 6-9 Fujimi 2-chome, Chiyoda-ku Tokyo Japan. LC PL730.

SENTEI JIDO TOSHO MOKUROKU. JA. Japanese. ir. Nagoya-shi Jido Tosho Sentei Kyogikai, c/o Nagoya-shi Tsurumai Chuo Toshokan 1-55, Tsurumai 1-chome Showa-ku Nagoya Japan 466. LC Z1037.8.J3, PN1009.J3.

SEQUOIA. Began with Winter 1956 issue. 0037-2420. Periodical. US. English. ty. $9.75. Storke Student Publications, Publications Building, Stanford CA 94305. Tel (415)326-0477. LC PS508.C6. DD 810.8.

THE SERIF SERIES : BIBLIOGRAPHIES AND CHECKLISTS. See Bibliographies.

SEVENTEENTH-CENTURY NEWS. VFOAT SCN. V. 1- 1942-. 0037-3028. Periodical. US. English. qt. $6.00 US, Canada; $9.00 Others. Texas A & M University, c/o H T Meseroele, Department of English, College Station TX 77843. Tel (409)845-3400. Ed Harrison T Meseroele and J Max Patrick. Ind/Abst MLA Int. Bibliogr. Books Artic. Mod. Lang. Lit., Years Work Eng. Stud. LC PR1. bk rev. adv acc. Circ 1,300. Covers all aspects of Seventeenth century culture. English, American and European, with emphasis on literature and history.

THE SEWANEE REVIEW. V. 1- Nov. 1892-. 0037-3052. Periodical. US. English. ir. $18.00. Sewanee Review, University of the South, Sewanee TN 37375-4009. Tel (615)598-1245. Ed George Core. Ind/Abst Humanit. Index, Abstr. Engl. Stud., MLA Int. Bibliogr. Books Artic. Mod. Lang. Lit., Annu. Bibliogr. Engl. Lang. Lit., Book Rev. Index, Index Book Rev. Humanit., Index Am. Period. Verse, Int. Index, Soc. Sci. Index, Years Work Eng. Stud. LC AP2. (cum index). bk rev. adv acc. Circ 3,560. American and English literature: short fiction, poetry, literary essays and criticism, book reviews, and book notices.

SEZ. No. 1 (Winter 1978)-. 0190-3640. Monographic Series. US. English. ir. $8.50. Sez /A Multi-Racial Journal of Poetry, PO Box 8803, Minneapolis MN 55408. Tel (612)822-3488. Ed Jim Dochniak. bk rev. adv acc. Circ 2,000. (ctrl). Multicultural, working class literary magazine. Poetry, fiction, reviews, interviews, and articles on progressive culture. International and regional.

SHAKESPEARE JAHRBUCH. See Yearbooks, Almanacs, Directories.

THE SHAKESPEARE NEWSLETTER. V. 1- (No. 1-). 0037-3214. Periodical. US. English. qt. $7.00 Domestic, $8.00 Foreign. Shakespeare Newsletter, 1217 Ashland Avenue, Evanston IL 60202. Ed Louis Marder. Ind/Abst Abstr. Engl. Stud., MLA Int. Bibliogr. Books Artic. Mod. Lang. Lit., Annu. Bibliogr. Engl. Lang. Lit., Years Work Eng. Stud. LC PR2885. DD 822.33. bk rev. adv acc. Circ 1,800. A wide-ranging survey of all biographical critical interpretation. Theatrical Shakespeare studies in digest form, book reviews, authorship, news, scholarly trends, festivals, meetings, etc., with annual index.

SHAKESPEARE QUARTERLY. V. 1- Jan. 1950-. 0037-3222. Periodical. US. English. qt. $40.00. Folger Library, 201 East Capitol Street Southeast, Washington DC 20003. Tel (202)544-4600. Ed Barbara A Mowat. Ind/Abst Abstr. Engl. Stud., Annu. Bibliogr. Engl. Lang. Lit., Film Lit. Index, Index Book Rev. Humanit., Humanit. Index, MLA Int. Bibliogr. Books Artic. Mod. Lang. Lit., Soc. Sci. Index, Years Work Eng. Stud. LC PR2885. DD 822.33. (cum index). bk rev. adv acc. Circ 3,400. A scholarly periodical published in one volume of five issues for 1986, plus one supplement- World Shakespeare Bibliography. *Shakespeare Association Bulletin*, 0270-8604.

SHAKESPEARE STUDIES. 1- 1965-. 0582-9399. US. English. an. Bert Franklin & Company Inc, 235 East 44th Street, New York NY 10017. Tel (212)687-5250. Ind/Abst MLA Int. Bibliogr. Books Artic. Mod. Lang. Lit., Years Work Eng. Stud., Humanit. Index. LC PR2885. DD 822.33. (cum index).

SHAKESPEARE SURVEY. 0080-9152. UK. English. ir. 21.00. Cambridge University Press, Edinburg Building, Shaftesbury Road, Cambridge CB2 2RU England. Tel 0223-312393. Ed Stanley Wells. Ind/Abst Abstr. Engl. Stud., MLA Int. Bibliogr. Books Artic. Mod. Lang. Lit., Annu. Bibliogr. Engl. Lang. Lit., Humanit. Index, Years Work Eng. Stud. LC PR2888. DD 822.33. (cum index). bk rev. adv acc. Circ 3,000. A yearbook of scholarly articles, with a different theme each year, based on all aspects of Shakespeare and the reading and performance of his works.

SHAKESPEARE TRANSLATION. V. 1- 1974-. JA. English (Multilingual). ir. Yushoda Shoten Ltd, 29 San-ei-cho Shinjuku-ku, Tokyo Japan. LC PR2881. DD 822.33.

SHAN CHA. Began with Apr. 1980 issue. Periodical. CC. Chinese. bm. $3.11. China Publication Centre, PO Box 2820, Beijing China. LC PL2515.5.M56. DD 895.108.

SHAN-HSI WEN HSUEH. VFOAT Shanxi Wenxue. 1982, 1-. Periodical. CC. Chinese. mo. $8.64. China Publication Centre, PO Box 2820, Beijing China. LC PL3031.S32. DD 895.10995117. *Fen Shui.*

SHAN-TUNG WEN HSUEH. Periodical. CH. Chinese. mo. 0.35. Chung-Kuo Kuo Chi Shu Tien, PO Box 399, Peking China. LC PL3031.S3. DD 895.109095114.

SHANG-HAI WEN HSUEH. VFOAT Shanghai Wenxue. Began with Oct. 1959 issue. Periodical. CC. Chinese. mo. China Publication Centre, PO Box 2820, Beijing China. *Wen I Yueh Pao.*

SHANTIH. V. 1- Winter 1971-. 0037-329X. Periodical. US. English. qt $8.00. Shantih, PO Box 125 Bay Ridge Station, Brooklyn NY 11220. LC PN6010.5. DD 808.8004.

SHAW. Vol. 1-. 0741-5842. Periodical. US. English. an. $22.50. Penn State University Press, 215 Wagner Building, c/o Jane Dietz, University Park PA 16802. Tel (814)865-1327. Ed Stanley Weintraub. Ind/Abst Abstr. Engl. Stud., MLA Int. Bibliogr. Books Artic. Mod. Lang. Lit., Index Book Rev. Humanit. LC PR5366. DD 822.912. Devoted to studying Shaw. Odd numbered volumes have a theme; even numbered volumes are general studies of Shaw. *Shaw Review*, 0037-3354.

SHEKSPIROVSKIE CHTENIIA. VFOAT Shakespeare Readings. 1976-. Periodical. UR. Russian. 1.80. Izdatelstvo Nauka, V-485 Profsoiusznaia Ul 90, 117864 GSP-7 Moskva Russia. LC PR2885. DD 822.33.

SHEN HUA. Periodical. CH. Chinese. mo. 0.30. Post Office, Chang-Chun Shih China. LC PL2513. DD 895.109005.

SHENANDOAH. V. 1- Spring 1950-. 0037-3583. Periodical. US. English. qt. $21.60. Washington Lee University, Box 722, Lexington VA 24450. Tel (703)463-8765. Ed James Boatwright. Ind/Abst Annu. Bibliogr. Engl. Lang. Lit., Abstr. Engl. Stud., MLA Int. Bibliogr. Books Artic. Mod. Lang. Lit., Index Am. Period. Verse. LC AP2. DD 051. (cum index) bk rev. adv acc. Circ 1,000. A literary magazine publishing first-rate fiction, poetry, essays, and reviews since 1950.

THE SHERLOCK HOLMES JOURNAL. Began in 1952. 0037-3621. Periodical. UK. English. sa. Sherlock Holmes Society of London, Old Crown Inn Lopen, Somerset TA13 5JX England. LC PR4623. DD 823.8.

Literature

SHIH CHIEH WEN HSUEH. VFOAT Shijie Wenxue. Periodical. CC. Chinese (table of contents also in English). bm. $7.83. China Publication Centre, PO Box 2820, Beijing China. LC PN9. DD 809. / Wen.

SHIH YUEH. VFOAT Shiyue. Periodical. CC. Chinese. bm. $11.34. China Publication Centre, PO Box 2820, Beijing China. LC PL2513. DD 895.109005.

SHIKYO KENKYU. VFOAT Journal of Shi-Jing. No. 1-. Periodical. Japanese. ir. 800. Shikyogaku Kenkyu Senta, c/o Waseda, Daigaku/Bungakubu/Murayama, Kenkyushitsu Toyamacho Shinjuku-Ku, Tokyo Japan. LC PL2466.Z7.

SHIMANE DAIGAKU HOBUNGAKUBU KIYO. BUNGAKUKA HEN. VFOAT Memoirs of the Faculty of Law and Literature. Periodical. JA. English (Japanese). ir. Shimane Daigaku Hobungakubu, 1060 Nishi Kawazumachi Matsue-Shi, Shimane-Ken Japan. LC PN9.

SHIMAZAKI TOSON KENKYU. Sokango-1976-. JA. Japanese. ir. 4-3 Shibuya, Shibuya 2-Chome 150 Japan. LC PL816.H55. Fusetsu.

SHINMATSU SHOSETSU KENKYU. No. 1-. JA. Japanese. ir. 980. Shinmatsu Shosetsu Kenkyukai, Heijo Dai 2 Danchi 19-208, Ukyo 2-Chome Nara Japan 631. LC PL2437.

SHISHA. Ed. - 1979-Year Spring. Periodical. JA. Japanese. ir. 3800. Shogaukkan, 3-1 Hitotsubashi 2, Chiyoda-Ku 101, Tokyo Japan. LC PL755.8.

SHOE TREE. Vol. 1, No. 1 (Fall 1985)-. 0883-2668. Periodical. US. English. qt. $15.00 Domestic, $19.00 Foreign. Pequest Publications, PO Box 356, Belvidere NJ 07823. DD 808.

SHORT STORY INDEX. See Indexes/Abstracts.

SHU LIN. VFOAT Shu Lin. Began with Sept. 1979 issue. Periodical. CC. Chinese. bm. 0.32. Hsin Hua Shu Tien Shang-Hai Fa Hsing So, Shanghai China. LC Z1035.A1. DD 028.105.

SI QUE. (SI QUE —). 1-. 0229-5776. CN. French. an. $5.00 Per Volume. Directeur de si que Dep des Etudes Francaises, Universite de Moncton, Moncton New Brunswick E1A 3E9 Canada. DD 840.9.

SIARA. VFOAT Siaar. Periodical. Panjabi. ir. 1.00 Single Issue. Pasha, Talwandi Salem, Jalandhara India. LC PK2650.

SIDETREKKED. (SIDETREKKED : THE STAR TREK ONTARIO FANZINE). 0715-3007. Periodical. CN. English. bm. $5.00. Science Fiction London, 419 Beachwood Avenue, London Ontario N6J 3J9 Canada. DD 809.387605.

SIEGENER PERIODICUM ZUR INTERNATIONALEN EMPIRISCHEN LITERATURWISSENSCHAFT. VFOAT S.P.I.E.L. Vol. 1, No. 1 (1982)-. 0722-7833. Periodical. GW. German. sa. Verlag Peter Lang, Wolfgangstrasse 92, D-6000 Frankfurt AM Main West Germany. LC PN4. DD 805.

SIGMA. IT. Italian. $5.35. Guida Editori SRL, V-Port Alba 19, 80134 Napoli Italy. LC PQ4001. DD 809.

SIGNATURE. Periodical. US. English. ir. $3.00. Sumter High School, Haynsworth Street, Sumter SC 29150. LC PS559.S9. DD 810.809283.

SIJILL AL-UDABA. Journal 1. (1979)-. Arabic. an. 2.50. LC Z3014.L56, PJ7510.

SILLAGES. Vol. 1 1972-. FR. French (English or Portuguese). ir. Universite de Poitiers, 95 Avenue du Recteur-Pineau, 86022 Poities France. LC PQ9004. DD 869.09.

SILVER VAIN. 1- Spring 1977-. 0147-6122. Periodical. US. English. ty. Silver Vain, PO Box 2366, Park City UT 84060. Tel (801)649-8866. LC PS501. DD 810.80054.

SIMAN KERIAH. 1- September 1972-. IS. Hebrew. 28. Siman Kria, POB 39267, Tel Aviv Israel 61392. Tel (03)420995. Ed M Perry. LC HJ5001. bk rev. adv acc. Circ 3,000. Fiction, poetry, criticism, poetics of literature. criticism, essays, theory of literature, reviews, articles.

SIMANTIKA. VFOAT Seemantika. April 1984-. 8755-7517. Periodical. US. Hindi. mo. $20.00. Folklore Institute, PO Box 1142, Berkeley CA 94701. Ed Ved Prakash Vatuk. DD 891. bk rev. adv acc. Circ 1,000. Articles, poetry, book reviews, and short stories, by Hindi writers world over.

SIMPLY STATED. No. 8 (July/Aug. 1980)-. 0731-2016. Periodical. US. English. m. American Institute for Research, 1055 Thomas Jefferson Street NW, Washington DC 20007. Tel (202)342-5000. Ed Robbin M Battison. bk rev. Circ 10,000. Articles on readability, plain language laws, and research on effective writing. Fine Print.

SIMUNHAK. Periodical. KO. Korean. ir. 3,000. Simunhak Sa, 190 Migun-dong, Sodaemun-ku, Seoul Korea. LC PL972.7.

SIN NOMBRE. V. 1- 1970-. 0037-5527. Periodical. PR. Spanish. qt. $20.00. Sin Nombre, Apartado 4391, San Juan Puerto Rico 00905. Ind/Abst Am. Hist. Life, Hist. Abstr., Part A, Mod. Hist. Abstr., Hist. Abst., Part B, Twent. Century Abstr., MLA Int. Bibliogr. Books Artic. Mod. Lang. Lit., Index Am. Period. Verse, Hist. Abstr. LC AP63. DD 860.5.

SING HEAVENLY MUSE. No. 1 (Spring 1978)-. 0198-9855. Periodical. US. English. sa. $21.00. Sing Heavenly Muse, c/o S Martinson Box 14059, Minneapolis MN 55414. Tel (612)822-8713. Ed Sue Ann Martinson. LC PS508.W7. DD 810.809287. adv acc. Circ 1,000. A women's publication of poetry and prose. We encourage women to range freely, honestly, and imaginatively over all subjects, philosophies, and styles.

SINISTER WISDOM. Began with July 1976 issue. 0196-1853. Periodical. US. English. qt. $26.00. Sinister Wisdom, PO Box 1023, Rockland ME 04841. Tel (207)596-0680. Ed Melanie Kaye/Kantrowitz. Ind/Abst Altern. Press Index. LC PS508.W7. DD 810.809287. bk rev. adv acc. The best of contemporary women's writing, emphasis on new voices, feminist perspective.

SINN UND FORM. Vol. 1-. 0037-5756. Periodical. German. bm. $23.06. Kunst & Wissen Erich Bieber, Dufourstrasse 51, CH-8008 Zurich Switzerland. Ind/Abst Annu. Bibliogr. Engl. Lang. Lit., MLA Int. Bibliogr. Books Artic. Mod. Lang. Lit. LC AP30. DD 053.1.

SIVAM. Periodical. II. Hindi. mo. 20.00. Miss Tripta Tivari, E-114/12 Shivaji Nagar, Bhopal 462006 India. LC PK2103.M3.

THE SLACKWATER REVIEW. V. 1- Spring 1976-. 0160-7677. Periodical. US. English. an. $6.00. Confluence Press, Spalding Hall, LC Campus, Lewiston ID 83501. Tel (208)743-0470. LC PS1. DD 810.9005.

SLOVENSKA LITERATURA. Vol. 1- 1954-. 0037-6973. Periodical. GW. Czech. bm. Kubon and Sagner, Postfach 34 01 08, D8 Munchen 34 West Germany. Tel (089)52 20 27. Ind/Abst MLA Int. Bibliogr. Books Artic. Mod. Lang. Lit. LC PG5400. The older classical Slovak literature as well works and problems of the contemporary Socialistic literature are equally being treated. Literarnohistoricky Sbornik.

SLOVO A SLOVESNOST. Vol. 1- 1935-. 0037-7031. Periodical. CS. Czech. qt. Kubon and Sagner, Postfach 34 01 000, D-8000 Munchen West Germany. Tel (089)52 20 27. Ind/Abst MLA Int. Bibliogr. Books Artic. Mod. Lang. Lit., Annu. Bibliogr. Engl. Lang. Lit., Sociol. Abstr., Lang. Lang. Behav. Abstr. LC PG4004. A journal of discussion of grammar, lexicography, phonemic, and phonetic studies, problems of stylistics and semantics, and of translation of prose and verse.

THE SMALL POND MAGAZINE OF LITERATURE. VFOAT Small Pond Magazine. 1964. 0737-1535. Periodical. US. English. ty. $5.50. Small Pond Magazine, PO Box 664, Stratford CT 06497. Tel (203)378-4066. Ind/Abst Index Am. Period. Verse. bk rev. adv acc. Circ 300. Contemporary poetry, short prose (usually fiction), poetry book reviews, and editorial opinions on various current topics. Small Pond.

SMASH. V. 1- 1974-. 0360-6074. US. English. Editorial Offices, 62 West 83rd Street, New York NY 10024. LC AP201. DD 051.

SMOKE SIGNALS. (SMOKE SIGNALS : A COLLECTION OF PRIZE-WINNING ENTRIES FROM THE SASKATCHEWAN WRITERS' GUILD LITERARY COMPETITION). 1973/74-. 0228-8672. CN. English. be. $2.00. Saskatchewan Writers' Guild, PO Box 3986, Regina Sasaktoon S4P 3R9 Canada. DD C810.8097123.

SNAPDRAGON. V. 1- Fall 1977-. 0160-5305. Periodical. US. English. sa. $4.50. University of Idaho Library, Moscow ID 83843. Tel (208)885-6584. Ed Gail Eckwright, Tina Foriyes, and Ron McFarland. adv acc. Circ 200. Personal experience and humorous essays, experimental, humorous mainstream and literary fiction, novel excerpts, and poetry. Also drawings, prints and black and white photographs.

SOBESEDNIK. Vol. 1-. UR. Russian. an. 0.90. Izdatelstvo Sovremennik, 121351 Moskva, G-351 Iartsevskai, Moskva Russian SFSR. LC PG2910. DD 891.709.

SOCIOLOGIA DELLA LETTERATURA. 1977-. Periodical. Italian. ir. $10.00. C C P 31054000 Intestato A, Bulzoni Editore Roma. LC PN51.

SOLAIRE CEASED. 1- May 1973-. Periodical. French. ir. 25.00. Les Editions Federop, Eglise Neuve d'Issac, 24400 Mussidan France. Tel 53.80.10.74. LC PQ1100.

SOLARIS. V. 5, No 3 (No 28-)- Aug./Sept. 1979-. 0709-8863. Periodical. CN. French. bm. $14.70. Solaris, 266 rue Belleau, Chicoutimi Quebec G7H 2Y8 Canada. Tel (418)549-2559. Ed Elisabeth Vonarburg. DD 808.83876. bk rev. adv acc. Circ 800. Science fiction, fantasy in literature, graphic arts, cinema; essays, reviews, stories and information. Requiem, 0317-5324.

SOLZHENITSYN STUDIES. Vol. 1, No. 1 (Spring 1980)-. 0731-2261. Periodical. US. English. qt. $10.50. University Lancaster, Russian Soviet, Studies Department, c/o Professor Nicholson, Lancaster LA1 4YN England. LC Z8825.76, PG3488.O4. DD 891.7344.

SOSOL MUNHAK. Periodical. KO. Korean. mo. 24.00. 61-2 Kyonam-Dong, Chongno-Ku Seoul 110 South Korea. LC PL980.A1.

SOUCHE. (LA SOUCHE). 1981-. 0712-6956. CN. French. an. Souche, a/s G Belanger, Dep de Francais, Universite Laurentienne, Sudbury Ontario P3C 2C6 Canada. DD C840.8092375.

SOUNDINGS EAST. V. 2- Spring 1979-. Periodical. US. English. sa. $4.00. Soundings East, Salem State College, Salem MA 01970. Tel (617)745-0556. Ed Claire Keyes. Circ 2,000. Publishes short fiction and poetry. 64 pages, perfect-bound. Feature poet section. Photographs and original illustrations. College literary magazine. Soundings.

SOUTH DAKOTA REVIEW. V. 1- Dec. 1963-. 0038-3368. Periodical. US. English. qt. $10.00. University of South Dakota, Vermillion SD 57069. Tel (605)677-5966. Ed John R Milton. Ind/Abst Abstr. Engl. Stud., MLA Int. Bibliogr. Books Artic. Mod. Lang. Lit., Annu. Bibliogr. Engl. Lang. Lit., Index Am. Period. Verse, Years Work Eng. Stud. LC AP2. DD 051. (cum index). Circ 500. Fiction, poetry, essays, critical articles often with emphasis on writers in the American west. Occasional special issues on one subject or one writer.

SOUTH EAST ARTS REVIEW. Periodical. UK. English. qt. Free to South East Arts Association Members, Universities, and Libraries, 1.20 Others. South East Arts, 9-10 Crescent Road, Tunbridge Wells Kent TN1 2LU England. LC PR8389.S6245. DD 820.8099422.

SOUTHEAST ASIAN REVIEW OF ENGLISH. See Linguistics.

THE SOUTHERN LITERARY JOURNAL. V. 1- Autumn 1968-. 0038-4291. Periodical. US. English. sa. $10.00. University of North Carolina Press, Box 2288, Chapel Hill NC 27514. Tel (919)966-3561. Ind/Abst Abstr. Engl. Stud., MLA Int. Bibliogr. Books Artic. Mod. Lang. Lit., Index Book Rev. Humanit., Humanit. Index, Am. Hist. Life, Hist. Abstr., Part A, Mod. Hist. Abstr., Hist. Abst., Part B, Twent. Century Abstr., Years Work Eng. Stud., Hist. Abstr. LC PS261. DD 810.9975. (cum index).

THE SOUTHERN REVIEW. V. 1-7, July 1935-Spring 1942. 0038-4534. Periodical. US. English. qt. $12.00. Southern Review, 43 Allen Hall, Louisiana State University, Baton Rouge LA 70803. Tel (504)388-5108. Ed James Olney and Lewis P Simpson. Ind/Abst Annu. Bibliogr. Engl. Lang. Lit., Abstr. Engl. Stud., Am. Hist. Life, Humanit. Index, Book Rev. Index, MLA Int. Bibliogr. Books Artic. Mod. Lang. Lit., Index Book Rev. Humanit., Index Am. Period. Verse, Ocean. Abstr., Hist. Abstr., Part A, Mod. Hist. Abstr., Hist. Abst., Part B, Twent. Century Abstr., Years Work Eng. Stud., Hist. Abstr. LC AP2. DD 051. (cum index). bk rev. adv acc. Circ 3,000. Available on microfilm from University Microfilms and on microfiche from Johnson Associates, Inc. Fiction, poetry, essays, and reviews with emphasis on contemporary literature in the United States and abroad and with special interest in Southern culture and history.

Literature

THE SOU'WESTER. New Ser. V. 1- Winter 1973-. 0038-4976. Periodical. US. English. ty. $3.00. Southern Illinois University, Edwardsville, Edwardsville IL 62026-1438. **Tel** (616)692-2289. **Ed** Dickie Spurgeon. LC PS501. DD 810.80054. Poetry and fiction, up to 10,000 words. Sou'wester Literary Quarterly.

SOVESTSKAIA LITVA. Periodical. UR. Russian. ir. $37.00. Victor Kamkin Inc (67214), 12224 Parklawn Drive, Rockville MD 20852. **Tel** (301)881-5973. LC PG8771.R1.

SOVETAKAN GRAKANUTYUN. SOVETSKAIA LITERATURA. 1933-. Periodical. UR. Armenian. mo. $31.50. Victor Kamkin Inc (77823), 12224 Parklawn Drive, Rockville MD 20852. **Tel** (301)881-5973.

SOVETSKAIA TIURKOLOGIIA. 1970-. Periodical. US. Russian. bm. $42.50. Victor Kamkin Inc (70927), 12224 Parklawn Drive, Rockville MD 20852. **Tel** (301)881-5973. **Ind/Abst** MLA Int. Bibliogr. Books Artic. Mod. Lang. Lit. LC PL21. Voprosy Dialektologii Tiurkskikh Iazykov.

SOVIET LITERATURE. V. 1- 1931-. Periodical. UR. English (Russian). mo. Soviet Literature, #70836. **Ind/Abst** MLA Int. Bibliogr. Books Artic. Mod. Lang. Lit. Literature of the World Revolution.

THE SOVIET REVIEW. See Literary and Political Reviews.

SOVIET STUDIES IN LITERATURE. V. 1- Winter 1964/65-. 0038-5875. Periodical. US. English (Russian). qt. $178.50. M E Sharpe Inc, 80 Business Park Drive, Armonk NY 10504. **Tel** (914)273-1800. **Ed** Bernard L Koten. **Ind/Abst** MLA Int. Bibliogr. Books Artic. Mod. Lang. Lit. LC PN2. adv acc. **Circ** 200. Devoted to literary history and theory, criticism and controversy by Soviet writers and scholars, covering pre-revolutionary and Soviet works.

SOVREMENNAIA LITERATURA ZA RUBEZHOM. Vol. 1-. 0584-5750. Periodical. UR. Russian. ir. 2.60. Izd-Vo Sovetskii Pisatel 121069, Ul Vorovskogo 11, Moskva USSR.

SOVREMENNAIA VOSTOCHNAIA NOVELLA; SBORNIK PEREVODOV. Vol. 1-. UR. Russian. 0.42. Nauka, Tsentr Armianskii Per, Moskva 2 Russia. LC PJ486.

SOZVEZDIE. UR. Russian. 0.55 Each Issue. Mordovskoe Kniznhoe Izd-vo, Moskovskaia 115, Saransk USSR. LC PG3504.M59.

SPACE. 1-. UK. English. Transatlantic Arts, North Village Green, Levittown NY 11756. LC PZ1, PR1309.S3. DD 823.0876.

THE SPECTRUM. V. 1- 1955-. Periodical. English. an. LC LH5.I7.

SPECULUM. See History (General) - History of Europe.

SPHINX. (THE SPHINX). No. 1- Winter 1974-. 0319-0188. CN. English. sa. $5.81. University of Regina, English Department, Regina Campus, Regina Saskatchewan S4S 0A2 Canada. **Tel** (306)584-4311. **Ind/Abst** MLA Int. Bibliogr. Books Artic. Mod. Lang. Lit., Years Work Eng. Stud. DD 809.

SPICILEGIO MODERNO. 1- 1972-. 0391-4216. IT. English, French, German or Italian. an. 6500. Editrice Libreria Goliardica, Via Oberdan 2-4, Pisa 56100 Italy. **Ind/Abst** MLA Int. Bibliogr. Books Artic. Mod. Lang. Lit. LC PN5.

SPIEGEL DER LETTEREN. 1- Yearly volume. Periodical. BE. Dutch. qt. 19.37. Editions Peeters, Bondgenotenlaan 153 Box 41, B-3000 Leuven Belgium. LC PT6000. adv acc. (ctrl).

SPINDRIFTER. (THE SPINDRIFTER). Vol. 1, No. 1 (Mar. 1981)-. 0711-4826. Periodical. CN. English. qt. $2.50 Each Number. Spindrift Writers, Parksville British Columbia V0R 2S0 Canada. DD C810.80971134.

THE SPIRIT THAT MOVES US. V. 2- Fall 1976-. 0364-4014. Periodical. US. English. ir. $9.60. The Spirit that Moves Us Press, PO Box 1585, Iowa City IA 52244. **Tel** (319)338-7502. **Ed** Morty Sklar. **Ind/Abst** Index Am. Period. Verse. LC PS580. DD 811.5408. **Circ** 3,000. Contemporary poetry, fiction and art. One of our authors, whose book we published as a special issue, won the 1984 Nobel Prize. Spirit That Moves Us Magazine, 0163-3880.

SPIT IN THE OCEAN. V. 1- 1974-. 0095-0459. US. English. $1.00. Intrepid Trips Information Service, Rt 8 Box 477, Plesant Hill OR 97401. LC PS501. DD 810.8005.

SPITBALL. Vol. 1, No. 1 (Spring 1981)-. 8755-741X. Periodical. US. English. qt. $10.00. Spitball The Literary Baseball Magazine, Spitball 1721 Scott Boulevard, Covington KY 41011. **Tel** (606)261-3024. **Ed** Mike Shannon. DD 810. bk rev. adv acc. **Circ** 2,000. We publish poetry, fiction, and literary prose exclusively about baseball. We are also the only periodical which reviews every new baseball book. We also sponsor the Casey Award for best baseball book.

SPLIT LEVEL. V. 1- Oct. 1974-. 0317-0039. Periodical. CN. English. sa. $1.50. Split Level House, No 1 277 River Avenue, Winnipeg Manitoba R3L 0B5 Canada. DD 810.80054.

SPRACHE UND LITERATUR IN WISSENSCHAFT UND UNTERRICHT. See Linguistics.

SQUATCHBERRY JOURNAL. (THE SQUATCHBERRY JOURNAL). Brew No. 1- June 1975-. 0383-283X. Periodical. CN. English. sa. $2.00 Each Number. Squatchberry Journal, PO Box 205, Geraldton Ontario P0T 1M0 Canada. DD C810.80054.

SRASHTA. VFOAT Sarashta. Periodical. Nepali. bm. 1.50. Paschim Sikkim Sahitya Prakashan Samiti Gejing Bazar, W Sikkim In, Gejinga Bajara India. LC PK2597.5.

SRAVNITELNO LITERATUROZNANIE. VFOAT Litterature Comparee. V. 1, Kn. 1-. 0205-0390. Periodical. Bulgarian (summaries in English, French, German, and Russian). ir. 1.671 Each Issue. LC PN851. DD 809.

SSI. SHORT STORY INTERNATIONAL. (SSI, SHORT STORY INTERNATIONAL). VFOAT Short Story International. VAT Short Story International. V. 1- April 1977-. 0147-7706. Periodical. US. English. bm. $20.00. Short Story International, PO Box 405, Great Neck NY 11022. **Tel** (516)466-4166. **Ed** Sylvia Tankel. LC PZ1.A1, PN6010.5. DD 808.831. **Circ** 75,000. Contemporary short stories from all lands for the college level adult reader. Stories for pleasurable reading and insight into many cultures around the world.

STAND MAGAZINE. VFOAT Stand. Vol. 24, No. 4 (Autumn 1983)-. Periodical. UK. English. qt. 7.80. Stand Magazine, 179 Wingrove Road, New Castle on Tyne NE4 9DA England. **Tel** (091)273-3280. **Ed** Jon Silkin. **Ind/Abst** Abstr. Engl. Stud., Index Am. Period. Verse, Index Book Rev. Humanit. bk rev. adv acc. **Circ** 3,500. Is both British and international and publishes poetry, short stories, reviews, criticism and occasional short plays in English and English translation. Stand, 0038-9366.

STANFORD FRENCH AND ITALIAN STUDIES. Began publication in 1975. Monographic Series. US. English. ir. $25.00. Anma Libra and Company, PO Box 876, Saratoga CA 95070. **Tel** (415)851-3375. **Ed** A Suillaud. **Ind/Abst** MLA Int. Bibliogr. Books Artic. Mod. Lang. Lit. University research monographs in French and Italian literature.

STANFORD FRENCH REVIEW. See Literary and Political Reviews.

STAR-WEB PAPER. No. 1-. 0146-2105. Periodical. US. English. $15.00 Per 5 issues. Star-Web Paper, Regents 509 NMSU, Las Cruces NM 88003.

STARDOCK (OTTAWA SCIENCE FICTION SOCIETY). (STARDOCK). 0228-9326. Periodical. CN. English. $1.25 Each Number. c/o G Goracz, PO Box 4601, Station E, Ottawa Ontario K1S 5B3 Canada. DD C813.0876.

STEAUA. Periodical. RM. Romanian. mo. Ilexim Press Department, PO Box 1-136-1-137, Bucharest Romania. **Ind/Abst** MLA Int. Bibliogr. Books Artic. Mod. Lang. Lit. LC AP86.

STEINBECK QUARTERLY. V. 2, No. 3- Fall 1969-. 0039-100X. US. English. qt. Ball State University, English Department, c/o Dr Hayashi, Munice IN 47306. **Tel** (317)285-8389. **Ind/Abst** Abstr. Engl. Stud., MLA Int. Bibliogr. Books Artic. Mod. Lang. Lit., Years Work Eng. Stud. LC PS3537.T3234. DD 813.52. bk rev. adv acc. **Circ** 500. (ctrl). This journal is devoted to criticism of John Steinbeck, Nobel Prize novelist, and his great literature. We publish both critical and biographical essays, book reviews, bibliographical checklists, etc. Steinbeck Newsletter.

STENDHAL CLUB. 1.- Year (No. 1-). Periodical. FR. French. qt. Stendhall Club, 3 rue Maurice Gignoux, 38000 Grenoble France. **Ind/Abst** Recent Publ. Artic., Index Book Rev. Humanit., MLA Int. Bibliogr. Books Artic. Mod. Lang. Lit. LC PQ2436. DD 848.709.

STEPPINGSTONES. (STEPPINGSTONES (HARLEM, NEW YORK, N.Y.)). VFOAT Stepping Stones. Summer 1982-. 0735-4789. Periodical. US. English. ir. $15.00. Steppingstones, PO Box 1856, Harlem NY 10027. **Tel** (212)474-5063.

STING (CENTER SQUARE, PA.). (STING). Vol. 1, No. 1 (July/Aug. 1984)-. 8750-8974. Periodical. US. English. bm. $12.00 Domestic, $15.00 Canada. Alpine Publications, 1079 Route 202, Bluebell PA 19422. **Tel** (215)277-6342. **Ed** C Baker. Political, humor, and satire.

STOCKHOLM SLAVIC STUDIES. 1-. Monographic Series. SW. Swedish. ir. Almqvist & Wiksell, 108 Drottninggatan, PO Box 45150, S-104 30 Stockholm Sweden. **Tel** #85413160.

STONEY MONDAY. Issue No. 1- June 1978-. 0706-9006. Periodical. CN. English. qt. .50 Each Number. Stoney Monday Collective, 128 Keefer Street, Ottawa Ontario K1M 1T5 Canada. DD C810.80054.

STORIES. No. 1 (Sept.-Oct. 1982)-. Periodical. US. English. bm. $20.00. Stories, 14 Beacon Street, Boston MA 02108.

STORY ART. 1930-. 0039-1999. Periodical. US. English. ir. $5.00. Story Art, 872 High Street #5710, Canal Fulton OH 44614. **Tel** (216)854-3573.

STORY SO FAR. (THE STORY SO FAR). 1- 1971-. 0316-0645. CN. English. $3.00. Coach House Press, 401 Huron Street, Toronto Ontario M5S 2G5 Canada. LC PZ1.A1. DD 818.005.

STRAIGHT LINES. Periodical. UK. English. Straight Lines, 30 Mayfield Road, Mosley Birmingham 13 England. LC PR1098. DD 820.5.

STRANI JEZICI. 1- 1972-. Multilingual (Serbo-Croatian-R). ir. 30.00. Skolska Knjia, Masarykova 28, Zagreb Yugoslovia. **Ind/Abst** Lang. Teach. LC PB38.Y8.

STRELEC. (STRELETS). 1 (Jan. 1984)-. 0747-7287. Periodical. US. Russian. mo $40.00. Strelets, 286 Barrow Street, Jersey City NJ 07302. **Tel** (201)434-3274. **Ed** Alexander Glezer. LC PG3199. DD 891. bk rev. adv acc. **Circ** 500. (ctrl). Russian unofficial literature and art in USSR, in exile and political reviews.

STRUMENTI CRITICI. 1- Oct. 1966-. 0039-2618. Periodical. IT. Italian. Citta de Firenze, Via Ruffini 1, 50129 Firenze Italy. **Ind/Abst** Abstr. Engl. Stud., MLA Int. Bibliogr. Books Artic. Mod. Lang. Lit.

STUDI AMERICANI. No. 1-. 0085-6819. IT. Italian (English). ir. Edizioni di Storia e Letteratu, Via Lancellotti 18, Roma Italy. **Ind/Abst** Abstr. Engl. Stud., MLA Int. Bibliogr. Books Artic. Mod. Lang. Lit. LC PS1.

STUDI DI LETTERATURA FRANCESE. Series/Titl Biblioteca Dell'Archivum Romanicum. Serie 1: Storia, Letteratura, Paleografia. 1- 1967-. 0585-4768. Periodical. IT. Italian. an. Casa Editrice, Leo S Olschki, Casella Postale PO Box 66, 50100 Firenze Italy. **Ind/Abst** MLA Int. Bibliogr. Books Artic. Mod. Lang. Lit. LC PQ5.

STUDI DI LETTERATURA ISPANO-AMERICANA. V. 1- 1967-. 0585-4776. IT. Italian (Spanish). ir. Cisalpino-Goliardica, Via Bassini 17-2, 20133 Milan Italy.

STUDI FRANCESI. V. 1- (1-). 0039-2944. Periodical. IT. Italian (English, French and Italian). ir. 70.000 Domestic, 90.000 Europe, 126.000 Others. Rosenberg & Sellier, Via Andrea Doria 14, 10123 Torino Italy. **Tel** (011)8398131. **Ed** Sergio Cigada, Guiseppe di Stafano, Emanuele Kanceff, Gianni Mombello, Mario Richter, Cecillia Rizza, Corrado Rosso, and Lionello Sozzi. **Ind/Abst** MLA Int. Bibliogr. Books Artic. Mod. Lang. Lit. LC PQ5. (cum index). bk rev. adv acc. **Circ** 1,000. International forum of debate founded by Franco Simone. Wide bibliographic review.

STUDI GERMANICI. Began in 1935. 0039-2952. Periodical. IT. German (Italian). ty. Edizioni dell Ateneo, Casella Postale 7216, 00100 Rome Italy. **Tel** 7578853. **Ind/Abst** MLA Int. Bibliogr. Books Artic. Mod. Lang. Lit. LC PT5. DD 830.9.

STUDI GOLDONIANI. Book No. 1- 1968-. IT. Italian. ir. Casa Goldoni, San Toma 2794, 30125 Venezia Italy. **Ind/Abst** MLA Int. Bibliogr. Books Artic. Mod. Lang. Lit. **LC** PQ4698.

STUDI ISPANICI. 1976-. Periodical. Italian (Spanish). an. $172.27. Giardini Editorie Stampator, Via Santa Bibbiana 28 1, 56100 Pisa Italy. **Ind/Abst** MLA Int. Bibliogr. Books Artic. Mod. Lang. Lit. *Studi Ispanici.*

STUDI MEDIEVALI (TURIN, ITALY : 1928). (STUDI MEDIEVALI). New Series, Vol. 1, Issue. 1 (1928)-New Series, V. 18. 0391-8467. Periodical. IT. Italian. sa. Centro Studi Alto Medioevo, Palazzo Ancaianio Medioevo, I 06049 Spoleto Italy. **Ed** V Crescini and F Ermini. **Ind/Abst** MLA Int. Bibliogr. Books Artic. Mod. Lang. Lit. **LC** PN661. **DD** 809.02. *Nuovi Studi Medievali.*

STUDI TASSIANI. Year 1- 1951-. 0081-6256. IT. Italian. an. $5.94. Centro Di Studi Tassiani, Bib Civica Piazza Vecchia 15, 24100 Bergamo Italy. **Tel** 399430. **Ind/Abst** MLA Int. Bibliogr. Books Artic. Mod. Lang. Lit. **LC** PQ4646. **Circ** 350.

STUDIA CELTICA. *See* Linguistics.

STUDIA GERMANICA GANDENSIA. 1.- 1959-. 0081-6442. BE. text in Dutch, English or German. ir. 400. Studia Germanica Gandenica, Rozier 44, B-9000 Gent Belgium. **Tel** 00-32-91/25.75.71. **Ed** G De Smet. **Ind/Abst** MLA Int. Bibliogr. Books Artic. Mod. Lang. Lit. **Circ** 200. Studies on Germanic literature and languages.

STUDIA HIBERNICA. No. 1- 1961-. 0081-6477. IE. Multilingual (English or Irish). ir. 1.00 Each Issue. Colaiste Phadraig, Drumcondra 9, Baile Altha Cliath Ireland. **Tel** (01)376191. **Ed** S E Hannrachain. **Ind/Abst** Am. Hist. Life, Hist. Abstr., Part A, Mod. Hist. Abstr., Hist. Abst., Part B, Twent. Century Abstr., MLA Int. Bibliogr. Books Artic. Mod. Lang. Lit. **LC** PB1201. bk rev. **Circ** 1,000. A journal of Irish studies language, literature, history, archaeology, and long review section.

STUDIA NEOPHILOLOGICA. *See* Linguistics.

STUDIA POLONISTYCZNE. *See* Linguistics.

STUDIA ROMANICA ET ANGLICA ZAGRABIENSIA. *See* Linguistics.

STUDIA ROMANICA. SERIES LITTERARIA. **Main/Corp** Kossuth Lajos Tudomanyegyetem. No. 1.- 1962-. 0418-4572. Periodical. ir. Tankonyvkaido, Szalay u 10 14 Postfiok 20, H 1055 Budapest V Hungary. **LC** PC13.

STUDIEN ZUM FORTWIRKEN DER ANTIKE. Vol. 1- 1966-. 0585-5926. Monographic Series. GW. German. ir. Carl Winter Universitatsverlag, Postfach 1866/Lutherstrasse 59, D6900 Heidelberg West Germany. **Tel** 6221-49111. Studies of Greek and Roman literature and its influences on later authors.

STUDIEN ZUM FRUHNEUHOCHDEUTSCHEN. *See* Linguistics.

STUDIEN ZUR ALLGEMEINEN UND VERGLEICHENDEN LITERATURWISSENSCHAFT. 0585-5950. Monographic Series. GW. English. ir. J B Metzlersche Verlagsbuchhan, Kernerstrasse 43, 7000 Stuttgart 1 West Germany. **Ind/Abst** MLA Int. Bibliogr. Books Artic. Mod. Lang. Lit.

STUDIEN ZUR DEUTSCHEN LITERATUR. V. 1- 1966-. 0081-7236. Monographic Series. GW. German. ir. Max Niemeyer Verlag, Postfach 2140, 7400 Tuebingen 1 West Germany. **Ed** Richard Brinkmann. **Ind/Abst** MLA Int. Bibliogr. Books Artic. Mod. Lang. Lit. Monographs on German literature, especially 17th to 20th centuries.

STUDIEN ZUR GERMANISTIK, ANGLISTIK UND KOMPARATISTIK. Vol. 1- 1970-. Monographic Series. GW. German. ir. Vereinigte Verlag GMBH, Postfach 7777, 4830 Guetersloh 1 West Germany. **Tel** (05241)801. **Ind/Abst** MLA Int. Bibliogr. Books Artic. Mod. Lang. Lit.

STUDIENREIHE ROMANIA. V. 1-. Monographic Series. German. ir. Erich Schmidt Verlag GMBH, POB 7330-40/Viktoriastr 44-A, D4800 Bielefeld 1 West Germany. **Tel** 0521/66061. **Ed** E Leube and L Schrader. Roman literature studies.

STUDIES IN 20TH CENTURY LITERATURE. **VFOAT** Studies in Twentieth Century Literature. V. 1- Fall 1976-. 0145-7888. Periodical. US. English. sa. $15.00. Kansas State University, Department of Modern Languages, Eisenhower Hall, Manhattan KS 66506. **Tel** (913)539-8628. **Ed** Michael Ossar and Warren Motte. **Ind/Abst** MLA Int. Bibliogr. Books Artic. Mod. Lang. Lit. **LC** PN771. **DD** 809.04. adv acc. **Circ** 350. Articles on 20th Century literature and literary theory in any genre; primary emphasis on Europe and the Americas.

STUDIES IN AMERICAN FICTION. V. 1- Spring 1973-. 0091-8083. Periodical. US. English. sa. $4.00. Northeastern University, c/o James Nagel, Department of English, Boston MA 02115. **Ed** James Nagel. **Ind/Abst** Abstr. Engl. Stud., MLA Int. Bibliogr. Books Artic. Mod. Lang. Lit., Index Book Rev. Humanit. **LC** PS370. **DD** 813.009. bk rev. adv acc. **Circ** 1,100. Articles, notes and reviews on American fiction.

STUDIES IN AMERICAN HUMOR. V. 1.-V. 3, No. 3. 0095-280X. Periodical. US. English. qt. $15.00. Southwest Texas State University, Department of English, John Rosenbolm, San Marcos TX 78666. **Tel** (512)245-2615. **Ed** John O Rosenbolm. **Ind/Abst** Abstr. Engl. Stud., MLA Int. Bibliogr. Books Artic. Mod. Lang. Lit. **LC** PS430. **DD** 817.009. **Circ** 600. (ctrl). *American Humor, 0193-7146.*

STUDIES IN AMERICAN INDIAN LITERATURE. (STUDIES IN AMERICAN INDIAN LITERATURES : NEWSLETTER OF THE ASSOCIATION FOR STUDY OF AMERICAN INDIAN LITERATURES). **VFOAT** Newsletter of the Association for Study of American Indian Literatures. New Ser., Vol. 4, No. 1 (Winter 1980)-. 0730-3238. Periodical. US. English. ir. $4.00. Columbia University, Center for American Culture Studies 603 Lewisohn Hall, New York NY 10027. **Tel** (212)280-8253. Publishes book reviews, critical essays, and bibliographic information on contemporary native American poets and novelists and on traditional oral literatures and contemporary works in native American languages. *Newsletter of the Association for Study of American Indian Literatures.*

STUDIES IN AMERICAN JEWISH LITERATURE (ALBANY, N.Y.). (STUDIES IN AMERICAN JEWISH LITERATURE). No. 1 (1981)-. 0271-9274. US. English. an. $25.00. State University of New York Press, State University Plaza, Albany NY 12246. **Tel** (518)472-5000. **Ed** Daniel Walden. **Ind/Abst** MLA Int. Bibliogr. Books Artic. Mod. Lang. Lit., Abstr. Engl. Stud. **LC** PS153.J4. **DD** 810.98924. Journal designed to meet the long-felt need for a single publication that examines the American Jewish writer and the American Jewish experience. *Studies in American Jewish Literature, 0148-7663.*

STUDIES IN AMERICAN LITERATURE (NIHON AMERIKA BUNGAKKAI). (STUDIES IN AMERICAN LITERATURE). **VFOAT** Amerika Bungaku Kenkyu. 0385-6100. JA. English (Japanese). ir. American Literature Society of Japan, c/o Kyoto University, Sakyo Kyoto 606 Japan. **LC** PS1. **DD** 810.9.

STUDIES IN BLACK AMERICAN LITERATURE. Vol. 1-. 0738-0755. US. English. an. $15.00. Penkeville Publishing Company, Box 212, Greenwood FL 32443.

STUDIES IN BROWNING AND HIS CIRCLE. V. 1- Spring 1973-. 0095-4489. US. English. sa. $15.00. Armstrong Browning Library, Baylor University, Box 6336, Waco TX 76706. **Tel** (817)755-3566. **Ed** Jack W Herring. **Ind/Abst** MLA Int. Bibliogr. Books Artic. Mod. Lang. Lit., Index Book Rev. Humanit., Years Work Eng. Stud. **LC** PR4229. **DD** 821.8. bk rev. **Circ** 350. A journal of criticism, history, and bibliography of Robert Browning and Elizabeth Barrett Browning. *Browning Newsletter, 0007-2532.*

STUDIES IN CANADIAN LITERATURE. Monographic Series. CN. English. ir. Copp Clark Publishing Company, 35 Ames Circle, Don Mills Ontario M3B 3B9 Canada. **Ind/Abst** Abstr. Engl. Stud.

STUDIES IN CANADIAN LITERATURE (FREDERICTON, N.B.). (STUDIES IN CANADIAN LITERATURE). **VFOAT** S.C.L., SCL. Began with Winter 1976 issue. 0380-6995. Periodical. CN. English. sa. $11.61. University of New Brunswick, Department of English, Fredericton New Brunswick Canada. **Tel** (406)453-4598. **Ed** Barrie Davies. **Ind/Abst** Abstr. Engl. Stud., MLA Int. Bibliogr. Books Artic. Mod. Lang. Lit., Can. Period. Index. **LC** PR9180. **DD** 810.9971. **Circ** 400. (ctrl). Devoted to the scholarly and critical study of English and French-Canadian literature of all periods.

STUDIES IN COMPARATIVE LITERATURE. **Main/Corp** New York University. 1- 1967-. 0077-9504. Monographic Series. US. English. ir. Columbia University Press, 136 South Broadway, Irvington NY 10533.

STUDIES IN CONTEMPORARY SATIRE. Began with Spring 1974. 0163-4143. Periodical. US. English. an. $3.00. Clarion University of Pennsylvania, Department of English, C Pasquarette, Clarion PA 16214. **Tel** (814)226-2530. **Ed** C D Sheraw. **Ind/Abst** Abstr. Engl. Stud., MLA Int. Bibliogr. Books Artic. Mod. Lang. Lit. **LC** PN6149.S2. **DD** 808.87. bk rev. adv acc. **Circ** 100. (ctrl). Publishes critical articles, original poetry, prose, and reviews.

STUDIES IN ENGLISH LITERATURE. **VFOAT** Eibungaku Kenkyu. 0039-3649. Periodical. JA. English (three numbers a year are in Japanese). ir. $59.00. Japan Publishers Trading Company Ltd, PO Box 5030, Tokyo International, Tokyo 100-31 Japan. **Ind/Abst** MLA Int. Bibliogr. Books Artic. Mod. Lang. Lit., Annu. Bibliogr. Engl. Lang. Lit. **LC** PR1. **DD** 820.9.

STUDIES IN ENGLISH LITERATURE, 1500-1900. V. 1- Winter 1961-. 0039-3657. Periodical. US. English. qt. $20.00 Domestic, $25.00 Foreign. Studies in English Literature, Rice University, PO Box 1892, Houston TX 77251. **Tel** (713)527-8101. **Ed** Edward Doughtie. **Ind/Abst** Humanit. Index, Abstr. Engl. Stud., Annu. Bibliogr. Engl. Lang. Lit., MLA Int. Bibliogr. Books Artic. Mod. Lang. Lit., Years Work Eng. Stud., Recent Publ. Artic. **LC** PR1. **DD** 820.9. bk rev. adv acc. **Circ** 1,900. A journal of critical and scholarly studies. Each issue contains a review of the year's scholarship in the area covered by that issue.

STUDIES IN FRENCH LITERATURE. 0081-7937. Monographic Series. English or French. ir. Walter de Gruyter Inc, 200 Saw Mill River Road, Hawthorne NY 10532. **Tel** (914)747-0110.

STUDIES IN HAMITO-SEMITIC. *See* Linguistics.

STUDIES IN LITERATURE. **Main/Corp** Odense Universitet. V. 1- 1969-. 0078-3323. Monographic Series. DK. Danish (summaries in English). ir. Odense University Press, 36 Pjentedamsgade, DK 5000 Odense Denmark. **Tel** (09)14 16 11. **LC** PN35. **DD** 809. Scandinavian and especially Danish literature.

STUDIES IN LITERATURE. **VFOAT** U.H. Studies in Literature. V. 9, No. 2/3-. 0196-2280. Periodical. US. English. ir. $9.00. University of Hartford, 200 Bloomfield Avenue, West Hartford CT 06177. **Tel** (203)243-4315. **Ed** Charles Ross. **Ind/Abst** Abstr. Engl. Stud., MLA Int. Bibliogr. Books Artic. Mod. Lang. Lit. **LC** PN2. **DD** 809. bk rev. adv acc. **Circ** 300. Interdisciplinary criticism of literature. *Hartford Studies in Literature, 0017-7989.*

STUDIES IN MEDIEVALISM. V. 1- Spring 1979-. 0738-7164. Periodical. US. English. qt. University of Akron, Department of English, Associate Editor, Akron OH 44325. **Tel** (216)375-7606. **Ind/Abst** Am. Hist. Life, Hist. Abstr., Part A, Mod. Hist. Abstr., Hist. Abst., Part B, Twent. Century Abstr.

STUDIES IN MIDDLE EASTERN LITERATURES. No. 1- 1972-. Monographic Series. US. English. ir. Bibliotheca Islamica Inc, Box 14474 U Station, Minneapolis MN 55414. **Tel** (612)221-9883. Middle Eastern literatures in translation.

STUDIES IN MYSTICAL LITERATURE. **VFOAT** Ao Mi Wen Hsueh yen Chiu. Vol. 1, No. 1 (Fall 1980)-. Periodical. CH. English. qt. $15.00. Studies in Mystical Literature, Box 961, Tunghai University, Taichung Taiwan 400. **Ind/Abst** MLA Int. Bibliogr. Books Artic. Mod. Lang. Lit. **LC** PN49. **DD** 809.91.

STUDIES IN PHILOLOGY. V. 1- 1906-. 0039-3738. Periodical. US. English. qt. $20.00. University of North Carolina Press, Box 2288, Chapel Hill NC 27514. **Tel** (919)966-3561. **Ed** Jerry L Mills. **Ind/Abst** Abstr. Engl. Stud., MLA Int. Bibliogr. Books Artic. Mod. Lang. Lit., Annu. Bibliogr. Engl. Lang. Lit., Soc. Sci. Index, Humanit. Index, Years Work Eng. Stud. **LC** P25. **DD** 405. (cum index). adv acc. **Circ** 1,700. (ctrl). Articles on literary subjects before 1900, chiefly English, but including classical, Romance, and Germanic literatures.

Literature

STUDIES IN ROMANTIC AND MODERN LITERATURE. Vol. 1-. 0743-7889. Monographic Series. US. English. ir. Peter Lang Publishing Inc, 34 East 39th Street, New York NY 10016. LC UNC. DD 809.

STUDIES IN ROMANTICISM. V. 1- Autumn 1961-. 0039-3762. Periodical. US. English. qt. $15.00. Boston University, Scholarly Publications, 985 Commonwealth Avenue/Room 230, Boston MA 02115. Tel (617)353-4106. Ind/Abst Am. Hist. Life, Hist. Abstr., Part A, Mod. Hist. Abstr., Hist. Abst., Part B, Twent. Century Abstr., Abstr. Engl. Stud., MLA Int. Bibliogr. Books Artic. Mod. Lang. Lit., Women Stud. Abstr., Repert. Int. Litt. Art, Index Book Rev. Humanit., Soc. Sci. Index, Humanit. Index, Music Index, Hist. Abstr., Years Work Eng. Stud. LC PN751. DD 809.914. (cum index).

STUDIES IN SCOTTISH LITERATURE. V. 1- July 1963-. 0039-3770. US. English. an. University of South Carolina, English Department, Columbia SC 29208. Tel (803)777-2239. Ed G Ross Roy. Ind/Abst Abstr. Engl. Stud., MLA Int. Bibliogr. Books Artic. Mod. Lang. Lit., Annu. Bibliogr. Engl. Lang. Lit., Index Book Rev. Humanit., Years Work Eng. Stud. LC PR8500. DD 820.9411. bk rev. Circ 450. (ctrl). Devoted to all aspects of Scottish literary studies including bibliographies, checklists, unpublished documents and letters.

STUDIES IN SHORT FICTION. V. 1- Fall 1963-. 0039-3789. Periodical. US. English. qt. $21.00. Studies in Short Fiction, Newberry College, 2100 College Street, Newberry SC 29108. Tel (803)276-5010. Ed Steen H Spove. Ind/Abst Abstr. Engl. Stud., MLA Int. Bibliogr. Books Artic. Mod. Lang. Lit., Annu. Bibliogr. Engl. Lang. Lit., Women Stud. Abstr., Index Book Rev. Humanit., Humanit. Index, Years Work Eng. Stud. LC PN3311. bk rev. Circ 1,650. (ctrl). A scholarly international journal devoted exclusively to serious commentary on short fiction.

STUDIES IN THE AGE OF CHAUCER. Series/Titl Publications of the New Chaucer Society. Began in 1979. 0190-2407. US. English. an. $30.00. The New Chaucer Society, University of Tennessee, Department of English, Knoxville TN 37996. Tel (615)974-5401. Ed Thomas Heffernan. Ind/Abst MLA Int. Bibliogr. Books Artic. Mod. Lang. Lit., Years Work Eng. Stud. LC PR1901. DD 820.9001. bk rev. Circ 800. (ctrl). Studies relating to Chaucer and his contemporaries.

STUDIES IN THE AMERICAN RENAISSANCE. 1977-. 0149-015X. US. English. an. University Press of Virginia, Box 3608 University Station, Charlottesville VA 22903. Tel (804)924-3468. Ed J Myerson. Ind/Abst Am. Hist. Life, Hist. Abstr., MLA Int. Bibliogr. Books Artic. Mod. Lang. Lit., Am. Hist., Writ. Am. Hist., Relig. Index One, Period. LC PS201. DD 810.9003. Presents a wide range of scholarly articles including annotated list of the year's book publications.

STUDIES IN THE LITERARY IMAGINATION. V. 1- Apr. 1968-. 0039-3819. Periodical. US. English. sa. $5.00. Studies in the Literary Imagination, Department of English, Georgia State University, Atlanta GA 30303. Ind/Abst Abstr. Engl. Stud., MLA Int. Bibliogr. Books Artic. Mod. Lang. Lit., Humanit. Index, Years Work Eng. Stud. LC PR1.

STUDIES IN THE NOVEL. V. 1- Spring 1969-. 0039-3827. Periodical. US. English. qt. $15.00. North Texas State University, Box 13706, Denton TX 76203. Tel (817)387-6475. Ed Gerald A Kirk. Ind/Abst Abstr. Engl. Stud., MLA Int. Bibliogr. Books Artic. Mod. Lang. Lit., Index Book Review. Humanit., Humanit. Index, Years Work Eng. Stud. LC PN3311. DD 809.3305. bk rev. adv acc. Circ 1,500. Articles on novels and novelists.

STUDIES ON VOLTAIRE AND THE EIGHTEENTH CENTURY. V. 2 (1956)-. 0435-2866. Periodical. UK. English (French). ir. Voltaire Foundation, Taylor Institution Library, Oxford OX1 3NA England. Tel (865) 512931. Ed Hayden Mason. Ind/Abst MLA Int. Bibliogr. Books Artic. Mod. Lang. Lit., Years Work Eng. Stud. LC PQ2105.A2. (cum index). All aspects of Eighteenth Century culture and history, with particular emphasis upon the European Enlightenment. *Travaux sur Voltaire et le Dix-Huitieme Siecle.*

STUDII DE LITERATURA UNIVERSALA. RM. Romanian. an. Ilexim Press Department, PO Box 1-136-1-137, Bucharest Romania.

STUDIUM. V. 1/2- 1961/62-. 0585-766X. Periodical. IT. Spanish. ty. $20.00. Edizioni Studium, Via Crescenzio 63, 00193 Roma Italy. Tel 6565846. Ind/Abst Old Testam. Abstr., New Testam. Abstr. adv acc. Circ 3,000.

STUMP. (THE STUMP). Vol. 5, No. 1 (Fall/Winter 1980)-. 0229-2882. Periodical. CN. English. Creative Writing Club, Malaspina College, 900 Fifth Street, Nanaimo British Columbia V9R 5S5 Canada. DD C810.8092379. *Shorelines, 0229-2874.*

STUTTGARTER ARBEITEN ZUR GERMANISTIK. VFOAT S.A.G. No. 1- 1975-. Monographic Series. GW. German or English. Akademischer Verlag Stuttgart Heinz Steiermarkerstr 132, 7000 Stuttgart 30 West Germany. Tel (0711)812413. Ed Hans-Dieter Heinz. Ind/Abst MLA Int. Bibliogr. Books Artic. Mod. Lang. Lit. Monographs, text-books, and editions of German literature (15th century to present) and of general and German linguistics; festschriften and proceedings.

STYLE. V. 1- Winter 1967-. 0039-4238. Periodical. US. English. qt. $8.00. English Department, University of Arkansas Fayetteville AR 72701. Ind/Abst Abstr. Engl. Stud., MLA Int. Bibliogr. Books Artic. Mod. Lang. Lit., Lang. Lang. Behav. Abstr., Index Book Rev. Humanit. LC PE1.

SUB-STANCE. No. 1-. 0049-2426. Periodical. US. English (French). qt. $30.00. University of Wisconsin, 618 Van Hise Hall, Madison WI 53706. Tel (608)262-5816. Ed Sydney Levy and Michel Pierssens. Ind/Abst MLA Int. Bibliogr. Books Artic. Mod. Lang. Lit., Film Lit. Index. LC PN2. DD 805. bk rev. adv acc. Circ 400. An interdisciplinary journal promoting new thoughts by American and Europe authors which alter the perception of contemporary culture.

SUB-STANCE. No. 1- Fall 1971-. Periodical. US. English (French). ty. $32.00. University of Wisconsin Press Journal Division, 114 North Murray Street, Madison WI 53715. Tel (608)262-4952.

SUBH-I ADAB. Nov. 1974-. Periodical. Urdu. ir. 20.00. Nazir Ahmad Nuri, Mahmood Manzil Gwynne Road, Lakhnau India. LC PK2151.

SUBJECT INDEX TO SELECT PERIODICAL LITERATURE. See Indexes/Abstracts.

SUGANDHA. Periodical. Marathi. an. 8.00. Sugandha Prakasana, 271 V Patel Road, Bombay 400004 India. LC PK2400.

SULFUR (PASADENA, CALIF.). (SULFUR). 1 (1981)-. 0730-305X. Periodical. US. English. ty. $18.00 Domestic, $15.00 Foreign. Spring Publications, Dallas Institute of Humanities and Culture, 2719 Routh Street, Dallas TX 75201. Ind/Abst Index Am. Period. Verse. LC PS501. DD 810.8.

SUN (CHAPEL HILL, N.C.). (THE SUN). Began with 11th (Nov. 1975)-. 0744-9666. Periodical. US. English. mo. $25.00. The Sun/NC/, 412 West Rosemary Street, Chapel Hill NC 27514. Tel (919)942-5282. Ed Sy Safransky. LC AP2. DD 051. bk rev. adv acc. Circ 5,000. A magazine of ideas that prints a wide range of essays, articles, poetry, fiction, and photographs. *Chapel Hill Sun.*

SUNTRACKS. Began publication with Vol. 1, No. 1 (June 1971)-. 0300-788X. Periodical. US. English. ir. $5.00. Sun Tracks, University of Arizona, Department of English, Modern Languages Building #67, Tuscon AZ 85721. LC PS501. DD 810.80054.

SUNYATA. V. 1- May 1976-. 0384-8248. Periodical. CN. English. qt. $9.00. Sunyata Press, Box 278, Brentwood Bay British Columbia V0S 1A0 Canada. DD C810.80054.

SUOMALAIS-UGRILAISEN SEURAN AIKAKAUSKIRJA. VFOAT Journal de la Socette Finno-Ougrienne. 1- 1886-. Fl. Finnish (contributions in French, German, or English). ir. Akakeeminen-Kirjakuppa, PO Box 128, 00101 Helsinki Finland. LC PH1.

SURA SAURABHA. Periodical. II. Hindi. qt. 12.00. Sur Smarak Mandal, 15/230 Bhagatsingh Dvar, Agra 282002 India. LC PK1967.9.S9.

SUSA. Periodical. Marathi. an. 2.50. Suyoga Sadhana, Behind Maharashtra Mandal, Poona-30, Pune India. LC PK2400.

SVENSK LITTERATURTIDSKRIFT. V. 1-. 0039-663X. Periodical. SW. Swedish. qt. $9.10. Professor Knut Ahnland, Parkvagen 50, 183 51 Taby Sweden. Ind/Abst MLA Int. Bibliogr. Books Artic. Mod. Lang. Lit. LC PT9201. DD 839.709. (cum index).

SVERSTNIKI. Began with issue for 1977. Periodical. UR. Russian. an. 0.75. Izdatelstvo Sovremennik, 121351 Moskva, G-351 Iartsevskaia 4, Moskva Russian SFSR. LC PG3021.

SWALLOW'S TALE MAGAZINE. VFOAT Swallow's Tale. No. 1 (Spring 1983)-. 0735-9055. Periodical. US. English. sa. Swallows Tale Magazine, PO Box 4328, Tallahassee FL 32315. Tel (904)224-8859. LC PS501. DD 810.8.

SWEVEN. Sept. 1978-. 0707-2953. Periodical. CN. English. ir. Free. John Deutsch University Centre, Queen's University, Kingston Ontario K7L 3N6 Canada. DD C810.8092379. (ctrl).

SWISS PAPERS IN ENGLISH LANGUAGE AND LITERATURE. See Linguistics.

SYDNEY STUDIES IN ENGLISH. V. 1- 1975/76-. AT. English. an. $4.80. University of Sydney, English Department, New South Wales 2006 Australia. Ed G A Wilkes and A P Riemer. Ind/Abst Abstr. Engl. Stud., MLA Int. Bibliogr. Books Artic. Mod. Lang. Lit. Circ 1,000. Critical essays on literature and drama.

SYMPOSIUM. V. 1- Nov. 1946-. 0039-7709. Periodical. US. English. qt. $40.00. Heldref Publications, 4000 Albemarle Street NW/Suite 302, Washington DC 20016. Tel (202)362-6445. Ed Roberta Leboffe. Ind/Abst MLA Int. Bibliogr. Books Artic. Mod. Lang. Lit., Index Book Review. Humanit., Humanit. Index. LC PB1. DD 405. adv acc. Circ 697. A journal on modern, foreign languages and literatures, includes research on authors, themes, periods, genres, and works outside an exclusively American or British context.

SYMPOSIUM. Main/Corp German Canadian Studies (Association). Annalen 1 (1976)-. 0823-2458. CN. German. an. Etudes Allemandes Departement d'Etudes Anciennes et Modernes, Universite de Montreal, P O Box 6128 Station A, Montreal Quebec H3C 3J7 Canada. DD C830.9.

SYNTHESIS. Main/Corp Comitetul National Pentru Literatura Comparata. 1-. English (French, German, Italian, Russian, or Spanish). an. $42.00. Rompresfilatelia, PO Box 1362137, Bucharest Romania. Ind/Abst MLA Int. Bibliogr. Books Artic. Mod. Lang. Lit. LC PN855.

SZENE. Periodical. SZ. German. qt. Kunst & Wissen Erich Bieber, Dufourstrasse 51, CH-8700 Zurich Switzerland. LC PN2004.

LA TABLE RONDE. CAHIERS. Winter 1973-. Periodical. FR. French. ir. Les Editions de la Table Ronde, 40 rue de Bac, 75007 Paris France. LC PQ1100. DD 840.800914.

TAC PHAM MI. Periodical. VM. Vietnamese. ir. Xunhasaba, 32 Hai ba Trung, Hanoi Drv North Vietnam. LC PL4378.

TAGIM. 1- 1969-. Hebrew (summaries in English, V. 1-). ir.

TAI-WAN HSIAO SHUO HSUAN. VFOAT Tai-Wan Hsiao Shuo Nien Hsuan. 1982-. Periodical. JA. Chinese. an. 100.00. Chien Wei Chu Pan She, P O Box 562555, Taipei Taiwan. LC PL3031.T32. DD 895.135080951249.

TAI-WAN SAN WEN HSUAN. VFOAT Tai-Wan San Wen Nien Hsuan. 1982-. Periodical. CH. Chinese. an. 100.00. Chien Wei Chu Pan She, PO Box 562555, Taipei Taiwan. LC PL3031.T32. DD 895.145080951249.

TALLIN. Began in 1978. Periodical. UR. Russian. bm. 0.40 Each Issue. 200001 Estonskaia SSR, Tallin Piarnuskoe Shosse, 6 Tallin Estonian SSR. LC PG3504.E8.

TALLINSKIE TETRADI. Periodical. UR. Russian. 1.20. Izdatelstvo Eesti Raamat Piarnuskoe Shosse 10, Tallin 200090 USSR. LC PG3227.

TANASENA. VFOAT Tansen. V. 1, No. 1 (June/July/August 2035 Sept/Dec. 1978)-. Periodical. Nepali. ir. 2.00. LC PK2598.Z9.

TANG TAI (PEKING, CHINA). (TANG TAI). VFOAT Dang Dai. July 1979-. Periodical. CC. Chinese. bm. 1.00. Chung-Kuo Kyo CHitu Shu Mao I Tsung Kung Ssu, PO Box 2820, Pei-Ching China Mainland. LC PL2250. DD 895.109005.

TANG TAI WEN HSUEH. VFOAT Dang Dai Wen Xue. V. 1 (July 1981)-. Periodical. CC. Chinese. qt. 1.00. Kuang-Tung Sheng Hsin Hua Shu Tien Canton China. LC PN779.C5. DD 895.108005.

Literature

TANG TAI WEN HSUEH LUN TSUNG.
VFOAT Tang Tai Wen Hsueh. Periodical. CH. Chinese. ir. 1.05. Hsin Hua Shu Tien, Shan-Hsi Sheng China. **LC** PL2291. **DD** 895.109003. *Tang Tai Wen Hseuh (Sian, China).*

TANGUK MUNHAK. 1982-. Periodical. KO. Korean. ir. 3,500. Tanguk Munhakhoe San 8, Hannam-Dong Yongsan-Ku, Seoul South Korea. **LC** PL969.8.

TAP CHI VAN HOC. 0404-6928. Periodical. VM. Vietnamese. bm. Xunhasaba, 32 Hai ba Trung, Hanoi Drv North Vietnam. **Ind/Abst** Math. Rev. **LC** PL4378.

TARAKHARA : BHO. JI. SAM. SA. ANERASVAVIYU KO MUKHAPATRA. V. 1, No. 1-. NP. Nepali. ir. 4.00. Bhojpur District Coordination Committee of all Nepal National Independent Students' Union, Kathmandu Nepal. **LC** PK25998.A2.

TAY. VFOAT Thai. Periodical. Tamil. wk. 1.00. K Ravindran, 34 Nelson Manickam Street, Madras 600029 India. **LC** PL4758.45.

TEACHING LANGUAGE THROUGH LITERATURE. See Linguistics.

TECHNOSTYLE. Vol. 1, No. 1-. 0712-4627. Periodical. CN. English (French). ty. $10.00. J Pavelich, c/o Department of English, University of British Columbia, 2075 Wesbrook Place, Vancouver British Columbia V6T 1W5 Canada. **DD** 808.0666.

TEKSTY. 1-. 0324-8208. Periodical. PL. Polish. bm. ARS Polona, Krakowskie Przedmiescie 7, 00-068 Warsaw Poland. **Ind/Abst** MLA Int. Bibliogr. Books Artic. Mod. Lang. Lit. **LC** PN9.

TELESCOPE (IOWA CITY, IOWA). (TELESCOPE). 1 (Spring 1981)-. 0277-6146. Periodical. US. English. ty. $9.00. Galileo Press, PO Box 2177, Iowa City IA 52244. **LC** PS536.2.

TEMPERAMENTE. Periodical. German. qt. **Tel** 2093 27 65. **LC** PT3831. Contains stories, records, poems, essays, fueilletons, aphorisms, reviews, plays, letters, interviews, photos, graphics from still unknown as well as from well-known authors and artists.

TENDRIL. No. 1- Winter 1977/78-. 0197-890X. Periodical. US. English. ty. $12.00. Tendril, Box 512, Green Harbor MA 02041. **Tel** (617)834-4137. Ed George Murphy. **Ind/Abst** Index Am. Period. Verse. adv acc. **Circ** 1,800. Fiction and poetry.

TENGGARA. No. 1- 1967-. MY. English. sa. Dewan Bahasa dan Pustaka Mal Peti Surat 803, Kuala Lumpur Malaysia. **Ind/Abst** MLA Int. Bibliogr. Books Artic. Mod. Lang. Lit. **LC** PJ1.

TENNESSEE STUDIES IN LITERATURE. V. 1-. 0497-2384. Monographic Series. US. English. an. University of Tennessee Press, 293 Communications Building, Knoxville TN 37996. **Tel** (615)974-3321. **Ind/Abst** Abstr. Engl. Stud., MLA Int. Bibliogr. Books Artic. Mod. Lang. Lit., Annu. Bibliogr. Engl. Lang. Lit. **LC** PS1. **DD** 809. (cum index).

TENOR. 1- June 1978-. Periodical. English. ir. $3.00. M Sivaramkrishna Editor, Tenor 2-2-1137/4/2 Prashantnagar, Hyderbad 500 044 AP India. **LC** PR9480. **DD** 820.5.

TERMINUS (MONTREAL, QUEBEC). (TERMINUS). VFOAT Revue Terminus. Vol. 1, No. 1 (Feb. 1984)-. 0822-3394. Periodical. CN. French. bm. $10.00. Revue Terminus, CP 157 Succursale C, Montreal Quebec H2L 4K1 Canada. **DD** C840.80054.

TERRELL'S INDEX TO BLACK PERIODICAL LITERATURE. See Indexes/Abstracts.

TEXAS STUDIES IN LITERATURE AND LANGUAGE. VFOAT TSLL. V. 1- Spring 1959-. 0040-4691. Periodical. US. English. qt. $30.00. University of Texas Press, PO Box 7819, Austin TX 78712. **Tel** (512)471-4531. Ed William Scheick and Edwin Bowden. **Ind/Abst** Abstr. Engl. Stud., MLA Int. Bibliogr. Books Artic. Mod. Lang. Lit., Sociol. Abstr., Lang. Lang. Behav. Abstr., Annu. Bibliogr. Engl. Lang. Lit., Humanit. Index, Years Work Eng. Stud. **LC** AS30. **DD** 820.5. adv acc. **Circ** 950. (ctrl). Deals with all periods of literary history, while each issue focuses on a particular period, author, or stylistic problem. *Texas Studies in English, 0364-8656.*

TEXAS WRITER'S NEWSLETTER. No. 1- 1974?-. Periodical. US. English. qt. $5.00. Texas A & M University, Department of English, College Station TX 77843. **Tel** (915)677-7281.

TEXT. (TEXT : TRANSACTIONS OF THE SOCIETY FOR TEXTUAL SCHOLARSHIP). 1 (for 1981)-. 0736-3974. US. English. an. AMS Press Inc, 56 East 13th Street, New York NY 10003. **Tel** (212)777-4700. **DD** 808. International and interdisciplinary forum for the investigation of all forms of the transmission of communication through a text.

TEXT + KRITIK. (TEXT UND KRITIK). Began with: No. 1, in 1963. 0040-5329. Periodical. GW. German. qt. 36.-. Edition Text & Kritik GMBH, Levelingstrasse 6A, 8000 Munich 80 West Germany. **Tel** 089/43292929-29. Ed Heinz Ludwig Arnold. **Ind/Abst** MLA Int. Bibliogr. Books Artic. Mod. Lang. Lit. Texts, interpretations and critique. Each volume is dedicated to one contemporary author of the German literature with previously unpublished texts by that author plus interpretation and analysis.

TEXTE DES SPATEN MITTELALTERS UND DER FRUHEN NEUZEIT. No. 16-. 0563-3079. Monographic Series. GW. German. ir. Erich Schmidt Verlag GMBH, POB 7330, 40/ Viktoriastr 44A, D4800 Bielefeld 1 West Germany. **Tel** 0521/66061. Ed Karl Stackmann and Stanley N Werbow. **Ind/Abst** MLA Int. Bibliogr. Books Artic. Mod. Lang. Lit. Literature of the Middle Ages. *Texte des Spaten Mittelalters.*

TEXTE UND UNTERSUCHUNGEN ZUR GESCHICHTE DER ALTCHRISTLICHEN LITERATUR. 1- 1883-. 0082-3589. Monographic Series. GE. German. ir. Deutscher Buch Export-Import, Leninstrasse 16, DDR-7010 Leipzig East Germany. **Ind/Abst** MLA Int. Bibliogr. Books Artic. Mod. Lang. Lit. (cum index).

TEXTES LITTERAIRES FRANCAIS. Monographic Series. French. ir. Librairie Droz S A, 11 rue Massot, Geneva Switzerland. **Ind/Abst** MLA Int. Bibliogr. Books Artic. Mod. Lang. Lit. **Circ** 600. French literature.

TEXTES PUBLIES PAR L'INSTITUT D'ETUDES SLAVES. See Linguistics.

THALIA (OTTAWA, ONT.). (THALIA). Vol. 1, No. 1 (Spring 1978)-. 0706-5604. Periodical. CN. English (French). sa. $21.67. Thalia, Department of English, University of Ottawa, Ottawa Ontario K1N 6N5 Canada. **Tel** (613)564-2311. Ed J Tavernier-Courbin. **Ind/Abst** Abstr. Engl. Stud., MLA Int. Bibliogr. Books Artic. Mod. Lang. Lit. **LC** PN6147. **DD** 809.7. bk rev. adv acc. **Circ** 600. Critical studies on humor in literature, film, psychology, cartoons, illustrations, literary theory of humor, satire, clinical uses of humor, etc.

THERAPEUTISCHE DICHTUNG. 1972-. German. ir. 4.00 Each Issue. Verlag fur Schone Wissenschaften, CH-4143 Dornach Unterer Zielweg 36, Donarch Switzerland. **LC** PT2639.T28.

THESAURUS. See Linguistics.

THESIS AND DISSERTATION. 0253-9284. Monographic Series. English. ir. NLM W1 TH691.

THIRD RAIL. 1- 1975-. 0741-5958. Periodical. US. English. ir. $36.00. Third Rail, PO Box 46127, Los Angeles CA 90046. **Tel** (213)850-7548. Ed Uri Hertz. bk rev. adv acc. **Circ** 10,000. A review of international literature and the arts, published in Los Angeles once or twice a year. Includes poetry, interviews, translations, criticism.

THIS MAGAZINE. V. 7- May/June 1973-. 0381-3746. Periodical. CN. English. bm. $11.61. This Magazine, 70 The Esplanade 3rd Floor, Toronto Ontario M5E 1R2 Canada. **Tel** (416)364-2431. Ed Lorraine Filyer. **Ind/Abst** Women Stud. Abstr., Can. Period. Index, Altern. Press Index, New Period. Index. **LC** L11. **DD** 370.5. adv acc. **Circ** 6,500. A journal of culture and politics of Canadian and international affairs. Original graphics, short stories, poetry, controversial columns. *This Magazine is About Schools.*

THOMAS HARDY ANNUAL. No. 1-. 0731-8286. Periodical. US. English. an. Humanities Press, 171 First Avenue, Atlantic Highlands NJ 07716. Ed Norman Page. **LC** PR4752. **DD** 823.8. bk rev. A collection of essays by international Hardy scholars presenting wide ranging topics covering the whole corpus of Hardy's works.

THOMAS HARDY YEAR BOOK. See Yearbooks, Almanacs, Directories.

THOMAS-MANN-STUDIEN. GW. German. ir. A Francke Verlag GMBH, Postfach 2560, Dischingerweg 5, 7400 Tuebingen 5 West Germany.

Ind/Abst MLA Int. Bibliogr. Books Artic. Mod. Lang. Lit.

THE THOMAS WOLFE NEWSLETTER. V. 1-4. 0148-1789. Periodical. US. English. sa. **Ind/Abst** Abstr. Engl. Stud. **LC** PS3545.O337. **DD** 813.52.

THE THOMAS WOLFE REVIEW. See Bibliographies.

THOREAU JOURNAL QUARTERLY CEASED. V. 1-13. 0040-6392. Periodical. US. English. qt. $4.00. Thoreau Fellowship, PO 551, Old Town ME 04468. **LC** PS3053. **DD** 818.309.

THE THOREAU QUARTERLY. Vol. 14, No. 1 (Winter 1982)-. 0730-868X. Periodical. US. English. qt. $20.00. University of Minnesota, Department of Philosophy, 355 Ford Hall, Minneapolis MN 55455. **Tel** (612)373-3613. Ed John M Dolan and Wendell Glick. **Ind/Abst** Abstr. Engl. Stud., MLA Int. Bibliogr. Books Artic. Mod. Lang. Lit. **LC** PS3053. **DD** 818.309. bk rev adv acc. **Circ** 1,000. A journal of literary and philosophical studies. *Thoreau Journal Quarterly, 0040-6392.*

THE THOREAU SOCIETY BULLETIN. No. 1- Oct. 1941-. 0040-6406. Periodical. US. English. qt. $10.00. Thoreau Society Inc, 165 Belknap Street, Concord MA 01742. **Tel** (716)245-5513. Ed Walter Harding. **Ind/Abst** MLA Int. Bibliogr. Books Artic. Mod. Lang. Lit., Annu. Bibliogr. Engl. Lang. Lit. **LC** PS3053. (cum index). bk rev. **Circ** 1,600. Honoring Henry David Thoreau.

THE THORNDYKE FILE. No. 1- Spring 1976-. 0145-5575. Periodical. US. English. sa. $5.00. P T Asdell, Box 355, Frederick MD 21701. **LC** PR6011.R43. **DD** 823.912.

THRESHOLD. V. 1- Feb. 1957-. 0040-6562. Periodical. UK. English. sa. 1.50. Thelyric Players Theatre, 55 Ridgeway Street, Belfast 9 Northern Ireland. **Tel** (0232)669660. Ed John Boyd. **LC** AP4. **DD** 820.5. bk rev. **Circ** 600. (ctrl).

THRESHOLD OF FANTASY. No. 1-. 0277-7800. Periodical. US. English. ir. $2.00 Each Issue. Fandom Unlimited Enterprises, 3378 Valley Forge Way, San Jose CA 95117.

TIDEPOOL (HAMILTON, ONT.). (TIDEPOOL). No. 1 (1984)-. 0824-7579. CN. English. an. $2.50 Each Number. Hamilton Haiku Workshop Press, 4 East 23rd Street, Hamilton Ontario L8V 2W6 Canada. **DD** C811.0408.

TIFA SASTRA. Began in 1972?. Periodical. IO. Indonesian. ir. Kelompok Majalah Senat Mahasiswa Fsui, Kompleks Ui Rawamangun Kotakpos 001/Jng, Jakarta Indonesia. **LC** PL5080.

TIGHTROPE. V. 1- 1975-). Periodical. US. English. sa. Swamp Press, 300 Main Street, Oneonta NY 13820.

TIJDSCHRIFT VOOR NEDERLANDSCHE TAAL-EN LETTERKUNDE CEASED. Vol. 1-64. 0040-7550. Periodical. NE. Dutch. qt. 86.-. E J Brill, POB 9000, 2300 PA Leiden The Netherlands. **Tel** (071)312-624. Ed D M Bakker and D C Damsteegr. **Ind/Abst** MLA Int. Bibliogr. Books Artic. Mod. Lang. Lit. **LC** PF4. **DD** 439.3105. Index in last issue of volume - attached. (cum index). bk rev. **Circ** 600. Publishes original papers in Dutch linguistics, history of literature, and theory of literature. Its main stress is on the historical aspects within these fields.

TINTA (SANTA BARBARA, CALIF.). (TINTA). Vol. 1, No. 1 (May 1981)-. 0739-7003. Periodical. US. Portuguese (Spanish). sa. $8.00. Tinta, Department of Spanish and Portuguese, UCSB, Santa Barbara CA 93106. **Tel** (805)961-3161. Ed Sonia Zuniga-Lomeli. **LC** PQ6001. **DD** 860.008. bk rev. adv acc. **Circ** 200. Publishes original works concerning Latin American and peninsular literature written by graduate students.

TINTENFISCH. 1-. Periodical. GW. German. ir. $6.01. Verlag-Klaus Wagenbach, Ahornstrasse 4, D-1000 Berlin 30 West Germany. **Tel** (030)211-5060. **LC** PT1141.A2. **DD** 830.8.

TIPOLOGIIA I VZAIMOSVIAZI V RUSSKOI I ZARUBEZHNOI LITERATURE. Vol. 1-. Periodical. UR. Russian. 0.75. Redaktsionno-Izdatelskii Otdel, Ul Lebedevoi 89, 660017 Krasnoiarsk Russia. **LC** PG2981.E8.

TISTA-SUNAKOSA. VFOAT Tista Sunkosh. Periodical. Nepali. qt. 6.00. Sharada Sanskritik Sangha, Kalchini Out Division, PO Kalchini, Dist Jalpaiguri, Kalchini India. **LC** PK2597.5.

Literature

TOGIL MUNHAK. See Linguistics.

TOKYO-TO HAIKU REMMEI TAIKAI KUSHU. JA. Japanese. ir. Tokyo-To Haiku Remmei, 25-1 Higashi Nakano 1-Chome, Nakano-Ku 164, Tokyo Japan. LC PL759.A1.

TOMIS. US. Romanian. mo. Ilexim Press Department, PO Box 1-136-1-137, Bucharest Romania. LC PC800.

TONGIL MUNYE. VFOAT Tong Il Korean Literature. V. 1- March 1979-. Periodical. CN. Korean. Tongil Munye S A, 51 Oakwood Avenue, Toronto Ontario M6H 2V7 Canada. LC PL969.8.

TORONTO MEDIEVAL LATIN TEXTS. 1- 1972-. Monographic Series. CN. English. ir. Pontifical Institute of Mediaeval Studies, 59 Queens Park Cresent East, Toronto Ontario M55 2C4 Canada. Tel (416)926-7144. Ed A G Rigg. Editions of Latin texts based on a single manuscript, covering varied subject matter, intended as teaching texts for medieval Latin.

TORONTO SOUTH ASIAN REVIEW. (THE TORONTO SOUTH ASIAN REVIEW). Vol. 1, No. 1-. 0714-3508. Periodical. CN. English. ty. $11.61. Toronto South Asian Review, PO Box 6996/Station A, Toronto Ontario Canada M5W 1X7. Tel (416)923-5362. Ed M G Vassanji. DD C810.808914. bk rev. Circ 500. Literature that traces some part of its meaning to traditions, cultures and history of Indian subcontinent.

TOUCHSTONE (LOCKEPORT, N.S.). (TOUCHSTONE). Vol. 1, No. 1-. 0823-8456. Periodical. CN. English. bm. $12.00. Touchstone, PO Box 85, Lockeport Nova Scotia B0T 1L0 Canada. DD C810.5.

TRAC. Dec. 1976-. 0703-7147. CN. French. $2.50 Each Number. Trac, 320 East rue Notre-Dame, Montreal Quebec H2Y 1C6 Canada. DD C842.5408.

TRACES. 0248-496X. Periodical. FR. French. qt. 150. 52 rue Rene Boulanger, 75010 Paris France. LC DS101. DD 909.0492405.

TRACKS (MORNINGTON, MEATH). (TRACKS). No. 1-. Periodical. English. ir. 1.50 Each Issue. LC PN2. DD 808.8.

TRAITS : BULLETIN LITTERAIRE DE LA LIBRAIRIE LIBRIS. Periodical. BE. French. qt. 300. Traits, Avenue de la Toison d'Or 29, 1060 Bruxelles Belgium.

TRAJEKT. 1- 1970-. Periodical. German. ir. Hinstorff Verlag, DDR 2500 Rostock Kropeliner Strasse, 25 Rostock East Germany. Tel 34441. LC PT1141.A2. Informs own authors and her books which are edited by Hinstorff Verlag.

TRANSLATION. V. 1- Winter 1973-. 0093-9307. US. English. sa. $16.00. Columbia University, Translation Center, Mathematics Building, New York NY 10027. Tel (212)280-2305. Ed Diane G H Cook. Ind/Abst MLA Int. Bibliogr. Books Artic. Mod. Lang. Lit. LC PN241. DD 418.02. adv acc. Circ 1,000. A publication dedicated to finding and publishing the best translations of a significant work of foreign contemporary literature.

TRANSLATION REVIEW. See Linguistics.

TRANSLATIONS REGISTER-INDEX. See Indexes/Abstracts.

TRAVAUX DE LINGUISTIQUE ET DE LITTERATURE. See Linguistics.

TRAVESSIA. No. 1 (Second Semester 1980)-. Periodical. Portuguese. sa. Editora da UFSC, Caixa Postal 476, 88.000 Florianopolis SC Brazil. LC PQ9500. DD 869.080981.

TREE. No. 1- Winter 1970-. 0041-2171. Periodical. US. English. sa. $20.00. Tree Books, PO Box 9005, Berkeley CA 94709. Ed David Meltzer.

TREELINE. 1981-. 0710-4375. CN. English. an. $3.75 Each Volume. Treeline, Northern Lights College, 11401-8th Street, Dawson Creek British Columbia V1G 4G2 Canada. DD C810.8092379.

TRIBUNA LITERARIA. Periodical. Spanish. ir. $10.00. Rivadavia 4213, 1205 Capital Federal, Buenos Aires Argentina. LC PQ7600. DD 860.

TRIQUARTERLY. (TRI-QUARTERLY). Spring 1963-. 0041-3097. Periodical. US. English. ir. $40.00. Northwestern University, 1735 Benson Avenue, Evanston IL 60201. Tel (312)491-3490. Ed Reginald Gibbons. Ind/Abst MLA Int. Bibliogr. Books Artic. Mod. Lang. Lit., Annu. Bibliogr. Engl. Lang. Lit., Index Am. Period. Verse, Am. Hist. Life, Hist. Abstr., Years Work Eng. Stud. DD 805. bk rev. adv acc. Circ 3,500. Available also on microfilm from University Microfilms International. An international journal of art, writing, and cultural inquiry. "Perhaps the preeminent journal for literary fiction" (New York Times).

TRISTANIA. V. 1- Nov. 1975-. 0360-3385. Periodical. US. Multilingual (English with some French and German). sa. Lewis A M Sumberg Editor, PO Box 11091, Chattanooga TN 37401. Tel (502)636-6216. Ind/Abst MLA Int. Bibliogr. Books Artic. Mod. Lang. Lit. LC PN57.T8. DD 841.109351.

TRUCK. No. 1- Nov. 1970-. 0147-2445. US. English. $3.00 Each Issue. Truck Press, PO Box 86, Carrboro NC 27510. LC PS501. DD 811.505.

TRUE NORTH, DOWN UNDER. (TRUE NORTH/DOWN UNDER). No. 1-. 0823-1508. CN. English. an. $7.00. True North/Down Under, P O Box 55, Lantzville British Columbia V0R 2H0 Canada. DD C810.80054.

TSAO TANG. VFOAT Caotang. First published in 1981. Periodical. CH. Chinese. ir. Tsao Tang Pien Chi Pu, Cheng-Tu China. LC PL2675. DD 895.113.

TUAN PIEN HSIAO SHUO HSUAN. VFOAT Best Chinese Stories. 1968-. CN. Chinese. an. LC PL2653.

TUAN PIEN HSIAO SHUO HSUAN (PEKING, CHINA). (TUAN PIEN HSIAO SHUO HSUAN). 1980-. CC. Chinese. an. 1.75. Jen Min Wen Hsueh Chu Pan She, Hsin Hua Shu Tien Pei-Ching Fa Hsing So Pei-Ching, Pei-Ching China Mainland. LC PL2653.

TUAN PIEN HSIAO SHUO NIEN PIEN. 1980-. CH. Chinese. an. 1.69. Chiang-Su Sheng, Hsin Hua Shu Tien, Nan-Ching China. LC PL2653. DD 895.130108.

TULANE STUDIES IN ENGLISH. V. 1-. 0082-6758. Monographic Series. US. English. Department of English, Tulane University, New Orleans LA 70118. Ind/Abst MLA Int. Bibliogr. Books Artic. Mod. Lang. Lit., Annu. Bibliogr. Engl. Lang. Lit. LC PR13. DD 820.9. (cum index).

TULANE STUDIES IN ROMANCE LANGUAGES AND LITERATURE. No. 1- 1966-. 0564-4380. Monographic Series. US. English. ir. Newcomb College-Tulane University, Art Department, New Orleans LA 70118. Tel (504)865-5115. Ed Gloria Harris. Ind/Abst Abstr. Engl. Stud., MLA Int. Bibliogr. Books Artic. Mod. Lang. Lit. DD 440. adv acc. Volumes that come out periodically in the Romance languages and literature. The volumes deal with literature from the Middle Ages through the 20th century.

TULIMULD. Began with 1-. 0041-4034. Periodical. SW. Swedish. qt. 25.00. Tulimuld Sweden, B K Skordevagen, 222-38 Lund Sweden. Tel 119690. Ed B Kangro. Ind/Abst MLA Int. Bibliogr. Books Artic. Mod. Lang. Lit. LC AP95.E4. bk rev. Circ 1,000. Cultural magazine publishing poetry, short stories, book reviews, articles on art and literature in Estonian language.

TULSA STUDIES IN WOMEN'S LITERATURE. Vol. 1, No. 1 (Spring 1982)-. 0732-7730. Periodical. US. English. sa. $14.00. University of Tulsa, 600 South College Avenue, Tulsa OK 74104. Tel (918) 592-6000. Ed Shari Benstock. Ind/Abst MLA Int. Bibliogr. Books Artic. Mod. Lang. Lit. LC PN471. DD 809.89287. bk rev. adv acc. Circ 500. The only scholarly journal in the world devoted solely to women's literature. Includes articles and reviews on women's writing, from all times and places.

TUNG FANG (HANG-CHOU SHIH, CHINA). (TUNG FANG). VFOAT Dongfang. Periodical. CH. Chinese. ir. 1.00. Chung-Kuo Kuo Chi Shu Tien, PO Box 399, Pei-Ching China. LC PL2250. DD 895.108005.

TUNG HUA. VFOAT Tonghua. 1 (May 1980)-. Periodical. CH. Chinese. ir. 0.85. Hsin Hua Shu Tien, Tien-Chin Shih China. LC PZ10.24.

TUNG SU WEN HSUEH HSUAN KAN. Periodical. Chinese. ir. 0.45. Hsin Hua Shu Tien Tai-Yuan Shih, Shan-Hsi, Tai-Yuan Shih Japan. LC PL2446. DD 398.20951.

TUUMBA. Began with issue for Aug. 1976-. 0146-2083. Monographic Series. US. English. $6.00. Tuumba Press, PO Box 1075, Willits CA 95490. LC PS642. DD 813.008.

TVORCHESTVO A. P. CHEKHOVA. See Linguistics.

TVORCHOSTS. VFOAT Slovnik Serbskohorvatsko-Rusky. Vol. 1- 1975-. Slavic (other). ir. LC PG3898.Y8.

TWAYNE'S ENGLISH AUTHOR SERIES. V. 1-. 0564-559X. Monographic Series. US. English. ir. Twayne Publishing Inc, 70 Lincoln Street, Boston MA 02111. Tel (617)423-3990. Ed Athenaide Dallett. Ind/Abst MLA Int. Bibliogr. Books Artic. Mod. Lang. Lit., Years Work Eng. Stud. DD 823. Bio-critical studies of individual authors of the British Isles.

TWEED. V. 1- Sept. 1972-. Periodical. AT. English. qt. $7.34. Tweed, PO Box 304, Murwillimbah 2484 Australia.

TWENTIETH CENTURY INTERPRETATIONS. Monographic Series. US. English. ir. Prentice Hall Inc, Route 9 West, Englewood Cliffs NJ 07632. Ind/Abst MLA Int. Bibliogr. Books Artic. Mod. Lang. Lit.

TWENTIETH CENTURY LITERATURE. V. 1- Apr. 1955-. 0041-462X. Periodical. US. English. qt. Twentieth Century Literature, 49 Sheridan Avenue, Albany NY 12210. Tel (212)757-5530. Ed William McBrien. Ind/Abst Abstr. Engl. Stud., Annu. Bibliogr. Engl. Lang. Lit., Humanit. Index, Bibliogr. Index, MLA Int. Bibliogr. Books Artic. Mod. Lang. Lit., Years Work Eng. Stud. LC PN2. DD 809.04. Circ 2,000. Available on microfilm from University Microfilms. Concerns all aspects of modern and contemporary literature.

TWENTIETH CENTURY VIEWS. 0496-6058. Monographic Series. US. English. ir. Prentice Hall Inc, Route 9 West, Englewood Cliffs NJ 07632. Ind/Abst MLA Int. Bibliogr. Books Artic. Mod. Lang. Lit.

TWORCZOSC. Vol. 1- Sierp. 1945-. 0041-4727. Periodical. PL. Polish. mo. ARS Polona, Krakowskie Przedmiescie 7, 00-068 Warsaw Poland. Ind/Abst MLA Int. Bibliogr. Books Artic. Mod. Lang. Lit. LC PG7001.

TZU HSUEH. V. 1, (Nov. 1981)-. Periodical. CH. Chinese. ir. 0.90. Hsin Hua Shu Tien Shang-Hai fa Hsing so Shanghai China. LC PL2336. DD 895.1104.

UBU REPERTORY THEATER PUBLICATIONS. See Theater.

U.C. REVIEW. (U. C. REVIEW). Main/Corp University College, Toronto, Ont. VFOAT University College Literary Review. VAT University College Review, University College Literary Review. 0226-3440. CN. English. an. U C Review, University College, University of Toronto, Toronto Ontario M5S 1A1 Canada. DD C810.8092379.

UKRAINSKA MOVA I LITERATURA V SHKOLI. V. 13- Sept. 1963-. 0041-6096. Periodical. UR. Ukrainian. mo. Ind/Abst MLA Int. Bibliogr. Books Artic. Mod. Lang. Lit. LC PG3903. Ukrainska Mova V Shkoli, Literatura V Shkoli.

UKRAINSKE LITERATUROZNAVSTVO. Periodical. UR. Ukrainian. ir. Ind/Abst MLA Int. Bibliogr. Books Artic. Mod. Lang. Lit. LC PG3900.

ULAGASHEVSKIE CHTENIIA. Vol. 1-. UR. Russian. LC PL43.5.

UMI. No. 1- Ken (1- Go). Periodical. Japanese. mo. Kinokuniya Book Stores of America, 1581 Webster Street, San Francisco CA 94115. LC AP95.J2.

UNGA DIKTARE. Swedish. ir. Bokforlaget Inferi, Box 167 821 01 1, Bollnas Sweden. LC PT9547.

UNILETRAS : REVISTA DO DEPARTAMENTO DE LETRAS DA UEPG. See Linguistics.

THE UNIVERSAL BLACK WRITER. See Ethnic.

UNIVERSE. 0276-1033. US. English. Doubleday & Company Inc, 245 Park Avenue, New York NY 10017. Ed Terry Carr.

UNIVERSITY OF CALIFORNIA UNION LIST OF SERIALS. See Bibliographies.

THE UNIVERSITY OF MISSISSIPPI STUDIES IN ENGLISH. New Ser. V. 1 (1980)-. 0278-310X. US. English. an. University of Mississippi, College of Liberal Arts, University MS 38677. Ind/Abst Abstr. Engl. Stud., MLA Int. Bibliogr. Books Artic. Mod. Lang. Lit., Annu. Bibliogr. Engl.

Literature

Lang. Lit. **LC** PR5.M5. **DD** 820.9. *Studies in English (University of Mississippi. Dept. of English).*

UNIVERSITY OF NORTH CAROLINA. STUDIES IN COMPARATIVE LITERATURE. (STUDIES IN COMPARATIVE LITERATURE). 1950-. 0081-7775. Monographic Series. US. English. ir. University of North Carolina Press, University of North Carolina, Chapel Hill NC 27514. **Tel** (919)966-3561. **Ind/Abst** MLA Int. Bibliogr. Books Artic. Mod. Lang. Lit. **DD** 809.

UNIVERSITY OF TORONTO ROMANCE SERIES. V. 1- 1949-. 0082-5336. Monographic Series. CN. English (French). ir. University of Toronto Press, Front Campus, Toronto Ontario M5S 1A6 Canada. **Ind/Abst** MLA Int. Bibliogr. Books Artic. Mod. Lang. Lit. A series of monographic studies in the areas of Romance languages, consisting of books on French, Italian, Spanish, and Portuguese literature, language, and linguistics.

UNIVERSITY STUDIES IN MEDIEVAL AND RENAISSANCE LITERATURE. 0749-4149. Periodical. US. English. Peter Lang Publishing Inc, 34 East 39th Street, New York NY 10016.

THE UNSPEAKABLE VISIONS OF THE INDIVIDUAL. V. 1-. 0049-559X. Monographic Series. US. English. an. A W Knight, PO Box 439, California PA 15419. **Tel** (412)938-8956. Ed Arthur Winfield Knight and Kit Knight. **LC** PS536. **DD** 810.5. bk rev. adv acc. **Circ** 1,700. 'Best generation writings.'' Jack Kerouac.

UNTERSUCHUNGEN ZUR DEUTSCHEN LITERATURGESCHICHTE. V. 1 1962-. 0083-4564. Monographic Series. GW. German. ir. Max Niemeyer Verlag, Postfach 21 40, 7400 Tuebingen 1 West Germany. **Ind/Abst** MLA Int. Bibliogr. Books Artic. Mod. Lang. Lit. **DD** 830. Monographs on German literature from the beginnings of our times.

UNTERSUCHUNGEN ZUR SPRACH- UND LITERATURGESCHICHTE DER ROMANISCHEN VOLKER. 1- 1959-. 0083-4580. Monographic Series. GW. German. ir. Franz Steiner Verlag GMBH, Postfach 347, D7000 Stuttgart 1 West Germany. **Tel** (0711)2582229. Ed H H Christmann. Monographs about romance literatures and languages.

UNVEILLING. Vol. 2, No. 1 (Sept.-Nov. 1984)-. 0747-931X. Periodical. US. English (Spanish). qt. $6.00. Unveilling Cuba Inc, PO Box 170 Rockefeller Center Station, New York NY 10185. **DD** 860. *Unveiling Cuba, 0747-9328.*

URDU NAMAH. 0042-1065. Periodical. Urdu. ir. **LC** AP95.U7.

URGENCES. No. 1-. 0226-9554. Periodical. CN. French. ty. $9.00. Urgences, CP 54, Rimouski Quebec G5L 7B7 Canada. **DD** C840.80971477.

US 1 WORKSHEETS. **VFOAT** US1 Worksheets. **VAT** United States One Worksheets. 0362-7012. US. English. ir. US 1 Poets Cooperative, 21 Lake Drive, Roosevelt NJ 08555. **Tel** (609)448-5096. **Ind/Abst** Index Am. Period. Verse. **LC** PS501. **DD** 810.8005.

US WURK. See Linguistics.

THE USF LANGUAGE QUARTERLY. See Linguistics.

UTAH STUDIES IN LITERATURE AND LINGUISTICS. No. 1- 1974-. 0171-726X. Monographic Series. US. English (German, French or Spanish). ir. Peter Lang AG, Jupiterstrasse 15 PO Box 277, CH-3000 Berne 15 Switzerland. **Ind/Abst** MLA Int. Bibliogr. Books Artic. Mod. Lang. Lit. Monograph series on literature and linguistics.

UTTARA VARSHIKA. Gujarati. ir. 3.00. Sahitya Bharati Prakasana, 8 Navyug Society, N.S. Road No 4, Vile Parle (West), 56, Mumbai India. **LC** PK1855.

UTUNK. Periodical. US. Hungarian. wk. Ilexim Press, PO Box 1-136-1-137, Bucharest Romania. **LC** DR279.7.

V SELSKOM KLUBE. Vol. 1.-. Periodical. UR. Russian. an. 0.25. Izdatelstvo Iskusstvo, Sobinovskii Per 3, 103009 Moskva USSR. **LC** PG3227.5.

VALLEY VOICES. 0712-3752. CN. English. an. $5.00 Per Volume. Valley Voices, c/o Alberni Valley Creative Writer's, 34-4467 Wallace Street, Port Alberni British Columbia V9Y 3Y4 Canada. **DD** C810.80971134.

VAN NGHE. Periodical. VM. Vietnamese. ir. Xunhasaba 32 Hai Ba Trung Hanoi DRV North Vietnam. **LC** PL4378.

THE VANCOUVER LITERARY NEWS. 2/83-. 0826-4961. Periodical. CN. English. mo. Literary Storefront, 314 West Cordova Street, Vancouver British Columbia V6B 1E8 Canada. **DD** C810.5. *Literary Storefront Monthly, 0820-6678.*

VANCOUVER STREETS. Vol. 1, No. 1 (Spring 1982)-. 0714-8518. Periodical. CN. English. qt. $2.00 Per Number Domestic, $3.00 Others. Vancouver Streets, PO Box 46697/Station G, Vancouver British Columbia V6R 4KB Canada. **DD** C810.80054.

VARLK. Began publication in 1934?. Periodical. TU. Turkish. mo. $20.00. Varlik Yayinevi Cagaloglu, Yokusu 40, Ankara Caddesi, Istanbul Turkey. **Tel** 5226924. Ed Yasar Nabi Nayr. adv acc. **Circ** 5,000. Subject headings: literature, poetry and arts.

VECTOR (READING). (VECTOR). Began in Summer 1958. 0505-0448. Periodical. UK. English. ir. bk rev. adv acc. **Circ** 800. Reviews, interviews and analysis of science fiction and fantasy literature from a British perspective.

UN VERANO. Began publication with issue for Summer 1978. 0730-9708. US. English. an. $2.50. Latino Youth Alternative H/S, 1919 West Cullerton, Chicago IL 60608. **Tel** (312)829-0178. Journal of literature and art.

VERSANTS. No 1 (Autumn 1981)-. Periodical. SZ. French (German, Italian, Romanian, and Spanish). an. $17.32. Editions de la Baconniere SA, 19 Avenue du College, CH-2017 Boundry Switzerland. Ed Marc Eigelinger. **Circ** 800. The Swiss review of romance literatures. Publishes literary studies and documents related to the French, Spanish, Italian and Catalan languages.

VERSUS *CEASED*. No. 1, Summer 1976. Ceased with No. 4. 0384-868X. Periodical. CN. English. ty. Gruppo Editoriale Fabri, Via Mecanate 91, 20138 Milano Italy. **DD** C810.80054.

VERTEX. V. 1- Apr. 1973-. 0091-7257. Periodical. US. English. bm. $6.00. 8060 Melrose Avenue, Los Angeles CA 90046. **LC** PZ1, PS648.S3. **DD** 813.0876.

VERZEICHNIS DER ORIENTALISCHEN HANDSCHRIFTEN IN DEUTSCHLAND. SUPPLEMENTBAND. 1- 1965-. 0506-7944. Monographic Series. GW. German (English). ir. Franz Steiner Verlag GMBH, Postfach 347, D7000 Stuttgart 1 West Germany. **Tel** (0711)2582229. Ed D George. Catalogs of manuscripts in oriental and African languages to be found in German libraries and museums.

VES SVET. UR. Russian. 1.02. Molodaia Gvardiia K-30, Sushchevskaia 21, Moscow USSR. **LC** PN6065.R9.

VESTNIK LENINGRADSKOGO UNIVERSITETA. ISTORIJA, JAZYK, LITERATURA. See History (General).

VETERANS' VOICES. 1952. 0504-0779. Periodical. US. English. ty. $3.00. Veterans Voices, 5920 Nall/Room 117, Mission KS 66202. Ed Margaret Clark. **LC** PS508.V45. **DD** 810.80920697. **Circ** 5,000. (ctrl). Works by patients in veterans administration medical centers writing as therapy, an all volunteer project. Prose and poetry.

VIA. No. 1- May 1976-. 0147-8184. Periodical. US. English (Portuguese or Spanish). sa. $6.00. University of Berkeley, 103 Sproul Hall, Berkeley CA 94720. **LC** PN1. **DD** 805.

VICAKSANA. Periodical. Sinhalese. ir. **LC** PK2850.

THE VICTORIAN NEWSLETTER. No. 1- Apr. 1952-. 0042-5192. Periodical. US. English. sa. $5.00. Victorian Newsletter, c/o Ward Hollstrom, FAC 200, Western Kentucky University, Bowling Green KY 42101. Ed Ward Hellstrom. **Ind/Abst** Abstr. Engl. Stud., MLA Int. Bibliogr. Books Artic. Mod. Lang. Lit., Annu. Bibliogr. Engl. Lang. Lit., Years Work Eng. Stud. **LC** PR1. bk rev. **Circ** 1,000. (ctrl). Victorian literature criticism.

VIEW FROM THE SILVER BRIDGE. V. 1- June 1972-. 0703-5802. Periodical. CN. English. ir. $1.00 Each Number. B Standeven, 1928 Nunns Road, Campbell River British Columbia V9W 1H2 Canada. **DD** C810.80054.

VIGILIAE CHRISTIANAE. V. 1- Jan. 1947-. 0042-6032. Periodical. NE. English (French and German). qt. 108.-. E J Brill, PO Box 9000, 2300 PA Leiden The Netherlands. Ed A F J Klyn and C Mahrman. **Ind/Abst** MLA Int. Bibliogr. Books Artic. Mod. Lang. Lit., New Testam. Abstr., Recent Publ. Artic., Relig. Index One, Period. **LC** BR66. **DD** 270.105. bk rev. adv acc. **Circ** 850. Contains articles of a historical, cultural, linguistic or philological nature on Early Christian literature posterior to the New Testament in the widest sense of the word.

VII. VFOAT Seven. Vol. 1-. 0271-3012. US. English. an. Heffers Printers Ltd, c/o P Andrews, King Hedges Road, Cambridge CB4 2PQ England. **Ind/Abst** MLA Int. Bibliogr. Books Artic. Mod. Lang. Lit. **LC** PR471. **DD** 823.91209.

VIJAYA. V. 1- 2030- 1973-. Nepali. ir. 2.00 Single Issue. Vijaya Parivara, Vijay Parivar Vijaypur 11, Dharana Nepal. **LC** PK2598.A2.

VIMAN DAIJIST. Periodical. Urdu. ir. Mussarat Aziz, Gardi Building, Nepar Road, Lahor Pakistan. **LC** PK2151.

VINDUET. VFOAT Gyldendals Tidskrift for Litteratur. Vol. 1-. 0042-6288. Periodical. NO. Norwegian. qt. $15.32. Forlagsentralens Tidsskrift, Postboks 6005 Etterstad, Oslo 6 Norway. **Tel** 02 20 07 10. **Ind/Abst** MLA Int. Bibliogr. Books Artic. Mod. Lang. Lit. **LC** PN9. **DD** 808.8. (cum index).

VIRGINIA WOOLF QUARTERLY. V. 1- Fall 1972-. 0090-4546. Periodical. US. English. qt. $5.00. California State Univestty Press, School of Literature, San Diego CA 92115. **Ind/Abst** Abstr. Engl. Stud., MLA Int. Bibliogr. Books Artic. Mod. Lang. Lit., Women Stud. Abstr. **LC** PR6045.O72. **DD** 823.912.

VISHAYA VASTU. V. 1, No. 1- (July/August/September 1980)-. Periodical. II. Hindi. qt. 15.00. Vishayavastu Karyalays, J-11/7 Rajouri Garden, New Delhi 110027 India. **LC** PK2040.5.

VISHVESHVARANAND INDOLOGICAL JOURNAL. Vol. 1, No. 1 (Mar. 1963)-. 0507-1410. Periodical. II. English (text in Sanskrit, or Hindi). sa. Panjab University, PO Sadhu Ashram, Hoshiarpur Panjab India. **Ind/Abst** MLA Int. Bibliogr. Books Artic. Mod. Lang. Lit. **LC** PK101. **DD** 491.105. (cum index).

THE VISIONARY COMPANY. Vol. 1, No. 1 (Summer 1981)-. 0742-6119. Periodical. US. English. an. $6.00. Visionary Company, Mercy College, Dobbs Ferry NY 10522. **Ind/Abst** MLA Int. Bibliogr. Books Artic. Mod. Lang. Lit. **LC** PS223. **DD** 810.9. *Hart Crane Newsletter, 0147-7862.*

VITAL SPEECHES OF THE DAY. V. 1- Oct. 8, 1934-. 0042-742X. Periodical. US. English. sm. $25.00. City News Publishing Company, PO Box 606, Southold Long Island NY 11971. Ed Thomas F Daly. **Ind/Abst** ABI/Inform, Hospit. Lit. Index, Manage. Contents, Biogr. Index, Read. Guide Period. Lit., Energy Inf. Abstr., Environ. Abstr., Mag. Index, Pop. Mag. Rev. **LC** PN6121. **DD** 808.85. (cum index). **Circ** 20,000. Covers education, government, current events, history, economics, business and commerce, social progress, and politics.

VIVECANA (BOMBAY, INDIA). (VIVECANA). V. 1, No. 1 (January/March 1982)-. Periodical. II. Gujarati. qt. S N D T University, Bombay 400020 India. **LC** PK1850.

VOCES (BARCELONA, SPAIN). (VOCES). 1-. Periodical. SP. Spanish. bm. $18.00. Montesinos, Editor, c/o C Ronda San Pedro 11 6, Barcelona 10 Spain. **LC** PN6. **DD** 809.

VOIX ET IMAGES. VFOAT Etudes Quebecoises. V. 1- Sept. 1975-. 0318-9201. CN. French. ty. $17.99. University du Quebec a Montreal, CP 8888, Succursale A, Montreal Quebec H3C 3P8 Canada. **Tel** (514)282-4278. **Ind/Abst** MLA Int. Bibliogr. Books Artic. Mod. Lang. Lit., Point Repere. **LC** PQ3900. **DD** C840.9005. **Circ** 900. (ctrl). Exclusively studies of Quebec literature. An open journal dealing with modern theories (semiology, study of narratives, psycho-critique) as well as the history of literature. *Voix et Images du Pays, 0318-921X.*

VOPROSY LITERATURY. V. 1- 1957-. 0042-8795. Periodical. UR. Russian. mo. $44.00. Victor Kamkin Inc (70149), 12224 Parklawn Drive, Rockville MD 20852. **Tel** (301)881-5973. **Ind/Abst** Annu. Bibliogr. Engl. Lang. Lit., MLA Int. Bibliogr. Books Artic. Mod. Lang. Lit. **LC** PN9.

VOPROSY LITERATURY NARODOV SSSR. Vol. 1-. UR. Russian. 0.72. Izdatelskoe Obedinenie Vyshcha Shkola, Odessa Ostrovidova, 64, Kiev USSR. **LC** PN849.R9.

Literature

VOPROSY RUSSKOI LITERATURY. No. 1-. 0507-3871. Periodical. UR. Russian. ir. Victor Kamkin Inc, 12224 Parklawn Drive, Rockville MD 20852.

VOPROSY SIUZHETOSLOZHENIIA. 1.- 1969-. UR. Russian. 0.84 Single Issue. Zvaigzne, Ul Gorkogo 105, Riga USSR. LC PN218.

VOPROSY STRUKTURY GERMANSKIKH IAZYKOV. See Linguistics.

VORTEX (BHUBANESWAR, INDIA). (VORTEX). Periodical. US. English. qt. 10.00. 9/5 R Flats, Unit III, Bhubaneswar 751001 India. LC PN2. DD 808.8. *Probitas*.

VORTICE. See Linguistics.

THE VOYEUR. V. 1- Dec. 1974-. Periodical. US. English. mo. $3.50. Open Window Society, 566 Laguardia Place, New York NY 10012.

VREMJA I MY. (VREMIA I MY). No. 1- Noiabr 1975-. 0737-7061. Periodical. US. Russian (summaries in English). bm. Vremya i My, 409 Highwood Avenue, Leonia NJ 07605. Tel (212)684-3014. LC DS101.

W. D. THOMAS MEMORIAL LECTURE. 0083-6958. Monographic Series. UK. English. ir. University of Wales Press, Cathays Park, Cardiff Wales.

WAI KUO WEN HSUEH CHI KAN. 1981, 1-. Periodical. CC. Chinese. qt. 1.25. Hsin Hua Shu Tien Pei-Ching fa Hsing So, Peking China Mainland. LC PN9. DD 809.

WAI KUO WEN HSUEH YEN CHIU (WU-CHANG, HUPEH PROVINCE, CHINA). (WAI KUO WEN HSUEH YEN CHIU). VFOAT Studies in Foreign Literature. Began in 1978. Periodical. CC. Chinese. qt. 0.70. Chung-Kuo Kuo Chi Shu Tien, PO Box 2820, Peking China. LC PN9. DD 809.

A WAKE NEWSLITTER CEASED. No. 1 (Mar. 1962)-No. 18 (Dec. 1963). 0511-0866. Periodical. UK. English. bm. Ind/Abst MLA Int. Bibliogr. Books Artic. Mod. Lang. Lit., Annu. Bibliogr. Engl. Lang. Lit., Abstr. Engl. Stud. LC PR6019.O9. DD 823. (cum index).

WALTER PRESCOTT WEBB MEMORIAL LECTURES. 1- 1968-. 0083-713X. Monographic Series. US. English. an. Texas University Press, Drawer C, College Station TX 77843.

WAR, WERKGROEP ARBEIDERSLITERATUUR ROTTERDAM. Main/Corp Werkgroep voor Arbeidersliteratuur. VFOAT Tijdschrift voor Arbeidersliteratuur. VAT Werkgroep Arbeidersliteratuur Rotterdam, Werkgroep Arbeidersliteeratuur Rotterdam. Dutch. ir. 15.00. Weikgroep Voor Arbeidersliteratur, Kruisplein 30, Rotterdam Netherlands. LC PT5460.

WARD-PHILLIPS LECTURES IN ENGLISH LANGUAGE AND LITERATURE. See Linguistics.

WASCANA REVIEW. V. 1- 1966-. 0043-0412. Periodical. CN. English. sa. $3.86. University of Regina, Canadian Plains Research Center, Regina Saskatchewan S4S 0A2 Canada. Tel (306)584-4311. Ind/Abst Abstr. Engl. Stud., MLA Int. Bibliogr. Books Artic. Mod. Lang. Lit., Years Work Eng. Stud.

WASHINGTON AND JEFFERSON LITERARY JOURNAL. 1- 1966-. 0043-0455. Periodical. US. English. an. $1.00. Washington & Jefferson College, Washington PA 15301.

WASHINGTON REVIEW. See The Arts (General).

WASTELANDS. No. 1 Autumn 1980-. 0228-1937. Periodical. CN. English. qt. $6.50. Wastelands, PO Box 300, Station A, Ottawa Ontario J1B 8V3 Canada. DD C810.80054.

WATNO DUR. (THE WATNO DUR). V. 1- July 1973-. 0700-8163. Periodical. CN. Panjabi. mo. Watno Dur Punjabi, Post Box 1041, Coquitlam British Columbia Canada. Tel (604)734-1413. DD 971.10049142.

WAVES. V. 1- Spring 1972-. 0315-3932. Periodical. CN. English. qt. $9.28. Waves, 79 Denham Drive, Richmond Hill Ontario L4C 6H9 Canada. Tel (416)889-6703. Ed Bernice Lever. LC PR9229. DD 810.80054. bk rev. adv acc. Circ 1,000. Canadian focus with international writers: fiction, poetry, interviews, reviews, and graphics. An eclectic, prize winning 100 plus page of fine Canadian writing.

WDS FORUM. VAT Writer's Digest School Forum. 0275-9748. Periodical. US. English. mo. $3.00. Writer's Digest School, 9933 Alliance Road, Cincinnati OH 45242. DD 808.

WEE GIANT. V. 1- Autumn 1977-. 0702-4894. Periodical. CN. English. ty. $1.25 Each Number. Wee Giant Press, 178 Bond Street North, Hamilton Ontario L8S 3W6 Canada. DD C810.80054.

WEGZEICHEN. Vol. 1-. German. sa. LC PT3732. DD 830.809431.

WEIRDBOOK. See Romance and Adventure.

WELT DER SLAVEN. (DIE WELT DER SLAVEN). Vol. 1- 1956-. 0043-2520. Periodical. GW. German. be. Kubon & Sagner, Postfach 34 01 08, D8 Munchen 34 West Germany. Ind/Abst MLA Int. Bibliogr. Books Artic. Mod. Lang. Lit. LC PG1.

WEN CHI (TAIPEI, TAIWAN : 1983-). (WEN CHI). Vol. 1- (Apr. 1983)-. Periodical. CH. Chinese. bm. $16.00. Hsueh Sheng Ying Wen Tsa Chih, She Taipei Taiwan. LC PL3031.T3. DD 895.108951249.

I WEN HSI TSO CHI KAN. First published in 1982. Periodical. Chinese. ir. LC PL2513. DD 895.1080951249.

WEN HSUEH CHIEH. VFOAT Literary Taiwan. Vol. 1-. Periodical. CH. Chinese. ir. 90.00. Chung Hui Chu Pan She 8, Lane 3, Ling Ya Chu Cheng I Road, Kao-Hsiung Shih Taiwan. LC PL3031.T3. DD 895.108.

WEN HSUEH LUN TSUNG. 1 (Dec. 1983)-. Periodical. CC. Chinese. qt. 0.84. Hsin Hua Shu Tien, Ho-Nan Sheng China.

WEN HSUEH YUEH PAO (CHANG-SHA SHIH, CHINA). (WEN HSUEH YUEH PAO). 1984-4 (Apr. 1984)-. Periodical. CC. Chinese. mo. 0.35. Chung-Kuo Kuo Chi Tu Shu Mao I Tsung Kung SSU, PO Box 2820, Pei-Ching China. LC PL2250. DD 895.109. Hsiang-Chiang Wen Hsueh.

WEN HSUN. VFOAT Wen Hsun Yueh Kan. First published in 1983. Periodical. CH. Chinese. mo. $15.00. Wen Hsu Tsa Chih She, PO Box 588475, Taipei Taiwan China. LC PL3031.T3.

WEST BRANCH. No. 1-. 0149-6441. Periodical. US. English. sa. $5.00. West Branch Department of English, Bucknell University, Lewisburg PA 17837. Tel (717)524-1440. Ed Karl Patten and Robert Taylor. LC PN6010.5. DD 808.8105. bk rev. Circ 500. Poetry and fiction of the highest quality.

WESTERN AMERICAN LITERATURE. V. 1- Spring 1966-. 0043-3462. Periodical. US. English. qt. $20.00. Western American Literature, UMC 32-Utah State University, Logan UT 84322. Tel (801)750-1603. Ed Thomas J Lyon. Ind/Abst Am. Hist. Life, Hist. Abstr., Part A, Mod. Hist. Abstr., Hist. Abst., Part B, Twent. Century Abstr., Abstr. Engl. Stud., MLA Int. Bibliogr. Books Artic. Mod. Lang. Lit., Annu. Bibliogr. Engl. Lang. Lit., Women Stud. Abstr., Film Lit. Index, Book Rev. Index, Ref. Source, Index Book Rev. Humanit. LC PS271. DD 810.9978. bk rev. adv acc. Circ 900. Dedicated to the study and enjoyment of western regional literature, which is worthy of both scholarly and popular attention.

WESTERN HUMANITIES REVIEW. V. 3- Jan. 1949-. 0043-3845. Periodical. US. English. qt. $20.00. University of Utah, OSH 341 University of Utah, Salt Lake City UT 84112. Tel (801)581-7438. Ed Jack Garlington. Ind/Abst Abstr. Engl. Stud., MLA Int. Bibliogr. Books Artic. Mod. Lang. Lit., Annu. Bibliogr. Engl. Lang. Lit., Film Lit. Index, Book Rev. Index, Index Book Rev. Humanit., Index Am. Period. Verse, Media Rev. Dig., Am. Hist. Life, Hist. Abstr., Years Work Eng. Stud., Hist. Abstr., Part A, Mod. Hist. Abstr., Hist. Abst., Part B, Twent. Century Abstr. Circ 1,000. Articles on the humanities, fiction, poetry, book and film reviews. *Utah Humanities Review*.

WESTERN HUMOR AND IRONY MEMBERSHIP SERIAL YEARBOOK. See Yearbooks, Almanacs, Directories.

WESTERN ILLINOIS REGIONAL STUDIES. See History (General) - History of North, South, and Central America.

WHETSTONE. 1971-. 0318-1065. CN. English. sa. $3.86. University of Lethbridge, English Department, 4401 University Drive, Lethbridge Alberta T1K 3M4 Canada. Tel (403)329-2490. Ed Marlene Graveland. Circ 100. (ctrl). Fiction, artwork and poetry by new and established artists.

WHITE SPACE. V. 1- Jan. 1978-. 0705-2049. Periodical. CN. English. ir. $1.50 Each Number. D M Vereschagin, R R 2, New Sarepta Alberta T0B 3M0 Canada. DD 809.387605.

WHITE WALL REVIEW. 0712-8991. CN. English. an. $2.50 Each Number. Ryerson Literary Society, Ryerson Polytechnical Institute 5th Floor Jorgenson Hall 50 Gould Street, Toronto Ontario M5B 1E8 Canada. DD C810.80054.

WHITTIER NEWSLETTER. No. 1- Fall 1966-. 0511-8832. US. English. an. Free. Professor John B Pickard, Department of English University of Florida, Gainesville FL 32611. Tel (905)376-6829. Ed Howard W Carter. LC PS3279. DD 811.3 B. bk rev. Circ 500. (ctrl). Survey of works and articles about Whittier. Accounts of club activities, library holdings, and bibliographic, yearly review. Short articles on Whittier and his poetry.

WHIZ FUNNIES. Vol. 1, No. 1 (Oct. 1977)-. 0229-0804. Periodical. CN. English. ir. $0.50 Each Number. Whiz Funnies, 616-415 Edison Avenue, Winnipeg Manitoba R2G 0M3 Canada. DD C810.80054.

WIENER ZEITSCHRIFT FUR DIE KUNDE DES MORGENLANDES. See History (General).

THE WILSON QUARTERLY. See Social Sciences (General).

WIND. (WIND/LITERARY JOURNAL). Publication began with V. 1 (Spring 1971). 0361-2481. Periodical. US. English. ty. $6.00. Wind Magazine, Route 1 Box 809K, Pikeville KY 41501. Tel (606)631-1129. Ed Quentin R Howard. Ind/Abst Index Am. Period. Verse. LC PS501. DD 810.810054. bk rev. Circ 500. An eclectic literary periodical published three times yearly containing poetry, short stories and book reviews from small presses, only publishing beginners.

WINDOW (BETHESDA, MD.). (WINDOW). 1 (Spring 1976)-. 0275-2166. Periodical. US. English. qt. $2.50 Each Issue. Window Press, 7005 Westmoreland Drive, Takoma Park MD 20912. LC PS1. DD 810.8.

WINDSCRIPT. Vol. 1 (Sept. 1983)-. 0822-2363. Periodical. CN. English. ir. 6.00. Saskatchewan Writers Guild, 1-1861 Scarth Street, Regina Sask S4P 2G9 Canada. Tel 757-6332. Ed Paul Wilson. adv acc. Circ 4,000. (ctrl). Collection of prose, poetry, and artwork by Saskatchewan high school students.

THE WINESBURG EAGLE. Began with Nov. 1975 issue. 0147-3166. US. English. sa. $5.00. University of Richmond, Sherwood Anderson Society, Richmond VA 23173. Tel (804)285-6225. Ed Welford D Taylor. Ind/Abst MLA Int. Bibliogr. Books Artic. Mod. Lang. Lit. LC PS3501.N4. DD 813.52. bk rev. adv acc. Circ 150. Features articles and reviews with Sherwood Anderson as a central point of focus.

WINTER'S TALES. Monographic Series. US. English. an.

WINTER'S TALES FROM IRELAND. V. 1- 1970-. 0332-0014. IE. English. ir. Gill and MacMillan, 15 17 Eden Quay, Dublin 1 Ireland. LC PZ1.A1, PR8875. DD 823.01.

WIRKUNG DER LITERATUR. 0084-0467. GW. German. ir. C H Becksche Verlagsbchhndlg, Wilhelmstrasse 9, Postfach 400340, D-8 Munchen 40 West Germany. Ind/Abst MLA Int. Bibliogr. Books Artic. Mod. Lang. Lit.

WISCONSIN CHINA SERIES. No. 1-. 0084-053X. Monographic Series. US. English. ir. $40.00. University of Wisconsin, 1212 Van Hise Hall, East Asian Lan, Madison WI 53706. Tel (608)262-2291. Ed William H Nienhauser Jr. bk rev. adv acc. Circ 300. A journal on Chinese literature, modern and traditional.

WISCONSIN STUDIES IN LITERATURE. No.1- 1964-. Periodical. English. ir. LC PR1.

WISSENSCHAFTLICHE ZEITSCHRIFT DER UNIVERSITAT ROSTOCK. GESELLSCHAFTS- UND SPRACHWISSENSCHAFTLICHE REIHE. VFOAT WZ Rostock. Ceased with 1975. 0557-3548. Periodical. SZ. German (summaries in English, French, and Russian). mo. $100.93. Kunst & Wissen Erich Bieber, Dufourstrasse 51, CH-8008 Zurich Switzerland. Tel (011)411694420. Ind/Abst Phys. Abstr., Comput. Control Abstr., Electr. Electron. Abstr., Am. Hist. Life, Hist. Abstr., MLA Int. Bibliogr.

Literature

Books Artic. Mod. Lang. Lit. LC AS182. **CODEN** WZRGAC.

WITCH AND THE CHAMELEON. (THE WITCH AND THE CHAMELEON). 1- Aug. 1974-. 0382-0246. Periodical. CN. English. ir. $1.00 Per Number. A Bankier, 2 Paisley Avenue South Apartment 6, Hamilton Ontario L8S 1T7 Canada. **DD** 823.0876.

WOLGAN MUNHAK. VFOAT Munhak. Periodical. KO. Korean. ir. 6,000. Wolgan Munhak, 110 Insa-Dong, Chongno-Ku, Seoul South Korea. **LC** PL950.2.

WOMEN & LITERATURE. VAT Women and Literature. V. 3-7, Spring 1975-79. 0147-1759. US. English. an. Holmes & Meier Publishers Inc, 30 Irving Place, New York NY 10003. **Tel** (212)254-4100. **Ind/Abst** Abstr. Engl. Stud., MLA Int. Bibliogr. Books Artic. Mod. Lang. Lit., Women Stud. Abstr., Humanit. Index. **LC** PN481. **DD** 809.93352. *Mary Wollstonecraft Journal, 0193-7103.*

WORD LOOM. 1 (Winter 1981/82)-. 0714-3257. Periodical. CN. English. sa. $5.00 Each Number. Word Loom, Box 31, 242 Montrose Street, Winnipeg Manitoba R3M 3M7 Canada. **DD** 820.800914.

WORDS FROM INSIDE. 1971-. 0316-8670. Periodical. CN. English (includes some text in French). an. Prison Arts Foundation, 143 5th Avenue, Brantford Ontario N3S 1A3 Canada. **DD** C810.80054.

WORDSWORTH CIRCLE. (THE WORDSWORTH CIRCLE). V. 1- Winter 1970-. 0043-8006. Periodical. US. English. qt. $12.00. Temple University, Department of English, College of Liberal Arts, Philadelphia PA 19122. **Tel** (215)787-7344. **Ed** Marilyn Gaull. **Ind/Abst** Abstr. Engl. Stud., MLA Int. Bibliogr. Books Artic. Mod. Lang. Lit., Recent Publ. Artic., Index Book Rev. Humanit., Years Work Eng. Stud. **LC** PR1. **DD** 820.914. bk rev. adv acc. **Circ** 1,000. A learned journal devoted to the study of English romantic poets and prose writers especially Coleridge, Wordsworth, Hazlitt, de Quincey and others.

WORLD LITERATURE TODAY. V. 51- Winter 1977-.]196-3570. Periodical. US. English. qt. $35.00. World Literature Today, 630 Parrington Oval Room 109, Norman OK 73019. **Tel** (405)325-4531. **Ed** Ivar Ivask. **Ind/Abst** Abstr. Engl. Stud., MLA Int. Bibliogr. Books Artic. Mod. Lang. Lit., Lang. Lang. Behav. Abstr., Ref. Source, Soc. Sci. Index, Book Rev. Index, Int. Bibliogr. Book Rev., Humanit. Index. **LC** Z1007. **DD** 028.1. bk rev. adv acc. **Circ** 2,200. (ctrl). 10-15 essays plus 300 reviews of contemporary fiction, poetry, theatre, criticism, and biography from more than 50 languages around the world. *Books Abroad, 0006-7431.*

WORLD LITERATURE WRITTEN IN ENGLISH. VFOAT WLWE. No. 20, Nov. 1971. 0093-1705. Periodical. US. English. sa. $12.00. WLWE English Department, University of Guelph, Guelph Ontario N1G 2W1 Canada. **Ind/Abst** Abstr. Engl. Stud., MLA Int. Bibliogr. Books Artic. Mod. Lang. Lit. **LC** PR1. **DD** 820.9. *World Literature Written in English Newsletter, 0732-622X.*

WORLD'S WORD. Vol. 1, Winter 1983-. 8756-0631. Periodical. US. English (Multilingual). qt. Free. World's Word, c/o J P C da Silva, Room F-718/ The World Bank, Washington DC 20433. **DD** 808.

WOT. VFOAT W O T. V. 1- Spring 1979-. 0709-4035. Periodical. CN. English. sa. $4.00. Wot Publications, 657 Ardmore Drive, RR 2, Sidney British Columbia V8L 3S1 Canada. **DD** C810.80054.

WPA. WRITING PROGRAM ADMINISTRATION. (WPA, WRITING PROGRAM ADMINISTRATION). VFOAT Writing Program Administration. 0196-4682. US. English. $11.50. J Sargeant Reynolds Community College, A Dixon, Humanities and Social Sciences, PO Box C 32040, Richmond VA 23261. **LC** PE1404. **DD** 808.04205.

THE WRITER; A MONTHLY MAGAZINE FOR LITERARY WRITERS. V. 1- Apr. 1887-. 0043-9517. Periodical. US. English. $19.00. The Writer, 120 Boylston Street, Boston MA 02116. **Tel** (617)423-3157. **Ed** Sylvia K Burack. **Ind/Abst** Read. Guide Period. Lit., Mag. Index, Pop. Mag. Rev. **LC** PN101. **DD** 808.02505. adv acc. **Circ** 56,400. Practical instruction in all phases of writing for publication, including novels, short stories, articles, non-fiction books, poetry, plays, etc. Articles by famous writers plus lists of market for manuscripts.

WRITERS AT WORK. 1st- Series. 0510-9671. US. English. ir. Viking Press, 40 West 23rd Street, New York NY 10010.

WRITERS FORUM. 0163-9072. Periodical. US. English. an. $8.95. University of Colorado, Colorado Springs CO 80907. **Tel** (303)599-4023. **Ed** Alex Blackburn. **DD** 810.80054. adv acc. **Circ** 1,000. Fiction, poetry, some literary criticism. Features the best in contemporary American literature with emphasis upon serious Western literature.

WRITERS GUILD DIRECTORY. See Yearbooks, Almanacs, Directories.

WRITER'S NEWS. V. 2- June/July 1976-. 0705-0704. Periodical. CN. English. qt. Writers Federation Nova Scotia, PO Box 3608, Halifax South Nova Scotia 3BJ 3K6 Canada. **Tel** (902)423-8116. **Ed** Peggy Amirault. **DD** 808.042062716. adv acc. **Circ** 1,000. Provincial, regional and national news of interest to writers. How-to articles on the craft of writing. *Newsletter, 0705-0941.*

WRITER'S NEWSLETTER. July/Aug. 1977-. Periodical. US. English. mo $19.95. Writers Newsletter, High Point Mountain Road, West Shokan NY 12494. **Tel** (914)657-8092.

WRITER'S NOTES & QUOTES. VAT Writer's Notes and Quotes. 0043-955X. Periodical. US. English. qt. Writers Notes & Quotes, 142 West Bookdale Place, Fullerton CA 92632. *Amateur Notes & Quotes.*

THE WRITING CENTER JOURNAL. Vol. 1, No. 1 (Fall/Winter 1980)-. Periodical. US. English. sa. $5.00. The Writing Center Journal, Department of English UMC, 32 Utah State University, Logan UT 84322. **Tel** (801)750-2725. **Ed** Joyce Kinkead and Jeanette Harris. bk rev. adv acc. **Circ** 500. (ctrl). Focuses on writing centers in colleges and public schools including computers, collaborative learning and peer tutoring; also annual bibliographies plus book reviews.

WRITING IN PEEL. Issue 7 (June 1980). 0714-413X. Periodical. CN. English. sa. Free. Peel Board of Education, 73 King Street West, Mississauga Ontario L5B 1H5 Canada. **DD** C810.809282. (ctrl).

WRITING (TORONTO, ONT.). (WRITING). VFOAT Ecrits. VAT Ecrits (Toronto). '81-. 0712-1385. Periodical. CN. English (French). an. Writing, Information and Publications Department, Toronto Board of Education, 155 College Street, Toronto Ontario M5T 1P6 Canada. **DD** C811.540809283.

WRITINGS . . . FROM THE GREAT PLAINS. V. 1, No. 2- Spring 1978-. Periodical. US. English. sa. Panhandle Press, P O Box 1246, Scottsbluff NE 69361-1246. **Tel** (308)632-8624.

WRITTEN COMMUNICATION. Vol. 1, No. 1 (Jan. 1984)-. Periodical. US. English. qt. $50.00. Sage Publication Inc, 275 South Beverly Drive, Beverly Hills CA 90212.

WU HSIA SHIH CHIEH. Began in Mar. 1959. Periodical. Chinese. ir. $100.00. 7-13 Hsin Chieh 2nd Floor, Hong Kong China. **LC** PL2653.

WU MING WEN HSUEH. Periodical. CH. Chinese. bm. 0.30. Post Office, Tsang-Chou Shih China. **LC** PL2452. **DD** 895.105.

X-IT. VFOAT X-IT Magazine. VAT Exit (St. John's). Vol. 1, No. 1 (Jan./June 1984)-. 0824-2178. Periodical. CN. English. sa. $2.00 Each Issue. X-It, P O Box 102, St John's Newfoundland A1C 5H5 Canada. **DD** C810.80054.

XIN SHENG. (HSIN SHENG). First published in March 1972-. 0438-0797. Periodical. Chinese. ir. $0.30 Single Issue. Chinese Language and Literary Society, Nanyang University Jurong Road 22, Singapore. **LC** AP95.C4.

YA-LU CHIANG. VFOAT Yalujiang. Periodical. CC. Chinese. mo. $9.18. China Publication Centre, PO Box 2820, Beijing China. **LC** PL2303.

YADAM KWA SIRHWA. VFOAT Historical Romance & True Story. Periodical. KO. Korean. ir. 700 Each Issue. Popchisa, 30-21 Mukchong-Dong, Chung-Ku, Seoul South Korea. **LC** AP95.K6.

THE YALE LITERARY MAGAZINE. V. 148- May 1979-. 0044-0108. Periodical. US. English. qt. $40.00. Yale Literary Magazine, Box 243-A Yale Station, New Haven CT 06520. **LC** PS501. **DD** 810.5. *Yale Lit, 0196-7738.*

YALE STUDIES IN ENGLISH. See Linguistics.

THE YALE UNIVERSITY LIBRARY GAZETTE. See Library and Information Science.

HAI YANG WEN I. V. 1-. Periodical. Chinese. ir. $2.50 Single Issue. The Ocean Literary Press, No 3 on Ning Lane, Sai Ying Pun Hong Kong. **LC** PL2250.

YEARBOOK OF COMPARATIVE AND GENERAL LITERATURE. See Yearbooks, Almanacs, Directories.

THE YEAR'S BEST MYSTERY & SUSPENSE STORIES. VFOAT Year's Best Mystery and Suspense Stories. 1982-. 0741-0212. US. English. an. $12.95. Walker and Company, 720 Fifth Avenue, New York NY 10019. **Ed** E D Hoch. **LC** PZ1. **DD** 813.087208. *Best Detective Stories of the Year, 0067-625X.*

YEAR'S BEST SCIENCE FICTION (NEW YORK, N.Y.). (THE YEAR'S BEST SCIENCE FICTION). VFOAT Science Fiction. 1st Annual Collection-. 0743-1740. US. English. an. $9.95. Bluejay Books Inc, 130 West 42nd Street Room 504, New York NY 10036. **LC** PS648.S3. **DD** 813.087608.

THE YEAR'S SCHOLARSHIP IN SCIENCE FICTION, FANTASY AND HORROR LITERATURE. (THE YEAR'S SCHOLARSHIP IN SCIENCE FICTION, FANTASY, AND HORROR LITERATURE). 1980-. 0741-2231. US. English. an. Kent State University Press, Kent OH 44242. **Tel** (216)672-7913. **Ed** Marshall Tymn. **LC** Z5917.S36, PN3448.S45. **DD** 016.809387. Bibliographical listings of science fiction and fantasy scholarship. 1980, 1981, and 1982 are separate volumes. Beginning in 1983 the listings are included in the journal extrapolation. *Year's Scholarship in Science Fiction and Fantasy.*

YEAR'S WORK IN ENGLISH STUDIES. (THE YEAR'S WORK IN ENGLISH STUDIES). V. 1- 1919/20-. 0084-4144. UK. English. an. Humanities Press, Atlantic Highlands NJ 07716. **Ind/Abst** Humanit. Index, MLA Int. Bibliogr. Books Artic. Mod. Lang. Lit. **LC** PE58. bk rev. Team of scholars summarizes and evaluates all significant books and articles relating to study of English language and literature during the year. Comprehensive and worldwide in scope.

YEATS. Vol. 1 (1983)-. 0742-6224. Periodical. US. English. an. Cornell University Press, 124 Roberts Place, Ithaca NY 14853. **LC** PR5906. **DD** 821.8.

YELLOW BRICK ROAD. 0361-8552. Periodical. US. English. sa. Emerald City Press, 107 West 7th Street, Tempe AZ 85281. **Tel** (602)882-9409. **Ind/Abst** Index Am. Period. Verse.

YERUSHOLAYMER ALMANAKH. VFOAT Jerusalaimer Almanach. 2/3- 1974-. Yiddish. ir. Eygens, Shederot Eshkol 12/6, Yerushalayim Israel. **Ind/Abst** MLA Int. Bibliogr. Books Artic. Mod. Lang. Lit. **LC** PJ5161.5. *Almanakh: Yidishe Shrayber Fun Yerusholaim.*

YIDDISH. V. 1- Summer 1973-. 0364-4308. Periodical. US. English. qt. $9.00. Queens College, Kiely Hall 802, Flushing NY 11367. **Tel** (718)520-7076. **Ed** Joseph C Landis. **Ind/Abst** MLA Int. Bibliogr. Books Artic. Mod. Lang. Lit. **LC** PJ5120. **DD** 839.0905. bk rev. **Circ** 600. (ctrl). Accepts articles on Yiddish literature, language, folklore, the cultural context of Yiddish and translations of literature and criticism from Yiddish into English.

YIDISE QULTUR. (YIDDISHE KULTUR). VFOAT Yidishe Kultur. V. 1- Nov. 1938-. 0044-0426. Periodical. US. Yiddish. ir. $15.00. Kiddisher Kultur Farbound Inc, 1123 Broadway Room 203, New York NY 10010. **Tel** (212)691-0708. **Ed** Itche Goldberg. **Ind/Abst** MLA Int. Bibliogr. Books Artic. Mod. Lang. Lit. **LC** AP91. **Circ** 2,000. A literary magazine.

YONGHAK NONJIP. See Linguistics.

YOSONG MUNHAK. 1st Vol. (Jan. 1984)-. Periodical. KO. Korean. ir. 3,500 Each Issue. Chonyewon 569 Socho-Dong Kangnam-Ku, Seoul Korea. **LC** PL950.2.

YOUTH (FREDERICTON, N.B.). (YOUTH). 0712-1768. CN. English. an. Free. Youth New Brunswick Teachers' Association, PO Box 752, Fredericton New Brunswick E3B 5R6 Canada. **DD** C810.8092375. (ctrl). *Students' Creative Writing, 0712-1776.*

YU WEN YUEH KAN. See Linguistics.

YUGOPAYOGI. VFOAT Jugopajogi. Periodical. Oriya. mo. 2.00. B Das 43 Shitalatala Lane, Post Hind Motor 712233 Dist Hugli. **LC** PK2574.5.

Literature—Poetry

Z DZIEJOW FORM ARTYSTYCZNYCH W LITERATURZE POLSKIEJ. Vol. 1-. 0084-4411. Monographic Series. PL. Polish. ir. **Ind/Abst** MLA Int. Bibliogr. Books Artic. Mod. Lang. Lit. **LC** PG7001.

ZABAN O ADAB : BIHAR URDU AKADMI KA SIHMAHI JARIDAH. VFOAT Zoban O Adab. Periodical. Urdu. qt. 24.00. Bihar Urdu Academy, 6-A Rajindar Nagar, Patna 800001 India. **LC** PK2151.

ZAGADNIENIA RODZAJOW LITERACKICH. VFOAT Voprosy Literaturnykh Zhanrov, Problemes des Genres Litteraires. V. 1- (No. 1-). 0084-4446. PL. Polish (English and other languages). sa. ARS Polona, Krakowskie Przedmiescie 7, 00-068 Warsaw Poland. **Ind/Abst** Abstr. Engl. Stud., MLA Int. Bibliogr. Books Artic. Mod. Lang. Lit., Lang. Lang. Behav. Abstr., Sociol. Abstr. **LC** PN1.

ZAMLUNGEN. No. 1 (Jan.-March 1954)-. Periodical. US. Yiddish. qt. **LC** PJ5111. **DD** 839.0908.

ZAPIS. 1- Jan. 1977-. Periodical. UK. Polish. ir. Writers Scholars International Ltd, 39C Highbury Place, London N5 1QP England. **Tel** (01)359-0161. **LC** PG7368.

ZBORNIK ISTORIJE KNJIZEVNOSTI. VFOAT Recueil des Travaux de l'Histoire de la Litterature. Vol. 8-. YU. Serbo-Croatian -C (summaries in French or German). ir. Sprska Akademija Nauka I Umetnosti, Knez Mihailova 35, Beograd Yugoslavia. **Ind/Abst** MLA Int. Bibliogr. Books Artic. Mod. Lang. Lit. **LC** PG1400. *Zbornik Istorije Knjizevnosti.*

ZEHUT. 1 (May 1981)-. 0333-838X. Periodical. Hebrew. ir. $24.00 3 Issues. Agudat Zehut, POB 1544, Ramat Gan 52-115 Israel. **LC** PJ5001.

ZEITSCHRIFT FUR ANGLISTIK UND AMERIKANISTIK. Vol. 1-. 0044-2305. Periodical. English. qt. $23.95. Kunst & Wissen Erich Bieber, Dufourstrasse 51, CH-8008 Zurich Switzerland. **Tel** 011-41-1-69 44 20. **Ind/Abst** Abstr. Engl. Stud., MLA Int. Bibliogr. Books Artic. Mod. Lang. Lit., Sociol. Abstr., Years Work Eng. Stud., Annu. Bibliogr. Engl. Lang. Lit., Lang. Teach., Chem. Abstr., Lang. Lang. Behav. Abstr. **LC** PR1. **DD** 820.9. Index in last issue of volume - attached.

ZEITSCHRIFT FUR CELTISCHE PHILOLOGIE. See Linguistics.

ZEITSCHRIFT FUR DEUTSCHES ALTERTUM UND DEUTSCHE LITERATUR. Began publication in 1876. 0044-2518. Periodical. GW. German. qt. 128. Franz Steiner Verlag GMBH, Postfach 347, D7000 Stuttgart 1 West Germany. **Tel** 0711/2582-0. Ed Kurt Ruh. **Ind/Abst** MLA Int. Bibliogr. Books Artic. Mod. Lang. Lit., Index Book Rev. Humanit., Recent Publ. Artic. bk rev. adv acc. **Circ** 800. Also available on microfilm from General Microfilm, Cambridge, Mass. Reviews and articles in the field of Germanic (mostly German) literatures and languages in the Middle Ages. *Zeitschrift fur Deutschen Alterthum.*

ZEITSCHRIFT FUR FRANZOSISCHE SPRACHE UND LITERATUR. Began publication in 1889. 0044-2747. Periodical. GW. German (French). qt. 96. Franz Stiener Verlag GMBH, Postfach 347, D7000 Stuttgart 1 West Germany. **Tel** (0711)2582229. Ed A Noyer-Weidner and H Stimm. **Ind/Abst** MLA Int. Bibliogr. Books Artic. Mod. Lang. Lit. (cum index). bk rev. adv acc. **Circ** 450. Articles and reviews in the field of French language and literature. *Zeitschrift fur Neufranzosische Sprache und Literatur.*

ZEITSCHRIFT FUR ROMANISCHE PHILOLOGIE. BEIHEFTE. No. 1- 1905-. Periodical. GW. German. ir. Max Niemeyer Verlag, Postfach 21 40, 7400 Tuebingen 1 West Germany. Monographs on Romantic languages and literature (French, Spanish, Italian, etc.).

ZEST (NELSON, B.C.). (ZEST). 0824-3492. Periodical. CN. English. $2.50 Each Number. Zest, PO Box 339 Station P, Toronto Ontario M5S 2S8 Canada. **DD** C810.80054.

ZESZYTY LITERACKIE : ZL. VFOAT ZL. 1 (Winter 1983)-. Periodical. FR. Polish. qt. $26.00. Cahiers Litteraires, 44 rue Tiquetonne, 75002 Paris France. **Tel** 42463253. **LC** PG7001. **DD** 891.85008. bk rev. adv acc. **Circ** 3,000. (ctrl) Polish and East European literature.

ZESZYTY PRASOZNAWCZE. Vol. 1- (No. 1-). Periodical. PL. Polish (summaries in English and Russian (some also in French)). qt. ARS Polona, Krakowskie Przedmiescie 7, 00-068 Warsaw Poland. **Ind/Abst** Sociol. Abstr., Lang. Lang. Behav. Abstr. **LC** PN4705. *Prasa Wspoczesna I Dawna.*

ZET, DAS ZEICHENHEFT FUR LITERATUR UND GRAPHIK. VFOAT Zeichenheft fur Literatur und Graphik. Periodical. German. ir. 73.00. Wederplatz 17, D-69 Heidelberg West Germany. **LC** PT1141.A2.

ZHAR. Bulgarian. ir. 0.85. **LC** PG1000.

ZONA FRANCA. Began with Sept. 1964 issue. 0044-4987. Periodical. VE. Spanish. bm. $7.50. Apartado Postal 76978, El Marques Caracas Venezuela. **Ind/Abst** MLA Int. Bibliogr. Books Artic. Mod. Lang. Lit. **LC** PN6. **DD** 860.8.

ZONE (BROOKLYN, NEW YORK, N.Y.). (ZONE). 1-. 0162-1904. Periodical. US. English. ir. Zone Press, PO Box 194, Bay Station, Brooklyn NY 11235. **Tel** (212)499-3349. **LC** PS501. **DD** 810.8.

ZPRAVODAJ - CESKOSLOVENSKE NARODNI SDRUZENI V KANADE. ODBOCKA VANCOUVER. (ZPRAVODAJ - CESKOSLOVENSKE NARODNI SDRUZENI V KANADE, ODBOCKA VANCOUVER). **Main/Corp** Czechoslovak National Association of Canada. Vancouver Branch. Began with Apr. 1970 issue. 0701-0109. Periodical. CN. Czech. ir. Free to members, 0.25 Others. Zpravodaj, c/o J Klinka, 2720 Oyama Court, Vancouver British Columbia V6T 1N6 Canada. **DD** 057.86.

ZWOLSE DRUKKEN EN HERDRUKKEN VOOR DER MAATSCHAPPIJ DER NEDERLANDSE LETTERKUNDE TE LEIDEN. No. 1- 1953-. 0514-4787. NE. Dutch. ir. Maatschappy der Ned Letterkunde, Rapenburg 70 74, Leiden Netherlands.

ZYZZYVA. Vol. 1, No. 1 (Spring 1985)-. 8756-5633. Periodical. US. English. qt. $20.00. Zyzzyva, 55 Sutter Street Suite 400, San Francisco CA 94104. **Tel** (415)387-8389. Ed Howard Junker. **DD** 810. adv acc. **Circ** 3,000. Covers West Coast writers, artists, and excerpts from forthcoming books from West Coast publishers. Also includes black and white photographs and graphic arts.

POETRY

80 I.E. DELAPAN PULUH, BUKU PUISI. Indonesian. ir. 250. N/A Horison, Jalan Gereja Theresia 47, Jakarta Indonesia. **LC** PL5086.

AAG-AAG. VFOAT AAG AAG. 8756-7636. Periodical. US. English. be. $2.00 per issue. Two Magpie Press, PO Box 177, Kendrick ID 83537. **DD** 811.

ABATIS. 1-. 0882-9586. Periodical. US. English. an. $5.00. Duane Locke Abatis, University of Tampa, Tampa FL 33606. **Ind/Abst** Index Am. Period. Verse. **DD** 811. *UT Review.*

AGENDA (LONDON, ENGLAND). (AGENDA). Vol. 1, No. 1 (Jan. 1959)-. 0002-0796. UK. English. qt. $30.00. Agenda, 5-Cranbourne Court, Albert Bridge Road, London SW11 4PE England. **Tel** 01 228 0700. Ed William Cookson and Peter Dale. **Ind/Abst** Abstr. Engl. Stud., MLA Int. Bibliogr. Books Artic. Mod. Lang. Lit. bk rev. adv acc. **Circ** 1,000. Includes poems, critical and technical articles on poetry, book reviews. *Four Pages.*

AIR (VANCOUVER, B.C.). (AIR). 1 (Jan. 71)-. 0044-6947. Periodical. CN. English. bm. **DD** C811.5408.

AKROS. Began publication in 1966. 0002-3728. Periodical. UK. English. Ed Duncan Glen.

ALCHERINGA (NEW YORK, N.Y.) CEASED. (ALCHERINGA). No. 1 (Fall 1970) - No. 5 (Spring/Summer 1973). 0044-7218. Periodical. US. English. sa. **LC** PN1345. **DD** 398.205. Some issues have phonodiscs.

ALMANACCO DELLO SPECCHIO. See Yearbooks, Almanacs, Directories.

AMERICAN POETRY. 1922-. US. English. ty. $18.00. McFarland & Company, PO Box 611, Jefferson NC 28640. **Tel** (919)246-4460. Ed Robert Franklin. **LC** PS614. **DD** 811.008. bk rev. adv acc. **Circ** 500. Only periodical exclusively devoted to the critical appraisal of American poetry from its inception to the contemporary scene. *Miscellany of American Poetry.*

AMERICAN POETRY INDEX. See Indexes/Abstracts.

ANGEL EXHAUST. 0143-8050. Periodical. UK. English. 1.50. Islington Press, 59 Ilford House Dove Road, London N1 3NA England. **LC** PR1170. **DD** 821.91408.

THE ANGLO-SAXON POETIC RECORDS : A COLLECTIVE EDITION. Vol. 1-6. US. English. ir. Columbia University Press, 136 South Broadway, Irvington-on-Hudson NY 10533. Ed G P Krapp. **LC** PR1502.

ANTHOLOGY. English. ir. 1,000 Domestic, $5.00 Foreign. Ikuta Press, 1-5-3 Sumiyoshi-Yamate, Higashinada-Ku 658, Kobe Japan. **Tel** (078)811-1329. Ed Yoko Danno. **LC** PR9515.6. **DD** 811.0080952. bk rev. **Circ** 1,000. Publishes poetry of the contributions living in Japan and abroad.

ANTHOLOGY OF MAGAZINE VERSE AND YEARBOOK OF AMERICAN POETRY. See Yearbooks, Almanacs, Directories.

ANUARIO DE POETAS DO BRASIL. See Yearbooks, Almanacs, Directories.

APPLE. No. 1- Summer 1967-. 0003-6765. US. English. $1.25 Single Issue. D Curry, Box 2271, Springfield IL 62705. **LC** PS580. **DD** 811.5408.

AQUARIMANTIMA. Yearly V. 1- Oct/Dec 1973-. Periodical. Spanish. ir. Apartado Aereo 3845, Medellin Colombia. **LC** PQ8174.

ARC. 1- Spring 1978-. 0705-6397. Periodical. CN. English. sa. Arc Department of English, Carleton University, Colonel By Drive, Ottawa Ontario K1S 5B6 Canada. **DD** C811.5408.

ARGO. V. 1- Summer 1979-. 0143-0246. Periodical. UK. English. ir. 18. Argo, 40 George Street/Old Fire Station, Oxford OX1 2AQ England. Ed Hilary Davies and David Contantive. bk rev. adv acc. **Circ** 800. A leading British journal of contemporary poetry, especially from Britain, but also from the USA, Canada, and Israel, plus translations. *Delta.*

ARION (BUDAPEST, HUNGARY). (ARION). Began with 1 in 1966. 0572-4082. HU. Hungarian (English, German, French, and Russian). an. International Publications Service, 114 East 32nd Street, New York NY 10016. **LC** PN1010. **DD** 894.51108.

ARION'S DOLPHIN. No. 1- Autumn 1971-. 0044-8834. Periodical. US. English. qt. Arions Dolphin, PO Box 313, Cambridge MA 02138. **LC** PN6099.6. **DD** 808.8104.

ART AND POETRY TODAY. See The Arts (General).

ATHANOR. V. 1- Nov. 1979-. 0709-9592. Periodical. CN. English. qt. $1.00 Per No. Athanor, PO Box 562, Victoria Station, Westmount Quebec H3Z 2Y6 Canada. **DD** C811.5408.

AUSTRALIAN POETRY. Vol. 1 1941-. AT. English. an. **LC** PR9551.A1. **DD** 821.91082.

AVEGA. 0376-5296. in Hindi. ir. 5.00. 64 Biharilal Marg, Ratalama India. **LC** PK2057.

LA BARBACANE. Began in 1965. Periodical. French. sa. 50 Single Issue. Chateau de Banaguil, 500 Fumel, Saint-Front-Sur-Lemance 47 France. **LC** PQ1184. **DD** 841.91408.

BAYLOR BROWNING INTERESTS CEASED. Ceased in 1962. Monographic Series. US. English. ir. Baylor University Browning, Armstrong Browning Library, Waco TX 76706. **Tel** (817)755-3566. **LC** UNC. **Circ** 150. (ctrl). Monographs concerning the lives and works of Robert and Elizabeth Barrett Browning. *Baylor University Browning Interests (1927).*

THE BELOIT POETRY JOURNAL. Vol. 1, No. 1 (Fall 1950)-. 0005-8661. Periodical. US. English. qt. $6.00. Beloit Poetry Journal, Box 154 Rural Free Delivery 2, Ellswoth ME 04605. **Tel** (207)667-5598. Ed Marion K Stocking. **Ind/Abst** Index Am. Period. Verse, Am. Humanit. Index. **LC** PS301. **DD** 811.008. (cum index). bk rev. **Circ** 1,100. Microfilmed by AMS Film Service, New York. The growing tip of contemporary poetry in a wide range of forms, subjects and schools. Reviews and occasional chapbooks. Thirty-five years of discovering new poets.

BEPPU DAIGAKU KIYO. See History (General) - History of Asia.

BERKELEY POETS CO-OPERATIVE. VFOAT Berkeley Poets Cooperative. Began publication with: No. 1 (Sept. 1970). 0734-2489. US. English. ir. Berkeley Poets Workshop & Press, PO Box 459, Berkeley CA 94701. **Tel** (415)524-9797. Ed

Literature—Poetry

Charles Entrekin. **LC** PS501. **DD** 810.8. **Circ** 2,000. Eighty pages of poetry, fiction, and graphics.

BIRD EFFORT. No. 1/2-. Periodical. US. English. sa. Bird Effort, 25 Mudford Avenue, East Hampton NY 11937. **Tel** (516)324-4156.

BITS. No. 1- Jan. 1975-. 0197-7768. Periodical. English. sa. Ed R Wallace. **LC** PS580. **DD** 811.008.

BITTER OLEANDER. V. 1- 1975-. Periodical. US. English. ty. $5.00. Bitter Oleander Press, 310 Bradford Parkway, Syracuse NY 13224. **LC** PN6099.6. **DD** 808.810405.

BLACK BOX. 1- 1972-. Periodical. US. English. qt. Black Box, PO Box 50145, Washington DC 20004. **Tel** (202)347-4823.

BLACK WILLOW. **VFOAT** Black Willow Poetry. 1 (Fall '82)-. 0733-0073. Periodical. US. English. sa. $4.00. Black Willow, 3214 Sunset Avenue, Norristown PA 19403.

BLIND ALLEYS. Vol. 1, No. 1 (Spring/Summer 1982)-. 0737-9269. Periodical. US. English. sa. $9.00. Blind Alleys, 7th Son Press, PO Box 13224, Baltimore MD 21203. **LC** PS615. **DD** 811.008.

THE BLUE CLOUD QUARTERLY. Began in 1955?. 0006-5064. Monographic Series. US. English. qt. $4.00. Blue Cloud Quarterly, Blue Cloud Abbey, PO Box 98, Marvin SD 57251. **Tel** (605)432-5528. Ed Benet Tvedten. **LC** PS509.I5. **DD** 810.80352. **Circ** 1,000. (ctrl). A small magazine of native American poetry. Each issue is the work of a single poet.

BLUE UNICORN. V. 1- Oct. 1977-. 0197-7016. Periodical. US. English. ty. $9.00. Blue Unicorn, 22 Avon Road, Kensington CA 94707. **Tel** (415)526-8439. Ed Ruth G Iodice, B Jo Kinnick and Harold Witt. **LC** PS580. **DD** 811.008. **Circ** 500. (ctrl). We publish the best in poetry that is being written today, including work by established and new writers, in both traditional forms and free verse.

BLUEFISH. V. 1, No. 1 (Autumn 1983)-. 0741-5028. Periodical. US. English. sa. $6.00. Bluefish, Box 1601, Southampton NY 11968. **LC** PS615. **DD** 811.008.

BOREAL INTERNATIONAL. 0823-2679. Periodical. CN. Spanish. ir. Boreal International, PO Box 262 Victoria Station, Montreal Quebec H3Z 2V5 Canada. **DD** C861.6408. *Boreal, 0006-7717.*

BRICK. No. 1- Apr. 1977-. 0382-8565. Periodical. CN. English. ty. 12.00. Brick Books, Box 537 Station Q, Toronto Ontario M4T 2M5 Canada. **Tel** (416)921-4348. Ed Linda Spalding. **LC** Z1035.A1. **DD** 028.1, 028.105. bk rev. **Circ** 1,200. (ctrl). Intentionally eclectic, Brick favours books from small or alternate presses. Brick reviewers are passionate readers whose care shows in their writing.

BULLETIN BAUDELAIRIEN. V. 1- Aug. 1965-. 0007-4128. Periodical. US. French (English). sa. $5.00. Vanderbilt University, Box 6325, Station B, Nashville TN 37235. **Tel** (615)322-2807. Ed James S Patty and Claude Pichois. **Ind/Abst** MLA Int. Bibliogr. Books Artic. Mod. Lang. Lit. **DD** 841. (cum index). **Circ** 300. Short studies concerning the life and works of Charles Baudelaire.

C V 2. CONTEMPORARY VERSE TWO. (CV II, CONTEMPORARY VERSE/TWO). **VFOAT** Contemporary Verse/Two. V. 1- Spring 1975-. 0319-6879. Periodical. CN. English. qt. $5.00. CV II Publishers, Box 32 University Centre, University of Manitoba, Winnipeg Manitoba R3T 1E0 Canada. **Ind/Abst** Index Book Rev. Humanit. **LC** PR9195.1. **DD** 811.5409.

CADERNETA DE POESIA. 1- 1978-. Periodical. Portuguese. ir. Editora Brasiliense, 01042 rua Barao de Itapetininga, 93, Sao Paulo Brazil.

CAFE SOLO. No. 1- 1969-. 0007-9537. US. English. qt. $20.00. Solo Press, 7975 San Marcos Avenue, Atascadero CA 93422.

CAHIERS MAYNARD. No. 7- 1977-. Periodical. FR. French. Association des Amis Maynard, Epire 49170, St Geroges sur Loire France. **LC** PQ1820.M3. **DD** 841.4, B. *Cahier - Association des Amis de Maynard.*

CAHIERS POETIQUES DE L'ACADEMIE DES POETES CLASSIQUES DE FRANCE. Main/Corp Academie des Poetes Classiques de France. No 1-. French. ir. **LC** PQ1184. **DD** 841.9108.

CANADIAN POETRY JOURNAL. (THE CANADIAN POETRY ANNUAL). 1976-. 0383-1574. CN. English. an. $2.95 Per No. Musson Book Co, 30 Lesmill Road, Don Mills Ontario M3B 2T6 Canada. **DD** C811.5408.

CANADIAN POETRY (LONDON, ONT.). (CANADIAN POETRY). No. 1 (Fall/Winter 1977)-. 0704-5646. Periodical. CN. English. sa. 10.00. The Editors, Canadian Poetry, University of Western Ontario, Department of English, London Ontario N6A 3K7 Canada. **Tel** (519)679-3725. Ed D M R Bentley. **Ind/Abst** Abstr. Engl. Stud., MLA Int. Bibliogr. Books Artic. Mod. Lang. Lit., Index Book Rev. Humanit. **LC** PR9190.2. **DD** 811.009971. bk rev. **Circ** 400. Devoted to the study of poetry written in all periods and regions of Canada.

CAPE ISLAND SOUND. V. 1- Spring 1974-. 0094-9167. Periodical. US. English. qt. $4.00. PO Box 242, Cape May NJ 08204. **LC** PS580. **DD** 811.5408.

THE CAPE ROCK. V. 10, No.2- Summer 1975-. 0146-2199. Periodical. US. English. sa. $3.00. S E Missouri State University, Cape Girardeau Mo, Cape Girardeau MO 63701. **Tel** (314)651-2156. Ed Harvey Hecht. **Ind/Abst** Index Am. Period. Verse. **Circ** 500. Poetry journal with black and white photography. Pays $100.00 for photography, $200.00 for best poem, in each issue. *Cape Rock Journal.*

CHAYUSI. Periodical. KO. Korean. ir. 2,500. Chongha, 270 3-Ka Chungjongno Sodaemun-Ku, Seoul 120 Korea. **LC** PL974.A1.

CHIAROSCURO (ITHACA, N.Y.). (CHIAROSCURO). 1-. 0737-5182. Periodical. US. English. ir. $5.00. J Latta Ithaca House, PO Box 6484, Ithaca NY 14851. Ed John Latta. **LC** PS615. **DD** 810.8. bk rev. **Circ** 400. An annual magazine of contemporary poetry with translations, reviews, and fiction sometimes included.

CHICOREL INDEX TO POETRY IN ANTHOLOGIES AND COLLECTIONS IN PRINT. See Indexes/Abstracts.

CHINDAN SI. **VFOAT** Jindansi. V. 1-. Periodical. English. ir. Chindan Si Tonginhoe, 281-177 Pulgwang-Dong, Unpyong-Ku Seoul Korea. **LC** PL9974.A1.

CHING NIEN SHIH TAN. **VFOAT** Qingnianshitan. First published in 1983. Periodical. CC. Chinese. bm. 0.40. Kuang-Tung Sheng Hsin Hua Shu, Tien Kuang-chou Shih China. **LC** PL2543. **DD** 895.115.

CHOICE; A MAGAZINE OF POETRY AND GRAPHICS. V. 1, No. 1-Spring 1961-. 0009-4986. US. English. ir. Roger Aplon, PO Box 4858, Chicago IL 60680.

CHOOMIA. V. 1-. Periodical. US. English. ty. $3.00. Choomia, PO Box 107, Framingham MA 01701. **LC** PS615. **DD** 811.508.

CHUNG-HUA SHIH HSUEH. First published in April 1983. Periodical. CH. Chinese. qt. $1.50. Chung-Hua Shih Hsueh Yueh, Kan She 22-3, 88 Lane Hsin Sheng N Road, Section 2, Tai-Pei Shih Taiwan. **LC** PL2307. **DD** 895.11009. *Chung-Hua Shih Kan.*

CIRCLE; A PERIODICAL OF REVERSIBLE POETRY. V. 1, No. 1- Summer 1973-. Periodical. US. English. ir. Circle Forum, PO Box 176, Portland OR 97207.

CIRCULO POETICO. No. 1-. Periodical. US. English (Spanish). an. $8.00. Circulo de Cultura Panamerican, 16 Malvern Place, Verona NJ 07044. **LC** PQ7084.

CIRCUS MAXIMUS. V. 1- Dec. 1975-. 0145-5281. Periodical. US. English. qt. $6.00. Circus Maximus, PO Box 3251, York PA 17402. **LC** PS615. **DD** 811.008.

CIVIL SERVICE POETRY. UK. English. an. EMMA, Arden House Sunny Point, Walton-on-Naze Essex C014 8LD England.

CODA. (CODA : POETS & WRITERS NEWSLETTER). **VFOAT** Poets & Writers Newsletter. V. 1- May 1973-. 0091-5645. US. English. bm. $18.00. Poets & Writers Inc, 201 West 54th Street, New York NY 10019. **Tel** (212)757-1766. Ed Daryln Brewer. **Ind/Abst** New Period. Index. **LC** PS128. **DD** 810.9. adv acc. **Circ** 27,000. (ctrl). News and comments on publishing, grants, awards and other practical topics of interest to poets and fiction writers.

COLUMBIA, A MAGAZINE OF POETRY AND PROSE. 1977-. 0161-486X. Periodical. US. English. an. $4.50. School of the Arts, Writing Division, 404 Dodge Hall, Columbia University, New York NY 10027. **Tel** (212)280-4931. Ed Climeen Widoff and Patrick Goden. **LC** PN6010.5. **DD** 810.80054. adv acc. **Circ** 1,000. Articles and fiction to twenty-five typed pages. Includes poetry, pays in copies and annual awards.

CONCERNING POETRY. V. 1- Spring 1968-. 0010-5201. Periodical. US. English. an. $8.00. Western Washington University, Department of English, Virginia Sanborn, Bellingham WA 98225. **Tel** (206)676-3226. Ed Ellwood Johnson. **Ind/Abst** Abstr. Engl. Stud., MLA Int. Bibliogr. Books Artic. Mod. Lang. Lit., Index Am. Period. Verse, Index Book Rev. Humanit., Years Work Eng. Stud. **LC** PS301. **DD** 811.008. (cum index). bk rev. adv acc. **Circ** 400. (ctrl). A journal concerned with the history and criticism of poetry.

CONTEMPORARY POETS OF AMERICA. 1979-. 0734-4260. US. English. an. $7.50. Dorrance & Company Inc, Cricket Terance Center, Ardmore PA 19003. **LC** PS615. **DD** 811.008.

LA COQUILLE. Periodical. French. ir. Ed H Bazin. **LC** PQ1184.

CQ. CONTEMPORARY QUARTERLY. (CQ, CONTEMPORARY QUARTERLY). **VFOAT** Contemporary Quarterly. V. 1, No. 4- Autumn/Winter 1976/77-. 0162-7201. Periodical. US. English. qt. $8.00. CQ, PO Box 41110, Los Angeles CA 90041. **LC** PS501. **DD** 811.008. *CQ.*

CREATIVE WRITING. Began publication with first issue in 1950?. 0011-0930. Periodical. US. English. National Poetry Association, Box 218, Agoura CA 91301.

CREDENCES. Vol. 1-, No. 1-. 0740-4182. Periodical. US. English. ty. Credences, 434 Capen Hall SUNY, Buffalo NY 14260. **Ind/Abst** MLA Int. Bibliogr. Books Artic. Mod. Lang. Lit.

CREEPING BENT. No. 1 (Fall 1984)-. 8756-0291. Periodical. US. English. sa. $6.00. Creeping Bent, 433 West Market Street, Bethlehem PA 18018. **DD** 811.

CREOLIE. Began with 1978 Vol. 0245-6214. French (French Creole). an. Udir Mjc de Chateau-Morange, Bd Doret les Camelias, 97400 Saint-Denis la Reunion. **LC** PQ3988.5.R4. **DD** 841.008096981.

CROSS COUNTRY. **VAT** Crosscountry. No. 1- Winter 1975-. 0318-6075. Periodical. CN. English. ty. $8.00 (Two Years). Cross Country Press, 2365 Hampton Avenue No 7, Montreal Quebec H4A 2K Canada. **DD** C811'.5'408.

DA VINCI. **VFOAT** Davinci. No. 1- Winter 1973-. 0315-9914. Periodical. CN. English. ty. Vehicule Press, 61 St Catherine Street West, Montreal Quebec H2X 1Z7 Canada. **DD** C811.5405.

DACOTAH TERRITORY. V. 1- Jan. 1971-. 0084-9529. Periodical. US. English. Dacotah Territory, PO Box 775, Moorehead MN 56560. **DD** 8115408.

DALMO'MA. V. 1- July 1976-. 0191-7722. Periodical. US. English (Chinook or Nahuatl). sa. $5.00. Dalmo'Ma, PO Box 646, Port Townsend WA 98368. Ed Michael Daley and Francis Martin. **LC** PS591.I55. **DD** 811.5408. **Circ** 1,000. Periodical of "literature and responsibility" of northwest writing.

DAVIS' ANTHOLOGY OF NEWSPAPER VERSE. **VFOAT** Newspaper Verse. 1919-. Periodical. US. English. an. **LC** PS593.F7. **DD** 811.50822.

DICHTER UBER IHRE DICHTUNGEN. Monographic Series. GW. German. ir. Heimeran Verlag, Postfach 400824, D8000 Munchen West Germany.

A DIRECTORY OF AMERICAN POETS AND FICTION WRITERS. See Yearbooks, Almanacs, Directories.

DODECA. 0364-5207. Periodical. US. English. mo. $5.00. A M Warr, 11 Broadway, New York NY 10004. **LC** PS580. **DD** 811.5405.

ECRITIQUE. V. 1- Oct. 1978!-. 0226-6253. Periodical. CN. French. ty. 75. Per No. CEGEP, De St-Jerome455 rue Fournier, St Jerome Quebec J7Z 4V2 Canada. **DD** C840.8092375.

ECRITS HERITAGE. **VFOAT** Heritage Writing. 1978/79-. 0226-5850. CN. English (includes some text in French). an. London Free Press, Mr Dow, Canadian Heritage Writing Competition, Department of English, Faculty of Education, University of Western Ontario, London Ontario N6G 1G7 Canada. **DD** C810.809283. *My Canada, Heritage.*

EDITOR'S CHOICE. UK. English. Regency Press, 43 New Oxford Street, London WCIA 1BH England. **LC** PR1227. **DD** 821.9108.

ELECTRUM. Began in 1977. 8755-5824. Periodical. US. English. qt. $10.00. Medina Press, 2222 Silktree Drive, Tustin CA 92680. **Tel**

Literature—Poetry

(714)730-4046. Ed Roger Suva. DD 811. bk rev. adv acc. Circ 2,000. Special emphasis is given to a multi-cultural selection of work from around the country. Original art and photography is featured. Plus book reviews, letters, a calendar and contributors.

ENCORE. V. 1- Aug./Oct.? 1966-. 0013-7057. Periodical. US. English. qt. Encore Magazine, 1121 Major Avenue NW, Albuquerque NM 87107.

ENVOI. No. 1-. 0013-9394. Periodical. UK. English. ty. 5.00. Anne Lewis-Smith, Editor of Envoi, Pen Ffordd Newport, Dyfed SA42 0QT Great Britain. Tel 0239820285. Ed Anne Lewis-Smith. LC PR1225. DD 821.008. bk rev. adv acc. Circ 500. (ctrl). Publishes new poetry and reviews. All poems submitted, with SAE, have a free criticism from the editorial panel of thirty poets on return.

EQUIVALENCIAS. VFOAT Equivalences. 1 (Winter 1982)-. Periodical. English (Spanish). ir. Jorge Juan 102 2. B, Madrid 9 Espana Spain. LC PN1010. DD 808.81005.

EROS. Yearly V. 1- August 1973-. Periodical. Spanish. ir.

ESPLUMOIR. (L'ESPLUMOIR). V. 1- Feb. 1979-. 0706-0556. Periodical. CN. French. mo. $10.00. Cercle Litteraire Esoterique, Bureau 208/9408 rue Viau, Montreal Quebec H1R 3B5 Canada. DD C841.5408. Solitude-Inflexion.

ESTUAIRE. No. 1- May 1976-. 0700-365X. Periodical. CN. French. qt. Estuarie, Box 337 Succursale Outremont, Montreal Quebec H2V 4N1 Canada. Tel (418)271-1972. DD C841.54005. bk rev. adv acc. Publication of poetry, interviews, poems, and chronicles.

EXPERIMENT. V. 1- Apr. 1944-. 0014-4770. Periodical. US. English. ir. $13.00. Experiment, 6565 Windmere Road, Seattle WA 98105. Tel (202)527-4172. Ed Carol Ely Harper. LC PS301. DD 811.505. bk rev. adv acc. Original, intellectual, in content and form.

EXTRA VERSE. 0531-6243. Periodical. UK. English. ir. Extra Verse, 18 GT Percy St Islington, London WC 1 England.

FIELD. No. 1- Fall 1969-. 0015-0657. Periodical. US. English. sa. $7.00. Oberlin College, Rice Hall, Oberlin OH 44074. Tel (216)775-8408. Ed Friebert and Young. Ind/Abst MLA Int. Bibliogr. Books Artic. Mod. Lang. Lit., Index Am. Period. Verse, Index Book Rev. Humanit. LC PN6099.6. DD 808.8104. bk rev. Circ 2,200. (ctrl). Best contemporary poetry and poetics also symposia and translations.

FINE MADNESS. Vol. 1, No. 1 (Summer/Fall 1982)-. 0737-4704. Periodical. US. English. ty. $8.00. Fine Madness, PO Box 15176, Seattle WA 98115. Tel (206)526-2494. Ed Sean Bentley, Louis Bergsagel, Kathryn MacDonald, John Marshall and James Syndel. DD 811. bk rev. Circ 750. We publish among the best American and Welsh poems being written, ask for writing which shows that a mind is working, not just a tongue.

FLOATING ISLAND. 1 (Spring 1976)-. 0147-1686. US. English. ir. $12.95. Floating Island Publishing, PO Box 516, Point Reyes Station CA 94956. LC PS580. DD 811.5408.

FOMENTO LITERARIO : CUENTAS I POEMAS DE ARISTEO BRITO. Periodical. US. Spanish. an. Congreso Nacional Asuntos Cole 1, Dupont Circle Suite 400, Washington DC 20036. Tel (202)223-1174.

FOUR BY FOUR (MONTREAL, QUEBEC). (FOUR BY FOUR). No. 1 (Sept. 1982)-. 0714-9093. Periodical. CN. French. ir. $5.00. Villeneuve Publications, 4647 Hutchinson Street, Montreal Quebec H2V 4N4 Canada. DD C811.5408.

DER FROHLICHE TARZAN. Periodical. GW. German. ir. 12.00. May Offsetdruck, Hohenzollernring 97, 5 Koln 1 West Germany. LC PN1010.

FUKUSHIMA-KEN TANKA SENSHU. JA. Japanese. an. Fukushima-Ken Kajinkai, c/o Shiraki Aza Miyaminami, 108 Osamachi Tadano, Koriyama-Shi Japan. LC PL758.A1.

GALLERY WORKS. 0730-5206. US. English. an. Gallery Works, 1465 Hammeroley Avenue, Bronx NY 10469.

GANDAIA. Periodical. Portuguese. ir. rua Dr Noguchi, 271 - Casa 6 - Ramos, Rio de Janeiro Brazil. LC PQ9658. DD 869.1.

GEDICHT. Vol. 1-. Periodical. Dutch. ir. 30.00. De Bexige Bij, Van Miereveldstraat 1, Amsterdam Netherlands. LC PT5478.

GEGENSCHEIN QUARTERLY. No. 1-. Periodical. US. English. qt. $5.00. 350 East 9th Street/5, New York NY 10003. LC PS580. DD 811.5405.

GEKKAN POEMU. VFOAT Poemu, The Poem. 1st Ed. Oct., 1976-. JA. Japanese. ir. 450. Subaru Shobo, 5-24 Suido 1, Bunkyo-Ku 112, Tokyo Japan. LC PL726.65.

GEMS OF POETRY. 1982-. 0827-3138. CN. English. be. Gems of Poetry, c/o K Magnusson 14253 Vine Avenue, White Rock British Columbia V4B 2S9 Canada. Tel 531-7955. Ed Lynda James and Kristiana Magnusson. DD C811.54080971133. adv acc. (ctrl) Poetry, written by literary contestants, and by members of White Rock and Surrey Writer's Club.

GENDAI HAIKU NENKAN. JA. Japanese. an. 6000. Gendai Haiku Kyokai 6-10, Soto Kanda 4 Chiyoda-ku, Tokyo-to Japan.

GENDAI HAIKU SENSHU. Began in 1964. JA. Japanese. ir. 3500. Haijin Kyokai, c/o Karasumori Building/Room 601, 16-3 Shinbashi 3-Chome Minato-Ku, Tokyo 105 Japan. LC PL759.A1.

GERMINATION. V. 1- Spring 1976-. 0704-6286. Periodical. CN. English. ir. $6.00. Germination Owl's Head Press, 428 Yale Avenue, Riverview New Brunswick E1B 2B5 Canada. Tel (506)386-1687. Ed Allan Cooper and Leigh Faulkner. DD C811.5408. bk rev. adv acc. Circ 500. Publishes the best in contemporary Canadian and American poetry in addition, we publish some criticism and translations of foreign poetry.

GLASSWORKS. V. 1- Fall 1975-. 0145-6792. Periodical. US. English. ty. 6.00. Glassworks, PO Box 163 Rosebank Station, Staten Island NY 10305. LC PS580. DD 811.5405.

GLOBAL TAPESTRY. Periodical. UK. English. ir. Global Tapestry Journal, 1 Spring Bank, Salesbury Blacks Blackburn 49128 England.

GRANGER'S INDEX TO POETRY. See Indexes/Abstracts.

THE GREEN HORSE FOR POETRY. V. 1- 1973-. Periodical. US. English. ir. Bowling Green University, Creative Writing Program, Bowling Green OH 43403.

GRILLED FLOWERS. Vol. 1, No. 1 (Spring 1976)-. Periodical. US. English. ir. University of Arizona Poetry Center, 1086 North Highland Avenue, Tucson AZ 85719.

GROLIER POETRY PRIZE. Vol. 1 (1984)-. 0743-7242. US. English. an. $4.00. Ellen la Forge Memorial Poetry Foundation Inc, 6 Plympton Street, Cambridge MA 02138. LC PS615. DD 811.008.

GROUNDSWELL (CHATHAM, N.Y.). (GROUNDSWELL). Vol. 1, No. 1 (Fall 1984)-. 8756-9094. Periodical. US. English. te. $12.50. The Guild Press, PO Box 3, Chatham NY 12037. DD 811.

GROVE : CONTEMPORARY POETRY AND TRANSLATION. No. 1- Summer 1975-. Periodical. US. English. sa. Pitzer College/English Department, Claremont Colleges, Claremont CA 91711. Tel (714)626-8511.

GUAJANA. Vol. 1 1962-. 0017-498X. Periodical. Spanish. ir.

GUSTO. 0190-2253. Periodical. US. English. $5.00 4 Issues. M Karl Kulikowski, 2960 Philip Avenue, Bronx NY 10465.

HAPPINESS HOLDING TANK. No. 1- Oct. 1970-. 0046-6832. Periodical. US. English. ir. $3.50. Happiness Holding Tank, 1790 Grand River, Okemos MI 48864. LC PS615. DD 811.5408.

HARAUI. Yearly V. 1, No. 1 (September 1963)-. 0440-2987. Periodical. PE. Spanish. ir. Director, Francisco Carrillo, Bolivia 174, Chosica Peru. LC PN6108. DD 861.0080985.

HEJIRA (MONTREAL, QUEBEC). (HEJIRA). V. 1, No. 1 (Dec. 1983)-. 0826-0133. Periodical. CN. French. mo. $1.00 per no. Hejira, c/o M Berg Porter's Office Arts Building McGill University, Montreal Quebec Canada. DD C811.54092379.

HELICON. Periodical. II. English. ir. 10.00. 10/3C Nepal Bhattacharya Street, Calcutta -26 India. LC PN1010. DD 808.81.

HELIX. No. 1- Feb. 1978-. 0155-9044. Periodical. AT. English. ir. $14.75. Helix, 119 Maltravers Road, Ivanhoe 3079 Victoria Australia. Ed Les Harrop. bk rev. adv acc. Literary and arts review with emphasis on poetry. Canberra Poetry.

HOO-DOO. Began publication in 1972. US. English. ir. Energy Earth Communications, PO Box 1141, Galveston TX 77553.

HORA DE POESIA. 1- 1978-. Periodical. SP. Spanish. bm. $27.00. Hora de Poesia, Vigen de la Salud 78, 08024 Barcelona Spain. Tel 93-2195900. Ed Lentini. LC PQ6075. bk rev. adv acc. Circ 1,500. (ctrl). General poetry of Spain and different nationalities: England, France, Italy and Germany. Criticisms, essays, and edits from well known authors.

HSU SHIH SHIH TSUNG KAN. VFOAT Hsu Shih Shih. V. 1, (June 1980)-. Periodical. CH. Chinese. ir. 0.51. Hsing Hua Shu Tien, Cheng-Chou Shih China. LC PL2519.N47. DD 895.11508.

HWANGTO. Periodical. KO. Korean. ir. 500. Paeyongsa, 1-48 Sinmunno Chongno-Ku, Seoul 110 Korea. LC PL974.A1.

HYONDAESI. VFOAT Modern Poetry. V. 1-Series (Summer, 1984)-. Periodical. KO. Korean. ir. 3.000. Munhak Segyesa, 136 Pongik-Dong Chungno-Ku, Seoul Korea.

ICARUS. V. 1- Summer 1973-. 0163-0954. Periodical. US. English. qt. $2.00. Icarus Press, PO Box 8, Riderwood MD 21239. Ed M Diorio. LC PS580. DD 811.5408.

IMAGES (DAYTON, OHIO). (IMAGES). V. 1- 1974-. Periodical. US. English. ty. $3.00. Wright State University, English Department, Dayton OH 45431. Tel (513)873-2443. Ed Gary Pacernick. Ind/Abst Index Am. Period. Verse. DD 811.

IMAGINE (BOSTON, MASS.). (IMAGINE). Vol. 1, No. 1 (Summer 1984)-. 0747-489X. Periodical. US. Spanish or English (translations in various languages). sa. $12.00. Imagine Publishers, 645 Beacon Street/Suite 7, Boston MA 02215. Tel (617)267-2592. Ed Tino Villanueva and Luis Alberto Urrea. Ind/Abst Index Am. Period. Verse. DD 861. bk rev. Circ 1,500. (ctrl). Accepts texts in any language provided same are accompanied by the corresponding translations into either English or Spanish.

INDIAN VERSE. V. 1- Winter 1973-. Periodical. II. English. ir. Indian Verse, 9/3 Tamer Lane, Calcutta-9 India. LC PK2978.E5. DD 821.005.

INFLUX (MONTREAL, QUEBEC). (INFLUX). Mar. 1981-. 0712-6069. CN. French. an. $2.00 Per Volume. Influx, C P 595 Depot N, Montreal Quebec H2X 3M6 Canada. DD C841.5408092375.

INKSTONE. Vol. 1, No. 1 (Summer 1982)-. 0714-2870. Periodical. CN. English. qt. 15.00. Inkstone, PO Box 67 Station H, Toronto Ontario M4C 5H7 Canada. Tel (416)531-5688. Ed Keith Southward, Marshall Hryciuk, and Louise Fletcher. DD C811.0408. bk rev. Circ 100. Haiku; Haiku books in review and articles on subjects related to Haiku. Haiku may be traditional, modern or experimental in nature.

INSTANT. (INSTANT : UNE PRODUCTION DU THEATRE DU GANOUE). Series/Titl Instant de Parole. VAT Instant de Parole. 1 (1980)-. 0711-4648. CN. French. an. $5.00 Per Volume. Instant, c/o Theatre du Ganoue, St-Prosper, Beauce-Sud Quebec Canada. DD C841.5408.

INTERNATIONAL HOPKINS ASSOCIATION NEWSLETTER. (THE INTERNATIONAL HOPKINS ASSOCIATION NEWSLETTER). VFOAT IHA Newsletter. No. 1 (Summer 1979)-. 0227-5414. Periodical. CN. English. sa. Free to Members. R F Giles, International Hopkins Association, Department of English, Wilfrid Laurier University, Waterloo Ontario N2L 3C5 Canada. DD 821.8.

INTERNATIONAL JOURNAL OF SLAVIC LINGUISTICS AND POETICS. See Linguistics.

INTRINSIC. No. 1- Summer 1977-. 0704-7290. Periodical. CN. English. ir. $3.00. Intrinsic, Box 485 Postal Station P, Toronto Ontario M5S 2T1 Canada. DD C811.5408.

INVISIBLE CITY. No. 1- Feb. 1971-. 0147-4936. Periodical. US. English. ir. $5.00. Red Hill Press, PO Box 2853, San Francisco CA 94126. LC PN6099.6. DD 811.5408.

IRONWOOD. Began with No. 1, Spring 1972. 0047-150X. Periodical. US. English. sa. $8.50. Ironwood, Box 40907, Tucson AZ 85717. **Tel** (602)795-9928. **Ed** Michael Cuddihy. **LC** PN6099.6. **DD** 808.8L. adv acc. **Circ** 1,350. The best in contemporary poetry, including translations, interviews, reviews, special issues and features on individual poets or aspects of poetry. Perfect bound, approximately 200 pages.

ISLAND (LANTZVILLE, B.C.). (ISLAND). 1971. 0227-0773. Periodical. CN. English. ty. $11.61. Island, Box 256, Lantzville British Columbia V0R 2H0 Canada. **Tel** (604)390-3508. **Ed** John Marshall. **DD** C811.5408. bk rev. **Circ** 550. Canadian literary journal, poetry, prose, interviews, reviews.

L'ISLE SONANTE. 1 (Winter 1982)-. 0732-5886. Periodical. US. French (English). ty. $24.00. l'Isle Sonante, 473 Manoagian Hall/Wayne State University, Detroit MI 48202. **LC** PQ1170.E6. **DD** 841.008.

JOHN BERRYMAN STUDIES. V. 1- Jan. 1975-. 0098-2199. US. English. qt. $5.00. 805 West First Avenue, Derry PA 15627. **LC** PS3503.E744. **DD** 811.54.

JOURNAL OF CANADIAN POETRY. V. 1- Winter 1978-. 0705-1328. Periodical. CN. English. an. Journal of Canadian Poetry, 9 Ashburn Drive, Nepean Ontario Canada K2E 6N4. **Tel** (613)224-6937. **Ed** David Staines. **LC** PR9190.25. **DD** C811.009. bk rev. **Circ** 500. Scholarly research and criticism of the poetry of Canada from its origins to the present.

JOURNAL OF NEW JERSEY POETS. V. 1- Spring 1976-. 0363-4205. Periodical. US. English. an. $3.00. Florham-Madison Campus, Creative Writing, 285 Madison Avenue, Madison NJ 07940. **Ed** Marjorie Keyishian. **Ind/Abst** Index Am. Period. Verse. **LC** PS549.N5. **DD** 811.008. bk rev. **Circ** 250. (ctrl). Poetry written by poets connected with New Jersey. Review of poetry.

JUSHO KAJIN SHIRIZU. JA. Japanese. ir. 1000. Tanka Koron Sha, 18-4 Yamatocho 2 Nakano-Ku, Tokyo 165 Japan. **LC** PL758.A1.

KALO SURAJA. Periodical. Gujarati. ir. 1.00. **LC** PK1856.

KAVI. English. qt. $1.06. Kavi, PO Box #694, Bombay India. **LC** PR9494.5.I5. **DD** 821.008.

KAVI INDIA. Periodical. II. English. qt. 2.50 Single Issue. R Rao, Kavi India, Box No 694, Government Printing Office, Bombay India. **LC** PR9494.5.I5. **DD** 821. *Kavi.*

KAVILOKA. Periodical. Gujarati. ir. 8.00. Bacubhai Ravata, Kumar Printery, 1454 Raipur, Amadavada India. **LC** PK1852.

KAVITA (NEPALA RAJAKIYA PRAJNA-PRATISHTHANA : 1979). (KAVITA). Punahpravesanka 1 (July, August, Pausha 2036 Oct., Nov., Dec. Periodical. NP. Nepali. ir. 12.00. Nepal Rajakiya, Prajna-Pratishthan Prajna Bhavan Kamaladi, Kathmandu Nepal. **LC** PK2598.A2. *Kavita (Nepala Rajakiya Prajna-Pratishthana : 1964).*

KAYAK. -. 1- Autumn 1964-. 0022-9555. Periodical. US. English. qt. $3.00. Bonny Doon Road, Santa Cruz CA 95060. **Ind/Abst** Index Am. Period. Verse. **LC** PS580. **DD** 811.5408.

KIKAN HAIKU. **VFOAT** Haiku. No. 1-. JA. Japanese. ir. 1000. Chuo Shoin, 8 Saneicho Shinjuku-Ku, Tokyo Japan. **Ed** Horii Shunichiro. **LC** PL759.A1.

KISEKI. JA. Japanese. ir. Asaka Tankakai, c/o Koriyama Shiyakusho, 23-7 Asahi 1-Chome, Koriyama Japan. **LC** PL887.K67.

KUDZU. No. 1- July 1977-. 0194-424X. Periodical. US. English. qt. $4.00. Kudzu, PO Box 865, Cayce SC 29033. **LC** PS580. **DD** 811.008.

KUKSU. No. 3- Spring 1974-. Periodical. US. English. ir. Kuksu Press, Box 980/Alleghany Star Route, Nevada City CA 95959. **Tel** (916)265-6298. *Kyoi.*

LA-BAS. Began in 1976. 0193-7820. Periodical. US. English. bm. La-Bas: A Newsletter of La-Bas, PO Box 431, College Park MD 20840. **Tel** (301)864-6921. **LC** PS580.

LEVRES URBAINES. 1-. 0823-5112. Periodical. CN. French. bm. $10.00 for 4 months. Levres Urbaines, 3760 Av Parc la Fontaine, Montreal Quebec H2L 3M4 Canada. **DD** C841.5408.

LIGHT. V. 1-. 0147-121X. US. English. $3.00 (3 Issues). Box 1105 Stuyvesant Station, New York NY 10009. **LC** PS580. **DD** 811.5408.

LIGHT YEAR (CLEVELAND, OHIO). (LIGHT YEAR). '84-. 0743-913X. US. English. an. Bits Press, Department of English/Case Western Reserve University, Cleveland OH 44106. **LC** PS595.H8. **DD** 811.0708.

LIPS. No. 1-. 0278-0933. Periodical. US. English. ty. $9.00. Lips, PO Box 1345, Montclair NJ 07042.

LITMUS. 0024-4953. Periodical. US. English. bm. Litmus, 2209 California, Berkeley CA 94703.

LITORAL. No. 1- May. 1968-. Periodical. Spanish. qt. $40.00. Litoral, Urbanizacion la Roca 107 C Torremolinos Malaga Spain. **Tel** 38 42 00. **Ed** Jose Maria Amado. **LC** PN6054. bk rev. **Circ** 3,500. *Litoral.*

THE LITTLE MAGAZINE. V. 4- Spring 1970-. 0033-6300. Periodical. US. English. ir. Dragon Press, PO Box 78, Pleasantville NY 10570. **Tel** (914)769-5545. **Ed** David G Hartwell. bk rev. **Circ** 1,100. Primarily a poetry magazine, although we often publish fiction. *Quest.*

THE LITTLE WORD MACHINE. No. 1- 1972-. Periodical. UK. English. qt. $6.13. Little Word Machine Publs, 5 Beech Terrace/Undercliffe, Bradford BD3 OPY West York England.

LIVING POETS LIBRARY. 1- 1972-. Monographic Series. US. English. ir. Dragon Teeth Press, El Dorado National Forest, Georgetown CA 95634.

LOFTY TIMES. 1972. Periodical. US. English. ir. $12.00. Poetry Project, 10th Street & 2nd Avenue, New York NY 10003. **Tel** (212)674-0910. **Ed** Tim Dlugos. bk rev. adv acc. **Circ** 5,000. News, information, ideas, and reviews by, for, and about poets from America's most active poetry center.

THE LONG ISLAND POETRY COLLECTIVE NEWSLETTER. **Main/Corp** Long Island Poetry Collective. Periodical. US. English. bm. $7.00. Long Island Poetry Collective, Box 773, Huntington NY 11743. **Tel** (516)691-9253. **Ed** Sue Kain. bk rev. adv acc. **Circ** 300. (ctrl). We are a poetry information journal. Calendar for Long Island, NYC Area. Extensive poetry markets listings (USA and abroad) and reviews. Occasional contests.

THE LYRIC. Began in 1921. 0024-7820. Periodical. US. English. qt. Lyric, 307 Dunton Drive SW, Blacksburg VA 24060. **Tel** (703)552-3475. **Ed** Leslie Mellichamp. **LC** PS301. **Circ** 900. Poetry only. Prefer rhymed verse, traditional forms, 35 lines or so, upbeat, occasionally humorous, no grievances or current political/social problems. Accessible on at least second reading.

DIE MAINZER REIHE. Began with 1, 1956. 0076-2784. Periodical. German. ir. Verlag Hase & Koehler Verlag, Postfach 2269, 6500 Mainz 1 Germany. **Tel** 232334. The members of the academy have the possibility to publish manuscripts and poetry.

MAIRENA (RIO PIEDRAS, P.R.). (MAIRENA). Yearly V. 1, No. 1, (Spring 1979)-. Periodical. PR. Spanish. ty. Himalaya, 257 Urbanizacion Monterrey, Rio Peidras Puerto Rico 009. **LC** PQ7420. **DD** 861.008.

MAJALLAT AL-SHIR. **VFOAT** Shir. V. 1, No. 1 (Say 1982)-. Periodical. Arabic. qt. **LC** PN1010.

MAKER *CEASED.* Began publication in 1977. 0702-5092. Periodical. CN. English. ir. $3.00 for 6 issues. Maker, 1206 Seymour Avenue, Montreal Quebec H3H 2A5 Canada. **DD** C811.5408.

MALAYALAM LITERARY SURVEY. V. 1- Jan. 1977-. Periodical. II. English. ir. 12.-. Kerala Sahitya Akademi, Town Hall Road, Trichur 680 001 India. **Tel** 23569. **LC** PL4718. **DD** 894.81209. bk rev. adv acc. **Circ** 1,000. Publishes scholarly articles on various branches of Malayalam literature and language.

LA MANO EN EL CAJON; POESIA. Began in 1970. 0303-1152. Periodical. Spanish. qt. 100. Independencia 321 5, 2A Barcelona Spain. **LC** PQ6174.95.

MANROOT. No. 1- Aug. 1969-. 0025-2441. Periodical. US. English. ir. Man-Root, PO Box 982, South San Francisco CA 94080.

MANYO. **VFOAT** Manyo Bunko Nempo. JA. Japanese. ir. Nara Kenritsu Kashiwara Toshokan, 50 Unebicho 634, Kashiwara Japan. **LC** PL728.15.A1.

LA MANZANA MORDIDA. No. 1 (Set de 1975)-. Periodical. Spanish. sa. Esther Festini, 1486 Magdalena del Mar, Lima 17 Peru. **LC** PQ8448. **DD** 861.0080985.

MATRIX (URBANA, ILL.). (MATRIX). Began in 1976. 8755-7266. US. English. an. Red Herring Press, c/o Channing-Murray Foundation, 1209 West Oregon Street, Urbana IL 61801. **DD** 811.

MERIDIAN. Vol. 1, No. 1 (Mar. 1980)-. Periodical. US. English. mo. Meridian, 506 West 113th Street, New York NY 10025.

MERIDIAN POETRY MAGAZINE. 0306-3461. Periodical. UK. English. qt. 0.30 Each Issue. Rondo Publications, 10 Pall Mall, Liverpool L3 6HJ England. **LC** PR1170. **DD** 821.91408.

MESSIEURS, MES AMOURS. V. 1- Feb. 1978-. 0704-5719. Periodical. CN. French. mo. $2.75 Each Number. Les Entreprises Normand Vaughan, CP 274 Succursale M, Montreal Quebec H1V 3M3 Canada. **DD** C841.54080353.

MIDNIGHTSUN QUARTERLY. Began publication in 1965?. 0382-828X. Periodical. CN. English. qt. **DD** C811.5408.

THE MILL HUNK HERALD. **VFOAT** Punching Out With: the Mill Hunk Herald. Began with: Feb. 1979. Periodical. US. English. qt. $10.00. Mill Hunk Herald, 916 Middle Street, Pittsburgh PA 15212. **Tel** (412)321-4767. **Ed** Larry Evans. bk rev. **Circ** 8,000. (ctrl). Contains the views, stories, and poetry of working people.

MINAS GERAIS. SUPLEMENTO LITERARIO. **VFOAT** Suplemento Literario. Began with issue for Sept. 1, 1966. Periodical. BL. Portuguese. wk. 127.500. Imprensa Oficial do Estado de Minas Gerais, Av Augsto Delima, 270 Belo Horizonte Brazil. **Tel** (031)224-4088. **Ed** Pascoal Motta. **Ind/Abst** MLA Int. Bibliogr. Books Artic. Mod. Lang. Lit. **Circ** 5,000. (ctrl). Literary publication of poems. Analyses and discussion of art in general.

MR. COGITO. **VFOAT** Mister Cogito. Began with Vol. 1, No. 1 (Fall 1973). 0740-1205. Periodical. US. English. ir. $3.50. J Gogol, Pacific University Box 627, Forest Grove OR 97116. **Tel** (503)357-6151. **Ed** John M Gogol and Robert A Davies. adv acc. **Circ** 500. Poetry in English and in translation, line drawings.

MISTRAL. 1975-. 0318-2088. CN. English. qt. Mistral, 6023 Bliss Street, Halifax NS B3H 2A8 Canada. **DD** C811.5405.

MJP. MONTREAL JOURNAL OF POETICS. (MJP). **VFOAT** Montreal Journal of Poetics. **VAT** Montreal Journal of Poetics (1982). Series 2, # 1 (Fall/Winter 1982)-. 0823-1605. CN. English. ir. Free to Members, $10.00 Institutions. MJP, S Morrissey, R R #2, Huntingdon Quebec J0S 1H0 Canada. **DD** 808.105. *Montreal Journal of Poetics, 0228-0388.*

MODERN HAIKU. Vol. 1, No. 1 (Winter 1969)-. 0026-7821. Periodical. US. English. ty. $9.65. Modern Haiku, PO Box 1752, Madison WI 53701. **Tel** (608)233-2738. **Ed** Robert Spiess. **LC** PS593.H3. **DD** 811.04. bk rev. **Circ** 580. Foremost international English language haiku journal. Publishes haiku, haiku book reviews and articles on haiku aesthetics.

MODERN POETRY IN TRANSLATION. No. 1-. 0026-8291. Periodical. UK. English. an. Modern Poetry in Translation, 10B Arkwright Road, London NW3 England. **LC** PN6099.6. **DD** 808.81.

MODERN POETRY IN TRANSLATION . . . : AN ANNUAL SURVEY *CEASED.* 1983-. UK. English. an. Carcanet New Press Ltd, 330 Corn Exchange Building, Manchester M4 3BG England. *Modern Poetry in Translation, 0026-8291.*

MODERN POETRY STUDIES. V. 1- 1970-. 0026-8305. Periodical. US. English. ty. $9.00. Modern Poetry Studies, 207 Delaware Avenue, Buffalo NY 14202. **Ind/Abst** Abstr. Engl. Stud., MLA Int. Bibliogr. Books Artic. Mod. Lang. Lit., Index Am. Period. Verse, Index Book Rev. Humanit., Humanit. Index. **LC** PS301.

MOEBIUS. 1-. 0225-1582. Periodical. CN. French. qt. $6.00. Editions Triptyque, CP 670 Succursale N, Montreal Quebec Canada. **DD** C841.540809714.

MONTREAL NOW. 1st Quarterly 1984-. 0823-8944. Periodical. CN. English (French). qt. $2.00 Each Number. Montreal Now, 1A St-Etienne, Ste-Anne-de-Bellevue Quebec H9X 1E8 Canada. **DD** C841.5408.

MOONS AND LION TAILES. V. 1-. 0099-0264. Monographic Series. US. English. qt. $6.00. Editors, Lake Street Station, Box 8434, Minneapolis MN 55408. **LC** PN6099.6. **DD** 811.5408.

MORNING COFFEE CHAPBOOK. 0882-147X. Periodical. US. English. mo. $60.00. Coffee House Press, PO Box 546, West Branch IA 52358. **DD** 811.

Literature—Poetry

MOUTH OF THE DRAGON. No. 1- May 1974-. 0145-0042. Periodical. US. English. qt. $6.00. Box 107, Cooper Station, New York NY 10003. **LC** PS595.H65. **DD** 811.54080352.

MOYANGCHON. **VFOAT** Moyang Munhak Tongin Sahwajip. Periodical. KO. Korean. ir. 2,500. Mirae Munhaksa, 45-12 1-Ka Wonhyoro Yongsan-Ku, Seoul Korea. **LC** PL974.A1.

MULBERRY. No. 1- Nov. 1972-. 0090-4953. Periodical. US. English. bm. $6.00. 2070 Yale Station, New Haven CT 06520. **LC** PS580. **DD** 811.5408.

MUNCHAE. **VFOAT** Munchae, Tongin Sijip. Periodical. KO. Korean. ir. 1,500. Yonghak Chulpansa, 20-9 5-Ka Chungmuro Chung-Ku, Seoul 100 Korea. **LC** PL974.A1.

MUNHAK : KYONGBUSON. Periodical. Korean. ir. 350. 724-6 Taemyong-Dong, Taegu Korea. **LC** PL974.A1.

EL NAHUATZEN. 1-. 0162-9085. Periodical. US. English. sa. $6.00. University of Iowa, El Nahuatzen, Lowell Jaeger Editor, 308 Calvin Hall, Iowa City IA 52242. **LC** PS591 .M49. **DD** 811.0080897.

NARU SIJIP. V. 1- Series (1981)-. Periodical. KO. Korean. ir. 1,500. Hanguk Munhaksa, 195 Kwanhun-Dong, Chongno-Ku Seoul Korea. **LC** PL974.A1.

NENKAN GENDAI SHISHU. JA. Japanese. ir. 3000. Ninkan Gendai Shishu Henshu Iinkai, c/o Geifu Shoin, Bunkyo Shogaku Building 15-4, Hongo 1 Bunkyo-Ku Tokyo. **LC** PL763.8.

NEUE DEUTSCHE HEFTE. Vol. 1- (1-). 0028-3142. Periodical. GW. German. qt. 40.00. Neue Deutsche Hefte/Rechnungs, Dr Schmeisser, Elderstdterw 5B, D-1000 Berlin 38 West Germany. **Tel** (030)7112033. Ed Joachim Gunther. **Ind/Abst** MLA Int. Bibliogr. Books Artic. Mod. Lang. Lit., Annu. Bibliogr. Engl. Lang. Lit., Hist. Abstr., Am. Hist. Life, Hist. Abstr., Part A, Mod. Hist. Abstr., Hist. Abst., Part B, Twent. Century Abstr. **LC** AP30. **DD** 033.1. bk rev. adv acc. American literature and poetry, book reviews.

NEW COIN POETRY. **VFOAT** New Coin. V. 1- Jan. 1965-. 0028-4459. Periodical. SA. English. sa. $1.04. Institute-Study of English in Africa, I S E A/ Rhodes University, PO Box 94, Grahamstown 6140 South Africa.

NEW COLLAGE MAGAZINE. **VFOAT** New Collage. V. 1-. 0028-4467. Periodical. US. English. ty. $6.00. New College Press, 5700 North Trail, Sarasota FL 33580. **Tel** (813)355-2801. Ed A MCA Miller and Carol Mahler. bk rev. **Circ** 1,000. Poetry with clear focus and strong imagery; contemporary slants on traditional prosodies. Some interviews, book reviews and graphics.

NEW HEADLAND POETRY MAGAZINE. Periodical. UK. English. 1.00 per 4 issues. 27 Brook Road, Epping England. **LC** PR1170. **DD** 821.91408.

NEW POETRY. No. 28- 1975-. 0548-6505. Periodical. UK. English. qt. 3.00. Workshop Press, Accounts Department, 99 Pole Barn Lane, Frinton on Sea Essex CO13 9NQ England. **LC** PR1170. **DD** 821.005. Workshop New Poetry.

NEW POETS. UK. English. $7.00. Regency Press, 43 New Oxford Street, WCIA 1BH London England. **LC** PR1227. **DD** 821.91408.

NEW POET'S HANDBOOK. Spring 1984-. 0827-2425. CN. English. an. 6.00. League of Canadian Poets, 24 Ryerson Avenue, Toronto Ontario M5T 2P3 Canada. **Tel** 363-5047. Ed John Wilson and Marvyne Jenoff. **DD** 808.102371. **Circ** 3,000. (ctrl) A helpful tool for poets interested in launching themselves into the market place. Rich with advice on publishers and publishing.

THE NEW POETS SERIES. No. 1-. 0277-2752. Monographic Series. US. English. ir. New Poets Series, 541 Piccadilly Road, Baltimore MD 21204. **Tel** (301)828-0724. Ed Clarinda Harriss Lott. **Circ** 750. Publishes first books by outstanding younger poets who have not previously had a collection of their work published.

NEW QUARTERLY. (THE NEW QUARTERLY). Vol. 1, No. 1 (Spring 1981)-. 0227-0455. Periodical. CN. English. qt. $7.50. The New Quarterly, c/o Department of English, University of Waterloo, Waterloo Ont N2L 3G1 Canada. **DD** C810.80054.

NEW VOICES IN AMERICAN POETRY. 0735-4584. US. English. an. Vantage Press, 516 West 34th Street, New York NY 10001.

NEWS LETTER - CANADIAN POETS PEN CLUB CEASED. Main/Corp Canadian Poets Pen Club. V. 1, Jan. 1977. Ceased with Aug./Sept. 1978 issue (V. 2, No. 5)?. 0702-8563. Periodical. CN. English. Free to Members (Membership - $5.00). L R Grol Fonthill Studio, Trillium Books, 53 South Pelham Street, Fonthill Ontario L0S 1E0 Canada. **DD** C811.5406271.

NEWS POEMS. (NEW POEMS : A P.E.N. ANTHOLOGY). 1952-. 0548-6491. UK. English. an. Michael Joseph Ltd, 44 Bedford Square, London WCIB England. **LC** PR1225. **DD** 821.91082.

NEWSLETTER - EXECUTIVE COMMITTEE. LEAGUE OF CANADIAN POETS. (NEWSLETTER - EXECUTIVE COMMITTEE, LEAGUE OF CANADIAN POETS). Main/Corp League of Canadian Poets. No. 13- Fall/Winter 1974-. 0319-6658. Periodical. CN. English. qt. 20.00. League of Canadian Poets, 24 Ryerson Avenue, Toronto Ontario M5T 2P3 Canada. **Tel** (416) 363-5047. Ed Steven Smith. **DD** C811.006271. **Circ** 400. (ctrl). A comprehensive package on and about poetry in Canada. Poetry Canada, 0316-036X.

NEWSLETTER - MONTREAL POETS' INFORMATION EXCHANGE. (NEWSLETTER). **VFOAT** Bulletin. 0712-6239. Periodical. CN. English (text in French on inverted pages). mo. $10.00. Montreal Poets Information Exchange, 4050 MacKenzie, Chomedey Laval Quebec H7W 1M5 Canada. **DD** 808.105.

NEWSLETTER - PUBLIC PRESS. (NEWSLETTER). Vol. 1, No. 1 (Spring 1981)-. 0732-0051. Periodical. US. English. qt. Poetry Festival at Saint Clement's, 423 West 46th Street, New York NY 10036.

NICOTINE SOUP. V. 1- July 1976-). Periodical. US. English. ir. Nicotine Soup, Box 22613, San Francisco CA 94122. **Tel** (415)386-3768.

NIGHTSUN. No. 1 (1981)-. 0278-6079. Periodical. US. English. an. $6.00. Acheron Press, Bear Creek at the Kettle, Friendsville MD 21531. Ed J K Bramann.

NIHON KAIKO SHI SHI. Periodical. JA. Japanese. ir. Nihon Kaiko Shijinkai, 3-2 Higashi Komagata 4, Sumida-Ku 130 Tokyo Japan. **LC** PL757.A1.

NORTHERN LIGHT. No. 1- Winter 1974-. 0317-0586. CN. English. sa. $5.42. Box 162, St Francis Xavier University, Antigonish Nova Scotia B2G 1C0 Canada. **Tel** (902)867-2418. Ed Douglas Smith. **DD** C811.5405. adv acc. **Circ** 500. (ctrl.) An international magazine of poetry and poetics. Far Point, 0014-7621.

NORTHERN LIGHTS (CHELMSFORD, ONT.). (NORTHERN LIGHTS). Began with 1969 issue. 0822-0808. CN. English. an. $2.50. Northern Ontario Council Teachers of English, PO Box 278, Chelmsford Ontario P0M 1L0 Canada. **DD** C811.540809282.

NORTHERN POET. (THE NORTHERN POET). Summer '82-. 0713-4061. CN. English. qt. $11.00. Northern Poet, 1699 Paris Street, Sudbury Ontario P3E 3C4 Canada. **DD** C811.5408.

NOSTALGIA SCRAPBOOK. **VFOAT** Nostalgia Scrapbook Magazine. 8750-8923. Periodical. US. English. bm. $14.95. Nostalgia Scrapbook Magazine, 9401 West Beloit Road/Suite 303, Milwaukee WI 53227. **Tel** (414)545-3808. Ed V Mindel. Past and present manuscripts, articles, poems, pictures, and articles from different writers.

NOSTOC MAGAZINE. US. English. $8.00. Arts End Books, Box 162, Newton MA 02168. **Tel** (617)965-2478. Ed Marshall Brooks. **LC** PN2. **DD** 810.8. bk rev. adv acc. **Circ** 500. We publish good contemporary poetry and short fiction.

LA NOUVELLE TOUR DE FEU. No. 1 (Feb. 1982)-. 0294-4030. Periodical. FR. French. bm. $26.61. Editions du Soleil, 12 rue Elias Rebert, 91150 Etampes France. **Tel** 080 2433. Ed Eolivious Olu Soleil. **LC** PQ1184. **DD** 841.008. bk rev. adv acc. Poetry and philosophy. Tour de Feu.

A NOVA POESIA BRASILEIRA. BL. Portuguese. ir. Shogun Editora E Arte Ltda, Caixa Postal 43.021, CEP 22052 Rio de Janeiro Brazil.

NYQ. THE NEW YORK QUARTERLY. (THE NEW YORK QUARTERLY). **VFOAT** NYQ. No. 1- Winter 1970-. 0028-7482. Periodical. US. English. ty. $18.00. New York Quarterly, PO Box 2415 Grand Central Station, New York NY 10017. **Tel** (207)581-3814. Ed William Packard. **Ind/Abst** Abstr. Engl. Stud. **LC** PS580. **DD** 811.5408. (cum index). adv acc. **Circ** 700. Contemporary poetry. Some editorial commentary.

OCCURRENCE. 0146-9118. US. English. John Wilson, 928 Pine Street Apartment 12B, Philadelphia PA 19107. **LC** PS580. **DD** 811.505.

OINK. (OINK). No. 1-. 0883-8518. Periodical. US. English. an. $5.00. Oink Press, 1446 West Jarvis, Chicago IL 60626. **Tel** (312)764-1048. Ed Maxine Chernoff and Paul Hoover. bk rev. adv acc. **Circ** 500. Contemporary American poetry and non-fiction prose.

OLD TIME SONGS & POEMS. See Music.

OLIFANT. V. 1- Oct. 1973-. 0381-9132. Periodical. CN. English (includes some text in French). qt. $18.00. Olifant, St John College, University of Manitoba, Winnipeg Manitoba R3T 2M5 Canada. **Tel** (204)474-9122. **Ind/Abst** MLA Int. Bibliogr. Books Artic. Mod. Lang. Lit. **DD** 809.13.

OPEN PLACES. No. 1- Nov. 1966-. 0474-2389. Periodical. US. English. sa. $10.00. Open Places, Box 2085, Stephens College, Columbia MO 65125. **Tel** (314)442-2211. Ed Eleanor M Bender. **Ind/Abst** Index Am. Period. Verse. **LC** PS580. **DD** 810.8005. bk rev. adv acc. **Circ** 1,000. A magazine publishing poetry and reviews.

OPHIR. Periodical. US. English. ir. $3.00. Ravan Press, 1140 Avenue, New York NY 10036. **LC** PR9365.1. **DD** 821.

ORBIS (YOULGREAVE, DERBYSHIRE). (ORBIS). Began in July 1969. 0030-4425. Periodical. UK. English. qt $15.00. 199 The Long Shoot, Nuneaton Warwickshire CV11 6JQ England. A wide variety of poetry, prose and features aimed at general readers as well as literary specialists. Very suitable for libraries, colleges, schools, writers, groups, etc. Scrip (Chesterfield, Derbyshire), 0036-9659.

ORFEO. No. 1- Oct. 1963-. Periodical. Spanish. ir. **LC** PN1010.

ORPHIC LUTE. (THE ORPHIC LUTE). V. 1- June/July 1958-. 0030-5804. Periodical. US. English. qt. $10.00. Patricia Doherty Hinnebusch, 1021 E Lt Back River Road, PO Box 2815, Hampton VA 23669. **Tel** (804)850-0567. Ed Patricia Doherty Hinnebusch. bk rev. **Circ** 300. Contemporary and traditional poetry of high quality. Lyrical rather than polemic or political message poetry. Well crafted light verse welcome.

OUTPOSTS (WALTON-ON-THAMES) CEASED. (OUTPOSTS). No. 1 (1944)- No. 132 (Spring 1982). 0030-7297. Periodical. UK. English. qt. **LC** PR1225. **DD** 821.008.

OXFORD POETRY (OXFORD, OXFORDSHIRE). (OXFORD POETRY). Vol. 1, No. 1 (June 1983)-. Periodical. UK. English. ty. 4/50/-. Magdalen College, Oxford OX1 4AU England.

PADABALI. 1 (Vol. 1387 Jan. 1980!)-. Periodical. Bengali. ir. **LC** PK1714.

PAINTBRUSH. No. 1- Spring 1974-. 0094-1964. US. English. sa. $8.00. Georgia Southwestern College, Department of English, Americus GA 31709. **Tel** (912)928-0881. Ed Ben Bennani. **Ind/Abst** MLA Int. Bibliogr. Books Artic. Mod. Lang. Lit., Index Am. Period. Verse. **LC** PN6099.6. **DD** 808.81. bk rev. adv acc. **Circ** 500. (ctrl). Poetry, translations and letters.

THE PAINTED BRIDE QUARTERLY. V. 1- Fall 1973-. 0362-7969. Periodical. US. English. qt. $12.00. Painted Bride Art Center, 230 Vine Street, Philadelphia PA 19106. **Tel** (215)331-7389. Ed Louis McKee, Joanna D Paolo and Louis Camp. **LC** PS580. **DD** 811.5408. bk rev. adv acc. **Circ** 300. (ctrl). We wish to publish poetry, short fiction, essays, and reviews, from new as well as established writers.

PALMARES - ALL CANADA POETRY CONTESTS. (PALMARES). Summer 83-. 0822-1561. Periodical. CN. English (includes some text in French and Spanish). qt. Free. A.C.P.C., PO Box 5752/Station F, Ottawa Ontario K2C 3M1 Canada. **DD** C811.5408.

PAPER AIR. V. 1-. Periodical. US. English. ir. Paper Air, 825 Morris Road, c/o Gil Ott, Blue Bell PA 19422. **Tel** (215)925-9914. Ed Gil Ott. bk rev. adv acc. **Circ** 800. An occasional anthology of current poetry and poetics presented in an attractive format. The current volume is concerned with cross-cultural issues and translation.

PARNASSUS. POETRY IN REVIEW. See Literary and Political Reviews.

PASQUE PETALS. 0031-2649. Periodical. US. English. mo. $12.00. South Dakota State Poetry Society Inc, 909 East 34th Street, Sioux Falls SD 57105. **Tel** (605)338-9156. **Ed** Barbara Stevens. **Circ** 230. Only use poetry 44 lines long, or less; all types with no rough language; good taste is the criteria.

EN PASSANT, POETRY. 0271-5023. Periodical. US. English. sa. $3.50. c/o James A Costello, 1906 Brant Road, Wilmington DE 19810. **Ind/Abst** Index Am. Period. Verse. **LC** PS580. **DD** 811.5408. *En Passant Poetry Quarterly, 0363-3780.*

PENINSULA POETS. 0031-4307. Periodical. US. English. qt. $7.00. Poetry Society of Michigan, 8757 Berridge Road, Greenville MI 48838. **Tel** (616)754-8698. **Ed** Gwendolyn Niles. bk rev. **Circ** 300. (ctrl). Publication of Poetry Society of Michigan, a non-profit organization. Publishes only to members.

PIVOT. Began in 1951. 0554-2324. US. English. an. $5.00. Pivot Associates, Attn: Sibyl Grucci, 221 South Barnard Street, State College PA 16801. **Tel** (304)876-6745. **Ed** Georgia McElhaney.

PLAINS POETRY JOURNAL. No. 1-. 0730-6172. Periodical. US. English. qt. $14.00. Stronghold Press, PO Box 2337, Bismarck ND 58502. **Tel** (701)222-0728. **Ed** Jane Greer. **Circ** 400. Magazine for poetry that uses traditional constraints-meter, rhyme, alliteration, assonance, etc. in a vigorous finely-crafted, contemporary way.

PLAY THE RED. Vol. 1, No. 1 (Fall 1981)-. 0277-1098. Periodical. US. English. $3.00 Single Issue. Sisyphus Press, 192 Spring Street, New York NY 10012.

POEM. No. 1- Nov. 1967-. 0032-1885. Periodical. US. English. ty. $7.50. Huntsville Literary Association, PO Box 919, Huntsville, AL 35804. **Tel** (205)536-9038. **Ed** N R Dillard. **Ind/Abst** Index Am. Period. Verse. **LC** PS580. (ctrl). Brief lyric poems, compressed and intense with a high degree of verbal and dramatic tension.

POEMES INEDITS. **VFOAT** Inedits. V. 1- June 1970-. 0048-4520. Periodical. CN. French. ir. J Royer, 198 Av Royale, Ile d'Orleans, Comte Montmorency, Saint-Pierre Quebec Canada.

POESIA. Yearly V. 1- Dec. 1977-. Periodical. BL. Portuguese. ir. Clube de Poesicude Sao Paulo, rua Barao de Itapetininga, 262 30 S 305, Sao Paulo Brazil. **LC** PN1010. **DD** 808.81.

POESIA. No. 1- 1944-. Catalan, French, or Spanish. ir. Edicions Proa, Tuset 3, Barcelona Spain. **LC** PC3801.

POESIA. No. 1- March 1978-. Periodical. SP. Spanish. ir. $10.47. Rediccion y Administration, Torregalindo 10, Madrid 16 Spain. *Poesia Hispanica.*

POESIA DE VENEZUELA. No 1- May/June. 1963-. 0032-1893. Periodical. VE. Spanish (English and French). ir. $2.50. Apartado Postal 1114, Caracas Venezuela. **LC** PQ8544. **DD** 861.

POESIE 1. **VAT** Poesie Und. No 1-. 0302-297X. Periodical. FR. French. bm. $19.96. Librairie Armand Colin, 103 Boulevard Saint Michel, 75005 Paris Cedex 5 France. **Tel** 543-32-11.

POESIE DE MONTREAL. **VFOAT** Montreal Poems. No. 4- 1978-. 0708-6342. CN. English (includes some text in French). an. $3.00. Poesie de Montreal, Old Log House, Dewittville Quebec J0S 1C0 Canada. **DD** C811.5408. *Montreal Poems, 0702-7184.*

POESIE; LA POESIE FRANCAISE DE BELGIQUE. 0048-4555. Periodical. FR. French. ir. Sodis, 128 Av Marechal Lattre Tassign, 77400 Lagny France.

POESIE (PARIS, FRANCE : 1984). (POESIE). 1 (Jan./Feb. 1984)-. 0752-272X. Periodical. FR. French. bm. 185. Pierre Seghers, 228 Bd Raspail, 75014 Paris France. **LC** PQ1141. **DD** 841.9108.

POESIEALBUM. 1- 19 -. Periodical. English. mo. 0,90. Verlag Neues Leben, Leninstrasse 16, DDR-701 Leipzig Germany. **Tel** 209327165. Presents a contemporary author from the GDR or from abroad, a poet of world literature or a classic of literature.

POET. V. 1- 1960-. Periodical. English. mo. World Poetry Society, 118 Dr Seethapathi Nagar, Madras 42 India. **Tel** 434 186. **Ed** Krishna Srinivas. bk rev. microform. Devoted to poetry from all countries of the world.

POET AND CRITIC (AMES, IOWA). (POET AND CRITIC). **VFOAT** Poet & Critic. Vol. 1, No. 1 (Fall 1964)-. 0032-1958. Periodical. US. English. ir. $9.00. Iowa State University Press, English Department, Ross Hall, Ames IA 50011. **Tel** (515)294-2180. **Ed** Michael Martone. **Ind/Abst** Abstr. Engl. Stud., Index Am. Period. Verse. bk rev. **Circ** 500. Poetry and writing about poetry in changing formats. *Poet & Critic (Lafayette, Ind.), 0032-1958.*

POET LORE. V. 1- Jan. 1889-. 0032-1966. Periodical. US. English. qt. $20.00. Heldref Publications, 4000 Albemarle Street NW/Suite 100, Washington DC 20016. **Tel** (202)362-6445. **Ed** Edward Taylor. **LC** PN2. **DD** 808.805. (cum index). bk rev. adv acc. **Circ** 387. Each issue spotlights, with informative, lively reviews, new volumes of poetry, particularly small press publications. Presents the best work of both new and established writers.

THE POET PEU A PEU. **VFOAT** Poet. 0190-6682. Periodical. US. English. an. D I Nemeth 2314 West 6th Street, Mishawaka IN 46544. **Ed** Doris I Nemeth. **LC** PS615. **DD** 811.008.

POET (SHREVEPORT, LA.). (THE POET). Vol. 1, No. 1 (Fall 1984)-. 0748-4062. Periodical. US. English. qt. $15.00. The Poet, PO Box 44021, Shreveport LA, 71134-4021. **DD** 811.

POETI A GRADARA. 1970/71-. Italian. ir. 6.000. Eura Press, Via Lazzaro Papi 15, Milano 20135 Italy. **Tel** (02)5460353. **LC** PQ4214. **Circ** 1,500.

POETIC LICENCE. Began publication in March 1978?. 0708-9562. Periodical. CN. English. bm. $1.50 Per No. $9.00 Per Year. Poetic Licence, PO Box 3810 Station B, Calgary Alta T2M 4N6 Canada. **DD** C811.5408.

POETICA. 1- Apr. 1974-. Periodical. JA. English. sa. $53.00. Japan Publications Trading Company Limited, PO Box 5030, Tokyo International, Tokyo 100-31 Japan. **Tel** Telex J27161 JPTCO.

POETICS. 1- 1971-. 0304-422X. Periodical. NE. English (French or German). bm. Elsevier Science Publishers, P.O. Box 211, 1000 AE Amsterdam, Netherlands. **Tel** (020)5803.911. **Ind/Abst** Abstr. Engl. Stud., MLA Int. Bibliogr. Books Artic. Mod. Lang. Lit., Index Book Rev. Humanit. **LC** PN45. **DD** 801. (cum index).

POETICS JOURNAL. No. 1 (Jan. 1982)-. 0731-5236. Periodical. US. English. ir. $15.00. Poetics Journal, 2639 Russell Street, Berkeley CA 94705. **Tel** (415)535-1952. **Ed** Lyn Hejinian and Barrett Watten. bk rev. **Circ** 900. A journal of contemporary poetics by poets and prose writers and by other artists, critics, linguists, and political theorists. It features articles and reviews.

POETICS TODAY. Vol. 1, No. 1-2 (Autumn 1979)-. 0333-5372. Periodical. IS. English. ir. $35.00. Israel Science Publishing, PO Box 3115, Jerusalem 91030 Israel. **Tel** (02)637915. **Ed** B Hrushovski. **Ind/Abst** Index Book Rev. Humanit., Lang. Lang. Behav. Abstr., MLA Int. Bibliogr. Books Artic. Mod. Lang. Lit. bk rev. adv acc. (ctrl). An international journal for theory and analysis of literature and communication.

POETIQUE. 1- 1970-. 0032-2024. Periodical. French. ir. Editions du Seuil, BP 80 27 rue Jacob, 75261 Paris Cedex 06 France. **Ind/Abst** MLA Int. Bibliogr. Books Artic. Mod. Lang. Lit. **LC** PN3. **DD** 809.

POETISCHES JOURNAL. V. 1-. German. ir. **LC** PT1136.A2.

POETRY. V. 1- Oct. 1912-. 0032-2032. Periodical. US. English. mo. $22.00. Poetry, Box 4348, Chicago IL 60680. **Tel** (312)996-7803. **Ed** Joseph Parisi. **Ind/Abst** Abstr. Engl. Stud., Index Book Rev. Humanit., Read. Guide Period. Lit., Access, Book Rev. Index, Index Am. Period. Verse, Book Rev. Digest, Mag. Index. **LC** PS301. **DD** 811.005. (cum index). bk rev. adv acc. **Circ** 6,000. The mostly widely read, oldest monthly of verse. From Auden to Ashbery, Pound to Pinsky, Stevens to Soto-voices famous and new.

POETRY & AUDIENCE. **VAT** Poetry and Audience. 0032-2040. Periodical. UK. English. ir. 3. University of Leeds, School of English, Leeds 2 Yorks England. **Tel** (0532)742916. **Ed** Johnathon Ward and Barnaby Benson. bk rev. adv acc. **Circ** 280. Publishes 9,000 new poetry alongside the work of established poets. Past contributors include Seamus Heaney, Ted Hughs, Philip Larkin, and Stevie Smith.

POETRY AUDIT. 0737-1780. Periodical. US. English. Audit/Poetry, 314 Highland Avenue, Buffalo NY 14222. **LC** PS615. **DD** 811.008.

POETRY BOOK SOCIETY BULLETIN. No. 1- May 1955-. Periodical. UK. English. 15.50. The Poetry Book Society Ltd, 21 Earls Court Square, London SW5 9DE England. **Tel** (01)244-9792. **Ed** Medlin and Leach. **LC** PR604. **DD** 821.91209. adv acc. **Circ** 1,550. Britain's only poetry book club. All major titles at substantial discount.

POETRY DIMENSION ANNUAL. V. 4- 1976-. US. English. ir. Rowman and Littlefield, 81 Adams Drive, Totowa NJ 07512. **Ed** Homer Dickens. This seventh annual monograph includes among many others, memorable new poems by Alan Sillitoe, Roy Fisher and Peter Redgrove. *Poetry Dimension.*

POETRY EAST. No. 1- 1980-. 0197-4009. US. English. ty. $10.00. Poetry East, Star Rt 1 Box 50, Earlysville VA 22936. **Tel** (804)924-3509. **Ed** Richard Jones and Kate Daniels. **Ind/Abst** Index Am. Period. Verse. **LC** PN1271. **DD** 808.8105. bk rev. adv acc. **Circ** 1,000. An international magazine of poetry, criticism, translations, interviews and art. Features special issues on such topics as: surrealism, political poems, visual arts and etc.

POETRY FLASH. 0737-4747. Periodical. US. English. mo. $8.00. Poetry Flash, PO Box 4172, Berkeley CA 94704.

POETRY INDEX ANNUAL. *See* Indexes/ Abstracts.

POETRY INFORMATION *CEASED.* No. 1-20/ 21. 0048-4598. Periodical. UK. English. sa.

A POETRY MAG. No. 1 (Feb. 1982)-. 0730-8868. Periodical. US. English. qt. $8.00 Individual, $10.00 Institutions. Teri Fontaine, 39 Linden Place, Brookline MA 02146.

THE POETRY MAILING LIST. Periodical. US. English. ir. The Poetry Mailing List, 18 Cheshire Place, Staten Island NY 10301.

POETRY MARKETS IN CANADA. Fall 1982-. 0826-4708. CN. English. be. 5.00. League of Canadian Poets, 24 Ryerson Avenue, Toronto Ontario M5T 2P3 Canada. **Tel** (416)363-5047. **DD** 070.520971. **Circ** 3,000. (ctrl). Catalogue of poetry markets in Canada plus suggestions on how to approach them.

POETRY MONASH. 0314-6855. Periodical. AT. English. sa. 3.00. Monash University, English Department c/o Dr Dennis Davison, Clayton Victoria 3168 Australia. **Tel** 03 541 2135. **Ed** Dennis Davison. **Circ** 200. Current Australian poems.

POETRY MONTREAL. No. 1 (Feb. 1984)-. 0822-9937. Periodical. CN. English. mo. $1.00 Per No. Poetry Montreal, #1-3358 Lorne Avenue, Montreal Quebec H2X 2A6 Canada. **DD** C811.540809714281.

POETRY 'N' PROSE. 0821-5790. Periodical. CN. English. bm. $6.00 Canada and US, $7.00 other countries. Ahnene Publications, Box 3638 Station C, Ottawa Ontario K1Y 4J7 Canada. **DD** C811.5408.

POETRY NEWSLETTER. No. 1- Dec. 1971-. Periodical. US. English. an. $3.00. Temple University, Department of English, Philadelphia PA 19122. **Ed** Richard O'Connell.

POETRY NIPPON. 0032-2105. Periodical. JA. English. qt. 15.00. Poetry Society of Japan, 5-11 Nagaike-Cho Showa-Ku, Nagoya Japan. **Tel** (052)833-5724. **Ed** Onsey Nakagawa. bk rev. adv acc. **Circ** 500. Translation of Japanese poetry. poems by Japanese and foreigners, book reviews, poetics, essays on poets and poetry news home and abroad.

POETRY NORTHWEST. Began publication with June 1959 Issue. 0032-2113. Periodical. US. English. qt. University of Washington, 4045 Brooklyn Avenue NE JA 15, Seattle WA 98105. **Tel** (206)543-5900. **Ed** David Wagoner. **Ind/Abst** Index Am. Period. Verse. **LC** AP2. **DD** 811.005. **Circ** 1,500. Poetry from poets of the USA and foreign countries.

POETRY NOW (EUREKA, CALIF.). (POETRY NOW). V. 1, No. 1-. 0736-5551. Periodical. US. English. qt. $19.00. Poetry Now, 3118 K Street, Eureka CA 95501. **Ed** E V Griffith. **Ind/Abst** Index Am. Period. Verse. adv acc. **Circ** 3,000. Contemporary poetry (including 20th century poetry in translation), book reviews and new poetry volume listings.

POETRY OTTAWA YEARBOOK. *See* Yearbooks, Almanacs, Directories.

POETRY : PEOPLE. US. English. an. RVK Publishing Company, PO Box 264, Monomonee Falls WI 53051.

POETRY PILOT. 1- Aug. 1959-. 0554-3983. Periodical. US. English. mo. Academy of American Poets, 1078 Madison Avenue, New York NY 10028. **LC** PS301.

Literature—Poetry

POETRY SERIES (PRINCETON, N.J.). (POETRY SERIES). VFOAT Q.R.L. Contemporary Poetry Series. Vol. 24-. 0748-0865. Periodical. US. English. $20.00. Quarterly Review of Literature, 26 Haslet Avenue, Princeton NJ 08540. LC AP2. *Quarterly Review of Literature. Poetry Series, 0748-0873.*

POETRY SUPPLEMENT. 0551-1704. UK. English. an. Poetry Book Society, 9 Long Acre Covent Garden, London WC2E 9LH England. LC PR1227. DD 821.008.

POETRY TORONTO. No. 69 (Sept. 1981)-. 0381-6591. Periodical. CN. English. mo. 14.00. Poetry Toronto, 217 Northwood Drive, Willowdale Ontario M2M 2K5 Canada. Tel (416)222-4690. Ed Maria Jacobs. DD C811.54080971354. bk rev. adv acc. Circ 800. (ctrl). Poetry book reviews; events in realm of poetry in greater Toronto; calendar; regular column describing poets' literary activity; limited listing of poetry markets. *Poetry Toronto Newsletter, 0381-6591.*

POETRY TORONTO NEWSLETTER. 1-67/68. 0381-6591. Periodical. CN. English. mo. $9.28. Poetry Toronto, 217 Northwood Drive, Willowdale Ontario M2M 2K5 Canada. Tel (416)924-6329. Ed Maria Jacobs. DD C811.5408. Circ 700. Poetry, poetry reviews, calendar of events in greater Toronto, self-portraits of poets, markets. *Old Nun Newsletter.*

POETRY WALES. V. 1- Spring 1965-. 0032-2202. Periodical. UK. English (Welsh). qt. 6.75. Poetry Wales Press, 56 Parcau Avenue, Bridgend Mid-Glamorgan Wales. Tel (0056)880649. Ed Cary Archard. Ind/Abst Abstr. Engl. Stud. LC PR8954.5. bk rev. adv acc. Circ 800. (ctrl). Poetry, and articles about poetry, mostly with a Welsh interest. Also reviews of new poetry, critical books and biographies of poets.

POETRY/LA. VFOAT Poetry LA. No. 1 (Fall/Winter 1980)-. 0275-1739. Periodical. US. English. sa. $8.00. Poetry/LA, PO Box 84271, Los Angeles CA 90073. Tel (213)472-6171. Ed Helen Friedlan. LC PS1. DD 811.008. adv acc. Circ 500. Poems of literary value by Los Angeles-area poets without prior restraint on subject, style, or length.

POETS FROM OUR PLACE. V. 1- July 1979-. 0708-5524. Periodical. CN. English. Maverick Enterprises, PO Box 5805 Station A, Toronto Ont M5W 1P2 Canada. DD C811.54080920824.

POETS IN THE SOUTH. V. 1-. 0197-6338. Periodical. US. English. ir. Poets in the South, University of South Florida, Center Writers Let 141, Tampa FL 33620. LC PS551. DD 811.0080975.

POETS ON. V. 1- Winter 1977-. 0146-3136. Periodical. US. English. sa. $6.00. Poets On, Box 255, Chaplin CT 06235. Tel (203)455-9671. Ed Ruth Daigon. Circ 500. (ctrl). A theme-oriented poetry magazine interested in well-crafted poetry that explores basic human concerns.

THE POET'S VOICE (BATH, SOMERSETSHIRE). (THE POET'S VOICE). Periodical. UK. English. ir. 12.26. The Poet's Voice, 12 Dartmouth Avenue, Bath England. Ed Fred Beake. Presents an almost uniquely broad picture of English poetry as it is today. Includes a substantial retrospective on lesser known poets of merit.

DEN POEZII (LENINGRAD). (DEN POEZII). Began publication with 1966?. 0418-6176. UR. Russian. an. LC PG3505.L5. *Den Poezii.*

POINTS ET CONTREPOINTS. New Series, No. 13 April 1951-. 0032-2369. Periodical. French. ir. 45.00. Editions de la Revue Moderne, 14 rue de l'Armorique, Paris 15E France. *Points et Contrepoints-Ronsard.*

PORCH. V. 1- Spring 1977-. 0163-3872. Periodical. US. English. qt. $7.00. c/o James Cervantes Department of English, Arizona State University, Tempe AZ 85281. LC PS615. DD 811.008.

POSIE I.E. POESIE. No 1- 2. Quarter 1977-. 0152-0032. Periodical. French. ir. 160.00. Librairie Classique Eugene Belin, 8 rue Ferou, 75278 Paris France. Ind/Abst MLA Int. Bibliogr. Books Artic. Mod. Lang. Lit. LC PN1010. DD 808.81.

POT-HOOKS & HANGERS. V. 1- Summer 1973-. 0091-7230. Periodical. US. English. sa. $2.50. PO Box 718 Old Chelsea Station, New York NY 10014. LC PS580. DD 811.5405.

PRETEXTE. No. 1- Spring 1980-. 0226-367X. Periodical. CN. French. be. Pretexte, A.E.D.E.F., Universite de Montreal, Faculte des Arts et des Sciences, Departement d'Etudes Francaises, Salle 8146 rue Jean-Brillant, Montreal Quebec Canada. DD C840.8092375. *Versance, 0226-3661.*

PUDDING MAGAZINE. VFOAT Pudding. Began in 1980. 0196-5913. Periodical. US. English. ir. Pudding Magazine, 2384 Hardest Drive, South Columbus OH 43202.

RACCOON. No. 1- May 1977-. 0148-0162. Periodical. US. English. ir. $10.00. St Lukes Press, Suite 401/Mid-Memphis Tower 1407 Union, Memphis TN 38104. Tel (901)357-5441. Ed David Spicer. LC PS615. DD 811.5408. Circ 1,000. The best of contemporary poetry and criticism.

RAVEN. Issue 1- Fall 1979-. 0225-5855. Periodical. CN. English. $4.00 for 2 Issues. Raven, c/o S Lawrance, R R 1 Arbutus Road, Ganges British Columbia V0S 1E0 Canada. DD C811.5408.

REDUCCIONS. 1 (Gener 1977)-. Catalan. ir. 1.200. Llibreria la Tralla, C Riera 7, Vic Spain. LC PN1010. DD 849.91008.

REENBOU. No. 1- Dec. 1979-. 0225-2104. Periodical. CN. English (includes some text in French, Italian, German, Spanish and Portuguese). ir. $3.00 Each Number, $11.00 for 4 Issues. B Mogridge, Reenbou, c/o German Department, Carleton University, Ottawa Ontario K2S 5B6 Canada. DD 808.810405.

RETURNING. 1-3. 0318-5230. CN. English. $10.00. Returning, 2140 Yew Street, Vancouver British Columbia V6K 3G7 Canada. DD C811.5408.

REVISTA DE POESIA E CRITICA. Yearly V. 1- No. 1-. Periodical. Portuguese. ir. CLS 415 - Bloco B - Lote 2 Sobreloja, Brasilia Brazil. LC PQ9561.

REVUE PANIQUE. VFOAT Panique. Began with July 1974 issue. Monographic Series. French. ir. LC PQ3843. DD 841.9108 S.

RIVISTA DI ESTETICA. See *Philosophy.*

ROAD-HOUSE. (ROAD/HOUSE). No. 1- Fall 1975-. 0148-3730. Periodical. US. English. sa. $1.50. Road/House Press, 900 West 9th Street, Belvidere IL 61008. LC PS580. DD 811.5.

ROSH. No. 1- Jan. 1978-. Periodical. Hebrew. ir. LC PJ5042.

THE RUFUS. VFOAT Rufus Poetry. VAT The Raise Us Fools Up Serenely. V. 1- Fall 1972-. 0147-1163. Periodical. US. English. ty. $5.00. The RUFUS, PO Box 16, Pasadena CA 91102. LC PS580. DD 811.505.

SAGETRIEB. Vol. 1, No. 1 (Spring 1982)-. 0735-4665. Periodical. US. English. ty. $18.00. University of Maine, 305 Neville Hall, Orono ME 04469. Tel (207)581-3814. Ed Carroll F Terrell. Ind/Abst Abstr. Engl. Stud., MLA Int. Bibliogr. Books Artic. Mod. Lang. Lit. LC PS301. DD 811.509. bk rev. Circ 334. A journal devoted to poets in the Pound, H D Williams tradition.

SAITO MOKICHI TSUIBO KASHU. No. 1-. JA. Japanese. ir. Kaminoyama Shiritsu Saito Mokichi Kinenkan, Aza Benten 1421, Kitamachi, Kaminoyama-shi 999-31 Japan. LC PL758.A1.

SARCOPHAGUS. 0271-2342. Periodical. US. English. sa. $5.00. Ashford Press RRI, Box 128, Ashford CT 06278.

SASKATCHEWAN POETRY BOOK. 1936/37-. 0080-6560. Periodical. CN. English. be. Saskatchewan Poetry Society, 3104 College Avenue, Regina Saskatchewan S4T 1VT Canada. Tel 522-6321. DD C811.505. Contains short biographic notes on the poets, celebrating our 50th year as a society. *Saskatchewan Poetry Year Book.*

SCHIST. No. 1- Fall 1973-. 0092-9425. US. English. $5.00 for 4 Issues. PO Box 257, Willimantic CT 06226. LC PS615. DD 811.5408.

SCOPP. SATURDAY CENTRE OF PROSE & POETRY. Main/Corp Saturday Centre. VFOAT Saturday Centre of Prose & Poetry. VAT Saturday Centre of Prose and Poetry. 0313-685X. Periodical. AT. English. ty. $7.38. Saturday Centre, PO Box 140, Cammeray New South Wales 2062 Australia. *Saturday Club Book of Poetry.*

SCOTTISH POETRY. No. 1- 1966-. 0080-8156. UK. English. an. Edinburgh University Press, c/o Biblio District Court, 81 Adams Drive, Totowa NJ 07512. LC PR8658. DD 821.91408.

SEEMS. No. 1- Autumn 1971-. 0095-1730. US. English. an. $12.00. Seems c/o Karl Elder, Lakeland College, Sheboygan WI 53081. Tel (414)565-3871. Ed Karl Elder. LC PS501. DD 810.8005. Circ 350. Contemporary poetry and fiction.

SEMI-ANNUAL BOOKLIST. VFOAT Semiannual Booklist. Fall 1984-. US. English. sa. Academy of American Poets, 177 East 87th Street, New York NY 10128. *Semi-Annual Checklist of Poetry, 0147-1414.*

SENTENCES. Vol. 1, No. 1 (Apr., 1982)-. 0732-8907. Periodical. US. English. bm. $5.00. World Prison Poetry Center, 245 Whalley Avenue, New Haven CT 06511.

SEQUENCES. Began publication in 1958. 0559-4871. FR. French. an. $22.00. Jean Grassin Editeur, BP 75, 56340 Carnac France. Tel 97.52.93.63. LC PQ1160. DD 841.008. bk rev. adv acc. The only journal of contemporary French poetry.

SEVEN STARS. VFOAT Seven Stars Poetry. 0146-695X. Periodical. US. English. mo. Realities Library, PO Box 33512, San Diego CA 92103.

THE SEVENTIES. No. 1- Spring 1972-. 0037-5969. Periodical. US. English. ir. $3.00 (4 Issues). Seventies Press, Odin House, Madison MN 56256. LC PN1010. DD 808.8104. *Sixties, 0583-4570.*

SHELL. Fall/Winter 1976-. 0146-3985. Periodical. US. English. qt. 362 Waban Avenue, Waban MA 02168. LC PS580. DD 811.5408.

SHIH HSUAN. Periodical. CH. Chinese. an. 1.70. Hsin Hua Shu Tien, Pei-Ching Fa Hsing So, Peking China. LC PL2543. DD 895.11508.

SHIH HSUAN (TAIPEI, TAIWAN). (SHIH HSUAN). VFOAT Nieu tu Shih Hsuan. 1982-. CH. Chinese. an. $130.00. Erh Ya Chu Pan She, PO Box 30-190, Taipei Taiwan. LC PL3031.T32. DD 895.115080951249.

SHIH TAN SO. VFOAT Shi Tansuo. Periodical. CH. Chinese. ir. 0.65. Hsin Hua Shu Tien, Pei-Ching Fa Hsing So, Peking China. LC PL2307. DD 895.11009.

SHIKAI. Began with June 1960 issue. Periodical. JA. Japanese. ir. 200. 1-106 Nijigaoka Nishi Jutaku Chikusa-Ku, Nagoya Japan. LC PN1010.

SHIRIM : A JEWISH POETRY JOURNAL. Vol. 1 (Fall 1982)-. Periodical. US. English. sa. $5.00. c/o Hillel Hacor, 900 Hilgard Avenue, Los Angeles CA 90024. Tel (213)208-4427. Ed Marc Dworkin. Circ 700. Publishes poetry that reflects various life styles, attitudes and emotions of Jewish living. This journal has published some of America's finest poets.

SHOCKS. No. 1- 1972-. 0360-912X. US. English. $10.00. Momo's Press, Box 14061, San Francisco CA 94114. LC PS285.S3. DD 811.5405.

SIDNEY NEWSLETTER. V. 1- Spring 1980-. 0227-826X. Periodical. CN. English. sa. $7.00. Department of English, Wilfrid Laurier University, Waterloo Ontario N2L 3C5 Canada. Ind/Abst MLA Int. Bibliogr. Books Artic. Mod. Lang. Lit. DD 821.3.

SIGNAL. Began with Sept./Nov. 1970 issue. Croatian and English. ir. Dobrinjska 7, Beograd Yugoslavia. LC PN6110.C77.

SILVER. 1972-. 0090-5682. US. English. Sepharim (II), Box 244, Moorpark CA 93021. LC PS580. DD 811.5408.

SIMPLICISSIMUS (BURNABY, B.C.). (SIMPLICISSIMUS). Year. 1 (Apr. 1983)-. 0821-1604. CN. German (includes some text in English). an. Free. Simplicissimus German Division Department of Languages, Literatures & Linguistics, Simon Fraser University, Burnaby British Columbia V5A 1S6 Canada. Tel (604)291-3544. Ed L Kitching. DD C830.8. Circ 200. (ctrl). The undergraduate literary journal of students of German literature at Simon Fraser University; creative and critical pieces are published in the annual volume.

SIMSANG. VFOAT Image. V. 1- Dec. 1973-. Periodical. Korean. ir. 2500. 13-12 Kwanchol-Tong Chongno-Ku, Seoul Korea. LC PN1010.

Literature—Poetry

SKY-LETTERS. (SKY LETTERS). V. 1- 1977-. 0700-4834. Periodical. CN. English. ir. $3.10. Sunyata Press, Box 278, Brentwood Bay British Columbia V0S 1A0 Canada. DD C811.5408.

SKYLIGHT. 1978-. 0705-2790. CN. English. an. $1.50 Each Number. Skylight Student Union Building, Dalhousie University, Halifax Nova Scotia B3H 4J2 Canada. DD C811.5408.

SLOW DANCER. 1 (Late 1977)-. 0143-1412. Periodical. UK. English. sa. $8.00. Alan Brooks, Box 149A RR 1, Lubec ME 04652. LC PR1170. DD 821.008.

SLOW LORIS READER. V.1-. 0191-5703. Periodical. US. English. sa. $3.50. Slow Loris Press, 923 Highview Street, Pittsburgh PA 15206. **Ind/Abst** Index Am. Period. Verse. LC PS580. DD 811.008. *Rapport*, 0360-7895.

THE SMALL FARM. No. 1- Mar. 1975-. 0161-5270. Periodical. US. English. sa. $4.00. PO Box 563, Jefferson City TN 37760. Ed J D Marison. LC PS580. DD 811.5408.

SOCIETY OF CHRISTIAN POETS DIRECTORY. See Yearbooks, Almanacs, Directories.

SOJOURNER (CAMBRIDGE, MASS.). (SOJOURNER). Began in 1975. 0191-8699. Periodical. US. English. mo. $15.00. Sojourner, 143 Albany Street, Cambridge MA 02139. **Tel** (617)661-3567. Ed Shane Snowdon. bk rev. adv acc. **Circ** 45,000. National women's monthly offering nonfiction, fiction and poetry dealing with women's concerns including news, politics, personal experience, books, music and film.

SONG. (SONG : NGUYET-SAN THONG-TIN VAN-NGHE). V. 1 (April 6, 1982)-. 0822-4226. Periodical. CN. Vietnamese. mo. 34.00. Song, PO Box 317 Station H, Toronto Ontario M4C 5J2 Canada. **Tel** (416)421-4073. Ed Chuong Tang Nguyen. DD 059.95922. bk rev. adv acc. **Circ** 2,000. News, stories, and poems.

SOULDUST AND PEARLS. (SOULDUST AND PEARLS : OCTE . . . POETRY ANTHOLOGY). VFOAT OCTE . . . Poetry Anthology. VAT Ontario Council of Teachers of English Poetry Anthology. 1981-. 0821-5626. CN. English. an. $7.95 Each Volume. Belstein Publishing, Unit 7, 25 Planchet Road, Maple Ontario L0J 1E0 Canada. DD C811.5408.

SOUNDINGS. 1972-. UK. English. an. Blackstaff Press, 84 Wandsworth Road, Belfast BT4 3LW Northern Ireland. LC PR8848. DD 821.91408.

THE SOUTHERN CALIFORNIA ANTHOLOGY. Vol. 1, No. 1-. 0743-1406. US. English. an. $8.95. The Southern California Anthology, c/o Master of Professional Writing Program DDC 201, University of Southern California, Los Angeles CA 90089-0871. **Tel** (213)743-8255. Ed Carol Fuchs. LC PS571.C2. DD 810.8097949. A collection of the best previously unpublished prose and poetry from established and new authors. Also interviews with well-known writers.

SPARROW POVERTY PAMPHLETS. Began in 1977. 0885-9477. Periodical. US. English. ty. $7.50. Sparrow Press, 103 Waldon Street, West Lafayette IN 47906. **Tel** (317)743-1991. Ed Felix Stefanile. **Ind/Abst** Abstr. Engl. Stud. LC PS580. DD 811.008. **Circ** 850. Original poetry book form. *Sparrow*, 0361-8439.

SPEKTRUM. 0038-7274. Periodical. SZ. German. qt. Knebel Sven, Radaktion Spektrum Napfgasse 4, CH-8001 Zurich Switzerland. **Tel** #8531474. Ed Sven Knebel. bk rev. **Circ** 1,000. (ctrl). International quarterly publication for poetry and original graphics.

SPENSER NEWSLETTER. V. 1- 1970-. 0038-7347. Periodical. US. English. ty. $4.00 Domestic, $7.00 Foreign. State University of New York at Albany, Department of English, Albany NY 12222. **Tel** (518)442-4084. Ed Hugh MacLean. **Ind/Abst** Index Book Rev. Humanit. bk rev. **Circ** 575. Edmund Spenser career, poetry, art and related aspects of Renaissance history and culture.

SPENSER STUDIES. 1- 1980-. 0195-9468. US. English. an. $37.50. AMS Press Inc, 56 East 13th Street, New York NY 10003. **Tel** (212)777-4700. Ed Patrick Cullen and Thomas P Roche Jr. **Ind/Abst** MLA Int. Bibliogr. Books Artic. Mod. Lang. Lit. LC PR2362. DD 821.3. Historical investigations and critical studies on Spenser and other poets of the English Renaissance.

SPIRIT. V. 1- Mar. 1934-. 0038-7584. Periodical. US. English. ir. $4.00. Seton Hall, University, South Orange NJ 07079. **Tel** (201)761-9388. Ed David Rogers. **Ind/Abst** MLA Int. Bibliogr. Books Artic. Mod. Lang. Lit., Cathol. Period. Lit. Index. LC PS301. DD 811.505. bk rev. adv acc. **Circ** 600. Poetry and criticism of poetry.

SPRING. (SPRING : THE JOURNAL OF THE E. E. CUMMINGS SOCIETY). Vol. 1, No. 1 (Apr. 1981)-. 0735-6889. Periodical. US. English. qt. $4.00. D V Forrest Editor, 155 West 68th Street, New York NY 10023. LC PS3505.U334. DD 811.52.

STATIONS. 1- Fall 1972-. 0090-4171. Periodical. US. English. ir. Membrane Press, PO Box 11601, Shorrwood, Milwaukee WI 53211. LC PS501. DD 811.5408.

STEPPENWOLF. No. 1- Winter 1965/66-. 0081-5462. US. English. ty. Steppenwolf, Box 31773, Omaha NE 68131. (cum index).

STIKHI, STIKHI. Vol. 1.- 1967-. UR. Russian. Iskusstvo, Tsvetnoi Bulvar 25, Moskva USSR. LC PG3233.

THE STONE. V. 1- 1967-). Periodical. US. English. ir. Greenpeace, 125 Beach #44, Santa Cruz CA 95060.

STONE COUNTRY. 1974. 0146-1397. Periodical. US. English. sa. $9.50. Stone Country, PO Box 132, Menemsha MA 02552. **Tel** (617)693-5832. Ed Judith Neeld. **Ind/Abst** Index Am. Period. Verse. DD 811. bk rev. adv acc. **Circ** 900. In poetry, "An unusual, expressive voice of our times, this is recommended for all libraries.'Library Journal, April 1985. '. . . appreciation of the exuberance of poetry.'". *Patterns*.

STORYQUARTERLY. VFOAT Story Quarterly. 1- 1975-. US. English. qt. Story Quarterly, PO Box 1416, Northbrook IL 60062.

STUDIEN ZUR POETIK UND GESCHICHTE DER LITERATUR. Vol. 1- 1966-. 0585-6159. Monographic Series. GW. German or English. ir. W Kohlhammer Verlag GMBH, Hessbruhlstrasse 69, Postfach 800430, 7000 Stuttgart 80 West Germany.

SZEP VERSEK. Hungarian. ir. LC PH3152.

TAHAWWULAT. VFOAT Tahaoulat. 1 (Adad Al-Sayf 1983)-. Periodical. Arabic. ir. $60.00. Tahaoulat, BP 113/6043, Beyrouth Lebanon. LC PJ7541.

TAI-WAN SHIH CHI KAN. VFOAT Taiwan Poetry Quarterly. First published in 1983. Periodical. CH. Chinese. qt. 250.00. Lin Pai Chu Pan She, PO Box 14980, Taipei Taiwan.

TALISMAN (COLUMBUS, OHIO). (TALISMAN). Vol. 1, No. 1 (Summer '84)-. 0749-5994. Periodical. US. English. sa. $5.50. Talisman Publications, PO Box 44320, Columbus OH 44320. DD 811.

TAMARACK (AUSTERLITZ, N.Y.). (TAMARACK : JOURNAL OF THE EDNA ST. VINCENT MILLAY SOCIETY). Periodical. US. English. an. LC PS3525.I495. DD 811.52.

TANG TAI SHIH TZU. V. 1- July 1981-. Periodical. Chinese. qt. 0.32. Hua Cheng Chu Pan She, Hsin Hua Shu Tien, Kuang-Chou Kuang-Tung China Mainland. LC PL2543. DD 895.115008.

TANKA GENDAI. V. 1-. Periodical. Japanese. ir. 480. Tanka Shimbun Sha, 43-9 Koenji Minami 4, Suginami-Ku 166 Tokyo Japan. LC PL758.A1.

TANSY (LAWRENCE, KAN. : 1976). (TANSY). Began publication in 1976. Periodical. US. English. sa. John Morits, Route 4 Box 279, Lawrence KS 66044.

TEACHERS & WRITERS. See Education (General).

TELEPHONE. No. 1-. 0147-5452. Periodical. US. English. $6.00. Editor Maureen Owen, Box 672, Old Chelsea Station, New York NY 10011. Ed Maureen Owen. **Ind/Abst** Index Am. Period. Verse. LC PS580. DD 811.008.

TEMBLOR. VFOAT Temblor, Contemporary Poets. Issue No. 1 (1985)-. 0883-1599. Periodical. US. English. sa. $20.00. Temblor, 4624 Cahuenga Boulevard, #307, North Hollywood CA 91602. **Tel** (818)763-8249. Ed Leland Hickman. DD 808. bk rev. adv acc. **Circ** 1,000. (ctrl). Avant-garde and traditional poetry by contemporary American and international poets; some prose, mainly poets.

TENTH MUSE. (THE TENTH MUSE). 0094-162X. US. English. sa. 2942 West 5th Street, Brooklyn NY 11224. LC PS580. DD 811.5408.

THAMES POETRY. Vol. 1, No. 1 (Winter 1976)-. 0307-9562. Periodical. UK. English. sa. Thames Poetry, 160 High Road Wealdstone Harrow, Middlesex HA3 7AX England.

THERE IS. 1983-. 0823-3276. CN. English. an. $3.00 Each Number. Canadian Authors Association, Niagara Branch, 23 Pinecrest Street, St Catharines Ontario L2T 1C6 Canada. DD C811.54080971338.

THIRD EYE. 0198-800X. Periodical. US. English. ty. $2.50. The Third Eye, 189 Kewin Drive, Kenmore NY 14223. **Tel** (716)832-4097.

THIS ENGLAND. See General Interest - General Interest-Europe.

THREE RIVERS POETRY JOURNAL. 1-. 0362-4846. Monographic Series. US. English. sa. $10.00. Three River Press, PO Box 21, Carnegie Mellon University, Pittsburgh PA 15213. **Ind/Abst** Index Am. Period. Verse. LC PS580. DD 811.5405.

TICKLEACE. 0823-6399. Periodical. CN. English. ir. $2.50 Each Number. Tickleace, PO Box 4276, St John's Newfoundland A1C 6C4 Canada. DD C811.540809718.

TINDERBOX. 197 -. Periodical. US. English. qt. 334 Molasses Lane, Mt Pleasant SC 29464. Ed A R Cabaniss.

TOCHI SHISHU. JA. Japanese. ir. 1000. Hiroshima Shijinkai, 5633 Kaita Kaita-Cho Aki-Gun Hiroshima-Ken, Kaito-Cho Japan. LC PL886.H52.

TONGCHON. V. 5-Series (Spring 1980)-. Periodical. KO. Korean. ir. 1,300. Tongchon Tongin, 251-1 Singdang-Dong, Chung-Ku Seoul Korea. LC PL974.A1. *Mongsok*.

TONGGANG SI. 1-. Periodical. KO. Korean. ir. 2,500. Tonggang Si Tonginhoe, 34 Hap-Dong Sodaemun-ku, Seoul Korea. LC PL974.A1.

TOP STORIES. No. 1-. Periodical. US. English. Top Stories, 700 Main Street, Buffalo NY 14202.

TOWER. 1952-. 0495-9701. Periodical. CN. English. sa. Secretary Tower Poetry Society, School of Adult Education McMaster University, Hamilton Ontario Canada. DD C811.5408.

TREBLE POETS. 1-. Monographic Series. UK. English. ir. Chatto and Windus, 42 William IV Street, London WE2N 4DF England. DD 821.91408.

TWELFTH KEY. Began with issue No. 0, 1977. 0380-9919. Periodical. CN. English. ty. $3.50 Each Number. Applegarth Follies, PO Box 40 Station B, London Ontario N6A 4C3 Canada. DD C811.5408.

TWO O'CLOCK RAP. (2 O'CLOCK RAP). V. 1- 1972-. 0318-1189. Periodical. CN. English. an. Toronto Public Library, 40 St Clair Avenue East, Toronto Ontario M4T 1M9 Canada. Ed F Murray. DD 811.5408.

UNMUZZLED OX. V. 1- Nov. 1971-. 0049-5557. Periodical. US. English. ir. $20.00. Unmuzzled Ox Nss, 105 Hudson Street/Room 311, New York NY 10013. **Tel** (212)226-7170. Ed Michael Andre. **Ind/Abst** Index Am. Period. Verse. LC PS580. DD 811.5405. adv acc. **Circ** 20,000. The Cantos(121-150) Ezra Pound, being a serialized second folio by Cage, Sinsberg, Creeley, Fuller, Arbus et. al, in newspaper format.

UP FRONT. V. 1- Sept./Oct. 1979-. 0225-3577. Periodical. CN. English. $1.00 Each Number.

UROBOROS. 0146-8510. Periodical. US. English. ir. $4.00. Allegany Mountain Press, 111 North 10th Street, Olean NY 14760. **Tel** (716)372-0935.

VAGABONDAGES. Began with June 1978 issue. 0153-9620. Periodical. French. ir. 165. Atelier Marcel Jullian, 3 rue Seguier, 75006 Paris France. LC PQ1160. DD 841.008.

VANCOUVER POETRY CENTRE NEWSLETTER. VAT From the West: Vancouver Poetry Centre Newsletter. 0228-782X. Periodical. CN. English. Vancouver Poetry Centre, 3504 Bella Vista Street, Vancouver British Columbia V5N 3W9 Canada. DD C810.90054.

VICTORIA POETRY CHAPBOOK. 1935-. 0702-2298. CN. English. ir. John Wainscott, 8421 Central Saanich Road, Victoria British Columbia Canada.

Manufacturing

VICTORIAN POETRY. V. 1- Jan. 1963-. 0042-5206. Periodical. US. English. qt. $20.00. West Virginia University, Department of English, Morgantown WV 26506. **Tel** (304)293-3107. **Ed** John F Stasny. **Ind/Abst** Abstr. Engl. Stud., MLA Int. Bibliogr. Books Artic. Mod. Lang. Lit., Annu. Bibliogr. Engl. Lang. Lit., Index Book Rev. Humanit., Humanit. Index, Years Work Eng. Stud. **LC** PR500. bk rev. adv acc. **Circ** 1,300. Available on microfilm from University Microfilms. A journal of criticism and analysis of English poetry, written between 1830 and 1914.

VOICES INTERNATIONAL. V. 1- Spring 1966-. 0042-8280. Periodical. US. English. qt. $10.00. Clovita Rice-Editor, 1115 Gillette Drive, Little Rock AR 72207. **Tel** (501)225-0166. **Ed** Clovita Rice. **Circ** 350. Publishes literary quality poetry with haunting imagery and significant statement. Poetry that reminds the reader of something he knows and enriches those moments spent reading.

VOICES ISRAEL. Vol. 6 (Aug. 1978)-. Periodical. IS. English. an. R Rose Editor, Voices Israel, 38 Nehemia Street, Nave Shaanan, Haifa 32 296 Israel. **Ed** Reuben Rose. **LC** PR9510.45. **DD** 821.00805694. adv acc. **Circ** 400. (ctrl). A poetry anthology in English published in Israel taking in poetry from all over the world. *Voices (Haifa, Israel).*

VOYAGES TO THE INLAND SEA. 1- 1971-. 0095-5388. US. English. ir. University of Wisconsin, Murphy Library, Center of Contemporary Poetry, Lacrosse WI 54601. **LC** PS301. **DD** 811.5408.

VSTRECHI (PHILADELPHIA, PA.). (VSTRECHI : ALMANAKH). 1983-. Periodical. US. Russian. an. $7.00. Encounters, 7738 Woodbine Avenue, Philadelphia PA 19151. **Tel** (215)477-6172. **Ed** Valentina Sinkevich. **LC** PG3542. **Circ** 500. The only serial poetry and art publication printed outside of the Soviet Union in the Russian language. *Perekrestki, 0160-5534.*

VWA. VFOAT V.W.A. No 1 (Spring 1983)-. Periodical. French. ty. 45. Revue Litteraire VWA, C P 172, CH-2301 la Chaux-de-Fonds Switzerland. **Tel** (039)282418. **LC** PQ1141. **Circ** 800. (ctrl).

THE WALLACE STEVENS JOURNAL. V. 1- Spring 1977-. 0148-7132. Periodical. US. English. sa. $20.00 Foreign including Canada. Wallace Stevens Journal, Clarkson University, John Serio, Postdam New York 13676. **Tel** (315)268-3987. **Ed** John N Serio. **Ind/Abst** Abstr. Engl. Stud., MLA Int. Bibliogr. Books Artic. Mod. Lang. Lit. bk rev. adv acc. **Circ** 500. (ctrl). Criticism on the poetry of Wallace Stevens with book reviews, bibliography, and poetry.

WATCHWORDS (LONDON, ONT.). (WATCHWORDS). Vol. 1, No. 1 (Sept. 1982)-. 0714-6663. Periodical. CN. English. mo. $10.00. Watchwords, 9 Beaconsfield Avenue, London Ontario N6C 1B4 Canada. **DD** C811.5408097132.

THE WESLEYAN POETRY PROGRAM. 1959-. US. English. sa. Harper and Row, Keystone Industrial Park, Scranton PA 18512. **Tel** (717)343-4761.

THE WINDLESS ORCHARD. No. 1- Feb. 1970-. 0043-5716. Periodical. US. English. ir. $20.00. c/o Dr Robert Novak Editor, English Department, Indiana Purdue University, Fort Wayne IN 46805. **Tel** (219)482-5583. **Ed** Robert Novak. **Ind/Abst** Index Am. Period. Verse. **LC** PS580. **DD** 811.5408. bk rev. **Circ** 300. Contemporary poetry: original verse and criticism.

WOMAN POET (RENO, NEV.). (WOMAN POET). Vol. 1-. 0195-6183. US. English. ir. $16.95. Women in Literature Inc, PO Box 60550, Reno NV 89506. **Tel** (702)972-1671. **Ed** Elaine Dallman. **LC** PS589. **DD** 811.008. **Circ** 2,500. Regional anthologies study several featured poets through poems, criticism, interviews, biographies, photos. Poems, photos, biographical notes of 30-40 other key poets.

WOOD IBIS. 1- 1975-. 0275-6773. Periodical. US. English. ir. Place of Herons Press, 1002B East 13th Street, Austin TX 78702.

THE WORCESTER REVIEW. 8756-5277. Periodical. US. English. sa. $8.00. Worcester County Poetry Association, PO Box 2575, Worcester MA 01613. **DD** 811.

WORLD (ST. MARK'S CHURCH IN-THE-BOWERY (NEW YORK, N.Y.) POETRY PROJECT. (THE WORLD). No. 1 (1/67)-. 0043-8154. Periodical. US. English. ir. Poetry Project, St Mark's Church in the Bowery 2nd Avenue and 10th Streets, New York NY 10003.

WRITING (DAVID THOMPSON UNIVERSITY CENTRE. WRITING PROGRAM). (WRITING). No. 1 (Summer 1980)-. 0706-1889. Periodical. CN. English. ir. $12.38. Writing Magazine, Box 69609 Station K, Vancouver British Columbia V5K 4W7 Canada. **Tel** (604)732-1013. **Ed** Colin Browne. **DD** C810.80054. **Circ** 750. A literary magazine publishing the most exciting new writing in Canada and the United States. Read Writing for the latest in poetry, fiction, and drama.

XANADU. V. 1- Oct. 1975-. 0146-0463. Periodical. US. English. an. $5.00. Long Island Poetry Collective, PO Box 773, Huntington NY 11743. **Tel** (516)691-2376. **Ed** Anne-Ruth E Baehr, Mildred M Jeffrey, Barbara Lucas and Pat Fisher. adv acc. **Circ** 500. Poems that are well focused and finely crafted-work that grows out of keen immediate perceptions. We look for fresh, carefully chosen images.

YA-CHOU HSIEN TAI SHIH CHI. Vol. 1 (1982). Periodical. CH. Chinese (Japanese and Korean). an. 200.00. Shih Pao Wen Hua Chu Pan Shih Yeh Yu Hsien Kung Ssu, 132 Ta Li Chieh, Taipei Taiwan. **LC** PJ356. **DD** 895.

THE YALE SERIES OF YOUNGER POETS. Began with: Vol. 1 in 1919. 0084-3458. US. English. an. Yale University, 92A Yale Station, New Haven CT 06520. **Tel** (203)436-7584. **LC** UNC. **DD** 811.008.

THE YEARBOOK OF CONTEMPORARY POETRY. *See* Yearbooks, Almanacs, Directories.

YOUNG AMERICA SINGS... ANTHOLOGY OF PRIVATE SECONDARY SCHOOL POETRY. 1942-. US. English. ir. National High School Poetry Association, Box 218, Agoura CA 91301. **LC** PS591.S3. **DD** 811.50822.

YOUNG VOICES (WILLOWDALE, ONT.). (YOUNG VOICES). 0714-4431. CN. English. an. Free. North York Public Library, 5126 Yonge Street, Willowdale Ontario M2J 4S4 Canada. **DD** C811.540809282. (ctrl).

MANUFACTURING

33 METAL PRODUCING. *See* Metals & Metallurgy.

ABITIBI-PRICE. *See* Paper & Pulp Industry.

ABRASIVES MANUFACTURERS. Main/ Corp Statistics Canada. Manufacturing and Primary Industries Division. VFOAT Fabricants d'Abrasifs. 1970-. 0575-7851. CN. English (French). ir. Receiver General for Canada, Statistics Canada Publications, Ottawa Ontario K1A 0T6 Canada. *Abrasives Manufacturers, 0575-7851.*

ADVANCE REPORT ON DURABLE GOODS MANUFACTURERS' SHIPMENTS AND ORDERS. Periodical. US. English. mo. Bureau of the Census, Washington DC 20230.

ADVANCED MANUFACTURING TECHNOLOGY. Vol. 6, No. 1 (Jan. 14, 1985)-. 0885-5684. Periodical. US. English. sm. $317.00 Domestic, $365.00 Foreign. Technical Insights Inc, PO Box 1304, Fort Lee NJ 07024. **DD** 670. *Industrial Robots International, 0197-9280.*

AEROSOL. *See* Packaging.

AEROSOL AGE. *See* Packaging.

AEROSOL RELEASE AND TRANSPORT PROGRAM QUARTERLY PROGRESS REPORT. *See* Packaging.

AEROSOL-REPORT. *See* Packaging.

AEROSOL REVIEW. *See* Packaging.

AGMA DIRECTORY. *See* Yearbooks, Almanacs, Directories.

AIRCRAFT AND AIRCRAFT PARTS MANUFACTURERS. *See* Aeronautics, Astronautics.

ALABAMA DIRECTORY OF MINING AND MANUFACTURING. *See* Yearbooks, Almanacs, Directories.

ALBERTA MANUFACTURERS INDEX. *See* Indexes/Abstracts.

ALTES HANDWERK. Sammelband 4- (No. 31-). Monographic Series. GW. German. ir. Dr Rudolf Habelt GMBH, Am Buchenhang 1, 5300 Bonn 1 West Germany. *Sterbendes Handwerk.*

AMERICAN BLADE CEASED. (THE AMERICAN BLADE). 0097-8949. Periodical. US. English. bm. $10.00. Beinfeld Publishing, 12767 Saticoy Street, North Hollywood CA 91605. **LC** TS380. **DD** 621.93.

AMERICAN MACHINIST MANUFACTURING COST ESTIMATING GUIDE. 1982 Ed.-. 0731-5368. US. English. an. American Machinist, PO Box 416 Domestic AG, Hightstown NJ 08520. **LC** TS213. **DD** 671.

AMERICAN MACHINIST (NEW YORK, N.Y. : 1968). *See* Metals & Metallurgy.

AMERICAN SHOEMAKING. *See* Leather and Fur Industry.

AMERICAN SHOEMAKING DIRECTORY OF SHOE MANUFACTURERS. *See* Yearbooks, Almanacs, Directories.

AMERICAN TOOL, DIE & STAMPING NEWS. VAT American Tool, Die and Stamping News. 1973. 0192-5709. Periodical. US. English. bm. $50.00. American Tool Die and Stamping, 31505 Grand River Suite 1, Farmington MI 48024. **Tel** (313)474-8439. **Ed** Bonnie Paschke. bk rev. adv acc. **Circ** 22,000. Information on new products related to the tool and die and metal stamping industries.

ANNUAIRE DES CONCEPTEURS. *See* Yearbooks, Almanacs, Directories.

ANNUAL REPORT - AUSTRALIAN MANUFACTURING COUNCIL. Main/ Corp Australian Manufacturing Council. AT. English. an. Australian Government Publishing Service, PO Box 84, Canberra ACT 2600 Australia. **Tel** (062) 954-617.

ANNUAL REPORT - DENNISON MANUFACTURING COMPANY. Main/ Corp Dennison Manufacturing Company. 19 -. US. English. an. Free. Dennison Maufacturing Company, Farminghouse MA 01701. **LC** HD9829.D4.

ANNUAL REPORT - QUEENSLAND. DEPT. OF COMMERCIAL AND INDUSTRIAL DEVELOPMENT. Main/ Corp Queensland. Dept. of Commercial and Industrial Development. 1971/72-. English. ir. Free. The Director, Box 183, PO North Quay, 4000 Brisbane Australia. **Tel** (07)2242087. **LC** HC631. **DD** 354.9430082. **Circ** 6,000. (ctrl). The department is a government instrumentality and the report to Parliament contains the summary of industrial development in the state of Queensland during the previous year.

ANNUAL SURVEY OF MANUFACTURES. (ANNUAL SURVEY OF MANUFACTURES : ASM). Began with 1949-50. 0082-9307. US. English. be. US Department of Commerce, Bureau of Census, Washington DC 20233. **LC** HD9724. **DD** 338.4.

ANNUAL SURVEY OF MANUFACTURES. MANUFACTURERS' ALTERNATIVE ENERGY CAPABILITIES. VFOAT Manufacturers' Alternative Energy Capabilities. 1976-. US. English. an. 20233.

ANNUAL SURVEY OF MANUFACTURES. STATISTICS FOR STATES, STANDARD METROPOLITAN STATISTICAL AREAS, LARGE INDUSTRIAL COUNTIES, AND SELECTED CITIES. *See* Statistics.

ANNUAL SURVEY OF MANUFACTURES. VALUE OF MANUFACTURERS' INVENTORIES. VFOAT Value of Manufacturers' Inventories. US. English. an. Data User Services Division, Customer Services Publications, Bureau of the Census, Washington DC 20233.

APPAREL MANUFACTURER. Began publication in 1923. 0003-6692. Periodical. US. English. mo. **Ind/Abst** Predicasts. **LC** TT570. **DD** 687.05. *International Clothing Designer.*

Manufacturing

APPLIANCE MANUFACTURER. See Household Hardware & Appliances.

APPLIANCES, RADIO, AND TELEVISION MANUFACTURERS. VFOAT Fabricants d'Appareils Menagers, de Radios, et de Televiseurs. 1981-. 0319-8995. CN. English (French). an. $4.75 Canada, $5.70 Foreign. Publication Sales and Services, Statistics Canada, Ottawa Ontario K1A 0V7 Canada. LC HD9971.5.E543. DD 338.47683830971. *Manufacturers of Small Electrical Appliances, 0575-8939; Manufacturers of Major Appliances; Manufacturers of Household Radio and Television Receivers, 0527-5520.*

AQUA-FIELD SPORTSMAN. VFOAT Colt American Handgunning. 0742-910X. Periodical. US. English. qt. $2.50 Single Issue US, $2.95 Single Issue Canada. Aqua-Field Publications Inc, 656 Shrewsbury Avenue Suite 1, Shrewsbury NJ 07701. LC TS380. DD 621.93205.

ARCHIV FUR DAS EISENHUTTENWESEN. See Genealogy and Heraldry - Archives.

ASIAN MANUFACTURING. 0301-7117. Periodical. English. ir. $6.00. Far East Trade Press, 1908 Princes Building/des Voeux Road, Hong Kong China. LC TS191. DD 670.5.

ASIAN SOURCES. ELECTRONICS. See Engineering - Electricity, Electrical Engineering, Electronics.

ASPHALT ROOFING MANUFACTURERS. Main/Corp Statistics Canada. Manufacturing and Primary Industries Division. Series/Titl Annual Census of Manufactures. VFOAT Manufactures SIC de Papier-Toiture Asphalte. 1970-. 0384-2746. CN. English (French). ir. Receiver General for Canada, Statistics Canada Publications, Ottawa Ontario K1A 0T6 Canada.

ASSEMBLY ENGINEERING. See Engineering - Mechanical Engineering & Machinery.

AUSTRALIAN MACHINERY AND PRODUCTION ENGINEERING. See Engineering - Mechanical Engineering & Machinery.

AUTOMATION AND CONTROL. See Engineering - Electricity, Electrical Engineering, Electronics.

BACKLOG OF ORDERS FOR AEROSPACE COMPANIES. See Aeronautics, Astronautics.

BAR CODE MANUFACTURERS & SERVICES DIRECTORY. See Yearbooks, Almanacs, Directories.

BARRY FAIN'S PRIVATE BLUE BOOK OF GUN VALUES. VFOAT Blue Book of Gun Values. Vol. 1, No. 1-. 0273-2874. US. English. sa. Investment Rarities, 1 Appletree Square, Minneapolis MN 55420. LC TS532.4. DD 683.40075.

BEDRIJF EN TECHNIEK. 1- Yearly Volume. Periodical. NE. Dutch. sm. 135.-. Uitgeversmaatschappij C Misset BV/Postbus 3, 7000 BA, Doetinchem Netherlands. Tel N/08340-49502. Ed Wil Wynands. Ind/Abst Excerpta Med., CIS Abstr. bk rev. adv acc. Circ 4,500. New materials, high tech (CAD/CAM/Robotics) on a management level (implications etc) new processes production of discrete components.

BIRMINGHAM AREA INDUSTRIAL DIRECTORY. See Yearbooks, Almanacs, Directories.

BISCUIT MANUFACTURERS (FINAL). (BISCUIT MANUFACTURERS). Series/Titl Annual Census of Manufactures. VFOAT Fabricants de Biscuits, Manufacturiers de Biscuits. 1970-. 0527-4826. CN. text in English and French, English only, 1960-1966. an. Receiver General for Canada, Statistics Canada Publications, Ottawa Ontario K1A 0T6 Canada. DD 338.476647525. *Biscuit Industry, 0384-2789.*

THE BLACKPOWDER REPORT. VFOAT Black Powder Report. Vol. 11, No. 1 (Oct. 1983)-. 0746-3634. Periodical. US. English. mo. $15.00. The Buckskin Press Inc, Circulation Department, PO Box 789, Big Timber MT 59011. LC TS536.6.M8. DD 683.4. *Buckskin Report, 0145-4234; Black Powder Cartridge Rifles, 0273-6594.*

THE BLADE MAGAZINE. Vol. 9, No. 4 (June 1982)-. 0744-6179. Periodical. US. English. ir. $14.99. American Blade Inc, PO Box 22007, Chattanooga TN 37422. Tel (615)894-0339. Ed J Bruce Voyles. LC TS380. DD 621.932. bk rev. adv acc. Circ 16,000. The magazine of all aspects of the cuttery industry: sporting use, collecting, history, new products and innovations, legislation, knife making, art knives, official publication of the Knifemakers Guild. *American Blade, 0097-8949.*

BLUE BOOK. OFFICIAL LAWN MOWER TRADE-IN GUIDE. VFOAT Official Lawn Mower Trade-In Guide. US. English. ABOS Marine Publications, PO Box 12901, Overland Park KS 61212. LC HD9486.6.L373. DD 681.7631.

BNV DIJNYERTES TERMEKEI. Main/Corp Budapest. Vasar. VAT Budapesti Nemzetkozi Vasar Dijnyertes Termekei. Hungarian. ir. LC TS191.

BOILER AND PLATE WORKS CEASED. Main/Corp Statistics Canada. Manufacturing and Primary Industries Division. Series/Titl Annual Census of Manufactures. VFOAT Industrie des Chaudieres et des Plaques. 1970-1980. 0527-4842. CN. English (French). an. Receiver General for Canada, Statistics Canada Publications, Ottawa Ontario K1A 0T6 Canada. Tel (800)268-1511.

BOILER EXPLOSIONS ACTS, 1882 AND 1890, REPORT OF PRELIMINARY INQUIRY. (BOILER EXPLOSIONS ACTS, 1882 AND 1890). Main/Corp Great Britain. Board of Trade. UK. English. *Boiler Explosions Acts, 1882 and 1890.*

BRUSHWARE. 1898. 0007-2710. Periodical. US. English. bm. Centaur & Company, 5 Willowbrook Court, Potomac MD 20854. Tel (301)983-1152. Ed William D Magnes. DD 679. adv acc. Circ 2,000. A publication edited for key personnel in the brush, roller, broom, mop and applicator industry. A four language B's guide and manufacturing directory.

BUSINESS MONITOR. REPORT ON THE CENSUS OF PRODUCTION: WHEELED TRACTOR MANUFACTURING. See Business.

CALIFORNIA MANUFACTURERS REGISTER. 1968-. 0068-5739. US. English. an. Manufacturers News Inc, 4 East Huron Street, Chicago IL 60611. Tel (213)337-1084. Contains 16,000 manufacturers, 90,000 executives. Companies listed alphabetically by city and town, by product, geographically, numerically, by SIC key executives, SIC, number of employees, zip codes and telephone numbers. *California Manufacturers Annual Register, 0730-5818.*

CALZADO Y TENERIA. Periodical. MX. Spanish. mo. 2,500. Editorial Elizondo, Apartado Postal 7103, CP 06000 Mexico 1 DF Mexico. Tel 557-63-96. adv acc. Circ 3,500. (ctrl). Technical and literary articles on the shoe industry. Presentation of fashion trends in shoe-manufacturing materials as well as in completed shoes. Photographs and reports on events.

CANADIAN APPAREL MANUFACTURING. (THE CANADIAN APPAREL MANUFACTURER). V. 1- Dec. 1977-. 0705-3010. Periodical. CN. English. qt. Free. CTJ Inc, 1 Pacifique, Gardenvale Quebec H9X 1B0 Canada. Tel (514)457-2347. Ind/Abst World Text Abstr. DD 338.476870971. (ctrl).

CANADIAN CONTROLS AND INSTRUMENTATION. BUYERS' GUIDE. 1971-. CN. English. an. Southam Communications Limited, 1450 Don Mills Road, Don Mills Ontario M3B 2X7 Canada. Tel (416)445-6641. Ed Leslie M Burt. DD 629.802571. adv acc. Circ 40,000. (ctrl). Covers the latest in process control, industrial measurement, instrumentation and manufacturing automation in an editorial mix of articles and new product write-ups. *Control/Instrument Buyers' Guide.*

CANADIAN DESIGN CEASED. VFOAT Design Canadien. Began with issue for Jan. 1975. Ceased with issue for Jan. 1976?. Periodical. CN. English (text also in French). Ottawa Office of Design, Department of Industry, Ottawa Ontario K1A 0H5 Canada. LC TS171.A1. DD 745.20971. *Design Canada Newsletter = Design Canada Actualites.*

CANADIAN GAS ASSOCIATION. MANUFACTURERS' PRODUCT DIRECTORY. See Yearbooks, Almanacs, Directories.

CANADIAN REPRO-DRAFT MAGAZINE. VFOAT Repro-Draft. V. 1 or 2, (Dec./Jan.). 0824-7382. Periodical. CN. English. bm. $12.00. Canadian Repro-Draft Magazine, Unit 15/ 1121 Bellamy Road, Scarborough Ontario M1H 3B9 Canada. DD 681.605.

CANADIAN WELDER & FABRICATOR. See Metals & Metallurgy - Welding.

CAPACITY UTILIZATION, MANUFACTURING AND MATERIALS. Series/Titl Federal Reserve Statistical Release. Periodical. US. English. mo. Board of Governors of the Federal Reserve System, 20th Street & Constitution Avenue, Washington DC 20551. Ind/Abst Am. Stat. Index. *Capacity Utilization in Manufacturing, 0364-2860.*

CAPACITY UTILIZATION RATES IN CANADIAN MANUFACTURING. VFOAT Taux d'Utilisation de la Capacite dans les Industries Manufacturieres au Canada. Vol. 1, No. 1 (3rd Quarter 1976)-. 0700-1517. Periodical. CN. English (French). qt. Receiver General for Canada, Statistics Canada Publications, Ottawa Ontario K1A 0T6 Canada. LC HD9734.C2. DD 338.40971.

CARPET AND RUGS. (CURRENT INDUSTRIAL REPORTS. MQ-22Q. CARPET AND RUGS). 0364-1821. US. English. qt. $7.50. Data User Services Division, Customer Services Publication, Bureau of the Census, Washington DC 20233. Tel (301)763-4100. Ind/Abst Predicasts, Am. Stat. Index. LC HD9937.U5. DD 380.1456776430973. Presents timely data on the production, inventories, and orders of approximately 5,000 products, which represents 40 percent of all US manufacturing.

DIE CASTING ENGINEER. V. 1- Mar. 1957-. 0012-253X. Periodical. US. English. bm. Society of Die Casting Engineers, 2000 North 5th Avenue, River Grove IL 60171. Ind/Abst Eng. Index Mon., Eng. Index Bioeng. Abstr., Eng. Index Energy Abstr., Met. Abstr., World Alum. Abstr., Eng. Index Annu., Chem. Abstr. LC TS239. DD 671.25. CODEN DICEAB. Available on microfilm from University Microfilms.

CASTING ENGINEERING & FOUNDRY WORLD. VFOAT Casting Engineering and Foundry World. Began with issue for Sept. 1980. 0273-9607. Periodical. US. English. qt. $20.00. Casting Engineering, 1115 Main Street, Bridgeport CT 06604. Tel (203)377-5566. Ed W H Moore. Ind/Abst Eng. Index Annu., Eng. Index Mon., Eng. Index Bioeng. Abstr., Eng. Index Energy Abstr., Chem. Abstr., Met. Abstr., World Alum. Abstr. LC TS200. DD 671.205. CODEN CEFWDA. adv acc. Circ 70,000. (ctrl). Edited for the user and producer of metal castings. *Casting Engineering, 0008-7513; Foundry World, 0191-1767.*

DIE CASTING MANAGEMENT. Vol. 1, No. 1 (Jan./Feb. 1983)-. 0745-449X. Periodical. US. English. bm. $25.00. American Die Casting Institute, 2340 des Plaunes Avenue, Des Plaines IL 60018. Tel (312)298-1220. Ed John J Kolar. LC TS239. DD 671.253. adv acc. Circ 3,000. (ctrl). Edited for management decision makers in the diecasting industry and to contribute to the profitable management of the diecasting business.

CATV DIRECTORY OF EQUIPMENT, SERVICES, & MANUFACTURERS. See Yearbooks, Almanacs, Directories.

CEMENT INDUSTRIES. VFOAT Fabrication de Ciment. 1981-. 0319-9029. CN. English (French). an. $6.35 Domestic, $7.60 Foreign. Publication Sales and Services, Statistics Canada, Ottawa Ontario K1A 0V7 Canada. LC HD9622.C2. DD 338.47666890971. *Cement Manufacturers, 0384-2916.*

CENSO DE INDUSTRIAS MANUFACTURERAS DE PUERTO RICO. VFOAT Census of Manufacturing Industries of Puerto Rico. Began in 1946. PR. Spanish (English). ir. LC HD5744.

CENSUS OF MAINE MANUFACTURES. See Economics - Economics: Industry & Production.

CENSUS OF MANUFACTURING ESTABLISHMENTS. DETAILS OF OPERATIONS AND SMALL AREA STATISTICS, TASMANIA. See Statistics.

CENSUS OF MANUFACTURING SERIES B. CANTERBURY, OTAGO, SOUTHLAND STATISTICAL AREAS. See Statistics.

CENSUS OF MANUFACTURING SERIES B. GENERAL REGIONAL STATISTICS SUMMARY. VFOAT General Regional Statistics Summary. US. English. Department of Statistics, Private Bag, Wellington New Zealand. LC HD9738.N46. DD 338.470009931.

Manufacturing

CHATTANOOGA AND TRI-STATE AREA DIRECTORY OF MANUFACTURERS. See Yearbooks, Almanacs, Directories.

CHICAGO, COOK COUNTY, AND ILLINOIS INDUSTRIAL DIRECTORY. See Yearbooks, Almanacs, Directories.

CHICAGO GEOGRAPHIC EDITION OF THE ILLINOIS MANUFACTURERS DIRECTORY. See Yearbooks, Almanacs, Directories.

CHICAGO GEOGRAPHIC ZIP-CODED EDITION OF THE ILLINOIS MANUFACTURERS DIRECTORY. See Yearbooks, Almanacs, Directories.

CHONGUK CHUNGSO KWANGGONGOP TONGGYE CHOSA POGOSO. See Engineering - Mining Engineering.

CHUKEN HOKOKU. Main/Corp Waseda Daigaku, Tokyo. Imono Kenkyujo. VFOAT Transactions of the Castings Research Laboratory, Waseda University. VAT Waseda Daigaku Imono Kenkyujo Hokoku. No. 1-. Japanese (with synopses in English). ir. 8-26 Nishi Waseda 2, Shinjuku-Ku, Tokyo 160 Japan. Ind/Abst Chem. Abstr. LC TS236. CODEN CHHODH.

CHUNG-KUO CHIH LIANG KUAN LI. VFOAT China Quality Control. Began with Feb. 15, 1981 issue. Periodical. CH. Chinese. mo. 0.35. Pei-Ching Pao Kan Fa Hsing Chu, Peking Ching. LC TS156.A1. DD 620.004505.

CIEN. CANADIAN INDUSTRIAL EQUIPMENT NEWS. (C I E N, CANADIAN INDUSTRIAL EQUIPMENT NEWS). VFOAT Canadian Industrial Equipment News. Began publication in 1940. 0319-5902. Periodical. CN. English. mo. $62.00. Southam Communications Ltd, 1450 Don Mills Road, Don Mills Ontario M3B 1Z2 Canada. Tel (416)445-6641. Ed Olga Markovitch. adv acc. Circ 35,000. (ctrl). Provides up-to-date information on new and improved industrial products and technical literature. 0319-5910.

CIM (ELK GROVE VILLAGE, ILL.). See Computers and Computer Science.

CIM STRATEGIES. VFOAT C.I.M. Strategies. Vol. 1, No. 1 (Aug. 1984)-. 0748-9250. Periodical. US. English. sm. $187.00. Cahners Publishing Co, PO Box 716, Back Bay Annex, Boston MA 02117. DD 670.

CIMENTS, BETONS, PLATRES, CHAUX. See Building and Construction.

CIRCUITS MANUFACTURING. V. 4, No. 6- Nov./Dec. 1964-. 0009-7306. Periodical. US. English. mo. $50.00. Morgan Grampian Publishing, Berkshire Common, Pittsfield MA 01201. Tel (413)499-2550. Ind/Abst Excerpta Med., Comput. Control Abstr., Electr. Electron. Abstr., Sci. Abstr. Sect. A. Phys. Abstr., Met. Abstr., World Alum. Abstr., Phys. Abstr. CODEN CMFGAF. Electronic Production.

CLASSIFIED DIRECTORY OF WISCONSIN MANUFACTURERS. See Yearbooks, Almanacs, Directories.

COAL MINES - (STATISTICS CANADA). Main/Corp Statistics Canada. Manufacturing and Primary Industries Division. VFOAT Mines de Charbon. CN. Multilingual. an. 20.00 Domestic, 21.00 Foreign. Receiver General for Canada, Statistics Canada Publications, Ottawa Ontario K1A 0T6 Canada. Tel (800)268-1151. Presents statistics on the number of mines or plants, average number of employees, salaries and wages, cost of fuel and electricity, cost of materials and gross selling value of products, with comparative totals for earlier years for Canada and breakdown by province.

COLLECTIVE AGREEMENT SURVEY IN THE MANUFACTURING INDUSTRY. See Economics - Labor.

COMMUNICATIONS EQUIPMENT MANUFACTURERS. (COMMUNICATIONS EQUIPMENT MANUFACTURERS). Main/Corp Statistics Canada. Manufacturing and Primary Industries Division. VFOAT Fabricants d'Equipement de Telecommunication. VAT Manufacturiers de Materiel de Telecommunication. 1970-. 0527-494X. CN. English (French). an. $0.50. Statistics Canada, Publication Distribution, Ottawa Ontario K1A 0T6 Canada. LC HD9696.A3. DD 338.4762138. Communications Equipment Manufacturers, 0527-494X.

COMPUTERIZED MANUFACTURING. See Computers and Computer Science.

COMPUTERS IN MANUFACTURING. DISTRIBUTION MANAGEMENT. See Computers and Computer Science.

COMPUTERS IN MANUFACTURING. EXECUTION AND CONTROL SYSTEMS. See Computers and Computer Science.

COMPUTERS IN MANUFACTURING. MANUFACTURING RESOURCE PLANNING. See Computers and Computer Science.

COMPUTERS IN MANUFACTURING. MASTER PRODUCTION SCHEDULING. See Computers and Computer Science.

COMPUTERS IN MANUFACTURING. MATERIAL REQUIREMENTS PLANNING. See Computers and Computer Science.

CONCRETE PRODUCTS MANUFACTURERS. See Building and Construction.

CONCRETE PRODUCTS MANUFACTURERS. Main/Corp Statistics Canada. Manufacturing and Primary Industries Division. VFOAT Fabricants de Produits en Beton. VAT Fabricants de Produits en Beton (Ed. Provisorie). Began with issue for 1971?. 0708-6199. CN. English (text in French). an. Tel (800)268-1151.

CONFECTIONERY PRODUCTION. See Food & Drink.

CONNECTICUT MANUFACTURING DIRECTORY. See Yearbooks, Almanacs, Directories.

CONNECTICUT, RHODE ISLAND DIRECTORY OF MANUFACTURERS. See Yearbooks, Almanacs, Directories.

CONSUMPTION OF CONTAINERS AND OTHER PACKAGING SUPPLIES BY THE MANUFACTURING INDUSTRIES. See Packaging.

CONTRACT. V. 1- Nov. 1960-. 0010-7832. Periodical. US. English. mo. Contract, 1515 Broadway, New York NY 10036. Ed Len Corlin. Ind/Abst Hospit. Lit. Index. LC TS840.

COTTON FIBER AND PROCESSING TEST RESULTS. 0566-5469. US. English. ir. Agricultural Marketing Service, US Department of Commerce, Test Cotton Division, PO Box 67, Clemson SC 29631. Ind/Abst Am. Stat. Index. LC TS1542. DD 677.21305. Cotton Fiber and Processing Results.

CURRENT INDUSTRIAL REPORTS. M22D, CONSUMPTION ON THE WOOLEN SYSTEM AND WORSTED COMBING. VFOAT Consumption on the Woolen System and Worsted Combing. Publication began with Feb. 1978. US. English. an. $16.00. Data User Services Division, Customer Services Publication, Bureau of the Census, Washington DC 20233. Tel (301)763-4100. Ind/Abst Am. Stat. Index, Predicasts. Presents timely data on the production, inventories, and orders of approximately 5,000 products, which represents 40 percent of all US manufacturing. Current Industrial Reports. M22D, Consumption on the Woolen and Worsted Systems, 0364-1791.

CURRENT INDUSTRIAL REPORTS. MA-23F, WOMEN'S AND CHILDRENS' OUTERWEAR. VFOAT Women's and Childrens' Outerwear. 1981-. US. English. an. $1.50. Data User Services Division, Customer Services Publication, Bureau of the Census, Washington DC 20233. Tel (301)763-4100. LC HD9940.U3. DD 338.476871420973. Presents timely data on the production, inventories, and orders of approximately 5,000 products, which represents 40 percent of all US manufacturing. Current Industrial Reports. Series MA-23F, Women's and Childrens' Outerwear.

CURRENT INDUSTRIAL REPORTS. MA31A, FOOTWEAR. VFOAT Footwear. Began with 1977. US. English. an. $16.00. Data User Services Division, Customer Services Publication, Bureau of the Census, Washington DC 20233. Tel (301)763-4100. LC HD9787.U4. DD 338.476853F0973. Presents timely data on the production, inventories, and orders of approximately 5,000 products, which represents 40 percent of all US manufacturing.

CURRENT INDUSTRIAL REPORTS. SERIES MA-23G, UNDERWEAR AND NIGHTWEAR. VFOAT Underwear and Nightwear. 1980-. US. English. an. $1.25. Data User Services Division Customer Services Publication, Bureau of the Census, Washington DC 20233. Tel (301)763-4100. Presents timely data on the production, inventories, and orders of approximately 5,000 products, which represents 40 percent of all US manufacturing. Current Industrial Reports. Series MA-23A, Apparel.

DCAS MANUFACTURING COST CONTROL DIGEST. Main/Corp United States. Defense Contract Administration Services. VFOAT Manufacturing Cost Control Digest. VAT Defense Contract Administration Services Manufacturing Cost Control Digest. V. 1- 1975-. 0099-1961. US. English. an. Defense Supply Agency, Defense Contract Administration Services, Cameron Street, Alexandria VA 22314. LC TS165. DD 658.1552.

DESIGNERS' CHOICE. 26Th ('80)-. 0277-6685. Periodical. US. English. an. $7.95. Design Publications Inc, 717 5th Avenue Room 1201, New York NY 10022. LC TS23. DD 745.20973. Design Review, 0147-4944.

DEVELOPMENTS IN AUSTRALIAN MANUFACTURING INDUSTRY. Series Corp Australia. Department of Trade. Investment Series. 1955/56?-. 0404-164X. Periodical. AT. English. ir. Australia Manufacturing Division, Department of Trade and Industry, Melbourne Victoria 3000 Australia. LC HD9738.A8. DD 338.4. Developments in Australian Manufacturing Industry.

DEVICES & DIAGNOSTICS LETTER. VAT Devices and Diagnostics Letter. V. 1- Nov. 15, 1974-. 0098-7573. Periodical. US. English. wk. $417.00. Washington Business Information Inc, 1117 North 19 19th Street/Suite 200, Arlington VA 22209. Tel (703)247-3424. Ed Maria Rudensky. NLM W1 DE9992. For executives concerned with government regulation of medical devices and in vitro diagnostic products.

DIRECTORY, KOREA ELECTRONICS MANUFACTURERS. See Yearbooks, Almanacs, Directories.

DIRECTORY, MARYLAND MANUFACTURERS. See Yearbooks, Almanacs, Directories.

DIRECTORY, MARYLAND MANUFACTURERS. See Yearbooks, Almanacs, Directories.

DIRECTORY OF ARKANSAS MANUFACTURERS. See Yearbooks, Almanacs, Directories.

DIRECTORY OF CENTRAL ATLANTIC STATES MANUFACTURERS. See Yearbooks, Almanacs, Directories.

DIRECTORY OF COLORADO MANUFACTURERS. See Yearbooks, Almanacs, Directories.

DIRECTORY OF DISTRIBUTORS. See Yearbooks, Almanacs, Directories.

DIRECTORY OF FLORIDA INDUSTRIES. See Yearbooks, Almanacs, Directories.

DIRECTORY OF IOWA MANUFACTURERS. See Yearbooks, Almanacs, Directories.

DIRECTORY OF LOUISIANA MANUFACTURERS. See Yearbooks, Almanacs, Directories.

DIRECTORY OF MANUFACTURERS AND PROCESSORS. See Yearbooks, Almanacs, Directories.

DIRECTORY OF MANUFACTURERS, STATE OF HAWAII. See Yearbooks, Almanacs, Directories.

DIRECTORY OF MANUFACTURING INDUSTRIES OF ROCHESTER AND MONROE COUNTY, NEW YORK : INFORMATION AS SUPPLIED BY THE FIRMS LISTED, OR COMPILED FROM AVAILABLE SOURCES. See Yearbooks, Almanacs, Directories.

Manufacturing

DIRECTORY OF MONTANA MANUFACTURERS. See Yearbooks, Almanacs, Directories.

DIRECTORY OF NEBRASKA MANUFACTURERS AND THEIR PRODUCTS. See Yearbooks, Almanacs, Directories.

DIRECTORY OF NEW MEXICO MANUFACTURING & MINING. See Yearbooks, Almanacs, Directories.

DIRECTORY OF NORTH CAROLINA MANUFACTURING FIRMS. See Yearbooks, Almanacs, Directories.

DIRECTORY OF NORTH DAKOTA MANUFACTURERS. See Yearbooks, Almanacs, Directories.

DIRECTORY OF TENNESSEE MANUFACTURERS. See Yearbooks, Almanacs, Directories.

DIRECTORY OF TEXAS MANUFACTURERS. See Yearbooks, Almanacs, Directories.

DIXIE GUN WORKS BLACKPOWDER ANNUAL. VFOAT Blackpowder Annual. 0737-0105. Periodical. US. English. an. $2.50 Domestic, $2.95 Canada. Pioneer Press, PO Box 684 Gunpowder Lane, Union City TN 38261. **LC** TS536.6.M8. **DD** 683.4005.

DIY RETAILING. VFOAT D.I.Y. Retailing. VAT Do It Yourself Retailing. Vol. 147, No. 3 (Sept. 1984)-. 8750-2569. Periodical. US. English. mo. $4.00 Domestic $4.50 Foreign. National Retail Hardware Association, 770 North Highschool Road, Indianapolis IN 46224. **Ind/Abst** Trade Ind. Index. **LC** TS200. **DD** 338.476830973. Hardware Retailing, 0164-7695.

DODGE BUILDING COST AND SPECIFICATION DIGEST. US. English. sa. $176.50. McGraw Hill/FW Dodge Division, PO Box 28, Princeton NJ 08540. **Tel** (212)512-2000.

ECONOMIC CENSUSES : MANUFACTURING ESTABLISHMENTS CEASED. Main/Corp Australian Bureau of Statistics. Tasmanian Office. Series/Titl Statistics of Tasmania. 1972/73-. AT. English. ir. Australian Bureau of Statistics, Canberra 2600 Australia. **LC** HD9738.A83. **DD** 338.476709946. Economic Censuses: Manufacturing Establishments.

EDM DIGEST. See Engineering - Mechanical Engineering & Machinery.

EIC. ELECTRONIQUE, INDUSTRIELLE & COMMERCIALE. See Engineering - Electricity, Electrical Engineering, Electronics.

ELECTRIC LAMP AND SHADE MANUFACTURERS. See Engineering - Electricity, Electrical Engineering, Electronics.

ELECTRONIC INDUSTRY MANUFACTURERS REPRESENTATIVES LOCATOR. VFOAT Locator. 1981/82-. 0735-3316. US. English. an. Electronic Representatives Association, 20 East Huron Street, Chicago IL 60611. Electronics Industry Directory of Manufacturers Representatives.

ELECTRONICS KOREA. See Engineering.

ENERGY FOR INDUSTRY AND COMMERCE. See Energy.

ENTERPRISE. V. 1- Feb. 1977-. 0191-5215. Periodical. US. English. ir. $16.50. National Association of Manufacturers, 1776 F Street Northwest, Washington DC 20006. **Tel** (202)637-3091. Ed Richard W Flanagan. **Ind/Abst** Public Aff. Inf. Serv. Bull., Energy Inf. Abstr., Environ. Abstr. **LC** HC101. **DD** 330.973092. **Circ** 40,000. (ctrl) Articles deal with issues of public policy of interest to manufacturers. NAM Reports, 0027-5921.

EUROCLAY. July/Aug. 1973-. 0306-1841. UK. English. bm. 32.00. London & Sheffield Publishing Co Ltd, 5 Pond Street, London NW3 2PN England. **Tel** (01)794-0800. Ed Barry Lohan. **Ind/Abst** Coal Abstr. **LC** TP785. **DD** 666. bk rev. adv acc. **Circ** 2,800. Journal for management in heavy clay products production, makers of brick, tile, pipe and other industrial ceramics. Claycraft.

FDM, FURNITURE DESIGN & MANUFACTURING. See Interior Design - Home Furnishings.

FEDERAL SUPPLY CODE FOR MANUFACTURERS, UNITED STATES AND CANADA. NAME TO CODE AND CODE TO NAME. Series/Titl GSA-FSS H. Publication began with Dec. 1978. Periodical. US. English. bm. US Government Printing Office, Superintendent of Documents, Washington DC 20402. Federal Supply Code for Manufacturers, United States and Canada. Name to Code, 0145-0557.

FINISHED BROADWOVEN FABRIC PRODUCTION. (CURRENT INDUSTRIAL REPORTS. MA-22S, FINISHED BROADWOVEN FABRIC PRODUCTION). Began in 1976. 0276-3389. US. English. an. $1.25. Data User Services Division, Customer Services Publication, Bureau of the Census, Washington DC 20233. **Tel** (301)763-4100. **LC** HD9851. **DD** 338.4767700973. Presents timely data on the production, inventories, and orders of approximately 5,000 products, which represents 40 percent of all US manufacturing. Broadwoven Fabrics Finished.

FINISHED FABRICS. PRODUCTION, INVENTORIES, AND UNFILLED ORDERS. (CURRENT INDUSTRIAL REPORTS. M22A, FINISHED FABRICS, PRODUCTION, INVENTORIES, AND UNFILLED ORDERS). VFOAT Finished Fabrics, Production, Inventories, and Unfilled Orders. Jan. 1980-. 0272-5509. US. English. mo. $15.00. Data User Services Division, Customer Services Publication, Bureau of the Census, Washington DC 20233. **Tel** (301)763-4100. **Ind/Abst** Am. Stat. Index, Predicasts. **LC** HD9851. **DD** 338.4767700973. Presents timely data on the production, inventories, and orders of approximately 5,000 products, which represents 40 percent of all US manufacturers. Woven Fabrics, Production, Inventories, and Unfilled Orders, 0145-5028.

FINISHING INDUSTRIES CEASED. V. 1-6, No. 5. 0309-3018. Periodical. UK. English. mo. 16.00. UK Publishers, PO Box 36420, Fort Logan Denver CO 80236. **Ind/Abst** Electron. Commun. Abstr. J., ISMEC Bull., Pollut. Abstr. Indexes, Saf. Sci. Abstr. J., Eng. Index Annu., Eng. Index Mon., Eng. Index Energy Abstr., Predicasts, Excerpta Med., Chem. Abstr. **LC** TS670.A1. **DD** 671.705. **CODEN** FIINDP. Electroplating and Metal Finishing, 0013-5305; Industrial Finishing and Surface Coatings, 0039-6001.

FINOMMECHANIKA, MIKROTECHNIKA. (FINOMMECHANIKA-MIKROTECHNIKA). 12. Vol. - 1973-. 0231-2662. Periodical. HU. Hungarian. ir. 72.00. Lapkiado Vallalat, Lenin Korut 9-11, 1073 Budapest VII Hungary. **Ind/Abst** Excerpta Med., Int. Aerosp. Abstr., Comput. Control Abstr., Electr. Electron. Abstr., Sci. Abstr. Sect. A. Phys. Abstr. **LC** TS176. **CODEN** FNMKAY. Finommechanika.

FLEXIBLE AUTOMATION. Vol. 1, No. 1 (June 21, 1982). 0732-7471. US. English. mo. $162.00 US/Canada, $174.00 Others. Flexible Automation, PO Box 1175, Hohokus NJ 07423. **Tel** (201)562-4464. Ed Dora Merris. bk rev. Newsletter that covers programmable production and assembly equipment and the hardware and software that ties them together into computer integrated manufacturing systems.

FLORIDA MANUFACTURERS REGISTER. 0882-9438. US. English. an. Manufacturers' News Inc, 4 East Huron Street, Chicago IL 60611-2793. **Tel** (312)337-1084. Ed Louise West. adv acc. Up to 30 facts available about Florida manufacturers.

FMA'S JOURNAL OF THE FABRICATOR. Main/Corp Fabrication Manufacturers Association (U.S.). VFOAT Journal of the Fabricator. VAT Fabrication Manufacturers Association's Journal of the Fabricator. 1971. 0192-8066. Periodical. US. English. mo. Fabricator Manufacturing Association, 7811 North Alpine, Rockford IL 61111. **Tel** (815)654-1902. Ed John Nandzik. **Ind/Abst** Met. Abstr., World Alum. Abstr. adv acc. **Circ** 51,000. (ctrl). Serves the metal fabrication field, including coil, sheet metal, tube, pipe, plate and structural shapes.

FOLDING CARTON AND SET-UP BOX MANUFACTURERS CEASED. VFOAT Fabricants de Cartons Pliants et de Boites Montees. Began with issue for 1970. 0384-4668. CN. English (French). an. Receiver General for Canada, Statistics Canada Publications, Ottawa Ontario K1A 0T5 Canada.

FOLDING CARTON AND SET-UP BOX MANUFACTURERS (FINAL). See Packaging.

FONDERIE CEASED. V. 1- Jan. 1946-. 0015-6094. Periodical. FR. French. mo. **Ind/Abst** Excerpta Med., CIS Abstr. **LC** TS200. Bulletin d'Information de l'Association Technique de Fonderie et du Centre Technique des Industries de la Fonderie.

FONDERIE BELGE. (LA FONDERIE BELGE). 1911. 0015-6108. Periodical. BE. French (Dutch). qt. A T F B, Grote Steenweg Noord 12, B-9710 Zwijnaarde Belgium. Ed Vari Eeghem. **Ind/Abst** Eng. Index Annu., Eng. Index Mon., Eng. Index Bioeng. Abstr., Eng. Index Energy Abstr., CIS Abstr., Met. Abstr., World Alum. Abstr., Chem. Abstr. **LC** TS200. **CODEN** FNDRAA. bk rev. adv acc. **Circ** 1. (ctrl). Foundry research.

FORGING TOPICS. V. 24- 1965-. 0099-233X. US. English. qt. Forging Industry Association, 55 Public Square, Cleveland OH 44113. **LC** TS225. **DD** 671.33. Drop Forging Topics.

FORM (COLOGNE, GERMANY). (FORM). Vol. 1-. 0015-7678. Periodical. German. qt. 71.00. Verlag Form GMBH, Ernsthoferstrasse 12, D6104 Seeheim-Jugenheim. **Tel** 06257-81395. Ed Karlheinz Krug. **LC** TS149. bk rev. adv acc. **Circ** 7,000. (ctrl).

FOUNDRY CATALOG FILE. 0533-005X. US. English. be. $30.00. Penton Publishing Company, Penton Plaza, Cleveland OH 44114.

FRUIT AND VEGETABLE PROCESSING INDUSTRIES. See Food & Drink.

FUNK AND SCOTT INDEX OF CORPORATIONS AND INDUSTRIES. See Indexes/Abstracts.

FURNITURE DESIGN & MANUFACTURING. See Interior Design - Home Furnishings.

FURNITURE MANUFACTURER. See Interior Design - Home Furnishings.

FURNITURE MANUFACTURING MANAGEMENT. See Interior Design - Home Furnishings.

FURNITURE PRODUCTION. See Interior Design - Home Furnishings.

GEORGE D. HALL'S DIRECTORY OF CONNECTICUT MANUFACTURERS. See Yearbooks, Almanacs, Directories.

GEORGE D. HALL'S DIRECTORY OF MASSACHUSETTS MANUFACTURERS. See Yearbooks, Almanacs, Directories.

GEORGE D. HALL'S NEW JERSEY MANUFACTURERS DIRECTORY. See Yearbooks, Almanacs, Directories.

GEORGIA MANUFACTURING DIRECTORY. See Yearbooks, Almanacs, Directories.

GIJUTSU RENKAN CHOSA KENKYU HOKOKUSHO. Main/Corp Chusho Kigyo Shinko Jigyodan. 1974-. Japanese. ir. Chusho Kigyo Shinko Jigyodan, c/o Sankaido Building, 9-13 Akasaka 1-Chome Minato-Ku (107), Tokyo Japan. **LC** TS200.

GLASS AND GLASS PRODUCTS MANUFACTURERS. See Glass and Ceramics.

THE GMP LETTER. VAT Good Manufacturing Practices Letter. 1 (Feb. 1980)-. 0196-626X. Periodical. US. English. mo. $197.00. Washington Business Info Inc, 1117 North 19th Street/Suite 200, Arlington VA 22209. **Tel** (703)247-3400. Ed Sam Gilston. **DD** 344. Helps firms cope as federal regulations move into enforcement and actual practice. It also provides detailed and technical help in complying with these crucial rules.

GMP REPORT. VAT Good Manufacturing Practice Report. April/May 1979-. 0194-7788. Periodical. US. English. qt. GMP Institute, 3823 Pacific Avenue, Cincinnati OH 45212. **Tel** (513)631-3600.

GREAT SOUTHERN MANUFACTURERS DIRECTORY. See Yearbooks, Almanacs, Directories.

GREEN BOOK. See Beauty & Cosmetics.

GUIDE BOOK OF JAPANESE OPTICAL AND PRECISION INSTRUMENTS. VFOAT Japanese Optical and Precision Instruments. JA. English. ir. Japan Optical and Precision Instruments Manif's Association, 1-5

Manufacturing

Shiba Koen Minato-ku, Tokyo (105) Japan. LC TS516. DD 338.47681402552.

GUIDE DES ACHETEURS : HORLOGERIE, BIJOUTERIE ET BRANCHES ANNEXES. See Jewelry - Clocks and Watches.

HAN CHIEH HSUEH PAO. VFOAT Hanjie Xuebao. 0253-360X. Periodical. CC. Chinese. qt. $7.74. China Publication Centre, PO Box 2820, Beijing China. Ind/Abst Met. Abstr., World Alum. Abstr., Chem. Abstr. LC TS227.A1. DD 671.5205. CODEN HHPAD2.

HARDBOARD. Main/Corp Statistics Canada. Manufacturing and Primary Industries Division. VFOAT Panneaux Presses. V. 20- Jan. 1972-. 0318-790X. Periodical. CN. text in English and French. mo. Receiver General for Canada, Statistics Canada, Ottawa Ontario K1A 0T6 Canada. Hardboard.

HARRIS INDIANA INDUSTRIAL DIRECTORY. See Yearbooks, Almanacs, Directories.

HARRIS MICHIGAN INDUSTRIAL DIRECTORY (TWINSBURG, OHIO : 1984). See Yearbooks, Almanacs, Directories.

HARRIS MICHIGAN MARKETERS INDUSTRIAL DIRECTORY. See Yearbooks, Almanacs, Directories.

HARRIS PENNSYLVANIA INDUSTRIAL DIRECTORY. See Yearbooks, Almanacs, Directories.

HBG-MITTEILUNGEN. Main/Corp Holz-Berfusgenossenschaft. VFOAT Ihre Holz-Berufsgenossenschaft Informiert. VAT H. German. ir. Holz-Berufgenossenschaft, Am Knie 6, 8000 Munchen 60 West Germany. LC TS810.G3.

HINSHITSU. VFOAT Quality, J.S.Q.C. JA. Japanese. ir. Nihon Hinshitsu Kanri Gakkai, c/o Nihon Kagaku Gijutsu Renmei 10-11, Sendagaya 5 Shibuya-ku, Tokyo-to Japan. LC TS156.A1.

I.B.C.A.M. See Transportation - Automobiles.

IDENTIFICATION JOURNAL. Began in 1984. 0747-962X. Periodical. US. English. bm. $18.00. Marking Devices Publishing Company, 2640 North Halsted Street, Chicago IL 60614. Tel (312)528-6600. Ed David Hachmeister. DD 658. adv acc. Circ 23,000. (ctrl). This magazine deals with variable identification in a manufacturing setting including plant prooduct, and personnel identification system.

IEE PRODUCTRONIC. See Engineering - Electricity, Electrical Engineering, Electronics.

ILLINOIS MANUFACTURERS DIRECTORY. See Yearbooks, Almanacs, Directories.

ILLINOIS SERVICES DIRECTORY. See Yearbooks, Almanacs, Directories.

IMP. INDUSTRIAL MODELS & PATTERNS. (IMP, INDUSTRIAL MODELS & PATTERNS). VFOAT Industrial Models & Patterns. VAT Industrial Models and Patterns. 0146-0161. Periodical. US. English. bm. $15.00. National Association of Pattern Manufacturers, 21010 Center Ridge Road, Cleveland OH 44116. Tel (216)333-7417. Ed Ben J Imburgia. adv acc. Circ 1,200. (ctrl). Manufacturers of models, molds, patterns and plastic tooling for industry.

THE INDIAN FACTORIES JOURNAL. Vol. 1- 1949/50-. 0019-476X. Periodical. II. English. mo. Laws of India Private Ltd, Thyagarayanagar, Madras 17 India.

THE INDIANA INDUSTRIAL DIRECTORY. See Yearbooks, Almanacs, Directories.

INDIANA MANUFACTURERS DIRECTORY. See Yearbooks, Almanacs, Directories.

INDUSTRIAL DEVELOPMENT IN THE T.V.A. AREA. See Economics.

INDUSTRIAL DEVELOPMENT TENNESSEE VALLEY REGION. See Economics.

INDUSTRIAL LUBRICATION AND TRIBOLOGY. 0036-8792. Periodical. UK. English. bm $33.00. Peterson Publishing Company Ltd, High House/Vigo, Bromsgrove Worcs England. Tel 0905 77556. Ed Bernal Osborne. Ind/Abst Eng. Index Annu., Eng. Index Mon., Eng. Index Bioeng. Abstr., Eng. Index Energy Abstr., Fluidex, Ship Abstr. LC TJ1075.A2. DD 621.8905. CODEN ILTRA7. bk rev. adv acc. Circ 4,250. Covers the design manufacture operation and maintenance of plant and equipment, requiring efficient lubrication and protection against wear. Industrial Lubrication.

INDUSTRIAL MAINTENANCE AND PLANT OPERATION. VFOAT Impo Plant Operations. Began in 1953. 0192-8201. Periodical. US. English. mo. $36.00. Chilton Company, Chilton Way, Radnor PA 19089. Tel (215)964-4041. Ed Jerry Steinbrink. DD 658. adv acc. Circ 120,000. (ctrl). The leading product news tabloid serving the lucrative $368 billion plant engineering/MRO market. Industrial Maintenance.

INDUSTRIAL PROCESS RESEARCH AND DEVELOPMENT DIVISIONAL ANNUAL REPORT. Main/Corp New Zealand. Industrial Processing Division. English. an. LC T55.778. DD 670.9931.

INDUSTRIAL PRODUCT BULLETIN. VFOAT IPB. 0199-2074. Periodical. US. English. ir. $36.00. Gordon Publications, 13 Emery Avenue/Box 1952, Randolph NJ 07801-0952. Tel (201)361-9060. Ed Anita La Fond. adv acc. Circ 200,000. (ctrl). New product tabloid magazine devoted to the manufacturing related areas, including product design, production, maintenance, purchasing and management. Industrial Bulletin.

INDUSTRIAL PRODUCT IDEAS. 0820-6759. Periodical. CN. English. ir. Free to Canadian Manufacturers $12.00 Per Year Canada, $20.00 Per Year Others. Subscription Department, MacLean Hunter Business Publishing Company, PO Box 9100 Station A, Toronto Ontario M5W 1V5 Canada. DD 670.420294. Ideas in Canada's Manufacturing & Metalworking Industries, 0316-6813.

INDUSTRIAL PRODUCTS MASTER CATALOG. VFOAT IPMC. 0730-2630. US. English. an. Free to Qualified Recipients in the US, $10.00 Per Copy Others, US. United Technical Publications, 645 Stewart Avenue, Garden City NY 11530. LC TS191.6. DD 670.29473.

INDUSTRIE-FLASH. V. 11, No. 11-. Periodical. German. ir. LC TS1. Flash.

INDUSTRY. V. 1- 1918-. 0019-9435. Periodical. US. English. mo. $15.00. Associated Industries of Massachusetts, 462 Boylston Street/Box 763, Boston MA 02116. Tel (617)262-1180. Ed Angelo Alabiso. LC HC107.M4. adv acc. Circ 5,300. Non-technical monthly publication carries articles on all types of manufacturing firms, products, and operations in Massachusetts; material of interest to top industrial executives in the state.

INDUSTRY WAGE SURVEY. CIGARETTE MANUFACTURING. See Economics - Labor.

INSTRUMENTALNYE I PODSHIPNIKOVYE STALI. No. 1- 1973-. UR. Russian. 0.64 Single Issue. Metallurgiia, G-34 2-I Obydenskii Per 14, Moskva 119034 Russia. LC TS320.

INSTRUMENTS INDIA. 0047-0376. Periodical. English. mo. $15.00. Instruments India IMBA The Editor, A-32 Navyug Niwas 167 Dr D Bhadkamkar Road, Bombay 400-007 India. Ind/Abst Eng. Index Annu., Eng. Index Mon., Eng. Index Bioeng. Abstr., Eng. Index Energy Abstr., Comput. Control Abstr., Electr. Electron. Abstr., Sci. Abstr. Sect. A. Phys. Abstr., Chem. Abstr. CODEN ISIDBS. IMDA Journal.

INTERNATIONAL TEXTILE MANUFACTURING. V. 1- 1978-. English. an. 70. International Textile Manufacturers Federation, Postfach 289, CH-8039 Zurich Switzerland. Tel (01)2017080. Ed Herwig Strolz. Ind/Abst Eng. Index Annu., Eng. Index Mon., Eng. Index Bioeng. Abstr., Eng. Index Energy Abstr., World Text Abstr. LC HD9850.1. DD 338.47677005. CODEN ITXMAY. adv acc. Circ 800. Mainly statistics related to the International Textile Industry. Cotton and Allied Textile Industries.

INVENTORIES, SHIPMENTS AND ORDERS IN MANUFACTURING INDUSTRIES. VFOAT Stocks, Expeditions et Commandes des Industries Manufacturieres, Stocks, Livraisons et Commandes des Industries Manufacturieres. Feb. 1952-. 0707-7367. Periodical. CN. English (French). mo. Receiver General for Canada, Statistics Canada Publications, Ottawa Ontario K1A 0T6 Canada. DD 338.47670971.

Inventories & Shipments by Manufacturing Industries (Ottawa, Ont. : 1950), 0701-7375.

INVENTORIES, SHIPMENTS, AND ORDERS IN MANUFACTURING INDUSTRIES. ANNUAL SUPPLEMENT CEASED. (INVENTORIES, SHIPMENTS AND ORDERS IN MANUFACTURING INDUSTRIES, ANNUAL SUPPLEMENT). VFOAT Stocks, Livraisons et Commandes des Industries Manufacturieres, Supplement Annuel. 0225-3712. CN. English (French). an. LC HD9734.C2. DD 338.47670971.

INVESTMENT STATISTICS. MANUFACTURING SUB-INDUSTRIES AND SELECTED ENERGY RELATED INDUSTRIES. OUTLOOK. See Statistics.

IOWA MANUFACTURERS REGISTER. 1st Ed. (1983)-. 0737-7940. US. English. an. Manufacturers News, 4 East Huron Street, Chicago IL 60611-2793. Tel (312)337-1084. Ed Louise West. LC HD9727.I8. DD 338.47670294777. adv acc. Up to 30 facts available about Iowa manufacturers.

IRON AND STEEL FOUNDRIES AND STEEL INGOT PRODUCERS. (CURRENT INDUSTRIAL REPORTS. M33A, IRON AND STEEL FOUNDRIES AND STEEL INGOT PRODUCERS). 0732-8621. US. English. an. Superintendent of Documents, US Government Printing Office, Washington DC 20402. LC HD9511. DD 338.476720973.

ISA DIRECTORY OF INSTRUMENTATION (TRADE EDITION). See Yearbooks, Almanacs, Directories.

JENAER RUNDSCHAU. Periodical. GE. German. ir. 15.75. Veb Verlag Technik, Literarisches Buro des veb Carl Zeiss Jena, 69 Jena, Carl-Zeiss-Strasse 1 East Germany. Ind/Abst Excerpta Med., GeoRef, Energy Res. Abstr. LC TS510. CODEN JERUA2.

JOURNAL OF MANUFACTURING SYSTEMS. VFOAT Manufacturing Systems. Vol. 1, No. 1-. 0278-6125. Periodical. US. English. sa. $219.00. Society of Manufacturing Engineers, Computer and Automated Systems, PO Box 930/One SME Drive, Dearborn MI 48128. Ed John Bollinger. Ind/Abst Eng. Index. CODEN JMSYEB. bk rev. Circ 500. Highly technical information on the integration of manufacturing processes into systems.

JOURNAL OF QUALITY TECHNOLOGY. V. 1- Jan. 1969-. 0022-4065. Periodical. US. English. qt. $21.00. American Society of Quality Control, 230 West Wells Street/Suite 7000, Milwaukee WI 53203. Tel (414)272-8575. Ind/Abst Sci. Cit. Index, Abr. Ed., Phys. Abstr., Appl. Sci. Technol. Index, Electr. Electron. Abstr., Comput. Control Abstr., Int. Aerosp. Abstr., Sci. Abstr. Sect. A. Phys. Abstr., Eng. Index, Sel. Water Resour. Abstr., Energy Res. Abstr. LC TS156.Q3. DD 620.004508. CODEN JQUTAU. Industrial Quality Control, 0884-822X.

JOURNAL OF THE FLAGSTAFF INSTITUTE. See Economics - International Economics.

JOURNAL - Q.F.M.A. See Interior Design - Home Furnishings.

KANSAS NEW AND EXPANDING MANUFACTURERS. US. English. an. Topeka Department of Economic Development, 503 Kansas/6th Floor, Topeka KS 66603. Tel (913)296-3490. Ed Lisa Kraemer. LC HD9727.K2. Circ 400. Listing of new and expanding manufacturers in Kansas, including company location, product(s), and number of employees.

KENTUCKY MANUFACTURERS REGISTER. 1st Ed. (1985)-. 0741-9031. US. English. an. $40.00. Manufacturers New Inc, 4 East Huron Street, Chicago IL 60611-2793. Tel (312)337-1084. Ed Louise West. LC T12.3.K4. DD 670.25769. adv acc.

KEY COMPANY DIRECTORY, U.S. MANUFACTURING. See Yearbooks, Almanacs, Directories.

KEYNOTES (ASSOCIATED LOCKSMITHS OF AMERICA). (KEYNOTES). 0277-0792. US. English. mo. Associated Locksmiths of America, 3003 Live Oak Street, Dallas TX 75204. LC TS519. DD 683.305.

Manufacturing

KIKAI TO KOGU. *See* Engineering - Mechanical Engineering & Machinery.

KIT GUNS & HOBBY GUNSMITHING. VFOAT Kit Guns and Hobby Gunsmithing. 1st Ed.-. 0882-7362. US. English. an. $11.95. Balund Inc, 2409 Westlawn Drive, Kettering OH 45440. LC TS535. DD 683.405.

KNIFE DIGEST. US. English. an. $7.90. Knife Digest Publishers Company, PO Box 4596/Sather Gate Station, Berkeley CA 94704. LC TS380.

KNIVES. 1st Ed. (81)-. 0277-0725. US. English. an. $11.95. DBI Books Inc, 4092 Commercial Avenue, Northbrook IL 60062. **Tel** (312)272-6310. Ed Ken Warner. LC TS380. DD 621.93205.

KOMPASS. VFOAT Kompass. German (English, French, Italian, or Spanish). an. $175.00. Business Press International USA, 205 East 42nd Street, New York Ny 10017. **Tel** (212)867-2080.

KOZERDEKU TAJEKOZTATO ES HIRDETESEK. Hungarian. ir. Orszagos Anyag-Es Arhivatal, Lapkiado Vallalat, 1073 Lenin Krt 9-11, Budapest Hungary. LC TS191.6.

LABOUR COSTS IN CANADA. MANUFACTURING. *See* Economics - Labor.

LAND- UND FORSTWIRTSCHAFT, FISCHEREI. REIHE 4.3.2 : SCHLACHTTIER- UND FLEISCHBESCHAU. Main/Corp Germany (West). Statistiches Bundesamt. VAT Land- und Forstwirtschaft, Fischerei. Reihe Vier.Drei. Zwei: Schlachttier- und Fleischbeschau. 1976-. German. ir. 5.40. LC TS1975. *Land- und Forstwirtschaft, Fischerei. Reihe 3: Viehwirtschaft. IV. Schlachttier- und Fleischbeschau.*

THE LEATHER MANUFACTURER. 0023-9763. Periodical. US. English. mo. $27.00. Shoe Trade Publishing Company, PO Box 198, Cambridge MA 02140. **Tel** (617)492-2387. **Ind/Abst** Chem. Abstr. CODEN LEMAA7.

LIME MANUFACTURERS. Main/Corp Statistics Canada. Manufacturing and Primary Industries Division. **Series/Titl** Annual Census of Manufactures: Preliminary Bulletin. VFOAT Fabricants de Chaux. 0384-3246. CN. English (text in French). an. **Tel** (300)268-1151.

LONG ISLAND DIRECTORY OF MANUFACTURERS. *See* Yearbooks, Almanacs, Directories.

LOUISIANA DIRECTORY OF MANUFACTURERS. *See* Yearbooks, Almanacs, Directories.

LOUISVILLE AREA DIRECTORY OF MANUFACTURERS. *See* Yearbooks, Almanacs, Directories.

MAANDSTATISTIEK VAN DE INDUSTRIE. Main/Corp Netherlands (Kingdom, 1815-). Centraal Bureau Voor de Statistiek. VFOAT Monthly Statistical Bulletin of Manufacturing. Vol. 1- Jan. 1959-. 0470-6684. NE. Dutch. mo. 107.00. Staatsuitgeverij, Christoffel Plantijnstraat 1, 2515 TZ'S-Gravenhage Netherlands. LC HD9735.N2. *Maandstatistiek van de Nijverheid.*

MACRAE'S INDUSTRIAL DIRECTORY. *See* Yearbooks, Almanacs, Directories.

MACRAE'S VERIFIED DIRECTORY OF MANUFACTURERS' REPRESENTATIVES. *See* Yearbooks, Almanacs, Directories.

MAGAZINE L'OUTILITE. VFOAT Outilite. V. 1, No. 1 (June/July 1980)-. 0228-7889. Periodical. CN. French. bm. Free. 5 rue Chauvet, Charlesbourg Ouest Quebec G2K 1L1 Canada. DD 338.4767109714.

MAINE, VERMONT, NEW HAMPSHIRE DIRECTORY OF MANUFACTURERS. *See* Yearbooks, Almanacs, Directories.

MANA MEMBERSHIP DIRECTORY OF MANUFACTURER'S SALES AGENCIES. *See* Yearbooks, Almanacs, Directories.

MANUFACTURERS & PROCESSORS DIRECTORY. *See* Yearbooks, Almanacs, Directories.

MANUFACTURERS DIRECTORY. *See* Yearbooks, Almanacs, Directories.

MANUFACTURERS DIRECTORY (SAINT JOHN, N.B.). *See* Yearbooks, Almanacs, Directories.

MANUFACTURERS DIRECTORY, WINDSOR-ESSEX COUNTY, ONTARIO, CANADA. *See* Yearbooks, Almanacs, Directories.

MANUFACTURERS GUIDE. OHIO. (MANUFACTURERS GUIDE : OHIO). 1st- Ed. 0197-2723. US. English. an. $70.00. State Industrial Directories Corporation, 2 Penn Plaza, New York NY 10001. LC HD9727.O3. DD 338.0025771.

MANUFACTURERS OF CORRUGATED BOXES CEASED. VFOAT Manufacturiers de Boites en Carton Ondule. 1961-1964. 0575-8912. Periodical. CN. English (French). an. Receiver General for Canada, Statistics Canada Publications, Ottawa Ontario K1A 0T6 Canada. *Paper Box Manufacturers, 0575-9307.*

MANUFACTURERS OF ELECTRIC WIRE AND CABLE. Main/Corp Statistics Canada. Manufacturing and Primary Industries Division. VFOAT Fabricants de Fils et de Cables Electriques. VAT Fabricants de Fils et de Cables Electriques (Provisoire). Began with issue for 1971. 0700-0774. CN. English (French). an. 20.00 Domestic, 21.00 Foreign. Receiver General for Canada, Statistics Canada Publications, Ottawa Ontario K1A 0T6 Canada.

MANUFACTURERS OF ELECTRICAL INDUSTRIAL EQUIPMENT. Main/Corp Statistics Canada. Manufacturing and Primary Industries Division. **Series/Titl** Annual Census of Manufactures. VFOAT Fabricants d'Equipement Electrique Industriel. 0700-0782. CN. English (French). an. Receiver General for Canada, Statistics Canada/Publications, Ottawa Ontario K1A 0T6 Canada.

MANUFACTURERS OF INDUSTRIAL CHEMICALS. VFOAT Manufacturiers de Produits Chimiques Industriels. 1960-. 0527-5539. Periodical. CN. English and French. ir. Receiver General for Canada, Statistics Canada Publications, Ottawa Ontario K1A 0T6 Canada. DD 338.2.

MANUFACTURERS OF LIGHTING FIXTURES CEASED. **Main/Corp** Statistics Canada. Manufacturing and Primary Industries Division. **Series/Titl** (Annual Census of Manufactures = Recensement Annuel des Manufactures). VFOAT Fabricants d'Appareils d'Eclairage. 1970-. 0384-3793. CN. English (French). an. 0.70.

MANUFACTURERS OF MAJOR APPLIANCES (ELECTRIC AND NON-ELECTRIC). Main/Corp Statistics Canada. Manufacturing and Primary Industries Division. VFOAT Fabricants de Gros Appareils. 1960-. Periodical. CN. English (French). an. Statistics Canada, Publication Distribution, Ottawa Ontario K1A 0T6 Canada. *Electrical Apparatus and Supplies Industry.*

MANUFACTURERS OF MISCELLANEOUS ELECTRICAL PRODUCTS CEASED. **Main/Corp** Statistics Canada. Manufacturing and Primary Industries Division. VFOAT Fabricants de Produits Electriques Divers. VAT Fabricants de Produits Electriques Divers (Provisoire). Began with issue for 1970?. 0700-0766. CN. English (text in French). an. **Tel** (800)268-1151.

MANUFACTURERS OF MIXED FERTILIZERS CEASED. **Main/Corp** Statistics Canada. Manufacturing and Primary Industries Division. **Series/Titl** Annual Census of Manufactures. VFOAT Fabricants d'Engrais Composes. 1970-1980. 0090-0397. CN. English (French). an. 0.70. *Manufacturers of Mixed Fertilizers, 0090-0397.*

MANUFACTURERS OF PHARMACEUTICALS AND MEDICINES (FINAL). *See* Pharmacy.

MANUFACTURERS OF SMALL ELECTRIC APPLIANCES. FABRICANTS DE PETITS APPAREILS ELECTRIQUES. Main/Corp Statistics Canada. Manufacturing and Primary Industries Division. VFOAT Fabricants de Petits Appareils Electriques. 1960-. Periodical. CN. English (French). an. Statistics of Canada, Manufacturing and Primary Industries Division, Main Building/Tunneys Pasture, Ottawa Ontario K1H 0T6 Canada. *Electrical Apparatus and Supplies Industry.*

MANUFACTURERS OF SMALL ELECTRICAL APPLIANCES. *See* Household Hardware & Appliances.

MANUFACTURERS OF SOAP AND CLEANING COMPOUNDS (FINAL) CEASED. (MANUFACTURERS OF SOAP AND CLEANING COMPOUNDS). **Series/Titl** Annual Census of Manufactures. VFOAT Manufacturiers de Savons et de Composes de Nettoyage. 1960-1980. 4524-3912. CN. English. an. LC HD9999.S9. DD 338.4766810971. *Soaps, Washings i.e. Washing Compounds and Cleaning Preparations Industry, 0384-3920.*

MANUFACTURERS OF TOILET PREPARATIONS (FINAL) CEASED. (MANUFACTURERS OF TOILET PREPARATIONS). **Series/Titl** Annual Census of Manufactures. VFOAT Manufacturiers de Produits de Toilette. 1960-1980. 0384-3882. Periodical. CN. English. an. Receiver General for Canada, Statistics Canada Publications, Ottawa Ontario K1A 0T6 Canada. **Tel** (800)268-1151. DD 338.4766850971. *Toilet Preparations Industry, 0384-3890.*

MANUFACTURERS' SHIPMENTS, INVENTORIES, AND ORDERS. (CURRENT INDUSTRIAL REPORTS. M3-1, MANUFACTURERS' SHIPMENTS, INVENTORIES, AND ORDERS). 0364-1880. Periodical. US. English. mo. $28.00. Data User Services Division, Customer Services Publication, Bureau of the Census, Washington DC 20233. **Tel** (301)763-4100. **Ind/Abst** Predicasts, Am. Stat. Index. LC HD9724. DD 380.10973. Presents timely data on the production, inventories, and orders of approximately 5,000 products, which represents 40 percent of all US manufacturing.

MANUFACTURING & SERVICE INDUSTRIES. Main/Corp Great Britain. Health and Safety Executive. VFOAT Health and Safety. 1976-. UK. English. 2.50. Her Majesty's Stationery Office, 49 High Holborn Street, London WC1V 6HB England. LC T55.A1. DD 614.852.

MANUFACTURING CHEMIST AND AEROSOL NEWS. *See* Chemistry.

MANUFACTURING CHEMIST (LONDON, ENGLAND : 1983). *See* Chemistry.

MANUFACTURING COMMODITIES. PRINCIPAL ARTICLES PRODUCED. (MANUFACTURING COMMODITIES : PRINCIPAL ARTICLES PRODUCED). **Main/Corp** Australian Bureau of Statistics. 1971/73-. 0312-9578. AT. English. an. 2.80. Australian Bureau of Statistics, PO Box 84, Canberra Australian Capital Territory 2600 Australia. **Tel** (062)52 6778. LC HD9738.A8. DD 338.40994. Quantities produced, and quantities and values of sales and transfers out, of approximately 3,600 manufacturing commodities produced by establishments in the manufacturing census. *Manufacturing Commodities: Principal Articles Produced, 0312-9578.*

THE MANUFACTURING CONFECTIONER. (MC. THE MANUFACTURING CONFECTIONER). VFOAT Manufacturing Confectioner. V. 36, No. 10- Oct. 1956-. 0163-4364. Periodical. US. English. mo. $25.00. Manufacturing Confectioner, 175 Rock Road, Glen Rock NJ 07452. **Tel** (201)652-2655. **Ind/Abst** Life Sci. Collect. DD 338. *Manufacturing Confectioner, 0163-4364.*

MANUFACTURING DIRECTORY OF IDAHO. *See* Yearbooks, Almanacs, Directories.

MANUFACTURING ENGINEERING. *See* Engineering.

MANUFACTURING ENGINEERING TRANSACTIONS. *See* Engineering.

MANUFACTURING ESTABLISHMENTS. AUSTRALIAN CAPITAL TERRITORY. (MANUFACTURING ESTABLISHMENTS : AUSTRALIAN CAPITAL TERRITORY). **Main/Corp** Australian Bureau of Statistics. 1972/73-. 0310-0758. AT. English. an. Australian Bureau of Statistics, Ground Floor Wing, 5 Cameron Offices, Belconnen Australian Capital Territory 2617 Australia. **Tel** (062)52 6627. LC HD9738.A83. DD 338.409947. Structural variables: number of establishments, employment, wages and salaries, stocks, purchases, etc. *Manufacturing Establishments: Australian Capital Territory, 0310-0758.*

Manufacturing

MANUFACTURING ESTABLISHMENTS, DETAILS OF OPERATIONS BY INDUSTRY, SOUTH AUSTRALIA. English. an. 2.80. Australian Bureau of Statistics, Ground Floor Annexe City Mutual Centre, 10-20 Pulteney Street, Adelaide South 5000 Australia. **Tel** (08)228 9439. **LC** HD9738.A83. **DD** 338.4700099423. Final results from the manufacturing census for structural variables: number of establishments, employment, wages and salaries, turnover, stocks, purchases, etc. *Manufacturing Establishments, Details of Operations.*

MANUFACTURING ESTABLISHMENTS. NORTHERN TERRITORY. (MANUFACTURING ESTABLISHMENTS : NORTHERN TERRITORY). **Main/Corp** Australian Bureau of Statistics. 1972/73-. 0310-0766. AT. English. an. Australian Bureau of Statistics, 5th Floor MLC Building, 81 Smith Street, Darwin Northern Territory 5790 Australia. **Tel** (089)81 5222. **LC** HD9738.A83. **DD** 338.4099429. Structural variables: number of establishments, persons employed, wages and salaries, turnover, stocks, purchases, etc. *Manufacturing Establishments: Northern Territory, 0310-0766.*

MANUFACTURING ESTABLISHMENTS : SUMMARY OF OPERATIONS BY INDUSTRY CLASS : AUSTRALIA. **Main/Corp** Australian Bureau of Statistics. 1972/73-. AT. English. ir. Australian Bureau of Statistics, PO Box 84, Canberra Australian Capital Territory 2600 Australia. **LC** HD9738.A83. **DD** 338.409941. *Economic Censuses: Manufacturing Establishments, Summary of Operations by Industry Class.*

MANUFACTURING FORUM. V. 1- Fall 1976-. 0146-6550. Periodical. US. English. ty. $3.00. Department of Industry & Technology, Ball State University, Muncie IN 47306. **Tel** (317)285-5659. **Ed** Thomas Wright. **LC** LC1081. **DD** 607. **Circ** 425. Articles on teaching manufacturing technology to students in industrial arts/technology education programs in secondary schools and colleges.

MANUFACTURING IN MINNESOTA. **Main/Corp** Minnesota. Dept. of Economic Development. Research Division. 0149-9521. US. English. 480 Cedar Street, St Paul MN 55101. **LC** HD9727.M6. **DD** 338.409776.

MANUFACTURING INDUSTRIES OF CANADA. SUB-PROVINCIAL AREAS. (MANUFACTURING INDUSTRIES OF CANADA, SUB-PROVINCIAL AREAS). **VFOAT** Industries Manufacturieres du Canada, Niveau Infraprovincial. 1972-. 0382-4012. Periodical. CN. English (French). an. Receiver General for Canada, Statistics Canada Publications, Ottawa Ontario K1A 0T6 Canada. **LC** HD9734.C2. **DD** 33847670971. *Manufacturing Industries of Canada, Geographical Distribution, 0527-5636.*

MANUFACTURING INDUSTRIES OF CANADA. TYPE OF ORGANIZATION AND SIZE OF ESTABLISHMENTS *CEASED.* **VFOAT** Industries Manufacturieres du Canada. Forme d'Organization et Taille des Etablissements. 1969-1976. 0590-5737. CN. English (French). an. Receiver General for Canada, Statistics Canada Publications, Ottawa Ontario K1A 0T6 Canada. **LC** HD9734.C2. **DD** 338.40971.

MANUFACTURING MANAGEMENT SERIES. See Business - General Management.

MANUFACTURING + MARKETING OPPORTUNITIES; BULLETIN. 0706-0084. Periodical. CN. English. mo. Free. Ministry of Industry and Tourism, 900 Bay Street, Queen's Park, Toronto Ontario M7A 2E4 Canada. (ctrl). *Ontario Manufacturing & Diversification Opportunities.*

MANUFACTURING OPERATIONS. **VFOAT** Operations. Vol. 1, No. 1 Sept. 1983-. 0743-023X. Periodical. US. English. qt. Hitchcock Publishing Company, Hitchcock Building, Wheaton IL 60187.

MANUFACTURING OPPORTUNITIES. **Main/Corp** British Columbia. Dept. of Economic Development. CN. English. Department of Economic Development, Government of British Columbia, Parliament Buildings, Victoria British Columbia V8V 4R9 Canada. **LC** HF130.B7. **DD** 338.09711.

MANUFACTURING SERIES A. NO. 1, GENERAL STATISTICS. See Statistics.

MANUFACTURING SERIES C. NO. 7, BASIC METAL INDUSTRIES. See Metals & Metallurgy.

MANUFACTURING SYSTEMS. 0748-948X. Periodical. US. English. mo. $60.00. Hitchcock Publishing Company, Hitchcock Building, Wheaton IL 60188. **Tel** (312)665-1000. **Ed** Tom Inglesby. **DD** 338. bk rev. adv acc. **Circ** 131,000. (ctrl). Management oriented articles on application of information processing to increase manufacturing productivity including all computer and advanced manufacturing techniques as management philosophies.

MANUFACTURING TECHNOLOGY. See Technology (General).

MANUFACTURING TECHNOLOGY HORIZONS. See Technology (General).

MASHPRIBORINTORG. **Main/Corp** Vsesoiuznoe Obedinenie Mashpriborintorg. Periodical. UR. English. qt. V/O Mashpriborintory 121200, Moscow USSR. **LC** TS500. **DD** 681.40947.

MASSACHUSETTS DIRECTORY OF MANUFACTURERS. See Yearbooks, Almanacs, Directories.

MATERIALNO-TEKHNICHESKO SNABDIAVANE. Periodical. BU. Bulgarian. ir. Hemus, 6 Boulevard Rusky, Sofia Bulgaria. **LC** TS161.

MATTRESSES AND FOUNDATIONS. (CURRENT INDUSTRIAL REPORTS. MA-25E, MATTRESSES AND FOUNDATIONS). 0276-6418. US. English. an. Bureau of the Census, Data User Services Division Customer Services, Washington DC 20233. **LC** HD9971.5.M383. **DD** 338.47684150973.

MEAT PROCESSING. 0025-6390. Periodical. US. English. mo. Meat Processing, 1 East First Street, Duluth MN 55802. **Tel** (312)325-2930. **Ind/Abst** Bibliogr. Agric., Predicasts, Funk Scott Index Corp. Ind. **LC** TS1950. **DD** 664.9005. *MP.*

MECHANO BUYERS DIRECTORY. NORTHERN CALIFORNIA. See Yearbooks, Almanacs, Directories.

MEN'S AND BOYS' OUTERWEAR. (CURRENT INDUSTRIAL REPORTS. MA-23E, MEN'S AND BOYS' OUTERWEAR). 1981-. 0741-630X. US. English. an. $1.25. Data User Services Division, Customer Services Publication, Bureau of the Census, Washington DC 20233. **Tel** (301)763-4100. **LC** HD9940.U3. **DD** 338.476871410973. Presents timely data on the production, inventories, and orders of approximately 5,000 products, which represents 40 percent of all US manufacturing. *Current Industrial Reports. Series MA-23E, Men's and Boys' Outerwear, 0741-630X.*

METAL FABRICATING NEWS. 0026-055X. Periodical. US. English. bm. $6.00. Metal Fabricating Institution Inc, PO Box 1178, Rockford IL. **Tel** (815)965-4031. **Ed** Ronald L Fowler. **Ind/Abst** Met. Abstr., World Alum. Abstr. bk rev. adv acc. **Circ** 46,000. (ctrl). Edited for those in the metal fabricating, manufacturing plants, responsible for the plant operations.

METRO NEW YORK DIRECTORY OF MANUFACTURERS. See Yearbooks, Almanacs, Directories.

MICHIGAN MANUFACTURERS DIRECTORY. See Yearbooks, Almanacs, Directories.

MICROELECTRONIC MANUFACTURING AND TESTING. Sept./Oct. 1978-. 0161-7427. Periodical. US. English. mo. $60.00. Lake Publishing Corporation, PO Box 159, 17730 Peterson Road, Libertyville IL 60048. **Tel** (312)362-8711.

MICROELECTRONIC MANUFACTURING AND TESTING. DESK MANUAL. **VFOAT** Microelectronic Manufacturing and Testing Desk Manual. US. English. an. $60.00. Lake Publishing Corporation, PO Box 159, Libertyville IL 60048. **Tel** (312)362-8711. **Ed** Terrence Thompson. **LC** TK7874. **DD** 621.381705. bk rev adv acc. **Circ** 35,000. (ctrl). Serves manufacturers involved in the production, testing, design, development and use of microelectronic and solid state devices and circuits. Also served are a limited number of independent research firms, government agencies, universities, manufacturers' representatives and distributors.

MINNESOTA DIRECTORY OF MANUFACTURERS. See Yearbooks, Almanacs, Directories.

MINNESOTA MANUFACTURERS REGISTER. 1st Ed. (1984)-. 0738-1514. US. English. an. $65.00. Manufacturers News Inc, 4 East Huron Street, Chicago IL 60611-2793. **Tel** (312)337-1084. **Ed** Louise West. **LC** HD9727.M6. **DD** 338.47670294776. adv acc.

MIRROR NEWS. 0191-4677. Periodical. US. English. bm. $10.00. Wil Tiller, PO Box 471, Hopkins MN 55343. **Tel** (612)935-3666. **Ed** Wil L Tiller. bk rev. adv acc. **Circ** 9,700. (ctrl). Serves management in the manufacture and marketing of mirror products, glass frames and allied accessories. Coverage includes manufacturing retailing, wholesaling, interior designing and contract installation.

MISCELLANEOUS CHEMICAL INDUSTRIES. Series/Titl Annual Census of Manufactures. **VFOAT** Fabricants de Produits Chimiques Divers. 1970-. 0700-0464. CN. English (French). an. 70. Statistics Canada, Publication Distribution, Ottawa Ontario K1A 0T6 Canada. **LC** HD9655.C2. **DD** 338.4766. *0829-8475; Explosives and Ammunition Manufacturers, 0575-8467.*

MISCELLANEOUS MACHINERY AND EQUIPMENT MANUFACTURERS. **Main/Corp** Statistics Canada. Manufacturing and Primary Industries Division. Series/Titl Annual Census of Manufacturers: Preliminary Bulletin. **VFOAT** Fabricants de Machines et d'Equipement Divers. 0701-7383. CN. English (French). an. Receiver General for Canada, Statistics Canada Publications, Ottawa Ontario K1A 0T6 Canada.

MISCELLANEOUS VEHICLE MANUFACTURERS *CEASED.* **Main/Corp** Statistics Canada. Manufacturing and Primary Industries Division. Series/Titl Annual Census of Manufactures. **VFOAT** Fabricants de Vehicules Divers. 1970-1980. 0527-5741. CN. English (French). an. 70. *Miscellaneous Vehicle Manufacturers, 0527-5741.*

MISSISSIPPI MANUFACTURERS DIRECTORY. See Yearbooks, Almanacs, Directories.

MISSOURI DIRECTORY OF MANUFACTURING AND MINING. See Yearbooks, Almanacs, Directories.

MISSOURI—NEW AND EXPANDING MANUFACTURERS. **VFOAT** New and Expanding Manufacturers. 1976-. US. English. an. Missouri Division of Commerce & Industrial Development, Jefferson Building, Jefferson City MO 65101. **Tel** (314)751-3674. **Ed** Earl Cannon. **LC** HD9727.M8. **DD** 338.09778. **Circ** 3,000. A listing of Missouri's new and expanding manufacturers in each calendar year including statistical analysis and a section on office, warehouse, research and distribution facilities. *Missouri's New and Expanding Manufacturers.*

THE MOBILE HOME AND RECREATIONAL VEHICLE MANUFACTURERS OF THE UNITED STATES AND CANADA. **VFOAT** Manufacturers of Mobile Homes and Recreational Vehicles, of the United States and Canada. US. English. an. **LC** HD9715.7.U6. **DD** 338.4762922602573.

MOBILE/MANUFACTURED HOME BLUE BOOK. **VAT** Mobile, Manufactured Home Blue Book. Vol. 46, No. 1 (Jan. 1982)-. 0733-6497. US. English. sa. National Market Reports Inc, 300 West Adams Street, Chicago IL 60606. **Tel** (312)726-2802. **LC** TL297. **DD** 643.2. *Mobile Home Blue Book, 0733-6489.*

MODERN MACHINE SHOP. V. 1- June 1928-. 0026-8003. Periodical. US. English. mo. Gardner Publications Inc, 6600 Clough Pike, Cincinnati OH 45244. **Tel** (513)231-8020. **Ed** Kenneth M Gettelman. **Ind/Abst** Electron. Commun. Abstr. J., ISMEC Bull., Pollut. Abstr. Indexes, Saf. Sci. Abstr. J., Trade Ind. Index, Comput. Control Abstr., Electr. Electron. Abstr., Sci. Abstr. Sect. A. Phys. Abstr., Met. Abstr., World Alum. Abstr., Appl. Sci. Technol. Index, Funk Scott Index Corp. Ind., Phys. Abstr. **LC** TJ1. **DD** 621.7505. **CODEN** MMASAY. bk rev. adv acc. **Circ** 106,000. (ctrl). Edited for and distributed to production executives in the metal working industries.

MODERN MATERIALS HANDLING. 0026-8038. Periodical. US. English. ir. Cahners Publishing, 270 St Paul Street, Denver CO 80206. **Tel**

Manufacturing

(303)388-4511. **Ind/Abst** Manage. Contents, Trade Ind. Index, Appl. Sci. Technol. Index, Predicasts, Eng. Index Annu., Eng. Index Mon., Eng. Index Bioeng. Abstr., Eng. Index Energy Abstr., ABI/Inform, Comput. Control Abstr., Electr. Electron. Abstr., Sci. Abstr. Sect. A. Phys. Abstr., Int. Packag. Abstr., Energy Res. Abstr., Funk Scott Index Corp. Ind., Phys. Abstr., Eng. Index. **LC** TS149. **DD** 658.7805. **CODEN** MMHHA2. *Palletizer.*

MOTOR VEHICLE MANUFACTURERS *CEASED.* **Main/Corp** Statistics Canada. Manufacturing and Primary Industries Division. **VFOAT** Fabricants de Vehicules Automobiles. 1970-1980. 0575-9129. CN. English (French). an. 70.00. *Motor Vehicle Manufacturers, 0575-9129.*

MUZZLELOADERS' ANNUAL. (DIXIE GUN WORKS MUZZLELOADERS' ANNUAL). **Main/Corp** Dixie Gun Works. 0146-6143. US. English. an. $1.75. Aqua-Field Publications Inc, 342 Madison Avenue, New York NY 10017. **LC** TS536.6.M8. **DD** 683.42.

N.A.D.A. MOBILE HOME MANUFACTURED HOUSING APPRAISAL GUIDE. **VFOAT** NADA Mobile Home Manufactured Housing Appraisal Guide. Jan./Apr. 1982-. 0742-9274. US. English. ty. $49.00. N A D A Appraisal Guides, PO Box 1407, Covina CA 91722. **LC** HD9715.7.U62. **DD** 381.456908790973. *N.A.D.A. Mobile Home Appraisal Guide, 0095-6538.*

NARROW FABRICS. (CURRENT INDUSTRIAL REPORTS. MA-22G, NARROW FABRICS). Began with 1965. 0149-032X. US. English. an. $1.00. Data User Services Division, Customer Services Publication, Bureau of the Census, Washington DC 20233. **Tel** (301)763-4100. **LC** HD9851. **DD** 338.476770973. Presents timely data on the production, inventories, and orders of approximately 5,000 products, which represents 40 percent of all US manufacturing. *Current Industrial Reports. M22G, Narrow Fabrics.*

NATIONAL MANUFACTURERS REGISTER. V. 1- 1977-. 0163-2191. US. English. an. $50.00. 8672 Melrose, Los Angeles CA 90069. **LC** T12. **DD** 338.476702573.

NATURAL GAS PROCESSING PLANTS IN CANADA. See Petroleum and Natural Gas.

NAVY ARMS MUZZLELOADERS' JOURNAL. 0272-7854. US. English. $2.25 Domestic, $2.75 Canada. Aqua-Field Publications Inc, 728 Beaver Dam Road, Point Pleasant NJ 08742. **LC** TS536.6.M8. **DD** 683.4.

N/C COMMLINE. See Computers and Computer Science.

NEW BRUNSWICK MANUFACTURERS AND PRODUCTS. **VFOAT** Fabricants et Produits du Nouveau-Brunswick. 1974-. 0709-2342. Periodical. CN. English (text in French, 1978). be. Department of Commerce and Development, PO Box 6000, Fredericton New Brunswick E3B 5H1 Canada. **DD** 338.767025715. *Directory of Products and Manufacturers, 0709-2350.*

NEW EQUIPMENT NEWS. See Engineering - Mechanical Engineering & Machinery.

NEW JERSEY DIRECTORY OF MANUFACTURERS. See Yearbooks, Almanacs, Directories.

NEW MEXICO MANUFACTURING DIRECTORY. See Yearbooks, Almanacs, Directories.

NEW ZEALAND WHOLE EARTH CATALOGUE. 1st- 1972-. English. ir. $4.95. Alister Taylor Pub, Whole Earth Mail Order Department, Box 10-292, Wellington New Zealand. **LC** TS199. **DD** 381.456.

NEWS (MACHINE TOOL INDUSTRY RESEARCH ASSOCIATION). (NEWS). No. 1-. Periodical. UK. English. mo. $32.18. Machine Tool Industry Research Association, Hulley Road, MacClesfield Cheshire SK10 2NE England. **Tel** 0625 25421. List of articles from journals reports proceedings and translations relevant to manufacturing industry and production engineering.

NFPA LETTER. **VFOAT** N.F.P.A. Letter. **VAT** National Flaxseed Processors Association Letter. No. 1 (Aug. 1955)-. Periodical. US. English. mo.

NOPA MANUFACTURER SELLING COSTS SURVEY. See Office Equipment & Services.

OCCUPATIONAL PROFILE OF SELECTED NONMANUFACTURING INDUSTRIES. See Economics - Labor.

OCCUPATIONAL PROFILES OF OREGON'S MANUFACTURING INDUSTRIES. See Occupations and Careers.

OEM DESIGN. **VFOAT** Original Equipment Manufacture. V. 1- Oct.1971-. 0306-0381. Periodical. UK. English. mo. $30.65. Business Publications Ltd, Canada House, Kildare Close, Ruislip Middx HA4 9XB England. **Tel** (01)928-3388. **Ind/Abst** Fluidex, Ship Abstr., Comput. Control Abstr., Electr. Electron. Abstr., Sci. Abstr. Sect. A. Phys. Abstr. **LC** TA174. **CODEN** OEMDAF.

THE OFFICIAL PRICE GUIDE TO POCKET KNIVES. **VFOAT** Pocket Knives. 1st Ed. (1984)-. 0748-1152. US. English. an. $2.95. House of Collectibles Inc, Orlando Central Park, 1900 Premier Row, Orlando FL 32809. **LC** TS380. **DD** 621.932.

OHIO INDUSTRIAL BUYERS DIRECTORY. See Yearbooks, Almanacs, Directories.

OHIO MANUFACTURERS DIRECTORY. See Yearbooks, Almanacs, Directories.

OHIO REGISTER OF MANUFACTURERS. 1985-1986 Ed.-. US. English. an. $82.50. Commerce Register Inc, 190 Godwin Avenue, Midland Park NJ 07432. **Tel** (201)445-3000. Ed Joel Rosano. adv acc. Circ 3,000. Detailed listings of all manufacturing companies, including top executives, annual sales, number of employees, address, phone, and more. *Ohio Directory of Manufacturers, 0738-3711.*

THE OHIO STATE MANUFACTURERS GUIDE. 0275-1887. US. English. an. $93.75. Macrae's Blue Book, 87 Terminal Drive, Plainview NY 11803. **Tel** (800)622-7237.

OKLAHOMA DIRECTORY OF MANUFACTURERS AND PRODUCTS. See Yearbooks, Almanacs, Directories.

OTHER MISCELLANEOUS MANUFACTURING INDUSTRIES = AUTRES INDUSTRIES MANUFACTURIERES DIVERSES. **Main/Corp** Statistics Canada. Manufacturing and Primary Industries Division. Began with issue for 1971. 0384-398X. CN. English (French). an. 20.00. Industry Division Statistics, Canada Publications, Ottawa Ontario K1A 0T6 Canada. **Tel** (613)991-3514. Ed T R Wright. Circ 400. Statistics on miscellaneous manufacturing industries including, records, flooring, fur dressing, brooms, brushes, buttons, buckles, musical instruments, etc.

PAINT AND VARNISH MANUFACTURERS. **Main/Corp** Statistics Canada. Manufacturing and Primary Industries Division. **Series/Titl** Annual Census of Manufacturers : Preliminary Bulletin. **VFOAT** Fabricants de Peintures et Vernis. 0384-4706. Periodical. CN. English (French). an. Receiver General for Canada, Statistics Canada Publications, Ottawa Ontario K1A 0T6 Canada.

DAS PAPIER. See Paper & Pulp Industry.

PARTS MANUFACTURER APPROVALS. 0278-3088. US. English. an. Superintendent of Documents, US Government Printing Office, Washington DC 20402.

PEM. PLANT ENGINEERING AND MAINTENANCE. See Engineering - Mechanical Engineering & Machinery.

PENNSYLVANIA DIRECTORY OF MANUFACTURERS (HOHOKUS, N.J.). See Yearbooks, Almanacs, Directories.

PLANOVOE KHOZIAISTVO. Began in 1924. 0032-0757. Periodical. UR. Russian. mo $40.50. Victor Kamkin Inc (70696), 12224 Parklawn Drive, Rockville MD 20852. **Tel** (301)881-5973. Index in last issue of volume - attached. *Biulleteni Gosplana.*

PLANT ENGINEERING. V. 1- Nov. 1947-. 0032-082X. Periodical. US. English. bw. $50.00. Circulation Office, 1301 South Grove Avenue, PO Box 1030, Barrington IL 60010. **Tel** (312)381-1840. Ed Leo Spector. **Ind/Abst** Trade Ind. Index, Eng. Index Mon., Eng. Index Bioeng. Abstr., Eng. Index Energy Abstr., Excerpta Med., Predicasts, Energy Inf. Abstr., Environ. Abstr., CIS Abstr., Energy Res. Abstr., Chem. Abstr., Eng. Index Annu., Eng. Index, Appl. Sci. Technol. Index, Funk Scott Index Corp. Ind. **LC** TS155.A1. **DD** 658.205. **CODEN** PLENAV. bk rev. adv acc. Circ 115,510. (ctrl). Serves the plant engineering function in industry. Problem-solution articles on plant and equipment design, construction, operation, maintenance, systems, advanced technology, news, and management.

PLANT ENGINEERING PRODUCTS. See Engineering - Mechanical Engineering & Machinery.

PLANT SYSTEMS & EQUIPMENT. **VFOAT** Plant Systems and Equipment. Vol. 1, No. 1 (Jan./Feb. 1982)-. 0744-3900. Periodical. US. English. bm. $20.00. Plant Systems & Equipment, 35 East Wacker Drive, Chicago IL 60601. **Tel** (312)346-3074.

PLI KNOW HOW. No. 106- Feb. 1973-. Periodical. UK. English. mo. 10.50. Industrial Opportunities Ltd, 13-14 Homewell Havant Hampshire, Havant PO9 1EF England. **LC** TS1. **DD** 608.7. *Product Licensing Index.*

PRINCIPAL MANUFACTURING STATISTICS, ALBERTA. See Statistics.

PRINTED CIRCUIT FABRICATION. See Engineering - Electricity, Electrical Engineering, Electronics.

PRO METAL. Began in 1948. French (German). ir. **LC** TS620.

PROCEEDINGS OF THE ANNUAL TECHNICAL CONFERENCE - SOCIETY OF VACUUM COATERS. (PROCEEDINGS OF THE . . . ANNUAL TECHNICAL CONFERENCE). **Main/Corp** Society of Vacuum Coaters. 25th (1982)-. 0737-5921. US. English. an. **Ind/Abst** Eng. Index Annu., Eng. Index Mon., Eng. Index Bioeng. Abstr., Eng. Index Energy Abstr. **LC** TS695. **DD** 671.73505. **CODEN** PASVBF. *Annual Technical Conference Proceedings, 0731-1699.*

PROCEEDINGS - SMALLGOODS MANUFACTURING WORKSHOP. **Main/Corp** Smallgoods Manufacturing Workshop. Periodical. English. ir. Ed P A Baumgartner.

PROCEEDINGS - STEELMAKING CONFERENCE. See Metals & Metallurgy.

PRODUCT CANADA EXPORT JOURNAL. 0822-8906. Periodical. CN. English (includes some text in French). qt. $15.00. Product Canada Export Journal, Suite 601/2050 Mansfield, Montreal Quebec H3A 1Z2 Canada. **Tel** (514)842-5263. Ed Olaf Silva. **DD** 382.60971. adv acc. Circ 12,000. Import-export publication.

PRODUCT DESIGN & DEVELOPMENT. **VAT** Product Design and Development. V. 1- Nov. 1946-. Periodical. US. English. mo. $35.00. Chilton Company, Chilton Way, Radnor PA 19089. **Tel** (215)964-4000. **LC** TS1. **DD** 658.57505.

PRODUCT SAFETY LETTER. **VFOAT** PSL. 0098-7530. Periodical. US. English. wk. $497.00. Washington Business Information Inc, 1117 North 19th Street/Suite 200, Arlington VA 22209. **Tel** (202)247-3423. Ed Jan Simmons. Monitors the CPS and other agencies. The weekly offers vital advance notice of tough rules that hit production and sale of products ranging from TV's to toys, cleaners to clothing.

PRODUCTION ENGINEER. (THE PRODUCTION ENGINEER). V. 39- 1960-. 0032-9851. Periodical. UK. English. ir. $73.56. Institute of Production Engineers, Rochester House 66 L Ealin Lane, London W5 4XX England. **Tel** 01 579 9411. Ed Rory Baxter. **Ind/Abst** Electron. Commun. Abstr. J., ISMEC Bull., Pollut. Abstr. Indexes, Saf. Sci. Abstr. J., Eng. Index Mon., Eng. Index Bioeng. Abstr., Eng. Index Energy Abstr., Excerpta Med., Ship Abstr., Chem. Abstr., Eng. Index Annu., Eng. Index. **CODEN** PDENA9. bk rev. adv acc. Circ 20,000. (ctrl). How production engineering can help improve competitiveness of the manufacturing industry. *Journal.*

PRODUCTS FINISHING. V. 1- Oct. 1936-. 0032-9940. Periodical. US. English. $18.00. Sawell Publications, 127 Stanstead Road/Forest Hill, London SE23 1JE England. **Tel** 01-699 6792. Ed John Bean. **Ind/Abst** Eng. Index Mon., Eng. Index Bioeng. Abstr., Eng. Index Energy Abstr., World Surf. Coat. Abstr., Met. Abstr., World Alum. Abstr., Chem. Abstr., Eng. Index Annu., Eng. Index, Nucl. Sci. Abstr. **LC** TS200. **DD** 671.705. **CODEN** PRFCAB. adv acc. Illustrating materials methods and ways of completing the finishing processes of manufactured goods. The yearbook is a directory.

PRODUCTS SHIPPED BY CANADIAN MANUFACTURERS. **VFOAT** Produits Libres par les Fabricants Canadiens. 1961-. 0575-9455. CN. text in English and French, English only, 1961-1970.

Manufacturing

an. Receiver General for Canada, Statistics Canada Publications, Ottawa Ontario K1A 0T6 Canada. **DD** 380.145670971.

PROIZVODSTVO CHUGUNA. *See* Metals & Metallurgy.

PROMYSHLENNYI TRANSPORT. Began with Jan. 1972 issue. 0131-5560. Periodical. UR. Russian. mo. $40.50. Victor Kamkin Inc, 12224 Parklawn Drive, Rockville MD 20852. **Tel** (301)881-5731. **Ind/Abst** Coal Abstr. **LC** TS180.

PRZEGLAD ODLEWNICTWA. Began publication in 1951. 0033-2275. Periodical. PL. Polish (tables of contents also in Russian and English). bm. ARS Polona, Krakowskie Przedmiescie 7, 00-068 Warsaw Poland. **Ind/Abst** Coal Abstr., CIS Abstr., Met. Abstr., World Alum. Abstr., Chem. Abstr. **LC** TS200. **CODEN** PRZOAB.

QUALITY CONTROL REPORTS. VFOAT QC. 0163-2418. US. English. mo. $75.00. FDC Reports, 5550 Friendship Boulevard, Chevy Chase MD 20815. **Tel** (301)657-9830. Ed Bill Paulson. **Ind/Abst** Pharm. News Index. NLM W1 GO62. **CODEN** QUCRB6. For executives concerned with quality assurance and quality control procedures in the prescription and over-the-counter pharmaceutical, cosmetics, medical device industries (monthly).

QUARTERLY STATISTICS OF MANUFACTURERS' SALES. INDEX OF COMMODITIES. *See* Indexes/Abstracts.

RAPPORT D'ACTIVITE - CENTRE DE CREATION INDUSTRIELLE. Main/Corp Centre de Creation Industrielle. FR. French. ir. Centre de Creation Industrielle Service Documentation, Centre George Pompidou, 75191 Paris Cedex 04 France. **LC** TS71. **DD** 745.207.

REGISTER OF QUALITY ASSESSED UNITED KINGDOM MANUFACTURERS. 1st Ed.-. UK. English. 27.50. Her Majestys Stationery Office, 49 High Holburn, London WC1V 6HB England. **LC** TS156.6. **DD** 670.2541.

REPERTOIRE DES ETABLISSEMENTS MANUFACTURIERS. *See* Yearbooks, Almanacs, Directories.

REPERTOIRE DES MANUFACTURES DE LA PROVINCE DE QUEBEC. *See* Yearbooks, Almanacs, Directories.

REPERTOIRE . . . DES PRODUITS ET SERVICES, DOMAINE DE L'EAU. *See* Water Resources.

REPERTOIRE DES PRODUITS FABRIQUES AU QUEBEC. 1st Ed.- 1978-. 0704-7940. CN. French. an. $30.95. Cntr Rech Industrielle Quebec, CP 9038/333 rue Franquet Ste Foy, Quebec G1V 4C7 Canada. **Tel** (418)659-1550. **DD** 338'.0025'714. Directory of Quebec manufacturers: alphabetical list of manufacturers, classified list of products, index of products and English-French glossary.

REPORT - NATIONAL ASSOCIATION OF MANUFACTURERS OF THE UNITED STATES OF AMERICA. POSTWAR COMMITTEE. Main/Corp National Association of Manufacturers of the United States of America. Postwar Committee. US. English. mo. $147.00. National Association of Manufacturers of the United States, 1776 F Street NW, Washington DC 20006. **Tel** 26144.

RHODE ISLAND DIRECTORY OF MANUFACTURERS. *See* Yearbooks, Almanacs, Directories.

RIVISTA DI IMPIANTI INDUSTRIALI. VFOAT Impianti Industriali. V. 1- Apr. 1968-. Periodical. Italian. ir. 13,330. Dr A Barbieri, Via le Premuda 2, Milano 20129 Italy. **LC** TS155.A1.

RMA MONTHLY TIRE REPORT. Main/Corp Rubber Manufacturers Association. Jan. 1977-. Periodical. US. English. mo. $200.00. Rubber Manufacturers Association, 1400 K Street NW, Washington DC 20006. **Tel** (202)682-4860. *RMA Tire Report Statistical Highlights.*

ROBOTICS AND COMPUTER-INTEGRATED MANUFACTURING. *See* Computers and Computer Science.

THE ROOFER MAGAZINE. Vol. 1, Issue 1 (Sept./Oct. 1981)-. 0279-4616. Periodical. US. English. bm. D & H Publications, PO Box 06253, Ft Myers FL 33906. **Tel** (813)275-7663. Ed Karen S Parker. **LC** TH2391. **DD** 695.05. adv acc. **Circ** 15,500. (ctrl). Features the latest in roofing technology, equipment comparisons, product news, safety, legal and business columns. Format includes contractor interviews and photo essays.

RUBBER MANUFACTURERS ASSOCIATION INDUSTRY RUBBER REPORT. VFOAT Industry Rubber Report. Jan. 1983-. 0741-5621. Periodical. US. English. mo. Rubber Manufacturers Association, 1440 K Street NW, Washington DC 20006. *RMA Industry Rubber Report.*

RUBBERVERWERKENDE INDUSTRIE. Series/Titl Produktiestatistieken Industrie. VFOAT Manufacture of Rubber Products. 1981-. 0168-4965. NE. Dutch (summaries in English). an. 9.50. Centraal Bureau Voor de Statistiek, Prinses Beatrixlaan 428, Postbus 959, 2270 AZ Voorburg Netherlands. *Rubberver Werkende Industrie, Produktiestatistieken.*

SACHGUTERERZEUGUNG SCHNELLBERICHT. Main/Corp Osterreichisches Statistisches Zentralamt. AU. German. qt. 140.-. Osterreichisches Statistisches Zentralamt, Neue Hofburg Heldenplatz, A 1010 Wien Austria. **Tel** (0222)6628-0. **LC** HC26A.A29A. **DD** 338.09436. bk rev. adv acc. **Circ** 150. (ctrl). Index based on 1981 for produced goods.

SAN DIEGO COUNTY DIRECTORY OF MANUFACTURERS AND INDUSTRIAL DISTRIBUTORS. *See* Yearbooks, Almanacs, Directories.

SASKATCHEWAN MANUFACTURERS' GUIDE (1979). (SASKATCHEWAN MANUFACTURERS' GUIDE). 1979-. 0711-8899. CN. English. an. Saskatchewan Industry and Commerce, 7th Floor of the Saskatchewan Power Building, Regina Saskatchewan S4P 3V7 Canada. **LC** HD9734.C3. **DD** 338.470002947124. *Saskatchewan Manufacturers' Gude and Distributors' Index, 0704-0016.*

SCIENTIFIC AND PROFESSIONAL EQUIPMENT INDUSTRIES. VFOAT Fabrication de Materiel Scientifique et Professionnel. 1970-. 0384-4242. Periodical. CN. English (text in French). an. 20.00 Domestic, 21.00 Foreign. Receiver General for Canada, Statistics of Canada Publications, Ottawa Ontario K1A 016 Canada. **Tel** (800)268-1151. **DD** 338.47681. *Scientific and Professional Equipment Manufacturers, 0575-9692.*

SCOTT'S DIRECTORIES, WESTERN MANUFACTURERS. *See* Yearbooks, Almanacs, Directories.

SCOTT'S INDUSTRIAL DIRECTORY. ATLANTIC MANUFACTURERS. *See* Yearbooks, Almanacs, Directories.

SCOTT'S INDUSTRIAL DIRECTORY. ONTARIO MANUFACTURERS. *See* Yearbooks, Almanacs, Directories.

SCOTT'S INDUSTRIAL DIRECTORY. WESTERN MANUFACTURERS. *See* Yearbooks, Almanacs, Directories.

SEN'I KOBUNSHI ZAIRYO KENKYUJO NENPO. Began with the issue for I.E. 1949. Japanese. an. **LC** TS1548.5. *Sen'i Kogyo Shikenjo Nenpo.*

SENSOR AND TRANSDUCER DIRECTORY. *See* Yearbooks, Almanacs, Directories.

SHIKEN HOKOKU (NIHON SENBAI KOSHA. HIRATSUKA SEIZO SHIKENJO). (SHIKEN HOKOKU). 0389-2263. Japanese (summaries in English). ir. Nihon Senbai Kosha Hiratsuka Seizo Shikenjo, 1-31 Kurobegaoka Hiratsuka-Shi, Kanagawa-Ken Japan. **LC** TS2220.

SHIPMENTS TO FEDERAL GOVERNMENT AGENCIES. (CURRENT INDUSTRIAL REPORTS. MA-175, SHIPMENTS TO FEDERAL GOVERNMENT AGENCIES). VFOAT Shipments to Federal Government Agencies. 1978-. 0275-4533. US. English. an. Data User Services Division Customer Services Publication, Bureau of the Census, Washington DC 20233. **Tel** (301)763-4100. **LC** JK1673. **DD** 353.00712. Presents timely data on the production, inventories, and orders of approximately 5,000 products, which represents 40 percent of all US manufacturing. *Shipment of Defense-Oriented Industries.*

SHOE FACTORY BUYER' GUIDE. *See* Leather and Fur Industry.

SIGNS AND DISPLAYS INDUSTRY. Main/Corp Canada. Statistics Canada. Manufacturing and Primary Industries Division. VFOAT Fabrication d'Enseignes et d'Etalages. VAT Industrie des Enseignes et Etalages. 1970-. 0527-6187. Periodical. CN. English (French). an. Receiver General for Canada, Statistics Canada Publications, Ottawa Ontario K1A 0T6 Canada. **Tel** (800)268-1151. *Signs and Displays Industry, 0527-6187.*

SINGAPORE MANUFACTURERS AND PRODUCTS DIRECTORY. *See* Yearbooks, Almanacs, Directories.

THE SITE REPORT. Vol. 1, No. 1 (Jan. 1981)-. 0275-1488. Periodical. US. English. bm. $250.00. Conway Publishers, 1954 Airport Road NE, Atlanta GA 30341. **Tel** (404)458-6026. Ed George Adcock. **Circ** 650. State by state coverage of new industrial facilities. Also contains comprehensive statistical summaries.

THE SMA DIRECTORY. *See* Yearbooks, Almanacs, Directories.

SME TECHNICAL DIGEST. Main/Corp Society of Manufacturing Engineers. 1969-. Periodical. US. English. qt. $24.00. Society of Manufacturing Engineers, PO Box 930 One SME Drive, Dearborn MI 48121. **Tel** (313)271-1500. **Ind/Abst** Fluidex, Eng. Index. Each issue contains an index to its own contents - no vol index - loose. Abstracts of all technical papers and articles published by same throughout the year. *ASTME Technical Digest.*

SOFTWHERE. MANUFACTURING. VFOAT Manufacturing. 0882-7443. Periodical. US. English. sa. $49.95. Moore Data Management Services, 1660 South Highway 100, Minneapolis MN 55416. **DD** 001.

SOLID MODELING TODAY. Vol. 1, No. 1 (May 1986)-. 0888-1588. Periodical. US. English. mo. $327.00. Merritt Co, Subscription Office, 1661 9th Street/PO Box 955, Santa Monica CA 90406. **DD** 670.

SOLID STATE TECHNOLOGY. V. 11- 1968-. 0038-111X. Periodical. US. English. mo. $30.00. Technical Publishing Company, 875 3rd Avenue, New York NY 10022. **Tel** (516)883-6200. Ed S Marshall. **Ind/Abst** Eng. Index Mon., Eng. Index Bioeng. Abstr., Eng. Index Energy Abstr., Predicasts, Comput. Control Abstr., Electr. Electron. Abstr., Sci. Abstr. Sect. A. Phys. Abstr., Ref. Source, Chem. Abstr., Eng. Index Annu., Eng. Index Mon., Nuci. Sci. Abstr., Met. Abstr., World Alum. Abstr., Appl. Sci. Technol. Index, Humanit. Index, Phys. Abstr., Funk Scott Index Corp. Ind., Sci. Cit. Index, Abr. Ed., Eng. Index. **CODEN** SSTEAP. bk rev. adv acc. **Circ** 35,000. (ctrl). *Semiconductor Products and Solid State Technology, 0096-3631.*

SOUTH AUSTRALIAN MAJOR MANUFACTURING, MINING AND DEVELOPMENT PROJECTS. VFOAT Development. (1973/74-). Periodical. AT. English. sa. Major Manufacturing & Mining, 309 Pitt Street, Government Bookshop, Sydney New South Wales 2000 Australia. **Tel** (02)267-8455.

SPUN YARN PRODUCTION. (CURRENT INDUSTRIAL REPORTS. MA-22F.2, SPUN YARN PRODUCTION). Began in 1959. 0277-0733. US. English. an. $1.25. Data User Services Division, Customer Services Publication, Bureau of the Census, Washington DC 20233. **Tel** (301)763-4100. **LC** HD9909.Y3. **DD** 338.4767702862. Presents timely data on the production, inventories, and orders of approximately 5,000 products, which represents 40 percent of all US manufacturing.

STATE GUIDE FOR RV MANUFACTURERS. VFOAT State Guide for R.V. Manufacturers. US. English. an. Recreational Vehicle Industry Association, PO Box 204, 14650 Lee Road, Chantilly VA 22021. **LC** HD9710.37.U6. **DD** 343.7307862922, 347. 3037862922.

STEEL FABRICATION JOURNAL. Began with Nov. 1971 issue. 0311-015X. Periodical. AT. English. qt. Australian Institute of Steel Construction, Eagle House, 118 Alfred Street, Milsons Point New South Wales 2061 Australia. **LC** TS350. **DD** 672.

STEEL FOUNDERS' RESEARCH JOURNAL. *See* Metals & Metallurgy.

THE STORAGE BATTERY MANUFACTURING INDUSTRY. YEARBOOK. *See* Yearbooks, Almanacs, Directories.

Manufacturing

SURVEY OF PLANT CAPACITY. (CURRENT INDUSTRIAL REPORTS. MQ-C1, SURVEY OF PLANT CAPACITY). VFOAT Survey of Plant Capacity. 0744-1290. US. English. an. $1.75. Data User Services Division, Customer Services Publication, Bureau of the Census, Washington DC 20233. Tel (301)763-4100. LC HD69.C3. DD 338.060973. Presents timely data on the production, inventories, and orders of approximately 5,000 products, which represents 40 percent of all US manufacturing.

SWEET'S SHOWROOM. 0364-7021. US. English. $5.00. McGraw Hill Information Systems Company, 1221 Avenue of the Americas, New York NY 10020. LC TS887. DD 381.45684100973.

TAIWAN BUYERS' GUIDE. 0082-1470. US. English (Chinese). be. $120.00. US International Marketing Company, 17057 Bellflower Boulevard/Suite 205, Bellflower CA 90706. Tel (213)925-2918. Ed R M Heaton. adv acc. Circ 2,000. Directory listing and illustrating thousands of low cost products. Lists 12,000 Taiwan manufacturers, exporters, and trading firms. *Chung Hua Min Kuo Kung Shang Ming Lu.*

TAIWAN ENTERPRISE. *See* Business - Commerce.

TECHNICAL MONOGRAPH (AGGLOMERATION DE BRUXELLES). (TECHNICAL MONOGRAPH / INTERNATIONAL GROUP OF NATIONAL ASSOCIATIONS OF MANUFACTURERS OF AGROCHEMICAL PRODUCTS). BE. English. ir. GIFAP, Avenue Hamoir 12, 1180 Bruxelles Belgique.

TECHNICAL PAPER - SOCIETY OF MANUFACTURING ENGINEERS. (TECHNICAL PAPER - SOCIETY OF MANUFACTURING ENGINEERS. MF). **Main/Corp** Society of Manufacturing Engineers. 1952. 0191-085X. US. English. ir. $625.00. Society of Manufacturing Engineers, PO Box 930 One SME Drive, Dearborn MI 48121. Tel (313)271-1500. **Ind/Abst** Eng. Index Annu., Eng. Index Mon., Eng. Index Bioeng. Abstr., Eng. Index Energy Abstr., Chem. Abstr. CODEN TSMFD7. Conference papers covering the entire spectrum of manufacturing technology.

TECHNIQUES INDUSTRIELLES. French. ir. 48.00. Comite d Etudes Pedagogiques et Techniques, Sevpen, 29 rue Dulm, 75230 Cachan France. LC TS183. *Enseignants Techniques: Technique Industrielles.*

TECNICA INDUSTRIAL. 0040-1838. Periodical. Spanish. ir. 275. Asociacion Nacional de Peritos E Ingenieros Tenicos Industriales, Plaza Luca de Tena 1, Madrid Spain. **Ind/Abst** Chem. Abstr. LC TS191. CODEN TEINBD.

TENNESSEE DIRECTORY OF MANUFACTURERS. *See* Yearbooks, Almanacs, Directories.

TEXAS INDUSTRIAL EXPANSION. V. 6-1956-. 0040-4365. Periodical. US. English. mo. Bureau of Business Research, University of Texas at Austin Box 7459, Austin TX 78713. Tel (512)471-1616. Ed Patti Hudgens-Higginbotham. Circ 3,000. (ctrl). Lists new plants and expanding plants in Texas also covers other business: mergers, layoffs, office leases, and contracts. *Industrial Expansion in Texas.*

TEXAS MANUFACTURERS REGISTER. 1st Ed. (1985)-. 0743-1163. US. English. an. $110.00. Manufacturers' News Inc, 4 East Huron Street, Chicago IL 60611. Tel (312)337-1084. LC HD9727.T4. DD 338.47670294764. adv acc.

TEXTILE & APPAREL MANUFACTURER. VFOAT Textile and Apparel Manufacturer. Vol. 57, No. 5 (Aug./Sept. 1982)-. 0810-574X. Periodical. English. ir. $30.00. Yaffa Publishing Group, 432-436 Elizabeth Street, Surry Hills New South Wales Australia. **Ind/Abst** World Text Abstr. LC TS1300. DD 338.4767700994. *Textile Journal/Australia.*

TEXTURED YARN PRODUCTION. (CURRENT INDUSTRIAL REPORTS. MA-22F.1, TEXTURED YARN PRODUCTION). 0272-7439. US. English. an. $1.00. Data User Services Division, Customer Services Publication, Bureau of the Census, Washington DC 20233. Tel (301)763-4100. LC HD9909.Y3. DD 338.4767702862. Presents timely data on the production, inventories, and orders of approximately 5,000 products, which represents 40 percent of all US manufacturing.

THAILAND MANUFACTURERS AND PRODUCTS DIRECTORY. *See* Yearbooks, Almanacs, Directories.

THESAURUS, MANUFACTURING ENGINEERING TERMS. VFOAT Thesaurus. 1st Ed.-. 0739-8778. US. English. an. Society of Manufacturing Engineers, Publications/Marketing Division, One SME Drive, PO Box 930, Dearborn MI 48121. LC Z699.5.M26. DD 025.4967.

THOMAS REGISTER OF AMERICAN MANUFACTURERS AND THOMAS REGISTER CATALOG FILE. 1st- Ed. 0362-7721. US. English. an. $190.00. Thomas Publishing Company, One Penn Plaza, 250 West 34th Street, New York NY 10117. Tel (212)695-0500. LC T12. DD 338.7602573. NLM T 12 T461. (cum index).

TITANIUM DEVELOPMENT ASSOCIATION BUYERS GUIDE. *See* Metals & Metallurgy.

TKG : FACHZEITSCHRIFT FUR DIE TECHNIK IN DER KERAMIK, GLAS UND EMAIL INDUSTRIE. *See* Glass and Ceramics.

TODAY'S TRANSPORT INTERNATIONAL. *See* Transportation.

TOOL & MANUFACTURING ENGINEER. *See* Engineering - Mechanical Engineering & Machinery.

TOOLING. 0040-9227. Periodical. UK. English. mo. Sawell Publications Limited, 127 Stanstead Road Forest Hill, London SE23 1JE England. Tel 01-699 6792. Ed T Savage. **Ind/Abst** CIS Abstr., ISMEC Bull. LC TJ1180.A1. DD 621.90205. bk rev. adv acc. Circ 5,800. (ctrl). A magazine which is aimed at the toolmaking side of manufacturing. *Toolmaker.*

TOYO SODA KENKYU HOKOKU. VFOAT Scientific Report of Toyo Soda Manufacturing Company, Ltd. 0041-0144. Periodical. English (Japanese). ir. Tokyo Soda Kogyo, Kabushiki Kaisha 4560, Tonda Shinnanyo-Shi, Yamaguchi-Ken 746 Japan. **Ind/Abst** Chem. Abstr. CODEN TSKEAP.

TRAILER/BODY BUILDERS. *See* Transportation.

TRAVAIL ET METHODES. *See* Business - General Management.

TRUCK BODY AND TRAILER MANUFACTURERS. *See* Transportation - Automobiles.

TRUCK TRAILERS. (CURRENT INDUSTRIAL REPORTS. M37L, TRUCK TRAILERS). VFOAT Truck Trailers. 0145-5001. Periodical. US. English. mo. $16.00. Data User Services Division Customer Services Publication, Bureau of the Census, Washington DC 20233. Tel (301)763-4100. **Ind/Abst** Predicasts, Am. Stat. Index. Presents timely data on the production, inventories, and orders of approximately 5,000 products, which represents 40 percent of all US manufacturing.

TZ FUR METALLBEARBEITUNG. *See* Metals & Metallurgy.

UHREN UND SCHMUCK. Periodical. SZ. German. bm. Kunst & Wissen Erich Bieber, Dufourstrasse 51, CH-8008 Zurich Switzerland. LC TS720.

U.S. INDUSTRIAL DIRECTORY. *See* Yearbooks, Almanacs, Directories.

UPHOLSTERING TODAY. Vol. 93, No. 4 (Sept. 1981)-. 0744-138X. Periodical. US. English. mo. $39.00. Communications Today, PO Box 2754, High Point NC 27261. Tel (919889-0013. Ed Gary Evans. LC TT198. DD 338.768412. bk rev. adv acc. Circ 10,000. (ctrl). Edited for manufacturing management of upholstered seating manufacturers i.e., residential, contract, institutional, business and transportation seating. *Upholstering Industry, 0042-0700.*

UPHOLSTERY MANUFACTURING MANAGEMENT. 0746-5017. Periodical. US. English. bm. Associations Publications Inc, 740 Chaney Drive, Collierville TN 38017.

UPSTATE NEW YORK DIRECTORY OF MANUFACTURERS. *See* Yearbooks, Almanacs, Directories.

VEGETABLE OIL MILLS. Series/Titl Annual Census of Manufactures. VFOAT Moulins a Huile Vegetable. 1970-. 0527-6403. CN. English (French). an. Receiver General for Canada, Statistics Canada Publications, Ottawa Ontario K1A 0T6 Canada. *Vegtable Oils Industry, 0384-4897.*

VESTNIK KIEVSKOGO POLITEKHNICHESKOGO INSTITUTA. SERIIA PRIBOROSTROENIIA. **Main/Corp** Kiev. Politekhnichnyi Instytut. VFOAT Seriia Priborostroeniia. Began in 1970. 0321-2211. UR. Russian (summaries in English). Izdatelaskoe Ob'Edinenie Vyshcha Shkola, Kiev USSR. **Ind/Abst** Chem. Abstr. LC TS500. CODEN VKPPDI.

VIRGINIA INDUSTRIAL DIRECTORY. 15th Ed. (1981-82)-. 0882-3219. US. English. be. $50.00 Members and Public Libraries, $60.00 Nonmembers. Virginia Chamber of Commerce, 611 East Franklin Street, Richmond VA 23219. Tel (804)644-1607. Ed John R Broadway. LC HC107.V8. DD 338.74025755. Circ 5,000. A completely up-to-date publication describing Virginia manufacturing and mining firms. It is a valuable resource for anyone who does business in Virginia. *Industrial Directory of Virginia.*

WASHINGTON LETTER ON LATIN AMERICA. *See* Economics.

WASHINGTON MANUFACTURERS REGISTER. 1978/79-. 0148-5687. US. English. be. $75.00. Manufactures News Inc, 4 East Huron Street, Chicago IL 60611. Tel (312)337-1084. LC T12. DD 338.4767025797. Consists of about 4,000 firms with four or more employees. Companies listed alphabetically by city and town, giving address, key executives, product, SIC, telephone, employees, sales volume. *Directory of Washington Manufacturers, 0148-3641.*

WEST VIRGINIA MANUFACTURING DIRECTORY. *See* Yearbooks, Almanacs, Directories.

WESTERN AUSTRALIAN MANUFACTURERS DIRECTORY. *See* Yearbooks, Almanacs, Directories.

WESTERN AUSTRALIAN PRODUCTS DIRECTORY. *See* Yearbooks, Almanacs, Directories.

WINDSOR & ESSEX COUNTY MANUFACTURERS DIRECTORY. *See* Yearbooks, Almanacs, Directories.

WIRE AND WIRE PRODUCTS MANUFACTURERS. **Main/Corp** Statistics Canada. Manufacturing and Primary Industries Division. Series/Titl Annual Census of Manufactures : Preliminary Bulletin. VFOAT Industrie du Fil Metallique et de Ses Produits. 0384-4781. Periodical. CN. English (French). an. Receiver General for Canada, Statistics Canada Publications, Ottawa Ontario K1A 0T6 Canada.

WIRE JOURNAL INTERNATIONAL. Vol. 14, No. 4 (Apr. 1981)-. 0277-4275. Periodical. US. English. mo. Wire Association International, 1570 Boston Post Road PO Box H, Guilford CT 06437. Tel (203)453-2777. **Ind/Abst** Eng. Index Annu., Eng. Index Mon., Eng. Index Bioeng. Abstr., Eng. Index Energy Abstr., Excerpta Med., Comput. Control Abstr., Electr. Electron. Abstr., Sci. Abstr. Sect. A. Phys. Abstr., Chem. Abstr., Met. Abstr., World Alum. Abstr., Appl. Sci. Technol. Index. LC TS270.A1. DD 671.842. CODEN WJINDF. *Wire Journal, 0043-602X.*

WIRE TECH. 0745-7510. Periodical. US. English. bm. Free to Manufacturers or Workers of Wire Related Products, $25.00 Others. Wire Tech, 6521 Davis Industrial Parkway, Solon OH 44139. **Ind/Abst** Comput. Control Abstr., Electr. Electron. Abstr., Sci. Abstr. Sect. A. Phys. Abstr., Met. Abstr., World Alum. Abstr. LC TS270.A1. DD 671.84205. *Wire Technology, 0361-4565.*

WISCONSIN MANUFACTURERS REGISTER. 1st Ed. (1984)-. 0738-0070. US. English. an. $75.00. Manufacturers News Inc, 4 East Huron Street, Chicago IL 60611-2793. Tel (312)337-1084. Ed Louise West. LC HD9727.W6. DD 338.4767029477*5*. adv acc.

WORLD MOTOR VEHICLE DATA. VFOAT MVMA. World Motor Vehicle Data. 0085-8307. US. English. an. $35.00. Motor Vehicle Manufacturers Association, 300 New Center Building, Detroit MI 48202. Tel (313)872-4311. LC HD9710.A1. DD 338.4762922. Contains sections on vehicle production, sales, registration, ownership, usage, and economic and social impact.

Mathematics

WYOMING DIRECTORY OF MANUFACTURING AND MINING. See Yearbooks, Almanacs, Directories.

ZEITSCHRIFT FUR WIRTSCHAFTLICHE FERTIGUNG. (ZWF : ZEITSCHRIFT FUR WIRTSCHAFTLICHE FERTIGUNG). **VFOAT** ZWF. 0044-3743. Periodical. German. mo. Carl Hanser Verlag, Kolbgerstrasse 22, D-8000 Munchen 80 West Germany. **Ind/Abst** CIS Abstr., Excerpta Med., Chem. Abstr., Energy Res. Abstr. **CODEN** ZTWFAP. Determined by the editorial presentation of problems related to modern production. Focuses on production planning and factory equipment, material flow automation, thermal treatment and hardening technology.

MATHEMATICS

ABHANDLUNGEN AUS DEM MATHEMATISCHEN SEMINAR DER HAMBURGISCHEN UNIVERSITAT. Vol. 1, No. 1 (Sept. 1921)-. Periodical. GW. German. ir. $49.83. Vandenhoeck & Ruprecht, Postfach 3753/Theaterstr 13, D 3400 Goettingen West Germany. **Tel** (0551)65061. **Ind/Abst** Math. Rev. **LC** QA1. **DD** 510.62. **CODEN** AMHAAJ. (cum index).

ABHANDLUNGEN DER AKADEMIE DER WISSENSCHAFTEN DER DDR, ABTEILUNG MATHEMATIK, NATURWISSENSCHAFTEN, TECHNIK. **Main/Corp** Akademie der Wissenschafter der DDR. Abteilung Mathematik, Naturwissenschaften, Technik. **VAT** Abhandlungen der Akademie der Wissenschaften der Deutsche Demokratische Republik, Abteilung Mathematik, Naturwissenschaften, Technik. Yearly V. 1975-. 0138-1059. Monographic Series. GE. English (German). ir. Deutscher Buch Export-Import, Leninstrasse 1, DDR-701 Leipzig East Germany. **Ind/Abst** Math. Rev., Chem. Abstr. **LC** UNC. **CODEN** AAWTD2. *Abhandlungen.*

ABHANDLUNGEN DER AKADEMIE DER WISSENSCHAFTEN IN GOTTINGEN. MATHEMATISCH-PHYSIKALISCHE KLASSE. **Main/Corp** Akademie der Wissenschaften in Gottingen. 0341-9843. Monographic Series. GW. Multilingual (German, French, English). ir. Vandenhoeck & Ruprecht, Postfach 3753, Theaterstr 13, D 3400 Goettingen West Germany. **Tel** (0551)65061. **Ind/Abst** Math. Rev., GeoRef, Chem. Abstr., Bibliogr. Index Geol. **CODEN** AWGMAI. adv acc. *Abhandlungen der Gesellschaft der Wissenschaften zu Gottingen. Mathematisch-Physikalische Klasse.*

ABSTRACTS OF BULGARIAN SCIENTIFIC LITERATURE. MATHEMATICAL AND PHYSICAL SCIENCES. See Indexes/Abstracts.

ABSTRACTS OF PAPERS PRESENTED TO THE AMERICAN MATHEMATICAL SOCIETY. See Indexes/Abstracts.

ACTA ACADEMIAE ABOENSIS. MATHEMATICA ET PHYSICA. V. 1-23. FI. Multilingual. ir. ABO Akademis Bibliotek, 20500 ABO 50, A B O 2 Finland. **Tel** 21-654224. Ed Goran Hognas. **Ind/Abst** Math. Rev., Bibliogr. Index Geol. adv acc. **Circ** 500. Original papers, surveys and theses in mathematics, science and engineering.

ACTA APPLICANDAE MATHEMATICAE. Vol. 1, No. 1-. 0167-8019. Periodical. English. ir. $159.00. D Reidel Publishing Company, PO Box 17, 3300 AA Dordrecht Holland. **Tel** (31)78-334911. Ed Michiel Hazewinkel. **Ind/Abst** Math. Rev. **LC** QA1. **DD** 510.5. **CODEN** AAMADV. bk rev. adv acc. **Circ** 600. The art and techniques of applying mathematics and the development of new applicable mathematical theories.

ACTA ARITHMETICA. Vol. 1 1935/36. 0065-1036. Periodical. PL. Polish (English and German). ir. ARS Polona, Krakowskie Przedmiescie 7, 00-068 Warsaw Poland. **Ind/Abst** Math. Rev., GeoRef. **CODEN** AARIA9. (cum index).

ACTA CIENCIA INDICA. MATHEMATICS. **VFOAT** Mathematics. V. 5, No. 1 (1979)-. Periodical. in English. qt. 150.-. Pragati Prakashan, PO Box 62, 250001 Meerut India. **Tel** 73022. Ed S C Agarwal. **Ind/Abst** Math. Rev., Energy Res. Abstr., Comput. Control Abstr., Electr. Electron. Abstr., Sci. Abstr. Sect. A. Phys. Abstr. **LC** QD1. **DD** 500.205. bk rev. adv acc. **Circ** 1,000. *Acta Ciencia Indica, 0379-5411.*

ACTA FACULTATIS RERUM NATURALIUM UNIVERSITATIS COMENIANAE. MATHEMATICA CEASED. **VFOAT** Mathematica. Began in 1956. Ceased with 36 (1980). 0524-2339. CS. Slovak (summaries in English, French, German or Russian). ir. **Ind/Abst** Math. Rev. **LC** QA1. **DD** 510.5. **CODEN** AFNUAQ.

ACTA MATHEMATICA. Vol. 1-. 0001-5962. Periodical. SW. Swedish (contributions in English, French, and German). ir. $90.00. Institut Mittag-Leffler, Auravagen 17, c/o Karin Lindberg, S-182 62 Djursholm Sweden. **Tel** 08/755 1809. **Ind/Abst** Math. Rev., Energy Res. Abstr. **LC** QA1. **DD** 510.5. **CODEN** ACMAA8. (cum index).

ACTA MATHEMATICA ACADEMIAE SCIENTIARUM HUNGARICAE CEASED. Began with: V. 1, in 1950. Ceased with V. 40, No. 3-4. 0001-5954. Periodical. HU. English (French, German, and Russian). qt. $88.00. Akademiai Kiado, POB 24, 1363 Budapest Hungary. **Tel** 111-010. Ed K Tandori. **Ind/Abst** Math. Rev., Zentralbl. Math. Ihre Grenzgeb., Sci. Cit. Index, Abr. Ed. **LC** QA1. **DD** 510.5. **CODEN** ACMTAV. (cum index). **Circ** 1,299. *Hungarica Acta Mathematica.*

ACTA MATHEMATICA HUNGARICA. **VFOAT** Acta Mathematica. Vol. 41, No. 1-2-. 0236-5294. Periodical. English (French, German, or Russian). ir. **Ind/Abst** Math. Rev. **LC** QA1. **DD** 510.5. *Acta Mathematica Academiae Scientiarum Hungaricae.*

ACTA MATHEMATICA VIETNAMICA. Began with: V. 1, No. 1 (1976). Periodical. VM. English (French). sa. Institute of Mathematics in Hanoi, 11 rue Pieree et Marie Curie, 75005 Paris France. **Ind/Abst** Math. Rev. *Acta Scientiarum Vietnamicarum. Sectio Scientiarum Mathematicarum et Physicarum.*

ACTA SCIENTIARUM MATHEMATICARUM. **Main/Corp** Szeged, Hungary. Tudomanyegyetem (Founded 1940). **VFOAT** A M. Kir. Ferencz Jozsef-Tudomanyegyetem Tudomanyos Kozlemenyei. Mathematikai Tudomanyok. V. 1- 1922/23-. 0001-6969. Periodical. English, French or German. ir. $88.00 US. Akademiai Kiado, POB 24, 1363 Budapest Hungary. **Tel** 111-010. Ed K Tandori. **Ind/Abst** Math. Rev., Sci. Cit. Index, Abr. Ed. **LC** AS142. **DD** 510.82. adv acc. **Circ** 1,200. All branches of mathematics.

ACTA STEREOLOGICA. Vol. 1, 1 (Jan. 1982)-. 0351-580X. Periodical. English. sa. $30.00. Institute of Histology and Embryology Medical Faculty, University E Kardeljat Ljubljana Zaloska 4/1 P O B 10, 1105 Ljubljana Yugoslavia. **Tel** (061)317-153. Ed Miroslav Kalisnik. **Ind/Abst** Chem. Abstr., Met. Abstr., World Alum. Abstr. **NLM** W1 AC949KH. **CODEN** ASTLDL. bk rev. adv acc. **Circ** 500. (ctrl). Stereology, quantitative, image analysis, morphometry, mathematics, instrumentation materials, and life sciences pattern recognition. Newsletter in Stereology, *Stereologica Iugoslavica, 0350-3062.*

ACTA UNIVERSITATIS CAROLINAE. MATHEMATICA ET PHYSICA. 1959-. 0001-7140. Periodical. CS. English (text in French, German and Russian). sa. Artia, Ve-Smeckach 30, Praha 1 Czechoslovakia. **Ind/Abst** Astron. Astrophys. Abstr., Math. Rev., Ref. Z., Zentralbl. Math. Ihre Grenzgeb., Sociol. Abstr., Lang. Lang. Behav. Abstr. **CODEN** AUMMBZ.

ADVANCES IN APPLIED MATHEMATICS. V. 1- Mar. 1980-. 0196-8858. Periodical. US. English. qt. $85.00. Academic Press, 4805 Sand Lake Road, Orland FL 32819. **Ind/Abst** Math. Rev. **LC** QA1. **DD** 510.5.

ADVANCES IN APPLIED PROBABILITY. Vol. 1- Spring 1969-. 0001-8678. Periodical. UK. English. qt. 81.00 North, South and Central America, 66.00 others. Applied Probability University, Department of Probability and Statistics, Sheffield S3 7RH England. **Tel** (0742)787555. Ed J Gani. **Ind/Abst** Math. Rev., Electron. Commun. Abstr. J., ISMEC Bull., Pollut. Abstr. Indexes, Saf. Sci. Abstr. J., GeoRef, Eng. Index, Biol. Abstr., Comput. Control Abstr., Electr. Electron. Abstr., Phys. Abstr., Sci. Abstr., Abr. Ed., Sci. Abstr. Sect. A. Phys. Abstr., Eng. Index Annu., Eng. Index Mon. **LC** QA273. **DD** 519.105. **CODEN** AAPBBD. (cum index). adv acc. **Circ** 1,100. Review and expository papers in applied probability, also mathematical and scientific papers of interest to probabilists, and letters to the editor.

ADVANCES IN MATHEMATICS. V. 1-. 0001-8708. US. English. mo. Academic Press, 4805 Sand Lake Road, Orlando FL 32819. Ed H Busemann. **Ind/Abst** Math. Rev., Sci. Cit. Index, Abr. Ed. **LC** QA1. **CODEN** ADMTA4.

ADVANCES IN MATHEMATICS : SUPPLEMENTARY STUDIES. V. 1-. Monographic Series. US. English. be. Academic Press, 4805 Sand Lake Road, Orlando FL 32887. **Tel** (305)345-4100. Ed Victor Guillemin. **Ind/Abst** Math. Rev.

ADVANCES IN PROBABILITY AND RELATED TOPICS. V. 1-. 0065-3217. Monographic Series. US. English. ir. Marcel Dekker, 270 Madison Avenue, New York NY 10016. **Tel** (212)696-9000. Ed P Ney. **Ind/Abst** Math. Rev. **LC** QA273.A1. **DD** 519.2. This is an ongoing series. Each title has a different subject.

AEQUATIONES MATHEMATICAE. Vol. 1 (1968)-. 0001-9054. Periodical. English (French, German, Italian or Russian). bm. Birkhauser Boston Inc, 380 Green Street, PO Box 3005, Cambridge MA 02139. **Ind/Abst** Math. Rev., Int. Aerosp. Abstr., Energy Res. Abstr. **LC** QA1. **DD** 510.5. **CODEN** AEMABN.

ALGEBRA AND LOGIC. V. 7- Jan./Feb. 1968-. 0002-5232. Periodical. US. English (Russian). bm. $445.00 Domestic, $495.00 Foreign. Consultants Bureau, 233 Spring Street, New York NY 10013. **Tel** (212)620-8000. Ed Yu L Ershor. **Ind/Abst** Math. Rev., Electron. Commun. Abstr. J., ISMEC Bull., Pollut. Abstr. Indexes, Saf. Sci. Abstr. J., Philos. Index, Curr. Math. Publ., Index Math. Pap., Zentralbl. Math. Ihre Grenzgeb., Comput. Rev. **LC** QH150. **CODEN** ALL0A6. This journal reports results of the latest research in the areas of modern general algebra and logic considered primarily from an algebraic viewpoint.

ALGEBRA I LOGISKA. (ALGEBRA I LOGIKA, SEMINAR : SBORNIK TRUDOV). **Main/Corp** Akademiia Nauk SSSR. Sibirskor Otdelenie. Seminar Algebra I Logiki. V. 1- 1962-. Periodical. Russian. ir. Institute of Mathematics, Novosibirsk 90 USSR 630090. Ed Yu L Ershov, E N Kuzmin and Yu I Merzlyakov. **LC** QA1. Algebra and logic.

ALGEBRA UNIVERSALIS. V. 1-. 0002-5240. Periodical. CN. English. ir. $144.00. Birkhauser Boston Inc, 380 Green Street, PO Box 3005, Cambridge MA 02139. **Tel** (617)576-6638. **Ind/Abst** Math. Rev. **LC** QA251. **DD** 512. **CODEN** AGUVA9.

ALGEBRAS, GROUPS AND GEOMETRIES. (ALGEBRAS, GROUPS, AND GEOMETRIES). Vol. 1, No 1 (Mar. 1984)-. 0741-9937. Periodical. US. English. qt. $150.00. Hadronic Press, Nonantum MA 02195. **Ind/Abst** Math. Rev. **DD** 512.

ALKALMAZOTT MATEMATKAI LAPOK. (ALKALMAZOTT MATEMATKAI LAPEK). 1.- Vol. 0133-3399. HU. Hungarian (with summaries in English and Russian). qt. Akademiai Kiado, PO Box 24, 1363 Budapest Hungary. **Tel** 187-002. Ed A Prekopa. **Ind/Abst** Math. Rev., Comput. Control Abstr., Electr. Electron. Abstr., Sci. Abstr. Sect. A. Phys. Abstr. **LC** QA1. **CODEN** AMLAD8. Eng. Index. Applied mathematics. *Magyar Tudomanyos Akademia Matematikai es Fizikai Tudomanyok Oszstalyanak Kozlemenyai.*

AMERICAN JOURNAL OF MATHEMATICAL AND MANAGEMENT SCIENCES. Vol. 1, No. 1-. 0196-6324. Periodical. US. English. qt. $29.95. American Sciences Press, 20 Cross Road, Syracuse NY 13224. **Tel** (315)446-1843. Ed Edward J Dudewicz. **Ind/Abst** Math. Rev. **LC** T55.4. **DD** 658.4034. **CODEN** AMMSDX. bk rev. adv acc. **Circ** 1000. AJMMS brings together the best new work in the various areas of the mathematical and management sciences. Computer programs are included in articles, which are readable and usable.

AMERICAN JOURNAL OF MATHEMATICS. V. 1- 1878-. 0002-9327. Periodical. US. English. bm. $105.00. Johns Hopkins University Press, 701 West 40th Street/Suite 275, Baltimore MD 21211. **Tel** (301)338-6987. Ed Jun-Ichi Igusa and J H Simpson. **Ind/Abst** Math. Rev., Electron. Commun. Abstr. J., ISMEC Bull., Pollut. Abstr. Indexes, Saf. Sci. Abstr. J., Sci. Cit. Index, Abr.

Mathematics

Ed. LC QA1. DD 510.5. CODEN AJMAAN. (cum index). adv acc. Circ 1,521. Now in its second century, AJM is one of the oldest mathematical journals in the US. Contributions from theoretical mathematicians are published.

THE AMERICAN MATHEMATICAL MONTHLY. (THE AMERICAN MATHEMATICAL MONTHLY : THE OFFICIAL JOURNAL OF THE MATHEMATICAL ASSOCIATION OF AMERICA). Began publication Jan. 1894. 0002-9890. Periodical. US. English. $70.00. Mathematical Association of America Inc, 1529 Eighteenth Street NW, Washington DC 20036. Tel (202)387-5200. Ed Paul Halmos. Ind/Abst Math. Rev., Int. Aerosp. Abstr., Curr. Index J. Educ., Gen. Sci. Index, Sci. Cit. Index, Abr. Ed., Bibliogr. Index, Comput. Rev. LC QA1. DD 510.5. CODEN AMMYAE. bk rev. adv acc. Circ 18,000. Available on microfilm from University Microfilms International. Contains expository articles, pure and applied math, department of notes and the teaching of math, elementary and advanced problems and reviews.

AMERICAN SERIES IN MATHEMATICAL AND MANAGEMENT SCIENCES. VFOAT American Science Press Series in Mathematical and Management Sciences. 0883-6221. Monographic Series. US. English. $135.00. American Sciences Press Inc, 20 Cross Road, Syracuse NY 13224. Ed Edward J Dudewicz. Ind/Abst Math. Rev. DD 515. bk rev. adv acc. Seeks to bring together the best new work in the various areas of the mathematical and management sciences.

ANALELE. SERIA STIINTE MATEMATICE. Main/Corp Universitatea Din Timisoara. 7- 1969-. Periodical. RM. Romanian (English, French, German). ir. Cartimex, PO Box 134-135, Bucharest Romania. Analele. Seria Stiinte Matematice-Fizice.

ANALELE STIINTIFICE ALE UNIVERSITATII AL. I. CUZA DIN IASI. SERIE NOUA. SECTIUNEA I A: MATEMATICA. Main/Corp Jassy. Universitatea. Din Iasi. VFOAT Matematica. V. 10- 1964-. 0448-9047. Periodical. RM. Romanian (English, French, or Russian). an. Rompresfilatelia, PO Box 1362137, Bucharest Romania. Ind/Abst Math. Rev. LC QA1. Analele Stiintifice. Serie Noua. Sectiunea I: Matematica, Fizica, Chimie.

ANALES DEL INSTITUTO DE MATEMATICAS. See Yearbooks, Almanacs, Directories.

ANALIZ NA PROBLEMNYKH SETIAKH. Vol. 1-. 0130-9412. Periodical. UR. Russian. 0.40. LC QA63.

L'ANALYSE NUMERIQUE ET LA THEORIE DE L'APPROXIMATION. VFOAT Mathematica - Revue d'Analyse Numerique et de Theorie de l'Approximation. V. 4-. Periodical. RM. English (French, German or Russian). sa. Editions de l'Academie de la Republique Socialiste de Roumanie, Elena Popoviciu, Academia Republicii, Socialiste Romania, Filiala Din Cluj-Napoca Str Republicii Nr 9, Clu-Napoca Roumanie. Ind/Abst Math. Rev. LC QA297. DD 519.405. Revue d'Analyse Numerique et de la Theorie de l'Approximation.

ANALYSIS MATHEMATICA. V. 1-. 0133-3852. Periodical. HU. Multilingual (English and Russian). qt. $190.00. Pergamon Press, 395 Sawmill River Road, Elmsford NY 10523. Ind/Abst Math. Rev., Comput. Control Abstr., Electr. Electron. Abstr., Sci. Abstr. Sect. A. Phys. Abstr., Phys. Abstr. LC QA300. CODEN ANMADK.

ANALYSIS (WIESBADEN). (ANALYSIS). Vol. 1, No. 1-. 0174-4747. Periodical. English. ir. 216.-. R Oldenbourg Verlag, Postfach 801360, D-8000 Munchen 80 West Germany. Tel 089/4112. Ind/Abst Math. Rev.

ANNALES DE LA FACULTE DES SCIENCES DE TOULOUSE. (ANNALES DE LA FACULTE DES SCIENCES DE TOULOUSE. MATHEMATIQUES). Ser. 5, V. 1, Issue 1- – 79E Vol.-. 0240-2963. Periodical. FR. French (English). ty. 350. Annales de la Faculte des Sciences, Universite Paul Sabatier, 31077 Toulouse Cedex France. Ind/Abst Math. Rev., Comput. Control Abstr., Electr. Electron. Abstr., Sci. Abstr. Sect. A. Phys. Abstr. LC Q46. DD 510.5. CODEN AFSMDU. Annales de la Faculte des Sciences de l'Universite de Toulouse.

ANNALES DE LA SOCIETE SCIENTIFIQUE DE BRUXELLES. Main/Corp Societe Scientifique de Bruxelles. Vol. 1-. 0037-959X. Periodical. BE. French. qt. 1100. Societe Scientifique, 61 rue de Bruxelles, B 5000 Namur Belgium. Tel 081-229061. Ind/Abst Met. Abstr., World Alum. Abstr., Math. Rev., Phys. Abstr., Electr. Electron. Abstr., Comput. Control Abstr., Chem. Abstr. LC Q56. (cum index). Circ 400. Research papers on mathematics, physics, and chemistry.

ANNALES DE L'I.H.P. PHYSIQUE THEORIQUE. See Physics.

ANNALES DE L'I.H.P. PROBABILITES ET STATISTIQUES. VFOAT Annales de l'IHP. Vol. 19, No. 1-. 0246-0203. Periodical. FR. English (French). qt. 640. Gauthier-Villars, Centrale des Revues, 11 rue Gossin, 92543 Montrouge Cedex France. Ed J Neveu. Ind/Abst Math. Rev. bk rev. adv acc. Circ 750. This journal recently reorganized welcomes high standard manuscripts from all areas of the theory of probabilities. Annales de l'Institut Henri Poincare. Section B, Probabilites et Statistiques, 0020-2347.

ANNALES DE L'INSTITUT FOURIER. Vol. 1- 1949-. 0373-0956. Periodical. FR. French. qt. 940. Annales de l'Institut Fourier, B P 74, 38402 St Martin d'Heres France. Tel (76)51 46 57. Ind/Abst Math. Rev., Int. Aerosp. Abstr., Energy Res. Abstr. LC Q46. DD 505. CODEN AIFUA7. Circ 1,300. High quality papers in all branches of pure mathematics; main published fields: classical analysis, partial differential equations, differential geometry, theory of singularities and number theory. Annales de l'Universite de Grenoble. Section des Sciences Mathematiques et Physiques.

ANNALES DE L'INSTITUT HENRI POINCARE. SECTION A. PHYSIQUE THEORIQUE. See Physics.

ANNALES DE L'INSTITUT HENRI POINCARE. SECTION B, CALCUL DES PROBABILITES ET STATISTIQUE. See Statistics.

ANNALES DES SCIENCES MATHEMATIQUES DU QUEBEC. (LES ANNALES DES SCIENCES MATHEMATIQUES DU QUEBEC). V. 1-Jan. 1977-. 0707-9109. Periodical. CN. French. sa. 7.74. University of Montreal, Center Mathematiques, CP 6128 Succursale A, Montreal Quebec H3C 3J7 Canada. Ed Robert Cleroux. Ind/Abst Math. Rev. LC QA1. DD 510.5. Circ 300. Research papers on any subject related to mathematics.

ANNALES POLONICI MATHEMATICI. Vol. 1 1954-. 0066-2216. Periodical. PL. French, German, English, and other languages. ty. ARS Polona, Krakowskie Przedmiescie 7, 00-068 Warsaw Poland. Ind/Abst Math. Rev. LC QA1. CODEN APNMA4. (cum index). Annales de la Societe Polonaise de Mathematique.

ANNALES SCIENTIFIQUES DE L'ECOLE NORMALE SUPERIEURE. Main/Corp Ecole Normale Superieure (France). V. 1-7, 1864-1870. 0012-9593. Periodical. FR. French (English or German). qt. $95.52. Centrale des Revues-Gauthier Villars, 11 rue Gossin, 92543 Montrouge Cedex France. Tel (1)43 20 15 50. Ed M Herman. Ind/Abst Math. Rev., Sci. Cit. Index, Abr. Ed. CODEN ASENAH. (cum index). adv acc. Circ 900. Leading mathematics journal since 1864.

ANNALES SCIENTIFIQUES DE L'UNIVERSITE DE CLERMONT. MATHEMATIQUES. Main/Corp Universite de Clermont-Ferrand. Series/Titl Annales Scientifiques de l'Universite de Clermont. 8E- Issue. 0249-7042. FR. French. ir. 20.00 Per Issue. Universite de Clermont-Ferrand, 5 rue Kessler, 63000-Clermont-Ferrand France. LC QA1. DD 510.5. Annales de la Faculte des Sciences de l'Universite de Clermont. Mathematiques, 0069-472X.

ANNALES SOCIETATIS MATHEMATICAE POLONAE. SERIES 4. FUNDAMENTA INFORMATICAE. (ANNALES SOCIETATIS MATHEMATICAE POLONAE. SERIES IV : FUNDAMENTA INFORMATICAE). Main/Corp Polskie Towarzystwo Matematyczne. VFOAT Fundamenta Informaticae. V. 1-. 0324-8429. Periodical. GW. English. ir. $70.34. Wissenschaftliche Versandbuch, Hahnenkleerstrasse 14, 3394 Langelsheim 2 West Germany. Ind/Abst Math. Rev., Comput. Control Abstr., Electr. Electron. Abstr., Sci. Abstr. Sect. A. Phys. Abstr. LC QA267. DD 519.705. CODEN FUMAAJ.

ANNALES UNIVERSITATIS MARIAE CURIE-SKODOWSKA. SECTIO A. MATHEMATICA. Main/Corp Uniwersytet Marii Curie-Skodowskiej. VFOAT Roczniki Uniwersytetu Marii Curie-Skodowskiej. V. 1- 1946-. 0365-1029. Polish (French or other languages). an. Ind/Abst Math. Rev. LC QA1.L8. CODEN ACAMAI.

ANNALI DELLA SCUOLA NORMALE SUPERIORE DI PISA, CLASSE DI SCIENZE. Main/Corp Scuola Normale Superiore (Italy). Classe di Scienze. Ser. 4, V. 1- 1974-. 0391-173X. Periodical. IT. English. qt. Scuola Normale Superiore, Piazza dei Cavalieri 7, 56100 Pisa Italy. Ind/Abst Math. Rev. LC QA1. CODEN PSNAAI. Annali Della Scuola Normale Superiore di Pisa. Scienze Fisiche I Matematiche.

ANNALI DELL'UNIVERSITA DI FERRARA. SEZIONE 7. SCIENZE MATEMATICHE. (ANNALI DELL'UNIVERSITA DI FERRARA. SEZIONE 7 : SCIENZE MATEMATICHE). Main/Corp Ferrara. Universita. VAT Annali Dell'Universita di Ferrarae. Sezione Sette: Scienze Matemati. Began with Vol. for 1950/51. 0430-3202. Italian (summaries in English). ir. Istituto di Matematica, Via Savonarola 9, 44100 Ferrara Italy. Ind/Abst Math. Rev. LC QA1. DD 510. CODEN AUFMAX.

ANNALI DI MATEMATICA PURA ED APPLICATA. Vol. 1 (1858)-Vol. 7 (1865). 0373-3114. Periodical. IT. Italian (articles in English, French and German). ir. 40.000. Nicola Zanichelli Editore, Via Irnerio 34, 40126 Bologna Italy. Tel 051/293265. Ed B Tortolini and F Brioschi. Ind/Abst Math. Rev., Appl. Mech. Rev. CODEN ANLMAE. (cum index). Yearbooks of pure and applied mathematics. Annali di Scienze, Matematiche E Fisiche.

ANNALS OF DISCRETE MATHEMATICS. V.1-. Monographic Series. English. ir. Ind/Abst Math. Rev., Comput. Control Abstr., Electr. Electron. Abstr., Sci. Abstr. Sect. A. Phys. Abstr.

ANNALS OF MATHEMATICAL LOGIC. V. 1-23. 0003-4843. Periodical. English. ir. Ind/Abst Math. Rev., Electron. Commun. Abstr. J., ISMEC Bull., Pollut. Abstr. Indexes, Saf. Sci. Abstr. J., Philos. Index. LC QA1. DD 164.05. CODEN AMLOAD.

ANNALS OF MATHEMATICS STUDIES. No. 1-. 0066-2313. Monographic Series. US. English. ir. Princeton University Press, Box A 3175, Princeton Pike, Lawrenceville NJ 08648. Tel (609)896-2111. Ind/Abst Math. Rev. CODEN ANMAA.

ANNALS OF PROBABILITY. See Statistics.

ANNALS OF STATISTICS. See Statistics.

ANNALS OF THE INSTITUTE OF STATISTICAL MATHEMATICS. See Statistics.

APLIKACE MATEMATIKY. V. 1-. 0373-6725. Periodical. CS. Czech (English, Russian and other languages). bm. $235.00 Domestic, $362.00 Foreign. Plenum Publishing Company Ltd, 233 Spring Street, New York NY 10013. Tel (212)620-8000. Ed Zbynek Sidak. Ind/Abst Math. Rev., Int. Aerosp. Abstr., Comput. Control Abstr., Electr. Electron. Abstr., Sci. Abstr. Sect. A. Phys. Abstr., Phys. Abstr., Appl. Mech. Rev., Comput. Rev. LC QA1. CODEN APMTAK. Provides researchers with up-to-date research. Being conducted in mathematics by Czechoslovakian mathematicians.

APPLICABLE ANALYSIS. V. 1- Apr. 1971-. 0003-6811. Periodical. US. English. qt. $334.00. Harwood Academic Publishers, PO Box 197, London WC2E 9PX England. Ed R P Gilbert. Ind/Abst Math. Rev., Electron. Commun. Abstr., ISMEC Bull., Pollut. Abstr. Indexes, Saf. Sci. Abstr. J., Int. Aerosp. Abstr., Comput. Control Abstr., Electr. Electron. Abstr., Sci. Abstr. Sect. A. Phys. Abstr., Appl. Mech. Rev., Phys. Abstr. LC QA300. DD 515.05. CODEN APANCC. bk rev. adv acc.

APPLICATIONS OF MATHEMATICS. 1-. 0172-4568. Monographic Series. US. English. ir. Springer Verlag-New York Inc, 175 5th Avenue, New York NY 10010. Tel (212)460-1584. Ind/Abst Math. Rev., Comput. Control Abstr., Electr. Electron. Abstr., Sci. Abstr. Sect. A. Phys. Abstr. LC UNC. CODEN APMADY. Topics include methods of numerical mathematics, applied functional analysis, difference methods and their extrapolations.

APPLIED MATHEMATICAL SCIENCES. Vol. 1-. 0066-5452. Monographic Series. US. English. ir. Springer Verlag, 44 Hartz Way, Secaucus NJ 07094. Tel (201)348-4033. Ed F John. Ind/Abst Math. Rev., Electr. Electron. Abstr., Comput. Control Abstr., Phys. Abstr. LC QA1. CODEN AMSCDF. Oriented towards mathematicians interested in the application of their subject. Covers a

Mathematics

wide spectrum of current applied mathematics. Many volumes are suitable as undergraduate texts.

APPLIED MATHEMATICS AND COMPUTATION. V. 1- Jan. 1975-. 0096-3003. Periodical. US. English. $220.00. Elsevier Science Publishing Company Inc, PO Box 1663 Grand Central Station, New York NY 10163. **Ind/Abst** Math. Rev., Electron. Commun. Abstr. J., ISMEC Bull., Pollut. Abstr. Indexes, Saf. Sci. Abstr. J., Int. Aerosp. Abstr., Comput. Control Abstr., Electr. Electron. Abstr., Sci. Abstr. Sect. A. Phys. Abstr., Sci. Cit. Index, Abr. Ed., Phys. Abstr., Comput. Rev., Appl. Mech. Rev. **LC** QA1. **DD** 519.405. **NLM** W1 AP526. **CODEN** AMHCBQ.

APPLIED MATHEMATICS AND MECHANICS (NEW YORK, N.Y.). (APPLIED MATHEMATICS AND MECHANICS : AN INTERNATIONAL SERIES OF MONOGRAPHS). Began with: V. 1, in 1956. US. English. ir. Academic Press, Library Services, Orlando FL 32887. **Tel** (305)345-4500. Ed William K Blake. **Ind/Abst** Electr. Electron. Abstr., Eng. Index, Phys. Abstr., Comput. Control Abstr.

APPLIED MATHEMATICS & OPTIMIZATION. (APPLIED MATHEMATICS AND OPTIMIZATION). **VFOAT** Applied Mathematics Optimization. V. 1- 1974-. 0095-4616. Periodical. US. English. ty. $77.00. Springer Verlag New York Inc, 175 5th Avenue, New York NY 10010. **Tel** (212)460-1500. Ed A V Balakrisnan, J L Lions, G I Marchuk and L S Pontryagin. **Ind/Abst** Math. Rev., Eng. Index Annu., Eng. Index Mon., Eng. Index Bioeng. Abstr., Eng. Index Energy Abstr., Int. Aerosp. Abstr., Comput. Control Abstr., Electr. Electron. Abstr., Sci. Abstr., Sci. Abstr. Sect. A. Phys. Abstr., Sci. Cit. Index, Abr. Ed., Phys. Abstr., Comput. Rev., Eng. Index. **LC** QA402.5. **DD** 519.05. **CODEN** AMOMBN. Contains papers dealing with applied mathematical topics with a practical implication, reports concerning modeling and identification of systems, and critical surveys of new advances in theory and application.

APPLIED MATHEMATICS NOTES. **VFOAT** Notes de Mathematiques Appliquees. V. 1- Apr. 1975-. 0700-9224. Periodical. CN. English (includes some text in French). qt. $7.74. Canadian Mathematical Society, 577 King Edward Avenue, Ottawa Ontario K1N 6N5 Canada. **Tel** (613)564-2223. Ed G Sabin. **Ind/Abst** Math. Rev. **DD** 519.05. **Circ** 300. Expository and newsworthy material aimed at bridging the gap between professional mathematicians and the users of mathematics.

APPLIED MATHEMATICS SERIES. **Main/Corp** United States. National Bureau of Standards. 1-. Monographic Series. US. English. ir. US Department of Commerce, National Bureau of Standards, Washington DC 20402. **LC** QA3. **DD** 510.5.

APPLIED NUMERICAL MATHEMATICS : TRANSACTIONS OF IMACS. **VFOAT** Transactions of IMACS. Vol. 1, No. 1 (Jan. 1985)-. 0168-9274. Periodical. English. bm. $117.50. PO Box 1991, 1050 BZ Amsterdam Netherlands.

ARBEITEN ZUR ANGEWANDTEN STATISTIK. See Statistics.

ARCHIMEDE : RIVISTA PER GLI INSEGNANTI E I CULTORI MATEMATICHE PURE E APPLICATE. Yearly V. 1, No. 1 (Feb./Mar. 1949)-. 0003-8369. Periodical. IT. Italian. qt. $20.00. Casa Edit Felice le Monnier, Post Box 202, 50100 Firenze Italy. **Tel** 055-6813801. bk rev. adv acc. **Circ** 5,000. Outline of different branches of mathematics- historical development of concepts and theories of elementary mathematics- philosophy methodology and didactics of mathematics. Bollettino di Matematica.

ARCHIV DER MATHEMATIK. See Genealogy and Heraldry - Archives.

ARCHIV FUR MATHEMATISCHE LOGIK UND GRUNDLAGENFORSCHUNG. See Genealogy and Heraldry - Archives.

AREA MATEMATICAS. Series/Titl Contribuciones Cientificas Y Tecnologicas. 1-. Spanish (summaries in English). ir. Direccion de Investigaciones Cientificas y Tecnologicas de la Universidad Tecnica del Esado, Avda Ecuado 3469, Santiago Chile. **LC** QA1.

THE ARITHMETIC TEACHER. 0004-136X. Periodical. US. English. mo. $40.00. National Council of Teachers of Mathematics, 1906 Association Drive, Reston VA 22091. **Tel** (703)620-9840. Ed Harry B Tunis. **Ind/Abst** Except. Child Educ. Resour., Educ. Index, Curr. Index J. Educ., Media Rev. Dig. **LC** QA135. **DD** 510.7. bk rev. adv acc. **Circ** 33,251. (ctrl). Forum for exchange of ideas and source of techniques for teaching mathematics in grades kindergarten through eighth grade. It presents new developments in curriculum, instruction, learning and teacher education.

ARKHIMEDES. 1949-. 0004-1920. Periodical. Fl. Finnish (Swedish. summaries in English). ir. 73.-. Akakeeminen-Kirjakauppa, P O Box 128, 00101 Helsinki Finland. **Tel** (90)651 122. **Ind/Abst** Math. Rev., Chem. Abstr., Energy Res. Abstr. **CODEN** AKMDA5. (cum index).

ARKIV FOR MATEMATIK. V. 1- 1949/52-. 0004-2080. Periodical. SW. English (French or German). sa. $40.00. Institut Mittag-Leffler, Auravagen 17, c/o Karin Larin, S-182 62 Djursholm Sweden. **Tel** 08/755 1809. **Ind/Abst** Math. Rev., Int. Aerosp. Abstr., Comput. Control Abstr., Electr. Electron. Abstr., Sci. Abstr. Sect. A. Phys. Abstr., Sci. Cit. Index, Abr. Ed., Phys. Abstr. **LC** QA3. **CODEN** AKMTAJ. Arkiv For Matematik, Astronomi Och Fysik.

ASTERISQUE. 1-. 0303-1179. French (text in English with summaries in English or French). mo. 880.00. Offilib, 48 rue Gay-Lussac, 75240 Paris Cedex 05 France. **Tel** 329-21-32. **Ind/Abst** Math. Rev., Zentralbl. Math. Ihre Grenzgeb.

ATLANTIC MATHEMATICS BULLETIN. V. 1- May 1977-. 0705-9078. Periodical. CN. English. Limited Free Distribution. Z Star Mathematics Department, University of New Brunswick, Box 4400, Fredericton New Brunswick E3B 5A3 Canada. **DD** 510.711715. (ctrl).

ATTI - INSTITUTO VENETO DI SCIENZE, LETTRE ED ARTI. CLASSE DI SCIENZE FISICHE, MATEMATICHE E NATURALI. See Science (General).

AUSTRALIAN MATHEMATICS TEACHER. (THE AUSTRALIAN MATHEMATICS TEACHER). Vol. 39, No. 1 (March 1983)-. 0045-0685. Periodical. English. ir. **Ind/Abst** Curr. Index J. Educ.

BARRON'S REGENTS EXAMS AND ANSWERS, 9TH YEAR MATHEMATICS, ELEMENTARY ALGEBRA. (BARRON'S REGENTS EXAMS AND ANSWERS : NINTH YEAR MATHEMATICS, ELEMENTARY ALGEBRA). **Main/Corp** Barron's Educational Series, Inc. 0362-1413. US. English. $2.25. Barrons Educational Series Inc, 113 Crossways Park Drive, Woodbury NY 11797. **LC** QA157. **DD** 512.9042076. Exams and Answers: Elementary Algebra.

BARRON'S REGENTS EXAMS AND ANSWERS. 10TH YEAR MATHEMATICS. See Education (General).

BARRON'S REGENTS EXAMS AND ANSWERS. 11TH YEAR MATHEMATICS. (BARRON'S REGENTS EXAMS AND ANSWERS : 11TH YEAR MATHEMATICS). **Main/Corp** Barron's Educational Series, Inc. **VFOAT** Regents Exams' and Answers. **VAT** Barron's Regents Exams and Answers: Eleventh Year Mathematics. 0146-406X. US. English. $2.50. Barrons Educational Series, 113 Crossways Park Drive, Woodbury NY 11797. **LC** QA43. **DD** 510.76.

BARRON'S REGENTS EXAMS AND ANSWERS, BUSINESS MATHEMATICS. See Business.

BEITRAGE ZUR ALGEBRA UND GEOMETRIE. Series Corp Universitat Halle- Wittenberg. Wissenschaftliche Beitrage. No. 1- 1971-. Periodical. GE. German. an. 30. Deutscher Buch Export-Import, Leninstrasse 16, DDR-701 Leipzig East Germany. **Tel** 22900. Ed O H Keller, O Krotenheerdt, E T Schmidt and L Stammler. **Ind/Abst** Math. Rev. Articles by E Bohme, H Boseck, K Drechsler, U Sterz, B Goldschmidt, O H Keller, G Liebhold, B Renschuch, W Vogel, P Schreiber, B Schultz, L Stammler, G Geise and B Weibbach.

BEITRAGE ZUR ANALYSIS CEASED. Ceased with Vol. 18. Periodical. WB. German. sa. 310,20. Deutscher Buch Export-Import, Leninstrasse 16, DDR-701 Leipzig East Germany. **Tel** 22900. Ed R Kotzler. **Ind/Abst** Math. Rev. **LC** QA300. **CODEN** BEANDF. Publishes articles in English on the field of mathematical analysis. These include theory of functions, functional analysis, differential equations, mathematical, physics, and differential geometry.

BEITRAGE ZUR DIFFERENTIALGEOMETRIE. Series/Titl Bonner Mathematische Schriften. Monographic Series. German. ir. **LC** QA1.

BEITRAGE ZUR NUMERISCHEN MATHEMATIK CEASED. V. 1-. Periodical. GE. German. sa. Deutscher Buch Export-Import, Leninstrasse 16, DDR-701 Leipzig East Germany. Ed Frieder Kuhnert and Jochen W Schmidt. **Ind/Abst** Math. Rev.

BIBLIOGRAFIA BRASILEIRA DE MATEMATICA. V. 1- 1970-. 0067-6667. BL. Portuguese. ir. Insti Braslerio de Biblio Doc, Ave General Justo 171-3, Rio de Janeiro Brazil. **Tel** 242-2915. **LC** Z6653, QA36. **DD** 016.51. Bibliografia Brasileira de Matematica E Fisica.

BIOMATHEMATICS. See Biology.

BIULETYN LUBELSKIE TOWARZYSTWA NAUKOWEGO. MATEMATYKA, FIZYKA-CHEMIA. (BIULETYN. WYDZIA III : MATEMATYKA, FIZYKA-CHEMIA). **Main/Corp** Lubelskie Towarzystwo Naukowe. **VFOAT** Matematyka, Fizyka-Chemia. Began with Vol. for 1963/64. 0460-2366. Polish (summaries in English). ir. 15.00. Zakad Narodowy Im Ossolinskich, Plac Litewski 5, Lublin Poland. **Ind/Abst** Math. Rev., Chem. Abstr. **LC** QA1. **CODEN** BLTMDK. Biuletyn.

BOLETIM DA SOCIEDADE BRASILEIRA DE MATEMATICA. Main/Corp Sociedade Brasileira de Matematica. V. 1- 1970-. Periodical. BL. Portuguese (English, French). sa. Sociedade Brasileira de Matematica, Rua Luiz Camoes 68, 20.000 Rio de Janeiro Brazil. **Ind/Abst** Math. Rev. **LC** QA1. **CODEN** BSBMDD.

BOLETIN DE LA SOCIEDAD MATEMATICA MEXICANA. Main/Corp Sociedad Matematica Mexicana. Began in: Oct. 1943. 0037-8615. Periodical. Spanish. qt. 16.00. **Ind/Abst** Math. Rev. **LC** QA1. **CODEN** BSMXAU.

BOLLETTINO DI STORIA DELLE SCIENZE MATEMATICHE. V. 1, No. 1 (June 1981)-. Periodical. IT. English (French, German, Italian, and Latin). sa. 35.000. La Nuova Italia Editrice, Via A Giacomini 8, 50132 Firenze Italy. **Tel** 27981. Ed Enrico Giusti. **Ind/Abst** Math. Rev. **LC** QA21. **DD** 510.9. **Circ** 1,000. (ctrl).

BULETINUL UNIVERSITATII DIN GALATI. FASCICULA II, MATEMATICA, FIZICA, MECANICA TEORETICA. Began in 1978. 0254-4385. Periodical. English (French and German). an. Redactia Buletinului, 6200 Galati Str, Republicii Nr 47 Romania. **Ind/Abst** Math. Rev., Chem. Abstr. **LC** QA1. **DD** 510.5. **CODEN** BUGTD5.

BULLETIN AMQ. Main/Corp Association Mathematique du Quebec. V. 10- 1968-. 0316-8832. Periodical. CN. French. qt. $27.09. Association Mathematique du Quebec, CP 247, Montreal Quebec H1H 5L2 Canada. **Tel** (514)327-4745. Ed Jean-Marie Labrie. **Ind/Abst** Point Repere, Can. Educ. Index. adv acc. Articles on mathematics, class room experience from mathematics teachers, history of mathematic experience from high school, universities in mathematics and computer. Bulletin, 0044-9512.

BULLETIN - CALCUTTA STATISTICAL ASSOCIATION. See Statistics.

BULLETIN DE LA SOCIETE MATHEMATIQUE DE BELGIQUE. SER. B. **VFOAT** Tijdschrift van het Belgisch Wiskundig Genootschap. Reeks B. Vol. 29, No. 1 (1st Quarter 1977)-. Periodical. BE. English (French). qt. Guy Hirsch, 317 Avenue Charles Woeste, 1090 Brussels Belgium. **Ind/Abst** Math. Rev. **CODEN** BMBEAC. Bulletin de la Societe Mathematique de Belgique.

BULLETIN DE LA SOCIETE MATHEMATIQUE DE FRANCE. MEMOIRE. Main/Corp Societe Mathematique de France. No. 1-. 0583-8665. Periodical. French. ir. **Ind/Abst** Math. Rev.

BULLETIN DE L'ACADEMIE POLONAISE DES SCIENCES. SERIE DES SCIENCES MATHEMATIQUES. Vol. 27, No. 1-V. 30, No. 11-12. 0137-639X. Periodical. PL. English (French, and Russian). ARS Polona, Krakowskie Przedmiescie 7, 00-068 Warsaw Poland.

Mathematics

Ind/Abst Math. Rev., Met. Abstr., World Alum. Abstr., Chem. Abstr. **LC** QA1. **DD** 510.5. *Bulletin de l'Academie Polonaise des Sciences. Serie des Sciences Mathematiques, Astronomiques et Physiques.*

BULLETIN DE L'ASSOCIATION DES PROFESSEURS DE MATHEMATIQUES DE L'ENSEIGNEMENT PUBLIC. Main/Corp Association des Professeurs de Mathematiques de l'Enseignement Public, Paris. No. 1-. Periodical. FR. French. ir. 27.94. Association Professeurs Mathematiques, 13 rue de Jura, 75013 Paris France. **Tel** (1)43313405. bk rev. adv acc.

BULLETIN DE LIAISON DU GROUPE DES RESPONSABLES EN MATHEMATIQUE AU SECONDAIRE. (BULLETIN DE LIAISON). No. 2 (Nov. 1971)-. 0826-5879. Periodical. CN. French. ir. Free to members, $20.00 Others. Groupe des Responsables en Mathematique au Secondaire, CP 609, Saing-Basile-le-Grand Quebec J0L 1S0 Canada. **DD** 510.712714. *Bulletin de Liaison du Groupe des Responsables en Mathematique au Secondaire, 0826-5879.*

BULLETIN DES SCIENCES MATHEMATIQUES. Series 2, V. 9- 1885-. 0007-4497. Periodical. FR. French. qt. $75.83. Centrale des Revues/Gauthier Villars, 11 rue Gossin, 92543 Montrouge Cedex France. **Tel** (1)43 20 15 50. Ed P Malliavin. **Ind/Abst** Math. Rev. adv acc. **Circ** 700. Leading mathematics journal since 1870. *Bulletin des Sciences Mathematiques et Astronomiques.*

BULLETIN - INSTITUTE OF MATHEMATICAL STATISTICS. See Statistics.

BULLETIN - INSTITUTE OF MATHEMATICS AND ITS APPLICATIONS. Main/Corp Institute of Mathematics and Its Applications. V. 1- March 1965-. Periodical. UK. English. bm. $61.30. Institute of Math & Its Applications, Maitland House, Warrior Sq Sea Ex, Essex SS1 2JY England. **Ind/Abst** Math. Rev., Energy Res. Abstr. **CODEN** IMTABW.

BULLETIN, NEW SERIES, OF THE AMERICAN MATHEMATICAL SOCIETY. (BULLETIN (NEW SERIES) OF THE AMERICAN MATHEMATICAL SOCIETY). Vol. 1, No. 1 (Jan. 1979)-. 0273-0979. US. English. qt. $20.00 Members, $39.00 Nonmembers. American Mathematical Society, PO Box 6248, Providence RI 02940. **Ind/Abst** Math. Rev. **LC** QA1. **DD** 510.5. *Bulletin of the American Mathematical Society, 0002-9904.*

BULLETIN, NEW SERIES, OF THE AMERICAN MATHEMATICAL SOCIETY. GENERAL INDEX. See Indexes/Abstracts.

BULLETIN OF MATHEMATICAL STATISTICS CEASED. Ceased publication with V. 19, No. 3/4, Mar. 1981. 0007-4993. Periodical. JA. English. ir. **Ind/Abst** Math. Rev. **CODEN** TSUKBQ.

BULLETIN OF NUMBER THEORY AND RELATED TOPICS. VFOAT Boletin de Teoria de Numeros y Temas Conexos. Vol. 1- Jan. 1975-. English. ty. $25.00. Carlos Raitzin, Casilla Correo 298/Correo Centre, Buenos Aires Argentina. **Tel** 8548045. Ed Aldo Peretti and Carlos Raitzin. **Ind/Abst** Math. Rev. bk rev adv acc. **Circ** 150. Specialized publication in number theory.

BULLETIN OF THE AMERICAN MATHEMATICAL SOCIETY. Main/Corp American Mathematical Society. V. 1-3, 1891-94. Periodical. US. English. qt. American Mathematical Society, PO Box 6248, Providence RI 02940. **Ind/Abst** Math. Rev., Sci. Cit. Index, Abr. Ed. (cum index).

BULLETIN OF THE AUSTRALIAN MATHEMATICAL SOCIETY. V. 1- 1969-. 0004-9727. Periodical. AT. English. bm. 145.00 Domestic, 128.00 US. Australian Mathematical Society Association Inc, University of Queensland, St Lucia Queensland 4067 Australia. **Tel** 07 377 2149. Ed Sheila Williams. **Ind/Abst** Math. Rev., Comput. Control Abstr., Electr. Electron. Abstr., Sci. Abstr. Sect. A. Phys. Abstr., Phys. Abstr. **LC** QA1. **CODEN** ALNBAB. (cum index). **Circ** 700. Bulletin of the Australian Mathematical Society, commenced in 1969, aims at quick publication or original research in all branches of mathematics.

BULLETIN OF THE CALCUTTA MATHEMATICAL SOCIETY. Main/Corp Calcutta Mathematical Society. V. 1- Apr. 1909-. 0008-0659. Periodical. II. English. qt $36.00. Prints India, 11 Darya Ganj, New Delhi 110002 India. **Ind/Abst** Math. Rev., Int. Aerosp. Abstr. **LC** QA1. **CODEN** BCMSA5.

BULLETIN OF THE FACULTY OF SCIENCE, IBARAKI UNIVERSITY. SERIES A : MATHEMATICS. Main/Corp Ibaraki Daigaku. Rigakubu. Sugaku Kyoshitsu. VFOAT Ibaraki Daigaku Rigakubu Kiyo (Sugaku). No. 1- 1968-. English. ir. Ibaraki University, 1-1 Bunkyo 2-chome, Mito 310 Japan. **Ind/Abst** Math. Rev. **LC** QA1. **DD** 510.5. **CODEN** BFSMD7.

BULLETIN OF THE INSTITUTE OF MATHEMATICS, ACADEMIA SINICA. Main/Corp Chung Yang Yen Chiu Yuan. Shu Hsueh Yen Chiu So. V. 1- June 1973-. Periodical. CH. English. qt. $30.00. Institute of Mathematics, Academia Sinica, Nankang Taipai Taiwan. **Tel** (02)7821848. Ed Hsuan-Pei Lee and Chii-Ruey Hwang. **Ind/Abst** Math. Rev. **LC** QA1. **DD** 510.5. **CODEN** BIMSDG.

BULLETIN OF THE LONDON MATHEMATICAL SOCIETY. (THE BULLETIN OF THE LONDON MATHEMATICAL SOCIETY). Main/Corp London Mathematical Society. V. 1- (No. 1-). 0024-6093. Periodical. UK. English. bm. $100.00. CF Hodgson & Sons Limited, Unit 4, Central Trading Estate, Staines Middlesex TW18 4UR England. **Ind/Abst** Math. Rev., Sci. Cit. Index, Abr. Ed. **LC** QA1. **DD** 510.5. **CODEN** LMSBBT. bk rev. Short papers on higher mathematics including obituary notices and book reviews.

BULLETIN OF THE MALAYSIAN MATHEMATICAL SOCIETY. Main/Corp Malaysian Mathematical Society. 0126-6705. Periodical. MY. English. ty. $4.23. Malaysian Mathematical Society, University of Malaysia, Department of Mathematics, Kuala Lumpur Malaysia. Ed Tan Keng-Teh. **Ind/Abst** Math. Rev. **LC** QA1. **DD** 510.5. Publishes original research articles, expository review papers and abstracts of thesis in all branches of mathematics.

BULLETIN OF THE MATHEMATICAL ASSOCIATION OF INDIA. Vol. 2, Nos. 1, 2, 3, 4 (Jan.-Dec. 1970)-. Periodical. English. ir. $15.00. Indian Books & Periodicals, 4341 Christian Colony-Pyarey Lal Road, New Delhi 110005 India. **Ind/Abst** Math. Rev. **LC** QA11.A1. *Bulletin of Mathematical Association of India.*

BULLETIN OF THE POLISH ACADEMY OF SCIENCES. MATHEMATICS. VFOAT Mathematics. Vol. 31, No. 1-2-. 0239-7269. Periodical. English (French, German, and Russian). ir. $87.00. Foreign Trade Enterprise, ARS Polona-Ruch, Krakowskie Przedmiescie 7, PO Box 1001, 00-068 Warszawa Poland. **Ind/Abst** Math. Rev. *Bulletin de l'Academie Polonaise des Sciences. Serie des Sciences Mathematiques, 0137-639X.*

BULLETIN SIGNALETIQUE. 110. See Bibliographies.

CAHIERS DE TOPOLOGIE ET GEOMETRIE DIFFERENTIELLE. V. 8- 1966-. Periodical. FR. English (French). qt $27.27. Madame Ehresmann, U E R Mathematiques, 33 rue St Leu, Amiens France. Ed Mme Ehresmann. **Ind/Abst** Math. Rev. **LC** QA611.A1. **DD** 514.05. **CODEN** CTGDBR. bk rev. **Circ** 800. Original papers on category theory and its applications, e.g. in topology and differential geometry. From 1980 to 1983 supplements devoted to Charles Ehresmann's complete works. *Topologie et Geometrie Differentielle.*

CAMBRIDGE TRACTS IN MATHEMATICS. No. 64-. Monographic Series. UK. English. ir. Cambridge University Press, 510 North Avenue, New Rochelle NY 10801. **Ind/Abst** Math. Rev. *Cambridge Tracts in Mathematics and Mathematical Physics.*

CANADIAN JOURNAL OF MATHEMATICS. VFOAT Journal Canadien de Mathematiques. V. 1- 1949-. 0008-414X. Periodical. CN. English (includes some text in French). bm. 64.00. University Toronto Press, Journals Department, 5201 Dufferin Street, Downsview Ontario M3H 5T8 Canada. **Tel** (416)667-7781. Ed P C Greiner. **Ind/Abst** Math. Rev., Int. Aerosp. Abstr., Sci. Cit. Index, Abr. Ed. **CODEN** CJMAAB. adv acc. **Circ** 1,200. (ctrl). Research in all aspects of mathematics, with emphasis on pure mathematics.

CANADIAN MATHEMATICAL BULLETIN. VFOAT Bulletin Canadien de Mathematiques. V. 1- 1958-. 0008-4395. Periodical. CN. English. qt. 35.00. Canadian Mathematical Society, 577 King Edward Avenue, Ottawa Ontario K1N 6N5 Canada. **Tel** (613)564-2223. Ed J Fournier and D Sjerve. **Ind/Abst** Math. Rev., Electron. Commun. Abstr. J., ISMEC Bull., Pollut. Abstr. Indexes, Saf. Sci. Abstr. J. **Circ** 900. Research journal in mathematics.

CANADIAN MATHEMATICS TEACHER. (THE CANADIAN MATHEMATICS TEACHER). Winter 1982-. 0714-573X. Periodical. CN. English. ir. Canadian Mathematics Teacher, c/o L Dukowski, 3821/202A Street, Langley British Columbia V3A 1T3 Canada. **Ind/Abst** Can. Educ. Index. **DD** 510.7071.

CARLETON MATHEMATICAL LECTURE NOTES. V. 1- 1972-. 0318-6288. Monographic Series. CN. English. Carleton University, Department of Mathematics, Ottawa Ontario K1S 5B6 Canada. **Tel** 564-5500. Ed Brian Mortimer. **DD** 510.8. **Circ** 120. Mathematical lectures.

CARLETON MATHEMATICAL SERIES. 0069-0600. Monographic Series. CN. English. ir. Carlton University, Department of Mathematics, Ottawa Ontario K1S 5B6 Canada. **Tel** (613)564-5500. Ed Brian Mortimer. **LC** UNC. **DD** 510. **Circ** 200. Original research papers and expository surveys.

THE CARUS MATHEMATICAL MONOGRAPHS. (CARUS MATHEMATICAL MONOGRAPHS). No. 1- 1925-. 0069-0813. Monographic Series. US. English. ir. Mathematical Association of America, 1529 18th Street NW, Washington DC 20036. **Tel** (202)387-5200. **Ind/Abst** Math. Rev. **CODEN** CAMMDL.

CASOPIS PRO PESTOVANI MATEMATIKY. V. 76, No. 1-. 0528-2195. Periodical. CS. Czech. qt. $83.60. Kubon & Sagner, Postfach 34 01 08, 8000 Munchen 34 West Germany. **Tel** 0811 52 20 27. **Ind/Abst** Math. Rev., Int. Aerosp. Abstr. **LC** QA1. **CODEN** CPMTA8. Scientific publications covering the most important mathematical disciplines. Reviews, informations and bibliographical data. *Casopis Pro Pestovani Matematiky a Fysiky.*

CBMS-NSF REGIONAL CONFERENCE SERIES IN APPLIED MATHEMATICS. Main/Corp Conference Board of the Mathematical Sciences. VFOAT Regional Conference Series in Applied Mathematics. VAT Conference Board of the Mathematical Sciences-National Science Foundation Regional Conference Series in Applied Mathematics. V. 17- 1975-. 0163-9439. Monographic Series. US. English. ir. Society Industrial & Applied Mathematics, 1405 Architects Building, 117 South 17th Street, Philadelphia PA 19103. **Tel** (215)564-2929. **Ind/Abst** Math. Rev. *Regional Conference Series in Applied Mathematics, 0097-4455.*

CHICAGO LECTURES IN MATHEMATICS. 0069-3286. Monographic Series. US. English. ir. University of Chicago Press, PO Box 37005, Chicago IL 60637. **Ind/Abst** Math. Rev. **LC** UNC.

CHINESE ANNALS OF MATHEMATICS. SER. B. VFOAT Shu Hsueh Nien Kan. Vol. 4, No. 1 (Mar. 1983)-. 0252-9599. Periodical. English. bm. $120.00. J C Baltzer AG, Wettsteinplatz 10, CH-4058 Basel Switzerland. **Tel** 61 26 8925. **Ind/Abst** Math. Rev. **LC** QA1. **DD** 510.5. *Shu Hsueh Nien Kan, 0252-9599.*

CHINESE JOURNAL OF MATHEMATICS. VFOAT Chung-kuo Shu Hsueh Tsa Chih. V. 1- June 1973-. Periodical. CH. English (French). sa. $30.00. Mathematics Research Center, National Taiwan University, Taipei Taiwan China. **Ind/Abst** Math. Rev. **CODEN** CJMADE.

COLLECTANEA MATHEMATICA (BARCELONA). (COLLECTANEA MATHEMATICA). Vol. 1, Issue 1.-. 0010-0757. Periodical. SP. English (German, and Spanish). ir. $30.00. Universidad de Barcelona, Gran Cia 585 Ciencias Seminario, Barcelona-7 Spain. **Ind/Abst** Math. Rev. **LC** QD1. **CODEN** COLMBA.

COLLECTED ALGORITHMS FROM CACM CACM. Main/Corp Association for Computing Machinery. 0572-4260. US. English. qt. Association for Computing Machinery, PO Box 9209, Church Street Station, New York NY 10249.

Mathematics

THE COLLEGE MATHEMATICS JOURNAL. (THE COLLEGE MATHEMATICS JOURNAL : AN OFFICIAL PUBLICATION OF THE MATHEMATICAL ASSOCIATION OF AMERICA). Vol. 15, No. 1 (Jan. 1984)-. 0746-8342. Periodical. US. English. qt. $14.00. Mathematical Association of America, 1529 18th Street Northwest, Washington DC 20036. **Ind/Abst** Math. Rev., Educ. Index, Gen. Sci. Index. LC QA11.A1. DD 510.0711. *Two-Year College Mathematics Journal, 0049-4925.*

COLLOQUIA MATHEMATICA. Main/Corp Bolyai Janos Matematikai Tarsulat. Monographic Series. English. ir. Elsevier Science Publishers, PO Box 1663 Grand Central Station, New York NY 10163. **Ind/Abst** Math. Rev., Phys. Abstr., Electr. Electron. Abstr., Comput. Control Abstr., Sci. Abstr. Sect. A. Phys. Abstr.

COLLOQUIUM DOCUMENTS - JACOB MARSCHAK INTERDISCIPLINARY COLLOQUIUM ON MATHEMATICS IN THE BEHAVIORAL SCIENCES. Main/Conf Jacob Marschak Interdisciplinary Colloquium on Mathematics in the Behavioral Sciences. 1976/77-. 0160-7146. US. English. an. $5.50. Western Management Science Institute, Graduate School of Management, University of Southern California in Los Angeles, Los Angeles CA 90024. *Colloquium Documents - Interdisciplinary Colloquium on Mathematics in the Behavioral Sciences, 0146-3047.*

COLLOQUIUM MATHEMATICUM. Vol. 1-. 0010-1354. Periodical. PL. English (French, German, and Russian). sa. $62.10. Ars Polona, Krakowskie Przedmiescie 7, 00-068 Warsaw Poland. **Ind/Abst** Math. Rev., GeoRef. (cum index). Circ 2,000. (ctrl). Publishes communications on new results, survey articles, programs of research, open problems in all fields of mathematics and its applications.

COLLOQUIUM PUBLICATIONS. Vol. 6-. 0065-9258. Monographic Series. US. English. ir. American Mathematical Society, PO Box 1571 Annex Station, Providence RI 02901. Tel (401)272-9500. **Ind/Abst** Math. Rev. *Colloquiem Lectures.*

COMBINATORICA. (COMBINATORICA : AN INTERNATIONAL JOURNAL OF THE JANOS BOLYAI MATHEMATICAL SOCIETY). Vol. 1, No. 1-. 0209-9683. Periodical. English. qt. Elsevier Science Publishers, PO Box 211, 1000 AE Amsterdam Netherlands. Tel (020)5803.911. **Ind/Abst** Math. Rev., Comput. Control Abstr., Electr. Electron. Abstr., Sci. Abstr. Sect. A. Phys. Abstr. CODEN COMBDI.

COMBINED MEMBERSHIP LIST OF THE AMERICAN MATHEMATICAL SOCIETY, MATHEMATICAL ASSOCIATION OF AMERICA, AND THE SOCIETY FOR INDUSTRIAL AND APPLIED MATHEMATICS. Main/Corp American Mathematical Society. 0569-6461. US. English. an. American Mathematical Society, PO Box 1571, Annex Station, Providence RI 02901. Tel (401)272-9500.

COMMENTARII MATHEMATICI HELVETICI. V. 1, Issue Spring (1929)-. 0010-2571. Periodical. US. German (French). qt. $114.00. Birkhauser Boston Inc, 380 Green Street, PO Box 3005, Cambridge MA 02139. Tel (617)576-6638. Ed Rudolf Fueter.

COMMENTARII MATHEMATICI UNIVERSITATIS SANCTI PAULI. VFOAT Rikkyo Daigaku Sugaku Zassi. V. 1 (Dec. 1, 1952)-. 0010-258X. Periodical. English (Vols. for 1952- in French, or German). sa. **Ind/Abst** Math. Rev. LC QA1. CODEN COMAAC. (cum index).

COMMUNICATIONS FROM THE KAMERLINGH ONNES LABORATORY OF THE UNIVERSITY OF LEIDEN. See Physics.

COMMUNICATIONS IN ALGEBRA. V. 1- 1974-. 0092-7872. Periodical. US. English. bw. $475.00. Marcel Dekker Inc, 11305 Church Street Station, New York NY 10249. Tel (212)696-9000. Ed Earl J Taft. **Ind/Abst** Curr. Contents, Phys. Chem. Earth Sci., Compumath Citation Index, Sci. Cit. Index, Abr. Ed., Math. Rev., Phys. Briefs, Comput. Rev., Sci. Cit. Index, Abr. Ed. LC QA150. DD 512.005. CODEN COALDM. bk rev. adv acc. (ctrl). The one journal you need to remain thoroughly conversant with the main trends and ideas compromising the thrust of contemporary work in algebra.

COMMUNICATIONS IN MATHEMATICAL PHYSICS. See Physics.

COMMUNICATIONS IN PARTIAL DIFFERENTIAL EQUATIONS. V. 1- 1976-. 0360-5302. Periodical. US. English. mo. $255.00. Marcel Dekker Inc, PO Box 11305 Church Street Station, New York NY 10249. Tel (212)696-9000. Ed Baouendi and R Beals. **Ind/Abst** Math. Rev. LC QA377. DD 515.35305. CODEN CPDIDZ. bk rev. adv acc. (ctrl). A collection of articles addressing specific mathematical aspects of partial differential equations and applications, such as existence, uniqueness, and properties of solutions.

COMMUNICATIONS IN STATISTICS. SIMULATION AND COMPUTATION. See Statistics.

COMMUNICATIONS IN STATISTICS. THEORY AND METHODS. See Statistics.

COMMUNICATIONS OF THE DUBLIN INSTITUTE FOR ADVANCED STUDIES. SERIES A. VFOAT Sgribhinni Instituid Ard-Leiinn Bhaile Atha Cliath. Spaith A. Began in 1943. 0070-7414. Monographic Series. English. ir. Tel 680748. **Ind/Abst** Math. Rev., Comput. Control Abstr., Electr. Electron. Abstr., Sci. Abstr. Sect. A. Phys. Abstr. CODEN CDIAAH. Circ 500. Reports of research work in mathematics or theoretical physics done in School of Theoretical Physics of DIAS.

COMMUNICATIONS ON PURE AND APPLIED MATHEMATICS. V. 2- 1949-. 0010-3640. Periodical. US. English. bm. John Wiley & Sons Inc, 605 Third Avenue, New York NY 10158. Tel (800)526-5368. **Ind/Abst** Math. Rev., Int. Aerosp. Abstr. DD 510. CODEN CPMAMV. Index in last issue of volume - attached. *Communications on Applied Mathematics.*

COMPLEX VARIABLES, THEORY & APPLICATION. (COMPLEX VARIABLES THEORY AND APPLICATION). Vol. 1, No. 1 (Sept. 1982)-. 0278-1077. Periodical. US. English. ir. $266.00. Gordon & Breach, 1 Bedford Street, London WC2E 9HD England. Tel (01)836-5125. Ed Robert P Gilbert. **Ind/Abst** Math. Rev. LC QA331. DD 515.905. CODEN CVTADV. bk rev. adv acc.

COMPOSITIO MATHEMATICA. V. 1- Jan. 25, 1934-. 0010-437X. Periodical. English. ir. 904.00. Kluwer Academic Publishing Group, PO Box 322, 3300 AH Dordrecht Netherlands. Tel 078-172811. Ed J H M Steenbrink. **Ind/Abst** Math. Rev., Sci. Cit. Index, Abr. Ed. LC QA1. DD 510.5. CODEN CMPMAF. (cum index). adv acc. Circ 650. (ctrl). Aim of the journal is to further the development of mathematics and international mathematical co-operation as indicated by the international editorial board.

COMPTES RENDUS DE L'ACADEMIE DES SCIENCES. VFOAT Mathematique, Serie I, Mathematique. V. 298, No. 1 (Jan. 7, 1984)-. Periodical. French (summaries in English). ir. 1570. Gauthier-Villars CDR, Centrale des Revues, BP No 119, 93104 Montreuil Cedex France. *0249-6321.*

COMPTES RENDUS MATHEMATIQUES DE L'ACADEMIE DES SCIENCES. Main/Corp Royal Society of Canada. Academy of Science. VFOAT Mathematical Reports of the Academy of Science. Began in 1979. 0706-1994. Periodical. CN. English (includes some text in French). bm. $10.00. University of Waterloo, Department of Pure Mathematics, Waterloo Ontario N2L 3G1 Canada. Tel (519)885-1211. Ed G de B Robinson and P Ribenboin. **Ind/Abst** Math. Rev. LC QA1. DD 510.5. Circ 400. Quick publication of short papers summarizing important mathematical research. Also survey papers by fellows of the Royal Society of Canada on their fields of research.

COMPUMATH CITATION INDEX. See Indexes/Abstracts.

COMPUTATIONAL STATISTICS & DATA ANALYSIS. See Statistics.

COMPUTER SCIENCE AND APPLIED MATHEMATICS. V. 1- 1968?. 0884-2027. Monographic Series. US. English. ir. Academic Press, 4805 Sand Lake Road, Orlando FL 32819. Tel (305)345-4100. Ed Peter Lancaster and Miron Tismenetsky. **Ind/Abst** Math. Rev. DD 519.

COMPUTERS & MATHEMATICS, WITH APPLICATIONS. PART A. See Computers and Computer Science.

COMPUTERS & MATHEMATICS, WITH APPLICATIONS. PART B. See Computers and Computer Science.

CONFERENZE DEL SEMINARIO DI MATEMATICA DELL'UNIVERSITA DI BARI. Main/Corp Universita de Bari. Seminario di Matematica. 1-. 0374-2113. Monographic Series. IT. Italian. ir. Libreria Laterza, Via Sparano 134, Bari Italy. **Ind/Abst** Math. Rev. LC QA3. CODEN CSMUAW.

CONSTRUCTIVE APPROXIMATION. Vol. 1, No. 1-. 0176-4276. Periodical. US. English. qt. $79.00. Springer-Verlag New York Inc, 175 Fifth Avenue, New York NY 10010. Ed R A DeVore, E B Staff. **Ind/Abst** Curr. Contents, Math. Rev. New international mathematics journal devoted to significant research in approximations and expansions.

CONTEMPORARY MATHEMATICS (AMERICAN MATHEMATICAL SOCIETY). (CONTEMPORARY MATHEMATICS). V. 1-. 0271-4132. Monographic Series. US. English. ir. American Mathematical Society, PO Box 1571 Annex Station, Providence RI 02901. Tel (401)272-9500. **Ind/Abst** Math. Rev.

CONTENTS OF CONTEMPORARY MATHEMATICAL JOURNALS CEASED. V. 1-3. 0010-759X. Periodical. US. English. bw.

CONTRIBUTI DEL CENTRO LINCEO INTERDISCIPLINARE DI SCIENZE E LORO APPLICAZIONI. Main/Corp Accademia Nazionale dei Linceo, Roma. Centro Linceo Interdisciplinare di Scienze Matematiche e Loro Applicazioni. Monographic Series. IT. Italian. ir. Bardi Editore, Salita de Crescenzi 16, 00186 Rome Italy. **Ind/Abst** Math. Rev.

CRC HANDBOOK OF MATHEMATICAL SCIENCES. VFOAT C.R.C. Handbook of Mathematical Sciences. 5th- Ed.-. US. English. ir. CRC Press Inc, 2000 Corporate Boulevard NW, Boca Raton FL 33431. Tel (305)994-0555. *Handbook of Tables for Mathematics.*

CRUX MATHEMATICORUM. V. 3- 1977-. 0705-0348. Periodical. CN. English. mo. $19.35. Crux Mathematicorum, 200 Lees Avenue, Ottawa Ontario K1S 0C5 Canada. Tel (613)231-6772. Ed Leo Sauve. DD 510.5. Circ 650. A problem solving journal at the senior secondary and University undergraduate levels for those who practice, teach, or just enjoy mathematics. *Eureka, 0700-558X.*

CURRENT INDEX TO STATISTICS. See Indexes/Abstracts.

CURRENT MATHEMATICAL PUBLICATIONS. V. 7- Jan. 10, 1975-. 0361-4794. US. English. ir. American Mathematical Society, PO Box 1571 Annex Station, Providence RI 02901. **Ind/Abst** Math. Rev. LC Z6653, QA36. DD 016.51. CODEN CUMPBW. *Contents of Contemporary Mathematical Journals and New Publications.*

CURRENT TOPICS IN CHINESE SCIENCE. SECTION C, MATHEMATICS. Vol. 1 (1982)-. 0732-4405. Periodical. US. English. an. Gordon and Breach Science Publishers, PO Box 786, Cooper Station, New York NY 10276. DD 510.

CYBERNETICS AND SYSTEMS. See Computers and Computer Science.

CZECHOSLOVAK MATHEMATICAL JOURNAL. V. 19-. 0011-4642. English (French, German, or Russian). qt. $315.00 Domestic, $349.00 Foreign. Plenum Publishing Company, 233 Spring Street, New York NY 10013. Tel (212)620-8000. Ed Miroslav Fiedler. **Ind/Abst** Int. Aerosp. Abstr., Math. Rev., Comput. Rev. LC QA1. DD 510.5. This journal publishes original research papers in mathematics. *Chekhoslovatskii Matematicheskii Zhurnal, Czechoslovak Mathematical Journal.*

DEMONSTRATIO MATHEMATICA. V. 1- 1969-. 0420-1213. PL. Polish (English, French, German, and summaries in Russian). ir. ARS Polona, Krakowskie Przedmiescie 7, 00-068 Warsaw Poland. **Ind/Abst** Math. Rev., Int. Aerosp. Abstr. LC QA1. CODEN DEMADO.

DEVELOPMENTS IN STATISTICS. See Statistics.

DIFFERENCIALNYE URAVNENIJA. (DIFFERENTSIALNYE URAVNENIIA). No. 1-. UR. Russian. mo. $84.50. Victor Kamkin Inc (70254), 12224 Parklawn Drive, Rockville MD 20852. Tel (301)881-5973. **Ind/Abst** Math. Rev. LC QA371.

DIFFERENTIAL EQUATIONS. V. 1- Jan. 1965-. 0012-2661. Periodical. US. English (Russian). mo. $645.00 Domestic, $715.00 Foreign. Consultants

Bureau, 233 Spring Street, New York NY 10013. **Tel** (212)620-8000. **Ed** N P Ervgin. **Ind/Abst** Math. Rev., Electron. Commun. Abstr. J., ISMEC Bull., Pollut. Abstr. Indexes, Saf. Sci. Abstr. J., Int. Aerosp. Abstr., Appl. Mech. Rev., Contents Contemp. Math. J., Index Math. Pap., Zentralbl. Math. Ihre Grenzgeb., Comput. Rev. **LC** QA371. **CODEN** DIEQAN. This journal is devoted exclusively to differential equations and the associated in legal equations. Contents include stability theory, oscillation theory, operational calculus and skill theory.

DIFFERENTSIALNAIA GEOMETRIIA. No. 1-. UR. Russian. 0.50. IZD-VO Saratovskogo Universiteta, Universitetskaia 42, Saratov Russia. **LC** QA641.

DIRECTORY OF PROGRAMS IN STATISTICS AND RELATED AREAS IN CANADIAN UNIVERSITIES. *See* Yearbooks, Almanacs, Directories.

DIRECTORY OF WOMEN IN THE MATHEMATICAL SCIENCES. *See* Yearbooks, Almanacs, Directories.

DISCRETE APPLIED MATHEMATICS. V. 1- Sept. 1979-. 0166-218X. Periodical. English (French). qt. $224.50. Elsevier Science Publishers, PO Box 211, 1000 AE Amsterdam Netherlands. **Tel** (020) 5862 467. **Ed** Peter L Hammer. **Ind/Abst** Math. Rev., Electron. Commun. Abstr. J., ISMEC Bull., Pollut. Abstr. Indexes, Saf. Sci. Abstr. J., Eng. Index Annu., Eng. Index Mon., Eng. Index, Eng. Index Bioeng. Abstr., Eng. Index Energy Abstr., Comput. Control Abstr., Electr. Electron. Abstr., Sci. Abstr. Sect. A. Phys. Abstr., Phys. Abstr., Sci. Cit. Index, Abr. Ed., Comput. Rev. **LC** QA1. **DD** 510. **CODEN** DAMADU. adv acc. Major goal of this journal is to bring together research carried out in different areas of discrete applied mathematics.

DISCRETE MATHEMATICS. V. 1- May 1971-. 0012-365X. Periodical. NE. English. mo. 1090.00 Domestic, $403.75 US. Elsevier Science Publishers, Sara Burgerhartstraat 25, 1055 KV Amsterdam The Netherlands. **Tel** (020)5862 467. **Ed** Peter L Hammer. **Ind/Abst** Math. Rev., Electron. Commun. Abstr. J., ISMEC Bull., Pollut. Abstr. Indexes, Saf. Sci. Abstr. J., Int. Aerosp. Abstr., Comput. Control Abstr., Electr. Electron. Abstr., Sci. Abstr. Sect. A. Phys. Abstr., Energy Res. Abstr., Sci. Cit. Index, Abr. Ed., Phys. Abstr., Comput. Rev. **LC** QA1. **DD** 510.5. **CODEN** DSMHA4. (cum index). adv acc. (ctrl). The aim of the journal is to bring together research papers in different areas of discrete mathematics.

DISQUISITIONES MATHEMATICAE HUNGARICAE. 1- 1970-. Monographic Series. HU. Hungarian. Akademiai Kiado, POB 24, 1363 Budapest Hungary. **Ind/Abst** Math. Rev.

DISSERTATIONES MATHEMATICAE. **VFOAT** Rozprawy Matematyczne. No. 52-. 0012-3862. Monographic Series. PL. English. ir. ARS Polona, Krakowskie Przedmiescie 7, 00-068 Warsaw Poland. **Ind/Abst** Math. Rev. **CODEN** DSMAAH. *Rozprawy Matematyczne.*

THE DOLCIANI MATHEMATICAL EXPOSITIONS. (DOLCIANI MATHEMATICAL EXPOSITIONS). **VFOAT** Mathematical Expositions. No. 1-. 0884-4461. Monographic Series. US. English. Mathematical Association of America, 1529-18th Street NW, Washington DC 20036. **Ind/Abst** Math. Rev.

DONGWU SHULIXUE BAO. (SOOCHOW JOURNAL OF MATHEMATICAL & NATURAL SCIENCES). **VFOAT** Tung Wu Shu Li Hsueh Pao. V. 1- 1975-. 0250-3255. CH. English (with summaries in Chinese). ir. $5.00. Soochow University, Wai Shuange Hsi Shih Lin, Taipei Taiwan. **Ind/Abst** Math. Rev. **LC** QA1. **DD** 510.5.

DUKE MATHEMATICAL JOURNAL. Vol. 1, No. 1 (Mar. 1935)-. 0012-7094. Periodical. US. English. qt. $120.00. Duke University Press, College Station Box 6697, Durham NC 27708. **Tel** (919)684-2173. **Ed** Morris K Weisfeld. **Ind/Abst** Math. Rev., Int. Aerosp. Abstr., Sci. Cit. Index, Abr. Ed. **LC** QA1. **DD** 510.5. **CODEN** DUMJAO. (cum index). adv acc. **Circ** 1,200. Published under the auspices of Duke University since 1934, it has long been regarded as one of the leading mathematics journal in the world.

THE DUODECIMAL BULLETIN. Began with Vol. 1, No. 1 (Jan./Mar. 1945). 0046-0826. Periodical. US. English. sa. Duodecimal Society of America, 9728 Cielo Drive, Huntington Beach CA 92649. **LC** QA141. **DD** 513.56. (cum index).

THE DUODECIMAL BULLETIN. V. 27, No. 3- Fall 1982-. Periodical. US. English. qt.

ECONOMETRIC REVIEWS. Vol. 3, No. 1-. 0747-4938. Periodical. US. English. sa. $65.00. Marcel Dekker Journals, PO Box 11305 Church Street Station, New York NY 10249. **Ed** Dale J Poirier. **Ind/Abst** Math. Rev., Curr. Index Stat., Stat. Theory Method Abstr., Zentralbl. Math. Ihre Grenzgeb., Index Econ. Artic. J. Collect. Vol. **DD** 330. **CODEN** ECREEP. bk rev. adv acc. *Communications in Statistics. Econometric Reviews, 0731-1761.*

EDUCATIONAL STUDIES IN MATHEMATICS. Began with May 1968. 0013-1954. Periodical. English (French and German). qt. $70.00. Kluwer Academic Publishers Group, PO Box 322, 3300 AH Dordrecht Netherlands. **Tel** (31)78-334911. **Ed** Alan J Bishop. **Ind/Abst** Math. Rev., Comput. Control Abstr., Electr. Electron. Abstr., Sci. Abstr., Educ. Index, Curr. Index J. Educ., Phys. Abstr., Bibliogr. Index, Sci. Abstr. Sect. A. Phys. Abstr. **LC** QA1. **DD** 510.07. **CODEN** EDSMAN. bk rev. adv acc. **Circ** 1,150. New ideas and developments of major importance to workers in the field of mathematical education.

EKONOMICKO-MATEMATICKY OBZOR. *See* Economics - Economic Theory.

EKONOMIKA I MATEMATICHESKIE METODY. *See* Economics - Economic Theory.

ELEKTRONNOE MODELIROVANIE. *See* Computers and Computer Science.

ELEMENTE DER MATHEMATIK VOM HOHEREN STANDPUNKT AUS. V. 1- 1952-. 0422-9622. Monographic Series. German. ir. Birkhauser Boston Inc, 380 Green Street/PO Box 3005, Cambridge MA 02139.

EMPLOYMENT INFORMATION IN THE MATHEMATICAL SCIENCES. *See* Economics - Labor.

ENCYCLOPEDIA OF MATHEMATICS AND ITS APPLICATIONS. *See* Encyclopedias & General Reference Books.

ENSEIGNEMENT MATHEMATIQUE. (L'ENSEIGNEMENT MATHEMATIQUE). V. 1-40, 1899-1954. 0013-8584. Periodical. FR. French. qt. 140. Institute de Mathematiques, Paris France. **Ind/Abst** Math. Rev., Energy Res. Abstr. **LC** QA1. **CODEN** ENMAAR. Index published separately - free - automatically sent. (cum index). bk rev. adv acc. **Circ** 900. Research-expository papers, survey and historical articles in mathematics.

ERGEBNISSE DER MATHEMATIK UND IHRER GRENZGEBIETE. 0071-1136. Monographic Series. German (monographs are in English or French). ir. Springer Verlag-New York Inc, 175-5th Avenue, New York NY 10010. **Tel** (212)460-1584. **Ind/Abst** Math. Rev., Energy Res. Abstr. Numbered series.

ERGODIC THEORY AND DYNAMICAL SYSTEMS. Vol. 1, Pt. 1 (Mar. 1981)-. 0143-3857. Periodical. UK. English. qt. $180.00. Cambridge University Press, 510 North Avenue, New Rochelle NY 10801. **Tel** (914)235-0300. **Ed** Michel Herman, Anatole Katok, Klaus Schmidt and Peter Walters. **Ind/Abst** Math. Rev. **LC** QA611.5. **DD** 515.42. bk rev. Provides a focus for this important and rapidly developing area of mathematics and an opportunity to bring together many major contributions in the field.

EUREKA : THE ARCHIMEDEANS' JOURNAL. 1939. 0071-2248. Periodical. UK. English. an. 1-00. Cambridge University Math Society, The Arts School, Cambridge CB2 1TD England. **Ed** Edward Welbourne. adv acc. **Circ** 1,000. The appeal of Eureka spans in the mathematical world. Articles vary from a light-hearted approach to serious expositions of new mathematical ideas.

EUROPEAN JOURNAL OF COMBINATORICS. **VFOAT** Journal Europeen de Combinatoire, Europaische Zeitschrift fur Kombinatorik. V. 1- Mar. 1980-. 0195-6698. Periodical. UK. English. qt. $130.00. Academic Press, 4805 Sand Lake Road, Orlando FL 32819. **Tel** (305)345-4100. **Ind/Abst** Math. Rev., Comput. Control Abstr., Electr. Electron. Abstr., Sci. Abstr. Sect. A. Phys. Abstr., Phys. Abstr. **CODEN** EJOCDI.

EXPOSITIONES MATHEMATICAE. Vol. 1, No. 1-. Periodical. GW. English (French and German). qt. 234.-. Bibliographisches Institut, Postfach 311, D-6800 Mannheim West Germany. **Tel** (621)3901-389. **Ed** S D Chatterji. **Ind/Abst** Math. Rev. bk rev. adv acc. **Circ** 300. International journal of pure and applied mathematics. Original research articles, surveys, expository essays, historical studies, new results, novel points of view.

THE FIBONACCI QUARTERLY. V. 1- Feb. 1963-. 0015-0517. Periodical. US. English. qt. $25.00. Fibonacci Association, University of Santa Clara, Santa Clara CA 95053. **Tel** (408)554-4525. **Ed** G E Bergum. **Ind/Abst** Math. Rev., Sci. Cit. Index, Abr. Ed. **LC** QA1. **CODEN** FIBQA. adv acc. **Circ** 850. (ctrl). The official journal of the Fibonacci Association devoted to the study of integers with special properties.

FIZIKO-MATEMATICHESKO SPISANIE. *See* Physics.

FOCUS - MATHEMATICAL ASSOCIATION OF AMERICA. (FOCUS). **VFOAT** MAA Focus. Vol. 1, No. 1 (Mar. 1981)-. 0731-2040. Periodical. US. English. bm. $1.00 Members, Included in Dues. Mathematical Association of America, 1529 18th Street Northwest, Washington DC 20036. **DD** 510.

FOCUS ON LEARNING PROBLEMS IN MATHEMATICS. Began with Jan. 1979 issue. 0272-8893. Periodical. US. English. qt. $40.00. Center for Teaching and Learning Mathematics, PO Box 3149, Framingham MA 01701. **Tel** (617)877-7895. **Ed** Mahesh C Sharma. **LC** QA11.A1. **DD** 371.9044. bk rev. adv acc. **Circ** 2,000. To make available the current research, methods of identification, diagnosis and remediation of learning problems in mathematics. Reports research from education, psychology and other related fields.

FOR THE LEARNING OF MATHEMATICS. *See* Education (General) - Theory, Practice of Education.

FUN WITH MATHEMATICS. No. 1- Apr. 1972-. 0380-2930. Periodical. CN. English. ir. 15.48. Ontario Institute for Studies in Education, 252 Bloor Street West, Toronto Ontario MS5 1V6 Canada. **Tel** (416)926-6641. **Ed** Kathy Corrigan. **DD** 510.5. **Circ** 400. A 4-page booklet for students from grade 7 to 10. Eight issues per year from September to May (March excepted). Fun is sold in batches of ten copies per issue.

FUNCTIONAL ANALYSIS AND ITS APPLICATIONS. V. 1- Jan./Mar. 1967-. 0016-2663. Periodical. US. English (Russian). qt. $495.00 Domestic, $550.00 Foreign. Consultants Bureau, 233 Spring Street, New York NY 10013. **Tel** (212)620-8000. **Ed** I M Gelfand. **Ind/Abst** Math. Rev., Contents Contemp. Math. J., Index Math. Pap., Zentralbl. Math. Ihre Grenzgeb., Comput. Rev. **CODEN** FAAPBZ. This journal is devoted to current problems of functional analysis. Covers representation theory, theory of operators, spectral theory, theory of operator equations and theory of normed rings.

FUNCTIONES ET APPROXIMATIO COMMENTARII MATHEMATICI. 1-. 0208-6573. English. ir. **Ind/Abst** Math. Rev. **LC** QA331.

FUNCTIONS. (FUNCTIONS : THE PUBLICATION OF THE MATHEMATICS COUNCIL OF THE NEW BRUNSWICK TEACHERS' ASSOCIATION). Vol. 11, No. 2 (Jan. 1982)-. 0821-2708. Periodical. CN. English. ir. New Brunswick Teachers Association, Mathematics Council, PO Box 752, Fredericton New Brunswick E3B 5R6 Canada. **Tel** (506)753-5196. **Ed** John Jewett. **Ind/Abst** Can. Educ. Index. **DD** 510.712. bk rev. adv acc. (ctrl). Articles on puzzles, methodology, and motivation, some computer topics with math applications. *Mathematics (New Brunswick Teachers' Association. Mathematics Council), 0711-1193.*

FUNDAMENTA MATHEMATICAE. Began in 1920. 0016-2736. Periodical. PL. English (French, German, and Italian). ir. $124.20. Ars Polona, Krakowskie Przedmiescie 7, 00-068 Warsaw Poland. **Ind/Abst** Math. Rev. **LC** QA1. (cum index). **Circ** 2,000. (ctrl). Publishes papers devoted to set theory, topology, mathematical logic and foundations, real functions, measure and integration and abstract algebra.

FUNKCIALAJ EKVACIOJ. (FUNKCIALAJ EKVACIOJ. SERIO INTERNACIA). Began with April 1958 issue. 0532-8721. JA. Multilingual (contents in English, French, German, and Esperanto). ty. $75.00. Kinokuniya Book Stores, 1581 Webster Street, San Francisco CA 94115. **Tel** (415)567-7625. **Ind/Abst**

Mathematics

Math. Rev. LC QA431. **CODEN** FESIAT. Analysis mathematics.

FUNKCIONALNYJ ANALIZ I EGO PRILOZENIJA. (FUNKTIONALNYI ANALIZ I EGO PRILOZHENIIA). V. 1- Jan/March 1967-. 0374-1990. Periodical. UR. Russian. qt. $25.00. Victor Kamkin Inc (71036), 12224 Parklawn Drive, Rockville MD 20852. **Tel** (301)881-5973. **Ind/Abst** Math. Rev. LC QA320. DD 510.

FUZZY SETS AND SYSTEMS. Vol. 1, No. 1-. 0165-0114. Periodical. NE. English. bm. Elsevier Science Publishers, PO Box 211, 1000 AE Amsterdam The Netherlands. **Tel** (020)5803.911. **Ind/Abst** Math. Rev., Comput. Control Abstr., Electr. Electron. Abstr., Sci. Abstr. Sect. A. Phys. Abstr. LC QA248. DD 511.32. **CODEN** FSSYD8.

GACETA MATEMATICA. Began publication in 1949. 0016-3805. Periodical. SP. Spanish. ir. $10.31. Real Sociedad Matematica Espan, Serrano 123, Madrid 14 Spain. **Ind/Abst** Math. Rev. LC QA1.

GAKUJUTSU KENKYU : SUGAKUHEN. VFOAT Scientific Researches. No. 24-. Japanese or English. ir. Waseda Daigaku Kyoikugakubu, 6-1 Nishi Waseda Shinjuku-Ku, Tokyo Japan. LC QA1. *Gakujutsu Kenkyu: Sogohen.*

GANITA. V. 1- June 1950-. 0046-5402. II. English (title also in Hindi). an. Bharata Ganita Parisad, Mathematics and Astronomy, University of Lucknow, Lucknow India. **Ind/Abst** Math. Rev. LC QA1. **CODEN** GNTAAG.

GAZETA DE MATEMATICA. (GAZETA DE MATEMATICA. JORNAL DOS CONCORRENTES DO EXAME DE APTIDAO E DOS ESTUDANTES DE MATEMATICA DAS ESCOLAS SUPERIORES). No. 1- Jan. 1940-. 0373-2681. Periodical. PO. Portuguese. qt. Livraria sa da Costa Editora, Rua Garrett 100 102, Lisbon 2 Portugal. **Ind/Abst** Math. Rev., Comput. Control Abstr., Electr. Electron. Abstr., Sci. Abstr. Sect. A. Phys. Abstr. LC QA1. DD 510.5. **CODEN** GZMTAK.

GAZETA MATEMATICA. SERIA A. V. 69-79, No.6. 0016-5433. Periodical. RM. Romanian. mo. $40.00. Rompresfilatelia, PO Box 1362137, Bucharest Romania. **Ind/Abst** Math. Rev. *Gazeta Matematica si Fizica. Seria A.*

GAZETTE - AUSTRALIAN MATHEMATICAL SOCIETY. Main/Corp Australian Mathematical Society. V. 1- 1974-. 0311-0729. Periodical. AT. English. ty. 25.00. Australian Mathematical Society, University of Queensland, Department of Mathematics, St Lucia Queensland 4067 Australia. **Tel** (02)218-9969. **Ed** Graeme Cohen. **Ind/Abst** Math. Rev., Appl. Mech. Rev. **Circ** 800. Carries news items, mathematical articles of on tertiary mathematical teaching.

GEODEZJA I KARTOGRAFIA; KWARTALNIK NAUKOWY. V. 1- 1952-. 0016-7134. Periodical. PL. Polish (tables of contents also in Russian and French). qt. ARS Polona, Krakowskie Przedmiescie 7, 00-068 Warsaw Poland. LC QB275. **CODEN** GEJKAZ.

GEOMETRIAE DEDICATA. V. 1- Nov. 1972-. Periodical. English or German. bm. 156. Kluwer Academic Publishers Group, PO Box 322, 3300 AH Dordrecht Netherlands. **Tel** (31)78-334911. **Ed** K Strambach and F D Veldkamp. **Ind/Abst** Math. Rev. LC QA440. DD 516.005. **CODEN** GEMDAT. bk rev. adv acc. **Circ** 600. Classical problems, geometrisation of mathematical language, penetration of geometrical ideas in analysis and algebra.

GEOMETRICHESKII SBORNIK. Series/Titl Seriia Mekhaniko-Matematicheskaia. Began in 1962. UR. Russian. IZD-VO Tomskogo Universiteta, Ul Nikitina, Tomsk 17 Russia. LC QA440.

THE GLIM NEWSLETTER. Periodical. UK. English. sa. $15.33. Numerical Algorithms Group, 256 Banbury Road, Oxford OX2 7DE England. **Tel** (0865) 511245. **Circ** 400. Newsletter for users of the Generalised Linear Modelling (GLIM).

GOTTINGER WIRTSCHAFTS- UND SOZIALWISSENSCHAFTLICHE STUDIEN. See Economics.

GRADUATE TEXTS IN MATHEMATICS. 1-. 0072-5285. Monographic Series. US. English. ir. Springer Verlag-New York Inc, 175 5th Avenue, New York NY 10010. **Tel** (212)460-1584. **Ind/Abst** Math. Rev. LC UNC. Contains articles on all types and courses of mathematics.

GRAPH THEORY NEWSLETTER. V. 1- 1971-. 0161-3324. Periodical. US. English. bm. $6.00. Western Michigan University, Mathematics Department GTN, Kalamazoo MI 49009. **Tel** (616)383-6165. **Ed** Ortrud R Oellermann. **CODEN** GTNED9. **Circ** 180. Abstracts of recent papers in graph theory; announcements relating to graph theory, conferences, changes of addresses, and announcements of recent books in graph theory.

GROUPE D'ETUDE D'ALBEBRE. EXPOSES. V. 1-. FR. French. ir. Secretariat Mathematique, 11 rue Pierre et Marie Curie, 75231 Paris Cedex 05 France. **Ed** Marie-Paule Malliavin. *Seminaire P. Dubreil, F. Aribaud et M. P. Malliavin. Algebre.*

GROUPE D'ETUDE D'ANALYSE ULTRAMETRIQUE. EXPOSES. Began with 1973/74 Vol. French. ir. Secretariat Mathematique, 11 rue Pierre et Marie Curie, 75231 Paris Cedex 05 France. LC QA300. DD 515.1.

DIE GRUNDLEHREN DER MATHEMATISCHEN WISSENSCHAFTEN. Vol. 1- 1921-. 0072-7830. Monographic Series. German. ir. Springer Verlag-New York Inc, 175-5th Avenue, New York NY 10010. **Tel** (212)460-1584. **Ind/Abst** Math. Rev.

GRUNDLEHREN DER MATHEMATISCHEN WISSENSCHAFTEN. (GRUNDLEHREN DER MATHEMATISCHEN WISSENSCHAFTEN IN EINZELDARSTELLUNGEN MIT BESONDERER BERUCKSICHTIGUNG DER ANWENDUNGSGEBIETE). Began in 1921. 0072-7830. Monographic Series. German. ir. **Tel** (212)460-1584. **Ind/Abst** Math. Rev.

GUIDE BOOK TO DEPARTMENTS IN THE MATHEMATICAL SCIENCES IN THE UNITED STATES AND CANADA. 1st- Ed. Periodical. US. English. **Ed** R Hailpern.

GUJARAT STATISTICAL REVIEW. See Statistics.

HANDBOOK OF TABLES FOR MATHEMATICS. VFOAT CRC Handbook of Tables for Mathematics. 3rd Ed. 0362-8191. US. English. CRC Press, 18901 Cranwood Parkway, Cleveland OH 44128. LC QA47. DD 510.212. *Handbook of Mathematical Tables.*

HISTORIA MATHEMATICA. V. 1- Feb. 1974-. 0315-0860. Periodical. US. English (no language are excluded, and authors give summaries in the language of their choice). qt. Academic Press, 4805 Sand Lake Road, Orlando FL 32819. **Tel** (305)345-4100. **Ind/Abst** Math. Rev., Am. Hist. Life, Hist. Abstr., Part A, Mod. Hist. Abstr., Hist. Abst., Part B, Twent. Century Abstr., Recent Publ. Artic. LC QA21. DD 510.9. **CODEN** HIMADS.

HOKKAIDO MATHEMATICAL JOURNAL. V. 1- Oct. 1972-. 0385-4035. Periodical. JA. English. ty. $102.00. North Oxford Academic Publishing Company, 242 Banbury Road, Oxford OX2 7DR England. **Tel** 0865-51-1166. **Ind/Abst** Math. Rev. LC QA1. DD 510.5. **CODEN** HMAJDN. *Journal of the Faculty of Science, Hokkaido University. Series I. Mathematics.*

HOUSTON JOURNAL OF MATHEMATICS. V. 1- 1975-. 0362-1588. Periodical. US. English. qt. $70.00 Domestic, $75.00 Foreign. University of Houston, Department of Mathematics, Houston TX 77004. **Tel** (713)749-2112. **Ed** Gordon G Johnson. **Ind/Abst** Math. Rev., Comput. Control Abstr., Electr. Electron. Abstr., Sci. Abstr. Sect. A. Phys. Abstr., Phys. Abstr. LC QA1. DD 510.5. **CODEN** HJMADZ. **Circ** 525. Original research from all areas of mathematics.

ILLINOIS INVENTORY OF EDUCATIONAL PROGRESS. MATHEMATICS ITEM RESULTS. See Education (General) - Theory, Practice of Education.

ILLINOIS JOURNAL OF MATHEMATICS. V. 1- Mar. 1957-. 0019-2082. Periodical. US. English (French). qt. $50.00. University of Illinois Press, 54 East Gregory Drive, Champaign IL 61820. **Tel** (217)333-0950. **Ed** Mahlon M Day. **Ind/Abst** Math. Rev., Int. Aerosp. Abstr., Sci. Cit. Index, Abr. Ed. LC QA1. DD 510.5. **CODEN** IJMTAW. **Circ** 1,000. Basic research in all fields of pure and applied mathematics.

IMA JOURNAL OF APPLIED MATHEMATICS. VFOAT Journal of Applied Mathematics. Vol. 27, No. 1 (Jan. 1981)-. 0272-4960. Periodical. UK. English. bm. $233.20. Academic Press, 4805 Sand Lake Road, Orlando FL 32819. **Tel** (305)345-4100. **Ind/Abst** Math. Rev., Electron. Commun. Abstr. J., ISMEC Bull., Pollut. Abstr. Indexes, Saf. Sci. Abstr. J., Fluidex, Int. Aerosp. Abstr., Comput. Control Abstr., Electr. Electron. Abstr., Sci. Abstr. Sect. A. Phys. Abstr. LC QA1. DD 505. **CODEN** IJAMDM. *Journal of the Institute of Mathematics and its Applications, 0020-2932.*

IMA JOURNAL OF NUMERICAL ANALYSIS. Began with Jan. 1981 issue. 0272-4979. Periodical. UK. English. qt. $172.70. Academic Press, 4805 Sand Lake Road, Orlando FL 32819. **Tel** (305)345-4100. **Ind/Abst** Math. Rev., Electron. Commun. Abstr. J., ISMEC Bull., Pollut. Abstr. Indexes, Saf. Sci. Abstr. J., Fluidex, Int. Aerosp. Abstr., Comput. Control Abstr., Electr. Electron. Abstr., Sci. Abstr. Sect. A. Phys. Abstr. LC QA297. DD 519.405. **CODEN** IJNADH. *Journal of the Institute of Mathematics and its Applications, 0020-2932.*

INDAGATIONES MATHEMATICAE. 0019-3577. NE. Dutch (English, French, or German). qt. Elsevier Science Publishers, PO Box 211, 1000 AE Amsterdam Netherlands. **Tel** (020)5803.911. **Ind/Abst** Math. Rev. LC QA1. DD 510.58. **CODEN** IMTHBJ.

INDEX OF MATHEMATICAL PAPERS. See Indexes/Abstracts.

INDEX TO TRANSLATIONS SELECTED BY THE AMERICAN MATHEMATICAL SOCIETY. See Indexes/Abstracts.

INDIAN JOURNAL OF PURE AND APPLIED MATHEMATICS. Vol. 1, No. 1 (Jan. 1970)-. 0019-5588. Periodical. II. English. mo. $100.00. Asia Books and Periodicals Company, 11-3 Darya Ganj Ansari Road, New Delhi 110002 India. **Tel** 268645,271378,275542. **Ind/Abst** Math. Rev., Comput. Control Abstr., Electr. Electron. Abstr., Sci. Abstr. Sect. A. Phys. Abstr., Sci. Cit. Index, Abr. Ed., Phys. Abstr. LC QA1. DD 510.5. **CODEN** IJMHAU.

INDIANA UNIVERSITY MATHEMATICS JOURNAL. VFOAT Mathematics Journal. Vol. 20, No. 1 (July 1970)-. 0022-2518. US. English (articles in French, German, or Italian). qt. $95.00. Indiana University Mathematics Journal, Swain Hall East 22, Bloomington IN 47405. **Tel** (812)335-2252. **Ed** John Brothers. **Ind/Abst** Math. Rev., Int. Aerosp. Abstr., Sci. Cit. Index, Abr. Ed. LC QA1. DD 510.5. **CODEN** IUMJAB. Significant research articles in both pure and applied mathematics. *Journal of Mathematics and Mechanics, 0095-9057.*

INDUSTRIAL MATHEMATICS. V. 1- 1950-. 0019-8528. Periodical. US. English. sa. $15.00. Industrial Mathematics Society, PO Box 159, Roseville MT 48066. **Tel** (313)927-1367. **Ed** Robert Schmidt. **Ind/Abst** Eng. Index Mon., Eng. Index Bioeng. Abstr., Eng. Index Energy Abstr., Comput. Control Abstr., Electr. Electron. Abstr., Sci. Abstr. Sect. A. Phys. Abstr., Eng. Index Annu., Eng. Index Mon., Math. Rev., Phys. Abstr., Appl. Mech. Rev., Eng. Index. **CODEN** IMTHAI. (cum index). bk rev. adv acc. **Circ** 300. Publishes original papers in applied mathematics; preliminary notes containing novel items of mathematical, scientific, and technical interest; etc.

INFO-MATHS. Vol. 1, No. 1 (1st Sept. 1978)-. 0710-0027. Periodical. CN. French. ir. Free. Commission Scolaire Regionale Orleans, CP 5160, Quebec Quebec G1E 6B6 Canada. DD 510.71271447. (ctrl).

INFORMATION BULLETIN (ERIC CLEARINGHOUSE FOR SCIENCE, MATHEMATICS AND ENVIRONMENTAL EDUCATION). See Education (General).

INSTANTANES MATHEMATIQUES. First issue in Oct. 1964. 0226-2061. Periodical. CN. French. ir. $10.00. Instantanes Mathematiques, Apame C P 433, Succursale Westmount Montreal Quebec H3Z 2T5 Canada. DD 372.73044.

THE INSTITUTE OF MATHEMATICAL STATISTICS DIRECTORY. See Yearbooks, Almanacs, Directories.

INTEGRAL EQUATIONS AND OPERATOR THEORY. V. 1-. 0378-620X. Periodical. English. bm. $110.00. Birkhauser Boston Inc, 380 Green Street, PO Box 3005, Cambridge MA

Mathematics

02139. **Tel** (617)576-6638. **Ind/Abst** Math. Rev. **LC** QA431. **DD** 515.4505.

INTERDISCIPLINARY MATHEMATICS. Vol. 1/2-. Monographic Series. US. English. an. Math Science Press, 53 Jordan Road, Brookline MA 02146. Ed R Hermann.

INTERNATIONAL JOURNAL OF GAME THEORY. Began with: V. 1, in 1971. 0020-7276. Periodical. AU. English. qt. $79.62. Physica Verlag, Seilerstaette 18, A-1010 Vienna Austria. **Ind/Abst** Math. Rev., Comput. Control Abstr., Electr. Electron. Abstr., Sci. Abstr. Sect. A. Phys. Abstr., Phys. Abstr., Comput. Rev. **LC** QA269. **DD** 519.305. **CODEN** IJGTA2.

INTERNATIONAL JOURNAL OF MATHEMATICAL EDUCATION IN SCIENCE AND TECHNOLOGY. VFOAT Mathematical Education in Science and Technology. V. 1- Jan./Mar. 1970-. 0020-739X. Periodical. UK. English. bm. $176.00. Taylor & Francis Ltd, 242 Cherry Street, Philadelphia PA 19106. **Tel** (215)238-0939. Ed A C Bajpai. **Ind/Abst** Math. Rev., Int. Aerosp. Abstr., Comput. Control Abstr., Electr. Electron. Abstr., Sci. Abstr. Sect. A. Phys. Abstr., Educ. Index, Curr. Index J. Educ., Phys. Abstr. **CODEN** IJMEBM. Provides a medium by which a wide range of experience in mathematical education can be presented, assimilated and eventually adapted to everyday needs in schools, colleges, polytechnics, universities, industry and commerce.

INTERNATIONAL JOURNAL OF MATHEMATICS AND MATHEMATICAL SCIENCES. V. 1- Mar. 1978-. 0161-1712. Periodical. US. English. qt. $25.00. University of Central Florida, Department of Mathematics, c/o Dr Debnath, Orlando FL 32816. **Tel** (305)275-2754. Ed Dr L Debnath. **Ind/Abst** Math. Rev. **LC** QA1. **DD** 510.8. **Circ** 325. (ctrl). A journal devoted to publication of original research papers, research notes, research expository and survey articles with emphasis on unsolved problems and open questions in mathematics and mathematical sciences.

INTERNATIONAL SERIES IN MODERN APPLIED MATHEMATICS AND COMPUTER SCIENCE. Began with: Vol. 1, published 1981. 0733-1932. Monographic Series. UK. English. ir. Oxford University Press, 16-00 Pollitt Drive, Fairlawn NJ 07410. **Ind/Abst** Math. Rev.

INTERNATIONAL SERIES OF NUMERICAL MATHEMATICS. INTERNATIONALE SCHRIFTENREIHE ZUR NUMERISCHEN MATHEMATIK. SERIE INTERNATIONALE D'ANALYSE NUMERIQUE. VFOAT Internationale Schriftenreihe zur Numerischen Mathematik. Began publication with V. 3, 1961. 0539-0141. Monographic Series. US. English (French or German). ir. Birkhauser Boston Inc, 380 Green Street, PO Box 3005, Cambridge MA 02139. **Ind/Abst** Math. Rev.

INTERNATIONALE MATHEMATISCHE NACHRICHTEN. VFOAT Internationale Mathematical News, Nouvelles Mathematique Internationales. Periodical. AU. Multilingual (English, German, and French). ir. $10.25. Oesterreichische Math Geslshft Technische University, Karlsplatz 13, A-1040 Vienna Austria. **Tel** 0222-56015387. **Ind/Abst** Math. Rev. bk rev. adv acc. **Circ** 1,500. (ctrl). News in the mathematical world, book reviews of new mathematical books, and personalities.

INTRODUCTORY MATHEMATICS FOR SCIENTISTS AND ENGINEERS. 0275-259X. Monographic Series. UK. English. ir. John Wiley & Sons Inc, 1 Wiley Drive, Somerset NJ 08873.

INVENTIONES MATHEMATICAE. V. 1- Feb. 1966-. 0020-9910. Periodical. WB. English (French or German). mo. Springer Verlag-New York Inc, 175 5th Avenue, New York NY 10010. **Tel** (212)460-1500. Ed M Berger, A Borel, J Coates, A Connes, A A Kirillov, B Magur, R Remmert, J P Serre, J Sjostrand, T A Springer and S T Yau. **Ind/Abst** Math. Rev., Int. Aerosp. Abstr. **LC** QA1. **CODEN** INVMBH. Index in last issue of volume - attached. A forum for leading fundamental and authoritative papers on mathematics.

ISRAEL JOURNAL OF MATHEMATICS. Vol. 1 (Mar. 1963)-. 0021-2172. Periodical. English. mo. **Ind/Abst** Math. Rev., Int. Aerosp. Abstr., Comput. Control Abstr., Electr. Electron. Abstr., Sci. Abstr. Sect. A. Phys. Abstr., Energy Res. Abstr. **LC** QA1. **CODEN** ISJMAP. Bulletin of the Research Council of Israel. Section F, Mathematics and Physics.

ITOGI NAUKI I TEHNIKI - VSESOJUZNYI INSTITUT NAUCNOJ I TEHNICESKOJ INFORMACII. SERIJA TEORIJA VEROJATNOSTEJI, MATEMATICESKAJA STATISTIKA, TEORETICESKAJA KIBERNETIKA. (ITOGI NAUKI I TEKHNIKI : TEORIIA VEROIATNOSTEI, MATEMATICHESKAKIA STATISTIKA, TEORETICHESKAIA KIBERNETIKA). VFOAT Itogi Nauki i Tekhniki. V. 10-. UR. Russian. Liubertsy Oktiabrskii Prospekt 403, Moskva USSR. **LC** QA273. *Itogi Nauki: Teoriia Veroiatnostei. Matematicheskai a Statistika.*

ITOGI NAUKI I TEKHNIKI : ALGEBRA, TOPOLOGIIA, GEOMETRIIA. VFOAT Itogi Nauki I Tekhinki: Seriia Algebra, Topologiia, Geometriia. V. 10-. UR. Russian. 1.78. Vsesoiuznyu Institut, Nauchoni I Tecknhicheskoi, Informastsii Liubertsy, Oktiabrskii Prospekt Moskva 303 USSR. **LC** QA1. *Itogi Nauki: Algebra. Topologiia. Geometriia.*

ITOGI NAUKI I TEKHNIKI : MATEMATICHESKII ANALIZ. VFOAT Itogi Nauki I Tekhniki: Seriia Matematicheskii Analiz. V. 10- 1973-. UR. Russian. Liubertsy, Oktiabrskii Pr, Moskva 403 Russia. **LC** QA300. *Itogi Nauki: Matematicheskii Analiz.*

ITOGI NAUKI I TEKHNIKI : PROBLEMY GEOMETRII. VFOAT Problemy Geometrii. Periodical. UR. Russian (summaries in English). 1.87 Single Issue. A-219 Baltiiskaia Ulitsa 14, Moskva Russian SFSR. **LC** QA443. *Trudy.*

ITOGI NAUKI I TEKHNIKI : SOVREMENNYE PROBLEMY MATEMATIKI. VFOAT Itogi Nauki i Tekhniki. V. 1- 1973-. Periodical. UR. Russian. ir. 1.32. Proizvodstvenno-Izdatelskii, Kombinat Viniti Liubertsy Oktiabrsloi Pr 403, Moskva USSR. **LC** QA1.

IZVESTIIA AKADEMII NAUK ARMIANSKOI SSR. (SOVIET JOURNAL OF CONTEMPORARY MATHEMATICAL ANALYSIS). Vol. 14, No. 1-. 0735-2719. Periodical. US. English (Russian). bm. Allerton Press Inc, 150 5th Avenue, New York NY 10011. **Tel** (212)924-3950. **Ind/Abst** Math. Rev. **LC** QA297. **DD** 515.3505.

IZVESTIIA. MATEMATIKA. Main/Corp Akademiia Nauk Arminaskoi SSR, Erivan. V. 1- 1966-. 0002-3043. Periodical. Russian. ir. **Ind/Abst** Int. Aerosp. Abstr. *Izvestiia: Fisiko-Matematicheskie, Estestvennye I Tekhnicheskie Nauki.*

IZVESTIIA. SERIIA FIZIKO-MATEMATICHESKIKH NAUK. See Physics.

IZVESTIIA VYSSHIKH UCHEBNYKH ZAVEDENII. MATEMATIKA. VFOAT Matematika. Began in 1957. 0021-3446. Periodical. UR. Russian. mo. Victor Kamkin Inc, 12224 Parklawn Drive, Rockville MD 20852. **Tel** (301)881-5973. **Ind/Abst** Math. Rev., Comput. Control Abstr., Electr. Electron. Abstr., Sci. Abstr. Sect. A. Phys. Abstr., Sci. Cit. Index, Abr. Ed. **LC** QA1. **CODEN** IVUMBY.

JAHRESBERICHT DER DEUTSCHEN MATHEMATIKER-VEREINIGUNG. Main/Corp Deutsche Mathematiker-Vereinigung. Vol. 1- (1890/91)-. 0012-0456. Periodical. GW. German. qt. 94.—. BG Teubner GMBH, Postfach 80 10 69, Industriestr 15, D7000 Stuttgart 80 West Germany. **Tel** 0711/78901-17. Ed K Jacobs and W D Geyer. **Ind/Abst** Math. Rev., Energy Res. Abstr. **CODEN** JDMVA7. (cum index). bk rev adv acc. Official journal of the German Mathematical Society. Contains partly main lectures of the annual conferences and special contributions.

JAHRESTAGUNG - GESELLSCHAFT FUR INFORMATIK E.V. (JAHRESTAGUNG). Main/Corp Gesellschaft fur Informatik. **Series/Titl** Lecture Notes in Economics and Mathematical Systems. VFOAT Proceedings. 0343-3110. English or German. ir. Springer-Verlag, 175 Fifth Avenue, New York NY 10010. **LC** QA76. **DD** 001.64.

JAPANESE JOURNAL OF MATHEMATICS. Vol. 1, Nos. 1/2-. 0075-3432. JA. English (with some articles in German and French; title also in Japanese). sa. $92.00. North Oxford Academic Publishing Company, 242 Banbury Road, Oxford OX2 7DR England. **Tel** (0865)51-1166. **Ind/Abst** Electron. Commun. Abstr. J., ISMEC Bull., Pollut. Abstr. Indexes, Saf. Sci. Abstr. J., Sci. Cit. Index, Abr. Ed., Index Med., Chem. Abstr. **LC** QA1. **CODEN** JJMAAK.

JOURNAL D'ANALYSE MATHEMATIQUE. V. 1- 1951-. 0021-7670. Periodical. IS. English (French). ir. $47.00. Weizmann Science Press Israel, PO Box 801, Jerusalem 91007 Israel. **Ind/Abst** Math. Rev., Int. Aerosp. Abstr., Sci. Cit. Index, Abr. Ed. **LC** QA1. **CODEN** JOAMAV.

JOURNAL DE MATHEMATIQUES PURES ET APPLIQUEES. Periodical. FR. French. qt. 856. Centrale des Revues-Gauthier Villars, 11 rue Gossin, 92543 Montrouge Cedex France. **Tel** 1 (43 20 25 50). Ed Jacques Louis Lions. **Ind/Abst** Appl. Mech. Rev., Math. Rev., Sci. Cit. Index, Abr. Ed. adv acc. **Circ** 1,000. Leading mathematics journal since 1836.

JOURNAL FOR RESEARCH IN MATHEMATICS EDUCATION. Began with V. 1, Jan. 1970. 0021-8251. Periodical. US. English. ir. National Council of Teachers of Mathematics, 1906 Association Drive, Reston VA 22091. **Tel** (703)620-9840. **Ind/Abst** Educ. Index, Curr. Index J. Educ., Psychol. Abstr. **LC** QA11.A1. **DD** 510.071. **CODEN** JRMEDN. ERIC version for July 1982 distributed to depository libraries in microfiche.

JOURNAL FUR DIE REINE UND ANGEWANDTE MATHEMATIK. Vol. 1- 1826-. 0075-4102. Periodical. German. ir. $750.00. Walter de Gruyter & Company, 200 Saw Mill River Road, Hawthorne NY 10532. **Tel** (914)747-0110. Ed W Jaeger, M Kneser, H Leptin, S J Patterson and P Roquette. **Ind/Abst** Math. Rev., Sci. Cit. Index, Abr. Ed. **LC** QA1. **CODEN** JRMAA8. (cum index). adv acc. **Circ** 900. Contains original investigations in all branches of pure and applied mathematics.

JOURNAL OF ALGEBRA. V. 1- Apr. 1964-. 0021-8693. Periodical. US. English. mo. Academic Press, 4805 Sand Lake Road, Orlando FL 32819. **Tel** (305)345-4100. **Ind/Abst** Math. Rev., Electron. Commun. Abstr. J., ISMEC Bull., Pollut. Abstr. Indexes, Saf. Sci. Abstr. J., Int. Aerosp. Abstr., Sci. Cit. Index, Abr. Ed. **CODEN** JALGA4.

JOURNAL OF APPLIED PROBABILITY. 0021-9002. Periodical. UK. English. qt. 81.00 North, South and Central America, 66.00 Others. Applied Probability University, Department of Probability and Statistics, Sheffield S3 7RH England. **Tel** (0742)78555. Ed J Gani. **Ind/Abst** Sci. Cit. Index, Abr. Ed., Eng. Index, Phys. Abstr., Math. Rev., Electr. Electron. Abstr., Comput. Control Abstr. adv acc. **Circ** 1,500. Research papers and notes on applications of probability theory to the biological, physical, social and technological sciences.

JOURNAL OF APPROXIMATION THEORY. V. 1- June 1968-. 0021-9045. Periodical. US. English (articles in German). mo. Academic Press, 4805 Sand Lake Road, Orlando FL 32819. **Tel** (305)345-4100. **Ind/Abst** Math. Rev., Comput. Control Abstr., Electr. Electron. Abstr., Sci. Abstr. Sect. A. Phys. Abstr., Sci. Cit. Index, Abr. Ed., Phys. Abstr., Comput. Rev., Sci. Cit. Index, Abr. Ed. **LC** QA221. **DD** 511.405. **CODEN** JAXTAZ.

JOURNAL OF CLASSIFICATION. Vol. 1, No. 1-. 0176-4268. Periodical. US. English. ty. $45.00. Springer-Verlag New York Inc, Service Center Secaucus, 44 Hartz Way, Secaucus NJ 07094. Ed P Arabie. adv acc. **Circ** 101. Classification, numerical taxonomy and other ordination techniques as applied in a wide range of disciplines, including biology, psychology information sciences.

JOURNAL OF COMBINATORIAL THEORY. SERIES A. Vol. 10- Jan. 1971-. 0097-3165. Periodical. US. English. bm. Academic Press, 4805 Sand Lake Road, Orlando FL 32819. **Tel** (305)345-4100. **Ind/Abst** Math. Rev., Comput. Control Abstr., Electr. Electron. Abstr., Sci. Abstr. Sect. A. Phys. Abstr., Sci. Cit. Index, Abr. Ed., Comput. Rev., Phys. Abstr. **CODEN** JCBTA7. *Journal of Combinatorial Theory, 0021-9800.*

JOURNAL OF COMBINATORIAL THEORY. SERIES B. V. 10- Feb. 1971-. 0095-8956. Periodical. US. English. bm. $56.00 Domestic, $62.00 Foreign. Academic Press, 4805 Sand Lake Road, Orlando FL 32819. **Tel** (305)345-4100. **Ind/Abst** Math. Rev., Sci. Cit. Index, Abr. Ed., Phys. Abstr., Comput. Control Abstr., Electr.

Electron. Abstr. **CODEN** JCBTB8. *Journal of Combinatorial Theory, 0021-9800.*

JOURNAL OF COMBINATORICS, INFORMATION & SYSTEM SCIENCES. **VAT** Journal of Combinatorics, Information and System Sciences. Began with V. 1, No. 1, 1976. 0250-9628. Periodical. II. English. qt. $60.00. Asia Books & Periodicals Company, 11 Darya Ganj, New Delhi 110002 India. **Ind/Abst** Math. Rev. **LC** QA164.

JOURNAL OF COMPLEXITY. Vol. 1, No. 1 (Oct. 1985)-. 0885-064X. Periodical. US. English. qt. $80.00. Academic Press, 6277 Sea Harbor Drive, Orlando FL 32887. **DD** 511.

JOURNAL OF COMPUTATIONAL AND APPLIED MATHEMATICS. V. 1- Mar. 1975-. 0377-0427. Periodical. BE. English. qt. Elsevier Science Publishers, PO Box 211, 1000 AE Amsterdam Netherlands. **Tel** (020)5803911. **Ind/Abst** Math. Rev., Electron. Commun. Abstr. J., ISMEC Bull., Pollut. Abstr. Indexes, Saf. Sci. Abstr. J., Eng. Index Annu., Eng. Index Mon., Eng. Index Bioeng. Abstr., Eng. Index Energy Abstr., Int. Aerosp. Abstr., Appl. Mech. Rev., Comput. Abstr., Comput. Rev., Eng. Index. **LC** QA1. **DD** 519.405. **CODEN** JCAMDI.

JOURNAL OF DIFFERENTIAL EQUATIONS. V. 1- Jan. 1965-. 0022-0396. Periodical. US. English. ir. Academic Press, 4805 Sand Lake Road, Orlando FL 32819. **Tel** (305)345-4100. **Ind/Abst** Math. Rev., Int. Aerosp. Abstr., Comput. Control Abstr., Electr. Electron. Abstr., Sci. Abstr. Sect. A. Phys. Abstr., Appl. Mech. Rev., Phys. Abstr., Sci. Cit. Index, Abr. Ed., Comput. Rev. **LC** QA371. **CODEN** JDEQAK. *Contributions to Differential Equations, 0589-5839.*

JOURNAL OF DIFFERENTIAL GEOMETRY. V. 1- Mar. 1967-. 0022-040X. Periodical. US. English. qt. American Math Society, PO Box 6248, Providence RI 02940. **Tel** (401)272-9500. **Ind/Abst** Math. Rev. **LC** QA641. **DD** 516.36005. **CODEN** JDGEAS.

JOURNAL OF ENGINEERING MATHEMATICS. 0022-0833. Periodical. NE. English. qt. 288.- Domestic, $102.00 US. Kluwer Academic Publishing Group, Distribution Center, PO Box 322, AH Dordrecht Netherlands. **Tel** 078-172811. **Ed** H W Hoogstraten. **Ind/Abst** Appl. Mech. Rev., Eng. Index, Int. Aerosp. Abstr., Math. Rev., Sci. Cit. Index, Abr. Ed., Phys. Abstr., Comput. Control Abstr., Electr. Electron. Abstr. adv acc. **Circ** 600. (ctrl). Original work in engineering science in which mathematical method of solution is essential, promote application of mathematics to engineering problems and stress intrinsic unity of fundamental problems of different branches of engineering.

JOURNAL OF FUNCTIONAL ANALYSIS. Periodical. US. English. ir. Academic Press, 4805 Sand Lake Road, Orlando FL 32819. **Tel** (305)345-4100. **Ind/Abst** Math. Rev., Sci. Cit. Index, Abr. Ed., Electr. Electron. Abstr., Phys. Abstr., Comput. Control Abstr., Comput. Rev.

JOURNAL OF FUNCTIONAL ANALYSIS. V. 1- May 1967-. 0022-1236. Periodical. US. English. mo. $54.00 Per Volume/US, $63.00 Per Volume/Foreign. Academic Press, 4805 Sand Lake Road, Orlando FL 32819. **Ind/Abst** Math. Rev., Electron. Commun. Abstr. J., ISMEC Bull., Pollut. Abstr. Indexes, Saf. Sci. Abstr. J., Comput. Control Abstr., Electr. Electron. Abstr., Sci. Abstr. Sect. A. Phys. Abstr. **LC** QA320. **DD** 517.505. **CODEN** JFUAAW.

JOURNAL OF GEOMETRY. V. 1- 1971-. 0047-2468. Periodical. US. English (German, with summaries in English). ir. Birkhauser Boston Inc, 380 Green Street/PO Box 3005, Cambridge MA 02139. **Tel** (617)576-6638. **Ind/Abst** Math. Rev. **LC** QA443. **DD** 516.2005.

JOURNAL OF GRAPH THEORY. V. 1- Spring 1977-. 0364-9024. Periodical. US. English. qt. John Wiley & Sons, 605 Third Avenue, New York NY 10158. **Tel** (800)526-5368. **Ind/Abst** Math. Rev., Comput. Control Abstr., Electr. Electron. Abstr., Sci. Abstr. Sect. A. Phys. Abstr., Bibliogr. Agric. **LC** QA166. **DD** 510.505. **CODEN** JGTHDO.

JOURNAL OF INFORMATION & OPTIMIZATION SCIENCES. (JOURNAL OF INFORMATION & OPTIMIZATION SCIENCES : A JOURNAL DEVOTED TO ADVANCES IN INFORMATION SCIENCES, OPTIMIZATION SCIENCES AND RELATED ASPECTS). **VFOAT** Journal of Information and Optimization Sciences. Vol. 1, No. 1 (Jan. 1980)-. 0252-2667. Periodical. II. English. ty. $45.00. Asia Books and Periodicals Company, 11 Darya Ganj, New Delhi 110002 India. **Ind/Abst** Math. Rev., Electron. Commun. Abstr. J., ISMEC Bull., Pollut. Abstr. Indexes, Saf. Sci. Abstr. J., Comput. Control Abstr., Electr. Electron. Abstr., Sci. Abstr. Sect. A. Phys. Abstr. **LC** QA75.5. **DD** 001.5. **CODEN** JIOSDC.

JOURNAL OF INTEGRAL EQUATIONS. V. 1- May 1979-. 0163-5549. Periodical. US. English. ir. Elsevier Science Publishers Company Inc, PO Box 1663, Grand Central Station, New York NY 10163. **Ind/Abst** Math. Rev., Eng. Index Annu., Eng. Index Mon., Eng. Index Bioeng. Abstr., Eng. Index Energy Abstr., Int. Aerosp. Abstr. **LC** QA431. **DD** 515.4505. **CODEN** JIEQDO.

JOURNAL OF MATHEMATICAL ANALYSIS AND APPLICATIONS. Periodical. US. English. ir. Academic Press, 4805 Sand Lake Road, Orlando FL 32819. **Tel** (305)345-4100. **Ind/Abst** Appl. Mech. Rev., Eng. Index, Math. Rev., Sci. Cit. Index, Abr. Ed., Phys. Abstr., Comput. Rev., Comput. Control Abstr., Electr. Electron. Abstr.

JOURNAL OF MATHEMATICAL ANALYSIS AND APPLICATIONS. V. 1- June 1960-. 0022-247X. Periodical. US. English. mo. Academic Press, 4805 Sand Lake Road, Orlando FL 32819. **Ed** R Bellman. **Ind/Abst** Electron. Commun. Abstr. J., ISMEC Bull., Pollut. Abstr. Indexes, Saf. Sci. Abstr. J., Eng. Index Mon., Eng. Index Bioeng. Abstr., Eng. Index Energy Abstr., Comput. Control Abstr., Electr. Electron. Abstr., Sci. Abstr. Sect. A. Phys. Abstr., Eng. Index Mon., Eng. Index Annu., Int. Aerosp. Abstr., Math. Rev., Nuci. Sci. Abstr., Energy Res. Abstr. **LC** QA1. **CODEN** JMANAK.

JOURNAL OF MATHEMATICAL AND PHYSICAL SCIENCES. V. 1- June 1967-. 0047-2557. Periodical. II. English. bm. $20.00. Journal of Mathematical and Physical Science, Editorial Office, Room # H5B 249/Humanities and Sciences Building, Indian Institute of Technology, Madras 600036 India. **Tel** 414769. **Ed** K Swaminathan. **Ind/Abst** Math. Rev., Int. Aerosp. Abstr., Comput. Control Abstr., Electr. Electron. Abstr., Sci. Abstr. Sect. A. Phys. Abstr., Appl. Mech. Rev., Phys. Abstr. **LC** QC20. **DD** 530.15005. **CODEN** JMPSB9. bk rev. **Circ** 300. Mathematical sciences-continuum mechanics, analysis, probability, combinatorial mathematics, theoretical physics, astrophysics, differential educations and numerical anlysis.

THE JOURNAL OF MATHEMATICAL BEHAVIOR. Vol. 3, No. 1 (Autumn 1980)-. 0732-3123. Periodical. US. English. ty. $59.50. Ablex Publishing Corporation, 355 Chestnut Street, Norwood NJ 07648. **Tel** (201)767-8450. **Ed** Robert B Davis. **Ind/Abst** Psychol. Abstr. bk rev. adv acc. **Circ** 500. Articles addressed toward improving mathematics education either from a theoretical or practical viewpoint. *Journal of Children's Mathematical Behavior, 0160-0133.*

JOURNAL OF MATHEMATICAL BIOLOGY. *See* Biology.

JOURNAL OF MATHEMATICAL ECONOMICS. *See* Economics.

JOURNAL OF MATHEMATICAL PSYCHOLOGY. *See* Psychology.

JOURNAL OF MATHEMATICAL SCIENCES. Began with: Vol. 1, published in 1966. 0449-2757. II. English. an. $15.00. Asia Books and Periodicals, 11/3 Darya Ganj Ansari Road, New Delhi 110002 India. **Ind/Abst** Math. Rev., Comput. Rev. **LC** QA1. **DD** 510.5. **CODEN** JOMSB8.

THE JOURNAL OF MATHEMATICAL SOCIOLOGY. *See* Sociology: General Works, Theory.

JOURNAL OF MATHEMATICS OF KYOTO UNIVERSITY. Periodical. English. qt. $82.00. North Oxford Academic, 242 Banbury Road, Oxford OX 2 7DR England. **Tel** 0865-51-1166. **Ind/Abst** Math. Rev.

JOURNAL OF MATHEMATICS, TOKUSHIMA UNIVERSITY. **Main/Corp** Tokushima Daigaku. V. 1- 1967-. JA. English. ir. Publishing Committee of Journal of Mathematics, Tokushima University, Tokushima Japan 770. **Ind/Abst** Math. Rev. **LC** QA1. **DD** 510.5. **CODEN** JMTUBZ. *Journal of Gakugei, Tokushima University Mathematics.*

JOURNAL OF MULTIVARIATE ANALYSIS. **VFOAT** Multivariate Analysis. V. 1- Apr. 1971-. 0047-259X. Periodical. US. English. bm. Academic Press, 4805 Sand Lake Road, Orlando FL 32819. **Tel** (305)345-4100. **Ind/Abst** Electron. Commun. Abstr. J., ISMEC Bull., Pollut. Abstr. Indexes, Saf. Sci. Abstr. J., Comput. Control Abstr., Electr. Electron. Abstr., Sci. Abstr. Sect. A. Phys. Abstr., Eng. Index, Eng. Index Mon., Math. Rev., Comput. Rev., Sci. Cit. Index, Abr. Ed., Phys. Abstr., Eng. Index Annu. **LC** QA278. **DD** 519.53. **CODEN** JMVAAI.

JOURNAL OF NUMBER THEORY. 0022-314X. Periodical. US. English. bm. Academic Press, 4805 Sand Lake Road, Orlando FL 32819. **Tel** (305)345-4100. **Ind/Abst** Math. Rev., Sci. Cit. Index, Abr. Ed., Phys. Abstr., Comput. Rev., Comput. Control Abstr., Electr. Electron. Abstr.

JOURNAL OF OPERATOR THEORY. Vol. 1, No. 1 (Winter 1979)-. 0379-4024. Periodical. US. English (French, German and Russian). qt. American Mathematical Society, PO Box 1571/Annex Station, Providence RI 02901. **Tel** (401)272-9500. **Ind/Abst** Math. Rev.

JOURNAL OF OPTIMIZATION THEORY AND APPLICATIONS. V. 1- July 1967-. 0022-3239. Periodical. US. English. mo. $460.00 Domestic, $12.00 Foreign. Plenum Publishing Corporation, 233 Spring Street, New York NY 10013. **Tel** (212)620-8000. **Ed** A Miele. **Ind/Abst** Electron. Commun. Abstr. J., ISMEC Bull., Pollut. Abstr. Indexes, Saf. Sci. Abstr. J., Eng. Index Mon., Eng. Index Bioeng. Abstr., Eng. Index Energy Abstr., Int. Aerosp. Abstr., Comput. Control Abstr., Electr. Electron. Abstr., Sci. Abstr. Sect. A. Phys. Abstr., Appl. Mech. Rev., Contents Contemp. Math. J., Curr. Contents, Eng. Index Annu., Int. Abstr. Oper. Res., Math. Rev., Zentralbl. Math. Ihre Grenzgeb., Energy Res. Abstr., Eng. Index, Sci. Cit. Index, Abr. Ed. **LC** QA402.5. **CODEN** JOTABN. bk rev. adv acc. Publishes carefully selected papers covering mathematical optimization techniques and their application to science and engineering.

JOURNAL OF PURE AND APPLIED ALGEBRA. **VFOAT** Pure and Applied Algebra. V. 1- Jan. 1971-. 0022-4049. Periodical. NE. English. ir. Elsevier Science Publishers, PO Box 211, 1000 AE Amsterdam Netherlands. **Tel** (020) 5862 467. **Ed** P J Freyd and A Heller. **Ind/Abst** Math. Rev., Sci. Cit. Index, Abr. Ed. **LC** QA150. **DD** 512.005. **CODEN** JPAAA2. adv acc. The journal concentrates on that part of algebra likely to be of general mathematical interest.

JOURNAL OF RECREATIONAL MATHEMATICS. V. 1- Jan. 1968-. 0022-412X. Periodical. US. English. qt. $40.00. Baywood Publishing Company Inc, 120 Marine Street/PO Box D, Farmingdale NY 11735. **Tel** (516)249-2464. **Ed** Joseph S Madachy. **Ind/Abst** Math. Rev., Gen. Sci. Index. **LC** QA95. **CODEN** JRMAB9. bk rev. Puzzles, problems and challenges to the solvers' ingenuity. Alphametics, games, polyhedra, topology, map coloring, and more for the math enthusiast.

JOURNAL OF SOVIET MATHEMATICS. V. 1- Jan./Feb. 1973-. 0090-4104. Periodical. US. English. sm. $1345.00 Domestic, $1485.00 Foreign. Consultants Bureau, 233 Spring Street, New York NY 10013. **Tel** (212)620-8000. **Ed** N N Ural Tseva. **Ind/Abst** Math. Rev., ISMEC Bull., Electron. Commun. Abstr. J., Pollut. Abstr. Indexes, Saf. Sci. Abstr. J., Comput. Inf. Syst. Abstr. J., Curr. Math. Publ., Index Math. Pap., Math. Rev., Zentralbl. Math. Ihre Grenzgeb. **LC** QA1. **DD** 510.5. **CODEN** JOSMAR. This journal provides a single medium for reports on current mathematical advances, surveys wide range of topics including mathematical analyses, probability statistics, cybernetics, algebra, geometry, mathematical physics and wave propagation. *Progress in Mathematics, Problems in Mathematical Analysis; Seminars in Mathematics, 0080-8813.*

JOURNAL OF STATISTICAL COMPUTATION AND SIMULATION. **VFOAT** JSCS. V. 1- Jan. 1972-. 0094-9655. US. English. qt. $334.00. Harwood Academic Publishers, 50 West 23 Street, New York NY 10010. **Ed** R Krutchkoff. **Ind/Abst** Math. Rev., Excerpta Med., Comput. Control Abstr., Electr. Electron. Abstr., Sci. Abstr. Sect. A. Phys. Abstr., Phys. Abstr., Sci. Cit. Index, Abr. Ed., Comput. Rev. **LC** QA276.A1. **DD** 519.502854. **CODEN** JSCSAJ. bk rev. adv acc.

JOURNAL OF STATISTICAL PLANNING AND INFERENCE. *See* Statistics.

Mathematics

JOURNAL OF STATISTICAL RESEARCH. See Statistics.

JOURNAL OF SYMBOLIC COMPUTATION. Vol. 1, No. 1 (Mar. 1985)-. 0747-7171. Periodical. UK. English. qt. $95.00. Academic Press, 111 5th Avenue, New York NY 10003. **DD** 511.

THE JOURNAL OF SYMBOLIC LOGIC. V. 1- Mar. 1936-. 0022-4812. Periodical. US. English. qt. $65.00. Association for Symbolic Logic, PO Box 70557, Pasadena CA 91107. **Tel** (800)577-7233. **Ind/Abst** Math. Rev., Philos. Index, Comput. Control Abstr., Electr. Electron. Abstr., Sci. Abstr. Sect. A. Phys. Abstr., Index Book Rev. Humanit., Humanit. Index, Comput. Rev., Sci. Cit. Index, Abr. Ed., Phys. Abstr. **LC** BC1. **CODEN** JSYLA6.

JOURNAL OF THE AUSTRALIAN MATHEMATICAL SOCIETY. SERIES A, PURE MATHEMATICS AND STATISTICS. VFOAT Pure Mathematics and Statistics. Vol. 29, Pt. 1 (Feb. 1980)-. 0263-6115. Periodical. UK. English. bm. 150.00 Domestic, 133.00 US. Australian Mathematical Publishing Association Inc, University of Queensland, St Lucia Queensland 4067 Australia. **Tel** (03)541-2612. **Ed** T E Hall. **Ind/Abst** Math. Rev. **CODEN** JAMADS. Index in last issue of volume - attached. **Circ** 860. Commenced in 1959, publishes papers on pure mathematics and statistics. *Journal of the Australian Mathematical Society. Series A, Pure Mathematics.*

JOURNAL OF THE AUSTRALIAN MATHEMATICAL SOCIETY. SERIES B. APPLIED MATHEMATICS. (JOURNAL OF THE AUSTRALIAN MATHEMATICAL SOCIETY. SERIES B : APPLIED MATHEMATICS). VFOAT Applied Mathematics. V. 19-June 1975-. 0334-2700. Periodical. AT. English. bm. 84.74. Australian Mathematical Publishing Association Inc, University of Queensland, St Luica Queensland 4067 Australia. **Tel** 03 228 5136. **Ed** E O Tuck. **Ind/Abst** Math. Rev., Int. Aerosp. Abstr., Comput. Control Abstr., Electr. Electron. Abstr., Sci. Abstr. Sect. A. Phys. Abstr., Appl. Mech. Rev., Phys. Abstr. **CODEN** JAMMDU. **Circ** 830. Publishes papers in any field of applied mathematics and related mathematical sciences, excluding statistics. *Journal of the Australian Mathematical Society.*

THE JOURNAL OF THE INDIAN ACADEMY OF MATHEMATICS. Main/Corp Indian Academy of Mathematics. V. 1- Mar. 1979-. Periodical. English. ir. $15.00. Indian Academy of Mathematics Editor, 41 Shankarbag, Indore 452006 India. **Ind/Abst** Math. Rev. **LC** QA1. **DD** 510.5.

JOURNAL OF THE INDIAN MATHEMATICAL SOCIETY. (THE JOURNAL OF THE INDIAN MATHEMATICAL SOCIETY). V. 3 (1911)-V. 20 (1933). 0019-5839. Periodical. II. English. qt. $40.00. Indian Mathematical Society, Professor Bhanu Murthy, University of Madras, Madras 600005 India. **Ind/Abst** Math. Rev. **LC** QA1. **DD** 510.6254. **CODEN** JIMTA2. (cum index). *Journal of the Indian Mathematical Club.*

JOURNAL OF THE INTERNATIONAL ASSOCIATION FOR MATHEMATICAL GEOLOGY. See Earth Sciences - Geology.

JOURNAL OF THE KOREAN MATHEMATICAL SOCIETY. VFOAT Taehan Suhakhoe Chi. 0304-9914. Periodical. English (summaries in Korean). sa. **Ind/Abst** Math. Rev. **LC** QA1. **DD** 510.5. **CODEN** JKMSDG.

JOURNAL OF THE LONDON MATHEMATICAL SOCIETY. Main/Corp London Mathematical Society. V. 1-44, 1926-69. 0024-6107. Periodical. UK. English. bm. $200.00. C F Hodgson & Son Ltd, Unit 4/Central Trading Estate, Staines Middlesex England. **Ind/Abst** Int. Aerosp. Abstr., Math. Rev., Zentralbl. Math. Ihre Grenzgeb., Sci. Cit. Index, Abr. Ed., Appl. Mech. Rev. **LC** QA1. **DD** 510.5. **CODEN** JLMSAK. Index in last issue of volume - attached. (cum index). bk rev. Short papers on higher mathematics.

JOURNAL OF THE MATHEMATICAL SOCIETY OF JAPAN. Main/Corp Nihon Sugakkai. V. 1- Sept. 1948-. 0025-5645. Periodical. JA. English. mo. Japan Publs Trading Company Ltd, PO Box 5030, Tokyo International, Tokyo 100-31 Japan. **Ind/Abst** Math. Rev. **LC** QA1. **DD** 510.6252. **CODEN** NISUBC. (cum index). *Proceedings of the Physico-Mathematical Society of Japan. Nippon Suugaku-Buturigakkwai Kizi.*

JOURNAL OF TIME SERIES ANALYSIS. Vol. 1, No. 1 (1980)-. 0143-9782. Periodical. UK. English. qt. $80.00. Tieto Ltd, Bank House/8-A Hill Road, Clevedon Avon B521 7HH England. **Ind/Abst** Math. Rev., Comput. Control Abstr., Electr. Electron. Abstr., Sci. Abstr. Sect. A. Phys. Abstr. **LC** QA280. **DD** 519.5505. **CODEN** JTSADL.

JOURNAL OF UNDERGRADUATE MATHEMATICS. V. 1- Mar. 1969-. 0022-5339. Periodical. US. English. sa. $6.00. Guilford College, Department of Mathematics, Greensboro NC 27410. **Tel** (919)292-5511. **LC** QA1.

JOURNAL - SASKATCHEWAN MATHEMATICS TEACHERS' SOCIETY. (JOURNAL). VFOAT S.M.T.S. News/Journal. **VAT** S.M.T.S. News/Journal (Spring, Summer 1980) Saskatchewan Mathematics Teachers' Society News/Journal (Spring, Summer 1980), News/Journal - Saskatchewan Mathematics Teachers' Society (1980). Vol. 17, No. 4 (Spring/Summer 1980)-. 0714-7082. Periodical. CN. English. ty. $8.00. Saskatchewan Mathematics Teachers Society, 2317 Arlington Avenue/Box 1108, Saskatoon Saskatchewan S7J 2H8 Canada. **Ind/Abst** Can. Educ. Index. **DD** 510.7. *News/Journal, 0316-5779.*

KEIRYO KOKUGOGAKU. VFOAT Mathematical Linguistics. Began with May 1957 issue. Periodical. JA. Japanese (summaries in English). qt. Japan Publishing Trade Company Ltd, PO Box 5030, Tokyo International, Tokyo 100-31 Japan. **Ind/Abst** MLA Int. Bibliogr. Books Artic. Mod. Lang. Lit., Lang. Lang. Behav. Abstr., Sociol. Abstr. **LC** P9.

KENKYU KIYO (SUGAKU KYOIKU GAKKAI (JAPAN)). (KENKYU KIYO). VFOAT Yen Chiu Chi Yao. Chinese (Japanese). ir. **LC** QA11.A1.

KLEINE ERGANZUNGSREIHE ZU DEN HOCHSCHULBUCHERN FUR MATHEMATIK. 1- 1954-. 0453-9893. WB. German. ir. Deutscher Buch Export-Import, Leninstrasse 16, DDR-701 Leipzig East Germany. **Ind/Abst** Math. Rev. **LC** QA11.

KODAI MATHEMATICAL JOURNAL. V. 1- Mar. 1978-. Periodical. English. ty. $94.00. North Oxford Academic, 242 Banbury Road, Oxford OX2 7DR England. **Tel** 0865-51-1166. **Ind/Abst** Math. Rev. *Kodai Mathematical Seminar Reports.*

KOHO - KEIO GIJUKU DAIGAKU JOHO KAGAKU KENKYUJO. Main/Corp Keio Gijuku Daigaku, Tokyo Joho Kagaku Kenkyujo. JA. Japanese. ir. Keio Gijuku Daigaku, 1-1 Hiyoshi 4 Kohoku-Ku (223), Yokohama Japan. **LC** QA74.

KONGELIGE DANSKE VIDENSKABERNES SELSKAB. MATEMATISK-FYSISKE MEDDELELSER. (MATEMATISK-FYSISKE MEDDELELSER). Vol. 1-. 0023-3323. Danish. ir. Munksgaard Limited, 35 Norre Sogade, DK-1370 Copenhagen K Denmark. **Ind/Abst** Math. Rev., Comput. Control Abstr., Electr. Electron. Abstr., Sci. Abstr., Chem. Abstr., Energy Res. Abstr., Sci. Cit. Index, Abr. Ed., Phys. Abstr., Sci. Abstr. Sect. A. Phys. Abstr. **CODEN** KDVSAK. Index published separately - free - automatically sent. *Oversigt over Selskabets Virksomhed.*

KONSTRUKTIVNAIA TEROIIA FUNKTSII I FUNKTSIONALNYI ANALIZ. Periodical. UR. Russian. 1.10. IZD-VO Kazanskogo Universiteta, Ul Lenina 4/5, 42011 G Kazan Russia. **LC** QA331.

KYUNGPOOK MATHEMATICAL JOURNAL. V. 1- Jan. 1958-. 0454-8124. Periodical. KO. English. sa. $20.00. Kyungpook University, Department of Mathematics, Taegu 630 Korea. **Ind/Abst** Math. Rev. **LC** QA1. **CODEN** KPMJAW.

LARGE SCALE SYSTEMS. Began with Vol. 1, No. 1 (Feb. 1980). 0165-0777. Periodical. NE. English. qt. North-Holland Publishers Company, PO Box 211, 1000 AC Amsterdam The Netherlands. **Ind/Abst** Chem. Abstr. **LC** QA402. **DD** 003. **CODEN** LSSAD2.

LATVIJSKIJ MATEMATICESKIJ EZEGODNIK. (LATVIISKII MATEMATICHESKII EZHEGODNIK). 1- 1965-. 0321-2270. Periodical. UR. Russian (summaries in English). an. Victor Kamkin Inc, 12224 Parklawn Drive, Rockville MD 20852. **Tel** (301)881-5973. **Ind/Abst** Math. Rev., Int. Aerosp. Abstr., Appl. Mech. Rev. **LC** QA1. *Trudy.*

LECTURE NOTES IN BIOMATHEMATICS. See Biology.

LECTURE NOTES IN ECONOMICS AND MATHEMATICAL SYSTEMS. See Economics.

LECTURE NOTES IN MATHEMATICS (SPRINGER-VERLAG). (LECTURE NOTES IN MATHEMATICS). 1-. 0075-8434. Monographic Series. English (German or French). ir. Springer Verlag, 44 Hartz Way, Secaucus NJ 07094. **Tel** (201)348-4033. **Ed** A Dold and B Eckmann. **Ind/Abst** Comput. Control Abstr., Electr. Electron. Abstr., Sci. Abstr. Sect. A. Phys. Abstr., Math. Rev., Phys. Abstr. **LC** QA3. **CODEN** LNMAA2. (cum index). Spans the entire range of modern mathematics. Serves as the model for all other Lecture Note series at Springer since 1964.

LECTURE NOTES IN NUMERICAL AND APPLIED ANALYSIS. Series/Titl North-Holland Mathematics Studies. 0168-1370. Monographic Series. US. English. ir. Elsevier Science Publishing Company Inc, 52 Vanderbilt Avenue, New York NY 10017. **Ind/Abst** Math. Rev. **LC** UNC.

LECTURE NOTES IN PURE AND APPLIED MATHEMATICS. US. English. ir. Marcel Dekker, Continuation Department, 270 Madison Avenue, New York NY 10016. **Tel** (212)696-9000. **Ed** Kobayashi, Hewitt and Taft. **Ind/Abst** Math. Rev. This is an ongoing series. Each title has a different subject.

LECTURE NOTES - INSTITUTE OF MATHEMATICAL STATISTICS, UNIVERSITY OF COPENHAGEN. See Statistics.

LECTURE NOTES SERIES. Main/Corp Aarhus, Denmark. Universitet. Matematisk Institut. 1962/63-. 0065-017X. DK. Danish. ir. Matematisk Institut, Aarhus Universitet, DK-8000 Aarhus C Denmark. **Ind/Abst** Math. Rev.

LECTURE NOTES SERIES. Main/Corp London Mathematical Society. 0076-0552. UK. English. ir. Blackwell Scientific Publishing Ltd, PO Box 88, Oxford OX2 0EL England.

LECTURES ON MATHEMATICS IN THE LIFE SCIENCES. V. 1-. 0075-8523. Monographic Series. US. English. ir. American Mathematical Society, PO Box 1571 Annex Station, Providence RI 02901. **Ind/Abst** Math. Rev., Chem. Abstr., Biol. Abstr. **LC** UNC. **NLM** W3 LE33. **CODEN** LMLSAA.

LEHRBUCHER UND MONOGRAPHIEN AUS DEM GEBIETE DER EXAKTEN WISSENSCHAFTEN. MATHEMATISCHE REIHE CEASED. VFOAT Mathematische Reihe. Began with V. 1, published in 1945. Ceased V. 77. Monographic Series. German. ir. **Ind/Abst** Math. Rev.

LETTERS IN MATHEMATICAL PHYSICS. See Physics.

LIBERTAS MATHEMATICA. V. 1-. 0278-5307. US. English (French). an. $40.00. ARA Publications, 4310 Finley Avenue/#6, Los Angeles CA 90027. **Ind/Abst** Math. Rev. **LC** QA1. **DD** 510.5.

LINEAR ALGEBRA AND ITS APPLICATIONS. V. 1- Jan. 1968-. 0024-3795. Periodical. US. English. ir. $792.00. Elsevier Science Publishing Company Ltd, PO Box 1663, Grand Central Station, New York NY 10163. **Tel** (212)370-5520. **Ind/Abst** Math. Rev., Electron. Commun. Abstr. J., ISMEC Bull., Pollut. Abstr. Indexes, Saf. Sci. Abstr. J., Int. Aerosp. Abstr., Comput. Control Abstr., Electr. Electron. Abstr., Sci. Abstr. Sect. A. Phys. Abstr., Phys. Abstr., Sci. Cit. Index, Abr. Ed. **LC** QA251. **DD** 512.897. **CODEN** LAAPAW.

LINEAR AND MULTILINEAR ALGEBRA. V. 1- 1973-. 0308-1087. Periodical. US. Mathematics. qt. $334.00. Gordon & Breach, PO Box 197, London WC2E 9PX England. **Ed** M Marcus. **Ind/Abst** Math. Rev. **LC** QA184. **DD** 512.505. **CODEN** LNMLAZ. bk rev. adv acc.

LITHUANIAN MATHEMATICAL JOURNAL. V. 15- Jan./Mar. 1975-. 0363-1672. Periodical. US. English (translated from Russian). qt. $325.00 Domestic, $365.00 Foreign. Consultants Bureau, 233 Spring Street, New York NY 10013. **Tel** (212)620-8000. **Ed** P Katilius. **Ind/Abst** Math. Rev., Electron. Commun. Abstr. J., ISMEC Bull., Pollut. Abstr. Indexes, Saf. Sci. Abstr. J., Zentralbl. Math.

Mathematics

Ihre Grenzgeb. **LC** QA1. **DD** 510.5. **CODEN** LMJTD6. This journal focuses on a number of fundamental problems on a wide variety of topics in theoretical mathematics. *Lithuanian Mathematical Transactions, 0148-8279.*

LITOVSKII MATEMATICHESKII SBORNIK. VFOAT Lietuvos Matematikos Rinkinys. 1- 1961-. 0024-2977. Periodical. UR. Russian (summaries in Lithuanian, and English, French or German). qt. $39.00. Victor Kamkin Inc (76716), 12224 Parklawn Drive, Rockville MD 20852. **Tel** (301)881-5973. **Ind/Abst** Math. Rev., Int. Aerosp. Abstr. **LC** QA1.

LOGIK UND GRUNDLAGEN DER MATHEMATIK. Monographic Series. German. ir. **Ind/Abst** Math. Rev. **LC** QA9.

LOGIQUE ET ANALYSE. See Indexes/ Abstracts.

MC VARIA. VAT Mathematisch Centrum Varia. 1-. Monographic Series. Dutch. ir. Mathematical Center, PO Box 4079 Kruislaan 413, 1009 AB Amsterdam Netherlands. **Ind/Abst** Math. Rev.

MANITOBA MATHEMATICS TEACHERS. See Education (General) - Theory, Practice of Education.

MANUSCRIPTA MATHEMATICA. V. 1- Feb. 14, 1969-. 0025-2611. Periodical. English (French, or German with summaries in English). bm. $289.00. Springer Verlag-New York Inc, 175 5th Avenue, New York NY 10010. **Tel** (212)460-1500. Ed M Barnes, H Brezis, P M Cohn, S Dold, S Hildebrandt, E Hlawka, T Kats, H Kraft, S Prestel, P Roquette and J Tits. **Ind/Abst** Math. Rev., Sci. Cit. Index, Abr. Ed. **LC** QA1. **DD** 510.05. **CODEN** MSMHB2. Covering all fields of mathematics. This journal gives you the opportunity to be informed of developments as they happen.

MARKETING SCIENCE. See Business - Marketing.

MAT SPECIAL ISSUE. Main/Corp Mathematical Association of Tanzania. VAT Mathematical Association of Tanzania Special Issue. English. ir. Institute of Education, University of Dar Es Salaam PO Box 35094, Dar Es Salaam Tanzania. **LC** QA1. **DD** 510.710678.

MATCH (MULHEIM AN DER RUHR, GERMANY). See Chemistry.

MATEKON. See Economics.

MATEMAATTISTEN AINEIDEN AIKAKAUSKIRJA. Began in 1937. 0025-5149. Periodical. Fl. Finnish (summaries in English). ir. $11.53. Maolry, Akavatalo Rautatielaisenk 6, 00520 Helsinki 52 Finland. **LC** QA1. **DD** 510.5.

MATEMATICESKAJA FIZIKA CEASED. (MATEMATICHESKAIA FIZIKA). Vol. 1-34. 0542-9986. UR. Russian. ir. **Ind/Abst** Math. Rev., Int. Aerosp. Abstr., Comput. Control Abstr., Electr. Electron. Abstr., Sci. Abstr. Sect. A. Phys. Abstr. **LC** QC19.2. **CODEN** MAFIAD.

MATEMATICESKIJ SBORNIK. (MATEMATICHESKII SBORNIK). VFOAT Receuil Mathematique. V. 1-42, 1866-1935. 0368-8666. Periodical. UR. Russian (summaries in English, French or German, or in one of these languages with a summary in Russian). mo. $99.00. Victor Kamkin Inc (70512), 12224 Parklawn Drive, Rockville MD 20852. **Tel** (301)881-5973. **Ind/Abst** Math. Rev., Int. Aerosp. Abstr. **LC** QA1. (cum index).

MATEMATICHESKIE ZAMETKI. V. 1- 1967-. 0025-567X. Periodical. UR. Russian. mo. $59.50. Victor Kamkin Inc (70560), 12224 Parklawn Drive, Rockville MD 20852. **Tel** (301)881-5973. **Ind/Abst** Math. Rev. **LC** QA1. (cum index).

MATEMATICKI VESNIK. New Series Vol. 1- 1964-. 0025-5165. Periodical. YU. Serbo-Croatian -C (some articles in English, French or German). qt. Jugoslovensak Knjica, PO Box 36, Beograd Yuguslavia. **Ind/Abst** Math. Rev., Int. Aerosp. Abstr. **LC** QA1. **CODEN** MVNSAQ. *Vesnik.*

MATEMATIKA. Main/Corp Kharkivskyi Derzhavnyi Universytet Imeni O.M. Horkoho. UR. Russian. 1.80 Each Issue. **LC** AS262.

MATEMATIKA. Periodical. BU. Bulgarian. bm. Hemus, 6 Boulevard Rusky, Sofia Bulgaria. **LC** QA1.

MATEMATIKAI LAPOK. V. 1- 1949-. 0025-519X. Periodical. HU. Hungarian (summaries and tables of contents in English and Russian). ir. $21.00. Akademiai Kiado, PO Box 24, 1363 Budapest Hungary. **Tel** (01136)1-187396. Ed A Csaszar. **Ind/Abst** Math. Rev., Zentralbl. Math. Ihre Grenzgeb. **LC** QA1. **CODEN** MTLPAR. bk rev. Circ 1,400. (ctrl). Covers algebra, analysis, combinatorics, geometry, number theory, probability and mathematical statistics, topology, mathematical logic and foundations of mathematics. *Matematikai Es Fizikai Lapok.*

MATEMATYKA. Began in 1956. Monographic Series. PL. Polish (summaries in English). bm. ARS Polona, Krakowskie Przedmiescie 7, 00-068 Warsaw Poland. **LC** QA1.

MATH MONOGRAPH. No. 4 (June 1976)-. 0711-2521. CN. English. an. Alberta Teachers' Association, 11010-142 Street, Edmonton Alberta T5N 2R1 Canada. **DD** 510.7. *Monograph, 0317-8579.*

MATH NOTEBOOK. V. 1- Nov. 1979-. 0272-8885. Periodical. US. English. mo. $13.00. Center for Teaching and Learning Mathematics, PO Box 3149, Framingham MA 01701. **Tel** (617)877-7895. Ed Mahesh C Sharma. **DD** 372. bk rev. adv acc. Circ 2,000. (ctrl). Information for the teachers and parents of children with learning problems in mathematics. Diagnostic, remedial and instructional strategies in learning disabilities in mathematics.

MATH NOTES. 0821-3143. Periodical. CN. English. Free. B C Association of Mathematics Teachers, 105-2235 Burrard Street, Vancouver British Columbia V6J 3H9 Canada. **DD** 510.70711. (ctrl).

MATHEMATICA. V. 1-23, 1929-48. 0025-5505. Periodical. RM. English (French, German, or Italian). an. $48.00. Rompresfilatelia, PO Box 1362137, Bucharest Romania. **Ind/Abst** Math. Rev., Appl. Mech. Rev., Comput. Rev. **CODEN** MTHCA2.

MATHEMATICA BALKANICA. 1- 1971-. Periodical. YU. English (French, German, or Russian) an. D R Kurep A Duro, Boegrad PP 550, Studentski TRG 16 Yogoslavia. **Ind/Abst** Math. Rev., Comput. Control Abstr., Electr. Electron. Abstr., Sci. Abstr. Sect. A. Phys. Abstr., Phys. Abstr. **LC** QA1. **CODEN** MTMBBP.

MATHEMATICA JAPONICAE. VFOAT Mathematica Japonica. V. 1, No. 1- May 1948-. 0025-5513. Periodical. JA. Multilingual (English, French, German). qt. $195.00. North Oxford Academic Publishing Company, 242 Banbury Road, Oxford OX2 7DR England. **Tel** 0865-51-1166. Ed T Shimizu. **Ind/Abst** Math. Rev. **LC** QA1. **DD** 510.5. **CODEN** MAJAA9.

MATHEMATICA NUMERICA SINICA. VFOAT Chi Suan Shu Hsueh. CC. English. qt. China Publication Centre, PO Box 2820, Beijing China. **Ind/Abst** Math. Rev., Comput. Control Abstr., Electr. Electron. Abstr., Sci. Abstr. Sect. A. Phys. Abstr. **CODEN** JSUXDP.

MATHEMATICA SCANDINAVICA. V. 1-. 0025-5521. Periodical. DK. English (text in French or German). qt. 690.-. Matematisk Institut and Aarhus Universitet, Ny Munkegade, DK-8000 Aarhus C Denmark. Ed Johan Dupont. **Ind/Abst** Math. Rev., Sci. Cit. Index, Abr. Ed., Comput. Rev. **LC** QA1. **CODEN** MTSCAN. Circ 1,100. *Matemetisk Tidsskrift. Series B.*

MATHEMATICA SCRIPTA. 1-. 0076-5309. Monographic Series. German. ir. Springer Verlag-New York Inc, 175 5th Avenue, New York NY 10010. **Tel** (212)460-1584.

MATHEMATICA SLOVACA. V. 26- 1976-. Periodical. CS. Czech, English, French, German, Russian, or Slovak. qt. Slovart Foreign Trade Company Ltd, Gottwaldovo Nam 6, 817 64 Bratislv Czechoslovakia. **Tel** 48841-49. **Ind/Abst** Math. Rev., Comput. Control Abstr., Electr. Electron. Abstr., Sci. Abstr. Sect. A. Phys. Abstr., Phys. Abstr. **LC** QA1. **DD** 510.5. **CODEN** MASLDM. *Matematicky Casopis.*

MATHEMATICAL CENTRE TRACTS. 1-. Monographic Series. NE. English. ir. Stichting Mathematisch Centrum, PO Box 4079, Estraat 49, 1009 AB Amsterdam Netherlands. **Tel** (020)592-9333. **Ind/Abst** Math. Rev.

MATHEMATICAL CHRONICLE. V. 1- Nov. 1969-. 0581-1155. NZ. English. ir. University of Auckland, Math Department, Private Bag, Auckland New Zealand. **Tel** 792-300. **Ind/Abst** Math. Rev. **LC** QA1. **CODEN** MTHCB3.

MATHEMATICAL ECONOMICS TEXTS. See Economics.

MATHEMATICAL EXPOSITIONS. No. 1- 1940-. 0076-5333. Monographic Series. CN. English. ir. University of Toronto Press, Front Campus, Toronto Ontario M5S 1A6 Canada. **Ind/Abst** Math. Rev.

MATHEMATICAL GAZETTE. (THE MATHEMATICAL GAZETTE). V. 1- April 1894-. 0025-5572. Periodical. UK. English. qt. 16.00. Mathematical Association, 259 London Road, Leicester LE2 3BE England. **Tel** (0533) 703877. Ed V Bryant. **Ind/Abst** Math. Rev. **LC** QA1. **CODEN** MAGAAS. Index published separately - free - automatically sent. (cum index). bk rev. adv acc. **Circ** 6,000. (ctrl). Offers articles on mathematical topics of wide appeal and mathematics teaching at the level of secondary school, college, and university.

MATHEMATICAL INTELLIGENCER (BERLIN, GERMANY : 1978). (THE MATHEMATICAL INTELLIGENCER). Vol. 1, No. 1-. 0343-6993. Periodical. WB. English. qt. $21.95. Springer-Verlag New York Inc, 175 5th Avenue, New York NY 10010. **Tel** (212)460-1500. Ed J Ewing. **Ind/Abst** Math. Rev., Energy Res. Abstr., Gen. Sci. Index. **LC** QA1. **DD** 510.5. **CODEN** MAINDC. Covers a wide range of topics, such as people, theorems, philosophy, and history relevant to mathematics, designed for researchers, students, teachers, and others concerned with mathematics. *Mathematical Intelligencer (Berlin, Germany : 1972).*

THE MATHEMATICAL LOG. 0025-5580. Periodical. US. English. ir. $2.00 Domestic, $3.50 Foreign. Mu Alpha Theta, 601 Elm Avenue/Room 423, Norman OK 73019. **Tel** (405)325-4489. Ed H Don Allen. **Circ** 30,000. (ctrl). Mathematical articles, problems and recreationals appropriate for secondary and junior college students.

MATHEMATICAL METHODS IN THE APPLIED SCIENCES. Vol. 1, No. 1-. 0170-4214. Periodical. English (French or German). qt. 328.—. B G Teubner GMBH, Postfach 80 10 69, Industriestr 15, D7000 Stuttgart 80 West Germany. **Tel** 0711/78901-17. Ed B Brosowski and G F Roach. **Ind/Abst** Math. Rev., Eng. Index Annu., Eng. Index Mon., Eng. Index, Eng. Index Bioeng. Abstr., Eng. Index Energy Abstr., Int. Aerosp. Abstr., Appl. Mech. Rev. **CODEN** MMSCDB. adv acc. Deals with problems arising in the engineering and physics sciences, the corresponding mathematical modelling and solutions using sophisticated analytical and numerical methods.

MATHEMATICAL MODELLING. Vol. 1, No. 1-. 0270-0255. Periodical. US. English. bm. $140.00. Pergamon Press, 395 Sawmill River Road, Elmsford NY 10523. **Tel** (914)592-7700. **Ind/Abst** Math. Rev., Fluidex, Excerpta Med., Abstr. Bull. Inst. Paper Chem., Comput. Control Abstr., Electr. Electron. Abstr., Sci. Abstr. Sect. A. Phys. Abstr. **LC** QA401. **DD** 001.434. **CODEN** MAMODZ. Also available in microfiche and microfilm.

MATHEMATICAL NOTES. 2-. Monographic Series. US. English. ir. Princeton University Press, 3175 Princeton Pike, Box A, Lawrenceville NJ 08648. **Tel** (609)896-2111. *Princeton Mathematical Notes.*

MATHEMATICAL NOTES OF THE ACADEMY OF SCIENCES OF THE USSR. VAT Mathematical Notes of the Academy of Sciences of the Union of Soviet Socialist Republics. V. 1, No. 1/2- Jan./Feb. 1967-. 0001-4346. Periodical. US. English (Russian). mo. $645.00 Domestic, $715.00 Foreign. Consultants Bureau, 233 Spring Street, New York NY 10013. **Tel** (212)620-8000. Ed S B Stechkin. **Ind/Abst** Math. Rev., Appl. Mech. Rev., Contents Contemp. Math. J., Index Math. Pap., Zentralbl. Math. Ihre Grenzgeb., Sci. Cit. Index, Abr. Ed. **LC** QA1. **CODEN** MTHNB2. Contains original papers in all branches of advanced contemporary math. Covers canonical subdivision of Lobackwuski space, regulatory of processing and piece wise polynomial interpolation.

MATHEMATICAL PROCEEDINGS OF THE CAMBRIDGE PHILOSOPHICAL SOCIETY. Main/Corp Cambridge Philosophical Society, Cambridge, Eng. V. 77- Jan. 1975-. 0305-0041. Periodical. UK. English. bm. $220.00. Cambridge University Press, 510 North Avenue, New Rochelle NY 10801. **Tel** (914)235-0300. Ed P T Johnstone. **Ind/Abst** Math. Rev., Eng. Index Annu., Eng. Index Mon., Eng. Index Bioeng. Abstr., Eng. Index Energy Abstr., Int. Aerosp. Abstr., GeoRef, Comput. Control Abstr., Electr. Electron. Abstr., Sci. Abstr. Sect. A. Phys. Abstr., Appl. Mech. Rev., Sci. Cit. Index, Abr. Ed., Phys. Abstr., Bibliogr. Index

Geol., Eng. Index. **LC** Q41. **DD** 510.5. **CODEN** MPCPCO. All branches of pure mathematics are covered, in particular set theory, classical and functional analysis, operators, differential equations, probability and statistics. *Proceedings of the Cambridge Philosophical Society, Mathematical and Physical Sciences.*

MATHEMATICAL PROGRAMMING. V. 1- Oct. 1971-. 0025-5610. Periodical. NE. English. bm. Elsevier Science Publishers, PO Box 211, 1000 AE Amsterdam The Netherlands. **Tel** (020)5803911. **Ind/Abst** Math. Rev., Electron. Commun. Abstr. J., ISMEC Bull., Pollut. Abstr. Indexes, Saf. Sci. Abstr. J., Eng. Index Annu., Eng. Index Mon., Eng. Index Bioeng. Abstr., Eng. Index Energy Abstr., Comput. Control Abstr., Electr. Electron. Abstr., Sci. Abstr. Sect. A. Phys. Abstr., Phys. Abstr., Sci. Cit. Index, Abr. Ed., Comput. Rev., Eng. Index. **LC** QA264. **DD** 519.7005. **CODEN** MHPGA4. (cum index).

MATHEMATICAL PROGRAMMING STUDY. No. 1- 1974-. 0303-3929. Monographic Series. NE. English. sa. Elsevier Science Publishers, PO Box 211, 1000 AE Amsterdam Netherlands. **Tel** (020)5803911. **Ind/Abst** Math. Rev., Eng. Index Annu., Eng. Index Mon., Eng. Index Bioeng. Abstr., Eng. Index Energy Abstr., Comput. Control Abstr., Electr. Electron. Abstr., Sci. Abstr. Sect. A. Phys. Abstr., Phys. Abstr., Sci. Cit. Index, Abr. Ed., Comput. Rev., Eng. Index. **CODEN** MPSTDF.

MATHEMATICAL REPORTS (CHUR, SWITZERLAND). (MATHEMATICAL REPORTS). Vol. 1, Pt. 1 (July 1983)-. 0275-7214. Monographic Series. US. English. ir. $136.00. Harwood Academic Publishers, PO Box 197, London WC2E 9PX England. **Tel** (212)242-4464. **Ed** J Dieudonne. **Ind/Abst** Math. Rev. bk rev. adv acc.

MATHEMATICAL RESEARCH = MATHEMATISCHE FORSCHUNGEN : WISSENSCHAFTEN BEITRAGE HERAUSGEGEBEN VON DER AKADEMIE DER WISSENSCHAFTEN DER DDR, ZENTRALINSTITUT FUR MATEMATIK UND MECHANIK. VFOAT Mathematische Forschung. BD. 1-. Monographic Series. English. ir. Deutscher Buch Export, Leninstrasse 16, DDR 701 Leipzig East Germany. **LC** UNC. Original contributions on all fields of mathematical research, e.g. research monographs, collections of papers to a single topic, reports on congresses to promote quick information and communication. *Schriftenreihe des Zentralinstituts fur Mathematik und Mechanik.*

MATHEMATICAL REVIEWS. V. 1- Jan. 1940-. 0025-5629. US. English. mo. American Mathematical Society, PO Box 1571 Annex Station, Providence RI 02901. **Tel** (401)272-9500. **Ind/Abst** Math. Rev., Appl. Mech. Rev., Comput. Rev. **LC** QA1. **DD** 510.5. **NLM** Z 6653 M426. **CODEN** MAREAR. (cum index).

MATHEMATICAL SCIENCES ADMINISTRATIVE DIRECTORY. *See* Yearbooks, Almanacs, Directories.

MATHEMATICAL SCIENCES PROFESSIONAL DIRECTORY. *See* Yearbooks, Almanacs, Directories.

MATHEMATICAL SCIENTIST. (THE MATHEMATICAL SCIENTIST). V. 1- Jan. 1976-. 0312-3685. Periodical. AT. English. sa. 12.93. Australian Mathematical Society, University of Queensland, Department of Mathematics, St Lucia Queensland 4067 Australia. **Ed** C B Rennie. **Ind/Abst** Math. Rev., Energy Res. Abstr. **LC** QA1. **DD** 510.5. bk rev. **Circ** 650. Commenced in 1976; publishes papers of general interest in all areas of mathematics.

MATHEMATICAL SOCIAL SCIENCES. *See* Social Sciences (General).

MATHEMATICAL SPECTRUM. Vol. 1- 1968/69-. 0025-5653. Periodical. UK. English. ty. 4.00 Britain, Europe, others, 8.00 North, South, and Central America, 8.00 Australia. Mathematical Spectrum, Editor, Hicks Building, The University, Sheffield 33 7RH England. **Tel** (0742) 78555. **Ed** David Sharpe. **Ind/Abst** Fluidex, Comput. Control Abstr., Electr. Electron. Abstr., Sci. Abstr. Sect. A. Phys. Abstr., Math. Rev., Phys. Abstr. **LC** QA1. **DD** 510.05. **CODEN** MSPEB8. bk rev. adv acc. **Circ** 1,800. Articles on all branches of mathematics, book reviews, computer column, problems and solutions. Suitable for students and general readers.

MATHEMATICAL SURVEYS *CEASED.* No. 1-18. 0076-5376. Monographic Series. US. English. ir. American Mathematical Society, PO Box 1571, Annex Station, Providence RI 02901. **Tel** (401)272-9500. **Ind/Abst** Math. Rev. **DD** 510.

MATHEMATICAL SYSTEMS IN ECONOMICS. Monographic Series. GW. English, French or German. ir. Athenaeum Verlag/Anton Hain, PF 1220, Adelheidstrasse 2, 6240 Koenigstein West Germany. **Tel** 06174/3021. **Ed** R Henn, W Eichhorn, S N Afriat, G Bamberg. **Ind/Abst** Math. Rev. bk rev. adv acc. A survey of one particular subject within the context of mathematical economics, operations research and computer science.

MATHEMATICAL SYSTEMS THEORY. V. 1- Jan./Feb. 1967-. 0025-5661. Periodical. US. English. qt. Springer Verlag-New York Inc, 175 5th Avenue, New York NY 10010. **Tel** (212)460-1500. **Ed** S A Greibach. **Ind/Abst** Math. Rev., Electron. Commun. Abstr. J., ISMEC Bull., Pollut. Abstr. Indexes, Saf. Sci. Abstr. J., Comput. Control Abstr., Electr. Electron. Abstr., Sci. Abstr. Sect. A. Phys. Abstr., Sci. Cit. Index, Abr. Ed., Phys. Abstr., Comput. Rev. **LC** QA1. **CODEN** MASTBA. (cum index). Examines the various mathematical aspects of everyday problems in engineering, computer science, and other areas, such as economics and biology, which rely on direct applications of systems ideas.

MATHEMATICIANS OF OUR TIME. V. 1-. Monographic Series. US. English. ir. Massachusetts Institute of Technology, 28 Carlton Street, Cambridge MA 02142.

MATHEMATICS AND COMPUTER EDUCATION. Vol. 16, No. 1 (Winter 1982)-. 0730-8639. Periodical. US. English. ty. $25.00 Domestic, $35.00 Foreign. Mathematics and Computer Education, Nassau Community College, Department of Mathematics and Computer Processing, Garden City NY 11530. **Ind/Abst** Comput. Control Abstr., Electr. Electron. Abstr., Sci. Abstr. Sect. A. Phys. Abstr., Curr. Index J. Educ., Math. Rev., Zentralbl. Didakt. Math. **LC** QA13. **DD** 510.711. **CODEN** MCEDDA. Available on microfilm and microfiche through University Microfilms International. *MATYC Journal, 0092-1424.*

MATHEMATICS AND COMPUTERS IN SIMULATION. V. 19- Mar. 1977-. 0378-4754. Periodical. NE. English (French). bm. 339.00 Domestic, $117.00 Foreign. Elsevier Science Publishers, PO Box 211, 1000 AE Amsterdam Netherlands. **Tel** 020- 5862911. **Ed** A Sevenster. **Ind/Abst** Math. Rev., Electron. Commun. Abstr. J., ISMEC Bull., Pollut. Abstr. Indexes, Saf. Sci. Abstr. J., Eng. Index Annu., Eng. Index Mon., Eng. Index Bioeng. Abstr., Eng. Index Energy Abstr., Coal Abstr., GeoRef, Comput. Control Abstr., Electr. Electron. Abstr., Sci. Abstr. Sect. A. Phys. Abstr., Energy Res. Abstr. **LC** QA76.4. **DD** 001.424. **CODEN** MCSIDR. bk rev. adv acc. **Circ** 600. Bimonthly official organ of International Association for Mathematics and Computers in Simulation. *Transactions of the International Association for Mathematics and Computers in Simulation.*

MATHEMATICS AND ITS APPLICATIONS. 0543-0941. Monographic Series. US. English. ir. Gordon & Breach, 50 West 23rd Street, New York NY 10010. **Tel** (212)206-8900. **Ind/Abst** Math. Rev. **LC** UNC.

MATHEMATICS AND STATISTICS RESEARCH DEPARTMENT PROGESS REPORT. *See* Statistics.

MATHEMATICS COUNCIL NEWSLETTER. VFOAT MCATA Newsletter. **VAT** Mathematics Council Alberta Teachers' Association Newsletter. Vol. 1, No. 1 (Jan. 1983)-. 0823-1117. Periodical. CN. English. mo. Free. Alberta Teachers Association, 11010-142 Street, Edmonton Alberta T5N 2R1 Canada. **DD** 510.607123. (ctrl).

THE MATHEMATICS EDUCATION. 0047-6269. Periodical. English. qt. $20.00. J B Prasad Editor, Nlrala Nagar PO, Siwan 841226 Biha India. **Ind/Abst** Math. Rev., Ref. Source. **LC** QA1. **DD** 510.5.

MATHEMATICS IN SCHOOL. Vol. 1- Nov. 1971-. 0305-7259. Periodical. UK. English. ir. 15.00 Domestic, $30.00. Longman Group Ltd, Fourth Avenue, Harlow Essex CM19 5AA England. **Tel** (0279)442601. **Ed** David M Neal. **Ind/Abst** Curr. Index J. Educ. bk rev. adv acc. **Circ** 6,600. Provides a specialist service to mathematics teachers of the 7-16 age group, with practical advice on teaching methods and ideas for class work.

MATHEMATICS IN SCIENCE AND ENGINEERING. Began publication with Vol. 1 in 1961. 0076-5392. Monographic Series. US. English. ir. Academic Press, 4805 Sand Lake Road, Orlando FL 43887. **Tel** (305)345-4100. **Ed** Yoshikazu Sawaragi, Hirotaka Namayama and Tetsuyo Tanino. **Ind/Abst** Math. Rev.

MATHEMATICS INTERNATIONAL. (MATHEMATICS INTERNATIONAL MICROFORM). V. 2- 1981-. 0091-7214. US. English (Russian). Gordon & Breach Science Publishers, 440 Park Avenue, New York NY 10016. **Tel** (212)689-0360. **LC** QA1. **DD** 510.8. *Mathematics International.*

MATHEMATICS MAGAZINE. V. 21- Sept./Oct. 1947-. 0025-570X. Periodical. US. English. ir. Math Association of Americas, 1529 Eighteenth Street NW, Washington DC 20036. **Tel** (202)387-5200. **Ind/Abst** Math. Rev., Int. Aerosp. Abstr., Gen. Sci. Index. **CODEN** MAMGA8. (cum index). *National Mathematics Magazine.*

MATHEMATICS OF COMPUTATION. V. 14- 1960-. 0025-5718. Periodical. US. English. qt. American Mathematical Society, PO Box 1571, Annex Station, Providence RI 02901. **Tel** (401)272-9500. **Ind/Abst** Math. Rev., Abstr. Bull. Inst. Paper Chem., Int. Aerosp. Abstr., Comput. Control Abstr., Electr. Electron. Abstr., Sci. Abstr. Sect. A. Phys. Abstr., Energy Res. Abstr., Spin, Appl. Mech. Rev., Comput. Abstr., Sci. Cit. Index, Abr. Ed., Phys. Abstr., Comput. Rev. **NLM** W1 MA96. **CODEN** MCMPAF. (cum index). Available on microfilm. *Mathematical Tables and Other Aids to Computation.*

THE MATHEMATICS OF FINITE ELEMENTS AND APPLICATIONS. 0271-1982. UK. English. ir. Academic Press, 4805 Sand Lake Road, Orlando FL 32887. **Tel** (305)345-4100. **Ed** J R Whiteman. **Ind/Abst** Chem. Abstr. **CODEN** MFEADM.

MATHEMATICS OF OPERATIONS RESEARCH. V. 1- Feb. 1976-. 0364-765X. Periodical. US. English. qt. Operations Research Society America, Circulation Department, PO Box 64237, Baltimore MD 21264. **Tel** (401)274-2525. **Ind/Abst** Math. Rev., Electron. Commun. Abstr. J., ISMEC Bull., Pollut. Abstr. Indexes, Saf. Sci. Abstr. J., Manage. Contents, Eng. Index Mon., Eng. Index Bioeng. Abstr., Eng. Index Energy Abstr., ABI/Inform, Comput. Control Abstr., Electr. Electron. Abstr., Sci. Abstr. Sect. A. Phys. Abstr., Eng. Index Annu., Phys. Abstr., Sci. Cit. Index, Abr. Ed., Comput. Rev., Eng. Index. **LC** T57.6.A1. **DD** 658.4034. **CODEN** MOREDQ.

MATHEMATICS OF THE USSR. IZVESTIJA. (MATHEMATICS OF THE USSR : IZVESTIJA). **VAT** Mathematics of the Union of Soviet Socialist Republics. Izvestija. V. 1- Jan./Feb. 1967-. 0025-5726. Periodical. US. English (Russian). bm. American Mathematical Society, PO Box 1571, Annex Station, Providence RI 02901. **Ind/Abst** Math. Rev., Sci. Cit. Index, Abr. Ed. **LC** QA1. **CODEN** MUSIAE. Available on microfilm from American Mathematical Society.

MATHEMATICS OF THE USSR. SBORNIK. (MATHEMATICS OF THE USSR : SBORNIK). **VAT** Mathematics of the Union of Soviet Socialist Republics. Sbornik. V. 1- Jan. 1967-. 0025-5734. Periodical. US. English (Russian). bm. American Mathematical Society, PO Box 1571, Annex Station, Providence RI 02901. **Ind/Abst** Math. Rev., Sci. Cit. Index, Abr. Ed. **CODEN** MUSBBS.

MATHEMATICS REPORTS, TOYAMA UNIVERSITY. Began with 1978 vol. 0386-832X. Periodical. JA. English. an. Department of Mathematics, Faculty of Science, Toyama University Gofuku, Toyama 930 Japan. **Ind/Abst** Math. Rev., Comput. Control Abstr., Electr. Electron. Abstr., Sci. Abstr. Sect. A. Phys. Abstr. **LC** QA1. **DD** 510.5. **CODEN** MRTUD3.

THE MATHEMATICS STUDENT. Began publication with Vol. 1 in Mar. 1933. 0025-5742. Periodical. II. English. qt. $35.00. Indian Mathematical Society, B 33 Panki, Kanpur 2080 20 UP India. **Ed** A Narasinga Rao. **Ind/Abst** Math. Rev. **LC** QA1. **DD** 510.5. **CODEN** MTHSBH. *Journal of the Indian Mathematical Society.*

MATHEMATICS STUDENT *CEASED.* (THE MATHEMATICS STUDENT). V. 21-28, No. 6. 0095-7089. Periodical. US. English. mo. $2.50. 1906 Association Drive, Reston VA 22091. **LC** QA1. **DD** 510.5. *Mathematics Student Journal.*

THE MATHEMATICS TEACHER. V. 1- Sept. 1908-. 0025-5769. Periodical. US. English. mo. $40.00. National Council Teachers of Mathematics, 1906 Association Drive, Reston VA 22091. **Tel** (703)620-9840. **Ed** Harry B Tunis. **Ind/Abst** Except. Child Educ. Resour., Educ. Index, Curr. Index J. Educ., Media Rev. Dig., Comput. Rev. **LC** QA1. **DD**

Mathematics

510.7. (cum index). bk rev. adv acc. **Circ** 39,600. (ctrl). Devoted to the improvement of mathematics instruction in the junior high schools, senior high schools, two year colleges and teacher education colleges.

MATHEMATICS TEACHING. No. 1- 1955-. 0025-5785. Periodical. UK. English. qt. $24.52. Association of Teachers of Math, Kings Chambers/ Queen Street, Derby DE1 3DA England. **Ed** Dick Tahra and Ray Hemmings. **Ind/Abst** Educ. Index, Curr. Index J. Educ. bk rev. adv acc. **Circ** 4,000. (ctrl). Issues Relating to the Teaching and Learning of Mathematics.

MATHEMATIKA. V. 1- (No. 1-). 0025-5793. Periodical. UK. English. sa. 27.00. University College of London, Department of Mathematics, Gower Street, London WC1E 6BT England. **Tel** (01)387-7050. **Ed** C A Rogers. **Ind/Abst** Math. Rev., Sci. Cit. Index, Abr. Ed., Appl. Mech. Rev. **LC** QA1. **DD** 510.5. **CODEN** MTKAAB. Index in last issue of volume - attached. (cum index). bk rev. **Circ** 700. Research articles on pure and applied mathematics, short reviews of advanced books on mathematics.

MATHEMATIQUES ET SCIENCES HUMAINES. Began publication in 1962. 0025-5815. Periodical. FR. French. sm. 243.00 Domestic, 265.50 Foreign. Europeriodiques SA, BP 104, 78191 Trappes Cedex France. **Tel** (1)30 62 93 86. **Ind/Abst** Math. Rev., Psychol. Abstr.

MATHEMATISCH-PHYSIKALISCHE SEMESTERBERICHTE ZUR PFLEGE DES ZUSAMMENHANGS VON SCHULE UND UNIVERSITAT CEASED. V. 1-27. 0025-5823. Periodical. GW. German. sa. **Ed** H Behnke and others. **Ind/Abst** Math. Rev. **LC** QA1. **CODEN** MPYSA5. Semesterberichte zur Pflege des Zusammenhangs von Universitat und Schule aus den Mathematischen Seminaren.

MATHEMATISCHE NACHRICHTEN. V. 1-. 0025-584X. Periodical. SZ. German. ir. $221.65. Kunst und Wissen Erich Bieber, Dufourstrasse 51, CH-8008 Zurich Switzerland. **Tel** 011-41-1-69 44 20. **Ind/Abst** Math. Rev., Sci. Cit. Index, Abr. Ed. **LC** QA1. **DD** 510.5. **CODEN** MTMNAQ. (cum index).

MATHEMATISCHE SEMESTERBERICHTE. V. 28, No. 1-. 0720-728X. Periodical. GW. German. sa. $24.43. Vandenhoeck & Ruprecht, Postfach 3753, Theaterstr 13, D 3400 Goettingen West Germany. **Tel** 0551/65061. **Ind/Abst** Math. Rev., Energy Res. Abstr. Mathematisch-Physikalische Semesterberichte zur Pflege des Zusammenhangs von Schule und Universitat.

MATHEMATISCHE ZEITSCHRIFT. Vol. 1-. 0025-5874. Periodical. German. mo. $577.00. Springer Verlag New York Inc, 175 5th Avenue, New York NY 10010. **Tel** (212)460-1500. **Ed** W P Barth, E Becker, K Diederich, G Faltings, H Heyer, W Klingenberg, C C Moore, H H Schaefer, L Smith and W van Wahl. **Ind/Abst** Math. Rev., Int. Aerosp. Abstr., Sci. Cit. Index, Abr. Ed. **LC** QA1. **CODEN** MAZEAX. (cum index). Contributions range from topics such as: algebra to analysis including applied disciplines. Guaranteed high standard of work published.

MATHNEWS. (MATHNEWS : A NEW WEEKLY PUBLISHED AT THE UNIVERSITY OF WATERLOO). Jan. 25, 1973-. 0705-0410. Periodical. CN. English. bw. Free. Mathnews M&C 3038, University of Waterloo, Waterloo Ontario N2L 3G1 Canada. **DD** 378.71344.

MATRIX AND TENSOR QUARTERLY. (THE MATRIX AND TENSOR QUARTERLY). Began with Sept. 1950 issue. 0025-5998. Periodical. UK. English. qt. $15.33. Power System Studies, PO Box 27, Stafford ST17 4LN England. **Ind/Abst** Math. Rev., Eng. Index Annu., Eng. Index Mon., Eng. Index Bioeng. Abstr., Eng. Index Energy Abstr., Comput. Control Abstr., Electr. Electron. Abstr., Sci. Abstr. Sect. A. Phys. Abstr., Sci. Cit. Index, Abr. Ed., Phys. Abstr., Appl. Mech. Rev., Eng. Index. **LC** QA401. **DD** 512.896. **CODEN** MATQA5.

MEMBERSHIP DIRECTORY - INSTITUTE OF MATHEMATICAL STATISTICS. See Yearbooks, Almanacs, Directories.

MEMOIRE - SOCIETE MATHEMATIQUE DE FRANCE. Main/ Corp Societe Mathematique de France. VFOAT Memoire de la Societe Mathematique de France. No. 1-63, 1964-79. 0583-8665. Monographic Series. FR. French. qt. Gauthier Villars, Central des Revues BP 119, 93104 Montreuil Cedex France. **Ind/Abst** Math. Rev.

MEMOIRS OF THE AMERICAN MATHEMATICAL SOCIETY. Main/Corp American Mathematical Society. No. 1-. 0065-9266. Periodical. US. English. bm. American Mathematical Society, PO Box 1571, Annex Station, Providence RI 02901. **Ind/Abst** Math. Rev., Int. Aerosp. Abstr., Sci. Cit. Index, Abr. Ed. **LC** QA3. **DD** 510.82. **CODEN** MAMCAU.

MEMOIRS OF THE FACULTY OF SCIENCE. KYUSHU UNIVERSITY. SERIES A. MATHEMATICS. (MEMOIRS OF THE FACULTY OF SCIENCE, KYUSHU UNIVERSITY. SERIES A, MATHEMATICS). VFOAT Kyushu Daigaku Rigakubu Kiyo. Began in July 1949. 0373-6385. Periodical. English (French and German). sa. Kyushu University, Faculty of Science, Exchange Librarian, 33 Fukuoka 812 Japan. **Ind/Abst** Math. Rev. **LC** QA1. **DD** 510.5. **CODEN** MFKAAF. Memoirs of the Faculty of Science, Kyushu Imperial University. Series A, Mathematics.

METRIKA. Began in 1958. 0026-1335. Periodical. AU. English (German). bm. $107.03. Physica Verlag, Seilerstaette 18, A-1010 Vienna Austria. **Ind/Abst** Math. Rev., Comput. Control Abstr., Electr. Electron. Abstr., Sci. Abstr. Sect. A. Phys. Abstr., Energy Res. Abstr., Soc. Sci. Citation Index, Phys. Abstr. **LC** QA276.A1. **DD** 519.505. **CODEN** MTRKA8. Mitteilungsblatt fur Mathematische Statistik, Statistische Vierteljahrsschrift.

METRON. V. 1- July 1920-. 0026-1424. Periodical. IT. Italian (English, French, and German). sa. $47.00. E S I A, SRVZ Abbonamenti, Via Palestro 30, I-00185 Rome RM Italy. **Tel** 6-4750050. **Ed** Carlo Benedetti. **Ind/Abst** Math. Rev., Avery Index Archit. Period. **LC** HA1. **DD** 310.5. **CODEN** MRONAM. bk rev. **Circ** 1,000. Contributions of most significant mathematicians, statisticians and economists. Topics in statistics applied to demography, physics, biology and medicine.

THE MICHIGAN MATHEMATICAL JOURNAL. V. 1-. 0026-2285. Periodical. US. English. ty. $30.00. University of Michigan, 3220 Angell Hall, Ann Arbor MI 48109. **Tel** (313)764-0337. **Ed** Carl Pearcy. **Ind/Abst** Math. Rev., Int. Aerosp. Abstr., Sci. Cit. Index, Abr. Ed. **LC** QA1. **DD** 510.5. **Circ** 800. (ctrl). Math research journal.

MITTEILUNGEN DER MATHEMATISCHEN GESELLSCHAFT IN HAMBURG. Began in May 1881. GW. German. ir. 38.00. Math Gesellschaft in Hamburg, Bundesstrasse 55, 2000 Hamburg 13 West Germany. **Ed** H Muller. **Ind/Abst** Math. Rev. **Circ** 500. (ctrl). Contains mathematical research, biographies of mathematicians, teaching of mathematics.

MMU, DER MATHEMATISCHE UND NATURWISSENSCHAFTLICHE UNTERRICHT. (MATHEMATISCHE UND NATURWISSENSCHAFTLICHE UNTERRICHT). V. 1-, Sept. 1948-. 0025-5866. Periodical. GW. German. ir. Ferd Dummler Verlag, Kaiserstr 31-37 Postfach 1480, 5300 Bonn 1 West Germany. **Ind/Abst** Energy Res. Abstr., Chem. Abstr. **CODEN** MNWUAL.

MO HU SHU HSUEH. VFOAT Fuzzy Mathematics. First published in (Sept. 1981)-. Periodical. CH. Chinese (summaries in English). qt. 0.60. Post Office, Wu-Chang China. **Ind/Abst** Math. Rev. **LC** QA248. **DD** 511.322.

MODERNE MATHEMATIK IN ELEMENTARER DARSTELLUNG. GW. German. ir. Vandenhoeck & Ruprecht, Postfach 3753, Theaterstr 13, D 3400 Goettingen West Germany. **Tel** 0551/65061. **Ed** Arnold Virsch and Hans G Steiner. **Ind/Abst** Math. Rev. bk rev. adv acc. **Circ** 3,500.

MONATSHEFTE FUR MATHEMATIK. V. 1- 1890-. 0026-9255. German. ir. $169.00. Springer Verlag New York Inc, 175 5th Avenue, New York NY 10010. **Tel** (212)460-1500. **Ed** S Grober, J Hejtmanek, E Hlawka, N Hofreiter, V Losert, H Reiter, L Schmetter, W M Schmidt and K Sigmund. **Ind/Abst** Math. Rev., Sci. Cit. Index, Abr. Ed. **CODEN** MNMTA2. (cum index). Contains reviews of significant recent books in the fields of pure and applied mathematics and mathematical physics. Of interest to mathematical libraries and research institutes.

MONOGRAFIE MATEMATYCZNE. V. 1-. 0077-0507. Monographic Series. PL. English (French, German, or Polish). ir. ARS Polona, Krakowskie Przedmiescie 7, 00-068 Warsaw Poland. **Ind/Abst** Math. Rev. **LC** UNC.

MONOGRAPHIES DE L'ENSEIGNEMENT MATHEMATIQUE. VFOAT Monographie No. de l'Enseignement Mathematique. No. 1-. Monographic Series. SZ. English (French or German). ir. Institut di Mathematiques, 2-4 rue dv li Vre Cp 240, 1211 Geneva Switzerland. **Ind/Abst** Math. Rev. Monographs on various subjects in mathematics.

MONOGRAPHS AND STUDIES IN MATHEMATICS. Began with: Vol. 1, published 1977. 0743-0329. Monographic Series. US. English. ir. Pitman Publishers Inc, 1020 Plain Street, Marshfield MA 02050. **Ind/Abst** Math. Rev.

MOSCOW UNIVERSITY MATHEMATICS BULLETIN. Main/Corp Moskovskii Gosudarstvennyi Universitet IM. M. V. Lomonosova. VFOAT Mathematics Bulletin. 0027-1322. Periodical. US. English (Russian). bm. Allerton Press Inc, 150 Fifth Avenue, New York NY 10011. **Tel** (212)924-3950. **Ind/Abst** Math. Rev., Appl. Mech. Rev. **CODEN** MUMBA.

MULTIPLE LINEAR REGRESSION VIEWPOINTS. 1970. 0195-7171. US. English. qt. $5.00. Southern Illinios University, Guidance & Ed Psych Department, Dr John Pohlmann, Carbondale IL 62901. **Tel** (618)536-7763. **Ed** Isadore Newman. **LC** QA278.2. **DD** 519.536. bk rev. adv acc. **Circ** 200. Published to facilitate communication, authorship, creativity and exchange of ideas relating to the teaching, theory and application of MLR.

NACHRICHTEN DER AKADEMIE DER WISSENSCHAFTEN IN GOTTINGEN. 2. MATHEMATISCH-PHYSIKALISCHE KLASSE. (NACHRICHTEN DER AKADEMIE DER WISSENSCHAFTEN IN GOTTINGEN. II, MATHEMATISCH-PHYSIKALISCHE KLASSE). 1958, Issue 9-. 0065-5295. Monographic Series. GW. German. ir. Vandenhoeck & Ruprecht, Postfach 3753, Theaterstr 13, D 3400 Goettingen West Germany. **Tel** 0551/65061. **Ind/Abst** Math. Rev. **CODEN** NAAKA5. Index published separately - free - automatically sent. Nachrichten der Akademie der Wissenschaften in Gottingen. Mathematisch-Physikalische Klasse. IIA.

NAGOYA MATHEMATICAL JOURNAL. V. 1- June 1950-. 0027-7630. Periodical. UK. English (French and German). qt. North Oxford Academic Publishing Company, 242 Banbury Road, Oxford OX2 7DR England. **Tel** 0865-51-1166. **Ind/Abst** Math. Rev., Sci. Cit. Index, Abr. Ed. **LC** QA1. **DD** 510.5. **CODEN** NGMJA2. (cum index).

NATO ADVANCED STUDY INSTITUTES SERIES. SERIES C, MATHMATICAL AND PHYSICAL SCIENCES. Vol. 1-. 0377-2071. Monographic Series. US. English. ir. Kluwer Boston Inc, 190 Old Derby Street, Hingham MA 02043. **Ind/Abst** Eng. Index Annu., Eng. Index Mon., Eng. Index Bioeng. Abstr., Eng. Index Energy Abstr., Life Sci. Collect., Comput. Control Abstr., Electr. Electron. Abstr., Sci. Abstr. Sect. A. Phys. Abstr., GeoRef, Chem. Abstr. **CODEN** NASCD6.

NATO ASI SERIES. SERIES C, MATHEMATICAL AND PHYSICAL SCIENCES. VFOAT Mathematical and Physical Sciences. Monographic Series. US. English. ir. Kluwer Academic Publisher, 190 Old Derby Street, Hingham MA 02043. **Ind/Abst** Chem. Abstr. **CODEN** NSCSDW. NATO Advanced Study Institutes Series. Series C, Mathematical and Physical Sciences.

NCTM NEWS BULLETIN. See Education (General).

NEW TRENDS IN MATHEMATICS TEACHING. VFOAT Tendances Nouvelles de l'Enseignement des Mathematiques. 1- 1966-. 0077-8893. Periodical. US. English (French). ir. UNIPUB, PO Box 1222, Ann Arbor MI 48106. **Tel** (800)521-8110. **LC** QA11.A1. **DD** 510.71.

NEW ZEALAND MATHEMATICS MAGAZINE. (THE NEW ZEALAND MATHEMATICS MAGAZINE). V. 1- Nov. 1963-. NZ. English. qt. $13.50. Auckland Math Association Inc, PO Box 6855, Auckland 1 New Zealand. **Ind/Abst** Math. Rev. **LC** QA11.A1.

NEWS BULLETIN (NATIONAL COUNCIL OF TEACHERS OF MATHEMATICS). See Education (General) - School Organization and Administration.

Mathematics

NEWS/JOURNAL - SASKATCHEWAN MATHEMATICS TEACHERS' SOCIETY CEASED. Main/Corp Saskatchewan Mathematics Teachers' Society. VFOAT SMTS News/Journal. V. 11, No. 1-V. 17, No. 3. 0316-5779. Periodical. CN. English. qt. $5.00. Saskatchewan Mathematics Teachers' Society, 2317 Arlington Avenue, PO Box 1108, Saskatoon Saskatchewan S7J 2H8 Canada. DD 510.7.

NEWSLETTER - ASSOCIATION FOR WOMEN IN MATHEMATICS. Main/Corp Association for Women in Mathematics. Periodical. US. English. ir. Wellesley College, Box 178, Wellesley MA 02181. Tel (617)235-0320. Ed 1,500. adv acc. (ctrl). Our letter encourages women to enter and be active in careers in mathematics and related areas, and to promote equal opportunity and equal treatment of women in the mathematical community.

NONLINEAR ANALYSIS. VFOAT Nonlinear Analysis, Theory, Methods and Applications. Began with Sept. 1976 issue. 0362-546X. Periodical. UK. English. mo. Pergamon Press, Attn Cashier, 395 Sawmill River Road, Elmsford NY 10523. Ind/Abst Math. Rev., Electron. Commun. Abstr. J., ISMEC Bull., Pollut. Abstr. Indexes, Saf. Sci. Abstr. J., Int. Aerosp. Abstr., Comput. Control Abstr., Electr. Electron. Abstr., Sci. Abstr. Sect. A. Phys. Abstr. LC QA299.6. DD 515.05. CODEN NOADD. Also issued on microfilm and microfiche.

NORMAT. VFOAT Nordisk Matematisk Tidskrift. V. 27, 1979-. Periodical. Danish (articles in Norwegian or Swedish). qt. 80.00. Universitetsforlaget, Postboks 7508 Skillebekk, Oslo 2 Norway. Ind/Abst Math. Rev. Nordisk Matematisk Tidskrift.

NORTH-HOLLAND MATHEMATICAL LIBRARY. See Library and Information Science.

NORTH-HOLLAND MATHEMATICS STUDIES. 1-. 0304-0208. Monographic Series. English. ir. Elsevier Science Publishing, PO Box 1663, Grand Central Station, New York NY 10163. Ind/Abst Comput. Control Abstr., Electr. Electron. Abstr., Sci. Abstr. Sect. A. Phys. Abstr., Phys. Abstr., Math. Rev. LC UNC. CODEN NMSTD5.

NORTH-HOLLAND SERIES IN STATISTICS AND PROBABILITY. See Statistics.

NORTHPOINT. V. 1- July 1964-. 0380-0881. Periodical. CN. English. qt. $11.61. Association of Certified Survey Technicians, 6070 Yonge Street/Suite 102, Willowdale M2M 3W6 Canada. Tel (416)222-5481. Ed William Mates. bk rev. adv acc. Circ 1,000. (ctrl). Articles for the education and technical advancement of the survey technician both field and office.

NOTES AND REPORTS IN COMPUTER SCIENCE AND APPLIED MATHEMATICS. See Computers and Computer Science.

NOTES - CANADIAN MATHEMATICAL CONGRESS. Main/Corp Canadian Mathematical Congress. V. 1-10, No. 8. 0823-0587. Periodical. CN. English (includes some text in French). ir. $7.74. Canadian Mathematical Society, 577 King Edward Avenue, Ottawa Ontario K1N 6N5 Canada. Tel (613)564-2223. Ed Y Cuttle. adv acc. Circ 1,200. Primary organ for the dissemination of information to the members of the C.M.S. General news items and information of mathematical activities in Canada. Includes problem section.

NOTES - CANADIAN MATHEMATICAL SOCIETY. (NOTES). Main/Corp Canadian Mathematical Society. VFOAT Nouvelles & Commentaries. Vol. 10, No. 9 (May 1978)-. 0045-5164. Periodical. CN. English (includes some text in French). mo. $10.00. Canadian Mathematical Society, 577 King Edward Avenue, Ottawa Ontario K1N 6N5 Canada. DD 510.971. Notes, 0823-0587.

NOTES ON PURE MATHEMATICS. No. 1-. Monographic Series. AT. English. ir. PO Box 4, Canberra 2600 Australia. Ind/Abst Math. Rev.

NOTICES OF THE AMERICAN MATHEMATICAL SOCIETY. Main/Corp American Mathematical Society. V. 1- Feb. 1954-. 0002-9920. US. English. $25.00 Members, $50.00 Nonmembers. American Mathematical Society, PO Box 1571, Annex Station, Providence RI 02940. LC UNC. CODEN AMNOAN.

NOTICES OF THE AMERICAN MATHEMATICAL SOCIETY. Main/Corp American Mathematical Society. V. 11, No.1, Pt. 2- Jan. 1964-. Periodical. US. English. ir. American Mathematical Society, PO Box 1571 Annex Station, Providence RI 02901. Notices - American Mathematical Society.

NOVA MATH. Vol. 1, No. 1 1982-. 0715-3457. Periodical. CN. English. ty. $5.00. Nova Math c/o Department of Mathematics, Dalhousie University, Halifax Nova Scotia B3H 4H8 Canada. Ind/Abst Can. Educ. Index. DD 510.712715.

NOVINKY LITERATURY : MATEMATIKA-FYZIKA. See Bibliographies.

NUMBER THEORY. (NUMBER THEORY, INCLUDING ALGEBRAIC GEOMETRY). Began in 1981. 0720-2563. Periodical. English (French and German). mo. $63.00. Zentralblatt Fur Mathematik, Hardenbergstrasse 29C, D1000 Berlin 1 West Germany. LC QA241. DD 512.705.

NUMERICAL ANALYSIS. Main/Conf Dundee Conference on Numerical Analysis. Series/Titl Lecture Notes in Mathematics (Berlin). 1st- 1965-. 0720-258X. English. mo. $52.00. Springer Verlag New York Inc, 175-5th Avenue, New York NY 10010. Tel (212)460-1500. Ed B Wegner. Index available. (cum index). Draws on a worldwide pool of several thousands of distinguished reviewers. Users are assured rapid, easy access to the abstracts and reviews they acquire.

NUMERICAL FUNCTIONAL ANALYSIS AND OPTIMIZATION. V. 1- 1979-. 0163-0563. Periodical. US. English. ir. $86.00. Marcel Dekker Inc/Journals Department, PO Box 11305 Church Street Station, New York NY 10249. Ed M Z Nashed. Ind/Abst Math. Rev., Eng. Index Mon., Eng. Index Bioeng. Abstr., Eng. Index Energy Abstr., Comput. Control Abstr., Electr. Electron. Abstr., Sci. Abstr. Sect. A. Phys. Abstr., Eng. Index Annu. LC QA320. DD 515.7. CODEN NFAODL. bk rev. adv acc. Original research papers on the development and application of functional analysis and operator theoretic methods within the fields of approximation theory, optimization, control and systems.

NUMERICAL METHODS FOR PARTIAL DIFFERENTIAL EQUATIONS. Vol. 1, No. 1 (Spring 1985)-. 0749-159X. Periodical. US. English. qt. $96.00. John Wiley, 605 Third Avenue, New York NY 10158. DD 515.

NUMERICAL SOLUTION OF PARTIAL DIFFERENTIAL EQUATIONS. Main/Conf Symposium on the Numerical Solution of Partial Differential Equation. 1st- 1965-. 0362-3017. US. English. ir. Academic Press, 4805 Sand Lake Road, Orlando FL 32887. Tel (305)345-4100. Ed Bert Hubbard. LC QA374. DD 515.62.

NUMERISCHE MATHEMATIK. 1- Vol. 0029-599X. Periodical. English (German or French). bm. $285.00. Springer Verlag-New York Inc, 175-5th Avenue, New York NY 10010. Tel (212)460-1500. Ed F L Bauer, R Bulirsch, G H A S Golub, A S Householder, H B Keller, G W Stewart, J Stoer, J Todd, R S Varga, J H Wilkinson and C Zenger. Ind/Abst Math. Rev., Int. Aerosp. Abstr., Comput. Control Abstr., Electr. Electron. Abstr., Sci. Abstr. Sect. A. Phys. Abstr., Appl. Mech. Rev., Comput. Abstr., Comput. Rev., Sci. Cit. Index, Abr. Ed., Phys. Abstr. LC QA76.5. CODEN NUMMA7. Fields of interest: numerical solution of differential equations, numerical linear algebra, approximation and control theory and numerical solution of non-linear problems.

OBZORNIK ZA MATEMATIKO IN FIZIKO. Vol. 1- Mar. 1951-. 0473-7466. Periodical. YU. Serbo-Croatian -R (tables of contents also in English). bm. 20. Komisija Za Tisk MFA Srs, Jadranska 19 Soba 316, 61111 Ljubljana Yugoslavia. Tel (061)265-061. Ed Jamez Strnad. Ind/Abst Math. Rev., Int. Aerosp. Abstr., Chem. Abstr. LC Q4. CODEN OBMFAY. bk rev. adv acc. Circ 1,500. (ctrl). Professional journal of the Society of Mathematicians, Physicists and Astronomer of the federal state of Slovenia containing, review articles, pedagogical articles, news, etc.

ONTARIO MATHEMATICS GAZETTE. V. 1- Feb. 1962-. 0030-3011. Periodical. CN. English. ir. 12.00 Domestic, 14.00 US, 16.00 Others. Ontario Association of Mathematics Education, 247 Bright Street, Sarnia Ontario N7T 4E9 Canada. Tel (519)337-8382. Ind/Abst Can. Educ. Index. bk rev. Circ 1,500. An updating of the Education Acts of the Province of Ontario, lesson strategies for teachers grade K P-University. Summaries of changes in mathematical education in the world over.

ONTARIO SECONDARY SCHOOL MATHEMATICS BULLETIN. V. 1- Sept. 1965-. 0380-6235. Periodical. CN. English. ir. Ontario Secondary School Mathematics Bulletin, Faculty of Mathematics, University of Waterloo, Waterloo Ontario N2L 3G1 Canada. Tel (519)885-1211.

OPERATIONS RESEARCH-VERFAHREN. See Economics - Economic Theory.

OPSEARCH. See Business - General Management.

OPTIMIZATION. V. 8-. Periodical. English (German). ir. Ind/Abst Math. Rev., Comput. Control Abstr., Electr. Electron. Abstr., Sci. Abstr. Sect. A. Phys. Abstr. LC QA402.5. DD 519.705. CODEN OPTZDQ. Mathematische Operationsforschung und Statistik.

ORDER. Vol. 1, No. 1-. 0167-8094. Periodical. English. D Reidel Publishing Company, PO Box 17, 3300 AA Dordrecht Holland. Tel (31)78-334911. Ind/Abst Math. Rev. bk rev adv acc. Circ 500. Theory or ordered sets and its applications throughout mathematics, operations, research, computer science and physical and social sciences.

OSAKA JOURNAL OF MATHEMATICS. V. 1- Aug. 1964-. 0030-6126. Periodical. UK. English (some articles in French). qt. $132.00. North Oxford Academic Publishers, 242 Banbury Road, Oxford OX2 7DR England. Tel 0865/51-1166. Ind/Abst Math. Rev., Math. Rev., Zentralbl. Math. Ihre Grenzgeb. LC QA1. DD 510.05. CODEN OJMAA7. Osaka Mathematical Journal, Journal of Mathematics, Osaka City University.

PACIFIC JOURNAL OF MATHEMATICS. VFOAT Journal of Mathematics. V. 1- March 1951-. 0030-8730. Periodical. US. English. mo. Pacific Journal of Mathematics, PO Box 969, Carmel Valley CA 93924. Tel (408)659-4634. Ed Donald Babbitt. Ind/Abst Math. Rev., Electron. Commun. Abstr. J., ISMEC Bull., Pollut. Abstr. Indexes, Saf. Sci. Abstr. J., Int. Aerosp. Abstr., Sci. Cit. Index, Abr. Ed. LC QA1. DD 510.5. CODEN PJMAAI. (cum index). Circ 1,500. (ctrl). Mathematics research.

PAPERS PRINTED FOR MID-YEAR EXAMINATIONS. SECTION 2. MATHEMATICS, SCIENCES. Main/Corp Harvard University. Faculty of Arts and Sciences. VFOAT Mid-Year Examinations. Jan. 1967-. US. English. an. Harvard University Printing Office, Lucy Robinson, Registrar's Office, Holyoke 827, Cambridge MA 02138.

PENTAGON. 1941. 0031-4870. Periodical. US. English. sa. $2.50. Dr Gerald White, Department of Mathematics, The Pentagon Western Illinois University, Macomb IL 60455. Tel (309)298-1383. Ed Kent Harris. bk rev. Circ 3,000. Articles of interest for undergraduate students of mathematics.

PERIODICA MATHEMATICA HUNGARICA. 0031-5303. Periodical. HU. English (French or German). qt. 70.00. D Reidel Publishing Co, PO Box 17, 3300 AA Dordrecht Netherlands. Tel (31)78-334911. Ed P Erdos. Ind/Abst Math. Rev., Comput. Control Abstr., Electr. Electron. Abstr., Sci. Abstr. Sect. A. Phys. Abstr. LC QA1. CODEN PMHGAW. bk rev adv acc. Circ 550. Corners pure and applied mathematics.

PERSPECTIVES IN MATHEMATICAL LOGIC. 0172-6641. Monographic Series. English. ir. Springer Verlag-New York Inc, 175 5th Avenue, New York NY 10010. Tel (212)460-1584. Contains topics on: admissable sets and structures, constructability, general recursion theory, recursion - theoretic, hierarchies, degrees of unsolvability, and basic set theory.

PHASE TRANSITIONS AND CRITICAL PHENOMENA. See Physics.

PHILOSOPHIA MATHEMATICA. V. 1- June 1964-. 0031-8019. Periodical. US. English (French and German). sa. $25.00. J Fang Editor, Philosophy Department, Old Dominion University, Norfolk VA 23508. Tel (804)440-4378. Ed J Fang. Ind/Abst Math. Rev., Philos. Index. LC QA9. DD 510.01. CODEN PHMAB5. bk rev adv acc. Circ 600. (ctrl). Concerns the main current of philosophy, history, and sociology of mathematics.

PHILOSOPHICAL TRANSACTIONS OF THE ROYAL SOCIETY OF LONDON, SERIES A: MATHEMATICAL AND PHYSICAL SCIENCES. (PHILOSOPHICAL TRANSACTIONS. SERIES A. MATHEMATICAL AND PHYSICAL SCIENCES). Main/Corp Royal Society (Great Britain). V. 234- 1935-. 0080-4614. UK. English. ir. 352.00. The Royal Society, 6 Carlton House Terrace, London SW1Y 5AG England. Tel

Mathematics

(01)839-5561. **Ind/Abst** Chem. Abstr., Coal Abstr., Comput. Control Abstr., Electr. Electron. Abstr., Fluidex, GeoRef, Int. Aerosp. Abstr., Life Sci. Collect., Math. Rev., Met. Abstr., Sci. Abstr. Sect. A. Phys. Abstr., World Alum. Abstr., Appl. Mech. Rev., Sci. Cit. Index, Abr. Ed., Phys. Abstr. **NLM** W1 PH605Z. **CODEN** PTRMAD. Index published separately - free - automatically sent. (cum index). **Circ** 630. Original papers at post graduate levels on biological subjects. *Philosophical Transactions of the Royal Society of London. Series A. Containing Papers of a Mathematical or Physical Character.*

PI MU EPSILON JOURNAL. V. 1- Nov. 1949-. 0031-952X. Periodical. US. English. sa. $12.00. Mathematics and Computer Science Department, Macalester College, St Paul MN 55105. **Tel** (612)696-6057. Ed J D E Konhauser. **Ind/Abst** Math. Rev. **LC** QA1. **DD** 371.85451. **CODEN** PMEJBR. bk rev. **Circ** 5,000. (ctrl). Mathematics for the undergraduate and beginning graduate student.

PM. PRAXIS DER MATHEMATIK. (PRAXIS DER MATHEMATIK). Vol. 1-. 0032-7042. Periodical. GW. German. ir. 78.40. Aulis Verlag Deubner & Company, Antwerpenerstrasse 6-12, 5 Koeln 1 West Germany. **Tel** (0221)518051. **Ind/Abst** Math. Rev., Energy Res. Abstr. **LC** QA1. Index in last issue of volume - loose - separately paged. bk rev. adv acc. **Circ** 3,000.

POPULAR LECTURES IN MATHEMATICS. 0079-3841. Monographic Series. US. English. ir. University of Chicago Press, PO Box 37005, Chicago IL 60637. **Ind/Abst** Math. Rev.

PORTUGALIAE MATHEMATICA. V. 1- 1937-. 0032-5155. Periodical. English (contributions in French, German, Italian or Portuguese). qt. $55.00. Portugaliae Mathematica, Av da Republica 37 #4, 1000 Lisboa Portugal. Ed A Monteiro. **Ind/Abst** Math. Rev. **LC** QA1. **DD** 510.5. **CODEN** POMAAJ. (cum index).

PRACE IPI PAN. See Computers and Computer Science.

PRACE MATEMATYCZNE. Main/Corp Krakow. Wyzsza Szkota Pedagogiczna. **Series Corp** Its #T Rocznik Nauko-Dydaktyczny. 4-. 0454-4994. Monographic Series. Polish (summaries in Russian, and English or French). ir. **LC** AS142.K66. *Matematyka.*

PRACE MATEMATYCZNE. Main/Corp Uniwersytet Jagiellonski. **Series Corp** Its Zeszyty Naukowe. **VFOAT** Schedae Mathematicae. No. 5- 1959-. Periodical. PL. Polish. sa. ARS Polona, Krakowskie Przedmiescie 7, 00-068 Warsaw Poland. **Ind/Abst** Math. Rev. *Serie Nauk Matematyczno-Przyrodniczych: Matematyka, Fizyka, Chemia.*

PRACE NAUKOWE INSTYTUTU MATEMATYKI POLITECHNIKI WROCAWSKIEJ. Main/Corp Wrocawska. Instytut Matematyki. **VFOAT** Scientific Papers of the Institute of Mathematics of Wrocaw Technical University. Monographic Series. PL. English, Polish, or Russian, with summaries in the other languages. ir. 20.00. ARS Polona, Krakowskie Przedmiescie 7, 00-068 Warsaw Poland. **LC** TJ260.A1.

PREPRINT SERIES OF THE DEPARTMENT OF MATHEMATICS. No. 14 (1976)-. Periodical. English. an. Institute of Mathematics Physics and Mechanics, PO Box 543, Ljubljana Yugoslavia. *Publications of the Department of Mathematics.*

PRIKLADNAIA MATEMATIKA I MEKHANIKA. Main/Corp Kharkivskyi Derzhavnyi Universytet Imeni O.M. Horkoho. Vol. 42-. UR. Russian. Vyscha Shkola, Ul Universytetskaia 16, Kharkov Russia. **LC** AS262, QA1. *Matematika i Mekhanika.*

PRIKLADNAJA MATEMATIKA I MEHANIKA. (PRIKLADNAIA MATEMATIKA I MEKHANIKA). **VFOAT** Applied Mathematics and Mechanics, Zhurnal Prikladnoi Matematiki I Mekhaniki, Novaia Seriia. V. 1- 1937-. 0032-8235. Periodical. UR. Russian (some articles in English, summaries in English, French or German). bm. $71.00. Victor Kamkin Inc (70706), 12224 Parklawn Drive, Rockville MD 20852. **Tel** (301)881-5973. **Ind/Abst** Int. Aerosp. Abstr., Comput. Control Abstr., Electr. Electron. Abstr., Sci. Abstr. Sect. A. Phys. Abstr., Chem. Abstr., Math. Rev., Appl. Mech. Rev., Phys. Abstr. **CODEN** PMAMAF. (cum index).

PRIMARY MATHEMATICS. V. 6- Spring 1968-. 0032-8294. Periodical. UK. English. ty. $5.00. Pergamon Press, 44-01 21st Street, Long Island City NY 11101. **LC** QA135. **DD** 372.705. *Teaching Arithmetic.*

PRINCETON MATHEMATICAL SERIES. 1-. 0079-5194. Monographic Series. US. English. ir. Princeton University Press, Box A/3175 Princeton Pike, Lawrenceville NJ 08648. **Tel** (609)896-2111. **Ind/Abst** Math. Rev.

PROBABILISTIC METHODS IN APPLIED MATHEMATICS. Periodical. US. English. ir. Academic Press, 4805 Sand Lake Road, Orlando FL 32887. **Tel** (305)345-4100. Ed A T Bharucha-Reid.

PROBABILITY AND MATHEMATICAL STATISTICS. See Statistics.

PROBABILITY AND MATHEMATICAL STATISTICS (INSTYTUT MATEMATYCZNY (POLSKA AKADEMIA NAUK)). (PROBABILITY AND MATHEMATICAL STATISTICS). Vol. 1, No. 1-. 0208-4147. Periodical. English (French, German or Russian). ir. $42.00. Pl Grunwaldzki Nr 2/4, 50-384 Wroclaw Poland. **Tel** 21-15-00. Ed Kazimeierz Urbanik. **Ind/Abst** Math. Rev. **LC** QA273.A1. **DD** 519.205. adv acc. **Circ** 1,000. Publishes original contributions to the theory of probability and mathematical statistics (e.g. random measures, testing of hypotheses, decision theory).

PROBLEMY KIBERNETIKI. See Communication.

PROCEEDINGS - AMERICAN MATHEMATICAL SOCIETY. Main/Corp American Mathematical Society. V. 1- Feb. 1950-. Periodical. US. English. mo. American Mathematical Society, Box 6248, Providence RI 02940. **Tel** (401)272-9500. **Ind/Abst** Math. Rev., Sci. Cit. Index, Abr. Ed.

PROCEEDINGS. MATHEMATICAL SCIENCES - INDIAN ACADEMY OF SCIENCES. Main/Corp Indian Academy of Sciences. **VFOAT** Proceedings of the Indian Academy of Sciences (Mathematical Sciences). Vol. 89, No. 1 (Jan. 1980)-. 0370-0089. Periodical. English. ir. $94.00. J C Baltzer, Wettsteinplatz 10, CH 4058 Basel Switzerland. **Tel** 61 26 8925. *Proceedings. Section A.*

PROCEEDINGS OF SYMPOSIA IN PURE MATHEMATICS. V. 1-. 0082-0717. Monographic Series. US. English. ir. American Mathematical Society, PO Box 1571 Annex Station, Providence RI 02901. **Tel** (401)272-9500. **Ind/Abst** Math. Rev. **LC** UNC.

PROCEEDINGS OF THE BERKELEY SYMPOSIUM ON MATHEMATICAL STATISTICS AND PROBABILITY. Main/Conf Berkeley Symposium on Mathematical Statistics and Probability. 1st- 1945/46-. 0097-0433. Monographic Series. US. English. University of California Press, 1428 Harbour Way South, Richmond CA 94804. **LC** QA276. **DD** 311.2. **NLM** W3 BE512.

PROCEEDINGS OF THE CONFERENCE ON PROBABILITY THEORY. Main/Conf Conference on Probability Theory. 4th- 1971-. English. ir. **LC** QA273.A1. **DD** 519.205.

PROCEEDINGS OF THE EDINBURGH MATHEMATICAL SOCIETY. Main/Corp Edinburgh Mathematical Society. V. 1-44, 1883-1925/ 26. 0013-0915. Periodical. UK. English. ty. $75.00. Scottish Academic Press Limited, 33 Montgomery Street, Edinburgh EH7 5JX Scotland. **Tel** 031/ 556-2796. **Ind/Abst** Math. Rev., Sci. Cit. Index, Abr. Ed. **CODEN** PEMSA3. (cum index).

PROCEEDINGS OF THE LONDON MATHEMATICAL SOCIETY. Main/Corp London Mathematical Society. V. 1-35 (No. 1-819) Jan. 1865-Jan. 1903. 0024-6115. Periodical. UK. English. ir. Oxford University Press, Journals Department, Walton Street, Oxford OX2 6DP England. **Tel** 0865/ 56767. **Ind/Abst** Math. Rev., Sci. Cit. Index, Abr. Ed., Appl. Mech. Rev. **LC** QA1. **DD** 510.08. **CODEN** PLMTAL. (cum index).

PROCEEDINGS OF THE MATHEMATICAL AND PHYSICAL SOCIETY OF U.A.R. (EGYPT). VFOAT Majmuat Abhath Jamiyat Al-Ulum Al-Riyadiyah Wa-Al-Fizyaiyah Bi-Al-Jumhuriyah Al-Arabiyah Al-Muttahidah. Periodical. English. ir. c/o University of Cairo, Faculty of Science, Cairo Egypt.

PROCEEDINGS OF THE ROYAL SOCIETY OF EDINBURGH. SECTION A. MATHEMATICA. (PROCEEDINGS A : MATHEMATICS). **VFOAT** Proceedings of the Royal Society of Edinburgh. Vol. 72, Pt. 1-. 0308-2105. Periodical. UK. English. qt. **Tel** 225-6057. **Ind/Abst** Int. Aerosp. Abstr. **LC** Q41. **DD** 510.5. *Proceedings. Section A, Mathematical and Physical Sciences.*

PROCEEDINGS OF THE SOUTHEASTERN CONFERENCE ON COMBINATORICS, GRAPH THEORY, AND COMPUTING. Main/Corp Southeastern Conference on Combinatorics, Graph Theory, and Computing. 3rd-. 0316-1382. Periodical. CN. English. an. Utilitas Mathematica Publishing Inc, PO Box 7, University Centre, University of Manitoba, Winnipeg Manitoba R3T 2N2 Canada. **DD** 511.6. *Proceedings of the Louisiana Conference on Combinatorics, Graph Theory, and Computing, 0316-1390.*

PROCEEDINGS OF THE STATISTICAL COMPUTING SECTION. See Statistics.

THE PROCEEDINGS OF THE TOPOLOGY CONFERENCE. Main/Conf Topology Conference. **Series/Titl** Topology Proceedings. 0196-3880. US. English. an. Topology Proceedings, Mathematics Department, Auburn University, Auburn AL 36830. **Tel** (205)826-4290. Ed Zenor Gruenhage. **LC** QA611.A1. **DD** 514 S, 514. **Circ** 350. Refereed papers presented at the annual topology conference with questions and answers sections at the end.

PROCEEDINGS - SYMPOSIUM ON NONLINEAR ESTIMATION THEORY AND ITS APPLICATIONS. Main/Conf Symposium on Nonlinear Estimation Theory and its Applications. 1st- 1970-. US. English. Western Periodicals Company, 13000 Raymer Street, North Hollywood CA 91605. **LC** QA402.3. **DD** 519.54.

PROFESSIONAL OPPORTUNITIES IN THE MATHEMATICAL SCIENCES. 10th Ed. (Nov. 1978)-. 0732-2127. US. English. ir. Mathematical Association of America, 1529 18th Street Northwest, Washington DC 20036. *Professional Opportunities in Mathematics, 0882-1550.*

PROGRESS OF MATHEMATICS. V. 1- Mar. 1967-. 0555-4330. Periodical. II. English. sa. University of Allahabad, Academy for Progress in Mathematics, Allahabad India. **Ind/Abst** Math. Rev. **LC** QA1. **DD** 510.05. **CODEN** PMTHBS.

PUBBLICAZIONI - ISTITUTO PER LE APPLICAZIONI DEL CALCOLO. Main/ Corp Rome (City). Istituto Nazionale per le Applicazioni del Calcolo. Monographic Series. Italian. ir. **LC** QA3.

PUBLICATION OF THE MATHEMATICS RESEARCH CENTER, THE UNIVERSITY OF WISCONSIN-MADISON. (PUBLICATION ... OF THE MATHEMATICS RESEARCH CENTER, THE UNIVERSITY OF WISCONSIN). No. 25-. 0273-4559. US. English. ir. Academic Press, 111 5th Avenue, New York NY 10003. **Ind/Abst** Chem. Abstr. **LC** QA3. **DD** 510.5. **CODEN** PMRWDV. *Publication ... of the Mathematics Research Center, United States Army, the University of Wisconsin.*

PUBLICATION ... OF THE MATHEMATICS RESEARCH CENTER, UNITED STATES ARMY, THE UNIVERSITY OF WISCONSIN. No. 1-No. 24. Monographic Series. US. English. ir. Academic Press, 4805 Sand Lake Road, Orlando FL 32819. **Tel** (305)345-4100. **LC** QA3. **DD** 510.72.

PUBLICATIONES MATHEMATICAE. Main/Corp Kossuth Lajos Tudomanyegyetem. Matematikai Intezet. Vol. 1- 1949-. 0033-3883. Periodical. HU. Hungarian (English, French, and German). qt. $44.00. Debrecen, Institute Mathematique de Universite, Debrecen 10 Hungary. **Tel** 388-511. Ed B Barna. **Ind/Abst** Math. Rev. **CODEN** PUMAAR. adv acc. Covers mathematics.

PUBLICATIONS DE L'INSTITUT MATHEMATIQUE. Vol. 1 (1947)-V. 14 (1960). 0350-1302. YU. Multilingual (English, French, German, and Russian). ir. Matematicki Institut, Knez Mihailova 35, Beograd Yugoslavia. **Ind/Abst** Math. Rev., Appl. Mech. Rev. *Publications Mathematiques de l'Universite de Belgrade.*

PUBLICATIONS DU CENTRE DE RECHERCHES EN MATHEMATIQUES PURES. SERIE I. Began in 1975. FR. French. an. Centre de Recherches en Mathematiques Pures, PR Gare 2,

CH-2002 Neuchatel Switzerland. **Ind/Abst** Math. Rev. **LC** QA1. **DD** 510.5. *Publications du Seminaire de Geometrie de l'Universite de Neuchatel. Serie I.*

PUBLICATIONS DU DEPARTEMENT DE MATHEMATIQUES. No. 1 (1980)-. Periodical. French. ir. U.E.R. des Sciences, 124 Avenue Albert Thomas, 87060 Limoges Cedex France. **Ind/Abst** Math. Rev.

PUBLICATIONS DU DEPARTEMENT DE MATHEMATIQUES. New Series 1 (1982)-. 0076-1656. Periodical. FR. French. qt. Lyons Universite, C Bernard, 43 Boulevard du 11 Novembre 1918, 69622 Villeurbanne France. **Ind/Abst** Math. Rev. *Publications du Departement de Mathematiques.*

PUBLICATIONS DU SEMINAIRE DE GEOMETRIE DE L'UNIVERSITE DE NEUCHATEL. SERIE I. Began in 1958. Periodical. SZ. French. ir. Centre du Recherches en Math Pure, Ave du Ier Mars 24, CH-2002 Neuchatel Switzerland. **LC** QA1. **DD** 510.5.

PUBLICATIONS MATHEMATIQUES. French (English). an. Springer Verlag-New York Inc, 175 5th Avenue, New York NY 10010. **Tel** (212)460-1500. **Ed** Jacques Tits. Appearing in two hardcover volumes each year, this outstanding journal presents many of the best papers in pure mathematics.

PUBLICATIONS OF THE RAMANUJAN INSTITUTE. Began in 1969. II. English. ir. University of Madras/Registrar, University Buildings, Chepauk, Madras 600 005 India. **LC** UNC. **DD** 510.5.

PUBLICATIONS OF THE RESEARCH INSTITUTE FOR MATHEMATICAL SCIENCES. SERIES A. (PUBLICATIONS OF THE RESEARCH INSTITUTE FOR MATHEMATICAL SCIENCES). Vol. 5, No. 1 (July 1969)-. 0454-7845. Periodical. UK. English. bm. $143.00. North Oxford Academic Publ Company, 242 Banbury Road, Oxford OX2 7DR England. **Tel** 0865-51-1166. **Ind/Abst** Math. Rev. **CODEN** KRMPBV. *Publications of the Research Institute for Mathematical Sciences. Series A.*

PUBLIKACIJE ELEKTROTEHNICKI FAKULTET. UNIVERZITET U BEOGRADU. SERIJA: MATEMATIKA I FIZIKA. (PUBLIKACIJE. SERIJA : MATEMATIKA I FIZIKA). **Main/Corp** Univerzitet u Beogradu. Elektrotehnicki Fakultet. No. 1- 1956-. 0522-8441. Periodical. YU. Serbo-Croatian -R. ir. Matematika I Fizika, Univerzitet u Beogradu, Beograd Yugoslavia. **Ind/Abst** Math. Rev., Comput. Control Abstr., Electr. Electron. Abstr., Sci. Abstr. Sect. A. Phys. Abstr. **LC** QA1. **DD** 510.

PURE AND APPLIED MATHEMATICS. 0079-8177. US. English. ir. Marcel Dekker/ Continuation Department, 270 Madison Avenue, New York NY 10016. **Tel** (212)696-9000. **Ed** Earl J Taft and Edwin Hweitt. This is an ongoing series, each title has a different subject.

PURE AND APPLIED MATHEMATICS (ACADEMIC PRESS). (PURE AND APPLIED MATHEMATICS). V. 1-. 0079-8169. Monographic Series. US. English. ir. Academic Press, 4805 Sand Lake Road, Orlando FL 32887. **Tel** (305)345-4100. **Ed** Charalambos D Aliprantis and Owen Burkinshaw. **Ind/Abst** Math. Rev. **LC** QA3. **DD** 510.82.

PURE AND APPLIED MATHEMATIKA SCIENCES. Periodical. II. English. sa. 80.00. Impex India, 2118 Ansari Road, New Delhi 110002 India. **Tel** 278034. **Ed** P L Maggu. **Ind/Abst** Math. Rev. **CODEN** PASIDC. bk rev. adv acc. **Circ** 500. Covers research in operations research, management sciences, computer science, and industrial engineering. *Mathematika Sciences.*

QUAESTIONES MATHEMATICAE : JOURNAL OF THE SOUTH AFRICAN MATHEMATICAL SOCIETY : TYDSKRIF VAN DIE SUID-AFRIKAANSE WISKUNDEVERENIGING. VFOAT Journal of the South African Mathematical Society. 1 (1976)-. Periodical. SA. English. ir. $24.78. SA Math Society, Department of Mathematics, Potchefstroom University for C.H.E., Potchefstroom 2520 South Africa. **LC** QA1. **DD** 510.5. **Circ** 500. This journal publishes research papers as well as survey and expository articles in the mathematical sciences.

QUARTERLY CHECK-LIST OF MATHEMATICA. V.1- Jan. 1961-. 0481-1372. Periodical. English. ir. **LC** Z6653.

QUARTERLY JOURNAL OF MATHEMATICS. (THE QUARTERLY JOURNAL OF MATHEMATICS. OXFORD SERIES). V. 1-20 (No. 1-80). 0033-5606. Periodical. UK. English. qt. Oxford University Press, Journals Department, Walton Street, Oxford OX2 6DP England. **Tel** 0865/ 56767. **Ind/Abst** Math. Rev., Sci. Cit. Index, Abr. Ed., Stat. Theory Method Abstr. **LC** QA1. **DD** 510.5. **CODEN** QJMAAT. (cum index). *Quarterly Journal of Pure and Applied Mathematics, Messenger of Mathematics.*

QUARTERLY JOURNAL OF MECHANICS AND APPLIED MATHEMATICS. (THE QUARTERLY JOURNAL OF MECHANICS AND APPLIED MATHEMATICS). V. 1- March 1948-. 0033-5614. Periodical. UK. English. qt. 90.00. Oxford University Press, Journals Department/Walton Street, Oxford OX2 6DP England. **Tel** 0865 56767. **Ed** R Shail. **Ind/Abst** Eng. Index Mon., Eng. Index Bioeng. Abstr., Eng. Index Energy Abstr., Fluidex, Ship Abstr., Comput. Control Abstr., Electr. Electron. Abstr., Sci. Abstr. Sect. A. Phys. Abstr., Chem. Abstr., Math. Rev., Nuci. Sci. Abstr., Int. Aerosp. Abstr., Eng. Index Annu., Eng. Index Mon., Appl. Mech. Rev., Sci. Cit. Index, Abr. Ed., Phys. Abstr., Eng. Index. **LC** QA1. **DD** 510.5. **CODEN** QJMMAV. **Circ** 334. Contains original papers in general fields of mechanics, i.e. theoretical, continuum (all branches of fluids and solids, classical electromagnetism, non linear dynamics, magnetohydrodynamics, etc.).

QUARTERLY OF APPLIED MATHEMATICS. V. 1- Apr. 1943-. 0033-569X. Periodical. US. English. qt. Maruzen Company Ltd, PO Box 5050, 100-31 Tokyo Japan. **Tel** (901)272-9500. **Ind/Abst** Eng. Index Mon., Eng. Index Bioeng. Abstr., Eng. Index Energy Abstr., Comput. Control Abstr., Electr. Electron. Abstr., Sci. Abstr. Sect. A. Phys. Abstr., Energy Res. Abstr., Biol. Abstr., Chem. Abstr., Eng. Index Annu., Eng. Index Mon., Int. Aerosp. Abstr., Math. Rev., Nuci. Sci. Abstr., Spin, Appl. Mech. Rev., Sci. Cit. Index, Abr. Ed., Pet. Abstr., Phys. Abstr., Comput. Rev., Eng. Index. **LC** QA1. **DD** 510.5. **NLM** W1 QU421. **CODEN** QAMAAY.

QUEEN'S PAPERS IN PURE AND APPLIED MATHEMATICS. **Main/Corp** Queen's University (Kingston, Ont.). No. 1- 1966-. 0079-8797. Periodical. CN. English. ir. Queens University, Campus Bookstore, Kingston Ontario K7L 3N6 Canada. **Ind/Abst** Math. Rev. Mathematics.

R.A.I.R.O. ANALYSE NUMERIQUE. (RAIRO : ANALYSE NUMERIQUE). **VFOAT** Analyse Numerique, RAIRO : Numerical Analysis. **VAT** Revue Francaise d'Automatique, d'Informatique et de Recherche Operationnelle: Analyse Numerique. V. 11-. 0399-0516. Periodical. English or French. qt. 180.00. Centrale des Revues, Dunod-Gauthier-Villars, BP 119, 93104 Montreuil Cedex France. **Ind/Abst** Math. Rev., Comput. Control Abstr., Electr. Electron. Abstr., Sci. Abstr. Sect. A. Phys. Abstr., Energy Res. Abstr. **LC** QA1. **DD** 519.4. **CODEN** RFANDS. *Revue Francaise d'Automatique, Informatique, Recherche Operationelle, Sommaire: Analyse Numerique.*

RAIRO : AUTOMATIQUE. **VFOAT** Automatique, Systems Analysis and Control, RAIRO : Systems Analysis and Control, RAIRO, Revue Francaise d'Automatique, d'Informatique et de Recherche Operationnelle. **VAT** Revue Francaise d'Automatique, d'Informatique, et de Recherche Operationnelle: Automatique. V. 11-. 0399-0524. FR. French (summaries in English). qt. 180.00. Central des Revues, Dunod-Gauthier-Villars, BP 119, 93104 Montreuil Cedex France. **Ind/Abst** Math. Rev., Excerpta Med., Comput. Control Abstr., Electr. Electron. Abstr., Sci. Abstr. Sect. A. Phys. Abstr., Energy Res. Abstr. **LC** QA267.5.S4. **DD** 003.05. **CODEN** RFAADN. *Revue Francaise d'Automatique, Informatique, Recherche Operationnelle: Automatique.*

R.A.I.R.O. INFORMATIQUE THEORIQUE. (RAIRO : INFORMATIIQUE THEORIQUE). **VFOAT** Informatique Theorique, RAIRO : Theoretical Computer Science. V. 11-. 0399-0540. Periodical. FR. English (French). qt. 190.00. Centrale des Revuew, Dunod-Gauthier-Villars, BP 119, 93104 Montreuil Cedex France. **Ind/Abst** Math. Rev., Comput. Control Abstr., Electr. Electron. Abstr., Sci. Abstr. Sect. A. Phys. Abstr., Energy Res. Abstr. **LC** QA1. **DD** 001.6. **CODEN** RSITD7. *Revue Francaise d'Automatique, Informatique, Recherche Operationelle, Sommaire: Informatique Theorique.*

RAPPORT NATIONAL DE CONJONCTURE SCIENTIFIQUE : MATHEMATIQUES PURES ET METHODOLOGIE MATHEMATIQUE. **Main/Corp** France. Centre National de la Recherche Scientifique. Comite National de la Recherche Scientifique. FR. French. ir. 15 Quai Anatole, Paris France 75700. **LC** QA11.A1. **DD** 510.72044.

RAY DE CRANE'S CUT YOUR OWN TAXES. (PROCEEDINGS). **Main/Conf** Conference on Compact Transformation Groups. First conference was held in 1967. English. ir. 32.-. Springer-Verlag, 175 Fifth Avenue, New York NY 10010. **LC** QA3, QA387. **DD** 510.8 S, 512.55.

REAL ANALYSIS. Began in 1981. 0720-2601. English (French and German). mo. $63.00. Zentralblatt fur Mathematik, Hardenbergstrasse 29C, D1000 Berlin 1 West Germany. **LC** QA299.6. **DD** 515.05.

REAL ANALYSIS EXCHANGE. V. 1- 1976-. 0147-1937. Periodical. US. English. sa. $10.00. Michigan State University, Department of Math, East Lansing MI 48824. **Tel** (517)353-8489. **Ed** Clifford E Weil. **Ind/Abst** Math. Rev. **LC** QA331.5. **DD** 515.805. **Circ** 400. Research in roads and survey articles in real variables, real set theory, and real measure theory.

RECHENTECHNIK DATENVERARBEITUNG. 0300-3450. German. mo. $37.71. Kunst & Wissen Erich Bieber, Dufourstrasse 51, CH-8008 Zurich Switzerland. **Tel** 011-41-1-69 44 20. **Ind/Abst** Comput. Control Abstr., Electr. Electron. Abstr., Sci. Abstr. Sect. A. Phys. Abstr., Phys. Abstr. **CODEN** RTDVAQ.

REFERATIVNYI ZHURNAL : MATHEMATIKA. Oct. 1953-. 0034-2467. Periodical. UR. Russian. mo. **Ind/Abst** Math. Rev. **LC** QA1. (cum index).

REGIONAL CONFERENCE SERIES IN MATHEMATICS. No. 1-. 0160-7642. Monographic Series. US. English. ir. American Mathematical Society, PO Box 1571, Annex Station, Providence RI 02901. **Tel** (401)272-9500. **Ind/Abst** Math. Rev. **LC** QA1. **DD** 510.8.

RENDICONTI DEL CIRCOLO MATEMATICO DI PALERMO. Publication began with V. 1 (1884-87). 0009-725X. Periodical. IT. Italian (text in English, French or German). ir. $44.85. Circolo Matematico de Palermo, SCLA Matematica V, Archirafi 34, 90123 Palermo Italy. **Ind/Abst** Math. Rev., Appl. Mech. Rev. **CODEN** RCMMAR. (cum index).

RENDICONTI DEL SEMINARIO MATEMATICO. **Main/Conf** Seminario Matematico, Turin. Began in 1930. IT. Italian (English). ty. 100,000 Domestic, 135,000 Europe, 190,000 all other countries. Rosenberg & Sellier, Levrotto E Della, 10123 Torino Italy. **Tel** 011 532150. **Ed** Fulvio Ricci. **LC** QA1. **DD** 510.82. (cum index). **Circ** 500. Original articles containing relevant results in mathematics.

RENDICONTI DEL SEMINARIO MATEMATICO E FISICO DI MILANO. **Main/Corp** Milan. Seminario Matematico E Fisico. V. 1 (1927)-. 0370-7377. IT. Italian. ir. Tamburini Editore, Via C Pascoli 55, 20133 Milano Italy. **Ind/Abst** Math. Rev., Int. Aerosp. Abstr., Appl. Mech. Rev. **LC** QA1. **DD** 510.62452. **CODEN** RSMFAG.

RENDICONTI DI MATEMATICA E DELLE SUE APPLICAZIONI (ISTITUTO MATEMATICO GUIDO CASTELNUOVO : 1981). (RENDICONTI DI MATEMATICA E DELLE SUE APPLICAZIONI : RIVISTA TRIMESTRALE PUBBLICATA DA UNIVERSITA DEGLI STUDI DI ROMA (ISTITUTO MATEMATICO GUIDO CASTELNUOVO, ISTITUTO DI MATEMATICA APPLICATA) E ISTITUTO NAZIONALE DI ALTA MATEMATICA). Series 7, V. 1, No. 1 (Jan./ March 1981)-. Periodical. IT. Italian (English). qt. $74.00. E.S.I.A., SRVZ Abbonamenti, Via Sommacampagna 13, I-00185 Roma Italy. **Ind/Abst** Math. Rev. *Rendiconti di Matematica.*

RENDICONTI - SEMINARIO MATEMATICO DELLA UNIVERSITA DI PADOVA. (RENDICONTI DEL SEMINARIO MATEMATICO DELLA UNIVERSITA DI PADOVA). **Main/Corp** Padua. Universita. Seminario Matematico. V. 1- 1930-. 0041-8994. Periodical. IT. Italian (also in English, French or German). sa. $56.43. Cedam Casa Editrice, Via Jappelli 5, 35100 Padova Italy. **Ind/Abst** Math. Rev., Appl. Mech. Rev. **LC** QA1. **DD** 510.5.

REPORT FROM THE DEPARTMENT OF MATHEMATICS AND STATISTICS. *See* Statistics.

REPORT OF THE RESEARCH COMMITTEE ON THE SUMMER RESEARCH INSTITUTE. **Main/Corp** Canadian Mathematical Congress. Research Committee. First session held in 1950. 0380-5921. CN.

Mathematics

English (includes some text in French). an. Canadian Mathematical Congress, 3421 Drummond Street, Montreal Quebec H3G 1X7 Canada. **DD** 510.5.

REPORT TW. Main/Corp Matematisch Centrum (Amsterdam, Netherlands). No. 1- 1950?-. English. ir. Mathematical Center, 49-2E Boerhadvestraat, Amsterdam Netherlands. **Ind/Abst** Appl. Mech. Rev.

REPORTS ON MATHEMATICAL LOGIC. V. 1-. 0137-2904. PL. English, French, German or Russian. sa. ARS Polona, Krakowskie Przedmiescie 7, 00-068 Warsaw Poland. **Ind/Abst** Math. Rev., Philos. Index. **LC** QA9.A1. **CODEN** RMLODX. *Prace Z Logiki.*

RESULTATE DER MATHEMATIK. **VFOAT** Mathematical Results. Began in 1978. 0378-6218. Periodical. German (English). sa. $55.00. Birkhauser Boston Inc, 380 Green Street, PO Box 3005, Cambridge MA 02139. **Tel** (617)576-6638. **Ind/Abst** Math. Rev. **LC** QA1. **DD** 510.5.

REVISTA COLOMBIANA DE MATEMATICAS. V. 1- Mar. 1967-. 0034-7426. Periodical. CK. Spanish (text in English and French). qt. 20.00. Societe Colombiana de Matematicas, Apartado Nacional #2521, Bogota Colombia. **Tel** 686465. Ed Xavier Caicedo. **Ind/Abst** Math. Rev. **LC** QA1. **CODEN** RCMABQ. bk rev. adv acc. Circ 600. Articles and works in mathematics, pure and applied.

REVISTA COMPACTA. Spanish. ir. **LC** QA1.

REVISTA DE LA UNION MATEMATICA ARGENTINA. Main/Corp Union Matematica Argentina. Began publication with volume for 1936/37. 0041-6932. Periodical. AG. Spanish (English). ir. Union Matematica Argentina, Casilla de Correo 3588, 1000 Buenos Aires Argentina. **Ind/Abst** Math. Rev. **LC** QA1. **DD** 510.5. **CODEN** RMAFAG.

REVISTA MATEMATICA HISPANO-AMERICANA. Vol. 1-7, Jan./Feb. 1919-Dec, 1925. 0373-0999. Periodical. SP. Spanish. bm. Consejo Super Invest Cientific, Vitruvio 8, Apartado 14 458, 28006 Madrid Spain. **Ind/Abst** Math. Rev. **LC** QA1.

REVUE DE MATHEMATIQUES SPECIALES. Vol. 1- 1890-. 0035-1504. Periodical. FR. French. mo. $45.89. Librairie Vuibert, 63 BD Saint Germain, 75240 Paris Cedex 05 France. **Tel** 01-325-61-00. Ed B Niewenglowski. **LC** QA1. **DD** 510.5.

REVUE ROUMAINE DE MATHEMATIQUES PURES ET APPLIQUEES. V. 9- 1964-. 0035-3965. Periodical. English (chiefly French). ir. 92.00. Str Academiei 14, R-70109 Bucuresti Romania. **Tel** (90)507680. **Ind/Abst** Math. Rev., Int. Aerosp. Abstr., Comput. Rev., Appl. Mech. Rev. **LC** QA1. **CODEN** RRMPB6. bk rev. adv acc. Circ 1,000. Research papers in mathematics and applications of mathematics. *Revue de Mathematiques Pures et Appliquees.*

RICERCHE DI MATEMATICA. V. 1- 1952-. 0035-5038. Periodical. IT. Italian. sa. Libreria Commissionaria Liquor, Mezzocannone 21-23, 80134 Naples Italy. **Ind/Abst** Math. Rev. **CODEN** RCMTAE. Index in last issue of volume - attached.

RIVISTA DI MATEMATICA PER LE SCIENZE ECONOMICHE E SOCIALI. Year 1, No. 1 (1. half-yearly 1978)-. Periodical. IT. English (Italian). sa. 54,000. Assn Per Matematica Applicata, Via Conservatorio 7, 20122 Milano Italy. **Tel** 02798985. **Ind/Abst** Math. Rev. **LC** H61.25. **DD** 300.724. bk rev. adv acc. Circ 2,000. Applied mathematics to social and economical sciences.

RIVISTA DI MATEMATICA DELLA UNIVERSITA DI PARMA. SERIE 4. Began publication in 1975. Italian (French, English, German, Russian). an. **Ind/Abst** Math. Rev.

THE ROCKY MOUNTAIN JOURNAL OF MATHEMATICS. V. 1- Winter 1971-. 0035-7596. Periodical. US. English. qt. $115.00. Rocky Mountain Math Consortium, Arizona State University, Department of Math, Tempe AZ 85287. **Tel** (602)965-3788. Ed W R Scott. **Ind/Abst** Math. Rev., Energy Res. Abstr., Spin. **LC** QA1. **DD** 510.5. **CODEN** RMJMA. Circ 650.

ROCZNIKI POLSKIEGO TOWARZYSTWA MATEMATYCZNEGO. SERIA 1. PRACE MATEMATYCZNE. (ANNALES SOCIETATIS MATHEMATICAE POLONAE). **Main/Corp** Polskie Towarzystwo Matematyczne. **VFOAT** Roczniki Polskiego Towarzystwa Matematycznego, Commentationes Mathematicae. 14- 1970-. 0373-8299. chiefly in English. ir. PAAC Kultury i Nauka, Osrodek Rozpowszechniania Wydawnictw Naukowych Pan, 00-091 Warszawa Poland. **Ind/Abst** Math. Rev. **LC** QA1. *Roczniki. Seria 1.: Prace Matematyczne.*

ROCZNIKI POLSKOGO TOWARZYSTWA MATEMATYCZNEGO, SERIA 2. WIADOMOSCI MATEMATYCZNE. (ROCZNIKI. SERIA 2 : WIADOMOSCI MATEMATYCZNE). **Main/Corp** Polskie Towarzystwo Matematyczne. **VFOAT** Wiadomosci Matematiczne. 1- 1955-. PL. Polish. sa. ARS Polona, Krakowskie Przedmiescie 7, 00-068 Warsaw Poland. **Ind/Abst** Math. Rev. **LC** QA1.

ROCZNIKI POLSKOGO TOWARZYSTWA MATEMATYCZNEGO, SERIA 3: MATEMATYKA STOSOWANA. (ROCZNIKI. SERIA III : MATEMATYKA STOSOWANA). **Main/Corp** Polskie Towarzystwo Matematyczne. **VFOAT** Matematyka Stosowana. 1- 1973-. 0137-2890. PL. Polish. ir. 22.00. Panstwowe Wydawn, Pac Kultury I Nauki, Warszawa Poland. **Ind/Abst** Math. Rev. **LC** QA1.

ROSTOCKER MATHEMATISCHES KOLLOQUIUM. Periodical. German. ir. Wilhelm-Pieck-Universitat Sektion Mathematik, 25 Rostock Vogelsand 13/14, Rostock German Democratic Republic. **Tel** 0081-369-334. **Ind/Abst** Math. Rev. **LC** QA1. Publication of original papers (research results). Main topics: mathematical analysis, discrete mathematics, numerical mathematics, and mathematical statistics.

RUSSIAN MATHEMATICAL SURVEYS. V. 15- Jan./Feb. 1960-. 0036-0279. Periodical. UK. English (Russian). bm. $183.89. Royal Society of Chemistry, Blackhorse Road, Letchworth Herts SG6 1HN England. **Tel** (01)636-1544. Ed J L B Cooper. **Ind/Abst** Int. Aerosp. Abstr., Math. Rev. **LC** QA1.

SAITAMA MATHEMATICAL JOURNAL. Vol. 1 (1983)-. 0289-0739. Periodical. English. ir. Saitama University, Department of Mathematics, Faculty of Science, Urawa 338 Japan. **Ind/Abst** Math. Rev. **LC** QA1. **DD** 510.5. *Science Reports of Saitama University. Series A, Mathematics, Physics, Chemistry and Biochemistry.*

SBORNIK RABOT PO TEORII OPTIMALNYKH PROTSESSOV. V. 1- 1973-. UR. Russian. Kaliningradskii Gos Universitet, Univerisitetskaia 23, Kalinigrad USSR. **LC** QA402.5.

SCANDINAVIAN JOURNAL OF STATISTICS. See Statistics.

SCHOLASTIC DYNAMATH. VFOAT Dynamath. Vol. 1, No. 1 (Sept. 1982)-. 0732-7773. Periodical. US. English. mo. $19.00. 730 Broadway, New York NY 10003. **Tel** (212)505-3134. Circ 210,000. Also available on microfilm. A classroom magazine for children in grades 5 and 6. Includes articles, games, and puzzles which give children a chance to practice math skills.

SCHOLASTIC MATH MAGAZINE. V. 1- Sept. 19, 1980-. 0198-8379. Periodical. US. English. ir. $19.00. Scholastic Magazines, PO Box 644, Lyndhurst NJ 07071.

SCHRIFTENREIHE DER INSTITUTE FUR MATHEMATIK BEI DER DEUTSCHEN AKADEMIE DER WISSENSCHAFTEN ZU BERLIN. REIHE A: REIHE MATHEMATIK. Main/Corp Deutsche Akademie der Wissenschaften zu Berlin. Began with No. 1, 1965. 0568-4188. Periodical. German. Deutscher Buch Export, Leninstrasse 16, DDR 701 Leipzig East Germany. *Schriftenreihe des Forschunginstituts fur Mathematik Bei der Deutschen Akademie der Wissenschaften zu Berlin.*

SCIENCE OF COMPUTER PROGRAMMING. See Computers and Computer Science.

SCIENCES ET TECHNIQUES EN PERSPECTIVE. See Science (General).

SCRIPTA FACULTATIS SCIENTIARUM NATURALIUM UNIVERSITATIS PURKYNIANAE BRUNENSIS. MATHEMATICA. (MATHEMATICA). **Main/Corp** Univerzita J.E. Purkynev Brne. Prirodovedecka Fakulta. 1971-. CS. Czech (English or German; Russian summaries). ir. 6.50 Single Issue. Univerzita J E Purkyne, Janackovo Nam 2A, Brno Czechoslovakia. **Ind/Abst** Math. Rev. **LC** Q1.A1, QA1. **DD** 510.8.

SCRIPTA MATHEMATICA CEASED. V. 1-29. 0036-9713. Periodical. US. English. ir. Academic Press, 4805 Sand Lake Road, Orlando FL 32819. **Tel** (305)345-4100.

SCRIPTA SERIES IN MATHEMATICS. 0276-9670. Monographic Series. US. English. ir. John Wiley & Sons, 605 Third Avenue, New York NY 10158.

SELECTA MATHEMATICA SOVIETICA. Vol. 1, No 1-. 0272-9903. Periodical. US. English (Russian). qt. Birkhauser Boston Inc, 380 Green Street, PO Box 3005, Cambridge MA 02139. **Tel** (617)576-6638. **Ind/Abst** Math. Rev., Comput. Control Abstr., Electr. Electron. Abstr., Sci. Abstr. Sect. A. Phys. Abstr. **LC** QA1. **DD** 510.5. **CODEN** SMSODB.

SELECTED TABLES IN MATHEMATICAL STATISTICS. V. 1- 1973-. 0094-8837. US. English. ir. American Mathematical Society, PO Box 1571 Annex Station, Providence RI 02901. **Tel** (401)272-9500. **LC** QA276.25. **DD** 519.50212.

SELECTED TOPICS IN GRAPH THEORY. 1-. UK. English. Academic Press, 111 5th Avenue, New York NY 10003. **LC** QA166. **DD** 511.505.

SELECTED TRANSLATIONS IN MATHEMATICAL STATISTICS AND PROBABILITY. V. 1- 0065-9274. US. English. ir. American Mathematical Society, PO Box 1571 Annex Station, Providence RI 02901. **LC** QA273. **DD** 519.082. **CODEN** SMSRB.

SEMIGROUP FORUM. V. 1- Mar. 1970-. 0037-1912. Periodical. US. English (articles in French, German or Russian). bm. $231.00. Springer Verlag New York Inc, 175 5th Avenue, New York NY 10010. **Tel** (212)460-1500. Ed K H Hoffman, P S Mostert, G J Lallement and N R Reilly. **Ind/Abst** Math. Rev., Sci. Cit. Index, Abr. Ed. **LC** QA171. **CODEN** SMGFA. Contains survey and research articles, announcements of new results, research problems, short notes, and abstracts and bibliographic items of complete work.

SEMINAIRE CHOQUET. EXPOSES. 1.- Year. English or French. ir. Secretariat Mathematique, 11 rue Pierre et Marie Curie, 75231 Paris Cedex 05 France. **LC** QA300. **DD** 515.05.

SEMINAIRE DE THEORIE DES NOMBRES. 1979-80-. US. English (French). an. **LC** QA24. **DD** 512.705. *Seminaire Delange-Pisot-Poitou : Exposes.*

SEMINAIRE DE THEORIE DU POTENTIEL, PARIS : EXPOSES. No. 1 (1972-1974)-. GW. French. an. Springer-Verlag New York Inc, 175 5th Avenue, New York NY 10016. Ed F Hirsch and G Mokobodzki. **LC** QA3, QA404.7. **DD** 510 S, 515.7. *Seminaire de Theorie du Potentiel Exposes, Seminaire de Theorie du Potentiel. Exposes.*

SEMINAIRE PAUL KREE. EXPOSES. Yearly V. 1-. French. ir. Secretariat Mathematique, 11 rue Pierre et Marie Curie, 75231 Paris Cedex 05 France. **LC** QA377. **DD** 515.35308.

SEMINAIRE SUR LES EQUATIONS AUX DERIVEES PARTIELLES. 1962/63-. 0553-2264. Periodical. French. ir. **LC** QA374.

SEQUENTIAL ANALYSIS. Vol. 3, No 1-. 0747-4946. Periodical. US. English. qt. $100.00. Marcel Dekker Journals, PO Box 11305 Church Street Station, New York NY 10249. Ed G K Ghosh. **Ind/Abst** Stat. Theory Method Abstr., Math. Rev. **DD** 519. **CODEN** SEANEX. bk rev. adv acc. *Communications in Statistics. Sequential Analysis, 2173-177X.*

SERDICA. VFOAT Serdika. V. 1-. 0204-4110. Periodical. English, German, or Russian. qt. $57.00. Hemus, 6 Boulevard Rusky, Sofia Bulgaria. **Ind/Abst** Math. Rev., Int. Aerosp. Abstr. **LC** QA1. *Izvestiia.*

SERIA CHEMIA. No. 11-. Polish (summaries in English). ir. 21.00. Ul Krakowski Azedmiescie 7, 00-068 Warszawa Poland. **Ind/Abst** Chem. Abstr. **LC** QA1. **CODEN** SCUCDH. *Prace. Seria Chemia.*

SERIA MATEMATYKA. V. 1- 1963-. 0551-6625. Monographic Series. Polish. ir. **LC** QA1.

SERIA MONOGRAFIE - POLITEKHNIKA WROCAWSKA, INSTYTUT MATEMATYKI. Main/Corp Politekhnika Wrocawska. Instytut Matematyki. **VFOAT** Monografie - Politekhnika Wrocawska, Instytut

Matematyki. Began in 1974. Monographic Series. PL. Polish (summaries in English and Russian). ir. 20.00. ARS Polona, Krakowskie Przedmiescie 7, 00-068 Warsaw Poland. **Ind/Abst** Math. Rev. **LC** TJ260.A1.

SERIA STUDIA I MATERIAY - POLITECHNIKA WROCAWSKA, INSTYTUT MATEMATYKI. **Main/Corp** Politechnika Wrocawska. Instytut Matematyki. **VFOAT** Studies and Research - Wrocaw Technical University, Institute of Mathematics. No. 10-. Monographic Series. PL. Polish (English or Russian with summaries in all three languages). ir. 20.00. ARS Polona, Krakowskie Przedmiescie 7, 00-068 Warsaw Poland. **Ind/Abst** Math. Rev. **LC** TJ260.A1. *Studia I Materiay.*

SERIIA MATEMATICHESKIKH NAUK. **VFOAT** Mathematical Sciences Series. Monographic Series. UR. Russian. 1.58 Single Issue. Izdatelstvo Lgu Im, A A Zhdanova 199164, Leningrad Universitetskaia Nab 7/9, Leningrad Russian SFSR. **LC** AS262.

SHU HSUEH HSUEH PAO. **VFOAT** Acta Mathematica Sinica. Began in 1951. 0583-1431. Periodical. CC. Chinese (added table of contents in English). bm. $27.54. China Publication Centre, PO Box 2820, Beijing China. **Ind/Abst** Math. Rev.

SHU HSUEH NIEN KAN. Periodical. Chinese (English). bm. 1.10. Scientific Publishing Company, Wettsteinplatz 10, CH-4058 Basel Switzerland. **Ind/Abst** Math. Rev. **LC** QA1. **DD** 510.5. *Su Hsueh Nien Pao.*

SHU HSUEH WU LI HSUEH PAO. *See* Physics.

SHU HSUEH YEN CHIU YU PING LUN. **VFOAT** Journal of Mathematical Research and Exposition. Began in 1981. Periodical. Chinese (English). qt. $16.00. China National Publishing of Import-Export, PO Box 88, Beijing China. **Tel** P08-21-84. **Ind/Abst** Math. Rev. **LC** QA1. **DD** 510.5.

SIAM-AMS PROCEEDINGS. **VFOAT** S.I.A.M.-A.M.S. Proceedings. V. 1-. 0080-5084. Monographic Series. US. English. ir. American Mathematical Society, PO Box 1571, Annex Station, Providence RI 02901. **Tel** (401)272-9500. **Ind/Abst** Math. Rev., Chem. Abstr., Eng. Index. **CODEN** SAMPBY.

SIAM JOURNAL ON ALGEBRAIC AND DISCRETE METHODS. **Main/Corp** Society for Industrial and Applied Mathematics. **VFOAT** Journal on Algebraic and Discrete Methods. V. 1- Mar. 1980-. 0196-5212. Periodical. US. English. qt. $60.00. Business Manager SIAM Publications, 1406 Architects Building, 117 South 17th Street, Philadelphia PA 19103. **Tel** (215)564-2929. **Ed** Carl D Meyer Jr. **Ind/Abst** Math. Rev., Electron. Commun. Abstr. J., ISMEC Bull., Pollut. Abstr. Indexes, Saf. Sci. Abstr. J., Comput. Control Abstr., Electr. Electron. Abstr., Sci. Abstr. Sect. A. Phys. Abstr., Comput. Rev., Sci. Cit. Index, Abr. Ed. **LC** QA1. **DD** 510.5. **CODEN** SJAMDU. adv acc. **Circ** 1,000. Contains research and survey papers in linear algebra (including matrix methodology), combinatorics, and line graphs.

SIAM JOURNAL ON APPLIED MATHEMATICS. **Main/Corp** Society for Industrial and Applied Mathematics. **VFOAT** Applied Mathematics. **VAT** Society for Industrial and Applied Mathematics Journal on Applied Mathematics. V. 14- Jan. 1966-. 0036-1399. Periodical. US. English. bm. $13.00. Business Manager SIAM Publications, 1405 Architects Building, 117 South 17th Street, Philadelphia PA 19103. **Tel** (215)564-2929. **Ed** Norman R Lebovitz. **Ind/Abst** Electron. Commun. Abstr. J., ISMEC Bull., Pollut. Abstr. Indexes, Saf. Sci. Abstr. J., Eng. Index Mon., Appl. Mech. Rev., Comput. Rev., Eng. Index Energy Abstr., Excerpta Med., Coal Abstr., Abstr. Bull. Inst. Paper Chem., Comput. Control Abstr., Electr. Electron. Abstr., Sci. Abstr. Sect. A. Phys. Abstr., Chem. Abstr., Eng. Index Annu., Phys. Abstr., Int. Aerosp. Abstr., Math. Rev., Nuci. Sci. Abstr., Appl. Sci. Technol. Index, Sci. Cit. Index, Abr. Ed., Eng. Index. **CODEN** SMJMAP. adv acc. **Circ** 3,000. Contains research articles in the applied (analytical, stochastic, statistical, numerical, and discrete) of the physical engineering, biological, medical and social sciences. *Journal of the Society for Industrial and Applied Mathematics, 0368-4245.*

SIAM JOURNAL ON COMPUTING. **Main/Corp** Society for Industrial and Applied Mathematics. **VFOAT** Journal on Computing. **VAT** Society for Industrial and Applied Mathematics Journal on Computing. V. 1- Mar. 1972-. 0097-5397. Periodical. US. English. qt. $98.00. Business Manager SIAM Publications, 1405 Architects Building, 117 South 17th Street, Philadelphia PA 19103. **Tel** (215)564-2929. **Ed** S Rao Kosaraju. **Ind/Abst** Math. Rev., Electron. Commun. Abstr. J., ISMEC Bull., Pollut. Abstr. Indexes, Saf. Sci. Abstr. J., Int. Aerosp. Abstr., Comput. Control Abstr., Electr. Electron. Abstr., Sci. Abstr. Sect. A. Phys. Abstr., Appl. Sci. Technol. Index, Appl. Mech. Rev., Comput. Abstr., Sci. Cit. Index, Abr. Ed., Phys. Abstr., Humanit. Index, Comput. Rev. **LC** QA76. **DD** 001.6405. **CODEN** SMJCAT. adv acc. **Circ** 2,000. Contains research articles in mathematics that apply to the problems of computer science and the non-numerical aspects of computing.

SIAM JOURNAL ON CONTROL AND OPTIMIZATION. **Main/Corp** Society for Industrial and Applied Mathematics. **VFOAT** Journal on Control and Optimization, Control and Optimization. **VAT** Society for Industrial and Applied Mathematics Journal on Control and Optimization. V. 14- Jan. 1976-. 0363-0129. Periodical. US. English. bm. $130.00. Society for Industrial and Applied Mathematics, 1405 Architects Building, 33 South 17th Street, Philadelphia PA 19103. **Tel** (215)564-2929. **Ed** H T Banks. **Ind/Abst** Math. Rev., Electron. Commun. Abstr. J., ISMEC Bull., Pollut. Abstr. Indexes, Saf. Sci. Abstr. J., Eng. Index Mon., Eng. Index Bioeng. Abstr., Eng. Index Energy Abstr., Int. Aerosp. Abstr., Comput. Control Abstr., Electr. Electron. Abstr., Sci. Abstr. Sect. A. Phys. Abstr., Eng. Index Annu., Appl. Sci. Technol. Index, Appl. Mech. Rev., Comput. Rev., Sci. Cit. Index, Abr. Ed., Phys. Abstr., Humanit. Index, Eng. Index. **LC** QA402.3. **DD** 629.831205. **CODEN** SJCODC. adv acc. **Circ** 2,000. Contains papers on mathematical theory of control and its applications in system theory, optimization (including continuous and discrete mathematical programming), and game theory. *SIAM Journal on Control, 0036-1402.*

SIAM JOURNAL ON MATHEMATICAL ANALYSIS. **Main/Corp** Society for Industrial and Applied Mathematics. **VFOAT** Journal on Mathematical Analysis. **VAT** Society for Industrial and Applied Mathematics Journal on Mathematical Analysis. V. 1- Feb. 1970-. 0036-1410. Periodical. US. English. bm. $156.00. Business Manager SIAM Publications, 1405 Architects Building, 117 South 17th Street, Philadelphia PA 19103. **Tel** (215)564-2929. **Ed** Donald G Saari. **Ind/Abst** Math. Rev., Electron. Commun. Abstr. J., ISMEC Bull., Pollut. Abstr. Indexes, Saf. Sci. Abstr. J., Int. Aerosp. Abstr., Comput. Control Abstr., Electr. Electron. Abstr., Sci. Abstr. Sect. A. Phys. Abstr., Appl. Mech. Rev., Comput. Rev., Math. Rev., Phys. Abstr., Sci. Cit. Index, Abr. Ed. **LC** QA300. **DD** 517.05. **CODEN** SJMAAH. adv acc. **Circ** 1,500. Contains research articles on the part of mathematical analysis that bridges abstract pure mathematics and numerical, physical, and engineering applications.

SIAM JOURNAL ON NUMERICAL ANALYSIS. **Main/Corp** Society for Industrial and Applied Mathematics. V. 3- 1966-. 0036-1429. Periodical. US. English. bm. $136.00. Business Manager SIAM Publications, 1405 Architects Building, 117 South 17th Street, Philadelphia PA 19103. **Tel** (215)564-2929. **Ed** Eugene Isaacson. **Ind/Abst** Math. Rev., Electron. Commun. Abstr. J., ISMEC Bull., Pollut. Abstr. Indexes, Saf. Sci. Abstr. J., Int. Aerosp. Abstr., Comput. Control Abstr., Electr. Electron. Abstr., Sci. Abstr. Sect. A. Phys. Abstr., Appl. Sci. Technol. Index, Appl. Mech. Rev., Comput. Abstr., Comput. Rev., Sci. Cit. Index, Abr. Ed., Phys. Abstr. **LC** QA297. **DD** 519. **CODEN** SJNAAM. adv acc. **Circ** 3,000. Contains research articles on the development and analysis of numerical methods, including their convergence, stability and error analysis, along with related results in functional analysis and approximation theory. *Journal of the Society for Industrial and Applied Mathematics. Series B. Numerical Analysis, 0887-459X.*

SIAM JOURNAL ON SCIENTIFIC AND STATISTICAL COMPUTING. *See* Statistics.

SIAM NEWS : A PUBLICATION OF SOCIETY FOR INDUSTRIAL AND APPLIED MATHEMATICS. V. 6- Feb. 1973-. Periodical. US. English. bm. $8.00. Society for Industrial and Applied Mathematics, 1405 Architects Building, 117 South 17th Street, Philadelphia PA 19103. **Tel** (215)564-2929. **Ed** Lloyd W Black. bk rev. adv acc. **Circ** 7,500. (ctrl). A news-journal for the applied mathematics community; reports on research in academe and industry, federal activities, SIAM activities; lists conferences, meetings, positions, etc. *SIAM Newsletter (1968).*

SIAM REVIEW. **Main/Corp** Society for Industrial and Applied Mathematics. **VAT** Society for Industrial and Applied Mathematics Review. V. 1- Jan. 1959-. 0036-1445. Periodical. US. English. qt. $82.00. Business Manager of SIAM Publications, 1405 Architects Building, 117 South 17th Street, Philadelphia PA 19103. **Tel** (215)564-2929. **Ed** John A Burns. **Ind/Abst** Appl. Sci. Technol. Index, Excerpta Med., Int. Aerosp. Abstr., Comput. Control Abstr., Electr. Electron. Abstr., Sci. Abstr. Sect. A. Phys. Abstr., Math. Rev., Comput. Rev., Sci. Cit. Index, Abr. Ed., Phys. Abstr., Appl. Mech. Rev. **LC** QA1. **DD** 519. **CODEN** SIREAD. bk rev. adv acc. **Circ** 8,000. Contains primarily expository and survey papers on the applied mathematics of the physical and biological sciences.

SIBERIAN MATHEMATICAL JOURNAL. V. 7- Jan./Feb. 1966-. 0037-4466. Periodical. US. English (Russian). bm. $795.00 Domestic, $880.00 Foreign. Consultants Bureau, 233 Spring Street, New York NY 10013. **Tel** (212)260-8000. **Ed** S L Sobeler. **Ind/Abst** Math. Rev., Electron. Commun. Abstr. J., ISMEC Bull., Pollut. Abstr. Indexes, Saf. Sci. Abstr. J., Int. Aerosp. Abstr., Contents Contemp. Math. J., Index Math. Pap., Zentralbl. Math. Ihre Grenzgeb. **LC** QA1. **CODEN** SMTJAW. This outstanding mathematics journal provides the English-speaking scientific community with an authoritative translation of math work being done in the educational and research center near Novo Sibirisk in Siberia.

SIBIRSKII MATEMATICHESKII ZHURNAL. V. 1- May/June 1960-. 0037-4474. Periodical. UR. Russian. bm. $85.50. Victor Kamkin Inc, 12224 Parklawn Drive, Rockville MD 20852. **Tel** (301)881-5973. **Ind/Abst** Math. Rev., Int. Aerosp. Abstr. **LC** QA1.

SIGMAP BULLETIN. *See* Computers and Computer Science.

SIGNUM NEWSLETTER. *See* Computers and Computer Science.

SIGSAM BULLETIN. *See* Computers and Computer Science.

SIMON STEVIN; WIS- EN NATUURKUNDIG TIJDSCHRIFT. 25-Yearly volume. 0037-5454. Periodical. BE. Multilingual (Flemish, Dutch and English). qt. $19.76. Simon Stevin Wis-en, Krijgslaan 281, B-9000 Gent Belgium. **Tel** 091/225715. **Ed** J A Ohao Irygolaan. **Ind/Abst** Math. Rev., Comput. Control Abstr., Electr. Electron. Abstr., Sci. Abstr. Sect. A. Phys. Abstr., Phys. Abstr. **LC** QA1. **CODEN** SSWNAX. bk rev. (ctrl). Pure and applied mathematics. *Christiaan Huygens, Mathematica B, Wis- En Natuurkundig Tijdschrift.*

SITZUNGSBERICHTE - OSTERREICHISCHE AKADEMIE DER WISSENSCHAFTEN,. Vol. 156, 3/4. Issue-190, 8/10. 0029-8816. Periodical. German. ir. 456.-. Springer Verlag-Wien, Postfach 367, Moelderbastei 5, A-1011 Vienna Austria. **Ed** H Reiter, L Schmetterer, W M Schmidt, K Sigmund, S Grober, J Hejtmanek, E Hiawka, N Hofreiter, and V Losert. **Ind/Abst** Biol. Abstr., Life Sci. Collect. **CODEN** OAWBAV. bk rev. This international journal is devoted to research in pure mathematics in its broadest significance. *Sitzungsberichte - Osterreichische Akademie der Wissenschaften.*

SOME MATHEMATICAL QUESTIONS IN BIOLOGY. *See* Biology.

SOURCES IN THE HISTORY OF MATHEMATICS AND PHYSICAL SCIENCES. 1-. 0172-6315. Monographic Series. English. ir. Springer Verlag-New York Inc, 175 5th Avenue, New York NY 10010. **Tel** (212)460-1584. **Ind/Abst** Math. Rev. Contains articles on the history and study of mathematics and physical sciences.

SOUTH AFRICAN STATISTICAL JOURNAL. *See* Statistics.

SOUTHEAST ASIAN BULLETIN OF MATHEMATICS. V. 1- 1977-. Periodical. SI. English. sa. 24.00. Department of Math, NAT University of Singapore, Kent Ridge, Republic of Singapore 0511. **Tel** 0-635211. **Ed** R F Turner-Smith. **Ind/Abst** Math. Rev. bk rev. adv acc. **Circ** 450. Research and expository articles in mathematics.

SOVIET MATHEMATICS. **Main/Corp** Russia (1923- U.S.S.R.). Ministerstvo Vysshego I Srednego Spetsial Nogo Obrazovaniia. V. 18- 1974-. 0197-7156. Periodical. US. English (translated from Russian). mo. Allerton Press Inc, 150 Fifth Avenue, New York NY

Mathematics

10011. **Tel** (212)924-3950. **Ind/Abst** Math. Rev., Comput. Control Abstr., Electr. Electron. Abstr., Sci. Abstr. Sect. A. Phys. Abstr., Phys. Abstr., Comput. Rev. **LC** QA1. **DD** 510.5. **CODEN** SOMADL.

SOVIET MATHEMATICS - DOKLADY. V. 20- Jan./Feb.1979-. 0197-6788. Periodical. US. English (Russian). bm. American Mathematical Society, PO Box 1571 Annex Station, Providence RI 02901. **Ind/Abst** Math. Rev. **LC** QA1. **DD** 510.5. *Soviet Mathematics, 0038-5573.*

STATE, DISTRICT, AND REGIONAL REPORT OF STATEWIDE ASSESSMENT RESULTS. *See* Education (General) - Theory, Practice of Education.

STATE SUMMARY OF RESULTS, MICHIGAN EDUCATIONAL ASSESSMENT PROGRAM. **Main/Corp** Michigan. Dept. of Education. **VFOAT** Michigan Educational Assessment Program. 0361-2139. US. English. Michigan Department of Education, PO Box 673, East Lansing MI 48823. **LC** LB1573. **DD** 372.126.

STATISTICAL SOFTWARE NEWSLETTER. *See* Statistics.

STATISTICS. *See* Statistics.

STOCHASTIC ANALYSIS AND APPLICATIONS. Vol. 1, No. 1-. 0736-2994. Periodical. US. English. qt. $75.00. Marcel Dekker Inc, PO Box 11305/Church Street Station, New York NY 10249. **Ind/Abst** Math. Rev., Curr. Index Stat., Int. Bibliogr. Zeitschriftenliteratur Allen Gebieten Wissens, Zentralbl. Math. Ihre Grenzgeb. **LC** QA274.2. **DD** 519.2. **CODEN** SAAPDA.

STOCHASTIC PROCESSES AND THEIR APPLICATIONS. V. 1- Jan. 1973-. 0304-4149. Periodical. NE. English. bm. Elsevier Science Publishers, PO Box 211, 1000 AE Amsterdam Netherlands. **Tel** (020)5803911. **Ind/Abst** Math. Rev., Comput. Control Abstr., Electr. Electron. Abstr., Sci. Abstr. Sect. A. Phys. Abstr., Phys. Abstr., Comput. Rev. **LC** QA274.A1. **DD** 519.205. **CODEN** STOPB7.

STOCHASTICA. 0210-7821. Catalan (Spanish). ir. Departamento de Estadistica Matematica de la Universidad de Barcelona, Ediciones de Promocion Cultural, c/o Rocafort 256-258, Barcelona Spain. **Ind/Abst** Math. Rev. **LC** QA1. **DD** 510.5.

STOCHASTICS. V. 1- 1973-. 0090-9491. Periodical. US. English. qt. $334.00. Gordon & Breach, PO Box 197, London WC2E 9PX England. **Ed** Mark H A Davis. **Ind/Abst** Math. Rev., Eng. Index Annu., Eng. Index Mon., Eng. Index Bioeng. Abstr., Eng. Index Energy Abstr., Comput. Control Abstr., Electr. Electron. Abstr., Sci. Abstr. Sect. A. Phys. Abstr., Phys. Abstr., Eng. Index. **LC** QA274.A1. **DD** 519.205. **CODEN** STOCB2. bk rev. adv acc.

STUDENT MATHEMATICS. No. 1-6. 0085-6800. CN. English. an. $0.16. Student Mathematics, Faculty of Education, 371 Bloor Street West, Toronto Ontario M5S 2R7 Canada. **DD** 510.71271.

STUDIA CARTESIANA . . . . 1(1979)-. NE. French (English, German and Italian, with summaries in English and French). an. Quadrature, Postbus 6463, Amsterdam Netherlands.

STUDIA MATHEMATICA. Vol. 1-. 0039-3223. Periodical. PL. Polish. ir. ARS Polona, Krakowskie Przedmiescie 7, 00-068 Warsaw Poland. **Ind/Abst** Math. Rev., Sci. Cit. Index, Abr. Ed. **LC** QA1. **CODEN** SMATAZ. (cum index).

STUDIA UNIVERSITATIS BABES-BOLYAI. MATHEMATICA. (STUDIA UNIVERSITATIS BABES-BOLYAI : MATHEMATICA). **Main/Corp** Universitatea Babes-Bolyai. 0373-1227. Romanian (English and French). ir. 10.00. **Ind/Abst** Math. Rev., Int. Aerosp. Abstr., Chem. Abstr. **LC** QA1. **DD** 510. **CODEN** SUBMDA. *Studia Universitatis Babes-Bolyai. Series Mathematica-Mechanica, 0370-8659.*

STUDIES IN APPLIED MATHEMATICS. V. 48- Mar. 1969-. 0022-2526. Periodical. US. English. bm. $126.00. Elsevier Science Publishing Company Inc, PO Box 1663 Grand Central Station, New York NY 10163. **Tel** (212)370-5520. **Ind/Abst** Math. Rev., Eng. Index Annu., Eng. Index Mon., Eng. Index Bioeng. Abstr., Eng. Index Energy Abstr., Excerpta Med., Int. Aerosp. Abstr., Comput. Control Abstr., Electr. Electron. Abstr., Sci. Abstr. Sect. A. Phys. Abstr., Ship Abstr., Sci. Cit. Index, Abr. Ed., Phys. Abstr., Appl. Mech. Rev., Comput. Rev., Eng. Index. **LC** QA1. **DD** 500.205. **CODEN** SAPMB6. *Journal of Mathematics and Physics, 0097-1421.*

STUDIES IN LOGIC AND THE FOUNDATIONS OF MATHEMATICS. 0049-237X. Monographic Series. English. ir. Elsevier Science Publishing Company Ltd, PO Box 1663 Grand Central Station, New York NY 10163. **Tel** (212)370-5520. **Ind/Abst** Comput. Control Abstr., Electr. Electron. Abstr., Sci. Abstr. Sect. A. Phys. Abstr., Phys. Abstr., Math. Rev. **CODEN** SLFMDZ.

STUDIES IN MATHEMATICAL AND MANAGERIAL ECONOMICS. *See* Economics.

STUDIES IN MATHEMATICS AND ITS APPLICATIONS. 1-. 0168-2024. Monographic Series. English. ir. Elsevier Science Publishing Company Ltd, PO Box 1663 Grand Central Station, New York NY 10163. **Tel** (212)370-5520. **Ind/Abst** Math. Rev., Comput. Control Abstr., Electr. Electron. Abstr., Sci. Abstr. Sect. A. Phys. Abstr. **CODEN** SMIADL.

STUDIES IN THE HISTORY OF MATHEMATICS AND PHYSICAL SCIENCES. 1-. 0172-570X. Monographic Series. US. English. ir. **Tel** (212)460-1500. **Ind/Abst** Math. Rev. Numbered series.

STUDII SI CERCETARI MATEMATICE. Vol. 1- 1950-. 0039-4068. Periodical. RM. Romanian (English, French, German, or Russian, with summaries in Romanian, English, French, German, and Russian). bm. $72.00. Rompresfilatelia, PO Box 1362137, Bucharest Romania. **Ind/Abst** Int. Aerosp. Abstr., Math. Rev., Appl. Mech. Rev., Comput. Rev. *Disquisitiones Mathematicae et Physicae, Bulletin Mathematique, 0007-4691.*

SUGAKUSHI KENKYU. **VFOAT** Journal of History of Mathematics, Japan. 0386-9555. Periodical. JA. Japanese. ir. Nihon Sugakushi Gakkai c/o Fuji Tanki Daigaku Kagaku-Shi Kyoshitsu 7-7, Shimoochiai 1 Shinjuku-Ku, Tokyo-To 161 Japan. **Ind/Abst** Math. Rev. **LC** QA27.J3.

SZIGMA. *See* Economics.

TAMKANG JOURNAL OF MATHEMATICS. V. 1- Mar. 1970-. Periodical. CH. English. sa. $48.00. Chinese Materials Service Center, 1716 Ocean Avenue/Suite 103, San Francisco CA 94112. **Tel** (886)752-9255. **Ed** Ching Mu Wu. **Ind/Abst** Math. Rev. **LC** QA1. **DD** 510.5. **Circ** 1,000. (ctrl). Research articles by Chinese and western experts on mathematics. *Tan-Chiang Shu Hsueh.*

THE TANZANIAN MATHEMATICAL BULLETIN. **VFOAT** Mathematical Bulletin. Vol. 1-. Periodical. TZ. English (Kiswahili). ir. Mathematical Association of Tanzania, PO Box 35062, Dar es Salaam Tanzania. **LC** WMLC L 83/520. (cum index).

TAP CHI TOAN HOC. Vol. 4- 1976-. Periodical. VM. Vietnamese. qt. **Ind/Abst** Math. Rev. **LC** QA1. *Tap San Toan Hoc.*

TECHNICAL REPORT SERIES OF THE LABORATORY FOR RESEARCH IN STATISTICS AND PROBABILITY. *See* Statistics.

TECHNOMETRICS. V. 1- Feb. 1959-. 0040-1706. Periodical. US. English. qt. $10.00 Members, $15.00 Nonmembers. Technometrics, PO Box 587 Benjamin Franklin Station, Washington DC 20044. **Ind/Abst** Eng. Index Mon., Eng. Index Bioeng. Abstr., Eng. Index Energy Abstr., World Text Abstr., Abstr. Bull. Inst. Paper Chem., Int. Aerosp. Abstr., GeoRef, Eng. Index Annu., Eng. Index Mon., Math. Rev., Nuci. Sci. Abstr., Sel. Water Resour. Abstr., Appl. Sci. Technol. Index. **LC** QA276. **DD** 310.5. **NLM** W1 TE211P. **CODEN** TCMTA2. (cum index). Available on microfilm from University Microfilms.

TENSOR. No. 1-9, 1938-49. 0040-3504. Periodical. JA. English. ir. $160.00. Maruzen Company Ltd, PO Box 5050, 100-31 Tokyo Japan. **Tel** 0467-86-4713. **Ind/Abst** Math. Rev. **LC** QA1. **DD** 517.2. **CODEN** TNSRAZ. (ctrl).

TEORIIA FUNKTSII, FUNKTSIONALNYI ANALIZ I IKH PRILOZHENIIA. 0497-2708. Periodical. UR. Russian. **Ind/Abst** Int. Aerosp. Abstr., Math. Rev. **LC** QA331.

TEORIIA FUNKTSII KOMPLEKSNOGO PEREMENNOGO I KRAEVYE ZADACHI. UR. Russian. 0.80. Chuvashskii Gos. Universitet, Moskovskii Prospekt 15, Cheboksary USSR. **LC** QA331.

TEORIJA SLUCAINYH PROCESSOV. (TEORIIA SLUCHAINYKH PROTSESSOV). Vol. 1- 1973-. 0321-3900. UR. Russian. ir. $4.00. Victor Kamkin Inc, 12224 Parklawn Drive, Rockville MD 20852. **Tel** (301)881-5973. **Ind/Abst** Int. Aerosp. Abstr. **LC** QA274.A1.

TEORIJA VEROJATNOSTEJ I EE PRIMENENIJA. (TEORIIA VEROIATNOSTEI I EE PRIMENENIIA). Vol. 1- 1956-. 0040-361X. Periodical. UR. Russian (tables of contents also in English, French, and German). qt. $57.00. Victor Kamkin Inc (70965), 12224 Parklawn Drive, Rockville MD 20852. **Tel** (301)881-5973. **Ind/Abst** Math. Rev., Comput. Control Abstr., Electr. Electron. Abstr., Sci. Abstr. Sect. A. Phys. Abstr. **LC** QA273. **CODEN** TVPRA8. (cum index).

TEXAS MATHEMATICS TEACHER. V. 1- 1954-. 0277-030X. Periodical. US. English. ir. $5.00. c/o J W Brown, 100 South Glasgow Drive, Dallas TX 75214. **Tel** (214)824-3267. **Ed** J William Brown. adv acc. **Circ** 1,200. (ctrl). Articles concerning elementary, secondary and college level mathematics - Texas mathematics teacher journal.

THEORETICAL AND MATHEMATICAL PHYSICS. V. 1- Oct. 1969-. 0040-5779. Periodical. US. English (Russian). mo. $625.00 Domestic, $695.00 Foreign. Consultants Bureau, 233 Spring Street, New York NY 10013. **Tel** (212)620-8000. **Ed** N N Bogolyubov. **Ind/Abst** Math. Rev., Electron. Commun. Abstr. J., ISMEC Bull., Pollut. Abstr. Indexes, Saf. Sci. Abstr. J., Comput. Control Abstr., Electr. Electron. Abstr., Sci. Abstr. Sect. A. Phys. Abstr., Appl. Mech. Rev., Chem. Abstr., Phys. Abstr., Zentralbl. Math. Ihre Grenzgeb., Sci. Cit. Index, Abr. Ed., Phys. Abstr. **LC** QC20. **DD** 530.0151. **CODEN** TMPHAH. This journal reports on current developments in theoretical physics as well as mathematical problems related to theoretical physics.

THEORETICAL COMPUTER SCIENCE. *See* Computers and Computer Science.

THEORY OF PROBABILITY AND ITS APPLICATIONS. V. 1- Mar. 1956-. 0040-585X. Periodical. UK. English (Russian). qt. $216.00. Society Industrial & Applied Mathematics, 1405 Architects Building, 117 South 17th Street, Philadelphia PA 19103. **Tel** (215)564-2929. **Ind/Abst** Math. Rev., Electron. Commun. Abstr. J., ISMEC Bull., Pollut. Abstr. Indexes, Saf. Sci. Abstr. J., Int. Aerosp. Abstr., Comput. Control Abstr., Electr. Electron. Abstr., Sci. Abstr. Sect. A. Phys. Abstr., Phys. Abstr., Sci. Cit. Index, Abr. Ed., Appl. Mech. Rev. **LC** QA273. **DD** 519.1. **CODEN** TPRBAU. adv acc. **Circ** 1,100. Contains papers on theory and application of probability, statistics, and stochastic processes.

THEORY OF PROBABILITY AND MATHEMATICAL STATISTICS. No. 1-. 0094-9000. Periodical. US. English. ir. American Mathematical Society, PO Box 1571, Annex Station, Providence RI 02901. **Tel** (401)272-9500. **Ind/Abst** Math. Rev. **LC** QA273.A1. **DD** 519.205. **CODEN** TPMSCO.

THEORY OF STOCHASTIC PROCESSES. No. 1- 1974-. 0095-7380. US. English. John Wiley & Sons, 605 3rd Avenue, New York NY 10158. **LC** QA274.A1. **DD** 519.205.

TODAY'S EDUCATION. MATHEMATICS/SCIENCE EDITION. (TODAY'S EDUCATION. MATHEMATICS/ SCIENCE EDITION : THE JOURNAL OF THE NATIONAL EDUCATION ASSOCIATION). **VAT** Today's Education. Mathematics Science Edition. Vol. 70, No. 2, (April/ May 1981)-. 0272-4111. Periodical. US. English. qt. $1.75. National Education Association of the United States, 1201 16th Street Northwest, Washington DC 20036. **LC** LA210. **DD** 370.5.

TOHOKU MATHEMATICAL JOURNAL. Began with: Ser. 1, V. 1 (July 1911). 0040-8735. Periodical. JA. English (French, German, Italian or Japanese). qt. 104.00. Maruzen Company Ltd, PO Box 5050, 100-31 Tokyo Japan. **Tel** 03/278 9224. **Ed** T Hayashi. **Ind/Abst** Math. Rev. **LC** QA1. **CODEN** TOMJAM. (cum index). (ctrl). Receiving good reputations from the learned peoples for its editorial principle that it accepts valuable articles of the contributors aiming at the international academic level.

TOIMITUKSIA. SARJA A. I : MATHEMATICA. **Main/Corp** Suomalainen Tiedeakatemia. **VFOAT** Annales Academiae Scientiarum Fennicae. Series A. I : Mathematica. 235-305. Monographic Series. FI. English (German). ir. Akakeeminen-Kirjakuppa, PO Box 128, 00101

Mathematics

Helsinki Finland. *Suomalaisen Tiedeakatemia Toimituksia. Sarja A. I: Mathematica-Physica.*

TOKEI SURI KENKYUJO NEMPO. Main/Corp Tokei Suri Kenkyujo, Tokyo. JA. Japanese. ir. Tokei Suri Kenkyujo, 6-7 Minami Azabu 4-Chome Minato-Ku, Tokyo 106 Japan. LC QA276.A1.

TOPOLOGIE STRUCTURALE. VFOAT Structural Topology. 1. (1979)-. 0226-9171. Periodical. CN. English (French). ty. 37.00. Department of Mathematics University of Quebec, PO Box 8888 Station A, Montreal Quebec H3C 3P8. **Tel** (514)282-7710. **Ind/Abst** Math. Rev. DD 624.105. bk rev. **Circ** 250. An interdisciplinary journal on the applications of classical and contemporary mathematics, especially geometry to the solution of morphological and structural problems.

TOPOLOGY. V. 1- Jan./Mar. 1962-. 0040-9383. Periodical. UK. English (French, German, or Italian). qt. Pergamon Press, 395 Sawmill River Road, Elmsford NY 10523. **Ind/Abst** Math. Rev. LC QA611. DD 514.05. **CODEN** TPLGAF. Available on microfilm.

TOPOLOGY AND ITS APPLICATIONS. V. 11- Jan. 1980-. 0166-8641. Periodical. English. ir. 146.00. North-Holland Publishing Company, Journal Division, 335 Jan Van Galenstraat, PO Box 211, 1000 AE Amsterdam Netherlands. **Ind/Abst** Math. Rev., Electron. Commun. Abstr. J., ISMEC Bull., Pollut. Abstr. Indexes, Saf. Sci. Abstr. J. LC QA611.A1. DD 514. **CODEN** TIAPD9. *General Topology and its Applications.*

TOPOLOGY (BERLIN, GERMANY). (TOPOLOGY). Began in 1981. 0720-2571. English (French and German). ir. Zentralblatt Fur Mathematik, Hardenburgstrasse 29C, D1000 Berlin 1 West Germany. LC QA611.A1. DD 514.05.

TOPOLOGY PROCEEDINGS. V. 1-. 0146-4124. Monographic Series. US. English. an. Auburn University, Mathematics Department, Auburn AL 36830. **Tel** (205)826-4290. Ed Gruenhage, Kuperberg, and Zenor. **Ind/Abst** Math. Rev. LC QA611.A1. DD 514. **Circ** 350. Refereed papers presented at the Annual Topology Conference.

TRANSACTIONS OF THE AMERICAN MATHEMATICAL SOCIETY. Main/Corp American Mathematical Society. V. 1- Jan. 1900-. 0002-9947. Periodical. US. English. mo. American Mathematical Society, PO Box 1571, Annex Station, Providence RI 02901. **Tel** (401)272-9500. **Ind/Abst** Math. Rev., Electron. Commun. Abstr. J., ISMEC Bull., Pollut. Abstr. Indexes, Saf. Sci. Abstr. J., Int. Aerosp. Abstr., Sci. Cit. Index, Abr. Ed. LC QA1. DD 510.5. **CODEN** TAMTAM. (cum index).

TRANSACTIONS OF THE MOSCOW MATHEMATICAL SOCIETY. Main/Corp Moskovskoe Matematicheskoe Obshchestvo. 0077-1554. US. English (Russian). sa. American Mathematical Society, PO Box 1571, Annex Station, Providence RI 02901. **Tel** (401)272-9500. **Ind/Abst** Math. Rev. LC QA1. DD 510.5. **CODEN** TMMSD4.

TRANSACTIONS OF THE . . . PRAGUE CONFERENCE ON INFORMATION THEORY, STATISTICAL DECISION FUNCTIONS, RANDOM PROCESSES. Main/Conf Conference on Information Theory, Statistical Decision Functions, Random Processes. 1st-. 0573-3634. US. English (text in French, German and Russian). ir. Kluwer Boston Inc, 190 Old Derby Street, Hingham MA 02043. LC QA273.

TRANSLATIONS - AMERICAN MATHEMATICAL SOCIETY. Main/Corp American Mathematical Society. No. 1-105. 0065-9290. US. English (Russian). ir. American Mathematical Society, PO Box 1571, Annex Station, Providence RI 02901. **Ind/Abst** Math. Rev. LC QA3.

TRANSLATIONS OF MATHEMATICAL MONOGRAPHS. 1- 1962-. 0065-9282. Monographic Series. US. English. ir. American Math Society, PO Box 1571, Annex Station, Providence RI 02901. **Tel** (401)272-9500. **Ind/Abst** Math. Rev.

TRUDY. Main/Corp Voronezh, Russia (City). Universitet. Matematicheskii Fakultet. UR. Russian. 0.20 Each Issue. **Ind/Abst** Math. Rev. LC QA1.

TRUDY. Main/Corp Akademiia Nauk SSSR. Matematicheskii Institut Im. V. A. Steklova. 1- 1932-. Periodical. UR. English (French, German or Russian). ir. Victor Kamkin Inc, 12224 Parklawn Drive, Rockville MD 20852. **Tel** (301)881-5973.

TRUDY FIZIKO-MATEMATICHESKOGO INSTITUTA IMENI V.A. STEKLOVA / TRAVAUX DE L'INSTITUT PHYSICO-MATHEMATIQUE STEKLOFF. VFOAT Travaux de l'Institut Mathematique Stekloff. 1- 1933-. UR. Russian (English, French, German with a table of contents in French). ir. **Ind/Abst** Math. Rev., Int. Aerosp. Abstr.

TRUDY ORDENA LENINA MATEMATICHESKOGO INSTITUTA IMENI V. A. STEKLOVA. (PROCEEDINGS OF THE STEKLOV INSTITUTE OF MATHEMATICS). 0081-5438. Monographic Series. US. English (Russian). qt. American Mathematical Society, PO Box 1571, Annex Station, Providence RI 02901. **Tel** (401)272-9500. **Ind/Abst** Math. Rev.

TRUDY SEMINARA IMENI I. G. PETROVSKOGO. Main/Corp Seminar Imeni I. G. Petrovskogo. Vol. 1- 1975-. 0321-2971. UR. Russian. an. 3.60. Izdatelstvo Moskovskogo Universiteta, 103009 Moskva Ul Gertsena 5/7, Moskva USSR. **Ind/Abst** Math. Rev., Int. Aerosp. Abstr., Chem. Abstr. LC QA370. **CODEN** TSIPDH.

TSUKUBA JOURNAL OF MATHEMATICS. V. 1- Dec. 1977-. 0387-4982. Periodical. JA. English. ir. Institute of Mathematics, University of Tsukuba, Ibaraki 300-31 Sakura-Mura Japan. **Ind/Abst** Math. Rev. LC QA1. DD 510.5. *Science Reports of the Tokoy Kyoiku Daigaku.*

THE TWO-YEAR COLLEGE MATHEMATICS JOURNAL CEASED. (TWO-YEAR COLLEGE MATHEMATICS JOURNAL). V. 1-14. 0049-4925. Periodical. US. English. The Mathematical Association of America, 1529 18th Street NW, Washington DC 20036. **Ind/Abst** Math. Rev., Educ. Index, Curr. Index J. Educ., Gen. Sci. Index. LC QA11.A1. DD 510.0711.

TZU HSUEH (PEKING, CHINA). (TZU HSUEH). VFOAT Zi Xue. Periodical. CC. Chinese. ir. 0.36. Chung-kuo Kuo Chi Shu Tien, PO Box 2820, Pei-ching China.

UKRAINIAN MATHEMATICAL JOURNAL. V. 19- Jan./Feb. 1967-. 0041-5995. Periodical. US. English (Russian). bm. $625.00 Domestic, $695.00 Foreign. Plenum Publishing, 227 West 17th Street, New York NY 10011. **Tel** (212)620-8000. Ed Yu A Mitropolskii. **Ind/Abst** Math. Rev., Electron. Commun. Abstr. J., ISMEC Bull., Pollut. Abstr. Indexes, Saf. Sci. Abstr. J., Contents Contemp. Math. J., Index Math. Pap., Zentralbl. Math. Ihre Grenzgeb. LC QA1. **CODEN** UKMJB6. This journal publishes articles and brief communications in various areas of pure and applied mathematics. Contains sections devoted to science information, criticism, bibliographies, reviews of problems of current interest.

UKRAINSKIJ MATEMATICSKIJ ZURNAL. (UKRAINSKII MATEMATICHESKII ZHURNAL). V. 1- 1949-. 0041-6053. Periodical. UR. Ukrainian. bm. **Tel** (301)881-5973. **Ind/Abst** Math. Rev., Int. Aerosp. Abstr. LC QA1.

THE UMAP JOURNAL. VFOAT U.M.A.P. Journal. VAT Undergraduate Mathematics Applications Project Journal. Vol. 1, No. 1 (Spring 1980)-. 0197-3622. Periodical. US. English. qt. $60.00 Domestic, $66.50 Foreign. Comap Inc, 271 Lincoln Street/Suite #4, Lexington MA 02173. **Tel** (617)863-1930. Ed Phillip Straffin and Paul Campbell. **Ind/Abst** Educ. Index. bk rev. adv acc. **Circ** 2,000. Math modules, articles and reviews on math applications and the contemporary use and application of math in our world today.

UNDERGRADUATE TEXTS IN MATHEMATICS. Began in 1974. 0172-6056. Monographic Series. US. English. ir. Springer Verlag-New York Inc, 175 5th Avenue, New York NY 10010. **Tel** (212)460-1584. Contains articles on analytic number theory, linear algebra, general topology, mathematical logic, applied abstract algebra and calculus.

UPORIADOCHENNYE MNOZHESTVA I RESHETKI. UR. Russian. 0.70 Each Issue. Izd-Vo Saratovskogo Universiteta, Universiteskaia 42, Saratov USSR. LC QA248.

USPEKHI MATEMATICHESKIKH NAUK. V. 1- 1936-. 0042-1316. UR. Russian. bm. $71.00. Victor Kamkin Inc (71002), 12224 Parklawn Drive, Rockville MD 20852. **Tel** (301)881-5973. **Ind/Abst** Math. Rev. LC QA1.

U.S.S.R. COMPUTATIONAL MATHEMATICS AND MATHEMATICAL PHYSICS. VAT Union of Soviet Socialist Republics Computational Mathematics and Mathematical Physics. 0041-5553. Periodical. UK. English (Russian). bm. Pergamon Press, 395 Sawmill River Road, Elmsford NY 10523. **Tel** (914)592-7700. **Ind/Abst** Math. Rev., Life Sci. Collect., Int. Aerosp. Abstr., Comput. Control Abstr., Electr. Electron. Abstr., Sci. Abstr. Sect. A. Phys. Abstr., Phys. Abstr., Comput. Rev., Appl. Mech. Rev. LC QA297. DD 517.6. **CODEN** CMMPA9. Available on microfilm from Microfilms International Marketing Co.

UTILITAS MATHEMATICA. V. 1- May 1972-. 0315-3681. Periodical. CN. English. sa. $29.00. Utilitas Mathematica Publishers Inc, University of Manitoba Box 7, University Center, Winnipeg Manitoba R3T 2N2 Canada. **Tel** (204)474-8313. Ed R G Stanton. **Ind/Abst** Math. Rev., Int. Aerosp. Abstr., Comput. Rev. A Canadian journal of applied mathematics, computer science, and statistics.

VARIOUS PUBLICATIONS SERIES - AARHUS UNIVERSITET. MATEMATISK INSTITUT. (VARIOUS PUBLICATIONS SERIES). Main/Corp Aarhus Universitet. Matematisk Institut. No. 1-. English. ir. Matematisk Institut Publ, Aarhus Universitet, DK-8000 Aarhus C Denmark. **Ind/Abst** Math. Rev.

VECSI AKADEMII NAVUK BSSR. SERYJA FIZIKA-MATEMATYCNYH NAVUK. (VESTSI AKADEMII NAUK BSSR. SERYIA FIZIKA-MATEMATYCHNYKH NAUK). Main/Corp Akademiia Navuk Belaruskai SSR. VFOAT Izvestiia Akademii Nauk, BSSR. 1965-. 0002-3574. Periodical. UR. Belorussian (White Russian or Russian). bm. **Ind/Abst** Math. Rev., Chem. Abstr., Met. Abstr., World Alum. Abstr. LC QC1. **CODEN** VBSFA5.

VESTNIK. LENINGRAD UNIVERSITY. MATHEMATICS. (VESTNIK, LENINGRAD UNIVERSITY. MATHEMATICS). V. 1- 1974-. 0146-924X. US. English (Russian). qt. $225.00. Allerton Press Inc, 150 Fifth Avenue, New York NY 10011. **Tel** (212)924-3950. **Ind/Abst** Math. Rev. LC QA1.

VESTNIK MOSKOVSKOGO UNIVERSITETA. (MOSCOW UNIVERSITY COMPUTATIONAL MATHEMATICS AND CYBERNETICS). VFOAT Computational Mathematics and Cybernetics. Began in 1979. 0278-6419. US. English (Russian). qt. Allerton Press, 150 Fifth Avenue, New York NY 10011. **Tel** (212)924-3950. **Ind/Abst** Eng. Index, Electr. Electron. Abstr., Comput. Control Abstr., Phys. Abstr., Sci. Abstr. Sect. A. Phys. Abstr., Eng. Index Annu., Eng. Index Mon., Eng. Index Bioeng. Abstr., Eng. Index Energy Abstr. LC QA1. DD 510.5. **CODEN** MUCTD4.

VESTNIK MOSKOVSKOGO UNIVERSITETA, SERIJA 1 : MATEMATIKA, MEKHANIKA. (VESTNIK MOSKOVSKOGO UNIVERSITETA SERIIA I, MATEMATIKA, MEKHANIKA). VFOAT Matematika, Mekhanika. 1960-. 0579-9368. Periodical. UR. Russian. bm. Victor Kamkin Inc, 12224 Parklawn Drive, Rockville MD 20852. **Tel** (301)881-5973. **Ind/Abst** Math. Rev., Int. Aerosp. Abstr., Comput. Control Abstr., Electr. Electron. Abstr., Sci. Abstr. Sect. A. Phys. Abstr., Energy Res. Abstr. **CODEN** VMMMA5. *Vestnik Moskovskogo Universiteta. Seriia Matematiki, Mekhaniki, Astronomii, Fiziki, Khimii.*

VESTNIK MOSKOVSKOGO UNIVERSITETA. SERIJA 15. VYCISLITELNAJA MATEMATIKA I KIBERNETIKA. (VESTNIK MOSKOVSKOGO UNIVERSITETA. SERIIA XV : VYCHISLITELNAIA MATEMATIKA I KIBERNETIKA). Main/Corp Moskovskii Gosudarstvennyi Universitet. VFOAT Vychislitelnaia Matematika i Kibernetika. 1977-. 0137-0782. Periodical. UR. Russian (summaries in English). qt. 0.05 Single Issue. IZD-Vo Moskovskogo Universiteta, 103009 Ul Gertsena 5/7, Moskva Russian SFSR. **Ind/Abst** Math. Rev., Comput. Control Abstr., Electr. Electron. Abstr., Sci. Abstr. Sect. A. Phys. Abstr. LC QA75.5. **CODEN** VMUKD8.

VISNIK LVIVSKOGO ORDENA LENINA DERZARNOGO UNIVERSITETU IM. IV. FRANKA. SERIJA MEHANIKO-MATEMATICNA. (VISNIK LVIVSKOGO ORDENA LENINA DERZARNOGO UNIVERSITETU. SERIIA MEKHANIKO-MATEMATICHNA). Main/Corp Lvov. Universitet. Vol. 1-. 0320-6572. Periodical. UR.

Medicine

Ukrainian (summaries in Russian). **Ind/Abst** Math. Rev. **LC** QA1.

VOPROSY PRIKLADNOI MATEMATIKI I MEKHANIKI. UR. Russian. 1.00 Single Issue. **LC** QA1.

VYCHISLITELNAIA I PRIKLADNAIA MATEMATIKA. Vol. 1-. 0321-4117. Monographic Series. UR. Russian.

WAVE MOTION (NORTH-HOLLAND PUBLISHING COMPANY). (WAVE MOTION). Vol. 1, No. 1 (Jan. 1979)-. 0165-2125. Periodical. English. bm. Elsevier Science Publishers, PO Box 211, 1000 AE Amsterdam The Netherlands. **Tel** (020)5803.911. **Ind/Abst** Math. Rev., Eng. Index Annu., Eng. Index Mon., Eng. Index, Eng. Index Bioeng. Abstr., Eng. Index Energy Abstr., Life Sci. Collect., Int. Aerosp. Abstr., Comput. Control Abstr., Electr. Electron. Abstr., Sci. Abstr. Sect. A. Phys. Abstr., Energy Res. Abstr., Phys. Abstr., Sci. Cit. Index, Abr. Ed., Appl. Mech. Rev. **LC** QA927. **DD** 531.1133. **CODEN** WAMOD9.

WIADOMOSCI MATEMATYCZNE. Ser. 2, V. 1-. Periodical. PL. Polish. sa. ARS Polona, Krakowskie Przedmiescie 7, 00-068 Warsaw Poland. **Ind/Abst** Math. Rev. *Prac Mathmatyczno-Fizycznych, Wiadomosci Matematycznych.*

WILEY SERIES IN PURE AND APPLIED OPTICS. 0277-2493. Monographic Series. US. English. ir. John Wiley & Sons Inc, 1 Wiley Drive, Somerset NJ 08873. **Ind/Abst** Math. Rev.

WORLD DIRECTORY OF HISTORIANS OF MATHEMATICS. See Yearbooks, Almanacs, Directories.

WORLD DIRECTORY OF MATHEMATICIANS. See Yearbooks, Almanacs, Directories.

WU-HAN TA HSUEH HSUEH PAO. TZU JAN KO HSUEH PAN. VFOAT Journal of Wuhan University. Natural Sciences Edition. Periodical. Chinese (abstracts in English). qt. 0.60. Chung-Kuo Kuo Chi Shu Tien, PO Box 2820, Pei-Ching China. **Ind/Abst** Math. Rev. **LC** Q4. **DD** 505.

YALE MATHEMATICAL MONOGRAPHS. Vol. 1-. 0084-3377. Monographic Series. US. English. ir. Yale University Press, 92A Yale Station, New Haven CT 06520. **Tel** (203)436-7583. **Ind/Abst** Math. Rev. **LC** UNC.

YEARBOOK - NATIONAL COUNCIL OF TEACHERS OF MATHEMATICS. See Yearbooks, Almanacs, Directories.

YEARBOOK OF ADULT AND CONTINUING EDUCATION. See Yearbooks, Almanacs, Directories.

YING YUNG SHU HSUEH. First published in June 1976-. Chinese. ir. **LC** QAL.

YING YUNG SHU HSUEH HO LI HSUEH. (APPLIED MATHEMATICS AND MECHANICS). VFOAT Ying Yung Shu Hsueh ho li Hsueh. Began in 1980. Periodical. HK. English. bm. $72.00. Techmodern Business Promotion Centre, 10/F Bank of China Building/Bank Street, Central Hong Kong HK. **Ind/Abst** Math. Rev. **LC** QA1. **DD** 620.0042.

YING YUNG SHU HSUEH HSUEH PAO. VFOAT Acta Mathematicae Applicatae Sinica. Began with Feb. 1978 issue. Periodical. CC. Chinese (abstracts in English). qt. $125.00. D Reidel Publishing Center, PO Box 17, 3300 AA Dordrecht Netherlands. **Tel** (31)78-334911. **Ed** Hua Luogeng. **Ind/Abst** Math. Rev., Comput. Control Abstr., Electr. Electron. Abstr., Sci. Abstr. Sect. A. Phys. Abstr. **LC** QA1. **DD** 510.5. **CODEN** YYSPDS. adv acc. **Circ** 500. Advance and development of applied mathematics in China. An international journal publishing original works in English.

YOKOHAMA MATHEMATICAL JOURNAL. (THE YOKOHAMA MATHEMATICAL JOURNAL). V. 1- May 1953-. 0044-0523. Periodical. JA. English. sa. $11.00. Japan Publishers Trading Company Ltd, PO Box 5030, Tokyo International, Tokyo 100-31 Japan. **Ind/Abst** Math. Rev., Chem. Abstr. **LC** QA1.

YUN CHOU HSUEH TSA CHIH. VFOAT Chinese Journal of Operations Research : OR. Vol. 1- (Oct. 1982)-. Periodical. CC. Chinese. sa. 0.53. Hsin Hua Shu Tien, Shang-Hai Fa Hsing So, Shanghai China. **Ind/Abst** Math. Rev. **LC** T57.6.A1. **DD** 001.42405.

ZAMP : ZEITSCHRIFT FUR ANGEWANDTE MATHEMATIK UND PHYSIK. VFOAT Z.A.M.P., Journal of Applied Mathematics and Physics, Journal de Mathematiques et de Physique Appliquees. Vol. 33, No. 1 (Jan. 1982)-. Periodical. English (French, German, or Italian). bm. $262.00. Birkhauser Boston Inc, 380 Green Street/PO Box 3005, Cambridge MA 02139. **Tel** (617)576-6638. *Zeitschrift fur Angewandte Mathematik und Physik.*

ZASTOSOWANIA MATEMATYKI. Vol. 1-. 0044-1899. PL. Polish (English and German with table of contents and summaries also in Russian and English). qt. ARS Polona, Krakowskie Przedmiescie 7, 00-068 Warsaw Poland. **Ind/Abst** Math. Rev., Int. Aerosp. Abstr., Appl. Mech. Rev. **LC** QA1. **CODEN** ZAMTAK.

ZDM. ZENTRALBLATT FUR DIDAKTIK DER MATHEMATIK. VFOAT Zentralblatt fur Didaktik der Mathematik. 1- June 1969-. GW. German. bm. $66.35. W E Saarbach GMBH, Postfach 101610, D5000 Koln 1 West Germany. **LC** QA11.

ZEITSCHRIFT FUR ANALYSIS UND IHRE ANWENDUNGEN. Vol. 1, No. 1. 0232-2064. Periodical. SZ. German (English and Russian). bm. $119.53. Kunst & Wissen Erich Bieber, Dufourstrasse 51, Ch-8008 Zurich Switzerland. **Tel** 011-41-1-69 44 20. **Ind/Abst** Math. Rev.

ZEITSCHRIFT FUR ANGEWANDTE MATHEMATIK UND MECHANIK. Vol. 1- Feb. 1921-. 0044-2267. Periodical. SZ. German. mo. $179.70. Kunst & Wissen Erich Bieber, Dufourstrasse 51, CH-8008 Zurich Switzerland. **Tel** (011)411694420. **Ind/Abst** Math. Rev., Eng. Index Annu., Eng. Index Mon., Eng. Index Bioeng. Abstr., Eng. Index Energy Abstr., GeoRef, Int. Aerosp. Abstr., Comput. Control Abstr., Electr. Electron. Abstr., Sci. Cit. Index, Abr. Ed., Phys. Abstr., Eng. Index. **LC** TA3. **DD** 510.5. **CODEN** ZAMMAX. (cum index).

ZEITSCHRIFT FUR MATHEMATISCHE LOGIK UND GRUNDLAGEN DER MATHEMATIK. Vol. 1-. 0044-3050. Periodical. SZ. German (some articles in English, French or Russian). bm. $85.89. Kunst & Wissen Erich Bieber, Dufourstrasse 51, CH-8008 Zurich Switzerland. **Tel** 011-41-1-69 44 20. **Ed** G Asser and K Schroter. **Ind/Abst** Math. Rev., Philos. Index, Comput. Control Abstr., Electr. Electron. Abstr., Sci. Abstr. Sect. A. Phys. Abstr., Phys. Abstr., Sci. Cit. Index, Abr. Ed., Comput. Rev. **LC** QA1. **DD** 510.5. **CODEN** ZMLGAQ. (cum index).

ZEITSCHRIFT FUR NATIONALOKONOMIE. SUPPLEMENTUM. 0084-537X. Monographic Series. German. ir. 258.-. Springer Verlag, Postfach 367, Moelkerbastei 5, A-1011 Vienna Austria. **Ed** D Bos. Specializes in mathematical economic theory. It also centers on microeconomic theory but also publishes papers on macroeconomic topics.

ZEITSCHRIFT FUR WAHRSCHEINLICHKEITSTHEORIE UND VERWANDTE GEBIETE. Vol. 1- 1962/63-. 0044-3719. Periodical. German (English and French). mo. Springer Verlag-New York Inc, 175 5th Avenue, New York NY 10010. **Tel** (212)460-1500. **Ind/Abst** Math. Rev., Int. Aerosp. Abstr., Math. Rev., Sci. Cit. Index, Abr. Ed. **LC** QA273. **NLM** W1 ZE685N.

ZENTRALBLATT FUR MATHEMATIK UND IHRE GRENZGEBIETE. See Indexes/Abstracts.

ZESZYTY NAUKOWE. SERIA 2. NAUKI MATEMATYCZNO PRZYRODNICZE. Main/Corp Odz, Poland. Uniwersytet. VFOAT Nauki Matematyczno Przyrodnicze. No. 1- 1955-. 0076-0366. Periodical. PL. Polish. ir. ARS Polona, Krakowskie Przedmiescie 7, 00-068 Warsaw Poland.

ZURNAL VYCISLITELNOJ MATEMATIKI I MATEMATICESKOJ FIZIKI. (ZHURNAL VYCHISLITELNOI MATEMATIKI I MATEMATICHESKOI FIZIKI). Vol. 1- 1961-. 0044-4669. Periodical. UR. Russian. bm. $83.00. Victor Kamkin Inc, 12224 Parklawn Drive, Rockville MD 20852. **Tel** (301)881-5973. **Ind/Abst** Math. Rev., Int. Aerosp. Abstr., Comput. Control Abstr., Electr. Electron. Abstr., Sci. Abstr. Sect. A. Phys. Abstr., Phys. Abstr. **LC** QA297. **CODEN** ZVMFAN. (cum index).

MEDICINE

483 VALIDATION MONITOR FOR STERILE, NON-STERILE AND MEDICAL DEVICES. Began with Vol. 2nd-1 (Jan. 15, 1981). Periodical. US. English. bw. Bureau of Pharmaceutical Research Inc, PO Box 068, Pinellas Park FL 33565. *483 Validation Monitor for Sterile Products, 483 Validation Monitor for Non-Sterile Products; 483 Validation Monitor for Medical Devices.*

A. C. P. D. Q. BULLETIN. See Dentistry.

AAB NEWS BRIEFS. VFOAT News Briefs. VAT American Association of Blood Banks News Briefs. 8756-6095. Periodical. US. English. mo. Free to members, $60.00 Physicians, $40.00 Others. American Association of Blood Banks, 1117 North 19th Street Suite 600, Arlington VA 22209. **Tel** (703)528-8200. **Ed** Jackie Campbell. **DD** 616. adv acc. **Circ** 10,000. Blood banking and transfusion therapy news and information regarding technical and administrative aspects, government regulation, and continuing education as well as research.

AAMC CURRICULUM DIRECTORY. See Yearbooks, Almanacs, Directories.

AAMC DIRECTORY OF AMERICAN MEDICAL EDUCATION. See Yearbooks, Almanacs, Directories.

AAMI MEMBERSHIP DIRECTORY. See Yearbooks, Almanacs, Directories.

AAMI NEWS. (AAMI NEWS : THE OFFICIAL NEWSLETTER OF THE ASSOCIATION FOR THE ADVANCEMENT OF MEDICAL INSTRUMENTATION). VAT Association for the Advancement of Medical Instrumentation News. 0739-0270. Periodical. US. English. bm. $70.00. Association for the Advancement of Medical Instrumentation, 1901 North Fort Meyer Drive/Suite 602, Arlington VA 22209.

AAMI TECHNOLOGY ASSESSMENT REPORT. No. 1-81-. Monographic Series. US. English. sa. **NLM** W1.

AAMT NEWSLETTER. Main/Corp American Association for Medical Transcription. VAT American Association for Medical Transcription Newsletter. 1978. 0279-7917. Periodical. US. English. bm. $20.00. American Association for Medical Transcription, PO Box 634, Modesta CA 95353. **Tel** (209)57600883. adv acc. **Circ** 10,000. (ctrl). News pertinent to the profession of medical transcription, listings of coming events, job openings.

ABMAC BYLINES. VAT American Bureau for Medical Advancement in China Bylines. 8756-2138. Periodical. US. English. mo. Abmac, 2 East 103rd Street, New York NY 10029. **DD** 610.

ABMS COMPENDIUM OF CERTIFIED MEDICAL SPECIALTIES. See Biographies.

ABMS DIRECTORY OF CERTIFIED ALLERGY/IMMUNOLOGY PHYSICIANS. See Yearbooks, Almanacs, Directories.

ABMS DIRECTORY OF CERTIFIED ANESTHESIOLOGISTS. See Yearbooks, Almanacs, Directories.

ABMS DIRECTORY OF CERTIFIED EMERGENCY PHYSICIANS. See Yearbooks, Almanacs, Directories.

ABMS DIRECTORY OF CERTIFIED FAMILY PRACTITIONERS. See Yearbooks, Almanacs, Directories.

ABMS DIRECTORY OF CERTIFIED NUCLEAR MEDICINE SPECIALISTS. See Yearbooks, Almanacs, Directories.

ABMS DIRECTORY OF CERTIFIED PREVENTIVE MEDICINE PHYSICIANS. See Yearbooks, Almanacs, Directories.

ABRIDGED INDEX MEDICUS. See Indexes/Abstracts.

ABSTRACTS OF BULGARIAN SCIENTIFIC MEDICAL LITERATURE. See Indexes/Abstracts.

Medicine

ABSTRACTS OF CONTRIBUTED PAPERS - MEDICAL CARE SECTION. See Indexes/Abstracts.

ABSTRACTS OF UPPSALA DISSERTATIONS FROM THE FACULTY OF MEDICINE. See Indexes/Abstracts.

ABSTRACTS ON WORLD MEDICINE. See Indexes/Abstracts.

THE ACADEMY BOOKMAN. See Bibliographies.

ACMC FORUM. Main/Corp Association of Canadian Medical Colleges. VFOAT AFMC Forum. V. 7, No. 2- Mar./Apr. 1974-. 0317-5006. Periodical. CN. English (includes some text in French). ir. Association of Canadian Medical Colleges, 151 Slater Street, Ottawa Ontario K1P 0S9 Canada. Tel (613)237-0070. Ed De G Vaillancourt. NLM W1 A1136H. bk rev. adv acc. Circ 1,200. Forum deals mainly with medical education in Canada, major activities of the 16 medical schools, and any other news of interest to medical educators. ACMC Newsletter.

ACTA ACADEMIAE MEDICINAE WUHAN. VAT Wuhan Yixueyuan Xuebao. Vol. 1, No. 1-. 0253-3316. Periodical. English (articles also in German). qt. $42.80. Springer Verlag-New York Inc, 175 5th Avenue, New York NY 10010. Tel (212)477-8200. Ind/Abst Excerpta Med., Index Med. NLM W1 AC7394.

ACTA ANAESTHESIOLOGICA BELGICA. Vol. 1-. 0001-5164. Periodical. BE. French (articles in English or Dutch). qt. 2000. Association Society Scientifique Medical Beld, 43 rue des Champs Elysees, B 1050 Brussels Belgium. Tel 091-225741. Ed G Rolly. Ind/Abst Excerpta Med., Index Med., Biol. Abstr., Chem. Abstr., Hospit. Lit. Index. NLM W1 AC749. CODEN AABEAJ. bk rev. adv acc. Circ 800. All aspects related to anesthesiology, (anesthesia, pain treatment, intensive care, emergency medicine, etc.), basic research and clinical practice.

ACTA ANAESTHESIOLOGICA ITALICA. V. 23- Jan./Feb. 1972-. 0374-4965. Periodical. English (articles in French, German, or Italian, summaries also in English). bm. 35.64. La Garangola, Via Montona 4, 35100 Padova Italy. Tel 049/20667. Ind/Abst Excerpta Med., Biol. Abstr., Chem. Abstr. NLM W1 AC751C. CODEN AANIBO. bk rev. adv acc. Circ 2,000.

ACTA BIO-MEDICA DE L'ATENEO PARMENSE. (ACTA BIO-MEDICA DE L'ATENEO PARMENSE : ORGANO DELLA SOCIETA DI MEDICINA E SCIENZE NATURALI DI PARMA). Vol. 52, N. 1-. 0392-4203. Periodical. IT. Italian. bm. $11.88. L Ateneo Parmense, Ospedale Maggiroe, Parma Italy. Ind/Abst Excerpta Med., Index Med., Biol. Abstr., Chem. Abstr. NLM W1 AC7631P. CODEN ABPADJ. Ateneo Parmense. Acta Bio-Medica, 0004-6351.

ACTA BIOLOGICA ET MEDICA GERMANICA. See Biology.

ACTA CLINICA BELGICA. V. 1- Jan./Feb. 1946-. 0001-5512. BE. Dutch (articles in French and Flemish). bm. $45.00. Academisch Zeikenhuis, Avenue Emmanuel Mounier 52, B-1200 Brussels Belgium. Ind/Abst Life Sci. Collect., Pestdoc, Ringdoc, Vetdoc, Excerpta Med., Biol. Abstr., Chem. Abstr., Nuci. Sci. Abstr., Index Med., Sci. Cit. Index, Abr. Ed., Hospit. Lit. Index. NLM W1 AC7835. CODEN ACCBAT. Bulletins et Comptes Rendus de la Societe Clinique dans Hopitaux de Bruxelles.

ACTA JUTLANDICA. MEDICINE SERIES. Series/Titl Acta Jutlandica. VFOAT Medicine Series. 21-. Monographic Series. English. ir. NLM W1. Acta Jutlandica. Medicinsk Serie.

ACTA LEIDENSIA. (ACTA LEIDENSIA. MEDEDELINGEN UIT HET INSTITUUT VOOR TROPISCHE GENEESKUNDE TE LEIDEN). VFOAT Mededelingen Uit Het Instituut Voor Tropische Geneeskunde te Leiden. V. 1- 1926-. 0065-1362. Monographic Series. NE. Dutch (English, French and German). Universitaire Pers Leiden, Pieterskerkhof 38, The Netherlands. Ind/Abst Excerpta Med., Bibliogr. Agric., Biol. Abstr., Chem. Abstr., Index Med. LC RC960. NLM W1 AC816. CODEN ALSMAZ.

ACTA MEDICA. 0001-5989. HU. English (articles in French, German or Russian, with summaries in Russian). qt. $44.00. Akademiai Kiado, POB 24, 1363 Budapest Hungary. Tel 111-010. Ed E Stark. Ind/Abst Index Med. Index published separately - free - upon request. bk rev. adv acc. Circ 700. (ctrl). Publishes original research papers in the field of clinial experimental medicine covering primarily fundamental and applied pathophysiology. Hungarica Acta Medica.

ACTA MEDICA. V. 1- Jan./Mar. 1965-. 0001-5997. Periodical. MX. Spanish. ir. Direct Consejo Editoral, Apartado Postal 42-200, Mexico 4 DF Mexico. Ind/Abst Chem. Abstr. NLM W1 AC824J. CODEN ACMDBI.

ACTA MEDICA COSTARRICENSE. 0001-6012. Periodical. CR. Spanish. ir $3.00. Acta Medica Costarricense, Apartado 4054, San Jose Costa Rica C/A. Ind/Abst Life Sci. Collect., Excerpta Med., Biol. Abstr., Chem. Abstr. NLM W1 AC8333. CODEN ATCTAW.

ACTA MEDICA ET BIOLOGICA. V. 1- Mar. 1953-. 0567-7734. Periodical. JA. Contributions in English or German. qt. Japan Publishers Trading Co Ltd, PO Box 5030 Tokyo International, Tokyo 100-31 Japan. Ind/Abst Life Sci. Collect., Excerpta Med., Biol. Abstr., Chem. Abstr., Nuci. Sci. Abstr., Sel. Water Resour. Abstr. NLM W1 AC835. CODEN AMBNAS.

ACTA MEDICA HUNGARICA. VFOAT Acta Medica. Vol. 40, No. 1-. 0236-5286. Periodical. English. ir. Ind/Abst Index Med., Life Sci. Collect., Excerpta Med. NLM W1 AC839J. Acta Medica Academiae Scientiarum Hungaricae, 0001-5989.

ACTA MEDICA IRANICA. 0044-6025. Periodical. IR. English (articles in French or English with summaries in one or both of these languages). ir. $15.00. University of Teheran, Faculty of Medicine, Teheran Iran. Ind/Abst Biol. Abstr., Chem. Abstr., Nuci. Sci. Abstr., Index Med. NLM W1 AC84D. CODEN AMEIAS.

ACTA MEDICA IUGOSLAVICA. 1- 1947-. 0375-8338. Periodical. YU. English (articles in Croatian, French, Serbian with summaries in French and German). ir. Mladost Export Import, PO Box 1028, Ilica 30, 41000 Zagreb Yugoslavia. Ind/Abst Excerpta Med., Life Sci. Collect., Biol. Abstr., Chem. Abstr., Index Med., Nuci. Sci. Abstr. NLM W1 AC842. CODEN AMIUAG.

ACTA MEDICA PHILIPPINA. V. 1-19, 1939-1963. 0001-6071. Periodical. PH. English. sa. University of the Philippines, College of Medicine and Institute of Hygiene, 547 Herran Street, Manila Philippines. Ind/Abst Excerpta Med. NLM W1 AC8493. Proceedings of the College of Medicine, University of the Philippines.

ACTA MEDICA POLONA. V. 1- 1960-. 0001-608X. Periodical. PL. English (text also in French). sa. ARS Polona, Krakowskie Przedmiescie 7, 00-068 Warsaw Poland. Ind/Abst Life Sci. Collect., Excerpta Med., Index Med., Biol. Abstr., Chem. Abstr., Hospit. Lit. Index. NLM W1 AC851. CODEN AMDPAA. Annals of the Medical Section of the Polish Academy of Sciences.

ACTA MEDICA ROMANA. (ACTA MEDICA ROMANA : ANNALI DELLA FACOLTA DI MEDICINE E CHIRURGIA). Yearly V. 1, No. 1(July- Dec. 1963)-. 0001-6098. Periodical. IT. Italian. qt. Soc Edit Vita e Pensiero, Largo Agostino Gemelli 1, 20102 Milano Italy. Ind/Abst Biol. Abstr., Chem. Abstr., Excerpta Med. NLM W1 AC853. CODEN AMROBA.

ACTA MEDICA SCANDINAVICA. V. 52- 1919-. 0001-6101. Periodical. SW. English (articles in English, French and German). mo. $113.00. Almqvist & Wiksell, PO Box 62, S-101 20 Stockholm Sweden. Tel Telex 85413160. Ind/Abst Life Sci. Collect., Pestdoc, Ringdoc, Vetdoc, Excerpta Med., CIS Abstr., Biol. Abstr., Chem. Abstr., Nuci. Sci. Abstr., Index Med., Energy Res. Abstr., Sci. Cit. Index, Abr. Ed., Hospit. Lit. Index. NLM W1 AC8551. CODEN AMSVAZ. (cum index). Nordiskt Medicinskt Arkiv. Avd. 2. Arkiv Foer Inre Medicin, 0365-3250.

ACTA MEDICAE HISTORIAE PATAVINA. V. 1- 1954/55-. 0065-1389. IT. Italian. an. $4.76. Inst Storia Medicina Universit, Via G Falloppia 50, 35100 Padova Italy.

ACTA MEDICOTECHNICA. VFOAT AM. Acta Medicotechnica. Yearly V. 27, No. 5- Oct. 1979-. 0172-6099. Periodical. GW. articles in English or German. sm. $38.15. Fischer & Pflaum Verlag GMBH, Postfach 10 57 67, 6900 Heidelberg 1 West Germany. Ind/Abst Excerpta Med., Energy Res. Abstr., Comput. Control Abstr., Electr. Electron. Abstr., Sci. Abstr. Sect. A. Phys. Abstr. NLM W1 AC8624. Technik in der Medizin, Medizinal-Markt, 0025-8423.

ACTA MORPHOLOGICA. 1-. 0204-9139. Periodical. English (Russian, German, French). qt. Ind/Abst Excerpta Med., Chem. Abstr. LC QH351. NLM W1 AC8637. CODEN ACMODJ. Izvestiia, 0068-3817.

ACTA MORPHOLOGICA ACADEMIAE SCIENTIARUM HUNGARICAE CEASED. VFOAT Acta Morphologica. Began in 1951. Ceased with V. 30, No. 3-4. 0001-6217. Periodical. HU. English (with summaries in German and Russian). qt. Ind/Abst Life Sci. Collect., Excerpta Med., Biol. Abstr., Chem. Abstr. NLM W1. CODEN AMSHAR. Index published separately - free - automatically sent.

ACTA MORPHOLOGICA HUNGARICA. See Biology - Physiology.

ACTA PATHOLOGICA ET MICROBIOLOGICA SCANDINAVICA. SECTION C. IMMUNOLOGY CEASED. (ACTA PATHOLOGICA ET MICROBIOLOGICA SCANDINAVICA. SECTION C : IMMUNOLOGY). V. 83C-89C. 0304-1328. Periodical. UK. chiefly in English. bm $51.80. Munksgaard Ltd, 35 Norre Sogade, DK 1370 K Copenhagen Denmark. Ind/Abst Excerpta Med., Life Sci. Collect. NLM W1 AC9111H. Acta Pathologica et Microbiologica Scandinavica. Section B : Microbiology and Immunology, 0365-5571.

ACTA PATHOLOGICA, MICROBIOLOGICA ET IMMUNOLOGICA SCANDINAVICA. SECTION C. IMMUNOLOGY. (ACTA PATHOLOGICA, MICROBIOLOGICA ET IMMUNOLOGICA SCANDINAVICA. SECTION C, IMMUNOLOGY). VFOAT Immunology. Vol. 90, No. 1 (Feb. 1982)-. 0108-0202. Periodical. bm. 1,834.00 Domestic, $204.00 US. Munksgaard International Publishers Limited, 35 Norre Sogade, DK-1370 Copenhagen K Denmark. Tel 45 12 70 30. Ed Jorgen Rygaard. Ind/Abst Excerpta Med., Biol. Abstr., Chem. Abstr., Energy Res. Abstr., Index Med., Life Sci. Collect., Pestdoc, Ringdoc, Vetdoc. NLM W1 AC913F. CODEN APMIDO. Circ 1,200. Acta Pathologica et Microbiologica Scandinavica. Section C, Immunology, 0304-1328.

ACTA PATHOLOGICA, MICROBIOLOGICA, ET IMMUNOLOGICA SCANDINAVICA. SUPPLEMENT. See Medicine - Pathology.

ACTA STOMATOLOGICA BELGICA. Vol. 57- 1960-. 0001-7000. Periodical. BE. Text in French or Dutch, summaries in Dutch, English or German. qt $33.59. Association for the Society of Scientifique Medica Belgica, 43 rue des Champs Elysees, B-1050 Brussels Belgium. Ind/Abst Life Sci. Collect., Excerpta Med., Index Med., Biol. Abstr., Nuci. Sci. Abstr. NLM W1 AC949L. CODEN ASBEBA. Index published separately - free - automatically sent. Revue Belge de Stomatologie.

ACTA STOMATOLOGICA CROATICA. V. 1- 1966-. 0001-7019. Periodical. YU. Serbo-Croatian -R. qt. $32.40. Acta Stomatologica Croatica, Ilica 30-1 Mladost Export Import, Zagreb 41000 Yugoslavia. Ind/Abst Index Dent. Lit. NLM W1 AC949N.

ACTA TROPICA. V. 1-. 0001-706X. Periodical. SZ. English (text in German; summaries in English and French). qt. 160.00. Schwabe & Company, Steinentorstrasse 13, CH-4000 Basel 10 Switzerland. Tel (061)235523. Ed R Geigy, R Gigon, F Speiser, and R Tschudi. Ind/Abst Life Sci. Collect., Pestdoc, Ringdoc, Vetdoc, Excerpta Med., Bibliogr. Agric., Biol. Abstr., Chem. Abstr., Index Med., Sci. Cit. Index, Abr. Ed. LC Q3. DD 505. NLM W1 AC951. CODEN ACTRAQ. bk rev. adv acc. International journal of biomedical sciences which gives attention to every aspect of this field relevant to human health, including veterinary medicine and biology in the tropics.

ACTA TROPICA. SUPPLEMENTUM CEASED. 1-11. 0365-1541. Monographic Series. English (text in French, or German). ir. LC UNC. NLM W1 AC9511.

ACTA UNIVERSITATIS CAROLINAE. MEDICA CEASED. V. 1- 1954-. 0001-7116. Periodical. CS. Czech (summaries in English, German, or Russian). ir. Artia, Ve-Smeckach 30, Praha 1 Czechoslovakia. Ind/Abst Excerpta Med., Index Med., CIS Abstr., Biol. Abstr., Chem. Abstr. NLM W1 AC954K. CODEN AUNCA9. Index published separately - free - automatically sent. Acta Universitatis Carolinae.

Medicine

ACTA UNIVERSITATIS CAROLINAE. MEDICA. MONOGRAPHIA. 10- 1961-. 0567-8250. Monographic Series. CS. Czech (text in English, or German with summaries in Russian, English or Czech). Artia, VE-Smeckach 30, Praha 1 Czechoslovakia. **Ind/Abst** Index Med., Biol. Abstr. **NLM** W1 AC954M. **CODEN** AUCMBJ.

ACTA UNIVERSITATIS OULUENSIS. SER. D, MEDICA. No. 1- 1972-. Monographic Series. articles in English or Finnish. ir. **Ind/Abst** Psychol. Abstr. **NLM** W1 AC954NM.

ACTAS DE LA FACULTAD DE MEDICINA. VFOAT Actas de la Facultad de Medicina de la Universidad Autonoma de Guadalajara. Series 5, V. 1, No. 1, (Jan./April/80)-. Periodical. Spanish. ty. $150.00. **NLM** W1 AC959E.

ACTUALITE MEDICALE. (L'ACTUALITE MEDICALE). Vol. 1, No. 1 (Nov. 4, 1980)-. 0229-9429. Periodical. CN. French. bw. $30.00. L'Actualite Medicale Inc, Bureau 324/50 Place Cremazie, Montreal Quebec H2P 2S9 Canada. **DD** 610.9714.

ACUPUNCTURE. V. 1- 1800/1972-. 0092-5047. US. English. National Acupuncture Association, 1033 Gayley Avenue Suite 200, Los Angeles CA 90024. **LC** Z6665.A45. **DD** 016.615892. **NLM** ZWB 369 A189.

ACUPUNCTURE & ELECTRO-THERAPEUTICS RESEARCH. VAT Acupuncture and Electro-Therapeutics Research. V. 1-. 0360-1293. Periodical. UK. English. qt. Pergamon Press, 395 Sawmill River Road, Elmsford NY 10523. **Ind/Abst** Life Sci. Collect., Cumul. Index Nurs. Allied Health Lit., Excerpta Med., Index Med., Biol. Abstr., Chem. Abstr., Psychol. Abstr. **LC** RM184. **DD** 615.892. **NLM** W1 AC999K. **CODEN** AERDS.

THE ACUPUNCTURE LETTER. V. 1- Jan. 1974-. 0163-1314. Periodical. US. English. mo. $20.00 Residents, Interns & Students, $30.00 Others. Acupuncture Letter, 2567 Washington Avenue, Oceanside NY 11572. **NLM** W1 AC999M.

ACUPUNCTURE RESEARCH QUARTERLY. VFOAT Chen Chiu Yen Chiu Chi k'An. V. 1- 1977-. Periodical. CH. English. ir. Acupuncture Research Quarterly, PO Box 84-223, Taipei Taiwan.

ACUPUNCTURE TODAY. V. 1- Aug. 1977-. 0706-9812. Periodical. CN. English. bm. Free to members, $12. Others. Acupuncture Foundation of Canada, Suite 503 10 Mary Street, Toronto Ontario M4Y 1P9 Canada. **DD** 615.89205.

ACUTE CARE MEDICINE. Began with: Vol. 1, No. 1 (Jan. 1984). 0742-1567. Periodical. US. English. mo. $35.00 US, $40.00 Canada. Acute Care Medicine Pub, 149 Fifth Avenue, New York NY 10010. **DD** 610. **NLM** W1.

ADLER MUSEUM BULLETIN. See Museums.

ADOLESCENT MEDICINE. V. 1- 1976-. 0160-8231. Periodical. US. English. Spectrum Publications, 175-20 Wexford Terrace, Jamaica NY 11432. Ed R I Lopez. **NLM** W1 AD37HC.

ADRENAL MEDULLA. (THE ADRENAL MEDULLA). Series/Titl Annual Research Reviews. V. 1- 1979-. 0704-4917. CN. English. ir. Eden Press, 4626 St Catherine Street West, Montreal Quebec H3Z 1S3 Canada. Ed S W Carmichael. **DD** 612.45. **NLM** W1 AD388.

ADVANCES FOR MEDICINE. V.1-. US. English. qt. Hewlett-Packard Company, 175 Wyman Street, Waltham MA 02154.

ADVANCES IN BIOMATERIALS. Vol. 1-. 0272-3840. Monographic Series. UK. English. ir. John Wiley & Sons Inc, 605 3rd Avenue, New York NY 10158. Ed George D Winter and Jenny Upton. **Ind/Abst** Chem. Abstr. **NLM** W3 AD23. **CODEN** ABIODQ.

ADVANCES IN BIOMEDICAL ENGINEERING. V. 1- 1971-. 0300-161X. US. English. an. Academic Press, 4805 Sand Lake Road, Orlando FL 32819. **Ind/Abst** Comput. Control Abstr., Electr. Electron. Abstr., Sci. Abstr. Sect. A. Phys. Abstr., Energy Res. Abstr. **LC** R856.A1. **DD** 610.28. **NLM** W1 AD448. **CODEN** ABEGBE.

ADVANCES IN DISEASE PREVENTION. Vol. 1-. 0277-0687. Periodical. US. English. an. Springer Publishing Company, 200 Park Avenue South, New York NY 10003. Ed Charles B Arnold. **NLM** W1 AD548H.

ADVANCES IN EXPERIMENTAL MEDICINE AND BIOLOGY. VFOAT Experimental Medicine and Biology. V. 1-. 0065-2598. Monographic Series. US. English. ir. Plenum Press, c/o H Feldman, 233 Spring Street, New York NY 10013. **Tel** (212)620-8000. **Ind/Abst** Life Sci. Collect., Index Med., Biol. Abstr., Chem. Abstr., Energy Res. Abstr., Sci. Cit. Index, Abr. Ed., Hospit. Lit. Index. **LC** UNC. **NLM** W1 AD559. **CODEN** AEMBAP.

ADVANCES IN IMMUNOLOGY. V. 1- 1961-. 0065-2776. US. English. an. Academic Press, 4805 Sand Lake Road, Orlando FL 32819. Ed W H Taliferro and J H Humphrey. **Ind/Abst** Life Sci. Collect., Index Med., Biol. Abstr., Chem. Abstr., Energy Res. Abstr. **LC** QR180. **DD** 615.3705. **NLM** W1 AD647. **CODEN** ADIMAV.

ADVANCES IN INFLAMMATION RESEARCH. V. 1-. 0197-8322. Monographic Series. US. English. Raven Press, 1140 Avenue of the Americas, New York NY 10036. **Tel** (212)575-0335. Ed G Weissmann, B Samuelsson and R Paoletti. **Ind/Abst** Life Sci. Collect., Biol. Abstr., Chem. Abstr. **NLM** W1 AD648. **CODEN** ADIRDF.

ADVANCES IN MEDICAL SOCIAL SCIENCE. See Social Sciences (General).

ADVANCES IN PEDODONTICS. V. 1- 1970-. US. English. an. **NLM** ZWU 480 A244.

ADVANCES IN SHOCK RESEARCH. V. 1- 1979-. 0195-878X. Periodical. US. English. sa. Alan R Liss Inc, 150 Fifth Avenue, New York NY 10011. **Ind/Abst** Index Med., Chem. Abstr. **NLM** W3 AD243M. **CODEN** ADSRDV.

ADVANCES IN THE STUDY OF BIRTH DEFECTS. V. 1-. 0196-4992. Monographic Series. US. English. ir. Alan R Liss Inc, 41 East 11th Street, New York NY 10003. **Tel** (212)475-7700. Ed T V N Persaud and M P Persaud. **Ind/Abst** Chem. Abstr. **NLM** W1 AD88H. **CODEN** ASBDD9. A scholarly book series covering all topics in the area of birth defects.

ADVANCES IN VIRUS RESEARCH. See Biology - Microbiology.

AEGEAN MEDICAL JOURNAL. V. 1- 1972-. 0304-4939. Periodical. English (summaries in Turkish). bm. Ege Universitesi, School of Medicine, Bornova Izmir Turkey. **Ind/Abst** Excerpta Med. **NLM** W1 AE14.

AEROSPACE MEDICINE AND BIOLOGY. See Aeronautics, Astronautics.

AFRICA HEALTH. V. 1- Oct. 1978-. 0141-9536. Periodical. UK. English. bm. $50.00. Bryan Pearson, 9 Heneage Street, London E1 England. **Tel** 44 (1) 377-9262. Ed Bryan Pearson. **NLM** W1 AF513. bk rev. adv acc. **Circ** 5,500. (ctrl). An update on health and medicine for doctors in Africa. Covers a broad range of tropical medicine as well as health education and medico/political issues.

AFRICAN JOURNAL OF CLINICAL AND EXPERIMENTAL IMMUNOLOGY. V. 1- Jan. 1980-. 0253-052X. Periodical. English. qt. Editor-in-Chief Fac Med UOFS, PO Box 339, G1 ZA-9300 Bloemfontein Republic of South Africa. **Ind/Abst** Life Sci. Collect., Biol. Abstr., Chem. Abstr. **NLM** W1 AF518. **CODEN** AJCIDY.

AFRICAN JOURNAL OF MEDICINE AND MEDICAL SCIENCES. V. 5- Mar. 1976-. 0309-3913. Periodical. UK. articles in English or French with summaries in both languages. qt. $97.50. Blackwell Scientific Publishing Co, PO Box 88, Osney Mead, Oxford OX9 0EL England. Ed L A Salako. **Ind/Abst** Life Sci. Collect., Excerpta Med., Index Med., Biol. Abstr. **NLM** W1 AF524. **CODEN** AJMSDC. **Circ** 473. All aspects of medicine, treatment, education, tribal lores, etc. in Nigeria. African Journal of Medical Sciences, 0002-0028.

AFRIQUE MEDICALE. V. 1- (No. 1-). 0002-0516. Periodical. French. ir. 200. Africa, 10 rue A Karim Bourgi BP 1826, Dakar Senegal. **Tel** 21 08 80 22 07 76. Ed Joel Decupper. **NLM** W1 AF628. bk rev. adv acc.

AISPICH CHAKWAN. (AISPICH CHAKWAN : THE INFORMATION BULLETIN OF THE CONSEIL CRI DE LA SANTE ET DES SERVICES SOCIAUX DE LA BAIE JAMES). VFOAT Information Bulletin of the Conseil Cri de la Sante et des Services Sociaux de la Baie James, The Information Bulletin of the Cree Board of Health and Social Services of James Bay. Vol. 1, No. 1 (May 1983)-. 0824-4715. Periodical. CN. English. bm. Cree Board of Health and Social Services of James Bay, Documentation Centre, Chisasibi Quebec J0M 1E0 Canada. **Tel** (819)855-2844. Ed Martine Nadia Halle. **DD** 361.97141. **Circ** 2,000. (ctrl). Issues which are of interest to the native population, special programmes of activities performed by the Cree Board of Health and Social Services of James Bay for the population.

AKTUALNYE PROBLEMY REVMATOLOGII. Series/Titl Trudy Volgogradskogo Gosudarstvennogo Meditsinskogo Instituta. V. 4- 1972-. UR. Russian. **NLM** W1 AK989DD. Problemy Revmatologii.

AKTUELLE PROBLEME DER INTENSIVMEDIZIN (LEIPZIG, GERMANY). (AKTUELLE PROBLEME DER INTENSIVMEDIZIN). V. 1- German. an. Ed L Engelmann, D Schneider, H Wegner. **NLM** W1.

AKTUELLE RHEUMATOLOGIE. V. 1- Sept. 1976-. 0341-051X. Periodical. German. bm. Thieme-Stratton Inc, 381 Park Avenue South, New York NY 10016. **Tel** (212)683-5088. **Ind/Abst** Life Sci. Collect., Excerpta Med., Curr. Contents, Sci. Cit. Index, Abr. Ed., Energy Res. Abstr. **NLM** W1 AK996.

AKTUELLE TRAUMATOLOGIE. V. 4- Feb. 1974-. 0044-6173. Periodical. in German. bm. Thieme-Stratton Inc, 381 Park Avenue, New York NY 10016. **Tel** (212)683-5088. **Ind/Abst** Life Sci. Collect., Excerpta Med., Index Med. **NLM** W1 AK996J. Actuelle Traumatologie.

AL-FAYSAL AL-TIBBIYAH. VFOAT Alfaisal Medical Journal. Periodical. Arabic (English). bm. 50. Majallat Al-Faysal Al-Tibbiyah, S B 2114, Al-Dammam Saudia Arabia. **LC** R97.7.A7.

AL-JAMIYAH AL-ILMIYAH AL-TULLABIYAH-TIBB AL-AZHAR. V. 1, No. 1, (September 1979)-. Periodical. Arabic (English). ty. Mustashfa Al-Husayn Al-Jamii Al-Markaz Al-Dawli Lil-Dirasat Al-Islamiyah, S B 1894, Al-Qahirah United Arab Emirates. **LC** R97.7.A7. **DD** 610.5.

AL-MAGALLA AL-TIBBIYYA AL-URDUNIYYA. VFOAT Jordon Medical Journal. 0446-9283. Periodical. Multilingual. ir. **Ind/Abst** Excerpta Med., Chem. Abstr. **CODEN** JOMJAE.

AL-MAGHRIB AL-TIBBI. VFOAT Maroc Medical. V. 1- Oct. 1978-. 0025-388X. Periodical. French. ir. Maroc Medical Hopital, Avicenne, Rabat Morocco. **Ind/Abst** Excerpta Med., Index Med. **NLM** W1 MA66B. Maroc Medical, 0025-388X.

AL-MAJALLAH AL-TIBBIYAH AL-SAUDIYAH. Periodical. Arabic. bm. 3 Single Issue. Wizarat Al-Sihhah Al-Alaqat Al-Ammah, PO Box 10062, Al-Riyad Saudi Arabia. **LC** R97.7.A7.

THE ALABAMA JOURNAL OF MEDICAL SCIENCES. V. 1- Jan. 1964-. 0002-4252. Periodical. US. English. qt. $15.00. Alabama Journal of Medical Science, Box 310 University Station, Birmingham AL 35294. **Tel** (205)934-4807. Ed Myra Crawford. **Ind/Abst** Life Sci. Collect., Cumul. Index Nurs. Allied Health Lit., Index Med., Biol. Abstr., Chem. Abstr., Energy Res. Abstr., Sci. Cit. Index, Abr. Ed., Am. Hist. Life, Hist. Abstr., Hospit. Lit. Index, Hist. Abstr., Part A, Mod. Hist. Abstr., Hist. Abst., Part B, Twent. Century Abstr. **NLM** W1 AL152C. **CODEN** AJOMAZ. bk rev. adv acc. **Circ** 8,000. (ctrl). Geared to the practicing physician.

ALABAMA MEDICAID. See Insurance.

ALABAMA MEDICINE. (ALABAMA MEDICINE : JOURNAL OF THE MEDICAL ASSOCIATION OF THE STATE OF ALABAMA). Vol. 53, No. 1 (July 1983)-. 0738-4947. Periodical. US. English. mo. $15.00 Member, $30.00 Non-Member. Medical Association of the State of Alabama, 19 South Jackson Street, Montgomery AL 36197-4201. **Ind/Abst** Index Med., Cumul. Index Nurs. Allied Health Lit., Excerpta Med., Hospit. Lit. Index. **NLM** W1 AL55T. Journal of the Medical Association of the State of Alabama, 0025-7044.

ALASKA MEDICINE. V. 1- Mar. 1959-. 0002-4538. Periodical. US. English. bm. $40.00. Alaska State Medical Association, 4107 Laurel Street 1, c/o M MacDermaid, Anchorage AK 99508. **Tel** (907)562-2662. Ed William Bowers. **Ind/Abst** Life Sci. Collect., Hospit. Lit. Index, Index Med., ASTIS Bibliogr., ASTIS Curr. Aware. Bull., Energy Res. Abstr. **NLM** W1 AL193. adv acc. **Circ** 800. (ctrl). Official journal of the Alaska State Medical Association.

THE ALBERTA HERITAGE FOUNDATION FOR MEDICAL RESEARCH ESTIMATES OF PROPOSED INVESTMENT. Main/Corp Alberta Heritage Savings Trust Fund. Capital Projects Division. CN. English. **LC** R854.C3. **DD** 610.7207123.

ALBERTA MEDICAL BULLETIN. V. 1- Apr. 1935-. 0002-4848. Periodical. CN. English. qt. Alberta Medical Association, 304 C.M.A. Alberta House, 9901-108 Street, Edmonton Alberta T5K 1G8 Canada. **NLM** W1 AL258.

ALBERTA PHYSICIANS AND SURGEONS. PROVINCE OF ALBERTA. (ALBERTA PHYSICIANS AND SURGEONS, PROVINCE OF ALBERTA). 1975-. 0319-5031. Periodical. CN. English. College of Physicians and Surgeons of Alberta, 9901-108 Street, Edmonton Alberta T5K 1G9 Canada. **DD** 610.69520257123. *List of Members of the College of Physicians and Surgeons of Alberta, 0318-157X.*

ALFRED BENZON SYMPOSIUM. 1-. 0105-3639. Monographic Series. English. ir. 33.25. Munksgaard Ltd, 35 Norre Sogade, DK-1370 Copenhagen K Denmark. **Tel** 451127030. **Ind/Abst** Biol. Abstr., Chem. Abstr. **NLM** W3 AL36. **CODEN** ABSYB2. Scientific research within medicine and pharmacology. Each volume is dealing with a specific subject.

ALIVE (VANCOUVER, B.C.). *See* Nutrition and Dietetics.

ALL ABOUT MEDICAID. *See* Insurance.

ALL ABOUT MEDICARE. *See* Insurance.

ALLERGOLOGIA ET IMMUNOPATHOLOGIA. V. 1- Jan./Feb. 1973-. 0301-0546. Periodical. SP. Spanish (articles in English). bm. $32.14. Editorial Garsi, Londres 17, Madrid 28 Spain. **Ind/Abst** Life Sci. Collect., Cumul. Index Nurs. Allied Health Lit., Excerpta Med., Index Med., Chem. Abstr. **NLM** W1 AL563. **CODEN** AGIMBJ. Index in last issue of volume - attached.

ALLERGY ALERT. No. 19 (Spring 1980)-. 0824-1333. Periodical. CN. English. qt. 9.00. Allergy Foundation of Canada, PO Box 1904, Saskatoon Saskatchewan S7K 3S5 Canada. **Tel** 664-4618. **Ed** Michelle Agnerian. **DD** 616.97005. bk rev. **Circ** 650. Allergy information on foods, products, environmental information, book reviews, and doctor information. *Newsletter (Allergy Foundation of Canada), 0824-1325.*

ALLIED HEALTH EDUCATION DIRECTORY. *See* Yearbooks, Almanacs, Directories.

ALLIED HEALTH EDUCATION NEWSLETTER. Began publication with No. 101 (Sept. 1, 1977). Periodical. US. English. mo. $10.00. American Medical Association, 535 North Dearborn Street, Chicago IL 60610. **Tel** (312)645-4695. **Ed** John Boberg. bk rev. **Circ** 1,500. A multidisciplinary national resource for studies, projects, conferences, and publications, as well as a summation of information and activities relating to allied health education and accreditation.

ALLIED HEALTH EDUCATION PROGRAMS IN JUNIOR AND SENIOR COLLEGES. HEALTH PLANNERS EDITION. **Series/Titl** Health Manpower References. 1973-. 0148-5067. Periodical. US. English. $18.50. **NLM** W 22 AA1 A34. *Allied Health Education Programs in Junior Colleges, Allied Health Education Programs in Senior Colleges, 0090-3442.*

ALLIED MEDICAL EDUCATION NEWSLETTER. 1968-74. 0002-6115. Periodical. US. English. mo. Free. American Medical Association, 535 Dearborn Street, Chicago IL 60610. **Tel** (312)645-4695. **Ed** John T Boberg. **NLM** W1 AL83K. bk rev. **Circ** 4,200. With its multidisciplinary national perspective, the newsletter provides a timely topical monthly summation of activities, information, and publications related to allied health education and accreditation.

ALLIED MEDICAL EDUCATION NEWSLETTER. (ALLIED MEDICAL EDUCATION NEWSLETTER : A PERIODIC PUBLICATION OF THE CONJOINT ACCREDITATION SERVICE OF THE CMA). No. 1 (Sept. 1979)-. 0821-6584. Periodical. CN. English (includes some text in French). ty. Free. Canadian Medical Association/ Conjoint Accreditation Service, PO Box 8650, Ottawa Ont K1G 0G8 Canada. **Tel** (613)731-9331. **Ed** Charlotte Hicks-Innes. **DD** 610.7. bk rev. **Circ** 1,500. (ctrl). Matters of interest to medical technology groups and their educators and accreditors.

ALUMNI DIRECTORY - UNIVERSITY OF PITTSBURGH, SCHOOL OF MEDICINE. *See* Yearbooks, Almanacs, Directories.

AMA DIRECTORY OF OFFICIALS AND STAFF - AMERICAN MEDICAL ASSOCIATION. *See* Yearbooks, Almanacs, Directories.

AMA DRUG EVALUATIONS. **Main/Corp** American Medical Association. Dept. of Drugs. **VFOAT** Drug Evaluations. **VAT** American Medical Association Drug Evaluations. 1971-. 0065-9304. US. English. American Medical Association, 535 Dearborn Street, Chicago IL 60610. **LC** RM300. **DD** 615.1. **NLM** QV 740 AA1 A17. *AMA Drug Evaluations, 0065-9304.*

AMA GAZETTE. **Main/Corp** Australian Medical Association. Began in 1968. 0300-4708. Periodical. AT. English. ir. $47.22. Australasian Medical Publ Company, 77 79 Arundel Street Glebe, Sydney New South Wales 2037 Australia. **Tel** (02)660 6055. **Ed** John Connell. adv acc. **Circ** 27,000. (ctrl). General interest to medical profession including travel, finance, medico-political, car features, computers, law, world medical news.

AMA MEDICAL HEALTH FILM LIBRARY. **Main/Corp** American Medical Association. **VFOAT** Medical Health Film Library. **VAT** American Medical Association Medical Health Film Library. 0197-7148. US. English. American Medical Association, 535 North Dearborn Street, Chicago IL 60610. *List of Films Available From the Film Library.*

AMB. **Main/Corp** Associacao Medica Brasileira. **VFOAT** Revista da Associacao Medica Brasileira. V. 14- March 1968-. 0004-5241. Periodical. BL. Portuguese (some summaries in English and French). mo. AMB Revista da Associacao, Antonio 278-9, PO Box 8904, Avda Brig Luiz, Sao Paulo Brazil. **Ind/Abst** Excerpta Med., Index Med., Chem. Abstr. **NLM** W1 A1397N. **CODEN** AMRTBP. *Revista.*

AMEDD SPECTRUM. **Main/Corp** United States. Army Medical Dept. **VAT** Army Medical Department Spectrum. V. 1- 1974-. 0093-9684. Periodical. US. English. qt. $7.00. Superintendent of Documents, US Government Printing Office, Washington DC 20402. **LC** UH223. **DD** 355.3450973. **NLM** W1 A13972M. **CODEN** AMESDR.

THE AMERICAN ACADEMY OF ACUPUNTURE MEDICINE. (THE AMERICAN ACADEMY OF ACUPUNCTURE MEDICINE : JOURNAL). Vol. 1, No. 1 (May 1980)-. 0278-8918. US. English. sa. T Gencheff MD, c/o The American Academy of Acupuncture Medicine, 2718 Dryden Drive, Madison WI 53704. **NLM** W1 AM109T.

AMERICAN CLINICAL PRODUCTS REVIEW. **VFOAT** Clinical Products Review. Began in 1982. 8750-9490. Periodical. US. English. mo. $126.00 Domestic, $162.00 Foreign. International Scientific Communications Inc, 808 Kings Highway/ PO Box 827, Fairfield CT 06430. **Tel** (203)576-0500. **Ed** Brian Howard. **NLM** W1. **Circ** 80,000.

AMERICAN FAMILY PHYSICIAN (KANSAS CITY, MO. : 1970). (AMERICAN FAMILY PHYSICIAN). V. 2, No. 6- Dec. 1970-. 0002-838X. Periodical. US. English. mo. $45.00. American Family Physician, 1740 West 92nd Street, Kansas City MO 64114. **Tel** (816)333-9700. **Ed** Walter H Kemp. **Ind/Abst** Trade Ind. Index, Hospit. Lit. Index, Life Sci. Collect., Excerpta Med., Index Med., CIS Abstr., Gen. Sci. Index, Sci. Cit. Index, Abr. Ed. **NLM** W1 AM397T. bk rev. adv acc. **Circ** 130,000. (ctrl). A clinical publication for family physicians. *American Family Physician/GP, 0572-3612.*

AMERICAN HOSPITAL ASSOCIATION GUIDE TO THE HEALTH CARE FIELD. **VFOAT** Guide to the Health Care Field, A.H.A. Guide to the Health Care Field, AHA Guide to the Health Care Field. 1974 Ed.-. 0094-8969. Periodical. US. English. an. $80.00. American Hospital Association, PO Box 99376, Chicago IL 60693. **Tel** (312)280-6029. **LC** RA977.A1. **DD** 362.1102573. **NLM** WX 22 AA1 A53. *AHA Guide to the Health Care Field.*

AMERICAN HOSPITAL FORMULARY SERVICE. **Main/Corp** American Society of Hospital Pharmacists. Committee on Pharmacy and Pharmaceuticals. Vol. 1 1959-. Monographic Series. US. English. qt. American Society of Hospital Pharmacists, 4630 Montgomery Avenue, Bethesda MD 20814. **Tel** (301)657-3000. **Ed** G K McEvoy. **NLM** QV 740 AA1 A53A. The authority on drug information. Monographs contain comprehensive information on uses, cautions, pharmacology, drug interactions, dosage and administration, pharmacokinetics and lists of products.

AMERICAN JOURNAL OF ACUPUNCTURE. V. 1- Jan./Mar. 1973-. 0091-3960. Periodical. US. English. qt. $58.00. American Journal Acupuncture, 1400 Lost Acre Drive, Felton CA 95018. **Ed** John W Nawratil. **Ind/Abst** Life Sci. Collect., Excerpta Med., Biol. Abstr. **NLM** W1 AM447. **CODEN** AJAPB9. bk rev. adv acc. **Circ** 3,000. Devoted to reporting new and original experimental and theoretical findings of interest to health professionals and acupuncturists.

AMERICAN JOURNAL OF ANATOMY. *See* Biology.

THE AMERICAN JOURNAL OF CHINESE MEDICINE. **VFOAT** Mei-Chou Chung-Kuo I Hsueh Tsa Chih. V. 7, No. 2- Spring 1979-. 0192-415X. Periodical. US. English. qt. $35.00. The American Journal of Chinese Medicine, PO Box 555, Garden City NY 11530. **Ind/Abst** Life Sci. Collect., Excerpta Med., Index Med., Biol. Abstr., Chem. Abstr., Psychol. Abstr., Energy Res. Abstr. **LC** R601. **DD** 615.0951. **NLM** W1 AM449MB. **CODEN** AJCMBA. *Comparative Medicine East and West, 0147-2917.*

THE AMERICAN JOURNAL OF EMERGENCY MEDICINE. **VFOAT** A.J.E.M. Vol. 1, No. 1 (July 1983)-. 0735-6757. Periodical. US. English. bm. $55.00. W B Saunders Company, c/o President, PO Box 465, Hanover PA 17331. **Tel** (215)574-4762. **Ed** William Burns. **NLM** W1 AM451C. bk rev. adv acc. **Circ** 3,000. Timely authoritative articles. Original research, work in progress, case reports, regular features. An independent journal covering important issues and developments from many sources and perspectives.

THE AMERICAN JOURNAL OF GASTROENTEROLOGY. V. 21- Jan. 1954-. 0002-9270. Periodical. US. English. mo. $80.00. Williams & Wilkins, 428 East Preston Street, Baltimore MD 21202. **Tel** (301)528-4000. **Ed** Arthur E Lindner. **Ind/Abst** Life Sci. Collect., Pestdoc, Ringdoc, Vetdoc, Excerpta Med., Index Med., Biol. Abstr., Chem. Abstr., Energy Res. Abstr., Sci. Cit. Index, Abr. Ed. **NLM** W1 AM452. **CODEN** AJGAAR. adv acc. **Circ** 4,500. Practical, clinically oriented original articles and major reviews of current topics in gastroenterology, for gastroenterologists and internists. *Review of Gastroenterology, 0096-2929.*

AMERICAN JOURNAL OF HEMATOLOGY. V. 1- 1976-. 0361-8609. Periodical. US. English. mo. Alan R Liss Inc, 41 East 11th Street, New York NY 10003. **Tel** (212)741-2515. **Ind/Abst** Life Sci. Collect., Excerpta Med., Index Med., Biol. Abstr., Chem. Abstr., Energy Res. Abstr., Curr. Contents. Life Sci., Curr. Contents Clin. Pract., Soc. Sci. Index. **LC** QP91. **DD** 616.1505. **NLM** W1 AM452J. **CODEN** AJHEDD.

AMERICAN JOURNAL OF INDUSTRIAL MEDICINE. Vol. 1, No. 1-. 0271-3586. Periodical. US. English. mo. $323.00. Alan R Liss Inc, 41 East 11th Street, New York NY 10003. **Tel** (212)741-2515. **Ind/Abst** Life Sci. Collect., Coal Abstr., Excerpta Med., Index Med., Biol. Abstr., Chem. Abstr. **NLM** W1 AM468H. **CODEN** AJIMD8.

AMERICAN JOURNAL OF MEDICAL TECHNOLOGY. (AMERICAN JOURNAL OF MEDICAL TECHNOLOGY : MICROFORM). **VFOAT** Medical Technology. Began publication with Vol. 43, No. 3 in Mar. 1977. 0148-8759. Periodical. US. English. an. University Microfilms International, 300 North Zeeb Road, Ann Arbor MI 48106. *Medical Technology (American Society for Medical Technology), 0146-8596.*

THE AMERICAN JOURNAL OF MEDICINE. V. 1- July 1946-. 0002-9343. Periodical. US. English. $59.00. Technical Publishing Company, 875 3rd Avenue, New York NY 10022. **Tel** (212)605-9400. **Ind/Abst** Life Sci. Collect., Pestdoc, Ringdoc, Vetdoc, Excerpta Med., Index Med., CIS Abstr., Biol. Abstr., Chem. Abstr., Bibliogr. Agric., Energy Res. Abstr., Sci. Cit. Index, Abr. Ed., Hospit. Lit. Index. **LC** RC60. **DD** 610.5. **NLM** W1 AM493. **CODEN** AJMEAZ. (cum index).

AMERICAN JOURNAL OF REPRODUCTIVE IMMUNOLOGY *CEASED.* (AMERICAN JOURNAL OF REPRODUCTIVE IMMUNOLOGY : AJRI : OFFICIAL JOURNAL OF THE AMERICAN SOCIETY FOR THE IMMUNOLOGY OF REPRODUCTION AND THE INTERNATIONAL COORDINATION COMMITTEE FOR IMMUNOLOGY OF REPRODUCTION). **VFOAT** AJRI, A.J.R.I. Vol. 1, No. 1-V. 6, No. 4 (Dec. 1984). 0271-7352. Periodical. US. English. mo. $198.00. Alan R Liss Inc, 41 East 11th Street, New York NY 10003. **Tel** (212)741-2515. **Ind/Abst** Excerpta Med., Life Sci. Collect., Index Med., Chem. Abstr. **LC** QP252.5. **DD** 616.65079. **NLM** W1 AM521N. **CODEN** AAJID6.

Medicine

AMERICAN JOURNAL OF SPORTS MEDICINE. (THE AMERICAN JOURNAL OF SPORTS MEDICINE). V. 4- Jan./Feb. 1976-. 0363-5465. Periodical. US. English. bm. $60.00. Williams & Wilkens, 428 East Preston Street, Baltimore MD 21202. Tel (301)528-4000. Ind/Abst Excerpta Med., Cumul. Index Nurs. Allied Health Lit., Index Med., Educ. Index, Abstr. Anthropol., Hospit. Lit. Index. LC RC1200. DD 617.1027. NLM W1 AM522M. CODEN AJSMDO. adv acc. Available on Microfilm from Williams & Wilkens. Covers the diagnosis, surgical treatment, rehabilitation, and prevention of a wide range of sports-related injuries for orthopaedic surgeons. *Journal of Sports Medicine, 0090-4201.*

THE AMERICAN JOURNAL OF THE MEDICAL SCIENCES. VFOAT Medical Sciences. V. 1-26 (No. 1-52), Nov. 1827-Aug. 1840. 0002-9629. Periodical. US. English (summaries in interlingua, July 1955-). mo. $42.00 Domestic, 57.00 Foreign. Slack Inc, 6900 Grove Road, Thorofare NJ 08086. Ind/Abst Life Sci. Collect., Pestdoc, Ringdoc, Vetdoc, Excerpta Med., Index Med., Int. Aerosp. Abstr., CIS Abstr., Chem. Abstr., Energy Res. Abstr. LC R11. DD 610.5. NLM W1 AM524. CODEN AJMSA9. Available on microfilm from University Microfilms. *Philadelphia Journal of the Medical and Physical Sciences, Philadelphia Monthly Journal of Medicine and Surgery; American Medical Recorder.*

THE AMERICAN JOURNAL OF TROPICAL MEDICINE AND HYGIENE. V. 1- Jan. 1952-. 0002-9637. Periodical. US. English. bm. $90.00 Domestic, $95.00 Foreign. The Allen Press, 1041 New Hampshire Street, PO Box 368, Lawrence KS 66044. Tel (913)843-1234. Ed W D Tigertt. Ind/Abst Index Med., Biol. Abstr., Life Sci. Collect., Pestdoc, Ringdoc, Vetdoc, Sci. Cit. Index, Abr. Ed., Hospit. Lit. Index, Chem. Abstr., Excerpta Med., Recent Publ. Artic. LC RC960. DD 616.988305. NLM W1 AM527. CODEN AJTHAB. bk rev. Circ 3,800. (ctrl). Publishes original research papers, reviews, book reviews, etc., which contribute to the advancement of knowledge of tropical medicine and hygiene. *American Journal of Tropical Medicine, 0096-6746.*

AMERICAN MEDICAL DIRECTORY. See Yearbooks, Almanacs, Directories.

AMERICAN MEDICAL DIRECTORY UPDATE. See Yearbooks, Almanacs, Directories.

AMERICAN MEDICAL NEWS. V. 12, No. 26- July 1969-. 0001-1843. Periodical. US. English. wk. American Medical Association, 535 Dearborn Street, Chicago IL 60610. Tel (312)645-4927. Ind/Abst Trade Ind. Index, Hospit. Lit. Index, Med. Socioecon. Res. Source. NLM W1 AM629G. *AMA News.*

AMERICAN MEN AND WOMEN OF SCIENCE. MEDICAL AND HEALTH SCIENCES. (AMERICAN MEN AND WOMEN OF SCIENCE : MEDICAL AND HEALTH SCIENCES). 0145-9996. US. English. Bowker, 1180 Avenue of the Americas, New York NY 10036. LC R153. DD 610.922, B. NLM W 22 AA1 A53.

AMERICAN MEN AND WOMEN OF SCIENCE. THE MEDICAL SCIENCES. (AMERICAN MEN AND WOMEN OF SCIENCE : THE MEDICAL SCIENCES). 0097-6148. US. English. an. R R Bowker Company, 1180 Avenue of the Americas, New York NY 10036. LC R153. DD 610.922, B. NLM W 22 DA2 A6.

AMRA MEMBERSHIP ROSTER. Main/Corp American Medical Record Association. VAT American Medical Record Association Membership Roster. 0363-4876. US. English. $2.00. American Medical Record, 875 North Michigan Avenue Suite 1850, Chicago IL 60611. LC RA976. DD 651.5.

ANAESTHESIA. V. 1- Oct. 1946-. 0003-2409. Periodical. UK. English. mo. Academic Press, 4805 Sand Lake Road, Orlando FL 32819. Tel (305)345-4100. Ind/Abst Pestdoc, Ringdoc, Vetdoc, Excerpta Med., Life Sci. Collect., Chem. Abstr., Index Med., Nuci. Sci. Abstr., Sci. Cit. Index, Abr. Ed., Hospit. Lit. Index. NLM W1 AN103R. CODEN ANASAB.

ANAESTHESIA AND INTENSIVE CARE. V. 1- Aug. 1972-. 0310-057X. Periodical. AT. English. qt. $22.13. Australian Society of Anaesthetists, PO Box 355, Paddington New South Wales 2021 Australia. Tel 331-3211. Ed B F Horan. Ind/Abst Cumul. Index Nurs. Allied Health Lit., Excerpta Med., Life Sci. Collect., Index Med., Sci. Cit. Index, Abr. Ed. NLM W1 AN103T. bk rev. adv acc. Clinical and research papers on anesthesia and related disciplines.

ANAESTHESIA (EDINBURGH, LOTHIAN). (ANAESTHESIA). VFOAT Anaesthesia Review. Review 1-. 0263-1512. UK. English. Ed Leon Kaufman. NLM W1 AN103G.

ANAESTHESIOLOGICA. Series/Titl Acta Universitatis Ouluensis: Series D Medica. No. 1-. 0358-4836. Monographic Series. Fl. English (Finnish). ir. Prof Sakari Piha, 90100 Oulu 10 Finland. Tel 358-81-332133. Ed Leo Hirvonen. Ind/Abst NLM W1 AC954NM NO.12 ETC. adv acc. Circ 500. (ctrl). Monographs, reviews, and dissertation in the field of surgical anesthesiology.

ANAESTHESIOLOGIE UND REANIMATION. V. 1- 1976-. 0323-4983. Periodical. SZ. German. bm. Kunst & Wissen Erich Bieber, Dufourstrasse 51, CH-8008 Zurich Switzerland. Ind/Abst Excerpta Med., Chem. Abstr. NLM W1 AN103Z. CODEN ANREDN.

ANAIS DO INSTITUTO DE HIGIENE E MEDICINA TROPICAL. (ANAIS DO INSTITUTO DE HIGIENE E MEDICINA TROPICAL). V. 1- Jan./Dec. 1973-. 0303-7762. Periodical. text in Portuguese or English. ir. Instituto de Medicina Tropical, Lisboa Portugal. Ind/Abst Excerpta Med. NLM W1 AN111E. *Anais da Escola Nacional de Saude Publica e de Medicina Tropical, 0075-9767.*

ANAIS DO INSTITUTO DE MEDICINA TROPICAL CEASED. V. 1-23. 0365-3307. Periodical. PO. articles mainly in Portuguese, with some in English or French. ir. Instituto de Medicina Tropical, Lisboa Portugal. Ind/Abst Index Med. NLM W1 AN111K.

ANALES CHILENOS DE HISTORIA DE LA MEDICINA. See Yearbooks, Almanacs, Directories.

ANALES DE LA REAL ACADEMIA NACIONAL DE MEDICINA, MADRID. See Yearbooks, Almanacs, Directories.

ANALES DE MEDICINA. See Yearbooks, Almanacs, Directories.

ANALYTISCHE METHODEN ZUR PRUFUNG GESUNDHEITSSCHADLICHER ARBEITSSTOFFE. BAND 1, LUFTANALYSEN. (ANALYTISCHE METHODEN ZUR PRUFUNG GESUNDHEITSSCHADLICHER ARBEITSSTOFFE). V. 1- 1976-. 0172-1240. Monographic Series. German. ir. NLM W1 AN1919G.

ANASTHESIE, INTENSIVTHERAPIE, NOTFALLMEDIZIN. 15- Yearly Vol. 0174-1837. Periodical. German. bm. $98.00. Thieme Stratton Inc, 381 Park Avenue, New York NY 10016. Tel (212)683-5088. Ind/Abst Life Sci. Collect., Excerpta Med., Index Med., Chem. Abstr., Sci. Cit. Index, Abr. Ed., Curr. Contents, Energy Res. Abstr. NLM W1 AN301XI. CODEN AINNDT. *Praktische Anasthesie, Wiederbelebung und Intensivtherapie, 0302-7600.*

THE ANATOMICAL RECORD. V. 1- Nov. 24, 1906-. 0003-276X. Periodical. US. English. mo. $132.00. Alan R Liss Inc, 150 Fifth Avenue, New York NY 10011. Ind/Abst Life Sci. Collect., Excerpta Med., Index Med., Int. Aerosp. Abstr., Biol. Abstr., Chem. Abstr., Bibliogr. Agric. LC QL801. DD 611.05. NLM W1 AN193. CODEN ANREAK.

ANATOMISCHER ANZEIGER. Vol. 1-. 0003-2786. Periodical. GE. German (articles in English). $188.00. VCH Publishers Inc, 303 Northwest 12th Avenue, Deerfield Beach FL 33442. Tel (305)428-5566. Ed K von Bardelehen. Ind/Abst Life Sci. Collect., Excerpta Med., Index Med., Biol. Abstr., Chem. Abstr., Sci. Cit. Index, Abr. Ed. LC QL801. NLM W1 AN207. CODEN ANANAU. Index published separately - free - automatically sent. (cum index).

ANATOMY AND EMBRYOLOGY. Began in 1974. 0340-2061. Periodical. GW. articles in English, French or German. ir. Springer Verlag-New York Inc, 175 5th Avenue, New York NY 10010. Tel (212)460-1500. Ed R Bellairs, K Fleischhauer, W G Forssmann and W Kriz. Ind/Abst Excerpta Med., Index Med., Biol. Abstr., Life Sci. Collect., Sci. Cit. Index, Abr. Ed. LC QL951. DD 596.03. NLM W1 AN211. CODEN ANEMDG. adv acc. Original articles on anatomy, neuro-anatomy, histology, morphological endocrinology and embryology. *0044-2232.*

ANDROLOGIA. (ANDROLOGIA : OFFICIAL JOURNAL OF COMITE INTERNACIONAL DE ANDROLOGIA (CIDA)). Began with: Vol. 6, No. 1, 1974. 0303-4569. Periodical. GW. English (German, with summaries also in French or Spanish). bm. Grosse Verlag, Kurfurstendamm 152, D1000 Berlin 31 West Germany. Ind/Abst Life Sci. Collect., Pestdoc, Ringdoc, Vetdoc, Excerpta Med., Index Med., Biol. Abstr., Chem. Abstr., Sci. Cit. Index, Abr. Ed. NLM W1 AN215P. CODEN ANDRDQ. *Andrologie, 0303-4569.*

ANESTEZJA, REANIMACJA, INTENSYWNA TERAPIA. V. 5- Jan./Mar. 1973-. 0324-8216. Periodical. PL. Polish (summaries and tables of contents in English, and Russian). qt. ARS Polona, Krakowskie Przedmiescie 7, 00-068 Warsaw Poland. Ind/Abst Chem. Abstr. NLM W1 AN217Y. CODEN ARITCG. *Anestezja I Reanimacja.*

ANESTHESIA AND ANALGESIA. Began with issue for Aug. 1922. 0003-2999. Periodical. US. English. mo. $90.00. Elsevier Science Publishing Co Inc, PO Box 1663 Grand Central Station, New York NY 10163. Tel (212)370-5520. Ed Nicholas M Greene. Ind/Abst Chem. Abstr., Excerpta Med., Index Med. LC RD81.A1. DD 617.9605. bk rev. adv acc. Circ 17,000. The official journal of the International Anesthesia Research Society. This journal publishes original research and clinical articles for practicing physicians and allied medical personnel.

ANESTHESIE, ANALGESIE, REANIMATION. Began with V. 14- 1957. Ceased with V. 38, No. 11/12, 1981?. 0003-3014. Periodical. French (summary of some articles in English, German, Spanish, and Italian). bm. Ind/Abst Biol. Abstr., Chem. Abstr., Nuci. Abstr., Index Med., Life Sci. Collect., Excerpta Med., Biol. Abstr. NLM W1 AN22. CODEN AAREAV. *Anesthesie et Analgesie, 0301-4452.*

ANESTHESIOLOGY. V. 1- July 1940-. 0003-3022. Periodical. US. English. mo. $40.00. J B Lippincott Company, East Washington Square, Philadelphia PA 19105. Tel (215)574-4200. Ed Lawrence J Saidman. Ind/Abst Life Sci. Collect., Hospit. Lit. Index, Pestdoc, Ringdoc, Vetdoc, Excerpta Med., Index Med., Int. Aerosp. Abstr., Biol. Abstr., Chem. Abstr., Sci. Cit. Index, Abr. Ed. DD 617. NLM W1 AN22H. CODEN ANESAV. (cum index). bk rev. adv acc. Circ 32,768. Editorials, articles, laboratory reports, clinical and case reports, reports from scientific meetings.

ANESTHESIOLOGY BIBLIOGRAPHY. See Bibliographies.

ANESTHESIOLOGY REVIEW. V. 1- Feb. 1974-. 0093-4437. Periodical. US. English. mo. $55.00. Macor Publishing Company, 116 West 32nd Street 8th Floor, New York NY 10001. Tel (212)736-6688. Ed Andrew Voynow. Ind/Abst Excerpta Med. LC RD78.3. DD 617.9605. NLM W1 AN22K. Index in last issue of volume - attached. bk rev. adv acc. Circ 6,000. Presents fresh informative scientific, original, and review articles as well as symposia and news reports on matters of concern to the practicing anesthesiologist.

ANGEIOLOGIE : REVUE INTERNATIONALE DE DOCUMENTATION SCIENTIFIQUE. Yearly V. 11, No. 5- Nov. 1959-. 0003-3049. Periodical. English (text also in French). ir. Ind/Abst Excerpta Med. NLM W1 AN221. *Angeiologie et Annales.*

ANKARA TIP BULTENI. VFOAT Journal of Ankara Medical School. 1- 1979-. 0252-970X. Periodical. Turkish (the journal welcomes contributions also in English, French, and German. An abstract. . . must be written in English, French, or German). qt. Ankara Universitesi Tip, Fakultesi Yayn Komisyonu Baskanlg, Ankara Turkey. Ind/Abst Excerpta Med. NLM W1 AN2301.

ANNALES ACADEMIAE SCIENTIARUM FENNICAE. SERIE A.5. MEDICA-ANTHROPOLOGICA. (SUOMALAISEN TIEDEAKATEMIAN TOIMITUKSIA. SAR. A.5, MEDICA-ANTHROPOLOGICA). VFOAT Annales Academiae Scientiarum Fennicae. 1-85. 0374-5198. Monographic Series. Fl. Articles in English, French, or German. ir. Akakeeminen-Kirjakuppa, PO Box 128, 00101 Helsinki Finland. Ind/Abst Index Med. NLM W1 SU591. *Annales Academiae Scientiarum Fennicae. Series A, 0365-673X.*

ANNALES ACADEMIAE SCIENTIARUM FENNICAE. SERIES A. 5.MEDICA. (ANNALES ACADEMIAE SCIENTIARUM FENNICAE. SER. A.5, MEDICA). VFOAT Suomalaisen Tiedeakatemian Toimituksia. 86-

Medicine

1961-. 0066-1996. Monographic Series. Fl. articles in English, French, or German. ir. Akakeeminen-Kirjakuppa, PO Box 128, 00101 Helsinki Finland. **Ind/Abst** Index Med., Energy Res. Abstr., Excerpta Med., MLA Int. Bibliogr. Books Artic. Mod. Lang. Lit. **NLM** W1 AN307N. *Annales Academiae Scientiarum Fennicae. Series A. 5. Medica-Anthropologica, 0374-5198.*

ANNALES DE LA SOCIETE BELGE DE MEDECINE TROPICALE. VFOAT Annales Van de Belgische Vereniging Voor Tropische Geneeskunde. V. 52- 1972-. 0365-6527. Periodical. BE. articles in English, French, or Dutch, with summaries in all three languages. qt. $55.33. Annales Societe Belge de Grensstratt 21, c/o J Goemaere, 1030 Brussels Belgium. **Ind/Abst** Life Sci. Collect., Excerpta Med., Index Med., Biol. Abstr., Chem. Abstr., Bibliogr. Agric., Sci. Cit. Index, Abr. Ed., Hospit. Lit. Index. **NLM** W1 AN341T. **CODEN** ASBMAX.

ANNALES DE L'INSTITUT PASTEUR. IMMUNOLOGIE. VFOAT Immunologie. V. 136C, No. 1 (Jan/Feb 1985)-. Periodical. English (with some articles in French). bm. **Ind/Abst** Biol. Abstr., Chem. Abstr., Index Med. **NLM** W1. *Annales d'Immunologie, 0300-4910.*

ANNALES DE L'UNIVERSITE DE MADAGASCAR. BIOLOGIE-CLINIQUE-SANTE PUBLIQUE. *See Biology.*

ANNALES DE MEDECINE VETERINAIRE. V. 1- 1852-. 0003-4118. Periodical. English summaries. ir. $35.57. Faculte de Medecine Veterinaire de l'Universite, 45 rue des Veterinaires, Brussels 7 Belgium. **Tel** (312)944-6780. **Ind/Abst** Life Sci. Collect., Pestdoc, Ringdoc, Vetdoc, Biol. Abstr., Curr. Contents, Chem. Abstr., Sci. Cit. Index, Abr. Ed. **NLM** W1 AN373. **CODEN** AMVRA4. *Repertoire de Medecine.*

ANNALES DE VIROLOGIE. Series/Titl Collection des Annales de l'Institut Pasteur. V. 131 E, No. 1 (Jan/March 1980)-V. 135 E, No. 4 (Oct./Dec. 1984). 0242-5017. Periodical. FR. French (articles also in English). qt. **Ind/Abst** Life Sci. Collect., Biol. Abstr., Excerpta Med., Chem. Abstr., Energy Res. Abstr. **NLM** W1. **CODEN** ANVIDL. *Annales de Microbiologie, 0300-5410.*

ANNALES FRANCAISES D'ANESTHESIE ET DE REANIMATION. Vol. 1, 1-. 0750-7658. Periodical. French. bm. $115.00. Masson Publishing USA Inc, 211 East 43rd Street/Room 1306, New York NY 10017. **Tel** (212)370-1937. **Ind/Abst** Excerpta Med., Chem. Abstr., Index Med., Life Sci. Collect., Pestdoc, Ringdoc, Vetdoc. **NLM** W1 AN408S. **CODEN** AFAREO. *Anesthesie, Analgesie, Reanimation, 0003-3014; Annales de l'Anesthesiologie Francaise, 0003-4061.*

ANNALES IMMUNOLOGIAE HUNGARICAE. V. 1- 1958-. 0570-1708. English (French, or German). ir. **Ind/Abst** Life Sci. Collect., Chem. Abstr. **LC** QR180. **NLM** W1 AN423. **CODEN** AIMHA3.

ANNALES MEDICALES DE NANCY CEASED. V. 1-17. 0003-4460. Periodical. FR. French. ir. Universite of Nancy Faculte de Medicine, 16 Avenue de la Garenne, Nancy France. **Ind/Abst** CIS Abstr. *Revue Medicale de Nancy.*

ANNALES SCIENTIFIQUES DE L'UNIVERSITE DE FRANCHE-COMTE -BESANCON. *See Pharmacy.*

ANNALES SOCIETATIS DOCTRINAE STUDENTIUM ACADEMIAE MEDICAE SILESIENSIS. Periodical. articles in English or Russian. ir. **NLM** W1 AN47KS.

ANNALES UNIVERSITATIS SARAVIENSIS. MEDICINAE. SUPPLEMENT. 1-. 0173-6973. Monographic Series. German. ir. **NLM** W1 AN47R.

ANNALES UNIVERSITATIS SARAVIENSIS. MEDIZIN. V. 1- 1953-. 0003-4533. Periodical. GW. in German. ir. Verlag Ermer KG, Postfach 1155, D665 Homburg-Saar West Germany. **Tel** 068 41/ 781 86. **Ind/Abst** Excerpta Med., CIS Abstr. **NLM** W1 AN47S.

ANNALS (ACADEMY OF MEDICINE, SINGAPORE). (ANNALS OF THE ACADEMY OF MEDICINE, SINGAPORE). New Ser., Vol. 1 (Jan. 1972)-. 0304-4602. Periodical. SI. English. qt. 60.00. Academy of Medicine Singapore, Medical Center 4-1 College Road, Singapore 0316 Singapore. **Tel** 2245166. **Ed** Tan Ngoh Chuan. **Ind/Abst** Excerpta Med., Index Med. **NLM** W1 AN626JS. bk rev. adv acc. **Circ** 1,500. (ctrl). Original and review articles on topical medical subjects. *Annals of the Academy of Medicine, Singapore.*

ANNALS OF BIOMEDICAL ENGINEERING. VFOAT Biomedical Engineering. V. 1- Sept. 1972-. 0090-6964. Periodical. US. English. bm. $266.00. Pergamon Press, 395 Sawmill River Road, Elmsford NY 10523. **Tel** (914)592-7700. **Ind/Abst** Excerpta Med., Life Sci. Collect., Eng. Index Mon., Eng. Index Bioeng. Abstr., Eng. Index Energy Abstr., Index Med., Int. Aerosp. Abstr., Biol. Abstr., Eng. Index Annu., Chem. Abstr., Energy Res. Abstr., Comput. Control Abstr., Electr. Electron. Abstr., Sci. Abstr. Sect. A. Phys. Abstr., Phys. Abstr., Hospit. Lit. Index, Sci. Cit. Index, Abr. Ed. **LC** R856.A1. **DD** 610.28. **NLM** W1 AN564. **CODEN** ABMECF. *Journal of Bioengineering, 0145-3068.*

ANNALS OF EMERGENCY MEDICINE. V. 9- Jan. 1980-. 0196-0644. Periodical. US. English. mo. $55.00. Annals of Emergency Medicine, PO Box 619911, Dallas TX 75261. **Tel** (214)659-0911. **Ed** Ronald L Krome. **Ind/Abst** Life Sci. Collect., Excerpta Med., Cumul. Index Nurs. Allied Health Lit., Index Med., Biol. Abstr., Energy Res. Abstr., Hospit. Lit. Index. **LC** RC86. **DD** 616.02505. **NLM** W1 AN574M. **CODEN** AEMED3. bk rev. adv acc. **Circ** 15,000. Original clinical and research articles, case reports, methods and techniques in emergency medicine and emergency medical services. Peer-reviewed. *JACEP, 0361-1124.*

ANNALS OF INDIAN ACADEMY OF MEDICAL SCIENCES. V. 1- Jan. 1965-. 0019-4263. Periodical. II. English. ir. Indian Books & Periodical, 3341 Christian Colony-Pyarey Lal Road, New Delhi 110005 India. **Ind/Abst** Biol. Abstr., Chem. Abstr. **NLM** W1 AN604G. **CODEN** AIADAX.

ANNALS OF LIFE INSURANCE MEDICINE. *See Insurance.*

ANNALS OF SPORTS MEDICINE. Vol. 1, No. 1-. 0734-1997. Periodical. US. English. qt. $42.00. Oxford University Press, 200 Madison Avenue c/o B Weisserman, New York NY 10016. **Tel** (212)679-7300. **Ed** Otto Appenzeller. bk rev. adv acc. **Circ** 1,500. (ctrl). Concerned with the clinical application of scientifically valid research, with a strong emphasis on clinical and basic studies of sports medicine.

ANNALS OF THE NATIONAL ACADEMY OF MEDICAL SCIENCES (INDIA). **Main/Corp** National Academy of Medical Sciences (India). V. 13- Jan./Mar. 1977-. 0379-038X. Periodical. English. qt. $10.00. Prints India, 11 Darya Ganj, New Delhi 110002 India. **Tel** 26 86 45. **Ind/Abst** Excerpta Med., Chem. Abstr. **NLM** W1 AN626YG. **CODEN** ANAIDI. *Annals of Indian Academy of Medical Sciences, 0019-4263.*

ANNALS OF THE ROYAL COLLEGE OF PHYSICIANS AND SURGEONS OF CANADA. **Main/Corp** Royal College of Physicians and Surgeons of Canada. VFOAT Annales du College Royal des Medecins et Chirurgiens du Canada. V. 1- Jan. 1968-. 0035-8800. Periodical. CN. English (includes some text in French). ir. College Physicians & Surgeons, 74 Stanley Avenue, Ottawa Ontario K1M 1P4 Canada. **Tel** (613)746-8177. **Ed** Robert Gourdeau. **Ind/Abst** Life Sci. Collect., Excerpta Med. **LC** R15. **DD** 610.5. **NLM** W1 AN627D. bk rev. adv acc. **Circ** 23,000. (ctrl). Includes updates in internal medicine, pediatrics, psychiatry, bioethics, continuing medical education, general surgery, obstetrics and gynecology. Lab medicine—symposia—news.

ANNALS OF TROPICAL MEDICINE AND PARASITOLOGY. V. 1- Feb. 1907-. 0003-4983. Periodical. UK. English. bm. $147.00. Grune & Stratton, 111 Fifth Avenue, New York NY 10003. **Tel** (212)614-3232. **Ind/Abst** Life Sci. Collect., Pestdoc, Ringdoc, Vetdoc, Excerpta Med., Bibliogr. Agric., Biol. Abstr., Chem. Abstr., Index Med., Nuci. Sci. Abstr., Sci. Cit. Index, Abr. Ed., Hospit. Lit. Index. **LC** RC960. **NLM** W1 AN627P. **CODEN** ATMPA2. *Memoir.*

L'ANNEE DU MEDECIN. 1976-. 0399-3914. Periodical. FR. French. ir. Flammarion Medecine-Sciences, 20 rue de Vaugirard, 75 Paris Vie France. **Ed** P Milliez. **NLM** W1 AN646H.

ANNEE EN REANIMATION MEDICALE. (LANNEE EN REANIMATION MEDICALE). 1970-. 0376-6306. FR. French. ir. Flammarion Medecine-Sciences, 20 rue de Vaurigard, 75006 Paris France. **NLM** W1 AN648.

ANNOTATED STUDENT AFFAIRS BIBLIOGRAPHY. *See Bibliographies.*

ANNUAL ACTIVITIES SUMMARY - DIVISION OF MEDICAL SERVICES, TENNESSEE VALLEY AUTHORITY. **Main/Corp** Tennessee Valley Authority. Division of Medical Services. 1974/75-. Periodical. US. English. an. **NLM** W2 A T17A. *Annual Report - Division of Medical Services, Tennessee Valley Authority.*

ANNUAL FINANCIAL REPORT - TEXAS STATE BOARD OF MEDICAL EXAMINERS. **Main/Corp** Texas State Board of Medical Examiners. US. English. an. Texas State Board of Medical Examiners, Southwest Tower Building Suite 900/211 East 7th Street, Austin TX 78701. **LC** RA396.A4. **DD** 354.9764007231.

ANNUAL FINANCIAL STATEMENT - ANATOMICAL BOARD OF THE STATE OF TEXAS. **Main/Corp** Anatomical Board of the State of Texas. US. English. an. University of Texas, Medical Branch, Galveston TX 77550. **LC** QM33.2.T4. **DD** 354.97640072236841.

ANNUAL HEALTH MANPOWER CONFERENCE. (ANNUAL HEALTH MANPOWER CONFERENCE. PROCEEDINGS). **Main/Conf** Health Manpower Conference. 0094-8942. US. English. an. No 1 Camino Sobrante, Orinda CA 94563. **LC** RA410.8.C2. **DD** 331.7616106909794.

ANNUAL MEDICAL REPORT FOR THE YEAR . . . - RAND MINES, LIMITED, HEALTH DEPARTMENT. (ANNUAL MEDICAL REPORT FOR THE YEAR). **Main/Corp** Rand Mines Limited. Health Dept. 0254-2986. English. an. **NLM** W1 RA484C. *Report for the Year, 0254-2978.*

ANNUAL MEDICAL REPORT - SOUTH DAKOTA. DEPT. OF SOCIAL SERVICES. PROGRAM ANALYSIS AND EVALUATION. *See Insurance.*

ANNUAL MEDICARE PROGRAM STATISTICS. *See Statistics.*

ANNUAL PLAN OF THE ILLINOIS DEPARTMENT OF MENTAL HEALTH AND DEVELOPMENTAL DISABILITIES. *See Sociology: General Works, Theory - Social Pathology, Welfare, Criminology.*

ANNUAL PROGRESS REPORT - UNIVERSITY OF CALIFORNIA, LABORATORY OF NUCLEAR MEDICINE AND RADIATION BIOLOGY. 0193-5224. Periodical. US. English. an. **NLM** W1 AN7581.

ANNUAL PROGRESS REPORT (WALTER REED ARMY INSTITUTE OF RESEARCH). (ANNUAL PROGRESS REPORT). US. English. an. Walter Reed Army Institute of Research, Walter Reed Army Medical Center, Washington DC 20307. *Research in Biological and Medical Sciences, 0161-3685.*

ANNUAL REPORT - ADULT DEVELOPMENT AND AGING RESEARCH COMMITTEE, NATIONAL INSTITUTES OF HEALTH. **Main/Corp** National Institute of Child Health and Human Development. Adult Development and Aging Research Committee. US. English. an. National Institute of Child Health and Human Development, National Institutes of Health, 9000 Rockville Pike, Bethesda MD 20014.

ANNUAL REPORT - AMERICAN BUREAU FOR MEDICAL ADVANCEMENT IN CHINA, INC. **Main/Corp** American Bureau for Medical Advancement in China. 1978-. 0197-0909. US. English. an. American Bureau for Medical Advancement in China Inc, 1790 Broadway, New York NY 10019. **NLM** W1 AM292D. *Annual Report - American Bureau for Medical Aid to China, Inc., 0197-0917.*

ANNUAL REPORT & REFERENCE HANDBOOK. **Main/Corp** American Board of Medical Specialties. VAT Annual Report and Reference Handbook. 1980-. 0272-9741. US. English. an. American Board of Medical Specialties, 1603 Orrington Avenue/Suite 1160, Evanston IL 60201. **LC** R729.5.S6. **DD** 610.6073. **NLM** W1 AM282T. *Annual Report - American Board of Medical Specialties, 0146-5872.*

ANNUAL REPORT AND STATEMENT OF ACCOUNTS - PERSATUAN BAGI MENCHEGAH PENYAKIT TIBI MALAYSIA. **Main/Corp** Persatuan Bagi Menchegah Penyakit Tibi Malaysia. 1949-. Periodical. MY. text in Malay and English. ir. **NLM** W1 PE842.

Medicine

ANNUAL REPORT - ARIZONA BOARD OF MEDICAL EXAMINERS. Main/Corp Arizona Board of Medical Examiners. US. English. an. Arizona Board of Medical Examiners, 5060 North 19th Avenue/Suite 300, Phoenix AZ 85015.

ANNUAL REPORT - BASEL INSTITUTE FOR IMMUNOLOGY. (ANNUAL REPORT). Main/Corp Basel Institute for Immunology. 1972-. 0301-3782. English. ir. LC QR180. DD 596.02905. NLM W1 BA785.

ANNUAL REPORT - BOSTON UNIVERSITY MEDICAL CENTER. Main/Corp Boston University Medical Center. 1962/63-. 0520-6677. Periodical. US. English. an. Boston University, 765 Commonwealth Avenue, Boston MA 02215.

ANNUAL REPORT - CENTRAL COUNCIL FOR RESEARCH IN UNANI MEDICINE (INDIA). Main/Corp Central Council for Research in Unani Medicine (India). 1978-79 & 1979-80-. English. ir. NLM W2 JI4 C39. *Annual Report.*

ANNUAL REPORT - CHARLES A. DANA FOUNDATION. Main/Corp Charles A. Dana Foundation. 0739-5345. US. English. an. LC R852. DD 610.72073.

ANNUAL REPORT - CLINICAL APPLICATIONS AND PREVENTION ADVISORY COMMITTEE, NATIONAL INSTITUTES OF HEALTH. Main/Corp National Heart, Lung, and Blood Institute. Clinical Applications and Prevention Advisory Committee. US. English. an. National Heart Lung and Blood Institute, National Institutes of Health, 9000 Rockville Pike, Bethesda MD 20014.

ANNUAL REPORT - DIVISION OF LONG-TERM CARE. Main/Corp United States. Health Resources Administration. Division of Long-Term Care. 1975/76-. 0149-1539. US. English. an. US Department of Health Education & Welfare, 5600 Fishers Lane, Rockville MD 30852. LC RA644.6. DD 353.008416.

ANNUAL REPORT - EDUCATIONAL COMMISSION FOR FOREIGN MEDICAL GRADUATES. Main/Corp Educational Commission for Foreign Medical Graduates. 1974-. 0145-2037. US. English. an. 3624 Market Street, Philadelphia PA 19104. LC RA396.A3. DD 610.6952. NLM W1 ED857. *Annual Report - Educational Council for Foreign Medical Graduates, 0160-7189.*

ANNUAL REPORT, EXCHANGE OF MEDICAL INFORMATION PROGRAM. VFOAT Exchange of Medical Information Program Annual Report. US. English. an. Veterans Administration Department of Medicine & Surgery, Office of Academic Affairs, 810 Vermont Avenue, Washington DC 20420. LC R118. DD 353.00841. NLM W2 A V58A.

ANNUAL REPORT FOR THE YEAR ENDED - MEXIA STATE SCHOOL. Main/Corp Mexia State School. US. English. an. Mexia State School, Box 1132, Mexia TX 76667. LC HV3006.T42. DD 353.9764007232.

ANNUAL REPORT - FOUNDATION FOR MEDICAL RESEARCH FUNGO. Main/Corp Stichting Voor Medisch Weterschappelijk Onderzoek Fungo. 0376-7337. English. ir. NLM W1 ST497.

ANNUAL REPORT - GENERAL MEDICINE A STUDY SECTION, NATIONAL INSTITUTES OF HEALTH. Main/Corp United States. National Institutes of Health. General Medicine A Study Section. US. English. an. National Institutes of Health, 9000 Rockville Pike, Bethesda MD 20014.

ANNUAL REPORT - GENERAL MEDICINE B STUDY SECTION, NATIONAL INSTITUTES OF HEALTH. Main/Corp United States. National Institutes of Health. General Medicine B Study Section. US. English. an. National Institutes of Health, 9000 Rockville Pike, Bethesda MD 20014.

ANNUAL REPORT - HAWAII MEDICAL ASSOCIATION. EMERGENCY MEDICAL SERVICES PROGRAM. (ANNUAL REPORT FOR THE FISCAL YEAR ENDED JUNE 30 . . .). Main/Corp Hawaii Medical Association. Emergency Medical Services Program. 0748-7738. US. English. an. LC RA645.6.H3. DD 353.996900841.

ANNUAL REPORT. HOSPITAL INSURANCE AND DIAGNOSTIC SERVICES (1976). See Insurance.

ANNUAL REPORT - HOWARD UNIVERSITY COLLEGE OF MEDICINE. See Education (General) - Higher Education.

ANNUAL REPORT - INTERAGENCY COMMITTEE ON EMERGENCY MEDICAL SERVICES, HEALTH SERVICES ADMINISTRATION. Main/Corp United States. Interagency Committee on Emergency Medical Services. US. English. an. Department of Health Education and Welfare, Interagency Committee on Emergency Medical Services, 5600 Fishers Lane, Rockville MD 20857.

ANNUAL REPORT - INTERNATIONAL CENTRE FOR DIARRHOEAL DISEASE RESEARCH. (ANNUAL REPORT). Main/Corp International Centre for Diarrhoeal Disease Research, Bangladesh. 1979-. 0253-5386. English. an. NLM W1 IN719R. *Annual Report of the Cholera Research Laboratory.*

ANNUAL REPORT - JOSIAH MACY, JR. FOUNDATION. (ANNUAL REPORT FOR THE YEAR - JOSIAH MACY, JR. FOUNDATION). Main/Corp Josiah Macy, Jr. Foundation. VFOAT Report for the Year - Josiah Macy, Jr. Foundation. VAT Annual Report- Josiah Macy, Junior Foundation. 1968-. 0160-2888. Periodical. US. English. an. Josiah Macy Jr Foundation, One Rockefeller Plaza, New York NY 10020. NLM W1 JO22. *Report - Josiah Macy, Jr. Foundation, 0160-7073.*

ANNUAL REPORT - MANITOBA HEALTH RESEARCH COUNCIL. Main/Corp Manitoba Health Research Council. 1982-1983-. US. English. an. Manitoba Health Research Council, Room S107 759 Bannatyne Avenue, Winnipeg Manitoba R3E 0W3 Canada. LC RA185.M3. DD 610.79.

ANNUAL REPORT - MEDICAL DEVICES APPLICATIONS COMMITTEE, NATIONAL INSTITUTES OF HEALTH. Main/Corp National Heart and Lung Institute. Medical Devices Applications Committee. US. English. an. National Heart Lung and Blood Institute, National Institutes of Health, 9000 Rockville Pike, Bethesda MD 20014.

ANNUAL REPORT - MEDICAL RESEARCH COUNCIL (GREAT BRITAIN). INSTITUTE OF HEARING RESEARCH. Main/Corp Medical Research Council (Great Britain) Institute of Hearing Research. 1st-. Periodical. UK. English. an. Medical Research Council, Institute of Hearing Research, University of Nottingham, University Park, Nottingham NG7 2RD England.

ANNUAL REPORT - MEDICAL RESEARCH COUNCIL OF NIGERIA. Main/Corp Medical Research Council of Nigeria. 1973-. 0331-3719. Periodical. English. ir. NLM W1 ME4496.

ANNUAL REPORT - MISSISSIPPI MEDICAID COMMISSION. See Insurance.

ANNUAL REPORT - NATIONAL BOARD OF MEDICAL EXAMINERS. Main/Corp National Board of Medical Examiners. 1975-. 0146-1524. US. English. an. National Board of Medical Examiners, 3930 Chestnut Street, Philadelphia PA 19104. NLM W1 NA3284N.

ANNUAL REPORT - NATIONAL INSTITUTE FOR MEDICAL RESEARCH (NIGERIA). Main/Corp Nigeria. National Institute for Medical Research. Series/Titl NIMR Publications. Monographic Series. English. ir. NLM W2 HN5 N22A. *Annual Report - Medical Research Council of Nigeria, 0331-3719.*

ANNUAL REPORT - NATIONAL INSTITUTE OF GENERAL MEDICAL SCIENCES. Main/Corp United States. National Institute of General Medical Sciences. Periodical. US. English. an. National Institute of General Medical Sciences, 9000 Rockville Pike, Bethesda MD 20014.

ANNUAL REPORT - NATIONAL INSTITUTES OF HEALTH (U.S.). BIOMEDICAL ENGINEERING AND INSTRUMENTATION BRANCH. (ANNUAL REPORT FY . . .). Main/Corp National Institutes of Health (U.S.) Biomedical Engineering and Instrumentation Branch. 8756-8144. US. English. an. LC R856.4. DD 610.28. *Annual Report, 0730-8892.*

ANNUAL REPORT - NATIONAL INSTITUTES OF HEALTH (U.S.). DIVISION OF RESEARCH GRANTS. (ANNUAL REPORT). Main/Corp National Institutes of Health (U.S.). Division of Research Grants. 8756-9035. US. English. an. LC R854.U5. DD 610.72073.

ANNUAL REPORT - NATIONAL INSTITUTES OF HEALTH (U.S.). DIVISION OF RESEARCH SERVICES. Main/Corp National Institutes of Health (U.S.). Division of Research Services. 1977-. Periodical. US. English. an. NLM W2 A N212A.

ANNUAL REPORT - NATIONAL MEDICAL FELLOWSHIPS. (ANNUAL REPORT). Main/Corp National Medical Fellowships. 0733-4389. US. English. an. NLM W1 NA513.

ANNUAL REPORT - NATIONAL MEDICAL LIBRARIES ASSISTANCE ADVISORY BOARD, NATIONAL INSTITUTES OF HEALTH. See Library and Information Science.

ANNUAL REPORT - NATIONAL PROFESSIONAL STANDARDS REVIEW COUNCIL. Main/Corp United States. National Professional Standards Review Council. 0361-9052. US. English. an. US Department of Health Education & Welfare, Professional Standard Review, Washington DC 20202. LC RA399.A3. DD 353.008243. NLM W1 NA567.

ANNUAL REPORT - NEW ZEALAND. DEPT. OF HEALTH. MANAGEMENT SERVICES AND RESEARCH UNIT. Main/Corp New Zealand. Dept. of Health. Management Services and Research Unit. English. an. New Zealand Department of Health Management Services and Research Unit, PO Box 5013, Wellington New Zealand. LC RA373. DD 354.93100841.

ANNUAL REPORT OF BOARD OF MEDICAL EXAMINERS. Main/Corp Board of Medical Examiners of Maryland. 0734-337X. US. English. an. Board of Medical Examiners of Maryland, 201 West Preston Street, Baltimore MD 21201.

ANNUAL REPORT OF THE AFRICAN MEDICAL AND RESEARCH FOUNDATION. (ANNUAL REPORT). Main/Corp African Medical and Research Foundation. 0379-6981. English. ir. NLM W1 AF544. *Annual Field Report, 0253-5912.*

ANNUAL REPORT OF THE RESEARCH INSTITUTE OF ENVIRONMENTAL MEDICINE, NAGOYA UNIVERSITY. Main/Corp Nagoya Daigaku. Kankyo Igaku Kenkyujo. 0469-4759. JA. English. an. Nagoya University, Research Institute of Environmental Medicine, Furo Cho Chikusa Nagoya Japan. Ind/Abst Excerpta Med., Chem. Abstr. NLM W1 AN761. CODEN ARINAU.

ANNUAL REPORT ON MEDICARE. (ANNUAL REPORT ON MEDICARE COVERING FISCAL YEAR . . . : PURSUANT TO SEC. 1875(B)). Main/Corp United States. Health Care Financing Administration. VFOAT Medicare Annual Report. Began with 13th, 1978/79. 0196-5972. US. English. an. Department of Health & Human Services, Health Care Financing Administration, Washington DC 20201. LC HD7102.U4. DD 353.008256. NLM W2 A H23A. *Annual Report on Medicare, 0196-5972.*

ANNUAL REPORT - STATE OF NEW JERSEY, DEPARTMENT OF INSTITUTIONS AND AGENCIES, DIVISION OF MEDICAL ASSISTANCE AND HEALTH SERVICES-MEDICAID. See Insurance.

ANNUAL REPORT, THE SURGEON GENERAL, UNITED STATES ARMY. See Military Science.

ANNUAL REPORT TO THE CALIFORNIA LEGISLATURE. See Economics - Labor.

ANNUAL REPORT TO THE GOVERNOR AND LEGISLATURE ON PREPAID HEALTH PLANS, PHPS (CALIFORNIA). Main/Corp California. Dept. of Health. 0145-9171. US. English. an. LC RA413.5.U6. DD 353.979400841.

ANNUAL REPORT TO THE GOVERNOR, LEGISLATURE, COMMISSIONER OF EDUCATION AND THE BOARD OF REGENTS FROM THE COMMUNITY HOSPITAL EDUCATION COUNCIL (FLORIDA). Main/Corp Community Hospital Education Council (Fla.). 0735-5203. US. English. an. State University

Medicine

System of Florida, 107 West Gaines Street, Tallahassee FL 32304. **LC** R845. **DD** 610.715.

ANNUAL REPORTS ON THE EXCHANGE OF MEDICAL INFORMATION AND SHARING MEDICAL RESOURCES. **VFOAT** Exchange of Medical Information and Sharing Medical Resources. Began with 1976/77. 0190-5031. US. English. an. **LC** RA11. **DD** 353.00841. **NLM** W2 A V49Al. *Annual Report on Exchange of Medical Information, 0363-5635; Annual Report on Sharing Medical Resources, 0362-0123.*

ANNUAL REPORTS - ZAMBIA FLYING DOCTOR SERVICE. **Main/Corp** Zambia Flying Doctor Service. 1973/74/75/76/77/78-. English. an. **LC** RA996.5. **DD** 354.689400841.

ANNUAL REVIEW OF IMMUNOLOGY. Vol. 1 (1983)-. 0732-0582. US. English. an. $31.00 Domestic, $34.00 Foreign. Annual Reviews Inc, 4139 El Camino Way, Palo Alto CA 94306. **Tel** (415)493-4400. **Ed** William E Paul. **Ind/Abst** Life Sci. Collect., Biol. Abstr., Chem. Abstr., Index Med. **LC** QR180. **DD** 616.07905. **NLM** W1 AN772H. **CODEN** ARIMDU. Comprehensive, thorough coverage of latest advances in immunology, written by acknowledged experts in the field. Extensive literature citations included.

ANNUAL REVIEW OF MEDICINE. V. 1- 1950-. 0066-4219. US. English. an. $31.00 Domestic, $34.00 Foreign. Annual Reviews Inc, 4139 El Camino Way, Palo Alto CA 94306. **Tel** (415)493-4400. **Ed** William P Creger. **Ind/Abst** Life Sci. Collect., Index Med., Biol. Abstr., Chem. Abstr., Psychol. Abstr., Bibliogr. Agric., Energy Res. Abstr., Sci. Cit. Index, Abr. Ed., Hospit. Lit. Index. **DD** 610.58. **NLM** W1 AN773. **CODEN** ARMCAH. Comprehensive, thorough coverage of latest advances in medicine, written by acknowledged experts in the field. Extensive literature citations included.

ANNUAL STATISTICAL REPORT - AMERICAN ASSOCIATION OF COLLEGES OF OSTEOPATHIC MEDICINE. See Statistics.

ANNUARIO SEAT. VOL. C, CHIMICA, MATERIE PLASTICHE, MEDICINE. See Yearbooks, Almanacs, Directories.

ANTIBIOTICS. No. 1-. 0097-4668. Monographic Series. US. English. ir. Springer Verlag-New York Inc, 175 5th Avenue, New York NY 10010. **Tel** (212)460-1500. **Ind/Abst** Chem. Abstr. **LC** UNC. **NLM** W1 AN854B. **CODEN** ANTBDO. Study of antibiotics.

ANTIBIOTICS. **VFOAT** Antibiotiki. V. 4, No. 1- Jan./Feb. 1959-. Periodical. US. English (translated from Russian). bm. Consultants Bureau, 233 Spring Street, New York NY 10013. **LC** RM265. **DD** 615.329.

ANTIBIOTICS AND CHEMOTHERAPY. 0066-4758. Periodical. English. ir. S Karger Ag, PO Box, CH-4009 Basel Switzerland. **Tel** 061-39 08 80. **Ed** H Schonfeld and F E Hahn. **Ind/Abst** Index Med., Chem. Abstr. Reports relevant to progress in laboratories, clinics, and hospitals.

ANTIBIOTIKI. V. 1-29. 0003-5637. Periodical. UR. 5233247 (summaries in English and French). mo. $61.00. Victor Kamkin Inc (70018), 12224 Parklawn Drive, Rockville MD 20852. **Tel** (301)881-5973. **Ind/Abst** Excerpta Med., Index Med., Biol. Abstr., Chem. Abstr., Life Sci. Collect., Ringdoc, Pestdoc, Vetdoc, Curr. Abstr. Chem. Index Chem., Sci. Cit. Index, Abr. Ed., Index Med. **NLM** W1 AN8582. **CODEN** ANTBAL.

ANTIBIOTIKI I MEDITSINSKAIA BIOTEKHNOLOGIIA. **VFOAT** Antibiotics and Medical Biotechnology. V. 30, 1 (Jan. 1985)-. 0233-7525. Periodical. UR. Russian (with summaries in English). mo. 9.60. Izd-Vo Meditsina, Nauchnyi Proezd 6, 117819 GSP-7 Moskva B-246 Russia. *Antibiotiki, 0003-5637.*

ANTIMICROBIAL CHEMOTHERAPY RESEARCH STUDIES SERIES. 1-. 0278-8284. Monographic Series. UK. English. ir. John Wiley & Sons, 605 Third Avenue, New York NY 10158. **Ed** R N Gruneberg. **NLM** W1 AN875.

THE ANTIMICROBIC NEWSLETTER. See Biology - Microbiology.

ANTISEPTIC. (THE ANTISEPTIC). Began publication in 1904. 0003-5998. Periodical. II. English. mo. $7.91. Antiseptic, 144 Thambu Chetty Street, Georgetown Madras 600001 India. **Ind/Abst** Excerpta Med. **LC** R97. **DD** 610.5. **NLM** W1 AN888.

ANTIVIRAL RESEARCH. Vol. 1, No. 1 (Mar. 1981)-. 0166-3542. Periodical. US. English. bm. Elsevier Science Publishers, PO Box 211, 1000 AE Amsterdam Netherlands. **Tel** (020)5803.911. **Ind/Abst** Life Sci. Collect., Excerpta Med., Index Med., Biol. Abstr., Chem. Abstr., Bibliogr. Agric. **NLM** W1 AN869Q. **CODEN** ARSRDR.

ANTONIE VAN LEEUWENHOEK. See Biology - Microbiology.

APMA NEWS. (APMA NEWS : NEWS FROM THE AMERICAN PODIATRIC MEDICAL ASSOCIATION). **VFOAT** A.P.M.A. News. **VAT** American Podiatric Medical Association News. V. 5, No. 9 (Sept. 15, 1984)-. 8750-2585. Periodical. US. English. mo. $8.00 Non-Members US, $13.00 Non-Members Foreign. APMA News, 20 Chevy Chase Circle NW, Washington DC 20015-2979. **DD** 617. *APA Report, 0272-7722.*

APPLICATION OF OPTICAL INSTRUMENTATION IN MEDICINE. Series/Titl Proceedings of the Society of Photo-Optical Instrumentation Engineers. 1- 1972-. 0362-5443. US. English. Society of Photo-Optical Instrumentation Engineers, 338 Telon Place, Palos Verdes Estates CA 90274. **LC** R857.O6. **DD** 616.075028. **NLM** W1 AP49P.

APPLICATIONS TO THE PROFESSIONAL SCHOOLS AND COLLEGES FOR THE FALL TERM 1948 : MEDICINE, DENTISTRY, VETERINARY MEDICINE, PHARMACY, OPTOMETRY, OSTEOPATHY, LAW. 1949-. US. English. ir. Ohio State University, College of Arts and Sciences, Columbus OH 43210. **LC** R745. **DD** 610.71173.

ARBEITEN AUS DEM PAUL-EHRLICH-INSTITUT, DEM GEORG-SPEYER-HAUS UND DEM FERDINAND-BLUM-INSTITUT ZU FRANKFURT A.M. (ARBEITEN AUS DEM PAUL-EHRLICH-INSTITUT, DEM GEORG-SPEYER-HAUS UND DEM FERDINAND-BLUM-INSTITUT). **Main/Corp** Paul-Ehrlich-Institut (Bundesamt fur Sera und Impfstoffe). 0066-5665. Monographic Series. German. ir. VCH Publishers Inc, 303 NW 12th Avenue, Deerfield Beach FL 33442. **Ind/Abst** Chem. Abstr., Index Med. **NLM** W1 AR115E. **CODEN** AESBAL. *Arbeiten Aus Dem Staatlichen Institut fur Experimentelle Therapie und Dem Georg Speyer-Hause zu Frankfurt A.M.*

ARBEITSMEDIZIN, SOZIALMEDIZIN, PRAVENTIVMEDIZIN. 8.- Yearly Volume. 0300-581X. Periodical. GW. German. mo. 190.80. A W Gentner Verlag, Postfach 688, Forststr 131, 7000 Stuttgart 1 West Germany. **Tel** (0711)638356. **Ind/Abst** Life Sci. Collect., Coal Abstr., Excerpta Med., CIS Abstr., Biol. Abstr., Energy Res. Abstr. **LC** RC963. **NLM** W1 AR125QP. **CODEN** ASPVAS. bk rev. adv acc. **Circ** 6,500. *Arbeitsmedizin, Sozialmedizin, Arbeitshygiene, 0003-7753.*

ARCHIVES BELGES DE MEDECINE SOCIALE HYGIENE, MEDECINE DU TRAVAIL ET MEDECINE LEGALE. See Genealogy and Heraldry - Archives.

ARCHIVES D'ANATOMIE, D'HISTOLOGIE ET D'EMBRYOLOGIE. See Genealogy and Heraldry - Archives.

ARCHIVES D'ANATOMIE MICROSCOPIQUE ET DE MORPHOLOGIE EXPERIMENTALE. See Genealogy and Heraldry - Archives.

ARCHIVES DE L'INSTITUT PASTEUR D'ALGERIE. See Genealogy and Heraldry - Archives.

ARCHIVES DE L'UNION MEDICALE BALKANIQUE ET BULLETIN DE L'UNION MEDICALE BALKANIQUE. See Genealogy and Heraldry - Archives.

ARCHIVES DES MALADIES DU COEUR ET DES VAISSEAUX. See Genealogy and Heraldry - Archives.

ARCHIVES DES MALADIES PROFESSIONNELLES DE MEDECINE DU TRAVAIL ET SECURITE SOCIALE. See Genealogy and Heraldry - Archives.

ARCHIVES OF FAMILY PRACTICE. See Genealogy and Heraldry - Archives.

ARCHIVES OF PODIATRIC MEDICINE AND FOOT SURGERY. See Genealogy and Heraldry - Archives.

ARCHIVES OF PODIATRIC MEDICINE AND FOOT SURGERY. SUPPLEMENT. See Genealogy and Heraldry - Archives.

ARCHIVIO DE VECCHI PER L'ANATOMIA PATOLOGICA E LA MEDICINA CLINICA. See Genealogy and Heraldry - Archives.

ARCHIVIO ITALIANO DI ANATOMIA E DI EMBRIOLOGIA. See Genealogy and Heraldry - Archives.

ARCHIVIO ITALIANO DI SCIENZE MEDICHE TROPICALI E DI PARASSITOLOGIA. See Genealogy and Heraldry - Archives.

ARCHIVOS DE BIOLOGIA Y MEDICINA EXPERIMENTALES. See Genealogy and Heraldry - Archives.

ARCHIVOS DE INVESTIGACION MEDICA. See Genealogy and Heraldry - Archives.

ARCHIVUM HISTOLOGICUM JAPONICUM. See Genealogy and Heraldry - Archives.

ARCHIVUM IMMUNOLOGIAE ET THERAPIAE EXPERIMENTALIS. See Genealogy and Heraldry - Archives.

ARCHIVUM IMMUNOLOGII ET THERAPIAE EXPERIMENTALIS. See Genealogy and Heraldry - Archives.

ARCHIWUM HISTORII MEDYCYNY. See Genealogy and Heraldry - Archives.

ARHEIA IATRIKON ETAIREION. See Genealogy and Heraldry - Archives.

ARHIV PATOLOGIJ. (ARKHIV PATOLOGII). V. 8- 1946-. 0004-1955. Periodical. UR. Russian (table of contents and summaries also in English). mo. $68.50. Victor Kamkin Inc (70021), 12224 Parklawn Drive, Rockville MD 20852. **Tel** (301)881-5973. **Ind/Abst** CIS Abstr., Life Sci. Collect., Excerpta Med., Index Med., Int. Aerosp. Abstr., Biol. Abstr., Chem. Abstr., Ringdoc, Pestdoc, Vetdoc. **NLM** W1 AR8287. **CODEN** ARPTAF. Index in last issue of volume - attached. *Arkhiv Patologicheskoi Anatomifi i Patologicheskoi Fiziologii.*

ARIZONA MEDICINE. V. 1- Jan./Feb. 1944-. 0004-1556. Periodical. US. English. mo. $20.00. Arizona Medical Association Inc, 810 West Bethany Home Road, Phoenix AZ 85013. **Tel** (602)246-8901. **Ind/Abst** Electron. Commun. Abstr. J., ISMEC Bull., Pollut. Abstr. Indexes, Saf. Sci. Abstr. J., Life Sci. Collect., Hospit. Lit. Index, Excerpta Med., Index Med., Chem. Abstr., Energy Res. Abstr. **NLM** W1 AR796. **CODEN** ARMEAN. *Southwestern Medicine.*

ARKANSAS HEALTH MANPOWER STATISTICS. OSTEOPATHS. See Statistics.

ARKANSAS HEALTH MANPOWER STATISTICS. PHYSICIANS. See Statistics.

ARKANSAS HEALTH MANPOWER STATISTICS. PODIATRISTS. See Statistics.

ARKANSAS HEALTH MANPOWER STATISTICS, SUMMARIES OF LICENSED HEALTH MANPOWER PROFESSIONALS BY COUNTY. See Statistics.

ARKHIV ANATOMII, GISTOLOGII I EMBRIOLOGII. **VFOAT** Archives Russes d'Anatomie, d'Histologie et D'Embryologie. V. 10- 1931-. 0004-1947. Periodical. UR. Russian (summaries in English). mo. $64.00. Victor Kamkin Inc (70020), 12224 Parklawn Drive, Rockville MD 20852. **Tel** (301)881-5973. **Ind/Abst** Int. Aerosp. Abstr., Biol. Abstr., Index Dent. Lit., Chem. Abstr., Index Med. **NLM** W1 AR828. **CODEN** AAGEAA. *Russkii Arkhiv Anatomii, Gistologii I Embryologii.*

ARQUIVOS CATARINENSES DE MEDICINA. (ACM. ARQUIVOS CATARINENSES DE MEDICINA). V. 3- Dec. 1974-. 0004-2773. Periodical. Portuguese. ir. **Ind/Abst** Index Med. **NLM** W1 A1136D. *Arquivos Catarinense de Medicina, 0004-2773.*

ARS MEDICI, MONATSSCHRIFT FUR ALLGEMEINMEDIZIN. V. 1- 1911-. 0004-2897. Periodical. SZ. German. mo. $44.53. Novapress AG, Spitalgasse 5 Postfach, 8025 Zurich Switzerland. **Tel** 01/252 12 42. **Ind/Abst** Excerpta Med. **NLM** ZW 1 A782.

ART THERAPY. See Psychology.

ARTERY. Dec. 1974-. 0098-6127. Periodical. US. English. mo. $40.00 Domestic, $45.00 Foreign. Artery, 13998 W Avenue East, Fulton MI 49052. **Tel**

(616)649-4681. **Ed** Charles E Day. **Ind/Abst** Excerpta Med., Index Med., Life Sci. Collect., Biol. Abstr., Chem. Abstr., Sci. Cit. Index, Abr. Ed. **LC** RC691. **DD** 616.13005. **NLM** W1 AR9515K. **CODEN** ARTEDR. Scientific journal on the research of atherosclerosis.

ARTS & WERELD. **VAT** Arts en Wereld. 0165-5299. Periodical. NE. Dutch. mo. $23.36. Arts en Wereld BV, Traay 186A, 3971 GV Driebergen Netherlands. **NLM** W1 AR959.

ARZT IM KRANKENHAUS UND IM GESUNDHEITSWESEN (ERLANGEN, GERMANY : 1981). (DER ARZT IM KRANKENHAUS UND IM GESUNDHEITSWESEN : MONATSSCHRIFT DES MARBURGER BUNDES). BEGAN IN 1981. Periodical. German. mo. **NLM** W1 AR973DC. *Arzt Im Krankenhaus, 0175-7822.*

ARZT UND PATIENT. 1/80-. 0173-5764. Periodical. German. qt. **NLM** W1 AR982.

ARZTE. **VFOAT** Medecins, Medici. Began with: June 6, 1979 issue. 0253-0341. Periodical. French (articles in German, or Italian). wk. **Ind/Abst** CIS Abstr. **NLM** W1 AE153M. *Schweizerische Aerztezeitung.*

ARZTEBLATT BADEN-WURTTEMBERG. Year 22-. 0001-947X. Periodical. GW. German. mo. A W Gentner Verlag, Postfach 688, Forststr 131, 7000 Stuttgart 1 West Germany. **NLM** W1 AE153S. *Arzteblatt Baden-Wurttemberg, 0001-947X.*

ARZTEZITSCHRIFT FUR NATURHEILVERFAHREN. (ARZTEZEITSCHRIFT FUR NATURHEILVERFAHREN : ORGAN DES ZENTRALVERBANDES DER ARZTE FUR NATURHEILVERFAHREN E.V). Year 22, No. 1 (Jan. 1981)-. 0720-6003. Periodical. German. mo. **Ind/Abst** Excerpta Med. **NLM** W1. *Physikalische Medizin und Rehabilitation.*

ARZTLICHE KOSMETOLOGIE. **VFOAT** Medical Cosmetology. Began in 1975. 0340-5702. GW. German. bm. G Braun, Karl-Friederichstr 14-18, 7500 Karlsruhe 1 West Germany. **Ind/Abst** Chem. Abstr., Excerpta Med. **CODEN** AEKODN. *Kosmetologie.*

ARZTLICHE LABORATORIUM. (DAS ARZTLICHE LABORATORIUM). V. 1-. 0001-9526. Periodical. GW. German. mo. 80. Medicus Verlag GMBH, Klingsorstrasse 21, D-1000 Berlin 41 West Germany. **Tel** 030 179 3091. **Ed** Medicus Verlag GMBH. **Ind/Abst** Excerpta Med., Chem. Abstr., Energy Res. Abstr. **NLM** W1 AE229. **CODEN** AELAAH. bk rev. adv acc. **Circ** 4,842. Clinical laboratory science journal for the medical laboratory.

ARZTLICHE PRAXIS. 0001-9534. Periodical. GW. German. sw. 98.-. Werk Verlag, Dr E Banaschewski, Hans Corneliusstrasse 4, D-8032 Munich West Germany. **Ed** Edmund Banaschewski. **Ind/Abst** CIS Abstr. **NLM** W1 AE412. bk rev. adv acc. **Circ** 49,000. The newspaper for the physician in clinics or practice.

ASA NEWSLETTER. **Main/Corp** American Society of Anesthesiologists. **VAT** American Society of Anesthesiologists Newsletter. V. 29, No. 11- Nov. 1965-. 0270-5877. Periodical. US. English. ir. $6.00. American Society of Anesthesiologists, 515 Busse Highway, Park Ridge IL 60068. **NLM** W1 A15V. *Newsletter - American Society of Anesthesiologists.*

ASAIO JOURNAL *CEASED.* **Main/Corp** American Society for Artificial Internal Organs. **VAT** American Society for Artificial Internal Organs Journal. V. 1- July/Aug. 1978-. 0162-1432. Periodical. US. English. qt. Lippincott/Harper, 2350 Virginia Avenue, Hagerstown MD 21740. **Tel** (301)824-7300. **Ind/Abst** Excerpta Med., Chem. Abstr. **LC** RD130. **DD** 617.95. **NLM** W1 AS111D. **CODEN** ASJODE.

ASCLEPIO. V. 16- 1964-. 0210-4466. Periodical. SP. Spanish. ir. Consejo Super Invest Cientific Vitruvio, 8 Apartado 14 458, 28006 Madrid Spain. *Archivo Iberoamericano de Historia de la Medicina y Antropologia Medica.*

ASIAN MEDICAL JOURNAL. V. 1- Oct. 1958-. 0004-461X. Periodical. JA. English. mo. $48.00. Kyowa Book Company Inc, 1-38 Kanda Jinbo-Cho Chiyoda-Ku, Tokyo 101 Japan. **Ind/Abst** Life Sci. Collect., Excerpta Med., Chem. Abstr. **NLM** W1 AS14. **CODEN** ASMJAB.

ASMT NEWS. **Main/Corp** American Society for Medical Technology. Began publication in 1965. 0001-2564. Periodical. US. English. bm. American Society of Medical Technology, 330 Meadowfern Drive, Houston TX 77067. **Tel** (713)893-7072. **Ed** Margo L Diggs. bk rev. adv acc. **Circ** 25,000. (ctrl). News about society and health.

LES ASSISES DE MEDECINE. **VFOAT** Medecine Genrale Francaise. Yearly V. 9-26, No. 5-. Periodical. French. ir. **NLM** W1 AS3605. *Medecine Generale Francaise.*

ASSOCIATION MONDIALE DES MEDECINS FRANCOPHONES. (ASSOCIATION MONDIALE DES MEDECINS FRANCOPHONES : BULLETIN). No. 8 (July 1982)-. 0820-7399. CN. French. sa. Free to Members. Association Mondiale des Medecins Francophones, 9 Chemin, Beckenham Ottawa Ontario K1J 7J5 Canada. **DD** 610.69520601. *AMMF, 0820-7380.*

ATENCION MEDICA. **VFOAT** Patient Care en Mexico. MX. Spanish. mo. 50.00. Intersistemas sa de Cv, Fernando Alencastre No 110, Lomas Virreyes Mexico 10 Mexico. **Tel** 540 5600. **Ed** Martha Castilleja. **NLM** W1 AT212H. bk rev. adv acc. **Circ** 16,500. (ctrl). Continuous medical education articles for general practitioners on day to day practice. Editorial features round table and flow charts.

ATTI - ACCADEMIA MEDICA LOMBARDA. **Main/Corp** Accademia Medica Lombarda. V. 25, N. 2/3- 1970-. Periodical. IT. Italian (summaries in English). sa. $7.12. Accademia Medica Lombarda, 3 Clinica Chirurgica Via F Sforza 35, 20100 Milano Italy. **Ind/Abst** Index Med., Chem. Abstr. **LC** R61. **DD** 610.5.

ATTI DELLA ACCADEMIA PELORITANA DEI PERICOLANTI. CLASSE DI SCIENZE MEDICO-BIOLOGICHE. Periodical. Italian (some summaries in English). ir. **LC** R106. **DD** 610.5. **NLM** W1 AC645.

ATUALIDADES MEDICAS. **VFOAT** AM. V. 5- April 1969-. Periodical. Portuguese. ir. **NLM** W1 AT875B. *AM. Revista de Atualidades Medicas.*

AUDIO-DIGEST. 0571-8600. Periodical. US. English. sm. $192.72. Audio-Digest Foundation, 1577 Chevy Chase Drive, Glendale, CA 91206. **Tel** (213)245-8505. **Ed** Claron L Oakley. A twice-monthly interactive system of audio cassette postgraduate medical education, with each one-hour program eligible for two Category I credit hours.

AUDIO-DIGEST. FAMILY PRACTICE. Periodical. US. English. sm. $192.72. Audio-Digest Foundation, 1577 Chevy Chase Drive, Glendale CA 91206. **Tel** (213)245-8505. **Ed** Claron L Oakley. A four-time monthly interactive system of audio cassette postgraduate medical education, with each one-hour program eligible for two Category I credit hours.

AUDIT ACTION LETTER. (THE AUDIT ACTION LETTER). V. 1- Nov. 1, 1975-. 0363-5473. Periodical. US. English. sm. Patient Care Institute, 16 Thorndal Circle, Darien CT 06820. **NLM** W1 AU202.

THE AUDIT ACTION LETTER INFORMATION BONUS. *See* Business - Accounting.

AUDIT REPORT, BOARD OF MEDICAL EXAMINERS (TENNESSEE). **Main/Corp** Tennessee. Division of State Audit. 0148-3439. US. English. an. Tennessee Comptroller of the Treasury, Nashville TN 37202. **LC** RA396.A4. **DD** 353.976800841.

AUDIT REPORT, BOARD OF PODIATRY (TENNESSEE). **Main/Corp** Tennessee. Division of State Audit. 0149-1903. US. English. Division of State Audit, Andrew Jackson State Office Building, Nashville TN 37219. **LC** RD563. **DD** 353.97680084197585.

AUSTRALASIAN PHYSICAL & ENGINEERING SCIENCES IN MEDICINE. (AUSTRALASIAN PHYSICAL & ENGINEERING SCIENCES IN MEDICINE). **VFOAT** Australasian Physical and Engineering Sciences in Medicine. New Ser., V. 3, No. 1 (Jan/Feb 1980)- – Serial No. 86-. 0158-9938. Periodical. AT. English. qt. 35.00. Cancer Institute, c/o Department of Physical Science, 481 Little Lonsdale Street, Melbourne Victoria 3000 Australia. **Tel** (03)602-1333. **Ed** Kenneth H Clarke. **Ind/Abst** Electron. Commun. Abstr. J., ISMEC Bull., Pollut. Abstr. Indexes, Saf. Sci. Abstr. J., Index Med., Chem. Abstr. **NLM** W1 AU335H. **CODEN** AUPMDI. bk rev. adv acc. **Circ** 500. Application of the physical sciences and engineering to medical and clinical problems. *Australasian Physical Sciences in Medicine, 0157-9738.*

AUSTRALIAN CLINICAL REVIEW. No. 1 (May 1981)-. 0726-3139. Periodical. AT. English. qt. $19.92. AMA/ACHS Peer Review Resource Centre, 71 Arundel Street, Glebe New South Wales 2037 Australia. **Tel** (02)660 0333. **Ed** John Best. **Ind/Abst** Hospit. Lit. Index, Cumul. Index Nurs. Allied Health Lit., Index Med. **NLM** W1 AU5185M. **Circ** 850. Keeps the medical and allied health professions up-to-date with what is happening in peer review, quality assurance, criteria auditing, utilization review and continuing medical education throughout Australia.

AUSTRALIAN FAMILY PHYSICIAN. V. 1- Feb. 1972-. 0300-8495. Periodical. AT. English. mo. $44.27. Royal Australian College of GP, 70 Joilmont Street 4th Floor, Melbourne Vic 3002 Australia. **Tel** (03)654 3000. **Ind/Abst** Excerpta Med., Index Med., Biol. Abstr., Hospit. Lit. Index. **NLM** W1 AU53K. **CODEN** AFPHCX. *Annals of General Practice.*

AUSTRALIAN JOURNAL OF EXPERIMENTAL BIOLOGY AND MEDICAL SCIENCE. *See* Biology.

THE AUSTRALIAN JOURNAL OF MEDICAL LABORATORY SCIENCE. V. 1- Feb. 1980-. 0158-4960. Periodical. AT. English. qt. 40.00. Australian Journal of Medical Laboratory Science, National Secretary, PO Box 450, Toowong Queensland 4066 Australia. **Tel** 378-4210. **Ed** J S Welch. **Ind/Abst** Excerpta Med., Chem. Abstr. **NLM** W1 AU613B. **CODEN** AJMLDP. bk rev. adv acc. **Circ** 2,250. (ctrl). Medical and clinical pathology laboratory practice. *Australian Journal of Medical Technology, 0312-956X.*

AUSTRALIAN JOURNAL OF SPORTS MEDICINE AND EXERCISE SCIENCES : THE OFFICIAL JOURNAL OF THE AUSTRALIAN SPORTS MEDICINE FEDERATION. **VFOAT** Sports Medicine and Exercise Sciences. Vol. 14, No. 2-. Periodical. English. qt. **NLM** W1. *Australian Journal of Sports Medicine, 0045-0650.*

AUSTRALIAN PRESCRIBER. 0312-8008. Periodical. AT. English. qt. Free. Australian Government Publishing Service, The Editor, Australian Prescriber, PO Box 100, Woden Australian Capital Territory 2606 Canberra Australia. **Tel** (6162)897038. **Ed** R Hall. **NLM** W1 AU644E. bk rev. **Circ** 45,000. (ctrl). Review of medical management and medications available in Australia.

AUTOMEDICA. V. 1- Jan. 1974-. 0095-0963. Periodical. US. English. qt. Gordon & Breach, 1 Bedford Street, London WC2E 9HD England. **Tel** (01)836-5125. **Ind/Abst** Eng. Index Annu., Eng. Index Mon., Eng. Index Bioeng. Abstr., Eng. Index Energy Abstr., Biol. Abstr., Energy Res. Abstr., Comput. Control Abstr., Electr. Electron. Abstr., Sci. Abstr. Sect. A. Phys. Abstr., Phys. Abstr., Eng. Index. **LC** R858.A1. **DD** 610.2854. **NLM** W1 AU873P. **CODEN** AUMDC9.

AVIATION MEDICINE. 1951. 0250-5045. Periodical. II. English. sa. 10.00 Pounds. Air Headquarters, Medical Directorate, R K Puram West Block VI, New Delhi 110066 India. **Tel** 606611. **Ed** Avm J Vasudevan. **Ind/Abst** Int. Aerosp. Abstr. **NLM** W1 AV453M. (cum index). bk rev. adv acc. **Circ** 700. (ctrl). Original works in the field of aerospace medicine are published. Applied studies, aviation, and medicine are also catered to. *Journal of Aero Medical Society of India, 0515-5207.*

AVIATION, SPACE, AND ENVIRONMENTAL MEDICINE. (AVIATION SPACE AND ENVIRONMENTAL MEDICINE). V. 46- Jan. 1975-. 0095-6562. Periodical. US. English. mo. $55.00. Aerospace Medical Association, Washington National Airport, Washington DC 20001. **Tel** (703)892-2240. **Ed** Sidney D Leverett. **Ind/Abst** Excerpta Med., Life Sci. Collect., Cumul. Index Nurs. Allied Health Lit., Index Med., Int. Aerosp. Abstr., CIS Abstr., Biol. Abstr., Ref. Source, Chem. Abstr., Psychol. Abstr., Energy Res. Abstr., Hospit. Lit. Index, Sci. Cit. Index, Abr. Ed. **LC** RC1050. **DD** 616.98. **NLM** W1 AV47. **CODEN** ASEMCG. bk rev. adv acc. **Circ** 5,000. Edited for those involved in protecting the health of man in hostile environments. It contains original articles on clinical, investigative and applied medicine. *Aerospace Medicine, 0001-9402.*

AYU. 0005-2469. English or Hindi. ir. 6.00. Gujarata Ayurveda Yunivarsiti, Registrar Dhanvantari Mandir, Jamanagara India. **LC** R606. **NLM** W1 AY966. *Ayurvedaloka.*

THE BABOON IN MEDICAL RESEARCH. (THE BABOON IN MEDICAL RESEARCH : PROCEEDING OF THE FIRST INTERNATIONAL SYMPOSIUM ON THE BABOON

Medicine

AND ITS USE AS AN EXPERIMENTAL ANIMAL). **Main/Conf** International Symposium on the Baboon and its Use as an Experimental Animal. 1st (1963)-. 0074-8919. US. English. University of Texas Press, Box 7819/University Station, Austin TX 78712. **DD** 619.98.

BANGLADESH MEDICAL RESEARCH COUNCIL BULLETIN. V. 1- 1975-. 0377-9238. Periodical. BG. English. sa. Bangladesh Medical Research Council, Mahakhali, Dacca-12 Bangladesh. **Ind/Abst** Excerpta Med., Index Med., Biol. Abstr., Hospit. Lit. Index. **NLM** W1 BA644F. **CODEN** BMRBDI.

BASIC AND CLINICAL CARDIOLOGY. Vol. 1-. 0731-1672. Monographic Series. US. English. ir. Marcel Dekker Inc, 270 Madison Avenue, New York NY 10016. **Tel** (212)696-9000. **Ed** Denolin and Swan. **Ind/Abst** Chem. Abstr. **LC** UNC. **DD** 616.12005. **NLM** W1 BA813ST. **CODEN** BACCDW. This is an ongoing series. Each title has a different subject.

BASIC AND CLINICAL IMMUNOLOGY. 1976-. Periodical. US. English. be. $25.00. Lange Medical Publications, Drawer L, Los Altos CA 94023. **Tel** (415)948-4526. **Ed** Daniel R Stites, John D Stobo, H Huge Fundenberg and J Vivian Wells. Each issue contains an index to its own contents - no vol index - loose. Comprehensive text covering the fundamentals of cellular immunology, immunobiology, molecular immunology, immunochemistry, and immunologic laboratory test.

BASIC AND CLINICAL IMMUNOLOGY. 0195-4261. Monographic Series. US. English. ir. John Wiley & Sons Inc, 1 Wiley Drive, Somerset NJ 08873.

BASIC DATA RELATING TO THE NATIONAL INSTITUTES OF HEALTH CEASED. Ceased with 1981. US. English. an. US Government Printing Office, Superintendent of Documents, Washington DC 20402. **NLM** W2 A N208B.

BASLER VEROFFENTLICHUNGEN ZUR GESCHICHTE DER MEDIZIN UND DER BIOLOGIE. No. 1- 1953-. 0067-4524. Periodical. SZ. German. ir. Schwabe & Company, Steinentorstrasse 13, CH-4000 Basel 10 Switzerland. **Tel** 061 23 55 23. **Circ** 500. Serial about the history of medicine and biology of local interest (Basler Switzerland).

BAYER-SYMPOSIUM. 1-. Monographic Series. US. English. ir. Springer Verlag-New York Inc, 175 5th Avenue, New York NY 10010. **Tel** (212)460-1500.

BEDSIDE CARE. 0147-6254. Periodical. US. English. qt. $5.00. American Health Care Association, 1200 15th Street NW, Washington DC 20005. **Tel** (202)833-2050.

BEHAVIORAL MEDICINE ABSTRACTS. See Indexes/Abstracts.

BEIHEFT ZU LEISTUNGSSPORT. (LEISTUNGSSPORT. BEIHEFT). 0341-7492. Monographic Series. German. ir. **NLM** W1 LE67SB.

BEITRAGE ZUR ANAESTHESIOLOGIE UND INTENSIVMEDIZIN : SCHRIFTENREIHE DES LUDWIG BOLTZMANN-INSTITUTES FUR EXPERIMENTELLE ANAESTHESIOLOGIE UND INTENSIVMEDIZINISCHE FORSCHUNG. 1-. German. ir. **Ed** Karl Steinbereithner and Hans Bergmann. **NLM** W1.

BEITRAGE ZUR ORTHOPADIE UND TRAUMATOLOGIE. V. 7- 1960-. 0005-8149. Periodical. WB. German. mo. Kunst & Wissen Erich Bieber, Dufourstrasse 51, CH-8008 Zurich Switzerland. **Tel** 01/69 44 20. **Ind/Abst** Excerpta Med., Index Med., CIS Abstr., Biol. Abstr. **NLM** W1 BE163. **CODEN** BOTRAJ. Beitrage aus dem Gesamten Arbeitsbereich der Orthopadie und Chirurgisch-Medizinischen Technik.

BERETNING FOR . . . . **Main/Corp** Centrale Videnskabsetiske Komite (Denmark). 1980-81-. 0107-9786. DK. Danish. an. Forskningssekretariatet, 7 Holmens Kanal, DK-1060 Copenhagen Denmark. **LC** R724. **DD** 174.209489.

BERITA PMI. **VFOAT** Berita P.M.I. **VAT** Berta Pelang Merah Indonesia. Began in 1972. 0216-2210. Periodical. Indonesian. mo. **NLM** W1 BE659J.

THE BERKS COUNTY MEDICAL RECORD. Began with: Vol. 72, No. 7 (Sept. 1981). 0736-7333. Periodical. US. English. mo. **NLM** W1 BE671U. Medical Record (Reading, PA.).

BERLINER ARZTEBLATT. Began in 1956. Periodical. German. sm. 78.-. CB-Verlag Carl Boldt, Baseler Strabe 80, 1 Berlin 45 West Germany. **Tel** (030)833 60 66. **Ed** CB-Verlag Carl Boldt. **NLM** W1 BE804. bk rev. adv acc. (ctrl). Independent magazine for health-politics. Zeitschrift fur Arztliche Fortbildung (Berlin), Gross-Berliner Arzteblatt, Arztliches Mitteilungsblatt fur Berlin; Berliner Arzt.

THE BEST OF LAW AND MEDICINE. See Law.

BEVOLKERUNG UND KULTUR. REIHE 7 : GESUNDHEITSWESEN. IV. STERBEFALLE NACH TODESURSACHEN. **Main/Corp** Germany (West). Statistisches Bundesamt. GW. German. an. 3.20. **LC** RA407.5.G4.

BHPR SUPPORT. See Yearbooks, Almanacs, Directories.

BI-ANNUAL REVIEW OF ALLERGY. 1979-1980. 0278-9566. US. English. ir. $32.02. Medical Examination Publishing Co, 3003 New Hyde Park Road, New Hyde Park NY 11040. **Tel** (516)328-6200. **Ed** C A Frazier. **LC** RC583. **DD** 616.97005. **NLM** W1 B112. Review of recent allergy research and literature with commentary by noted specialists. Annual Review of Allergy, 0090-1083.

BIBLIOGRAFIA URUGUAYA DE MEDICINA : PUBLICACIONES PERIODICAS. See Bibliographies.

BIBLIOGRAPHY OF BIOETHICS. See Bibliographies.

BIBLIOGRAPHY OF MEDICAL REVIEWS. See Bibliographies.

BIBLIOGRAPHY OF MEDICAL TRANSLATIONS. See Bibliographies.

BIBLIOGRAPHY OF THE HISTORY OF MEDICINE. See Bibliographies.

BIBLIOTEK FOR LAGER. 0006-1786. Periodical. Danish. qt. Munksgaard Ltd, 35 Norre Sogade, DK-1370 Copenhagen K Denmark. **Ind/Abst** Excerpta Med. **NLM** W1 BI345. NYT Bibliotek for Lager.

BIBLIOTHECA ANATOMICA. Vol. 1- 1961-. 0067-7833. Periodical. English (articles in German or French). ir. S Karger AG, PO Box, CH-4009 Basel Switzerland. **Tel** 061-39 08 80. **Ed** W Lierse. **Ind/Abst** Life Sci. Collect., Index Med., Biol. Abstr., Chem. Abstr., Bibliogr. Agric., Hospit. Lit. Index. **NLM** W1 BI394. **CODEN** BIANA6. Important additions to literature documenting advances in the anatomical sciences.

BIBLIOTHECA HAEMATOLOGICA. Vol. 1 1955-. 0067-7957. Monographic Series. German. ir. S Karger AG, PO Box CH-4009, Basel Switzerland. **Tel** (061)39 08 80. **Ind/Abst** Excerpta Med., Biol. Abstr., Chem. Abstr., Nuci. Sci. Abstr., Index Med. **NLM** W1 BI412. **CODEN** BIHAA2.

BIBLIOTHECA MEDICA CANADIANA. See Library and Information Science.

BIENNIAL REPORT - GORGAS MEMORIAL LABORATORY. **Main/Corp** Gorgas Memorial Laboratory. 1979-1980-. US. English. be. Gorgas Memorial Institute, 2001 Wisconsin Avenue North West, Washington DC 20235. **LC** RC960. **DD** 616.988305.

BIENNIAL REPORT OF EXAMINING AND LICENSING BOARDS - MINNESOTA BOARD OF PODIATRY. **Main/Corp** Minnesota Board of Podiatry. US. English. be. 717 Delaware Street Se, Minneapolis MN 55440. **LC** RD563. **DD** 353.977600841.

BIENNIAL REPORT OF EXAMINING AND LICENSING BOARDS - MINNESOTA. EMERGENCY MEDICAL TECHNICIAL ADVISORY COUNCIL. **Main/Corp** Minnesota. Emergency Medical Technician Advisory Council. 1978-80-. US. English. be. Emergency Medical Technician Advisory Council, 717 Delaware Street Se, Minneapolis MN 55440. **LC** RA645.6.M6. **DD** 353.9776008243.

BIO-MEDICAL INSIGHT. V. 1- 1970-. 0090-161X. Periodical. US. English. bw. Intl Bio-Medical Inform SVC, PO Box 756, Miami FL 33156. **Tel** (305)271-7272. **NLM** W1 BI854L.

BIO-MEDICAL SCOREBOARD. V. 1- Sept. 1974-. 0095-0971. Periodical. US. English. mo. Intl Bio-Medical Info Service, PO Box 756, Miami FL 33156. **Tel** (305)271-7272.

BIOCHEMICAL MEDICINE. See Biology - Biochemistry.

BIOCYBERNETICS AND BIOMEDICAL ENGINEERING. Vol. 1, No. 1/2-. 0208-5216. Periodical. English. ir. **NLM** W1 BI662M.

BIOELECTROMAGNETICS. V. 1-. 0197-8462. Periodical. US. English. qt. Alan R Liss Inc, 41 East 11th Street, New York NY 10003. **Tel** (212)741-2515. **Ind/Abst** Life Sci. Collect., Excerpta Med., Index Med., Biol. Abstr., Chem. Abstr., Comput. Control Abstr., Electr. Electron. Abstr., Sci. Abstr. **LC** QP82.2.E43. **DD** 591.1917. **NLM** W1 BI663N. **CODEN** BLCTDO.

BIOENGINEERING CURRENT AWARENESS NOTIFICATION : BECAN. **VFOAT** BECAN. 0142-0674. Periodical. UK. English. mo. **LC** R856.A1. **DD** 610.28.

BIOGENIC AMINES. See Biology - Biochemistry.

BIOGRAPHICAL DIRECTORY OF THE AMERICAN PODIATRY ASSOCIATION. See Yearbooks, Almanacs, Directories.

BIOLOGIA ET IMMUNOLOGIA REPRODUCTIONIS. See Biology.

BIOLOGY AND MEDICINE DIVISION ANNUAL REPORT. See Biology.

BIOMATERIALS, MEDICAL DEVICES AND ARTIFICIAL ORGANS. (BIOMATERIALS, MEDICAL DEVICES, AND ARTIFICIAL ORGANS). V. 1- 1973-. 0090-5488. US. English. qt $139.00. Marcel Dekker Inc, 11305 Church Street Station, New York NY 10249. **Tel** (212)696-9000. **Ed** T F Yen. **Ind/Abst** Eng. Index Mon., Eng. Index Bioeng. Abstr., Eng. Index Energy Abstr., Life Sci. Collect., Excerpta Med., Biol. Abstr., Met. Abstr., World Alum. Abstr., Chem. Abstr., Eng. Index Annu., Eng. Index, Index Med., Energy Res. Abstr., Comput. Control Abstr., Electr. Electron. Abstr., Sci. Abstr. Sect. A. Phys. Abstr., Phys. Abstr., Sci. Cit. Index, Abr. Ed. **LC** R856.A1. **DD** 610.28. **NLM** W1 BI852S. **CODEN** BMDOAI. bk rev. adv acc. (ctrl). Medical electronic systems, plastic and reconstructive surgery, principles and methodology as well as applications, and religious, psychological, plus legal impact of use of artificial organs.

BIOMEDICA BIOCHIMICA ACTA. See Biology - Biochemistry.

BIOMEDICAL BUSINESS INTERNATIONAL. See Business.

BIOMEDICAL ELECTRONICS CEASED. Began with V. 1, No. 1 (Jan. 1965). Ceased with V. 16, No. 14 (July 25, 1981). 0006-338X. Periodical. US. English. sm. **NLM** W1 BI854F.

BIOMEDICAL ENGINEERING. V. 1- Jan. 1967-. 0006-3398. Periodical. US. English (Russian). bm. $545.00 Domestic, $605.00 Foreign. Consultants Bureau, 227 West 17th Street, New York NY 10011. **Tel** (212)260-8000. **Ed** V A Uktoror. **Ind/Abst** Eng. Index Mon., Eng. Index Bioeng. Abstr., Eng. Index Energy Abstr., Biol. Abstr., Chem. Abstr., Eng. Index Annu., Eng. Index Mon., Excerpta Med., Index Med., Energy Res. Abstr. **LC** R856. **DD** 610.28. **NLM** W1 BI854I. **CODEN** BIOEAF. Covers recent advances in the growing field of biomedical technology, instrumentation, and administration.

BIOMEDICAL ENGINEERING AND COMPUTATION SERIES. Vol. 1-. 0194-2778. Monographic Series. US. English. ir. Harwood Academic Publishers, PO Box 786 Cooper Station, New York NY 10276. **Ed** Dhanjoo N Ghista. **NLM** W1 BI854IH.

BIOMEDICAL ENGINEERING AND HEALTH SYSTEMS. 0190-0951. Monographic Series. US. English. ir. John Wiley & Sons Inc, 1 Wiley Drive, Somerset NJ 08873. **Ind/Abst** Math. Rev.

BIOMEDICAL ENGINEERING AND INSTRUMENTATION. See Engineering.

BIOMEDICAL ETHICS REVIEWS. See Ethics.

BIOMEDICAL LABORATORY TECHNICAL REPORT. 0730-8027. Monographic Series. US. English. US Army Medical Research and Development Command, Biomedical Laboratory, Aberdeen Proving Ground MD 21010. **Ind/Abst** Chem. Abstr. **CODEN** BLTRDZ.

BIOMEDICAL PRODUCTS. 0192-1266. Periodical. US. English. mo. $12.00. Gordon Publications, Box 1952/13 Emory Avenue, Dover NJ 07801-0952. **Tel** (201)361-9060.

Medicine

BIOMEDICAL RESEARCH. Vol. 1, No. 1 (Feb. 1980)-. 0388-6107. Periodical. JA. English. bm. Maruzen Co Ltd, PO Box 5050 Tokyo International, Tokyo 100-31 Japan. Tel (03)278-9224. Ind/Abst Life Sci. Collect., Excerpta Med., Biol. Abstr., Chem. Abstr. NLM W1 BI856C. CODEN BRESD5.

BIOMEDICAL TECHNOLOGY INFORMATION SERVICE. V. 4- Jan. 31, 1977-. 0147-2682. Periodical. US. English. sm. $118.00. Quest Publishing Co, 1351 Titan Way, Brea CA 92621. Tel (714)738-6400. Ed Allan F Pacela and Lon Richardson. NLM W1 BI856T. Index available. bk rev. Covers advances in medical technology and instrumentation. *Advanced Biomedical Technology, 0094-0100; Biomedical Inventions Reporter, 0094-0119; Government Documents Review, 0094-0127; Health Care Statistics Report, 0094-0135.*

BIOMEDICAL TECHNOLOGY TODAY. (BIOMEDICAL TECHNOLOGY TODAY : FROM THE ASSOCIATION FOR THE ADVANCEMENT OF MEDICAL INSTRUMENTATION). Nov./Dec. 1985-. 0883-9093. Periodical. US. English. bm. $60.00 Domestic, $72.00 Foreign. Hanley & Belfus Inc, 210 South 13th Street, Philadelphia PA 19107. DD 681.

BIOMEDICINE. VFOAT Biomedicine. V. 18-35. 0300-0893. Periodical. English (title, text and summaries in French). ir. Masson, 120 Boulevard Saint-Germain, Paris France. Ind/Abst CIS Abstr., Biol. Abstr., Life Sci. Collect. NLM W1 BI857. CODEN BIMDB3. *Revue Europeenne d'Etudes Cliniques et Biologiques, 0035-3019.*

BIOMEDICINE & PHARMACOTHERAPY. VFOAT Biomedecine & Pharmacotherapie. V. 36, No. 1 (Jan. 1982)-. 0753-3322. Periodical. US. English (articles also in French). bm. Masson Publ USA Inc, 211 East 43rd Street/Room 1306, New York NY 10017. Tel (212)370-1937. Ind/Abst Life Sci. Collect., Pestdoc, Ringdoc, Vetdoc, Excerpta Med., Index Med., Biol. Abstr., Chem. Abstr., Energy Res. Abstr. NLM W1 BI857J. CODEN BIPHEX. *Biomedicine, 0300-0893; Biomedicine Express, 0300-0855.*

BIOMEDICINE EXPRESS CEASED. VFOAT Biomedicine. Began with 1935-. 0300-0885. Periodical. FR. English (title, text and summaries in French). bm. Masson Publishing USA, 14 East 60th Street, New York NY 10016. Ind/Abst Life Sci. Collect. *Revue Europeenne d'Etudes Cliniques et Biologiques, 0035-3019.*

BIOMEDICINE (TRIVANDRUM, INDIA). See Biology.

BIOMEDIZINISCHE TECHNIK. (BIOMEDIZINISCHE TECHNIK). VFOAT Biomedical Engineering. Vol. 16- Feb. 1971-. 0013-5585. Periodical. WB. German (English or with occasional summaries in both languages). bm. Fachverlag Schiele & Schoen, Markgrafenstrasse 11, D1000 Berlin 61 West Germany. Tel (030)2516029. Ind/Abst Life Sci. Collect., Excerpta Med., Index Med., CIS Abstr., Chem. Abstr., Energy Res. Abstr., Comput. Control Abstr., Electr. Electron. Abstr., Sci. Abstr. Sect. A. Phys. Abstr., Sci. Cit. Index, Abr. Ed., Phys. Abstr. LC R856.A1. NLM W1 BI858. CODEN BMZTA7. *Elektromedizin.*

BIORESEARCH TODAY. ADDICTION. VFOAT Addiction. 0149-1008. US. English. mo. $100.00. Bioscience Information Service, 2100 Arch Street, Philadelphia PA 19103. Tel (215)587-4800. Ed BIOSIS. Current awareness journal covering drug addiction.

BIORESEARCH TODAY. BIRTH DEFECTS. VFOAT Birth Defects. 0149-0982. US. English. mo. $100.00. Bioscience Information Service, 2100 Arch Street, Philadelphia PA 19103. Tel (215)587-4800. Current awareness journal covering birth defects.

BIOSIS/CAS SELECTS. INTERFERON. See Indexes/Abstracts.

BIOSIS/CAS SELECTS. MAMMALIAN BIRTH DEFECTS. See Indexes/Abstracts.

BIOSIS/CAS SELECTS. VITAMINS. See Indexes/Abstracts.

BIRTH DEFECTS ORIGINAL ARTICLE SERIES. VFOAT Birth Defects. Vol. 1-. 0547-6844. Monographic Series. US. English. mo. Alan R Liss Inc, 41 East 11th Street, New York NY 10003. Tel (212)475-7700. Ed D Bergsma. Ind/Abst Life Sci. Collect., Excerpta Med., Biol. Abstr., Chem. Abstr., Index Med., Hospit. Lit. Index, Sociol. Abstr. LC RG626. DD 616.04305. NLM W1 BI966. CODEN BTHDAK. (cum index). A scholarly book series concerning birth defects.

BITAMIN (VITAMIN). See Chemistry.

THE BLACK BAG. (BLACK BAG). V. 1- 1972-. 0196-1594. Periodical. US. English. qt. $10.00. Student National Medical Association, 4400 Stamp Road Suite 208, Temple Hill MD 20748. Tel (301)899-0775. NLM W1 BL21.

BLACK'S MEDICAL DICTIONARY. See Yearbooks, Almanacs, Directories.

BLOOD. V. 1- Jan. 1946-. 0006-4971. Periodical. US. English (some summaries in Interlingua). mo. Grune & Stratton Inc, 111 Fifth Avenue, New York NY 10003. Tel (212)614-3232. Ind/Abst Life Sci. Collect., Pestdoc, Ringdoc, Vetdoc, Excerpta Med., Index Med., Int. Aerosp. Abstr., Biol. Abstr., Chem. Abstr., Energy Res. Abstr., Hospit. Lit. Index. DD 616. NLM W1 BL661. CODEN BLOOAW.

BLOOD BANK WEEK. Vol. 1, No. 1 (Mar. 9, 1984)-. 0747-2420. Periodical. US. English. wk. $70.00 Members, $95.00 Non-Members. American Association of Blood Banks, Suite 600/1117 North 19th Street, Arlington VA 22209. *Federal Register Excerpts Program.*

BLOOD LEAD, PROFICIENCY TESTING. US. English. mo. Centers for Disease Control, Atlanta GA 30333.

BLOOD THERAPY JOURNAL. INTERNATIONAL. (BLOOD THERAPY JOURNAL INTERNATIONAL). Vol. 1, No. 1 (Jan. 1980)-. 0006-5005. Periodical. II. English. bm. BTJ Verlag and Scientific News Service, 4 Pusa Road, PO Box 2544, New Delhi 110005 India. NLM W1 BL6615B. *Blood Therapy Journal.*

BLUT. Vol. 1- Mar. 1955-. 0006-5242. Periodical. GW. German (articles in French or English). mo. $198.00. Springer Verlag-New York Inc, 175 5th Avenue, New York NY 10010. Tel (212)460-1500. Ed H Heimpel, D Huhn, C Mueller-Eckhardt and G Ruhenstroth-Bauer. Ind/Abst Life Sci. Collect., Excerpta Med., Index Med., Biol. Abstr., Curr. Contents, Chem. Abstr., Energy Res. Abstr., Hospit. Lit. Index, Sci. Cit. Index, Abr. Ed. NLM W1 BL959. CODEN BLUTA9. Index published separately - free - automatically sent. Covers the whole spectrum of clinical and experimental hematology, hemostaseology and blood transfusion, including the diagnosis and treatment of hemopoietic and lymphatic neoplasias and bone marrow transplantation. *Folia Haematologica.*

BOERHAAVE SERIES FOR POSTGRADUATE MEDICAL EDUCATION. No. 10- 1975-. 0304-9167. Monographic Series. NE. English. ir. Leiden University Press, PO Box 566, 2501 CN The Hague Netherlands. Ind/Abst Chem. Abstr. NLM W3 BO672. CODEN BSPEDP.

BOLETIM CLINICO DES HOSPITAIS CIVIS DE LISBOA. V. 7- March/June 1946-. 0374-6070. PO. Portuguese. ir. 60.00. Livraria Sa da Costa, Rua Garrett, Lisboa 102 Portugal. LC RC31.L5. *Boletim Clinico e de Estatistica Dos Hospitais Civis de Lisboa.*

BOLETIM DE BIOESTATISTICA E EPIDEMIOLOGIA. Main/Corp Fundacao Servicos de Saude Publica. Portuguese. ir. Fundacao Servicious de Saude Publica, Av Rio Branco 251 Caixa Postal 1530, Guanabara Brazil. LC RA407.5.B7. NLM W1 BO162.

BOLETIN DA ACADEMIA NACIONAL DE MEDICINA. V. 1- April/June 1971-. 0001-3838. Periodical. Portuguese. ir. Av General Justo 365 90 Andar, 20 021 Rio de Janeiro Brazil. NLM W1 BO15F. *Boletim da Academia Nacional de Medicina, 0001-3838.*

BOLETIN DE LA ASOCIACION MEDICA DE PUERTO RICO. (BOLETIN). Main/Corp Asociacion Medica de Puerto Rico. 0004-4849. Periodical. English. mo. Puerto Rican Medical Association, Box 9378, Santurce Puerto Rico 00908. Tel (809)721-6969. Ind/Abst Life Sci. Collect., Cumul. Index Nurs. Allied Health Lit., Index Med. NLM W1 BO197H.

BOLETIN DEL ANO. Periodical. CL. Spanish. an. Academia Chilena de Medicina Clasificador, 1349 Correo Central, Santiago de Chile. LC R482.C5. DD 362.10983.

BOLETIN DEL CENTRO PANAMERICANO DE FIEBRE AFTOSA. Main/Corp Pan American Foot and Mouth Disease Center. No. 1- Jan./Mar. 1971-. 0009-0131. Periodical. BL. Spanish (English). ir. Centro Pan Am Fiebre, Aftosa Caixa Postal 589, Rio de Janerio Brasil.

BOLETIN HOSPITAL DE VINA DEL MAR. VFOAT Boletin del Hospital de Vina del Mar. V. 1- Jan. 1945-. Periodical. Spanish (some summaries in English). ir. NLM W1 BO44N.

BOLETIN INFORMATION - CEBIDE. (BOLETIN). VFOAT Boletin Informativo, Cebide. VAT Boletin Information - Centro Bibliografico de Enfermedades Endemicas. 0325-8645. Periodical. English (Spanish). ir. NLM ZWC 705 B688B.

BOLLETTINO DELLA SOCIETA MEDICO CHIRURGICA E DEGLI OSPEDALI PROVINCIA DI CREMONA. Year 30- 1976-. 0391-5999. Periodical. Italian. ir. NLM W1 BO558Z. *Bollettion - Societa Medico Chirurgica Cremona.*

BOLLETTINO DELL'ISTITUTO SIEROTERAPICO MILANESE. Main/Corp Istituto Sieroterapico Milanese Serafino Belfanti. V. 19- Jan. 1940-. Periodical. IT. Italian (English). bm. Isti Sieroterapico Milanese, Via Darwin 20/22, 20143 Milano Italy. Ind/Abst Index Med., Sci. Cit. Index, Abr. Ed. *Bollettino dell'Istituto Sieroterapico Milanese.*

BORDEAUX MEDICAL. Vol. 1- Jan. 1968-. 0021-7867. Periodical. FR. French (summaries in English, German, Spanish, and Italian). ir. 400,000. Bordeaux Medical, 153 rue de Pessac, 33000 Bordeaux France. Tel 96 01 33. Ind/Abst Life Sci. Collect., Excerpta Med., CIS Abstr., Biol. Abstr., Chem. Abstr., Energy Res. Abstr. NLM W1 BO741P. CODEN BOMEBE. *Journal de Medecine de Bordeaux et du Sud-Ouest.*

BPT-BERICHT. VFOAT BPT Bericht. VAT B. Began with: 1/77, issued May 1977. 0721-9245. Periodical. German. ir. Ind/Abst Chem. Abstr. NLM W1. CODEN BPTBDF.

BRATISLAVSKE LEKARSKE LISTY. Vol. 1 1921-. 0006-9248. Periodical. CS. Czech and English with added table of contents in French, German, and Russian. ir. Ind/Abst Life Sci. Collect., Coal Abstr., Excerpta Med., CIS Abstr., Nuci. Sci. Abstr., Index Med., Chem. Abstr., Biol. Abstr. NLM W1 BR129. CODEN BLLIAX.

BRAZILIAN JOURNAL OF MEDICAL AND BIOLOGICAL RESEARCH. VFOAT Revista Brasileira de Pesquisas Medicas e Biologicas. Vol. 14, 1 (Apr. 1981)-. 0100-879X. Periodical. English. qt. $25.00. Ind/Abst Life Sci. Collect., Excerpta Med., Biol. Abstr., Index Med., Chem. Abstr., Curr. Contents. NLM W1 BR189N. CODEN BJMRDK. *Revista Brasileira de Pesquisas Medicas e Biologicas.*

BREAST DISEASE. 0888-6008. Periodical. US. English. bm. Elsevier Science Publishing Co, 52 Vanderbilt, New York NY 10017.

BRISTOL ADVANCES IN THERAPEUTICS. VFOAT Advances in Therapeutics. Vol. 1-. 0262-8732. Monographic Series. UK. English. ir. NLM W1 BR256.

BRITISH COLUMBIA MEDICAL JOURNAL. V. 1-15, No. 5. 0007-0556. Periodical. CN. English. mo. $26.32. British Columbia Medical Journal, 1807 West 10th Avenue, Vancouver British Columbia V6J 2A9 Canada. Tel (604)736-5551. Ed Rosemary Rogan. NLM W1 BR362. adv acc. Circ 6,095. (ctrl). Official publication of the British Columbia Medical Association. Publishes medical reports and articles by British Columbia physicians and news and views on the medical scene. *Bulletin of the Vancouver Medical Association, 0366-4821.*

BRITISH JOURNAL OF ANAESTHESIA. Vol. 1 1923-. 0007-0912. Periodical. UK. English. mo. $118.00. Professional and Scientific Publishing, Travistock House E/ Travistock Square, London WC 1H 9JR England. Ind/ Abst Life Sci. Collect., Pestdoc, Ringdoc, Vetdoc, Excerpta Med., Nuci. Sci. Abstr., Index Med., Biol. Abstr., Chem. Abstr., Art Index, Hospit. Lit. Index, Sci. Cit. Index, Abr. Ed., Years Work Eng. Stud. NLM W1 BR503. CODEN BJANAD.

BRITISH JOURNAL OF CLINICAL PRACTICE. (THE BRITISH JOURNAL OF CLINICAL PRACTICE). Began with: Vol. 10, No. 10 (Oct. 1956). 0007-0947. Periodical. UK. English. mo. $61.30. Medical News Group, Tower House, Southampton Street, London WC2E 7LS England. Ind/Abst Life Sci. Collect., Pestdoc, Ringdoc, Vetdoc, Excerpta Med., Index Med., Hospit. Lit. Index, Sci. Cit. Index, Abr. Ed. LC R11. DD 610.5. NLM W1 BR519RP. *Medicine Illustrated.*

BRITISH JOURNAL OF HOSPITAL MEDICINE. V 1- Oct. 1968-. 0007-1064. Periodical. UK. English. mo $80.00. International Thomson Publishing Company, 23-29 Emerald Street,

London WC1N 3QJ England. **Ind/Abst** Life Sci. Collect., Excerpta Med., Index Med., Biol. Abstr., Chem. Abstr., Nucl. Sci. Abstr., Comput. Control Abstr., Electr. Electron. Abstr., Sci. Abstr. Sect. A. Phys. Abstr., Phys. Abstr., Hospit. Lit. Index, Sci. Cit. Index, Abr. Ed. **DD** 610. **NLM** W1 BR537N. **CODEN** BJHMAB. Index in first issue of next volume - loose - separately paged. *Hospital Medicine.*

BRITISH JOURNAL OF INDUSTRIAL MEDICINE. No. 1- Jan. 1944-. 0007-1072. Periodical. UK. English. qt. $105.74. British Medical Journal, Tavistock Square, London WC1H 9JR England. **Ind/Abst** Life Sci. Collect., World Text Abstr., World Surf. Coat. Abstr., Coal Abstr., Excerpta Med., Energy Inf. Abstr., Environ. Abstr., CIS Abstr., Biol. Abstr., Nucl. Sci. Abstr., Chem. Abstr., Index Med., Hospit. Lit. Index, Sci. Cit. Index, Abr. Ed. **LC** RC963. **DD** 331.82205. **NLM** W1 BR539. **CODEN** BJIMAG. (cum index).

BRITISH JOURNAL OF PARENTERAL THERAPY. **VFOAT** Parenteral Therapy. Vol. 4, No. 14 (May 1983)-. 0264-7494. Periodical. UK. English. bm. 18 Domestic, 23 Europe, 25 Others. The Medical News Group, Tower House, Southampton Street, London WC2E 7LS England. **Tel** (01)379-6005. **Ed** Michael Rennie. **NLM** W1. bk rev. adv acc. **Circ** 11,500. (ctrl). Reviews, original papers, book reviews, news on all aspects of administration and efficacy of parenteral therapy, relating to intravenous, intramuscular injections and other invasive routes. *British Journal of Intravenous Therapy, 0144-879X.*

BRITISH JOURNAL OF SEXUAL MEDICINE. V. 1- Sept./Oct. 1973-. 0301-5572. Periodical. UK. English. mo. 38 Domestic, 30 United Kingdom and 40 Foreign. Medical News-Tribune Ltd, Tower House Southampton Street, London WC2E 7LS England. **Tel** 01-379 6005. **Ed** Alan Riley. **Ind/Abst** Excerpta Med., Biol. Abstr. **NLM** W1 BR628. **CODEN** BJMEDF. bk rev. adv acc. **Circ** 20,000. (ctrl). Clinical papers, news and comment on sexual medicine. Principally papers on urology, gynecology, endocrinology, sexually transmitted diseases, reproductive medicine, psychosexual medicine.

BRITISH JOURNAL OF SPORTS MEDICINE. V. 4- 1969-. 0306-3674. Periodical. UK. English. qt. $30.00. British Association of Sports & Medicine, 29 Linkfield Road, Mountsorrel NR Loughborough LE12 7DJ England. **Tel** 0533-303436. **Ed** H E Robson. **Ind/Abst** Cumul. Index Nurs. Allied Health Lit., Index Med., Ref. Source, Chem. Abstr., Hospit. Lit. Index. **NLM** W1 BR637K. **CODEN** BJSMDZ. bk rev. adv acc. **Circ** 2,100. Fitness, exercise, physiology, injury prevention and treatment, doping, anthropometry including various ethnic groups. Sports psychology vehicle for communication with our members. *Bulletin - British Association of Sport and Medicine, 0306-3690.*

BRITISH MEDICAL BULLETIN. V. 1- Mar. 1943-. 0007-1420. Periodical. UK. English. ty. $75.00. British Medical Bulletin, PO Box 11318, Birmingham AL 35202. **Tel** (205)991-6920. **Ed** C A Mims. **Ind/Abst** Life Sci. Collect., Pestdoc, Ringdoc, Vetdoc, Excerpta Med., CIS Abstr., Biol. Abstr., Chem. Abstr., Nucl. Sci. Abstr., Index Med., Sci. Cit. Index, Abr. Ed. **LC** R31. **DD** 610.5. **NLM** W1 BR687. **CODEN** BMBUAQ. adv acc. Each issue covers a different medical topic. Experts worldwide review current knowledge and the latest research in a particular field.

BRITISH MEDICAL JOURNAL. V. 1- 1857-. 0007-1447. Periodical. UK. English. wk. $137.92. British Medical Journal, Tavistock Square, London WC1H 9JR England. **Ind/Abst** Excerpta Med., Bibliogr. Agric., Biol. Abstr., CIS Abstr., Coal Abstr., Cumul. Index Nurs. Allied Health Lit., Life Sci. Collect., Pestdoc, Popul. Index, Ringdoc, Vetdoc, Women Stud. Abstr., Chem. Abstr., Lang. Lang. Behav. Abstr., Hospit. Lit. Index, Sociol. Abstr., Index Med., Sci. Cit. Index, Abr. Ed. **LC** R31. **NLM** W1 BR69. **CODEN** BMJOAE. (cum index). *Association Medical Journal.*

BRITISH MEDICINE. V. 1- Jan. 1972-. 0140-2722. Periodical. UK. English. mo. $55.00. Medical Department British Council, 10 Spring Gardens, London SW1A England. **NLM** ZW 1 B863. *British Medical Book List, British Medical Index.*

BULLETIN. **Main/Corp** Association des Anatomistes. No. 1- Oct./Dec. 1926-. Periodical. FR. French. qt. $46.57. Association des Anatomists, BP 184, 54505 Vandoeuvre Nancy France.

BULLETIN - ACADEMIE NATIONALE DE MEDECINE, PARIS. **Main/Corp** Academie Nationale de Medecine, Paris. 0001-4079. French. mo. Imprimeries Reunies Chambery, 266 Route d'Apremont, 73490 la Ravoire France. **Ind/Abst** Index Med.

BULLETIN - ASSOCIATION DES MEDECINS DE LANGUE FRANCAISE DU CANADA. **Main/Corp** Association des Medecins de Langue Francaise du Canada. V. 11, No. 1- Jan./Feb. 1977-. 0702-7656. Periodical. CN. French. Association des Medecins de Langue Francaise du Canada, 5064 Avenue de Parc, Montreal Quebec H2V 4G2 Canada. **DD** 610.6271. *A M L F C, 0383-9516.*

BULLETIN - AUSTRALIAN DRUG AND MEDICAL INFORMATION GROUP. *See* Pharmacy.

BULLETIN CANADIEN D'HISTOIRE DE LA MEDECINE. **VFOAT** Canadian Bulletin of Medical History. Vol. 1, No. 1 (Jan. 1984)-. 0823-2105. Periodical. CN. English (text also in French). ir. Free to Members. Canadian Bulletin of Medical History, c/o Dr K B Roberts, Faculty of Medicine, Memorial University, St John's Newfoundland A1B 3V6 Canada. **DD** 610.971. *Newsletter (Canadian Society for the History of Medicine).*

BULLETIN - CORPORATION PROFESSIONNELLE DES MEDECINS DU QUEBEC. (BULLETIN - PROFESSIONAL CORPORATION OF PHYSICIANS OF QUEBEC). **Main/Corp** Professional Corporation of Physicians of Quebec. V. 14- Feb. 1974-. 0315-2979. Periodical. CN. English (French). mo. Free. Professional Corporation of Physicians of Quebec, 1440 rue Ste-Catherine Ouest #914, Montreal Quebec H3G 1S5 Canada. **Tel** (514)878-4441. **Ind/Abst** Point Repere. **Circ** 16,500. Pertaining to medicine and legislation. *Bulletin, 0069-5599.*

BULLETIN DE L'A. C. M. D. Q *CEASED.* **Main/Corp** Association des Conseils des Medecins et Dentistes du Quebec. V. 1-5, No. 1. 0384-5923. Periodical. CN. French. ir. Secretariat de l'Association des Conseils des Medecins et Dentistes du Quebec, 306 Est Boul St-Joseph, Montreal Quebec H2T 1J2 Canada. **DD** 610.6952062714.

BULLETIN DE LA SOCIETE FRANCAISE DE MYCOLOGIE MEDICALE. *See* Biology.

BULLETIN ET MEMOIRES DE L'ACADEMIE ROYALE DE MEDECINE DE BELGIQUE. V. 130- Jan. 1975-. 0377-8231. Periodical. BE. French. mo. $59.28. Academie Royale de Medecine de Belgique, 1 rue Ducale, Bruxelles Belgium. **Tel** (02)511-2471. **Ind/Abst** Excerpta Med., Index Med., Biol. Abstr., Chem. Abstr., Recent Publ. Artic. **NLM** W1 BU652P. **CODEN** BMABDZ. bk rev. *Bulletin de l'Academie Royale de Medecine de Belgique, 0001-4168; Memoires de l'Academie Royale de Medecine de Belgique, 0065-0595.*

BULLETIN - FEDERATION DES MEDECINS RESIDENTS ET INTERNES DU QUEBEC. (BULLETIN). Vol. 1, No. 1 (Sept. 1977)-. 0821-2406. Periodical. CN. French. mo. Free to Members. Federation des Medecins Residents et Internes du Quebec Bureau 303, 65 Est rue Sherbrooke, Montreal Quebec H2X 1C4 Canada. **DD** 610.6952060714.

THE BULLETIN - KING COUNTY MEDICAL SOCIETY. Began with V. 1, 1922. 0023-1592. Periodical. US. English. mo. $12.95. Journal & Bulletin Agency Inc, PO Box 10249, Bainbridge Island WA 98110. **Tel** (206)623-7325. **NLM** W1 BU671M. adv acc. **Circ** 4,000. Monthly bulletin and yearly photo roster.

BULLETIN - LUZERNE COUNTY MEDICAL SOCIETY. (THE BULLETIN - LUZERNE COUNTY MEDICAL SOCIETY). V. 3- Oct. 1931-. 0098-5880. Periodical. US. English. qt. $15.00. Luzerene County Medical Society, 130 South Franklin Street, Wilks Barre PA 18701. **Tel** (717)823-0917. **Ed** Edward Lottick. **NLM** W1 BU674. adv acc. **Circ** 675. Brief, socio-economic, up-to-date information on medicine and health care on a national, state, and local basis. Includes editorial, new members roster and committees listed.

BULLETIN - NEW JERSEY ASSOCIATION OF OSTEOPATHIC PHYSICIANS & SURGEONS. (BULLETIN). **Main/Corp** New Jersey Association of Osteopathic Physicians & Surgeons. 0028-5528. Periodical. US. English. mo. New Jersey Association Osteopathic Physicians & Surgeons, 1212 Stuyvesant Avenue, Trenton NJ 08618. *NJAOPS Journal (Trenton, N.J. : 1963).*

BULLETIN OF EXPERIMENTAL BIOLOGY AND MEDICINE. **VFOAT** Biulleten Eksperimentalnoi Biologii I Meditsiny. V. 41- Jan. 1956-. 0007-4888. Periodical. US. English. mo. $745.00 Domestic, $825.00 Foreign. Consultants Bureau Inc, 233 Spring Street, New York NY 10013. **Tel** (212)620-8000. **Ed** A D Ado. **Ind/Abst** Electron. Commun. Abstr. J., ISMEC Bull., Pollut. Abstr. Indexes, Saf. Sci. Abstr. J., Life Sci. Collect., Excerpta Med., Biol. Abstr., Chem. Abstr., Excerpta Med., Curr. Contents, Int. Abstr. Biol. Sci., Index Med., Sci. Cit. Index, Abr. Ed. **LC** R850. **DD** 619.05. **NLM** W1 BU772. **CODEN** BEXBAN. This important Soviet journal publishes accounts of experimental research on urgent problems of modern biology and medicine. Conducted by members of the Academy of Medical Science of the USSR.

BULLETIN OF THE ACADEMY OF MEDICINE TORONTO. (BULLETIN OF THE ACADEMY OF MEDICINE, TORONTO). **Main/Corp** Academy of Medicine, Toronto, Ont. V. 1- 1927-. 0001-4311. Periodical. CN. English. ir. Academy of Medicine, 288 Bloor Street West, Toronto Ontario M5S 1V8 Canada. **NLM** W1 BU84L.

BULLETIN OF THE CLINICAL RESEARCH INSTITUTE. V. 1- 1973-. 0304-1441. Periodical. English. ir. **NLM** W1 BU845L.

THE BULLETIN OF THE ESSEX COUNTY MEDICAL SOCIETY. 1934?-. 0014-0937. Periodical. US. English. mo. Essex County Medical Society of New Jersey, 144 South Harrison Street, East Orange NJ 07018. **NLM** W1 BU846M.

BULLETIN OF THE HISTORY OF MEDICINE. V. 1- Jan. 1933-. 0007-5140. Periodical. US. English. qt. $36.00. Johns Hopkins University Press, 701 West 40th Street/Suite 275, Baltimore MD 21211. **Tel** (301)338-6987. **Ed** Caroline Hannaway. **LC** R11. **DD** 610.9. Index received separately bound from publisher. (cum index). bk rev. adv acc. **Circ** 2,198. The leading scholarly journal in the history of medicine. It presents articles, documents and commentary about every aspect of medical history.

BULLETIN OF THE HONG KONG MEDICAL ASSOCIATION. (THE BULLETIN OF THE HONG KONG MEDICAL ASSOCIATION). **VFOAT** Hsiang-Kang I Hsueh Hui I K'an. V. 23- Oct. 1971-. 0304-954X. Periodical. HK. English. an. Hong Kong Medical Association, 15 Hennesy Road, Windsor Building/5th Floor, Hong Kong. **Ind/Abst** Excerpta Med. **NLM** W1 BU851I. *Bulletin of the Hong Kong Chinese Medical Association, 0304-9469.*

BULLETIN OF THE MASON CLINIC. **Main/Corp** Mason Clinic, Seattle. V. 1- Mar. 1947-. 0025-4657. Periodical. US. English. qt. The Mason Clinic, 1100 Ninth Avenue, PO Box 900, Seattle WA 98111. **Ind/Abst** Excerpta Med. **LC** RC31.S4. **DD** 610.5. **NLM** W1 BU856. *Clinics of the Virginia Mason Hospital, 0097-1863.*

BULLETIN OF THE MEDICAL STAFF OF THE METHODIST HOSPITALS OF DALLAS. **Main/Corp** Methodist Hospitals of Dallas. **VFOAT** Bulletin - Methodist Hospitals of Dallas Medical Staff. 0045-9550. Periodical. US. English. sa. Methodist Hospital of Dallas, PO Box 225999, Dallas TX 75265. **Tel** (214)944-8457. **Ind/Abst** Chem. Abstr. **NLM** W1 BU857GB. **CODEN** BMSDDT.

BULLETIN OF THE NATIONAL SOCIETY FOR MEDICAL RESEARCH. **Main/Corp** National Society for Medical Research. **VFOAT** NSMR Bulletin. V. 16- 1966-. 0028-0186. Periodical. US. English. mo. National Society for Medical Research, 1000 Vermont Avenue Northwest, Washington DC 20005. *Bulletin for Medical Research of the National Society for Medical Research, 0097-1855.*

BULLETIN OF THE NEW YORK ACADEMY OF MEDICINE. 2nd Series, V. 1- Mar. 1925-. 0028-7091. Periodical. US. English. mo. $18.00. New York Academy of Medicine, 2 East 103rd Street, New York NY 10029. **Tel** (212)876-8200. **Ed** William D Sharpe. **Ind/Abst** Hospit. Lit. Index, Biol. Abstr., Chem. Abstr., Cumul. Index Nurs. Allied Health Lit., Energy Res. Abstr., Excerpta Med., Index Med., Life Sci. Collect., Writ. Am. Hist., Ringdoc, Pestdoc, Vetdoc. **NLM** W1 BU874. **CODEN** BNYMAM. bk rev. **Circ** 4,000. (ctrl). The bulletin is a scholarly and scientific journal. It publishes papers presented at meetings, abstracts of original investigation, essays on medical history, book reviews, case reports, etc. *Transactions of the New York Academy of Medicine.*

BULLETIN OF THE OCMA. (THE BULLETIN OF THE OCMA). **Main/Corp** Orange County Medical Association. **VFOAT** The Bulletin of the Orange County Medical Association. 0199-7378. Periodical. US. English. mo. $24.00. Orange County Medical Association, 300 South Flower Street, Orange CA 92668. **NLM** W1 BU88. *Bulletin of the Orange County Medical Association, 0272-9059.*

BULLETIN OF THE ORIENTAL HEALING ARTS INSTITUTE OF U.S.A. **VFOAT** Mei-Kuo Chung I Yao Yen Chiu So Hui Pao. **VAT** Bulletin of the Oriental Healing Arts Institute of United States of America. Vol. 1, No. 1-. 0278-5315. US. English (Chinese, and Japanese). bm. 8820 South Sepulveda Boulevard/Suite 210, Los Angeles CA 90045. **NLM** W1 BU882P.

BULLETIN OF THE OSAKA MEDICAL SCHOOL. **Main/Corp** Osaka Ika Daigaku, Takatsuki. V. 1- April, 1954-. 0030-6142. Periodical. JA. English. sa. Osaka Medical College, 2-7 Daigakumachi Takatsuki, Osaka Japan. **Ind/Abst** Excerpta Med., Index Med., Biol. Abstr., Chem. Abstr. **NLM** W1 BU883. **CODEN** BUOSA5.

BULLETIN OF THE WORLD HEALTH ORGANIZATION. **Main/Corp** World Health Organization. **VFOAT** Bulletin de l'Organisation Mondiale de la Sante. 1742-9686. Periodical. SZ. English. bm. $60.00. World Health Organization, 49 Sheridan Avenue, Albany NY 12210. **Tel** (518)436-9686. **Ind/Abst** Life Sci. Collect., Pestdoc, Ringdoc, Vetdoc, Excerpta Med., Index Med., Biol. Abstr., CIS Abstr., Chem. Abstr., Bibliogr. Agric., Sel. Water Resour. Abstr., Hospit. Lit. Index, Sci. Cit. Index, Abr. Ed. **LC** R5. **DD** 610.82. **NLM** W1 BU896N. **CODEN** BWHOA6. Reviews progress in medical and related sciences and bringing to light new knowledge by publishing original papers on scientific research in the laboratory and field.

BULLETIN (RAJENDRA MEMORIAL RESEARCH INSTITUTE OF MEDICAL SCIENCES). (BULLETIN). Periodical. English. sa. **NLM** W1 BU478HD.

BULLETIN SIGNALETIQUE. 349, ANESTHESIE, REANIMATION. **VFOAT** Anesthesie, Reanimation. 0223-4017. French. mo. 500.00. Service des Abonnements, 26 rue Boyer, 75971 Paris Cedex 20 France. **LC** Z6667.A6, RD81. **DD** 016.61796. *Bulletin Signaletique. 349, Anesthesie, Reanimation, Choc.*

BULLETIN SIGNALETIQUE - CENTRE NATIONAL DE LA RECHERCHE SCIENTIGIQUE. 310, GENIE BIOMEDICAL, INFORMATIQUE BIOMEDICALE, PHYSIQUE BIOMEDICALE. (BULLETIN SIGNALETIQUE. 310, GENIE BIOMEDICAL, INFORMATIQUE BIOMEDICALE, PHYSIQUE BIOMEDICALE). **VFOAT** Genie Biomedical, Informatique Biomedicale, Physique Biomedicale. **VAT** Bulletin Signaletique - Centre National de la Recherche Scientifique. Trois Cent Dix, Genie Biomedical, Informatique Biomedicale, Physique Biomedicale. Vol. 42, No. 1-. 0240-852X. Periodical. French. mo. 460. **LC** Z6660, R856.A1. **DD** 016.574. **NLM** ZQ 1 B936RE. *Bulletin Signaletique. 310, Genie Biomedical, Informatique Biomedicale, 0398-9941.*

THE BULLETIN - ST LOUIS PARK MEDICAL CENTER. RESEARCH FOUNDATION. (THE BULLETIN). **VAT** Bulletin - Saint Louis Park Medical Center. Research Foundation. Vol. 20, No. 2 (Autumn 1976)-. 0741-8965. Periodical. US. English. St Louis Park Medical Center, Research Foundation, 4959 Excelsior Boulevard, Minneapolis MN 55416. **NLM** W1 BU478ID. *Bulletin (St. Louis Park Medical Center).*

BULLETIN - UNIVERSITY OF MARYLAND *CEASED.* (BULLETIN OF THE UNIVERSITY OF MARYLAND SCHOOL OF MEDICINE AND COLLEGE OF PHYSICANS AND SURGEONS). V. 1- Aug. 1916-. 0025-438X. Periodical. US. English. bm. $5.00. Medical Alumni Association of the University of Maryland Inc, University of Maryland, School of Medicine, Davidge Hall/Room 202, 522 West Lombard Street, Baltimore MD 21201. **NLM** W1 BU916. *Hospital Bulletin of the University of Maryland, Baltimore Medical College News; Journal of the Alumni Association of the College of Physicians and Surgeons, Baltimore.*

BULLETTINO DELLE SCIENZE MEDICHE. V. 1-. 0007-5787. Periodical. IT. Italian. qt. Soc Medica Chirugica Bologna Archiginnasio/Piazza Galvani 1 Bologna Italy.

BUREAU OF MEDICAL DEVICES STANDARDS SURVEY. **Main/Corp** United States. Bureau of Medical Devices and Diagnostic Products. **VFOAT** Standards Survey. Monographic Series. US. English. an.

BUREAU OF MEDICAL DEVICES STANDARDS SURVEY. INTERNATIONAL EDITION. (BUREAU OF MEDICAL DEVICES STANDARDS SURVEY). **VFOAT** Medical Devices Standards Survey. 0733-4028. US. English. an. US Food and Drug Administration, Bureau of Medical Devices, Office of the Associate Director for Standards, Washington DC 20036. **NLM** W 22.1 S785.

BUREAU OF MEDICAL DEVICES STANDARDS SURVEY. NATIONAL EDITION. (BUREAU OF MEDICAL DEVICES STANDARDS SURVEY). **VFOAT** Standards Survey. 0276-7368. US. English. an. US Government Printing Office, Superintendent of Documents, Washington DC 20402. **NLM** W 22 AA1 S7. *Bureau of Medical Devices Standards Survey (United States. Bureau of Medical Devices and Diagnostic Products), 0276-7368.*

BURNS. (BURNS, INCLUDING THERMAL INJURY). V. 1- Sept. 1974-. 0305-4179. Periodical. UK. English. 40.00 Domestic, 45.00 Foreign. John Wright and Sons Ltd, 823-825 Bath Road, Bristol B54 5NW England. **Tel** (617)486-8971. **Ed** J W L Davies. **Ind/Abst** Life Sci. Collect., Index Med., Excerpta Med. **NLM** W1 BU9732. bk rev. adv acc. Published six times per year, Burns is the only periodical to focus entirely on the scientific, clinical and social aspects of burns.

BYOIN NI OKERU KIGAI JOHO SHUSHU YOBI CHOSA HOKOKU. 1977-. Periodical. Japanese. ir. **NLM** W1 BY994U.

C. S. L. T. SPECTRUM. (THE C. S. L. T. SPECTRUM). **Main/Corp** Canadian Society of Laboratory Technologists. Alberta Branch. Dec. 1976-. 0701-1121. Periodical. CN. English. qt. C S L T Alberta Branch, PO Box 4165, Edmonton Alberta T6E 4T2 Canada. **DD** 610.69530627123. *Newsletter, 0318-062X.*

CADUCEUS. (CADUCEUS : A MUSEUM QUARTERLY FOR THE HEALTH SCIENCES). Vol. 1, No. 1 (Spring 1985)-. 0882-6447. Periodical. US. English. qt. $30.00. Department of Medical Humanities/Southern Illinois University, School of Medicine, PO Box 3926, Springfield IL 62708. **Tel** (217)782-4261. **Ed** Glen W Davidson. **DD** 362. adv acc. **Circ** 150. Focus on medical artifacts, medical practice, and institutions for health care delivery to inform readers about contexts from which contemporary health care issues have emerged.

CAEP REVIEW. (CAEP REVIEW : A CANADIAN ASSOCIATION OF EMERGENCY PHYSICIANS PUBLICATION). **VAT** Canadian Association of Emergency Physicians Review. Vol. 1, No. 1 (Fall 1980)-. 0228-8559. Periodical. CN. English. qt. Free to Members, $20.00 Nonmembers. c/o P Lane, Department of Emergency Services, Sunnybrook Medical Centre, 2075 Bayview Avenue, Toronto Ontario M4N 3M5 Canada. **DD** 616.025. **NLM** W1 CA1314.

CAHIERS D'ANESTHESIOLOGIE. 1- Apr. 1953-. 0007-9685. Periodical. FR. French. ir. $70.00. Librairie Arnette, 2 rue Casimir Delavigne, Paris VIE France. **Ind/Abst** Excerpta Med., Chem. Abstr. **NLM** W1 CA134. **CODEN** CAANBU.

CAHIERS DE BIOETHIQUE. 1- 1979-. Monographic Series. CN. French. ir. Presses de l'Universite Laval, CP 2447/Avenue de la Medecine, Ste-Foy Quebec G1K 7R4 Canada. **Tel** (418)656-5106. **NLM** W1 CA134N.

CAHIERS INTEGRES DE MEDECINE. No. 1- Oct. 10, 1970-. Periodical. FR. French. ir. S P P I F, Zi de Vineuil, BP 22, F-41350 Vineuil France.

CAHIERS MEDICAUX LYONNAIS. Ceased publication with V. 51, No. 24, June 20, 1975. 0008-0357. Periodical. FR. French. mo. $113.75. SIMEP Editions, 38-46 rue de Bruxelles, BP 1214, 69611 Villeubranne CDX France. **Ind/Abst** CIS Abstr. **NLM** W1 CA146V.

CALCIFIED TISSUE ABSTRACTS. *See* Indexes/Abstracts.

CALCIUM ANTAGONISMUS AKTUELL. **VFOAT** Calcium-Antagonismus Aktuell. Vol. 1-. 0724-7141. Periodical. German. ty. **NLM** W1.

CALIFORNIA PHYSICIAN. Vol. 1, No. 1 (Sept. 1984)-. 8750-1813. Periodical. US. English. mo. California Physician, 44 Gough Street, San Francisco CA 94103. *CMA NEWS, 0273-8244.*

CANADA DISEASES WEEKLY REPORT. **VFOAT** Rapport Hebdomadaire des Maladies au Canada. V. 1- May 10, 1975-. 0382-232X. Periodical. CN. English (French). wk. Free. Health & Welfare Canada, Health Protection Branch, Ottawa Ontario K1A 0L2 Canada. **Tel** (613)990-8964. **Ed** S E Acres. **Circ** 7,000. Current information on infectious and other diseases for surveillance purposes. *Epidemiological Bulletin, 0425-1474; Bulletin Epidemiologique, 0382-2311.*

CANADIAN ANAESTHETISTS' SOCIETY JOURNAL. (THE CANADIAN ANAESTHETISTS' SOCIETY JOURNAL. ANESTHESISTES). **VFOAT** Journal de la Societe Canadienne des Anesthesistes. V. 1- July 1954-. 0008-2856. Periodical. CN. English (French summaries). bm. $80.00. Canadian Anaesthetist Society, 94 Cumberland Street/Suite 901, Toronto Ontario M5R 1A3 Canada. **Tel** (416)923-1449. **Ed** Douglas B Craig. **Ind/Abst** Life Sci. Collect., Hospit. Lit. Index, Excerpta Med., Cumul. Index Nurs. Allied Health Lit., Nuci. Sci. Abstr., Biol. Abstr., Chem. Abstr., Index Med., Sci. Cit. Index, Abr. Ed. **NLM** W1 CA522. **CODEN** CANJAE. bk rev. adv acc. **Circ** 4,600. Also available in microfilm format. International anaesthesia medical journal publishing reports of current investigation, informative review article, editorials, clinical and technical reports, abstracts from the literature, and book reviews.

CANADIAN DOCTOR. *See* Law.

CANADIAN EMERGENCY SERVICES NEWS. V. 1- July/Aug. 1978-. 0706-9278. Periodical. CN. English. bm. 15.00. Canadian Emergency Service & News, 2116 27th Avenue Northeast/Suite 105, Calgary Alberta T2E 7A6 Canada. **Tel** (403)250-5575. **Ed** H G Gunderson. **DD** 362.10425. bk rev. adv acc. **Circ** 4,000. (ctrl). The magazine serves the need of the pre-hospital health latest news, events, and technological changes in the profession.

CANADIAN FAMILY PHYSICIAN. **VFOAT** Medecin de Famille Canadien. V. 13, No. 7- July 1967-. 0008-350X. Periodical. CN. English (includes some text in French). mo. $13.93. College of Family Physicians of Canada, 4000 Leslie Street, Willowdale Ontario M2K 2R9 Canada. **Tel** (416)493-7513. **Ed** Margaret McCaffery. **Ind/Abst** Life Sci. Collect., Sci. Cit. Index, Abr. Ed. **NLM** W1 CA553P. bk rev. adv acc. **Circ** 20,000. (ctrl). A medical journal produced by family physicians for family physicians.

CANADIAN JOURNAL OF APPLIED SPORT SCIENCES. *See* Recreation, Leisure - Sports.

CANADIAN JOURNAL OF MEDICAL TECHNOLOGY. V. 1- Oct. 1938-. 0008-4158. Periodical. CN. English (includes some text in French). qt. $15.48. Canadian Society of Laboratory Technologists, Box 830, Hamilton L8N 3N8 Ont Canada. **Tel** (416)528-8642. **Ed** Leslie D Mellor. **Ind/Abst** Life Sci. Collect., Hospit. Lit. Index, Cumul. Index Nurs. Allied Health Lit., Biol. Abstr., Chem. Abstr., Index Med., Sci. Cit. Index, Abr. Ed., Nuci. Sci. Abstr. **NLM** W1 CA594L. **CODEN** CJMTAY. bk rev. adv acc. **Circ** 21,000. (ctrl). Medical laboratory technology subjects, human interest, membership information including clinical chemistry, hematology, microbiology, histopathology, and immunohematology. *News Bulletin.*

CANADIAN JOURNAL OF OCCUPATIONAL THERAPY. **VFOAT** Revue Canadienne d'Ergotherapie. V. 6, No. 2- Oct. 1939-. 0008-4174. Periodical. CN. English (some text in French). ir. $27.09. Canadian Association of Occupational Therapy/Box 660, Hudson Heights, Quebec J0P 1J0 Canada. **Tel** (416)789-2689. **Ed** Geraldine Moore. **Ind/Abst** Hospit. Lit. Index, Excerpta Med., Cumul. Index Nurs. Allied Health Lit. **NLM** W1 CA597. bk rev. adv acc. Publishes articles and information which contribute to occupational therapy practice, theory, research and education. *Canadian Journal of Occupational Therapy and Physiotherapy, 0315-1034.*

CANADIAN LOCATIONS OF JOURNALS INDEXED FOR MEDLINE. *See* Indexes/Abstracts.

CANADIAN MEDICAL ASSOCIATION JOURNAL. **VFOAT** Journal de l'Association Medicale Canadienne. V. 1- Jan. 1911-. 0008-4409. Periodical. CN. English (includes some text in French). bw. Canadian Medical Association, PO Box 8650, Ottawa Ontario K1G 0G8 Canada. **Tel** (613)731-9331. **Ind/Abst** Hospit. Lit. Index, Pestdoc, Ringdoc, Vetdoc, Excerpta Med., Cumul. Index Nurs.

Medicine

Allied Health Lit., Energy Inf. Abstr., Environ. Abstr., CIS Abstr., Sel. Water Resour. Abstr., Nuci. Sci. Abstr., Biol. Abstr., Chem. Abstr., Index Med., Sci. Cit. Index, Abr. Ed., Sociol. Abstr., Lang. Lang. Behav. Abstr. **NLM** W1 CA624R. **CODEN** CMAJAX. *Montreal Medical Journal, 0319-6046; Maritime Medical News.*

CANADIAN MEDICAL DIRECTORY. See Yearbooks, Almanacs, Directories.

CANADIAN MEDICAL EDUCATION STATISTICS. See Statistics.

CANADIAN PODIATRIST CEASED. (THE CANADIAN PODIATRIST). V. 5-19, No. 1. 0008-4786. Periodical. CN. English. qt. The Canadian Podiatrist c/o Dr R Steiner, Suite 10 Main Square, 2615 Danforth Avenue, Toronto Ontario M4C 1L6 Canada. **DD** 617.585005. *Canadian Podiatry Journal, 0576-5927.*

CANADIAN PODIATRY ASSOCIATION NEWSLETTER. Fall 1981-. 0820-8212. Periodical. CN. English. qt. Canadian Podiatry Association, Suite 801/586 Elinton Avenue East, Toronto Ont M4P 1P2 Canada. **DD** 617.5850971. *Canadian Podiatrist, 0008-4786.*

C.A.R. SCOPE. Main/Corp Canadian Arthritis and Rheumatism Society. **VFOAT** Carscope. V. 1- Jan. 1960-. 0068-8258. Periodical. CN. English. mo. Canadian Arthritis and Rheumatism Society, 920 Yonge Street, Toronto Ont M4W 3J7 Canada.

CARLE SELECTED PAPERS. V. 27- Fall 1974-. 0098-0153. Periodical. US. English. sa. Carle Clinic Association, 6111 West Park Street, Urbana IL 61801. **Tel** (217)337-3327. **Ind/Abst** Chem. Abstr. **NLM** W1 CA793. **CODEN** CCCFAT. *Selected Papers of the Carle Clinic and Carle Foundation, 0093-5565.*

CASE STUDIES IN EMERGENCY MEDICINE. Vol. 1, No. 1 (Dec. 1984)-. 0748-027X. Periodical. US. English. mo. $95.00. Fulfillment Operations, Aspen Systems Corporation, 16792 Oakmont Avenue, Gaithersburg MD 20877. **DD** 616.

CASOPIS LEKARU CESKYCH. Vol. 1 1862-. 0008-7335. Periodical. CS. Czech (table of contents and summaries in English, French, German and Russian). wk. $132.40. Artia, Smecky 30, PO Box 790, Praha 1 Czechoslovakia. **Ind/Abst** Life Sci. Collect., Excerpta Med., Index Med., CIS Abstr., Chem. Abstr., Sociol. Abstr., Lang. Lang. Behav. Abstr. **NLM** W1 CA919. **CODEN** CLCEAL.

CATALOG - ARTHRITIS INFORMATION CLEARINGHOUSE (U.S.). (CATALOG). 1979-. 0277-9552. US. English. an. Arthritis Information Clearinghouse, PO Box 34427, Bethesda MD 20817. **LC** Z6664.A74, RC933.A1. **DD** 016.616722. **NLM** ZWE 344 C357C.

CATALOGO COLETIVO DE PUBLICACOES PERIODICAS EM CIENCIAS BIOMEDICAS. See Bibliographies.

CATHOLIC MEDICAL QUARTERLY : JOURNAL OF THE GUILD OF CATHOLIC DOCTORS. Began in Oct. 1947. 0008-8226. Periodical. UK. English. qt. $15.00. Guild of Catholic Doctors, Broad Towers, Caerleon Newport Guent England. **NLM** W1 CA972. *Catholic Medical Guardian.*

CAUSES OF DEATH. CANADA STATISTICS CANADA. VITAL STATISTICS SECTION. (CAUSES OF DEATH; PROVINCES BY SEX AND CANADA BY SEX AND AGE). Main/Corp Canada. Statistics Canada. Vital Statistics Section. **VFOAT** Causes de Deces par Province Selon le Sexe et le Canada Selon le Sexe et l'Age. 1970-. 0380-7533. Periodical. CN. English (text in French). an. $2.80. Number of deaths by three-digit categories and four-digit subcategories of the International Classification of Diseases, Injuries and Causes of Death, by sex for the provinces, and by sex and five-year age groups for Canada. *Causes of Death.*

C.C.R.U.M. PUB. **VFOAT** CCRUM Pub. Monographic Series. English (Multilingual). ir. **LC** UNC. **DD** 610.954. **NLM** W1 CC115.

CDC LIBRARY SERIAL HOLDINGS. See Library and Information Science.

CEARA MEDICO. (CEARA MEDICO : ORGAO DO CENTRO MEDICO CEARENSE). Began with: Yearly V. 5, March 1917. 0101-1782. Periodical. Portuguese. qt. **Ind/Abst** Excerpta Med. **NLM** W1 CE113. *Norte Medico.*

CENTER (NEW YORK, N.Y. : 1984). (CENTER). **VFOAT** C.E.N.T.E.R. No. 1- 1984. 0741-7144. Periodical. US. English. qt. $40.00. National Center for Health Education, 30 East 29th Street, New York NY 10016. **Tel** (212)689-1886. **Ed** Gerald Delamey. bk rev. adv acc. **Circ** 50,000. Describes education for health news, programs, and issues in patient care, and workplace. Purpose is to develop and sustain a network among all who educate for health.

CENTRAL AFRICAN JOURNAL OF MEDICINE. Vol. 1 Jan. 1955-. 0008-9176. Periodical. RH. English. mo. $35.00. Central African Journal of Medicine, PO Box 2073, 11 Lawson Avenue, Milton Park Salisbury Rhodesia. **Tel** 790340. **Ed** M Gelfand. **Ind/Abst** Excerpta Med., Biol. Abstr., Chem. Abstr., Index Med., Nuci. Sci. Abstr., Sci. Cit. Index, Abr. Ed., Hospit. Lit. Index. **NLM** W1 CE301. **CODEN** CAJMA3. bk rev. adv acc. **Circ** 1,300. General medicine pertaining to Africa and Zimbabwe in particular.

CENTRE MEDICAL. Yearly Vol. 37-. 0008-9826. Periodical. French. ir. **NLM** W1 CE485. (cum index). *Le Centre Medical et Pharmaceutique.*

CERRAHPASA MEDICAL REVIEW. Vol. 1-. 0254-4113. English. an. Free. **Ind/Abst** Excerpta Med. **NLM** W1 CE856.

CEYLON MEDICAL JOURNAL. New Series, V. 1- May 1952-. 0009-0875. Periodical. CE. English. qt. Ceylon Medical Association, 6 Wijerama Mawalha, Colombo 7 Ceylon. **Ind/Abst** Excerpta Med., Index Med. **NLM** W1 CE945. (cum index).

CHAMBLEE FACILITY SERIAL HOLDINGS. **VFOAT** Serial Holdings. 0748-9161. US. English. Department of Health & Human Services, Public Health Service, Centers for Disease Control, Atlanta GA 30333. **LC** Z6660. **DD** 016.6105.

CHANG KENG I HSUEH. **VFOAT** Chang Gung Medical Journal. Began with: Vol. 1, 1976. Periodical. Chinese (English). ir. **NLM** W1 CH1233R.

CHANGING MEDICAL MARKETS. See Business - Marketing.

CHE-CHIANG CHUNG I HSUEH YUAN HSUEH PAO. **VFOAT** Journal of Zhejiang Traditional Chinese Medical College, Zhejiang Zhongyi Xueyuan Xuebao. Began in 1977. Periodical. CH. Chinese. bm. Chung-Kuo Kuo Chi Shu Tien, PO Box 2820, Pei-Ching China. **LC** R97.7.C5. **DD** 610.951.

CHE-CHIANG I KO TA HSUEH HSUEH PAO. **VFOAT** Journal of Zhejiang Medical University. Periodical. Chinese. ir. **NLM** W1.

CHE VUOI?. **VFOAT** Che Vuoi. 1 (Fall 1984)-. 0749-906X. Periodical. US. English. qt. $20.00. Che Vuoi, 63 Duke Ellington Boulevard No 5, New York NY 10025. **DD** 616.

CHEMOTHERAPY. V. 13- 1968-. 0009-3157. Periodical. SZ. English. bm. $150.00. S Karger AG, PO Box, CH-4009 Basel Switzerland. **Tel** (061)39 08 80. **Ed** H Schonfeld. **Ind/Abst** Excerpta Med., Index Med., Life Sci. Collect., Index Dent. Lit., Chem. Abstr., Pestdoc, Ringdoc, Vetdoc, Sci. Cit. Index, Abr. Ed., Hospit. Lit. Index. **NLM** W1 CH399. **CODEN** CHTHBK. adv acc. Publishes the results of investigations into the mode of action and pharmacologic properties of antibacterial, antiviral and antitumor substances used in chemotherapy. *Chemotherapia.*

CHI SHENG CHUNG HSUEH YU CHI SHENG CHUNG PING TSA CHIH. **VFOAT** Journal of Parasitology & Parasitic Diseases. Vol. 1-, No. 1-. Periodical. Chinese. ir. **Ind/Abst** Index Med. **NLM** W1.

CHICAGO MEDICINE. V. 63, No. 28- 1961-. 0009-3637. Periodical. US. English. sm. $10.00. Chicago Medical Society, 515 North Dearborn, Chicago IL 60610. **Tel** (412)670-2550. **NLM** W1 CH5992.

CHILD AND FAMILY POLICY. Vol. 2-. 0741-2312. Monographic Series. US. English. ir. Ablex Publishing Corporation, 355 Chestnut Street, Norwood NJ 07648. **Tel** (201)767-8450. **Ed** Ron Haskins and James J Gallagher. **NLM** W1 CH643DC. Five book series on various aspects of social policy as it affects children. *Advances in Child and Family Policy.*

CHINA MEDICAL ABSTRACTS. See Indexes/Abstracts.

CHINA MEDICAL REPORTER. V. 1- Feb. 1973-. 0090-5003. Periodical. US. English. mo. PO Box 2342, Palo Alto CA 94305. **NLM** W1 CH755.

CHOESIN UIHAK. **VFOAT** The New Medical Journal. Began in 1958. Periodical. KO. Korean (with some summaries in English). ir. 12,000. Choesin Uihak SA, 25-9 3-ka Chungmu-ro Chung-ku, Seoul Korea. **LC** R97.7.K6. **DD** 610.5. **NLM** W1 CH881.

CHOKSIPCHA PYONGWON CHI. Main/Corp Soul Chsksipcha Pyongwon. **VFOAT** Medical Journal of the Red Cross Hospital. Periodical. KO. Korean (summaries in English). ir. Taehan Choksipcha Sa, 32 3-ka Namsan-dong Chung-ku, Seoul Korea. **LC** R97.7.K6. **DD** 610.5.

CHOONPA IGAKU. **VFOAT** Japanese Journal of Medical Ultrasonics. Periodical. JA. Japanese. sa. **NLM** W1 CH908. *Nippon Choonpa Igakkai Kenkyu Happyokai Koen Ronbun Shu.*

CHUCHE UIHAK. **VFOAT** Juche Uihak. V. 1, No. 1(1982)-. Periodical. KO. Korean (with summaries in English). Kwahak, Paekkwa Sajon Chulpansa, Changgyong 2-Dong Sosong-Kuyok, Pyongyang-Si North Korea. **LC** R97.7.K6.

CHUNG-HUA CH'I KUAN I CHIH TSA CHIH. **VFOAT** Zhonghua Qiguan Yizhi Zazhi. Vol. 1. 0254-1785. Periodical. CC. Chinese. qt. $5.04. China Publication Centre, PO Box 2820, Beijing China. **NLM** W1 CH977M.

CHUNG-HUA HSUEH YEH HSUEH TSA CHIH. **VFOAT** Zhonghua Xueyexue Zazhi. 0253-2727. Periodical. CC. Chinese. mo. $25.92. China Publication Centre, PO Box 2820, Beijing China. **Ind/Abst** Chem. Abstr. **NLM** W1 CH9819H. **CODEN** CHTCD7.

CHUNG-HUA I HSUEH TSA CHIH. **VFOAT** Chinese Medical Journal. Chuan 1- Yueh 1954-. 0578-1337. Periodical. Chinese (table of contents also in English). ir. **Ind/Abst** Excerpta Med., Chem. Abstr. **NLM** W1 CH982E. **CODEN** CIHCDM.

CHUNG-HUA LI LIAO TSA CHIH. **VFOAT** Zhonghua Liliao Zazhi. 0254-1408. Periodical. CC. Chinese. qt. 68394. China Publication Centre, PO Box 2820, Beijing China. **Ed** 23905-287. **NLM** W1 CH982KH. bk rev. adv acc. **Circ** 17,097. Original articles, clinicopathologica conference, basic sciences, lecturers and reviews, short reports, case reports, questions and answers, etc.

CHUNG-HUA NEI KO TSA CHIH. **VFOAT** Chinese Journal of Internal Medicine, Zhonghua Neike Zazhi. 1- 1953?-. 0578-1426. Periodical. CC. Chinese. ir. PO Box 2820, Beijing China. **Ind/Abst** Index Med., Chem. Abstr. **NLM** W1 CH983. **CODEN** CHHNAB.

CHUNG I YAO HSUEH PAO. **VFOAT** Zhongyiyaoxuebao. Periodical. CC. Chinese. qt. 0.30. Hei-Lung-Chiang Chung I Hsueh Yuan, Ha-Erh-Pin Shih yu Chu, Harbin Heilungkiang China Mainland. **LC** R97.7.C5. **DD** 610.951.

CHUNG-KUO I HSUEH KO HSUEH YUAN NIEN PAO. **VFOAT** Annual Report. Chinese (English). ir. **NLM** ZW 1.

CHUNG-KUO SHENG WU I HSUEH KUNG CHENG HSUEH PAO. **VFOAT** Chinese Journal of Biomedical Engineering. Vol. 1, (Nov. 1982)-. Periodical. CH. Chinese (abstracts in English). qt. Chung-Kuo Tu Shu Shin Chu Kou Tsung Kung SSU, 137 Chao Nei Ta Chieh, Peking China. **LC** R856.A1. **DD** 610.28. **NLM** W1.

CHUNG-SHAN I HSUEH YUAN HSUEH PAO. **VFOAT** Acta Academiae Medicinae Zhong Shan. V. 1-. Periodical. CC. Chinese. qt. 0.60. Hsin I Hsueh Pien Chi Shih, Chugn-Shan I Hsueh Yuan, Canton China Mainland. **NLM** W1 CH991G.

CHUNG YAO T'UNG PAO. **VFOAT** Zhongyao Tongbao. V. 1-5, No. 3. 0578-2031. Periodical. CC. Chinese. mo. $7.29. China Publication Centre, PO Box 2820, Beijing China.

CICLOS SOBRE EL AVANCE CONTINUO DE LA MEDICINA. 0185-1020. Monographic Series. Spanish. ir. **NLM** W3 C162BG.

CIENCIAS MEDICAS. 1968-. Periodical. Portuguese. ir. **Ind/Abst** Excerpta Med. **NLM** W1 CI263.

CIENCIAS MEDICAS (NITEROI, RIO DE JANEIRO, BRAZIL). (CIENCIAS MEDICAS). V. 1, N. 1 (July/Dec. 1981)-. 0101-4501. Periodical. Portuguese. ir. **NLM** W1 CI262V.

CINCINNATI MEDICINE. V. 1- Fall 1978-. 0163-0075. Periodical. US. English. qt. $8.00. Academy Journal Publishing Co, 320 Broadway, Cincinnati OH 45202. **NLM** W1 CI334V. *Cincinnati Journal of Medicine, 0009-6873.*

CIOMS CALENDAR OF INTERNATIONAL AND REGIONAL CONGRESSES OF MEDICAL SCIENCES. (CIOMS CALENDAR). **VFOAT** Calendar of Congresses of Medical Sciences. **VAT** Council for International Organizations of Medical

Sciences Calendar of International and Regional Congresses of Medical Sciences. 0379-8100. SZ. English (French). an. 10.-. C I O M S Publications, Avenue Appia, 1211 Geneva 27 Switzerland. **Tel** 91 34 06. **NLM** W 3.5 C143. adv acc. **Circ** 2,000. Calendar of congresses of medical sciences. *CIOMS Calendar of International and Regional Congresses of Medical Sciences, 0379-8100.*

CIRCUIT (NEW BRUNSWICK HOSPITALS MEDICAL ENGINEERING PROGRAM). (CIRCUIT). Vol. 1-. 0715-4828. Periodical. CN. English (text also in French and in parallel columns). bm. Free. Circuit, c/o Bio-Engineering Institute, University of New Brunswick, PO Box 4400, Fredericton New Brunswick E3B 5A3 Canada. **DD** 610.2809715. *Newsletter, 0383-0586; Circulaire, 0383-0594.*

CIRCULATION RESEARCH. V. 1- Jan. 1953-. 0009-7330. Periodical. US. English. mo. $86.00 Domestic, $105.00 Foreign. American Heart Association, 7320 Greenville Avenue, Dallas TX 75231. **Tel** (214)750-5466. **Ed** Francois M Abboud. **Ind/Abst** Life Sci. Collect., Pestdoc, Ringdoc, Vetdoc, Excerpta Med., Index Med., Int. Aerosp. Abstr., Biol. Abstr., Chem. Abstr., Energy Res. Abstr., Sci. Cit. Index, Abr. Ed. **LC** RC681.A1. **DD** 616.105. **NLM** W1 CI741. **CODEN** CIRUAL. **Circ** 3,300. (ctrl). Basic research in the cardiovascular field, publishing original articles and editorials for clinicians interested in basic science and for research workers in anatomy and etc.

CIRCULATION RESEARCH. SUPPLEMENT. Aug. 1964-. 0069-4185. Periodical. US. English. mo. American Heart Association, 44 East 23rd Street, New York NY 10010. **Ind/Abst** Life Sci. Collect., Chem. Abstr. **NLM** W1 CI741A. **CODEN** CIRSAF.

CLEVELAND PHYSICIAN. Periodical. US. English. mo. Bulletin of the Academy of Medicine, 11001 Cedar Avenue, Cleveland OH 44106. *Bulletin.*

CLIN-ALERT. Began in 1962. 0069-4770. Periodical. US. English. sm. $69.95. Science Editors Inc, PO Box 7185, Louisville KY 40207. **Tel** (502)897-5310. **Ed** Ramona M Scheible. **NLM** ZQZ 42 C641. Adverse drug reaction and interaction bulletin service. Current information on therapeutic hazards. All back issues from 1962 available. Binders, quarterly, cumulative indexes provided free.

CLINICA. 0144-7777. Periodical. UK. English. wk. $376.00. Pharmabooks Ltd, 82 Riverside Drive, New York NY 10024. **Tel** (212)580-82700. **Ed** Peter Charlish. **Ind/Abst** Pharm. News Index, Predicasts. **CODEN** CLNCD5. adv acc. **Circ** 10,000. Offers information on medical/surgical equipment, specialties, disposables, reagents and instrumentation. Covers all aspects of the medical device market place as a weekly international publication.

CLINICA CHEMICA. No. 1-. 0358-4879. Monographic Series. FI. English (Finnish). ir. Professor Sakari Piha, University of Oulu, 90100 Oulu 10 Finland. **Tel** 358-81-332133. **Ed** Leo Hirvonen. **NLM** W1 AC954NM NO.33 ETC. adv acc. **Circ** 500. (ctrl). Monographs, reviews and dissertations in the field of clinical chemistry.

CLINICA E LABORATORIO. 0391-2035. Periodical. IT. Italian. qt. Il Pensiero Scientifico Edit, Via Panama 48, 00198 Rome Italy. **Ind/Abst** Chem. Abstr. **NLM** W1 CL366V. **CODEN** CLLADN.

CLINICA EUROPEA. 0009-9007. Periodical. IT. Italian. bm. $64.00. Clinica Europea, Via Concordia 20, Rome Italy. **Tel** 06/7543927. **Ed** Federici Fausto. **Ind/Abst** Excerpta Med., Chem. Abstr. **NLM** W1 CL372. **CODEN** CLEUAB. bk rev. adv acc. **Circ** 3,000.

CLINICA TERAPEUTICA *CEASED.* (LA CLINICA TERAPEUTICA). May 1951-. 0009-9074. Periodical. IT. Italian. mo. $95.05. Societa Editrice Universo, Via G B Morgagni 1, Roma Italy 00161. **Tel** 06/85-9063. **Ind/Abst** Pestdoc, Ringdoc, Vetdoc, Excerpta Med., Index Med., Biol. Abstr., Chem. Abstr. **NLM** W1 CL582. **CODEN** CLTEA4.

CLINICAL AND EXPERIMENTAL HYPERTENSION. PART A, THEORY AND PRACTICE. **VFOAT** Theory and Practice. Vol. A4, No. 1 & 2 (1982)-. 0730-0077. Periodical. US. English. mo. $375.00. Marcel Dekker Journals, PO Box 11305 Church Street Station, New York NY 10249. **Ed** Irvin H Stater. **Ind/Abst** Life Sci. Collect., Arch. Environ. Health, Biol. Abstr., Biol. Dig., Chem. Abstr., Curr. Contents, Vetdoc, Ringdoc, Excerpta Med., Index Med., Int. Pharm. Abstr., Sci. Cit. Index, Abr. Ed., Pestdoc, Ringdoc, Vetdoc, Autom. Subj. Citation Alert. **LC** RC685.H8. **NLM** W1 CL658B. **CODEN** CEHADM. bk rev. adv acc. *Clinical and Experimental Hypertension, 0148-3927.*

CLINICAL AND EXPERIMENTAL IMMUNOLOGY. V. 1- 1966-. 0009-9104. Periodical. UK. English. mo. 200 Domestic, 450 Foreign. Blackwell Scientific Publishing, PO Box 88, Oxford OX2 0EL England. **Tel** 0865 240201. **Ed** J L Turk. **Ind/Abst** Life Sci. Collect., Pestdoc, Ringdoc, Vetdoc, Excerpta Med., Energy Inf. Abstr., Environ. Abstr., Biol. Abstr., Chem. Abstr., Index Med., Bibliogr. Agric. **LC** RC583. **DD** 616.0705. **NLM** W1 CL664. **CODEN** CEXIAL. adv acc. **Circ** 1,740. Publishes material describing original research on the role of immunology in the diagnosis and pathogenesis of disease, including allergy.

CLINICAL AND EXPERIMENTAL RHEUMATOLOGY. **VFOAT** Rheumatology. V. 1, No. 1 (Jan./March 1983)-. Periodical. English. qt. $15.75. Clinical and Experimental Rheumatology, Via S Marie 31, 56100 Pisa Italy. **Ind/Abst** Excerpta Med., Chem. Abstr. **NLM** W1 CL664F. **CODEN** CERHDP.

CLINICAL AND INVESTIGATIVE MEDICINE. **VFOAT** Medicine Clinique et Experimentale. V. 1-. 0147-958X. Periodical. UK. English (summaries in French). qt. $92.86. University of Toronto Press, 5201 Dufferin Street, Downsview Ontario M3H 5T8 Canada. **Tel** (514)931-0745. **Ed** Carl A Goresky. **Ind/Abst** Life Sci. Collect., Excerpta Med., Index Med., Biol. Abstr., Chem. Abstr. **NLM** W1 CL664G. **CODEN** CNVMDL. bk rev. adv acc. **Circ** 1,200. Available on microfilm and microfiche. Research and review articles dealing with clinical investigation, laboratory research, epidemiologic, analysis, health care research, medical education, studies, symposia, clinical science conferences.

CLINICAL AND LABORATORY HAEMATOLOGY. V. 1-. 0141-9854. Periodical. UK. English. qt. $137.50. Blackwell Scientific Publ Ltd, PO Box 88, Oxford OX2 OEL England. **Tel** 240201. **Ed** J M England. **Ind/Abst** Excerpta Med., Index Med., Chem. Abstr., Sci. Cit. Index, Abr. Ed., Hospit. Lit. Index. **NLM** W1 CL664L. **CODEN** CLHAD3. bk rev. adv acc. **Circ** 650. (ctrl). Publishes a broad spectrum of work related to the practice of haematology and blood transfusion.

CLINICAL ANTIBIOTIC SELECTION. V. 1. 0091-8881. Monographic Series. US. English. an. Futura Publishing Company, 295 Main Street, PO Box 298, Mount Kisco NY 10549. **Tel** (914)666-3505. **NLM** W1 CL668E.

CLINICAL BIOMECHANICS. V. 1-. 0191-7870. Monographic Series. US. English. ir. Clinical Biomechanics Coorporation, PO Box 35185, Los Angeles CA 90035. **LC** UNC. **NLM** W1 CL668U.

CLINICAL DIAGNOSIS BY LABORATORY METHODS. US. English. ir. W B Saunders, West Washington Square, Philadelphia PA 19105. **Tel** (800)523-0713.

CLINICAL ECOLOGY. *See* Genealogy and Heraldry - Archives.

CLINICAL ENGINEERING INFORMATION SERVICE. **VFOAT** CEIS. Vol. 1, No. 1 (Jan./Feb.). 0277-0393. Periodical. US. English. bm. $85.00. Scientific Enterprises Inc, 5104 Randolph Road, North Little Rock AR 72116. **Tel** (501)771-1775. **Ed** David Simmons. **Ind/Abst** Hospit. Lit. Index. **NLM** W1. Topics in management and technology for clinical engineering. Contains practical, usable material written by and for clinical engineers and Bmet'S.

CLINICAL EXPERIENCE. Vol. 1, No. 1 (March 1984)-. 0747-7724. Periodical. US. English. qt. $32.00. Hospital Practice, HP Publishing Company Inc, 575 Lexington Avenue, New York NY 10022. **Ed** Gene H Stollerman. **DD** 616.

CLINICAL HEMORHEOLOGY. Vol. 1, No. 1-. 0271-5198. Periodical. US. English. bm. Pergamon Press, 395 Sawmill River Road, Elmsford NY 10523. **Tel** (914)592-7700. **Ind/Abst** Excerpta Med., Chem. Abstr. **LC** QP105. **DD** 612.1181. **NLM** W1 CL71F. **CODEN** CLHEDF. Available on microfiche and microfilm.

CLINICAL IMMUNOLOGY AND IMMUNOPATHOLOGY. V. 1- Oct. 1972-. 0090-1229. Periodical. US. English. mo. Academic Press, 4805 Sand Lake Road, Orlando FL 32819. **Ind/Abst** Life Sci. Collect., Excerpta Med., Index Med., Biol. Abstr., Chem. Abstr., Energy Res. Abstr. **LC** RC583. **DD** 616.07905. **NLM** W1 CL715. **CODEN** CLIIAT.

CLINICAL IMMUNOLOGY NEWSLETTER. V. 1- Jan. 7, 1980-. 0197-1859. Periodical. US. English. mo. $58.00. Elsevier Science Publishing Company Inc, PO Box 1663/Grand Central Station, New York NY 10163. **Tel** (212)370-5520. **Ed** Herman Friedman. **Ind/Abst** Life Sci. Collect., Chem. Abstr. **NLM** W1 CL715G. **Circ** 1,000. This newsletter brings readers concise and practical reports on topics of immediate importance in immunology.

CLINICAL IMMUNOLOGY REVIEWS. Vol. 1, No. 1-. 0277-9366. Periodical. US. English. qt. $90.00. Marcel Dekker, 270 Madison Avenue, New York NY 10016. **Ind/Abst** Life Sci. Collect., Index Med., Biol. Abstr., Chem. Abstr. **NLM** W1. **CODEN** CIMRDO.

CLINICAL IMMUNOLOGY UPDATE. **Series/Titl** Reviews for Physicians. 1979-. 0163-1683. US. English. an. $62.00. Elsevier-North Holland Inc, 52 Vanderbilt Avenue, New York NY 10017. **Ed** Herman Friedman, Mario Escobar and Nael Rose. **LC** RC582. **DD** 616.079. **NLM** W1 CL715L. **Circ** 1,000. Each issue contains concise and practical reports on topics of immediate importance, focusing on seriodiagnosis and immunopathology. Features include original reports, case studies, guest editorials, and announcements.

CLINICAL JOURNAL. V. 1- Spring 1978-. 0366-6743. Periodical. US. English. sa. $11.00. North Shore University Hospital, 300 Community Drive, Manhasset NY 11030. **Tel** (516)562-0100. **NLM** W1 CL72B.

CLINICAL LAB PRODUCTS. 1972. 0192-1282. Periodical. US. English. mo. $42.50. Clinical Lab Products Inc, PO Box 69, Amherst NH 03031. **Tel** (603)673-7555. **Ed** Jane Pluke. adv acc. **Circ** 53,000. (ctrl). New products in the clinical diagnostic field.

CLINICAL LABORATORY REFERENCE. **VFOAT** CLR. 1st- Ed. 0093-8076. US. English. an. Litton Publishing, 550 Kinderkamack Road, Oradell NJ 07649. **Ed** Robert J Fitzgibbon. **LC** RB36.2. **DD** 338.47616075. **NLM** QY 26 C641. adv acc. **Circ** 50,000. A source for comparing and evaluating products and machinery used in clinical labs. Indexed by manufacturer, product, and test. Also lists professional groups, meetings, etc.

CLINICAL MEDICINE. V. 47, No. 9- Sept. 1940-. 0412-7994. Periodical. US. English. ir. $80.00. Lippincott Harper, 2350 Virginia Avenue, Hagerstown MD 21740. **Tel** (800)638-3031. **NLM** W1 CL73TC. *Clinical Medicine and Surgery, 0092-6477; Southern General Practitioner; Mississippi Valley Medical Journal, 0096-5480; Antibiotics & Chemotherapy, 0570-3123.*

CLINICAL MONOGRAPHS IN HEMATOLOGY. V. 1- 1979-. 0193-1547. Monographic Series. US. English. ir. Thieme-Stratton, 381 Park Avenue South, New York NY 10016. **Tel** (212)683-5088/89. **Ed** T F Necheles. **LC** UNC. **NLM** W1 CL731M.

CLINICAL RESEARCH. V. 6- Jan. 1958-. 0009-9279. Periodical. US. English. qt. $25.00 Domestic, $26.50 Foreign. American Federation for Clinical Research, 6900 Grove Road, Thorofare NJ 08086. **Ind/Abst** Life Sci. Collect., Hospit. Lit. Index, Pestdoc, Ringdoc, Vetdoc, Excerpta Med., Index Med., Biol. Abstr. **NLM** W1 CL778. **CODEN** CLREAS. *Clinical Research Proceedings, 0096-0004; Journal of Clinical Investigation, 0021-9738.*

CLINICAL RESEARCH ASSOCIATES NEWSLETTER. Periodical. US. English. $31.00. Clinical Research Associates, 3707 North Canyon Road, Suite 6, Provo UT 84601.

CLINICAL RHEUMATOLOGY. Vol. 1, No. 1 (March 1982)-. 0770-3198. Periodical. English. qt. $41.50. Association Society of Scientifique Medica Belgica, 43 rue des Champs Elysees, B1050 Brussels Belgium. **Ind/Abst** Excerpta Med., Index Med., Chem. Abstr. **NLM** W1 CL779L. **CODEN** CLRHD6. *Acta Rhumatologica, 0250-4642.*

CLINICAL STUDIES. 1- 1971-. Periodical. US. English. ir. Elsevier Science Publishing Co, PO Box 1663, Grand Central Station, New York NY 10163.

CLINICAL SYMPOSIA. V. 1- Spring 1948-. 0009-9295. Periodical. US. English. ir. $18.97. Clinical Symposia, 420 Madison Avenue, New York NY 10017. **Ind/Abst** Index Med., Cumul. Index Nurs. Allied Health Lit. **LC** R11. **DD** 616.05.

Medicine

CLINICAL THERAPEUTICS. V. 1-. 0149-2918. Periodical. US. English. qt. $46.00. Excerpta Medica, PO Box 3085, Princeton NJ 08540. **Tel** (609)896-9450. Ed George E Farrar Jr. **Ind/Abst** Life Sci. Collect., Excerpta Med., Index Med., Biol. Abstr., Chem. Abstr. **LC** RM260. **DD** 615.5805. **NLM** W1 CL796I. **CODEN** CLTHDG. **Circ** 2,000. (ctrl). Dedicated to the prompt publication of clinical studies and results of on-going research of new and existing therapeutic agents. Distributed to medical schools, teaching hospitals, and individuals worldwide.

CLINICAL TRIALS JOURNAL. See Biology - Biochemistry.

CLINICAL UPDATE. VFOAT Mayo Clinical Update. Vol. 1, No. 1 (Winter 1985)-. 0882-6617. Periodical. US. English. qt. Mayo Clinic, Rochester MN 55905. **DD** 616.

CLINICAL UPDATE, SPORTS MEDICINE. (CLINICAL UPDATE. SPORTS MEDICINE). VFOAT Sports Medicine. V. 1, No. 1 (Jan./Feb. 1984)-. 0740-7238. Periodical. US. English. bm. $20.00. Circulation Manager, Aurora Publishing Company, PO Box 54594, Atlanta GA 30308.

CLINICS IN CHEST MEDICINE. V. 1- Jan. 1980-. 0272-5231. Monographic Series. US. English. qt. $55.00. W B Saunders Co, West Washington Square, Philadelphia PA 19105. **Tel** (215)574-3395. Ed Susan Plummer. **Ind/Abst** Excerpta Med., Life Sci. Collect., Index Med., Sci. Cit. Index, Abr. Ed. **LC** UNC. **NLM** W1 CL831AG. **Circ** 4,000. Practical updates for the clinician on the latest advances plus topics of current interest.

CLINICS IN CRITICAL CARE MEDICINE. 1-. 0262-1614. Monographic Series. UK. English. ir. Churchill Livingstone Inc, 1560 Broadway, New York NY 10036. **Tel** (212)819-5400. Ed Iain Mca Ledingham and Ake Grenvik. **Ind/Abst** Chem. Abstr. **NLM** W1 CL831AI. **CODEN** CCCMDJ.

CLINICS IN DIAGNOSTIC ULTRASOUND. V. 1-. 0193-743X. Monographic Series. US. English. ir. Longman Inc, 95 Church Street, White Plains NY 10601. **Tel** (212)764-3950. **NLM** W1 CL831BC.

CLINICS IN EMERGENCY MEDICINE. Vol. 1-. 0733-4354. Monographic Series. US. English. ir. Churchill Livingstone Inc, 1560 Broadway, New York NY 10036. **Tel** (212)819-5400. **LC** UNC. **NLM** W1 CL831BCI.

CLINICS IN GASTROENTEROLOGY. V. 1- Jan. 1972-. 0300-5089. Monographic Series. UK. English. ty. $60.00. WB Saunders Company, West Washington Square, Philadelphia PA 19105. **Tel** (215)574-3395. Ed Sean Duggan. **Ind/Abst** Life Sci. Collect., Excerpta Med., Index Med., Biol. Abstr., Chem. Abstr., Sci. Cit. Index, Abr. Ed. **LC** RC799. **DD** 616.3005. **NLM** W1 CL831BG. **CODEN** CGSTA9. Each issue contains an index to its own contents - no vol index - loose. **Circ** 2,400. Practical updates for the clinician on the latest advances plus topics of current interest.

CLINICS IN HAEMATOLOGY. VFOAT Haematology. Began with: Vol. 1, No. 1 (Feb. 1972)-. 0308-2261. Periodical. UK. English. ty. $60.00. W B Saunders Company, West Washington Square, Philadelphia PA 19105. **Tel** (215)574-3395. Ed Nicholas Dunton. **Ind/Abst** Life Sci. Collect., Index Med., Biol. Abstr., Chem. Abstr., Sci. Cit. Index, Abr. Ed. **NLM** W1 CL831C. **CODEN** CLHMB3. **Circ** 2,000. Practical updates for the clinician on the latest advances plus topics of current interest.

CLINICS IN LABORATORY MEDICINE. VFOAT Laboratory Medicine. Vol. 1, No. 1 (March 1981)-. 0272-2712. Periodical. US. English. qt. $45.00. W B Saunders Co, West Washington Square, Philadelphia PA 19105. **Tel** (215)574-3395. Ed Edward Yeager. **Ind/Abst** Excerpta Med., Index Med. **NLM** W1 CL831CC. **Circ** 2,200. Practical updates for the clinician on the latest advances plus topics of current interest.

CLINICS IN PERINATOLOGY. V. 1- March 1974-. 0095-5108. Periodical. US. English. ty. $45.00. W B Saunders Co, West Washington Square, Philadelphia PA 19105. **Tel** (215)574-3395. Ed Barbara Conover. **Ind/Abst** Life Sci. Collect., Excerpta Med., Index Med., Biol. Abstr., Chem. Abstr., Energy Res. Abstr., Hospit. Lit. Index, Sci. Cit. Index, Abr. Ed. **NLM** W1 CL831CH. **CODEN** CLPEDL. **Circ** 4,000. Practical updates for the clinician on the latest advances and topics of current interest.

CLINICS IN PODIATRY. Vol. 1, No. 1 (April 1984)-. 0742-0668. Periodical. US. English. ty. $36.00. W B Saunders Co, West Washington Square, Philadelphia PA 19105. **LC** RD563. **DD** 617.585005. **NLM** W1.

CLINICS IN SPORTS MEDICINE. VFOAT Sports Medicine. Vol. 1, No. 1 (March 1982)-. 0278-5919. Monographic Series. US. English. qt. $50.00. W B Saunders Company, West Washington Square, Philadelphia PA 19105. **Tel** (215)574-3395. Ed Edward Yeager. **Ind/Abst** Index Med. **LC** UNC. **DD** 617.1027. **NLM** W1. **Circ** 4,000. Practical updates for the clinician on the latest advances plus topics of current interest.

CLINIMED. (CLINIMED ENREGISTREMENT SONORE). V. 1, No. 1 (Jan. 27, 1976)-. 0825-3005. Periodical. CN. French. ir. Medifacts Ltee, 472 Ch Richmond, Ottawa Ontario K2A 0G3 Canada. **DD** 610.

CLIO MEDICA. VFOAT Acta Academiae Internationalis Historiae Medicinae. V. 1- Nov. 1965-. 0366-676X. Periodical. NE. English (French or German). qt. 120.-. Editions Rodopi, Keizersgracht 302-304, 1016 EX Amsterdam Netherlands. **Tel** (020)227507. Ed Putscher. **Ind/Abst** Am. Hist. Life, Hist. Abstr., Part A, Mod. Hist. Abstr., Hist. Abst., Part B, Twent. Century Abstr., Excerpta Med., Index Med., Am. Hist. Life, Hist. Abstr., Hospit. Lit. Index. **LC** R131.A1. **NLM** W1 CL933. bk rev. adv acc. **Circ** 350. (ctrl).

CLUJUL MEDICAL. 1- Feb. 1920-. Periodical. RM. Romanian. qt. Ilexim Press Department, PO Box 1-136-1-137, Bucharest Romania. **Ind/Abst** Biol. Abstr., Chem. Abstr. **NLM** W1 CL934. **CODEN** CLUMBY.

CMD, CURRENT MEDICAL DIALOG. VFOAT Current Medical Dialog. 0007-862X. Periodical. US. English. mo. Williams & Wilkins, PO Box 64025, Baltimore MD 21264. **LC** R11. **DD** 610.5. **NLM** W1 C402. **CODEN** CMDIDE. CMD.

CME NEWS. (C M E NEWS). **Main/Corp** University of Saskatchewan. Continuing Medical Education. 1969. 0701-4880. Periodical. CN. English. ir. $10.00. University of Saskatchewan, 408 Ellis HL Department Continuing Medical Education, Saskatoon Saskatchewan S7N 0W0 Canada. **Tel** (306)966-7790. Ed Mona Chappell and K Stakiw. **Circ** 1,800. (ctrl) A variety of medical topics covering diagnostics and their specialties.

COLLANA DI AGGIORNAMENTI IN ANESTESIA E RIANIMAZIONE. 0390-6310. Periodical. Italian. ir. **NLM** W1 CO167CR.

COLLECTIONS. See Genealogy and Heraldry - Archives.

THE COLLEGE REVIEW. (THE COLLEGE REVIEW : A PUBLICATION OF THE AMERICAN COLLEGE OF MEDICAL GROUP ADMINISTRATORS). Vol. 1, No. 1 (Spring 1984)-. 0742-8057. Periodical. US. English. sa. Free to ACMGA Fellows, $18.00 ACMGA Nominees & Candidates, $22.00 Others. American College of Medical Group Administrators, 1355 South Colorado Boulevard/Suite 900, Denver CO 80222. **Ind/Abst** Hospit. Lit. Index. **NLM** W1.

COLORADO MEDICINE. V. 77- Jan. 1980-. 0199-7343. Periodical. US. English. sm. $12.00. Colorado Medical Society, 1601 East 19th Avenue, Denver CO 80218. **Ind/Abst** Hospit. Lit. Index, Excerpta Med., Index Med. **LC** R11. **DD** 610.5. **NLM** W1 CO25LD. Rocky Mountain Medical Journal, 0035-760X.

COLORADO MEDICINE. DIRECTORY OF PHYSICIANS. See Yearbooks, Almanacs, Directories.

COMMENTARIES ON RESEARCH IN BREAST DISEASE. V. 1-. 0194-1666. Periodical. US. English. ir. Alan R Liss Inc, 41 East 11th Street, New York NY 10003. **Tel** (212)475-7700. Ed RD Bulbrook and D Jane Taylor. **Ind/Abst** Chem. Abstr. **NLM** W1 CO37I. **CODEN** CRBDDO. A book series concerning the research in breast disease.

COMMUNICATIVE DISORDERS CEASED. V. 1-6. Periodical. US. English. mo. Ed Larry J Bradford. **NLM** W1 CO4279I.

COMMUNITY MEDICINE. V. 1- Feb. 1979-. 0142-2456. Periodical. UK. English. qt. PSG Publications, 545 Great Road, Littleton MA 01460. **Tel** (617)486-8971. **Ind/Abst** Excerpta Med., Index Med., Cumul. Index Nurs. Allied Health Lit., Hospit. Lit. Index. **NLM** W1 CO429LC.

COMPARATIVE STUDIES IN HEALTH SYSTEMS AND MEDICAL CARE. VFOAT Comparative Studies of Health Systems and Medical Care. No. 1- 1978-. Monographic Series. US. English. Ed C Leslie. **NLM** W1 CO437S.

COMPENDIA RHEUMATOLOGICA. 1-. 0379-7996. Monographic Series. SZ. German. ir. Eular Verlag, Postfach 146 Oberwilerstr 23, CH-4011 Basel Switzerland. Ed H Mathies, and F J Wagenhauser. **NLM** W1 CO439R.

COMPENDIUM DE INVESTIGACIONES CLINICAS LATINOAMERICANAS. Periodical. MX. Spanish. bm. $90.00. Intersistemas sa de Cv, Ferando Alencastre #110, Lomas Virreyes Mexico 10 Mexico. **Tel** 540 5600/540 07 98. Ed Juan del Rio H. **Ind/Abst** Excerpta Med., Biol. Abstr. **NLM** W1 CO448. **CODEN** CLATDP. **Circ** 5,500. (ctrl). Clinical and pharmacological research studies and clinical therapeutic trials.

COMPENSATION REPORT ON HOSPITAL-BASED PHYSICIANS. 1976/1977-. 0275-5211. US. English. an. Hospital Compensation Service, 115 Watchung Drive/PO Box 321, Hawthorne NJ 07507. **Tel** (201)427-2221. **LC** R728.5. **DD** 331.2816106952. **NLM** W1.

COMPLEMENT (BASEL, SWITZERLAND). (COMPLEMENT). 1/1/84 (March 1984)-. 0253-5076. Periodical. SZ. English. qt. $97.00. S Karger AG, 150 Fifth Avenue, New York NY 10011. Ed U E Nydegger. **Ind/Abst** Life Sci. Collect., Chem. Abstr., Index Med. **NLM** W1. **CODEN** CMPLDF. adv acc. Provides a single source for basic research results, anticipating that this concentration will encourage interest in the development of clinical applications.

COMPREHENSIVE DISSERTATION INDEX. See Indexes/Abstracts.

COMPREHENSIVE IMMUNOLOGY. V. 1-. 0149-1148. Monographic Series. US. English. ir. Plenum Press, 233 Spring Street, New York NY 10013. **Tel** (212)620-8000. Ed R A Good and S B Day. **Ind/Abst** Life Sci. Collect., Chem. Abstr. **LC** UNC. **NLM** W1 CO4523. **CODEN** COIMDV. Index published separately - free - upon request.

COMPREHENSIVE PLAN FOR EMERGENCY MEDICAL SERVICES - (INDIANA). Main/Corp Indiana. Emergency Medical Services Commission. US. English. State of Indiana, Emergency Medical Services Commission, 315 State Office Building, Indianapolis IN 46204. **LC** RA645.6.I5. **DD** 362.1809772.

COMPREHENSIVE THERAPY. V. 1- May 1975-. 0098-8243. Periodical. US. English. mo. $125.10. Laux Company Inc, PO Box 700, Ayer MA 01432. **Tel** (617)772-2584. Ed John G Bellows and Randall T Bellows. **Ind/Abst** Excerpta Med., Cumul. Index Nurs. Allied Health Lit., Index Med., Energy Res. Abstr., Hospit. Lit. Index. **LC** R11. **DD** 610.5. **NLM** W1 CO453K. **Circ** 2,300. Continuing medical education journal. Offers opportunity to earn Category 1 credits. Each issue covers different area of medicine.

COMPREHENSIVE VIROLOGY. V. 1- 1974-. Periodical. US. English. ir. Plenum Press, c/o H Feldman, 233 Spring Street, New York NY 10013. **Tel** (212)620-8000. **Ind/Abst** Life Sci. Collect., Bibliogr. Agric.

COMPUTER APPLICATIONS IN THE BIOSCIENCES : CABIOS. See Biology.

COMPUTER PROGRAMS IN BIOMEDICINE. See Computers and Computer Science.

COMPUTERS AND BIOMEDICAL RESEARCH. See Computers and Computer Science.

COMPUTERS AND MEDICINE. See Computers and Computer Science.

COMPUTERS IN BIOLOGY AND MEDICINE. See Computers and Computer Science.

COMPUTING PHYSICIAN. Vol. 1, No. 1 (April 1983)-. 0737-8556. Periodical. US. English. mo. $80.00. PW Communications Inc, 515 Madison Avenue, New York NY 10022. **NLM** W1.

CONCOURS MEDICAL. Vol. 1 1879-. 0010-5309. Periodical. FR. French. wk. $106.43. Concours Medical, 37 rue de Bellefond, 75009 Paris France. Ed Jacque Pouletty. **Ind/Abst** Excerpta Med.,

Medicine

Coal Abstr., CIS Abstr., Nucl. Sci. Abstr., Chem. Abstr., Biol. Abstr., Energy Res. Abstr. **NLM** W1 CO462. **CODEN** COMEAO. bk rev. adv acc. **Circ** 55,000. (ctrl). Medical review regarding continuous information on therapeutic medicine and ethics.

CONFERENCE ON RESEARCH IN MEDICAL EDUCATION : PROCEEDINGS. **VFOAT** Research in Medical Education, Proceedings of the . . . Annual Conference. Began in 1962. 0573-3960. US. English. an. $15.00. Association of American Medical Colleges, 1 Dupont Circle NW/Suite 200, Washington DC 20036. **Tel** (202)828-0549. **NLM** W3 C8832B.

CONFERENCE PROCEEDINGS IN THE HEALTH SCIENCES. **VFOAT** Comptes Rendus des Conferences sur les Sciences de la Sante. V. 1- 1925/73-. Periodical. CN. English (French). an. **NLM** ZW 3 C748. Conference Proceedings in the Health Sciences Held by the National Science Library.

CONNECTICUT MEDICINE. V. 22, No. 8- Aug. 1958-. 0010-6178. Periodical. US. English. mo. Connecticut Medicine, 160 St Ronan Street, New Haven CT 06511. **Tel** (203)865-0587. **Ind/Abst** Life Sci. Collect., Hospit. Lit. Index, Excerpta Med., Cumul. Index Nurs. Allied Health Lit., Index Med., CIS Abstr., Energy Res. Abstr. **NLM** W1 CO711N. Connecticut State Medical Journal, 0096-0179.

CONNECTIVE ISSUES. 8756-9086. Periodical. US. English. bm. $20.00. The National Marfan Foundation, 54 Irma Avenue, Port Washington NY 11050. **Tel** (516)883-8712. **Ed** Priscilla Ciccariello. **DD** 616. adv acc. **Circ** 2,000. (ctrl). Articles by, about, and for people, and their families, with the Marfan Syndrome. Information for the layman and the professional. Human interest stories and information regarding research.

CONN'S CURRENT THERAPY. 1984-. 8755-8823. US. English. an. W B Saunders Company, West Washington Square, Philadelphia PA 19105. **LC** RM101. **DD** 615.505. Current Therapy, 0070-2102.

CONSULTANT. V. 1- April 1961-. 0010-7069. Periodical. US. English. ir. Consultant Publishing Division, Cliggott, PO Box 4010, Greenwich CT 06830. **Tel** (203)661-0600. **Ind/Abst** Cumul. Index Nurs. Allied Health Lit. **LC** R11. **DD** 616.005. **NLM** W1 CO752.

CONTACT. 1- 1972-. Periodical. SZ. English. bm. $7.43. Christian Medical Commission, 150 Route de Ferney, 1211 Geneva Switzerland. **Ed** Eric Ram. bk rev. **Circ** 25,000. Bulletin of the Christian Medical Commission reporting topical, innovative approaches to the promotion of health.

CONTEMPORARY ANESTHESIA PRACTICE. 1-. 0191-247X. Monographic Series. US. English. **Ed** B R Brown Jr. **Ind/Abst** Index Med. **LC** UNC. **NLM** W1 CO769ME. Clinical Anesthesia.

CONTEMPORARY DIALYSIS CEASED. Began with Vol. 1 (Sept. 1980). 0273-6535. Periodical. US. English. mo. $35.00. Contemporary Dialysis Inc, 17901 Ventura Boulevard, Suite D, Encino CA 91316. **Tel** (818)344-4200. **Ed** Jerry Fisher. **DD** 616. **NLM** W1 CO769MG.

CONTEMPORARY ISSUES IN CLINICAL ONCOLOGY. **VFOAT** Contemporary Issues in Oncology. Vol. 1-. Monographic Series. US. English. **Ed** Peter H Wiernik. **NLM** W1.

CONTEMPORARY ISSUES IN FETAL AND NEONATAL MEDICINE. 1-. Monographic Series. US. English. **NLM** W1.

CONTEMPORARY ISSUES IN INFECTIOUS DISEASES. Vol. 1-. Monographic Series. US. English. **Ed** Merle A Sande and Richard K Root. **NLM** W1.

CONTEMPORARY RESEARCH IN CHINESE ACUPUNCTURE. 1- Spring 1974-. 0704-0830. Periodical. CN. English (Chinese). qt. $24. Academy of Oriental Heritage, PO Box 3507 Station E, Vancouver BC Canada. **LC** RM184. **DD** 615.89205.

CONTEMPORARY TOPICS IN MOLECULAR IMMUNOLOGY. V. 2-. 0090-8800. US. English. ir. Plenum Press, 233 Spring Street, New York NY 10013. **Tel** (212)620-8000. **Ind/Abst** Index Med., Chem. Abstr., Energy Res. Abstr., Sci. Cit. Index, Abr. Ed. **LC** QR180. **DD** 574.2905. **NLM** W1 CO77K. **CODEN** CTMIB4. Contemporary Topics in Immunochemistry, 0161-4304.

CONTINUING EDUCATION FOR THE FAMILY PHYSICIAN. **VFOAT** Continuing Education. V. 1- Aug. 1973-. 0092-735X. Periodical. US. English. mo. $80.00. Le Jacq Publishing Inc, 53 Park Place, New York NY 10007. **Tel** (212)766-4300. **Ed** Gayle Stephens. **LC** R11. **DD** 610.5. **NLM** W1 CO775N. adv acc. **Circ** 78,000. (ctrl).

CONTINUING MEDICAL EDUCATION NEWSLETTER. V. 1- Aug. 1968-. 0163-805X. Periodical. US. English. mo. American Medical Association, 535 Dearborn Street, Chicago IL 60616. **Tel** (312)645-5000. **NLM** W1 CO776J.

CONTRIBUTIONS IN MEDICAL HISTORY. No. 1-. 0147-1058. Monographic Series. US. English. ir. Greenwood Press, 88 Post Road West, Box 5007, Westport CT 06881. **Tel** (203)226-3571. **Ed** John C Burnham. **LC** UNC. **NLM** W1 CO778NH.

CONTROLLED CLINICAL TRIALS. V. 1- May 1980-. 0197-2456. Periodical. US. English. qt. $52.00. Elsevier Science Publishing Company Inc, PO Box 1663 Grand Central Station, New York NY 10163. **Tel** (212)370-5520. **Ed** C L Meinert. **Ind/Abst** Life Sci. Collect., Pestdoc, Ringdoc, Vetdoc, Excerpta Med., Index Med., Sci. Cit. Index, Abr. Ed. **LC** R850.A1. **DD** 616.0072. **NLM** W1 CO779F. **CODEN** CCLTDH. bk rev. adv acc. **Circ** 1,750. This international journal provides authoritative coverage of the design, methods and operational aspects of prospective follow-up studies with clinical trials.

CONVENTION REPORTER. 0882-5319. US. English. ir. PW Communications Inc, 400 Plaza Square, Secaucus NJ 07094. **DD** 610.

CONVERGENCES MEDICALES. V. 1, No. 1-. 0750-0785. Periodical. French. ir. **Ind/Abst** Excerpta Med., Chem. Abstr. **NLM** W1. **CODEN** COMEES.

COOPERATION. 0192-4842. Periodical. US. English. bm. $20.00. Missouri Osteopathic Association, PO Box 748, Jefferson City MO 65102. **Ed** E H Borman. **NLM** W1 CO816. adv acc. **Circ** 1,800. (ctrl). Policy update in health care, government-bills, rules and regulations, new medical trends, scientific and management articles, association news.

CORE JOURNALS IN CLINICAL PHARMACOLOGY. **VFOAT** Clinical Pharmacology. Vol. 1, No. 1 (Jan. 1983)-. 0167-8965. Periodical. English. mo. Elsevier Scientific Publishers, PO Box 211, 1000 AE Amsterdam Netherlands. **CODEN** CJCPD9.

CORE JOURNALS IN GASTROENTEROLOGY. 0165-8719. English. mo. Elsevier Science Publishers, PO Box 211, 1000 AE Amsterdam Netherlands. **NLM** ZWI 100 C797. **CODEN** CJGADI.

CORPUS MEDICORUM GRAECORUM SUPPLEMENTUM ORIENTALE. 1- 1963-. 0589-8072. Periodical. ir. Deutscher Buch Export-Import, Leninstrasse 16, DDR-701 Leipzig East Germany.

COST AND PRODUCTION SURVEY REPORT. See Economics - Economics: Industry & Production.

COST CONTAINMENT. See Medicine - Medical Centers, Hospitals.

COST EFFECTIVENESS RESOURCE PERSONNEL DIRECTORY. See Yearbooks, Almanacs, Directories.

COUNCIL NOTES - INDIANA FAMILY HEALTH COUNCIL, INC. (COUNCIL NOTES). **Main/Corp** Indiana Family Health Council. No. 1- Winter 1977-. 0146-1117. Periodical. US. English. qt. Indiana Family Health Council, 21 Beachway Drive/Suite B, Indianapolis IN 46224. **Tel** (317)247-9151.

CRANIOFACIAL GROWTH SERIES. Monograph No. 1-. 0162-7279. Monographic Series. US. English. ir. Center Human Growth & Development, 300 North Ingalls Building, Ann Arbor MI 48106. **Tel** (313)764-4485. **LC** UNC. **NLM** W1 CR118.

CRC CRITICAL REVIEWS IN CLINICAL LABORATORY SCIENCES. **VFOAT** Critical Reviews in Clinical Laboratory Sciences. **VAT** Chemical Rubber Company Critical Reviews in Clinical Laboratory Sciences. V. 1- Jan. 1970-. 0590-8191. Periodical. US. English. qt. CRC Press Inc, 2000 Corporate Boulevard NW, Boca Raton FL 33431. **Ind/Abst** Life Sci. Collect., Index Med., Biol. Abstr., Chem. Abstr., Energy Res. Abstr. **DD** 610. **NLM** W1 C555B. **CODEN** CRCLBH.

CRC CRITICAL REVIEWS IN IMMUNOLOGY. **VFOAT** Critical Reviews in Immunology. V. 1- Nov. 1979-. 0197-3355. Periodical. US. English. ir. $116.00. CRC Press Inc, 2000 Corporate Boulevard NW, Boca Raton FL 33431. **Tel** (305)994-0555. **Ind/Abst** Life Sci. Collect., Index Med., Biol. Abstr., Chem. Abstr., Sci. Cit. Index, Abr. Ed. **LC** QR180. **DD** 574.2905. **NLM** W1 CR1243. **CODEN** CCRIDE. Seeks to present a balanced overview of contemporary immunology and held together with molecular immunology and immunobiology.

CRC CRITICAL REVIEWS IN ONCOLOGY/HEMATOLOGY. **VFOAT** C.R.C. Critical Reviews in Oncology/Hematology. Vol. 1, Issue 1-. 0737-9587. Periodical. US. English. qt. $116.00. CRC Press Inc, 2000 Corporate Boulevard NW, Boca Raton FL 33431. **Tel** (305)994-0555. **Ind/Abst** Life Sci. Collect. **LC** RC254.A1. **DD** 616.992005. Subject matter pertaining to etiology, epidemiology, diagnosis, treatment, pathophysiology, immunology, and cell biology will be discussed in a critical and analytical manner.

CRC HANDBOOK OF ENGINEERING IN MEDICINE AND BIOLOGY. See Engineering.

CRC HANDBOOK SERIES IN CLINICAL LABORATORY SCIENCE. SECTION A. NUCLEAR MEDICINE. (CRC HANDBOOK SERIES IN CLINICAL LABORATORY SCIENCE. SECTION A : NUCLEAR MEDICINE). **VAT** Chemical Rubber Company Handbook Series in Clinical Laboratory Science. Section A. Nuclear Medicine. V. 1- 1977-. 0160-4406. US. English. CRC Press Inc, 18901 Cranwood Parkway, Cleveland OH 44128. **Ed** R P Spencer. **NLM** W1 C56N.

CRC HANDBOOK SERIES IN CLINICAL LABORATORY SCIENCE. SECTION D. BLOOD BANKING. (CRC HANDBOOK SERIES IN CLINICAL LABORATORY SCIENCE. SECTION D : BLOOD BANKING). **VFOAT** Handbook Series in Clinical Laboratory Science. **VAT** Chemical Rubber Company Handbook Series in Clinical Laboratory Science. Section D. Blood Banking. V. 1- 1977-. 0160-4414. US. English. CRC Press Inc, 18901 Cranwood Parkway, Cleveland OH 44128. **Ed** T J Greenwalt and E A Steane. **NLM** W1 C56Q.

CRC HANDBOOK SERIES IN CLINICAL LABORATORY SCIENCE. SECTION I. HEMATOLOGY. **VFOAT** Handbook Series in Clinical Laboratory Science. V. 1-. 0270-4722. US. English. **NLM** W1 C56SE.

CRC HANDBOOK SERIES IN ZOONOSES. SECTION C, PARASITIC ZOONOSES. **VFOAT** Parasitic Zoonoses. Vol. 1-. 0739-7372. US. English. CRC Press, 2000 Corporate Boulevard NW, Boca Raton FL 33431. **NLM** W1 CR1243F.

CREATION AND DETECTION OF THE EXCITED STATE. V. 2- 1974-. 0097-1405. US. English. ir. Marcel Dekker/Continuation Department, PO Box 11305, Church Street Station, New York NY 10249. **NLM** W1 CR125.

CRITICAL CARE. **Main/Corp** Society of Critical Care Medicine. V. 1- 1980-. 0270-7462. US. English. an. $37.00. Society of Critical Care Medicine, 223 East Imperial Highway/Suite 110, Fullerton CA 92635. **Tel** (714)870-5243. **LC** RC86. **DD** 616.028. **NLM** W1 CR216D.

CRITICAL CARE MEDICINE. V. 1- Jan./Feb. 1973-. 0090-3493. Periodical. US. English. mo. $75.00. Williams & Wilkins Company, 428 East Preston Street, Baltimore MD 21202. **Tel** (301)528-4000. **Ed** William C Shoemaker. **Ind/Abst** Life Sci. Collect., Excerpta Med., Cumul. Index Nurs. Allied Health Lit., Index Med., Energy Res. Abstr., Sci. Cit. Index, Abr. Ed. **LC** RC86. **DD** 616.02505. **NLM** W1 CR216K. adv acc. **Circ** 9,300. Cross-disciplinary journal for hospital-based specialists who treat patients in the ICU and CCU, including anaesthesiologists and critical care nurses.

CRITICAL CARE QUARTERLY. V. 1- May 1978-. 0160-2551. Monographic Series. US. English. qt. Aspen Systems Corporation, PO Box 6018, Gaithersburg MD 20760. **Tel** (301)251-5000. **Ind/Abst**

Medicine

Hospit. Lit. Index, Excerpta Med., Cumul. Index Nurs. Allied Health Lit., Biol. Abstr. **LC** RC86. **DD** 616.02505. **NLM** W1 C23L. **CODEN** CCCQDV.

CRITICAL CARE UPDATE CEASED. V. 10, No. 9. 0162-7252. Periodical. US. English. mo. $35.00 Membership. Critical Care Update, PO Box 5828, Orange CA 92667. **Ind/Abst** Cumul. Index Nurs. Allied Health Lit., Int. Nurs. Index. **NLM** W1 CR216U.

CRITICAL LIST. (THE CRITICAL LIST). V. 1- Aug. 1975-. 0380-1446. Periodical. CN. English. bm. $8. The Critical List, 32 Sullivan Street, Toronto Ontario M5T 1B9 Canada. **DD** 610.5.

CRITICAL REVIEWS IN CLINICAL LABORATORY SCIENCES. VFOAT CRC Critical Reviews in Clinical Laboratory Sciences. V. 4- 1973-. Periodical. US. English. qt. $116.00. CRC Critical Review Journals, CRC Press Inc, Arvida Executive Center, 2000 North West 24th Street, Boca Raton FL 33431. **Tel** (305)994-0555. Provides a detailed, critical evaluation of new concepts, methods, and data by recognized leaders. *CRC Critical Reviews in Clinical Laboratory Sciences.*

CRITICAL REVIEWS IN THERAPEUTIC DRUG CARRIER SYSTEMS. VFOAT C.R.C. Critical Reviews In Therapeutic Drug Carrier Systems. Vol. 1, Issue 1-. 0743-4863. Periodical. US. English. an. $116.00. CRC Press Inc, 2000 Corporate Boulevard NW, Boca Raton FL 33431. **Tel** (305)994-0555. **DD** 615. Publishes authoritative, objective, and comprehensive, multidisciplinary critical review papers which encompass the basic biological, medical, and pharmaceutical sciences.

CRITICAL REVIEWS IN TROPICAL MEDICINE. Vol. 1-. 0737-609X. US. English. ir. Plenum Publishing Corporation, 233 Spring Street, New York NY 10013. **Tel** (212)620-8000. Ed R K Chandra. **LC** RC960. **DD** 616.9883. **NLM** W1 CR216Y.

CUADERNOS VALENCIANOS DE HISTORIA DE LA MEDICINA Y DE LA CIENCIA. 16- 1975-. Monographic Series. SP. Spanish. ir. Instituto Historia de la Medecina, Paseo al Mar, Valencia Spain. **NLM** W1 CU142MA. *Cuadernos Hispanicos de Historia de la Medicina Y de la Ciencia.*

CUMULATED ABRIDGED INDEX MEDICUS. See Indexes/Abstracts.

CUMULATED INDEX MEDICUS. See Indexes/Abstracts.

CUR. V. 1- 1970-. 0010-0226. Periodical. FR. French. qt. 350.00. Librairie Maloine, 27 rue de l'Ecole de Medecine, 75006 Paris France. **NLM** W1 CO107E.

CURA ANIMARUM : A JOURNAL FOR THE ADVANCEMENT OF RELIGIOUS CARE OF TROUBLED PERSONS. Vol. 36, No. 1 (May 1984)-. Periodical. US. English. ir. Kutztown Publishing Co, PO Box 346, Route 222 & Sharadin Road, Kutztown PA 19530. *AMHC Forum, 0883-0401.*

CURE SYSTEMS: UV-IR-EB. (BUYER'S GUIDE TO REACTIVE CURE SYSTEMS, UV-IR-EB). VFOAT Reactive Cure Systems, UV-IR-EB. 0734-7200. Periodical. US. English. an. $110.00. Captan Associates, 218 Stuyvesant Avenue, Lyndhurst NJ 07071.

CURRENT ADVANCES IN IMMUNOLOGY. Vol. 1, No. 1 (Jan. 1984)-. 0741-1650. UK. English. mo. $295.00. Pergamon Press Inc, Maxwell House, Fairview Park, Elmsford NY 10532. **Tel** (914)592-7700. Ed H Smith. **LC** Z6663.I4, QR180. **DD** 016.59129. Circ 1,200. Gives listings of titles of immunological papers published throughout the world classified into 50 main areas and provides a comprehensive listing of review articles.

CURRENT CONCEPTS IN ALLERGY AND CLINICAL IMMUNOLOGY. Began with: Vol. 1 (1971). 0736-4350. Periodical. US. English. ty. New York Allergy Society, 428 West 59th Street, Roosevelt Hospital, New York NY 10019. **Tel** (212)554-7192. **NLM** W1 CU7873.

CURRENT CONCEPTS IN TRAUMA CARE. V. 1- Nov/Dec 1977-. 0193-7286. Periodical. US. English. qt. MacMillan Professional ournal, 640 North LaSalle Street, Suite 380, Chicago IL 60610. **Tel** (312)944-5888. **NLM** W1 CU788B.

CURRENT CONTENTS. YOUR TWICE MONTHLY SURVEY OF PHARMACEUTICAL PUBLICATIONS CEASED. (CURRENT CONTENTS). 0272-1430. US. English. sm. **NLM** ZW 1 C9592.

CURRENT DIAGNOSIS. 1966-. 0070-1912. Periodical. US. English. ir. WB Saunders Co, Fulfillment Department, West Washington Square, Philadelphia PA 19105. **LC** RC71. **DD** 616.075. **NLM** W1 CU788CX.

CURRENT EMERGENCY THERAPY. '84-. 0739-8573. Periodical. US. English. an. Appleton-Century-Crofts, 25 Van Zant Street East, Norwalk CT 06855. Ed Richard F Edlich and Daniel A Spyker. **LC** RC86. **DD** 616.025. **NLM** W1.

CURRENT ESTIMATES FROM THE HEALTH INTERVIEW SURVEY, UNITED STATES CEASED. Series/Titl Vital and Health Statistics. Ser. 10: Data from the National Health Survey, No. 5, etc. 1962/63-1980. 0502-2673. Periodical. US. English. an. **NLM** W2 A N148VJ NO.5 ETC.

CURRENT LITERATURE OF BLOOD. Began with Vol. 1 in 1968. 0001-7108. Periodical. US. English. wk. **NLM** ZWH 100 C976.

CURRENT MEDICAL DIAGNOSIS & TREATMENT. VAT Current Medical Diagnosis and Treatment. 1974-. 0092-8682. US. English. an. $29.50. Lange Medical Publications, Drawer L, Los Altos CA 94023. **Tel** (415)948-4526. Ed Marcus A Krupp, Milton J Chatton and Lawrence M Tierney, Jr. **LC** RC71. **DD** 616.07505. **NLM** W1 CU788M. Provides the most useful and comprehensive single source of information available on currently accepted methods of diagnosis and treatment of medical diseases and disorders. *Current Diagnosis & Treatment.*

CURRENT MEDICAL RESEARCH AND OPINION. V. 1- 1972. 0300-7995. Periodical. UK. English. ir. Clayton-Wray Publishers Ltd, 1A High Street, Alton Hants GU34 1BA England. **Ind/Abst** Life Sci. Collect., Pestdoc, Ringdoc, Vetdoc, Excerpta Med., Index Med., Chem. Abstr., Sci. Cit. Index, Abr. Ed., Hospit. Lit. Index. **NLM** W1 CU794. **CODEN** CMROCX.

CURRENT MEDICINE. Series/Titl Wiley Medical Publication. Vol. 1-. 0734-9939. Periodical. US. English. ir. John Wiley and Sons Inc, 605 Third Avenue, New York NY 10158. Ed Gary L Gitnick. **LC** R11. **DD** 616.005. **NLM** W1 CU796F.

CURRENT MEDICINE FOR ATTORNEYS. Vol. 1, No. 1 (Sept. 1953)-. 0011-3719. Periodical. US. English. qt. Current Medicine for Attorneys, Box 806, South Miami FL 33143. **Ind/Abst** Leg. Resour. Index. **LC** UNC. **DD** 614.1. **NLM** W1 CU799. (cum index).

CURRENT OPINIONS OF THE JUDICIAL COUNCIL OF THE AMERICAN MEDICAL ASSOCIATION. See Ethics.

CURRENT PODIATRY. V. 8- Jan. 1959-. 0011-3824. Periodical. US. English. mo. Current Podiatry Publications, PO Box 13828, Orlando FL 32859. **Tel** (305)352-1102. **NLM** W1 CU786. *Current Chiropody.*

CURRENT PROBLEMS IN ANESTHESIA AND CRITICAL CARE MEDICINE. V. 1- July 1977-. 0147-197X. Monographic Series. US. English. mo. $35.00. Year Book Medical Publishers, 35 East Wacker Drive, Chicago IL 60601. **LC** UNC. **NLM** W1 CU804E.

CURRENT PROBLEMS IN EPILEPSY. 1-. Monographic Series. UK. English. **NLM** W1.

CURRENT PULMONOLOGY. V. 1- 1979-. 0163-7800. US. English. ir. John Wiley & Sons, One Wiley Drive, Somerset NJ 08873. **LC** RC756. **DD** 616.24. **NLM** W1 CU807M.

CURRENT REVIEWS IN BIOMEDICINE. 1-. 0167-7209. Monographic Series. US. English. ir. Elsevier North-Holland Inc, 52 Vanderbilt Avenue, New York NY 10017. **Ind/Abst** Chem. Abstr. **NLM** W1 CU8093L. **CODEN** CRBID5.

CURRENT THERAPEUTIC RESEARCH. See Pharmacy.

CURRENT THERAPY IN SPORTS MEDICINE. See Recreation, Leisure - Sports.

CURRENT TOPICS IN ANAESTHESIA. VFOAT Current Topics in Anaesthesia Series. 1-. 0144-8684. Monographic Series. UK. English. **NLM** W1 CU82.

CURRENT TOPICS IN CHINESE SCIENCE. SECTION G, MEDICAL SCIENCE. VFOAT Medical Science. Vol 1 (1982)-. 0732-4448. US. English. an. Gordon and Breach Science Publishers, PO Box 786, Cooper Station, New York NY 10276. **LC** R97. **DD** 610.5. **NLM** W1.

CURRENT TOPICS IN CRITICAL CARE MEDICINE. V. 1- 1976-. 0376-4249. English. ir. S Karger, CH-4009 Basel Switzerland. **Ind/Abst** Chem. Abstr. **NLM** W1 CU82FM. **CODEN** CTCMD2.

CURRENT TOPICS IN IMMUNOLOGY. No. 1- 1974-. Monographic Series. US. English.

CURRENT WORK IN THE HISTORY OF MEDICINE. No. 1- Jan./Mar. 1954-. 0011-3999. Periodical. UK. English. qt. $30.65. Professional & Scientific Publications, Tavistock House, East Tavistock Square, London WC1H 9JR England. **LC** R131.A1.

CYSTIC FIBROSIS CLUB ABSTRACTS. See Indexes/Abstracts.

CYSTIC FIBROSIS (NATIONAL INSTITUTE OF ARTHRITIS, DIABETES, AND DIGESTIVE AND KIDNEY DISEASES (U.S.)). (CYSTIC FIBROSIS). VFOAT NIADDK Research Advances. US. English. an. National Institutes of Health, Bethesda MD 20205. *Cystic Fibrosis (National Institute of Arthritis, Metabolism, and Digestive Diseases.*

CYSTIC FIBROSIS; QUARTERLY ANNOTATED REFERENCES. V. 1- Jan. 1962-. 0011-4510. Periodical. US. English. qt. National Cystic Fibrosis Research Foundation, 6000 Executive Boulevard/Suite 309, Rockville MD 20852. **NLM** ZWI 820 C997.

CZECHOSLOVAK MEDICINE. V. 1- 1978-. 0139-9179. Periodical. SZ. English. qt. $52.00. Karger Libri AG, Petersgraben 31, CH-4009 Basel 11 Switzerland. **Tel** 061/390880. **Ind/Abst** Life Sci. Collect., Excerpta Med., Index Med., Chem. Abstr., Hospit. Lit. Index. **NLM** W1 CZ34H. **CODEN** CZMED2. *Review of Czechoslovak Medicine.*

D-J-M ENZYME REPORT. See Biology.

DAKAR MEDICAL. V. 24- 1979-. 0049-1101. Periodical. French. qt. 20.000. Society Medical d'Afrique Noire Langue, Boite Postale 450, Dakar CCP 007 40 Senegal. **Tel** 21-55-88. **Ind/Abst** Excerpta Med., Index Med. **NLM** W1 DA243M. bk rev. Publications on tropical diseases. *Bulletin de la Societe Medicale d'Afrique Noire de Langue Francaise, 0049-1101.*

DALLAS MEDICAL JOURNAL. Began with 1, 1901. 0011-586X. Periodical. US. English. bm. $5.00. Dallas County Medical Society, 3630 Noble, Dallas TX 75201. **NLM** W1 DA353.

DANISH MEDICAL BULLETIN. VFOAT DMB. V. 1- Mar. 1954-. 0011-6092. Periodical. DK. English (some summaries multilingual). ir. 175.-. Danish Medical Association, Trondhjemsgade 9, DK-2100 Copenhagen OE Denmark. **Tel** 01 38 55 00. Ed John Philip. **Ind/Abst** Electron. Commun. Abstr. J., ISMEC Bull., Pollut. Abstr. Indexes, Saf. Sci. Abstr., Life Sci. Collect., Excerpta Med., Index Med., Chem. Abstr. **NLM** W1 DA545. **CODEN** DDMBDK. adv acc. Circ 5,200. Scientific publication.

DAS OSTERREICHISCHE KNEIPP-MAGAZIN. (DAS OESTERREICHISCHE KNEIPP-MAGAZIN). 0250-5428. Periodical. German. ir. **NLM** W1 OE45M. *Oesterreichisches Kneipp Jahrbuch.*

DATA PROCESSING IN MEDICINE. VFOAT Datenverarbeitung in der Medizin. 1-. 0070-2889. Monographic Series. SZ. English. ir. S Karger, CH-4009 Basel Switzerland. **NLM** W1 DA915. *Datenverarbeitung in der Medizin.*

DDARSAKER.HOVEDTABELLER. See Statistics.

DELAWARE MEDICAL JOURNAL. V. 32, No. 2- Feb. 1960-. 0011-7781. Periodical. US. English. mo. $15.00. Medical Society of Delaware, 1925 Lovering Avenue, Wilmington DE 19806. **Tel** (302)652-6512. Ed B Z Paulshock. **Ind/Abst** Life Sci. Collect., Hospit. Lit. Index, Index Med., Energy Res. Abstr. **NLM** W1 DE1234. bk rev. adv acc. Circ 1,300. (ctrl). A medical journal covering both scientific material and health-related issues of importance to physicians. *Delaware State Medical Journal, 0092-7959.*

LES DEPENSES OBLIGATOIRES DE SANTE, STATISTIQUES DEPARTEMENTALES. French. ir. **LC** RA410.55.F8. **DD** 338.4336210944021.

DER ANAESTHESIST. (ANAESTHESIST). 0003-2417. Periodical. WB. German. mo. Springer Verlag-New York Inc, 175 5th Avenue, New York NY

Medicine

10010. **Tel** (212)460-1500. **Ind/Abst** Pestdoc, Ringdoc, Vetdoc, Excerpta Med., Life Sci. Collect., Int. Aerosp. Abstr., Biol. Abstr., Chem. Abstr., Nucl. Sci. Abstr., Index Med., Energy Res. Abstr., Sci. Cit. Index, Abr. Ed. **NLM** W1 AN1046. **CODEN** ANATAE. adv acc. Numbered series for the anesthetist.

DER NUKLEARMEDIZINER. (DER NUKLEARMEDIZINER : ORGAN DES BERUFSVERBANDES DEUTSCHER NUKLEARMEDIZINER). Began with: Mar. 1977. 0723-7065. English (articles in German). qt. **Ind/Abst** Chem. Abstr., Energy Res. Abstr. **NLM** W1. **CODEN** NKLZD8.

DERMATO-VENEROLOGIE. V. 1-18. 0011-9024. RM. Romanian. qt. Ilexim Press, PO Box 1-136-1-137, Bucharest Romania. **Ind/Abst** Excerpta Med. **NLM** W1 DE509V.

DESCRIPTIVE STUDY OF MEDICAL SCHOOL APPLICANTS. **Main/Corp** Association of American Medical Colleges. Division of Student Studies. 1974/75-. 0147-9423. US. English. an. Association of American Medical Colleges, One Dupont Circle Northwest, Washington DC 20036. **LC** R838.4. **DD** 610.71173.

DESK REFERENCE - AMERICAN PODIATRY ASSOCIATION. (DESK REFERENCE). **Main/Corp** American Podiatry Association. Began with Vol. for 1958. 0364-7226. US. English. an. American Podiatry Association, 20 Chevy Chase Circle Northwest, Washington DC 20014. **LC** RD563. **DD** 617.585005. **NLM** WE 22 AA1 A55D.

DEUTSCHE GESUNDHEITSWESEN. (DAS DEUTSCHE GESUNDHEITSWESEN). **VFOAT** DG. Vol. 1- No. 1 & 2-. 0012-0219. Periodical. GE. German (summaries in Russian, English, and French). wk. $128.74. Kunst & Wissen Erich Bieber, Dufourstrasse 51, CH-8008 Zurich Switzerland. **Ind/Abst** Excerpta Med., Biol. Abstr., CIS Abstr., Chem. Abstr., Life Sci. Collect., Sci. Cit. Index, Abr. Ed. **LC** R51. **DD** 610.5. **NLM** WI DE709. **CODEN** DEGEA3.

DEUTSCHE MEDIZINISCHE WOCHENSCHRIFT. **VFOAT** German Medical Monthly, DMW, Deutsche Medizinische Wochenschrift. **VAT** DMW. Vol. 1- Sept 25, 1875-. 0012-0472. Periodical. GW. German (some summaries in English and Spanish). wk. $122.00. Thieme-Stratton Inc, 381 Park Avenue South, New York NY 10016. **Tel** (212)683-5088. **Ind/Abst** Life Sci. Collect., Pestdoc, Ringdoc, Vetdoc, Excerpta Med., Index Med., CIS Abstr., Chem. Abstr., Curr. Contents, Sci. Cit. Index, Abr. Ed. **NLM** W1 DE758. **CODEN** DDMWDF. Index published separately - free - automatically sent.

DEUTSCHE ZEITSCHRIFT FUR SPORTMEDIZIN. 29.- Vol. 0344-5925. Periodical. GW. German. mo. 66.00. Deutscher Arzte-Verlag GMBH, Dieselstrabe 2, 5000 Koln 40 West Germany. **Ind/Abst** Chem. Abstr. **NLM** W1 DE909. **CODEN** DZSPD8. Sportarzt und Sportmedizin.

DEUTSCHES ARZTEBLATT. 0012-1207. Periodical. GW. German. wk. 423.00. Deutscher Arzte-Verlag GMBH, Dieselstrabe 2, 5000 Koln 40 West Germany.

DEVELOPMENTAL AND COMPARATIVE IMMUNOLOGY. **VFOAT** Journal of Developmental and Comparative Immunology. V. 1- Jan. 1977-. 0145-305X. Periodical. US. English. qt. Pergamon Press, 395 Sawmill River Road, Elmsford NY 10523. **Ind/Abst** Life Sci. Collect., Excerpta Med., Index Med., Biol. Abstr., Chem. Abstr., Bibliogr. Agric., Energy Res. Abstr., Sci. Cit. Index, Abr. Ed. **LC** QR180. **DD** 591.2905. **NLM** W1 DE997PM. **CODEN** DCIMDQ.

DEVELOPMENTAL NEUROPSYCHOLOGY. Vol. 1, No. 1 (1985)-. 8756-5641. Periodical. US. English. qt. $50.00. Erlbaum Associates Inc, 365 Broadway, Hillsdale NJ 07642. **DD** 618.

DEVELOPMENTS IN IMMUNOLOGY. V. 1-. 0163-5921. Monographic Series. US. English. ir. Elsevier Science Publ Co Inc, PO Box 1663 Grand Central Station, New York NY 10163. **Tel** (212)370-5520. **Ind/Abst** Life Sci. Collect., Biol. Abstr., Chem. Abstr. **LC** UNC. **NLM** W1 DE997WM. **CODEN** DEIMD6.

DEVELOPMENTS IN PERINATAL MEDICINE. Vol. 1-. 0167-6385. Monographic Series. US. English. ir. Kluwer Boston Inc, 190 Old Derby Street, Hingham MA 02043. **Ind/Abst** Chem. Abstr. **LC** UNC. **DD** 618.32. **NLM** W1. **CODEN** DPMDD8.

DEVICE TECHNIQUES. 1980. 0273-3137. Periodical. US. English. bm. DEVTEQ, PO Box 3175, Walnut Creek CA 94598. **Tel** (415)945-0137. **Ed** Marvin Shepherd. **Circ** 300. Practical guidelines in the safe and proper use of medical devices for nurses and engineers.

DEVICES & DIAGNOSTICS LETTER. See Manufacturing.

DG : ORGAN DER GESELLSCHAFT FUR KLINISCHE MEDIZIN DER DDR. 36, 1/81-. 0012-0219. Periodical. German (summaries in English and Russian). wk. VEB Verlag Volk und Gesundheit Berlin, Neue Grunestrasse 18, DDR - 1020 Berlin West Germany. **Ind/Abst** Chem. Abstr., Biol. Abstr., Life Sci. Collect. **LC** R51. **DD** 610.5. Deutsche Gesundheitswesen.

EL DIA MEDICO. **VFOAT** Dia Medico. Yearly V. 1- August 6, 1928-. 0012-1762. Periodical. Spanish. tm. **NLM** W1 DI132.

DIABETES. Yearly V. 1- 1976-. 0378-6277. Periodical. Spanish. ir. **NLM** W1 DI152N.

DIABETES LITERATURE INDEX. See Indexes/Abstracts.

DIABETIC MEDICINE. (DIABETIC MEDICINE : A JOURNAL OF THE BRITISH DIABETIC ASSOCIATION). **Series/Titl** A Wiley Medical Publication. Vol. 1, No. 1 (May 1984)-. 0742-3071. Periodical. UK. English. bm. $69.00. John Wiley & Sons, Baffin Lane, Chichester Sussex England. **DD** 616. **NLM** W1. **CODEN** DIMEEV.

DIABETOLOGIA. V. 1- Aug. 1965-. 0012-186X. Periodical. German (English or French with summaries in all three languages). **Tel** (212)460-1500. **Ind/Abst** Excerpta Med., Index Med., Biol. Abstr., Chem. Abstr., Energy Res. Abstr., Life Sci. Collect., Pestdoc, Ringdoc, Vetdoc, Nuci. Sci. Abstr. **LC** RC660.A1. **NLM** W1 DI217. **CODEN** DBTGAJ. Publishes reports of clinical and experimental work on all aspects of diabetes research and related subjects.

DIAGNOSIS. Mar./Apr. 1979-. 0163-3228. Periodical. US. English. ir. $41.00. Medical Economics Inc, 680 Kinderkamack Road, Oradell NJ 07649. **Tel** (201)262-3030. **Ed** Evelyn Gross. **LC** RC71. **DD** 616.0705. **NLM** W1 DI258B. adv acc. **Circ** 100,000. (ctrl). A journal totally devoted to helping the office-based physician with the most important aspect of health care - diagnosing medical diseases and illnesses.

DIAGNOSIS (CANADIAN ED.). (DIAGNOSIS). Vol. 1, No. 1 (June 1984)-. 0825-4656. Periodical. CN. English. bm. Free. STA Communications, 63 Place Frontenac, Pointe-Claire Quebec H9R 4Z7 Canada. **DD** 616.07505. (ctrl).

DIAGNOSTIC DIALOG. See Chemistry.

DIAGNOSTIC IMMUNOLOGY. Vol. 1, No. 1-. 0735-3111. Periodical. US. English. qt. $90.00. Alan R Liss, 41 East 11th Street, New York NY 10003. **Tel** (212)741-2515. **Ind/Abst** Life Sci. Collect. **NLM** W1 DI258F.

DIAGNOSTIC MEDICINE. V. 1- Feb. 1978-. 0147-8893. Periodical. US. English. $39.50 Domestic, $46.00 Foreign. Medical Economics Co, Box 555, Oradell NJ 07649. **Ind/Abst** Cumul. Index Nurs. Allied Health Lit. **LC** RB37.A1. **DD** 616.075. **NLM** W1 DI258J.

DIAGNOSTICS INDEX. See Indexes/Abstracts.

DIAGNOSTIK. 0340-5680. Periodical. GW. German. George Thieme Verlag Stuttgart, Postfach 732, Herdweg 63, D7000 Stuttgart 1 West Germany. **Ind/Abst** Excerpta Med., Chem. Abstr. **NLM** W1 DI259AF. **CODEN** DGNKA2.

DIALYSIS & TRANSPLANTATION. **VAT** Dialysis and Transplantation. V. 1- Apr./May 1972-. 0090-2934. Periodical. US. English. mo. Creative Age Publications, 7628 Densmore Avenue, Van Nuys CA 91406. **Tel** (213)782-7328. **Ind/Abst** Life Sci. Collect., Excerpta Med., Chem. Abstr. **NLM** W1 DI261N. **CODEN** DITRD2.

THE DIGEST OF CHIROPRACTIC ECONOMICS. **VFOAT** Chiropractic Economics. 0415-8407. Periodical. US. English. bm. $18.00. Chiropractic News Publishing Corporation, 29229 West 6 Mile Road, Livonia MI 48152. **Tel** (313)427-5720. **Ed** George M Davidson. **NLM** W1 DI539. bk rev. adv acc. **Circ** 20,000. All topics of interest to chiropractors including techniques, finances, business management, books, nutrition, sports injuries, etc.

THE DIGEST OF EMERGENCY MEDICAL CARE. Vol. 1, No. 1-. 0731-1362. Periodical. US. English. mo. Emergency Medical Care Digest, PO Box 2160, Van Nuys CA 91404. **Tel** (213)873-4399. **Ed** Jerome R Hoffman and Joel Geederman. **NLM** W1 DI539M. bk rev. **Circ** 2,500. Authoritive review for emergency clinicians.

DIGEST OF OFFICIAL ACTIONS. **Main/Corp** American Medical Association. 1846/1958-. 0273-0456. US. English. ir. American Medical Association, PO Box 821, Monroe WI 53566. **NLM** W1 DI541.

DIGESTIVE DISEASES. **VFOAT** NIAMDD Research Advances. Began with 1979. US. English. an. National Institutes of Health, Bethesda MD 20205. **NLM** W1 DI572.

DIPLOMATE DIRECTORY - AMERICAN BOARD OF FAMILY PRACTICE. See Yearbooks, Almanacs, Directories.

DIRECT DIAGNOSIS BY IMAGING. 0882-441X. Periodical. US. English. UMDNJ-Rutgers Medical School, Department of Radiology, Academic Health Science Center CN 19, New Brunswick NJ 08903. **DD** 616.

DIRECTORIO MEDICO PANAMENO. See Yearbooks, Almanacs, Directories.

DIRECTORY - AAMC GROUP ON MEDICAL EDUCATION. See Yearbooks, Almanacs, Directories.

DIRECTORY - AMERICAN GROUP PRACTICE ASSOCIATION. See Yearbooks, Almanacs, Directories.

DIRECTORY, AVIATION MEDICAL EXAMINERS. See Yearbooks, Almanacs, Directories.

DIRECTORY - INTERNATIONAL REHABILITATION MEDICINE ASSOCIATION. See Yearbooks, Almanacs, Directories.

DIRECTORY OF BIOMEDICAL ENGINEERS. See Yearbooks, Almanacs, Directories.

DIRECTORY OF BLOOD ESTABLISHMENTS REGISTERED UNDER SECTION 510 OF THE FOOD, DRUG, AND COSMETIC ACT. See Yearbooks, Almanacs, Directories.

DIRECTORY OF CLINICAL FELLOWSHIPS IN MEDICINE. UNITED STATES AND CANADA. See Yearbooks, Almanacs, Directories.

DIRECTORY OF CLINICAL LABORATORIES, CLINICAL LABORATORY PERSONNEL. See Yearbooks, Almanacs, Directories.

DIRECTORY OF DOCTORS OF MEDICINE, DOCTORS OF OSTEOPATHY, CLINICAL AUDIOLOGISTS, SPEECH PATHOLOGISTS, SPEECH PATHOLOGISTS & CLINICAL AUDIOLOGISTS, PROFESSIONAL PHYSICAL THERAPISTS, AND PSYCHOLOGISTS. See Yearbooks, Almanacs, Directories.

DIRECTORY OF DOCTORS OF OSTEOPATHY LICENSED AND REGISTERED IN TENNESSEE. See Yearbooks, Almanacs, Directories.

DIRECTORY OF FEDERAL HEALTH/MEDICINE GRANTS AND CONTRACTS PROGRAMS. See Yearbooks, Almanacs, Directories.

DIRECTORY OF KOREAN PHYSICIANS. DISTRICT OF COLUMBIA, MARYLAND, AND VIRGINIA. See Yearbooks, Almanacs, Directories.

DIRECTORY OF LICENTIATES AND REGISTRATION LAW. See Yearbooks, Almanacs, Directories.

Medicine

DIRECTORY OF MEDICAL MANUFACTURER'S REPRESENTATIVES. See Yearbooks, Almanacs, Directories.

DIRECTORY OF MEDICAL PRODUCTS DISTRIBUTORS. See Yearbooks, Almanacs, Directories.

DIRECTORY OF MEDICAL SPECIALISTS. See Yearbooks, Almanacs, Directories.

DIRECTORY OF MEMBERS. See Yearbooks, Almanacs, Directories.

DIRECTORY OF MEMBERS - AMERICAN HOLISTIC MEDICAL ASSOCIATION. See Yearbooks, Almanacs, Directories.

DIRECTORY OF MEMBERS - LOS ANGELES COUNTY MEDICAL ASSOCIATION. See Yearbooks, Almanacs, Directories.

DIRECTORY OF OSTEOPATHIC PHYSICIANS AND SURGEONS LICENSED BY THE STATE OF CALIFORNIA. See Yearbooks, Almanacs, Directories.

DIRECTORY OF PARA MEDICAL INSTITUTIONS OF INDIA. See Yearbooks, Almanacs, Directories.

DIRECTORY OF PODIATRISTS LICENSED IN TENNESSEE. See Yearbooks, Almanacs, Directories.

DIRECTORY OF REGISTERED LICENSEES, BOARD OF MEDICAL EXAMINERS OF THE STATE OF OREGON. See Yearbooks, Almanacs, Directories.

DIRECTORY OF RESIDENCY TRAINING PROGRAMS ACCREDITED BY THE ACCREDITATION COUNCIL FOR GRADUATE MEDICAL EDUCATION. See Yearbooks, Almanacs, Directories.

DIRECTORY OF RESIDENCY TRAINING PROGRAMS ACCREDITED BY THE LIAISON COMMITTEE ON GRADUATE MEDICAL EDUCATION. See Yearbooks, Almanacs, Directories.

DIRECTORY OF WOMEN PHYSICIANS IN THE U.S. See Yearbooks, Almanacs, Directories.

DIRECTORY - ROYAL COLLEGE OF PHYSICIANS OF EDINBURGH. See Yearbooks, Almanacs, Directories.

DIRECTORY - STATE BOARD OF MEDICAL EXAMINERS OF SOUTH CAROLINA. See Yearbooks, Almanacs, Directories.

DIRECTORY - TEXAS OSTEOPATHIC MEDICAL ASSOCIATION. See Yearbooks, Almanacs, Directories.

DISASTER MEDICINE. (DISASTER MEDICINE : THE OFFICIAL JOURNAL OF THE CLUB OF MAINZ FOR EMERGENCY AND DISASTER MEDICINE WORLDWIDE AND THE INTERNATIONAL LEAGUE OF RED CROSS SOCIETIES). Vol. 1, No. 1 (Spring 1983)-. 0736-8070. Monographic Series. US. English. qt. $45.00. Centrum Philadelphia, 3508 Market Street/Suite 230, Philadelphia PA 19104. **NLM** W1.

DISCHARGE PLANNING UPDATE. Began with: V. 1, No. 1 (Fall 1980). 0276-4652. Periodical. US. English. qt. American Hospital Association, PO Box 99376, Chicago IL 60693. **Tel** (312)280-6029. **NLM** W1 DI742V.

DISEASE-A-MONTH. (DM, DISEASE-A-MONTH). Oct. 1954-. 0011-5029. Periodical. US. English. mo. $65.00. Yearbook Medical Publishers, 35 East Wacker Drive, Chicago IL 60601. **Ind/Abst** Life Sci. Collect., Index Med., Excerpta Med. **LC** R11. **DD** 610.5. **NLM** W1 D116.

DISEASE MARKERS. Series/Titl A Wiley Medical Publication. Vol. 1, No. 1 (Mar. 1983)-. 0278-0240. Periodical. UK. English. qt. $95.00. John Wiley & Sons, Baffins Lane, Chichester Sussex DO19 1UD England. **DD** 616. **CODEN** DMARD3.

THE DISPENSING OPTICIAN. V. 27, No. 6-July 1976-. 0194-2174. Periodical. US. English. mo. $17.00. Opticians Association of America, 10341 Democracy Lane, Fairfax VA 22030. **Tel** (703)691-8355. **Ed** James H McCormick. **DD** 617. bk rev. adv acc. **Circ** 11,300. (ctrl). Directed primarily to key executives and branch managers of optical firms who influence and make purchasing decisions as well as to state-level dispensing opticians. *RXO, Journal of Opticianry.*

DISTRIBUTION OF PRIMARY CARE PHYSICIANS IN MAINE. Began with: Jan. 1, 1976. 0740-0896. US. English. an. Bureau of Health Planning and Development, Division of Data and Research, Augusta ME 04333. **LC** RA410.8.M2. **DD** 331.1251610695209741021. **NLM** W2 AM2 D8M.

DM & S ADP PLAN. Main/Corp United States. Veterans Administration. Dept. of Medicine and Surgery. Medical Information Resources Management Office. **VFOAT** DM and S ADP Plan. **VAT** Department of Medicine and Surgery Automated Data Processing Plan. 8756-5447. US. English. an. Veterans Administration, Department of Medicine and Surgery, Washington DC 20420. **LC** UB369. **DD** 353.00812.

THE DNAGENTS. VFOAT DNA Agents. 1- – Vol. 1, No. 1 (March 1983)-. 0737-6162. US. English. mo. Eclipse Enterprises, 81 Delaware Street, Staten Island NY 10304.

DOKUMENTATION DATENVERARBEITUNG, DATENSCHUTZ IN DER MEDIZIN. (DOKUMENTATION- DATENVERARBEITUNG DATENSCHULTZ IN DER MEDIZIN). V. 1-. 0720-1885. Monographic Series. German. ir. **NLM** W1 DO641L.

DOKUMENTATION MEDIZIN IM UMWELTSCHUTZ. (DOKUMENTATION : MEDIZIN IM UMWELTSCHUTZ). **VFOAT** Medizin im Umweltschutz. V. 1- Jan. 1977-. 0342-0795. English (text in German). ir. **NLM** ZW 1 D658. *Dokumentation: Reinhaltung der Luft + Medizin.*

DORLAND'S ILLUSTRATED MEDICAL DICTIONARY. See Encyclopedias & General Reference Books.

DORLAND'S MEDICAL DIRECTORY OF PHILADELPHIA AND METROPOLITAN AREA. See Yearbooks, Almanacs, Directories.

DORLAND'S POCKET MEDICAL DICTIONARY. See Encyclopedias & General Reference Books.

DRAFT, FULL DESIGNATION RENEWAL APPLICATION. (DRAFT OF FULL DESIGNATION RENEWAL APPLICATION HEALTH PLANNING AND DEVELOPMENT SOUTH CAROLINA AREA II). **Main/Corp** Three Rivers Health Systems Agency, Inc. **VFOAT** Full Designation Renewal Application. 197 -). US. English. ir. 3325 Medical Park Road, Columbia SC 29203.

DRG : DIRECTORY OF RESEARCH GRANTS. See Yearbooks, Almanacs, Directories.

DRUG DESIGN. See Chemistry.

DYNAMIS (GRANADA, SPAIN). (DYNAMIS). Vol. 1 (1981)-. Periodical. Spanish. an. $14.00. Secretariado de Publicaciones, Universidad de Granada, Hospital Real Granada, Espana Spain. **Ind/Abst** Am. Hist. Life, Hist. Abstr., Part A, Mod. Hist. Abstr., Hist. Abst., Part B, Twent. Century Abstr. **LC** R131.A1. **DD** 610.9.

DYSLEXIA REVIEW. 0308-6275. UK. English. ir. **NLM** W1 DY99.

E ENDOCURIETHERAPY/HYPERTHERMIA ONCOLOGY. (ENDOCURIETHERAPY/HYPERTHERMIA ONCOLOGY : THE OFFICIAL JOURNAL OF THE AMERICAN ENDOCURIETHERAPY SOCIETY). **VFOAT** Endocurietherapy Hyperthermia Oncology. Vol. 1, No. 1 (Jan. 1985)-. 8756-1689. Periodical. US. English. qt. $40.00 Members, $60.00 Nonmembers, $100.00 Institutions. Endocurietherapy Research Foundation, 1750 Ocean Boulevard/Suite 208, Long Beach CA 90802. **DD** 616.

EAR AND HEARING. V. 1- Jan./Feb. 1980-. 0196-0202. Periodical. US. English. bm. $50.00. Williams & Wilkins Company, 428 East Preston Street, Baltimore MD 21202. **Tel** (30)528-4000. **Ed** Robert W Keith. **Ind/Abst** Life Sci. Collect., Excerpta Med., Index Med., Energy Res. Abstr., Sci. Cit. Index, Abr. Ed. **LC** RF286. **DD** 617.8005. **NLM** W1 EA59. adv acc. **Circ** 3,200. Original articles focus on assessment, diagnosis, and management of auditory disorders for audiologists. *Journal of the American Auditory Society, 0164-5080.*

EAST AFRICAN MEDICAL JOURNAL. (THE EAST AFRICAN MEDICAL JOURNAL). V. 9-April 1932-. 0012-835X. Periodical. KE. English. mo. $65.00. East African Medical Journal, Box 41632, Nairobi Kenya East Africa. **Tel** 724711/724617. **Ed** M L Oduori. **Ind/Abst** Life Sci. Collect., Excerpta Med., Index Med., Chem. Abstr., Bibliogr. Agric., Sci. Cit. Index, Abr. Ed., Hospit. Lit. Index. **LC** R98. **DD** 610.5. **NLM** W1 EA824. **CODEN** EAMJAV. bk rev. adv acc. **Circ** 2,500. (ctrl). Medical subjects based on clinical findings. *Kenya and East African Medical Journal.*

EDUCATION FOR ALLIED HEALTH CAREERS. See Occupations and Careers.

EDUCATIONAL REQUIREMENTS AND SCHOOLS OF STUDY FOR HEALTH CAREERS. 1973-. 0318-9503. Periodical. CN. English. an. Ontario Hospital Association, 150 Ferrand Drive, Don Mills Ontario M3C 1H6 Canada. **DD** 610.711713. *Hospital Careers, 0318-949X.*

EDUCATIONAL SERIES ON CHINESE MEDICINE. No. 1-. Monographic Series. US. English (summaries in Chinese). **NLM** W1.

E.D.V. IN MEDIZIN UND BIOLOGIE. (EDV IN MEDIZIN UND BIOLOGIE). **VFOAT** EDV. Began in Oct. 1970. 0300-8282. Periodical. German. qt.

EEG-EMG. VAT E. V. 1- 1970-. 0012-7590. Periodical. German. qt $89.00. Thieme-Stratton Inc, 381 Park Avenue South, New York NY 10016. **Tel** (212)683-5088. **Ind/Abst** Excerpta Med., Index Med., Energy Res. Abstr. **NLM** W1 E22.

DAS EEG-LABOR. V. 1.- 1979-. 0170-8287. Periodical. German. qt. $48.00. VCH Publishers Inc, 303 NW 12th Avenue, Deerfield Beach FL 33442. **Tel** (305)428-5566. **Ind/Abst** Excerpta Med. **NLM** W1 E22L.

EGE UNIVERSITESI TP FAKULTESI MECMUAS. (TP FAKULTESI MECMUAS - EGE UNIVERSITESI). **VFOAT** Journal of the Medical Faculty of Ege University. Vols. 1-11. 0536-0927. Periodical. TU. articles mainly in Turkish with some in English or French. qt. 2600. Ege Universitesi Tip Fakultesi Bornova, Izmir Turkey. **Tel** 18 18 80/13. **Ed** Nahide H Altan. **NLM** W1 TI81M. bk rev. **Circ** 3,000. (ctrl). Contains every subjects included under medicine of the list on reverse side.

THE EINSTEIN QUARTERLY. (THE EINSTEIN QUARTERLY JOURNAL OF BIOLOGY AND MEDICINE). **VFOAT** Einstein Quarterly. Began with Vol. 1, No. 1 (Spring 1982). 0724-6706. Periodical. US. English. qt $79.00. Springer Verlag-New York Inc, 175-5th Avenue, New York NY 10010. **Tel** (212)460-1500. **Ed** J A Hannafin and P Quartararo. **NLM** W1 EI507. Available in microform from University Microfilms International. Presents investigations into disciplines at the interface of medicine and the social sciences-medico-legal and ethical studies, epidemiology and public policy, and the history of medicine.

ELDORADO. (L'ELDORADO). Vol. 1, No. 1 June 74 Vol. 7, No. 22 May/June 1981. 0712-7030. Periodical. CN. French. ir. Free. Association Canadienne de l'Ataxie de Friedreich, 5620 rue C A Jobin, Montreal Quebec H1P 1H8 Canada. **DD** 616.838006071. Yes.

ELECTROMEDICA. 1967-. 0013-4724. Periodical. GW. English. qt. $14.05. Mencke Blaesing, Postfach 2140, 08520 Erlangen West Germany. **Tel** 9131-26062. **Ind/Abst** Excerpta Med., Biol. Abstr., Energy Res. Abstr., Comput. Control Abstr., Electr. Electron. Abstr., Sci. Abstr. Sect. A. Phys. Abstr., Phys. Abstr. **NLM** W1 EL331. **CODEN** ELMCBK. *SRW News.*

ELECTRON MICROSCOPY IN HUMAN MEDICINE. V. 1- 1978-. 0271-1877. US. English. an. **Ind/Abst** Chem. Abstr. **CODEN** EMHMDY. Each issue contains an index to its own contents - no vol index - loose.

EMERGENCY DEPARTMENT NEWS. (EMERGENCY DEPARTMENT NEWS : EDN). **VFOAT** EDN. Began with Vol. 1, Oct. 1979. 0195-3281. Periodical. US. English. mo. $24.00. Herlitz Publicaitons Inc, 404 Park Avenue South, New York NY 10016. **Tel** (212)532-9400. **Ed** Jonathan S Wood. **Ind/Abst** Hospit. Lit. Index. **NLM** W1 EM662AA. bk rev. adv acc. **Circ** 28,000. (ctrl). Independent publication dedicated to the dissemination of news in

Medicine

all areas of emergency medicine and emergency departments.

EMERGENCY HEALTH SERVICES REVIEW. VFOAT Emergency Health Services Quarterly. Vol. 2, No. 1 (Fall 1983)-. 0738-6192. Periodical. US. English. ty. $93.00. Haworth Press, 28 East 22nd Street, New York NY 10010. Tel (212)228-2800. Ed Ralph B D'Agostino. **Ind/Abst** Abstr. Health Care Manage. Stud., Bibliogr. Index Health Educ. Period., Hospit. Abstr., Hospit. Lit. Index, Med. Care Rev., Saf. Sci. Abstr. J., Soc. Work Res. Abstr., Excerpta Med. LC RA645.5. DD 362.1805. **NLM** W1. adv acc. **Circ** 436. Covers heart diseases, cardiac death, prehospital care, personnel and transfer of trauma patients. *Emergency Health Services Quarterly*, 0163-9358.

EMERGENCY MEDICAL SERVICES. V. 1- Nov./Dec. 1972-. 0094-6575. Periodical. US. English. ir. $38.00. Creative Age Publ, 7628 Densmore Avenue, Van Nuys CA 91406. Tel (818)782-7328. Ed Barbara Feiner. **Ind/Abst** Hospit. Lit. Index. **NLM** W1 EM661V. bk rev. adv acc. **Circ** 46,000. (ctrl) Professional journal with clinical features for paramedics, EMTS, physicians, nurses, rescue personnel, administrators. Covers prehospital and emergency department card.

EMERGENCY MEDICAL SERVICES RESEARCH METHODOLOGY WORKSHOP. Series/Titl NCHSR Research Proceedings Series. 1- Apr. 20/21, 1978-. 0193-7448. US. English. ir. **NLM** W3 EM51.

EMERGENCY MEDICINE. 0013-6654. Periodical. US. English. ir. $32.50. Cahners Publishing Company c/o Medical Care Group, 475 Park Avenue South, New York NY 10016. Tel (212)686-0555. Ed Douglas W E Wagner. **Ind/Abst** Hospit. Lit. Index, Cumul. Index Nurs. Allied Health Lit. adv acc. **Circ** 140,000. (ctrl). The source for practical, clinical information on acute medical problems for primary-care physicians.

EMERGENCY MEDICINE CLINICS OF NORTH AMERICA. Vol. 1, No. 1 (Apr. 1983)-. 0733-8627. Periodical. US. English. qt. $50.00. W B Saunders Company, West Washington Square, Philadelphia PA 19105. Tel (215)574-4821. Ed William J Lamsback. **Ind/Abst** Excerpta Med. **NLM** W1 EM661J. bk rev. **Circ** 5,100. Each issue contains 13 to 17 practice applicable articles, in a symposium format, on important, current topics and review topics in emergency medicine.

EMERGENCY MEDICINE REPORTS. Vol. 4, No. 14 (July 11, 1983)-. 0746-2506. Periodical. US. English. bw. $60.00. American Medical Reports, 410 Townsend Street/Suite 225, San Francisco CA 94107. **NLM** W1. *ER Reports*.

EMERGENCY MEDICINE SURVEY. Vol. 1, No. 1 (July/Aug. 1982)-. 0732-7390. Periodical. US. English. bm. $45.00. Williams & Wilkins, PO Box 64025, Baltimore MD 21202. **NLM** W1.

EMERGENCY MEDICOLOGAL DIGEST. 8756-727X. Periodical. US. English. mo. $125.00. Aspen Systems Corp, 1600 Research Boulevard, Rockville MD 20850.

EMIRATES MEDICAL JOURNAL. V. 1- Apr. 1980-. 0250-6882. Periodical. English. ty. **Ind/Abst** Excerpta Med. **NLM** W1 EM661VN.

EMS COMMUNICATOR. VAT Emergency Medical Services Communicator. 1974. 0275-0716. Periodical. US. English. bm. Emergency Care Information Center, PO Box 457, Wilton CT 06897. Tel (203)762-3911. Ed Stephanie I Ludewig. bk rev. News of developments in emergency medical services and emergency medicine.

ENCYCLOPEDIA OF HEALTH SCIENCES. See Encyclopedias & General Reference Books.

ENCYCLOPEDIA OF MEDICAL ORGANIZATIONS AND AGENCIES. See Encyclopedias & General Reference Books.

ENDAI NAIYO SHOROKU, NIHON KETSUGO SOSHIKI GAKKAI SOKAI. VFOAT Nihon Ketsugo Soshiki Gakkai Sokai Endai Naiyo Shoroku. Periodical. Japanese. ir. **Ind/Abst** Chem. Abstr. **NLM** W1 EN274S. **CODEN** NSSHDB.

ENDOSCOPY. V. 1- Apr. 1969-. 0013-726X. Periodical. GW. English (text in German with summaries in English). bm. $100.00. Thieme-Stratton Inc, 381 Park Avenue South/Suite 1501, New York NY 10016. Tel (212)683-5088. Ed L Demling. **Ind/Abst** Excerpta Med., Index Med., Biol. Abstr., Energy Res. Abstr., Hospit. Lit. Index, Soc. Sci. Citation Index, Sci. Cit. Index, Abr. Ed. **NLM** W1 EN42. **CODEN** ENDCAM. **Circ** 1,900. Information medium for the field of endoscopy.

ENGINEERING IN MEDICINE (INSTITUTION OF MECHANICAL ENGINEERS (GREAT BRITAIN). See Engineering.

THE ENGINEERING INDEX BIOENGINEERING ABSTRACTS. See Indexes/Abstracts.

ENTEROVIRUS SURVEILLANCE. (CENTERS FOR DISEASE CONTROL ENTEROVIRUS SURVEILLANCE). 1970-1979-. 0734-3531. US. English. Centers for Disease Control, c/o Enteric and Neurotropic Viral Diseases Branch, Viral Diseases Division, Center of Infectious Diseases, Atlanta GA 30333. LC RA644.E54. DD 614.57.

ENVIRONMENTAL MEDICINE : ANNUAL REPORT OF THE RESEARCH INSTITUTE OF ENVIRONMENTAL MEDICINE, NAGOYA UNIVERSITY. 26-. 0287-0517. Periodical. English. an. **Ind/Abst** Excerpta Med. LC RA565.A1. DD 616.98005. *Annual Report of the Research Institute of Environmental Medicine, Nagoya University*, 0469-4759.

THE EPIDEMIOLOGY MONITOR. 1980. 0744-0898. Periodical. US. English. mo. $40.00. The Epidemiology Monitor, 2861 Templar Knight Drive, Tucker GA 30084. Tel (404)939-9380. Ed Roger Bernier. bk rev. adv acc. **Circ** 2,000. News and information for epidemiologists, public health officials, preventive medicine and community health departments.

EPLB, EMERGENCY PHYSICIAN LEGAL BULLETIN. See Law.

ERFAHRUNGS-HEILKUNDE. 0014-0082. Periodical. GW. German. ir. 84. Karl F Haug Verlag GMBH, Blumenthalstrasse 38-40, Postfach 10 28 40, 6900 Heidelberg 1 Germany. **Ind/Abst** Chem. Abstr., Energy Res. Abstr. **NLM** W1 ER221. **CODEN** ERFAAK.

ESAO PROCEEDINGS. Main/Corp European Society for Artificial Organs. Meeting. Sept. 1-3, 1982-. UK. English. an. **NLM** W1. *Proceedings European Society for Artificial Organs (ESAO)*.

ESSAYS IN FUNDAMENTAL IMMUNOLOGY. 1-. 0301-4703. Monographic Series. UK. English. ir. Ed I Roitt. **Ind/Abst** Chem. Abstr. LC QR180. DD 616.079. **NLM** W1 ES674RF. **CODEN** EFIMAL.

ESTIMATES. PART III, MEDICAL RESEARCH COUNCIL. CN. English (French). $3.00 Domestic, $3.60 Foreign. Canadian Government Publishing Centre, Supply and Services Canada, Ottawa Ontario K1A 0S9 Canada. LC RA184. DD 354.7100841.

ETHICS AND MEDICS. V. 1- Jan./Feb. 1976-. Periodical. US. English. mo. $12.00. Pope John Center, 186 Forbes Road, Braintree MA 02184. Tel (617)848-6965. Ed Albert S Moraczewski. **Circ** 27,000. Covers medical-moral issues.

ETHIOPIAN MEDICAL JOURNAL. 0014-1755. Periodical. ET. English. qt. $40.00. Ethiopian Medical Association, Box 3472, Addis Ababa Ethiopia. Tel Addis Ababa 15 81 74. **Ind/Abst** Life Sci. Collect., Excerpta Med., Index Med., Biol. Abstr. **NLM** W1 ET439. **CODEN** EMDJA2. bk rev. adv acc. **Circ** 450. Publishes papers containing original observations or research of relevance to clinical medicine and public health in Ethiopia and other developing countries.

ETTORE MAJORANA INTERNATIONAL SCIENCE SERIES. LIFE SCIENCES. V. 1-. 0199-9966. Monographic Series. US. English. ir. Plenum Press, 277 West 17th Street, New York NY 10011. Ed A Zichichi. **Ind/Abst** Chem. Abstr. **NLM** W1 ET712M. **CODEN** EMISDN.

EULAR BULLETIN. MONOGRAPH SERIES. VFOAT Monograph Series. No. 1-. 0253-0333. Monographic Series. English (French and German). ir. 94.-. Eular Verlag, Mionssstr 36, CH-4012 Basel Switzerland. Tel (061)251317. Ed K Chlud. LC UNC. **NLM** W1 EU471. bk rev. adv acc. **Circ** 22,000. Official journal of the European League against Rheumatism.

EUROHEALTH HANDBOOK. See Medicine - Medical Centers, Hospitals.

EUROPEAN ACADEMY OF ANAESTHESIOLOGY (SERIES). (EUROPEAN ACADEMY OF ANAESTHESIOLOGY). Vol. 1-. 0174-7401. Monographic Series. English. ir. **NLM** W1 EU612.

EUROPEAN JOURNAL OF CHIROPRACTIC. Vol. 30, No. 2 (June 1982)-. 0263-9114. Periodical. UK. English. qt. $60.00. Blackwell Scientific Publications, PO Box 88, Oxford England. Tel 0865-240201. Ed S Leyson. **NLM** W1 EU72BN. bk rev. adv acc. **Circ** 1,000. Scholarly articles fully backed up by sound research are accepted. Journal also encourages postgraduate work in chiropractic and education. *Bulletin of the European Chiropractors' Union*, 0423-6793.

EUROPEAN JOURNAL OF IMMUNOLOGY. V. 1- Jan. 1971-. 0014-2980. Periodical. GW. English. mo. VCH Publishers Inc, 303-12th Avenue NW, Deerfield Beach FL 33442. Tel (305)428-5566. **Ind/Abst** Life Sci. Collect., Pestdoc, Ringdoc, Vetdoc, Excerpta Med., Energy Inf. Abstr., Environ. Abstr., Nuci. Sci. Abstr., Biol. Abstr., Chem. Abstr., Index Med., Bibliogr. Agric., Energy Res. Abstr., Sci. Cit. Index, Abr. Ed. LC QR180. DD 616.07905. **NLM** W1 EU72DG. **CODEN** EJIMAF.

EUROPEAN JOURNAL OF MEDICINAL CHEMISTRY. VFOAT Chimica Therapeutica. V. 9- Jan./Feb. 1974-. 0223-5234. Periodical. FR. English (French and German, with some summaries in English and German). bm. Societe d'Etudes Chimie Therapeutique, 3 rue J Baptiste Clement, F92290 Chatenay Malabry France. Tel (1)6613325. **Ind/Abst** Life Sci. Collect., Pestdoc, Ringdoc, Vetdoc, Excerpta Med., Biol. Abstr., Chem. Abstr., Energy Res. Abstr., Curr. Abstr. Chem. Index Chem. **NLM** W1 EU72DI. **CODEN** EJMCA5. *Chimica Therapeutica*, 0009-4374.

EUROPEAN JOURNAL OF NUCLEAR MEDICINE. V. 1- 1976-. 0340-6997. Periodical. GW. English. mo. $125.00. Springer Verlag-New York Inc, 175-5th Avenue, New York NY 10010. Tel (212)460-1500. Ed H Hundeshagen. **Ind/Abst** Life Sci. Collect., Excerpta Med., Coal Abstr., Index Med., Comput. Control Abstr., Electr. Electron. Abstr., Sci. Abstr. Sect. A. Phys. Abstr., Chem. Abstr., Energy Res. Abstr., Sci. Cit. Index, Abr. Ed., Hospit. Lit. Index, Phys. Abstr. **NLM** W1 EU72DJ. **CODEN** EJNMD9. Covers developments in nuclear medicine, including original articles on such vital topics as diagnosis, therapy with "open" radionuclides, in-vitro investigations, and methods of radiobiological and radiation protection studies.

EVALUATION & THE HEALTH PROFESSIONS. VFOAT EHP. VAT Evaluation and the Health Professions. V. 1- Spring 1978-. 0163-2787. Periodical. US. English. qt. Sage Publications Inc, 275 South Beverly Drive, Beverly Hills CA 90212. Tel (213)274-8003. **Ind/Abst** Hospit. Lit. Index, Excerpta Med., Curr. Index J. Educ. LC RA399.A1. DD 362.1. **NLM** W1 EV13F.

EXCERPTA MEDICA. LIST OF JOURNAL ABSTRACTED. See Indexes/Abstracts.

EXCERPTA MEDICA. SECTION 1. ANATOMY, ANTHROPOLOGY, EMBRYOLOGY AND HISTOLOGY. See Indexes/Abstracts.

EXCERPTA MEDICA. SECTION 6. INTERNAL MEDICINE. (EXCERPTA MEDICA. SECTION 6 : INTERNAL MEDICINE). VFOAT Internal Medicine. VAT Excerpta Medica. Section Six. Internal Medicine. V. 1- Oct. 1947-. 0014-410X. English. ir. 391.00. Elsevier Science Publishers, Biomedical Division, PO Box 1527, 1000 BM Amsterdam The Netherlands. Tel (020)5803911. **Ind/Abst** Chem. Abstr. **NLM** ZW 1 E959. **CODEN** IMDCBQ. Index published separately - free - automatically sent. adv acc. **Circ** 350. This abstract journal provides abstracts of the most important articles on diseases affecting the various organ systems in adults.

EXCERPTA MEDICA. SECTION 15. CHEST DISEASES, THORACIC SURGERY AND TUBERCULSOIS. 0014-4193. Periodical. English. ir. 315.50. Elsevier Science Publishers Biomedical Division, PO Box 1527, 1000 BM Amsterdam The Netherlands. Tel (020)5803911. adv acc. **Circ** 300. The abstract journal covers all aspects on chest diseases and is organized on an etiopathological basis.

Medicine

EXCERPTA MEDICA. SECTION 19. REHABILITATION AND PHYSICAL MEDICINE. VFOAT Rehabilitation and Physical Medicine. V. 7- Jan. 1964-. 0014-4231. Periodical. English. ir. $106.75. Elsevier Science Publishers, Biomedical Division, PO Box 1527, 1000 BM Amsterdam The Netherlands. Tel (020) 5003911. NLM ZW 1 E973. adv acc. Circ 350. This abstract journal reflects the multiplicity of aspects of physical medicine and the care of the disabled. *Excerpta Medica. Section 19. Rehabilitation.*

EXCERPTA MEDICA. SECTION 24. ANESTHESIOLOGY. See Indexes/Abstracts.

EXCERPTA MEDICA. SECTION 26, IMMUNOLOGY, SEROLOGY AND TRANSPLANTATION. See Indexes/Abstracts.

EXCERPTA MEDICA. SECTION 35. OCCUPATIONAL HEALTH AND INDUSTRIAL MEDICINE. See Indexes/Abstracts.

EXCERPTA MEDICA. SECTION 61. TRANSPLANTATION IMMUNOLOGY. LITERATURE INDEX. See Indexes/Abstracts.

EXERCISE AND SPORT SCIENCES REVIEWS. V. 1- 1973-. 0091-6331. US. English. an. MacMillan Publishing Co, Front & Brown Streets, Riverside NJ 08075. Tel (416)362-6483. Ind/Abst Index Med. LC RC1200. DD 612.7605. NLM W1 EX203. Sportsmedicine.

EXPENDITURES OF THE HEALTH CARE SYSTEM IN ONTARIO. 0715-819X. CN. English. ir. $6.50. Ontario Government Bookstore, 880 Bay Street, Toronto Ontario M7A 1N8 Canada. LC RA410.55.C2. DD 338.43362109713. Also available on microfiche. *Estimated Expenditure on Health Care, Ontario, 0380-3031.*

EXPERIMENTAL BIOLOGY AND MEDICINE. See Biology.

EXPERIMENTAL HEMATOLOGY. V. 1- 1973-. 0301-472X. Periodical. US. English. $150.00. Springer Verlag New York Inc, 175-5th Avenue, New York NY 10010. Tel (212)460-1500. Ed E Cronkite. Ind/Abst Life Sci. Collect., Excerpta Med., Index Med., Biol. Abstr., Chem. Abstr., Nuci. Sci. Abstr., Sci. Cit. Index, Abr. Ed. NLM W1 EX504K. CODEN EXHMA6. Publishes papers strictly related to international experimentation in hematology. In addition, it has periodic supplements dealing with thematic issues such as bone marrow transplantation. *Experimental Hematology.*

EXPERIMENTAL HEMATOLOGY TODAY. 1977-. 0251-0170. SZ. English. ir. S Karger AG, PO Box CH 4009, Basel Switzerland. Ind/Abst Chem. Abstr., Index Med. LC RB145. DD 612.11. NLM W1 EX504P. CODEN EHTODV.

EXTRAMURAL RESEARCH PROGRAMS SUPPORTED BY THE FOOD AND DRUG ADMINISTRATION. Main/Corp United States. Food and Drug Administration. Office of Science. Extramural Research Staff. VFOAT FDA Extramural Research Programs. 0149-9742. US. English. US Department of Health Education and Welfare, Public Health Service, Food and Drug Administration, Office of Science Extramural Research, 5600 Fishers Lane, Rockville MD 20857. LC R854.U5. DD 610.72073.

EZHEGODNIK NAUCHNYKH RABOT - ALMA-ATINSKII INSTITUT USOVERSHENSTVOVANIIA VRACHEI. V. 2- 1966-. 0569-0781. UR. Russian. an. NLM W1 EZ32. *Ezhegodnik Nauchnykh Rabot - Institut Usovershenstvovaniia Vrachei.*

F M O Q NEWS. Main/Corp Federation of General Practitioners of Quebec. V. 1- Aug. 1972-. 0318-0557. Periodical. CN. English. ir. Federation of General Practitioners of Quebec, 1440 St Catherine Street West/Room 1100, Montreal Quebec H3G 1R8 Canada. DD 362.109714.

FAC. (FAC : REVISTA PRACTICA DE MEDICINA). VFOAT Revista Pratica de Medicina. 0210-8852. Spanish. ir. NLM W1 FA171.

FACHDOKUMENTATION ARBEITSWISSENSCHAFT, ARBEITSSCHUTZ, ARBEITSMEDIZIN. 0344-0656. German. ir. Bundesanstalt fur Arbeitsschutz und Unfallforschung Offentlichkeitsarbeit, Vogelpothsweg 50-52, 4600 Dortmund-Dorsfeld West Germany. NLM ZWA 400 F139. *Fachdokumentation Arbeitsschutz, Zentralblatt fur Arbeitsmedizin, Arbeitsschutz und Prophylaxe, 0340-7047.*

FACT BOOK - UNITED STATES. NATIONAL INSTITUTE OF GENERAL MEDICAL SCIENCES. Main/Corp National Institute of General Medical Sciences (U.S.). US. English. an. LC R854.U5. DD 353.00841.

FAMILY HEALTH CEASED. V. 1-13, No. 6. 0014-7249. Periodical. US. English. mo. $12.00. Family Health, 149 Fifth Avenue, New York NY 10010. Ind/Abst Cumul. Index Nurs. Allied Health Lit., Women Stud. Abstr. LC RA773. DD 613.05. NLM W1 FA449G. *Today's Health, 0040-8514.*

FAMILY HEALTH BULLETIN. 1- 1958-. 0014-7257. Periodical. US. English. qt. Free. Maternal and Child Health Branch of the California State Department of Health Services/Room 350 OB 8, Sacramento CA 95814. NLM W1 FA432BR.

FAMILY MEDICINE. Began with: Vol. 13, No. 1 (Jan./Feb. 1981). 0742-3225. Periodical. US. English. bm. $30.00. Family Medicine, 1740 West 92nd Street, Kansas City MO 64114. Tel (800)821-2512. Ed John J Frey. NLM W1 FA45N. bk rev. adv acc. Circ 3,000. (ctrl). Family medicine education and research. Society of Teachers of Family Medicine journal. *Family Medicine Teacher.*

THE FAMILY MEDICINE REVIEW. V. 1, No. 1 (Winter 1980)-. 0197-6974. Periodical. US. English. qt. Editor Family Medicine Review, Department of Family Medicine, Trailer 15, University of North Carolina, Chapel Hill NC 27514. NLM W1 FA4504.

FAMILY PRACTICE JOURNAL. Dec. 1977-. 0191-2461. Periodical. US. English. NLM W1 FA454CDB.

A FAMILY PRACTICE MONOGRAPH. 1-. 0191-1279. Monographic Series. US. English. ir. NLM W1 FA454CE. *Monograph - American Academy of Family Physicians, 0093-9323.*

FAMILY PRACTICE NEWS. V. 1- Oct. 1971-. 0300-7073. Periodical. US. English. sm. International Medical News Group, 12230 Wilkins Avenue, Rockville MD 20852. NLM W1 FA454CF.

FAMILY PRACTICE RECERTIFICATION. V. 1- Apr. 1979-. 0163-6642. Periodical. US. English. mo. $90.00. Medical Recertification Association, 2 Park Avenue 4th Floor, New York NY 20016. Tel (212)689-3777. Ed Peggy Ann Chevalier. LC R11. DD 616.005. NLM W1 FA454CM. bk rev. adv acc. (ctrl). Clinical journal with constantly updated articles on most frequent patient problems in family practice, keeping current departments, 20 hours Category I CME credits.

THE FAMILY PRACTICE RESEARCH JOURNAL. V. 1, No. 1 (Fall 1981)-. 0270-2304. Periodical. US. English. qt. Human Sciences Press, 72 5th Avenue, New York NY 10011. Ind/Abst Cumul. Index Nurs. Allied Health Lit., Famli, Fam. Med. Lit. Index, Psychol. Abstr. NLM W1 FA454CP. CODEN FPRJD5.

FAMILY PRACTICE SURVEY. Vol. 1, No. 1 July/Aug. 1983-. 0736-2196. Periodical. US. English. bm. $45.00 US, $55.00 Foreign. Williams & Wilkins, 428 East Preston Street, Baltimore MD 21202. NLM W1.

FAMILY PRACTITIONER. (THE FAMILY PRACTITIONER : THE PUBLICATION OF COLLEGE OF GENERAL PRACTITIONERS MALAYSIA). Vol. 1, No. 1 (June 1973)-. 0301-2093. Periodical. English. ir. NLM W1 FA454D.

THE FAMILY PRACTITIONER SERVICES. V. 1- May 1974-. 0305-9669. Periodical. UK. English. mo. 1/25/-. NLM W1 FA454DF.

FAMLI. FAMILY MEDICINE LITERATURE INDEX. See Indexes/Abstracts.

FARMAKOLOGIIA I TOKSIKOLOGIIA. Began in 1938. 0014-8318. Periodical. UR. English. bm. $45.50. Victor Kamkin Incorporated (71020), 12224 Parklawn Drive, Rockville MD 20852. Tel (301)881-5973. Ind/Abst Excerpta Med., Index Med., Biol. Abstr., Chem. Abstr., Psychol. Abstr., Pestdoc, Ringdoc, Vetdoc, Sci. Cit. Index, Abr. Ed. NLM W1 FA87. CODEN FATOAO. *Farmakologiia.*

FDA DEVICE EXPERIENCE NETWORK REPORT. VFOAT Device Experience Network Report. VAT Food and Drug Administration Device Experience Network Report. Dec. 1979-. 0196-6944. Periodical. US. English. mo. $180.00. FOI Services, 12315 Wilkens Avenue, Rockville MD 20852. Tel (301)881-0410. Lists all adverse reactions for medical devices voluntarily reported to FDA.

FEDERAL PERSONNEL MANUAL SYSTEM. FPM SUPPLEMENT 339-31. REVIEWING AND ACTING ON MEDICAL INFORMATION. See Economics - Labor.

FEDERAL RESEARCH REPORT. See Education (General) - Special Aspects of Education.

FERTILITY ASSISTANCE. 0740-3178. Periodical. US. English. mo. $72.00. Third Wave Publications, 216 South State Street/Suite No 1, Ann Arbor MI 48104. DD 304. *Surrogate Parenting News, 0736-7325.*

FILIPINO PHYSICIANS IN AMERICA. V. 1-. 0739-8131. US. English. Philippine Heritage Endowment Publications, PO Box 1606, Indianapolis IN 46206. LC R697.F6. DD 610.922, B.

FILM REFERENCE GUIDE FOR MEDICINE AND ALLIED SCIENCES. June 1956-. 0071-4909. US. English. an. Superintendent of Documents, US Government Printing Office, Washington DC 20402. LC R835. DD 610.84.

FINMED. Began in 1978?. 0357-7236. Periodical. English (introductory text in Finnish, and Swedish). ir. NLM ZW 1 FI598J.

FINSKA LAKARESALLSKAPETS HANDLINGAR. Main/Corp Finska Lakaresallskapet. Vol. 1- 1841-. 0015-2501. Periodical. Fl. Finnish. qt. Finska Lakaresallskapets, Snellmansg 9-11, Helsinki 17 Finland. Ind/Abst Excerpta Med. NLM W1 FI605C.

FLORIDA ARTHRITIS NEWS. V. 1- 1958-. 0428-7045. Periodical. US. English. ir. Florida Chapter, Arthritis & Rheumatism Foundation, 3205 Manatu Avenue West, Bradenton FL 33503.

FLORIDA FAMILY PHYSICIAN. V. 1- 1951-. 0015-4067. US. English. ir. Florida Academy of Family Physicians, Suite 229/4057 Carmichael Avenue, Jacksonville FL 32207. DD 610.

FLORIDA MEDICAL DIRECTORY. See Yearbooks, Almanacs, Directories.

FLORIDA RELATIVE VALUE STUDIES. Began in 1962. 0733-1223. US. English. ir. $17.50. Florida Medical Association Inc, 760 Riverside Avenue, Box 2411, Jacksonville FL 32203. LC R728.5. DD 338.436109759.

THE FMG. (THE FMG : THE NEWSLETTER FOR THE FOREIGN MEDICAL GRADUATE). VFOAT F.M.G. VAT Foreign Medical Graduate. Vol. 1, No. 1 (Apr. 1982)-. 0744-589X. Periodical. US. English. qt. Special Committee on Foreign Medical Graduates of the New York County Medical Society, 40 West 57th Street, New York NY 10019.

FMG NEWSLETTER. VAT Foreign Medical Graduates Newsletter. 0885-7032. Periodical. US. English. mo. $50.00. Civic Research Center Inc, PO Box 2124, Memphis TN 38101. DD 610.

FMSQ. FEDERATION DES MEDECINS SPECIALISTES DU QUEBEC. (FMSQ : BULLETIN D'INFORMATION DE LA FEDERATION DES MEDECINS SPECIALISTES DU QUEBEC). VFOAT Bulletin d'Information de la Federation des Medicins Specialistes du Quebec. Vol. 1, No 1 (19 Oct. 1981)-. 0820-6090. Periodical. CN. French. mo. Free. FMSQ, Porte 3000 2 Complexe Desjardins, C P 216 Succursale Desjardins, Montreal Quebec H5B 1G8 Canada. DD 610.60714.

FOCUS (BOSTON, MASS.). (FOCUS). Began in Sept. 1971. Periodical. US. English. wk. Harvard University News Office for the Medical Area, 25 Shattuck Street, Boston MA 02115. *Harvard Medical Area Newsletter and Focus on Medical Area Meetings.*

FOLIA HAEMATOLOGICA. INTERNATIONALES MAGAZIN FUR KLINISCHE UND MORPHOLOGISCHE HAMATOLOGIE. Vol. 1- 1904-. Periodical. German (texts in French or English). ir. $87.37. Kunst & Wissen Erich Bieber, Dufourstrasse 51, CH-8008 Zurich Switzerland. Tel 011-41-1-69 44 20. Ind/Abst Life Sci. Collect., Index Med., Excerpta Med., Biol. Abstr., Chem. Abstr. NLM W1 FO179. CODEN FOHEAW. Index published separately - free - automatically sent.

Medicine

FOLIA MEDICA CRACOVIENSIA. V. 1- 1959-. 0015-5616. Periodical. PL. Polish (with summaries in English). ir. ARS Polona, Krakowskie Przedmiescie 7, 00-068 Warsaw Poland. **Ind/Abst** Excerpta Med., Index Med., Biol. Abstr., Chem. Abstr. NLM W1 FO225. **CODEN** FMCRAW.

FOLIA MORPHOLOGICA. See Biology.

FOLIA MORPHOLOGICA. See Biology.

FOLIO'S MEDICAL DIRECTORY OF MASSACHUSETTS. See Yearbooks, Almanacs, Directories.

FORSCHUNG UND ERGEBNISSE DES BEREICHES MEDIZIN. Series/Titl Kongress- und Tagungsberichte der Martin-Luther-Universitat Halle-Wittenberg. 0440-1298. Periodical. German. ir. Martin-Luther-Universitat Halle-Wittenberg, August-Bebel-Strasse 13, DDR-4010 Halle West Germany.

FORSCHUNGSBERICHT KLINISCH-THEORETISCHE MEDIZIN. Series/Titl Forschungsberichte der Johannes Gutenberg-Universitat Mainz. 1. Feb. 1973/1. Aug. 1976-. Periodical. German. ir. Ed P Klein. NLM W1 FO686T.

FORTSCHRITT UND FORTBILDUNG IN DER MEDIZIN : JAHRBUCH. See Yearbooks, Almanacs, Directories.

FORTSCHRITTE DER MEDIZIN. Vol. 1-. 0015-8178. Periodical. GW. German (summaries in English and French). ir. $44.64. Verlag MB Schwappach, Postfach 1220, Wessobrunner Stras 4-8, D-8035 Gauting West Germany. **Ind/Abst** Life Sci. Collect., Excerpta Med., Index Med., Chem. Abstr. Sci. Cit. Index, Abr. Ed. NLM W1 FO86. **CODEN** FMDZAR.

FORUM ON IMMUNOTHERAPY. Vol. 1, No. 1-. 0309-5932. Periodical. UK. English. sa. Royal Society of Medicine, 1 Wimpole Street, London W1M 8AE England. NLM W1 FO957.

FORUM ON INFECTION. V. 1- June 1974-. 0148-4710. Monographic Series. US. English. bm. Biomedical Information Corporation, 919 Third Avenue, New York NY 10022. NLM W1 FO958G.

FOUNDATION ONE. 9952-5622. Periodical. US. English. $15.00. Editor Foundation News, 6 Lomond Avenue, Spring Valley NY 10977. **Tel** (914)624-8516. Ed Ivana Podvalova. NLM W1 FO985. bk rev. **Circ** 5,000. Devoted to biopsychosocial health, pastoral medicine, international health, biologos, health communications, and traditional cultures.

FRACASTORO. (IL FRACASTORO). Vol. 1- June 1905-. 0015-9271. Periodical. IT. Italian (summaries in French, English, and German). qt. $13.00. Istituti Ospitalieri Verona, Piazza a Stefani 1, Verona Italy. **Tel** (045)932370. **Ind/Abst** Excerpta Med., Biol. Abstr. NLM W1 FR138. **CODEN** FRACAC. bk rev. adv acc. **Circ** 2,000. (ctrl). Covers general medicine, clinical problems, laboratory epidemiology, and psychiatry.

FRONTIERS IN IMMUNOASSAY. V. 1- Apr. 1980-. 0270-0476. Periodical. US. English. mo. $60.00. Scientific Newsletters Inc, PO Box 4546, Anaheim CA 92803. **Tel** (714)497-3522. Ed I Fischer. bk rev. Latest developments in the non-isotopic immunoassay field. Covers new products, applications, bibliography, meetings, government regulations and book reviews.

FRONTIERS OF GASTROINTESTINAL RESEARCH. V. 1- 1975-. 0302-0665. English. ir. S Karger AG, PO Box 352, White Plains NY 10602. **Tel** 061-39 08 80. Ed P Rozen. **Ind/Abst** Chem. Abstr., Index Med., Hospit. Lit. Index. NLM W1 FR946E. **CODEN** FGREDT. A guide to leading investigations in the field of gastroenterology. Bibliotheca Gastroenterologica, 0067-7949.

FUKUOKA ACTA MEDICA. VFOAT Fukuoka Igaku Zasshi. V. 20- 1927-. Periodical. JA. Japanese (summaries in English). mo. Japan Publishing Trading Company Ltd, PO Box 5030 Tokyo International, Tokyo 100-31 Japan. **Ind/Abst** Index Med. Fukuoka-Ikwadaigaku-Zasshi.

FUND SOURCES IN HEALTH AND ALLIED FIELDS. July 1976-. 0145-6644. US. English. mo. $95.00. Oryx Press, 3930 East Camelback Road, Phoenix AZ 85018. NLM WA 20.5 F981.

FUNKTIONELLE BIOLOGIE & MEDIZIN. See Biology.

FUTURE HEALTH. VFOAT Perspectives Sante. V. 1- Dec. 1979-. 0225-395X. Periodical. CN. English (French). qt. $7.74. Canadians for Health Research, PO Box 1268, Westmount Quebec H3Z 2T1 Canada. **Tel** (514)392-4864. Ed Leonard Greenberg. **DD** 610.72071. NLM W1 FU612. bk rev. **Circ** 2,000. Health science research in Canada, articles by scientists, voluntary health associations, health workers, the public government departments. News, people items and book reviews. Newsletter, 0226-1340; Nouvelles des C R M, 0226-1332.

FYSIATRICKY A REUMATOLOGICKY VESTNIK. Vol. 44-. 0072-0038. Periodical. CS. Czech. bm. Artia, Smecky 30, PO Box 790, Praha 1 Czechoslovakia. **Ind/Abst** Excerpta Med. NLM W1 FY634. Fysiatricky Vestnik.

GACETA MEDICA DE BILBAO. V. 21-24. 0304-4858. Periodical. Spanish (added table of contents in English). ir. **Ind/Abst** Chem. Abstr. NLM W1 GA23N. **CODEN** GCMBA9. Gaceta Medica del Norte.

GACETA MEDICA DE CARACAS. Vol. 1- Apr. 1893-. 0367-4762. Periodical. Spanish (some summaries in English). ir. **Ind/Abst** Excerpta Med. NLM W1 GA231.

GACETA MEDICA DE MEXICO. 1864-1900. 0016-3813. Periodical. MX. Spanish. mo. Unidad de Cong Centro Med Nac, Bloque B Av Cuauhtemoc 330, Mexico 7 DF Mexico. **Ind/Abst** Life Sci. Collect., Index Med., Chem. Abstr. LC R21. **DD** 610.6272. NLM W1 GA258. **CODEN** GMMEAK. **Circ** 5,000.

GAP CONFERENCE REPORT. Main/Corp Cystic Fibrosis Foundation. Research Program. VFOAT G.A.P. Conference Report. Vol. 4, No. 1-. 0740-7025. US. English. ir. Cystic Fibrosis Foundation, 6000 Executive Boulevard/Suite 309, Rockville MD 20852. Cystic Fibrosis GAP Conference Report, 0196-2418.

GASTROINTESTINAL ENDOSCOPY. Began with V. 12 (Aug. 1965). 0016-5107. Periodical. US. English. qt. $55.00. Williams & Wilkins, 428 East Preston Street, Baltimore MD 21202. **Tel** (301)528-4000. Ed Bernard M Schuman. **Ind/Abst** Life Sci. Collect., Excerpta Med., Biol. Abstr., Nuci. Sci. Abstr., Index Med., Energy Res. Abstr., Sci. Cit. Index, Abr. Ed., Hospit. Lit. Index. LC RC804.E6. **DD** 616.3307544. NLM W1 GA459E. **CODEN** GAENBQ. adv acc. **Circ** 6,350. State-of-the-art clinical journal, publishing the most current papers in fiberoptic endoscopy for gastroenterologists and general surgeons. Bulletin of Gastrointestinal Endoscopy.

GAZETTE MEDICALE. V. 91 No. 1 (du 6 au 12/01/84)-. 0760-758X. Periodical. French. wk. NLM W1. Gazette Medicale de France (Paris, France : 1969), 0016-5557.

GAZETTE OF THE INSTITUTE OF MEDICAL LABORATORY SCIENCES. (THE GAZETTE OF THE INSTITUTE OF MEDICAL LABORATORY SCIENCES). V. 19, No. 8- Aug. 1975-. 0307-5656. Periodical. UK. English. mo. 12. Institute of Medical Laboratory Sciences, 12 Queen Anne Street, London W1M 0AU England. **Tel** 01-636 8192. Ed J K Fawcett. **Ind/Abst** Cumul. Index Nurs. Allied Health Lit. NLM W1 GA777PI. bk rev. adv acc. **Circ** 14,500. Articles on med lab sciences: profession, lab safety, management, NHS news, meetings, courses, job and product ads.

GAZZETTA MEDICA ITALIANA. Began 1936. 0016-5670. Periodical. Italian. mo. Edizioni Minerva Medica, Corso Bramante 83/85, Turin Italy 10126. **Tel** 078282. **Ind/Abst** Chem. Abstr., Excerpta Med. NLM W1 GA977. **CODEN** GMITAB. bk rev adv acc. Journal addresses to practitioners in Italy and abroad. It deals with experimental topics and clinical and experimental pharmacology. Gazzetta Medica Lombarda.

DIE GELBEN HEFTE. V. 1-. 0016-6006. Periodical. GW. German. qt. Dr Dietmar Neede Edit, Kennedyalle 123, 6 Frankfurt Main 70 West Germany.

GENEES- EN VERBANDMIDDELENINDUSTRIE. Series/Titl Produktiestatistieken Industrie. VFOAT Manufacture of Drugs, Medicines, and Dressings. 0168-437X. NE. Dutch (summaries in English). an. 9.50. Centraal Bureau Voor de Statistiek, Prinses Beatrixlaan 428, Postbus 959, 2270 AZ Voorburg Netherlands. Genees- en Verbandmiddelenindustrie Produktiestatistieken.

GENEESKUNDE EN SPORT. See Recreation, Leisure - Sports.

GENEESKUNDIG ADRESBOEK VOOR NEDERLAND. 1984/85-. NE. Dutch. an. Blok Uitgeverij, Postbus 208, 3100 AE Schiedam Netherlands. Geneeskundig Adresboek.

GENEESKUNDIG JAARBOEK MEDICIJNEN. See Yearbooks, Almanacs, Directories.

GENEESKUNDIGE GIDS (1969-). 0016-6464. Periodical. NE. German. bw. Geneeskundige Gids, Misset Amersfoort, Box 26, Amersfoort The Netherlands.

GENERAL PRACTICE ADVISER. (THE GENERAL PRACTICE ADVISER). VFOAT Adviser. VAT Adviser (General Practice Ed.) Vol. 1, No. 1 (Jan. 1983)-. 0821-6274. Periodical. CN. English. mo. $20.00 Domestic, $32.00 Foreign. General Practice Adviser, 1300 Bay Street/Suite 400, Toronto Ontario M5R 3K8 Canada. **DD** 332.024616.

GENERAL PRACTITIONER. VFOAT GP. Began in June 1971. 0046-5607. Periodical. UK. English. wk. $96.54. Haymarket Publishing Ltd, 1214 Annsdell Street, Kensington London W85TR England. **Tel** 01 937 7288. NLM W1 GE265C. GP.

GENERAL REGISTER OF MEDICAL PRACTITIONERS. PART 1, FULLY REGISTERED MEDICAL PRACTITIONERS AS AT . . . . VFOAT Fully Registered Medical Practitioners as at . . . . Periodical. English. ir. NLM W 22. Medical Register of Ireland.

GEORGETOWN MEDICAL BULLETIN. V. 1- June/July 1947-. 0016-8106. Periodical. US. English. qt. Georgetown Medical Bulletin, 3800 NW Reservoir Road, Washington DC 20007. **Ind/Abst** Chem. Abstr., Biol. Abstr. LC RLL. **CODEN** GTMBAQ.

GESNERUS. 1- 1943-. 0016-9161. Periodical. SZ. German. qt. $37.10. Sauerlaender AG, Postfach, CH-5001 Aarau Switzerland. **Tel** 064 22 12 64. **Ind/Abst** Math. Rev., Index Med., Recent Publ. Artic., Writ. Am. Hist. NLM W1 GE823. (cum index).

GEZONDHEID & SAMENLEVING. VFOAT Gezondheid en Samenleving. Vol. 1, No. 1 (March 1980)-. 0167-1642. Periodical. Dutch. ir. NLM W1 GE982.

GHANA MEDICAL JOURNAL. V. 1- 1962-. 0016-9560. Periodical. English. ir. Ghana Medical Journal, Box 297, Accra Ghana. **Ind/Abst** Excerpta Med., Curr. Contents Clin. Pract., Biol. Abstr. NLM W1 GH377. **CODEN** GHMJAY.

GIORNALE DI BATTERIOLOGIA, VIROLOGIA ED IMMUNOLOGIA ED ANNALI DELL'OSPEDALE MARIA VITTORIA DI TORINO. V. 51-63. 0017-0267. Periodical. IT. Italian. ir. $14.20. Giornale di Batteriologia Virologia Ed Immunologia Ed Annali Dell'Ospedale Maria Vittoria di Torino, Via Gibrario 72, Torino Italy. Giornale di Batteriologia e Immunologia.

GIORNALE DI CLINICA MEDICA. 0017-0275. Periodical. IT. Italian. mo. $64.70. Giornale di Clinica Medica, Via Gualandi 1, 40136 Bologna Italy. **Ind/Abst** Excerpta Med., Index Dent. Lit., Biol. Abstr., Chem. Abstr., Index Med. NLM W1 GI509. **CODEN** GCMEAI.

GIORNALE DI MEDICINA MILITARE. Began 1908. 0017-0364. Periodical. IT. Italian. bm. $30.00. Comando Corpo Sanita Escercito, Giornale di Medicina Militar Stef Rot 4, 00184 Rome Italy. **Tel** 06-4735-4105. **Ind/Abst** Chem. Abstr., Excerpta Med. NLM W1 GI617H. **CODEN** GMMIAW. bk rev. adv acc. (ctrl). Military medicine and pharmacy, emergency war survey, preventive medicine, health-care of large communities, medical and surgical specialities, ophthalmology, ENT, etc. veterinary medicine and food survey and supply. Giornale Medico del Regio Esercito.

GIORNALE ITALIANO DI CHEMIOTERAPIA. 1- 1954-. 0017-0445. Periodical. IT. Italian (summaries in also in English). an. 40.00. Edizioni Minerva Medica, Corso Bramante 83/85 POB 491, Torino Italy 10126. **Tel** 67 82 82. Ed C Grassi. **Ind/Abst** Excerpta Med., Index Med., Index Dent. Lit., Chem. Abstr. NLM W1 GI769. **CODEN** GICTAL. adv acc. Journal addressed to practitioners and specialists in chemotherapy in Italy and abroad. It deals with topics in chemotherapy, scientific practice and research.

Medicine

GIORNALE ITALIANO DI MEDICINA DEL LAVORO. V. 1- July 1979-. 0391-9889. Periodical. IT. Italian. bm. $25.70. Centro Stamp Multiprinte, Via Goffredo Mameli 3, 27100 Pavia Italy. **Ind/Abst** Excerpta Med., Index Med., Biol. Abstr., Chem. Abstr. **NLM** W1 GI779. **CODEN** GIMLDG.

GIORNALE ITALIANO DI SENOLOGIA. (GIORNALE ITALIANO DI SENOLOGIA : ORGANO UFFICIALE DELLA SOCIETA ITALIANA DI SENOLOGIA). **VFOAT** Senologia. Vol. 1, No. 1 (Jan./Mar.1980)-. 0391-9056. Periodical. Italian. qt. **Ind/Abst** Excerpta Med. **NLM** W1 GI814M.

GLAS K O H T-A. **Main/Corp** Koordinacijski Odbor Hrvata Toronta. Began publication in 1972. 0700-8139. Periodical. CN. Serbo-Croatian -R. mo. GLAS K O H T-A, PO Box 235/Station T, Toronto Ontario M6B 4A1 Canada. **Tel** (416)781-0359. **DD** 971.00491823. **Circ** 1,000. We list past and coming events i.e. mainly lectures, write-ups on lectures, and health, tidbits about members, write-ups about our health fair outlines and outings.

GOVERNMENT RELATIONS NOTE. V. 1- Jan. 16, 1975-. Periodical. US. English. **NLM** W1 GO879N.

GP. THE AUSTRALIAN & NEW ZEALAND GENERAL PRACTITIONER. **VFOAT** GP. **VAT** General Practitioner. The Australian and New Zealand General Practitioner. 0158-0787. Periodical. English. ir. **NLM** W1 G626H. *Australian and New Zealand General Practitioner, 0045-0227.*

GRADUATE EDUCATION BULLETIN. *See* Education (General) - Higher Education.

GRADUATE MEDICAL EDUCATION IN THE EUROPEAN REGION. SUPPLEMENTARY REPORT. *See* Education (General) - Higher Education.

GRANTS AND AWARDS GUIDE - MEDICAL RESEARCH COUNCIL. (GRANTS AND AWARDS GUIDE). **Main/Corp** Medical Research Council (Canada). **VFOAT** Guide de Subventions et Bourses. 1970-. 0703-2595. Periodical. CN. English (French in parallel columns). an. Medical Research Council, General Purpose Building, Ottawa Ontario K1A 0W9 Canada. **DD** 610.72071.

GROUP PRACTICE IN CANADA. V. 1- Jan./Feb. 1973-. 0319-3209. Periodical. CN. English. Canadian Association of Medical Clinics, PO Box 8244, Ottawa Ontario K1G 3H7 Canada. *Bulletin, 0045-4389.*

GROUP PRACTICE JOURNAL. V. 29- Jan. 1980-. 0199-5103. Periodical. US. English. bm. Free to Qualified Professionals, $30.00 Domestic, $40.00 Foreign. Physicians World Communications, 400 Plaza Drive, Secaucus NJ 07094. **Ind/Abst** Hospit. Lit. Index, Excerpta Med. **DD** 610. **NLM** W1 GR8586F. *Group Practice, 0017-4726.*

GROWTH. *See* Biology.

DIE GRUPPENPRAXIS. V. 1-. 0344-7344. Periodical. GW. German. Arzte Infound Verlag, Postfach 222, Stuttgart 70 West Germany. **NLM** W1 GR937.

GUIA DE MEDICAMENTOS. UY. Spanish. ir. Editorial Publifarma, Juan B Blanco 861, AP 201, Montevideo Uruguay.

GUIDE ROSENWALD. FR. French. ir. Expansion Scientifique Francaise, 15 rue Saint-Benoit, 75278 Paris Cedex 06 France. **LC** R713.43.A6. **DD** 616.002544. *Guide Medical et Pharmaceutique Rosenwald.*

GUIDE TO BIOMEDICAL STANDARDS. (THE GUIDE TO BIOMEDICAL STANDARDS). **VFOAT** Biomedical Standards. 1st- Ed. 0085-1353. US. English. ir. Quest Publishing Company, PO Box 4141, Diamond Bar CA 91765. **Ed** A F Pacela and H A Von der Mosel. **LC** R856.6. **DD** 610.28. **NLM** ZW 26 G946.

GUIDE TO POSTGRADUATE DEGREES, DIPLOMAS AND COURSES IN MEDICINE. *See* Education (General) - Higher Education.

GUIDE TO U.S. MEDICAL AND SCIENCE NEWS CORRESPONDENTS AND CONTACTS. *See* Journalism.

GUIDELINES IN MEDICINE. V. 1-. 0270-0646. Monographic Series. US. English. University Park Press, 223 East Redwood Street, Baltimore MD 21202. **LC** UNC. **NLM** W1 GU78Y.

THE GUTHRIE BULLETIN OF THE DONALD GUTHRIE FOUNDATION FOR MEDICAL RESEARCH. **VFOAT** Guthrie Bulletin. 0735-4592. Periodical. US. English. qt. Guthrie Foundation, Sayre PA 18840. **Tel** (717)888-6666. **Ind/Abst** CIS Abstr., Life Sci. Collect., Excerpta Med. **NLM** W1 GU829. *Guthrie Bulletin of the Donald Guthrie Medical Center, 0094-369X.*

HAEMATOLOGIA. V. 1- 1976-. 0133-4883. Monographic Series. English. ir. **Ed** I Bernat. **NLM** W1 HA155R.

HAEMATOLOGICA. V. 59- March 1974-. 0390-6078. Periodical. articles chiefly in Italian, some in English. bm. Il Pensiero Scientifico Edit, Via Panama 48, 00198 Rome Italy. **Tel** 863-633. **Ind/Abst** Life Sci. Collect., Index Med., Excerpta Med., Biol. Abstr., Nucl. Sci. Abstr., Index Med., Chem. Abstr., Sci. Cit. Index, Abr. Ed. **CODEN** HAEMAX. *Haematologica.*

AL HAKEEM. Vol. 6- Nov. 1965-. 0253-9691. Periodical. English (with some in Arabic). ir. **NLM** W1 HA266. (cum index). *Hakeim, 0438-413X.*

HAKUSHI GAKUI RONBUN (AKITA DAIGAKU). (HAKUSHI GAKUI RONBUN). No. 1- (1980)-. Japanese. ir. **LC** R97.7.J3.

HAMDARD (KARACHI, PAKISTAN : 1980). (HAMDARD). **VFOAT** Hamdard Medicus. Vol. 23, No. 1-2 (Jan./March 1980)-. Periodical. English. qt. **LC** R97. **DD** 610.5. **NLM** W1 HA479M. *Hamdard Medicus.*

HAMOSTASEOLOGIE. V. 1, No. 1, (March 1981)-. 0720-9355. Periodical. GW. German. qt. $41.76. F K Schattauer Verlag, Postfach 2945/Lenzhalde 3, D7000 Stuttgart 1 West Germany. **Ind/Abst** Excerpta Med., Chem. Abstr. **NLM** W1 HA155W. **CODEN** HAEMD2.

HANDBOOK - FACULTY OF MEDICINE. UNIVERSITY OF NEW SOUTH WALES. (HANDBOOK - FACULTY OF MEDICINE, UNIVERSITY OF NEW SOUTH WALES). **Main/Corp** New South Wales. University, Kensington. Faculty of Medicine. Began in 1961. 0312-6137. English. an. 20.00. Faculty of Medicine, University of New South Wales, PO Box 1 2033, Kensington Australia. **Tel** (02)697-2450. **LC** R831.N46. **DD** 610.711944. **Circ** 10,000. General information relating to course content, rules and procedures for undergraduate and postgraduate studies in medicine. Also student services and staff listing.

HANDBOOK - LONDON. ROYAL COLLEGE OF SURGEONS OF ENGLAND. **Main/Corp** London. Royal College of Surgeons of England. UK. English. ir. Lincoln's Inn Fields, London WC2A 3PN England. **LC** R773. **DD** 610.71142132.

HANDBOOK OF ANTIMICROBIAL THERAPY. **VFOAT** Medical Letter Handbook of Antimicrobial Therapy. 1972-. 0190-3454. Periodical. US. English. ir. The Medical Letter Inc, 56 Harrison Street, New Rochelle NY 10801. **Tel** (914)235-0500. **NLM** W1 HA51H.

HANDBOOK OF BRITISH ANAESTHESIA. **VFOAT** British Journal of Anaesthesia. 1979/80-. 0260-2873. UK. English. an. **NLM** W1 HA51IG.

HANDBOOK OF ELECTROENCEPHALOGRAPHY AND CLINICAL NEUROPHYSIOLOGY. US. English. ir. Elsevier Science Publishing Co Inc, PO Box 1663/Grand Central Station, New York NY 10163. **Ind/Abst** Excerpta Med. **NLM** WL 150 H236.

HANDBOOK OF HYPERTENSION. Vol. 1-. Monographic Series. English. ir. **Ed** W H Birkenhager and H L Reid. **NLM** W1.

HANDBOOK OF MEDICAL EDUCATION. 0253-7621. English. an. Association of Indian Universities, Rouse Avenue, New Delhi-110002 India. **LC** R814.A6. **DD** 610.71154. **NLM** W 22 J14 H2.

HANDBOOK OF MEDICAL TREATMENT. 0072-9841. Periodical. US. English. ir. Jones Medical Publications, 355 Los Cerros Drive, Greenbra CA 94904. **Tel** (415)461-3749.

HANDBUCH DER HAUT- UND GESCHLECHTSKRANKHEITEN. ERGANZUNGSWERK. Monographic Series. US. English. bm. Springer Verlag, 44 Hartz Way, Secaucus NJ 07094. **Tel** (201)348-4033. **Ed** J Jadassohn.

HANGGONG UIHAK. Korean. ir. **LC** RC1054.K6. **NLM** W1 HA524.

HANGUG NUIHAG DOSEGWAN. *See* Library and Information Science.

HANGUK UIKWAHAK : THE OFFICIAL JOURNAL OF RESEARCH INSTITUTE OF MEDICAL SCIENCE OF KOREA. Began with Jan. 1969 issue. 0379-1521. Periodical. English (Korean). qt. Chungang Taehakkyo Pusok Hanguk Uikwahak Yonguso, 82-1 2-Ka Pil-Dong, Chung-Ku, Seoul South Korea. **Ind/Abst** Chem. Abstr., Energy Res. Abstr. **LC** R97.7.K6. **NLM** W1 HA524K. **CODEN** HAUID2.

HANGUK YOJA UISAHOE CHI. Periodical. Korean (English). ir. **LC** R97.7.K6.

HANSENOLOGIA INTERNATIONALIS. V. 1-. 0100-3283. Periodical. Portuguese (with some articles in English). sa. **Ind/Abst** Excerpta Med., Index Med., Biol. Abstr. **NLM** W1 HA538. **CODEN** HAINDP. *Revista Brasileira de Leprologia.*

HAREFUAH. 0017-7768. Periodical. IS. Hebrew (summaries in English). bw. $75.00. Medical Association, 39 IBN Gvirol Street, Tel Aviv Israel. **Ind/Abst** Life Sci. Collect., Excerpta Med., Biol. Abstr., Chem. Abstr., Index Med., Nucl. Sci. Abstr. **NLM** W1 HA579. **CODEN** HAREA6.

HARVARD MEDICAL ALUMNI BULLETIN. V. 6- 1931-. 0191-7757. Periodical. US. English. bm. Harvard Medical Alumni Bulletin, 25 Shattuck Street, Boston MA 02115. **NLM** W1 HA636. *Bulletin of the Harvard Medical School Alumni Association.*

THE HARVARD MEDICAL SCHOOL HEALTH LETTER. Began in Nov. 1975. 0161-7486. Periodical. US. English. mo. $35.00. Harvard Medical School, 79 Garden Street, Cambridge MA 02138. **Tel** (617)495-5234. **Ed** William I Bennett. **Ind/Abst** Mag. Index, Bibliogr. Agric. **NLM** W1 HA636S. Index published separately - free - automatically sent. **Circ** 315,000. Monthly newsletter of general health information written by doctors of Harvard Medical School for the public. Treats serious medical topics with in-depth analysis.

THE HASTINGS CENTER REPORT. *See* Ethics.

HAWAII MEDICAL JOURNAL. V. 21, No. 4- Mar./Apr. 1962-. 0017-8594. Periodical. US. English. mo. Hawaii Medical Association, 320 Ward Avenue, Honolulu HI 96814. **Tel** (808)536-7702. **Ed** J I Frederick. **Ind/Abst** Life Sci. Collect., Hospit. Lit. Index, Excerpta Med., Biol. Abstr., Chem. Abstr., Index Med., Energy Res. Abstr. **NLM** W1 HA968. **CODEN** HWMJAE. bk rev. adv acc. **Circ** 1,500. Contains health related scientific articles relative to Hawaii and the Pacific, news of local physicians, editorials, continuing medical education events. *Hawaii Medical Journal and Inter-Island Nurses Bulletin, 0097-1030.*

HAYES DIRECTORY OF PHYSICIAN AND HOSPITAL SUPPLY HOUSES. *See* Yearbooks, Almanacs, Directories.

THE HEALING HAND. *See* Religion, Mythology, Rationalism.

HEALTH & MEDICAL HORIZONS. *See* Public Health and Safety.

HEALTH CARE DIGEST. V. 1- Mar. 1974-. 0316-2141. Periodical. CN. English. bm. $6.00 Domestic, $8.00 US, $5.00 Foreign. Health Care Digest, 1450 Don Mills Road, Don Mills Ontario M3B 2X7 Canada. **DD** 338.4761028.

THE HEALTH CARE DIRECTORY. *See* Yearbooks, Almanacs, Directories.

HEALTH CARE FINANCING ADMINISTRATION RULINGS ON MEDICARE, MEDICAID, PROFESSIONAL STANDARDS REVIEW, AND RELATED MATTERS. **Main/Corp** United States. Health Care Financing Administration. **VFOAT** Rulings on Medicare, Medicaid, Professional Standards Review, and Related Matters. Began with Nov. 1978. 0197-4246. US. English. ir. Superintendent of Documents, US Government Printing Office, Washington DC 20402. **LC** KF3608.A4. **DD** 344.7303210425. **NLM** W 32.5 AA1 H36.

HEALTH CARE MANAGEMENT REVIEW. *See* Business - General Management.

Medicine

HEALTH CARE MARKETER. *See* Business - Marketing.

HEALTH CARE RESOURCES IN PENNSYLVANIA, LONG TERM CARE FACILITIES. VFOAT Long Term Care Facilities. 1981-. 0883-900X. US. English. an. State Health Data Center, Pennsylvania Department of Health, PO Box 90, Harrisburg PA 17108. *Long Term Care Facilities, 0883-7414.*

THE HEALTH CARE SUPERVISOR. 1:1 (Oct. 1982)-. 0731-3381. Periodical. US. English. qt. $52.00. Aspen Systems Corporation, PO Box 6018, Gaithersburg MD 20877. **Tel** (800)638-8437. **Ind/Abst** Hospit. Lit. Index, Cumul. Index Nurs. Allied Health Lit., ABI/Inform. **NLM** W1.

HEALTH CARE SYSTEMS (NEW YORK, N.Y.). (HEALTH CARE SYSTEMS). Vol. 19, No. 10 (Oct. 1982)-. 0745-1717. Periodical. US. English. mo. $30.00. Gralla Publications, 1515 Broadway, New York NY 10036. **NLM** W1 HE302T. *Health Care Product News, 0018-5566.*

HEALTH CAREERS. 1975/76-. 0362-8337. US. English. United Hospital Fund of New York, 3 East 54th Street, New York NY 10022. **LC** R690. **DD** 362.1023.

HEALTH CAREERS. EDUCATIONAL REQUIREMENTS AND PROGRAM LOCATIONS. (HEALTH CAREERS : EDUCATIONAL REQUIREMENTS AND PROGRAM LOCATIONS). VAT Health Careers. Educational Requirements, Program Locations. 1975-. 0381-6435. CN. English. an. Ontario Hospital Association, 150 Ferrand Drive, Don Mills Ontario M3G 1H6 Canada. **DD** 610.711713.

HEALTH CAREERS NEWS. *See* Occupations and Careers.

HEALTH COMPUTER APPLICATIONS IN CANADA. VFOAT L'Ordinateur au Service de la Sante Canadienne. V. 1- 1974-. 0318-286X. CN. Multilingual (text in English and French). qt. Health Computer Information Bureau, 274 Friel Street, Ottawa Ontario K1N 7W1 Canada. **Tel** (613)232-2687. **DD** 610.2854. **NLM** W 22 DC2 H4.

HEALTH COST REPORT TO THE RHODE ISLAND GENERAL ASSEMBLY. Main/Corp Rhode Island. Governor. VFOAT Health Care Costs. 1975-. 0145-9821. US. English. **LC** RA410.54.R4. **DD** 658.155.

HEALTH DEVICES. V. 1- Jan. 1971-. 0046-7022. Periodical. US. English. mo. $975.00 Membership. ECRI, 5200 Butler Pike, Plymouth Meeting PA 19462. **Tel** (215)825-6000. Ed R Mosenkis. **LC** R856.A1. **DD** 610.28. **NLM** W1 HE317K. bk rev. A journal reporting comparative medical device evaluations with brand-name ratings, and reporting hazards and problems with hospital devices.

HEALTH DEVICES ALERTS. V. 1- Apr. 15, 1977-. 0163-0458. US. English. wk. $195.00. Emergency Care Research Institute, 5200 Butler Pike, Plymouth Meeting PA 19462. **Tel** (215)825-6000. Ed R Mosenkis. **NLM** ZW 26 H434. **Circ** 2,500. Abstracts of reported problems with medical devices and equipment, often with recommendation action.

HEALTH DEVICES SOURCEBOOK. 0278-3452. US. English. an. $115.00 Domestic, $140.00 Foreign. Emergency Care Research Institute, 5200 Butler Pike, Plymouth Meeting PA 19462. **Tel** (215)825-6000. Ed Robert Mosenkis. **LC** R856.48. **DD** 681.761029473. **NLM** W 26 H433. Directory of medical devices and products and who manufactures them. Cross-referenced in six sections.

HEALTH FUNDS DEVELOPMENT LETTER. 1978. 0193-7928. Periodical. US. English. mo. $135.00. Health Funds Development, PO Box 1442, Wall Township NJ 07719. **Tel** (201)681-1133. Ed Robert K Jenkins. (ctrl). Information on federal and foundation fund sources.

HEALTH INDUSTRY BUYERS GUIDE : HIBG. VFOAT HIBG. 44th Ed. (1983-1984)-. US. English. an. $30.00 Domestic, $35.00 Foreign. Cassak Publications Inc, 454 Morris Avenue, Springfield NJ 07081. **NLM** W 26. *Surgical Trade Buyer's Guide.*

HEALTH LAW IN CANADA. *See* Law.

HEALTH LAW PROJECT. LIBRARY BULLETIN. *See* Law.

HEALTH LAWYERS NEWS REPORT. 1971. 0145-4129. US. English. mo. $34.00. National Health Lawyers Association, 522 21st Street NW/ Suite 708, Washington DC 20006. **Tel** (202)833-1100. Ed Cynthia Barvin. **LC** KF3821.A15. **DD** 344.730405. **NLM** W1 HE405. **Circ** 4,500. (ctrl). Newsletter reporting on the latest developments in the health care field.

HEALTH LETTER (WASHINGTON, D.C.). (HEALTH LETTER). Vol. 1, No. 1 (Mar./Apr. 1985). 0882-598X. Periodical. US. English. $9.00. Public Citizen Health Research, Group 2000 P Street NW, Washington DC 20036. **Tel** (202)872-0320. Ed Sidney M Wolfe. **DD** 361. bk rev. **Circ** 28,000. (ctrl). The medical field from a consumer advocacy viewpoint.

HEALTH LIBRARIES REVIEW. *See* Library and Information Science.

HEALTH MANPOWER LITERATURE. V. 1- July 1977-. 0160-0222. Periodical. US. English. sa. $8.00. Northeastern University, Center for Medical Manpower Studies, 301 Lake Hall, Boston MA 02115. **LC** RA410.7. **DD** 331.11.

HEALTH NEWS (UNIVERSITY OF TORONTO. FACULTY OF MEDICINE). (HEALTH NEWS). Vol. 1, No. 1 (Feb. 1983)-. 0821-3925. Periodical. CN. English. bm. 9.00. University of Toronto, Faculty of Medicine, Toronto Ontario M5S 1A8 Canada. **Tel** (416)978-5411. Ed June V Engel. **DD** 610.5. Publication of the University of Toronto Medical Faculty, information.

HEALTH ORGANIZATIONS OF THE UNITED STATES, CANADA AND INTERNATIONALLY. VFOAT Health Organizations. 2nd Ed.-. 0440-5609. US. English. ir. **DD** 610.6073. **NLM** W 22 DA2 H4. *Health Organizations of the United States and Canada, National, Regional, and State.*

HEALTH PHYSICS. V. 1- June 1958-. 0017-9078. Periodical. US. English. mo. Pergamon Press, 395 Sawmill River Road, Elmsford NY 10523. **Tel** (914)592-7700. **Ind/Abst** Electron. Commun. Abstr. J., ISMEC Bull., Life Sci. Collect., Excerpta Med., Coal Abstr., Energy Inf. Abstr., Environ. Abstr., Index Med., Mintec, Min. Technol. Abstr., Minproc, Int. Aerosp. Abstr., CIS Abstr., GeoRef, Comput. Control Abstr., Electr. Electron. Abstr., Sci. Abstr. Sect. A. Phys. Abstr., Biol. Abstr., Chem. Abstr., Nuci. Sci. Abstr., Sel. Water Resour. Abstr., Bibliogr. Agric., Energy Res. Abstr., Appl. Mech. Rev., Sci. Cit. Index, Abr. Ed., Pollut. Abstr. Indexes, Ocean. Abstr. **LC** QH505.A1. **NLM** W1 HE4705. **CODEN** HLTPAO. (cum index).

HEALTH PROFESSIONS SCHOOLS. SELECTED ENROLLMENT DATA. US. English. an. Department of Health, Education and Welfare, Public Health Service, 3700 East-West Highway, Hyattsville MD 20782. **NLM** W 19 H434.

HEALTH PSYCHOLOGY. (HEALTH PSYCHOLOGY : THE OFFICIAL JOURNAL OF THE DIVISION OF HEALTH PSYCHOLOGY, AMERICAN PSYCHOLOGICAL ASSOCIATION). V. 1, No. 1 (Winter 1982)-. 0278-6133. Periodical. US. English. bm. $80.00. Lawrence Earlbaum Associates, 365 Broadway/Suite 102, Hillsdale NJ 07642. **Tel** (201)666-4110. **Ind/Abst** Psychol. Abstr. **LC** R726.5. **DD** 610.19. **NLM** W1 HE488.

HEALTH RESOURCES MEDICAL MANPOWER. Series/Titl Western Australia Health Statistics. Series G. English. an. **LC** RA410.9.A8. **DD** 331.12916109941.

HEALTH SCIENCE REVIEW (KRP INFOR/MEDIA). (HEALTH SCIENCE REVIEW). Vol. 1, No. 1 (Apr. 1982)-. 0731-5694. Periodical. US. English. ir. KPR Infor/Media Corporation, 605 Third Avenue, New York NY 10158. **Tel** (212)878-3700. Ed Linda Stanley. **NLM** W1 HE534M. (ctrl). Various topics of interest to physicians and the medical community.

HEALTH SCIENCES INFORMATION IN CANADA. LIBRARIES. *See* Library and Information Science.

HEALTH SCIENCES SERIALS. (HEALTH SCIENCES SERIALS MICROFORM). **Main/Corp** National Library of Medicine (U.S.). Jan. 1979-. 0162-0843. Periodical. US. English. qt. Superintendent of Documents, US Government Printing Office, Washington DC 20402. **NLM** ZW 1 H435.

THE HEALTH SCIENCES VIDEOLOG : A DIRECTORY OF VIDEO CASSETTE PROGRAMS. *See* Yearbooks, Almanacs, Directories.

HEALTH SERVICES MANPOWER REVIEW. *See* Economics - Labor.

HEALTH STATISTICS REPORT : HOSPITAL AND SELECTED MORBIDITY DATA. *See* Statistics.

HEALTH SYSTEMS AND ANNUAL IMPLEMENTATION PLANS. Main/Corp South Dakota Health Systems Agency. 0730-7195. US. English. an. **LC** RA395.A4. **DD** 362.109783.

HEALTH SYSTEMS REPORT ALMANAC ON FEDERAL HEALTH ISSUES, PROPOSALS, ADMINISTRATIVE ACTIONS, LEGISLATION, PUBLIC LAWS. *See* Yearbooks, Almanacs, Directories.

HEALTH TECHNOLOGY ASSESSMENT REPORTS. Series/Titl DHHS Publication. VFOAT Health Technology Assessment Series. 8755-9765. US. English. an. Office of Health Technology Assessment, National Center for Health Services Research, Park Building/Room 310, 5600 Fishers Lane, Rockville MD 20857. **LC** R854.U5. **DD** 610.28.

HEALTH TECHNOLOGY CASE STUDY. VFOAT Case Study Series. 22 (Mar. 1983)-. Monographic Series. US. English. **NLM** W1.

HEALTH VALUES. *See* Education (General) - Special Aspects of Education.

THE HEALTH VISITOR. 0017-9140. Periodical. UK. English. mo. $53.63. B Edsall & Company Ltd, 124 Belgrave Road, London SW1V 2BL England. **Tel** 01-834 0451. Ed June Thompson. bk rev. adv acc. **Circ** 16,000. (ctrl). Socio-Medical matters including health education, child care, child health, developmental pediatrics, community nursing. *Woman Health Officer.*

HEALTHCARE EXECUTIVE. VFOAT Health Care Executive. Vol. 1, No. 1 (Nov./Dec. 1985)-. 0883-5381. Periodical. US. English. bm. $20.00 Domestic, $25.00 Foreign. Foundation of the American College of Healthcare Executives, PO Box 95639, Chicago IL 60694. **Tel** (312)943-0544. **DD** 362. adv acc. **Circ** 21,000. Magazine focusing on critical professional development issues in healthcare management. Designed for executives, trustees, physicians, executives staff and business leaders.

HEALTHWAYS MAGAZINE DIGEST CEASED. 0192-6675. Periodical. US. English. bm.

HEFTE ZUR UNFALLHEILKUNDE. *See* Industrial Health & Safety.

DIE HEILBERUFE. V. 1-. 0017-9604. Periodical. German. mo. Kunst & Wissen Erich Bieber, Dufourstrasse 51, CH-8008 Zurich Switzerland. **Tel** 011-41-1-69 44 20. **NLM** W1 HE733.

HEMATOLOGY CASE STUDIES. V. 1- 1973-. 0091-2336. US. English. Medical Examination Company, 65-36 Fresh Meadow Lane, Flushing NY 11365. **LC** RC633.A1. **DD** 616.150905.

HEMATOLOGY REVIEWS AND COMMUNICATIONS. 0882-8083. Periodical. English. ir. Harwood Acacemic Publishers, 1 Bedford Street, London WC2E 9PP England.

HEMOPHILIA ONTARIO. Vol. 15, No. 2 (June 1983)-. 0822-5974. Periodical. CN. English. bm. 25.00. Canadian Hemophilia Society Ontario Chapter, 1643 Yonge Street, Toronto Ontario M4T 2A1 Canada. **Tel** (416)488-2244. Ed Frank Terpstra. **DD** 616.1572009713. bk rev. **Circ** 2,000. (ctrl). Medical and informational articles to inform hemophiliacs, families, medical personnel and interested people in Ontario. *Ontario Chapter Bulletin, 0045-4923.*

HEMOPHILIE DE NOS JOURS. (L'HEMOPHILIE DE NOS JOURS). V. 14, No. 2- 2nd Quarterly, 1977-. 0226-6644. Periodical. CN. French. qt. Societe Canadienne de l'Hemophilie, 460 Jarvis, Toronto Ontario M4Y 2H5 Canada. **DD** 616.157200971.

THE HENRY E. SIGERIST SUPPLEMENTS TO THE BULLETIN OF THE HISTORY OF MEDICINE. No. 1-. 0194-1100. Monographic Series. US. English. ir. Johns Hopkins University Press, 701 West 40th Street/Suite 275, Baltimore MD 21211. **Tel**

Medicine

(301)338-6987. **Ind/Abst** Index Med. **NLM** W1 HE896. *Bulletin of the History of Medicine. Supplements.*

HEPATOLOGY. **VFOAT** Hepatology Rapid Literature Review. 0171-6123. Periodical. GW. Undetermined. ir. Falk Foundation, Habsburgerstrasse 8, D-7800 Freiburg I Br West Germany.

HEPATOLOGY. (HEPATOLOGY : OFFICIAL JOURNAL OF THE AMERICAN ASSOCIATION FOR THE STUDY OF LIVER DISEASES). Vol. 1, No. 1 (Jan./Feb. 1981)-. 0270-9139. Periodical. US. English. bm. $100.00. Williams & Wilkens, 428 East Preston Street, Baltimore MD 21202. **Tel** (301)528-4000. **Ed** Steven Schenker. **Ind/Abst** Excerpta Med., Index Med., Biol. Abstr., Chem. Abstr. **LC** RC845. **DD** 616.362005. **NLM** W1 HE912. **CODEN** HPTLD9. adv acc. **Circ** 3,5000. State-of-the-art clinical journal publishes the best current papers in fiberoptic endoscopy for gastroenterologists and general surgeons.

HER WORLD ANNUAL. English. an. $3.39. Times Periodicals Pte Ltd, 422 Thomson Road, Singapore 1129 Malaysia.

HERZ + GEFASSE. **VFOAT** Herz und Gefassse. Began with: Jan. 1981. 0720-0730. Periodical. German. ir. **NLM** W1 HE986UF.

HEXAGON ROCHE. Vol. 1-. 0376-9550. Periodical. German. ir. F Hoffmann la Roche AG, CH 400 Basel Switzerland. **NLM** W1 HE999N. *Literatur-Eildienst Roche*, 0024-4635.

HILEIA MEDICA. Vol. 1, No. 1 (Oct. 1979)-. 0101-9597. Periodical. Portuguese. ir. **NLM** W1 HI406G.

HILEIA MEDICA. SUPLEMENTO. No. 1, (August 1980)-. 0101-9600. Periodical. BL. Portuguese. ir. Centro de Ciencias da Saude, Praca Camelo Salgarda 1 66 000 Belem-Para Brasil. **NLM** W1 HI406H.

HIMIKO-FARMACEVTICESKIJ ZHURNAL. (KHIMIKO-FARMA T SEVTICHESKII ZHURNAL). Vol. 1- Jan. 1967-. 0023-1134. Periodical. UR. Russian (table of contents also in English). mo. $80.50. Victor Kamkin Inc (71053), 12224 Parklawn Drive, Rockville MD 20852. **Tel** (301)881-5973. **Ind/Abst** Life Sci. Collect., Excerpta Med., Pestdoc, Ringdoc, Vetdoc, Biol. Abstr., Chem. Abstr., Bibliogr. Agric., Sci. Cit. Index, Abr. Ed. **LC** RS402. **NLM** W1 KH508. **CODEN** KHFZAN.

HINDUSTAN ANTIBIOTICS BULLETIN. See Pharmacy.

HISPALIS MEDICA. 0018-2125. Periodical. SP. Spanish. mo. 25.00. Hispalis Medica, Gravina 29, Seville Spain. **Tel** 954-221751. **Ed** M Rios Mozo. bk rev. adv acc. **Circ** 2,000.

HISTOIRE DES SCIENCES MEDICALES. V. 1- Jan/Mar. 1967-. 0440-8888. Periodical. FR. French. qt. $24.00. Ed de Medecine Pratique, 4 rue Louis Armand, 92600 Asnieres France.

HLABC FORUM. **Main/Corp** Health Libraries Association of B.C. **VAT** Forum - Health Libraries Association of B.C. Vol. 6, No. 4 (Nov. 1983)-. 0826-0125. Periodical. CN. English. bm. Free to Members. HLABC Forum, c/o Kathy Ellis, HLABC Treasurer Disabled Living Resources Centre, Kinsmen Rehabilitation Foundation of British Columbia, 2256 West 12th Avenue, Vancouver British Columbia V6K 2N5 Canada. **DD** 026.6109711. *BCHLA News*, 0225-6142.

H.M. QUEEN ELIZABETH THE QUEEN MOTHER FELLOWSHIP. **VFOAT** HM Queen Elizabeth the Queen Mother Fellowship. Monographic Series. UK. English. an. **NLM** W1.

HOKKAIDO DAIGAKU MEN'EKI KAGAKU KENKYUJO KIYO. **VFOAT** Bulletin of the Institute of of Immunological Science, Hokkaido University. Weekly 35- 1975-. 0385-504X. Periodical. JA. Japanese (table of contents in English). ir. **NLM** W1 HO4881. *Kekkaku No Kenkyu*, 0075-5354.

HOKURIKU MASUIGAKU ZASSHI. **VFOAT** Hokuriku Journal of Anesthesiology. V. 1- Nov. 1967-. 0367-5947. Periodical. Japanese. ir. **Ind/Abst** Excerpta Med. **NLM** W1 HO491K.

HOLISTIC HEALTH. 0882-8148. Periodical. US. English. qt. Holistic Health, PO Box 955, Mill Valley CA 94942.

HOME HEALTH JOURNAL. 0734-7588. Periodical. US. English. mo $70.00. Home Health Journal, 1539 Parental Home Road, Jacksonville FL 32216. **Tel** (904)725-7100. **Ed** Jacelyn W Griffo. **Ind/Abst** Hospit. Lit. Index. adv acc. **Circ** 1,500. (ctrl). Home health care information for HHC administrators, nurses and aides, hospital administrators, health departments, durable medical equipment suppliers, medical libraries, and other professionals.

THE HOMECARE MARKET REPORT. (THE ... HOMECARE MARKET REPORT). 0882-9152. US. English. $40.00 Domestic, $60.00 Foreign. Homecare, 2048 Cotner Avenue, Los Angeles CA 90025. **Tel** (213)477-1033. **Ed** Andria Segedy. **LC** HD9995.H563. **DD** 381.45681761. adv acc. **Circ** 11,400. (ctrl). A business magazine devoted to the home health care market.

HORMONE AND METABOLIC RESEARCH. SUPPLEMENT SERIES. 1-. 0170-5903. Monographic Series. English. ir. Thieme-Stratton, 381 Park Avenue South, New York NY 10016. **Tel** (212)683-5088. **Ed** R Levine and E F Pfeiffer. **Ind/Abst** Index Med., Chem. Abstr., Hospit. Lit. Index. **NLM** W1 HO63Q. **CODEN** HMRSAU.

HOSHASEN IGAKU SOGO KENKYUJO NEMPO. Japanese. ir. Hoshasen Igaku Sogo Kenkyujo, 9-1 Anakawa 4-Chome (280), Chiba Japan. **LC** R895.A1. **NLM** W1 HO69FE.

HOSPICES COAST TO COAST. 1982-1983-. 0743-5029. US. English. $17.00. National Hospice Organization, 1901 North Forth Myer Drive, Arlington VA 22209. **Tel** (703)243-5900. **NLM** WX 22.1 H828.

HOSPITAL MEDICINE. V. 1- Sept. 1964-. 0441-2745. Periodical. US. English. mo. $75.00. Hospital Publications Inc, 90 Park Avenue, New York NY 10016. **Tel** (212)682-5430. **Ind/Abst** Cumul. Index Nurs. Allied Health Lit. **LC** R11. **NLM** W1 HO817J.

HOSPITAL PHYSICIAN CEASED. V. 1- July 1965-. 0018-5795. Periodical. US. English. mo $45.00. F & F Publications, 515 Madison Avenue, New York NY 10022. **Tel** (201)865-7500. **Ind/Abst** Hospit. Lit. Index. **DD** 610. **NLM** W1 HO869F. **CODEN** HOPYA.

HOSPITAL PHYSICIAN (RESIDENT-STAFF EDITION). (HOSPITAL PHYSICIAN). **VFOAT** Hospital Physician (Staff-Resident Edition). 8750-7560. Periodical. US. English. mo. Physician World Communications, 515 Madison Avenue, New York NY 10022. **DD** 610. Issued also in microfilm by University Microfilms International. *Hospital Physician*, 0018-5795.

HOSPITAL PRACTICE (OFFICE EDITION). (HOSPITAL PRACTICE). Vol. 16, No. 1 (Jan. 1981)-. 8750-2836. Periodical. US. English. mo. $45.00. Hospital Practice, 575 Lexington Avenue, New York NY 10022. **Tel** (212)421-7320. **Ed** David Fisher. **Ind/Abst** Cumul. Index Nurs. Allied Health Lit., Hospit. Lit. Index, Index Med. **DD** 616. **NLM** W1. adv acc. **Circ** 190,000. (ctrl). Clinical medicine and biomedical research. *Hospital Practice*, 0018-5809.

HOSPITAL PRODUCTS AND TECHNOLOGY. Vol. 1, No. 1 (May 1983)-. 0823-6798. Periodical. CN. English. qt. MaClean Hunter Ltd, PO Box 9100/Station A, Toronto Ontario M5W 1V5 Canada. **DD** 381.4568176105.

HOSPITAL THERAPY. Vol. 10, No. 1 (Jan. 1985)-. 8750-6831. Periodical. US. English. mo. $42.00. Biomedical Information Corporation, 800 Second Avenue, New York NY 10017. **DD** 615. **NLM** W1. *Drug Therapy. Clinical Therapeutics in the Hospital*, 0887-4433.

HOST/PATHOGEN NEWS. **VFOAT** Host Pathogen News. 0747-6116. Periodical. US. English. qt. $16.00 Domestic, $20.00 Foreign. Host/Pathogen News, 5 Center Avenue, Little Falls NJ 07424. **DD** 616.

HSL NEWSLETTER. See Library and Information Science.

HSUEH PAO (SHAN-TUNG CHUNG I HSUEH YUAN). (HSUEH PAO). **VFOAT** Journal of Shandong College of Traditional Chinese Medicine. Periodical. CH. Chinese. qt. $2.79. China Publication Centre, PO Box 2820, Beijing China. **LC** R97.7.C5. **DD** 610.5.

HUMAN EXPERIMENTATION ABSTRACTS. See Indexes/Abstracts.

HUNAN YIXUEYUAN XUEBAO. (HU-NAN I HSUEH YUAN HSUEH PAO). **VFOAT** Bulletin of Hunan Medical College. 0253-3170. Periodical. CC. Chinese. qt. $7.20. China Publication Centre, PO Box 2820, Beijing China. **Ind/Abst** Excerpta Med., Chem. Abstr. **NLM** W1 HU428M. **CODEN** HYHPDO.

HYPERBARIC OXYGEN REVIEW. **VFOAT** HBO Review. V. 1- Jan. 1980-. 0195-9263. Periodical. US. English. qt. Plenum Publishing Corporation, 233 Spring Street, New York NY 10013. **Tel** (212)620-8000. **Ed** Eric P Kindwall. **LC** RM666.O8. **DD** 615.836q. **NLM** ZWB 342 H998. **CODEN** HOXRD6. adv acc. Features articles that highlight both the clinical applications of hyperbaric oxygen and current research in this field. Also included are abstracts on research oxygen toxicity treatment chambers.

HYPERTENSION. V. 1- Jan./Feb. 1979-. 0194-911X. Periodical. US. English. bm. $55.00. American Heart Association, 8320 Greenville Avenue, Dallas TX 75231. **Tel** (214)750-5466. **Ed** Edgar Haber. **Ind/Abst** Excerpta Med., Index Med., Biol. Abstr., Chem. Abstr., Cumul. Index Nurs. Allied Health Lit., Pestdoc, Ringdoc, Vetdoc, Hospit. Lit. Index, Sci. Cit. Index, Abr. Ed. **LC** RC685.H8. **DD** 616.132005. **NLM** W1 HY841M. **CODEN** HPRTDN. adv acc. **Circ** 3,000. (ctrl). Publishing reports of clinical and experimental investigation in hypertension. Designed for clinicians, clinical investigators, laboratory scientists. *Circulation Research*, 0009-7330.

ICA UPDATE VIROLOGY/HEPATITIS. **Main/Corp** Information Company of America. **VFOAT** Update Virology/Hepatitis. **VAT** Information Company of America Update Virology/Hepatitis. 1973/1-. 0273-0529. Periodical. US. English. ir. Information Company of America, PO Box 8329, Philadelphia PA 19101. *Update/Virology*.

ICPM. SERIES 1. **VAT** Illinois College of Podiatric Medicine. Series One. No. 1- June 1975-. 0196-4925. Monographic Series. US. English. ir. **NLM** W1 I216.

ICU FORUM. **VAT** Intensive Care Unit Forum. 8756-7857. Periodical. US. English. bm. Free. ICU Forum, PO Box 8025/Wainwright Station, San Antonio TX 78208. **DD** 616.

IDF BULLETIN. **VAT** International Diabetes Foundation Bulletin. V. 19- Apr. 1974-. 0306-4980. Periodical. UK. English. ty. $10.73. American Diabetes Association, Two Park Avenue, New York NY 10016. **Tel** (212)683-7444. **Ed** Leo P Krali.Boskar. **Ind/Abst** Chem. Abstr. **NLM** W1 I219K. **CODEN** IDFBD6. bk rev. adv acc. **Circ** 2,200. Review articles on aspects of living with diabetes. Federation and national association news. *News Bulletin - International Diabetes Federation*, 0534-9753.

IEEE ENGINEERING IN MEDICINE AND BIOLOGY MAGAZINE. See Engineering - Electricity, Electrical Engineering, Electronics.

IEEE TRANSACTIONS ON BIOMEDICAL ENGINEERING. See Engineering.

IEEE TRANSACTIONS ON MEDICAL IMAGING. See Engineering - Electricity, Electrical Engineering, Electronics.

I.F.I.P. MEDICAL INFORMATICS MONOGRAPH SERIES. (IFIP MEDICAL INFORMATICS MONOGRAPH SERIES). V. 1- 1974-. 0303-870X. Periodical. English. ir. Elsevier Science Publishing Company Inc, PO Box 1663, Grand Central Station, New York NY 10163. **NLM** W1 I227M.

IGAKU SENSUI. No. 1-. 0385-1591. Periodical. Japanese. bm. **NLM** W1 IG3906.

ILLINOIS CONFERENCE ON MEDICAL INFORMATION SYSTEMS. 1st- 1974-. 0147-0191. Periodical. US. English. an. **NLM** W3 IL37.

ILLINOIS MEDICAL JOURNAL. (IMJ, ILLINOIS MEDICAL JOURNAL). V. 123- Jan. 1963-. 0019-2120. Periodical. US. English. mo. $12.00. Illinois Medical Journal, 20 North Michigan Avenue/Suite 700, Chicago IL 60602. **Tel** (312)782-1654. **Ind/Abst** Energy Res. Abstr., Hospit. Lit. Index, Index Med., Life Sci. Collect., Soc. Welf. Soc. Plan./Policy Soc. Dev., Sociol. Abstr., Biol. Abstr., Chem. Abstr., Sci. Abstr., Curr. Contents Clin. Pract., Nuci. Sci. Abstr. **NLM** W1 I261J. Available on microfilm from University Microfilms. *Illinois Medical Journal*, 0019-2120.

IMAGE. 1971. 0383-9710. Periodical. CN. English. qt. Free. Kinsmen Rehabilitation Foundation of British Columbia, 2256 West 12th Avenue, Vancouver British Columbia V6K 2N5 Canada. **Tel** (604)736-8841. **Ed** Thomas Ferguson. **DD** 362.4062711. bk rev. adv acc.

Medicine

Circ 20,000. (ctrl). Articles on medical, social service and technological advances and issues of interest to physically disabled people, health care, and social service professionals, and the general public. *Image 5, 0315-324X*.

IMMUNE INTERVENTION. Vol. 1-. Monographic Series. UK. English. Ed I M Roitt. **Ind/Abst** Chem. Abstr. **NLM** W1. **CODEN** IMMIEO.

IMMUNOASSAY. SUPPLEMENT. 1-. 0262-8740. Monographic Series. UK. English. ir. University of Sheffield, Biomedical Information Service, Sheffield S10 2TN England. **Ind/Abst** Chem. Abstr. **CODEN** ISUPDO.

IMMUNOASSAY TECHNOLOGY. Vol. 1-. English. ir. Walter De Gruyter Inc, 200 Sawmill River Road, Hawthorne NY 10532. **NLM** W1.

IMMUNOGENETICS. Vol. 1- Feb. 1974-. 0093-7711. Periodical. US. English. bm. $261.00. Springer Verlag-New York Inc, 175 5th Avenue, New York NY 10010. **Tel** (212)460-1500. Ed J Klein and J Dausset. **Ind/Abst** Life Sci. Collect., Excerpta Med., Energy Inf. Abstr., Environ. Abstr., Index Med., Biol. Abstr., Chem. Abstr., Bibliogr. Agric., Sci. Cit. Index, Abr. Ed. **LC** QR184. **DD** 574.29. **NLM** W1 IM485. **CODEN** IMNGBK. Covers such topics as immunogenetics of cell interaction, immunogenetics of tissue differentiation and development, phylogeny of alloantigens and immune response and genetics and biochemistry of alloantigens.

IMMUNOLOGIA CLINICA E SPERIMENTALE. (IMMUNOLOGIA CLINICA E SPERIMENTALE : ORGANO UFFICIALE DELLA SOCIETA ITALIANA DI IMMUNOLOGIA E IMMUNOPATOLOGIA). Vol. 1, No.1 (May 1982)-. 0392-6702. Periodical. English (articles in Italian). qt. Masson Publishing USA Inc, 211 East 43rd Street/Room 1306, New York NY 10017. **Tel** (212)370-1937. **Ind/Abst** Excerpta Med. **NLM** W1 IM494.

IMMUNOLOGIA POLSKA. 1-. 0324-8534. PL. Polish (summaries in English). qt. ARS Polona, Krakowskie Przedmiescie 7, 00-068 Warsaw Poland. **Ind/Abst** Excerpta Med., Biol. Abstr., Chem. Abstr., Energy Res. Abstr. **LC** QR180. **NLM** W1 IM495q. **CODEN** IMPODM. *Annals of Immunology, 0044-8338*.

IMMUNOLOGICAL COMMUNICATIONS CEASED. V. 1- 1972. Ceased with Vol. 13, No. 6 Dec. 1984. 0090-0877. Periodical. US. English. bm. **Ind/Abst** Excerpta Med., Life Sci. Collect., Index Med., Biol. Abstr., Ref. Source, Chem. Abstr., Bibliogr. Agric., Energy Res. Abstr. **DD** 616. **NLM** W1 IM51. **CODEN** IMLCAV.

IMMUNOLOGICAL METHODS. Vol. 1-. 0277-7894. US. English. sm. $603.00. American Association of Immunologists, 9650 Rockville Pike, Bethesda MD 10014. **Ind/Abst** Chem. Abstr. **CODEN** IMETDG.

IMMUNOLOGICAL REVIEWS. Began with Vol 33. 0105-2896. Periodical. English. bm. 115.98. Munksgaard Ltd, 35 Norre Sogade, DK-1370 Copenhagen K Denmark. **Tel** 45-1-127030. Ed Goran Moller. **Ind/Abst** Life Sci. Collect., Excerpta Med., Index Med., Biol. Abstr., Chem. Abstr., Sci. Cit. Index, Abr. Ed. **LC** PAR. **NLM** W1 IM512. **CODEN** IMRED2. adv acc. Circ 2,000. Publishes invited reviews within the fields of clinical and experimental immunology. *Transplantation Reviews, 0082-5948*.

IMMUNOLOGIIA. (SOVIET IMMUNOLOGY). 1982, No. 1-. 0739-8433. Periodical. US. English (Russian). bm. $270.00. Allerton Press Inc, 150 Fifth Avenue, New York NY 10011. **LC** QR181q. **DD** 616.079. **NLM** W1.

IMMUNOLOGY & ALLERGY PRACTICE. VAT Immunology and Allergy Practice. V. 1- Mar./Apr. 1979-. 0194-7508. Periodical. US. English. mo. $55.00. Macor Publishing Company, 116 West 32nd Street/8th Floor, New York NY 10001. **Tel** (212)736-6688. Ed Sidney Friedlaender. **Ind/Abst** Excerpta Med. **LC** RC581. **DD** 616.97005. **NLM** W1 IM53B. bk rev. adv acc. Circ 19,000. (ctrl). Original, review and state-of-the art articles covering important aspects of clinical immunology and allergy.

IMMUNOLOGY LETTERS. V. 1- July 1979-. 0165-2478. Periodical. English. mo. Elsevier Science Publishers, PO Box 211, 1000 AE Amsterdam Netherlands. **Tel** (020)5803.911. **Ind/Abst** Life Sci. Collect., Excerpta Med., Energy Inf. Abstr., Environ. Abstr., Index Med., Biol. Abstr., Chem. Abstr., Sci. Cit. Index, Abr. Ed. **NLM** W1 IM53D. **CODEN** IMLED6.

IMMUNOLOGY SERIES. V. 1-. 0092-6019. Monographic Series. US. English. ir. Marcel Dekker, Continuation Department, 270 Madison Avenue, New York NY 10016. **Tel** (212)696-9000. Ed N Rose. **Ind/Abst** Life Sci. Collect., Chem. Abstr., Chem. Abstr., Math. Rev. **LC** UNC. **NLM** W1 IM53K. **CODEN** IMSED7. This is an ongoing series. Each title has a different subject.

IMMUNOLOGY TODAY. V. 1- July 1980-. 0167-4919. Periodical. US. English. mo. $43.00. Elsevier Science Publishers, 52 Vandervilt Avenue, New York NY 10017. **Tel** 223-315961. Ed John R Inglis. **Ind/Abst** Life Sci. Collect., Biol. Abstr., Chem. Abstr. **NLM** W1 IM53P. **CODEN** IMTOD8. bk rev. adv acc. Circ 6,200. Basic immunology, aspects of clinical medicine with immunological dimension, infection, cell and molecular biology, the organization, administration and history of medical research.

IMMUNOLOGY TRIBUNE. Vol. 1- Feb. 1979-. 0271-3284. Periodical. US. English. mo. $60.00. MDT Publications, 2915 Bissonnet, Houston TX 77005. **NLM** W1 IM53T.

IMMUNOTHERAPY AND CLINICAL CANCER IMMUNOLOGY. Main/Corp International Cancer Research Data Bank. Series/Titl ICRDB Cancergram. Periodical. US. English. Department of Health Education and Welfare, Public Health Service, National Institutes of Health, National Cancer Institute, Springfield VA 22161.

IN VITRO. MONOGRAPH. *See* Biology.

INDEX MEDICUS FOR WHO SOUTH-EAST ASIA REGION. *See* Indexes/Abstracts.

INDEX MEDICUS LATINO-AMERICAN. *See* Indexes/Abstracts.

INDEX MEDICUS (NATIONAL LIBRARY OF MEDICINE (U.S.)). *See* Indexes/Abstracts.

INDEX OF NLM SERIAL TITLES. *See* Indexes/Abstracts.

INDEX TO AUDIOVISUAL SERIALS IN THE HEALTH SCIENCES. *See* Indexes/Abstracts.

INDIAN JOURNAL OF HISTORY OF MEDICINE. V. 1- June 1956-. 0019-5677. Periodical. II. English. ir. Hindustan Book Agency, 17 UB Jawahar Nagar, Delhi 7 India. **LC** R131.A1.

INDIAN JOURNAL OF MEDICAL EDUCATION. 0019-5332. Periodical. II. English. mo. $24.00. Indian Association for the Advancement of Medical Education, Madras Medical College, Madras 3 India.

INDIAN JOURNAL OF MEDICAL RESEARCH. 1913. 0019-5340. Periodical. II. English. mo. $70.00. Indian Council of Medical Research, PO Box 4508 Ansari Nagar, New Delhi 110016 India. **Tel** 663001. Ed G V Satyavati. **Ind/Abst** Life Sci. Collect., Excerpta Med., CIS Abstr., Chem. Abstr., Biol. Abstr., Nuci. Sci. Abstr., Index Med., Sel. Water Resour. Abstr., Sci. Cit. Index, Abr. Ed., Hospit. Lit. Index. **NLM** W1 IN214G. **CODEN** IJMRAQ. bk rev. Circ 1,000. Journal publishing all aspects of medical research that contribute significantly to the advancement of knowledge in medical sciences. *Paludism*.

INDIAN JOURNAL OF MEDICAL SCIENCES. V. 1- July 1947-. 0019-5359. Periodical. II. English. mo. $25.00. Indian Journal Medical Science, Back Bay VW #3-A Mama Parm Marg, Bombay 400 004 India. **Ind/Abst** Life Sci. Collect., Excerpta Med., Biol. Abstr., Chem. Abstr., Nuci. Sci. Abstr., Index Med. **NLM** W1 IN215. **CODEN** INJMAO. *Medical Bulletin*.

INDIAN JOURNAL OF OCCUPATIONAL HEALTH. Began with Aug. 1958 issue. 0019-5391. Periodical. II. English. mo. Society for the Study of Industrial Medicine, 243 Kerwadi Main Road, Bombay 4 Maharashtra India. **Ind/Abst** CIS Abstr. **LC** RC963. **NLM** W1 IN2225.

INDIAN MEDICAL GAZETTE. V. 1- May 1961-. 0019-5863. Periodical. II. English. mo. $30.00. Savory Chambers, Wallace Street, 40001 Bombay India. **Ind/Abst** Excerpta Med., Chem. Abstr. **NLM** W1 IN25. **CODEN** IMGAAY.

INDIAN MEDICAL JOURNAL. 0019-5871. Periodical. II. English. mo. $10.00. Indian Books and Periodical, 3341 Christian Colony-Pyarey Lal Road, New Delhi 110005 India. **Ind/Abst** Chem. Abstr., Excerpta Med. **NLM** W1 IN252. **CODEN** IMJUA7.

INDIAN PRACTITIONER. 1947. 0019-6169. Periodical. II. English. mo. 230.-. The Indian Practitioner, David Sassoon Building/3rd Floor, 143 Mahatma Gandhi Road, Bombay 400 023 India. **Tel** 27 38 09. Ed S A Nanivadekar. bk rev. adv acc. Circ 17,000. Journal devoted to medicine, public health and surgery.

INDIANA MEDICINE. (INDIANA MEDICINE : THE JOURNAL OF THE INDIANA STATE MEDICAL ASSOCIATION). Vol. 77, No. 1 (Jan. 1984)-. 0746-8288. Periodical. US. English. mo. $18.00. Indiana Medicine, 3935 North Meridian Street, Indianapolis IN 46208. **Tel** (317)925-7545. Ed Frank Ramsey. **Ind/Abst** Life Sci. Collect., Index Med., Cumul. Index Nurs. Allied Health Lit., Excerpta Med., Hospit. Lit. Index, Energy Res. Abstr. **NLM** W1. bk rev. adv acc. Circ 6,500. (ctrl). Devoted to the interests of the medical profession and public health in Indiana since 1908. *Journal of the Indiana State Medical Association, 0019-6770*.

INDICE MEDICO ESPANOL. *See* Indexes/Abstracts.

INFECTION. VFOAT Zeitschrift fur Klinik und Therapie der Infektionen, Journal for the Clinical Study and Treatment of Infections. 1.- Volume. 0300-8126. Periodical. GW. German (English, summaries in both languages). qt. 240.00. MMV Medizin Verlag, Postfach 860529, 8000 Munchen 86 West Germany. **Tel** 957170. **Ind/Abst** Life Sci. Collect., Excerpta Med., Index Med., Biol. Abstr., Chem. Abstr., Pestdoc, Ringdoc, Vetdoc. **NLM** W1 IN405K. **CODEN** IFTNAL. Journal for the study and treatment of infectious diseases, includes supplements.

INFECTION CONTROL DIGEST. Vol. 1, No. 1 (Jan. 1980)-. 0275-0236. Periodical. US. English. mo. $50.00. American Hospital Association, PO Box 99376, Chicago IL 60693. **Tel** (312)280-6029. **NLM** W1 IN406B.

INFECTIOUS DISEASE ALERT. Vol. 1, No. 1 (Oct. 1, 1981)-. 0739-7348. Periodical. US. English. sm. $59.00. International Thomson Medical Information, 680 K Kinderkamack Road, Oradell NJ 07649. **Tel** (215)925-7060. **NLM** W1 IN406HM.

INFECTIOUS DISEASE PRACTICE. 0162-6493. Periodical. US. English. mo. $74.00. Laux Company Inc, PO Box 700, Ayer MA 01432. **Tel** (617)772-2584. Ed Dean Laux. bk rev. Circ 1,500. Medical information for physicians in infectious diseases.

INFLUENZA SURVEILLANCE (ATLANTA, GA. : 1976). (INFLUENZA SURVEILLANCE). VFOAT Influenza Surveillance Report, Influenza Report. No. 90 (1973-1974 and 1974-1975)-. 0362-3351. US. English. ir. US Department of Health and Human Services, Public Health Service Centers for Disease Control, Atlanta GA 30333. **LC** RA644.I6. **DD** 614.5180973021. **NLM** W2 A C7Cl. Vols. for July 1979-June 1981- distributed to depository libraries in microfiche. *Influenza-Respiratory Disease Surveillance, 0362-3343*.

INFORM-APIQ. *See* Economics - Labor.

INFORMATION MEDICALE ET PARAMEDICALE CEASED. (L'INFORMATION MEDICALE ET PARAMEDICALE). First issued in 1948. 0020-014X. Periodical. CN. French. bw. **NLM** W1 IN422.

INFUSION. V. 1- Sept. 1977-. 0160-757X. Periodical. US. English. bm. $12.00. Artemis Publishing, 12 High Street, Andover MA 01810.

IN'GAN KWAHAK. VFOAT Human Science. Periodical. KO. English (Korean). ir. Songsim Chungang Yuji Chaedan, 94-195 Yongdungpo-dong Yongdungpo-ku, Seoul South Korea. **Ind/Abst** Chem. Abstr. **LC** R97.7.K6. **NLM** W1 IN447E. **CODEN** INKWDS.

INJURED ATHLETE. (THE INJURED ATHLETE). V. 1- 1977-. 0705-369X. Periodical. CN. English. qt. Free. The Injured Athlete, 559 Jarvis Street, Toronto Ontario M4Y 2J1 Canada. **DD** 617.1027602713. (ctrl).

INORGANIC PERSPECTIVES IN BIOLOGY AND MEDICINE. *See* Biology.

INQUIRY. V. 1- Aug. 1963-. 0046-9580. Periodical. US. English. qt. $35.00. Blue Cross Association, PO Box 527, Glenview IL 60025. **Tel** (312)440-6182. **Ind/Abst** Excerpta Med., Hospit. Lit. Index, Index Med.,

Medicine

Public Aff. Inf. Serv. Bull., Bus. Period. Index, Energy Res. Abstr., Cumul. Index Nurs. Allied Health Lit., Abstr. Soc. Work., Soc. Sci. Citation Index. **LC** RA410.A1. **NLM** W1 IN456K. **CODEN** INQYA. (cum index).

INSEMINATOR. Vol. 12, No. 1-. Periodical. Polish. ir.

INSERM SYMPOSIUM. Main/Corp Institut Nacional de la Sante et de la Recherche Medicale. **VAT** Institut National de la Sante et de la Recherche Medicale Symposium. No. 1-. 0378-0546. Monographic Series. English. ir. Elsevier Science Publishing Company Inc, PO Box 1663 Grand Central Station, New York NY 10163. **Ind/Abst** Chem. Abstr. **NLM** W3 I328E. **CODEN** INSSDM.

INSTAND SCHRIFTENREIHE. V. 1-. Periodical. German. ir. **NLM** W1.

INSTANTANES MEDICAUX. (LES INSTANTANES MEDICAUX). No. 1, (Dec. 1949)-. 0020-2142. Periodical. FR. French. mo. Encyclopedie Medico-Chururgica, 18 rue Seguier, Paris 6E France. **Ind/Abst** CIS Abstr.

INTENSIVBEHANDLUNG. V. 1- 1, Quarter 1976-. 0341-3063. Periodical. German. qt. $38.00. Dustri Verlag, Dr Karl Feistle, Bahnofstrasse 9 Postfach 49, 8024 Deisenhofen - West Germany. **Ind/Abst** Energy Res. Abstr., Excerpta Med., Life Sci. Collect., Biol. Abstr. **NLM** W1 IN652ZU. **CODEN** NTNSDQ.

INTENSIVE CARE MEDICINE. V. 3- 1977-. 0342-4642. Periodical. GW. English. bm. $87.00. Springer Verlag New York Inc, 175 5th Avenue, New York NY 10010. **Tel** (212)460-1500. **Ed** J Tinker, F Lemaire, P M Suter, G Wolff, W M Zapol and D Bihari. **Ind/Abst** Excerpta Med., Index Med., Chem. Abstr., Energy Res. Abstr. **NLM** W1 IN6523. **CODEN** ICMED9. Current work and ideas intended for all involved in intensive medical care, physicians, anesthetists, surgeons, pediatricians, and all concerned with the pre-clinical subjects and medical sciences. *European Journal of Intensive Care Medicine, 0340-0964.*

INTENSIVMEDIZIN CEASED. Vol. 9-20, No. 3. 0303-6251. Periodical. German (summaries in English). bm. Springer Verlag-New York Inc, 175 5th Avenue, New York NY 10010. **Tel** (212)460-1500. **Ind/Abst** Excerpta Med., Biol. Abstr., Chem. Abstr. **NLM** W1. **CODEN** ITMZBJ. *Wiederbelebung, Organersatz, Intensivmedizin, 0043-5252.*

INTER-CLINIC INFORMATION BULLETIN. VFOAT ICIB. V. 1- Oct. 1961-. 0028-7911. Periodical. US. English. mo. New York University, Post-Graduate Medical School, Prosthetics and Orthotics, 317 East 34th Street, New York NY 10016. **Ind/Abst** Excerpta Med. **NLM** W1 I213S. **CODEN** ICIBA.

INTERNATIONAL ANESTHESIA & CRITICAL CARE REPORTER. VAT International Anesthesia and Critical Care Reporter. V. 1-. 0147-3034. Periodical. US. English. ir. $47.00. International Medical Reporter, 326 Suffolk Road, Baltimore MD 21218. **Tel** (301)889-4441. **NLM** ZWO 200 I61.

INTERNATIONAL BIBLIOGRAPHY ON BURNS. See Bibliographies.

INTERNATIONAL CLINICAL PRODUCTS REVIEW. Began with: Vol. 1, No. 1 Nov. 1982). Periodical. US. English. qt. $32.00. **NLM** W1.

INTERNATIONAL CONGRESS AND SYMPOSIUM SERIES - ROYAL SOCIETY OF MEDICINE. (INTERNATIONAL CONGRESS AND SYMPOSIUM SERIES). No. 1-. 0142-2367. Monographic Series. UK. English. Academic Press, 4805 Sand Lake Road, Orlando FL 32819. **Tel** (305)345-4100. **Ind/Abst** Chem. Abstr. **NLM** W3 IN207. **CODEN** RMISDU.

INTERNATIONAL CONGRESS SERIES. (EXCERPTA MEDICA. INTERNATIONAL CONGRESS SERIES). No. 1- 1952-. 0531-5131. Monographic Series. NE. Multilingual. ir. Elsevier Science Publishing Company Inc, PO Box 1663, Grand Central Station, New York NY 10163. **Ind/Abst** Excerpta Med., Int. Aerosp. Abstr., Life Sci. Collect., Chem. Abstr. **NLM** W 3 EX89. **CODEN** EXMDA4.

INTERNATIONAL CONVOCATION ON IMMUNOLOGY. PROCEEDING. 1st- 1968-. 0074-4220. SZ. English. ir. S Karger, PO Box, CH-4009 Basel Switzerland. **Tel** 061-39 08 80.

INTERNATIONAL HOSPITAL EQUIPMENT : IHE. VFOAT IHE. Periodical. US. English. ir. $30.00. Pan Europena Publishing Company, c/o H Briels, rue Verte 216, 1030 Brussels Belgium.

INTERNATIONAL JOURNAL OF BIO-MEDICAL COMPUTING. See Computers and Computer Science.

INTERNATIONAL JOURNAL OF HOLISTIC HEALTH & MEDICINE. VAT International Journal of Holistic Health and Medicine. Began with Sept.-Oct. 1982 issue?. 0737-9560. Periodical. US. English. qt. $8.00 Domestic, $13.00 Foreign. International Journal of Holistic Health and Medicine, PO Box 955, Mill Valley CA 94942.

INTERNATIONAL JOURNAL OF OBESITY. V. 1- 1977-. 0307-0565. Periodical. UK. English. bm. $150.00. John Libbey & Company, 80/84 Bondway, London SW8 1SF England. **Tel** 01 582 5266. **Ed** Per Bjorntorp. **Ind/Abst** Life Sci. Collect., Excerpta Med., Index Med., Chem. Abstr., Bibliogr. Agric. **NLM** W1 IN77P. **CODEN** IJOBDP. bk rev. adv acc. **Circ** 1,000. All aspects of obesity research.

THE INTERNATIONAL JOURNAL OF ORAL AND MAXILLOFACIAL IMPLANTS. (THE INTERNATIONAL JOURNAL OF ORAL AND MAXILLAFACIAL IMPLANTS). 0882-2786. Periodical. US. English. qt. Quintessence Publishing Company, 8 South Michigan Avenue/Suite 2301, Chicago IL 60503.

INTERNATIONAL JOURNAL OF PEPTIDE AND PROTEIN RESEARCH. See Chemistry.

INTERNATIONAL JOURNAL OF SPORTS MEDICINE. V. 1- 1980-. 0172-4622. Periodical. English. bm. **Tel** (212)683-5088. **Ind/Abst** Excerpta Med., Index Med., Chem. Abstr. **NLM** W1 IN791E. **CODEN** IJSMDA. **Circ** 5,000. Promotes world-wide communication in sports medicine.

INTERNATIONAL JOURNAL OF ZOONOSES. V. 1- June 1974-. 0377-0168. Periodical. CH. English. sa. $118.00. International Laboratory for Zoonoses, Number 2 Lane 7 Tsingtien Street, Taipei Taiwan Republic of China. **Ind/Abst** Life Sci. Collect., Excerpta Med., Index Med., Biol. Abstr., Chem. Abstr., Bibliogr. Agric. **NLM** W1 IN792. **CODEN** IJZODH.

INTERNATIONAL MEDICINE. V. 1- July 1979-. 0143-4853. Periodical. UK. English. qt. $56.00. Franklin Scientific Publishing, 371 Kennington Lane, London SE11 5QY England. **Ed** D Geoffrey Brandon. **NLM** W1 IN823U. **Circ** 5,000. Review articles of general medical interest to doctors working in all fields of medicine.

INTERNATIONAL MEDICINE. SUPPLEMENT. No. 1-. 0143-4853. Monographic Series. UK. English. ir. $60.00. Franklin Scientific Publications, 371 Kennington Lane, London SE11 5RA England. **Tel** 582-5344. **Ed** D Geoffrey Brandon. **NLM** W1. **Circ** 5,000. Topics in all branches of medicine written with the non-specialist in mind.

INTERNATIONAL PORTFOLIO. Vol. 1, No. 1 (Spring 1983)-. Periodical. US. English. qt. $55.00. Cortlandt Group Inc, 175 Main Street, Ossining NY 10562. **LC** RZA 0449.

INTERNATIONAL REHABILITATION MEDICINE. VFOAT Rehabilitation Medicine. V. 1-. 0379-0797. Periodical. SZ. English. qt. 95.-. Eular Verlag, Postfach 146, Oberwilerstr 23, CH-4011 Basel Switzerland. **Tel** 061-25 13 11. **Ed** Philip H N Wood. **Ind/Abst** Excerpta Med., Cumul. Index Nurs. Allied Health Lit., Index Med. **NLM** W1 IN828C. bk rev. adv acc. **Circ** 2,000. Official journal of the International Rehabilitaiton Medicine Association.

INTERNATIONAL REVIEWS OF IMMUNOLOGY. 0883-0185. Periodical. UK. English. qt. Harwood Academic, c/o STBS, 1 Bedford Street, London WC2E 9PP England.

INTERNATIONAL SPORT SCIENCES. Vol. 1, No. 1 (Apr. 1979)-. 0190-9541. Periodical. US. English. mo. $95.00. Franklin Research Center, Benjamin Franklin Parkway, Philadelphia PA 19103. **LC** RC1200. **DD** 617.102705. **NLM** ZQT 260 I61. **CODEN** ISSCD9.

INTERNISTISCHE PRAXIS. V. 1- 1961-. 0020-9570. Periodical. GW. German. qt. Marseille Verlag, Burkleinstr 12, D8000 Munich 22 West Germany. **Tel** 89-227988. **Ed** H Feiereis. **Ind/Abst** Excerpta Med. **NLM** W1 IN968. Index published separately - free - automatically sent. (cum index). Information and continued education of the internist in practice of hospital-with numerous illustrations, some in color.

INVENTORY OF HEALTH CARE FACILITY SURVEYORS, UNITED STATES. 1972-. 0190-3500. Periodical. US. English. be. **NLM** W1 IN993V.

INVESTIGACION CLINICA. No. 1 (July 1960)-. 0535-5133. Periodical. VE. Spanish. qt. Investigacion Clinica, Apartado 1151, Maracaibo Venezuela. **Ind/Abst** Excerpta Med., Chem. Abstr. **NLM** W1 IN993W. **CODEN** ICLIAD.

INVESTIGACION MEDICA INTERNACIONAL. V. 1- 1974-. 0377-0206. Periodical. MX. Spanish (with summaries in English and Spanish). ir. $60.00. Investigacion Medica International, Matias Romero 116, Mexico 12 DF Mexico. **Ind/Abst** Life Sci. Collect., Excerpta Med., Chem. Abstr. **NLM** W1 IN993X. **CODEN** IMEIDH.

IOWA MEDICINE. (IOWA MEDICINE : JOURNAL OF THE IOWA MEDICAL SOCIETY). Vol. 74, No. 1 (Jan. 1984)-. 0746-8709. Periodical. US. English. mo. $15.00. Iowa Medical Society, 1001 Grand Avenue West, Des Moines IA 50265. **Tel** (515)223-1401. **Ed** M E Alberts. **Ind/Abst** Index Med., Hospit. Lit. Index, Energy Res. Abstr. **LC** R15. **DD** 610.5. **NLM** W1. bk rev. adv acc. **Circ** 3,700. Contains articles on scientific and socio economic side of medicine plus public health material. *Journal of the Iowa Medical Society, 0021-0587.*

IRB. VAT Institutional Review Boards. V. 1- Mar. 1979-. 0193-7758. Periodical. US. English. bm. $56.20. Hastings Center, 360 Broadway, Hastings-on-Hudson NY 10706. **Tel** (914)478-0500. **Ed** Robert J Levin. **NLM** W1 I268G. bk rev. **Circ** 1,000. Mainly directed toward members and institutional review boards who are involved with protocols in human subjects research.

IRCS JOURNAL OF MEDICAL SCIENCE. VFOAT I.R.C.S. Journal of Medical Science. **VAT** International Research Communications System Journal of Medical Science. V. 3- Jan. 1975-. 0305-6481. Periodical. UK. English. mo. IRCS Medical Science, PO Box 500, St Leonards House, Lancaster LA1 1PF England. **Tel** 0524/68116. **NLM** W1 I268L. *IRCS Journal of International Research Communications, 0300-5569.*

IRCS MEDICAL SCIENCE. CLASSIFIED LIST. (IRCS MEDICAL SCIENCE : CLASSIFIED LIST). **VFOAT** International Research Communications System. V. 3- Jan. 1975-. 0305-649X. Periodical. UK. English. mo. IRCS Medical Science, PO Box 500, St Leonards House, Lancaster LA1 1PF England. **Tel** 0524/68116. *Classified List of International Research Communications Medical Science, 0305-2567.*

IRCS MEDICAL SCIENCE. SOCIAL AND OCCUPATIONAL MEDICINE. (IRCS MEDICAL SCIENCE : SOCIAL AND OCCUPATIONAL MEDICINE). **VFOAT** Social and Occupational Medicine. V. 3- Jan. 1975-. 0305-6945. Periodical. UK. English. qt. $50.00. IRCS Medical Science, PO Box 500/St Leonards House, Lancaster LA1 1PF England. **Tel** (0524)68116. **Ed** S Johnson. bk rev. Publishes results of original research into social aspects of all branches of medicine within weeks of completion. Papers fully refereed. *Research on Social and Occupational Medicine, 0305-2931.*

IRISH JOURNAL OF MEDICAL SCIENCE. 1832. 0021-1265. Periodical. IE. English. mo. 36.00 Domestic, 42.00 Foreign. Royal Academy of Medicine Ireland, 6 Kildare Street, Dublin 1 Ireland. **Tel** 767650. **Ed** John F Murphy. **Ind/Abst** Life Sci. Collect., Pestdoc, Ringdoc, Vetdoc, Excerpta Med., Biol. Abstr., Chem. Abstr., Nucl. Sci. Abstr., Index Med., Curr. Contents, Sci. Cit. Index, Abr. Ed. **NLM** W1 IR429. **CODEN** IJMSAT. bk rev. adv acc. **Circ** 1,500. (ctrl). Medical and allied sciences research.

IRISH MEDICAL JOURNAL CEASED. **VFOAT** Journal of the Irish Medical Association. V. 67, No. 13 (July 12, 1974)-. 0332-3102. Periodical. IE. English. mo. 66 Domestic/UK, 75.00 Foreign. Irish Medical Association, 10 Fitzwilliam Place, Dublin Ireland. **Tel** 767273. **Ed** Norm O'Brien. **Ind/Abst** Life Sci. Collect., Excerpta Med., Index Med., Chem. Abstr., Sci. Cit. Index, Abr. Ed., Hospit. Lit. Index. **NLM** W1 IR449E. **CODEN** IMDJBD. bk rev. adv acc. (ctrl). *Journal of the Irish Medical Association of Eire, 0368-2986.*

Medicine

ISOZYMES; CURRENT TOPICS IN BIOLOGICAL AND MEDICAL RESEARCH. See Biology - Biochemistry.

ISRAEL JOURNAL OF MEDICAL SCIENCES. V. 1- Jan. 1965-. 0021-2180. Periodical. IS. English (some articles have summaries in French and Spanish). mo. $140.00. Israel Journal of Medical Sciences, PO Box 1435, Jerusalem 91 013 Israel. **Tel** 02-227085. **Ed** M Prywes. **Ind/Abst** Life Sci. Collect., Pestdoc, Ringdoc, Vetdoc, Excerpta Med., Index Med., Biol. Abstr., Chem. Abstr., Sci. Cit. Index, Abr. Ed., Hospit. Lit. Index. **LC** R97. **NLM** W1 IS63TU. **CODEN** IJMDAI. bk rev. adv acc. **Circ** 5,000. We publish articles on experimental and chemical medicine, epidemiology and public health, as well as periodic special issues on specific subjects and international proceedings. *Israel Medical Journal, Israel Journal of Experimental Medicine.*

ISSUES IN HEALTH CARE TECHNOLOGY. 1981-. 8756-8721. Periodical. US. English. bm. $145.00. ECRI, 5200 Butler Pike, Plymouth Meeting PA 19462. **Tel** (215)825-6000. **Ed** Malin Van Antwerp. **DD** 620. Overview of health care topics for hospital executives and planners.

ISSUES IN LAW & MEDICINE. See Law.

ISTANBUL TIP FAKULTESI MECMUASI. MONOGRAFI SERISINDEN. No. 28- 1961-. 0379-1173. Monographic Series. Turkish (text mainly in English). ir. **NLM** W1 IS782M. *Istanbul Ueniversitesi Tip Fakultesi Mecmuasi. Monografi Serisi, 0379-1181.*

ITALIAN JOURNAL OF SPORTS TRAUMATOLOGY. V. 1- Jan./Mar. 1979-. 0391-4089. Periodical. IT. English (text in Italian). qt. $50.00. Editrice Kurtis SRL, Via G Rotondi 2, 20145 Milano Italy. **Tel** 02/4396583. **Ind/Abst** Excerpta Med. **NLM** W1 IT136M.

IYO DENSHI TO SEITAI KOGAKU. See Engineering.

IZOBRETENIIA I RATSIONALIZATORSKIE PREDLOZHENIIA V OBLASTI MEDITSINY. Vol. 1- 1973-. UR. Russian. 0.20 Single Issue. Vses Nauchno-issl, In-t Med I Medko-Tekhn, Informatsii, Moskva USSR. **LC** R856.A1. **NLM** W1 IZ65G.

JAARVERSLAG - STICHTING VOOR MEDISCH WETENSCHAPPELIJK ONDERZOEK FUNGO. Main/Corp Stichting Voor Medisch Wetenschappelijk Onderzoek Fungo. 0166-400X. Dutch. ir. **NLM** W1 ST497D.

JAHRBUCH DER DISSERTATIONEN - RUPRECHT-KARLS-UNIVERSITAT HEIDELBERG, MEDIZINISCHE FAKULTAT. See Yearbooks, Almanacs, Directories.

JAHRESSTATISTIK ... DER AMBULANTEN BERATUNGS- UND BEHANDLUNGSSTELLEN FUR SUCHTKRANKE IN DER BUNDESREPUBLIK DEUTSCHLAND. See Statistics.

JAMA EN CENTROAMERICA. VFOAT Journal of the American Medical Association en Centroamerica. V. 1- Oct. 1978-. 0185-1217. Periodical. Spanish. mo.

JAMA EN ESPANOL. VFOAT Journal of the American Medical Association en Espanol. V. 1- Jan. 1975-. 0211-4445. Periodical. SP. Spanish. mo. Editorial Eco S A, c/ de la Cruz 44, Barcelona-34 Spain. **NLM** W1 J221D.

JAMA, THE JOURNAL OF THE AMERICAN MEDICAL ASSOCIATION. (JAMA : THE JOURNAL OF THE AMERICAN MEDICAL ASSOCIATION). VFOAT Journal of the American Medical Association. Vol. 173, No. 9 (July 2, 1960)-. 0098-7484. Periodical. US. English. ir. American Medical Association, 535 North Dearborn Street, Chicago IL 60610. **Tel** (312)645-4927. **Ind/Abst** Bibliogr. Agric., Biol. Abstr., Chem. Abstr., Energy Res. Abstr., Index Med., Life Sci. Collect., Nuci. Sci. Abstr., Psychol. Abstr., Hospit. Lit. Index, Gen. Sci. Index, Lang. Lang. Behav. Abstr., Sociol. Abstr., Abstr. Soc. Work. **LC** R15. **DD** 610.5. **NLM** W1 J221. **CODEN** JAMAAP. Available in microform from University Microfilms International. *Journal of the American Medical Association, 0002-9955.*

JAMA. THE JOURNAL OF THE AMERICAN MEDICAL ASSOCIATION. NIHONGOBAN. Vol. 1- Jan. 1980-. Periodical. Japanese. ir.

JANUS. Vol. 1-. 0021-4264. Periodical. French (contributions in German, or English). qt. **Ind/Abst** Math. Rev. **LC** R131.A1. **NLM** W1 JA864. **CODEN** JNUSA6. (cum index).

JAOA. THE JOURNAL OF THE AMERICAN OSTEOPATHIC ASSOCIATION. (JAOA. THE JOURNAL OF THE AMERICAN OSTEOPATHIC ASSOCIATION). VFOAT Journal AOA. V. 72, No. 5- Jan. 1973-. 0098-6151. Periodical. US. English. mo. $10.00. JAOA, 212 East Ohio Street, Chicago IL 60611. **Tel** (312)280-5800. **Ed** George W Northup. **Ind/Abst** Biol. Abstr., Chem. Abstr., Nuci. Sci. Abstr., Index Med. **NLM** W1 J222F. **CODEN** JOAAZ. bk rev. adv acc. **Circ** 28,500. (ctrl). The official scientific publication of the American Osteopathic Association. It documents osteopathic contributions in all scientific and clinical medical fields. *Journal of the American Osteopathic Association, 0003-0287.*

JAPAN MEDICAL RESEARCH FOUNDATION PUBLICATION. Monographic Series. US. English. **Ind/Abst** Chem. Abstr. **NLM** W1 JA883. **CODEN** JMRPDC.

JAPANESE ANAESTHESIA JOURNALS' REVIEW. Vol. 1, No. 1-. 0169-1066. Periodical. English. qt. **Tel** (0)3046 3737. **NLM** W1. A journal enhancing the accessibility of research and clinical data in anaesthesia originating in Japan and containing the most important articles and latest findings.

THE JAPANESE JOURNAL OF EXPERIMENTAL MEDICINE. Vol. 7, No. 1 (Nov. 10, 1928)-. 0021-5031. Periodical. JA. Japanese. bm. Japan Publishing Trading Company Ltd, PO Box 5030, Tokyo International, Tokyo 100-31 Japan. **Ind/Abst** Index Med., Biol. Abstr., Index Dent. Lit., Chem. Abstr., Bibliogr. Agric., Hospit. Lit. Index, Sci. Cit. Index, Abr. Ed., ISMEC Bull., Excerpta Med., Pollut. Abstr. Indexes, Saf. Sci. Abstr. J., Life Sci. Collect., Electron. Commun. Abstr. J. **LC** R97. **NLM** W1 JA952. **CODEN** JJEMAG. *Scientific Reports from the Government Institute for Infectious Diseases, The Tokyo Imperial University.*

JAPANESE JOURNAL OF MEDICAL SCIENCE & BIOLOGY. VAT Japanese Journal of Medical Science and Biology. V. 5- 1952-. 0021-5112. Periodical. JA. English. bm. Maruzen Company Limited, PO Box 5050, 100-31 Tokyo Japan. **Ind/Abst** Life Sci. Collect., Excerpta Med., Nuci. Sci. Abstr., Biol. Abstr., Chem. Abstr., Index Med., Bibliogr. Agric., Sci. Cit. Index, Abr. Ed. **NLM** W1 JA975. **CODEN** JJMCAQ. (ctrl). Publishes full communications, reviews, epidemiological reports dealing with all aspects of medical science and biology. *Japanese Medical Journal, 0368-3095.*

JAPANESE JOURNAL OF MEDICINE. V. 1, No. 1- Mar. 1962-. 0021-5120. Periodical. JA. English (some in Japanese). qt. $44.07. Tokyo International, PO Box 5272, Tokyo Japan. **Tel** 03 811 7238. **Ind/Abst** Excerpta Med., Index Med., Chem. Abstr., Nuci. Sci. Abstr., Biol. Abstr. **NLM** W1 JA9619. **CODEN** JJMDAT. Index in last issue of volume - attached. bk rev. adv acc. **Circ** 15,000. Most reputational general medical journal in Japan. *Abstracts of Papers of the Journal.*

J.C.U. JOURNAL OF CLINICAL ULTRASOUND. (JCU : JOURNAL OF CLINICAL ULTRASOUND). VFOAT Journal of Clinical Ultrasound. V. 1- March 1973-. 0091-2751. Periodical. US. English. John Wiley & Sons, Medical Division, 605 Third Avenue, New York NY 10158. **Tel** (800)526-5368. **Ind/Abst** Life Sci. Collect., Excerpta Med., Index Med., Biol. Abstr., Comput. Control Abstr., Electr. Electron. Abstr., Sci. Abstr. Sect. A. Phys. Abstr., Energy Res. Abstr., Sci. Cit. Index, Abr. Ed., Phys. Abstr., Hospit. Lit. Index. **LC** RM862.7. **DD** 616.075. **NLM** W1 J223Y. **CODEN** JCULDD.

JEMS. (JEMS : A JOURNAL OF EMERGENCY MEDICAL SERVICES). VFOAT J.E.M.S. VAT Journal of Emergency Medical Services. Began with: V. 5, No. 1 (Mar. 1980). 0197-2510. Periodical. US. English. mo. $17.95. JEMS Publishing Company, PO Box 1026, Solana Beach CA 92075. **Tel** (619)481-1128. **Ed** Keith Griffiths. **Ind/Abst** Hospit. Lit. Index. **NLM** W1 JO637. bk rev. adv acc. **Circ** 30,000. Serves the providers and administrators of emergency medical care and rescue with the latest news and educational information relevant to this field. *Paramedics International, 0191-6351.*

J.E.M.U. JOURNAL D'ECHOGRAPHIE ET DE MEDECINE ULTRASONORE. (JOURNAL D'ECHOGRAPHIE ET DE MEDECINE ULTRASONORE : JEMU). VFOAT JEMU. Vol. 1, 1-. 0245-5552. Periodical. French. bm. Masson Publishing USA Inc, 211 East 43rd Street/Room 1306, New York NY 10017. **Tel** (212)370-1937. **NLM** W1 JO237B.

JHP. JOURNAL OF HOMEOPATHIC PRACTICE. (JHP, JOURNAL OF HOMEOPATHIC PRACTICE). VFOAT Journal of Homeopathic Practice. V. 1- Spring 1978-. 0190-1818. Periodical. US. English. qt. $10.00 US/Mexico/Canada, $20.00 Others. Journal of Homeopathic Practice, PO Box 5015, Berkeley CA 94705. **LC** RX1. **DD** 615.53205.

JIANGSU ZHONGYI ZAZHI. (CHIANG-SU CHUNG I TSA CHIH). VFOAT Jiangsu Journal of Traditional Chinese Medicine. Began with: V. 1, No. 1 in 1980. 0253-9799. Periodical. Chinese. bm. **Ind/Abst** Chem. Abstr. **NLM** W1 CH423BD. **CODEN** CIYCD5.

JIKEIKAI MEDICAL JOURNAL. V. 1- 1954-. 0021-6968. Periodical. JA. English (Japanese). qt. Jikeikai Medical Journal, Takagi Memorial Hall/2nd Floor, The Jekei University School of Medicine Nishi Shinbashi, Minato-Ku Tokyo 105 Japan. **Ind/Abst** Biol. Abstr., Chem. Abstr. **NLM** W1 JI612. **CODEN** JMEJAS.

JIKKEN DOBUTSU. VFOAT Experimental Abstracts. V. 17- 1968-. 0007-5124. Periodical. JA. Japanese (with summaries in English). qt. Japan Publishing Trading Company Ltd, PO Box 5030/Tokyo International, Tokyo 100-31 Japan. **Ind/Abst** Excerpta Med., Index Med., Biol. Abstr. **NLM** W1 JI625. **CODEN** JIDOAA. *Jikken Dobutsu. Bulletin of the Experimental Animals.*

JILINYIKE DAXUE XUEBAO. (CHI-LIN I KO TA HSUEH HSUEH PAO). VFOAT Jilinyikedaxue Xuebao. Vol. 1-. 0253-2719. Periodical. CC. Chinese. qt. Chi-Lin Ko Ta Hsueh, Chang-Chun China. **Ind/Abst** Chem. Abstr. **LC** R97.7.C5. **CODEN** CIKPD8.

JMCI. JOURNAL OF MOLECULAR AND CELLULAR IMMUNOLOGY. See Biology.

JOM. JOURNAL OF OCCUPATIONAL MEDICINE. VFOAT Journal of Occupational Medicine. V. 10- Jan. 1968-. 0096-1736. Periodical. US. English. mo. American Occupational Medicine Association, 2340 South Arlington Heights Road, Arlington Heights IL 60005. **Tel** (312)228-6850. **Ind/Abst** Excerpta Med., Trade Ind. Index, Chem. Abstr., CIS Abstr., Coal Abstr., Energy Inf. Abstr., Energy Res. Abstr., Environ. Abstr., Hospit. Lit. Index, Life Sci. Collect., Index Med., Biol. Abstr., Int. Aerosp. Abstr., Nuci. Sci. Abstr., Sociol. Abstr., Sci. Cit. Index, Abr. Ed., Lang. Lang. Behav. Abstr. **NLM** W1 JO802. **CODEN** JJOMDZ. *Journal of Occupational Medicine, 0022-3212.*

JONCTIONS (PARIS, FRANCE : 1972). (JONCTIONS). No. 1 (May 1972)-. 0300-0478. Periodical. FR. French. mo. $26.07. Doin Editeurs, 8 Place de l' Odeon, 75006 Paris France. **Tel** 325.34.02.

JONXIS LECTURES. (THE JONXIS LECTURES). V. 1-. 0166-2430. Monographic Series. English. ir. Excerpta Medica, PO Box 1126, 1000 BC Amsterdam Netherlands. **Ind/Abst** Chem. Abstr. **NLM** W3 JO44. **CODEN** JOLEDV.

JOURNAL - AMERICAN ASSOCIATION OF MEDICAL DOSIMETRISTS. (JOURNAL). VFOAT AAMD Journal. 0739-0211. Periodical. US. English. qt. $30.00. American Association of Medical Dosimetrists, 925 Chestnut Street, Philadelphia PA 19107. *Treatment Planning.*

JOURNAL (ARZTEKAMMER FUR STEIERMARK). (JOURNAL : MITTEILUNGEN DER ARZTEKAMMER FUR STEIERMARK). VFOAT AK Journal. V. 34, 1 (Jan. 1983)-. Periodical. German. mo. **NLM** W1. *Mitteilungen.*

JOURNAL - CHRISTIAN MEDICAL SOCIETY. (CHRISTIAN MEDICAL SOCIETY JOURNAL). VFOAT CMS Journal. V. 1- Winter 1970-. 0009-546X. Periodical. US. English. qt. $16.00. Christian Medical Society, PO Box 689, Richardson TX 75080. **Tel** (214)783-8384. **Ed** Sidney S MacAuley. **Ind/Abst** Christ. Period. Index. **NLM** W1 CH934. bk rev. **Circ** 7,000. (ctrl). The journal presents a Christian perspective on the relationship between Jesus Christ and medicine. *Christian Medical Society Journal.*

JOURNAL - COLLEGE OF MEDICINE, THE OHIO STATE UNIVERSITY. (COLLEGE OF MEDICINE JOURNAL). V. 14- Autumn 1963-. 0030-1132. Periodical. US. English. ir. Medical Administration Center, Ohio State University, 370 West 9th Avenue, Columbus OH 43210. **Tel** (614)422-5672. **Ed** Ernest W Johnson. **NLM** W1. bk rev. **Circ** 13,200. (ctrl). *Health Center Journal.*

JOURNAL DE GENETIQUE HUMAINE. V. 1- June 1952-. 0021-7743. Periodical. SZ. French (some articles in English, summaries in German). qt. 130.00 Domestic, $61.00 Foreign. Editions Medecine and Hygiene, Case Postale 229, CH-1211 Geneve 4 Switzerland. **Tel** (022) 46 93 55. **Ind/Abst** Life Sci. Collect., Excerpta Med., Energy Inf. Abstr., Environ. Abstr., Index Med., Biol. Abstr., Chem. Abstr., Nuci. Sci. Abstr., Recent Publ. Artic. **NLM** W1 JO307. **CODEN** JGHUAY.

JOURNAL DE TRAUMATOLOGIE. Vol. 1, No.1-. 0245-5811. Periodical. US. English (articles in French). qt. Masson Publishing USA Inc, 14 East 60th Street, New York NY 10022. **Ind/Abst** Excerpta Med. **NLM** W1 JO366C.

JOURNAL - FEDERATION DES MEDECINS SPECIALISTES DU QUEBEC. (LE JOURNAL - FEDERATION DES MEDECINS SPECIALISTES DU QUEBEC). **Main/Corp** Federation des Medecins Specialistes du Quebec. V. 1- April 1978-. 0706-9936. Periodical. CN. French (text in English). mo. Free. Federation des Medecins Specialistes du Quebec, CP 216 Succursale Desjardins, Montreal Quebec H5B 1G8 Canada. **DD** 610.695209714.

JOURNAL OF AFFECTIVE DISORDERS. V. 1- Mar. 1979-. 0165-0327. Periodical. English. qt. Elsevier Science Publishers, PO Box 211, 1000 AE Amsterdam Netherlands. **Tel** (020)5803.911. **Ind/Abst** Life Sci. Collect., Excerpta Med., Index Med., Biol. Abstr., Chem. Abstr., Psychol. Abstr., Sci. Cit. Index, Abr. Ed. **NLM** W1 JO534B. **CODEN** JADID7.

JOURNAL OF AMBULATORY CARE MARKETING. 0886-9723. Periodical. US. English. bm. The Haworth Press, 75 Griswold Street, Binghampton NY 13904. *Emergency Health Services Review, 0738-6192.*

JOURNAL OF AMERICAN COLLEGE HEALTH. (JOURNAL OF AMERICAN COLLEGE HEALTH : J OF ACH). **VFOAT** J of ACH. Vol. 30, No. 5 (April 1982)-. 0744-8481. Periodical. US. English. bm. $35.00. Heldref Publications, 4000 Albemarle Street NW/Suite 100, Washington DC 20016. **Tel** (202)362-6445. **Ed** Mary Anna Bloch. **Ind/Abst** Cumul. Index Nurs. Allied Health Lit., Index Med., Educ. Index, Excerpta Med., Curr. Index J. Educ., Psychol. Abstr. **LC** RA564.5. **DD** 613.088375. **NLM** W1 JO535D. adv acc. **Circ** 1,434. Provides a forum on college health care. Covers developments and research in this broad field; it features research articles and the practical help of clinical and program notes. *Journal of the American College Health Association, 0164-4300.*

JOURNAL OF ANTIMICROBIAL CHEMOTHERAPY. (THE JOURNAL OF ANTIMICROBIAL CHEMOTHERAPY). V. 1- March 1975-. 0305-7453. Periodical. UK. English. mo. Academic Press, 4805 Sand Lake Road, Orlando FL 32819. **Tel** (305)345-4100. **Ind/Abst** Life Sci. Collect., Pestdoc, Ringdoc, Vetdoc, Excerpta Med., Energy Inf. Abstr., Environ. Abstr., Index Med., Biol. Abstr., Chem. Abstr., Hospit. Lit. Index, Sci. Cit. Index, Abr. Ed. **NLM** W1 JO538M. **CODEN** JACHDX.

JOURNAL OF APPLIED MEDICINE. V. 1- Jan. 1975-. 0377-0400. Periodical. II. English. mo. $20.00. Living Media India Limited, POB 29/9K Clock Connaught Circle, New Delhi 110001 India. **Tel** 2026152. **Ed** G S Sainani. **Ind/Abst** Chem. Abstr. **NLM** W1 JO541H. **CODEN** JAMED6. bk rev. adv acc. **Circ** 10,000. (ctrl). A medical review journal to keep Indian doctors abreast with international developments in the field of medicine.

JOURNAL OF APPLIED REHABILITATION COUNSELING. **VFOAT** JARC. V. 1- 1970-. 0047-2220. Periodical. US. English. qt. $30.00. National Rehabilitation Counseling, 633 South Washington Street, Alexandria VA 22314. **Tel** (703)836-7677. **Ed** Arnold Wolf. **Ind/Abst** Psychol. Abstr. **NLM** W1 JO544D. **CODEN** JRCOD3. bk rev. adv acc. **Circ** 450. (ctrl). Publishes articles with practical applications for professional practice, as well as research and theory articles.

JOURNAL OF AUDIOVISUAL MEDIA IN MEDICINE. (THE JOURNAL OF AUDIOVISUAL MEDIA IN MEDICINE). V. 1- Feb. 1978-. 0140-511X. Periodical. UK. English. qt. Update Publications, 33/34 Alfred Place, London WC1E 7DP England. **Ind/Abst** Life Sci. Collect., Index Med. **NLM** W1 JO546T. *Medical and Biological Illustration, 0025-6978.*

JOURNAL OF AYURVEDA (JAIPUR, INDIA). (JOURNAL OF AYURVEDA). **VFOAT** Ayurveda Thraimasiki. Vol. 1, No. 1 (Jan. 1981)-. Periodical. English (articles in Hindi and Orsanskrit). qt. $10.00. **NLM** W1.

JOURNAL OF BEHAVIORAL MEDICINE. **VFOAT** Behavioral Medicine. V. 1- Mar. 1978-. 0160-7715. Periodical. US. English. qt. $36.00 Domestic, $37.80 Foreign. Plenum Press, 227 West 17th Street, New York NY 10011. **Ind/Abst** Sociol. Abstr., Soc. Welf. Soc. Plan./Policy Soc. Dev., Excerpta Med., Cumul. Index Nurs. Allied Health Lit., Index Med., Biol. Abstr., Psychol. Abstr. **LC** R726.5. **DD** 616.0019. **NLM** W1 JO555P. **CODEN** JBMEDD.

JOURNAL OF BIOCOMMUNICATION. (THE JOURNAL OF BIOCOMMUNICATION). V. 1- June 1974-. 0094-2499. Periodical. US. English. qt. $47.00. Journal of Biocommunication, 3215 Haddon Road, Durham NC 27705. **Tel** (919)966-1161. **Ind/Abst** Hospit. Lit. Index, Index Med., Curr. Index J. Educ., Energy Res. Abstr. **LC** R118. **DD** 610.78. **NLM** W1 JO563I.

JOURNAL OF BIOELECTRICITY. Vol. 1, No. 1-. 0730-823X. Periodical. US. English. sa. $100.00. Marcel Dekker, PO Box 11305, Church Street Station, New York NY 10249. **Tel** (318)674-6180. **Ed** Andres A Marino. **Ind/Abst** Life Sci. Collect., Excerpta Med., Biol. Abstr., Comput. Control Abstr., Electr. Electron. Abstr., Sci. Abstr. Sect. A. Phys. Abstr., Chem. Abstr. **LC** QP341. **DD** 574.191705. **NLM** W1 JO563V. **CODEN** JOUBDX.

JOURNAL OF BIOMEDICAL ENGINEERING. V. 1- Jan. 1979-. 0141-5425. Periodical. UK. English. qt. 162.00. Butterworth Scientific Limited, PO Box 63, Westbury House/Bury Street, Guilford GU2 5BH England. **Tel** 31261. **Ed** G H Byford. **Ind/Abst** Eng. Index Annu., Eng. Index Mon., Eng. Index, Eng. Index Bioeng. Abstr., Eng. Index Energy Abstr., Excerpta Med., Index Med., Biol. Abstr., Comput. Control Abstr., Electr. Electron. Abstr., Sci. Abstr. Sect. A. Phys. Abstr., Chem. Abstr., Phys. Abstr., Hospit. Lit. Index, Sci. Cit. Index, Abr. Ed. **NLM** W1 JO564N. **CODEN** JBIEDR. bk rev. adv acc. Physical sciences and mathematics are applied to medical situations. This journal provides communication of technology in health care to both engineers and clinicians.

JOURNAL OF BIOMEDICAL MATERIALS RESEARCH. Periodical. US. English. ir. John Wiley & Sons Inc, 605 Third Avenue, New York NY 10158. **Tel** (800)526-5368. **Ind/Abst** Sci. Cit. Index, Abr. Ed., Hospit. Lit. Index, Chem. Abstr., Eng. Index, Index Med., Appl. Mech. Rev.

JOURNAL OF BIOMEDICAL MATERIALS RESEARCH. V. 1- Mar. 1967-. 0021-9304. Periodical. US. English. mo. John Wiley & Sons, 605 3rd Avenue, New York NY 10158. **Ind/Abst** Eng. Index Mon., Eng. Index Bioeng. Abstr., Eng. Index Energy Abstr., Life Sci. Collect., Excerpta Med., Int. Aerosp. Abstr., Biol. Abstr., Chem. Abstr., Eng. Index Annu., Eng. Index Mon., Nuci. Sci. Abstr., Index Med., Energy Res. Abstr. **LC** R856. **DD** 610.28. **NLM** W1 JO564P. **CODEN** JBMRBG.

THE JOURNAL OF BLOODLESS MEDICINE AND SURGERY. (THE JOURNAL OF BLOODLESS MEDICINE AND SURGERY : THE OFFICIAL PUBLICATION OF THE INSTITUTE OF BLOODLESS MEDICINE AND SURGERY). Vol. 1, No. 1 (Winter 1983)-. 0882-1364. Periodical. US. English. qt. Journal of Bloodless Medicine and Surgery, 1505 North San Fernando Boulevard, Burbank CA 91504. **DD** 617. **NLM** W1.

THE JOURNAL OF BURN CARE & REHABILITATION. **VFOAT** Journal of Burn Care and Rehabilitation. Vol. 1, No. 1 (Sept/Oct 1980)-. 0273-8481. Periodical. US. English. bm. $28.00. JBC Publisher Inc, PO Drawer 36329, Dallas TX 75235. **Tel** (214)688-3523. **Ed** Charles R Baxter. **Ind/Abst** Excerpta Med., Cumul. Index Nurs. Allied Health Lit., Chem. Abstr. **NLM** W1 JO57R. **CODEN** JBCRD2. bk rev. adv acc. **Circ** 5,000. (ctrl). Provides most recent information about care of burn patients from emergency treatment through rehabilitation. Articles of report findings of researchers, clinicians and other burn specialists.

THE JOURNAL OF CHINESE MEDICINE. No. 1 (Summer 1979)-. 0143-8042. Periodical. UK. English. ty. 11.00. 68 Prince Edward Road, Lewes Sussex BN7 1BH England. **NLM** W1 JO583J.

JOURNAL OF CHIROPRACTIC. Vol. 19, No. 1 (Jan. 1982)-. 0744-9984. Periodical. US. English. mo. $80.00. American Chiropractic Association, 8229 Maryland Avenue, St Louis MO 63105. **Tel** (314)862-7800. **Ed** Kathleen Z Brown. **NLM** W1 JO5842. bk rev. adv acc. **Circ** 19,000. Journal carrying professional papers, association activities, letters, editorials, book reviews, and various news items of interest to the chiropractic profession. *ACA Journal of Chiropractic, 0044-7609.*

JOURNAL OF CHROMATOGRAPHY. BIOMEDICAL APPLICATIONS. **Series/Titl** Journal of Chromatography. V. 1- Jan. 1977-. 0378-4347. Periodical. NE. English. bm. Elsevier Science Publishers, PO Box 211, 1000 AE Amsterdam The Netherlands. **Tel** (020)5803.911. **Ind/Abst** Pestdoc, Ringdoc, Vetdoc, Excerpta Med., Biol. Abstr. **NLM** W1 JO5845. **CODEN** JCBADL.

JOURNAL OF CHRONIC DISEASES. Vol. 1, No. 1 (Jan. 1955)-. 0021-9681. Periodical. US. English. mo. Pergamon Press, 395 Sawmill River Road, Elmsford NY 10523. **Tel** (914)592-7700. **Ind/Abst** Electron. Commun. Abstr. J., ISMEC Bull., Pollut. Abstr. Indexes, Saf. Sci. Abstr. J., Life Sci. Collect., Excerpta Med., Cumul. Index Nurs. Allied Health Lit., CIS Abstr., Biol. Abstr., Chem. Abstr., Index Med., Nuci. Sci. Abstr., Energy Res. Abstr., Sci. Cit. Index, Abr. Ed., Hospit. Lit. Index. **LC** RB156. **DD** 616.05. **NLM** W1 JO585H. **CODEN** JOCDAE.

JOURNAL OF CLINICAL APHERESIS. Vol. 1, No. 1-. 0733-2459. Periodical. US. English. qt. Alan R Liss Inc, 41 East 11th Street, New York NY 10003. **Tel** (212)741-2515. **Ind/Abst** Life Sci. Collect., Excerpta Med. **NLM** W1 JO587AG.

JOURNAL OF CLINICAL ENGINEERING. V. 1- Oct./Dec. 1976-. 0363-8855. Periodical. US. English. qt. $40.00. Quest Publishing Company, 1351 Titan Way, Brea CA 92621. **Tel** (714)738-6400. **Ed** Allan F Pacela and Peggy Browneller. **Ind/Abst** Eng. Index Mon., Eng. Index Bioeng. Abstr., Eng. Index Energy Abstr., Hospit. Lit. Index, Excerpta Med., Biol. Abstr., Comput. Control Abstr., Electr. Electron. Abstr., Sci. Abstr. Sect. A. Phys. Abstr., Ref. Source, Eng. Index Annu. **LC** R856.A1. **DD** 610.28. **NLM** W1 JO588C. **CODEN** JCEND7. Index available. bk rev. adv acc. Featuring the latest technical and professional information in biomedical and clinical engineering.

JOURNAL OF CLINICAL IMMUNOLGY. Vol. 1, No. 1 (Jan. 1981)-. 0271-9142. Periodical. US. English. bm. $145.00 Domestic, $163.00 Foreign. Plenum Publishing Company, 233 Spring Street, New York NY 10013. **Tel** (212)620-8000. **Ind/Abst** Life Sci. Collect., Excerpta Med., Index Med., Biol. Abstr., Chem. Abstr., Curr. Contents. **LC** RC581. **DD** 616.07905. **NLM** W1 JO588DE. **CODEN** JCIMDO. This journal is devoted exclusively to clinical immunology and its application to the practice of medicine.

THE JOURNAL OF CLINICAL INVESTIGATION. V. 1- Oct. 1924-. 0021-9738. Periodical. US. English. mo. Rockefeller University Press, PO Box 5108, Church Street Station, New York NY 10249. **Tel** (212)570-8572. **Ind/Abst** Life Sci. Collect., Pestdoc, Ringdoc, Vetdoc, Excerpta Med., Int. Aerosp. Abstr., CIS Abstr., Biol. Abstr., Chem. Abstr., Index Med., Nuci. Sci. Abstr., Bibliogr. Agric., Energy Res. Abstr., Sci. Cit. Index, Abr. Ed. **LC** R11. **DD** 616.005. **NLM** W1 JO588H. **CODEN** JCINAO. (cum index).

JOURNAL OF CLINICAL LABORATORY IMMUNOLOGY. 1978. 0141-2760. Periodical. UK. English. mo. Teviot Kimpton Books, 205 Great Portland Street, London W1N 6LR England. **Tel** 031-447-9411. **Ed** James Irvine. **Ind/Abst** Sci. Cit. Index, Abr. Ed. bk rev. adv acc. An international journal concerning immunology in all areas relevant to understanding the role of immunology in health and disease.

THE JOURNAL OF EMERGENCY MEDICINE. Vol. 1, No. 1-. 0736-4679. Periodical. S. English. bm. $75.00. Pergamon Press, Maxwell House/Fairview Park, Elmsford NY 10523. **Ind/Abst**

Electron. Commun. Abstr. J., ISMEC Bull., Pollut. Abstr. Indexes, Saf. Sci. Abstr. J., Life Sci. Collect. **NLM** W1.

THE JOURNAL OF ENERGY MEDICINE. VFOAT Energy Medicine. 0196-1330. Periodical. US. English. qt. $100.00. The Energy Center Inc, 1175 NE 125th Street, North Miami FL 33161. **NLM** W1 JO643M.

JOURNAL OF EXPERIMENTAL & CLINICAL CANCER RESEARCH : CR. VFOAT Journal of Experimental and Clinical Cancer Research. Began with: V. 1, No. 1 (Jan./March 1982). Periodical. US. English. qt. $70.00. Lippincott/Harper, East Washington Square, Philadelphia PA 19105. **Ed** Ercole Sega. **Ind/Abst** Excerpta Med. **NLM** W1 JO44FR. Contains original articles with new scientific data on immunological, epidemiological, pathological, biological, and clinical aspects of oncology.

JOURNAL OF EXPERIMENTAL MEDICAL SCIENCES. Began publication in 1957. 0022-099X. Periodical. II. English. qt. Society of Experimental Medical Sciences, 50-2 Dharamtala Street, Calcutta 13 India. **Ind/Abst** Index Med.

THE JOURNAL OF EXPERIMENTAL MEDICINE. V. 1- Jan. 1896-. 0022-1007. Periodical. US. English. mo. Rockefeller University Press, PO Box 5108/Church Street Station, New York NY 10249. **Tel** (212)570-8572. **Ind/Abst** Life Sci. Collect., Pestdoc, Ringdoc, Vetdoc, Excerpta Med., Biol. Abstr., Chem. Abstr., Nuci. Sci. Abstr., Index Med., Energy Res. Abstr., Sci. Cit. Index, Abr. Ed. **NLM** W1 JO644Q. **CODEN** JEMEAV. (cum index).

JOURNAL OF FAMILY PRACTICE. (THE JOURNAL OF FAMILY PRACTICE). V. 1- May 1974-. 0094-3509. Periodical. US. English. mo. $40.00. Appleton Century Croft, 25 Van Zant Street, East Norwalk CT 06855. **Tel** (203)838-4400. **Ed** John P Geyman. **Ind/Abst** Hospit. Lit. Index, Life Sci. Collect., Excerpta Med., Index Med., Cumul. Index Nurs. Allied Health Lit., Psychol. Abstr., Energy Res. Abstr., Sci. Cit. Index, Abr. Ed. **LC** R11. **DD** 610. **NLM** W1 JO6444. bk rev. adv acc. **Circ** 74,000. (ctrl). Original articles and clinical research of interest to the family practitioner and related health professionals.

THE JOURNAL OF HEAD TRAUMA REHABILITATION. 0885-9701. Periodical. US. English. qt. $60.00. Aspen Systems Corporation, 16792 Oakmont Avenue, Gaithersburg MD 20877.

JOURNAL OF HEALTH CARE TECHNOLOGY. Vol. 1, No. 1 (Summer 1984)-. 0748-075X. Periodical. US. English. qt. $80.00. ECRI, 5200 Butler Pike, Plymouth Meeting PA 19462. **Tel** (215)825-6000. **Ed** Malin Van Antwerp. **DD** 338. **NLM** W1. Health care technology assessments, planning, and value analysis.

JOURNAL OF HEALTH POLITICS, POLICY AND LAW. V. 1- Spring 1976-. 0361-6878. Periodical. US. English. qt. $60.00. Duke University Press, Box 3018, Durham NC 27710. **Tel** (919)684-4188. **Ed** Lawrence D Brown. **Ind/Abst** Leg. Resour. Index, Hospit. Lit. Index, Sociol. Abstr., Soc. Welf. Soc. Plan./Policy Soc. Dev., Excerpta Med., Index Med., Biol. Abstr., Curr. Law Index, Soc. Sci. Citation Index, Public Aff. Inf. Serv. Bull. **LC** RA395.A3. **DD** [38.4736210973. **NLM** W1 JO67BL. **CODEN** JHPLDN. bk rev. adv acc. **Circ** 1,900. Initiation, formulation, and implementation of health policy, drawing from politics, sociology, economics, public administration, law and ethics.

JOURNAL OF HOLISTIC MEDICINE. 0195-5977. Periodical. US. English. sa. Human Sciences Press, 72 5th Avenue, New York NY 10011. **Tel** (212)243-6000. **Ind/Abst** Excerpta Med., Psychol. Abstr. **LC** R733. **DD** 613.05. **NLM** W1 JO671G. **CODEN** JHMEDL. *American Journal of Holistic Medicine, Holistic Health Review, 0163-8491.*

JOURNAL OF HYPERBARIC MEDICINE. 0884-1225. Periodical. US. English. qt. Free to Members, $60.00 Nonmembers. Plenum Publishing Corporation, 9650 Rockville Pike, Bethesda MD 20814. *Hyperbaric Oxygen Review, 0195-9263.*

JOURNAL OF HYPERTENSION. Vol. 1, No. 1 (June 1983)-. 0263-6352. Periodical. UK. English. bm. $60.00. Gower Medical Publishing Ltd, 101 5th Avenue, New York NY 10003. **Ed** J D Swales. **Ind/Abst** Excerpta Med., Chem. Abstr. **NLM** W1 JO674R. **CODEN** JOHYD3. bk rev. adv acc. **Circ** 2,000. Original clinical and scientific research which contribute to the advancement of knowledge in hypertension.

JOURNAL OF IMMUNOLOGY. (THE JOURNAL OF IMMUNOLOGY : OFFICIAL JOURNAL OF THE AMERICAN ASSOCIATION OF IMMUNOLOGISTS). Vol. 64, No. 1 (Jan. 1950)-. 0022-1767. Periodical. US. English. mo. Journal of Immunology, PO Box 64471, Baltimore MD 21264. **Tel** (301)528-4105. **Ind/Abst** Life Sci. Collect., Excerpta Med., Pestdoc, Ringdoc, Vetdoc, Energy Inf. Abstr., Environ. Abstr., Index Med., Int. Aerosp. Abstr., Biol. Abstr., Chem. Abstr., Nuci. Sci. Abstr., Bibliogr. Agric., Energy Res. Abstr., Sci. Cit. Index, Abr. Ed. **LC** QR180. **NLM** W1 JO677. **CODEN** JOIMA3. *Journal of Immunology, Virus-Research & Experimental Chemotherapy.*

JOURNAL OF IMMUNOPHARMACOLOGY. V. 1- 1978/79-. 0163-0571. Periodical. US. English. qt. $125.00. Marcel Dekker Journals, PO Box 11305, Church Street Station, New York NY 10249. **Ed** Michael A Chirigas. **Ind/Abst** Life Sci. Collect., Excerpta Med., Pestdoc, Ringdoc, Vetdoc, Index Med., Biol. Abstr., Chem. Abstr. **NLM** W1 JO679. **CODEN** JOIMD6. bk rev. adv acc.

THE JOURNAL OF INFECTION. V. 1- Mar. 1979-. 0163-4453. Periodical. UK. English. bm. $113.50. Academic Press, 4805 Sand Lake Road, Orlando FL 32819. **Tel** (305)345-4100. **Ind/Abst** Life Sci. Collect., Excerpta Med., Pestdoc, Ringdoc, Vetdoc, Index Med., Chem. Abstr. **NLM** W1 JO706M. **CODEN** JINFD2.

THE JOURNAL OF INFECTIOUS DISEASES. V. 1- Jan. 1904-. 0022-1899. Periodical. US. English. mo. University Chicago Press, PO Box 37005, Chicago IL 60637. **Tel** (312)753-3347. **Ind/Abst** Life Sci. Collect., Excerpta Med., Pestdoc, Ringdoc, Vetdoc, Energy Inf. Abstr., Environ. Abstr., Biol. Abstr., Chem. Abstr., Nuci. Sci. Abstr., Index Med., Energy Res. Abstr., Hospit. Lit. Index, Sci. Cit. Index, Abr. Ed. **NLM** W1 JO707. **CODEN** JIDIAQ. (cum index).

THE JOURNAL OF INTER-AMERICAN MEDICINE. V. 1- Mar. 1976-. 0363-2768. Periodical. US. English (Spanish with some summaries in English and Spanish). qt. American Hospital of Miami, 11750 Bird Road, Miami FL 33175. **NLM** W1 JO716E.

JOURNAL OF INTERNATIONAL BIOMEDICAL INFORMATION AND DATA. IBID. (THE JOURNAL OF INTERNATIONAL BIOMEDICAL INFORMATION AND DATA : IBID). VFOAT IBID. Vol. 1, No. 1-. 0260-0765. Periodical. UK. English. ir. 35.00. MCS Consultants, 33 Vale Road, Turnbridge Wells Kent TN1 BP England. **Tel** 27282. **Ed** B P Hughes. **Ind/Abst** Chem. Abstr. **NLM** W1 JO717. **CODEN** JIBDD4.

JOURNAL OF INTERNATIONAL MEDICAL RESEARCH. (THE JOURNAL OF INTERNATIONAL MEDICAL RESEARCH). V. 1- 1972-. 0300-0605. Periodical. UK. English (summaries in French, German, and Spanish). bm. $60.00. Cambridge Medical Publishers Ltd, 435/437 Wellingborough Road, Northampton WN1 4EZ England. **Tel** (0604)32559. **Ed** J Eric Murphy. **Ind/Abst** Electron. Commun. Abstr. J., ISMEC Bull., Pollut. Abstr. Indexes, Saf. Sci. Abstr. J., Life Sci. Collect., Excerpta Med., Pestdoc, Ringdoc, Vetdoc, Index Med., Biol. Abstr., Curr. Contents Clin. Pract., Chem. Abstr., Hospit. Lit. Index, Sci. Cit. Index, Abr. Ed. **NLM** W1 JO718K. **CODEN** JIMRBV. **Circ** 4,000. (ctrl). Medical research predominately comparative drug evaluation.

JOURNAL OF INTERNATIONAL PHYSICIANS. V. 1- 1976-. 0161-7702. Periodical. US. English. bm. $30.00. Pacifica Ventures, 1030 North Kings Highway, Cherry Hill NJ 08034. **NLM** W1 JO719.

JOURNAL OF INTRAVENOUS THERAPY. VFOAT Journal of I.V. Therapy. Jan./Feb. 1977-. 0194-1658. Periodical. US. English. bm. $24.00. Journal of Intravenous Therapy, Box 67159/Century City, Los Angeles CA 90067. **Tel** (213)475-5141. bk rev. adv acc. **Circ** 3,000. (ctrl). All aspects of intravenous therapy. *Western States IV Therapy Journal, 0363-4302.*

THE JOURNAL OF LABORATORY AND CLINICAL MEDICINE. V. 1- Oct. 1915-. 0022-2143. Periodical. US. English. mo. $100.00. C V Mosby, c/o R K Kinnes, 11830 Westline Industrial Drive, St Louis MO 63146. **Tel** (314)872-8370. **Ed** Norton J Greenberger. **Ind/Abst** Life Sci. Collect., Excerpta Med., Pestdoc, Ringdoc, Vetdoc, CIS Abstr., Biol. Abstr., Chem. Abstr., Index Med., Nuci. Sci. Abstr., Energy Res. Abstr., Sci. Cit. Index, Abr. Ed. **LC** R11. **NLM** W1 JO734. **CODEN** JLCMAK. adv acc. **Circ** 4,663. Advanced information for directories of clinical and pathology laboratories, laboratory consultants, laboratory technologists, physicians interested in diagnosis, and those with a related interested in investigation and research.

JOURNAL OF LONG TERM CARE ADMINISTRATION. (THE JOURNAL OF LONG TERM CARE ADMINISTRATION). VFOAT Journal of Long-Term Care Administration. 1972. 0093-4445. Periodical. US. English. qt. $60.00. American College Health Care Administration, 8012 Woodmont Avenue/Suite 200, Bethesda MD 20814. **Tel** (301)652-8384. **Ed** Kathleen M Griffin. **Ind/Abst** Hospit. Lit. Index, Cumul. Index Nurs. Allied Health Lit., Biol. Abstr. **LC** RA997.A1. **DD** 362.1605. **NLM** W1 JO746. **CODEN** JLTAD4. bk rev. adv acc. **Circ** 7,200. Offers thorough, researched articles and series on issues and developments in the fields of long-term health care and administration.

JOURNAL OF LOW-TEMPERATURE PLASMA CHEMISTRY. 0747-9352. Periodical. US. English. qt. $145.00. Technomic Publishing Company, 851 New Holland Avenue/Box 3535, Lancaster PA 17604.

JOURNAL OF MANIPULATIVE AND PHYSIOLOGICAL THERAPEUTICS. VFOAT Manipulative and Physiological Therapeutics. V. 1- Mar. 1978-. 0161-4754. Periodical. US. English. qt. $45.00. Journal of Manipulative and Physiological Therapeutics, PO Box 64025, Baltimore MD 21264. **Tel** (301)528-4105. **Ind/Abst** Index Med. **LC** RM724. **DD** 615.53405. **NLM** W1 JO748F.

JOURNAL OF MEDICAL AND HEALTH LABORATORY TECHNOLOGY, MALAYSIA. 0126-7752. MY. English. an. Institute of Medical and Health, Laboratory of Technology, Institute of Medical Research, Jalan Pahang Kuala Lumpur Malaysia. **NLM** W1 JO749NV.

JOURNAL OF MEDICAL ENGINEERING & TECHNOLOGY. VAT Journal of Medical Engineering and Technology. Vol. 1, No. 1 (Jan. 1977)-. 0309-1902. Periodical. UK. English. bm. $110.00. Taylor & Francis Ltd, 242 Cherry Street, Philadelphia PA 19106. **Tel** (215)238-0939. **Ed** R E Trotman and S J Meldrum. **Ind/Abst** Eng. Index Annu., Eng. Index Mon., Eng. Index, Eng. Index Bioeng. Abstr., Eng. Index Energy Abstr., Excerpta Med., Index Med., Comput. Control Abstr., Electr. Electron. Abstr., Sci. Abstr. Sect. A. Phys. Abstr., Chem. Abstr., Energy Res. Abstr., Appl. Mech. Rev., Sci. Cit. Index, Abr. Ed., Phys. Abstr., Hospit. Lit. Index. **LC** R856.A1. **DD** 610.28. **NLM** W1 JO75C. **CODEN** JMTEDN. An international and independent bi-monthly for engineers, physicians, scientists, hospital staff, teachers, and industry and government personnel. *Biomedical Engineering (London, England), 0006-2898.*

JOURNAL OF MEDICAL ETHICS. *See* Ethics.

THE JOURNAL OF MEDICAL HUMANITIES AND BIOETHICS. *See* Ethics.

THE JOURNAL OF MEDICAL PRACTICE MANAGEMENT. (MEDICAL PRACTICE MANAGEMENT). VFOAT MPM. Began in 1985. 8755-0229. Periodical. US. English. qt. $40.00 Domestic, $50.00 Foreign. Williams & Wilkins, 428 East Preston Street, Baltimore MD 21202. **Tel** (301)528-4000. **DD** 658. adv acc. **Circ** 2,500. Perspectives on legislation, litigation, office management and other key issues that affect the medical practice of office-based physicians and health care professionals.

JOURNAL OF MEDICAL TECHNOLOGY. (JOURNAL OF MEDICAL TECHNOLOGY : OFFICIAL PUBLICATION OF AMERICAN MEDICAL TECHNOLOGISTS AND AMERICAN SOCIETY FOR MEDICAL TECHNOLOGY). VFOAT Medical Technology. Vol. 1, No. 1 (Jan. 1984)-. 0741-5397. Periodical. US. English. mo. $48.00 Domestic, $53.00 Canada, $66.00 Others. American Society for Medical Technology, 330 Meadowfern Drive, Houston TX 77067. **Tel** (713)872-7072. **Ed** Diana Mass and Gerard P Boe. **Ind/Abst** Cumul. Index Nurs. Allied Health Lit., Excerpta Med., Hospit. Lit. Index, Life Sci. Collect., Curr. Contents. bk rev. adv acc. (ctrl). Technical, scientific and professional information for supervisory and staff level technologists in clinical laboratory science/medical technology. *American Journal of Medical Technology, 0148-8759; Journal of the American Medical Technologists (1966), 0002-9963.*

JOURNAL OF MEDICINE. V. 1- 1970-. 0025-7850. Periodical. US. English. bm. $90.00. PJD Publishing Limited, PO Box 966, Westbury NY 11590. **Tel** (516)626-0650. **Ed** J L Ambrus and Siva Sankar. **Ind/Abst** Excerpta Med., Pestdoc, Ringdoc, Vetdoc, CIS Abstr., Biol. Abstr., Chem. Abstr., Index Med., Nuci. Sci. Abstr., Energy Res. Abstr., Sci. Cit. Index, Abr. Ed., Leg. Resour. Index, Curr. Law Index, Lang. Lang. Behav. Abstr., Sociol. Abstr. **NLM** W1 JO758T. **CODEN** JNMDBO. bk rev. adv acc. A highly important refereed journal covering all areas of medicine. Recommended to universities and medical libraries. *Medicina Experimentalis.*

JOURNAL OF MEDICINE. V. 1- 1970-. English. ir. **Ind/Abst** Life Sci. Collect. **LC** R11. **DD** 610.5. *Medicina Experimentalis.*

JOURNAL OF MEDICINE & BIOLOGY. **VFOAT** Journal of Medicine and Biology. Periodical. US. English. qt. Alin Foundation Press, 2107 Dwight Way, Berkeley CA 94704.

THE JOURNAL OF MEDICINE AND PHILOSOPHY. V. 1- Mar. 1976-. 0360-5310. Periodical. NE. English. qt. 37. Kluwer Academic Publishers Group, PO Box 322, 3300 AH Dordrecht Netherlands. **Tel** (31)78-334911. **Ed** H Tristram Engelhardt. **Ind/Abst** Sociol. Abstr., Soc. Welf. Soc. Plan./Policy Soc. Dev., Energy Res. Abstr., Hospit. Lit. Index, Index Med., Philos. Index, Humanit. Index, Soc. Sci. Citation Index, Guide Soc. Sci. Relig. Period. Lit. **LC** R723. **DD** 610.1. **NLM** W1 JO758G. bk rev. adv acc. **Circ** 1,850. Shared themes and concerns of philosophy and the medical sciences.

JOURNAL OF NUCLEAR MEDICINE AND ALLIED SCIENCES. (THE JOURNAL OF NUCLEAR MEDICINE AND ALLIED SCIENCES). **VFOAT** Minerva Mediconucleare. V. 21 - Jan/June 1977-. 0392-0208. Periodical. IT. English. qt. 60.00. Edizioni Minerva Medica, Corso Bramante 83-855, Torino Italy. **Tel** 678282. **Ed** G Mariami. **Ind/Abst** Life Sci. Collect., Excerpta Med., Index Med., Comput. Control Abstr., Electr. Electron. Abstr., Sci. Abstr. Sect. A. Phys. Abstr., Chem. Abstr., Energy Res. Abstr. **NLM** W1 JO796C. **CODEN** JNMSD3. bk rev. adv acc. Journal addressed to practitioners and specialists in nuclear medicine. It deals with topics in scientific practice and research. *Journal of Nuclear Biology and Medicine, 0368-3249.*

JOURNAL OF NUCLEAR MEDICINE. SUPPLEMENT. 0075-4315. US. English. ir. Society of Nuclear Medicine, 136 Madison Avenue, New York NY 10016. **Ind/Abst** Energy Res. Abstr., Chem. Abstr.

JOURNAL OF NUCLEAR MEDICINE TECHNOLOGY. V. 1- Mar. 1973-. 0091-4916. Periodical. US. English. qt. $55.00. Society of Nuclear Medicine, 136 Madison Avenue, New York NY 10016. **Tel** (212)889-0717. **Ed** Paul E Christian. **Ind/Abst** Phys. Abstr., Comput. Control Abstr., Electr. Electron. Abstr. **LC** R895.A1. **DD** 616.0757505. **NLM** W1 JO796E. **CODEN** JNMTB4. bk rev. adv acc. **Circ** 5,430. Articles are devoted to topics that explore the various facets of nuclear medicine technology.

JOURNAL OF ORAL MEDICINE. 0022-3247. Periodical. US. English. qt. $55.00. American Academy of Oral Medicine, 829 Hanamoor Court, St Louis MO 63122. **Ind/Abst** Hospit. Lit. Index, Index Med.

THE JOURNAL OF ORGONOMY. V. 1- Nov. 1967-. 0022-3298. Periodical. US. English. sa. $20.00. Orgonomic Publs, PO Box 565/Ansonia Station, New York NY 10023. **Tel** (212)772-0857. **Ed** Elsworth F Baker. **LC** RZ460. **NLM** W1 JO804MK. bk rev. **Circ** 1,000. (ctrl). Available on microfilm from University Microfilms. Continues the work of Wilhelm Reich with translations. Clinical and research papers on psychiatry, medicine, physics, childrearing, and education.

JOURNAL OF PODIATRIC MEDICAL EDUCATION. V. 5- Spring 1974-. 0093-7339. Periodical. US. English. sa. $8.00. American Association of Colleges in Podiatric Medicine, 6110 Executive Boulevard 204, Rockville MD 20852-3903. **Tel** (301)984-9351. **Ed** Suzanne H Howard. **Ind/Abst** Curr. Index J. Educ. **NLM** W1 JO837E. **Circ** 1,300. (ctrl). Dedicated to publishing information and studies pertaining to the field of podiatric medical education. *Journal of Podiatric Education, 0092-4024.*

JOURNAL OF POSTGRADUATE MEDICINE. (JOURNAL OF POST GRADUATE MEDICINE). V. 1- April 1955-. 0022-3859. Periodical. II. English. qt. $18.00. Journal of Postgraduate Medicine, Kem Hospital, Bombay 12 India. **Tel** 4460501. **Ed** S D Bhandarkar. **Ind/Abst** Index Med., Chem. Abstr. **NLM** W1 JO838. **CODEN** JPMDA3. bk rev. adv acc. **Circ** 1,000. We publish original articles describing clinical and experimental work and case reports on various subspecialties of modern medicine.

THE JOURNAL OF PRE-HOSPITAL CARE. (THE JOURNAL OF PRE-HOSPITAL CARE : THE OFFICIAL PUBLICATION OF THE NATIONAL ASSOCIATION OF EMERGENCY MEDICAL TECHNICIANS). Vol. 1, No. 1 (Mar. 1984)-. 0747-5004. Periodical. US. English. bm. $20.00. The Journal of Pre-Hospital Care, 434 West Nakoma Avenue, San Antonio TX 78216. **Tel** (512)341-9228. **Ed** John Siga Foos. **DD** 616. **NLM** W1. bk rev. adv acc. **Circ** 20,000. The journal offers the latest ideas and advances in the field of pre-hospital care. The official publication of NAEMT.

JOURNAL OF PREVENTIVE AND SOCIAL MEDICINE : JOPSOM : A BI-ANNUAL JOURNAL OF THE NATIONAL INSTITUTE OF PREVENTIVE AND SOCIAL MEDICINE. **VFOAT** JOPSOM. Vol. 1, No. 1 (May 1982)-. Periodical. English. sa. **NLM** W1.

JOURNAL OF REPRODUCTIVE IMMUNOLOGY. V. 1- Jan./Feb. 1979-. 0165-0378. Periodical. English. bm. $75.50. **Ind/Abst** Life Sci. Collect., Excerpta Med., Index Med., Biol. Abstr., Chem. Abstr. **NLM** W1 JO868N. **CODEN** JRIMDR.

JOURNAL OF RESEARCH IN AYURVEDA & SIDDHA. **VFOAT** Journal of Research in Ayurveda and Siddha. Vol. 1, No. 1 (Mar. 1980)-. 0254-3478. Periodical. II. English. qt. $30.00. Central Council for Research in Ayurveda and Siddha, S-10 Dharma Bhawan Green Park Extension Market, New Delhi-110016 India. **LC** R605. **DD** 615.89. **NLM** W1 JO868V. *Journal of Research in Indian Medicine, Yoga and Homoeopathy, 0250-4790.*

JOURNAL OF SPORTS MEDICINE AND PHYSICAL FITNESS. *See* Recreation, Leisure - Sports.

JOURNAL OF THE AMERICAN ANALGESIA SOCIETY. **Main/Corp** American Analgesia Society. 0002-7243. Periodical. US. English. sa. Dr Norman Menken, 11 Stratford Road, New Rochelle NY 10804. **Ind/Abst** Chem. Abstr. **NLM** W1 JO222TK. **CODEN** JAASBK.

THE JOURNAL OF THE AMERICAN COLLEGE HEALTH ASSOCIATION *CEASED.* Began with V. 11, No. 1 in Oct. of 1962. Ceased with V. 30, No. 4 in Feb. of 1982. 0164-4300. US. English. bm. **Ind/Abst** Excerpta Med., Cumul. Index Nurs. Allied Health Lit., CIS Abstr., Educ. Index, Energy Res. Abstr. **NLM** W1 JO908J. *Student Medicine, 0096-7149.*

JOURNAL OF THE AMERICAN COLLEGE OF TRADITIONAL CHINESE MEDICINE. (JOURNAL OF THE AMERICAN COLLEGE OF TRADITIONAL MEDICINE). Began in 1982. 0739-571X. Periodical. US. English. qt. $40.00. American College of Traditional Chinese Medicine, 2400 Geary Boulevard, San Francisco CA 94115.

JOURNAL OF THE AMERICAN MEDICAL ASSOCIATION. **Main/Corp** American Medical Association. V. 1- July 1883-. Periodical. English. ir.

JOURNAL OF THE AMERICAN MEDICAL ASSOCIATION EN ARGENTINA. **VFOAT** Revista de la Asociacion Medica Americana en Argentina. Vol. 1- March 1979-. 0325-9226. Periodical. Spanish. mo. Editorial Eco Sa, De la Cruz 44, Barcelona Spain.

JOURNAL OF THE AMERICAN MEDICAL WOMEN'S ASSOCIATION. **Main/Corp** American Medical Women's Association. **VFOAT** JAMWA. V. 27, No. 3- Mar. 1972-. 0098-8421. US. English. bm. $49.00. American Medical Women's Association, 465 Grand Street, New York NY 10002. **Tel** (212)533-5104. **Ind/Abst** Hospit. Lit. Index, Life Sci. Collect., Index Med., Women Stud. Abstr., Ref. Source, Energy Res. Abstr. **LC** R15. **DD** 610.5. **NLM** W1 JO909S. adv acc. *Woman Physician, 0002-7103.*

JOURNAL OF THE AMERICAN PODIATRIC MEDICAL ASSOCIATION. Vol. 75, No. 1 (Jan. 1985)-. 8750-7315. Periodical. US. English. mo. $31.00. American Podiatric Medical Association, 20 Chevy Chase Circle NW, Washington DC 20015. **Ind/Abst** Index Med., Excerpta Med. **DD** 617. **NLM** W1. *Journal of the American Podiatry Association, 0003-0538.*

JOURNAL OF THE AMERICAN PODIATRY ASSOCIATION *CEASED.* **Main/Corp** American Podiatry Association. V. 48-74. 0003-0538. Periodical. US. English. mo. **Ind/Abst** Hospit. Lit. Index, Life Sci. Collect., Index Med., Energy Res. Abstr. **LC** RD563.A2. **DD** 617.585005. **NLM** W1 JO91H. **CODEN** JPDAA. *Journal of the National Association of Chiropodists, 0360-1684.*

JOURNAL OF THE ANATOMICAL SOCIETY OF INDIA. **Main/Corp** Anatomical Society of India. V. 1- June 1952-. 0003-2778. Periodical. II. English. ir. $20.00. Anatomical Society of India, Medical College/Department of Anatomy, Allahabad II Auramgabad India. **Ind/Abst** Chem. Abstr. **LC** QM1. **DD** 611.06254. **NLM** W1 JO911Q. **CODEN** JAINAA.

JOURNAL OF THE ARKANSAS MEDICAL SOCIETY. (THE JOURNAL OF THE ARKANSAS MEDICAL SOCIETY). V. 3- June 1906-. 0004-1858. Periodical. US. English. mo. $22.00 Domestic, $27.00 Foreign. Business Office, PO Box 1208, Fort Smith AR 72902. **Tel** (501)782-8218. **Ed** Alfred Kahn Jr. **Ind/Abst** Hospit. Lit. Index, Life Sci. Collect., Index Med., Chem. Abstr., Energy Res. Abstr. **NLM** W1 JO911W. **CODEN** JAMSAB. **Circ** 3,100. (ctrl). Scientific articles and news items pertaining to the medical profession. *Monthly Bulletin of the Arkansas Medical Society.*

JOURNAL OF THE ASSOCIATION OF PHYSICIANS OF INDIA. (THE JOURNAL OF THE ASSOCIATION OF PHYSICIANS OF INDIA). **Main/Corp** Association of Physicians of India. 1953? Ceased with Vol. 29, No. 12 (Dec. 1981). 0004-5772. Periodical. II. English. mo. $100.00. Association of Physicians of India, Laud Mansion/21 M Karve Road 3rd, Bombay 400004 India. **Tel** 35 93 48. **Ed** G S Sainani. **Ind/Abst** Index Med., Chem. Abstr., Hospit. Lit. Index. **NLM** W1 JO912N. **CODEN** JPHIAR. bk rev. adv acc. **Circ** 5,000. (ctrl). Discusses editorials, original articles, update articles, methods in medicine, postgraduate clinics, vignettes in medicine, clippings, quiz case reports, correspondence and book reviews.

THE JOURNAL OF THE BRITISH ASSOCIATION FOR IMMEDIATE CARE. Periodical. UK. English. qt. Basics, 14 Princess Gate, London SW7 1PU England. **NLM** W1 JO913M.

JOURNAL OF THE CANADIAN ATHLETIC THERAPISTS ASSOCIATION. (THE JOURNAL OF THE CANADIAN ATHLETIC THERAPISTS ASSOCIATION). **VAT** Journal - Canadian Athletic Therapists Association, C.A.T.A. Journal, Canadian Athletic Therapists Association Journal. 1972. 0225-9877. Periodical. CN. English. qt. $15.48. Canada Athletic Therapists Association, 333 River Road, Ontario L6H 2L1 Canada. **Tel** (613)748-5671. **Ed** Evert van Beek. **DD** 617.102706071. bk rev. adv acc. **Circ** 500. (ctrl). Publication of the CATA dealing specifically with the prevention and care of athletic injuries in the area of sports medicine.

JOURNAL OF THE CHRISTIAN MEDICAL ASSOCIATION OF INDIA. **Main/Corp** Christian Medical Association of India. V. 1- 1926-. Periodical. II. English. qt. $8.00. Hindustan Book Agency, 17 UB Jawahar Nagar, Delhi 7 India. *Medical Missions in India.*

THE JOURNAL OF THE DELTA SOCIETY. Vol. 1, No. 1 (Fall 1984)-. 8755-5883. Periodical. US. English. an. $10.00. Delta Society, 212 Wells Avenue South/Suite C, Renton WA 98055. **Tel** (206)226-7357. **Ed** Aaron Katcher. **DD** 636. bk rev. adv acc. **Circ** 1,000. Research results of studies about the effects of animals on human health and well being, the meaning of animals and the environment in human life.

JOURNAL OF THE FLORIDA MEDICAL ASSOCIATION. (THE JOURNAL OF THE FLORIDA MEDICAL ASSOCIATION). V. 61- Jan. 1974-. 0015-4148. Periodical. US. English. mo. **Tel** (904)356-1571. **Ind/Abst** Life Sci. Collect., Excerpta

Med., Cumul. Index Nurs. Allied Health Lit., Chem. Abstr., Index Med., Nuci. Sci. Abstr., Energy Res. Abstr. **NLM** W1 JO922M. **CODEN** JFMAAQ. bk rev. adv acc. **Circ** 15,500. A scientific publication sent primarily to our members. *J.F.M.A., Journal of the Florida Medical Association, 0091-6757.*

JOURNAL OF THE HISTORY OF MEDICINE AND ALLIED SCIENCES. V. 1- Jan. 1946-. 0022-5045. Periodical. US. English. qt. Journal History of Medicine, c/o Gryphon Editions Ltd, PO 76108, Birmingham AL 35253. **Tel** (212)675-7480. **Ind/Abst** Life Sci. Collect., Writ. Am. Hist., Soc. Sci. Citation Index, Ref. Source, Biol. Abstr., Chem. Abstr., Index Med., Energy Res. Abstr., Am. Hist. Life, Hist. Abstr., Part A, Mod. Hist. Abstr., Hist. Abst., Part B, Twent. Century Abstr., Sci. Cit. Index, Abr. Ed., Am. Hist. Life, Recent Publ. Artic., Hist. Abstr. **LC** R131.A1. **DD** 610.9. **NLM** W1 JO928Q. **CODEN** JHMAA6.

JOURNAL OF THE INDIAN MEDICAL ASSOCIATION. V. 1- Sept. 1931-. 0019-5847. Periodical. II. English. mo. $35.00. Journal of the Indian Medical Association, 53 Creek Row, Calcutta 700 014 India. **Ind/Abst** Life Sci. Collect., Excerpta Med., Nuci. Sci. Abstr., Biol. Abstr., Chem. Abstr., Index Med., Hospit. Lit. Index. **NLM** W1 JO931. **CODEN** JIMAAD. *Indian Medical World.*

JOURNAL OF THE INDIAN MEDICAL PROFESSION. **VFOAT** JIMP Annual. V. 1- 1954-. 0022-507X. Periodical. II. English. mo. United Asis Publishers Private Ltd, 12 Rampart Row, Bombay 1 India.

THE JOURNAL OF THE INDIANA STATE MEDICAL ASSOCIATION *CEASED.* Began Jan. 15, 1908. Ceased Dec. 1983, -V. 76, No. 12. 0019-6770. Periodical. US. English. mo. **Ind/Abst** Hospit. Lit. Index, Life Sci. Collect., Excerpta Med., Cumul. Index Nurs. Allied Health Lit., Energy Res. Abstr. **NLM** W1 JO931L. *Fort Wayne Medical Journal-Magazine, Transactions of the Indiana State Medical Association.*

JOURNAL OF THE INTERNATIONAL ACADEMY OF PREVENTIVE MEDICINE. (THE JOURNAL OF THE INTERNATIONAL ACADEMY OF PREVENTIVE MEDICINE). **Main/Corp** International Academy of Preventive Medicine. V. 1- Spring 1974-. 0094-324X. Periodical. US. English. bm. $24.00. International Academy of Preventive Medicine, 10950 Grandview/ Suite 469, Overland Park KS 66210. **Tel** (913)648-8720. **Ed** Leon R Pomeroy. **Ind/Abst** Excerpta Med., Chem. Abstr., Psychol. Abstr. **LC** RA421. **DD** 613. **NLM** W1 JO931V. **CODEN** JIAMDQ. bk rev. adv acc. **Circ** 3,000. Concerns preventive and/or alternative medicine.

JOURNAL OF THE IOWA MEDICAL SOCIETY *CEASED.* Vol. 51, No. 9 (Sept. 1961)-Vol. 73, No. 12 (Dec. 1983). 0021-0587. Periodical. US. English. mo. **Ind/Abst** Hospit. Lit. Index, Energy Res. Abstr. **NLM** W1. *Journal of the Iowa State Medical Society, 0096-6983.*

JOURNAL OF THE JOHN BASTYR COLLEGE OF NATUROPATHIC MEDICINE. **Main/Corp** John Bastry College of Naturopathic Medicine. V. 1- May 1, 1979-. 0192-2548. Periodical. US. English. sa. $17.00. Journal of John Bastyr College, 1408 NE 45th Street, Seattle WA 98105. **Tel** (206)632-0165.

THE JOURNAL OF THE KANSAS MEDICAL SOCIETY *CEASED.* **Main/Corp** Kansas Medical Society. V. 1- June 1901-. 0022-8699. Periodical. US. English. mo. Kansas Medical Society, 1300 Topeka Avenue, Topeka KS 66612. **Ind/Abst** Hospit. Lit. Index, Life Sci. Collect., Cumul. Index Nurs. Allied Health Lit., Biol. Abstr., Chem. Abstr., Index Med., Nuci. Sci. Abstr., Energy Res. Abstr. **LC** R15. **DD** 610.62781. **NLM** W1 JO934I. **CODEN** JKMSAD. *Western Medical Journal, Wichita Journal.*

THE JOURNAL OF THE KENTUCKY MEDICAL ASSOCIATION. **Main/Corp** Kentucky Medical Association. 62, No. 11- Nov. 1964-. 0023-0294. Periodical. US. English. mo. $15.00. Kentucky Medical Association, 3532 Ephraim McDowell Drive, Louisville KY 40205. **Ed** A Evan Overstreet. **Ind/Abst** Hospit. Lit. Index, Excerpta Med., Cumul. Index Nurs. Allied Health Lit., Biol. Abstr., Chem. Abstr., Index Med., Energy Res. Abstr. **NLM** W1 JO934KN. **CODEN** JKMAB5. bk rev. adv acc. **Circ** 4,500. (ctrl). Scientific articles, membership news, socioeconomic articles, and CME courses. *Journal of the Kentucky State Medical Association.*

THE JOURNAL OF THE KUWAIT MEDICAL ASSOCIATION. **VFOAT** Magalla Al-Gamiyya At-Tibiyya Al-Kuwaitiyya. V. 1- Mar. 1967-. 0023-5776. Periodical. English (title also in Arabic). ir. **Ind/Abst** Excerpta Med., Chem. Abstr. **NLM** W1 JO934T. **CODEN** KMAJAJ.

JOURNAL OF THE LIBERIAN MEDICAL ASSOCIATION. Vol. 1, No. 1 (Nov. 1964)-. Periodical. English. qt. **NLM** W1 JO936D.

THE JOURNAL OF THE LOUISIANA STATE MEDICAL SOCIETY. (JOURNAL). **VFOAT** Journal of the Louisiana State Medical Society. Vol. 135, No. 1 (Jan. 1983)-. 0024-6921. Periodical. US. English. mo. $12.00 Domestic, $15.00 Foreign. Louisiana State Medical Society, 1700 Josephine Street, New Orleans LA 70113-1596. **Tel** (800)462-9508. **Ed** Mannie D Paine Jr. **Ind/Abst** CIS Abstr., Life Sci. Collect., Biol. Abstr., Chem. Abstr., Nuci. Sci. Abstr., Index Med., Energy Res. Abstr., Hospit. Lit. Index. **NLM** W1. **CODEN** JLSMAW. Index in last issue of volume - attached. bk rev. adv acc. **Circ** 6,300. (ctrl). Includes scientific manuscripts, editorial column, book reviews, medical student section, calendar, new members, auxiliary report, EKG of the month; occassional special issues. *Journal of the Louisiana State Medical Society, 0024-6921.*

THE JOURNAL OF THE MAINE MEDICAL ASSOCIATION *CEASED.* V. 30-71. 0025-0694. Periodical. US. English. mo. **Ind/Abst** Life Sci. Collect., Excerpta Med., Nuci. Sci. Abstr., Biol. Abstr., Chem. Abstr., Index Med., Energy Res. Abstr. **NLM** W1 JO938G. **CODEN** JMMAA7. *Maine Medical Journal (1930), 0092-7007.*

JOURNAL OF THE MEDICAL ASSOCIATION OF GEORGIA. **Main/Corp** Medical Association of Georgia. V. 1- Aug. 1911-. 0025-7028. Periodical. US. English. mo. $15.00. Medical Association of Georgia, 938 Peachtreet Street NE, Atlanta GA 30309. **Tel** (404)876-7535. **Ind/Abst** Life Sci. Collect., Index Med., Cumul. Index Nurs. Allied Health Lit., Energy Res. Abstr., Hospit. Lit. Index. **LC** R15. **DD** 610.62758. **NLM** W1 JO939H.

JOURNAL OF THE MEDICAL ASSOCIATION OF THAILAND. Began in 1941. 0025-7036. Periodical. English (Thai). mo. Antituberculosis Association of Thailand, Paholyothin Road, Bankok Thailand. **Ind/Abst** Index Med., Biol. Abstr., Chem. Abstr. **NLM** W1 JO939P. **CODEN** JMTHBU. *Medical Journal of the Medical Association of Thailand.*

JOURNAL OF THE MEDICAL ASSOCIATION OF THE STATE OF ALABAMA *CEASED.* (THE JOURNAL OF THE MEDICAL ASSOCIATION OF THE STATE OF ALABAMA). Began with: Vol. 1, in July 1931. Ceased with V. 52, No. 12 (June 1983). 0025-7044. Periodical. US. English. mo. $30.00. Medical Association of the State of Alabama, 19 South Jackson Street, Montgomery AL 36104. **Tel** (205)263-6441. **Ed** William L Smith and William H McDonald. **Ind/Abst** Hospit. Lit. Index, Excerpta Med., Cumul. Index Nurs. Allied Health Lit., Energy Res. Abstr., Index Med. **NLM** W1 JO939S. adv acc. **Circ** 4,400. (ctrl). Written for more than 4,300 physician members of the Association. Features scientific and socio-economic articles, columns by the president, executive director and auxiliary president. Human interest profiles.

JOURNAL OF THE MEDICAL SOCIETY OF NEW JERSEY *CEASED.* **Main/Corp** Medical Society of New Jersey. Began with Vol. 1, 1904 Ceased with Vol. 82, No. 7. 0025-7524. Periodical. US. English. Medical Society of New Jersey, PO Box 904, Trenton NJ 08605. **Tel** (609)896-1766. **Ind/Abst** Hospit. Lit. Index, Life Sci. Collect., Sociol. Abstr., Excerpta Med., Index Med., Cumul. Index Nurs. Allied Health Lit., Energy Res. Abstr., Lang. Lang. Behav. Abstr. **LC** R15. **DD** 610.62749. **NLM** W1 JO94.

THE JOURNAL OF THE MICHIGAN DENTAL ASSOCIATION. *See* Dentistry.

JOURNAL OF THE MISSISSIPPI STATE MEDICAL ASSOCIATION. **Main/Corp** Mississippi State Medical Association. V. 1- Jan. 1960-. 0026-6396. Periodical. US. English. mo. $25.00. Mississippi State Medical Association Journal, 735 Riverside Drive, Jackson MS 39216. **Tel** (601)354-5433. **Ed** Myron W Lockey. **Ind/Abst** Hospit. Lit. Index, Index Med., Energy Res. Abstr. **NLM** W1 JO94N. **CODEN** MSMJB8. bk rev. adv acc. **Circ** 2,700. Contains scientific articles, socioeconomic issues and association news. *Mississippi Doctor.*

JOURNAL OF THE NATIONAL INTEGRATED MEDICAL ASSOCIATION. V. 14, No. 4- Apr. 1972-. 0377-0621. Periodical. II. English. mo. $20.00. National Integrated Medical Association, G/2 Mohan Kunj Jyotiba Phule Marg, Dadar Bombay-400 014 India. **Tel** 453-608. **NLM** W1 JO941K. *National Medical Journal Amalgamating with Journal of the National Integrated Medical Association, 0377-0621.*

JOURNAL OF THE NATIONAL MEDICAL ASSOCIATION. V. 1- Jan./Mar. 1909-. 0027-9684. Periodical. US. English. mo. $97.00. Appleton Century Crofts, 25 Van Zant Street East, Norwalk CT 06855. **Tel** (203)838-4400. **Ed** Calvin Sampson. **Ind/Abst** Hospit. Lit. Index, Life Sci. Collect., Excerpta Med., Cumul. Index Nurs. Allied Health Lit., Biol. Abstr., Chem. Abstr., Index Med., Nuci. Sci. Abstr., Psychol. Abstr., Energy Res. Abstr. **NLM** W1 JO941N. **CODEN** JNMAAE. bk rev. adv acc. **Circ** 24,000. (ctrl). The primary source for information on specialized clinical research related to the health problems of the urban patient through peer-reviewed medical literature.

JOURNAL OF THE NATIONAL REYE'S SYNDROME FOUNDATION. Vol. 1, No. 1-. 0276-2293. Periodical. US. English. National Reye's Syndrome Foundation, PO Box 829, Bryan OH 43506. **NLM** W1 JO941PI.

THE JOURNAL OF THE PENNSYLVANIA OSTEOPATHIC MEDICAL ASSOCIATION. **VFOAT** POMA Journal. 1956. Periodical. US. English. bm. $10.00. Pennsylvania Osteopathic Association, 1330 Eisenhower Boulevard, Harrisburg PA 17111. **Tel** (717)939-9318. **Ed** Leonard H Finkelstein. adv acc. Professional articles of interest to osteopathic physicians on medicine, surgery; news from osteopathic colleges, hospitals, current legislation.

JOURNAL OF THE ROYAL ARMY MEDICAL CORPS. **Main/Corp** Great Britain. Army. Royal Army Medical Corps. V. 1- July 1903-. 0035-8665. Periodical. UK. English. ty. 8.00. Royal Army Medical College, Millbank, London SW1P 4RJ, England. **Tel** 01-834-9060. **Ed** Brigadier P Abraham. **Ind/Abst** Excerpta Med., Index Med. **LC** UH201. **NLM** W1 JO95Q. bk rev. adv acc. **Circ** 1,500. Medical articles and case reports on various diseases, medical book reviews, reports on medical lectures, publications, abstracts and summaries by Royal Army Medical Corps Officers.

JOURNAL OF THE ROYAL COLLEGE OF GENERAL PRACTITIONERS. (THE JOURNAL OF THE ROYAL COLLEGE OF GENERAL PRACTITIONERS). V. 13, No. 3- (No. 62-). 0035-8797. Periodical. UK. English. mo. $100.00. Royal College General Practitioner, 14 Princes Gate, Hyde Park London SW7 1PU England. **Tel** 031 225 7629. **Ed** E G Buckley. **Ind/Abst** Excerpta Med., Index Med., Cumul. Index Nurs. Allied Health Lit., Hospit. Lit. Index, Sci. Cit. Index, Abr. Ed. **NLM** W1 JO95S. bk rev. adv acc. **Circ** 15,000. (ctrl). Reviews, comments and original papers relevant to family practice. *Journal of the College of General Practitioners, 0307-4749.*

JOURNAL OF THE ROYAL COLLEGE OF PHYSICIANS OF LONDON. **Main/Corp** Royal College of Physicians of London. V. 1- Oct. 1966-. 0035-8819. Periodical. UK. English. qt. 15.00 UK/Republic of Ireland, 25.00 US/Canada, 17.00 all other countries. Royal College of Physicians, 11 St Andrews Place, London, NW1 4LE England. **Tel** 935 1174. **Ed** A Stuart Mason. **Ind/Abst** Life Sci. Collect., Excerpta Med., Cumul. Index Nurs. Allied Health Lit., CIS Abstr., Biol. Abstr., Index Med., Hospit. Lit. Index. **LC** R31. **NLM** W1 JO95U. **CODEN** RCPJAX. bk rev. adv acc. **Circ** 8,000. Medicine and the medical specialties.

JOURNAL OF THE ROYAL NAVAL MEDICAL SERVICE. Vol. 1, No. 1 (Jan. 1915)-. 0035-9033. Periodical. UK. English. qt. $18.00. Institute of Naval Medicine, PO 122 DL, Alverstoke Hants PO12 2DL England. **Tel** 9705 822351. **Ed** J W Richardson. **Ind/Abst** Excerpta Med., CIS Abstr., Nuci. Sci. Abstr., Chem. Abstr., Biol. Abstr., Index Med., Hospit. Lit. Index. **NLM** W1 JO951E. **CODEN** JRNMAF. bk rev. adv acc. **Circ** 1,100. Articles on clinical and occupational medicine of relevance to The Royal Navy.

JOURNAL OF THE ROYAL SOCIETY OF MEDICINE. **Main/Corp** Royal Society of Medicine (Great Britain). V. 71- Jan. 1978-. 0141-0768. Periodical. UK. English. mo. $110.00.

Medicine

Oxford University Press, Journals Department, Walton Street, Oxford OX2 6DP England. Tel 0865 56767. Ed Victor Bloom. Ind/Abst Life Sci. Collect., Excerpta Med., Pestdoc, Ringdoc, Vetdoc, Index Med., Cumul. Index Nurs. Allied Health Lit., Chem. Abstr. LC R35. DD 610.8. NLM W1 JO951H. CODEN JRSMD9. bk rev. adv acc. Circ 415. Covers general medicine especially clinical reporting original work with editorials, review papers, preliminary communications, discussion papers, case reports and correspondence column. *Proceedings of the Royal Society of Medicine, 0035-9157.*

JOURNAL OF THE ROYAL SOCIETY OF MEDICINE. SUPPLEMENT. Began publication in 1982. Monographic Series. UK. English. The Royal Society of Medicine, 1 Wimpale Street, London W1M 8AE England.

JOURNAL OF THE SOCIETY OF OCCUPATIONAL MEDICINE. (THE JOURNAL OF THE SOCIETY OF OCCUPATIONAL MEDICINE). V. 23- Jan. 1973-. 0301-0023. Periodical. UK. English. qt. 16.50 Domestic, 20.00 Foreign. John Wright & Sons Ltd, 823-825 Bath Road, Bristol BS4 5NW England. Tel (617)486-8971. Ed A N B Stott. Ind/Abst Electron. Commun. Abstr. J., ISMEC Bull., Pollut. Abstr. Indexes, Saf. Sci. Abstr. J., Life Sci. Collect., Excerpta Med., Coal Abstr., Index Med., CIS Abstr., Chem. Abstr., Biol. Abstr., Hospit. Lit. Index. NLM W1 JO955C. CODEN JSOMBS. bk rev. adv acc. A summary of latest clinical and research developments. Exposure to chemical vapors, employment of diabetics, occupational psychology of back injury are samples of topics discussed. *Transactions of the Society of Occupational Medicine, 0037-9972.*

JOURNAL OF THE SOUTH CAROLINA MEDICAL ASSOCIATION. (THE JOURNAL OF THE SOUTH CAROLINA MEDICAL ASSOCIATION). Vol. 71, No. 10 (Oct. 1975)-. 0038-3139. Periodical. US. English. mo. South Carolina Medical Association, PO Box 11888/Capitol Station, Columbia SC 29211. Tel (803)798-6207. Ed Charles S Bryan. Ind/Abst Hospit. Lit. Index, Energy Res. Abstr. DD 610. Index in last issue of volume - attached. bk rev. adv acc. Circ 3,000. (ctrl) A scientific publication for practicing physicians, containing scientific articles and association news with some socioeconomic information. *Journal (South Carolina Medical Association), 0038-3139.*

JOURNAL OF THE TENNESSEE MEDICAL ASSOCIATION. V. 56, No. 5- May 1963-. 0040-3318. Periodical. US. English. mo. $16.00 Domestic, $22.00 Foreign. Tennessee Medical Association, 112 Louise Avenue, Nashville TN 37203. Tel (615)327-1451. Ed John B Thomison. Ind/Abst Hospit. Lit. Index, Life Sci. Collect., Excerpta Med., Index Med., Energy Res. Abstr. NLM W1 JO957M. adv acc. Circ 6,000. (ctrl). Scientific information and news about legislative, socioeconomic, educational, and medical activities in the state. *Journal of the Tennessee State Medical Association, 0735-7338.*

JOURNAL OF THE WORLD ASSOCIATION FOR EMERGENCY AND DISASTER MEDICINE. VFOAT J.W.A.E.D.M. Vol. 1, No. 1, (Spring 1985)-. 0882-7397. Periodical. US. English. qt. $60.00 Members, $70.00 Nonmembers. University of Pittsburgh, 3434 5th Avenue, Pittsburgh PA 15260. DD 616.

THE JOURNAL OF TRADITIONAL ACUPUNCTURE. Vol. 1, No. 1 (Summer 1977)-. 0270-661X. Periodical. US. English. ty. $40.00. Traditional Acupuncture, Foundation American City Building/Suite 108, Columbia MD 21044. LC RM184. DD 615.89205. NLM W1 JO966KE.

JOURNAL OF TRADITIONAL CHINESE MEDICINE. (CHUNG I TSA CHIH). VFOAT Journal of Traditional Chinese Medicine. Began in 1955. 0529-5858. Periodical. CC. Chinese. mo. China Publication Centre, PO Box 2820, Beijing China. LC R97.7.C5. DD 610. NLM W1 CH985R. *Pei-Ching Chung I.*

JOURNAL OF TRADITIONAL CHINESE MEDICINE. VFOAT Chung I Ysa Chih Ying wen Pan. Vol. 1, No. 1 (Sept. 1981)-. 0254-6272. CC. English. bm. $66.00 US. China National Publication Import and Export Corporation, PO Box 88, Beijing China. Tel 446661-402. Ed Chen Jorui. Ind/Abst Index Med., Biol. Abstr. NLM W1 JO966KF. CODEN JTCMEC. bk rev. adv acc. The journal provides the latest information of clinical and basic investigation on traditional Chinese medicine and acupuncture, together with Chinese medical history and lectures on acupuncture.

JOURNAL OF TROPICAL MEDICINE AND HYGIENE. V. 1- 1898-. 0022-5304. Periodical. UK. English. bm. $78.00. Blackwell Scientific Publisher, PO Box 88, Oxford OX2 0EL England. Ind/Abst Hospit. Lit. Index, Chem. Abstr.

JOURNAL OF ULTRASOUND IN MEDICINE. (JOURNAL OF ULTRASOUND IN MEDICINE : OFFICIAL JOURNAL OF THE AMERICAN INSTITUTE OF ULTRASOUND IN MEDICINE). Vol. 1, No. 1 (Jan.-Feb. 1982)-. 0278-4297. Periodical. US. English. mo. $75.00. Journal of Ultrasound in Medicine, Box 465, Hanover PA 17331. Tel (215)574-3395. Ed Robin Hipple. Ind/Abst Excerpta Med., Index Med. NLM W1 JO968C. bk rev. adv acc. Circ 9,000. Original articles on basic and clinical aspects of ultrasound, advances in the field, techniques, and equipment modifications.

JOURNAL OF VIROLOGICAL METHODS. V. 1-. 0166-0934. Periodical. English. ir. Elsevier Science Publishers, PO Box 211, 1000 AE Amsterdam The Netherlands. Tel (020)5803.911. Ind/Abst Life Sci. Collect., Excerpta Med., Index Med., Biol. Abstr., Chem. Abstr. NLM W1 JO97T. CODEN JVMEDH.

JOURNAL - OKLAHOMA STATE MEDICAL ASSOCIATION. V. 1- June 1908-. 0030-1876. Periodical. US. English. mo. $10.00. Oklahoma State Medical Association, 601 NW Expressway, Oklahoma City OK 73118. Tel (405)843-9571. Ed Mark R Johnson. Ind/Abst Hospit. Lit. Index, Index Med. LC R15. DD 610.62766. NLM W1 JO976D. bk rev adv acc. Circ 3,700. (ctrl). A scientific publication written by and for the physicians of Oklahoma.

JPMA : JOURNAL OF THE PHILIPPINE MEDICAL ASSOCIATION. VFOAT Journal of the Philippine Medical Association. Vol. 58, No. 3 (June-July 1982)-. Periodical. English. qt. $30.00. Philippine Medical Association, North Avenue Diliman, Quezon City Philippines. *Journal of the Philippine Medical Association, 0031-7748.*

KANSAS MEDICINE. Vol. 86, No. 1 (Jan. 1985)-. 8755-0059. Periodical. US. English. mo. $40.00. Kansas Medical Society, 1300 Topeka Avenue, Topeka KS 66612. Tel (913)235-2383. Ind/Abst Index Med., Hospit. Lit. Index. DD 610. NLM W1. bk rev. adv acc. Circ 3,650. Issued also on microfilm by University Microfilm Services. We publish scientific/medical material and articles on practice management and socio-economic issues of interest to Kansas physicians. *Journal of the Kansas Medical Society, 0022-8699.*

KARADA NO KAGAKU. VFOAT Popular Medicine. Began in 1965. Periodical. Japanese. mo. China Publication Centre, PO Box 2820, Beijing China. Ind/Abst Chem. Abstr. CODEN Karkan.

KAWASAKI IGAKKAISHI. (KAWASAKI IGAKKAI SHI). VFOAT Kawasaki Medical Journal. 1- 1975-. 0386-5924. Periodical. Japanese. ir. NLM W1 KA93KI.

KAWASAKI MEDICAL JOURNAL. V. 1-. 0385-0234. Periodical. JA. English. ir. Kawasaki Medical Journal, Kawasaki Medical School, Kurashiki Japan 701-01. Ind/Abst Excerpta Med., Biol. Abstr., Chem. Abstr. NLM W1 KA93L. CODEN KAMJDW.

KAZANSKII MEDITSINSKII ZHURNAL. V. 1- Jan./Feb. 1901-. 0368-4814. Periodical. UR. Russian. bm. $18.00. Victor Kamkin Inc (73205), 12224 Parklawn Drive, Rockville MD 20852. Tel (301)881-5973. Ind/Abst Int. Aerosp. Abstr., Biol. Abstr., Chem. Abstr. NLM W1 KA98. CODEN KAMZA9.

KEIO JOURNAL OF MEDICINE. V. 1. 0022-9717. Periodical. JA. English (Japanese). qt. Keio University, School of Medicine, Shinanomachi Shinjuku Ku, Tokyo Japan 160. Ed Toyomi Fiijino. Ind/Abst Index Med., Biol. Abstr., Chem. Abstr. NLM W1 KE381. CODEN KJMEA9. (cum index). Circ 1,000. (ctrl). General medicine and surgery basic medicine.

KEITHWOOD DIRECTORY OF HOSPITAL & SURGICAL SUPPLY DEALERS. See Yearbooks, Almanacs, Directories.

KEYS TO HEALTH. 0823-9827. Periodical. CN. English. qt. Free to Members. Saskatchewan Council for Alternate Therapy, PO Box 2437, Prince Albert Saskatchewan Canada. DD 610.5.

THE KILLERS AND CRIPPLERS. US. English. an. National Health Education Commission, 866 United Nations Plaza, New York City NY 10017. *Facts on the Major Killing and Crippling Diseases in the United States Today.*

KING ABDULAZIZ MEDICAL JOURNAL. VFOAT Majallat Al-Malik Abd Al-Aziz Al-Tibbiyah. Vol. 1, No. 1 (Mar. 1981)-. 0254-413X. Periodical. English (articles chiefly in Arabic). qt. Ind/Abst Chem. Abstr. NLM W1 KI65. CODEN KAMJEX.

KING FAISAL SPECIALIST HOSPITAL MEDICAL JOURNAL. (THE KING FAISAL SPECIALIST HOSPITAL MEDICAL JOURNAL). Vol. 1, No. 1 (July 1981)-. 0253-4770. Periodical. English. qt. NLM W1 KI6683D.

KING'S GAZETTE. 0085-2546. Periodical. UK. English. ty. NLM W1 KI714S. *King's College Hospital Gazette, 0309-7366.*

KITA KANTO IGAKU. VFOAT The Kitakanto Medical Journal. Began in 1951. 0023-1908. Periodical. JA. Japanese (summaries in English). bm. Gumma Daigaku Igakubu, 3-39-22 Showa-machi, Maebashi-shi Gumma Japan. Ind/Abst Excerpta Med., CIS Abstr., Chem. Abstr. CODEN KKAIA2.

KITASATO ARCHIVES OF EXPERIMENTAL MEDICINE. See Genealogy and Heraldry - Archives.

KLINICHESKAIA MEDITSINA. V. 1- 1923-. 0023-2149. Periodical. UR. Russian. mo. $47.50. Victor Kamkin Inc (70432), 12224 Parklawn Drive, Rockville MD 20852. Tel (301)881-5973. Ind/Abst Excerpta Med., Pestdoc, Ringdoc, Vetdoc, Index Med., Biol. Abstr., Chem. Abstr., Sci. Cit. Index, Abr. Ed. NLM W1 KL187. CODEN KLMIAZ. (cum index).

DER KLINIKARZT. Yearly V. 1- June 28, 1972-. 0341-2350. Periodical. German. ir. NLM W1 KL313. *Med. Assn, 0341-2466.*

KOKUBYO GAKKAI ZASSHI. VFOAT Journal of the Japan Stomatological Society. Vol. 1- June 1927-. 0300-9149. Periodical. JA. Japanese (summaries in German, 1934-44). qt. Japan Publishers Trading Company Limited, PO Box 5030, Tokyo International, Tokyo 100-31 Japan. Ind/Abst Index Med., Index Dent. Lit., Chem. Abstr. NLM W1 KO296. CODEN KOGZA9.

KOKUNAI IGAKU ZASSHI KIJI SAKUIN. VFOAT Index of Japanese Medical Periodicals. Vol. 5- Jan. 1974-. Periodical. Japanese. ir. NLM ZW 1. *Kokunai Igaku Zasshi Kiji Sakuin.*

KOKURITSU TAMA KENKYUJO NEMPO. Began with the report for 1955. Japanese. ir. Kokuritsu Tama Kenkyujo, 2-1 Aobacho 4-Chome, Higashimurayama Japan. LC RC154.A1.

KOLNER MEDIZINHISTORISCHE BEITRAGE. VFOAT Arbeiten der Forschungsstelle des Instituts fur Geschichte der Medizin der Universitat zu Koln. V. 1-. 0172-7036. Monographic Series. German. ir. NLM W1 KO282MS.

KOPFSCHMERZ. Series/Titl Reihe Zwangloser Darstellungen zur Kopfschmerz Forschung des Arbeitskreises fur Kopfschmerz-Forschung Im Deutschen Sprachraum. 0723-5364. Monographic Series. English. ir. G Braun GMBH, Karl-Friedrich-Strasse 14-18, Karlsruhe 1 West Germany.

KOROTH. See History (General).

KOSMICESKAJA BIOLOGIJA I AVIAKOSMICESKAJA MEDICINA. See Aeronautics, Astronautics.

THE KUMAMOTO MEDICAL JOURNAL. V. 1- July 1938-. 0023-5326. Periodical. JA. English (issued 1938-1943 in German). Kumamoto Diaguku Igakubu Library, Kumamoto Japan. Ind/Abst Excerpta Med., Chem. Abstr., Index Med. NLM W1 KU699. CODEN KUMJAX.

KUO CHIA I HSUEH TSA CHIH. VFOAT Kuo Chia I Hsueh. First published in 1983. Periodical. CH. Chinese. qt. $200.00. Kuo Chia I Hsueh Tsa Chih She, PO Box 44-45, Tai-Pei Shih Taiwan. LC R97.7.C5. DD 610.951.

KURORTO-FIZIOTERAPIIA I LFK PRI ZABOLEVANIIAKH VNUTRENNIKH ORGANOV, NERVNOII SISTEMY I OPORNO-DVIGATEL'NOGO APPARATA. V. 10- 1976-. Monographic Series. UR. Russian. NLM W1 KU708Q. *Voprosy Kurortologii.*

KURUME MEDICAL JOURNAL. V. 1- Jan./Mar. 1954-. 0023-5679. Periodical. JA. English. qt. Kurume University, School of Medicine, Kurume Shi Japan. Ind/Abst Excerpta Med., Index Med., Biol. Abstr., Chem. Abstr. NLM W1 KU722. CODEN KRMJAC.

Medicine

KYOBU SHIKKAN NO KANBETSU SHINDAN SHIRIIZU. Ed. 1 March 1973-. Monographic Series. Japanese. ir. **NLM** W1 KY941S.

LAAKARIT. See Dentistry.

LAB. VFOAT Laboratory Medicine for Practicing Physicians. V. 1- May/June 1978-. 0192-7698. Periodical. US. English. bm. $15.00. Peer Communications Group, Box 691, 615 Franklin Turnpike, Ridgewood NJ 07451. **NLM** W1 LA123.

LAB. Vol. 1- 1974-. 0390-069X. Periodical. Italian (English). bm. $68.00. Editrice Kurtis SRL, Via G Rotondi 2, 20145 Milano Italy. **Tel** (02)4396583. **Ed** A Burlina. **Ind/Abst** Chem. Abstr. **NLM** W1 LA122. **CODEN** LABMDV. bk rev. adv acc. **Circ** 5,000. Publishes original studies concerning clinical chemistry hematology, immunology and molecular biology.

LAB REPORT FOR PHYSICIANS. Began with issue for Nov. 1979. 0278-5161. Periodical. US. English. mo. $60.00. Lab Report for Physicians, 648 Beacon Street, Boston MA 02215. **Tel** (614)267-1513. **Ed** Ray Gambino. **DD** 616. **NLM** W1 LA131F. **Circ** 2,500. The only newsletter bridging the gap between practicing physician and clinical laboratory by providing timely information on which tests are best and why which lab tests are outdated.

LABOR-PRAXIS IN DER MEDIZIN. (LABORPRAXIS IN DER MEDIZIN). **VAT** Labor Praxis in der Medizin. Began with: Feb. 20, 1978. 0171-4279. Periodical. GW. German. sa. $8.11. Vogel Verlag, Postfach 67 40, D-8700 Wurzburg 1 West Germany. **Ind/Abst** Energy Res. Abstr. **NLM** W1 LA236L.

LABORATORIUMSMEDIZIN. VFOAT Laboratoriums Medizin. Vol. 1- May 1977-. 0342-3026. Periodical. GW. German (summaries in English). mo. 102.00. Verlag Kirchheim Mainz, Kaiserstrasse 41, Postfach 2524, D-6500 Mainz 1 West Germany. **Tel** 06131/67 10 81. **Ind/Abst** Chem. Abstr. **NLM** W1 LA2055D. **CODEN** LABOD3. bk rev. adv acc. **Circ** 8,500. (ctrl). Clinical chemistry, haematology, microscopy, laboratory automation, immunology, bacteriology, haemostaseology, serology, chromatography, RIA (radioimmunassay), epidemiology. *Medizinische Laboratorium.*

LABORATORY AND RESEARCH METHODS IN BIOLOGY AND MEDICINE. See Biology.

LABORATORY ANIMAL HANDBOOKS. Began publication with No. 2 in 1969. 0458-5933. Monographic Series. UK. English. ir. 1 Thrifts Mead, Theydon Bois Epping, Essex CM16 7NF England. **Tel** 037 881 4141. **Ed** David Morton. bk rev. adv acc. **Circ** 1,700. All aspects of laboratory animal science including microbiology, nutrition, pathology, toxicology, etc. *Laboratory Animal Symposia.*

LABORATORY MEDICINE. V. 1- Jan. 1970-. 0007-5027. Periodical. US. English. ir. American Society of Clinical Pathologists, 2100 West Harrison Street, Chicago IL 60612. **Tel** (312)738-1336. **Ind/Abst** Chem. Abstr., Energy Inf. Abstr., Environ. Abstr. **LC** RB37.A1. **NLM** W1 LA219R. **CODEN** LBMEBX. bk rev. adv acc. **Circ** 154,000. *Bulletin of Pathology, Technical Bulletin of the Registry of Medical Technologists, 0097-0654.*

LABORMEDIZIN UND KLINIK. Vol. 1-. 0175-386X. German. ir. **NLM** W1.

LACMA PHYSICIAN. Main/Corp Los Angeles County Medical Association. **VAT** Los Angeles County Medical Association Physician. V. 108, No. 16- Aug. 17, 1978-. 0162-7163. Periodical. US. English. ir. $15.00. Los Angeles County Medical Association, PO Box 3465, Los Angeles CA 90041-1465. **Tel** (213)483-1581. **Ed** Howard Bender. **Ind/Abst** Cumul. Index Nurs. Allied Health Lit. **NLM** W1 L1P. bk rev. adv acc. **Circ** 10,500. Socioeconomic non-clinical journal published by the Association for its membership. Contains health care news and information as well as continuing medical education notices, etc. *Los Angeles County Medical Association Bulletin, 0047-5076.*

LANCET (NORTH AMERICAN EDITION). (THE LANCET). No. 7453 (2 July 1966)-. 0099-5355. Periodical. US. English. wk. $68.00. Little Brown and Company, 34 Beacon Street, Boston MA 02106. **Tel** (617)227-0730. **Ed** Ian Munro. **Ind/Abst** Biol. Abstr., Sel. Water Resour. Abstr., Cumul. Index Nurs. Allied Health Lit., Life Sci. Collect., Popul. Index, Index Med., Sci. Cit. Index, Abr. Ed., Hospit. Lit. Index, Chem. Abstr. **LC** R31. **DD** 610.5. **NLM** W1 LA453B. **CODEN** LANAA1. bk rev. adv acc. **Circ** 15,000. Published every week since 1823. Serves worldwide audiences in every area of medicine.

LANDSFORENINGEN MOT KREFT. VFOAT Aarsberetning - Landsforeningen Mot Kreft. 0250-6629. Periodical. Norwegian. ir. **NLM** W1 LA598B.

LARC MEDICAL. VFOAT L.A.R.C. Medical. Vol. 1, No. 1 (Oct. 1981)-. Periodical. FR. French (summaries in English). mo. $46.57. Larc Medical, 19 Bis rue d'Inkermann, 59000 Lille France. **Tel** (20)57 67 06. **Ind/Abst** Life Sci. Collect., Excerpta Med., Index Med., Chem. Abstr., Coal Abstr. **NLM** W1 LA774M. bk rev. Original articles, clinical observations, review, brief reports, pages for the practitioner, etc. *Lille Medical, 0024-3507.*

LASER APPLICATIONS IN MEDICINE AND BIOLOGY. V. 1- 1971-7505. Monographic Series. US. English. ir. Plenum Press, 233 Spring Street, New York NY 10013. **Tel** (212)620-8000. **Ind/Abst** Biol. Abstr. **LC** R857.L37. **DD** 610.28. **NLM** W1 LA78F. **CODEN** LAMBBH.

LASER- + ELEKTRO-OPTIK CEASED. (LASER + I.E. UND ELEKTRO-OPTIK). **VAT** Laser und Elektro-Optik. Vol. 1-. 0344-5186. Periodical. GW. English (German). qt. 36. AT-Fachverlag, Postfach 50 01 80, 7000 Stuttgart 50 West Germany. **Ind/Abst** Excerpta Med. **LC** TA1671. **NLM** W1 LA78S. **CODEN** LELOAA.

LASER MEDICINE & SURGERY NEWS. (LASER MEDICINE & SURGERY NEWS : THE OFFICIAL NEWSLETTER OF THE AMERICAN SOCIETY FOR LASER MEDICINE AND SURGERY). **VFOAT** Laser Medicine and Surgery News. Vol. 1, No. 1 (Mar. 1983)-. 0736-9417. Periodical. US. English. bm. $57.00 Domestic, $73.00 Foreign. Mary Ann Liebert Inc, 157 East 86th Street, New York NY 10028. **NLM** W1 LA78T.

LAUGHING MATTERS. See Business.

LAW, MEDICINE & HEALTH CARE. See Law.

LAWS RELATING TO THE PRACTICE OF MEDICINE AND SURGERY PODIATRY DISPENSING OPTICIANS SPEECH PATHOLOGY. See Law.

LAWYERS' GUIDE TO MEDICAL PROOF. See Law.

LAWYERS' MEDICAL DIGEST. See Law.

LAWYER'S MEDICAL JOURNAL. See Law.

LE JOURNAL INTERNATIONAL DE MEDECINE. (LE JOURNAL INTERNATIONAL DE MEDECINE : JIM). **VFOAT** JIM. Vol. 1, No. 1 (Oct. 1979)-. 0241-0109. Periodical. FR. French. ir. $17.96. S. E. P. I., 10 rue Sainte Anastase, 75003 Paris France. **NLM** W1 JO479D.

LEBANESE MEDICAL JOURNAL. (LE JOURNAL MEDICAL LIBANAIS). **VFOAT** The Lebanese Medical Journal. V. 3- Jan. 1950-. 0023-9852. Periodical. LE. French (articles in English, or Arabic). bm. Inter Commerce Center, PO Box 11-9450, Beirut Lebanon. **Ind/Abst** Index Med. **NLM** W1 JO517. **CODEN** LMJJA7. Index in last issue of volume - attached. *Revue Medicale Libanaise.*

LECTURE NOTES IN MEDICAL INFORMATICS. 1-. 0172-7788. Monographic Series. English. ir. Springer Verlag-New York Inc, 175 5th Avenue, New York NY 10010. **Tel** (212)460-1500. **Ed** D A B Lindberg and P L Reichertz. **Ind/Abst** Math. Rev. **LC** UNC. **NLM** W1 LE334N. Contains articles on therapeutic studies, decision-making systems approach in acute diseases, and topics in image science.

LEGAL ASPECTS OF MEDICAL PRACTICE. See Law.

LEGAL MEDICAL QUARTERLY. See Law.

LEGAL MEDICINE. See Law.

LEGAL MEDICINE ANNUAL. See Law.

THE LEGAL SIDE OF MEDICINE REPORT. See Law.

LEISTUNGSSPORT. Vol. 1-. 0341-7387. Periodical. GW. German (summaries in English and French). bm. $17.04. Philippka Verlag, Steinfurter Strasse 104, D-4400 Muenster West Germany. **NLM** W1 LE67S.

LEKARSKY OBZOR. Began 1952. 0457-4214. Periodical. Slovak (summaries and table of contents in English, German and Russian). mo. Artia, PO Box 790, Smech 30, Praha Czechoslovakia. **Ind/Abst** Excerpta Med., CIS Abstr., Chem. Abstr. **NLM** W1 LE685. **CODEN** LEOBAK.

LENGTH OF STAY BY OPERATION, NORTHEASTERN REGION. VFOAT Length of Stay by Operation, United States, Northeastern Region. 1981-. US. English. an. **NLM** W1. *Length of Stay in PAS Hospitals by Operation, United States, Northeastern Region.*

LENS RESEARCH. Vol. 1, No. 1 & 2-. 0738-1441. Periodical. US. English. $100.00. Marcel Dekker Journals, PO Box 11305 Church Street Station, New York NY 10249. **Ed** Sidney Lerman. **NLM** W1. **CODEN** LERSDL. bk rev. adv acc.

LEPRA REPORT. Main/Corp British Leprosy Relief Association. UK. English. an. **NLM** W1 BR662. *Report of the British Empire Leprosy Relief Association.*

LEPROSY REVIEW. V. 1- Jan. 1930-. 0305-7518. Periodical. UK. English. qt. 15.00. Lepra, c/o Irene Allen, Fairfax House, Causton Road, Colchester Essex CO1 1PU England. **Ed** A C McDougall. **Ind/Abst** Life Sci. Collect., Excerpta Med., Index Med., Biol. Abstr., Chem. Abstr., Sci. Cit. Index, Abr. Ed. **NLM** W1 LE872. **CODEN** LEREAA. adv acc. **Circ** 1,500. Research and control of leprosy. *Leprosy Notes.*

LET'S LIVE. 0024-1288. Periodical. US. English. mo. $8.50 US, $11.50 Canada. Lets Live, 444 North Larchmont Boulevard, Los Angeles CA 90004. **Tel** (213)469-3901. **Ed** Keith Stepro. bk rev. adv acc. **Circ** 125,000. Information on natural living, preventive medicine, nutrition, diet, longevity, health foods, physical fitness, environmental protection, vitamins, minerals, protein and related food supplements, recipes, exercise, etc.

LIFE SUPPORT. V. 1- Mar. 1976-. 0383-8099. Periodical. CN. English. bm. $5. Association of Casualty Care Personnel, PO Box 901, Oshawa L1H 7N1 Ontario Canada. **DD** 362.10425.

LIFE SUPPORT SYSTEMS. (LIFE SUPPORT SYSTEMS : THE JOURNAL OF THE EUROPEAN SOCIETY FOR ARTIFICIAL ORGANS). Vol. 1, (No. 1 Jan./Mar. 1983). 0261-989X. Periodical. UK. English. ir. $73.56. W B Saunders Company Ltd, 1 Vincent Square, London SWIP 2 PN England. **Tel** 01-630 7881. **Ed** M Black. **Ind/Abst** Excerpta Med., Index Med. **LC** RC86. **DD** 616.028. **NLM** W1 LI407I. bk rev. adv acc. **Circ** 350. Artificial organs, orthopedics, transplants, bioengineering, biomaterials, bioprostheses, intensive care, fluid delivery systems, dialysis, instrumentation, organ preservation, and regeneration.

THE LIGAND REVIEW. V. 1- Fall 1979-. 0197-4041. Periodical. US. English. qt. $20.00. Technical & Professional Services Inc, 1015 North Austin Street, Seguin TX 78155. **Ind/Abst** Chem. Abstr. **NLM** W1 LI468B. **CODEN** LRVWD8.

LIJECNICKI VJESNIK. VFOAT Liecnicki Viestnik. 0024-3477. Periodical. YU. Serbo-Croatian(R) (summaries in English, French, German and Russian). mo. 3000. Lijecnicki Vjesnik, Subiceva 9, Zagreb Yugoslavia. **Tel** (041)440-621. **Ind/Abst** Index Med., Chem. Abstr. bk rev. adv acc. **Circ** 6,400. Official journal of the Medical Association of Croatia publishing articles from clinical and experimental medicine.

LIN CHUANG I HSUEH. VFOAT Clinical Medicine. Began Jan. 1978-. Periodical. Chinese. mo. **NLM** W1 LI623L.

THE LINACRE QUARTERLY. See Ethics.

LINSCOTT'S DIRECTORY OF IMMUNOLOGICAL AND BIOLOGICAL REAGENTS. See Yearbooks, Almanacs, Directories.

LIST OF CERTIFIED HEALTH CARE PRODUCTS AND SERVICES. Main/Corp Canadian Standards Association. 1980-. 0824-7536. CN. English. Canadian Standards Association, Health Care Technology Program, 178 Rexdale Boulevard, Ontario M9W 1R3 Canada. **DD** 381.4561028.

LIST OF JOURNALS INDEXED IN INDEX MEDICUS. See Indexes/Abstracts.

Medicine

LIST OF MEDICAL PRACTITIONERS CURRENTLY LICENSED TO PRACTISE IN THE PROVINCE. Main/Corp College of Physicians and Surgeons of Manitoba. Sept. 8th, 1981-. 0823-6909. Periodical. CN. English. sa. College of Physicians and Surgeons of Manitoba, 1410-155 Carlton Street, Winnipeg Manitoba R3C 3H8 Canada. **DD** 610.69520257127. *List of Medical Practitioners Currently Registered and Entitled to Practise in the Province, 0823-6666.*

LIST OF REGISTERED DOCTORS OF MEDICINE AND SURGERY, DOCTORS OF OSTEOPATHY LICENSED TO PRACTICE MEDICINE AND SURGERY, DOCTORS OF OSTEOPATHY LICENSED TO PRACTICE OSTEOPATHY, DOCTORS OF CHIROPRACTIC, DOCTORS OF PODIATRY. Mar. 1978-. 0276-2250. US. English. te. Kansas State Board of Healing Arts, Licensed to Practice, Topeka KS. **NLM** W 22 AK3 L7. *List of Registered Doctors of Medicine and Surgery, Doctors of Osteopathy Licensed to Practice Medicine and Surgery, Doctors to Practice Osteopathy, Doctors of Chiropractic.*

LIST OF SERIALS INDEXED FOR ONLINE USERS. See Indexes/Abstracts.

LIST OF THE MEMBERS OF THE ROYAL COLLEGES OF PHYSICIANS OF THE UNITED KINGDOM. 1971-. 0307-7462. UK. English. te. Royal College of Physicians of Edinburgh, 11 St Andrews PL Regents Park, London NW1 4LE England. **LC** R713.29. **DD** 610.6241. **NLM** W 22 FA1 L7.

LITERATURE AND MEDICINE. Vol. 1-. 0278-9671. Periodical. US. English. an. $26.25. Johns Hopkins University Press, 701 West 40th Street/Suite 275, Baltimore MD 21211. **Tel** (301)338-6987. Ed Anne Hudson Jones. bk rev. adv acc. Circ 600. A journal focusing on an emerging specialty of the medical humanities. Devoted to examining the connections between the two disciplines.

LITERATURE SCAN: TRANSPLANTATION. (LITERATURE SCAN. TRANSPLANTATION). Vol. 1, No. 1 (July 1985)-. 0883-8410. Periodical. US. English. qt. $60.00 Domestic, $80.00 Foreign. World Medical Communications Organization Inc, 5 Center Avenue, Little Falls NJ 07424. **DD** 617.

LITERATURE SEARCH. VFOAT NLM Literature Search. No. 7-67-. 0083-2251. Monographic Series. US. English. ir. National Library of Medicine, Reference Section/8600 Rockville Pike, Bethesda MD 20209. **Tel** (301)496-6308. **NLM** ZW 1 N272. *National Library of Medicine Literature Search, 0278-6885.*

LONG TERM CARE (DON MILLS, ONT.). (LONG TERM CARE). Vol. 1, No. 1 (Mar. 1985)-. Periodical. English. sa. $38.00. **Ind/Abst** Hospit. Lit. Index. **NLM** W1.

LONG TERM CARE MANAGEMENT. Vol. 13, No. 8 (Mar. 1, 1984)-. 0743-1422. Periodical. US. English. bw. $257.00. McGraw Hill Inc, 1120 Vermont Avenue NW/Suite 1200, Washington DC 20005. **NLM** W1. *Long Term Care, 0192-7701.*

LOUVAIN MEDICAL. V. 86- Jan. 1967-. 0024-6956. Periodical. French. mo. $29.64. UCL-5265, 52 Avenue E Mounier, 1200 Bruxelles Belgium. **Ind/Abst** Life Sci. Collect., Excerpta Med., Chem. Abstr. **NLM** W1 LO956. **CODEN** LOMEAL. *Revue Mediale de Louvain, Recipe.*

LR. LEGISLATIVE ROUNDUP. VFOAT Legislative Roundup. VAT LR. V. 19, LR7- Mar. 10, 1978-. Periodical. US. English. bm. American Medical Association, 535 North Dearborn Street, Chicago IL 60610. **Tel** (312)645-4927. *Legislative Roundup, 0024-0494.*

LUNG BIOLOGY IN HEALTH AND DISEASE. V. 1-. 0362-3181. Monographic Series. US. English. ir. Marcel Dekker/Continuation Department, 270 Madison Avenue, New York NY 10016. **Tel** (212)696-9000. Ed C Lenfant. **Ind/Abst** Chem. Abstr. **NLM** W1 LU62. **CODEN** LBHDD7. This is an ongoing series, each title has a different subject.

LYMPHOKINE RESEARCH. See Biology.

LYMPHOLOGY. V. 1- Mar. 1968-. 0024-7766. Periodical. US. German. qt. $75.00. Lymphology, Department of Surgery, Arizona Health Services Center, Tucson AR 85749. **Tel** (602)626-6118. Ed Charles L Witte. **Ind/Abst** Excerpta Med., Life Sci. Collect., Energy Res. Abstr., Biol. Abstr., Chem. Abstr., Nucl. Sci. Abstr., Index Med., Sci. Cit. Index, Abr. Ed. **LC** RC646. **NLM** W1 LY528. **CODEN** LYMPBN. bk rev. Circ 500. Covers the study of lymphatics, lymph, lymph nodes and lymphocytes in normal and diseased states.

LYON MEDICAL. V. 237, No. 11- June 15, 1977-. 0024-7790. Periodical. FR. French. sm. Medipharly, 12 rue de la Barre, 69002 Lyon France. **Tel** 07 837-06-15. **Ind/Abst** Curr. Contents. bk rev. adv acc. Circ 5,000. (ctrl). Medical science and practice editorials; report of cases, reviews, therapeutic, continuous education. *Lyon Medical-la Revue Lyonnaise de Medecine.*

M D OF CANADA. VFOAT M D. V. 1- Jan. 1960-. 0047-5246. Periodical. CN. English. mo. MD Publications (Canada) Ltd, 1310 Greene Avenue, Montreal Quebec H3Z 2B3 Canada. **LC** R11. **DD** 610.5. **NLM** W1 M294.

MCGILL MEDICAL JOURNAL. 0024-905X. Periodical. CN. includes some text in French. ir. $3.86. McGill Medical Science Center, 3655 Drummond Street, McIntyre Medical Sci, Montreal Quebec H3A 1W8 Canada. **Ind/Abst** Excerpta Med. **NLM** W1 MA158E. *McGill Medical Undergraduate Journal, 0381-0720.*

MCGRAW-HILL'S MEDICAL UTILIZATION REVIEW. VFOAT Medical Utilization Review. V. 10, No. 15 (Aug. 1, 1982)-. 0734-1970. Periodical. US. English. sm. $297.00. McGraw-Hill's Medical Utilization, 1220 Vermont Avenue/Room 1200, Washington DC 20005. **Tel** (202)624-7558. *PSRO Letter, 0149-5844.*

MACROMUSE. VFOAT Macro Muse. 0737-8084. Periodical. US. English. $15.00. Macromuse, PO Box 40012, Washington DC 20016. **Tel** (301)656-4313. Ed P Rossoff. Marobiotic, treating illnesses with Yiy Yang technics.

MAGNES LECTURE SERIES. V. 1-. Monographic Series. US. English. **NLM** W1.

MAGYAR ORVOSI BIBLIOGRAFIA. See Bibliographies.

MAGYAR REUMATOLOGIA. Began with: V. 21, 1 (Jan. 1980)-. 0139-4495. Periodical. Hungarian. qt. **Ind/Abst** Excerpta Med., Energy Res. Abstr. **NLM** W1 MA408D. *Rheumatologia, Balneologia, Allergologia.*

MAITOMAISHIN RINSHO KENKYUKAI HOKKAIDO BUKAI KOENSHU. 1st 1967-. Periodical. JA. Japanese. ir. **NLM** W1.

MAJALAH KEDOKTERAN INDONESIA. VFOAT Journal of the Indonesian Medical Association. 197?-. 0377-1121. Periodical. IO. articles mainly in Indonesian with some in English. ir. **NLM** W1 MA492K. *Madjalah Kedokteran Indonesia, 0464-3196.*

MAJALLAH-I NIZAM-I PIZISHKI-I IRAN. VFOAT The Journal of the Iranian Medical Council. 0254-4571. Periodical. IR. Persian, Modern. ir. Iranian Medical Council, 40 Shirin Avenue/PO Box 3474, Ehran Iran. **Tel** 821111-821113. **NLM** W1 JO9315.

MAJOR MEDICAL PLANS. SELECTED COLLECTIVE BARGAINING AGREEMENTS, CALIFORNIA. See Economics - Labor.

MAJOR PROBLEMS IN ANAESTHESIA. V. 1- 1973-. Monographic Series. UK. English. be. W B Saunders Company, West Washington Square, Philadelphia PA 19105. **Tel** (800)523-0713. **NLM** W1 MA492M. Index in last issue of volume - attached.

MALPRACTICE PREVENTION FOR PHYSICIANS. See Law.

THE MALPRACTICE REPORTER. See Law.

THE MALPRACTICE REPORTER. ANESTHESIOLOGY. See Law.

THE MALPRACTICE REPORTER. HOSPITALS. See Law.

THE MALPRACTICE REPORTER. PODIATRY. See Law.

MAN AND MEDICINE. See Ethics.

MANAGING PAIN. Periodical. US. English. mo. *Aches & Pains, 0273-7663.*

MANHATTAN MEDICINE. (MANHATTAN MEDICINE : OFFICIAL PUBLICATION OF THE NEW YORK COUNTY MEDICAL SOCIETY). Vol. 1, No. 1 (Jan. 1982)-. 0744-4966. Periodical. US. English. ir. $10.00. New York County Medical Society, 40 West 57th Street, New York NY 10019. **Tel** (212)399-9055. Ed Nancy L Adams. bk rev. adv acc. Circ 6,000. (ctrl). Contains articles about political issues confronting doctors in Manhattan (malpractice insurance costs, etc.), not technical material. About goings-on at the Medical Society, the AMA, the State Medical Society, etc.

MANITOBA MEDICAL REGISTER. Began with 1951? issue. 0382-5221. CN. English. an. College of Physicians and Surgeons of Manitoba, 371 Broadway Avenue, Winnipeg Manitoba R3O 0T9 Canada. **DD** 610.69520257127.

MANITOBA MEDICAL REVIEW. V. 13- Jan. 1933-. 0025-2255. Periodical. CN. English. mo. Manitoba Medical Association, 201 Kennedy Street, Winnipeg Manitoba Canada. **DD** 610.5.

MANUAL OF MEDICAL THERAPEUTICS. US. English. ir. $17.95. Little, Brown & Company, 200 West Street, Medical Division, Waltham MA 02154. **Tel** (617)890-0250.

MANUELLE MEDIZIN. 0025-2514. Periodical. German. bm. Springer Verlag-New York Inc, 175 5th Avenue, New York NY 10010. **Tel** (212)460-1500. Ed H Baumgartner and H D Wolff. **Ind/Abst** Excerpta Med. **NLM** W1 MA635. Orthopedics, general medicine, internal medicine therapy, contributions on practical manual medicine, works on scientific research, convention calendar and job market.

MARKER (NEW YORK, N.Y.). (THE MARKER). 0882-3634. Periodical. US. English. ty. Free. The Marker, 250 West 57th Street, New York NY 10107. **DD** 616. *Newsletter (Committee to Combat Huntington's Disease), 0882-3642.*

MARYLAND STATE MEDICAL JOURNAL CEASED. V. 1-33. 0025-4363. Periodical. US. English. mo. Maryland Medical Journal, 1211 Cathedral Street, Baltimore MD 21201. **Tel** (301)539-0872. Ed James G Zimmerly. **Ind/Abst** Hospit. Lit. Index, Life Sci. Collect., Excerpta Med., Cumul. Index Nurs. Allied Health Lit., Energy Res. Abstr., Index Med., Biol. Abstr., Chem. Abstr., Nucl. Sci. Abstr. **LC** R11. **DD** 610.5. **NLM** W1 MA791. **CODEN** MSMJA7. bk rev. adv acc. Circ 7,000. (ctrl). Educational, scientific and informative articles, meeting notices, and news pertinent to Maryland physicians.

MASSACHUSETTS MEDICINE. Vol. 1, No. 1 (Jan./Feb. 1986)-. 0886-6546. Periodical. US. English. bm. $15.00. Massachusetts Medicine, 1440 Main Street, Waltham MA 02254. **DD** 610.

MATERIALY PROBLEMNOI KOMISSII AKADEMII MEDITSINSKIKH NAUK SSSR KOR, VIRUSNYE ENTSEFALITY, POLIOMIELIT. Began with: Vol. 3, 1968. Monographic Series. UR. Russian. **NLM** W1 MA944C. *Materialy Problemnoi Komissii Akademii Meditsinskikh Nauk SSSR Poliomielit I Virusnye Entsefality.*

MATERIALY SIMPOZIUMOV PO OBSHCHEI IMMUNOLOGII. VFOAT Voprosy Immunologii. Began in 1967. UR. Russian. **NLM** W1 MA944L.

MAURITIUS MEDICAL JOURNAL. V. 1- Dec. 1975-. 0377-9270. Periodical. articles mainly in English with some in French. ir. **NLM** W1 MA997G. *Mauritian Medical Journal, 0543-1492.*

M.C.V.Q. MEDICAL COLLEGE OF VIRGINIA QUARTERLY. (MCV/Q, MEDICAL COLLEGE OF VIRGINIA QUARTERLY). Main/Corp Medical College of Virginia. School of Medicine. VFOAT Medical College of Virginia Quarterly. Began with V. 1-, Spring 1965. 0025-7141. Periodical. US. English. qt. **Ind/Abst** Life Sci. Collect., Excerpta Med., Biol. Abstr. **NLM** W1 M231. **CODEN** MCVQAT.

MD. VAT Medical Doctor. V. 1- Jan. 1957-. 0024-8010. Periodical. US. English. mo. MD Publications Inc, 30 East 60th Street, New York NY 10022. **Tel** (212)355-5432. Ed A J Vogl. **Ind/Abst** Hospit. Lit. Index, Media Rev. Dig. **LC** R11. **DD** 610.5. **NLM** W1 M256. (ctrl). *MD.*

M.D. COMPUTING. See Computers and Computer Science.

MD/PC. See Law.

Medicine

MEAD JOHNSON ADVANCES IN THERAPEUTICS. VFOAT Advances in Therapeutics. 0264-1410. Monographic Series. UK. English. ir. **NLM** W1 ME103M.

MED DEV. VFOAT Medical Devices. 0883-1750. Periodical. US. English. qt. $50.00. Biellambe, PO Box 21451, Sarasota FL 33583. **Tel** (813)922-6353. **Ed** John J Lamb. **DD** 681. adv acc. **Circ** 50. Basis of information is Food and Drug Administration publications on medical devices. Other interests are materials used in implants and testing of medical devices.

MEDAL. 1969-. 0318-0735. CN. English. an. Dalhousie Medical Alumni Association, Dalhousie University, Halifax Nova Scotia Canada. **DD** 610.71171622.

MEDECIN DU QUEBEC. (LE MEDICIN DU QUEBEC). V. 1- June 1965-. 0025-6692. Periodical. CN. French. mo. $50.00. Federation of General Practitioners of Quebec, 1440 St Catherine Street/Suite 1100, Montreal 107 Quebec Canada. **Tel** (514)878-1911. **Ed** Georges Boileau. **Ind/Abst** Point Repere. **NLM** W1 ME118C. bk rev. adv acc. **Circ** 16,500. (ctrl). Socio-economic content addressed to the Quebec medical profession.

MEDECINE AERONAUTIQUE ET SPATIALE. V. 21, No. 81 (1st Quarterly 1982)-. 0294-0817. Periodical. FR. French. ir. Regies Edition Publicite, 46 Avenue Rene Coty, 75014 Paris France. **Tel** 321-31-41. **Ind/Abst** CIS Abstr., Int. Aerosp. Abstr., Chem. Abstr. **LC** RC1050. **DD** 616.9802105. *Medecine Aeronautique et Spatiale, Medecine Subaquatique et Hyperbare.*

MEDECINE & CHIRURGIE DIGESTIVES. VFOAT MCD. VAT Medecine et Chirurgie Digestives, MCD. V. 1- 1972-. 0047-6412. Periodical. FR. French (articles in English). ir. $19.96. Editions Ouranos, 12 Bis rue Jean-Jaures, 92807 Puteaux France. **Ind/Abst** Life Sci. Collect., Excerpta Med., Chem. Abstr., Index Med., Nuci. Sci. Abstr., Biol. Abstr. **NLM** W1 ME139N. **CODEN** MCDGBC. *Revue Medico-Chirurgicale de Maladies du Foie.*

MEDECINE DU SPORT. V.42- 1968-. 0025-6722. Periodical. FR. French. bm. 320. Medecine du Sport, 17 rue du 8 Mai 1945, F 75010 Paris France. **Tel** 1.46.07.64.28. **Ed** Robert J Lederer. **Ind/Abst** Biol. Abstr. **NLM** W1 ME136F. **CODEN** MNSPBL. bk rev. adv acc. **Circ** 3,000. Medicine of sports, surgery, traumatology, physiology, biology, rehabilitation and public health. *Medecine, Education Physique et Sport.*

MEDECINE ET ARMEES. See Military Science.

MEDECINE ET HYGIENE. (MEDECINE & HYGIENE). Vol. 1- (No. 1-). 0025-6749. Periodical. French. ir. **Tel** (022) 46 93 55. **Ind/Abst** Excerpta Med., Index Dent. Lit., Chem. Abstr. **NLM** W1 ME1393. **CODEN** MEHGAB:

MEDECINE MODERNE DU CANADA. First issued in 1946?. 0025-6803. Periodical. CN. French. mo $54.17. Southam Communications Ltd, 1450 Don Mills Road, Don Mills Ontario M3B 1X2 Canada. **Tel** (416)445-6641. **Ind/Abst** Chem. Abstr. **NLM** W1 ME147G. **CODEN** MMCNAT.

MEDECINE NATURELLE. (MEDECINE NATURELLE : LA SANTE SANS DROGUES). Fall 1981-. 0710-0892. Periodical. CN. French. qt. Free. Medecine Naturelle, 6655 rue St-Denis, Montreal Quebec H2S 2S1 Canada. **DD** 615.53505.

MEDECINE TRADITIONNELLE CHINOISE ET ACUPUNCTURE. (MEDECINE TRADITIONNELLE CHINOISE ET ACUPUNCTURE : ORGANE OFFICIEL DE L'ASSOCIATION INTERNATIONALE DE MEDECINE TRADITIONNELLE CHINOISE ET DE L'ASSOCIATION D'ACUPUNCTURE DU QUEBEC). Vol. 4, No. 1-. 0228-409X. Periodical. CN. English (French). qt. $6.00 Inside Quebec, $10.00 Outside Quebec. Acupuncture Association of Quebec, 4251 Hochelaga Street East, Montreal Quebec H1V 1C1 Canada. **DD** 610.951. *Acupuncture (Montreal, Quebec), 0228-4081.*

MEDECINE TROPICALE. Began publication with V. 1, 1941. 0025-682X. Periodical. FR. French. bm. 140 Domestic, 160 Foreign. Institut de Medecine Tropicale, Parc du Pharo, 13007 Marseille France. **Tel** (91)52.30.46. **Ed** J J Pico. **Ind/Abst** Life Sci. Collect., Excerpta Med., Chem. Abstr., Nuci. Sci. Abstr., Biol. Abstr., Index Med. **NLM** W1 ME149. **CODEN** METRA2. bk rev. **Circ** 1,500. Original works in tropical medicine, epidemiology and public health. *Annales de Medecine et de Pharmacie Coloniales.*

MEDEQUIP. Began in 1982. 0253-7419. Periodical. English (articles in German). ir. Brueder Hollinek, Gallgasse 40 A, A-1130 Wien XIII Austria. **NLM** W 26 M488.

MEDI-US. V. 1- Fall 1975-. 0382-8808. Periodical. CN. French. ir. Association des Etudiants en Medecine, Universite de Montreal, CP 6128, Montreal Quebec H3C 3J7 Canada. **DD** 610.711714281.

MEDICA (STUTTGART, GERMANY). (MEDICA). V. 1, No. 1 (15. Jan. 1980)-. 0172-9160. Periodical. German. sm. **NLM** W1 ME156T.

MEDICAID DATA REPORT. See Insurance.

MEDICAID MANAGEMENT REPORTS. ANNUAL REPORT. See Insurance.

MEDICAID MEDICARE EXCHANGE. See Insurance.

MEDICAL 911. VAT Medical Nine Eleven. 1974. 0275-2735. US. English. bm. Emergency Care Information Center, PO Box 457, Wilton CT 06897. **Tel** (203)762-3911. **Ed** Stephanie I Ludewig. A resource guide to reports, books, films, instructional materials, journal articles and organizations related to emergency medical services.

MEDICAL ABSTRACTS JOURNAL. See Indexes/Abstracts.

MEDICAL ABSTRACTS NEWSLETTER. See Indexes/Abstracts.

MEDICAL ADVERTISING NEWS. See Business - Advertising & Public Relations.

MEDICAL ALMANAC. See Yearbooks, Almanacs, Directories.

MEDICAL & BIOLOGICAL ENGINEERING & COMPUTING. See Engineering.

MEDICAL AND HEALTH ANNUAL. 1977-. 0363-0366. US. English. an. $12.95. Encyclopaedia Britannica, 425 North Michigan Avenue, Chicago IL 60611. **LC** R5. **DD** 362.105.

MEDICAL AND HEALTH CARE BOOKS AND SERIALS IN PRINT. See Publishing - Books and Bookmaking.

MEDICAL AND HEALTH INFORMATION DIRECTORY. See Yearbooks, Almanacs, Directories.

MEDICAL AND HEALTH RELATED SCIENCES THESAURUS. See Encyclopedias & General Reference Books.

THE MEDICAL AND HEALTHCARE MARKETPLACE GUIDE. See Economics - Industry & Production.

MEDICAL ANTHROPOLOGY. See Anthropology.

MEDICAL ANTHROPOLOGY NEWSLETTER. See Anthropology.

MEDICAL ANTHROPOLOGY QUARTERLY. See Anthropology.

MEDICAL ASPECTS OF HUMAN SEXUALITY. See Sexual Life.

MEDICAL ASSISTANCE PROGRAM ANNUAL REPORT. Main/Corp Illinois. Dept. of Public Aid. US. English. an. Illinois Department of Public Aid, 316 South Second Street, Springfield IL 62762. **LC** HD7102.U5. **DD** 353.977300841045.

MEDICAL ASSISTANCE : UTAH REPORT OF MEDICAID & INDIGENT MEDICAL PROGRAMS. VFOAT Utah Report of Medicaid & Indigent Medical Programs. Vol. 6 (FY 1982-83)-. US. English. an. Bureau of Cost Management Division of Health Care Financing and Standards, Box 2500, Salt Lake City UT 84110-2500. **LC** HD7102.U5. **DD** 353.979200841045. *Report of Utah's Medicaid and County Indigent Medical Programs.*

MEDICAL BIOLOGY. See Biology.

MEDICAL BOOK GUIDE. Series/Titl Computext Book Guide Series. 1974-. 0091-7877. Periodical. US. English. an. G K Hall, 70 Lincoln Street, Boston MA 02111. **LC** Z6660, R129. **DD** 016.61.

MEDICAL BULLETIN (UNITED STATES. ARMY. MEDICAL COMMAND, 7TH). (MEDICAL BULLETIN). VFOAT Medical Bulletin of the U.S. Army, Europe. Began with V. 27, No. 11, Nov. 1970. Periodical. US. English. mo. Commander in Chief, United States Army, Europe and Seventh Army, Attention Office of the Chief Surgeon Editor, Medical Bulletin APO NY 09102. **LC** RC970. **DD** 616.9802305. **NLM** W2 A2 E73M4. *Medical Bulletin of the U.S. Army, Europe.*

MEDICAL CARE. V. 1, No. 1- Jan./Mar. 1963-. 0025-7079. Periodical. US. English. mo. $78.00. J B Lippincott Company, East Washington Square, Philadelphia PA 19105. **Ed** Duncan Neuhauser. **Ind/Abst** Life Sci. Collect., Hospit. Lit. Index, Sociol. Abstr., Index Med., Excerpta Med., Cumul. Index Nurs. Allied Health Lit., Energy Res. Abstr., Soc. Sci. Citation Index, Sci. Cit. Index, Abr. Ed. **LC** RA1. **DD** 362.10973. **NLM** W1 ME25L. **CODEN** MELAA. adv acc. **Circ** 2,926. International journal for original articles describing significant current developments in medical care.

MEDICAL CARE REVIEW. V. 24- (No. 1-). 0025-7087. Periodical. US. English. qt. $32.50. University of Michigan, 1021 East Huron, Ann Arbor MI 48109. **Tel** (313)764-1380. **Ed** Roice Luke and Jean Thorby. **Ind/Abst** Hospit. Lit. Index. **LC** RA410. **DD** 362.10973. **NLM** ZWA 100 P973. **CODEN** MDCRB. bk rev. **Circ** 1,300. Review articles and abstracts related to medical care organization and financing. *Public Health Economics and Medical Care Abstracts.*

MEDICAL CATALOG OF SELECTED AUDIOVISUAL MATERIALS PRODUCED BY THE UNITED STATES GOVERNMENT. Main/Corp National Audiovisual Center. VFOAT Medical Catalog, National Audiovisual Center. Began with: 1979. 0734-0303. US. English. an. National Audiovisual Center, National Archives and Records Service, General Services Administration, Washington DC 20402. **NLM** W 18 N276M.

MEDICAL COMPUTER JOURNAL. See Computers and Computer Science.

MEDICAL COMPUTING SERIES. See Computers and Computer Science.

MEDICAL DECISION MAKING. (MEDICAL DECISION MAKING : AN INTERNATIONAL JOURNAL OF THE SOCIETY FOR MEDICAL DECISION MAKING). Vol. 1, No. 1-. 0272-989X. Periodical. US. English. qt. $78.00 Domestic, $86.00 Foreign. Hanley & Belfus Inc, 210 South 13th Street, Philadelphia PA 19107. **Tel** (215)546-7293. **Ed** Dennis G Fryback. **Ind/Abst** Excerpta Med., Index Med. **NLM** W1 ME2966D. bk rev. adv acc. **Circ** 1,000. Devoted to analysis of decision making in clinical practice, health outcomes, computer-aided diagnosis, cost control and health policy, health care technology assessment.

MEDICAL DEVICE & DIAGNOSTIC INDUSTRY. VAT Medical Device and Diagnostic Industry. V. 1- June 1979-. 0194-844X. Periodical. US. English. mo. Cannon Communications, 2422 Wilshire Boulevard, Santa Monica CA 90403. **Tel** (213)829-0315. **Ind/Abst** Eng. Index, Chem. Abstr. **NLM** W1 ME2966I. **CODEN** MDIIDI.

MEDICAL DEVICE REGISTER. 1981-. 0278-808X. US. English. an. Directory Systems Order Processing, PO Box 50, Smithtown NY 11787. **Tel** (203)346-6319. **Ed** Heidi Garrett. **LC** R856.48. **DD** 681.7610294. Each issue contains an index to its own contents - no vol index - loose. adv acc. **Circ** 11,000. The official directory of hospital suppliers, a 2,300 page hard cover book with complete information on medical equipment, supplies and their suppliers.

MEDICAL DEVICES. Main/Corp United States. Food and Drug Administration. VFOAT Pocket Supplement to Preamble Compilation. Apr. 1978-Mar. 1980-. US. English. an. Superintendent of Documents, US Government Printing Office, Washington DC 20402.

MEDICAL DEVICES AND DIAGNOSTIC PRODUCTS STANDARDS SURVEY. VFOAT Standards Survey. Monographic Series. US. English. an.

MEDICAL DEVICES, DIAGNOSTICS & INSTRUMENTATION REPORTS. VFOAT Gray Sheet. VAT Medical Devices, Diagnostics and Instrumentation Reports. 0163-2426. Periodical. US. English. wk. $340.00. FDC Reports, 5550 Friendship Boulevard/Suite 1, Chevy Chase MD 20815. **Tel** (301)657-9830. **Ed** Meg Bryant and Cole Palmer Werber. **Ind/Abst** Pharm. News Index. **CODEN**

Medicine

MDDIDR. Review of medical devices, diagnostics and instrumentation industries; Regulatory Agency (national and state) actions and impact; industry developments and investor/financial news.

MEDICAL DEVICES REPORT. 0748-4852. Periodical. US. English. wk. $250.00. Medical Devices Report, PO Box 28096, Washington DC 20005.

MEDICAL DIMENSIONS. V. 1- Mar. 1972-. 0047-648X. Periodical. US. English. bm. $12.00 Domestic, $14.00 Foreign. MBA Communications, 730 Third Avenue, New York NY 10017. **LC** R707. **DD** 362.1. **NLM** W1 ME2991.

MEDICAL DIRECTORY. See Yearbooks, Almanacs, Directories.

MEDICAL DIRECTORY - COLLEGE OF PHYSICIANS AND SURGEONS OF ALBERTA. See Yearbooks, Almanacs, Directories.

MEDICAL DIRECTORY OF AUSTRALIA. See Yearbooks, Almanacs, Directories.

MEDICAL DIRECTORY OF NEW YORK STATE. See Yearbooks, Almanacs, Directories.

MEDICAL EDUCATION. See Education (General).

MEDICAL ELECTRONIC PRODUCTS. See Engineering - Electricity, Electrical Engineering, Electronics.

MEDICAL ELECTRONIC SERVICE JOURNAL. See Engineering - Electricity, Electrical Engineering, Electronics.

MEDICAL ELECTRONICS. See Engineering - Electricity, Electrical Engineering, Electronics.

MEDICAL ELECTRONICS AND COMMUNICATIONS ABSTRACTS. See Indexes/Abstracts.

THE MEDICAL EQUIPMENT CLASSIFIED. 0162-816X. Periodical. US. English. mo. GOVESCO Publications, Box 29268, Minneapolis MN 55429.

MEDICAL EXAMINING BOARD. See Yearbooks, Almanacs, Directories.

MEDICAL FOCUS (WURZBURG, GERMANY). (MEDICAL FOCUS). 1/1983 (May 1983)-. Periodical. English. qt. **Tel** 931-4102312. **NLM** W1. bk rev. adv acc. **Circ** 15,000. (ctrl). the international trade journal for medical, laboratory and hospital supplies. Export Markt. Physicians' and Hospital Supply.

MEDICAL FORUM (OXFORD, OXFORDSHIRE). (MEDICAL FORUM). No. 1-. 0261-3646. Periodical. UK. English. qt. $15.33. Medicine Group, Pembroke House/36 37 Pembroke Street, Oxford OX1 1BL England. **Tel** 0865-724631. **NLM** W1 ME322E.

MEDICAL GROUP MANAGEMENT. V. 8- 1960-. 0025-7257. Periodical. US. English. bm. $32.00. Medical Group Management Association, 4101 East Louisiana Avenue, Denver CO 80222. **Tel** (303)753-1111. Ed Fred E Graham and Barbara Hoagland. **Ind/Abst** Hospit. Lit. Index. **LC** R729.5.G6. **DD** 658.9136212. **NLM** W1 ME334G. (cum index). bk rev. adv acc. **Circ** 8,000. (ctrl). Ideas and techniques for group practice management including building, personnel management, finance, marketing, and general management. Bulletin of the National Association of Clinic Managers.

MEDICAL GROUP NEWS. V. 1- 1968-. 0025-7265. Periodical. US. English. bm. $24.00. Global Medical Press, Box 36, Glencoe IL 60022. **Tel** (312)441-6474. Ed Milton Golin. **LC** R11. **NLM** W1 ME334K. adv acc. **Circ** 54,000. (ctrl). News and features specifically for physicians and administrators in group practice.

MEDICAL HISTORY. Vol. 1- Jan. 1957-. 0025-7273. Periodical. UK. English. qt. $30.00. The Welcome Institute for the History of Medicine, 183 Euston Road, London NW1 2BP England. Ed W J Bishop. **Ind/Abst** Am. Hist. Life, Hist. Abstr., Part A, Mod. Hist. Abstr., Hist. Abst., Part B, Twent. Century Abstr., Life Sci. Collect., Excerpta Med., Ref. Source, Biol. Abstr., Index Med., Recent Publ. Artic. **LC** R131.A1. **DD** 610.9. **NLM** W1 ME338. **CODEN** MDHIAA.

MEDICAL HOTLINE. 0274-614X. Periodical. US. English. mo. Medical Hotline, PO Box 1700, Bergenfield NJ 07621. **Tel** (212)889-4600.

MEDICAL HYPOTHESES. V. 1- Jan./Feb. 1975-. 0306-9877. Periodical. UK. English. mo. $228.00. Longman Group Ltd, 4th Avenue Harlow, Essex CM19 5AA England. **Ind/Abst** Life Sci. Collect., Excerpta Med., Index Med., Biol. Abstr., Chem. Abstr., Sci. Cit. Index, Abr. Ed., Hospit. Lit. Index. **LC** R5. **DD** 610.5. **NLM** W1 ME341D. **CODEN** MEHYDY.

MEDICAL INDUSTRY ANALYSIS SERVICE. Apr. 1980-. 0275-1461. Monographic Series. US. English. mo. Creative Strategies International, 4340 Stevens Creek Boulevard/Suite 275, San Jose CA 95129. **NLM** W1 ME341U. Medical Industry Analysis.

MEDICAL INFORMATICS. VFOAT Medecine et Informatique. Vol. 1, No. 1 (Apr. 1976)-. 0307-7640. Periodical. UK. English (summaries in French). qt. $45.00. Taylor & Francis Ltd, 10-14 Macklin Street, London WC2B 5NF England. **Ind/Abst** Electron. Commun. Abstr. J., ISMEC Bull., Pollut. Abstr. Indexes, Saf. Sci. Abstr. J., Hospit. Lit. Index, Excerpta Med., Life Sci. Collect., Index Med., Cumul. Index Nurs. Allied Health Lit., Biol. Abstr., Comput. Control Abstr., Electr. Electron. Abstr., Sci. Abstr. Sect. A. Phys. Abstr. **NLM** W1. **CODEN** MINFDZ.

MEDICAL INSTRUMENTATION. V. 1- July/Aug. 1966-. 0090-6689. Periodical. US. English. bm. $75.00. **Tel** (215)574-3395. Ed Gail Corbett. **Ind/Abst** Cumul. Index Nurs. Allied Health Lit., Life Sci. Collect., Hospit. Lit. Index, Eng. Index Mon., Eng. Index Bioeng. Abstr., Eng. Index Energy Abstr., Excerpta Med., Comput. Control Abstr., Electr. Electron. Abstr., Sci. Abstr. Sect. A. Phys. Abstr., Energy Res. Abstr., Ref. Source, Biol. Abstr., Eng. Index Annu., Eng. Index Mon., Index Med., Phys. Abstr., Sci. Cit. Index, Abr. Ed. **LC** R856A1. **DD** 610.28. **NLM** W1 ME342I. **CODEN** MLISBY. bk rev. adv acc. **Circ** 5,500. Leading authorities provide data on biomedical and biotechnical applications of medical instrumentation and articles exploring the tools and techniques used in a host of medical situations. JAAMI. Journal of the Association for the Advancement of Medical Instrumentation, 0004-5446.

MEDICAL INVESTIGATOR (BLOOMINGTON, IND.). (MEDICAL INVESTIGATOR). Vol. 1, No. 1 (Jan. 1847)-V. 1, No. 12 (Dec. 1847). Periodical. US. English. qt. $5.17. Geelong Historical Society, 23 Cook Street, Newton Victoria 3220 Australia.

MEDICAL JOURNAL. ARMED FORCES INDIA. (MEDICAL JOURNAL, ARMED FORCES INDIA). V. 30, No. 4- Oct. 1974-. 0377-1237. Periodical. English. ir. **Ind/Abst** Energy Res. Abstr. **NLM** W1 ME344M. Armed Forces Medical Journal, India, 0004-2218.

MEDICAL JOURNAL OF AUSTRALIA. V. 1- July 1914-. 0025-729X. Periodical. AT. English. sm. $132.07. Australasian Medical Publishing Company, 77-79 Arundel Street, PO Box 116, New South Wales 2037 Australia. **Tel** (02)660 6055. Ed Alister Brass. **Ind/Abst** Life Sci. Collect., Excerpta Med., Pestdoc, Ringdoc, Vetdoc, Cumul. Index Nurs. Allied Health Lit., CIS Abstr., Nuci. Sci., Biol. Abstr., Chem. Abstr., Index Med., Sci. Cit. Index, Abr. Ed., Hospit. Lit. Index. **NLM** W1 ME345. **CODEN** MJAUAJ. bk rev. adv acc. **Circ** 22,000. (ctrl). Medical and scientific plus book reviews, letters, meetings, classified advertising supplement. Australasian Medical Gazette, 0314-5158; Australian Medical Journal, 0314-514X.

THE MEDICAL JOURNAL OF ST. JOSEPH HOSPITAL, HOUSTON. V. 10, No. 3- Sept. 1975-. 0361-4093. Periodical. US. English. qt. St Joseph Hospital, 1919 LaBranch, Houston TX 77002. **NLM** W1 ME352M. St. Joseph Hospital Medical Surgical Journal, 0361-4107.

MEDICAL LABORATORY SCIENCES. V. 33- Jan. 1976-. 0308-3616. Periodical. UK. English. qt. $80.00US and Canada. Blackwell Scientific Publishers Ltd, PO Box 88, Oxford United Kingdom. **Tel** 240201. Ed A D Farr. **Ind/Abst** Life Sci. Collect., Excerpta Med., Index Med., Cumul. Index Nurs. Allied Health Lit., Biol. Abstr., Chem. Abstr., Sci. Cit. Index, Abr. Ed. **NLM** W1 ME361E. **CODEN** MLASDU. bk rev. adv acc. **Circ** 18,300. Worldwide papers are published on all aspects of medical laboratory sciences with particular emphasis on the major disciplines of blood transfusion, cellular pathology, clinical chemistry, haematology, immunology and microbiology. Medical Laboratory Technology, 0022-2607.

MEDICAL LABORATORY SCIENTIFIC OFFICERS REGISTER. (THE MEDICAL LABORATORY SCIENTIFIC OFFICERS REGISTER). 1979-. 0263-8568. UK. English. an. **NLM** QZ 22 FA1 M489L. Medical Laboratory Technicians Register.

MEDICAL LABORATORY WORLD. V. 1- Sept. 1977-. 0140-3028. Periodical. UK. English. mo. 30 UK. United Trade Press Ltd, 33/35 Bowling Green Lane, London EC1R 0DA England. **Tel** 01-837-1212. Ed Susan Pearson. **Ind/Abst** Chem. Abstr. **NLM** W1 ME361KR. **CODEN** MLWODQ. adv acc. **Circ** 10,000. (ctrl). Covers all equipment and techniques associated with all aspects of medical laboratory sciences. News, comments, and articles of general interest are also covered.

THE MEDICAL LAW LETTER FOR PHYSICIANS, SURGEONS & HEALTH PROFESSIONALS. See Law.

MEDICAL LIABILITY ADVISORY SERVICE. See Law.

MEDICAL LIABILITY MONITOR. See Insurance.

MEDICAL LIBRARY NEWS - MCGILL UNIVERSITY. See Library and Information Science.

MEDICAL MALPRACTICE. See Insurance.

MEDICAL MALPRACTICE LAW & STRATEGY. See Law.

MEDICAL MALPRACTICE LAW & STRATEGY. See Law.

MEDICAL MALPRACTICE LITIGATION REPORTER. See Law.

MEDICAL MANPOWER IN NEW ZEALAND. STATISTICS. See Statistics.

MEDICAL MARKETING & MEDIA. See Business - Marketing.

MEDICAL MEETINGS. V. 1- 1973-. 0093-1314. Periodical. US. English. $22.00. Laux Company Inc, Po Box 700, Ayer MA 01432. **Tel** (617)772-2584. Ed Betsy Bair Cassidy. **DD** 610. **NLM** W1 ME384K. adv acc. **Circ** 95,000. (ctrl). Reports on healthcare meetings industry with news, departments, informative features, and updates on destinations where medical meetings are held.

MEDICAL MONOGRAPH. Series/Titl Publication. VFOAT National Drug Abuse Center Medical Monograph Series, and NDAC Medical Monograph Series. V. 1-. 0198-9235. Monographic Series. US. English. ir. **NLM** W1 ME3939.

THE MEDICAL-MORAL NEWSLETTER. V. 2, No. 5- Jan. 1966-. 0025-7397. Periodical. US. English. $20.00. Ayd Medical Communications, 1130 East Cold Spring Lane, Baltimore MD 21239. **Tel** (301)433-9220. Ed Frank J Ayd Jr. bk rev. **Circ** 800. In-depth analysis of medical/ethical topics with special emphasis on the background, present status, and possible ramifications of current thinking. Medical Newsletter for Religious.

MEDICAL NEWS & INTERNATIONAL REPORT. VFOAT Medical News and International Report. Vol. 1, No. 1 (Feb. 28, 1977)-. Periodical. US. English. ir. $25.00. International Medical Press Inc, 257 Park Avenue South 19th Floor, New York NY 10010. **Tel** (212)674-8500.

MEDICAL OPINION. V. 1- May 1972-. 0090-1474. Periodical. US. English. mo. $14.00 Domestic, $18.00 Foreign. Weston Communications Inc, 575 Madison Avenue, New York NY 10022. **LC** R11. **DD** 610.5. **NLM** W1 ME409C. Medical Opinion.

MEDICAL PHYSICS. See Physics.

MEDICAL PHYSICS HANDBOOKS. See Physics.

MEDICAL PHYSICS MONOGRAPH. See Physics.

MEDICAL POST. (THE MEDICAL POST). V. 1- Sept. 14, 1965-. 0025-7435. Periodical. CN. English. bw. $34.83. MacLean Hunter, PO Box 100, Station A, Toronto Ontario M5W 1A7 Canada. **NLM** W1 ME412M.

MEDICAL PROBLEMS OF PERFORMING ARTISTS. 0885-1158. Periodical. US. English. qt. Hanley & Belfus Inc, 210 South 13th Street, Philadelphia PA 19107.

MEDICAL PRODUCTS MARKETERS DIRECTORY. See Yearbooks, Almanacs, Directories.

MEDICAL PRODUCTS SALES. (MEDICAL PRODUCTS SALES : MPS : THE OFFICIAL JOURNAL OF THE AMERICAN SURGICAL TRADE ASSOCIATION). VFOAT MPS. Began with: Vol. 12, No. 5 (May 1981). 0279-4802. Periodical. US. English.

Medicine

mo. $20.00. McKnight Medical Communications Inc, 550 Frontage Road/Suite 3015, Northfield IL 60093. **Ind/Abst** Hospit. Lit. Index. **NLM** W1 ME4173. *MPS. Medical Products Salesman, 0192-432X.*

MEDICAL PRODUCTS SALESMAN. (MPS. MEDICAL PRODUCTS SALESMAN). V. 5, No. 9- Sept. 1974-. 0192-432X. Periodical. US. English. mo. $25.00. McKnight Medical Communication, 550 Frontage Road, Northfield IL 60093. **Tel** (312)446-1622. **Ed** Christopher Bale. **NLM** W1 M387L. adv acc. **Circ** 10,000. (ctrl). Covers product distribution over the entire health care marketplace. *Medical Products Salesman, American Surgical Dealer.*

MEDICAL PROGRESS. 0377-9963. Periodical. English. mo. $180.00. Medpro Pacific Ltd, 19 F Tung Sun Commercial Center, 194-200 Lockhardt Road Hong Kong. **Ind/Abst** Chem. Abstr. **CODEN** MEPRDJ.

MEDICAL PROGRESS THROUGH TECHNOLOGY. VFOAT Medical Progress Technology. V. 1- Mar. 1972-. 0047-6552. Periodical. NE. English. qt. $88.00. Martinus Nijhoff Publishers, PO Box 163, 3300 AD Dordrecht Netherlands. **Tel** 078-334233. **Ed** H Hutten. **Ind/Abst** Eng. Index Annu., Eng. Index Mon., Eng. Index, Bioeng. Abstr., Eng. Index Energy Abstr., Excerpta Med., Index Med., Cumul. Index Nurs. Allied Health Lit., Energy Res. Abstr., Comput. Control Abstr., Electr. Electron. Abstr., Sci. Abstr. Sect. A. Phys. Abstr., Hospit. Lit. Index, Sci. Cit. Index, Abr. Ed., Phys. Abstr., Eng. Index. **NLM** W1 ME4198. **CODEN** MDPTBG. Index in last issue of volume - attached. bk rev. adv acc. **Circ** 1,000. Supports the exchange of information between the medical sciences and the engineering and physical sciences. Promotes understanding of interdisciplinary problems originating from applied medicine.

MEDICAL RECORD. V. 1- 1955-. 0025-7478. Periodical. UK. English. qt. 6.00 Domestic, 8.00 Foreign. Association of Health Care Information, Barncoose Hospital, Redruth Cornwall England. **Tel** 0209-213021. **Ed** R D Knight. **Ind/Abst** Excerpta Med., Hospit. Lit. Index. **NLM** W1 ME431. bk rev. adv acc. **Circ** 1,500. A professional journal covering medical records administration and health care information. Topics covered are management of patient services, medical statistics and general management medical record and health care information journal.

MEDICAL RECORD NEWS CEASED. Vol. 33 (1962)-V. 51, No. 3 (June 1980). 0025-7486. Periodical. US. English. bm. **Ind/Abst** Life Sci. Collect., Excerpta Med., Cumul. Index Nurs. Allied Health Lit. **NLM** W1 ME433. **CODEN** MERNB. *Journal of the American Association of Medical Record Librarians.*

THE MEDICAL REGISTER. 1858. Periodical. UK. English. an. $126.16. General Medical Council, 44 Hallam Street, London W1N 6AE England. **Tel** 01-580-7642. Lists doctors registered in principal list of register on first January in year of publication and gives general information on medical registration. *The Medical Register, Printed and Published under the Direction of the General Council of Medical Education and Registration of the United Kingdom... Comprising the Names and Addresses of Medical Practitioners....*

MEDICAL RESEARCH (CANBERRA, A.C.T. : 1982). (MEDICAL RESEARCH). 1982-. 0811-6199. English. ir. **NLM** W 20. *Medical Research Projects.*

MEDICAL RESEARCH COUNCIL ANNUAL REPORT. Apr. 1965-Mar. 1966-. 0141-2256. UK. English. an. Her Majestys Stationery Office, PO Box 276, London SW8 5DT England. **NLM** W2. *Report of the Medical Research Council.*

MEDICAL RESEARCH COUNCIL MEMORANDUM. VFOAT Memorandum - Medical Research Council. No. 18- 1948-. Monographic Series. UK. English. ir. H M Stationery Office, PO Box 276, London SW8 5DT England. **LC** R111. *War Memorandum - Medical Research Council.*

MEDICAL RESEARCH ENGINEERING. See Engineering.

MEDICAL RESEARCH FUNDING BULLETIN. 1972-. Periodical. US. English. tm. $52.00. Medical Research Funding Bulletin, Science Supplement Center, Box 587, Bronxville NY 10708. **Tel** (212)371-3398. **Ed** Carroll Jordon. **Circ** 3,000. (ctrl). Publishes every ten days, complete information on government and private agency grants and contracts available to support health science programs at universities and medical centers.

MEDICAL RESEARCH IN THE VETERANS' ADMINISTRATION. **Main/Corp** United States. Veterans Administration. 1962/63-. 0083-3541. US. English. US Government Printing Office, Superintendent of Documents, Washington DC 20402. **LC** RA11. **DD** 610.72073. **NLM** W2 A V54MO. *Medical Research in the Veteran's Administration, 0083-3541.*

MEDICAL RESEARCH INDEX. See Indexes/Abstracts.

MEDICAL RESEARCH PROJECTS CEASED. 0313-6949. English. ir. **NLM** W2 KA8 N2RE. *Medical Research, 0313-6930.*

MEDICAL SCHOOL ADMISSION REQUIREMENTS, UNITED STATES AND CANADA. See Education (General) - Higher Education.

MEDICAL SELF-CARE. VAT Medical Self Care. Began publicaiton with No. 1 (Summer 1976). 0162-2285. Periodical. US. English. bm. $27.50. Medical Self-Care Magazine, PO Box 718, Inverness CA 94937. **Tel** (415)663-8462. **Ed** Michael Castleman. **Ind/Abst** Altern. Press Index. **NLM** W1 ME462W. bk rev. adv acc. **Circ** 30,000. Empowers readers to stay healthy, reduce medical expenses, and deal with illnesses and the medical system with a new degree of confidence assertiveness, and control.

MEDICAL SERIES BULLETIN. (MEDICAL SERIES, BULLETIN). **Main/Corp** Industrial Hygiene Foundation of America. Began publication on Apr. 15, 1937. 0073-7518. US. English. ir. $75.00. Industrial Health Foundation, 34 Penn Circle West, Pittsburgh PA 15206. **Tel** (412)363-6600. **Ed** Gene W Kennedy. **LC** HD7260. bk rev. **Circ** 2,000. (ctrl).

MEDICAL SERVICE DIGEST. VFOAT Digest. Began with June 1950 issue. 0041-7491. Periodical. US. English. qt. Superintendent of Documents, US Government Printing Office, Washington DC 20402. **Tel** (202)783-3238. **Ind/Abst** Index U.S. Gov. Period. **LC** RC1050. **DD** 616.980213. Index in last issue of volume - attached.

MEDICAL SOCIOECONOMIC CURRENT AWARENESS. See Economics.

MEDICAL SOCIOECONOMIC RESEARCH SOURCES. See Bibliographies.

MEDICAL STAFF DIRECTORY. See Yearbooks, Almanacs, Directories.

THE MEDICAL STAFF FELLOWSHIP PROGRAM AT THE NATIONAL INSTITUTES OF HEALTH : CATALOG. **Main/Corp** National Institutes of Health (U.S.). Began with 1982. US. English. an. National Institutes of Health, Building 31/Room 4804, Bethesda MD 20205. **Tel** (301)496-2427. *Associate Training Programs in the Medical and Biological Sciences at the National Institutes of Health.*

MEDICAL STAFF FORUM. AHA, AMERICAN HOSPITAL ASSOCIATION. 0735-2514. Periodical. US. English. bm. $18.00. American Hospital Association, PO Box 99376, Chicago IL 60693. **Tel** (800)621-6902. **Ed** Daniel Schechter. **Circ** 20,000. News and analysis related to the relationship between hospitals and their medical staffs.

MEDICAL STAFF NEWS. Vol. 14, No. 3 (Mar. 1985)-. 8756-680X. Periodical. US. English. mo. $18.00. American Hospital Association, PO Box 99376, Chicago IL 60693. **Tel** (800)621-6902. **Ed** Daniel Schechter. **DD** 658. **Circ** 20,000. News and analysis related to the relationship between hospitals and their medical staff. *Hospital Medical Staff, 0090-0710.*

MEDICAL STUDENT. V. 1-. 0360-7623. Periodical. US. English. qt. Mark Powley Associates Inc, 88 Main Street, New Canaan CT 06840. **Tel** (203)972-1902. **NLM** W1 ME4985D.

MEDICAL SUBJECT HEADINGS. ANNOTATED ALPHABETIC LIST. See Library and Information Science.

MEDICAL SUBJECT HEADINGS. TREE ANNOTATIONS. Began with 1977. 0161-3278. US. English. an. $18.00. National Technical Information Service, 5285 Port Royal Road, Springfield VA 22161. **Ed** T Charen. **NLM** Z 695.9 M489. Vols. for 1983-1984 distributed to depository libraries in microfiche.

THE MEDICAL TECHNOLOGIST AND SCIENTIST. V. 5, No. 11- Nov. 1975-. 0309-2666. Periodical. UK. English. mo. 23. A E Morgan Publications Ltd, Stanley House, 9 West Street, Epsom Surrey KT187RL England. **Tel** 03727-4141. **Ed** Guy Kingslety. **NLM** W1 ME518T. bk rev. adv acc. (ctrl). Laboratory instrumentation (medical). Analytical and diagnostic equipment and processes. *Medical Technologist, 0300-5879.*

MEDICAL TRIBUNE AND MEDICAL NEWS CEASED. VFOAT Medical Tribune. Began with Vol. 4, No. 26 Apr. 1, 1963. Ceased V. 21, No. 16 Apr. 23, 1980. 0098-6240. Periodical. US. English. wk. **NLM** W1 ME5283. *Medical Tribune, 0025-7605.*

MEDICAL TRIBUNE (NEW YORK, N.Y. : 1980). (MEDICAL TRIBUNE). Began in 1980. 0279-9340. Periodical. US. English. ir. $65.00. Medical Tribune Inc, 257 Park Avenue South, New York NY 10010. **Tel** (212)674-8500. **Ed** William Ingram. **LC** R5. **DD** 610.5. **NLM** W1 ME5268. bk rev. adv acc. **Circ** 160,000. (ctrl). Written by professionals for professionals. 25 years serving the medical community. Coverage on medical news, medicolegal drug hearings, meetings, infection control, and more. *Medical Tribune and Medical News, 0098-6240.*

MEDICAL ULTRASOUND. V. 1- Jan. 1977-. 0147-6742. Periodical. US. English. qt. John Wiley & Sons Medical Division, 605 3rd Avenue, New York NY 10158. **Tel** (800)526-5368. **Ind/Abst** Excerpta Med., Biol. Abstr., Eng. Index. **LC** R857.U48. **DD** 616.0754. **NLM** W1 ME532I. **CODEN** MEULDQ.

MEDICAL UPDATE. (MEDICAL UPDATE : THE WORLD BOOK FAMILY HEALTH ANNUAL). 1982-. 0732-0183. US. English. an. $14.95. World Book Inc, Merchandise Mart Plaza, Chicago IL 60654. **LC** RC81.A1. **DD** 610.5.

MEDICAL WIRE SERVICE. Vol. 1, No. 1 (July 1984)-. 0748-190X. Periodical. US. English. mo. $125.00. PM Inc, PO Box 2160, Van Nuys CA 91404-2160. **DD** 338.

MEDICAL WORLD ANNUAL. Began in 1963. US. English. an. McGraw Hill Book Company, 1221 Avenue of the Americas, New York NY 10020. **LC** R101. **DD** 610.5.

MEDICAL WORLD (LONDON, ENGLAND : 1969). (MEDICAL WORLD). Vol. 107, No. 1 (Jan. 1969)-. Periodical. UK. English. mo. $4.82. Subscription Department, 10-26A Jamestown Road, London NW1 7DT England. *Medical World and Newsletter, 0260-3101.*

MEDICAL WORLD NEWS. V. 1- Apr. 22, 1960-. 0025-763X. Periodical. US. English. sm. $36.50. HEI Publications Inc, PO Box 200796, Houston TX 77216. **Tel** (713)780-2299. **Ed** Annette Ostreicher. **Ind/Abst** Hospit. Lit. Index, Predicasts, Cumul. Index Nurs. Allied Health Lit., Women Stud. Abstr., Bibliogr. Agric., Funk Scott Index Corp. Ind. **LC** R11. **DD** 610.5. **NLM** W1 ME5472. **CODEN** MDWNA. adv acc. **Circ** 115,000. (ctrl). The latest medical update reports. The latest material for doctors (most important for them).

MEDICAL WORLD NEWS REVIEW. Series/Titl A McGraw-Hill Publication. V. 1- May 1974-. 0094-5811. Periodical. US. English. qt. $10.00. McGraw Hill, 1221 Avenue of the Americas, New York NY 10020. **LC** R11. **DD** 6105. **NLM** W1 ME5473.

MEDICALDISC REPORTER. VFOAT Medical Disc Reporter. Began in 1985. 0882-4665. Periodical. US. English. bm. $55.00. 6471 Merrittet, Alexandria VA 22312. **Tel** (703)354-8155. **Ed** Scott Stewart. **DD** 610. adv acc. Newsletter covering videodisc, optical disk and compact disk applications in the health sciences.

MEDICARE CONTRACTORS' CONFERENCE REPORT. See Insurance.

THE MEDICARE DIRECTORY OF PREVAILING CHARGES. See Yearbooks, Almanacs, Directories.

MEDICARE EXPLAINED. See Insurance.

MEDICARE. USE OF SKILLED NURSING FACILITIES. See Insurance.

MEDICINA. 0025-7680. Periodical. AG. Spanish (most articles have summaries in English, French, and German). bm. $50.00. Medicina Argentina, Donato Alvarez 3150, 1427 Buenos Aires Argentina. **Tel** 52-0061/64. **Ind/Abst** Excerpta Med., Life Sci. Collect., Biol. Abstr., Chem. Abstr., Nucl. Sci. Abstr.,

Medicine

Index Med. **LC** R21. **DD** 610.5. **NLM** W1 ME551K. **CODEN** MEDCAD. bk rev. **Circ** 5,000. (ctrl). Contains scientific research, and articles about different subjects of medicine.

MEDICINA CLINICA. 0025-7753. Periodical. SP. Spanish. ir. $36.00. Ediciones Doyma SA, Travesera de Gracia 17-21, 08021 Barcelona Spain. **Ind/Abst** Life Sci. Collect., Excerpta Med., Index Med., Biol. Abstr., Chem. Abstr., Nuci. Sci. Abstr. **NLM** W1 ME569. **CODEN** MCLBA2.

MEDICINA DE POSTGRADO. 0300-3833. Periodical. MX. Spanish. mo. $30.00. Novaro International Sa Calle 5 No 12, Naucaplpan Mexico.

MEDICINA DEI LAVORATORI. 0390-0703. Periodical. IT. Italian (summaries in English and French). bm. $23.76. Medicina dei Laboratori, Via Gaeta 15, 00185 Roma Italy. **Ind/Abst** CIS Abstr. **NLM** W1 ME578H. *Rassegna di Medicina Dei Lavoratori.*

MEDICINA DEL LAVORO. V. 16- 1925-. 0025-7818. Periodical. IT. Italian (summaries in English, German). bm. $41.58. Instituti Clinici Perfezioname, Via Daverio 6, 20122 Milano Italy. **Ind/Abst** Excerpta Med., CIS Abstr., Nutr. Abstr. Rev., Chem. Abstr., Nuci. Sci. Abstr., Biol. Abstr., Index Med. **NLM** W1 ME578T. **CODEN** MELAAD. *Lavoro.*

MEDICINA DELLO SPORT. V. 1- 1938-. Periodical. IT. Italian. bm. 80.00. Ediz Minerva Medica, Corso Bramante 83-85, Turin Italy 10126. **Tel** 67 82 82. **Ed** A Vemerando. adv acc. Journal addressed to practitioners and specialists and abroad. It deals with topics in sports medicine, scientific practice and research.

MEDICINA NEI SECOLI. V. 1- 1964-. 0025-7877. Periodical. IT. Italian (English, French, German and Spanish). ty. $11.88. Institut di Storia Della, Medicina-Viale del Univ 34 A, 00185 Roma Italy. **Ind/Abst** Chem. Abstr., Index Med. **LC** R5. **NLM** W1 ME605. **CODEN** MDSCAD. *Tribuna Sanitaria.*

MEDICINA OSPEDALIERA ROMANA. (MEDICINA OSPEDALIERA ROMANA : ORGANO UFFICIALE DELLA SOCIETA DI MEDICINA OSPEDALIERA). Vol. 1, N. 1 (Mar. 1980)- 0391-7231. Periodical. English (articles in Italian). qt. **NLM** W1 ME5926F.

MEDICINA TERMALE E CLIMATOLOGIA. Began in 1969. 0580-9320. Periodical. IT. English (Italian and German with summaries in English and Italian). qt. $35.00. Libreria Dello Studente, Viale Romagna 37, 20133 Milano Italy. **Ind/Abst** Chem. Abstr. **NLM** W1 ME629E. **CODEN** MTCLD7.

MEDICINAL RESEARCH. VFOAT Medicinal Research Series. V. 1- 1967-. 0076-6062. Monographic Series. US. English. ir. Marcel Dekker, Continuation Department, 270 Madison Avenue, New York NY 10016. **Tel** (212)696-9000. **Ed** G L Gronewald. **NLM** W1 ME64H. **CODEN** MRSMA. This is an ongoing series. Each title has a different subject.

MEDICINALSTATISTISKE MEDDELELSER. 0106-0759. Monographic Series. Danish. ir. **NLM** W2 GD4 S9MC.

MEDICINE. V. 1- May 1922-. 0025-7974. Periodical. US. English. bm. **Tel** (301)528-4000. **Ind/Abst** Excerpta Med., Energy Res. Abstr., Biol. Abstr., Chem. Abstr., Index Med., Life Sci. Collect., Nuci. Sci. Abstr., Energy Inf. Abstr., Environ. Abstr. **LC** R11. **DD** 610.5. **NLM** W1 ME648. **CODEN** MEDIAV. (cum index). adv acc. **Circ** 7,900. Available on microfilm from Williams & Wilkins. The only general medicine review journal to cover areas of interest to the internists, including literature review and and follow-up studies.

MEDICINE & COMPUTER. VFOAT Medicine and Computer. Vol. 1, No. 1 (Oct./Nov. 1983)-. 0739-2044. Periodical. US. English. bm. $20.00 Domestic, $25.00 Canada. Medicine & Computer, 470 Mamaroneck Avenue, White Plains NY 10605. **NLM** W1.

MEDICINE AND LAW. See Law.

MEDICINE AND SCIENCE IN SPORTS AND EXERCISE. See Recreation, Leisure - Sports.

MEDICINE AND SPORT SCIENCE. See Recreation, Leisure - Sports.

MEDICINE D'AFRIQUE NOIRE. Yearly V. 1- March 11, 1954)-. Periodical. FR. French. ir. $26.61. Medecine d'Afrique Noire, 25 rue Charles Poncy, 83000 Toulon France. **Tel** (16 94) 92 98 38.

MEDICINE DIGEST. V. 1- 1974-. Periodical. UK. English. mo. $38.00. York House, 37 Queen Square, London WC1 England. **Tel** 681 6806. **Ed** H de Glanville. bk rev. adv acc. **Circ** 23,000. (ctrl). General medicine for tropical countries.

MEDICINE NORTH AMERICA. 1st Ser., No. 1- Mar. 1980-. 0225-3895. Periodical. CN. English. mo. $46.43. C M E Publications, 4342 Sherbrooke Street West, Westmount Quebec H3Z 1E3 Canada. **Tel** (514)937-9514. **Ed** Ian R Hart. **DD** 610.5. **NLM** W1 ME6533T. adv acc. **Circ** 32,000. Textbook of general medicine in journal format published a chapter at a time over a 3 year publishing cycle.

MEDICINSKAJA PARAZITOLOGIJA I PARAZITARNYE BOLEZNI. (MEDITSINSKAIA PARAZITOLOGIIA I PARAZITARNYE BOLEZNI). VFOAT Medical Parasitology and Parasitic Diseases. V. 1- 1932-. 0025-8326. Periodical. UR. Russian (summaries in English). bm. $38.00. Victor Kamkin Inc (70514), 12224 Parklawn Drive, Rockville MD 20852. **Tel** (301)881-5973. **Ind/Abst** Life Sci. Collect., Sel. Water Resour. Abstr., Excerpta Med., Pestdoc, Ringdoc, Vetdoc, Index Med., Biol. Abstr., Chem. Abstr. **LC** RC960. **NLM** W1 ME796. **CODEN** MPPBAB. *Tropicheskaia Meditsina I Veterinariia.*

MEDICINSKAJA TEHNIKA. (MEDITSINSKAIA TEKHNIKA). V. 1- Jan./Feb. 1967-. 0025-8075. Periodical. UR. Russian (added table of contents in English). bm. $24.50. Victor Kamkin Inc (70563), 12224 Parklawn Drive, Rockville MD 20852. **Tel** (301)881-5973. **Ind/Abst** Index Med., Int. Aerosp. Abstr., Comput. Control Abstr., Electr. Electron. Abstr., Sci. Abstr. Sect. A. Phys. Abstr., Chem. Abstr. **NLM** W1 ME804. **CODEN** MEDTBV.

MEDICINSKI CASOPIS. VFOAT Medical Journal. 1961-. 0350-1221. Periodical. Serbo-Croatian -R (summaries in English, French, German, or Russian). ir. **NLM** W1.

MEDICINSKI PREGLED. 1948. 0025-8105. Periodical. YU. Serbo-Croatian -C. mo. $30.00. Serbian Medical Society, Vase Stajica 9, 21000 Novi Sas Yugoslavia. **Tel** 021-28767. **Ind/Abst** Biol. Abstr., Chem. Abstr., Index Med., Nuci. Sci. Abstr. **NLM** W1 ME74655. **CODEN** MEPEAB. bk rev. adv acc. **Circ** 1,300. (ctrl). Original articles from all medical fields, case reports.

MEDICINSKI RAZGLEDI. See Biology.

MEDICO INTERAMERICANO. Yearly V. 1, No. 1, (January 1982)-. 0278-9779. Periodical. US. Spanish. mo. $30.00. Colegio Interamericano de Medicos Cirujanos, 299 Madison Avenue, New York NY 10017. **NLM** W1.

MEDICOLEGAL NEWS. See Law.

MEDICOM. Vol. 1, No. 1 (July-Sept. 1979)-. 0253-0961. Periodical. English. an. Les Amis Alexander Brown Hall University, College Hospital, Ibadan Nigeria. **NLM** W1 ME776.

MEDIFACTS. (MEDIFACTS SOUND RECORDING). 1971. 0317-7017. Periodical. CN. English. ir. 65.00. Medifacts Ltd, 471 Richmond Road, Ottawa Ontario K2A 0G3 Canada. **Tel** (613)728-4655. **Ed** Les Johnson. **DD** 610. **NLM** W1 ME787FK. adv acc. **Circ** 9,000. (ctrl). Continuing medical education on audio cassettes for family physicians and specialists.

MEDIGUIDE TO PAIN. Vol. 1, Issue 1-. 0738-2995. Periodical. US. English. qt. $24.00. Lawrence Dellacorte Publications Inc, 767 Lexington Avenue, New York NY 10021. **NLM** W1 ME787GH.

MEDIKO-BIOLOGICHESKII ZHURNAL. V. 1- 1925-. Periodical. UR. Russian. **LC** R91.

MEDIKON. VFOAT Medikon National. 1st- 1972-. 0304-4823. Periodical. articles and summaries in Dutch, English, or French. ir. **Ind/Abst** Life Sci. Collect., Curr. Contents. **NLM** W1 ME7884M.

MEDILAG. Periodical. English. sa. Students Union, University of Lagos, College of Medicine, PMB 12003, Lagos Nigeria.

MEDIQUIZ ANNUAL. V. 1- 1975-. 0363-3926. US. English. an. Pierson, 80 Shore Road, Port Washington NY 11050. **Ed** C A Ragan Jr and F Coulston. **NLM** W1 ME7887.

MEDISCH BIOLOGISCH PERSPEKTIEF. 0167-8515. Monographic Series. Dutch. ir. **NLM** W1 ME7889.

HET MEDISCH JAAR. 1975-. 0167-6601. NE. Dutch. an. Libresso BV, Postbus 23, 7400 GA Deventer Netherlands. **Tel** 030-511274. **Ed** Bohn Schelrema and Molhena. **NLM** W1 ME7895. (cum index). **Circ** 3,000. The best medical news of the previous year.

MEDISCHE INSTRUMENTEN- EN ORTHOPEDISCHE ARTIKELENINDUSTRIE, TANDTECHNISCHE WERKPLAATSEN. Series/Titl Produktiestatistieken Industrie. VFOAT Medical Instruments and Orthopedical Articles Industry, Dental Technical Workshops. 1980 and 1981-. Dutch (summaries in English). an. Centraal Bureau voor de Statistiek, Prinses Beatrixlaan 428 Postbus 959, 2270 AZ Voorburg Netherlands.

MEDISPHERE. Began publication in 1976. 0707-6193. Periodical. CN. English. ir. Free. Faculty of Medicine, University of Toronto, Toronto Ontario M5S 1A1 Canada. **DD** 610.711713541.

MEDITERRANEE MEDICALE. No.1-. 0302-9263. Periodical. FR. French. sm. $26.61. Mediterrannee Medicale, 58 Avenue de la Marne, 92600 Asnieres France. **Ind/Abst** Biol. Abstr. **NLM** W1 ME794M. **CODEN** MDTMBF. *Corse Medicale, Sud Medical; Marseille Chirurgical, 0025-4045; Marseille Medical; Archives de Medecine.*

MEDITSINSKA TEKHNIKA. 0324-1440. Periodical. Bulgarian. qt. $20.40. Hemus, 6 Boulevard Rusky, Sofia Bulgaria. **CODEN** MDTEDR.

MEDITSINSKI RABOTNIK. Vol. 18- 1979-. 0204-8442. BU. Bulgarian. ir. $24.00. Hemus, 6 Boulevard Rusky, Sofia Bulgaria. **NLM** W1 ME808J. *Sreden Meditsinski Rabotnik.*

MEDITSINSKII ZHURNAL UZBEKISTANA. Began in 1957-. 0025-830X. Periodical. UR. Russian. mo. $25.50. Victor Kamkin Inc, 12224 Parklawn Drive, Rockville MD 20852. **Tel** (301)881-5973. **Ind/Abst** Biol. Abstr., Chem. Abstr. **NLM** W1 ME8085. **CODEN** MZUZA8. Index in last issue of volume - attached.

MEDIZIN AKTUELL. V. 1-. 0323-5386. Periodical. SZ. German (table of contents also in English and Russian). mo. Kunst & Wissen Erich Bieber, Dufourstrasse 51, CH-8008 Zurich Switzerland. **NLM** W1 ME81N.

DIE MEDIZIN IN WEST-BERLIN. GW. German. ir. 33.-. J Kugler, 1000 Berlin 37 Schutzallee 45, West Berlin West Germany. **Tel** (030)8018096. **Ed** Joachim Kugler. **LC** R713.45. adv acc. **Circ** 4,300. Directory of health service of Berlin (West) medical practitioners, hospitals, pharmacies, etc. Remedial gymnastics, midwifes, and domestic nursing, etc.

MEDIZIN UND GESELLSCHAFT. V. 1-. 0323-6153. Monographic Series. German. ir. **Ind/Abst** Excerpta Med. **NLM** W1 ME814GH. *Zeitschrift fur Arztliche Fortbildung. Beiheft, 0323-8970.*

MEDIZIN UND SPORT. Vol. 1-. 0025-8415. Periodical. German (summaries in English, French, and Russian). mo. $47.60. Kunst & Wissen Erich Bieber, Dufourstrasse 51, CH-8008, Zuerich Switzerland. **Tel** (011)41-1-69 44 20. **Ind/Abst** Excerpta Med., Biol. Abstr., Chem. Abstr. **NLM** W1 ME8145. **CODEN** MESPBQ.

MEDIZINHISTORISCHES JOURNAL. VAT Medizin Historisches Journal. Vol. 1- 1966-. 0025-8431. Periodical. German (some articles in English). qt. $54.00. VCH Publishers Inc, 303 NW 12th Avenue, Deerfield Beach FL 33442. **Tel** (305)428-5566. **Ind/Abst** Recent Publ. Artic. **LC** R131.A1. **DD** 610.9. **NLM** W1 ME818M.

MEDIZINISCHE KLINIK. Year 1-40, No. 39/40, 1. Dec. 1904-Sept. 1944. 0025-8458. Periodical. GW. German. ir. Urban & Vogel, Postfach 15 22 09, 8000 Munchen 15 West Germany. **LC** R51. **DD** 610.5.

MEDIZINISCHE KLINIK (MUNICH, GERMANY : 1983). (MEDIZINISCHE KLINIK). V. 78, 1 (21 Jan. 1983)-. 0723-5003. Periodical. German. ir. **Ind/Abst** Excerpta Med., Life Sci. Collect., Pestdoc, Ringdoc, Vetdoc, CIS Abstr., Energy Res. Abstr. **NLM** W1 ME8236TC. *Medizinische Klinik (Klinik-Ausg.), 0722-9321.*

MEDIZINISCHE LANDERKUNDE. VFOAT Geomedical Monograph Series. 1-. 0076-6115. Monographic Series. English (German). Springer Verlag-New York Inc, 175 5th Avenue, New York NY 10010. **Tel** (212)460-1500. **Ed** Helmut J Jusatz. **NLM** W1 ME825N. Numbered series on regional studies in geographical medicine.

MEDIZINISCHE MITTEILUNGEN SCHERING. No. 1-. German. ir. **NLM** W1. *Medizinische Mitteilungen.*

Medicine

MEDIZINISCHE MONATSSCHRIFT. (MEDIZINISCHE MONATSSCHRIFT, ZEITSCHRIFT FUR ALLGEMEINE MEDIZIN UND THERAPIE). Vol. 1-. 0025-8474. Periodical. GW. German. mo. 99.-. Wissenschaftliche Verlagsgesellschaft, Postfach 40, D7000 Stuttgart 1 West Germany. Tel (0711)2582-0. Index in last issue of volume - attached. bk rev. adv acc. Circ 12,000. (ctrl).

MEDIZINISCHE PRAXIS (MUNICH, GERMANY). (MEDIZINISCHE PRAXIS). 79. Vol., 1 (13. Jan. 1984)-. 0175-6125. Periodical. German. ir. Verlag Urban & Schwarzenberg, Postfach 202440, 8000 Muenchen 2 West Germany. NLM W1. Medizinische Klinik & Praxis, 0723-4996.

MEDIZINISCHE UND PADAGOGISCHE JUGENDKUNDE. Vl. 1-8. 0076-6186. Periodical. German. ir. S Karger AG, PO Box 352, White Plains NY 10602. NLM W1.

MEDIZINTECHNIK. See Technology (General).

MEDOC. See Indexes/Abstracts.

MEDYCYNA PRACY. Vol. 1-2 ?, 1948-49. 0465-5893. Periodical. PL. Polish (summaries in Polish, Russian, and English). bm. ARS Polona, Krakowskie Przedmiescie 7, 00-068 Warsaw Poland. Ind/Abst Coal Abstr., Index Med., CIS Abstr., Chem. Abstr. NLM W1 ME8697. CODEN MEPAAX.

MEMBERSHIP DIRECTORY - AMERICAN ASSOCIATION OF PHYSICISTS IN MEDICINE. See Yearbooks, Almanacs, Directories.

MEMBERSHIP DIRECTORY - AMERICAN COLLEGE OF SPORTS MEDICINE. See Yearbooks, Almanacs, Directories.

MEMBERSHIP DIRECTORY - AMERICAN MEDICAL WOMEN'S ASSOCIATION. See Yearbooks, Almanacs, Directories.

MEMBERSHIP DIRECTORY - AMERICAN OCCUPATIONAL MEDICAL ASSOCIATION. See Yearbooks, Almanacs, Directories.

MEMBERSHIP DIRECTORY OF THE AMERICAN SOCIETY FOR HOSPITAL PUBLIC RELATIONS. See Yearbooks, Almanacs, Directories.

MEMBERSHIP DIRECTORY OF THE BIOFEEDBACK SOCIETY OF AMERICA. See Yearbooks, Almanacs, Directories.

MEMOIRS OF NATIONAL INSTITUTE OF POLAR RESEARCH. SERIES E : BIOLOGY AND MEDICAL SCIENCE. See Biology.

MENNONITE MEDICAL MESSENGER (WINNIPEG, MAN.). (MENNONITE MEDICAL MESSENGER). 0824-3093. Periodical. CN. English. qt. 8.00. Mennonite Medical Association, 600 Shaftesbury Boulevard, Winnipeg Manitoba R3P 0M4 CAnada. Tel (204)888-6781. Ed Bernie Wiebe. DD 289.7. bk rev. Circ 2,000. (ctrl). Information, promotion and theological treatment of a holistic approach to health care. The magazine addresses health care professionals, especially doctors, nurses and administrators.

MEN'S HEALTH. Vol. 1, No. 1 (Feb. 1983)-. 0747-8461. Periodical. US. English. mo. $24.00. Rodale Press, 33 East Minor Street, Emmaus PA 18049.

MENTAL HEALTH SERVICE SYSTEM REPORTS. SERIES DN. HEALTH/ MENTAL HEALTH RESEARCH. (MENTAL HEALTH SERVICE SYSTEM REPORTS. SERIES DN, HEALTH/MENTAL HEALTH RESEARCH). VFOAT Health/Mental Health Research. Began with: No. 1. 0730-1588. Monographic Series. US. English. LC UNC. DD 362.20973. NLM W1 ME928EP.

THE MERCK MANUAL OF DIAGNOSIS AND THERAPY. 8th Ed.-. 0076-6526. Periodical. US. English. ir. Merck & Company, PO Box 2000, Rahway NJ 07065. Tel (201)574-5403. LC RC55. DD 615.5805. NLM WB 100 M555M. Merck Manual of Therapeutics and Materia Medica.

MERIDIAN. V. 1- Nov. 1973-. 0093-0997. Periodical. US. English. ir. Acupuncture Research Institute, PO Box 31194, Los Angeles CA 90031. NLM W1 ME951E.

METHODS OF INFORMATION IN MEDICINE. VFOAT Methodik der Information in der Medizin. V. 1- Jan. 1962-. 0026-1270. Periodical. GW. English (in German with summaries in both languages). qt. F K Schattauer Verlag, Postfach 2945, Lenzhalde 3, Stuttgart 1 West Germany. Ind/Abst Hospit. Lit. Index, Life Sci. Collect., Excerpta Med., Index Med., Comput. Control Abstr., Electr. Electron. Abstr., Sci. Abstr. Sect. A. Phys. Abstr., Energy Res. Abstr., Biol. Abstr., Sci. Cit. Index, Abr. Ed., Phys. Abstr. LC R51. DD 025.066105. NLM W1 ME9617M. CODEN MIMCAI. (cum index). Medizinische Dokumentation.

METHOTREXATE UPDATE. Summer 1983-. 0738-856X. Periodical. US. English. qt. $3.00 Single Issue. Postgraduate Institute of Medical Education, 210 Summit Avenue, Montvale NJ 07645.

MEYLER AND PECK'S DRUG-INDUCED DISEASES. Vol. 5-. 0167-5885. Monographic Series. US. English. ir. Elsevier/North-Holland Inc, 52 Vanderbilt Avenue, New York NY 10017. Ind/Abst Chem. Abstr. NLM W1 ME996J. CODEN MPDID9. Drug-Induced Diseases.

MI. MEDICINA ILLUSTRATA. (MI. MEDICINA). VFOAT Medicina Illustrata. 0391-2043. Periodical. IT. Italian. qt. Il Pensiero Scientifico Edit, Via Panama 48, 00198 Rome Italy. Tel 863 633. NLM W1 M386G.

MIAMI MEDICINE. V. 43. Periodical. US. English. mo. Dade County Medical Association, 444 Bricknell Avenue, Miami FL 33131. Tel (305)324-8717. Bulletin of the Dade County Medical Association.

MICHIGAN MEDICINE. VFOAT Michigan Medicine/Medigram. V. 63, No. 7- 1964-. 0026-2293. Periodical. US. English. mo. $30.00. Michigan State Medical Society, 120 West Saginaw Street, East Lansing MI 48823. Tel (517)337-1351. Ed Judith E Marr. Ind/Abst Hospit. Lit. Index, Index Med., Cumul. Index Nurs. Allied Health Lit., CIS Abstr., Energy Res. Abstr. NLM W1 MI22J. adv acc. Circ 10,000. Nonscientific medical news. Journal - Michigan State Medical Society, 0098-7522.

MICROCIRCULATION. Vol. 1, No. 1-. 0275-4177. Periodical. US. English. qt. $55.00. Marcel Dekker Journals, PO Box 11305 Church Street Station, New York NY 10249. Ind/Abst Excerpta Med., Biol. Abstr., Chem. Abstr. LC QP106.6. DD 612.135. NLM W1 MI298. CODEN MCCRD8.

MICROCIRCULATION, ENDOTHELIUM, AND LYMPHATICS. Vol. 1, No. 1 (Feb. 1984)-. 0740-9451. Periodical. US. English. bm. $135.00. VCH Publishers Inc, 303 NW 12th Avenue, Deerfield Beach FL 33442. NLM W1.

MIDDLE EAST HEALTH. Vol. 5, No. 8 (Sept. 1981)-. 0263-1016. Periodical. UK. English. mo. $130.00. Business Press International Ltd, Perrymount Road, Haywards Heath West Sussex RH16 3BR England. NLM W1 MI32K. MEH. Middle East Health Supply & Service, 0309-2003.

MIKROOKOLOGIE UND THERAPIE. VFOAT Microecology and Therapy. V. 7-. 0720-0536. German (articles in English or with summaries in both languages). ir. NLM W1 MI424. Uber die Behandlungen mit Physiologischen Bakterien, 0720-1648.

MILITARY MEDICINE. V. 116- Jan. 1955-. 0026-4075. Periodical. US. English. mo. $33.50 US and Canada. Association of Military Surgeons of US, 10605 Concord Street/Suite 306, Kensington MD 20895. Tel (301)933-2801. Ed John C Duffy. Ind/Abst Hospit. Lit. Index, Life Sci. Collect., Excerpta Med., Cumul. Index Nurs. Allied Health Lit., CIS Abstr., Energy Res. Abstr., Biol. Abstr., Chem. Abstr., Index Med., Nuci. Sci. Abstr., Psychol. Abstr., Sci. Cit. Index, Abr. Ed. NLM W1 MI488. CODEN MMEDA9. bk rev. adv acc. Circ 14,500. (ctrl). Knowledge concerning medical activities of the Federal Medical Services. A means of communication among members. An exchange of scientific, technological and developments of medicine. Military Surgeon (Washington, D.C. : 1907), 0096-6827.

MIMS. See Indexes/Abstracts.

MIND, THE MEETINGS INDEX. SERIES SEMT, SCIENCE, ENGINEERING, MEDICINE, TECHNOLOGY. See Indexes/Abstracts.

MINERVA ANESTESIOLOGICA. Vol. 19- Jan. 1953-. 0375-9393. Periodical. IT. Italian. mo. 80.00. Edizoni Minerva Medica, Corso Bramante 83-85, Torino Italy 10126. Tel 67 82 82. Ed O Zaffiiu.

Ind/Abst Excerpta Med., Index Med., Chem. Abstr. NLM W1 MI631. CODEN MIANAP. bk rev. adv acc. Giornale Italiano di Anestesiologia.

MINNESOTA MEDICINE. V. 1- Jan. 1918-. 0026-556X. Periodical. US. English. mo. $18.00. Minnesota State Medical Association, 2221 University Avenue/Suite 400, Minneapolis MN 55414. Tel (612)378-1875. Ed Richard L Reece. Ind/Abst Hospit. Lit. Index, Life Sci. Collect., Excerpta Med., Index Med., Energy Res. Abstr., Biol. Abstr., Chem. Abstr., Nuci. Sci. Abstr., Sci. Cit. Index, Abr. Ed. LC R15. DD 610.5. NLM W1 MI699. CODEN MIMDAL. bk rev adv acc. Circ 7,200. Medical.

MINORITY BIOMEDICAL SUPPORT PROGRAM : A DIRECTORY OF THE RESEARCH PROJECTS. See Yearbooks, Almanacs, Directories.

MINORITY STUDENT OPPORTUNITIES IN UNITED STATES MEDICAL SCHOOLS. 1969/70-. 0085-3488. US. English. an. $5.00. Association of American Medical College, 1 Dupont Circle NW, Washington DC 20036. LC R745. DD 610.71173. NLM W 22 AA1 M67.

MISSOURI MEDICINE. V. 50- Jan. 1953-. 0026-6620. Periodical. US. English. mo. $15.00. Missouri State Medical Association, 113 Madison Box 1028, Jefferson City MO 65101. Tel (314)636-5151. Ed Jordan W Burkey. Ind/Abst Hospit. Lit. Index, Life Sci. Collect., Excerpta Med., Index Med., Sci. Cit. Index, Abr. Ed. NLM W1 MI878. adv acc. Circ 7,200. Published for Missouri physicians. Scientific articles are previously unpublished clinical, review, and investigative articles. News articles cover organizational, economic, political, legislative, social and personal medical activities.

MITGLIEDER DER DEUTSCHEN GESELLSCHAFT FUR INNERE MEDIZIN. Main/Corp Deutsche Gesellschaft fur Innere Medizin. German. ir. LC R713.45. DD 610.695202543.

MITTEILUNGEN DER ARBEITSSTELLE FUR ETHNOMEDIZIN. Main/Corp Arbeitsstelle fur Ethnomedizin. No.1-. Periodical. German. ir. Arbeitsstelle fur Ethnomedizin, 2 Hamburg West Germany, Curschmannstr 33, Hamburg West Germany.

MJ. BRITISH COLUMBIA MEDICAL JOURNAL. (MJ : BRITISH COLUMBIA MEDICAL JOURNAL). VFOAT British Columbia Medical Journal. VAT British Columbia Medical Journal (1973), B.C. Medical Journal (1973). Vol. 15, No. 6 (July 1973)-. 0824-3301. Periodical. CN. English. mo. 30.00 Domestic, 34.00 Foreign. British Columbia Medical Association, 1807 West 10th Avenue, Vancouver British Columbia V6J 2A9 Canada. Tel 736-5551. Ed A F Hardyment. DD 610.9711. bk rev. adv acc. Circ 6,200. (ctrl). To provide educational service through scientific articles and inform membership of current medical affairs in British Columbia and provide information regarding BCMA and its activities. British Columbia Medical Journal, 0007-0556.

MLO. MEDICAL LABORATORY OBSERVER. (MLO, MEDICAL LABORATORY OBSERVER). VFOAT Medical Laboratory Observer. V. 1- July 1969-. 0580-7247. US. English. mo. $34.75. Medical Economics Inc, 680 Kinderkamack Road, Oradell NJ 07649. Tel (201)262-3030. Ed Robert J Fitzgibbon. Ind/Abst Trade Ind. Index, Hospit. Lit. Index, Cumul. Index Nurs. Allied Health Lit. LC RB36. DD 610.28. NLM W1 M386R. adv acc. Circ 60,000. (ctrl). Devoted to improving the management skills of clinical laboratory directors, managers, and supervisors.

MMW. MUNCHENER MEDIZINISCHE WOCHENSCHRIFT. VFOAT Munchener Medizinische Wochenschrift. Vol. 116-. 0341-3098. Periodical. GW. German (summaries in English). wk. 154.00. MMV Medizin Verlag, Postfach 860529, Rosen Kavalier Pl 4, D-80 Muenchen 80 West Germany. Tel 957170. Ind/Abst Chem. Abstr., CIS Abstr., Energy Res. Abstr., Excerpta Med., Life Sci. Collect., Pestdoc, Ringdoc, Vetdoc, Sci. Cit. Index, Abr. Ed. NLM W1 M386Z. CODEN MMMWD7. Weekly medical journal of Munich. Munchener Medizinische Wochenschrift, 0027-2973.

MOBIUS. (MOBIUS : A JOURNAL FOR CONTINUING EDUCATION PROFESSIONALS IN HEALTH SCIENCES). Vol. 1, No. 1 (Jan. 1981)-. 0272-3425. Periodical. US. English. qt. $30.00. University of California Press 2120 Berkeley Way,

Medicine

Berkeley CA 94720. **Tel** (415)642-4191. **Ed** Lucy Ann Geiselman. **Ind/Abst** Hospit. Lit. Index, Cumul. Index Nurs. Allied Health Lit., Curr. Index J. Educ. **LC** R845. **DD** 610.715. **NLM** W1 MO186. bk rev. adv acc. **Circ** 7,000. National forum for the exploration of current knowledge related to development, conduct and evaluation of continuing education programs in the health sciences.

MODERN CONCEPTS IN IMMUNOLOGY. Vol. 1-. Monographic Series. US. English. **NLM** W1.

MODERN MEDICINE. V. 1- Oct. 1932-. 0026-8070. Periodical. US. English. mo. $35.00. Harcourt Bruce Tovanovick Publishing, 1 East First Street, Duluth MN 55802. **Tel** (218)723-9516. **Ed** Kristi Thomsen. **LC** R11. **DD** 616.005. **NLM** W1 MO142. adv acc. **Circ** 118,945. (ctrl). A doctor's business journal serving medical and osteopathic physicians.

MODERN MEDICINE. VFOAT Modern Medicine of Australia. V. 15- Jan. 1972-. 0312-875X. Periodical. English. ir. Free to doctors in Australia and the Territory of Papua and New Guinea. Modern Medicine of Australia Party Ltd, 457 Pacific Highway, 2064 Artarmon New South Wales Australia. **NLM** W1 MO14. *Modern Medicine of Australia, 0026-8089.*

MODERN MEDICINE. V. 16- Jan. 1971-. 0262-4273. Periodical. UK. English. mo. **NLM** W1 MO139M. *Modern Medicine of Great Britain Ltd.*

MODERN MEDICINE OF CANADA. V. 1- Oct. 1946-. 0026-8097. Periodical. CN. English. mo. $54.17. Southam Communications Ltd, 1450 Don Mills Road, Don Mills Ontario M3B 1X2 Canada. **Tel** (416)445-6641. **NLM** W1 MO161.

MODERN MEDICINE OF IRELAND. 0306-6657. Periodical. UK. English. mo. **NLM** W1 MO165l.

MODULE D'AUTOFORMATION. No. 1-. 0825-0464. Periodical. CN. French. bm. $7.00 Each Number. Federation des Medecins Omnipraticiens du Quebec, Bureau 1100/1440 rue Ste-Catherine, Montreal Quebec H3G 1R8 Canada. **DD** 610.715.

MOLECULAR ASPECTS OF MEDICINE. V. 1-. 0098-2997. Periodical. UK. English. ir. Pergamon Press, 395 Sawmill River Road, Elmsford NY 10523. **Ind/Abst** Life Sci. Collect., Excerpta Med., Index Med., Biol. Abstr., Chem. Abstr., Sci. Cit. Index, Abr. Ed. **LC** RB112. **DD** 616.07. **NLM** W1 MO195H. **CODEN** MAMED5.

MOLECULAR IMMUNOLOGY. V. 16- Jan. 1979-. 0161-5890. Periodical. UK. English. mo. Pergamon Press, 395 Sawmill River Road, Elmsford NY 10523. **Ind/Abst** Life Sci. Collect., Excerpta Med., Pestdoc, Ringdoc, Vetdoc, Index Med., Biol. Abstr., Energy Res. Abstr., Chem. Abstr. **LC** QR180. **DD** 574.29. **NLM** W1 MO196K. **CODEN** MOIMD5. available on microfilm and microfiche. *Immunochemistry.*

MONOCLONAL ANTIBODY NEWS. Vol. 1, No. 1 & 2-. 0272-4588. Periodical. US. English. qt. Mary Ann Liebert Inc, 157 East 86th Street, New York NY 10028. **Tel** (212)289-2300. **Ind/Abst** Excerpta Med. **NLM** QW 539 M751.

MONOGRAPH SERIES - OKLAHOMA. UNIVERSITY. MEDICAL CENTER, OKLAHOMA CITY. LIBRARY. Main/Corp Oklahoma. University. Medical Center, Oklahoma City. Library. **VFOAT** University of Oklahoma Medical Center Library Monograph Series. No. 1- 1967-. Monographic Series. US. English. **NLM** W1 OK7925.

MONOGRAPHS IN VIROLOGY. Began in 1968. 0077-0965. Monographic Series. English. ir. S Karger Ag, PO Box, CH-4009 Basel Switzerland. **Tel** 061-39 08 80. **Ed** J L Melnick. **Ind/Abst** Life Sci. Collect., Biol. Abstr., Chem. Abstr., Index Med. **NLM** W1 MO569P. **CODEN** MONVAK. Compact but thorough reference tools for virologists and non-virologists alike.

MONTEFIORE MEDICINE. V. 1- Summer 1976-. 0149-6735. Periodical. US. English. qt. Montefiore Hospital and Medical Center, 111 East 210 Street, Bronx NY 10467. **NLM** W1 MO583P.

MONTHLY PRESCRIBING REFERENCE. 0883-0266. Periodical. US. English. mo. $60.00. Prescribing Reference Inc, 53 Park Place, New York NY 10017. **Tel** (212)766-7200. **Ed** Susan E Di Georgio. adv acc. **Circ** 115,000. (ctrl). A unique prescribing reference for office based physicians, updated every month and including essential information on the top 2,000 prescribed drugs.

MORPHOLOGIA MEDICA. Vol. 1, No. 1 (Feb. 1981)-. 0172-9187. Periodical. German. bm. $118.00. Verlag Chemie International Inc, Plaza Centre, Suite E/1020 NW Sixth Street, Deerfield Beach FL 33441. **Ind/Abst** Excerpta Med., Index Med. **NLM** W1 MO915H. **CODEN** MOMDDW.

MORPHOLOGIAI ES IGAZSAGUGYI ORVOSI SZEMLE. 0540-889X. Periodical. HU. Hungarian (summaries in English, German and Russian). qt. Akademiai Kiado, POB 24, 1363 Budapest Hungary. **Ind/Abst** Excerpta Med., Index Med., Energy Res. Abstr., Chem. Abstr. **LC** R96.H8. **NLM** W1 MO915J. **CODEN** MIOSA8.

MOTPOL. V. 54, No. 5- 1976-. 0347-0989. Periodical. SW. Swedish. ir. Motpol, Box 3306, 10366 Stockholm Sweden. **NLM** W1 MO949F. *MFT. Medicinska Foreningarnas Tidskrift.*

THE MOUNT SINAI JOURNAL OF MEDICINE. (THE MOUNT SINAI JOURNAL OF MEDICINE, NEW YORK). V. 37- Jan./Feb. 1970-. 0027-2507. Periodical. US. English. $25.00. Mount Sinai Medical Center, Annenberg Building, 5th Avenue and 100th Street, New York NY 10029. **Ind/Abst** Life Sci. Collect., Excerpta Med., Energy Res. Abstr., Biol. Abstr., Chem. Abstr., Index Med., Nuci. Sci. Abstr. **LC** R11. **DD** 610.5. **NLM** W1 MO95KG. **CODEN** MSJMAZ. *Journal of the Mount Sinai Hospital, New York, 0099-9695.*

MOUSE NEWS LETTER. 1949. 0580-0811. Periodical. UK. English. sa. $20.00. Mouse News Letter, Jackson Laboratory, Bar Harbor ME 04609. **Tel** (207)288-337. **Ed** Josephine Peters. (ctrl). A newsletter for investigators who work with or are interested in inbred strains of mice.

MRZH. MEDITSINSKII REFERATIVNYI ZHURNAL. VFOAT Meditsinskii Referativnyi Zhurnal. V. 19- 1975-. UR. Russian (added table of contents in English). **NLM** ZW 1 M4915. *Meditsinskii Referativnyi Zhurnal.*

MS QUARTERLY REPORT. (MS QUARTERLY REPORT : A PUBLICATION OF THE EASTERN PARALYZED VETERANS ASSOCIATION). **VFOAT** M.S. Quarterly Report. **VAT** Multiple Sclerosis Quarterly Report. 0738-3967. Periodical. US. English. qt. Eastern Paralyzed Veterans Association, 432 Park Avenue South, New York NY 10016. *MS Quarterly, 0195-2285.*

MTA-JOURNAL. VFOAT MTA Journal. Began in 1979. 0171-8037. Periodical. GW. German. mo. Umschau Verlag Breidenstein GMBH, Postfach 110262 Stuttgarter Strasse 18-24, D-6000 Frankfurt Am Main 1 West Germany. **Ind/Abst** Chem. Abstr. **CODEN** MTJODH.

MUG'M NEWSLETTER. See Library and Information Science.

MULTIPLE SCLEROSIS INDICATIVE ABSTRACTS. See Indexes/Abstracts.

MYKOSEN. 0027-5557. Periodical. GW. German. mo. Grosse Verlag, Kurfeurstendamm 152, D1000 Berlin 31 West Germany. **Ind/Abst** Life Sci. Collect., Excerpta Med., Pestdoc, Ringdoc, Vetdoc, Biol. Abstr., Chem. Abstr., Nuci. Sci. Abstr., Index Med., Bibliogr. Agric., Sci. Cit. Index, Abr. Ed. **LC** QR145. **NLM** W1 MY736. **CODEN** MYKSAW.

NAGOYA MEDICAL JOURNAL. V. 1- Jan. 1953-. 0027-7649. Periodical. JA. English. qt. Nagoya City University Medical School, Mizhuo Ward, Nagoya Japan. **Ind/Abst** Biol. Abstr., Chem. Abstr. **NLM** W1 NA115. **CODEN** NMJOAA.

NAPHT NEWS. Oct. 1969-. 0363-4701. Periodical. US. English. qt. **NLM** W1 N117.

NARA IGAKU ZASSHI. VFOAT Journal of Nara Medical Association. Began 1949. 0469-5550. Periodical. Japanese (English). bm. Japan Publications Trading Company, PO Box 5030/Tokyo International, Tokyo 100-31 Japan. **Ind/Abst** Biol. Abstr., Chem. Abstr. **NLM** W1 NA171. **CODEN** NAIZAM. Index in last issue of volume - attached.

NARODNA ZDRAVSTVENA KULTURA U SR SRBIJI. Series/Titl Posebna Izdanja - Naucno Drustvo za Istoriju Zdravstvene Kulture Jugoslavije. **VFOAT** Folk Health Culture in the Socialist Republic of Serbia. Vol. 1- 1976-. Monographic Series. Serbo-Croatian -R. ir. **Ed** J Tucakov. **NLM** W1 PO863.

THE NATIONAL BOARD EXAMINER. V. 1- 1954-. 0027-8785. Periodical. US. English. qt. National Board of Medical Examiners, 3930 Chestnut Street, Philadelphia PA 19104. **Tel** (215)349-6400. **LC** R745. **NLM** W1 NA328. *Diplomate, 0096-0209.*

NATIONAL DIRECTORY OF HEALTH/MEDICINE ORGANIZATIONS. See Yearbooks, Almanacs, Directories.

THE NATIONAL DIRECTORY OF HOLISTIC HEALTH PROFESSIONALS. See Yearbooks, Almanacs, Directories.

NATIONAL DIRECTORY OF MEDICARE HOME HEALTH AGENCIES. See Yearbooks, Almanacs, Directories.

NATIONAL DISEASE AND THERAPEUTIC INDEX. See Indexes/Abstracts.

NATIONAL DISEASE AND THERAPEUTIC INDEX (NDTI). DIAGNOSIS. See Indexes/Abstracts.

NATIONAL DISEASE AND THERAPEUTIC INDEX (NDTI). DRUG NATIONAL ESTIMATES. See Indexes/Abstracts.

NATIONAL DISEASE AND THERAPEUTIC INDEX (NDTI). NON-HOSPITAL. See Indexes/Abstracts.

NATIONAL HEALTH PRACTITIONER PROGRAM PROFILE. Began with Vol. for 1979-80. 0277-3376. US. English. an. Association of Physician Assistant Programs, 2341 Jefferson Davis Highway/Suite 700, Arlington VA 22202. **LC** R847.5. **DD** 610.737. **NLM** W 22 AA1 N275. *National New Health Practitioner Program Profile, 0145-3793.*

NATIONAL HEALTH SERVICE (SCOTLAND) ACTS 1947 TO 1968, ACCOUNTS, SUMMARISED ACCOUNTS OF REGIONAL HOSPITAL BOARDS (INCLUDING BOARD OF MANAGEMENT) AND EXECUTIVE COUNCILS (INCLUDING DRUG ACCOUNTS COMMITTEE) AND THE ACCOUNT OF THE DENTAL ESTIMATES BOARD, FOR SCOTLAND, BOARD, FOR SCOTLAND, TOGETHER WITH THE REPORT OF THE COMPTROLLER AND AUDITOR GENERAL THEREON. Main/Corp Great Britain. Exchequer and Audit Dept. UK. English. an. 0.26. Her Majesty's Stationery Office, PO Box 276, London SW8 5DT England. **LC** RA243. **DD** 354.41100841. **NLM** W2 FS2 D4N.

THE NATIONAL HEART, LUNG, AND BLOOD INSTITUTE'S FACT BOOK. Series/Titl Dhew Publication. **VFOAT** Fact Book - National Heart, Lung, & Blood Institute. 1975/76-. Periodical. US. English. an. **NLM** W 22 AA1 N274. *National Heart and Lung Institute Fact Book.*

NATIONAL INSTITUTES OF HEALTH INTERNATIONAL AWARDS FOR BIOMEDICAL RESEARCH AND RESEARCH TRAINING. Main/Corp John E. Fogarty International Center for Advanced Study in the Health Sciences. International Cooperation and Geographic Studies Branch. **VFOAT** International Awards for Biomedical Research and Research Training. US. English. an. John E Fogarty International Center for Advanced Study in The Health Sciences, International Coordination and Liaison Branch, 9000 Rockville Pike, Bethesda MD 20205. **LC** R852. **DD** 610.79. **NLM** WA 22 AA1 N36. *International Awards for Biomedical Research and Research Training.*

NATIONAL INTELLIGENCE REPORT. CLINICAL LABS/BLOOD BANKS. VFOAT Clinical Labs/Blood Banks. **VAT** National Intelligence Report. Clinical Labs Blood Bank. 0270-6768. Periodical. US. English. sm. $132.00. Washington G-2 Reports, 1511 K Street NW/Suite 539, Washington DC 20005. **Tel** (202)789-1034.

NATIONAL JOURNAL OF MEDICINE & MEDICAL RESEARCH. VFOAT National Journal of Medicine and Medical Research. Vol. 1-. 0733-9844. Periodical. US. English. mo. $156.00. National Journal of Medicine and Medical Research/Suite 232-303 E Semoran Boulevard, Altamonte Springs FL 32701. **NLM** W1 NA486SM.

Medicine

NATIONAL LEGAL BIBLIOGRAPHY. SUBJECT AREA LIST. MEDICINE AND HEALTH LAW. See Bibliographies.

NATIONAL LIBRARY OF MEDICINE AUDIOVISUALS CATALOG. See Library and Information Science.

NATIONAL LIBRARY OF MEDICINE AVLINE CATALOG. See Library and Information Science.

NATIONAL LIBRARY OF MEDICINE CURRENT CATALOG. ANNUAL CUMULATION. See Library and Information Science.

NATIONAL LIBRARY OF MEDICINE CURRENT CATALOG. CUMULATIVE LISTING. See Library and Information Science.

NATIONAL LIBRARY OF MEDICINE PROGRAMS AND SERVICES. See Library and Information Science.

NATIONAL LISTING OF PROVIDERS FURNISHING KIDNEY DIALYSIS AND TRANSPLANT SERVICES. Began with Jan. 1981. 0882-0015. US. English. an. Superintendent of Documents, US Government Printing Office, Washington DC 20402. **NLM** WJ 22. Renal Provider List, 0195-8771.

NATIONAL MEDICAL AUDIOVISUAL CENTER CATALOG. 1974-. 0094-551X. US. English. Superintendent of Documents, US Government Printing Office Washington DC 20402. **LC** R835. **DD** 016.61. **NLM** W 18. National Medical Audiovisual Center Motion Picture and Videotape Catalog, 0093-7363.

NATIONAL MEDICAL JOURNAL OF CHINA. Periodical. CH. English. mo. China Publication Centre, PO Box 2820, Beijing China. **Tel** 55,1918. **Ed** Xu Hongdao. bk rev. adv acc. **Circ** 21,000. Our serial is a superior comprehensive medical journal, chiefly reflecting the new advances, achievements and techniques in the studies of medical sciences in China.

NATIONAL NEW HEALTH PRACTITIONER PROGRAM PROFILE. Main/Corp Association of Physician Assistant Programs. 0145-3793. US. English. an. Association of Physician Assistant, 2341 Jefferson Davis Highway, Arlington VA 22202. **Tel** (202)920-5730. **LC** R847.5. **DD** 610. **NLM** W 22 AA1 N275.

NATIONAL NEWS MEDIA DIRECTORY. MEDICINE/HEALTH. See Yearbooks, Almanacs, Directories.

THE NATIONAL PHYSICIAN ASSISTANT PROGRAM PROFILE. Main/Corp Association of Physician Assistant Programs. 1st- Ed. 0363-7174. US. English. Association of Physician Assistant Programs, 2120 L Street NW/Suite 210, Washington DC 20037. **LC** R847.5. **DD** 610.737071.

NDC PAPER. 1- 1974-. 0306-5464. Periodical. UK. English. ir. **NLM** W1.

THE NEBRASKA MEDICAL JOURNAL. V. 56, No. 12- Dec. 1971-. 0091-6730. Periodical. US. English. mo. $18.00. Nebraska Medical Association Inc, 1512 First National Bank Building, Lincoln NE 68508. **Tel** (402)474-4472. **Ed** Alan Forker. **Ind/Abst** Life Sci. Collect., Hospit. Lit. Index, Energy Res. Abstr., Chem. Abstr., Index Med. **NLM** W1 NE1145. **CODEN** NBMJAZ. adv acc. **Circ** 2,200. Nebraska State Medical Journal, 0028-1956.

NEDERLANDS MILITAIR GENEESKUNDIG TIJDSCHRIFT. 1.- Vol. Periodical. Dutch. ir. **LC** RC971. **NLM** W1 NE138.

NEDERLANDS TIJDSCHRIFT VOOR GENEESKUNDE. 0028-2162. Periodical. NE. Dutch. wk. Libresso BV, Postbus 878, 7400 AW Deventer Netherlands. **Ind/Abst** Life Sci. Collect., Excerpta Med., Pestdoc, Ringdoc, Vetdoc, Index Med., CIS Abstr., Index Dent. Lit., Chem. Abstr. **NLM** W1 NE147. **CODEN** NETJAN. Nederlandsch Tijdschfift Voor Geneeskunde.

NETHERLANDS JOURNAL OF MEDICINE. V. 16- 1973-. 0300-2977. Periodical. NE. English. mo. Libresso BV, Postbus 878, 7400 AW Deventer Netherlands. **Ind/Abst** Excerpta Med., Life Sci. Collect., Index Med., Biol. Abstr., Chem. Abstr., Sci. Cit. Index, Abr. Ed. **NLM** W1 NE229J. **CODEN** NLJMAV. Folia Medica Neerlandica, 0015-5624.

NEUE MUNCHNER BEITRAGE ZUR GESCHICHTE DER MEDIZIN UND NATURWISSENSCHAFTEN. MEDIZINHISTORISCHE REIHE. Vol. 1- 1970-. 0300-8371. Periodical. GW. German. ir. Werner Fritish Verlag, Promenadeplatz 11, 8000 Munchen 2 West Germany. **Ed** H Goerke. **NLM** W1 NE264E.

NEUE SCHRIFTENREIHE DES VERBANDES SCHWEIZER BADEKURORTE. No. 1-. Periodical. French (articles in German). ir. **NLM** W1.

NEURALTHERAPIE NACH HUNEKE. VFOAT Freudenstadter Vortrage. Vol. 1- 1974-. 0172-9225. German. ir. **NLM** W1 NE323D.

NEUROLOGIC ILLNESS: DIAGNOSIS & TREATMENT. See Medicine - Neurology.

NEUROPATOLOGIA POLSKA. 1- 1963-. 0028-3894. Periodical. PL. Polish (summaries in English and Russian). qt. ARS Polana, Krakowskie Przedmiescie 7, 00-068 Warsaw Poland. **Ind/Abst** Excerpta Med., Index Med., Chem. Abstr. **NLM** W1 NE337P. **CODEN** NUPOBT.

THE NEW DIRECTORY OF MEDICAL SCHOOLS. See Yearbooks, Almanacs, Directories.

NEW DYNAMICS OF PREVENTIVE MEDICINE. V. 1- 1974-. 0360-2613. Monographic Series. US. English. ir. Symposia Specialists, 1480 NE 129 Street, Miami FL 33161. **NLM** W1 NE374J.

THE NEW ENGLAND JOURNAL OF MEDICINE. V. 198- Feb. 23, 1928-. 0028-4793. Periodical. US. English. wk. $60.00 Domestic, $75.00 Foreign. New England Journal of Medicine Manager, Circulation Marketing, 1440 Main Street, Waltham MA 02254. **Tel** (617)893-3800. **Ed** Arnold S Relman. **Ind/Abst** Pestdoc, Energy Inf. Abstr., Environ. Abstr., Index Med., Cumul. Index Nurs. Allied Health Lit., Popul. Index, Pop. Mag. Rev., Women Stud. Abstr., Int. Aerosp. Abstr., Biol. Abstr., CIS Abstr., Energy Res. Abstr., Chem. Abstr., Sociol. Abstr., Nuci. Sci. Abstr., Hospit. Lit. Index, Psychol. Abstr., Sel. Water Resour. Abstr., Bibliogr. Agric., Gen. Sci. Index, Sci. Cit. Index, Abr. Ed., Lang. Lang. Behav. Abstr., Abstr. Soc. Work. **LC** R11. **DD** 610.5. **NLM** W1 NE388. **CODEN** NEJMAG. (cum index). bk rev. adv acc. **Circ** 215,000. World's leading general medical journal. One of most respected sources of new medical knowledge. Largest paid circulation of any English language medical journal. Boston Medical and Surgical Journal, 0096-6762.

A NEW IMAGE OF MAN IN MEDICINE. Vol. 1-. 0270-7748. US. English. ir. Futura Publishing Company, PO Box 298, Mount Kisco NY 10549. **Ind/Abst** Chem. Abstr. **DD** 306. **CODEN** NIMED4.

NEW MEDICAL SCIENCE. Vol. 1, No. 1 (July 1984)-. 0748-8777. Periodical. US. English. mo. New Medical Science, 2333 Waukegan Road, Suite S-280, Bannockburn IL 60015. **DD** 610.

NEW MEXICO STATE MEDICAL FACILITIES PLAN. Main/Corp New Mexico. State Health Planning and Development Bureau. 1978/79-. 0196-4852. US. English. an. **NLM** W2 AN5 H5NA. New Mexico State Plan for Hospitals and Health Facilities Survey, Construction and Modernization, 0192-1053.

NEW PHYSICIAN. 1951. 0028-6451. Periodical. US. English. $15.00. American Medical Student Association, 1910 Association Drive, Reston VA 22091. **Tel** (703)620-6600. **Ed** Renie Schapiro. **Ind/Abst** Hospit. Lit. Index. **NLM** W1 NE484I. bk rev. adv acc. **Circ** 80,000. (ctrl). News and feature coverage on social, political, and ethical issues in medical education and health care delivery, primary care clinical columns, etc.

NEW TITLES IN BIOETHICS. See Ethics.

NEW VISTAS IN COUNSELING SERIES. V. 1-. 0160-7162. Monographic Series. US. English. ir. Human Sciences Press, 72-5th Avenue, New York NY 10011. **LC** UNC. **NLM** W1 NE513K.

NEW YORK AND NEW JERSEY REGIONAL MEDICAL LIBRARY NEWS. See Library and Information Science.

NEW YORK FAMILY PHYSICIAN. Began with Vol. 24, No. 4 (July/Aug. 1972). Periodical. US. English. qt. New York State Academy of Family Physicians, 84 Main Street, Binghamton NY 13905. New York FP.

THE NEW YORK MEDICAL QUARTERLY. V. 1- Summer 1979-. 0196-6871. Periodical. US. English. qt. New York Medical Publ. Company, 370-7th Avenue, New York NY 10001. **Ind/Abst** Chem. Abstr. **LC** R11. **DD** 610.5. **NLM** W1 NE697AL. **CODEN** NYMQDG.

NEW YORK STATE JOURNAL OF MEDICINE. V. 1- Jan. 1901-. 0028-7628. Periodical. US. English. mo. $25.00. Medical Society of the State of New York, 420 Lakeville Road, PO Box 5404, Lake Success NY 11040. **Tel** (516)488-6100. **Ed** Alan Blum. **Ind/Abst** Life Sci. Collect., Excerpta Med., Pestdoc, Ringdoc, Vetdoc, Cumul. Index Nurs. Allied Health Lit., Int. Aerosp. Abstr., CIS Abstr., Energy Res. Abstr., Biol. Abstr., Chem. Abstr., Index Med., Nuci. Sci. Abstr., Hospit. Lit. Index, Psychol. Abstr., Sci. Cit. Index, Abr. Ed. **LC** R11. **DD** 610.5. **NLM** W1 NE885. **CODEN** NYSJAM. bk rev. adv acc. **Circ** 30,000. Peer reviewed general medical journal; independent editorial content emphasis on commentary, research, and news.

NEW ZEALAND JOURNAL OF MEDICAL LABORATORY TECHNOLOGY. (THE NEW ZEALAND JOURNAL OF MEDICAL LABORATORY TECHNOLOGY). V. 17- Apr. 1963-. 0028-8349. Periodical. NZ. English. ir. **Ind/Abst** Excerpta Med., Cumul. Index Nurs. Allied Health Lit., Chem. Abstr. **NLM** W1 NE973N. **CODEN** NZJMAR. Journal of the New Zealand Institute of Medical Laboratory Technology.

THE NEW ZEALAND JOURNAL OF SPORTS MEDICINE. V. 1- Nov. 1969-. 0110-6384. Periodical. NZ. English. qt. 40.00. New Zealand Foundation for Sports Medicine, L Dey National Section, PO Box 6171, Dunedin New Zealand. **Tel** 776733. **Ed** N Roydhouse. **Ind/Abst** Index New Z. Period. **NLM** W1 NE974. bk rev. adv acc. **Circ** 1,300. (ctrl). Sports medicine, the study of all the health implications of man in activity, physiology, psychology, illness and injury rehabilitation. Sports Medicine Bulletin.

NEW ZEALAND MEDICAL JOURNAL. 0028-8446. Periodical. NZ. English. sm. $85.00. New Zealand Medical Journal, 26 The Terrace, PO Box 156, Wellington New Zealand. **Tel** 724-741. **Ed** R G Robinson. **Ind/Abst** Life Sci. Collect., Excerpta Med., Pestdoc, Ringdoc, Vetdoc, Cumul. Index Nurs. Allied Health Lit., CIS Abstr., Biol. Abstr., Chem. Abstr., Nuci. Sci. Abstr., Index Med., Cumul. Index Nurs. Allied Health Lit., Index Dent. Lit., Biol. Abstr., Chem. Abstr., Nuci. Sci. Abstr., Index Med., Sci. Cit. Index, Abr. Ed. **NLM** W1 NE977. **CODEN** NZMJAX. bk rev. adv acc. **Circ** 5,500. Journal of New Zealand Medical Association. Original clinical articles, related to medical practice and health care. Includes correspondence and news.

NEW ZEALAND MEDICAL MANPOWER STATISTICS. See Statistics.

NEW ZEALAND MEDICAL REGISTER. See Yearbooks, Almanacs, Directories.

NEW ZEALAND REGISTER OF SPECIALISTS. 0300-2217. English. ir. Medical Council of New Zealand, PO Box 5135, Wellington New Zealand. **LC** R713.93. **DD** 616.0025931. **NLM** W 22 KN4 N5.

NEWFOUNDLAND MEDICAL DIRECTORY. See Yearbooks, Almanacs, Directories.

NEWS - BRITISH COLUMBIA MEDICAL ASSOCIATION. (NEWS). 0715-5379. Periodical. CN. English. British Columbia Medical Association, 1807 West Tenth Avenue, Vancouver British Columbia V6J 2A9 Canada. **DD** 362.109711.

NEWS FROM ABMAC. Main/Corp American Bureau for Medical Advancement in China. VAT News from American Bureau for Medical Advancement in China. V. 40- Sept. 1979-. 0196-3856. US. English. bm. American Bureau of Medical Advancement in China, 1790 Broadway, New York NY 10019. **LC** HV688.C4. **DD** 362.104250951. ABMAC Bulletin, 0001-0529.

NEWS - MANITOBA HEALTH LIBRARIES ASSOCIATION. (NEWS). Vol. 1, No. 1 (1979)-. 0821-1310. Periodical. CN. English. ir. Free. Manitoba Health Libraries Association, 202-880 Portage Avenue, Winnipeg Manitoba R3G 0P1 Canada. **DD** 026.61. (ctrl).

Medicine

NEWS - NATIONAL LIBRARY OF MEDICINE. (NEWS). V. 11, No. 10- Oct. 1956-. 0027-965X. Periodical. US. English. bw. National Library of Medicine, 8600 Rockville Pike, Bethesda MD 20209. **Tel** (301)496-6308. **Ind/Abst** Cumul. Index Nurs. Allied Health Lit. *News of the U.S. Armed Forces Medical Library.*

NEWS OF NEW YORK. 0028-9264. Periodical. US. English. sm. $5.00. Medical Society State of NY, 420 Lakeville Road, Lake Success NY 11042. **Tel** (516)488-6100. Ed Brian Quinn. **NLM** W1 ME493A. adv acc. **Circ** 29,000. Social, political and economic news of the Medical Society of New York State, with emphasis on the people of the society.

NEWSLETTER - AMBULANCE & MEDICAL SERVICES ASSOCIATION OF AMERICA. **VAT** Newsletter - Ambulance and Medical Services Association of America. V. 1- July 1978-. 0192-6055. Periodical. US. English. **NLM** W1 NE997TM.

NEWSLETTER - AMERICAN ASSOCIATION OF TISSUE BANKS. **Main/Corp** American Association of Tissue Banks. 0270-2673. Periodical. US. English. qt. Free. American Association of Tissue Banks, 12111 Parklawn Drive, Rockville MD 20852.

NEWSLETTER - ASSOCIATION OF TEACHERS OF PREVENTIVE MEDICINE. **Main/Corp** Association of Teachers of Preventive Medicine. V. 4, No. 3- Apr. 1955-. 0519-170X. Periodical. US. English. ty. **NLM** W1 CO469. *Newsletter.*

NEWSLETTER - CANADIAN ACADEMY OF PODIATRIC SPORTS MEDICINE. **Main/Corp** Canadian Academy of Podiatric Sports Medicine. V. 1- Spring 1978-. 0705-6915. Periodical. CN. English. Free. Canadian Academy of Podiatric Sports Medicine, Suite 801, 586 Eglinton Avenue East, Toronto Ontario M4P 1P2 Canada. **DD** 617.585. (ctrl).

NEWSLETTER - CANADIAN ACADEMY OF SPORT MEDICINE. (NEWSLETTER). 0715-3422. Periodical. CN. English. Canadian Academy of Sport Medicine Group, Box 85 Hospital Medical Centre, Huntsville Ontario P0A 1K0 Canada. **DD** 617.102706071. *Journal (Canadian Academy of Sport Medicine), 0715-3422.*

NEWSLETTER - CANADIAN ATHLETIC THERAPISTS ASSOCIATION. (NEWSLETTER). **VAT** CATA Newsletter, Canadian Athletic Therapists Association Newsletter. 0822-7578. Periodical. CN. English (includes some text in French). Canadian Athletic Therapists Association, 333 River Road, Ottawa Ontario K1L 8B9 Canada. **DD** 617.102706071.

NEWSLETTER - CANADIAN MEDICAL AND BIOLOGICAL ENGINEERING SOCIETY. **Main/Corp** Canadian Medical and Biological Engineering Society. Began with Jan. 1966? issue. 0384-1820. Periodical. CN. English. ir. Free. Canadian Medical and Biological Engineering Society, c/o A Quanbury, 633 Wellington Crescent, Winnipeg Manitoba R3M 0A8 Canada. **DD** 610.2806271. (ctrl).

NEWSLETTER - CANADIAN PHYSIOTHERAPY ASSOCIATION. SPORTS PHYSIOTHERAPY DIVISION. (NEWSLETTER). **VFOAT** Sports Physiotherapy Newsletter. **VAT** Newsletter - Sports Physiotherapy Division. Vol. 7, No. 1 (Nov. 1981)-. 0824-2917. Periodical. CN. English. ir. Canadian Physiotherapy Association, Sports Physiotherapy Division, PO Box 1625, Saskatoon Saskatchewan S7K 3R8 Canada. **DD** 617.102705. *Sports Medicine Division Newsletter, 0715-3880.*

NEWSLETTER - CANADIAN PODIATRIC SPORTS MEDICINE ACADEMY. **Main/Corp** Canadian Podiatric Sports Medicine Academy. V. 1, No. 3- Fall/Winter 1978-. 0709-5554. Periodical. CN. English. ty. $15.00. Canadian Podiatric Sports Medicine Academy, Suite 801/586 Eglinton Avenue East, Toronto Ontario M4P 1P2 Canada. **DD** 617.585. *Newsletter, 0705-6915.*

NEWSLETTER - COMMITTEE TO COMBAT HUNTINGTON'S DISEASE. (NEWS LETTER). No. 1 (Spring 1968)-. 0882-3642. Periodical. US. English. CCHD, West 57th Street/Suite 2016, New York NY 10106. **DD** 616.

NEWSLETTER - HUNTINGTON SOCIETY OF CANADA. (NEWSLETTER). 1-. 0712-2136. Periodical. CN. English. ir. Huntington Society of Canada, PO Box 333, Cambridge Ontario N1R 5T8 Canada. **DD** 616.85106071. *Newsletter (Committee to Combat Huntington's Disease. Ontario Chapter).*

NEWSLETTER - INSTITUTE OF MEDICINE. Dec. 1972-. 0363-4671. Periodical. US. English. bm. $5.00. National Academy of Sciences, 2101 Constitution Avenue NW, Washington DC 20418. **Tel** (202)389-6958. **NLM** W1 NE998JH.

NEWSLETTER - MEDICAL RESEARCH COUNCIL. **Main/Corp** Medical Research Council (Canada). **VFOAT** Actualites - Conseil de Recherches Medicales. V. 1- Oct. 15, 1970-. 0047-6560. Periodical. CN. text in English and French. Medical Research Council of Canada, Jeanne Mance Building, 20th Floor, Ottawa Ontario K1A 0W9 Canada.

NEWSLETTER OF BIOMEDICAL SAFETY & STANDARDS CEASED. **VFOAT** Biomedical Safety & Standards. **VAT** Newsletter of Biomedical Safety and Standards. Began with: V. 1, in 1971-V. 14, No. 12 (Dec. 15, 1984). 0048-0282. Periodical. US. English. mo. $104.00. Quest Publishing Company, 1351 Titan Way, Brea CA 92621. **Tel** (714)738-6400. Ed Allan F Pacela and Bill Bayless. **NLM** W1 NE998P. **CODEN** NBSSB. Index available. bk rev. Covers medical product hazards and recalls, hospital safety, standards activities, and government regulations.

NEWSLETTER ON DENGUE, YELLOW FEVER, AND AEDES AEGYPTI IN THE AMERICAS. V. 5, No. 2- Aug. 1976-. 0378-6781. Periodical. US. English. qt. **LC** RA644.D4. **DD** 614.571097. **NLM** W1 NE998WM. *Dengue Newsletter for the Americas, 0376-818X.*

NEWSLETTER - SPECIAL PROGRAMME FOR RESEARCH AND TRAINING IN TROPICAL DISEASES. (NEWSLETTER). Began with: No. 1 (Sept. 1975). 0253-0163. Periodical. English. ir. **NLM** W1 NE9981E.

NHRC REPORT. **Main/Corp** Naval Health Research Center. **VAT** Naval Health Research Center Report. 0161-1607. US. English. Naval Health Research Center, San Diego CA 95152. **Ind/Abst** Psychol. Abstr. **LC** RC981. **DD** 613.088359. **NLM** W2 A5 N19N. *Abstracts of Completed Research - Naval Health Research Center, 0164-0518.*

NIANBAO - ZHONGGUO YIXUE KEXUEYUAN, ZHONGLIU YANJIUSUO, RITAN YIYUAN. (NIEN PAO). 1978-. 0254-9018. Chinese. an. **NLM** W1 NI376S.

NIEREN- UND HOCKDRUCKKRANKHEITEN. 0300-5224. Periodical. GW. German. bm. $97.00. Dustri Verlag, Dr Karl Feistle, Bahnofstrasse 9 Postfach 49, 8024 Deisenhofen West Germany. **Ind/Abst** Life Sci. Collect., Excerpta Med., Chem. Abstr. **NLM** W1 NI376V. **CODEN** NIHOD9.

NIGERIAN JOURNAL OF MEDICAL SCIENCES. V. 1- Jan./Mar. 1979-. 0331-4316. Periodical. English. qt. **Ind/Abst** Chem. Abstr. **NLM** W1 NI392E. **CODEN** NJMSDJ.

NIGERIAN MEDICAL JOURNAL. V. 1- Jan. 1971-. 0300-1652. Periodical. NR. English. qt. Nigerian Medical Association, PO Box 1108, Lagos Nigeria. **Ind/Abst** Index Med. **NLM** W1 NI41. *Journal of the Nigeria Medical Association, 0300-1652.*

THE NIGERIAN MEDICAL PRACTITIONER. SUPPLEMENT. No. 1 (May 1982)-. 0189-0964. Periodical. English. ir. $8.00. **NLM** W1 NI41H.

NIGMS RESEARCH GRANTS. **Main/Corp** National Institute of General Medical Sciences (U.S.). Data Management Systems Unit. **VFOAT** Research Grants. **VAT** National Institute of General Medical Sciences Research Grants. Began with Sept. 30, 1983, Pt. 1. 8756-6877. US. English. an. Data Management Systems Unit, Financial & Data Management Section, Office of Administrative Management, National Institute of General Medical Sciences NIH, Bethesda MD 20205. **LC** R854.U5. **DD** 610.72073. *Research Grants.*

NIH ALMANAC. See Yearbooks, Almanacs, Directories.

NIH DATA BOOK. (NIH DATA BOOK : BASIC DATA RELATING TO THE NATIONAL INSTITUTES OF HEALTH). **VFOAT** N.I.H. Data Book. **VAT** National Institutes of Health Data Book. 1982-. 8755-4674. US. English. an. Division of Public Information, Office of Communications, National Institutes of Health, 9000 Rockville Pike, Bethesda MD 20205. **DD** 362. **NLM** W2 A N208B. *Basic Data Relating to the National Institutes of Health.*

NIH FACTBOOK : GUIDE TO NATIONAL INSTITUTES OF HEALTH PROGRAMS AND ACTIVITIES. **VAT** National Institutes of Health Factbook. 1- 1976-. US. English. ir. Marquis Whos Who Inc, 200 East Ohio Street, Chicago IL 60611. **Tel** (317)298-5400.

NIH-NIMH INTRAMURAL RESEARCH INDEX. See Indexes/Abstracts.

NIH PEER REVIEW NOTES. **Main/Corp** National Institutes of Health (U.S.). Division of Research Grants. **VFOAT** Peer Review Notes. **VAT** National Institutes of Health Peer Review Notes. Periodical. US. English. ir. National Institutes of Health, Division of Research Grants, Office of Grant Inquiries, Westwood Building Room 455, Bethesda MD 20205.

NIH PUBLIC ADVISORY GROUPS. **Main/Corp** National Institutes of Health (U.S.). Committee Management Staff. **VAT** National Institutes of Health Public Advisory Groups. 0566-8301. Periodical. US. English. sa. Committee Management Office, National Institutes of Health, Building 1 Room 300, Bethesda MD 20205. **LC** RA11. **DD** 353.0077025. **NLM** WA 22 AA1 N13.

NIH PUBLICATIONS LIST. See Bibliographies.

NIH RESEARCH ADVANCES. Series/Titl DHEW Publication. **VAT** National Institutes of Health Research Advances. 1976-. 0164-162X. Periodical. US. English. an. **NLM** W1 N317C. *Research Advances, 0098-6593.*

NIHON HOIGAKU ZASSHI. **VFOAT** The Japanese Journal of Legal Medicine. Began in 1944. 0047-1887. Periodical. JA. Japanese. bm. Japan Publishing Trading Company Ltd, PO Box 5030, Tokyo International, Tokyo 100-31 Japan. **Ind/Abst** Excerpta Med., Index Med., Chem. Abstr. **CODEN** NHOZAX.

NIHON KAGAKU RYOHO GAKKAI SOKAI SHOROKUSHU. Japanese. ir. Nihon Kagaku Ryoho Gakkai, 20-8 Kami Osaki 2-chome, Shinagawa-ku (141) Tokyo Japan. **LC** RM260.

NIHON RAIGAKKAI ZASSHI. (NIPPON RAI GAKKAI ZASSHI). **VFOAT** Japanese Journal of Leprosy. V. 46- Jan./Mar. 1977-. 0386-3980. Periodical. JA. Japanese. qt. $29.37. Japanese Leprosy Association, 2-1 4-Chome Aobacho Higashi, Murayama-Shi Tokyo Japan. **Tel** 0423/91-8211. **Ind/Abst** Excerpta Med., Index Med., Biol. Abstr., Chem. Abstr. **NLM** W1 NI927V. **CODEN** NRGZDW. *Repura, 0024-1008.*

NIHON RINSHO. **VFOAT** Japanese Journal of Clinical, Nippon Rinsho, Japanese Journal of Clinical Medicine. Began 1943. 0047-1852. Periodical. JA. Japanese. mo. Japan Publishing Trading Co Ltd, PO Box 5030 Tokyo International, Tokyo 100-31 Japan. **Ind/Abst** Index Med. **NLM** W1 NI928M. *Chuo Igaku, Gendai No Igaku; Jikken Chiryo; Osaka Iji Shinshi; Rinko; Tenbo to Yakubutsu; Yuseigaku.*

THE NINCDS NEUROMUSCULAR DISORDERS RESEARCH PROGRAM. **Main/Corp** National Institute of Neurological and Communicative Disorders and Stroke. **VAT** National Institute of Neurological and Communicative Disorders and Stroke Neuromuscular Disorders Research Program. Periodical. US. English. an. $0.90. US Department of Health Education and Welfare, Public Health Service, National Institute of Health, Washington DC 20402. *NINCDS Muscular Dystrophy and the Neuromuscular Disorders Research Program, 0161-3057.*

NITA. **Main/Corp** National Intravenous Therapy Association. **VAT** National Intravenous Therapy Association. V. 1- Jan. 1978-. 0160-3930. Periodical. US. English. bm. $35.00. J B Lippincott Company, East Washington Square, Philadelphia PA 19105. **Tel** (215)238-4273. Ed Mary Larkin. **Ind/Abst** Cumul. Index Nurs. Allied Health Lit., Int. Nurs. Index. **NLM** W1 N143. bk rev. adv acc. **Circ** 4,672. I.V. related articles, studies, reports, and reviews for continuing education of professionals in I.V. therapy. Also correspondence and an employment placement service.

NJAOPS JOURNAL (TRENTON, N.J. : 1981). (NJAOPS JOURNAL). **VAT** New Jersey Association of Osteopathic Physicians and Surgeons Journal. Began in 1981. 8756-7024. Periodical. US. English. mo.

NLM CATALOG. SUPPLEMENT. (NLM CATALOG. SUPPLEMENT MICROFORM). **Main/Corp** National Library of Medicine (U.S.). **VAT** National

Library of Medicine Catalog. Supplement. Jun. 1985-. 0883-7538. Periodical. US. English. qt. **NLM** Z 675.M4.

NORTH CAROLINA MEDICAL JOURNAL. V. 1- Jan. 1940-. 0029-2559. Periodical. US. English. mo. **Ind/Abst** CIS Abstr., Life Sci. Collect., Hospit. Lit. Index, Index Med., Cumul. Index Nurs. Allied Health Lit. **LC** R11. **DD** 610.5. **NLM** W1 NO407.

NOTFALL-MEDIZIN. (NOTFALLMEDIZIN). Vol. 1-. 0341-2903. Periodical. GW. German. mo. $38.96. Peri Med Verlag, Vogelherd 35 Postfach 3740, D-8520 Erlangen West Germany. **Tel** 09131/609-1. **Ed** Ahnefeld, Dick, Schuster, and Lemburg. **Ind/Abst** Excerpta Med. **NLM** W1 NO763P. bk rev. adv acc. **Circ** 45,000. (ctrl). First-aid measures in emergency situations and first-aid equipment.

NOTRE HOPITAL. SUPPLEMENT SCIENTIFIQUE. No. 1- Fall 1972-. 0704-013X. Periodical. CN. French. ir. Free. Hotel-Dieu de Montreal, Centre de Documentation, 3840 rue Saint-Urbain, Montreal Quebec H2W 1T8 Canada. **DD** 610.5. (ctrl).

NOUKOGUDE EESTI TERVISHOID. ZDRAVOOKHRNENIE SOVETSKOI ESTONII. **VFOAT** Zdravookhrnenie Sovetskoi Estonii. Began in 1958. Periodical. UR. Estonian (with summaries in Russian). bm. $18.00. Victor Kamkin Inc (78191), 12224 Parklawn Drive, Rockville MD 20852. **Tel** (301)881-5973. **LC** R96.E8. **NLM** W1 NO825.

NOUVELLE PRESSE MEDICALE *CEASED.* (LA NOUVELLE PRESSE MEDICALE). Vol. 1, No. 1 (1 Jan. 1972)- Vol. 11, No. 52 (25 Dec. 1982). 0301-1518. Periodical. FR. French (table of contents and some summaries also in English). wk. **Ind/Abst** Life Sci. Collect., Excerpta Med., Coal Abstr., CIS Abstr., Pestdoc, Ringdoc, Vetdoc, Curr. Contents. **NLM** W1 NO834F. Index published separately - free - automatically sent. *Presse Medicale.*

NOUVELLE REVUE FRANCAISE D'HEMATOLOGIE (BERLIN, GERMANY : 1978). (NOUVELLE REVUE FRANCAISE D'HEMATOLOGIE). Vol. 20, No. 1-. 0029-4810. Periodical. GW. French (English). bm. Springer Verlag-New York Inc, 175-5th Avenue, New York NY 10010. **Tel** (212)460-1500. **Ed** J L Binet and J P Caen. **Ind/Abst** Life Sci. Collect., Excerpta Med., Index Med., Biol. Abstr., Energy Res. Abstr., Chem. Abstr., Sci. Cit. Index, Abr. Ed. **NLM** W1 NO834LB. **CODEN** NRFHA4. International journal of the French Society of Hematology and its study groups; editorials, original articles, and a list of events. Works are submitted to the study group. *Nouvelle Revue Francaise d'Hematologie, Blood Cells.*

NOUVELLES DE LA F M O Q. **Main/Corp** Federation des Medecins Omnipraticiens du Quebec. V. 1- Aug. 1972-. 0318-0530. CN. French. ir. Federation des Medecins Omnipraticiens du Quebec, Bureau 1100, 1440 Ouest rue Ste-Catherine, Montreal Quebec H3G 1R8 Canada. **DD** 610.62714.

NOUVELLES DE LA F M O Q. **Main/Corp** Federation des Medecins Omnipraticiens du Quebec. V. 4- Apr. 1975-. 0318-0549. Periodical. CN. English. ir. Federation of General Practitioners of Quebec, 1440 St Catherine Street/Room 1100, Montreal Quebec H3G 1R8 Canada. **DD** 362.109714. *F M O Q News, 0318-0557.*

NOVA SCOTIA MEDICAL BULLETIN. V. 4- Jan. 1925-. 0029-5094. Periodical. CN. English. bm. $11.61. Medical Society of Nova Scotia, 6080 Young Street/Suite 305, Halifax NS B3K 5L2 Canada. **Tel** (902)453-0205. **Ed** J F O'Connor. **Ind/Abst** Excerpta Med. **NLM** W1 NO921. bk rev. adv acc. **Circ** 2,000. (ctrl). Articles on medicine, all aspects, but mostly geared to the family practictioner. Considered to be the official organ of the Medical Society of Nova Scotia. *Bulletin - Medical Society of Nova Scotia.*

N.P.N. MEDECINE. (NPN MEDECINE). V. 1, No. 1 (Jan./1, 1981)-. 0248-9635. Periodical. French. sm. **Ind/Abst** Excerpta Med. **NLM** W1 NP404. *Medecine, Revue Medicale Inter-Regionale du Nord & de l'Est, 0153-8748.*

NUC COMPACT, COMPACT NEWS IN NUCLEAR MEDICINE. (NUC COMPACT : COMPACT NEWS IN NUCLEAR MEDICINE). **VFOAT** N.U.C. Compact. Began in 1970. 0344-3752. Periodical. GW. English (German). bm. G I T Verlag Ernst Giebler, Alsfelder Strasse 10 Postfach 110572, D-6100 Darmstadt 11 West Germany. **Ind/Abst** Excerpta Med., Chem. Abstr., Energy Res. Abstr. **NLM** W1. **CODEN** CNNMAC.

NUCLEAR MEDICINE ANNUAL. 1980-. 0272-0108. US. English. an. Raven Press, 1140 Avenue of the Americas, New York NY 10036. **Ind/Abst** Biol. Abstr., Chem. Abstr. **LC** R895.A1. **DD** 616.0757. **NLM** W1 NU124M. **CODEN** NMANDX.

NUCLEAR-MEDIZIN. (NUKLEARMEDIZIN). **VFOAT** Nuclear Medicine. V. 15- Feb. 1976-. 0029-5566. Periodical. GW. English (German). bm. FK Schattauer Verlag, Postfach 2945, Lenzhalde 3, D7000 Stuttgart 1 West Germany. **Ind/Abst** Life Sci. Collect., Index Med., Biol. Abstr., Energy Res. Abstr., Excerpta Med., Chem. Abstr. **LC** R895.A1. **DD** 616.0757505. **NLM** W1 NU183. **CODEN** NMIMAX. *Nuclear-Medizin, 0029-5566.*

NYEIBAN NUIHAG HOI JI. (YEBANG UIHAKHOE CHI). **Main/Corp** Taehan Yebank Uihakhoe. **VFOAT** The Korean Journal of Preventive Medicine. Began in 1968. 0254-5985. Periodical. KO. English (Korean). ir. 28 Yong On-dong Chongno-ku, Seoul South Korea. **Ind/Abst** Chem. Abstr. **LC** RA421. **CODEN** YUHCA5.

OBSERVER. (AMERICAN COLLEGE OF PHYSICIANS OBSERVER). **VFOAT** Observer. Vol. 1, No. 1/2 (Jan./Feb. 1981)-. 0279-9529. Periodical. US. English. mo. $12.00. American College of Physicians, 4200 Pine Street, Philadelphia PA 19104. **Ind/Abst** Hospit. Lit. Index. **NLM** W1 AM326R. *Forum on Medicine.*

OCHANOMIZU IGAKU ZASSHI. **VFOAT** The Ochanomizu Medical Journal. Began in 1952. 0472-4674. Periodical. JA. Japanese. qt. Tokyo Ikashika Daigaku, 3 Yushima, Bunkyo-ku Tokyo Japan. **Ind/Abst** Chem. Abstr. **CODEN** OCIZAD. *Ochanomizu Gakkai Shi.*

THE OFFICE LAB LETTER. Vol. 1, No. 1 (May 1986)-. 0887-7882. Periodical. US. English. mo. $88.00. American Health Consultant, 67 Peachtree Park Drive NE, Atlanta GA 30309. **DD** 616.

OFFICIAL DIRECTORY OF REGISTERED DOCTORS OF MEDICINE, MEDICAL CORPORATIONS AND DOCTORS OF CHIROPODY-PODIATRY. *See* Yearbooks, Almanacs, Directories.

THE OHIO STATE MEDICAL JOURNAL. V. 1- July 1905-. 0030-1124. Periodical. US. English. mo. Ohio State Medical Association, 600 South High Street, Columbus OH 43215. **Tel** (614)228-6971. **Ed** Karen S Edwards. **Ind/Abst** Life Sci. Collect., Hospit. Lit. Index, Excerpta Med., Energy Res. Abstr., Biol. Abstr., Chem. Abstr., Nuci. Sci. Abstr., Index Med. **NLM** W1 OH842. **CODEN** 0SMJAT. bk rev. adv acc. **Circ** 19,000. Articles on socio-economic issues facing medicine with emphasis on how they affect Ohio physicians; clinical and scientific articles, organization news, special features, legislative update, second opinion, etc.

OKAJIMAS FOLIA ANATOMICA JAPONICA. Vol. 14, Issue 3- June 1936-. 0030-154X. Periodical. JA. English (German). bm. $93.00. Japan Publishers Trading Company Ltd, PO Box 5030, Tokyo International, Tokyo 100-31 Japan. **Ind/Abst** Life Sci. Collect., Excerpta Med., Index Med., Biol. Abstr., Bibliogr. Agric., Chem. Abstr., Index Med. **NLM** W1 OK102. **CODEN** OFAJAE. (cum index). *Folia Anatomica Japonica.*

OMNIA MEDICA ET THERAPEUTICA. ARCHIVIO. *See* Genealogy and Heraldry - Archives.

ONTARIO CHAPTER BULLETIN *CEASED.* **Main/Corp** Canadian Hemophilia Society. Ontario Chapter. V. 1-15, No. 1. 0045-4923. Periodical. CN. English. bm.

ONTARIO MEDICAL REVIEW. V. 10, No. 3- June 1943-. 0030-302X. Periodical. CN. English. mo. 25.00. Ontario Medical Association, Suite 600/250 Bloor Street East, Toronto Ontario M4W 3P8 Canada. **Tel** (416)963-9383. **Ed** Ronald E Brownridge. **NLM** W1 ON672. adv acc. **Circ** 17,000. (ctrl). Contains articles on health care delivery; medical economics, politics, education; physicians' lifestyles, medico-legal matters.

ONTARIO MEDICAL TECHNOLOGIST. **VFOAT** Technologist. Vol. 1, No. 1 (March 1980)-. 0228-877X. Periodical. CN. English. qt. $8.00. Ontario Medical Technologist, Suite 206/234 Eglinton Avenue East, Toronto Ontario M4P 1K5 Canada. **DD** 610.73705. *Newsletter (Ontario Society of Medical Technologists), 0380-1888.*

ONTARIO MEDICINE. Vol. 1, No. 1 (Nov. 15, 1982)-. 0712-6689. Periodical. CN. English. ir. $45.00. Ontario Medicine, 1425 de la Montagne/Suite 350, Montreal Quebec H3G 2R7 Canada. **DD** 610.9713.

OPM NEWS (LONDON, ENGLAND). (OPM NEWS : OFFSHORE PARA-MEDICINE NEWSLETTER). **VFOAT** Offshore Para-Medicine Newsletter. Periodical. UK. English. mo. **NLM** W1.

OPUSCULA MEDICA. Vol. 1- Jan. 1956-. 0030-414X. Periodical. SW. Swedish. qt. Opuscula Medica, Sodersjukuset, Stockholm 38 Sweden. **Ind/Abst** Excerpta Med., CIS Abstr. **NLM** W1 OP94. **CODEN** OPMEAR.

ORVOSI HETILAP. **VFOAT** OH. V. 1-. 0030-6002. Periodical. HU. Hungarian (some summaries in English, German, and Russian). wk. Akademiai Kiado, POB 24, 1363 Budapest Hungary. **Ind/Abst** Excerpta Med., Index Med. **NLM** W1 OR877.

ORVOSKEPZES. Began with issue for 1911. 0030-6037. Periodical. HU. Hungarian. bm. Akademiai Kiado, POB 24, 1363 Budapest Hungary. **Ind/Abst** Excerpta Med., Biol. Abstr., Energy Res. Abstr. **LC** R91. **NLM** W1 OR881. **CODEN** ORVOAE.

OSAKA IKA DAIGAKU ZASSHI. **VFOAT** The Journal of Osaka Medical College. 0030-6118. Periodical. JA. Japanese. qt. Japan Publications Trading Company Ltd, PO Box 5030/Tokyo International, Tokyo 100-31 Japan. **Ind/Abst** Chem. Abstr. **CODEN** OIDZAU. *Osaka Koto Igaku Senmon Gakko Zasshi.*

OSSA. V. 1- 1974-. 0345-8865. Monographic Series. SW. English (articles in German with summaries in Russian). an. University of Stockholm-Ossa, Professor Gejvall, Gnejsvagen 1, S-310 40 Harplinge Sweden. **Ind/Abst** Biol. Abstr., GeoRef. **NLM** W1 OS548. **CODEN** OIJRD5.

OSTEOPATHIC ANNALS. V. 1- Oct. 1973-. 0092-9336. Periodical. US. English. mo. $32.00. Ronald Park Davis Publishing Co Inc, 139 Harristown Road, Glen Rock NJ 07452. **Ind/Abst** Excerpta Med. **LC** RZ301. **NLM** W1 OS801.

OSTEOPATHIC MEDICINE *CEASED.* Began with V. 1- July 1976-. Ceased with June 1981. 0363-7360. Periodical. US. English. mo. $20.00 US, $30.00 Canada. A Retlaw & Associates, Suite 2080/1633 Orrington Avenue, Evanston IL 60201. **LC** RZ301. **DD** 615.53305. **NLM** W1 OS872.

OUTLOOK (EDUCATIONAL COMMISSION FOR FOREIGN MEDICAL GRADUATES). *See* Education (General) - Higher Education.

OUTREACH. V. 1- March/April 1980-. 0270-207X. US. English. bm. $35.00. American Hospital Association, PO Box 99376, Chicago IL 60693. **Tel** 94258,000. **Ed** Diane M Howard. **NLM** W1 OU56. bk rev. (ctrl). Ambulatory care management issues into homecare hospice PPO's, HMO's ambulatory surgery and emergency services.

OVERVIEW OF BLOOD. 0093-9404. US. English. Blood Information Service, 508 Getzville Road, Buffalo NY 14226. **Ed** C Bishop. **LC** RC633.A1. **DD** 612.1105.

OXFORD MEDICAL SCHOOL GAZETTE. V. 1- 1949-. 0030-7661. Periodical. UK. English. sa. **NLM** W1 OX621. (cum index).

P & S. **VFOAT** P and S. Began with: Vol. 1, No. 1, issued 1981. 0743-507X. Periodical. US. English. Free. P & S Editor, Office of the Dean, College of Physicians and Surgeons, 630 West 168th Street, New York NY 10032. **Tel** (212)305-3900. **Ed** Donald F Tapley. **NLM** W1 P129C. bk rev. **Circ** 19,000. (ctrl). A non-technical news and features publication reporting on scholarly activities, educational policy, and discussion of contemporary issues in medicine. *P&S Alumni Journal.*

THE PACIFIC JOURNAL OF ORIENTIAL MEDICINE. (THE PACIFIC JOURNAL OF ORIENTAL MEDICINE : A PUBLICATION OF THE SAN FRANCISCO COLLEGE OF ACUPUNCTURE & ORIENTAL MEDICINE). **VAT** Pac. J. Orient. Med. Vol. 1, No. 1 (Fall 1984)-. 8756-0321. Periodical. US. English. qt. $20.00, $10.00 Students. San Francisco College of Acupuncture and Oriental Medicine, 2409 19th Avenue at Taraval, San Francisco CA 94116. **DD** 615.

PAFAMS UPDATE. **VAT** Panamerican Federation of Associations of Medical Schools Update. Vol. 1, No. 1 (Apr. 1984)-. 8756-2650. Periodical. US. English. qt. Free. Educational

Medicine

Commission for Foreign Medical Graduates, 2100 Pennsylvania Avenue NW/Suite 738, Washington DC 20037. Tel (202)293-9320. DD 610. Medical education throughout the Americas.

PANMINERVA MEDICA. V. 1- May 1959-. 0031-0808. Periodical. IT. English. qt. $60.00. Lippincott Harper, East Washington Square, Philadephia PA 19105. Tel (215)238-42957. Ed Tomaso Oliaro. Ind/Abst Life Sci. Collect., Biol. Abstr., Chem. Abstr., Nuci. Sci. Abstr., Index Med., Sociol. Abstr., Lang. Lang. Behav. Abstr. NLM W1 PA494. CODEN PMMDAE. A review journal survey which summarizes the entire original articles and abstracts of articles published in European journals.

PAPUA NEW GUINEA MEDICAL JOURNAL. Vol. 14, No. 3 (Sept. 1971)-. Periodical. PP. English. qt. 40.00. Medical Society-Papua New Guinea, Box 60, Goroka EHP Papua New Guinea. Tel 712200. Ed Michael Alpers. Ind/Abst Excerpta Med., Index Med., Biol. Abstr. CODEN PGMJBP. bk rev. adv acc. Circ 400. (ctrl). Articles on health, medicine and human brology in Papua, New Guinea and elsewhere. *Papua and New Guinea Medical Journal.*

PARASITE IMMUNOLOGY. V. 1- Spring 1979-. 0141-9838. Periodical. UK. English. bm. $197.50. Blackwell Scientific Publ Ltd, PO Box 88, Oxford OX2 0EL England. Tel 240201. Ed G A T Targett and Bridget M Ogilvie. Ind/Abst Life Sci. Collect., Excerpta Med., Index Med., Biol. Abstr., Chem. Abstr., Bibliogr. Agric., Sci. Cit. Index, Abr. Ed. NLM W1 PA635U. CODEN PAIMD8. Circ 500. (ctrl). Research on parasite immunology in the general sense, emphasis on how hosts control parasites and the immunopathological reactions in parasitic infections.

PARKINSON NETWORK. Bulletin # 27 (March 1984)-. 0824-7315. Periodical. CN. English. bm. 10.00. Parkinson Foundation of Canada, Suite 232/Manulife Centre, 55 Bloor Street West, Toronto Ontario M4W 1A6 Canada. Tel (416)964-1155. Ed Jacqueline Hampton. DD 616.833006071. Circ 5,500. (ctrl). Facts, theories, and hopes for future cure research. Reports of activities pleas for help either financially or as volunteers. *Bulletin (Parkinson Foundation of Canada), 0711-236X.*

PATH FINDER. Feb. 1978-. 0707-8617. Periodical. CN. English. bm. Free. R A Rockerbie, Editor, Intersociety Council of Laboratory Medicine of Canada, 7755 Jensen Place, Burnaby British Columbia V5A 2A7 Canada. DD 616.0750971.

PATIENT CARE. V. 1- Jan. 1967-. 0031-305X. Periodical. US. English. ir. $45.00. Patient Care Communications, 16 Thorndale Circle, PO Box 1245, Darien CT 06820. Tel (203)655-8951. Ed Clayton Raker Hasser. Ind/Abst Trade Ind. Index, Hospit. Lit. Index, Cumul. Index Nurs. Allied Health Lit. LC R11. DD 610.5. NLM W1 PA963N. adv acc. Circ 114,000. (ctrl). Advice for the primary care physician on the diagnosis and treatment of conditions encountered in office practice.

PATIENT CARE FLOW CHART MANUAL. Main/Corp Patient Care Publications, Inc. Special Publications Group. 0270-1553. US. English. an. Patient Care Publications Inc, Special Publications Group, 16 Thorndal Circle, Darien CT 06820. LC RC59. DD 616. NLM W1 PA963R.

PATIENT EDUCATION AND COUNSELING. Vol. 5, No. 1 (1983)-. 0738-3991. Periodical. US. English. qt. $44.00. Excerpta Medica, PO Box 3085, Princeton NJ 08540. Ind/Abst Hospit. Lit. Index, Excerpta Med., Cumul. Index Nurs. Allied Health Lit. LC R727.4. DD 362.17. NLM W1. *Patient Counselling and Health Education, 0190-2040.*

PATIENT EDUCATION IN THE PRIMARY CARE SETTING. (PATIENT EDUCATION IN THE PRIMARY CARE SETTING : PROCEEDINGS). Began with vol. for 1977. 0736-7813. US. English. an. LC R727.4. DD 610.696.

PATIENT MANAGEMENT. V. 1- June 1972-. 0110-4578. Periodical. English. ir. NLM W1 PA9634. *Medical Equipment.*

PATIENT MANAGEMENT (SEAFORTH, N.S.W.). (PATIENT MANAGEMENT). Vol. 1, No. 1 (June 1977)-. 0314-660X. Periodical. English. mo. $59.03. Adis Press Pty Ltd, Private Bag, Mairangi Bay Auckland New Zealand. Tel 419-1040. Ed Graeme S Avery and Sandra Wilson. NLM W1 PA9632G. bk rev. adv acc. Circ 5,000. (ctrl). Discusses the place and interrelationship of diagnostic, therapeutic and supportive measures in the overall treatment of disease states. Aimed at the general and hospital practitioner.

PATIENTORIENTIERTE ALLGEMEINMEDIZIN. V. 1-. German. ir. NLM W1 PA965H.

THE PEARSON MUSEUM MONOGRAPH SERIES. Ser. No. 81/1-. Monographic Series. US. English. qt. $10.00. Department of Medical Humanities, Southern Illinois University, School of Medicine, PO Box 3926, Springfield IL 62708. Ed Glen W Davidson. NLM W1.

A PECSI ORVOSTUDOMANYI EGYETEM EVKONYVE. 0556-3542. Periodical. Hungarian. ir. NLM W1 PE105.

PENNSYLVANIA MEDICINE. V. 69, No. 3- Mar. 1966-. 0031-4595. Periodical. US. English. mo. $20.00. Pennsylvania Medical Society, 20 Erford Road, Lemoyne PA 17043. Tel (717)763-7151. Ed Mary L Uehlein. Ind/Abst CIS Abstr., Life Sci. Collect., Hospit. Lit. Index, Excerpta Med., Cumul. Index Nurs. Allied Health Lit., Biol. Abstr., Chem. Abstr., Index Med. NLM W1 PE385K. CODEN PNMDAL. adv acc. Circ 17,000. Socioeconomic and political news affecting the practice of medicine in Pennsylvania. *Pennsylvania Medical Journal (1928), 0096-0667.*

PERIODICUM BIOLOGORUM. See Biology.

PERSISTENT PAIN: MODERN METHODS OF TREATMENT. VFOAT Modern Methods of Treatment. V. 1- 1977-. Monographic Series. UK. English. ir. Grune & Stratton, 111 5th Avenue, New York NY 10003. Tel (212)614/3232. Ed S Lipton.

PERSONAL INJURY DESKBOOK. See Law.

PERSONALSITUATIONEN. Main/Corp Svenska Landstingsforbundet. SW. Swedish. ir. Landstingsforbundet, Box 6606, 113 84 Stockholm Sweden. LC RA410.9.S8. DD 331.12516109485.

PERSONS ENROLLED FOR MEDICARE. See Insurance.

PERSPECTIVES IN BIOLOGY AND MEDICINE. See Biology.

PERSPECTIVES IN BIOMECHANICS. Vol. 1, Pt. A-. 0272-6327. US. English. ir. Harwood Academic Publishers, PO Box 786 Cooper Station, New York NY 10276. Ed D N Ghista. NLM W3 PE871AG.

PERSPECTIVES IN LONG-TERM CARE. V. 1- Jan./Feb. 1970-. 0018-4195. Periodical. US. English. bm. NLM W1 PE871AT. *Homemaker-Home Health Aide Bulletin, 0441-1153; Chronic Illness News Letter, 0578-0349.*

PERSPECTIVES IN MEDICINE CEASED. 1-7. 0079-1024. Monographic Series. SZ. English. ir. S Karger, PO Box, CH 4009 Basel Switzerland. Ed L Van der Reis. LC UNC. NLM W1 PE871B.

PERSPECTIVES IN NEPHROLOGY AND HYPERTENSION. V. 1- 1973-. 0092-2900. Periodical. US. English. ir. John Wiley & Sons, 605 Third Avenue, New York NY 10158. Tel (212)692-6034. Ind/Abst Energy Res. Abstr., Index Med. NLM W1 PE871C.

PERSPECTIVES IN VIROLOGY. Main/ Conf Gustav Stern Symposium. V. 1- 1958-. 0072-9086. US. English. ir. Alan R Liss, 41 East 11th Street, New York NY 10003. Tel (212)475-7700. Ed Morris Pollard. Ind/Abst Biol. Abstr., Chem. Abstr., Bibliogr. Agric. LC QR360. DD 616.019. NLM W3 PE58. CODEN PEVIAI. Proceedings of the Gustav Stern Symposium.

PEST MEGYEI ORVOS-GYOGYSZERESZ NAPOK TUDOMANYOS KOZLEMENYEI. 1978-. 0139-4215. Hungarian. an. NLM W3 PE66. *Pest Megyei Orvosi Napok Tudomanyos Kozlemenyei 0200-1225.*

THE PHAROS OF ALPHA OMEGA ALPHA HONOR MEDICAL SOCIETY. (THE PHAROS OF ALPHA OMEGA ALPHA-HONOR MEDICAL SOCIETY). Main/Corp Alpha Omega Alpha. VFOAT Pharos. V. 1- 1938-. 0031-7179. Periodical. US. English. qt. $10.00. Alpha Omega Alpha Honor Medical Society, 515 Middlefield Road, Suite 200, Menlo Park CA 94025. Tel (415)329-0291. Ed Robert J Glaser. Ind/Abst Index Med., Energy Res. Abstr. LC LJ105.A6. DD 378.1985461. NLM W1 PH328. bk rev. Circ 54,000. (ctrl). Non-technical articles relating to medicine.

PHILADELPHIA MEDICINE. V. 37, No. 43- June 13, 1942-. 0031-7306. Periodical. US. English. mo. $10.50. Philadelphia County Medical Society, 2100 Spring Garden Street, Philadelphia PA 19130. Tel (215)564-3059. Ed William Weiss. NLM W1 PH414. adv acc. Circ 4,000. (ctrl). Medical oriented article news and classified ads. *Weekly Roster and Medical Digest, Medical Digest.*

PHILOSOPHY AND MEDICINE. See Philosophy.

PHILSOM/S: PERIODICAL HOLDINGS IN THE LIBRARY OF THE SCHOOL OF MEDICINE BY SUBJECT. See Library and Information Science.

PHYSICAL FITNESS/SPORTS MEDICINE. (PHYSICAL FITNESS/SPORTS MEDICINE : A PUBLICATION OF THE PRESIDENT'S COUNCIL ON PHYSICAL FITNESS AND SPORTS). VFOAT Physical Fitness, Sports Medicine. Began with V. 1, No. 1, Winter 1978. 0163-2582. Periodical. US. English. qt. $6.00 Domestic, $7.50 Foreign. US Government Printing Office, Superintendent of Documents, Washington DC 20402. LC Z6664.6. DD 016.6171027. NLM ZQT 255 P578.

PHYSICAL TECHNIQUES IN MEDICINE. V. 1-. 0162-2528. UK. English. ir. John Wiley & Sons Inc, 605 Third Avenue, New York NY 10158. Ed J T McMullan. NLM W1 PH748.

PHYSICIAN & PATIENT. VFOAT Physican and Patient. Vol. 1, No. 1 (June 1982)-. 0745-0885. Periodical. US. English. $25.00. D & G Publishing Corporation, Box 377, 32 North Cottenet Street, Irvington-on-Hudson NY 10533. Tel (914)591-7100. Ed Leonard H Gross. bk rev. adv acc. Circ 110,000. (ctrl). Foster physician-patient communication and understanding of psychosocial influences on health.

PHYSICIAN AND SPORTSMEDICINE. (THE PHYSICIAN AND SPORTSMEDICINE). VFOAT Sportsmedicine. V. 1- June 1973-. 0091-3847. Periodical. US. English. mo. $39.00. Physician & Sportsmedicine, 4530 West 77th Street, Minneapolis MN 55435. Tel (612)835-3222. Ed Richard H Strauss. Ind/Abst Trade Ind. Index, Excerpta Med., Gen. Sci. Index. LC RC1200. DD 617.1027. NLM W1 PH773M. bk rev. adv acc. Circ 140,000. (ctrl). Scientific articles dealing with all medical aspects of participation in recreational and competitive sports.

PHYSICIAN ASSISTANT. (PHYSICIAN ASSISTANT : THE OFFICIAL JOURNAL OF THE AMERICAN ACADEMY OF PHYSICIAN ASSISTANTS). VFOAT Physician Assistant & Health Practitioner, Physician Assistant and Health Practitioner. Vol. 7, No. 1 (Jan. 1983)-. 8750-7544. Periodical. US. English. mo. $40.00 Domestic, $48.00 Foreign. Physician Assistant, 400 Plaza Drive, Secaucus NJ 07094. Ind/Abst Hospit. Lit. Index, Cumul. Index Nurs. Allied Health Lit. LC R697.P45. DD 610. *Physician Assistant, Health Practitioner, 0197-713X.*

PHYSICIAN ASSISTANT, HEALTH PRACTITIONER. VFOAT Health Practitioner. VAT Physician Assistant and Health Practitioner. V. 3, No. 8-V. 6. 0197-713X. Periodical. US. English. mo. $40.00. P W Communications Inc, 400 Plaza Drive, Secaucus NJ 07094. Tel (201)865-7500. Ed Carol Ann Murphy. Ind/Abst Cumul. Index Nurs. Allied Health Lit. LC R697.P45. DD 610.737. NLM W1 PH774S. adv acc. Circ 16,200. (ctrl). Clinical and practice related information geared to the physician assistant profession. The official jounral of the American Academy of P. A.'s. *Health Practitioner, Physician Assistant, 0192-7310.*

PHYSICIAN CHARACTERISTICS AND DISTRIBUTION IN THE U.S. VAT Physician Characteristics and Distribution in the United States. 1981 Ed.-. 0731-0315. US. English. an. American Medical Association, PO Box 821, Monroe WI 53566. LC RA410.7. DD 331.119161069520973. NLM W1 PH775. *Physician Distribution and Medical Licensure in the U.S., 0364-6610.*

PHYSICIAN EAST. V. 1- Jan. 1979-. 0192-2963. Periodical. US. English. mo. $36.00. Physician East, 60 State Street/Suite 3330, Boston MA 02109. NLM W1 PH776. *Massachusetts Physician, 0025-4851.*

PHYSICIAN MANPOWER FOR MISSOURI. See Economics - Labor.

PHYSICIAN MANPOWER IN OREGON DATA BOOK. See Economics - Labor.

PHYSICIANS' CURRENT PROCEDURAL TERMINOLOGY. (PHYSICIANS' CURRENT PROCEDURAL TERMINOLOGY : CPT). **VFOAT** CPT. 3rd Ed.-. 0276-8283. US. English. ir. American Medical Association, 535 North Dearborn, Chicago IL 60610. **Tel** (312)645-4927. **LC** RB155. **DD** 616.0014. *Current Procedural Terminology, 0590-4129.*

PHYSICIAN'S HANDBOOK. 1st-. 0079-192X. US. English. te. $16.50. Lange Medical Publications, Drawer L, Los Altos CA 94023. **Tel** (415)948-4526. **Ed** Marcus A Krupp, Lawrence M Tierney Jr, Robert L Roe and Carlos A Camargo. **LC** RC55. **DD** 616.075. Describes the most serviceable diagnostic tests and emphasizes anatomic, physiologic, and pharmacologic bases for understanding diagnostic data and therapeutic interventions.

THE PHYSICIAN'S LEGAL ALERT. *See* Law.

PHYSICIAN'S MANAGEMENT. Began in 1961. 0031-9066. Periodical. US. English. mo. $35.00. Harcourt Brace Jovanovich Publishing, 1 East First Street, Duluth MN 55802. **Tel** (218)773-9516. **Ed** Robert A Feigenbaum. **Ind/Abst** Hospit. Lit. Index. **LC** R728. **NLM** W1 PH828. adv acc. **Circ** 110,885. (ctrl). Serves medical and osteopathic physicians, the doctors business journal. *Surgeon's Management.*

PHYSICIAN'S MANAGEMENT MANUALS. Fall 1976-. 0705-6311. Periodical. CN. English. mo. 60.00. Physicians Management Manual, 777 Bay Street, Toronto Ontario M5W 1A7 Canada. **Tel** (416)596-5724. **Ed** Oleu Edur. **DD** 658'.91'610971. adv acc. **Circ** 33,000. (ctrl). Written to serve the practice and financial needs of Canadian physicians. Topics covered include: taxes, personal finance, retirement, law, real estate.

PHYSICIAN'S MARKETING. *See* Business - Marketing.

PHYSICIAN'S WORLD. 0091-200X. Periodical. US. English. mo. $15.00. 400 Madison Avenue, New York NY 10017. **LC** R11. **DD** 610.5. **NLM** W1 PH835.

PHYSIFAX. **Main/Corp** Meducation International. US. English. Meducation International Ltd, Multimedia Communications in Medical Education, Montclair NJ 07042. **LC** RC55. **DD** 616.00202.

PHYSIOLOGICAL CHEMISTRY AND PHYSICS *CEASED.* V. 1-14. 0031-9325. Periodical. US. English. qt. $80.00. Meridional Publications, Rt 2 Box 28A, Wake Forest NC 27587. **Ed** William Negendank. **Ind/Abst** Index Med., Biol. Abstr., Energy Res. Abstr., Chem. Abstr., Bibliogr. Agric., Sci. Cit. Index, Abr. Ed., Int. Aerosp. Abstr. **LC** QP501. **DD** 574.192. **NLM** W1 PH926J. **CODEN** PLCHB4. adv acc. Original research in biophysics, biochemistry and cellular physiology. Basic knowledge to human studies including NMR imaging.

PHYSIOTHERAPY CANADA. **VFOAT** Physiotherapie Canada. V. 24, No. 3- July 1972-. 0300-0508. Periodical. CN. English (text also in French). bm. 25.00 Domestic, 30.00 Foreign. Canadian Physiotherapy Association, 3600 Barclay Avenue/Suite 300, Montreal Quebec J7A 3S6 Canada. **Tel** (514)731-4002. **Ed** Joan Cleather. **Ind/Abst** Hospit. Lit. Index, Excerpta Med., Cumul. Index Nurs. Allied Health Lit., Biol. Abstr. **DD** 615.805. **NLM** W1 PH968. **CODEN** PTHCAZ. bk rev. adv acc. **Circ** 7,140. (ctrl). Articles on research, clinical practice, education and administration relevant to physical rehabilitation. Also book reviews, abstracts, coming events and news reports. *Journal of the Canadian Physiotherapy Association, 0008-4751.*

PLASMA QUARTERLY. *See* Biology.

PLASMA THERAPY. V. 1-V. 1, No. 4. 0196-4267. Periodical. US. English. qt. Haemonetics Research Institute, 400 Wood Road, Braintree MA 02182. **Tel** (617)848-7100. **NLM** W1 PL111T.

PLASMAPHERESIS AND PLASMA EXCHANGE. **Series/Titl** Annual Research Reviews. V. 1-. 0225-4212. CN. English. an. $18.00 Per Number. Eden Press, Suite 10/245 Victoria Avenue, Westmount Quebec H3Z 2M6 Canada. **DD** 615.65.

PLZENSKY LEKARSKY SBORNIK. **VFOAT** Pilezenskii Meditsinskii Sbornik. Began in 1956. 0551-1038. Periodical. CS. Czech (summaries in English and Russian). ir. Charles University Medical Facility, Lidicka 21, Plzen Czechoslovakia.

P.M.B.R. PHYSICIAN'S MEDICAL BOOK REFERENCE. (PMBR, PHYSICIANS'S MEDICAL BOOK REFERENCE). **VFOAT** Physician's Medical Book Reference. 1974-. 0093-2248. US. English. an. $25.95. Medi-Facts Publishing Co, 2337 Lemoine Avenue, Fort Lee NJ 07024. **LC** Z6658. **DD** 016.61. **NLM** ZWB 100 P114.

POLIMERY W MEDYCYNIE. **VFOAT** Polimery V Meditsine, Polymere in der Medizin, Polymers in Medicine. Vol. 1- 1970-. 0370-0747. PL. Multilingual (articles in Polish, English, German, and Russian). ARS Polona, Krakowskie Przedmiescie 7, 00-068 Warsaw Poland. **Ind/Abst** Index Med., Chem. Abstr. **NLM** W1 PO213M. **CODEN** PMYMAX.

POLSKI TYGODNIK LEKARSKI. V. 15- Jan. 1960-. 0032-3756. Periodical. PL. Polish. wk. ARS Polona, Krakowskie Przedmiescie 7, 00-068 Warsaw Poland. **Ind/Abst** Excerpta Med., Index Med., CIS Abstr. **NLM** W1 PO29. *Polski Tygodnik Lekarski I Wiadomosci Lekarskie.*

POLYMERS IN BIOLOGY AND MEDICINE. *See* Biology.

PORTLAND PHYSICIAN. 0032-4930. Periodical. US. English. mo. Multnomah County Medical Society, 2188 SW Park Place, Portland OR 97205. **Tel** (503)222-3326.

POSTGRADUATE DOCTOR. AFRICA. 0142-7946. Periodical. UK. English. mo. 30.00. Barker Publishing Ltd, 539 London Road Barker House, Middlesex TW7 4DA United Kingdom. **Tel** (01)847-1774. **Ed** D Harvey and W Styles. **NLM** W1 PO955H. bk rev. adv acc. **Circ** 9,000. (ctrl). Review articles on clinical medicine in primary care.

POSTGRADUATE DOCTOR. ASIA. **VFOAT** Asia. Vol. 1, No. 1 (Jan. 1981)-. 0144-8455. Periodical. UK. English. mo. Barker Publications Limited, 539 London Road, Barker House, Mddx TW7 4DA United Kingdom. **Tel** (01)847-1774. **NLM** W1 PO955HC.

POSTGRADUATE DOCTOR. MIDDLE EAST EDITION. (POSTGRADUATE DOCTOR. MIDDLE EAST). 0140-7724. Periodical. UK. English. mo. 30.00. Barker Publications Limited, 539 London Road/Barker House, Middlesex TW7 4DA United Kingdom. **Tel** (01)847-1774. **Ed** D Harvey and W Styles. **NLM** W1 PO955HD. bk rev. adv acc. **Circ** 20,000. (ctrl). Review articles on clinical medicine in primary care.

POSTGRADUATE MEDICAL JOURNAL. V. 1- (No. 1-) 1925-. 0032-5473. Periodical. UK. English. mo. $155.00. H Holt MacMillan Journals, Houndmills, Basingstoke Hants RG21 2XS United Kingdom. **Tel** (0256)29242. **Ed** B I Hoffbrand. **Ind/Abst** Life Sci. Collect., Excerpta Med., Pestdoc, Ringdoc, Vetdoc, Biol. Abstr., Chem. Abstr., Nuci. Sci. Abstr., Index Med., Sci. Cit. Index, Abr. Ed. **NLM** W1 PO957H. **CODEN** PGMJAO. bk rev. adv acc. Provides a compendium of current clinical research and practice invaluable to the graduate in training.

POSTGRADUATE MEDICAL JOURNAL. SUPPLEMENT. Monographic Series. UK. English. ir. Lippincott/Harper, 2350 Virginia Avenue, Hagerstown MD 21740. **Ind/Abst** Chem. Abstr.

POSTGRADUATE MEDICINE. V. 1- Jan. 1947-. 0032-5481. Periodical. US. English. $44.00. Postgraduate Medicine, 4530 West 77th Street, Minneapolis MN 55435. **Tel** (612)835-3222. **Ed** Robert B Howard. **Ind/Abst** Life Sci. Collect., Excerpta Med., Cumul. Index Nurs. Allied Health Lit., CIS Abstr., Energy Res. Abstr., Biol. Abstr., Chem. Abstr., Index Med., Nuci. Sci. Abstr., Sci. Cit. Index, Abr. Ed. **LC** R11. **DD** 616.05. **NLM** W1 PO958. **CODEN** POMDAS. bk rev. adv acc. **Circ** 133,000. (ctrl). Journal of applied medicine for the primary care physician.

PRACOVNI LEKARSTVI. V. 1- Zari 1949-. 0032-6291. Periodical. CS. Czech. ir. Artia, PO Box 790, Praha 1 Czechoslovakia. **Ind/Abst** Excerpta Med., Coal Abstr., CIS Abstr., Chem. Abstr. **NLM** W1 PR135. **CODEN** PRLFAG.

PRACTICAL METHODS IN CLINICAL IMMUNOLOGY. (PRACTICAL METHODS IN CLINICAL IMMUNOLOGY SERIES). 1-. 0262-8783. Monographic Series. UK. English. ir. Churchill Livingstone Inc, 19 West 44th Street, New York NY 10036. **Ed** R C Nairn. **LC** UNC. **DD** 616.07905. **NLM** W1 PR142K.

PRACTITIONER. (THE PRACTITIONER). V. 1- July 1868-. 0032-6518. Periodical. UK. English. mo. Morgan Grampian, Royal Sovereign House, 40 Beresford, London SE18 6BQ England. **Tel** (01)854 2200. **Ind/Abst** Cumul. Index Nurs. Allied Health Lit., Excerpta Med., Index Med., Life Sci. Collect., Pestdoc, Ringdoc, Vetdoc, Sci. Cit. Index, Abr. Ed., Abstr. Anthropol. **NLM** W1 PR158. (cum index).

LA PRATIQUE MEDICALE. Began with: 1 (Jan. 8 1982). 0750-6155. Periodical. French. ir. $58.00. **NLM** W1 PR299D. *Psychiatrie du Praticien, 0248-1758; Gynecologie Obstetrique du Praticien; Dermatologie du Praticien, 0248-9686.*

PRAXIS DER ALLGEMEINMEDIZIN. V. 1-. Monographic Series. German. ir. **Ed** D Klaus, D Tetzlaff, and W Vogler. **NLM** W1 PR311.

PRAXIS KURIER, KONGRESS-SYNOPSE AKTUELL : PK. **VFOAT** Praxis Kurier, Kongress Synopse Aktuell. No. 1 (22. June 1983)-. Periodical. GW. German. wk. $30.44. Selecta Verlag, Pasinger Str 8, 8033 Planegg West Germany. **NLM** W1 PR328D.

PRAXIS KURIER. MEDIZIN-REPORT AKTUELL : PK. **VFOAT** PK. No. 1 (29. Feb. 1984)-. Periodical. German. ir. **NLM** W1.

PRAXISHILFEN. No. 1-. German. ir. **NLM** W1.

PRENSA MEDICA ARGENTINA. V. 1- 10 June 1914-. 0032-745X. Periodical. AG. Spanish. ir. $60.00. Prensa Medica Argentina, Junin 845, Buenos Aires Argentina. **Tel** 839796. **Ed** Pablo Lopez. **Ind/Abst** Life Sci. Collect., Excerpta Med., Biol. Abstr., Chem. Abstr., Nuci. Sci. Abstr. **NLM** W1 PR405. **CODEN** PMARAU. bk rev. adv acc. **Circ** 8,000.

PRESSE MEDICALE (PARIS, FRANCE : 1983). (LA PRESSE MEDICALE). V. 12, No. 1 (8 Jan. 1983)-. 0755-4982. Periodical. French (with summaries in French and English). ir. Masson Italia Periodici, Via Pinturicchio 1, 20133 Milano Italy. **Tel** 02/276268-273940. **Ed** Claudio Ortolani. **Ind/Abst** Excerpta Med., Life Sci. Collect., Pestdoc, Ringdoc, Vetdoc, Index Med., CIS Abstr., Energy Res. Abstr., Chem. Abstr. **NLM** W1 PR455. **CODEN** PRMEEM. bk rev. adv acc. **Circ** 40,000. A reference publication for all hospital doctors. *Nouvelle Presse Medicale, 0301-1518.*

PREVENT. V. 1- 1972/73-. 0300-2659. Periodical. UK. English. bm. $28.00. Experts Publishers, (Business Manager Prevent) 124 Upton Lane, London E7 England. **LC** RA421. **DD** 614.44. **NLM** W1 PR493.

PREVENTIVE MEDICINE. V. 1- Mar. 1972-. 0091-7435. Periodical. US. English. bm. Academic Press, 4805 Sand Lake Road, Orlando FL 32819. **Tel** (305)345-4100. **Ind/Abst** Excerpta Med., Life Sci. Collect., Hospit. Lit. Index, Coal Abstr., Energy Res. Abstr., Biol. Abstr., Chem. Abstr., Index Med., Sci. Cit. Index, Abr. Ed. **LC** RA421. **DD** 613. **NLM** W1 PR507K. **CODEN** PVTMA3.

PREVENTIVE MEDICINE. (PREVENTIVE MEDICINE : THE OFFICIAL PUBLICATION OF NORTHWEST ACADEMY OF PREVENTIVE MEDICINE). 0741-0662. Periodical. US. English. mo. $20.00 Domestic, $25.00 Foreign. Northwest Academy of Preventive Medicine, 15615 Bellevue-Redmond Road/Suite E, Bellevue WA 98008.

PREVENTIVE MEDICINE NEWSLETTER. 0199-2481. Periodical. US. English. qt. $20.00. American College of Preventive Medicine, 1015 18th Street NW, Washington DC 20036. **Tel** (202)789-0003. **DD** 610. *Newsletter - American College of Preventive Medicine, 0002-8029.*

PREVENTIVE MEDICINE QUARTERLY. V. 1- Spring 1977-. 0270-9961. Periodical. US. English. qt. Editor DHEC, 2600 Bull Street, Columbia SC 29201. **NLM** W1 PR507W.

PRIMARY CARE. V. 1, No. 1 (Mar. 1974)-. 0095-4543. Periodical. US. English. qt. $40.00. W B Saunders Company, West Washington Square, Philadelphia PA 19105. **Tel** (215)574-3395. **Ed** Karen McFadden. **Ind/Abst** Excerpta Med., Life Sci. Collect., Index Med., Energy Res. Abstr. **LC** R11. **DD** 610.5. **NLM** W1 PR522A. **Circ** 5,000. Practical updates for the clinician on the latest advances plus topics of current interest.

PRIMATES IN MEDICINE. *See* Zoology- Vertebrate and Invertebrate.

PRINCIPLES AND TECHNIQUES OF HUMAN RESEARCH AND THERAPEUTICS. V. 1- 1974-. 0094-9264. Periodical. US. English. ir. Futura Publishing Company Inc, 295 Main Street/POB 298, Mount Kisco NY 10549/0549. **Tel** (914)666-3505. **Ed** F G McMahon. **NLM** W1 PR524E.

Medicine

PRINTOUT. June 1974-. 0316-5582. Periodical. CN. English and French. Health Computer Information Bureau, 274 Friel Street, Ottawa Ontario K1N 7W1 Canada. DD 610.2854.

PRISM. V. 1- Apr. 1973-. 0091-2670. Periodical. US. English. mo. $10.00. American Medical Association, 535 North Dearborn Street, Chicago IL 60610. **Ind/Abst** Public Aff. Inf. Serv. Bull. LC RA418. DD 362.105. NLM W1 PR526E.

PRIVATE PRACTICE. V. 1- Feb. 1969-. 0032-891X. Periodical. US. English. mo. $24.00. Private Practice, PO Box 12489, Oklahoma City OK 73157. Tel (405)943-2318. Ed Brian Sherman. LC R11. DD 610.5. NLM W1 PR532. adv acc. Circ 190,000. Social-economic journal.

PROBLEMS AND PROGRESS IN MEDICAL CARE; ESSAYS ON CURRENT RESEARCH. VFOAT Portfolio for Health. 1st- Ser. Periodical. UK. English. ir. Oxford University Press, 200 Madison Avenue, New York NY 10016. Ed G McLachlan.

PROBLEMY MEDYCYNY WIEKU ROZWOJOWEGO. Vol. 1- 1972-. 0303-2264. Periodical. PL. Polish (summaries in English). sa. ARS Polona, Krakowskie Przedmiescie 7, 00-068 Warsaw Poland. **Ind/Abst** Index Med., Chem. Abstr. NLM W1 PR5806. CODEN PMWRA4.

PROBLEMY SZKOLNICTWA I NAUK MEDYCZNYCH. See Education (General).

PROCEEDINGS, ANNUAL MEETING OF THE MEDICAL SECTION OF THE AMERICAN LIFE INSURANCE ASSOCIATION. See Insurance.

PROCEEDINGS OF THE ADVANCED COMPONENT SEMINAR. Main/Conf Advanced Component Seminar. V. 1- 1972-. 0160-4376. US. English. an. Haemonetics Research Institute Inc, PO Box 186, Cochituate Station, Wayland MA 01778. NLM W3 AD193.

PROCEEDINGS OF THE AMERICAN ASSOCIATION FOR AUTOMOTIVE MEDICINE CONFERENCE. VFOAT Proceedings, American Association for Automotive Medicine. 22d- 1978-. Periodical. US. English. an. American Association Automotive Medicine, #40 2nd Avenue, Arlington Hights IL 60005. Tel (312)640-8440. Ed D F Huelke. NLM W1 PR584l. *Proceedings of the Conference of the American Association for Automotive Medicine.*

PROCEEDINGS OF THE ANNUAL AAMI-FDA CONFERENCE ON MEDICAL DEVICE REGULATION. (PROCEEDINGS OF THE ANNUAL AAMI/FDA CONFERENCE ON MEDICAL DEVICE REGULATION). **Main/Corp** Association for the Advancement of Medical Instrumentation. VAT Proceedings of the Annual Association for the Advancement of Medical Instrumentation-Food and Drug Administration Conference on Medical Device Regulation. 1st- 1974-. 0146-146X. US. English. an. NLM W3 AS759.

PROCEEDINGS OF THE ANNUAL COCCIDIOIDOMYCOSIS STUDY GROUP MEETING. 0191-1856. English. ir. NLM W1 PR584LTG.

PROCEEDINGS OF THE ANNUAL CONFERENCE ON ENGINEERING IN MEDICINE AND BIOLOGY. (PROCEEDINGS OF THE ANNUAL CONFERENCE ON ENGINEERING IN MEDICINE AND BIOLOGY). **Main/Conf** Annual Conference on Engineering in Medicine and Biology Proceedings. 15th- 1962-. 0589-1019. US. English. an. $35.00. Alliance for Engineering in Medicine and Biology, 1101 Connecticut Avenue NW/Suite 700, Washington DC 20036. Tel (202)857-1199. **Ind/Abst** Eng. Index Mon., Eng. Index Bioeng. Abstr., Eng. Index Energy Abstr., Chem. Abstr., Eng. Index Annu., Eng. Index Mon. LC R856. NLM W3 C62. CODEN CEMBAD. Circ 1,000. *Digest of the . . . Annual Conference on Engineering in Medicine and Biology.*

PROCEEDINGS OF THE ANNUAL MEETING OF THE SOCIETY OF PROSPECTIVE MEDICINE. (PROCEEDINGS OF THE . . . ANNUAL MEETING OF THE SOCIETY OF PROSPECTIVE MEDICINE). **Main/Corp** Society of Prospective Medicine., Meeting. 16th (Oct.-Nov. 1, 1980)-. 0276-1483. Periodical. US. English. an. Society of Prospective Medicine, 1101 Connecticut Avenue NW/Suite 700, Washington DC 20036. Tel (202)857-1199. *Proceedings of the Annual Meeting on Prospective Medicine and Health Hazard Appraisal.*

PROCEEDINGS OF THE BIOFEEDBACK SOCIETY OF AMERICAN ANNUAL MEETING. (PROCEEDINGS OF THE BIOFEEDBACK SOCIETY OF AMERICA . . . ANNUAL MEETING). **Main/Conf** Biofeedback Society of America Meeting. 10th (Feb. 23-27, 1979)-13th (Mar. 5-8, 1982.). 0276-2838. US. English. an. $16.00. Biofeedback Research Society, 4301 Owens Street, Wheat Ridge CO 80033. Tel (303)422-8436. Ed Francine Butler. NLM W1 PR5847KB. Circ 1,000. *Proceedings of the Biofeedback Society of America, 0162-5845.*

PROCEEDINGS OF THE EUROPEAN CONGRESS ON SLEEP RESEARCH. (SLEEP : PROCEEDINGS OF THE . . . EUROPEAN CONGRESS ON SLEEP RESEARCH). **Main/Conf** European Congress on Sleep Research. 1st (Oct. 3-6, 1972)-. 0302-5128. Periodical. SZ. English. be. S Karger AG, PO Box 352, White Plains NY 10602. **Ind/Abst** Chem. Abstr. DD 612. NLM W3. CODEN SLEPD5.

PROCEEDINGS OF THE GREENWOOD GENETIC CENTER. Vol. 1 (1982)-. 0733-124X. US. English. ir $15.00. Greenwood Genetic Ceneter, 1 Gregor Merdel Circle, Greenwood SC 29646. Tel (803)223-9411. Ed Robert A Saul. LC RB155. DD 616.04205. NLM W1 PR585IG. Genetic articles and abstracts.

PROCEEDINGS OF THE INTERNATIONAL CONGRESS - INTERNATIONAL SOCIETY FOR THE STUDY OF VULVAR DISEASES. 1st- 1973-. English. ir. NLM W1 PR5852J.

PROCEEDINGS OF THE INTERNATIONAL CONGRESS OF CHEMOTHERAPY. Main/Conf International Congress of Chemotherapy. 3rd-. 0074-3577. US. English. ir. American Society of Microbiology, 19131 Street NW, Washington DC 20006. Tel (202)833-9680. *Proceedings, International Symposium of Chemotherapy.*

PROCEEDINGS OF THE INTERNATIONAL CONGRESS ON MEDICAL RECORDS. Main/Conf International Congress on Medical Records. 1st- 1952-. 0534-9354. UK. English. ir. Canadian Health Records Association, 187 King Street East, Oshawa Ontario L1H 1C3 Canada. Tel (416)728-9743. LC RA976.

PROCEEDINGS OF THE KONINKLIJKE NEDERLANDSE AKADEMIE VAN WETENSCHAPPEN. SERIES C : BIOLOGICAL AND MEDICAL SCIENCES. See Biology.

PROCEEDINGS OF THE NATIONAL HEALTH LAWYERS ASSOCIATION'S HEALTH LAW UPDATE. See Law.

PROCEEDINGS OF THE SAN DIEGO BIOMEDICAL SYMPOSIUM. Main/Conf San Diego Biomedical Symposium. V. 9- 1970-. 0095-5876. US. English. an. $20.00. San Diego Biomedical Symposium, PO Box 965, San Diego CA 92112. LC R856. DD 610.28. NLM W3 SA305.

PROCEEDINGS OF THE SANTA BARBARA MEDICAL FOUNDATION CLINIC. Vol. 1, No. 1-. Periodical. US. English. ir.

PROCEEDINGS OF THE WORLD CONGRESS. Main/Conf World Congress on Fertility and Sterility. 1st- 1953-. 0084-1641. NE. English (Spanish, French, and German). ir. Excerpta Medica, PO Box 1126, 1000 BC Amsterdam The Netherlands. LC RC889. DD 612.6.

PROCEEDINGS - SYMPOSIUM ON COMPUTER APPLICATION IN MEDICAL CARE. See Computers and Computer Science.

PROCOF MEDICAL : ANNUAIRE MEDICAL ET PHARMACEUTIQUE DE FRANCE. See Yearbooks, Almanacs, Directories.

PROFESSIONAL LIABILITY. See Law.

PROFESSIONAL LIABILITY NEWSLETTER. See Insurance.

THE PROFESSIONAL MEDICAL ASSISTANT. V. 1- July/Aug. 1968-. 0033-0140. Periodical. US. English. bm. $12.00. American Association Medical Assistant, 20 North Wacker Drive/Suite 1575, Chicago IL 60606. Tel (312)899-1500. Ed Margaret R Ring. **Ind/Abst** Cumul. Index Nurs. Allied Health Lit. LC R728.8. DD 610.695305. NLM W1 PR59. bk rev. adv acc. Circ 15,000. Articles by and for medical assistants (medical secretaries, clinical assistants technicians) stressing their importance in helping doctors respond successfully to the demands for medical services. *AAMA Bulletin.*

PROFESSIONAL MEMBERSHIP DIRECTORY. See Yearbooks, Almanacs, Directories.

PROFESSIONALS. VFOAT Ambulance, Rescue, Fire and Police. Your Community. 0744-3471. Periodical. US. English. bm. Wisconsin Emergency Medical Technicians Association, 453 5th Street, Random Lake WI 53075. *WEMTA Journal, 0194-519X.*

PROFESSIONS EDUCATION RESEARCHER NOTES. See Education (General) - Theory, Practice of Education.

PROFILE OF MEDICAL PRACTICE. 1978-. 0194-2921. US. English. an. American Medical Association, Order Department, OP 011, PO Box 821, Monroe WI 53566. LC RA410.7. DD 338.43610973. NLM W1 PR623R. *Reference Data on Profile of Medical Practice, 0734-0354.*

PROFILES OF FINANCIAL ASSISTANCE PROGRAMS. 1978-. 0191-197X. US. English. be. NLM WA 22 AA1 P85. *Profiles of Grant Programs, 0094-3088.*

PROGRAM HIGHLIGHTS. Main/Corp National Institutes of Health (U.S.). Division of Research Resources. 1979-. 0278-5374. US. English. an. Free. Office of Science and Health Reports, Division of Research Resources, National Institute of Health, Bethesda MD 20205. Tel (301)496-5545. Ed Edward Post. LC R854.U5. DD 610.72073. NLM W2 A N167P. Circ 12,000. (ctrl). Review of biomedical research performed in research centers supported by the NIH Division of Research Resources.

PROGRES EN HEMATOLOGIE. 1 (Oct. 1980)-. 0246-0149. Monographic Series. French. ir. NLM W1 PR64M.

PROGRESS IN ANATOMY. Vol. 1-. UK. English. Press Syndicate of the University of Cambridge, 32 East 57th Street, New York NY 10022. **Ind/Abst** Biol. Abstr. LC QL801. DD 599.04. NLM W1 PR666FE. CODEN PANTDK.

PROGRESS IN APPLIED MICROCIRCULATION. Vol. 1-. Monographic Series. English. ir. Tel (061)39 08 80. Ed K Messmer and F Hammersen. **Ind/Abst** Chem. Abstr. NLM W1. CODEN MFKLDH. Series that confronts some of the most challenging problems of microcirculation research - and show how their solutions may alter clinical practices.

PROGRESS IN BIOMEDICAL ENGINEERING. See Engineering.

PROGRESS IN CLINICAL MEDICINE. Vol. 1-. UK. English. LC R31. DD 616.005. NLM W1.

PROGRESS IN CRITICAL CARE MEDICINE. Vol. 1-. 0254-623x. Monographic Series. SZ. English. ir. S Karger Ag, 150 5th Avenue, New York NY 10011. Tel 061-39 08 80. Ed W H Massion. NLM W1. Books featured in this series are intended to provide an up-to-date presentation of new knowledge gained from research and clinical experience in the rapidly developing field of critical care medicine.

PROGRESS IN HEMATOLOGY. V. 1- 1956-. 0079-6301. US. English. ir. Grune & Stratton, 111 5th Avenue, New York NY 10003. Tel (212)614-3232. **Ind/Abst** Energy Res. Abstr., Biol. Abstr., Chem. Abstr., Index Med., Nuci. Sci. Abstr., Sci. Cit. Index, Abr. Ed. LC RB145. DD 616.15082. NLM W1 PR67E. CODEN PRHMAH.

PROGRESS IN IMMUNOLOGY. Main/Conf International Congress of Immunology. 1- 1971-. US. English. ir. North-Holland Publishing Company, PO Box 1663 Grand Central Station, New York NY 10163. LC QR1803. DD 574.29. NLM W3 PR947F.

PROGRESS IN MEDICAL VIROLOGY. VFOAT Fortschritte der Medizinischen Virusforschung, Progres en Virologie Medicale, Medical Virology. V. 1- 1958-. 0079-645X. Periodical.

Medicine

US. English. ir. S Karger AG, PO Box 352, White Plains NY 10602. **Tel** 061-39 08 80. **Ed** J L Melnick. **Ind/Abst** Life Sci. Collect., Biol. Abstr., Chem. Abstr., Nucl. Sci. Abstr., Index Med., Bibliogr. Agric., Sci. Cit. Index, Abr. Ed. **NLM** W1 PR6712. **CODEN** PMVIA6. New knowledge arising from virologic research is regularly consolidated and interpreted in this series.

PROGRESS OF DIGESTIVE ENDOSCOPY. V. 1- 1972-. Periodical. Japanese. ir. **NLM** W1 PR687R.

PROGRESS REPORT - STATE UNIVERSITY OF NEW YORK AT BUFFALO. HEALTH SCIENCES LIBRARY. See Library and Information Science.

PROMOTING COMMUNITY HEALTH. 0161-6471. US. English. an. $1.20. Health Services Administration, Bureau of Community Health Services, Rockville MD 20402. **LC** RA445. **DD** 362.1.

PROSTAGLANDINS & THERAPEUTICS. Series/Titl Guidelines to Medical Science Series. **VAT** Prostaglandins and Therapeutics. V. 1- Spring 1975-. 0162-9352. Periodical. US. English. qt. Prostaglandins & Therapeutics, 666 Fifth Avenue/6th Floor, New York NY 10019. **NLM** W1 PR77T.

THE PROSTAGLANDINS : BIBLIOGRAPHY. SUPPLEMENT. See Bibliographies.

PROSTAGLANDINS LEUKOTRIENES AND MEDICINE. (PROSTAGLANDINS, LEUKOTRIENES, AND MEDICINE). Vol. 8, No. 1 (Jan. 1982)-. 0262-1746. Periodical. UK. English. mo. $450.00. Churchill Livingstone, 19 West 44th Street, New York NY 10036. **Ed** D F Horrobin, M Karmazyn, M S Marku, P Sirois and P Borgeat. **Ind/Abst** Life Sci. Collect., Excerpta Med., Index Med., Energy Res. Abstr., Chem. Abstr. **NLM** W1 PR77TM. **CODEN** PLMEDD. adv acc. **Circ** 650. Publishes all types of work on prostaglandins and leukotrienes. Features studies related to clinical medical practice. Publishes a large number of international submissions. *Prostaglandins and Medicine, 0161-4630.*

THE PROSTATE. Vol. 1, No. 1-. 0270-4137. Periodical. US. English. bm. $198.00. Alan R Liss Inc, 41 East 11th Street, New York NY 10003. **Tel** (212)741-2515. **Ind/Abst** Life Sci. Collect., Excerpta Med., Index Med., Biol. Abstr., Chem. Abstr. **LC** RC899. **NLM** W1 PR77V. **CODEN** PRSTDS.

PRZEGLAD EPIDEMIOLOGICZNY. Began publication with V. 1, 1947. 0033-2100. Periodical. PL. Polish (articles have summaries in English or French). qt. ARS Polona, Krakowskie Przedmiescie 7, 00-068 Warsaw Poland. **Ind/Abst** Life Sci. Collect., Excerpta Med., Index Med. **NLM** W1 PR929.

PRZEGLAD LEKARSKI. (PRZEGLAD LEKARSKI : ORGAN TOWARZYSTWA LEKARSKIEGO KRAKOWSKIEGO, ODDZIAU, PTL). Began 1945. 0033-2240. Periodical. Polish (summaries and table of contents also in English and Russian). mo. ARS Polona, Krakowskie Przedmiescie 7, 00-068 Warsaw Poland. **Ind/Abst** Excerpta Med., Index Med., CIS Abstr., Chem. Abstr. **NLM** W1 PR932. **CODEN** PRLKAV.

PSYCHOSOMATIC MEDICINE : PROCEEDINGS OF THE . . . INTERNATIONAL CONGRESS OF THE ACADEMY OF PSYCHOSOMATIC MEDICINE. Main/Conf International Congress of the Academy of Psychosomatic Medicine. Series/Titl International Congress Series. 1st-. English. ir. S Karger, CH-4009 Basel Switzerland.

PUBLICATION - MORRIS FISHBEIN CENTER FOR THE STUDY OF THE HISTORY OF SCIENCE AND MEDICINE. (PUBLICATION). No. 1 (1979)-. 0196-6855. Monographic Series. US. English. an. **LC** UNC. **DD** 509. **NLM** W1 PU679M.

PUBLICATION OF THE HANNAH INSTITUTE FOR THE HISTORY OF MEDICINE. Main/Corp Hannah Institute for the History of Medicine. V. 1- 1979-. 0704-0148. Periodical. CN. English. ir. Free. The Hannah Institute for the History of Medicine, Suite 105/50 Prince Arthur Avenue, Toronto Ontario M5R 1B5 Canada. **DD** 610.5. **NLM** W1 PU69.

PUBLICATIONS IN INDIANA MEDICAL HISTORY. No. 1-. 0743-6017. Monographic Series. US. English. ir. Indiana Historical Society, 315 West Ohio Street, Indianapolis IN 46202. **LC** UNC.

PUBLICATIONS (NATIONAL LIBRARY OF MEDICINE (U.S.)). See Bibliographies.

PUBLICATIONS OF THE SOCIAL INSURANCE INSTITUTION, FINLAND. M. See Insurance.

PUBLIKATIES VAN DE GEZONDHEIDSORGANISATIE T.N.O. SERIE A. ALGEMENE ONDERWERPEN. (PUBLIKATIES VAN DE GEZONDHEIDSORGANISATIE T. N. O. SERIE A : ALGEMENE ONDERWERPEN). **VFOAT** Proceedings of the Organization for Health Research T. N. O. No. 1- 1958-. 0165-7259. Monographic Series. articles mainly in Dutch with some in English. ir. **NLM** W1 PU7393.

PUBLIKATION - INSTITUT FOR SOCIAL MEDICIN, KBENHAVNS UNIVERSITET. (PUBLICATION - INSTITUTE OF SOCIAL MEDICINE, UNIVERSITY OF COPENHAGEN). 5- 1974-. 0105-4139. Monographic Series. DK. Danish. ir. **NLM** W1 PU676. *Publikation - Institut for Social Medicin, Kbenhavns Universitet, 0105-4139.*

PUBLISHED SEARCH BIBLIOGRAPHIES FROM THE NTIS BIBLIOGRAPHIC DATA BASE. HEALTH AND MEDICINE. See Bibliographies.

PUERTO RICO HEALTH SCIENCES JOURNAL. Vol. 1, No. 1 (Mar. 1982)-. 0738-0658. Periodical. English. qt. $15.00. Puerto Rico Health Sciences Journal, Medical Sciences Campus, Office of the Editor, Deanship for Academic Affairs, GPO Box 5067, San Juan PR 00936. **NLM** W1 PU787JR.

PUNJAB MEDICAL JOURNAL. 1- 1951-. 0033-4340. Periodical. II. English. ir. Hindustan Book Agency, 17 UB Jawahar Nagar, New Delhi 7 India.

PUSAN UISAHOE CHI. **VFOAT** The Journal of the Busan Medical Association. Periodical. KO. Korean (with summaries in English). mo. Pusan-si Uisahoe, 2 UI 8 2-ka Kwangbok-dong/Pusan South Korea. **LC** R97.7.K6.

QUALITY ASSURANCE NEWS FOR THE CLINICAL LABORATORY. (QUALITY ASSURANCE NEWS FOR THE CLINICAL LABORATORY : QAN). **VFOAT** Quality Assurance News. Vol. 1, No. 1 (Jan. 1983)-. 0734-5844. Periodical. US. English. mo. $125.00. Scientific Newsletter Inc, PO Box 4546, Anaheim CA 92803. **Tel** (714)497-3522.

QUANTITATIVE APPROACH TO LIFE SCIENCE. V. 1- 1970-. English. ir. Marcel Dekker, Continuation Department, PO Box 11305, Church Street Station, New York NY 10249.

QUARTERLY BIBLIOGRAPHY OF MAJOR TROPICAL DISEASES. See Bibliographies.

QUARTERLY INDEX TO CURRENT CONTENTS. LIFE SCIENCES. See Indexes/Abstracts.

QUARTERLY JOURNAL OF MEDICINE. (THE QUARTERLY JOURNAL OF MEDICINE). V. 1-24, Oct. 1907-July 1931. 0033-5622. Periodical. UK. English. qt. 125.00. Oxford University Press, Journals Department Walton Street, Oxford OX2 6DP England. **Tel** 0865 56767. **Ed** J M Holt. **Ind/Abst** Life Sci. Collect., Excerpta Med., Biol. Abstr., Chem. Abstr., Nucl. Sci. Abstr., Index Med., Sci. Cit. Index, Abr. Ed. **CODEN** QJMEA7. (cum index). adv acc. **Circ** 808. Publishes original work in all fields of both descriptive and scientific angles with emphasis on pathological or physiological clinical medicine.

QUARTERLY LABORATORY NEWSLETTER. No. 1 (Jan. 1981)-. 0711-0073. Periodical. CN. English. qt. Quarterly Laboratory Newsletter, c/o R Haggar, 50 Charleton Avenue East, Hamilton Ontario L8N 1Y4 Canada. **DD** 616.075. *Laboratory Newsletter, 0701-1563.*

QUARTERLY - PHI LAMBDA KAPPA MEDICAL FRATERNITY. (QUARTERLY). **VFOAT** Phi Lambda Kappa Quarterly. **VAT** Phi Lambda Kappa Medical Student's Aid Society Quarterly. Vol. 39, No. 1 (Mar. 1964)-. 0739-2079. Periodical. US. English. qt. Phi Lambda Kappa Medical Fraternity, Bucks County Office Center, 1200 New Rodgers Road/Suite B4A, Bristol PA 19007. **NLM** W1 QU158ML. *Phi Lambda Kappa Quarterly, 0733-4400.*

QUARTERLY/JOURNAL. Main/Corp American Association for Automotive Medicine. V. 1- Jan. 1979-. Periodical. US. English. qt. $20.00. American Association for Automotive Medicine, #40 Second Avenue, Arlington Heights IL 60005. **Tel** (312)640-8440. *Quarterly - American Association for Automotive Medicine, 0197-7725.*

RAD DISPANZERA ZA PLUCNE BOLESTI I TUBERKULOZU. 1973-. 0351-4331. Periodical. Serbo-Croatian -R. ir. **NLM** W2 GS4.1 V8I4R. *Rad Antituberkuloznih Dispanzera, 0485-8506.*

RADAR. V. 1- May, 1973-. 0380-8580. Periodical. CN. French. ir. Centre Hospitalier Bibliotheque Medicale, Harve de Gaspe, Gaspe Quebec G0C 1S0 Canada. **DD** 362.110971479.

RADIATION CARCINOGENESIS. Main/Corp International Cancer Research Data Bank. Series/Titl ICRDB Cancergram. Periodical. US. English. Department of Health Education and Welfare, Public Health Service, National Institutes of Health, National Cancer Institute, Springfield VA 22161.

RADIOASSAY NEWS. V. 1- Aug. 1974-. 0098-0889. Periodical. US. English. mo. $75.00. Scientific Newsletters Inc, 2421 West Broadway, PO Box 4536, Anaheim CA 92803. **Tel** (714)497-3522. **Ed** Imre Fischer. **NLM** W1 RA193. Index published separately - free - automatically sent. bk rev. Latest developments, products, services, highlights of meetings, scientific papers, government regulations, educational materials and books relating to radioassay.

RADIOIMMUNOASSAY SURVEY. 0727-6184. Periodical. English. qt. **NLM** W2 KA8 A93R.

RAPPORT ANNUEL SUR LE FONCTIONNEMENT TECHNIQUE - INSTITUT PASTEUR DU VIET-NAM. Main/Corp Institut Pasteur du Viet-Nam. 0486-8668. Periodical. VM. French. ir. **DD** 616.9. *Rapport Annuel Sur le Fonctionnement Technique de l'Institute Pasteur de Saigon.*

RAPPORT SUR LE FONCTIONNEMENT TECHNIQUE - INSTITUT PASTEUR DE SAIGON. Main/Corp Institut Pasteur de Saigon. 19 -1954. Periodical. VM. French. ir. Institut Pasteur de Saigon, Saigon Vietnam. **LC** Q74. **DD** 616.9.

RASSEGNA MEDICA (ENGLISH ED.). (RASSEGNA MEDICA. MONOGRAPHS). Monographic Series. English. ir. **NLM** W1 RA885EB.

RATE REVIEW TOPICS. V. 1- June 1, 1977-. 0190-5139. Periodical. US. English. sm. $85.00. Miller & Byrne Inc, 1370 Piscard Drive, Rockville MD 20850. **NLM** W1 RA9477.

REACH (CANADIAN DIABETIC ASSOCIATION. B.C. DIVISION). (REACH). 0712-5364. Periodical. CN. English. qt. Free to Members. Canadian Diabetic Association, British Columbia Division, 4480 Main Street, Vancouver British Columbia V5V 3R3 Canada. **DD** 616.462005.

REACTIONS. No. 1 (Jan. 25, 1980)-. 0157-7271. Periodical. US. English. bm. Adis Press, 401 South State Street, Newton PA 18940T. **Tel** (215)860-2000. **NLM** W1 RE1H. Index published separately - free - automatically sent. (cum index). **Circ** 800. Current international reports on adverse drug reactions, interactions, overdose, poisoning, abuse and drug addiction.

READINGS AND PERSPECTIVES IN MEDICINE. Booklet No. 1-. 0737-0822. Monographic Series. US. English. ir. Duke University Medical Center, Medical History Program and the Trent Collection, Durham NC 27710. **NLM** W1 RE103F.

REANIMATION ET MEDECINE D'URGENCE. **VFOAT** Conferenced de Reanimation et de Medecine d'Urgence de l'Hopital Raymond Poincare et de l'Hopital Henri Mondor. 1968-. Periodical. FR. French. Semaine des Hopitaux, 15 rue Saint Benoit, 75278 Paris Cedex 06 France. **Ind/Abst** Chem. Abstr. **NLM** W3 RE288. **CODEN** RMDUA8.

RECENT ADVANCES IN ANAESTHESIA AND ANALGESIA. 0309-2305. UK. English. ir. Longman Inc, 95 Church Street, White Plains NY 10601. **Ed** C L Hewer and R S Atkinson. **Ind/Abst** Chem. Abstr. **NLM** W1 RE105RG. **CODEN** RAAADM.

RECENT ADVANCES IN CLINICAL NEUROLOGY. See Medicine - Neurology.

RECENT ADVANCES IN CLINICAL NUCLEAR MEDICINE. No. 1- 1975-. 0308-2458. Periodical. UK. English. ir. Churchill Livingstone Inc, 1560 Broadway, New York NY 10036.

Medicine

Tel (212)819-5400. Ed W R Greig and F C Gillespie. **Ind/Abst** Chem. Abstr., Index Med. **NLM** W1 RE105TL. **CODEN** RACMDY.

RECENT ADVANCES IN CLINICAL ONCOLOGY. No. 1-. 0261-7013. UK. English. ir. $47.50 Per Number. Churchill Livingstone Inc, 19 West 44th Street, New York NY 10036. Ed C J Williams and J M A Whitehouse. **NLM** W1 RE105TN.

RECENT ADVANCES IN CLINICAL VIROLOGY. Began with: No. 1, published 1977. 0143-6775. UK. English. ir. Churchill Livingston, 1560 Broadway, New York NY 10036. **Tel** (212)819-5400. Ed A P Waterson. **NLM** W1 RE105UC.

RECENT ADVANCES IN NUCLEAR MEDICINE. V. 5-. 0163-6170. Periodical. US. English. ir. Grune & Stratton, 111 5th Avenue, New York NY 10003. **Tel** (212)614-3110. Ed J H Lawrence and T F Budinger. **LC** R895.A1. **DD** 616.075708. **NLM** W1 RE105VK. *Progress in Atomic Medicine, 0085-5189.*

RECENT ADVANCES IN OCCUPATIONAL HEALTH. No. 1-. 0261-1449. Periodical. UK. English. ir. Churchill Livingstone Inc, 19 West 44th Street, New York NY 10036. Ed J C McDonald. **NLM** W1 RE105VNM.

RECENT ADVANCES IN OTORHINOLARYNGOLOGY. See Medicine - Otorhinolaryngology.

RECENT ADVANCES IN ULTRASOUND IN BIOMEDICINE. **Series/Titl** Ultrasound in Biomedicine Series. V. 1-. 0148-2319. US. English. Research Studies Press, PO Box 92, Forest Grove OR 97116. **LC** R857.U48. **DD** 616.0754.

RECENT AND RECOMMENDED MEDICAL BOOKS. **Main/Corp** British Columbia Medical Library Service. **VAT** Selective List for Hospital Libraries. 1979-. 0228-0655. CN. English. an. $3.00. British Columbia Medical Library Service, 1807 West 10th Avenue, Vancouver British Columbia V6J 2A9 Canada. **DD** 016.61. *Recent and Recommended Texts, 0228-0647.*

RECENTI PROGRESSI IN MEDICINA. V. 1- Oct. 1946-. 0034-1193. Periodical. IT. Italian (summaries in English). mo. Il Pensiero Scientifico, Via Panama 48, 00198 Rome Italy. **Tel** 863 633. **Ind/Abst** Excerpta Med., Index Med., Chem. Abstr. **NLM** W1 RE106R. **CODEN** RPMDAN.

RECEPTORS AND LIGANDS IN INTERCELLULAR COMMUNICATION. Vol. 1-. 0742-4108. Monographic Series. US. English. ir. Marcel Dekker Inc, 270 Madison Ave, New York NY 10016. **Tel** (212)696-9000. Ed Bernard Cinader. **Ind/Abst** Chem. Abstr. **NLM** W1 RE107LM. This is an ongoing series. Each title has a different subject.

RECURRING BIBLIOGRAPHY. EDUCATION IN THE ALLIED HEALTH PROFESSIONS. See Bibliographies.

RECURRING BIBLIOGRAPHY OF HYPERTENSION. See Bibliographies.

REFERATIVNYJ ZURNAL - VSESOJUZNYJ INSTITUT NAUCNOJ I TEHNICESKOJ INFORMACII. 53. IMMUNOLOGIJA. ALLERGOLOGIJA. (REFERATIVNYI ZHURNAL. IMMUNOLOGIIA. ALLERGOLOGIIA). **VFOAT** Immunologiia. 1978-. 0202-9030. Periodical. UR. Russian. **NLM** ZQW 4 R332. *Referativnyi Zhurnal. Obshchie Voprosy Patologii.*

REFERENCE LIST OF HEALTH SCIENCE RESEARCH IN CANADA. **VFOAT** Repertoire de Recherches en Sante au Canada. 1969/70-. 0704-3899. CN. English (French), 1977/78-). an. **DD** 610'.7'2071. **NLM** W 22 DC2 R3. *Reference List of Medical Research Projects in Canada, 0527-6535.*

REFLECTIONS (LOS ANGELES, CALIF.). (REFLECTIONS). 0272-1368. Periodical. US. English. bm. Free to Members. c/o Director's Office of the Emergency Medicine Center UCLA Hospitals and Clinics, 10833 le Conte Avenue, Los Angeles CA 90024. **NLM** W1 RE1698M. *Weekly Reader (Los Angeles, Calif.).*

REFRESHER COURSES IN ANESTHESIOLOGY. **VFOAT** ASA Refresher Courses in Anesthesiology. V. 2- 1974-. 0363-471X. Periodical. US. English. an. $15.00. Lippincott/Harper, 2350 Virginia Avenue, Hagerstown MD 21740. Ed S G Hershey. **NLM** W1 RE1717. *Regional Refresher Courses in Anesthesiology, 0093-7401.*

REGAN REPORT ON MEDICAL LAW. See Law.

REGIONAL-ANASTHESIE. (REGIONAL-ANAESTHESIE). **VAT** Regional Anasthesie. V. 1, No. 1, (Jan. 1978)-. 0171-1946. Periodical. German. qt. **Ind/Abst** Excerpta Med., Index Med., Biol. Abstr., Chem. Abstr. **NLM** W1 AN1046 Bd.27 No.1 Etc. **CODEN** REANDL.

REGIONAL ANESTHESIA. V. 1- Oct./Dec. 1976-. 0146-521X. Periodical. US. English. qt. $49.00. J B Lippincott Company, East Washington Square, Philadelphia PA 19105. **Tel** (215)238-4273. Ed Benjamin Coving. **Ind/Abst** Excerpta Med., Chem. Abstr. **LC** RD84. **DD** 617.96405. **NLM** W1 RE173BI. **CODEN** RGANDZ. adv acc. **Circ** 4,988. Original articles, case reports, clinical workshops, and other data for local anesthetics.

REGISTERED PHYSICIANS IN THE STATE OF NEVADA. US. English. **LC** R712.A2. **DD** 614.24. **NLM** W 22 AN2 S7R.

REGULATORY AFFAIRS/M.D. **VAT** Regulatory Affairs Doctor of Medicine, Regulatory Affairs M.D. V. 1- Oct. 1978-. 0192-107X. Periodical. US. English. bm. $22.50. Communications Media for Education Inc, PO Box 712, Princeton Junction NJ 08550. **NLM** QV 32.5 AA1 R3.

REHABILITATION. Vol. 15- 1962-. 0034-3536. Periodical. English (articles in German, or French, with summaries in all three languages). qt. $47.00. Thieme-Stratton Inc, 381 Park Avenue, New York NY 10016. **Tel** (212)683-5088. **Ind/Abst** Excerpta Med., Index Med. **NLM** W1 RE173U. *Internationale Zeitschrift fur Physikalische Medizin und Rehabilitation.*

RENAL PROSTAGLANDINS. **Series/Titl** Annual Research Reviews. V. 1- 1977-. 0706-3539. CN. English. ir. Eden Press, 4626 St Catherine Street West, Montreal Quebec H3Z 1S3 Canada. **Ind/Abst** Chem. Abstr. **DD** 599.044. **NLM** W1 RE198H. **CODEN** RPRODG.

REPORT - INSTITUTE ON HUMAN VALUES IN MEDICINE. See Ethics.

REPORT - MEDICAL RESEARCH COUNCIL. **Main/Corp** Canada. Medical Research Council. **VFOAT** Rapport - Conseil de Recherches Medicales. No. 1- 1966-. Monographic Series. CN. English (text also in French with No 4 1970-). ir. Receiver General for Canada, Supply and Services Canada, Ottawa Ontario K1A 0S9 Canada. **Tel** (819)997-2560. **LC** R854.C3. *Rapport, No. 4, 1970.*

REPORT - NATIONAL COUNCIL ON HEALTH CARE TECHNOLOGY (U.S.). (REPORT). **Main/Corp** National Council on Health Care Technology (U.S.). 0278-6354. US. English. an. National Center for Health Care Technology, 5600 Fishers Lane, Rockville MD 20857. **LC** R854.U5. **DD** 353.00841.

REPORT - NAVAL SUBMARINE MEDICAL RESEARCH LABORATORY. (REPORT). **VFOAT** Naval Submarine Medical Center Report. Began in 1972. 0363-0765. Monographic Series. US. English. ir. **NLM** W2 A5 N3R. **CODEN** XNSRAB. *Report (U.S. Naval Submarine Medical Center), 0730-8515.*

REPORT OF SCIENTIFIC ACTIVITIES. **Main/Corp** Polska Akademia Nauk. Centrum Medycyny Doswiadczalnej I Klinicznej. 1967/71-. PL. Polish (English). ir. Orpan Palace of Culture and Science, Warsaw Poland. **LC** R854.P6.

REPORT OF THE PRESIDENT - MEDICAL RESEARCH COUNCIL. **Main/Corp** Medical Research Council (Canada). **VFOAT** Rapport du President - Conseil de Recherches Medicales. **VAT** Rapport du President - Conseil de Recherches Medicales (Ottawa), MRC Report of the President, Medical Research Council Report of the President, Rapport du President du CRM, Rapport du President du Conseil de Recherches Medicales. 1969/70-. 0384-2029. Periodical. CN. English (French). an. Medical Research Council, Jeanne Mance Building/20th Floor, Ottawa Ontario K1A 0W9 Canada. **Tel** (613)996-8182. *Annual Report, 0384-2215; Annual Review on Support of University Research. Compte Rendu Annuel sur l'Aide Apportee a la Recherche Scientifique dans les Universites, 1970/71, 0384-2010.*

REPORT OF THE PRESIDENT - MEDICAL RESEARCH COUNCIL OF CANADA. **Main/Corp** Medical Research Council of Canada. **VFOAT** Rapport du President. 1969/70-. CN. English (and French in parallel columns). an.

Information Canada, Receiver General Canada/Statistics Publisher Canada, Ottawa Ontario K1A 0T6 Canada.

REPORT ON AMA MEMBERSHIP OPINION POLL. **Main/Corp** American Medical Association. Center for Health Services Research and Development. **VFOAT** Opinions of AMA Members. **VAT** Report on American Medical Association Membership Opinion Poll. 1972-. 0090-1172. US. English. American Medical Association, 535 North Dearborn Street, Chicago IL 60610. **LC** R728. **DD** 301.154336210973. **NLM** W1 OP379H.

REPORT ON AUDIT - STATE OF MONTANA. DEPARTMENT OF PROFESSIONAL AND OCCUPATIONAL LICENSING. BOARD OF MEDICAL DOCTORS. (DEPARTMENT OF PROFESSIONAL AND OCCUPATIONAL LICENSING, BOARD OF MEDICAL DOCTORS). **Main/Corp** Montana. Office of the Legislative Auditor. 0092-2927. US. English. State of Montana, Office of the Legislative Auditor, State Capitol, Helena MT 59601. **LC** RA101. **DD** 353.9786008243.

A REPORT ON RESEARCH IN THE FACULTY OF MEDICINE, UNIVERSITY OF MANITOBA. (A REPORT ON RESEARCH CONDUCTED IN THE FACULTY OF MEDICINE, UNIVERSITY OF MANITOBA). **Main/Corp** University of Manitoba. Faculty of Medicine. **VFOAT** Report on Research in the Faculty of Medicine, University of Manitoba. 1971/72-. 0700-9305. Periodical. CN. English. bm. Faculty of Medicine University of Manitoba, 753 McDermot, Winnipeg Manitoba R3E 0W3 Canada. **DD** 610.72. **NLM** W1 RE212E.

REPORT - SMITH, KLINE AND FRENCH FOUNDATION. **Main/Corp** Smith, Kline and French Foundation. 0583-6506. US. English. an.

REPORT TO THE CONGRESS - LISTER HILL NATIONAL CENTER FOR BIOMEDICAL COMMUNICATIONS. (REPORT TO THE CONGRESS). **Main/Corp** Lister Hill National Center for Biomedical Communications. 0095-0831. US. English. 8600 Rockville Pike, Bethesda MD 20014. **LC** R118. **DD** 610.7.

REPORT - UNIVERSITY OF IBADAN, VIRUS RESEARCH LABORATORY. **VFOAT** Report - Virus Research Laboratory. 8th- 1971/72-. 0331-9849. English. be. **NLM** W1 RE212MN. *University of Ibadan Arbovirus Research Project.*

RESEARCH AND CLINICAL FORUMS. V. 1-. 0143-3083. Periodical. UK. English. ir. MCS Consultants, 33 Vale Road/Turnbridge Wells, Kent TN1 1BP England. **Ind/Abst** Chem. Abstr. **NLM** W3 RE457. **CODEN** RCLFD4. Proceedings of medico-scientific meetings.

RESEARCH AND DEVELOPMENT CONTRACTS. **VFOAT** NIH Research and Development Contracts. 0363-583X. US. English. an. US Department of Health and Human Services, Public Health Service, National Institutes of Health, Building WB/Room 449, Bethesda MD 20205. **LC** R854.U5. **DD** 610.72073. **NLM** WA 22 AA1 R44. *Public Health Service Grants and Awards, 0502-4749.*

RESEARCH AND DEVELOPMENT MONOGRAPH - UNIVERSITY OF NEW SOUTH WALES, CENTRE FOR MEDICAL EDUCATION, RESEARCH AND DEVELOPMENT. (RESEARCH AND DEVELOPMENT MONOGRAPH). 0157-745X. Monographic Series. English. ir. **NLM** W1 RE215BM.

RESEARCH AWARDS INDEX. See Indexes/Abstracts.

RESEARCH IN ACTION. **VFOAT** Actualites-Recherches. No. 1- Nov. 1976-. 0703-9603. CN. English (French). Free. Faculty of Graduate Studies and Research of McGill University, W D Croft Director, Office of Industrial Research, 853 Sherbrooke Street West, Montreal Quebec H3A 2T6 Canada. **DD** 613.620720714281.

RESEARCH IN MOLECULAR BIOLOGY. See Biology.

RESEARCH IN THE SOCIOLOGY OF HEALTH CARE. See Sociology: General Works, Theory.

RESEARCH MONOGRAPHS IN IMMUNOLOGY. Vol. 1-. 0167-6091. Monographic Series. English. ir. Elsevier North-Holland Inc, 52 Vanderbilt Avenue, New York NY

Medicine

10017. **Ind/Abst** Life Sci. Collect., Chem. Abstr. **LC** UNC. **DD** 616.079. **NLM** W1 RE232GS. **CODEN** RMIMDC.

RESEARCH PROGRAMS IN THE MEDICAL SCIENCES. 1st Ed. (1981)-. 0197-0372. US. English. be. Jaques Cattell Press, PO Box 25001, Tempe AZ 85282. **LC** R854.U5. **DD** 610.72073. **NLM** W 22.1 R432.

RESEARCH PUBLICATIONS - WELLCOME UNIT FOR THE HISTORY OF MEDICINE. (RESEARCH PUBLICATIONS OF THE WELLCOME UNIT FOR THE HISTORY OF MEDICINE). **VFOAT** Research Publications. No. 2-. 0143-7984. Monographic Series. UK. English. ir. **NLM** W1 RE233Q. *Research Publications (Wellcome Unit for the History of Medicine).*

RESEARCH REPORT - HEALTH SERVICES MOBILITY STUDY. No.1- 1968-. 0161-942X. Monographic Series. US. English. ir. **NLM** W1 RE234DM.

RESEARCH REPORT - OKLAHOMA MEDICAL RESEARCH FOUNDATION. V. 1- 1977-. 0193-2209. Periodical. US. English. ir. **NLM** W1 RE234G. *Research Reporter.*

RESEARCH RESOURCES REPORTER. Began with V. 1, No. 1, Jan. 1977. 0160-807X. Periodical. US. English. mo. $23.00. Superintendent of Documents, US Government Printing Office, Washington DC 20402. **Tel** (202)783-3238. **NLM** W1 RE234U.

RESIDENT & STAFF PHYSICIAN. (RESIDENT AND STAFF PHYSICIAN). V. 15, No. 7- July 1969-. 0034-5555. Periodical. US. English. mo. $39.00. Romaine Pierson Publishers Inc, 80 Shore Road, Port Washington NY 11050. **Tel** (516)883-6350. Ed Alfred Jay Bollet. **Ind/Abst** Hospit. Lit. Index. **NLM** W1 RE245. bk rev. adv acc. **Circ** 100,000. (ctrl). We are a clinical journal directed toward residents and full-time hospital staff. *Resident Physician.*

RESMEDICA. **VFOAT** Res Medica. Began with: Vol. 1, No. 2 (Aug. 1983). 0738-0496. Periodical. US. English. qt $10.00. Res Medicus Magazine, 505 Doctor's Building, St John's Mercy Medical Center, 615 South New Ballas Road, St Louis MO 63141. **NLM** W1. *Resmedicus.*

REUMATOLOGIA. V. 1, No. 1, (1963)-. 0034-6233. Periodical. PL. Polish (summaries in English and Russian). qt. ARS Polona, Krakowskie Przedmiescie 7, 00-068 Warsaw Poland. **Ind/Abst** Excerpta Med., Biol. Abstr., Chem. Abstr. **NLM** W1 RE251H. **CODEN** RMTOA2. Index in first issue of next volume - loose - separately paged.

REVIEW PAPER - UNIVERSITY OF NEW SOUTH WALES, CENTRE FOR MEDICAL EDUCATION RESEARCH AND DEVELOPMENT. (REVIEW PAPER). 1979, 1-. 0157-9347. Monographic Series. English. ir. **NLM** W1 RE257CC.

REVIEWS OF HEMATOLOGY. Vol. 1-. 0272-507X. Monographic Series. US. English. an. PJD Publications, PO Box 966, Westbury NY 11590. **Tel** (516)626-0650. Ed Julian L Ambrus. **Ind/Abst** Chem. Abstr. **NLM** W1. **CODEN** REHEDT.

REVIEWS OF MAGNETIC RESONANCE IN MEDICINE. 0883-8291. Periodical. US. English. sa. Pergamon Press, Fairview Park, Maxwell House, Elmsford NY 10523.

REVIEWS OF RESEARCH FOR PRACTITIONERS AND PARENTS. No. 1-. US. English. ir. Institute for Child Development, University of Minnesota, Center for Early Education, Minneapolis MN 55455. **Tel** (612)376-3229.

REVISTA BRASILEIRA DE CLINICA E TERAPEUTICA. (CLINICA E TERAPEUTICA). **VFOAT** Revista Brasileira de Clinica e Terapeutica. Yearly V. 6- Jan. 1977-. 0100-3232. Periodical. Portuguese. mo. **Ind/Abst** Excerpta Med., Chem. Abstr. **NLM** W1 CL367T. **CODEN** CLTRDC. *Revista Brasileira de Clinica e Terapeurica.*

REVISTA BRASILEIRA DE MALARIOLOGIA E DOENCAS TROPICAIS. V. 1- Jan. 1949-. 0034-7256. Periodical. Portuguese (summaries in English). qt. S U C A M Esplan Ministerios, Bloco G, 2000 Rio de Janeiro Brazil. **Ind/Abst** Index Med.

REVISTA BRASILEIRA DE MEDICINA. V. 1- Jan. 1944-. 0034-7264. Periodical. BL. Portuguese (summaries in English). mo. $120.00. Revista Brasileira de Medicina, Rua Pinheiros 504, 01000 Sao Paulo Brazil. **Tel** 881-3422. Ed Americo Moreira Jr. **Ind/Abst** Life Sci. Collect., Excerpta Med., Chem. Abstr., Sci. Cit. Index, Abr. Ed. **NLM** W1 RE3429. **CODEN** RBMEAU. adv acc. **Circ** 25,000. (ctrl). Scientific articles.

REVISTA BRASILEIRA DE PESQUISAS MEDICAS E BIOLOGICAS *CEASED.* **VFOAT** Brazilian Journal of Medical and Biological Research. Began with: Vol. 1 (Jan./Feb. 1968). 0034-7310. Periodical. Portuguese (English). ir. **LC** R850.A1. **NLM** W1 RE345F.

REVISTA CLINICA ESPANOLA. Began with V. 1, July 1940. 0014-2565. Periodical. SP. Spanish (most articles summarized in English, French, and German). sm. $60.00. Idepsa, Principe de Bergara 112 1 G, 28002 Madrid Spain. Ed E Lopez Garcia. **Ind/Abst** Life Sci. Collect., Excerpta Med., Index Med., CIS Abstr., Chem. Abstr. **NLM** W1 RE355F. **CODEN** RCESA5. bk rev. adv acc. **Circ** 6,000.

REVISTA COSTARRICENSE DE CIENCIAS MEDICAS. Vol. 1, No. 1 (June 1980)-. 0253-2948. Spanish. sa. $15.00. Caja Costarricense Seguro Socl, Apartado 10105, San Jose Costa Rica. **Tel** (516)216193. Ed Jessie Orlich. **Ind/Abst** Excerpta Med. **NLM** W1 RE359BL. bk rev. adv acc. **Circ** 2,500. Covers all medical subjects, especially clinical applications and laboratory practice and research. General essays may be accepted if applicable to clinical practice.

REVISTA CUBANA DE MEDICINA. V. 1-. 0034-7523. Periodical. CU. Spanish. bm. Empresa Ediciones Cubanas, Sub-Direccion Exportacion Oreilly, 407 Ciudad, Havana Cuba. **Ind/Abst** Life Sci. Collect., Excerpta Med., Chem. Abstr. **NLM** W1 RE362. **CODEN** RCBMA6.

REVISTA CUBANA DE MEDICINA TROPICAL. V. 18, No. 1 (August 1966)-. Periodical. CU. Spanish. ir. $12.38. Empresa Ediciones Cubanas, Sub-Direccion Exportacion Oreilly, 407 Ciudad, Havana Cuba. **Ind/Abst** Index Med., Biol. Abstr., Chem. Abstr. **NLM** W1 RE362L. **CODEN** RCMTBF. *Revista Kuba de Medicina Tropical y Parasitologia.*

REVISTA DE BIOLOGIA Y MEDICINA NUCLEAR. Periodical. AG. Multilingual (English and Spanish Portuguese). ty. Revista de Biologia y Medicina Nuclear, Casilla de Correo No 13 Suc, 53 Buenos Aires Argentina. **LC** R895.A1.

REVISTA DE LA ASOCIACION MEDICA ARGENTINA. **Main/Corp** Asociacion Medica Argentina. V. 23, No. 130- 1915-. 0004-4830. Periodical. AG. Spanish. bm. $60.00. Premsa Medica Argentina, Junin 845, 1113 Buenos Aires Argentina. *Revista.*

REVISTA DE LA FACULTAD DE CIENCIAS MEDICAS DE CORDOBA. Yearly V. 12- 1954-. 0014-6722. Periodical. Spanish. ir. **NLM** W1 RE408. *Revista de la Facultad de Ciencias Medicas de la Universidad Nacional de Cordoba.*

REVISTA DE LA SANIDAD DE LAS FUERZAS POLICIALES. V. 41, No. 1 (Jan./June 1980)-. 0254-3435. Periodical. PE. Spanish. ir. $30.00. F Raul Jeri, Apartment 5281, Lima 100 Peru. **Tel** 412410. Ed F Raul Jeri. **Ind/Abst** Energy Res. Abstr. **NLM** W1 RE41S. bk rev. adv acc. **Circ** 4,000. (ctrl). Original articles in areas of health and military medicine, pharmacy, dentistry, nursing, special and review articles. *Revista de la Sanidad del Ministerio del Interior, 0379-3907.*

REVISTA DE SANIDAD MILITAR. Spanish. ir. Escuela de Aplicacion de Sanidad Militar, Camino de los Ingenieros 6, 19 Madrid Spain. **LC** RC970. **NLM** W1 RE496D. *Medicina y Cirugia de Guerra.*

REVISTA DEL VIERNES MEDICO. **Main/Corp** Viernes Medico. V. 1, No. 1-. Periodical. Spanish. ir.

REVISTA DO HOSPITAL DAS CLINICAS. **VFOAT** HC. V. 1- Jan. 1946-. 0041-8781. Periodical. BL. Portuguese. bm. $45.00. Revista do Hospital das Clinicas, Caixa Postal 8091, Sao Paulo Brazil. **Tel** 0055-011-282-2811. **Ind/Abst** Life Sci. Collect., Excerpta Med., Index Med., Biol. Abstr., Chem. Abstr. **NLM** W1 RE52. **CODEN** RHCFAP. adv acc. **Circ** 6,000. (ctrl). Medicine in general.

REVISTA DO INSTITUTO DE MEDICINA TROPICAL DE SAO PAULO. (REVISTA). **Main/Corp** Instituto de Medicina Tropical de Sao Paulo. 1- 1959-. 0036-4665. Periodical. BL. Portuguese. bm. Inst Medicina Tropical Sao Paulo, Caixa Postal 2921, Sao Paulo 01000 Brazil. **Tel** 143 853-6011. **Ind/Abst** Life Sci. Collect., Excerpta Med., Index Med., Chem. Abstr. **NLM** W1 RE521H. **CODEN** RMTSAE.

REVISTA ECUATORIANA DE HIGIENE Y MEDICINA TROPICAL. Yearly V. 1-. 0048-7775. Periodical. EC. Spanish. ir. Instituto Nacional de Higiene, Casilla de Correos No 3961, Guayaquil Ecuador.

REVISTA ECUATORIANA DE MEDICINA Y CIENCIAS BIOLOGICAS. V. 1, No. 1-. 0034-9313. Periodical. EC. Spanish (contains English summaries). ir. Ctr Nac Documentos Contoficos, Casa de la Cultura Ecatoriana, Quito Ecuador. **Ind/Abst** CIS Abstr. **NLM** W1 RE524M.

REVISTA ESPANOLA DE ANESTESIOLOGIA Y REANIMACION. 0034-9356. Periodical. SP. Spanish. bm. $20.00. Ediciones Doyma SA, Traversera de Gracia 17-21, 08021 Barcelona Spain. **Ind/Abst** Excerpta Med., Index Med., Chem. Abstr. **NLM** W1 RE527. **CODEN** REANBJ. *Revista Espanola de Anesthsiologia.*

REVISTA ESPANOLA DE REUMATISMO Y ENFERMEDADES OSTEOARTICULARES. Began June 1945. 0048-7791. Periodical. SP. Spanish. qt. $17.00. Editorial EC0, Cruz 44, Barcelona 34 Spain. **Ind/Abst** Life Sci. Collect., Excerpta Med., CIS Abstr.

REVISTA MEDICA. V. 1- Jan./April 1977-. 0482-6760. Periodical. Spanish. ir. **NLM** W1 RE606GD.

REVISTA MEDICA DE COSTA RICA. Began publication Oct. 1933. 0034-9909. Periodical. CR. Spanish. qt. Revista Medica de Costa Rica, Apartado 978, San Jose Costa Rica. **NLM** W1 RE617G.

REVISTA MEDICA DE PANAMA. V. 1- Jan./April 1976-. 0379-1629. Periodical. PN. Spanish. Academia Panamena Medicina Cir, Apartado 1815, Panama 1. **Ind/Abst** Index Med. **NLM** W1 RE612M. *Revista Medica de Panama.*

REVISTA MEDICA DE VALPARAISO. **VAT** RMV. V. 1- Feb. 1948-. Periodical. Spanish. ir. **NLM** W1 RE6284.

REVISTA MEDICA DEL HOSPITAL COLONIA. 0018-5604. Periodical. Spanish. bm. Avenida Ejercito Nacional, No 884-201, Mexico 5 DF Mexico. **NLM** W1 RE631D.

REVISTA MEDICA DO ESTADO DO RIO DE JANEIRO. **VFOAT** RM. Revista Medica do Estado do Rio de Janeiro. V. 1- Jan./April 1977-. 0100-0195. Periodical. Portuguese. bm. **Ind/Abst** Excerpta Med. **NLM** W1 RE635U. *RM. Revista Medica do Estado do Rio de Janeiro, 0100-0195.*

REVISTA MEDICO-CHIRURGICALA A SOCIETATII DE MEDICI SI NATURALISTI DIN IASI. *See* Medicine - Surgery.

REVISTA PARAENSE DE MEDICINA. Yearly V. 1, No. 1 (Jan./July 1979)-. 0101-5907. Periodical. Portuguese. sa. **NLM** W1 RE712B.

REVISTA PAULISTA DE HOSPITAIS. 0048-7864. Periodical. BL. Portuguese. mo. $70.00. Association Paulista de Medicina, CX Postal 2103, Sao Paulo SP Brasil. **Tel** 37-4581/5. **Ind/Abst** Excerpta Med. **NLM** W1 RE7125. adv acc. **Circ** 20,000. (ctrl). General medicine.

REVMATOLOGIIA (MOSCOW, R.S.F.S.R.). (REVMATOLOGIIA). 1'83-. UR. Russian. qt. **Ind/Abst** Index Med. **NLM** W1 RE74K. *Voprosy Revmatizma.*

REVUE BELGE D'ACUPUNCTURE. **VFOAT** Belgisch Tijdschrift der Akupunktuur. No 1- March 1978-. 0250-488X. Periodical. French (articles in Dutch). qt. $22.00. Association Belge Medecins Acupuncture, Av de 1 Yser 10, 1040 Brussels Belgium. **NLM** W1 RE741L.

Medicine

REVUE DE L'ATHEROSCLEROSE. V. 1-7. Periodical. FR. French. ir. J B Bailliere et Fils, 10 rue Thenard, 75005 Paris France. **Ind/Abst** Index Med. **NLM** W1 RE785. *Revue de l'Atherosclerose et des Arteriopathies Peripheriques, 0556-7459.*

REVUE DE MEDECINE DE TOULOUSE. 0556-753X. Periodical. FR. French. sm. Revue de Medecine de Toulouse, 37 Allees Jules Guesde, Toulouse 31 France. **Ind/Abst** Life Sci. Collect., Excerpta Med., Chem. Abstr., Sci. Cit. Index, Abr. Ed. **NLM** W1 RE794M. **CODEN** RMDTA5.

REVUE D'HISTOIRE DE LA MEDECINE HEBRAIQUE. VFOAT Ketav-at Lahakirat Toledot Ha-Refuah Ha-Ivrit. Yearly V. 1- (No. 1-). 0035-2330. Periodical. FR. French (summaries in Hebrew). qt. $11.31. 177 BD Malesherbes, Paris 17E France. **Tel** 227 97 11. **Ed** Simon Isidore. (cum index). bk rev. History of Hebrew medicine, medical ethic.

REVUE DU PRACTICIEN. (LA REVUE DU PRACTICIEN). V. 1- Oct. 1951-. 0035-2640. Periodical. FR. French. $113.09. J B Bailliere et Fils Edit, 10 rue Thenard, 75005 Paris France. **Ind/Abst** Excerpta Med., CIS Abstr., Energy Res. Abstr. **NLM** W1 RE8391. *Journal des Practiciens, Paris Medical.*

REVUE FRANCAISE DE TRANSFUSION ET IMMUNOHEMATOLOGIE. (REVUE FRANCAISE DE TRANSFUSION ET IMMUNO-HEMATOLOGIE). Vol. 18- March 1975-. 0338-4535. Periodical. FR. French. sa. $65.19. Librarie Arnette, 2 rue Casimir Dalavigne, Paris 6E France. **Ind/Abst** Life Sci. Collect., Excerpta Med., Index Med., Biol. Abstr., Chem. Abstr., Hospit. Lit. Index, Sci. Cit. Index, Abr. Ed. **NLM** W1 RE848E. **CODEN** RFTID6. *Revue Francaise de Transfusion, 0035-2977.*

REVUE INTERNATIONALE DES SERVICES DE SANTE DES ARMEES DE TERRE, DE MER ET DE L'AIR. VFOAT International Review of the Army, Navy, and Air Force Medical Services. 31.-Year. 0035-3469. Periodical. BE. French (English). mo. $37.05. Comite International Medicine-Pharmacie Militaires, rue St Laurent 79, B-4000 Leige Belgium. **Tel** (41)22 21 83. **Ed M** Cools. **Ind/Abst** Life Sci. Collect., Biol. Abstr. **NLM** W1 RE895I. **CODEN** RSSAAV. bk rev. adv acc. Circ 2,000. (ctrl). All matters interesting the armed forces medical service.

REVUE INTERNATIONALE D'OCEANOGRAPHIE MEDICALE. VFOAT R.I.O.M. V. 1-. 0035-3493. Periodical. FR. French (French or English). qt. $37.25. Centre Etudes Recherch Biologi, 1 Avenue Jean Lorrain, 06300 Nice France. **Tel** 89.32.92/89.72.49. **Ind/Abst** Life Sci. Collect., Excerpta Med., GeoRef, Biol. Abstr., Energy Res. Abstr., Chem. Abstr., Bibliogr. Index Geol., Ocean. Abstr., Pollut. Abstr. Indexes. **LC** RA600. **NLM** W1 RE898T. *Cahiers du C.E.R.B.O.M.*

REVUE INTERNATIONALE DU TRACHOME ET DE PATHOLOGIE OCULAIRE TROPICALE ET SUBTROPICALE ET DE SANTE PUBLIQUE : ORGANE DE LA LIGUE CONTRE LE TRACHOME AVEC LA COLLABORATION DE L'INTERNATIONAL ORGANIZATION AGAINST TRACHOMA ET DES ORGANISATIONS NATIONALES ET INTERNATIONALES DE SANTE PUBLIQUE. 58th Year, New Ser., No. 1-2-. 0249-7026. FR. French (English). ir. Laboratoires H Faure, BP 131, 07104 Annonay France. **Ind/Abst** Index Med., Excerpta Med. **NLM** W1 RE899LA. *Revue Internationale du Trachome et de Pathologie Oculaire Tropicale et Subtropicale, 0249-7026.*

REVUE MAROCAINE DE MEDECINE ET SANTE. VFOAT Tibb Wa-Al-Sihhah. 1- 1979-. 0251-0758. Periodical. French. qt. **Ind/Abst** Life Sci. Collect., Excerpta Med., Chem. Abstr. **NLM** W1 RE902L. **CODEN** RMMSDG.

REVUE MEDICALE DE BRUXELLES. 0035-3639. Periodical. BE. French. ir. ULB-FAC Medecine Bureau Info Medicale, 2 rue Evers, 1000 Bruxelles Belgium. **Tel** 02/539.23.12. **Ind/Abst** Excerpta Med., Index Med. **NLM** W1 RE907Z. bk rev. adv acc. Covers original or review articles for postgraduate and general practitioners.

REVUE MEDICALE DE LA SUISSE ROMANDE. V. 1- Jan. 1881-. 0035-3655. Periodical. SZ. French. mo. $44.53. Societe Medicale de la Suisse, 2 Bellefontaine, CH-1003 Lausanne Switzerland. **Tel** 21 20 32 51. **Ind/Abst** Life Sci. Collect., Excerpta Med., Index Med., CIS Abstr. **NLM** W1 RE907S. adv acc. Circ 3,800. Medical journal of the Medical Society of Switzerland. *Bulletin de la Societe Medicale Romande.*

REVUE MEDICALE DE LIEGE. V. 1- July 1946-. 0370-629X. Periodical. BE. French. sm. $35.57. University de Liege, Institut de Medicine rue Alex, Bouvy 13, B-4000 Liege Belgium. **Tel** 041 437572. **Ind/Abst** Life Sci. Collect., Excerpta Med., Index Med., Biol. Abstr., CIS Abstr., Chem. Abstr. **NLM** W1 RE9087. **CODEN** RMLIAC.

REVUE MEDITERRANEENNE DES SCIENCES MEDICALES CEASED. V. 1, No. 1-V. 5, No. 6. 0397-1724. Periodical. French. ir. **NLM** W1 RE937L. *Journal de Medecine de Montpellier, 0021-7891; Marseille Medical; Nice Medical.*

REVUE ROUMAINE DE MEDECINE. VIROLOGIE. VFOAT Virologie, Romanian Journal of Medicine. Virology. Periodical. RM. Romanian (English, French, or German). qt. Ilexim Press Department, PO Box 1-136-1-137, Bucharest Romania. **Ind/Abst** Index Med. *Revue Roumaine de Virologie.*

RHODE ISLAND MEDICAL JOURNAL. V. 59- Jan. 1976-. 0363-7913. Periodical. US. English. mo. $15.00. Rhode Island Medical Journal, 106 Francis Street, Providence RI 02903. **Ed** Wendy J Smith. **Ind/Abst** Life Sci. Collect., Hospit. Lit. Index, Index Med., Cumul. Index Nurs. Allied Health Lit., Energy Res. Abstr. **NLM** W1 RH48B. bk rev. adv acc. Circ 1,575. Medical journal, clinical papers, case reports, newsletter editorials, and annual index. *R.I. Medical Journal, 0360-067X.*

RHUMATOLOGIE (CENTRE D'ETUDES DES MALADIES RHUMATISMALES D'AIX-LES-BAINS). (RHUMATOLOGIE). Began publication in 1949. 0249-7581. Periodical. FR. French. ir. $46.57. Publ Periodiques Specialisees, 11 rue d'Algerie, 69001 Lyon France. **Tel** 28-82-25. **Ind/Abst** Excerpta Med., CIS Abstr.

RICERCA IN CLINICA E IN LABORATORIO. (LA RICERCA IN CLINICA E IN LABORATORIO). VFOAT Research in Clinic and Laboratory. V. 1- 1971-. 0390-5748. Periodical. IT. Vols. for 1971-74 in English and Italian. qt. Casa Editrice il Ponte SRL, Piazzale Stefano Turr 5, 20149 Milano Italy. **Ind/Abst** Life Sci. Collect., Biol. Abstr., Bull. Signal., Chem. Abstr., Excerpta Med., Index Med., Ref. Z., Sci. Cit. Index, Abr. Ed. **NLM** W1 RI101T. **CODEN** RCLADN.

RINSHO TO KAIBO SEMINA. VFOAT Readings on Advanced Functional Anatomy Seminar. V. 1 (July/Sept. 1983)-. Japanese. ir. **Ed** Hoshino Kazumasa. **NLM** W3 RI195L.

THE RISK MANAGEMENT REPORT, MEDICAL RECORDS. VFOAT Medical Records. Vol. 1, No. 1 (Apr. 1983)-. 0273-3617. Periodical. US. English. bm. $125.00. Cox Publications, PO Box 958, El Cerrito CA 94530. **Tel** (415)527-2552. **Ed** Meridith B Cox. Legal liability involving medical records and ways to reduce liability risks.

RIVISTA DEGLI INFORTUNI E DELLE MALATTIE PROFESSIONALI. Began 1941. 0035-5836. Periodical. IT. Italian. bm. $13.37. Rivista Degli Infortuni e Delle Malattie Professionali, Via IV Novembre 144, 00187 Roma Italy. **Ind/Abst** CIS Abstr. **NLM** W1 RI349. *Rassegna Della Providenza Sociale.*

ROCK CARLING FELLOWSHIP. 1964?-. Monographic Series. UK. English. an.

ROLLCALL. Series/Titl Report R (University of British Columbia. Division of Health Services Research and Development). 1974-. 0707-3542. CN. English. ir. $5.00. Office of the Coordinator Division of Health Services Research and Development, Health Sciences Centre University of British Columbia, Vancouver British Columbia V6T 1W5 Canada. **DD** 610.6909711.

ROMANIAN MEDICAL REVIEW. V. 9, No. 2- 1966-. 0048-8585. Periodical. English (Romanian). qt. Medical Publishing House, 7 Aristide Briand Street, Bucharest Romania. **Ind/Abst** Life Sci. Collect. **NLM** W1 RO329. *Rumanian Medical Review.*

ROSTER - CANADIAN SOCIETY OF LABORATORY TECHNOLOGISTS CEASED. **Main/Corp** Canadian Society of Laboratory Technologists. Began with 1952 issue? Ceased in 1982. 0318-1561. CN. text in English and French. an. Free to members. Canadian Society of Laboratory Technologists, PO Box 830, Hamilton Ontario L8N 3N8 Canada. **DD** 610.695306071. **NLM** QZ 22 DC2 C6R.

ROSTER DE L'ACTL. Main/Corp Canadian Society of Laboratory Technologists. VFOAT CSLT Roster. VAT Roster de l'Association Canadienne des Technologistes de Laboratoire, Canadian Society of Laboratory Technologists. 1 Mar. 1983-. 0823-4639. CN. English (French). an. Canadian Society of Laboratory Technologists, PO Box 830, Hamilton Ontario L8N 3N8 Canada. **DD** 610.695306071. *Roster, 0318-1561.*

ROSTER OF MEMBERS - ASSOCIATION FOR HOSPITAL MEDICAL EDUCATION. Main/Corp Association for Hospital Medical Education. 0160-9440. US. English. an. Association for Hospital Medical Education, 1911 Jefferson Davis Highway/ Suite 1003, Arlington VA 22202. **LC** R735.A1. **DD** 610.71073. **NLM** WX 22.1 A849R.

ROSTER OF REGISTERED PRACTITIONERS OF THE HEALING ARTS LICENSED AND REGISTERED IN THE STATE OF VIRGINIA. Main/Corp Virginia State Board of Medicine. VFOAT Roster of Practitioners of the Healing Arts Licensed and Registered in the Commonwealth of Virginia. 0097-9147. US. English. an. Virginia State Board of Medicine, 505 Washington Street/No 200, Portsmouth VA 23704. **LC** R712.A2. **DD** 610.25755. **NLM** W 22 AV8 S7R. *Roster of Registered Practitioners of the Healing Art, in Active Practice in Virginia.*

RX HOME CARE. V. 1- June/July 1979-. 0191-961X. Periodical. US. English. mo. $80.00. Brentwood Publishing Company, PO Box 49045, Los Angeles CA 90049. **Tel** (213)826-8388. **LC** RA645.3. **DD** 649.8028.

SAARLANDISCHES ARZTEBLATT. Vol. 1-. 0340-644X. Periodical. German. ir. **Ind/Abst** Excerpta Med. **NLM** W1 SA104.

ST. LOUIS METROPOLITAN MEDICINE. V. 1- 1979-. Periodical. US. English. mo. $25.00. St Louis Metropolitan Medical Society, 3839 Lindell Boulevard, St Louis MO 63108. **Tel** (314)371-5225. **Ed** John Payne Roberts. bk rev. adv acc. Circ 3,500. (ctrl). Association business matters relating to medicine. *St. Louis County Medical Society Bulletin, St. Louis Medicine.*

ST. THOMAS'S HOSPITAL GAZETTE (1981). (ST. THOMAS'S HOSPITAL GAZETTE). VFOAT Saint Thomas's Hospital Gazette. Vol. 78, No. 3 (Winter 1980)-. 0263-3507. Periodical. UK. English. ir. $13.00. St Thomas Hospital Gazette, Albert Embankment, London SE 1 England. **Tel** 01 928 9292. **Ed** A J Grimes. **NLM** W1 ST121. bk rev. adv acc. Circ 1,400. Articles on medical education, history of medicine relating particularly to St. Thomas Hospital and medical school. *STH Gazette.*

SAN DIEGO PHYSICIAN. V. 55- Jan. 1969-. Periodical. US. English. mo. $12.00. San Diego County Medical Society 3702 Ruffin Road, San Diego CA 92123. **Tel** (714)565-8888. *Bulletin- San Diego County Medical Society.*

SAN FRANCISCO MEDICINE. V. 49- Jan. 1976-. 0361-705X. Periodical. US. English. mo. San Francisco Medical Society, 250 Masonic Avenue, San Francisco CA 94118. **NLM** W1 SA5768. *Bulletin - San Francisco Medical Society, 0036-4142.*

SANITAR UND HEIZUNGTECHNIK. 0036-4401. Periodical. GW. German. mo. Krammer Verlag, Hermannstrasse 3, D4000 Duesseldorf West Germany. **Ind/Abst** Energy Res. Abstr. **NLM** W1 SA653N.

SANOP MISAENGMUL HAKHOE CHI. VFOAT Korean Journal of Applied Microbiology and Bioengineering. Periodical. English (Korean). ir. Hanguk Sanop Misaengmul Hakhoe Sasoham, 131 Tongdaemun Ucheguk, Seoul South Korea. **LC** QR53.

SANTE 2000 MEDECINE. VFOAT Sante Deux Mille Medecine. Began with: V. 1, No. 1 (March/April 1982). 0293-5945. Periodical. French. qt. **NLM** W1 SA834.

SARCOIDOSIS. Vol. 1, No. 1 (Sept. 1984)-. 0393-1447. Periodical. English. sa. $60.00. **NLM** W1.

SASEBO SHIRITSU SOGO BYOIN IGAKU GYOSEKI SHU. Periodical. Japanese. ir. **NLM** W1 SA943C. *Sasebo Shiritsu Shimin Byoin Igaku Gyoseki Shu.*

SAUDI MEDICAL JOURNAL. V. 1- July 1979-. 0379-5284. Periodical. English. qt. 18. Saudi Medical Journal, PO Box 4522, Riyadh Kingdom of

Medicine

Saudi Arabia. **Tel** 4649482. **Ed** Rashid Al Kuhaymi. **Ind/Abst** Life Sci. Collect., Excerpta Med. **NLM** W1 SA966. bk rev. adv acc. **Circ** 26,000. (ctrl). General medical journal.

SBORNIK LEKARSKY. VFOAT Archives Bohemes de Medecine. Began in 1887. 0036-5327. Periodical. CS. Slovak (summaries in English and Russian). mo. Artia, Ve Smeckach 30 PO Box 790, Praha 1 Czechoslovakia. **Ind/Abst** Life Sci. Collect., Excerpta Med., Index Med., CIS Abstr., Chem. Abstr. **NLM** W1 SB471. **CODEN** SBLEA2.

SBORNIK NAUCHNO-PRAKTICHESKIKH RABOT - MINISTERSTVO ZDRAVOOKHRANENIIA RSFSR, CHETVERTOE GLAVNOE UPRAVLENIE. V. 1- 1970-. UR. Russian. **NLM** W1 SB471X.

SBORNIK NAUCHNYKH TRUDOV IV. KLINICHESKOI BOLNITSI. V. 1- 1970-. Periodical. UR. Russian (articles and summaries in Armenian). **NLM** W1 SB51E.

SBORNIK TRUDOV - NAUCHNO-ISSLEDOVATELSKII INSTITUT GIGIENY TRUDA I PROFZABOLEVANII IM. N. MAKHVILADZE. V. 3/4- 1976-. Periodical. UR. Georgian (articles in Russian). **NLM** W1 SB693LM. *Trudy - Nauchno-Issledovatelskii Institut Gigieny Truda I Professionalnykh Zabolevanii.*

SBORNIK VEDECKYCH PRACI LEKARSKE FAKULTY UNIVERZITY KARLOVY V HRADCI KRALOVE. (SBORNIK VEDECKYCH PRACI). **Main/Corp** Prague. Universita Karlova Lekarska Fakulta v Hdadci Kralove. 0049-5514. Periodical. CS. Czech. ir. Artia, PO Box 790, VE Smeckach 90, Prague Czechoslovakia. **Ind/Abst** Chem. Abstr., Excerpta Med., Index Med., Bibliogr. Index Geol. **LC** R95.P7. **NLM** W1 SB702P. **CODEN** SVLKAO.

SCALPEL (BRONXVILLE, N.Y.). (THE SCALPEL). **VFOAT** Scalpel of Alpha Epsilon Delta. Vol. 1, No. 1 (Jan. 1931). Periodical. US. English. sa. $3.50. Scalpel, 7 Brookside Circle, c/o Dr M Moore, Bronxville NY 10708. **NLM** W1 SC141.

SCANDINAVIAN JOURNAL OF CLINICAL AND LABORATORY INVESTIGATION. SUPPLEMENT. VFOAT Scandinavian Journal of Clinical & Laboratory Investigation. 150 (1978)-. 0085-591X. Periodical. UK. English. ir. **Ind/Abst** Index Med., Life Sci. Collect., Energy Res. Abstr. *Scandinavian Journal of Clinical and Laboratory Investigation. Supplementum.*

SCANDINAVIAN JOURNAL OF IMMUNOLOGY. V. 1- Feb. 1972-. 0300-9475. Periodical. UK. English. mo. 215. Blackwell Scientific Publishers Ltd, PO Box 88, Oxford OX2 0EL England. **Tel** (0865)240201. **Ed** M Harboe and J B Natvig. **Ind/Abst** Life Sci. Collect., Excerpta Med., Index Med., Biol. Abstr., Energy Res. Abstr., Chem. Abstr., Bibliogr. Agric. **LC** QR180. **DD** 574.2905. **NLM** W1 SC15E. **CODEN** SJIMAX. adv acc. **Circ** 1,250. International papers within the various fields of cellular and molecular immunology (all in English).

SCANDINAVIAN JOURNAL OF REHABILITATION MEDICINE. V. 1- 1969-. 0036-5505. Periodical. English. qt. $41.00. Almqvist & Wiksell, 108 Drottninggatan, PO Box 45150, S-104 30 Stockholm Sweden. **Tel Telex** 85413160. **Ind/Abst** Life Sci. Collect., Excerpta Med., Index Med., Cumul. Index Nurs. Allied Health Lit., Biol. Abstr., Hospit. Lit. Index, Sci. Cit. Index, Abr. Ed. **NLM** W1 SC153N. **CODEN** SJRMAA.

SCANDINAVIAN JOURNAL OF WORK, ENVIRONMENT & HEALTH. VAT Scandinavian Journal of Work, Environment and Health. V. 1- Mar. 1975-. 0355-3140. Periodical. Fl. English. bm. 500.00. Haartmaninkatu 1, SF00290 Helsinki Finland. **Tel** (0)47471. **Ed** Sven Hernberg. **Ind/Abst** Coal Abstr., Index Med., Cumul. Index Nurs. Allied Health Lit., Biol. Abstr., CIS Abstr., Energy Res. Abstr., Chem. Abstr. **LC** RC963.A1. **DD** 616.980305. **NLM** W1 SC154K. **CODEN** SWEHDO. bk rev. **Circ** 1,450. (ctrl). Original scientific articles and reviews concerning occupational health and the work environment in the fields of medicine, toxicology, epidemiology, hygiene, safety, ergonomics, sociology, psychology, and physiology. *Nordisk Hygienisk Tidskrift, 0029-1374; Work. Environment. Health, 0300-3221.*

SCHEDULE OF FEES. Main/Corp Ontario Medical Association. CN. English. mo. Ontario Medical Association, 240 St George Street, Toronto Ontario M5R 2P4 Canada.

SCHEDULE OF NIH CONFERENCES. Main/Corp National Institutes of Health (U.S.). Division of Research Grants. **VFOAT** Schedule of N.I.H. Conferences. **VAT** Schedule of National Institutes of Health Conferences. Began with Oct. 1969. 0733-4397. Periodical. US. English. qt. Division of Research Grants, National Institutes of Health, Bethesda MD 20205. **NLM** W 3.5 S414.

SCHISTO UPDATE. July 1977/Dec. 1978-. 0197-7210. Periodical. US. English. qt. Edna McConnell Clark Foundation, 250 Park Avenue, New York NY 10017. **NLM** ZWC 810 S3365.

SCHMERZSTUDIEN. V. 1-. 0170-0596. Monographic Series. German. ir. VCH Publishers Inc, 303 NW 12th Avenue, Deerfield Beach FL 33442. **Tel** (305)428-5566. **Ind/Abst** Chem. Abstr. **NLM** W1 SC18M. **CODEN** SCHMDG.

SCHOOL IMMUNIZATION SURVEY REPORT. US. English. an. **LC** RJ240. **DD** 362.19892905.

SCHRIFTEN ZUR PSYCHOANALYSE UND PSYCHOSOMATISCHEN MEDIZIN. 0582-0464. Monographic Series. German. ir. **Ed** W Loch, A Mitscherlich, T von Uexkull. **NLM** W1 SC303.

SCHRIFTENREIHE DER AKADEMIE FUR AERZTLICHE FORTBILDUNG DER DDR. VAT Schriftenreihe der Akademie fur Arztliche Fortbildung der Deutsche Demokratische Republik. 43- 1972-. 0138-1806. Monographic Series. GE. German. ir. Deutscher Buch Export-Import, Leninstrasse 16, DDR-701 Leipzig East Germany. **Ind/Abst** Excerpta Med. **NLM** W1 SC326. *Schriftenreihe.*

SCHRIFTENREIHE DER DEUTSCHEN GESELLSCHAFT FUR MEDIZINISCHE DOKUMENTATION, INFORMATIK UND STATISTIK E. V. No. 1-. 0174-4771. Monographic Series. German. ir. **Ed** G Wagner. **NLM** W1 SC329F.

SCHRIFTENREIHE INFANS CEREBROPATHICUS. V. 1-. German. ir. **Ed** A Rett. **NLM** W1.

SCHUMPERT MEDICAL QUARTERLY. Vol. 1, No. 1 (June 1982)-. 0731-5406. Periodical. US. English. qt. Free. Schumpert Medical Center, 915 Margaret Place, Shreveport LA 71120. **Tel** (318)227-6602. **Ed** Merrilee S Leatherman. **NLM** W1 SC373. adv acc. **Circ** 5,000. (ctrl). Each issue devoted to one specialty. Provides forum for exchange of ideas and gives practical clinical information from various specialties for primary care physicians treating various patients.

SCHWEIZERISCHE MEDIZINISCHE WOCHENSCHRIFT. VFOAT Journal Suisse de Medecine. Vol. 50- 1 Jan. 1920-. 0036-7672. Periodical. SZ. German (contains articles in French). wk. 103.-. Schwabe & Company, Steinentorstrasse 13, CH-4000 Basel 10 Switzerland. **Tel** 061 23 55 23. **Ind/Abst** Life Sci. Collect., Excerpta Med., Pestdoc, Ringdoc, Vetdoc, Index Med., Biol. Abstr., CIS Abstr., Index Dent. Lit., Chem. Abstr., Sci. Cit. Index, Abr. Ed. **NLM** W1 SC485. **CODEN** SMWOAS. Index in last issue of volume - attached. bk rev. adv acc. **Circ** 5,300. (ctrl). Gives precise information about all fields of medicine. *Correspondenz-Blatt fur Schweizer Artze.*

SCHWEIZERISCHE ZEITSCHRIFT FUR MILITAR- UND KATASTROPHENMEDIZIN. VFOAT Revue Suisse de Medecine Militaire et de Catastrophes. V. 52- May 1975-. 0377-8347. Periodical. SZ. articles in French and German with some summaries in both languages. qt. 50.00 Domestic, $25.00 Foreign. Editions Medecine et Hygiene, Case Postale 229, CH-1211 Geneva 4 Switzerland. **Tel** (022) 46 93 55. **Ind/Abst** Excerpta Med. **NLM** W1 SC591. *Schweizerische Zeitschrift fur Militarmedizin, 0036-8024.*

SCHWEIZERISCHE ZEITSCHRIFT FUR SPORTMEDIZIN. *See* Recreation, Leisure - Sports.

SCHWERPUNKT MEDIZIN. (SCHWERPUNKT MEDIZIN : S.M). **VFOAT** S.M. Began with 1978. 0722-3625. Periodical. German (summaries in English and German). ir. **NLM** W1 SC643H.

THE SCIENCE AND PRACTICE OF CLINICAL MEDICINE. V. 1. 0197-1719. Periodical. US. English. ir. Grune & Stratton Inc, 111 Fifth Avenue, New York NY 10003. **Tel** (212)614-3110. **CODEN** SPCMDE.

SCIENCE, MEDICINE, AND TECHNOLOGY IN EAST ASIA. Vol. 1-. 0737-612X. Monographic Series. US. English. an. University of Michigan, Lane Hall Center, Chinese Street, Ann Arbor MI 48109. **Ed** Nathan Sivin. **NLM** W1 SC744.

SCIENTIA VETERUM. VFOAT Collana di Studi di Storia Della Medicina. 1- 1958-. Periodical. Italian. ir. **LC** R131.A1.

SCIENTIFIC REPORT. Main/Corp Scripps Clinic and Research Foundation. 0361-3054. US. English. an. Scripps Clinic and Research Foundation, 10666 North Torrey Pines Road, La Jolla CA 92037. **LC** R862.S37. **DD** 616.005.

SCOTTISH MEDICAL JOURNAL. V. 1- Jan. 1956-. 0036-9330. Periodical. UK. English. qt. $58.00. Scottish Academic Press Ltd, 33 Montgomery Street, Edinburgh EH7 5JX Scotland. **Tel** 031/556 2796. **Ind/Abst** Life Sci. Collect., Excerpta Med., Pestdoc, Ringdoc, Vetdoc, Energy Inf. Abstr., Environ. Abstr., Index Med., Biol. Abstr., Chem. Abstr., Curr. Contents. Life Sci., Sci. Cit. Index, Abr. Ed., Excerpta Med., Pestdoc, Ringdoc, Vetdoc, Energy Inf. Abstr., Environ. Abstr., Index Med., Biol. Abstr., Chem. Abstr., Sci. Cit. Index, Abr. Ed., Pestdoc, Ringdoc, Vetdoc, Energy Inf. Abstr., Environ. Abstr., Index Med., Biol. Abstr., Chem. Abstr., Sci. Cit. Index, Abr. Ed., Hospit. Lit. Index. **NLM** W1 SC902. **CODEN** SMDJAK. *Glasgow Medical Journal, Edinburgh Medical Journal.*

SCRIPTA MEDICA FACULTATUM MEDICINAE UNIVERSITATIS MASARYKIANAE ET PALACKYANAE. VFOAT Spisy Lekarsksch Fakult University Masarykovy a Palackeho. Czech. ir. (cum index).

SCRIPTA SCIENTIFICA MEDICA. V. 4, No. 2- 1965-. 0582-3250. Periodical. Bulgarian (sometimes issued in English with added title: Annual Scientific Papers; tables of contents and summaries in English and Russian). ir. **Ind/Abst** Chem. Abstr., CIS Abstr. **NLM** W1 SC938. **CODEN** SSCMBX. *Nauchni Trudove of the Vissh Meditsinski Institut, Varna.*

SEAMIC INFORMATION RETRIEVAL ON CURRENT LITERATURE. SERIES H, ENTEROTOXIGENIC E. COLI. Series/Titl SEAMIC-IR. No. 1 (Dec. 1980)-. English. ir. **NLM** ZWC 260 S106H.

SEAMIC INFORMATION RETRIEVAL ON CURRENT LITERATURE. SERIES I, CAMPYLOBACTER. Series/Titl SEAMIC-IR. No. 1-. English. ir. **NLM** ZQW 154 S438.

SEAMIC INFORMATION RETRIEVAL ON CURRENT LITERATURE. SERIES K, DYSENTERY, BACILLARY. VFOAT S.E.A.M.I.C Information Retrieval on Current Literature. No. 1 (Dec. 1981)-. Periodical. English. ir. **NLM** ZWC 282 S438.

SEAMIC INFORMATION RETRIEVAL ON CURRENT LITERATURE. SERIES M, MALARIA. VFOAT S.E.A.M.I.C. Information Retrieval on Current Literature. No 1 (Dec. 1981)-. Periodical. English. ir. **NLM** ZWC 750 S438.

SEAMIC PUBLICATION. No. 1- 1975-. Monographic Series. English. ir. **NLM** W1 S48H.

THE SECRETORY PROCESS. Vol. 1-. 0167-8523. Monographic Series. US. English. Elsevier Science Publishing Company Inc, PO Box 1663, Grand Central Station, New York NY 10163. **Tel** (212)370-5520. **Ed** A M Poisner and J M Trifaro. **Ind/Abst** Chem. Abstr. **LC** UNC. **NLM** W1 SE2205. **CODEN** SEPREI.

SEITAI JOHO KAGAKU KENKYU. VFOAT Biomedical Information Science. 1- 1976-. Japanese. ir. c/o Kobe Daigaku Igakubu, Dai/2 Seirigabu Kyoshitsu Kusunokicho 6-chome Ikuta-ku (650), Koba Japan. **LC** RA409.5.

SELECTA (PLANEGG, GERMANY). (SELECTA. SUPPLEMENT). No. 1 (Sept. 7, 1981)-. Periodical. German. ir. **NLM** W1.

Medicine

SELECTED MEDICAL CARE STATISTICS. See Statistics.

SELECTED STUDIES IN MEDICAL CARE AND MEDICAL ECONOMICS. 0361-3046. US. English. an. Blue Cross Association, 840 North Lake Shore Drive, Chicago IL 60611. **LC** RA410.53. **DD** 362.105. **NLM** W 22 AA1 S4.

SEMANA MEDICA (BUENOS AIRES, ARGENTINA : 1894). (LA SEMANA MEDICA). Began in 1894. Periodical. AG. Spanish. ir. $150.00. La Semana Medica, Arenales 3574, Buenos Aires 1425 Argentina. **NLM** W1 SE44.

SEMANA MEDICA DE MEXICO. 0037-1823. Periodical. English. sm. $40.00. Semana Medica SA, Queeretaro 183, Mexico 7 DF Mexico. **Tel** 574-50-33.

SEMINARS IN FAMILY MEDICINE. V. 1- Feb. 1980-. 0194-0465. Periodical. US. English. qt. $24.50 Domestic, $27.50 Foreign. Grune & Stratton, 111 5th Avenue, New York NY 10003. Ed L R Martin. **Ind/Abst** Excerpta Med., Biol. Abstr. **NLM** W1 SE488M. **CODEN** SFAMD2.

SEMINARS IN INFECTIOUS DISEASE. V. 1- 1978-. 0162-5454. US. English. an. $54.00. Thieme-Stratton Inc, 381 Park Avenue South/Suite 1501, New York NY 10016. **Tel** (212)683-5088. Ed L Weinstein and B N Fields. **Ind/Abst** Biol. Abstr., Chem. Abstr. **LC** RC110. **DD** 616.905. **NLM** W1 SE489BI. **CODEN** SEIDD8. Each issue contains an index to its own contents - no vol index - loose.

SEMINARS IN NUCLEAR MEDICINE. VFOAT Nuclear Medicine. V. 1- Jan. 1971-. 0001-2998. Monographic Series. US. English. qt. Grune & Stratton Inc, 111 Fifth Avenue, New York NY 10003. **Tel** (212)614-3110. **Ind/Abst** Life Sci. Collect., Excerpta Med., Comput. Control Abstr., Electr. Electron. Abstr., Sci. Abstr. Sect. A. Phys. Abstr., Energy Res. Abstr., Biol. Abstr., Chem. Abstr., Index Med., Nucl. Sci. Abstr., Phys. Abstr., Sci. Cit. Index, Abr. Ed. **LC** UNC. **NLM** W1 SE489D. **CODEN** SMNMAB.

SEMINARS IN OCCUPATIONAL MEDICINE. 0882-5815. Periodical. US. English. qt. Thieme-Stratton Inc, 318 Park Avenue South, New York NY 10016. **Tel** (212)683-5088. In-depth look at topics vital to the practice of occupational medicine.

SEMINARS IN ULTRASOUND. V. 1- Mar. 1980-. 0194-1720. Periodical. US. English. qt. $65.00. Grune & Stratton, 111 Fifth Avenue, New York NY 10003. **Tel** (212)614-3110. **Ind/Abst** Excerpta Med., Biol. Abstr. **NLM** W1 SE498Q. **CODEN** SEULDO.

SENSORY INTEGRATION SPECIAL INTEREST SECTION NEWSLETTER. 0279-4128. Periodical. US. English. qt. American Occupational Therapy Association, 1383 Piccard Drive, Rockville MD 20850. **Tel** (301)948-9626. Newsletter - Sensory Integration Specialty Section, American Occupational Therapy Association, 0194-6358.

SERIAL HOLDINGS - B. C. MEDICAL LIBRARY SERVICE. See Library and Information Science.

SERONO SYMPOSIA PUBLICATIONS FROM RAVEN PRESS. Vol. 1-. 0733-897X. Monographic Series. US. English. Raven Press, 1140 Avenue of the Americas, New York NY 10036. **Ind/Abst** Biol. Abstr., Chem. Abstr. **NLM** W3 SE4779YM. **CODEN** SPRPDU.

SGA JOURNAL - (SOCIETY OF GASTROINTESTINAL ASSISTANTS (U.S.). (SGA JOURNAL). VAT Society of Gastrointestinal Assistants Journal. 0744-1126. Periodical. US. English. qt. $45.00. Williams & Wilkens, 428 East Preston Street, Baltimore MD 21202. **Tel** (301)528-4000. Ed Susan Triivits. **DD** 616. **NLM** W1 SG91. adv acc. The only professional journal specifically for gastrointestinal assistants. Describes new procedures, techniques, and equipment. Journal of the Society of Gastrointestinal Assistants.

SHAN-HSI HSIN I YAO. VFOAT Shanxi Xin Yiyao. Began in 1972. 0253-9853. Periodical. CH. Chinese. mo. 0.25. Hsi-An Shih Yu Chu China Mainland. **Ind/Abst** Chem Abstr. **LC** R97.7.C5. **DD** 610.5. **CODEN** SHIYDO.

SHANG-HAI CHEN CHIU TSA CHIH. First published in (Feb. 1982)-. Periodical. Chinese (abstracts in English). qt. 0.30. Guozi Shudian, PO Box 2820, Peking China. **Tel** 383453. Ed Chao Tsen-Wu. **LC** RM184. **DD** 615.89205. bk rev. adv acc. **Circ** 20,000. Covers clinical studies on neurophysiological and biochemical basis of acupuncture analgesia, and clincal study on acupuncture treatment for gastric and duodenal ulcers.

SHANG-HAI I HSUEH. VFOAT Shanghai Yixue. 0253-9934. Periodical. Chinese. mo. $0.35. **Ind/Abst** Chem. Abstr. **LC** R97.7.C5. **NLM** W1 SH127K. **CODEN** SIHSD8.

SHANG-HAI I HSUEH. VFOAT Shanghai Medical Journal. Periodical. CC. Chinese. mo. $11.34. China Publication Centre, PO Box 2820, Beijing China. **NLM** W1 SH127K.

SHANGHAI DIYI YIXUEYUAN XUEBAO. (SHANG-HAI TI I I HSUEH YUAN HSUEH PAO). VFOAT Hankukilbo, Acta Academiae Medicinae Primae Shanghai. Began with: V. 2, July 1, 1964. 0003-3650. Periodical. CH. Chinese. bm. $8.10. China Publication Centre, PO Box 2820, Beijing China. **Ind/Abst** Excerpta Med., Chem. Abstr. **NLM** W1 SH127U. **CODEN** SIIPD4. Shang I Hsueh Pao, 0559-7374.

SHANGONG YIXUEYUAN XUEBAO. See Biology.

SHIKOKU ACTA MEDICA. Periodical. JA. English. bm. Japan Publishing Trading Company Ltd, PO Box 5030 Tokyo International, Tokyo 100-31 Japan.

SHINSHA IGAKU ZASSHI. VFOAT Shinshu Medical Journal. 0037-3826. Periodical. JA. English. bm. Japan Publishing Trading Company Ltd, PO Box 5030, Tokyo International, Tokyo 100-31 Japan.

SHITSUGI OTO. No. 1-. JA. Japanese. ir. 4800. Nihon Iji Shimpo Sha, 9 Kanda Surugsdai 2 Chiyoda-ku (101-9), Tokyo Japan. **LC** R97.7.J3.

SICHUAN YIXUEYUAN XUEBAO. (SSU-CHUAN I HSUEH YUAN HSUEH PAO). VFOAT Acta Academiae Medicinae Sichuan. 0253-4290. Periodical. CC. Chinese. qt. $6.30. China Publication Centre, PO Box 2820, Beijing China. **Ind/Abst** Excerpta Med., Biol. Abstr., Chem. Abstr. **NLM** W1 SS18. **CODEN** CIYPDA.

SILI ZHONGGUO YIYAO XUEYUAN YANJIU NIANBAO. See Education (General) - Higher Education.

SINGAPORE MEDICAL JOURNAL. 0037-5675. Periodical. SI. English. bm. $80.00. Periodicals & Magazines Pty Ltd, 100 Beach Road, 33-10 Shaw Towers, Singapore 0718 Singapore. **Tel** 297-2377. **Ind/Abst** Life Sci. Collect., Excerpta Med., Index Med., Cumul. Index Nurs. Allied Health Lit., Biol. Abstr., Hospit. Lit. Index. **NLM** W1 SI523. **CODEN** SIMJA3.

SLEEP WATCHERS. 0748-5352. Periodical. US. English. qt. $25.00. Sleep Disorders Center OVMC, Wheeling WV 26003. **DD** 616.

SOCIAL SCIENCE & MEDICINE (1982). See Social Sciences (General).

SOCIEDAD MEXICANA DE HISTORIA Y FILOSOFIA DE LA MEDICINA MONOGRAFIAS. 1- 1976-. Periodical. Spanish. ir. **NLM** W1 SO254H.

SOCIETY FOR ANCIENT MEDICINE NEWSLETTER. VFOAT SAM Newsletter. No. 1- Apr. 1976-. Periodical. US. English. University of Kentucky, History Department/Society for Ancient Medicine, Lexington KY 40506. **Tel** (606)257-1731.

SOCIOECONOMIC CHARACTERISTICS OF MEDICAL PRACTICE. 1983-. 0742-2709. US. English. an. American Medical Association, PO Box 10946, Chicago IL 60610. **LC** R729. **DD** 338.473621720973.

SOCIOECONOMIC REPORT. Main/Corp California Medical Association. Bureau of Research and Planning. 0575-5964. Periodical. US. English. bm. California Medical Association, Bureau of Research and Planning, 731 Market Street, San Francisco CA 94103.

SOUTH DAKOTA JOURNAL OF MEDICINE. V. 18, No. 3- Mar. 1965-. 0038-3317. Periodical. US. English. mo. $15.00. South Dakota State Medical Association, 608 West Avenue North, Sioux Falls SD 57104. **Tel** (605)336-1965. Ed Robert E Vandemark. **Ind/Abst** Hospit. Lit. Index, Energy Res. Abstr., Biol. Abstr., Index Med., Index Med. **NLM** W1 SO917. **CODEN** SDMEAL. adv acc. **Circ** 1,100. (ctrl). Scientific articles. South Dakota Journal of Medicine and Pharmacy, 0096-8420.

THE SOUTHEAST ASIAN JOURNAL OF TROPICAL MEDICINE AND PUBLIC HEALTH. See Public Health and Safety.

SOUTHERN MEDICAL JOURNAL. V. 1- July 1908-. 0038-4348. Periodical. US. English. mo. $45.00. Southern Medical Association, 2151 Highland Avenue/Suite 207, PO Box 190088, Birmingham AL 35219-0088. **Tel** (205)945-1840. Ed John B Thomison. **Ind/Abst** Life Sci. Collect., Excerpta Med., Hospit. Lit. Index, Coal Abstr., Cumul. Index Nurs. Allied Health Lit., CIS Abstr., Energy Res. Abstr., Biol. Abstr., Chem. Abstr., Nucl. Sci. Abstr., Index Med., Pestdoc, Ringdoc, Vetdoc, Sci. Cit. Index, Abr. Ed. **LC** R11. **NLM** W1 S0955. **CODEN** SMJOAV. adv acc. **Circ** 26,000. (ctrl) Official journal publishing more than 450 original clinical articles annually. All articles are directed to the practicing physician and surgeon. Gulf States Journal of Medicine and Surgery, Mobile Medical and Surgical Journal.

SOVETSKAJA MEDICINA. (SOVETSKAIA MEDITSINA). VFOAT SM. 15 June 1937-. 0038-5077. Periodical. UR. Russian (some articles have summaries in English, June 1959-). mo. $45.00. Victor Kamkin Inc (73365), 12224 Parklawn Drive, Rockville MD 20852. **Tel** (301)881-5973. **Ind/Abst** Excerpta Med., Index Med., Int. Aerosp. Abstr., Life Sci. Collect., Biol. Abstr., CIS Abstr., Sci. Cit. Index, Abr. Ed. **NLM** W1 S0976. **CODEN** SOMEAU.

SPACE BIOLOGY AND AEROSPACE MEDICINE. See Aeronautics, Astronautics.

SPECIAL REPORT SERIES - INDIAN COUNCIL OF MEDICAL RESEARCH. Main/Corp Indian Council of Medical Research. No. 18- 1951-. Periodical. English. ir. Indian Council of Medical Research, PO Box 4508, Ansari Nagar New Delhi 16 India.

SPECIAL REPORT SERIES - MEDICAL RESEARCH COUNCIL (GREAT BRITAIN). Main/Corp Medical Research Council (Gt. Brit.). No. 50- 1920-. UK. English. ir. Her Majestys Stationery Office, PO Box 276, London SW8 5DT England. **Tel** 01-622 3316. Special Report Series.

SPECTRUM (ROCKVILLE, MD.). (SPECTRUM). Vol. 1, No. 1 (Feb. 1981)-. 0738-470X. Periodical. US. English. an. Cystic Fibrosis Foundation, 6000 Executive Boulevard, Suite 309, Rockville MD 20852. **Tel** (301)881-9130. **NLM** W1 SP32R.

SPINE. V. 1- Mar. 1976-. 0362-2436. Periodical. US. English. mo. $112.00. J B Lippincott Company, East Washington Square, Philadelphia PA 19105. **Tel** (215)238-4273. Ed Henry LaRocca. **Ind/Abst** Excerpta Med., Life Sci. Collect., Index Med., Biol. Abstr., Energy Res. Abstr., Chem. Abstr. **LC** RD768. **DD** 617.375005. **NLM** W1 SP47. **CODEN** SPINDD. adv acc. **Circ** 8,223. Information gathered from a variety of disciplines dealing with the human spine, research, case reports. Treatments and practice methods are also included.

SPORT HEALTH : OFFICIAL GAZETTE OF AUSTRALIAN SPORTS MEDICINE FEDERATION. Vol. 1, No. 1 (May/June 1983)-. Periodical. English. bm. 20.00. **NLM** W1.

SPORT MEDICINE DIRECTORY. See Yearbooks, Almanacs, Directories.

SPORTMEDINFO. See Recreation, Leisure - Sports.

SPORTS MEDICINE. Series/Titl Archives of Podiatric Medicine and Foot Surgery. Supplement. 1978-. 0271-2857. Periodical. US. English. an. Futura Publishing Company, 295 Main Street, Mount Kisco NY 10549. **Ind/Abst** Life Sci. Collect. **LC** RD560. **DD** 617.585.

SPORTS MEDICINE (AUKLAND, (N.Z.). (SPORTS MEDICINE). Began in 1984. 0112-1642. Periodical. US. English. bm. $110.00. Adis Press International, 401 South State Street, Newtown PA 18940. **Tel** (215)860-2000. **CODEN** SPMEE7. **Circ** 900. Independent review journal of applied science and medicine in sport and exercise.

SPORTSMEDICINE DIGEST. V. 1- Sept. 1979-. 0194-0295. Periodical. US. English. mo. $64.00. PM Inc, PO Box 2160, Van Nuys CA 91404. **Tel** (213)843-4399. Ed Gerald McKee and Lewis Yocum. bk rev. **Circ** 2,500. Newsletter for health care professionals. Publication is dedicated to the prevention, treatment and rehabilitation of sports and recreational injuries.

Medicine

SPRI RAD. 1. (SPRI RAD 1). VFOAT Effektiviseringsemtodik, Terminologi M. M. 1- Jan. 1972-. 0303-6553. Periodical. text in Swedish. ir. **NLM** W1 SP682H.

SRPSKI ARHIV ZA CELOKUPNO LEKARSTVO. See Genealogy and Heraldry - Archives.

STANDARD MEDICAL ALMANAC. See Yearbooks, Almanacs, Directories.

STANDARDS FOR BLOOD BANKS AND TRANSFUSION SERVICES. 0730-6865. US. English. $3.00. Committee on Standards, American Association of Blood Banks, 1828 L Street NW, Suite 608, Washington DC 20036. **LC** RM172. **DD** 615.39. **NLM** W1 ST149. Standards for a Blood Transfusion Service, 0272-2038.

STANDARDS MONITOR. (STANDARDS MONITOR : AAMI STANDARDS AND RECOMMENDED PRACTICES, A PROGRESS REPORT AND NOTIFICATION OF PROPOSED ACTION). **Main/Corp** Association for the Advancement of Medical Instrumentation. 0739-0564. Periodical. US. English. bm. $70.00. Association for the Advancement of Medical Instrumentation, 1901 North Fort Meyer Drive, Suite 602, Arlington VA 22209.

STANDARDS SURVEY. **Main/Corp** United States. Bureau of Medical Devices. 1977-. 0146-9207. US. English. an. Department of Health, Education and Welfare, Public Health Service, Food and Drug Administration, Division of Medical Device Standards and Research, Bureau of Medical Devices, 5600 Fishers Lane, Rockville MD 20857. **LC** R856.6. **DD** 610.28. **NLM** W 22 AA1 S7. Medical Devices and Diagnostic Products Standards Survey.

STAT. V. 1- Spring 1979-. 0272-555X. Periodical. US. English. qt. Janzen Johnston and Rockwell, 1520 Arizona Avenue, Santa Monica CA 90404. **LC** RC86. **DD** 616.025. **NLM** W1 ST292B.

STATE OF THE ART REVIEWS. OCCUPATIONAL MEDICINE. (STATE OF THE ART REVIEW : OCCUPATIONAL MEDICINE). VFOAT Occupational Medicine. Vol. 1, No. 1 (Jan./Mar. 1985 I.E. 1986)-. 0885-114X. Periodical. US. English. qt. Hanley & Belfus Inc, 210 South 13th Street, Philadelphia PA 19107. **DD** 615.

STATE SUMMARY DATA ON PHYSICIANS. 1981-. 0882-2468. US. English. American Medical Association, PO Box 10946, Chicago IL 60610. **LC** RA410.7. **DD** 331.76161069520973021.

STATISTICS IN MEDICINE. See Statistics.

STATISTICS OF NAVY MEDICINE. See Statistics.

STATISTISCHE GEGEVENS BETREFFENDE HET GENEESHERENKORPS. DONNEES STATISTIQUES CONCERNANT LE CORPS MEDICAL. **Main/Corp** Belgium. Ministere de la Sante Publique et de la Famille. Centre de Traitement de l'Information. Dutch (French). ir. **LC** RA410.9.B4.

STATISTISCHER JAHRESBERICHT DES GESUNDHEITS- UND SOZIALWESENS BEZIRK MAGDEBURG. **Main/Corp** Magdeburg (Bezirk). Bureau fur Medizinische Statistik und Datenverarbeitung. German. ir. **LC** RA407.5.G42.

STATUS REPORT - UNITED STATES. HEALTH CARE FINANCING ADMINISTRATION. OFFICE OF RESEARCH AND DEMONSTRATIONS. (STATUS REPORT). **Series/Titl** Health Care Financing. HCFA Pub. Apr. 1983-. 0742-8871. Periodical. US. English. sa. US Department of Health and Human Services/Health Care Financing, Administration Office of Research and Demonstrations, 6325 Security Boulevard, Baltimore MD 21207. **LC** RA410.53. **DD** 338.4336210973. **NLM** W 20.5. Research and Demonstrations in Health Care Financing.

STEDMAN'S MEDICAL DICTIONARY. Periodical. US. English. ir. $70.49. J A Majors Medical Book Company, PO Box 47552 8911 Directors, Dallas TX 75247. A Practical Medical Dictionary.

STRAUB PROCEEDINGS. Vol. 47, No. 1-4 (Dec. 1982)-. 0741-8930. Periodical. US. English. mo. Straub Clinic & Hospital, Office of Professional Activities, 888 South King Street, Honolulu HI 96813. **Ind/Abst** Life Sci. Collect. **NLM** W1 ST794F. Straub Clinic Proceedings, 0039-2251.

STRESS MEDICINE. 0748-8386. Periodical. UK. English. qt. John Wiley & Sons, Baffins Lane, Chichester Sussex United Kingdom.

STRUKTURA I ROL' VODY V ZHIVOM ORGANIZME. SB. 1- 1966-. Periodical. Russian. ir. **NLM** W1 ST825.

STUDI SULLA TOSCANA MEDICEA. 1-. Monographic Series. IT. Italian. ir. Casa Editrice, Leo S Olschki, Casella Postale PO Box 66, 50100 Firenze Italy.

STUDIEN ZUR MEDIZINGESCHICHTE DES NEUNZEHNTEN JAHRHUNDERTS. 0081-7333. Monographic Series. GW. German. ir. Vandenhoeck & Ruprecht, Postfach 3753/Theaterstr 13, D-3400 Goettingen West Germany. **Tel** 0551/65061. **Ed** Walter Heischvel-Artelt and and Edith Maun. **Ind/Abst** Chem. Abstr. **NLM** W1 ST913K. **CODEN** SMNJA2. adv acc.

STUDIENMATERIAL ZUR WEITERBILDUNG MEDIZINISCH-TECHNISCHER LABORASSISTENTEN. VFOAT Studienmaterial. 0323-4126. Periodical. GW. German. ir. Institut fur Weiterbildung Mittlerer Medizinischer, Fachkrafte Rubensstrasse, 1500 Potsdam DDR East Germany. **Ind/Abst** Chem. Abstr. **NLM** W1 ST915B. **CODEN** SWMTAT.

STUDIES IN HISTORY OF MEDICINE. V. 1- Mar. 1977-. 0379-3915. Periodical. II. English. qt. $15.00. Institute in History of Medicine & Medical Research, New Delhi 110062 India. **LC** R131.A1. **NLM** W1 ST92Q.

STUDIES IN MEDICAL GEOGRAPHY. 0585-6906. Monographic Series. US. English. ir. $175.00. Hafner Press, 866 Third Avenue, New York NY 10022. **Tel** (212)702-4200. **Ed** David Loiterstein. **Ind/Abst** Biol. Abstr. **NLM** W1 ST921. **CODEN** SMDGAB.

SUDHANIDHI. V. 1- Jan. 1973-. Periodical. Hindi. ir. 8.00. **LC** R97.7.H5.

SUGGESTED LIST OF MEDICAL BOOKS & JOURNALS. See Publishing - Books and Bookmaking.

SUID-AFRIKAANSE MEDIESE TYDSKRIF. VFOAT South African Medical Journal. 1884. Periodical. SA. English (with some Afrikaans). wk. $53.69. Medical Association of South Africa, Medical House Central Square, Pinelands 7405 South Africa. **Tel** 53-3081. **Ed** Dr S S B Gilder. **Ind/Abst** Excerpta Med., Life Sci. Collect., CIS Abstr., Cumul. Index Nurs. Allied Health Lit., Sel. Water Resour. Abstr., Pestdoc, Ringdoc, Vetdoc. **LC** R98. **DD** 610.5. **NLM** W1 SO906H. bk rev. adv acc. **Circ** 12,000. Original research, "state of the art" news, medical information and opinions. South African Medical Journal.

SUOMEN LAAKARILEHTI. FINLANDS LAKARTIDNING. VFOAT Finlands Lakartidning. 1946-. 0039-5560. Periodical. Finnish. tm. **NLM** W1 SU605. Index published separately - free - automatically sent. Suomen Laakari - Liiton Aikauslehiti.

SUPPLEMENT ONE, HEALTH SCIENCES BOOKS & JOURNALS. See Publishing - Books and Bookmaking.

SURGICAL GASTROENTEROLOGY. Vol. 1, No. 1-. 0730-2681. Periodical. US. English. qt. Masson Publications USA Inc, 211 East 43rd Street Room 1306, New York NY 10017. **Tel** (212)370-1937. **NLM** W1 SU765K.

SURINAAMS MEDISCH BULLETIN. VFOAT Surinam Medical Bulletin. V. 1- 1977-. 0379-1637. Periodical. Dutch (English). ir. **NLM** W1 SU8754.

SURVEY OF ANESTHESIOLOGY. V. 1- Feb. 1957-. 0039-6206. Periodical. US. English. bm. $50.00. Williams & Wilkins Company, 428 East Preston Street, Baltimore MD 21202. **Tel** (301)528-4000. **Ed** Burnell R Brown Jr. **Ind/Abst** Life Sci. Collect. **LC** RD81.A1. **DD** 615.78105, 617.9605. **NLM** ZWO 200 S963. **CODEN** SANEA5. adv acc. **Circ** 5,350. Available on microfilm. In-depth condensations with critical comments of the most important anaesthesiology-related literature from around the world.

SURVEY OF IMMUNOLOGIC RESEARCH. 1/1/82 (Mar. 1982)-. 0252-9564. Periodical. English. qt. S Karger AG, PO Box 10, CH-4009 Basel Switzerland. **Tel** (061)390880. **Ind/Abst** Life Sci. Collect., Excerpta Med., Index Med., Biol. Abstr., Chem. Abstr. **NLM** W1. **CODEN** SIMRDU.

SUVREMENNA MEDICINA. (SUVREMENNA MEDITSINA). VFOAT Savremenna Meditsina. Vol. 1- Jan./Feb. 1950-. 0562-7192. Periodical. BU. Russian (added tables of contents and some summaries in Bulgarian and English). mo. $40.00. Medicina I Fizkultru, Pl Slaveikov 11, Sofiya Bulgaria. **Ind/Abst** Excerpta Med., CIS Abstr., Chem. Abstr. **NLM** W1 SU926. **CODEN** SUMEA4. Suvremenna Meditsina.

SWISS MED. 0251-1665. Periodical. SZ. German. mo. $34.64. Verlag Dr Felix Wuest AG, Seestrasse 5/Postfach, CH-8700 Kuesnacht Switzerland. **Tel** (01)9110055. **Ind/Abst** Excerpta Med. **NLM** W1 SW406M.

SYMPOSIA MEDICA HOECHST. 7- 1973-. 0341-6321. Monographic Series. GW. English. an. $68.00. F K Schattauer Verlag, Postfach 2945, Lenzhalde 3, D7000 Stuttgart 1 West Germany. **Tel** (0711)221733. **Ed** E Lindenlaub. **Ind/Abst** Chem. Abstr. **NLM** W3 SY1055. **CODEN** SMHODO. (ctrl).

SYNAPSE. 0147-6661. US. English. University of Utah, Medical Science, Library, Salt Lake City UT 84112. **LC** Z6676, R129. **DD** 016.61.

TAEHAN HAEK UIHAKHOE CHAPCHI. VFOAT Korean Journal of Nuclear Medicine. 0378-8725. Periodical. KO. Korean (English). ir. Taehan Haek Uihakhoe, c/o Soul Taehakkyo Uikwa Taehak Haek Uihakkwa, Seoul South Korea. **LC** R895.A1. **NLM** W1 TA392F.

TAEHAN HANUI HAKHOE CHI. VFOAT The Journal of Korean Oriental Medical Society. Periodical. KO. Korean. ir. Taehan Hanui Hakhoe, 929-4 Chegi-dong Tongdaemun-ku, Seoul Korea. **LC** R97.7.K6.

TAEHAN UIHAK HYOPHOE CHI. VFOAT Journal of the Korean Medical Association. Periodical. KO. Korean. ir. Taehan Uihak Hyophoe, CPO Box 2062, Seoul Korea. **Ind/Abst** Excerpta Med. **LC** R97.7.K6. **DD** 610.5. **NLM** W1 TA396.

TAGLICHE PRAXIS. 1960-. 0494-464X. Periodical. GW. German. qt. Hans Marseille Verlag, Burkleinstrasse 12, D8000 Munich 22 West Germany. **Ind/Abst** Excerpta Med. **NLM** W1 TA39. Index published separately - free - automatically sent.

TAIWAN REVIEW. 8756-212X. Periodical. US. English. Abmac, 2 East 103rd Street, New York NY 10029. **DD** 610. **NLM** W1.

TANG TAI I HSUEN. VFOAT Medicine Today. No. 1- 1973-. Periodical. Chinese. ir. **Ed** Y F Liao and C H Chou. **NLM** W1 TA5398I.

LE TECHNICIEN BIOLOGISTE. Began with V. 1, No. 1, (April 1975). 0337-9965. Periodical. FR. French. bm. 100.00. 22-24 rue du Chateau des Rentiers, 75013 Paris France. **Ind/Abst** CIS Abstr., Chem. Abstr. **NLM** W1 TE152C. **CODEN** TBIODV.

TECHNIQUES IN IMMUNOCYTOCHEMISTRY. Vol. 1-. 0742-9878. UK. English. Academic Press Inc, 4805 Sand Lake Road, Orlando FL 32819. **LC** QR183.6. **DD** 574.876042.

TECHNOLOGY FOR ANESTHESIA. 8756-8578. Periodical. US. English. mo. $70.00. ECRI, 5200 Butler Pike, Plymouth Meeting PA 19462. **Tel** (215)825-6000. **Ed** J Nobel. **DD** 617. A newsletter for anesthesiologists and anesthetists summarizing health care technology issues and reporting product recalls, hazards, and problems. Health Devices Update. Anesthesia.

TECHNOLOGY FOR EMERGENCY MEDICINE. 8756-8594. Periodical. US. English. mo. $70.00. ECRI, 5200 Butler Pike, Plymouth Meeting PA 19462. **Tel** (215)835-6000. **Ed** J Nobel. **DD** 362. bk rev. A newsletter for EMS specialists summarizing health care technology issues and reporting product recalls, hazards, and problems. Health Devices Update. Emergency Medicine.

TECHNOLOGY FOR MATERIALS MANAGEMENT. Vol. 5, No. 7 (Jan. 1985)-. 8756-8608. Periodical. US. English. mo. $70.00. ECRI, 5200 Butler Pike, Plymouth Meeting PA 19462. **Tel** (215)825-6000. **Ed** J Nobel. **DD** 658. bk rev. A newsletter for materials managers, purchasing agents, and CSR supervisors summarizing health care technology issues, product recalls, hazards, and problems. *Health Devices Update. Materials Management.*

TERAPEVTICESKIJ ARHIV. (TERAPEVTICHESKII ARKHIV). Vol. 1- 1923-. 0040-3660. Periodical. UR. Russian (summaries in English, 1959-). mo. $57.00. Victor Kamkin Inc (70969), 12224 Parklawn Drive, Rockville MD 20852. **Tel** (301)881-5973. **Ind/Abst** Life Sci. Collect., Excerpta Med., Pestdoc, Ringdoc, Vetdoc, Index Med., Biol. Abstr., Chem. Abstr., Sci. Cit. Index, Abr. Ed. **NLM** W1 TE511. **CODEN** TEARAI.

TERAPIA MODERNA. 0040-3695. Periodical. IT. Italian. ir. 35.00. Il Pensiero Scientifico, Via Panama, 48 - 00198 Roma Italy. **Ind/Abst** Chem. Abstr. **CODEN** TPMDAB.

TERATOGENESIS, CARCINOGENESIS, AND MUTAGENESIS. Vol. 1, No. 1- (1980)-. 0270-3211. Periodical. US. English. bm. Alan R Liss Inc, 41 East 11th Street, New York NY 10003. **Tel** (212)741-2515. **Ind/Abst** Life Sci. Collect., Excerpta Med., Pestdoc, Ringdoc, Vetdoc, Index Med., Biol. Abstr., Chem. Abstr. **NLM** W1 TE5697. **CODEN** TCMUD8.

TESTNEVELES- ES SPORTEGESZSEGUGYI SZMELE. 1960?. 0563-2013. Periodical. HU. Hungarian (table of contents and summaries in English and Russian). qt. Akademiai Kiado, POB 24, 1363 Budapest Hungary. **NLM** W1 TE631.

TEXAS DO. **VAT** Texas Doctor of Osteopathy. V. 37, No.7- Aug. 1980-. 0275-1453. Periodical. US. English. mo. $5.00. Texas Osteopathic Medical Association, 226 Bailey Avenue, Fort Worth TX 76107. **NLM** W1 TE694. *Texas Osteopathic Physicians Journal, 0275-1445.*

TEXAS FAMILY PHYSICIAN. V. 26- Jan./Feb. 1975-. 0098-1052. Periodical. US. English. bm. Texas Academy of Family Physicians, 1905 North Lamar, Austin TX 78705. **NLM** W1 TE724. *GP Press, 0098-0994.*

TEXAS MEDICINE. V. 62- May 1966-. 0040-4470. Periodical. US. English. mo. $20.00. Texas Medical Association, Business Office, 1801 North Lamar Boulevard, Austin TX 78701. **Tel** (512)477-6704. **Ed** Rae Vajgert. **Ind/Abst** Life Sci. Collect., Excerpta Med., Hospit. Lit. Index, Cumul. Index Nurs. Allied Health Lit., CIS Abstr., Energy Res. Abstr., Chem. Abstr., Index Med. **NLM** W1 TE787. **CODEN** TXMDAX. adv acc. **Circ** 24,000. Clinical medical journal and organizational publication for Texas Medical Association. *Texas State Journal of Medicine, 0096-7165.*

TEXAS OSTEOPATHIC PHYSICIANS JOURNAL. V.1-37, No. 6. 0275-1445. Periodical. US. English. mo. **NLM** W1 TE818.

TEXAS REPORTS ON BIOLOGY AND MEDICINE *CEASED.* V. 1-41. 0040-4675. Periodical. US. English. ir. **Ind/Abst** Life Sci. Collect., Excerpta Med., Energy Res. Abstr., Biol. Abstr., Chem. Abstr., Index Med. **LC** R11. **DD** 610.5. **NLM** W1 TE85. **CODEN** TRBMAV. (cum index). *Bulletin of the John Sealy Hospital and the School of Medicine of the University of Texas.*

TEXTE ZUR GESCHICHTE DER PRAVENTIVMEDIZIN : TGP. **VFOAT** TGP. V. 1-. Monographic Series. German (text in French and Latin). ir. **NLM** W1.

THEORETICAL MEDICINE. Vol. 4, No. 1 (Feb. 1983)-. 0167-9902. Periodical. English. ty. 63. Kluwer Academic Publishers Group, PO Box 322, 3300 AH Dordrecht Netherlands. **Tel** (31)78-334911. **Ed** K Sadegh-Zadeh and D Thomasma. **Ind/Abst** Energy Res. Abstr., Philos. Index. **LC** R723. **DD** 610.1. **NLM** W1. bk rev. adv acc. **Circ** 450. Interdisciplinary studies in the philosophy and methodology of medical practice and research. *Metamedicine, 0166-2031.*

THERAPIE. (THERAPIE. REVUE DE THERAPEUTIQUE ET DE PHARMACOLOGIE CLINIQUE). Began with Vol. 1, 1946. 0040-5957. Periodical. FR. French (summaries in English). bm. Doin Editeurs, 8 Place de l'Odeon, F 75006 Paris France. **Tel** 325.34.02. **Ind/Abst** Excerpta Med., Index Med., Biol. Abstr., Chem. Abstr., Life Sci. Collect., Pestdoc, Ringdoc, Vetdoc, Sci. Cit. Index, Abr. Ed. **NLM** W1 TH641. **CODEN** THERAP.

THERAPIE DER GEGENWART. (DIE THERAPIE DER GEGENWART : MEDIZINISCH-CHIRURGISCHE RUNDSCHAU FUR PRAKTISCHE ARZTE). Vol. 36 (Jan. 1895)-. 0040-5965. Periodical. German. mo. Urban & Vogel, Postfach 15 22 09, 8000 Munchen 15 West Germany. **Tel** (301)539-2550. **Ind/Abst** Life Sci. Collect., Excerpta Med., Pestdoc, Ringdoc, Vetdoc, Chem. Abstr., Energy Res. Abstr., Index Med. **NLM** W1 TH643. **CODEN** THGEAU. *Medizinisch-Chirurgische Rundschau.*

THORAX. V. 1- 1946-. 0040-6376. Periodical. UK. English. mo. $137.92. British Medical Journal, Tavistock Square, London WC1H 9JR England. **Tel** (01)387-4499. **Ed** R A L Brewis and H Matthews. **Ind/Abst** Life Sci. Collect., Excerpta Med., Coal Abstr., Index Med., Biol. Abstr., CIS Abstr., Chem. Abstr., Sci. Cit. Index, Abr. Ed., Hospit. Lit. Index. **NLM** W1 TH898. **CODEN** THORA7. (cum index). bk rev. adv acc. **Circ** 4,000. Intended primarily for the publication of original work on diseases of the thorax and of relevant anatomical and physiological studies.

THROMBOSIS AND HAEMOSTASIS. V. 35- Feb. 29, 1976-. 0340-6245. Periodical. GW. English (IN). ir. FK Schattauer Verlag, Postfach 2945, Lenzhalde 3, D7000 Stuttgart 1 West Germany. **Ind/Abst** Life Sci. Collect., Excerpta Med., Pestdoc, Ringdoc, Vetdoc, Index Med., Biol. Abstr., Energy Res. Abstr., Chem. Abstr. **NLM** W1 TH923. **CODEN** THHADQ. *Thrombosis et Diathesis Haemorrhagica, 0340-5338.*

TIANJIN YIYAO. (TIEN-CHIN I YAO). 0253-9896. Periodical. CC. Chinese. mo. $7.83. China Publication Centre, PO Box 2820, Beijing China. **Ind/Abst** Chem. Abstr., Biol. Abstr. **LC** R97.7.C5. **NLM** W1 TI345. **CODEN** TIYADG.

TIDSSKRIFT FOR DEN NORSKE LAEGEFORENING. **Main/Corp** Norske Laegeforening. **VFOAT** Journal of the Norwegian Medical Association. Vol. 10-. 0029-2281. Periodical. NO. Norwegian. ir. $64.64. Tidsskrift for den Norske, Inkognitogt 26, Oslo Norway. **Tel** 472552000. **Ed** Arne Bjoruevoll. **Ind/Abst** Index Med. **NLM** W1 NO266. **CODEN** TNLAAH. bk rev. adv acc. **Circ** 13,500. (ctrl). Membership news and advertisements. *Tidsskrift for Praktisk Medicine.*

TIJDSCHRIFT VOOR DE GESCHIEDENIS DER GENEESKUNDE, NATUURWETENSCHAPPEN WISKUNDE EN TECHNIEK. (TIJDSCHRIFT VOOR DE GESCHIEDENIS DER GENEESKUNDE, NATUURWETENSCHAPPEN, WISKUNDE EN TECHNIEK). Began with Vol. 1, published in 1978. 0167-2088. Periodical. NE. Dutch. qt. Editions Rodopi Nv, Keizersgracht 302-304, Amsterdam The Netherlands. **NLM** W1 TI65M.

TIJDSCHRIFT VOOR PARAMEDICI. (TIJDSCHRIFT VOOR PARAMEDICI : TVP). **VFOAT** TVP. Vol. 1, No. 1 (Jan. 1980)-. 0167-5737. Periodical. Dutch. mo. 20.00. De Tijdstroom, Postbus 14, 7240 BA Lochem Netherlands. **NLM** W1 TI714M.

TIMISOARA MEDICALA. Began in 1956. 0493-3079. Periodical. Romany. ir.

TIP DUNYASI. **VFOAT** Tib Dunyasi. V. 1- Jan. 1928. Periodical. Turkish. ir. **NLM** W1 TI1002.

TITLE MASTER. **Main/Corp** American Overseas Book Company. 0747-6418. Periodical. US. English. an. $12.75 Domestic, $17.60 Foreign. American Overseas Book Company, 550 Walnut Street, Norwood NJ 07648. **Tel** (201)767-7600. **Ed** Chitty. Medicine and medical updates.

TMA ACTION. **Main/Corp** Texas Medical Association. **VAT** Texas Medical Association Action. Periodical. US. English. mo. Texas Medical Association, 1801 North Lamar Boulevard, Austin TX 78701. **Tel** (512)477-6704. **Ed** Jon R Hornaday. **Circ** 25,000. Information on non-clinical activities, policies, and news of interest to physicians and medical student members of the Texas Medical Association.

TODAY'S CLINICIAN. (TODAY'S CLINICIAN AND POSTGRADUATE EDUCATION AT COMMUNITY HOSPITALS). V. 1- Sept. 1977-. 0147-4782. Periodical. US. English. mo. $20.00. Weston Communications, 575 Madison Avenue, New York NY 10022. **LC** R11. **DD** 610.5. **NLM** W1 TO161K.

TODAY'S THERAPEUTIC TRENDS. (TODAY'S THERAPEUTIC TRENDS : THE JOURNAL OF NEW DEVELOPMENTS IN CLINICAL MEDICINE). **VFOAT** Journal of New Developments in Clinical Medicine. Vol. 1, No. 1 (Apr. 1983)-. 0741-2320. Periodical. US. English. ir. $20.00. Todays Therapeutic Trends, PO Box 712, Princeton Junction NJ 08550. **Tel** (609)799-2300. **Ind/Abst** Excerpta Med. **NLM** W1 TO172M. **Circ** 3,500. Reviews of clinical experience with new or existing drug products or medical instrumentation, applicable to clinicians and medical investigators.

TOHO IGAKKAI ZASSHI. **VFOAT** Journal of the Medical Society of Toho University. 0040-8670. Periodical. JA. Japanese (tables of contents and summaries in English, 1956-). bm. Japan Publications Trading Company, PO Box 5030, Tokyo International, Tokyo 100-31 Japan. **Ind/Abst** Chem. Abstr., Excerpta Med. **NLM** W1 TO182. **CODEN** TOIZAG.

TOHOKU JOURNAL OF EXPERIMENTAL MEDICINE. (THE TOHOKU JOURNAL OF EXPERIMENTAL MEDICINE). **VFOAT** Tohoku Jikkenigaku. V. 1- 1920-. 0040-8727. Periodical. JA. English (English or German, 1920-45). mo. 200.00. Maruzen Company Ltd, PO Box 5050, 100-31 Tokyo Japan. **Tel** 03/278 9224. **Ind/Abst** Life Sci. Collect., Excerpta Med., Index Med., Biol. Abstr., CIS Abstr., Chem. Abstr., Sci. Cit. Index, Abr. Ed. **NLM** W1 TO182U. **CODEN** TJEMAO. (cum index). (ctrl). Official publication of the Tohoku University for all original works in all branches of medical sciences, containing original articles only. *Arbeiten, Mitteilungen Uber Allgemeine Pathologie und Pathologische Natomie.*

TOPICS IN ACUTE CARE AND TRAUMA REHABILITATION. 0885-971X. Periodical. US. English. qt. $44.00. Aspen Systems Corporation, 16792 Oakmont Avenue, Gaithersburg MD 20877.

TOPICS IN ALLERGY AND CLINICAL IMMUNOLOGY. Vol. 1, No. 1 (Jan. 1983)-. 0734-2780. Periodical. US. English. mo. $35.00 Domestic, $45.00 Foreign. PSG Inc, Topics in Allergy and Clinical Immunology, 545 Great Road, Littleton MA 01460. **NLM** W1.

TOPICS IN EMERGENCY MEDICINE. V. 1- May 1979-. 0164-2340. Monographic Series. US. English. qt. $47.50. Aspen Systems Corporation, PO Box 6018 Gaithersburg MD 20760. **Tel** (301)251-5000. **Ind/Abst** Excerpta Med., Hospit. Lit. Index, Cumul. Index Nurs. Allied Health Lit. **LC** UNC. **NLM** W1 TO539LL.

TOPICS IN HEALTH CARE FINANCING. Vol. 1, No. 1 (Fall 1974)-. 0095-3814. Periodical. US. English. qt. Aspen Systems Corporation, PO Box 6018, Gaithersburg MD 20760. **Tel** (301)251-5000. **Ind/Abst** Manage. Contents, Excerpta Med., Hospit. Lit. Index, Index Med., ABI/Inform, Bus. Period. Index. **LC** RA410.A1. **DD** 338.43362105. **NLM** W1 TO539MN. **CODEN** THCFDG.

TOPICS IN HEALTH RECORD MANAGEMENT. **VFOAT** THRM. Vol. 1, No. 1 (Sept. 1980)-. 0270-5230. Periodical. US. English. qt. Aspen Systems Corporation, PO Box 6018, Gaithersburg MD 20760. **Tel** (301)251-5000. **Ed** Melanie M Pariser. **Ind/Abst** Manage. Contents, Hospit. Lit. Index. **LC** UNC. **NLM** W1 TO539MP. bk rev. adv acc. One topic covered in-depth each issue, with facts, approaches, techniques, and strategies for medical record professionals.

TOPICS IN PAIN MANAGEMENT. Vol. 1, No. 1 (June 1985)-. 0882-5645. Periodical. US. English. mo. $35.00. Topics in Pain Management, Managing Editor, 545 Great Road, Littleton MA 01460. **Tel** (617)486-8971. **DD** 616. Provides a succinct review of relevant and practical pain therapy.

TOPICS IN THERAPEUTICS. 1- 1979-. 0141-1071. Monographic Series. US. English. an. Medical Publications Division, 70 Lincoln Street, Boston MA 02111. **NLM** W1 TO54W.

TP FAKULTESI MECMUASI *CEASED.* **Main/Corp** Istanbul Universite. TP Fakultesi. V. 1-14, 1919-1932. 0047-1623. Periodical. TU. Turkish. mo. Istanbul Universites, Istanbul Turkey. **Ind/Abst** Excerpta Med. **LC** R97.7.T8. **NLM** W1 TI81.

TRAINING HEALTH PROFESSIONALS. **Main/Corp** United States. Health Resources Administration. Bureau of Health Professions. 1978/79-. 0273-3331. US. English. an. US Department of Health & Human Services, 200 Independence Avenue SW, Washington DC 20201. **LC** R745. **DD** 353.00841.

TRANSACTIONS. **Main/Corp** Medical Society of London. V. 13- 1889/90-. 0076-6011. UK. English. an. 10. Medical Society of London, 11 Chandos Street, Cavendish Square, London W1 England. **Tel** (01)580 1043. **Ed** R P Rosswick. **Ind/Abst** Index Med. **Circ** 700. Papers presented to the Society in each year.

Medicine

TRANSACTIONS & STUDIES OF THE COLLEGE OF PHYSICIANS OF PHILADELPHIA. Main/Corp College of Physicians of Philadelphia. VFOAT Transactions and Studies of the College of Physicians of Philadelphia. Ser. 4, V. 6, No. 1- June 1938-. 0010-1087. US. English. qt. $30.00. College of Physicians of Philadelphia, 19 South 22 Street, Philadelphia PA 19103. Tel (215)561-0360. Ed John L McClenahan. Ind/Abst Biol. Abstr., Hospit. Lit. Index, Energy Res. Abstr., Chem. Abstr., Index Med. NLM W1 TR2231. CODEN TSCPAI. bk rev. Circ 2,300. Current medical topics, medical ethics, and medical history. *Transactions of the College of Physicians of Philadelphia, 0093-2949.*

TRANSACTIONS - NORTH CAROLINA MEDICAL SOCIETY. Main/Corp North Carolina Medical Society. 0361-5537. US. English. an. 222 North Person Street, Raleigh NC 27611. LC R15. DD 610.62756. *Transactions of the Medical Society of the State of North Carolina.*

TRANSACTIONS OF THE AMERICAN CLINICAL AND CLIMATOLOGICAL ASSOCIATION. Main/Corp American Clinical and Climatological Association. V. 49- 1933-. 0065-7778. US. English. an. American Clinical & Climatological Association, 720 Rutland Avenue, 522 Taylor Boulevard, Baltimore MA 21205. Ind/Abst Excerpta Med., Energy Res. Abstr., Chem. Abstr., Biol. Abstr., Index Med., Nucl. Sci. Abstr., Hospit. Lit. Index. NLM W1 TR224L. CODEN TACCAN. *Transactions of the American Climatological and Clinical Association, 0732-3255.*

TRANSACTIONS OF THE ASSOCIATION OF AMERICAN PHYSICIANS. Main/Corp Association of American Physicians. V. 1- 1886-. 0066-9458. US. English. an. Transactions of the Association of American Physicians, PO Box 64025, Baltimore MD 21264. Tel (301)528-4105. Ind/Abst Excerpta Med., Energy Res. Abstr., Chem. Abstr., Index Med., Sci. Cit. Index, Abr. Ed. LC R15. NLM W1 TR225J. CODEN TAAPAI. (cum index).

TRANSACTIONS OF THE ASSOCIATION OF LIFE INSURANCE MEDICAL DIRECTORS OF AMERICA - ANNUAL MEETING. See Insurance.

TRANSACTIONS OF THE BRITISH MYCOLOGICAL SOCIETY. See Biology.

TRANSACTIONS OF THE ROYAL SOCIETY OF TROPICAL MEDICINE AND HYGIENE. Main/Corp Royal Society of Tropical Medicine and Hygiene. V. 14- May 1920-. 0035-9203. Periodical. UK. English. bm. 65.00. Royal Society of Tropical Medicine, Manson House/26 Portland Place, London W1N 4EY England. Tel (01)580 2127. Ed S Willmott. Ind/Abst Life Sci. Collect., Excerpta Med., Index Med., Chem. Abstr., Bibliogr. Agric., Sci. Cit. Index, Abr. Ed. NLM W1 TR227M. CODEN TRSTAZ. bk rev. adv acc. Circ 4,000. (ctrl). Articles on research and treatment of diseases in man and other animals in warm climates. *Transactions of the Society of Tropical Medicine and Hygiene.*

TRENDS IN BHPR PROGRAM STATISTICS. GRANTS, AWARDS, LOANS. See Statistics.

TROPICA-CANADA. (TROPICA-CANADA : NEWSLETTER OF THE INTERNATIONAL HEALTH COMMITTEE, CANADIAN SOCIETY FOR TROPICAL MEDICINE AND INTERNATIONAL HEALTH). VFOAT Newsletter of the International Health Committee, Canadian Society for Tropical Medicine and International Health. Vol. 1, No. 1 (Winter 1982/83)-. 0715-7614. Periodical. CN. English. qt. Free. Canadian Society for Tropical Medicine and International Health, Suite 210/1335 Carling Avenue, Ottawa Ontario K1Z 8N8 Canada. DD 616.988305.

TROPICA-CANADA. (TROPICA-CANADA : NEWSLETTER OF THE INTERNATIONAL HEALTH COMMITTEE, CANADIAN SOCIETY FOR TROPICAL MEDICINE AND INTERNATIONAL HEALTH). VFOAT Newsletter of the International Health Committee, Canadian Society for Tropical Medicine and International Health, Bulletin du Comite de la Sante Internationale, Societe Canadienne pour la Medecine Tropicale et la Sante Internationale. Vol. 1, No. 1 (Autumn 1983)-. 0823-5848. Periodical. CN. French. qt. Free. Societe Canadienne pour la Medecine Tropicale et la Sante Internationale, Bureau 210/1335 Ave Carling, Ottawa Ontario K1Z 8N8 Canada. DD 616.988305.

TROPICAL AND GEOGRAPHICAL MEDICINE. V. 10- 1958-. 0041-3232. Periodical. English (summaries in Spanish). qt. $57.00. Foris Publications, PO Box 509, 3300 AM Dordrecht Netherlands. Tel (78)510454. Ed L C Vogel. Ind/Abst Life Sci. Collect., Excerpta Med., Index Med., Bibliogr. Agric., Hospit. Lit. Index. NLM W1 TR878M. bk rev. adv acc. Circ 1,100. Tropical diseases and disease in the tropics; tropical public health and geographical pathology; pathology and parasitology in the tropics and medical care in developing countries. *Documenta de Medicine Geographica et Tropica.*

TROPICAL DISEASES BULLETIN. V. 1- Nov. 15, 1912-. 0041-3240. Periodical. UK. English. mo. $131.00. Bureau of Hygiene and Tropical Diseases, Keppel Street, London WC1E 7HT England. Ind/Abst Index Med. LC RC960. DD 616. Index in last issue of volume - attached. *Bulletin of the Sleeping Sickness Bureau and the Kala Azar Bulletin.*

TROPICAL DISEASES RESEARCH SERIES. No. 1-. 0252-9750. Monographic Series. English. ir. LC UNC. NLM W3 TR856.

TROPICAL DOCTOR. V. 1-Jan. 1971-. 0049-4755. Periodical. UK. English. qt. $40.00. Oxford University Press, Journals Department, Walton Street, Oxford OX2 6DP England. Tel 0865 56767. Ed M J Colbourne and A B Laing. Ind/Abst Life Sci. Collect., Excerpta Med., Index Med., Cumul. Index Nurs. Allied Health Lit., Biol. Abstr., Hospit. Lit. Index. LC RC960. DD 616.988305. NLM W1 TR88G. CODEN TPDCAV. Contains contributions on prevention, management and treatment of prevalent diseases providing a postgraduate course in the practice of medicine in tropical countries.

TROPICAL MEDICINE AND PARASITOLOGY. Vol. 36, No. 1 (Mar. 1985)-. 0177-2392. Periodical. GW. English. qt. 160.00 Members, 208.00 Nonmembers. Ind/Abst Index Med. NLM W1. CODEN TMPAEY. *Tropenmedizin und Parasitologie, 0303-4208.*

TROPICAL MEDICINE RESEARCH STUDIES SERIES. 1-. 0276-797X. Monographic Series. UK. English. ir. Research Studies Press, 8 Willian Way Letchworth, Herts SG6 2HG England. Ed K N Brown. NLM W1 TR883F.

TRUDY KLINICHESKOGO OTDELA INSTITUTA. Vol. 1- 1970-. UR. Russian. NLM W1 TR956G.

TUBERCULOSIS STATISTICS. STATES AND CITIES. See Statistics.

TUNISIE MEDICALE. (LA TUNISIE MEDICALE). Began in 1929?. 0041-4131. Periodical. TI. French. bm. Tunisie Medicale, 18 rue de Russie, Tunis Tunisie. Ind/Abst Excerpta Med., Index Med. NLM W1 TU726. *Revue Tunisienne des Sciences Medicales.*

TURK TP DERNEGI DERGISI. VFOAT Journal of the Turkish Medical Society. Vol. 39 No. 9- 1973-. 0377-2497. Periodical. Turkish. mo. NLM W1 TU565I. *Turk TP Cemiyeti Mecmaus, 0494-2736.*

U C L A FORUM IN MEDICAL SCIENCES. Main/Corp California. University. University at Los Angeles. 0082-7134. US. English. ir. University of California Press, PO Box 1588, Richmond CA 94802.

UGESKRIFT FOR LAGER. Vol. 1- 1839-. 0041-5782. DK. Danish. wk. 12 A Kristianiagade, DK 2100 Copenhagen Denmark. Ind/Abst Life Sci. Collect., Excerpta Med., Index Med., Biol. Abstr., CIS Abstr., Art Archaeol. Tech. Abstr., Chem. Abstr., Energy Res. Abstr. NLM W1 UG13. CODEN UGLAAD.

UIHAK YONGU. VFOAT Medical Research. Periodical. KO. Korean (with summaries in English). ir. Choson Taehakkyo Uihak Yonguso, 17 Pullo-dong, Tong-ku Kwangju-si Korea. LC R97.7.K6.

UIRUSU. VFOAT Virus. V. 1- April 1951-. 0042-6857. Periodical. JA. Japanese. sa. $46.50. Japan Publishers Trading Company Ltd, PO Box 5030, Tokyo International, Tokyo 100-31 Japan. Ind/Abst Life Sci. Collect., Excerpta Med., Biol. Abstr., Chem. Abstr., Index Med. NLM W1 UI332U. CODEN UIRUAF.

ULSTER MEDICAL JOURNAL. V. 1- Jan. 1932-. 0041-6193. Periodical. UK. English. sa. $15.33. Ulster Medical Journal, Institute of Clinical Science, Grosvenor Road, Belfast BT12 6BJ North Ireland. Tel (0232) 222043. Ed D R Hadden. Ind/Abst Life Sci. Collect., Excerpta Med., Index Med., Sci. Cit. Index, Abr. Ed., Hospit. Lit. Index. NLM W1 UL72X. bk rev. adv acc. Circ 1,000. Medicine in general; medicine in Ireland. *Transactions of the Ulster Medical Society.*

ULTRASCHALL IN DER MEDIZIN. (ULTRASCHALL IN DER MEDIZIN : ORGAN DER DEUTSCHEN GESELLSCHAFT FUR ULTRASCHALL IN DER MEDIZIN, DER OSTERREICHISCHEN GESELLSCHAFT FUR ULTRASCHALL IN DER MEDIZIN, DER SCHWEIZERISCHEN GESELLSCHAFT FUR ULTRASCHALL IN MEDIZIN UND BIOLOGIE. BIOLOGIE). V. 1, No.1, (May 80)-. 0172-4614. Periodical. German. bm. $70.00. Thieme-Stratton Inc, 381 Park Avenue, New York NY 10016. Tel (212)683-5088. Ind/Abst Excerpta Med., Index Med. NLM W1 UL7301.

ULTRASOUND IN BIOMEDICINE RESEARCH SERIES. 0277-254X. Monographic Series. UK. English. ir. Research Studies Press, 8 William Way, Letchworth Herts SG6 2HG England. Ind/Abst Comput. Control Abstr., Electr. Electron. Abstr., Sci. Abstr. Sect. A. Phys. Abstr.

ULTRASOUND IN MEDICINE. Main/Corp American Institute of Ultrasound in Medicine. V. 1- 1975-. 0098-0382. US. English. an. Plenum Press, 227 West 17th Street, New York NY 10011. LC RC78.7.U4. DD 616.0754. NLM W3 UL849. *Annual Scientific Conference of the American Institute of Ultrasound Medicine, 0065-8871.*

ULTRASOUND IN MEDICINE & BIOLOGY. VAT Ultrasound in Medicine and Biology. V. 1- Sept. 1973-. 0301-5629. Periodical. US. English. bm. Pergamon Press, 395 Sawmill River Road, Elmsford NY 10523. Tel (914)592-7700. Ind/Abst Electron. Commun. Abstr. J., ISMEC Bull., Pollut. Abstr. Indexes, Saf. Sci. Abstr. J., Life Sci. Collect., Excerpta Med., Index Med., Int. Aerosp. Abstr., Biol. Abstr., Comput. Control Abstr., Electr. Electron. Abstr., Sci. Abstr. Sect. A. Phys. Abstr., Bibliogr. Agric., Appl. Mech. Rev., Phys. Abstr., Hospit. Lit. Index, Sci. Cit. Index, Abr. Ed. LC RM862.7. DD 616.0754. NLM W1 UL751. CODEN USMBA3.

UNDERWATER MEDICINE. Vol. 1, No. 1 (Jan./Feb. 1986)-. 0886-3474. Periodical. US. English. bm. $60.00. Undersea Medical Society Inc, 9650 Rockville Pike, Bethesda MD 20814. DD 612. *Underwater Physiology Abstracts.*

UNDERWATER MEDICINE AND RELATED SCIENCES. V. 1- 1968/71-. 0191-2534. Periodical. US. English. Ed M F Werts and C W Shilling. NLM ZWD 650 S556AB.

UNIFORMED SERVICES MEDICAL/ DENTAL FACILITIES IN THE U.S.A. Series/Titl DOD PA. US. English. ir. American Forces Information Service, Department of Defense, Arlington VA 22209.

UNION LIST OF SERIALS IN MONTREAL HOSPITAL LIBRARIES. See Bibliographies.

UNION MEDICALE DU CANADA. (UNION MEDICALE DU CANADA). V. 1- Jan. 1872-. 0041-6959. Periodical. CN. French (summaries in French and English). mo. 60.00 Domestic, 75.00 US, 80.00 Foreign. Association des Medicale Langue Francaise Canada, 1440 Ste Catherine Ouest/Suite 510, Montreal Quebec H3G 2P9 Canada. Tel (514)866-2053. Ed Marcel Cadotte. Ind/Abst Life Sci. Collect., Excerpta Med., Index Med., Point Repere, Chem. Abstr. NLM W1 UN208. CODEN UMCAAA. bk rev. adv acc. Circ 13,000. (ctrl). Medical journal containing clinical and research papers, review articles, continuing medical education. Read by general practitioners, certified specialists, interns and residents.

U.S. ALPHABETICAL PHYSICIAN REFERENCE LISTING. VAT United States Alphabetical Physician Reference Listing. 0098-8413. US. English. Fisher-Stevens Inc, 120 Brighton Road, Clifton NJ 07012. LC R712.A1. DD 610.695202573.

U.S. MEDICAL DIRECTORY. See Yearbooks, Almanacs, Directories.

U.S. MEDICAL LICENSURE STATISTICS AND LICENSURE REQUIREMENTS. See Statistics.

U.S. MEDICINE. VAT United States Medicine. 1964. 0191-6246. Periodical. US. English. sm. $75.00. US Medicine Inc, 2033 M Street NW/Suite 505, Washington DC 20036. Tel (202)463-6000. Ed Nancy Tomich. Ind/Abst Hospit. Lit. Index. NLM W1 U752. bk rev. adv acc. Circ 32,000. (ctrl). Clinical, political

Medicine

U.S. NAVY MEDICINE. Series/Titl Navmed P. **VAT** United States Navy Medicine. Began with V. 56, No. 3, Sept. 1970. 0364-6807. Periodical. US. English. bm. Superintendent of Documents, US Government Printing Office, Washington DC 20402. **Ind/Abst** Life Sci. Collect., Index Dent. Lit., Index U.S. Gov. Period. **LC** R11. **DD** 359.3450973. **NLM** W2 A5 B9ME. *Navy Medical Newsletter.*

U.S. PHYSICIAN REFERENCE LISTING. VAT United States Physician Reference Listing. 1973-. 0098-986X. US. English. Fisher-Stevens Inc, 120 Brighton Road, Clifton NJ 07012. **LC** R712.A1. **DD** 610.2573. **NLM** W 22 AA1 U59. *AMA Physician Reference Listing, 0360-0998.*

UNIVERSITAS. CIENCIAS BIOLOGICAS. Periodical. Spanish. sa. **LC** R21.

THE UNIVERSITY OF CHICAGO SICKLE CELL CENTER HEMOGLOBIN SYMPOSIA. VFOAT Symposia. Vol. 1-. 0736-7406. Monographic Series. US. English. an. **LC** UNC. **DD** 616.1527005. **NLM** W3 UN94.

UNIVERSITY OF MINNESOTA CONTINUING MEDICAL EDUCATION. Series/Titl Publications in the Health Sciences. Vol. 1-. 0737-1276. Monographic Series. US. English. University of Minnesota Press, 2037 University Avenue SE, Minneapolis MN 55414. **LC** UNC. **DD** 610. **NLM** W1 UN944T.

UNIVERSITY OF MINNESOTA MEDICAL BULLETIN. Vol. 27 -. Periodical. US. English. qt. Minnesota Medical Foundation, Box 193 Mayo, Minneapolis MN 55455. **Tel** (218)373-8023. Ed Elaine Cunningham. **NLM** W1 MI773. **Circ** 15,000. (ctrl). Informs readers about the medical school. Features faculty, students, alumni and medical advances. *Bulletin of the University of Minnesota Hospitals and the Minnesota Medical Foundation.*

UNIVERSITY OF TORONTO MEDICAL JOURNAL. 0042-0239. Periodical. CN. English. qt. $9.28. University of Toronto Medical Journal, Medical Society of University Toronto, Toronto Ontario M5S 1A8 Canada. **Tel** (416)978-8730. **NLM** W1 UN961. adv acc.

UPDATE. V. 1- Oct. 1968-. 0301-5718. Periodical. UK. English. sm. $101.14. Update Publications Ltd, So Down House Station Road/Petersfield, Hampshire GU32 3ET England. **Ind/Abst** Excerpta Med. **NLM** W1 UP51. *Update Plus.*

UPDATE: COMPUTERS IN MEDICINE. (UPDATE, COMPUTERS IN MEDICINE). VFOAT Computers in Medicine. Vol. 1, No. 2 (Sept./Oct. 1983)-. 0738-0216. Periodical. US. English. bm. $24.00 Domestic, $30.00 Canada. Medical Market Communications, PO Box 2156, Princeton NJ 08540. **NLM** W1.

UPSALA JOURNAL OF MEDICAL SCIENCES. 0300-9734. Periodical. SW. English. ty. $30.00. Almqvist & Wiksell, 108 Drottninggatan, PO Box 45150, S-104 30 Stockholm Sweden. **Tel** 85413160. **Ind/Abst** Life Sci. Collect., Excerpta Med., Index Med., Biol. Abstr., Chem. Abstr., Sci. Cit. Index, Abr. Ed. **NLM** W1 UP67K. **CODEN** UJMSAP. *Acta Societas Medicorum Upsaliensis.*

UREMIA INVESTIGATION. Vol. 8, No. 1-. 0740-1353. Periodical. US. English. qt. $125.00. Marcel Dekker Journals, PO Box 11305 Church Street Station, New York NY 10249. Ed Kurt H Stengel and Albert L Rubin. **Ind/Abst** Life Sci. Collect., Chem. Abstr., Index Med. **DD** 617. **NLM** W1. **CODEN** URINDF. bk rev. adv acc. *Clinical and Experimental Dialysis and Apheresis, 0276-5497.*

URGENTIS CHIRURGIAE COMMENTARIA. (URGENTIS CHIRURGIAE COMMENTARIA : ORGANO DELLA SOCIETA ITALIANA DI CHIRURGIA D'URGENZA, DI PRONTO SOCCORSO, DI TERAPIA INTENSIVA CHIRURGICA). Vol. 1, N. 1 (Jan. 1978)-. 0392-8101. Periodical. Italian (articles in English or French). ty. **NLM** W1 UR246.

USSR REPORT. SPACE BIOLOGY AND AEROSPACE MEDICINE. V. 13, No. 4- Oct. 9, 1979-. 0196-9269. Periodical. US. English. ir. **NLM** W1 U758. *Space Biology and Aerospace Medicine, 0149-8762.*

UWO MEDICAL JOURNAL. (U W O MEDICAL JOURNAL). VFOAT University of Western Ontario Medical Journal. V. 26, No. 4-40, No. 4. 0315-4378. Periodical. CN. English. qt. $9.28. University of Western Ontario, London Ontario Canada. **NLM** W1 U78. *University of Western Ontario Medical Journal.*

VACCINATION CERTIFICATE REQUIREMENTS FOR INTERNATIONAL TRAVEL AND HEALTH ADVICE TO TRAVELLERS. *See* Travel.

VACCINE. Vol. 1, No. 1 (Dec. 1983)-. 0264-410X. Periodical. UK. English. qt. $162.00. Butterworths Scientific Ltd, Box 63 Westbury House Bury Street, Guilford GU1 5BH England. Ed R E Spier (0483) 31261. **Ind/Abst** Life Sci. Collect., Index Med., Chem. Abstr. **NLM** W1. **CODEN** VACCDE. bk rev. adv acc. Covers design, production and testing of human and veterinary vaccines. Control of vaccines, public health, social and ethical considerations are also covered.

VANDERBILT MEDICAL ALUMNI DIRECTORY. *See* Yearbooks, Almanacs, Directories.

VASCULAR DIAGNOSIS & THERAPY. VFOAT Vascular Diagnosis and Therapy. Began with Vol. 1 (Oct./Nov. 1980). 0273-7140. Periodical. US. English. bm. $30.00. Barrington Publications Inc, 825 South Barrington Avenue, Los Angeles CA 90049. **NLM** W1 VA919.

VASCULAR MEDICINE. Vol. 1, No. 1 (Jan.-Mar. 1983)-. 0738-4580. Periodical. US. English. qt. $50.00 Domestic, $55.00 Foreign. Westminster Publications, 320 Northern Boulevard, Great Neck NY 11021. **NLM** W1 VA92J.

VASCULAR VIEWS. 8756-3401. Periodical. US. English. mo. $18.00. Vascular Training Center, 2001 West Orange Grove Road/Suite 262, Tucson AZ 85704. **DD** 616.

VERHANDLUNGEN DER ANATOMISCHEN GESELLSCHAFT. 1.-. 0066-1562. Periodical. German. ir. VCH Publishers Inc, 303 NW 12th Avenue, Deerfield Beach FL 33442. **Tel** (212)683-5088. **Ind/Abst** Biol. Abstr., Chem. Abstr., Index Med. **NLM** W1 VE483K. **CODEN** VHAGAS.

VERHANDLUNGEN DER DEUTSCHEN GESELLSCHAFT FUR HERZ- UND KREISLAUFFORSCHUNG. *See* Medicine - Cardiovascular Diseases.

VERHANDLUNGSBERICHT DER DEUTSCHEN GESELLSCHAFT FUR LASERMEDIZIN E.V. Main/Conf Deutsche Gesellschaft fur Lasermedizin. 1. (3.-6. Nov. 1982)-. 0724-6765. German. ir. **NLM** W1.

VEROFFENTLICHUNGEN. Main/Corp Schweizerische Gesellschaft fur Geschichte der Medizin und der Naturwissenschaften. 1- 1922-. Monographic Series. SZ. German. ir. Sauerlaender AG, CH-5001 Aarau Switzerland.

VEROFFENTLICHUNGEN AUS DEM INSTITUT FUR WEHRMEDIZIN UND HYGIENE, ERNST-RODENWALDT-INSTITUT. VFOAT Veroffentlichungen Wehr Med Inst. 0720-8480. Periodical. English (German). ir. Wehrmedinst, Viktoriastrasse 11-13, 5400 Koblenz West Germany. **LC** RC970. **DD** 616.98023.

VIATA MEDICALA. V. 22- Aug. 1974-. 0042-5036. Periodical. RM. Romanian. mo. **Ind/Abst** CIS Abstr., Int. Nurs. Index. **NLM** W1 VI169C. *Munca Sanitara, 0027-318X.*

VIDA MEDICA. Began publication in 1963. Periodical. Spanish. ir. **NLM** W1 VI189H. *Colegio Medico - Vida Medica.*

VIEWPOINT. *See* Insurance.

VIRGINIA FAMILY PHYSICIAN. V. 26- Jan. 1976-. 0194-1119. Periodical. US. English. bm. $15.00. Virginia Academy of Family Physicians, 4211 Dover Road, Richmond VA 23221. **NLM** W1 VI777L. *Virginia Family Practice News, 0091-2050.*

VIRGINIA LIFELINE. (VIRGINIA LIFELINE : OFFICIAL PUBLICATION OF VIRGINIA ASSOCIATION OF VOLUNTEER RESCUE SQUADS). 0279-6023. Periodical. US. English. mo. $7.50. Virginia Association Volunteer Rescue Squad, 2015 Staples Mill Road/Suite 429, Richmond VA 23230. **Tel** (804)355-5757. *First Aid Bulletin, 0273-8309.*

VIRGINIA MEDICAL. V. 103, No. 8- Aug. 1976-. 0146-3616. Periodical. US. English. mo. $12.00. Virginia Medical, 4205 Dover Road, Virginia Medical Monthly 23221. **Tel** (804)353-2721. Ed Ann Gray. **Ind/Abst** Excerpta Med., Hospit. Lit. Index, Index Med., Energy Res. Abstr. **NLM** W1 VI799I. bk rev. adv acc. **Circ** 7,200. (ctrl). Medical journal of the Medical Society of Virginia. *Virginia Medical Monthly, 0042-6644.*

VIRUS RESEARCH : AN INTERNATIONAL JOURNAL OF MOLECULAR AND CELLULAR VIROLOGY. Vol. 1, No. 1 (Jan. 1984)-. 0168-1702. Periodical. NE. English. bm. Elsevier Science Publishers, PO Box 211, 1000 AE Amsterdam The Netherlands. **Tel** (20)5803.911. **Ind/Abst** Life Sci. Collect., Chem. Abstr., Index Med. **NLM** W1 VI836D. **CODEN** VIREDF.

VITAL & HEALTH STATISTICS. SERIES 3, ANALYTICAL AND EPIDEMIOLOGICAL STUDIES. *See* Statistics.

VITAL NOTES ON MEDICAL PERIODICALS : A PUBLICATION OF THE MEDICAL LIBRARY ASSOCIATION CEASED. Began with V. 1, No. 1 (Oct, 1952). Ceased with V. 30, No. 3, (Dec. 1982). 0042-7411. Periodical. US. English. ty. **LC** Z6660, Z6658. **DD** 016.6105. **NLM** ZW 1 V836. Index in last issue of volume - attached. (cum index).

VITAL STATISTICS (QUARTERLY). *See* Statistics.

VOENNO-MEDICINSKIJ ZURNAL. (VOENNO-MEDITSINSKII ZHURNAL). 0026-9050. Periodical. UR. Russian. mo. $26.00. Victor Kamkin Inc (70138), 12224 Parklawn Drive, Rockville MD 20852. **Tel** (301)881-5973. **Ind/Abst** Chem. Abstr., Index Med., Int. Aerosp. Abstr. **NLM** W1 VO22. **CODEN** VMEZA4.

VOLUNTARY EFFORT QUARTERLY. V. 1- Feb. 1979-. 0193-2179. Periodical. US. English. qt. The Voluntary Effort, 840 North Lake Shore Drive, Chicago IL 60611. **NLM** W1 VO594F.

VOPROSY KLINICESKOJ MEDICINY. (VOPROSY KLINICHESKOI MEDITSINY). Vol. 1- 1970-. 0137-0618. UR. Russian. **NLM** W1 VO634L.

VOPROSY KURORTOLOGII, FIZIOTERAPII I LECEBNOJ FIZICESKOJ KULTURY. (VOPROSY KURORTOLOGII, FIZIOTERAPII I LECHEBNOI FIZICHESKOI KULTURY). Began 1955. 0042-8787. Periodical. UR. Russian. bm. Victor Kamkin Inc, 12224 Parklawn Drive, Rockville MD 20852. **Tel** (301)881-5973. **Ind/Abst** Index Med., Int. Aerosp. Abstr., Chem. Abstr. **NLM** W1 VO636. **CODEN** VKFLAL. *Voprosy Kurortologii.*

VRACEBNOE DELO CEASED. (VRACHEBNOE DELO, NAUCHNYI MEDITSINSKII ZHURNAL). 0049-6804. Periodical. UR. Russian. mo. $40.50. Victor Kamkin Inc (74088), 12224 Parklawn Drive, Rockville MD 20852. **Tel** (301)881-5973. **Ind/Abst** Chem. Abstr., Excerpta Med., Index Med., Biol. Abstr. **NLM** W1 VR181. **CODEN** VRDEA5.

WADLEY MEDICAL BULLETIN. 0097-5427. Periodical. US. English. qt. Wadley Institute of Molecular Medicine, 9000 Harry Mines Boulevard, Dallas TX 75235. **Ind/Abst** Chem. Abstr. **NLM** W1 WA204. **CODEN** WDMBAM.

WAKAYAMA IGAKU. VFOAT Journal of the Wakayama Medical Society. Began 1950. 0043-0013. Periodical. Japanese (with summaries in English). qt. The Wakayama Medical Society, 9 Kyuban-Cho, Wakayama-Shi 640 Japan. **Ind/Abst** Excerpta Med., Chem. Abstr. **NLM** W1 WA215. **CODEN** WKMIAO.

WARASAN KROMKANPAET LAE ANAMAI. (JOURNAL OF THE DEPARTMENT OF MEDICAL AND HEALTH SERVICES). V. 1, No. 3- May 1973-. 0125-1643. Periodical. Thai. ir. **NLM** W1 JO918X. *Warasan Kromkanpaet Lae Anamai, 0125-1643.*

WASHINGTON HEALTH COSTS LETTER. *See* Insurance.

THE WASHINGTON PHYSICIANS DIRECTORY. *See* Yearbooks, Almanacs, Directories.

WASHINGTON REPORT ON MEDICINE & HEALTH. VAT Washington Report on Medicine and Health. No. 1107- Sept. 16, 1968-. 0043-0730. Periodical. US. English. wk. $297.00. McGraw Hill Publishers National Press, 1120 Vermont Avenue NW Suite 1200, Washington DC 20005. **Tel** (202)463-1700. **Ind/Abst** Hospit. Lit. Index. **NLM** W1 WA621. *Washington Report on the Medical Sciences.*

Medicine

WESLEY W. SPINK LECTURES ON COMPARATIVE MEDICINE. US. English. ir. University of Minnesota Press, 2037 University Avenue, Minneapolis MN 55455.

WEST INDIAN MEDICAL JOURNAL. (THE WEST INDIAN MEDICAL JOURNAL). V. 1-, 1951-. 0043-3144. Periodical. JM. English. qt. $30.00. West Indian Medical Journal, University of West Indies, Mona Kingston Jamaica. **Tel** (809)927-6214. Ed Vasil Persaud. **Ind/Abst** Life Sci. Collect., Excerpta Med., Index Med., Chem. Abstr., Hospit. Lit. Index. **NLM** W1 WE389. **CODEN** WIMJAD. bk rev. adv acc. **Circ** 2,000. Medical research in clinical and community medicine in the English speaking Caribbean. *Jamaica Medical Journal.*

WEST VIRGINIA DOCTORS OF MEDICINE. 0743-1333. US. English. West Virginia Statistics Center, 1800 Washington Street, East Charleston WV 25305. **LC** RA410.8.W4. **DD** 331.12516109754.

WEST VIRGINIA MEDICAL JOURNAL. V. 1- Aug. 1906-. 0043-3284. Periodical. US. English. mo. $10.00. West Virginia Medical Journal, PO Box 4106-4307, MacCorkle Avenue, Charleston WV 25364. **Tel** (304)925-0342. Ed Stephen Ward. **Ind/Abst** Life Sci. Collect., Excerpta Med., Hospit. Lit. Index, Index Med., Energy Res. Abstr. **NLM** W1 WE456. bk rev. adv acc. **Circ** 2,627. (ctrl). Scientific, socio-economic news of medicine in West Virginia. Official journal of West Virginia State Medical Association.

WESTERN JOURNAL OF MEDICINE. (THE WESTERN JOURNAL OF MEDICINE). V. 120- Jan. 1974-. 0093-0415. Periodical. US. English. mo. $30.00. California Medical Association, 44 Gough Street, San Francisco CA 94103. **Tel** (415)863-5522. Ed Malcolm S M Watts. **Ind/Abst** Life Sci. Collect., Excerpta Med., Hospit. Lit. Index, Coal Abstr., Index Med., Cumul. Index Nurs. Allied Health Lit., Chem. Abstr., Bibliogr. Agric., Energy Res. Abstr., Sci. Cit. Index, Abr. Ed. **LC** R15. **DD** 610.5. **NLM** W1 WE632J. **CODEN** WJMDA2. bk rev. adv acc. **Circ** 51,000. Contains articles for physicians on medical practice and research. Content is of interest to general physicians, specialists and health-care workers. Also publishes medical socioeconomics. *California Medicine, 0008-1264.*

WEST'S PERSONAL INJURY NEWS. **VFOAT** Personal Injury News. Vol. 1, No. 1 (Mar. 8, 1983)-. 0746-1526. Periodical. US. English. bw. $80.00. West Publishing Company, 50 West Kellogg Boulevard, PO Box 3526, St Paul MN 55166.

WHO'S WHO IN MEDICINE. English. ir. Who's Who International Red Series, Postfach 1150, D-8031 Woerthsee West Germany. **LC** R512.A1. **DD** 610.922B. **NLM** W 22 GG4 WG.

WIADOMOSCI MELIORACYJNE I LAKARSKIE. V. 2- 1959-. 0510-4262. Periodical. PL. Polish. mo. ARS Polona, Krakowskie Przedmiescie 7, 00-068 Warsaw Poland. **Ind/Abst** Bibliogr. Agric.

WID NEWS. See Communication.

WIENER KLINISCHE WOCHENSCHRIFT. 0043-5325. Periodical. AU. German. sm. Springer Verlag-New York Inc, 175 5th Avenue, New York NY 10010. **Tel** (212)460-1500. Ed O Kraupp and E Deutsch. **Ind/Abst** Life Sci. Collect., Excerpta Med., Pestdoc, Ringdoc, Vetdoc, Index Med., Biol. Abstr., CIS Abstr., Chem. Abstr., Curr. Contents, Sci. Cit. Index, Abr. Ed. **NLM** W1 WI28. **CODEN** WKWOAO. Main purpose is the continued education of physicians and the documentation of medical research findings. Reviews and original works in all areas of clinical medicine and new drugs (with supplements).

WISCONSIN MEDICAL ALUMNI QUARTERLY. 8755-1519. Periodical. US. English. qt. 758 Warf Building, 610 North Walnut Street, Madison WI 53706. **DD** 610.

WISCONSIN MEDICAL JOURNAL. V. 1- Jan. 1903-. 0043-6542. Periodical. US. English. mo. $25.00 Foreign. State Medical Society of Wisconsin, PO Box 1109, Madison WI 53701. **Tel** (608)257-6781. Ed Mary Angell. **Ind/Abst** Life Sci. Collect., Excerpta Med., Hospit. Lit. Index, Index Med., Cumul. Index Nurs. Allied Health Lit., Energy Res. Abstr. **LC** R11. **DD** 610.5. **NLM** W1 WI801G. bk rev. adv acc. **Circ** 6,000. (ctrl). Contains scientific articles, socioeconomic organizational, medical meetings, classified advertisements, physical news, and special articles.

WISCONSIN PHYSICIANS, DESCRIPTION AND DISTRIBUTION. (WISCONSIN PHYSICIANS : DESCRIPTION AND DISTRIBUTION). 0361-817X. US. English. an. Wisconsin Department of Health & Social Services, PO Box 309, Madison WI 53701. **LC** RA410.8.W6. **DD** 331.11.

WISCONSIN PUBLICATIONS IN THE HISTORY OF SCIENCE AND MEDICINE. No. 1-. 0736-4318. Monographic Series. US. English. ty. University of Wisconsin Press, PO Box 1379, Madison WI 53701. Ed William Coleman, David C Lindberg, and Ronald L Numbers. **NLM** W1 WI805.

WISSENSCHAFTLICHE ZEITSCHRIFT - ERNST-MORITZ-ARNDT-UNIVERSITAT GREIFSWALD. MEDIZINISCHE REIHE. VAT Wissenschaftliche Zeitschrift der Ernst Moritz Arndt Universitat Griefswald. Medizinische Reihe. Volume 21- 1972-. 0138-1067. German. qt. Deutscher Buch Export Import, Leninstrasse 16, DDR-701 Leipzig East Germany. **Ind/Abst** Chem. Abstr., Am. Hist. Life, Hist. Abstr., MLA Int. Bibliogr. Books Artic. Mod. Lang. Lit. **NLM** W1 WI984. **CODEN** WZERDH.

WOLGAN HANUIYAK CHONGBO. **VFOAT** Hanuiyak Chongbo, Oriental Medicine Information. Periodical. KO. Korean. ir. 7,400. Hanuiyak Chongbo Sa, 145 Chongjin-dong, Chongno-ku, Seoul South Korea. **LC** R97.7.K6.

WOMEN IN MEDICAL ACADEMIA. V. 1- Winter 1977-. 0162-6892. Periodical. US. English. American Medical Women's Association/Professional Resources Research Center, 2302 E Speedway Boulevard Suite 206A, Tucson AZ 85719. **NLM** W1 WO481.

WORCESTER MEDICAL NEWS. V. 1- Feb. 1937-. 0043-7905. Periodical. US. English. bm. $10.00. Worcester Dis Medical Society, 321 Main Street, Worcester MA 01608. **Tel** (617)753-1579. **Ind/Abst** Energy Res. Abstr. **NLM** W1 WO845N.

WORKING PAPER - UNIVERSITY OF NEWCASTLE, FACULTY OF MEDICINE. (WORKING PAPER). No. 1-. 0813-4472. Monographic Series. English. ir. **NLM** W1 WO848DS.

WORKSHOP CONFERENCES HOECHST. Series/Titl Excerpta Medica : International Congress Series. V. 1- 1973-. Periodical. English. ir. **Ind/Abst** Biol. Abstr. **CODEN** WCHODW.

WORLD DIRECTORY OF MEDICAL SCHOOLS. See Yearbooks, Almanacs, Directories.

WORLD DIRECTORY OF SCHOOLS FOR MEDICAL ASSISTANTS. See Yearbooks, Almanacs, Directories.

WORLD MEDICAL JOURNAL. V. 1- Jan. 1954-. 0049-8122. Periodical. US. English (French and Spanish). bm. $9.00. American Medical Association, 535 North Dearborn Street, Chicago IL 60610. **Tel** (312)645-4927. **Ind/Abst** Life Sci. Collect., Hospit. Lit. Index. **LC** R5. **DD** 610.621. **NLM** W1 WO895. *Bulletin - World Medical Association.*

WORLD MEETINGS. MEDICINE. V. 1- Jan. 1978-. 0161-2875. US. English. qt. $145.00. MacMillan Publishing Company, 866 3rd Avenue, New York NY 10022. **Tel** (800)257-8247. Ed Clark Hansen. **NLM** W 3.5 W921. **CODEN** WMMEDT. **Circ** 400. A two year registry of future meetings on the subject of medicine, psychiatry, biology, clinical research, pharmacology, pediatrics and other pertinent topics.

THE WORLDWIDE GUIDE TO MEDICAL ELECTRONICS MARKETING REPRESENTATION. 1st- Ed. 0146-8014. Periodical. US. English. be. International Bio-Medical Information Service, PO Box 756, Miami FL 33156. Ed Adeline B Hale and Arthur B Hale. **NLM** QT 22.1 W927.

THE YALE JOURNAL OF BIOLOGY & MEDICINE. (THE YALE JOURNAL OF BIOLOGY AND MEDICINE). V. 1- Oct. 1928-. 0044-0086. Periodical. US. English. bm. $50.00 Domestic, $55.00 Foreign. Yale Journal of Biology and Medicine, 333 Cedar Street, New Haven CT 06510. **Tel** (203)785-4251. Ed Philip K Bondy. **Ind/Abst** Life Sci. Collect., Excerpta Med., Index Med., Biol. Abstr., Chem. Abstr., Energy Res. Abstr., Sci. Cit. Index, Abr. Ed., Hospit. Lit. Index. **LC** R11. **DD** 610.5. **NLM** W1 YA454. **CODEN** YJBMAU. bk rev. adv acc. **Circ** 600. Original contributions, medical reviews, case reports, medical history symposia related to biomedical matters.

YEAR BOOK HEMATOLOGY. 0882-5998. Periodical. US. English. an. $39.95. Year Book Medical Publishers Inc, 35 East Wacker Drive, Chicago IL 60601.

THE YEAR BOOK OF CRITICAL CARE MEDICINE. See Yearbooks, Almanacs, Directories.

THE YEAR BOOK OF DRUG THERAPY. See Yearbooks, Almanacs, Directories.

THE YEAR BOOK OF EMERGENCY MEDICINE. See Yearbooks, Almanacs, Directories.

THE YEAR BOOK OF FAMILY PRACTICE. See Yearbooks, Almanacs, Directories.

YEAR BOOK OF INFECTIOUS DISEASES. See Yearbooks, Almanacs, Directories.

YEAR BOOK OF MEDICINE. See Yearbooks, Almanacs, Directories.

THE YEAR BOOK OF SPORTS MEDICINE. See Yearbooks, Almanacs, Directories.

YEAR BOOK - ROYAL SOCIETY OF TROPICAL MEDICINE AND HYGIENE. See Yearbooks, Almanacs, Directories.

YEARBOOK AND DIRECTORY OF OSTEOPATHIC PHYSICIANS. See Yearbooks, Almanacs, Directories.

YEARBOOK OF PODIATRIC MEDICINE AND SURGERY. See Yearbooks, Almanacs, Directories.

YOKOHAMA MEDICAL BULLETIN. V. 1- Oct. 1950-. 0044-0531. Periodical. JA. English (contributions in French or German). bm. University School of Medicine, Yokohama Japan. **Ind/Abst** Excerpta Med., Biol. Abstr., Chem. Abstr. **NLM** W1 YO671. **CODEN** YMBUA7.

YONSEI MEDICAL JOURNAL. V. 1- 1960-. 0513-5796. Periodical. KO. English. sa. Yonsei University International, PO Box 1010, Seoul Korea. **Ind/Abst** Excerpta Med., Index Med., Chem. Abstr. **NLM** W1 YO682. **CODEN** YOMJA9.

YONSEI REPORTS ON TROPICAL MEDICINE. V. 1- 1970-. 0375-5207. Periodical. KO. English. an. Institute of Tropical Medicine, Central PO Box 1010, Seoul Korea. **Ind/Abst** Life Sci. Collect., Excerpta Med., Chem. Abstr. **NLM** W1 YO683. **CODEN** YRTMA6.

YOUR HEALTH AND MEDICAL BULLETIN. 0745-4627. Periodical. US. English. wk. Summit Publishing Company, Rouses Point NY 12979. *Medical Bulletin, 0273-5342.*

ZBORNIK RADOVA PRIRODNO-MATEMATICKOG FAKULTETA. SERIJA ZA BIOLOGIJU. See Biology.

ZDOROVE. 1955-. 0044-1945. Periodical. UR. Russian. mo. $17.00. Victor Kamkin Inc (70328), 12224 Parklawn Drive, Rockville MD 20852. **Tel** (301)881-5973. **Ind/Abst** Int. Aerosp. Abstr. **NLM** W1 ZD832.

ZEITSCHRIFT FUR ARZTLICHE FORTBILDUNG. Vol. 1- 1904-. 0044-2178. Periodical. GE. German. sm. $39.00. VCH Publishers Inc, 303 Northwest 12th Avenue, Deerfield Beach FL 33442. **Tel** (305)428-5566. **Ind/Abst** Excerpta Med., Index Med., CIS Abstr. **NLM** W1 ZE2302.

ZEITSCHRIFT FUR BADER- UND KLIMAHEILKUNDE. Vol. 27-. 0720-0587. Periodical. German. bm. Futura Media Services Inc, 295 Main Street, PO Box 298, Mount Kisco NY 10549. **Ind/Abst** Excerpta Med. **NLM** W1 ZE237C. *Zeitschrift fur Agewandte Bader- und Klimaheilkunde, 0084-5280.*

ZEITSCHRIFT FUR DIE GESAMTE INNERE MEDIZIN UND IHRE GRENZGEBIETE. Vol. 1- 1946-. 0044-2542. Periodical. GE. German (summaries and table of contents in English or Russian). sm. $69.96. Kunst & Wissen Erich Bieber, Dufourstrasse 51, CH-8008

Medicine—Allergic, Metabolic, Nutritional Diseases

Zurich Switzerland. Tel 011-41-1-69 44 20. **Ind/Abst** Life Sci. Collect., Excerpta Med., Index Med., Chem. Abstr. **NLM** W1 ZE266. **CODEN** ZGIMAL. Index published separately - free - automatically sent.

ZEITSCHRIFT FUR KLINISCHE MEDIZIN. VFOAT ZKM. V. 40, No. 1 (Jan. 1985)-. 0233-1608. Periodical. German (summaries in English and Russian). sa. Futura Media Services Inc, 295 Main Street, Mount Kisco NY 10549. Tel (914)666-3505. **Ind/Abst** Chem. Abstr. **NLM** W1. **CODEN** ZKMEEF. *Deutsche Gesundheitswesen.*

ZEITSCHRIFT FUR LYMPHOLOGIE. VFOAT Journal of Lymphology. V. 1- Sept. 1977-. 0343-8554. Periodical. English (articles in English or German). sa. Futura Media Services Inc, 295 Main Street, Mount Kisco NY 10549. Tel (914)666-3505. **Ind/Abst** Life Sci. Collect., Excerpta Med., Index Med., Biol. Abstr., Chem. Abstr., Sci. Cit. Index, Abr. Ed. **NLM** W1 ZE445D. **CODEN** ZELYDR.

ZEITSCHRIFT FUR MEDIZINISCHE LABORATORIUMSDIAGNOSTIK. Vol. 18- 1977-. 0323-5637. Periodical. SZ. German. bm. $49.28. Kunst & Wissen Erich Bieber, Dufourstrasse 51, CH-8008 Zurich Switzerland. Tel 011-41-1-69 44 20. **Ind/Abst** Excerpta Med., Index Med., Chem. Abstr. **NLM** W1 ZE461. **CODEN** ZMLADB. *Zeitschrift fur Medizinische Labortechnik, 0044-3069.*

ZEITSCHRIFT FUR MILITARMEDIZIN. 0514-8782. Periodical. SZ. German. bm. Kunst & Wissen Erich Bieber, Dufourstrasse 51, CH-8008 Zurich Switzerland. **Ind/Abst** Chem. Abstr. **LC** RC970. **NLM** W1 ZE465. **CODEN** ZEMIAF.

ZEITSCHRIFT FUR PARASITENKUNDE. VFOAT Parasitologic Research. Vol. 46 (27 Mar. 1975)-. 0044-3255. Periodical. English (some articles in German or French). bm. $265.00. Springer Verlag-New York Inc, 175 5th Avenue, New York NY 10010. Tel (212)460-1500. Ed B M Honigberg, H Mehlorn, H M Seitz and W Wulker. bk rev. Presents information on the latest developments in parasitology research, with a special emphasis on practical aspects such as immunodiagnosis, chemotherapy, and epidemiology. *Zeitschrift fur Parasitenkunde.*

ZEITSCHRIFT FUR PHYSIOTHERAPIE. Vol. 23-. 0003-9357. Periodical. SZ. German. bm. $34.43. Kunst & Wissen Erich Bieber, Dufourstrasse 51, CH-8008 Zurich Switzerland. Tel 011-41-1-69 44 20. **Ind/Abst** Excerpta Med. **NLM** W1 ZE54. **CODEN** ZPYTAF. *Archiv fur Physikalische Therapie, Balneologie und Klimatologie.*

ZEITSCHRIFT FUR TROPENMEDIZIN UND PARASITOLOGIE. Vol. 1-24. 0044-359X. Periodical. Multilingual (English and German with summaries in English). qt. $108.00. Thieme-Stratton Inc, 381 Park Avenue, New York NY 10016. Tel (212)683-5088. **Ind/Abst** CIS Abstr., Index Med., Sci. Cit. Index, Abr. Ed. **NLM** W1 ZE629.

ZEITSCHRIFT FUR UNFALLCHIRURGIE, VERSICHERUNGSMEDIZIN UND BERUFSKRANKHEITEN : OFFIZIELLES ORGAN DER SCHWEIZERISCHEN GESELLSCHAFT FUR UNFALLMEDIZIN UND BERUFSKRANKHEITEN. MALADI. Vol. 76, Issue 1 (March 1983)-. Periodical. French (German). qt. 97.-. Hans Huber Ag, Laenggasstr 76, CH 3000 Bern 9 Switzerland. Tel 031 24 25 33. Ed E Baur. **Ind/Abst** CIS Abstr., Excerpta Med., Index Med. **NLM** W1 ZE629T. bk rev. adv acc. Circ 700. Official journal of the Swiss Society for Accident-Medicine and Occupational Diseases. *Zeitschrift fur Unfallmedizin und Berufskrankheiten.*

ZENTRALBLATT FUR ARBEITSMEDIZIN, ARBEITSSCHUTZ, PROPHYLAXE UND ERGONOMIE. Vol. 30, No. 4- April 1980-. 0173-3338. German. ir. **Ind/Abst** Excerpta Med., Coal Abstr., Chem. Abstr., Energy Res. Abstr. **NLM** W1 ZE767M. **CODEN** ZAAEDK. *Zentralblatt fur Arbeitsmedizin, Arbeitsschutz und Prophylaze, 0340-7047.*

ZENTRALBLATT FUR BAKTERIOLOGIE MIKROBIOLOGIE UND HYGIENE. 1. ABT. ORIGINALE A: MEDIZINISCHE MIKROBIOLOGIE, INFEKTIONSKRANKHEITEN UND PARASITOLOGIE. See Biology - Microbiology.

ZENTRALBLATT GASTROENTEROLOGIE STOFFWECHSEL ENDOKRINOLOGIE. Periodical. Multilingual (English and German). mo. Springer Verlag-New York Inc, 175 5th Avenue, New York NY 10010. Tel (212)460-1500.

ZENTRALBLATT HAUT- UND GESCHLECHTSKRANKHEITEN. 138.- Vol. 0343-3048. English (German). mo. Springer Verlag-New York Inc, 175 5th Avenue, New York NY 10010. Tel (212)460-1500. Ed P Altmeyer and R Clorius. **NLM** ZWR 100 Z56. bk rev. Covers dermatology, venereology, andrology, diseases and therapy, diagnostic methods, convention meeting reports and book reviews. *Zentralblatt fur Haut- und Geschlechtskrankheiten, Sowie Deren Grenzgebieten.*

ZENTRALBLATT IMMUNOLOGIE, TRANSPLANTATION CEASED. VFOAT Zentralblatt fur die Gesamte Innere Medizin. 0301-5882. Periodical. German (articles in English). ir. **NLM** ZQW 504 Z56. *Kongresszentralblatt fur die Gesamte Innere Medizin und Ihre Grenzgebiete, 0024-9998.*

ZFA. ZEITSCHRIFT FUR ALLGEMEINMEDIZIN. VFOAT Zeitschrift fur Allgemeinmedizin. Vol. 52-. 0341-9835. Periodical. GW. German. ir. $81.00. Thieme-Stratton Inc, 381 Park Avenue South, New York NY 10016. Tel (212)683-5088. **Ind/Abst** Excerpta Med. **NLM** W1 Z11. *Zeitschrift fur Allgemeinmedizin, 0300-8673.*

ZHONGGUO YIXUE KEXUEYUAN XUEBAO. (CHUNG-KUO I HSUEH K'O HSUEH YUAN HSUEH PAO = ACTA ACADEMIAE MEDICINAE SINICAE). VFOAT Acta Academiae Medicinae Sinicae. V. 1, 1979-. 0253-3774. Periodical. CC. Chinese. bm. $14.31. China Publication Centre, PO Box 2820, Beijing China. **Ind/Abst** Index Med., Chem. Abstr. **NLM** W1 CH988CE. **CODEN** CIHPDR.

ZHONGGUO YIXUE WENZHAI. ZHONGYI. See Indexes/Abstracts.

ZHONGHUA XIAOHUA ZAZHI. (CHUNG-HUA HSIAO HUA TSA CHIH). VFOAT Chinese Journal of Digestion. Vol. 1-. 0254-1432. Periodical. CC. Chinese. qt. $4.50. China Publication Centre, PO Box 2820, Beijing China. **NLM** W1 CH9818M.

ZHONGHUA YISHI ZAZHI. (CHUNG-HUA I SHIH TSA CHIH). Aug. 1980-. 0255-7053. Periodical. Chinese. qt. $9.90. China Publication Centre, PO Box 2820, Beijing China. **LC** R601. **NLM** W1 CH982HM. *I Hsueh Shih Yu Pao Chien Tsa Chih.*

ZHONGHUA YIXUE ZAZHI. YINGWEBAN. (CHINESE MEDICAL JOURNAL). VFOAT Chung-Hua Hsueh Tsa Chih. New Series V. 1-4, Jan. 1975-Dec. 1978. 0366-6999. Periodical. CH. English (Chinese). mo. $113.00. China Books & Periodicals Inc, 2929 24th Street, San Francisco CA 94110. Tel (415)282-2994. **Ind/Abst** Biol. Abstr., Chem. Abstr., Coal Abstr., Excerpta Med., Index Med., Sci. Cit. Index, Abr. Ed., Hospit. Lit. Index. **NLM** W1 CH775B. **CODEN** CMJODS.

ZHONGHUA YUFANG-YIXUE ZAZHI. (CHUNG-HUA YU FANG I HSUEH TSA CHIH). VFOAT Zhonghua Yufangyixue Zazhi. 0253-9624. Periodical. Chinese (table of contents also in English). qt. **Ind/Abst** Index Med., Chem. Abstr. **NLM** W1 CH985H. **CODEN** CHYCDW.

ZHONGUA MINGUO MAZUI XUEHUI ZAZHI. (CHUNG-HUA MIN KUO MA TSUI HSUEH HUI TSA CHIH). VFOAT Acta Anaesthesiologica Sinica. Began with: Vol. 1, 1961. 0529-5769. Periodical. English (articles also in Chinese). qt. **NLM** W1 CH982R.

ZHONGXI YI JIEHE ZAZHI. (CHUNG HSI I CHIEH HO TSA CHIH). VFOAT Chinese Journal of Modern Developments in Traditional Medicine. Vol. 1, No. 1 (July 1981)-. 0254-9034. Periodical. CC. Chinese (summaries in English). qt. **Ind/Abst** Index Med. **LC** R97.7.C5. **DD** 610.5. **NLM** W1 CH977J.

ZHONGYAO TONGBAO. (CHUNG YAO TUNG PAO). Began with: Vol. 6, 1981. 0254-0029. Periodical. Chinese. bm. **Ind/Abst** Index Med., Chem. Abstr. **NLM** W1 CH991SB. **CODEN** CYTPDT.

ZHURNAL EKSPERIMENTAL'NOI I KLINICHESKOI MEDITSINY. Vol. 1- 1961. 0514-7484. Periodical. UR. Russian (title in Armenian precedes title). bm. $20.50. Victor Kamkin Inc, 12224 Parklawn Drive, Rockville MD 20852. Tel (301)881-5973. **Ind/Abst** Biol. Abstr., Chem. Abstr. **NLM** W1 ZH418E. **CODEN** ZKMAAX.

ZOONOSES. V. 1- Mar./June 1978-. Periodical. English. ir. Pan American Zoonoses Center, Casilla de Correo 23, Ramos Mejia Argentina. **LC** RC113.5. **DD** 616.9505. **NLM** W1 ZO614R.

ALLERGIC, METABOLIC, NUTRITIONAL DISEASES

ADVANCES IN METABOLIC DISORDERS. V. 1- 1964-. 0065-2903. US. English. ir. Academic Press, Library Services, Orlando FL 32887. Tel (305)345-2000. Ed Rachmiel Levine and Rolf Luft. **Ind/Abst** Life Sci. Collect., Energy Res. Abstr., Index Med. **LC** RC620.A1. **DD** 616.39. **NLM** W1 AD68.

ADVANCES IN METABOLIC DISORDERS. SUPPLEMENT. Latest Vol. No. 23, 1983. 0587-4394. Monographic Series. US. English. $65.00. Academic Press Inc, Library Services, Orlando FL 32887. Tel (305)345-2000. Ed Rachmiel Levine and Rolf Luft. **Ind/Abst** Life Sci. Collect., Chem. Abstr. **LC** Unc. **NLM** W1 AD68A. **CODEN** ADMDBP.

ALERGIA. 0002-5151. MX. Spanish. qt. $40.00. Alergia/Revista Iberoamericana c/o Dr J P Martin, F Emperador 6, Tecamachalo Edo de Mexico. Ed Jesus Perez Martin. **Ind/Abst** Biol. Abstr., Index Med. **NLM** W1 AL316C. **CODEN** ALEGAF. Circ 3,500. Allergy and clinical immunology. Abstracts of allergy original articles.

ALLERGIE UND IMMUNOLOGIE. Vol. 17- 1971-. 0323-4398. Periodical. GE. German. bi. $62.80. Deutscher Buch Export-Import, Leninstrasse 16, DDR-701 Leipzig East Germany. Tel 70131. Ed H Ambrosius Kleine-Natrop, and Lunzenauer. **Ind/Abst** Life Sci. Collect., Excerpta Med., Index Med., Biol. Abstr., Chem. Abstr. **NLM** W1 AL557E. **CODEN** ALIMCL. bk rev. adv acc. (ctrl). Publishes original articles and survey reports of the entire field of immunology and allergology. Experimental immunological investigations are also taken into consideration as clinical immunological and allergological ones. *Allergie und Asthma.*

ALLERGOLOGIE. Yearly V. 1, No. 1 (1. Quarterly 1978)-. 0344-5062. Periodical. GW. German. bm. $97.00. Dustri Verlag/Dr Karl Feistle, Bahnofstrasse 9 Postfach 49, 8024 Deisenhofen-West Germany. **Ind/Abst** Excerpta Med., Chem. Abstr. **NLM** W1. **CODEN** ALLRDI.

ALLERGY. VFOAT Acta Allergologica. V. 33- Feb. 1978-. 0105-4538. Periodical. DK. English. 930.00 Domestic, 1,054.00 US/Canada 1,006.00 Other Countries. Munksgaard Ltd, 35 Norre Sogade, DK-1370 Copenhagen K Denmark. Tel 1 12 70 30. Ed Gunnar Bendixen. **Ind/Abst** CIS Abstr., Life Sci. Collect., Pestdoc, Ringdoc, Vetdoc, Excerpta Med., Index Med., Biol. Abstr., Chem. Abstr., Energy Res. Abstr. **NLM** W1 AL564. **CODEN** LLRGDY. bk rev. adv acc. Circ 1,000. Covers allergology and immunology. *Acta Allergologica, 0001-5148.*

ALLERGY RELIEF. 0883-7767. Periodical. US. English. mo. $24.00. Rodale Press, 33 East Miner Street, Emmaus PA 18049.

ALLERGY SHOT. VFOAT A.I.A. Newsletter. V. 16- Winter 1979/80-. 0227-7387. Periodical. CN. English. qt. $10.00 Membership, Free to Members. Allergy Information Association, Suite 7, 25 Poynter Drive, Weston Ont M9R 1K8 Canada. **DD** 616.97. *Newsletter, 0705-0984.*

ANNALS OF ALLERGY. V. 1- July/Aug. 1943-. 0003-4738. Periodical. US. English (summaries of many articles in Spanish). mo. American College of Allergists, 800 East North West Highway, Mount Prospect IL 60056. Tel (202)625-2671. Ed J A Bellanti. **Ind/Abst** Life Sci. Collect., Pestdoc, Ringdoc, Vetdoc, Excerpta Med., CIS Abstr., Biol. Abstr., Chem. Abstr., Index Med., Nuci. Sci. Abstr., Sci. Cit. Index, Abr. Ed., Hospit. Lit. Index. **DD** 616. **NLM** W1 AN56. **CODEN** ANAEA3. bk rev. adv acc. Circ 6,100. Diagnosis, prognosis, treatment of allergic disorders, case reports, some papers on immunology, CME articles, abstracts, clinical allergy-immunology rounds, book reviews, editorials, and news items are included.

ANNALS OF NUTRITION AND METABOLISM. See Nutrition and Dietetics.

ANNUAL CONTRACTORS' CONFERENCE : PROGRAM. Main/Conf Contractors' Conference of the Artificial Kidney Program of the National Institute of Arthritis, Metabolism, and Digestive Diseases. 6th- 1973-. US.

English. an. Department of Health Education and Welfare, National Institutes of Health, 9000 Rockville Pike, Bethesda MD 20014. *Annual Contractors' Conference.*

ARERUGI. Began 1952. 0021-4884. Periodical. JA. Japanese (includes English summaries). mo. $99.00. Japan Publs Trading Co Ltd, PO Box 5030 Tokyo Intl, Tokyo 100-31 Japan. **Ind/Abst** Index Med., Biol. Abstr., Chem. Abstr. **NLM** W1 AR7563. **CODEN** ARERAM.

ASIAN PACIFIC JOURNAL OF ALLERGY AND IMMUNOLOGY. Vol. 1, No. 1 (June 1983)-. 0125-877X. Periodical. English. ir. $50.00. **NLM** W1 AS14F.

ASTHMA UPDATE. Winter 1985-. 8756-4734. Periodical. US. English. qt. $8.00. Asthma Update, 123 Monticello Avenue, Annapolis MD 21401. **Tel** (301)267-0309. **Ed** David C Jamison. **DD** 616. bk rev. **Circ** 250. Newsletter for people with asthma reporting current developments in asthma research and treatment from medical journals.

BEITRAGE ZU INFUSIONSTHERAPIE UND KLINISCHE ERNAHRUNG. Vol. 1-. 0378-8679. Monographic Series. SZ. English (articles and summaries in German). ir. S Karger AG, CH-4009 Basel Switzerland. **Tel** (61)390880. **Ed** H Reissigl, K H Bassler, U Henneberg and A Grunert. **Ind/Abst** Index Med., Chem. Abstr., Biol. Abstr. **NLM** W1 BE168M. **CODEN** BKEPDF. Series for all physicians interested in problems of nutrition. Experimental and clinical information concerning nutrition, health and treatment of nurtitional diseases. *Infusionstherapie und Klinische Ernahrung. Sonderheft, 0379-4938.*

CLINICA DIETOLOGICA. (LA CLINICA DIETOLOGICA). Began with 1970. 0392-7318. Periodical. IT. Italian. bm. Free. Societa Editrice Universo, Via G B Morgagni, Roma Italy 00161. **Tel** (06)862835. **Ed** Michelangelo Cairella. **Ind/Abst** Biol. Abstr. **NLM** W1 CL366K. **CODEN** CLDID7. bk rev. adv acc. **Circ** 3,000. Covers nutrition dietetics, metabolic diseases, obesity, diabetes, hellitus, and preventive medicine.

CLINICAL ALLERGY. **VFOAT** Journal of the British Allergy Society, Journal of the British Society for Allergy and Clinical Immunology. V. 1- March 1971-. 0009-9090. Periodical. UK. English. bm. $145.00. Blackwell Scientific Publishers Limited, PO Box 88, Osney Mead, Oxford OX2 OEL England. **Ind/Abst** Life Sci. Collect., Pestdoc, Ringdoc, Vetdoc, Excerpta Med., Curr. Contents, Biol. Abstr., Chem. Abstr., Index Med., Sci. Cit. Index, Abr. Ed. **NLM** W1 CL65K. **CODEN** CLAGBI. Asthma, food allergies, allergias to all allergens.

CLINICAL ALLERGY. SUPPLEMENT. 0263-4848. Monographic Series. UK. English. ir. Blackwell Scientific Publications Ltd, Osney Mead, Oxford OX2 OEL England.

CLINICAL REVIEWS IN ALLERGY. Vol. 1, No. 1 (Mar. 1983)-. 0731-8235. Periodical. US. English. qt. $46.00. Elsevier Science Publishing Co, PO Box 1663, Grand Central Station, New York NY 10163. **Tel** (212)370-5520. **Ed** M Eric Gershwin. **Ind/Abst** Index Med. **NLM** W1. **CODEN** CRVADD. adv acc. **Circ** 500. Each issue publishes scholarly review articles devoted to a single topic of critical importance to allergists in an attempt to provide comprehensive treatment.

CLINICS IN IMMUNOLOGY AND ALLERGY. Vol. 1, No. 1 (Feb. 1981)-. 0260-4639. Periodical. UK. English. ty. W B Saunders Co, West Washington Square, Philadelphia PA 19105. **Tel** (215)574-3395. **Ed** David Dickens. **Ind/Abst** Excerpta Med., Chem. Abstr. **NLM** W1. **CODEN** CIALDE. **Circ** 800. Practical updates for the clinician on the latest advances plus topics of current interest.

CONTEMPORARY ISSUES IN CLINICAL IMMUNOLOGY AND ALLERGY. 1-. Monographic Series. UK. English. **NLM** W1 CO769MQD.

CRC HANDBOOK SERIES IN NUTRITION AND FOOD. SECTION E. NUTRITIONAL DISORDERS. (CRC HANDBOOK SERIES IN NUTRITION AND FOOD. SECTION E : NUTRITIONAL DISORDERS). **VFOAT** Handbook Series in Nutrition and Food. V. 1- 1978-. 0192-6241. Monographic Series. US. English. ir. **NLM** W1 C58A.

CURRENT TOPICS IN NUTRITION AND DISEASE. V. 1-. 0191-2453. Monographic Series. US. English. ir. Alan R Liss Inc, 41 East 11th Street, New York NY 10003. **Tel** (212)475-7700. **Ed** Anthony Albanese and David Kritchevsky. **Ind/Abst** Biol. Abstr., Chem. Abstr. **LC** UNC. **NLM** W1 CU82R. **CODEN** CTNDDU. A scholarly book series concerning all aspects of nutrition and nutritional diseases.

DIGESTION. V. 1-. 0012-2823. Periodical. SZ. English. mo. $194.00. S Karger AG, PO Box, CH-4009 Basel Switzerland. **Tel** (061)39 08 80. **Ed** W Creutzfeldt. **Ind/Abst** Life Sci. Collect., Excerpta Med., Biol. Abstr., Chem. Abstr., Nuci. Sci. Abstr., Index Med., Bibliogr. Agric., Sci. Cit. Index, Abr. Ed. **LC** QP141.A1. **DD** 616.3005. **NLM** W1 DI57. **CODEN** DIGEBW. adv acc. Publishes research reports on diseases and pathophysiology of the gastrointestinal tract, liver and pancreas and on gastrointestinal endocrinology. *Gastroenterologia.*

EXPERIMENTAL AND CLINICAL IMMUNOGENETICS. 1/1/84 (Apr. 1984)-. 0254-9670. Periodical. English. qt. $97.00. S Karger AG, PO Box, CH-4009 Basel Switzerland. **Tel** (061)39 08 80. **Ed** K Bauer. **NLM** W1. adv acc. Experimental data on proteins, histocompatibility, blood group and other cell surface antigens. Recent advances in the evolution, ontogeny and antibody variations of immunoglobulins and the genetics of the immune response.

FOLIA ALLERGOLOGICA ET IMMUNOLOGICA CLINICA. V. 21- Jan/Feb 1974-. 0303-8432. Periodical. IT. Italian. bm. 100.000. Lombardo Editore, Via Verona 22, 00161 Roma Italia. **Tel** (06)428905. **Ed** Emanuele Errigo. **Ind/Abst** Excerpta Med., Biol. Abstr., Chem. Abstr. **NLM** W1 FO127C. **CODEN** FAICAZ. bk rev. adv acc. **Circ** 1,700. (ctrl). Editorials, reviews, original articles, case reports and clinical trials in the field of allergology and clinical immunology. *Folia Allergologica, 0015-5470.*

HORMONE AND METABOLIC RESEARCH. V. 1- Jan. 1969-. 0018-5043. Periodical. GW. English (French and German). mo. $134.00. Thieme-Stratton Inc, 381 Park Avenue South/Suite 1501, New York NY 10016. **Tel** (212)683-5088. **Ed** E F Pfeiffer. **Ind/Abst** Life Sci. Collect., Excerpta Med., Nuci. Sci. Abstr., Index Med., Biol. Abstr., Chem. Abstr., Bibliogr. Agric., Curr. Contents, Sci. Cit. Index, Abr. Ed., Energy Res. Abstr., Pestdoc, Ringdoc, Vetdoc. **NLM** W1 HO63P. **CODEN** HMMRA2. **Circ** 16,000. Problems of diabetology in the widest sense emphasizing their endocrinologic mass disease aspect, etc.

IMMUNOLOGIJA. (IMMUNOLOGIIA). Jan./Feb. 1980-. 0206-4952. Periodical. UR. Russian. bm. $53.00. Victor Kamkin Inc (70421), 12224 Parklawn Drive, Rockville MD 20852. **Tel** (301)881-5973. **Ind/Abst** Biol. Abstr., Chem. Abstr. **NLM** W1 IM52B. **CODEN** IMUNDA.

IMMUNOLOGY & ALLERGY PRACTICE. *See* Medicine.

IMMUNOPATHOLOGY IMMUNOTHERAPY LETTER. Vol. 1, No. 1 (Apr. 1985)-. 0882-5262. Periodical. US. English. bm. $36.00 Domestic, $42.00 Foreign. Immunopathology Immunotherapy Letter, 5 Center Avenue, Little Falls NJ 07424. **Tel** (201)890-0500. **DD** 616. adv acc. **Circ** 10,000. (ctrl). Up-to-date information on developments and techniques in the field of immunopathology and immunotherapy written by leaders in these fields, with a tele-lecture presentation.

INTERNATIONAL ARCHIVES OF ALLERGY AND APPLIED IMMUNOLOGY. *See* Genealogy and Heraldry - Archives.

IRCS MEDICAL SCIENCE. IMMUNOLOGY AND ALLERGY. (IRCS MEDICAL SCIENCE IMMUNOLOGY AND ALLERGY). **VFOAT** International Research Communications System. V. 3- Jan. 1975-. 0305-666X. Periodical. UK. English. mo. $95.00. IRCS Medical Science, PO Box 500/St Leonards House, Lancaster LA1 1PF England. **Tel** (0524)68116. **Ed** S Johnson. bk rev. Publishes results of original research into all aspects of immunology including experimental work and transplantation and tumour immunology within weeks. Papers fully refereed. *Research on Immunology and Allergy, 0305-2788.*

IRCS MEDICAL SCIENCE. METABOLISM AND NUTRITION. (IRCS MEDICAL SCIENCE : METABOLISM AND NUTRITION). **VFOAT** Metabolism and Nutrition. V. 3- Jan. 1975-. 0305-6821. Periodical. UK. English. mo. $110.00. IRCS Medical Science, PO Box 500/St Leonards House, Lancaster LA1 1PF England. **Tel** (0524)68116. **Ed** S Johnson. bk rev. Publishes results of original research into all aspects of metabolism, both clinical and experimental, within weeks of completion. Papers fully refereed. *Research on Human Metabolism and Nutrition, 0305-2818.*

JOURNAL OF ALLERGY AND CLINICAL IMMUNOLOGY. (THE JOURNAL OF ALLERGY AND CLINICAL IMMUNOLOGY : OFFICIAL ORGAN OF AMERICAN ACADEMY OF ALLERGY). V. 48- July 1971-. 0091-6749. Periodical. US. English. mo. $83.50. C V Mosby, c/o R K Kinnes, 11830 Westline Industrial Drive, St Louis MO 63146. **Tel** (314)872-8370. **Ed** Elliott Middleton Jr. **Ind/Abst** Life Sci. Collect., Pestdoc, Ringdoc, Vetdoc, Excerpta Med., CIS Abstr., Biol. Abstr., Chem. Abstr., Nuci. Sci. Abstr., Index Med., Energy Res. Abstr., Sci. Cit. Index, Abr. Ed., Hospit. Lit. Index, Chem. Abstr. **NLM** W1 JO534S. **CODEN** JACIBY. adv acc. **Circ** 8,212. Serves the needs of the clinical allergist as well as those dermatologists, internists, general practitioners, and pediatricians concerned with clinical manifestations of allergies in their practice. *Journal of Allergy, 0021-8707.*

JOURNAL OF INHERITED METABOLIC DISEASE. **VFOAT** Inherited Metabolic Disease. V. 1- 1978-. 0141-8955. Periodical. UK. English. bm. 275. Kluwer Academic Publishers Group, PO Box 322, 3300 AH Dordrecht Netherlands. **Tel** 0524 78765. **Ed** R A Harkness, R J Pollitt and G M Addison. **Ind/Abst** Life Sci. Collect., Excerpta Med., Index Med., Biol. Abstr., Chem. Abstr., Sci. Cit. Index, Abr. Ed. **NLM** W1 JO709. **CODEN** JIMDDP. bk rev. adv acc. **Circ** 1,000. Reviews, current research clinical reports on inborn errors of metabolism in humans.

METABOLISM, CLINICAL AND EXPERIMENTAL. V. 1- Jan. 1952-. 0026-0495. Periodical. US. English. mo. Grune and Stratton Inc, 111 Fifth Avenue, New York NY 10003. **Tel** (212)614-3232. **Ed** S Soskin. **Ind/Abst** Excerpta Med., Life Sci. Collect., Pestdoc, Ringdoc, Vetdoc, Energy Res. Abstr., Biol. Abstr., Chem. Abstr., Nuci. Sci. Abstr., Index Med., Bibliogr. Agric., Sci. Cit. Index, Abr. Ed. **LC** RB147. **DD** 616.39. **NLM** W1 ME961P. **CODEN** METAAJ.

MINERAL AND ELECTROLYTHE METABOLISM. (MINERAL AND ELECTROLYTE METABOLISM). V. 1- 1978-. 0378-0392. Periodical. SZ. English. bm. $199.00. S Karger AG, PO Box, CH-4009 Basel Switzerland. **Ed** S G Massry. **Ind/Abst** Life Sci. Collect., Excerpta Med., Index Med., Biol. Abstr., Chem. Abstr. **NLM** W1 MI624E. **CODEN** MELMDI. adv acc. Reports present new findings concerning calcium, potassium, sodium, magnesium, phosphorus, acid-base and water metabolism as well as hormones, trace metals and vitamins.

MONOGRAPHS IN ALLERGY. V. 1-. 0077-0760. Monographic Series. US. English. ir. S Karger AG, PO Box, CH-4009 Basel Switzerland. **Tel** 061-39 08 80. **Ed** P Dukor, P Kallos, Z Trnka, BH Waksman and A L de Weck. **Ind/Abst** Life Sci. Collect., Index Med., Chem. Abstr., Sci. Cit. Index, Abr. Ed. **DD** 616. **NLM** W1 MO567E. **CODEN** MOALAR. Focuses on areas of allergy and immunology characterized by exceptional importance and growth.

NEW ENGLAND AND REGIONAL ALLERGY PROCEEDINGS. **VFOAT** NER Allergy Proc. **VAT** New England and Regional Allergy Proc. Vol. 4, No. 1 (Winter 1983)-. 0742-2814. Periodical. US. English. qt. $45.00. New England Society of Allergy, 95 Pitman Street, Providence RI 02906. **Tel** (401)331-2510. **Ed** G Settipane. **Ind/Abst** Chem. Abstr. **NLM** W1 NE374L. **CODEN** NRAPD6. adv acc. **Circ** 2,300. (ctrl). Original research reports and review articles in allergy and immunology. *New England Society of Allergy Proceedings, 0276-7511.*

THE NEW ENGLAND SOCIETY OF ALLERGY PROCEEDINGS. **VFOAT** NESA Proceedings. Vol. 1, No. 1 (Spring 1980)- V. 3, No. 4 (Fall 1982). 0276-7511. Periodical. US. English. qt. New England Society of Allergy, 95 Pitman Street, Providence RI 02906. **Tel** (401)331-2510. **Ed** Guy A Settipane. **Ind/Abst** Chem. Abstr. **NLM** W1 NE394M. **CODEN** NESPD5. adv acc. **Circ** 2,200. Reviews, articles on allergy and immunology. We are the official Journal of Regional and State Allergy Societies.

NIAID MANUAL OF TISSUE TYPING TECHNIQUES. **Main/Corp** United States. National Institute of Allergy and Infectious Diseases. Allergic and Immunologic Diseases Program. **VAT**

National Institute of Allergy and Infectious Diseases Manual of Tissue Typing Techniques. 0147-7277. US. English. United States National Institute of Allergy and Infectious Diseases, Immunology Allergic and Immunologic Diseases Program, Bethesda MD 20205. **LC** QR184.3. **DD** 616.079. *NIAID Manual of Tissue Typing Techniques, 0147-7277.*

PROCEEDINGS - ANNUAL CONTRACTOR'S CONFERENCE OF THE ARTIFICIAL KIDNEY PROGRAM OF THE NATIONAL INSTITUTE OF ARTHRITIS, METABOLISM, AND DIGESTIVE DISEASES. (ANNUAL CONTRACTOR'S CONFERENCE OF THE ARTIFICIAL KIDNEY PROGRAM OF THE NATIONAL INSTITUTE OF ARTHRITIS, METABOLISM, AND DIGESTIVE DISEASES). **Main/Conf** Contractor's Conference of the Artificial Kidney Program of the National Institute of Arthritis, Metabolism, and Digestive Diseases. 0147-5258. US. English. an. US National Institutes of Health, 9000 Rockville Pike, Bethesda MD 20014. **LC** RC901.7.A7. **DD** 617.461. **NLM** W1 PR583CGB. *Annual Contractor's Conference.*

PROCEEDINGS - NEW ENGLAND SOCIETY OF ALLERGY. **Main/Corp** New England Society of Allergy. V. 1, No. 1- Spring 1980-. Periodical. US. English. qt. $35.00. New England Society of Allergy, 95 Pitman Street, Providence RI 02906.

PROGRESS IN ALLERGY. Began with: Vol. 2, published in 1949. 0079-6034. SZ. English. ir. S Karger AG, PO Box 352, White Plains NY 10602. **Tel** 061-39 08 80. Ed K Ishizaka, P Kallos and B H Waksman. **Ind/Abst** Life Sci. Collect., Excerpta Med., Nucl. Abstr., Biol. Abstr., Chem. Abstr., Index Med., Sci. Cit. Index, Abr. Ed. **LC** RC583. **NLM** W1 PR666F. **CODEN** PRALAD. (cum index). The series that pioneered the concept of review articles in the field of immunology. *Fortschritte der Allergielehre, 0253-0376.*

PROGRESS IN CLINICAL AND BIOLOGICAL RESEARCH. See Biology.

RECENT ADVANCES IN ENDOCRINOLOGY AND METABOLISM. No. 1-. 0140-9123. Periodical. UK. English. Churchill Livingston Inc, 1560 Broadway, New York NY 10036. **Ind/Abst** Life Sci. Collect., Chem. Abstr. **LC** RC648.A1. **DD** 616.4005. **NLM** W1 RE105UL. **CODEN** RAEMDA.

A REPORT FROM THE DIRECTOR, NATIONAL INSTITUTE OF ALLERGY AND INFECTIOUS DISEASES. (REPORT FROM THE DIRECTOR, NATIONAL INSTITUTE OF ALLERGY AND INFECTIOUS DISEASES). **Main/Corp** United States. National Institute of Allergy and Infectious Diseases. VFOAT NIAID Report of the Director. 0161-3618. US. English. **LC** RC583. **DD** 616.079072073. **NLM** W1 RE212TN.

REVUE FRANCAISE D'ALLERGOLOGIE ET D'IMMUNOLOGIE CLINIQUE. Yearly V. 14-. 0335-7457. Periodical. FR. French (table of contents and summaries in English). ir. $75.83. Expansion Scientifique Francaise, 15 rue Saint-Benoit, 75278 Paris Cedex 06 France. **Tel** 548-42-60. **Ind/Abst** Life Sci. Collect., Excerpta Med., CIS Abstr., Sci. Cit. Index, Abr. Ed. **NLM** W1 RE844E. *Revue Francaise d'Allergologie, 0035-2845.*

REVUE FRANCAISE D'ENDOCRINOLOGIE CLINIQUE, NUTRITION ET METABOLISME. V. 1- Jan./Feb. 1960-. 0048-8062. Periodical. FR. French (some summaries in English). bm. $56.28. Editions de Medecine Pratique, 4 rue Louis-Armand, 92600 Asnieres France. **Ind/Abst** CIS Abstr., Excerpta Med., Biol. Abstr., Chem. Abstr. **NLM** W1 RE848N. **CODEN** RECNAS.

RHEUMATOLOGIA, BALNEOLOGIA, ALLERGOLOGIA. V. 1-20. 0035-4554. Periodical. HU. Hungarian (summaries in English, German and Russian). qt. Akademiai Kiado, POB 24, 1363 Budapest Hungary. **Ind/Abst** Excerpta Med. **NLM** W1 RH361.

THYROID TODAY. V. 1- Aug. 1977-. 0190-0625. Periodical. US. English. bm. Flint Laboratories, 1 Baxter Parkway, Deerfield IL 60015. **Ind/Abst** Chem. Abstr. **NLM** W1 TH96. **CODEN** THTODQ.

TOPICS IN INFECTIOUS DISEASES. V. 1-. 0171-2160. Monographic Series. US. English. ir. Springer Verlag-New York Inc, 175 5th Avenue, New York NY 10010. **Tel** (212)480-1584. **Ind/Abst** Life Sci. Collect., Chem. Abstr. **NLM** W1 TO539P. **CODEN** TIDID3. Topics include drug receptor R-factors, and influenza virus Hemagglutinin.

VERHANDELINGEN - KONINKLIJKE ACADEMIE VOOR GENEESKUNDE VAN BELGIE. **Main/Corp** Koninklijke Academie voor Geneeskunde van Belgie. 0302-6469. Periodical. BE. Dutch (English and French). ir. 2400. Verhandelingen Koninklijke, Hortogelijkestr 1, Brussels 1 Belgium. **Tel** (02)5117897. **Ind/Abst** Index Med., Chem. Abstr. **NLM** W1 VE475KA. **CODEN** VKGBAU. **Circ** 400. (ctrl). *Verhandelingen van de Koninklijke Vlaamse Academie voor Geneeskunde van Belgie.*

ZENTRALBLATT IMMUNOLOGIE, KLINISCHE RHEUMATOLOGIE. VFOAT Immunology, Rheumatology. Vol. 334, No. 1-. 0722-3048. Periodical. English (abstracts in German). mo. Springer Verlag-New York Inc, 175 5th Avenue, New York NY 10010. **Tel** (212)460-1500. **NLM** ZQW 504 Z56. *Zentralblatt Immunologie-Transplantation, 0301-5882.*

CARDIOVASCULAR DISEASES

ACTA CARDIOLOGICA. 0001-5385. French (articles in French or English with summaries in both languages). bm. $53.35. Acta Cardiologica, rue des Champs-Elysees 43, 1050 Bruxelles Belgium. **Tel** 02/648 35 93. **Ind/Abst** Life Sci. Collect., Pestdoc, Ringdoc, Vetdoc, Excerpta Med., Index Med., Int. Aerosp. Abstr., Biol. Abstr., Chem. Abstr., Sci. Cit. Index, Abr. Ed., Hospit. Lit. Index. **NLM** W1 AC775. **CODEN** ACCAAQ. Devoted to the study of cardiovascular diseases. Publishes original papers about physiology, anatomy and clinics. *Bulletin de la Societe Belge de Cardiologie.*

ADVANCES IN CARDIOLOGY. V. 4- 1970-. 0065-2326. Periodical. English. ir. S Karger Ag, PO Box, CH-4009 Basel Switzerland. **Tel** 061-39 08 80. Ed J J Kellermann. **Ind/Abst** Excerpta Med., Biol. Abstr., Chem. Abstr., Index Med., Cumul. Index Nurs. Allied Health Lit. **LC** RC681.A25. **NLM** W1 AD53C. **CODEN** ACDYB2. A tradition of well-documented scientific studies adding process in the management of cardiac disease. *Fortschritte der Kardiologie.*

ADVANCES IN CARDIOVASCULAR PHYSICS. V. 1-. 0378-6900. Monographic Series. SZ. English. ir. S Karger Ag, PO Box, CH-4009 Basel Switzerland. **Tel** 061-39 08 80. Ed D N Ghista. **Ind/Abst** Chem. Abstr., Index Med. **NLM** W1 AD53F. **CODEN** ACAPDU. Instructive texts covering technical innovations useful in the monitoring, diagnosis and rehabilitation of patients with cardiovascular disease.

ADVANCES IN CLINICAL CARDIOLOGY. Vol. 1-. 0272-9237. Monographic Series. US. English. ir. Yorke Medical Books, 875 3rd Avenue, New York NY 10022. **Tel** (212)605-9400. Ed H W Heiss. **Ind/Abst** Chem. Abstr. **NLM** W1 AD539. **CODEN** ACCADT.

ADVANCES IN HEART DISEASE. Series/Titl Clinical Cardiology Monographs. V. 1-. 0160-1601. Periodical. US. English. ir. Ed D T Mason. **NLM** W1 AD622.

ADVANCES IN MICROCIRCULATION. V. 1-. 0065-2938. English. ir. S Karger AG, PO Box, CH-4009 Basel Switzerland. **Tel** 061-39 08 80. Ed B M Altura and E Davis. **Ind/Abst** Chem. Abstr., Biol. Abstr., Index Med., Sci. Cit. Index, Abr. Ed. **LC** QP101. **DD** 574.11. **NLM** W1 AD682. **CODEN** ADVMBT. This series creates new bases for understanding how the microcirculation is involved in various states of health and disease.

ADVANCES IN THE MANAGEMENT OF CARDIOVASCULAR DISEASE. V. 1- 1980-. 0198-103X. US. English. ir. Yearbook Medical Publishers, 35 East Wacker Drive, Chicago IL 60801. **LC** RC666. **DD** 616.1005. **NLM** W1 AD8792T.

ADVANCES IN THE MANAGEMENT OF CLINICAL HEART DISEASE. V. 1-. 0146-8790. Monographic Series. US. English. Futura Publishing Company, 295 Main Street/PO Box 298, Mt Kisco NY 10549. Ed J I Haft and C P Bailey. **LC** RC681.A1. **DD** 616.12. **NLM** W1 AD8793.

THE AMERICAN HEART JOURNAL. V. 1- Oct. 1925-. 0002-8703. Periodical. US. English. mo. $89.50. C V Mosby Company, c/o R K Kinnes 11830 Westline Industrial Drive, St Louis MO 63141. **Tel** (314)872-8370. Ed Dean T Mason. **Ind/Abst** Life Sci. Collect., Pestdoc, Ringdoc, Vetdoc, Excerpta Med., Index Med., Int. Aerosp. Abstr., CIS Abstr., Biol. Abstr., Chem. Abstr., Energy Res. Abstr., Sci. Cit. Index, Abr. Ed., Hospit. Lit. Index. **LC** RC681.A1. **DD** 616.12005. **NLM** W1 AM423. **CODEN** AHJOA2. adv acc. **Circ** 11,158. Serves the university affiliated clinician who lectures and treats, and the cardiologist and internist responsible for advanced treatment and teaching of cardiovascular and renal disorders.

THE AMERICAN JOURNAL OF CARDIOLOGY. V. 1- Jan. 1958-. 0002-9149. Periodical. US. English. ir. $106.00. Technical Publishing Company, 875 3rd Avenue, New York NY 10022. **Tel** (212)605-9400. **Ind/Abst** Life Sci. Collect., Pestdoc, Ringdoc, Vetdoc, Excerpta Med., Index Med., Int. Aerosp. Abstr., CIS Abstr., Biol. Abstr., Bibliogr. Agric., Energy Res. Abstr., Hospit. Lit. Index, Sci. Cit. Index, Abr. Ed. **LC** RC681.A1. **DD** 616.105. **NLM** W1 AM449. **CODEN** AJCDAG. *Transactions of the American College of Cardiology.*

AMERICAN REVIEW OF DIAGNOSTICS. V. 1, No. 1 (Nov./Dec.1982)-. 0735-1283. Periodical. US. English. bm. $36.00. Degram Communications Inc, PO Box 617, Encino CA 91426. **Tel** (213)501-6167. **Ind/Abst** Excerpta Med. **NLM** W1 AM747.

ANGINA PECTORIS. Series/Titl Annual Research Reviews. V. 1- 1977-. 0707-3070. CN. English. ir. Eden Press, 4626 St Catherine Street West, Montreal Quebec H3Z 1S3 Canada. **DD** 616.122005. **NLM** W1 AN224.

ANGIOLOGIA. V. 1- Jan./Feb. 1949-. 0003-3170. Periodical. Spanish. bm. $16.72. Angiologia, C Laforja 138, 08021 Barcelona Spain. **Tel** (200)13-89. **Ind/Abst** Life Sci. Collect., Excerpta Med., Biol. Abstr., Chem. Abstr., Nucl. Sci. Abstr., Index Med. **NLM** W1 AN225. **CODEN** ANGOAT.

ANNALES DE CARDIOLOGIE ET D'ANGEIOLOGIE. 17.- Yearly Vol. 0003-3928. Periodical. FR. French. ir. $90.47. Expansion Scientifique Francaise, 15 rue Saint-Benoit, 75278 Paris Cedex 06 France. **Tel** 548-42-60. **Ind/Abst** Life Sci. Collect., Excerpta Med., Index Med. **NLM** W1 AN327C. Index Published Separately - Free - automatically sent. *Actualities Cardiologiques et Angeiologiques Internationales.*

THE ANNALS OF THORACIC SURGERY. See Medicine - Surgery.

ANNUAL REPORT - ARTERIOSCLEROSIS AND HYPERTENSION ADVISORY COMMITTEE, NATIONAL INSTITUTES OF HEALTH. **Main/Corp** National Heart, Lung, and Blood Institute Arteriosclerosis and Hypertension Advisory Committee. 1975/76-. US. English. an. National Heart Lung and Blood Institute, National Institutes of Health, 9000 Rockville Pike, Bethesda MD 20014. *Annual Report -Arteriosclerosis and Hypertension Advisory Committee, National Institutes of Health.*

ANNUAL REPORT - CARDIOVASCULAR AND PULMONARY STUDY SECTION, NATIONAL INSTITUTES OF HEALTH. **Main/Corp** United States. National Institutes of Health. Cardiovascular and Pulmonary Study Section. US. English. an. National Institutes of Health, 9000 Rockville Pike, Bethesda MD 20014.

ANNUAL REPORT - NATIONAL HEART, LUNG, AND BLOOD INSTITUTE. (ANNUAL REPORT). **Main/Corp** National Heart, Lung, and Blood Institute. VFOAT Intramural Research. 0278-0577. US. English. an. National Heart Lung and Blood Institute, National Institutes of Health 9000 Rockville Pike, Bethesda MD 20205. **LC** RC666. **DD** 616.10072073. **NLM** W 22 AA1 I61.

AORTA (NEW YORK, N.Y.). (AORTA). 1 (1982)-. Periodical. US. English. PO Box 30A, Brooklyn NY 11202.

APPLIED CARDIOLOGY. V. 12, No. 4 (June/July 1984)-. 8750-0426. Periodical. US. English. bm. $40.00. Brentwood Publishing Corp, 825 South Barrington Avenue, Los Angeles CA 90049. **Ind/Abst** Hospit. Lit. Index, Cumul. Index Nurs. Allied Health Lit. **LC** RC681.A1. **DD** 616.1005. **NLM** W1. *CVP, 0091-4738.*

ARCHIVIO DI CHIRURGIA TORACICA E CARDIOVASCOLARE. See Genealogy and Heraldry - Archives.

ARQUIVOS BRASILEIROS DE CARDIOLOGIA. V. 1- Mar. 1948-. 0066-782X. Periodical. BL. Portuguese. mo. $70.00. Sociedade Brasileira de Cardio, Rua Itapeva 574 80 Conj 81-B,

Medicine—Cardiovascular Diseases

01332 Sao Paulo Brazil. **Ind/Abst** Excerpta Med., Index Med., Chem. Abstr. **NLM** W1 AR867. **CODEN** ABCAAJ. Index in last issue of volume - attached.

ARTERIOSCLEROSIS. (ARTERIOSCLEROSIS : AN OFFICIAL JOURNAL OF THE AMERICAN HEART ASSOCIATION, INC) **VFOAT** Journal of Vascular Biology and Disease. Vol. 1, No. 1 (Jan.-Feb. 1981)-. 0276-5047. Periodical. US. English. bm. $60.00 US, $75.00 Foreign. American Heart Association, 7320 Greenville Avenue, Dallas TX 75231. **Tel** (214)750-5466. Ed Edwin L Bierman. **Ind/Abst** Excerpta Med., Energy Inf. Abstr., Environ. Abstr., Index Med., Biol. Abstr., Chem. Abstr. **LC** RC692. **DD** 616.136. **NLM** W1 AR9515D. **CODEN** ARTRDW. adv acc. **Circ** 1,500. (ctrl). Designed for physicians and investigators interested in studies of vascular biology. It includes research papers.

ATHEROGENESIS. **VFOAT** Atherogenese. 1-. 0250-4677. Monographic Series. English (German). ir. **NLM** W1 AT383. **CODEN** ATRGD3.

ATHEROSCLEROSIS REVIEWS. V. 1-. 0362-1650. US. English. ir. Raven Press, 1140 Avenue of the Americas, New York NY 10036. **Ind/Abst** Biol. Abstr., Chem. Abstr., Sci. Cit. Index, Abr. Ed. **LC** RC692. **DD** 616.136005. **NLM** W1 AT385. **CODEN** ATHEDF.

BASIC RESEARCH IN CARDIOLOGY. V. 68- Jan./Feb. 1973-. 0300-8428. Periodical. GW. English (German). bm. $183.00. Springer Verlag-New York Inc, 175 5th Avenue, New York NY 10010. **Tel** (212)460-1500. Ed R Jacob, T H Kenner and W Schaper. **Ind/Abst** Life Sci. Collect., Excerpta Med., Index Med., Biol. Abstr., Chem. Abstr., Energy Res. Abstr., Sci. Cit. Index, Abr. Ed. **LC** RC633.A1. **DD** 616.994005. **NLM** W1 BA814N. **CODEN** BRCAB7. This journal keeps scientists in several fields abreast of results in fundamental cardiology research. *Archiv fur Kreislaufforschung, 0003-9217.*

BIBLIOTHECA CARDIOLOGICA. 1- 1939-. 0067-7906. Monographic Series. English (German and French). ir. S Karger AG, PO Box CH-4009, Basel Switzerland. **Tel** 061-39 08 80. Ed J J Kellermann. **Ind/Abst** Biol. Abstr., Chem. Abstr., Nuci. Sci. Abstr., Index Med., Hospit. Lit. Index. **NLM** W1 BI396. **CODEN** BCSCAL. Information on how new technical developments can aid the assessment of cardiovascular function.

BIULLETEN' VSESOIUZNOGO KARDIOLOGICHESKOGO NAUCHNOGO TSENTRA AMN SSSR. 1978-. Periodical. UR. Russian. sa. $20.50. Victor Kamkin Inc, 12224 Parklawn Drive, Rockville MD 20852. **Tel** (301)881-5973. **Ind/Abst** Index Med. **NLM** W1 BI99LU.

BLOOD PRESSURE CONTROL. Vol. 1-. 0713-5548. CN. English. ir. Eden Press, 4626 St Catherine Street West, Montreal Quebec H3Z 1S3 Canada. **NLM** W1 BL661R.

BOLLETTINO, DELLA SOCIETA ITALIANA DI CARDIOLOGIA. Main/Corp Societa Italiana di Cardiologia. V. 1- 1956-. 0037-878X. Periodical. IT. Italian (summaries in French, German, and English). mo. $70.00. Italian Society of Cardiology, Corso Francia 197, 00191 Rome Italy. **Ind/Abst** Index Med., Biol. Abstr. Chem. Abstr. **NLM** W1 BO475. **CODEN** BOTLAZ.

BRITISH HEART JOURNAL. Began with Vol. 1 (Jan. 1939). 0007-0769. Periodical. UK. English. mo. $140.98. British Medical Journal, Tavistock Square, London WC1H 9JR England. **Ind/Abst** Life Sci. Collect., Pestdoc, Ringdoc, Vetdoc, Excerpta Med., Index Med., Int. Aerosp. Abstr., CIS Abstr., Biol. Abstr., Sci. Cit. Index, Abr. Ed., Hospit. Lit. Index. **NLM** W1 BR455G. **CODEN** BHJUAV. (cum index). Available on microfilm.

BRITISH JOURNAL OF DISEASES OF THE CHEST. See Medicine - Respiratory Diseases.

BULLETIN. Vol. 1, No. 1 (July 1957)-. 0495-7792. JA. English. ir. Tokyo Women's Medical College, Tokyo Japan.

BULLETIN - CARDIOVASCULAR RESEARCH CENTER. Main/Corp Cardiovascular Research Center. V. 1-22, No. 1. 0008-6371. Periodical. US. English. qt. Baylor College of Medicine, 1200 Moursund Boulevard, Cardiovascular Research Center, Houston TX 77030. **Tel** (713)664-8381. **Ind/Abst** Excerpta Med., Index Med., Chem. Abstr., Energy Res. Abstr., Hospit. Lit. Index. **NLM** W1 CA773. **CODEN** CRCBAK.

BUTTERWORTHS INTERNATIONAL MEDICAL REVIEWS. CARDIOLOGY. **VFOAT** Cardiology. 1-. 0260-0064. Monographic Series. UK. English. ir. **NLM** W1 BU98J.

CARDIAC ALERT. V. 1- 1979-. 0194-2557. Periodical. US. English. mo $60.00. Phillips Publishing Inc, 7811 Montrose Road, Potomac MD 20854. **Tel** (301)340-2100. Ed Jorge C Rios. **NLM** W1 CA763C. bk rev. (ctrl). Personal advice on every aspect of heart health with emphasis on case histories, recent cardiac developments, diet, exercise, lifestyle, subscriber questions, news, studies and reviews.

CARDIAC REHABILITATION CEASED. V. 1 - V. 12, No. 4. 0147-3875. Periodical. US. English. qt. $4.00. New York State Heart Assembly, 3 West 29th Street, New York NY 10001. **LC** RC669. **NLM** W1 CA764C.

CARDIAC/THORACIC SURGERY. See Medicine - Surgery.

CARDIO. Began with: V. 1, No. 1 (Jan. 1984). 0742-9622. Periodical. US. English. mo. Free to Qualified Physicians in US, $35.00 Domestic, $42.00 Foreign. Miller Freeman Publications, Circulation Department/500 Howard Street, San Francisco CA 94105. **NLM** W1.

CARDIO-VASCULAR NURSING. See Medicine - Nursing.

CARDIOLOGIC CONSULTATION. 0741-7454. Periodical. US. English. qt. Free. HP Publishing Company, 575 Lexington Avenue, New York NY 10022.

CARDIOLOGIE TROPICALE. **VFOAT** Tropical Cardiology. 0253-5580. Periodical. English (articles also in French, with summaries in both languages). ir. **NLM** W1 CA7698.

THE CARDIOLOGIST'S COMPENDIUM OF DRUG THERAPY. (THE CARDIOLOGIST'S COMPENDIUM OF DRUG THERAPY : A PUBLICATION OF BIOMEDICAL INFORMATION CORPORATION). **VFOAT** Compendium of Drug Therapy. 1981/1982-. 0276-4296. US. English. an. Biomedical Information Corporation, 800 2nd Avenue, New York NY 10017.

CARDIOLOGISTS' LEGAL LETTER. See Law.

CARDIOLOGY. 55- 1970-. 0008-6312. Periodical. SZ. English. bm. $132.00. S Karger AG, PO Box, CH-4009 Basel Switzerland. **Tel** (061)39 08 80. Ed J J Kellermann. **Ind/Abst** Life Sci. Collect., Pestdoc, Ringdoc, Vetdoc, Excerpta Med., Index Med., Biol. Abstr., Chem. Abstr., Nuci. Sci. Abstr., Int. Aerosp. Abstr., Index Med., Sci. Cit. Index, Abr. Ed. **LC** RC681.A1. **DD** 616.12005. **NLM** W1 CA77F. **CODEN** CAGYAO. adv acc. Describes and offers critical appraisals of new developments in non-invasive, invasive, diagnostic and therapeutic methods. Reports the functions and metabolism of the heart and the morphology and physiology of cardiovascular disease. *Cardiologia, 0366-5313.*

CARDIOLOGY CLINICS. Vol. 1, No. 1 (Feb. 1983)-. 0733-8651. Periodical. US. English. qt. WB Saunders Company, West Washington Square, Philadelphia PA 19105. **Ind/Abst** Index Med. **LC** RC681.A1. **DD** 616.12005. **NLM** W1 CA77G.

CARDIOLOGY DIGEST. V. 14, No. 8/9- Aug./Sept. 1979-. 0008-6347. Periodical. US. English. mo. Medical Digest Inc, 445 Central Avenue, Northfield IL 60093. **NLM** W1 CA77H. Available on microfilm or microfiche from University Microfilms. *Journal of Continuing Education in Cardiology, 0148-5199.*

CARDIOLOGY IN PRACTICE. Vol. 1, No. 1 (May 1982)-. 0262-5547. Periodical. UK. English. bm. 18 Domestic, 21 Europe, 24 Others. The Medical News Group, Tower House/Southampton Street, London WC2E 7LS England. **Tel** (01)279-6005. Ed Philip Poole-Wilson and Kim Fox. **NLM** W1 CA77I. bk rev. adv acc. **Circ** 20,000. (ctrl). Articles on management and treatment of cardiovascular diseases, investigative procedures, research, case reports, book reviews, news for GPs and cardiologists.

CARDIOLOGY IN PRACTICE (NEW YORK, N.Y.). (CARDIOLOGY IN PRACTICE). Vol. 1, No. 2 (May/June 1984)-. 8750-0647. Periodical. US. English. bm $40.00. Le Jacq Publishing Inc, 53 Park Place, New York NY 10007. **DD** 616. *Clinical Cardiology in Practice, 0742-6976.*

CARDIOLOGY TIMES. Began in 1982?. 0278-4157. Periodical. US. English. mo. $35.00. Cardiology Times, 95 Madison Avenue/Suite 1407, New York NY 10016.

CARDIOLOGY UPDATE. 1979-. 0163-1675. US. English. ir. Elsevier Science Publishing Co Inc, PO Box 1663 Grand Central Station, New York NY 10163. **Tel** (212)370-5520. **LC** RC681.A1. **DD** 616.12005. **NLM** W1 CA77KE.

CARDIOLOGY WORLD NEWS. Began in 1985?. 0883-4946. Periodical. US. English. mo. $29.00. Medical Publishing Enterprises, One Bridge Plaza/Suite 270, Ft Lee NJ 07024. **DD** 616.

CARDIOLOGY (YORKE MEDICAL BOOKS). (CARDIOLOGY). 1981-. 0275-0066. US. English. an. $49.50. Yorke Medical Books, 875 3rd Avenue, New York NY 10022. **Tel** (212)605-9621. Ed William C Roberts. **LC** RC681.A1. **DD** 616.12005. **NLM** W1 CA77FE. **Circ** 5,000. Publication covering the most recent developments in cardiovascular medicine and surgery.

CARDIOPULMONARY MEDICINE. V. 14, No. 3- Oct. 1975-. 0149-6719. Periodical. US. English. qt. $72.00. American College of Chest Physicians, 911 Busse Highway, Park Ridge IL 60068. **Tel** (312)698-2200. Ed Alfred Soffer and Sylvia Peterson. **NLM** W1 CA77M. bk rev. adv acc. **Circ** 20,000. Peer review journal for the cardiopulmonary specialties, clinical and surgical. *Bulletin of the American College of Chest Physicians, 0002-7960.*

CARDIOVASCULAR AND INTERVENTIONAL RADIOLOGY. See Medicine - Radiology.

CARDIOVASCULAR CLINICS. Vol. 1-. 0069-0384. Monographic Series. US. English. ir. F A Davis, 1915 Arch Street, Philadelphia PA 19103. **Tel** (215)568-2270. Ed Albert N Brest. **Ind/Abst** Excerpta Med., Index Med., Chem. Abstr., Energy Res. Abstr. **LC** RC681.A1. **DD** 616.1. **NLM** W1 CA77N. **CODEN** CCLIBG. (ctrl). On going series which extends concepts in the diagnosis and management of a wide range of cardiovascular disorders. Each book covers a topic of major interest in cardiology. Acclaimed series.

CARDIOVASCULAR DISEASES CEASED. V. 1-8. 0093-3546. Periodical. US. English. qt. The Bulletin of the Texas Heart Institute of St Luke's Episcopal and Texas Children's Hospitals, PO Box 20269, Houston TX 77225. **Ind/Abst** Excerpta Med., Chem. Abstr. **NLM** W1 CA77T. **CODEN** CADIDW.

CARDIOVASCULAR DRUGS. V. 1-. 0161-5734. Monographic Series. US. English. University Park Press, 233 East Redwood Street, Baltimore MD 21202. **Ind/Abst** Chem. Abstr. **LC** RM345. **DD** 615.71. **NLM** W1 CA77V. **CODEN** CADRDP.

CARDIOVASCULAR MEDICINE (NEW YORK, N.Y. : 1984). (CARDIOVASCULAR MEDICINE). Vol. 9, No. 10 (Oct. 1984)-. 8756-4211. Periodical. US. English. mo. Cardiovascular Medicine, 475 Park Avenue South, New York NY 10016. **DD** 616. *Journal of Cardiovascular Medicine, 0199-6614.*

CARDIOVASCULAR NEWS. Vol. 1, No. 1 (Jan. 1982)-. 0747-461X. Periodical. US. English. mo. $36.00. McMahon Publishing Company, 121 South Gertrude Avenue, Paramus NJ 07652. **Tel** (203)544-9343.

CARDIOVASCULAR PHYSIOLOGY. 1-. 0363-387X. Periodical. US. English. be. University Park Press, 300 North Charles Street, Baltimore MD 21201. Ed A C Guyton. **LC** QP1, QP101.2. **DD** 599.011. **NLM** W1 IN834F V.9 ETC. WG 102 C2672.

CARDIOVASCULAR RESEARCH. V. 1- Jan. 1967-. 0008-6363. Periodical. UK. English. mo. $174.69. British Medical Journal, Tavistock Square, London WC1H 9JR England. **Ind/Abst** Life Sci. Collect., Pestdoc, Ringdoc, Vetdoc, Excerpta Med., Biol. Abstr., Chem. Abstr., Index Med., Int. Aerosp. Abstr., Nuci. Sci. Abstr., Sci. Cit. Index, Abr. Ed. **NLM** W1 CA772. **CODEN** CVREAU.

CARDIOVASCULAR REVIEW. 1979-. 0271-4779. US. English. an. Williams & Wilkins, 428 East Preston Street, Baltimore MD 21202. **LC** RC666. **DD** 616.1005. **NLM** W1 CA773E.

CARDIOVASCULAR REVIEWS & REPORTS. VAT Cardiovascular Reviews and Reports. V. 1- April 1980-. 0197-3118. Periodical. US. English. mo. $65.00. Le Jacq Publishing Inc, 53 Park Place, New York NY 10007. **Tel** (212)766-4300. Ed

Medicine—Cardiovascular Diseases

John Laragh. **Ind/Abst** Excerpta Med. **NLM** W1 CA773H. bk rev. adv acc. **Circ** 110,000. (ctrl). Peer review articles on the treatment of cardiovascular diseases.

CARDIOVASCULAR SURGERY. See Medicine - Surgery.

CATHETERIZATION AND CARDIOVASCULAR DIAGNOSIS. V. 1-. 0098-6569. Periodical. US. English. bm. Alan R Liss Inc, 41 East 11th Street, New York NY 10003. **Tel** (212)741-2515. **Ind/Abst** Life Sci. Collect., Excerpta Med., Index Med., Biol. Abstr., Energy Res. Abstr., Sci. Cit. Index, Abr. Ed., Hospit. Lit. Index. **LC** RC683. **DD** 616.120757205. **NLM** W1 CA967. **CODEN** CCDID.

CHEST. V. 57- Jan. 1970-. 0012-3692. Periodical. US. English. mo. $72.00. Chest, PO Box 93760, Chicago IL 60670. **Tel** (312)698-2200. Ed Alfred Soffer. **Ind/Abst** Coal Abstr., Excerpta Med., Index Med., Cumul. Index Nurs. Allied Health Lit., Int. Aerosp. Abstr., Biol. Abstr., CIS Abstr., Life Sci. Collect., Chem. Abstr., Energy Res. Abstr., Sci. Cit. Index, Abr. Ed., Hospit. Lit. Index. **NLM** W1 CH415. **CODEN** CHETBF. bk rev. adv acc. **Circ** 19,500. (ctrl). The journal for pulmonologists, cardiologists, cardiothoracic surgeons and related specialists. *Diseases of the Chest, 0096-0217.*

CIRCULATION. V. 1- Jan. 1950-. 0009-7322. Periodical. US. English. mo. $56.00 Domestic, $72.00 Foreign. American Heart Association, 7320 Greenville Avenue, Dallas TX 75231. **Tel** (214)750-5466. Ed Burton E Sobel. **Ind/Abst** Excerpta Med., Index Med., Int. Aerosp. Abstr., Life Sci. Collect., Biol. Abstr., CIS Abstr., Chem. Abstr., Energy Res. Abstr., Ringdoc, Pestdoc, Vetdoc. **LC** RC681.A1. **DD** 616.105. **NLM** W1 CI743. **CODEN** CIRCAZ. (cum index). adv acc. **Circ** 23,000. (ctrl). A devoted to clinical research and advances in the cardiovascular field. Original articles in cardiovascular, clinical and laboratory investigation.

CIRCULATORY SHOCK. SUPPLEMENT. 1-. 0193-7545. Monographic Series. US. English. Alan R Liss, 41 East 11th Street, New York NY 10003. **Tel** (212)741-2515. **Ind/Abst** Index Med. **NLM** W1 CI745KB.

CLINICAL CARDIOLOGY. V. 1- April 1978-. 0160-9289. Periodical. US. English. mo. $50.00. Clinical Cardiology Publ Co Inc, The JBI Building, Box 521, Mahwah NJ 07430. **Tel** (201)529-3883. Ed H W Heiss. **Ind/Abst** Excerpta Med., Index Med. **NLM** W1 CL673. bk rev. adv acc. **Circ** 22,000. (ctrl). Dissemination of latest information on cardiovascular disease, treatment, prevention.

CLINICAL CARDIOLOGY ALERT. Began in 1982. 0741-4218. Periodical. US. English. mo. $59.00. Intl Thomson Medical Information, 680 Kinderkamack Road, Oradell NJ 07649. **Tel** (215)925-7060. *Cardiology Alert.*

CLINICAL PROGRESS IN ELECTROPHYSIOLOGY AND PACING. Vol. 3, No. 1 (Feb. 1985)-. 8756-9264. Periodical. US. English. bm. $55.00. Futura Publishing Company Inc, 295 Main Street, PO Box 330, Mount Kisco NY 10549. **Tel** (914)666-7528. **DD** 616. **NLM** W1. adv acc. **Circ** 3,000. Communicates knowledge which has immediate clinical relevance to physicians and surgeons who require timely overviews on topics which are pertinent to daily practice. *Clinical Progress in Pacing and Electrophysiology, 0736-6108.*

CLINICAL PROGRESS IN PACING AND ELECTROPHYSIOLOGY. Vol. 1, No. 1 (Mar. 1983)-. 0736-6108. Periodical. US. English. qt. $40.00 Domestic, $50.00 Foreign. Futura Publishing Company Inc, 295 Main Street, PO Box 330, Mt Kisco NY 10549. **NLM** W1 CL768CNF.

COMBINED CUMULATIVE INDEX TO CARDIOLOGY. See Indexes/Abstracts.

COMPUTERS IN CARDIOLOGY. Oct. 2-4, 1974-. 0276-6574. US. English. an. $60.00. IEEE Computer Society, 10662 Los Vaqueros Circle, Los Alamitos CA 90720. **Ind/Abst** Index IEEE Publ., Eng. Index Annu., Eng. Index Mon., Eng. Index Bioeng. Abstr., Eng. Index Energy Abstr., Eng. Index. **LC** RC683.5.D36. **DD** 616.1202854. **NLM** W3 C185. **CODEN** COCADX. bk rev. (ctrl). Covers engineering details of clinically useful systems for applications such as arrhythmia monitoring, intensive care, information displays, etc.

CONTEMPORARY PROBLEMS IN CARDIOLOGY. V. 1- 1974-. 0093-5166. US. English. Futura Publishing Company Inc, 295 Main Street, PO Box 298, Mount Kisco NY 10549. **Tel** (914)666-3505. **Ind/Abst** Chem. Abstr. **NLM** W1 CO769T. **CODEN** CPCAD6.

COR ET VASA = INTERNATIONAL JOURNAL OF CARDIOLOGY. Vol. 1 1959-. 0010-8650. Periodical. text in English, French or German. sm. $101.00. Karger Libri AG, Petersgraben 31, CH-4009 Basel 11 Switzerland. **Tel** (061)390880. **Ind/Abst** Biol. Abstr., Chem. Abstr., Excerpta Med., Index Med., Life Sci. Collect., Hospit. Lit. Index. **NLM** W1 CO8496. **CODEN** COVAAN.

CORE JOURNALS IN CARDIOLOGY. V. 1, No. 1 (Sept. 1980)-. 0165-9405. Periodical. English. mo. Elsevier Science Publishers, PO Box 211, 1000 AE Amsterdam Netherlands. **NLM** ZWG 100 C797. **CODEN** CJCADW.

THE CORONARY CLUB BULLETIN. Vol. 3, No. 2 (Sept. 1974)-. 8755-5271. Periodical. US. English. mo. $15.00 Domestic, $17.00 Foreign. The Coronary Club Bulletin, 3659 Green Road #200, Cleveland OH 44122. **DD** 616. *Bulletin - The Coronary Club, Incorporated, 8755-6308.*

CURRENT CARDIOLOGY. V. 1- 1979-. 0163-9501. Periodical. US. English. ir. John Wiley & Sons, One Wiley Drive, Somerset NJ 08873. **LC** RC681.A1. **DD** 616.12005. **NLM** W1 CU71.

CURRENT PROBLEMS IN CARDIOLOGY. VFOAT CPC, Current Problems in Cardiology. V. 1- Apr. 1976-. 0146-2806. Monographic Series. US. English. mo. $65.00. Yearbook Medical Publishers, 35 East Wacker Drive, Chicago IL 60601. **Ind/Abst** Index Med. **DD** 616. **NLM** W1 CU804J.

C.V.P. (CVP). V. 1- May/June 1973-. 0091-4738. Periodical. US. English. bm. $80.00. Brentwood Publishing Corp, PO Box 49045, Los Angeles CA 90049. **Ind/Abst** Cumul. Index Nurs. Allied Health Lit. **LC** RC681.A1. **DD** 616.1005. **NLM** W1 C955. **CODEN** CVPJA.

DEVELOPMENTS IN CARDIOPULMONARY RESEARCH. Vol. 1-. Monographic Series. US. English. Ed G Cumming. **NLM** W1 DE997VMC (P.

DEVICES AND TECHNOLOGY BRANCH CONTRACTORS MEETING PROCEEDINGS. Began with: 1978. 0276-9921. US. English. an. National Heart Lung and Blood Institute, Division of Heart and Vascular Diseases, Devices and Technology Branch, 7550 Wisconsin Avenue, Bethesda MD 20205. **LC** RC681.A2. **DD** 616.120028. **NLM** W3 DE616B. Vol. for 1980- distributed to depository libraries in microfiche. *Devices and Technology Branch Contractors Conference Proceedings, 0191-6564.*

DOMYAKU KOKASHO KENKYU NO SHINPO. Main/Conf Domyaku Koka Semina. Vol. 1-. Periodical. Japanese. an. **NLM** W3 DO66.

DRUGS IN CARDIOLOGY (POINTE-CLAIRE, QUEBEC). See Pharmacy.

ECHOCARDIOGRAPHY (MOUNT KISCO, N.Y.). (ECHOCARDIOGRAPHY). Vol. 1, No. 1 (Jan. 1984)-. 0742-2822. Periodical. US. English. qt. $65.00 US and Canada, $77.00 Foreign. Futura Publishing Company, 295 Main Street/PO Box 330, Mount Kisco NY 10549. **Tel** (914)666-7528. Ed Vincent Friedewald. **DD** 616. **NLM**. adv acc. **Circ** 2,000. Provides a single source of the information that is vital to maintaining current knowledge for performing and interpreting M Mode, 2-D and Doppler echocardiograms for adults and children.

EUROPEAN HEART JOURNAL. V. 1- Feb. 1980-. 0195-668X. Periodical. UK. English. mo. $157.00. Academic Press, 4805 Sand Lake Road, Orlando FL 32819. **Tel** (305)345-4100. **Ind/Abst** Life Sci. Collect., Pestdoc, Ringdoc, Vetdoc, Excerpta Med., Index Med., Chem. Abstr., Sci. Cit. Index, Abr. Ed. **NLM** W1 EU636. **CODEN** EHJODF.

EUROPEAN JOURNAL OF CARDIOLOGY CEASED. V. 1-12. 0301-4711. Periodical. English. **Ind/Abst** Life Sci. Collect., Excerpta Med., Chem. Abstr. **NLM** W1 EU72BE. **CODEN** EJCDBR.

EXCERPTA MEDICA. SECTION 18. CARDIOVASCULAR DISEASES AND CARDIOVASCULAR SURGERY. See Indexes/Abstracts.

GIORNALE DI EMODINAMICA. Vol. 1, N. 1 (Jan./June 1981)-. Periodical. Italian (English). sa. 60.00. Edizioni Minerva Medica, Corso Bramente 83/85, Turin Italy 10126. **Tel** 67 82 82. Ed G Biffani. **NLM** W1. bk rev. adv acc.

GIORNALE ITALIANO DI CARDIOLOGIA. V. 1- 1971-. 0046-5968. Periodical. IT. Italian (some summaries in English). mo. $100.00. Edizioni Luigi Pozzi, Via Panama 68, Rome Italy. **Ind/Abst** Life Sci. Collect., Excerpta Med., Index Med., Biol. Abstr., Index Dent. Lit., Chem. Abstr. **NLM** W1 GI767. **CODEN** GICDA7. *Cuore e Circolazione, Folia Cardiologica; Malattie Cardiovascolari.*

HAEMOSTASIS. V. 1- 1972-. 0301-0147. Periodical. English. bm. 314.-. S Karger AG, PO Box, CH-4009 Basel Switzerland. **Tel** (061)390880. Ed H C Hemker. **Ind/Abst** Life Sci. Collect., Excerpta Med., Index Med., Biol. Abstr., Chem. Abstr., Sci. Cit. Index, Abr. Ed. **NLM** W1 HA1653. **CODEN** HMTSB7. adv acc. Original papers report the latest findings on the pathology, physiology and biochemistry of nemorrhagic disease and thrombosis. *Coagulation, 0009-9902.*

HART BULLETIN. Vol. 1- 1970-. 0301-8202. Periodical. NE. Dutch. 40.-. Uitgeversmij Vewe Bv, Postbus 50, 3640 AB Mijdrecht The Netherlands. **Tel** 02979-1251. **NLM** W1 HA599. Index published separately - free - automatically sent. bk rev. (ctrl).

HEART AND VESSELS. Vol. 1, No. 1 (Feb. 1985)-. 0910-8327. Periodical. English. $60.00. **Tel** 03-812-0331. **NLM** W1. **Circ** 1,000.

HEART FAILURE. V. 1, No. 1 (Jan./Feb. 1985)-. 8755-7673. Periodical. US. English. bm. $24.00 Individuals, U.S., $30.00 Individuals, Foreign, $40.00 Institutions, U.S., $48.00 Institutions, Foreign. Le Jacq Publishing Inc, 53 Park Place, New York NY 10007. **DD** 616.

HEART TALK. 0882-1836. Periodical. US. English. $6.00. Heart Talk Queen and Company, 218-F West Rockrimmon Boulevard, Colorado Springs CO 80919. **DD** 616.

HEART TRANSPLANTATION. See Medicine - Surgery.

HEMOPHILIA TODAY. V. 1, No. 2 (Mar./Apr. 1964)-. 0046-7251. Periodical. CN. English. bm. **DD** 616.157200971. *Report (Canadian Hemophilia Society), 0822-6636.*

HERZ-KREISLAUF. V. 1- 1969-. 0046-7324. Periodical. German. ir. **Ind/Abst** Life Sci. Collect., Excerpta Med., Chem. Abstr., Energy Res. Abstr. **CODEN** HZKLAV.

HIGH BLOOD PRESSURE HIGHLIGHTS. V. 1- Sept. 1978-. 0164-758X. Periodical. US. English. qt. State of California, Department of Health Services, 714 P Street, Sacramento CA 95814.

HYPERLIPOPROTEINAEMIAS AND ATHEROSCLEROSIS. (THE HYPERLIPOPROTEINAEMIAS AND ATHEROSCLEROSIS). Series/Titl Annual Research Reviews. V. 1-. 0709-8618. CN. English. ir. Eden Press, 4626 St Catherine Street West, Montreal Quebec Canada H3Z 1S3. **DD** 616.136005. **NLM** W1 HY841G.

HYPERTENSIE IN DE HUISARTSENPRAKTIJK. Began with: V. 1, 1971. Monographic Series. Dutch. ir. Ed K P C Amery. **NLM** W1 HY841L.

HYPERTENSION. 0362-4323. Periodical. US. English. mo. $25.00. Hypertension Publishing Company, 79 Madison Avenue, New York NY 10016. **LC** RC685.H8. **DD** 616.132005.

INDEX OF FEDERALLY SUPPORTED PROGRAMS IN HEART, BLOOD VESSEL, LUNG, AND BLOOD DISORDERS. See Indexes/Abstracts.

INDIAN HEART JOURNAL. V. 1- Jan. 1949-. 0019-4832. Periodical. II. English. bm. $60.00. Dr Shantilal Shah, 534 Sandhurst Bridge, Bombay 7 India. **Ind/Abst** Excerpta Med., Index Med. **NLM** W1 IN206.

INDIAN HEART JOURNAL. TEACHING SERIES. (INDIAN HEART JOURNAL : TEACHING SERIES). V. 1- June 1976-. 0378-6315. Monographic Series. English. ir. **NLM** W1 IN206B.

INDIAN JOURNAL OF CHEST DISEASES & ALLIED SCIENCES. (THE INDIAN JOURNAL OF CHEST DISEASES & ALLIED SCIENCES). **VAT** Indian Journal of Chest Diseases and Allied Sciences. V. 18- Jan. 1976-. 0377-9343. Periodical. II. English. qt. $18.00. The Director V P Chest Institute, University of Delhi, Delhi 7 India. **Tel** 2517027. Ed A S Paintal. **Ind/Abst** Life

Sci. Collect., Index Med. **NLM** W1 IN206S. bk rev. adv acc. **Circ** 1,000. (ctrl). Advancement of knowledge in the field of cardiorespiratory diseases and allied sciences. *Indian Journal of Chest Diseases.*

L'INFORMATION CARDIOLOGIQUE. Began with: Vol. 1, No. 1 Oct. 1978). 0220-2476. Periodical. FR. French. ir. $39.91. MME Pino, 3 rue Charles Peguy, 77500 Chelles France. **Tel** 820-63-21. **NLM** W1 IN416ED.

INTELLIGENCE REPORTS IN CARDIOVASCULAR DISEASE. Vol. 1, No. 1 (Nov./Dec. 1980)-. 0271-1141. Periodical. US. English. bm. $30.00. Healthscan Inc, Valley Road at Copper Avenue, Upper Montclair NJ 07043. **Tel** (201)744-4755. **LC** RC666. **DD** 616.1005.

INTERNAL MEDICINE NEWS & CARDIOLOGY NEWS. *See* Medicine - Internal Medicine.

INTERNATIONAL CARDIOLOGICAL REPORTER. V. 1-. 0147-3042. Periodical. US. English. mo. $47.00. International Medical Reporter, 325 Suffolk Road, Baltimore MD 21218. **Tel** (301)243-2777. *International Cardiological & Respiratory Disease Reporter.*

INTERNATIONAL JOURNAL OF CARDIAC IMAGING. Vol. 1, No. 1-. 0167-9899. Periodical. US. English. qt. $80.00. Martinus Nijoff Publishers, c/o Kluwer Academic Publishers, 190 Old Derby Street, Hingham MA 02043. **NLM** W1.

INTERNATIONAL JOURNAL OF CARDIOLOGY. Vol. 1, No. 1-. 0167-5273. Periodical. English. mo. Elsevier Science Publishers, PO Box 211, 1000 AE Amsterdam Netherlands. **Tel** (020)5803.911. **Ind/Abst** Life Sci. Collect., Pestdoc, Ringdoc, Vetdoc, Excerpta Med., Index Med., Biol. Abstr., Chem. Abstr. **NLM** W1 IN766C. **CODEN** IJCDD5. *European Journal of Cardiology, 0301-4711.*

IRCS MEDICAL SCIENCE. CARDIOVASCULAR SYSTEM. (IRCS MEDICAL SCIENCE : CARDIOVASCULAR SYSTEM). **VFOAT** Cardiovascular System. V. 3- Jan. 1975-. 0305-6732. Periodical. UK. English. mo. $95.00. IRCS Medical Science, PO Box 500, St Leonards House, Lancaster LA1 1PF England. **Tel** (0524)68116. **Ed** S Johnson. bk rev. Publishes results of original research into all aspects of cardiovascular disease in man and animals within weeks of completion. Papers fully refereed. *Research on the Cardiovascular System, 0305-2656.*

JAPANESE CIRCULATION JOURNAL. **VFOAT** Nippon Junkankigaku Shi. V. 24- Jan. 1960-. 0047-1828. Periodical. JA. English (articles also in Japanese). mo. Japanese Circulation Society, 14 Yoshida Kawaharacho, Sokyo Ku Kyoto 606 Japan. **Tel** 075-751-8643. **Ed** Satoru Murad. **Ind/Abst** Life Sci. Collect., Excerpta Med., Index Med., Biol. Abstr., Chem. Abstr., Sci. Cit. Index, Abr. Ed. **NLM** W1 JA949C. **CODEN** JCIRA2. adv acc. **Circ** 9,000. *Nippon Junkankigaku Shi.*

JAPANESE HEART JOURNAL. V. 1- Jan. 1960-. 0021-4868. Periodical. JA. English (Japanese). bm. $112.00. JC Baltzer AG Scientific Publishing Company, Wettsteinplatz 10, CH-4058 Basel Switzerland. **Tel** 61-26 89 25. **Ind/Abst** Life Sci. Collect., Excerpta Med., Index Med., Int. Aerosp. Abstr., Biol. Abstr., Chem. Abstr., Sci. Cit. Index, Abr. Ed. **NLM** W1 JA95. **CODEN** JHEJAR.

JOURNAL DES MALADIES VASCULAIRES. V. 1- 1976-. 0398-0499. Periodical. French. qt. Masson Publishing USA Inc, 211 East 43rd Street/Room 1306, New York NY 10017. **Tel** (212)370-1937. **Ind/Abst** Excerpta Med., Index Med. **NLM** W1 JO371M.

JOURNAL OF CARDIAC REHABILITATION. Vol. 1, No. 1 (Mar. 1981)-. 0275-1429. Periodical. US. English. bm. $60.00. Le Jacq Publishing, 53 Park Place, New York NY 10007. **Ind/Abst** Excerpta Med. **NLM** W1 JO574N.

JOURNAL OF CARDIAC SURGERY. *See* Medicine - Surgery.

JOURNAL OF CARDIOPULMONARY REHABILITATION. **VFOAT** JCR. Vol. 5, No. 5 (May 20, 1985)-. 0883-9212. Periodical. US. English. mo. $65.00. Le Jacq Publishing Inc, 53 Park Place, New York NY 10007. **Tel** (212)766-4300. **DD** 616. **NLM** W1. bk rev. adv acc. **Circ** 17,000. (ctrl). Peer reviewed articles on the subject of cardiovascular and pulmonary rehabilitation. *Journal of Cardiac Rehabilitation, 0275-1429.*

THE JOURNAL OF CARDIOVASCULAR MEDICINE. V. 5- Jan. 1980-. 0199-6614. Periodical. US. English. mo. $29.00. Cahners Publishing Company, Medical and Health Care Group, 475 Park Avenue South, New York NY 10016. **Tel** (212)686-0555. **Ed** Edwin Bayrd. **Ind/Abst** Life Sci. Collect., Excerpta Med., Biol. Abstr., Chem. Abstr. **LC** RC666. **DD** 616.1005. **NLM** W1 JO575M. **CODEN** JCMEDK. adv acc. **Circ** 120,000. (ctrl). Concise, clearly written, appropriately illustrated articles on cardiovascular disease and related circulatory disorders, written by national and international authorities specifically for primary care physicians. *Cardiovascular Medicine, 0145-403X.*

JOURNAL OF CARDIOVASCULAR PHARMACOLOGY. Vol. 1, No. 1 (Jan./Feb. 1979)-. 0160-2446. Periodical. US. English. bm. Raven Press, 1140 Avenue of the Americas, New York NY 10036. **Tel** (212)575-0335. **Ind/Abst** Life Sci. Collect., Pestdoc, Ringdoc, Vetdoc, Excerpta Med., Index Med., Chem. Abstr. **LC** RM345. **DD** 616.1061. **NLM** W1 JO576. **CODEN** JCPCDT.

JOURNAL OF CARDIOVASCULAR SURGERY. V. 1- July 1960-. 0021-9509. Periodical. US. English. bm. $80.00. Lippincott/Harper, East Washington Square, Philadelphia PA 19105. **Tel** (215)238-4295. **Ed** R A Deterling Jr and S S Rose. **Ind/Abst** Life Sci. Collect., Excerpta Med., Index Med., Nuci. Sci. Abstr., Index Med., Biol. Abstr., Chem. Abstr., Sci. Cit. Index, Abr. Ed. **NLM** W1 JO577. **CODEN** JCVSA2. Covers clinical, experimental, and surgical aspects of diseases of the heart and the entire vascular system.

JOURNAL OF CARDIOVASCULAR ULTRASONOGRAPHY. Vol. 1, No. 1-. 0730-8396. Periodical. US. English. qt. $118.00. Mary Ann Liebert Inc, 157 East 86th Street/2nd Floor, New York NY 10028. **Tel** (212)289-2300. **Ind/Abst** Excerpta Med. **NLM** W1. bk rev. adv acc. Promulgates information on the diagnostic applications of M-Mode, 2-D and Doppler ultrasonography to diseases of the heart and blood vessels of the adult, child and fetus.

JOURNAL OF CLINICAL HYPERTENSION. Vol. 1, No. 1 (Mar. 1985)-. 0748-450X. Periodical. US. English. qt. $90.00. Elsevier Science Publishing Company Inc, 52 Vanderbilt Avenue, New York NY 10017. **Tel** (212)370-5520. **Ed** Walter Flamenbaum. **DD** 616. **CODEN** JCHYEM. bk rev. adv acc. Provides original articles and critical reviews on the pathogenesis, pathophysiology, and treatment of hypertension.

JOURNAL OF ELECTROCARDIOLOGY. Vol. 1, No. 1-. 0022-0736. Periodical. US. English. qt. $50.00. Research in Electrocardiology Inc, PO Box 90505/Pacific Beach Station, San Diego CA 92109. **Tel** (619)459-1918. **Ed** Ronald H Selvester. **Ind/Abst** Life Sci. Collect., Excerpta Med., Index Med., Int. Aerosp. Abstr., Biol. Abstr., Energy Res. Abstr., Hospit. Lit. Index, Sci. Cit. Index, Abr. Ed. **LC** RC681.A1. **DD** 616.120754705. **NLM** W1 JO628R. **CODEN** JECAB4. adv acc. **Circ** 1,400. Research papers in electrocardiology and case reports.

THE JOURNAL OF EXTRA-CORPOREAL TECHNOLOGY. V. 1-. 0022-1058. Periodical. US. English. qt. $30.00. American Society of Extra Corporeal Technology, 1980 Issac Newton Square South, Reston VA 22090. **Tel** (703)435-8556. **Ed** James P Dearing. **Ind/Abst** Excerpta Med., Chem. Abstr., Curr. Contents, Cumul. Index Nurs. Allied Health Lit. **LC** QP110.A7. **DD** 617.412059. **NLM** W1 J06442. **CODEN** JEXCBD. **Circ** 2,600. Forerunner for international scientific articles, case studies and techniques re: extracorporeal (perfusion) technology.

JOURNAL OF ST. LUKE'S HEART INSTITUTE. **VFOAT** Journal of Saint Luke's Heart Institute. 0748-8238. Periodical. US. English. qt. Free. St Luke's Heart Institute, St Luke's Hospitals, 5535 Delmar Boulevard, St Louis MO 63112. **DD** 616.

JOURNAL OF SOVIET CARDIOVASCULAR RESEARCH. Vol. 1, No. 1 (Jan.-Mar. 1980)-. 0270-630X. Periodical. US. English (translations of articles in soviet publications). qt. $75.00 US, $87.50 Domestic. Plenum Publishers Corporation, 227 West 17th Street, New York NY 10011. **Ind/Abst** Biol. Abstr. **LC** QP101.2. **DD** 616.1005. **NLM** W1 JO901V. **CODEN** JSCRDJ.

JOURNAL OF THE AMERICAN COLLEGE OF CARDIOLOGY. **VFOAT** JACC. Vol. 1, No. 1 (Jan. 1983)-. 0735-1097. Periodical. US. English. mo. $100.00. Elsevier Science Publishers Company Inc, PO Box 1663, Grand Central Station, New York NY 10163. **Tel** (212)370-5520. **Ed** Simon Dack. **Ind/Abst** Life Sci. Collect., Excerpta Med., Index Med. **NLM** W1 JO908K. bk rev. adv acc. **Circ** 17,400. Provides timely reports on the latest advances in adult and pediatric cardiology, diagnostic procedures, drug therapy, cardiovascular surgery, and basic research.

JOURNAL OF THORACIC AND CARDIOVASCULAR SURGERY. *See* Medicine - Surgery.

JOURNAL OF VASCULAR SURGERY. *See* Medicine - Surgery.

KARDIOLOGIA POLSKA. V. 1- 1957-. 0022-9032. Periodical. PL. Polish. mo. ARS Polona, Krakowskie Przedmiescie 7, 00-068 Warsaw Poland. **Ind/Abst** Excerpta Med., Index Med. **NLM** W1 KA759.

KARDIOLOGIIA. **VFOAT** Cardiology. V. 1- Jan./Feb. 1961-. 0022-9040. Periodical. UR. Russian (summaries in English). mo. $56.00. Victor Kamkin Inc (70425), 12224 Parklawn Drive, Rockville MD 20852. **Tel** (301)881-5973. **Ind/Abst** Index Med., Int. Aerosp. Abstr., Biol. Abstr., Chem. Abstr. **NLM** W1 KA775. **CODEN** KARDA2.

KOKURITSU JUNKANKIBYO SENTA GYOSEKI NEMPO. Ed. (1977-1978)-. Periodical. JA. Japanese. an. Kokuritsu Junkankibyo Senta, 5-125 Fujishirodai, Suita 565 Japan. **LC** RC666.

KREDSLBS SYGDOMME. RAPPORT. (KREDSLBS SYGDOMME; RAPPORT). 0106-1267. Periodical. Danish. ir. **NLM** W1 KR348.

KROVOOBRASCENIE. (KROVOOBRASHCHENIE). 1970-. 0368-6736. Periodical. UR. Russian (added title in Armenian). bm. $11.50. Victor Kamkin Inc (77786), 12224 Parklawn Drive, Rockville MD 20852. **Tel** (301)881-5973. **Ind/Abst** Biol. Abstr., Chem. Abstr. **NLM** W1 KR599. **CODEN** KROVAO.

L.E.R.S. MONOGRAPH SERIES. **VFOAT** LERS Monograph Series. **VAT** Laboratoires d'Etudes et de Recherches-Synthelabo Monograph Series. Vol. 1-. 0742-3896. Monographic Series. US. English. ir. Raven Press, 1140 Avenue of the Americas, New York NY 10036. **Ind/Abst** Chem. Abstr. **NLM** W1. **CODEN** LMSED6.

MEDIGUIDE TO CARDIOLOGY. Vol. 1, No. 1-. 0738-2979. Periodical. US. English. qt. Lawrence Dellacorte Publications, 767 Lexington Avenue, New York NY 10021. **NLM** W1 ME787FKE.

METABOLIC ASPECTS OF CARDIOVASCULAR DISEASE. Vol. 1-. 0167-725X. Monographic Series. US. English. ir. American Elsevier Publishing Company Inc, 52 Vanderbilt Avenue, New York NY 10017. **Ind/Abst** Chem. Abstr. **LC** UNC. **NLM** W1 ME961KN (P). **CODEN** MACDDK.

MINERVA CARDIOANGIOLOGICA. Yearly V. 1- Nov/Dec 1953-. 0026-4725. Periodical. IT. Italian. mo. 80.00. Edizoni Minerva Medica, Corso Bramante 83-85, Torino Italy 10126. **Tel** 67 82 82. **Ed** F Spadaccimi. **Ind/Abst** Life Sci. Collect., Excerpta Med., Index Med. **NLM** W1 MI634. bk rev. adv acc.

MONOGRAPHS ON ATHEROSCLEROSIS. V. 1- 1969-. 0077-099X. Monographic Series. English. ir. S Karger AG, PO Box, CH-4009 Basel Switzerland. **Tel** 061-39 08 80. **Ed** D Kritchevsky and O J Pollak. **Ind/Abst** Index Med., Chem. Abstr., Biol. Abstr. **NLM** W1 MO569T. **CODEN** MOATAH. Designed to quickly and conveniently communicate laboratory findings to medical practitioners as well as other investigators involved with disorders of the cardiovascular system.

MULTIPLE RISK FACTOR INTERVENTION TRIAL. PUBLIC ANNUAL REPORT. **Main/Corp** National Heart, Lung, and Blood Institute. Division of Heart and Vascular Diseases. **VFOAT** Public Annual Report. 0164-0577. US. English. an. National Heart Lung and Blood Institute, National Institutes of Health, 9000 Rockville Pike, Bethesda MD 20014. *Multiple Risk Factor Intervention Trial. Public Annual Report, 0146-4884.*

MYOCARDIAL PROTECTION IN REGIONAL AND GLOBAL ISCHEMIA. **Series/Titl** Annual Research Reviews. Vol. 1-. 0229-9070. Periodical. CN. English. ir. Eden Press, 4626 St Catherine Street West, Montreal Quebec H3Z 1S3 Canada. **DD** 616.1237.

Medicine—Dermatology

NAUHEIMER FORTBILDUNGS-LEHRGANGE. Vol. 11- 1935-. 0077-6173. Monographic Series. German. ir. **Ind/Abst** Chem. Abstr. **NLM** W3 NA846. **CODEN** NFBLBF.

NEW CONCEPTS IN CARDIAC IMAGING. VFOAT Cardiac Imaging. 1985-. 0743-9237. US. English. an. G K Hall Medical Publishers, 70 Lincoln Street, Boston MA 02111. **DD** 616. **NLM** W1.

NEW DRUGS ANNUAL, CARDIOVASCULAR DRUGS. Vol. 1-. 0742-387X. US. English. an. Raven Press, 1140 Avenue of the Americas, New York NY 10036. **Tel** (212)575-0335. Ed Alexander Scriabine. **Ind/Abst** Chem. Abstr. **LC** RM345. **DD** 615.7105. **NLM** W1. **CODEN** NDADD8.

PACING AND CLINICAL ELECTROPHYSIOLOGY. (PACE. PACING AND CLINICAL ELECTROPHYSIOLOGY). V. 1- Jan. 1978-. 0147-8389. Periodical. US. English. bm. $62.00 US and Canada, $80.00 Foreign. Futura Publishing Co, 295 Main Street, PO Box 330, Mount Kisco NY 10549. **Tel** (914)666-7528. Ed Seymour Furman. **Ind/Abst** Excerpta Med., Life Sci. Collect., Index Med. **LC** RC684.P3. **DD** 617.412. **NLM** W1 P114T. bk rev. adv acc. Circ 4,800. Welcomes communications in laboratory and clinical cardiac pacing, electrophysiology and the electro-stimulation of other organs which affect the cardiovascular system.

PAEDIATRIC CARDIOLOGY. See Medicine - Pediatrics.

PAROI ARTERIELLE. VFOAT Arterial Wall. V. 1- June 1973-. 0398-7655. Periodical. FR. French (articles in English or with summaries in both languages). qt. $34.15. Centre Recherches Cardiologiqu, 78 rue de la Convention, Paris 1 5E France. **Ind/Abst** Excerpta Med., Index Med., Sci. Cit. Index, Abr. Ed. **NLM** W1 PA864H.

PEDIATRIC CARDIOLOGY. See Medicine - Pediatrics.

PERFUSION LIFE. Began with Jan. 1984 issue?. 0747-3079. Periodical. US. English. mo. Free to Members, $20.00 Nonmembers. AMSECT, Reston International Center, 11800 Sunrise Valley Drive/Suite 808, Reston VA 22091. **Tel** (703)435-8556. bk rev. adv acc. Circ 2,300. In-depth backgrounders on key issues, resources, events, and professional development opportunities for perfusionists.

PERSPECTIVES IN CARDIOVASCULAR RESEARCH. V. 1-. 0361-0527. Monographic Series. US. English. ir. Raven Press, 1140 Avenue of the Americas, New York NY 10036. **Ind/Abst** Life Sci. Collect., Biol. Abstr., Chem. Abstr. **NLM** W1 PE871AL. **CODEN** PCRED9.

PHLEBOLOGIE. (PHLEBOLOGIE : BULLETIN DE LA SOCIETE FRANCAISE DE L'UNION INTERNATIONALE DE PHLEBOLOGIE). Began with Jan./Mar. 1952. 0031-8280. Periodical. French. qt. **Ind/Abst** Excerpta Med., Index Med. **NLM** W1 PH62K. Bulletin of the Societe Francaise de Phlebologie.

PRACTICAL CARDIOLOGY. V. 1- Oct. 1975-. 0361-3372. Periodical. US. English. mo. $45.00. Medical Publishing Inc, 50 Route 9, Morganville NJ 07751. **Tel** (201)536-3600. **Ind/Abst** Excerpta Med. **LC** RC681.A1. **DD** 616.12005. **NLM** W1 PR1382. adv acc.

PRIMARY CARDIOLOGY. 0363-5104. Periodical. US. English. mo. $45.00. PW Communications Inc, 400 Plaza Drive, Secaucus NJ 07094. **Tel** (201)865-7500. **Ind/Abst** Excerpta Med. **LC** RC681.A1. **DD** 616.1005. **NLM** W1 PR521R.

PRINCIPLES OF CLINICAL ELECTROCARDIOGRAPHY. VFOAT Clinical Electrocardiography. 1st Ed. (1956)-. US. English. te. $19.00. Lange Medical Publications, Drawer L, Los Altos CA 94023. **Tel** (415)948-4526. Ed Mervin J Goldman. **LC** RC683.5.E5. **DD** 616.12075. Offers a concise explanation of the normal electrocardiogram and changes associated with clinical abnormalities.

PROCEEDINGS - ASSOCIATION OF EUROPEAN PAEDIATRIC CARDIOLOGISTS. See Medicine - Pediatrics.

PROCEEDINGS OF THE MEETING ON CARDIOVASCULAR EPIDEMIOLOGY AND BIOSTATISTICS TRAINING PROGRAMS. Main/Conf Meeting on Cardiovascular Epidemiology and Biostatistics Training Programs. Series/Titl NIH Publication. 4th- 1979-. Periodical. US. English. **NLM** W3 ME427SP.

Proceedings of the Workshop on Cardiovascular Epidemiology and Biostatistics Training Programs.

PROGRESS IN CARDIAC REHABILITATION. V. 1-. 0195-9530. Monographic Series. US. English. **LC** UNC. **NLM** W1 PR667N.

PROGRESS IN CARDIOLOGY. 1- 1972-. 0097-109X. US. English. an. Lea & Febiger, 600 Washington Square, Philadelphia PA 19106-4198. **Tel** (800)433-3850. Ed Paul N Yu and John F Goodwin. **Ind/Abst** Biol. Abstr. **LC** RC681.A1. **DD** 616.12005. **NLM** W1 PR667P. **CODEN** PGCDAO. The editors pick interesting, exciting, and sometimes controversial topics in cardiology, carefully written by shrewdly chosen experts from all over the globe.

PROGRESS IN CARDIOVASCULAR DISEASES. V. 1- June 1958-. 0033-0620. Periodical. US. English. bm. $78.00. Grune & Stratton Inc, 111 Fifth Avenue, New York NY 10003. **Tel** (212)614-3232. **Ind/Abst** Life Sci. Collect., Excerpta Med., Energy Res. Abstr., Biol. Abstr., Chem. Abstr., Index Med., Sci. Cit. Index, Abr. Ed. **DD** 616. **NLM** W1 PR6671. **CODEN** PCVDAN.

PROGRESS IN STROKE RESEARCH. 1-. 0144-865X. UK. English. ir. Ed R M Greenhalgh and F C Rose. **NLM** W1 PR681K.

PSYCHOSOZIALER STRESS UND KORONARE HERZKRANKHEIT. English (articles in German). ir. **NLM** W3 PS966.

PUBLIC ANNUAL REPORT - MULTIPLE RISK FACTOR INTERVENTION TRIAL. Main/Corp Multiple Risk Factor Intervention Trial. Series/Titl DHEW Publication. 1974/75-. Periodical. US. English. an. **NLM** W2 A M9P.

PULMONARY DISEASE REVIEWS. V. 1- 1980-. 0272-7900. US. English. ir. John Wiley & Sons, 1 Wiley Drive, Somerset NJ 08873. **LC** RC756. **DD** 616.24. **NLM** W1 PU884.

QUALITY OF LIFE AND CARDIOVASCULAR CARE. Vol. 1, No. 1 (Oct. 1984)-. 0748-6901. Periodical. US. English. bm. $40.00 Domestic, $48.00 Foreign. Le Jacq Publishing Inc, 53 Park Place, New York NY 10007. **DD** 616.

RECENT ADVANCES IN CARDIAC ARRHYTHMIAS. 1-. Monographic Series. UK. English. ir. **Ind/Abst** Chem. Abstr. **NLM** W1. **CODEN** RACAEX.

REVISTA ARGENTINA DE CARDIOLOGIA. (REVISTA ARGENTINA DE CARDIOLOGIA : ORGANO DE LA SOCIEDAD ARGENTINA DE CARDIOLOGIA). Began with: Vol. 1, published in 1934. 0034-7000. Periodical. AG. Spanish (summaries in English). bm. Sociedad Argentina de Cardiologia, Gia Larrea 1132, Buenos Aires Argentina. **Ind/Abst** Excerpta Med. **NLM** W1 RE267L. **CODEN** RACDA4.

REVISTA DE MEDICINA DE LA UNIVERSIDAD DE NAVARRA. V. 7- March 1963-. 0556-6177. Periodical. SP. Spanish. qt. Free. Ed Universidad Navarra SA, Plaza los Sauces, Apartado 396, Baranain Pamplona Spain. **Tel** (48)25 68 50. Ed Eduardo Alegria. **Ind/Abst** Life Sci. Collect., Excerpta Med., Index Med. **NLM** W1 RE423H. bk rev. adv acc. Circ 12,000. (ctrl). Describes the important research that is being conducted at the University of Navarra Medical School. Revista de Medicina del Estudio General de Navarra.

REVISTA LATINA DE CARDIOLOGIA. Vol. 1, No. 1 (Jan. 1980)-. 0210-8755. Periodical. Spanish. ir. Edit Cientifico Medica, Via Layetana 53, Barcelona 3 Spain. **NLM** W1.

SCANDINAVIAN JOURNAL OF THORACIC AND CARDIOVASCULAR SURGERY. See Medicine - Surgery.

SCHRITTMACHER. VFOAT Herzschrittmacher. V. 1, 1/81 (Oct. 29, 1981)-. 0721-5479. Periodical. GW. German. qt. EBM Medizinischer Verlag, Elektrstr 5, 8000 Munchen 81 West Germany. **NLM** W1 SC365T.

SEMINARS IN THROMBOSIS AND HEMOSTASIS. V. 1- July 1974-. 0094-6176. Periodical. US. English. qt. $68.00. Thieme-Stratton Inc, 381 Park Avenue South/Suite 1501, New York NY 10016. **Tel** (212)683-5088. Ed Eberband F Mannen. **Ind/Abst** Life Sci. Collect., Excerpta Med., Index Med., Biol. Abstr., Energy Res. Abstr., Chem. Abstr., Sci. Cit. Index, Abr. Ed. **NLM** W1 SE489P. **CODEN** STHMBV. adv acc. Circ 1,478. (ctrl). Topic-oriented journal for the practitioner specializing in areas of vascular diseases, blood clots and metabolism.

SOINS. CARDIOLOGIE. VFOAT Cardiologie. No 1 (March 83)-. 0755-1916. Periodical. French. mo. **Ind/Abst** Int. Nurs. Index. **NLM** W1.

SUNHWANGI. VFOAT Korean Circulation Journal. Periodical. KO. Korean (summaries in English). ir. Taehan Sunhwangi Hakhoe, 28 Yongon-Dong Chongno-Ku, Seoul Korea. **LC** RC666. **DD** 616.12005.

TECHNOLOGY FOR CARDIOLOGY. 8756-8586. Periodical. US. English. mo. $70.00. ECRI, 5200 Butler Pike, Plymouth Meeting PA 19462. **Tel** (215)825-6000. Ed J Novel. **DD** 616. bk rev. A newsletter for cardiologists and cardiovascular specialists summarizing health care technology issues and reporting product recalls, hazards, and problems. Health Devices Update. Cardiology.

TEXAS HEART INSTITUTE JOURNAL. Vol. 9, No. 1 (Mar. 1982)-. 0730-2347. Periodical. US. English. qt. $25.00. Texas Heart Institute, PO Box 20269, Houston TX 77025. **Tel** (713)791-4209. **Ind/Abst** Life Sci. Collect., Excerpta Med., Index Med. **NLM** W1 TE778. **CODEN** THIJDO. Cardiovascular Diseases, 0093-3546.

THROMBOSIS RESEARCH. V. 1- Feb. 1972-. 0049-3848. Periodical. US. English (French, German, or Russian, summaries in English). sm. Pergamon Press, 395 Sawmill River Road, Elmsford NY 10523. **Tel** (914)592-7700. **Ind/Abst** Life Sci. Collect., Excerpta Med., Pestdoc, Ringdoc, Vetdoc, Index Med., Biol. Abstr., Energy Res. Abstr., Chem. Abstr., Sci. Cit. Index, Abr. Ed. **NLM** W1 TH94. **CODEN** THBRAA. Index published separately - free - automatically sent. Available on microfilm or microfiche.

UPDATE : CARDIOLOGY. V. 1- 1976-. 0162-0975. Periodical. US. English. ir. **NLM** W1 UP511.

VASA. ZEITSCHRIFT FUR GEFASSKRANKHEITEN. VFOAT Journal for Vascular Diseases. Vol. 1- 1972-. Periodical. SZ. German (articles also in English). qt. 48.00 Domestic, $39.00 US. Hogrefe International Inc, 12-14 Bruce Park Avenue, Toronto Ontario M4P 2S3 Canada. **Tel** (416)482-6339. Ed H J Leu. **Ind/Abst** Biol. Abstr., Curr. Contents Clin. Pract., Index Med. **NLM** W1 V101C. **CODEN** VASAAH. bk rev. adv acc. Circ 1,200. This journal of vascular diseases is directed not only toward angiologists, phlebologists and circulation physiologists but also toward general and specialist physicians who are frequently confronted with vascular problems. Zentralblatt fur Phlebologie.

VASCULAR REPORTS. Vol. 1, No. 1 (July-Aug. 1984)-. 0748-8971. Periodical. US. English. bm. $82.50. Appleton Davies Inc, 32 South Raymond Avenue/Suite 10, Pasadena CA 91105. **Tel** (818)792-3046. Ed Wiley F Barker. **DD** 617. bk rev. adv acc. Circ 1,500. Covers articles, case reports, patient problems in diagnosis and treatment of vascular disease. Includes educational reviews and self-assessment exams, book reviews and announcements.

VERHANDLUNGEN DER DEUTSCHEN GESELLSCHAFT FUR HERZ- UND KREISLAUFFORSCHUNG. V. 45-. 0174-2817. Monographic Series. GW. German. ir. free. Dr Dietrich Steinkopff Verlag, PO Box 1008, Saalbaustrasse 12, 6100 Darmstadt 11 West Germany. **Tel** 06151-26538. Ed P Lichtlen and F Loogan. **Ind/Abst** Excerpta Med., Index Med., Chem. Abstr. **LC** RC667. **NLM** W1 VE483MK. **CODEN** VDGKDB. adv acc. Circ 3,000. (ctrl). Publicates the contributions of the conferences of German Society of Cardiology. Verhandlungen der Deutschen Gesellschaft fur Kreislaufforschung, 0070-4075.

WELLCOME TRENDS IN CARDIOLOGY. VFOAT Cardiology. V. 1- Apr. 1979-. Periodical. US. English. ir. Park Row Publishing, 15 Park Row/23rd Floor, New York NY 10038. Clinical Trends in Cardiology, 0733-4893.

THE YEAR BOOK OF CARDIOLOGY. See Yearbooks, Almanacs, Directories.

DERMATOLOGY

ABMS DIRECTORY OF CERTIFIED DERMATOLOGISTS. See Yearbooks, Almanacs, Directories.

ACTA DERMATO-VENEREOLOGICA. V. 1- 1920-. 0001-5555. Periodical. SW. articles in German, English or French with summaries in the other two languages. bm. 370.-. Almqvist & Wiksell, 108 Drottninggatan, PO Box 45150, S-104 30 Stockholm Sweden. **Tel** (018)118740. **Ed** Nils Thyresson. **Ind/Abst** Life Sci. Collect., Pestdoc, Ringdoc, Vetdoc, Excerpta Med., CIS Abstr., Biol. Abstr., Chem. Abstr., Nuci. Sci. Abstr., Index Med., Sci. Cit. Index, Abr. Ed., Hospit. Lit. Index. **NLM** W1 AC7921. **CODEN** ADVEA4. adv acc. **Circ** 1,500. Clinical and experimental research in the field of dermatology and venereology.

ACTA DERMATO-VENEREOLOGICA. SUPPLEMENTUM. 1- 1929-. 0365-8341. Periodical. English (contributions in German). ir. **Ind/Abst** Life Sci. Collect., Biol. Abstr., Index Med., Chem. Abstr. **NLM** W1 AC7922. **CODEN** AVSUAR.

AKTUELLE DERMATOLOGIE. V. 1- Feb. 1975-. 0340-2541. Periodical. German. bm. Thieme-Stratton Inc, 381 Park Avenue South, New York NY 10016. **Tel** (212)683-5088. **Ind/Abst** Excerpta Med. **NLM** W1 AK991P.

THE AMERICAN JOURNAL OF DERMATOPATHOLOGY. V. 1- Spring 1979-. 0193-1091. Periodical. US. English. ir. $98.00. Raven Press, 1140 Avenue of the Americas, New York NY 10036. **Tel** (212)575-0335. **Ind/Abst** Life Sci. Collect., Excerpta Med., Index Med., Chem. Abstr., Sci. Cit. Index, Abr. Ed. **LC** RL95. **DD** 616.5005. **NLM** W1 AM45NH. **CODEN** AJODDB.

ANAIS BRASILEIROS DE DERMATOLOGIA. 0365-0596. Periodical. BL. Portuguese. bm. $80.00. ECN-Editora Cientifica Nacion, Caixa Postal 590, 20001-Rio de Janeiro RJ Brazil. **Ed** Nacional. **Ind/Abst** Excerpta Med. **NLM** W1 AN106. bk rev. adv acc. **Circ** 2,600. (ctrl). Covers diseases of the skin.

ANNALES DE DERMATOLOGIE ET DE VENEREOLOGIE. V. 104- Jan. 1977-. 0151-9638. Periodical. French. $140.00. Masson Publishing USA Inc, 211 East 43rd Street/Room 1306, New York NY 10017. **Tel** (212)370-1937. **Ind/Abst** CIS Abstr., Life Sci. Collect., Excerpta Med., Index Med., Biol. Abstr. **NLM** W1 AN334B. **CODEN** ADVED7. *Annales de Dermatologie et de Syphiligraphie, 0003-3979.*

ANNUAL REPORT - NATIONAL PSORIASIS FOUNDATION (U.S.). (ANNUAL REPORT). **Main/Corp** National Psoriasis Foundation (U.S.). 8756-2243. US. English. an. National Psoriasis Foundation, 6415 SW Canyon Court/Suite 200, Portland OR 97221. **DD** 616.

ANNUAL REPORT - ORENTREICH FOUNDATION FOR THE ADVANCEMENT OF SCIENCE, INC. **Main/Corp** Orentreich Foundation for the Advancement of Science. **VAT** Annual Report - Orentreich Foundation for the Advancement of Science, Incorporated. 0145-9139. US. English. an. Orentreich Foundation for the Advancement of Science Inc, 909 Fifth Avenue, New York NY 10021. **LC** RL49.O7. **DD** 616.5007207471.

ARCHIVES OF DERMATOLOGICAL RESEARCH. *See* Genealogy and Heraldry - Archives.

ARCHIVES OF DERMATOLOGY. *See* Genealogy and Heraldry - Archives.

AUSTRALASIAN JOURNAL OF DERMATOLOGY. (THE AUSTRALASIAN JOURNAL OF DERMATOLOGY). V. 9- 1967-. 0004-8380. Periodical. AT. English. ty. 20.00. Australasian College of Dermatology, 271 Bridge Road, Glebe New South Wales 2037 Australia. **Tel** (02)660-5392. **Ed** Rex Becke. **Ind/Abst** Life Sci. Collect., Excerpta Med., Index Med., Biol. Abstr., Hospit. Lit. Index. **NLM** W1 AU248. **CODEN** AJDEBP. bk rev. adv acc. **Circ** 500. (ctrl). Original articles, case reports; research reports in dermatology, etc. *Australian Journal of Dermatology.*

BEITRAGE ZUR DERMATOLOGIE. V. 1-. 0171-0184. Monographic Series. German. ir. Verlag Mr Med D Straube, D-8520 Erlangen West Germany. **NLM** W1 BE221.

BRITISH JOURNAL OF DERMATOLOGY. V. 63- 1951-. 0007-0963. Periodical. UK. English. mo. $137.50. Blackwell Scientific Publications Ltd, PO Box 88/Osney Mead, Oxford OX2 0EL England. **Tel** Oxford 240201. **Ed** R M Mackie. **Ind/Abst** Life Sci. Collect., Pestdoc, Ringdoc, Vetdoc, Excerpta Med., Index Med., CIS Abstr., Biol. Abstr., Nuci. Sci. Abstr., Index Med., Chem. Abstr., Sci. Cit. Index, Abr. Ed. **NLM** W1 BR526. **CODEN** BJDEAZ. bk rev. adv acc. **Circ** 4,100. Publishes original articles on all aspects of the biology and pathology of the skin. Attracts contributions from all countries in which research is carried out. *British Journal of Dermatology and Syphilis.*

CESKOSLOVENSKA DERMATOLOGIE. Vol. 22, No. 2- 1946-. 0009-0514. Periodical. CS. Czech (some summaries in Russian, English, or French). bm. $56.10. Artia, Ve Smeckach 30, PO Box 790, Praha 1 Czechoslovakia. **Ind/Abst** Life Sci. Collect., Excerpta Med., CIS Abstr., Chem. Abstr., Biol. Abstr., Index Med. **NLM** W1 CE879. **CODEN** CEDEAB.

CHUNG-HUA PI FU KO TSA CHIH. **VFOAT** Chinese Journal of Dermatology. 1- 1953?-. 0412-4030. Periodical. CC. Chinese (table of contents and some abstracts also in English). qt. $8.64. China Publication Centre, PO Box 2820, Beijing China.

CLINICAL AND EXPERIMENTAL DERMATOLOGY. V. 1- March 1976-. 0307-6938. Periodical. UK. English. bm. $172.50. Blackwell Scientific Publishing Ltd, PO Box 88, Oxford OX2 0EL England. **Ed** Griffitus. **Ind/Abst** Life Sci. Collect., Pestdoc, Ringdoc, Vetdoc, Excerpta Med., Index Med., Biol. Abstr., Chem. Abstr., Sci. Cit. Index, Abr. Ed. **NLM** W1 CL656. **CODEN** CEDEDE. bk rev. adv acc. **Circ** 911. Articles of interest to practicing dermatologists articles on the history of dermatology controversies and unusual observations. *Transactions of the St. John's Hospital Dermatological Society, 0036-2891.*

CLINICS IN DERMATOLOGY. Vol. 1, No. 1 (July-Sept. 1983)-. 0738-081X. Periodical. US. English. qt. $81.00 Domestic, $90.00 Foreign. J B Lippincott Co, 2350 Virginia Avenue, Hagerstown MD 21740. **Tel** (301)824-7300 Maryland, (800)638-3030 outside Maryland. **Ed** Lawrence C Parish. **DD** 616. **NLM** W1. **Circ** 825. A series of symposia for discriminiating clinicians, each hardbound issue focuses on a specific topic in dermatology and related specialities.

CONTACT DERMATITIS. V. 1- 1975-. 0105-1873. Periodical. DK. English. $95.88. Munksgaard Ltd, 35 Norre Sogade, DK-1370 Copenhagen K Denmark. **Tel** 1 12 70 30. **Ed** C D Calnan. **Ind/Abst** Life Sci. Collect., Excerpta Med., Index Med., Biol. Abstr., Art Archaeol. Tech. Abstr., Chem. Abstr., Sci. Cit. Index, Abr. Ed., Hospit. Lit. Index. **NLM** W1 CO768CH. **CODEN** CODEDG. bk rev. adv acc. **Circ** 1,500. Environmental and occupational dermatitis- allergy, clinical immunology, and chemistry.

CURRENT CONCEPTS IN SKIN DISORDERS. **VFOAT** Skin Disorders. Began with V. 1, No. 1 (Spring 1980). 0199-8757. Periodical. US. English. qt. Professional Communications Associates, 625 North Michigan Avenue, Chicago IL 60611. **NLM** W1 CU788AZ.

CURRENT ISSUES IN DERMATOLOGY. Vol. 1-. 0738-7865. US. English. an. $30.00. G K Hall Medical Publishers, 70 Lincoln Street, Boston MA 02011. **NLM** W1.

CURRENT PROBLEMS IN DERMATOLOGY. V. 2- 1968-. 0070-2064. English. ir. S Karger Ag, PO Box, CH-4009 Basel Switzerland. **Tel** (061)390880. **Ed** J W H Mali. **Ind/Abst** Index Med., Chem. Abstr. **NLM** W1 CU804L. **CODEN** APDEBX. Superb editing uncovers the right topics and the right authors and has produced well-referenced and timely expositions from the most active areas of skin research.

CUTIS. V. 1- Feb. 1965-. 0011-4162. Periodical. US. English. mo. $65.00. Technical Publishing Co, 875 3rd Avenue, New York NY 10022. **Tel** (212)605-9400. **Ind/Abst** Life Sci. Collect., Excerpta Med., Index Med., Biol. Abstr., Energy Res. Abstr., Sci. Cit. Index, Abr. Ed., Hospit. Lit. Index. **LC** RL1. **DD** 616.5005. **NLM** W1 CU97. **CODEN** CUTIB.

DERMATOLOGIC CAPSULE & COMMENT. **VFOAT** Dermatologic Capsule and Comment. 0741-7489. US. English. mo. Free. HP Publishing Co, 575 Lexington Avenue, New York NY 10022.

DERMATOLOGIC CLINICS. Vol. 1, No. 1 (Jan. 1983)-. 0733-8635. Periodical. US. English. qt. $70.20. W B Saunders Company Publ, West Washington Square, Philadelphia PA 19105. **Tel** (800)523-0713. **Ind/Abst** Excerpta Med. **LC** RL1. **DD** 616.5005. **NLM** W1 DE501B.

DERMATOLOGICA. V. 79- 1939-. 0011-9075. Periodical. SZ. German (text in English or French with summaries in English, French and German). mo. **Ind/Abst** Life Sci. Collect., Pestdoc, Ringdoc, Vetdoc, Excerpta Med., Index Med., CIS Abstr., Biol. Abstr., Chem. Abstr., Nuci. Sci. Abstr. **NLM** W1 DE501G. **CODEN** DERAAC. Available on microfilm from University Microfilms International. *Dermatologische Zeitschrift, 0366-8878.*

DERMATOLOGISCHE STUDIEN *CEASED.* Periodical. German. ir. Deutscher Buch Export-Import, Leninstrasse 16, DDR-701 Leipzig East Germany.

THE DERMATOLOGIST'S COMPENDIUM OF DRUG THERAPY. (THE DERMATOLOGIST'S COMPENDIUM OF DRUG THERAPY : A PUBLICATION OF BIOMEDICAL INFORMATION CORPORATION). **VFOAT** Compendium of Drug Therapy. 1981/1982-. 0276-430X. US. English. an. Biomedical Information Corp, 800-2nd Avenue, New York NY 10017.

DERMATOLOGY & ALLERGY. **VAT** Dermatology and Allergy. Began with Mar. 1980 issue. 0273-2254. Periodical. US. English. mo. $20.00 US, $30.00 Domestic. Circulation Department, Dermatology & Allergy, Suite 2080/1603 Orrington Avenue, Evanston IL 60201. **LC** RL1. **DD** 616.5005. **NLM** W1 DE5085M. *Dermatology, 0162-5446.*

DERMATOLOGY DIGEST. V. 18, No. 8/9- Aug./Sept. 1979-. 0198-6643. Periodical. US. English. mo. $27.50. Medical Digest Inc, 445 Central Avenue, Northfield IL 60093. **NLM** W1 DE509G. Available in microfilm or microfiche from Xerox University Microfilm. *Journal of Continuing Education in Dermatology, 0160-7685.*

DERMATOLOGY IN PRACTICE (LONDON, ENGLAND). (DERMATOLOGY IN PRACTICE). 0262-5504. Periodical. UK. English. bm. **Tel** 01-379 6005. **NLM** W1 DE509H. bk rev. adv acc. **Circ** 20,700. (ctrl). Articles on management and treatment of skin diseases, book review, news for general practitioners and dermatologists.

DERMATOLOGY (NEW YORK, N.Y.). (DERMATOLOGY). Vol. 1-. 0742-3217. Monographic Series. US. English. Marcel Dekker Inc, 270 Madison Avenue, New York NY 10016. **Ed** Charles C Calnan and Howard Maibach. **NLM** W1 DE5084.

DERMATOLOGY TIMES. 0196-6197. Periodical. US. English. mo. $35.00. Dermatology Times Inc, 95 Madison Avenue, New York NY 10016.

DERMATOLOGY UPDATE. **Series/Titl** Reviews for Physicians. 1979- Ed. 0163-1691. US. English. an. Elsevier-North Holland Inc, 52 Vanderbilt Avenue, New York NY 10017. **LC** RL1. **DD** 616.5005. **NLM** W1 DE509K.

DERMATOSEN IN BERUF UND UMWELT. **VFOAT** Occupational and Environmental Dermatoses. V. 26- 1978-. 0343-2432. Periodical. GW. German. bm. 51.00. Editio Cantor, Postfach 12 55, D-7960 Aulendorf West Germany. **Tel** 07525/ 431. **Ed** H Ippen, K H Schulz and H Tronnier. **Ind/Abst** Excerpta Med., Index Med., Chem. Abstr., Energy Res. Abstr. **NLM** W1 DE509L. **CODEN** DBUMDB. bk rev. adv acc. **Circ** 4,500. The modern journal for question concerning skin lesions induced by occupation and environment, intended for the dermatologists, industrial medical officer and specialist in internal medicine. *Berufs-Dermatosen, 0005-9498.*

DERMOFARMACIA. V. 1- Jan./Apr. 1974-. 0303-8890. Periodical. IT. Italian (summaries in English). ir. Edizioni Minerva Medica, Corso Bramante 83, 10126 Torino Italy. **NLM** W1 DE509M.

DIRECTORY - AMERICAN ACADEMY OF DERMATOLOGY. *See* Yearbooks, Almanacs, Directories.

DRUGS IN DERMATOLOGY. **Series/Titl** PRM : Physicians' Reference Manuals. No. 1 (1982)-. 0824-7048. Periodical. CN. English. sa. 50.00. Drugs in Dermatology, c/o STA Communications 63 Place Frontenac, Pointe-Claire Quebec H9R 4Z7 Canada. **Tel** (514)695-6723. **Ed** Paul Brand. **DD** 616.5061. adv acc. **Circ** 500. (ctrl). Drug reference manuals.

EUPHORIA ET CACOPHORIA. No. 1- May 1974-. English (German). ir. Aldo Castellani Memorial Research, PO Box No 120, Gifu Japan. **LC** RL1. **DD** 616.5005. **NLM** W1 EU51. *Bulletin of Pharmaceutical Research Institute.*

Medicine—Endocrinology

EXCERPTA MEDICA. SECTION 13. DERMATOLOGY AND VENEREOLOGY. See Indexes/Abstracts.

GIORNALE ITALIANO DI DERMATOLOGIA E VENEREOLOGIA. (GIORNALE ITALIANO DI DERMATOLOGIA E VENEREOLOGIA : ORGANO UFFICIALE SOCIETA ITALIANA DI DERMATOLOGIA E SIFILOGRAFIA). Vol. 115, No. 1-2 (Jan./Feb. 1980)-. 0392-0488. Periodical. IT. Italian (English). bm. 80.00. Edizioni Minerva Medica, PO Box 491, 10100 Torino Italy. Tel 678282. Ed G Zirla. Ind/Abst Life Sci. Collect., Excerpta Med., Index Med., Chem. Abstr. NLM W1 GI777A. CODEN GIDVDZ. bk rev. adv acc. Addressed to practitioners and specialists in dermatology in Italy and abroad; deals with topics in scientific practice and research. *Giornale Italiana di Dermatologia. Minerva Dermatologica, 0533-7712.*

H + G ZEITSCHRIFT FUR HAUTRANKHEITEN. (ZEITSCHRIFT FUR HAUTKRANKHEITEN). **VFOAT** H + G. V. 48, No. 13-1973-. 0301-0481. Periodical. GW. German. bw. Grosse Verlag GMBH, Kurfuerstendamm 152, D1000 Berlin 31 West Germany. Ind/Abst Life Sci. Collect., Excerpta Med., Pestdoc, Ringdoc, Vetdoc, Index Med., CIS Abstr., Energy Res. Abstr. NLM W1 ZE361H. *Zeitschrift fur Haut- und Geschlechtskrankheiten, 0044-2844.*

HAUTARZT. (HAUTARZT, ZEITSCHRIFT FUR DERMATOLOGIE, VENEROLOGIE UND VERWANDTE GEBIETE). 0017-8470. Periodical. GW. German. mo. $109.00. Springer Verlag-New York Inc, 175 5th Avenue, New York NY 10010. Tel (212)460-1500. Ed O Braun-Falco, D Petzoldt, U W Schneyder and K Wolff. Ind/Abst Life Sci. Collect., Pestdoc, Ringdoc, Vetdoc, Excerpta Med., Chem. Abstr., Biol. Abstr., Nuci. Sci. Abstr., Index Med., Energy Res. Abstr., Curr. Contents, Sci. Cit. Index, Abr. Ed., INIS Atomindex. NLM W1 HA899. CODEN HAUTAW. bk rev. Directed at the dermatologist in the hospital and in practice as well as researchers and the pharmaceutical industry. Original works, book reviews, questions, answers and meeting reports.

HIFU = SKIN RESEARCH. Periodical. JA. Japanese (abstracts also in English). bm. Osaka Dermatological Association, 1-1-50 Fukushima, Osaka-Shi Japan. Tel (06)451-0051. Ed Minoru Yasuhara. Ind/Abst Biol. Abstr., Chem. Abstr. NLM W1 HI192. CODEN HIFUAG. adv acc. Circ 1,200. (ctrl). Clinical electronmicroscopic atlas, review and original article including all parts of dermatology.

HIFUKA KIYO. VFOAT Acta Dermatologica. V. 1-1923-. 0065-1176. Periodical. JA. Japanese (with some English and German). qt. $33.50. Japan Publications Trading Company, PO Box 5030, Tokyo International, Tokyo 100-31 Japan. Ind/Abst Excerpta Med. NLM W1 HI198.

INDIAN JOURNAL OF DERMATOLOGY. Began with Oct. 1955. 0019-5154. Periodical. II. English. qt. $16.00. Dermatological Society, 78 Dharamtala Street, Calcutta 13 India. Tel 24-4547. Ed A K Dutta. Ind/Abst Excerpta Med., Biol. Abstr., Index Med. NLM W1 IN2075. CODEN IJDEAA. bk rev. adv acc. Circ 500. Subjects include: dermatology, venereology, and leprology.

INDIAN JOURNAL OF DERMATOLOGY, VENEREOLOGY, AND LEPROLOGY. (INDIAN JOURNAL OF DERMATOLOGY, VENEREOLOGY AND LEPROLOGY). V. 42- Jan./Feb. 1976-. 0378-6323. Periodical. II. English. bm. $20.00. Indian Association of Dermatology Venereology and Leprology, c/o Dr Mathai CMC Hospital, Vellore 632004 India. Ind/Abst Life Sci. Collect., Excerpta Med. NLM W1 IN208F. *Indian Journal of Dermatology and Venereology, 0019-5162.*

INTERNATIONAL JOURNAL OF DERMATOLOGY. V. 9- Jan./Mar. 1970-. 0011-9059. Periodical. US. English (French, and Spanish, with summaries in the three languages). ir. $66.00. J B Lippincott Company, East Washington Square, Philadelphia PA 19105. Tel (215)238-4273. Ed Lawrence Charles. Ind/Abst Life Sci. Collect., Excerpta Med., Chem. Abstr., Biol. Abstr., Index Med., Energy Res. Abstr., Sci. Cit. Index, Abr. Ed., Hospit. Lit. Index. LC RL1. DD 616.5005. NLM W1 IN766G. CODEN IJDEBB. bk rev. adv acc. Circ 9,214. Includes new important relevant information written with clinical concerns and continuing education needs in mind offers a worldwide view of skin disorders and current treatment. *Dermatologia Internationalis, 0096-1108.*

INTERNATIONAL PSORIASIS BULLETIN. V. 1-. 0190-5074. Periodical. US. English. qt. Psoriasis Research Institute, PO Box V/Editorial Office, Stanford CA 94305. Ed Lexie Nay. NLM W1 IN827T. Circ 9,000. (ctrl). Recent advances in research efforts directed toward identifying the cause and subsequent cure of psoriasis.

ITALIAN GENERAL REVIEW OF DERMATOLOGY. VFOAT Revue Generale Italienne de Dermatologie. 0021-292X. Periodical. IT. Multilingual (English and French). bm. Clinica Dermatologica University, Via Degi Alfani 31, Firenze Italy. Ind/Abst Index Med.

JOURNAL OF CUTANEOUS PATHOLOGY. VFOAT Cutaneous Pathology. V. 1- 1974-. 0303-6987. Periodical. DK. English. bm. Munksgaard Ltd, 35 Norre Sogade, DK-1370 Copenhagen K Denmark. Tel 1.12.70.30. Ed Evan R Farmer. Ind/Abst Life Sci. Collect., Excerpta Med., Index Med., Biol. Abstr., Chem. Abstr., Energy Res. Abstr., Hospit. Lit. Index, Sci. Cit. Index, Abr. Ed. NLM W1 JO612P. CODEN JCUPBN. adv acc. Circ 1,600. Diseases of the epidermis, dermis and cutaneous appendages, light and electron microscopy, histochemistry, microbiology, biochemistry, immunology, pharmacology, tissue culture, embryology and genetics.

JOURNAL OF DERMATOLOGY. (THE JOURNAL OF DERMATOLOGY). V. 1- March 1974-. 0385-2407. Periodical. JA. English. qt. Japan Publishers Trading Company Ltd, PO Box 5030, Tokyo International, Tokyo 100-31 Japan. Ind/Abst Excerpta Med., Index Med., Chem. Abstr., Biol. Abstr. NLM W1 JO619R. CODEN JDMYAG. *Japanese Journal of Dermatology. Ser. B.*

JOURNAL OF INVESTIGATIVE DERMATOLOGY. (JOURNAL OF INVESTIGATIVE DERMATOLOGY). V. 1 Feb. 1938-. 0022-202X. Periodical. US. English. mo. $95.00. Williams & Wilkins Company, PO Box 64025, Baltimore MD 21264. Tel (301)528-4000. Ind/Abst Chem. Abstr., Index Med., Sci. Cit. Index, Abr. Ed., Life Sci. Collect., Excerpta Med., Pestdoc, Vetdoc, Ringdoc, CIS Abstr., Biol. Abstr., Chem. Abstr., Nuci. Sci. Abstr., Index Med., Bibliogr. Agric., Energy Res. Abstr. LC RL1. DD 616.505. NLM W1 JO73. CODEN JIDEAE. Available on microfilm. *Advances in Biology of Skin, 0065-2253.*

JOURNAL OF THE AMERICAN ACADEMY OF DERMATOLOGY. Vol. 1, No. 1 (July 1979)-. 0190-9622. Periodical. US. English. mo. $93.00. C V Mosby Company, R W Kinnes, 11830 Westline Industrial Drive, St Louis MO 63146. Tel (314)872-8370. Ed J Graham Smith. Ind/Abst Life Sci. Collect., Excerpta Med., Index Med., Biol. Abstr. LC RL1. DD 616.5005. NLM W1 JO907WL. CODEN JAADDB. bk rev. adv acc. Circ 11,485. Provides for the continuing education needs of dermatologists and those family practitioners, internists, and pediatricians concerned with clinical manifestations of skin diseases. *Bulletin of the American Academy of Dermatology.*

KOSMETIK INTERNATIONAL. See Beauty & Cosmetics.

LUPUS NEWS. (LUPUS NEWS : LN). VFOAT LN. 0732-0280. Periodical. US. English. qt. Free. The Lupus Foundation of America Inc, 11673 Holly Springs Drive, St Louis MO 63141.

MAJOR PROBLEMS IN DERMATOLOGY. V. 1- 1974-. 0301-7842. Periodical. UK. English. ir. Lloyd Luke Medical Books Ltd, 49 Newman Street, London W1P 4BX England. NLM W1 MA492S.

MASSON MONOGRAPHS IN DERMATOPATHOLOGY. 1-. 0733-9178. Monographic Series. US. English. ir. Masson Distribution Inc, Box C-762, Brooklyn NY 11205. Tel (800)221-4530. Ed A Bernard Ackerman. LC UNC. DD 616.507. NLM W1 MA9209RF.

MEDICINA CUTANEA IBERO-LATINO-AMERICANA. V. 1- 1973-. 0377-1245. Periodical. PO. articles in Portuguese or Spanish with summaries in English, French and German. bm. $50.00. Colegio Ibero-Latino-Americano de Dermatologica, Lisboa Portugal. Ind/Abst Excerpta Med., Index Med. NLM W1 ME575CI. *Dermatologia Ibero Latino-Americana, 0011-9040; Medicina Cutanea, 0025-7788.*

MEDIGUIDE TO SKIN CONDITIONS. Vol. 1, Issue 1-. 0737-6081. Periodical. US. English. bm. Dellacorte Publications, 767 Lexington Avenue, New York NY NY 10021. NLM W1 ME787GHD.

MINERVA DERMATOLOGICA. Periodical. IT. Italian. mo. $60.00. Edizioni Minerva Medica, Corso Bramante 83-85, 10126 Torino Italy.

MONOGRAFIA DEL COLEGIO IBERO-LATINO-AMERICANO DE DERMATOLOGIA. 3-. 1977-. 0210-5268. Monographic Series. Spanish. ir. NLM W1 MO5415T. *Monografia de Dermatologia Ibero Latino-Americana.*

PEDIATRIC DERMATOLOGY. Vol. 1, No. 1 (July 1983)-. 0736-8046. Periodical. US. English. qt. $105.00. Blackwell Scientific Publishing Co, 52 Beacon Street, Boston MA 02108. Tel (617)720-0761. Ed Nancy Esterley and Lawrence Solomon. NLM W1. adv acc. Circ 1,000. Official publication of Society for Pediatric Dermatology. Original articles on research and clinical findings pertaining to genetics, infectious diseases; dysmorphic disorders and diseases of unknown enology.

PHOTO-DERMATOLOGY. VFOAT Photodermatology. Vol. 1, No. 1 (Feb. 1984)-. 0108-9684. Periodical. English. bm. $65.00. Munksgaard International Publishers Limited, 35 Norre Sogade, DK-1370 Copenhagen K Denmark. Tel 45 12 70 30. NLM W1.

PIBU SONGBYONG : TAEHAN PIBUKWA HAKHOE PO. VFOAT Bulletin of Dermatology & Venereology. Periodical. KO. Korean. bm. NLM W1 PI748.

PRZEGLAD DERMATOLOGICZNY. V. 46- 1959-. 0033-2526. Periodical. PL. Polish. bm. ARS Polona, Krakowskie Przedmiescie 7, 00-068 Warsaw Poland. Ind/Abst Excerpta Med., Index Med., Chem. Abstr. NLM W1 PR925. CODEN PRDEA7. *Przeglad Dermatologii I Wenerologii.*

RECENT ADVANCES IN DERMATOLOGY. 0309-2747. Periodical. UK. English. ir. Churchill Livingstone Inc, 1560 Broadway, New York NY 10036. Tel (212)819-5400. Ed A J Rook. NLM W1 RE105UJ.

THE SCHOCH LETTER. 0487-6520. Periodical. US. English. mo. Free to Members, $20.00 Non-Members. American Academy of Dermatology, 820 Davis Street, Evanston IL 60201. NLM W1 SC225. *Current News in Dermatology, 0191-796X.*

SCHRIFTTUM UND PRAXIS. Began in 1969. 0586-7703. Periodical. German. qt. NLM ZWR 100.

SEMINARS IN DERMATOLOGY. Vol. 1, No. 1 (Mar. 1982)-. 0278-145X. Periodical. US. English. qt. $52.00. Thieme-Stratton Inc, 381 Park Avenue South/Suite 1501, New York NY 10016. Tel (212)683-5088. Ed Rook and Maibach. Ind/Abst Excerpta Med. NLM W1. Circ 1,124. A clinical journal devoted to assessment and treatment of disorders in dermatology.

SKIN & ALLERGY NEWS. VAT Skin and Allergy News. V. 1- May 1970-. 0037-6337. Periodical. US. English. mo. $45.00. International Medical News Service, 12230 Wilkins Avenue, Rockville MD 20852. Tel (212)421-0707. Ed William Rubin. NLM W1 SK59. bk rev. adv acc. Circ 35,772. (ctrl). Information of specific or general interest to the dermatologist, allergist, and pediatric allergist, and those GP's and FP's prescribing in these specialties.

VESTNIK DERMATOLOGII I VENEROLOGII. V. 31- 1957-. 0042-4609. Periodical. UR. Russian (some articles have summaries in English). mo. $33.50. Victor Kamkin Inc (70118), 12224 Parklawn Drive, Rockville MD 20852. Tel (301)881-5973. Ind/Abst Life Sci. Collect., Excerpta Med., Index Med., Biol. Abstr., Chem. Abstr., Sci. Cit. Index, Abr. Ed. NLM W1 VE821. CODEN VDVEAV.

THE YEAR BOOK OF DERMATOLOGY AND SYPHILOLOGY. See Yearbooks, Almanacs, Directories.

YEARBOOK OF DERMATOLOGY. See Yearbooks, Almanacs, Directories.

ENDOCRINOLOGY

ACTA ENDOCRINOLOGICA. V. 1- 1948-. 0001-5598. Periodical. DK. English (vol. for 1948- contains articles in English, French, or German with

Medicine—Endocrinology

summaries in English). mo. $154.42. Periodica, 12 Skolegade, DK-2500 Valby Copenhagen Denmark. **Tel** 01-305300. **Ed** Jorgen Starup. **Ind/Abst** Life Sci. Collect., Pestdoc, Ringdoc, Vetdoc, Excerpta Med., CIS Abstr., Biol. Abstr., Chem. Abstr., Nuci. Sci. Abstr., Index Med., Bibliogr. Agric., Energy Res. Abstr., Chem. Abstr., Sci. Cit. Index, Abr. Ed. **NLM** W1 AC798. **CODEN** ACENA7. **Circ** 2,300.

ADVANCES IN PROSTAGLANDIN AND THROMBOXANE RESEARCH CEASED. V. 1-8. 0361-5952. Monographic Series. US. English. 1140 Avenue of the Americas, New York NY 10036. **Ed** B Samuelsson and R Paoletti, with P Ramwell. **Ind/Abst** Chem. Abstr. **LC** QP801.P68. **DD** 599.01. **NLM** W1 AD787. **CODEN** APTRDI.

ADVANCES IN PROSTAGLANDIN, THROMBOXANE, AND LEUKOTRIENE RESEARCH. Vol. 9-. 0732-8141. Periodical. US. English. ir. Raven Press, 1140 Avenue of the Americas, New York NY 10036. **Ind/Abst** Index Med., Biol. Abstr., Chem. Abstr. **LC** QP801.P68. **DD** 612.015. **NLM** W1 AD788. **CODEN** ATLRD6. *Advances in Prostaglandin and Thromboxane Research, 0361-5952.*

ADVANCES IN SEX HORMONE RESEARCH CEASED. Began with V. 1. Ceased with V. 4, 1980. 0098-0137. Monographic Series. US. English. Urban & Schwarzenberg, 7 East Redwood Street, Baltimore MD 21202. **LC** QP572.S4. **DD** 599.016. **NLM** W1 AD845H.

AKTUELLE ENDOKRINOLOGIE UND STOFFWECHSEL. V. 1- Jan. 1980-. 0172-4606. German. qt. $68.00. Thieme-Stratton Inc, 381 Park Avenue, New York NY 10016. **Tel** (212)683-5088. **Ind/Abst** Excerpta Med., Chem. Abstr. **NLM** W1 AK992AE. **CODEN** AENSDG.

AMERICAN JOURNAL OF PHYSIOLOGY : ENDOCRINOLOGY AND METABOLISM. See Biology - Physiology.

ANNALES D'ENDOCRINOLOGIE. V. 1- March 1939-. 0003-4266. Periodical. French (English). bm. $140.00. Masson Publishing USA Inc, 211 East 43rd Street Room 1306, New York NY 10017. **Tel** (212)370-1937. **Ind/Abst** Life Sci. Collect., Excerpta Med., Index Med., Biol. Abstr., Chem. Abstr., Energy Res. Abstr. **NLM** W1 AN396H. **CODEN** ANENAG.

ANNEE ENDOCRINOLOGIQUE. (L'ANNEE ENDOCRINOLOGIQUE). Vol. 1 25th Year. 0365-1940. Periodical. French. ir. Masson Publishing USA Inc, 211 East 43rd Street/Room 1306, New York NY 10017. **Tel** (212)370-1937. **Ind/Abst** Index Med. **LC** RC648.A1. **NLM** W1 AN649. (cum index).

ANNUAL REPORT TO THE DIRECTOR, NATIONAL INSTITUTES OF HEALTH. Began with 1st, 1973/74. 0363-4914. US. English. an. US Department of Health, Washington DC 20202. **LC** RC660.A1. **DD** 362.19646200973. **NLM** W2 A N167D.

ARQUIVOS BRASILEIROS DE ENDOCRINOLOGIA E METABOLOGIA. V. 5- 1955-. 0004-2730. Periodical. BL. Portuguese. ir. Inst de Endocrinologia, rua Santa Luzia 206ZC-39, Rio de Janeiro GB Brazil. **Ind/Abst** Excerpta Med., Chem. Abstr. **NLM** W1 AR869. **CODEN** ABENAY. *Arquivos Brasileiros de Endocrinologia, 0301-5343.*

BASIC AND CLINICAL ENDOCRINOLOGY. 1-. 0277-7886. Monographic Series. US. English. ir. Marcel Dekker Inc, 270 Madison Avenue, New York NY 10016. **Tel** (212)696-9000. **Ed** London, Sonsken, Lasen, and Reed. **Ind/Abst** Chem. Abstr. **LC** UNC. **DD** 616.4005. **NLM** W1 BA813T. **CODEN** BCLEDT. This is an ongoing series. Each title has a different subject.

BETA RELEASE. (BETA RELEASE : BRINGING EDUCATION TO ALL). 0710-0248. Periodical. CN. English. qt. $15.48. Canadian Diabetes Association, 78 Bond Street, Toronto Ontario M5G 2J8 Canada. **Tel** (416)362-4440. **DD** 616.462005.

BIBLIOGRAPHIA NEUROENDOCRINOLOGICA. See Bibliographies.

BIOSIS/CAS SELECTS. HORMONES & HORMONE RECEPTOR INTERACTIONS. See Indexes/Abstracts.

CLINICAL ENDOCRINOLOGY. V. 1- Jan. 1972-. 0300-0664. Periodical. UK. English. mo. 114 Domestic, 255 Foreign. Blackwell Scientific Publishing Ltd, PO Box 88, Oxford OX2 0EL England. **Tel** 0865-240201. **Ed** D C Anderson and J S Jenkins. **Ind/Abst** Life Sci. Collect., Excerpta Med., Index Med., Biol. Abstr., Chem. Abstr., Pestdoc, Ringdoc, Vetdoc. **NLM** W1 CL696. **CODEN** CLECAP. bk rev. adv acc. **Circ** 1,360. Publishes material which contributes directly to understanding of the human endocrine disorder, its pathogenesis, diagnosis and treatment.

CLINICS IN ENDOCRINOLOGY AND METABOLISM. V. 1- 1972-. 0300-595X. Periodical. UK. English. ty. $60.00. W B Saunders Co, West Washington Square, Philadelphia PA 19105. **Tel** (215)574-3395. **Ed** Nicholas Dunton. **Ind/Abst** Life Sci. Collect., Excerpta Med., Index Med., Biol. Abstr., Chem. Abstr., Sci. Cit. Index, Abr. Ed. **LC** RC648.A1. **DD** 616.4005. **NLM** W1 CL831BD. **CODEN** CEDMB2. **Circ** 2,500. Practical updates for the clinician on the latest advances plus topics of current interest.

COMPREHENSIVE ENDOCRINOLOGY. 0160-242X. US. English. ir. Raven Press, 1140 Avenue of the Americas, New York NY 10036. *Comprehensive Endocrinology Series, 0271-1850.*

CONTEMPORARY ENDOCRINOLOGY. V. 1- 1979-. 0196-8653. Periodical. US. English. an. Plenum Publishing Corp, 227 West 17th Street, New York NY 10011. **Ed** S H Ingbar. **Ind/Abst** Chem. Abstr. **LC** QP187.A1. **DD** 612.4005. **NLM** W1 CO769MPE. **CODEN** CNEND7. *Year in Endocrinology, 0146-4078.*

CURRENT ADVANCES IN ENDOCRINOLOGY. Vol. 1, No. 1 (Jan. 1984)-. 0741-1634. UK. English. mo. $215.00. Pergamon Press Inc, Maxwell House, Fairview Park, Elmsford NY 10523. **Tel** (914)592-7700. **Ed** H Smith. **LC** QP187.A1. **DD** 599.01405. **Circ** 1,200. Gives listings of titles of endocrinological papers published throughout the world classified into 73 major areas. Full bibliographical citations and reprint addresses are included.

CURRENT TOPICS IN EXPERIMENTAL ENDOCRINOLOGY. V. 1- 0091-7397. US. English. ir. Academic Press, 4805 Sand Lake Road, Orlando FL 32887. **Tel** (305)345-4100. **Ed** L Martini and V H T James. **Ind/Abst** Biol. Abstr., Chem. Abstr., Nuci. Sci. Abstr., Energy Res. Abstr., Index Med. **LC** RC648.A1. **DD** 616.4027. **NLM** W1 CU82H. **CODEN** CTEEAJ.

CURRENT TOPICS IN MOLECULAR ENDOCRINOLOGY. V. 1- 1974-. 0094-6761. Periodical. US. English. ir. Plenum Press Inc, 233 Spring Street, New York NY 10013. **Tel** (212)620-8000. **Ind/Abst** Index Med., Energy Res. Abstr. **NLM** W1 CU82M.

CURRENT TOPICS IN NEUROENDOCRINOLOGY. Vol. 1-. 0723-1229. Monographic Series. English. ir. **Ind/Abst** Chem. Abstr. **LC** UNC. **NLM** W1 CU82Q. **CODEN** CTNEEY.

CURRENT TOPICS IN REPRODUCTIVE ENDOCRINOLOGY. VFOAT Wiley Series on Current Topics in Reproductive Endocrinology. Vol. 1-. 0742-3616. Monographic Series. UK. English. **Ed** S L Jeffcoate. **LC** UNC. **NLM** W3 CU614.

DEVELOPMENTS IN ENDOCRINOLOGY. V. 1-. 0165-1900. Monographic Series. English. an. Elsevier Science Publ Co Inc, PO Box 1663 Grand Central Station, New York NY 10163. **Tel** (212)370-5520. **Ind/Abst** Chem. Abstr. **NLM** W1 DE997VW. **CODEN** DENDD4.

DEVELOPMENTS IN ENDOCRINOLOGY (HAGUE, NETHERLANDS) (MARTINUS NIJHOFF PUBLISHERS). (DEVELOPMENTS IN ENDOCRINOLOGY). Vol. 1-. 0167-6334. Monographic Series. US. English. ir. Kluwer Boston Inc, 190 Old Derby Street, Hingham MA 02043. **Ind/Abst** Chem. Abstr. **LC** UNC. **NLM** W1 DE997VWB. **CODEN** DVEND6.

DIABETES. V. 1- Jan./Feb. 1952-. 0012-1797. Periodical. US. English. mo. $60.00. American Diabetes Association, Two Park Avenue, New York NY 10016. **Tel** (212)683-7444. **Ind/Abst** Life Sci. Collect., Excerpta Med., Index Med., Chem. Abstr., Bibliogr. Agric., Pestdoc, Ringdoc, Vetdoc, Sci. Cit. Index, Abr. Ed. **LC** RC660.A1. **DD** 616. **NLM** W1 DI151. **CODEN** DIAEAZ. *Proceedings of the American Diabetes Association, 0097-1472; Diabetes Abstracts.*

DIABETES CARE. V. 1- Jan./Feb. 1978-. 0149-5992. Periodical. US. English. bm. American Diabetes Association, Two Park Avenue, New York NY 10016. **Tel** (212)683-7444. **Ed** F John Service. **Ind/Abst** Excerpta Med., Cumul. Index Nurs. Allied Health Lit., Index Med., Chem. Abstr., Bibliogr. Agric. **LC** RC660.A1. **DD** 616.462005. **NLM** W1 DI161Q. **CODEN** DICAD2. bk rev. adv acc. **Circ** 10,300. Primary research journal with focus on clinical and applied research in diabetes and related disorders.

DIABETES DATELINE : THE NDIC BULLETIN. Vol. 1, No. 1 (Sept. 1979)-. Periodical. US. English. bm. National Diabetes Information Clearinghouse, Box NDIC, Bethesda MD 20205. **Tel** (301)496-7433. **Ed** Beatrice Jakubowski. bk rev. **Circ** 3,000. Announcements of meetings, new materials, research studies, and other topics relevant to diabetes care.

DIABETES DIALOGUE. V. 24- 1st Quarter 1977-. 0703-5764. Periodical. CN. English. qt. Canadian Diabetic Association, 1491 Yonge Street, Toronto Ontario M4T 1Z5 Canada. **DD** 616.462005. Newsletter, 0007-8018.

THE DIABETES EDUCATOR. 0145-7217. Periodical. US. English. qt. A J Jannetti Inc, c/o L Thompson, Box 56 North Woodbury Road, Pitman NJ 08071. **Tel** (609)589-4831. **Ind/Abst** Cumul. Index Nurs. Allied Health Lit., Int. Nurs. Index. **LC** RC660.A1. **DD** 616.462005. **NLM** W1 DI161R.

DIABETES FORECAST. V. 27, No. 6- Nov./Dec. 1974-. 0095-8301. Periodical. US. English. bm. $15.00. American Diabetes Association, Two Park Avenue, New York NY 10016. **Tel** (212)683-7444. **Ed** Ralph Boneheim. **LC** RC660.A1. **DD** 616.462005. **NLM** W1 DI161T. adv acc. **Circ** 215,455. (ctrl). Geared towards diabetics and their families. Offers articles with all problems of diabetes. *ADA Forecast, 0001-0847.*

DIABETES IN THE NEWS. VFOAT DITN. V. 1- 1962-. 0012-1800. Periodical. US. English. bm. $16.00. Diabetes in the News, 1165 North Clark Street/Suite 311, Chicago IL 60616. **Tel** (312)664-9782. **Ed** Morton B Stone. **NLM** W1 DI162. bk rev. adv acc. **Circ** 105,000. Provides diabetics and health professionals with interesting stories and features which deal with all aspects of modern diabetes management, in clear, easy-to-understand language.

DIABETIC NEPHROPATHY. (DIABETIC NEPHROPATHY : DN). VFOAT DN. Vol. 1, No. 1 (Nov. 1982)-. 0739-7380. Periodical. US. English. qt. Travenol Laboratories, 1 Baxter Parkway, Deerfield IL 60045. **DD** 616. **NLM** W1 DI165.

DIABETOLOGIE-INFORMATIONEN. V. 1-. 0171-8045. Periodical. German. ir. Martinus Nijhoff, PO Box 269, 2501 AX, The Hague The Netherlands. **NLM** W1 DI219.

DITN. VFOAT D.I.T.N. VAT Diabetes in the News. Began in 1984. 8750-1244. Periodical. US. English. bm. $4.98. DITN, PO Box 3105, Elkhart IN 46515. **Tel** (312)664-9782. **Ed** Morton B Stone. **DD** 616. bk rev. adv acc. **Circ** 100,000. Helps diabetics learn to live with their disease. Written for the diabetic in simple, easy-to-understand language. *Diabetes in the News, 0012-1800.*

DOMESTIC ANIMAL ENDOCRINOLOGY. Vol. 1, No. 1 (Jan. 1984)-. 0739-7240. Periodical. US. English. qt $40.00 Domestic, $55.00 Foreign. Department of Physiology and Pharmacology, School of Veterinary Medicine Auburn University, Auburn AL 36849. **Tel** (205)826-4425. **Ed** James L Sartin. adv acc. **Circ** 200. A journal to promote basic and clinical endocrine research in domestic animal species.

ENDOCRINE PHYSIOLOGY. Began with Vol. issued in 1974. 0732-6262. US. English. Universtiy Park Press International Publishers in Science Medicine and Education, 300 North Carles Street, Baltimore MD 21201. **Ed** S M McCann. **LC** QP1. **DD** 612.4005.

ENDOCRINE RESEARCH. Vol. 10, No. 1-. 0743-5800. Periodical. US. English. qt. $125.00. Marcel Dekker Journals, PO Box 11305 Church Street Station, New York NY 10249. **Ed** Paul J Davis. **Ind/Abst** Bull. Signal., Chem. Abstr., Index Med., Excerpta Med., Sci. Cit. Index, Abr. Ed., Curr. Contents. **DD** 616. **NLM** W1. **CODEN** ENRSE8. bk rev. adv acc. *Endocrine Research Communications, 0093-6391.*

ENDOCRINE RESEARCH COMMUNICATIONS CEASED. V. 1-9. 0093-6391. Periodical. US. English. qt. $125.00. Marcel Dekker Inc, PO Box 11305/Church Street Station, New York NY 10249. **Tel** (212)696-9000. **Ed**

Paul J Davis. **Ind/Abst** Life Sci. Collect., Excerpta Med., Biol. Abstr., Chem. Abstr., Bibliogr. Agric., Energy Res. Abstr., Index Med., Sci. Cit. Index, Abr. Ed. **LC** RC648.A1. **DD** 616.4005. **NLM** W1. **CODEN** EDRCAM. bk rev. adv acc. (ctrl). Detailed research evaluated in terms of experimental design, originality, and significance, plus a new section, techniques, reporting on methodological developments in hormone quantitation.

ENDOCRINE REVIEWS. V. 1- Winter 1980-. 0163-769X. Periodical. US. English. qt. $50.00. Williams & Wilkins Company, 428 East Preston Street, Baltimore MD 21202. **Tel** (301)528-4000. **Ed** Pentti Siiteri. **Ind/Abst** Energy Inf. Abstr., Environ. Abstr., Index Med., Chem. Abstr. **LC** QP187.A1. **DD** 612.4. **NLM** W1 EN367R. **CODEN** ERVIDP. adv acc. **Circ** 3,970. Clinical and experimental endocrinology covered through in-depth review articles focusing on current topics of high interest.

THE ENDOCRINE SOCIETY - ANNUAL MEETING, PROGRAM AND ABSTRACTS. *See* Indexes/Abstracts.

ENDOCRINOLOGIA (BARCELONA, SPAIN). (ENDOCRINOLOGIA : ORGANO DE LA SOCIEDAD ESPANOLA DE ENDOCRINOLOGIA). Began in 1953. Periodical. English (articles in Spanish). bm. $20.00. Ediciones Doyma S A, Travesera de Gracia 17-21, 08021 Barcelona Spain. **Tel** 200 07 11. **NLM** W1 EN385T.

ENDOCRINOLOGIA EXPERIMENTALIS. V. 1- 1967-. 0013-7200. Periodical. English. ir. **Ind/Abst** Life Sci. Collect., Excerpta Med., Index Med., Biol. Abstr., Chem. Abstr. **NLM** W1 EN392. **CODEN** ENEXAM. Index in last issue of volume - attached. *Endocrinologia Experimentalis, 0013-7200.*

ENDOCRINOLOGY ABSTRACTS. *See* Indexes/Abstracts.

ENDOCRINOLOGY AND METABOLISM SERIES. Vol. 1-. 0264-0767. Monographic Series. UK. English. **LC** UNC. **NLM** W1 EN396U.

ENDOCRINOLOGY (PHILADELPHIA, PA.). (ENDOCRINOLOGY). Began with: Vol. 1, in 1917. 0013-7227. Periodical. US. English. mo. $100.00. Williams & Wilkins, 428 East Preston Street, Baltimore MD 21202. **Tel** (301)528-4000. **Ed** Nicholas S Halmi. **Ind/Abst** Life Sci. Collect., Excerpta Med., Chem. Abstr., Biol. Abstr., Nuci. Sci. Abstr., Int. Aerosp. Abstr., Index Med., Bibliogr. Agric., Energy Res. Abstr., Energy Inf. Abstr., Environ. Abstr., Pestdoc, Ringdoc, Vetdoc, Sci. Cit. Index, Abr. Ed. **LC** QP187. **DD** 612.4005. **NLM** W1 EN396S. **CODEN** ENDOAO. (cum index). adv acc. **Circ** 6,150. Broad-focus journal covering all aspects of research on endocrine glands and their hormones for the endocrinologist and internist. *Transactions of the American Goiter Association, 0096-7173.*

ENDOKRINOLOGIE *CEASED.* Vol. 1-80. 0013-7251. Periodical. GE. articles in English and German. bm. **Ind/Abst** Life Sci. Collect., Excerpta Med., Biol. Abstr., Chem. Abstr., Bibliogr. Agric. **LC** QP187.A1. **NLM** W1 EN396V. **CODEN** ENDKAC. Index in first issue of next volume - loose - separately paged.

ENDOKRYNOLOGIA POLSKA. Began with: V. 1, in 1950. 0423-104X. Periodical. Polish (summaries in English, French, and Russian and Russian). bm. ARS Polona, Krakowskie Przedmiescie 7, 00-068 Warsaw Poland. **Ind/Abst** Excerpta Med., Index Med., Chem. Abstr. **NLM** W1 EN397. **CODEN** EDPKA2.

EUROPEAN JOURNAL OF CLINICAL INVESTIGATION. V. 1- Mar. 1970-. 0014-2972. Periodical. UK. English. bm. $150.00. Blackwell Scientific Publishing Ltd, PO Box 88, Oxford OX2 0EL England. **Tel** 0685 240201. **Ed** R Arnold. **Ind/Abst** Life Sci. Collect., Pestdoc, Ringdoc, Vetdoc, Excerpta Med., Nuci. Sci. Abstr., Biol. Abstr., Chem. Abstr., Index Med., Energy Res. Abstr., Sci. Cit. Index, Abr. Ed. **LC** R850.A1. **DD** 616.005. **NLM** W1 EU72C. **CODEN** EJCIB8. adv acc. **Circ** 1,473. Cultivation of clinical research by methods of natural science. *Archiv fur Klinische Medizin, 0365-3773.*

EXCERPTA MEDICA. SECTION 3, ENDOCRINOLOGY. **VFOAT** Endocrinology. 0014-407X. Periodical. English. ir. Elsevier Science Publishers Biomedical Division, PO Box 1527, 1000 BM Amsterdam Netherlands. Index published separately - free - automatically sent. *Excerpta Medica. Section 3. Endocrinology, Experimental and Clinical.*

EXCERPTA MEDICA. SECTION 64. DIABETES MELLITUS. LITERATURE INDEX. *See* Indexes/Abstracts.

EXPERIMENTAL AND CLINICAL ENDOCRINOLOGY. Vol. 81, No. 1 (Jan. 1983)-. 0232-7384. Periodical. English (German). ir. $59.18. Kunst & Wissen Erich Bieber, Dufourstrasse 51, CH-8008 Zuerich Switzerland. **Tel** 011-41-1-69 44 20. **Ind/Abst** Life Sci. Collect., Pestdoc, Ringdoc, Vetdoc, Excerpta Med., Index Med., Chem. Abstr. **LC** QP187.A1. **DD** 599.0142. **NLM** W1 EX464. **CODEN** EXCEDS. *Endokrinologie.*

FOLIA ENDOCRINOLOGICA JAPONICA. Periodical. JA. Multilingual (Japanese and English). mo. Japan Publications Trading Company, PO Box 5030, Tokyo 100-31 Japan. *Collected Papers of Thyroid Gland.*

FRONTIERS IN DIABETES. Vol. 1-. 0251-5342. Monographic Series. English. ir. S Karger AG, PO Box 352, White Plains NY 10602. **Tel** 061-39 08 80. **Ed** F Belfiore. **Ind/Abst** Biol. Abstr. **NLM** W1 FR945X. **CODEN** FDIADJ. Volumes in this series provide a unique reference tool for workers who need convenient, well-ordered access to the newest information.

FRONTIERS IN NEUROENDOCRINOLOGY. V. 1- 1969-. 0091-3022. US. English. ir. Raven Press, 1140 Avenue of the Americas, New York NY 10036. **Ed** W F Ganong and L Martin. **Ind/Abst** Biol. Abstr., Chem. Abstr. **LC** QP187.A1. **DD** 599.044. **NLM** W1 FR946B. **CODEN** FNEDA7.

FRONTIERS OF HORMONE RESEARCH. 0301-3073. Periodical. English. ir. S Karger AG, PO Box 352, White Plains NY 10602. **Tel** 061-39 08 80. **Ed** Tj B van Wimersma Greidanus. **Ind/Abst** Index Med., Sci. Cit. Index, Abr. Ed., Chem. Abstr. Information on how findings from hormone research can be used in clinical medicine.

HORMONE RESEARCH. V. 4- 1973-. 0301-0163. Periodical. SZ. English. bm. $194.00. S Karger AG, PO Box, CH-4009 Basel Switzerland. **Tel** (061)39 08 80. **Ed** J Girard. **Ind/Abst** Life Sci. Collect., Pestdoc, Ringdoc, Vetdoc, Excerpta Med., Index Med., Chem. Abstr., Biol. Abstr., Sci. Cit. Index, Abr. Ed., Hospit. Lit. Index. **LC** QP187.A1. **DD** 574.192705. **NLM** W1 HO63T. **CODEN** HRMRA3. adv acc. Papers provide a background of experimental data on the pathology, cytology, histology, biochemistry, pharmacology and regulation of hormones. Topical problems such as growth, diabetes, sexual development and hormone-dependent cancers are covered. *Hormones, 0018-5051.*

HORMONES AND BEHAVIOR. V. 1- Apr. 1969-. 0018-506X. Periodical. US. English. qt. Academic Press, 4805 Sand Lake Road, Orlando FL 32819. **Tel** (305)345-4100. **Ind/Abst** Life Sci. Collect., Excerpta Med., Index Med., Biol. Abstr., Chem. Abstr., Psychol. Abstr., Bibliogr. Agric., Energy Res. Abstr., Sci. Cit. Index, Abr. Ed. **LC** QP187.A1. **DD** 591.192705. **NLM** W1 HO656F. **CODEN** HOBEAO.

HORUMON TO RINSHO. **VFOAT** Clinical Endocrinology. Vol. 1- Apr. 1953-. 0045-7167. Periodical. JA. Japanese (table of contents in English). mo. Japan Publishers Trading Company Limited, PO Box 5030, Tokyo International, Tokyo 100-31 Japan. **Ind/Abst** Chem. Abstr., Index Med. **NLM** W1 HO688. **CODEN** HORIAE.

INTERNATIONAL WORKSHOP ON DIABETES AND CAMPING. 3rd 1976-. 0161-7524. Periodical. US. English. an. **NLM** W3 IN9324Q.

IRCS MEDICAL SCIENCE. ENDOCRINE SYSTEM. (IRCS MEDICAL SCIENCE : ENDOCRINE SYSTEM). **VFOAT** Endocrine System. V. 3- Jan. 1975-. 0305-6783. Periodical. UK. English. mo. $145.00. IRCS Medical Science, PO Box 500/St Leonards House, Lancaster LA1 1PF England. **Tel** (0524) 68116. **Ed** S Johnson. bk rev. Publishes results of original research into all aspects of endocrinology, both clinical and experimental, within weeks of completion. Papers fully refereed. *Research on the Endocrine System.*

THE JOURNAL OF CLINICAL ENDOCRINOLOGY AND METABOLISM. V. 1- Jan. 1941-. Periodical. US. English. mo. C C Thomas, 301-327 East Lawrence Avenue, Springfield IL 62717. **LC** RC648. **DD** 615.3605.

THE JOURNAL OF CLINICAL ENDOCRINOLOGY AND METABOLISM. (THE JOURNAL OF CLINICAL ENDOCRINOLOGY & METABOLISM). Vol. 46, No. 1 (Jan. 1978)-. 0021-972X. Periodical. US. English. mo. $100.00. Williams & Wilkins Company, 428 East Preston Street, Baltimore MD 21202. **Tel** (301)528-4000. **Ed** Robert D Utiger. **Ind/Abst** Biol. Abstr., Excerpta Med., Life Sci. Collect., Energy Inf. Abstr., Environ. Abstr., Index Med., Nuci. Sci. Abstr., Energy Res. Abstr., Pestdoc, Ringdoc, Vetdoc. **NLM** W1 JO588. **CODEN** JCEMAZ. adv acc. **Circ** 9,055. The latest information on the clinical applications of endocrine research for internists, endocrinologists, obstetrics/gynecologist's physiologists. *Journal of Clinical Endocrinology and Metabolism, 0021-972X.*

JOURNAL OF CLINICAL IMMUNOASSAY. (JOURNAL OF CLINICAL IMMUNOASSAY : OFFICIAL PUBLICATION OF THE CLINICAL LIGAND ASSAY SOCIETY). Vol. 6, No. 1 (Spring 1983)-. 0736-4393. Periodical. US. English. qt. $42.00 Domestic, $47.00 Foreign. Clinical Ligand Assay Society Inc, PO Box 67, Wayne MI 48184. **Tel** (313)722-6290. **Ed** Carolyn S Feldkamp. **Ind/Abst** Chem. Abstr. **NLM** W1 JO588DC. bk rev. adv acc. **Circ** 1,650. (ctrl). Contains articles related to ligand methodology (advances and reviews) and associated problems such as data reduction, equipment, quality control and related clinical information. *Ligand Quarterly, 0199-4794.*

JOURNAL OF ENDOCRINOLOGICAL INVESTIGATION. Vol. 1- Jan. 1978-. 0391-4097. Periodical. English. bm. $77.00. Editrice Kurtis SRL, Via G Rotondi 2, 20145 Milano Italy. **Tel** (02)4396583. **Ed** Aldo Pinchera. **Ind/Abst** Life Sci. Collect., Excerpta Med., Index Med., Biol. Abstr., Chem. Abstr., Sci. Cit. Index, Abr. Ed. **NLM** W1 JO641. **CODEN** JEIND7. adv acc. **Circ** 4,000. Publication devoted to original studies on clinical and experimental research in endocrinology and related fields.

JOURNAL OF ENDOCRINOLOGY. (THE JOURNAL OF ENDOCRINOLOGY). V. 1- June 1939-. 0022-0795. Periodical. UK. English. mo. $275.00. Stonebridge Distributors, 823-825 Bath Road, Bristol BS4 5NU England. **Tel** (0272)732060. **Ed** G P Vinson. **Ind/Abst** Life Sci. Collect., Pestdoc, Ringdoc, Vetdoc, Excerpta Med., Nuci. Sci. Abstr., Biol. Abstr., Chem. Abstr., Index Med., Bibliogr. Agric., Hospit. Lit. Index, Sci. Cit. Index, Abr. Ed. **LC** QP187.A1. **NLM** W1 JO642. **CODEN** JOENAK. (cum index). adv acc. **Circ** 2,200. All aspects of the nature and functions of the endocrine systems.

JOURNAL OF REPRODUCTIVE ENDOCRINOLOGY. 0731-3039. Periodical. US. English. qt. Mary Ann Liebert Inc, 500 East 85th Street, New York NY 10028.

JOURNEES ANNUELLES DE DIABETOLOGIE DE L'HOTEL-DIEU. **VFOAT** Journees de Diabetologie de l'Hotel-Dieu. 0075-4439. FR. French. ir. Dawson-France SA, BP 40 F-9L, Palaiseau France. **Tel** 009-0122. **Ind/Abst** Chem. Abstr., Biol. Abstr., Index Med., Nuci. Sci. Abstr. **NLM** W1 JO994D. **CODEN** JDBHAC.

MEMOIRS OF THE SOCIETY FOR ENDOCRINOLOGY. **Main/Corp** Society for Endocrinology. No. 1- July 1953-. 0081-136X. Monographic Series. UK. English. ir. Cambridge University Press, 510 North Avenue, New Rochelle NY 10801. **Ind/Abst** Biol. Abstr., Chem. Abstr. **NLM** W1 ME895V. **CODEN** MSENAD.

METHODS IN HORMONE RESEARCH. V. 1- 1962-). 0543-6133. Periodical. US. English. ir. Academic Press, 4805 Sand Lake Road, Orlando FL 32819. **Tel** (305)345-4100.

MOLECULAR AND CELLULAR ENDOCRINOLOGY. V. 1- Mar. 1974-. 0303-7207. Periodical. English. mo. Elsevier Scientific Publishers Ltd, PO Box 85, Limerick Ireland. **Ind/Abst** Excerpta Med., Index Med., Biol. Abstr., Chem. Abstr., Life Sci. Collect., Bibliogr. Agric., Sci. Cit. Index, Abr. Ed. **LC** QP187.A1. **DD** 574.14. **NLM** W1 MO194V. **CODEN** MCEND6.

MONOGRAPHS ON ENDOCRINOLOGY. V. 1-. 0077-1015. Monographic Series. US. English. ir. Springer Verlag New York Inc, 44 Hartz Way, Secaucus NJ 07094. **Tel** (212)460-1500. **Ind/Abst** Index Med., Chem. Abstr., Biol. Abstr. **LC** UNC. **NLM** W1 MO57. **CODEN** MOENBK.

NEURO-ENDOCRINOLOGY LETTERS. (NEURO ENDOCRINOLOGY LETTERS). 0172-780X. Periodical. US. English. bm. $104.00. VCH Publishers

Medicine—Forensic Medicine, Medical Jurisprudence

Inc, 303 NW 12th Avenue, Deerfield Beach FL 33442. **Tel** (305)428-5566. **Ind/Abst** Excerpta Med., Chem. Abstr. **NLM W1** NE328E. **CODEN** NLETDU.

NEUROENDOCRINE PERSPECTIVES. Vol. 1-. US. English. an. Elsevier Science Publishing Co, PO Box 1663 Grand Central Station, New York NY 10163. **Tel** (212)370-5520. Ed Eugenio E Muller and Robert M MacLeod. **LC** QP356.4. **DD** 612.814. **NLM W1** NE328C.

NEUROENDOCRINOLOGY. See Medicine - Neurology.

PEDIATRIC AND ADOLESCENT ENDOCRINOLOGY. V. 1- 1976-. 0304-4254. Monographic Series. English. ir. S Karger Ag, PO Box 352, White Plains NY 10602. **Tel** 061-39 08 80. Ed Z Laron. **Ind/Abst** Biol. Abstr., Chem. Abstr. **NLM W1** PE163H. **CODEN** PAENDP. Collects basic and clinical research designed to improve the understanding and management of pediatric and adolescent diseases and disorders involving the endocrine system.

PERSPECTIVES IN NEUROENDOCRINE RESEARCH. V. 1- 1975-. 0361-0225. Monographic Series. US. English. ir. Plenum Press, Attn H Feldman, 233 Spring Street, New York NY 10013. **Tel** (212)620-8000. **Ind/Abst** Chem. Abstr. **NLM W1** PE871H.

PLEIN SOLEIL. V. 18- Jan./Mar. 1976-. 0384-7810. Periodical. CN. French. qt. 15.00. Association du Diabete du Quebec, 1111 rue St Dominique, Montreal Quebec H2X 3V6 Canada. **Tel** (514)879-1191. **Ind/Abst** Point Repere. **DD** 616.462005. adv acc. **Circ** 15,000. (ctrl) Bulletin of medical information on diabetes in a proper manner for diabetics. Survivre, 0562-7087.

PRACTICAL DIABETOLOGY. Vol. 1, No. 1 (Jan./Feb. 1982)-. 0730-3491. Periodical. US. English. bm. Pharmaceutical Communications, 42-15 Crescent Street, Long Island City NY 11101. **Tel** (212)937-4283. **NLM W1** PR139S.

PROBLEMY ENDOKRINOLOGII. Vol. 13- Jan./Feb. 1967-. 0375-9660. Periodical. UR. Russian. bm. $25.00. Victor Kamkin Inc (70744), 12224 Parklawn Drive, Rockville MD 20852. **Tel** (301)881-5973. **Ind/Abst** Life Sci. Collect., Excerpta Med., Pestdoc, Ringdoc, Vetdoc, Index Med., Int. Aerosp. Abstr., Biol. Abstr., Chem. Abstr. **NLM W1** PR5784. **CODEN** PROEAS. Problemy Endokrinologii I Gormonoterapii.

PROCEEDINGS - ENDOCRINE SOCIETY OF AUSTRALIA. VFOAT Proceedings of the Annual Meeting - Endocrine Society of Australia. 0312-4738. Periodical. AT. English. an. $4.87. Endocrine Society of Royal Adelaide Hospital, Adelaide SA 5000 Australia. **Ind/Abst** Excerpta Med. **NLM W1** PR583W.

PROCEEDINGS OF THE ASIA & OCEANIA CONGRESS OF ENDOCRINOLOGY. Main/Conf Asia & Oceania Congress of Endocrinology. English. ir. Transactions of the Asia and Oceania Regional Congress of Endocrinology.

PSYCHONEUROENDOCRINOLOGY. V. 1- July 1975-. 0306-4530. Periodical. UK. English. qt. $237.50. Pergamon Press, 395 Sawmill River Road, Elmsford NY 10523. **Ind/Abst** Excerpta Med., Pestdoc, Ringdoc, Vetdoc, Index Med., Life Sci. Collect., Biol. Abstr., Chem. Abstr., Psychol. Abstr., Sci. Cit. Index, Abr. Ed. **NLM W1** PS748G. **CODEN** PSYCDE.

RECENT ADVANCES IN DIABETES. No. 1-. 0264-7397. Periodical. UK. English. Churchill Livingston Inc, 1560 Broadway, New York NY 10036. Ed Malcolm Nattrass and Julio V Santiago. **LC** RC660.A1. **DD** 616.462. **NLM W1** RE105UK.

RECENT ADVANCES IN ENDOCRINOLOGY AND METABOLISM. See Medicine - Allergic, Metabolic, Nutritional Diseases.

RECENT PROGRESS IN HORMONE RESEARCH. V. 1- 1947-. 0079-9963. US. English. ir. Academic Press, 4805 Sand Lake Road, Orlando FL 32887. **Tel** (305)345-4100. Ed Gregory Pincus. **Ind/Abst** Excerpta Med., Life Sci. Collect., Chem. Abstr., Index Med., Bibliogr. Agric., Biol. Abstr., Nucl. Sci. Abstr., Sci. Cit. Index, Abr. Ed. **LC** QP187. **DD** 612.4058. **NLM W1** RE106E. **CODEN** RPHRA6. (cum index).

RESEARCH PROGRAMS OF THE NATIONAL INSTITUTE OF CHILD HEALTH AND HUMAN DEVELOPMENT. NUTRITION AND ENDOCRINOLOGY. See Nutrition and Dietetics.

REVISTA DE LA SOCIEDAD COLOMBIANA DE ENDOCRINOLOGIA. V. 1, No. 1, (Dec. 1955)-. 0120-1182. Periodical. Spanish. ir. **NLM W1** RE412P.

REVUE FRANCAISE D'ENDOCRINOLOGIE CLINIQUE, NUTRITION ET METABOLISME. See Medicine - Allergic, Metabolic, Nutritional Diseases.

SEMINARS IN REPRODUCTIVE ENDOCRINOLOGY. Vol. 1, No. 1 (Feb. 1983)-. 0734-8630. Periodical. US. English. qt. $64.00. Thieme Inc, 381 Park Avenue South, New York NY 10016. **Tel** (212)683-5088. Ed Leon Speroff. **NLM W1** SE489H. adv acc. **Circ** 1,200. Topic-oriented journal for the practitioner specializing in reproductive functions and diseases.

SPECIAL TOPICS IN ENDOCRINOLOGY AND METABOLISM. Vol. 1-. 0193-0982. US. English. Alan R Liss, 41 East 11th Street, New York NY 10003. **Tel** (212)475-7700. Ed Margo P Cohen and Piero P Foa. **Ind/Abst** Index Med., Biol. Abstr., Chem. Abstr. **LC** RC648.A1. **DD** 616.4005. **NLM W1** SP302. **CODEN** SEMTD8. A book series concerning endocrinology and metabolism.

VITAMINS AND HORMONES; ADVANCES IN RESEARCH AND APPLICATIONS. V. 1- 1943-. 0083-6729. US. English. ir. Academic Press, 4805 Sand Lake Road, Orlando FL 32887. **Tel** (305)345-4100. Ed Robert S Harris. **Ind/Abst** Excerpta Med., Pestdoc, Ringdoc, Vetdoc, Index Med., Chem. Abstr., Energy Res. Abstr. **LC** QP801.V5. **DD** 612.05058. **NLM W1** VI985. **CODEN** VIHOAQ. (cum index).

THE YEAR BOOK OF ENDOCRINOLOGY. See Yearbooks, Almanacs, Directories.

FORENSIC MEDICINE, MEDICAL JURISPRUDENCE

ACTA MEDICINAE LEGALIS ET SOCIALIS CEASED. V. 1-20, No. 1. 0065-1397. Periodical. BE. Multilingual (articles in English, French, German, or Italian, usually with summaries in one or more of these languages). an. 1,500. 39 rue dos Fachon, B-4020 Liege Belgium. Ed G Brahy. **Ind/Abst** Index Med. **NLM W1** AC857. (cum index). bk rev. **Circ** 500.

ADVANCES IN FORENSIC PSYCHOLOGY AND PSYCHIATRY. Vol. 1-. 0747-6353. US. English. an. Ablex Publishing Corp, 355 Chestnut Street, Norwood NJ 07648. **Tel** (201)767-8450. Ed Robert W Rieber. **DD** 347. Book series focusing on current research in forensic psychology and psychiatry.

THE AMERICAN JOURNAL OF FORENSIC MEDICINE AND PATHOLOGY. V. 1- Mar. 1980-. 0195-7910. Periodical. US. English. qt. $89.00 Domestic, $99.00 Foreign. Raven Press, 1140 Avenue of the Americas, New York NY 10036. **Tel** (212)575-0335. Ed William G Eckert. **Ind/Abst** Life Sci. Collect., Excerpta Med., Index Med., Abstr. Anthropol. **LC** RA1001. **DD** 614.105. **NLM W1** AM451R. bk rev. adv acc. **Circ** 1,700. Devoted to the latest development in forensic science reported from development in research and clinical practice.

AMERICAN JOURNAL OF LAW & MEDICINE. See Law.

ANNUAL REPORT AND FINANCIAL STATEMENT - MEDICAL AND DENTAL DEFENCE UNION OF SCOTLAND LIMITED. Main/Corp Medical and Dental Defence Union of Scotland. 0144-8730. UK. English. an. **NLM W1** ME179B. Annual Report - Medical and Dental Defence Union of Scotland Limited, 0144-8749.

ANNUAL REPORT - CENTER FOR LAW AND HEALTH SCIENCES. Main/Corp Boston University. Center for Law and Health Sciences. 1970/71-. 0162-9417. US. English. an. **NLM W1** CE185.

ARCHIVES BELGES DE MEDECINE SOCIALE, HYGIENE, MEDECINE DU TRAVAIL ET MEDECINE LEGALE. See Genealogy and Heraldry - Archives.

ARCHIVIO DI MEDICINA LEGALE E DELLE ASSICURAZIONI. See Genealogy and Heraldry - Archives.

ARZTRECHT. Year 12-. 0343-5733. Periodical. GW. German. mo. Verlag fur Arztrecht, Schinnrainstrasse 15, Karlsruhe 41 West Germany. **NLM W1** AR996. Arzt + Arzneimittelrecht, 0340-5532.

ATTORNEYS' DICTIONARY OF MEDICINE. US. English. an. Matthew Bender & Company Inc, 1275 Broadway, Albany NY 12201. **Tel** (800)833-9844.

ATTORNEYS' TEXTBOOK OF MEDICINE. US. English. ir. Matthew Bender & Company Inc, 1275 Broadway, Albany NY 12201. **Tel** (800)833-9844.

AUSTRALIAN JOURNAL OF FORENSIC SCIENCES. (THE AUSTRALIAN JOURNAL OF FORENSIC SCIENCES). 0045-0618. Periodical. AT. English. qt. Butterworths-Australia, c/o EBSCO Bennett, 35 Mitchell, North Sydney 2060 New South Wales Australia. **Ind/Abst** Leg. Resour. Index, Excerpta Med., APAIS, Aust. Public Aff. Inf. Serv., Chem. Abstr. **LC** K1. **DD** 340.605. **NLM W1** AU611R. **CODEN** AJFSB9.

BEITRAGE ZUR GERICHTLICHEN MEDIZIN. Began in 1911. 0067-5016. AU. German. an. Franz Deuticke Verlag, Helferstorferstrasse 4, PO Box 761/1, 1011 Wien Austria. **Ind/Abst** Excerpta Med., Index Med., Chem. Abstr. **LC** RA1001. **NLM W1** BE27. **CODEN** BEGMA5. Beytrage Zur Gerichtlichen Arzneykunde.

BOLETIM DE MEDICINA LEGAL E TOXICOLOGIA FORENSE. (BOLETIM DE MEDICINA LEGAL E TOXICOLOGIA FORENSE : COLECTANEA DE PUBLICACOES CIENTIFICAS DO INSTITUTO DE MEDICINA LEGAL DO PORTO). Vol. 1, No. 1-. 0253-0554. Periodical. Portuguese. sa. **NLM W1** BO160M.

CANADIAN SOCIETY OF FORENSIC SCIENCE JOURNAL. V. 1- March 1968-. 0008-5030. Periodical. CN. English (includes some text in French). qt. $38.69. Canadian Society Forensic Science, 2660 Southvale Cresc Suite 215, Ottawa Ontario K1B 4W5 Canada. **Tel** (613)731-2096. Ed Brian M Dixon. **Ind/Abst** Excerpta Med., Art Archaeol. Tech. Abstr., Chem. Abstr. **CODEN** JCFSBP. bk rev. adv acc. **Circ** 1,000. (ctrl). Original papers, chemistry, blood, alcohol, analysis, toxicology, questioned documents, odontology, firearms examination, pathology, biology, law enforcement and jurisprudence.

COLLECTION DE MEDECINE LEGALE ET DE TOXICOLOGIE MEDICALE. No. 53-. 0398-9119. Monographic Series. French. ir. **Ind/Abst** Excerpta Med., Chem. Abstr. **NLM W1** CO17Q. **CODEN** CMLMDW.

EXCERPTA MEDICA. SECTION 49. FORENSIC SCIENCE ABSTRACTS. See Indexes/Abstracts.

THE EXPERT AND THE LAW. See Law.

FEDERATION BULLETIN. Main/Corp Federation of State Medical Boards of the United States. V. 7- Jan. 1921-. 0014-9306. Periodical. US. English. mo. $25.00. Federation of State Medical Boards of the United States, 2630 West Freeway/Suite 138, Ft Worth TX 76102. **Tel** (817)335-1141. Ed Ray L Casterline. **Ind/Abst** Hospit. Lit. Index. **NLM W1** FE272. **Circ** 3,378. Medical licensure; requirements for licensure; state board policies. Monthly Bulletin of the Federation of State Medical Boards of the United States.

FORENSIA. 0724-844X. German. qt. Springer Verlag-New York Inc, 175 5th Avenue, New York NY 10010. **Tel** (212)460-1500. Ed G Harrer and CH Frank. **DD** 345.06605, 342.56605. Interdisciplinary exchange of ideas on current questions of law theory and practice of criminology, forensic medicine, psychiatry and psychology, original articles, convention reports and notices.

FORENSIC SCIENCE INTERNATIONAL. V. 12- July/Aug. 1978-. 0379-0738. Periodical. English (French, or German with summaries in English). mo. Elsevier Scientific Publishers Irelands Limited, PO Box 85, Limerick Ireland. **Ind/Abst** Electron. Commun. Abstr. J., ISMEC Bull., Pollut. Abstr. Indexes, Saf. Sci. Abstr. J., Leg. Resour. Index, Life Sci. Collect., Excerpta Med., Index Med., Biol. Abstr., Chem. Abstr., Energy Res. Abstr., Leg. Resour. Index, Abstr. Anthropol., Curr. Law Index. **LC** RA1001. **DD** 614.19. **NLM W1** FO615I. **CODEN** FSINDR. Index in last issue of volume - attached. Forensic Science.

FORENSIC SEROLOGY NEWS. 0739-7658. Periodical. US. English. qt. $7.50. Forensic Sciences Foundation, 225 South Academy Boulevard/Suite 201, Colorado Springs CO 80910.

THE INTERNATIONAL BIBLIOGRAPHY OF THE FORENSIC SCIENCES. *See* Bibliographies.

INTERNATIONAL JOURNAL OF MEDICINE AND LAW. (THE INTERNATIONAL JOURNAL OF MEDICINE AND LAW : IJML). Vol. 1, No. 1 (Summer 1979)-. 0334-3049. Periodical. UK. English. qt. $50.00. Turtledove Publishing, 15 Kinneret Street/PO Box 1337, Ramat Gan Israel. **Ind/Abst** Excerpta Med. **LC** K9. **DD** 344.04105. **NLM** W1 IN769S.

JOURNAL DE MEDECINE LEGALE, DROIT MEDICAL. **VFOAT** Medecine Legale, Droit Medical. V. 24, No. 1 (Jan./Feb. 1981)-. 0249-6208. Periodical. US. English (French). bm. Masson Publishing USA Inc, 211 East 43rd Street/ Room 1306, New York NY 10017. **Tel** (212)370-1937. **Ind/Abst** Life Sci. Collect., Excerpta Med., Chem. Abstr. **LC** RA1001. **DD** 614.105. **NLM** W1 JO322M. **CODEN** JMLMD7. *Medecine Legale, Toxicologie, 0241-6751.*

JOURNAL OF CHIROPRACTIC JURISPRUDENCE. Vol. 1, No. 1 (Dec. 1985)-. 0885-8497. Periodical. US. English. mo. $180.00. Clay-Jen Publishers, PO Box 59221/5140 Crowley Drive, Birmingham AL 35259-9221. **DD** 346. **NLM** W1.

JOURNAL OF FORENSIC SCIENCES. V. 1- Jan. 1956-. 0022-1198. Periodical. US. English. qt. $53.00. **Tel** (215)299-5400. **Ind/Abst** Leg. Resour. Index, Excerpta Med., Abstr. Bull. Inst. Paper Chem., Int. Aerosp. Abstr., Biol. Abstr., Chem. Abstr., Nucl. Sci. Abstr., Index Med., Bibliogr. Agric., Energy Res. Abstr., Sci. Cit. Index, Abr. Ed., Curr. Law Index, Hospit. Lit. Index, Abstr. Anthropol. **LC** RA1001. **DD** 340.6. **NLM** W1 JO659. **CODEN** JFSCAS. Index in last issue of volume - attached. Available in microfilm.

JOURNAL OF LEGAL MEDICINE (CHICAGO, ILL.). (THE JOURNAL OF LEGAL MEDICINE). Began in Apr. 1979. 0194-7648. Periodical. US. English. qt. $102.00. Pharmaceutical Communications, 42-15 Crescent Street, Long Island City NY 11101. **Tel** (212)937-4283. **Ind/Abst** Hospit. Lit. Index, Index Med., Index Leg. Period., Cumul. Index Nurs. Allied Health Lit., Curr. Law Index, Leg. Resour. Index, Soc. Sci. Citation Index. **LC** K10. **DD** 344.7304105, 347.3044105. **NLM** W1 JO745B.

MEDICAL TRIAL TECHNIQUE QUARTERLY. V. 1- Sept. 1954-. 0025-7591. Periodical. US. English. qt. $98.50. Callaghan and Company, 3201 Old Glenview Road, Wilmette IL 60091. **Ind/Abst** Leg. Resour. Index, Index Leg. Period., Energy Res. Abstr. **DD** 614.105. **NLM** W1 ME5278.

MEDICINE, SCIENCE, AND THE LAW. Vol. 1, No. 1 (Oct. 1960)-. 0025-8024. Periodical. UK. English. qt. $44.45. Kluwer Publishing Ltd, 1 Harlequin Avenue, Great West Road, Brentford Middlesex TW8 9EW England. **Tel** 01/ 568 6441. **Ed** J M Cameron. **Ind/Abst** Life Sci. Collect., Excerpta Med., Coal Abstr., Index Med., CIS Abstr., Chem. Abstr., Soc. Sci. Citation Index, Hospit. Lit. Index, Leg. Resour. Index, Curr. Law Index, Sci. Cit. Index, Abr. Ed. **LC** K13. **DD** 614.105. **NLM** W1 ME655. **CODEN** MDSLA6. Index in last issue of volume - attached. bk rev. adv acc. **Circ** 2,000. (ctrl). Academic journal featuring topics associated with forensic science: medicine, science, law forensic odontology etc. Contains information on recent cases of coronorship and pathology.

MEDICOLEGAL-GRAM. Vol. 1, No. 1 (July 1980)-. Periodical. US. English. mo. Board of Medicolegal Investigations, Office of the Chief Medical Examiner, 901 North Stonewall, Oklahoma City OK 73117. **LC** RA1001. **DD** 614.105. *Oklahoma Journal of Forensic Medicine, 0363-2679.*

MEDIZIN IN RECHT UND ETHIK. V. 12-. German. ir. **Ed** Albin Eser and Eduard Seidler. **NLM** W1 ME811F. *Medizin und Recht, 0340-9511.*

MINERVA MEDICOLEGALE. V. 70-. 0026-4849. IT. Italian. qt. 40.00. Edizoni Minerva Medica, Corso Bramante 83-85, Torino Italy 10126. **Tel** 67 82 82. **Ed** T Oliaro. **Ind/Abst** CIS Abstr. **NLM** W1 MI648. bk rev. adv acc. Journal addressed to practitioners and specialists in forensic medicine and criminal anthropology in Italy and abroad. It deals with topics in scientific practice and research. *Archivio di Antropologia Criminale, Psichiatria, e Medicina Legale.*

OKLAHOMA JOURNAL OF FORENSIC MEDICINE. 0363-2679. US. English. ir. Board of Medicolegal, PO Box 26901/800 Northeast 13th Street, Oklahoma City OK 73190. **LC** RA1001. **DD** 614.19.

ORTHOPEDIC SURGEONS' LEGAL LETTER. **VFOAT** Legal Letter. 0741-7470. Periodical. US. English. Free. Merck Sharp and Dohme, PO Box 2000, Rahway NJ 07065. **LC** KF2910.O78. **DD** 344.730412, 347.304412.

PROCEEDINGS OF THE NATIONAL CONFERENCE ON THE MEDICOLEGAL IMPLICATIONS OF EMERGENCY MEDICAL CARE. **Main/Conf** National Conference on the Medicolegal Implications of Emergency Medical Care. 1st- 1975-. 0190-700X. US. English. ir. American Heart Association, 7320 Greenville Avenue, Dallas TX 57231. **NLM** W3 NA512.

RECHT UND MEDIZIN. **VFOAT** RECHT & MEDIZIN. V. 1-. 0172-116X. Monographic Series. German. ir. **Ed** E Deutsch, A Laufs, and H L Schreiber. **LC** UNC. **NLM** W1 RE1093.

REVISTA DEL INSTITUTO NACIONAL DE MEDICINA LEGAL DE COLOMBIA. **Main/Corp** Instituto Nacional de Medicina Legal de Colombia. Began in 1975. 0120-0097. Spanish. sa. Carrera 13 No 7-46, Bogota Colombia. **Ind/Abst** Excerpta Med., Chem. Abstr. **LC** RA1001. **DD** 614.1905. **NLM** W1 RE513EI. **CODEN** RINCDD. *Revista de Medicina Legal de Colombia.*

RIVISTA DI MEDICINA DEL LAVORO ED IGIENE INDUSTRIALE. Jan.-Mar. 1977-. 0391-2825. Periodical. Italian. qt. $60.00. Casa Editrice Libraria Idelson, Via a de Gasperi 55, 80133 Napoli Italy. **Tel** 081/324733. **Ed** Luigi Ambrosi. **Ind/Abst** Excerpta Med., Chem. Abstr. **NLM** W1 RI53F. **CODEN** RMLIDF. bk rev. *Folia Medica (Naples, Italy).*

SCIENTIFIC SLEUTHING NEWSLETTER (1983). (SCIENTIFIC SLEUTHING NEWSLETTER). Vol. 7, No. 1 (Jan. 1983)-. 0749-1395. Periodical. US. English. qt. $20.00. Scientific Sleuthing Newsletter, POB 196, McLean VA 22101. **Tel** (301)540-0684. **Ed** Rick Tontarski. **DD** 345. **Circ** 800. Review of legal decisions involving forensic evidence. Implications and impact discussed. *Science in Criminal Law Newsletter.*

THE SOLBERG HEALTH LAW LETTER. Began in 1981. 0740-3259. Periodical. US. English. bm. $30.00. Patrice Solberg, 211 North Columbia Street, Chapel Hill NC 27515. **LC** KFN7760.A15. **DD** 344.75604105, 347.56044105.

SPECIALTY LAW DIGEST. HEALTH CARE. (SPECIALTY LAW DIGEST : HEALTH CARE). **VFOAT** Health Care. Mar. 1979-. 0198-8778. Periodical. US. English. ir. $219.00. Bureau of National Affairs Inc, 1231 25th Street NW, Washington DC 20037. **Tel** (301)258-1033. **Ind/Abst** Hospit. Lit. Index. **LC** KF3821.A59. **DD** 344.7304102648. **NLM** W 32.5 AA1 S7S.

SPECIALTY LAW DIGEST. HEALTH CARE (ANNUAL). (SPECIALTY LAW DIGEST. HEALTH CARE). **VFOAT** Health Care. Digest V. 1 (Mar. 1979 through Feb. 1980)-. 0276-3079. US. English. an. Bureau of National Affairs, 1231 25th Street NW, Washington DC 20037. **LC** KF3821.A59. **DD** 344.7304102648, 347. 3044102648. **NLM** W 32.5 AA1.

STATE HEALTH LEGISLATION REPORT. Began with issue for Dec. 1973. 0094-6400. US. English. qt. American Medical Association, 535 N Dearborn Street, Chicago IL 60690. **LC** KF3821.Z95. **DD** 344.7304105, 347.3044105. **NLM** W1 ST314G.

STATE LEGISLATIVE REPORT (KANSAS CITY, MO.). (STATE LEGISLATIVE REPORT). 8756-5994. Periodical. US. English. qt. $25.00. Center for Research, American Nurses' Association, 2420 Pershing Road, Kansas City MO 64108. **LC** KF2915.N8. **DD** 344.73041405, 347.30441405. **NLM** W1.

SUDEBNOMEDICINSKAJA EKSPERTIZA. (SUDEBNOMEDITSINSKAIA EKSPERTIZA). Vol. 1- 1958-. 0039-4521. Periodical. UR. Russian (summaries in English). qt. $13.50. Victor Kamkin Inc (70889), 12224 Parklawn Drive, Rockville MD 20852. **Tel** (301)881-5973. **Ind/Abst** Excerpta Med., Index Med., Biol. Abstr., Chem. Abstr. **NLM** W1 SU167. **CODEN** SMEZA5.

TOPICS IN HOSPITAL LAW. Vol. 1, No. 1 (Dec. 1985)-. 0883-7147. Periodical. US. English. qt. $59.50. Aspen Systems Corporation, 16792 Oakmont Avenue, Gaithersburg MD 20877. **Ed** Robert D Miller. **DD** 344.

TRAUMA. V. 1- June 1959-. 0564-1470. Periodical. US. English. bm. Matthew Bender & Company Inc, 1275 Broadway, Albany NY 12201. **Tel** (800)833-9844. **Ed** M Houts. **Ind/Abst** Curr. Law Index, Leg. Resour. Index. **LC** RA1001. **DD** 340.6. **NLM** W1 TR257. (cum index).

WASHINGTON REPORT ON HEALTH LEGISLATION. V. 1- Jan. 29, 1975-. 0098-2512. Periodical. US. English. wk. $327.00. McGraw-Hill, 457 National Press Building, Washington DC 20045. **LC** KF3821.A15. **DD** 344.7304105. **NLM** W1 WA619G.

ZEITSCHRIFT FUR RECHTSMEDIZIN. **VFOAT** Journal of Legal Medicine. 0044-3433. GW. German (English). bm. Springer Verlag-New York Inc, 175 5th Avenue, New York NY 10010. **Tel** (212)460-1500. **Ed** J Gerchow. **Ind/Abst** Life Sci. Collect., Excerpta Med., Index Med., Biol. Abstr., Chem. Abstr., Curr. Contents, Sci. Cit. Index, Abr. Ed. **LC** RA1001. **NLM** W1 ZE58F. **CODEN** ZRMDAN. Reviews and original works in forensic pathology, trauma, treatment, forensic toxicology, medical jurisprudence, abuse of alcohol and drugs. Furthers international exchange of ideas. *Deutsche Zeitschrift fur die Gesamte Gerichtliche Medizin.*

ZENTRALBLATT FUR DIE GESAMTE RECHTSMEDIZIN UND IHRE GRENZGEBIETE *CEASED.* (ZENTRALBLATT FUR DIE GESAMTE RECHTSMEDIZIN UND IHRE GRENZGEBIET : REFERATENORGAN DER DEUTSCHEN GESELLSCHAFT FUR RECHTSMEDIZIN). **VFOAT** Legal Medicine. Began in 1970. Ceased 23. V., No. 6 (Sept. 1983). 0044-4154. Periodical. German. ir. Springer Verlag-New York Inc, 175 5th Avenue, New York NY 10010. **NLM** W1 ZE777JR. *Deutsche Zeitschrift fur die Gesamte Gerichtliche Medizin.*

ZENTRALBLATT RECHTSMEDIZIN. **VFOAT** Rechtsmedizin, Legal Medicine. 24. Vol., No. 1-. 0722-3056. German (English). mo. Springer Verlag-New York Inc, 175 5th Avenue, New York NY 10010. **Tel** (212)460-1500. **Ed** G Schmidt. **NLM** ZW 700 Z56. Meeting reports, reviews, suicide, accidental deaths on trains, ships and airplanes, unexpected death through natural causes, injuries, poisonings, criminology, psychiatry and legal psychology. *Zentralblatt fur die Gesamte Rechtsmedizin und Ihre Grenzgebiete, 0044-4154.*

GERIATRICS

ACTA GERONTOLOGICA JAPONICA. (YOKUFUKAI CHOSA KENKYU KIYO). **VFOAT** Acta Gerontologica Japonica. Week 56 Nov. 1972-. 0001-5768. Periodical. Japanese (summaries in English). ir. **NLM** W1 YO675A. *Acta Gerontologica Japonica, 0001-5768.*

ACTIVITIES, ADAPTATION, & AGING. (ACTIVITIES, ADAPTATION & AGING). **VAT** Activities, Adaptation, and Aging. Vol. 1, No. 1 (Fall 1980)-. 0192-4788. Periodical. US. English. qt. $98.00. The Haworth Press Inc, 149 Fifth Avenue, New York NY 10010. **Tel** (212)228-2800. **Ed** Phyllis M Foster. **Ind/Abst** Sociol. Abstr., Soc. Welf. Soc. Plan./Policy Soc. Dev., Biol. Abstr., Soc. Work Res. Abstr., Psychol. Abstr. **LC** RC952.5. **DD** 362.605. **NLM** W1 AC9802. **CODEN** AADADK. bk rev. adv acc. **Circ** 1,326. Provides timely and useful case studies, program evaluations, research, and theory for activities directors, coordinators in nursing homes and community centers.

ADVANCED GERIATRIC MEDICINE. **VFOAT** Geriatric Medicine. 1-. 0261-2763. UK. English. Pitman Books Ltd, 39 Parker Street, London WC2B 51B England. **Ed** F I Caird and J Grimley Evans. **NLM** W1 AD404.

AGE. (AGE : THE JOURNAL OF THE AMERICAN AGING ASSOCIATION). Vol. 1, No. 1 (Jan. 1978)-. 0161-9152. Periodical. US. English. qt. $25.00 Domestic, $29.00 Foreign. Age, 42nd & Dewey Avenue, Omaha NB 68105. **Tel** (402)559-4416. **Ed** Denham Harman. **Ind/Abst** Excerpta Med., Int. Aerosp. Abstr., Life Sci. Collect., Biol. Abstr., Chem. Abstr. **NLM** W1 AG299. **CODEN** AGEEDB. bk rev. **Circ** 400. Papers pertinent to biomedical aging research. Subject areas include effect of age on DNA, RNA hormones, mitochondria, connective tissue, lipid metabolism, central nervous system, etc.

AGE AND AGEING. V. 1- Feb. 1972-. 0002-0729. Periodical. UK. English. bm. Bailliere Tindall, 1 St Annes Road, Eastbourne East Sussex BN21 EUN England. **Ind/Abst** Life Sci. Collect., Excerpta Med., Index Med., Biol. Abstr., Chem. Abstr., Soc. Sci. Index, Sci. Cit. Index, Abr. Ed., Hospit. Lit. Index. **LC** RC952. **DD** 618.97005. **NLM** W1 AG31. **CODEN** AANGAH.

Medicine—Geriatrics

AGEING INTERNATIONAL. V. 1- Winter 1973/74-. 0163-5158. Periodical. US. English. qt. $22.00. International Federation of Aging, 1909 K Street NW Suite 512, Washington DC 20049. Tel (202)728-4717. Ed Charlotte Nusberg. NLM W1 AG326I. bk rev. adv acc. Circ 2,000. Covers developments in aging around the world with emphasis on innovations in policies and programs for the elderly.

AGING. V. 1-. 0160-2721. Monographic Series. US. English. ir. Raven Press, 1140 Avenue of the Americas, New York NY 10036. Ind/Abst Chem. Abstr., Biol. Abstr. LC UNC. DD 612. NLM W1 AG342E. CODEN AGNYDE.

AGING. VFOAT Annual Editions: Aging. 0272-3808. Periodical. US. English. an. Dushkin Publishing Group, Sluice Dock, Guilford CT 06437. Tel (203)453-4351. Ed Harold Cox. LC HQ1060. DD 305.26. Annually updated collection of public press articles covering current issues on aging. Includes topic guide and complete index. *Annual Editions. Focus: Aging, 0162-3621.*

AGING NEWS. VFOAT Aging Research and Training News. Began with: Apr. 1978. 0197-4017. Periodical. US. English. mo. Business Publishers Inc, 951 Pershing Drive, Silver Spring MD 20910. Tel (301)587-6300. Ed Nancy Aldrich. NLM W1 AG326M. Newsletter highlighting funds (grants and contracts) available for research and programs in gerontology-health care, housing, transportation, nutrition, geriatric medicine and more.

AKTUELLE GERONTOLOGIE. V. 4- Jan. 1974-. 0300-5704. Periodical. GW. German. bm. Georg Thieme Verlag Stuttgart, Postfach 732 Herdweg 63, D7000 Stuttgart 1 West Germany. Tel 0711/89 31 298. Ind/Abst Life Sci. Collect., Excerpta Med., Chem. Abstr., Energy Res. Abstr. NLM W1 AK995D. CODEN AKGRAH. *Actuelle Gerontologie.*

ANNUAL EDITIONS : FOCUS : AGING CEASED. VFOAT Focus: Aging. 1978-. 0162-3621. US. English. an. Dushkin Publishing Group, Sluice Dock Box 426, Guilford CT 06437. Tel (203)463-4351. LC HQ1060. DD 305.26.

ANNUAL REVIEW OF GERONTOLOGY AND GERIATRICS. Vol. 2 (1981)-. 0198-8794. US. English. an. Springer Publishing Company, 200 Park Avenue South, New York NY 10003. Ind/Abst Index Med. LC RC952.A1. NLM W1 AN772. *Annual Review of Gerontology & Geriatrics, 0198-8794.*

AOA OCCASIONAL PAPERS IN GERONTOLOGY. Series/Titl Dhew Publication. VAT Administration on Aging Occasional Papers in Gerontology. No. 1-. 0191-7854. Monographic Series. US. English. ir. NLM W1 A14V.

ARCHIVES OF GERONTOLOGY AND GERIATRICS. See Genealogy and Heraldry - Archives.

ARECO'S QUARTERLY INDEX TO PERIODICAL LITERATURE ON AGING. See Indexes/Abstracts.

BEITRAGE ZUR GERONTOLOGIE UND ALTENARBEIT. Began with: 13, published in 1977?. 0175-8365. Monographic Series. German. ir. NLM W1 BE273.

BIORESEARCH TODAY. HUMAN & ANIMAL AGING. VFOAT Human & Animal Aging. VAT Bioresearch Today. Human and Animal Aging. 0149-0966. Periodical. US. English. mo. $100.00. Bioscience Information Service, 2100 Arch Street, Philadelphia PA 19103. Tel (215)587-4800. Current awareness journal covering human and animal aging.

CANADIAN JOURNAL ON AGING. VFOAT Revue Canadienne du Vieillissement. Vol. 1, No. 1/2 (1982)-. 0714-9808. Periodical. CN. English (includes some text in French). qt. $35.00. Canadian Association on Gerontology, c/o Publishing and Printing Services Unit 7/25 Planchet Road, Maple Ontario L0J 1E0 Canada. Ind/Abst Psychol. Abstr. DD 612.6705.

CARING. (CARING : NATIONAL ASSOCIATION FOR HOME CARE MAGAZINE). Oct. 1982-. 0738-467X. Periodical. US. English. mo. $45.00. National Association for Home Care, 311 Massachusetts NE, Washington DC 20002. Tel (202)547-7424. Ind/Abst Hospit. Lit. Index, Cumul. Index Nurs. Allied Health Lit. NLM W1 CA789J.

CLINICAL GERONTOLOGIST. Vol. 1, No. 1 (Fall 1982)-. 0731-7115. Periodical. US. English. qt. Haworth Press, 28 East 22nd Street, New York NY 10010. Tel (212)228-2800. Ed T L Brink. Ind/Abst Electron. Commun. Abstr. J., ISMEC Bull., Pollut. Abstr. Indexes, Saf. Sci. Abstr. J., Life Sci. Collect., Hospit. Lit. Index, Sociol. Abstr., Excerpta Med., Psychol. Abstr. NLM W1 CL71D. bk rev. adv acc. Circ 1,816. The journal presents timely material which is relevant to the needs of mental health professionals and all practitioners who deal with the aged client.

CLINICS IN GERIATRIC MEDICINE. 0749-0690. Periodical. US. English. qt $40.00. W B Saunders, West Washington Square, Philadelphia PA 19105.

CONTEMPORARY GERIATRIC MEDICINE. Vol. 1-. 0748-2760. US. English. be. Plenum Publishing Corporation, 233 Spring Street, New York NY 10013. Ed Steven R Gambert. LC RC952.A1. DD 618.97005. NLM W1 CO769MPJ.

CONTRIBUTIONS TO THE STUDY OF AGING. No. 1-. 0732-085X. Monographic Series. US. English. ir. Greenwood Press, 88 Post Road West, Westport CT 06881. LC UNC. NLM W1 CO778W.

EXCERPTA MEDICA. SECTION 20. GERONTOLOGY AND GERIATRICS. See Indexes/Abstracts.

EXPERIMENTAL AGING RESEARCH. V. 1- Sept. 1975-. 0361-073X. Periodical. US. English. qt. $90.00. PO Box 136, Southwest Harbor ME 04679. Tel (207)244-3931. Ed Merrill F Elias. Ind/Abst Life Sci. Collect., Excerpta Med., Cumul. Index Nurs. Allied Health Lit., Index Med., Biol. Abstr., Chem. Abstr., Psychol. Abstr., Energy Res. Abstr., Sci. Cit. Index, Abr. Ed., Hospit. Lit. Index. LC QP86. NLM W1 EX46. CODEN EAGRDS. bk rev. adv acc. Circ 1,000. (ctrl). An interdisciplinary scientific journal dealing with all aspects of the aging process and the aged.

EXPERIMENTAL GERONTOLOGY. V. 1- July 1964-. 0531-5565. Periodical. UK. English. bm. Pergamon Press, 395 Sawmill River Road, Elmsford NY 10523. Tel (914)592-7700. Ind/Abst Life Sci. Collect., Excerpta Med., Int. Aerosp. Abstr., Biol. Abstr., Nuci. Sci. Abstr., Index Med., Bibliogr. Agric., Chem. Abstr., Sci. Cit. Index, Abr. Ed. QP86. DD 612.6705. NLM W1 EX504D. CODEN EXGEAB. Available on microfilm from Microforms International Marketing Corporation.

FRONTIERS IN AGING SERIES. V. 1-. 0271-955X. Monographic Series. US. English. ir. Human Sciences Press, 72 5th Avenue, New York NY 10011. Ed G Lesnoff-Caravaglia. Ind/Abst Hospit. Lit. Index. NLM W1 FR945T.

GENERATIONS. (GENERATIONS : THE JOURNAL OF THE WESTERN GERONTOLOGICAL SOCIETY). VFOAT Journal of the Western Gerontological Society. 0738-7806. Periodical. US. English. qt $25.00. Western Gerontological Society, 833 Market Street/Suite 516, San Francisco CA 94103.

GERIATRIC CONSULTANT. Vol. 1, No. 1 July/Aug. 1982. 0745-1202. Periodical. US. English. bm. $19.00. Medical Publishing Enterprises Inc, One Bridge Plaza North, Fort Lee NJ 07024. DD 618.

GERIATRIC MEDICINE. V. 9, No. 4- Apr. 1979-. 0143-3628. Periodical. UK. English. mo. $20.00. Modern Medicine Publications, Findlay Publishings Ltd, 1 Copers Cope Road, Beckenham Kent BR3 1NB England. NLM W1 GE457BC. *Modern Geriatrics.*

GERIATRIC MEDICINE CURRENTS. Vol. 1, No. 1 (May/June 1980)-. Periodical. US. English. bm. Ross Laboratories, 625 Cleveland Avenue, Columbus OH 43216.

GERIATRIC MEDICINE JOURNAL. 0882-4614. Periodical. US. English. an. Medical Economic Books, Box C-779 Pratt Station, Brooklyn NY 11205. DD 618.

GERIATRIC MEDICINE TODAY. Vol. 1, No. 1 (Sept. 1982)-. 0745-1709. Periodical. US. English. mo $45.00. Geriatric Medicine Today, 50 Route 9, Morganville NJ 07757. Tel (201)536-7800.

GERIATRICS. V. 1- Jan. 1946-. 0016-867X. Periodical. US. English. mo. $25.00. Geriatrics, 1 East First Street, Duluth MN 55802. Tel (218)723-9516. Ed Richard L Peck. Ind/Abst Life Sci. Collect., Hospit. Lit. Index, Pestdoc, Ringdoc, Vetdoc, Excerpta Med., Biol. Abstr., Chem. Abstr., Nuci. Sci. Abstr., Index Med., Energy Res. Abstr., Gen. Sci. Index, Lang. Lang. Behav. Abstr., Sci. Cit. Index, Abr. Ed., Sociol. Abstr. LC RC952.A1. DD 618.97005. NLM W1 GE457H. CODEN GERTAZ. adv acc. Circ 55,367. (ctrl). A medical journal for physicians who treat older patients.

GERIATRICS SURVEY. Vol. 1, No. 1 (July 1983)-. 0736-9042. Periodical. US. English. $50.00 Domestic. Williams & Wilkins, 428 East Preston Street, Baltimore MD 21202. NLM W1.

GERODONTOLOGY. Vol. 1, No. 1 (Summer 1982)-. 0734-0664. Periodical. US. English. ty. Beech Hill Publishing Company, PO Box 136, Southwest Harbor ME 04679. Tel (207)244-3931. Ind/Abst Life Sci. Collect., Excerpta Med., Chem. Abstr. NLM W1 GE569. CODEN GRDND6. bk rev. Publication of original-basic experimental research, clinical studies, methodological comments and review articles dealing with the aging process as it pertains to dentition, its supporting tissue, and associated structures.

GERONTOLOGICAL ABSTRACTS. See Indexes/Abstracts.

GERONTOLOGY. V. 22- 1976-. 0304-324X. Periodical. SZ. English (French). bm. S Karger AG, PO Box 352, White Plains NY 10602. Tel (061)39 08 80. Ed H P von Hahn. Ind/Abst Life Sci. Collect., Excerpta Med., Index Med., Biol. Abstr., Chem. Abstr., Sci. Cit. Index, Abr. Ed., Hospit. Lit. Index. NLM W1 GE585K. CODEN GERNDJ. adv acc. Draws experimental contributions from diverse medical, biological and behavioral disciplines to provide a primary source of high quality papers covering all aspects of aging in man, animals, and plants. *Gerontologia, 0016-898X; Gerontologia Clinica, 0016-8998.*

GERONTOLOGY & GERIATRICS EDUCATION. VAT Gerontology and Geriatrics Education. Vol. 1, No. 1 (Fall 1980)-. 0270-1960. Periodical. US. English. qt. Haworth Press, 28 East 22nd Street, New York NY 10010. Tel (212)228-2800. Ed John F Santos. Ind/Abst Sociol. Abstr., Soc. Welf. Soc. Plan./Policy Soc. Dev., Excerpta Med., Cumul. Index Nurs. Allied Health Lit., Index Med., Index Dent. Lit. LC RC952.5. DD 362.605. NLM W1 GE585KF. bk rev. adv acc. Circ 658. A source of practical curriculum information for educators, trainers, and supervisors in the aging field.

GERONTOLOGY GRADUATE PROGRAM DIRECTORY. See Yearbooks, Almanacs, Directories.

GERONTOLOGY SPECIAL INTEREST SECTION NEWSLETTER. 0279-4101. Periodical. US. English. qt. $15.00. American Occupational Therapy Association, 1383 Piccard Drive, Rockville MD 20850. Tel (215)898-8088. Ed Nancy Ellis. bk rev. Circ 3,500. (ctrl). Health care, rehabilitation, independent living in late adulthood. *Newsletter - Gerontology Specialty Section, American Occupational Therapy Association, 0194-6366.*

GERONTOPICS CEASED. VFOAT New England Gerontology Center's Gerontopics. 0192-740X. Periodical. US. English. qt. Human Sciences Press, 75 5th Avenue, New York NY 10011. Tel (212)243-6000.

GIORNALE DI GERONTOLOGIA. 0017-0305. Periodical. IT. Italian. mo. Soc Italiana di Gerontologiae, Via G C Vanini N 5, 50129 Firenze Italy. Ind/Abst Life Sci. Collect., Excerpta Med., Biol. Abstr., Chem. Abstr., Nuci. Sci. Abstr. NLM W1 GI515. CODEN GIGEAU.

GUIDELINES FOR PREPARATION OF GRANT APPLICATIONS. RESEARCH AND DEVELOPMENT PROJECTS IN AGING, TITLE IV-B OF THE OLDER AMERICANS ACT. Main/Corp United States. Administration on Aging. VFOAT Research and Development Projects in Aging, Title IV-B of the Older Americans Act. 1978-. US. English. Administration on Aging, 330 Independence Avenue Southwest, Washington DC 20201. *Guidelines for Preparation of Grant Applications. Research and Development Projects in Aging, Title IV-B of the Older Americans Act.*

INDEX OF CURRENT RESEARCH GRANTS AND CONTRACTS ADMINISTERED BY THE NATIONAL INSTITUTE ON AGING. See Indexes/Abstracts.

INDIAN JOURNAL OF GERONTOLOGY. V. 1- Jan 1969-. Periodical. English. ir.

INTERDISCIPLINARY TOPICS IN GERONTOLOGY. V. 1- 1968-. 0074-1132. Monographic Series. English. ir. S Karger AG, PO Box, CH-4009 Basel Switzerland. Tel (061)390880. Ed H P von Hahn. Ind/Abst Biol. Abstr., Chem. Abstr. NLM W1 IN679. CODEN ITGEAR. Aims at a comprehensive and integrated approach to the

Medicine—Gynecology & Obstetrics

problems of aging as a whole and presents pertinent data from studies in animal and human gerontology.

INTERDISZIPLINARE GERONTOLOGIE. 1-. 0723-8800. Monographic Series. German. ir. **Ind/Abst** Chem. Abstr. **NLM** W1 IN681. **CODEN** INGRDR.

INTERNATIONAL JOURNAL OF BEHAVIORAL GERIATRICS. See Medicine - Psychiatry, Psychopathology.

JOURNAL FOR GERIATRIC CARE STAFF MEMBER. V. 1- Feb. 1974-. 0093-7320. Periodical. US. English. mo. American Geriatrics Society, 10 Columbus Circle, New York NY 10019. **NLM** W1 JO38M.

JOURNAL OF APPLIED GERONTOLOGY. (JOURNAL OF APPLIED GERONTOLOGY : THE OFFICIAL JOURNAL OF THE SOUTHERN GERONTOLOGICAL SOCIETY). **VFOAT** J.A.G. Vol. 1 (June 1982)-. 0733-4648. Periodical. US. English. sa. $18.00. University of South Florida, PO Box 3183, Tampa FL 33620. **Tel** (813)974-2414. **Ed** Wiley Mangum and Tom Rich. **Ind/Abst** Psychol. Abstr. LC HQ1061. DD 362.6042. bk rev. adv acc. **Circ** 600. Contributions which focus explicitly on the application of knowledge to the improvement of the quality of life of older persons.

JOURNAL OF CLINICAL AND EXPERIMENTAL GERONTOLOGY. **VFOAT** Gerontology. V. 1-. 0192-1193. Periodical. US. English. qt. $109.25. Marcel Dekker Inc, Journal Department, 11305 Church Street Station, New York NY 10249. **Tel** (212)696-9000. **Ed** F I Caird. **Ind/Abst** Excerpta Med., Biol. Abstr., Chem. Abstr. **LC** RC952.A1. DD 618.97005. **NLM** W1 JO5852. **CODEN** JCEGDK. bk rev. adv acc. (ctrl). Emphasizes the biology of aging and its clinical applications, focusing on scientific explorations. Encompasses cardiology, pharmacy, immunology, pathology, neurology, nutrition, and psychology.

JOURNAL OF GERIATRIC DRUG THERAPY. 8756-4629. Periodical. US. English. qt. $32.00 Institutions, $42.00 Libraries. Haworth Press, 75 Griswold Street, Binghamton NY 13904.

JOURNAL OF THE AMERICAN GERIATRICS SOCIETY. V. 1- Jan. 1953-. 0002-8614. US. English. mo. $88.00. American Geriatrics Society, 10 Columbus Circle, New York NY 10019. **Tel** (717)632-3535. **Ind/Abst** Hospit. Lit. Index, Life Sci. Collect., Sociol. Abstr., Soc. Welf. Soc. Plan./Policy Soc. Dev., Pestdoc, Ringdoc, Vetdoc, Excerpta Med., Cumul. Index Nurs. Allied Health Lit., Women Stud. Abstr., Int. Aerosp. Abstr., CIS Abstr., Soc. Work Res. Abstr., Biol. Abstr., Chem. Abstr., Psychol. Abstr., Nuci. Sci. Abstr., Index Med., Energy Res. Abstr., Soc. Sci. Citation Index, Sci. Cit. Index, Abr. Ed., Hospit. Lit. Index, Lang. Lang. Behav. Abstr., Abstr. Soc. Work. **NLM** W1 JO909F. **CODEN** JAGSAF. Transactions of the American Therapeutic Society, 0096-686X.

KENKYU KIYO - TOKYO-TO ROJIN SOGO KENKYUJO, TOKYO-TO YOIKUIN FUZOKU BYOIN. Main/Corp Tokyo-To Rojin Sogo Kenkyujo. **VFOAT** Collected Papers - Tokyo Metropolitan Institute of Gerontology & Tokyo Metropolitan Geriatric Hospital. Began with 1972 issue. JA. Japanese (English). ir. Tokyo-To Rojin Sogo Kenkyujo, 35-2 Sakaecho, Itabashi 173, Tokyo Japan. LC RC952.A1.

LECTURES ON GERONTOLOGY. Vol. 1-. Monographic Series. UK. English. Each issue contains an index to its own contents - no vol index - loose.

LONG LIFE MAGAZINE. V. 2, No. 2- (Issue No. 7-). 0191-1864. Periodical. US. English. bm. $9.00. Society for Life Extension, 627 West Berry 3-N, Chicago IL 60657. **NLM** W1 LO73. Life Extension Managine.

MADUREZ. Spanish (summaries in English and French). ir. Instituto de Seguridad del Estado de Mexico, Allende 101 - 1 Piso, Toluca Mexico. **LC** RC952.A1.

MATURITAS. V. 1- June 1978-. 0378-5122. Periodical. English. qt. Elsevier Science Publishers, PO Box 211, 1000 AE Amsterdam Netherlands. **Tel** (020)5803.911. **Ind/Abst** Life Sci. Collect., Excerpta Med., Index Med., Biol. Abstr., Chem. Abstr. **NLM** W1 MA99. **CODEN** MATUDK.

MODERN AGING RESEARCH. Vol. 1-. 0275-360X. Monographic Series. US. English. ir. Alan R Liss Inc, 41 East 11th Street, New York NY 10003. **Tel** (212)475-7700. **Ed** Richard Adelman, George Baker III, Vincent Cristofalo, and Jay Roberts. **Ind/Abst** Biol. Abstr., Chem. Abstr. **NLM** W1 MO117. **CODEN** MARDDR. A scholarly book series covering aspects of aging such as visual functions, intervention in aging process, comparative pathobiology of major age related diseases, altered endocrine status, etc.

NEWSLETTER - AMERICAN GERIATRICS SOCIETY. Main/Corp American Geriatrics Society. V. 1- 1972-. Periodical. US. English. mo. American Geriatrics Society, 10 Columbus Circle, New York NY 10019.

NEWSLETTER (MISSISSIPPI GERONTOLOGICAL SOCIETY). (NEWSLETTER). Vol. 1, No. 1 (June 1980)-. Periodical. US. English. Mississippi Gerontological Society, Drawer HV, Mississippi State MS 39762.

OCCASIONAL PAPERS ON AGING. VFOAT Occasional Papers on Gerontology. 1980/81-. 0711-5873. CN. English (includes some text in French). an. Free. Committee for the Studies on Aging, c/o School of Social Work/McGill University, 3506 University Street, Montreal Quebec H3A 2A7 Canada. DD 305.2605. (ctrl).

OLD AGE. Periodical. UK. English. National Corporation for the Care of Old People, Nuffield Lodge, Regent's Park, London NW1 4RS England. LC HQ1064.G7. DD 362.6072041.

PERSPECTIVE ON AGING. V. 1- Spring 1972-. 0096-2740. Periodical. US. English. bm. 1828 L Street NW, Washington DC 20036. LC HQ1060. DD 301.43505. **NLM** W1 PE8705E.

PHYSICAL & OCCUPATIONAL THERAPY IN GERIATRICS. **VAT** Physical and Occupational Therapy in Geriatrics. Vol. 1, No. 1 (Fall 1980)-. 0270-3181. Periodical. US. English. qt. $102.00. Haworth Press, 28 East 22nd Street, New York NY 10010. **Tel** (212)228-2800. **Ed** Ellen Taira. **Ind/Abst** Electron. Commun. Abstr. J., ISMEC Bull., Pollut. Abstr. Indexes, Saf. Sci. Abstr. J., Excerpta Med., Cumul. Index Nurs. Allied Health Lit., Psychol. Abstr. LC RC952.A1. DD 615.82. **NLM** W1 PH683M. bk rev. adv acc. **Circ** 1,296. It is designed to provide a forum for all allied health professionals to share information, clinical expertise and research on therapeutic practice in geriatrics.

PROBIN HITAISHI. VFOAT Bangladesh Journal of Geriatrics, Prabina Hitaishi. Periodical. Bengali (articles also in English). qt. Bangladesh Association for the Aged, 78 Dhanmandi Residential Area Road No 5, Dacca Bangladesh. **NLM** W1 PR552G. Pakistan Journal of Geriatrics.

PROCEEDINGS OF THE AUSTRALIAN ASSOCIATION OF GERONTOLOGY. Main/Corp Australian Association of Gerontology. V. 1- 1969-. 0311-9297. Periodical. AT. English. ir. **NLM** W1.

RECENT ADVANCES IN GERIATRIC MEDICINE. VFOAT Geriatric Medicine. No. 1-. 0144-0519. Periodical. UK. English. ir. Churchill Livingstone Inc, 1560 Broadway, New York NY 10036. **Tel** (212)819-5400. **Ed** B Isaacs. **Ind/Abst** Chem. Abstr. **NLM** W1 RE105ULB. **CODEN** RAGMDK.

REPORT FROM THE WHITE HOUSE CONFERENCE ON AGING. Main/Conf White House Conference on Aging. Began with: No. 1 (April 1980). 0278-517X. Periodical. US. English. mo. The White House Conference on Aging, 330 Independence Avenue SW, Washington DC 20201. **NLM** W1 RE209BQC.

REPORT ON THE . . . ANNUAL MEETING OF THE NIA GERIATRIC MEDICINE ACADEMIC AWARDEES. 1st (June 16-17, 1980)-. US. English. an. National Institute of Aging, National Institutes of Health, Bethesda MD 20205. LC RC952.5. DD 618.9700711. **NLM** W1 RE212HD.

RESEARCH HIGHLIGHTS IN AGING. Main/Corp United States. National Institutes of Health. Center for Aging Research. 1959-. 0499-9797. Periodical. US. English. an. Natl Institutes of Health, Ctr Aging Research, Bethesda MD 20014. LC QP86. DD 612.67072.

RESEARCH ON AGING. V. 1- Mar. 1979-. 0164-0275. Periodical. US. English. qt. Sage Publications Inc, 275 South Beverly Drive, Beverly Hills CA 90212. **Ind/Abst** Excerpta Med., Sociol. Abstr., Soc. Sci. Citation Index. LC HQ1060. DD 301.4350973. **NLM** W1 RE232L.

RESEARCH SERIES - UNIVERSITY OF FLORIDA. CENTER FOR GERONTOLOGICAL STUDIES. (RESEARCH SERIES). Vol. 1-. 0740-0861. Monographic Series. US. English. University Presses of Florida, 15 NW 15th Street, Gainesville FL 32603. **NLM** W1 RE234VM.

REVIEW OF BIOLOGICAL RESEARCH IN AGING. Vol. 1-. 0736-5055. US. English. ir. Alan R Liss, 41 East 11 Street, New York NY 10003. Ed Morton Rothstein. **Ind/Abst** Biol. Abstr., Chem. Abstr. LC QP86. DD 599.0372. **NLM** W1 RE252N. **CODEN** RBRADC. A book series concerning the biological research in aging.

REVISTA ESPANOLA DE GERIATRIA Y GERONTOLOGIA. V. 15- Jan./Feb. 1980-. 0211-139X. Periodical. SP. Spanish. bm. Editorial Garsi, Londres 17, Madrid 28 Spain. **Ind/Abst** Excerpta Med. **NLM** W1 RE534G. Revista Espanola de Gerontologia y Geriatria, 0210-6175.

LA REVUE DE GERIATRIE. V. 1- Sept. 1976-. 0397-7927. Periodical. FR. French. mo. 20.00. Les Editions de la Vie Medicale, 133 Bis rue de l'Universite, 75007 Paris France. Tel 45.55.95.52. **Ind/Abst** Excerpta Med. **NLM** W1 RE778EN. Revue de Gerontologie d'Expression Francaise, 0035-2896.

ROMANIAN JOURNAL OF GERONTOLOGY AND GERIATRICS. V. 1, 1-. 0254-2307. English (articles also in French). sa. $56.00. Ilexim Press Department, PO Box 1-136-1-137, Bucharest Romania. **Ind/Abst** Excerpta Med., Chem. Abstr. **NLM** W1 RO327. **CODEN** RJGGDV.

SCRIPTUM GERIATRICUM. 0172-1364. Periodical. German. ir. **NLM** W3 SC65.

SPRINGER SERIES ON ADULTHOOD AND AGING. V. 1-. 0272-5835. Monographic Series. US. English. ir. Springer Publishing Company Inc, 536 Broadway, New York NY 10012. **Tel** (212)431-4370. **Ed** L F Jarvik and B D Starr. **NLM** W1 SP685N.

TOPICS IN GERIATRIC REHABILITATION. 0882-7524. Periodical. US. English. qt $60.00. Aspen Systems Corporation, 16792 Oakmont Avenue, Gaithersburg MD 20877.

TOPICS IN GERIATRICS. (TOPICS IN GERIATRICS : MASSACHUSETTS GENERAL HOSPITAL NEWSLETTER). Began with Vol. 1, No. 1 (May 1982). 0732-1139. Periodical. US. English. mo. $35.00. PSG Inc, c/o John Wright, 545 Great Road, Littleton MA 01460. **Tel** (617)486-8971. **Ed** Michael A Jenike. **NLM** W1 MA858V. **Circ** 900. Addresses the specific health care issues which can help in management of geriatric patients.

ZEITSCHRIFT FUR GERONTOLOGIE. Vol. 1- Jan./Feb. 1968-. 0044-281X. Periodical. GW. German. bm. $75.08. Dr Dietich Steinkopff Verlag, PO Box 11 10 08, 6100 Darmstadt 11 West Germany. **Tel** 06151-26538. **Ed** I Falck and U Lehr. **Ind/Abst** Life Sci. Collect., Excerpta Med., Index Med., Chem. Abstr., Psychol. Abstr., Soc. Sci. Citation Index, Sci. Cit. Index, Abr. Ed. LC RC952. **NLM** W1 ZE357T. **CODEN** ZGERAG. bk rev. adv acc. **Circ** 1,500. (ctrl). European journal for geriatrics and gerontology, regarding all disciplines.

ZFA. ZEITSCHRIFT FUR ALTERNSFORSCHUNG. Vol. 29- 1974-. Periodical. GE. articles in English or German. bm. $45.82. Kunst & Wissen Erich Bieber, Dufourstrasse 51, CH-8008 Zurich Switzerland. **Tel** 011-41-1-69 44 20. **Ind/Abst** Index Med. **NLM** W1 Z115. Zeitschrift fur Alternsforschung.

ZHONGHUA LAONIAN YIZAZHI. (CHUNG-HUA LAO NIEN I HSUEH TSA CHIH). (Feb. 1982)-. 0254-9026. Periodical. CH. Chinese. qt. $6.30. China Publication Centre, PO Box 2820, Beijing China. **NLM** W1 CH982KD.

GYNECOLOGY & OBSTETRICS

ACOG NEWSLETTER. VFOAT ACOG. **VAT** American College of Obstetricians and Gynecologists Newsletter. V. 1956-. 0400-048X. Periodical. US. English. mo. **NLM** W1 A103.

ACOG TECHNICAL BULLETIN. No. 1- Jan. 1965-. Periodical. US. English. **NLM** W1 A1136S. Index in first issue of next volume - loose - unpaged. (cum index).

ACTA OBSTETRICIA ET GYNECOLOGICA SCANDINAVICA. V. 4- 1926-. 0001-6349. Periodical. SW. English (German and French). ir. $99.00. Acta Obstetricia et Gynecologica Scandinavica, PO Box 443, S-901 09 Umea Sweden. **Ind/Abst** Life Sci. Collect., Pestdoc,

Medicine—Gynecology & Obstetrics

Ringdoc, Vetdoc, Excerpta Med., Biol. Abstr., Nucl. Sci. Abstr., Index Med., Chem. Abstr., Energy Res. Abstr., Sci. Cit. Index, Abr. Ed., Hospit. Lit. Index. **NLM** W1 AC8731. **CODEN** AOGSAE. (cum index). *Acta Gynecologica Scandinavica.*

ACTIVITES DE PROTECTION MATERNO-INFANTILE ET DE PLANIFICATION FAMILIALE : RAPPORT ANNUEL. **Main/Corp** Haiti (Republic). Division d'Hygiene Familiale. Unite de Statistiques. French. ir. **LC** RG963.H2. **DD** 362.1982.

ADVANCES IN FERTILITY RESEARCH. Vol. 1. 0732-8060. US. English. Raven Press, 1140 Avenue of the Americas, New York NY 10036. **Ind/Abst** Chem. Abstr. **NLM** W1 AD571P. **CODEN** ADFRDY.

ADVANCES IN INTERNATIONAL MATERNAL AND CHILD HEALTH. Series/Titl Oxford Medical Publications. Vol. 1-. 0262-8244. UK. English. an. $45.00. Oxford University Press, Journals Department/Walton Street, Oxford OX2 6DP England. **Tel** 0865/ 56767. Ed D B Jelliffe and E F P Jelliffe. **NLM** W1 AD653J.

ADVANCES IN PERINATAL MEDICINE. Vol. 1-. 0731-1400. US. English. ir. $35.00. Plenum Publishing Corp, 227 West 17th Street, New York NY 10011. Ed Aubrey Milunsky, Emanuel A Friedman and Louis Gluck. **Ind/Abst** Chem. Abstr. **DD** 618.32. **NLM** W1 AD73T. **CODEN** APMDD9.

AKUSERSTVO I GINEKOLOGIJA. (AKUSERSTVO I GINEKOLOGIIA). 1936-. 0300-9092. Periodical. UR. Russian. mo. $30.50. Victor Kamkin Inc (70011), 12224 Parklawn Drive, Rockville MD 20852. **Tel** (301)881-5973. **Ind/Abst** Excerpta Med., Index Med., Chem. Abstr. **NLM** W1 AK998. **CODEN** AKGIAO. *Zhurnal Akusherstva i Zhenskikh Boleznei, Ginekologiia i Akusherstva.*

AMERICAN BABY'S CHILDBIRTH EDUCATOR. VFOAT Childbirth Educator. Vol. 1, No. 1 (Fall 1981)-. 0279-490X. Periodical. US. English. qt. $10.00. Childbirth Educator, 575 Lexington Avenue, New York NY 10022. **Tel** (212)752-7005. Ed Marsha Rehns. bk rev. adv acc. **Circ** 22,000. (ctrl). Labor and birth, fetal development, pregnancy, child care, and teaching techniques for teachers of childbirth classes.

AMERICAN DIRECTORY OF OBSTETRICIANS AND GYNECOLOGISTS. 1st- Ed. US. English. be. American Directory of Obstetricians and Gynecologists, 5710 Kingston Pike, Knoxville TN 37919.

AMERICAN JOURNAL OF OBSTETRICS AND GYNECOLOGY. V. 1- Oct. 1920-. 0002-9378. Periodical. US. English. sm. $97.50. C V Mosby, c/o R K Kinnes, 11830 Westline Industrial Drive, St Louis MO 63146. **Tel** (314)872-8370. Ed John I Brewer, E J Quilligan and Frederick P Zuspan. **Ind/Abst** Life Sci. Collect., Pestdoc, Ringdoc, Vetdoc, Cumul. Index Nurs. Allied Health Lit., Excerpta Med., Energy Inf. Abstr., Environ. Abstr., Index Med., Int. Aerosp. Abstr., Biol. Abstr., Chem. Abstr., Bibliogr. Agric., Energy Res. Abstr., Sci. Cit. Index, Abr. Ed., Hospit. Lit. Index. **NLM** W1 AM496E. **CODEN** AJOGAH. (cum index). adv acc. **Circ** 21,006. Available on microfilm. Edited for physicians specializing in obstetrics and gynecology and those in general practice. Scientific material published represents original contributions. Clinical and investigative reports are also published. *American Journal of Obstetrics and Diseases of Women and Children.*

AMERICAN JOURNAL OF PERINATOLOGY. Vol. 1, No. 1 (Oct. 1983)-. 0735-1631. Periodical. US. English. qt. $50.00. Thieme-Stratton Inc, 381 Park Avenue South/Suite 1501, New York NY 10016. **Tel** (212)683-5088. Ed Peter A M Auld, Steven G Gabbe, Alfred N Krauss and Jennifer R Niebyl. **Ind/Abst** Index Med., Excerpta Med. **NLM** W1. adv acc. **Circ** 700. Topic-oriented journal for the practitioner specializing in gynecology and obstetrics and perinatal medicine.

AMERICAN JOURNAL OF REPRODUCTIVE IMMUNOLOGY AND MICROBIOLOGY. (AMERICAN JOURNAL OF REPRODUCTIVE IMMUNOLOGY AND MICROBIOLOGY : AJRIM). VFOAT AJRIM. Vol. 7, No. 1 (Jan. 1985)-. 8755-8920. Periodical. US. English. mo. $165.00 Domestic, $198.00 Foreign. Alan R Liss Inc, 150 Fifth Avenue, New York NY 10011. **Ind/Abst** Chem. Abstr., Curr. Contents. Life Sci., Index Med., Life Sci. Collect., Soc. Sci. Citation Index, Excerpta Med. **DD** 616. **NLM** W1. **CODEN** AJRMEK. *American Journal of Reproductive Immunology, 0271-7352.*

ANNALES CHIRURGIAE ET GYNAECOLOGIAE. See Medicine - Surgery.

ANNALI DI OSTETRICIA, GINECOLOGIA, MEDICINA PERINATALE. Yearly V. 93- Jan. 1972-. 0300-0087. Periodical. IT. Italian. bm. $38.61. Istituti Clinici d'Perfezionam, Via Daverio 6, 20122 Milano Italy. **Ind/Abst** Life Sci. Collect., Excerpta Med., Index Med., Chem. Abstr. **NLM** W1 AN501. **CODEN** AOGMAU. *Annali di Ostetricia E Ginecologia, 0003-4657.*

ARCHIVES OF ANDROLOGY. See Genealogy and Heraldry - Archives.

ARCHIVES OF GYNECOLOGY. See Genealogy and Heraldry - Archives.

ARCHIVIO DI OSTETRICIA E GINECOLOGIA. See Genealogy and Heraldry - Archives.

AUDIO-DIGEST. OBSTETRICS AND GYNECOLOGY. 0571-8635. Periodical. US. English. sm. $192.72. Audio-Digest Foundation, 1577 Chevy Chase Drive, Glendale CA 91206. **Tel** (213)245-8505. Ed Claron L Oakley. A twice-monthly interactive system of audio cassette postgraduate medical education, with each one-hour program eligible for two Category I credit hours.

AUSTRALIAN & NEW ZEALAND JOURNAL OF OBSTETRICS & GYNAECOLOGY. (AUSTRALIAN AND NEW ZEALAND JOURNAL OF OBSTETRICS AND GYNAECOLOGY). V. 1- March 1961-. 0004-8666. Periodical. AT. English. qt. 35.00 Domestic, 40.00 Foreign. Australian & New Zealand, 254 Albert Street, East Melbourne 3002 Victoria Australia. **Tel** 417-1699. Ed N A Beischer. **Ind/Abst** Life Sci. Collect., Excerpta Med., Chem. Abstr., Biol. Abstr., Nucl. Sci. Abstr., Index Med., Hospit. Lit. Index. **DD** 618.05. **NLM** W1 AU497. **CODEN** AZOGBS. bk rev. adv acc. **Circ** 3,000. (ctrl). The only Australasian journal specializing in this field, and the official organ of the Royal Australian College of Obstetricians and Gynaecologists.

AVANCES EN OBSTETRICIA Y GINECOLOGIA. 0210-7171. Periodical. Spanish. ir. Ed J Gonzalez-Merlo and I Burzaco. **NLM** W3 AV13.

BABY TALK (1977). (BABY TALK). Began with: Vol. 42, No. 4 (Apr. 1977)?. 0749-971X. Periodical. US. English. mo. $9.00. Blessing Corporation, 185 Madison Avenue, New York NY 10016. **Tel** (212)679-4400. Ed P D Irons. **DD** 649. adv acc. (ctrl). Information on pregnancy, infant care and child growth and development during the first two years of life. *New Baby Talk, 0364-1554.*

BERICHTE GYNAKOLOGIE, GEBURTSHILFE. VFOAT Gynaecology, Obstetrics. 118. V., No.1-. 0722-9852. Periodical. German (English). ir. Springer-Verlag New York Inc, 175 Fifth Avenue, New York NY 10010. **NLM** ZWP 100 B511. *Berichte uber die Gesamte Gynakologie und Geburtshilfe Sowie Deren Grenzgebiete, 0005-9064.*

BERICHTE UBER DIE GESAMTE GYNAKOLOGIE UND GEBURTSHILFE SOWIE DEREN GRENZGEBIETE CEASED. VFOAT Gynecology - Obstetrics. Began 1, 1923. Ceased in 1982. 0005-9064. Periodical. German. ir. **NLM** ZWP 100 B511. *Zentralblatts fur die Gesamte Gynaekologie Und Geburtshilfe.*

BIOLOGICAL RESEARCH IN PREGNANCY AND PERINATOLOGY. Vol. 4, No. 1 (1st Quarter 1983)-. 0724-438X. Periodical. English. qt. $76.00. Dustri-Verlag/Dr Karl Feistle, Bahnofstr 9, Postfach 49, D8024 Deisenhofen West Germany. **Tel** 089/613 50 41. **Ind/Abst** Excerpta Med., Index Med. **NLM** W1. *International Journal of Biological Research in Pregnancy, 0173-8593.*

BIOLOGY OF THE NEONATE. V. 15- 1970-. 0006-3126. Periodical. SZ. English (French and German). mo. 336.-. S Karger AG, PO Box, CH-4009 Basel Switzerland. **Tel** (061)39 08 80. Ed A Minkowski. **Ind/Abst** Life Sci. Collect., Excerpta Med., Nucl. Sci. Abstr., Biol. Abstr., Chem. Abstr., Bibliogr. Agric., Index Med., Sci. Cit. Index, Abr. Ed. **LC** RJ251. **DD** 612.65205. **NLM** W1 BI852P. **CODEN** BNEOBV. adv acc. Presents laboratory findings from both human and animal studies covering the physiological and biochemical events taking place during the period leading up to and immediately following birth, whether full-term or premature. *Biologia Neonatorum.*

BIRTH (BERKELEY, CALIF.). (BIRTH). Vol. 9 1 (Spring 1982)-. 0730-7659. Periodical. US. English. qt. $20.00. Blackwell Scientific Publications Inc, 52 Beacon Street, Boston MA 02108. **Tel** (617)720-0761. Ed Madeleine H Shearer. **Ind/Abst** Life Sci. Collect., Int. Nurs. Index, Cumul. Index Nurs. Allied Health Lit., Curr. Contents, Curr. Contents, Soc. Behav. Sci., Int. Nurs. Index, Psychol. Abstr., Soc. Sci. Citation Index. **LC** RG651. **DD** 618.1005. **NLM** W1 BI963B. bk rev. adv acc. **Circ** 6,000. Issues in perinatal care and education such as obstetric practices, childbirth, parent education, contraception and abortion, breastfeeding, and family life. *Birth and the Family Journal, 0098-860X.*

BIRTH PSYCHOLOGY BULLETIN. Vol. 1, No. 1 (Jan. 1980)-. 0734-3124. Periodical. US. English. sa. $8.00 Domestic, $9.00 Foreign. Association for Birth Psychology, 444 East 82nd Street, New York NY 10028. **Ind/Abst** Psychol. Abstr. **LC** RG658. **DD** 618.20019.

BREAST, DISEASES OF THE BREAST CEASED. Began with 1, Oct/Dec. 1975. Ceased in 1983. 0361-3828. Periodical. US. English. qt. $25.00. CPC Communications, PO Box 4010, 55 Holly Hill Lane, Greenwich CT 06830. **Tel** (203)661-0600. **Ind/Abst** Excerpta Med., Chem. Abstr. **LC** RC280.B8. **DD** 618.19005. **NLM** W1 BR192. **CODEN** BDBRD5.

BRIEFS (THOROFARE, N.J.) CEASED. (BRIEFS). Began in Dec. 1936. Ceased with V. 47, No. 10 Dec. 1983. 0007-0068. Periodical. US. English. mo. **NLM** W1 BR205.

BRITISH JOURNAL OF OBSTETRICS AND GYNAECOLOGY. V. 82- Jan. 1975-. 0306-5456. Periodical. UK. English. mo. 51 Domestic, 107.50 Foreign. Blackwell Scientific Publishing Ltd, PO Box 88, Oxford OX2 0EL England. **Tel** 0865 240201. Ed F Hytten. **Ind/Abst** Life Sci. Collect., Pestdoc, Ringdoc, Vetdoc, Excerpta Med., Index Med., Biol. Abstr., Chem. Abstr., Sci. Cit. Index, Abr. Ed., Hospit. Lit. Index. **NLM** W1 BR586. **CODEN** BJOGAS. bk rev. adv acc. **Circ** 4,700. An international journal aimed at both the practicing clinician and research scientist. *Journal of Obstetrics and Gynaecology of the British Commonwealth, 0022-3204.*

BUCHEREI DES FRAUENARZTES. 0068-337X. GW. German. ir. Ferdinand Enke Verlag, 1-1 Postfach 1304, D7000 Stuttgart 1 West Germany. **Tel** (0711)8931-0. Ed G Martius and M Schmidt-Gollwitzer. Deals with practical and clinical relevant subjects from the whole subject of gynecology and obstetrics. The volumes are supplements of the journal "Zeitschrift fur Geburtshilfe und Perinatologie".

THE BULLETIN OF THE KANDANG KERBAU HOSPITAL, SINGAPORE, MALAYSIA. Began in 1956?. Periodical. English. sa. **NLM** W1 BU854HB.

BULLETIN OFFICIEL DE LA SOCIETE FRANCAISE DE PSYCHO-PROPHYLAXIE OBSTETRIQUE. No. 14- June 1963-. Periodical. FR. French. an. $6.66. Societe International Psycho- Prophylaxie Obstetrical, 31 rue Street, Guillaume Paris 7E France. **Tel** 548 59 93. **NLM** W1. *Bulletin Trimestriel - Societe Francaise de Psycho-Prophylaxie Obstetrique.*

BULLETIN OFFICIEL DE LA SOCIETE INTERNATIONALE DE PSYCHO-PROPHYLAXIE OBSTETRICALE. V. 1- Oct./Dec. 1959-. 0037-9468. Periodical. FR. French (summaries of articles in English, Spanish, and German). Ed de Medical Pratique, 31 rue Louis Armad, 92600 Paris France. **NLM** W1 BU901J.

THE CERVIX AND THE LOWER FEMALE GENITAL TRACT. V. 1, No. 1 (Jan.-April 1983)-. Periodical. English (Italian). ir. $20.00. **NLM** W1.

CESKOSLOVENSKA GYNAEKOLOGIE. V. 1- Jan. 1936-. 0374-6852. Periodical. CS. Czech. ir. $72.30. Artia, Ve Smeckach 30, PO Box 790, Praha 1 Czechoslovakia. **Ind/Abst** Excerpta Med., Index Med. **NLM** W1 CE885F. *Rozhledy v Chirurgii a Gynaekologii.*

CHILDBIRTH ALTERNATIVES QUARTERLY. 0272-6319. Periodical. US. English. qt. $10.00. Childbirth Alternatives, c/o Janet Isaacs Ashford, 14230 Elva Avenue, Saratoga CA

95070. **Tel** (408)867-7022. **Ed** Janet Isaacs Ashford. bk rev. adv acc. **Circ** 500. Articles, news, and reviews on home birth midwifery, consumer advocacy, and issues in maternal/child health.

CHUNG-HUA FU CHAN KO TSA CHIH. **VFOAT** Zhonghua Fu-Chanke Zhazhi, Chinese Journal of Obstetrics and Gynecology. 1- 1953?-. 0529-567X. Periodical. CC. Chinese (tables of contents and some abstracts also in English). bm. $13.50. China Publication Centre, PO Box 2820, Beijing China. **Ind/Abst** Index Med., Chem. Abstr. **NLM** W1 CH982. **CODEN** CHFCA2.

CLINICA E INVESTIGACION EN GINECOLOGIA Y OBSTETRICIA. 0210-573X. Periodical. SP. Spanish. bm. $25.00. Ediciones Doyma SA, Travesera de Gracia 17-21, 08021 Barcelona Spain. **Ind/Abst** Excerpta Med. **NLM** W1 CL366T.

CLINICA GINECOLOGICA. (LA CLINICA GINECOLOGICA). V. 1- 1959-. 0529-9608. Periodical. IT. Italian. bm. Clinica Ginecologica, Via Del Plebiscito 632, Catania Italy. **Ind/Abst** Index Med.

CLINICAL AND EXPERIMENTAL HYPERTENSION. PART B, HYPERTENSION IN PREGNANCY. **VFOAT** Hypertension in Pregnancy. V. B1, No. 1 (1982)-. 0730-0085. Periodical. US. English. qt. $139.00. Marcel Dekker Inc, PO Box 11305 Church Street Station, New York NY 10249. **Tel** (212)696-9000. **Ed** Frederick P Zuspan, E Malcolm Symonds. **Ind/Abst** Life Sci. Collect., Excerpta Med., Chem. Abstr., Pestdoc, Ringdoc, Vetdoc, Biol. Abstr. **LC** RG580.H9. **DD** 618.3. **NLM** W1 CL658C. **CODEN** CEHBDP. bk rev. adv acc. (ctrl). Covers all the important and vital issues relating to the safe and effective management of all forms of pregnancy hypertension: Beta Blocker therapy, reciprocal embryo transfers, heart size, etc. *Clinical and Experimental Hypertension, 0148-3927.*

CLINICAL AND EXPERIMENTAL OBSTETRICS & GYNECOLOGY. **VAT** Clinical and Experimental Obstetrics and Gynecology. V. 1- Jan. 1974-. 0390-6663. Periodical. English. qt. $85.00. SOG/SRL, Galleria Storione 2A, 35128 Padua Italy. **Tel** (049)36505. **Ed** A Onnis. **Ind/Abst** Excerpta Med., Index Med., Biol. Abstr., Chem. Abstr. **NLM** W1 CL664C. **CODEN** CEOGA4. bk rev. adv acc. **Circ** 500. (ctrl). Experimental and clinical research in every field of obstetrics and gynecology. Neonatology-Family Planning.

CLINICAL OBSTETRICS AND GYNECOLOGY. V. 1- Mar. 1958-. 0009-9201. Periodical. US. English. qt. $83.00. Lippincott/Harper, 2350 Virginia Avenue, Hagerstown MD 21740. **Tel** (800)242-7737. **Ind/Abst** Life Sci. Collect., Excerpta Med., Index Med., Biol. Abstr., Chem. Abstr., Energy Res. Abstr., Hospit. Lit. Index, Sci. Cit. Index, Abr. Ed. **LC** RG101. **DD** 618.05. **NLM** W1 CL742. **CODEN** COGYAK.

CLINICAL REPRODUCTION AND FERTILITY. Vol. 1, No. 1 (Mar. 1982)-. 0725-556X. Periodical. UK. English. bm. $116.00. Blackwell Scientific Publications Ltd, 107 Barry Street, Carlton Victoria Australia. **Ind/Abst** Excerpta Med., Index Med., Chem. Abstr. **NLM** W1 CL774F. **CODEN** CRFEDD.

CLINICS IN OBSTETRICS AND GYNAECOLOGY. V. 1- April 1974-. 0306-3356. Monographic Series. UK. English. ty. $60.00. W B Saunders Co, West Washington Square, Philadelphia PA 19105. **Tel** (215)574-3395. **Ed** Barbara Conover and Geoffrey Smaldon. **Ind/Abst** Life Sci. Collect., Excerpta Med., Index Med., Biol. Abstr., Hospit. Lit. Index. **NLM** W1 CL831CE. **CODEN** COBGBA. **Circ** 3,000. Practical updates for the clinician on the latest advances in OB/GYN-written by experts in the field.

COLLECTED LETTERS OF THE INTERNATIONAL CORRESPONDENCE SOCIETY OF OBSTETRICIANS, GYNECOLOGISTS. **Main/Corp** International Correspondence Society of Obstetricians and Gynecologists. 1960. 0443-9058. Periodical. US. English. sm. $57.00. International Correspondence Society of Obstetricians & Gynecologists, PO Box 947, Lakeland FL 33802. **Tel** (813)688-2157. **Ed** James M Ingram. **NLM** W1 CO169D. **Circ** 3,000. Ob/Gyn medical letters.

COLPOSCOPY & GYNECOLOGIC LASER SURGERY. *See* Medicine - Surgery.

CONGENITAL MALFORMATIONS SURVEILLANCE. 0092-5594. Periodical. US. English. qt. US Department of Health and Human Services, Public Health Service, Centers for Disease Control, Atlanta GA 30333. **Ind/Abst** Am. Stat. Index. **LC** RG627. **DD** 616.04305. **NLM** W2 A C15C. *Metropolitan Atlanta Congenital Defects Program, 0190-2504.*

CONTEMPORARY OB/GYN. **VAT** Contemporary Obstetrics-Gynecology. V. 1- Jan. 1973-. 0090-3159. Periodical. US. English. $48.00. Medical Economics Inc, 680 Kinderkamack Road, Oradell NJ 07649. **Tel** (201)262-3030. **Ed** James Swan. **Ind/Abst** Life Sci. Collect., Excerpta Med., Energy Inf. Abstr., Environ. Abstr. **LC** RG1. **DD** 618.05. **NLM** W1 CO769NK. adv acc. **Circ** 31,000. (ctrl). Original articles covering latest clinical/socioeconomic developments affecting practice of obstetrics/gynecology with emphasis on problems of diagnosis treatment and delivery of care.

CONTRIBUTIONS TO GYNECOLOGY AND OBSTETRICS. V. 1- 1976-. 0304-4246. Monographic Series. English. ir. S Karger Ag, PO Box, CH-4009 Basel Switzerland. **Tel** 061-39 08 80. **Ed** P J Keller. **Ind/Abst** Life Sci. Collect., Excerpta Med., Index Med., Biol. Abstr., Chem. Abstr. **NLM** W1 CO778RG. **CODEN** CGOBD6. Original data and reviews of current information on problems in all fields of gynecology. *Fortschritte der Geburtshilfe und Gynakologie.*

CORE JOURNALS IN OBSTETRICS/GYNECOLOGY. V. 1- 1977-. 0376-5059. Periodical. English. mo. $52.00. Excerpta Medica BV, 3131 Princeton Pike, Princeton NJ 08648. **Tel** (609)896-9450. **Ind/Abst** Chem. Abstr. **NLM** ZWP 100 C797. **CODEN** CJOGD8.

CURRENT LITERATURE REVIEW IN OBSTETRICS & GYNECOLOGY. **VFOAT** Current Literature Review in Obstetrics and Gynecology. 1980-. 0733-8643. US. English. an. Appleton-Century-Crofts, 25 Van Zant Street, East Norwalk CT 06855.

CURRENT OBSTETRIC & GYNECOLOGIC DIAGNOSIS & TREATMENT. **Series/Titl** Concise Medical Library for Practitioner and Student. **VAT** Current Obstetric and Gynecologic Diagnosis and Treatment. 1st- Ed. 0197-582X. US. English. be. $26.50. Lange Medical Publications, Drawer L, Los Altos CA 94023. **Tel** (415)948-4526. **Ed** Ralph C Benson. **NLM** W1 CU799G. Discusses basic information and recent developments affecting the diagnosis and treatment of all diseases and disorders of women and of the female generative organs.

CURRENT PROBLEMS IN OBSTETRICS AND GYNECOLOGY *CEASED.* **VFOAT** CPO. V. 1, Sept. 1977. Ceased with V. 7. 0147-1988. Monographic Series. US. English. mo. $65.00. Yearbook Medical Publishers, 35 East Wacker Drive, Chicago IL 60601. **Tel** (312)726-9733. **LC** UNC. **DD** 618. **NLM** W1 CU804NG.

CURRENT THERAPY OF INFERTILITY. 1982-83-. Periodical. US. English. be. B C Decker Inc, 3 Belmont Circle, Trenton NJ 08618. **Ed** Celso-Ramon Garcia. **NLM** W1.

DES LITIGATION REPORTER. *See* Law.

DEVELOPMENTAL PHARMACOLOGY AND THERAPEUTICS. *See* Pharmacy.

DEVELOPMENTS IN OBSTETRICS AND GYNECOLOGY. 0167-8302. US. English. ir. Kluwer Boston Inc, 190 Old Derby Street, Hingham MA 02043. **Ind/Abst** Chem. Abstr. **CODEN** DOGYDY.

DIRECTORY - AMERICAN SOCIETY FOR PSYCHOPROPHYLAXIS IN OBSTETRICS. *See* Yearbooks, Almanacs, Directories.

DRUGS IN OBSTETRICS/GYNECOLOGY. **Series/Titl** PRM : Physicians' Reference Manuals. No. 1 (1983)-. 0824-1694. Periodical. CN. English. sa. Free. Drugs in Obstetrics/Gynecology, c/o STA Communications 63 Place Frontenac, Pointe-Claire Quebec H9R 4Z7 Canada. **DD** 618. (ctrl).

EARLY HUMAN DEVELOPMENT. V. 1- June 1977-. 0378-3782. Periodical. English. bm. $97.93. Elsevier Science Publishers BV, PO Box 1527 Biomedical Division, 1000 BM Amsterdam Netherlands. **Tel** (020)5803911. **Ed** John Dobbing. **Ind/Abst** Life Sci. Collect., Excerpta Med., Cumul. Index Nurs. Allied Health Lit., Index Med., Biol. Abstr., Chem. Abstr., Psychol. Abstr. **LC** RG600. **DD** 618.3005. **NLM** W1 EA753. **CODEN** EHDEDN. bk rev. adv acc. **Circ** 350. The journal emphasizes continuum of fetal life, the problems of the perinatal period and aspects of postnatal growth.

ELEVAGE ET INSEMINATION. (ELEVAGE INSEMINATION). Periodical. FR. French. bm. Union Natl de Coop d'Elevage, 149 rue de Bercy, 75579 Paris France Cedex 12. **Tel** 346-12-20. **Ind/Abst** Bibliogr. Agric. **NLM** W1 EL454B.

ENDOMETRIUM. 1976-. 0145-9937. US. English. an. Scientia Press, 11071 Delmar Avenue, Richland MI 49083. **LC** RG316. **DD** 618.14. **NLM** ZWP 400 E56.

EUROPEAN JOURNAL OF GYNAECOLOGICAL ONCOLOGY. Vol. 1, No. 1-. 0392-2936. Periodical. IT. English. ty. $40.96. S.O.G S.R.L., Galleria Storione 2A, 35128 Padua Italy. **Tel** (049) 36505. **Ed** A Onnis. **Ind/Abst** Excerpta Med., Index Med., Biol. Abstr. **NLM** W1 EU72DF. **CODEN** EJGODE. bk rev. adv acc. **Circ** 500. (ctrl). Clinical and experimental research in the field of gynecological oncology with particular reference to multimodality approach to the treatment of cancer and clinical treatment.

EUROPEAN JOURNAL OF OBSTETRICS, GYNECOLOGY AND REPRODUCTIVE BIOLOGY. V. 3- 1973-. 0301-2115. Periodical. NE. English. bm. Elsevier Science Publishers, PO Box 211, 1000 AE Amsterdam Netherlands. **Tel** (020)5803911. **Ind/Abst** Life Sci. Collect., Excerpta Med., Index Med., Biol. Abstr., Chem. Abstr., Sci. Cit. Index, Abr. Ed. **NLM** W1 EU72DK. **CODEN** EOGRAL. *European Journal of Obstetrics and Gynecology, 0028-2243.*

EXCERPTA MEDICA. SECTION 10. OBSTETRICS AND GYNECOLOGY. *See* Indexes/Abstracts.

FELDSER I AKUSERKA. (FELDSHER I AKUSHERKA). Began in 1940. 0014-9772. Periodical. UR. Russian. mo. $15.50. Victor Kamkin Inc (71021), 12224 Parklawn Drive, Rockville MD 20852. **Tel** (301)881-5973. **Ind/Abst** Int. Nurs. Index.

THE FEMALE PATIENT. V. 1- Feb. 1976-. 0364-1198. Periodical. US. English. mo. $45.00. PW Communications Inc, 400 Plaza Drive, Secaucus NJ 07094. **Tel** (201)865-7500. **LC** RG1. **DD** 618.1005. **NLM** W1 FE543.

FERTILITY AND STERILITY. V. 1- Jan. 1950-. 0015-0282. Periodical. US. English. mo. $40.00 US, $47.00 Foreign. American Fertility Society, 1608 13th Avenue South/Suite 101, Birmingham AL 35205. **Ind/Abst** Life Sci. Collect., Pestdoc, Ringdoc, Vetdoc, Excerpta Med., Energy Inf. Abstr., Environ. Abstr., Int. Aerosp. Abstr., Chem. Abstr., Biol. Abstr., Nucl. Sci. Abstr., Index Med., Bibliogr. Agric., Energy Res. Abstr. **LC** RC889. **DD** 616.69. **NLM** W1 FE839. **CODEN** FESTAS. (cum index).

FERTILITY OF AMERICAN WOMEN . . . ADVANCE REPORT. **Series/Titl** Current Population Reports. Series P-20. Began with June 1977. US. English. an. Superintendent of Documents, US Government Printing Office, Washington DC 20402. *Prospects for American Fertility.*

FORTSCHRITTE DER FERTILITATSFORSCHUNG. 0344-6204. Monographic Series. German. ir. **NLM** W1 FO853S.

FRIEND INDEED. (A FRIEND INDEED : FOR WOMEN IN THE PRIME OF LIFE). Vol. 1, No. 1 (Apr. 1984)-. 0824-1961. Periodical. CN. English (French). mo. $18.00. A Friend Indeed, 4180 Wilson Avenue, Montreal Quebec H4A 2T9 Canada. **Tel** (514)481-9886. **Ed** Janine O'Leary Cobb. **DD** 618.175005. bk rev. **Circ** 1,800. Newsletter of information, support and exchange for women during menopause and/or midlife.

FRP REPORT. **VFOAT** F.R.P. Report. **VAT** Fertility Research Project Report. Began with No. 1 (Jan. 1975). 0253-5475. Monographic Series. English. ir. **DD** 363.96. **NLM** W1 FR946I.

GEBURTSHILFE UND FRAUENHEILKUNDE. (GEBURTSHILFE UND FRAUENHEILKUNDE : ERGEBNISSE DER FORSCHUNG FUR DIE PRAXIS). Vol. 1-. 0016-5751. Periodical. GW. German (summaries in English and Spanish). mo. $105.00. Georg Thieme Verlag, PO Box 732, Herdweg 63, D7000 Stuttgart 1 West Germany. **Tel** (212)683-5088. **Ind/Abst** Life Sci. Collect., Pestdoc, Ringdoc, Vetdoc, Excerpta Med., Index Med., Chem. Abstr., Energy Res. Abstr., Sci. Cit. Index, Abr. Ed. **NLM** W1 GE103. **CODEN** GEFRA2.

GENESIS (WASHINGTON, D.C.). (GENESIS). 0744-0596. Periodical. US. English. bm. $30.00. Genesis, 1840 Wilson Boulevard, Arlington VA 22201. **Tel** (703)524-7802. **Ed** Alice Berman. bk rev. adv acc. **Circ** 6,200. (ctrl). Membership magazine of

Medicine—Gynecology & Obstetrics

ASPO/Lamaze. Serves to keep childbirth educators, physicians and parents informed regarding the world of childbirth, child health and maternal health.

GINECOLOGIA Y OBSTETRICIA DE MEXICO. V. 1- Jan./March 1946-. 0300-9041. Periodical. MX. Spanish. mo. $80.00. Revista Medica Mensual, Amsterdam No 214-PH2, Col Hipodromo 06100 Mexico DF. Tel 564-54-63. Ed Luis Ricaud Rothiot. Ind/Abst Excerpta Med., Index Med., Chem. Abstr. NLM W1 GI214. CODEN GOMEAY. adv acc. Circ 3,000. (ctrl). We publish articles in cardiovascular diseases, geriatrics, endocrinology, preservatives, etc. All in relation with gynecology and obstetrics.

GINEKOLOGIA POLSKA. SUPLEMENT. No. 1- 1972-. Periodical. Polish. ir. NLM W1 GI212U.

GYNAKOLOGISCHE RUNDSCHAU. V. 1- 1964-. 0017-6001. Periodical. German (French). qt. 154.-. S Karger AG, PO Box, CH-4009 Basel Switzerland. Tel (061)39 08 80. Ed M Berger, E Gitsch and H A Hirsch. Ind/Abst Life Sci. Collect., Index Med., Biol. Abstr., Curr. Contents. NLM W1 GY555N. CODEN GYRUA7. Index published separately - free - automatically sent. adv acc. Microfilm, microfiche. Selected original works and praxis-oriented studies to specific topics of obstetrics and gynecology-important works from international journals are discussed-several supplements per year with reports on conventions.

GYNECOLOGIC AND OBSTETRIC INVESTIGATION. V. 9-. 0378-7346. Periodical. SZ. English. mo. 154.00. S Karger AG, PO Box, CH-4009 Basel Switzerland. Tel (061)39 08 80. Ed G Zador. Ind/Abst Life Sci. Collect., Excerpta Med., Index Med., Biol. Abstr., Chem. Abstr., Sci. Cit. Index, Abr. Ed. NLM W1 GY556U. CODEN GOBIDS. adv acc. Reports selected experimental and clinical investigations in all fields related to gynecology, obstetrics and reproduction. *Gynecologic Investigation, 0017-5986.*

GYNECOLOGIC ONCOLOGY. See Medicine - Neoplasma, Neoplastic.

HEALTH CARE FOR WOMEN INTERNATIONAL. Vol. 5, No. 1-3-. 0739-9332. Periodical. US. English. bm. $56.00. Hemisphere Publishing Corp, 1010 Vermont Avenue NW/Suite 612, Washington DC 20005. Tel (202)783-3958. Ed Phyllis Stern. Ind/Abst Cumul. Index Nurs. Allied Health Lit. DD 362. NLM W1. CODEN HCWIDQ. bk rev. adv acc. Circ 880. Interdisciplinary journal covering a wide variety of clinical and theoretical women's medical and psychological health issues. *Issues in Health Care of Women, 0161-5246.*

HEALTHRIGHT. See Birth Control.

HUMAN REPRODUCTIVE MEDICINE. V. 1-. 0165-7100. Monographic Series. English. ir. Elsevier North-Holland Inc, 52 Vanderbilt Avenue, New York NY 10017. Ed S E Hafez. Ind/Abst Chem. Abstr. LC UNC. NLM W1 HU462. CODEN HRMEDZ.

ICEA NEWS : OFFICIAL PUBLICATION OF THE INTERNATIONAL CHILDBIRTH EDUCATION ASSOCIATION. VFOAT I.C.E.A. News. VAT International Childbirth Education Association News. US. English. qt. International Childbirth Education Association, PO Box 20048, Milwaukee WI 55420. Tel (612)881-9194. NLM W1 I213M.

ICRDB CANCERGRAM. GYNECOLOGIC TUMORS: DIAGNOSIS, TREATMENT. See Medicine - Neoplasma, Neoplastic.

INFECTIOUS DISEASE LETTERS FOR OBSTETRICS-GYNECOLOGY. (INFECTIOUS DISEASE LETTERS FOR OBSTETRICS, GYNECOLOGY). V. 1- July 1979-. 0196-500X. Periodical. US. English. mo. $36.00. Infectious Disease Letter, 3003 SW First Way, Gainesville FL 32601. Ed G R G Monif. NLM W1 IN406I. Circ 1,200. (ctrl). Latest medical information in obstetrics and gynecology.

INFERTILITY. V. 1-. 0160-7626. Periodical. US. English. qt. $20.00. Marcel Dekker Inc, 270 Madison Avenue, New York NY 10016. Ind/Abst Excerpta Med., Biol. Abstr., Chem. Abstr. LC RC889. DD 618.178005. NLM W1 IN408K. CODEN INFEDH.

L'INSEMINATION ARTIFICIELLE EN FRANCE. VFOAT Elevage Insemination. 1967-. Periodical. French. ir.

INTERNATIONAL JOURNAL OF FERTILITY. V. 1- Oct./Dec. 1955-. 0020-725X. Periodical. US. English (summaries in Spanish, and French). qt $32.00. International Journal of Fertility, 112-44 69th Street, Forest Hill NY 11375. Tel (718)544-7599. Ed Maxwell Roland. Ind/Abst Life Sci. Collect., Pestdoc, Ringdoc, Vetdoc, Excerpta Med., Energy Inf. Abstr., Environ. Abstr., Index Med., Biol. Abstr., Chem. Abstr., Bibliogr. Agric., Sci. Cit. Index, Abr. Ed. LC QP251. DD 612.6. NLM W1 IN766J. CODEN INJFA3. bk rev. adv acc. Circ 26,000. (ctrl). Field of reproduction, fertility and sterility.

INTERNATIONAL JOURNAL OF GYNAECOLOGY AND OBSTETRICS. (INTERNATIONAL JOURNAL OF GYNAECOLOGY & OBSTETRICS). V. 7- 1969-. 0020-7292. Periodical. US. English. ir. Elsevier Scientific Publishers of Ireland Ltd, PO Box 85, Limerick Ireland. Tel (919)549-0517. Ind/Abst Life Sci. Collect., Excerpta Med., Index Med., Biol. Abstr., Chem. Abstr., Energy Res. Abstr., Sci. Cit. Index, Abr. Ed., Hospit. Lit. Index. NLM W1 IN766T. CODEN IJGOAL.

INTERNATIONAL JOURNAL OF GYNECOLOGICAL PATHOLOGY. See Medicine - Pathology.

IRCS MEDICAL SCIENCE. REPRODUCTION, OBSTETRICS AND GYNECOLOGY. (IRCS MEDICAL SCIENCE : REPRODUCTION, OBSTETRICS AND GYNECOLOGY). VFOAT Reproduction, Obstetrics and Gynecology. V. 3- Jan. 1975-. 0305-6929. Periodical. UK. English. mo. $120.00. IRCS Medical Science, PO Box 500/St Leonards House, Lancaster LA1 1PF England. Tel (0524) 68116. Ed S Johnson. bk rev. Publishes results of original research into all aspects of reproduction, both clinical and experimental, within weeks of completion. Papers fully refereed. *Research on Reproduction, Obstetrics and Gynecology, 0305-2915.*

JOGN NURSING. See Medicine - Nursing.

JORNAL BRASILEIRO DE GINECOLOGIA. VAT JBG. V. 69- Jan. 1970-. 0368-1416. Periodical. Portuguese. ir. Ind/Abst Biol. Abstr. NLM W1 JO193P. CODEN JBGCA8. *Anais Brasileiros de Ginecologia.*

JOURNAL DE GYNECOLOGIE, OBSTETRIQUE ET BIOLOGIE DE LA REPRODUCTION. V. 1- Jan./Feb. 1972-. 0368-2315. Periodical. French. ir. Masson Publishing USA Inc, 211 East 43rd Street/Room 1306, New York NY 10017. Tel (212)370-1937. Ind/Abst Life Sci. Collect., Excerpta Med., Biol. Abstr., Chem. Abstr., Index Med. NLM W1 JO308. CODEN JGOBAC. *Gynecologie et Obstetrique, 0017-601X; Bulletin de la Federation des Societes de Gynecologie et d'Obstetrique de Langue Francaise, 0046-3515.*

JOURNAL OF IN VITRO FERTILIZATION AND EMBRYO TRANSFER. (JOURNAL OF IN VITRO FERTILIZATION AND EMBRYO TRANSFER : IVF). VFOAT IVF. Vol. 1, No. 1 (Mar. 1984)-. 0740-7769. Periodical. US. English. qt. $80.00. Plenum Publishing Corporation, 233 Spring Street, New York NY 10013. LC RG135. DD 618.178. NLM W1. CODEN JFETDC.

JOURNAL OF NURSE-MIDWIFERY. See Medicine - Nursing.

JOURNAL OF OBSTETRICS AND GYNAECOLOGY. Vol. 1, No. 1 (Aug. 1980)-. 0144-3615. Periodical. UK. English. qt. 25.00 Domestic, 32.00 Foreign. John Wright & Sons Ltd, 823-825 Bath Road, Bristol B54 5NW England. Tel (617)486-8971. Ed D F Hawkins. Ind/Abst Excerpta Med., Chem. Abstr. NLM W1 JO798M. CODEN JOGYDW. bk rev. adv acc. Provides an international arena for original material relevant to the entire field of obstetrics and gynecology, from laboratory research to clinical reports.

JOURNAL OF OBSTETRICS AND GYNAECOLOGY OF INDIA. Began publication in 1951. 0022-3190. Periodical. II. English. bm. $35.00. Asia Books and Periodicals Company, 11 Darya Ganju, New Delhi 110002 India. Ind/Abst Life Sci. Collect., Chem. Abstr. NLM W1 JO799. CODEN JOBYA4.

JOURNAL OF PAEDIATRICS, OBSTETRICS, AND GYNAECOLOGY. Periodical. English. ir. $42.00. NLM W1.

JOURNAL OF PERINATAL MEDICINE. Began with Vol. 1, published in 1973. 0300-5577. Periodical. GW. English (with summaries in German and French). bm. $120.00. Walter de Gruyter Inc, 200 Saw Mill River Road, Hawthorne NY 10532. Tel (914)747-0110. Ed J W Dudenhausen. Ind/Abst Life Sci. Collect., Excerpta Med., Index Med., Biol. Abstr., Chem. Abstr., Sci. Cit. Index, Abr. Ed., Hospit. Lit. Index. NLM W1 JO828I. CODEN JPEMAO. adv acc. Circ 2,000. The journal features contributions from specialists worldwide in this new and developing field of perinatal medicine.

JOURNAL OF PERINATOLOGY. (JOURNAL OF PERINATOLOGY : OFFICIAL JOURNAL OF THE CALIFORNIA PERINATAL ASSOCIATION). Vol. 4, No. 3 (Summer 1984)-. 0743-8346. Periodical. US. English. qt. $20.00 Includes Subscription to Quarterly: Periscope. Sheridan Press, PO Box 465, Hanover PA 17331. DD 618. NLM W1. *Journal of the California Perinatal Association, 0733-334X.*

JOURNAL OF PSYCHOSOMATIC OBSTETRICS AND GYNAECOLOGY. Vol. 1, No. 1 (May 1982)-. Periodical. English. ir. $74.48. Elsevier Science Publishers, PO Box 211, 1000 AE Amsterdam The Netherlands. Ind/Abst Excerpta Med. NLM W1 JO858VF.

JOURNAL OF REPRODUCTIVE MEDICINE. V. 2- Jan. 1969-. 0024-7758. Periodical. US. English. mo. $85.00. Journal of Reproductive Medicine, 2 Jacklynn Court, St Louis MO 63132. Tel (314)991-4440. Ed George L Wied. Ind/Abst Life Sci. Collect., Excerpta Med., Chem. Abstr., Index Med., Biol. Abstr., Energy Res. Abstr., Sci. Cit. Index, Abr. Ed., Hospit. Lit. Index. LC RG1. DD 618.05. NLM W1 JO868S. CODEN JRPMAP. bk rev. adv acc. Circ 26,500. (ctrl). Clinical obstetrics and gynecology. Original articles and review articles including invitational symposia with in-depth coverage of a clinical topic. *Lying-In, 0096-7033.*

KEADAAN KESEHATAN ANAK DAN IBU : HASIL SURVEI SOSIAL EKONOMI NASIONAL. VFOAT Health Conditions of the Children and Mothers : Results of National Socio-Economic Survey. English (Indonesian). ir. Biro Pusat Statistik, Jl Dr Sutomo No 8, Jakarta Indonesia. Tel 372808. LC RG965.I5. DD 362.19820099598. bk rev. adv acc. (ctrl).

KVINNOVETENSKAPLIG TIDSKRIFT. V. 1, No. 1-. 0348-8365. Periodical. Swedish. ir. 90.00. Kvinnovetenskaplig Tidskrift, Klostergatan 9, 222 22 Lund Sweden.

THE LACTATION REVIEW. V. 1- 1976-. 0362-3173. Periodical. US. English. $35.00. Human Lactation Center, 666 Sturges Highway, Westport CT 06880. Tel (203)259-5995. Ed Dana Raphael. NLM W1 LA245. bk rev. adv acc. Circ 5,000. Books and research articles on breastfeeding, infant feeding practices, family planning, women in development, nutrition and cultural patterns.

LAMAZE IN ONTARIO. 0714-3680. Periodical. CN. English. bm. $10.00. Lamaze Childbirth Association of Ontario, 48 Drakefield Road, Markham Ontario L3P 1G7 Canada. DD 618.4505.

MCN, THE AMERICAN JOURNAL OF MATERNAL CHILD NURSING. See Medicine - Nursing.

MAJOR PROBLEMS IN OBSTETRICS AND GYNECOLOGY. V. 1- 1970-. 0076-2873. US. English. ir. WB Saunders, c/o Fullfillment Department, West Washington Square, Philadelphia PA 19105. Tel (800)523-0713. Ed E A Friedman. Ind/Abst Energy Res. Abstr., Index Med. LC RG39. NLM W1 MA492V.

THE MALPRACTICE REPORTER. OB/GYN. See Law.

MASTITIS NEWSLETTER. No. 1- May 1977-. Periodical. English. ir.

MATERNAL & CHILD HEALTH (RICHMOND, SURREY). (MATERNAL & CHILD HEALTH). VFOAT Journal of Maternal and Child Health. Vol. 6, No. 3 (Mar. 1981)-. 0262-0200. Periodical. UK. English. mo. 30.00. Barker Publications Limited, 539 London Road/Barker House, Middlesex TW7 4DA United Kingdom. Tel (01)847-1774. Ed D Harvey and W Styles. NLM W1 MA946XA. bk rev. adv acc. Circ 18,000. (ctrl). Review articles on family medicine with special emphasis on the care of women and children for medical practitioners. *Journal of Maternal and Child Health, 0308-4426.*

Medicine—Gynecology & Obstetrics

MATERNAL AND CHILD HEALTH STATISTICS : NORTH CAROLINA. See Statistics.

MATERNAL/NEWBORN ADVOCATE. VAT Maternal Newborn Advocate. V. 1- July 1974-. 0190-0757. Periodical. US. English. qt. March of Dimes Birth Defects Foundation, Box 2000, White Plains NY 10602. **NLM** W1 MA947MC.

MEDICAL EXAMINATION REVIEW BOOK. OBSTETRICS AND GYNECOLOGY SPECIALTY BOARD REVIEW. VFOAT Obstetrics and Gynecology Specialty Board Review. 1st- Ed. 0091-4223. US. English. ir. Medical Exam Publishing Company, 3003 New Hyde Park Road, New Hyde Park NY 10040.

MEDIGUIDE TO OB/GYN. VAT Mediguide to Obstetrics Gynecology. Vol. 1, Issue 1-. 0738-2987. US. English. qt. Lawrence Della Corte Publications Inc, 767 Lexington, New York NY 10021. **NLM** W1 ME787FLC.

MIDLIFE WELLNESS. Vol. 1, No. 3-. 0740-6150. Periodical. US. English. qt $12.00. Center for Climacteric Studies, University of Florida, 901 NW 8th Avenue/Suite B-1, Gainesville FL 32601. LC RG186. DD 613.04244. *Menopause Update, 0734-9009.*

MIDWIVES CHRONICLE AND NURSING NOTES. VFOAT Midwives Chronicle. 0026-3524. Periodical. UK. English. mo. Royal College of Midwives, 15 Mansfield Street, London England. Ind/Abst Cumul. Index Nurs. Allied Health Lit., Int. Nurs. Index. **NLM** W1 MI333. *Midwives Chirugical Nursing.*

MINERVA GINECOLOGICA. Vol. 1- Oct. 1949-. 0026-4784. Periodical. IT. Italian. mo. 80.00. Edizoni Minerva Medica, Corso Bramante 83-85, Torino Italy 10126. Tel 678282. Ed T Oliaro. Ind/Abst Excerpta Med., Index Med. **NLM** W1 MI643. bk rev. adv acc. Addressed to practitioners and specialists in gynecology and obstetrics in Italy and abroad; deals with topics in scientific practice and research. *Folia Gynaecologica, Ginecologia.*

MODERN TRENDS IN INFERTILITY AND CONCEPTION CONTROL. VFOAT Fertility and Sterility. V.1- 1979-. Monographic Series. US. English. Ed Edward E Wallach and Robert D Kempers. Each issue contains an index to its own contents - no vol index - loose.

MOTHER & CHILD. VAT Mother and Child. 0379-2617. Periodical. PK. English. qt. 14.00. Maternity & Child Welfare Association, MCH House 30-F Gulberg-II, Lahore Pakistan. Tel 882146. Ed A K Awan. **NLM** W1 MO941J. bk rev. adv acc. Circ 2,500. (ctrl). Concerned mainly with activities (both medical and social) related to mothers and children. In our own way it's our contribution for the upliift of the section of society.

MOTHERS TODAY. Vol. 19, No. 1 (Jan./Feb. 1983)-. 0745-8371. Periodical. US. English. bm. $1.00 Single Issue. Mothers Today, PO Box 243, Franklin Lakes NJ 07417. LC RG525. DD 649.105. *Mothers Manual (Franklin Lakes, N.J.), 0027-1551.*

NAPSAC DIRECTORY OF ALTERNATIVE BIRTH SERVICES AND CONSUMER GUIDE. See Yearbooks, Almanacs, Directories.

NATIONAL ADVISORY COUNCIL ON MATERNAL, INFANT, AND FETAL NUTRITION . . . BIENNIAL REPORT. Main/Corp United States. National Advisory Council on Maternal, Infant, and Fetal Nutrition. US. English. be. Superintendent of Documents, US Government Printing Office, Washington DC 20402.

NEONATOLOGY LETTER. 0747-6132. Periodical. US. English. bm. Neonatology Letter, 5 Center Parkway, Little Falls NJ 07424. Tel (201)890-0500. Ed John W Scanlon. DD 618. adv acc. Circ 20,000,000. (ctrl). Up-to-date information on developments and techniques in the fields of neonatology and obstetrics/gynecology, written by leaders in these fields, with tele-lecture presentation.

NIPPON FUNIN GAKKAI ZASSHI. VFOAT Japanese Journal of Fertility and Sterility. Maki 1- 1956-. 0029-0629. Periodical. JA. Japanese (English). qt. Japanese Society of Fertiltiy and Sterlity, 1 Ichigaya Sadoharacho 1 Chome, Shinjuku Ku Tokyo 162 Japan. Ind/Abst Biol. Abstr., Chem. Abstr. **NLM** W1 NI893. CODEN NFGZAD.

NIPPON SANKA FUJINKA GAKKAI ZASSHI. VFOAT Journal of the Japanese Obstetrical and Gynecological Society. Vol. 1- July 1949-. 0300-9165. Periodical. JA. Japanese. mo. $90.00. Japan Publishers Trading Company Limited, PO Box 5030, Tokyo International, Tokyo 100-31 Japan. Ind/Abst Index Med., Chem. Abstr. **NLM** W1 NI931N. CODEN NISFAY. *Nippon Fujinka Gakkai Zasshi., Sanka Fujinka Kiyo Zasshi.*

OB. GYN. NEWS. VAT Obstetrics Gynecology News. 0029-7437. Periodical. US. English. sm. $70.00. International Medical News Service, 12230 Wilkins Avenue, Rockville MD 20852. Tel (212)421-0707. LC RG1. **NLM** W1 OB402P. bk rev. adv acc. Circ 27,638. (ctrl). Coverage of clinical meetings, symposia, and conventions to report clinical developments in the fields of obstetrics and gynecology.

OB-GYN OBSERVER. V. 1- Dec. 1961-. 0029-7445. Periodical. US. English. bm. **NLM** W1 OB4024.

OBG DIAGNOSIS. VFOAT O.B.G. Diagnosis. VAT Obstetrics Gynecology Diagnosis. Vol. 1, No. 1 0738-3029. Periodical. US. English. qt. Free. Lawrence Dellacorte Publications Inc, 767 Lexington Avenue, New York NY 10021. **NLM** W1 OB402KF.

OB/GYN CLINICAL ALERT. VFOAT OBGYN Clinical Alert. Vol. 1, No. 1 (May 1984)-. 0743-8354. Periodical. US. English. mo $49.00. International Thomson Medical Information Inc, 600 Chestnut Street/Suite 426, Philadelphia PA 19106. DD 618. *Advances in Reproductive Medicine, 0741-420X.*

OB/GYN LITIGATION REPORTER. See Law.

OB/GYN-PED-DERM ADVISER. (THE OB/GYN-PED-DERM ADVISER). VFOAT Adviser. VAT Advicer (Ob/Gyn-Ped-Derm Ed.). Vol. 1, No. 1 (Jan. 1984)-. 0824-6750. Periodical. CN. English. mo. $30.00. Ob/Gyn-Ped-Derm Adviser, 1300 Bay Street, Toronto Ontario M5R 3K8 Canada. DD 332.024610971.

OB/GYN TRENDS AT MOUNT SINAI SCHOOL OF MEDICINE. VFOAT OB/GYN Trends. VAT Obstetrics Gynecology Trends at Mount Sinai School of Medicine. Vol. 1, No. 1 (Mar. 1985)-. 0883-492X. Periodical. US. English. qt. $19.00. Medical Publishing Enterprises, One Bridge Plaza North/Suite 270, Fort See NJ 07024. DD 618.

OBSTETRIC ANESTHESIA DIGEST. Vol. 1, No. 1 (Mar. 1981)-. 0275-665X. Periodical. US. English. qt. $60.00. University of Texas, Department of Anesthesiology, R Hodgkinson, 7703 Floyd Curld Drive, San Antonio TX 78284. Tel (512)695-9198. Ed G T Marx and Robert Hodgkinson. **NLM** W1 OB495. CODEN OADIDS. bk rev. Circ 800. Abstracts of obstetrics, obstetrics anesthesia and neonatology.

OBSTETRICA ET GYNECOLOGICA. Series/Titl Acta Universitatis Ouluensis: Series D Medica. No. 1-. 0358-4844. Monographic Series. FI. English (Finnish). ir. Professor Sakari Piha, University of Oulu, 90100 Oulu 10 Finland. Tel 358-81-332133. Ed Leo Hirvonen. **NLM** W1 AC954MN No.8 Etc. adv acc. Circ 500. (ctrl). Monographs, reviews and dissertations in the field of obstetrics and gynecology.

OBSTETRICAL & GYNECOLOGICAL SURVEY. VAT Obstetrical and Gynecological Survey. V. 1- Feb. 1946-. 0029-7828. Periodical. US. English. mo. $70.00. Williams & Wilkins, 428 East Preston Street, Baltimore MD 21202. Tel (301)528-4000. Ed E Stewart Taylor. Ind/Abst Life Sci. Collect., Excerpta Med., Index Med., Energy Res. Abstr., Biol. Abstr., Chem. Abstr. LC RG1. DD 618.1. **NLM** ZWP 100 O14. CODEN OGSUA8. (cum index). adv acc. Circ 12,100. Review articles and in-depth condensations of important obstetric/gynecology articles from nearly 100 US and international journals.

THE OBSTETRICIAN'S & GYNECOLOGIST'S COMPENDIUM OF DRUG THERAPY. VFOAT Compendium of Drug Therapy. VAT Obstetrician's and Gynecologist's Compendium of Drug Therapy. 1980/81-. 0272-9369. US. English. an. Biomedical Information Corporation, 800 2nd Avenue, New York NY 10017. LC RG131. DD 618.

OBSTETRICS AND GYNAECOLOGY SOUND RECORDING. 0824-7404. Periodical. CN. English. ir. Medifacts Ltd, 471 Richmond Road, Ottawa Ontario K2A 0G3 Canada. DD 618.05.

OBSTETRICS AND GYNECOLOGY. Vol. 1- Jan. 1953-. 0029-7844. Periodical. US. English. mo. $94.00. Elsevier Science Publications Company Inc, PO Box 1663, Grand Central Station, New York NY 10163. Tel (212)370-5520. Ed Richard F Mattingly. Ind/Abst Life Sci. Collect., Excerpta Med., Biol. Abstr., Chem. Abstr., Nuci. Sci. Abstr., Index Med., Energy Res. Abstr., Pestdoc, Ringdoc, Vetdoc, Sci. Cit. Index, Abr. Ed. LC RG1. DD 618.05. **NLM** W1 OB488. CODEN OBGNAS. (cum index). bk rev. adv acc. Circ 30,075. Official journal of the American College of Obstetricians and Gynecologists, publishes news on scientific advances, new medical and surgical techniques, obstetric management, keeps clinical evaluation of drugs and instruments in the field.

OBSTETRICS & GYNECOLOGY. VAT Obstetrics and Gynecology (New York. 1970). 0078-298X. US. English. an. Medical World News, 299 Park Avenue, New York NY 10017. LC RG1. DD 618.05.

OBSTETRICS AND GYNECOLOGY ANNUAL. V. 1- 1972-. 0091-3332. US. English. an. $57.26. Appleton Century Crofts, 25 Van Zant Street, East Norwalk CT 06855. Tel (203)833-4400. Ed Ralph Wynn. Ind/Abst Excerpta Med., Index Med., Biol. Abstr., Energy Res. Abstr., Chem. Abstr. **NLM** W1 OB49. CODEN OGYAAC. Collection of original articles in obstetrics and gynecology.

PATOLOGIA E CLINICA OSTETRICA E GINECOLOGICA. V. 1- 1973-. 0304-0313. Periodical. IT. Italian (summaries in English). bm. 80.00. Piccin Editore, Via Atlinate 107, 35121 Padua Italy. Tel 049/655566. Ind/Abst Life Sci. Collect., Excerpta Med. **NLM** W1 PA969G. Circ 2,087. Italian translation of the American Journal Clinical Obstetrics and Gynecology. *Clinica Ostetrica e Ginecologica, 0009-9031.*

PEDIATRIC AND ADOLESCENT GYNECOLOGY. See Medicine - Pediatrics.

PERINATAL CARE. V. 1- June 1977-. 0160-3701. Periodical. US. English. mo. $25.00. Neomed Publishing Inc, 420 Lexington Avenue, New York NY 10170. LC RG1. DD 618.2005. **NLM** W1 PE788B.

PERINATAL MEDICINE. V. 1- 1976-. 0364-4545. Periodical. US. English. ir. Ed F C Battaglia, G Meschia and E J Quilligan. **NLM** ZWQ 610 P445.

PERINATAL PRACTICE. Series/Titl A Wiley Medical Publication. VFOAT Wiley Series on Perinatal Practice. Vol. 1-. Monographic Series. UK. English. ir. Ed Geoffrey Chamberlain and Forrester Cockburn. **NLM** W1.

PERINATOLOGY-NEONATOLOGY. (PERINATOLOGY/NEONATOLOGY). VFOAT P/N. VAT Perinatology Neonatology. V. 1- July/Aug. 1977-. 0147-7927. Periodical. US. English. bm. $80.00. Brentwood Publishing Corporation, 825 Barrington Avenue, Los Angeles CA 90049. Tel (213)826-8388. Ed Esther Gross. Ind/Abst Cumul. Index Nurs. Allied Health Lit. LC RG1. DD 618.32. **NLM** W1 PE788L. bk rev. adv acc. Circ 17,854. (ctrl). For medical professionals involved in the management of high-risk pregnancy and births. Integrates the work being done by obstetricians, pediatricians, perinatologists, neonatologists, etc.

PHILIPPINE JOURNAL OF OBSTETRICS & GYNECOLOGY : OFFICIAL PUBLICATION, PHILIPPINE OBSTETRICAL AND GYNECOLOGICAL SOCIETY. VFOAT Philippine Journal of Obstetrics and Gynecology. Began in 1977. Periodical. English. qt. **NLM** W1.

POSTGRADUATE OBSTETRICS & GYNECOLOGY. VAT Postgraduate Obstetrics and Gynecology. 0194-3898. Monographic Series. US. English. bw. $160.00. Postgraduate Obstetrics & Gynecology, PO Box 673, Glennside PA 19038. Tel (215)885-2643.

THE PRACTICING MIDWIFE. 1977. 0733-8317. Periodical. US. English. qt. $38.00. Ina May Gaskin, 42 The Farm, Summertown TN 38483. Tel (615)964-2519. Ed Ina May Gaskin. bk rev. adv acc. Circ 1,500. Articles, interviews, news items, pictures, opinions, reviews, advertisements and other features of interest to midwives, physicians, nurses, childbirth educators, parents, and students.

PRENATAL DIAGNOSIS. Vol. 1, No. 1 (Jan. 1981)-. 0197-3851. Periodical. UK. English. bm. 180.00. John Wiley & Son, Baffins Lane Chichester,

Medicine—Gynecology & Obstetrics

Sussex PO19 1UD England. **Tel** 0243 784531. **Ed** M A Ferguson-Smith. **Ind/Abst** Excerpta Med., Index Med., Biol. Abstr., Chem. Abstr., Sci. Cit. Index, Abr. Ed. DD 618. **NLM** W1 PR397M. **CODEN** PRDIDM. bk rev. adv acc. Circ 1,000. Results of original research in clinical and scientific specialities concerned with in utero diagnosis of fetal abnormaility in man resulting from genetic and environmental.

PROGRESS IN GYNECOLOGY. V. 1-. 0079-6298. US. English. ir. Grune & Stratton, 111 5th Avenue, New York NY 10003. **Tel** (212)614-3232. **Ind/Abst** Chem. Abstr. LC RG39. DD 618.1082. **NLM** W1 PR668Y. **CODEN** PGYNAS.

PROGRESS IN OBSTETRICS AND GYNAECOLOGY. Vol. 1-. 0261-0140. UK. English. an. $26.00. Churchill Livingstone, 1560 Broadway, New York NY 10036. **Tel** (212)819-5400. **Ed** John Studd. **NLM** W1 PR675P.

RECENT ADVANCES IN OBSTETRICS AND GYNAECOLOGY. Began in 1926. 0143-6848. Periodical. UK. English. ir. Churchill Livingstone Inc, 1560 Broadway, New York NY 10036. **Tel** (212)819-5400. LC RG1. DD 618.05. **NLM** W1 RE105YJ.

RECENT ADVANCES IN PERINATAL MEDICINE. No. 1-. 0264-2417. UK. English. Churchill Livingstone Inc, 1560 Broadway, New York NY 10036. LC RG626. DD 618.32005. **NLM** W1 RE105XR.

REPORT - LIAISON MEETING WITH NURSING/MIDWIFERY ASSOCIATIONS. **Main/Conf** Liaison Meeting with Nursing/Midwifery Associations on Who's European Nursing/Midwifery Programme. English. ir.

REPRODUCTIVE MEDICINE. Vol. 1-. 0732-1279. Monographic Series. US. English. ir. Marcel Dekker Inc, 270 Madison Avenue, New York NY 10016. **Tel** (212)696-9000. Ed Symonds and Zuspan. LC UNC. DD 618.05. **NLM** W1 RE213P. This is an ongoing series. Each title has a different subject.

RESOURCES IN HUMAN NURTURING MONOGRAPH. VFOAT RHNI Monograph. No. 1-. 0198-9774. Monographic Series. US. English. ir. Resources in Human Nurturing International, 3885 Forest Street, PO Box 6861, Denver CO 80206. **NLM** W1 RE248BM.

REVISTA BRASILEIRA DE GINECOLOGIA E OBSTETRICIA. (REVISTA BRASILEIRA DE GINECOLOGIA E OBSTETRICIA : REVISTA DA FEDERACAO BRASILEIRA DAS SOCIEDADES DE GINECOLOGIA E OBSTETRICIA). 0100-7203. Periodical. BL. Portuguese. bm. $100.00. Avenida Armando Lombardi, 800 Sala 233 Barra da Tijuca, CEP 22 600 Rio de Janeiro RJ Brazil. **Tel** (021)399-4705. Ed Carlos Andre Henriques. **Ind/Abst** Chem. Abstr. **CODEN** RBGODX. adv acc. (ctrl). Original works, case reports, communication in brief.

REVISTA COLOMBIANA DE OBSTETRICIA Y GINECOLOGIA. 0034-7434. Periodical. CK. Spanish. bm. Societe Colombiana de Obstetricia y Ginecologia, PO Box 34188, Y 14961 Bogota Colombia. **Ind/Abst** Excerpta Med. **NLM** W1 RE357.

REVISTA CUBANA DE OBSTETRICIA Y GINECOLOGIA. V. 1- Jan./April 1975-. Periodical. CU. Spanish. qt. Empresa Ediciones Cubanas, Sub-Direccion Exportacion Oreilly, 407 Ciudad, Havana Cuba. **Ind/Abst** Energy Res. Abstr. **NLM** W1 RE363F.

REVISTA DE PEDIATRIE, OBSTETRICA SI GINECOLOGIE. PEDIATRIA. VFOAT Pediatria. V. 23, No. 4- July/Sept. 1974-. 0303-8416. Periodical. RM. Romanian. qt. Ilexim Press Dept, PO Box 1-136-1-137, Bucharest Romania. **Ind/Abst** Excerpta Med., Index Med., Chem. Abstr. **NLM** W1 RE458T. **CODEN** RPOPD4. Pediatria, 0031-3904.

REVISTA ECUATORIANA DE MEDICINA PERINATAL. (REVISTA ECUATORIANA DE MEDICINA PERINATAL : ORGANO OFICIAL DE LA ASOCIACION ECUATORIANA DE MEDICINA PERINATAL). Vol. 1, No. 1-. 0253-5874. Periodical. EC. Spanish. qt. **NLM** W1 RE524K.

REVISTA ESPANOLA DE OBSTETRICIA Y GINECOLOGIA. 0034-9445. Periodical. SP. Spanish. bm. $40.00. Revista Espanola de Obste, Avellanas No 4 Entlo, Valencia 4 Spain. **Ind/Abst** Chem. Abstr., Excerpta Med. **NLM** W1 RE5465. **CODEN** REOGAX.

REVISTA MEXICANA DE CIRUGIA, GINECOLOGIA Y CANCER. Yearly V. 1- August 1933-. 0034-9984. Periodical. MX. Spanish. bm. Revista Mexicana de Cirugia, Marsella 11, Mexico 6 DF Mexico. **NLM** W1 RE6828.

REVISTA OBSTETRICIA Y GINECOLOGIA DE VENEZUELA. VFOAT Revista de Obstetricia y Ginecologia de Venezuela. V. 20- 1960-. 0048-7732. Periodical. Spanish. ir. **Ind/Abst** Excerpta Med. **NLM** W1 RE4534. Revista de Obstetricia y Ginecologia.

REVUE FRANCAISE DE GYNECOLOGIE ET D'OBSTETRIQUE. Yearly V. 14, No. 8- Aug. 1919-. 0035-290X. Periodical. FR. French. ir. $105.10. Expansion Scientifique Francaise, 15 rue Saint-Benoit, 75278 Paris Cedex 06 France. **Tel** 548-42-60. **Ind/Abst** Life Sci. Collect., Excerpta Med., Chem. Abstr. **NLM** W1 RE845C. **CODEN** RFGOAO. Revue Mensuelle de Gynecologie, d'Obstetrique, et de Pediatrie, 0301-8458.

RIVISTA DI OSTETRICIA GINECOLOGIA PRATICA E MEDICINA PERINATALES. V. 54- Jan. 1973/74-. 0391-0970. Periodical. IT. Italian. bm. Rivista d'Ostetrica e, Via l'Spallanzani 11, 00161 Roma Italy. **Ind/Abst** Excerpta Med. **NLM** W1 RI574I. Rivista d'Ostetricia e Ginecologia Pratica e di Medicina Perinatale, 0391-0970.

SAGES FEMMES. V. 1 - 1977-. 0180-0612. Periodical. French. ir. **NLM** W1 SA127.

SANFUJINKA CHIRYO. VFOAT Obstetrical and Gynecological Therapy. Began in 1960. 1908-471X. Periodical. JA. Japanese. mo. Nagai Shoten, 21-15 8-chome Fukushima, Fukushima Osaka 553 Japan. **Tel** 06-452-1881. Ed Tadao Nagai. **Ind/Abst** Chem. Abstr. **CODEN** SACHAR. Circ 10,000.

THE SEARLE REVIEW OF OBSTETRIC & GYNECOLOGIC LITERATURE. VFOAT Searle Review of Obstetric and Gynecologic Literature, Obstetric & Gynecologic Literature. 1971-. US. English. an. Science and Medicine Publishing Company, 515 Madison Avenue, New York NY 10022. LC RG101. DD 618.08. **NLM** ZWQ 100 S439.

SEMINARS IN PERINATOLOGY. V. 1- Jan. 1977-. 0146-0005. Periodical. US. English. qt. $60.00. Grune & Stratton Inc, 111 Fifth Avenue, New York NY 10003. **Tel** (212)614-3110. **Ind/Abst** Life Sci. Collect., Excerpta Med., Index Med., Biol. Abstr., Energy Res. Abstr., Hospit. Lit. Index, Sci. Cit. Index, Abr. Ed. DD 618. **NLM** W1 SE489F. **CODEN** SEMPDU.

SEMINARS IN REPRODUCTIVE ENDOCRINOLOGY. See Medicine - Endocrinology.

SEXUAL MEDICINE TODAY. V. 1- Oct. 1977-. 0149-2926. Periodical. US. English. mo. $25.00. International Medical News Service, 600 New Hampshire Avenue North West, Washington DC 20036. LC RC556. DD 616.6.

SEXUALMEDIZIN. Yearly V. 1-. 0341-4884. Periodical. GW. German. ir. $33.27. Medical Tribune, Rheinstrasse 19, D-62 Wiesbaden 1 West Germany. **NLM** W1 SE99W.

SHENGZHI YU BIYUN. (SHENG CHIH YU PI YUN). VFOAT Reproduction and Contraception. Began in 1980. 0253-357X. Periodical. Chinese (English). qt. China Publication Centre, PO Box 2820, Beijing China. **Ind/Abst** Chem. Abstr. **CODEN** SCYYDZ.

SINGAPORE JOURNAL OF OBSTETRICS & GYNAECOLOGY. VAT Singapore Journal of Obstetrics and Gynaecology. V. 8- 1977-. 0129-3273. Periodical. SI. English. ir. $14.82. Obstetrics-Gynaecology Society of Singapore, Kandang Kerbau Hospital, Singapore 0821 Singapore. Ed S R Kottegoda. **Ind/Abst** Life Sci. Collect., Chem. Abstr. **NLM** W1 SI52M. **CODEN** SJOGDE. bk rev adv acc. Circ 1,000. Studies and editorials relevant to the practice of obstetrics and gynecology in Asia and Africa in general, and Singapore and Malaysia in particular. Proceedings of the Obstetrical and Gynaecological Society, Singapore, 0377-2942.

SOINS. GYNECOLOGIE, OBSTETRIQUE, PUERICULTURE. VFOAT Gynecologie, Obstetrique, Puericulture. 1 (Nov. 1980)-. 0151-6655. Periodical. French. bm. $103.90. OPISA, 33 Chemin des Hutins Anieres, 1247 Geneve Switzerland. **Tel** 512347. **Ed** SFIREC. **NLM** W1 SO8862R. adv acc. Gynecology, obstetrics, infant and child care.

SOINS. GYNECOLOGIE, OBSTETRIQUE, PUERICULTURE, PEDIATRIE. VFOAT Gynecologie, Obstetrique, Puericulture, Pediatrie. 7 (Nov. 1981)-. Periodical. French. mo. **NLM** W1 SO8862S. Soins. Gynecologie, Obstetrique, Puericulture, 0151-6655.

SPECIAL CARE. Vol. 1, No. 1 (May/June 1985)-. 0883-1882. Periodical. US. English. bm. $12.00 Domestic, $22.00 Canada. Neonatal Network, PO Box 4516, Petaluma CA 94953. DD 618.

SURGERY, GYNECOLOGY & OBSTETRICS. See Medicine - Surgery.

SURGICAL STERILIZATION SURVEILLANCE. TUBAL STERILIZATION AND HYSTERECTOMY IN WOMEN AGED 15-44. VFOAT Tubal Sterilization and Hysterectomy in Women Aged 15-44. 1979-1980-. 0743-6173. US. English. be. US Department of Health and Human Services, Public Health Service, Center for Disease Control, Center for Health Promotion and Education, Division of Reproductive Health, Atlanta GA 30333. LC RG138. DD 363.970973. Centers for Disease Control Surgical Sterilization Surveillance. Hysterectomy in Women Aged 15-44, 0277-3430; 0743-6165.

TIELINES. Vol. 1, No. 1 (Fall 1982)-. 0737-0474. Periodical. US. English. qt. $12.00 Domestic, $18.00 Foreign. Center for Birth Defects, Information Services, 171 Harrison Avenue, Box 403, Boston MA 02111.

TRANSACTIONS OF THE PACIFIC COAST OBSTETRICAL AND GYNECOLOGICAL SOCIETY. Main/Corp Pacific Coast Obstetrical and Gynecological Society. V. 14- 1944/46-. 0078-7442. US. English. an. $33.50. C V Mosby c/o Leadbetter, 11830 Westline Industrial Drive, St Louis MO 63141. **Ind/Abst** Energy Res. Abstr., Hospit. Lit. Index, Index Med. LC RG1. DD 618.05. **NLM** W1 TR227A.

ULTRASUONI IN OSTETRICIA E GINECOLOGIA : ORGANO UFFICIALE DELLA SOCIETA ITALIANA DI ECOGRAFIA OSTETRICO-GINECOLOGICA. 0392-7741. Periodical. Italian. qt. **NLM** W1.

UNE A L'AUTRE. (L'UNE A L'AUTRE : LE JOURNAL DE NAISSANCE-RENAISSANCE). Vol. 1, No 1 (Winter 1983)-. 0824-8230. Periodical. CN. French. qt. 10.00. Naissance-Renaissance, C P 249 Succursale E, Montreal Quebec H2T 3A7 Canada. **Tel** (514)325-5895. DD 612.6305. bk rev acc. Circ 2,000. (ctrl) Information on birth humanisation issues and rights of women on the legalization of midwifery, and holistics medicine.

VOIE LACTEE. (LA VOIE LACTEE). Vol. 1, No. 1 Jan/ Feb. 1978. 0710-5479. Periodical. CN. French. bm. $4.65. Ligue la Leche, CP 874, Ville St Laurent Quebec H4L 4E Canada. DD 649.3.

WOMEN & HEALTH. VAT Women and Health. V. 1- Jan./Feb. 1976-. 0363-0242. Periodical. US. English. qt. $102.00. Haworth Press, 28 East 22nd Street, New York NY 10010. **Tel** (212)228-2800. Ed Jeanne H Stellman. **Ind/Abst** Sociol. Abstr., Soc. Welf. Soc. Plan./Policy Soc. Dev., Hospit. Lit. Index, Index Med., Cumul. Index Nurs. Allied Health Lit., Biol. Abstr., Altern. Press Index, Psychol. Abstr., Public Aff. Inf. Serv. Bull., Soc. Sci. Citation Index. LC RG1. DD 613.0424405. **NLM** W1 WO478. **CODEN** WOHEDI. bk rev. adv acc. Circ 1,473. The journal covers material involving the physical and psychological well-being of women, and also concerns itself with sociocultural factors that lead to health problems.

THE YEAR BOOK OF OBSTETRICS AND GYNECOLOGY. See Yearbooks, Almanacs, Directories.

ZEITSCHRIFT FUR GEBURTSHILFE UND PERINATOLOGIE. VFOAT Geburtshilfe und Perinatologie. 0300-967X. Periodical. German (summaries in English). bm. $154.00. Thieme-Stratton Inc, 381 Park Avenue, New York NY 10016. **Tel** (212)683-5088. **Ind/Abst** Life Sci. Collect., Excerpta Med., Index Med., Biol. Abstr., Chem. Abstr., Energy Res. Abstr., Sci. Cit. Index, Abr. Ed. LC RG1. DD 618.2005. **NLM** W1 ZE357C. **CODEN** ZGPRA3. Zeitschrift fur Geburtshilfe und Gynakologie.

ZENTRALBLATT FUR GYNAKOLOGIE.
Vol. 27-. 0044-4197. Periodical. GE. German
(summaries in English). sm. $59.57. Kunst & Wissen
Erich Bieber, Dufourstrasse 51, CH-8008 Zurich
Switzerland. Tel 011-41-1-69 44 20. Ind/Abst Life Sci.
Collect., Excerpta Med., Index Med., Biol. Abstr.,
Chem. Abstr., Curr. Contents, Energy Res. Abstr., Sci.
Cit. Index, Abr. Ed. NLM W1 ZE777N. CODEN
ZEGYAX.

HOMEOPATHY

AMERICAN HOMEOPATHY (SPRINGFIELD, VA. : 1984).
(AMERICAN HOMEOPATHY). Vol. 1, No. 1
(July-Aug.1984)-. 0747-606X. Periodical. US. English.
$20.00. United States Homeopathic Association, 6560
Backlick Road/Suite 211, Springfield VA 22150. DD
615. American Homeopathy (Consumer Edition),
0741-6857; American Homeopathy (Professional
Edition), 0741-6865; American Homeopathy (Affiliate
Edition), 0741-6873.

BIOLOGICAL THERAPY. No. 1 (Jan. 1983)-.
0733-2661. Periodical. US. English (French and
German). qt. $12.50. Menaco Publishing Company,
PO Box 13677, Albuquerque MN 87192. Tel
(505)293-3843. Ed Lex E O'Brient. DD 615. NLM W1.
bk rev. adv acc. Circ 2,000. (ctrl). Articles relating to
various homeopathic combined remedies as well as
other holistic forms of medical treatment.

COMMON GROUND (VANCOUVER, B.C.). (COMMON GROUND). Issue No. 1 (Winter
1982/83)-. 0824-0698. Periodical. CN. English. qt.
$6.00. Common Ground, PO Box 34090 Station D,
Vancouver British Columbia V6J 4M1 Canada. DD
615.8025711.

THE HAHNEMANNIAN. V. 84, No. 2- 1949-.
Periodical. US. English. qt. $6.00. Homeopathic
Medical Society, Neffsville, Lancaster PA 17601. Ed
Arland Lebo. bk rev. adv acc. Circ 300. Homeopathic
medical recommendations-update on reliable
nutritional information and new drugs and medicine
for the sick and suffering. Hahnemannian Monthly.

HOMEOTHERAPY. V. 1- Aug. 1974-. 0363-2776.
Periodical. US. English. bm. State Homoeopathic
Medical Society, PO Box 31100, San Francisco CA
94131. NLM W1 HO519C. Pacific Coast Homopathic
Bulletin, 0363-2784.

THE HOMOPATHIC SANDESH. V. 1-28.
0018-4446. Periodical. II. English (articles mainly in
Hindi). ir. Hindustan Book Agency of India,
Subscription Division, 17 UB Jawahhar Nagar Delhi 7
India. NLM W1 HO541.

JOURNAL OF THE AMERICAN INSTITUTE OF HOMEOPATHY. Began
with: Vol. 1, Jan. 1909. 0002-8967. Periodical. US.
English. qt. $30.00. American Institute of
Homeopathy, 1500 Massachusetts Avenue NW/#41,
Washington DC 20005. Tel (202)223-6182. Ed Karl
Robinson. LC RX1. DD 615.5320973. NLM W1
JO909I. bk rev. adv acc. Circ 500. (ctrl). A scholarly
journal containing articles written by homeopathic
practitioners on unusual cases and treatments,
philosophy, research, education and recent
developments in the field. Transactions, Homeopathic
Recorder.

INTERNAL MEDICINE

ABMS DIRECTORY OF CERTIFIED INTERNISTS. See Yearbooks, Almanacs,
Directories.

ABSTRACTS, ANNUAL MEETING - AMERICAN SOCIETY FOR ARTIFICIAL INTERNAL ORGANS. See
Indexes/Abstracts.

ACTA ENDOSCOPICA. V. 8- 1978-.
0240-642X. Periodical. English (text in French and
Spanish). bm. $69.18. Dr F Vicari, 127 rue St Dizier,
54000 Nancy France. Tel 8337.44.38. Ed F Vicari.
Ind/Abst Excerpta Med. NLM W1 AC8012G. bk rev.
adv acc. Circ 5,000. Original articles about
endoscopy in its medical and surgical applications-
experimental studies of endoscopic instrumentation,
bibliographical analysis, confrontations with other
techniques. Acta Endoscopica Et
Radiocinematographica.

ACTA GASTRO-ENTEROLOGICA BELGICA. Began publication with V. 9, 1946.
0001-5644. Periodical. BE. French (articles and
summaries in English, French, Dutch and German).
$54.35. Association for the Society of Scientifique
Medica Belgique, 43 rue des Champs Elysses, B-1050
Brussels Belgium. Ind/Abst Life Sci. Collect.,
Excerpta Med., Index Med. NLM W1 AC804. Index
published separately - free - automatically sent.
Journal Belge de Gastro-Enterologie, 0301-7354.

ACTA GASTROENTEROLOGICA BOLIVIANA. (ACTA GASTROENTEROLOGICA
BOLIVIANA : PUBLICACION OFICIAL DE LOS
INSTITUTOS DE GASTROENTEROLOGIA
BOLIVIANO-JAPONES). Vol. 1, No. 1 (Jan./April
1981)-. 0253-5513. Periodical. BO. English (articles
also in Spanish). ty. Administrador Acta
Gastroenterologica, Boliviana Casilla No 8578, La Paz
Bolivia. Ind/Abst Chem. Abstr. NLM W1 AC804G.
CODEN AGBODQ.

ACTA GASTROENTEROLOGICA LATINOAMERICANA. 0300-9033. AG.
Spanish. ir. Acta Gastroenterologica, Juncal 2134 PB
B, 1125 Buenos Aires Republica Argentina. Ind/Abst
Biol. Abstr., Chem. Abstr., Index Med., Excerpta Med.
NLM W1 AC804H. CODEN AGLTBL.

ACTA MEDICA AUSTRIACA. Vol. 1- 1974-.
0303-8173. Periodical. AU. German (articles with
summaries in German and English). bm. 680.00.
Bruder Hollinek, Gallgasse 40 A, A-1130 Wien X11
Austria. Tel (0222)845346. Ind/Abst Life Sci. Collect.,
Excerpta Med., Index Med., Biol. Abstr., Sci. Cit.
Index, Abr. Ed. NLM W1 AC831K. CODEN AMAUBB.
bk rev. Austrian internal medicine. Weiner Zeitschrift
Fur Innere Medizin Und Ihre Grenzgebiete,
0043-5376.

ADVANCES IN INTERNAL MEDICINE.
V. 1-. 0065-2822. US. English. an. Yearbook Medical
Publ, 35 East Wacker Drive, Chicago IL 60601. Ed J
M Steele and others. Ind/Abst Index Med., Chem.
Abstr., Energy Res. Abstr., Sci. Cit. Index, Abr. Ed. LC
RC46. DD 616. NLM W1 AD653. CODEN AIMNAL.

AIDS RESEARCH. VFOAT A.I.D.S. Research.
Vol. 1, No. 1-. 0737-6006. Periodical. US. English. bm.
$95.00 Domestic, $117.00 Foreign. M A Liebert, 157
East 86th Street, New York NY 10028. LC RC607.A26.
DD 616.9. NLM W1 AI696F.

AMERICAN JOURNAL OF PROCTOLOGY, GASTROENTEROLOGY & COLON & RECTAL SURGERY CEASED. VAT American
Journal of Proctology, Gastroenterology and Colon
and Rectal Surgery. V. 29-36, No. 2. 0162-6566.
Periodical. US. English. mo. McMahon Publishing
Company, 121 South Gertrude Avenue, Paramus NJ
07652. Tel (203)544-9343. Ind/Abst Excerpta Med.,
Life Sci. Collect. LC RC864.A1. DD 616.3005. NLM
W1 AM511B. American Journal of Proctology,
0002-9521.

ANGIOLOGY. V. 1- Feb. 1950-. 0003-3197.
Periodical. US. English. mo. $80.00. Westminster
Publications Inc, 1044 Northern Boulevard, Roslyn NY
11576. Tel (516)484-6880. Ind/Abst Life Sci. Collect.,
Pestdoc, Ringdoc, Vetdoc, Excerpta Med., Index
Med., CIS Abstr., Biol. Abstr., Chem. Abstr., Energy
Res. Abstr., Sci. Cit. Index, Abr. Ed. LC RC691. DD
616.105. NLM W1 AN227. CODEN ANGIAB.

ANNALES DE MEDECINE INTERNE.
Vo1. 120-. 0003-410X. Periodical. FR. French. mo.
$180.00. Masson Publishing USA Inc, 211 East 43rd
Street Room 1306, New York NY 10017. Tel
(212)370-1937. Ind/Abst Life Sci. Collect., Excerpta
Med., Index Med., CIS Abstr., Chem. Abstr., Energy
Res. Abstr. NLM W1 AN352N. CODEN AMDIBO.
Bulletins et Memoires de la Societe Medicale des
Hopitaux de Paris, 0366-1334.

ANNALS OF CLINICAL RESEARCH. V.
1- May 1969-. 0003-4762. Periodical. Fl. English. bm.
$140.00. Finnish Medical Society Duodecim,
Kalevankatu 11 A, 00100 Helsinki Finland. Tel
358-0-611050. Ed J Huttunen. Ind/Abst Life Sci.
Collect., Excerpta Med., Biol. Abstr., Chem. Abstr.,
Index Med., Nuci. Sci. Abstr., Psychol. Abstr., Sci. Cit.
Index, Abr. Ed. NLM W1 AN571K. CODEN ACLRBL.
Circ 2,000. All branches of internal medicine. Annales
Paediatriae Fenniae, 0570-1732; Annales Medicinae
Internae Fenniae, 0365-4362.

ANNALS OF INTERNAL MEDICINE. V.
1- July 1927-. 0003-4819. US. English. mo. $21.00.
American College of Physicians, 4200 Pine Street,
Philadelphia PA 19104. Ind/Abst Life Sci. Collect.,
Hospit. Lit. Index, Pestdoc, Ringdoc, Vetdoc, Coal
Abstr., Excerpta Med., Cumul. Index Nurs. Allied
Health Lit., CIS Abstr., Ref. Source, Biol. Abstr.,
Chem. Abstr., Index Med., Nuci. Sci. Abstr., Energy
Res. Abstr. LC R11. NLM W1 AN605. CODEN
AIMEAS. (cum index). Available on microfilm from
University Microfilms. Annals of Clinical Medicine,
0095-9944.

ANNUAL REPORT OF THE DIGESTIVE DISEASES COORDINATING COMMITTEE TO THE SECRETARY, U.S. DEPARTMENT OF HEALTH AND HUMAN SERVICES. Main/Corp United
States. Digestive Diseases Coordinating Committee.
2nd (Fiscal year 1978)-. US. English. an. National
Institute of Arthritis Metabolism and Digestive
Diseases, Coordinating Committee, 9000 Rockville
Pike, Bethesda MD 20014. NLM W2. Annual Report of
the Digestive Diseases Coordinating Committee to the
Secretary, U.S. Department of Health, Education, and
Welfare.

ARCHIVES OF INTERNAL MEDICINE.
See Genealogy and Heraldry - Archives.

ARQUIVOS DE GASTROENTEROLOGIA. See Genealogy
and Heraldry - Archives.

ARTHRITIS NEWS. (ARTHRITIS NEWS : AN
INFORMATION PUBLICATION OF THE ARTHRITIS
SOCIETY). Vol. 3, No. 4 (Sept. 1981)- Vol. 4, No. 5
(Sept. l982)-. 0820-9006. Periodical. CN. English. qt.
Free. Arthritis Society, 920 Yonge Street/Suite 420,
Toronto Ontario M4W 3J7 Canada. DD
616.722006071. Arthritis Society News, u 0227-8146.

AUDIO-DIGEST. INTERNAL MEDICINE. 0571-8627. Periodical. US. English.
sm. $192.72. Audio-Digest Foundation, 1577 Chevy
Chase Drive, Glendale CA 91206. Tel (213)245-8505.
Ed Claron L Oakley. A twice-monthly interactive
system of audio cassette postgraduate medical
education, with each one-hour program eligible for
two Category I credit hours.

AUSTRALIAN AND NEW ZEALAND JOURNAL OF MEDICINE. V. 1- Feb.
1971-. 0004-8291. Periodical. AT. English. bm. 40
Domestic, $45.00 US. Royal Australian College of
Physicians, 145 Macquarie Street, Sydney New South
Wales 2000 Australia. Tel (02)27 4461. Ed Michael F
O'Rourke. Ind/Abst Life Sci. Collect., Pestdoc,
Ringdoc, Vetdoc, Excerpta Med., Nuci. Sci. Abstr.,
Biol. Abstr., Index Med., Chem. Abstr., Sci. Cit. Index,
Abr. Ed., Hospit. Lit. Index. NLM W1 AU495. CODEN
ANZJB8. bk rev. adv acc. Circ 5,000. Accounts of
original research in internal medicine and the
biomedical sciences. Australasian Annals of
Medicine, 0571-9283.

BIBLIOGRAPHY OF ACUTE DIARRHOEAL DISEASES. See
Bibliographies.

BIFIDOBACTERIA AND MICROFLORA MICROFLORA : BM. VFOAT BM. Vol. 1, No.
1 (Mar. 1982)-. 0286-9306. Periodical. English. ir.
Subscription Department, Business Center for
Academic Societies Japan, 20-6 Mukogaoka 1-chome
Bunkyo-ku, Tokyo 113 Japan. Ind/Abst Life Sci.
Collect., Chem. Abstr. NLM W1. CODEN BIMIDK.

BLOOD PURIFICATION. 1/1/83 (Sept.
1983)-. 0253-5068. Periodical. English. qt. $97.00. S
Karger AG, PO Box, CH-4009 Basel Switzerland. Tel
(061)39 08 80. Ed K Shaefer and L W Henderson.
Ind/Abst Life Sci. Collect., Chem. Abstr. NLM W1.
CODEN BLPUDO. adv acc. Features information on
hemodialysis, hemotiltration, peritoneal dialysis and
plasma filtration. Particular emphasis on reports
drawn from a wide range of fields, describing
technical advances and improvements in
methodology.

BRITISH JOURNAL OF HAEMATOLOGY. V. 1- Jan. 1955-. 0007-1048.
Periodical. UK. English. mo. $187.50 US, Canada and
Mexico. Blackwell Scientific Publ Ltd, PO Box 88,
Oxford OX2 0EL England. Tel 0865-260201. Ed E C
Gordon-Smith. Ind/Abst Life Sci. Collect., Excerpta
Med., Biol. Abstr., Chem. Abstr., Index Med., Int.
Aerosp. Abstr., Nuci. Sci. Abstr., Hospit. Lit. Index,
Sci. Cit. Index, Abr. Ed. NLM W1 BR535. CODEN
BJHEAL. bk rev. adv acc. Clinical laboratory and
experimental haematology.

BRUIT. (BRUIT : OFFICIAL JOURNAL OF THE
SOCIETY OF NON-INVASIVE VASCULAR
TECHNOLOGY). 0739-8670. Periodical. US. English.

Medicine—Internal Medicine

qt. $20.00. SNIVT, 5300 East Main Street Suite 206, Columbus OH 43213. **NLM** W1.

BULLETIN - CANADIAN LUNG ASSOCIATION. **Main/Corp** Canadian Lung Association. **VFOAT** Bulletin - Association Pulmonaire du Canada. V. 56, No. 2- Summer 1977-. 0709-0463. Periodical. CN. English (French). ty. Canadian Lung Association, 75 Albert Street/Suite 908, Ottawa Ontario K1P 5E7 Canada. **Tel** (613)237-1208. **Ed** Pamela Murray. **LC** RC306. **DD** 614.592400971, 616.24006271. (ctrl). Provincial update and news on fund-raising health education and public relations programs focusing on lung disease and health education information. *Bulletin*, 0008-5235.

BULLETIN ON RHEUMATIC DISEASES. (BULLETIN ON THE RHEUMATIC DISEASES). Began with Sept. 1966 issue?. 0007-5248. US. English. ir. Free Domestic, $10.00 Foreign. Arthritis Foundation, 1314 Spring Street NW, Atlanta GA 30309. **Tel** (404)872-7100. **Ed** Evelyn V Hess. **Ind/Abst** Life Sci. Collect., Excerpta Med., Index Med., Biol. Abstr., Chem. Abstr., Energy Res. Abstr. **LC** RC927. **DD** 616.723005. **NLM** W1 BU903J. **CODEN** BRDIAZ. **Circ** 21,000. Geared for primary care physicians, each issue contains a concise discussion by a distinguished authority on current topics in management and research in rheumatic diseases. *Bulletin on Rheumatic Diseases*, 0007-5248.

CANDID FACTS. **VFOAT** A Propos. Began publication in 1960. 0226-2347. Periodical. CN. English (text in French, Spring 1979-). Free. Canadian Cystic Fibrosis Foundation, Suite 503/161 Eglinton Avenue, Toronto Ontario M4P 1J5 Canada. **DD** 616.37. (ctrl).

CESKOSLOVENSKA GASTROENTEROLOGIA A VYZIVA. Vol. 9 1955-. 0009-0565. Periodical. CS. Czech. ir. $75.50. Artia, VE Smeckach 30, PO Box 790, Praha 1 Czechoslovakia. **Ind/Abst** Excerpta Med., Biol. Abstr., CIS Abstr., Chem. Abstr., Index Med. **NLM** W1 CE885C. **CODEN** CKGAAM. *Sbornik Pro Pathofysiologii Traveni a Vyzivu*.

CHAIRMAN'S REPORT - NATIONAL ARTHRITIS ADVISORY BOARD. **Main/Corp** United States. National Arthritis Advisory Board. 0196-2728. US. English. United States Department of Health, Education, and Welfare, National Arthritis Advisory Board, PO Box 30286, Bethesda MD 20014. **LC** RC933.A1. **DD** 362.196722.

CHEST DISEASES, THORACIC SURGERY AND TUBERCULOSIS. Series/Titl Excerpta Medica, Section 15. 0014-4193. English. ir. $96.00. Excerpta Medica, Journals Division, Amsterdam Netherlands. **LC** RC306. **DD** 617.54005. **NLM** ZW 1 E968. *Chest Diseases*.

CIRCULATORY SHOCK. Vol. 1- March 1974-. 0092-6213. Periodical. US. English. bm. Alan R Liss Inc, 41 East 11th Street, New York NY 10003. **Tel** (212)741-2515. **Ind/Abst** Life Sci. Collect., Excerpta Med., Index Med., Biol. Abstr., Chem. Abstr., Energy Res. Abstr., Sci. Cit. Index, Abr. Ed. **LC** RC685.C18. **DD** 616.047. **NLM** W1 CI745K. **CODEN** CRSHAG.

LA CLINICA. Periodical. IT. Italian (summaries in English, French and German). bm. 40.00. Casa Editrice L Cappelli Spa, Via Marsili 9, 40124 Bologna Italy. **Tel** 330411. bk rev. adv acc. **Circ** 2,000. Covers general medicine.

CLINICAL EXERCISES IN INTERNAL MEDICINE. V. 1-. 0164-0852. Monographic Series. US. English. ir. W B Saunders Company, West Washington Square, Philadelphia PA 19105. **Tel** (800)523-0713. **NLM** WB 18 C641.

CLINICAL ULTRASOUND REVIEW. Series/Titl A Wiley Medical Publication. Vol. 1-. 0275-4541. Periodical. US. English. ir. John Wiley and Sons, One Wiley Drive, Somerset NJ 08873. **Tel** (201)469-4400. **LC** RC78.7.U4. **DD** 616.07543. **NLM** W1 CL799R.

CLINICAL UPDATE IN NEPHROLOGY. 0883-0339. Periodical. US. English. bw. $245.00. Nassau Publications Inc, 11 Forest Street, New Canaan CT 06840. **DD** 616.

COEUR ET MEDECINE INTERNE CEASED. V. 1, No. 1, (Jan. 1962)- V. 19, No. 2 (April/June 1980). 0010-0234. Periodical. French. qt. **Ind/Abst** CIS Abstr., Life Sci. Collect., Excerpta Med. **NLM** W1 CO107.

CONTEMPORARY ISSUES IN GASTROENTEROLOGY. Vol. 1-. 0739-7305. Monographic Series. US. English. Churchill Livingston, 1560 Broadway, New York NY 10036. Ed Sidney Cohen and Roger D Soloway. **LC** UNC. **NLM** W1 CO769MQR.

CONTEMPORARY METABOLISM. V. 1-. 0193-340X. US. English. ir. Plenum Publishing Corporation, 233 Spring Street, New York NY 10013. **Tel** (212)620-8000. **Ed** N Freinkel. **Ind/Abst** Chem. Abstr. **LC** RC627.5. **DD** 616.39005. **NLM** W1 CO769MV. **CODEN** CONMDM. *Year in Metabolism*, 0147-4189.

CRC CRITICAL REVIEWS IN CLINICAL NEUROBIOLOGY. VFOAT C.R.C. Critical Reviews in Clinical Neurobiology. Vol. 1, No. 1. 0742-941X. US. English. an. $96.00. CRC Press, 2000 Corporate Boulevard NW, Boca Raton FL 33431. **Ind/Abst** Life Sci. Collect. **DD** 616.

CURRENT CONCEPTS IN GASTROENTEROLOGY. V. 1- May 1976-. 0363-6526. Periodical. US. English. bm. $50.00. Sieber & McIntyre Publishing Division, 625 North Michigan Avenue, Chicago IL 60611. **Tel** (312)266-9200. **LC** RC799. **DD** 616.3005. **NLM** W1 CU7877.

CURRENT GASTROENTEROLOGY. Series/Titl A Houghton Mifflin Medical Publication. Vol. 1-. 0198-8085. US. English. an. Houghton Mifflin Professional Publishers Medical Division, 2 Park Street, Boston MA 02107. **Ind/Abst** Chem. Abstr. **LC** RC799. **DD** 616.3. **NLM** W1 CU788JAD. **CODEN** CUGADR.

CURRENT HEMATOLOGY AND ONCOLOGY. Vol. 3-. 0739-4810. Periodical. US. English. an. John Wiley, 605 3rd Avenue, New York NY 10158. Ed Virgil F Fairbanks. **LC** RC633.A1. **DD** 616.15005. *Current Hematology*, 0272-085X.

CURRENT HEPATOLOGY. Series/Titl A Houghton Mifflin Medical Publication. Vol. 1-. 0198-8093. US. English. an. Houghton Mifflin Professional Publishers, Medical Division, 2 Park Street, Boston MA 02107. **LC** RC845. **DD** 616.362005. **NLM** W1 CU788JAN.

CYSTIC FIBROSIS FOUNDATION ANNUAL REPORT FOR THE FISCAL YEAR . . . . Began with: 1975. Periodical. US. English. an. **NLM** W1 CY751C. *Report*.

DATELINE HYPERTENSION. 0747-6124. Periodical. US. English. bm. $18.00 Domestic, $24.00 Foreign. Dateline Hypertension, 5 Center Avenue, Little Falls NJ 07424. **Tel** (201)890-0500. Ed Norman M Kaplan. **DD** 616. adv acc. **Circ** 55,000,000. (ctrl). Up-to-date information on developments and techniques in the field of hypertension, written by leaders in this field, with a tele-lecture presentation.

DEISTVIE PROIZVODSTVENNYKH FAKTOROV NA ORGANIZM I MERY ZASHCHITY. 1976-. UR. Multilingual (Russian). bm. 0.28 Single Issue. Akademiia Nauk SSR, UI Voskhod 15, Novosibirsk USSR. **LC** Z6675.I5, RC963.A1.

DER INTERNIST. (INTERNIST). 0020-9554. Periodical. GW. German. mo. Springer Verlag-New York Inc, 175 5th Avenue, New York NY 10010. **Tel** (212)460-1500. Ed M Broglie, E Buchborn, and W Doelle. **Ind/Abst** CIS Abstr., Excerpta Med., Chem. Abstr., Biol. Abstr., Nucl. Sci. Abstr., Index Med., Energy Res. Abstr., Sci. Cit. Index, Abr. Ed. **NLM** W1 IN962. **CODEN** INTEAG. (cum index). All areas of internal medicine. Each issue is dedicated to one specific area, articles are coordinated for a comprehensive coverage of the subject, diagnosis and therapy take priority. *Aertzliche Wochenschrift*.

DEUTSCHE ZEITSCHRIFT FUER VERDAUUNGS- UND STOFFWECHSELKRANKHEITEN. Began with 1, Jan. 1938. 0323-522X. Periodical. GE. German. bm. Kunst & Wissen Erich Bieber, Dufourstrasse 51, CH-8008 Zurich Switzerland. **Tel** 01/69 44 20. **Ind/Abst** Excerpta Med., Index Med., Chem. Abstr. **NLM** W1 DE912. **CODEN** DZVSAT.

DIAGNOSTIC DYNAMICS. Vol. 1, No. 1 (July 1983)-. 0749-7725. Periodical. US. English. Biodynamics, 9115 Hague Road, Indianapolis IN 46250. **DD** 616.

DIGESTIVE DISEASES AND SCIENCES. New Ser., V. 24- Jan. 1979-. 0163-2116. Periodical. US. English. mo. $125.00 Domestic, $144.00 Foreign. Plenum Press, 233 Spring Street, New York NY 10013. **Tel** (212)620-8000. Ed Frank P Brooks. **Ind/Abst** Life Sci. Collect., Pestdoc, Ringdoc, Vetdoc, Excerpta Med., Biol. Abstr., Chem. Abstr., Curr. Contents, Index Med., Sci. Cit. Index, Abr. Ed., Bibliogr. Agric., Energy Res. Abstr., Curr. Surg. **LC** RC799. **DD** 616.3005. **NLM** W1 DI573. **CODEN** DDSCDJ. bk rev. adv acc. *American Journal of Digestive Diseases*, 0002-9211.

DIRECTORY OF SUBSPECIALTY FELLOWSHIP TRAINING PROGRAMS. See Yearbooks, Almanacs, Directories.

DISEASES OF THE COLON & RECTUM. VAT Diseases of the Colon and Rectum. V. 1- Jan./Feb. 1958-. 0012-3706. Periodical. US. English. mo. $92.00. J B Lippincott Company, East Washington Square, Philadelphia PA 19105. **Tel** (215)238-4273. Ed John R Hill. **Ind/Abst** Life Sci. Collect., Excerpta Med., Cumul. Index Nurs. Allied Health Lit., Index Med., Biol. Abstr., Energy Res. Abstr., Sci. Cit. Index, Abr. Ed., Hospit. Lit. Index. **NLM** W1 DI755. **CODEN** DICRAG. bk rev. adv acc. **Circ** 4,379. Original manuscripts devoted to a review of protogologic diseases and surgery.

DUODENAL ULCER. Series/Titl Annual Research Reviews. 1976-. 0703-1637. Periodical. CN. English. an. $20.00 (1976). Eden Press, Suite 201/1538 Sherbrooke Street West, Montreal Quebec H3G Canada. Ed K G Wormsley. **NLM** W1 DU707.

ELECTROMYOGRAPHY AND CLINICAL NEUROPHYSIOLOGY. Began in 1972. 0301-150X. BE. English (some summaries in French, or German). bm. $25.00. Nauwelaerts Publishing House, Mgr Ladeuzeplein 2, Louvain Belgium. **Ind/Abst** Excerpta Med., Index Med., Biol. Abstr. **LC** RC77.5. **DD** 616.740754. **NLM** W1 EL332E. **CODEN** EMCNA9. *Electromyography*.

END-STAGE RENAL DISEASE PROGRAM MEDICAL INFORMATION SYSTEM, FACILITY SURVEY TABLES. 0738-0267. US. English. an. Superintendent of Documents, US Government Printing Office, Washington DC 20402.

ENDOSCOPY REVIEW. Began in 1984. 8756-968X. Periodical. US. English. qt. Free. Island Publishing Group Inc, PO Box 508, Lawrence NY 11559. **Tel** (516)239-2372. Ed Harold Jacob. **DD** 616. bk rev. adv acc. **Circ** 13,000. (ctrl). A guide to techniques and products in the application of diagnostic and therapeutic endoscopy to the science of gastroenterology.

ERGEBNISSE DER INNEREN MEDIZIN UND KINDERHEILKUNDE. Vol. 1-65, 1908-1945. 0071-111X. Periodical. German. ir. Springer Verlag-New York Inc, 175-5th Avenue, New York NY 10010. **Tel** (212)460-1584. **Ind/Abst** Index Med. **NLM** W1 ER281. Advances in internal medicine and pediatrics.

EXCERPTA MEDICA. SECTION 25. HEMATOLOGY. See Indexes/Abstracts.

EXCERPTA MEDICA. SECTION 48. GASTROENTEROLOGY. See Indexes/Abstracts.

EXTRACTA GASTROENTEROLOGICA. V. 9, No. 1 (Feb. 1980)-. 0173-1629. Periodical. GW. German (summaries in English and German). bm. $15.83. Acron Verlag, Potsdamer Strasse 89, 1000 Berlin 30 West Germany. **Tel** 030/262-20-21. Ed K Cremer. **Ind/Abst** Excerpta Med. **NLM** W1 EX752F. bk rev. adv acc. *Aktuelle Gastrologie*.

G. E. N. VAT GEN. V. 1- July/Sept. 1946-. 0016-3503. Periodical. VE. Spanish. qt. $50.00. Apartado 51890, Sabana Grande, Caracas 1050-A Venezuela. **Tel** 979-9380. Ed Marta Rodriguez de Gozalez. **Ind/Abst** Index Med. **NLM** W1 G425. (cum index). adv acc. **Circ** 1,900. Original papers and review articles concerning all aspects of gastroenterology and hepatology.

GASTROENTEROLOGIA JAPONICA. 1-. 0435-1339. Periodical. JA. English. bm. $36.00. Japanese Society of Gastroenterology, G Orient Building 9-13, Ginza 8 Chome Chuo-Ku, Tokyo 104 Japan. **Tel** 03-573-4297. Ed Keiichi Kawai. **Ind/Abst** Index Med., Biol. Abstr., Chem. Abstr. **NLM** W1 GA455N. **CODEN** GAJABC. adv acc. **Circ** 3,000. Original articles on gastroenterology, including case records, short communications, editorials, proceedings, etc.

GASTROENTEROLOGIA Y HEPATOLOGIA. 0210-5705. Periodical. Spanish. mo. $35.00. **Ind/Abst** Excerpta Med. **NLM** W1.

GASTROENTEROLOGIE CLINIQUE ET BIOLOGIQUE. V. 1- Jan. 1977-. 0399-8320. Periodical. FR. articles in English or French. mo. Masson Publishing USA Inc, 211 East 43rd Street/

Room 1306, New York NY 10017. **Tel** (212)370-1937. **Ind/Abst** Life Sci. Collect., Excerpta Med., Index Med., Biol. Abstr., Chem. Abstr. **NLM** W1 GA456L. **CODEN** GCBIDC. *Archives Francaises des Maladies de l'Appareil Digestif, 0003-9772; Biologie et Gastro-Enterologie, 0006-3258.*

DAS GASTROENTEROLOGISCHE KOMPENDIUM. Began with: 1, in 1977. Monographic Series. German. ir. **NLM** W1 GA457K.

GASTROENTEROLOGY. **Series/Titl** Excerpta Medica, Section 48. V. 1- Apr. 1971-. NE. English. ir. Excerpta Medica, PO Box 126, 1000 BC Amsterdam Netherlands. **LC** RC799. **DD** 616.3005.

GASTROENTEROLOGY. V. 1- Jan. 1943-. 0016-5085. Periodical. English. ir. $118.00. Elsevier Science Publishing Company Inc, PO Box 1663/ Grand Central Station, New York NY 10163. **Tel** (212)370-5520. **Ed** Robert K Ockner. **Ind/Abst** Biol. Abstr., Chem. Abstr., Nuci. Sci. Abstr., Index Med., Sci. Cit. Index, Abr. Ed., Hospit. Lit. Index. **DD** 616.305. **CODEN** GASTAB. bk rev. adv acc. **Circ** 15,000. The world's most prestigious gastroenterological journal covers all aspects of the digestive tract and liver in clinical and basic science articles, brief reviews, and clinical case reports.

GASTROENTEROLOGY ABSTRACTS AND CITATIONS. *See* Indexes/Abstracts.

GASTROENTEROLOGY (MARCEL DEKKER, INC.). (GASTROENTEROLOGY). Vol. 1-. Monographic Series. US. English. **Ed** Jules Dienstag and Anthony L Imbembo.

GASTROINTESTINAL ENDOSCOPY (LONDON, ENGLAND). (GASTROINTESTINAL ENDOSCOPY : ADVANCES IN DIAGNOSIS AND THERAPY). Vol. 1-. 0262-8996. Periodical. UK. English. **Ed** P R Salmon. **NLM** W1.

GASTRONOMIE. 0323-4762. Periodical. German. bm. Kunst & Wissen Erich Bieber, Dufourstrasse 51, CH-8008 Zurich Switzerland.

GUT. V. 1- Mar. 1960-. 0017-5749. Periodical. UK. English. mo. $136.39. British Medical Journal, Tavistock Square, London WC1H 9JR England. **Ind/Abst** Life Sci. Collect., Excerpta Med., Index Med., Biol. Abstr., Chem. Abstr., Pestdoc, Ringdoc, Vetdoc, Hospit. Lit. Index, Sci. Cit. Index, Abr. Ed. **NLM** W1 GU821. **CODEN** GUTTAK.

HAEMATOLOGIA. (HAEMATOLOGIA. INTERNATIONAL QUARTERLY OF HAEMATOLOGY). V. 1- 1967-. 0017-6559. Periodical. NE. English (articles in French, German and Russian). qt. $113.22. Proost & Brandt Distribution BV, 63 Strijkviertel, 3454 PK de Meern Netherlands. **Tel** (0)3406 3737. **Ed** S R Hollan. **Ind/Abst** Excerpta Med., Biol. Abstr., Chem. Abstr., Nuci. Sci. Abstr., Index Med. **NLM** W1 HA155P. **CODEN** HAEMBY. bk rev. adv acc. **Circ** 300. Journal publishing papers in haematology and related fields such as immunology, blood transfusion, transplantation and oncology. *Haematologia Hungarica, 0367-5599.*

HAMATOLOGIE UND BLUTTRANSFUSION. Vol. 1-19. 0440-0607. Monographic Series. German. ir. Springer Verlag-New York Inc, 175 5th Avenue, New York NY 10010. **Tel** (212)460-1500. **Ind/Abst** Chem. Abstr., Nuci. Sci. Abstr., Index Med. **NLM** W1 HA1655. **CODEN** HABLAF. Numbered series supplement to the journal Blut.

HEMOGLOBIN. V. 1-. 0363-0269. Monographic Series. US. English. bm. $166.75. Marcel Dekker Inc, PO Box 11305 Church Street Station, New York NY 10249. **Ed** T H J Huisman. **Ind/Abst** Life Sci. Collect., Biol. Abstr., Bull. Signal., Chem. Abstr., Curr. Aware. Biol. Sci., Curr. Contents. Life Sci., Curr. Lit. Blood, Excerpta Med., Index Med., Sci. Cit. Index, Abr. Ed., Energy Res. Abstr., Autom. Subj. Citation Alert. **LC** RC641.7.H35. **DD** 616.15. **NLM** W1 HE878. **CODEN** HEM0D8. bk rev. adv acc. (ctrl). A primary current source for hematologists, clinicians, enzymologists, pathologists, medical technicians, and all researchers seeking up-to-date blood research findings.

HEMOSTASIS AND THROMBOSIS; A BIBLIOGRAPHY. *See* Bibliographies.

HEPATO-GASTROENTEROLOGY. V. 27- Feb. 1980-. 0172-6390. Periodical. English. bm. $80.00. Thieme-Stratton Inc, 381 Park Avenue South/ Suite 1501, New York NY 10016. **Tel** (212)683-5088. **Ed** H W Altman. **Ind/Abst** Life Sci. Collect., Excerpta Med., Index Med., Chem. Abstr., Energy Res. Abstr. **NLM** W1 HE91. **CODEN** HEGAD4. **Circ** 1,350. Contains original papers, editorials, abstract and critical reviews. *Acta Hepato-Gastroenterologica, 0300-970X.*

HEPATOLOGY. SHORT FORM. (HEPATOLOGY; RAPID LITERATURE REVIEW, SHORT FORM). 0171-9645. US. English. qt. Charles B Slack Inc, 6900 Grove Road, Thorofare NJ 08086. **NLM** ZWI 700 H529.

THE HLB NEWSLETTER. **VAT** Heart, Lung, Blood Newsletter. Began in 1985?. 0887-3712. Periodical. US. English. mo. $97.00. Suite 306/1001-3rd Street SW, Washington DC 20024-4408. **DD** 616.

HODGKIN'S DISEASE AND THE LYMPHOMAS. 1977-. 0703-1653. Periodical. CN. English. an. Eden Press, 4626 St Catherine Street West, Montreal Quebec H3Z 1S3 Canada. **Ed** C R Taylor. **Ind/Abst** Life Sci. Collect. **DD** 616.42. **NLM** W1 HO459D.

IMMUNOPHARMACOLOGY. Began with: Vol. 1, published in Dec. 1978. 0162-3109. Periodical. US. English. bm. $195.86. Marcel Dekker Inc, PO Box 11305/Church Street Station, New York NY 10249. **Ed** Michael A Chirigos. **Ind/Abst** Life Sci. Collect., Pestdoc, Ringdoc, Vetdoc, Excerpta Med., Index Med., Biol. Abstr., Chem. Abstr. **NLM** W1 IM56. **CODEN** IMMUDP. bk rev. adv acc. (ctrl). Studies interrelating the modulation of the immune system with agents which may affect this modulation. An interface between disciplines of immunology and pharmacology.

INDIAN JOURNAL OF GASTROENTEROLOGY : OFFICIAL JOURNAL OF THE INDIAN SOCIETY OF GASTROENTEROLOGY. Began with: Vol. 1, No. 1 (Apr. 1982). Periodical. English. qt. $20.00. Prints India, 11 Darya Ganj, New Delhi 110002 India. **Ind/Abst** Excerpta Med. **NLM** W1.

INFLAMMATION. V. 1- Mar. 1975-. 0360-3997. Periodical. US. English. qt. $105.00 Domestic, $118.00 Foreign. Plenum Press, 233 Spring Street, New York NY 10013. **Tel** (212)620-8000. **Ed** Gerald Weissmann. **Ind/Abst** Life Sci. Collect., Excerpta Med., Index Med., Biol. Abstr., Chem. Abstr., Energy Res. Abstr., Pestdoc, Ringdoc, Vetdoc, Sci. Cit. Index, Abr. Ed. **LC** RB131. **DD** 616.047. **NLM** W1 IN41KR. **CODEN** INFLD4. bk rev. adv acc. An international journal devoted to experimental and clinical studies of the physiology, biochemistry, cell biology and pharmacology of inflammation.

DER INFORMIERTE ARZT. Vol. 1- 1973-. 0342-2593. Periodical. German. ir. 60.-. I M P Verlagsgesellschaft MBH, Beethovenstrasse 2 Postfach 266, 6078 Neu-Isenberg West Germany. **Tel** (089)472086. **Ed** Lisa Carr. **NLM** W1 IN443. bk rev. adv acc. **Circ** 50,000. (ctrl). We provide continuing education to general practitioners by means of original articles on a variety of medical topics pertaining to everyday practice for relevant background information.

INFUSIONSTHERAPIE UND KLINISCHE ERNAHRUNG. Vol. 2- Feb. 1975-. 0378-0791. Monographic Series. SZ. Multilingual (articles in German or English, with summaries and table of contents in both languages). bm. 116.-. S Karger AG, PO Box, CH-4009 Basel Switzerland. **Tel** (061)39 08 80. **Ed** H Reissigl, K H Bassler, A Grunert and G Kleinberger. **Ind/Abst** Life Sci. Collect., Index Med., Chem. Abstr., Excerpta Med., Curr. Contents, Sci. Cit. Index, Abr. Ed. **NLM** W1 IN447C. **CODEN** IKEFAP. adv acc. Microfilm, microfiche. Newest findings in the area of clinical nutrition and research in digestion-metabolic problems of patients are discussed, questions of blood transfusions and blood replacements and techniques are discussed. *Infusionstherapie, 0301-3243.*

INNERE MEDIZIN. V. 1-. 0303-4305. Periodical. GW. German (summaries in English). ir. Verlag Gerhard Witzstrock GMBH, Bismarckstrasse 9, 7570 Baden Baden Germany. **Ind/Abst** Excerpta Med., Energy Res. Abstr., Sci. Cit. Index, Abr. Ed. **NLM** W1 IN454N.

INTERNAL MEDICINE ADVISER. (THE INTERNAL MEDICINE ADVISER). **VAT** Adviser (Internal Medecine Ed.). Vol. 1, No. 1 (Apr. 1983)-. 0823-6534. Periodical. CN. English. mo. $20.00. Internal Medicine Adviser, 1300 Bay Street, Toronto Ontario M5R 3K8 Canada. **DD** 332.024616.

INTERNAL MEDICINE ALERT. V. 1- Mar. 15, 1979-. 0195-315X. Periodical. US. English. sm. $55.00. International Thompson Medical Information, 680 Kinderkamack Road, Oradell NJ 07649. **Tel** (215)925-7060. **NLM** W1 IN698M.

INTERNAL MEDICINE FOR THE SPECIALIST. (INTERNAL MEDICINE FOR THE SPECIALIST : IM). **VFOAT** IM. Issue 1 (Sept. 1980)-. 0273-6608. Periodical. US. English. ir. IM—Internal Medicine for the Specialist, 50 Route 9, Morganville NJ 07751. **Tel** (201)536-3600. **LC** R11. **DD** 616. **NLM** W1 IN699M. adv acc.

INTERNAL MEDICINE NEWS & CARDIOLOGY NEWS. **VAT** Internal Medicine News and Cardiology News. V. 13, No. 9- May 1, 1980-. 0274-5542. Periodical. US. English. sm. $70.00. Diagnosis News Inc, 12230 Wilkins Avenue, Rockville MD 20852. **Tel** (301)770-6170. *Internal Medicine News, 0099-152X.*

INTERNATIONAL BLOOD/PLASMA NEWS. **VFOAT** International Blood, Plasma News. 0742-7719. Periodical. US. English. mo. $295.00 Domestic, $315.00 Foreign. International Blood/ Plasma News, 352 3rd Street/#308, Laguna Beach CA 92651. **Tel** (714)497-6522. **Ed** Jack Reasor. **Circ** 150. Covers business and general information regarding what is happening around the world regarding blood/plasma/genetic about these subjects. We also list a patent section covering blood/plasma products and a list of meetings that maybe of interest to our readership.

INTERNATIONAL JOURNAL OF ARTIFICIAL ORGANS. (THE INTERNATIONAL JOURNAL OF ARTIFICIAL ORGANS). V. 1- Jan. 1978-. 0391-3988. Periodical. IT. English. bm. $56.00. Wichtig Editore, 3 Via Rovani, 20123 Milano Italy. **Ind/Abst** Life Sci. Collect., Excerpta Med., Index Med., Chem. Abstr. **NLM** W1 IN7655H. **CODEN** IJAODS.

THE INTERNATIONAL JOURNAL OF EATING DISORDERS. Vol. 1, No. 1 (Autumn 1981)-. 0276-3478. Periodical. US. English. qt. $96.00. John Wiley & Sons Inc, 605 Third Avenue, New York NY 10158. **Tel** (212)850-6000. **Ind/Abst** Electron. Commun. Abstr. J., ISMEC Bull., Pollut. Abstr. Indexes, Saf. Sci. Abstr. J., Life Sci. Collect., Excerpta Med., Biol. Abstr., Psychol. Abstr. **LC** RC815.2. **DD** 616.89. **NLM** W1. **CODEN** INDIDJ.

INTERNISTISCHE WELT. V. 1-. 0344-4201. Periodical. German. mo. Futura Media Services Inc, 295 Main Street, Mount Kisco NY 10549. **Tel** (914)666-3505. **Ind/Abst** Excerpta Med., Energy Res. Abstr. **NLM** W1 IN968C.

INTRAVENOUS THERAPY NEWS. Vol. 11, No. 6 (June 1984)-. 8750-3182. Periodical. US. English. mo. $32.00. Intravenous Therapy News, 121 South Gertrude Avenue, Paramus NJ 07652. **Ind/Abst** Life Sci. Collect. **DD** 615. **NLM** W1. *American Journal of Intravenous Therapy & Clinical Nutrition, 0195-0282.*

IRCS MEDICAL SCIENCE. ALIMENTARY SYSTEM. (IRCS MEDICAL SCIENCE : ALIMENTARY SYSTEM). **VFOAT** Alimentary System. V. 3- Jan. 1975-. 0305-6678. Periodical. UK. English. bm. $70.00. IRCS Medical Science, PO Box 500, St Leonards House, Lancaster LA1 1PF England. **Tel** (0524)68116. **Ed** S Johnson. bk rev. Publishes results of original research into gastroenterology and gut physiology and biochemistry within weeks of completion. Papers fully refereed. *Research on the Alimentary System, 0305-2575.*

IRCS MEDICAL SCIENCE. HEMATOLOGY. (IRCS MEDICAL SCIENCE : HEMATOLOGY). **VFOAT** Hematology. V. 3- Jan. 1975-. 0305-6805. Periodical. UK. English. mo. $95.00. IRCS Medical Science, PO Box 500/St Leonards House, Lancaster LA1 1PF England. **Tel** (0524)68116. **Ed** S Johnson. bk rev. Publishes results of original research into all aspects of hematology, both clinical and experimental, within weeks of completion. Papers fully refereed. *Research on Hematology, 0305-277X.*

THE ITALIAN JOURNAL OF GASTROENTEROLOGY. V. 10- Apr. 1978-. 0392-0623. Periodical. English. qt. Masson Italia Periodici, Via Pinturicchio 1, 20133 Milano Italy. **Tel** 02/276268. **Ed** Aldo Torsoli. **Ind/Abst** Excerpta Med., Chem. Abstr. **NLM** W1 IT1355. **CODEN** ITJGDH. bk rev. adv acc. **Circ** 2,000. Official organ of the Societa Italiana di Gastroenterologia (Italian Association of Gastroenterology) and of the Italian Association for the Study of the Liver. *Rendiconti di Gastro-Enterologia, 0389-4849.*

THE JOHNS HOPKINS MEDICAL JOURNAL *CEASED.* V. 120-151. 0021-7263. US. English. mo. $34.00 Domestic, $39.00 Foreign. Journals Department, The Johns Hopkins University Press, Baltimore MD 21205. **Ind/Abst** Excerpta Med., Life Sci. Collect., Energy Inf. Abstr., Environ. Abstr., Biol. Abstr., Chem. Abstr., Energy Res. Abstr., Nuci. Sci. Abstr., Index Med. **LC** RC31.B2. **NLM** W1

Medicine—Internal Medicine

JO158G. CODEN JHMJAX. *Bulletin of the Johns Hopkins Hospital, 0097-1383.*

THE JOHNS HOPKINS UNIVERSITY SCHOOL OF MEDICINE POSTGRADUATE COURSE IN INTERNAL MEDICINE. (THE JOHNS HOPKINS UNIVERSITY SCHOOL OF MEDICINE POSTGRADUATE COURSE IN INTERNAL MEDICINE. KIT). VFOAT Johns Hopkins Postgraduate Course in Internal Medicine. V. 1- (Program 1- April 1975)-. 0360-5914. Periodical. US. English. mo. Johns Hopkins University, School of Medicine, 1721 East Madison Street, Baltimore MD 21205. **Tel** (301)955-3988. **NLM** AV KIT 103.

JOURNAL OF CLINICAL GASTROENTEROLOGY. V. 1- Mar. 1979-. 0192-0790. Periodical. US. English. bm. $72.00. Raven Press, 1140 Avenue of the Americas, New York NY 10036. **Tel** (212)575-0335. **Ind/Abst** Life Sci. Collect., Excerpta Med., Index Med., Sci. Cit. Index, Abr. Ed. **LC** RC799. **DD** 616.3005. **NLM** W1 JO588CM.

JOURNAL OF GENERAL INTERNAL MEDICINE. 0884-8734. Periodical. US. English. bm. $70.00. Hanley & Belfus Inc, 210 South 13th Street, Philadelphia PA 19107.

JOURNAL OF HEPATOLOGY. Vol. 1, No. 1-. 0168-8278. Periodical. NE. English. bm. $100.75. **Ind/Abst** Chem. Abstr., Index Med. **NLM** W1. **CODEN** JOHEEC.

JOURNAL OF MEDICAL VIROLOGY. V. 1-. 0146-6615. Periodical. US. English. bm. Alan R Liss Inc, 150 5th Avenue, New York NY 10011. **Tel** (212)741-2515. **LC** RC114.5. **DD** 616.019405. **NLM** W1 J0756V. **CODEN** JMVIDB.

KEKKAKU TOROKUSHA CHOSA. Main/Corp Japan. Koseisho. Koshu Eiseikyoku. No. 6-Issue. JA. Japanese. ir. 1000. Kekkaku Yobokai, 3-12 Misakucho, Chiyoda-Ku 101, Tokyo Japan. **LC** RC317.J26. *Kekkaku Jittai Chosa.*

KEYWORD INDEX IN INTERNAL MEDICINE. See Indexes/Abstracts.

KLINISCHE WOCHENSCHRIFT. V. 1- 1922-. 0023-2173. Periodical. WB. German. sm. Springer Verlag-New York Inc, 175 5th Avenue, New York NY 10010. **Tel** (212)460-1584. Ed N Zoellner. **Ind/Abst** Life Sci. Collect., Excerpta Med., Pestdoc, Ringdoc, Vetdoc, Index Med., Int. Aerosp. Abstr., Biol. Abstr., Chem. Abstr., Energy Res. Abstr., Sci. Cit. Index, Abr. Ed. **NLM** W1 KL581. **CODEN** KLWOAZ. Journal of Association of German Natural Scientists and Doctors, Clinical and Experimental Medicine. Publishes research findings in medicine and related areas, with special emphasis on internal medicine. *Therapeutische Halbmonatshefte, Berliner Klinische Wochenschrift.*

KOKU IGAKU JIKKENTAI KENKYU SEIKA GAIYO. Main/Corp Japan. Kioku Igaku Jikkentai. Japanese. ir. 2-10 Sakaecho 1, Tachikawa Japan. **LC** RC050.

LEBER, MAGEN, DARM. 1-Yearly Volume. 0300-8622. Periodical. GW. German. bm. $28.40. Gerhard Witzstrock, Bismarckstr 9, D 7570 Baden-Baden East Germany. **Ind/Abst** Life Sci. Collect., Excerpta Med., Index Med., Chem. Abstr., Sci. Cit. Index, Abr. Ed. **NLM** W1 LE324. **CODEN** LBMDAT.

LIVER. Vol. 1, No. 1 (Mar. 1981)-. 0106-9543. Periodical. English. bm. $79.08. Munksgaard Ltd, 35 Norre Sogade, DK-1370 Copenhagen K Denmark. **Tel** 1.12.70.30. Ed Hemming Poulsen and Per Christoffersen. **Ind/Abst** Excerpta Med., Index Med., Biol. Abstr. **NLM** W1 LI919N. **CODEN** Liver. bk rev. adv acc. **Circ** 800. Liver pathology, hepatology and diseases of the liver.

LIVER (AMSTERDAM, NETHERLANDS) CEASED. (THE LIVER). VFOAT Liver Annual. V. 1 (1981)-. Periodical. US. English. an. Elsevier North-Holland, 52 Vanderbilt Avenue, New York NY 10017. Ed I M Arias, M Frenkel and J H P Wilson. **NLM** W1 LI919M.

MAGNETIC RESONANCE IMAGING. V. 1, No. 1-. 0730-725X. Periodical. US. English. qt. $120.00. Pergamon Press, c/o Cashier, 395 Sawmill River Road, Elmsford NY 10523. **Ind/Abst** Electron. Commun. Abstr. J., ISMEC Bull., Pollut. Abstr. Indexes, Saf. Sci. Abstr. J., Excerpta Med., Biol. Abstr., Chem. Abstr. **LC** RC78.7.N83. **DD** 616.0757. **NLM** W1 MA34H. **CODEN** MRIMDQ. Issued also in microform.

MAGNETIC RESONANCE IN MEDICINE. (MAGNETIC RESONANCE IN MEDICINE : OFFICIAL JOURNAL OF THE SOCIETY OF MAGNETIC RESONANCE IN MEDICINE). Began with Vol. 1, No. 1 (Feb. 1984)-. 0740-3194. Periodical. US. English. bm. $85.00. Academic Press, 4805 Sand Lake Road, Orlando FL 32819. **Ind/Abst** Chem. Abstr. **DD** 616. **NLM** W1. **CODEN** MRMEEN.

MAJOR PROBLEMS IN INTERNAL MEDICINE. V. 1- 1971-. 0090-6956. US. English. ir. W B Saunders Company, West Washington Square, Philadelphia PA 19105. **Tel** (800)523-0713. **Ind/Abst** Energy Res. Abstr., Index Med. **NLM** W1 MA492T.

MANUAL FOR LABORATORY WORKLOAD RECORDING METHOD. 0747-9158. US. English. an. College of American Pathologists, 7400 North Skokie Boulevard, Skokie IL 60077-3388. **DD** 616. *Laboratory Workload Recording Method.*

MEDICAL GRAND ROUNDS (NEW YORK, N.Y.). (MEDICAL GRAND ROUNDS). Vol. 1, No. 1 (Mar. 1982)-. 0277-805X. Periodical. US. English. qt. $95.00 Domestic, $107.00 Foreign. Plenum Publishing Corporation, 233 Spring Street, New York NY 10013. **Tel** (212)620-8000. Ed Sidney H Ingbar. **Ind/Abst** Excerpta Med. **NLM** W1 ME334C. **CODEN** MGRODY. adv acc. This journal translates into written form. The current and style of the time tested format. Contains presentation and discussion of actual cases in each of ten areas of internal medicine.

MEDICINA INTERNA. V. 7-26, Vol. 6. 0025-7869. Periodical. RM. Romanian (summaries in English, French, German, and Russian). bm. Ilexim Press Department, PO Box 11361137, Bucharest Romania. **Ind/Abst** Excerpta Med., Biol. Abstr., Chem. Abstr., Nuci. Sci. Abstr., Index Med. **NLM** W1 ME598. **CODEN** MINTA6. *Revista Stiintelor Medicale: Medicina.*

MEDICINE. US. English. an. John Wiley, 605 Third Avenue, New York NY 10016. **LC** R5. **DD** 610.5.

MEMBERSHIP DIRECTORY - AMERICAN SOCIETY OF INTERNAL MEDICINE. See Yearbooks, Almanacs, Directories.

METABOLISMO. V. 1- Jan./Feb. 1965-. 0026-0509. Periodical. IT. chiefly Italian. bm. C E P I, Via G B Martini 6, Rome Italy. **LC** RC620.A1. *Archivo del Ricambio.*

METHODS IN HEMATOLOGY. Vol. 1-. 0277-8599. Monographic Series. US. English. ir. Churchill Livingstone Inc, 1560 Broadway, New York NY 10036. **Tel** (212)819-5400. **Ind/Abst** Chem. Abstr. **NLM** W1 ME9615L. **CODEN** MHEMD4.

MICROVASCULAR RESEARCH. VFOAT MVR. V. 1- June 1968. 0026-2862. Periodical. US. English. bm. Academic Press, 4805 Sand Lake Road, Orlando FL 32819. **Tel** (305)345-4100. **Ind/Abst** Life Sci. Collect., Excerpta Med., Energy Res. Abstr., Nuci. Sci. Abstr., Index Med., Biol. Abstr., Chem. Abstr., Sci. Cit. Index, Abr. Ed. **LC** RC681.A1. **DD** 612.135072. **NLM** W1 MI313N. **CODEN** MIVRA6.

MINERVA DIETOLOGICA E GASTROENTEROLOGICA. V. 23, No. 2- April/June 1977-. 0391-1993. Periodical. IT. Italian (summaries in English). qt. 80.00. Edizoni Minerva Medica, Corso Bramante 83-85, Torino Italy 10126. **Tel** 67 82 82. Ed A Oliaro. **Ind/Abst** Excerpta Med., Index Med., Chem. Abstr. **LC** RC799. **NLM** W1 MI6395C. **CODEN** MDGADI. bk rev. adv acc. Journal addressed to practitioners and specialists in gastroenterology and diet. It deals with topics in scientific practice and research. *Minerva Dietologica, Minerva Gastroenterologica.*

MINERVA MEDICA. 0026-4806. IT. Italian. wk. 100.00. Edizioni Minerva Medica, Corso Brabante 83-85, Torino Italy 10126. **Tel** 67 82 82. Ed A Oliaro. **Ind/Abst** Chem. Abstr., CIS Abstr., Index Med., Life Sci. Collect., Excerpta Med., Pestdoc, Ringdoc, Vetdoc. **LC** R61. **NLM** W1 MI646. **CODEN** MIMEAO. bk rev. adv acc. Journal addressed to practitioners and specialists in internal medicine in Italy and abroad. It deals with topics in medicine, scientific practice and research.

NAIKA. VFOAT Internal Medicine. Vol. 1- Jan.1958-. 0547-1729. Periodical. JA. Japanese. mo. $154.37. Nankodo Company Ltd, Hongo 3 Chome 42-6 Bunkyo Ku, Tokyo Japan. **NLM** W1 NA11695.

NAIKA HOKAN = JAPANESE ARCHIVES OF INTERNAL MEDICINE. See Genealogy and Heraldry - Archives.

NEWSLETTER - NORTHWESTERN SOCIETY OF INTESTINAL RESEARCH. (NEWSLETTER). 0715-3236. Periodical. CN. English. ir. Free to Members. Northwestern Society of Intestinal Research, Box 80838, South Burnaby British Columbia V5H 3Y1 Canada. **DD** 616.34005. *Newsletter to all Members (Northwestern Society of Intestinal Research), 0715-3228.*

NIHON NAIKA GAKKAI ZASSHI. VFOAT Journal of the Japanese Society of Internal Medicine. Vol. 1- July 1913-. 0021-5384. Periodical. JA. Japanese (summaries in English, 1956-). mo. Japan Publications Trading Co, PO Box 5030 Tokyo International, Tokyo 100-31 Japan. **Ind/Abst** Index Med., Chem. Abstr. **NLM** W1 NI923P. **CODEN** NNGAAS. Index in last issue of volume - attached. *Nihon Naika Gakkaishi.*

NIPPON KETSUEKI GAKKAI ZASSHI. VFOAT Acta Haematologica Japonica, Journal of Japan Hematological Society. V. 1- 1937-. 0001-5806. Periodical. JA. Japanese (text also in English). ir. Japan Publishers Trading Company Ltd, PO Box 5030/Tokyo International, Tokyo 100-31 Japan. **Ind/Abst** Life Sci. Collect., Index Med., Excerpta Med., Biol. Abstr., Chem. Abstr., Sci. Cit. Index, Abr. Ed. **NLM** W1 NI919P. **CODEN** NKGZAE.

PERSPECTIVES IN ASTHMA. 1-. 0738-4688. Monographic Series. UK. English. Academic Press Inc, 4805 Sand Lake Road, Orlando FL 32819. **Ind/Abst** Chem. Abstr. **LC** UNC. **DD** 616.238005. **NLM** W1 PE8705L. **CODEN** PEASDE.

PHLEBOLOGIE UND PROKTOLOGIE. (PHLEBOLOGIE UND PROKTOLOGIE : ORGAN DER DEUTSCHEN GESELLSCHAFT FUR PHLEBOLOGIE UND PROKTOLOGIE). Began with: V. 1, No. 1, (1972). 0340-305X. Periodical. German. ir. Futura Media Services Inc, 295 Main Street PO Box 298, Mount Kisco NY 10549. **Tel** (914)666-3505. **Ind/Abst** Excerpta Med. **NLM** W1 PH62M.

POLSKIE ARCHIWUM MEDYCYNY WEWNETRZNEJ. See Genealogy and Heraldry - Archives.

PRACTICAL GASTROENTEROLOGY. Vol. 4, No. 9 (Oct. 1980)-. 0277-4208. Periodical. US. English. bm. $114.00. Pharmaceutical Communications, 45-15 Crescent Street, Long Island City NY 11101. **Tel** (212)937-4283. **NLM** W1 PR141N. *Primary Care Physician's Guide to Practical Gastroenterology, 0163-7894.*

PROGRAM REPORT - NATIONAL HEART, LUNG, AND BLOOD INSTITUTE, DIVISION OF LUNG DISEASES. (PROGRAM REPORT). 0192-9305. US. English. an. National Institutes of Health, National Heart Lung and Blood Institute, Division of Lung Diseases, 533 Westbard Avenue, Bethesda MD 20205. **LC** RC756. **DD** 353.00841. **NLM** WF 20 P964.

PROGRESS IN CLINICAL RHEUMATOLOGY. Vol. 1-. 0742-745X. US. English. ir. Grune & Stratton Inc, Orlando FL 32887. **DD** 616.

PROGRESS IN GASTROENTEROLOGY. V. 1-. 0079-6271. US. English. ir. Grune & Stratton, 111 5th Avenue, New York NY 10003. Ed G B J Glass. **Ind/Abst** Life Sci. Collect., Biol. Abstr., Chem. Abstr. **LC** RC801. **DD** 616.3. **NLM** W1 PR668W. **CODEN** PGGAAZ.

PROGRESS IN LIVER DISEASES. V. 1-. 0079-6409. US. English. Grune & Stratton, 111 5th Avenue, New York NY 10003. **Ind/Abst** Life Sci. Collect., Energy Res. Abstr., Biol. Abstr., Chem. Abstr., Index Med. **LC** RC845. **DD** 616.362. **NLM** W1 PR67085. **CODEN** PLVDAI.

RECENT ADVANCES IN GASTROENTEROLOGY. Began with 1965 Vol. 0141-5581. Periodical. UK. English. ir. Churchill Livingstone Inc, 1560 Broadway, New York NY 10036. **Tel** (212)819-5400. Ed John Badenoch, Bryan N Brooke. **Ind/Abst** Chem. Abstr. **LC** RC799. **DD** 616.33005. **NLM** W1 RE105ULA. **CODEN** RAGADI.

RECENT ADVANCES IN HAEMATOLOGY. No. 1 - 0143-697X. UK. English. ir. Churchill Livingstone Inc, 1560 Broadway, New York NY 10036. **Tel** (212)819-5400. Ed A

Goldbert and M C Brain. **Ind/Abst** Chem. Abstr. **DD** 616.15. **NLM** W1 RE105UM. **CODEN** RAHADN.

RECENT ADVANCES IN HEPATOLOGY. No. 1-. Periodical. UK. English. Churchill Livingstone Inc, 1560 Broadway, New York NY 10036. **Ed** Howard C Thomas and Roderick N M MacSween. **NLM** W1.

REFERENCE SERIES. HEMATOLOGY. HE-1-. 0824-6882. Monographic Series. CN. English. Toronto Institute of Medical Technology, 222 St Patrick Street, Toronto Ontario M5T 1V4 Canada. **DD** 616.15.

REFLECTIONS. 0098-9223. Periodical. US. English. qt. $10.00. Oklahoma Institute of Ultrasound in Medicine, PO Box 26901, Oklahoma City OK 73190. **LC** RC78.7.U4. **DD** 616.0754.

REPORT - CANADIAN RENAL FAILURE REGISTER. (REPORT). **Main/Corp** Canadian Renal Failure Register. 1981-. 0821-784X. Periodical. CN. English. an. $2.50 Each Volume. Canadian Renal Failure Register, c/o Kidney Foundation of Canada, Ottawa Valley Chapter, 230-739B Ridgewood Avenue, Ottawa Ontario K1V 6M8 Canada. **DD** 616.61400971. *Report of the Canadian Renal Failure Registry, 0821-7823.*

REPORT OF THE PATIENT REGISTRY. **Main/Corp** Cystic Fibrosis Foundation. 1977-. 0197-7423. US. English. ir. Cystic Fibrosis Foundation, 6000 Executive Boulevard/Suite 309, Rockville MD 20852. **LC** RC858.C95. **DD** 614.5937. **NLM** W1 CY751F. *Report on Survival Studies of Patients with Cystic Fibrosis, 0161-472X.*

REVISTA DE INVESTIGACION CLINICA. V. 1- 1948-. 0034-8376. Periodical. MX. Spanish (English). qt. 20.00. Instituto Nacionale Nutricion, Salvador Zubiran Vasco de Quiroga No 15, Tlalpan 1400 Mexico DF. **Tel** 573-12-00. **Ed** Ruben Liskery and Enrique Wolpert. **Ind/Abst** Life Sci. Collect., Index Med., Sci. Cit. Index, Abr. Ed. **NLM** W1 RE403T. **CODEN** RICLAG. Index published separately - free - automatically sent. bk rev. adv acc. **Circ** 1,500. Most papers relate to clinical research in internal medicine. Case reports and review articles are generally included. Medical education and quality control often published.

REVISTA ESPANOLA DE LAS ENFERMEDADES DEL APARATO DIGESTIVO. **Series/Titl** Archivos Espanolas de Enfermedades del Aparato Digestivo y de la Nutricion 4.- Epoca. V. 27- Jan. 1968-. 0034-9437. Periodical. SP. English. bm. 100. Editorial Garsi, Londres 17, Madrid 28 Spain. **Tel** 2556800. **Ed** Arias Vallejo. **Ind/Abst** Life Sci. Collect., Excerpta Med., Index Med., Chem. Abstr. **NLM** W1 RE544. **CODEN** READBN. bk rev. adv acc. **Circ** 3,500. Gastroenterology, nutrition, clinical and surgical treatment of sickness of the digestive system.

REVISTA ESPANOLA DE LAS ENFERMEDADES DEL APARATO DIGESTIVO Y DE LA NUTRICION. Periodical. SP. Spanish. mo. Revista Espanola de las Londres 1F, Madrid 28 Spain. **Tel** 2556800. bk rev. adv acc. **Circ** 3,500.

REVISTA MEDICA DE CHILE. Vol. 1- July 1872-. 0034-9887. Periodical. CL. Spanish (some summaries in English). mo. $60.00. Revista Medica de Chile, Esmeralda 678 Int Casilla 23-D, Santiago Chile. **Tel** 56-2-392944. **Ed** Alejandro Goic. **Ind/Abst** Life Sci. Collect., Index Med., Chem. Abstr., Sci. Cit. Index, Abr. Ed. **NLM** W1 RE616L. **CODEN** RMCHAW. bk rev. adv acc. **Circ** 2,500. Contains research on education, ethics, health respectures, history, news.

REVUE ROUMAINE DE MEDECINE. MEDECINE INTERNE. (MEDECINE INTERNE). **VFOAT** Internal Medicine. Vol. 13- 1975-. 0377-1202. Periodical. RM. articles and summaries in English or French. qt. Ilexim Press Department, PO Box 1-136-1-137, Bucharest Romania. **Ind/Abst** Life Sci. Collect., Excerpta Med., Index Med., Biol. Abstr., Chem. Abstr. **NLM** W1 ME144C. **CODEN** RMMIDK. *Revue Roumaine de Medecine, 0303-822X.*

RIFORMA MEDICA. Yearly V. 1- Jan. 1885-. 0035-5259. Periodical. IT. Italian (some summaries in French, English, and German). sa. 60.00. Edizioni Minerva Medica, Corso Bramante 83-85, Torino Italy 10126. **Tel** 678282. **Ed** T Oliaro. **Ind/Abst** CIS Abstr., Chem. Abstr. **NLM** W1 RI168L. **CODEN** RIMEAB. bk rev. adv acc. Journal addressed to practitioners in Italy and abroad. It deals with topics in medicine and pharmachology, scientific practice and research.

SANGRE. V. 1- 1956-. 0036-4355. Periodical. SP. Spanish (English and French). qt. $48.60. Sangre, Paseo de le Constitucion 10, 50008 Zaragoza Spain. **Tel** (967)22 80 50. **Ind/Abst** Excerpta Med., Index Med., Biol. Abstr., Chem. Abstr. **LC** RC633.A1. **NLM** W1 SA6455. **CODEN** SNGRAW. bk rev. adv acc. **Circ** 2,000. Official organ of Spanish Society of Hematology and Blood Transfusions.

SCANDINAVIAN JOURNAL OF GASTROENTEROLOGY. V. 1- Sept. 1966-. 0036-5521. Periodical. English. ir. 216.-. Universitetsforlaget, PO Box 2959-Toyen, Oslo 6 Norway. **Tel** (45)-2-27 60 60. **Ed** J Myren. **Ind/Abst** Life Sci. Collect., Pestdoc, Ringdoc, Vetdoc, Index Med., Biol. Abstr., Energy Res. Abstr., Chem. Abstr., Excerpta Med., Sci. Cit. Index, Abr. Ed., Hospit. Lit. Index. **NLM** W1 SC149G. **CODEN** SJGRA4. adv acc. **Circ** 1,700. Papers are concerned with clinical problems, and experimental work on animals.

SCANDINAVIAN JOURNAL OF HAEMATOLOGY. Began in 1964. 0036-553X. Periodical. DK. English (Danish). Munksgaard Ltd, 35 Norre Sogade, DK-1370 Copenhagen K Denmark. **Tel** 1.12.70.30. **Ed** Aage Videbak. **Ind/Abst** Life Sci. Collect., Excerpta Med., Index Med., Biol. Abstr., Energy Res. Abstr., Chem. Abstr., Sci. Cit. Index, Abr. Ed., Hospit. Lit. Index. **NLM** W1 SC15. **CODEN** SJHAAQ. bk rev. adv acc. **Circ** 1,300. Original articles on clinical and experimental haematology and related subjects.

SCHWEIZERISCHE RUNDSCHAU FUR MEDIZIN PRAXIS. **VFOAT** Revue Suisse de Medicine Praxis. 59. Year. 1 (6. Jan. 1970)-. 0369-8394. Periodical. SZ. German (articles in French). wk. 127.-. Hallwag AG, Nordring 4, CH-3001 Bern Switzerland. **Tel** 031 42 31 31. **Ind/Abst** CIS Abstr., Life Sci. Collect., Excerpta Med., Pestdoc, Ringdoc, Vetdoc, Index Med., Chem. Abstr. **NLM** W1. **CODEN** SRMPDJ. bk rev. adv acc. **Circ** 4,500. Editorials, original articles with bibliographies, question-answer page, CPC, book and journal reviews. *Praxis.*

SCIENTIFIC AMERICAN MEDICINE. 0194-9063. Periodical. US. English. mo. $220.00. Scientific American, 415 Madison Avenue, New York NY 10017. **Tel** (212)754-0550. **Ed** Edward Rubenstein. **Circ** 29,000. Contains current patient-care information in the 15 subspecialties of medicine.

SEAMIC INFORMATION RETRIEVAL ON CURRENT LITERATURE. SERIES J, VIRAL DIARRHEA. **VFOAT** S.E.A.M.I.C. Information Retrieval on Current Literature. No. 1 (Dec. 1981)-. Periodical. English. ir. **NLM** ZWI 407 S438.

SEMINARS IN HEMATOLOGY. Vol. 1, No. 1 (Jan. 1964)-. 0037-1963. Periodical. US. English. qt. Grune & Stratton Inc, 111 Fifth Avenue, New York NY 10003. **Tel** (212)614-3110. **Ind/Abst** Life Sci. Collect., Excerpta Med., Energy Res. Abstr., Biol. Abstr., Chem. Abstr., Index Med., Nuci. Sci. Abstr., Sci. Cit. Index, Abr. Ed. **LC** RC633.A1. **DD** 616.1505. **NLM** W1 SE489. **CODEN** SEHEA3.

SEMINARS IN LIVER DISEASE. Vol. 1, No. 1 (Feb. 1981)-. 0272-8087. Periodical. US. English. qt. $68.00. Thieme-Stratton Inc, 381 Park Avenue South/Suite 1501, New York NY 10016. **Tel** (212)683-5088. **Ed** Paul Berk. **Ind/Abst** Index Med. **DD** 616. **NLM** W1 SE489C. adv acc. **Circ** 1,800. Topic-oriented journal for the practitioner specializing in hepatic diseases and advances.

SONIX. V. 1- Apr. 1975-. 0177-6008. Periodical. US. English. mo. $2.00. Norman House, 1569 South Pearl, Denver CO 80210. **LC** RC78.7.U4. **DD** 616.0754. **NLM** W1 SO88845. **CODEN** SONIDG.

SPECIAL PUBLICATION (INTERNATIONAL CENTRE FOR DIARRHOEAL DISEASE RESEARCH, BANGLADESH). (SPECIAL PUBLICATION). No. 4 (Jan. 1980)-. Monographic Series. English. ir. **NLM** W1 SP295DL. *Special Publications (International Centre for Diarrhoeal Disease Research, Bangladesh).*

SPECIAL PUBLICATIONS - INTERNATIONAL CENTRE FOR DIARRHEOAL DISEASE RESEARCH, BANGLADESH. **Main/Corp** International Centre for Diarheoal Disease Research, Bangladesh. No. 1- 1977-. English. ir. *Special Publication (Cholera Research Laboratory), 0255-6650.*

SURVEY OF DIGESTIVE DISEASES. 1/1/83 (May 1983)-. 0253-4398. Periodical. SZ. English. qt. S Karger AG, 150 Fifth Avenue/Suite 1105, New York NY 10011. **Tel** 061-39 08 80. **Ind/Abst** Chem. Abstr. **NLM** W1 SU92H. **CODEN** SDDIDP. Also available on microform.

THERAPEUTIQUE. 0040-5922. Periodical. French. ir. **Tel** 45.39.22.91. **Circ** 9,000. (ctrl).

THYMUS. V. 1- Sept. 1979-. 0165-6090. Periodical. NE. English. bm. $92.00. Martinus Nijhoff Publishers, PO Box 163, 3300 AD Dordrecht Netherlands. **Tel** 078-334233. **Ed** Jean-Louis Touraine. **Ind/Abst** Life Sci. Collect., Excerpta Med., Index Med., Biol. Abstr., Sci. Cit. Index, Abr. Ed. **NLM** W1 TH958. **CODEN** THYMDB. bk rev. adv acc. **Circ** 1,000. Devoted to the rapid publication of papers (original papers, review articles, short communications and letters to the editor), within the fields of thymology, immunobiology and clinical immunology.

TIJDSCHRIFT VOOR GENEESKUNDE. Vol. 22- 1966-. 0005-8440. Periodical. BE. Dutch. sm. 900. Tijdschrift Voor Geneeskunde, de Pintelaan 185, B-9000 Gent Belgium. **Tel** 091-22 57 41. **Ind/Abst** Excerpta Med. **NLM** W1 TI653C. bk rev. adv acc. (ctrl). Journal of medicine, internal medicine, general practice. *Belgisch Tijdschrift Voor Geneeskunde, 0366-368X; Luevens Geneeskunde Tijdschrift.*

TISSUE ANTIGENS. V. 1- Jan. 1971-. 0001-2815. Periodical. DK. English. 1120. Munksgaard Ltd, 35 Norre Sogade, DK-1370 Copenhagen K Denmark. **Tel** 1 12 70 30. **Ed** Flemming Kissmeyer. **Ind/Abst** Life Sci. Collect., Excerpta Med., Index Med., Biol. Abstr., Energy Res. Abstr., Chem. Abstr., Sci. Cit. Index, Abr. Ed. **LC** QR180. **DD** 591.29205. **NLM** W1 TI827K. **CODEN** TSANA2. adv acc. **Circ** 1,000. Transplantation compatability, histocompatability and immunogenetics.

TRANSACTIONS - AMERICAN SOCIETY FOR ARTIFICIAL INTERNAL ORGANS *CEASED.* **Main/Corp** American Society for Artificial Internal Organs. **VFOAT** ASAIO. V. 1- 1955-. 0066-0078. US. English. an. $60.00. ASAIO National Office, Post Office Box C, Boca Raton FL 33429. **Tel** (305)391-8589. **Ed** George E Schreiner. **Ind/Abst** Life Sci. Collect., Excerpta Med., Energy Res. Abstr., Biol. Abstr., Chem. Abstr., Index Med., Nuci. Sci. Abstr., Eng. Index, Hospit. Lit. Index, Sci. Cit. Index, Abr. Ed. **LC** RD130. **DD** 617.95. **NLM** W1 TR223Q. **CODEN** TAIOAL. (cum index). **Circ** 3,000. Hardbound. Artificial organs.

TREATMENT IN GENERAL PRACTICE. 1st- Ed. US. English. ir. W B Saunders Company, West Washington Square, Philadelphia PA 19105. **LC** RC46. **DD** 616.

TROPICAL GASTROENTEROLOGY. (TROPICAL GASTROENTEROLOGY : OFFICIAL JOURNAL OF THE DIGESTIVE DISEASES FOUNDATION). 0250-636X. Periodical. II. English. qt. $18.00. Asia Books & Periodicals Company, 11 Darya Ganj, New Delhi 110002 India. **Tel** 268645. **Ind/Abst** Index Med. **NLM** W1 TR88L.

ULTRASONIC IMAGING. V. 1- Jan. 1979-. 0161-7346. Periodical. US. English. qt. $84.00. Academic Press, 4805 Sand Lake Road, Orlando FL 32819. **Tel** (305)345-4100. **Ind/Abst** Excerpta Med., Index Med., Int. Aerosp. Abstr., Comput. Control Abstr., Electr. Electron. Abstr., Sci. Abstr. Sect. A. Phys. Abstr. **LC** RC78.7.U4. **DD** 616.0754. **NLM** W1 UL745. **CODEN** ULIMD4.

VERHANDLUNGEN DER DEUTSCHEN GESELLSCHAFT FUR INNERE MEDIZIN. 1921-. 0070-4067. German. ir. **Tel** (212)460-1500. **Ind/Abst** Excerpta Med., Index Med., Chem. Abstr. **NLM** W1 VE483Q. **CODEN** VDGIA2. (cum index). Annual congress. *Verhandlungen.*

VITAL SIGN. (THE VITAL SIGN). Issue #37 (July 1983)-. 0826-0303. Periodical. CN. English. mo. Free to Members. I.F.A.A.A. of British Columbia, PO Box 46108 Station G, Vancouver British Columbia V6R 4G5 Canada. **DD** 616.025205. *Association News (Industrial First Aid Attendants Association of British Columbia), 0715-4607.*

VOX SANGUINIS. V. 3-5, March 1953-Dec. 1955. 0042-9007. Periodical. SZ. articles in English, Dutch, French, or German with summaries in one or more of these languages. mo. $176.00. S Karger AG, PO Box 352, White Plains NY 10602. **Tel** (061)39 08 80. **Ed** C P Engelfriet. **Ind/Abst** Life Sci. Collect., Excerpta Med., Index Med., Biol. Abstr., Chem. Abstr., Bibliogr. Agric., Sci. Cit. Index, Abr. Ed., Hospit. Lit. Index. **DD** 616.1. **NLM** W1 VO87. **CODEN** VOSAAD. Index in last issue of volume - attached. adv acc. Contains outstanding papers on new techniques in transfusion and plasma exchange, preparation

Medicine—Medical Centers, Hospitals

procedures of blood cell concentrates and plasma derivatives, and the storage of blood products. *Bulletin van het Centraal Laboratorium van de Bloedtransfusiedienst van het Nederlandse Rode Kruis.*

WARREN-TEED G.I. TRACT. VFOAT G.I. Tract. VAT Warren-Teed Gastrointestinal Tract, Gastrointestinal Tract. V. 1- 1970-. 0360-7666. Periodical. US. English. qt. $5.00. 582 West Goodale Street, Columbus OH 43215. NLM W1 WA265.

WORKING PAPER - CHOLERA RESEARCH LABORATORY. (WORKING PAPER). Began in 1976. 0253-5505. Monographic Series. English. ir. LC UNC. DD 616.932. NLM W1 WO848E.

YEAR BOOK OF DIGESTIVE DISEASES. See Yearbooks, Almanacs, Directories.

THE YEAR BOOK OF NUCLEAR MEDICINE. See Yearbooks, Almanacs, Directories.

ZEITSCHRIFT FUR GASTROENTEROLOGIE. Began publication with Vol. 1, 1963. 0044-2771. Periodical. GW. German. mo. 114.00. Karl Demeter Verlag, Wuermstrasse 13 Postfach, D-8032 Graefelfing West Germany. Tel (089)85 20 33. Ed N Henning. Ind/Abst Life Sci. Collect., Excerpta Med., Index Med., Chem. Abstr., Energy Res. Abstr., Sci. Cit. Index, Abr. Ed. NLM W1 ZE356. CODEN ZGASAX. bk rev. adv acc. Circ 2,400.

ZENTRALBLATT PRAKTISCHE INNERE MEDIZIN. VFOAT Internal Medicine. 332. V., No. 1-. 0722-9860. Periodical. German (English). mo. Springer-Verlag New York Inc, 175 Fifth Avenue, New York NY 10010. Tel (212)460-1500. NLM ZW 1. *Zentralblatt Praktische Innere Medizin Und Grenzgebiete.*

ZENTRALBLATT PRAKTISCHE INNERE MEDIZIN UND GRENZGEBIETE CEASED. VFOAT Internal Medicine. Began with V. 310-331. 0301-584X. Periodical. English (German). ir. NLM ZW 1 Z58. *Kongresszentralblatt fur die Gesamte Innere Medizin und Ihre Grenzgebiete, 0024-9998.*

MEDICAL CENTERS, HOSPITALS

1ST READING. See Law.

1199 NEWS. See Economics - Labor.

ABSTRACTS OF HEALTH CARE MANAGEMENT STUDIES. See Indexes/Abstracts.

ABSTRACTS OF HOSPITAL MANAGEMENT STUDIES. See Indexes/Abstracts.

ACCREDITATION MANUAL FOR HOSPITALS. VFOAT Hospital Accreditation Program. 1970-. US. English. an. Joint Commission on Accreditation of Hospitals, 875 North Michigan Avenue, Chicago IL 60611. NLM WX 15 A187. Each issue contains an index to its own contents - no vol index - loose.

ACHA NEWS. V. 1- 1938-. 0001-0707. Periodical. US. English. mo. $12.00. American College of Healthcare Executives, 840 Lake Shore Drive, Chicago IL 60611. Tel (312)943-0544.

ADMINISTRATEUR HOSPITALIER. (L'ADMINISTRATEUR HOSPITALIER). V. 1- Jan. 1978-. 0704-9528. Periodical. CN. French. qt. $5.00. Association des Hopitaux du Canada, 410 Ouest Avenue, Laurier Ottawa K1R 7T6 Canada. DD 658.9136110971.

ADMINISTRATION HOSPITALIERE ET SOCIALE. V. 20- Jan. 1974-. 0317-3739. Periodical. CN. French. bm. $11.23. Editions Delmas, C P 308 Succursale Longueuil, Longueuil Que J4K 4Y3 Canada. Tel (514)674-4914. NLM W1. bk rev adv acc. Circ 3,000. (ctrl). The magazine publishes articles that are directed to public health and social service managers. The only. *Hopital d'Aujourd'Hui, 0018-4853.*

ADMINISTRATIVE BRIEFS. V. 1- 1967-. 0147-524X. Periodical. US. English. qt.

ADMINISTRATOR'S COLLECTION. Began with Vol. for 1972. 0149-3280. US. English. an. American Hospital Association, 840 North Lake Shore Drive, Chicago IL 60611. LC Z6673.4, RA393. DD 016.658913621.

AGGREGATE HOSPITAL DATA FOR CALIFORNIA. 1979-1980-. 0739-9162. US. English. an. $15.00. California Health Facilities Commission, 717 K Street/Suite 100, Sacramento CA 95814. LC RA981.C3. DD 338.433621109794 S, 338.433621109794. *Inventory of Financial and Statistical Information for California Hospitals.*

AHA HOSPITAL TECHNOLOGY ALERTS. See Technology (General).

AHA HOSPITAL TECHNOLOGY SERIES. See Technology (General).

AKTIVITETEN I SYGEHUSVSENET. Series/Titl Sygehusstatistik. 1979-. Danish. ir. 25.00. LC RA989.D4.

ALBERTA HOSPITAL ASSOCIATION'S HOSPITALTA. (THE ALBERTA HOSPITAL ASSOCIATION'S HOSPITALTA). VFOAT Hospitalta. 0821-2015. Periodical. CN. English. mo. Free to Members. Alberta Hospital Association, 10025-108 Street, Edmonton Alta T5J 1K9 Canada. Tel (403)423-1776. Ed Ellen Chesney. DD 362.11097123. adv acc. Circ 2,600. Newsmagazine providing information on all matters of interest to the Alberta healthcare setting, including hospital profiles, topical features, government news and education schedules.

THE AMERICAN JOURNAL OF HOSPICE CARE. Vol. 1, No. 1 (Winter 1984)-. 0749-1565. Periodical. US. English. bm. $46.00 Canada. R A De Vito, 470 Boston Post Road, Weston MA 02193. Tel (617)899-2702. Ed Bernard Smith. DD 362. NLM W1. bk rev. adv acc. Circ 6,000. Professional journal for healthcare providers serving terminally ill patients. For doctors, nurses, theologians, social workers, administrators, pharmacists and occupational therapists.

AMERICAN JOURNAL OF HOSPITAL PHARMACY. See Pharmacy.

ANALYSES OF HOSPITAL RUNNING COSTS, RELATED INCOME AND STATISTICS. See Statistics.

ANNALES DE LA SOCIETE BELGE D'HISTOIRE DES HOPITAUX. Main/Corp Societe Belge d'Histoire des Hopitaux. VFOAT Annalen van de Belgische Vereniging voor Hospitaal-Geschiedenis. 1- 1963-. 0583-8142. BE. French (Dutch). ir. Societe Belge d'Histoire Hospital, rue Haute 298A, B-1000 Brussels Belgium. LC RA989.B4.

ANNUAL FINANCIAL REPORT - TEXAS HEALTH FACILITIES COMMISSION. Main/Corp Texas. Health Facilities Commission. VFOAT Audit Report - Texas Health Facilities Commission. US. English. an. Texas Health Facilities Commission, Jefferson Building Suite 305 1600 West 38th Street, Austin TX 78731. LC RA981.T4. DD 353.9764007231.

ANNUAL HOSPITAL REPORT. VFOAT South Dakota Annual Hospital Report. 0277-9579. US. English. an. South Dakota Department of Health, State Center of Health Statistics, Foss Building, Pierre SD 57501. LC RA981.S62. DD 362.1109783.

ANNUAL REPORT - ALASKA NATIVE MEDICAL CENTER. Main/Corp Alaska Native Medical Center. 0362-6849. US. English. an. PO Box 7-741, Anchorage AK 99510. LC RA982.A382. DD 362.84.

ANNUAL REPORT - ALBERTA HOSPITALS & MEDICAL CARE. Main/Corp Alberta. Alberta Hospitals & Medical Care. 1978/79-. 0227-7883. CN. English. an. Hospitals and Medical Care, PO Box 2222, 10035 - 108 Street, Edmonton Alberta Canada. LC RA983.A4. DD 351.0841097123. *Annual Report, 0701-6514.*

ANNUAL REPORT AND FINANCIAL STATEMENTS - ALASKA MEDICAL FACILITY AUTHORITY. (ANNUAL REPORT AND FINANCIAL STATEMENTS). Main/Corp Alaska Medical Facility Authority. 0737-0601. US. English. an. Alaska Medical Facility Authority, c/o Alaska Department of Revenue/Treasury Division, Pouch SB, Juneau AK 99811. LC RA981.A58. DD 353.00841.

ANNUAL REPORT FOR FISCAL YEAR - VERMONT STATE HOSPITAL. Main/Corp Vermont State Hospital. US. English. an. Department of Mental Health, Osgood Building/103 South Main Street, Waterbury VT 05676. LC RC445.V43. DD 362.2109743.

ANNUAL REPORT FOR THE FISCAL YEAR - SOUTH CAROLINA STATE BOARD OF EXAMINERS FOR NURSING HOME ADMINISTRATORS. Main/Corp South Carolina State Board of Examiners for Nursing Home Administrators. US. English. an. South Carolina State Board of Examiners for Nursing Home Administrators, 221 Devine Street/Suite 201 PO Box 11477, Columbia SC 29211. LC RA997.5.S6. DD 353.9757008243.

ANNUAL REPORT - GENERAL CLINICAL RESEARCH CENTERS COMMITTEE, NATIONAL INSTITUTES OF HEALTH. Main/Corp National Institutes of Health. General Clinical Research Centers Committee. US. English. an. National Institutes of Health, 9000 Rockville Pike, Bethesda MD 20014.

ANNUAL REPORT - HALIFAX INFIRMARY. Main/Corp Halifax Infirmary. 0709-6232. CN. English. an. The Halifax Infirmary, 1335 Queen Street, Halifax NS B3J 2H6 Canada.

ANNUAL REPORT - HOSPITALS AND HEALTH SERVICES COMMISSION (AUSTRALIA). Main/Corp Australia. Hospitals and Health Services Commission. 1973/74-. AT. English. ir. $0.60. Hospitals and Health Services Commission, PO Box 392 Woden, Canberra Australian Capital Territory 2600 Australia. LC J905, RA371. DD 354.9940084105.

ANNUAL REPORT - ILLINOIS HEALTH FACILITIES AUTHORITY. Main/Corp Illinois Health Facilities Authority. US. English. Illinois Health Facilities Authority, 35 East Wacker Drive, Chicago IL 60601. LC RA981.I4. DD 353.977300841.

ANNUAL REPORT - ILLINOIS HEALTH FINANCE AUTHORITY. Main/Corp Illinois Health Finance Authority. 1979-. US. English. an. Illinois Health Finance Authority, 524 South 2nd Street/Room 577, Springfield IL 62706. LC RA981.I4. DD 353.977300841045.

ANNUAL REPORT - KERRVILLE STATE HOSPITAL. (ANNUAL REPORT). Main/Corp Kerrville State Hospital. 0730-6997. US. English. an. Kerrville State Hospital, Box 1468, Kerrville TX 78028. LC RC445.T4. DD 362.2109764884.

ANNUAL REPORT - MASSACHUSETTS GENERAL HOSPITAL. Main/Corp Massachusetts General Hospital. V. 1-. US. English. an. Massachusetts General Hospital, Boston MA 02114. LC RA982.B7.

ANNUAL REPORT - NEW CASTLE STATE HOSPITAL. Main/Corp New Castle State Hospital. 0145-773X. US. English. an. LC HV3006.I62. DD 362.210977264.

ANNUAL REPORT - NEW YORK STATE MEDICAL CARE FACILITIES FINANCE AGENCY. Main/Corp New York State Medical Care Facilities Finance Agency. 1973-. 0361-4018. US. English. an. New York State Medical Care Facilities Finance Agency, 1250 Broadway, New York NY 10001. LC RA981.N7. DD 353.9747008243.

ANNUAL REPORT - NURSING HOME OMBUDSMEN OFFICE (CONNECTICUT). Main/Corp Connecticut. Nursing Home Ombudsmen Office. 1977/78-. US. English. an. LC RA997.5.C8. DD 353.974600846.

ANNUAL REPORT OF THE WASHINGTON STATE HOSPITAL COMMISSION. Main/Corp Washington State Hospital Commission. US. English. an. Washington State Hospital Commission, 206 Evergreen Plaza, 711 Capitol Way, Olympia WA 98504. LC RA981.W2. DD 353.979700841.

ANNUAL REPORT ON ALBERTA HEALTH FACILITIES REVIEW COMMITTEE. (ANNUAL REPORT ... OF ALBERTA HEALTH FACILITIES REVIEW COMMITTEE). Main/Corp Alberta Health Facilities Review Committee. 0713-1887. CN. English. an. Alberta Health Facilities Review Committee, 108 Street Building, 9942 - 108 Street, Edmonton Alberta Canada. LC RA983.A4. DD 354.712300841. *Annual Report, 0706-9804.*

ANNUAL REPORT - PINELAND HOSPITAL AND TRAINING CENTER. (ANNUAL REPORT - PINELAND HOSPITAL & TRAINING CENTER). Main/Corp Pineland Hospital

Medicine—Medical Centers, Hospitals

and Training Center. 0464-5685. US. English. an. Box C, Pownal ME 04069. LC RJ506.M4. **DD** 362.210974191.

ANNUAL REPORT - SOURIS VALLEY EXTENDED CARE HOSPITAL CEASED. **Main/Corp** Souris Valley Extended Care Hospital. 1st-10th. 0702-8113. CN. English. an. Souris Valley Extended Care Hospital, Box 2001, Weyburn Saskatchewan S4H 2L7 Canada. LC RA983.W462. **DD** 362.110971244.

ANNUAL REPORT : STATE HOSPITALS FOR THE MENTAL DISORDERS (CALIFORNIA). Main/Corp California. Center for Health Statistics. US. English. an. 744 P Street/Room 777, Sacramento CA 95814. LC RC445.C178. **DD** 362.2109794. **NLM** W2 AC2 C3A.

ANNUAL REPORT - STATE OF CONNECTICUT HEALTH & EDUCATIONAL FACILITIES AUTHORITY. Main/Corp Connecticut. Health and Educational Facilities Authority. **VAT** Annual Report - State of Connecticut Health and Educational Facilities Authority. 0098-4167. US. English. an. State of Connecticut Health & Educational Facilities Authority, 60 Washington Street, Hartford CT 06106. LC RA981.C6. **DD** 353.974600841.

ANNUAL REPORT - TERRELL STATE HOSPITAL. Main/Corp Terrell State Hospital. US. English. an. Terrell State Hospital, Box 70, Terrell TX 75160. LC RC445.T4. **DD** 362.2109764277.

ANNUAL REPORT - TEXAS BOARD OF LICENSURE FOR NURSING HOME ADMINISTRATORS. (ANNUAL REPORT). **Main/Corp** Texas Board of Licensure for Nursing Home Administrators. 0277-0571. US. English. an. Texas Board of Licensure for Nursing Home Administrators, PO Box 9706, Austin TX 78766. LC RA997.5.T4. **DD** 353.976400722368243.

ANNUAL REPORT - TEXAS HEALTH FACILITIES COMMISSION. Main/Corp Texas. Health Facilities Commission. 0162-9921. US. English. an. Texas Health Facilities Commission, Jefferson Building, Suite 305, 1600 West 38th Street, Austin TX.

ANNUAL REPORT TO THE GOVERNOR AND GENERAL ASSEMBLY - STATE OF CONNECTICUT, COMMISSION ON HOSPITALS & HEALTH CARE. (ANNUAL REPORT TO THE GOVERNOR AND GENERAL ASSEMBLY). **Main/Corp** Connecticut. Commission on Hospitals and Health Care. 1st- 1973/74-. 0146-7077. US. English. an. Commission on Hospitals & Health Care, 340 Capitol Avenue, Hartford CT 06115. LC RA395.A4. **NLM** W2 AC8 C75A.

ANNUAL REPORT TO THE GOVERNOR AND LEGISLATURE - FLORIDA. HOSPITAL COST CONTAINMENT BOARD. (ANNUAL REPORT . . . TO THE GOVERNOR AND LEGISLATURE). **Main/Corp** Florida. Hospital Cost Containment Board. 0735-4118. US. English. an. Larson Building, 200 East Gaines Street, Tallahassee FL 32301. LC RA981.F4. **DD** 338.433621109759.

ANNUAL REPORT - WARM SPRINGS STATE HOSPITAL. Main/Corp Warm Springs State Hospital. US. English. an. Warm Springs State Hospital, Warm Springs MT 59756. LC RC445.M9. **DD** 362.110978687.

ANNUAL REPORTS OF PROGRESS - REHABILITATION ENGINEERING CENTER AT RANCHO LOS AMIGOS HOSPITAL. VFOAT Annual Progress Report - Rehabilitation Engineering Center at Rancho Los Amigos Hospital. No. 1- Dec. 1971/Nov. 1972-. 0147-0876. Periodical. US. English. an. **NLM** W1 AN769GT.

ANNUAL STATISTICAL REPORT - EMILY P. BISSELL HOSPITAL (DELAWARE). See Statistics.

ARIZONA UNIFORM REPORTING SYSTEM HOSPITALS. 1978-9-. US. English. an. LC RA971.3. **DD** 338.433621109791021.

ARKANSAS HEALTH MANPOWER STATISTICS. NURSING HOME ADMINISTRATORS. See Statistics.

ARTERE. Oct. 1983-. 0823-4124. Periodical. CN. French. ir. 35.00. AHQ Direction des Communications, Bureau 400 505 Ouest Boulevard de Maisonneuve, Montreal Quebec H3A 3C2 Canada.

Tel (514)842-4861. Ed Danielle Racette. **DD** 362.11068. adv acc. **Circ** 6,000. (ctrl). A French publication distributed to all senior executives in the Quebec hospital sector with a capital expenditure of over $900,000,000.

ASSOCIATION DES STOMISES DES BASSES LAURENTIDES. (ASSOCIATION DES STOMISES DES BASSES LAURENTIDES : BULLETIN). Vol. 1, No. 1 (June 1983)-. 0820-9995. Periodical. CN. French. qt. Free to Members. Association des Stomises des Basses Laurentides, 126 31E Avenue, St-Eustache Quebec J7P 2X4 Canada. **DD** 362.197554.

ASSOCIATION REGULATIONS OF THE AMERICAN HOSPITAL ASSOCIATION. Main/Corp American Hospital Association. 0364-748X. US. English. ir.

AUDIT REPORT, HARLINGEN STATE CHEST HOSPITAL. Main/Corp Harlingen State Chest Hospital. US. English. an. LC RA982.H19. **DD** 362.1975409764495.

AUDIT REPORT. TEXAS BOARD OF LICENSURE FOR NURSING HOME ADMINISTRATORS. Main/Corp Texas Board of Licensure for Nursing Home Administrators. **VFOAT** Texas Board of Licensure for Nursing Home Administrators. US. English. State Auditor/John H Reagan, State Office Building, PO Box 12067, Austin TX 78711. LC RA997.5.T4. **DD** 353.976400841.

AUSTRALIAN HEALTH REVIEW. (AUSTRALIAN HEALTH REVIEW : A PUBLICATION OF THE AUSTRALIAN HOSPITAL ASSOCIATION). Began in 1978. 0156-5788. Periodical. AT. English. qt. 33.00. Australian Hospital Association, PO Box 344, Kingston Australian Capital Territory 2064 Australia. Tel (062) 851844. Ed Jonathan Tribe. **Ind/Abst** Hospit. Lit. Index. **NLM** W1 AU453T. bk rev. **Circ** 1,000. (ctrl). A journal for hospital administrators, medical and nursing directors students in health administration and anyone interested in keeping informed in the health field, in particular management.

AUSTRALIAN HOSPITAL. No. 1- Oct. 1976-. 0314-0024. Periodical. AT. English. ir. $12.92. Peter Isaacson Publ Pty Ltd, 46-50 Porter Street, Box 172, Prahran Victoria 3181 Australia. Tel 03 520 5555. **Ind/Abst** Hospit. Lit. Index. **NLM** W1 AU533C. National Hospital and Health Care, 0312-794X.

BED USE STATISTICS. See Statistics.

BULLETIN - ASSISTANCE MEDICALE INTERNATIONALE. (BULLETIN DE L'ASSISTANCE MEDICALE INTERNATIONALE). **VAT** AMI (International Medical Assistance (Society)). V. 1, No. 1, (Fall 1982)-. 0382-4462. Periodical. CN. French. sa. Assistance Medicale Internationale, 3540 Ave de Lorimier, Montreal Quebec H2K 3X6 Canada. **DD** 362.10425. Bulletin, 0382-4462.

THE BULLETIN - UNIVERSITY OF KANSAS MEDICAL CENTER. Main/Corp Kansas. University. Medical Center. 0199-1256. Periodical. US. English. qt. Free. University of Kansas Medical Center, 39th Rainbow Boulevard, Kansas City KS 66103.

BYOIN KANRI KENKYUJO. Main/Corp Byoin Kanri Kenkyujo. **VFOAT** Annual Report of the National Institute of Hospital Administration. JA. Japanese. ir. Byoin Kanri Kenkyujo, 1 Toyamamachi, Shinjuku-ku 162, Tokyo Japan. LC RA971.

BYOIN YORAN. See Yearbooks, Almanacs, Directories.

CADASTRO DE ESTABELECIMENTOS DE SAUDE, BRASIL. Series/Titl Serie G, Estatistica e Informacao em Saude. 1981, V. 1-. Portuguese. ir. LC RA978.B6. **DD** 362.110981.

CADASTRO HOSPITALAR BRASILEIRO. Main/Corp Brazil. Coordenacao de Assistencia Medica e Hospitalar. Portuguese. ir. LC RA984.B8.

CADASTROS : ESTABELECIMENTOS HOSPITALARES, ESTABELECIMENTOS PARA-HOSPITALARES, ESTABELECIMENTOS DE SERVICOS OFICIAIS DE SAUDE PUBLICA. BL. Portuguese. ir. Instituto Estadual de Estatistica, Av Afonso Pena 867 - 200. Andar, Belo Horizonte Brazil. LC RA984.B83.

CANADIAN HOSPITAL DIRECTORY. See Yearbooks, Almanacs, Directories.

CANADIAN HOSPITAL ENGINEERING JOURNAL. VAT Quarterly Journal - Canadian Hospital Engineering Society. Vol. 1, No. 1 (Oct. 1981)-. 0821-2236. Periodical. CN. English (includes some text in French). qt. Canadian Hospital Engineering Journal, PO Box 5658/Station F, Ottawa Ontario K2C 3M1 Canada. **DD** 362.110682.

CANADIAN HOSPITALS AND RELATED FACILITIES CEASED. **VFOAT** Hopitaux Canadiens et Installations Connexes. 1975-76. 0319-8014. CN. English (French). an. Receiver General for Canada, Statistics Canada Publications, Ottawa Ontario K1A 0T6 Canada. LC RA983.A1. **DD** 362.110971. **NLM** W2 DC2 S8C. List of Canadian Hospitals and Related Institutions and Facilities, 0319-8022.

CANADIAN JOURNAL OF HOSPITAL PHARMACY. See Pharmacy.

CANADIAN PALLIATIVE CARE DIRECTORY. See Yearbooks, Almanacs, Directories.

THE CANCER BULLETIN OF THE UNIVERSITY OF TEXAS M.D. ANDERSON HOSPITAL AND TUMOR INSTITUTE AT HOUSTON. See Medicine - Neoplasma, Neoplastic.

CARCH NEWS. Main/Corp California Association of Residential Care Homes. **VAT** California Association of Residential Care Homes News. 0163-2213. Periodical. US. English. mo. California Association of Residential Care Homes, 2530 J Street/Suite 302, Sacramento CA 95816. Tel (916)447-8885.

CARREFOUR DES ADMINISTRATEURS DE CENTRE HOSPITALIER. V. 1- Jan. 1975-. 0383-1426. Periodical. CN. French. Association des Hopitaux de la Province de Quebec, Bureau 324 276 Ouest rue St-Jacques, Montreal Quebec H2Y 1N3 Canada. **DD** 362.11062714. A-Propos, 0383-1434.

CATALOG OF HOSPITAL MANAGEMENT ENGINEERING TECHNICAL PAPERS. Main/Corp Clearinghouse for Hospital Management Engineering (U.S.). 1982-. 0738-1271. US. English. American Hospital Association, Clearinghouse for Hospital Management Engineering, 840 North Lake Shore Drive, Chicago IL 60611. **NLM** ZWX 150 C623C.

CATHOLIC HOSPITAL ASSOCIATION OF CANADA DIRECTORY. See Yearbooks, Almanacs, Directories.

CENTRES HOSPITALIERS. GUIDE BUDGETAIRE. (CENTRES HOSPITALIERS : GUIDE BUDGETAIRE . . . : STANDARDS BUDGETAIRES). **Main/Corp** Quebec (Province). Ministere des Affaires Sociales. **VFOAT** Guide Budgetaire. 0712-3108. CN. French. an. Gouvernement du Quebec, 600 St Amable 4E Etage, Quebec G1R 4Z1 Canada. **DD** 362.110681.

CERTIFIED PUBLIC HOSPITAL LIST. VFOAT Liste des Hopitaux Publics Certifies. 0828-0967. CN. English (French). an. $1.00. Technical Information Section Excise, Department of National Revenue/Customs and Excise, Ottawa Ontario K1A 0L5 Canada. LC RA983.A1. **DD** 362.1102571.

CHA NEWS. VAT California Hospital Association News. V. 1- May 2, 1969-. Periodical. US. English. wk. $50.00. California Hospital Association, PO Box 1100, Sacramento CA 95805. Tel (916)443-7401. Ed Ted Fourhas. **Circ** 12,000. (ctrl).

C.H.A.C. REVIEW. (C. H. A. C. REVIEW). **Main/Corp** Catholic Health Association of Canada. **VAT** Catholic Health Association of Canada Review. V. 8, No. 1- Jan./Feb. 1980-. 0226-5923. Periodical. CN. English. bm. 12.00. Catholic Health Association of Canada, 312 Daly Avenue, Ottawa Ontario K1N 6G7 Canada. **Ind/Abst** Hospit. Lit. Index. **DD** 362.110971. **NLM** W1 C342. Catholic Hospital, 0008-8099.

CHFC REPORT. VFOAT C.H.F.C. **VAT** California Health Facilities Commission Report. 0739-9154. Monographic Series. US. English. 717 K Street, Suite 100, Sacramento CA 95814. LC RA981.C3. **DD** 338.433621109794.

CLARK'S DIRECTORY OF SOUTHERN HOSPITALS. See Yearbooks, Almanacs, Directories.

CLINICAL PROCEEDINGS - CHILDREN'S HOSPITAL NATIONAL MEDICAL CENTER. Main/Corp Children's Hospital National Medical Center. V. 28- Jan. 1972-. 0092-7813. Periodical. US. English. bm. Children Hospital National Medical Center, 111 Michigan Avenue NW, Washington DC 20010. Tel

Medicine—Medical Centers, Hospitals

(202)745-3000. Ind/Abst Life Sci. Collect. LC RJ1. DD 618.920005. NLM W1 CL768CK. *Clinical Proceedings - Children's Hospital of the District of Columbia, 0009-4129.*

CODING CLINIC FOR ICD-9-CM. (CODING CLINIC FOR ICD-9-CM : A BIMONTHLY PUBLICATION OF THE AMERICAN HOSPITAL ASSOCIATION). V. 1, No. 1 (May/June 1984)-. 0742-9800. Periodical. US. English. bm. $135.00 Nonmembers, $85.00 Members. American Hospital Association, 840 North Lake Shore Drive, Chicago IL 60611. DD 651.

COLLECTIVE AGREEMENT SURVEY IN NOVA SCOTIA HOSPITALS. See Economics - Labor.

COMMITTEE RESEARCH REPORT - CANADIAN HOSPITAL ASSOCIATION. (CANADIAN HOSPITAL ASSOCIATION COMMITTEE RESEARCH REPORT). 0228-8907. Monographic Series. CN. English. ir. NLM W1 CA563.

COMMUNITY CANCER PROGRAMS IN THE UNITED STATES : THE DELEGATE ROSTER OF THE ASSOCIATION OF COMMUNITY CANCER CENTERS. See Medicine - Neoplasma, Neoplastic.

COMPENSATION REPORT, MANAGEMENT EMPLOYEES IN HOSPITAL & NURSING HOME MANAGEMENT COMPANIES. See Business - Personnel Management.

COMPENSATION REPORT. MANAGEMENT EMPLOYEES IN HOSPITAL MANAGEMENT COMPANIES. See Business - Personnel Management.

COMPENSATION SURVEY FOR CHICAGO AREA HOSPITALS. US. English. Chicago Hospital Council, 840 North Lake Shore Drive, Chicago IL 60611. LC RA982.C45. DD 331.281362110977311021.

COMPUTERS IN HEALTHCARE. See Computers and Computer Science.

CONNECTICUT'S PRIVATE MENTAL HOSPITALS : INPATIENT STATISTICS FOR YEAR ENDING . . . . See Statistics.

CONSOLIDATED STANDARDS MANUAL FOR CHILD, ADOLESCENT, AND ADULT PSYCHIATRIC, ALCOHOLISM, AND DRUG ABUSE FACILITIES. Began in 1979. Periodical. US. English. an. $35.00. Joint Commission on Accredited Hospitals, 875 North Michigan Avenue, Chicago IL 60611. Tel (312)642-6061.

CONTACT. V. 1- Nov. 1976-. 0705-0771. Periodical. CN. French. bm. Free. Conseil Regional de la Sante et des Services Sociaux de la Region, 04 364 des Forges, Trois-Rivieres Quebec G9A 2H1 Canada. DD 362.971445.

CONTINUING EDUCATION IN NURSING HOME ADMINISTRATION. V. 1- 1974-. 0094-6192. Periodical. US. English. ir. Futura Publishing Co, 295 Main Street, Mount Kisco NY 10549. Tel (914)666-3505. Ed S D Wallace. NLM W1 CO775R.

COST CONTAINMENT. V. 1- Jan. 9, 1979-. 0198-9782. Periodical. US. English. sm. $185.00. William H White Publications, 475 Park Avenue South, 30th Floor, New York NY 10016-6901. Tel (212)685-7570. Ed Jacqueline Thompson. Ind/Abst Hospit. Lit. Index. NLM W1 CO937. Circ 600. (ctrl). Newsletter for hospital administrators and financial managers on containing costs of medical care.

COTH REPORT. VAT Council of Teaching Hospitals Report. V. 1- July 1967-. 0146-2814. Periodical. US. English. mo. $30.00. Association of the American Medical Colleges, 1 Dupont Circle NW/Suite 200, Washington DC 20036. NLM W1 C544T.

COTH SURVEY OF HOUSE STAFF STIPENDS, BENEFITS, AND FUNDING. VFOAT Survey of House Staff Stipends, Benefits, and Funding. VAT Council of Teaching Hospitals Survey of House Staff Stipends, Benefits, and Funding. Began in 1978. 0272-9148. US. English. an. $3.75. Association of the American Medical Colleges, 1 Dupont Circle NW/Suite 200, Washington DC 20036. LC RA975.T43. DD 331.281610973. NLM W1 CO544Z. *COTH Survey of House Staff Policy & Related Information, 0272-9156.*

COUGH. COMPUTERIZED ONLINE UNIVERSITY OF GUELPH HOSPITAL. (COUGH : COMPUTERIZED ONLINE UNIVERSITY OF GUELPH HOSPITAL). VFOAT Computerized Online University of Guelph Hospital. Vol. 1, Issue 1 (Apr. 1982)-. 0823-7654. Periodical. CN. English. ir. COUGH Computer Group, Ontario Veterinary College, University of Guelph, Guelph Ontario N1G 2W1 Canada. DD 636.0890285.

CRITICAL CARE CLINICS. Vol. 1, No. 1 (Mar. 1985)-. 0749-0704. Periodical. US. English. ty. $36.00. W B Saunders Co, West Washington Square, Philadelphia PA 19105. DD 616.

CUMULATIVE INDEX OF HOSPITAL LITERATURE. See Indexes/Abstracts.

CURRENT CHARGES FOR SELECTED HOSPITAL SERVICES . . . . Main/Corp Florida. Hospital Cost Containment Board. VFOAT Annual Report, Current Charges for Selected Services. US. English. an. $8.63. Florida Hospital Cost, Containment Board/Larson Building, Tallahassee FL 32301. LC RA981.F4. DD 338.433621109759.

DIMENSIONS IN HEALTH SERVICE. V. 51- Jan. 1974-. 0317-7645. Periodical. CN. English (includes some text in French). mo. 31.00 Canada, $41.00 US. Canadian Hospital Association, 17 York Street/Suite 100, Ottawa Ontario K1N 9J6 Canada. Tel (613)238-8005. Ed Ruta Klicius. Ind/Abst Hospit. Lit. Index, Index Med., Cumul. Index Nurs. Allied Health Lit., Can. Bus. Index. NLM W1 DI593. bk rev. adv acc. Circ 13,000. (ctrl). A forum which publishes news, articles about management techniques, programs and services that will help to improve patient care in Canadian facilities. *Canadian Hospital, 0008-3798.*

DIRECTORY - AMERICAN COLLEGE OF HOSPITAL ADMINISTRATORS. See Yearbooks, Almanacs, Directories.

DIRECTORY - ASSOCIATION OF ACADEMIC HEALTH CENTERS (U.S.). See Yearbooks, Almanacs, Directories.

DIRECTORY, LICENSED & CERTIFIED HEALTH CARE FACILITIES. See Yearbooks, Almanacs, Directories.

DIRECTORY. LICENSED HOSPITALS AND AMBULATORY SURGICAL TREATMENT CENTERS IN TENNESSEE. See Yearbooks, Almanacs, Directories.

DIRECTORY, LICENSED NURSING HOMES AND HOMES FOR AGED IN TENNESSEE. See Yearbooks, Almanacs, Directories.

DIRECTORY OF HEALTH CARE FACILITIES. See Yearbooks, Almanacs, Directories.

DIRECTORY OF HOSPITALS AND RELATED HEALTH SERVICES LICENSED OR CERTIFIED BY MISSOURI DIVISION OF HEALTH. See Yearbooks, Almanacs, Directories.

DIRECTORY OF HOSPITALS IN INDIA. See Yearbooks, Almanacs, Directories.

DIRECTORY OF INPATIENT FACILITIES FOR THE MENTALLY RETARDED. See Yearbooks, Almanacs, Directories.

DIRECTORY OF INVESTOR-OWNED HOSPITALS AND HOSPITAL MANAGEMENT COMPANIES. See Yearbooks, Almanacs, Directories.

DIRECTORY OF LICENSED HOSPITALS AND RELATED FACILITIES. See Yearbooks, Almanacs, Directories.

DIRECTORY OF LICENSED NURSING HOMES, STATE OF LOUISIANA. See Yearbooks, Almanacs, Directories.

DIRECTORY OF LONG TERM CARE CENTRES IN CANADA. See Yearbooks, Almanacs, Directories.

DIRECTORY OF MEDICAL FACILITIES. ALL REGIONS. See Yearbooks, Almanacs, Directories.

DIRECTORY OF MEDICAL FACILITIES. REGION VIII, DENVER. See Yearbooks, Almanacs, Directories.

DIRECTORY OF MULTIHOSPITAL SYSTEMS. See Yearbooks, Almanacs, Directories.

DIRECTORY OF NURSING HOME ADMINISTRATORS LICENSED AND REGISTERED IN TENNESSEE. See Yearbooks, Almanacs, Directories.

DIRECTORY OF NURSING HOMES IN THE UNITED STATES, U. S. TERRITORIES, AND CANADA. See Yearbooks, Almanacs, Directories.

DIRECTORY OF NURSING HOMES IN THE UNITED STATES, U.S. POSSESSIONS AND CANADA. See Yearbooks, Almanacs, Directories.

DIRECTORY OF SHARED SERVICES ORGANIZATIONS AND CONSORTIA OF HEALTH CARE INSTITUTIONS. See Yearbooks, Almanacs, Directories.

D'UN ETAGE A L'AUTRE. VFOAT Menusuel de l'Hopital St-Joseph de Rimouski. V. 1, No. 2- Dec. 1978-. 0709-3934. Periodical. CN. French. mo. Free. Hopital St-Joseph de Rimouski, 150 rue Rouleau, Rimouski Quebec G5L 5T1 Canada. DD 362.1109714771. (ctrl). *Journal, 0709-3942.*

EASY BREATHING. V. 1- May 1974-. 0315-2421. Periodical. CN. English. bm. Sanatorium Board of Manitoba, 1625 Dublin Avenue, Winnipeg Manitoba R3H Canada.

EDINBURGH DENTAL HOSPITAL GAZETTE. See Dentistry.

ENSEMBLE. V. 1- Feb. 1977-. 0705-5005. Periodical. CN. French. mo. Centre Hospitalier de Lachine, 650-16E Avenue, Lachine Quebec H8S 3N5 Canada. DD 362.110971428.

ESTADISTICA DE ESTABLECIMIENTOS SANITARIOS CON REGIMEN DE INTERNADO. See Statistics.

ESTATISTICAS DE SAUDE. ASSISTENCIA MEDICO-SANITARIA. See Statistics.

EUROHEALTH HANDBOOK. VFOAT Statistical Health and Hospital Data for Fourteen West European Countires. 1971-. 0094-9361. Periodical. US. English. an. Robert S First Inc, 405 Lexington Avenue, New York NY 10017. NLM W1 EU578.

EXCERPTA MEDICA. SECTION 36. HEALTH ECONOMICS AND HOSPITAL MANAGEMENT. (HEALTH ECONOMICS AND HOSPITAL MANAGEMENT). Series/Titl Excerpta Medica, Section 36. VAT Excerpta Medica. Section Thirty-Six. Health Economics and Hospital Management. V. 3-. 0300-5321. NE. English. ir. Elsevier Science Publishers, PO Box 211, 1000 AE Amsterdam Netherlands. LC RA410.A1. DD 362.105. NLM ZW 1 E978R. *Health Economics, 0014-4401.*

FACTS ABOUT HOSPITALS IN METROPOLITAN CHICAGO. Main/Corp Chicago Hospital Council. US. English. LC RA982.C45. DD 362.110977311.

FEDERAL MEDICAL CENTERS, HOSPITALS, AND MEDICAL CLINICS WITH REPORTED MORBIDITY DATA. 0192-2211. US. English. an. $20.00. Association of Military Surgeons of the United States, 10605 Concord Street, Suite 306, PO Box 104, Kensington MD 20795. LC UH463. DD 355.3450973.

FIRST AND READMISSIONS TO STATE AND COUNTY PSYCHIATRIC HOSPITALS BY COUNTY, MUNICIPALITY OF RESIDENCE, AND SERVICE AREA. Main/Corp New Jersey. Bureau of Statistical Analysis and Social Research. 1975/76-. US. English. an. LC RC445.N48. DD 362.2109749.

FUHREN UND WIRTSCHAFTEN IM KRANKENHAUS : F&W. VFOAT F&W. 1/84-. 0175-4548. Periodical. German. bm. NLM W1. *Privatkrankenanstalt.*

Medicine—Medical Centers, Hospitals

GESCHICHTE DES HOSPITALS. V. 2- 1971-. Monographic Series. German. ir. Ed D Jetter. NLM W1 GE693. *Geschichte des Hospitals.*

GROUP PRACTICE. 0190-440X. Periodical. US. English. sm. $48.00. American Group Practice Association, 20 South Quaker Lane, Alexandria VA 22314. Tel (703)838-0033. Ed Timothy A Stalker. adv acc. Circ 40,000. (ctrl) Medical journal for physicians practicing in medical group practices.

GUY'S HOSPITAL GAZETTE. 0017-5870. Periodical. UK. English. ir. $15.33. Gazette Office, Mary Sheridan House, Guy's Hospital, London SE1 9RT England. Ind/Abst Index Med.

HANDBOOK FOR STAFF PHYSICIANS. Main/Corp National Institutes of Health (U.S.). Clinical Center. US. English. an. Deputy Director/Clinical Center, Room 2C146 Building 10, National Institutes of Health, Bethesda MD 20205.

HAS/MONITREND SIX-MONTH NATIONAL DATA BOOK. (HAS/MONITREND SIX-MONTH NATIONAL DATA BOOK FOR PERIOD ENDING . . .). VFOAT H.A.S./M.O.N.I.T.R.E.N.D. Six-Month National Data Book for Period Ending . . . . 0737-7487. US. English. sa. American Hospital Association, Hospital Administrative Services Division, 840 North Lake Shore Drive, Chicago IL 60611. LC RA981.A2. DD 362.10973.

HCMT NEWSLETTER. VAT Hospital Council of Metropolitan Toronto Newsletter. Vol. 1, No. 1 (Apr. 1981)-. 0826-5976. Periodical. CN. English. mo. Hospital Council of Metropolitan Toronto, Suite 1305 2 Carlton Street, Toronto Ontario M5B 1J3 Canada. DD 362.11060713541.

HEALTH CARE FACILITIES. V. 3- Winter 1975-. 0098-8219. US. English. bm. $8.00. North American Publishing Company, 134 North 13th Street, Philadelphia PA 19107. NLM W1 HE299H. *Health Care Engineering, 0091-5173.*

HEALTH CARE FACILITIES : EXISTING AND NEEDED. HILL-BURTON STATE PLAN DATA. Series/Titl HB Health Facilities Series. HEW Publication. 1969-. US. English. an. US Department of Health Education and Welfare, 5600 Fisher Lane, Rockville MD 20857. DD 362.10973. *Hill-Burton State Plan Data : A National Summary.*

HEALTH CARE NEWS. V. 4, No. 20- Sept. 12, 1979-. 0745-2438. Periodical. US. English. bw. $20.00. Health Care News, PO Box 2459, Detroit MI 48202. Tel (313)965-0388. *Medical Center News.*

HEALTH CARE STRATEGIC MANAGEMENT. Vol. 1, No. 1 (Oct. 1983)-. 0742-1478. Periodical. US. English. mo. $70.00. Health Care Strategic Management, PO Box 8626, Ann Arbor MI 48107. Tel (313)761-3912. Ed Darrell P Thorpe. Ind/Abst Hospit. Lit. Index. NLM W1. bk rev. adv acc. Circ 2,000. (ctrl) Professional journal for hospital administrators, planners, marketers department directors, Includes articles on timely topics, interviews with health care leaders, case studies, book and meeting reviews.

HEALTH FACILITIES DIRECTORY. See Yearbooks, Almanacs, Directories.

HEALTH FACILITIES ENERGY REPORT. See Energy.

HEALTH MANAGEMENT FORUM. VAT Forum (Toronto. 1980). 0712-5046. Periodical. CN. English. qt. $30.00. Health Management Forum, c/o Extendicare Ltd, 1 Yonge Street, Toronto Ont M5E 1E5 Canada. Ind/Abst Hospit. Lit. Index. LC RA971. DD 362.1068. NLM W1 HE413P.

HEALTH MATRIX. See Law.

HEALTH PROGRESS (SAINT LOUIS, MO.). (HEALTH PROGRESS). Vol. 65, No. 8 (Sept. 1984)-. 0882-1577. Periodical. US. English. mo. $30.00 US/Canada, $35.00 Foreign. Catholic Health Association of the United States, 4455 Woodson Road, St Louis MO 63134. Tel (314)427-2500. Ed Judy Cassidy. Ind/Abst Abstr. Hospit. Manage. Stud., Cathol. Period. Index, Cumul. Index Nurs. Allied Health Lit., Hospit. Lit. Index, Index Med., Med. Socioecon. Res. Source, Nurs. Stud. Index. NLM W1. bk rev. adv acc. Circ 14,000. Issued also in microform. *Hospital Progress, 0018-5817.*

HEALTH SERVICES MANAGER. See Business - General Management.

HEALTHCARE FINANCIAL MANAGEMENT. (HEALTHCARE FINANCIAL MANAGEMENT : JOURNAL OF THE HEALTHCARE FINANCIAL MANAGEMENT ASSOCIATION). VFOAT H.F.M. Vol. 36, No. 6 (June 1982) -. 0735-0732. Periodical. US. English. mo. $80.00. Healthcare Financial Management, 1900 Spring Road/Suite 500, Oak Brook IL 60521. Tel (312)655-4600. Ed Ronald E Keener. Ind/Abst Manage. Contents, Trade Ind. Index, Excerpta Med., Account. Index. Suppl., ABI/Inform, Comput. Control Abstr., Electr. Electron. Abstr., Sci. Abstr. Sect. A. Phys. Abstr., Hospit. Lit. Index, Bus. Period. Index. LC HF5686.H7. DD 362.10681. NLM W1 HE608. CODEN HFMAD7. bk rev adv acc. Circ 27,000. (ctrl) Accounting and financial management of hospitals and healthcare providers. *Hospital Financial Management, 0018-5639.*

HEBDO AHPQ. (HEBDO A H P Q). Main/Corp Association des Hopitaux de la Province de Quebec. VAT Hebdo. Association des Hopitaux de la Province de Quebec. V. 1- Dec. 17, 1976-. 0707-204X. Periodical. CN. French. wk. Free to Members. Association des Hopitaux de la Province de Quebec, Bureau 324 276 rue Saint-Jacques, Montreal Quebec H2Y 1N3 Canada. DD 362.1109714.

HEMLOCK QUARTERLY. Issue 1 (Oct. 1980)-. 0742-5376. Periodical. US. English. qt. $15.00. Hemlock Society, PO Box 66218, Los Angeles CA 90066. LC R726. DD 362.175.

HENRY FORD HOSPITAL MEDICAL JOURNAL. V. 15, No. 2-Summer 1967-. 0018-0416. US. English. qt. Free. Henry Ford Hospital, Editor of Medical Journal, Detroit MI 48202. Tel (313)876-2028. Ed Raymond C Mellinger. Ind/Abst Life Sci. Collect., Excerpta Med., Index Med., CIS Abstr., Biol. Abstr., Chem. Abstr., Nucl. Sci. Abstr. NLM W1 HE901H. CODEN HFHJA6. bk rev. Circ 9,500. Work of current Henry Ford Hospital staff, alumni, participants in sponsored symposia. Broad scientific forum for all areas: clinical, research, technical, administrative, and patient care delivery. *Henry Ford Hospital Medical Bulletin, 0096-1868.*

HOMES FOR THE AGED. 0229-415X. CN. English. be. $3.00 Per No. Community Information Centre of Metropolitan Toronto, 34 King Street East/3rd Floor, Toronto Ontario M5C 1E5 Canada. DD 362.61025713541.

HOSPICE LETTER. 1979. 0193-6816. Periodical. US. English. mo $88.00. Hospice Letter, PO Box 1442, Wall Township NJ 07719. Tel (201)681-1133. Ed Marshall Sewell Jr. Circ 1,000. Developments in the care of the terminally ill through hospice. Accreditation, reimbursement, raising money, nursing care, counseling programs, regulations, and legislation.

EL HOSPITAL. Vol. 1- July 1945-. 0018-5485. Periodical. US. Spanish. bm. $40.00. Brentwood Publishing Corporation, PO Box 49045, Los Angeles CA 90049. Tel (213)826-8388. Ed Nigel Sylvester. NLM W1 HO812. bk rev. adv acc. Circ 15,235. (ctrl). Contains information about recent medical research, techniques and equipment of interest to the Spanish-speaking world.

HOSPITAL ABSTRACTS. See Indexes/Abstracts.

HOSPITAL ADMINISTRATION. Began publcation with Vol. 1, 1964. 0018-5531. Periodical. II. English. qt. $4.58. Indian Hospital Association, C-II-72 Shajahan Road, New Delhi 110011 India. Tel 382602. Ed P N Ghei. Ind/Abst Hospit. Lit. Index, Excerpta Med. NLM W1 HO7S. Circ 1,000. Deals with hospital and health administration aspects, particularly in planning, management, evaluation and primary health care.

HOSPITAL ADMITTING MONTHLY. Began with: Vol. 1, No. 1 (July 1982) 0745-1466. Periodical. US. English. mo. American Health Consultants, 67 Peachtree Park Drive NE/Suite 2625, Atlanta GA 30309. Tel (404)351-4523. NLM W1 HO71K.

HOSPITAL AND HEALTH CARE REPORT. Main/Corp American Management Association. Executive Compensation Service. 1st-Ed. 0146-7360. US. English. Amacom, 135 West 50th Street, New York NY 10020. LC RA981.A2. DD 331.281362110973.

HOSPITAL & HEALTH SERVICES ADMINISTRATION. (HOSPITAL & HEALTH SERVICES ADMINISTRATION : THE JOURNAL OF THE FOUNDATION OF THE AMERICAN COLLEGE OF HOSPITAL ADMINISTRATORS). VFOAT Hospital and Health Services Administration. Vol. 29, No. 5 (Sept./Oct. 1984)-. 8750-3735. Periodical. US. English. bm. $25.00. American College of Healthcare Executives, 840 Lake Shore Drive, Chicago IL 60611. Tel (312)943-0544. Ed Joyce Flory. Ind/Abst Manage. Contents, Excerpta Med., Hospit. Lit. Index, Abstr. Health Care Manage. Stud. LC RA971. DD 362.11068. NLM W1. bk rev. Circ 21,000. Available on microform from University Microfilms. Publishes articles on new developments, innovations, and trends in healthcare management. Subject areas include strategy planning and policy, board/medical staff administrative relations and others. *ACHA/Journal, 0749-1913.*

HOSPITAL & HEALTH SERVICES ADMINISTRATION (CHICAGO, ILL. : 1976) CEASED. (HOSPITAL & HEALTH SERVICES ADMINISTRATION : QUARTERLY JOURNAL OF THE AMERICAN COLLEGE OF HOSPITAL ADMINISTRATORS). VFOAT Hospital and Health Services Administration. VAT Hospital and Health Services Administration. Began with V. 21 (Winter 1976). 0364-4553. Periodical. US. English. bm $25.00. American College Hospital Administrators, 840 North Lake Shore Drive, Chicago IL 60611. Tel (312)943-0544. Ed Joyce Flory. Ind/Abst Excerpta Med., Cumul. Index Nurs. Allied Health Lit., Account. Index. Suppl., Hospit. Lit. Index, Abstr. Hospit. Manage. Stud., Soc. Sci. Citation Index, Manage. Contents. LC RA971. DD 362.11068. NLM W1 HO71PY. bk rev. Circ 22,000. Available on microform from University Microfilms. Articles and research studies on practical issues in healthcare management. Includes manuscripts, case studies, essays, speeches, commentaries, articles from healthcare executives welcomed. *Hospital Administration, 0018-5523.*

HOSPITAL & HEALTH SERVICES PURCHASING. See Business - Purchasing.

HOSPITAL AND HEALTH SERVICES PURCHASING GUIDE TO EQUIPMENT AND SUPPLIES. 1967. UK. English. mo. $26.82. T G Scott and Son Ltd, 30-32 Southampton Street, London WCZE 7HR England. Ed Stuart Farr. NLM W1 HO71QAC. adv acc. Circ 6,500. (ctrl). Features of health service supplies, new product on market, purchasing customers in NHS. *Hospital Supplement HPG.*

THE HOSPITAL AND HEALTH SERVICES REVIEW. V. 1- 1904-. 0308-0234. Periodical. UK. English. bm. $50.00. Longman Group Limited, Fourth Avenue, Harlow Essex CM19 5AA England. Ind/Abst Hospit. Lit. Index.

HOSPITAL AND NURSING YEAR BOOK OF SOUTHERN AFRICA (JOHANNESBURG (SOUTH AFRICA) : 1971)). See Yearbooks, Almanacs, Directories.

HOSPITAL ANNUAL STATISTICS. See Statistics.

HOSPITAL BUILDING NOTE. Main/Corp Great Britain. Ministry of Health. Vol. 1 1961-. 0434-4871. UK. English. ir. H M Stationery Office, PO Box 276, London SW8 5DT England.

HOSPITAL BUYER'S GUIDE. (THE HOSPITAL BUYER'S GUIDE). VFOAT Guide des Acheteurs de Produits et Services Hospitaliers. 1981-. 0820-9421. CN. English (some text in French). an. Canadian Hospital Association, 410 Laurier Avenue/Suite 800 West, Ottawa Ontario K1R 7T6 Canada. DD 381.45681761029471.

HOSPITAL CAPITAL FINANCE. Vol. 1, No. 1 (Winter 1984)-. 0742-5708. Periodical. US. English. qt $30.00 Members, $40.00 Others. American Hospital Association, 840 North Lake Shore Drive, Chicago IL 60611. Ind/Abst Hospit. Lit. Index. NLM W1.

HOSPITAL CENTRAL SERVICE. V. 1- July 1967-. 0197-0712. Periodical. US. English. bm. American Hospital Association, 840 North Lake Shore Drive, Chicago IL 60611. NLM W1 HO754J.

HOSPITAL CONTRACTS MANUAL. See Law.

HOSPITAL DEVELOPMENT. V. 1- Jan./Feb. 1973-. 0300-5720. Periodical. UK. English. ir. United Trade Press Ltd, 33/35 Bowling Green Lane, London EC1R 0DA England. Tel 01-404 5531. Ind/Abst Hospit. Lit. Index, Excerpta Med. NLM W1 HO77T. *Hospital Building & Engineering, 0018-5582.*

HOSPITAL DIRECTORY OF INDIA. See Yearbooks, Almanacs, Directories.

HOSPITAL EMPLOYEE HEALTH. See Economics - Labor.

HOSPITAL ENGINEERING. 0163-3465. Periodical. US. English. bm. American Hospital Association, 840 North Lake Shore Drive, Chicago IL 60611. NLM W1 HO772K. *Hospital Engineer's Newsletter.*

Medicine—Medical Centers, Hospitals

HOSPITAL ENGINEERING. 0309-7498. Periodical. UK. English. ir. $53.63. Tully Goad Vinall, 40 Earl Street, Maidstone Kent ME14 1PF England. **Tel** 0622 678310. **Ind/Abst** Hospit. Lit. Index, Excerpta Med., Electr. Electron. Abstr., Comput. Control Abstr., Phys. Abstr. **NLM** W1 HO772R. *HE. Hospital Engineering, 0309-7501.*

HOSPITAL ENTREPRENEURS' NEWSLETTER. Began in 1985. 8756-7253. Periodical. US. English. mo. $125.00. Aspen Systems Corporation, 16792 Oakmont Avenue, Gaithersburg MD 20877. **DD** 362.

HOSPITAL EQUIPMENT NOTE. No. 1- Oct. 1962-. 0072-6028. Monographic Series. UK. English. ir. Her Majestys Stationery Office, PO Box 276, London SW8 5DT England. **Tel** 01-622 3316.

HOSPITAL FINANCIAL MANAGEMENT. *See* Business - Accounting.

HOSPITAL FINANCIAL MANAGEMENT ASSOCIATION ANNUAL REPORT. 1978/79-. 0271-406X. US. English. an. **NLM** W1 HO776D.

HOSPITAL FOOD & NUTRITION FOCUS. VFOAT Hospital Food and Nutrition Focus. Began in 1984. 0747-7376. Periodical. US. English. mo. $75.00 Domestic, $90.00 Foreign. Aspen Systems Corporation, 16792 Oakmont Avenue, Gaithersburg MD 20877. **DD** 641.

HOSPITAL FOOD SERVICE. V. 1- Nov. 1967-. 0046-7979. Periodical. US. English. qt. American Hospital Association, 840 North Lake Shore Drive, Chicago IL 60611. **NLM** W1 HO777L.

HOSPITAL FORUM. *See* Business - General Management.

HOSPITAL FUND RAISING NEWSLETTER. 1979. 0193-9939. Periodical. US. English. bm. $36.00. Hospital Fund Raising, PO Box 1442, Wall Township NJ 07719. **Tel** (201)681-1133. Ed Robert K Jenkins. Summary of ways to raise funds to meet competitive pressures and demands for services.

HOSPITAL GRAPHICS. *See* The Arts (General) - Graphic Arts.

HOSPITAL HIGHLIGHTS (DON MILLS, ONT. : 1981). (HOSPITAL HIGHLIGHTS). Summer 1981-. 0711-5652. Periodical. CN. English. qt. Ontario Hospital Association, 150 Ferrand Drive, Don Mills Ontario M3C 1H6 Canada. **Tel** (416)429-2661. **DD** 362.1109713. *Highlights, 0225-7602.*

HOSPITAL IN-PATIENT ENQUIRY. Series/Titt Series MB4. VFOAT Hospital in Patient Enquiry. 1974-. UK. English. an. Her Majesty's Stationery Office, 49 High Holburn, London WC1V 6HB England. **LC** RA407.G7. **DD** 362.110942. **NLM** W2 FA1 M6R. *Report on Hospital in-Patient Enquiry.*

HOSPITAL IN-PATIENT STATISTICS, WESTERN AUSTRALIA. *See* Statistics.

HOSPITAL INDICATORS. Main/Corp Statistics Canada. Health Division. Institutional Statistics Section. VFOAT Indicateurs des Hopitaux. V. 9, No. 2- Jan./June 1977-. 0046-7995. CN. English (French). qt. Statistics Canada, Publications Distribution, Ottawa Ontario K1A 0T6 Canada. **LC** RA983.A1. **DD** 362.110971. *Hospital Indicators, 0046-7995.*

HOSPITAL INFECTION CONTROL. V. 1- Nov. 1974-. 0098-180X. Periodical. US. English. mo. American Health Consultants, 67 Peachtree Park Drive, Atlanta GA 30307. **Tel** (404)351-4523. **Ind/Abst** Hospit. Lit. Index. **NLM** W1 HO799.

HOSPITAL LAW. *See* Law.

HOSPITAL LAW MANUAL. ADMINISTRATORS VOLUME. *See* Law.

HOSPITAL LITERATURE INDEX. *See* Indexes/Abstracts.

HOSPITAL MANAGEMENT REVIEW. Began with Jan. 1982? 0737-903X. Periodical. US. English. mo. $39.00. COR Research Inc, PO Box 6295, Torrance CA 90504. **Tel** (213)833-3316. Ed Dean H Anderson. bk rev. **Circ** 4,200. Informative summaries of key articles and research reports selected from more than 60 publications in the health care and management fields.

HOSPITAL MANAGEMENT SERIES. 1-. 0363-390X. Monographic Series. US. English. Catholic Hospital Association, St Louis MO 63104. **NLM** W1 HO817CM.

THE HOSPITAL MANAGER. *See* Business - General Management.

HOSPITAL MARKET ATLAS. UNITED STATES. *See* Encyclopedias & General Reference Books.

HOSPITAL MATERIALS MANAGEMENT NEWS. (HOSPITAL MATERIALS MANAGEMENT NEWS : THE BIMONTHLY NEWSLETTER OF ASHMM REPRESENTING PURCHASING MANAGEMENT, LOGISTICS MANAGEMENTS, AND INVENTORY AND DISTRIBUTION MANAGEMENT SECTIONS). Vol. 27, No. 1 (Jan.-Feb. 1983)-. 0749-6672. Periodical. US. English. bm. $60.00 Members, $90.00 Nonmembers. ASHMM, 840 North Lake Shore Drive, Chicago IL 60611. **Tel** (312)280-6155. Ed Cheryl L Ritzi. **DD** 362. bk rev. **Circ** 1,700. (ctrl). A membership newsletter which includes industry developments and changes. *Hospital Purchasing (Chicago, ILL.).*

HOSPITAL MATERIEL MANAGEMENT QUARTERLY. VFOAT HMMQ. V. 1- Aug. 1979-. 0192-2262. Periodical. US. English. qt. Aspen Systems Corporation, PO Box 6018, Gaithersburg MD 20760. **Tel** (301)251-5000. **Ind/Abst** Manage. Contents, Hospit. Lit. Index, Excerpta Med., ABI/Inform. **LC** RA971.33. **DD** 362.110687. **NLM** W1 HO817E.

HOSPITAL MORBIDITY, QUEENSLAND. (QUEENSLAND HOSPITAL MORBIDITY). 0725-4857. English. an. 2.10. Australian Bureau of Statistics, Ground Floor Statistics House, 345 Ann Street, Brisbane Queensland 4000 Australia. **Tel** (07)222 6351. **NLM** W2 KA8.1 Q3B9Q. Patients discharged: principal condition treated by numbers and rates; age group and sex, total and average stay (public/private hospitals), selected durations of stay; external cause (type of accident, etc.) by age group and sex; principal operation performed by age group and sex. *Patients Treated in Hospitals.*

HOSPITAL PEER REVIEW. V. 1- Aug.? 1976-. 0149-2632. Periodical. US. English. mo. American Health Consultants, 67 Peachtree Park Drive/Suite 110, Atlanta GA 30309. **Tel** (404)351-4523. **NLM** W1 HO864.

THE HOSPITAL PHONE BOOK. 1980-81-. 0278-5153. US. English. an. $37.95. US Directory Service, PO Box 86-1700, Miami FL 33168. **Tel** (305)769-1700. Ed S Alperin and B E Shaw. **NLM** WX 22 AA1 H8392. **Circ** 150,000. A complete name and address book of hospitals in all fifty states.

HOSPITAL PLANNING. V. 1- Jan./Feb. 1980-. 0270-2096. Periodical. US. English. bm. American Hospital Association, 840 North Lake Shore Drive, Chicago IL 60611. **NLM** W1 HO869K.

HOSPITAL PLANNING AND MARKETING : THE BIMONTHLY NEWSLETTER OF THE SOCIETY FOR HOSPITAL PLANNING AND MARKETING. *See* Business - Marketing.

HOSPITAL PRACTICE CEASED. V. 1-15. 0018-5809. Periodical. US. English. mo. $10.00. 485 Madison Avenue, New York NY 10022. **Ind/Abst** Life Sci. Collect., Excerpta Med., Cumul. Index Nurs. Allied Health Lit., Hospit. Lit. Index, Biol. Abstr., Nuci. Sci. Abstr., Energy Res. Abstr. **LC** R11. **DD** 616.005. **NLM** W1 HO87G. **CODEN** HOPRBW.

HOSPITAL PRACTICE (HOSPITAL EDITION). (HOSPITAL PRACTICE). 8755-4542. Periodical. US. English. mo. $32.00 US, $40.00 Foreign. HP Publishing Company, 575 Lexington Avenue, New York NY 10022. **Ind/Abst** Index Med., Hospit. Lit. Index. **DD** 616. *Hospital Practice, 0018-5809.*

HOSPITAL PROGRESS. V. 1-65, No. 7. 0018-5817. Periodical. US. English. ir. $30.00. Catholic Health Association of the US, 4455 Woodson Road, St Louis MO 63134. **Tel** (314)427-2500. Ed Judy Cassidy. **Ind/Abst** Hospit. Lit. Index, Excerpta Med., Energy Inf. Abstr., Environ. Abstr., Cumul. Index Nurs. Allied Health Lit., Soc. Work Res. Abstr., Energy Res. Abstr., Cathol. Period. Lit. Index. **LC** RA960. **DD** 362.05. **NLM** W1 HO871. **CODEN** HOPRA. bk rev. adv acc. **Circ** 14,000. Health care administration.

HOSPITAL PUBLIC RELATIONS. *See* Business - Advertising & Public Relations.

HOSPITAL PURCHASING MANAGEMENT. *See* Business - Purchasing.

HOSPITAL PURCHASING NEWS. (HOSPITAL PURCHASING NEWS : HPN). VFOAT HPN. Vol. 5, No. 9 (Sept. 1981)-. 0279-4799. Periodical. US. English. mo. $25.00. McKnight Medical Communication, 550 Frontage Road/Suite 3015, Northfield IL 60093. **Tel** (312)446-1622. Ed Christopher Bale. **Ind/Abst** Hospit. Lit. Index. adv acc. **Circ** 20,000. (ctrl). The magazine of choice by materials management professionals at every hospital. HPN reaches materials managers, purchasing directors and central service managers. *Purchasing Administration, 0192-4311.*

HOSPITAL RISK MANAGEMENT. *See* Business - General Management.

HOSPITAL SAFETY INFORMATION SERVICE. Vol. 1, No. 1 (Mar./Apr. 1979)-. 0276-2323. Periodical. US. English. bm. $160.00. Scientific Enterprises Inc, 5104 Randolph Road, North Little Rock AK 72116. **Tel** (501)771-1775. Ed James O Wear. **NLM** W1 HO877. Topics on hospital safety regulations and problems, interpretation of JCAH, OSHA, and NFPA standards and how to meet these standards.

HOSPITAL SALARY SURVEY REPORT ON DEPARTMENT HEAD POSITIONS. VFOAT Hospital Salary Survey Report. 1971-. 0277-2353. US. English. an. $92.50. Hospital Compensation Service, 115 Watchung Drive/PO Box 321, Hawthorne NJ 07506. **Tel** (201)427-2221. **LC** RA981.A2. **DD** 331.281362110973. **NLM** W1.

HOSPITAL SECURITY AND SAFETY MANAGEMENT. Vol. 3, No. 5 (Sept. 1982)-. 0745-1148. Periodical. US. English. mo. $180.00. Rusting Publications, 402 Main Street, Port Washington NY 11050. **Tel** (516)883-1440. Ed Victoria Nelsen. **Ind/Abst** Hospit. Lit. Index. **Circ** 1,100. Programs, ideas, and trends for preventing, reducing, and dealing with employee theft, violent crime, accidents and fires in hospitals. *Health Care Security and Safety Management, 0279-3466.*

HOSPITAL STATISTICS. *See* Statistics.

HOSPITAL STATISTICS : PRELIMINARY ANNUAL REPORT. *See* Statistics.

HOSPITAL STATISTICS. PUBLIC AND PRIVATE HOSPITALS. MENTAL HEALTH SERVICES. *See* Statistics.

HOSPITAL STATISTICS. VOLUME 1. BEDS, SERVICES, PERSONNEL. *See* Statistics.

HOSPITAL SUPERVISOR'S BULLETIN. *See* Business - Personnel Management.

HOSPITAL SURVEY PROFILE. US. English. ir. Joint Commission Accredited Hospital, 875 North Michigan Avenue, Chicago IL 60611. **Tel** (312)642-6061.

HOSPITAL TECHNOLOGY SERIES. VFOAT Executive Briefing. Began with: Vol. 2, No. 25, published in 1983. Periodical. US. English. mo. **Ind/Abst** Hospit. Lit. Index. **NLM** W1. *AHA Hospital Technology Series.*

HOSPITAL TOPICS. V. 29, No. 9- Sept. 1951-. 0018-5868. Periodical. US. English. bm. $35.00. The Hospital Topics Inc, 1308 Casey Key Road, Nokomis FL 33555. **Tel** (813)488-0905. Ed Gordon M Marshall. **Ind/Abst** Life Sci. Collect., Hospit. Lit. Index, Index Med., Cumul. Index Nurs. Allied Health Lit., Energy Res. Abstr. **NLM** W1 HO893. bk rev. adv acc. **Circ** 5,000. How-to-do-it short, illustrated to the point articles for the busy hospital managers, C.S., infection control, financial management. New techniques and systems. *Hospital Topics and Buyer's Guide, 0093-173X.*

HOSPITAL TOPICS. V. 1- Sept. 1922-. Periodical. US. English. mo.

HOSPITAL TRIBUNE. V. 1- 1967-. 0018-5876. Periodical. US. English. ir. $22.73. Medical Tribune, Rheinstrasse 19, D-62 Wiesbaden 1 West Germany. **NLM** W1 HO894.

HOSPITAL TRUSTEE. V. 1- May 1977-. 0704-0407. Periodical. CN. English. bm. $41.02. Canadian Hospital Association, 17 York Street/Suite 100, Ottawa Ontario K1N 9J6 Canada. **Tel** (613)238-8005. Ed Ruta Klicius. **Ind/Abst** Hospit. Lit. Index, Cumul. Index Nurs. Allied Health Lit. **DD** 658.42. **NLM** W1 HO894D. adv acc. **Circ** 6,000. Material to help members of hospital governing boards to conduct their business.

HOSPITAL UPDATE. 0305-4136. Periodical. UK. English. mo. $58.23. Update Publishing Ltd, South Down House/Station Road, Petersfield

Medicine—Medical Centers, Hospitals

Hampshire GU21 3ET England. **Ind/Abst** Life Sci. Collect. **NLM** W1 HO894K.

HOSPITAL UTILIZATION DATA, WISCONSIN. Main/Corp Wisconsin. Bureau of Health Statistics. **Series/Titl** Wisconsin Health Facility Statistics, Resources and Utilization. **VFOAT** Hospitals, Wisconsin. 1974-. US. English. an. Bureau of Health Statistics, Box 309, Madison WI 53701. *Hospital Inventory and Utilization Data, Wisconsin.*

HOSPITAL WAGE, SALARY AND BENEFITS SURVEY. (HOSPITAL WAGE, SALARY, AND BENEFITS SURVEY). **Main/Corp** Kentucky Hospital Research and Education Foundation. 0198-6384. US. English. Kentucky Hospital Association, Suite 407/1951 Bishop Lane, Louisville KY 40218. **LC** RA981.K4. **DD** 331.2813621109769.

HOSPITAL WEEK. Vol. 6-. 0149-6352. Periodical. US. English. wk. $8.00. American Hospital Publishing, PO Box 91497, Chicago IL 60693. **Tel** (312)951-1100. **NLM** W1 HO895. *Week for Hospitals.*

HOSPITAL/COMMUNITY RELATIONS PROFESSIONAL. VFOAT Hospital, Community Relations Professional. Aug. 1983-. 0740-3674. Periodical. US. English. mo. $50.00. Hospital/Community Relations Professional, PO Box 590, Naperville IL 60566.

HOSPITALS. (HOSPITALS : THE JOURNAL OF THE AMERICAN HOSPITAL ASSOCIATION). Began with: Vol. 10, No. 1 (Jan. 1936). 0018-5973. Periodical. US. English. sm. American Hospital Publishing Company, PO Box 91497, Chicago IL 60611. **Ind/Abst** Life Sci. Collect., Hospit. Lit. Index, Excerpta Med., Index Med., Cumul. Index Nurs. Allied Health Lit., Account. Index. Suppl., Energy Res. Abstr., Sci. Cit. Index, Abr. Ed., Soc. Sci. Citation Index. **LC** RA960. **DD** 362.110973. **NLM** W1 HO934. *Bulletin of the American Hospital Association, American Hospital Directory.*

HOSPITALS. (HOSPITALS : A COUNTY AND METROPOLITAN AREA DATA BOOK). **Series/Titl** DHHS Publication. 0093-3732. US. English. Superintendent of Documents, US Government Printing Office, Washington DC 20402. **LC** RA981.A2. **DD** 362.110973. **NLM** WX 22 AA1 H85.

HOSPITALS & HEALTH SERVICES YEARBOOK AND DIRECTORY OF HOSPITAL SUPPLIERS. See Yearbooks, Almanacs, Directories.

HOSPITALS & HEALTH SERVICES YEARBOOK AUSTRALIA. See Yearbooks, Almanacs, Directories.

HOSPITALS AND NURSING HOMES. Main/Corp Australian Bureau of Statistics. 0312-4940. AT. English. ir. Australian Bureau of Statistics, Government Printing Office, Sydney New South Wales 2001 Australia. **LC** RA992.A1. **DD** 362.110994. *Hospitals and Nursing Homes.*

HOSPITALS, NURSING HOMES AND RELATED HEALTH FACILITIES. (HOSPITALS, NURSING HOMES AND RELATED HEALTH FACILITIES LICENSED BY THE STATE OF CALIFORNIA, DEPARTMENT OF HEALTH, HEALTH QUALITY SYSTEMS, FACILITIES LICENSING SECTION). 1973-. 0094-9833. Periodical. US. English. an. **NLM** WX 22 AC2 H8. *Hospitals, Nursing Homes and Related Health Facilities Licensed by the State of California, Department of Public Health, Bureau of Health Facilities Licensing and Certification, 0094-9833.*

INFORMA 7200. V. 1- May/June 1970-. 0380-3880. Periodical. CN. French. Hospital Riviere-des-Prairies, 7200 East Boulevard Gouin, Montreal Quebec Canada.

INFORMACIONES ESTADISTICAS. See Statistics.

INPATIENT HEALTH FACILITIES STATISTICS, UNITED STATES. See Statistics.

INTERBLOCS. No. 1- Oct. 1977-. 0705-0828. Periodical. CN. French. ir. Free. Hopital Sainte-Justine, 3175 Chemin Sainte-Catherine, Montreal Quebec H3T 1C5 Canada. **DD** 362.1109714281. (ctrl).

INTERNATIONAL JOURNAL OF PARTIAL HOSPITALIZATION. VFOAT Partial Hospitalization. Vol. 1, No. 1 (Jan. 1982)-. 0272-4308. Periodical. US. English. qt. $65.00 Domestic, $74.00 Foreign. Plenum Publishing Corporation, 233 Spring Street, New York NY 10013. **Ind/Abst** Hospit. Lit. Index, Excerpta Med., Cumul. Index Nurs. Allied Health Lit., Curr. Contents, Psychol. Abstr. **NLM** W1 IN771ND. **CODEN** IPHOD3. This journal has the primary intent of stimulating and communicating information regarding research programming and administrative issues in all types of partial hospitalization as well as other community based residential or rehabilitation settings.

INVENTORY OF FINANCIAL AND STATISTICAL INFORMATION FOR CALIFORNIA LONG-TERM CARE FACILITIES. See Statistics.

INVENTORY OF HOSPITAL FACILITIES. US. English. an. 908 Standard Building, Cleveland OH 44113.

IRYO. VFOAT Medical Journal of National Hospitals and Sanitoriums of Japan. Vol. 1-. 0021-1699. Periodical. JA. table of contents and summaries in English. mo. $79.50. Japan Publishers Trading Company Ltd, PO Box 5030, Tokyo International, Tokyo 100-31 Japan. **Ind/Abst** Life Sci. Collect., Excerpta Med., Biol. Abstr., Chem. Abstr. **NLM** W1 IR629. **CODEN** IRYOAV.

JAHRESBERICHT - DIE BEHANDLUNGSEINRICHTUNGEN DER ALLGEMEINEN UNFALLVERSICHERUNGSANSTALT. (JAHRESBERICHT : DIE BEHANDLUNGSEINRICHTUNGEN DER ALLGEMEINEN UNFALLVERSICHERUNGSANSTALT). **Main/Corp** Allgemeine Unfallversicherungsanstalt (Vienna, Austria). Began in 1971. 0253-9233. German. an. **NLM** WX 2 GA8 A4J. *Jahresbericht der Arbeitsunfallkrankenhauser Graz, Klagenfurt, Linz, Salzburg, Wien XII, Wien XX, 0379-7430.*

JCAH PERSPECTIVES. Main/Corp Joint Commission on Accreditation of Hospitals. **VFOAT** J.C.A.H. Perspectives. **VAT** Joint Commission on Accreditation of Hospitals Perspectives. Vol. 1 (July/Aug. 1981)-. 0277-8327. Periodical. US. English. bm. $26.25. Joint Commission on Accreditation of Hospitals, 875 North Michigan Avenue, Chicago IL 60611. **Tel** (312)642-6061. **Ind/Abst** Hospit. Lit. Index. **NLM** W1 JO1786D. *Perspectives on Accreditation, 0099-2402.*

JOURNAL DES TRAVAILLEURS D'HOPITAUX. V. 1- Mar. 1978-. 0707-7858. Newspaper. CN. French. mo. $4.00. L'Association Ouvriere Canadienne, C P 666 Succursale C, Montreal Quebec H2L 4L5 Canada. **DD** 331.2041362110971.

JOURNAL - NATIONAL ASSOCIATION FOR HOSPITAL DEVELOPMENT. (JOURNAL). **VFOAT** NAHD Journal. Vol. 1, No. 1-. 0360-0599. Periodical. US. English. sa. National Association of Hospital Development, 8300 Greenboro Drive/Suite 1110, McLean VA 22102. **Tel** (703)556-9555. **LC** RA981.A2. **DD** 362.110973. **NLM** W1 JO523.

JOURNAL - NATIONAL ASSOCIATION OF PRIVATE PSYCHIATRIC HOSPITALS CEASED. V. 1-13, No. 1. 0027-8629. US. English. qt. $16.00. National Association of Private Psychiatric Hospitals, 1319 F Street NW/Suite 1000, Washington DC 20004. **Tel** (202)393-6700. **Ind/Abst** Psychol. Abstr., Hospit. Lit. Index. **NLM** W1. **CODEN** JNAPB. bk rev. adv acc. Circ 7,000. (ctrl).

THE JOURNAL OF AMBULATORY CARE MANAGEMENT. VFOAT Ambulatory Care Management. V. 1- Jan. 1978-. 0148-9917. Periodical. US. English. qt. Aspen Systems Corporation, PO Box 6018, Gaithersburg MD 20760. **Tel** (301)251-5000. Ed Seth B Goldsmith and Norbert Goldfield. **Ind/Abst** Excerpta Med., Hospit. Lit. Index, Cumul. Index Nurs. Allied Health Lit. **LC** RA411. **DD** 362.12. **NLM** W1 JO535CM. bk rev. adv acc. (ctrl). Devoted exclusively to the management information needs of ambulatory care professionals cutting costs, marketing, regulations, increasing productivity, and more are addressed.

JOURNAL OF CLINICAL COMPUTING. See Computers and Computer Science.

THE JOURNAL OF HOSPITAL INFECTION. V. 1- Mar. 1980-. 0195-6701. Periodical. US. English. qt. $81.00. Academic Press, 4805 Sand Lake Road, Orlando FL 32819. **Tel** (305)345-4100. **Ind/Abst** Life Sci. Collect., Excerpta Med., Index Med. **NLM** W1 JO673N.

JOURNAL OF HOSPITAL MARKETING. 0883-7570. Periodical. US. English. qt. $32.00 Institutions, $42.00 Libraries. Haworth Press, 73 Griswold Street, Binghamton NY 13904.

JOURNAL OF HOSPITAL RESEARCH. 0022-1627. Periodical. US. English. ir. Educational Department of American Sterilizer Company, 2424 West 23rd Street, Erie PA 16512.

JOURNAL OF HOSPITAL SUPPLY, PROCESSING, AND DISTRIBUTION. VFOAT Journal HSPD. Vol. 1, No. 1-. 0738-2928. Periodical. US. English. bm. $28.00 US, $36.00 Canada. Mayworm Associates Inc, PO Box 999, Libertyville IL 60048. **Ind/Abst** Hospit. Lit. Index.

JOURNAL OF MEDICAL SYSTEMS. V. 1-. 0148-5598. Periodical. US. English. bm. Plenum Press, 233 Spring Street, New York NY 10013. **Tel** (212)620-8000. Ed Ralph P Grahms. **Ind/Abst** Hospit. Lit. Index, Excerpta Med., Index Med., Biol. Abstr., Energy Res. Abstr., Cumul. Index Nurs. Allied Health Lit. **LC** R858.A1. **DD** 362.102854. **NLM** W1 JO756T. **CODEN** JMSYDA. bk rev. adv acc. This journal is designed to provide a forum for presentation and discussion of the increasingly extensive applications of new systems techniques and methods in hospitals, clinics and doctors' office administrations. *Journal of Medical Systems.*

JOURNAL OF THE AMERICAN MEDICAL RECORD ASSOCIATION. (JOURNAL). **VFOAT** Journal of A.M.R.A. 54/1 (Jan. 1983)-. 0273-9976. Periodical. US. English. mo. $40.00. AMRA, 875 North Michigan Drive/Suite 1850, Chicago IL 60611. **Tel** (312)787-2672. Ed Jill Callahan Dennis. **Ind/Abst** Hospit. Lit. Index, Excerpta Med., Cumul. Index Nurs. Allied Health Lit., Life Sci. Collect. **NLM** W1. bk rev. adv acc. Circ 27,000. Professional association journal for those interested in health data, health information management. *Journal of the American Medical Record Association, 0273-9976.*

KENTUCKY HOSPITAL FACTS. US. English. an. Kentucky Hospital Association, 1951 Bishop Lane/Suite 407, Louisville KY 40218. **LC** RA981.K4. **DD** 362.1109769.

KOKURITSU RYOYOJO YORAN. JA. Japanese. ir. Koseisho Imukyoku Kokuritsu Ryoyojoka, 2-2 Kasumigaseki 1, Chiyoda-Ku 100, Tokyo Japan. **LC** RA990.J4.

KORHAZ- ES ORVOSTECHNIKA. (KORHAZ- ES ORVOSTECHNIKA : AZ ORSZAGOS KORHAZ- ES ORVOSTECHNIKAI INTEZET TUDOMANYOS FOLYOIRATA). V. 18, 1 (Jan. 1980)-. 0139-4509. Periodical. HU. Hungarian. bm. $22.00. Akademiai Kiado, POB 24, 1363 Budapest Hungary. **Ind/Abst** Energy Res. Abstr. **NLM** W1 KO611V. *Orvos es Technika, 0473-4424.*

THE LEARNING RESOURCES DIRECTORY FOR HEALTHCARE EXECUTIVES : LRD. See Yearbooks, Almanacs, Directories.

LENGTH OF STAY IN P.A.S. HOSPITALS, UNITED STATES. (LENGTH OF STAY IN PAS HOSPITALS IN THE UNITED STATES). **Main/Corp** Commission on Professional and Hospital Activities. **VAT** Length of Stay in Professional Activity Study Hospitals in the United States. Began with Vol. for 1969. 0096-3348. US. English. an. Commission on Professional and Hospital Activities, 1968 Green Road, Ann Arbor MI 48105. **Tel** (313)769-6511. **LC** RA981.A2. **DD** 362.110973. **NLM** W1 LE772NL. Length of stay in short-term general hospitals published for the US and four census regions, also by geriatric, pediatric and Canada.

LENGTH OF STAY IN P.A.S. HOSPITALS, UNITED STATES, EASTERN REGION. (LENGTH OF STAY IN PAS HOSPITALS, UNITED STATES, EASTERN REGION). **Main/Corp** Commission on Professional and Hospital Activities. **VAT** Length of Stay in Professional Activity Study Hospitals, United States, Eastern Region. 1973-. 0096-1329. Periodical. US. English. an. Commission on Professional and Hospital Activities, 1968 Green Road, PO Box 1809, Ann Arbor MI 48106. **Tel** (313)769-6511. **LC** RA981.N86. **DD** 362.110974. **NLM** W1 LE772NR. *Length of Stay in PAS Hospitals, United States, Regional, 0097-904X.*

LICENSED & CERTIFIED HEALTH CARE FACILITIES : DIRECTORY. See Yearbooks, Almanacs, Directories.

LICENSED HEALTH CARE FACILITIES IN IOWA. Began with Vol. for 1973. 0098-3454. US. English. an. Iowa State Department of Health, Divison of Health Facilities, Des Moines IA 50319. **LC** RA997.5.I6. **DD** 362.1609777. **NLM** WX 22 AI8 S7L. *Licensed Nursing and Custodial Health Care Facilities in Iowa, 0090-581X.*

Medicine—Medical Centers, Hospitals

LIST OF ACCREDITED HOSPITALS AND OTHER HEALTH CARE INSTITUTIONS. (LIST OF ACCREDITED HOSPITALS AND OTHER HEALTH CARE INSTITUTIONS AT CONCLUSION . . . SURVEY YEAR). VFOAT Liste des Hopitaux et Autres Etablissements de Sante Agrees A la Conclusion du Programme pour l'Annee. 1980-. 0710-4936. CN. English (French). an. Free. Canadian Council on Hospital Accreditation, 1815 Alta Vista Drive, Ottawa Ontario K1G 3Y6 Canada. **DD** 362.1102571.

LIST OF CANADIAN HOSPITALS AND SPECIAL CARE FACILITIES. VFOAT Liste des Hopitaux Canadiens et des establissements de Soins Speciaux. 0225-5642. CN. French (English). an. **DD** 362.102571. **NLM** W2 DC2 S827L.

LISTE DES PERIODIQUES - HOPITAL RIVIERE-DES-PRAIRIES, BIBLIOTHEQUE DU PERSONNEL. See Bibliographies.

LONG TERM CARE. V. 1- Sept. 1, 1972-. 0192-7701. US. English. wk. $187.00. National Press Building, Washington DC 20045. **NLM** W1 LO789.

LONG-TERM CARE ADMINISTRATOR. V. 9, No. 2- Feb. 1975-. 0146-275X. Periodical. US. English. ir. $35.00. American College Health Care Administration, 8120 Woodmont Avenue/Suite 200, Bethesda MD 20814. **Tel** (301)652-8384. Ed Kathleen Griffen. **NLM** W1 LO7899. bk rev. adv acc. **Circ** 7,000. Scholarly peer review journal on long term health care administration, any health care administrator should subscribe. *Newsletter - American College of Nursing Home Administrators.*

LONG TERM CARE AND HEALTH SERVICES ADMINISTRATION QUARTERLY. (LONG TERM CARE & HEALTH SERVICES ADMINISTRATION QUARTERLY). V. 1- Spring (March 1977)-. 0161-6773. Periodical. US. English. qt. $36.00. Panel Publishers, 14 Plaza Road, Greenvale NY 11548. LC RA997.A1. **DD** 362.16068. **NLM** W1 LO7899J.

MCLEAN HOSPITAL JOURNAL. V. 1- Winter 1976-. 0363-0226. Periodical. US. English. qt. McLean Hospital, c/o Evelyn M Stone, 115 Mill Street, Belmont MA 02178. **Ind/Abst** Excerpta Med., Biol. Abstr. **NLM** W1 MA165H. **CODEN** MHJODZ.

MAINE HEALTH FACILITIES, RESOURCES, AND UTILIZATION. 1979-. US. English. Bureau of Health Planning and Development, Department of Human Services, Station 1/State House, Augusta ME 04333. LC RA981.M2. **DD** 362.1109741.

MALPRACTICE PREVENTION FOR HOSPITALS. See Law.

MAYO CLINIC PROCEEDINGS. V. 39- Jan. 1964-. 0025-6196. Periodical. US. English. mo. Mayo Clinic Proceedings, Plummer Building/Room 1035, Mayo Clinic, Rochester MN 55905. **Tel** (507)284-2154. Ed Robert G Siekert. **Ind/Abst** Hospit. Lit. Index, Life Sci. Collect., Excerpta Med., Cumul. Index Nurs. Allied Health Lit., Energy Res. Abstr., Biol. Abstr., Chem. Abstr., Index Med., Nucl. Sci. Abstr., Sci. Cit. Index, Abr. Ed. **NLM** W1 MA997V. **CODEN** MACPAJ. bk rev. adv acc. **Circ** 124,000. (ctrl). New information about clinical and research activities of the Mayo Clinic and Mayo Foundation, plus review articles and reports written by Mayo Clinic staff members. *Proceedings of the Staff Meetings of the Mayo Clinic, 0092-699X.*

MEDICAL CENTER. VFOAT UAB Medical Center. Vol. 16, No.3 (March 1972)-. 0745-4910. Periodical. US. English. qt. UAB Medical Center, University Station, Birmingham AL 35294. *University of Alabama Medical Center News Bulletin.*

THE MEDICAL CLINICS OF NORTH AMERICA. V. 1- July 1917-. 0025-7125. Monographic Series. US. English. bm. $45.00. W B Saunders, West Washington Square, Philadelphia PA 19105. **Tel** (215)574-3395. Ed Susan Plummer. **Ind/Abst** Life Sci. Collect., Excerpta Med., Pestdoc, Ringdoc, Vetdoc, Energy Res. Abstr., Biol. Abstr., Chem. Abstr., Index Med., Nucl. Sci. Abstr., Hospit. Lit. Index, Sci. Cit. Index, Abr. Ed. LC RC60. **NLM** W1 ME252R. **CODEN** MCNAA9. (cum index). **Circ** 23,000. Clinical updates on management and techniques written by experts in the field. Topics are those of current concerns to internists. *Medical Clinics of Chicago, 0096-7041.*

MEDICAL DIRECTORY. See Yearbooks, Almanacs, Directories.

MEMBERSHIP ROSTER OF THE AMERICAN SOCIETY OF HOSPITAL ATTORNEYS. See Law.

MEMORIAL SLOAN-KETTERING CANCER CENTER. 1972-. 0162-0967. US. English. an. Memorial Sloan-Kettering Cancer Center, 1275 York Avenue, New York NY 10021. **NLM** WX 2 AN7 M45R. *Report - Memorial Sloan-Kettering Cancer Center, 0543-4440.*

MICHIGAN HOSPITALS. V. 1- 1965-. 0026-220X. Periodical. US. English. mo. $20.00. Michigan Hospitals Association, 6215 West Street, St Joseph Highway, Lansing MI 48917. **Tel** (517)323-3443. Ed Maryanne Butt. **Ind/Abst** Hospit. Lit. Index, Hospit. Lit. Index. **NLM** W1 MI203. adv acc. **Circ** 2,400. Each edition examines in detail a timely health care issue affecting hospitals.

MIDDLESEX HOSPITAL JOURNAL. 0026-3222. Periodical. UK. English. ty. Middlesex Hospital Journal, Mortimer Street, London W 1 England. **Ind/Abst** Bibliogr. Index Geol.

MINNESOTA MEDICAL ASSISTANCE (TITLE XIX) FOR FISCAL YEAR. Main/Corp Minnesota. Dept. of Public Welfare. Operations Review Division. Reports and Statistics. 1980/81-. US. English. an. Department of Public Welfare Reports and Statistics, Space Center Building, St Paul MN 55101. LC HD7102.U5. **DD** 362.10425209776. *Minnesota Medical Assistance (Title XIX) Biennium Report for Fiscal Years . . . .*

MINUTES OF ANNUAL MEETING - BRITISH COLUMBIA ASSOCIATION OF HOSPITALS AND HEALTH ORGANIZATIONS. Main/Corp British Columbia Association of Hospitals and Health Organizations. 1974-. 0384-9481. Periodical. CN. English. an. **NLM** W1 MI7804B. *Minutes of Annual Meeting and Conference - British Columbia Hospitals' Association, 0317-3755.*

MISSOURI HOSPITAL PROFILES. Series/Titl Missouri Center for Health Statistics Publication. Began with Vol. for 1978. 0192-6543. US. English. an. Missouri Center for Health Statistics, PO Box 570, Jefferson City MO 65102. LC RA981.M8. **DD** 362.1109778. **NLM** W2 AM8 B8M. *Missouri Hospital Profiles for . . . .*

MODERN HEALTHCARE. V. 7- Jan. 1977-. 0160-7480. Periodical. US. English. bw. $75.00. Crain Communications, 740 Rush Street, Chicago IL 60611. **Tel** (312)649-5200. **Ind/Abst** Manage. Contents, Hospit. Lit. Index, Predicasts, Cumul. Index Nurs. Allied Health Lit., Account. Index. Suppl., Energy Res. Abstr., Soc. Work Res. Abstr. LC RA960. **DD** 338.4736210973. **NLM** W1 MO132T. *Modern Healthcare, Modern Healthcare, 0093-7061.*

MONOGRAPHIES DE LA FEDERATION DES INSTITUTIONS HOSPITALIERES. Monographic Series. French. ir. **NLM** W1 MO567BY.

MULTIS. Vol. 1, No. 1 (Mar. 1, 1983)-. 0749-1611. Periodical. US. English. qt. American Hospital Publishing Inc, 211 East Chicago Avenue/Suite 700, Chicago IL 60611. **Ind/Abst** Hospit. Lit. Index. **NLM** W1.

NATIONAL INSTITUTES OF HEALTH ANNUAL REPORT OF INTERNATIONAL ACTIVITIES. Main/Corp John E. Fogarty International Center for Advanced Study in the Health Sciences. Began with 1968/69. 0146-6690. US. English. an. John E Fogarty International, Center for Advanced Study in the Health Sciences, National Institutes of Health, Bethesda MD 20205. LC RA11. **DD** 610.72. **NLM** W2 A N206N.

NATIONAL SURVEY OF HOSPITAL AND MEDICAL SCHOOL SALARIES. See Economics - Labor.

NCI FACT BOOK. See Medicine - Neoplasma, Neoplastic.

NEBRASKA HEALTH MANPOWER REPORTS. NURSING HOME ADMINISTRATORS. (NEBRASKA HEALTH MANPOWER REPORTS : NURSING HOME ADMINISTRATORS). Main/Corp Nebraska. Division of Health Data and Statistical Research. 0148-9321. US. English. an. LC RA997.5.N2. **DD** 331.11. **NLM** W2 AN1 D34NN.

NEW JERSEY STATE PLAN FOR THE CONSTRUCTION AND MODERNIZATION OF HOSPITALS AND OTHER MEDICAL FACILITIES. Main/Corp New Jersey. Bureau of Medical Facility Construction and Planning. US. English. an. Bureau of Medical Facility Construction and Planning, PO Box 1540, John Fitch Plaza, Trenton NJ 08625. LC RA981.N5. **DD** 362.1109749. *New Jersey State Plan for the Construction of Hospitals and Related Medical Facilities.*

NEWS - HOSPITAL ASSOCIATION OF NEW YORK STATE. Main/Corp Hospital Association of New York State. 1970. 0018-5574. Periodical. US. English. wk. Hospital Association of New York State, 15 Computer Drive West, Albany NY 12205. **Tel** (518)458-7940. **Circ** 2,608. (ctrl). Information of current interest concerning health care institutions.

NEWSLETTER (NATIONAL ASSOCIATION OF PRIVATE PSYCHIATRIC HOSPITALS). (NEWSLETTER). Began publication in 1950. 0027-8637. Periodical. US. English. bm. National Association of Private Psychiatric Hospitals, 1319 NW, Suite 1000, Washington DC 20004.

NEWSLINES - ST. BONIFACE GENERAL HOSPITAL. (NEWSLINES : ST. BONIFACE GENERAL HOSPITAL COMMUNITY AND STAFF NEWS). Main/Corp St. Boniface General Hospital. Vol. 1, No. 1 (Sept. 1983)-. 0822-8132. Periodical. CN. English. qt. Free. St Boniface General Hospital, Public Relations Department, 409 Tache Avenue, Winnipeg Manitoba R2H 2A6 Canada. **DD** 362.11097127.4.

NIPPON BYOINKAI ZASSHI. VFOAT Journal of Japan Hospital Association. Maki 22- Ichigatsu 1975-. Periodical. Japanese. ir. **NLM** W1 NI8833. *Nippon Byoin Kyokai Zasshi.*

NLP HEALTH LABOR RELATIONS ALERT. See Law.

NOTRE HOPITAL. First issue, Dec. 1965. 0704-8815. Periodical. CN. French. ir. Free. Hotel-Dieu de Montreal, Centre de Documentation, 3840 rue Saint-Urbain, Montreal Quebec H2W 1T8 Canada. **DD** 362.1109714281. (ctrl).

NOUVEAUTES - BIBLIOTHEQUE DU PERSONNEL, HOSPITAL RIVIERE-DES-PRAIRIES. (NOUVEAUTES). Main/Corp Hopital Riviere-des-Prairies. Bibliotheque du Personnel. Sept. 1981-. 0714-4016. Periodical. CN. French. mo. Free. Nouveautes, c/o Bibliotheque du Personnel Hopital Riviere des Prairies, 1070 Boulevard Perras, Montreal Quebec H1E 1A4 Canada. **DD** 016.61689. *Liste des Nouveautes, 0228-6270.*

NOUVELLES ARCHIVES HOSPITALIERES. See Genealogy and Heraldry - Archives.

NURSING HOME SALARY & BENEFITS REPORT. VAT Nursing Home Salary and Benefits Report. Began with 1979 issue. 0275-1070. US. English. an. $125.00. John R Zabka Associates, 115 Watchung Drive, Hawthorne NJ 07506. **Tel** (201)487-2221. Ed John R Zabca. LC RA997.A1. **DD** 331.281362160973. **Circ** 13,00. (ctrl). Salary and fringe benefit data on nursing home employees.

NURSING HOMES. 1957. 0029-649X. Periodical. US. English. bm. $25.00. Centaur & Company, 5 Willowbrook Court, Potomac MD 20854. **Tel** (301)983-1152. Ed William D Magnes. **Ind/Abst** Hospit. Lit. Index, Cumul. Index Nurs. Allied Health Lit., Bus. Period. Index, Account. Index. Suppl. **NLM** W1 NU6095. bk rev. adv acc. **Circ** 2,000. Magazine for nursing home administrators. Academic and human interest articles. Columns on nutrition, legal briefs, pharmacology, government (federal and state). New products and marketing information.

NURSING HOMES. (NURSING HOMES : A COUNTY AND METROPOLITAN AREA DATA BOOK). 1967-. 0093-3260. Monographic Series. US. English. an. **NLM** WT 22 AA1 N9.

NURSING HOMES IN WASHINGTON STATE. VFOAT Report, Nursing Homes ih Washington State. 0278-7059. US. English. Center for Health Statistics, MS LL-15 Health Services Division, Department of Social and Health Services, Olympia WA 98504. LC RA997.5.W3. **DD** 362.1609797.

NURSING HOMES (TORONTO, ONT.). (NURSING HOMES). VFOAT Nursing Homes in Metropolitan Toronto. 0712-1342. Periodical. CN. English. be. $3.00 Per Issue. Community Information Centre of Metropolitan Toronto, 3rd Floor/34 King Street East, Toronto Ontario M5C 1E5 Canada. **Ind/Abst** Trade Ind. Index. **DD** 362.61.

OHARA SOGO BYOIN NENPO. VFOAT Annual Report of Ohara General Hospital. Vol. 1- Oct. 1957-. Periodical. Japanese. ir. **NLM** W1 OH19.

Medicine—Medical Centers, Hospitals

ONTARIO HOSPITALS DIRECTORY. See Yearbooks, Almanacs, Directories.

ONTARIO NURSING HOMES. Vol. 5, No. 12 (Autumn,1974)-. 0712-9971. Periodical. CN. English. ir. $6.00. Ontario Nursing Home Association, 6075 Yonge Street, Willowdale Ontario M2M 3W2 Canada. DD 362.6109713. *Ontario Nursing Home News.*

OSPEDALE MAGGIORE. 0369-7843. Periodical. IT. Italian. qt. $11.88. Direzione Redazione Amm Publ, Via F Sforza 28, 20122 Milano Italy. Tel 88 20. Ind/Abst Excerpta Med. NLM W1 OS527.

OSTEOPATHIC HOSPITALS. (OH. OSTEOPATHIC HOSPITALS). VFOAT Osteopathic Hospitals. V. 19, No. 4- April 1975-. 0161-0007. Periodical. US. English. mo. American Osteopathic Hospital Association, 55 West Seegers Road, Arlington Heights IL 60005. Tel (312)952-8900. Ed Finlayson. Ind/Abst Hospit. Lit. Index, Med. Socioecon. Res. Source, Cumul. Index Nurs. Allied Health Lit., Abstr. Hospit. Manage. Stud. NLM W1 O252. bk rev. adv acc. Circ 1,800. (ctrl). Available on microfilm from University Microfilms. Concerns hospital governance and management. *Osteopathic Hospital, 0048-2293.*

PATIENT ACCOUNTS. Began with Vol. 1, No. 1 (Feb. 10, 1978). 0195-7775. Periodical. US. English. mo. $115.00. Healthcare Financial Management Association, 1900 Spring Road, Suite 500, Oak Brook IL 60521. Tel (312)655-4600. Ind/Abst Hospit. Lit. Index. NLM W1 PA963M.

PATIENT CARE REVIEW. V. 1- Aug. 1975-. 0147-3913. Periodical. US. English. mo. Illinois Hospital Association, 1200 Jorie Boulevard, Oak Brook IL 60521. NLM W1 PA9632.

PATIENT ORIGIN DATA FOR NORTH DAKOTA HOSPITALS AND NURSING HOMES. Main/Corp North Dakota. Division of Health Facilities. 0147-0957. US. English. North Dakota Division of Health Facilities, 1200 Missouri Avenue, Bismarck ND 58505. LC RA981.N85. DD 362.109784. NLM W2 AN8 D65P.

PENNSYLVANIA HOSPITALS. Vol. 1, No. 1 (Spring 1982)-. 0744-5636. Periodical. US. English. qt. Hospital Association of Pennsylvania, PO Box 608, Camp Hill PA 17011. *Hospital Issues & Trends, 0162-520X.*

LA PHARMACIE HOSPITALIERE FRANCAISE. 0369-9579. Periodical. FR. French. qt. Syn Prefh, c/o J Allaz, Pharmacien-Chef, Hopital Saint-Eloi C H R U Avenue, Bertin Sans 34059 Montpellier Cedex France. Ind/Abst Excerpta Med., Chem. Abstr. CODEN PHHFAS.

PLAN FOR HEALTH CARE FACILITIES. Main/Corp Rhode Island. Division of Medical Care Standards. 0148-7221. US. English. LC RA981.R4. DD 353.974500841. NLM W2 AR4 D35R. *Rhode Island State Plan for Health Care Facilities, 0080-276X.*

PRESIDENTIAL PAPER - ALBERTA HOSPITAL ASSOCIATION. (PRESIDENTIAL PAPER). 1981-. 0712-5534. CN. English. an. Alberta Hospital Association, 10025 108 Street, Edmonton Alberta T5J 1K9 Canada. Tel (403)434-9531. Ed A Judith Prowse. DD 362.1097123. Circ 2,000. Hospital trustees, administrators and other health professionals are challenged to evaluate the current status of their rehabilitation services and to examining the priority given rehabilitation.

PRIVATE PSYCHIATRIC HOSPITALS. Main/Corp United States. National Institute of Mental Health. 0162-9913. US. English. National Institute of Mental Health, 5600 Fishers Lane, Rockville MD 20857.

PROCEEDINGS OF THE ... ANNUAL CONFERENCE OF THE HEALTH SERVICES DIVISION OF THE INSTITUTE OF INDUSTRIAL ENGINEERS. Main/Corp Institute of Industrial Engineers (1981-) Health Services Division. 0194-1135. US. English. an. Hospital Management Systems Society and the American Hospital Association, 840 North Lake Shore Drive, Chicago IL 60611. Tel (312)280-6023. Ed Richard P Covert. LC RA971. DD 362.11068. NLM W3 AM537. Circ 800. A collection of technical papers describing management engineering and information systems case studies in health care. *Proceedings of the Annual Conference of the American Institute of Industrial Engineers, Health Services Division, 0194-1135.*

PROCEEDINGS OF THE ANNUAL CONFERENCE OF THE HOSPITAL MANAGEMENT SYSTEMS SOCIETY. (PROCEEDINGS OF THE . . . ANNUAL CONFERENCE OF THE HOSPITAL MANAGEMENT SYSTEMS SOCIETY). Main/Corp Hospital Management Systems Society. Conference. Began with: 1st, 1972. 0193-0486. US. English. an. Center for Hospital Management Engineering American Hospital Association, 840 North Lake Shore Drive, Chicago IL 60611. LC RA971. DD 658.9136211. NLM W3 HO823R.

PROCEEDINGS OF THE MUMPS USERS' GROUP MEETING. Main/Conf Mumps Users' Group.*Meeting. VFOAT MUGM. VAT Proceedings of the Massachusetts General Hospital Utility Multiprograming System User's Group Meeting. 0276-699X. US. English. an. Free to Members, $15.00 Nonmembers. Mumps Users' Group, PO Box 37247, Washington DC 20013.

PROFILES IN HOSPITAL MARKETING. See Business - Marketing.

PROGRAM NOTES - ASSOCIATION OF UNIVERSITY PROGRAMS IN HEALTH ADMINISTRATION. Main/Corp Association of University Programs in Health Administration. No. 54- June 1973-. 0098-1559. Periodical. US. English. ir. NLM W1. *Program Notes - Association of University Programs in Hospital Administration, 0098-1567.*

PROGRAM STATUS REPORT ... TO THE GOVERNOR AND LEGISLATURE. Main/Corp Florida. Hospital Cost Containment Board. VFOAT Annual Report, Program Status. US. English. an. $8.50. Florida Hospital Cost, Containment Board/Larson Building, Tallahassee FL 32301. LC RA981.F4. DD 362.1.

A PROSPECTIVE REIMBURSEMENT SYSTEM BASED ON PATIENT CASE-MIX FOR NEW JERSEY HOSPITALS. (A PROSPECTIVE REIMBURSEMENT SYSTEM BASED ON PATIENT CASE-MIX FOR NEW JERSEY HOSPITALS . . . . ANNUAL REPORT). Main/Corp New Jersey. State Dept. of Health. VFOAT Annual Report. Began in 1977. 0737-5913. US. English. an. LC RA981.N5. DD 362.110681.

PROVISIONAL DATA ON FEDERALLY FUNDED COMMUNITY MENTAL HEALTH CENTERS. 1972/73-. Periodical. English. ir. NLM W2 A N204P. *0163-2523.*

THE PSYCHIATRIC HOSPITAL. Vol. 13, No. 2 (Spring 1982)-. Periodical. US. English. qt. $16.00. Ind/Abst Hospit. Lit. Index, Psychol. Abstr. NLM W1. *Journal - National Association of Private Psychiatric Hospitals, 0027-8629.*

PUBLICATIONS CATALOG - AMERICAN HOSPITAL ASSOCIATION. (PUBLICATIONS CATALOG). Main/Corp American Hospital Association. 0569-5090. US. English. ir.

QRB. QUALITY REVIEW BULLETIN. VFOAT Quality Review Bulletin. V. 1- Sept. 1974-. 0097-5990. Periodical. US. English. mo. Joint Commission on Accreditation of Hospitals, 875 North Michigan Avenue, Chicago IL 60611. Tel (312)642-6061. Ind/Abst Excerpta Med., Hospit. Lit. Index, Index Med., Cumul. Index Nurs. Allied Health Lit., Soc. Work Res. Abstr. NLM W1 Q65.

THE REGAN REPORT ON HOSPITAL LAW. See Law.

REGISTRO DE HOSPITALES Y OTRAS FACILIDADES DE SALUD. VFOAT Registry of Hospitals and Other Health Facilities. English (Spanish). an. LC RA984.P8. DD 362.11097295. NLM WX 22 DP8 B9R.

REHABILITATION FACILITIES PLAN, ADDENDUM FOR THE ESTABLISHMENT AND IMPROVEMENT OF WORKSHOPS, MEDICALLY ORIENTED CENTERS, COMMUNITY BASED AUDIOLOGICAL FACILITIES, WORK ACTIVITY CENTERS, WORK STUDY PROGRAMS. See Physical Therapy.

REPORT - COMMISSION ON ACCREDITATION OF REHABILITATION FACILITIES. VFOAT CARF Report. June 1968-. 0045-7590. Periodical. US. English. ir. Commission on Accreditation of Rehabilitation Facilities, 4001 West Devon Avenue, Chicago IL 60646. Ind/Abst Hospit. Lit. Index. NLM W1 RE209AN.

REPORT - HOSPITAL DESIGN AND EVALUATION UNIT, DEPARTMENT OF HEALTH. (REPORT - HOSPITAL DESIGN AND EVALUATION UNIT, DEPARTMENT OF HEALTH, NEW ZEALAND). No. 1-. 0110-6929. Monographic Series. NZ. English. ir. NLM W1 RE209CJ.

REPORT OF THE MISSISSIPPI STATE HOSPITAL COMMISSION. Main/Corp Mississippi. State Hospital Commission. 18th- 1969/ 70-. 0147-2607. US. English. an. Mississippi State University, State Hospital Commission, Mississippi State MS 39762. LC RA981.M7. DD 338.43. *Biennial Report of the Mississippi State Hospital Commission.*

REPORT OF THE OHIO NURSING HOME COMMISSION TO THE GOVERNOR AND OHIO GENERAL ASSEMBLY. Main/Corp Ohio. Nursing Home Commission. 1978-. US. English. an. Ohio Nursing Home Commission, Statehouse, Columbus OH 43210. LC RA997.5.O3. DD 362.1609771.

REPORT - PREVENTION RESEARCH CENTER. (REPORTS). Main/Corp Prevention Research Center. VFOAT Prevention Research Center Reports. Vol. 1, No. 1 (Spring 1985)-. 0883-1769. Periodical. US. English. ty. Free. Prevention Research Center, 2532 Durant Avenue, Berkeley CA 94704. DD 362.

REPORTS - BRITISH COLUMBIA ASSOCIATION OF HOSPITALS AND HEALTH ORGANIZATIONS. Main/Corp Brirish Columbia Association of Hospitals and Health Organizations. 1973/74-. 0384-0883. CN. English. an. British Columbia Association of Hospitals and Health Organizations, 440 Cambie Street, Vancouver British Columbia V6B 2N6 Canada. DD 362.1062711.

RESEARCH DIRECTORY OF THE REHABILITATION RESEARCH AND TRAINING CENTERS : FISCAL YEAR . . . . See Yearbooks, Almanacs, Directories.

RESEARCH PROJECTS AND INVESTIGATIONS RELATED TO HOSPITALS, CANADA. 0709-8774. Periodical. CN. English. ir. NLM WX 22 DC2 R4.

REVIEW - FEDERATION OF AMERICAN HOSPITALS. Main/Corp Federation of American Hospitals. V. 9, No. 3- June 1976-. 0148-9496. Periodical. US. English. bm. $50.00. Federation of American Hospitals, 1405 North Pierce/ Suite 305, Little Rock AK 72207. Tel (501)661-9555. Ind/Abst Hospit. Lit. Index, Excerpta Med. NLM W1 RE252H. *Investor-Owned Hospital Review, 0093-7312.*

REVUE A.C.C.S. (REVUE A. C. C. S). Main/Corp Association Catholique Canadienne de la Sante. VAT Revue Association Catholique Canadienne de la Sante. V. 8, No 1- Jan./Feb. 1980-. 0226-5931. Periodical. CN. French. bm. $12.00. Association Catholique Canadienne de la Sante, 312 Av Daly, Ottawa Ontario K1N 6G7 Canada. DD 362.110971. *Hopital Catholique, 0315-4858.*

REVUE HOSPITALIERE DE FRANCE. 0397-4626. Periodical. FR. French. ir. Revue Hospitaliere de France, 33 A 87 Avenue d'Italie, Paris 13E France. Ind/Abst CIS Abstr., Excerpta Med. NLM W1 RE865. (ctrl). Hospital science in France.

RIVISTA DEGLI OSPEDALI. Vol. 1- Sept./ Oct. 1969-. 0035-5844. Periodical. IT. Italian. bm. Il Pensiero Scientifico, Via Panama 48, 00198 Rome Italy. Ind/Abst Excerpta Med., Chem. Abstr. NLM W1 RI35K. CODEN RIOSDW.

RODO EISEI KENKYUJO NEMPO. Japanese. ir. Rodosho Rodo Eisei Kenkyujo, 2051 Kizuki Sumiyoshicho, Kawasaki 211 Japan. LC RA963. NLM W2 JJ3 R57N.

ROSTER OF MEMBERSHIP - HOSPITAL MANAGEMENT SYSTEMS SOCIETY. (ROSTER OF MEMBERSHIP). Main/Corp Hospital Management Systems Society. Began with: 1969?. 0731-1826. US. English. an. Hospital Management Systems Society, 840 North Lake Shore Drive, Chicago IL 60611. NLM WX 22 AA1 H828R. *Hospital Management Systems Society. Roster of Board of Directors and Membership.*

A SAUDE NO BRASIL. Vol. 1, No. 1 (Jan./ March 1983)-. 0101-8973. Periodical. Portuguese. qt. Centro de Documenta Cao do Ministerio da Saude, Esplanada dos Ministerios Block G Terreo, 70058 Brasilia DF Brazil. LC RA463. DD 362.10981.

Medicine—Musculoskeletal Diseases

SCHWEIZER SPITAL. 44. Vol. 1980/1-. 0304-4432. Periodical. French (articles in German). mo. $42.05. Verlag Schweizer Spital, Postfach 689, CH-5001 Aarau Switzerland. Tel 064 24 72 22. Ed Veska. Ind/Abst Excerpta Med. NLM W1 SC399. bk rev. adv acc. Circ 3,000. Management in health care hospitals. *Veska.*

SEMAINE DES HOPITAUX. (LA SEMAINE DES HOPITAUX DE PARIS). VFOAT La Semaine des Hopitaux. Yearly V. 1- Jan. 2, 1925-. 0037-1777. Periodical. FR. French. wk. $183.59. Semaine des Hopitaux, 15 rue Saint Benoit, 75278 Paris Cedex 06 France. Tel 548-42-60. Ind/Abst Pestdoc, Ringdoc, Vetdoc, CIS Abstr., Index Dent. Lit., Energy Res. Abstr., Chem. Abstr., Bull. Signal., Index Med., Biol. Abstr. NLM W1 SE39. CODEN SHPAAI.

SEMAINE DES HOPITAUX. THERAPEUTIQUE. (LA SEMAINE DES HOPITAUX. THERAPEUTIQUE). Yearly V. 49-. 0302-9271. Periodical. FR. French. ir. Semaine des Hopitaux, 15 rue Saint Benoit, 75278 Paris Cedex 06 France. NLM W1 SE416D. *Therapeutique.*

SMALL AND RURAL HOSPITAL REPORT. Began with: Sept. 1977. 0731-1338. Periodical. US. English. bm. Center for Small and Rural Hospitals, American Hospital Association, 840 North Lake Shore Drive, Chicago IL 60611. NLM W1 SM759M.

SODEQ INFO DE LANAUDIERE. Vol. 1, No. 1, (May 1981)-. 0227-0870. Periodical. CN. French. ir. Free. Sodeq de Lanaudiere, 1232 rue Notre Dame, Joliette Quebec J6E 3K5 Canada. DD 338.006071441.

SOUTHERN HOSPITALS. Began publication in 1942. 0038-4178. Periodical. US. English. ir. $70.00. Billan Publishing Company, 2100 Powers Ferry Road, Suite 125, Atlanta GA 30339. Tel (404)955-5656. Ind/Abst Hospit. Lit. Index, Cumul. Index Nurs. Allied Health Lit. DD 658. NLM W1 SO953E. *Southern Hospital.*

STATE MEDICAL FACILITIES PLAN (RICHMOND, VA.). (STATE MEDICAL FACILITIES PLAN). US. English. LC RA981.V8. DD 362.109755021.

STATE MENTAL HOSPITALS. OMH 1.13- 1971-. 0162-2374. US. English. an. NLM W2 AP4 O3S. *State Mental Hospital Patients.*

STATE PLAN FOR CONSTRUCTION AND MODERNIZATION OF HOSPITAL AND MEDICAL FACILITIES. (SOUTH CAROLINA STATE PLAN FOR CONSTRUCTION AND MODERNIZATION OF HOSPITAL AND MEDICAL FACILITIES). Main/Corp South Carolina. State Board of Health. 1965/66-. 0081-2692. US. English. an. LC RA981.S6. DD 362.1109757. NLM W2 AS6 S7S. *South Carolina State Plan: Hospital and Medical Facilities Construction Program, P. L. 725-P. L. 482 with Amendments.*

STATE PLAN FOR HOSPITAL AND MEDICAL FACILITIES CONSTRUCTION. Main/Corp North Dakota. State Dept. of Health. 0091-1585. US. English. North Dakota State Department Health, 320 Avenue B East, Bismarck ND 58501. LC RA981.N85. DD 362.109784.

STATISTICAL REPORT - DIV. OF THE WOMEN'S HOSPITAL. See Statistics.

STATISTICAL REPORT - LOUISIANA, HEALTH AND SOCIAL AND REHABILITATION SERVICES ADMINISTRATION. See Statistics.

STATISTICAL REPORT OF SASKATCHEWAN PUBLIC HOSPITALS. See Statistics.

STATISTICAL SUMMARY - LOUISIANA STATE DEPARTMENT OF HOSPITALS. See Statistics.

STATISTICS OF HOSPITAL CASES DISCHARGED. BRITISH COLUMBIA. See Statistics.

STRATEGIC HEALTH CARE MARKETING. Vol. 1, No. 1 (Oct. 1984)-. 0749-5153. Periodical. US. English. mo. $180.00. Health Care Communications, 211 Midland Avenue PO Box 594, Rye NY 10580. Tel (914)967-6741. Ed Michele Von Dambrowski. DD 362. bk rev. Newsletter includes marketing news, case histories and applications in hospitals, group practices, HMOS and other settings.

SUOMEN SAIRAALATILASTO. VFOAT Finlands Sjukhusstatistik. Finnish (Swedish). an. LC RA989.F3.

SURVEY OF HOSPITAL SEMI-PRIVATE ROOM CHARGES. Main/Corp Health Insurance Association of America. 0147-2232. US. English. Health Insurance Association of America, 919 3rd Avenue, New York NY 10022. LC RA981.A2. DD 338.43362110973.

TEXAS HOSPITALS. V. 1- June 1945-. 0040-4357. Periodical. US. English. mo. $18.00. Texas Hospitals, PO Box 15587, Austin TX 78761. Tel (512)453-7204. Ed Ann Ward Rogers. Ind/Abst Hospit. Lit. Index. NLM W1 TE767. adv acc. Circ 7,400. Editorially, the magazine covers managerial aspects of health care. Its purpose is to aid health care professionals maintain and improve management skills and keep abreast of new trends.

TODAY'S NURSING HOME. Began with: May/June 1980. 0274-5089. Periodical. US. English. mo. $25.00. McKnight Medical Communication, 550 Frontage Road/Suite 386, Northfield IL 60093. Tel (312)446-1622. Ed James Bowe. Ind/Abst Hospit. Lit. Index. NLM W1 TO172H. adv acc. Circ 30,000. (ctrl). The news source for nursing home administrative and patient care management at every long term care facility in the US and Canada.

TRANSPLANT NEWS. V. 1- Apr. 1979-. 0709-8871. Periodical. CN. English. qt. $2.50. Human Parts Banks of Canada, 5326 Ada Boulevard, Edmonton Alberta T5W 4N7 Canada. DD 362.17.

TRUSTEE. Vol. 1- Oct. 1947-. 0041-3674. Periodical. US. English. mo. American Hospital Publishing Company, PO Box 91497, Chicago IL 60693. Tel (312)951-1100. Ind/Abst Hospit. Lit. Index. LC RA960. DD 362.11. NLM W1 TR985. CODEN TRSTB.

TUBERCULOSIS BEDS IN HOSPITALS. See Medicine - Respiratory Diseases.

UTILIZATION OF SHORT-STAY HOSPITALS. UNITED STATES, ANNUAL SUMMARY. (UTILIZATION OF SHORT-STAY HOSPITALS. UNITED STATES ... ANNUAL SUMMARY). Series/Titl DHHS Publication. 1981-. 0748-4798. US. English. an. Superintendent of Documents, US Government Printing Office, Washington DC 20402. LC RA407.3. DD 362.110973. *Utilization of Short-Stay Hospitals. Annual Summary for the United States, 0145-9732.*

UTILIZATION OF SHORT-TERM GENERAL AND SPECIALTY HOSPITALS IN METROPOLITAN CHICAGO FOR THE ... QUARTER OF .... VFOAT C.H.C. Utilization Report, Metro Chicago. 0748-5816. US. English. qt. Chicago Hospital Council, 840 North Lake Shore Drive, Chicago IL 60611.

UTILIZATION OF SHORT-TERM GENERAL AND SPECIALTY HOSPITALS IN METROPOLITAN CHICAGO FOR THE YEAR ENDING DECEMBER 31 .... 1982-. 0882-6943. US. English. an. Chicago Hospital Council, 840 North Lake Shore Drive, Chicago IL 60611.

VERMONT STATE PLAN FOR CONSTRUCTION AND MODERNIZATION OF HOSPITAL AND MEDICAL FACILITIES. Main/Corp Vermont. Dept. of Health. VFOAT Vermont State Plan for Hospitals and Related Health Facilities. US. English. State of Vermont Department of Health, 115 Collchester, Burlington VT 05401. LC RA981.V5. DD 362.109743.

THE VOICE (WAUWATOSA, WIS.). (THE VOICE). Periodical. US. English. bm. $25.00. Wisconsin Medical Credit Association, 4934 North Mohawk Avenue, Glendale WI 53217. Tel (414)962-2106.

THE VOLUNTEER LEADER. V. 10- 1969-. 0005-1861. Periodical. US. English. qt. $8.00. American Hospital Publishing Company, PO Box 91497, Chicago IL 60693. Tel (312)951-1100. Ind/Abst Hospit. Lit. Index. NLM W1 VO597K. *Auxiliary Leader.*

VOLUNTEER NEWSPAPER. Periodical. US. English. qt. California Hospital Association, PO Box 1100, Sacramento CA 95805. Tel (916)443-7401.

WASHINGTON MEMO (AMERICAN HOSPITAL ASSOCIATION). (WASHINGTON MEMO). 0746-472X. Periodical. US. English. wk. $250.00. American Hospital Association, PO Box 99376, Chicago IL 60693. Tel (202)638-1100.

WASHINGTON REPORT ON LONG TERM CARE. 0091-7311. Periodical. US. English. sm. $287.00. McGraw Hill Publications, 1120 Vermont Avenue NW Suite 1200, Washington DC 20005. Tel (202)463-1672. Ed Donna M Jablonski. NLM W1 WA619L. bk rev. Congressional, administration, state, legal, and business developments affecting long term health care.

WASHINGTON WATCH. V. 1, No. 2- Oct. 1976-. 0191-3816. Periodical. US. English. mo. American Protestant Hospital Association, 840 North Lake Shore Drive, Chicago IL 60611. NLM W1 WA688J.

WORLD HOSPITALS. VFOAT Hopital Dans le Monde. V. 1- July 1964-. 0512-3135. Periodical. UK. English (French with summaries in German and Spanish). qt. 19 Domestic, 21 Foreign. International Hospital Federation, 2 St Andre's Place, London NW1 4LB England. Tel 935-9487. Ed Leslie Paine. Ind/Abst Excerpta Med., Hospit. Lit. Index, Cumul. Index Nurs. Allied Health Lit. NLM W1 WO88C. Index published separately - free - automatically sent. bk rev. adv acc. Circ 2,000. Reports on papers from the activities of the International Hospital Federation and other health-related events.

YONBO. Main/Corp Soul Choksipcha Pyongwon. VFOAT Annual Report. V. 1- (1981)-. KO. Korean (English). an. Soul Choksipcha Pyongwon, 32 3-Ka Namsan-Dong, Chung-Ku, Seoul South Korea. LC RA990.K64.

HET ZIEKENHUIS. Vol. 1. 0044-4715. Periodical. NE. Dutch. sm. Nationale Ziekenhuistraad, Postbus 9696/3506 GR, 3506 GR Utrecht Netherlands. Ind/Abst Excerpta Med. NLM W1 ZI431H.

MUSCULOSKELETAL DISEASES

ALS NEWS. VAT Amyothrophic Lateral Sclerosis News. Vol. 4, No. 1 (Spring 1981)-. 0715-3139. Periodical. CN. English. ALS News, Suite 305/234 Eglinton Avenue East, Toronto Ontario M4P 1K5 Canada. DD 616.83. *ALSSOC News, 0715-3147.*

ANNALS OF THE RHEUMATIC DISEASES. Vol. 1, No. 2 (1939)-. 0003-4967. Periodical. UK. English. mo. $140.98. British Medical Journal, Tavistock Square, London WC1H 9JR England. Ind/Abst Biol. Abstr., Chem. Abstr., CIS Abstr., Excerpta Med., Index Med., Life Sci. Collect., Pestdoc, Ringdoc, Vetdoc, Cumul. Index Nurs. Allied Health Lit. NLM W1 AN627. CODEN ARDIAO. *Rheumatic Diseases.*

ANNUAL REPORT - NATIONAL ARTHRITIS ADVISORY BOARD. (ANNUAL REPORT OF THE NATIONAL ARTHRITIS ADVISORY BOARD). Main/Corp United States. National Arthritis Advisory Board. Began with 1978. 0190-5422. US. English. an. National Arthritis Advisory Board, PO Box 30286, Bethesda MD 20814. LC RC933. DD 353.008419672. NLM W1 AN759FD. *Annual Report.*

ANNUAL REPORT - NATIONAL MULTIPLE SCLEROSIS SOCIETY. Main/Corp National Multiple Sclerosis Society. Began publication 1946/51. Periodical. US. English. ir. $10.00. National Multiple Sclerosis Society, 205 East 42nd Street, New York NY 10017. Tel (212)986-3240. Ed Shirley Silverlerg. LC RC377.A1. Circ 400,000. (ctrl). A report on the services provided by and the financial status within a given fiscal year of the National Multiple Sclerosis Society.

ARTHRITIS AND RHEUMATISM. V. 1- Feb. 1958-. 0004-3591. Periodical. US. English. mo. $65.00. Arthritis Foundation, 3400 Peachtree Road NE, Atlanta GA 30309. Tel (404)872-7100. Ed William J Koopman. Ind/Abst Life Sci. Collect., Excerpta Med., Index Med., CIS Abstr., Biol. Abstr., Chem. Abstr., Energy Res. Abstr., Ringdoc, Pestdoc, Vetdoc, Sci. Cit. Index, Abr. Ed., Hospit. Lit. Index. LC RC927.A1. DD 616.706273. NLM W1 AR95163. CODEN ARHEAW. bk rev. adv acc. Circ 8,000. Laboratory research and clinical reports on the rheumatic diseases. Topics include immunology, biochemistry, pharmacology, cell biology,

Medicine—Musculoskeletal Diseases

bioengineering, radiology, epidemiology. World's leading rheumatology journal.

ARTHRITIS AND RHEUMATISM. V. 1-. 0014-4355. English. ir. $88.00. Excerpta Medica, PO Box 1126, Amsterdam Netherlands. LC RC933.A1. DD 616.72. NLM ZW 1 E978K.

ARTHRITIS FOUNDATION ANNUAL REPORT. 1964/65-. 0191-2836. US. English. an. Arthritis Foundation, 3400 Peachtree Road NE/Suite 1101, Atlanta GA 30326. NLM W1 AR953H. *Interim Report - Arthritis Foundation.*

ARTHRITIS INTERAGENCY COORDINATING COMMITTEE ANNUAL REPORT TO THE SECRETARY, U.S. DEPARTMENT OF HEALTH, EDUCATION, AND WELFARE. Main/Corp United States. Arthritis Interagency Coordinating Committee. VFOAT Annual Report to the Secretary, U.S. Department of Health, Education, and Welfare. VAT Arthritis Interagency Coordinating Committee Annual Report to the Secretary, United States Department of Health, Education, and Welfare. 0198-7216. US. English. an. United States Department of Health, Education, and Welfare, Bethesda MD 20205. LC RC933.A1. DD 362.196722. NLM W2 A A6R.

THE ARTHRITIS PROGRAM. (THE ARTHRITIS PROGRAM : ANNUAL REPORT OF THE DIRECTOR, NATIONAL INSTITUTE OF ARTHRITIS, METABOLISM, AND DIGESTIVE DISEASES). VFOAT Annual Report of the Director, National Institute of Arthritis, Metabolism, and Digestive Diseases. Began with 1st, 1977. 0191-0337. US. English. an. National Institute of Arthritis Diabetes and Digestive and Kidney Diseases, National Institutes of Health 9000 Rockville Pike, Bethesda MD 20205. LC RC933.A1. DD 362.19672. NLM W2 AN167A.

ARTHRITIS, RHEUMATIC DISEASES, AND RELATED DISORDERS. Main/Corp National Institute of Arthritis, Metabolism, and Digestive Diseases. US. English. an. National Institute of Arthritis Metabolism and Digestive Diseases, National Institutes of Health 9000 Rockville Pike, Bethesda MD 20014. NLM W1 AR953W.

BACK TO BACK (TORONTO, ONT.). (BACK TO BACK). V. 1, Issue 1 (June 15, 1981)-. 0712-9122. Periodical. CN. English. qt. Free to Members, $12.00 Others. Back to Back, Back Association of Canada, Concourse Level, 111 Avenue Road, Toronto Ontario M5R 3J8 Canada. DD 616.7306071.

BEITRAGE ZUR RHEUMATOLOGIE. Vol. 1- 1958-. 0067-5199. Periodical. GE. German. ir. Deutscher Buch Export-Import, Leninstrasse 16, DDR-701 Leipzig East Germany. Tel 27332. Ind/Abst Excerpta Med., Index Med. NLM W1 BE457. bk rev.

BIBLIO-PROFILE. Began with: No. 1, published 1983. Monographic Series. US. English. ir. NLM ZWE 300.

BONE. Vol. 6, No. 1-. 8756-3282. Periodical. US. English. bm. $275.00. Pergamon Press, Fairview Park, Elmsford NY 10523. Ind/Abst Index Med. DD 616. NLM W1. *Metabolic Bone Disease & Related Research, 0221-8747.*

BONE AND MINERAL RESEARCH. V. 1 (1983)-. 0168-051X. US. English. an. $73.00. Elsevier Science Publishing Company, PO Box 1663/Grand Central Station, New York NY 10163. Tel (212)370-5520. Ed William A Peck. NLM W1 BO707D.

BRITISH JOURNAL OF RHEUMATOLOGY. Vol. 22, No. 1 (Feb. 1983)-. 0263-7103. Periodical. UK. English. qt. 32.00. Bailliere Tindall, 1 St Annes Road, Eastbourne E Sussex BN21 3UN England. Tel (01)630-7881. Ed T Gibson. Ind/Abst Pestdoc, Ringdoc, Vetdoc, Excerpta Med., Index Med., Life Sci. Collect. bk rev. adv acc. Circ 2,600. International clinical laboratory research, editorials, correspondence and official journal of British Society for Rheumatology. *Rheumatology and Rehabilitation.*

CLINICAL RHEUMATOLOGY IN PRACTICE. Vol. 1, No. 1 Jan./Feb. 1983. 0736-2803. Periodical. US. English. bm. $40.00 Domestic, $48.00 Foreign. Lejacq Publishing Inc, 53 Park Place, New York NY 10007. NLM W1.

CLINICS IN RHEUMATIC DISEASES. V. 1- April 1975-. 0307-742X. Monographic Series. UK. English. ty. 15.00. W B Saunders Company, West Washington Square, Philadelphia PA 19105. Ind/Abst Life Sci. Collect., Excerpta Med., Index Med., Biol.

Abstr., Chem. Abstr. LC RC927. DD 616.723. NLM W1 CL831DJ. CODEN CRHDDK.

COMMUNIQUE - SOCIETE D'ARTHRITE. (COMMUNIQUE). V. 1 (Dec. 1982)-. 0824-4154. Periodical. CN. French. ir. Free. Societe d'Arthrite, Bureau 420 920 rue Yonge, Toronto Ontario 37J M4W Canada. DD 616.722006071.

EUROPEAN JOURNAL OF RHEUMATOLOGY AND INFLAMMATION. V. 1- Jan. 1978-. 0140-1610. Periodical. UK. English. ir. $60.00. Cameron Publishing Ltd, 33 Malew Street/Castletown, Isle of Man British Isles. Tel 0624 823748. Ind/Abst Excerpta Med., Index Med., Biol. Abstr., Chem. Abstr. NLM W1 EU72EM. CODEN EJRIDH. Original work reviews and any other material which represents a useful contribution to the literature.

FORTBILDUNGSKURSE FUR RHEUMATOLOGIE. 1.- 1971-. 0071-7851. Monographic Series. SZ. German. ir. S Karger, PO Box 352, White Plains NY 10602. Tel (61)390880. Ed G Kaganas, W Muller, and F Wagenhauser. Diagnosis and therapy of musculoskeletal diseases. Provides valuable information to rheumatologists and neurologists and also to internists, orthopedic surgeons and general practitioners.

INFO ALS. VAT Info Amyotrophic Lateral Sclerosis. Vol. 1, No. 1 Winter 1980/81. 0715-3120. Periodical. CN. English. ir. ALS Professional Newsletter, 234 Eglinton Avenue East/Suite 305, Toronto Ontario M4P 1K5 Canada. DD 616.83.

IRCS MEDICAL SCIENCE. CONNECTIVE TISSUE, SKIN AND BONE. (IRCS MEDICAL SCIENCE : CONNECTIVE TISSUE, SKIN AND BONE). VFOAT Connective Tissue, Skin and Bone. V. 3- Jan. 1975-. 0305-6767. Periodical. UK. English. qt. $50.00. IRCS Medical Science, PO Box 500/St Leonards House, Lancaster LA1 1PF England. Tel (0524)68116. Ed S Johnson. bk rev. Publishes results of original research into all aspects of connective tissue and mineral metabolism, both clinical and experimental, within weeks of completion. Papers fully refereed. *Research on Connective Tissue, Skin and Bone, 0305-2672.*

JORNADAS DE TRABAJO SOBRE SUSTITUCIONES ARTICULARES. Series/Titl Serie Monografias Medicas de la Seguridad Social. 0210-8240. Spanish. an. NLM W3 JO528K.

JOURNAL OF RHEUMATOLOGY. (THE JOURNAL OF RHEUMATOLOGY). V. 1- March 1974-. 0315-162X. Periodical. CN. English. bm. 75.00 Domestic, 80.00 Foreign. Journal of Rheumatology, 250 Bloor Street/Suite 401, Toronto Ontario M4W 3P2 Canada. Tel (416)967-1414. Ed D A Gordon. Ind/Abst Life Sci. Collect., Excerpta Med., Index Med., Biol. Abstr., Chem. Abstr. NLM W1 JO87H. CODEN JRHUA9. bk rev. adv acc. Circ 3,000. Issued also in microform by University Microfilms. Original research and clinical reports on rheumatology and related disorders irrespective of the geographical origin.

THE JOURNAL OF RHEUMATOLOGY. SUPPLEMENT. No. 1- 1974-. 0380-0903. CN. English. ir. Journal of Rheumatology, 45 Charles Street East, Toronto Ontario M4Y 1S2 Canada. Ind/Abst Index Med., Chem. Abstr. DD 616.72005. NLM W1 JO87HD. CODEN JRSUDX.

O L A NEWSLETTER. Main/Corp Ontario Lupus Association. VAT Ontario Lupus Association Newsletter (1979). V. 1, No. 3- Winter 1979-. 0225-5634. Periodical. CN. English. qt. Free. Ontario Lupus Association, Suite 420/920 Yonge Street, Toronto Ontario M4W 3J7 Canada. DD 616.77005. (ctrl). *Ontario Lupus Association Newsletter, 0225-5626.*

MDA NEWS. Main/Corp Muscular Dystrophy Association. VAT Muscular Dystrophy Association News. V. 26 No. 3-. 0279-0742. Periodical. US. English. bm. Muscular Dystrophy Association, 810 7th Avenue, New York NY 10019. *Association, 0027-3759.*

MDA NEWSMAGAZINE. VFOAT MDA News Magazine. VAT Muscular Dystrophy Association Newsmagazine. Vol. 1, No. 1 (Aug. 1984)-. 8750-2321. Periodical. US. English. qt. MDA, 810 Seventh Avenue, New York NY 10019. DD 616. *MDA News, 0279-0742.*

MEDIGUIDE TO RHEUMATOLOGY. Began in 1982-. 0738-3002. Periodical. US. English. qt. Lawrence Dellacorte Publications Inc, 676 Lexington Avenue, New York NY 10021.

MEMBERSHIP DIRECTORY - AMERICAN RHEUMATISM ASSOCIATION. See Yearbooks, Almanacs, Directories.

MICHIGAN OSTEOPATHIC JOURNAL. 1901. 0026-2374. Periodical. US. English. ir. Michigan Association of Osteopathic Physicians and Surgeons, 33100 Freedom Road, Farmington MI 48024. Tel (313)476-2800. Ed Ted Montgomery. NLM W1 MI222. adv acc. Circ 3,300. (ctrl). The official publication of the Michigan Osteopathic Association. Up-to-date scientific news pertinent to the osteopathic profession.

MUSCULAR DYSTROPHY ABSTRACTS. See Indexes/Abstracts.

MUSCULAR DYSTROPHY REPORTER CEASED. V. 1-23, No. 4. 0580-2512. Periodical. CN. English (includes some text in French). qt. Muscular Dystrophy Association of Canada, Suite 203/387 Bloor Street East, Toronto Ontario M4W 1H7 Canada. NLM W1 MU967.

MUSCULOSKELETAL UPDATE. Vol. 1, No. 1-. 0277-3007. Periodical. US. English. qt. Biomedical Information Corporation, 800 2nd Avenue, New York NY 10017.

THE NATIONAL ARTHRITIS NEWS. Began in 1980. 0882-9705. Periodical. US. English. qt. Arthritis Foundation, 1314 Spring Street Northwest, Atlanta GA 30309. DD 616.

NEWSLETTER - FLORIDA ARTHRITIS FOUNDATION. Main/Corp Florida. Arthritis Foundation. 19 -. US. English. qt. Arthritis Foundation, 3205 Manatee Avenue W, Bradenton FL 33505. Tel (813)748-1300.

NEWSLETTER, PROSTHETICS AND ORTHOTICS CLINIC. VFOAT Prosthetics and Orthotics Clinic. Vol. 1, No. 1 (Oct. 1976)-. 0279-6910. Periodical. US. English. qt. Am Academy of Orthotists & Prosthetics, 717 Pendleton Street, Alexandria VA 22314. Tel (703)836-7114. NLM W1 NE998Y. *Newsletter, Amputee Clinics.*

RECENT ADVANCES IN RHEUMATOLOGY. No. 1- 1976-. 0309-2283. Periodical. UK. English. ir. Churchill Livingstone Inc, 1560 Broadway, New York NY 10036. Tel (212)819-5400. Ed W W Buchanan and W C Dick. Ind/Abst Chem. Abstr. NLM W1 RE105YH. CODEN RARHDQ.

REPORT TO THE SECRETARY, DEPARTMENT OF HEALTH, EDUCATION, AND WELFARE. Main/Corp United States. Arthritis Interagency Coordinating Committee. 1976-. 0193-9998. Periodical. US. English. NLM W2 A A6R.

REPORTER - MUSCULAR DYSTROPHY ASSOCIATION OF CANADA. (REPORTER). VFOAT Muscular Dystrophy Reporter. VAT Muscular Dystrophy Reporter (1981). Vol. 24, No. 1 (June 15, 1981)-. 0827-3251. Periodical. CN. English (includes some text in French). ir. Free. Muscular Dystrophy Association of Canada, 357 Bay Street/10th Floor, Toronto Ontario M5H 2T7 Canada. DD 616.748006071. *Muscular Dystrophy Reporter, 0580-2512.*

REPORTS ON RHEUMATIC DISEASES. 1959. 0048-7279. Periodical. UK. English. sa. free. Arthritis & Rheumatism Council, 41 Eagle Street, London WC14 4AR England. Tel 01-405 8572. Ed Clifford Hawkins, Harry Currey, Paul Dieppe. Ind/Abst Index Med. Circ 40,000. (ctrl). Two reports on rheumatic diseases. Practical problems give advice on diagnosis and treatment. Topical reviews are on areas of clinical and research interest.

REVUE DU RHUMATISME ET DES MALADIES OSTEO-ARTICULAIRES. Vol. 13- Jan. 1946-. 0035-2659. Periodical. FR. French (summaries in English, German, or Spanish). mo. $113.09. Expansion Scientifique Francaise, 15 rue Saint-Benoit, 75278 Paris Cedex 06 France. Tel 548-42-60. Ind/Abst Excerpta Med., Index Med., CIS Abstr., Life Sci. Collect., Chem. Abstr., Sci. Cit. Index, Abr. Ed. NLM W1 RE841. CODEN RRMOA2. Index published separately - free - automatically sent. (cum index). *Revue du Rhumatisme, 0301-8474.*

RHEUMATOID ARTHRITIS AND RELATED CONDITIONS. Series/Titl Annual Research Reviews. V. 1- 1975/76-. 0703-2994. CN. English. Eden Press, 4626 St Catherine Street West, Montreal Quebec Canada H3Z 1S3. DD 616.72. NLM W1 RH359I.

Medicine—Neoplasma, Neoplastic

RHEUMATOLOGY. (RHEUMATOLOGY, AN ANNUAL REVIEW). V. 1- 1967-. 0080-2727. English. ir. S Karger Ag, PO Box, CH-4009 Basel Switzerland. Tel 061-39 08 80. Ed M Schattenkirchner. Ind/Abst Biol. Abstr., Chem. Abstr., Index Med. NLM W1 RH42G. CODEN RHEUBD. Features extensive reviews covering clinical and pathophysiologic aspects of rheumatology.

RHEUMATOLOGY AND REHABILITATION CEASED. V. 12-21. 0300-3396. Periodical. UK. English. qt. Ind/Abst Life Sci. Collect., Excerpta Med., Cumul. Index Nurs. Allied Health Lit. NLM W1 RH39H. *Rheumatology and Physical Medicine, 0003-4908.*

RHEUMATOLOGY IN PRACTICE. 0262-5512. Periodical. UK. English. ir. 18 Domestic, 21 Europe, 24 outside Europe. Medical News Group, 1 Bedford Street, London WC2E 7LS England. Tel (01)379-6005. Ed Peter Fowler. NLM W1 RH39M. bk rev. adv acc. Circ 20,000. (ctrl). Clinical papers, comments, news, and book reviews on rheumatology and musculoskeletal disorders.

RHEUMATOLOGY INTERNATIONAL. Vol. 1, No. 1-. 0172-8172. Periodical. US. English. qt. $56.00. Springer Verlag-New York Inc, 175 5th Avenue, New York NY 10010. Tel (212)460-1500. Ed B Bresnihan, E G L Bywaters, K Fehr, J R Kalden, E M Lennel, K D Muirden, J B Natvig, C Steffen, R Winchester and M Ziff. Ind/Abst Excerpta Med., Index Med., Chem. Abstr. NLM W1 RH42H. CODEN RHINDE. Covers all modern trends in clinical and experimental research as well as in the management of rheumatic diseases.

RYUMACHI. VFOAT The Ryumachi : Official Journal of the Japan Rheumatism Association. 0300-9157. Periodical. JA. Japanese (summaries in English). qt. Japan Rheumatism Association, 401 Pare-Nogizaka, 9-5-26 Akasa, Minato-ku Tokyo 107 Japan. Ind/Abst Excerpta Med., Index Med., Chem. Abstr. NLM W1 RY659. CODEN RYMCAF.

SCANDINAVIAN JOURNAL OF RHEUMATOLOGY. V. 1- 1972-. 0300-9742. Periodical. SW. English. qt. $55.00. Almqvist & Wiksell, 108 Drottninggatan, PO Box 45150, S-104 30 Stockholm Sweden. Tel 85413160. Ind/Abst Life Sci. Collect., Excerpta Med., Pestdoc, Ringdoc, Vetdoc, Index Med., Biol. Abstr., Energy Res. Abstr., Chem. Abstr., Sci. Cit. Index, Abr. Ed. LC RC927. DD 616.72005. NLM W1 SC154B. CODEN SJRHAT. *Acta Rheumatologica Scandinavica.*

SEMINARS IN ARTHRITIS AND RHEUMATISM. VFOAT Arthritis and Rheumatism. V. 1- May 1971-. 0049-0172. Periodical. US. English. qt. $73.00. Grune and Stratton, 111 5th Avenue, New York NY 10003. Tel (212)614-3110. Ind/Abst Life Sci. Collect., Excerpta Med., Energy Res. Abstr., Biol. Abstr., Chem. Abstr., Index Med. LC RC933.A1. DD 616.72005. NLM W1 SE487. CODEN SAHRBF.

SPINA BIFIDA THERAPY. Vol. 1, No. 1 (July 1978)-. 0160-9475. Periodical. US. English. qt. $30.00. Eterna Press, PO Box 1344, Oak Brook IL 60521. Tel (312)969-0318. Ed Stephen B Parrish. NLM W1 SP466.

VERHANDLUNGEN DER DEUTSCHEN GESELLSCHAFT FUR RHEUMATOLOGIE. Main/Corp Deutsche Gesellschaft fur Rheumatologie. VFOAT Zeitschrift fur Rheumatologie. 1- 1969-. 0070-4121. Monographic Series. GW. German (summaries in English and French). ir. Steinkopff, PO Box 1008 Saal Baustrasse 12, 6100 Darmstadt 11 West Germany. Ind/Abst Excerpta Med., Index Med., Chem. Abstr. NLM W1 VE483MR. CODEN VDGRAT.

VOPROSY REVMATIZMA. V. 1- 1961-. 0042-885X. Periodical. UR. Russian (summaries in English). qt. Victor Kamkin Inc (70155), 12224 Parklawn Drive, Rockville MD 20852. Tel (301)881-5973. Ind/Abst Excerpta Med., Biol. Abstr., Chem. Abstr., Index Med. NLM W1 VO644A. CODEN VOREAK. *Voprosy Revmatizma.*

ZEITSCHRIFT FUR RHEUMATOLOGIE. V. 33- 1974-. 0340-1855. Periodical. GW. German (summaries in English and French). bm. $77.00. Springer Verlag New York Inc, 175 5th Avenue, New York NY 10010. Tel (212)460-1500. Ed W H Hauss, V R Ott and K L Schmidt. Ind/Abst Life Sci. Collect., Excerpta Med., Pestdoc, Ringdoc, Vetdoc, Index Med., Biol. Abstr., Chem. Abstr., Energy Res. Abstr., Sci. Cit. Index, Abr. Ed. NLM W1 ZE583. CODEN ZRHMBQ. Official organ of the German Society of Rheumatology, the Austrian Society of Rheumatology, the Swiss Society of Rheumatology, and the German Association of Practicing Rheumatologists. *Zeitschrift fur Rheumaforschung.*

NEOPLASMA, NEOPLASTIC

ACCOMPLISHMENTS IN ONCOLOGY. 0887-056X. Periodical. US. English. ir. Lippincott/Harper, 2350 Virginia Avenue, Hagerstown MD 21740.

ACTA ONCOLOGICA BRASILEIRA. V. 1- July/Sept. 1977-. 0100-3127. Periodical. Portuguese. ir. Ind/Abst Excerpta Med. NLM W1 AC877E.

ACTIVATION AND METABOLISM OF CARCINOGENS. Main/Corp International Cancer Research Date Bank. Series/Titl ICRDB Cancergram. Periodical. US. English. Department of Health Education and Welfare, Public Health Service, National Institutes of Health National Cancer Institute, Springfield VA 22161.

ACTUALITES DE CARCINOLOGIE CERVICOFACIALE. (ACTUALITES DE CARCINOLOGIE CERVICO-FACIALE). 1-. 0338-3784. Monographic Series. French. ir. NLM W1 AC991C.

ADVANCES IN CANCER CHEMOTHERAPY. V. 1-. 0190-4817. US. English. ir. Marcel Dekker, Continuation Department, 270 Madison Avenue, New York NY 10016. Tel (212)696-9000. Ed A Rosowsky. Ind/Abst Pestdoc, Ringdoc, Vetdoc, Chem. Abstr. LC RC271.C5. DD 616.994061. NLM W1 AD511M. CODEN ACEMD7. This is an ongoing series each title has a different subject.

ADVANCES IN CANCER RESEARCH. V. 1-. 0065-230X. US. English. ir. Academic Press, 4805 Sand Lake Road, Orlando FL 32887. Tel (305)345-4100. Ed Jesse P Greenstein and Alexander Haddow. Ind/Abst Life Sci. Collect., Pestdoc, Ringdoc, Vetdoc, Index Med., Chem. Abstr., Energy Res. Abstr., Sci. Cit. Index, Abr. Ed. LC RC267. DD 616.994. NLM W1 AD512. CODEN ACRSAJ.

ADVANCES IN TUMOUR PREVENTION, DETECTION AND CHARACTERIZATION. V.1 (1974)-. Monographic Series. US. English. ir. Elsevier Science Publishing Co PO Box 1663 Grand Central Station, New York NY 10163.

ADVANCES IN VIRAL ONCOLOGY. Vol. 1-. 0735-0104. Monographic Series. US. English. ir. Raven Press, 1140 Avenue of the America, New York NY 10036. Tel (212)575-0335. Ind/Abst Life Sci. Collect., Biol. Abstr., Chem. Abstr. LC UNC. NLM W1 AD888. CODEN AVONDN.

AGGIORNAMENTI IN ONCOLOGIA CLINICA. V. 1- 1975-. 0390-0517. Monographic Series. IT. Italian. ty. Il Pensiero Scientifico Edit, Via Panama 48, 00198 Rome Italy. NLM W1 AG336F.

AKTUELLE ONKOLOGIE. 1-. 0174-2744. Monographic Series. German. ir. NLM W1 AK995GOB.

AMERICAN CANCER SOCIETY ANNUAL REPORT. 0190-5147. US. English. an. American Cancer Society, 4 West 35th Street, New York NY 10001. LC RC261. DD 616.99406273. NLM W1 AM292K.

AMERICAN JOURNAL OF CLINICAL ONCOLOGY. (AMERICAN JOURNAL OF CLINICAL ONCOLOGY : CANCER CLINICAL TRIALS). Vol. 5, No. 1 (Feb. 1982)-. 0277-3732. Periodical. US. English. bm. $72.00. Raven Press, 1140 Avenue of the Americas, New York NY 10036. Tel (212)575-0335. Ind/Abst Pestdoc, Ringdoc, Vetdoc, Excerpta Med., Index Med., Life Sci. Collect., Biol. Abstr., Chem. Abstr. NLM W1 AM45K. CODEN AJCODI. *Cancer Clinical Trials, 0190-1206.*

THE AMERICAN JOURNAL OF PEDIATRIC HEMATOLOGY/ONCOLOGY. See Medicine - Pediatrics.

ANNUAL MEETING OF THE AMERICAN ASSOCIATION FOR CANCER RESEARCH. PROCEEDINGS. Main/Corp American Association for Cancer Research. V. 23 (March 1982)-. US. English. an. $20.00. Williams & Wilkins, PO Box 64025, Baltimore MD 21202.

ANNUAL PLAN, NATIONAL CANCER PROGRAM. (ANNUAL PLAN : NATIONAL CANCER PROGRAM). Main/Corp United States. National Cancer Institute. 0145-7276. US. English. an. LC RC267. DD 616.9940072073. NLM W2 A N1476A.

ANNUAL PROGRESS REPORT - NATIONAL FOUNDATION FOR CANCER RESEARCH (U.S.). (ANNUAL PROGRESS REPORT). Main/Corp National Foundation for Cancer Research. 0735-4428. US. English. an. LC RC267. DD 616.994005.

ANNUAL REPORT - BIOHAZARD CONTROL AND CONTAINMENT WORKING GROUP, NATIONAL INSTITUTES OF HEALTH. Main/Corp United States. National Cancer Institute. Biohazard Control and Containment Working Group. US. English. an. National Cancer Institute, National Institutes of Health 9000 Rockville Pike, Bethesda MD 20014.

ANNUAL REPORT - BOARD OF SCIENTIFIC COUNSELORS, DCBD, NCI, NATIONAL INSTITUTES OF HEALTH. Main/Corp United States. National Cancer Institute. Division of Cancer Biology and Diagnosis. Board of Scientific Counselors. VAT Annual Report - Board of Scientific Counselors, Division of Cancer Biology and Diagnosis, National Cancer Institute, National Institutes of Health. US. English. an. National Cancer Institute, National Institutes of Health 9000 Rockville Pike, Bethesda MD 20014.

ANNUAL REPORT - BOARD OF SCIENTIFIC COUNSELORS, DIVISION OF CANCER TREATMENT, NATIONAL CANCER INSTITUTE, NATIONAL INSTITUTES OF HEALTH. Main/Corp National Cancer Institute Division of Cancer Treatment. Board of Scientific Counselors. US. English. an. National Cancer Institute, National Institutes of Health 9000 Rockville Pike, Bethesda MD 20014.

ANNUAL REPORT - CANCER CONTROL ADVISORY COMMITTEE, NATIONAL INSTITUTES OF HEALTH. Main/Corp United States. National Cancer Institute. Cancer Control Advisory Committee. US. English. an. National Cancer Institute, National Institutes of Health 9000 Rockville Pike, Bethesda MD 20014.

ANNUAL REPORT - CANCER CONTROL GRANT REVIEW COMMITTEE, NATIONAL INSTITUTES OF HEALTH. Main/Corp United States. National Cancer Institute. Cancer Control Grant Review Committee. US. English. an. National Cancer Institute, National Institutes of Health, 9000 Rockville Pike, Bethesda MD 20014.

ANNUAL REPORT - CANCER RESEARCH CAMPAIGN. Main/Corp Cancer Research Campaign. 48th- 1970-. Periodical. UK. English.

ANNUAL REPORT - CANCER SPECIAL PROGRAM ADVISORY COMMITTEE, NATIONAL INSTITUTES OF HEALTH. Main/Corp United States. National Cancer Institute. Cancer Special Program Advisory Committee. US. English. an. National Cancer Institute, National Institutes of Health, 9000 Rockville Pike, Bethesda MD 20014.

ANNUAL REPORT - CARCINOGENESIS PROGRAM SCIENTIFIC REVIEW COMMITTEE B, NATIONAL INSTITUTES OF HEALTH. Main/Corp United States. National Cancer Institute. Carcinogenesis Program Scientific Review Committee B. 1973/74-. US. English. an. National Cancer Institute, National Institutes of Health 9000 Rockville Pike, Bethesda MD 20014.

ANNUAL REPORT - DAMON RUNYON-WALTER WINCHELL CANCER FUND. (ANNUAL REPORT). Main/Corp Damon Runyon-Walter Winchell Cancer Fund. 1st- 1973-. 0095-6775. US. English. an. Damon Runyon-Walter Winchell Cancer Fund, 33 West 56th Street, New York NY 10019. LC RC267. DD 362.196994006273. *Annual Report - Damon Runyon Memorial Fund for Cancer Research, 0416-6639.*

ANNUAL REPORT - DIAGNOSTIC RESEARCH ADVISORY GROUP, NATIONAL INSTITUTES OF HEALTH. Main/Corp National Cancer Institute. Diagnostic Research Advisory Committee. Periodical. US. English. an. National Cancer Institute, National

Medicine—Neoplasma, Neoplastic

Institutes of Health 9000 Rockville Pike, Bethesda MD 20014.

ANNUAL REPORT - DIVISION OF CANCER CONTROL AND REHABILITATION. Main/Corp National Cancer Institute (U.S.). Division of Cancer Control and Rehabilitation. US. English. an. National Cancer Institute, National Institutes of Health, 9000 Rockville Pike, Bethesda MD 20014.

ANNUAL REPORT FOR THE PERIOD - CANCER FOUNDATION OF WESTERN AUSTRALIA. Main/Corp Cancer Foundation of Western Australia. 3rd Jan. 1983 to 31st Dec. 1983-. English. an. NLM W1. Annual Report.

ANNUAL REPORT - MANITOBA CANCER TREATMENT AND RESEARCH FOUNDATION. (ANNUAL REPORT - THE MANITOBA CANCER TREATMENT AND RESEARCH FOUNDATION). Main/Corp Manitoba Cancer Treatment and Research Foundation. 1973-. 0227-3497. Periodical. CN. English. an. NLM W1 MA6148C. Report, 0076-3802.

ANNUAL REPORT - NATIONAL CANCER ADVISORY BOARD. Main/Corp United States. National Cancer Advisory Board. 0739-8905. US. English. an. National Institutes of Health, National Cancer Institute, 9000 Rockville Pike, Bethesda MD 20205. LC RC267. DD 616.9940072073.

ANNUAL REPORT - NATIONAL CANCER INSTITUTE. (ANNUAL REPORT). 0195-8690. US. English. an. National Cancer Institute, 9000 Rockville Pike, Bethesda MD 20014. LC RC267. DD 616.9940072073.

ANNUAL REPORT - NATIONAL CANCER INSTITUTE, DIVISION OF CANCER BIOLOGY AND DIAGNOSIS. (ANNUAL REPORT). 0148-8333. US. English. an. US Department of Health and Human Services/National Institutes of Health, National Cancer Institute/Division of Cancer Biology and Diagnosis, 9000 Rockville Pike, Bethesda MD 20205. LC RC267. DD 616.9940072073. Vols. for 1982/1983- distributed to depository libraries in microfiche.

ANNUAL REPORT - NATIONAL CANCER INSTITUTE, DIVISION OF CANCER RESEARCH RESOURCES AND CENTERS. Main/Corp United States. National Cancer Institute. Division of Cancer Research Resources and Centers. 0196-8645. US. English. an. National Cancer Institute, Division of Cancer Research Resources and Centers, Bethesda MD 20014. LC RC267. DD 616.9940072073. NLM W2 A N1474A.

ANNUAL REPORT - NATIONAL CANCER INSTITUTE (U.S.). DIVISION OF CANACER PREVENTION AND CONTROL. (ANNUAL REPORT). Main/Corp National Cancer Institute (U.S.). Division of Cancer Prevention and Control. 0883-3176. US. English. an. United States Department of Health and Human Services, National Institutes of Health, National Cancer Institute, Bethesda MD 20205. Annual Report, 0730-1650.

ANNUAL REPORT - NATIONAL CANCER INSTITUTE (U.S.). DIVISION OF CANCER CAUSE AND PREVENTION. (ANNUAL REPORT). Main/Corp National Cancer Institute (U.S.) Division of Cancer Cause and Prevention. 0735-8970. US. English. an. National Cancer Institute, Division of Cancer Cause and Prevention, 9000 Rockville Pike, Bethesda MD 20205. LC RC268.5. DD 616.994071. Vols. for (1980/81-) distributed to depository libraries in microfiche. Report of the Division of Cancer Cause and Prevention, 0194-0228.

ANNUAL REPORT - NATIONAL CANCER INSTITUTE (U.S.) DIVISION OF CANCER TREATMENT. Main/Corp National Cancer Institute (U.S.) Division of Cancer Treatment. VFOAT DCT . . . Annual Report. US. English. an. National Institutes of Health, National Cancer Institute, Division of Cancer Treatment, Bethesda MD 20205. LC RC261.A1. DD 616.994061072073. NLM W2 A N1475A. Vols. for 1982/1983- distributed to depository libraries in microfiche. Report of the Division of Cancer Treatment, NCI, 0145-7268.

ANNUAL REPORT - NATIONAL CANCER INSTITUTE (U.S.). DIVISION OF EXTRAMURAL ACTIVITIES. (ANNUAL REPORT - NATIONAL CANCER INSTITUTE). Main/Corp National Cancer Institute (U.S.) Division of Extramural Activities. 0738-0372. US. English. an. United States Department of Health and Human Services, National Institutes of Health, National Cancer Institute Division of Extramural Activities, 9000 Rockville Pike, Bethesda MD 20205. LC RC261.A1. DD 353.00841. Vols. for 1981/1982-(1982/1983) distributed to depository libraries in microfiche.

ANNUAL REPORT - NATIONAL CANCER INSTITUTE (U.S.). FIELD STUDIES AND STATISTICS PROGRAM. (ANNUAL REPORT). Main/Corp National Cancer Institute U.S. Field Studies and Statistics Program. Oct. 1, 1980 through Sept. 30, 1981-. 0730-6911. US. English. an. LC RC276. DD 614.5999. Report of the Field Studies and Statistics Program, 0277-8629.

ANNUAL REPORT OF CANCER INCIDENCE IN MASSACHUSETTS. VFOAT Annual Report, Cancer Incidence in Massachusetts. 1982-. US. English. an. NLM W2.

ANNUAL REPORT OF THE SASKATCHEWAN CANCER FOUNDATION. Main/Corp Saskatchewan Cancer Foundation. VAT Annual Report - Saskatchewan Cancer Foundation. Aug. 1, 1979 to Mar. 31, 1980-. 0715-013X. CN. English. an. LC RC261. DD 354.712400841. NLM W2 DC2.1 S2C2A.

ANNUAL REPORT OF THE UNIVERSITY OF TEXAS SYSTEM CANCER CENTER TO THE CHANCELLOR AND BOARD OF REGENTS OF THE UNIVERSITY OF TEXAS SYSTEM. Main/Corp University of Texas System. Cancer Center. Sept. 1, 1980 through Aug. 31, 1981-. US. English. an. NLM WX 2 AT4 H8M2A.

ANNUAL REPORT ON CARCINOGENS. 1st (1980)-. 0272-2836. US. English. an. Public Information Office, National Toxicology Program, B2-04 PO Box 12233, Research Triangle Park NC 27709. LC RC268.6. DD 616.994071. NLM W1 AN762T. Vol. for 1981 distributed to depository libraries in microfiche.

ANNUAL REPORT ON NATIONAL CANCER INSTITUTE AND ENVIRONMENTAL PROTECTION AGENCY PROJECTS. (ANNUAL REPORT ON NATIONAL CANCER INSTITUTE AND ENVIRONMENTAL PROTECTION AGENCY PROJECTS : NCI/EPA COLLABORATIVE PROGRAM ON ENVIRONMENTAL CARCINOGENESIS). Began with 1st, 1980. 0270-5591. US. English. an. National Institutes of Health, Department of Health and Human Services, 9000 Rockville Pike, Bethesda MD 20014. LC RC268.5. DD 616.9940072073. NLM W1 AN763.

ANNUAL REPORT ON THE RESULTS OF TREATMENT IN GYNECOLOGICAL CANCER. Vol. 17-1969/72-. 0348-8799. English. ir. International Federation of Gynecology & Obstetrics, Radiumhemmet, S104 01 Stockholm 60 Sweden. Tel 46 8 328752. Ed Folke Pettersson. NLM W1 AN768BD. adv acc. Circ 2,000. (ctrl). Presentation of five-year results of treatment in gynecological cancer. Annual Report on the Results of Treatment in Carcinoma of the Uterus, Vagina, and Ovary, 0346-7503.

ANNUAL REPORT-THE FRANKLIN MCLEAN MEMORIAL RESEARCH INSTITUTE. Main/Corp Franklin McLean Memorial Research Institute. 1975-. Periodical. US. English. an.

ANNUAL SYMPOSIUM ON FUNDAMENTAL CANCER RESEARCH. (SYMPOSIUM ON FUNDAMENTAL CANCER RESEARCH). Main/Corp M.D. Anderson Hospital and Tumor Institute. 1st- 1947-. 0190-1214. US. English. ir. Raven Press, 1140 Avenue of the Americas, New York NY 10036. Ind/Abst Index Med., Biol. Abstr., Chem. Abstr. NLM W3 SY5177. CODEN AFCPDR.

ANTICANCER RESEARCH. Vol. 1, No. 1-. 0250-7005. Periodical. GR. English. bm. $224.00 Domestic, $240.00 US. Anticancer Research, 5 Argyropoulou S/Kato Patissia, Athens Gr-111 45 Greece. Ed John G Delinassios. Ind/Abst Life Sci. Collect., Excerpta Med., Index Med., Biol. Abstr., Chem. Abstr. NLM W1 AN859T. CODEN ANTRD4. bk rev. adv acc. Circ 1,150. (ctrl). Rapid publication within 2-5 months of original high quality works and reviews on all aspects of experimental and clinical cancer research.

ARCHIV FUR GESCHWULSTFORSCHUNG. See Genealogy and Heraldry - Archives.

ATLAS OF TUMOR RADIOLOGY. See Medicine - Radiology.

BANGLADESH CANCER REPORTS. 0253-5394. English. tw. NLM W1 BA642D.

BEITRAGE ZUR ONKOLOGIE. Vol. 1-. 0250-3220. Monographic Series. SZ. German. ir. S Karger AG, CH-4009 Basel Switzerland. Tel (61)390880. Ed S Eckhardt, J H Holgner, and G A Nagel. Ind/Abst Biol. Abstr., Chem. Abstr. NLM W1 BE444N. CODEN BEONDH. Contains all aspects of research and treatment of cancer. Discusses types of tumors, diagnosis, treatments, and gives precise overall view of the current knowledge in this field.

BIENNIAL REPORT - NEW HAMPSHIRE CANCER COMMISSION. Main/Corp New Hampshire. Cancer Commission. US. English. be. LC RC261.A1.

BIOLOGICAL RESPONSES IN CANCER. (BIOLOGICAL RESPONSES IN CANCER : PROGRESS TOWARD POTENTIAL APPLICATIONS). Vol. 1-. 0736-7414. US. English. an. Plenum Press, 233 Spring Street, New York NY 10013. Ed Enrico Mihich. Ind/Abst Chem. Abstr. NLM W1 BI754PB. CODEN BRECDP.

BIOMEDICAL ADVANCES IN CARCINOGENESIS. Vol. 1-. Monographic Series. US. English. Ed Merle Mizell. NLM W1.

BIORESEARCH TODAY. CANCER A. CANCEROGENESIS. VFOAT Cancer A. Carcinogenesis. 0149-1016. US. English. mo. $100.00. Bioscience Information Service, 2100 Arch Street, Philadelphia PA 19103. Tel (215)587-4800. Current awareness journal covering cancer/carcinogenesis.

BIORESEARCH TODAY. CANCER B. ANTICANCER AGENTS. VFOAT Cancer B. Anitcancer Agents. 0149-1024. US. English. mo. $100.00. Bioscience Information Service, 2100 Arch Street, Philadelphia PA 19103. Tel (215)587-4800. Current awareness journal covering cancer and anticancer agents.

BIORESEARCH TODAY. CANCER C. IMMUNOLOGY. VFOAT Cancer C. Immunology. 0149-1032. US. English. mo. $100.00. Bioscience Information Service, 2100 Arch Street, Philadelphia PA 19103. Tel (215)587-4800. Current awareness journal covering cancer/immunology.

BIOSIS/CAS SELECTS. CANCER & NUTRITION. See Biology - Biochemistry.

BIOSIS/CAS SELECTS. CANCER IMMUNOLOGY. See Indexes/Abstracts.

BREAST CANCER. V. 1-. 0161-0112. US. English. Plenum Publishing Corp, 233 Spring Street, New York NY 10013. Tel (212)620-8000. Ind/Abst Chem. Abstr. LC RC280.B8. DD 616.99449. NLM W1 BR191. CODEN BCATDJ.

BREAST CANCER RESEARCH AND TREATMENT. Vol. 1, No. 1-. 0167-6806. Periodical. English. bm. Kluwer Academic Publishers, PO Box 322, 3300 AH Dordrecht Netherlands. Ind/Abst Excerpta Med., Index Med., Chem. Abstr. NLM W1 BR191R. CODEN BCTRD6.

BREAST CANCER TASK FORCE PROGRAM REPRINTS. 1972-1974-. Periodical. English. ir. NLM W1 BR191S.

BRISTOL-MYERS CANCER SYMPOSIA. 1-. 0197-8756. Monographic Series. US. English. ir. Academic Press, 4805 Sand Lake Road, Orlando FL 32887. Tel (305)345-4100. Ed U Veronesi and G Bonadonna. Ind/Abst Biol. Abstr., Chem. Abstr. NLM W3 BR429. CODEN BCSYDM.

BRITISH JOURNAL OF CANCER. (THE BRITISH JOURNAL OF CANCER). V. 1- March 1947-. 0007-0920. Periodical. UK. English. mo. $260.00. H Holt MacMillan Journals, Houndmills, Basingstoke Hants RG21 2XS United Kingdom. Tel (0256) 29242. Ed Michael Moore. Ind/Abst Life Sci. Collect., Pestdoc, Ringdoc, Vetdoc, Excerpta Med., Energy Inf. Abstr., Environ. Abstr., CIS Abstr., Ref. Source, Biol. Abstr., Chem. Abstr., Nuci. Sci. Abstr., Index Med., Sci. Cit. Index, Abr. Ed. NLM W1 BR509. CODEN BJCAAI. bk rev. adv acc. Circ 2,000. Available on microfilm and microfiche from University Microfilms International. Publishes articles on all aspects of oncology, basic research, animal studies, clinical trials, and case reports from all parts of the world.

THE BRITISH JOURNAL OF CANCER. SUPPLEMENT. No. 1-. 0306-9443. Monographic Series. UK. English. ir. H K Lewis & Company, PO Box 66136, Glower Lane, London WC2

England. **Ind/Abst** Index Med., Chem. Abstr. **DD** 616.9. **NLM** W1 BR509A. **CODEN** BJCSB5.

BULLETIN DU CANCER. V. 53- 1966-. 0007-4551. Periodical. FR. French. Masson Publishing USA Inc, 211 East 43rd Street/Room 1306, New York NY 10017. **Tel** (212)370-1937. **Ind/Abst** Life Sci. Collect., Pestdoc, Ringdoc, Vetdoc, Excerpta Med., Index Med., Biol. Abstr., Chem. Abstr., Energy Res. Abstr. **NLM** W1 BU647K. **CODEN** BUCABS. *Bulletin de l'Association Francaise pour l'Etude du Cancer, 0004-5497.*

BULLETIN - INTERNATIONAL UNION AGAINST CANCER *CEASED.* **Main/Corp** International Union Against Cancer. 0041-5111. Periodical. English. ir. **Ind/Abst** Energy Res. Abstr.

BULLETIN SIGNALETIQUE. 251, CANCEROLOGIE, CANCERNET. **VFOAT** Cancerologie, Cancernet, Cancernet, Oncology. Vol. 28, No. 1-. 0245-9566. FR. French (English). mo. 850. Service des Abonnements, 26 rue Boyer, 75971 Paris Cedex 20 France. **LC** Z6664.C2, RC261.A1. **DD** 016.616994. *Bulletin Signaletique. 351, Cancer.*

BULLETIN SIGNALETIQUE. 351, CANCER. **VFOAT** Cancer. V. 17-. 0007-5477. Periodical. FR. French. ir. $147.00. Institut Gustave Roussy, 16 Bis Ave Paul Vaillant Cout, 94800 Villejuif France. Index published separately - free - automatically sent. *Cancer.*

BULLETIN VIES A VIES. **VFOAT** Vies A Vies. V. 2, No. 1, (April 1984)-. 0826-4570. Periodical. CN. French. qt. Free. Organisation Montrealaise des Personnes Atteintes de Cancer, 4366B rue St Hubert, Montreal Quebec H2J 2W8 Canada. **DD** 616.9940060714281. (ctrl). *Bulletin de Liaison (Organisation Montrealaise des Personnes Atteintes de Cancer), 0828-5233.*

CA. V. 1- Nov. 1950-. 0007-9235. Periodical. US. English. bm. American Cancer Society/Int Activities, c/o Gerry de Harven, 90 Park Avenue, New York NY 10016. **Tel** (212)736-3030. **Ed** C S Cameron. **Ind/Abst** Life Sci. Collect., Cumul. Index Nurs. Allied Health Lit., Index Med., Chem. Abstr., Curr. Contents Clin. Pract., Biol. Abstr., Excerpta Med., Abstr. World Med., Med. Socioecon. Res. Source, Energy Res. Abstr. **LC** RC261. **DD** 616.99405. **NLM** W1 C103. **CODEN** CAMCAM.

CANCER. V. 1- May 1948-. 0008-543X. Periodical. US. English. sm. $84.00. J B Lippincott Company, East Washington Square, Philadelphia PA 19105. **Tel** (215)238-4273. **Ed** Jonathan E Rhods. **Ind/Abst** Excerpta Med., Index Med., Int. Aerosp. Abstr., Life Sci. Collect., Biol. Abstr., CIS Abstr., Chem. Abstr., Ringdoc, Pestdoc, Vetdoc, Energy Inf. Abstr., Environ. Abstr., Sci. Cit. Index, Abr. Ed., Hospit. Lit. Index. **LC** RC261. **DD** 616.99405. **NLM** W1 CA671K. **CODEN** CANCAR. (cum index). adv acc. **Circ** 21,216. Contains original articles oriented toward clinical research seeking to bridge the gap between the investigator and the clinician.

CANCER BIOCHEMISTRY BIOPHYSICS. V. 1- Nov. 1974-. 0305-7232. Periodical. US. English. qt. $314.00. Gordon & Breach, PO Box 197, London WC2E 9PX England. **Tel** (01)836-5125. **Ed** H D Brown. **Ind/Abst** Life Sci. Collect., Excerpta Med., Index Med., Biol. Abstr., Chem. Abstr., Sci. Cit. Index, Abr. Ed. **LC** RC261.A1. **DD** 599.019024616. **NLM** W1 CA673. **CODEN** CABCD4. bk rev. adv acc.

CANCER BIOLOGY. **Series/Titl** Advances in Pathobiology. 1-. 0363-017X. Monographic Series. US. English. an. Stratton Intercontinental Medical Book Corporation, 381 Park Avenue South, New York NY 10016. **LC** RC254. **DD** 616.994. **NLM** W1 AD716 V.2 ETC.

CANCER BIOLOGY REVIEWS. V. 1-. 0198-6473. US. English. Marcel Dekker, 270 Madison Avenue, New York NY 10016. **Ed** J J Marchalonis, M G Hanna and I J Fidler. **Ind/Abst** Chem. Abstr. **LC** RC261.A1. **DD** 616.994005. **NLM** W1 CA674. **CODEN** CBRVDC.

THE CANCER BULLETIN *CEASED.* V. 1-32. 0008-5448. Periodical. US. English. bm. Medical Arts Publishing Foundation, 1603 Oakdale, Houston TX 77004. **Tel** (713)529-7371. **Ed** Glenn R Knotts. **Ind/Abst** Excerpta Med. **NLM** W1 CA677. **CODEN** CBTEA. bk rev. **Circ** 25,000. (ctrl). Cancer information. *Texas Cancer Bulletin.*

THE CANCER BULLETIN OF THE UNIVERSITY OF TEXAS M.D. ANDERSON HOSPITAL AND TUMOR INSTITUTE AT HOUSTON. **VFOAT** Cancer Bulletin. Vol. 33, No. 1 (Jan.-Feb. 1981)-. 0740-820X. Periodical. US. English. bm. $12.00. Medical Arts Publishing Foundation, 1603 Oakdale, Houston TX 77004. **Tel** (713)521-3314. **Ed** R Lee Clark. **Ind/Abst** Excerpta Med. bk rev. **Circ** 23,000. Clinical and research articles on cancer which are of interest to the physician. *Cancer Bulletin, 0008-5448.*

CANCER CELLS. 1/1984-. 0743-2194. Monographic Series. US. English. ir. Cold Spring Harbor Laboratory, PO Box 100, Cold Spring Harbor NY 11724. **Tel** (516)367-8470. **NLM** W1. *Cold Spring Harbor Conferences on Cell Proliferation.*

CANCER CHEMOTHERAPY. (CANCER CHEMOTHERAPY : THE EORTC CANCER CHEMOTHERAPY ANNUAL). **VFOAT** EORTC Cancer Chemotherapy Annual. 1 (1979)-. 0167-7853. English. an. **Ed** H M Pinedo. **NLM** W1 CA677BM.

CANCER CONTROL JOURNAL. V. 1- May/June 1973-. 0191-3794. Periodical. US. English. bm. $8.00. Cancer Control Society, 2043 North Berendo, Los Angeles CA 90027. **NLM** W1 CA6779.

CANCER CYTOLOGY *CEASED.* V. 1-20. Periodical. US. English. sa. **Ind/Abst** Excerpta Med. **NLM** W1 CA6783.

CANCER DETECTION AND PREVENTION. V. 1-. 0361-090X. Periodical. US. English. sa. $27.50 Domestic, $29.80 Foreign. Marcel Dekker Journals, PO Box 11305 Church Street Station, New York NY 10249. **Ind/Abst** Life Sci. Collect., Excerpta Med., Index Med., Chem. Abstr. **LC** RC268. **DD** 616.99405. **NLM** W1 CA6785K. **CODEN** CDPRD4.

CANCER DRUG DELIVERY. Vol. 1, No. 1-. 0732-9482. Periodical. US. English. qt. $110.00. Mary Ann Liebert Inc, 157 East 86th Street, New York NY 10028. **Ind/Abst** Life Sci. Collect., Chem. Abstr., Index Med. **NLM** W1. **CODEN** CDDED7.

CANCER EN PUERTO RICO. English (text also in Spanish). an. **LC** RC279.P8. **DD** 614.5999. **NLM** W2 DP8 C3C.

CANCER FORUM. 1- Autumn 1974-. 0311-306X. Periodical. AT. English. ty. Australian Cancer Society, Government Printing Office, Box 4708, Sydney New South Wales 2001 Australia. **Tel** (02) 231 3355. **Ed** L A Wright. **NLM** W1 CA679U. bk rev. **Circ** 3,000. (ctrl). Original and reprinted reports on cancer research education and patient welfare also reports on meetings, book reviews and meeting calendars.

CANCER GENETICS AND CYTOGENETICS. V. 1- July 1979-. 0165-4608. Periodical. US. English. ir. $495.00. Elsevier Science Publishing Co, PO Box 1663 Grand Central Station, New York NY 10163. **Tel** (212)370-5520. **Ed** A A Sandberg. **Ind/Abst** Life Sci. Collect., Excerpta Med., Index Med., Biol. Abstr., Chem. Abstr., Sci. Cit. Index, Abr. Ed. **LC** RC268.4. **DD** 616.994042. **NLM** W1 CA697UD. **CODEN** CGCYDF. adv acc. **Circ** 500. Original articles on human, animal, molecular, population and biomedical genetics and cytogenetics as they relate to broad fields of cancer.

CANCER IMMUNOLOGY AND IMMUNOTHERAPY. V. 1-. 0340-7004. Periodical. GW. English. qt. $186.00. Springer Verlag-New York Inc, 175 5th Avenue, New York NY 10010. **Tel** (212)460-1500. **Ed** G Mathe, R W Baldwin and E Mihich. **Ind/Abst** Life Sci. Collect., Excerpta Med., Index Med., Chem. Abstr., Energy Res. Abstr., Sci. Cit. Index, Abr. Ed. **NLM** W1 CA679UI. **CODEN** CIIMDN. Available on microfilm. Fields of interest: tumor immunology, tumor biology, drug research, clinical and experimental therapy and tumor diagnosis.

CANCER IN CANADA. **VFOAT** Le Cancer au Canada. 1976-. 0227-1788. CN. English (French). an. 35.00 Domestic, 36.50 Foreign. Receiver General for Canada, Statistics Canada Publications, Ottawa Ontario K1A 0T6 Canada. **Tel** (800)268-1151. **LC** RC279.C3. **DD** 614.59990971. Counts of new cases reported to provincial tumor registries by site of tumour, age, sex, and methods of diagnosis (Ontario excluded). *New Primary Sites of Malignant Neoplasms in Canada (as Reported by Provincial Tumour Registries).*

CANCER IN ILLINOIS. 0277-7215. US. English. an. American Cancer Society, Illinois Division Inc, 37 South Wabash Avenue, Chicago IL 60603. **LC** RC277.I3. **DD** 312.3994009773.

CANCER IN NEW SOUTH WALES. INCIDENCE AND MORTALITY. (CANCER IN NEW SOUTH WALES : INCIDENCE AND MORTALITY). 1972-. 0157-2547. AT. English. ir. **NLM** W2 KA8.1 N5C3C. *Interim Report - New South Wales Cancer Registry.*

CANCER IN ONTARIO. 1972/73-. 0315-9884. CN. English. an. **NLM** W1 CA679X. *Annual Report, 0078-4699.*

CANCER IN WEST VIRGINIA. **VFOAT** Cancer. Annual Report. US. English. an. **LC** RC277.W4. **NLM** W2 AW4 D7C.

CANCER INCIDENCE IN FIVE CONTINENTS. V. 1-. English. ir. **Ed** Richard Doll. **LC** RC275.

CANCER INVESTIGATION. Vol. 1, No. 1 (Jan./Feb. 1983). 0735-7907. Periodical. US. English. bm. $95.00. Marcel Dekker Inc, PO Box 11305/ Church Street Station, New York NY 10249. **Tel** (212)696-9000. **Ed** Yashar Hirshaut. **Ind/Abst** Excerpta Med., Index Med., Biol. Abstr., Bibliogr. Index Health Educ. Period., Biol. Dig., Chem. Abstr., Curr. Contents, Excerpta Med., Leukemia Abstr., Sci. Cit. Index, Abr. Ed. **LC** RC261.A1. **DD** 616.994005. **NLM** W1. **CODEN** CINVD7. bk rev. adv acc. (ctrl). Devoted to both the clinician and to the researcher. Provides in-depth view of ongoing cancer research.

CANCER LETTER. (THE CANCER LETTER). V. 1- Jan. 3, 1975-. 0096-3917. Periodical. US. English. wk. $160.00. The Cancer Letter Inc, PO Box 2370, Reston VA 22090. **Tel** (703)620-4646. **Ed** Jerry Boyd. **NLM** W1 CA68. bk rev. **Circ** 1,000. Program and policy development of cancer research. *Cancer Newsletter.*

CANCER LETTERS. V. 1- Sept. 1975-. 0304-3835. Periodical. NE. English. bm. Elsevier Scientific Publishing Company, PO Box 330, Amsterdam The Netherlands. **Ind/Abst** Life Sci. Collect., Excerpta Med., Index Med., Biol. Abstr., Art Archaeol. Tech. Abstr., Chem. Abstr., Sci. Cit. Index, Abr. Ed. **LC** RC261.A1. **DD** 616.994005. **NLM** W1 CA68E. **CODEN** CALEDQ.

CANCER MANAGEMENT. 1978-. 0193-1415. Monographic Series. US. English. ir. Masson Distribution Inc, Box C-762, Brooklyn NY 11205. **Tel** (212)838-8510. **NLM** W1 CA68S.

CANCER MARKERS DIGEST. **VFOAT** C.M.D. Vol. 1, No. 1 (May/June 1984)-. 0743-8427. Periodical. US. English. mo. $84.00. International Society for Innovations in Oncology, PO Box 6539, Silver Springs MD 20906. **DD** 616.

CANCER METASTASIS REVIEWS. Vol. 1, No. 1-. 0167-7659. Periodical. English. qt. Kluwer Academic Group, Distribution Center/PO Box 322, 3300 AH Dordrecht Netherlands. **Ind/Abst** Index Med., Chem. Abstr. **NLM** W1 CA68L. **CODEN** CMRED4.

CANCER MORTALITY STATISTICS. *See* Statistics.

CANCER NEWS. V. 1- 1947-. 0008-5464. Periodical. US. English. ty. Free. American Cancer Society, 777 Third Avenue, New York NY 10017. **DD** 616. **NLM** W1 CA683. **CODEN** CANEAX. *Bulletin of the American Cancer Society, Inc., Field Army News.*

CANCER NEWS JOURNAL. V. 1- Sept. 1965-. 0099-2372. Periodical. US. English. bm. $20.00. International Association of Cancer, 7740 West Manchester Avenue/Suite 110, Playa Del Rey CA 90291. **Tel** (213)822-5032. **Ed** Ann Cinquina. **LC** RC261.A1. **DD** 616.994005. **NLM** W1 CA683N. bk rev. adv acc. **Circ** 5,000. Cancer information regarding patient freedom of choice and alternative therapies. Exclusive articles quarterly.

CANCER NEWSLINE. V. 1- Sept. 1976-. 0276-3974. Periodical. US. English. qt. Minnesota Cancer Council, 2750 Park Avenue, Minneapolis MN 55407.

CANCER NURSING NEWS. *See* Medicine - Nursing.

THE CANCER PHARMACOLOGY ANNUAL. 1983-. NE. English. an. Elsevier Science Publishing Company, 52 Vanderbilt Avenue, New York NY 10017. **Ed** B A Chabner and H M Pinedo. **LC** RC271.C5. **DD** 616.994061. **NLM** W1.

CANCER REPORT. No. 1- March 1977-. 0190-5112. Periodical. US. English. Cancer Report/ New York University Medical Center, Room 1WS Bellevue 550 First Avenue, New York NY 10016. **NLM** W1 CA687E.

CANCER RESEARCH. V. 1- Jan. 1941-. 0008-5472. Periodical. US. English. mo. $15.00 Members, $75.00 Non-Members. Waverly Press, 428 East Preston Street, Baltimore MD 21202. **Ind/Abst** Life Sci. Collect., Excerpta Med., Index Med., Biol. Abstr., Chem. Abstr., Energy Res. Abstr., Energy Inf.

Medicine—Neoplasma, Neoplastic

Abstr., Environ. Abstr., Pestdoc, Ringdoc, Vetdoc. LC RC261. DD 616.99405. NLM W1 CA688. CODEN CNREA8. (cum index). *American Journal of Cancer.*

CANCER RESEARCH SAFETY MONOGRAPH SERIES. V. 1-. 0190-2466. Monographic Series. US. English. ir. Cancer Research Safety Symposium Coordinator/Monograph Series Editor Bioharard and Environment Control Litton Bionetics Inc, Frederick Cancer Research Center, Box B, Frederick MD 21701. Ed L S Idoine. NLM W3 C1164E.

CANCER SEMINAR. V. 1-4, No. 2. 0069-0171. Periodical. US. English. University of South Florida, College of Medicine, Tampa FL 33620.

CANCER SURVEYS. Vol. 1, No. 1 (Spring 1982)-. 0261-2429. Periodical. UK. English. qt. 95.00. Oxford University Press, Journals Department, Walton Street, Oxford OX2 6DP England. Tel 0865 56767. Ed L M Franks. Ind/Abst Excerpta Med. NLM W1 CA692D. adv acc. Circ 124. Comprehensive review of oncology including new research findings relative to epidemiology and laboratory research to clinical problems. This is of interest to clinicians and laboratory workers.

CANCER THERAPY ABSTRACTS. See Indexes/Abstracts.

CANCER TREATMENT AND RESEARCH. VFOAT CTAR. Vol. 1-. Monographic Series. English. ir. Ind/Abst Life Sci. Collect. NLM W1.

CANCER TREATMENT AND RESEARCH. LUNG CANCER. Series/Titl Cancer Treatment and Research. VFOAT Lung Cancer. 1-. English. ir. Ed R B Livingston. NLM W1 CA693 V. 1 etc.

CANCER TREATMENT AND RESEARCH. LYMPHOMAS INCLUDING HODGKIN'S DISEASE. Series/Titl Cancer Treatment and Research. VFOAT Lymphomas Including Hodgkin's Disease. 1-. Periodical. English. ir. Ed John M Bennett. NLM W1 CA693 V.4 ETC.

CANCER TREATMENT REVIEWS. V. 1- March 1974-. 0305-7372. Periodical. UK. English. qt. Academic Press, 4805 Sand Lake Road, Orlando FL 32819. Tel (305)345-4100. Ed K Hellmann and S K Carter. Ind/Abst Life Sci. Collect., Excerpta Med., Energy Inf. Abstr., Environ. Abstr., Index Med., Biol. Abstr., Sci. Cit. Index, Abr. Ed. NLM W1 CA695. CODEN CTREDJ.

CANCER TREATMENT SYMPOSIA. Vol. 1-. 0742-1761. Periodical. US. English. bm. R A Bloch International Cancer Information Center, Building 82 Room 235 National Institute of Health, Bethesda MD 20205. NLM W3.

CANCER UPDATE. Vol. 1, No. 1 (Dec. 1983)-. 0739-1692. Periodical. US. English. mo. $56.00. Mary Ann Liebert Inc, 157 East 86th Street, New York NY 10028. DD 616. NLM W1.

CANCEROLOGIE. 1976-. Periodical. FR. French. Editions du CNRS, 23 rue du Maroc, 75019 Paris France. Ed A Demaille. NLM W3 CA699N.

CARCINOGENESIS. V. 1- Jan. 1980-. 0143-3334. Periodical. US. English. mo. $275.00. IRL Press, Information Retrieval, 1911 Jefferson Davis Highway, Arlington VA 22202. Tel (703)998-2980. Ed A Dipple, T C Garner and C C Harris. Ind/Abst Life Sci. Collect., Excerpta Med., Index Med., Biol. Abstr., Chem. Abstr., Bibliogr. Agric., Energy Res. Abstr. LC RC268.5. DD 616.994071. NLM W1 CA7623. CODEN CRNGDP. bk rev. adv acc. Circ 800. A multidisciplinary journal covering all aspects of research leading ultimately to the prevention of cancer in man: viral, physical, chemical carcinogenesis and mutagenesis and modifying factors.

CARCINOGENESIS. A COMPREHENSIVE SURVEY. V. 1-. 0147-4006. Monographic Series. US. English. ir. Raven Press, 1140 Avenue of the Americas, New York NY 10036. Ind/Abst Life Sci. Collect., Index Med., Biol. Abstr., Chem. Abstr. LC RC268.5. DD 616.99407105. NLM W1 CA7624. CODEN CCSUDL.

CARCINOGENESIS ABSTRACTS. See Indexes/Abstracts.

CARCINOGENICITY OF AZO DYES, ARYL AMINES, AND RELATED COMPOUNDS. Main/Corp International Cancer Research Data Bank. Series/Titl ICRDB Cancergram. Periodical. US. English. Department of Health Education and Welfare, Public Health Service, National Institutes of Health National Cancer Institute, Springfield VA 22161.

CARCINOGENICITY OF NITROSO COMPOUNDS. Main/Corp International Cancer Research Data Bank. Series/Titl ICRDB Cancergram. Periodical. US. English. Department of Health, Education and Welfare, Public Health Service, National Institutes of Health, National Cancer Institute, Springfield VA 22161.

CARCINOGENICITY OF POLYCYCLIC AROMATIC HYDROCARBONS AND RELATED COMPOUNDS. Main/Corp International Cancer Research Data Bank. Series/Titl ICRDB Cancergram. Periodical. US. English. Department of Health, Education and Welfare, Public Health Service, National Institutes of Health, National Cancer Institute, Springfield VA 22161. *Polycyclic Aromatic Hydrocarbons and Related Compounds.*

CHEMICAL INDUCTION OF CANCER. US. English. ir. Academic Press, 4805 Sand Lake Road, Orlando FL 32887. Tel (305)345-4100.

CHEMIOTERAPIA : INTERNATIONAL JOURNAL OF THE MEDITERRANEAN SOCIETY OF CHEMOTHERAPY. Vol. 1, 1/82 (Feb. 1982)-. 0392-906X. Periodical. English. ir. $40.00. Ind/Abst Excerpta Med. NLM W1 CH303. *Chemioterapia Antimicrobica, Chemioterapia Oncologica.*

CHEMOTHERAPIA. V. 1-12. 0577-6384. Periodical. English (French or German). bm. LC RM260. NLM W1 CH398. (cum index).

CHIBA-KEN GAN SENTA NEMPO. No. 1-. Japanese. ir. Chiba-Ken Gan Senta, 666-2 Nitonacho, Chiba Japan. LC RC267.

CHILDHOOD SOLID TUMORS AND LYMPHOMAS. Main/Corp International Cancer Research Data Bank. Series/Titl ICRDB Cancergram. Periodical. US. English. Department of Health Education and Welfare, Public Health Service, National Institutes of Health, National Cancer Institute, Springfield VA 22161.

CLINICAL & EXPERIMENTAL METASTASIS. VFOAT Clinical and Experimental Metastasis. Vol. 1, No. 1 (Jan./March 1983)-. 0262-0898. Periodical. UK. English. qt. $92.00. Taylor & Francis Ltd, 4 John Street, London WC1N 2ET England. Ind/Abst Life Sci. Collect., Excerpta Med., Index Med., Chem. Abstr. NLM W1. CODEN CEXMD2.

THE CLINICAL CANCER LETTER. 1978. 0164-985X. Periodical. US. English. mo. $36.00 Domestic, $40.00 Foreign. Clinical Cancer Letter, Box 2370, Reston VA 22090. Tel (703)620-4646. Ed Jerry Boyd. Circ 2,000. Advances in clinical cancer research.

CLINICAL EVALUATION AND TREATMENT OF MULTIPLE MYELOMA AND OTHER MONOCLONAL GAMMOPATHIES. Main/Corp International Cancer Research Data Bank. Series/Titl ICRDB Cancergram. Periodical. US. English. Department of Health Education and Welfare, Public Health Service, National Institutes of Health, National Cancer Institute, Springfield VA 22161.

CLINICAL ONCOLOGY CEASED. V. 1- March 1975-. 0305-7399. Periodical. UK. English. qt. $26.00. Academic Press, 4805 Sand Lake Road, Orlando FL 32819. Ind/Abst Life Sci. Collect., Excerpta Med., Index Med. DD 616. NLM W1 CL745.

CLINICS IN ONCOLOGY. Vol. 1, No. 1 (March 1982)-. 0261-9873. Periodical. UK. English. ty. $55.00. W B Saunders Company, West Washington Square, Philadelphia PA 19105. Tel (215)574-3395. Ed Barbara Conover and Sean Duggan. Ind/Abst Excerpta Med., Chem. Abstr. NLM W1 CL831CG. CODEN CLONEA. Circ 1,500. Practical updates for the clinician on the latest advances plus topics of current interest.

COLLECTED PAPERS FROM THE NATIONAL CANCER RESEARCH INSTITUTE. V. 1- 1962/65-. 0077-3662. Periodical. JA. English. an. National Cancer Center Library, Tsukiju 5-Chrome Cho-KY, Tokyo Japan. NLM W1.

COMMUNIQUE - MANITOBA DIVISION, CANADIAN CANCER SOCIETY. Main/Corp Canadian Cancer Society. Manitoba Division. Began publication with Jan. 1978 issue?. 0707-5995. Periodical. CN. English. qt. Free. Canadian Cancer Society Manitoba Division, Suite 202, 960 Portage Avenue, Winnipeg Manitoba R3G 0R4 Canada. DD 362.1969940097127. *Cancer Comment, 0707-5987.*

COMMUNITY CANCER PROGRAMS IN THE UNITED STATES : THE DELEGATE ROSTER OF THE ASSOCIATION OF COMMUNITY CANCER CENTERS. Main/Corp Association of Community Cancer Centers. VFOAT ACCC Roster. 1980-81-. 0743-5061. US. English. an. NLM QZ 22 AA1 A849C.

CONTEMPORARY HEMATOLOGY/ONCOLOGY. VAT Contemporary Hematology, Oncology. V. 1-. 0197-3649. US. English. Plenum Publishing Corp, 227 West 17th Street, New York NY 10011. Ind/Abst Chem. Abstr. LC RB145. DD 616.15005. NLM W1 CO769MQ. CODEN CHONDF. *Year in Hematology, 0160-7014.*

CURRENT ARTICLES ON NEOPLASIA. Began publication Feb. 19, 1971. Periodical. US. English. ir. University of Texas, MD Anderson Hospital Res Med Library, Houston TX 77030. Tel (713)792-2282.

CURRENT CONCEPTS IN ONCOLOGY. 0199-4697. Periodical. US. English. qt. MacMillan Professional Journal, 640 North LaSalle Street/Suite 380, Chicago IL 60610. Tel (312)944-5888. NLM W1 CU788ASB.

CURRENT ONCOLOGY. Began in 1984. 0743-930X. US. English. an. Elsevier Science Publishing Co Inc, 52 Vanderbilt Avenue, New York NY 10017. DD 616.

CURRENT PROBLEMS IN CANCER. VFOAT CPCA. Current Problems in Cancer. V. 1- July 1976-. 0147-0272. Monographic Series. US. English. mo. $65.00. Yearbook Medical Publishers, 35 East Wacker Drive, Chicago IL 60601. Ind/Abst Index Med., Biol. Abstr., Energy Res. Abstr. DD 616. NLM W1 CU804HI. CODEN CPRCDJ.

DCT BULLETIN. VAT Division of Cancer Treatment Bulletin. Mar. 1979-. 0194-1283. Periodical. US. English. ir. National Institutes of Health, National Cancer Institute, Division of Cancer Treatment, Bethesda MD 20205. NLM W1 D109F. *DCT Newsletter, 0162-6930.*

THE DETECTION, DIAGNOSIS, AND THERAPY, AND PRE-CLINICAL BIOLOGY OF BREAST CANCER. Main/Corp International Cancer Research Data Bank. Series/Titl ICRDB Cancergram. Periodical. US. English. Department of Health, Education and Welfare, Public Health Service, National Institutes of Health, National Cancer Institute, Springfield VA 22161.

THE DETECTION, DIAGNOSIS, AND THERAPY OF LUNG CANCER. Main/Corp International Cancer Research Data Bank. Series/Titl ICRDB Cancergram. Periodical. US. English. Department of Health, Education and Welfare, Public Health Service, National Institutes of Health, National Cancer Institute, Springfield VA 22161.

DEVELOPMENTS IN CANCER RESEARCH. V. 1-. 0163-6146. Monographic Series. US. English. ir. Elsevier Science Publ Co Inc, PO Box 1663 Grand Central Station, New York NY 10163. Tel (212)370-5520. Ind/Abst Chem. Abstr. LC UNC. NLM W1 DE997VM. CODEN DCREDD.

DEVELOPMENTS IN ONCOLOGY. V. 1-. 0167-4927. Monographic Series. English. ir. Ind/Abst Chem. Abstr. LC UNC. NLM W1 DE998N. CODEN DEOND5.

DIAGNOSIS AND TREATMENT OF ACUTE AND CHRONIC LEUKEMIA. Main/Corp International Cancer Research Data Bank. Series/Titl ICRDB Cancergram. Periodical. US. English. Department of Health, Education and Welfare, Public Health Service, National Institutes of Health, National Cancer Institute, Springfield VA 22161.

DIAGNOSIS AND TREATMENT OF HODGKIN'S DISEASE. Main/Corp International Cancer Research Data Bank. Series/Titl ICRDB Cancergram. Periodical. US. English. Department of Health, Education and Welfare, Public Health Service, National Institutes of Health, National Cancer Institute, Springfield VA 22161.

DIAGNOSIS AND TREATMENT OF NON-HODGKIN'S LYMPHOMAS. Main/Corp International Cancer Research Data Bank. Series/Titl ICRDB Cancergram. Periodical. US.

Medicine—Neoplasma, Neoplastic

English. Department of Health Education and Welfare, Public Health Service, National Institutes of Health, National Cancer Institute, Springfield VA 22161.

DIAGNOSIS AND TREATMENT OF SARCOMAS AND RELATED TUMORS. Main/Corp International Cancer Research Data Bank. Series/Titl ICRDB Cancergram. Periodical. US. English. Department of Health, Education and Welfare, Public Health Service, National Institutes of Health, National Cancer Institute, Springfield VA 22161.

DIAGNOSTIC TUMOUR BIBLIOGRAPHIES. See Bibliographies.

DIRECTIONS IN ONCOLOGY. 0883-0312. Periodical. US. English. bw. $295.00. Nassau Publications Inc, 11 Forest Street, New Canaan CT 06840. **DD** 616.

DIRECTOR'S REPORT - PAPANICOLAOU CANCER RESEARCH INSTITUTE AT MIAMI FLORIDA. (DIRECTOR'S REPORT). Main/Corp Papanicolaou Cancer Research Institute. 0090-7359. US. English. Papanicolaou Cancer Research Institute, Miami FL 33135. **LC** RC261. **DD** 616.9940072075938.

DIRECTORY OF CANCER RESEARCH INFORMATION RESOURCES. See Yearbooks, Almanacs, Directories.

DIRECTORY OF MEMBERS - AMERICAN ASSOCIATION FOR CANCER RESEARCH. See Yearbooks, Almanacs, Directories.

DIRECTORY OF ON-GOING RESEARCH IN CANCER EPIDEMIOLOGY. See Yearbooks, Almanacs, Directories.

THE ECHO. 0046-1067. Periodical. US. English. qt.

EKSPERIMENTALNAJA ONKOLOGIJA. (EKSPERIMENTALNAIA ONKOLOGIIA). **VFOAT** Experimental Oncology. Began in: 1979. 0204-3564. Periodical. UR. Russian (summaries in English). bm. $33.50. Victor Kamkin Inc (71097), 12224 Parklawn Drive, Rockville MD 20852. **Tel** (301)881-5973. **Ind/Abst** Life Sci. Collect., Biol. Abstr., Chem. Abstr., Energy Res. Abstr., Index Med. **NLM** W1. **CODEN** EKSODD.

ENVIRONMENTAL AND OCCUPATIONAL CARCINOGENESIS. Main/Corp National Cancer Institute. International Cancer Research Data Bank Program. Series/Titl ICRDB Cancergram. Jan. 1978-. Periodical. US. English. mo. Price upon application. Department of Health, Education and Welfare, Public Health Service, National Institutes of Health, National Cancer Institute, Springfield VA 22161. *Etiology of Cancer in the General Population.*

ERGEBNISSE DER CHIRURGISCHEN ONKOLOGIE. (ERGEBNISSE DER CHIRURGISCHEN ONKOLOGIE : VERHANDLUNGEN DER CHIRURGISCHEN ARBEITSGEMEINSCHAFT FUR ONKOLOGIE (CAO) DER DEUTSCHEN GESELLSCHAFT FUR CHIRURGIE E.V). 1-. 0720-3462. German. ir. **NLM** W1 ER264D.

ETIOLOGY OF CANCER IN THE GENERAL POPULATION. Main/Corp International Cancer Research Data Bank. Series/Titl ICRDB Cancergram. Periodical. US. English. Price Upon Application. Department of Health Education and Welfare, Public Health Service, National Institutes of Health, National Cancer Institute, Springfield VA 22161.

EUROPEAN JOURNAL OF CANCER. CEASED. **VFOAT** Journal Europeen de Cancerologie. Began with V. 1-17, No. 6. 0014-2964. Periodical. UK. English (French or German). mo. **Ind/Abst** Nucl. Sci. Abstr., Biol. Abstr., Chem. Abstr., Index Med. **DD** 616.9. **NLM** W1 EU72. **CODEN** EJCAAH. (cum index).

EUROPEAN JOURNAL OF CANCER & CLINICAL ONCOLOGY. **VFOAT** European Journal of Cancer and Clinical Oncology. Vol. 17, No. 7 (July 1981)-. 0277-5379. Periodical. UK. English. mo. Pergamon Press, 395 Sawmill River Road, Elmsford NY 10523. **Tel** (914)592-7700. **Ind/Abst** Electron. Commun. Abstr. J., ISMEC Bull., Pollut. Abstr. Indexes, Saf. Sci. Abstr. J., Life Sci. Collect., Pestdoc, Ringdoc, Vetdoc, Excerpta Med., Energy Inf. Abstr., Environ. Abstr., Index Med., Biol. Abstr., Chem. Abstr., Energy Res. Abstr. **NLM** W1 EU72M. **CODEN** EJCODS. *European Journal of Cancer, 0014-2964.*

EUROPEAN JOURNAL OF GYNAECOLOGICAL ONCOLOGY. See Medicine - Gynecology & Obstetrics.

EXCERPTA MEDICA. SECTION 16. CANCER. See Indexes/Abstracts.

EXCERPTA MEDICA. SECTION 65, CANCER IMMUNOLOGY. LITERATURE INDEX. See Indexes/Abstracts.

FLORIDA CANCER NEWS. 1- 1960-. US. English. qt. American Cancer Society, Florida Division, 1001 South MacDill Avenue, Tampa FL 33609. **Tel** (813)253-0541.

FOREFRONT. V. 1- Spring 1976-. 0162-7260. Periodical. US. English. ty. Forefront, Memorial Sloan-Kettering Cancer Center, 1275 York Avenue, New York NY 10021. **NLM** W1 FO558I.

FORTSCHRITTE DER ONKOLOGIE. V. 1-. 0323-5084. Monographic Series. German. ir. **Ind/Abst** Chem. Abstr. **NLM** W1 FO86W. **CODEN** FONKDF.

FRONTIERS OF RADIATION THERAPY AND ONCOLOGY. See Medicine - Radiology.

FUNDACION CIENTIFICA DE LA ASOCIACION ESPAÑOLA CONTRA EL CANCER INFORMA. Periodical. Spanish. an. **LC** RC261.A1. **DD** 616.994005.

FUNDAMENTALS OF CANCER MANAGEMENT. 1-. 0739-7364. Monographic Series. US. English. ir. Marcel Dekker Continuation Department, 270 Madison Avenue, New York NY 10016. **Tel** (212)696-9000. Ed Bleehan and Glatstein. **NLM** 11 FU5395. This is an ongoing series. Each title has a different subject.

GAN NO RINSHO. **VFOAT** Japanese Journal of Cancer Clinics. V. 1- 1954-. 0021-4949. Periodical. JA. Japanese. mo. Japan Publishing Trading Company Ltd, 5030 Tokyo International, 100-31 Tokyo Japan. **Ind/Abst** Life Sci. Collect., Index Med., Chem. Abstr. **NLM** W1 GA41E. **CODEN** GANRAE.

GAN TO KAGAKU RYOHO. **VFOAT** Cancer & Chemotherapy. 0385-0684. Periodical. JA. Japanese. ir. $132.00. Kyowa Book Company Inc, 1-38 Kanda Junbocho Chiyoda-ku, Tokyo 101 Japan. **Tel** 293-0727. **Ind/Abst** Index Med., Excerpta Med., Chem. Abstr. **NLM** W1 GA411. **CODEN** GTKRDX.

GANN. V. 1- 1907-. 0016-450X. Periodical. JA. Multilingual (English and Japanese). bm. $160.35. Elsevier Science Publishers, PO Box 211, 1000 AE Amsterdam The Netherlands. **Ind/Abst** Life Sci. Collect., Excerpta Med., Biol. Abstr., Chem. Abstr., Nucl. Sci. Abstr., Index Med. **NLM** W1 GA407. **CODEN** GANNA2.

GANN MONOGRAPH ON CANCER RESEARCH. V. 11- 1971-. Monographic Series. English. ir. **Ind/Abst** Excerpta Med., Biol. Abstr., Chem. Abstr., GeoRef. **NLM** W3 GA163. **CODEN** GMCRDC. *Gann Monograph, 0072-0151.*

GASTROINTESTINAL CARCINOGENESIS. Main/Corp International Cancer Research Data Bank. Series/Titl ICRDB Cancergram. Periodical. US. English. Department of Health Education and Welfare, Public Health Service, National Institutes of Health/National Cancer Institute, Springfield VA 22161.

GYNECOLOGIC ONCOLOGY. V. 1- Nov. 1972-. 0090-8258. Periodical. US. English. mo. Academic Press, 4805 Sand Lake Road, Orlando FL 32819. **Tel** (305)345-4100. **Ind/Abst** Life Sci. Collect., Excerpta Med., Index Med., Chem. Abstr. Biol. Abstr., Energy Res. Abstr., Sci. Cit. Index, Abr. Ed., Hospit. Lit. Index. **LC** RC280.G5. **DD** 616.9926505. **NLM** W1 GY557N. **CODEN** GYNOA3.

THE HANDBOOK OF CANCER IMMUNOLOGY. **VFOAT** Cancer Immunology. Vol. 1 (1978)-. 0736-8674. US. English. ir. Garland Publishing Inc, 136 Madison Avenue, New York NY 10016. **Tel** (212)686-7492. Ed Harold Waters. **LC** RC268.3. **DD** 616.994079. Comprehensive reference guide to cancer immunology.

HEALTH STATISTICS REPORT. CANCER DATA. See Statistics.

HEMATOLOGICAL ONCOLOGY. V. 1, No. 1 (Jan./Mar. 1983)-. 0278-0232. Periodical. UK. English. qt. 62 Domestic, 120 Foreign. John Wiley & Sons Ltd, Baffins Lane Chichester, Sussex PO19 1UD England. **Tel** (0243) 784531. Ed J W Parker, R J Lukes, G P Canellos and J M A Whitehouse. **Ind/Abst** Excerpta Med., Index Med., Chem. Abstr. **DD** 616. **NLM** W1 HE87E. **CODEN** HAONDL. bk rev. adv acc. A multi-disciplinary approach to solving problems of neoplasms of the hematopoietic system. Original articles and continuing updates of progress in various fields.

IARC INTERNAL TECHNICAL REPORT. Monographic Series. English (text in French). ir. **NLM** W1 I21E.

IARC MONOGRAPHS ON THE EVALUATION OF THE CARCINOGENIC RISK OF CHEMICALS TO HUMAN. Main/Corp International Agency for Research on Cancer. Working Group on the Evaluation of The Carcinogenic Risk of Chemicals to Humans. Monographic Series. English. ir. World Health Organization, 49 Sheridan Avenue, Albany NY 12210. **Tel** (518)436-9686. **Ind/Abst** Index Med. *IARC Monographs on the Evaluation of the Carcinogenic Risk of Chemicals to Man.*

IARC SCIENTIFIC PUBLICATIONS. VAT International Agency for Research on Cancer Scientific Publication. 1979-. 0300-5038. Monographic Series. US. English. ir. Oxford University Press, 16-00 Pollitt Drive, Fair Lawn NJ 07410. **Tel** (201)796-8000. **Ind/Abst** Index Med., Bibliogr. Agric. **NLM** W1 I21K. *IARC Publications, 0254-2730.*

ICRBD CANCERGRAM. CELL BIOLOGY: GROWTH REGULATION, DIFFERENTIATION. (ICRDB CANCERGRAM. SERIES CB16, CELL BIOLOGY. GROWTH REGULATION, DIFFERENTIATION). **VFOAT** Cell Biology Regulation, Differentiation. Began with Apr. 1978. 0190-3446. Periodical. US. English. mo. US Department of Commerce, National Technical Information Service, 5285 Port Royal Road, Springfield VA 22161. **NLM** ZQZ 202 I11CG.

ICRDB CANCERGRAM. ACUTE AND CHRONIC LEUKEMIA: DIAGNOSIS, TREATMENT. (ICRDB CANCERGRAM. SERIES CT03, ACUTE AND CHRONIC LEUKEMIA. DIAGNOSIS, TREATMENT). **VFOAT** Acute and Chronic Leukemia. Began with Jan. 1978. 0164-1921. Periodical. US. English. mo. US Department of Commerce, National Technical Information Service, 5285 Port Royal Road, Springfield VA 22161. **NLM** ZWH 250 C23D. *ICRDB Cancergram. NCI/ICRDB/CT03, Diagnosis and Treatment of Acute and Chronic Leukemia, 0190-0056.*

ICRDB CANCERGRAM. ANTITUMOR AND ANTIVIRAL AGENTS: EXPERIMENTAL THERAPEUTICS, TOXICOLOGY, PHARMACOLOGY. (ICRDB CANCERGRAM. SERIES CB20, ANTITUMOR AND ANTIVIRAL AGENTS. EXPERIMENTAL THERAPEUTICS, TOXICOLOGY, PHARMACOLOGY). **VFOAT** Antitumor and Antiviral Agents. Began with May 1978. 0164-193X. Periodical. US. English. mo. US Department of Commerce, National Technical Information Service, 5285 Port Royal Road, Springfield VA 22161. **NLM** ZQZ 267 I11AC.

ICRDB CANCERGRAM. ANTITUMOR AND ANTIVIRAL AGENTS: MECHANISMS OF ACTION. (ICRDB CANCERGRAM. SERIES CB19, ANTITUMOR AND ANTIVIRAL AGENTS. MECHANISMS OF ACTION). **VFOAT** Mechanisms of Action. Began with May 1978. 0164-1948. Periodical. US. English. mo. US Department of Commerce, National Technical Information Service, 5285 Port Royal Road, Springfield VA 22161. **NLM** ZQV 269 I35.

ICRDB CANCERGRAM. BREAST CANCER: DIAGNOSIS, TREATMENT, PRE-CLINICAL BIOLOGY. (ICRDB CANCERGRAM. SERIES CT09, BREAST CANCER. DIAGNOSIS, TREATMENT, PRE-CLINICAL BIOLOGY). **VFOAT** Breast Cancer. Began with Jan. 1978. 0164-1956. Periodical. US. English. mo. US Department of Commerce, National Technical Information Service, 5285 Port Royal Road, Springfield VA 22161. **NLM** ZWP 870 I11DP. *ICRDB Cancergram. NCI/ICRDB/CT09, The Detection, Diagnosis, Therapy, and Pre-Clinical Biology of Breast Cancer, 0190-0161.*

ICRDB CANCERGRAM. CANCER DETECTION AND MANAGEMENT: BIOLOGICAL MARKERS. (ICRDB CANCERGRAM. SERIES CT01, CANCER DETECTION AND MANAGEMENT. BIOLOGICAL MARKERS). **VFOAT** Cancer Detection and Management. 0190-3438. Periodical. US. English. mo. US

Medicine—Neoplasma, Neoplastic

Department of Commerce, National Technical Information Service, 5285 Port Royal Road, Springfield VA 22161. **NLM** ZQZ 206 I11BB.

ICRDB CANCERGRAM. CANCER DETECTION AND MANAGEMENT: DIAGNOSTIC RADIOLOGY. See Medicine - Radiology.

ICRDB CANCERGRAM. CANCER DETECTION AND MANAGEMENT, NUCLEAR MEDICINE. (ICRDB CANCERGRAM. SERIES CT02, CANCER DETECTION AND MANAGEMENT. NUCLEAR MEDICINE). **VFOAT** Cancer Detection and Management. Began with Jan. 1978. 0164-1980. Periodical. US. English. mo. US Department of Commerce, National Technical Information Service, 5285 Port Royal Road, Springfield VA 22161. **NLM** ZQZ 241 C24N. *ICRDB Cancergram. NCI/ICRDB/CT02, Nuclear Medicine in Cancer Diagnosis and Management, 0190-0129.*

ICRDB CANCERGRAM. CELL BIOLOGY, CELL KINETICS. (ICRDB CANCERGRAM. SERIES CB09, CELL BIOLOGY. CELL KINETICS). **VFOAT** Cell Biology. **VAT** International Cancer Research Data Bank Cancergram. Cell Biology, Cell Kinetics. Began with Jan. 1978. 0164-1972. Periodical. US. English. mo. US Department of Commerce, National Technical Information Service, 5285 Port Royal Road, Springfield VA 22161. **NLM** ZQZ 206 C24R. *ICRDB Cancergram. Series CB09, Regulation of Cell Kinetics In Vitro and In Vivo, 0164-2979.*

ICRDB CANCERGRAM. CELL BIOLOGY, CYTOGENETICS. (ICRDB CANCERGRAM. SERIES CB12, CELL BIOLOGY. CYTOGENETICS). **VFOAT** Cell Biology. Began with Jan. 1978. 0164-2065. Periodical. US. English. mo. US Department of Commerce, National Technical Information Service, 5285 Port Royal Road, Springfield VA 22161. **NLM** ZQZ 206 C24C. *ICRDB Cancergram. NCI/ICRDB/CB12, Cytogenetics and Cancer, 0190-0048.*

ICRDB CANCERGRAM. CHEMICAL CARCINOGENESIS: AZO DYES, ARYL AMINES, AND RELATED COMPOUNDS. (ICRDB CANCERGRAM. SERIES CK10, CHEMICAL CARCINOGENESIS. AZO DYES, ARYL AMINES, AND RELATED COMPOUNDS). **VFOAT** Chemical Carcinogenesis. Azo Dyes, Aryl Amines, and Related Compounds. Began with Jan. 1978. 0164-2073. Periodical. US. English. mo. US Department of Commerce, National Technical Information Service, 5285 Port Royal Road, Springfield VA 22161. **NLM** ZQZ 202 I11C. *ICRDB Cancergram. NCI/ICRDB/CK10, Carcinogenicity of Azo Dyes, Aryl Amines, and Related Compounds, 0198-9529.*

ICRDB CANCERGRAM. CHEMICAL CARCINOGENESIS: MISCELLANEOUS AGENTS. (ICRDB CANCERGRAM. SERIES CK13, CHEMICAL CARCINOGENESIS. MISCELLANEOUS AGENTS). **VFOAT** Chemical Cacinogenesis. Publication began with June 1978. 0190-3411. Periodical. US. English. mo. US Department of Commerce, National Technical Information Service, 5285 Port Royal Road, Springfield VA 22161. **NLM** ZQZ 202 I11CM.

ICRDB CANCERGRAM. CHEMICAL CARCINOGENESIS. POLYCYCLIC AROMATIC HYDROCARBONS AND RELATED COMPOUNDS. (ICRDB CANCERGRAM. SERIES CK07, CHEMICAL CARCINOGENESIS. POLYCYCLIC AROMATIC HYDROCARBONS AND RELATED COMPOUNDS). **VFOAT** Chemical Carcinogenesis. Polycyclic Aromatic Hydrocarbons and Related Compounds. **VAT** International Cancer Research Data Bank Cancergram. Chemical Carcinogenesis. Polycyclic Aromatic Hydrocarbons and Related Compound. Began with Jan. 1978. 0190-003X. Periodical. US. English. mo. US Department of Commerce, National Technical Information Service, 5285 Port Royal Road, Springfield VA 22161. **NLM** ZQZ 202 C23P. *ICRDB Cancergram. NCI/ICRDB/CK07, Carcinogenicity of Polycyclic Aromatic Hydrocarbons and Related Compounds, 0164-2952.*

ICRDB CANCERGRAM. CHEMICAL CARCINOGENS: NITROSO COMPOUNDS. (ICRDB CANCERGRAM. SERIES CK01, CHEMICAL CARCINOGENESIS. NITROSO COMPOUNDS). **VFOAT** Nitroso Compounds. Began with Jan. 1978. 0164-2081. Periodical. US. English. mo. US Department of Commerce, National Technical Information Service, 5285 Port Royal Road, Springfield VA 22161. **NLM** ZQZ 202 C23N. *ICRDB Cancergram. Carcinogenicity of Nitroso Compounds, 0164-2960.*

ICRDB CANCERGRAM. CLINICAL CANCER IMMUNOLOGY AND IMMUNOTHERAPY. (ICRDB CANCERGRAM. SERIES CT06, CLINICAL CANCER IMMUNOLOGY AND IMMUNOTHERAPY). **VFOAT** Clinical Cancer Immunology and Immunotherapy. Began with Jan. 1978. 0164-209X. Periodical. US. English. mo. US Department of Commerce, National Technical Information Service, 5285 Port Royal Road, Springfield VA 22161. **NLM** ZQZ 266 C24I. *ICRDB Cancergram. Series CT06, Immunotherpay and Clinical Cancer Immunology, 0190-0102.*

ICRDB CANCERGRAM. CLINICAL EVALUATION AND TREATMENT OF MULTIPLE MYELOMA AND OTHER GAMMOPATHIES. (ICRDB CANCERGRAM. SERIES CT13, CLINICAL EVALUATION AND TREATMENT OF MULTIPLE MYELOMA AND OTHER GAMMOPATHIES). **VFOAT** Clinical Evaluation and Treatment of Multiple Myeloma and Other Gammopathies. Began with Jan. 1978. 0164-2138. Periodical. US. English. mo. US Department of Commerce, National Technical Information Service, 5285 Port Royal Road, Springfield VA 22161. **NLM** ZWH 540 I11CE. *ICRDB Cancergram. NCI/ICRDB/CT13, Clinical Evaluation and Treatment of Multiple Myeloma and Other Monoclonal Gammopathies, 0164-2936.*

ICRDB CANCERGRAM. CLINICAL TREATMENT OF CANCER: RADIATION THERAPY. (ICRDB CANCERGRAM. SERIES CT15, CLINICAL TREATMENT OF CANCER. RADIATION THERAPY). **VFOAT** Clinical Treatment of Cancer. Began with Feb. 1978. 0164-2146. Periodical. US. English. mo. US Department of Commerce, National Technical Information Service, 5285 Port Royal Road, Springfield VA 22161. **NLM** ZQZ 269 I11CR.

ICRDB CANCERGRAM. CNS MALIGNANCIES: DIAGNOSIS, TREATMENT. (ICRDB CANCERGRAM. SERIES CT18, CNS MALIGNANCIES: DIAGNOSIS, TREATMENT). **VFOAT** CNS Malignancies. Diagnosis, Treatment. Began with Apr. 1978. 0190-342X. Periodical. US. English. mo. US Department of Commerce, National Technical Information Service, 5285 Port Royal Road, Springfield VA 22161. **NLM** ZWL 358 I11.

ICRDB CANCERGRAM. COLO-RECTAL CANCERS: DIAGNOSIS, TREATMENT. (ICRDB CANCERGRAM. SERIES CT07, COLO-RECTAL CANCERS. DIAGNOSIS, TREATMENT). **VFOAT** Colo-Rectal Cancers. Began with Jan. 1978. 0164-2405. Periodical. US. English. mo. US Department of Commerce, National Technical Information Service, 5285 Port Royal Road, Springfield VA 22161. **NLM** ZWI 520 C23DE. *ICRDB Cancergram. Series CT07, The Detection, Diagnosis, and Therapy of Human Colo-Rectal Cancers.*

ICRDB CANCERGRAM. CYTOLOGY: TECHNIQUES, APPLICATIONS. (ICRDB CANCERGRAM. SERIES CB21, CYTOLOGY. TECHNIQUES, APPLICATIONS). **VFOAT** Cytology. Began with Mar. 1978. 0164-2413. Periodical. US. English. mo. US Department of Commerce, National Technical Information Service, 5285 Port Royal Road, Springfield VA 22161. **NLM** ZQZ 241 I11CT.

ICRDB CANCERGRAM. DIETARY ASPECTS OF CARCINOGENESIS. (ICRDB CANCERGRAM. SERIES CK03, DIETARY ASPECTS OF CARCINOGENESIS). Began with May 16, 1977. 0164-2162. Periodical. US. English. mo. US Department of Commerce, National Technical Information Service, 5285 Port Royal Road, Springfield VA 22161. **NLM** ZQZ 202 C23D. *Cancergram on Dietary Aspects of Carcinogenesis, 0164-0992.*

ICRDB CANCERGRAM. DNA TUMOR VIRUSES IN NONPRIMATE SYSTEMS. (ICRDB CANCERGRAM. SERIES CB11, DNA TUMOR VIRUSES IN NON-PRIMATE SYSTEMS). **VFOAT** DNA Tumor Viruses in Non-Primate Systems. Began with June 16, 1977. 0164-2154. Periodical. US. English. mo. US Department of Commerce, National Technical Information Service, 5285 Port Royal Road, Springfield VA 22161. **NLM** ZQW 166 C21D.

Cancergram on DNA Tumor Viruses in Non-Primate Systems, 0164-1166.

ICRDB CANCERGRAM. ENDOCRINE TUMORS: DIAGNOSIS, TREATMENT PATHOPHYSIOLOGY. (ICRDB CANCERGRAM. SERIES CT21, ENDOCRINE TUMORS. DIAGNOSIS, TREATMENT, PATHOPHYSIOLOGY). **VFOAT** Endocrine Tumors. Began with Nov. 1978. 0191-6661. Periodical. US. English. mo. US Department of Commerce, National Technical Information Service, 5285 Port Royal Road, Springfield VA 22161. **NLM** ZWK 100.3 I11.

ICRDB CANCERGRAM. ENVIRONMENTAL AND OCCUPATIONAL CARCINOGENESIS. (ICRDB CANCERGRAM. SERIES CK02, ENVIRONMENTAL AND OCCUPATIONAL CARCINOGENESIS). **VFOAT** Environmental and Occupational Carcinogenesis. Began with Jan. 1978. 0164-2421. Periodical. US. English. mo. US Department of Commerce, National Technical Information Service, 5285 Port Royal Road, Springfield VA 22161. **NLM** ZQZ 202 C23E. *ICRDB Cancergram. NCI/ICRDB/CK 02, Etiology of Cancer in the General Population, 0190-0080.*

ICRDB CANCERGRAM. GENITO-URINARY CANCERS: DIAGNOSIS, TREATMENT. (ICRDB CANCERGRAM. SERIES CT16, GENITO-URINARY CANCERS. DIAGNOSIS, TREATMENT). **VFOAT** Genito-Urinary Cancers. Began with Jan. 1978. 0164-243X. Periodical. US. English. mo. US Department of Commerce, National Technical Information Service, 5285 Port Royal Road, Springfield VA 22161. **NLM** ZWJ 160 I11DG. *ICRDB Cancergram. Series CT16, The Detection, Diagnosis, and Treatment of Genitourinary Cancers, 0190-0153.*

ICRDB CANCERGRAM. GYNECOLOGIC TUMORS: DIAGNOSIS, TREATMENT. (ICRDB CANCERGRAM. SERIES CT17, GYNECOLOGIC TUMORS. DIAGNOSIS, TREATMENT). **VFOAT** Gynecologic Tumors. Began with Jan. 1978. 0164-2367. Periodical. US. English. mo. US Department of Commerce, National Technical Information Service, 5285 Port Royal Road, Springfield VA 22161. **NLM** ZWP 145 I11G.

ICRDB CANCERGRAM. HORMONES IN CANCER-RELATED BIOLOGY: NON-STEROID HORMONES. (ICRDB CANCERGRAM. SERIES CB24, HORMONES IN CANCER-RELATED BIOLOGY. NON-STEROID HORMONES). **VFOAT** Non-Steroid Hormones. Began with July 1978. 0190-4442. Periodical. US. English. mo. US Department of Commerce, National Technical Information Service, 5285 Port Royal Road, Springfield VA 22161. **NLM** ZQZ 206 I11H.

ICRDB CANCERGRAM. HORMONES IN CANCER-RELATED BIOLOGY: STEROID HORMONES. (ICRDB CANCERGRAM. SERIES CB07, HORMONES IN CANCER-RELATED BIOLOGY. STEROID HORMONES). **VFOAT** Hormones in Cancer-Related Biology. Began with Jan. 1978. 0164-2375. Periodical. US. English. mo. US Department of Commerce, National Technical Information Service, 5285 Port Royal Road, Springfield VA 22161. **NLM** ZQZ 206 C24SH. *ICRDB Cancergram. Series CB07, Steroid Hormones in Cancer-Related Biology, 0164-2987.*

ICRDB CANCERGRAM. IMMUNOBIOLOGY AND CANCER: ANTIBODIES AND HUMORAL IMMUNITY. (ICRDB CANCERGRAM. SERIES CB08, IMMUNOBIOLOGY AND CANCER. ANTIBODIES AND HUMORAL IMMUNITY). **VFOAT** Immunobiology and Cancer. Began with Jan. 1978. 0164-2324. Periodical. US. English. mo. US Department of Commerce, National Technical Information Service, 5285 Port Royal Road, Springfield VA 22161. **NLM** ZQZ 206 C24TK. *ICRDB Cancergram. Series CB08, Tumor Antibodies, 0190-0196.*

ICRDB CANCERGRAM. IMMUNOBIOLOGY AND CANCER: FUNCTIONAL ASPECTS OF CELLULAR IMMUNITY. (ICRDB CANCERGRAM. SERIES CB15, IMMUNOBIOLOGY AND CANCER. FUNCTIONAL ASPECTS OF CELLULAR IMMUNITY). **VFOAT** Immunobiology and Cancer. Functional Aspects of Cellular Immunity. Began with Mar. 1978. 0190-3543. Periodical. US. English. mo. US Department of Commerce, National

Medicine—Neoplasma, Neoplastic

Technical Information Service, 5285 Port Royal Road, Springfield VA 22161. **NLM** ZQZ 206 I11J.

ICRDB CANCERGRAM. IMMUNOBIOLOGY AND CANCER: IDENTIFICATION AND CHARACTERIZATION OF IMMUNE CELLS. (ICRDB CANCERGRAM. SERIES CB17, IMMUNOBIOLOGY AND CANCER. IDENTIFICATION AND CHARACTERIZATION OF IMMUNE CELLS). **VFOAT** Immunobiology and Cancer. **VAT** International Cancer Research Data Bank Cancergram. Immunobiology and Cancer: Identification and Characterization of Immune Cells. Began with Mar. 1978. 0190-3551. Periodical. US. English. mo. US Department of Commerce, National Technical Information Service, 5285 Port Royal Road, Springfield VA 22161. **NLM** ZQZ 206 I11JE.

ICRDB CANCERGRAM. IMMUNOBIOLOGY AND CANCER: THE MAJOR HISTOCOMPATIBILITY COMPLEX. (ICRDB CANCERGRAM. SERIES CB03, IMMUNOBIOLOGY AND CANCER. THE MAJOR HISTOCOMPATIBILITY COMPLEX). **VFOAT** Immunobiology and Cancer. Began with Jan. 1978. 0164-2391. Periodical. US. English. mo. US Department of Commerce, National Technical Information Service, 5285 Port Royal Road, Springfield VA 22161. **DD** Cancer. **NLM** ZQZ 206 C24TH. *ICRDB Cancergram. Series CB03, The Major Histocompatibility Complex, 0190-017X.*

ICRDB CANCERGRAM. IMMUNOBIOLOGY AND CANCER: TUMOR-ASSOCIATED ANTIGENS. (ICRDB CANCERGRAM. SERIES CB05, IMMUNOBIOLOGY AND CANCER. TUMOR-ASSOCIATED ANTIGENS). **VFOAT** Immunobiology and Cancer. Tumor-Associated Antigens. Began with Jan. 1978. 0164-2332. Periodical. US. English. mo. US Department of Commerce, National Technical Information Service, 5285 Port Royal Road, Springfield VA 22161. **NLM** ZQZ 206 C24TL. *ICRDB Cancergram. NCI/ICRDB/CB05, Tumor Associated Antigens, 0198-9537.*

ICRDB CANCERGRAM. LUNG CANCER: DIAGNOSIS, TREATMENT. (ICRDB CANCERGRAM. SERIES CT08, LUNG CANCER. DIAGNOSIS, TREATMENT). **VFOAT** Lung Cancer. Began with Jan. 1978. 0164-2359. Periodical. US. English. mo. US Department of Commerce, National Technical Information Service, 5285 Port Royal Road, Springfield VA 22161. **NLM** ZWF 658 C23TD. *ICRDB Cancergram. NCI/ICRDB/CT08: The Detection, Diagnosis, and Therapy of Lung Cancer, 0190-0145.*

ICRDB CANCERGRAM. LYMPHOMAS: DIAGNOSIS, TREATMENT. (ICRDB CANCERGRAM. SERIES CT05, LYMPHOMAS. DIAGNOSIS, TREATMENT). Began with Jan. 1978. 0164-2464. Periodical. US. English. mo. US Department of Commerce, National Technical Information Service, 5285 Port Royal Road, Springfield VA 22161. **NLM** ZWH 525 I11L. *ICRDB Cancergram. NCI/ICRDB/CT04, Diagnosis and Treatment of Hodgkin's Disease, 0190-0064; ICRDB Cancergram. NCI/ICRDB/CT05, Diagnosis and Treatment of Non-Hodgkin's Lymphomas, 0190-0072.*

ICRDB CANCERGRAM. MECHANISMS OF CARCINOGENESIS: ACTIVATION AND METABOLISM OF CARCINOGENS. (ICRDB CANCERGRAM. SERIES CK08, MECHANISMS OF CARCINOGENESIS. ACTIVATION AND METABOLISM OF CARCINOGENS). **VFOAT** Mechanisms of Carcinogenesis. Began with Jan. 1978. 0164-2383. Periodical. US. English. mo. US Department of Commerce, National Technical Information Service, 5285 Port Royal Road, Springfield VA 22161. **NLM** ZQZ 202 I11A. *ICRDB Cancergram. NCI/ICRDB/CK08, Activation and Metabolism of Carcinogens, 0164-1913.*

ICRDB CANCERGRAM. MECHANISMS OF CARCINOGENESIS: MACROMOLECULAR ALTERATION AND REPAIR. (ICRDB CANCERGRAM. SERIES CK11, MECHANISMS OF CARCINOGENESIS. MACROMOLECULAR ALTERATION AND REPAIR). **VFOAT** Mechanisms of Carcinogenesis. Began with Jan. 1978. 0164-2251. Periodical. US. English. mo. US Department of Commerce, National Technical Information Service, 5285 Port Royal Road, Springfield VA 22161. **NLM** ZQZ 202 I11M. *ICRDB Cancergram. Series CK11, Macromolecular Alteration and Repair in Carcinogenesis, 0190-0110.*

ICRDB CANCERGRAM. MECHANISMS OF CARCINOGENESIS: ONCOGENIC TRANSFORMATION. (ICRDB CANCERGRAM. SERIES CK14, MECHANISMS OF CARCINOGENESIS. ONCOGENIC TRANSFORMATION). **VFOAT** Oncogenic Transformation. Began with June 1978. 0190-4485. Periodical. US. English. mo. US Department of Commerce, National Technical Information Service, 5285 Port Royal Road, Springfield VA 22161. **NLM** ZQZ 202.3 I11LM.

ICRDB CANCERGRAM. MELANOMA AND OTHER SKIN CANCER: DIAGNOSIS TREATMENT. (ICRDB CANCERGRAM. SERIES CT22, MELANOMA AND OTHER SKIN CANCER. DIAGNOSIS, TREATMENT). **VFOAT** Melanoma and Other Skin Cancer. Diagnosis Treatment. Began with Dec. 1978. 0191-667X. Periodical. US. English. mo. US Department of Commerce, National Technical Information Service, 5285 Port Royal Road, Springfield VA 22161. **NLM** ZWR 500 I11.

ICRDB CANCERGRAM. MODIFICATION OF CARCINOGENESIS. (ICRDB CANCERGRAM. SERIES CK04, MODIFICATION OF CARCINOGENESIS). Began with May 1978. 0164-226X. Periodical. US. English. mo. US Department of Commerce, National Technical Information Service, 5285 Port Royal Road, Springfield VA 22161. **NLM** ZQZ 202.3 I11M.

ICRDB CANCERGRAM. MOLECULAR BIOLOGY: CYCLIC NUCLEOTIDES. (ICRDB CANCERGRAM. SERIES CB14, MOLECULAR BIOLOGY. CYCLIC NUCLEOTIDES). **VFOAT** Molecular Biology. Began with Jan. 1978. 0164-2278. Periodical. US. English. mo. US Department of Commerce, National Technical Information Service, 5285 Port Royal Road, Springfield VA 22161. **NLM** ZQZ 206 I11C. *ICRDB Cancergram. Series CB14, Cyclic Nucleotides and Cancer, 0164-2928.*

ICRDB CANCERGRAM. MOLECULAR BIOLOGY: PROTEINS, POLYPEPTIDES, AMINO ACIDS. (ICRDB CANCERGRAM. SERIES CB27, MOLECULAR BIOLOGY. PROTEINS, POLYPEPTIDES, AMINO ACIDS). **VFOAT** Proteins, Polypeptides, Amino Acids. Began with Dec. 1978. 0191-3956. Periodical. US. English. mo. US Department of Commerce, National Technical Information Service, 5285 Port Royal Road, Springfield VA 22161. **NLM** ZQZ 206 I11CA.

ICRDB CANCERGRAM. MOLECULAR BIOLOGY: RNA. (ICRDB CANCERGRAM. SERIES CB26, MOLECULAR BIOLOGY. RNA). **VFOAT** Molecular Biology. **VAT** International Cancer Research Data Bank Cancergram. Molecular Biology: Ribonucleic Acid. Began with Oct. 1978. 0190-4450. Periodical. US. English. mo. US Department of Commerce, National Technical Information Service, 5285 Port Royal Road, Springfield VA 22161. **NLM** ZQZ 206 I11MB.

ICRDB CANCERGRAM. NEOPLASIA OF THE HEAD AND NECK. (ICRDB CANCERGRAM. SERIES CT11, NEOPLASIA OF THE HEAD AND NECK. DIAGNOSIS, TREATMENT). **VFOAT** I.C.R.D.B. Cancergram. Began with May 25, 1977. 0164-2170. Periodical. US. English. mo. US Department of Commerce, National Technical Information Service, 5285 Port Royal Road, Springfield VA 22161. **NLM** ZWE 707 C23N. *Cancergram on Neoplasia of the Head and Neck, 0164-1034.*

ICRDB CANCERGRAM. ONCOFETAL PROTEINS. (ICRDB CANCERGRAM. SERIES CB01, ONCOFETAL PROTEINS). **VFOAT** Oncofetal Proteins. Began with June 17, 1977. 0164-2189. Periodical. US. English. mo. US Department of Commerce, National Technical Information Service, 5285 Port Royal Road, Springfield VA 22161. **NLM** ZQZ 206 C24P. *Cancergram on Oncofetal Proteins, 0164-0976.*

ICRDB CANCERGRAM. ORGAN SITE CARCINOGENESIS. KIDNEY AND URINARY TRACT. (ICRDB CANCERGRAM. SERIES CK17, ORGAN SITE CARCINOGENESIS. KIDNEY AND URINARY TRACT). **VFOAT** Kidney and Urinary Tract. Publication began with Dec. 1978. 0198-9480. Periodical. US. English. mo. US Department of Commerce, National Technical Information Service, 5285 Port Royal Road, Springfield VA 22161. **NLM** ZWJ 160 I11DK.

ICRDB CANCERGRAM. ORGAN SITE CARCINOGENESIS: LIVER. (ICRDB CANCERGRAM. SERIES CK16, ORGAN SITE CARCINOGENESIS. LIVER). Publication began with Apr. 1978. 0164-2197. Periodical. US. English. mo. US Department of Commerce, National Technical Information Service, 5285 Port Royal Road, Springfield VA 22161. **NLM** ZWI 735 I11NS.

ICRDB CANCERGRAM. ORGAN SITE CARCINOGENESIS: LYMPHATIC AND HEMATOPOIETIC TISSUES. (ICRDB CANCERGRAM. SERIES CK20, ORGAN SITE CARCINOGENESIS. LYMPHATIC AND HEMATOPOIETIC TISSUES). **VFOAT** Lymphatic and Hematopoietic Tissues. Nov. 1979-. 0271-9568. Periodical. US. English. mo. US Department of Commerce, National Technical Information Service, 5285 Port Royal Road, Springfield VA 22161. **NLM** ZWH 250 I102.

ICRDB CANCERGRAM. ORGAN SITE CARCINOGENESIS: MAMMARY GLAND. (ICRDB CANCERGRAM. SERIES CK12, ORGAN SITE CARCINOGENESIS. MAMMARY GLAND). **VFOAT** Organ Site Carcinogenesis. Publication began with Feb. 1978. 0164-2294. Periodical. US. English. mo. US Department of Commerce, National Technical Information Service, 5285 Port Royal Road, Springfield VA 22161. **NLM** ZWP 870 I11MG.

ICRDB CANCERGRAM. ORGAN SITE CARCINOGENESIS. REPRODUCTIVE TRACT. (ICRDB CANCERGRAM. SERIES CK18, ORGAN SITE CARCINOGENESIS. REPRODUCTIVE TRACT). **VFOAT** Organ Site Carcinogenesis. **VAT** International Cancer Research Data Bank Cancergram. Organ Site Carcinogenesis. Reproductive Tract. Began with July 1979. 0195-9573. US. English. mo. US Department of Commerce, National Technical Information Service, 5285 Port Royal Road, Springfield VA 22161. **NLM** ZWJ 700 I105.

ICRDB CANCERGRAM. ORGAN SITE CARCINOGENESIS: RESPIRATORY TRACT. (ICRDB CANCERGRAM. SERIES CK15, ORGAN SITE CARCINOGENESIS. RESPIRATORY TRACT). **VFOAT** Respiratory Tract. Began with July 1979. 0193-7553. Periodical. US. English. mo. US Department of Commerce, National Technical Information Service, 5285 Port Royal Road, Springfield VA 22161. **NLM** ZWF 450 I101.

ICRDB CANCERGRAM. PEDIATRIC ONCOLOGY. (ICRDB CANCERGRAM. SERIES CT10, PEDIATRIC ONCOLOGY). **VFOAT** I.C.R.D.B. Cancergram. Began with Jan. 1978. 0164-2308. Periodical. US. English. mo. US Department of Commerce, National Technical Information Service, 5285 Port Royal Road, Springfield VA 22161. **NLM** ZQZ 200 C23C. *ICRDB Cancergram. Series CT10, Childhood Solid Tumors and Lymphomas, 0164-2944.*

ICRDB CANCERGRAM. RADIATION CARCINOGENESIS. (ICRDB CANCERGRAM. SERIES CK06, RADIATION CARCINOGENESIS). **VFOAT** Radiation Carcinogenesis. Began with June 17, 1977. 0164-2200. Periodical. US. English. mo. US Department of Commerce, National Technical Information Service, 5285 Port Royal Road, Springfield VA 22161. **NLM** ZQZ 202 C23R. *Cancergram on Radiation Carcinogenesis, 0164-1190.*

ICRDB CANCERGRAM. REHABILITATION AND SUPPORTIVE CARE. (ICRDB CANCERGRAM. SERIES CT20, REHABILITATION AND SUPPORTIVE CARE). Began with Dec. 1978. 0198-9502. Periodical. US. English. mo. US Department of Commerce, National Technical Information Service, 5285 Port Royal Road, Springfield VA 22161. **NLM** ZQZ 200.3 I11.

ICRDB CANCERGRAM. SARCOMAS AND RELATED TUMORS: DIAGNOSIS, TREATMENT. (ICRDB CANCERGRAM. SERIES CT12, SARCOMAS AND RELATED TUMORS. DIAGNOSIS, TREATMENT). **VFOAT** Sarcomas and Related Tumors. Began with Jan. 1978. 0164-2219. Periodical. US. English. mo. US Department of Commerce, National Technical Information Service, 5285 Port Royal Road, Springfield VA 22161. **NLM** ZQZ 345 I11D. *ICRDB Cancergram Diagnosis and Treatment of Sarcomas and Related Tumors, 0164-2995.*

ICRDB CANCERGRAM. SERIES CK09, ORGAN SITE CARCINOGENESIS. GASTROINTESTINAL TRACT AND PANCREAS. **VFOAT** Organ Site Carcinogenesis. No. 80/08 (Aug. 1980)-. 0737-6138. Periodical. US. English. mo. US Department of

Medicine—Neoplasma, Neoplastic

Commerce, National Technical Information Service, 5285 Port Royal Road, Springfield VA 22161. **NLM** ZWI 149 I11G. *ICRDB Cancergram. Series CK09, Organ Site Carcinogenesis. Gastrointestinal Tract, 0164-2286.*

ICRDB CANCERGRAM. SHORT TERM TEST SYSTEMS FOR CARCINOGENICITY AND MUTAGENICITY. (ICRDB CANCERGRAM. SERIES CK19, SHORT TERM TEST SYSTEMS FOR CARCINOGENICITY AND MUTAGENICITY). **VFOAT** Short Term Test Systems for Carcinogenicity and Mutagenicity. Publication began with June 1979. 0196-2612. Periodical. US. English. mo. US Department of Commerce, National Technical Information Service, 5285 Port Royal Road, Springdfield VA 22161. **NLM** ZQZ 202 I11S.

ICRDB CANCERGRAM. STRUCTURAL AND FUNCTIONAL ASPECTS OF CELL MEMBRANES. (ICRDB CANCERGRAM. SERIES CB06, STRUCTURAL AND FUNCTIONAL ASPECTS OF CELL MEMBRANES). **VFOAT** Structural and Functional Aspects of Cell Membranes. Began with June 9, 1977. 0164-2235. Periodical. US. English. mo. US Department of Commerce, National Technical Information Service, 5285 Port Royal Road, Springfield VA 22161. **NLM** ZQZ 206 C24SM. *Cancergram on Structural and Functional Aspects of Cell Membranes, 0164-1182.*

ICRDB CANCERGRAM. UPPER GASTROINTESTINAL TUMORS. (ICRDB CANCERGRAM. SERIES CT19, UPPER GASTROINTESTINAL TUMORS. DIAGNOSIS, TREATMENT). **VFOAT** Upper Gastrointestinal Tumors. Began with Sept. 1978. 0190-4477. Periodical. US. English. mo. US Department of Commerce, National Technical Information Service, 5285 Port Royal Road, Springfield VA 22161. **NLM** ZWI 149 I11U.

ICRDB CANCERGRAM. VIRAL IMMUNOLOGY. (ICRDB CANCERGRAM. SERIES CB13, VIRAL IMMUNOLOGY). **VFOAT** Viral Immunology. Began with Jan. 1978. 0164-2243. Periodical. US. English. mo. US Department of Commerce, National Technical Information Service, 5285 Port Royal Road, Springfield VA 22161. **NLM** ZQZ 206 I11A. *ICRDB Cancergram. Series CB13, Antigens Associated with Cancer-Related Viruses, 0198-9545.*

ICRDB CANCERGRAM. VIRUS STUDIES IN HUMANS AND OTHER PRIMATES. (ICRDB CANCERGRAM. SERIES CB04, VIRUS STUDIES IN HUMANS AND OTHER PRIMATES). **VFOAT** I.C.R.D.B. Cancergram. Began with June 3, 1977. 0164-2316. Periodical. US. English. mo. US Department of Commerce, National Technical Information Service, 5285 Port Royal Road, Springfield VA 22161. **LC** Virus Studies in Humans and Other Primates. **NLM** ZQW 166 C21V. *Cancergram on Virus Studies in Humans and Other Primates, 0164-1115.*

IMPORTANT ADVANCES IN ONCOLOGY. 1985-. 0883-5896. US. English. an. J B Lippincott Company, East Washington Square, Philadelphia PA 19105. Ed Vincent T Devita Jr, Samuel Hellman and Steven A Rosenberg.

INDIAN JOURNAL OF CANCER. V. 1- Oct. 1963-. 0019-509X. Periodical. II. English. bm. $40.00. Indian Cancer Society, Borges Marg, Parel Bombay 400 012 India. **Tel** 9925671. Ed D J Jussawalla. **Ind/Abst** Life Sci. Collect., Excerpta Med., Biol. Abstr., Chem. Abstr., Nucl. Sci. Abstr., Index Med., Hospit. Lit. Index. **NLM** W1 IN206PT. **CODEN** IJCAAR. bk rev. adv acc. **Circ** 800. Preventive oncology and cancer treatment.

INTERNATIONAL ADVANCES IN SURGICAL ONCOLOGY. *See* Medicine - Surgery.

INTERNATIONAL JOURNAL OF CANCER. **VFOAT** Journal International du Cancer. V. 1- Jan. 1966-. 0020-7136. Periodical. SZ. English (French). mo. $250.00. Alan R Liss Inc, 41 East 11th Street, New York NY 10003. **Tel** (212)741-2515. **Ind/Abst** Life Sci. Collect., Pestdoc, Ringdoc, Vetdoc, Excerpta Med., Energy Inf. Abstr., Environ. Abstr., Biol. Abstr., Chem. Abstr., Nucl. Sci. Abstr., Index Med., Sci. Cit. Index, Abr. Ed. **NLM** W1 IN766B. **CODEN** IJCNAW. *Acta - Unio Internationalis Contra Cancrum, 0365-3056.*

INTERNATIONAL JOURNAL OF RADIATION ONCOLOGY, BIOLOGY, PHYSICS. V. 1- Oct./Nov. 1975-. 0360-3016. Periodical. US. English. mo. Pergamon Press, 395 Sawmill River Road, Elmsford NY 10523. **Ind/Abst** Electron. Commun. Abstr. J., ISMEC Bull., Pollut. Abstr. Indexes, Saf. Sci. Abstr. J., Life Sci. Collect., Excerpta Med., Comput. Control Abstr., Electr. Electron. Abstr., Sci. Abstr. Sect. A. Phys. Abstr., Curr. Contents, Biol. Abstr., Chem. Abstr., Index Med., Energy Res. Abstr., Hospit. Lit. Index, Phys. Abstr., Sci. Cit. Index, Abr. Ed. **LC** RC271.R3. **DD** 616.994064205. **NLM** W1 IN785R. **CODEN** IOBPD3.

INVESTIGATIONAL NEW DRUGS. **VFOAT** Journal of New Anticancer Agents. Vol. 1, No. 1-. 0167-6997. Periodical. US. English. qt. Kluwer Academic Group, PO Box 322, 3300 AH Dordrecht Netherlands. **Ind/Abst** Index Med., Chem. Abstr. **NLM** W1 IN949R. **CODEN** INNDDK.

IRCS MEDICAL SCIENCE. CANCER. (IRCS MEDICAL SCIENCE : CANCER). **VFOAT** Cancer. V. 3- Jan. 1975-. 0305-6724. Periodical. UK. English. mo. $95.00. IRCS Medical Science, PO Box 500/St Leonards House, Lancaster LA1 1PF England. **Tel** (0524)68116. Ed S Johnson. bk rev. Publishes results of original research into all aspects of cancer in man and animals within weeks of completion. Papers fully refereed. *Research on Cancer, 0305-2648.*

JAPANESE JOURNAL OF CLINICAL ONCOLOGY. V. 1- Jan. 1971-. 0368-2811. Periodical. JA. English. sa. $63.00. Japan Publishing Trading Company, PO Box 5030/Tokyo Internatioal Tokyo 100-31 Japan. **Ind/Abst** Life Sci. Collect., Index Med., Biol. Abstr. **NLM** W1 JA95R. **CODEN** JJCOAC.

JNCI, JOURNAL OF THE NATIONAL CANCER INSTITUTE. **Main/Corp** National Cancer Institute (U.S.). **VFOAT** Journal of the National Cancer Institute. V. 61- July 1978-. Periodical. US. English. mo. US Government Printing Office, Superintendent of Documents, Washington DC 20402. **Tel** (202)783-3238. **Ind/Abst** Chem. Abstr. **CODEN** JJIND8. *Journal of the National Cancer Institute, 0027-8874.*

JOURNAL OF CANCER. **VFOAT** Taj Pahlavi Cancer Bulletin. 0378-2360. Periodical. English. ir. **Ind/Abst** Chem. Abstr. **NLM** W1 JO572J. **CODEN** JCANDL. *Cancer Bulletin, 0304-145X.*

JOURNAL OF CANCER AND VIROLOGY. English. mo. Academic Press, 4805 Sand Lake Road, Orlando FL 32819. **Tel** (305)345-4100. **Ind/Abst** Sci. Cit. Index, Abr. Ed., Chem. Abstr.

THE JOURNAL OF CANCER EDUCATION. 0885-8195. Periodical. US. English. qt. Maxwell House, Fairview Park, Elmsford NY 10523.

JOURNAL OF CANCER RESEARCH AND CLINICAL ONCOLOGY. **VFOAT** Cancer Research and Clinical Oncology. V. 93-. 0171-5216. Periodical. English (articles also in German). bm. $345.00. Springer Verlag-New York Inc, 175 5th Avenue, New York NY 10010. **Tel** (212)460-1500. Ed H Busch, H Fujiki, D M Goldenbert, E Grundmann, E Hecker, H M Pinedo, and C G Schmidt. **Ind/Abst** Life Sci. Collect., Pestdoc, Ringdoc, Vetdoc, Excerpta Med., Index Med., Biol. Abstr., Curr. Contents, Chem. Abstr., Energy Res. Abstr., Sci. Cit. Index, Abr. Ed. **NLM** W1 JO574E. **CODEN** JCROD7. Index in last issue of volume - attached. Available in microform edition from publisher. Covers recent developments in tumor therapy, general diagnosis, laboratory diagnosis, diagnostic and experimental pathology, oncologic surgery and epidemiology. *Zeitschrift fur Krebsforschung und Klinische Onkologie, 0084-5353.*

JOURNAL OF CLINICAL HEMATOLOGY AND ONCOLOGY. **VFOAT** Wadley Medical Bulletin. V. 7-. 0162-9360. Monographic Series. US. English. qt. Free to Libraries and Medical Professions. Wadley Institution Molecular Medicine, 9000 Harry Hines Boulevard, Dallas TX 75232. **Tel** (214)351-8571. Ed Amanullah Khan. **Ind/Abst** Life Sci. Collect., Excerpta Med., Biol. Abstr., Chem. Abstr., Sci. Cit. Index, Abr. Ed. **LC** UNC. **NLM** W1 JO588D. **CODEN** JCHODP. bk rev. **Circ** 9,000. (ctrl). All articles pertaining to hematology and oncology and reviewed for publication in the journal. *Wadley Medical Bulletin, 0097-5427.*

JOURNAL OF CLINICAL ONCOLOGY. (JOURNAL OF CLINICAL ONCOLOGY : OFFICIAL JOURNAL OF THE AMERICAN SOCIETY OF CLINICAL ONCOLOGY). Vol. 1, No. 1 (Jan. 1983)-. 0732-183X. Periodical. US. English. mo. $145.00. Grune & Stratton Inc, 111 5th Avenue, New York NY 10003. **Tel** (212)614-3232. **Ind/Abst** Excerpta Med., Index Med., Chem. Abstr. **NLM** W1 JO5895. **CODEN** JCONDN.

JOURNAL OF ENVIRONMENTAL PATHOLOGY, TOXICOLOGY AND ONCOLOGY. (JOURNAL OF ENVIRONMENTAL PATHOLOGY, TOXICOLOGY AND ONCOLOGY : OFFICIAL ORGAN OF THE INTERNATIONAL SOCIETY FOR ENVIRONMENTAL TOXICOLOGY AND CANCER). **VFOAT** JEPTO. Vol. 5, No. 4/5 (July 1984)-. 0731-8898. Periodical. US. English. bm. $115.00 US, $85.00 Others. Chem-Orbital, Box 134, Park Forest IL 60466. **DD** 615. **NLM** W1. *Journal of Environmental Pathology and Toxicology, 0146-4779.*

JOURNAL OF ENVIRONMENTAL SCIENCE AND HEALTH. PART C, ENVIRONMENTAL CARCINOGENESIS REVIEWS. *See* Sanitation, Environmental Technology.

JOURNAL OF NUTRITION, GROWTH AND CANCER. **VFOAT** F.N.P. Journal of Nutrition, Growth, and Cancer. Vol. 1, No. 1 (Mar. 1983)-. 0736-8283. Periodical. US. English. qt. $80.00. Food and Nutrition Press, 155 Post Road East/Suite 6, Westport CT 06881. **LC** RC261.A1. **DD** 616.994. **NLM** W1.

JOURNAL OF SOVIET ONCOLOGY. Vol. 1, No. 1 (Jan.-Mar. 1980)-. 0270-6296. Periodical. US. English (Russian). qt. $75.00 Domestic, $87.50 Foreign. Plenum Publishers Corporation, 227 West 17th Street, New York NY 10011. **Ind/Abst** Biol. Abstr., Curr. Contents. **LC** RC261.A1. **DD** 616.99400947. **NLM** W1 JO901VP. **CODEN** JSONDX.

JOURNAL OF THE NATIONAL CANCER INSTITUTE. (JOURNAL OF THE NATIONAL CANCER INSTITUTE : JNCI). **VFOAT** JNCI, J.N.C.I. Began with V. 1, No. 1, Aug. 1940. 0027-8874. Periodical. US. English. mo. US Government Printing Office, Superintendent of Documents, Washington DC 20402. **Ind/Abst** CIS Abstr., Biol. Abstr., Chem. Abstr., Index Med., Int. Aerosp. Abstr., Nuci. Sci. Abstr., Index U.S. Gov. Period., Energy Res. Abstr. **NLM** W1 JO941C. **CODEN** JNCIAM. (cum index).

JOURNAL OF TUMOR MARKER ONCOLOGY. 0886-3849. Periodical. US. English. qt. $90.00. Mary Ann Liebert Inc, 157 East 86th Street, New York NY 10028.

KLINISCH-ONKOLOGISCHES SEMINAR. V. 1-. 0344-595X. Monographic Series. GW. German. George Thieme Verlag, Postfach 732, Herdweg 63, D7000 Stuttgart 1 West Germany. **LC** UNC. **NLM** W3 KL61.

KOKURITSU GAN SENTA NEMPO. JA. Japanese. ir. Kokuritsu Gan Senta, 1-1 Tsukiji 5-Chome Chuo-Ku, Tokyo 104 Japan. **LC** RC267. **NLM** W2 JJ3 K86N.

KREBSBEKAMPFUNG. V. 1-. 0342-8907. Monographic Series. German. ir. VCH Publishers Inc, 303 NW 12th Avenue, Deerfield Brach FL 33442. **Tel** (305)428-5566. Ed E Grundmann. **NLM** W1 KR339L.

KREBSGESCHEHEN. 0340-5672. Periodical. GW. German. bm. Karl F Haug Verlag/Dr Fischer, Postfach 10 28 40, 6900 Heidelberg West Germany. **Ind/Abst** Excerpta Med. **NLM** W1 KR342.

LEUKEMIA. 0887-6924. Periodical. US. English. mo. Williams & Wilkins Co, 428 East Preston Street, Baltimore MD 21202.

LEUKEMIA ABSTRACTS. *See* Indexes/Abstracts.

LEUKEMIA REVIEWS INTERNATIONAL. Vol. 1-. 0737-7673. US. English. ir. Marcel Dekker Inc, 270 Madison Avenue, New York NY 10016. Ed Marvin A Rich. **LC** UNC. **DD** 616.99419. **NLM** W1 LE928H.

LUDWIG SYMPOSIA. 1-. 0737-142X. Monographic Series. English. ir. **NLM** W3 LU96D.

MACROMOLECULAR ALTERATION AND REPAIR IN CARCINOGENESIS. **Main/Corp** International Cancer Research Data Bank. **Series/Titl** ICRDB Cancergram. Periodical. US. English. Department of Health Education and Welfare, Public Health Service, National Institutes of Health, National Cancer Institute, Springfield VA 22161.

MAGYAR ONKOLOGIA. Vol. 1-. 0025-0244. Periodical. HU. Hungarian. qt. Akademiai Kiado, POB 24, 1363 Budapest Hungary. **Ind/Abst** Excerpta Med., Chem. Abstr. **NLM** W1 MA4045. **CODEN** MGONAD. Index in last issue of volume - loose - separately paged.

Medicine—Neoplasma, Neoplastic

THE MANAGEMENT OF MALIGNANT DISEASE SERIES. 1-. 0144-8692. Monographic Series. UK. English. ir. Year Book Medical Publishers, 35 East Wacker Drive, Chicago IL 60601. Ed M J Peckham and R L Carter. NLM W1 MA57P.

MEDICAL AND PEDIATRIC ONCOLOGY. V. 1- 1975-. 0098-1532. Periodical. US. English. bm. Alan R Liss Inc, 41 East 11th Street, New York NY 10003. Tel (212)741-2515. Ind/Abst Life Sci. Collect., Excerpta Med., Index Med., Biol. Abstr., Chem. Abstr., Sci. Cit. Index, Abr. Ed., Hospit. Lit. Index. LC RC261.A1. DD 616.992005. NLM W1 ME18L. CODEN MPONDB.

MEDICAL AND PEDIATRIC ONCOLOGY. SUPPLEMENT. 1 (1982)-. 0740-8226. Monographic Series. US. English. ir. Ind/Abst Index Med. NLM W1 ME18LA.

MEDICAL ONCOLOGY AND TUMOR PHARMACOTHERAPY. Vol. 1, No. 1-. 0736-0118. Periodical. UK. English. qt. $85.00. Pergamon Press, 395 Sawmill River Road, Elmsford NY 10523. Ind/Abst Life Sci. Collect., Chem. Abstr., Index Med. NLM W1. CODEN MOTPE2.

MEDIGUIDE TO ONCOLOGY. Vol. 1, Issue 1-. 0278-2480. Periodical. US. English. bm. Dellacorte Publications, 767 Lexington Avenue, New York NY 10021. Tel (212)751-2806. NLM W1 ME787FM.

MEMBERSHIP ROSTER, CANCER CLINICAL TRIALS GROUPS AND PROJECTS. Began with issue for Aug. 1977. 0161-8679. US. English. an. National Cancer Institute, NIH Landow Building/Room 4C33, Bethesda MD 20205. LC RC276. DD 616.994002573. NLM QZ 22.1 M533. *Membership Roster, Cancer Clinical Cooperative Groups.*

MEMORIAL SLOAN-KETTERING CANCER CENTER. See Medicine - Medical Centers, Hospitals.

METASTASIS. 1-. 0272-5819. Monographic Series. US. English. ir. G K Hall, 70 Lincoln Street, Boston MA 02111. LC UNC. NLM W1 ME9611BT.

METHODS IN CANCER RESEARCH. V. 1-. 0076-6852. Periodical. US. English. ir. Academic Press, 4805 Sand Lake Road, Orlando FL 32887. Tel (305)345-4100. Ed Harris Busch. Ind/Abst Life Sci. Collect., Biol. Abstr., Chem. Abstr., Sci. Cit. Index, Abr. Ed. LC RC267. DD 616.99400724. NLM W1 ME9615B. CODEN MECRBK.

NATIONAL CANCER INSTITUTE MONOGRAPH. No. 1- Dec. 1959-. 0083-1921. Monographic Series. US. English. Ind/Abst Excerpta Med., Life Sci. Collect., Energy Res. Abstr., Biol. Abstr., Chem. Abstr., Index Med., Nucl. Sci. Abstr. LC RC261. NLM W1 NA34P. CODEN NCIMAV.

NATIONAL CANCER PROGRAM. (NATIONAL CANCER PROGRAM : REPORT OF THE NATIONAL CANCER ADVISORY BOARD SUBMITTED TO THE SECRETARY OF THE DEPARTMENT OF HEALTH AND HUMAN SERVICES FOR SIMULTANEOUS TRANSMITTAL TO THE PRESIDENT OF THE UNITED STATES AND TO THE CONGRESS). Main/Corp United States. National Cancer Advisory Board. VFOAT Report of the National Cancer Advisory Board. Began with issue for 1973. 0196-7029. US. English. an. US Department of Health and Human Services, Public Health Service National Institutes of Health and National Cancer Institute, 9000 Rockville Pike, Bethesda MD 20014. LC RC267. DD 616.99400973. NLM W2 A N1473N.

NATIONAL CANCER PROGRAM. DIRECTOR'S REPORT AND ANNUAL PLAN. (DIRECTOR'S REPORT AND ANNUAL PLAN FOR FY . . . , NATIONAL CANCER PROGRAM). Main/Corp National Cancer Institute (U.S.). VFOAT National Cancer Program. 1979-. 0278-1972. US. English. an. US Department of Health & Human Services, 200 Independence Avenue SW, Washington DC 20201. LC RC276. DD 353.00841. *National Cancer Program, Report of the Director Submitted to the President of the United States for Transmittal to the Congress of the United States, 0095-1781.*

NCI FACT BOOK. Main/Corp National Cancer Institute (U.S.). VFOAT N.C.I. Fact Book. VAT National Cancer Institute Fact Book. Began with 1979. 0270-7950. US. English. an. National Cancer Institute, 9000 Rockville Pike, Bethesda MD 20205. LC RC267. DD 353.00841. Vols. for 1980-1983 distributed to depository libraries in microfiche. *National Cancer Institute Fact Book, 0196-8149.*

NCI GRANT SUPPORTED LITERATURE INDEX. See Indexes/Abstracts.

NCI GRANTS AWARDED. VFOAT N.C.I. Grants Awarded. VAT National Cancer Institute Grants Awarded. Began with 1977/78. 0272-9695. US. English. an. National Cancer Institute, Division of Extramural Activities Grants Financial and Data Analysis Branch, 9000 Rockville Pike, Bethesda MD 20014. NLM QZ 22 AA1 N14.

NCI GRANTS AWARDED BY STATE, CITY, INSTITUTION, AND GRANT NUMBER. Main/Corp National Cancer Institute. Division of Cancer Research Resources and Centers. Grants Financial and Data Analysis Branch. VAT National Cancer Institute Grants Awarded by State, City, Institution, and Grant Number. US. English. an. National Cancer Institute, National Institutes of Health 9000 Rockville Pike, Bethesda MD 20014.

NEOPLASMA. VFOAT Journal of Experimental and Clinical Oncology. Vol. 4- 1957-. 0028-2685. Periodical. CS. Multilingual (articles in English or German, with summaries in Czech, Slovak, English, German or Russian). bm. $108.00. Karger Libri AG, Petersgraben 31, CH-4009 Basel 11 Switzerland. Tel (061)390880. Ind/Abst Life Sci. Collect., Excerpta Med., Index Med., Biol. Abstr., CIS Abstr., Chem. Abstr., Sci. Cit. Index, Abr. Ed. NLM W1 NE199F. CODEN NEOLA4. *Ceskoslovenska Onkologia.*

NEWSLETTER - UNIVERSITY OF TEXAS SYSTEM CANCER CENTER M.D. ANDERSON HOSPITAL AND TUMOR INSTITUTE. (NEWSLETTER - THE UNIVERSITY OF TEXAS SYSTEM CANCER CENTER M.D. ANDERSON HOSPITAL AND TUMOR INSTITUTE). V. 18, No. 4- Nov. 1973-. 0190-2113. Periodical. US. English. bm. NLM W1 NE9983C. *News Letter - University of Texas M.D. Anderson Hospital and Tumor Institute, Houston, 0517-7316.*

NFCR CANCER SYMPOSIA. VFOAT N.F.C.R. Cancer Symposia. VAT National Foundation for Cancer Research Cancer Symposia. No. 1. 0737-6049. Monographic Series. UK. English. ir. Academic Press, 4805 Sand Lake Road, Orlando Fl 32887. Tel (305)345-4100. Ed David C H McBrien. LC UNC. NLM W3 NF575.

NOWOTWORY. V. 1- 1950-. 0029-540X. Periodical. PL. Polish. qt. ARS Polona, Krakowskie Przedmiescie 7, 00-068 Warsaw Poland. Ind/Abst Excerpta Med., Index Med., Biol. Abstr., Chem. Abstr. NLM W1 NO979. CODEN NOWOAL.

NUCLEAR MEDICINE IN CANCER DIAGNOSIS AND MANAGEMENT. Main/Corp International Cancer Research Data Bank. Series/Titl ICRDB Cancergram. Periodical. US. English. Department of Health Education and Welfare, Public Health Service, National Institutes of Health, National Cancer Institute, Springfield VA 22161.

NUTRITION AND CANCER. See Nutrition and Dietetics.

ONCODEVELOPMENTAL BIOLOGY AND MEDICINE. (ONCODEVELOPMENTAL BIOLOGY AND MEDICINE : THE JOURNAL OF THE INTERNATIONAL SOCIETY FOR ONCODEVELOPMENTAL BIOLOGY AND MEDICINE). Vol. 1, No. 1 (Aug. 1980)-. 0167-1618. Periodical. English. bm. $84.75. Elsevier/North-Holland Biomedical Press, PO Box 211, 1000 AE Amsterdam The Netherlands. Ind/Abst Excerpta Med., Biol. Abstr., Chem. Abstr. NLM W1 ON102. CODEN OBIMD4.

ONCOLOGY. V. 21-. 0030-2414. Periodical. SZ. English (French, German or Italian). bm. 496.- Domestic, $237.00 US. S Karger AG, Arnold-Bocklin-Strasse 25, CH-4001 Basel Switzerland. Tel (061)39 08 80. Ed S Eckhardt, K Munk, G P Murphy and H Wrba. Ind/Abst Life Sci. Collect., Excerpta Med., Index Med., Int. Aerosp. Abstr., Biol. Abstr., Chem. Abstr., Curr. Contents, Sci. Cit. Index, Abr. Ed. LC RC261. NLM W1 ON107. CODEN ONCOBS. adv acc. Circ 1,125. Microfilm and microfiche. Findings from basic research are integrated with current theoretic knowledge and discussed in terms of their relevance to the detection and treatment of cancer. *Oncologia.*

ONCOLOGY ABSTRACTS (BETHESDA, MD.). See Indexes/Abstracts.

ONCOLOGY LITERATURE NEWS. V. 1- July 1979-. 0196-6863. US. English. mo. Med Publishing Inc, 50 Route 9 North, Morganville NJ 07751. Tel (201)536-3600. Ed Paul Sherlock. NLM W1 ON107I.

ONCOLOGY NURSING FORUM. See Medicine - Nursing.

ONCOLOGY OVERVIEW. See Indexes/Abstracts.

ONCOLOGY TIMES. Began with: V. 1, 1979. 0276-2234. Periodical. US. English. mo. $24.00. Herlitz Publications Inc, 404 Park Avenue South, New York NY 10016. Tel (609)547-7284. NLM W1 ON107R.

ONCOLOGY UPDATE. Vol. 1-. 0883-4903. Periodical. US. English. an. Medical Publishing Enterprises, One Bridge Plaza North/Suite 270, Fort Lee NJ 07024. DD 616.

ONKOLOGIE. Vol 1- Feb. 1978-. 0378-584X. Periodical. SZ. German. bm. 116.- Domestic. S Karger AG, PO Box, CH-4009 Basel Switzerland. Tel (061)39 08 80. Ed S Eckhardt, JH Holzner and GA Nagel. Ind/Abst Life Sci. Collect., Excerpta Med., Index Med., Biol. Abstr., Chem. Abstr., Curr. Contents. NLM W1 ON167. CODEN ONKOD2. Microfilm, microfiche. An overview of all aspects of cancer and cancer treatment containing contributions to all problems of cancer: from basic research to clinical questions, prevention, early detection, psychological counseling and chemotherapie. *Osterreichische Zeitschrift fur Onkologie, 0377-2004.*

ONKOLOGIJA. (ONKOLOGIIA). 0369-7436. Monographic Series. UR. Russian. mo. $13.50. Victor Kamkin Inc (57957), 12224 Parklawn Drive, Rockville MD 20852. Tel (301)881-5973. Ind/Abst Chem. Abstr. LC UNC. NLM W1 ON172E. CODEN OKLGAR.

OPUKHOLI OPORNO-DVIGATEL'NOGO APPARATA. Periodical. UR. Russian. NLM W1 OP938.

PLASMA THERAPY & TRANSFUSION TECHNOLOGY. VFOAT Plasma Therapy and Transfusion Technology. Began with Vol. 2, No. 1 (Apr. 1981). 0278-6222. Periodical. US. Medicine. qt. $107.00. Laux Company, PO Box 700, Ayer MA 01432. Tel (617)772-2584. Ed Donna Peterson. Ind/Abst Excerpta Med., Chem. Abstr. NLM W1 PL111U. CODEN PTTTDD. bk rev. Circ 700. Medical magazine dedicated to preparation of plasma or cellular components, and therapeutic treatment. *Plasma Therapy, 0196-4267.*

PLEINE FORME. Vol. 1, No 1 (Hiver 1981)-. 0714-735X. Periodical. CN. French. ir. Pleine Forme, a/s Societe Canadienne du Cancer, Bureau 1001/130 Ouest rue Bloor, Toronto Ontario M5S 2V7 Canada. DD 613.8505. *Route au Tabac (Societe Canadienne du Cancer), 0227-6895; Souffle Nouveau, 0229-5075.*

POLYNUCLEAR AROMATIC HYDROCARBONS. 1st-. 0191-2232. US. English. an. Raven Press, 1140 Avenue of the Americas, New York NY 10036. LC RC268.7.H9. DD 616.994071. NLM W3 IN921K.

PRIMARY CARE & CANCER. VFOAT Primary Care and Cancer. Vol. 4, No. 7 (July 1984)-. 0743-8176. Periodical. US. English. mo. $30.00. Dominus Publishing Company Inc, 79 Powerhouse Road, PO Box 67, Roslyn Heights NY 11577. LC RC261.A1. DD 616.994005. *Your Patient & Cancer, 0272-6905.*

PROCEEDINGS - AMERICAN SOCIETY OF CLINICAL ONCOLOGY. Main/Conf American Society of Clinical Oncology. V. 1 (Mar. 1982)-. Periodical. English. ir.

PROCEEDINGS - AMERICAN SOCIETY OF CLINICAL ONCOLOGY. MEETING. (PROCEEDINGS : ANNUAL MEETING OF THE AMERICAN SOCIETY OF CLINICAL ONCOLOGY). Main/Corp American Society of Clinical Oncology. Meeting. VFOAT Proceedings of the American Society of Clinical Oncology. Vol. 1 (Mar. 1982)- – 18th (Apr. 25-27, 1982)-. 0736-7589. US. English. an. Waverly Press Inc, Baltimore MD 21202. Ind/Abst Excerpta Med., Pestdoc, Ringdoc, Vetdoc. DD 616. NLM W1 AM785M. *Annual Meeting of the American Association for Cancer Research. Proceedings, 0197-016X.*

PROCEEDINGS - AMERICAN SOCIETY OF CLINICAL ONCOLOGY. MEETING. Main/Corp American Society of Clinical Oncology. Meeting. Vol. 1 (1982)-. US. English. an. $15.00. Williams & Wilkins, PO Box 64025, Baltimore MD 21264. *Proceedings, 0197-016X.*

Medicine—Neoplasma, Neoplastic

PROCEEDINGS OF INVITATIONAL SYMPOSIUM ON THE SERODIAGNOSIS OF CANCER. Main/Conf Invitational Symposium on the Serodiagnosis of Cancer. 1st- Sept. 1973-. 0190-7581. US. English. NLM W3 IN997.

PROCEEDINGS OF THE ... INTERNATIONAL CONGRESS OF VIRAL ONCOLOGY OF THE T. AND L. DE BEAUMONT BONELLI FOUNDATION FOR CANCER RESEARCH. (THE ROLE OF VIRUSES IN HUMAN CANCER : PROCEEDINGS OF THE ... INTERNATIONAL CONGRESS OF VIRAL ONCOLOGY OF THE T. AND L. DE BEAUMONT BONELLI FOUNDATION FOR CANCER RESEARCH). Main/Conf International Congress of Viral Oncology. V. 1 (1979)-. 0270-2118. US. English. te. Elsevier North Holland, 52 Vanderbilt Avenue, New York NY 10017. NLM W3 IN588.

PROCEEDINGS - ONCOLOGY NURSING SOCIETY. CONGRESS. See Medicine - Nursing.

PROGRESS IN CANCER RESEARCH AND THERAPY. V. 1-. 0145-3726. Monographic Series. US. English. ir. Raven Press, 1140 Avenue of the Americas, New York NY 10036. Ind/Abst Life Sci. Collect., Biol. Abstr., Chem. Abstr. NLM W1 PR667M. CODEN PCRTDK.

PROGRESS IN CLINICAL CANCER. VFOAT Clinical Cancer. V. 1- 1965-. 0079-6166. US. English. ir. Harcourt Brace & Jovanivich, 6377 Sea Harbour Drive, Orlando FL 32887. Tel (305)345-2000. Ind/Abst Energy Res. Abstr., Chem. Abstr., Index Med., Nuci. Sci. Abstr. NLM W1 PR668F. CODEN PCLCA4.

PROGRESS IN EXPERIMENTAL TUMOR RESEARCH. VFOAT Fortschritte der Experimentellen Tumorforschung. 0079-6263. Monographic Series. English. ir. S Karger AG, PO Box, CH-4009 Basel Switzerland. Tel 061-39 08 80. Ed F Homburger. Ind/Abst Life Sci. Collect., CIS Abstr., Nuci. Sci. Abstr., Index Med., Biol. Abstr., Chem. Abstr., Sci. Cit. Index, Abr. Ed. NLM W1 PR668T. CODEN PEXTAR. Overviews of experimental work in key areas of tumor research. Scientists eager to take part in novel approaches to cancer research rely upon this series as a major information source.

PROGRESS REPORT - U.S.-JAPAN COOPERATIVE CANCER RESEARCH PROGRAM. (PROGRESS REPORT). Main/Corp U.S.-Japan Cooperative Cancer Research Program. Began with 1976/77. 0278-5382. US. English. an. National Cancer Institute Office of International Affairs, U S Japan Cooperative Cancer Research Program, 9000 Rockville Pike, Bethesda MA 20205. LC RC267. DD 616.9940072073. NLM W1 UN63703. Report.

PUBLIC EDUCATION ABOUT CANCER : RECENT RESEARCH AND CURRENT PROGRAMMES. Series/Titl UICC Technical Report Series. English. an. Ed Patricia Hobbs. LC RC261, RC266.5. DD 616.994 S, 616.994052.

RADIATION ONCOLOGY ANNUAL. 1983-. 0748-0296. Periodical. US. English. an. Raven Press, 1140 Avenue of the Americas, New York NY 10036. Ed Theodore L Phillips. LC RC271.R3. DD 616.9940642. NLM W1.

RECENT RESULTS IN CANCER RESEARCH. 0080-0015. Periodical. US. English. ir. Springer Verlag, 44 Hartz Way, PO Box 2485, Secaucus NJ 07094. Tel (212)460-1584. Ind/Abst Index Med., Sci. Cit. Index, Abr. Ed., Chem. Abstr. Contains articles on cancer - lung, breast, ovary, and leukemia.

REPORT - FLORIDA. UNIVERSITY, GAINESVILLE. CANCER RESEARCH LABORATORY. Main/Corp Florida. University, Gainesville. Cancer Research Laboratory. 1949-52-. US. English. ir. University of Florida, Cancer Research Laboratory, Gainesville FL 32601. LC RC261.

REPORT OF THE CARCINOGENESIS PROGRAM. Main/Corp United States. National Cancer Institute. Division of Cancer Cause and Prevention. VFOAT Carcinogenesis Program. 1974/75-. 0090-2403. US. English. Office of the Associate Director, Carcinogenesis Program, Division of Cancer Cause and Prevention, National Cancer Institute, Bethesda MD 20014. LC RC268.5. DD 616.994071. Report of the Carcinogenesis Program, 0090-2403.

REPORT OF THE CHAIRMAN - UNITED STATES. PRESIDENT'S CANCER PANEL. (REPORT OF THE CHAIRMAN - UNITED STATES. PRESIDENT'S CANCER PANEL). Main/Corp United States. President's Cancer Panel. 0739-9987. US. English. National Institutes of Health, Bethesda MD 20014. LC RC267. DD 616.9940072073. Vols. for (Oct. 1982-Sept. 1984-) distributed to depository libraries in microfiche.

RESEARCH REPORT - UNIVERSITY OF TEXAS SYSTEM CANCER SYSTEM, M.D. ANDERSON HOSPITAL AND TUMOR INSTITUTE AT HOUSTON. (RESEARCH REPORT - THE UNIVERSITY OF TEXAS SYSTEM CANCER CENTER M. D. ANDERSON HOSPITAL AND TUMOR INSTITUTE). Sept. 1971/Aug. 1973-. 0363-2814. Periodical. US. English. be. NLM W1 RE234HL. Research Report - University of Texas at Houston M. D. Anderson Hospital and Tumor Institute, 0066-1635.

REVIEWS IN CANCER EPIDEMIOLOGY. Vol. 1-. 0166-8544. US. English. Elsevier/North Holland, 52 Vanderbilt Avenue, New York NY 10017. Ed A M Lilienfeld. LC RC261.A1. DD 614.599905. NLM W1 RE257CEF.

REVIEWS IN LEUKAEMIA AND LYMPHOMA. VFOAT Leukaemia and Lymphoma. Vol. 1-. 0377-7855. Monographic Series. English. ir. Elsevier Science Publishing Company Inc, PO Box 1663/Grand Central Station, New York NY 10163. NLM W1 RE251CF.

REVIEWS ON CANCER. Series/Titl Biochimica et Biophysica Acta. Vol. CR1, No. 1-. 0304-419X. Periodical. English. ir. $58.60. Elsevier/North Holland, PO Box 1345, NL-1000 BH Amsterdam Netherlands. Ind/Abst Ringdoc, Pestdoc, Vetdoc. LC QD1.

REVISTA ESPANOLA ONCOLOGIA. Began with 1952 issue. 0482-640X. Periodical. SP. English (Spanish). qt. Inst Nacional de Oncologia, Ciudad Universitaria, Madrid 3 Spain. Ind/Abst Index Med. LC RC261.A1. DD 616.994005.

REVISTA MEXICANA DE CIRUGIA, GINECOLOGIA Y CANCER. See Medicine - Gynecology & Obstetrics.

THE ROLE OF SYNTHETIC AND NATURAL HORMONES IN CARCINOGENESIS. Main/Corp International Cancer Research Data Bank. Series/Titl ICRDB Cancergram. Periodical. US. English. Price upon application. Department of Health Education and Welfare, Public Health Service, National Institutes of Health National Cancer Institute, Springfield VA 22161.

SAARLANDISCHE KREBSDOKUMENTATION. Main/Corp Saarland. Statistisches Amt. German. ir. 9.-. Ger Statistisches Amt, Hardenbergstrasse 3, 6600 Saarbrucken 1 West Germany. Tel (0681)505-969. LC HA1320, RC279.G3. adv acc. (ctrl). The number of cases of human cancer in the Saarland and incidencerates and data about mortality of cancer in this region are published for all sites.

SCHRIFTENREIHE KREBSGESCHEHEN. VFOAT Krebsgeschehen. V. 5-. 0172-0066. Monographic Series. German. ir. NLM W1 SC343G.

SCIENTIFIC REPORT - CANCER INSTITUTE, CANCER INSTITUTE HOSPITAL, CANCER CHEMOTHERAPY CENTER. Main/Corp Gan Kenkyusho. 1973/75-. Periodical. English. ir. NLM W1 GA407R. Selected Papers from Cancer Institute.

SEMINARS IN ONCOLOGY. V. 1- Mar. 1974-. 0093-7754. Periodical. US. English. qt. $69.00. Grune & Stratton Inc, 111 Fifth Avenue, New York NY 10003. Tel (212)614-3110. Ind/Abst Life Sci. Collect., Excerpta Med., Index Med., Cumul. Index Nurs. Allied Health Lit., Biol. Abstr., Energy Res. Abstr., Chem. Abstr., Sci. Cit. Index, Abr. Ed., Hospit. Lit. Index. LC RC261. DD 616.992005. NLM W1 SE489E. CODEN SOLGAV.

SEMINARS IN ONCOLOGY NURSING. See Medicine - Nursing.

SENOLOGIA. V. 1-. 0395-0506. Periodical. French. ir. Masson Publishing USA Inc, 14 East 60th Street, New York NY 10022. Ind/Abst Chem. Abstr. NLM W1 SE58. CODEN SENODW.

SOCIAL ONCOLOGY NETWORK NEWSLETTER. (SOCIAL ONCOLOGY NETWORK . . . NEWSLETTER). VFOAT Social Oncology Network. Vol. 1, No. 1 (Jan. 1985)-. 0882-4398. Periodical. US. English. qt. Social Oncology Network Newsletter, c/o Dr E Claric, Department of Health Professions, Montclair State College, Upper Montclair NJ 07043. DD 616.

SUBJECT INDEX OF EXTRAMURAL RESEARCH ADMINISTERED BY THE NATIONAL CANCER INSTITUTE. See Indexes/Abstracts.

SYOPA. VFOAT Cancer. Vol. 1-9. 0356-3081. Periodical. Fl. Finnish. ir. Free to physicians, 20 Others. Suomen Ayopayhdistys, Liisankatu 21 B, 00170 Helsinki 17 Finland. NLM W1 SY66Q. Syovantorjunta, 0049-2787.

TECHNICAL REPORT - INTERNATIONAL UNION AGAINST CANCER. Main/Corp International Union Against Cancer. V. 1-. 0535-3513. SZ. English. ir. International Union Against Cancer, 3 rue de Conseil- General, 1205 Geneva Switzerland. Ind/Abst Chem. Abstr.

TUMORDIAGNOSTIK & THERAPIE. VFOAT Tumordiagnostik und Therapie. Vol. 3, No. 1-. 0722-219X. Periodical. English (German). ir. $30.00. Ind/Abst Excerpta Med., Energy Res. Abstr., Life Sci. Collect. NLM W1. Tumordiagnostik.

TUMORI. Vol. 1- July-Aug. 1911-. 0300-8916. Periodical. IT. Italian. bm. 90.000. Casa Editrice Ambrosiana, Via Frue 6, 20148 Milano Italy. Tel 0039-2-2390. Ind/Abst Life Sci. Collect., Excerpta Med., Index Med., Biol. Abstr., Chem. Abstr., Sci. Cit. Index, Abr. Ed. NLM W1 TU723. CODEN TUMOAB. bk rev. Circ 2,000. Clinical and experimental aspects of oncology.

UICC MONOGRAPH SERIES. 1-. 0074-9214. Monographic Series. English. ir. Springer Verlag-New York Inc, 175 5th Avenue, New York NY 10010. Tel (212)460-1500. NLM W1 U412.

ULTRASTRUCTURAL PATHOLOGY OF HUMAN TUMORS. Series/Titl Annual Research Reviews. V. 1-2. 0709-2989. CN. English. Eden Press, 4626 St Catherine Street West, Montreal Quebec H3Z 1S3 Canada. DD 616.992005. NLM W1 UL754.

UPPER GASTROINTESTINAL TUMORS, DIAGNOSIS, TREATMENT. Main/Corp National Cancer Institute. International Cancer Research Data Bank Program. Series/Titl ICRDB Cancergram. Oct. 1978-. US. English. mo. Department of Health Education and Welfare, Public Health Service, National Institutes of Health, National Cancer Institute, Springfield VA 22161. ICRDB Cancergram. Upper Gastrointestinal Tumors, 0190-4477.

VOPROSY EPIDEMIOLOGII ZLOKACHESTVENNYKH OPUKHOLEI. Series/Titl Nauchnyi Obzor, Zlokachestvennye Novoobrazovaniia. Vol. 1- 1967-. Periodical. UR. Russian. an. Ed A M Merkov. NLM W1 NA962N VYP.6 Etc.

VOPROSY ONKOLOGII. V. 1- 1955-. 0507-3758. Periodical. UR. Russian. mo. $47.50. Victor Kamkin Inc (70152), 12224 Parklawn Drive, Rockville MD 20852. Tel (301)881-5973. Ind/Abst Life Sci. Collect., Excerpta Med., Pestdoc, Ringdoc, Vetdoc, Index Med., Biol. Abstr., Chem. Abstr., Sci. Cit. Index, Abr. Ed. NLM W1 VO6405. CODEN VOONAW.

WILEY SERIES ON CANCER INVESTIGATION AND MANAGEMENT. VFOAT Cancer Investigation and Management. Vol. 1-. 0749-5935. Monographic Series. UK. English. ir. Wiley, 605 3rd Avenue, New York NY 10158. Ed J M A Whitehouse, C J Williams, and G Canellos. DD 616. NLM W1 WI53H (P).

WILEY SERIES ON NEW HORIZONS IN ONCOLOGY. VFOAT New Horizons in Oncology. Vol. 1-. Monographic Series. UK. English. John Wiley & Sons Inc, 605 Third Avenue, New York NY 10158. Ed Basil A Stoll. NLM W1.

THE YEAR BOOK OF CANCER. See Yearbooks, Almanacs, Directories.

Medicine—Neurology

ZEITSCHRIFT FUR ANTIMIKROBIELLE, ANTINEOPLASTISCHE CHEMOTHERAPIE : ZAC. VFOAT ZAC. Vol. 1, No. 1 and 2 (1983)-. 0724-9004. Periodical. German (with summaries in English). ir. NLM W1.

ZENKOKU HAIGAN KANJA TOROKU. Japanese. ir. LC RC280.L8.

ZENTRALBLATT HAMATOLOGIE, KLINISCHE ONKOLOGIE. (ZENTRALBLATT HAMATOLOGIE-KLINISCHE ONKOLOGIE). VFOAT Haematology-Clinical Oncology. 320- Vol. 0341-2598. Periodical. US. English and German. bm. Springer Verlag-New York Inc, 175 5th Avenue, New York NY 10010. **Tel** (212)460-1500. **NLM** ZWH 100 Z56. *Zentralblatt Hamatologie, 0301-5890.*

ZHONGHUA ZHONGLIU ZAZHI. (CHUNG-HUA CHUNG LIU TSA CHIH). VFOAT Chinese Journal of Oncology. Vol. 1- 1979-. 0253-3766. Periodical. Chinese. qt. **Ind/Abst** Excerpta Med., Index Med., Biol. Abstr., Chem. Abstr. **NLM** W1 CH979ID. **CODEN** CCLCDY.

NEUROLOGY

ABMS DIRECTORY OF CERTIFIED NEUROLOGICAL SURGEONS. See Yearbooks, Almanacs, Directories.

ABMS DIRECTORY OF CERTIFIED NEUROLOGISTS. See Yearbooks, Almanacs, Directories.

ACTA NEUROBIOLOGIAE EXPERIMENTALIS. V. 30- 1970-. 0065-1400. Periodical. PL. English. bm. ARS Polona, Krakowskie Przedmiescie 7, 00-068 Warsaw Poland. **Ind/Abst** Life Sci. Collect., Excerpta Med., Index Med., Biol. Abstr., Chem. Abstr., Psychol. Abstr., Bibliogr. Agric., Sci. Cit. Index, Abr. Ed. **LC** QP351. **NLM** W1 AC8655. **CODEN** ANEXAC. *Acta Biologiae Experimentalis.*

ACTA NEUROLOGICA. V. 33, No. 6 (Dec. 1978). 0001-6276. Periodical. IT. English (Italian). bm. $80.00. Clinica Neurologica, Via Sergio Pansini 5, 80131 Napoli Italy. **Tel** (081)466052. Ed G A Buscaino. **Ind/Abst** Life Sci. Collect., Excerpta Med., Biol. Abstr., Chem. Abstr., Nuci. Sci. Abstr., Psychol. Abstr., Index Med. **NLM** W1 AC871. **CODEN** ACNLAC. bk rev. adv acc. **Circ** 40. Reports in English in all areas in the field of neurosciences: neurology, neurobiology, neurochemistry, neuropathology, neuropharmacology, neurophysiology, neuropsychology and behavioral sciences.

ACTA NEUROLOGICA BELGICA. V. 70- 1970-. 0300-9009. Periodical. BE. French (summaries in English). bm. $46.00. Associational Society of Scientifique Medica Belgica, 43 rue des Champs, B 1050 Brussels Belgium. Ed A Capon. **Ind/Abst** Life Sci. Collect., Excerpta Med., GeoRef, Biol. Abstr., Chem. Abstr., Index Med., Nuci. Sci. Abstr., Psychol. Abstr., Sociol. Abstr., Lang. Lang. Behav. Abstr., Bibliogr. Index Geol. **NLM** W1 AC872B. **CODEN** ANUBBR. bk rev. adv acc. **Circ** 500. Neurological sciences-clinical and research. *Acta Neurologica et Psychiatrica Belgica, 0001-6284.*

ACTA NEUROLOGICA LATINOAMERICANA. V. 1- Jan./Mar. 1955-. 0001-6306. Periodical. UY. Spanish (articles also in English with summaries in both languages occasionally in French or German). qt. Acta Neurologica Latinoamericana, Instituto de Neurologia Piso 2, Montevideo Uruguay. **Ind/Abst** Biol. Abstr., Chem. Abstr., Nuci. Sci. Abstr., Index Med. **NLM** W1 AC872F. **CODEN** ANLAAC. (cum index).

ACTA NEUROLOGICA SCANDINAVICA. V. 37- 1961-. 0001-6314. Periodical. English (articles in English, French and German). mo. 1110.00 Domestic, 1266.00 Foreign, 1346.00 US/Canada. Munksgaard International Publishers Limited, 35 Norre Sogade, DK-1370 Copenhagen K Denmark. **Tel** 45 12 70 30. Ed H H Pakkenberg. **Ind/Abst** Life Sci. Collect., Pestdoc, Ringdoc, Vetdoc, Excerpta Med., Biol. Abstr., Chem. Abstr., Nuci. Sci. Abstr., Index Med., Psychol. Abstr., Energy Res. Abstr., Sci. Cit. Index, Abr. Ed. **NLM** W1 AC872I. **CODEN** ANRSAS. bk rev. adv acc. **Circ** 1,400. Neurology, neuro-surgery and basic neurological sciences. *Acta Psychiatrica et Neurologica Scandinavica, 0365-5598.*

ACTIVITAS NERVOSA SUPERIOR. V. 1- May 1959-. 0001-7604. Periodical. Czech (text and summaries in English and Russian). qt. **Ind/Abst** Life Sci. Collect., Excerpta Med., Index Med., CIS Abstr., Chem. Abstr., Psychol. Abstr. **LC** QP351.S65. **NLM** W1 AC973. **CODEN** ACNSAX.

ACTUALITES NEUROPHYSIOLOGIQUES. VFOAT Trends in Neurophysiology. Ser. 1- 1959-. 0567-882X. Periodical. articles in English or French, with summaries in the alternate language. ir. Masson 120, Boulevard Saint-Germain, Paris VI France. Ed A M Monnier. **LC** QP351. **DD** 612.805. **NLM** W1 AC9955.

ADVANCES IN BIOCHEMICAL PSYCHOPHARMACOLOGY. V. 1-. 0065-2229. Monographic Series. US. English. ir. Raven Press, 1140 Avenue of the Americas, New York NY 10036. **Tel** (212)575-0335. Ed E Costa and P Greengard. **Ind/Abst** Index Med., Biol. Abstr., Chem. Abstr., Energy Res. Abstr., Sci. Cit. Index, Abr. Ed. **LC** RM315. **DD** 615.78. **NLM** W1 AD437. **CODEN** ABPYBL.

ADVANCES IN CELLULAR NEUROBIOLOGY. V. 1- 1980-. 0270-0794. US. English. ir. Academic Press, 4805 Sand Lake Road, Orlando FL 32887. **Tel** (305)345-4100. Ed Sergey Fedoroff and Leif Hertz. **Ind/Abst** Biol. Abstr., Chem. Abstr. **LC** QP351. **DD** 599.0188. **NLM** W1 AD53IT. **CODEN** ADCND7.

ADVANCES IN CLINICAL NEUROPSYCHOLOGY. Vol. 1-. 0748-4410. US. English. Plenum Press, 233 Spring Street, New York NY 10013. Ed Gerald Goldstein. **LC** QP360. **DD** 616.890705. **NLM** W1.

ADVANCES IN EPILEPTOLOGY. 1977-. Monographic Series. English. ir. **NLM** W1 AD556M.

ADVANCES IN NEURAL AND BEHAVIORAL DEVELOPMENT. Vol. 1-. 8755-0032. US. English. Ablex Publishing Company, 355 Chestnut Street, Norwood NJ 07648. Ed Richard N Aslin. **DD** 591.

ADVANCES IN NEUROCHEMISTRY. V.1-. 0098-6089. Periodical. US. English. ir. Plenum Press, 233 Spring Street, New York NY 10013. **Tel** (212)620-8000. **Ind/Abst** Chem. Abstr. **LC** QP356.3. **DD** 612.8042. **NLM** W1 AD684E. **CODEN** ADNEDZ.

ADVANCES IN NEUROGERONTOLOGY. V. 1-. 0272-0787. Monographic Series. US. English. ir. Praeger Publishers, 521 Fifth Avenue, New York NY 10175. **Tel** (212)599-8410. **Ind/Abst** Chem. Abstr. **LC** UNC. **NLM** W1 AD684F. **CODEN** ANEUD6.

ADVANCES IN NEUROLOGY. V. 1-. 0091-3952. Monographic Series. US. English. ir. Raven Press, 1140 Avenue of the Americas, New York NY 10036. **Tel** (212)575-0335. **Ind/Abst** Life Sci. Collect., Index Med., Biol. Abstr., Chem. Abstr., Energy Res. Abstr., Hospit. Lit. Index. **LC** RC321. **DD** 616.805. **NLM** W1 AD684H. **CODEN** ADNRA3.

ADVANCES IN NEUROPSYCHOLOGY AND BEHAVIORAL NEUROLOGY. Vol. 1-. 0741-8957. US. English. Guilford Press, 200 Park Avenue South, New York NY 10003. Ed Kenneth M Heilman and Paul Satz. **LC** QP401. **DD** 612.8. **NLM** W1 AD684J.

ADVANCES IN PAIN RESEARCH AND THERAPY. V. 1-. 0146-0722. Monographic Series. US. English. ir. Raven Press, 1140 Avenue of the Americas, New York NY 10036. Ed J J Bonica and D G Albe-Fessard. **Ind/Abst** Biol. Abstr., Chem. Abstr., Sci. Cit. Index, Abr. Ed. **NLM** W1 AD706. **CODEN** APRTDE.

ADVANCES IN STEREOENCEPHALOTOMY. V. 1- 1962-. 0065-3381. Monographic Series. SZ. English. ir. S Karger Ag, PO Box, CH-4009 Basel Switzerland. **Tel** 061-39 08 80. Ed Ph L Gildenberg. **Ind/Abst** Index Med. **NLM** W1 AD874 (P. Fascinating technical advances applied in the treatment of neurologic disease.

AKTUELLE FRAGEN DER PSYCHIATRIE UND NEUROLOGIE. See Medicine - Psychiatry, Psychopathology.

AMERICAN JOURNAL OF E.E.G. TECHNOLOGY. (THE AMERICAN JOURNAL OF EEG TECHNOLOGY). VAT American Journal of Electroencephalography Technology. V. 1- March 1961-. 0002-9238. Periodical. US. English. qt. $28.00. American Society of EEG Technologists, 6th at Quint, Carroll IA 51401. **Tel** (712)792-2978. Ed Sharon Franklin. **Ind/Abst** Hospit. Lit. Index, Excerpta Med., Psychol. Abstr., Comput. Control Abstr., Electr. Electron. Abstr., Sci. Abstr. Sect. A. Phys. Abstr., Phys. Abstr. **LC** RC386.5. **NLM** W1 AM451. **CODEN** AJETA6. bk rev. adv acc. **Circ** 3,200. (ctrl). Presents papers on clinical and scientific levels and book reviews on EEG, evoked potential, and related neurodiagnostic topics.

ANNALS OF NEUROLOGY. V. 1- Jan. 1977-. 0364-5134. Periodical. US. English. mo. $74.50. Little Brown & Company, 34 Beacon Street, Boston MA 02106. **Tel** (617)227-0730. Ed Arthur K Asbury. **Ind/Abst** Life Sci. Collect., Excerpta Med., Index Med., Biol. Abstr., Chem. Abstr., Energy Res. Abstr., Hospit. Lit. Index, Sci. Cit. Index, Abr. Ed. **LC** RC321. **DD** 616.8005. **NLM** W1 AN6151. **CODEN** ANNED3. bk rev. adv acc. **Circ** 8,800. A leading voice in the community of physicians and scientists interested in the human nervous and neuromuscular systems and their diseases.

ANNUAL REPORT - BOARD OF SCIENTIFIC COUNSELORS, NINDS, NATIONAL INSTITUTES OF HEALTH. Main/Corp National Institute of Neurological Diseases and Stroke. Board of Scientific Counselors. US. English. an. National Institute of Neurological Diseases and Stroke, National Institutes of Health 9000 Rockville Pike, Bethesda MD 20014.

ANNUAL REPORT - EPILEPSY ADVISORY COMMITTEE, NATIONAL INSTITUTES OF HEALTH. Main/Corp National Institute of Neurological and Communicative Disorders and Stroke. Epilepsy Advisory Committee. US. English. an. National Institute of Neurological and Communicative Disorders and Stroke, 9000 Rockville Pike, Bethesda MD 20014. *Annual Report - Epilepsy Advisory Committee, National Institutes of Health.*

ANNUAL REPORT - NATIONAL ADVISORY NEUROLOGICAL AND COMMUNICATIVE DISORDERS AND STROKE COUNCIL. Main/Corp National Advisory Neurological and Communicative Disorders and Stroke Council (U.S.). US. English. an. National Advisory Neurological and Communicative Disorders and Stroke Council, National Institutes of Health 9000 Rockville Pike, Bethesda MD 20014.

ANNUAL REPORT - NATIONAL INSTITUTE OF NEUROLOGICAL AND COMMUNICATIVE DISORDERS AND STROKE. (ANNUAL REPORT). Main/Corp National Institute of Neurological and Communicative Disorders and Stroke. 0733-4508. US. English. an. National Institute of Neurological and Communicative Disorders and Stroke, 9000 Rockville Pike, Bethesda MD 20205. **LC** RC346. **DD** 353.00841.

ANNUAL REPORT - NEUROLOGICAL DISORDERS PROGRAM-PROJECT REVIEW A COMMITTEE, NATIONAL INSTITUTES OF HEALTH. Main/Corp National Institute of Neurological Diseases and Stroke. Neurological Disorders Program-Project Review A Committee. -1973/74. US. English. an. National Institute of Neurological Diseases and Stroke, National Institutes of Health 9000 Rockville Pike, Bethesda MD 20014.

ANNUAL REPORT - NEUROLOGICAL DISORDERS PROGRAM-PROJECT REVIEW B COMMITTEE, NATIONAL INSTITUTES OF HEALTH. Main/Corp National Institute of Neurological and Communicative Disorders and Stroke. Neurological Disorders Program-Project Review B Committee. 1974/75-. US. English. an. National Institute of Neurological and Communicative Disorders and Stroke, National Institutes of Health, 9000 Rockville Pike, Bethesda MD 20014. *Annual Report - Neurological Disorders Program-Project Review B Committee, National Institutes of Health.*

ANNUAL REVIEW OF NEUROSCIENCE. V. 1- 1978-. 0147-006X. Periodical. US. English. an. $31.00 Domestic, $34.00 Foreign. Annual Reviews Inc, 4139 El Camino Way, Palo Alto CA 94306. **Tel** (415)493-4400. Ed W Maxwell Cowan. **Ind/Abst** Life Sci. Collect., Excerpta Med., Index Med., Comput. Control Abstr., Electr. Electron. Abstr., Sci. Abstr. Sect. A. Phys. Abstr., Biol. Abstr., Chem. Abstr., Psychol. Abstr. **LC** QP351. **DD** 591.18805. **NLM** W1 AN778B. **CODEN** ARNSD5. Comprehensive, thorough coverage of latest advances in neuroscience, written by acknowledged

Medicine—Neurology

experts in the field. Extensive literature citations included.

APPLIED NEUROPHYSIOLOGY. V. 38-. 0302-2773. Periodical. SZ. English. $97.00. S Karger AG, PO Box 352, White Plains NY 10602. Ed L Gildenberg. **Ind/Abst** Life Sci. Collect., Excerpta Med., Index Med., Biol. Abstr., Chem. Abstr., Psychol. Abstr., Lang. Lang. Behav. Abstr., Sociol. Abstr., Sci. Cit. Index, Abr. Ed. **NLM** W1 AP528F. **CODEN** ANPHCL. adv acc. Topics include epilepsy, pain, Parkinson's and Alzheimer's disease, and dyskinesias. Communicates new findings from neuropathology, neurochemistry, neuroendocrinology and basic neurophysiology. *Confinia Neurologica, 0010-5678.*

ARCHIV FUR PSYCHIATRIE UND NERVENKRANKHEITEN. See Genealogy and Heraldry - Archives.

ARCHIVES OF NEUROLOGY. See Genealogy and Heraldry - Archives.

ARCHIVIO DI PSICOLOGIA, NEUROLOGIA E PSICHIATRIA. See Genealogy and Heraldry - Archives.

ARCHIVOS DE NEUROBIOLOGIA. See Genealogy and Heraldry - Archives.

ARQUIVOS DE NEURO-PSIQUIATRIA. V. 1- 1943-. 0004-282X. BL. Portuguese (articles in English, French, Italian or Spanish with summaries in the various languages). qt. Arquivos de Neuro-Psiquiatria, Caixa Postal 30 657, 01000 Sao Paulo Sp Brazil. **Tel** (011)287 9726. Ed O Lange. **Ind/Abst** Psychol. Abstr., Index Med., Sociol. Abstr., Hospit. Lit. Index, Lang. Lang. Behav. Abstr., Excerpta Med. **NLM** W1 AR917. **CODEN** ANPIAM. bk rev. adv acc. **Circ** 1,000. (ctrl). Original papers on: neurology, psychiatry and neurosciences.

AUBE. (L'AUBE). No. 1 (Jan. 1981)-. 0229-3587. Periodical. CN. French (English). qt. Free. Fondation Parkinson du Quebec, 110 Ouest Av des Pins, Montreal Quebec H2W 1R7 Canada. **DD** 616.833060714.

BEHAVIOURAL BRAIN RESEARCH. Vol. 1, No. 1 (Feb. 1980)-. 0166-4328. Periodical. English. mo. Elsevier Science Publishers, PO Box 211, 1000 AE Amsterdam Netherlands. **Tel** (020)5803.911. **Ind/Abst** Life Sci. Collect., Excerpta Med., Index Med., Biol. Abstr., Chem. Abstr., Psychol. Abstr. **NLM** W1 BE135DE. **CODEN** BBREDI.

BEITRAGE ZUR KLINISCHEN NEUROLOGIE UND PSYCHIATRIE. V. 49-. 0138-5097. English (articles principally in German, occasionally in English). an. Ed Karl Seidel. **Ind/Abst** Index Med. **NLM** W1 BE35TH. *Sammlung Zwangloser Abhandlungen Aus Dem Gebiete der Psychiatrie Und Neurologie.*

BIBLIOTECA DE NEUROLOGIA Y CONDUCTA. Monographic Series. Spanish. ir. **NLM** W1 BI336B.

BIOLOGICAL PSYCHIATRY. See Medicine - Psychiatry, Psychopathology.

BIOSIS/CAS SELECTS. HORMONES & GENE EXPRESSION. See Biology - Genetics.

BIOSIS/CAS SELECTS. NEURORECEPTORS. See Indexes/Abstracts.

BOLETIN DE ESTUDIOS MEDICOS Y BIOLOGICOS. See Biology.

BRAIN; A JOURNAL OF NEUROLOGY. V. 1- 1878-. 0006-8950. Periodical. UK. English. qt. Oxford University Press, Press Road, Neasden London NW10 0DD England. **Ind/Abst** Life Sci. Collect., Pestdoc, Ringdoc, Vetdoc, Excerpta Med., Index Med., Chem. Abstr. **LC** RC321. **NLM** W1 BR112. **CODEN** BRAIAK.

BRAIN & DEVELOPMENT. VFOAT Brain and Development. V. 1-. 0387-7604. Periodical. JA. English. qt. $70.00. Japan Publishing Trading Company Ltd, PO Box 5030 Tokyo International, Tokyo 100-31 Japan. **Ind/Abst** Life Sci. Collect., Excerpta Med., Index Med., Sci. Cit. Index, Abr. Ed., Index Med., Excerpta Med. **NLM** W1 BR112H. *No To Hattatsu, 0029-0831.*

BRAIN AND NERVE. VFOAT No to Shinkei. Vol. 1- Nov. 1948-. 0006-8969. Periodical. JA. English (Japanese). mo. 1,950. Igaky Shoin Ltd, 5-24-3 Hongo Bunkyo-Ku, Tokyo 113 91 Japan. **Tel** (03)817-5600. **Ind/Abst** Excerpta Med., Index Med., Biol. Abstr., Chem. Abstr. **NLM** W1 NO102K. **CODEN** BRNED8. bk rev. adv acc. **Circ** 5,000.

BRAIN, BEHAVIOR AND EVOLUTION. V. 1- 1968-. 0006-8977. Periodical. SZ. English. bm. Albert J Phiebig Inc, PO Box 352, White Plains NY 10602. **Tel** (061)39 08 80. Ed G Northcutt and W Riss. **Ind/Abst** Life Sci. Collect., Excerpta Med., GeoRef, Biol. Abstr., Psychol. Abstr., Index Med., Curr. Contents. **LC** QL750. **DD** 596.018. **NLM** W1 BR113. **CODEN** BRBEBE. Topics range from the neurology of speech in man to sensory and motor mechanisms in jawless fish.

BRAIN MIND BULLETIN. VFOAT Brain/Mind Bulletin. V. 1-. 0273-8546. Periodical. US. English. ir. $35.00. Interface Press, PO Box 42211, Los Angeles CA 90042. **Tel** (213)223-2500. Ed Marilyn Ferguson. **Ind/Abst** New Period. Index. bk rev. **Circ** 10,000. A concise report on breakthroughs in learning, psychology, creativity and brain function.

BRAIN RESEARCH. V. 1- 1966-. 0006-8993. Periodical. NE. English. wk. Elsevier Science Publishers, PO Box 211, 1000 AE Amsterdam Netherlands. **Tel** (020)5803-911. **Ind/Abst** Life Sci. Collect., Pestdoc, Ringdoc, Vetdoc, Excerpta Med., Index Med., Int. Aerosp. Abstr., Biol. Abstr., Chem. Abstr., Psychol. Abstr., Sci. Cit. Index, Abr. Ed., Abstr. Anthropol. **LC** QP376. **DD** 599. **NLM** W1 BR114S. **CODEN** BRREAP.

BRAIN RESEARCH BULLETIN. V. 1- Jan./Feb. 1976-. 0361-9230. Periodical. US. English. mo. $420.00. Ankho International Inc, PO Box 380227, San Antonio TX 78280. **Tel** (315)463-0182. Ed Matthew J Wayner. **Ind/Abst** Life Sci. Collect., Excerpta Med., Index Med., Int. Aerosp. Abstr., Biol. Abstr., Chem. Abstr., Psychol. Abstr., Energy Res. Abstr., Sci. Cit. Index, Abr. Ed. **LC** QP376. **DD** 599.0188. **NLM** W1 BR1141. **CODEN** BRBUDU. bk rev. adv acc. Publishes original reports on all aspects of the nervous system: biochemistry, physiology, anatomy, ultrastructure, electrophysiology, neurology, pathology and behavior. Features rapid communications and laboratory instrumentation and computing sections.

BULLETIN - LIGUE DE L'EPILEPSIE DU QUEBEC. (BULLETIN). 0712-2497. Periodical. CN. French (text in English). ir. Ligue de l'Epilepsie du Quebec, 493 Ouest rue Sherbrooke, Montreal Quebec H3A 1B6 Canada. **DD** 616.8530060714.

BULLETIN OF CLINICAL NEUROSCIENCES. Vol. 48 (1983)-. 0736-3583. Periodical. US. English. qt. $50.00. Academic Press, Sand Lake Road, Orlando FL 32819. **NLM** W1. *Bulletin of the Los Angeles Neurological Societies, 0024-659X.*

BULLETIN OF THE LOS ANGELES NEUROLOGICAL SOCIETIES CEASED. V. 31-47. 0024-659X. Periodical. US. English. qt. Harbor-UCLA Medical Center, c/o Hugh B McIntyre, 1000 West Carson Street, Torrance CA 90509. **Ind/Abst** Index Med. **DD** 616. **NLM** W1 BU854R. *Bulletin of the Los Angeles Neurological Society, 0024-659X.*

BULLETIN SIGNALETIQUE 356 : MALADIES DU SYSTEME NERVEUX, MYOPATHIES. VFOAT Maladies du Systeme Nerveux, Myopathies. V. 34- 1973-. Periodical. FR. French. ir. Centre National de la Recherche Scientifique Centre de Documentation, Humaines 54 Blvd Raspail, 75260 Paris Cedex 06 France. Index published separately - free - automatically sent.

CANADIAN JOURNAL OF NEUROLOGICAL SCIENCES. (THE CANADIAN JOURNAL OF NEUROLOGICAL SCIENCES). VFOAT Journal Canadien des Sciences Neurologiques. V. 1- Feb. 1974-. 0317-1671. Periodical. CN. English (includes some text and summaries in French). qt. $20.00. Canadian Journal of Neurological Sciences, 1516-233 Kennedy Street, Winnipeg Manitoba R3C 3J5 Canada. **Ind/Abst** Life Sci. Collect., Excerpta Med., Index Med., Biol. Abstr., Chem. Abstr. **LC** RC321. **DD** 616.805. **NLM** W1 CA596I. **CODEN** CJNSA2.

CELLULAR AND MOLECULAR NEUROBIOLOGY. Vol. 1, No. 1 (March 1981)-. 0272-4340. Periodical. US. English. qt. $115.00 Domestic, $124.00 Foreign. Plenum Publishing Corp, 233 Spring Street, New York NY 10013. **Tel** (212)620-8000. Ed David O Carpenter. **Ind/Abst** Life Sci. Collect., Excerpta Med., Index Med., Biol. Abstr., Chem. Abstr. **LC** QP351. **DD** 599.0188. **NLM** W1 CE1287. **CODEN** CMNEDI. This journal publishes original research abstract neuronal and brain function at the cellular or subcellular levels. Articles use anatomy, physiologic, pharmacologic, and biochemical approaches.

CENTRAL NERVOUS SYSTEM PHARMACOLOGY SERIES. Monographic Series. US. English. ir. Raven Press, 1140 Avenue of the Americas, New York NY 10036. **Tel** (212)575-0335. **NLM** W1 CE35M (P).

CEPHALALGIA. Began with March 1981 issue. 0333-1024. Periodical. English. qt. 93.-. Universitetsforlaget, PO Box 2959-Toyen, Oslo 6 Norway. **Tel** (45)2-27 60 60. Ed John Graham, James W Lance and Federigo Sicuteri. **Ind/Abst** Excerpta Med., Index Med., Biol. Abstr., Chem. Abstr. **NLM** W1 CE565. **CODEN** CEPHDF. adv acc. **Circ** 600. Provides an international forum for original research papers, review articles, and short communications on every aspect of headache.

CEREBROVASCULAR DISEASES. Main/Conf Princeton Conference on Cerebrovascular Diseases. 10th- 1976-. 0146-6917. US. English. ir. Raven Press, 1140 Avenue of the Americas, New York NY 10036. **Tel** (212)741-6800. **Ind/Abst** Chem. Abstr. **LC** RC388.5. **DD** 616.81005. **NLM** W3 C131. **CODEN** CERDDD. *Cerebral Vascular Diseases.*

CESKOSLOVENSKA NEUROLOGIE. Began in 1956. 0009-0581. Periodical. CS. Czech (table of contents and summaries in Russian and English). bm. $56.10. Artia, Ve Smeckach 30, PO Box 790, Praha 1 Czeschoslovakia. **Ind/Abst** Chem. Abstr., Index Med. **NLM** W1 CE897E. *Neurologie a Psychiatrie Ceskoslovenska.*

CHEMICAL DEPENDENCIES. Vol. 4, No. 1-. 0276-5608. Periodical. US. English. qt. $50.00 Domestic, $39.50 Foreign. Spectrum Publications Inc, 175-20 Wexford Terrace, Jamaica NY 11432. **Ind/Abst** Excerpta Med., Index Med., Psychol. Abstr. **LC** RC566.A1. **DD** 616.863005. **NLM** W1 CH246E. *Addictive Diseases, 0094-0267.*

CHILD'S BRAIN. V. 1- 1975-. 0302-2803. Periodical. SZ. English. bm. $128.00. Albert J Phiebig Inc, PO Box 352, White Plains NY 10602. **Ind/Abst** Life Sci. Collect., Excerpta Med., Index Med., Biol. Abstr., Curr. Contents. **NLM** W1 CH705. **CODEN** CHBRAR.

CLINICAL AND EXPERIMENTAL NEUROLOGY. V. 14- 1977-. 0196-6383. US. English. ir. $56.08. PSG Inc, c/o John Wright, 545 Great Road, Littleton MA 01460. **Tel** (800)638-7511. Ed J H Tyrer and M J Eadie. **Ind/Abst** Index Med., Chem. Abstr. **LC** QP351. **DD** 616.805. **NLM** W1 CL664BN.

CLINICAL APHASIOLOGY; PROCEEDINGS OF THE CONFERENCE. Main/Conf Conference on Clinical Aphasiology. 1972. 0195-7015. US. English. an. $22.50. BRK Publishers, Box 17036, Nokomis Station, Minneapolis MN 55417. **LC** RC425. **DD** 616.8552005. **NLM** W3 C5698. Diagnosis and treatment of neurologically-based speech and language disorders.

CLINICAL EEG ELECTROENCEPHALOGRAPHY. (CLINICAL ELECTROENCEPHALOGRAPHY). V. 1- Jan. 1970-. 0009-9155. Periodical. US. English. qt. $35.00. American Medical Electroencephalographic Association, 1824 Wilmette Avenue, Box 558, Wilmette IL 60091. **Tel** (312)256-0080. Ed Frederic H Gibbs. **Ind/Abst** Life Sci. Collect., Excerpta Med., Index Med., Biol. Abstr., Sci. Cit. Index, Abr. Ed. **NLM** W1 CL695. **CODEN** CEEGA. bk rev. adv acc. **Circ** 3,000. (ctrl). The goal of this journal is to convey clinically relevant research and development in electroencephalography to physicians, EEG labs, hospitals and medical libraries. libraries.

CLINICAL NEUROLOGY AND NEUROSURGERY. V. 77- Sept. 1974-. 0303-8467. Periodical. NE. English. qt. 120.00. Van Gorcum & Company BV, PO Box 43, 9400 AA Assen Netherlands. **Tel** 05920/46846. Ed J M Minderhoud. **Ind/Abst** Life Sci. Collect., Excerpta Med., Index Med., Biol. Abstr., Sci. Cit. Index, Abr. Ed. **NLM** W1 CL731Q. **CODEN** CNNSBV. bk rev. adv acc. **Circ** 1,250. (ctrl). An international journal publishing papers and reports on the clinical aspects of neurology and neurosurgery. *Psychiatria, Neurologia, Neurochirurgia, 0033-2666.*

COGNITIVE REHABILITATION. V. 1, Issue 1 (Jan./Feb. 1983). 0738-1069. Periodical. US. English. bm. $25.00. B & B Publishing Co, PO Box 29344, Indianapolis IN 46229. **NLM** W1.

Medicine—Neurology

COLLABORATIVE STUDY ON CEREBRAL PALSY, MENTAL RETARDATION, & OTHER NEUROLOGICAL & SENSORY DISORDERS OF INFANCY & CHILDHOOD. No. 6- July 1972/June 1973-. 0361-3267. Periodical. US. English. US National Institute of Neurological Disease & Strokes, Bethesda MA 20014. Tel (301)496-4000. NLM ZWS 340 B582. Bibliography: The Collaborative Study on Cerebral Palsy, Mental Retardation, and Other Neurological and Sensory Disorders of Infancy and Childhood, 0361-3259.

CONCEPTS IN PEDIATRIC NEUROSURGERY. VFOAT Pediatric Neurosurgery. 1-. 0251-2068. English. ir S Karger Ag, PO Box, CH-4009 Basel Switzerland. Tel 061-39 08 80. Ind/Abst Biol. Abstr. NLM W1 CO459RM. CODEN COPNDZ. Featuring the best academic work contributed by members of the American Society for Pediatric Neurosurgery.

CONNECTICUT STATE DEPARTMENT OF MENTAL HEALTH FACILITIES. INPATIENT STATISTICS. See Statistics.

CONTEMPORARY NEUROLOGY SERIES. V. 1- 1966-. 0069-9446. US. English. ir F A Davis Publishing Co, 1915 Arch Street, Philadelphia PA 19103. Tel (215)5680-2270. Ed Fred Plum. Ind/Abst Chem. Abstr., Energy Res. Abstr. NLM W1 CO769N. CODEN CNRSAG. Presents the latest therapeutic and management methods as well as the most up-to-date research and clinical findings on the major diseases and disorders confronting neurology.

CONTEMPORARY NEUROLOGY SYMPOSIA. V. 1- 1964-. 0069-9454. Monographic Series. US. English. Grune & Stratton, 111 Fifth Avenue, New York NY 10003.

CORE JOURNALS IN CLINICAL NEUROLOGY. Began with Vol. 1, No. 1 Jan. 1978. 0165-1056. Periodical. English. mo. $94.83. Excerpta Medica/Core Journals, PO Box 1126, 1000 BC Amsterdam Netherlands. NLM ZWL 100 C797.

CORTEX. V. 1- June 1964-. 0010-9452. Periodical. IT. English (text in French, German, Italian and Spanish). qt. Masson Publishing Inc, 211 East 43rd Street, Room 1306, New York NY 10017. Tel (516)349-1080. Ind/Abst Life Sci. Collect., Excerpta Med., Index Med., Biol. Abstr., Psychol. Abstr. NLM W1 CO911U. CODEN CRTXAX.

COURANT. (LE COURANT). 0712-3086. Periodical. CN. French. bm. Association de Paralysie Cerebrale du Quebec, Chapitre Mauricie, Bureau 030/1055 Boulevard des Forges, Trois-Rivieres Quebec G8Z 4J8 Canada. DD 362.1968360060714465.

CSA NEUROSCIENCES ABSTRACTS. See Indexes/Abstracts.

CURRENT ADVANCES IN NEUROSCIENCE. Began in 1984. 0741-1677. UK. English. mo. $295.00. Pergamon Press Inc, Maxwell House, Fairview Park, Elmsford NY 10523. Tel (914)592-7700. Ed H Smith. LC QP351. DD 599.0188. Circ 1,200. Gives listings of titles of neuroscientific papers published throughout the world classified into 134 major areas. Full bibliographical citations and reprint addresses are included.

CURRENT NEUROLOGY. V. 1-. 0161-780X. US. English. an. Houghton Mifflin Professional Publishers Medical Division, 2 Park Street, Boston MA 02107. Ind/Abst Chem. Abstr. LC RC321. DD 616.805. NLM W1 CU799F. CODEN CNEUDS.

CURRENT TOPICS IN MEMBRANES AND TRANSPORT. V. 1-. 0070-2161. US. English. ir Academic Press, 4805 Sand Lake Road, Orlando FL 32887. Tel (305)345-41000. Ed Felix Bronner and Arnust Kleinzeller. Ind/Abst Life Sci. Collect., Chem. Abstr., Sci. Cit. Index, Abr. Ed. LC QH601. DD 574.875. NLM W1 CU82J. CODEN CTMTA2.

CURRENT TOPICS IN NEUROBIOLOGY. V. 1-. 0093-4747. Monographic Series. US. English. ir Plenum Publ Corp, 233 Spring Street, New York NY 10013. Tel (212)620-8000. Ind/Abst Chem. Abstr. NLM W1 CU82P. CODEN CTNEDX.

DEVELOPMENTAL BRAIN RESEARCH. Series/Titl Brain Research. Vol. 1, No. 1 (Jan. 1981)-. 0165-3806. Periodical. English. ir. Elsevier Science Publishers, PO Box 211, 1000 AE Amsterdam Netherlands. Ind/Abst Life Sci. Collect., Pestdoc, Ringdoc, Vetdoc, Excerpta Med., Biol. Abstr., Chem. Abstr., Psychol. Abstr. LC QP376. DD 599.0188. CODEN DBRRDB.

DEVELOPMENTAL MEDICINE AND CHILD NEUROLOGY. V. 4- 1962-. 0012-1622. Periodical. UK. English. bm. Lippincott-Harper, 2350 Virginia Avenue, Hagerstown MD 21740. Ind/Abst Life Sci. Collect., Excerpta Med., Women Stud. Abstr., Except. Child Educ. Resour., Biol. Abstr., Index Med., Psychol. Abstr., Lang. Lang. Behav. Abstr., Sci. Cit. Index, Abr. Ed., Sociol. Abstr., Women Stud. Abstr. NLM W1 DE997T. CODEN DMCNAW. (cum index). Available on microfilm. Cerebral Palsy Bulletin.

DEVELOPMENTAL MEDICINE AND CHILD NEUROLOGY. SUPPLEMENT. V. 5- 1962-. 0419-0238. Periodical. UK. English. Blackwell Scientific Publ Ltd, PO Box 88, Osney Mead, Oxford OX2 0EL England. Ind/Abst Life Sci. Collect., Index Med. NLM W1 DE997U. Cerebral Palsy Bulletin. Supplement.

DEVELOPMENTAL NEUROBIOLOGY. V.1- Jan. 1977-. 0146-8227. Periodical. US. English. mo. $28.00. NLM ZWL 100 D489.

DEVELOPMENTAL NEUROSCIENCE. V. 1-. 0378-5866. Periodical. SZ. English. bm. 254.-. S Karger AG, PO Box, CH-4009 Basel Switzerland. Tel (061)39 08 80. Ed B Baumann. Ind/Abst Life Sci. Collect., Excerpta Med., Index Med., Biol. Abstr., Chem. Abstr. NLM W1 DE997UN. CODEN DENED7. adv acc. Publishes neuroscience papers covering all stages of vertebrate, invertebrate and human development.

DEVELOPMENTS IN NEUROSCIENCE. V. 1-. 0165-7003. Monographic Series. English. Elsevier Science Publ Co Inc, PO Box 1663 Grand Central Station, New York NY 10163. Tel (212)370-5520. Ind/Abst Chem. Abstr. NLM W1 DE998K. CODEN DNEUD5.

DIRECTORY OF MEMBERS - SOCIETY FOR NEUROSCIENCE. See Yearbooks, Almanacs, Directories.

DRUGS IN NEUROLOGY. Series/Titl PRM : Physicians' Reference Manuals. No. 1 (1984)-. 0824-7080. Periodical. CN. English. sa. 50.00. Drugs in Neurology, c/o STA Communications 63 Place Frontenac, Pointe-Claire Quebec H9R 4Z7 Canada. Tel (514)695-7623. Ed Paul Brand. DD 615.78. adv acc. Circ 500. (ctrl). Drug reference manuals.

THE EMISSARY. Periodical. US. English. mo. Texas Research Institute of Mental Sciences, 1300 Moursund Street, Houston TX 77030.

ENCEPHALE. (L'ENCEPHALE). Yearly Vol. 1-62, Jan./Feb. 1906-1973 New Series 1973-. 0013-7006. Periodical. FR. French (summaries in English). bm. $63.86. Doin Editeurs, 8 Place de Lodean, Paris 6 France. Tel 325.34.02. Ind/Abst Excerpta Med., Index Med., Chem. Abstr., Biol. Abstr., Psychol. Abstr., Lang. Lang. Behav. Abstr., Sociol. Abstr. NLM W1 EN223. CODEN ENCEAN.

ENCEPHALITIS SURVEILLANCE. (ENCEPHALITIS SURVEILLANCE, ANNUAL SUMMARY). 1976-. 0191-6955. US. English. an. US Department of Health and Human Services, Public Health Service, Center for Disease Control, Atlanta GA 30333. LC RA644.E52. DD 614.59832. NLM W2 A C2M. Neurotropic Viral Diseases Surveillance. Encephalitis, Annual Summary, 0566-7003.

ENDORPHINS. (ENDORPHINS : ENGODENOUS MORPHINOMIMETIC LIGANDS AND OPIATE RECEPTORS IN THE CENTRAL NERVOUS SYSTEM). July/Dec. 1976-. 0161-4584. US. English. NLM ZWL 104 E56.

EPILEPSIA. (EPILEPSIA : THE JOURNAL OF THE INTERNATIONAL LEAGUE AGAINST EPILEPSY). Began with: Ser. 1, Vol. 1, in 1909. 0013-9580. Periodical. NE. English (summaries in French). bm. Raven Press, 1140 Avenue of the Americas, New York NY 10036. Tel (212)575-0335. Ind/Abst Life Sci. Collect., Excerpta Med., Biol. Abstr., Chem. Abstr., Psychol. Abstr., Nuci. Sci. Abstr., Index Med., Sci. Cit. Index, Abr. Ed. LC RC395. DD 616.85305. NLM W1 EP453. CODEN EPILAK.

EPILEPSY. VFOAT Perspectives on Epilepsy,. '78-. 0141-965X. UK. English. an. British Epilepsy Association, Crowthorne House/New Wokingham Road, Wokingham Berkshire England. NLM W1 EP454.

EPILEPSY ABSTRACTS. See Indexes/Abstracts.

ESSAYS IN NEUROCHEMISTRY AND NEUROPHARMACOLOGY. V. 1-. 0147-0205. Periodical. UK. English. ir. John Wiley and Sons, 1 Wiley Drive, Somerset NJ 08873. Tel (212)867-9800. Ind/Abst Index Med., Chem. Abstr. NLM W1 ES674ST. CODEN ENNEDD.

ETAPE. (L'ETAPE). V. 1- Winter 1978-. 0708-1987. Periodical. CN. French. qt. Free to Members. Association de Paralysie Cerebrale du Quebec, 4765 1re Avenue/Bureau 300, Charlesbourg Quebec G1H 2T3 Canada. DD 616.8305.

EUROPEAN ARCHIVES OF PSYCHIATRY AND NEUROLOGICAL SCIENCES. See Genealogy and Heraldry - Archives.

EUROPEAN NEUROLOGY. V. 1, No. 1- 1968-. 0014-3022. Periodical. English. bm. 396.-. S Karger AG, PO Box, CH-4009 Basel Switzerland. Tel (061)39 08 80. Ed H E Kaeser. Ind/Abst Life Sci. Collect., Excerpta Med., Biol. Abstr., Index Med., Nuci. Sci. Abstr., Chem. Abstr., Sci. Cit. Index, Abr. Ed., Sociol. Abstr., Lang. Lang. Behav. Abstr. NLM W1 EU721L. CODEN EUNEAP. adv acc. Papers cover clinical aspects of diseases of the nervous system and muscles, as well as their neuropathological, biochemical, and electrophysiological basis. Psychiatria et Neurologia.

EXCERPTA MEDICA. SECTION 8: NEUROLOGY AND NEUROSURGERY. See Indexes/Abstracts.

EXPERIMENTAL BRAIN RESEARCH. VFOAT Experimentelle Hirnforschung, Experimentation Cerebale. V. 1- 1966-. 0014-4819. Periodical. English (contributions in French or German). mo. $738.00. Springer Verlag New York Inc, 175-5th Avenue, New York NY 10010. Tel (212)460-1500. Ed O Creutzfeldt. Ind/Abst Life Sci. Collect., Excerpta Med., Biol. Abstr., Chem. Abstr., Nuci. Sci. Abstr., Index Med., Int. Aerosp. Abstr. NLM W1 EX485. CODEN EXBRAP. Covers the whole field of experimental brain research such as neurophysiology, sensory physiology, neuroanatomy, developmental neurobiology, neuropharmacology, histochemistry, neuroplasticity, neuroendocrinology, behavioural sciences, and neuropsychology.

EXPERIMENTAL NEUROLOGY. V. 1- Apr. 1959-. 0014-4886. Periodical. US. English. mo. Academic Press, 4805 Sand Lake Road, Orlando FL 32819. Tel (305)345-4100. Ind/Abst Life Sci. Collect., Sociol. Abstr., Excerpta Med., Int. Aerosp. Abstr., Chem. Abstr., Biol. Abstr., Nuci. Sci. Abstr., Psychol. Abstr., Index Med., Energy Res. Abstr., Sci. Cit. Index, Abr. Ed., Lang. Lang. Behav. Abstr. LC RC321. DD 612.8072. NLM W1 EX507. CODEN EXNEAC.

FACT BOOK - NATIONAL INSTITUTE OF NEUROLOGICAL AND COMMUNICATIVE DISORDERS AND STROKE (U.S.). (FACT BOOK - NATIONAL INSTITUTE OF NEUROLOGICAL AND COMMUNICATIVE DISORDERS AND STROKE). Main/Corp National Institute of Neurological and Communicative Disorders and Stroke. Began with 1979. 0278-2502. US. English. an. National Institute of Neurological and Communicative Disorders and Strokes, National Institutes of Health, Bethesda MD 20205. NLM W2 A N2052F.

FOLIA PSYCHIATRICA ET NEUROLOGICA JAPONICA. See Medicine - Psychiatry, Psychopathology.

FORTSCHRITTE DER NEUROLOGIE, PSYCHIATRIE. V. 49, No. 1 (Jan. 1981)-. 0720-4299. Periodical. German. mo. Ind/Abst Excerpta Med., Index Med., Life Sci. Collect., Psychol. Abstr. NLM W1 FO86G. CODEN FNPGA3. Fortschritte der Neurologie, Psychiatrie und Ihrer Grenzgebiete.

FORTSCHRITTE DER NEUROLOGIE, PSYCHIATRIE UND IHRER GRENZGEBIETE CEASED. Vol. 1-48. 0015-8194. Periodical. German. mo. Ind/Abst Life Sci. Collect., Energy Res. Abstr. NLM W1 FO86H.

HANDBOOK OF BEHAVIORAL NEUROBIOLOGY. V. 1-. 0194-0880. Monographic Series. US. English. ir. Plenum Publishing Corporation, 227 West 17th Street, New York NY 10011. Tel (212)620-8000. LC UNC. NLM W1 HA51I.

HANDBOOK OF CHEMICAL NEUROANATOMY. Vol. 1-. Monographic Series. English. ir. Ed F Bjorklund and T Hokfelt. NLM W1.

HANDBOOK OF CLINICAL NEUROLOGY. US. English. ir. Elsevier Science Publishing Co, PO Box 1663 Grand Central Station, New York NY 10163. **Tel** (212)370-5520.

HANDBOOK OF NEUROCHEMISTRY. US. English. ir. Plenum Press, 233 Spring Street, New York NY 10013. **Tel** (212)620-8000.

HEADACHE. V. 1- Apr. 1961-. 0017-8748. Periodical. US. English. bm. $30.00. Headache, 5252 North Western Avenue, Chicago IL 60625. **Tel** (312)878-8977. **Ed** John Edmeads. **Ind/Abst** Life Sci. Collect., Excerpta Med., Index Med., Chem. Abstr., Biol. Abstr., Energy Res. Abstr., Sci. Cit. Index, Abr. Ed., Hospit. Lit. Index. **LC** RC392. **DD** 616.072. **NLM** W1 HE13. **CODEN** HEADAE. bk rev. adv acc. **Circ** 5,000. (ctrl). Available on microfilm from University Microfilms. Contains original articles and papers, abstracts with diagnosis and treatment of headache and related pain.

HUMAN ETHOLOGY NEWSLETTER. 0739-2036. Periodical. US. English. qt. $20.00. Human Ethology Newsletter, Joan Lockard/Department of Neurological Surgery, Eastern Kentucky University, Richmond KY 40475.

HUMAN NEUROBIOLOGY. Vol. 1, No. 1 (Mar. 1982)-. 0721-9075. Periodical. US. English. qt. $62.00. Springer Verlag-New York Inc, 175 5th Avenue, New York NY 10010. **Tel** (212)460-1500. **Ed** D H Ingvar and I Rentschler. **Ind/Abst** Life Sci. Collect., Excerpta Med., Index Med., Chem. Abstr., Psychol. Abstr. **LC** QP360. **DD** 612.805. **NLM** W1. **CODEN** HUNEDR. bk rev. Fields of interest: neuropsychology, sensory physiology,neurology, neuroendocrinology, neurosurgery, neurophysiology, neuropsychiatry, neurolinguistics, neuroethology, developmental neurobiology, neurochemistry, neuropharmacology and neuroanatomy.

INTERNATIONAL BRAIN RESEARCH ORGANIZATION MONOGRAPH SERIES. **VFOAT** IBRO Monograph Series. V. 1-. 0361-0462. Monographic Series. US. English. ir. Raven Press, 1140 Avenue of the Americas, New York NY 10036. **Ind/Abst** Biol. Abstr., Chem. Abstr. **NLM** W1 IN71S. **CODEN** IBRSDZ.

INTERNATIONAL JOURNAL OF DEVELOPMENTAL NEUROSCIENCE. (INTERNATIONAL JOURNAL OF DEVELOPMENTAL NEUROSCIENCE : THE OFFICIAL JOURNAL OF THE INTERNATIONAL SOCIETY FOR DEVELOPMENTAL NEUROSCIENCE). Vol. 1, No. 1-. 0736-5748. Periodical. UK. English. bm. $150.00. Pergamon Press, Maxwell House/Fairview Park, Elmsford NY 10523. **Ind/Abst** Life Sci. Collect., Psychol. Abstr. **LC** QP363.5. **DD** 591.18805. **NLM** W1.

INTERNATIONAL JOURNAL OF NEUROLOGY. **VFOAT** Internationale Zeitschrift fur Neurologie, Revista Internacional de Neurologia, Revue International de Neurologie. Vol. 1, No. 1 (Dec. 1959)-. 0020-7446. Periodical. UY. English (French, German or Spanish). qt. $80.00. International Journal of Neurology, Calle Buenos Aires 363, Montevideo Uruguay. **Ind/Abst** Index Med., Chem. Abstr. **NLM** W1 IN77. **CODEN** IJONAO.

INTERNATIONAL JOURNAL OF NEUROSCIENCE. **VFOAT** Neuroscience. V. 1- Oct. 1970-. 0020-7454. Periodical. US. English. qt. Gordon & Breach, 1 Bedford Street, London WC2E 9HD England. **Ind/Abst** Math. Rev., Life Sci. Collect., Excerpta Med., Index Med., Biol. Abstr., Chem. Abstr., Int. Aerosp. Abstr., Nuci. Sci. Abstr., Sci. Cit. Index, Abr. Ed. **LC** QP351. **DD** 612.805. **NLM** W1 IN77K. **CODEN** IJNUB7.

INTERNATIONAL REVIEW OF NEUROBIOLOGY. V. 1-. 0074-7742. US. English. ir. Academic Press, 4805 Sand Lake Road, Orlando FL 43887. **Tel** (305)345-4100. **Ed** Carl C Pfeiffer. **Ind/Abst** Excerpta Med., Chem. Abstr., Index Med., Energy Res. Abstr., Biol. Abstr., Sci. Cit. Index, Abr. Ed. **LC** RC341. **DD** 612.8082. **NLM** W1 IN834. **CODEN** IRNEAE.

ITALIAN JOURNAL OF NEUROLOGICAL SCIENCES. **VFOAT** Neurological Sciences. V. 1- Nov. 1979-. 0392-0461. Periodical. US. English. qt. Masson Publishing USA Inc, 211 East 43rd Street/Room 1306, New York NY 10017. **Tel** (212)370-1937. **Ind/Abst** Life Sci. Collect., Excerpta Med., Index Med., Chem. Abstr. **NLM** W1 IT357. **CODEN** IJNSD3.

JOURNAL FUR HIRNFORSCHUNG. V. 1- 1954-. 0021-8359. Periodical. GE. German (articles in English and French). bm. $121.02. Kunst & Wissen Erich Bieber, Dufourstrasse 51, CH-8008, Zurich Switzerland. **Tel** 011-41-1-69 44 20. **Ed** C Vogt and O Vogt. **Ind/Abst** Excerpta Med., Index Med., Energy Res. Abstr., Sci. Cit. Index, Abr. Ed., Hospit. Lit. Index. **NLM** W1 JO449. *Journal fur Psychologie und Neurologie.*

JOURNAL OF CHILD NEUROLOGY. Vol. 1, No. 1 (Jan. 1986)-. 0883-0738. Periodical. US. English. qt. $75.00. PSG Publishing Company, 545 Great Road, Littleton MA 01460. **Tel** (617)486-8971. **DD** 618. bk rev. adv acc. A journal devoted to publishing results of investigations of the developing nervous system and clinical and basic studies of children with nervous system disorders.

JOURNAL OF CLINICAL NEUROPHYSIOLOGY. (JOURNAL OF CLINICAL NEUROPHYSIOLOGY : OFFICIAL PUBLICATION OF THE AMERICAN ELECTROENCEPHALOGRAPHIC SOCIETY). Vol. 1, No. 1 (Jan. 1984)-. 0736-0258. Periodical. US. English. qt. $84.00. Raven Press, 1140 Avenue of the Americas, New York NY 10036. **Tel** (212)575-0335. **Ind/Abst** Life Sci. Collect., Index Med. **DD** 616. **NLM** W1. *Journal of the American EEG Society.*

JOURNAL OF COMPARATIVE NEUROLOGY (PHILADELPHIA, P.A. : 1911). (JOURNAL OF COMPARATIVE NEUROLOGY). Vol. 21, No. 1 (Mar. 1911)-. 0021-9967. Periodical. US. English. wk. $1,920.00. Alan R Liss Inc, 150 5th Avenue, New York NY 10011. **Ind/Abst** Life Sci. Collect., Excerpta Med., Int. Aerosp. Abstr., Biol. Abstr., Chem. Abstr., Index Med., Nuci. Sci. Abstr., Energy Res. Abstr. **LC** QL1. **DD** 616. **NLM** W1 JO595E. **CODEN** JCNEAM. (cum index). *Journal of Comparative Neurology and Psychology, 0092-7015.*

JOURNAL OF MENTAL DEFICIENCY RESEARCH. V. 1- July 1957-. 0022-264X. Periodical. UK. English. qt. 32.00 Domestic, 38.50 Foreign, $62.50 US and Canada. Blackwell Scientific Publishing Ltd, PO Box 88, Oxford OX2 0EL England. **Tel** 031 226 7232. **Ed** W I Fraser. **Ind/Abst** Biol. Abstr., Chem. Abstr., Psychol. Abstr., Index Med. **LC** RC321. **CODEN** JMDRAD. bk rev. adv acc. **Circ** 1,050. (ctrl). Contains clinical case reports, pathological reports, biochemical investigations, genetics and cytogenetics, psychological, educational and sociological studies, and the results of animal experiments that may increase knowledge of mental deficiency.

JOURNAL OF NEURAL TRANSMISSION. V. 33- Nov. 1972-. 0300-9564. Periodical. US. English (some summaries in French and German). bm. $272.00. Springer Verlag-New York Inc, 175 5th Avenue, New York NY 10010. **Tel** (212)460-1500. **Ed** A Carlsson. **Ind/Abst** Life Sci. Collect., Excerpta Med., Pestdoc, Ringdoc, Vetdoc, Index Med., Biol. Abstr., Chem. Abstr., Sci. Cit. Index, Abr. Ed. **LC** QP364.5. **DD** 599.018805. **NLM** W1 JO781. **CODEN** JNTMAH. Covers topics dealing with clinical investigation focusing on the pathogenic factors of neurological and psychiatric disorders. *Journal of Neuro-Visceral Relations, 0022-3026.*

JOURNAL OF NEURAL TRANSMISSION. SUPPLEMENTUM. 11- 1974-. 0303-6995. Monographic Series. contributions in English or German, with summaries in English. ir. Springer Verlag, 44 Hartz Way, Secaucus NJ 07094. **Tel** (201)348-4033. **Ed** A Carlsson. **Ind/Abst** Index Med., Chem. Abstr. **NLM** W1 JO781A. **CODEN** JNTSD4. The supplements mainly aspects related to clinical neuropharmacology and basic principles of the brain's neurotransmission including receptor biochemistry. *Journal of Neuro-Visceral Relations. Supplementum, 0075-4323.*

JOURNAL OF NEUROCHEMISTRY. Periodical. UK. English. mo. $184.00. Raven Press, 1140 Avenue of the Americas, New York NY 10036. **Tel** (212)575-0335. **Ind/Abst** Index Med., Sci. Cit. Index, Abr. Ed., Chem. Abstr.

JOURNAL OF NEUROCHEMISTRY. V. 1- May 1956-. 0022-3042. Periodical. US. English. mo. $275.00 Libraries, $30.00 ISN Members. Raven Press, 1140 Avenue of the Americas, New York NY 10036. **Ind/Abst** Life Sci. Collect., Excerpta Med., Pestdoc, Ringdoc, Vetdoc, Int. Aerosp. Abstr., Biol. Abstr., Chem. Abstr., Nuci. Sci. Abstr., Index Med. **LC** QP351. **NLM** W1 JO786. **CODEN** JONRA9. Available on microfilm from Microforms international Marketing Corporation.

JOURNAL OF NEUROGENETICS. Vol. 1, No. 1 (Sept. 1983)-. 0167-7063. Periodical. English. bm. Elsevier Science Publishers, PO Box 211, 1000 AE Amsterdam The Netherlands. **Tel** (020)5803.911. **Ind/Abst** Life Sci. Collect. **NLM** W1. **CODEN** JLNEDK.

JOURNAL OF NEUROIMMUNOLOGY. Vol. 1, No. 1 (Mar. 1981)-. 0165-5728. Periodical. English. mo. 807 Domestic, 299 Foreign. Elsevier Science Publishers, PO Box 211, 1000 AE Amsterdam Netherlands. **Ed** C S Raine. **Ind/Abst** Life Sci. Collect., Excerpta Med., Index Med., Biol. Abstr., Chem. Abstr., Psychol. Abstr. **NLM** W1 JO787M. **CODEN** JNRIDW. bk rev. adv acc. Neuroimmunology (research, articles, short communications, reviews) in neurology, neuroscience, cell biology.

JOURNAL OF NEUROLOGY. 0340-5354. Periodical. Multilingual (English and German summaries in English). bm. $226.00. Springer Verlag New York Inc, 175 5th Avenue, New York NY 10010. **Tel** (212)460-1500. **Ed** R A C Hughes and K Poeck. **Ind/Abst** Index Med., Sociol. Abstr., Lang. Lang. Behav. Abstr., Chem. Abstr. Concerned with description of organic neurological disorders. Publishes original investigations comprising full papers on clinical neurology and related basic research.

JOURNAL OF NEUROLOGY NEUROSURGERY AND PSYCHIATRY. (JOURNAL OF NEUROLOGY, NEUROSURGERY AND PSYCHIATRY). New Ser. V. 7- 1944-. 0022-3050. Periodical. UK. English. mo. $140.98. British Medical Journal, Tavistock Square, London WC1H 9JR England. **Ind/Abst** Life Sci. Collect., Excerpta Med., Index Med., Cumul. Index Nurs. Allied Health Lit., Int. Aerosp. Abstr., Biol. Abstr., Chem. Abstr., Psychol. Abstr., Sociol. Abstr., Lang. Lang. Behav. Abstr., Sci. Cit. Index, Abr. Ed., Nuci. Sci. Abstr. **LC** RC321. **DD** 616.8005. **NLM** W1 JO788. **CODEN** JNNPAU. *Journal of Neurology and Psychiatry.*

JOURNAL OF NEUROPATHOLOGY AND EXPERIMENTAL NEUROLOGY. V. 1- Jan. 1942-. 0022-3069. Periodical. US. English. bm. $65.00 Domestic, $71.00 Foreign. Journal of Neuropathology and Experimental Neurology, PO Box 368, Lawrence KS 66044. **Tel** (913)843-1234. **Ed** John and Yvonne Moossy. **Ind/Abst** Life Sci. Collect., Excerpta Med., Int. Aerosp. Abstr., Biol. Abstr., Chem. Abstr., Nuci. Sci. Abstr., Index Med., Energy Res. Abstr., Sci. Cit. Index, Abr. Ed. **LC** RC321 616.805. **NLM** W1 JO793. **CODEN** JNENAD. (cum index). adv acc. **Circ** 1,600. (ctrl). The journal publishes original articles on neuropathology and experimental neurology, book reviews, letters, and news of the Association.

JOURNAL OF NEUROPHYSIOLOGY. **VFOAT** Neurophysiology. V. 1- Jan. 1938-. 0022-3077. Periodical. US. English. mo. $225.00. American Physiological Society, 9650 Rockville Pike, Bethesda MD 20814. **Tel** (301)530-7070. **Ed** L M Mendell. **Ind/Abst** Life Sci. Collect., Excerpta Med., Pestdoc, Ringdoc, Vetdoc, Int. Aerosp. Abstr., Biol. Abstr., Chem. Abstr., Nuci. Sci. Abstr., Index Med., Psychol. Abstr., Energy Res. Abstr., Sci. Cit. Index, Abr. Ed. **LC** QP351. **DD** 612.805. **NLM** W1 JO794. **CODEN** JONEA4. adv acc. **Circ** 2,000. Neurophysiology.

THE JOURNAL OF NEUROSCIENCE. (THE JOURNAL OF NEUROSCIENCE : THE OFFICIAL JOURNAL OF THE SOCIETY FOR NEUROSCIENCE). **VFOAT** Neuroscience. Vol. 1, No. 1 (Jan. 1981)-. 0270-6474. Periodical. US. English. mo. $265.00. Williams & Wilkins, 428 East Preston Street, Baltimore MD 21202. **Tel** (301)528-4000. **Ind/Abst** Life Sci. Collect., Excerpta Med., Index Med., Chem. Abstr. **LC** QP351. **DD** 599.018805. **NLM** W1 JO795BN. **CODEN** JNRSDS. adv acc. A broad-focus, interdisciplinary journal, bringing together findings in neural systems and all areas of neuroscience: molecular, cellular, developmental, and behavioral.

JOURNAL OF NEUROSCIENCE METHODS. V. 1- Mar. 1979-. 0165-0270. Periodical. English. mo. 792.00 Domestic, $293.00 Foreign. Elsevier Science Publishers, PO Box 211, 1000 AE Amsterdam The Netherlands. **Tel** (020)5803.911. **Ed** John S Kelley. **Ind/Abst** Life Sci. Collect., Excerpta Med., Index Med., Biol. Abstr., Comput. Control Abstr., Electr. Electron. Abstr., Sci. Abstr. Sect. A. Phys. Abstr., Chem. Abstr., Sci. Cit. Index, Abr. Ed., Phys. Abstr. **NLM** W1 JO795BS. **CODEN** JNMEDT. bk rev. adv acc. Neuroscience methodology; reviews; original research articles; letters.

JOURNAL OF NEUROSCIENCE RESEARCH. V. 1-. 0360-4012. Periodical. US. English. bm. Alan R Liss Inc, 41 East 11th Street, New York NY 10003. **Tel** (212)741-2515. **Ind/Abst** Life Sci.

Collect., Excerpta Med., Index Med., Biol. Abstr., Chem. Abstr., Energy Res. Abstr., Sci. Cit. Index, Abr. Ed. **LC** QP351. **DD** 599.018805. **NLM** W1 JO795C. **CODEN** JNREDK.

THE JOURNAL OF SOMATIC EXPERIENCE. 0275-9624. Periodical. US. English. sa. $53.63. Human Science Press, 72 Fifth Avenue, New York NY 10011. **LC** QP401. **DD** 150.5. **CODEN** JSOED6. *Journal of Biological Experience.*

JOURNAL OF THE AUTONOMIC NERVOUS SYSTEM. Vol. 1, No. 1 (Oct. 1979)-. 0165-1838. Periodical. English. mo. Elsevier Science Publishers, PO Box 211, 1000 AE Amsterdam Netherlands. **Tel** (020)5803.911. **Ind/Abst** Excerpta Med., Index Med., Life Sci. Collect., Biol. Abstr., Chem. Abstr., Sci. Cit. Index, Abr. Ed. **NLM** W1 JO912VD. **CODEN** JASYDS.

JOURNAL OF THE NEUROLOGICAL SCIENCES. V. 1- Jan./Feb. 1964-. 0022-510X. Periodical. NE. English (French or German with summaries in Russian and Spanish). mo. Elsevier Science Publishers, PO Box 211, 1000 AE Amsterdam Netherlands. **Tel** (020)5803911. **Ind/Abst** Excerpta Med., Life Sci. Collect., Ref. Source, Biol. Abstr., Chem. Abstr., Nuci. Sci. Abstr., Index Med., Lang. Lang. Behav. Abstr., Sociol. Abstr. **LC** RC321. **NLM** W1 JO941U. **CODEN** JNSCAG.

JOURNAL OF THEORETICAL NEUROBIOLOGY. Vol. 1, No. 1 (Aug. 1981)-. 0727-761X. Periodical. AT. English. ty. $65.00. Australian Scientific Press, PO Box 154, Toorak Victoria 3142 Australia. **Tel** 03 541 2574. **Ed** Henry C Tuckwell. **Ind/Abst** Math. Rev., Excerpta Med., Chem. Abstr. **NLM** W1 JO966D. **CODEN** JTHND5. bk rev. adv acc. **Circ** 500. Theoretical studies of all aspects of the nervous system: analysis of neuroscience data or theoretical work with focus on neurobiology.

KOKURITSU MUSASHI RYOYOJO SHINKEI SENTA NENPO. Japanese. an. Kokuritsu Musashi Ryoyojo Shinkei Senta, 2620 Ogawa Higashicho, Kodaira-Shi 187 Japan. **LC** RC321.

M S ONTARIO. **VAT** Multiple Sclerosis Ontario. No. 1- Feb. 1977-. 0707-0934. Periodical. CN. English. ir. Free. Multiple Sclerosis Society Ontario Division, 130 Bloor Street West, Toronto Ontario M5S 1N5 Canada. **DD** 616.8340062713.

MAGYAR BELORVOSI ARCHIVUM. *See* Genealogy and Heraldry - Archives.

MAJOR PROBLEMS IN NEUROLOGY. V. 1-. 0301-5602. Monographic Series. UK. English. ir. W B Saunders Company, Fullfillment Department, West Washington Square, Philadelphia PA 19105. **Tel** (800)523-0713. **NLM** W1 MA492U.

MEDICAL EXAMINATION REVIEW BOOK. NEUROLOGY SPECIALTY BOARD REVIEW. **VFOAT** Neurology Specialty Board Review. 1st- Ed. 0090-7073. US. English. ir. Medical Exam Publishing Company, 3003 New Hyde Park Road, New Hyde Park NY 11040.

MEMBERSHIP DIRECTORY - AMERICAN ACADEMY OF NEUROLOGY. *See* Yearbooks, Almanacs, Directories.

MODERN APPROACHES TO THE DIAGNOSIS AND INSTRUCTION OF MULTI-HANDICAPPED CHILDREN. English. ir. Swets Publishing Service, PO Box 800, 2160 SZ Lisse Holland. **Tel** 09 31252119113. **Ed** Klaus T Plasterle. Series of monographs devoted to speech pathology and speech physiology, with special emphasis on neurological disorders that entail language disturbances.

MONOGRAPHIEN AUS DEM GESAMTGEBIETE DER PSYCHIATRIE. V. 1-. 0077-0671. Monographic Series. German. ir. Springer Verlag-New York Inc, 175 5th Avenue, New York NY 10010. **Tel** (212)460-1584. **Ind/Abst** Index Med., Chem. Abstr., Psychol. Abstr. **NLM** W1 MO561B. **CODEN** MGGPBE. Contains articles on neurology and psychiatry. *Monographien aus dem Gesamtgebiete der Neurologie und Psychiatrie, 0376-0464.*

MONOGRAPHS IN NEURAL SCIENCES. V. 1-. 0300-5186. Monographic Series. English. ir. S Karger Ag, PO Box, CH-4009 Basel Switzerland. **Tel** (061)390880. **Ed** M M Cohen. **Ind/Abst** Index Med., Biol. Abstr., Chem. Abstr. **NLM** W1 MO568C. **CODEN** MNUSB6. Makes fundamental and vital information available to clinicians active in the diagnosis, evaluation, and treatment of neurological diseases.

MONTAGE (TORONTO MENSA). (MONTAGE). Vol. 5, No. 6 (June 1981)-. 0710-0159. Periodical. CN. English. $5.00 Domestic, $8.00 Foreign. Montage, c/o 496 Dufferin Avenue, Toronto Ontario M5A 2J9 Canada. **DD** 367.9713. *Tan, 0227-3314.*

MOTRICITE CEREBRALE. (MOTRICITE CEREBRALE, READAPTATION, NEUROLOGIE DU DEVELOPPEMENT). V. 1- 1980-. 0245-5919. Periodical. French. qt. Masson Publishing USA Inc, 211 East 43rd Street/Room 1306, New York NY 10017. **Tel** (212)370-1937. **Ind/Abst** Excerpta Med. **NLM** W1 MO949N. *Cahier du Cercle de Documentation et d'Information pour la Reeducation des Infirmes Moteurs Cerebraux, 0150-0511.*

MS CANADA. **VFOAT** SP Canada. **VAT** Multiple Sclerosis Canada. V. 1- Feb. 1974-. 0315-1131. Periodical. CN. English (with some text in French, Feb. 1974-Summer 1980). qt. $3.86. Multiple Sclerosis Society of Canada, 130 Bloor Street West/Suite 700, Toronto Ontario M5S IN5 Canada.

MS TORONTO. **VAT** Multiple Sclerosis Toronto. Vol. 1, No. 1 (Fall 1982)-. 0714-7996. Periodical. CN. English. Multiple Sclerosis Society of Canada, Metropolitan Toronto Chapter, 130 Bloor Street West, Toronto Ontario M5S 1N5 Canada. **DD** 616.8340060713541. *MS Key-Notes, 0827-4185.*

MULTIPLE SCLEROSIS IN ICELAND. **Series/Titl** Studies in Multiple Sclerosis, 6. Acta Neurologica Scandinavica. Supplementum 2. Periodical. English. ir.

MUSCLE & NERVE. **VAT** Muscle and Nerve. V. 1- Jan./Feb. 1978-. 0148-639X. Periodical. US. English. $50.00 Domestic, $55.00 Foreign. John Wiley & Sons Medical Division, 605 Third Avenue, New York NY 10158. **Tel** (800)526-5368. **Ind/Abst** Excerpta Med., Life Sci. Collect., Index Med., Biol. Abstr., Chem. Abstr. **LC** RC925.A1. **DD** 616.74. **NLM** W1 MU925. **CODEN** MUNEDE.

NATIONAL SPOKESMAN. V. 4, No. 2- Spring 1971-. 0091-2387. Periodical. US. English. mo. Epilepsy Foundation of America, 4351 Garden City Drive/Suite 406, Landover MD 20785. **Tel** (301)459-3700. *National News.*

NEIROKHIMIIA. (NEUROCHEMISTRY). **Series/Titl** Archives of Soviet Science. V. 3, No. 1-. 0749-4300. Periodical. English (summaries in Russian). qt. $280.00 US. Harwood Academic Publishers, c/o Stbs Ltd, One Bedford Street, London WC2E 9PP UK. **LC** QP356.3. **DD** 591.188. **CODEN** NECHE4.

NEJROFIZIOLOGIJA. (NEIROFIZIOLOGIIA). **VFOAT** Neurophysiology. V. 1- July/Aug. 1969-. 0028-2561. UR. Russian (summaries in English). bm. $39.50. Victor Kamkin Inc (70629), 12224 Parklawn Drive, Rockville MD 20852. **Tel** (301)881-5973. **Ind/Abst** Excerpta Med., Index Med., Int. Aerosp. Abstr., Biol. Abstr., Chem. Abstr. **LC** QP361. **NLM** W1 NE195K. **CODEN** NEFZB2.

NERVENARZT. V. 1- 1928-. 0028-2804. Periodical. GW. German. mo. Springer Verlag-New York Inc, 175 5th Avenue, New York NY 10010. **Tel** (212)460-1500. **Ind/Abst** Excerpta Med., Life Sci. Collect., Pestdoc, Ringdoc, Vetdoc, Energy Res. Abstr., Nuci. Sci. Abstr., Psychol. Abstr., Biol. Abstr., Chem. Abstr., Index Med., Sci. Cit. Index, Abr. Ed. **NLM** W1 NE207H. **CODEN** NERVAF. Covers all areas of neurological research and practice. Journal of the German and Austrian Societies for Psychiatry and Neurology. Furthers continued education and reports latest research findings.

NERVENHEILKUNDE. 82/1 (Feb. 1982)-. 0722-1541. Periodical. German. qt. $50.00. Futura Media Services Inc, 295 Main Street, Mount Kisco NY 10549. **Tel** (914)666-3505. **Ind/Abst** Excerpta Med. **NLM** W1 NE207J.

THE NERVOUS SYSTEM AND ELECTRIC CURRENTS; PROCEEDINGS. **Main/Corp** Neuro-Electric Society. V. 1- 1970-. US. English. 227 West 17th Street, New York NY 10011. **Ed** N L Wulfsohn and A Sances Jr. **LC** QP341. **DD** 599.0188.

NEUROBIOLOGIA. Volume 1- June 1938-. 0028-3800. Periodical. BL. Portuguese. qt. $20.00. Neurobiologia/Revista de, Caix Postal 651, Recife Brazil. **Tel** (081)222-4359. **Ed** A Codeceira Jr. **Ind/Abst** Biol. Abstr., Psychol. Abstr. **LC** RC321. **NLM** W1 NE323G. **CODEN** NURBAX. bk rev. adv acc. **Circ** 800. Neurology, psychiatry, neurosurgery and psychology analysis abstracts of medical news.

NEUROCHEMICAL RESEARCH. V. 1- Feb. 1976-. 0364-3190. Periodical. US. English. mo. $320.00 Domestic, $358.00 Foreign. Plenum Publishing Corp, 233 Spring Street, New York NY 10013. **Tel** (212)620-8000. **Ed** Abel Lajtha. **Ind/Abst** Life Sci. Collect., Biol. Abstr., Energy Res. Abstr., Chem. Abstr., Curr. Contents, Excerpta Med., Index Med., Ref. Z., Sci. Cit. Index, Abr. Ed. **LC** QP356.3. **DD** 591.188. **NLM** W1 NE3235. **CODEN** NEREDZ. bk rev. adv acc. This journal is devoted to the rapid publication of studies which use neurochemical methodology in research of the nervous system serves as a bridge between neurochem and all other fields.

NEUROCHEMISTRY INTERNATIONAL. Began in 1980. 0197-0186. Periodical. US. English. ir. $150.00. Pergamon Press, 395 Sawmill River Road, Elmsford NY 10523. **Ind/Abst** Life Sci. Collect., Excerpta Med., Biol. Abstr., Chem. Abstr., Sci. Cit. Index, Abr. Ed. **LC** QP356.3. **DD** 599.0188. **NLM** W1 NE3237. **CODEN** NEUIDS.

NEUROENDOCRINOLOGY. V. 1- 1965/66-. 0028-3835. Periodical. English (summaries in French and German). mo. $285.00. S Karger AG, PO Box, CH-4009 Basel Switzerland. **Tel** (061)39 08 80. **Ed** S M McCann. **Ind/Abst** Excerpta Med., Life Sci. Collect., Pestdoc, Ringdoc, Vetdoc, Int. Aerosp. Abstr., Bibliogr. Agric., Biol. Abstr., Chem. Abstr., Index Med., Nuci. Sci. Abstr., Sci. Cit. Index, Abr. Ed. **LC** QP187.A1. **DD** 616.4005. **NLM** W1 NE328D. **CODEN** NUNDAJ. adv acc. Publishes papers reporting original research in basic and clinical neuroendocrinology. Topics range through the multiple, complex interactions between the endocrine system and the nervous system.

NEUROEPIDEMIOLOGY. 1/1/82 (Apr. 1982)-. 0251-5350. Periodical. SZ. English. qt. $74.00. S Karger AG, PO Box, CH-4009 Basel Switzerland. **Tel** (061)39 08 80. **Ed** F Clifford Rose. **Ind/Abst** Excerpta Med., Life Sci. Collect., Biol. Abstr. **NLM** W1 NE328F. **CODEN** NEEPD3. adv acc. Soley concerned with descriptive, analytical, and experimental aspects of neurologic epidemiology.

NEUROIMMUNOLOGY. Issue No. 1- Jan./Apr. 1973-. 0196-2787. US. English. qt. UCLA Brain Information Service, University of California, Los Angeles CA 90024. **NLM** ZWL 100 N494.

NEUROLOGIA EN COLOMBIA. V. 1- 1977-. 0120-1034. Periodical. CK. articles in Spanish. ir. $25.00. Fundacion Institute of Neurologia in Columbia, PO Box 90303, Bogota 8 Columbia. **Tel** (91) 232-61-31. **Ed** Edwin Ruiz Alarcon. **NLM** W1 NE328P. bk rev. **Circ** 2,000. (ctrl). Neurosurgery, clinical neurology, neuropsychiatric advances and new trends in neurosciences. Neuropathology infections of central nervous system, epilepsy, brain tumors and immunotherapy.

NEUROLOGIA ET PSYCHIATRIA. 0253-9446. Periodical. English (articles in German or Greek). qt. **NLM** W1 NE328R.

NEUROLOGIA I NEUROCHIRURGIA POLSKA. Vol. 1- 1967-. 0028-3843. Periodical. PL. Polish. bm. ARS Polona, Krakowskie Przedmiescie 7, 00-068 Warsaw Poland. **Ind/Abst** Excerpta Med., Index Med., Chem. Abstr. **NLM** W1 NE328T. **CODEN** NNPOBE. Index published separately - free - automatically sent. *Neurologia, Neurochirurgia I Psychiatria Polska.*

NEUROLOGIC CLINICS. Vol. 1, No. 1 (Feb. 1983)-. 0733-8619. Periodical. US. English. qt. W B Saunders, West Washington Square, Philadelphia PA 19105. **Tel** (800)523-0713. **Ind/Abst** Index Med. **LC** RC321. **DD** 616.8005. **NLM** W1 NE329T.

NEUROLOGIC ILLNESS: DIAGNOSIS & TREATMENT. (NEUROLOGIC ILLNESS). Vol. 1-. 0736-9263. Monographic Series. US. English. Spectrum Publications Inc, 175-20 Wexford Terrace, Jamaica NY 11432. **Tel** (718)658-0888. **Ed** Michael I Weintraub. **LC** UNC. **NLM** W1 NE329V. Clinical monographs in neurological illness: diagnosis and treatment.

NEUROLOGICAL RESEARCH. V. 1- 1979-. 0161-6412. Periodical. UK. English. qt. 130.00. Butterworths Scientific Ltd, Box 63, Westbury House, Bury Street, Guildford GU2 5BH England. **Tel** 31261. **Ed** G W Austin. **Ind/Abst** Excerpta Med., Life Sci. Collect., Index Med., Chem. Abstr. **LC** RC321. **DD** 612.805. **NLM** W1 NE33N. **CODEN** NRESDZ. bk rev. adv acc. A microform edition is available from

University Microfilms. Neurological research reports original fundamental; basic and clinical research in neurosurgery and the neurosciences underlying medical disciplines.

NEUROLOGY. V. 1- Jan./Feb. 1951-. 0028-3878. Periodical. US. English. mo. Neurology, 1 East First Street, Duluth NM 55802. **Tel** (218)723-9200. **Ind/Abst** Sociol. Abstr., Soc. Welf. Soc. Plan./Policy Soc. Dev., Excerpta Med., Life Sci. Collect., Int. Aerosp. Abstr., CIS Abstr., Biol. Abstr., Chem. Abstr., Index Med., Nuci. Sci. Abstr., Psychol. Abstr., Sci. Cit. Index, Abr. Ed., Lang. Lang. Behav. Abstr. **LC** RC321. **DD** 616.805. **NLM** W1 NE337. **CODEN** NEURAI.

NEUROLOGY ALERT. Began with Vol. 1, No. 1 (Sept. 1982). 0741-4234. Periodical. US. English. mo. $42.50. International Thomson Medical Information, 210 South Street, Boston MA 02111. **Ed** Fred M Plum. **DD** 616. Index published separately - free - automatically sent. (cum index).

NEUROLOGY AND NEUROBIOLOGY. Vol. 1-. 0736-4563. Monographic Series. US. English. Alan R Liss, 41 East 11th Street, New York NY 10003. **Tel** (212)475-7700. **Ed** Victoria Chan-Palay and Sanford Paylay. **Ind/Abst** Biol. Abstr., Chem. Abstr. **LC** UNC. **NLM** W1 NE337B. **CODEN** NEUND9. A scholarly book series covering topics such as sensorimotor activity, catecholamines, nervous systems, excitable cells, and anorexia nervosa.

NEUROLOGY INDIA. (NEUROLOGY, INDIA). V. 12- Jan./March 1964-. 0028-3886. Periodical. II. English. qt. $35.00. Neurological Society of India, 534 Sandhurst Bridge, Bombay 7 India. **Ind/Abst** Life Sci. Collect., Excerpta Med. **NLM** W1 NE337D. Index published separately - free - automatically sent. *Neurology.*

NEUROONCOLOGY. V. 1-. 0166-3518. Monographic Series. English. ir. **Ind/Abst** Chem. Abstr. **NLM** W1 NE337J. **CODEN** NRNCDW.

NEUROPADIATRIE. *See* Medicine - Pediatrics.

NEUROPATHOLOGY AND APPLIED NEUROBIOLOGY. *See* Medicine - Pathology.

NEUROPEDIATRICS. **VFOAT** Journal of Pediatric Neurobiology, Neurology and Neurosurgery. Vol. 11, No. 3 (Aug. 1980)-. 0174-304X. Periodical. English (German). qt. Hippokrates Verlag GMBH, Stuttgart West Germany. **Ind/Abst** Excerpta Med., Life Sci. Collect., Index Med., Energy Res. Abstr., Chem. Abstr. **NLM** W1 NE337SD. **CODEN** NRPDDB. *Neuropadiatrie, 0028-3797.*

NEUROPEPTIDES. Vol. 1, No. 1 (July 1980)-. 0143-4179. Periodical. UK. English. bm. $185.00. Neuropeptides, PO Box 1584, Birmingham AL 35202. **Tel** (205)991-6920. **Ed** M J Brownstein and J Hughes. **Ind/Abst** Excerpta Med., Life Sci. Collect., Index Med., Chem. Abstr. **NLM** W1 NE337SL. **CODEN** NRPPDD. Publishes original research and reviews articles on the structure, distribution, actions and functions of peptides in the central and peripheral nervous systems.

NEUROPSICHIATRIA. 0028-3916. Periodical. IT. Italian. mo. Instituto Psichiatrico, Via Redipuglia 95, Genoa Italy.

NEUROPSYCHIATRIE DE L'ENFANCE ET DE L'ADOLESCENCE. 27.- Year. 0222-9617. Periodical. FR. French (summaries in English, German, and Spanish). ir. $94.45. Expansion Scienfifique Fran, 15 rue Saint Benoit, 75278 Paris Cedex 06 France. **Tel** 548-42-60. **Ind/Abst** Excerpta Med., Index Med., Psychol. Abstr., Sci. Cit. Index, Abr. Ed. **NLM** W1 NE339L. *Revue de Neuropsychiatrie Infantile et d'Hygiene Mentale de l'Enfance, 0035-1628.*

NEUROPSYCHOBIOLOGY. V. 1- 1975-. 0302-282X. Periodical. SZ. English. bm. $166.60. S Karger AG, PO Box 352, White Plains NY 10602. **Tel** (061)390880. **Ed** J Mendlewicz, C H Pull, W Janke and H Kunkel. **Ind/Abst** Excerpta Med., Life Sci. Collect., Index Med., Biol. Abstr., Chem. Abstr., Psychol. Abstr., Pestdoc, Ringdoc, Vetdoc, Curr. Contents. **NLM** W1 NE3412. **CODEN** NPBYAL. adv acc. Features original and fundamental data on neurophysiology, neurochemistry, neuroendocrinology and genetics. A complete record of strategies and methodologies employed to study mental functions.

NEUROPSYCHOLOGIA. V. 1-. 0028-3932. Periodical. UK. English (French or German). bm. Pergamon Press, 395 Sawmill River Road, Elmsford NY 10523. **Tel** (914)592-7700. **Ind/Abst** Excerpta Med., Life Sci. Collect., Int. Aerosp. Abstr., Biol. Abstr., Psychol. Abstr., Index Med., Sci. Cit. Index, Abr. Ed., Sociol. Abstr., Lang. Lang. Behav. Abstr. **LC** RC321. **DD** 616.805. **NLM** W1 NE342. **CODEN** NUPSA6.

NEURORADIOLOGY. V. 1- Apr. 1970-. 0028-3940. Periodical. GW. German (English). $129.00. Springer Verlag-New York Inc, 175 5th Avenue, New York NY 10010. **Tel** (212)460-1500. **Ed** G du Boulay, T Naidich, M Takahashi, A Wackenheim, S Wende, and M M Schechter. **Ind/Abst** Excerpta Med., Life Sci. Collect., Index Med., Energy Res. Abstr., Sci. Cit. Index, Abr. Ed. **LC** RC349.R3. **DD** 616.80475705. **NLM** W1 NE342K. Fields of interest in neuroradiology, neurology, and neurosurgery.

NEUROSCIENCE. V. 1- 1976-. 0306-4522. Periodical. UK. English. mo. Pergamon Press, 395 Sawmill River Road, Elmsford NY 10523. **Ind/Abst** Excerpta Med., Life Sci. Collect., Index Med., Biol. Abstr., Chem. Abstr., Sci. Cit. Index, Abr. Ed. **LC** QP351. **DD** 591.18805. **NLM** W1 NE342M. **CODEN** NRSCDN.

NEUROSCIENCE AND BIOBEHAVIORAL REVIEWS. V. 2- Spring 1978-. 0149-7634. Periodical. US. English. qt. $175.00. Ankho International Inc, PO Box 380227, San Antonio TX 78280. **Tel** (315)463-0182. **Ed** Matthew J Wayner. **Ind/Abst** Excerpta Med., Life Sci. Collect., Index Med., Biol. Abstr., Chem. Abstr., Psychol. Abstr. **LC** QP360. **DD** 599.0188. **NLM** W1 NE342PB. **CODEN** NBREDE. bk rev. adv acc. Publishes original reviews in anatomy, biochemistry, embryology, endocrinology, genetics, pharmacology, physiology, and all aspects of biological sciences when relevance to problems of the nervous system or the investigation of behavior is clearly established. *Biobehavioral Reviews, 0147-7552.*

NEUROSCIENCE LETTERS. V. 1- July 1975-. 0304-3940. Periodical. NE. English. sm. Elsevier Scientific Publishers Ireland Ltd, PO Box 85, Limerick Ireland. **Ind/Abst** Excerpta Med., Life Sci. Collect., Index Med., Biol. Abstr., Chem. Abstr., Sci. Cit. Index, Abr. Ed. **LC** QP351. **DD** 599.0188. **NLM** W1 NE342S. **CODEN** NELED5.

NEUROSCIENCE RESEARCH : THE OFFICIAL JOURNAL OF THE JAPAN NEUROSCIENCE SOCIETY. **VFOAT** Shinkei Kagaku. Vol. 1, No. 1 (Feb. 1984)-. 0168-0102. Periodical. English. bm. $106.50. Elsevier Scientific Publishers of Ireland, PO Box 85, Limerick Ireland. **Ind/Abst** Life Sci. Collect. **NLM** W1.

NEUROSCIENCES ABSTRACTS. *See* Indexes/Abstracts.

NEUROSCIENCES RESEARCH PROGRAM BULLETIN *CEASED.* **Main/Corp** Neurosciences Research Program. **VFOAT** NRP Bulletin. V. 1-20. 0028-3967. Periodical. US. English. ir. $35.00. NRP Bulletin, The MIT Press, 28 Carleton Street, Cambridge MA 02142. **Ind/Abst** Excerpta Med., Biol. Abstr., Chem. Abstr. **LC** QP351. **DD** 616.8. **NLM** W1 NE343. **CODEN** NRPBA2. (cum index).

NEUROUROL. URODYN. (NEUROUROLOGY AND URODYNAMICS). Vol. 1, No. 1-. 0733-2467. Periodical. US. English. qt. Alan R Liss, 41 East 11th Street, New York NY 10003. **Tel** (212)741-2515. **Ind/Abst** Excerpta Med., Life Sci. Collect. **NLM** W1 NE3495M.

NEWSLETTER - CANADIAN ASSOCIATION OF ELECTROENCEPHALOGRAPH TECHNOLOGISTS. (THE CANADIAN ASSOCIATION OF ELECTROENCEPHALOGRAPH TECHNOLOGISTS : . . . NEWSLETTER). 0715-4658. Periodical. CN. English. bm. Free to Members. Donna Gregory, E E G Department WMCH, 392 South Street, London Ontario N6B 1B8 Canada. **DD** 616.8047547.

NIMHANS JOURNAL. *See* Medicine - Psychiatry, Psychopathology.

THE NINCDS CEREBRAL PALSY RESEARCH PROGRAM. **Main/Corp** National Institute of Neurological and Communicative Disorders and Stroke. **VAT** National Institute of Neurological and Communicative Disorders and Stroke Cerebral Palsy Research Program. 0161-2980. US. English. an. Superintendent of Documents, US Government Printing Office, Washington DC 20402. **NLM** W2 A N2052NC.

THE NINCDS PARKINSON'S DISEASE RESEARCH PROGRAM. **Main/Corp** National Institute of Neurological and Communicative Disorders and Stroke. **VAT** National Institute of Neurological and Communicative Disorders and Stroke Parkinson's Disease Research Program. 0161-3022. US. English. an. Superintendent of Documents, US Government Printers Office, Washington DC 20402. **NLM** W2 A N2052NP.

THE NINCDS RESEARCH PROGRAM. AMYOTROPHIC LATERAL SCLEROSIS. **Main/Corp** National Institute of Neurological and Communicative Disorders and Stroke. **VFOAT** Amyotrophic Lateral Sclerosis. **VAT** National Institute of Neurological and Communicative Disorders and Stroke Research Program. Amyotrophic Lateral Sclerosis. US. English. National Institute of Neurological and Communicative Disorders and Stroke, National Institutes of Health 9000 Rockville Pike, Bethesda MD 20014. *NINCDS Amyotrophic Lateral Sclerosis Research Program.*

THE NINCDS RESEARCH PROGRAM. EPILEPSY. **Main/Corp** National Institute of Neurological and Communicative Disorders and Stroke. **VFOAT** Epilepsy. **VAT** National Institute of Neurological and Communicative Disorders and Stroke Research Program. Epilepsy. 1980-. US. English. an. National Institute of Neurological and Communicative Disorders and Stroke, National Institutes of Health, 9000 Rockville Pike, Bethesda MD 20014. *NINCDS Epilepsy Research Program, 0161-3014.*

THE NINCDS RESEARCH PROGRAM. MULTIPLE SCLEROSIS. **VFOAT** Multiple Sclerosis. Began with 1980. US. English. an. National Institutes of Health, Bethesda MD 20205. **NLM** W2. *NINCDS Multiple Sclerosis Research Program, 0161-3030.*

THE NINCDS RESEARCH PROGRAM. MUSCULAR DYSTROPHY AND OTHER NEUROMUSCULAR DISORDERS. **Main/Corp** National Institute of Neurological and Communicative Disorders and Stroke. **VFOAT** Muscular Dystrophy and other Neuromuscular Disorders. 1980-. US. English. an. National Institute of Neurological and Communicative Disorders and Stroke, National Institutes of Health, 9000 Rockville Pike, Bethesda MD 20014. *NINCDS Muscular Dystrophy and the Neuromuscular Disorders Research Program, 0161-3057.*

THE NINCDS RESEARCH PROGRAM. STROKE. **VFOAT** Stroke. **VAT** National Institute of Neurological and Communicative Disorders and Stroke Research Program. Stroke. Began with 1980. US. English. an. National Institutes of Health, 9000 Rockville Pike, Bethesda MD 20205. **NLM** W2. *NINCDS Stroke Research Program, 0161-3006.*

NUTRITION AND THE BRAIN. *See* Nutrition and Dietetics.

P.B.N. PICCOLA BIBLIOTECA DI NEUROLOGIA E PSICHIATRIA. (P. B. N. PICCOLA BIBLIOTECA DI NEUROLOGIA E PSICHIATRIA). **VFOAT** Piccola Biblioteca di Neurologia e Psichiatria. 0303-7428. Periodical. Italian. ir. Il Pensiero Scientifico Editore, Via Panama 48, 00198 Rome Italy. **NLM** W1 P135. *PBN. Piccola Biblioteca de Neuropsichiatria, 0391-9927.*

PLEIN FEU. V. 1- May 1976-. 0381-1115. Periodical. CN. French. bm. Free. Association de Paralysie Cerebrale du Quebec, 265 Ouest Boulevard, St Cyrille Quebec G1R 2A7 Canada. **DD** 362.1968360062714. (ctrl).

PROCEEDINGS - INTERNATIONAL CONGRESS OF NEURO-PSYCHOPHARMACOLOGY. **Main/Corp** International Congress of Neuro-Psychopharmacology. 1st- 1958-. 0069-5769. Periodical. English (French, German, or Italian). ir. International Congress of Neuro-Psychopharmacology, Elsevier Publishing Company, PO Box 211, 1000 AE Amsterdam Netherlands. **LC** RC327. **DD** 615.780631.

PROCEEDINGS OF THE CAJAL CLUB. (PROCEEDINGS). **Main/Corp** Cajal Club. V. 1- 1973-. 0092-6930. US. English. University of Texas Medical Branch(Editor Glenn V Russell), 301 University Boulevard, Galveston TX 77550. **LC** QP351. **DD** 612.806273. **NLM** W1 PR5848N.

PROGRESS IN BRAIN RESEARCH. V. 1-. 0079-6123. Monographic Series. English. ir. Elsevier Science Publishing Company Inc, PO Box 1663, Grand Central Station, New York NY 10163. **Tel** (212)370-5520. **Ind/Abst** Life Sci. Collect., Biol. Abstr., Chem. Abstr., Nuci. Sci. Abstr., Index Med., Sci. Cit. Index, Abr. Ed. **NLM** W1 PR667J. **CODEN** PBRRA4.

Medicine—Neurology

PROGRESS IN CLINICAL NEUROPHYSIOLOGY. V. 1-. 0378-4045. Periodical. English. ir. S Karger Ag, PO Box, CH-4009 Basel Switzerland. Tel 061-39 08 80. Ed J E Desmedt. Ind/Abst Chem. Abstr. NLM WL 102 P963. CODEN PCNEDN. Volumes covering one of the most promising areas now under study in the neurological sciences.

PROGRESS IN MIGRAINE RESEARCH. Series/Titl Progress in Neurology Series. 1-. 0262-6330. Monographic Series. UK. English. Ind/Abst Chem. Abstr. NLM W1 PR6718. CODEN PMIRD5.

PROGRESS IN NEUROBIOLOGY. V. 1- 1973-. 0301-0082. UK. English. ir. $437.00. Pergamon Press, 395 Sawmill River Road, Elmsford NY 10523. Ed G A Kerkut and J W Phillis. Ind/Abst Life Sci. Collect., Excerpta Med., Index Med., Biol. Abstr., Chem. Abstr., Sci. Cit. Index, Abr. Ed. LC QP356. DD 612.805. NLM W1 PR672K. CODEN PGNBA5.

PROGRESS IN NEUROPATHOLOGY. V. 1-. 0099-9016. US. English. Raven Press, 1140 Avenue of the Americas, New York NY 10036. Tel (212)741-6800. Ind/Abst Biol. Abstr., Chem. Abstr. LC RC347. DD 616.8047. NLM W1 PR674K. CODEN PRNPAM.

PSYCHIATRIE, NEUROLOGIE UND MEDIZINISCHE PSYCHOLOGIE. BEIHEFTE. See Medicine - Psychiatry, Psychopathology.

PSYCHIATRY AND THE HUMANITIES. V. 1- 1976-. 0363-8952. US. English. an. $12.50. Yale University Press, 92A Yale Station, New Haven CT 06520. LC RC321. DD 616.89005. NLM W1 PS354T.

RECENT ACHIEVEMENTS IN RESTORATIVE NEUROLOGY. 1-. Monographic Series. SZ. English. ir. NLM W1.

RECENT ADVANCES IN CLINICAL NEUROLOGY. No. 1- 1975-. 0307-7403. Periodical. UK. English. ir. Churchill Livingstone Inc, 1560 Broadway, New York NY 10036. Tel (212)819-5400. Ed W B Matthews. NLM W1 RE105T. Recent Advances in Neurology and Neuropsychiatry.

RECENT ADVANCES IN EPILEPSY. No. 1-. 0264-7400. Periodical. UK. English. ir. Churchill Livingstone, 1560 Broadway, New York NY 10036. Tel (212)819-5400. Ed Timothy A Pedley and Brian S Meldrum. LC RC372.A1. DD 616.853. NLM W1 RE105ULAH.

RECENT ADVANCES IN NEUROPATHOLOGY. No. 1-. 0144-0535. UK. English. ir. Ed W T Smith and J B Cavanagh. Ind/Abst Chem. Abstr. NLM W1 RE105VH. CODEN RADND8.

RECENT DEVELOPMENTS OF NEUROBIOLOGY IN HUNGARY. V. 1-. 0079-9955. US. English. an. Heyden & Son Inc, 247 South 41st Street, Philadelphia PA 19104. Ind/Abst Biol. Abstr., Chem. Abstr. LC RC346. DD 616.8'05. NLM W1 RE106B. CODEN RDNHAO.

RESEARCH GRANTS, TRAINING AWARDS, FELLOWSHIP AWARDS : SUMMARY BY STATE AND INSTITUTION. VFOAT Geographical Summary Book. 0192-3447. US. English. an. National Institute of Neurological and Communicative Disorders and Stroke, 9000 Rockville Pike, Bethesda MD 20014. LC RC337. DD 616.80079. NLM WL 22 AA1 R41.

RESEARCH GRANTS, TRAINING AWARDS : SUMMARY BY GRANT NUMBER AND GRANTEE. VFOAT Numerical Summary Book. 0192-3366. US. English. an. National Institute of Neurological and Communicative Disorders and Stroke, 9000 Rockville Pike, Bethesda MD 20014. LC RC346. DD 616.80079. NLM WL 22 AA1 R43.

RESEARCH GRANTS, TRAINING AWARDS, SUMMARY TABLES. (RESEARCH GRANTS, TRAINING AWARDS . . . SUMMARY TABLES). VFOAT Research Grants, Training Awards, Fellowship Awards. FY 1980-. 0277-3090. US. English. an. Office of Data Analysis and Reports, NINCDS Extramural Activities Program, National Institute of Neurological and Communicative Disorders and Stroke, National Institutes of Health, Bethesda MD 20205. LC RC321. DD 616.80072073.

RESEARCH METHODS IN NEUROCHEMISTRY. V 1-. 0096-2902. US. English. ir. Plenum Press, c/o H Feldman, 233 Spring Street, New York NY 10013. Tel (212)620-8000. Ind/Abst Chem. Abstr. LC QP356.3. DD 612.8042. NLM W1 RE232D. CODEN RMNUBP.

RESEARCH PROGRAM REPORTS. (RESEARCH PROGRAM REPORTS - NATIONAL INSTITUTE OF NEUROLOGICAL DISEASES AND STROKE). Main/Corp National Institute of Neurological Diseases and Stroke. VFOAT NINDS Research Program Reports. 1974-. 0094-9582. US. English. $1.45. Superintendent of Documents, Government Printing Office, Washington DC 20402. LC RC337.N33A. DD 616.8072. NLM W2 A N2053NR. NINDS Research Profiles, 0083-2162.

RESEARCH PUBLICATIONS - ASSOCIATION FOR RESEARCH IN NERVOUS AND MENTAL DISEASE. Main/Corp Association for Research in Nervous and Mental Disease. V. 20- 1939-. 0091-7443. US. English. ir. Raven Press, 1140 Avenue of the Americas, New York NY 10036. Ind/Abst Biol. Abstr., Chem. Abstr., Index Med. NLM W1 RE233P. CODEN RPARA5. Series of Research Publications.

REVISTA DE NEURO-PSIQUIATRIA. Vol. 1- March 1938-. 0034-8597. Periodical. PE. Spanish (summaries in English, French, and German). qt. Directores Honorio Delgado, Casilla 1589, Lima Peru. Ind/Abst Index Med.

REVISTA ESPANOLA DE OTO-NEURO-OFTALMOLOGIA Y NEUROCIRUGIA. V. 1- 1944-. 0034-9453. Periodical. SP. Spanish. ir. $21.50. Redaccion y Administracion, Avellanas 4, Valencia 3 Spain. Ind/Abst Excerpta Med. NLM W1 RE5469.

REVUE D'ELECTROENCEPHALOGRAPHIE ET DE NEUROPHYSIOLOGIE CLINIQUE. VFOAT Revue d'Electroencephalographie et de Neurophysiologie Clinique de Langue Francaise. V. 1- Jan./Mar. 1971-. 0035-1857. Periodical. French. qt. $98.00. Edition Scientifique Elsevier, 91 rue de Rennes, 75006 Paris France. Tel 1/549 14 98. Ind/Abst Life Sci. Collect., Excerpta Med., Index Med., Biol. Abstr. NLM W1 RE785S. CODEN RENCBH.

REVUE NEUROLOGIQUE. Vol. 1- 28 Feb. 1893-. 0035-3787. Periodical. FR. French (summaries in English). mo. Masson Publications USA Inc, 211 East 43rd Street/Room 1306, New York NY 10017. Tel (212)370-1937. Ind/Abst Life Sci. Collect., Excerpta Med., Index Med., Biol. Abstr., CIS Abstr. NLM W1 RE943. CODEN RENEAM. Index published separately - free - automatically sent.

REVUE ROUMAINE DE NEUROLOGIE ET DE PSYCHIATRIE. 0301-7303. Periodical. RM. French. qt. Ilexim Press Department, PO Box 1-136-1-137, Bucharest Romania. Ind/Abst Index Med., Chem. Abstr.

RINSHO SHINKEIGAKU. VFOAT Clinical Neurology. V.1- 1960-. 0009-918X. Periodical. JA. Japanese (English). mo. 10,000. Japanese Society of Neurology, Aoido Bldg 2-40-6 Hongo, Bunkyo-ku Tokyo 113 Japan. Tel (03)815-1080. Ed Eijiro Satoyoshi. Ind/Abst Excerpta Med., Index Med. NLM W1 RI2167R. adv acc. Circ 5,100. (ctrl). A journal of clinical neurology containing original articles of research, case reports, diagnosis and treatment for neurological diseases.

RIVISTA DI NEUROBIOLOGIA. IT. Italian (French). qt. $23.00. Learning Press Publisher, Via Campo Marzio 12, 00186 Rome Italy. Tel 06-6780598. bk rev. adv acc. Clinical neurology, neuroradiology and neurosurgery.

RIVISTA DI NEUROLOGIA. V. 1- 1928-. 0035-6344. Periodical. IT. Italian. bm. Il Pensiero Scientifico Edit, Via Panama 48, 00198 Rome Italy. Tel 863 633. Ind/Abst Excerpta Med., Index Med. NLM W1 RI548.

RIVISTA ITALIANI DI ELETTROENCEFOLOGRAFIA E NEUROFISIOLOGIA CLINICA. (RIVISTA ITALIANI DI ELETTROENCEFOLOGRAFIA E NEUROFISIOLOGIA CLINICA : ORGANO OFFICIALE DELLA SOCIETA ITALIANA DI ELETTROENCEFALOGRAFIA ENEUROFISIOLOGIA). 0392-4793. Periodical. IT. Italian. ir. 23.08. Aulo Gaggi Editore, Via Andrea Costa 131/5, 40134 Bologna Italy. Ind/Abst Excerpta Med., Chem. Abstr. NLM W1 RI769E. CODEN RIECD2. Rivista Italiana di Elettroencefalografia e Neurofisiologia, 0391-3872.

SCHRIFTENREIHE NEUROLOGIE. VFOAT Neurology Series. Vol. 1- 1969-. 0080-715X. Periodical. German. ir. Springer Verlag-New York Inc, 175 5th Avenue, New York NY 10010. Tel (212)460-1584. Ind/Abst Index Med. NLM W1 SC344. Numbered series. Monographien aus dem Gesamtgebiete der Neurologie und Psychiatrie.

SCHWEIZER ARCHIV FUR NEUROLOGIE UND PSYCHIATRIE (ZURICH, SWITZERLAND : 1985). See Genealogy and Heraldry - Archives.

SEARA MEDICA NEUROCIRURGICA. VFOAT Neurocirurgica. Year 1- Sept. 1972-. 0037-0169. Periodical. BL. Portuguese (summaries in English). qt. 40. Sears Medica Neurocirurgica, Caixa Postal 20-389, 04034 Sao Paulo SP Brazil. Ed A Mattos Pimenta. Ind/Abst Chem. Abstr. NLM W1 SE15G. CODEN SMNCAF. bk rev. adv acc. Circ 1,000. (ctrl). Medicine and neurology. Seara Medica.

SEISHIN SHINKEIGAKU ZASSHI. See Medicine - Psychiatry, Psychopathology.

SEMINARS IN NEUROLOGY. Vol. 1, No. 1 (Mar. 1981)-. 0271-8235. Periodical. US. English. qt. $68.00. Thieme-Stratton Inc, 381 Park Avenue South/Suite 1501, New York NY 10016. Tel (212)683-5088. Ed Robert Joynt aned David Goldblatt. LC UNC. NLM W1 SE489CS. adv acc. Circ 1,400. Topic-oriented journal devoted to case reports and subjects in neurology and designed for the practitioner.

SERVICE DE LA BIBLIOTHEQUE. SUPPLEMENT AU GUIDE DE L'USAGER. See Bibliographies.

SHEN CHING CHING SHEN CHI PING TSA CHIH. VFOAT Journal of Nervous and Mental Diseases. Periodical. Chinese. ir. NLM W1.

SOCIETY FOR NEUROSCIENCE SYMPOSIA. V. 2- 1976-. 0161-7737. Monographic Series. US. English. an. NLM W3 SO59N. Neuroscience Symposia, 0160-7170.

SOMATOSTATIN. Series/Titl Annual Research Reviews. V. 1- 1977-. 0708-238X. CN. English. ir. Eden Press, 4626 St Catherine Street West, Montreal Quebec H3Z 1S3 Canada. DD 591.1927. NLM W1 SO887M.

SOUTH AFRICAN JOURNAL OF COMMUNICATION DISORDERS. (THE SOUTH AFRICAN JOURNAL OF COMMUNICATION DISORDERS). VFOAT Die Suid-Afrikaanse Tydskrif vir Kommunikasieafwykings. V. 24- 1977-. 0379-8046. SA. Afrikaans (or English). an. S A Speech & Hearing Association, PO Box 31782, Braamfontein 2017 South Africa. Tel 716-2374. Ed M L Aron. Ind/Abst Index Med., Biol. Abstr., Index Dent. Lit. LC RC423.A1. DD 616.855005. NLM W1 SO9044M. CODEN SAJDDJ. adv acc. Circ 700. (ctrl). Academic research and therapeutic applications in the field of speech therapy and audiology. Journal of the South African Speech and Hearing Association, 0300-9874.

SOVIET NEUROLOGY & PSYCHIATRY. VAT Soviet Neurology and Psychiatry. V. 1- Spring 1968-. 0038-559X. Periodical. US. English (Russian). qt. $178.50. International Arts and Sciences Press, 901 North Broadway, White Plains NY 10603. Tel (914)273-1800. Ed Gordon Mangan. Ind/Abst Excerpta Med., Curr. Contents Behav. Soc. Educ. Sci., Biol. Abstr., Psychol. Abstr. LC RC321. DD 616.8005. NLM W1 SO996M. adv acc. Circ 150. Reflects current developments in Soviet psychiatric and neurological theory and practice. Soviet Psychology and Psychiatry, 0584-5610.

SP QUEBEC. (MS QUEBEC). VAT Sclerose en Plaques Quebec Multiple Sclerosis Quebec. Vol. 6, No. 18 (Spring 1981)-. 0822-5702. Periodical. CN. English (French on inverted pages). qt. Free. Multiple Sclerosis Society of Canada, Quebec Division, 1455 Peel Street, Montreal Quebec H3A 1T5 Canada. DD 616.8340060714. (ctrl). SP Quebec, 0822-5702.

SPINAL CORD SOCIETY. (SPINAL CORD SOCIETY : SCS). VFOAT SCS. 0279-1137. Periodical. US. English. mo. $24.00 Domestic, $30.00 Foreign. Spinal Cord Society, 6203 Bellaire Avenue, North Hollywood CA 91606. Tel (818)762-4057. Ed Charles E Carson. Circ 25,000. Treatment and cure-research for spinal cord injury, other neurological disorders (MS, palsy, etc.) and their related disorders (renal, urological, circulatory, etc.).

STROEZH I FUNKTSII NA MOZUKA. VFOAT Structure and Functions of the Brain. Vol. 1-. 0204-4560. Periodical. Bulgarian (English, French, German, and Russian). ir. 1.10. Izdatelstvo No Ban, Ul Akad G Bonchev Por No 33, 1113 Sofiia Bulgaria. Tel 72-09-22. Ed A Varbanova. Ind/Abst Chem. Abstr. LC QP376. DD 612.8205. CODEN SFMODY. bk rev. adv acc. Circ 500. (ctrl). Research of functions, structure, and disease of the brain.

Medicine—Nursing

STROKE. V. 1- Jan./Feb. 1970-. 0039-2499. Periodical. US. English. bm. $50.00 Domestic, $65.00 Foreign. American Heart Association, 7320 Greenville Avenue, Dallas TX 75231. **Tel** (214)750-5466. Ed H J M Barnett. **Ind/Abst** Life Sci. Collect., Excerpta Med., Energy Res. Abstr., Biol. Abstr., Chem. Abstr., Index Med., Pestdoc, Ringdoc, Vetdoc, Sci. Cit. Index, Abr. Ed. **LC** RC388.5. **DD** 616.81005. **NLM** W1 ST81K. **CODEN** SJCCA7. adv acc. **Circ** 5,000. (ctrl). It is of interest to the practicing physician, internist, cardiologist and neurologist. Articles include clinical conferences and deal with prevention, diagnosis, treatment and rehabiltation.

STUDIES IN NEUROLINGUISTICS. 1976-. Monographic Series. US. English. ir. **Tel** (305)345-4100. Ed Haiganoosh Whitaker and Harry A Whitaker. **LC** RC423. **DD** 616.8552.

STUDIES OF BRAIN FUNCTION. V. 1-. 0172-5742. Monographic Series. English. ir. Springer Verlag-New York Inc, 175 5th Avenue, New York NY 10010. **Tel** (212)460-1584. **NLM** W1 ST937KF. Studies operation of the visual cortex, and vision in drosophila.

STUDIES ON THE DEVELOPMENT OF BEHAVIOR AND THE NERVOUS SYSTEM. V. 1- 1973-. 0093-3317. Periodical. US. English. ir. Academic Press, 4805 Sand Lake Road, Orlanda FL 32887. **Tel** (305)345-4100. Ed Gilbert Gottlieb. **NLM** W1 ST937M.

SVREMENNI PROBLEMI NA NEVROMORFOLOGIJATA. (SUVREMENNI PROBLEMI NA NEVROMORFOLOGIIATA). **VFOAT** Contemporary Problems of Neuromorphology. Vol. 1- 1973-. 0324-0258. Bulgarian (summaries in Russian and English). ir. 2.00 Each Issue. **Ind/Abst** Chem. Abstr. **LC** QP355.2. **NLM** W1 SU931. **CODEN** SPNEDB.

THERAPIE ET REEDUCATION PSYCHOMOTRICE. 0154-473X. French. an. Ed J Defontaine. **NLM** W1 TH644I.

TOKYO-TO SEISHIN IGAKU SOGO KENKYUJO KENKYU KIYO. No. 1-. JA. Japanese or English. ir. 1-8 Kami Kitazawa 1-Chome Setagaya-ku (156), Tokyo Japan. **LC** RC331.

TOKYO-TO SEISHIN IGAKU SOGO KENKYUJO NEMPO. 1977-. JA. Japanese. ir. Tokyo-To Seishin Igaku Sogo Kenkyujo, 1-8 Kami Kitazawa 2, Setagaya-Ku 156, Tokyo Japan. **LC** RC337.

TOKYO-TO SHINKEI KAGAKU SOGO KENKYUSHO NENPO. (TOKYO-TO SHINKEI KAGAKU SOGO KENKYUJO NEMPO). No. 1-. 0301-5041. JA. Japanese. ir. 6 Ban Musashidai 2-Chome Fuchushi, Tokyo Japan. **LC** RC329. **NLM** TO2145E.

TRAINING AWARDS, FELLOWSHIP AWARDS . . . DATA BOOK. Main/Corp National Institute of Neurological and Communicative Disorders and Stroke. **VFOAT** NINCDS Training and Fellowship Awards. US. English. an. National Institute of Neurological and Communicative Disorders and Stroke, Office of Planning and Analysis, Management Information and Data Section, 9000 Rockville Pike, Bethesda MD 20014.

TRANSACTIONS OF THE AMERICAN NEUROLOGICAL ASSOCIATION CEASED. (TRANSACTIONS OF THE AMERICAN NEUROLOGICAL ASSOCIATION. ANNUAL MEETING). Began with V. 1-106, for 1875. 0065-9479. US. English. an. **Ind/Abst** Biol. Abstr., Chem. Abstr., Index Med., Nuci. Sci. Abstr., Energy Res. Abstr. **LC** RC326. **DD** 616.8082. **NLM** W1 TR2244. **CODEN** TANAA4.

TRANSACTIONS OF THE AMERICAN SOCIETY FOR NEUROCHEMISTRY. Main/Corp American Society for Neurochemistry. V. 1- 1970-. 0066-0132. US. English. an. Free to Members. American Society for Neurochemistry, Veterans Administration Medical Center, Department of Neurology/127A, Palo Alto Ca 94304. **LC** QP356.3. **DD** 596.0188. **NLM** W1 TR225D.

TRENDS IN NEUROSCIENCES. **VFOAT** Tins. V. 1- 1978-. 0378-5912. Periodical. English. mo. $49.00. Elsevier Science Publishers, 52 Vanderbilt Avenue, New York NY 10017. **Tel** (212)916-1050. **Ind/Abst** Sci. Cit. Index, Abr. Ed., Psychol. Abstr., Chem. Abstr.

VERHANDLUNGEN DER GESELLSCHAFT FUR NEUROOTOLOGIE UND AEQUILIBRIOMETRIE E.V. (1981). (VERHANDLUNGEN DER GESELLSCHAFT FUR NEUROOTOLOGIE UND AEQUILIBRIOMETRIE E.V).

VFOAT Proceedings of the Neurootological and Equilibriometric Society Reg. V. 8-. German (articles in English, French, or Spanish). ir. **NLM** W1. Equilibrium in Patients and Research.

WORLD DIRECTORY OF NEUROLOGICAL SURGEONS. PART 1, UNITED STATES OF AMERICA AND CANADA. See Yearbooks, Almanacs, Directories.

THE YEAR BOOK OF NEUROLOGY AND NEUROSURGERY. See Yearbooks, Almanacs, Directories.

THE YEAR BOOK OF PSYCHIATRY AND APPLIED MENTAL HEALTH. See Yearbooks, Almanacs, Directories.

ZENTRALBLATT FUR DIE GESAMTE NEUROLOGIE UND PSYCHIATRIE CEASED. Began with V. 25, No. 1/2 (April 1, 1921). Ceased with 1982. 0044-412X. Periodical. GW. German. ir. **NLM** ZWL 100 Z56. Neurologische Centralblatt.

ZENTRALBLATT NEUROLOGIE, PSYCHIATRIE. **VFOAT** Neurology, Psychiatry. **VAT** Zentralblatt Neurologie-Psychiatrie. 238. Vol., No. 1-. 0722-3064. Periodical. German (English). mo. Springer Verlag-New York Inc, 175 5th Avenue, New York NY 10010. **Tel** (212)460-1500. Ed O Hallen, G Huber and F Funk. **NLM** ZWL 100 Z56. Reviews, meeting reports, all areas of psychiatry and neurology, special areas of neurology, birth defects of nervous system, nervous diseases, special areas of psychiatry and neuroses-psychoses. Zentralblatt fur die Gesamte Neurologie und Psychiatrie, 0044-412X.

ZURNAL VYSSEJ NERVNOJ DEJATELNOSTI IMENTI I P PAVLOVA. (ZHURNAL VYSSHEI NERVNOI DEIATELNOSTI IMENI I P PAVLOVA). Vol. 1- Jan./Feb. 1951-. 0044-4677. Periodical. UR. Russian (summaries in English). bm. $70.00. Victor Kamkin Inc, 12224 Parklawn Drive, Rockville MD 20852. **Tel** (301)881-5973. **Ind/Abst** Life Sci. Collect., Excerpta Med., Index Med., Biol. Abstr., Int. Aerosp. Abstr., Chem. Abstr., Psychol. Abstr., Sci. Cit. Index, Abr. Ed., Sociol. Abstr., Lang. Lang. Behav. Abstr. **NLM** W1 ZH425. **CODEN** ZVNDAM. (cum index).

NURSING

A. A. N. A. JOURNAL. (AANA JOURNAL). V. 42- Feb. 1974-. 0094-6354. Periodical. US. English. bm. $24.00. American Association of Nurse Anesthetists, 216 Higgins Road, Park Ridge IL 60068. **Tel** (312)692-7050. Ed Betty A Colitti. **Ind/Abst** Excerpta Med., Hospit. Lit. Index, Cumul. Index Nurs. Allied Health Lit., Int. Nurs. Index, Index Med. **NLM** W1 A1026T. bk rev. adv acc. **Circ** 22,400. It focuses on the clinical in the form of both practical and theoretical editorial matter provided by various specialists (principally in nursing and medicine). Journal of the American Association of Nurse Anesthetists, 0002-7448.

A A R N NEWSLETTER. Main/Corp Alberta Association of Registered Nurses. Began with Sept. 1945 issue. 0001-0197. Periodical. CN. English. mo. $20.00 Domestic, $25.00 Foreign. AARN News Letter, 10256-112 Street, Edmonton Alberta Canada. **Tel** (403)426-0160. Ed Evelyn Henderson. **Ind/Abst** Cumul. Index Nurs. Allied Health Lit., Int. Nurs. Index. **NLM** W1 A1028. adv acc. (ctrl). Official publication of the registered nurses of Alberta. Nursing topics/information in specific interest to registered nurses. Health promotion and illness prevention.

AANA NEWSBULLETIN. Main/Corp American Association of Nurse Anesthetists. **VFOAT** A. A. N. A. News Bulletin. **VAT** American Association of Nurse Anesthetists News Bulletin. V. 1- Sept. 1947-. 0199-2554. Periodical. US. English. mo. $1.00 Members. American Association of Nurse Anesthetists, 216 Higgins Road, Park Ridge IL 60068.

AARNA PULSE. (A A R N A PULSE). Main/Corp Alberta Association of Registered Nursing Assistants. V. 2, No. 5- May 1978-. 0706-2192. Periodical. CN. English. Alberta Association of Registered Nursing Assistants, 11435 107th Avenue, Edmonton Alberta T5H 0Y6 Canada. **DD** 610.7306980627123.

AICHI KENRITSU KANGO TANKI DAIGAKU ZASSHI. No. 1. JA. Japanese. ir. Kenritsu Kango Tanki Daigaku, Oaza Kami-Shidami Moriyama-Ku, Nagoya Japan. **LC** RT1.

A.I.I.S.T.Q. ASSOCIATION DES INFIRMIERES ER INFIRMIERS EN SANTE DU TRAVAIL DU QUEBEC. (A. I. I. S. T. Q). Main/Corp Association des Infirmieres et Infirmiers en Sante du Travail du Quebec. **VAT** Association des Infirmieres et Infirmiers en Sante du Travail du Quebec. V. 1, No. 2- June 1978-. 0708-2347. Periodical. CN. French. Association des Infirmieres en Sante en Travail du Quebec, Universite de Montreal, 2050 Edouard Montpetit Porte 077, Montreal Quebec H3T 1J4 Canada. **DD** 610.73069209714. A I S T Q, 0708-2339.

THE AJN GUIDE. **VFOAT** A.J.N. Guide. 1982-. English. ir.

AJN NURSING BOARDS REVIEW FOR THE NCLEX-RN EXAMINATION. (AJN . . . NURSING BOARDS REVIEW FOR THE NCLEX-RN EXAMINATION). **VFOAT** A.J.N. . . . Nursing Boards Review for the NCLEX-RN Examination. **VAT** American Journal of Nursing Nursing Boards Review for the NCLEX-RN Examination. 1st Ed (1983)-. 0737-3058. US. English. an. $14.95. Nuresco, PO Box 145, Pacific Palisades CA 90272. **Tel** (213)454-6597. **NLM** WY 18 A312. **Circ** 50,000. Review for NCLEX examination.

THE ALASKA NURSE. 0002-4546. Periodical. US. English. qt. $7.00. Alaska Nurses Association, 237 East Third Avenue, Anchorage AK 99501. **Tel** (907)274-0827. Ed Daryl Young. **Ind/Abst** Int. Nurs. Index. **NLM** W1 AL194. adv acc. **Circ** 500. (ctrl). Nursing topics.

THE ALUMNI MAGAZINE - ALUMNI ASSOCIATION OF THE JOHNS HOPKINS HOSPITAL SCHOOL OF NURSING. (THE ALUMNI MAGAZINE). V. 71- 1972-. 0149-2608. Periodical. US. English. sa. Alumni Association, 624 North Broadway, Baltimore MD 21205. **Ind/Abst** Cumul. Index Nurs. Allied Health Lit., Int. Nurs. Index. **NLM** W1 AL996V. Alumnae Magazine - Alumnae Association of the Johns Hopkins Hospitals of Nursing, 0002-6700.

THE AMERICAN JOURNAL OF PSYCHIATRIC NURSING. 0883-9417. Periodical. US. English. bm. Grune & Stratton, 6277 Sea Harbor Drive, Orlando FL 32821.

THE AMERICAN NURSE. V. 4- Feb. 1972-. 0098-1486. Periodical. US. English. ir. $10.00. American Nurses Association, 2420 Pershing Road, Kansas City MO 64108. **Tel** (816)474-5720. Ed Patricia McCarty. **Ind/Abst** Hospit. Lit. Index, Cumul. Index Nurs. Allied Health Lit., Int. Nurs. Index. **NLM** W1 AM6635. adv acc. **Circ** 185,000. A broad range of professional, economic, political, ethical and legal issues and events that affect nursing. ANA in Action.

ANA CLINICAL SESSIONS. 1966-. 0065-9495. Periodical. US. English. be. Appleton-Century-Crofts, 25 Van Zant Street, East Norwalk CT 06855. **LC** RT3. **DD** 610.73. **NLM** W1 A1398P.

ANNA JOURNAL. **VFOAT** A.N.N.A. Journal. **VAT** American Nephrology Nurses Association Journal. Vol. 11, No. 4 (June 1984)-. 8750-0779. Periodical. US. English. bm. $18.00 Domestic, $21.00 Foreign. American Nephrology Nurses Association Journal, North Woodbury Road Box 56, Pitman NJ 08071. **NLM** W1. AANNT Journal, 0744-1479.

ANNUAL CONVENTION. 74th (Oct. 22, 23, 24, 1980)-. Periodical. US. English. an. **NLM** W1 KE692E.

ANNUAL NURSING HOME SURVEY. **VFOAT** South Dakota Annual Nursing Home Report. US. English. an. South Dakota Department of Health, State Center for Health Statistics, Foss Building, Pierre SD 57501. **LC** RA997.5.S8. **DD** 362.1609783.

ANNUAL REPORT - BOARD OF NURSE REGISTRATION AND NURSING EDUCATION. Main/Corp Oklahoma. Board of Nurse Registration and Nursing Education. 0360-4624. US. English. an. Board of Nursing Education, Suite 76 Lincoln Office Plaza 4545 Lincoln Boulevard, Oklahoma City OK 73105. **LC** RT5.O5. **DD** 610.7309766.

ANNUAL REPORT - BOPHUTHATSWANA (SOUTH AFRICA) NURSING DIVISION. Main/Corp Bophuthatswana (South Africa) Nursing Division. Vol. 1 (1980)-. English. an. **LC** RT97. **DD** 354.6829400841.

ANNUAL REPORT - MISSOURI BOARD OF NURSING. Main/Corp Missouri Board of Nursing. US. English. an. State Board of Nursing, PO Box 656, 3523 North Ten Mile Drive, Jefferson City MO 65102. **LC** RT5.M62. **DD** 353.9778008243.

ANNUAL REPORT TO THE GOVERNOR AND GENERAL ASSEMBLY - STATE BOARD OF NURSING FOR SOUTH CAROLINA. Main/Corp State Board of Nursing for South Carolina. US. English. an. 1777 St Julian Place/Suite

Medicine—Nursing

102, Columbia SC 29204. **LC** RT5.S6. **DD** 353.9757008243.

ANNUAL REPORT - WYOMING STATE BOARD OF NURSING. **Main/Corp** Wyoming. State Board of Nursing. 0098-2679. US. English. an. Wyoming State Board of Nursing, Room 214/1902 Thomes Avenue, Cheyenne WY 82001. **LC** RT81.U6. **DD** 353.9787008416.

ANNUAL REVIEW OF NURSING RESEARCH. **VFOAT** Review of Nursing Research. Vol. 1 (1983)-. 0739-6686. US. English. an. Springer Publishing Company, 200 Park Avenue South, New York NY 10003. **Ed** Harriet H Werley and Joyce J Fitzpatrick. **LC** RT81.5. **DD** 610.73072. **NLM** W1.

ANNUAL SALARIES, NURSES, MAJOR HOSPITAL AGREEMENTS, CANADA. **VFOAT** Salaires Annuels, Infirmieres et Infirmieres, Conventions Signees dans les Principaux Hopitaux, Canada. 1983-. 0825-2815. Periodical. CN. English (French). ir. $3.00. Canadian Nurses Association, 50 The Driveway, Ottawa Ontario K2P 1E2 Canada. **DD** 331.281610730971.

ANS. ADVANCES IN NURSING SCIENCE. (ANS, ADVANCES IN NURSING SCIENCE). **VFOAT** Advances in Nursing Science. V. 1- Oct. 1978-. 0161-9268. Periodical. US. English. qt. $53.00. Aspen Systems Corporation, PO Box 6018, Gaithersburg MD 20760. **Tel** (301)251-5449. **Ind/Abst** Cumul. Index Nurs. Allied Health Lit., Index Med., Int. Nurs. Index. **LC** RT1. **DD** 174.2. **NLM** W1 A14SH.

AORN JOURNAL. **Main/Corp** Association of Operating Room Nurses. **VAT** Association of Operating Room Nurses Journal. V. 1- Jan./Feb. 1963-. 0001-2092. Periodical. US. English. mo. AORN Journal, 10170 East Mississippi Avenue, Denver CO 80231. **Ind/Abst** Hospit. Lit. Index, Cumul. Index Nurs. Allied Health Lit., Index Med., Int. Nurs. Index. **LC** RD99.A1. **NLM** W1 A142. Issued also in microform by University Microforms International. *OR Nursing.*

ARIZONA NURSE. 1947. 0004-1599. Periodical. US. English. bm. $15.00. Arizona Nurses Association, 4525 North 12th Street, Phoenix AZ 85014. **Tel** (602)277-4401. **Ed** Hazel Bennett. **Ind/Abst** Cumul. Index Nurs. Allied Health Lit., Int. Nurs. Index. **DD** 610. **NLM** W1 AR797. bk rev. adv acc. **Circ** 2,500. (ctrl). Continuing education for nurses, state legislation, organization activities, clinical articles, resources, book-review.

ARKANSAS HEALTH MANPOWER STATISTICS. LICENSED PRACTICAL NURSES. *See* Statistics.

ARKANSAS HEALTH MANPOWER STATISTICS. REGISTERED NURSES. *See* Statistics.

ARN JOURNAL *CEASED.* **Main/Corp** Association of Rehabilitation Nurses. **VAT** Association of Rehabilitation Nurses Journal. V. 1-5. 0362-3505. Periodical. US. English. bm. $18.00. ARN Journal, 2506 Gross Point Road, Evanston IL 60201. **Ind/Abst** Cumul. Index Nurs. Allied Health Lit. **LC** RT120.R4. **DD** 610.736. **NLM** W1 A15P.

ARNN NEWS NEWS NEWS. **Main/Corp** Association of Registered Nurses of Newfoundland. **VAT** Association of Registered Nurses of Newfoundland News News News. 0822-7160. Periodical. CN. English. bm. Association of Registered Nurses of Newfoundland, ARNN House, PO Box 4185, St John's Newfoundland A1C 6A1 Canada. **Tel** (709)753-6040. **Ed** Violet D Ruelokke. **DD** 610.73060718. **Circ** 5,300. (ctrl). Contains information on provincial and national professional nursing issues. *News News News, 0319-7611.*

THE ASPEN ADVISOR FOR NURSE EXECUTIVES. **VFOAT** Aspen's Advisor. 0883-9743. Periodical. US. English. mo. $95.00. Aspen Systems Corporation, 16792 Oakmont Avenue, Rockville MD 20877.

ASSOCIATE DEGREE EDUCATION FOR NURSING. **Main/Corp** National League for Nursing. Division of Associate Degree Programs. 0077-5118. US. English. $0.75. National League for Nursing, Ten Columbus Circle, New York NY 10019. **LC** RT74.5. **DD** 610.73071173. **NLM** WY 22 AA1 A8.

ASSOCIATE DEGREE EDUCATION FOR NURSING. CURRENT ISSUES. (ASSOCIATE DEGREE EDUCATION FOR NURSING—CURRENT ISSUES). **Main/Corp** National League for Nursing. Council of Associate Degree Programs. 0190-5198. US. English. $2.50. National League for Nursing, 10 Columbus Circle, New York NY 10019. **LC** RT81.U6. **DD** 610.73071173.

AUSTRALASIAN NURSES JOURNAL. (THE AUSTRALASIAN NURSES JOURNAL). V. 1- July 1971-. Periodical. AT. English. ir. $5.00. Messenger Publications, Box 197, Port Adelaide South Australia 5015. **Ind/Abst** Cumul. Index Nurs. Allied Health Lit., Int. Nurs. Index. **NLM** W1 AU333. *S.A. Nurses Journal.*

AUSTRALIAN NURSES' JOURNAL. (THE AUSTRALIAN NURSES' JOURNAL). V. 1- July 1971-. 0045-0758. Periodical. AT. English. mo. 35.00. Royal Australian Nursing Federation, 132-136 Albert Road, South Melbourne Victoria Australia 3205. **Tel** (03)690-8611. **Ed** George Thallon. **Ind/Abst** Cumul. Index Nurs. Allied Health Lit. **NLM** W1 AU643A. bk rev. adv acc. **Circ** 43,000. (ctrl). The official publication of the sole national organization representing nursing at both the professional and industrial levels-Royal Australian Nursing Federation.

AUXILIAIRE. (L'AUXILIAIRE). V. 50, No. 2-V. 55, No. 3. 0703-9484. Periodical. CN. French (English). qt. $4.00. L'Auxiliaire, 1380 rue Gilford, Montreal Quebec H2J 1R8 Canada. **DD** 610.73069309714. **NLM** W1 AU923. *La Revue des Infirmieres et Infirmiers Auxiliaires du Quebec, 0316-411X.*

BAYLOR NURSING EDUCATOR. V. 1-. 0270-7799. US. English. School of Nursing, Baylor University, 3616 Worth Street, Dallas TX 75246. **Ind/Abst** Cumul. Index Nurs. Allied Health Lit., Int. Nurs. Index. **NLM** W1 BA964.

BIENNIAL REPORT OF EXAMINING AND LICENSING BOARDS - MINNESOTA BOARD OF NURSING. **Main/Corp** Minnesota Board of Nursing. 1974-6-. US. English. be. Minnesota Board of Nursing, 717 Delaware Street SE, Minneapolis MN 55414. **LC** RT5.M6. **DD** 353.977600841. *Biennial Report to Governor, State of Minnesota.*

BULLETIN - TENNESSEE NURSES ASSOCIATION. **Main/Corp** Tennessee Nurses Association. 0040-3342. Periodical. US. English. bm. $20.00. Tennessee Nurses Association, 1720 West End Building/Room 400, Nashville TN 37203. **Tel** (615)329-2511. **Ind/Abst** Cumul. Index Nurs. Allied Health Lit., Int. Nurs. Index. **NLM** W1 BU934D.

CALIFORNIA NURSE. V. 65, No. 7- July/Aug. 1969-. 0008-1310. Periodical. US. English. mo. $3.50 Domestic, $4.00 Foreign. California Nurses' Association, 790 Market Street, San Francisco CA 94102. **Ind/Abst** Cumul. Index Nurs. Allied Health Lit., Int. Nurs. Index. **NLM** W1 CA402V. *CNA Bulletin.*

CANA. **VFOAT** News Bulletin - California Association of Nurse Anesthetists. **VAT** California Association of Nurse Anesthetists. 0196-2752. Periodical. US. English. qt. $8.00. California Association of Nurse Anesthetists, PO Box 1528, Eureka CA 95502. **Tel** (707)442-3621. **Ind/Abst** Int. Nurs. Index. **NLM** W1 C123.

CANADIAN CRITICAL CARE NURSING JOURNAL. **VFOAT** Critical Care. Vol. 1, No. 1 (Sept. 1984)-. 0826-6778. Periodical. CN. English. bm. 20.00. Canadian Critical Care Nursing Journal, 3rd Floor 25 Imperial Street, Toronto Ontario M5P 1C1 Canada. **Tel** (416)483-5116. **Ed** F Fagan. **DD** 610.736105. adv acc. **Circ** 4,500. (ctrl). Critical care nursing, intensive care, cardial care, post anaesthetic, etc.

CANADIAN JOURNAL OF PSYCHIATRIC NURSING. (THE CANADIAN JOURNAL OF PSYCHIATRIC NURSING). **VFOAT** Psychiatric Nursing. V. 7, No. 6- June/July 1966-. 0008-4247. CN. English. bm. $12.00 Domestic, $15.00 Foreign. Psychiatric Nurses Association of Canada, 1854 Portage Avenue, Winnipeg Manitoba R3J 0G9 Canada. **Tel** (204)885-1298. **Ed** Paul Tataryn. **Ind/Abst** Cumul. Index Nurs. Allied Health Lit., Int. Nurs. Index, Int. Nurs. Index. **DD** 610.736805. **NLM** W1 CA602U. bk rev. adv acc. **Circ** 5,400. (ctrl). *Psych Nurse, 0317-5774.*

CANADIAN NURSE. (THE CANADIAN NURSE). **VFOAT** Infirmiere Canadienne. Began in 1924. 0008-4581. Periodical. CN. English (includes some text in French). mo. Canadian Nurses Association, 50 The Driveway, Ottawa Ontario K2P 1E2 Canada. **Tel** (613)237-2133. **Ed** Anne Besharah. **Ind/Abst** Life Sci. Collect., Cumul. Index Nurs. Allied Health Lit., Can. Period. Index, Int. Nurs. Index, Index Med. **NLM** W1 CA63F. bk rev. adv acc. **Circ** 129,000. Professional, national nursing journal offering up-to-date information on nursing issues and practice. *Canadian Nurse and Hospital Review, 0315-1018.*

CANADIAN OPERATING ROOM NURSING JOURNAL. **VFOAT** Operating Room Nursing Journal. Vol. 1, No. 1 (Feb. 1983)-. 0712-6778. Periodical. CN. English (includes some text in French). bm. 12.00 Domestic, 27.00 US. Canadian Operating Room Nursing Journal, c/o Health Media Inc, 25 Imperial Street, Toronto Ontario M5P 1C1 Canada. **Tel** (416)483-5116. **Ed** Frank Fagan. **DD** 610.7367705. adv acc. **Circ** 5,000. (ctrl). Operating room technology, procedures, asepsis.

CANCER NURSING. V. 1- Feb. 1978-. 0162-220X. Periodical. US. English. bm. Raven Press, 1140 Avenue of the Americas, New York NY 10036. **Tel** (212)575-0335. **Ind/Abst** Cumul. Index Nurs. Allied Health Lit., Int. Nurs. Index. **LC** RC266. **DD** 610.736. **NLM** W1 CA683NG.

CANCER NURSING NEWS. (CANCER NURSING NEWS : AMERICAN CANCER SOCIETY NEWSLETTER FOR NURSES). V. 1, No. 1 (Sept./Oct. 1982)-. 0734-1873. Periodical. US. English. bm. American Cancer Society Inc, 777 Third Avenue, New York NY 10017.

CAPITAL NURSING. Vol. 1, No. 1 (May 1984)-. Periodical. US. English. bm. **Ind/Abst** Int. Nurs. Index.

CAPNA NEWS. (C A P N A NEWS). **Main/Corp** Canadian Association of Practical Nursing Assistants. 1977/78-. 0705-9159. CN. English. an. $1.00 Per Number. CAPNA, c/o F Paulmartin, 528 Cambian Crescent, Thunder Bay Ontario P7C 5B9 Canada. **DD** 610.73069806271.

CARDIO-VASCULAR NURSING. V. 1- Winter 1965-. 0008-6355. Periodical. US. English. bm. American Heart Association Inc, 7320 Greenville Avenue, Dallas TX 75231. **Ind/Abst** Cumul. Index Nurs. Allied Health Lit., Int. Nurs. Index. **DD** 610. **NLM** W1 CA771.

CAREERS IN NURSING AND OTHER HEALTH SERVICE PROFESSIONS. 0309-2399. Periodical. UK. English. ir. **NLM** W1 CA786C. *Careers in Nursing, 0309-2327.*

CHART. V. 53, No. 6- June/July 1956-. 0069-2778. Periodical. US. English. mo. $15.00. Illinois Nurses Association, 20 North Wacker Drive, Suite 2520, Chicago IL 60606. **Tel** (312)236-9708. **Ed** Pamela Towne. **Ind/Abst** Cumul. Index Nurs. Allied Health Lit., Int. Nurs. Index. **NLM** W1 CH147L. adv acc. **Circ** 8,200. (ctrl). Professional publication for members of the Illinois Nurses Association. Topics include INA news, nursing and health care issues, research and display advertising. *ISNA.*

CHICAGO NURSE. 0199-2066. Periodical. US. English. bm. Chicago Nurses Association, 180 North Michigan, Chicago IL 60601.

CHRISTIAN NURSE. 1933-. 0009-5540. Periodical. English. ir. **Ind/Abst** Cumul. Index Nurs. Allied Health Lit.

CLINICAL AND SCIENTIFIC SESSIONS (AMERICAN NURSES' ASSOCIATION). **Main/Corp** American Nurses' Association. 0197-6958. US. English. American Nurses' Association, 2420 Pershing Road, Kansas City MO 64108. **LC** RT3. **DD** 610.73. **NLM** W1 CL664R.

CLINICAL NURSING (COLLEGEVILLE COLLEGEVILLE, PA.). (CLINICAL NURSING). Vol. 1, No. 1 (Jan. 1985)-. 8756-761X. Periodical. US. English. mo. $19.00. Clinical Nursing, PO Box 186, Collegeville PA 19426. **DD** 616.

COLORADO NURSE. (COLORADO NURSE : OFFICIAL BULLETIN OF THE COLORADO NURSES' ASSOCIATION). Vol. 1, No. 4 (Feb. 25, 1985)-. 8750-846X. Periodical. US. English. mo. $20.00. Colorado Nurses' Association, 5453 East Evans Place, Denver CO 80222. **Tel** (303)757-7483. **Ed** Lola M Fehr. **Ind/Abst** Int. Nurs. Index. **DD** 610. **NLM** W1. adv acc. **Circ** 2,300. Contains association activities, nursing issues, legislative reports, continuing education listings. *Colorado Nurse Update, 8750-8451.*

COMMUNICATING NURSING RESEARCH. V. 1-. 0160-1652. Monographic Series. US. English. an. Western Interstate Commission on Higher Education, PO Drawer P, Boulder CO 80302. **Tel** (303)497-0290. **Ind/Abst** Cumul. Index Nurs. Allied Health Lit., Int. Nurs. Index. **NLM** W3 C1746.

Medicine—Nursing

THE COMMUNIQUE' (MILWAUKEE, WIS.). (THE COMMUNIQUE'). Began publication with issue for Spring, 1979?. Periodical. US. English. qt. Wisconsin League for Nursing, 9040 North Rexleigh Drive, Milwaukee WI 53217. **Ind/Abst** Int. Nurs. Index. *Newsletter (Wisconsin League for Nursing).*

COMPILATION OF PROVINCIAL NURSES' ACTS AND RELATED LEGISLATION. Main/Corp Canadian Nurses' Association. Library. VFOAT Compilation des Lois Regissant les Infirmieres et de la Legislation Qui S'y Rapporte. Began with 1972 or 1973 issue. 0706-3881. CN. English (French). an. Canadian Nurses' Association, 50 The Driveway, Ottawa Ontario K2P 1E2 Canada. DD 016.34471041. *Compilation of Provincial Nurses' Acts and Related Legislation, 0706-3881.*

CONA JOURNAL. Main/Corp Canadian Orthopaedic Nurses' Association. V. 1- Dec. 1978-. 0708-6474. Periodical. CN. English. qt. $15.48. Canadian Orthopaedic Nurses Association, 43 Wellesley Street East, Toronto Ontario M4Y 1H1 Canada. Tel (416)967-8622. Ed Susie Thibeault. **Ind/Abst** Cumul. Index Nurs. Allied Health Lit. DD 610.73677. bk rev. adv acc. Circ 400. Official publication of CONA-reflects current trend in ortho nursing and related fields in Canada.

CONNECTICUT NURSING NEWS. Began with Feb. 1980 issue. 0278-4092. Periodical. US. English. mo. $15.00. Connecticut Nurses Association, 1 Prestige Drive, Meriden CT 06450. Tel (203)238-1207. Ed R Helfferidi. **Ind/Abst** Cumul. Index Nurs. Allied Health Lit., Int. Nurs. Index. bk rev. adv acc. Circ 2,000. (ctrl). Information about nursing issues aimed at professional nurses concerns. *Nursing News, 0029-652X.*

CONTINUING EDUCATION FOR NURSES. SHORT-TERM NURSING COURSES IN CANADA. (CONTINUING EDUCATION FOR NURSES : SHORT-TERM NURSING COURSES IN CANADA). VFOAT Formation Continue des Infirmieres et Infirmiers. Fall 1982-. 0715-0075. Periodical. CN. English (French). sa. Free. Canadian Nurses Association, 50 The Driveway, Ottawa Onario K2P 1E2 Canada. DD 610.730771171.

COUNTDOWN; CANADIAN NURSING STATISTICS. See Statistics.

CRITICAL CARE NURSE. Vol. 1, No. 1 (Nov./Dec. 1980)-. 0279-5442. Periodical. US. English. bm. Critical Care Nurse, 300 Harmon Meadow Boulevard, Secaucus NJ 07094. Tel (201)231-0900. Ed Vee Rice and Penny Vaughan. **Ind/Abst** Hospit. Lit. Index, Cumul. Index Nurs. Allied Health Lit., Int. Nurs. Index. NLM W1 CR216N. bk rev. adv acc. Circ 28,000. Written by and for practicing professionals. It addresses the challenge of critical care from every aspect of this nursing specialty.

CUMULATIVE INDEX TO NURSING & ALLIED HEALTH LITERATURE. See Indexes/Abstracts.

CURRENT PERSPECTIVES IN NURSING MANAGEMENT. V. 1-. US. English. $12.50. C V Mosby Co, C Leadbetter, 11830 Westline Industrial Drive, St Louis MO 63141. Tel (800)325-4177. NLM WY 105 C976.

CURRENT PRACTICE IN FAMILY-CENTERED COMMUNITY NURSING. Series/Titl Mosby's Current Practice and Perspectives in Nursing Series. V. 1- 1977-. Periodical. US. English. ir. C V Mosby Company, C Leadbetter, 11830 Westline Industrial Drive, St Louis MO 63141. NLM W1 CU803AN.

CURRENT PRACTICE IN GERONTOLOGICAL NURSING. V. 1- 1979-. US. English. $10.50. C V Mosby Co, C Leadbetter, 11830 Westline Industrial Drive, St Louis MO 63141. Tel (314)872-8370.

CURRENT PRACTICE IN NURSING CARE OF THE ADULT. Series/Titl Mosby's Current Practice and Perspectives in Nursing Series. V. 1- 1979-. 0190-6771. Periodical. US. English. NLM W1 CU803AZ.

CURRENT PRACTICE IN PEDIATRIC NURSING CEASED. Series/Titl Mosby's Current Practice and Perspectives in Nursing Series. Began with V. 1- 1976-. Ceased with V. 3, 1980. 0361-9257. Periodical. US. English. ir. **Ind/Abst** Int. Nurs. Index. NLM W1 CU803F.

CURRENT REVIEWS FOR NURSE ANESTHETISTS. V. 1-. 0164-310X. Monographic Series. US. English. bw. $120.00. Current Reviews for Nurse Anesthetists, 7880 Fairway Drive/Suite 106, Miami Lakes FL 33014. Tel (305)822-1415. **Ind/Abst** Cumul. Index Nurs. Allied Health Lit. NLM W1 CU8093K.

CURRENT REVIEWS FOR RECOVERY ROOM NURSES. V. 1- 1979-. 0164-3118. Periodical. US. English. bw. $140.00. Current Reviews for Recovery Room Nurses, 7480 Fairway Drive/Suite 106, Miami Lakes FL 33014. Tel (305)822-1414. **Ind/Abst** Cumul. Index Nurs. Allied Health Lit. NLM W1 CU8093H.

DEUTSCHE KRANKENPFLEGE-ZEITSCHRIFT. (DEUTSCHE KRANKENPFLEGEZEITSCHRIFT). 24.- Volume. 0012-074X. Periodical. GW. German. mo. 69.-. W Kohlhammer Verlag GMBH, Hessbruhlstrasse 69 PF 800430, 7000 Stuttgart 80-West Germany. Tel 0711-7863. Ed Antje Grauhan and Paul W Schreiner. **Ind/Abst** Int. Nurs. Index. NLM W1 DE735R. bk rev. adv acc. Circ 20,000. (ctrl). All aspects of nursing: administration, legislation, research. Each issue contains a supplement with a larger comprehensive article. *Deutsche Schwesternzeitung.*

DIMENSIONS IN ONCOLOGY NURSING. Vol. 1, No. 1 (Winter 1985)-. 0885-6192. Periodical. US. English. qt. $10.00. Dimensions in Oncology Nursing, Division of Nursing, PO Box 82, 6723 Bertner Avenue/Room L1025, Houston TX 77030. DD 610. *Nursing Neogram.*

DIMENSIONS OF CRITICAL CARE NURSING. (DIMENSIONS OF CRITICAL CARE NURSING : DCCN). VFOAT DCCN. Vol. 1, No. 1 (Jan./Feb. 1982)-. 0730-4625. Periodical. US. English. bm. $42.00. J B Lippincott Company, East Washington Square, Philadelphia PA 19105. Tel (215)238-4273. Ed Suzanne Hall Johnson. **Ind/Abst** Cumul. Index Nurs. Allied Health Lit., Int. Nurs. Index. NLM W1 DI594. bk rev. adv acc. Circ 5,742. Articles discuss new techniques, medication and equipment in all areas of critical care nursing; also features, editorial, book reviews, product news and research abstracts.

DIRECTORY - COUNCIL OF SPECIALISTS IN PSYCHIATRIC AND MENTAL HEALTH NURSING. See Yearbooks, Almanacs, Directories.

DIRECTORY OF AGENCIES EMPLOYING COMMUNITY HEALTH NURSES IN MICHIGAN. See Yearbooks, Almanacs, Directories.

DIRECTORY OF CERTIFIED NURSES. See Yearbooks, Almanacs, Directories.

A DIRECTORY OF EXPANDED ROLE PROGRAMS FOR REGISTERED NURSES. See Yearbooks, Almanacs, Directories.

DIRECTORY OF LICENSED VOCATIONAL NURSES IN TEXAS. See Yearbooks, Almanacs, Directories.

DIRECTORY OF NURSES WITH DOCTORAL DEGREES. See Yearbooks, Almanacs, Directories.

DIRECTORY OF REGISTERED PROFESSIONAL NURSES AND LICENSED PRACTICAL NURSES. See Yearbooks, Almanacs, Directories.

DIRECTORY OF SOUTH DAKOTA REGISTERED NURSES AND LICENSED PRACTICAL NURSES. See Yearbooks, Almanacs, Directories.

EDUCATION FOR NURSING, THE DIPLOMA WAY. (EDUCATION FOR NURSING—THE DIPLOMA WAY). 1966- Ed. 0070-9166. Periodical. US. English. an. National League for Nursing, 10 Columbus Circle, New York NY 10019. LC RT79. DD 610.73071173. NLM WY 22 AA1 E17.

EDUCAZIONE SANITARIA E MEDICINA PREVENTIVA. V. 1- Jan./March 1978-. 0391-6200. Periodical. IT. Italian (With summaries in English). qt. 50.000. Il Pensiero Scientifico Edit, Via Panama 48, 00198 Rome Italy. Tel (06)863633. Ed Maria A Modolo. LC RA440.A1. NLM W1 ED89G. bk rev. adv acc. Circ 1,500. *Educazione Sanitaria.*

EMERGENCY NURSING REPORTS. 0885-8284. Periodical. US. English. mo. $75.00. Aspen Systems Corporation, 16792 Oakmont Avenue, Gaithersburg MD 20877.

ENFERMERA AL DIA. 1976. 0185-0970. Periodical. MX. Spanish. bm. $8.00. Intersistemas SA de CV, Fernando Alencastre #110 Mexico DF Mexico. Tel (905)540 07 98. Ed Abel Castorena. NLM W1 EN593. bk rev. adv acc. Circ 13,750. Continuous education for nurses: general practice, emergencies, and general information.

ENLB, EMERGENCY NURSE LEGAL BULLETIN. VFOAT Emergency Nurse Legal Bulletin. V. 1- 1975-. 0098-1516. Periodical. US. English. qt. $20.00. Medical Law Publishing, PO Box 293, Westville NJ 08093. Ed James E George. **Ind/Abst** Cumul. Index Nurs. Allied Health Lit., Int. Nurs. Index. LC KF2915.N8. DD 344.73041. NLM W1 E385. (ctrl). Covers mediolegal aspects of emergency nursing.

ENTRANCE REQUIREMENTS FOR DIPLOMA SCHOOLS OF NURSING AND SCHOOLS OF PRACTICAL NURSING. VFOAT Conditions d'Admission aux Ecoles Decernant de Diplome d'Infirmiere et d'Infirmiere Auxiliaire. 1981/82-. 0710-2976. CN. English (text in French). an. Free. Canadian Nurses' Association, 50 Driveway, Ottawa Ontario K2P 1E2 Canada. DD 610.73071171. (ctrl). *General Entrance Requirements for Schools of Nursing and Schools of Practical Nursing, 0706-3865.*

FAMILY-CENTERED COMMUNITY NURSING. VAT Family Centered Community Nursing. V. 2-. 0273-3544. US. English. ir. Ed A M Reinhardt and M D Quinn. NLM W1 FA432BN. *Current Practice in Family-Centered Community Nursing.*

THE FLESCHNER SERIES IN CRITICAL CARE NURSING. Began with: 1 (1981). 0732-9644. Monographic Series. US. English. Fleschner Publishing Company, 41 Village Lane, Bethany CT 06525. LC UNC. DD 610.7361. NLM W1 FL627.

THE FLORIDA NURSE. V. 1- 1953-. 0015-4199. Periodical. US. English. mo. $1.00 Members, $3.00 Nonmembers. Office of Publication, 1235 East Concord Street, Orlando FL 32803.

THE FLORIDA NURSE. 0015-4199. Periodical. US. English. mo. $12.00. Florida Nurses Association, 1235 East Concord Street, PO Box 6985, Orlando FL 32803. Tel (305)896-3261. Ed Paula Massey. **Ind/Abst** Cumul. Index Nurs. Allied Health Lit., Int. Nurs. Index. NLM W1 FL882. bk rev. adv acc. Circ 6,400. (ctrl). Information and news relevant to health care and nursing. *Bulletin of the Florida State Nurses Association.*

FOCUS ON CRITICAL CARE. Vol. 10, No. 1 (Feb. 1983)-. 0736-3605. Periodical. US. English. bm. $58.00. C V Mosby, c/o R K Kinnes, 11830 Westline Industrial Drive, St Louis MO 63146. Tel (314)872-8370. Ed Marguerite Kinney. **Ind/Abst** Cumul. Index Nurs. Allied Health Lit., Int. Nurs. Index. NLM W1 FO1003H. bk rev. adv acc. Circ 54,663. Provides information to the critical care nurse actively engaged in practice, making her aware of issues that affect nursing in general and critical care in particular. *Focus on AACN.*

FRONTIER NURSING SERVICE QUARTERLY BULLETIN. VFOAT Annual Report - Frontier Nursing Service. V. 4- June 1928-. 0016-2116. Periodical. US. English. qt. $5.00. Frontier Nursing Service Inc, Hyden KY 41749. Tel (606)672-2312. Ed David M Watfield. **Ind/Abst** Cumul. Index Nurs. Allied Health Lit., Int. Nurs. Index. NLM W1 FR945K. Circ 6,200. (ctrl). Articles on activities of frontier nursing service: rural health care, nurse-midwifery, nursing education, etc. *Quarterly Bulletin of the Kentucky Committee for Mothers and Babies.*

GEORGIA NURSING. V. 1- Aug. 1945-. 0016-8335. Periodical. US. English. bm. $12.00. Georgia Nurses Association, 1362 West Peach Street NW, Atlanta GA 30309. Tel (404)876-4624. Ed Ruth Martin. **Ind/Abst** Cumul. Index Nurs. Allied Health Lit., Int. Nurs. Index. NLM W1 GE444. bk rev. adv acc. Circ 4,000. Provides up-to-date coverage ofthe latest nursing news and issues in the state of Georgia.

GERIATRIC NURSING. V. 1- May/June 1980-. 0197-4572. Periodical. US. English. bm. $37.00. American Journal of Nursing Company, 555 West 57th Street, New York NY 10019. Tel (212)582-8820. Ed Cynthia H Kelly. **Ind/Abst** Cumul. Index Nurs.

Medicine—Nursing

Allied Health Lit., Int. Nurs. Index, Psychol. Abstr. **LC** RC954. **DD** 610.736505. **NLM** W1 GE457CB. bk rev. adv acc. **Circ** 28,000. Available in microform. Articles by professionals on clinical problems of old, drug/nutrition columns, relevant legislation, profiles of outstanding elders-Claude Pepper, Eric Sevarcid, Maggie Kahn, letters and editorials.

HAEOE HANIN KANHOWON CHONGNAM. *See* Yearbooks, Almanacs, Directories.

HEART & LUNG. VAT Heart and Lung. V. 1- Jan./Feb. 1972-. 0147-9563. Periodical. US. English. bm. $61.00. C V Mosby Company, c/o R K Kinnes, 11830 Westline Industrial Drive, St Louis MO 63146. **Tel** (314)872-8370. **Ed** Kathleen Dracup and Sylvan Lee Weinberg. **Ind/Abst** Life Sci. Collect., Excerpta Med., Index Med., Cumul. Index Nurs. Allied Health Lit., Biol. Abstr., Int. Nurs. Index, Chem. Abstr., Energy Res. Abstr., Hospit. Lit. Index, Sci. Cit. Index, Abr. Ed. **LC** RC681.A1. **DD** 616.12. **NLM** W1 HE644J. **CODEN** HELUAI. bk rev. adv acc. **Circ** 61,840. Concerned with the nurse's role and responsibility in the care and management of critically ill patients.

HOME HEALTHCARE NURSE. VFOAT Home Health Care Nurse. Vol. 1, No. 1 (Sept./Oct. 1983)-. Periodical. US. English. bm. $17.00. Home Healthcare Nurse Inc, 680 Route 206 North, Bridgewater NJ 08807. **Ind/Abst** Cumul. Index Nurs. Allied Health Lit. **NLM** W1. *Nephrology Nurse, 0164-4386.*

HOSPITAL AND NURSING YEAR BOOK OF SOUTHERN AFRICA (JOHANNESBURG (SOUTH AFRICA) : 1971)). *See* Yearbooks, Almanacs, Directories.

HOSPITAL-HEALTH CARE TRAINING MEDIA PROFILES *CEASED.* (HOSPITAL/HEALTH CARE TRAINING MEDIA PROFILES). V. 1- 1974-. 0095-0580. Periodical. US. English. **Ind/Abst** Media Rev. Dig. **NLM** WX 18 H824.

HOUSE OF DELEGATES REPORTS. **Main/Corp** American Nurses' Association. 1966/68-. 0195-5713. US. English. ir. American Nurses Association, 2420 Pershing Road, Kansas City MO 64108. **NLM** W1 AM6639C. *House of Delegates, Sections Reports, 0195-5721.*

IMAGE—THE JOURNAL OF NURSING SCHOLARSHIP. Vol. 15, No. 1 (Winter 1983). 0743-5150. Periodical. US. English. qt. $15.00. Sigma Theta Tau School of Nursing, 1100 Waterway Boulevard, Indianapolis IN 46202. **Tel** (317)634-8171. **Ed** Sister Rosemary Donky and Nell Watts. **Ind/Abst** Cumul. Index Nurs. Allied Health Lit., Int. Nurs. Index, Psychol. Abstr. **NLM** W1 IM457H. adv acc. **Circ** 65,000. Publishes research and scholarly articles on advances in nursing and health. *Image, 0363-2792.*

IMPRINT. V. 15- Jan. 1968-. 0019-3062. Periodical. US. English. ir. $29.00. National Student Nurses Association, 555 West 57th Street, New York NY 10019. **Tel** (212)581-2221. **Ed** Rita Didrichsons. **Ind/Abst** Cumul. Index Nurs. Allied Health Lit., Int. Nurs. Index, Energy Res. Abstr. **NLM** W1 IM66. bk rev. adv acc. **Circ** $15.00. Association news and articles on current issues and trends in nursing and nursing education. Features include reports on legislation, career planning, clinical news highlights, etc.

INDIAN NURSING YEAR BOOK. *See* Yearbooks, Almanacs, Directories.

INDUSTRY WAGE SURVEY. NURSING AND PERSONAL CARE FACILITIES. *See* Economics - Labor.

INFIRMIERE AUXILIAIRE. (L'INFIRMIERE AUXILIAIRE : REVUE DE LA CORPORATION PROFESSIONNELLE DES INFIRMIERES ET INFIRMIERS AUXILIAIRES DU QUEBEC). 0822-8558. Periodical. CN. French (English). qt. $3.00 Students. Corporation Professionnelle des Infirmieres et Infirmiers Auxiliaires du Quebec, Bureau 300/65 Ouest rue de Castelneau, Montreal Quebec H2R 2W3 Canada. **Ind/Abst** Int. Nurs. Index. **DD** 610.730693060714. **NLM** W1. *Auxiliaire, 0703-9484.*

INFIRMIERE CANADIENNE. (L'INFIRMIERE CANADIENNE). First issued in June 1959. 0019-9605. Periodical. CN. French. mo. $27.00. Canadian Nurses Association, 50 The Driveway, Ottawa Ontario K2P 1E2 Canada. **Tel** (613)237-2133. **Ind/Abst** Point Repere, Int. Nurs. Index. **NLM** W1 IN409G. bk rev. adv acc. **Circ** 125,000. For nurses.

INFO. VFOAT Info. V. 6, No. 4- July 1975-. 0382-5574. Periodical. CN. English (text in French). ir. New Brunswick Association of Registered Nurses, 231 Saunders Street, Fredericton New Brunswick E3B 1N6 Canada. **DD** 610.73062715. *N B A R N News, 0382-5566.*

INFORMATIONEN FRESENIUS FUR KRANKENSCHWESTERN UND KRANKENPFLEGER. Began in 1973?. German. ir. **NLM** W1.

INFORMES DE ENFERMERIA. (INFORME DE ENFERMERIA). Began in 1966. 0479-3439. Monographic Series. US. Spanish. ir. **NLM** W1 IN41. *Informes Sobre Enfermeria.*

INTERNATIONAL DIRECTORY OF NURSES WITH DOCTORAL DEGREES. *See* Yearbooks, Almanacs, Directories.

INTERNATIONAL JOURNAL OF NURSING STUDIES. Began with V. 1 In 1963. 0020-7489. Periodical. UK. articles in English, French, or German, with summaries in Russian and Spanish. qt. Pergamon Press, 395 Sawmill River Road, Elmsford NY 10523. **Tel** (914)592-7700. **Ind/Abst** Hospit. Lit. Index, Index Med., Cumul. Index Nurs. Allied Health Lit., Int. Nurs. Index, Psychol. Abstr., Soc. Sci. Citation Index. **NLM** W1 IN77N. **CODEN** IJNUA6.

INTERNATIONAL NURSING INDEX. *See* Indexes/Abstracts.

INTERNATIONAL NURSING REVIEW. VFOAT Revue Internationale des Infirmieres, Internationale Schwesternumschau, Revista de Enfermeria. V. 1- Apr. 1954-. 0020-8132. Periodical. SZ. English (articles in French, German or Spanish). bm. International Council of Nurses, 3 rue de l'Ancien-Port, 1201 Geneva Switzerland. **Tel** 022/31 29 60. **Ed** P D Nuttall. **Ind/Abst** Hospit. Lit. Index, Excerpta Med., Index Med., Cumul. Index Nurs. Allied Health Lit., Int. Nurs. Index. **NLM** W1 IN827A. (cum index). adv acc. **Circ** 2,500. Includes news of nursing throughout the world; articles of global interest involving nurses. *International Nursing Bulletin, 0141-5557; ICN Calling.*

ISSUES IN COMPREHENSIVE PEDIATRIC NURSING. Began with May/June 1976 issue. 0146-0862. Monographic Series. US. English. bm. $57.50. Hemisphere Publishing Corporation, 79 Madison Avenue Suite/1110, New York NY 10016. **Tel** (202)783-3958. **Ed** G M Scipien and M U Barnard. **Ind/Abst** Cumul. Index Nurs. Allied Health Lit., Int. Nurs. Index, Psychol. Abstr. **NLM** W1 IS6675. **CODEN** ICNUDS. bk rev. adv acc. **Circ** 2,000. Refereed journal addressing the specific needs of children and their families from the perspective of nurses and other health care providers.

ISSUES IN MENTAL HEALTH NURSING. VFOAT Mental Health Nursing. V. 1- Spring 1978-. 0161-2840. Periodical. US. English. qt. $49.50. Hemisphere Publishing Corporation, 79 Madison Avenue/Suite 110, New York NY 10016. **Tel** (202)783-3958. **Ed** Phyllis Stern. **Ind/Abst** Cumul. Index Nurs. Allied Health Lit., Int. Nurs. Index, Psychol. Abstr. **NLM** W1 IS669. **CODEN** IHNUDT. bk rev. adv acc. **Circ** 660. Refereed quarterly publishing practical information about the psychosocial and mental health aspects of nursing and patient care.

JAMAICAN NURSE. 0021-4140. Periodical. JM. English. qt. $15.00. Nurses Association of Jamaica, 72 Arnold Road, Kingston 5 Jamaica. **Ind/Abst** Cumul. Index Nurs. Allied Health Lit., Int. Nurs. Index. **NLM** W1 JA74.

JEN, JOURNAL OF EMERGENCY NURSING. VFOAT Journal of Emergency Nursing. V. 1- Jan./Feb. 1975-. 0099-1767. Periodical. US. English. bm. $62.50. C V Mosby, c/o R K Kinnes, 11830 Westline Industrial Drive, St Louis MO 63146. **Tel** (314)872-8370. **Ed** Gail Pisarcik-Lenehan. **Ind/Abst** Hospit. Lit. Index, Cumul. Index Nurs. Allied Health Lit., Int. Nurs. Index. **LC** RT120.E4. **DD** 610.736. **NLM** WL J26. bk rev. adv acc. **Circ** 18,654. Recognizes the nurse's role and responsibility in the care and management of the patient in the emergency department.

JOGN NURSING *CEASED.* VFOAT Journal of Obstetric, Gynecologic and Neonatal Nursing. V. 1-13, No. 6. 0090-0311. Periodical. US. English. bm. $36.00. J B Lippincott Company, East Washington Square, Philadelphia PA 19105. **Tel** (215)328-4273. **Ed** Judith Servino. **Ind/Abst** Hospit. Lit. Index, Excerpta Med., Index Med., Cumul. Index Nurs. Allied Health Lit., Int. Nurs. Index. **LC** RG951. **NLM** W1 J513. bk rev. adv acc. **Circ** 24,324. (ctrl). For nurses in obstetrics, gynecological and neonatal nursing. Research, new practices, current policies are published.

JOURNAL OF ADVANCED NURSING. Began with V. 1, No. 1 in 1976. 0309-2402. Periodical. UK. English. bm. 38.00 Domestic, 45.50 Foreign, $87.50 US and Canada. Blackwell Scientific Publishing Ltd, PO Box 88, Oxford OX2 0EL England. **Tel** (01)404-4101. **Ed** J P Smith. **Ind/Abst** Excerpta Med., Cumul. Index Nurs. Allied Health Lit., Int. Nurs. Index, Index Med., Hospit. Lit. Index, Soc. Sci. Citation Index. **NLM** W1 JO533U. bk rev. adv acc. **Circ** 2,000. (ctrl). Publishes scholarly contributions on all aspects of nursing care and nursing education, management and research which have a sound scientific, theoretical or philosophical base.

JOURNAL OF CHRISTIAN NURSING. (JOURNAL OF CHRISTIAN NURSING : A QUARTERLY PUBLICATION OF NURSES CHRISTIAN FELLOWSHIP). Vol. 1, No. 1 (Spring 1984)-. 0743-2550. Periodical. US. English. qt. $12.95. Journal of Christian Nursing, PO Box 1650, Downers Grove IL 60515. **Tel** (312)964-5700. **Ed** Ramona Cass. **NLM** W1. bk rev. adv acc. **Circ** 11,000. (ctrl). Deals with patient's spiritual needs and spiritual care, missions and crosscultural nursing, bioethical issues, personal and spiritual growth, and professional nursing issues. *Nurses Lamp, 0885-5854.*

JOURNAL OF COMMUNITY HEALTH NURSING. Vol. 1, No. 1-. 0737-0016. Periodical. US. English. qt. $40.00. Lawrence Erlbaum Associates, 365 Broadway, Hillsdale NJ 07642. **DD** 610. **NLM** W1.

JOURNAL OF CONTINUING EDUCATION IN NURSING. 0022-0124. Periodical. US. English. bm. Slack Inc, 6900 Grove Road, Thorofare NJ 08086. **Tel** (609)848-1000. **Ind/Abst** Cumul. Index Nurs. Allied Health Lit., Hospit. Lit. Index, Educ. Index.

THE JOURNAL OF CONTINUING EDUCATION IN NURSING. VFOAT Continuing Education in Nursing. V. 1- May 1970-. 0022-0124. Periodical. US. English. bm. C B Slack Inc, 6900 Grove Road, Thorofare NJ 08086. **Ind/Abst** Hospit. Lit. Index, Cumul. Index Nurs. Allied Health Lit., Int. Nurs. Index, Educ. Index, Ref. Source, Curr. Index J. Educ. **LC** RT90. **DD** 610.730711. **NLM** W1 JO595X.

JOURNAL OF ENTEROSTOMAL THERAPY. V. 7- Jan./Feb. 1980-. 0270-1170. Periodical. US. English. bm. $67.75. C V Mosby, c/o R K Kinnes, 11830 Westline Industrial Drive, St Louis MO 63146. **Tel** (314)872-8370. **Ed** Patricia M Kyne. **Ind/Abst** Cumul. Index Nurs. Allied Health Lit., Int. Nurs. Index, Index Med. **LC** RD540.6. **DD** 617.554. **NLM** W1 JO644AF. bk rev. adv acc. **Circ** 2,926. Serves an international network of enterostomal therapy practitioners and provides data related to the care of persons with ostomies, draining wounds, fistulae, and pressure ulcers. *ET Journal, 0195-9883.*

JOURNAL OF GERONTOLOGICAL NURSING. Began in 1975. 0098-9134. Periodical. US. English. mo. $30.00. Slack Inc, 6900 Grove Road, Thorofare NJ 08086. **Tel** (609)848-1000. **Ed** Edna M Stilwell. **Ind/Abst** Cumul. Index Nurs. Allied Health Lit., Int. Nurs. Index, Psychol. Abstr., Energy Res. Abstr. **LC** RC954. **DD** 610.736505. **NLM** W1 JO669NG. bk rev. adv acc. **Circ** 13,000. Gerontology-nursing care aspects of clinical research. How-to columns on pharmacology, skin care, nutrition. Consideration of well-elderly topics, social issues, health promotion.

JOURNAL OF NEPHROLOGY NURSING. Vol. 1, No. 1 (July/Aug. 1984)-. 0748-5328. Periodical. US. English. bm. $18.00 Domestic, $26.00 Canada, $32.00 Foreign. Phoenix Educational Systems Inc, Bear Wallow Road/Route 2 Box 101C, Ashland City TN 37015. **Tel** (615)792-5986. **Ed** Lowanna S Binkley. **DD** 610. **NLM** W1. bk rev. adv acc. **Circ** 4,000. A professional journal for the practicing nephrology nurse who is interested in clinically current information in order to provide improved care to the renal patient/family.

JOURNAL OF NEUROSURGICAL NURSING. 0047-2603. Periodical. US. English. bm. Journal of Neurosurgical Nursing, PO Box 64025, Baltimore MD 21264. **Tel** (301)528-4105. **Ind/Abst** Cumul. Index Nurs. Allied Health Lit., Index Med., Hospit. Lit. Index, Int. Nurs. Index, Energy Res. Abstr. **NLM** W1 JO795EE.

JOURNAL OF NURSE-MIDWIFERY. V. 18, No. 1- Spring 1973-. 0091-2182. Periodical. US. English. bm. $54.00. Elsevier Science Publishers, PO

Box 1663, Grand Central Station, New York NY 10163. **Tel** (212)370-5520. **Ed** Mary Ann Shah. **Ind/Abst** Cumul. Index Nurs. Allied Health Lit., Int. Nurs. Index, Soc. Sci. Citation Index. **NLM** W1 JO796K. bk rev. adv acc. Presents the latest developments and research in the fields of nurse-midwifery, parent-child health, obstetrics, family planning, neonatology and well-woman gynecology. *Bulletin of the American College of Nurse-Midwives.*

THE JOURNAL OF NURSING ADMINISTRATION. VFOAT JNA. V. 1- Jan. 1971-. 0002-0443. Periodical. US. English. mo. $40.00. J B Lippincott Company, East Washington Square, Philadelphia PA 19105. **Tel** (215)238-4273. **Ed** Suzanne Smith Coletta. **Ind/Abst** Excerpta Med., Cumul. Index Nurs. Allied Health Lit., Index Med., Int. Nurs. Index, Hospit. Lit. Index, Soc. Sci. Citation Index, Curr. Index J. Educ. **LC** RT89. **DD** 610.7305. **NLM** W1 JO796R. **CODEN** JNUAA. adv acc. **Circ** 14,751. Provides sound knowledge, strategies, and ideas for nurse administrators, only pertinent sophisticated articles are accepted, contents are aimed at upper level nursing exectives.

JOURNAL OF NURSING EDUCATION. Vol. 22, No. 8 (Oct. 1983)-. 0148-4834. Periodical. US. English. ir. Slack Inc, 6900 Grove Road, Thorofare NJ 08086. **Tel** (609)848-1000. **Ind/Abst** Hospit. Lit. Index, Cumul. Index Nurs. Allied Health Lit., Sci. Cit. Index, Abr. Ed., Index Med., Int. Nurs. Index. *JNE. Journal of Nursing Education.*

THE JOURNAL OF NURSING ETHICS. *See* Ethics.

JOURNAL OF OPHTHALMIC NURSING & TECHNOLOGY. VFOAT Journal of Ophthalmic Nursing and Technology. Vol. 1, No. 1 (May 1982)-. 0744-7132. Periodical. US. English. bm. Slack Inc, 6900 Grove Road, Thorofare NJ 08086. **Tel** (609)848-1000. **Ind/Abst** Int. Nurs. Index. **DD** 617. **NLM** W1 JO803I.

THE JOURNAL OF PRACTICAL NURSING. 0022-3867. Periodical. US. English. qt. $23.00. Journal of Practical Nursing, 10801 Pair Tree Lane/Suite 151, St Louis MO 63074. **Tel** (314)426-2665. **Ed** Rob Watson. **Ind/Abst** Hospit. Lit. Index, Cumul. Index Nurs. Allied Health Lit., Int. Nurs. Index. **NLM** W1 JO842M. adv acc. **Circ** 27,000. This publication provides information and education for licensed practical nurses. *Practical Nursing.*

JOURNAL OF PROFESSIONAL NURSING. (JOURNAL OF PROFESSIONAL NURSING : OFFICIAL JOURNAL OF THE AMERICAN ASSOCIATION OF COLLEGES OF NURSING). 8755-7223. Periodical. US. English. bm. $65.00. W B Saunders Company, Journals Department, PO Box 53489, Philadelphia PA 19105. **Tel** (215)574-3395. **Ed** Robin Hipple. bk rev. adv acc. **Circ** 5,000. Covers the practice, research, policy-making roles of nurses with baccalaureate and graduate degrees. Relevant for nurse educators, students, and practicing nurses concerned with above.

JOURNAL OF PSYCHIATRIC NURSING AND MENTAL HEALTH SERVICES *CEASED.* V. 5-19, No. 7. 0360-5973. Periodical. US. English. mo. $12.00. Charles B Slack, 6900 Grove Road, Thorofare NJ 08086. **Ind/Abst** Cumul. Index Nurs. Allied Health Lit. **LC** RC440. **DD** 610.736805. **NLM** W1 JO853I. **CODEN** JPNSDM. *Journal of Psychiatric Nursing, 0277-2973.*

JOURNAL OF PSYCHOSOCIAL NURSING AND MENTAL HEALTH SERVICES. Vol. 19, No. 8 (Aug. 1981)-. 0279-3695. Periodical. US. English. mo. $24.00. Slack Inc, 6900 Grove Road, Thorofare NJ 08086. **Tel** (609)848-1000. **Ed** Shirley A Smoyak. **Ind/Abst** Index Med., Hospit. Lit. Index, Int. Nurs. Index, Cumul. Index Nurs. Allied Health Lit. **LC** RC440. **DD** 610.736805. **NLM** W1 JO858V. bk rev. adv acc. **Circ** 12,000. Clinical information for psychosocial nurses and other mental health professionals. *Journal of Psychiatric Nursing and Mental Health Services, 0360-5973.*

JOURNAL OF THE ASSOCIATION OF PEDIATRIC ONCOLOGY NURSES. VFOAT Japon. Vol. 1, No. 1 (Winter 1984)-. 0748-1802. Periodical. US. English. qt. $20.00 Domestic, $25.00 Foreign. JAPON, PO Box 47079, Chicago IL 60647. **DD** 618. **NLM** W1. *APON Newsletter.*

JOURNAL OF THE AUSTRALIAN CONGRESS OF MENTAL HEALTH NURSES. Vol. 1, No. 1 (Sept. 1980)-. 0727-4173. English. ir. **NLM** W1 JO912U.

JOURNAL - ONTARIO OCCUPATIONAL HEALTH NURSES ASSOCIATION. (JOURNAL : THE OFFICIAL PUBLICATION OF THE ONTARIO OCCUPATIONAL HEALTH NURSES ASSOCIATION). Vol. 5, No. 2 (June 84)-. 0828-542X. Periodical. CN. English. ty. $12.00. Ontario Occupational Health Nurses Association, 1009-60 Ruddington Drive, Willowdale Ontario M2K 2R9 Canada. **DD** 610.734605. *Commoohnacator, 0228-6009.*

KAIIN JITTAI CHOSA. **Main/Corp** Nihon Kango Kyokai. **VFOAT** Report on Status of Member of Japanese Nursing Association. First 4- Issues. JA. Japanese (summaries in English). ni. Nihen Kango Kyokai, 8-2 Jingymae 5-Chome Shibuya-Ku, Tokyo 150 Japan. **LC** RT1, RT13.J3.

THE KANSAS NURSE. 1950. 0022-8710. Periodical. US. English. mo. $24.00. Kansas Nurse, 820 Quincy Street, Topeka KS 66612. **Tel** (913)233-8638. **Ed** Lynelle King. **Ind/Abst** Cumul. Index Nurs. Allied Health Lit. bk rev. adv acc. **Circ** 2,500. (ctrl). Nursing and health care.

KENTUCKY NURSE. Vol. 31, No. 1 (Jan./Feb. 1983)-. 0742-8367. Periodical. US. English. bm. $18.00. Kentucky Nurses Association, PO Box 8342/ Station E, Louisville KY 40208. **Tel** (502)637-2546. **Ed** Jean P Duncan. **Ind/Abst** Cumul. Index Nurs. Allied Health Lit., Int. Nurs. Index. **NLM** W1 KE69T. adv acc. **Circ** 1,847. (ctrl). News regarding nurses, the nursing profession, and health care in general. *Newsletter (Kentucky Nurses' Association : 1978).*

KRANKENPFLEGE. VFOAT Soins Infirmiers. Began with July 1979 issue. 0253-0465. German (French). ir. **Ind/Abst** Int. Nurs. Index. **NLM** W1 KR263M. *Zeitschrift fur Krankenpflege, 0044-2941.*

KRANKENPFLEGE-JOURNAL. (KRANKENPFLEGE JOURNAL). V. 18-. 0174-108X. Periodical. German. ir. **Ind/Abst** Int. Nurs. Index. **NLM** W1 KR263I. *Schwestern Revue.*

KURINIKARU SUTADI. Began with: V. 1, No. 1, (April 1980). 0388-5585. Periodical. Japanese. mo. **Ind/Abst** Int. Nurs. Index. **NLM** W1 KU706LC.

LAMP. (THE LAMP). V. 1- 1943-. 0047-3936. Periodical. AT. English. ir. $24.20. New South Wales Nurses Association, PO Box 231, 188-192 Goulburn Street, Darlinghurst New South Wales 2010 Australia. **Ed** Jerry Havies. **Ind/Abst** Cumul. Index Nurs. Allied Health Lit., Int. Nurs. Index. **NLM** W1 LA444. bk rev. adv acc. **Circ** 6,000. (ctrl). Includes nursing issues, industrial issues, award matters, medical issues, inter-union matters, wage indexes.

LEGISLATIVE NETWORK FOR NURSES. *See* Law.

LIBRARY CATALOGUE - REGISTERED NURSES' ASSOCIATION OF BRITISH COLUMBIA. **Main/Corp** Registered Nurses' Association of British Columbia. Library. 1970-. 0319-0234. Periodical. CN. English. Free to members and libraries. Registered Nurses' Association of British Columbia Library, 2130 West 12th Avenue, Vancouver British Columbia V6L 2N3 Canada. **DD** 016.61073.

LIEN. (LE LIEN). V. 5, No. 2, (Aug. 1980)-. 0711-7418. Periodical. CN. French (English). ir. Free to Members. Lien, c/o Ciiro, CP 271 Succursale A, Hull Quebec J8Y 6M9 Canada. **DD** 610.730607142. *Link (Hull, Quebec), 0714-3753.*

MCN, THE AMERICAN JOURNAL OF MATERNAL CHILD NURSING. VFOAT American Journal of Maternal Child Nursing. **VAT** Maternal Child Nursing, the American Journal of Maternal Child Nursing. V. 1- Jan./Feb. 1976-. 0361-929X. Periodical. US. English. bm. American Journal of Nursing Company, 555 West 57th Street, New York NY 10019. **Ind/Abst** Hospit. Lit. Index, Cumul. Index Nurs. Allied Health Lit., Int. Nurs. Index. **LC** RG951. **DD** 610.73678. **NLM** W1 M225.

MAINLINES. (MAINLINES : THE NEWSLETTER FOR THE MIDWEST ALLIANCE IN NURSING). **VFOAT** Main Lines. 0278-9450. Periodical. US. English. bm. $15.00. Indiana University, 1226 West Michigan Street, Midwest Alliance in Nursing, Indianapolis IN 46223. **Tel** (317)264-3255. **Ed** Barbara B Minckley. bk rev. adv acc. **Circ** 5,000. Regional nursing news related to clinical practice, education and research in nursing. Health care and legislative issues related to improving health care in the Midwest.

THE MARYLAND NURSE. V. 1- July/Aug. 1970-. 0047-6080. Periodical. US. English. bm. Maryland Nurses Association, 5820 Southwestern Boulevard, Baltimore MD 21227. **Tel** (301)242-7300. **Ed** Mary Lloyd Zusy. **Ind/Abst** Cumul. Index Nurs. Allied Health Lit., Int. Nurs. Index. **NLM** W1 MA76SD. adv acc. **Circ** 7,000. News and views of Maryland nurses and the Maryland Nurses Association. *Maryland Nursing News.*

THE MASSACHUSETTS NURSE. VFOAT MNA Bulletin. **VAT** Massachusetts Nurses Association Bulletin. V. 45- Mar. 1976-. 0163-0784. Periodical. US. English. mo. $12.00. Mass Nurses Association, 376 Boylston Street, Boston MA 02116. **Tel** (617)482-5465. **Ed** Denise M Sullivan. **Ind/Abst** Cumul. Index Nurs. Allied Health Lit., Int. Nurs. Index. **NLM** W1 MA913. bk rev. adv acc. **Circ** 13,000. (ctrl). Health care, legislation and broad range of nursing issues confronting nurses in Massachusetts book reviews. Nursing history articles. *Bulletin - Massachusetts Nurses Association, 0025-4843.*

MATERNAL-CHILD NURSING JOURNAL. V. 1- Spring 1972-. 0090-0702. Periodical. US. English. qt. $15.00 Domestic, $18.00 Canada, $20.00 Foreign. Maternal Child Nursing Journal, 3505 Fifth Avenue, Pittsburgh PA 15261. **Tel** (412)624-3844. **Ed** Corine M Barnes and Olive J Rich. **Ind/Abst** Excerpta Med., Index Med., Cumul. Index Nurs. Allied Health Lit., Int. Nurs. Index, Energy Res. Abstr., Cumul. Index Nurs. Allied Health Lit., Psychol. Abstr., Hospit. Lit. Index. **LC** RJ245. **DD** 610.736205. **NLM** W1 MA947M. **CODEN** MCNJA2. bk rev. **Circ** 1,800. Descriptive case studies, literature reviews, and research reports furthering professional knowledge of the expert nurse practitioner/clinician in care of mothers and children.

MEDICARE. USE OF SKILLED NURSING FACILITIES. *See* Insurance.

MEDICINSKAJA SESTRA. (MEDITSINSKAIA SESTRA). Began 1942. 0025-8342. Periodical. UR. Russian. mo. $9.00. Victor Kamkin Inc (73248), 12224 Parklawn Drive, Rockville MD 20852. **Tel** (301)881-5973. **Ind/Abst** Int. Nurs. Index. **NLM** W1 ME803. Index in last issue of volume - attached.

MICHIGAN NURSE. VFOAT Michigan Nurse Newsletter. Began with Vol. 1, 1928. 0026-2366. Periodical. US. English. mo. Michigan Nurses Association, 120 Spartan Avenue, East Lansing MI 48823. **Ind/Abst** Cumul. Index Nurs. Allied Health Lit., Int. Nurs. Index. **NLM** W1 MI221.

MIDWIFE HEALTH VISITOR & COMMUNITY NURSE. (MIDWIFE, HEALTH VISITOR & COMMUNITY NURSE). V. 11- Jan. 1975-. 0306-9699. Periodical. UK. English. mo. $28.35. Newbourne Publishing, Recorder House, 91 Stoke Newington Church Street, London N16 England. **Tel** 01-254-7231. **Ind/Abst** Cumul. Index Nurs. Allied Health Lit., Int. Nurs. Index. **NLM** W1 MI331H. *Midwife and Health Visitor, 0026-3516.*

MILWAUKEE PROFESSIONAL NURSE. 0026-4369. Periodical. US. English. qt. $4.00. Milwaukee District Nurses Association, 904 South 104 Street West, Allis WI 53214. **Tel** (414)453-8436. **Ed** Genee Brukwitzki. bk rev. adv acc. **Circ** 800. (ctrl). Nursing and health care issues, particularly those with local (Milwaukee) ramifications.

THE MISSISSIPPI RN. **VAT** Mississippi Registered Nurse. V. 1- 1969-. 0026-6388. Periodical. US. English. bm. $18.00 Domestic, $25.00 Foreign. Mississippi Nurses Association, 135 Bound Street/ Suite 100, Jackson MS 39206. **Tel** (601)982-9182. **Ed** Patricia O'Bannon Muse. **Ind/Abst** Cumul. Index Nurs. Allied Health Lit., Int. Nurs. Index. **NLM** W1 MI828. bk rev. adv acc. **Circ** 2,500. (ctrl). Covers nursing issues, clinical topics and other health care related information. Research articles and features are regular items.

THE MISSOURI NURSE. 0026-6655. Periodical. US. English. ir. $8.00. Missouri State Nurses Association, 206 East Dunklin, Jefferson City MO 65101. **Tel** (314)636-4623. **Ed** Caroline Davis. **Ind/Abst** Cumul. Index Nurs. Allied Health Lit., Int. Nurs. Index. **NLM** W1 MI882. adv acc. **Circ** 3,500. (ctrl). Educational information for registered professional nurses.

MLN BULLETIN-NEWSLETTER. **Main/Corp** Minnesota League for Nursing. **VAT** Minnesota League for Nursing Bulletin Newsletter. V. 1- Jan. 1975-. 0198-862X. Periodical. US. English. ty. $3.00. Minnesota League for Nursing, PO Box 35, Rosemount MN 55068. **Ind/Abst** Energy Res. Abstr. *MLN Bulletin, 0047-7508.*

MNA ACCENT. **Main/Corp** Minnesota Nurses Association. V. 48, No. 3- Mar. 1976-. Periodical. US. English. ir. $10.00. Minnesota Nursing Accent, 1821

University Avenue, Griggs Midway Building/Suite N-377, St Paul MN 55104. **Tel** (612)646-4807. **Ed** Ruth Lunde. adv acc. **Circ** 11,500. (ctrl). Nursing issues in Minnesota. *Minnesota Nursing Accent.*

MONOGRAPH - SIGMA THETA TAU. Ser. 75-. 0147-5223. Monographic Series. US. English. **NLM** W1 MO56K.

NATIONAL OFFICE NEWSLETTER - VICTORIAN ORDER OF NURSES FOR CANADA. **Main/Corp** Victorian Order of Nurses for Canada. **VFOAT** VON National Office Newsletter. **VAT** Victorian Order of Nurses for Canada National Office Newsletter. Apr. 1971-. 0228-0906. Periodical. CN. English. qt. Free. Victorian Order of Nurses for Canada, 5 Blackburn Avenue, Ottawa Ontario N1N 8A2 Canada. **DD** 610.7306071. (ctrl). *News from National Office, 0228-0892.*

NATNEWS. (NATNEWS : THE OFFICIAL JOURNAL OF THE NATIONAL ASSOCIATION OF THEATRE NURSES). **VAT** National Association of Theatre Nurses News. 0027-6049. Periodical. UK. English. mo. $30.65. Newton Mann Ltd, Sherwood House Holt Lane, Matlock Derbyshire DE4 3LY England. **Tel** 0629-3941. **Ed** I D Curry. **Ind/Abst** Cumul. Index Nurs. Allied Health Lit., Int. Nurs. Index. **NLM** W1 N119K. bk rev. adv acc. **Circ** 5,000. (ctrl). All aspects of theatre nursing techniques from patient to the latest surgery instruments, reports and articles.

NEBRASKA HEALTH MANPOWER REPORTS : REGISTERED NURSES. **Main/Corp** Nebraska. Division of Health Data and Statistical Research. 1976-. US. English. Nebraska Department of Health, 1003 O Street, Lincoln NE 68508. **LC** RT5.N2. **DD** 331.11. **NLM** W2 AN1 D34NR.

NEBRASKA NURSE. V. 1- June 1946-. 0028-1921. Periodical. US. English. qt. $10.00. Nebraska Nurses Association, 941 O Street, Lincoln NE 68508. **Tel** (402)475-3859. **Ed** Mary Ann Sak. **Ind/Abst** Int. Nurs. Index. **NLM** W1 NE117. adv acc. **Circ** 1,250. (ctrl). Nursing practice, nursing education, legislation and professional association issues and economic and general welfare of nurses.

NEHW HEALTH WATCH. **VFOAT** Health Watch. **VAT** Nurses' Environmental Health Watch Health Watch. 8756-0356. Periodical. US. English. qt. $50.00. Nurses' Environmental Health Watch, 24-14 21 Avenue, Astoria NY 11105. **Tel** (718)726-9219. **Ed** Diane J Mancino. **DD** 610. **Circ** 1,000. (ctrl). Issues related to environmental health nursing including air and water pollution; solid waste and toxic waste disposal; radioactive materials; and occupational health hazards.

NEONATAL NETWORK. (NEONATAL NETWORK : NN). **VFOAT** N.N. Vol. 1, No. 1 (Oct. 1981)-. 0730-0832. Periodical. US. English. bm. $30.00. Neonatal Network, 1640 Wynoochee Way, Petaluma CA 94952. **Tel** (707)762-2646. **Ed** Charles Rait. **Ind/Abst** Cumul. Index Nurs. Allied Health Lit. bk rev. adv acc. **Circ** 9,000. Practical and theoretical information for nurses working in level II and level III neonatal intensive care units.

NEPHROLOGY NURSE. V. 1-5. 0164-4386. Periodical. US. English. bm. $17.00. Home Healthcare Nurse, 300 Harmon Meadow Boulevard, Secaucus NJ 07094. **Tel** (201)864-4000. **Ed** Lucille Barisonek and Elana Zucker. **Ind/Abst** Cumul. Index Nurs. Allied Health Lit., Int. Nurs. Index. **NLM** W1 NE204FN. bk rev. adv acc. **Circ** 10,000. (ctrl). Clinical level patient care articles for nurses engaged in all areas of home care or non-institutional care: rehabilitation, chronic hospice, for community nurses, rural, visiting nurses, etc.

NERF STUDIES IN NURSING. No. 3- 1977-. 0111-1965. Monographic Series. English. ir. **NLM** W1 N125H. *Studies in Nursing, 0110-1455.*

NEW JERSEY NURSE. V. 8- Feb./Mar. 1978-. 0196-4895. Periodical. US. English. bm. $10.00. New Jersey State Nurses Association, 320 West State Street, Trenton NJ 08618. **Tel** (609)392-4884. **Ed** Barbara W Wright. **Ind/Abst** Cumul. Index Nurs. Allied Health Lit., Int. Nurs. Index, Nurs. Allied Health Index. **NLM** W1 NE446T. adv acc. (ctrl). Publication for all members of the New Jersey State Nurses Association. Covers all areas affecting nursing in New Jersey.

NEW MEXICO BOARD OF NURSING ANNUAL REPORT TO GOVERNOR. (ANNUAL REPORT TO GOVERNOR). 0362-7438. US. English. an. Board of Nursing, 505 Marquette NW, Albuquerque NM 87102. **LC** RT5.N44. **DD** 331.11.

NEW MEXICO NURSE. 0028-6273. Periodical. US. English. qt. $5.00. New Mexico Nurses Association, 525 San Padro NE, Albuquerque NM 87108. **Tel** (505)268-7744. **Ind/Abst** Cumul. Index Nurs. Allied Health Lit., Int. Nurs. Index. **NLM** W1 NE461.

NEW ZEALAND NURSING FORUM. **VFOAT** Nursing Forum. V. 5- Apr./May 1977-. 0110-7968. Periodical. NZ. English. qt. $8.44. Nurses Society of New Zealand, PO Box 3195, Auckland 1 New Zealand. **Tel** 09-817-8412. **Ed** David J Wills. **Ind/Abst** Cumul. Index Nurs. Allied Health Lit., Int. Nurs. Index. **NLM** W1 NE977P. bk rev. adv acc. **Circ** 11,000. (ctrl). Small journal for original papers on nursing and related areas, abstracts and book reviews. *Nursing Forum.*

NEW ZEALAND NURSING JOURNAL. (THE NEW ZEALAND NURSING JOURNAL). **VFOAT** Kaitiaki. V. 22, No. 3-. 0028-8535. Periodical. NZ. English. mo. 20.00. New Zealand Nurses Association, Westbrook House, 8th Floor, 181-183 Willis Street, Wellington New Zealand. **Tel** 64-4-850847. **Ed** Ann Cherrington. **Ind/Abst** Int. Nurs. Index, Cumul. Index Nurs. Allied Health Lit. bk rev. adv acc. **Circ** 17,500. (ctrl). Articles relating to professional and industrial welfare nursing issues. Information from the New Zealand Nurses Association head office to its members. *Kai Tiaki.*

NEWS BULLETIN - SASKATCHEWAN REGISTERED NURSES' ASSOCIATION. **Main/Corp** Saskatchewan Registered Nurses' Association. Began publication in 1972. 0319-8499. CN. English. ir. Saskatchewan Registered Nurses Association, 2066 Retakkack Street, Regina Saskatchewan S4T 2KS Canada. **DD** 610.730627124.

NEWS NEWS NEWS *CEASED.* **Main/Corp** Association of Registered Nurses of Newfoundland. V. 1-7, No.1. 0319-7611. CN. English. Association of Registered Nurses of Newfoundland, A.R.N.N. House, PO Box 4185, St John's Newfoundland A1C 6A1 Canada. **DD** 610.73062718.

NEWSLETTER - ONTARIO NURSES' ASSOCIATION. **Main/Corp** Ontario Nurses' Association. **VAT** O N A Newsletter (Ottawa), Ontario Nurses' Association Newsletter. V. 1- Mar. 1975-. 0704-8009. Periodical. CN. English. mo. Ontario Nurses' Association, c/o I F Robinson, Education Co-Ordinator, 885 Meadowlands Drive East/Suite 406, Ottawa Ontario K2C 3N2 Canada. **DD** 610.73062713.

NIGERIAN NURSE. Periodical. English. sm. Literamed Publications Nigeria, Oregun Village Private Bag 1068, Ikeja Nigeria Africa. **Ind/Abst** Cumul. Index Nurs. Allied Health Lit.

NIHON KANGO KYOKAI CHOSA KENKYU HOKOKU. JA. Japanese. ir. Nihon Kango Kyokai, 8-2 Jingumae 5 Shibuya-Ku, Tokyo 150 Japan. **LC** RT1.

NOTES ET NOUVELLES DE L'ORDRE DES INFIRMIERES ET INFIRMIERS DU QUEBEC. **Main/Corp** Order of Nurses of Quebec. **VFOAT** News and Notes from the Order of Nurses of Quebec. Feb./March 1974-. 0319-2636. Periodical. CN. English (French). ir. 10.00 Domestic, 15.00 Foreign. Order of Nurses of Quebec, 4200 Dorchester Boulevard West, Montreal Quebec H3Z 1V4 Canada. **Tel** (514)935-2501. **Ed** Nicole Rodrigue. **DD** 610.73069209714. adv acc. **Circ** 65,983. (ctrl). Expectations and needs of Quebec nursing population; scope of the nurse's concerns and work; report on health issues; priorities and preoccupations of the Order des Infirmieres et Infirmiers du Quebec. *Notes et Nouvelles, 0319-261X.*

NUEVA ENFERMERIA. Began in 1979. 0210-8275. Periodical. SP. Spanish. mo. Nueva Enfermeria, Cuesta de Santo Domingo, 6-20 Madrid 13 Spain. **Ind/Abst** Int. Nurs. Index. **NLM** W1 NU143. *Boletin Cultural e Informativo de A.T.S.*

NURSCENE. V. 1- July 1974-. 0382-8476. Periodical. CN. English. ir. $7.74. Nurscene, 647 Broadway, Winnipeg Manitoba R3C 0X2 Canada. **Tel** (204)774-3477. **Ed** J L Cummings. **DD** 610,73.0627127. bk rev. **Circ** 9,600. (ctrl). Professional association affairs, continuing education in health care. *M A R News, 0382-8484.*

NURSE EDUCATOR. V. 1- May/June 1976-. 0363-3624. Periodical. US. English. qt. $36.00 Domestic, $40.00 Foreign. Nurse Educator, 2350 Virginia Avenue, Hagerstown MD 21740. **Tel** (800)638-3030. **Ed** Suzanne Smith Coletta. **Ind/Abst** Hospit. Lit. Index, Cumul. Index Nurs. Allied Health Lit., Int. Nurs. Index, Curr. Index J. Educ. **LC** RT71. **DD** 610.730711. **NLM** W1 NU5524. **Circ** 4,300. A high-level resource for academic educators on both the practical and the theoretical aspects of nursing education.

THE NURSE PRACTITIONER. V. 1- Sept./Oct. 1975-. 0361-1817. Periodical. US. English. $40.00. Vernon Publications, 109 West Mercer Street, Seattle WA 98119. **Tel** (206)285-2050. **Ed** Linda Pearson. **Ind/Abst** Index Med., Energy Res. Abstr., Int. Nurs. Index, Cumul. Index Nurs. Allied Health Lit., Hospit. Lit. Index, Int. Pharm. Abstr. **LC** RT1. **DD** 610.7305. **NLM** W1 NU555. bk rev. adv acc. **Circ** 11,000. A principal source of clinical information for the primary health care provider.

THE NURSE RECRUITER. **VFOAT** Nurserecruiter. 0732-8729. Periodical. US. English. mo. $36.00. Creative Marketing Concepts, PO Box 8531, Prairie Village KS 66208. **Tel** (913)642-2357.

THE NURSE, THE PATIENT & THE LAW. **VAT** Nurse, the Patient and the Law. 1977. 0196-6790. Periodical. US. English. mo. $65.00. Cox Publications, PO Box 958, El Cerrito CA 94530. **Tel** (415)527-2552. **Ed** Meredith B Cox. **LC** KFC615.A15. **DD** 344.79404105. adv acc. Nursing law and risk management cases and articles.

NURSE TRAINING. (NURSE TRAINING : REPORT TO THE CONGRESS). **Main/Corp** United States. Bureau of Health Resources Development. Division of Nursing. 0364-0698. US. English. **LC** RT79. **DD** 610.73071173.

NURSES' DRUG ALERT. V. 1- Sept. 1976-. 0191-2291. Periodical. US. English. mo. $32.00. Nurses Drug Alert, 374 Millburn Avenue, Millburn NJ 07041. **Tel** (201)467-4556. **Ed** Rhoda M Michaels. **Ind/Abst** Cumul. Index Nurs. Allied Health Lit.

NURSING. V. 1- Nov. 1971-. 0360-4039. Periodical. US. English. mo. Intermed Communications Inc, 1 Health Road, Box 2023, Marion OH 43302. **Tel** (614)383-3141. **Ind/Abst** Cumul. Index Nurs. Allied Health Lit., Energy Res. Abstr., Hospit. Lit. Index, Int. Nurs. Index, Gen. Sci. Index. **LC** RT1. **DD** 610.7305. **NLM** W1 NU584K.

NURSING. 1st- Ser. 0142-0372. Periodical. UK. English. mo. $55.17. Medicine Group, Pembroke House, 36/37 Pembroke Street, Oxford 0X1 1BL England. **Tel** 01 630 7881. **Ed** Scilla Erskine. **Ind/Abst** Cumul. Index Nurs. Allied Health Lit., Int. Nurs. Index. **NLM** W1 NU584D. bk rev. adv acc. **Circ** 20,000. Add-on clinical nursing text.

NURSING ABSTRACTS. *See* Indexes/Abstracts.

NURSING ADMINISTRATION QUARTERLY. V. 1- Fall 1976-. 0363-9568. Periodical. US. English. qt. $49.75. Aspen Systems Corp, PO Box 6018, Gaithersburg MD 20760. **Tel** (301)251-5000. **Ind/Abst** Hospit. Lit. Index, Cumul. Index Nurs. Allied Health Lit., Int. Nurs. Index. **LC** RT89. **DD** 658.913621. **NLM** W1 NU585.

NURSING ALLIED HEALTH INDEX. *See* Indexes/Abstracts.

NURSING & HEALTH CARE. (NURSING & HEALTH CARE : OFFICIAL PUBLICATION OF THE NATIONAL LEAGUE FOR NURSING). **VFOAT** Nursing and Health Care. Vol. 1, No. 1 (July/Aug. 1980). 0276-5284. Periodical. US. English. mo. $45.00. National League for Nursing, 10 Columbus Circle, New York NY 10019. **Tel** (212)582-1022. **Ed** Laura Clark. **Ind/Abst** Hospit. Lit. Index, Cumul. Index Nurs. Allied Health Lit., Int. Nurs. Index. **LC** RT1. **DD** 610.7305. **NLM** W1 NU5853. bk rev. adv acc. **Circ** 20,000. (ctrl). Official journal of the National League for Nursing. Reports on nursing education, management, practice and research, as well as political, social, and economic issues affecting health care. *NLN News.*

NURSING AND HEALTH CARE. Vol. 1, No. 1 (Aug. 1983)-. 0740-3992. Periodical. US. English. mo. $11.00. Crowder-Courtland Publications, 15445 Venture Boulevard, Suite 29, Sherman Oaks CA 91403. **Ind/Abst** Hospit. Lit. Index.

NURSING ASSISTANT : OFFICIAL PUBLICATION OF THE AMERICAN ASSOCIATION OF NURSING ASSISTANTS. Began with: Vol. 1, No. 1 (Jan.-Mar. 1983). Periodical. US. English. qt. $17.00. **NLM** W1.

NURSING CAREER DIRECTORY. *See* Yearbooks, Almanacs, Directories.

THE NURSING CLINICS OF NORTH AMERICA. Vol. 1, No. 1 (Mar. 1966)-. 0029-6465. Periodical. US. English. qt. $30.00. W B Saunders, West Washington Square, Philadelphia PA 19105. **Tel** (215)574-3395. **Ed** Lisa McAllister. **Ind/Abst** Life Sci. Collect., Excerpta Med., Cumul. Index Nurs. Allied Health Lit., Hospit. Lit. Index, Int. Nurs. Index, Energy Res. Abstr., Chem. Abstr., Index Med. **LC** RT1. **DD** 610.7305. **NLM** W1 NU587G. **CODEN** NCNAAK. **Circ** 6,200. Practical updates for the clinician on the latest advances plus topics of current interest.

NURSING DIGEST *CEASED.* **VAT** Nurs. Dig. V. 1-6, No. 4. 0091-4215. Periodical. US. English. qt. **NLM** W1 NU587K.

NURSING DIMENSIONS EDUCATION SERIES. Series/Titl Nursing Dimensions Series. Began with: Vol. 1, No. 1. 0731-5961. Monographic Series. US. English. qt. **NLM** W1 NU587R.

NURSING DRUG HANDBOOK. (NURSING . . . DRUG HANDBOOK). **VFOAT** Drug Handbook. 1981-. 0273-320X. US. English. an. Intermed Communications, 132 Welsh Road, Horsham PA 19044.

NURSING ECONOMIC$. VFOAT Nursing Economics. Vol. 1, No. 1 (July/Aug. 1983)-. 0746-1739. Periodical. US. English. bm. $28.00. Nursing Economics, North Woodbury Road Box 56, Pitman NJ 08071. **Tel** (609)589-0319. **Ed** Karen Mitchell. **Ind/Abst** Cumul. Index Nurs. Allied Health Lit., Int. Nurs. Index, Nurs. Allied Health Index. **NLM** W1. bk rev. adv acc. **Circ** 7,000. (ctrl). Journal for nurse executives regarding practical approaches to nursing economics.

NURSING EXAMINATION REVIEW BOOK. US. English. ir. Medical Exam Publ Co, 3003 New Hyde Park Road, New Hyde Park NY 11040. **Tel** (212)463-1052.

NURSING EXECUTIVE (HOSPITAL EDITION). (NURSING EXECUTIVE). 8756-7598. Periodical. US. English. mo. $139.00. Springhouse Corp, 1111 Bethlehem Pike, Springhouse PA 19477. **Tel** (215)646-8700. **Ed** William J Moran. bk rev. News and information that helps nurse executives contain health care costs, improve productivity, and add revenues.

NURSING FOCUS. V. 1- Sept. 1979-. 0144-4069. Periodical. UK. English. bm. International Thomson Publ, Northwood House 93-99 Goswell Road, London EC1V 7QA England. **Tel** 01-254-7231. **Ind/Abst** Cumul. Index Nurs. Allied Health Lit., Int. Nurs. Index. **NLM** W1 NU596.

NURSING FORUM. V. 1- Winter 1961/62-. 0029-6473. Periodical. US. English. ir. $25.00. Nursing Publ Inc, PO Box 218, Hillsdale NJ 07642. **Tel** (201)391-7845. **Ind/Abst** Excerpta Med., Index Med., Cumul. Index Nurs. Allied Health Lit., Int. Nurs. Index. **LC** RT1. **NLM** W1 NU597. **CODEN** NUFOA.

NURSING JOB NEWS NURSING JOB GUIDE TO OVER 7,000 HOSPITALS. VFOAT Nursing Job News, Guide Issue. **VAT** Nursing Job News Nursing Job Guide to Over Seven Thousand Hospitals. 1979-. 0162-9069. US. English. an. $48.00. Prime National Publishing Corp, 470 Boston Post Road, Weston MA 02193. **Tel** (617)899-2702. **Ed** Ira Alterman. bk rev. adv acc. **Circ** 3,500. Listings of all US hospitals and some Canadian. Most complete listing of over 7,200 hospitals and medical centers.

NURSING JOURNAL OF INDIA. 1910. 0029-6503. Periodical. II. English. mo. $20.00. Trained Nurses Association, L-17 Green Park, New Delhi 110016 India. **Tel** 666665. **Ed** Narender Nagpal. **Ind/Abst** Int. Nurs. Index, Cumul. Index Nurs. Allied Health Lit. **NLM** W1 NU632. bk rev. adv acc. **Circ** 18,500. (ctrl). The organ of the Trained Nurses Association of India, educates nurses and mothers who form its largest readership. It is popular in the nursing and medical profession.

THE NURSING JOURNALS INDEX. *See* Indexes/Abstracts.

NURSING LEADERSHIP *CEASED.* V. 1-6. 0164-7865. Periodical. US. English. mo. $25.00. Slack Inc, 6900 Grove Road, Thorofare NJ 08086. **Tel** (609)848-1000. **Ed** Lynne Stanwood. **Ind/Abst** Int. Nurs. Index, Cumul. Index Nurs. Allied Health Lit. **DD** 610. **NLM** W1 NU639. bk rev. adv acc. **Circ** 3,000. A general information magazine geared specifically toward nurses.

NURSING MANAGEMENT. Vol. 12, No. 9 (Sept. 1981)-. 0744-6314. Periodical. US. English. mo. S-N Publications, 600 South Federal, Suite 700, Chicago IL 60605. **Tel** (312)341-1014. **Ind/Abst** Cumul. Index Nurs. Allied Health Lit., Int. Nurs. Index, Hospit. Lit. Index. **NLM** W1 NU641N. *Supervisor Nurse, 0039-5870.*

NURSING MIRROR INCORPORATING MIDWIVES JOURNAL & QUEENS NURSING JOURNAL. Vol. 144, No. 26 (June 30, 1977)-. Periodical. UK. English. wk. Business Press International Ltd, Perrymount Road, Haywards Heath, West Sussex RH16 3BR England. *Nursing Mirror Incorporating Midwives Journal.*

NURSING MONTREAL. Vol. 1, No. 1 (June 76)-. 0710-6157. Periodical. CN. English (French). ir. 15.00. Corporation of Nurses of the Montreal District, Suite 1004/666 Sherbrooke Street West, Montreal Quebec H3A 1E7 Canada. **Tel** 288-5388. **Ind/Abst** Cumul. Index Nurs. Allied Health Lit., Int. Nurs. Index. **DD** 610.73060714281. **NLM** W1 NU642F. adv acc. (ctrl). Informs our members of what it's corporation does for them, how it helps it's members and informs them about conferences for them. *Format XI, 0710-6149.*

NURSING OUTLOOK. V. 1- Jan. 1953-. 0029-6554. Periodical. US. English. bm. American Journal of Nursing Company, 555 West 57th Street, York NY 10019. **Tel** (212)582-8820. **Ed** Lucie Kelly. **Ind/Abst** Hospit. Lit. Index, Excerpta Med., Index Med., Cumul. Index Nurs. Allied Health Lit., CIS Abstr., Int. Nurs. Index, Curr. Index J. Educ., Media Rev. Dig., Soc. Sci. Citation Index, Soc. Work Res. Abstr., Abstr. Soc. Work. **LC** RT1. **DD** 610.7305. **NLM** W1 NU655. (cum index). bk rev. adv acc. Issues and trends in health care, particularly as they affect nursing. *Public Health Nurisng.*

NURSING PAPERS. VFOAT Perspectives en Nursing. Began with Apr. 1969 issue. 0318-1006. Periodical. CN. English (includes some text in French). qt. 22.00. School of Nursing/McGill University, Wilson Hall-3506 University Street, Montreal Quebec H3A 2A7 Canada. **Tel** (514)392-5028. **Ed** Mary Ellen Jeans. **Ind/Abst** Cumul. Index Nurs. Allied Health Lit., Point Repere, Int. Nurs. Index. **NLM** W1 NU657. adv acc. **Circ** 900. Research and scholarly manuscripts of relevance to nursing and health care.

NURSING PRACTICE. Vol. 1, No. 1 (June 1983)-. 0828-4660. Periodical. CN. English. qt. Free. Hotel Dieu Hospital Nursing Department, 123 Sydenham Street, Kingston Ontario K7L 3H6 Canada. **DD** 610.730971372. (ctrl).

NURSING PROGRAMS AND ENTRANCE REQUIREMENTS AT CANADIAN UNIVERSITIES. VFOAT Programmes des Sciences Infirmieres et Conditions d'Admission aux Universites du Canada. 1981/82-. 0229-7345. CN. English (French). an. 3.00. Canadian Nurses Association, 50 The Driveway, Ottawa Ontario K2P 1E2 Canada. **Tel** (613)237-2133. **DD** 610.73071171. *Nursing Programs Offered at Canadian Universities, 0706-3873; Outline of General Academic Entrance Requirements for Basic Programs in Nursing at Canadian Universities, 0708-7683.*

NURSING PROGRAMS OFFERED AT CANADIAN UNIVERSITIES. Main/Corp Association des Infirmieres et Infirmiers du Canada. **VFOAT** Programmes d'Etudes en Sciences Infirmieres Offerts par les Universites Canadiennes. 1977/78-. 0706-3873. CN. French (text in English). an. Association des Infirmieres Canadiennes, 50 The Driveway, Ottawa Ontario K2P 1E2 Canada. **DD** 610.73071171. *Nursing Programs Offered at Canadian Universities, 0706-3873.*

NURSING QUEBEC. V. 1- June 1976-. 0381-6419. Periodical. CN. English (French). 10.00 Domestic, 15.00 Foreign. Order of Nurses of Quebec, 4200 Dorchester Boulevard West, Montreal Quebec H3Z 1V4 Canada. **Tel** (514)935-2501. **Ed** Nicole Rodrigue. **Ind/Abst** Point Repere, Int. Nurs. Index. **DD** 610.73069209714. adv acc. **Circ** 65,983. Expectations and needs of Quebec nursing population; scope of the nurse's concerns and work; report on health issues; priorities and preoccupations of the Ordre des Infirmieres et Infirmiers du Quebec.

NURSING RESEARCH. 1-. 0098-0358. Periodical. US. English. Little Brown & Company, 34 Beacon Street, Boston MA 02106. **Ed** P J Verhonick. **Ind/Abst** Life Sci. Collect. **LC** RT81.5. **DD** 610.73072. **NLM** W1 NU751C.

NURSING RESEARCH. V. 1- June 1952-. 0029-6562. Periodical. US. English. bm. $35.00. American Journal of Nursing, 555 West 57th Street, New York NY 10019. **Tel** (212)582-8820. **Ed** Florence S Downs. **Ind/Abst** Excerpta Med., Index Med., Cumul. Index Nurs. Allied Health Lit., Hospit. Lit. Index, Int. Nurs. Index, Energy Res. Abstr., Psychol. Abstr., Soc. Sci. Citation Index, Sci. Cit. Index, Abr. Ed., Women Stud. Abstr., Abstr. Soc. Work. **LC** RT1. **DD** 610.73. **NLM** W1 NU751. **CODEN** NURNA. (cum index). bk rev. adv acc. **Circ** 12,000. Results of clinical, educational, administrative, and research studies in nursing by means of articles, book reviews, letters, news, items, and abstracts.

NURSING RESEARCH ABSTRACTS. *See* Indexes/Abstracts.

NURSING STUDIES INDEX. *See* Indexes/Abstracts.

NURSING SUCCESS TODAY. Vol. 1, No. 1 (Jan./Feb. 1984)-. 0743-6726. Periodical. US. English. mo. $24.00 US, $39.00 Foreign. Slack Incorporated, 6900 Grove Road, Thorofare NJ 08086. **Ind/Abst** Cumul. Index Nurs. Allied Health Lit., Int. Nurs. Index. **DD** 610. **NLM** W1. *Nursing Leadership, 0164-7865.*

NURSING TIMES. V. 1- May 16, 1905. 0029-6589. Periodical. UK. English. wk. $120.00. MacMillan Journals Ltd, 4 Little Essex Street, London WC2R 3LF England. **Tel** 0256 29242. **Ind/Abst** Cumul. Index Nurs. Allied Health Lit., CIS Abstr., Int. Nurs. Index. **NLM** W1 NU761. Also available on microfilm from University Microfilms. *Nursing Times and Journal of Widwifery, Nursing Mirror.*

THE NURSING WORKFORCE IN NEW ZEALAND. VFOAT Nursing Work Force in New Zealand. English. ir. **LC** RT16. **DD** 331.12516107309931021.

NURSINGLIFE. VFOAT Nursing Life. Vol. 1, Issue 1 (July/Aug. 1981)-. 0279-3091. Periodical. US. English. bm. $25.00. Intermed Communications Inc, 1 Health Road/PO Box 1010, Monasquan NJ 08736. **Tel** (614)383-3141. **Ind/Abst** Cumul. Index Nurs. Allied Health Lit., Int. Nurs. Index. **DD** 610. **NLM** W1 NU639M.

NURSINGWORLD JOURNAL. VFOAT Nursing World Joural. 0745-8630. Periodical. US. English. mo. Nursingworld Journal, Weston MA 02193. **Tel** (617)899-2702. bk rev. adv acc. **Circ** 45,000. (ctrl). Reviews of all nursing literature. *Nursing Job News, 0163-223X; Nursingworld Digest, 0733-317X.*

OCCUPATIONAL HEALTH NURSING. 0029-7933. Periodical. US. English. mo. Slack Inc, 6900 Grove Road, Thorofare NJ 08086. **Tel** (609)848-1000. **Ind/Abst** Excerpta Med., Cumul. Index Nurs. Allied Health Lit., Int. Nurs. Index, Index Med. **LC** RC966. **DD** 610.734605. **NLM** W1 OC573. **CODEN** OHNUAO. *American Association of Industrial Nurses Journal, 0098-6097.*

OFFICIAL DIRECTORY OF REGISTERED NURSES AND LICENSED PRACTICAL NURSES. *See* Yearbooks, Almanacs, Directories.

THE OKLAHOMA NURSE. 0030-1787. Periodical. US. English. ir. $16.00. Oklahoma Nurses Association, 6416 North Santa Fe Suite A, Oklahoma City OK 73116. **Tel** (405)840-3476. **Ed** Frances I Waddle. **Ind/Abst** Cumul. Index Nurs. Allied Health Lit., Int. Nurs. Index. **NLM** W1 OK615. adv acc. **Circ** 1,200. (ctrl). Professional association for RNs; activities include nursing practice, legislation, nursing education, convention and conferences, focus on nursing leaders.

OMVARDAREN. 1/82-. 0280-4123. Periodical. Swedish. **Ind/Abst** Int. Nurs. Index. **NLM** W1. *Tidskrift for Sjukvardspedagoger, 0364-2722.*

ONCOLOGY NURSING FORUM. V. 4, No. 4- Oct. 1977-. 0190-535X. Periodical. US. English. bm. $44.00. Oncology Nursing Society, 3111 Banksville Road/Suite 200, Pittsburgh PA 15216. **Tel** (412)344-3899. **Ed** Susan Baird. **Ind/Abst** Cumul. Index Nurs. Allied Health Lit., Int. Nurs. Index. **NLM** W1 ON107N. bk rev. adv acc. **Circ** 11,000. Concerns nursing care of persons with cancer, early detection and prevention of cancer; and oncology nursing society news. *Oncology Nursing Society Newsletter.*

ONE ON ONE. V. 1- Oct. 1979-. 0270-6628. Periodical. US. English. bm. $12.00 Domestic, $16.00 Foreign. Utah State Nurses Association, 1058 East 9th South, Salt Lake City UT 84105. **Tel** (801)322-3439. **Ed** Colleen Price. **Ind/Abst** Int. Nurs.

Medicine—Nursing

Index. NLM W1 ON135. adv acc. Circ 2,400. (ctrl). Professional news, topics of interest and research findings. *UNA Communique, 0162-7287.*

OREGON NURSE. V. 1- 1931?-. 0030-4751. Periodical. US. English. bm. $6.00. Oregon Nurses Association, 9700 SW Capitol Highway/Suite 200, Portland OR 97219. Tel (503)293-0011. Ed Paula McNeil and Martha Haggland. Ind/Abst Cumul. Index Nurs. Allied Health Lit., Int. Nurs. Index. NLM W1 OR531. adv acc. Circ 4,500. (ctrl). News and information about and for registered nurses in Oregon. Includes educational offerings and reports.

ORTHOPAEDIC NURSING. Vol. 2, No. 1 (Jan./Feb 1983)-. Periodical. US. English. bm. $18.00. NLM W1. *Orthopedic Nursing, 0744-6020.*

PATIENT CARE LAW. *See* Law.

PEDIATRIC NURSING. *See* Medicine - Pediatrics.

PELICAN NEWS. V. 1-. 0031-4161. Periodical. US. English. qt. $8.00. Louisiana State Nurses Association, PO Box 837, Metairie LA 70004. Ind/Abst Cumul. Index Nurs. Allied Health Lit., Int. Nurs. Index.

PENNSYLVANIA NURSE. (THE PENNSYLVANIA NURSE). V. 1- 1946-. 0031-4617. Periodical. US. English. mo. $15.00. Pennsylvania Nurses Association, PO Box 8525, Harrisburg PA 17105. Tel (717)234-7935. Ed David R Ranck. Ind/Abst Cumul. Index Nurs. Allied Health Lit., Int. Nurs. Index. NLM W1 PE411. bk rev. adv acc. Circ 10,000. (ctrl). Official publication of the Nursing Organization in Pennsylvania. News, features of interest to nurses especially members.

PERIODICAL HOLDINGS - HELEN K. MUSSALLEM LIBRARY. CANADIAN NURSES ASSOCIATION. *See* Bibliographies.

PERIOPERATIVE NURSING QUARTERLY. VFOAT PNQ. Vol. 1, No. 1 (Mar. 1985)-. 8755-9935. Periodical. US. English. qt. $45.00. Aspen Systems Corp, 16792 Oakmont Avenue, Gaithersburg MD 20877. DD 610. NLM W1. Issued also in microform by University Microfilms International.

PERSPECTIVES IN PSYCHIATRIC CARE. V. 1- Jan./Feb. 1963-. 0031-5990. Periodical. US. English. qt. Nursing Publications, Box 218, Hillsdale NJ 07642. Tel (201)391-7845. Ed Alice Clarke. Ind/Abst Excerpta Med., Index Med., Cumul. Index Nurs. Allied Health Lit., Hospit. Lit. Index, Int. Nurs. Index, Psychol. Abstr. LC RC475. NLM W1 PE871E. CODEN PEPYA. adv acc. Circ 5,000. (ctrl). Educational material on psychiatric nursing.

PHARMACOLOGY IN NURSING. 7th Ed.-. 0737-8882. US. English. ir. C V Mosby Company, c/o C Leadbetter, 11830 Westline Industrial Drive, St Louis MO 63141. LC RM125. DD 615.1. *Introduction to Materia Medica and Pharmacology.*

PLASTIC SURGICAL NURSING. (PLASTIC SURGICAL NURSING : OFFICIAL JOURNAL OF THE AMERICAN SOCIETY OF PLASTIC AND RECONSTRUCTIVE SURGICAL NURSES). Vol. 3, No. 1 (Spring 1983)-. 0741-5206. Periodical. US. English. qt. $14.00 Individual, $17.00 Institution. ASPRSN National Office, 23341 North Milwaukee Avenue, Half Day IL 60069. Ind/Abst Int. Nurs. Index, Cumul. Index Nurs. Allied Health Lit. NLM W1. *Journal of Plastic and Reconstructive Surgical Nursing, 0273-3285.*

PLEJERBLADET (COPENHAGEN, DENMARK : 1978). (PLEJERBLADET). V. 64, No. 9, (Sept. 1978)-. 0106-6897. Periodical. Danish. mo. NLM W1 PL255. *Dansk Hospitalsforbunds Medlemsblad.*

PN. PRACTICAL NURSING CAREER. (PRACTICAL NURSING CAREER). Series Corp National League for Nursing. Publication. 1973/74-. 0145-8981. Periodical. US. English. an. NLM WY 22 AA1 P8. *Let's be Practical About a Nursing Career.*

POINT OF VIEW. 0098-4345. Periodical. US. English. bw. Free. Ethicon Inc, Somerville NJ 08876. Ind/Abst Cumul. Index Nurs. Allied Health Lit. NLM W1 PO18.

POLITICAL ISSUES IN NURSING: PAST, PRESENT AND FUTURE. (POLITICAL ISSUES IN NURSING, PAST, PRESENT AND FUTURE). 0883-4504. UK. English. an. John Wiley & Sons, Baffins Lane, Chichester, West Sussex England.

THE PRAIRIE ROSE. 1931. 0032-6666. Periodical. US. English. qt. $10.00. North Dakota State Nurses Association, 212 North 4th Green Tree Square, Bismarck ND 58501. Tel (701)223-1385. Ed Betty Maher. Ind/Abst Cumul. Index Nurs. Allied Health Lit., Int. Nurs. Index. NLM W1 PR2418. adv acc. Circ 8,000. (ctrl). Published quarterly tab size 24 pages sent to all licensed nurses, student nurses and legislators in North Dakota.

PRN FORUM. VFOAT Pain Research News. VAT Pain Research Nurse Forum. Vol. 1, No. 1 (Feb./Mar. 1982)-. 0743-345X. Periodical. US. English. bm. $24.00. Center for Health Sciences, Department of Anesthesiology B6/387 600 Highland Avenue, Madison WI 53792. Ind/Abst Int. Nurs. Index.

PROBLEMI DELLA PROFESSIONE INFERMIERISTICA. 1-. 0392-0526. Monographic Series. Italian. ir. Ed C Iandolo. NLM W1 PR571DG.

PROCEEDINGS OF MEETING OF COUNCIL ON COLLEGIATE EDUCATION FOR NURSING. VFOAT Proceedings, Meeting - SREB Council on Collegiate Education for Nursing. 10th. 0270-7764. Periodical. US. English. sa. NLM WY 18 P9625. *Proceedings of Conference of Council on Collegiate Education for Nursing, 0196-8025.*

PROCEEDINGS - ONCOLOGY NURSING SOCIETY. CONGRESS. (PROCEEDINGS). VFOAT Annual Congress of the Oncology Nursing Society. Began with 1st, 1976. 0738-1298. US. English. an. $6.00. Oncology Nursing Society, 3111 Banksville Road/Suite 200, Pittsburgh PA 15216. Tel (301)294-0333. Ed Susan B Baird. NLM W1 PR5821O. adv acc. Circ 10,000. (ctrl). Published as supplement to Oncology Nursing Forum, official journal of the Oncology Nursing Society. Focus is clinical practice and research in cancer nursing.

PROGRAM PLANS. NURSING BASIC SERIES. VFOAT Nursing Basic Series. 1979. 0734-1431. Periodical. US. English. mo. $57.00. EPSCO/Education Planning Service Corporation, Box 182, Newton Highland MA 02161. Tel (617)235-8101. Ed Jessica Terrill. Circ 3,000. (ctrl). Prepared inservice education programs for nursing staff. Each program thirty minutes, written material intended for presentation by the training director.

PROGRAM PLANS. NURSING MANAGEMENT SERIES. *See* Business - General Management.

PUBLIC HEALTH NURSING (BOSTON, MASS.). (PUBLIC HEALTH NURSING). Vol. 1, No. 1 (Mar. 1984)-. 0737-1209. Periodical. US. English. qt. $42.50. Blackwell Scientific Publications 52 Beacon Street, Boston MA 02108. Tel (617)720-0761. Ed Sherry Shamansky. DD 362. NLM W1. bk rev. adv acc. Circ 1,000. Public health nursing publishers original material having application in the areas of public health nursing practice, research, theory development, and education.

R N A N S BULLETIN. Main/Corp Registered Nurses' Association of Nova Scotia. V. 3, No. 4- Nov. 1971-. 0319-4604. CN. English. ir. Registered Nurses' Association of Nova Scotia, 6035 Coburg Road, Halifax Nova Scotia B3H 1Y8 Canada. Tel (902)423-6156. Ed M J Emms. DD 610.73062716. bk rev. adv acc. Circ 9,000. (ctrl). News of professional association activities and of the profession and practice of nursing. *Bulletin, 0319-4590.*

R N A O NEWS. Main/Corp Registered Nurses Association of Ontario. V. 21, No. 5- Sept./Oct. 1965-. 0048-7112. Periodical. CN. English. ir. $9.28. Registered Nurses Association Ontario, 33 Price Street, Toronto Ontario M4W 1Z2 Canada. Tel (416)923-3523. Ed Peggy Wysong. Ind/Abst Cumul. Index Nurs. Allied Health Lit., Int. Nurs. Index. NLM W1 R119. adv acc. Circ 43,000. (ctrl). 4-color glossy magazine for registered nurses in Ontario and allied health organizations, government and media. The voice of the professional nurse on issues and action. *News Bulletin, 0380-922X.*

RECENT ADVANCES IN NURSING. 1-. 0144-6592. Monographic Series. UK. English. Ed M C Cahoon, L A Copp, and L Hockey. LC UNC. NLM W1 RE105VN.

REGAN REPORT ON NURSING LAW. *See* Law.

REGISTERED NURSING ORDERLY. (THE REGISTERED NURSING ORDERLY). V. 18- Dec. 1975-. 0380-1861. Periodical. CN. English. qt. Alberta Association of Registered Nursing Orderlies, C-10112-124 Street, Edmonton Alberta T5N 1P6 Canada. DD 610.7306980627123. *Nursing Orderly, 0380-187X.*

REHABILITATION NURSING. Vol. 6, No. 1 (Jan./Feb. 1981)-. 0278-4807. Periodical. US. English. bm. $25.00. Rehabilitation Nursing, 2506 Gross Point Road, Evanston IL 60201. Tel (312)475-7510. Ed Barbara A McHugh. Ind/Abst Cumul. Index Nurs. Allied Health Lit., Int. Nurs. Index. LC RT120.R4. DD 617. NLM W1 RE1479D. bk rev. adv acc. Circ 4,400. Provides scientific and professional data to nurses working with physically or emotionally disabled clients. Features cover nursing care techniques, nursing process, rehabilitation team functions, research and education. *ARN Journal, 0362-3505.*

REPORT - LOUISIANA STATE BOARD OF NURSING. Main/Corp Louisiana. State Board of Nursing. 1976-. 0149-0346. US. English. State Board of Nursing, 907 Pere Marquette Building, 150 Baronne Street, New Orleans LA 70112. LC RT5.L8. DD 610.7309763. *Report - Louisiana State Board of Nurse Examiners, 0095-5884.*

REPORT OF NURSE POPULATION IN OKLAHOMA. *See* Economics - Labor.

REPORT OF THE WEST VIRGINIA BOARD OF EXAMINERS FOR REGISTERED PROFESSIONAL NURSES TO THE GOVERNOR . . . FOR THE BIENNIUM PERIOD ENDING DECEMBER 31 . . . . Main/Corp West Virginia Board of Examiners for Registered Professional Nurses. VFOAT West Virginia Board of Registered Professional Nursing Biennium Report . . . to the Governor . . . of the State of West Virginia. US. English. be. West Virginia Board of Examiners for Registered Professional Nurses, Suite 309/Embleton Building, 922 Quarrier Street, Charleston WV 25301. LC RT5.W4. DD 362.17309754. *Report of the West Virginia Board of Examiners for Registered Nurses, 0362-1855.*

REPORT ON NURSING FACULTY SALARIES IN COLLEGES AND UNIVERSITIES. *See* Economics - Labor.

REPORT ON SALARIES OF NURSING DEANS IN COLLEGES AND UNIVERSITIES. *See* Economics - Labor.

REPORT TO THE CONGRESS, NURSE TRAINING ACT OF 1975. Main/Corp United States. Dept. of Health and Human Services. Office of the Secretary. Series/Titl DHHS Publication. VFOAT Nurse Training Act of 1975. 3rd (Feb. 17, 1982)-. US. English. US Department of Health and Human Services, Public Health Service Health Resources Administration, Bureau of Health Professions, Division of Nursing, Hyattsville MD 20782. *Report to the Congress, Nurse Training Act of 1975, 0161-8210.*

REPORT - VIRGINIA. STATE BOARD OF NURSING. (REPORT). Main/Corp Virginia. State Board of Nursing. July 1, 1978-June 30, 1981-. 0749-3746. US. English. LC RT5.V8. DD 353.975500841. *Annual Report, 0749-3738.*

THE REPORTER WB (WILMINGTON, DEL.). (THE REPORTER). V. 1-10, 1968-Nov./Dec. 1976. Periodical. US. English. mo. Delaware Nurses Association, 1003 Delaware Avenue, Wilmington DE 19806. Tel (302)655-6297. Ind/Abst Int. Nurs. Index. *Delaware Nurse.*

RESEARCH IN NURSING & HEALTH. VAT Research in Nursing and Health. V. 1- Apr. 1978-. 0160-6891. Periodical. US. English. qt. John Wiley & Sons, 605 Third Avenue, New York NY 10158. Tel (800)526-5368. Ind/Abst Index Med., Cumul. Index Nurs. Allied Health Lit., Int. Nurs. Index, Energy Res. Abstr., Psychol. Abstr. LC RT81.5. DD 610.7305. NLM W1 RE227IC.

REVISTA ROL DE ENFERMERIA. (REVISTA DE ENFERMERIA). VFOAT Revista Rol de Enfermeria, Barcelona. Began with: No. 1 (July 1978). 0210-5020. Monographic Series. Spanish. ir. Ind/Abst Int. Nurs. Index. NLM W1 RE394J. (cum index).

REVUE DE L'INFIRMIERE. VFOAT Informations. Began with June 1974. 0397-7897. Periodical. FR. French. ir. 370. Expansion Scientifique Francaise, 15 rue Saint-Benoit, 75278 Paris Cedex 06 France. Tel (1)45 48 42 60. Ind/Abst Int. Nurs. Index, Point Repere. NLM W1 RE789H. An efficient tool containing articles on nursing care, it is an introduction to health care. Precise information, a permanent almanac for health care.

RN. VFOAT RN Magazine. VAT Registered Nurse. V. 1- Oct. 1937-. 0033-7021. Periodical. US. English. mo. $30.00. Medical Economics Inc, 680 Kinderkamack Road, Oradell NJ 07649. Tel (201)262-3030. Ed James A Reynolds. Ind/Abst Trade Ind. Index, Hospit. Lit. Index, Gen. Sci. Index, Cumul. Index Nurs. Allied Health Lit., Int. Nurs. Index. LC RT1. DD 610.7305. NLM W1 R118. bk rev. adv acc. Circ 325,000. (ctrl). Available on microfilm from University Microfilms. Three quarters clinical; one quarter professional; with emphasis on events and current developments.

RN IDAHO. VAT Registered Nurse Idaho. V. 1- Aug. 1977-. 0192-298X. Periodical. US. English. bm. $10.00. Idaho Nurses Association, 1134 North Orchard/#8, Boise ID 83706. Tel (208)323-0103. Ed Nancy Leslie. Ind/Abst Int. Nurs. Index. NLM W1 R118D. adv acc. Circ 700. (ctrl). Newspaper sent to RN's in Idaho schools of nursing, and libraries. Current issues of interest to health professionals. *Gem State RN News Letter, 0072-0569.*

R.P.N.A.M. UPDATE. VAT Registered Psychiatric Nurses Association of Manitoba Update. Feb. 1983-. 0822-4048. Periodical. CN. English. bm. Registered Psychiatric Nurses Association of Manitoba, 1854 Portage Avenue, Winnipeg Manitoba R3J 0G9 Canada. DD 610.73680607127. *Prism, 0380-2442.*

SANTO TOMAS NURSING JOURNAL. V.1-. Periodical. PH. English. sa. University of Santo Tomas, College of Nursing, Malila Phillippines.

SCHOOLS OF NURSING, RN, LPN-LVN. (SCHOOLS OF NURSING—RN-LPN/LVN). 1974/75-. 0098-3268. US. English. $0.50. National League for Nursing, 10 Columbus Circle, New York NY 10019. LC RT81.U6. DD 610.73071173. NLM WY 22 AA1 S31. *Schools of Nursing / RN, 0090-1466.*

SCI NURSING : A PUBLICATION OF THE AMERICAN ASSOCIATION OF THE SPINAL CORD INJURY NURSES. Vol. 1, No. 1 (Winter 1984)-. Periodical. US. English. qt. Ind/Abst Int. Nurs. Index. NLM W1.

SCNA NEWSLETTER. Main/Corp South Carolina Nurses' Association. VAT South Carolina Nurses' Association Newsletter. 0199-3399. Periodical. US. English. bm. $12.00. South Carolina Nurses Association, 1821 Gadson Street, Columbia SC 29201. Tel (803)252-4781. Ed Judith Thompson. Ind/Abst Int. Nurs. Index. adv acc. Circ 1,500. A newsletter designed for the South Carolina nursing community updates on health issues. Legislation regulation workshops, education trends and policy issues.

SEMINARS IN ONCOLOGY NURSING. Vol. 1, No. 1 (Feb. 1985)-. 0749-2081. Periodical. US. English. qt. $50.00. Grune & Stratton, 111 5th Avenue, New York NY 10003. DD 616.

SENIOR NURSE. Vol. 1, No. 1 (Apr. 4, 1984)-. 0265-9999. Periodical. UK. English. wk. 25.00 Domestic, $53.00 US. International Thomson Pub Ltd, Northwood House 93-99 Goswell Road, London EC1V 7QA England. Ind/Abst Cumul. Index Nurs. Allied Health Lit. NLM W1. *Nursing Focus.*

THE SOCIETY FOR NURSING HISTORY GAZETTE. Began with: Vol. 1, No. 1 (Spring 1981). Periodical. US. English. sa. $20.00. NLM W1.

SOME STATISTICS ON BACCALAUREATE AND HIGHER DEGREE PROGRAMS IN NURSING. *See* Statistics.

SPECIAL PROJECTS FOR IMPROVEMENT IN NURSE TRAINING. 1978-. 0196-660X. US. English. NLM WY 22 AA1 S55. *Special Project Grants and Contracts Awarded for Improvement in Nurse Training, 0095-2141.*

STAT. 1933. 0038-9986. Periodical. US. English. sm. $45.00. Wisconsin Nurses Association, 206 East Olin Avenue, Madison WI 53713. Tel (608)221-0383. Ed Angela Apostoloff. Ind/Abst Cumul. Index Nurs. Allied Health Lit., Int. Nurs. Index. Circ 2,200. (ctrl). Membership information; legislative and nursing issues.

STATE-APPROVED SCHOOLS OF NURSING, L.P.N.-L.V.N. (STATE-APPROVED SCHOOLS OF NURSING. LPN/LVN). Main/Corp National League for Nursing. 1st- 1959-. 0081-4423. US. English. an. $10.95. National League for Nursing, 10 Columbus Circle, New York NY 10019. Tel (212)582-1022.

STATE-APPROVED SCHOOLS OF NURSING-R.N. VAT State Approved Schools of Nursing Registered Nurse. 25th- Ed. 0081-4431. US. English. an. $11.95. National League for Nursing, 10 Columbus Circle, Ms Currere, New York NY 10019. Tel (212)582-1022. NLM WY 22 AA1 S7. *State Approved Schools of Professional Nursing.*

STATE NURSING LEGISLATION QUARTERLY. *See* Law.

STATISTIQUES. LES INFIRMIERES AU CANADA *CEASED.* (STATISTIQUES; LES INFIRMIERES AU CANADA). 1973-1974. 0315-2618. CN. French. an. Association des Infirmieres Canadiennes, 50 The Driveway, Ottawa Ontario K2P 1E2 Canada. DD 331.761610730971.

STUDIES IN NURSING MANAGEMENT. No. 1-. 0739-7291. Monographic Series. US. English. UMI Research Press, Ann Arbor MI 48106. Ed Philip A Kalisch and Beatrice J Kalisch. NLM W1 ST929N.

SUMMARY OF PROCEEDINGS - AMERICAN NURSES' ASSOCIATION. CONVENTION. (SUMMARY OF PROCEEDINGS). Main/Corp American Nurses' Association., Convention. 52nd (1980)-. 0744-2580. US. English. be. American Nurses' Association, 2420 Pershing Road, Kansas City MO 64108. LC RT1. DD 610.7306073. *Summary Proceedings.*

SUPERVISOR NURSE *CEASED.* V. 1-12, No. 8. 0039-5870. Periodical. US. English. mo. Supervisor Nurse, 8 South Michigan Avenue, Chicago IL 60603. Ind/Abst Cumul. Index Nurs. Allied Health Lit., Int. Nurs. Index, Hospit. Lit. Index. NLM W1 SU69.

SURVEY OF CANADIAN NURSERY TRADES INDUSTRY. Main/Corp Canada. Statistics Canada. Horticultural Crops Unit. VFOAT Enquete sur l'Industrie des Pepinieres Canadiennes. 1972/73-. 0318-5184. Periodical. CN. English (French). an. 20.00 Domestic, 21.00 Foreign. Receiver General for Canada, Statistics Canada Publications, Ottawa Ontario K1A 0T6 Canada. LC SB29.C2. DD 338.17590971. Sales and purchases of fruit and ornamental nursery stock, financial statistics, for Canada and the provinces. *Survey of Canadian Nursery Trades Industry = Enquete sur l'Industrie des Pepinieres Canadiennes, 0318-5184.*

SYGEPLEJERSKEN. Vol. 72- Jan. 1972-. 0106-8350. Periodical. DK. Danish. wk. 545,00. Dansk Sygeplejerads, Vimmelskaftet 38 Postbox 1084, 1008 Kobenhavn K Denmark. Tel 01- 15 15 55. Ed Peter Hjorth. Ind/Abst Int. Nurs. Index. NLM W1 SY424. bk rev. adv acc. Circ 58,917. (ctrl). *Tiksskrift for Sygeplejersker, 0049-3856.*

SYKEPLEIEN. 1914. 0039-7628. Periodical. NO. Norwegian. ir. $41.98. Norwegian Nurses Association, PO Box 3649 Gamlebyen, 0135 Oslo 1 Norway. Tel (02)688890. Ed Berit Onarheim. Ind/Abst Int. Nurs. Index. bk rev. adv acc. Circ 34,000. (ctrl). Covers nursing.

TAEHAN KANHO. VFOAT Korean Nurse. Periodical. KO. Korean. ir. Taehan Kanho Hyophoe, 88-7 Sang Lim Dong, Choong Ku, Seoul Korea. Ind/Abst Int. Nurs. Index. LC RT1. NLM W1 TA392R.

TAR HEEL NURSE. Vol. 1- 1939-. 0039-9620. Periodical. US. English. bm. $12.00. North Carolina State Nurses Association, PO Box 12025, Raleigh NC 27605. Tel (919)821-4250. Ed Francis N Miller. Ind/Abst Int. Nurs. Index, Cumul. Index Nurs. Allied Health Lit. DD 610. NLM W1 TA597. adv acc. Circ 3,500. (ctrl). Information about nursing in North Carolina, including educational programs and legislative reviews.

TEHY. Year 1, 1 (13.1.1981)-. 0358-4038. Periodical. Finnish. ir. NLM W1 TE29. *Laboratoriohoitaja, Lastenhoitajalehti; Sairaanhoitaja.*

TEST SERVICES FOR SCHOOLS OF NURSING. 1978/79-. US. English.

TEXAS NURSING. V. 47, No. 4- Apr. 1973-. 0095-036X. Periodical. US. English. mo. $9.00. Texas Nurses Association, 314 Highland Mall Boulevard/ Suite 504, Austin TX 78752. Tel (512)452-0645. Ed John L Brown. Ind/Abst Cumul. Index Nurs. Allied Health Lit., Int. Nurs. Index. NLM W1 TE789. bk rev. adv acc. Circ 5,000. (ctrl). News about Association members, developments in nursing in Texas, health related issues, entry level nursing, etc. *Bulletin - Texas Nurses Association, 0040-4500.*

THIS MONTH *CEASED.* Began publication in 196-. Ceased with V. 13, No. 2, Apr./Aug. 1981. 0382-6341. Periodical. CN. English. mo. Psychiatric Nurses' Association of British Columbia, 602-7th Avenue, New Westminister British Columbia V3M 2J3 Canada. DD 610.7368062711. *Psych News, 0555-5345.*

TIDSKRIFT FOR SJUKVARDSPEDAGOGER *CEASED.* 0346-2722. Periodical. Swedish. NLM W1. *Pedagogiska Sektionens Medlemsblad - Svensk Sjukskoterskeforening.*

TIJDSCHRIFT VOOR ZIEKENVERPLEGING. Vol. 22, No. 14-15 July 1969-. 0303-6456. Periodical. NE. Dutch. ir. De Tijdstroom BV, Postbus 19300, 1000 GH Amsterdam Netherlands. Ind/Abst CIS Abstr., Int. Nurs. Index. NLM W1 TI793. *TVZ. Tijdschrift Voor Ziekencerpleging, 0049-2809.*

TODAY'S OR NURSE. VAT Today's Operating Room Nurse. V. 1- Mar. 1979-. 0194-5181. Periodical. US. English. mo. $56.00. Slack Inc, 6900 Grove Road, Thorofare NJ 08086. Tel (609)848-1000. Ind/Abst Cumul. Index Nurs. Allied Health Lit., Int. Nurs. Index. NLM W1 TO172I.

TOPICS IN CLINICAL NURSING. VFOAT Clinical Nursing. V. 1- Apr. 1979-. 0164-0534. Monographic Series. US. English. qt. $53.00. Aspen Systems Corporation, PO Box 6018, Gaithersburg MD 20760. Tel (301)251-5000. Ind/Abst Hospit. Lit. Index, Cumul. Index Nurs. Allied Health Lit., Int. Nurs. Index. LC UNC. NLM W1 TO539LC.

VERMONT REGISTERED NURSE. 0191-1880. Periodical. US. English. bm. $15.00. Vermont State Nurses Association, 500 Dorset Street South, Burlington VT 05401. Tel (802)864-9390. Ed Alan Sousie. Ind/Abst Cumul. Index Nurs. Allied Health Lit., Int. Nurs. Index. NLM W1 VE682. adv acc. Circ 400. (ctrl). Local, state, and national news. Feature articles of interest to professional nurses.

VERPLEEGKUNDIGE STUDIES. VFOAT Reeks Verpleegkundige Studies. V. 1-. 0167-4706. Monographic Series. Dutch. ir. NLM W1 VE785S.

VIRGINIA NURSE. V. 45- 1976-. 0270-7780. Periodical. US. English. qt. $10.00. Virginia Nurses Association, 1311 High Point Avenue, Richmond VA 23230. Tel (804)353-7311. Ed Deborah A Shetton. Ind/Abst Cumul. Index Nurs. Allied Health Lit., Int. Nurs. Index. NLM W1 VI81K. bk rev. adv acc. Circ 3,000. Information on nursing issues, health care, activities of the association and news in the state, national and international nursing community. *Virginia Nurse Quarterly.*

WASHINGTON STATE JOURNAL OF NURSING. VFOAT WSJN. V. 1- 1928-. 0043-0781. Periodical. US. English. mo. $10.00. Washington State Nurses Association, 2615 Fourth Avenue, Suite 380, Seattle WA 98121. Tel (206)622-3613. Ed Gigi Molvar. Ind/Abst Int. Nurs. Index, Cumul. Index Nurs. Allied Health Lit. NLM W1 WA66H. adv acc. Circ 9,500. (ctrl). A newsmagazine for nurses and related organizations in our state. *Bulletin (Washington State Graduate Nurses Association).*

THE WEATHER VANE. 0043-1664. Periodical. US. English. bm. West Virginia Nurses Association, 723 Kan Boulevard, University Building/Suite 511, Charleston WV 25301. Tel (304)342-7978. Ed Mary Angel. Ind/Abst Cumul. Index Nurs. Allied Health Lit., Int. Nurs. Index. NLM W1 WE119. adv acc. Circ 1,500. Professional nursing journal.

WESTERN JOURNAL OF NURSING RESEARCH. V. 1- Winter 1979-. 0193-9459. Periodical. US. English. qt. $16.00 WSRN Member, $35.00 Others. Phillips-Allen Publishers, 1330 South State College Boulevard, Anaheim CA 92806. Ind/Abst Cumul. Index Nurs. Allied Health Lit., Int. Nurs. Index. NLM WL WE635.

WILEY SERIES ON DEVELOPMENTS IN NURSING RESEARCH. VFOAT Developments in Nursing Research. Vol. 1-. 0737-6065. Monographic Series. UK. English. LC UNC. NLM W1 WI53LF.

ZHONGHUA HULI ZAZHI. (CHUNG-HUA HU LI TSA CHIH). VFOAT Chinese Journal of Nursing. 0254-1769. Periodical. Chinese (English). bm. Ind/Abst Int. Nurs. Index. NLM W1 CH9819M.

THE ZIMBABWE NURSE. 1980-. English. an. NLM W1. *Zimbabwe Rhodesia Nurse.*

Medicine—Ophthalmology

OPHTHALMOLOGY

ABHANDLUNGEN AUS DEM GEBIETE DER AUGENHEILKUNDE. V. 34- 1967-. Periodical. GE. German. ir. Deutscher Buchexport, Postfach 160, DDR 7010 Leipzig East Germany. **Tel** 27332. **Ind/Abst** Excerpta Med. **NLM** W1 AB458. bk rev. *Sammlung Zwangloser Abhandlungen Aus Dem Gebiete der Augenheilkunde.*

ABMS DIRECTORY OF CERTIFIED OPHTHALMOLOGISTS. See Yearbooks, Almanacs, Directories.

ACTA OPHTHALMOLOGICA. V. 1- 1923-. 0001-639X. Periodical. DK. English (articles in French or German). bm. 720.00. Scriptor Publisher APS, Gasvaerksvej 15, DK-1656 Copenhagen V Denmark. **Tel** (01) 22 92 01. **Ind/Abst** Life Sci. Collect., Excerpta Med., Biol. Abstr., Chem. Abstr., Nuci. Sci. Abstr., Index Med., Energy Res. Abstr., Sci. Cit. Index, Abr. Ed. **NLM** W1 AC8811. **CODEN** ACOPAT. (cum index). bk rev. adv acc. **Circ** 2,000.

ADVANCES IN OPHTHALMOLOGY *CEASED.* VFOAT Fortschritte der Augenheilkunde, Progres en Ophtalmologie. Began with 21-42. 0065-3004. Monographic Series. English (articles in French and German). ir. **Ind/Abst** Life Sci. Collect., Chem. Abstr., Biol. Abstr., Index Med. **NLM** W1 AD686M. **CODEN** AVOMBI. *Fortschritte der Augenheilkunde.*

AFRO-ASIAN JOURNAL OF OPHTHALMOLOGY. VFOAT Ophthalmology. Vol. 1, No. 1 (June 1982)-. 0254-0517. Periodical. English. qt. $40.00. **Ind/Abst** Excerpta Med., Chem. Abstr. **NLM** W1 AF629. **CODEN** AAJODO.

AGGIORNAMENTI DI TERAPIA OFTALMOLOGICA. 1- 1949-. 0002-0915. Periodical. IT. Italian. ty. Via Dietro la Corte 7/R, Pisa 56100 Italy.

AL-KAHHAL. VFOAT Alkahhal. Journal 1- Festival Year 1980-. Periodical. chiefly Arabic. qt. 35.00 Medical Students, 75.00 Others. Majallat Al-Kahhal, Ittihad Al-Kuttab Al-Arab, Dimashq Syria. **LC** RE1.

ALBRECHT VON GRAEFES ARCHIV FUR KLINISCHE UND EXPERIMENTELLE OPHTHALMOLOGIE. See Genealogy and Heraldry - Archives.

AMERICAN ACADEMY OF OPHTHALMOLOGY DIRECTORY. See Yearbooks, Almanacs, Directories.

AMERICAN JOURNAL OF OPHTHALMOLOGY. V. 1-34, 1884-1917. 0002-9394. Periodical. US. English. mo. $37.00. Ophthalmic Publishing Company, 435 North Michigan Avenue/Suite 1415, Chicago IL 60611. **Tel** (312)787-3853. Ed Frank W Newell. **Ind/Abst** Pestdoc, Ringdoc, Vetdoc, Life Sci. Collect., Excerpta Med., Index Med., Int. Aerosp. Abstr., Biol. Abstr., Chem. Abstr., Energy Res. Abstr., Sci. Cit. Index, Abr. Ed. **LC** RE1. **CODEN** AJOPAA. (cum index). bk rev. adv acc. **Circ** 19,000. (ctrl). Original articles written and reviewed by ophthalmologists. Contains letters, book reviews, correspondence, clip and file abstracts from other publications and news items. *Annals of Ophthalmology, Ophthalmic Record; Annals of Oftamologia; Ophthalmology; Ophthalmic Yearbook; Ophthalmic Literature.*

AMERICAN ORTHOPTIC JOURNAL. V. 1- 1951-. 0065-955X. Periodical. US. English. an. $25.00. University of Wisconsin Press, 114 North Murray Street, Madison WI 53715. **Ind/Abst** Excerpta Med., Energy Res. Abstr. **NLM** W1 AM674. (cum index). Available on microfilm from University Microfilms International.

AMIS DE LA BANQUE D'YEUX DU QUEBEC. (LES AMIS DE LA BANQUE D'YEUX DU QUEBEC : JOURNAL). Vol. 1, No. 1 (Jan. 1981)-. 0710-1368. Periodical. CN. French. qt. Free. Banque d'Yeux du Quebec, 5689 Boul Rosemont, Montreal Quebec G1T 2H1 Canada. **DD** 362.17. (ctrl).

ANNALS OF OPHTHALMOLOGY. Began with June/July 1969 issue. 0003-4886. Periodical. US. English. mo. $37.00 Domestic, $57.00 Foreign. American Society of Contemporary Ophthalmology, 211 East Chicago Avenue/Suite 1044, Chicago IL 60611. **Ind/Abst** Life Sci. Collect., Excerpta Med., Biol. Abstr., Chem. Abstr., Index Med., Energy Res. Abstr. **LC** RE1. **DD** 617.7005. **NLM** W1 AN617G. **CODEN** ANOPB5.

ANNEE THERAPEUTIQUE ET CLINIQUE EN OPHTALMOLOGIE. (L'ANNEE THERAPEUTIQUE ET CLINIQUE EN OPHTALMOLOGIE). Began publication with: V. 7 (1957). 0301-4495. FR. French. an. $54.37. Diffusion Generale de Librarie, 21 rue Paradis, 13231 Marseille Cedex France. **Ind/Abst** Index Med. **NLM** W1 AN679. *Annee Therapeutique en Ophtalmologie.*

ANNUAL REPORT - NATIONAL EYE INSTITUTE. (ANNUAL REPORT). **Main/Corp** National Eye Institute. Began with 1969/70. 0161-7699. US. English. an. National Eye Institute, National Instiute of Health, 9000 Rockville Pike, Bethesda MD 20205. **LC** RE1. **DD** 353.00841. **NLM** W2 A N157A. Vols. for 1981-(1983) distributed to depository libraries in microfiche.

ARCHEIA OPHTHALMOLOGIKES HETAIREIAS BOREIOU HELLADOS. See Genealogy and Heraldry - Archives.

ARCHIVES OF OPHTHALMOLOGY. See Genealogy and Heraldry - Archives.

ARCHIVOS DE LA SOCIEDAD AMERICANA DE OFTALMOLOGIA Y OPTOMETRIA. See Genealogy and Heraldry - Archives.

ARCHIVOS DE LA SOCIEDAD CANARIA DE OFTALMOLOGIA. See Genealogy and Heraldry - Archives.

ARCHIVOS DE OFTALMOLOGIA DE BUENOS AIRES. See Genealogy and Heraldry - Archives.

ARGUS. 0194-8172. Periodical. US. English. mo. $24.00. American Academy Ophthalmology, 655 Beach Street, Box 7424, San Francisco CA 94109-7424. **Tel** (415)561-8500. Ed Bruce E Spivey. bk rev. adv acc. **Circ** 14,000. (ctrl). Presents news, trends, opinions, and features affecting ophthalmology. Also serves as the official member publication for the American Academy of Ophthalmology.

ARQUIVOS BRASILEIROS DE OFTALMOLOGIA. V.1 (June 1938)-. 0004-2749. Periodical. Portuguese. ir. **Ind/Abst** Excerpta Med. **NLM** W1 AR8786.

ATTI DEL CONVEGNO - SOCIETA OFTALMOLOGICA MERIDIONALE. 1.- 1968-. 0392-0410. Periodical. Italian. ir. **NLM** W1 AT759K.

AUDIO-DIGEST. OPHTHALMOLOGY. Periodical. US. English. sm. $138.00. Audio-Digest Foundation, 1577 Chevy Chase Drive, Glendale CA 91206. **Tel** (213)245-8505. Ed Claron L Oakley. An interactive system of audio casette postgraduate medical education, with each one-hour program eligible for two Category I credit hours.

DER AUGENOPTIKER. 1.-Yearly volume. 0004-7929. Periodical. GW. German. mo. 76.80. Verlag Willy Schrickel GMBH, Ernst Mey Strasse 8 Postfach 10 02 52, 7022 Leinfelden West Germany. **Tel** 0711/7594-0. Ed Konrad Kohlhammer. bk rev. adv acc. **Circ** 11,500. Specialized journal for ophthalmic optics and optometry.

AUSTRALIAN AND NEW ZEALAND JOURNAL OF OPHTHALMOLOGY. Vol. 13, No. 1 (Feb. 1985)-. 0814-9763. Periodical. AT. English. ir. Royal Australian College of Ophthalmologists, 27 Commonwealth Street, Sydney 2010 Australia. **Ind/Abst** Biol. Abstr., Chem. Abstr., Index Med., Index Med. **NLM** W1. *Australian Journal of Ophthalmology, 0310-1177; Transactions of the Ophthalmological Society of New Zealand, 0300-8983.*

AUSTRALIAN ORTHOPTIC JOURNAL. 1967. AT. English. an. $11.07. Orthoptic Association of Association, PO Box E 47, St James NSW 2000 Australia. **Tel** 02/3372810. Ed Margaret Doyle. **NLM** W1 AU643G. (cum index). bk rev. adv acc. **Circ** 1,000. (ctrl). Orthoptics, binocular vision, ocular motility, strabismus, heterophoria, diplopia, visual acuity, amblyopia, electro diagnostic techniques, research case studies, visual screening and visual rehabilitation.

BIOMEDICAL FOUNDATIONS OF OPHTHALMOLOGY. 0732-3484. US. English. ir. Lippincott/Harper, 2350 Virginia Avenue, Hagerstown MD 21740. **Tel** (800)638-3031.

BOLLETTINO DI OCULISTICA. Began with: Yearly V. 51, published 1972. Periodical. Italian. mo. **NLM** W1. *Bollettino d'Oculistica.*

BOLLETTINO D'OCULISTICA *CEASED.* Year 1- 1922-. 0006-677X. Periodical. IT. Italian. mo. 50.00. Casa Editrice L Cappelli Spa, Via Marsili 9, 40124 Bologna Italy. **Tel** 330411. Ed F D Ermo. **Ind/Abst** Biol. Abstr., Chem. Abstr. **NLM** W1 BO58. **CODEN** BOOCAH. bk rev. adv acc. **Circ** 3,000. Ocular surgery and general ophthalmology.

BRITISH JOURNAL OF OPHTHALMOLOGY. Began with: Vol. 1 In 1917. 0007-1161. Periodical. UK. English. mo. $140.98. British Medical Journal, Tavistock Square, London WC1H 9JR England. **Ind/Abst** Life Sci. Collect., Excerpta Med., Index Med., Biol. Abstr., Sci. Cit. Index, Abr. Ed., Hospit. Lit. Index. **NLM** W1 BR589. **CODEN** BJOPAL. (cum index). *Ophthalmoscope, Ophthalmic Review; Reports.*

BRITISH ORTHOPTIC JOURNAL. No. 1- Dec. 1939-. 0068-2314. Periodical. UK. English. an. $16.09. British Orthoptic Society, Tavistock House, North Tavistock Square, London WC1H 9HX England. **Tel** 01-387-7992. Ed J V Plenty. **Ind/Abst** Excerpta Med. **NLM** W1 BR746. (cum index). bk rev. adv acc. **Circ** 1,600. (ctrl). The learned journal of the British Orthoptic Society. Articles on the management, treatment, and diagnosis of squints and other eye conditions.

BUCHEREI DES AUGENARZTES. Vol. 1-. 0068-3361. GW. German. ir. 108. Ferdinand Enke Verlag, 1-1 Postfach 1304, D7000 Stuttgart 1 West Germany. **Tel** (0711)8931-0. Ed G O H Naumann, H J Merte, F Hollwich and B Gloor. Deals with practical and clinical relevant subjects from the whole subject of ophthalmology. The volumes are supplements of the journal "Klinische Monatsblatter fur Augenheilkunde".

BULLETIN DES SOCIETES D'OPHTALMOLOGIE DE FRANCE. 1949-. 0081-1270. Periodical. FR. French. mo. $80.00. Librairie D L E S, 11 rue Moliere, 13001 Marseille ler France. **Ind/Abst** Index Med., Biol. Abstr., Chem. Abstr., Nuci. Sci. Abstr. **NLM** W1 BU612. **CODEN** BSOFAK. *Bulletin de la Societe d'Ophtalmologie de Paris, 0366-3485.*

BULLETINS ET MEMOIRES - SOCIETE FRANCAISE D'OPHTHALMOLOGIE. **Main/Corp** Societe Francaise d'Ophtalmologie. V. 1- 1883-. 0081-1092. French. ir. Scientific & Medical Publishing France, 16 East 34th Street, New York NY 10016. **Tel** (212)683-4441. **Ind/Abst** Index Med. (cum index).

BUTTERWORTHS INTERNATIONAL MEDICAL REVIEWS. OPHTHALMOLOGY. VFOAT Ophthalmology. 1-. 0260-0145. Monographic Series. UK. English. ir. **NLM** W1 BU99BD.

CANADIAN JOURNAL OF OPHTHALMOLOGY. VFOAT Journal Canadien d'Ophtalmologie. V. 1- Jan. 1966-. 0008-4182. Periodical. CN. English (includes some text and summaries in French). bm. Canadian Ophthalmological Society, PO Box 8844, Alta Vista Drive, Ottawa Ontario K1G 3J2 Canada. **Tel** (613)731-6493. Ed David J Addison. **Ind/Abst** Life Sci. Collect., Excerpta Med., Nuci. Sci. Abstr., Biol. Abstr., Chem. Abstr., Index Med., Hospit. Lit. Index, Sci. Cit. Index, Abr. Ed. **NLM** W1 CA598. **CODEN** CAJOBA. bk rev. adv acc. **Circ** 1,500. *Transactions of the Canadian Ophthalmological Society, Annual Meeting, 0068-9408.*

CATARACT (NEW YORK, N.Y.). (CATARACT). Nov. 1983-. 0740-6967. Periodical. US. English. bm. $35.00. Park Row Publishers Inc, 15 Park Row, New York NY 10038. **NLM** W1.

CESKOSLOVENSKA OFTALMOLOGIE. Vol. 1- 1933-. 0009-059X. Periodical. CS. Czech (some summaries in English, Russian, French, or German). bm. $56.10. Artia, VE Smeckach 30, PO Box 790, Praha 1 Czechoslovakia. **Ind/Abst** Excerpta Med., Index Med. **NLM** W1 CE897P.

THE CLAO JOURNAL. (THE CLAO JOURNAL : OFFICIAL PUBLICATION OF THE CONTACT LENS ASSOCIATION OF OPHTHALMOLOGISTS, INC). VFOAT C.L.A.O. Journal, Ophthalmologists Journal. VAT Contact Lens Association of Ophthalmologists Journal. V. 9, No. 1 (Jan./March 1983)-. 0733-8902. Periodical. US. English. qt. $35.00. Contact Lens Association of Ophthalmologists, 2620 Jena Street, New Orleans LA 70115. **Ind/Abst** Excerpta Med., Index Med., Chem. Abstr. **LC** RE977.C6. **DD** 617.752305. **NLM** W1 CL113. **CODEN** CLAJEU.

Medicine—Ophthalmology

Contact and Intraocular Lens Medical Journal, 0360-1358.

CLINICAL OPHTHALMOLOGY UPDATE. 0883-0320. Periodical. US. English. bw. $295.00. Nassau Publications Inc, 11 Forest Street, New Canaan CT 06840. DD 617.

CLINICAL RESEARCH REPORT. Main/Corp Detroit. Optometric Research Institute. No. 1-1937-. Periodical. US. English. Optometric Research Institute, Detroit MI 48219. LC RE46. DD 617.7072.

CLINIQUE OPHTALMOLOGIQUE. V. 1-32, No. 12. Periodical. FR. French. qt. $55.87. Laboratoires Martinet, 222 Boulevard Pereire, Paris 17 France.

CONTACT LENS FORUM. V. 1- May 1976-. 0363-1621. Periodical. US. English. mo. Advisory Enterprise, 5 North Greenwich Road, Armonk NY 10504. Tel (914)273-6666. LC RE977.C6. DD 617.752305. NLM W1 CO768CL.

CONTACT LENS JOURNAL. V. 8- June 1974-. 0096-2716. Periodical. US. English. mo. 36. The Contact Lens Journal, 14 Fairfield Avenue, Datchet Berks SL3 9NQ England. Tel (01)0753-46662. Ed W Grummer. LC RE977.C6. DD 617.752305. NLM W1 CO768D. bk rev. adv acc. Circ 2,000. (ctrl). Learned articles relating to contact lens, fitting, development problems effects trade development and news. Personalities, abstracts, social effects on wearers etc. general contact lens news. *Journal - Contact Lens Society of America*, 0589-5065.

CONTACT LENS MEDICAL SEMINAR PROCEEDINGS. V. 1- 1968-. 0591-0307. US. English. be. C C Thomas, 301-327 East Lawrence Avenue, Springfield IL 62717. Ed W G Sampson. LC RE977.C6. DD 617.552305. NLM W3 CO978SH.

CONTACTO (CHICAGO, ILL.). (CONTACTO). Vol. 1, No. 1 (Jan. 1957)-. 0045-8317. Periodical. US. English. bm. Ind/Abst Excerpta Med. LC RE977.C6. DD 617.752305. NLM W1 CO769E. *Universal Abstracts*.

CONTEMPORARY ISSUES IN OPHTHALMOLOGY. Vol. 1-. Monographic Series. US. English. Ed Frederick C Blodi. NLM W1.

CORNEA. Vol. 1, No. 1. 0277-3740. Periodical. US. English. qt. $72.00. Raven Press, 1140 Avenue of the Americas, New York NY 10036. Tel (212)575-0335. Ind/Abst Excerpta Med. NLM W1 CO8595M.

CUADERNOS MONOGRAFICOS - CRUZADA DE PROTECCION OCULAR. (CUADERNOS MONOGRAFICOS). 0211-1063. Monographic Series. Spanish. ir. NLM W1 CU14M.

CURRENT CANADIAN OPHTHALMIC PRACTICE. Vol. 1, No. 1 (Nov. 1983)-. 0823-4744. Periodical. CN. English. qt. $40.00. Current Canadian Ophthalmic Practice c/o Medicopea International, 1440 St Catherine Street West Suite 428, Montreal Quebec H3G 1R8 Canada. Tel (514)340-9157. Ed Inara Gaelis. DD 617.7005. bk rev. adv acc. (ctrl). Practical, state of the art, editorial content designed to be of immediate use in the everyday practice of ophthalmology.

CURRENT CONCEPTS IN OPHTHALMOLOGY. V. 1- 1967-. 0097-8353. US. English. ir. $45.00. C V Mosby Co, C Leadbetter, 11830 Westline Industrial Drive, St Louis MO 63141. LC RE1. DD 617.7008. NLM W1 CU788AT.

CURRENT EYE RESEARCH. Vol. 1, No. 1-. 0271-3683. Periodical. UK. English. mo. $95.00. IRL Press, 1911 Jeff Davis Highway/Suite 907, Arlington VA 22202. Tel (703)998-2980. Ed C A Paterson and N A Delamere. Ind/Abst Life Sci. Collect., Excerpta Med., Index Med., Biol. Abstr., Chem. Abstr. LC QP476. DD 599.01823. NLM W1 CU788H. CODEN CEYRDM. bk rev. adv acc. Circ 450. Clinical and basic research on the anatomy, physiology, biophysics, biochemistry, pharmacology, developmental biology, microbiology and immunology of the eye.

CURRENT RESEARCH IN OPHTHALMIC ELECTRON MICROSCOPY. Began with: 1 (1977). 0173-7082. English. ir. NLM W1 CU8092.

CURRENT TOPICS IN EYE RESEARCH. V. 1- 1979-. 0190-2970. Periodical. US. English. ir. Academic Press, 4805 Sand Lake Road, Orlando FL 32887. Tel (305)345-4100. Ed Jose A Zadunaisky and Hugh Davson. Ind/Abst Index Med., Chem. Abstr. LC QP476. DD 599.01823. NLM W1 CU82HH. CODEN CTERDR.

DEUTSCHE OPTIKERZEITUNG. (DOZ, DEUTSCHE OPTIKERZEITUNG). Began with issue for Jan. 15, 1978. 0344-7103. Periodical. German. mo. 76.-. Optische Fachveroffentlichung GMBH, Postfach 104443, Rohrbacher Str 57, 6900 Heidelberg West Germany. Tel (06221)14081. Ind/Abst Chem. Abstr. LC RE1. DD 617.752. NLM W1 D129E. CODEN DDOPD4. bk rev. adv acc. Circ 9,000. (ctrl). Our journal contents also economics, contact lenses, physiology, workshop equipment, practice, shop design, contact lens chemics, interviews with VIPs, etc. SOZ, *Suddeutsche Optikerzeitung*, 0344-7170.

DEVELOPMENTS IN OPHTHALMOLOGY. Vol. 1-. 0250-3751. Monographic Series. English. ir. S Karger Ag, PO Box, CH-4009 Basel Switzerland. Tel 061-39 08 80. Ed W Straub. Ind/Abst Index Med., Biol. Abstr., Chem. Abstr. NLM W1 DE998NG. CODEN DEOPDB. Expert summaries of international developments vital to the progress of this field. *Advances in Ophthalmology*, 0065-3004; *Bibliotheca Ophthalmologica*; *Modern Problems in Ophthalmology*, 0077-0078.

DOCUMENTA OPHTHALMOLOGICA. V. 1-. 0012-4486. English (also in French, German and Italian). mo. $300.00. Martinus Nijhoff Publishers, PO Box 163, 3300 AD Dordrecht Netherlands. Tel 078-334233. Ed H E Henkes. Ind/Abst Life Sci. Collect., Excerpta Med., Index Med., Biol. Abstr., Chem. Abstr., Sci. Cit. Index, Abr. Ed., Hospit. Lit. Index. LC RE14. NLM W1 DO489. CODEN DOOPAA. bk rev. adv acc. Circ 1,000. Publishes original articles in the field of ophthalmology.

EXCERPTA MEDICA. SECTION 12. OPTHALMOLOGY. See Indexes/Abstracts.

EXPERIENTIA OPHTHALMOLOGICA. VFOAT Experientia Ophthalmologica (Coimbra). 0253-0643. English (articles in Portuguese). ir. Ind/Abst Excerpta Med. NLM W1 EX23R.

EXPERIMENTAL EYE RESEARCH. V. 1- Sept. 1961-. 0014-4835. Periodical. UK. English. mo. $453.50. Academic Press, 4805 Sand Lake Road, Orlando FL 32819. Ind/Abst Life Sci. Collect., Excerpta Med., Biol. Abstr., Chem. Abstr., Index Med., Nuci. Sci. Abstr., Sci. Cit. Index, Abr. Ed. LC QP474. NLM W1 EX504. CODEN EXERA6.

FOLIA OPHTHALMOLOGICA. 1.- Year. 0323-4932. Periodical. SZ. German. bm. $88.36. Kunst & Wissen Erich Bieber, Dufourstrasse 51, CH-8008 Zurich Switzerland. Tel (011)41-1-69 44 20. Ind/Abst Excerpta Med., Biol. Abstr. NLM W1 FO268. CODEN FOOPDZ.

FORTSCHRITTE DER AUGENHEILKUNDE. VFOAT Advances in Ophthalmology, Progres d'Ophtalmologie. 0723-8045. Periodical. German. bm. Springer Verlag-New York Inc, 175 5th Avenue, New York NY 10010. Tel (212)460-1584. Ed W Jaeger and W Doden. Reports of the conventions of the German Ophthalmological Society, important results of research at German eye clinics and research institutes. Current questions and latest research findings.

GLAUCOMA. V. 1- Feb. 1979-. 0164-4645. Periodical. US. English. bm. $55.00. Le Jacq Publishing Inc, 53 Park Place/8th Floor, New York NY 10007. Tel (212)766-4300. Ed John G Bellows. Ind/Abst Biol. Abstr. LC RE871. DD 617.741005. NLM W1 GL359. CODEN GLAUD4. bk rev. adv acc. Circ 15,000. (ctrl). An ophthalmic journal for practicing ophthalmologists which concentrates on glaucoma.

GRAEFE'S ARCHIVE FOR CLINICAL AND EXPERIMENTAL OPHTHALMOLOGY. See Genealogy and Heraldry - Archives.

HIGHLIGHTS OF OPHTHALMOLOGY. Began in 1956. 0440-7911. Periodical. PN. English. mo. $65.00. Highlights of Ophthalmology, Box 1189, Panama 1 Republic of Panama. Ed B F Boyd. NLM W1 HI2843. adv acc. Each issue covers a single subject in the field of ophthalmology with an in-depth information and illustration on the most recent advances. Written for the practicing ophthalmologist.

HIGHLIGHTS OF OPHTHALMOLOGY : SILVER ANNIVERSARY. Series/Titl Highlights of Ophthalmology. Periodical. English. ir.

INDIAN JOURNAL OF OPHTHALMOLOGY. 0301-4738. Periodical. II. English. bm. $70.00. Indian Books and Periodical Syndicate, B-5/62 Dev Nagar, PC Road Karol Bagh, New Delhi 110005 India. Tel 660110/243. Ed Madan Mohan. Ind/Abst Index Med., Chem. Abstr., Hospit. Lit. Index. NLM W1 IN223N. CODEN IJOMBM. bk rev. adv acc. Circ 2,400. Ophthalmic scientific Indian national journal—clinical and experimental. *Journal of The All-India Ophthalmological Society*, 0044-7307.

INTERNATIONAL EYECARE. VFOAT International Eye Care. Vol. 1, No. 1 (June 1985)-. 0884-4577. Periodical. US. English. mo. International Eyecare, 5615 West Cermack Road, Cicero IL 60650. LC RE977.C6. DD 617.752305. *International Contact Lens Clinic*, 0094-1840; *Optometric Monthly*, 0160-9254.

INTERNATIONAL OPHTHALMOLOGICAL REPORTER. V. 1-. 0145-370X. US. English. ir. $31.50. Intercontinental Publications, Box 5026, Westport CT 06880. NLM Z 6669 I61.

INTERNATIONAL OPHTHALMOLOGY. V. 1- Sept. 1978-. 0165-5701. Periodical. NE. English. qt. $74.00 (1-6), $92.00 (7-8). Martinus Nijhoff Publishers, PO Box 163, 3300 AD Dordrecht Netherlands. Tel 078-334233. Ed A F Deutman, E L Greve and J J de Lacey. Ind/Abst Life Sci. Collect., Excerpta Med., Index Med., Biol. Abstr., Chem. Abstr., Energy Res. Abstr., Sci. Cit. Index, Abr. Ed. NLM W1 IN827D. CODEN INOPDR. bk rev. adv acc. Circ 1,000. Aims at providing clinician articles on all sub-specialities in ophthalmology relevant to clinicians.

INTERNATIONAL OPHTHALMOLOGY CLINICS. V. 1- 1961-. 0020-8167. Monographic Series. US. English. qt. $65.00. Little Brown & Company, 34 Beacon Street, Boston MA 02106. Tel (617)227-0730. Ed Carmen D Wiseman. Ind/Abst Life Sci. Collect., Excerpta Med., Biol. Abstr., Nuci. Sci. Abstr., Index Med., Energy Res. Abstr., Hospit. Lit. Index. LC UNC. DD 617.7005. NLM W1 IN827E. CODEN IOPCAV. Circ 2,600. Features eminent guest editors and contributors who focus on one topic per issue that is of significant clinical importance in ophthalmology.

INVESTIGATIVE OPHTHALMOLOGY & VISUAL SCIENCE. VAT Investigative Ophthalmology and Visual Science. V. 16- Jan. 1977-. 0146-0404. Periodical. US. English. mo. $163.53. Investigative Ophthalmology and Visual Science, 2350 Virginia Avenue, Hagerstown MD 21740. Ind/Abst Life Sci. Collect., Excerpta Med., Index Med., Biol. Abstr., Chem. Abstr., Energy Res. Abstr., Hospit. Lit. Index. LC RE1. DD 617.7005. NLM W1 IN994Z. CODEN IOVSDA. *Investigative Ophthalmology*, 0020-9988.

IRCS MEDICAL SCIENCE. THE EYE. (IRCS MEDICAL SCIENCE : THE EYE). VFOAT Eye. V. 3- Jan. 1975-. 0305-6791. Periodical. UK. English. qt. IRCS Medical Science, PO Box 500/St Leonards House, Lancaster LA1 1PF England. Tel (0524)68116. Ed S Johnson. Publishes results of original research into all aspects of the eye and visual system, both clinical and experimental within weeks of completion. Papers fully refereed. *Research on the Eye*, 0305-2761.

JAPANESE JOURNAL OF OPHTHALMOLOGY. Vol. 1, No. 1 (Apr. 1957)-. 0021-5155. Periodical. JA. English. qt. Kyowa Book Company Inc, 1-38 Kanda Jinbo Cho, Chiyoda-Ku Tokyo 101 Japan. Tel 293-0727. Ind/Abst Life Sci. Collect., Excerpta Med., Index Med., Chem. Abstr., Sci. Cit. Index, Abr. Ed. NLM W1 JA97J. CODEN JJOPA7.

JOURNAL - AMERICAN INTRA-OCULAR IMPLANT SOCIETY. Main/Corp American Intra-Ocular Implant Society. VFOAT American Intra-Ocular Implant Society Journal. V. 2- Oct. 1976-. 0146-2776. Periodical. US. English. qt. $35.00. American Intra-Ocular Implant Society, PO Box 3140, Santa Monica CA 90403. Tel (213)829-7317. Ind/Abst Index Med., Excerpta Med., Chem. Abstr., Energy Res. Abstr., Hospit. Lit. Index. NLM W1 JO222V. CODEN AIIJDQ. *Newsletter - American Intra-Ocular Implant Society*, 0361-235X.

JOURNAL FRANCAIS D'OPHTALMOLOGIE. V. 1- Jan. 1978-. 0181-5512. Periodical. FR. articles in French. Masson Publishers USA Inc, 211 East 43rd Street/Room 1306, New York NY 10017. Tel (212)370-1937. Ind/Abst Life Sci. Collect., Excerpta Med., Index Med. NLM W1 JO442F. *Archives d'Ophtalmologie*, 0399-4236; *Annales d'Oculistique*, 0003-4371.

JOURNAL OF CATARACT AND REFRACTIVE SURGERY. Vol. 12, No. 1 (Jan. 1986)-. 0886-3350. Periodical. US. English. bm. $35.00 US, $50.00 Foreign. American Society of

1907

Cataract and Refractive Surgery, 3700 Pender Drive/ Suite 108, Fairfax VA 22030. **Ind/Abst** Index Med. **DD** 616. **NLM** W1. *Journal - American Intra-Ocular Implant Society, 0146-2776.*

JOURNAL OF CLINICAL NEURO-OPHTHALMOLOGY. Vol. 1, No. 1 (Mar. 1981)-. 0272-846X. Periodical. US. English. qt. $68.00. Raven Press, 1140 Avenue of the Americas, New York NY 10036. **Tel** (212)575-0335. **Ind/Abst** Excerpta Med., Index Med. **DD** 617. **NLM** W1 JO5893N.

JOURNAL OF OCULAR PHARMACOLOGY. Vol. 1, No. 1 (Spring 1985)-. 8756-3320. Periodical. US. English. qt. $80.00. Mary Ann Liebert Inc, 157 East 86th Street, New York NY 10028. **Tel** (212)289-2300. **Ed** George C Y Chiou. **DD** 617. bk rev. adv acc. **Circ** 500. Research on all aspects of drug activity pertaining to preventing or controlling diseases of the eye.

JOURNAL OF OCULAR THERAPY & SURGERY *CEASED.* (JOURNAL OF OCULAR THERAPY & SURGERY : AN OFFICIAL PUBLICATION OF THE AMERICAN SOCIETY OF CONTEMPORARY OPHTHALMALOGY). **VFOAT** Journal of Ocular Therapy and Surgery. Vol. 1, No. 1A (Jan.-Feb. 1982)-. 0730-0883. Periodical. US. English. bm. $37.00 Domestic, $57.00 Foreign. c/o Colonial Publishing Inc, 501 Colonial Drive, St Joseph MI 49085. **Ind/Abst** Excerpta Med. **DD** 617. **NLM** W1 JO802PF.

THE JOURNAL OF OPHTHALMIC PHOTOGRAPHY. 1978. 0198-6155. US. English. sa. $15.00. Ophthalmic Photographers Society, c/o Cabrini Medical Center, J Rousseau, 227 East 19 Street, New York NY 10003. **Tel** (212)725-7592. **Ed** Kenneth Fong. **LC** RE79.P54. **DD** 617.71545. bk rev. adv acc. **Circ** 1,000. (ctrl). All papers pertaining to techniques of ophthalmic photography and/or ophthalmology.

JOURNAL OF PEDIATRIC OPHTHALMOLOGY AND STRABISMUS. V. 15- Jan./Feb. 1978-. 0191-3913. Periodical. US. English. bm. Charles B Slack Inc, 6900 Grove Road, Thorofare NJ 08086. **Tel** (609)848-1000. **Ind/Abst** Life Sci. Collect., Excerpta Med., Index Med., Biol. Abstr., Energy Res. Abstr. **NLM** W1 JO828FD. **CODEN** JPOSDR. *Journal of Pediatric Ophthalmology, 0022-345X.*

JOURNAL OF THE BRITISH CONTACT LENS ASSOCIATION. (THE JOURNAL OF THE B.C.L.A). **Main/Corp** British Contact Lens Association. V. 1-. 0141-7037. Periodical. UK. English. qt. 25. British Contact Lens Association, 14 Perceval Avenue, Hampstead London NW3 England. **Ed** Judith A Morris. **NLM** W1 JO913B. adv acc. **Circ** 1,200. (ctrl). Refereed papers and conference transactions of contact lens related subjects.

KLINIKA OCZNA. **VFOAT** Acta Opthalmologica Polonica. Vol. 25- 1923-. 0023-2157. Periodical. PL. Polish. mo. ARS Polona, Krakowskie Przedmiescie 7, 00-068 Warsaw Poland. **Ind/Abst** Index Med., Chem. Abstr. **NLM** W1 KL303. **CODEN** KOAOAE. *Postep Okulistyczny.*

KLINISCHE MONATSBLATTER FUR AUGENHEILKUNDE. 0023-2165. Periodical. German. mo. $240.00. Thieme-Stratton Inc, 381 Park Avenue South, New York NY 10016. **Tel** (212)683-5088. **Ind/Abst** Life Sci. Collect., Excerpta Med., Index Med., Biol. Abstr., Chem. Abstr., Nuci. Sci. Abstr., Sci. Cit. Index, Abr. Ed., Energy Res. Abstr. **NLM** W1 KL47. **CODEN** KMAUAI. *Klinische Monatsblatter fur Augenheilkunde und fur Augenarztliche Fortbildung, 0344-6360.*

MAJOR PROBLEMS IN OPHTHALMOLOGY. V. 1- 1975-. 0309-2410. Monographic Series. UK. English. ir. W B Saunders Co Ltd, West Washington Square, Philadelphia PA 19105. **Ed** P D Trevor-Roper. **NLM** W1 MA492W.

MEMBERSHIP DIRECTORY & RESOURCE MANUAL - AMERICAN ACADEMY OF OPHTHALMOLOGY. *See* Yearbooks, Almanacs, Directories.

METABOLIC OPHTHALMOLOGY (NEW YORK, N.Y. : 1984). (METABOLIC OPHTHALMOLOGY : OFFICIAL PUBLICATION OF THE INTERNATIONAL SOCIETY ON METABOLIC EYE DISEASE). Vol. 8, No. 1-. Periodical. US. English. qt. $120.00. **NLM** W1. *Metabolic, Pediatric, and Systemic Ophthalmology.*

METABOLIC, PEDIATRIC AND SYSTEMIC OPHTHALMOLOGY. Vol. 6, No. 1-. 0277-9382. Periodical. US. English. qt. $45.00. Opto Ed Inc, 1200 Fifth Avenue, New York NY 10029. **Tel** (212)427-1246. **Ind/Abst** Excerpta Med., Index Med., Life Sci. Collect., Chem. Abstr. **NLM** W1 ME961N. **CODEN** MPSODY. *Metabolic and Pediatric Ophthalmology, 0191-2771.*

MINERVA OFTALMOLOGICA. V. 1- July/ Sept. 1959-. 0026-4903. Periodical. IT. Italian. qt. 60.00. Edizoni Minerva Medica, Corso Bramante 83, Torino 10126 Italy. **Tel** 67 82 82. **Ed** T Oliado. **Ind/Abst** Excerpta Med. **NLM** W1 MI6489. bk rev. adv acc. Journal addressed to practitioners and specialists in ophthalmology in Italy and abroad. It deals with topics in scientific practice and research.

MINUTES OF MEETING - NATIONAL ADVISORY EYE COUNCIL. Apr. 3, 1969-. 0192-771X. Periodical. US. English. **NLM** W1 MI7806.

MODERN TRENDS IN OPHTHALMOLOGY. V. 1-. UK. English. ir. Butterworth and Company Publishers Ltd, 88 Kingsway, London WC2B 6AB England. **Ed** F Ridley and A Sorsby. **LC** RE45. **DD** 617.7. **NLM** W1 MO1750.

NEURO-OPHTHALMOLOGY (AEOLUS PRESS). (NEURO-OPHTHALMOLOGY). Vol. 1, No. 1 (Sept. 1980)-. 0165-8107. Periodical. NE. English. qt. $129.00. Aeolus Press, PO Box 740, 4116 ZJ Buren Netherlands. **Tel** 03447/2055. **Ind/Abst** Excerpta Med., Curr. Contents. **NLM** W1.

NIHON GANKA GAKKAI ZASSHI. (NIPPON GANKA GAKKAI ZASSHI). **Main/Corp** Nippon Ganka Gakkai. **VFOAT** Acta Societatis Ophthalmologicae Japonicae. Vol. 1- April 1897-. 0029-0203. Periodical. JA. Japanese (summaries in English and German, (1929-43)). sa. $110.00. Maruzen Company Ltd, PO Box 5050, 100-31 Tokyo Japan. **Tel** 03-295-2360. **Ed** Tsamu Tsukahara. **Ind/Abst** Index Med., Excerpta Med., Biol. Abstr., Chem. Abstr. **NLM** W1 NI896M. **CODEN** NGZAA6. **Circ** 8,000. (ctrl). The organ of Societas Ophthalmologica Japonica introduces dissertations and reports of activity. *Ganka Zasshi.*

NIPPON GANKA KIYO. **VFOAT** Folia Ophthalmologica Japonica, Bulletin of Japanese Ophthalmology. Vol. 1 (1950)-. 0015-5667. Periodical. JA. Japanese (abstracts in English). mo. $144.00. Japan Publishers Trading Company Ltd, PO Box 5030 Tokyo International, Tokyo 100-31 Japan. **Ind/Abst** Excerpta Med., Biol. Abstr., Chem. Abstr., Life Sci. Collect. **NLM** W1 NI897. **CODEN** NGKYA3.

OCULAR INFLAMMATION AND THERAPEUTICS. Vol. 1, No. 1 (Spring 1983)-. 0736-2374. Periodical. US. English. qt. $59.00 US and Canada, $65.00 Others. Ocular Inflammation and Therapeutics, Subscription Fulfillment Department, 20th and Northampton Streets, Easton PA 18042. **NLM** W1.

OFTALMOLOGICESKIJ ZURNAL. (OFTALMOLOGICHESKII ZHURNAL). 1- 1946-. 0030-0675. Periodical. UR. Russian. bm. $27.00. Victor Kamkin Inc (74358), 12224 Parklawn Drive, Rockville MD 20852. **Tel** (301)881-5973. **Ind/Abst** Excerpta Med., Index Med., Chem. Abstr. **NLM** W1 OF892. **CODEN** OFZHAV.

OFTALMOLOGIIA. Vol. 12- 1964-. 0374-2105. Periodical. BU. Bulgarian (table of contents and summaries in English). ty. $14.00. Hemus, 6 Boulevard Rusky, Sofia Bulgaria. **Ind/Abst** Excerpta Med., CIS Abstr., Chem. Abstr. **NLM** W1 OF895. **CODEN** OPTMAI. *Oftalmologichen Pregled.*

OPHTHALMIC FORUM. Vol. 1, No. 1 (Fall 1982)-. 0734-1652. Periodical. US. English. qt. $25.00. Silver Press Inc, PO Box 09724, Columbus OH 43209. **Tel** (614)421-4960. **Ed** Frederick H Davedorf. **NLM** W1 OP217F. adv acc. **Circ** 15,000. (ctrl). Articles focusing on topics having clinical relevance for the general ophthalmologist and optometrist.

OPHTHALMIC LITERATURE. V. 1- June 1947-. 0030-3720. Periodical. UK. English. qt. Institute of Ophthalmology, Circulation Manager, Judd Street, London WC1H 9GS England. **Ed** J H Kelsey. **LC** Z6669. **DD** 016.6177. **NLM** ZWW 100 O56. bk rev. adv acc. Abstracts ophthalmology and related sciences. *British Journal of Ophthalmology.*

OPHTHALMIC OBSERVER. 0743-6378. Periodical. US. English. qt. Free to Medical Personnel. Ophthalmic Observer, POB 19587, Irvine CA 92713.

OPHTHALMIC PAEDIATRICS AND GENETICS. *See* Medicine - Pediatrics.

OPHTHALMIC RESEARCH. V. 1-. 0030-3747. Periodical. English. bm. **Ind/Abst** Life Sci. Collect., Excerpta Med., Index Med., Int. Aerosp. Abstr., Biol. Abstr., Chem. Abstr., Int. Aerosp. Abstr. **LC** RE58. **DD** 617.7005. **NLM** W1 OP238P. **CODEN** OPRSAQ.

OPHTHALMOLOGICA. **VFOAT** International Journal of Ophthalmology. V. 96- 1938-. 0030-3755. Periodical. German (articles and summaries in English and French). bm. 214.-. S Karger AG, PO Box, CH-4099 Basel Switzerland. **Tel** (061)39 08 80. **Ed** F C Blodi, C Gailloud, H Neubauer, M J Roper-Hall, N M J Schweitzer and R Witener. **Ind/Abst** Life Sci. Collect., Excerpta Med., Index Med., Nuci. Sci. Abstr., Biol. Abstr., Chem. Abstr., Sci. Cit. Index, Abr. Ed. **LC** RE1. **NLM** W1 OP337. **CODEN** OPHTAD. (cum index). bk rev. adv acc. Each issue contains a selection of patient-oriented reports covering the etiology of eye diseases, diagnostic techniques, and advances in medical surgical treatment. *Zeitschrift fur Augenheilkunde.*

OPHTHALMOLOGICA ET OTO-RHINO-LARYNGOLOGICA. **Series/Titl** Acta Universitatis Ouluensis: Series D, Medica. No. 1-. 0358-4852. Monographic Series. FI. English (Finnish). ir. Professor Sakari Piha, University of Oulu, 90100 Oulu 10 Finland. **Tel** 358-81-332133. **Ed** Leo Hirvonen. **NLM** W1 AC954NM No. 18 Etc. adv acc. **Circ** 500. (ctrl). Monographs, reviews, and dissertations in the fields of ophthalmology and otorhinolaryngology.

OPHTHALMOLOGY. V. 81, No. 3- May/June 1976-. 0161-6420. Periodical. US. English. mo. $88.00. J B Lippincott Company, East Washington Square, Philadelphia PA 19105. **Tel** (215)238-4273. **Ed** Paul Henkind. **Ind/Abst** Life Sci. Collect., Excerpta Med., Index Med., Energy Res. Abstr., Chem. Abstr., Cumul. Index Nurs. Allied Health Lit., Biol. Abstr. **DD** 617. **NLM** W1 OP371P. **CODEN** 0PHTDG. adv acc. **Circ** 17,082. Original articles of practical value for the clinician. Also includes presentations given at the annual meeting of the Academy. *Transactions - American Academy of Ophthalmology and Otolaryngology, 0161-6978.*

OPHTHALMOLOGY ANNUAL. 0743-751X. US. English. an. Appleton-Century-Crofts, 25 Van Zant Street, Norwalk CT 06855.

OPHTHALMOLOGY DIGEST. V. 4L, No. 8/ 9- Aug./Sept. 1979-. 0048-1955. Periodical. US. English. mo. $27.50. Medical Digest Inc, 455 Central Avenue, Northfield IL 60093. **NLM** W1 OP371T. *Journal of Continuing Education in Ophthalmology, 0149-4260.*

OPHTHALMOLOGY MANAGEMENT. Vol. 1, No. 1 (Apr. 1983)-. 0746-1070. Periodical. US. English. $18.00 Domestic, $24.00 Foreign. Ophthalmology Management, Five North Greenwich Road, Armonk NY 10504. **DD** 617.

OPHTHALMOLOGY TIMES. 0193-032X. Periodical. US. English. mo. $100.00. Harcourt Brace Jovanovich Publishers, 1 East First Street, Duluth MN 55802. **Tel** (218)723-9516. **Ed** Cathy Chiaramonte. adv acc. **Circ** 14,594. (ctrl). A scientific tabloid providing accurate news of ophthalmology.

OPTICAL WORLD. **VFOAT** Optische Welt. Began publication with No. 1, Mar. 1972. Periodical. English (summaries in French and German). ir. $24.00. Optical World Ltd, 121 Pall Mall, Leigh-on-Sea Essex 559 IRF United Kingdom. **DD** 338.476177505.

ORBIT (AMSTERDAM, NETHERLANDS). (ORBIT). Vol. 1, No. 1 (Jan. 1982)-. 0167-6830. Periodical. English. qt. $79.00. Aeolus Press, PO Box 740, 4116 ZJ Buren The Netherlands. **Ind/Abst** Excerpta Med. **NLM** W1 OR146M.

PERSPECTIVES IN OPHTHALMOLOGY. V. 1- Mar. 1977-. 0161-8792. Periodical. US. English. qt. $85.00. Ankho International, PO Box 426, Fayetteville NY 13066. **Ind/Abst** Excerpta Med. **LC** RE1. **DD** 617.7005. **NLM** W1 PE871CN.

PHILIPPINE JOURNAL OF OPHTHALMOLOGY. Vol. 1, No. 1 (Jan.-Mar. 1969)-. 0031-7659. Periodical. PH. English. qt. $20.00. Philippine Ophthalmology Society, Philippine General Hospital, Taft Avenue, Manila Philippines D-406. **Ed** Romeo V Fajardo. **Ind/Abst** Excerpta Med. **NLM** W1 PH57T. bk rev. adv acc. **Circ** 1,000. Contains original articles, case reports, clinical and book reviews, and society proceedings.

PHYSICIANS' DESK REFERENCE FOR OPHTHALMOLOGY. **VFOAT** PDR for Ophthalmology. 1st- Ed. 0091-6803. US. English. an. $23.95. Medical Economics Inc, 680 Kinderkamack

Road, Oradell NJ 07649. Tel (201)262-3030. LC RE994. DD 617.706105. NLM QV 772 P576.

RECENT ADVANCES IN OPHTHALMOLOGY. No. 1- 1927-. 0309-2437. Periodical. UK. English. ir. Churchill Livingstone Inc, 1560 Broadway, New York NY 10036. Tel (212)819-5400. Ed W S Duke-Elder and A J B Goldsmith. NLM W1 RE105VP.

THE RED BOOK OF OPHTHALMOLOGY. 32d- Ed. 0146-4582. US. English. be. $15.00. Professional Press Inc, 101 East Ontario Street, Chicago IL 60611. LC RE22. DD 617.7002573. NLM WW 22 AA1 R3. *Red Book of Eye, Ear, Nose and Throat Specialists, 0146-4590.*

REPORT - NATIONAL SOCIETY TO PREVENT BLINDNESS. Main/Corp National Society to Prevent Blindness. 1978/79-. 0270-4234. US. English. an. National Society to Prevent Blindness, 79 Madison Avenue, New York NY 10016. LC RE1. DD 362.19712006073. NLM W1 NA752. *Report.*

RETINA. V. 1- (No. 1-). Periodical. Spanish. ir. Impresora Monterrey, Condomino Acero Monterrey, Zaragoza 1000 Sur, Despacho 1405, Monterrey NL Mexico.

RETINA (PHILADELPHIA, PA.). (RETINA). Vol. 1, No. 1 (Winter 1981)-. 0275-004X. Periodical. US. English. qt. $69.00. J B Lippincott Company, East Washington Square, Philadelphia PA 19105. Tel (215)238-4273. Ed Alexander J Brucker. Ind/Abst Excerpta Med., Index Med. NLM W1 RE2498. adv acc. Circ 2,107. Features articles on surgical and other techniques and an office reference system of abstracts from current literature.

REVISTA BRASILEIRA DE OTTALMOLOGIA. V. 1- 1942-. 0034-7280. Periodical. BL. Portuguese. qt. Revista Brasileira de rue Sao Salvador, 107 Laranjers, Rio de Janeiro Gua ZC01 Brasil.

REVUE CHIBRET D'OPHTALMOLOGIE. 0338-9987. Monographic Series. French. ir. Laboratoires Chibret, 100 Boulevard Clementel, 63018 Clermont-Ferr France. NLM W1 RE7455D. *Revue Chibret, 0338-9979.*

REVUE D'OTO-NEURO-OPHTALMOLOGIE. V. 5- Jan. 1927-. 0035-2497. Periodical. FR. French. qt. Ind/Abst Excerpta Med., Index Med. NLM W1 RE833V. *Revue d'Oto-Neuro-Oculistique, 0035-2497.*

REVUE INTERNATIONALE DU TRACHOME ET DE PATHOLOGIE OCULAIRE TROPICALE ET SUBTROPICALE CEASED. VFOAT Revue Internationale du Trachome. Nos. 52-57. 0249-7026. Periodical. FR. articles in English or French with summaries in German. sa. Ind/Abst Excerpta Med. NLM W1 RE899L. *Revue Internationale du Trachome, 0301-5017.*

SIGHTSAVING. VFOAT Sight Saving. Vol. 51, No. 1-. 0735-5688. Periodical. US. English. qt. $30.00 Domestic, $31.00 Foreign. National Society to Prevent Blindness, 79 Madison Avenue, New York NY 10016. Tel (212)684-3505. Ed Robert M Randall. Ind/Abst Except. Child Educ. Resour., Ref. Source, Energy Res. Abstr. LC RE1. DD 362.4170973. NLM W1 SI381M. Circ 10,000. (ctrl). Microform. Includes medical eye sciences, health and safety. Magazine covering blindness prevention for professionals and volunteers. *Sight-Saving Review, 0037-4822.*

SOUTH AFRICAN ARCHIVES OF OPHTHALMOLOGY. See Genealogy and Heraldry - Archives.

SURVEY OF OPHTHALMOLOGY. V. 1- Feb. 1956-. 0039-6257. Periodical. US. English. bm. $95.00. Survey of Ophthalmology Inc, 7 Kent Street Suite/4, Brookline MA 02146. Tel (617)566-2138. Ed Bernard Schwartz. Ind/Abst Life Sci. Collect., Excerpta Med., Index Med., Energy Res. Abstr., Biol. Abstr., Chem. Abstr., Nuci. Sci. Abstr., Sci. Cit. Index, Abr. Ed., Hospit. Lit. Index. LC UNC. DD 617. NLM ZWW 100 S963. CODEN SUOPAD. bk rev. adv acc. Circ 7,200. A review journal directed to practical needs of clinical ophthalmologists.

SYMPOSIUM ON OCULAR THERAPY. V. 3- 1967-. 0082-0873. US. English. J Wiley, 605 3rd Avenue, New York NY 10158. Ind/Abst Chem. Abstr. LC RE991. DD 617.706105. NLM W3 SY5365. CODEN SYOTAJ. *Ocular Therapy, Complications and Management, 0473-775X.*

TOPICS IN OCULAR PHARMACOLOGY AND TOXICOLOGY. Vol. 1, No. 1 (Jan. 1985)-. 8755-0970. Periodical. US. English. mo. $30.00 Domestic, $38.00 Canada. PSG Publishing Company Inc, 545 Great Road, Littleton MA 01460. Tel (617)486-8971. DD 617. Provides facts and information about drug issues related to the ocular physician.

TRANSACTIONS OF THE AMERICAN OPHTHALMOLOGICAL SOCIETY ANNUAL MEETING. Main/Corp American Ophthalmological Society. V. 1- 1864-. 0065-9533. US. English. an. $50.00. Johnson Printing Company, PO Box 7167, Rochester MN 55903. Tel (507)288-7788. Ed Robert B Welch. Ind/Abst Excerpta Med., Biol. Abstr., Chem. Abstr., Index Med., Nuci. Sci. Abstr., Energy Res. Abstr., Hospit. Lit. Index. LC RE1. DD 617.706273. NLM W1 TR2247. CODEN TAOSAT. (cum index). Circ 500. (ctrl). Includes membership listing, papers, theses, minutes of annual meeting, American Ophthalmological Society.

TRANSACTIONS OF THE . . . ANNUAL SCIENTIFIC PROGRAM OF THE COLLEGE OF VETERINARY OPHTHALMOLOGISTS. 11th (Nov. 2nd and 3rd, 1980)-. English. an. NLM W1. *Annual Scientific Program - American College of Veterinary Ophthalmologists.*

TRANSACTIONS OF THE NEW ORLEANS ACADEMY OF OPHTHALMOLOGY. Main/Corp New Orleans Academy of Ophthalmology. 0077-8605. US. English. ir. C V Mosby, c/o C Leadbetter, 11830 Westline Industrial Drive, St Louis MO 63141. Tel (314)872-8370. Ind/Abst Index Med., Chem. Abstr. NLM W1 TR226S. CODEN TNOOA6.

TRANSACTIONS OF THE OPHTHALMOLOGICAL SOCIETIES OF THE UNITED KINGDOM. Main/Corp Ophthalmological Society of the United Kindgom. V. 82- 1962-. 0078-5334. Periodical. UK. English. ir. $168.57. Professional & Scientific Publications, Tavistock House East, Tavistock Square, London WC1H 9JR England. Ind/Abst Life Sci. Collect., Excerpta Med., Index Med., Biol. Abstr. NLM W1 TR2261. CODEN TOSUAH. *Transactions of the Ophthalmological Society of the United Kingdom.*

TRANSACTIONS OF THE PACIFIC COAST OTO-OPHTHALMOLOGICAL SOCIETY. (TRANSACTIONS OF THE ANNUAL MEETING). Main/Corp Pacific Coast Oto-Ophthalmological Society. VFOAT Transactions of the Pacific Coast Oto-Ophthalmological Society Annual Meeting. 1st-35th. 0097-0093. Periodical. US. English. ir. Pacific Coast Oto-Ophthal Society, PO Box 49412, Los Angeles CA 90049. Ind/Abst Energy Res. Abstr., Index Med. NLM W1 TR227D. (cum index).

TRANSACTIONS - PENNSYLVANIA ACADEMY OF OPHTHALMOLOGY AND OTOLARYNGOLOGY. See Medicine - Otorhinolaryngology.

VESTNIK OFTALMOLOGII. 0042-465X. Periodical. UR. Russian (summaries in English). bm. $19.50. Victor Kamkin Inc (70122), 12224 Parklawn Drive, Rockville MD 20852. Tel (301)881-5973. Ind/Abst Excerpta Med., Index Med., Int. Aerosp. Abstr., Chem. Abstr. NLM W1 VE841. CODEN VEOFA6. *Sovetskii Vestnik Oftalmologii.*

VIEWS & VISIONS. (VIEWS & VISIONS : THE PUBLICATION OF THE HERMANN EYE CENTER). VFOAT Views and Visions. 0882-469X. Periodical. US. English. qt. Free. Hermann Eye Center, 1203 Ross Sterling Avenue, Houston TX 77030. DD 617.

VISION (SINGAPORE). (VISION : AN OFFICIAL PUBLICATION OF THE INTERNATIONAL AGENCY FOR THE PREVENTION OF BLINDNESS). Vol. 1-. 0217-1090. Monographic Series. English. ir. NLM W1 VI 838B.

VOPROSY OFTAL'MOLOGII. Series/Titl Trudy Volgogradskogo Meditsinskogo Instituta. Monographic Series. UR. Russian. NLM W1 VO6397.

VOZRASTNYE OSOBENNOSTI ORGANA ZRENIIA V NORME I PRI PATOLOGII U DETEI. Vol. 1- 1968-. UR. Russian. NLM W1 VO936.

WELLCOME TRENDS IN OPHTHALMOLOGY. VFOAT Ophthalmology. V. 1- Apr. 1979-. Periodical. US. English. Wellcome Trends in Ophthalmology 15 Park Row, New York NY

10038. *Clinical Trends in Ophthalmology, Otolaryngology, Allergy, 0529-9675.*

THE YEAR BOOK OF OPHTHALMOLOGY. See Yearbooks, Almanacs, Directories.

ZENTRALBLATT OPHTHALMOLOGIE. VFOAT Ophthalmology. 123. Vol., No. 1-. 0722-9933. Periodical. German (abstracts in English). mo. Springer Verlag-New York Inc, 175 5th Avenue, New York NY 10010. Tel (212)460-1500. Ed O Kaefer, W Jaeger, G Meyer-Schwickerath and E Schreck. NLM ZWW 100 Z56. Features reviews, meeting reports, monographs and handbooks, general and experimental ophthalmology, specific and clinical ophthalmology, glasses, lenses, other visual aids, the eye in general. *Zentralblatt fur die Gesamte Ophthalmologie und Ihre Grenzgebiete, 0044-4138.*

ZPA. ZEITSCHRIFT FUR PRAKTISCHE AUGENHEILKUNDE. (ZEITSCHRIFT FUR PRAKTISCHE AUGENHEILKUNDE : ZPA). VFOAT ZPA. No. 1 (Feb. 1980)-. 0173-2595. Periodical. GW. German. ir. 70-. Dr Alfred Huethig Verlag GMBH, Postfach 102869, IM Weiher 10, D-69 Heidelberg 1 West Germany. Tel (06221)10313. Ed R Kaden. NLM W1 ZE55J. bk rev. adv acc. Circ 3,500. News and scientific papers concerning the work in ophthalmology.

ORTHOPEDICS

5-YEAR CUMULATED BIBLIOGRAPHY OF ORTHOPAEDIC SURGERY. See Bibliographies.

ABMS DIRECTORY OF CERTIFIED ORTHOPAEDIC SURGEONS. See Yearbooks, Almanacs, Directories.

ACTA ORTHOPAEDICA BELGICA. Vol. 12- 1946-. 0001-6462. Periodical. BE. French. bm. $63.23. Association Societe Scientific Medica Belgica, 43 rue des Champs Elysees, B-1050 Brussels Belgium. Ind/Abst Life Sci. Collect., Excerpta Med., Index Med. NLM W1 AC8896. Index in last issue of volume - attached. *Bulletin de la Societe Belge d'Orthopedie et de Chirurgie de l'Appareil Moteur.*

ACTA ORTHOPAEDICA SCANDINAVICA. V. 1- 1930-. 0001-6470. Periodical. DK. English (articles in French or German). bm. 600.00 Domestic, 796.00 US and Canada, 720.00 all other countries. Munksgaard International Publishers Limited, 35 Norre Sogade, DK-1370 Copenhagen K Denmark. Tel 45 12 70 30. Ed Goran H C Bauer. Ind/Abst Life Sci. Collect., Excerpta Med., Biol. Abstr., Chem. Abstr., Nuci. Sci. Abstr., Index Med., Energy Res. Abstr., Sci. Cit. Index, Abr. Ed., Hospit. Lit. Index. NLM W1 AC8924. CODEN AOSAAK. (cum index). adv acc. Circ 4,200. Orthopedic surgery and traumatology.

AKTUAL'NYE VOPROSY TRAVMATOLOGII I ORTOPEDII. Periodical. UR. Russian. NLM W1 AK99RS.

THE AMERICAN ACADEMY OF ORTHOPAEDIC SURGEONS BULLETIN. VFOAT Academy Bulletin. Periodical. US. English. 222 South Prospect Avenue, Park Ridge IL 60068. Tel (312)823-7186. Ed Bill Spelbring. Circ 18,00. (ctrl). Membership publication of the academy. Reports news, current developments and educational programs of the academy, as well as socio-economic items of interest to orthopaedists.

ANNUAL REPORT - INTERNATIONAL CENTER FOR THE DISABLED. See Physically Impaired.

ANNUAL REPORT OF THE OXFORD ORTHOPAEDIC ENGINEERING CENTRE. Began with: 1 (1974). UK. English. an. NLM W1.

BUCHEREI DES ORTHOPADEN. 1- 1969-. 0068-3388. Periodical. GW. German. ir. Ferdinand Enke Verlag, Rudigerstr 14, Postfach 1304, 7 Stuttgart 1 West Germany. Tel (0711)8931-0. Ed P Otte and K F Schlegel. Deals with practical and clinical relevant subjects from the whole subject of orthopedics. The volumes are supplement of the journal "Zeitschrift fur Orthopadie".

BULLETIN OF THE HOSPITAL FOR JOINT DISEASES ORTHOPAEDIC INSTITUTE. Vol. 41 (1981)-. Periodical. US. English. sa. $20.00. Hospital for Joint Diseases Orthopaedic Institute, 301 East 17th Street, New York

NY 10003. **Ind/Abst** Excerpta Med., Index Med. **NLM** W1 BU851PD. *Bulletin of the Hospital for Joint Diseases (New York, N.Y. : 1962).*

CANADIAN ORTHO-PROS. (THE CANADIAN ORTHO-PROS). 0714-878X. Periodical. CN. English. sa. $8.00. Canadian Ortho-Pros, Canadian Association of Prosthetists and Orthotists, c/o E Cameron, 827 Glenwood Avenue, Burlington Ontario L7T 2J8 Canada. **DD** 617.307.

CLINICAL ORTHOPAEDICS AND RELATED RESEARCH. No. 1- Spring 1953-. Periodical. US. English. **Ed** A F de Palma and others. **LC** RD701. (cum index).

CLINICAL PROSTHETICS & ORTHOTICS. **VFOAT** Clinical Prosthetics and Orthotics. Vol. 6, No. 2 (Spring 1982)-. 0735-0090. Periodical. US. English. qt. $15.00 Domestic, $20.00 Foreign. American Academy of Orthotists and Prosthetists, 717 Pendleton Street, Alexandria VA 22314. **Tel** (703)836-7116. **Ed** Chris Colligan. **NLM** W1 CL768CP. adv acc. **Circ** 2,300. A scientific publication concerned with philosophical issues which arise in the clinical atmosphere of the profession. What every health-care professional needs to keep abreast of what is happening in the fields of orthotics and prosthetics. *Newsletter, Prosthetics and Orthotics Clinic, 0279-6910.*

CONTEMPORARY ORTHOPAEDICS. Began with: Vol. 1 (Feb. 1979). 0194-8458. Periodical. US. English. mo. $25.00. Bobit Publishing Company, 2500 Artesia Boulevard, Redondo Beach CA 90278. **Tel** (213)376-8788. **NLM** W1 CO769NN.

DIRECTORY OF DIPLOMATES. *See* Yearbooks, Almanacs, Directories.

EGYPTIAN ORTHOPEDIC JOURNAL. V. 1- Dec. 1966-. 0013-242X. Periodical. English (title and table of contents also in Arabic). sa. Egyptian Orthopaedic Journal, PO Box 4, Alexandria Egypt UAR.

FACIAL ORTHOPEDICS AND TEMPOROMANDIBULAR ARTHROLOGY. Vol. 1, No. 1-. 0749-0399. Periodical. US. English. mo. $225.00. Facial Orthopedics, Box 649, Evans GA 30809. **Ed** Eugene H Williamson. **DD** 617. bk rev. **Circ** 1,000. (ctrl). The journal is devoted to a comprehensive review and digest of the world literature on the scientific basis and clinical practice of the diagnosis prognosis and treatment of facial orthopedic dysfunction, disorders and diseases.

FOOT & ANKLE. (FOOT & ANKLE : THE OFFICIAL JOURNAL OF THE AMERICAN ORTHOPAEDIC FOOT SOCIETY). **VFOAT** Foot and Ankle. Vol. 1, No. 1 (July 1980)-. 0198-0211. Periodical. US. English. bm. $65.00. Williams & Wilkins, 428 East Preston Street, Baltimore MD 21202. **Tel** (301)528-4000. **Ed** Melvin H Jahss. **Ind/Abst** Excerpta Med., Index Med. **LC** RD781. **DD** 617.585. **NLM** W1. adv acc. **Circ** 3,400. Authoritative international articles on new approaches to foot and ankle disorders and surgical treatment, for orthopedic surgeons and podiatrists.

GIORVALE ITALIANO DI ORTOPEDIA E TRAUMATOLOGIA. V. 1- 1975-. 0390-0134. Monographic Series. Italian. ir. **NLM** W1 GI814.

HIP. (THE HIP). 1973-. 0095-7216. US. English. an. $56.95. C V Mosby Company, C Leadbetter, 11830 Westline Industrial Drive, St Louis MO 63141. **Tel** (314)872-8370. **Ind/Abst** Index Med. **LC** RD549. **DD** 617.58. **NLM** W1 HI409N.

INTERNATIONAL ORTHOPAEDICS. V. 1- 1977-. 0341-2695. Periodical. GW. articles in English or French with summaries in both languages. qt. $88.00. Springer Verlag New York Inc, 175 5th Avenue, New York NY 10010. **Tel** (212)460-1500. **Ed** P Masse, J Evrard and F T Horan. **Ind/Abst** Life Sci. Collect., Excerpta Med., Index Med., Energy Res. Abstr. **NLM** W1 IN827H. Publishes original papers from all over the world dealing with clinical orthopaedic surgery or basic research directly connected with orthopaedic surgery.

ITALIAN JOURNAL OF ORTHOPAEDICS AND TRAUMATOLOGY. V. 1- Apr. 1975-. 0390-5489. Periodical. IT. English (Italian). ty. $56.00. H Stillman Publishers Inc, 21405 Wood Chuck Lane, Boca Raton FL 33433. **Tel** (305)482-6343. **Ed** H Stillman. **Ind/Abst** Excerpta Med., Index Med., Hospit. Lit. Index. **NLM** W1 IT136. **Circ** 500. Official publication of the Italian Society of Orthopedics and Traumatology. *Orthopaedica Italica.*

THE JOURNAL OF ORTHOPAEDIC AND SPORTS PHYSICAL THERAPY. V. 1- Summer 1979-. 0190-6011. Periodical. US. English. bm. $45.00. Williams & Wilkins Company, 428 East Preston Street, Baltimore MD 21202. **Tel** (301)528-4000. **Ed** James A Gould and George J Davies. **Ind/Abst** Electron. Commun. Abstr. J., ISMEC Bull., Pollut. Abstr. Indexes, Saf. Sci. Abstr. J., Life Sci. Collect., Excerpta Med., Cumul. Index Nurs. Allied Health Lit. **LC** RD701. **DD** 617.3005. **NLM** W1 JO804S. adv acc. **Circ** 12,000. The latest clinical developments in sports medicine for practicing PT's athletic trainers, and orthopaedic surgeons.

JOURNAL OF ORTHOPAEDIC RESEARCH. (JOURNAL OF ORTHOPAEDIC RESEARCH : OFFICIAL PUBLICATION OF THE ORTHOPAEDIC RESEARCH SOCIETY). Vol. 1, No. 1-. 0736-0266. Periodical. US. English. qt. $80.00. Raven Press, 1140 Avenue of the Americas, New York NY 10036. **Tel** (212)575-0335. **NLM** W1.

JOURNAL OF THE AMERICAN OSTEOPATHIC ACADEMY ORTHOPEDICS. Vol. 1, No. 1 (1982)-. 0740-0926. US. English. an. $10.00. American Osteopathic Academy of Orthopedics, 1217 Salem Avenue, Dayton OH 45406. **NLM** W1 JO909Z.

JOURNAL OF THE ASSOCIATION OF CHILDREN'S PROSTHETIC-ORTHOTIC CLINICS. (JOURNAL OF THE ASSOCIATION OF CHILDREN'S PROSTHETIC-ORTHOTIC CLINICS). **VFOAT** JACPOC. Vol. 20, No. 3 (Autumn 1985)-. 0884-8424. Periodical. US. English. qt. $15.00. Prosthetics and Orthotics, NYU Postgraduate Medical School, 317 East 34th Street, New York NY 10016. **DD** 617. bk rev. **Circ** 1,100. (ctrl). Prosthetic-orthotic management of orthopedically disabled children, including book reviews and proceedings of annual meetings of the Association of Children's Prosthetic-Orthotic Clinics. *Inter-Clinic Information Bulletin, 0028-7911.*

JOURNAL OF THE WESTERN PACIFIC ORTHOPAEDIC ASSOCIATION. (THE JOURNAL OF THE WESTERN PACIFIC ORTHOPAEDIC ASSOCIATION). V. 1- Mar. 1964-. 0043-4019. Periodical. PH. English. sa. Western Pacific Orthopedic Association, Orthopedic Department, Queen Elizabeth Hospital, Kowloon Hong Kong. **Tel** 5-8176388. **Ed** S F Lam. **Ind/Abst** Excerpta Med. **NLM** W1 JO963I. bk rev. adv acc. **Circ** 1,000. (ctrl). To enable orthopedic surgeons of the Western Pacific area to exchange views, discuss new discoveries and new methods of handling orthopedic problems.

MEDIGUIDE TO ORTHOPAEDICS. Vol. 3, Issue 1-. 0737-6073. Periodical. US. English. bm. Dellacorte Publications, 767 Lexington Avenue, New York NY 10021. **NLM** W1 ME787GC. *Mediguide to Orthopedics, 0737-6073.*

MINERVA ORTOPEDICA; REVISTA MENSILE DI ORTOPEDIA ETRAUMATOLOGIA. Vol. 1- Sept. 1950-. 0026-4911. Periodical. IT. Italian (summaries in English). mo. 80.00. Edizoni Minerva Medica, Corso Bramante 83, Torino 10126 Italy. **Tel** 678282. **Ed** A Oliaro. **Ind/Abst** Excerpta Med. **NLM** W1 MI649. bk rev. adv acc. Addressed to practitioners and specialists in orthopedics and traumatology; deals with topics in scientific practice and research.

MODERN TRENDS IN ORTHOPAEDICS. 1st-. 0077-0159. Periodical. English. ir. **NLM** W1 MO175P.

NIPPON SEIKEIGEKAGGAKKAI ZASSHI. (NIPPON SEIKEIGEKA GAKKAI ZASSHI). **VFOAT** Journal of the Japanese Orthopaedic Association, Zeitschrift der Japanischen Orthopadisch-Chirurgischen Gesellschaft. Vol. 1- 1926-. 0021-5325. Periodical. JA. Japanese (with some articles in English or German). mo. $118.50. Japan Publishing Trading Co Ltd, PO Box 5030 Tokyo International, Tokyo 100-31 Japan. **Ind/Abst** Excerpta Med., Index Med., Biol. Abstr., Chem. Abstr. **NLM** W1 NI932F. **CODEN** NSGZA2.

ORTHOP. SURV *CEASED.* (ORTHOPAEDIC SURVEY). V. 1-6. 0147-6793. Periodical. US. English. bm. $30.00. Orthopaedic Survey, 428 Preston Street, Baltimore MD 21202. **Ind/Abst** Excerpta Med. **LC** RD701. **DD** 617.3005. **NLM** ZWE 168 O77.

DER ORTHOPADE. 1- April 1972-. 0085-4350. Periodical. German. qt. Springer Verlag-New York Inc, 175-5th Avenue, New York NY 10010. **Tel** (212)460-1500. **Ed** R Bauer, N Gschwend, and D Hohmann. **Ind/Abst** Excerpta Med., Index Med., Curr. Contents, INIS Atomindex. **NLM** W1 OR79KN. **CODEN** ORHPBG. Each issue is dedicated to one specific subject of orthopedics or related areas and gives a clear review of current knowledge. Special emphasis on diagnosis, prophylaxis and therapy.

ORTHOPAEDIC KNOWLEDGE UPDATE . . . HOME STUDY SYLLABUS. **VFOAT** Home Study Syllabus. 1-. US. English. **NLM** WE 39.

THE ORTHOPAEDIC PRACTITIONER. V. 1- 1978-. 0170-6004. GW. English. ir. Medizinisch Literarische Verlagsgesselschaft MBH, PO Box 120/140, D3110 Uelzen 1 West Germany. **NLM** W1 OR811L.

ORTHOPAEDIC REVIEW. V. 1- July 1972-. 0094-6591. Periodical. US. English. mo. $55.00. Macor Publishing Company, 116 West 32nd Street/8th Floor, New York NY 10001. **Tel** (212)736-6688. **Ed** William Kitay. **Ind/Abst** Excerpta Med. **LC** RD701. **DD** 617.3005. **NLM** W1 OR796R. **CODEN** ORTRDG. bk rev. adv acc. **Circ** 29,000. (ctrl). Clinical/surgical journal that meets the needs of the practicing orthopaedic surgeon.

ORTHOPAEDIC TRANSACTIONS. V. 1- May 1977-. 0162-9379. Periodical. US. English. ir. $14.00. Journal of Bone & Joint Surgery Inc, 10 Shattuck Street, Boston MA 02115. **Ind/Abst** Biol. Abstr. **NLM** W1 OR796T. **CODEN** ORTTDM.

ORTHOPAEDICS. **VFOAT** Audio-Digest. Orthopaedics Sound Recording. V. 1- 1978-. Periodical. US. English. mo. $100.67. Audio Digest Foundation, 1577 Chevy Chase Drive, Glendale CA 91206. **Tel** (213)245-8505. Ed Claron L Oakley. A once-monthly interactive system of audio cassette postgraduate medical education, with each one-hour program eligible for two Category I credit hours.

THE ORTHOPEDIC CLINICS OF NORTH AMERICA. V. 1- 1970-. 0030-5898. Monographic Series. US. English. qt. $60.00. WB Saunders, West Washington Square, Philadelphia PA 19105. **Tel** (215)574-3395. Ed Karen McFadden. **Ind/Abst** Life Sci. Collect., Excerpta Med., Index Med., Cumul. Index Nurs. Allied Health Lit., Biol. Abstr., Energy Res. Abstr., Sci. Cit. Index, Abr. Ed. **LC** UNC. **NLM** W1 OR81K. **CODEN** OCLNAQ. **Circ** 6,600. Clinical updates on surgical techniques and management written by experts in the field.

THE ORTHOPEDIC SURGEON'S COMPENDIUM OF DRUG THERAPY. (THE ORTHOPEDIC SURGEON'S COMPENDIUM OF DRUG THERAPY : A PUBLICATION OF BIOMEDICAL INFORMATION CORPORATION). **VFOAT** Compendium of Drug Therapy. 1981/1982-. 0276-4350. US. English. an. Biomedical Information Corporation, 800 2nd Avenue, New York NY 10017.

ORTHOPEDICS. V. 1- Jan./Feb. 1978-. 0147-7447. Periodical. US. English. bm. $60.00. Charles B Slack Inc, 6900 Grove Road, Thorofare NJ 08086. **Tel** (609)848-1000. **Ed** Linda L Jones. **Ind/Abst** Excerpta Med., Energy Res. Abstr. **LC** RD701. **DD** 617.3005. **NLM** W1 OR812A. bk rev. adv acc. **Circ** 26,000. (ctrl). Original, clinical papers on orthopedic and related subjects involving case presentations, studies and reports.

ORTHOPEDICS TODAY. Began with: Vol. 1, No. 1 (Jan./Feb. 1981). 0279-5647. Periodical. US. English. bw. Slack Inc, 6900 Grove Road, Thorofare NJ 08086. **Tel** (800)257-8290. **NLM** W1 OR813.

ORTOPEDIJA, TRAVMATOLOGIJA I PROTEZIROVANIE. (ORTOPEDIIA, TRAVMATOLOGIIA I PROTEZIROVANIE). Jan./Feb. 1955-. 0030-5987. Periodical. UR. Russian. mo. $40.50. Victor Kamkin Inc (70671), 12224 Parklawn Drive, Rockville MD 20852. **Tel** (301)881-5973. **Ind/Abst** Excerpta Med., Index Med. **NLM** W1 OR875. *Ortopediia i Travmatologiia, 0473-4378.*

PROCEEDINGS OF THE ANNUAL CONFERENCE ON REHABILITATION ENGINEERING. (PROCEEDINGS). **Main/Conf** Conference on Rehabilitation Engineering. **VFOAT** Proceedings of the . . . Annual Conference on Rehabilitation Engineering. 0733-5482. US. English. an. $20.00 Members, $25.00 Nonmembers. Rehabilitation Engineering Society of North America, Suite 210/4405 East-West Highway, Bethesda MD 20814. **LC** RD792. **DD** 617.

PROSTHETICS AND ORTHOTICS INTERNATIONAL. *See* Physically Impaired.

RECENT ADVANCES IN ORTHOPAEDICS. No. 1- 1969-. 0308-4914. Periodical. UK. English. ir. Churchill Livingstone Inc, 1560 Broadway, New York NY 10036. Tel (212)819-5400. Ed A G Apley. NLM W1 RE105W.

REGISTRY OF THE AMERICAN BOARD FOR CERTIFICATION IN ORTHOTICS AND PROSTHETICS, INC. (REGISTRY OF THE AMERICAN BOARD FOR CERTIFICATION IN ORTHOTICS AND PROSTHETICS). VFOAT Registry - American Board for Certification in Orthotics and Prosthetics. 1976-. 0164-0526. Periodical. US. English. an. NLM WE 22 AA1 R27. *Registry of Accredited Facilities and Certified Individuals in Orthotics and Prosthetics, 0190-5090.*

SAUNDERS MONOGRAPHS IN CLINICAL ORTHOPAEDICS. V. 1-. 0195-9565. Monographic Series. US. English. ir. WB Saunders Company, West Washington Square, Philadelphia PA 19105. Tel (800)523-0713. LC UNC. NLM W1 SA975.

SCHRIFTENREIHE MANUELLE MEDIZIN. VFOAT Manuelle Medizin. V. 3-. 0172-9233. Monographic Series. German. ir. NLM W1 SC343J.

SEIKEI GEKA MOOK. 1- 1978-. Monographic Series. Japanese. ir. NLM W1 SE2516G.

SEMINARS IN ORTHOPAEDICS. Periodical. US. English. qt. Grune & Stratton Inc, Orlando FL 32887.

TAEHAN CHONGHYONG OEKWA HAKHOE CHI. VFOAT The Journal of the Korean Orthopedic Association. Periodical. KO. Korean (with summaries in English). bm. Taehan Chonghyong Oekwa Hakhoe, 302-75 Tongbu Ichondong Yongsan-ku, Seoul Korea. *Taehan Chonghyong Oekwa Hakhoe Chapchi.*

TECHNIQUES IN ORTHOPAEDICS (ROCKVILLE, MD.). (TECHNIQUES IN ORTHOPAEDICS : TIO). VFOAT TIO. Vol. 1, No. 1 (Apr. 1986)-. 0885-9698. Periodical. US. English. qt. $79.00. Aspen Systems Corp, 16792 Oakmont Avenue, Gaithersburg MD 20877. DD 617.

TRUDY - BAKINSKII NAUCHNO-ISSLEDOVATEL'SKII INSTITUT TRAVMATOLOGII I ORTOPEDII. UR. Russian. NLM W1 TR947T.

UNFALLHEILKUNDE. VFOAT Traumatology. Volume 79- Jan. 1976-. 0341-5694. Periodical. US. German. mo. Springer Verlag-New York Inc, 175 5th Avenue, New York NY 10010. Tel (212)460-1500. Ind/Abst Biol. Abstr., Energy Res. Abstr., Life Sci. Collect., Excerpta Med. NLM W1 UN1035. CODEN UNFADZ. *Monatsschrift fur Unfallheilkunde, 0340-1669.*

ZEITSCHRIFT FUR ORTHOPADIE UND IHRE GRENZGEBIETE. V. 64- Oct. 1935-. 0044-3220. Periodical. GW. German. bm. $225.00. Thieme-Stratton Inc, 381 Park Avenue, New York NY 10016. Tel (212)683-5088/89. Ind/Abst Life Sci. Collect., Excerpta Med., Index Med., Biol. Abstr., CIS Abstr., Sci. Cit. Index, Abr. Ed. NLM W1 Z3529. CODEN ZOIGAP. *Zeitschrift fur Orthopadische Chirurgie Einschliesslich der Heilgymnastik and Massage.*

ZHONGHUA GUKE ZAZHI. (CHUNG-HUA KU KO TSA CHIH). VFOAT Chinese Journal of Orthopedics. Vol. 1, 1981-. 0253-2352. Periodical. CC. Chinese. bm. $6.52. China Publication Centre, PO Box 2820, Beijing China. NLM W1 CH982K.

OTORHINOLARYNGOLOGY

ABMS DIRECTORY OF CERTIFIED OTOLARYNGOLOGISTS. See Yearbooks, Almanacs, Directories.

ACADEMIC AND CLINICAL REPORTS - INSTITUTE OF LARYNGOLOGY AND OTOLOGY ASSOCIATED WITH THE ROYAL NATIONAL THROAT, NOSE AND EAR HOSPITAL. (ACADEMIC AND CLINICAL REPORTS). V. 21- 1973/74-. 0309-698X. Periodical. UK. English. ir. NLM W1 AC33N.

ACTA OTO-LARYNGOLOGICA. V. 1- 1918-. 0001-6489. Periodical. SW. English (articles in French or German). bm. $92.00. Almqvist & Wiksell, 108 Drottninggatan PO Box 45150, S-104 30 Stockholm Sweden. Tel Telex 85413160. Ind/Abst Life Sci. Collect., Lang. Lang. Behav. Abstr., Pestdoc, Ringdoc, Vetdoc, Excerpta Med., Int. Aerosp. Abstr., CIS Abstr., Biol. Abstr., Chem. Abstr., Psychol. Abstr., Nuci. Sci. Abstr., Index Med., Energy Res. Abstr., Sci. Cit. Index, Abr. Ed., Sociol. Abstr. NLM W1 AC8941. CODEN AOLAAJ. *Nordisk Tidskrift for Oto-Rhino-Laryngologi.*

ACTA OTO-RHINO-LARYNGOLOGICA BELGICA. 0001-6497. Periodical. BE. French. bm. $73.11. Association Societe Scientific Medica Belgica, 43 rue des Champs Elysees, B1050 Brussels Belgium. Ind/Abst Biol. Abstr., Excerpta Med., Index Med., Life Sci. Collect., Lang. Lang. Behav. Abstr., Hospit. Lit. Index, Sociol. Abstr., Chem. Abstr. NLM W1 AC897. CODEN AORLAE.

ACTA OTORHINO-LARYNGOLOGICA ITALICA. (ACTA OTORINOLARYNGOLOGICA ITALICA : ORGANO UFFICIALE DELLA SOCIETA ITALIANA DI OTORINOLARINGOLOGIA E CHIRURGIA CERVICO-FACCIALE). Vol. 1, No. 1 July-Aug. 1981-. 0392-100X. Periodical. Italian. ir. Ind/Abst Excerpta Med., Index Med. NLM W1 AC898N. *Annali di Laringologia, Otologia, Rinologia, E Faringologia.*

ACTA OTORRINOLARINGOLOGICA ESPANOLA. Yearly V. 1- Oct. 1949-. 0001-6519. Periodical. SP. Spanish. bm. $75.00. D I P S A, Francisco Aranda 43, Barcelona 5 Spain. Ind/Abst Life Sci. Collect., Excerpta Med. NLM W1 AC898L.

ADVANCES IN OTO-RHINO-LARYNGOLOGY. VFOAT Bibliotheca Oto-Rhino-Laryngologica, Fortschritte der Hals-Nasen-Ohren-Heilkunde, Progres en Oto-Rhino-Laryngologie. V. 15-. 0065-3071. Periodical. SZ. English. ir. S Karger AG, PO Box 352, White Plains NY 10602. Tel 061-39 08 80. Ed C R Platz. Ind/Abst Life Sci. Collect., Index Med., Biol. Abstr., Chem. Abstr., Sci. Cit. Index, Abr. Ed. NLM W1 AD701. CODEN ADORB9. Results from research and clinical studies pertaining to the pathophysiology, diagnosis, clinical symptoms, course, prognosis, and therapy of a variety of ear, nose, and throat disorders. *Fortschritte der Hals-Nasen-Ohren-Heilkunde.*

AKTUELLE OTO-RHINO-LARYNGOLOGIE. No. 1- 1969-. Periodical. German. ir. Thieme-Stratton, 381 Park Avenue South, New York NY 10016. Tel (212)683-5088.

AMERICAN JOURNAL OF OTOLARYNGOLOGY. V. 1- Fall 1979-. 0196-0709. Periodical. US. English. bm. $65.00. WB Saunders Co, West Washington Square, Philadelphia PA 19105. Tel (215)574-3395. Ed William Burns. Ind/Abst Cumul. Index Nurs. Allied Health Lit., Excerpta Med., Index Med., Chem. Abstr., Sci. Cit. Index, Abr. Ed. LC RF1. DD 616.21. NLM W1 AM497N. CODEN AJOTDP. bk rev. adv acc. Circ 8,300. Original articles cover the latest clinical findings of interest to otolaryngologists, otologists, allergists, plastic surgeons, maxillofacial surgeons, and speech scientists.

THE AMERICAN JOURNAL OF OTOLOGY. V. 1- July 1979-. 0192-9763. Periodical. US. English. bm. $79.00. Thieme-Stratton Inc, 381 Park Avenue South Suite 1501, New York NY 10016. Tel (212)683-5088. Ed Michael Glasscock III. Ind/Abst Excerpta Med., Index Med., Biol. Abstr. DD 617. NLM W1 AM497V. CODEN AJOTBN. bk rev. adv acc. Circ 1,500. A clinically-oriented journal devoted to otology, neurology and audiology and designed for the practitioner.

ANALES OTORRINOLARINGOLOGICOS IBERO-AMERICANOS. See Yearbooks, Almanacs, Directories.

THE ANNALS OF OTOLOGY, RHINOLOGY & LARYNGOLOGY. VAT Annals of Otology, Rhinology and Laryngology. V. 6- Feb. 1897-. 0003-4894. Periodical. US. English. bm. $60.00 Domestic, $75.00 Foreign. Annals Publishing Company, 4507 Lacided Avenue, St Louis MO 63108. Tel (314)367-4987. Ed Brian F McCabe. Ind/Abst Life Sci. Collect., Lang. Lang. Behav. Abstr., Excerpta Med., Int. Aerosp. Abstr., Biol. Abstr., Chem. Abstr., Index Med., Nuci. Sci. Abstr., Index Med., Energy Res. Abstr., Sci. Cit. Index, Abr. Ed., Sociol. Abstr., Hospit. Lit. Index. LC RF1. NLM W1 AN617L. CODEN AORHA2. (cum index). bk rev. adv acc. Circ 5,980. (ctrl). Over 90 years of excellence, publishing peer-reviewed clinical and research papers in the field of otolaryngology. *Annals of Ophthalmology and Otology.*

ARCHIVES OF OTO-RHINO-LARYNGOLOGY. See Genealogy and Heraldry - Archives.

Medicine—Otorhinolaryngology

ARCHIVES OF OTOLARYNGOLOGY (CHICAGO, ILL. : 1960). See Genealogy and Heraldry - Archives.

ASHA REPORTS. Began in 1965. 0569-8553. Monographic Series. US. English. ir. ASHA, 10801 Rockville Pike, Rockville MD 20852. NLM W1 A152E.

AUDIO-DIGEST. OTORHINOLARYNGOLOGY. V. - 19 -. Periodical. US. English. sm. $192.72. Audio Digest Foundation, 1577 Chevy Chase Drive, Glendale CA 91206.

AUDIOLOGY. VFOAT Audiologie. V. 10- Jan./Feb. 1971-. 0020-6091. Periodical. SZ. English (occasional articles in French). bm. $154.00. S Karger AG, PO Box 352, White Plains NY 10602. Tel (061)39 08 80. Ed J M Aran. Ind/Abst Excerpta Med., Biol. Abstr., Index Med., Life Sci. Collect., Energy Res. Abstr., Psychol. Abstr., Sci. Cit. Index, Abr. Ed., Lang. Lang. Behav. Abstr., Sociol. Abstr. NLM W1 AU201H. CODEN AUDLAK. adv acc. Includes major advances in the scientific, clinical and social aspects of hearing. Reflects the interdisciplinary nature of audiological study and practice. *International Audiology.*

BULLETIN SIGNALETIQUE - CENTRE NATIONAL DE LA RECHERCHE SCIENTIFIQUE. 347. OTO-RHINO-LARYNGOLOGIE, STOMATOLOGIE, PATHOLOGIE. (BULLETIN SIGNALETIQUE. 347 : OTO-RHINO-LARYNGOLOGIE, STOMATOLOGIE, PATHOLOGIE CERVICOFACIALE). VFOAT Oto-Rhino-Laryngologie, Stomatologie, Pathologie. 0301-3375. FR. French. ir. Editions du Cost-CNRS, 26 rue Boyer, 75971 Paris Cedex 20 France. Tel (1)43583559. LC Z6669. DD 617.52. NLM ZQ 1 B936RP. (ctrl). Medicine of ear, nose and throat, stomatology, and cervical pathology. *Bulletin Signaletique. 347: Otorhinolaryngologie.*

BUTTERWORTHS INTERNATIONAL MEDICAL REVIEWS. OTOLARYNGOLOGY. VFOAT Otolaryngology. 1-. 0260-0102. Monographic Series. UK. English. ir. Ind/Abst Biol. Abstr. NLM W1 BU99D. CODEN BIRODT.

LES CAHIERS D'OTO. RHINO. LARYNGOLOGIE, DE CHIRURGIE CERVICO. FACIALE ET D'AUDIOPHONOLOGIE. VFOAT Cahiers d'Oto, Rhino, Laryngologie, de Chirurgie Cervico Faciale et d'Audiophonologie. Began in 1976?. Periodical. FR. French. mo. $33.26. Editions la Simarre, #2 rue Joseph Cugnot, 37300 Joue-les-Tours France. Tel 53 53 66. Ind/Abst Chem. Abstr. CODEN CCCADH. *Cahiers de' O.R.L. et de Chirurgie Cervico-Faciale.*

CLINICAL OTOLARYNGOLOGY AND ALLIED SCIENCES. (CLINICAL OTOLARYNGOLOGY). V. 1- 1976-. 0307-7772. Periodical. UK. English. bm. 36.00 Domestic, 75.50 Foreign, $137.50 US and Canada. Blackwell Scientific Publishing Ltd, PO Box 88, Oxford OX2 0EL England. Tel (01)404-4101. Ed J Hibbert. Ind/Abst Excerpta Med., Index Med., Biol. Abstr., Sci. Cit. Index, Abr. Ed. NLM W1 CL761M. CODEN COTSD2. bk rev. adv acc. Circ 935. (ctrl). Research papers of the highest scientific standards dealing with current otorhinolaryngological practice and with audiology, speech pathology, head and neck oncology, head and neck plastic and reconstructive surgery.

EAR CLINICS INTERNATIONAL. Vol. 1-. 0739-733X. Monographic Series. US. English. Williams & Wilkins Co, 428 East Preston Street, Baltimore MD 21202. Ed Michael M Paparella and William L Meyerhoff. DD 617.8. NLM W3 EA117. Each issue contains an index to its own contents - no vol index - loose.

EAR, NOSE, & THROAT JOURNAL. (EAR, NOSE & THROAT JOURNAL). VAT Ear, Nose, and Throat Journal. V. 55, No. 7- July 1976-. 0145-5613. Periodical. US. English. mo. $32.00. Ronald Park Davis Publishing Co Inc, 139 Harristown Road, Glen Rock NJ 07452. Ind/Abst Life Sci. Collect., Excerpta Med., Index Med., Energy Res. Abstr. NLM W1 EA65. *Eye, Ear, Nose & Throat Monthly, 0014-5491.*

EXCERPTA MEDICA. SECTION 11. OTO-, RHINO-, LARYNGOLOGY. (OTO-, RHINO-, LARYNGOLOGY). VAT Excerpta Medica. Section Eleven. Oto-, Rhino-, Laryngology. V. 1- Jan. 1948-. 0014-4150. Periodical. NE. English. ir. Elsevier Science Publishers, PO Box 211, 1000 AE Amsterdam Netherlands. Ed M W Woerdeman. Ind/

Abst Chem. Abstr. **LC** RF1. **DD** 616.2005. **NLM** ZW 1 E964. **CODEN** ORLGA8.

FOLIA PHONIATRICA. V. 1- 1947-. 0015-5705. Periodical. SZ. English, French and German. bm. $97.00. S Karger AG, PO Box 352, White Plains NY 10602. **Tel** (061)39 08 80. **Ed** E Loebell. **Ind/Abst** MLA Int. Bibliogr. Books Artic. Mod. Lang. Lit., Life Sci. Collect., Lang. Lang. Behav. Abstr., Excerpta Med., Index Med., Biol. Abstr., Chem. Abstr., Psychol. Abstr., Soc. Sci. Citation Index, Sociol. Abstr. **LC** RC423. **NLM** W1 FO281. **CODEN** FOPHAD. adv acc. Provides a survey of international research in physiology and pathology of speech and the voice organs. Reports recent findings in the assessment of vocal functions and in the detection, therapy, and rehabilitation of speech disorders.

FUL-, ORR-, GEGEGYOGYASZAT. V. 1-. 0016-237X. Periodical. HU. Hungarian. qt. Akademiai Kiado, POB 24, 1363 Budapest Hungary. **Ind/Abst** Excerpta Med. **NLM** W1 FU495. **CODEN** FOGGAX.

HANDBOOK OF HEARING AID MEASUREMENT. 0362-7349. US. English. Veterans Administration, Washington DC 20420. **LC** RF300. **DD** 681.761. **NLM** W1 HA51ME. Vol. for (1982) distributed to depository libraries in microfiche. *Hearing Aid Performance Measurement Data and Hearing Aid Selection Procedures.*

HEARING INSTRUMENTS. V. 24, No. 8- Aug. 1973-. 0092-4466. Periodical. US. English. mo. $20.00. Hearing Instruments, 131 East First Street, Duluth MN 55802. **Tel** (218)723-9345. **Ed** Marjorie D Skafte. **LC** RF310. **DD** 617.89. **NLM** W1 HE6415I. bk rev. adv acc. **Circ** 18,500. (ctrl). Feature articles detailing new research and products utilized in hearing health care. Other articles detail marketing methods, news of industry, product reviews, listings of industry events. *Hearing Dealer, 0017-9205.*

THE HEARING JOURNAL. Vol. 36, No. 1 (Jan. 1983)-. 0745-7472. Periodical. US. English. mo. $16.00. Laux Company Inc, PO Box 7007, Ayer MA 01432. **Tel** (617)772-4890. **Ed** William Mohen. **Ind/Abst** Psychol. Abstr. bk rev. adv acc. **Circ** 18,000. (ctrl). *Hearing Aid Journal, 0091-2166.*

HEARING RESEARCH. V. 1- 1978-. 0378-5955. Periodical. NE. English. mo. $357.24. Elsevier Science Publishers, PO Box 211, 1000 AE Amsterdam Netherlands. **Tel** (020)5803.911. **Ind/Abst** Life Sci. Collect., Excerpta Med., Index Med., Biol. Abstr., Chem. Abstr. **NLM** W1 HE6419. **CODEN** HERED3.

HEARING RESEARCH AND THEORY. V. 1-. 0730-1480. US. English. ir. Academic Press, 4805 Sand Lake Road, Orlando FL 32887. **Tel** (305)345-4100. **Ed** Jerry V Tobias. **LC** QP460. **DD** 617.8. **NLM** W1 HE64192.

HNO. **VAT** Hals- Nasen- Ohrenheilkunde. 0017-6192. GW. German. mo. Springer Verlag-New York Inc, 175 5th Avenue, New York NY 10010. **Tel** (212)460-1500. **Ed** E Lehnhardt. **Ind/Abst** Excerpta Med., Biol. Abstr., Chem. Abstr., Nuci. Sci. Abstr., Index Med., Energy Res. Abstr., Curr. Contents, INIS Atomindex. **NLM** W1 H143. **CODEN** HBZHAS. Covers ear, nose and throat medicine; head and neck surgery. The latest scientific findings, continued education in diagnostic and therapeutic problems, summaries on conventions and symposiums.

HNO-PRAXIS. 1.- Year. 0323-5033. Periodical. GE. German. qt. 130. VEB Georg Thieme, Hainstrasse 17 19, 7010 Leipzig East Germany. **Tel** 291656. **Ed** H J Gerhardt. **Ind/Abst** Excerpta Med. **NLM** W1 H143F. bk rev. **Circ** 1,000. All what is related to otorhinolaryngology, audiometry, phoniatrics, head and neck surgery, and plastic surgery.

HNO PRAXIS HEUTE. **VFOAT** H.N.O. Praxis Heute. 1-. 0173-9859. German. an. **Ed** H Ganz. **NLM** W1 HN677. *HNO-Erkrankungen.*

INDIAN JOURNAL OF OTOLARYNGOLOGY. Began in 1949. 0019-5421. Periodical. II. English. qt. $32.00. Association Otolaryngologists India, 32 Ballygunge Circular Road Block Flat 4, Calcutta 700 019 India. **Tel** 47-8025. **Ed** Shyamal Kumar. **Ind/Abst** Biol. Abstr. **LC** RF1. **DD** 616.2105. **NLM** W1 IN224. **CODEN** IJOLBJ. bk rev. adv acc. **Circ** 2,500. (ctrl). Official publication of Association of Otolaryngologists of India containing scientific papers on ear, nose, and throat from authors of India and abroad.

INTERNATIONAL JOURNAL OF PEDIATRIC OTORHINOLARYNGOLOGY. **VFOAT** Pediatric Otorhinolaryngology. V. 1- July 1979-. 0165-5876. Periodical. English. bm. Elsevier Science Publishers, PO Box 211, 1000 AE Amsterdam Netherlands. **Tel** (020)5803.911. **Ind/Abst** Life Sci. Collect., Excerpta Med., Index Med., Biol. Abstr., Sci. Cit. Index, Abr. Ed. **NLM** W1 IN771P. **CODEN** IPOTDJ.

INTERNATIONAL OTORHINOLARYNGOLOGICAL REPORTER. **VFOAT** Otorhinolaringological Reporter. V. 1-. 0147-3026. Periodical. US. English. mo. $31.50. Intercontinental Publications, Box 5026, Westport CT 06880.

JIBI TO RINSHO. **VFOAT** Otologia. Began in 1954. 0447-7227. Periodical. Japanese. bm. Kushu Daigaku Igakubu, 1276 Kataksu Fukvoka-shi, Fukvoka Japan. **Ind/Abst** Excerpta Med., Sociol. Abstr., Lang. Lang. Behav. Abstr., Biol. Abstr., Chem. Abstr. **CODEN** JIRIAS.

JOURNAL FRANCAIS D'OTO-RHINO-LARYNGOLOGIE. **VFOAT** Journal Francais d'Oto-Rhino-Laryngologie. V. 26- Jan. 1977-. 0398-9771. Periodical. French. ir. **Ind/Abst** Excerpta Med., Index Med. **NLM** W1 JO442Z. *JFORL. Journal Francais d'Oto-Rhino-Laryngologie.*

THE JOURNAL OF AUDITORY RESEARCH. V. 1- Sept. 1960-. 0021-9177. Periodical. US. English. qt. $12.00. Journal of Auditory Research, PO Box N, Groton CT 06340. **Tel** (203)536-8865. **Ed** J Donald Harris. **Ind/Abst** Lang. Lang. Behav. Abstr., Index Med., Biol. Abstr., Psychol. Abstr., Nuci. Sci. Abstr., Energy Res. Abstr., Sociol. Abstr. **LC** QP461.A1. **DD** 612.8505. **NLM** W1 JO547. **CODEN** JAURAE. (cum index). **Circ** 1,500. Experimental papers on any topic of interest to serious students of the sciences of hearing.

JOURNAL OF LARYNGOLOGY AND OTOLOGY. V. 36- 1921-. 0022-2151. Periodical. UK. English. mo. 45.00 Domestic, $110.00 Foreign. Headley Brothers, 109 Kingsways, London WC2B 6PX England. **Tel** (0233) 23131. **Ed** J C Ballantyne. **Ind/Abst** Life Sci. Collect., Lang. Lang. Behav. Abstr., Excerpta Med., Int. Aerosp. Abstr., Biol. Abstr., Chem. Abstr., Index Med., Sci. Cit. Index, Abr. Ed., Sociol. Abstr., Hospit. Lit. Index. **NLM** W1 JO736. **CODEN** JLOTAX. (cum index). adv acc. **Circ** 2,500. (ctrl). A leading international journal, published monthly and containing original scientific articles and clinical records in all fields of otology, rhinology and laryngology. Includes occasional supplements. *Journal of Laryngology, Rhinology, and Otology.*

JOURNAL OF OTOLARYNGOLOGY. (THE JOURNAL OF OTOLARYNGOLOGY). **VFOAT** Journal d'Otolaryngologie. V. 5- Feb. 1976-. 0381-6605. Periodical. CN. English (includes some text in French). bm. $23.00 Domestic, $24.00 US, $25.00 Foreign. Canadian Journal of Otolaryngology, 600 University Avenue, Toronto Ontario M5G 1X5 Canada. **Ind/Abst** Life Sci. Collect., Excerpta Med., Index Med., Biol. Abstr. **DD** 616.2105. **NLM** W1 JO812. **CODEN** JOTODX. *Canadian Journal of Otolaryngology, 0045-5083.*

THE JOURNAL OF OTOLARYNGOLOGY. SUPPLEMENT. **VFOAT** Journal d'Oto-Rhino-Laryngologie. Supplement. No. 3- 1977-. 0707-7270. Monographic Series. CN. English (summaries in French). ir. $10.00. Journal of Otolaryngolgy, 289 Rutherford Road South/Suite 11, Brampton Ontario L6W 3R9 Canada. **Tel** (416)457-8009. **Ed** Derek Birt. **Ind/Abst** Index Med. **DD** 616.21005. **NLM** W1 JO812A. bk rev. adv acc. **Circ** 1,200. (ctrl). Official journal of the Canadian Otolaryngology Society - Head and Neck Surgery. *Canadian Journal of Otolaryngology. Journal Canadien d'Otolaryngologie Supplement.*

THE JOURNAL OF SPEECH AND HEARING DISORDERS. *See* Physically Impaired.

JOURNAL OF THE ACADEMY OF REHABILITATIVE AUDIOLOGY. Began with: Vol. 3, No. 2 (Oct. 1978)-. 0149-8886. Periodical. US. English. an. $8.00. Middle Tennessee State University, PO Box 436, M Bor TN 37132. **LC** RF297. **DD** 362.4205. **NLM** W1 JO907CH. *Newsletter (Academy of Rehabilitative Audiology), 0149-8878.*

JOURNAL OF THE OTO-LARYNGOLOGICAL SOCIETY OF AUSTRALIA. V. 1- Mar. 1961-. 0030-6614. Periodical. AT. English. ir. 30.00 Domestic. Otolaryngological Society of Australia, 33-35 Atchison Street, St Leonards 2065 Australia. **Tel** (02) 43.5141. **Ed** Rory C Willis. **Ind/Abst** Excerpta Med. **NLM** W1 JO944P. adv acc. **Circ** 400. (ctrl). Medical journal containing articles on diseases of ear, nose and throat region and surgery including head and neck surgery.

LA NUOVA CLINICA OTORINOLARINGOIATRICA. (LA NUOVA CLINICA OTORINOLARINGOIATRICA : ORGANO UFFICIALE DEL GRUPPO SICILIANO DI O.R.L. E PATOLOGIA CERVICO-FACCIALE, GRUPPO PUGLIESE DI O.R.L. E PATOLOGIA CERVICO-FACCIALE). **VFOAT** La Nuova Clinica O.R.L. No. 1 1978 – V. 30. 0392-1433. Italian. ir. **NLM** W1 NU236. *Clinica Otorinolaringoiatrica.*

LARYNGOLOGIE, RHINOLOGIE, OTOLOGIE. Vol. 54-. 0340-1588. Periodical. GW. German (summaries in English). mo. $111.00. Thieme-Stratton Inc, 381 Park Avenue, New York NY 10016. **Tel** (212)683-5088. **Ind/Abst** Life Sci. Collect., Excerpta Med., Index Med., CIS Abstr., Energy Res. Abstr., Lang. Lang. Behav. Abstr., Sociol. Abstr. **NLM** W1 LA776V. *Laryngologie, Rhinologie, Otologie und Ihre Grenzgebiete, 0302-9379; Monatsschrift fur Ohrenheilkunde und Laryngo-Rhinologie, 0026-9328.*

THE LARYNGOSCOPE. V. 1- July 1896-. 0023-852X. Periodical. US. English. mo. Laryngoscope, 9216 Clayton Road/Room 18, St Louis MO 63124. **Tel** (314)997-5070. **Ind/Abst** Life Sci. Collect., Excerpta Med., Int. Aerosp. Abstr., Chem. Abstr., Index Med., Nuci. Sci. Abstr., Energy Res. Abstr., Sci. Cit. Index, Abr. Ed., Sociol. Abstr., Hospit. Lit. Index, Lang. Lang. Behav. Abstr. **NLM** W1 LA78. **CODEN** LARYA8.

THE LARYNGOSCOPE. SUPPLEMENT. No. 1- 1974-. Periodical. US. English. ir. $60.00. The Laryngoscope, Business Office, 9216 Clayton Road/Suite 17, St Louis MO 63124. **Tel** (314)997-5070. **Ed** Gershon J Spector. bk rev. adv acc. **Circ** 8,000. Clinical and research contributions in otolaryngology, head and neck medicine and surgery.

MINERVA OTORINOLARINGOLOGICA *CEASED.* V. 1-30. 0026-4938. Italian. ir. **Ind/Abst** Excerpta Med. **NLM** W1 MI651.

MONOGRAPHS IN CONTEMPORARY AUDIOLOGY. Began with: Vol. 1, No. 1, published 1978. Periodical. US. English. qt. $6.00. **NLM** W1.

NEBRASKA HEALTH MANPOWER REPORTS, AUDIOLOGISTS. *See* Economics - Labor.

NUOVO ARCHIVIO ITALIANO DI OTOLOGIA, RINOLOGIA E LARINGOLOGIA. *See* Genealogy and Heraldry - Archives.

OPHTHALMOLOGICA ET OTO-RHINO-LARYNGOLOGICA. *See* Medicine - Ophthalmology.

O.R.L. & ALLERGY DIGEST. **VAT** Otorhinolaryngology and Allergy Digest. V. 41, No. 8/ 9- Aug./Sept. 1979-. 0198-7038. Periodical. US. English. mo. $27.50. O.R.L. & Allergy Digest, 445 Central Avenue, Northfield IL 60093. **NLM** W1 O532. Available on microfilm from University Microfilms. *Journal of Continuing Education in O.R.L. & Allergy, 0148-5180.*

O.R.L. JOURNAL FOR OTO-RHINO-LARYNGOLOGY AND ITS BORDERLANDS. (ORL). V. 34- 1972-. 0301-1569. Periodical. English. bm. 274.-. S Karger AG, PO Box, CH-4009, Basel Switzerland. **Tel** (061)39 08 80. **Ed** W Arnold. **Ind/Abst** Excerpta Med., Index Med., Life Sci. Collect., Chem. Abstr., Biol. Abstr., Sci. Cit. Index, Abr. Ed., Lang. Lang. Behav. Abstr., Sociol. Abstr. **NLM** W1 O524. **CODEN** ORLJAH. adv acc. Covers new knowledge on the anatomy, pathology, pathophysiology and immunology of the auditory and vestibular system and of the upper respiratory and digestive tract. *Practica Oto-Rhino-Laryngologica.*

OTO REVIEW. V. 1- 1966-. 0197-0674. Periodical. US. English. qt. Ear Research Institute, 256 South Lake Street, Los Angeles CA 90057. **NLM** W1 OT483.

OTO-RINO-LARINGOLOGIA ITALIANA. 0030-6630. Periodical. Italian (some summaries in French and English). ir.

OTO-RINO-LARINGOLOGIJA. (OTO-RINO-LARINGOLOGIIA). 1- 1964-. 0473-5609. Periodical. BU. Bulgarian. ty. Hemus, 6 Blvd Rusky, Sofia Bulgaria. **Ind/Abst** Excerpta Med. **NLM** W1 OT72.

OTOLARYNGOLOGIC CLINICS OF NORTH AMERICA. (THE OTOLARYNGOLOGIC CLINICS OF NORTH AMERICA). V. 1- June 1968-. 0030-6665. Monographic Series. US. English. qt. $60.00. WB

Saunders, West Washington Square, Philadelphia PA 19105. Tel (215)574-3395. Ed Lisa McAllister. Ind/Abst Life Sci. Collect., Excerpta Med., Index Med., Biol. Abstr., Energy Res. Abstr., Sci. Cit. Index, Abr. Ed. LC RF1. DD 616.21005. NLM W1 OT518. CODEN OCNAB. Circ 4,600. Practical clinical updates on topics of current interest written by experts in the field.

OTOLARYNGOLOGY AND HEAD AND NECK SURGERY. (OTOLARYNGOLOGY— HEAD AND NECK SURGERY : OFFICIAL JOURNAL OF AMERICAN ACADEMY OF OTOLARYNGOLOGY—HEAD AND NECK SURGERY). Vol. 89, No. 1 (Jan.-Feb. 1981)-. 0194-5998. Periodical. US. English. bm. $111.00. C V Mosby, c/o R K Kinnes, 11830 Westline Industrial Drive, St Louis MO 63146. Tel (314)872-8370. Ed Bruce Pearson. Ind/Abst Excerpta Med., Life Sci. Collect., Index Med., Biol. Abstr. NLM W1. adv acc. Circ 8,291. Serves the clinical and continuing education needs of specialists in otolaryngology-head and neck surgery. Otolaryngology and Head and Neck Surgery, 0194-5998.

PROGRESS REPORT - EAR RESEARCH INSTITUTE. Main/Corp Ear Research Institute. 0197-3657. US. English. an. Ear Research Institute, 256 South Lake Street, Los Angeles CA 90057. NLM W1 EA68. Progress Report - Los Angeles Foundation of Otology.

RECENT ADVANCES IN OTORHINOLARYNGOLOGY. 1st- Ed. 0143-6813. UK. English. ir. Churchill Livingstone Inc, 1560 Broadway, New York NY 10036. Tel (212)819-5400. Ed J Ransome. NLM W100 R212R.

RESEARCH BULLETIN - HOUSE EAR INSTITUTE. (RESEARCH BULLETIN). Began with: Vol. 1, No. 1 (Fall 1982). 0740-7599. Periodical. US. English. sa. $35.00. Research Bulletin c/o Fred H Linthicum Jr MD House Ear Institute, 256 South Lake Street, Los Angeles CA 90057. NLM W1 RE2157R.

REVISTA ORL. VFOAT Revista O.R.L. VAT Revista Otorhinolaringologia. V. 1, No. 1, (June 1982)-. Periodical. AG. Spanish. qt. $30.00. Fundacion de Ottorinolaringoli Parana, 759 Piso 1, 1017 Buenos Aires Argentina. Ed L C Barbon, I E Lazaro and S L Montes. NLM W1 RE711F. bk rev. adv acc. Circ 1,800. (ctrl). Concerns the diagnosis, treatment and surgery of otorhinolaryngologic diseases.

REVUE DE LARYNGOLOGIE, D'OTOLOGIE ET DE RHINOLOGIE. Vol. 36, No. 32/33- Aug. 15, 1915-. 0035-1334. Periodical. French. ir. Revue de Laryngologie, 114 Avenue d'Ares, 33074 Bordeaux Cedex France. Tel (56) 24.30.15. Ind/Abst Lang. Lang. Behav. Abstr., Index Med., Sociol. Abstr. NLM W1 RE783. bk rev. adv acc. Circ 2,200. Review founded in 1880 by E J Moure, published by Professor Michel Portmann, MD. Five issues per year and sometimes a supplementum about a particular subject.

RHINOLOGY. V. 8- 1970-. 0300-0729. Periodical. NE. English. qt. $41.33. Rhinology, University Hospital Utrecht, PO Box 16250, 3500 CG Utrecht Netherlands. Tel (206)259-1515. Ed E H Huizing. Ind/Abst Excerpta Med., Index Med., Biol. Abstr. NLM W1 RH43. CODEN RNGYA8. bk rev. adv acc. Circ 1,000. (ctrl). Physiology, diagnostics, pathology, medical therapy and surgery of the nose and paranasal sinuses, including allergology. International Rhinology, 0300-0737.

SCANDINAVIAN AUDIOLOGY. 0105-0397. English. qt. $60.00. Almqvist & Wiksell, 108 Drottninggatan, PO Box 45150, S-104 30 Stockholm Sweden. Tel 85413160. Ind/Abst Life Sci. Collect., Excerpta Med., Lang. Lang. Behav. Abstr., Index Med., Biol. Abstr., Comput. Control Abstr., Electr. Electron. Abstr., Sci. Abstr. Sect. A. Phys. Abstr., Psychol. Abstr., Sociol. Abstr., Sci. Cit. Index, Abr. Ed., Phys. Abstr. LC RF1. DD 617.8905. NLM W1 SC146A. CODEN SNADAS.

SEMINARS IN HEARING. Vol. 4, No. 1 (Feb. 1983)-. 0734-0451. Periodical. US. English. qt. $48.00. Thieme Inc, 381 Park Avenue South, New York NY 10016. Tel (212)683-5088. Ed Jerry L Northern and William H Perkins. NLM W1. adv acc. Circ 1,300. Topic oriented journal for the practitioner specializing in technical advances in audiology and otology. Seminars, Speech, Language, Hearing, 0196-108X.

TRANSACTIONS. Main/Corp American Laryngological, Rhinological and Otological Society. 0065-9037. US. English. an. Dr J H Ogura, American Laryngological Rhinological and Otological Society, 9126 Clayton Road, St Louis MO 63124. Tel (314)997-5070.

TRANSACTIONS OF THE AMERICAN OTOLOGICAL SOCIETY. Main/Corp American Otological Society. 0096-6851. US. English. an. $35.00. American Otological Society, 151 North Michigan Avenue, Chicago IL 60601. Tel (312)938-4327. Ed J D Clemis. Ind/Abst Chem. Abstr. LC RF1. NLM W1 TR2248. CODEN TAOTAW. Circ 350. Scientific papers dealing with the ear including business activities of the American otological society.

TRANSACTIONS OF THE ANNUAL MEETING OF THE AMERICAN LARYNGOLOGICAL ASSOCIATION. Main/Corp American Laryngological Association. VFOAT Transactions - American Laryngological Association. 1st- 1879-. 0065-9037. US. English. an. $35.00. American Laryngological Association, 3400 Spruce Street, c/o James B Snow Jr, Philadelphia PA 19104. Tel (215)662-2653. Ed James B Snow Jr. NLM W1 AM535. Index in last issue of volume - attached. (cum index). Circ 200. (ctrl). Scientific articles and business of the annual meeting of the American Laryngological Association.

TRANSACTIONS - PENNSYLVANIA ACADEMY OF OPHTHALMOLOGY AND OTOLARYNGOLOGY. Main/Corp Pennsylvania Academy of Ophthalmology and Otolaryngology. 0048-3206. US. English. sa. $15.00. Transactions of the Pennsylvania Academy of Ophthalmology & Otolaryngology, PO Box 1325, Reading PA 19603. Tel (215)375-4311. Ed Thomas Souders. Ind/Abst Excerpta Med., Index Med., Energy Res. Abstr., Hospit. Lit. Index. NLM W1 TR228A. CODEN TPOOA. bk rev. adv acc. Circ 1,000. (ctrl). Medical journal of the Pennsylvania Academy of Ophthalmology and Otolaryngology.

VESTNIK OTORINOLARINGOLOGII. V. 1- 1936-. 0042-4668. Periodical. UR. Russian. bm. $20.50. Victor Kamkin Inc (70121), 12224 Parklawn Drive, Rockville MD 20852. Tel (301)881-5973. Ind/Abst Excerpta Med., Index Med., Biol. Abstr., Int. Aerosp. Abstr. NLM W1 VE843. CODEN VORLA7. Vestnik Sovetskoi Otorinolaringologii.

THE YEAR BOOK OF OTOLARYNGOLOGY. See Yearbooks, Almanacs, Directories.

ZURNAL USNYH, NOSOVYH I GORLOVYH BOLEZNEJ. (ZHURNAL USHNYKH, NOSOVYKH I GORLOVYKH BOLEZNEI). VFOAT Journal of Otology, Rhinology, and Laryngology. V. 1- 1924-. 0044-4650. Periodical. UR. Russian. bm. $25.00. Victor Kamkin Inc (74184), 12224 Parklawn Drive, Rockville MD 20852. Tel (301)881-5973. Ind/Abst Life Sci. Collect., Excerpta Med., Int. Aerosp. Abstr., Chem. Abstr. NLM W1 ZH424. CODEN ZUNBA9.

PATHOLOGY

ABMS DIRECTORY OF CERTIFIED PATHOLOGISTS. See Yearbooks, Almanacs, Directories.

ACTA HAEMATOLOGICA. V. 1- 1948-. 0001-5792. Periodical. SZ. English (articles in French, or German with summaries in all three languages). mo. 294.00. S Karger AG, PO Box 352, White Plains NY 10602. Tel (061)39 08 80. Ed E A Beck, R S Hillman and H R Marti. Ind/Abst Life Sci. Collect., Excerpta Med., Index Med., Biol. Abstr., Curr. Contents, Chem. Abstr., Sci. Cit. Index, Abr. Ed. NLM W1 AC807. CODEN ACHAAH. (cum index). bk rev. adv acc. Concise reports summarizing the current status of international hematology research. Offers clinical researches and clinicians information on such diseases as anemia, leukemia, lymphoma, multiple myeloma and hereditary disorders.

ACTA NEUROPATHOLOGICA. V. 1- May 1961-. 0001-6322. articles and summaries in English, French or German. mo. $488.00. Springer Verlag-New York Inc, 175 5th Avenue, New York NY 10010. Tel (212)460-1500. Ed K Jellinger and F Seitelberger. Ind/Abst Life Sci. Collect., Excerpta Med., Index Med., Int. Aerosp. Abstr., Biol. Abstr., Chem. Abstr., Nuci. Sci. Abstr., Energy Res. Abstr., Sci. Cit. Index, Abr. Ed. NLM W1 AC872N. CODEN ANPTAL. bk rev. Information on subjects related to nerve-tissue research based on modern investigative techniques, including histochemistry, electron microscopy, immunology, tissue culture, biophysics, neurochemistry, and experimental neuropathology.

ACTA NEUROPATHOLOGICA. SUPPLEMENTUM. (ACTA NEUROPATHOLOGICA : SUPPLEMENTUM). 1962-. 0065-1435. English (articles also in German). ir.

Springer Verlag-New York Inc, 175 5th Avenue, New York NY 10010. Tel (212)460-1500. Ed K Jellinger and F Seitelberger. Ind/Abst Life Sci. Collect., Index Med., Biol. Abstr., Chem. Abstr. LC UNC. NLM W1 AC872NA. CODEN ANLSBX. adv acc. Nerve-tissue research, experimental and clinical.

ACTA PATHOLOGICA JAPONICA. V. 1- 1951-. 0001-6632. Periodical. JA. English (text in French or German). bm. Kyowa Book Company Inc, 1-38 Kanda Jinbo-Cho/Chiyoda-Ku, Tokyo 101 Japan. Tel 293-0727. Ind/Abst Life Sci. Collect., Excerpta Med., Index Med., Biol. Abstr., Chem. Abstr., Sci. Cit. Index, Abr. Ed. NLM W1 AC9126. CODEN APJAAG.

ACTA PATHOLOGICA, MICROBIOLOGICA ET IMMUNOLOGICA SCANDINAVICA. SECTION A. PATHOLOGY. (ACTA PATHOLOGICA, MICROBIOLOGICA ET IMMUNOLOGICA SCANDINAVICA. SECTION A, PATHOLOGY). VFOAT Pathology. Vol. 90 A, Issue 1 (Jan. 1982)-. 0108-0164. Periodical. DK. English (French or German). bm. 1,834.00 Domestic, $204.00 US. Munksgaard International Publishers Limited, 35 Norre Sogade, DK-1370.Copenhagen K Denmark. Tel 45 12 70 30. Ed Jorgen Rygaard. Ind/Abst Pestdoc, Ringdoc, Vetdoc, Life Sci. Collect., Excerpta Med., Index Med., Biol. Abstr., Chem. Abstr., Energy Res. Abstr. NLM W1 AC913. CODEN ACPADQ. Circ 1,200. Acta Pathologica et Microbiologica Scandinavica. Section A, Pathology, 0365-4184.

ACTA PATHOLOGICA, MICROBIOLOGICA, ET IMMUNOLOGICA SCANDINAVICA. SUPPLEMENT. No. 278-. 0108-0172. Monographic Series. English. ir. Ind/Abst Energy Res. Abstr., Biol. Abstr., Life Sci. Collect., Excerpta Med., Index Med., Chem. Abstr. NLM W1 AC913H. CODEN AMCSEI. Acta Pathologica et Microbiologica Scandinavica. Supplement.

ACTA PATHOLOGOCA ET MICROBIOLOGICA SCANDINAVICA. SECTION A. PATHOLOGY CEASED. (ACTA PATHOLOGICA ET MICROBIOLOGICA SCANDINAVICA. SECTION A : PATHOLOGY). V. 78A-89A. 0365-4184. Periodical. articles in Danish and English. bm. Munksgaard Ltd, 35 Norre Sogade, DK 1370 K Copenhagen Denmark. Ind/Abst Excerpta Med., Life Sci. Collect., Nuci. Sci. Abstr., Biol. Abstr., Chem. Abstr., Index Med., Bibliogr. Agric. NLM W1 AC9111B. CODEN AMBPBZ. Acta Pathologica et Microbiologica Scandinavica, 0365-5555.

ADVANCES IN HOST DEFENSE MECHANISMS. Vol. 1-. 0732-0566. Monographic Series. US. English. Raven Press, 1140 Avenue Of the Americas, New York NY 10036. Ind/Abst Life Sci. Collect., Biol. Abstr., Chem. Abstr. LC UNC. DD 616.079. NLM W1 AD636. CODEN AHDMD3.

ADVANCES IN PATHOBIOLOGY. 1-. 0099-1147. Monographic Series. US. English. ir. Thieme-Stratton, 381 Park Avenue South, New York NY 10016. Tel (212)683-5088. Ed C Fenoglio, C Borek, and D W King. Ind/Abst Energy Res. Abstr., Index Med. NLM W1 AD716.

ADVANCES IN THE BIOLOGY OF DISEASE. Vol. 1-. 0743-5592. US. English. an. $35.00. Williams & Wilkins, 428 East Preston Street, Baltimore MD 21202. Ed Emanuel Rubin, Ivan Damjanov. DD 616. NLM W1.

AKTUELLE PROBLEME DER NEUROPATHOLOGIE. (AKTUELLE PROBLEME DER NEUROPATHOLOGIE : AUSGEWAHLTE BEITRAGE). Main/Corp Osterreichische Arbeitsgemeinschaft fur Neuropathologie. Jahrestagung. Series/Titl Facultas-Texte fur Neuropathologie. V. 3 (28. Apr. 1976)-. 0253-5297. German (some articles in English). ir. Ed K Jellinger and H Gross. Ind/Abst Chem. Abstr. NLM W1. CODEN APRNDU. Aktuelle Probleme der Neuropathologie.

AMERICAN JOURNAL OF CLINICAL PATHOLOGY. V. 1- Jan. 1931-. 0002-9173. Periodical. US. English (summaries interlingual Jan. 1956-). mo. $75.00. J B Lippincott Company, East Washington Square, Philadelphia PA 19105. Tel (215)238-4273. Ed Myrton F Beeler. Ind/Abst Life Sci. Collect., Pestdoc, Ringdoc, Vetdoc, Excerpta Med., Index Med., Biol. Abstr., Chem. Abstr., Energy Res. Abstr., Sci. Cit. Index, Abr. Ed., Hospit. Lit. Index. LC RB. DD 616.05. NLM W1 AM45L. CODEN AJCPAI. bk rev. adv acc. Circ 15,200. Available on microfilm.

Medicine—Pathology

Latest reports on original studies and observations in clinical and anatomic pathology; also articles on laboratory use, management, and information.

THE AMERICAN JOURNAL OF FORENSIC MEDICINE AND PATHOLOGY. See Medicine - Forensic Medicine, Medical Jurisprudence.

THE AMERICAN JOURNAL OF PATHOLOGY. V. 1- (No. 1-). 0002-9440. Periodical. US. English. mo. $175.00. American Association of Pathologists and Bacteriologists, 2350 Virginia Avenue, Hagerstown MD 21740. Tel (215)238-4273. Ed Vincent T Marchesi. Ind/Abst Pestdoc, Ringdoc, Vetdoc, Excerpta Med., Life Sci. Collect., Energy Inf. Abstr., Environ. Abstr., Index Med., Biol. Abstr., Chem. Abstr., Energy Res. Abstr., Sci. Cit. Index, Abr. Ed., Hospit. Lit. Index. LC RB1. DD 616.0705. NLM W1 AM498. CODEN AJPAA4. (cum index). adv acc. Circ 5,103. Original experimental and non-experimental studies in histopathology and microbiology with emphasis on microscopic and biochemical observations. *Journal of Medical Research, 0097-3599.*

ANATOMICA, PATHOLOGICA, MICROBIOLOGICA. Series/Titi Acta Universitatis Ouluensis: Series D, Medica. No. 1-. 0358-4895. Fi. English (Finnish). ir. Prof Sakari Piha, University of Oulu, 90100 Oulu 10 Finland. Tel 358-81-332133. Ed Leo Hirvonen. NLM W1 AC954NM. adv acc. Circ 500. (ctrl). Monographs, reviews and dissertations in the fields of normal and pathological anatomy and microbiology.

ANNALES D'ANATOMIE PATHOLOGIQUE CEASED. V. 1-25. 0003-3871. Periodical. French. qt. Ind/Abst Excerpta Med., Biol. Abstr., Chem. Abstr., Nuci. Sci. Abstr., Index Med. NLM W1 AN315. CODEN ANAPA2. *Annales d'Anatomie Pathologique et d'Anatomie Normale Medico-Chirurgicale, 0365-0367.*

ANNALES DE BIOLOGIE CLINIQUE. Began in 1943. 0003-3898. Periodical. FR. French (summaries in English). bm. $99.78. Expansion Scientifique Francaise, 15 rue Saint-Benoit, 75278 Paris Cedex 06 France. Tel 548-42-60. Ind/Abst Life Sci. Collect., Excerpta Med., CIS Abstr., Biol. Abstr., Chem. Abstr., Nuci. Sci. Abstr., Index Med., Energy Res. Abstr., Sci. Cit. Index, Abr. Ed. LC RB1. DD 616.0705. NLM W1 AN327B. CODEN ABCLAI.

ANNALES DE PATHOLOGIE. Vol. 1, No. 1-. 0242-6498. Periodical. French (summaries in English). bm. $128.00. Masson Publishing USA Inc, 211 East 43rd Street/Room 1306, New York NY 10017. Tel (212)370-1937. Ind/Abst Life Sci. Collect., Excerpta Med., Index Med., Biol. Abstr., Chem. Abstr. NLM W1 AN374C. CODEN ASPAD2. *Annales d'Anatomie Pathologique, 0003-3871.*

ANNALS OF CLINICAL & LABORATORY SCIENCE. (ANNALS OF CLINICAL AND LABORATORY SCIENCE). V. 3, No. 3- May/June 1973-. 0091-7370. Periodical. US. English. bm. $45.00. Association of Clinical Scientists, 230 North Broad, Philadelphia PA 19102. Tel (215)568-6866. Ed J William Snuderman. Ind/Abst Life Sci. Collect., Excerpta Med., Chem. Abstr., Biol. Abstr., Index Med., Energy Res. Abstr., Sci. Cit. Index, Abr. Ed. LC RB37.A1. DD 616.0705. NLM W1 AN57K. CODEN ACLSCP. bk rev. adv acc. Circ 2,000. (ctrl). Research in clinical studies; critical reviews of subjects in clinical pathology, clinical chemistry, physiology, etc. *Annals of Clinical Laboratory Science, 0095-8905.*

ANNUAL RESEARCH PROGRESS REPORT - ARMED FORCES INSTITUTE OF PATHOLOGY. VFOAT Annual Research Progress Report for U.S. Army Medical Research and Development Command. 1965/66-. 0190-0641. Periodical. US. English. an. NLM W1 AN769HK. *Annual Progress Report - Armed Forces Institute of Pathology, 0190-2520.*

APPLIED PATHOLOGY. 1/1/83 (Jan.-Feb. 1983)-. 0252-1172. Periodical. English. qt. 234.-. S Karger AG, PO Box, CH-4009 Basel Switzerland. Tel (061)39 08 80. Ed A Ascenzi. Ind/Abst Life Sci. Collect., Excerpta Med., Index Med. NLM W1 AP528KR. CODEN APTHDM. adv acc. Aimed at improving the exchange of interdisciplinary information among pathologists, clinicians and basic researchers. Defines the role of pathology in modern medicine and its contribution to the understanding of disease mechanisms.

ARCHIVES D'ANATOMIE ET DE CYTOLOGIE PATHOLOGIQUES. See Genealogy and Heraldry - Archives.

ARCHIVES OF PATHOLOGY & LABORATORY MEDICINE. See Genealogy and Heraldry - Archives.

ARCHIVES ROUMAINES DE PATHOLOGIE EXPERIMENTALE ET DE MICROBIOLOGIE. See Genealogy and Heraldry - Archives.

ARCHIVIO DE VECCHI PER L'ANATOMIA PATOLOGICA E LA MEDICINA CLINICA. See Genealogy and Heraldry - Archives.

ARCHIVIO E MARAGLIANO DI PATOLOGIA E CLINICA. See Genealogy and Heraldry - Archives.

ARCHIVIO ITALIANO DI PATOLOGIA E CLINICA DEI TUMORI. See Genealogy and Heraldry - Archives.

ARQUIVO DE PATOLOGIA. (ARQUIVIO DE PATOLOGIA). 0004-2714. PO. Portuguese. ir. Inst Portuges de Oncologia de Francisco, Gentil Palhava, Lisbon Portugal. Ind/Abst Excerpta Med., Biol. Abstr., Chem. Abstr., Index Med., Nuci. Sci. Abstr. NLM W1 AR864. CODEN APALA4.

AUSTRALASIAN PLANT PATHOLOGY. VFOAT APP, Australasian Plant Pathology. V. 7, No. 2- June 1978-. 0156-0972. Periodical. AT. English. qt. Australasian Plant Pathology, Department of Agriculture, GPO Box 1671, Adelaide SA 5001 Australia. Tel 08 227 9911. Ed E C Marks. Ind/Abst Life Sci. Collect. Index in last issue of volume - attached. bk rev. adv acc. Circ 600. Research notes on plant pathology in Australasia including studies on disease control and descriptions of new diseases. *AAPS Newsletter, 0310-1266.*

BERICHTE PATHOLOGIE. V. 97, No. 1-. 0722-9674. Periodical. German (text also in English). ir. Springer-Verlag New York Inc, 175 Fifth Avenue, New York NY 10010. NLM ZQZ 4 B511. *Berichte Uber die Allgemeine Und Spezielle Pathologie.*

BIOLOGICAL TRACE ELEMENT RESEARCH. See Biology - Biochemistry.

BIOSIS/CAS SELECTS. LEUKOTRIENES & SLOW-REACTANTS SUBSTANCES. See Indexes/Abstracts.

BIOSIS/CAS SELECTS. LYMPHOKINES. See Biology - Biochemistry.

BRITISH JOURNAL OF EXPERIMENTAL PATHOLOGY. (THE BRITISH JOURNAL OF EXPERIMENTAL PATHOLOGY). VFOAT Experimental Pathology. V. 1- 1920-. 0007-1021. Periodical. UK. English. bm. 70.00 Domestic, $156.00 Foreign. Blackwell Scientific Publishing Ltd, PO Box 88, Osney Mead, Oxford OX2 0EL England. Tel (0865)240201. Ed R Marian Hicks. Ind/Abst Life Sci. Collect., Pestdoc, Ringdoc, Vetdoc, Excerpta Med., CIS Abstr., Biol. Abstr., Chem. Abstr., Nuci. Sci. Abstr., Index Med., Bibliogr. Agric., Sci. Cit. Index, Abr. Ed. LC RB1. DD 616.0705. NLM W1 BR529. CODEN BJEPA5. adv acc. Circ 1,050. Publishes original research into the bio-genesis and progression of pathological processes which afford new insights into the basic mechanisms underlying human disease.

BULLETIN - COLLEGE OF AMERICAN PATHOLOGISTS. V. 8-22. 0098-4450. Periodical. US. English. mo. Bulletin of the College of American Pathologists, 550 Munson, Traverse City MI 49684. NLM W1 BU491P. *Secretary's News Letter.*

BULLETIN DE LA SOCIETE DE PATHOLOGIE EXOTIQUE. (BULLETIN DE LA SOCIETE DE PATHOLOGIE EXOTIQUE ET DE SES FILIALES). V. 30, No. 7 (1937)-. 0037-9085. Periodical. French. ir. Masson Publishing USA Inc, 211 East 43rd Street/Room 1306, New York NY 10017. Tel (212)370-1937. Ind/Abst Excerpta Med., Index Med., Life Sci. Collect., Bibliogr. Agric. NLM W1 BU511P. *Bulletin de la Societe de Pathologie Exotique et Sa Filiale de l'Ouest-Africain.*

CATALOG OF CELL LINES. 1982-. 0737-7983. US. English. National Institute of Health, Bethesda MD 20014. LC RB155. DD 616.042. NLM QS 26 H918. *Human Genetic Mutant Cell Repository, 0148-835X.*

CESKOSLOVENSKE PATOLOGIE. (CESKOSLOVENSKA PATOLOGIE). Vol. 1- 1965-. 0009-0611. Periodical. CS. Czech (summaries in English and Russian). qt. Artia, Ve Smeckach 30, PO Box 790, Praha 1 Czechoslovakia. Ind/Abst Excerpta Med., Index Med., Chem. Abstr. NLM W1 CE902G. CODEN CPSLAE.

CHUNG-HUA PING LI HSUEH TSA CHIH. VFOAT Chinese Journal of Pathology, Zhonghua Binglixue Zazhi. 1955-. 0529-5807. Periodical. CC. Chinese (table of contents and some abstracts also in English). qt. $15.30. China Publication Centre, PO Box 2820, Beijing China. DD 616. NLM W1 CH984H.

CLINICAL INSTRUMENT SYSTEMS. (CLINICAL INSTRUMENT SYSTEMS : CIS). VFOAT CIS. Began with: V. 1, No. 1 (Aug. 1980). 0730-7578. Periodical. US. English. mo. $125.00. Macon Publishing Company, 116 West 32nd Street, 8th Floor, New York NY 10001. Tel (212)736-6688. Ed Nelson Alpert. NLM W1 CL715N. Circ 400. A technical information resource providing laboratory personnel and pathologists with in-depth information on a wide variety of instrumentation in fields of clinical chemistry, RIA, hematology, microbiology and blood banking.

CLINICAL LAB GUIDE. 1973/74-. 0091-472X. US. English. $5.00. American Chemical Society, 1155 Sixteenth Street NW, Washington DC 20036. LC RB36.2. DD 338.47616075028.

CLINICAL LAB LETTER. V. 1- Jan. 1, 1980-. 0197-8454. Periodical. US. English. sm. $120.00. Quest Publishing, 1351 Titan Way, Brea CA 92621. Tel (714)738-6400. Ed Allan F Pacela and Bill Bayless. NLM W1 CL726. Index available. bk rev. Written for hospital clinical laboratory personnel.

CLINICAL LABORATORY ANNUAL. Vol. 1 (1982)-. 0278-5870. US. English. an. $71.20. Appleton Century Crofts, 25 Van Zant Street, East Norwalk CT 06855. Ind/Abst Chem. Abstr. LC RB37.A1. DD 616.075. NLM W1 CL726D. CODEN CLAAD2.

CLINICAL NEUROPATHOLOGY. Vol. 1, No. 1 (1st Quarter, 1982)-. 0722-5091. Periodical. GW. English. ir. $65.00. Dustri-Verlag, Dr Karl Feistle, Bahnhofstrasse 5, Postfach 49, D-8024 Munchen Deisenhofen West Germany. Ind/Abst Excerpta Med., Index Med. NLM W1 CL731S. Also available on microfiche.

CLINICAL PATHOLOGY SEMINAR. 1- 1970-. Periodical. US. English. 2100 West Harrison Street, Chicago IL 606012.

COMPARATIVE PATHOBIOLOGY. V. 1-. 0161-6935. Monographic Series. US. English. ir. Plenum Press, Attn H Feldman, 233 Spring Street, New York NY 10013. Tel (212)620-8000. Ind/Abst Chem. Abstr. CODEN CPATDJ.

COMPARATIVE PATHOLOGY BULLETIN. V. 1- Nov. 1969-. Periodical. US. English. qt. $4.00. URAEP-Registry of Comparative Pathology, Armed Forces Institute of Pathology, Washington DC 20306. Tel (202)576-2452.

CONTEMPORARY TOPICS IN IMMUNOBIOLOGY. V. 1- 1972-. 0093-4054. US. English. ir. Plenum Press, Attn: H Feldman, 233 Spring Street, New York NY 10013. Tel (212)620-8000. Ind/Abst Life Sci. Collect., Index Med., Chem. Abstr., Bibliogr. Agric., Energy Res. Abstr., Sci. Cit. Index, Abr. Ed. LC QR180. DD 574.2905. NLM W1 CO77. CODEN CTIBBV.

CPT; PHYSICIANS' CURRENT PROCEDURAL TERMINOLOGY. VFOAT Physicians' Current Procedural Terminology. 1st- Ed. US. English. $2.00. American Medical Association, 535 North Dearborn Street, Chicago IL 60610. LC RB115. DD 616.0014.

CURRENT TOPICS IN HEMATOLOGY. V. 1-. 0190-1486. Periodical. US. English. Alan R Liss Inc, 41 East 11th Street, New York NY 10003. Tel (212)475-7700. Ed Sergio Piomelli and Stanley Yachnin. Ind/Abst Index Med., Chem. Abstr. LC RB145. DD 616.15005. NLM W1 CU82HN. CODEN CTHED3. A book series dealing with the blood and blood-forming organs.

CURRENT TOPICS IN PATHOLOGY. VFOAT Ergebnisse der Pathologie. V. 51- 1970-. 0070-2188. GW. English. ir. Springer Verlag-New York Inc, 175-5th Avenue, New York NY 10010. Tel (212)460-1584. Ind/Abst Life Sci. Collect., Chem. Abstr., Index Med., Nuci. Sci. Abstr. NLM W1 CU821H. CODEN CTPHBG. Topics include bone and joint disorders, drug-induced pathology, pulmonary diseases, and dermatopathology. *Ergebnisse der Allgemeinen Pathologie und Pathologischen Anatomie.*

DIRECTORY - CANADIAN ASSOCIATION OF PATHOLOGISTS. See Yearbooks, Almanacs, Directories.

Medicine—Pathology

DIRECTORY - LOUISIANA STATE BOARD OF EXAMINERS FOR SPEECH PATHOLOGY AND AUDIOLOGY. See Yearbooks, Almanacs, Directories.

DIRECTORY OF CLINICAL LABORATORIES, CLINICAL LABORATORY PERSONNEL. See Yearbooks, Almanacs, Directories.

DIRECTORY OF PATHOLOGY TRAINING PROGRAMS. See Yearbooks, Almanacs, Directories.

EXCERPTA MEDICA. SECTION 5. GENERAL PATHOLOGY AND PATHOLOGICAL ANATOMY. See Indexes/Abstracts.

EXPERIMENTAL AND MOLECULAR PATHOLOGY. V. 1- Feb. 1962-. 0014-4800. Periodical. US. English. bm. Academic Press, 4805 Sand Lake Road, Orlando FL 32819. Ind/Abst Life Sci. Collect., Excerpta Med., Chem. Abstr., Biol. Abstr., Nucl. Sci. Abstr., Bibliogr. Agric., Index Med., Energy Res. Abstr. LC RB1. DD 616.0705. NLM W1 EX47. CODEN EXMPA6.

EXPERIMENTAL PATHOLOGY. Vol. 19, No. 1-. 0232-1513. Periodical. English. ir. $141.89. Elsevier Scientific Publ of Ireland, PO Box 85, Limerick Ireland. Ind/Abst Life Sci. Collect., Excerpta Med., Index Med., Biol. Abstr., Chem. Abstr. NLM W1 EX511T. CODEN EXPADD. Experimentelle Pathologie.

EXPERIMENTELLE PATHOLOGIE. SUPPLEMENT. VFOAT Experimental Pathology. Supplement. 1-. 0323-6102. Monographic Series. GE. English. ir. Ind/Abst Life Sci. Collect., Index Med. LC UNC. DD 616.07. NLM W1 EX511TA.

FOLIA HEREDITARIA ET PATHOLOGICA. 0015-5578. Periodical. IT. Italian. qt. $18.00. Inst di Anatomie Istologia, Via Francesco Sforza 38, Milano Italy. Tel 02-8135366. Ind/Abst Excerpta Med., Life Sci. Collect. NLM W1 FO181. bk rev. adv acc. Circ 50. (ctrl). Congenital, malformations, hereditary diseases.

HANDBOOK OF INFLAMMATION. V. 1-. 0167-5567. Monographic Series. US. English. ir. Elsevier Science Publishing Co Inc, PO Box 1663/Grand Central Station, New York NY 10163. Ed L E Glynn, J C Houck and G Weissmann. LC RB131. NLM W1 HA51PS.

HERMATOLOGIC PATHOLOGY. 0886-0238. Periodical. US. English. qt. Marcel Dekker Journals, PO Box 11305/Church Street Station, New York NY 10249.

HISTOPATHOLOGY. V. 1-. 0309-0167. Periodical. UK. English. bm. $197.50. Blackwell Scientific Publishing Ltd, PO Box 88, Oxford OX2 0EL England. Tel 0865-240201. Ed R N M MacSween. Ind/Abst Excerpta Med., Index Med., Life Sci. Collect., Biol. Abstr. NLM W1 HI774. CODEN HISTDD. bk rev. adv acc. Circ 2,100. Original histopathological material with clinical application to human disease of practical importance to diagnostic histopathologists and workers in clinicopathological research.

HUMAN PATHOLOGY; A CLINICOPATHOLOGIC QUARTERLY. V. 1- Mar. 1970-. 0046-8177. Periodical. US. English. mo. $75.00. W B Saunders, West Washington Square, Philadelphia PA 19105. Tel (215)574-3392. Ed Gail Corbett. Ind/Abst Life Sci. Collect., Excerpta Med., Coal Abstr., Energy Inf. Abstr., Environ. Abstr., Index Med., Biol. Abstr., Chem. Abstr., Energy Res. Abstr., Sci. Cit. Index, Abr. Ed., Hospit. Lit. Index. NLM W1 HU46K. CODEN HPCQA4. bk rev. adv acc. Circ 9,000. Articles are drawn from morphologic and clinical laboratory studies relevant to the understanding of disease in man - including theoretical and experimental pathology and molecular biology.

IMMUNOLOGICAL PARAMETERS OF HOST-TUMOR RELATIONSHIPS. US. English. ir. Academic Press, 4805 Sand Lake Road, Orlando FL 32887. Tel (305)345-4100.

INDIAN JOURNAL OF PATHOLOGY & MICROBIOLOGY. V. 18, No. 2- Apr. 1975-. 0377-4929. Periodical. II. English. qt. 204. Indian Association of Pathologists & Microbiologists, J N Medical College, Belgaum 590 010 India. Ed S J Nagalotimath. Ind/Abst Life Sci. Collect., Excerpta Med., Index Med., Biol. Abstr., Hospit. Lit. Index. NLM W1 IN224H. CODEN IJPMDT. bk rev. adv acc. Circ 1,500. (ctrl). Covers diagnosis of diseases, laboratory diagnostic methods, cancer, experimental pathology, infectious diseases and blood disorders. Indian Journal of Pathology & Bacteriology, 0019-5448.

INTERNATIONAL JOURNAL OF GYNECOLOGICAL PATHOLOGY. (INTERNATIONAL JOURNAL OF GYNECOLOGICAL PATHOLOGY : OFFICIAL JOURNAL OF THE INTERNATIONAL SOCIETY OF GYNECOLOGICAL PATHOLOGISTS). Vol. 1, No. 1-. 0277-1691. Periodical. US. English. qt. Raven Press, 1140 Avenue of the Americas, New York City NY 10036. Tel (212)575-0335. Ind/Abst Excerpta Med., Index Med. NLM W1 IN766U.

INTERNATIONAL JOURNAL OF THE BREAST AND MAMMARY PATHOLOGY, SENOLOGIA (ENGLISH ED.). (THE INTERNATIONAL JOURNAL OF THE BREAST AND MAMMARY PATHOLOGY, SENOLOGIA). VFOAT Senologia, Journal Internatonal du Sein et de la Pathologie Mammaire, Senologia. Vol. 1, No. 1-. 0733-0847. Periodical. US. English. qt. Masson Publishing USA Inc, 211 East 43rd Street/Room 1306, New York NY 10017. Tel (212)370-1937.

INTERNATIONAL REVIEW OF EXPERIMENTAL PATHOLOGY. V. 1- 1962-. 0074-7718. US. English. ir. Academic Press, 4805 Sand Lake Road, Orlando FL 32887. Tel (305)345-4100. Ed J B Cragg. Ind/Abst Life Sci. Collect., Excerpta Med., Chem. Abstr., Biol. Abstr., Nucl. Sci. Abstr., Index Med., Energy Res. Abstr., Hospit. Lit. Index, Sci. Cit. Index, Abr. Ed. LC RB6. DD 616.07. NLM W1 IN832M. CODEN IRXPAT.

ISTOCITOPATOLOGIA. V. 1-. 0391-7452. Periodical. IT. Italian. qt. 50.00. Edi Ermes Srl, Via Timavo 12, Milano 20124 Italy. Tel 02/6073892. Ed Piero Canevini. Ind/Abst Excerpta Med. NLM W1 IS901. bk rev. adv acc. Circ 1,000. Publishes significative and rare cases in the field of pathological anatomy.

JOURNAL DE PSYCHOLOGIE NORMALE ET PATHOLOGIQUE. See Psychology.

THE JOURNAL OF CLINICAL LABORATORY AUTOMATION. Vol. 1, No. 1 (July/Aug. 1981)-. 0276-8860. Periodical. US. English. bm. $35.00 US and Canada, $42.00 Foreign. Appleton-Century-Crofts, 25 Van Zant Street, East Norwalk CT 06855. Ind/Abst Excerpta Med., Comput. Control Abstr., Electr. Electron. Abstr., Sci. Abstr. Sect. A. Phys. Abstr. LC RB37.A1. DD 616.07502854. NLM W1 JO588K. CODEN JOAUDO.

JOURNAL OF CLINICAL PATHOLOGY. V. 1- 1947-. 0021-9746. Periodical. UK. English. mo. $153.24. British Medical Journal, Tavistock Square, London WC1H 9JR England. Ind/Abst Life Sci. Collect., Pestdoc, Ringdoc, Vetdoc, Excerpta Med., Cumul. Index Nurs. Allied Health Lit., Biol. Abstr., CIS Abstr., Nucl. Sci. Abstr., Chem. Abstr., Index Med., Sci. Cit. Index, Abr. Ed., Hospit. Lit. Index. NLM W1 JO5896. CODEN JCPAAK.

JOURNAL OF CLINICAL PATHOLOGY. SUPPLEMENT. ROYAL COLLEGE OF PATHOLOGISTS SYMPOSIA. (JOURNAL OF CLINICAL PATHOLOGY. SUPPLEMENT (ROYAL COLLEGE OF PATHOLOGISTS)). VFOAT Journal of Clinical Pathology. 0144-0330. Monographic Series. UK. English. ir. British Medical Journal, Tavistock Square, London WC1H 9JH England. Ind/Abst Index Med. NLM W1 JO5896C.

JOURNAL OF COMPARATIVE PATHOLOGY. V. 75- Jan. 1965-. 0021-9975. Periodical. UK. English. qt. Academic Press, 4805 Sand Lake Road, Orlando FL 32819. Tel (305)345-4100. Ind/Abst Life Sci. Collect., Pestdoc, Ringdoc, Vetdoc, Excerpta Med., Biol. Abstr., Chem. Abstr., Nucl. Sci. Abstr., Index Med., Bibliogr. Agric., Sci. Cit. Index, Abr. Ed. NLM W1 JO595H. CODEN JCVPAR. Journal of Comparative Pathology and Therapeutics.

JOURNAL OF EXPERIMENTAL PATHOLOGY. Vol. 1, No. 1-. 0730-8485. Periodical. US. English. qt. $123.00. Mary Ann Liebert Inc, 157 East 86th Street, New York NY 10028. Tel (212)289-2300. Ind/Abst Life Sci. Collect. NLM W1 JO644R.

JOURNAL OF HEAD & NECK PATHOLOGY. VFOAT Journal of Head and Neck Pathology. Vol. 1, No. 1-. 0770-9471. Periodical. Dutch (articles in English or French). qt. 1,000 Belgium Institutions, 1,200 European Institutions, 1,500 Other Institutions. Centre Tete et Cou Hoofd en Hals Centrum, Av du Duc Jean 71-73, 1080 Bruxelles Belgium. Tel (02)428.80.00. Ed DI de Lathouwer. NLM W1. bk rev. adv acc. Circ 10,000. (ctrl). The aim is to elucidate all aspects of current knowledge concerning head and neck pathology. Moreover it plans to stimulate the mutual interest of all different disciplines involved directly or indirectly. Postgraduate Journal for Mouth, Head and Neck Pathology.

JOURNAL OF HUMAN STRESS. V. 1- Mar. 1975-. 0097-840X. Periodical. US. English. qt. $50.00. Helen Dwight Reid Educational Foundation, 4000 Albemarle Street NW, Washington DC 20016. Tel (202)362-6445. Ed Margaret Pearson. Ind/Abst Life Sci. Collect., Int. Aerosp. Abstr., Biol. Abstr., Curr. Contents, Soc. Behav. Sci., Excerpta Med., Index Med., Psychol. Abstr., Soc. Sci. Citation Index, Abstr. Anthropol., Hospit. Lit. Index. LC RB152. DD 616.071. NLM W1 JO673XH. adv acc. Circ 1,100. Issued also in microform. Focuses on research and management of today's unavoidable problem: stress. It also publishes evaluation studies, case reports, and major review articles.

JOURNAL OF MOLECULAR MEDICINE CEASED. V. 1-4. 0377-046X. Periodical. NE. English. ir. $34.47. Elsevier Scientific Publishing Company, PO Box 211, Amsterdam The Netherlands. Ind/Abst Excerpta Med., Chem. Abstr. LC RB113. DD 616.070157488. NLM W1 JO7732. CODEN JMMEDM.

JOURNAL OF PATHOLOGY. V. 97- 1969-. 0022-3417. Periodical. UK. English. mo. 102 Domestic, 185 Foreign. John Wiley and Sons Ltd, Baffins Lane Chichester, Sussex PO19 1UD England. Tel (0243)784531. Ed D H Wright. Ind/Abst Life Sci. Collect., Excerpta Med., Energy Inf. Abstr., Environ. Abstr., CIS Abstr., Biol. Abstr., Chem. Abstr., Nucl. Sci. Abstr., Index Med., Bibliogr. Agric., Sci. Cit. Index, Abr. Ed. DD 616. NLM W1 JO828B. CODEN JPTLAS. bk rev. adv acc. Published on behalf of Pathological Society of Great Britain. Covers whole range of experimental and diagnostic histopathology. Journal of Pathology and Bacteriology, 0368-3494.

K.V.P. MANITOBA NEWS. VAT MAMRT News, Manitoba Association of Medical Radiation Technologists News. Vol. 20, No. 3 (Sept. 1984)-. 0828-5942. Periodical. CN. English. Manitoba Association of Medical Radiation Technologists, Suite 215/819 Sargent Avenue, Winnipeg Manitoba R3E 0B9 Canada. DD 616.07570607127. K V P News, 0022-7439.

LAB WORLD. Began with Dec. 1949 issue. 0023-6454. Periodical. US. English. mo. $18.00. North American Publishing Co, 401 North Broad Street, Philadelphia PA 19108. Ind/Abst Cumul. Index Nurs. Allied Health Lit. LC R860. DD 616.075. NLM W1 LA138. Available in microfilm from University Microfilms.

LABORATORNOE DELO. 1955-. 0023-6748. Periodical. UR. Russian (table of contents also in French). mo. $25.00. Victor Kamkin Inc (70480), 12224 Parklawn Drive, Rockville MD 20852. Tel (301)881-5973. Ind/Abst Index Med., Int. Aerosp. Abstr., Biol. Abstr., Chem. Abstr., Chem. Abstr. NLM W1 LA204. CODEN LABDAZ.

LABORATORY INVESTIGATION. V. 1- Spring 1952-. 0023-6837. Periodical. US. English. mo. $105.00. Williams & Wilkins Co, PO Box 64025, Baltimore MD 21264. Tel (301)528-4000. Ed Emanuel Rubin. Ind/Abst Life Sci. Collect., Excerpta Med., Int. Aerosp. Abstr., Biol. Abstr., Chem. Abstr., Index Med., Nucl. Sci. Abstr., Bibliogr. Agric., Energy Res. Abstr., Sci. Cit. Index, Abr. Ed. LC RB1. NLM W1 LA208. CODEN LAINAW. Index in last issue of volume - attached. adv acc. Circ 6,100. Experimental, anatomical, and comparative pathology; cytologic and histologic methods, and tissue culturing for pathologists and laboratory technicians. Bulletin of the International Association of Medical Museums, 0160-452X.

LIVER: NORMAL FUNCTION AND DISEASE. (LIVER, NORMAL FUNCTION AND DISEASE). V. 1-. 0163-9021. Monographic Series. US. English. ir. Marcel Dekker, 270 Madison Avenue, New York NY 10016. Tel (212)696-9000. Ed Frederick F Becker. Ind/Abst Chem. Abstr. LC UNC. NLM W1 LI921. CODEN LNFDDD. This is an ongoing series each title has a different subject.

MAJOR PROBLEMS IN PATHOLOGY. Vol. 1-. 0076-2881. Monographic Series. US. English. ir. W B Saunders Co Fulfillment Department, West Washington Square, Philadelphia PA 19105. Tel (800)523-0713. Ed J L Bennington. Ind/Abst Energy Res. Abstr., Index Med. NLM W1 MA492X. Each issue contains an index to its own contents - no vol index - loose.

MASSON MONOGRAPHS IN DIAGNOSTIC PATHOLOGY. 1-. Monographic Series. English. ir. **Ed** Stephen S Sternberg. **NLM** W1 MA9309S.

MEDICAL EXAMINATION REVIEW BOOK. PATHOLOGY SPECIALTY BOARD REVIEW. **VFOAT** Pathology Specialty Board Review. 1st- Ed. 0090-7065. US. English. ir. Medical Exam Publishing Company, 3003 New Hyde Park Road, New Hyde Park NY 11040.

MEDICAL LABORATORY PRODUCTS. (MEDICAL LABORATORY PRODUCTS : MLP). **VFOAT** MLP. Vol. 1, No. 1 (Jan. 1986)-. 0887-0799. Periodical. US. English. mo. MLP, Box 555, Oradell NJ 07649. **Ind/Abst** Cumul. Index Nurs. Allied Health Lit. **LC** RB37.A1. **DD** 616.075. *Diagnostic Medicine, 0147-8893.*

METHODS AND ACHIEVEMENTS IN EXPERIMENTAL PATHOLOGY. V. 1- 1966-. 0076-681X. Periodical. English. ir. S Karger Ag, PO Box, CH-4009 Basel Switzerland. **Tel** 061-39 08 80. **Ed** G Jasmin and R Simard. **Ind/Abst** Biol. Abstr., Chem. Abstr., Index Med. **LC** RB125. **DD** 616.07. **NLM** W1 ME9613. **CODEN** MAEPBU. A convenient source of reliable information on methodology and new concepts in the microscopic study of diseases.

MONOGRAPHS IN PATHOLOGY. **Main/Corp** International Academy of Pathology. **VFOAT** International Academy of Pathology Monograph. No. 1- 1960-. 0077-0922. Monographic Series. US. English. ir. Rittenhouse Book Distributors, 511 Feheley Drive, King of Prussia PA 19406. **Tel** (215)277-1414. **Ind/Abst** Index Med., Energy Res. Abstr., Biol. Abstr., Chem. Abstr. **NLM** W1 MO568H. **CODEN** IAPMAV.

NCCLS PUBLICATION. **Main/Corp** National Committee for Clinical Laboratory Standards. **VFOAT** N.C.C.L.S. Publication. **VAT** National Committee for Clinical Laboratory Standards Publication. Vol. 1, No. 1-. 0273-3099. Monographic Series. US. English. ir. $350.00. National Committee for Clinical Laboratory Standards, 771 East Lancaster Avenue, Villanova PA 19085. **Tel** (215)525-2423. **Ed** Charles Rossi. **NLM** W1 NA347W. **Circ** 3,000. (ctrl). Focus is on laboratory procedures, reference methods and scientific evaluation protocols: 75 standards and guidelines of interest to different segments of the clinical/diagnostic community.

NEUROCHEMICAL PATHOLOGY. Vol. 1, No. 1 (Spring 1983)-. 0734-600X. Periodical. US. English. qt. $100.00. Humana Press Inc, Crescent Manor, PO Box 2148, Clifton NY 07015. **Tel** (201)773-4389. **Ed** Lloyd Harrocks. **Ind/Abst** Life Sci. Collect. **NLM** W1 NE323T. bk rev. adv acc. Primary journal in the rapidly emerging field of biochemical neuropathology.

NEUROPATHOLOGY AND APPLIED NEUROBIOLOGY. V. 1- Jan. 1975-. 0305-1846. Periodical. UK. English. bm. $295.00. Blackwell Scientific Publishers Ltd, PO Box 88, Oxford OX2 0EL England. **Tel** 240201. **Ed** J B Cavanagh. **Ind/Abst** Excerpta Med., Life Sci. Collect., Index Med., Biol. Abstr., Chem. Abstr., Sci. Cit. Index, Abr. Ed. **NLM** W1 NE337R. **CODEN** NANEDL. bk rev. adv acc. **Circ** 400. (ctrl). Original clinical and experimental papers on problems and pathological processes in neuropathology and muscle disease.

NIHON GAN CHIRYO GAKKAI SHI. (NIPPON GAN CHIRYO GAKKAI SHI). **VFOAT** Journal of Japan Society for Cancer Therapy. Vol. 1- 1966-. 0021-4671. Periodical. JA. Japanese (title also in English: The Journal of Society for Cancer Therapy). qt. 90.00. Maruzen Co Ltd, PO Box 5050, 100-31 Tokyo Japan. **Tel** 975-751-7150. **Ed** Yovinovi Higasa. **Ind/Abst** Excerpta Med., Index Med., Biol. Abstr., Chem. Abstr. **NLM** W1 NI895E. **CODEN** NGCJAK. **Circ** 6,800. (ctrl). Monographs about cancer therapy, and report of society's activity.

PAIN. V. 1- Mar. 1975-. 0304-3959. NE. English. mo. Elsevier Science Publishers, PO Box 211, 1000 AE Amsterdam Netherlands. **Tel** (020)5803.911. **Ind/Abst** Life Sci. Collect., Excerpta Med., Pestdoc, Ringdoc, Vetdoc, Index Med., Cumul. Index Nurs. Allied Health Lit., Biol. Abstr., Chem. Abstr., Psychol. Abstr. **LC** RB127. **NLM** W1 PA29. **CODEN** PAINDB.

PATHOBIOLOGY OF CELL MEMBRANES. Vol. 1-. 0095-1757. Periodical. US. English. Academic Press Inc, Library Services, Orlando FL 32887. **Tel** (305)345-4500. **Ed** Benjamin F Trump and Antti U Arstila. **LC** RB1. **DD** 611.01815. **NLM** W1.

DER PATHOLOGE. Vol. 1- Nov. 1979-. 0172-8113. Periodical. German. bm. Springer Verlag-New York Inc, Subs Department 175-5th Avenue, New York NY 10010. **Tel** (212)460-1500. **Ed** V Becker. **Ind/Abst** Excerpta Med., Index Med., Curr. Contents. **NLM** W1 PA898D. Applied pathology. Also covers pathological anatomy for the practicing pathologist, discusses problems of classification, definitions, new syndromes, practical hints and convention reviews.

PATHOLOGICA. V. 1- (No. 1-). 0031-2983. Periodical. IT. English (text in Italian). mo. Pathologica, Via Alessandro Volta 8, Genova Italy. **Ind/Abst** Excerpta Med., CIS Abstr., Nuci. Sci. Abstr., Chem. Abstr., Biol. Abstr., Index Med. **NLM** W1 PA899. **CODEN** PATHAB.

PATHOLOGIE-BIOLOGIE. (PATHOLOGIE BIOLOGIE). V. 17- Jan. 1969-. 0031-3009. Periodical. FR. French (English). ir. $141.02. Semaine des Hopitaux, 15 rue Saint Benoit, 75278 Paris Cedex 06 France. **Tel** 548-42-60. **Ind/Abst** CIS Abstr., Life Sci. Collect., Excerpta Med., Index Med., Energy Res. Abstr., Chem. Abstr., Bibliogr. Agric. **NLM** W1 PA95. **CODEN** PTBIAN. *Pathologie et Biologie.*

PATHOLOGIST. V. 23- 1969-. 0031-3017. Periodical. US. English. mo. $15.00. College of American Pathologists, 5202 Old Orchard Road, Skokie IL 60077-1034. **Tel** (312)966-5700. **Ed** Henry Soloway. **Ind/Abst** Hospit. Lit. Index. **NLM** W1 PA962F. **CODEN** PTHLA. bk rev. adv acc. **Circ** 14,000. Ideas and information on quality control, legislation, management and technology as it relates to the practice of laboratory medicine. *Bulletin - College of American Pathologists, 0098-4450.*

PATHOLOGY. V. 1- 1969-. 0031-3025. Periodical. AT. English. qt. $55.34. Royal College of Pathologists of Australia, Druham Hall, 207 Albion St, Surry Hills New South Wales 2010 Australia. **Tel** (02)332-4266. **Ed** D S Nelson. **Ind/Abst** Life Sci. Collect., Excerpta Med., Biol. Abstr., Chem. Abstr., Index Med., Nuci. Sci. Abstr., Sci. Cit. Index, Abr. Ed. **NLM** W1 PA962G. **CODEN** PTLGAX. bk rev. adv acc. **Circ** 1,500. (ctrl). Clinical, anatomical, and experimental.

PATHOLOGY ANNUAL. V. 1- 1966-. 0079-0184. US. English. an. Appleton Century Crofts, 25 Van Zant Street, East Norwalk CT 06855. **Tel** (203)838-4400. **Ed** Sheldon C Sommers, Paul Peter Rosen and Robert Fechner. **Ind/Abst** Index Med., Biol. Abstr., Energy Res. Abstr., Chem. Abstr., Sci. Cit. Index, Abr. Ed. **NLM** W1 PA962H. **CODEN** PATABP. Collection of original articles in the field of pathology.

PATHOLOGY, RESEARCH AND PRACTICE. V. 162- 1978-. 0344-0388. Periodical. English (articles in French or German). ir. $306.00. VCH Publishers Inc, 303 12th Avenue Northwest, Deerfield Beach FL 33442-1705. **Tel** (305)428-5566. **Ed** J Diebold, S Falkmer, D Ferluga, J V Johannessen, W Jones-Williams, A Llombart-Bosch, G Seifert and C Thomas. **Ind/Abst** Life Sci. Collect., Excerpta Med., Index Med., Biol. Abstr., Energy Res. Abstr., Chem. Abstr., Curr. Contents. **NLM** W1 PA963D. **CODEN** PARPDS. Pursues the essential goal of providing the international foundation for the entire field of pathology. All aspects of the field are represented from pure theory to daily practice. *Beitrage zur Pathologie.*

PATOLOGIA POLSKA. Vol. 1- Jan. 1950-. 0031-3114. Periodical. PL. Polish. qt. ARS Polona, Krakowskie Przedmiescie 7, 00-068 Warsaw Poland. **Ind/Abst** Excerpta Med., Index Med., Biol. Abstr., Chem. Abstr. **NLM** W1 PA976. **CODEN** PAPOAC.

PATOLOGICHESKAIA ANATOMIIA. **Series/Titl** Itogi Nauki i Tekhniki. V. 1- 1978-. Monographic Series. UR. Russian. **NLM** W1 PA986.

PEDIATRIC PATHOLOGY. *See* Medicine - Pediatrics.

PERSPECTIVES IN PEDIATRIC PATHOLOGY. *See* Medicine - Pediatrics.

PROBLEMS OF INFECTIOUS AND PARASITIC DISEASES. 0204-9155. Periodical. English. ir. **Ind/Abst** Excerpta Med., Chem. Abstr. **NLM** W1 PR574P. **CODEN** PIPDD4.

PROBLEMY PATOLOGII POZVONOCHNIKA. UR. Russian. **NLM** W1 PR5808NJ.

PROCEEDINGS - AMERICAN SOCIETY OF CLINICAL PATHOLOGISTS. **Main/Corp** American Society of Clinical Pathologists. US. English. qt. British Medical Journal, Tavistock Square, London WC1H 9RJ England.

PROGRESS IN CLINICAL PATHOLOGY. **VFOAT** Clinical Pathology. V. 1-. 0079-6174. US. English. ir. Grune & Stratton, 111 5th Avenue, New York NY 10003. **Tel** (212)614-3232. **Ed** Stefanini. **Ind/Abst** Index Med., Energy Res. Abstr., Biol. Abstr., Chem. Abstr., Nuci. Sci. Abstr. **LC** RB37. **DD** 616.075508. **NLM** W1 PR668GE. **CODEN** PGCPAQ.

PROGRESS IN HEMOSTASIS AND THROMBOSIS. V. 1-. 0362-6350. US. English. ir. Grune & Stratton Inc, 111 Fifth Avenue, New York NY 10003. **Tel** (212)614-3110. **Ind/Abst** Index Med., Energy Res. Abstr., Chem. Abstr., Sci. Cit. Index, Abr. Ed. **LC** RB144. **DD** 616.157005. **NLM** W1 PR67F. **CODEN** PGHTAT.

RECENT ADVANCES IN PATHOLOGY. No. -9. 0141-3384. UK. English. ir. Churchill Livingstone Inc, 1560 Broadway, New York NY 10036. **Tel** (212)819-5400. **NLM** W1 RE105XP.

REPOSITORY OF CHROMOSOMAL VARIANTS AND ANOMALIES IN MAN. **Main/Corp** Johns Hopkins University. Division of Medical Genetics. 0148-7183. US. English. The Johns Hopkins University, School of Medicine, Division of Medical Genetics, Baltimore MD 21205. **LC** RB155. **DD** 616.042.

REVISTA BRASILEIRA DE PATOLOGIA CLINICA. 1950. 0034-7302. Periodical. BL. Portuguese. bm. Soc Brasil Pathologia Clinica, rua Sampaio Viana 92/Rio Compr, 20261 Rio de Janeiro Brazil. **Tel** (021) 248 9495. **Ed** Jose Pinheiro. **Ind/Abst** Chem. Abstr. **CODEN** RBPTBN. bk rev. adv acc. **Circ** 3,000. Clinical pathology, laboratory medicine, hematology, immunology, bacteriology, nuclear medicine, toxicology, virology, biochemistry, endocrinology, parsitology, etc.

RINSHO KENSA. **VFOAT** Journal of Medical Technology. Began in 1957. 0485-1420. Periodical. JA. Japanese. ir. $81.05. Igaku Shoin Ltd, 5-24-3 Hongo Bunkyo-ku, Tokyo 113 91 Japan. **Tel** (03)817-5600. **Ed** Manabu Yamanaka. **Ind/Abst** Chem. Abstr. **CODEN** RNKNAT.

RIVISTA DI ANATOMIA PATOLOGICA E DI ONCOLOGIA. **VFOAT** Latino-American Journal of Pathology. Began with: V. 1, in 1948. 0048-8364. Periodical. IT. Italian (English). an. 40.00. Piccin Editore, Via Altinate 107, 35121 Padua Italy. **Tel** (049)655566. **Ed** Antonino Ferrara. **Ind/Abst** Life Sci. Collect. **NLM** W1 RI363. adv acc. **Circ** 500. (ctrl).

RIVISTA DI PATOLOGIA VEGETALE. Vol. 1, N. 1 (Mar. 1892)-V. 10 (Mar. 1902). 0035-6441. Periodical. IT. Italian. qt. $50.00. Societe Italiana di Fitoiatria Casella Postale 230, 27100 Pavia Italy. **Ind/Abst** Life Sci. Collect., Biol. Abstr., Chem. Abstr., Bibliogr. Agric., Sci. Cit. Index, Abr. Ed. **CODEN** RPVGA9.

SABOURAUDIA. **VFOAT** Journal of Medical and Veterinary Mycology. V. 1- Jan. 1961-. 0036-2174. Periodical. UK. English (French with summaries in German, Portuguese and Spanish). qt. Carfax Publishing Company, PO Box 25, Abingdon Oxfordshire OX14 3UE England. **Ed** F C Odds. **Ind/Abst** Life Sci. Collect., Excerpta Med., Index Med., Biol. Abstr., Index Dent. Lit., Chem. Abstr., Bibliogr. Agric., Sci. Cit. Index, Abr. Ed. **LC** RC117. **NLM** W1 SA106. **CODEN** SABOA9. bk rev. adv acc. An international journal describing innovative research on all aspects of invasive fungal disease.

SEMINARS IN DIAGNOSTIC PATHOLOGY. Vol. 1, No. 1 (Feb. 1984)-. 0740-2570. Monographic Series. US. English. qt. $55.00 Individual; $75.00 Libraries & Institutions; $42.00 Students, Interns, etc. Grune & Stratton Inc, Orlando FL 32887. **DD** 616. **NLM** W1.

SPEZIELLE PATHOLOGISCHE ANATOMIE; EIN LETTER-UND NACHSCHLAGEWERK. 1966-. 0081-3699. German. ir. Springer Verlag-New York Inc, 175 5th Avenue, New York NY 10010. **Tel** (212)460-1500.

SPRINGER SEMINARS IN IMMUNOPATHOLOGY. **VFOAT** Seminars in Immunopathology. V. 1- 1978-. 0344-4325. Periodical. US. English. qt. $77.00. Springer Verlag-New York Inc, 175 5th Avenue, New York NY 10010. **Tel** (212)460-1500. **Ed** P A Miescher and Hans J Muller-Eberhard. **Ind/Abst** Life Sci. Collect., Excerpta Med., Index Med., Chem. Abstr., Curr. Contents. **NLM** W1 SP685J. **CODEN** SSIMDV. Aim of this journal is to keep clinicians and pathologists up-to-date on developments in the field of immunopathology.

SURVEY AND SYNTHESIS OF PATHOLOGY RESEARCH. 1/1-2/83 (Jan. 1983)-. 0253-438X. Periodical. SZ. English. qt. $106.00. Ind/Abst Life Sci. Collect., Chem. Abstr., Index Med. **NLM** W1. **CODEN** SSPREE.

SYNDROME IDENTIFICATION CEASED. V. 1-8. 0091-1747. Periodical. US. English. 1275 Mamaroneck Avenue, White Plains NY 10605. Ed D Bergsma. **Ind**/Abst Excerpta Med. LC RB155. DD 616.04305. **NLM** W1. **CODEN** SYIDD.

TAEHAN H OLAEK HAKHOE CHAPCHI. VFOAT Korean Journal of Hematology, The Korean Journal of Hematology. Began in 1966. 0301-4045. Periodical. KO. Korean (English). ir. Taehan Hy Olaek Hakhoe, 505 Panpodong, Kangnam Ku Sequl. LC RB145. **NLM** W1 TA392I.

TOXICOLOGIC PATHOLOGY. V. 6, No. 3/4-. 0192-6233. Periodical. US. English. ir. $120.00. c/o FA de la Iglesia, PO Box 368, Lawrence KS 66044. **Tel** (913)843-1234. Ed Felix de la Iglesia. **Ind**/Abst Life Sci. Collect., Excerpta Med., Chem. Abstr. LC RB1. DD 616.0705. **NLM** W1 TO892. **CODEN** TOPADD. bk rev. **Circ** 500. (ctrl) Deals with investigative toxicology pathology and factors. Mechanisms that modify pathological responses, experimental results that address carcinogenisis and clinical pathology studies. Bulletin of the Society of Pharmacological and Environmental Pathologists, 0094-1824.

ULTRASTRUCTURAL PATHOLOGY. V. 1- Jan./Mar. 1980-. 0191-3123. Periodical. US. English. bm. $269.50. Hemisphere Publishing Corporation, 79 Madison Avenue/Suite 1110, New York NY 10016. **Tel** (202(783-3958. Ed Jan Vincents Johannessen. **Ind/Abst** Life Sci. Collect., Excerpta Med., Index Med., Biol. Abstr., Chem. Abstr., Sci. Cit. Index, Abr. Ed. LC RB25. DD 616.07582. **NLM** W1 UL753. **CODEN** ULPAD3. bk rev. adv acc. **Circ** 1,100. Presents research in human pathology and electron microscopy including significant aspects of immunohistochemistry, cell biology, clinical medicine. Current coverage of electron microscopy in human disease and diagnosis.

AN ULTRASTRUCTURAL PATHOLOGY PUBLICATION. 0730-6482. US. English. ir. Hemisphere Publishing Corporation, 19th West 44th Street, New York NY 10036.

UNIVERSIDAD DE ANTIOQUIA. V. 1- (No. 1-). Periodical. CK. Spanish. ir. Universidad de Antioquia, Department of Pathologie and Faculte Med, Medellin Columbia. LC AP63. DD 056.1.

VERHANDLUNGEN DER DEUTSCHEN GESELLSCHAFT FUR PATHOLOGIE. VFOAT Verhandlungen Deutscher Pathologen. 32nd Meeting. 0070-4113. GW. German. an. VCH Publishers Inc, 303 NW 12th Avenue, Deerfield Beach FL 33442. **Tel** (305)428-5566. **Ind**/Abst Life Sci. Collect., Index Med., Chem. Abstr., Energy Res. Abstr. **NLM** W1 VE483T. **CODEN** VDGPAN. (cum index). Verhandlungen.

VEROFFENTLICHUNGEN AUS DER MORPHOLOGISCHEN PATHOLOGIE. Issue 56-94. 0372-6312. Monographic Series. German (summaries in English in later volumes). ir. VCH Publishers Inc, 303 NW 12th Avenue, Deerfield Beach FL 33442. **Tel** (305)428-5566. **Ind**/Abst Index Med. **NLM** W1 VE783. Veroffentlichungen Aus der Konstitutions- Und Wehrpathologie.

VIRCHOWS ARCHIV. A, PATHOLOGICAL ANATOMY AND HISTOPATHOLOGY. See Genealogy and Heraldry - Archives.

THE YEAR BOOK OF PATHOLOGY AND CLINICAL PATHOLOGY. See Yearbooks, Almanacs, Directories.

PEDIATRICS

ABMS DIRECTORY OF CERTIFIED PEDIATRICIANS. See Yearbooks, Almanacs, Directories.

ACTA PAEDIATRICA ACADEMIAE SCIENTIARUM HUNGARICAE CEASED. VFOAT Acta Paediatrica Hungarica, Acta Paediatrica. Began in 1960. Ceased with V. 23, No. 4. 0001-6527. Periodical. HU. English (German, French, and Russian). qt. **Ind/Abst** Life Sci. Collect., Excerpta Med., Biol. Abstr. **NLM** W1 AC903. **CODEN** APHNAB.

ACTA PAEDIATRICA HUNGARICA. VFOAT Acta Paediatrica. Vol. 24, No. 1-. 0231-441X. Periodical. English. qt. $44.00. Akademiai Kiado, POB 24, 1363 Budapest Hungary. Ed P V Veghelyi. **Ind/Abst** Excerpta Med., Index Med., Life Sci. Collect. **NLM** W1 AC904. bk rev. adv acc. Presents original communications on subjects connected with the theoretical and practical aspects of pediatrics, including the fields of perinatal medicine, clinical genetics, pediatric surgery, pediatric psychology, etc. Acta Paediatrica Academiae Scientiarum Hungaricae.

ACTA PAEDIATRICA JAPONICA. OVERSEAS EDITION. (ACTA PAEDIATRICA JAPONICA. OVERSEAS EDITION). V. 5- 1963-. 0374-5600. Periodical. JA. English. qt. Japan Publications Trading Co, PO Box 5030, Tokyo International, Tokyo 100-31 Japan. **Ind**/Abst Excerpta Med., Biol. Abstr., Chem. Abstr. **NLM** W1 AC905E. **CODEN** APDJBE.

ACTA PAEDIATRICA LATINA. Periodical. IT. Italian. qt. 15.000 Domestic, 25.000 Foreign. Acta Paediatrica Latina, Via Casorati 29, Reggio Emilia 42100 Italy. **Tel** (0522)42227. **Ind/Abst** Excerpta Med. **NLM** W1 AC905. bk rev. adv acc. **Circ** 3,200. Original articles about pediatrics. Books, notes, and news.

ADOLESCENT MEDICINE. V. 1- 1969-. 0044-6335. Periodical. US. English. mo. $110.00. Adolescent Medicine, 2128 Wyoming Avenue, Washington DC 20008. **Tel** (202)234-1897. Ed Nathaniel Polster. bk rev. Practical advice to physicians, nurses, athletic directors and medical staff on adolescent medicine. Research reports; news affecting adolescent physical and mental care.

ADVANCES IN DEVELOPMENTAL AND BEHAVIORAL PEDIATRICS. Vol. 3 (1982)-. 0737-7452. Periodical. US. English. ir. $52.50. JAI Press, PO Box 1678, Greenwich CT 06836. **Tel** (203)661-7602. Ed Mark Volraich and Donald K Routh. **Ind**/Abst Psychol. Abstr. LC RJ47.5. DD 618.9200019. **NLM** W1. Advances in Behavioral Pediatrics, 0198-7089.

ADVANCES IN INFANCY RESEARCH. Vol. 1-. 0732-9598. US. English. Ablex Publishing Corp, 355 Chestnut Street, Norwood NJ 07648. **Tel** (201)767-8450. Ed Lewis P Lipsitt and Carolyn Rovee-Collier. **Ind**/Abst Psychol. Abstr. LC BF719. DD 155.422. **NLM** W1 AD647M. A book series devoted exclusively to infancy research, both human and animal.

ADVANCES IN LEARNING AND BEHAVIORAL DISABILITIES. Vol. 1 (1982)-. 0735-004X. US. English. an. $49.50. Jai Press Inc, 36 Sherwood Place, PO Box 1678, Greenwich CT 06836. Ed Ken Gaslow. **Ind**/Abst Sociol. Abstr., Psychol. Abstr. LC RJ506.L4. DD 618.9289. **NLM** W1 AD655.

ADVANCES IN PEDIATRIC SPORT SCIENCES. Vol. 1-. 0748-6375. US. English. be. $22.00. Human Kinetics Publishers Inc, Box 5076 Champaign IL 61820. **Tel** (217)351-5076. Series of scholarly reviews examining the influence of exercise and sports participation upon children and youth. Examines from biological and behavioral perspectives.

ADVANCES IN PEDIATRICS. V. 1-. 0065-3101. US. English. ir. Yearbook Medical Publishers, 35 East Wacker Drive, Chicago IL 60601. Ed A G de Sanctis. **Ind/Abst** Cumul. Index Nurs. Allied Health Lit., Index Med., Energy Res. Abstr. LC RJ23. DD 618.9. **NLM** W1 AD722.

AMERICAN JOURNAL OF DISEASES OF CHILDREN. VFOAT AJDC. V. 100- July 1960-. 0002-922X. Periodical. US. English. mo. $56.00. American Medical Association, 535 North Dearborn Street, Chicago IL 60610. **Tel** (312)645-4927. **Ind/Abst** Excerpta Med., Life Sci. Collect., Hospit. Lit. Index, Pestdoc, Ringdoc, Vetdoc, Index Med., Biol. Abstr., Chem. Abstr., Bibliogr. Agric., Energy Res. Abstr., Comb. Cumul. Index Pediatr., Sci. Cit. Index, Abr. Ed., Sociol. Abstr., Lang. Lang. Behav. Abstr. DD 618. **NLM** W1 A118. **CODEN** AJDCAI. A.M.A. Journal of Diseases of Children, 0096-6916.

THE AMERICAN JOURNAL OF PEDIATRIC HEMATOLOGY/ ONCOLOGY. VAT American Journal of Pediatric Hematology Oncology. V. 1- Spring 1979-. 0192-8562. Periodical. US. English. qt. Raven Press, 1140 Avenue of the Americas, New York NY 10036. **Tel** (212)575-0335. **Ind/Abst** Sci. Cit. Index, Abr. Ed., Index Med., Funk Scott Index Corp. Ind., Excerpta Med., Life Sci. Collect. LC RJ411. DD 618.9215. **NLM** W1 AM498BJ.

AMERICAN JOURNAL OF PERINATOLOGY. See Medicine - Gynecology & Obstetrics.

AMERICAN PEDIATRIC DIRECTORY. See Yearbooks, Almanacs, Directories.

ANNALES DE PEDIATRIE. 0066-2097. French (table of contents and summaries in English). ir. $119.73. Semaine des Hopiteaux, 15 rue Saint Benoit, 75278 Paris Cedex 06 France. **Tel** 548-42-60. **Ind/Abst** Life Sci. Collect., Excerpta Med., Chem. Abstr., Curr. Contents, Bull. Signal., Index Med., Biol. Abstr., Energy Res. Abstr., Phys. Abstr., Sci. Cit. Index, Abr. Ed., Electr. Electron. Abstr., Comput. Control Abstr., Int. Aerosp. Abstr. **NLM** W1 AN374E. **CODEN** APSHAE.

ANNALS - INSTITUTE OF CHILD HEALTH. Main/Corp Institute of Child Health. V. 1- July 1972-. II. English. ir. $5.00. Institute of Child Health, 11 Dr Biresh Guha Road, Calcutta 17 India. LC RJ1. DD 618.920005.

ANNALS OF TROPICAL PAEDIATRICS. Vol. 1, No. 1 (Mar. 1981)-. 0692-4936. Periodical. UK. English. qt $115.50. Academic Press, 4805 Sand Lake Road, Orlando FL 32819. **Tel** (305)345-4100. **Ind**/Abst Excerpta Med., Index Med. **NLM** W1 AN627U.

ANNUAL PROGRESS IN CHILD PSYCHIATRY AND CHILD DEVELOPMENT. 1968-. 0066-4030. US. English. an. Brunner Mazel Publishing, 19 Union Square West, New York NY 10003. Ed S Chess and A Thomas. **Ind/Abst** Psychol. Abstr. LC RJ499.A1. DD 618.928905. **NLM** W1 AN758P.

ANNUAL VOLUME OF PEDIATRICS CLUB BY CONTRIBUTING MEMBERS. V. 1- 1979-. 0197-873X. Periodical. US. English. an. Ed R M Ehrlich. **NLM** W1 AN782R.

ARCHIVES FRANCAISES DE PEDIATRIE. See Genealogy and Heraldry - Archives.

ARCHIVES OF DISEASE IN CHILDHOOD. See Genealogy and Heraldry - Archives.

ARCHIVOS DE PEDIATRIA DEL URUGUAY. See Genealogy and Heraldry - Archives.

AUDIO-DIGEST. PEDIATRICS. 0571-8643. Periodical. US. English. sm. $138.00. Audio-Digest Foundation, 1577 Chevy Chase Drive, Glendale CA 91206. **Tel** (213)245-8505. Ed Claron L Oakley. A twice-monthly interactive system of audio cassette postgraduate medical education, with each one-hour program eligible for two Category I credit hours.

AUSTRALIAN PAEDIATRIC JOURNAL. VFOAT Australian Pediatric Journal. V. 1- 1965-. 0004-993X. Periodical. AT. English. qt. 27 Domestic, $47.00 US, 41 all other countries. Blackwell Scientific Publications Ltd, PO Box Osney Mead, Oxford OX2 0EL England. **Tel** (03)47 0300. Ed J M Court. **Ind/Abst** Life Sci. Collect., Excerpta Med., Biol. Abstr., Chem. Abstr., Index Med., Sci. Cit. Index, Abr. Ed., Hospit. Lit. Index. **NLM** W1 AU643H. **CODEN** AUPJB7. bk rev. adv acc. **Circ** 1,000. Official journal of Australian College of Paediatrics and Paediatric Society of Australia. Publishes reports from major academic paediatric services.

BABY TALK (1977). See Medicine - Gynecology & Obstetrics.

BIOGRAPHICAL DIRECTORY OF THE AMERICAN ACADEMY OF PEDIATRICS. See Yearbooks, Almanacs, Directories.

BIOLOGY OF THE NEONATE. See Medicine - Gynecology & Obstetrics.

BOLETIN DE LA SOCIEDAD VASCO-NAVARRA DE PEDIATR. V. 1- Jan./June 1966-. 0037-8658. Periodical. SP. articles in Spanish or French. bm. Editorial Garsi, Londres 17, Madrid 28 Spain. **NLM** W1 BO25T.

BOLETIN MEDICO DEL HOSPITAL INFANTIL DE MEXICO. Began in 1944. 0539-6115. Periodical. MX. Spanish (summaries in English). mo. $50.00. Hospital Infantil de Mexico, Calle del Dr Marquez No 162, Mexico City 7 D F Mexico. **Tel** (5) 7 61 03 33. Ed Luis Valasquez Jones. **Ind/Abst** Chem. Abstr., Index Med. **CODEN** BMHIAK.

bk rev. adv acc. **Circ** 3,500. Articles on pediatrics and related topics: original articles, clinical cases and reviews.

BUCHEREI DES PADIATERS. No. 67- 1972-. 0373-3165. Periodical. GW. German. ir. Ferdinand Enke Verlag, Ridigerstr 14, Postfach 1304, D 7000 Stuttgart West Germany. **Tel** (0711)8931-0. **Ed** W Burmeister, G Heimann and F C Sitzmann. Deals with practical and clinical relevant subjects from the whole subject of pediatrics. The volumes are supplements of the journal "Klinische Padiatrie". *Beihefte zur Archiv fur Kinderheildkunde, 0066-6378.*

BULLETIN OF THE INTERNATIONAL PEDIATRIC ASSOCIATION. **Main/Corp** International Pediatric Association. **VFOAT** Bulletin de l'Association Internationale de Pediatrie, Boletin de la Asociacion Internacional de Pediatria. No. 1- Jan. 1975-. 0245-9337. Periodical. FR. English (articles in French and Spanish). qt. $30.00 US. Prof Gavin C Arneil, c/o University Department of Child Health, Royal Hospital for Sick Children, Yorkhill Glasgow G3 8SJ Scotland. **Tel** 339-88-88. **Ed** Gavin C Arneil. **NLM** W1 BU853NI. adv acc. **Circ** 2,350. Articles of interest to pediatricians which includes reports of the International Pediatrics Association organized meetings, progress in pediatric specialties, special contributions. Major topics in pediatrics treated. *Bulletin - International Paediatric Association.*

BULLETIN OF THE ORTON SOCIETY *CEASED.* V. 1-31. 0474-7534. US. English. an. **Ind/Abst** Sociol. Abstr., Lang. Lang. Behav. Abstr. **LC** RJ496.A5. **DD** 618.928553005. **NLM** W1 OR868. **CODEN** ORSBBT.

BUTTERWORTHS INTERNATIONAL MEDICAL REVIEWS. PEDIATRICS. **VFOAT** Pediatrics. 1-. 0260-0161. Monographic Series. UK. English. ir. **Ind/Abst** Biol. Abstr. **NLM** W1 BU99E. **CODEN** BIMPD7.

CALIFORNIA PEDIATRICIAN. Vol. 1, No. 1 (Winter 1984/85)-. 0882-3421. Periodical. US. English. ty. California Pediatrician, 1125 A Street/Suite 210, San Rafael CA 94901. **DD** 618.

CHILD ADVOCACY PROGRAMS. **Series/Titl** DHEW Publication. 1975-. 0160-290X. Periodical. US. English. **NLM** WS 22 AA1 C4.

CHILD & FAMILY BEHAVIOR THERAPY. **VFOAT** Child and Family Behavior Therapy. Vol. 4, No. 1 (Spring 1982)-. 0731-7107. Periodical. US. English. qt. $112.00. Haworth Press, 28 East 22nd Street, New York NY 10010. **Tel** (212)228-2800. **Ed** Cyril M Franks. **Ind/Abst** Except. Child Educ. Resour., Curr. Contents, Soc. Behav. Sci., Soc. Sci. Citation Index, Psychol. Abstr. **LC** RJ504. **DD** 618.928914205. bk rev. adv acc. **Circ** 845. This exciting journal is devoted exclusively to research and clinical applications in behavior therapy with children and adolescents, as well as the enhancement of parenting. *Child Behavior Therapy, 0162-1416.*

CHILD CARE, HEALTH AND DEVELOPMENT. V. 1- Jan./Feb. 1975-. 0305-1862. Periodical. UK. English. bm. 42.50 Domestic, 90 Foreign. Blackwell Scientific Publishing Ltd, PO Box 88, Oxford OX2 0EL England. **Tel** (0865)240201. **Ed** R B Jones. **Ind/Abst** Life Sci. Collect., Excerpta Med., Cumul. Index Nurs. Allied Health Lit., Index Med., Biol. Abstr., Except. Child Educ. Resour., Psychol. Abstr., Soc. Sci. Citation Index, Hospit. Lit. Index. **NLM** W1 CH646D. **CODEN** CCHDDH. bk rev. adv acc. **Circ** 740. Publishes material on the development of all children, particularly those handicapped by physical, intellectual, emotional and social problems.

CHILD HEALTH AND DEVELOPMENT. Vol. 1-. 0251-2467. Monographic Series. SZ. English (French). ir. S Karger Ag, PO Box, CH-4009 Basel Switzerland. **Tel** 061-39 08 80. **Ed** M Manciaux. **NLM** W1 CH661T. This series focuses attention on problems of social and preventive medicine central to the practice of pediatrics.

CHILD PERSONALITY AND PSYCHOPATHOLOGY. (CHILD PERSONALITY & PSYCHOPATHOLOGY : CURRENT TOPICS). V. 1- 1974-. 0093-2175. US. English. John Wiley & Sons, 605 Third Avenue, New York NY 10016. **LC** RJ499.A1. **DD** 618.9289005. **NLM** W1 CH668G.

CHILDREN'S HEALTH CARE. **VFOAT** JACCH. Vol. 9, No. 2 (Fall 1980)-. 0273-9615. Periodical. US. English. qt. $23.00. Association of Child Care Hospitals, ACEI Building, 3615 Wisconsin Avenue, Washington DC 20016. **Tel** (202)244-1801. **Ed** William Rae. **Ind/Abst** Hospit. Lit. Index, Cumul. Index Nurs. Allied Health Lit., Psychol. Abstr. **LC** RJ242. **DD** 362.19892. **NLM** W1 CH696. bk rev. adv acc. **Circ** 4,000. (ctrl). Peer review journal articles address psychosocial aspects of pediatric care. Includes media and book reviews. Special theme issues occasionally. *Journal of the Association for the Care of Children's Health, 0274-8916.*

CHILDREN'S NEWS. (THE CHILDREN'S NEWS). **VFOAT** Nouvelles de l'Hopital Montreal Children's. **VAT** Nouvelles - Hopital de Montreal Pour Enfants. Vol. 1, No. 1-. 0821-7106. Periodical. CN. English (text also in French with French text on inverted pages). sa. Free. Montreal Children's Hospital, 2300 Tupper Street, Montreal Quebec H3H 1P3 Canada. **DD** 362.1109714281.

CHILD'S BRAIN. *See* Medicine - Neurology.

THE CHILD'S DOCTOR. (THE CHILD'S DOCTOR : JOURNAL OF THE CHILDREN'S MEMORIAL HOSPITAL). Vol. 1, No. 1 (Fall 1983)-. 0882-2301. Periodical. US. English. sa. Children's Memorial Hospital, 2300 Children's Plaza, Chicago IL 60614. **DD** 618.

CHILD'S NERVOUS SYSTEM : CHNS: OFFICIAL JOURNAL OF THE INTERNATIONAL SOCIETY FOR PEDIATRIC NEUROSURGERY. **VFOAT** CHNS. Vol. 1, No.1 (Feb. 1985)-. Periodical. English. ir. $136.00. **Ind/Abst** Index Med. **NLM** W1. *Child's Brain, 0302-2803.*

CHILDSCOPE. 0882-6390. Periodical. US. English. mo. $15.00 Domestic, $20.00 Foreign. Sundrops Enterprises, Childscope Box 837, Broken Arrow OK 74013. **Tel** (918)357-2061. **Ed** Judy A Rollins. **DD** 649. bk rev. **Circ** 250. (ctrl). Creative resources, programs, activities, news, reviews, events, playthings, people, and other information of interest to child health care professionals. Emphasis in on the hospitalized child.

CHIRURGIE PEDIATRIQUE. V. 19- 1978-. 0180-5738. Periodical. French. bm. Masson Publishing USA Inc, 211 East 43rd Street/Room 1306, New York NY 10017. **Tel** (212)370-1937. **Ind/Abst** Life Sci. Collect., Excerpta Med., Index Med. **NLM** W1 CH832D. *Annales de Chirurgie Infantile, 0003-3952.*

CHUNG-HUA ERH KO TSA CHI. **VFOAT** Chinese Journal of Pediatrics, Zhonghua Erke Zazhi. 1- July 1950-. 0578-1310. Periodical. CC. Chinese (table of contents and some abstracts also in English). qt. $13.50. China Publication Centre, PO Box 2820, Beijing China.

CLINICA PEDIATRICA. 1- 1919-. Periodical. IT. Italian. mo. $20.50. La Clinica Pediatrica, Via Siepelunga 48/2, 40141 Bologna Italy.

CLINICAL APPROACHES TO PROBLEMS OF CHILDHOOD. V. 1- 1965-. 0069-4797. Monographic Series. US. English. Science and Behavior Books, 599 College Avenue, Palo Alto CA 94306.

CLINICAL DISORDERS IN PEDIATRIC NUTRITION. *See* Nutrition and Dietetics.

CLINICAL PEDIATRICS. V. 1- Oct. 1962-. 0009-9228. Periodical. US. English. mo. $49.00. J B Lippincott Company, East Washington Square, Philadelphia PA 19105. **Tel** (215)238-4273. **Ed** David M Cornfeld. **Ind/Abst** Life Sci. Collect., Excerpta Med., Cumul. Index Nurs. Allied Health Lit., Index Med., Comb. Cumul. Index Pediatr., Psychol. Abstr., Bibliogr. Agric., Energy Res. Abstr., Hospit. Lit. Index, Sci. Cit. Index, Abr. Ed. **LC** RJ1. **DD** 618.920005. **NLM** W1 CL762. **CODEN** CPEDAM. adv acc. **Circ** 24,250. Recent advances in pediatrics relating to office practice emphasis on more commonly encountered conditions. *American Practitioner, 0517-4465; Archives of Pediatrics, 0096-6630; Quarterly Review of Pediatrics, 0097-0107.*

CLINICAL PEDIATRICS (MARCEL DEKKER, INC.). (CLINICAL PEDIATRICS). Vol. 1-. 0883-7198. Monographic Series. US. English. Marcel Dekker Inc, 270 Madison Avenue, New York NY 10016. **Ed** Fima Lifshitz. **DD** 618. **NLM** W1. **CODEN** CLPEEM.

CLINICAL PEDIATRICS, MATERNAL AND CHILD HEALTH. 0193-9742. Monographic Series. US. English. ir. John Wiley & Sons Inc, 1 Wiley Drive, Somerset NJ 08873.

CLINICAL PROGRAMS FOR MENTALLY RETARDED CHILDREN. **Main/Corp** United States. Health Services Administration. Bureau of Community Health Services. 0501-798X. US. English. Superintendent of Documents, US Government Printing Office, Washington DC 20402. **LC** RJ506.M4. **DD** 362.78302573. **NLM** WS 22 AA1 C6.

CLINICAL UPDATE IN PEDIATRICS. 0883-0290. Periodical. US. English. bw. $295.00. Nassau Publications, 11 Forest Street, New Canaan CT 06840. **DD** 618.

COMBINED CUMULATIVE INDEX TO PEDIATRICS. *See* Indexes/Abstracts.

CONCEPTS IN PEDIATRIC NEUROSURGERY. *See* Medicine - Neurology.

CORE JOURNALS IN PEDIATRICS. Began in 1977. 0376-5040. Periodical. English. mo. **Ind/Abst** Chem. Abstr. **NLM** ZWS 100 C797. **CODEN** CJPED7.

CURRENT DIAGNOSTIC PEDIATRICS. V. 1-. 0172-1232. Monographic Series. English. ir. Springer Verlag-New York Inc, 175-5th Avenue, New York NY 10010. **Tel** (212)460-1584. **LC** UNC. **NLM** W1 CU788DP. Contains articles on pediatric radiology, kidney and urinary tracts, and pediatric traumas.

CURRENT PEDIATRIC DIAGNOSIS & TREATMENT. 1st- Ed. 0093-8556. Periodical. US. English. be. $29.00. Lange Medical Publications, Drawer L, Los Altos CA 94023. **Tel** (415)948-4526. **Ed** C Henry Kempe, Henry K Silver, Donough O'Brien and Vincent A Fulginiti. **LC** RJ1. **DD** 618.920005. **NLM** W1 CU799H. Presents the essential principles of clinical diagnosis and treatment of pediatric disorders, including psychiatric disorders, the role of nutrition, and drug therapy.

CURRENT PEDIATRIC THERAPY. 1-. 0070-2021. US. English. an. $56.69. W B Saunders Co Fulfillment Department, West Washington Square, Philadelphia PA 19105. **Tel** (800)523-0713. **Ed** S S Gellis and B M Kagan. **LC** RJ52. **DD** 618.92006. **NLM** W1 CU799S. Each issue contains an index to its own contents - no vol index - loose.

CURRENT PRACTICE IN PEDIATRIC NURSING. *See* Medicine - Nursing.

CURRENT PROBLEMS IN PEDIATRICS. **VFOAT** CPP. V. 1- Nov. 1970-. 0045-9380. US. English. mo. $65.00. Yearbook Medical Publishers Inc, 35 East Wacker Drive, Chicago IL 60601. **Ind/Abst** Index Med., Energy Res. Abstr. **NLM** W1 CU804P.

DIALOGUES IN PEDIATRIC MANAGEMENT. Vol. 1, No. 1-. 8755-2701. Monographic Series. US. English. ty. $48.50. Appleton-Century-Crofts, 25 Van Zant Street East, Norwalk CT 06855. **Ed** David Cornfeld and Benjamin K Silverman. **LC** UNC. **DD** 618. **NLM** W1.

DIALOGUES IN PEDIATRIC UROLOGY. *See* Medicine - Urology.

DRUGS IN PEDIATRICS. **Series/Titl** PRM : Physicians' Reference Manuals. No. 1 (1983)-. 0824-703X. Periodical. CN. English. sa. 50.00. Drugs in Pediatrics, c/o STA Communications 63 Place Frontenac, Pointe-Claire Quebec H9R 4Z7 Canada. **Tel** (514)695-7623. **Ed** Paul Brand. **DD** 615.58088054. adv acc. **Circ** 1,500. (ctrl). Drug reference manuals.

L'ENFANT EN MILIEU TROPICAL. *See* Public Health and Safety.

ERGEBNISSE DER INNEREN MEDIZIN UND KINDERHEILKUNDE. *See* Medicine - Internal Medicine.

ETA EVOLUTIVA (FLORENCE, ITALY). (ETA EVOLUTIVA). N. 1 (Nov. 1978)-. 0392-0658. Periodical. IT. Italian. ty. 12.000. Giunti Barbera 34, Via Gioberti, Firenze Italy. **Ind/Abst** Psychol. Abstr. **LC** RJ131. **DD** 612.6505. **NLM** W1 ET35.

EUROPEAN JOURNAL OF PEDIATRICS. **VFOAT** Zeitschrift fur Kinderheilkunde. V. 121- 1975-. 0340-6199. Periodical. GW. English (Vols. for 1975- have articles in German with summaries in both languages). mo. $318.00. Springer Verlag-New York Inc, 175-5th Avenue, New York NY 10010. **Tel** (212)460-1500. **Ed** J Spranger and L Corkeel. **Ind/Abst** Life Sci. Collect., Pestdoc, Ringdoc, Vetdoc, Excerpta Med., Index Med., Biol. Abstr., Chem. Abstr., Energy Res. Abstr., Sci. Cit. Index, Abr. Ed. **NLM** W1 EU72DP. **CODEN** EJPEDT. Covers the whole broad field of pediatrics in all its aspects. *Zeitschrift fur Kinderheilkunde, 0044-2917; Acta Paediatrica Belgica, 0001-6535.*

EXCEPTIONAL INFANT. V. 1-4. 0071-3295. Monographic Series. US. English. ir. **Ed** Jerome Hellmuth. **NLM** WS 430 E96.

EXCERPTA MEDICA. SECTION 7. PEDIATRICS AND PEDIATRIC SURGERY. **VFOAT** Pediatrics and Pediatric Surgery. **VAT** Excerpta Medica. Section Seven. Pediatrics and Pediatric Surgery. V. 26-. 0373-6512. Periodical. English. ir. $331.50. Elsevier Science Publishers, Biomedical Division, PO Box 1527, 1000 BM Amsterdam Netherlands. **Tel** (020)5803911. **NLM** ZW 1 E96. **CODEN** PPSUDH. adv acc. **Circ** 400. Covers all aspects of development and disease in childhood and adolescence. *Excerpta Medica. Section 7. Pediatrics.*

FELLOWSHIP LIST. **Main/Corp** American Academy of Pediatrics. US. English. ir. American Academy of Pediatrics, 141 Northwest Point Road, Elk Grove Village 60007. **LC** RJ1.

FORTSCHRITTE DER SOZIALPADIATRIE. V. 1-. 0341-1508. Monographic Series. German. ir. Urban & Schwarzenberg Verlag, 7 East Redwood Street, Baltimore MD 21202. **Tel** 089/530181. **Ed** T Hellbrugge. **NLM** W1 FO892C.

GAZETTE OF THE EGYPTIAN PAEDIATRIC ASSOCIATION. **Main/Corp** Egyptian Paediatric Association. 0304-484X. Periodical. UA. English. qt. Egyptian Pediatrics Association, PO Box 1441, Cairo Egypt. **Ind/Abst** Chem. Abstr. **NLM** W1 GA777M. **CODEN** GEPAB2.

GYERMEKGYOGYASZAT. Vol. 1-. 0017-5900. Periodical. HU. Hungarian. qt. Akademiai Kiado, POB 24, 1363 Budapest Hungary. **Ind/Abst** Energy Res. Abstr. **NLM** W1 GY379. Index published separately - free - automatically sent.

HANDBOOK OF PEDIATRICS. 0440-1921. US. English. te. $16.50. Lange Medical Publications, Drawer L, Los Altos CA 94023. **Tel** (415)948-4526. **Ed** Henry K Silver, C Henry Kempe, Henry B Bruyn and Vincent A Fulginiti. Handy, pocket-sized presentation of information pertinent to the health care of children from infancy through adolescence. Emphasizes the clinical aspects of pediatric diagnosis and treatment.

HELVETICA CHIRURGICA ACTA. V. 12- 1945-. 0018-0181. Monographic Series. SZ. German (text also in French with summaries in English). ir. 165.-. Schwabe & Company, Steinentorstrasse 13, CH-4000 Basel 10 Switzerland. **Tel** 061 23 55 23. **Ind/Abst** Life Sci. Collect., Excerpta Med., Biol. Abstr., Chem. Abstr., Nuci. Sci. Abstr., Index Med., Sci. Cit. Index, Abr. Ed. **NLM** W1 HE851. **CODEN** HCATAE. bk rev. adv acc. **Circ** 1,400. (ctrl). The official organ of the Swiss Society of Pediatrics; original articles of the whole field of pediatrics. *Helvetica Medica Acta.*

ICRDB CANCERGRAM. PEDIATRIC ONCOLOGY. *See* Medicine - Neoplasma, Neoplastic.

INDIAN JOURNAL OF PEDIATRICS. 0019-5456. Periodical. II. English. bm. $40.00. Department of Pediatrics, All-India Institute of Medical Sciences, New Delhi 110 029 India. **Tel** 661123. **Ed** I C Verma. **Ind/Abst** Life Sci. Collect., Excerpta Med., Biol. Abstr., Chem. Abstr., Index Med., Hospit. Lit. Index. **NLM** W1 IN224J. **CODEN** IJPEA2. bk rev. adv acc. **Circ** 3,000. All aspects of child health.

INDIAN PEDIATRICS. V. 1- Jan. 1964-. 0019-6061. Periodical. II. English. mo. $100.00. K K Roy Private Ltd, PO Box 10210/55 Gariahat Road, Calcutta 700019 India. **Tel** 91 33-474872. **Ed** K K Roy. **Ind/Abst** Life Sci. Collect., Excerpta Med., Index Med., Biol. Abstr., Chem. Abstr., Hospit. Lit. Index. **NLM** W1 IN263F. **CODEN** INPDAR. Index published separately - free - automatically sent. bk rev. adv acc. **Circ** 3,000. Carries specialized articles on child health. *Indian Journal of Child Health, Journal of the Indian Pediatric Society.*

INFANT MENTAL HEALTH JOURNAL. V. 1- Spring 1980-. 0163-9641. Periodical. US. English. qt. $79.00. Clinical Psychology Publishing Company, 4 Conant Square, Brandon VT 05733. **Tel** (802)247-6871. **Ed** Hiram Fitzgerald PhD. **Ind/Abst** Psychol. Abstr. **LC** RJ502.5. **DD** 618.9289005. **NLM** W1 IN3996. **CODEN** IMHJDZ. adv acc. **Circ** 650. Research on infant mental health.

INSTANTANEAS CLINICAS. 0379-8178. Periodical. Spanish. ir. **NLM** W1 IN495.

INTERNATIONAL CHILDREN'S CENTRE COURRIER. Periodical. FR. Multilingual (French and English). bm. $33.26. Centre Intl de l'Enfant, Chatea du Longchamps, Bois de Boulogna, 75016 Paris France.

THE INTERNATIONAL JOURNAL OF PEDIATRIC NEPHROLOGY. Vol. 1, No. 1 (1980/Mar.)-. 0391-6510. Periodical. US. English. qt. $120.00. Wichtig Editore, PO Box C-350, Birmingham AL 35283. **Tel** (205)991-6925. **Ed** Carmelo Giodano. **Ind/Abst** Life Sci. Collect., Excerpta Med., Index Med., Chem. Abstr. **NLM** W1 IN771NJ. **CODEN** IJPNDW. bk rev. adv acc. Offers latest research and techniques in the field of pediatric nephrology. Articles in the areas of pharmacology, glomerulopathies, neonatal, nephrology, uremia, kidney in systemic disease, and hypertension.

INTERNATIONAL JOURNAL OF PEDIATRIC OTORHINOLARYNGOLOGY. *See* Medicine - Otorhinolaryngology.

ISSUES IN COMPREHENSIVE PEDIATRIC NURSING. *See* Medicine - Nursing.

JISSEN TO KENKYU. **Main/Corp** Aichi-Ken Shinshin Shogaisha Koroni. No. 1- 1973-. JA. Japanese. ir. Aichi-Ken Shinshin Shogaisha Koroni, 713-8 Kamiya-Cho, Kasugai 480-03 Japan. **LC** RJ506.M4.

JOURNAL OF ABNORMAL CHILD PSYCHOLOGY. Began with Jan./Mar. 1973 issue. 0091-0627. Periodical. US. English. qt. Plenum Publishing Corporation, 233 Spring Street, New York NY 10013. **Tel** (212)620-8000. **Ind/Abst** Excerpta Med., Index Med., Biol. Abstr., Except. Child Educ. Resour., Psychol. Abstr., Soc. Sci. Citation Index, Hospit. Lit. Index. **LC** RJ499.A1. **DD** 618.9289005. **NLM** W1 JO533L. **CODEN** JABCAA.

JOURNAL OF ADOLESCENT HEALTH CARE. (JOURNAL OF ADOLESCENT HEALTH CARE : OFFICIAL PUBLICATION OF THE SOCIETY FOR ADOLESCENT MEDICINE). Vol. 1, No. 1 (Sept. 1980)-. 0197-0070. Periodical. US. English. bm. $110.00. Elsevier Science Publishing Company Inc, PO Box 1663, Grand Central Station, New York NY 10163. **Tel** (212)372-5520. **Ed** H Verdain Barnes. **Ind/Abst** Life Sci. Collect., Excerpta Med., Cumul. Index Nurs. Allied Health Lit., Index Med., Biol. Abstr., Psychol. Abstr., Soc. Sci. Citation Index. **LC** RJ550. **DD** 616.005. **NLM** W1 JO533S. **CODEN** JAHCD9. adv acc. Devoted to developing an effective approach to the acute and chronic health care problems of the adolescent. *Society for Adolescent Medicine Newsletter.*

JOURNAL OF CHILD NEUROLOGY. *See* Medicine - Neurology.

JOURNAL OF CHILDHOOD COMMUNICATION DISORDERS. *See* Physically Impaired.

JOURNAL OF DEVELOPMENTAL AND BEHAVIORAL PEDIATRICS. (JOURNAL OF DEVELOPMENTAL AND BEHAVIORAL PEDIATRICS : JDBP). **VFOAT** JDBP. Vol. 1, No. 1 (Mar. 1980)-. 0196-206X. Periodical. US. English. bm. $75.00. Williams & Wilkins Company, 428 East Preston Street, Baltimore MD 21202. **Tel** (301)528-4000. **Ed** Stanford Friedman. **Ind/Abst** Excerpta Med., Psychol. Abstr., Index Med. **LC** RJ1. **DD** 618.920005. **NLM** W1. adv acc. **Circ** 1,500. Articles cover learning disabilities, behavioral reactions of childhood and family dynamics for pediatricians, child psychiatrists, and special educators.

JOURNAL OF PEDIATRIC GASTROENTEROLOGY AND NUTRITION. Vol. 1, No. 1-. 0277-2116. Periodical. US. English. bm. $113.00. Raven Press, 1140 Avenue of the Americas, New York NY 10036. **Ind/Abst** Excerpta Med., Index Med., Chem. Abstr. **NLM** W1 JO828E. **CODEN** JPGND6.

JOURNAL OF PEDIATRIC OPHTHALMOLOGY AND STRABISMUS. *See* Medicine - Ophthalmology.

JOURNAL OF PEDIATRIC ORTHOPEDICS. Vol. 1, No. 1 (1981)-. 0271-6798. Periodical. US. English. bm. $105.00. Raven Press, 1140 Avenue of the Americas, New York NY 10036. **Tel** (212)575-0335. **Ind/Abst** Excerpta Med., Biol. Abstr., Index Med., Curr. Contents. **NLM** W1 JO828FE. **CODEN** JPORDO.

JOURNAL OF PEDIATRIC PSYCHOLOGY. Began with Jan. 1976 issue. 0146-8693. Periodical. US. English. qt. $115.00 Domestic, $129.00 Foreign. Plenum Publishing Corporation, 233 Spring Street, New York NY 10013. **Tel** (212)620-8000. **Ed** Gerald P Koocher. **Ind/Abst** Excerpta Med., Index Med., Cumul. Index Nurs. Allied Health Lit., Biol. Abstr., Except. Child Educ. Resour., Psychol. Abstr., Behav. Med. Abstr., Child Youth Serv., Ref. Z., Sage Fam. Stud. Abstr., Soc. Work Res. Abstr., Sociol. Abstr., Psychol. Read. Guide, Child Dev. Abstr. Bibliogr. **LC** RJ503.3. **DD** 618.9289005. **NLM** W1 JO828FG. **CODEN** JPPSDW. bk rev. adv acc. Psychological issues related to the care of children in pediatric settings and psychological aspects of childhood illness. *Pediatric Psychology.*

JOURNAL OF PEDIATRIC SURGERY. V. 1- Feb. 1966-. 0022-3468. Periodical. US. English (summaries in Interlingua). bm. $80.00. Grune & Stratton Inc, 111 Fifth Avenue, New York NY 10003. **Tel** (212)614-3232. **Ind/Abst** Life Sci. Collect., Excerpta Med., Nuci. Sci. Abstr., Biol. Abstr., Index Med., Energy Res. Abstr., Sci. Cit. Index, Abr. Ed., Hospit. Lit. Index. **LC** RD137.A1. **DD** 617. **NLM** W1 JO828FH. **CODEN** JPDSA3.

THE JOURNAL OF PEDIATRICS. V. 1- July 1932-. 0022-3476. Periodical. US. English. mo. $85.50. C V Mosby, c/o R K Kinnes, 11830 Westline Industrial Drive, St Louis Mo 63146. **Tel** (314)872-8370. **Ed** Joseph M Garfunkel. **Ind/Abst** Hospit. Lit. Index, Life Sci. Collect., Excerpta Med., Pestdoc, Ringdoc, Vetdoc, Cumul. Index Nurs. Allied Health Lit., CIS Abstr., Except. Child Educ. Resour., Soc. Work Res. Abstr., Biol. Abstr., Chem. Abstr., Comb. Cumul. Index Pediatr., Nuci. Sci. Abstr., Index Med., Bibliogr. Agric., Energy Res. Abstr., Sci. Cit. Index, Abr. Ed., Abstr. Soc. Work. **LC** RJ1. **DD** 618.9205. **NLM** W1 JO828H. **CODEN** JOPDAB. bk rev. adv acc. **Circ** 26,980. Devoted to diseases of infants and children. Serves the clinical information needs of physicians in pediatric practice and those in allied medical practice. *Transactions - American Academy of Pediatrics.*

JOURNAL OF THE ASSOCIATION FOR THE CARE OF CHILDREN IN HOSPITALS *CEASED.* **Main/Corp** Association for the Care of Children in Hospitals. **VFOAT** JACCH. V. 1- Summer 1972-. 0145-3351. Periodical. US. English. qt. $8.00. **Ind/Abst** Psychol. Abstr. **LC** RJ242. **DD** 362.781105. **NLM** W1 JO912E.

JOURNAL OF THE ASSOCIATION FOR THE CARE OF CHILDREN'S HEALTH. **VFOAT** JACCH. Vol. 9, No 1 (Summer 1980). 0274-8916. Periodical. US. English. qt. $23.00 Domestic, $33.00 Foreign. Association of the Care Childrens Health, 3615 Wisconsin Avenue, Washington DC 20016. **Tel** (202)244-1801. **Ed** William A Rae. **Ind/Abst** Cumul. Index Nurs. Allied Health Lit., Psychol. Abstr. **LC** RJ242. **DD** 362.19892. **NLM** W1 JO912EM. bk rev. adv acc. **Circ** 4,000. (ctrl). Psychosocial aspects of health care for children and their families in all settings from a multidisciplinary perspective. *Journal of the Association for the Care of Children in Hospitals, 0145-3351.*

JOURNAL OF THE SINGAPORE PAEDIATRIC SOCIETY. **Main/Corp** Singapore Paediatric Society. V. 1- 1959-. 0037-5683. Periodical. SI. English. $50.00. University Department of Paediatrics, Singapore General Hospital, Outram Road, Singapore 0316 Singapore. **Ed** H B Wong. **Ind/Abst** Excerpta Med., Index Med. **NLM** W1 JO954I. adv acc. **Circ** 1,000. (ctrl). Clinical pediatric publication of physiological, epidemiological and common pediatric problems in Singapore.

JOURNAL OF TROPICAL PEDIATRICS. V. 26- Feb. 1980-. 0142-6338. Periodical. UK. English. bm. 80.00. Oxford University Press, Journal Department, Walton Street, Oxford OX2 6DP England. **Tel** 0865-56767. **Ed** G J Ebrahim. **Ind/Abst** Life Sci. Collect., Excerpta Med., Index Med., Bibliogr. Agric. **NLM** W1 JO966VC. bk rev. adv acc. Covers all aspects of child health and nutrition including locality and quality of environment. Reporting results of clinical and community research and programme development. *Journal of Tropical Pediatrics and Environmental Child Health, 0300-9920.*

KINDERARZTLICHE PRAXIS. Vol. 1- Sept. 1930-. 0023-1495. Periodical. GE. German. mo. $68.37. Kunst and Wissen Erich Bieber, Dufourstrasse 51, CH-8008 Zurich Switzerland. **Tel** 011-41-1-69 44 20. **Ind/Abst** Life Sci. Collect., Excerpta Med., Index Med. **NLM** W1 KI623.

KLINISCHE PADIATRIE. V. 184- 1972-. 0300-8630. Periodical. GW. German (summaries in English). bm. $161.00. Thieme-Stratton Inc, 381 Park Avenue South, New York NY 10016. **Tel** (212)683-5088. **Ind/Abst** Life Sci. Collect., Excerpta Med., Pestdoc, Ringdoc, Vetdoc, Biol. Abstr., Chem. Abstr., Curr. Contents, Sci. Cit. Index, Abr. Ed., Index Med., Energy Res. Abstr., Sci. Cit. Index, Abr. Ed. **NLM** W1 KL52. **CODEN** KLPDB2. *Archiv fur Kinderheilkunde, 0003-9179.*

Medicine—Pediatrics

MAGYAR PEDIATER. V. 1-. 0303-5042. Periodical. Hungarian. ir. NLM W1.

MAJOR PROBLEMS IN CLINICAL PEDIATRICS. V. 1-. Monographic Series. US. English. ir. WB Saunders, West Washington Square, Philadelphia PA 19105. Tel (800)523-0713. Ind/Abst Energy Res. Abstr., Index Med. NLM W1 MA492N.

MASSON MONOGRAPHS IN PEDIATRIC HEMATOLOGY/ONCOLOGY. VAT Masson Monographs in Pediatric Hematology Oncology. 1-. 0736-0088. Monographic Series. US. English. ir. Masson Distribution Inc, Box C-762, Brooklyn NY 11205. Ed Carl Pochedly and Denis R Miller. LC UNC. NLM W1 MA9309T.

MATERNAL & CHILD HEALTH (RICHMOND, SURREY). See Medicine - Gynecology & Obstetrics.

MATERNAL AND CHILD HEALTH STATISTICS : NORTH CAROLINA. See Statistics.

MATERNAL-CHILD NURSING JOURNAL. See Medicine - Nursing.

MEDICAL AND PEDIATRIC ONCOLOGY. See Medicine - Neoplasma, Neoplastic.

MEDICAL AND PEDIATRIC ONCOLOGY. SUPPLEMENT. See Medicine - Neoplasma, Neoplastic.

MEDICAL EXAMINATION REVIEW BOOK. VOLUME 11. PEDIATRICS. VFOAT Pediatrics. VAT Medical Examination Review Book. Volume Eleven. Pediatrics. 0090-7030. US. English. ir. Medical Exam Publishing Company, 3003 New Hyde Park Road, New Hyde Park NY 11040.

MINERVA PEDIATRICA. Vol. 1- Jan. 1949-. 0026-4946. Periodical. IT. Italian (summaries in English). sm. 100.00. Edizoni Minerva Medica, Corso Bramante 83, Torino Italy 10126. Tel 678282. Ed M Migro. Ind/Abst Life Sci. Collect., Excerpta Med., Index Med., Chem. Abstr., Lang. Lang. Behav. Abstr., Sociol. Abstr. NLM W1 MI652. CODEN MIPEA5. bk rev. adv acc. Journal addressed to practitioners and specialists in pediatrics in Italy and abroad. It deals with topics in pediatrics, scientific practice and research. Policlinico Infantile, Pediatria del Medico Practico; Medicina Italiana; Rivista di Clinica Pediatrica.

MODERN PROBLEMS IN PAEDIATRICS. V. 12- 1972-. 0077-0086. English (contributions in French). ir. S Karger Ag, PO Box, CH-4009 Basel Switzerland. Tel 061-39 08 80. Ed F Falkner, N Kretchmer and E Rossi. Ind/Abst Biol. Abstr., Chem. Abstr., Index Med., Lang. Lang. Behav. Abstr., Sociol. Abstr. NLM W3 MO71. CODEN MPPDBI. Each volume in this series is a problem-oriented collection of knowledge on a specific aspect of pediatrics. Moderne Probleme der Padiatrie, 0077-0086.

MONATSCHRIFT FUR KINDERHEILKUNDE. (MONATSSCHRIFT KINDERHEILKUNDE : ORGAN DER DEUTSCHEN GESELLSCHAFT FUR KINDERHEILKUNDE). 128 Vol. No. 8 (Aug. 1980)-. 0026-9298. Periodical. German. mo. Springer Verlag-New York Inc, 175 5th Avenue, New York NY 10010. Tel (212)460-1500. Ed H Ewerbeck and K H Schafer. Ind/Abst Index Med., Life Sci. Collect., Chem. Abstr., Energy Res. Abstr., Excerpta Med., Curr. Contents, INIS Atomindex. NLM W1 MO364. CODEN MOKIAY. Journal of the German Association for Pediatrics. Scientific information and continued education for the pediatrician in the hospital or practice. New and important developments, reviews of international works and difficult cases are discussed.

MONATSSCHRIFT FUR KINDERHEILKUNDE CEASED. V. 1-128, No. 7-. 0026-9298. Periodical. German. mo. Ind/Abst Excerpta Med., Life Sci. Collect., Energy Res. Abstr., Chem. Abstr., Biol. Abstr. NLM W1 MO359D. CODEN MOKIAY. (cum index).

MONOGRAPH (PEDIATRIC PROJECTS INC.). (MONOGRAPH). No. 1-. Monographic Series. US. English. NLM W1.

MONOGRAPHS IN DEVELOPMENTAL PEDIATRICS. V. 1-. 0162-6906. Monographic Series. US. English. University Park Press, 233 East Redwood Street, Baltimore MD 21202. LC UNC. NLM W1 MO567LP.

MONOGRAPHS IN PAEDIATRICS. V. 1- 1971-. 0077-0914. Monographic Series. English. ir. S Karger Ag, PO Box, CH-4009 Basel Switzerland. Tel 061-39 08 80. Ed F Falkner, N Kretchmer and E Rossi. Ind/Abst Life Sci. Collect., Biol. Abstr., Chem. Abstr., Index Med. NLM W1 MO568G. CODEN MNGPBT. Volumes in this series clarify and evaluate difficult and changing problems in pediatrics. Bibliotheca Paediatrica, 0301-357X.

MONOGRAPHS OF THE SOCIETY FOR RESEARCH IN CHILD DEVELOPMENT. V. 1-. 0037-976X. Monographic Series. US. English. ir. $51.00. University of Chicago Press, PO Box 37005, Chicago IL 60637. Tel (312)753-3347. Ind/Abst Sociol. Abstr., Energy Res. Abstr., Educ. Index, Biol. Abstr., Index Med., Curr. Index J. Educ., Psychol. Abstr., Index Med., Soc. Sci. Citation Index, Educ. Index, Lang. Lang. Behav. Abstr. NLM W1 MO569RK. CODEN MSCDA7.

MOTHER & CHILD. See Medicine - Gynecology & Obstetrics.

NEONATAL NETWORK. See Medicine - Nursing.

NEONATOLOGY LETTER. See Medicine - Gynecology & Obstetrics.

NEUROPADIATRIE. VFOAT Journal of Pediatric Neurobiology, Neurology and Neurosurgery. V. 1-11, Issue 2. 0028-3797. Periodical. contributions in German or English with summaries in other languages. qt. $99.00. Thieme-Stratton Inc, 381 Park Avenue South, New York NY 10016. Tel (212)683-5088. Ind/Abst Excerpta Med., Biol. Abstr., Chem. Abstr., Index Med., Sci. Cit. Index, Abr. Ed. NLM W1 NE337L. CODEN NEPPABB.

NEUROPEDIATRIA LATINOAMERICANA. Periodical. Spanish. ir. Avenida Italia, 2817 Casilla de Correo No 847, Montevideo Uruguay.

NEUROPEDIATRICS. See Medicine - Neurology.

NEW YORK PEDIATRICIAN. (NEW YORK PEDIATRICIAN : OFFICIAL PUBLICATION OF DISTRICT II, AMERICAN ACADEMY OF PEDIATRICS, STATE OF NEW YORK). Vol. 1, No. 1 (Winter 1983)-. 0737-4216. Periodical. US. English. sa. $15.00. Coney Island Hospital, Department of Pediatrics, 2601 Ocean Parkway, Brooklyn NY 11235. Tel (718)615-5378. Ed Henry A Schaeffer. adv acc. Circ 3,000. (ctrl). News and commentaries on matters that affect pediatric practice and practitioners of this region.

NEWSLETTER OF THE A.A.P.S.C. See Medicine - Psychiatry, Psychopathology.

NICHD ANNUAL REPORT. Main/Corp National Institute of Child Health and Human Development (U.S.). VFOAT N.I.C.H.D. Annual Report. VAT National Institute of Child Health and Human Development Annual Report. 0741-4684. US. English. an. National Institute of Child Health and Human Development, 9000 Rockville Pike, Bethesda MD 20205. LC RJ101. DD 618.920005. Vols. for 1980/1981-(1982/1983) distributed to depository libraries in microfiche.

NIHON SHONIKA GAKKAI ZASSHI. VFOAT Acta Paediatrica Japonica. Began in 1951. 0001-6543. Periodical. JA. Japanese. mo. Japan Publishing Trading Co Ltd, PO Box 5030, Tokyo International, Tokyo 100-31 Japan. Ind/Abst Life Sci. Collect., Chem. Abstr. CODEN NIPOAC.

NOTIZIARIO PEDIATRICO. V. 1- Jan./Mar. 1979-. 0392-0615. Periodical. IT. Italian. qt. $37.32. Edizioni Minervia Medica, Corso Bramante 83/PO Box 491, Torino 10126 Italy. Tel 67.82.82. NLM W1 NO819K. Notiziario della Societa Italiana di Pediatria.

OB/GYN-PED-DERM ADVISER. See Medicine - Gynecology & Obstetrics.

OPHTHALMIC PAEDIATRICS AND GENETICS. Vol. 1, No. 1 (Nov. 1981)-. 0167-6784. Periodical. NE. English. qt. $158.00. Aeolus Press, PO Box 740, 4116 ZJ Buren The Netherlands. Tel 03447 2055. Ind/Abst Excerpta Med., Index Med. NLM W1 OP235R.

PADIATRIE UND GRENZGEBIETE. Vol. 1- 1962-. 0030-932X. Periodical. SZ. German. bm. $67.59. Kunst & Wissen Erich Bieber, Dufourstrasse 51, CH-8008 Zurich Switzerland. Tel 011-41-1-69 44 20. Ind/Abst Excerpta Med., Index Med. NLM W1 PA264J. Index published separately - free - automatically sent.

PADIATRIE UND PADOLOGIE. Vol. 1- April, 1965-. 0030-9338. Periodical. AU. German (English or French, with some English summaries). qt. Springer Verlag-New York Inc, 175 5th Avenue, New York NY 10010. Tel (212)460-1500. Ed G Weippl. Ind/Abst Excerpta Med., Chem. Abstr., Biol. Abstr., Index Med., Curr. Contents. NLM W1 PA264P. CODEN PAPAB5. Covers all areas of pediatrics and other sciences as they relate to the nature and development of the child. Main part consists of original articles, also includes reviews and convention notices. Neue Osterreichische Zeitschrift fur Kinderheilkunde.

PADIATRIE UND PADOLOGIE. SUPPLEMENTUM. 0300-9556. Monographic Series. AU. German (summaries in English). ir. Springer Verlag, Postfach 367, Moelkerbastei 5, A-1011 Vienna Austria. Ind/Abst Index Med. NLM W1 PA264Q.

PADIATRISCHE NUKLEARMEDIZIN. V. 1-. 0724-732X. German. an. Ed K Hahn. NLM W1 PA242.

PAEDIATRIC CARDIOLOGY. Vol. 1 (1977)-. 0261-7021. Periodical. UK. English. an. Churchill Livingstone Inc, 1560 Broadway, New York NY 10036. NLM W1 PA263J.

PAEDIATRICA INDONESIANA. V. 1- 1961-. 0030-9311. Periodical. IO. Indonesian. bm. $30.00. University of Indonesia, Department of Child Health, Medical School, PO Box 3620, 6 Salemba Jakarta Indonesia. Ind/Abst Excerpta Med., Index Med. NLM W1 PA263P.

PAEDIATRISCHE FORTBILDUNGSKURSE FUR DIE PRAXIS. V. 1- 1962-. 0078-7795. Periodical. SZ. German. ir. S Karger AG, CH-4009 Basel Switzerland. Tel (61)390880. Ed E Rossi. Ind/Abst Biol. Abstr. NLM W1 PA2645. CODEN PFPXA6. Much practical and important information for the practicing pediatrician. Each issue deals with a different aspect of childhood diseases-prevention, chronic illnesses, handicaps, and infections.

PAEDONOSON. 0737-5158. Periodical. US. English. qt. $50.00. Paedonoson, PO Box 1344, Oak Brook IL 60521.

PEDIATRIA. 1- 1958-. 0375-9563. Periodical. CL. Spanish (contains some summaries in English, German, French and Italian). qt. $20.00. Universite of Chile, Faculte Medicina, Zanartu 1085, Santiago Chile. Ind/Abst Excerpta Med.

PEDIATRIA. V. 1- April 1977-. 0325-3767. Periodical. AG. Spanish. bm. $60.00. La Prensa Medica Argentina, Junin 845, Buenos Aires Argentina. Ind/Abst Excerpta Med. NLM W1 PE142C. Archivos Argentinos de Pediatria, 0004-0487.

PEDIATRIA. (PEDIATRIA (S. PAULO) : REVISTA DO CENTRO DE ESTUDOS PROF. PEDRO DE ALCANTARA, EM CONVENIO COM INSTITUTO DA CRIANCA, HOSPITAL DAS CLINICAS, FMUSP). Vol. 1, No. 1 (March 1979)-. 0101-3858. Periodical. BL. Portuguese. qt. NLM W1 PE163E.

PEDIATRIA (LIMA, PERU). (PEDIATRIA). V. 1, No. 1 (Jan./June 1976)-. Periodical. Spanish. ir. NLM W1 PE135L.

PEDIATRIA OGGI MEDICA E CHIRURGICA. 0391-898X. Periodical. Italian. bm. NLM W1.

PEDIATRIA POLSKA. V. 1- 1921-. 0031-3939. Periodical. Polish. ir. Ind/Abst Life Sci. Collect., Excerpta Med., Index Med., Biol. Abstr., Chem. Abstr. NLM W1 PE159. CODEN PEPOA6. Przeglad Pedyatryczny.

PEDIATRIA. RIVISTA D'IGIENE MEDICINA E CHIRURGIA DELL'INFANZIA. 0031-3890. Periodical. IT. Italian. qt. $24.00. Clinica Pediatrica, S Andrea Delle/Dame 4, 80138 Napoli Italy. Ind/Abst Index Med. NLM W1 PE137.

PEDIATRIC ALERT. 0160-0184. Periodical. US. English. bw. Pediatric Alert, PO Box 338, Newton Highlands MA 02161. Tel (617)699-8027.

PEDIATRIC AND ADOLESCENT ENDOCRINOLOGY. See Medicine - Endocrinology.

PEDIATRIC AND ADOLESCENT GYNECOLOGY. (PEDIATRIC AND ADOLESCENT GYNECOLOGY : OFFICIAL JOURNAL OF THE INTERNATIONAL FEDERATION OF

INFANTILE AND JUVENILE GYNECOLOGY). Vol. 1, No. 1-. 0737-3945. Periodical. US. English. sa. $95.00. Marcel Dekker Inc, PO Box 11305/Church Street Station, New York NY 10249. **Ed** John Dervhurst. **Ind/Abst** Excerpta Med. **NLM** W1. **CODEN** PAGYDY. bk rev. adv acc.

PEDIATRIC ANESTHESIA. CURRENT PRACTICE. (PEDIATRIC ANESTHESIA—CURRENT PRACTICE). Vol. 1-. 0734-4600. US. English. **Ed** M Ramez Salem. **NLM** W1 PE163J.

PEDIATRIC ANNALS. V. 1- Oct. 1972-. 0090-4481. Periodical. US. English. mo. $74.00. Slack Inc, c/o Donna Carpenter, 6900 Grove Road, Thorofare NJ 08086. **Tel** (609)848-1000. **Ed** Donna Carpenter. **Ind/Abst** Life Sci. Collect., Excerpta Med., Index Med., Cumul. Index Nurs. Allied Health Lit., Energy Res. Abstr., Comb. Cumul. Index Pediatr., Bibliogr. Agric. **LC** RJ1. **DD** 618.920005. **NLM** W1 PE163N. Index in last issue of volume - attached. bk rev. adv acc. **Circ** 30,000. (ctrl). Provides the pediatrician with new information on diagnosis and patient management that will be useful to him in his practice.

PEDIATRIC CARDIOLOGY. V. 1-. 0172-0643. Periodical. US. English. bm. $90.00. Springer Verlag-New York Inc, 175 5th Avenue, New York NY 10010. **Tel** (212)460-1500. **Ed** I Carr, G Graham, F Macartney and R A Miller. **Ind/Abst** Life Sci. Collect., Excerpta Med., Index Med., Sci. Cit. Index, Abr. Ed. **LC** RJ421. **DD** 618.9212. **NLM** W1 PE164L. **CODEN** PECAD4. Contains technical notes on the latest instruments, unusual electrocardiographic, echocardiographic, and surgical observations in children, letters to the editors, and editorials and reviews on important clinical and scientific issues.

THE PEDIATRIC CLINICS OF NORTH AMERICA. V. 1- Feb. 1954-. 0031-3955. Monographic Series. US. English. bm. $45.00. W B Saunders, West Washington Square, Philadelphia PA 19105. **Tel** (215)574-3395. **Ed** Barbara Conover. **Ind/Abst** Life Sci. Collect., Excerpta Med., Energy Res. Abstr., Biol. Abstr., Chem. Abstr., Comb. Cumul. Index Pediatr., Index Med., Nuci. Sci. Abstr., Sci. Cit. Index, Abr. Ed. **LC** RJ23. **DD** 618.92082. **NLM** W1 PE165. **CODEN** PCNAA8. (cum index). **Circ** 20,000. Clinical updates on topics of current interest to pediatricians.

PEDIATRIC CONFERENCES FROM THE CHILDREN'S HOSPITAL OF NEWARK. 1970-. 0097-5982. Periodical. US. English. Childrens Hospital of Newark, 15 South 9th Street, Newark NJ 07107. **NLM** W1 PE167. *Pediatric Conferences from the Babies' Hospital Unit, United Hospitals of Newark, New Jersey, 0031-3963.*

PEDIATRIC CONFERENCES WITH SYDNEY GELLIS. Periodical. US. English. bm. $44.11. W B Saunders Company Canada Ltd, One Goldthorne Avenue, Toronto Ontario M8Z 5T9 Canada.

PEDIATRIC DERMATOLOGY. *See* Medicine - Dermatology.

PEDIATRIC EMERGENCY CARE. Vol. 1, No. 1 (Mar. 1985)-. 0749-5161. Periodical. US. English. qt. $55.00 Domestic, $65.00 Foreign. Williams & Wilkins, 428 East Preston Street, Baltimore MD 21202. **Tel** (301)528-4400. **DD** 618. **NLM** W1. adv acc. **Circ** 2,300. Valuable clinical information for emergency physicians and pediatricians who care for acutely ill or injured children and adolescents.

PEDIATRIC HABILITATION. Vol. 1-. 0731-5902. Monographic Series. US. English. ir. Marcel Dekker Inc, 270 Madison Avenue, New York NY 10026. **Tel** (212)696-9000. **Ed** Alfred Scherzer. **DD** 618.92. **NLM** W1 PE167K. This is an ongoing series. Each title has a different subject.

PEDIATRIC INFECTIOUS DISEASE. Vol. 1, No. 1 (Jan/Feb 1982)-. 0277-9730. Periodical. US. English. bm. $50.00. Williams & Wilkins Company, 428 East Preston Street, Baltimore MD 21202. **Tel** (301)528-4000. **Ed** John D Nelson and George H McCracken. **Ind/Abst** Excerpta Med., Index Med. **NLM** W1 PE168F. adv acc. **Circ** 8,800. Articles for pediatricians, family practitioners and infectious disease specialists. Covers the treatment of viral and bacterial illness in children.

PEDIATRIC MENTAL HEALTH. Vol. 1, No. 1 (Jan./Feb. 1982)-. 0278-4998. Periodical. US. English. bm. $28.00. Pediatric Projects Inc, PO Box 1880, Santa Monica CA 90406. **Tel** (213)459-7710. **Ed** Pat Azarnoff. bk rev. A professional publication describing theory and practice of psychological preparation, therapeutic play, and supported parenting of children in health care.

PEDIATRIC NEPHROLOGY. V. 1-. 0097-5257. US. English. ir. University of Miami School of Medicine, PO Box 016960, c/o Director Dr Jose Strauss, Miami FL 33101. **Tel** (305)549-6726. **Ed** Jose Strauss. **Ind/Abst** Chem. Abstr. **LC** RJ466. **DD** 618.9261005. **NLM** W1 PE168K. **CODEN** PENED3. **Circ** 2,000. Current aspects of diagnosis and treatment of urological and renal disorders in pediatrics.

PEDIATRIC NETWORK. 0742-1605. Periodical. US. English. mo. $9.00. Thagard Enterprises, PO Box 8396, Calabasas CA 91302. **Tel** (213)884-0315.

PEDIATRIC NEWS. V. 1- Jan. 1967-. 0031-398X. Periodical. US. English. mo. International Medical News Group, 12230 Wilkins Avenue, Rockville MD 20852. **LC** RJ1. **DD** 618.92. **NLM** W1 PE168N. Also available on microfilm from University Microfilms.

PEDIATRIC NOTES. V. 1- 1977-. 0738-8691. Periodical. US. English. wk. $55.00. Pediatric Notes, PO Box 59, Newtonville MA 02160.

PEDIATRIC NURSING. V. 1- Jan./Feb. 1975-. 0097-9805. Periodical. US. English. bm. $18.00. Pediatric Nursing, North Woodbury Road, Box 56, Pitman NJ 08071. **Tel** (609)589-2319. **Ind/Abst** Cumul. Index Nurs. Allied Health Lit., Index Dent. Lit., Int. Nurs. Index. **LC** RJ245. **DD** 610.736205. **NLM** W1 PE169D.

PEDIATRIC PATHOLOGY. Vol. 1, No. 1 (Jan.-Mar. 1983. 0277-0938. Periodical. US. English. ir. $230.00. Hemisphere Publishing Corporation, 79 Madison Avenue/Suite 1110, New York NY 10016. **Tel** (207)783-3958. **Ed** William A Blanc. **Ind/Abst** Life Sci. Collect., Excerpta Med. **NLM** W1. **CODEN** PPATDQ. bk rev. adv acc. **Circ** 880. Refereed articles cover all aspects of pediatric pathology as practiced by hospital and academic pathologists. Pediatricians research new techniques, case reports, pathological correlations, electron microscopy.

PEDIATRIC PHARMACOLOGY (NEW YORK, N.Y.). (PEDIATRIC PHARMACOLOGY). Vol. 1, No. 1-. 0270-322X. Periodical. US. English. qt. Alan R Liss Inc, 41 East 11th Street, New York NY 10003. **Tel** (212)741-2515. **Ind/Abst** Life Sci. Collect., Excerpta Med., Index Med., Biol. Abstr., Chem. Abstr. **NLM** W1 PE17H. **CODEN** PPHAD4.

PEDIATRIC RADIOLOGY. V. 1- Mar. 1973-. 0301-0449. Periodical. WB. English. bm. $114.00. Springer Verlag-New York Inc, 175 5th Avenue, New York NY 10010. **Tel** (212)460-1500. **Ed** W E Berdon, A R Chrispin, K D Ebel, O A Eklof, C Faure, C A Gooding, G B C Harris, K Lassrich, B J Reilly and E Willich. **Ind/Abst** Life Sci. Collect., Excerpta Med., Index Med., Energy Res. Abstr., Sci. Cit. Index, Abr. Ed. **NLM** W1 PE173. **CODEN** PDRYA5. Index in last issue of volume - attached. bk rev. The only journal devoted exclusively to the various aspects of diagnostic imaging in children. Fields of interest are diagnostics, radiology, pediatrics and gynecology.

PEDIATRIC RESEARCH. V. 1- Jan. 1967-. 0031-3998. Periodical. US. English (French). mo. $110.00. Williams & Wilkins Company, 428 East Preston Street, Baltimore MD 21202. **Tel** (3021)528-4000. **Ed** Delbert A Fisher. **Ind/Abst** Life Sci. Collect., Excerpta Med., Lang. Lang. Behav. Abstr., Biol. Abstr., Chem. Abstr., Index Med., Nuci. Sci. Abstr., Energy Res. Abstr., Sociol. Abstr., Sci. Cit. Index, Abr. Ed. **LC** RJ1. **NLM** W1 PE175. **CODEN** PEREBL. adv acc. **Circ** 2,965. Covers the latest advances in the understanding and management of pediatric pulmonary, endocrinological, gastroenterological and nutrition disorders. *Annales Paediatrici.*

PEDIATRIC REVIEWS AND COMMUNICATION. 0882-9225. Periodical. UK. English. qt. $140.00. Harwood Academic, PO Box 197, London WC2E 9PX England. **Ed** David Burman. bk rev. adv acc.

PEDIATRIC SOCIAL WORK. Vol. 1, No. 1 (Jan. 1980)-. 0195-5926. Periodical. US. English. qt. $25.00. Eterna Press, PO 1344, Oak Brook IL 60521. **Tel** (312)531-3491. **NLM** W1 PE175R.

PEDIATRIC THERAPY. 1st- Ed. Periodical. US. English. ir. C V Mosby, c/o C Leadbetter, 11830 Westline Industrial Drive, St Louis MO 63141.

PEDIATRIC WORLD. V. 1- Jan. 1963-. 0479-785X. Periodical. US. English. ir. Ross Laboratories, 625 Cleveland Avenue, Columbus OH 43216.

PEDIATRICS. V. 1- Jan. 1948-. 0031-4005. Periodical. US. English (most articles accompanied by Spanish abstracts). mo. $55.00 Domestic, $65.00 Foreign. American Academy of Pediatrics, PO Box 1034, Evanston IL 60204. **Tel** (312)228-5005. **Ed** Jerold Lucey. **Ind/Abst** Life Sci. Collect., Excerpta Med., Energy Res. Abstr., Except. Child Educ. Resour., Soc. Work Res. Abstr., Biol. Abstr., Chem. Abstr., Comb. Cumul. Index Pediatr., Index Med., Nuci. Sci. Abstr., Bibliogr. Agric., Cumul. Index Nurs. Allied Health Lit., Pestdoc, Ringdoc, Vetdoc, Sci. Cit. Index, Abr. Ed., Sociol. Abstr., Abstr. Soc. Work. **LC** RJ1. **DD** 618.9205. **NLM** W1 PE191. **CODEN** PEDIAU. (cum index). adv acc. **Circ** 41,000. Original and up-to-date articles on all aspects of child and adolescent health, and development pediatrics. The official journal of the American Academy of Pediatrics.

PEDIATRICS. 0079-0400. Periodical. US. English. $2.50. Medical World News, 299 Park Avenue, New York NY 10017. **LC** RJ1. **DD** 618.920005.

PEDIATRICS DIGEST. V. 21, No. 8/9- Aug./Sept. 1979-. 0198-6341. US. English. mo. $27.50. Pediatrics Digest, 445 Central Avenue, Northfield IL 60093. **NLM** W1 PE193. *Journal of Continuing Education in Pediatrics, 0160-7766.*

PEDIATRICS FOR PARENTS : THE MONTHLY NEWSLETTER FOR CARING PARENTS. 1981. 0730-6725. Periodical. US. English. mo. $15.00. Pediatrics for Parents, 176 Mt Hope Avenue, Bangor ME 04401. **Tel** (207)942-6212. **Ed** Richard J Sagall. bk rev. **Circ** 1,500. Pediatric information for non-medical people emphasizing self-care and parental participation in their child's health care. Written by health care professionals.

PEDIATRICS IN REVIEW. Vol. 1, No. 1 (July 1979)-. 0191-9601. Periodical. US. English. mo. $75.00. American Academy of Pediatrics, 141 Northwest Point Road, Elk Grove Village IL 60007. **Tel** (312)228-5005. **Ed** R James McKay. **NLM** W1 PE193H. **Circ** 20,000. Contains timely review articles related to the practice of pediatric medicine, editorials, and abstracts.

PEDIATRICS (MARCEL DEKKER, INC.). (PEDIATRICS). Vol. 1-. Monographic Series. US. English. ir. Marcel Dekker Inc, 270 Madison Avenue, New York NY 10016. **Tel** (212)696-9000. **Ed** Bauer. **NLM** W1. This is an ongoing series. Each title has a different subject.

PEDIATRICS UPDATE. 1979-. 0163-1713. Periodical. US. English. ir. Elsevier Science Publishing, PO Box 1663/Grand Central Station, New York NY 10163. **Tel** (212)370-5520. **Ind/Abst** Chem. Abstr. **LC** RJ16. **DD** 618.9205. **NLM** W1 PE195. **CODEN** PEUPD3.

PEDIATRIE. Vol. 1-. 0031-4021. Periodical. FR. French (summaries in English). ir. Professor Larbre, Hospital Debrousse, 29 rue Soiurs Bouvie, 69005 Lyon France. **Tel** 009-0122. **Ind/Abst** Index Med., Chem. Abstr. **NLM** W1 PE203. **CODEN** PEDRAN.

PEDIATRIJA. (PEDIATRIIA). **VFOAT** Pediatria. Vol. 1- 1962-. 0479-7876. Periodical. BU. Bulgarian (with summaries of some articles in Russian and English). bm. $20.00. Hemus, 6 Boulevard Rusky, Sofia Bulgaria. **Ind/Abst** Excerpta Med., Chem. Abstr., Index Med. **NLM** W1 PE227. **CODEN** PDTAAB.

PERINATAL PRESS. V. 1- Jan. 1977-. 0160-7219. Periodical. US. English. ir. $17.00. Perinatal Press, 5275 F Streets, Sacramento CA 95819. **Tel** (916)454-3450. **Ed** D F Bulger. **Ind/Abst** Cumul. Index Nurs. Allied Health Lit. **NLM** W1 PE788H. bk rev. **Circ** 5,000. Practical information for those caring for the pregnant woman, fetus and newborn.

PERINATOLOGY-NEONATOLOGY. *See* Medicine - Gynecology & Obstetrics.

PERSPECTIVES IN PEDIATRIC PATHOLOGY. V. 1- 1973-. 0091-2921. US. English. qt. Masson Publishing USA Inc, 211 East 43rd Street/Room 1306, New York NY 10017. **Tel** (212)370-1937. **Ind/Abst** Index Med., Energy Res. Abstr. **LC** RJ49. **DD** 618.9200705. **NLM** W1 PE871D.

PHYSICAL & OCCUPATIONAL THERAPY IN PEDIATRICS. **VFOAT** Physical and Occupational Therapy in Pediatrics. Vol. 1, No. 1 (Fall 1980)-. 0194-2638. Periodical. US.

Medicine—Psychiatry, Psychopathology

English. qt. $102.00. Haworth Press Inc, 28 East 22nd Street, New York NY 10010. Tel (212)228-2800. Ed Suzann K Campbell and Irma J Wilhelm. Ind/Abst Excerpta Med., Cumul. Index Nurs. Allied Health Lit., Biol. Abstr., Psychol. Abstr. LC RJ53.P5. DD 615.82. NLM W1 PH683P. CODEN POTPDY. bk rev. adv acc. Circ 2,512. Designed for physical therapy and occupational therapy pediatric professionals in hospitals, rehabilitation centers, schools, community, and health and human service agencies. Providing latest clinical research and practical applications.

POCKETBOOK OF PEDIATRIC ANTIMICROBIAL THERAPY. VFOAT Pocket Book of Pediatric Antimicrobial Therapy. 8755-5476. Periodical. US. English. be. $3.50. Jodone Publishing Company, 3226 Oliver Street, Dallas TX 75205. Ed John D Nelson. DD 615.

PRACTICAL PEDIATRICS. Vol. 1-. US. English. Ed Richard H Rapkin. NLM ZWS 100 P894.

PROCEEDINGS - ASSOCIATION OF EUROPEAN PAEDIATRIC CARDIOLOGISTS. Main/Corp Association of European Paediatric Cardiologists. VFOAT Bulletin de l'Association des Cardiologues Pediatres Europeens. No. 1- 1966?-. Periodical. English (articles in French). ir.

PROGRESS IN PEDIATRIC HEMATOLOGY-ONCOLOGY. (PROGRESS IN PEDIATRIC HEMATOLOGY/ONCOLOGY). V. 1-. 0146-1540. Monographic Series. US. English. Ed C Pochedly and D R Miller. Ind/Abst Chem. Abstr. LC UNC. NLM W1 PR677E. CODEN PPHODC.

PROGRESS IN PEDIATRIC RADIOLOGY. Began with: Vol. 1, published in 1967. 0079-6646. English. an. S Karger AG, PO Box 352, White Plains NY 10602. Tel 061-39 08 80. Ed H S Kaufmann. LC RJ51.R3. DD 618.9200757. NLM W1 PR677H.

RECENT ADVANCES IN PAEDIATRIC SURGERY. No. 1-. 0308-4906. UK. English. Churchill Livingstone Inc, 1560 Broadway, New York NY 10036. Tel (212)819-5400. Ed A W Wilkinson. NLM W1 RE105X.

RECENT ADVANCES IN PAEDIATRICS. 0309-0140. UK. English. ir. Churchill Livingstone Inc, 1560 Broadway, New York NY 10036. Tel (212)819-5400. NLM W1 RE105XF.

REPORT, NEWBORN METABOLIC SCREENING PROGRAM. VFOAT Newborn Metabolic Screening Program. US. English. an. Washington State Department of Social and Health Services, 1704 NE 150th Street, Seattle WA 98155. LC RJ399.P5. DD 362.1989239. *PKU, Phenylketonuria, Detection and Treatment Program, 0146-8774.*

REVISTA CHILENA DE PEDIATRIA. Vol. 1 - Jan. 1930-. 0370-4106. Periodical. CL. Spanish (some summaries in Portugese, English and German). bm. $45.00. Sociedad Chilena de Pediatria, Av Eliodoro Yanez 1984, Department 405, Casilla 16257, Santiago Chile. Tel 225-4393. Ed Carlos Toro. Ind/Abst Index Med. NLM W1 RE351E. bk rev. adv acc. Circ 1,200. (ctrl). Basic sciences, clinical, educational, academic and public health aspects of pediatric medicine and health care.

REVISTA DE PEDIATRIA PREVENTIVA E SOCIALE. NIPIOLOGIA. (RIVISTA DI PEDIATRIA PREVENTIVA E SOCIALE, NIPIOLOGIA : ORGANO UFFICIALE TRIMESTRALE SOCIETA ITALIANA DI PEDIATRIA PREVENTIVA E SOCIALE, NIPIOLOGIA). VFOAT Pediatria Preventiva e Sociale, Nipiologia. Vol. 30, N. 1 (Jan-Mar 1980)-. 0392-4416. Periodical. IT. Italian. qt. 60.00. Edizioni Minerva Medica, P O Box 491, 10100 Torino Italy. Tel 67 82 82. Ed E Memsi. NLM W1 RI608P. bk rev. adv acc. Journal addressed to practitioners and specialists in social mediatrics in Italy and abroad. It deals with topics in scientific practice and research. *Minerva Nipiologica.*

REVISTA DEL HOSPITAL DE NINOS. (REVISTA DEL HOSPITAL DE NINOS (BUENOS AIRES)). V. 1- (No. 1-). 0521-517X. Periodical. Spanish. Ind/Abst Excerpta Med. NLM W1 RE51.

REVISTA MEXICANA DE PEDIATRIA. 0035-0052. Periodical. MX. Spanish. mo. $50.00. Org de la Soc Mex de Pediatria, Tehuantepec 86 Desp 503, Mexico 7 D F Mexico 06760. Tel 564-83-71. bk rev. adv acc. Circ 10,000. (ctrl). Covers preventive, medical and social pediatrics.

REVUE DE PEDIATRIE. (LA REVUE DE PEDIATRIE). Began in 1965. 0035-1644. Periodical. FR. French. mo. 650. La Revue de Pediatrie, 62 rue Ivan Tourgueniev, 78380 Bougival France. Tel 16.30.61.65.11. Ind/Abst Excerpta Med. NLM W1 RE798N. bk rev. adv acc. Circ 6,000. (ctrl). Scientific review on all subjects in pediatrics.

RIVISTA ITALIANA DI PEDIATRIA. VFOAT The Italian Journal of Pediatrics. 0390-671X. Periodical. IT. Italian. bm. Il Pensiero Scientifico Edit, Via Panama 48, 00198 Rome Italy. Tel 863 633. Ind/Abst Excerpta Med. NLM W1 RI78M.

SEMINARS IN ADOLESCENT MEDICINE. Vol. 1, No. 1 (Mar. 1985)-. 0748-6480. Periodical. US. English. qt. $50.00. Thieme-Stratton Inc, 381 Park Avenue South/Suite 1501, New York NY 10016. Tel (212)683-5088. Ed Robert Shearin. DD 612. adv acc. Circ 700. Topic-oriented journal for the practitioner specializing in adolescent medicine and issues.

SERIE PEDIATRIA. VFOAT Pediatria. V.1-. Periodical. Portuguese. ir.

SERIES PAEDOPSYCHIATRICA. See Medicine - Psychiatry, Psychopathology.

SHONI GEKA. See Medicine - Surgery.

SOAKWA. JOURNAL OF THE KOREAN PEDIATRIC ASSOCIATION. VFOAT Journal of the Korean Pediatric Association. Periodical. KO. Korean (with summaries in English). ir. 28 Yongon-Dong, Chongno-Ku Seoul. LC RJ1. NLM W1 SO101.

SOINS. GYNECOLOGIE, OBSTETRIQUE, PUERICULTURE. See Medicine - Gynecology & Obstetrics.

SOZIALPADIATRIE IN PRAXIS UND KLINIK. Vol. 1-: 15. Sept. 1979-. 0171-9327. Periodical. German. ir. NLM W1 SO999Q.

SURPRISE CEASED. (LA SURPRISE : JOURNAL DES ENFANTS DE L'HOPITAL SAINTE-JUSTINE). 0824-4162. Periodical. CN. French (comprend du texte en Anglais). sa. Free. Surprise, 3175 Cote Sainte-Catherine, Montreal Quebec H3T 1C5 Canada. DD 362.198920009714281. (ctrl).

TAGUNG DER DEUTSCHEN GESELLSCHAFT FUR KINDERHEILKUNDE. Series/Titl Alete-Reihe. 0343-4893. Periodical. German. ir. NLM W1 TA41NM.

THEORY AND RESEARCH IN BEHAVIORAL PEDIATRICS. Vol. 1-. 0735-6897. Periodical. US. English. be. Plenum Publishing Corporation, 233 Spring Street, New York NY 10013. Ed Hiram E Fitzgerald, Barry M Lester, and Michael W Yogman. LC RJ131. DD 618.92029. NLM W1 TH123Y (P.

TIJDSCHRIFT VOOR KINDERGENEESKUNDE. Vol. 44- Feb. 1976-. 0376-7442. Periodical. NE. Dutch (articles and summaries in English). bm. Libresso, Postbus 878, 7400 AW Deventer Netherlands. Ind/Abst Life Sci. Collect., Excerpta Med., Index Med., Chem. Abstr. NLM W1 TI654N. CODEN TIKID4. *Maandschrift Voor Kindetgeneeskunde.*

TOPICS IN PEDIATRICS. Vol. 1, No. 1 (Spring 1982)-. Periodical. US. English. sa. NLM W1.

TURKISH JOURNAL OF PEDIATRICS. (THE TURKISH JOURNAL OF PEDIATRICS). V. 1- 1958-. 0041-4301. Periodical. TU. English. qt. 50.00. Turkish Journal of Pediatrics, PO Box 06572, Maltepe Ankara Turkey. Tel (41)234822. Ed Ihsan Dogramaci. Ind/Abst Excerpta Med., Index Med. NLM W1 TU973. bk rev. Circ 1,500. General pediatrics-clinical and research.

VOPROSY AKUSHERSTVA I PEDIATRII. Vol. 1- 1956-. 0137-0162. UR. Russian. NLM W1 VO6061H.

VOPROSY OHRANY MATERINSTVA I DETSVA. (VOPROSY OKHRANY MATERINSTVA I DETSVA). Vol. 1- Jan./Feb. 1956-. 0042-8825. Periodical. UR. Russian. mo. $31.50. Victor Kamkin Inc (73065), 12224 Parklawn Drive, Rockville MD 20852. Tel (301)881-5973. Ind/Abst Excerpta Med., Biol. Abstr., Chem. Abstr. NLM W1 VO6401. CODEN VOMDAQ.

THE YEAR BOOK OF PEDIATRICS. See Yearbooks, Almanacs, Directories.

ZEITSCHRIFT FUR KINDERCHIRURGIE. See Medicine - Surgery.

ZEITSCHRIFT FUR KINDERCHIRURGIE UND GRENZGEBIETE. See Medicine - Surgery.

ZENTRALBLATT KINDERHEILKUNDE. VFOAT Paediatrics. 129. Vol., No. 1-. 0722-8953. Periodical. German (English). mo. Springer Verlag-New York Inc, 175 5th Avenue, New York NY 10010. Tel (212)460-1500. Ed D Feist, K Scharer, D Scheffner and E Willich. NLM ZWS 100 Z56. Preventive and social pediatrics, growth and development, genetics, birth defects, prenatal care, premature births, infectious diseases, immunizations, nutrition, surgery and anesthesiology. *Zentralblatt fur die Gesamte Kinderheilkunde.*

ZERO TO THREE. Began in 1980. 0736-8038. Periodical. US. English. qt. $15.00. National Center for Clinical Infant Programs, 733 15th Street Suite 912, Washington DC 20005. Tel (202)347-0308. Ed Jeree Pawl. bk rev. Circ 6,500. New research on infant and toddler health. Mental health and development as well as promising service approaches new publications training and funding opportunities.

PSYCHIATRY, PSYCHOPATHOLOGY

ABMS DIRECTORY OF CERTIFIED PSYCHIATRISTS. See Yearbooks, Almanacs, Directories.

THE ACADEMY FORUM. V. 22- Spring 1978-. 0192-1088. Periodical. US. English. qt. Free. Ann Ruth Turkel MD, 350 Central Park West, New York NY 10025. Tel (212)679-4105. Ed Ann Ruth Turkel. LC RC500. DD 616.891705. NLM W1 AC482. bk rev. adv acc. Circ 4,000. (ctrl). News and opinions on matters of interest of psychoanalysts. *Academy.*

ACTA PSIQUIATRICA Y PSICOLOGICA DE AMERICA LATINA. V. 10- 1964-. 0001-6896. Periodical. AG. Spanish. qt. $50.00. Acta Psiquiatrica Y Malabia, 2274 13 A, Buenos Aires 1425 Argentina. Tel 72-3286. Ed Guillermo Vidal. Ind/Abst Index Med., Psychol. Abstr., Soc. Sci. Citation Index. NLM W1 AC93H. CODEN APQPAS. bk rev. adv acc. Circ 5,000. (ctrl). Original papers from Latin America covering psychiatry and psychology. *Acta Psiquiatrica Y Psicologica Argentina.*

ACTA PSYCHIATRICA BELGICA. V. 70- Jan. 1970-. 0300-8967. Periodical. BE. French (some summaries in Dutch, English, German, Italian and Spanish). bm. $51.38. Acta Psychiatrica Belgica, Avenue de l'Exposition 341, B-1090 Bruxelles Belgium. Tel 02/648 21 10. Ind/Abst Excerpta Med., Biol. Abstr., Psychol. Abstr., Index Med., Sociol. Abstr., Lang. Lang. Behav. Abstr. NLM W1 AC93R. CODEN APBABB. *Acta Neurologica et Psychiatrica Belgica.*

ACTA PSYCHIATRICA SCANDINAVICA. V. 37- 1961-. 0001-690X. Periodical. English (contributions in French and German). mo. Munksgaard Ltd, 35 Norre Sogade, DK-1370 Copenhagen Denmark. Tel 1.12.70.30. Ed Jan-Otto Ottosson. Ind/Abst Life Sci. Collect., Sociol. Abstr., Soc. Welf. Soc. Plan./Policy Soc. Dev., Pestdoc, Ringdoc, Vetdoc, Excerpta Med., Biol. Abstr., Chem. Abstr., Nuci. Sci. Abstr., Psychol. Abstr., Index Med., Energy Res. Abstr., Hospit. Lit. Index, Soc. Sci. Citation Index, Sci. Cit. Index, Abr. Ed., Lang. Lang. Behav. Abstr. NLM W1 AC9325. CODEN APYSA9. bk rev. adv acc. Circ 1,400. Psychiatry and adjacent fields. *Acta Psychiatrica et Neurologica Scandinavica.*

ACTIVE PATIENTS AT STATE MENTAL HEALTH FACILITIES AS OF JUNE 30 . . . . US. English. an. MIS and Data Services Division, Department of Mental Health and Retardation, Box 1797, Richmond VA 23214. LC RC445.V78. DD 312.389009755. *Active Patients at State Mental Health Facilities on June 30 . . . .*

ADOLESCENT MENTAL HEALTH ABSTRACTS. See Indexes/Abstracts.

ADOLESCENT PSYCHIATRY. V. 1- 1971-. 0065-2008. Periodical. US. English. an. $32.50. University of Chicago Press, PO Box 37005, Chicago IL 60637. Tel (312)753-3347. Ind/Abst Cumul. Index Nurs. Allied Health Lit., Index Med., Psychol. Abstr.,

Medicine—Psychiatry, Psychopathology

Soc. Sci. Citation Index. LC RJ499.A1. DD 618.9289. NLM W1 AD37K. (cum index).

ADVANCES IN BIOLOGICAL PSYCHIATRY. V. 1- 1978-. 0378-7354. Monographic Series. SZ. English. ir. S Karger Ag, PO Box, CH 4009 Basel Switzerland. Tel 061-39 08 80. Ed J Mendlewicz and H M van Praag. Ind/Abst Biol. Abstr., Chem. Abstr., Psychol. Abstr., Sci. Cit. Index, Abr. Ed., Index Med. NLM W1 AD44. CODEN ABPSD5. Reports of data that promise to advance understanding of abnormal human behavior.

ADVANCES IN FAMILY INTERVENTION, ASSESSMENT AND THEORY. V. 1- 1980-. 0270-9228. US. English. ir. $49.50. JAI Press, PO Box 1678, Greenwich CT 06836. Tel (203)661-7602. Ed John P Vincent. Ind/Abst Psychol. Abstr. LC RC488.5. DD 616.89156. NLM W1 AD564.

ADVANCES IN FAMILY PSYCHIATRY. Vol. 1-. US. English. an. $65.00 Domestic, $73.00 Foreign. International University Press International, 80 Northfield Avenue Building #424, Edison NJ 08837. Ed John G Howells. Ind/Abst Psychol. Abstr. NLM W1 AD566. Its broad clinical approach covers aspects of family functioning and dysfunctioning as well as family diagnostic and treatment considerations.

ADVANCES IN FORENSIC PSYCHOLOGY AND PSYCHIATRY. See Medicine - Forensic Medicine, Medical Jurisprudence.

ADVANCES IN MENTAL HANDICAP RESEARCH. Vol. 1-. 0271-9266. UK. English. John Wiley & Sons, 605 3rd Avenue, New York NY 10158. Ed J Hogg and P J Mittler. LC RC569.7. DD 616.8588005. NLM W1 AD679R.

ADVANCES IN MENTAL RETARDATION AND DEVELOPMENTAL DISABILITIES. Vol. 1 (1983)-. 0742-6313. US. English. an. JAI Press Inc, 36 Sherwood Place, Greenwich CT 06836. LC RC569.7. DD 616.8588005. NLM W1.

THE AFRICAN JOURNAL OF PSYCHIATRY. VFOAT Le Journal Africain de Psychiatrie. 0331-0175. Periodical. articles in English, with some in French. qt. Literamed Publications Ltd, Oregun Village PMB 1068, Ikeja Lagos Nigeria. Ind/Abst Excerpta Med., Index Med., Psychol. Abstr. NLM W1 AF542.

AKTUELLE FRAGEN DER PSYCHIATRIE UND NEUROLOGIE. (AKTUELLE FRAGEN DER PSYCHIATRIE UND NEUROLOGIE). VFOAT Topical Problems in Psychiatry and Neurology. V. 1- 1964-. 0082-4917. Monographic Series. SZ. articles in English or German. ir. Verlag Hans Huber Ag, Laenggasstr 76, 3000 Bern 9 Switzerland. Tel 031 24 25 33. NLM W1 BI429 FASC.122 ETC.

AMERICAN ASSOCIATION FOR GERIATRIC PSYCHIATRY NEWSLETTER. 0734-6026. Periodical. US. English. qt. $20.00. American Association of Geriatric Psychiatry, 230 North Michigan Avenue/Suite 2400, Chicago IL 60601. Tel (312)252-8840.

AMERICAN JOURNAL OF CLINICAL BIOFEEDBACK CEASED. V. 1- Summer 1978-. 0190-4019. Periodical. US. English. sa. $8.00. Hogrefe International Inc, 12-14 Bruce Park Avenue, Toronto Ontario M4P 2S3 Canada. Ind/Abst Excerpta Med., Soc. Work Res. Abstr., Psychol. Abstr. LC RC489.B53. DD 615.8. NLM W1 AM449N.

THE AMERICAN JOURNAL OF FAMILY THERAPY. Vol. 7, No. 1 (Spring 1979)-. 0192-6187. Periodical. US. English. qt. $55.00. Brunner/Mazel, 19 Union Square, New York NY 10003. Tel (212)924-3344. Ed S Richard Sauber. Ind/Abst Sociol. Abstr., Soc. Welf. Soc. Plan./Policy Soc. Dev., Ref. Source, Psychol. Abstr., Curr. Index J. Educ., Soc. Work Res. Abstr., Soc. Sci. Citation Index, Abstr. Soc. Work. LC RC488.5. DD 616.89156. NLM W1 AM451I. bk rev. adv acc. Circ 2,800. Theory, research and clinical practice of family therapy. International Journal of Family Counseling, 0147-1775.

THE AMERICAN JOURNAL OF FORENSIC PSYCHIATRY. V. 1- May 1978-. 0163-1942. Periodical. US. English. qt. $25.00. Ronald Shlensky MD, 251 East Chicago Avenue, Chicago IL 60611. Ed R Shlensky. Ind/Abst Psychol. Abstr. LC RA1151. DD 614.105. NLM W1 AM451S.

AMERICAN JOURNAL OF MENTAL DEFICIENCY. V. 45- July 1940-. 0002-9351. Periodical. US. English. bm. American Association of Mental Deficiency, 1719 Kalorana Road NW, Washington DC 20009. Ind/Abst Sociol. Abstr., Soc. Welf. Soc. Plan./Policy Soc. Dev., Excerpta Med., Index Med., Women Stud. Abstr., Biol. Abstr., Book Rev. Index, Educ. Index, Ref. Source, Except. Child Educ. Resour., Soc. Work Res. Abstr., Psychol. Abstr., Curr. Index J. Educ. LC RC326. DD 362.30973. NLM W1 AM494. CODEN AJMDAW. (cum index). Available on microfilm. Proceedings and Addresses of the Annual Session of the American Association on Mental Deficiency.

AMERICAN JOURNAL OF ORTHOPSYCHIATRY. V. 1- Oct. 1930-. 0002-9432. Periodical. US. English. qt. $35.00. American Orthopsychiatry Association, 49 Sheridan Avenue, Albany NY 12210. Tel (212)354-5770. Ed Albert A Cain. Ind/Abst Sociol. Abstr., Hospit. Lit. Index, Excerpta Med., Index Med., Women Stud. Abstr., Except. Child Educ. Resour., Soc. Work Res. Abstr., Educ. Index, Psychol. Abstr., Soc. Sci. Index, Bibliogr. Index, Lang. Lang. Behav. Abstr., Sci. Cit. Index, Abr. Ed., Soc. Sci. Citation Index, Abstr. Soc. Work. LC RA790.A1. DD 150.5. NLM W1 AM497L. CODEN AJORAG. (cum index). bk rev. adv acc. Available on microfilm from University Microfilms. Promotes an interdisciplinary approach (psychiatry, psychology, social work, education, nursing, etc.) to mental health practice. Publishes research, theoretical, clinical, and administrative articles.

THE AMERICAN JOURNAL OF PSYCHIATRY. V. 78- July 1921-. 0002-953X. Periodical. US. English. mo. $50.00 Domestic, $65.00 Foreign and Canada. American Psychiatric Association, 1700 18th Street NW, Washington DC 20009. Tel (202)682-6158. Ed John C Nemiah. Ind/Abst Pestdoc, Cumul. Index Nurs. Allied Health Lit., Women Stud. Abstr., Int. Aerosp. Abstr., CIS Abstr., Soc. Work Res. Abstr., Sociol. Abstr., Biol. Abstr., Chem. Abstr., Excerpta Med., Hospit. Lit. Index, Index Med., Int. Nurs. Index, Psychol. Abstr., Soc. Sci. Index, Ref. Source, Vetdoc, Ringdoc, Sci. Cit. Index, Abr. Ed., Soc. Sci. Citation Index, Lang. Lang. Behav. Abstr., Nutr. Abstr. Rev., Abstr. Soc. Work. NLM W1 AM513. CODEN AJPSAO. bk rev. adv acc. Circ 41,000. For psychiatrists and other professionals, the journal presents clinical research and discussion of current psychiatric issues. American Journal of Insanity.

THE AMERICAN JOURNAL OF PSYCHOANALYSIS. (AMERICAN JOURNAL OF PSYCHOANALYSIS). V. 1- 1941-. 0002-9548. Periodical. US. English. qt. Agathon Press Inc, 49 Sheridan Avenue, Albany NY 12210. Tel (212)741-3087. Ind/Abst Excerpta Med., Index Med., Women Stud. Abstr., Biol. Abstr., Abstr. Soc. Work., Hospit. Lit. Index, Psychol. Abstr., Soc. Sci. Citation Index. LC RC321. DD 616.805. NLM W1 AM516. CODEN AJPYA8. (cum index). Available on microfilm from University Microfilms International.

AMERICAN JOURNAL OF PSYCHOTHERAPY. V. 1- Jan. 1947-. 0002-9564. Periodical. US. English. qt. $45.00. Association for Advance of Psychotherapy, PO Box 260, Monsey NY 10952. Ind/Abst Cumul. Index Nurs. Allied Health Lit., Excerpta Med., Index Med., Biol. Abstr., Soc. Work Res. Abstr., Psychol. Abstr., Soc. Sci. Citation Index, Sociol. Abstr., Hospit. Lit. Index, Lang. Lang. Behav. Abstr., Sci. Cit. Index, Abr. Ed., Abstr. Soc. Work. LC RC321. DD 616.805. NLM W1 AM518. CODEN AJPTAR.

THE AMERICAN JOURNAL OF SOCIAL PSYCHIATRY. Vol. 1, No. 1 (Apr. 1981)-. 0277-8173. Periodical. US. English. qt. $36.00. Brunner/Mazel Inc, c/o S K Cakar, 19 Union Square, New York NY 10003. Tel (212)924-3344. Ed John L Carleton. Ind/Abst Psychol. Abstr. LC RC455. DD 616.89. NLM W1 AM522G. bk rev. adv acc. Circ 800. Interdisciplinary coverage of psychiatry in relation to many areas of the human condition.

AMHCA JOURNAL. Main/Corp American Mental Health Counselors Association. VAT American Mental Health Counselors Association Journal. V. 1- Jan. 1979-. 0193-1830. Periodical. US. English. qt. $12.00. American Association of Counseling Development, 5999 Stevenson Avenue, Alexandria VA 22304. Tel (703)823-9800. Ed Linda Seilgman. Ind/Abst Psychol. Abstr., Curr. Index J. Educ. LC BF637.C6. DD 362.20425605. adv acc. Circ 139. (ctrl). Articles on theoretical and practical issues in mental health counseling.

THE ANNUAL OF PSYCHOANALYSIS. V. 1- 1973-. 0092-5055. US. English. an. $20.00. International Universities Press Inc, 315 5th Avenue, New York NY 10016. Tel (312)726-6300. Ed Mrs Miller. Ind/Abst Biol. Abstr. LC RC500. DD 616.891705. NLM W1 AN756P. CODEN APSACT. bk rev. Annual appearance of original articles devoted to the theoretical, clinical, educational, historical, and applied psychoanalysis from the world.

ANNUAL REPORT - DEPARTMENT OF PSYCHIATRY AND BEHAVIORAL SCIENCES (SOUTH CAROLINA). Main/Corp South Carolina. Medical University, Charleston. Department of Psychiatry and Behavioral Sciences. US. English. an. 171 Ashley Avenue, Charleston SC 29403.

ANNUAL REPORT - LAREDO STATE CENTER FOR HUMAN DEVELOPMENT. Main/Corp Laredo State Center for Human Development. US. English. an. Laredo State Center for Human Development, PO Box 1835, Laredo TX 78041. LC RC445.T4. DD 362.2209764462.

ANNUAL REPORT - MENTAL HYGIENE ADMINISTRATION (MARYLAND). Main/Corp Maryland. Mental Hygiene Administration. VFOAT Mental Hygiene Administration Annual Report. 1st- 1978-. 0270-3300. US. English. an. NLM W2 AM3 M5A. Annual Report - State of Maryland, Department of Mental Hygiene, 0461-1861.

ANNUAL REPORT - NATIONAL INSTITUTE OF MENTAL HEALTH (U.S.). DIVISION OF INTRAMURAL RESEARCH PROGRAMS. (ANNUAL REPORT). Main/Corp National Institute of Mental Health (U.S.). Division of Intramural Research Programs. VFOAT N.I.M.H. D.I.R.P. . . . Annual Report. Oct. 1, 1982-Sept. 30, 1983-. 0747-6531. US. English. an. LC RC337. DD 616.890072073. Annual Report, Mental Health Intramural Research Program—Division of Clinical and Behavioral Research, Division of Biological and Biochemical Research, and Division of Special Mental Health Research.

ANNUAL REPORT OF CONSULTATION AND EDUCATION PROGRAM OF THE COMMONWEALTH OF MASSACHUSETTS, DEPARTMENT OF MENTAL HEALTH AND BOSTON UNIVERSITY, COMMUNITY MENTAL HEALTH AND RETARDATION CENTER. Main/Corp Massachusetts. Dept. of Mental Health. 0099-0574. US. English. an. Department of Mental Health, 765 Commonwealth Avenue, Boston MA 02215. LC RC455. DD 362.2042509744.

ANNUAL REPORT OF THE BOARD OF VISITORS OF THE BUFFALO PSYCHIATRIC CENTER TO THE DEPARTMENT OF MENTAL HYGIENE. Main/Corp Buffalo Psychiatric Center. Board of Visitors. 105th- 1974/75-. 0198-8034. US. English. Buffalo Psychiatric Center, Board of Visitors, Buffalo NY 14203. LC RC445. DD 353.97479700842.

ANNUAL REPORT - REGION V MENTAL RETARDATION SERVICES (NEBRASKA). Main/Corp Nebraska. Region V Mental Retardation Services. VAT Annual Report - Region Five Mental Retardation Services. US. English. an. Region V Mental Retardation Services, 2311 North Cotner Boulevard, Lincoln NE 68507. LC HV3006.N2. DD 353.978200843.

ANNUAL REPORT - RESEARCH CENTER. ROCKLAND STATE HOSPITAL. (ANNUAL REPORT). Main/Corp New York (State). Rockland State Hospital, Orangeburg. Research Center. 0093-2434. US. English. an. LC RC337. DD 616.890072074728.

ANNUAL REPORT - TEXAS RESEARCH INSTITUTE OF MENTAL SCIENCES. Main/Corp Texas Research Institute of Mental Sciences. US. English. an. LC RC445.T4. DD 353.9764007232.

ANNUAL REPORT - THE ROYAL COLLEGE OF PSYCHIATRISTS. Main/Corp Royal College of Psychiatrists. UK. English. an. NLM W1 RO623A.

ANNUAL REVIEW - NATIONAL ASSOCIATION FOR MENTAL HEALTH (GREAT BRITAIN). Began with: 1971-72?. Periodical. UK. English. an. NLM W1 NA239A.

Medicine—Psychiatry, Psychopathology

ANNUAL REVIEW OF BEHAVIOR THERAPY. THEORY & PRACTICE. (ANNUAL REVIEW OF BEHAVIOR THERAPY : THEORY & PRACTICE). **VAT** Annual Review of Behavior Therapy. Theory and Practice. 1973-. 0091-6595. Monographic Series. US. English. an. $25.00. Brunner/Mazel, 64 University Place, New York NY 10003. **Ind/Abst** Biol. Abstr., Psychol. Abstr. **LC** RC489.B4. **DD** 616.8914. **NLM** W1 AN769N. **CODEN** ARBPD4.

ANNUAL REVIEW OF FAMILY THERAPY. Vol. 1-. 0198-9731. US. English. ir. Human Science Press, 72 5th Ave, New York NY 10011. **Tel** (212)243-6000. **LC** RC488.5. **DD** 616.89156. **NLM** W1 AN771D.

ANNUAL STATISTICS - DEPARTMENT OF MENTAL HEALTH, STATISTICS BRANCH (INDIANA). See Statistics.

APPLIED RESEARCH IN MENTAL RETARDATION. Vol. 1, No. 1/2-. 0270-3092. Periodical. US. English. qt. $133.00. Pergamon Press, 395 Sawmill River Road, Elmsford NY 10523. **Tel** (914)592-7700. **Ind/Abst** Index Med., Biol. Abstr., Psychol. Abstr. **LC** RC569.7. **DD** 616.8588. **NLM** W1 AP528V. **CODEN** ARMREW.

THE ARC. **VFOAT** The A.R.C. V. 29- Mar./Apr. 1980-. 0199-9435. Periodical. US. English. ir. $10.00. Association of Retarded Citizens US, 2501 J Avenue, PO Box 6109, Arlington TX 76011. **Tel** (817)640-0204. Ed Liz Moore. bk rev. adv acc. Reports information on program innovations, legislative developments, scientific breakthroughs, and stories of retarded persons nationally. *Mental Retardation News*.

ARCHIV FUR PSYCHIATRIE UND NERVENKRANKHEITEN. See Genealogy and Heraldry - Archives.

ARCHIVES OF GENERAL PSYCHIATRY. See Genealogy and Heraldry - Archives.

ARQUIVOS DA COORDENADORIA DE SAUDE MENTAL DO ESTADO DE SAO PAULO. V. 32- Jan./Dec. 1966-. 0101-1693. BL. Portuguese. an. **LC** RA790.7.S25. **DD** 362.2098161. **NLM** W1 AR89I.

ARQUIVOS DE NEURO-PSIQUIATRIA. See Medicine - Neurology.

THE ARTS IN PSYCHOTHERAPY. V. 7-. 0197-4556. Periodical. US. English. qt. $90.00. Ankho International Inc, PO Box 380227, San Antonio TX 78280. **Tel** (315)463-0182. Ed Myra F Levick. **Ind/Abst** Excerpta Med., Biol. Abstr., Artbibliogr. Mod., Except. Child Educ. Resour., Psychol. Abstr., Soc. Sci. Citation Index. **LC** RC489.A7. **DD** 616.89165. **NLM** W1 AR959M. **CODEN** APCYAJ. bk rev. adv acc. Publishes articles including illustrations by art, dance, movements, music, poetry and drama psychotherapists, psychiatrists and psychologists which reflect the theory and practice of these disciplines. *Art Psychotherapy, 0090-9092*.

THE ATTORNEY'S DIRECTORY OF FORENSIC PSYCHIATRISTS IN THE UNITED STATES AND CANADA. See Yearbooks, Almanacs, Directories.

AUDIO-DIGEST. PSYCHIATRY. Periodical. US. English. sm. $138.00. Audio-Digest Foundation, 1577 Chevy Chase Drive, Glendale CA 91206. **Tel** (213)245-8505. Ed Claron L Oakley. A twice-monthly interactive system of audiocassette postgraduate medical education, with each one-hour program eligible for two Category I credit hours.

AUSTRALIAN AND NEW ZEALAND JOURNAL OF PSYCHIATRY. V. 1- Mar. 1967-. 0004-8674. Periodical. AT. English. qt. $27.30. Prince of Wales Hospital c/o Dr G Parker/Psychiatry Unit, Randwich NSW 2031 Australia. **Tel** (02)399-0111. Ed Gordon Parker. **Ind/Abst** Life Sci. Collect., Excerpta Med., Women Stud. Abstr., Biol. Abstr., Psychol. Abstr., Index Med., Soc. Sci. Citation Index, Hospit. Lit. Index. **LC** RC321. **NLM** W1 AU498. **CODEN** ANZPBQ. bk rev. adv acc. **Circ** 2,500. (ctrl) Contains editorial comment, case reports, book reviews, letters to the editor, original articles, clinical research issues, advertising.

BEHAVIOR CHANGE. 1974-. 0360-0696. US. English. an. Aldine Publishing Co, 529 South Wabash Avenue, Chicago IL 60605. **LC** RC475. **DD** 616.891405. **NLM** W1 BE121. *Psychotherapy and Behavior Change, 0091-8172*.

BEHAVIORAL ASSESSMENT. V. 1- 1979-. 0191-5401. Periodical. US. English. qt. $152.00. Pergamon Press, 395 Sawmill River Road, Elmsford NY 10523. **Ind/Abst** Biol. Abstr., Psychol. Abstr., Soc. Sci. Citation Index. **LC** RC489.B4. **DD** 616.8914205. **NLM** W1 BE129T. **CODEN** BEHSDV.

BEHAVIORAL NEUROPSYCHIATRY. Began with: V. 1, No. 1 (April 1969). 0005-7932. Periodical. US. English. ir. Behavioral Neuropsychiatry, 61 East 86th Street, New York NY 10028. **LC** RC321. **DD** 616.89005. **NLM** W1 BE13K. *International Journal of Neuropsychiatry, 0538-8163*.

BEHAVIOUR RESEARCH AND THERAPY. V. 1- May 1963-. 0005-7967. Periodical. UK. English. bm. Pergamon Press, c/o Cashier, 395 Sawmill River Road, Road, Elmsford NY 10523. **Ind/Abst** MLA Int. Bibliogr. Books Artic. Mod. Lang. Lit., Life Sci. Collect., Sociol. Abstr., Soc. Welf. Soc. Plan./Policy Soc. Dev., Excerpta Med., Cumul. Index Nurs. Allied Health Lit., Women Stud. Abstr., Soc. Work Res. Abstr., Biol. Abstr., Psychol. Abstr., Index Med., Soc. Sci. Citation Index, Hospit. Lit. Index, Abstr. Soc. Work. **LC** RC321. **DD** 616.89005. **NLM** W1 BE135. **CODEN** BRTHAA.

BEHAVIOURAL BRAIN RESEARCH. See Medicine - Neurology.

BEITRAGE ZUR KLINISCHEN NEUROLOGIE UND PSYCHIATRIE. See Medicine - Neurology.

BIBLIOTHECA PSYCHIATRICA. V. 143- 1970-. 0067-8147. SZ. German. ir. S Karger AG, PO Box 352, White Plains NY 10602. **Tel** 061-39 08 80. Ed P Berner and E Gabriel. **Ind/Abst** Life Sci. Collect., Biol. Abstr., Chem. Abstr., Index Med., Nuci. Sci. Abstr., Lang. Lang. Behav. Abstr., Sociol. Abstr. **NLM** W1 BI429. **CODEN** BIBPBI. Problems of clinical psychiatry covered in a series that has helped pioneer the development of this field. *Bibliotheca Psychiatrica et Neurologica*.

BIOGRAPHICAL DIRECTORY - AMERICAN PSYCHIATRIC ASSOCIATION. See Yearbooks, Almanacs, Directories.

BIOGRAPHICAL DIRECTORY OF THE FELLOWS & MEMBERS OF THE AMERICAN PSYCHIATRIC ASSOCIATION. See Yearbooks, Almanacs, Directories.

BIOLOGICAL PSYCHIATRY. V. 1- Jan. 1969-. 0006-3223. Periodical. US. English. mo. $120.00. Elsevier Science Publ Co Inc, PO Box 1663 Grand Central Station, New York NY 10163. **Tel** (212)370-5520. Ed Joseph Wortis. **Ind/Abst** Life Sci. Collect., Int. Aerosp. Abstr., Biol. Abstr., Chem. Abstr., Excerpta Med., Index Med., Curr. Contents, Psychol. Abstr., Sci. Cit. Index, Abr. Ed., Hospit. Lit. Index. **LC** RC321. **DD** 616.89005. **NLM** W1 BI754L. **CODEN** BIPCBF. adv acc. **Circ** 1,200. The international journal contains contributions from psychiatric related research areas as pathology, pharmacology, electroencephalography, biochemistry, and genetics. *Recent Advances In Biological Psychiatry*.

BIOLOGICAL PSYCHIATRY (LONDON, ENGLAND). (BIOLOGICAL PSYCHIATRY). 1-. 0266-2124. Monographic Series. UK. English. **NLM** W1.

BIOLOGICAL THERAPIES IN PSYCHIATRY : MASSACHUSETTS GENERAL HOSPITAL NEWSLETTER. Periodical. US. English. mo $37.50. PSG Publishing Company Inc, 545 Great Road, Littleton MA 01460. **Tel** (617)468-8971. Ed Alan J Gelenberg. **Circ** 5,800. Designed to keep clinicians up-to-date with the important psychotrophic drugs affecting his practice. *Massachusetts General Hospital Biological Therapies in Psychiatry Newsletter, 0199-2716*.

BORDURES. (BORDURES ——). Vol. No 1 (Dec. 1982)-. 0715-741X. Periodical. CN. French. ir. 7.00. Bordures, C P 836 Succursale Notre-Dame-de-Grace, Montreal Quebec H4A 3S2 Canada. **DD** 616.891705.

BRITISH JOURNAL OF PSYCHIATRY. (THE BRITISH JOURNAL OF PSYCHIATRY). V. 109- (No. 458-). 0007-1250. Periodical. UK. English. mo. $230.00. Headley Brothers Limited, 109 Kingsways, London WC2B 6PX England. **Ind/Abst** Life Sci. Collect., Pestdoc, Ringdoc, Vetdoc, Excerpta Med., Women Stud. Abstr., Ref. Source, Biol. Abstr., Chem. Abstr., Psychol. Abstr., Nuci. Sci. Abstr., Index Med., Soc. Sci. Citation Index, Sci. Cit. Index, Abr. Ed., Hospit. Lit. Index, Sociol. Abstr., Lang. Lang. Behav. Abstr. **NLM** W1 BR616. **CODEN** BJPYAJ. (cum index). *Journal of Mental Science, 0368-315X*.

BRITISH JOURNAL OF PSYCHIATRY. SPECIAL PUBLICATION. No. 1- 1967-. 0068-2225. Periodical. UK. English. ir. Headley Bros Ltd, 109 Kingsways, London WC2B 6PX England. **Ind/Abst** Chem. Abstr., Soc. Sci. Citation Index, Women Stud. Abstr.

BRITISH JOURNAL OF PSYCHOTHERAPY. Vol. 1, No. 1 (Autumn 1984)-. 0265-9883. Periodical. UK. English. qt. $50.00. **NLM** W1.

THE BULLETIN - AREA II DISTRICT BRANCHES, AMERICAN PSYCHIATRIC ASSOCIATION. Main/Corp American Psychiatric Association. Area II District Branches. V. 18, No. 2- Sept. 1975-. US. English. bm. American Psychiatric Association, 420 East 76th Street, New York NY 10021. *Bulletin - New York State District Branches, American Psychiatric Association, 0003-0643*.

BULLETIN - ASSOCIATION FOR PSYCHOANALYTIC MEDICINE. Main/Corp Association for Psychoanalytic Medicine. 0004-542X. Periodical. US. English. ir. $10.00. Association of Psychoanalytic Medicine, 4560 Delafield Avenue, Riverdale NY 10471. **Tel** (212)548-6088. **LC** RC500. **DD** 616.8914005.

BULLETIN D'INFORMATION EN ANTHROPOLOGIE MEDICALE ET EN PSYCHIATRIE TRANSCULTURELLE. See Anthropology.

THE BULLETIN - NEW YORK STATE DISTRICT BRANCHES, AMERICAN PSYCHIATRIC ASSOCIATION. (THE BULLETIN - THE NEW YORK STATE DISTRICT BRANCHES, AMERICAN PSYCHIATRIC ASSOCIATION). Main/Corp American Psychiatric Association. New York State District Branches. V. 1-18, No. 1. 0003-0643. US. English. bm. $5.00. American Psychiatric, 420 East 76th Street, New York NY 10021.

BULLETIN OF THE AMERICAN ACADEMY OF PSYCHIATRY AND THE LAW. Main/Corp American Academy of Psychiatry and the Law. V. 1- Autumn 1972-. 0091-634X. US. English. qt. $25.00 Domestic, $40.00 Foreign. AAPL Bulletin, 1211 Cathedral Street, Baltimore MD 21201. **Tel** (301)539-0379. Ed Richard T Rada. **Ind/Abst** Excerpta Med., Index Med., Psychol. Abstr., Contents Curr. Leg. Period., Hospit. Lit. Index, Leg. Resour. Index, Curr. Law Index, Soc. Sci. Citation Index. **LC** RA1151. **DD** 614.19. **NLM** W1 BU841H. bk rev. **Circ** 1,300. (ctrl). Devoted to scholarly articles in the field of forensic psychiatry.

BULLETIN OF THE HAMPSTEAD CLINIC. V. 1- 1978-. 0263-9688. Periodical. UK. English. qt. Bulletin of the Hampstead Clinic, 21 Maresfield Gardens, London NW3 5SU England. **Ind/Abst** Psychol. Abstr. **NLM** W1 BU8467E.

BULLETIN OF THE MENNINGER CLINIC. Main/Corp Menninger Clinic, Topeka, Kan. V. 1- Sept. 1936-. 0025-9284. Periodical. US. English. bm. $50.00. Bulletin of the Menninger Clinic, PO Box 829, Topeka KS 66601. **Tel** (913)273-7500. Ed Paul W Pruyser. **Ind/Abst** Soc. Welf. Soc. Plan./Policy Soc. Dev., Sociol. Abstr., Excerpta Med., Index Med., Biol. Abstr., Psychol. Abstr., Lang. Lang. Behav. Abstr., Hospit. Lit. Index, Soc. Sci. Citation Index, Abstr. Soc. Work. **LC** RC321. **DD** 616.89005. **NLM** W1 BU858. **CODEN** BMCLA4. (cum index). bk rev. **Circ** 2,100. (ctrl). Is a peer-reviewed multidisciplinary journal publishing original, scholarly articles on psychiatry, psychology, psychoanalysis, and related subjects.

BULLETIN OF THE NATIONAL GUILD OF CATHOLIC PSYCHIATRISTS. See Religion, Mythology, Rationalism - Roman Catholic Church.

BULLETIN OF THE ROYAL COLLEGE OF PSYCHIATRISTS. Main/Corp Royal College of Psychiatrists. Jan. 1978-. 0140-0789. Periodical. UK. English. mo. $9.20. Headley Brothers Ltd, 109 Kingsway, London WC2B 6PX England. **NLM** W1 BU8872.

BULLETIN SIGNALETIQUE - CENTRE NATIONAL DE LA RECHERCHE SCIENTIFIQUE. 390. PSYCHOLOGIE ET PSYCHOPATHOLOGIE, PSYCHIATRIE. (BULLETIN SIGNALETIQUE. 390 : PSYCHOLOGIE ET PSYCHOPATHOLOGIE, PSYCHIATRIE). **VFOAT** Psychologie et

Medicine—Psychiatry, Psychopathology

Psychopathologie, Psychiatrie. V. 32-. 0007-5531. Periodical. FR. French. ir. $163.63. Editions du CNRS, 23 rue du Maroc, 75019 Paris France. LC Z7203. NLM ZQ 1 B936SLK. *Bulletin Signaletique. 390: Psychologie, Psychopathologie.*

BULLETIN - UNIVERSITY OF WESTERN ONTARIO, DEPT. OF PSYCHIATRY. (BULLETIN). No. 8201-. 0711-6012. Monographic Series. CN. English. D B Weldon Library, University of Western Ontario, London Ontario N6A 3K7 Canada. DD 610.

CAHIERS PEDOPSYCHIATRIQUES. No 1- Spring 1974-. 0315-9477. Periodical. CN. French. sa. Hopital Sainte Justine/CISE, 3175 Cote St Catherine, Montreal Quebec H3T 1C5 Canada. **Tel** (514)731-4931. **Ind/Abst** Excerpta Med., Point Repere. DD 618.9289005. NLM W1 CA149.

CALIFORNIA LAWS FOR PSYCHOTHERAPISTS. *See* Law.

CALOTTE. (LA CALOTTE). Vol. 1, No. 1 (Winter 83)-. 0823-3594. Periodical. CN. French. qt. $2.00 Per No. Groupe Auto-Psy #3, 332 rue St-Luc, Quebec Quebec G1N 2S8 Canada. DD 362.2109714.

CANADIAN JOURNAL OF PSYCHIATRIC NURSING. *See* Medicine - Nursing.

CANADIAN JOURNAL OF PSYCHIATRY. VFOAT Revue Canadienne de Psychiatrie. V. 24- Feb. 1979-. 0706-7437. Periodical. CN. English (articles in French). ir. $30.95. Lex Limited, 431 Alden Road, Markham Ontario L3R 3L4 Canada. **Tel** (416)477-2030. **Ind/Abst** Life Sci. Collect., Sociol. Abstr., Soc. Welf. Soc. Plan./Policy Soc. Dev., Excerpta Med., Cumul. Index Nurs. Allied Health Lit., Index Med., Psychol. Abstr., Hospit. Lit. Index, Soc. Sci. Citation Index. LC RC321. DD 616.8900971. NLM W1 CA602V. **CODEN** CPAJAK. Index in last issue of volume - attached. bk rev. adv acc. (ctrl). Articles on treatment of psychiatric patients. *Canadian Psychiatric Association Journal, 0008-4824.*

CAREER DIRECTIONS. V. 1- 1970-. Periodical. US. English. ir.

CESKOSLOVENSKA PSYCHIATRIE. 1956?-. 0069-2336. Periodical. CS. Czech (summaries in Russian and English). bm. $56.10. Artia, Ve Smeckach 30, PO Box 790, Praha 1 Czechoslovakia. **Ind/Abst** Excerpta Med., Index Med., CIS Abstr., Psychol. Abstr. DD 616.8. NLM W1 CE902P. **CODEN** CEPYAX. *Neurologie a Psychiatrie Ceska.*

CHICAGO PSYCHOANALYTIC LITERATURE INDEX. *See* Indexes/Abstracts.

CHICOREL INDEX TO MENTAL HEALTH BOOK REVIEWS. *See* Indexes/Abstracts.

CHILD PSYCHIATRY AND HUMAN DEVELOPMENT. V. 1- Fall 1970-. 0009-398X. Periodical. US. English. qt. Human Sciences Press, 72 Fifth Avenue, New York NY 10016. **Tel** (212)243-6000. **Ind/Abst** Life Sci. Collect., Biol. Abstr., Educ. Index, Except. Child Educ. Resour., Soc. Work Res. Abstr., Index Med., Excerpta Med., Psychol. Abstr., Child Dev. Abstr. Bibliogr., Curr. Index J. Educ., Women Stud. Abstr., Curr. Contents Clin. Pract., Curr. Contents, Soc. Behav. Sci., Soc. Sci. Citation Index, Curr. Contents Behav. Soc. Educ. Sci., Abstr. Soc. Work. LC RJ499.A1. DD 618.92891405. NLM W1 CH668K. **CODEN** CPHDA3.

CHILD PSYCHIATRY QUARTERLY. 0009-3998. Periodical. II. English. qt. $15.00. Community Mental Health Center Indira, 7th Road Banjara Hills, Hyderabad 500034 India. Ed Jaya Nagavaja. **Ind/Abst** Excerpta Med., Psychol. Abstr. NLM W1 CH668P. **CODEN** CPQUDY. bk rev. adv acc. Microform. Topics include child and adolescent psychiatry, research, and clinical family counseling.

CLINICA Y ANALISIS GRUPAL. 0210-0657. Periodical. SP. Spanish. bm. $23.00. Editorial Fundamentos Caracas, 15 Madrid 4 Espana. LC RC475. DD 616.891405. NLM W1 CL613W.

CLINICAL PSYCHIATRY NEWS. V. 1- NOV. 1973-. 0270-6644. Periodical. US. English. mo. $45.00. International Medical News Service, 12230 Wilkins Avenue, Rockville MD 20852. **Tel** (212)421-0707. Ed William Rubin. NLM W1 CL768CS. bk rev. adv acc. Circ 27,340. (ctrl). Coverage of clinical meetings, symposia, and conventions to report clinical developments in the fields of psychiatry and neurology.

COMBINED CUMULATIVE INDEX TO PSYCHIATRY. *See* Indexes/Abstracts.

COMPREHENSIVE PSYCHOTHERAPY. Vol. 1-. 0275-7222. Periodical. US. English. Gordon and Breach, Science Publishers Inc, One Park Avenue, New York NY 10016. Ed Paul Olsen. LC RC475. DD 616.891405. NLM W1 CO453F.

COMPUTERS IN PSYCHIATRY/PSYCHOLOGY. VFOAT CP/P. V. 2, No. 1 (June-July 1979)-. Periodical. US. English. bm. 26 Trumbull Street, New Haven CT 06511.

CONNEXIONS: PSYCHOSOCIOLOGIE, SCIENCES HUMAINES. 1972. 0337-3126. FR. French. sa. $22.62. Desclee de Brouwer, 83 rue Hoche, 92240 Malakoff Paris France. **Tel** 1/656 26 93. Ed Dodei se Brouvne. **Ind/Abst** Psychol. Abstr. NLM W1 CO728.

CONTEMPORARY PSYCHIATRY (NEW YORK, N.Y.). (CONTEMPORARY PSYCHIATRY). Vol. 1, No. 1 (Mar. 1982)-. 0277-8041. Periodical. US. English. qt. $80.00 Domestic, $90.00 Foreign. Plenum Press, 233 Spring Street, New York NY 10013. **Tel** (212)620-8000. Ed Seymour L Halleck. **Ind/Abst** Adolesc. Ment. Health Abstr. LC RC321. DD 616.89. NLM W1 CO769V. **CODEN** CPCHDR. bk rev. adv acc. This journal is devoted solely to the critical evaluation and review of those books of special interest to, and by psychiatric practitioners, psychiatry teachers and residents.

CONTEMPORARY PSYCHOANALYSIS. V. 1- Fall 1964-. 0010-7530. Periodical. US. English. qt. $57.50. Contemporary Psychoanalysis, PO Box 465, Hanover PA 17331. **Tel** (717)632-3535. **Ind/Abst** Sociol. Abstr., Excerpta Med., Psychol. Abstr., Soc. Work Res. Abstr., Soc. Sci. Citation Index, Lang. Lang. Behav. Abstr., Abstr. Soc. Work. LC RC500. DD 616.891705. NLM W1 CO769W. **CODEN** CPPSBL.

CORRECTIVE AND SOCIAL PSYCHIATRY AND JOURNAL OF BEHAVIOR TECHNOLOGY METHODS AND THERAPY. VFOAT Journal of Behavior Technology Methods and Therapy. V. 20- 1974-. 0093-1551. Periodical. US. English. qt. $35.00. Martin Psychiatric Research, 7360 El Camino Real/Suite A, Atascadero CA 93442. **Tel** (913)782-4282. **Ind/Abst** Excerpta Med., Psychol. Abstr., Soc. Sci. Citation Index. LC RC321. DD 616.89005. NLM W1 CO898R. *Corrective and Social Psychiatry and Journal of Applied Behavior Therapy, 0091-2611.*

CRISIS INTERVENTION. V. 1-. 0045-9046. Periodical. US. English. qt. $15.00. Crisis Intervention Institute, 3258 Main Street/University Heights, Buffalo NY 14214. **Ind/Abst** Psychol. Abstr. LC RC480.6. DD 362.2. NLM W1 CR203. **CODEN** CITVD3.

CSF NEWSLETTER. Main/Corp Canadian Schizophrenia Foundation. Began publication in 1970. Ceased with V. 4, No. 4 (Oct. 1973). 0318-8264. Periodical. CN. English. qt. $3.09. Canadian Schizophrenia Foundation, 2229 Broad Street, Regina Saskatchewan S4P 1Y7 Canada. **Tel** (306)527-7969.

CULTURE, MEDICINE AND PSYCHIATRY. V. 1- Apr. 1977-. 0165-005X. Periodical. English. qt. 59. Kluwer Academic Publishers Group, PO Box 322, 3300 AH Dordrecht Netherlands. **Tel** (31)78-334911. Ed Arthur Kleinman. **Ind/Abst** Sociol. Abstr., Soc. Welf. Soc. Plan./Policy Soc. Dev., Excerpta Med., Index Med., Biol. Abstr., Psychol. Abstr. LC RC455.4.E8. DD 616.89005. NLM W1 CU446. **CODEN** CMPSD2. bk rev. adv acc. Circ 750. Medical and psychiatric anthropology, cross-cultural psychiatry, and related cross-societal, clinical and epidemiological studies.

CURARE. V. 1- 1978-. 0344-8622. Periodical. English (articles in German or French with summaries in some or all languages). qt. 82.-. Friedr Vieweg Verlag, PTFH 5829/Faulbrunnenstrasse 13, D6200 Wiesbaden 1 West Germany. **Tel** (06121) 534-1. Ed Ekkehard Schroder. **Ind/Abst** Sociol. Abstr., Soc. Welf. Soc. Plan./Policy Soc. Dev. NLM W1 CU484. bk rev. adv acc. Circ 820. Journal for ethnomedicine and psychiatry.

CURRENT CONCEPTS IN PSYCHIATRY. V. 1- Oct. 1975-. 0360-7569. Periodical. US. English. bm. Professional Communications Association, 625 North Michigan Avenue, Chicago IL 60611. LC RC321. DD 616.89005. NLM W1 CU788AY.

CURRENT ISSUES IN PSYCHOANALYTIC PRACTICE. Vol. 1, No. 1 (Spring 1984)-. 0737-7851. Monographic Series. US. English. qt. $48.00. The Haworth Press, 28 East 22nd Street, New York NY 10010. **Tel** (212)228-2800. Ed Herbert S Strean. DD 616. NLM W1. adv acc. Circ 577. This remarkable journal is designed to enhance the growth and development of psychoanalysis as a therapy, as a personality theory, and as a research tool.

CURRENT PSYCHIATRIC THERAPIES. V. 1- 1961-. 0070-2080. US. English. ir. Grune & Stratton Inc, 111-5th Avenue, New York NY 10003. **Tel** (212)614-3232. Ed J H Masserman. **Ind/Abst** Index Med. LC RC475. DD 616.891. NLM W1 CU807. (cum index). *Progress in Psychotherapy, 0555-4241.*

CURRENT THEMES IN PSYCHIATRY. Began with Vol. 1 in 1978. 0144-316X. US. English. an. Spectrum Publications Inc, 175-20 Wexford Terrace, Jamaica NY 11432. **Tel** (718)658-0888. Ed Raghu N Gaind. LC RC321. DD 616.89005. NLM W1 CU814.

DASEINSANALYSE. 1/1/84 (Oct. 1983)-. 0254-6221. Periodical. German. ir. $45.00. **Ind/Abst** Life Sci. Collect. NLM W1.

DEVELOPMENTS IN PSYCHIATRY. V. 1-. 0166-2481. Monographic Series. English. ir. Elsevier North-Holland Inc, 52 Vanderbilt Avenue, New York NY 10017. **Ind/Abst** Chem. Abstr. LC UNC. NLM W1 DE998P. **CODEN** DPSYDX.

DIRECTORY - AMERICAN GROUP PSYCHOTHERAPY ASSOCIATION. *See* Yearbooks, Almanacs, Directories.

DIRECTORY - COUNCIL OF SPECIALISTS IN PSYCHIATRIC AND MENTAL HEALTH NURSING. *See* Yearbooks, Almanacs, Directories.

DIRECTORY OF CERTIFIED PSYCHIATRISTS AND NEUROLOGISTS. *See* Yearbooks, Almanacs, Directories.

DIRECTORY OF PSYCHIATRY RESIDENCY TRAINING PROGRAMS. *See* Yearbooks, Almanacs, Directories.

DIRECTORY OF PSYCHOSOCIAL INVESTIGATORS. *See* Yearbooks, Almanacs, Directories.

DISCHARGES FROM STATE MENTAL HEALTH FACILITIES FISCAL YEAR . . . . 1978/79-. US. English. an. MIS and Data Services Division, Department of Mental Health & Retardation, POB 1797, Richmond VA 23214. LC RC445.V78. DD 362.204220973.

DIVISION OF RESEARCH ANNUAL REPORT - (NEW YORK). Main/Corp New York (State). Dept. of Mental Hygiene. Division of Research. 1975-. 0148-3137. US. English. an. NY State Department of Mental Hygiene, Albany NY 12237. LC RC337. DD 616.858800720747. NLM W2 AN6 D42D.

THE DOWNSTATE SERIES OF RESEARCH IN PSYCHIATRY AND PSYCHOLOGY. *See* Psychology.

DRUGS IN PSYCHIATRY (POINTE-CLAIRE, QUEBEC). (DRUGS IN PSYCHIATRY). Series/Titl PRM : Physicians' Reference Manuals. Vol. 1, No. 1 (1982)-. 0824-7102. Periodical. CN. English. sm. 50.00. Drugs in Psychiatry, c/o STA Communications 63 Place Frontenac, Pointe-Claire Quebec H9R 4Z7 Canada. **Tel** (514)695-7623. Ed Paul Brand. DD 615.78. adv acc. Circ 2,600. (ctrl). Drug reference manuals.

DYNAMIC PSYCHOTHERAPY. (DYNAMIC PSYCHOTHERAPY : THE JOURNAL OF THE POSTGRADUATE CENTER FOR MENTAL HEALTH). Vol. 1, No. 1 (Spring/Summer 1983)-. 0736-508X. Periodical. US. English. sa. $32.00. Brunner/Mazel Inc, 19 Union Square West, New York NY 10003. **Tel** (212)924-3344. Ed Bernard F Riess. DD 616. NLM W1. bk rev. adv acc. Circ 800. The journal of the Postgraduate Center for Mental Health - reflects current thinking and clinical practice in many areas where dynamic psychotherapy contributes.

DYNAMISCHE PSYCHIATRIE. VFOAT Dynamic Psychiatry. 1- Apr. 1968-. 0012-740X. Periodical. WB. German. bm. $37.33. Pinel Publikationen, Wielandstrasse 27-28, 100 Berlin 15 West Germany. **Ind/Abst** Biol. Abstr., Psychol. Abstr., Soc. Sci. Citation Index, Excerpta Med. DD 616.8. NLM W1 DY989. **CODEN** DYPSAQ.

THE EGYPTIAN JOURNAL OF PSYCHIATRY. (THE EGYPTIAN JOURNAL OF PSYCHIATRY : OFFICIAL JOURNAL OF THE EGPYPTIAN PSYCHIATRIC ASSOCIATION).

Medicine—Psychiatry, Psychopathology

0254-136X. Periodical. English. ir. NLM W1 EG914R. CODEN JEMAAJ.

EMOTIONS AND BEHAVIOR MONOGRAPHS. VFOAT Emotions & Behavior. Monograph No. 1-. 0734-9890. Monographic Series. US. English. ir. International Universities Press, 315 Fifth Avenue, New York NY 10016. LC UNC.

EMPIRICAL STUDIES OF PSYCHOANALYTICAL THEORIES. Vol. 1-. 0743-071X. US. English. ir. Analytic Press, 365 Broadway c/o Lawrence Erlbaum, Hillsdale NJ 07642. Tel (201)666-4110. Ed Joseph Masling. NLM W1 EM682.

ENCEPHALE. See Medicine - Neurology.

EUROPEAN ARCHIVES OF PSYCHIATRY AND NEUROLOGICAL SCIENCES. See Genealogy and Heraldry - Archives.

EVOLUTION PSYCHIATRIQUE. (L'EVOLUTION PSYCHIATRIQUE). 1. New Series V. 1-2, 1925-27. 0014-3855. Periodical. FR. French. qt. 250 Domestic, 400 Foreign. Editions Privat, 14 rue des Arts, 31000 Toulouse France. Tel 1-581120. Ind/Abst Psychol. Abstr., Sociol. Abstr., Lang. Lang. Behav. Abstr. NLM W1 EV635. CODEN EVPSAG. (cum index). bk rev. adv acc. Circ 2,900. (ctrl). Original research in psychiatry and clinical psychopathology.

EXCERPTA MEDICA. SECTION 32, PSYCHIATRY. See Indexes/Abstracts.

EXPERIMENTAL AND CLINICAL PSYCHIATRY. V. 1-. 0272-6408. Monographic Series. US. English. ir. Marcel Dekker, 270 Madison Avenue, New York NY 10016. Tel (212)696-9000. Ed Van Praag. Ind/Abst Chem. Abstr., Psychol. Abstr. LC UNC. NLM W1 EX465. CODEN ECPSDM. This is an ongoing series, each title has a different subject.

FAMILY PROCESS. V. 1- Mar. 1962-. 0014-7370. Periodical. US. English. qt. Family Process Inc, 149 East 78th Street, New York NY 10021. Tel (212)861-6059. Ed Carlos E Sluzki. Ind/Abst Sociol. Abstr., Soc. Welf. Soc. Plan./Policy Soc. Dev., Excerpta Med., Index Med., Soc. Work Res. Abstr., Psychol. Abstr., Soc. Sci. Citation Index, Cumul. Index Nurs. Allied Health Lit., Hospit. Lit. Index, Lang. Lang. Behav. Abstr., Abstr. Soc. Work. LC RC488.5.A1. DD 616.8915. NLM W1 FA454E. CODEN FAPRA. (cum index). bk rev. adv acc. Circ 11,000. A multidisciplinary journal of family study research and treatment.

FEELINGS & THEIR MEDICAL SIGNIFICANCE. V. 1- Dec. 1958-. 0430-2869. Periodical. US. English. bm. NLM W1 FE399.

FIRST AND READMISSIONS TO STATE AND COUNTY PSYCHIATRIC HOSPITALS BY COUNTY, MUNICIPALITY OF RESIDENCE, AND SERVICE AREA. See Medicine - Medical Centers, Hospitals.

FOLIA PSYCHIATRICA ET NEUROLOGICA JAPONICA. 0015-5721. Periodical. JA. Multilingual (Japanese and English). qt. $58.50. Japan Publishers Trading Company Limited, Tokyo International, PO Box 5030, Tokyo 100-31 Japan. Ind/Abst Life Sci. Collect., Excerpta Med., Index Med., Biol. Abstr., Chem. Abstr., Lang. Lang. Behav. Abstr., Sociol. Abstr. NLM W1 FO284. CODEN FPNJAG.

FORMAZIONE PSICHIATRICA : PERIODICO TRIMESTRALE A CURA DELLA CLINICA PSICHIATRICA DELL'UNIVERSITA DI CATANIA. N. 1 (Jan./Mar. 1980)-. Periodical. Italian (summaries in English). qt. V Le Andrea Doria 6, 95125 Catania Italy. Ind/Abst Excerpta Med., Psychol. Abstr. LC RC321. DD 616.89005. NLM W1.

FORTSCHRITTE DER NEUROLOGIE, PSYCHIATRIE. See Medicine - Neurology.

FORTSCHRITTE DER NEUROLOGIE, PSYCHIATRIE UND IHRER GRENZGEBIETE. See Medicine - Neurology.

FORTSCHRITTE DER SOZIALPSYCHIATRIE. 1-. 0341-1532. Monographic Series. German. ir. Urban & Schwarzenberg Verlag, 7 East Redwood Street, Baltimore MD 21202. Tel 089/530181. NLM W1 FO892D.

GENERAL HOSPITAL PSYCHIATRY. V. 1- Apr. 1979-. 0163-8343. Periodical. US. English. qt. $56.00. Elsevier Science Publishing Company Inc, PO Box 1663 Grand Central Station, New York NY 10163. Tel (212)370-5520. Ed Don R Lipsitt. Ind/Abst Life Sci. Collect., Excerpta Med., Index Med., Cumul. Index Nurs. Allied Health Lit., Psychol. Abstr. NLM W1 GE249H. CODEN GHPSDB. bk rev. adv acc. Circ 800. Designed for members of the health care team at the junction of psychiatry, medicine and primary care, emphasizes a biopsychosocial approach to illness and health.

THE GESTALT JOURNAL. V. 1- Winter 1978-. 0190-0412. Periodical. US. English. sa. $15.00. The Gestalt Journal, PO Box 395, New York NY 10024. Ind/Abst Psychol. Abstr. NLM W1 GE826.

GROUP ANALYSIS. V. 1- 1967-. 0533-3164. Periodical. UK. English. ty. The Trust for Group Analysis, 1 Daleham Gardens, London NW3 5BY England. Ed Harold Behr. LC RC500. DD 616.891505. NLM W1 GR81. (cum index). bk rev. adv acc. (ctrl). Articles on group therapy.

GROUP AND FAMILY THERAPY. 1980-. 0276-5594. US. English. an. Brunner/Mazel Inc, 19 Union Square, New York NY 10003. LC RC488.A1. DD 616.891505. NLM W1 GR81F. Group Therapy, 0090-3957.

GROUP PROCESS. 0046-6468. Periodical. UK. English. sa. $18.00. Gordon & Breach, 1 Bedford St, London WC2E 9HD England. LC RC488.A1. DD 616.8915. NLM W1 GR6588. CODEN GPCSA. Journal of Group Psychoanalysis and Process.

GROUP PSYCHOTHERAPY, PSYCHODRAMA & SOCIOMETRY CEASED. VAT Group Psychotherapy, Psychodrama and Sociometry. V. 29-33. 0146-6178. Periodical. US. English. an. $14.00. Beacon House, PO Box 311, Beacon NY 12508. LC RC488.A1. DD 616.891505. NLM W1 GR861. Group Psychotherapy and Psychodrama, 0096-0586; Handbook of International Sociometry, 0160-4635.

GROUP STUDIES JOURNAL. V. 1- 1973-. 0363-714X. US. English. Psychiatric Institute Foundation, Michigan Avenue and Franklin Street Northwest, Washington DC 20017. LC RC488.A1. DD 616.8915. NLM W1 GR872.

H&CP : HOSPITAL AND COMMUNITY PSYCHIATRY. VFOAT Hospital and Community Psychiatry. Vol. 34, No. 1 (Jan. 1983)-. Periodical. US. English. mo. American Psychiatric Association, 1400 K Street Northwest, Washington DC 20005. Ind/Abst Cumul. Index Nurs. Allied Health Lit., Biol. Abstr. Hospital & Community Psychiatry.

HANZAIGAKU ZASSHI. VFOAT Archiv fur Gerichtlich Medizin und Kriminologie. Vol. 1- Sept. 1928-. 0302-0029. Periodical. JA. Japanese (summaries also in English 1951-). ir. $30.00. Japanese Association of Criminology, Kanda-Surugadai Chiyoda 2-3-10, Tokyo Japan. Ed Osamu Nakata. Ind/Abst Biol. Abstr., Chem. Abstr. NLM W1 HA552. CODEN HAZAAY. adv acc. Circ 6. The publishing of a thesis on the subject following, the result of a psychiatric test, an inquest, a study of blood type and etc.

THE HILLSIDE JOURNAL OF CLINICAL PSYCHIATRY. V. 1-. 0193-5216. Periodical. US. English. sa. $40.00. International Universities Press, 315 Fifth Avenue, New York NY 10016. Ind/Abst Excerpta Med., Index Med., Biol. Abstr., Psychol. Abstr. LC RC321. DD 616.89005. NLM W1 HI406U. CODEN HJCPDU. Journal of the Hillside Hospital.

HISTORY OF PSYCHOANALYSIS MONOGRAPH. (HISTORY OF PSYCHOANALYSIS). VFOAT History of Psychoanalysis Monograph Series. Monograph 1-. 0734-9831. Monographic Series. US. English. ir. International Universities, 315 Fifth Avenue, New York NY 10016. Tel (212)684-7900. LC UNC. DD 616. Presents original contributions reviewing the seminal work and lives of the pioneers of psychology, psychiatry, and psychoanalysis from a variety of scholarly and theoretical viewpoints.

HISTORY OF PSYCHOLOGY SERIES. See Psychology.

HOGG FOUNDATION NEWS. Periodical. US. English. qt. PO Box 7998, University Station, Austin TX 78712.

HOSPITAL & COMMUNITY PSYCHIATRY. (HOSPITAL & COMMUNITY PSYCHIATRY : A JOURNAL OF THE AMERICAN PSYCHIATRIC ASSOCIATION). VFOAT Hospital and Community Psychiatry. Began with Jan. 1966 issue. 0022-1597. Periodical. US. English. mo. $35.00. American Psychiatric Association, 1400 K Street NW, Washington DC 20005. Tel (202)682-6158. Ed John A Talbott. Ind/Abst Excerpta Med., Life Sci. Collect., Hospit. Lit. Index, Index Med., Cumul. Index Nurs. Allied Health Lit., Biol. Abstr., Soc. Work Res. Abstr., Psychol. Abstr., Media Rev. Dig., Soc. Sci. Citation Index, Abstr. Soc. Work. NLM W1 HO71L. CODEN HSCPAM. bk rev. adv acc. Circ 22,155. For mental health professionals and facilities. Takes an interdisciplinary approach to issues related to the delivery of mental health services in organized settings. Mental Hospitals, 0096-5502.

IN PURSUIT OF WELLNESS. Vol. 1 Mar. 1979-. 0197-9264. US. English. California Department of Mental Health, Office of Prevention, 2340 Irving Street/Suite 108, San Francisco CA 94122. NLM W1 IN103.

INDIAN JOURNAL OF PSYCHIATRY. V. 1- 1958-. 0019-5545. Periodical. II. English. qt. $35.00. Hindustan Book Agency, 17 UB Jawahar Nagar, Delhi 7 India. Ind/Abst Chem. Abstr., Psychol. Abstr. NLM W1 IN227. CODEN IJRPAB.

INSTITUTE ON MENTAL RETARDATION. Series/Titl A Johnstone Bulletin. US. English. an. LC HV3004.

INTEGRATIVE PSYCHIATRY. Began in 1983. 0735-3847. Periodical. US. English. qt. $87.00. Elsevier Science Publishing Company Inc, PO Box 1663, Grand Central Station, New York NY 10163. Tel (212)370-5520. Ed Alfred M Freedman. LC RC321. DD 616.89. adv acc. Circ 300. An interdisciplinary forum for publication of original and review articles which foster the interpretation of the biopsychosocial elements of psychiatry.

INTERACTION. V. 1- Summer 1977-. 0161-6749. Periodical. US. English. qt. Psychiatric Institute of America, 1825 K Street NW, Washington DC 20007. Tel (202)337-5600. NLM W1 IN654Q.

INTERCOM - REGISTERED PSYCHIATRIC NURSES' ASSOCIAITON OF BRITISH COLUMBIA. (INTERCOM). Vol. 1, No. 1 (Dec./Jan. 1983)-. 0822-5842. Periodical. CN. English. bm. Free to Members. Registered Psychiatric Nurses' Association of British Columbia, 508 Clark Road, Coquitlam British Columbia V3J 3X2 Canada. DD 610.7368060711. This Month, 0382-6341.

INTERNATIONAL DRUG THERAPY NEWSLETTER. See Pharmacy.

INTERNATIONAL JOURNAL OF BEHAVIORAL GERIATRICS. Vol. 1, No. 1 (Spring 1982)-. 0730-6695. Periodical. US. English. qt. $96.00. Van Nostrand Reinhold, 135 West 50th Street, New York NY 10020. Ind/Abst Life Sci. Collect., Excerpta Med., Cumul. Index Nurs. Allied Health Lit., Psychol. Abstr. LC RC451.4.A5. DD 618.97689005. NLM W1.

INTERNATIONAL JOURNAL OF FAMILY PSYCHIATRY. V. 1-. 0271-2679. Periodical. US. English. qt. $65.00 Domestic, $73.00 Foreign. International University Press Inc, 300 Raritan Center Parkway CN94, Edison NJ 08818. Tel (212)684-7900. Ed John G Howells. Ind/Abst Excerpta Med., Psychol. Abstr. LC RC488.5. DD 616.8915605. NLM W1 IN766IS. Serves as an international forum for all professionals interested in the family as a unit for evaluation and therapy.

INTERNATIONAL JOURNAL OF FAMILY THERAPY. VFOAT Family Therapy. V. 1- Spring 1979-. 0148-8384. US. English. qt. Human Sciences Press, 72 5th Avenue, New York NY 10011. Tel (212)243-6000. Ind/Abst Curr. Index J. Educ., Psychol. Abstr. LC RC488.5. DD 616.8915605. NLM W1 IN766IT. CODEN IJFTDY.

INTERNATIONAL JOURNAL OF GROUP PSYCHOTHERAPY. (THE INTERNATIONAL JOURNAL OF GROUP PSYCHOTHERAPY). V. 1- April 1951-. 0020-7284. Periodical. US. English. qt. $50.00. International University Press, 300 Raritan Center Parkway CN94, Edison NJ 08818. Tel (212)684-7900. Ind/Abst Sociol. Abstr., Soc. Welf. Soc. Plan./Policy Soc. Dev., Excerpta Med., Women Stud. Abstr., Biol. Abstr., Psychol. Abstr., Index Med., Soc. Work Res. Abstr., Soc. Sci. Citation Index, Hospit. Lit. Index, Lang.

Medicine—Psychiatry, Psychopathology

Lang. Behav. Abstr., Abstr. Soc. Work. LC RC488. DD 616.805. NLM W1 IN766N. CODEN IJGPAO.

INTERNATIONAL JOURNAL OF LAW AND PSYCHIATRY. See Law.

INTERNATIONAL JOURNAL OF PSYCHIATRY IN MEDICINE. (THE INTERNATIONAL JOURNAL OF PSYCHIATRY IN MEDICINE). V. 4- Winter 1973-. 0091-2174. Periodical. US. English. qt. $58.00. Baywood Publishing Company, 120 Marine Street/PO Box D, Farmingdale NY 11735. Tel (516)249-2464. Ed Donald R Sweeney. Ind/Abst Life Sci. Collect., Excerpta Med., Soc. Work Res. Abstr., Biol. Abstr., Index Med., Psychol. Abstr., Energy Res. Abstr., Soc. Sci. Citation Index, Hospit. Lit. Index, Abstr. Soc. Work. LC RC321. DD 616.89005. NLM W1 IN776J. CODEN IJMEDO. Committed to research within the conceptual framework of psychosomatic medicine, to foster research on psychobiological and psychosocial factors in the prevention, diagnosis and treatment of illness. *Psychiatry in Medicine, 0033-278X.*

INTERNATIONAL JOURNAL OF PSYCHO-ANALYSIS. See Psychology.

INTERNATIONAL JOURNAL OF PSYCHOANALYTIC PSYCHOTHERAPY. VFOAT IJPP, International Journal of Psychoanalytic Psychotherapy. V. 1- Feb. 1972-. 0146-356X. US. English. be. $40.00. Jason Aronson Inc, 59 Fourth Avenue, New York NY 10003. Ind/Abst Index Med., Psychol. Abstr. LC RC500. DD 616.891705. NLM W1 IN777D. CODEN IJPPD4. *I.J.C.P. International Journal of Child Psychotherapy, 0090-6891.*

INTERNATIONAL JOURNAL OF PSYCHOSOMATICS. (INTERNATIONAL JOURNAL OF PSYCHOSOMATICS : OFFICIAL PUBLICATION OF THE INTERNATIONAL PSYCHOSOMATICS INSTITUTE). Vol. 31, No. 1-. Periodical. US. English. $47.00. PO Box 1296, Philadelphia PA 19105. Tel (215)525-5511. Ed Donald R Morse. Ind/Abst Index Med., Biol. Abstr., Index Dent. Lit., Psychol. Abstr. NLM W1. bk rev. adv acc. Circ 1,000. (ctrl). Psychosomatic (mind/body) aspects of health and disease. *Journal of the American Society of Psychosomatic Dentistry and Medicine, 0003-1194.*

INTERNATIONAL JOURNAL OF SOCIAL PSYCHIATRY. (THE INTERNATIONAL JOURNAL OF SOCIAL PSYCHIATRY). V. 1- Summer 1955-. 0020-7640. Periodical. UK. English. qt $60.00. Avenue Publishing Company, 55 Woodstock Avenue, London NW11 9RG England. Tel 01-455-2940. Ed S Bierer. Ind/Abst Sociol. Abstr., Soc. Welf. Soc. Plan./Policy Soc. Dev., Excerpta Med., Index Med., Psychol. Abstr., Soc. Sci. Index, Lang. Lang. Behav. Abstr., Hospit. Lit. Index, Abstr. Soc. Work. LC RC321. DD 362.205. NLM W1 IN7888. bk rev. adv acc. Circ 800. Official journal of World Association Social Psychiatry, founded by the late Dr. Joshua Bierer, covering fields of mental health.

INTERNATIONAL JOURNAL OF THE ADDICTIONS. See Drug Abuse and Alcoholism.

INTERNATIONAL JOURNAL OF THERAPEUTIC COMMUNITIES. V. 1- Spring 1980-. 0196-1365. Periodical. US. English. qt. $50.00. c/o Mr R D Hinshelwood, 18 Artesian Road, London W2 England. Ed R D Hinshelwood. LC RC489.T67. DD 616.8914. NLM W1 IN791NJ. CODEN IJTCDJ. bk rev. adv acc. Circ 500. Original articles, community, studies and shorter pieces on therapeutic institutions and other social systems.

INTERNATIONAL PHARMACOPSYCHIATRY. V. 1- 1968-. 0020-8272. Periodical. SZ. English, French, or German with summaries in English. qt. $40.00. Albert J Phiebig Inc, PO Box 352, White Plains NY 10602. Ind/Abst Excerpta Med., Chem. Abstr., Biol. Abstr., Psychol. Abstr., Nuci. Sci. Abstr. LC RC483. DD 615.7805. NLM W1 IN827O. CODEN INPHB6.

INTERNATIONAL REVIEW OF RESEARCH IN MENTAL RETARDATION. VFOAT Research in Mental Retardation. V. 1- 1966-. 0074-7750. US. English. ir. Academic Press, 4805 Sand Lake Road, Orlando FL 32887. Tel (305)345-4100. Ed N Ellis. Ind/Abst Soc. Sci. Citation Index. LC RC570. DD 157.808. NLM W1 IN834N.

INTERPERSONAL DEVELOPMENT. Vol. 1-. 0373-3793. Periodical. English. qt S Karger, 10 P Box Allsehwilerstrasse, CH 4009 Basel Switzerland.

Ind/Abst Sociol. Abstr. LC RC488.A1. DD 616.891505. NLM W1 IN969.

IRCS MEDICAL SCIENCE. PSYCHIATRY AND CLINICAL PSYCHOLOGY. (IRCS MEDICAL SCIENCE : PSYCHIATRY AND CLINICAL PSYCHOLOGY). VFOAT Psychiatry and Clinical Psychology. V. 3- Jan. 1975-. 0305-6899. Periodical. UK. English. bm $70.00. IRCS Medical Science, PO Box 500/St Leonards House, Lancaster LA1 1PF England. Tel (0524)68116. Ed S Johnson. bk rev. Publishes results of original research into all aspects of psychology, both clinical and experimental, within weeks of completion. Papers fully refereed. *Research on Psychiatry and Clinical Psychology, 0305-2885.*

ISRAEL JOURNAL OF PSYCHIATRY AND RELATED SCIENCES. (THE ISRAEL JOURNAL OF PSYCHIATRY AND RELATED SCIENCES). Vol. 18, No. 1-. 0333-7308. Periodical. IS. English. qt. $35.00. Israel Science Publishers Ltd, POB 3115, Jerusalem 91030 Israel. Tel (02)637915. Ed E L Edelstein. Ind/Abst Excerpta Med., Index Med., Soc. Work Res. Abstr., Psychol. Abstr. LC RC321. DD 616.89005. NLM W1 IS636UD. CODEN IPRDAH. bk rev adv acc. (ctrl). Microform. Mental health problems of Jewish and Israeli interest. Empirical and theoretical research in general psychiatry and related fields. *Israel Annals of Psychiatry and Related Disciplines.*

JAHRBUCH DER PSYCHOANALYSE. See Yearbooks, Almanacs, Directories.

JORNAL BRASILEIRO DE PSIQUIATRIA. 0047-2085. Periodical. BL. Portuguese (summaries in English and French). bm. $80.00. ECN-Editora Cientifica Nacional, Caixa Postal 590, 20001 Rio de Janeiro Brazil. Tel (021). Ed E Carvalho Neto. Ind/Abst Excerpta Med., Biol. Abstr., Chem. Abstr., Nuci. Sci. Abstr., Psychol. Abstr. NLM W1 JO195. CODEN JBPSAX. bk rev. adv acc. Circ 3,000. (ctrl). Ecletic publication dedicated to psychiatry and psychology. *Anais do Instituto de Psiquiatria.*

JOURNAL - NATIONAL ASSOCIATION OF PRIVATE PSYCHIATRIC HOSPITALS. See Medicine - Medical Centers, Hospitals.

JOURNAL OF AUTISM AND DEVELOPMENTAL DISORDERS. V. 9- Mar. 1979-. 0162-3257. Periodical. US. English. qt. $125.00 Domestic, $140.00 Foreign. Plenum Publishing Corporation, 233 Spring Street, New York NY 10013. Tel (212)620-8000. Ed Eric Schopler. Ind/Abst Excerpta Med., Index Med., Biol. Abstr., Educ. Index, Except. Child Educ. Resour., Curr. Index J. Educ., Psychol. Abstr. NLM W1 JO547N. CODEN JADDDQ. bk rev. adv acc. This journal is devoted to all severe psychopathologies on childhood and is not necessarily limited to autism and childhood schizophrenia. *Journal of Autism and Childhood Schizophrenia, 0021-9185.*

JOURNAL OF BEHAVIOR THERAPY AND EXPERIMENTAL PSYCHIATRY. V. 1- Mar. 1970-. 0005-7916. Periodical. UK. English. qt $45.00. Pergamon Press, c/o Cashier, 395 Sawmill River Road, Elmsford NY 10523. Tel (914)592-7700. Ind/Abst Lang. Lang. Behav. Abstr., Sociol. Abstr., Soc. Sci. Citation Index, Psychol. Abstr., Excerpta Med., Cumul. Index Nurs. Allied Health Lit., Index Med., Biol. Abstr. LC RC489.B4. DD 616.891. NLM W1 JO555. CODEN JBTEAB. Available on microfilm from Microforms International Marketing Corp.

JOURNAL OF CHILD PSYCHOLOGY AND PSYCHIATRY AND ALLIED DISCIPLINES. See Psychology.

THE JOURNAL OF CLINICAL PSYCHIATRY. V. 39- Jan. 1978-. 0160-6689. Periodical. US. English. mo. $40.00 Domestic, $82.00 Foreign. Physicians Postgraduate Press, PO Box 240008, Memphis TN 38124. Tel (901)682-1001. Ed Ferris Pitts. Ind/Abst Electron. Commun. Abstr. J., ISMEC Bull., Pollut. Abstr. Indexes, Saf. Sci. Abstr. J., Life Sci. Collect., Sociol. Abstr., Soc. Welf. Soc. Plan./Policy Soc. Dev., Pestdoc, Ringdoc, Vetdoc, Excerpta Med., Index Med., Cumul. Index Nurs. Allied Health Lit., Biol. Abstr., Chem. Abstr., Psychol. Abstr. LC RC321. DD 616.89005. NLM W1 JO59I. CODEN JCLPDE. bk rev. adv acc. Circ 29,000. (ctrl). Clinical material dealing with psychiatric disorders. *Diseases of the Nervous System.*

JOURNAL OF CLINICAL PSYCHIATRY MONOGRAPH SERIES. (THE JOURNAL OF CLINICAL PSYCHIATRY MONOGRAPH SERIES). VFOAT JCP Monograph. Vol. 2, No. 1 (Mar. 1984)-.

0742-1915. Monographic Series. US. English. Physicians Postgraduate Press, PO Box 240008, Memphis TN 38124. NLM W1. *JCP Monograph Series.*

JOURNAL OF CLINICAL PSYCHOPHARMACOLOGY. VFOAT Clinical Psychopharmacology. Vol. 1, No. 1 (Jan. 1981)-. 0271-0749. Periodical. US. English. bm. $55.00. Williams & Wilkins Company, 428 East Preston Street, Baltimore MD 21202. Tel (301)528-4000. Ed Richard I Shader. Ind/Abst Excerpta Med., Index Med., Chem. Abstr. NLM W1 JO592M. CODEN JCPYDR. adv acc. Circ 4,500. Leading clinical papers in this field, with perspectives for psychiatrists on antipsychotics, antianxiety agents, antidepressants, and stimulants.

JOURNAL OF COLLEGE STUDENT PSYCHOTHERAPY. 8756-8225. Periodical. US. English. qt. Haworth Press, 75 Griswold Street, Binghamton NY 13904.

JOURNAL OF COMMUNICATION DISORDERS. V. 1- May 1967-. 0021-9924. Periodical. US. English. bm. $124.00. Elsevier Science Publishing Company, 52 Vanderbilt Avenue, New York NY 10017. Tel (212)370-5520. Ed R W Rieber. Ind/Abst Lang. Lang. Behav. Abstr., Index Med., Except. Child Educ. Resour., Biol. Abstr., Psychol. Abstr., Curr. Index J. Educ., Soc. Sci. Citation Index, Sociol. Abstr., Hospit. Lit. Index. LC RC423.A1. DD 616.855005. NLM W1 JO593N. CODEN JCDIAI. adv acc. Covers the biological foundations of communicative processes and their relationship to communicative disorders, emphasizing the psychological, anatomical, diagnostic and therapeutic aspects of the subject.

JOURNAL OF COMMUNICATION THERAPY. Vol. 1, No. 1-. 0734-4368. Periodical. US. English. an. $30.00. University of Houston, c/o Dr Saral, 2700 Bay Area Boulevard, Houston TX 77058. Tel (713)488-9500. Ed Tulsi B Saral. LC RC475. DD 616.8914. bk rev. adv acc. Circ 300. Interdisciplinary journal presenting theoretical articles, case studies, research reports and book reviews on the role and scope of intrapersonal, interpersonal, intercultural and transpersonal communication in the therapeutic process.

JOURNAL OF CONTEMPORARY PSYCHOTHERAPY. V. 1- Fall 1968-. 0022-0116. Periodical. US. English. sa. Human Sciences Press, 72 5th Avenue, New York NY 10011. Tel (212)896-3400. Ind/Abst Excerpta Med., Psychol. Abstr., Soc. Work Res. Abstr., Soc. Sci. Citation Index, Abstr. Soc. Work. LC RC475. DD 616.89105. NLM W1 JO595V. CODEN JCPTBA. *Journal of the Long Island Consultation Center.*

JOURNAL OF FAMILY THERAPY. V. 1, No. 1 (Feb. 1979)-. 0163-4445. Periodical. UK. English. qt. $66.00. Academic Press, 4805 Sand Lake Road, Orlando FL 32819. Tel (305)345-4100. Ind/Abst Sociol. Abstr., Soc. Welf. Soc. Plan./Policy Soc. Dev., Psychol. Abstr. LC RC488.5. DD 616.89156. NLM W1 JO6445H.

JOURNAL OF FLUENCY DISORDERS. V. 1- July 1974-. 0094-730X. Periodical. US. English. qt. $88.00. Elsevier Science Publishing Company Inc, 1663 Grand Central Station, New York NY 10163. Tel (212)370-5520. Ed Anthony A Zenner and P Helbert Damste. Ind/Abst Lang. Lang. Behav. Abstr., Biol. Abstr., Ref. Source, Psychol. Abstr., Soc. Sci. Citation Index. LC RC423.A1. DD 616.855005. NLM WI JO65M. CODEN JFDID8. adv acc. Provides coverage of clinical and theoretical aspects of stuttering, including the latest remediation techniques.

JOURNAL OF GERIATRIC PSYCHIATRY. VFOAT Geriatric Psychiatry. V. 1- Fall 1967-. 0022-1414. Periodical. US. English. sa. $50.00 Domestic, $58.00 Foreign. International University Press Inc, 300 Raritan Center/Parkway CN94, Edison NJ 08818. Tel (212)684-7900. Ed David Blay and Ralph J Kahana. Ind/Abst Excerpta Med., Index Med., Cumul. Index Nurs. Allied Health Lit., Psychol. Abstr., Soc. Sci. Citation Index, Sociol. Abstr., Lang. Lang. Behav. Abstr. LC RC451.4.A5. NLM W1 JO669N. CODEN JGPSBZ. The journal presents the latest thinking and most recent findings in the field of geriatric psychiatry.

JOURNAL OF GROUP PSYCHOTHERAPY, PSYCHODRAMA AND SOCIOMETRY. DELETEDRAMA AND SOCIOMETRY. Vol. 34 (1981)-. 0731-1273. Periodical. US. English. qt. Heldref Publications, 4000 Albemarle Street NW/Suite 100, Washington DC 20016. Tel (202)362-6445. Ind/Abst

Medicine—Psychiatry, Psychopathology

Psychol. Abstr. LC RC488.A1. DD 616.891505. NLM W1 JO669QH. *Group Psychotherapy, Psychodrama and Sociometry, 0146-6178.*

THE JOURNAL OF NERVOUS AND MENTAL DISEASE. V. 3- 1876-. 0022-3018. US. English. mo. Ind/Abst MLA Int. Bibliogr. Books Artic. Mod. Lang. Lit., Life Sci. Collect., Excerpta Med., Pestdoc, Ringdoc, Vetdoc, Women Stud. Abstr., Except. Child Educ. Resour., Biol. Abstr., Chem. Abstr., Index Med., Nuci. Sci. Abstr., Psychol. Abstr., Energy Res. Abstr. NLM W1 JO778. CODEN JNMDAN. adv acc. Circ 2,520. Available on microfilm. Studies in the social, behavioral, and neurological sciences relevant to the clinical practice of psychiatry. *Chicago Journal of Nervous and Mental Disease.*

JOURNAL OF NEURAL TRANSMISSION. See Medicine - Neurology.

JOURNAL OF NEUROLOGY NEUROSURGERY AND PSYCHIATRY. See Medicine - Neurology.

JOURNAL OF OPERATIONAL PSYCHIATRY. V. 1- Jan. 1970-. 0047-2638. Periodical. US. English. sa. University of Missouri at Columbia, Medical Center, Columbia MO 65201. Tel (314)882-3176. Ind/Abst Psychol. Abstr., Sociol. Abstr., Lang. Lang. Behav. Abstr. LC RC321. DD 616.89005. NLM W1 JO803G. CODEN JOPYB7.

JOURNAL OF ORTHOMOLECULAR PSYCHIATRY. V. 3, No. 1- 1974-. 0317-0209. Periodical. CN. English. qt $34.83. Canadian Schizophrenia Foundation, 2229 Broad Street, Regina Saskatchewan S4P 1Y7 Canada. Tel (306)757-7969. Ind/Abst Life Sci. Collect., Excerpta Med., Bibliogr. Agric., Psychol. Abstr., Soc. Sci. Citation Index. DD 616.8982005. NLM W1 JO804R. *Orthomolecular Psychiatry, 0317-0217.*

JOURNAL OF PERSONALITY DISORDERS. 0885-579X. Periodical. US. English. qt $50.00. Guilford Publications, 200 Park Avenue South, New York NY 10003.

JOURNAL OF PREVENTIVE PSYCHIATRY. Vol. 1, No. 1 (Spring 1981)-. 0197-9353. Periodical. US. English. qt $75.00. Mary Ann Liebert Inc, 157 East 68th Street, New York NY 10028. Tel (212)289-2300. Ed Gilbert N Kliman. Ind/Abst Psychol. Abstr. LC RA790.A1. DD 616.8905. NLM W1 JO844J. bk rev. adv acc. Devoted to the primary prevention of diseases for people in a high risk population and sets scientific standards.

JOURNAL OF PSYCHIATRIC EDUCATION. V. 1- Spring/Summer 1977-. 0363-1907. Periodical. US. English. qt. Human Sciences Press, 72 5th Avenue, New York NY 10011. Tel (212)243-6000. Ind/Abst Excerpta Med., Psychol. Abstr., Soc. Sci. Citation Index. LC RC336. DD 616.8900711. NLM W1 JO853E. CODEN JPSEDS.

JOURNAL OF PSYCHIATRIC NURSING AND MENTAL HEALTH SERVICES. See Medicine - Nursing.

JOURNAL OF PSYCHIATRIC RESEARCH. V. 1- Oct. 1961-. 0022-3956. Periodical. UK. English. qt. Pergamon Press, 395 Sawmill River Road, Elmsford NY 10523. Tel (914)592-7700. Ind/Abst Life Sci. Collect., Excerpta Med., Int. Aerosp. Abstr., Biol. Abstr., Chem. Abstr., Psychol. Abstr., Nuci. Sci. Abstr., Index Med., Soc. Sci. Citation Index, Sci. Cit. Index, Abr. Ed., Sociol. Abstr., Lang. Lang. Behav. Abstr., Hospit. Lit. Index, Psychol. Abstr. LC RC321. DD 616.89005. NLM W1 JO854. CODEN JPYRA3.

JOURNAL OF PSYCHIATRIC TREATMENT AND EVALUATION. V. 1-. 0195-8127. Periodical. US. English. bm. $60.00 General, $20.00 Individual. Pergamon Press Inc, Fairview Park, Elmsford NY 10523. Ind/Abst Life Sci. Collect., Excerpta Med., Cumul. Index Nurs. Allied Health Lit., Biol. Abstr., Psychol. Abstr. LC RC321. DD 616.89005. NLM W1 JO85. CODEN JPTEDA.

JOURNAL OF PSYCHIATRY & LAW. See Law.

JOURNAL OF PSYCHOSOCIAL NURSING AND MENTAL HEALTH SERVICES. See Medicine - Nursing.

JOURNAL OF PSYCHOSOMATIC RESEARCH. V. 1- Feb. 1956-. 0022-3999. Periodical. UK. English. bm. Pergamon Press, 395 Sawmill River Road, Elmsford NY 10523. Tel 00/914/5927700. Ed D Leigh. Ind/Abst Sci. Cit. Index, Abr. Ed., Index Med., Psychol. Abstr., Soc. Sci. Citation Index, Sociol. Abstr., Hospit. Lit. Index, Lang. Lang. Behav. Abstr., Women Stud. Abstr., Life Sci. Collect., Excerpta Med., Biol. Abstr., Chem. Abstr. LC RC52. DD 616.8, 616.08. NLM W1 JO850. CODEN JPCRAT.

JOURNAL OF RATIONAL EMOTIVE THERAPY. (JOURNAL OF RATIONAL EMOTIVE THERAPY : THE JOURNAL OF THE INSTITUTE FOR RATIONAL-EMOTIVE THERAPY). VFOAT Journal of Rational-Emotive Therapy. Vol. 1, No. 1 (Fall 1983)-. 0748-1985. Periodical. US. English. sa. $76.00. Human Sciences Press Inc, 72 Fifth Avenue, New York NY 10011. Tel (212)243-6000. Ind/Abst Psychol. Abstr. LC RC489.R3. DD 616.8914. *Rational Living, 0034-0049.*

JOURNAL OF RELIGION AND HEALTH. See Religion, Mythology, Rationalism.

JOURNAL OF RESEARCH AND TRAINING. (THE JOURNAL OF RESEARCH AND TRAINING). VFOAT IDMH Journal of Research & Training. V. 1- Summer 1973-. 0092-3931. Periodical. US. English. qt. Illinois Mental Health Institutes, 1601 West Taylor Street, Chicago IL 60612. LC RC321. DD 616.89005.

JOURNAL OF SEX & MARITAL THERAPY. VAT Journal of Sex and Marital Therapy. V. 1- Fall 1974-. 0092-623X. Periodical. US. English. qt. $30.00. Human Sciences Press, 72 Fifth Avenue, New York NY 10011. Ind/Abst Sociol. Abstr., Soc. Welf. Soc. Plan./Policy Soc. Dev., Index Med., Psychol. Abstr., Excerpta Med. LC RC556. DD 616.8583005. NLM W1 JO876F. CODEN JSMTB.

JOURNAL OF SEX EDUCATION & THERAPY. See Sexual Life.

JOURNAL OF STRATEGIC & SYSTEMATIC THERAPIES. (THE JOURNAL OF STRATEGIC AND SYSTEMIC THERAPIES). 0711-5075. Periodical. CN. English. ir. 37.00. Journal of Strategic and Systemic Therapies, Box 2481/Station A, London Ontario N6A 4C7 Canada. Tel 433-3101. Ed Don Efron. DD 615.505. bk rev. Circ 1,300. Specialized journal for therapists using strategic-systemic models in individual and family therapy. Example given Haley, Erickson, MRI, Milan. Emphasis on clinical usefulness and therapy. No research.

JOURNAL OF THE AMERICAN ACADEMY OF CHILD PSYCHIATRY. Main/Corp American Academy of Child Psychiatry. VFOAT Journal of Child Psychiatry. V. 1- Jan. 1962-. 0002-7138. Periodical. US. English. bm. $90.00. Williams & Wilkins, 428 East Preston Street, Baltimore MD 21202. Tel (301)528-4000. Ed Melvin Lewis. Ind/Abst Excerpta Med., Cumul. Index Nurs. Allied Health Lit., Index Med., Women Stud. Abstr., Educ. Index, Except. Child Educ. Resour., Psychol. Abstr., Soc. Work Res. Abstr., Soc. Sci. Citation Index, Sci. Cit. Index, Abr. Ed., Sociol. Abstr., Hospit. Lit. Index, Bibliogr. Index, Lang. Lang. Behav. Abstr., Abstr. Soc. Work. LC RJ499.A1. DD 618.9289005. NLM W1 JO907W. adv acc. Circ 5,900. Leading journal in child psychiatry publishing high quality original papers in psychiatric research and treatment of child and adolescent.

JOURNAL OF THE AMERICAN ACADEMY OF PSYCHIATRY AND NEUROLOGY. Main/Corp American Academy of Psychiatry and Neurology. VFOAT Journal of the AAPN. V. 1- Jan./Mar. 1976-. 0362-4870. Periodical. US. English. qt. $30.00. AAPN, 17 Kingston Road, Scarsdale NY 10583. LC RC321. DD 616.8005. NLM W1 JO907XG.

JOURNAL OF THE AMERICAN ACADEMY OF PSYCHOANALYSIS. (THE JOURNAL OF THE AMERICAN ACADEMY OF PSYCHOANALYSIS). V. 1- 1973-. 0090-3604. Periodical. US. English. qt. John Wiley & Sons Inc, 605 Third Avenue, New York NY 10158. Tel (800)526-5368. Ind/Abst Excerpta Med., Index Med., Women Stud. Abstr., Psychol. Abstr., Soc. Sci. Citation Index, Abstr. Soc. Work. LC RC500. DD 616.891705. NLM W1 JO907Y. CODEN JAAPCC.

JOURNAL OF THE AMERICAN PSYCHOANALYTIC ASSOCIATION. Main/Corp American Psychoanalytic Association. V. 1- Jan. 1953-. 0003-0651. Periodical. US. English. qt. $68.00 Domestic, $76.00 Foreign. International University Press Inc, 300 Raritan Cente/Parkway CN94, Edison NJ 08818. Tel (212)684-7900. Ed Theodore Shapiro. Ind/Abst Life Sci. Collect., Excerpta Med., Biol. Abstr., Psychol. Abstr., Index Med., Hospit. Lit. Index, Lang. Lang. Behav. Abstr., Sociol. Abstr. LC BF173.A2. DD 616.891705. NLM W1 JO91K. CODEN JAPOAE. Noted for the outstanding quality of its articles on all aspects of psychoanalysis, the journal continues to present contributions of vital concern to its readers.

JOURNAL OF THE BALINT SOCIETY. V. 1- June 1971-. 0307-4765. Periodical. UK. English. NLM W1 JO913C.

JOURNAL OF THE PHILADELPHIA ASSOCIATION FOR PSYCHOANALYSIS. Main/Corp Philadelphia Association for Psychoanalysis. V. 1- Mar. 1974-. 0094-1476. Periodical. US. English. qt. $7.00. 15 St Asaph's Road, Bala Cynwyd PA 19004. Ind/Abst Excerpta Med. LC RC500. DD 616.891705. NLM W1 JO946E. *Bulletin of the Philadelphia Association for Psychoanalysis, 0480-2780.*

JOURNEE DE PEDO-PSYCHIATRIE. Periodical. French. ir. NLM W1 JO994CP.

KARGER BIOBEHAVIORAL MEDICINE SERIES. Began with 1, published 1983. Monographic Series. English. ir. Tel (061)39 08 80. NLM W1 KA821M. Texts that communicate new strategies for treating physiologic conditions influenced by mental events.

KLINISCHE PSYCHOLOGIE UND PSYCHOPATHOLOGIE. V. 1-. 0343-9429. Monographic Series. German. ir. Ferdinand Enke Verlag, Herdweg 63 POB 1304, 7000 Stuttgart 1 West Germany. Ed H Remschmidt. NLM W1 KL55P.

KOKURITSU MUSASHI RYOYOJO SHINKEI SENTA NENPO. See Medicine - Neurology.

KYUSHU SHINKEI SEISHIN IGAKU. VFOAT Kyushu Neuro-Psychiatry. Began in 1949. 0023-6144. Periodical. Japanese (with summaries in English). ty. $16.00. Kyushu University Kyushu Association, Neuro Psychiatry, Fukuoka 812 3-1-Maidashi, Higashiku Japan. Ind/Abst Chem. Abstr., Psychol. Abstr. NLM W1 KY9975. CODEN KSSIAC.

LAFAYETTE CLINIC HANDBOOKS IN PSYCHIATRY. No. 1- 1967-. 0075-7608. Monographic Series. US. English. ir. Wayne State University Press, 5959 Woodward Avenue, Detroit MI 48202. Tel (313)577-4602. NLM W1 LA285. Circ 800. Focuses on teaching programs in psychiatry.

LEGAL ASPECTS OF PSYCHIATRIC PRACTICE. See Law.

MCLEAN HOSPITAL JOURNAL. See Medicine - Medical Centers, Hospitals.

MALADJUSTMENT AND THERAPEUTIC EDUCATION : THE JOURNAL OF THE ASSOCIATION OF WORKERS FOR MALADJUSTED CHILDREN. Vol. 1, No. 1 (Spring 1983)-. 0264-4614. Periodical. UK. English. sa. 12.00. Longview Lodge Road Caerleon, Newport Gwent Wales NP6 1QS UK. Tel 0633 421209. Ed Graham Upton. NLM W1. bk rev. adv acc. Circ 2,000. The journal covers the interests of disturbed children and aims to promote communication between all the professional workers involved in working with them. *New Growth.*

MASSACHUSETTS GENERAL HOSPITAL BIOLOGICAL THERAPIES IN PSYCHIATRY NEWSLETTER CEASED. VFOAT Biological Therapies in Psychiatry Newsletter. 0199-2716. Periodical. US. English. mo. $37.50. PSG Publishing Company Inc, 545 Great Road, Littleton MA 01460. Tel (617)468-8971. Ed Alan J Gelenberg. Circ 5,800. Designed to keep clinicians up-to-date with the important psychotrophic drugs affecting his practice. *Harbor Area Somatic Therapy Newsletter.*

MEDICAL WORLD NEWS FOR PSYCHIATRISTS. Vol. 2, No. 17 (Sept. 13, 1984)-. 8750-4014. Periodical. US. English. sm. $33.00 Domestic, $44.00 Canada. Medical World News for Psychiatrists, HEI Publishing, 7676 Woodway, Houston TX 77063. DD 616. *Medical World News (Psychiatry Edition), 0743-7765.*

MEDICINA PSICOSOMATICA. 0025-7893. Periodical. IT. Italian. qt. $34.46. Societa Editrice Universo, Via Morgagni 1, Rome Italy 00161. Ind/Abst Excerpta Med., Biol. Abstr., Psychol. Abstr. NLM W1 ME614. CODEN MDPSAC.

Medicine—Psychiatry, Psychopathology

MEMBERSHIP DIRECTORY - AMERICAN ORTHOPSYCHIATRIC ASSOCIATION. See Yearbooks, Almanacs, Directories.

MEMBERSHIP DIRECTORY - CANADIAN PSYCHIATRIC ASSOCIATION. See Yearbooks, Almanacs, Directories.

MEMBERSHIP LIST - ROYAL COLLEGE OF PSYCHIATRISTS. Main/Corp Royal College of Psychiatrists. 1977-. 0142-5447. UK. English. an. Royal College of Psychiatrists, 17 Belgrave Square, London SW1X 8PG England. NLM WM 22 FA1 R8Y. Yearbook.

MENNINGER PERSPECTIVE. V. 1- Apr./May 1970-. 0025-9292. Periodical. US. English. qt. $25.00. Menninger Foundation Office of Information, PO Box 829, Topeka KS 66601. Tel (913)273-7500. Ed Emlin E North Jr and Judith L Craig. LC RC321. DD 616.89005. NLM W1 ME9199K. CODEN MNPVB. Circ 17,000. Articles related to mental health topics such as: psychiatric treatment, research, professional education, public advocacy, and the work of the Menninger Foundation. Menninger Quarterly.

MENTAL DISABILITY LAW REPORTER. See Law.

MENTAL HEALTH AUDIT CRITERIA SERIES. Issue 1-. 0190-1672. Monographic Series. US. English. ir. Interqual, 740 North Rush Street, Chicago IL 60611. NLM W1 ME924F.

MENTAL HEALTH EMERGENCIES ALERT. 1-. 0364-7757. US. English. National Institute of Mental Health, 5600 Fishers Lane, Rockville MD 20852. LC Z6664.N5, RC480.6. DD 616.89025.

MENTAL HEALTH REPORTS. Began in 1977. 0191-6750. Periodical. US. English. bw. $167.00. Capitol Publications Inc, 1300 North 17th Street, Arlington VA 22209. Tel (703)528-1100. Ed Patrick Rogers. NLM W1 ME927E. Circ 900. Mental health policy issues; funding of mental health programs and geared to mental health administrators and information needs.

MENTAL HEALTH SERVICE SYSTEM REPORTS. SERIES AN, EPIDEMIOLOGY. VFOAT Epidemiology. No. 1-. 0276-6884. Monographic Series. US. English. NLM W1 ME928EN.

MENTAL HEALTH SERVICE SYSTEM REPORTS. SERIES CN, MENTAL HEALTH NATIONAL STATISTICS. See Statistics.

MENTAL HEALTH SERVICE SYSTEM REPORTS. SERIES GN. METHODOLOGY. (MENTAL HEALTH SERVICE SYSTEM REPORTS. SERIES GN : METHODOLOGY). No. 1- 1980-. 0273-3498. Monographic Series. US. English. NLM W1 ME928FD.

MENTAL HEALTH SPECIAL INTEREST SECTION NEWSLETTER. 0279-4136. Periodical. US. English. qt. $15.00. American Occupational Therapy Association, 1383 Piccard Drive, Rockville MD 20850. Tel (301)948-9626. Ed Virginia Dickie and Roann Barris. bk rev. Circ 2,000. Mental health issues relevant to occupational therapy. Newsletter - Mental Health Specialty Section, American Occupational Therapy Association, 0194-6382.

MENTAL HEALTH STATISTICS. VOLUME 3. INSTITUTIONAL FACILITIES, SERVICES AND FINANCES. See Statistics.

MENTAL RETARDATION ABSTRACTS. See Indexes/Abstracts.

MILIEU THERAPY. Vol. 1, No. 1 (Summer 1981)-. 0276-8887. Periodical. US. English. sa. $12.00. Avalon Press, Old Stockbridge Road, Lennox MA 01240. Ind/Abst Except. Child Educ. Resour., Psychol. Abstr.

MINERVA PSICHIATRICA. V. 17- Jan./Mar. 1976-. 0391-1772. Periodical. IT. Italian. qt. 60.00. Edizioni Minerva Medica, Corso Bramante 83-85, Torino 10126 Italy. Tel 678282. Ed G Campailla and A Petiziol. Ind/Abst Sociol. Abstr., Excerpta Med., Index Med. NLM W1 MI652G. bk rev. adv acc. Addressed to practitioners and specialists in psychiatry and psychology in Italy and abroad; deals with topics in scientific practice and research. Minerva Psichiatrica E Psicologica.

MODERN GROUP BOOK. V. 1- 1972-. US. English. $10.00. Jason Aronson Inc, 111 8th Avenue, New York NY 10011. LC RC488.A1. DD 616.8915.

MODERN PROBLEMS OF PHARMACOPSYCHIATRY. VFOAT Moderne Probleme der Pharmakopsychiatrie, Problemes Actuels de Pharmacopsychiatrie. Vol. 1-. 0077-0094. Periodical. English. ir. S Karger Ag, PO Box, CH-4009 Basel Switzerland. Tel 061-39 08 80. Ed T A Ban, P Pichot and L W Poldinger. Ind/Abst Index Med., Biol. Abstr., Chem. Abstr. LC RC483. DD 616.891805. NLM W1 MO168P. CODEN MPPPBK. Expert information on the development and uses of drugs for psychiatric practice.

MODERN PSYCHOTHERAPY. V. 1- May 1978-. 0163-2841. Periodical. US. English. Dr John B Snook, Westchester Institute for Training in Counseling and Psychotherapy, 260 Styvesant Avenue, Rye NY 10580. LC RC475. DD 616.8.914.

MONOGRAFIE DE IL LAVORO NEUROPSICHIATRICO. (LE MONOGRAFIE DE IL LAVORO NEUROPSICHIATRICO). VFOAT Lavoro Neuropsichiatrico. 196-?-. 0023-9097. Periodical. IT. Italian. bm. $20.00. Direzione Radazione Amministra, Piazza S Maria Della Pieta 5, 00135 Roma Italia. Ind/Abst Psychol. Abstr. NLM W1 MO543R.

MONOGRAPH - CHILDREN'S PSYCHIATRIC RESEARCH INSTITUTE. Main/Corp Children's Psychiatric Research Institute. No. 1-. 0227-8561. Periodical. CN. English. Children's Psychiatric Research Institute, PO Box 2460 London, Ontario Canada N6A 4G6. DD 362.2.

MONOGRAPH SERIES - AMERICAN GROUP PSYCHOTHERAPY ASSOCIATION. (MONOGRAPH SERIES). VFOAT AGPA Monograph Series. Monograph 1-. 0742-3187. Monographic Series. US. English. ir. International Universities Press Inc, 80 Northfield Avenue, Building #424, Edison NJ 08837. LC UNC. DD 616.89152. NLM W1 MO559PU.

MONOGRAPHIEN AUS DEM GESAMTGEBIETE DER PSYCHIATRIE. See Medicine - Neurology.

MONOGRAPHS OF THE JOURNAL OF THE AMERICAN ACADEMY OF CHILD PSYCHIATRY. Main/Corp American Academy of Child Psychiatry. No. 1-. 0065-6852. Monographic Series. US. English. qt. Yale University, 92A Yale Station, New Haven CT 06520. Tel 203-436-7583. LC UNC. NLM W1 MO569QS.

MONTAGE (TORONTO MENSA). See Medicine - Neurology.

NATIONAL CONFERENCE ON ASIAN-AMERICAN MENTAL HEALTH. Series/Titl DHEW Publication. 1st- 1972-. 0164-2677. US. English. NLM W3 NA436W.

NATIONAL DIRECTORY OF PROVIDERS OF PSYCHIATRIC SERVICES TO RELIGIOUS INSTITUTIONS. See Yearbooks, Almanacs, Directories.

NATIONAL REGISTRY OF COMMUNITY MENTAL HEALTH SERVICES. 1985-. US. English.

NERVENARZT. See Medicine - Neurology.

NERVENHEILKUNDE. See Medicine - Neurology.

NEUROLOGIA ET PSYCHIATRIA. See Medicine - Neurology.

NEUROPSICHIATRIA. See Medicine - Neurology.

NEUROPSYCHIATRIA CLINICA. Vol. 1, No. 1 (1 Sept. 1982)-. 0723-0931. Periodical. US. English (text in German table of contents and summaries in both languages). at. $75.00. VCH Publishers Inc, 303 NW 12th Avenue, Deerfield Beach FL 33442. Tel (305)428-5566. NLM W1 NE339G.

NEUROPSYCHOBIOLOGY. See Medicine - Neurology.

NEW DIMENSIONS IN MENTAL HEALTH. June 1976-. 0146-1451. Monographic Series. US. English. Alcohol Drug Abuse and Mental Health Administration, Printing and Publications Management Section 5600, Fishers Lane/Room 6-105, Rockville MD 20852. NLM W1 NE372N. Memo from the Director - National Institute of Mental Health.

NEW DIMENSIONS IN PSYCHIATRY. (NEW DIMENSIONS IN PSYCHIATRY : A WORLD VIEW). V. 1 -. 0148-7361. US. English. be. J Wiley & Sons, 605 Third Avenue, New York NY 10158. Ed Silvano Arieti and Gerard Chrzanowski. LC RC331. DD 616.89005. NLM W1 NE373. World Biennial of Psychiatry and Psychotherapy, 0084-1420.

NEW DIRECTIONS IN PSYCHOTHERAPY. V. 1-. 0192-5822. Monographic Series. US. English. ir. Human Sciences Press, 72 Fifth Avenue, New York NY 10011. Ed P Olsen. NLM W1 NE374FE.

NEW HAMPSHIRE COMMUNITY MENTAL HEALTH AGENCIES, DIRECTORY OF STAFFS AND BOARD OF DIRECTORS. See Yearbooks, Almanacs, Directories.

NEW RESEARCH IN MENTAL HEALTH. See Sociology: General Works, Theory - Social Pathology, Welfare, Criminology.

NEWSLETTER (AMERICAN ACADEMY OF PSYCHIATRY AND THE LAW). (NEWSLETTER). Vol. 6, No. 2 (Aug. 1981)-. Periodical. US. English. ty. $4.00. American Academy of Psychiatry and the Law, 1211 Cathedral Street, Baltimore MD 21201. Tel (301)539-0379. Ed Robert M Wettstein. adv acc. Circ 1,300. (ctrl). Articles on forensic psychiatry, updates on legal cases, topical columns including "The Isaac Ray Corner", "Ask The Experts", and "The Children's Corner". Newsletter of the American Academy of Psychiatry and the Law.

NEWSLETTER -MEN'S AWARENESS NETWORK. Main/Corp Men's Awareness Network. VFOAT MAN Newsletter. Periodical. US. English. qt. Mens Resource Center, 3534 Southeast Main, Portland OR 97214. Tel (503)235-3433.

NEWSLETTER (NATIONAL ASSOCIATION OF PRIVATE PSYCHIATRIC HOSPITALS). See Medicine - Medical Centers, Hospitals.

NEWSLETTER OF THE A.A.P.S.C. (NEWSLETTER). Main/Corp American Association of Psychiatric Services for Children. VFOAT AAPSC Newsletter. VAT Newsletter of the American Association of Psychiatric Services for Children. V. 17- Spring 1970-. 0093-0237. Periodical. US. English. qt. American Association of Psychiatric Services for Children, 1701-18th Street Northwest, Washington DC 20009. LC RJ501.A2. DD 618.928900973. Newsletter of the AAPCC.

NEWSLETTER OF THE AMERICAN ACADEMY OF PSYCHIATRY AND THE LAW CEASED. VFOAT Newsletter of the American Academy of Psychiatry & The Law. Vol. 1, No. 1 (Jan. 1976)-V. 6, No. 1 (Mar. 1981). Periodical. US. English.

NEWSLETTER - WORLD FEDERATION FOR MENTAL HEALTH. Main/Corp World Federation for Mental Health. VAT President's Newsletter - World Federation for Mental Health. V. 1- Feb. 1975-. 0319-6992. Periodical. CN. English. qt. $8.00. The Federation, C M H A Liaison Committee with D F M H, R R 2, Lambeth Ontario N0L 1S0 Canada. NLM W1 NE9985. Bulletin - World Federation for Mental Health, 0043-8456.

NIMHANS JOURNAL. VFOAT N.I.M.H.A.N.S. Journal. VAT National Institute of Mental Health and Neuro Sciences Journal. Vol. 1, No. 1 (Jan. 1983)-. English. sa. 80.00. National Institute of Mental Health and Neuro Sciences, Bangalore 560 029 India. Tel 41256. Ed G N Narayana Reddy. NLM W1. bk rev. adv acc. Papers in mental health and neuro sciences in its broadest sense including basic sciences are published.

OCCUPATIONAL MENTAL HEALTH NOTES CEASED. July 1965-June 1970. 0029-795X. Periodical. US. English. ir. NLM ZWA 495 O145.

ODENSE UNIVERSITY STUDIES IN PSYCHIATRY AND MEDICAL PSYCHOLOGY. V. 1- 1973-. 0105-0621. Monographic Series. DK. Danish. ir. Odense University, 36 Pjentedamsgade, DK-500 Denmark. Tel (09)141611. NLM W1 OD115. Psychiatrical diseases.

OPENMIND. VFOAT Open Mind. No. 1 (Feb./Mar. 1983)-. Periodical. UK. English. bm. NLM W1. Mind Out.

Medicine—Psychiatry, Psychopathology

L'ORDINAIRE DU PSYCHANALYSTE.
1- May 1973-. 0395-000X. Periodical. FR. French. ir. 80.00. Librairie les Mains Libres 2, rue de Pere Corentin, 75014 Paris France. LC RC500. DD 616.891705. NLM W1 OR271.

OREGON REVISED STATUTES RELATING TO MENTAL HEALTH. See Law.

PARENTS VOICE. V. 1- 1950-. 0031-1936. Periodical. UK. English. qt. 4.40. Royal Society for Mentally Handicapped Children & Adults, 123 Golden Lane, London EC1Y 0RT England. Tel 253 9433. Ed Alan Leighton. Ind/Abst Except. Child Educ. Resour. NLM W1 PA6428. bk rev. adv acc. Circ 20,000. Also available on microfilm from University Microfilms. Book advertisements of mental handicap courses. Advertising residential homes and holidays, with general updates on mental handicap.

PEOPLE. 0146-6593. Periodical. US. English. qt. Division of Mental Hygiene and Mental Retardation, 4600 Kietzke Lane/Suite 108, Reno NV 89502. LC RA790.65.N3. DD 362.205.

PERSONALITY AND PSYCHOPATHOLOGY. 0079-0931. Monographic Series. US. English. ir. Ind/Abst Chem. Abstr. NLM W1 PE861. CODEN PEPSDL.

PERSONATION AND PSYCHOTHERAPY. V. 1-. 0253-5254. Monographic Series. English (text in German or Italian). ir. NLM W1 PE864.

PERSONNEL NEEDS AND TRAINING FOR BIOMEDICAL AND BEHAVIORAL RESEARCH. Main/Corp National Research Council (U.S.). Committee on a Study of National Needs for Biomedical and Behavioral Research Personnel. 1975-. Periodical. US. English. be. National Academy of Sciences, 2101 Constitution Avenue NW, Washington DC 20418. NLM W2 A N296R.

PERSPECTIVES IN PSYCHIATRIC CARE. See Medicine - Nursing.

PHARMACOPSYCHIATRIA CEASED. 14. Year, Iss. 1 (Jan. 1981)- V. 16, No. 6 (Nov. 1983). 0720-4280. Periodical. US. English (text also in German, summaries in both languages). bm. $81.00. Thieme Stratton Inc, 381 Park Avenue South, New York NY 10016. Tel (212)683-5088/89. Ind/Abst Life Sci. Collect., Excerpta Med., Pestdoc, Ringdoc, Vetdoc, Chem. Abstr., Curr. Contents, Sci. Cit. Index, Abr. Ed. LC RM315. DD 615.78. NLM W1 PH289T. CODEN PHMCDD. P.

PHARMACOPSYCHIATRY. See Pharmacy.

PHOBIA THERAPY JOURNAL. 0883-9751. Periodical. US. English. qt. $69.00. Human Sciences Press, 72 Fifth Avenue, New York NY 10011. Tel (212)243-6000.

PHOENIX RISING (TORONTO, ONT.). (PHOENIX RISING). Vol. 1, No. 1 (Spring 1980)-. 0710-1457. Periodical. CN. English. qt. 15.00. Phoenix Rising c/o On Our Own, Box 7251/Station A, Toronto Ontario M5W 1X9 Canada. Tel (416)699-3194. Ind/Abst Altern. Press Index. DD 362.2109713. bk rev. adv acc. Circ 3,000. (ctrl). Antipsychiatry quarterly: critiques, features on psychiatric abuses including drugging, electroshock, involuntary commitment, rights issues, personal stories, poetry, book reviews, movement news (Canada and US).

PHYTIATRIE-PHYTOPHARMACIE. V. 1- 1952-. 0031-8876. Periodical. FR. French. ir. $19.96. Societe Francaise de Phy, 35 F Cnra-Rt de St Cyr 8, Versailles France. Ind/Abst Chem. Abstr., Bibliogr. Agric. NLM W1 PH987H. CODEN PHPHA6.

PRATT INSTITUTE CREATIVE ARTS THERAPY REVIEW. VFOAT Creative Arts Therapy Review. Vol. 1 (1980)-. 0196-8459. US. English. an. $5.00. Pratt Institute, 200 Willoughby Avenue, Brooklyn NY 11205. Tel (718)636-3428. Ed Estelle Peisach. Ind/Abst Psychol. Abstr. LC RC489.A7. DD 616.891656. Circ 400. (ctrl). Articles pertaining to issues such as transference, countertransference, the use of creative movement and the role of aggression as applied to the creative arts therapies.

PRAXIS DER KINDERPSYCHOLOGIE UND KINDERPSYCHIATRIE. 1.- Volume. 0032-7034. Periodical. GW. German. ir. $26.78. Vandenhoeck & Ruprecht, Postfach 3753, Theaterstr 13, D 3400 Goettingen West Germany. Tel (0511)65061. Ind/Abst Excerpta Med., Psychol.

Abstr., Biol. Abstr., Index Med., Soc. Sci. Citation Index, Sociol. Abstr., Lang. Lang. Behav. Abstr. NLM W1 PR319. CODEN PKIKAZ.

PRAXIS DER KINDERPSYCHOLOGIE UND KINDERPSYCHIATRIE BEIHEFT. 1- 1958-. Periodical. GW. German. ir. Vandenhoeck & Ruprecht, Postfach 3753, Theaterstr 13, D 3400 Goettingen West Germany. Tel 0551/65061. Ind/Abst Index Med. NLM W1 PR319E.

PRIMARY PREVENTION OF PSYCHOPATHOLOGY. V. 1- 1975-. 0161-8776. Periodical. US. English. ir. University Press of New England, Box 979, Hanover NH 03755. Ed G W Albee and J M Joffe. NLM W3 PR945CK. Source of up-to-date information on research and conceptualization in the field of primary prevention of psychopathology.

PRIORITY ISSUES IN MENTAL HEALTH : A BOOK SERIES PUBLISHED UNDER THE AUSPICES OF THE WORLD FEDERATION FOR MENTAL HEALTH. Vol. 1-. Monographic Series. US. English. ir. Kluwer Boston Inc, 190 Old Derby Street, Hingham MA 02043. NLM W1 PR524R.

PRIVATE PSYCHIATRIC HOSPITALS. See Medicine - Medical Centers, Hospitals.

PROCEEDINGS OF THE ANNUAL CONFERENCE ON PARTIAL HOSPITALIZATION. Main/Conf Conference on Partial Hospitalization. 1 (Sept. 18-20, 1976)-. 0270-7292. US. English. an. LC RC439.2. DD 362.21. NLM W3 C844.

PROGRESS IN NEURO-PSYCHOPHARMACOLOGY & BIOLOGICAL PSYCHIATRY. VFOAT Progress in Neuro-Psychopharmacology and Biological Psychiatry. Vol. 6, No. 1-. 0278-5846. Periodical. UK. English. ir. $342.00. Pergamon Press, 395 Sawmill River Road, Elmsford NY 10523. Ind/Abst Life Sci. Collect., Excerpta Med., Pestdoc, Ringdoc, Vetdoc, Index Med., Biol. Abstr., Energy Res. Abstr., Chem. Abstr., Psychol. Abstr. LC RM315. DD 615.7805. NLM W1 PR6745E. CODEN PNPPD7. *Progress in Neuro-Psychopharmacology, 0364-7722.*

PSIQUIS (MADRID, SPAIN). (PSIQUIS). Began in 1979. 0210-8348. Periodical. SP. Spanish. bm. $44.00. Instit Psicoter Invest Psicosm, Avenida de Filipinas 52-B, Madrid 3 Spain. Ind/Abst Psychol. Abstr. NLM W1 PS182T.

PSYCHIATRIA CLINICA CEASED. V. 1-16. 0033-264X. Periodical. SZ. English (French or German). bm. $64.00. Albert J Phiebig Inc, PO Box 352, White Plains NY 10602. Ind/Abst Life Sci. Collect., Excerpta Med., Biol. Abstr., Curr. Contents. LC RC321. NLM W1 PS238P. CODEN PSCLBV. Index in last issue of volume - attached. Available in microform. *Psychiatria et Neurologia.*

PSYCHIATRIA FENNICA. VFOAT Finnish Psychiatry. 1977-. 0079-7227. English (articles also in other languages). ir. Akakeeminen-Kirjakuppa, PO Box 128, 00101 Helsinki Finland. Ind/Abst Psychol. Abstr. DD 616.89005. NLM W1 PS239E. CODEN PSFNBI. *Psychiatria Fennica. Finnish Psychiatry. Suomalaista Psykiatriaa.*

PSYCHIATRIA FENNICAN JULKAISUSARJA. VFOAT Reports from Psychiatria Fennica. No. 24- 1977-. 0355-7693. Monographic Series. Finnish. ir. Ed K A Achte. NLM W1 PS239EB. *Helsingin Yliopistollisen Keskussairaalan Psykiatrian Klinikan Julkaisusarja.*

PSYCHIATRIA POLSKA. V. 1- Jan./Feb. 1967-. 0033-2674. Periodical. PL. Polish (added table of contents in English and Russian). bm. ARS Polona, Krakowskie Przedmiescie 7, 00-068 Warsaw Poland. Ind/Abst Excerpta Med., Index Med., Psychol. Abstr. NLM W1 PS239K. CODEN PSPOB3. Index published separately - free - automatically sent. *Neurologia, Neurochirurgia I Psychiatria Polska.*

PSYCHIATRIC ANNALS. V. 1- Sept. 1971-. 0048-5713. Periodical. US. English. mo. $74.00. Slack Inc, c/o Donna Carpenter, 6900 Grove Road, Thorofare NJ 08086. Tel (609)848-1000. Ed Donna Carpenter. Ind/Abst Excerpta Med., Psychol. Abstr., Soc. Sci. Citation Index. LC RC321. DD 616.89005. NLM W1 PS249. CODEN PSANCS. bk rev. adv acc. Circ 28,000. (ctrl). Features articles on new in-sights and new developments that will affect the practice of psychiatry in the U.S.

PSYCHIATRIC ASPECTS OF MENTAL RETARDATION NEWSLETTER. (NEWSLETTER). VFOAT P.A.M.R. Newsletter. Vol. 1, No. 1 (Jan. 1982)-. 0278-9493. Periodical. US. English. mo. Psychiatric Media Inc, 8 Griggs Terrace, Brookline MA 02146. Tel (617)277-2991. Ind/Abst Psychol. Abstr. bk rev. adv acc. Circ 800. Mental retardation.

THE PSYCHIATRIC CLINICS OF NORTH AMERICA. Vol. 1, No. 1 (Apr. 1978)-. 0193-953X. Monographic Series. US. English. qt. $48.00. W B Saunders Company, West Washington Square, Philadelphia PA 19105. Ind/Abst Excerpta Med., Index Med., Psychol. Abstr. LC RC321. DD 616.89. NLM W1 PS255.

PSYCHIATRIC DEVELOPMENTS. Vol. 1, No. 1 (Spring 1983)-. 0262-9283. Periodical. UK. English. qt. $80.00. Oxford University Press, Journals Department Walton Street, Oxford OX2 6DP England. Tel 0865 56767. Ed S B Guze and Sir M Roth. Ind/Abst Index Med. NLM W1 PS256F. adv acc. Circ 117. Contains primary reports on original research covering rapid developments in the scientific inquiry in epidemiological, clinical and neurobiological aspects of psychiatry.

THE PSYCHIATRIC FORUM. V. 1- Winter 1969-. 0033-2690. Periodical. US. English. sa. Free. WS Hall Psychiatric Institute, Box 202, Columbia SC 29202. Tel (803)758-7154. Ed Lucius C Pressley. Ind/Abst Excerpta Med., Cumul. Index Nurs. Allied Health Lit., Psychol. Abstr., Soc. Sci. Citation Index. LC RC321. NLM W1 PS256R. CODEN PSYFAK. bk rev. Circ 4,000. Contents are original articles related to mental health.

THE PSYCHIATRIC HOSPITAL. See Medicine - Medical Centers, Hospitals.

PSYCHIATRIC JOURNAL OF THE UNIVERSITY OF OTTAWA. Main/Corp University of Ottawa. Dept of Psychiatry. VFOAT Revue de Psychiatrie de l'Universite d'Ottawa. 1976. 0702-8466. Periodical. CN. English. qt. $38.69. Psychiatric Journal of University of Ottawa, 501 Smyth Road, Department of Psychiatry, Ottawa Ontario K1H 8l6. Tel (613)526-1690. Ed G J Sarwer-Foner. Ind/Abst Excerpta Med., Index Med., Biol. Abstr., Psychol. Abstr. LC RC321. DD 616.89005, 616.8'9'005. NLM W1 PS258. CODEN PJUODZ. bk rev. adv acc. Circ 5,000. (ctrl). Devoted to clinical and research papers in psychiatry and its related fields, including neurophysiology, psychopharmacology, biochemistry and psychoanalysis. Book reviews are a regular feature.

PSYCHIATRIC MEDICINE. Vol. 1, No. 1 (Jan. 1983)-. 0732-0868. Periodical. US. English. qt. $75.00. SP Medical & Scientific Books, 175-20 Wexford Terrace, Jamaica NY 11432. Tel (718)658-0888. Ed Richard C W Hall. NLM W1 PS26J. Circ 500. This journal leads the way for new directions in medical psychiatry.

PSYCHIATRIC MEDICINE UPDATE. 1979-. 0163-1721. US. English. an. Elsevier-North Holland Inc, 52 Vanderbilt Avenue, New York NY 10017. LC RC321. DD 616.89005. NLM W1 PS26K.

PSYCHIATRIC NEWS. V. 1- Jan. 1966-. 0033-2704. Periodical. US. English. sm. $52.00. American Psychiatric Association, 1400 K Street NW, Washington DC 20005. Tel (202)682-6000. Ind/Abst Hospit. Lit. Index. LC RC321. NLM W1 PS26T. *Newsletter - American Psychiatric Association.*

PSYCHIATRIC OPINION CEASED. V. 14-17, NO. 2. 0163-2655. Periodical. US. English. mo. $30.00. Opinion Publications Inc, Rural Route 1 Box 396, Shelburne Falls MA 01370. Ind/Abst Psychol. Abstr., Community Ment. Health Rev. Available on microfilm from University Microfilms. *PO. Psychiatric Opinion, 0033-2712.*

PSYCHIATRIC OUTPATIENT PROGRAM. Main/Corp Hawaii. Mental Health Division. Research & Records Services. 0091-0422. US. English. an. State of Hawaii, Department of Health, Mental Health Division, Honolulu HI 96813. LC RC445.H32. DD 362.21. NLM W2 AH3 M5PA.

PSYCHIATRIC QUARTERLY. V. 1- Jan. 1927-. 0033-2720. Periodical. US. English. qt. Human Science Press, 3 Henrietta Street, c/o M Gleean, London WC2E 8LU England. Tel 01-240 0856. Ind/Abst Excerpta Med., Hospit. Lit. Index, Index Med., Cumul. Index Nurs. Allied Health Lit., Biol. Abstr., Psychol. Abstr., Sociol. Abstr., Lang. Lang. Behav. Abstr. NLM W1 PS262. CODEN PSQUAP. *State Hospitals Quarterly.*

LA PSYCHIATRIE DE L'ENFANT. V. 1- 1958-. 0079-726X. Periodical. French (summaries in English and Spanish). ir. **Tel** (1)326-22-16. **Ind/Abst** Excerpta Med., Index Med. **NLM** W1 PS332. **CODEN** PSYEAH. Contemporary child psychiatry is explored in lengthy articles detailing original research, personal ideas and theory.

PSYCHIATRIE, NEUROLOGIE UND MEDIZINISCHE PSYCHOLOGIE. Began publication with V. 1, Jan./Feb. 1949. 0033-2739. GE. German (summaries in Russian, English and French). mo. $47.60. Kunst & Wissen Erich Bieber, Dufourstrasse 51, CH-8008 Zuerich Switzerland. **Tel** (011)41-1-69 44 20. **Ind/Abst** Excerpta Med., Index Med., Psychol. Abstr., Sociol. Abstr., Lang. Lang. Behav. Abstr. **NLM** W1 PS339. **CODEN** PNMPAN.

PSYCHIATRIE, NEUROLOGIE UND MEDIZINISCHE PSYCHOLOGIE. BEIHEFTE. No. 1/2- 1963-. Periodical. German. qt. Cambridge Entomological Club, 16 Divinity Avenue, Harvard University, Cambridge MA 02138. **Tel** (617)495-2316. **Ind/Abst** Index Med. **NLM** W1 PS338.

PSYCHIATRISCHE PRAXIS. V. 1- March 1974-. 0303-4259. Periodical. German (some summaries in English). bm. $41.00. Thieme-Stratton Inc, 381 Park Avenue, New York NY 10016. **Tel** (212)683-5088/89. **Ind/Abst** Excerpta Med., Index Med., Soc. Sci. Citation Index. **NLM** W1 PS348N.

THE PSYCHIATRIST'S COMPENDIUM OF DRUG THERAPY. (THE PSYCHIATRIST'S COMPENDIUM OF DRUG THERAPY : A PUBLICATION OF BIOMEDICAL INFORMATION CORPORATION). **VFOAT** Compendium of Drug Therapy. 1981/1982-. 0276-4393. US. English. an. Biomedical Information Corporation, 800 2nd Avenue, New York NY 10017.

PSYCHIATRY. V. 1- Feb. 1938-. 0033-2747. Periodical. US. English. qt. $45.00. Guilford Press, 200 Park Avenue South, New York NY 10003. **Tel** (202)667-3008. **Ed** David Reiss. **Ind/Abst** MLA Int. Bibliogr. Books Artic. Mod. Lang. Lit., Excerpta Med., Sci. Cit. Index, Abr. Ed., Soc. Sci. Citation Index, Soc. Welf. Soc. Plan./Policy Soc. Dev., Soc. Work Res. Abstr., Biol. Abstr., Chem. Abstr., Psychol. Abstr., Nuci. Sci. Abstr., Index Med., Soc. Sci. Index, Women Stud. Abstr., Am. Hist. Life, Hist. Abstr., Part A, Mod. Hist. Abstr., Hist. Abst., Part B, Twent. Century Abstr., Lang. Lang. Behav. Abstr., Sociol. Abstr., Hist. Abstr., Abstr. Soc. Work. **LC** RC321. **DD** 132.05, 159.9705. **NLM** W1 PS352. **CODEN** PSYCAB. (cum index). bk rev. adv acc. **Circ** 2,100. Interdisciplinary psychiatric journal emphasizing intergration of psychological, biological, and social viewpoints. Publishes research, critiques, surveys, reviews and clinical studies.

PSYCHIATRY *CEASED.* (PSYCHIATRY : THE AMERICAN PSYCHIATRIC ASSOCIATION ANNUAL REVIEW). 1982. 0734-8436. Periodical. US. English. an. American Psychiatric Association, 1400 K Street NW, Washington DC 20005. **Tel** (202)682-6000. **Ed** Lester Grinspoon. **LC** RC321. **DD** 616.89005. **NLM** W1 PS358G (P).

PSYCHIATRY DIGEST (NORTHFIELD, ILL. : 1979). (PSYCHIATRY DIGEST). Began with Aug./Sept. 1979 issue. 0278-4602. Periodical. US. English. qt. $20.00. Medical Digest Inc, PO Box 8021, Northfield IL 60093. **LC** RC321. **DD** 616.89005. **NLM** W1 PS356M. *Journal of Continuing Education in Psychiatry, 0149-0265.*

PSYCHIATRY IN PRACTICE. Began with: Vol. 1, No. 1 (Sept. 1981). 0262-5377. Periodical. UK. English. mo. 18 Domestic, 21 Europe, 24 Others. The Medical News Group, Tower House, Southampton Street, London WC2E 7LS England. **Tel** (01)379-6005. **Ed** George Beaumont. **NLM** W1 PS357M. bk rev. adv acc. **Circ** 20,800. (ctrl). Articles on management and treatment of psychiatric and neurological disease states, research, book reviews, news for psychiatrists and neurologists.

PSYCHIATRY RESEARCH. V. 1- July 1979-. 0165-1781. Periodical. English. mo. Elsevier Science Publishers, PO Box 211, 1000 AE Amsterdam Netherlands. **Tel** (020)5803.911. **Ind/Abst** Life Sci. Collect., Excerpta Med., Pestdoc, Ringdoc, Vetdoc, Index Med., Biol. Abstr., Chem. Abstr., Psychol. Abstr., Sci. Cit. Index, Abr. Ed. **NLM** W1 PS358. **CODEN** PSRSDR.

PSYCHIATRY SPECIALIST PROGRAM. **VFOAT** Psychiatry. **VAT** Psychiatry (Ottawa). No. 1 (1983)-. 0824-7684. Periodical. CN. English. ir. Medifacts, 471 Richmond Road, Ottawa Ontario K2A 0G3 Canada. **DD** 616.89005.

PSYCHIATRY UPDATE. (PSYCHIATRY UPDATE : THE AMERICAN PSYCHIATRIC ASSOCIATION ANNUAL REVIEW). Vol. 2-. 0736-1866. Periodical. US. English. an. $47.00. American Psychiatric Association, 1400 K Street NW, Washington DC 20005. **Tel** (202)682-6262. **LC** RC321. **DD** 616.89005. *Psychiatry (American Psychiatric Association), 0734-8436.*

PSYCHOANALYSIS AND CONTEMPORARY THOUGHT. V. 1-. 0161-5289. Periodical. US. English. qt. $62.50 Domestic, $70.50 Foreign. International University Press Inc, 300 Raritan Center Parkway CN94, Edison NJ 08818. **Tel** (212)684-7900. **Ed** Leo Goldberger. **Ind/Abst** Excerpta Med., Sociol. Abstr., Biol. Abstr., Psychol. Abstr. **LC** RC500. **DD** 616.891705. **NLM** W1 PS395M. **CODEN** PCTHDS. Aimed at broadening the scientific and intellectual horizons of psychoanalysis, the journal publishes original clinical, theoretical, experimental, and quantitative contributions.

PSYCHOANALYTIC INQUIRY. Vol. 1, No. 1-. 0735-1690. Periodical. US. English. qt. $42.00. International Universities Press Inc, 315 Fifth Avenue, New York NY 10016. **Ind/Abst** Excerpta Med., Psychol. Abstr. **LC** RC500. **DD** 616.891705. **NLM** W1 PS427.

PSYCHOANALYTIC INQUIRY BOOK SERIES. Vol. 1-. Monographic Series. US. English. qt. $55.00. Analytic Press Inc, 365 Broadway Avenue, Hillsdale NJ 07642. **Tel** (201)666-4110. **NLM** W1.

PSYCHOANALYTIC STUDY OF SOCIETY. *See* Social Sciences (General).

PSYCHOBIOLOGY AND PSYCHOPATHOLOGY. Vol. 1 -. 0278-1719. Monographic Series. US. English. **Ind/Abst** Chem. Abstr. **NLM** W1 PS498H. **CODEN** PPSYDT.

PSYCHODRAMA AND GROUP PSYCHOTHERAPY MONOGRAPHS. No. 28- 1955-. Monographic Series. US. English. ir. Beacon House Inc, PO Box 311, Beacon NY 12508. *Psychodrama Monographs.*

PSYCHOPATHOLOGY. Vol. 17, No. 1 (Jan/Feb 1984)-. 0254-4962. Periodical. English. bm. $124.00. S Karger AG, PO Box, CH-4009 Basel Switzerland. **Tel** (061)39 08 80. **Ed** P Berner and E Gabriel. **Ind/Abst** Index Med., Life Sci. Collect., Psychol. Abstr. **NLM** W1. Index in last issue of volume - attached. adv acc. Publishes studies designed to increase the reliability and precision of explanatory concepts applied in descriptive psychopathology, phenomenology, and clinical diagnostics. *Psychiatria Clinica, 0033-264X.*

PSYCHOPATHOLOGY AND PICTORIAL EXPRESSION. 0555-5795. English. ir. S Karger AG, CH-4009 Basel Switzerland.

PSYCHOPHARMACOLOGY ABSTRACTS. *See* Indexes/Abstracts.

PSYCHOSOCIAL REHABILITATION JOURNAL. V. 1- Fall 1976-. 0147-5622. Periodical. US. English. qt. $36.00. Boston University/ Center of Rehabilitation Res Training & Mental Health, 1019 Commonwealth, Boston MA 02215. **Tel** (617)353-3549. **Ed** LeRoy Spaniol. **Ind/Abst** Cumul. Index Nurs. Allied Health Lit. **LC** RC439.5. **DD** 362.205. **NLM** W1 PS81H. bk rev. adv acc. **Circ** 2,500. Is currently the only publication that deals exclusively with the rehabilitation of the severely psychiatrically disabled in the community.

PSYCHOSOMATIC MEDICINE. V. 1- Jan. 1939-. 0033-3174. Periodical. US. English. bm. $32.50 Interns and Residents, $83.00 Institutions. Michael Torzewski, Elsevier North Holland Inc, 52 Vanderbilt Avenue, New York NY 10017. **Ind/Abst** Excerpta Med., Life Sci. Collect., Sociol. Abstr., Soc. Welf. Soc. Plan./Policy Soc. Dev., Energy Res. Abstr., Ref. Source, Biol. Abstr., Chem. Abstr., Index Med., Psychol. Abstr. **LC** RC321. **NLM** W1 PS82. **CODEN** PSMEAP.

PSYCHOSOMATICS. V. 1- Jan./Feb. 1960-. 0033-3182. Periodical. US. English. mo. $30.00. Cliggott Publishing Company, 500 West Putman Avenue, Box 4010, Greenwich CT 06830. **Tel** (203)661-0600. **Ind/Abst** Excerpta Med., Cumul. Index Nurs. Allied Health Lit., Energy Res. Abstr., Life Sci. Collect., Soc. Work Res. Abstr., Biol. Abstr., Chem. Abstr., Index Med., Psychol. Abstr., Lang. Lang. Behav. Abstr., Sociol. Abstr., Hospit. Lit. Index, Sci. Cit. Index, Abr. Ed., Soc. Sci. Citation Index. **LC** RC49. **DD** 616.0805. **NLM** W1 PS822. **CODEN** PSYCBC.

PSYCHOTHERAPIE, PSYCHOSOMATIK, MEDIZINISCHE PSYCHOLOGIE. V. 30-. 0173-7937. Periodical. German. mo. $70.00. Thieme-Stratton Inc, 381 Park Avenue, New York NY 10016. **Tel** (212)683-5088/89. **Ind/Abst** Excerpta Med., Index Med., Psychol. Abstr. **NLM** W1 PS83E. *Psychotherapie und Medizinische Psychologie, 0302-8984.*

PSYCHOTHERAPY AND PSYCHOSOMATICS. Began with V. 13. 0033-3190. Periodical. English (articles in German, or French with summaries in English). ir. 194.-. S Karger AG, PO Box, CH-4009 Basel Switzerland. **Tel** (061)39 08 80. **Ed** P E Sifneos. **Ind/Abst** Life Sci. Collect., Excerpta Med., Women Stud. Abstr., Biol. Abstr., Nuci. Sci. Abstr., Index Med., Psychol. Abstr., Sociol. Abstr., Soc. Sci. Citation Index, Hospit. Lit. Index, Lang. Lang. Behav. Abstr. **LC** RC49. **DD** 616.08. **NLM** W1 PS86K. **CODEN** PSPSBF. adv acc. Papers discuss the etiology of psychosomatic illnesses, whether biochemical, developmental or sociocultural, and their diagnosis and treatment. *Acta Psychotherapeutica et Psychosomatica, 0365-5822.*

PSYCHOTHERAPY (CHICAGO, ILL.). (PSYCHOTHERAPY). Vol. 1, No. 1 (Aug. 1963)-. 0033-3204. Periodical. US. English. qt. Psychotherapy-Theory, 912 Kinderkamack Road, River Edge NJ 07661. **Tel** (201)261-6884. **Ed** Donald K Freedheim. **Ind/Abst** Excerpta Med., Women Stud. Abstr., Psychol. Abstr., Soc. Sci. Citation Index. **LC** RC475. **DD** 616.891405. **NLM** W1 PS88. **CODEN** PSYOAD. (cum index). bk rev. adv acc. **Circ** 7,500. Psychotherapy theory research practice training.

PSYCHOTHERAPY FINANCES. 0163-1543. Periodical. US. English. mo. Psychotherapy Finances, 75 Oak Street, Ridgewood NJ 07450.

THE PSYCHOTHERAPY PATIENT. Vol. 1, No. 1 (Fall 1984)-. 0738-6176. Monographic Series. US. English. qt. $42.00. Haworth Press Inc, 28 East 22nd Street, New York NY 10010. **Tel** (212)228-2800. **Ed** Mark E Stern. **DD** 616. **NLM** W1. adv acc. **Circ** 1,084. Each issue focuses on diagnostic, behavioral or phenomenological groupings of persons in psychotherapy that psychotherapists in clinical practice are increasingly likely to see.

PUBLICATION - GROUP FOR THE ADVANCEMENT OF PSYCHIATRY. **Main/Corp** Group for the Advancement of Psychiatry. V. 9- (No. 97-). 0149-2640. Monographic Series. US. English. ir. Group for the Advancement of Psychiatry, Publications Office, 419 Park Avenue South, New York NY 10016. **Ind/Abst** Index Med., Psychol. Abstr. **NLM** W1 PU675N. **CODEN** GPSRB9. *Report - Group for the Advancement of Psychiatry, 0072-775X; Symposium - Group for the Advancement of Psychiatry.*

RASSEGNA DI STUDI PSICHIATRICI. V. 1- 1958-. 0033-9636. Periodical. IT. Italian. qt. 40.000. Rassegna di Studi Psichiatrici, Via Roma 56, Siena Italy. **Tel** (0577)290059. **Ind/Abst** Excerpta Med. **NLM** W1 RA71. **Circ** 300. Journal publishes articles from medical journals concerning psychiatry and scientific notes for professionals in medicine.

RBM. PSIQUIATRIA. **VFOAT** Psiquiatria. **VAT** Revista Brasileira de Medicina. Psiquiatria. Portuguese (text and summaries and table of contents in Portuguese and English). bm. rua Pinheiros 504, CEP 05422 Sao Paulo SP Brazil.

REACHING OUT. 0034-0324. Periodical. US. English. qt. IL Department of Mental Health, 401 South Spring Street, Springfield IL 62706. **LC** RA790.65.I4. **DD** 362.209773. **NLM** W1 RE1C.

REGISTERED PROFESSIONAL SANITARIANS . . . ROSTER. Jan. 1984-. US. English. an. Texas Department of Health, 1100 West 49th Street, Austin TX 78756. *Roster of Registered Professional Sanitarians of the State of Texas.*

REIHE VERGLEICHENDE PSYCHOTHERAPIE. V. 1-. 0720-0560. Monographic Series. German. ir. **NLM** W1 RE1807.

REPORT (GROUP FOR THE ADVANCEMENT OF PSYCHIATRY : 1984). (REPORT). **VFOAT** Gap Report. No. 116-. Monographic Series. US. English. **NLM** W1. *Publication - Group for the Advancement of Psychiatry, 0149-2640.*

REPORT OF THE ADMINISTRATOR - ALCOHOL, DRUG ABUSE, AND MENTAL HEALTH ADMINISTRATION. *See* Drug Abuse and Alcoholism.

Medicine—Psychiatry, Psychopathology

RESEARCH BULLETIN - ST. THOMAS PSYCHIATRIC HOSPITAL. (RESEARCH BULLETIN). VFOAT St. Thomas Psychiatric Hospital Research Bulletin. Vol. 1, No. 1 (Jan. 1982)-. 0711-6926. Periodical. CN. English. ir. St Thomas Psychiatric Hospital, PO Box 2004, St Thomas Ontario N5P 3V9 Canada. DD 616.890072071335.

RESEARCH COMMUNICATIONS IN PSYCHOLOGY, PSYCHIATRY AND BEHAVIOR. See Psychology.

RESEARCH FELLOWSHIP PROGRAM OF THE NATIONAL INSTITUTE OF MENTAL HEALTH. (THE RESEARCH FELLOWSHIP PROGRAM OF THE NATIONAL INSTITUTE OF MENTAL HEALTH). Series/Titl Public Health Service Publication, No. 1303, etc. 196-?. 0097-0182. Periodical. US. English. an. NLM WM 20.

RESEARCH PUBLICATIONS - ASSOCIATION FOR RESEARCH IN NERVOUS AND MENTAL DISEASE. See Medicine - Neurology.

REVIEW OF EXISTENTIAL PSYCHOLOGY AND PSYCHIATRY. See Psychology.

REVIEWS OF RESEARCH AND PRACTICE OF THE INSTITUTE FOR RESEARCH INTO MENTAL AND MULTIPLE HANDICAP. Main/Corp Institute for Research into Mental and Multiple Handicap. VFOAT IRMMH Reviews of Research and Practice. 0307-238X. Monographic Series. UK. English. ir. Elsevier Science Publishing, PO Box 1663/Grand Central Station, New York NY 10163. Ind/Abst Chem. Abstr. NLM W3 RE96. CODEN RRPHDX. *IRMMH Symposium, 0305-7852.*

REVISTA BRASILEIRA DE MEDICINA. PSIQUIATRIA. VFOAT Psiquiatria. Began in 1979. 0100-7343. BL. Portuguese. bm. $82.00. Revista Brasileira de Medicina, rua Pinheiros 504, 05422 Sao Paula SP Brazil. NLM W1 RE343J.

REVISTA BRASILEIRA DE PSICANALISE. V. 1-. 0486-641X. Periodical. Portuguese. qt. Ind/Abst Psychol. Abstr. LC RC500. NLM W1 RE345I.

REVISTA DE NEURO-PSIQUIATRIA. See Medicine - Neurology.

REVISTA DEL DEPARAMENTO DE PSIQUITRIA DE LA FACULTAD DE MEDICINA DE BARCELONA. (REVISTA DEL DEPARTAMENTO DE PSIQUIATRIA, FACULTAD DE MEDICINA DE BARCELONA). 0210-1793. Periodical. SP. Spanish. ir. Ind/Abst Excerpta Med., Psychol. Abstr. NLM W1 RE508M.

REVISTA DEL HOSPITAL PSIQUIATRICO DE LA HABANA. Main/Corp Hospital Psiquiatrico de la Habana, Mazorra, Cuba. 0440-436X. Periodical. CU. Spanish (summaries of articles in English). ir. $15.77. Empresa Ediciones Cubanas, Sub-Direccion Exportacion, Oreilly 407 Ciudad Habana Cuba. Ind/Abst Excerpta Med., Psychol. Abstr. NLM W1 RE51T.

REVUE DE MEDECINE PSYCHOSOMATIQUE ET DE PSYCHOLOGIE MEDICALE. V. 8, No. 1-Jan./Mar. 1966-. 0397-930X. Periodical. FR. French. ir. 380. La Pense Sauvage, BP 141, 38002 Grenoble Cedex France. Tel 76 87 13 03. Ind/Abst Excerpta Med., Psychol. Abstr. NLM W1 RE796E. CODEN RMPPAJ. Circ 5,000. Treats psychological aspects of illnesses. *Revue de Medecine Psychosomatique.*

REVUE ROUMAINE DE NEUROLOGIE ET DE PSYCHIATRIE. See Medicine - Neurology.

RIVISTA DI PATOLOGIA NERVOSA E MENTALE. V. 1- Jan. 1896-. 0035-6433. Periodical. IT. Italian (some summaries in English, French and German). bm. $38.61. Clinica Malattie Nervose e Mentali, Viale Morgagni 85, 1 50134 Firenze Italy. Ind/Abst Excerpta Med., Index Med. NLM W1 RI608.

RIVISTA DI PSICHIATRIA. 196—. 0035-6484. Periodical. IT. Italian (summaries in English). bm. Il Pensiero Scientifico Edit, Via Panama 48, 00198 Rome Italy. Tel 863 633. Ind/Abst Excerpta Med., Psychol. Abstr. NLM W1 RI61. CODEN RPSID3.

ROSTER OF THE AMERICAN PSYCHOANALYTIC ASSOCIATION. Main/Corp American Psychoanalytic Association. US. English. be. $19.50. American Psychoanalytic Association, 1 East 57th Street, New York NY 10022. Tel (212)752-0450.

R.P.N.A.M. UPDATE. See Medicine - Nursing.

S P BULLETIN *CEASED.* Main/Corp Societe Canadienne de la Sclerose en Plaques. Division du Quebec. VAT Sclerose en Plagues Bulletin, Bulletin - Societe Canadienne de la Sclerose en Plagues, Division du Quebec. V. 1-5, No. 17. 0700-320X. Periodical. CN. French. qt. Free. Societe Canadienne de la Sclerose en Plaques, Division du Quebec, 3555 rue Berri/Bureau 1015, Montreal Quebec H2L 4G4 Canada. DD 616.834006271.

SAGE ANNUAL REVIEWS OF COMMUNITY MENTAL HEALTH. VFOAT Annual Reviews of Community Mental Health. Vol. 1-. 0739-7283. Monographic Series. US. English. an. Sage Publications Inc, 275 South Beverly Drive, Beverly Hills CA 90212. Ed Richard H Price and John Monahan. DD 362.2205. NLM W1 SA125TC.

SANTE MENTALE AU QUEBEC. V. 1- Sept. 1976-. 0383-6320. Periodical. CN. French. sa. $12.38. Centre Sante Mentale Communaut, 180 Est Dorchester/Suite 408, Montreal Quebec H2X 1N6 Canada. Tel (514)866-6974. Ind/Abst Point Repere. DD 614.5809714. bk rev. Circ 1,100. (ctrl). Research projects and ideas in mental health.

SCHIZOPHRENIA BULLETIN. Began with Dec. 1969. 0586-7614. Periodical. US. English. qt. Superintendent of Documents, US Government Printing Office, Washington DC 20402. Tel (202)783-3238. Ind/Abst Excerpta Med., Index Med., Cumul. Index Nurs. Allied Health Lit., Biol. Abstr., Index U.S. Gov. Period., Psychol. Abstr., Hospit. Lit. Index, Sci. Cit. Index, Abr. Ed., Soc. Sci. Citation Index. LC RC514. NLM W1 SC17E. CODEN SCZBB3.

SCHWEIZER ARCHIV FUR NEUROLOGIE UND PSYCHIATRIE (ZURICH, SWITZERLAND : 1985). See Genealogy and Heraldry - Archives.

SCIENCE, PSYCHOTHERAPY, AND ETHICS. Vol. 1-. 0741-8949. Monographic Series. US. English. Haven Publishing Corporation, 38-15 149th Street, Flushing NY 11354. Ed Raphael Stern and Louise Horowitz. NLM W1 SC695F.

SCIENCE REPORTS (NATIONAL INSTITUTE OF MENTAL HEALTH (U.S.)). (SCIENCE REPORTS). 1-. 0197-8713. Monographic Series. US. English. National Institute of Mental Health, Division of Scientific and Public Information, 5600 Fishers Lane, Rockville MD 20857. LC UNC. NLM W1 SC77.

SEISHIN SHINKEIGAKU ZASSHI. VFOAT Psychiatria et Neurologia Japonica. Began in 1935. 0033-2658. Periodical. JA. Japanese (summaries in English). mo. $116.50. Japan Publishing Trading Company Ltd, PO Box 5030 Tokyo International, Tokyo 100-31 Japan. Ind/Abst Excerpta Med., Index Med., Biol. Abstr., Chem. Abstr. NLM W1 SE259. CODEN SSHZAS. *Neurologia.*

SELF-IN-PROCESS SERIES. V. 1-. 0160-4430. Monographic Series. US. English. Human Sciences Press, 72 Fifth Avenue, New York NY 10011. LC UNC. NLM W1 SE354.

SERIAL HANDBOOK OF MODERN PSYCHIATRY. VFOAT Handbook of Modern Psychiatry. V. 1- 1974-. 0094-6184. Periodical. US. English. ir. Thieme-Stratton, 381 Park Avenue South, New York NY 10016. Tel (212)683-5088. NLM W1 SE711.

SERIES IN PSYCHOSOCIAL EPIDEMIOLOGY. Vol. 4-. Monographic Series. US. English. ir. Rutgers University Press, 109 Church Street, New Brunswick NJ 08901. Tel (201)932-8174. Ed Andrew Slaby. NLM W1 PS79E (P). Studies of psychosocial epidemiological research, findings, methodology, ethnics policy, on drug abuse, children, stressful life events, illness behavior, community psychiatric surveys, etc. *Monographs in Psychosocial Epidemiology.*

SERIES PAEDOPSYCHIATRICA. No. 1-. 0080-9012. Monographic Series. SZ. French (German with summaries in English, French, and Spanish). Schwabe & Company AG, Steinentorstrasse 13, CH-4000 Basel 10 Switzerland. Tel (061)235523. Ind/Abst Index Med. NLM W1 SE73.

SOCIAL PSYCHIATRY. VFOAT Sozialpsychiatrie, Psychiatrie Sociale. V. 1- 1966-. 0037-7813. Periodical. WB. English (summaries in French and German). qt. $84.00. Springer-Verlag New York Inc, 175 5th Avenue, New York NY 10010. Tel (212)460-1500. Ed B Cooper, R S Daniels, N Kreitman and Y Pelicier. Ind/Abst Excerpta Med., Index Med., Psychol. Abstr., Life Sci. Collect., Women Stud. Abstr., Soc. Sci. Citation Index. NLM W1 SO123N. CODEN SCOPBE. Provides medium for prompt publication of scientific contributions concerned with effects of social conditions upon behaviour and the relationship between psychiatric disorder and the social environment.

SOCIAL PSYCHIATRY. V. 1- 1974-. 0095-0858. US. English. an. Academic Press, 4805 Sand Lake Road, Orlando FL 32819. LC RC455. DD 362.204205. NLM W1 SO123L.

SOCIJALNA PSIHIJATRIJA. V. 1- 1973-. 0303-7908. Periodical. YU. articles and summaries in Serbo-Croatian or English. qt. $75.00. Socijalna Psihijatrija, Kispaticeva 12, 41000 Zagred Rebro Yugoslavia. Ind/Abst Psychol. Abstr. NLM W1 SO878J. CODEN SPSIDE.

SOINS. PSYCHIATRIE. VFOAT Psychiatrie. Began with: No 1 (Mar. 1980). 0241-6972. Periodical. SZ. French. bm. $207.80. OPISA, 33 Chemin des Hutins Anieres, 1247 Geneve Switzerland. Tel 512347. Ind/Abst Int. Nurs. Index. NLM W1 SO8862T. bk rev. adv acc. Psychiatric care and nursing.

SOVIET NEUROLOGY & PSYCHIATRY. See Medicine - Neurology.

SPECIAL PUBLICATION (GASKELL (PUBLISHER)). (SPECIAL PUBLICATION). 1-. Monographic Series. UK. English. ir. NLM W1 SP295DK.

SPRINGER SERIES ON PSYCHIATRY. 1-. 0740-4212. Monographic Series. US. English. ir. Springer Publishing Company, 536 Broadway, New York NY 10012. Tel (212)460-1500. Ed Carl Eisdorfer. NLM W1 SP685SFM. Contains articles on neurology and psychiatry.

STATISTICAL REPORT - MENTAL HEALTH PROGRAMS. DEPARTMENT OF HEALTH. See Statistics.

SUBJECT TO CHANGE. V. 1- Dec. 1978-. 0706-7992. Periodical. CN. English. ty. $5.00. Gestalt Institute of Toronto, 395 Markham Street, Toronto Ontario M6G 2K8 Canada. DD 616.8914.

SYNOPSIS OF FAMILY THERAPY PRACTICE. Main/Conf Maryland/D.C./Virginia Network Symposium Family Therapy Practice. VFOAT Synopsis of the Annual Maryland/D.C./Virginia Network Symposium Family Therapy Practice. 1978-. 0162-7171. US. English. an. $7.95. Family Therapy Practice Network Inc, 18114 Hillcrest Avenue, Olney MD 20832. LC RC488.5. DD 616.8915605.

TASK FORCE REPORT. No. 1- Apr. 1970-. US. English. ir. American Psychiatric Association, 1400 K Street NW, Washington DC 20005. Tel (202)682-6000.

TEMAS DE PSICOLOGIA Y PSIQUIATRIA DE LA NINEZ Y ADOLESCENCIA. V. 1- 1969-. 0325-4437. Periodical. Spanish. ir. NLM W1 TE305K.

TEXAS STATE PLAN FOR CONSTRUCTION OF COMMUNITY MENTAL HEALTH CENTERS. Main/Corp Texas. Dept. of Mental Health and Mental Retardation. 0364-4642. US. English. an. Texas Department of Mental Health, PO Box 12668 Capital Station, Austin TX 78711. LC RA790.65.T4. DD 362.2209764.

TEXTES - HOPITAL MAISONNEUVE - ROSEMONT. SERVICE DE PEDOPSYCHIATRIE. (TEXTES). No. 1-. 0824-4294. CN. French. an. Hopital Maisonneuve-Rosemont Service de Pedopshchiatrie, 5689 Boul Rosemont, Montreal Quebec H1T 2H1 Canada. DD 618.9289005.

THERAPIE FAMILIALE. Vol. 1, No. 1-. 0250-4952. Periodical. SZ. French (articles in English French summaries). qt. 75.00 Domestic, $38.00 Foreign. Editions Medecine & Hygiene, Case Postale 229, CH-1211 Geneve 4 Switzerland. Tel (022) 469355. NLM W1 TH644K.

TIJDSCHRIFT VOOR PSYCHIATRIE. 16.- Yearly. 0303-7339. Periodical. NE. Dutch (summaries in English). ir. 69. Uitg Boom, Postbus 58, 7940 AB Meppel Netherlands. Ed P T Tongerius. Ind/Abst Excerpta Med. NLM W1 TI715P. bk rev. adv acc. Circ 3,250. Official journal of the Dutch Society for

Psychiatry and Society of Flemish Psychiatrists (Belgium). *Nederlands Tijdschrift Voor Psychiatrie.*

TODAY IN PSYCHIATRY. V. 1- 1975-. 0197-3185. Periodical. US. English. mo. Today in Psychiatry, 1630 Pine Street, Philadelphia PA 19103.

TOKYO-TO SHINKEI KAGAKU SOGO KENKYUSHO NENPO. See Medicine - Neurology.

TOPIQUE. Yearly V. 1-. 0040-9375. Periodical. FR. French. sa. $26.61. Desclee de Brouwer, 83 rue Hoche, 92240 Malakoff, 92240 Paris France. Tel (1)6562693. LC BF173.A2. DD 616.891705. NLM W1 TO54X.

THE TRAINING QUARTERLY ON MENTAL RETARDATION. Main/Corp Woodhaven Center (Phila.). Fall '79-. Periodical. US. English. qt. Woodhaven Center, 2900 Southampton Road, Philadelphia PA 19154. Ind/Abst Except. Child Educ. Resour.

TRANSACTIONAL ANALYSIS JOURNAL. V. 1- Jan. 1971-. 0362-1537. Periodical. US. English. qt. $25.00. International Transaction Analysis, 1772 Vallejo Street, San Francisco CA 94123. Tel (415)885-5992. Ed Robin Fryer. Ind/Abst Psychol. Abstr., Soc. Sci. Citation Index. LC RC489.T7. DD 616.89005. NLM W1 TR223B. bk rev. adv acc. Circ 5,200. Scientific articles for transactional analysis. *Transactional Analysis Bulletin, 0041-1051.*

TRANSCAN. V. 1- June 1971-. 0318-0026. Periodical. CN. English. qt. Canadian Association for the Mentally Retarded, Kinsmen Nimr Building, York University, 4700 Keele Street, Downsview Ontario M3J 1P3 Canada.

TRANSCULTURAL PSYCHIATRIC RESEARCH REVIEW. V. 6- Apr. 1969-. 0041-1108. Periodical. CN. English. qt. $35.00. Trans Psychiatric Research Review, 1022 Pine Avenue West, Montreal Quebec H3A 1A1 Canada. Tel (514)842-1231. Ed Raymona H Prince. NLM W1 TR228QB. bk rev. adv acc. Circ 600. Overviews, book reviews and abstracts dealing with cultural effects upon psychiatric disorders and their management. *Transcultural Psychiatric Research.*

TRANSNATIONAL MENTAL HEALTH RESEARCH NEWSLETTER CEASED. Began with V. 18, Spring 1976. Ceased with V. 23, No. 2/3 (Summer/Fall 1981). 0148-8678. Periodical. US. English. qt. $6.00. Postgraduate Center for Mental Health, 124 East 28th Street, New York NY 10016. LC RC475. DD 616.891405. NLM W1 TR233. *International Mental Health Research Newsletter, 0020-7969.*

UCLA UAF BIBLIOGRAPHY IN MENTAL RETARDATION. See Bibliographies.

U.S. FACILITIES AND PROGRAMS FOR CHILDREN WITH SEVERE MENTAL ILLNESSES. DIRECTORY. See Yearbooks, Almanacs, Directories.

VOICES: THE ART AND SCIENCE OF PSYCHOTHERAPY. V. 1- Fall 1965-. 0042-8272. Periodical. US. English. qt. $55.00 Domestic, $60.00 Foreign. American Academy of Psychotherapists, 215 East 11 Street, New York NY 10003. Tel (212)533-3511. Ed E Mark Stern. LC RC475. NLM W1 VO341. bk rev. adv acc. Circ 2,100. Explores psychotherapy relationship through experimental accounts of the therapeutic process, editorials, interviews, theoretical articles, reviews, peer supervision, humor, and poetry.

WAKING AND SLEEPING CEASED. V. 1-4. 0340-0905. Periodical. GW. English (French or German). ir. $45.00. Pfarrer-Henniger-Weg 10, D-8702 Eisingen Wurzburg Federal Republic of Germany. Ind/Abst Life Sci. Collect., Excerpta Med., Int. Aerosp. Abstr., Chem. Abstr. LC RC547. DD 612.82105. NLM W1 WA237. CODEN WASLDU.

THE WASHINGTON PSYCHIATRIC SOCIETY DIRECTORY. See Yearbooks, Almanacs, Directories.

WEEKLY PSYCHIATRY UPDATE SERIES. 1- 1976-. 0161-4568. Periodical. US. English. wk. Continuing Professional Education Center, 1101 State Road, Building Q, Princeton NJ 08540. Tel (609)924-4500. NLM W1 WE156.

WEITERENTWICKLUNG DER PSYCHOANALYSE UND IHRER ANWENDUNGEN. VFOAT Recent Developments in Psychoanalysis, Theory and Practice. Vol. 5-. GW. English or German. ir. Verlag Vandenhoeck and Ruprecht, Akademie der Wissenschaften, Gottingen West Germany. LC RC500. DD 616.8917. NLM W1 WE24G. *Fortschritte der Psychoanalyse.*

WOMEN & THERAPY. VFOAT Women and Therapy. Vol. 1, No. 1 (Spring 1982)-. 0270-3149. Periodical. US. English. qt. $89.00. Haworth Press, 28 East 22nd Street, New York NY 10010. Tel (212)228-2800. Ed Esther D Rothblum and Ellen Cole. Ind/Abst Biol. Abstr., Altern. Press Index, Psychol. Abstr. LC RC451.4.W6. DD 616.89088042. NLM W1 WO433V. CODEN WOTHDJ. bk rev. adv acc. Circ 1,955. Feminist in orientation, this lively quarterly defines therapy as an educational, expanding process rather than focusing, more traditionally, on pathology.

WORLD JOURNAL OF PSYCHOSYNTHESIS. VFOAT Shiijiee Jingshenn Zonghexue Yueekan, Journal Mondiale de Psychosynthese. V. 1- Sept. 1969-. 0043-860X. Periodical. US. English. sa. $20.00. World Journal Press, Box 859, East Lansing MI 48823. Tel (517)372-4660. Ed H C Tien. LC RC475. DD 616.89105. NLM W1 WO88H. bk rev. adv acc. Circ 300. Topics include psychiatry, psychology, video techniques, family psychiatry, Chinese language and medicine. Covers a wide range of U.S. and international articles.

WYOMING STATE PLAN FOR MENTAL HEALTH. Main/Corp Wyoming. Mental Health and Mental Retardation Services. VFOAT Mental Health Plan. US. English. an. LC RA790.65.W8. DD 353.978700842.

THE YEARBOOK OF PSYCHOANALYSIS AND PSYCHOTHERAPY. See Yearbooks, Almanacs, Directories.

YEARBOOK OF THE INTERNATIONAL ASSOCIATION FOR CHILD AND ADOLESCENT PSYCHIATRY AND ALLIED PROFESSIONS. See Yearbooks, Almanacs, Directories.

ZAGADNIENIA WYCHOWAWCZE A ZDROWIE PSYCHICZNE. 0324-8526. Periodical. PL. Polish (summaries in English and Russian). bm. ARS Polona, Krakowsie Przedmiescie 7, 00-068 Warsaw Poland. LC RJ499.A1. NLM W1 ZA359BF.

ZEITSCHRIFT FUR KLINISCHE PSYCHOLOGIE UND PSYCHOTHERAPIE. See Psychology.

ZEITSCHRIFT FUR PSYCHOSOMATISCHE MEDIZIN UND PSYCHOANALYSE. Vol. 13-. 0340-5613. Periodical. GW. German. qt. $42.20. Vandenhoeck & Ruprecht, Postfach 3753, Theaterstr 13, D-3400 Goettingen West Germany. Tel (0511)65061. Ind/Abst Excerpta Med., Index Med., Biol. Abstr., Psychol. Abstr., Soc. Sci. Citation Index, Sci. Cit. Index, Abr. Ed. NLM W1 ZE566. CODEN ZPPSB2. *Zeitschrift fur Psycho-Somatische Medizin, 0375-5355.*

ZENTRALBLATT FUR DIE GESAMTE NEUROLOGIE UND PSYCHIATRIE. See Medicine - Neurology.

ZENTRALBLATT NEUROLOGIE, PSYCHIATRIE. See Medicine - Neurology.

RADIOLOGY

ABMS DIRECTORY OF CERTIFIED RADIOLOGISTS. See Yearbooks, Almanacs, Directories.

ACTA RADIOLOGICA. Vol. 1, Issue 1-V. 58. 0001-6926. Periodical. English (text in French, and German). mo. 755. Acta Radiologica, PO Box 7449, S-10391 Stockholm Sweden. Tel 08/201054. Ed Erik Boijsen. Ind/Abst Sci. Cit. Index, Abr. Ed., Chem. Abstr. (cum index). bk rev. adv acc. Circ 6,000. (ctrl). Six issues each of diagnosis and oncology. In diagnosis: medical imaging and all varieties of clinical and experimental radiology. In oncology: radiotherapy, radiobiology and physics.

ACTA RADIOLOGICA. SUPPLEMENTUM. VFOAT Supplementum. Vol. 1-. 0365-5954. Monographic Series. English (French and German). ir. Acta Radiologica, PO Box 7449, S-10391 Stockholm Sweden. Ind/Abst Excerpta Med., Index Med., Chem. Abstr. NLM W1 AC9412.

ACTA THERMOGRAPHICA. V. 1- 1976-. 0391-9846. Periodical. English. ir. Free. Department of Radiology, University Hospital, 37100 Verona Italy. Ind/Abst Excerpta Med. NLM W1 AC95U. Index in first issue of next volume - loose - unpaged.

ACTA THERMOGRAPHICA. SUPPLEMENT. VFOAT Supplement to Acta Thermographica. 1-. 0392-0712. Monographic Series. IT. English. ty. Free to members. Department of Radiology, University Hospital, 37100 Verona Italy. NLM W1 AC95UF.

ADMINISTRATIVE RADIOLOGY. (ADMINISTRATIVE RADIOLOGY : AR). VFOAT A.R. 0738-6974. Periodical. US. English. bm. $18.00 US, $36.00 Foreign. Glendale Publishing Corporation, 1125 North Pacific Avenue, Glendale CA 91202.

ADVANCED EXERCISES IN DIAGNOSTIC RADIOLOGY. 9-. 0160-1636. Monographic Series. US. English. ir. W B Saunders Company, Fulfillment Department, West Washington Square, Philadelphia PA 19105. Tel (800)523-0713. LC RC78. DD 616.075705. NLM W1 AD402E. *Excercises in Diagnostic Radiology.*

ADVANCES IN X-RAY ANALYSIS. (ADVANCES IN X-RAY ANALYSIS : PROCEEDINGS OF THE . . . ANNUAL CONFERENCE ON APPLICATION OF X-RAY ANALYSIS). Main/Conf Conference on Application of X-Ray Analysis. VFOAT Advances in X Ray Analysis, Proceedings of the . . . Annual Conference on Application on X-Ray Analysis. Vol. 1 (Aug. 7-9, 1957)-. 0376-0308. US. English. an. Plenum Press, 233 Spring Street, New York NY 10013. Tel (212)620-8000. Ind/Abst Eng. Index Annu., Eng. Index Mon., Eng. Index Bioeng. Abstr., Eng. Index Energy Abstr., Comput. Control Abstr., Electr. Electron. Abstr., Sci. Abstr. Sect. A. Phys. Abstr., GeoRef, Chem. Abstr., Energy Res. Abstr., Bibliogr. Index Geol., Phys. Abstr., Eng. Index. LC TA417.25. DD 539.7222. NLM W3 AD25. CODEN AXRAAA.

AJR. VFOAT AJR, American Journal of Roentgenology. V. 128- Jan. 1977-. Periodical. US. English. mo. $40.00. Charles C Thomas, 301-327 East Lawrence Avenue, Springfield IL 62717. *American Journal of Roentgenology.*

AMERICAN JOURNAL OF NEURORADIOLOGY. (AJNR, AMERICAN JOURNAL OF NEURORADIOLOGY). V. 1- Jan./Feb. 1980-. 0195-6108. Periodical. US. English. bm. $105.00. Williams and Wilkins Company, 428 East Preston Street, Baltimore MD 21202. Tel (301)528-4000. Ed Juan Taveras. Ind/Abst Life Sci. Collect., Excerpta Med., Index Med. LC RC349.R3. DD 616.804757. NLM W1 A117GE. adv acc. Circ 3,500. Original clinical articles on imaging diagnosis of the CNS, including the spine, for radiologists, neuroradiologists, neurosurgeons, and neurologists.

AMERICAN JOURNAL OF ROENTGENOLOGY. (AJR, AMERICAN JOURNAL OF ROENTGENOLOGY). VFOAT AJR. V. 126- Jan. 1976-. 0361-803X. Periodical. US. English. mo. $100.00. Williams & Wilkins, 428 East Preston Street, Baltimore MD 21202. Tel (301)528-4000. Ed Robert N Berk. Ind/Abst Biol. Abstr., Energy Res. Abstr., Index Med., Life Sci. Collect., Pestdoc, Ringdoc, Vetdoc, Excerpta Med., Curr. Contents. LC RM845. DD 616.075705. NLM W1 A117GE. CODEN AJROAM. adv acc. Circ 19,500. High quality original articles on all aspects of general and diagnostic radiology, covering all current modalities including MRI. *American Journal of Roentgenology, Radium Therapy, and Nuclear Medicine, 0002-9580.*

ANNALES DE RADIOLOGIE. V. 1- 1958-. 0003-4185. Periodical. FR. French. ir. $159.64. Semaine des Hopitaux, 15 rue Saint Benoit, 75278 Paris Cedex 06 France. Tel 548-42-60. Ind/Abst Life Sci. Collect., Excerpta Med., CIS Abstr., Chem. Abstr., Biol. Abstr., Nuci. Sci. Abstr., Index Med., Energy Res. Abstr., Hospit. Lit. Index, Sci. Cit. Index, Abr. Ed. NLM W1 AN377. CODEN ANLRAT.

ANNALS OF THE ICRP. VAT Annals of the International Commission on Radiological Protection. V. 1-. 0146-6453. Periodical. UK. English. qt. Pergamon Press, 395 Sawmill River Road, Elmsford NY 10523. Ind/Abst Eng. Index Annu., Eng. Index Mon., Eng. Index Bioeng. Abstr., Eng. Index Energy Abstr., Energy Inf. Abstr., Environ. Abstr., Excerpta Med., Index Med., CIS Abstr., Biol. Abstr., Chem. Abstr. LC RA1231.R2. DD 614.839. NLM W1 AN626U. CODEN ANICD6. Available on microfilm and microfiche.

ANNUAL REPORT OF THE DIVISION OF BIOLOGICAL EFFECTS, BUREAU OF RADIOLOGICAL HEALTH. Fiscal year 1979-. US. English. an. Bureau of Radiological Health Technical Information Staff, HFX-28, 5600

Medicine—Radiology

Fishers Lane, Rockville MD 20857. *Quadrennial Report of the Division of Biological Effects.*

ANNUAL REPORT - RADIOBIOLOGY LABORATORY. (ANNUAL REPORT). Series/Titl DOE Research and Development Report. Began with 1966. 0164-047X. US. English. an. National Technical Information Service, United States Department of Commerce, 5285 Port Royal Road, Springfield VA 22161. NLM W1 AN769CC.

APPLIED RADIOLOGY. V. 5, No. 4- July/Aug. 1976-. 0160-9963. Periodical. US. English. bm. $80.00. Brentwood Publishing Corp, PO Box 49045, Los Angeles CA 90049. Tel (213)826-8388. Ed Esther Gross. Ind/Abst Hospit. Lit. Index, Cumul. Index Nurs. Allied Health Lit. LC RM845. DD 616.075705. NLM W1 AP528TE. bk rev. adv acc. Circ 26,031. (ctrl). Professional interest in imaging modalities: technical advances, case histories, facility reports, equipment, supplies, etc. *Applied Radiology and Nuclear Medicine,* 0099-2364.

APPLIED RADIOLOGY AND NUCLEAR MEDICINE. Began with Jan./Feb. 1975 issue. 0099-2364. Periodical. US. English. bm. Brentwood Publishing Corporation, PO Box 49045, Los Angeles CA 90049. Ind/Abst Excerpta Med. LC RM845. DD 616.075705. NLM W1 AP528U. CODEN ARDYA. *Applied Radiology.*

ASRT SCANNER. Main/Corp American Society of Radiologic Technologists. VAT American Society of Radiologic Technologists Scanner. 0161-3863. Periodical. US. English. bm. $25.00. American Society of Radiologic Technologists, 55 East Jackson Boulevard/Suite 1820, Chicago IL 60604. Tel (312)922-3962.

ATLAS OF TUMOR RADIOLOGY. Monographic Series. US. English. ir. Yearbook Medical Publishers Inc, 33 E Wacker Drive, Chicago IL 60601. Tel (312)726-9733.

AUSTRALASIAN RADIOLOGY. V. 10- 1966-. 0004-8461. Periodical. AT. English. qt. 32.00. Royal Australian College of Radiologist, 37 Lower Fort Street, Millers Point, Sydney New South Wales 2000 Australia. Tel (02)277797. Ed James Ryan. Ind/Abst Life Sci. Collect., Excerpta Med., Biol. Abstr., Chem. Abstr., Nucl. Sci. Abstr., Index Med., Energy Res. Abstr. NLM W1 AU335N. CODEN AURDAW. bk rev. adv acc. Circ 1,700. (ctrl). Diagnostic radiology, radiology oncology and other sciences of direct or indirect importance to these medical specialties.

BIBLIOTHECA RADIOLOGICA. No. 1-. 0067-8155. Monographic Series. German (English). ir. S Karger AG, PO Box CH-4009, Basel Switzerland. Tel (061)39 08 80. Ind/Abst Life Sci. Collect., Energy Res. Abstr., Index Med. NLM W1 BI4292.

BIRDEM LABORATORY ANNUAL BULLETIN. 1 (1982)-. English. an. NLM W1.

BRH BULLETIN CEASED. VAT Bureau of Radiological Health Bulletin. Ceased with V. 16, No. 9, Sept. 13, 1982. 0364-1023. Periodical. US. English. mo. US Department of Health & Human Services, Public Health Service, Food and Drug Administration, Bureau of Radiological Health, Rockville MD 20857. NLM W1 B531. (cum index).

BRITISH JOURNAL OF RADIOLOGY. (THE BRITISH JOURNAL OF RADIOLOGY). Began with: Vol. 1 (Jan. 1928). 0007-1285. Periodical. UK. English. mo. $149.00. British Journal of Radiology, PO Box 2513, Birmingham AL 35201. Tel (205)991-6925. Ed J L Haybittle and J T Patton. Ind/Abst Life Sci. Collect., Pestdoc, Ringdoc, Vetdoc, Excerpta Med., CIS Abstr., Biol. Abstr., Nucl. Sci. Abstr., Index Med., Chem. Abstr., Energy Res. Abstr., Comput. Control Abstr., Electr. Electron. Abstr., Sci. Abstr. Sect. A. Phys. Abstr., Hospit. Lit. Index, Sci. Cit. Index, Abr. Ed., Phys. Abstr. LC QC1. NLM W1 BR624R. CODEN BJRAAP. bk rev. adv acc. This long-established interdisciplinary journal covers not only the clinical aspects of radiology but also medical physics, radiation, biology and radiation protection as related to radiology. *British Journal of Radiology. B. I. R. Section, British Journal of Radiology. Roentgen Society Section.*

BRITISH JOURNAL OF RADIOLOGY. SUPPLEMENT. No. 1- 1947. 0306-8854. Monographic Series. UK. English. ir. British Institute of Radiology, 36 Portland Place, London W1N 3DG England. Tel 01-580 4189. Ed Lynn Whitfield. Ind/Abst Life Sci. Collect., Index Med. NLM W1 BR6241. adv acc. Occasional publications on subjects related to radiology.

BUREAU OF RADIOLOGICAL HEALTH PUBLICATIONS SUBJECT INDEX. *See* Indexes/Abstracts.

BUREAU OF RADIOLOGICAL HEALTH RESEARCH GRANTS PROGRAM. (RESEARCH GRANTS PROGRAM). Main/Corp United States. Bureau of Radiological Health. 0093-5654. US. English. Bureau of Radiological Health, Superintendent of Documents, US Government Printing Office, Washington DC 20402. LC RA1231.R2. DD 616.98970072073.

CANADIAN JOURNAL OF RADIOGRAPHY RADIOTHERAPY NUCLEAR MEDICINE. (THE CANADIAN JOURNAL OF RADIOGRAPHY, RADIOTHERAPY, NUCLEAR MEDICINE). V. 5, No. 5- Sept. 1974-. 0319-4434. Periodical. CN. English. bm. 12.00. Canadian Association of Medical Radiation Technologists, 280 Metcalfe Street, Suite 410, Ottawa Ontario K2P 1R7 Canada. Tel (613)234-0012. Ed S Besner. Ind/Abst Hospit. Lit. Index, Cumul. Index Nurs. Allied Health Lit. DD 616.075706271. NLM W1 CA606. bk rev. adv acc. Circ 8,700. (ctrl). Also available in microfiche format. A scientific publication of the Canadian Association of Medical Radiation Technologists featuring topical research submissions, techniques and findings from medical radiation technologists of every discipline in the field. *Canadian Journal of Radiography, Radiotherapy, Nucleography,* 0015-4938.

CARDIOVASCULAR AND INTERVENTIONAL RADIOLOGY. V. 3- Feb. 1980-. 0174-1551. Periodical. US. English. bm. $106.00. Springer Verlag-New York Inc, 175 5th Avenue, New York NY 10010. Tel (212)460-1500. Ed H L Abrams and E Zeitler. Ind/Abst Life Sci. Collect., Excerpta Med., Index Med. NLM W1 CA77MI. CODEN CARADA. bk rev. Contains articles dealing with diagnostic and therapeutic applications of radiographic methods, ultrasound, nuclear, medicine, computed tomography, and nuclear magnetic resonance. *Cardiovascular Radiology,* 0342-7196.

CESKOSLOVENSKA RADIOLOGIE. Vol. 18- 1964-. 0069-2344. Periodical. CS. Czech (table of contents and summaries also in English and Russian). bm. $56.10. Artia, Ve Smeckach 30, PO Box 790, Praha 1 Czechosloviakia. Ind/Abst Life Sci. Collect., Excerpta Med., Index Med., Energy Res. Abstr. NLM W1 CE903. *Ceskoslovenska Rentgenologie.*

CLINICAL NUCLEAR MEDICINE. V. 1- June 1976-. 0363-9762. Periodical. US. English. mo. J B Lippincott Company, East Washington Square, Philadelphia PA 19105. Tel (301)824-7300. Ed Sheldon Baum. Ind/Abst Life Sci. Collect., Excerpta Med., Index Med., Biol. Abstr., Energy Res. Abstr., Sci. Cit. Index, Abr. Ed. LC R895.A1. DD 616.0757505. NLM W1 CL739. CODEN CNMEDK. bk rev. adv acc. Circ 3,166. Original manuscripts involving scanning, imaging, and related subjects also meeting announcements.

CLINICAL RADIOLOGY. V. 11- Jan. 1960-. 0009-9260. Periodical. UK. English. bm. $85.00. Clinical Radiology, PO Box 11318, Birmingham AL 35202. Tel (205)991-6920. Ed I H Kerr. Ind/Abst Life Sci. Collect., Excerpta Med., CIS Abstr., Nucl. Sci. Abstr., Index Med., Biol. Abstr., Chem. Abstr., Sci. Cit. Index, Abr. Ed., Hospit. Lit. Index. NLM W1 CL768GK. CODEN CLRAAG. bk rev. adv acc. Devoted to radiodiagnosis, radiotherapy, oncology and allied subjects, with emphasis on clinical aspects of radiology. An international forum for exchange of news, research, techniques, and case studies. *Journal of the Faculty of Radiologists.*

CLINICS IN COMPUTED TOMOGRAPHY. 1-. Monographic Series. English. ir. NLM W1 CL831AH (P).

COMPREHENSIVE MANUALS IN RADIOLOGY. Began in 1978. 0172-4843. Monographic Series. US. English. ir. Springer Verlag-New York Inc, 175 Fifth Avenue, New York NY 10010. Tel (212)460-1584. Contains articles on radiology of the heart.

COMPUTERIZED RADIOLOGY. (COMPUTERIZED RADIOLOGY : THE OFFICIAL JOURNAL OF THE COMPUTERIZED TOMOGRAPHY SOCIETY). Vol. 6, No. 1 (Jan./Feb. 1982)-. 0730-4862. Periodical. US. English. bm. Pergamon Press, 395 Sawmill River Road, Elmsford NY 10523. Ind/Abst Electron. Commun. Abstr. J., ISMEC Bull., Pollut. Abstr. Indexes, Saf. Sci. Abstr. J., Life Sci. Collect., Eng. Index Annu., Eng. Index Mon., Eng. Index Bioeng. Abstr., Eng. Index Energy Abstr., Excerpta Med., Index Med., Biol. Abstr., Comput. Control Abstr., Electr. Electron. Abstr., Sci. Abstr. Sect. A. Phys. Abstr., Energy Res. Abstr. NLM W1 CO457N. CODEN COMRDW. *Computerized Tomography,* 0363-8235.

COMPUTERIZED TOMOGRAPHY CEASED. V. 1-5. 0363-8235. Periodical. UK. English. qt. $120.00. Pergamon Press, Fairview Park, Elmsford NY 10523. Ind/Abst Eng. Index Mon., Eng. Index Annu., Eng. Index Energy Abstr., Life Sci. Collect., Excerpta Med. NLM W1 CO457P. CODEN CTOMDS. (cum index). Current subscriptions available on microfiche and on microfilm on completion of the annual index at the end of the subscription year.

CONTEMPORARY DIAGNOSTIC RADIOLOGY. 1-. 0149-9009. Periodical. US. English. bw. $175.00. Williams and Wilkins, 428 East Preston Street, Baltimore MD 21202. Tel (301)528-4000. Ed Robert Campbell. adv acc. Circ 1,000. Twenty-six series feature original articles offering an overview of radiology. *Radiologic Science Update.*

CONTEMPORARY ISSUES IN COMPUTED TOMOGRAPHY. Vol. 1-. Monographic Series. US. English. ir. Ed Stanley S Siegelman. NLM W1 CO769MQK.

CRC CRITICAL REVIEWS IN DIAGNOSTIC IMAGING CEASED. Main/Corp Chemical Rubber Company. VFOAT Critical Reviews in Diagnostic Imaging. VAT Chemical Rubber Company Critical Reviews in Diagnostic Imaging. V. 9- 1977-. 0147-6750. Periodical. US. English. qt. $116.00. CRC Press Inc, 2000 Corporate Boulevard NW, Boca Raton FL 33431. Tel (305)994-0555. Ind/Abst Index Med., Biol. Abstr. LC RC78.A1. DD 616.075705. NLM W1 C555CI. CODEN CRDIDF. Provides up-to-date comprehensive review articles contributed by authors with recognized expertise. *C.R.C. Critical Reviews in Clinical Radiology and Nuclear Medicine,* 0091-6536.

CSU-FDA COLLABORATIVE RADIOLOGICAL HEALTH LABORATORY ANNUAL REPORT. VFOAT C.S.U.-F.D.A. Collaborative Radiological Health Laboratory Annual Report. Began with 1975. 0191-2089. US. English. an. Bureau of Radiological Health, Technical Information Staff, HFX-28 5600 Fishers Lane, Rockville MD 20857. LC RA1231.R2. DD 616.9897. NLM W1 C94E. *CSU-PHS Collaborative Radiological Health Laboratory Annual Report,* 0090-368X.

CT. THE JOURNAL OF COMPUTED TOMOGRAPHY. (THE JOURNAL OF COMPUTED TOMOGRAPHY). VFOAT CT. V. 2, No. 1 (Mar. 1978)-. 0149-936X. Periodical. US. English. ty. $110.00. Elsevier Science Publishing Company, 52 Vanderbilt Avenue, New York NY 10017. Tel (800)370-5520. Ed Franklin L Angell. Ind/Abst Excerpta Med., Index Med., Curr. Contents, Biol. Abstr., Energy Res. Abstr. LC RC78.7.T6. DD 616.07572. NLM W1 C94G. CODEN CJCTDL. bk rev. adv acc. This journal publishes original articles on computed tomography of the head and body with an eye to the promotion of affective diagnosis and therapy. *Computed Axial Tomography,* 0145-7616.

CURRENT CONCEPTS IN RADIOLOGY. V. 1- 1972-. 0149-2454. Periodical. US. English. ir. C V Mosby Co, C Leadbetter, 11830 Westline Industrial Drive, St Louis MO 63141. LC RC78.A1. DD 616.0757. NLM WN 100 C976.

CURRENT PROBLEMS IN DIAGNOSTIC RADIOLOGY. VFOAT Diagnostic Radiology. V. 6- Jan./Feb. 1976-. 0363-0188. Monographic Series. US. English. bm. $65.00. Yearbook Medical Publishers, 35 East Wacker Drive, Chicago IL 60601. Tel (213)726-9733. Ind/Abst Index Med., Biol. Abstr., Energy Res. Abstr., Hospit. Lit. Index. NLM W1 CU804M. CODEN CPDRDS. *Current Problems in Radiology,* 0045-9399.

CURRENT RADIOLOGY. V. 1-. 0161-7818. US. English. an. John Wiley & Sons Inc, 1 Wiley Drive, Somerset NJ 08873. Tel (617)725-5000. LC RC78.A1. DD 616.075705. NLM W1 CU808.

DENTO-MAXILLO-FACIAL RADIOLOGY. (DENTO MAXILLO FACIAL RADIOLOGY). V. 1-. 0250-832X. Monographic Series. US. English. sa. $25.00. Iadmfrl Hollender/Dentistry, School of Oral Radiology, Box 33070, S-400 Goteborg Sweden. Tel (213)825-5711. Ed Stuart C White. Ind/

Medicine—Radiology

Abst Index Dent. Lit. **NLM** W1 DE439F. adv acc. **Circ** 600. Publishes scientific articles pertaining to radiology in dentistry.

DEVELOPMENTS IN NUCLEAR MEDICINE. Vol. 1-. 0167-9074. Monographic Series. US. English. **Ind/Abst** Chem. Abstr. LC UNC. **NLM** W1. **CODEN** DNMDDS.

DIAGNOSTIC IMAGING. V. 1- Nov. 1979-. 0194-2514. Periodical. US. English. mo. $45.00. Miller Freeman Publ Inc, 500 Howard Street Attn Colleen M Y Rodgers, San Francisco CA 94105. **Tel** (415)397-1881. Ed Peter Ogle. **NLM** W1 DI258ID. adv acc. **Circ** 25,000. (ctrl). Newsmagazine for radiology, ultrasound, nuclear medicine, CT scanning, magnetic resonance imaging.

DIAGNOSTIC IMAGING (BASEL, SWITZERLAND). (DIAGNOSTIC IMAGING). Vol. 48, No. 1-. 0378-9837. Periodical. SZ. English. bm. $130.00. S Karger AG, PO Box, CH 4009 Basel Switzerland. **Ind/Abst** Life Sci. Collect., Excerpta Med., Biol. Abstr., Curr. Contents, Energy Res. Abstr., Index Med., Sci. Cit. Index, Abr. Ed. **NLM** W1 DI2581. **CODEN** DIIMDY. Index in last issue of volume - attached. Radiologia Clinica (1975), 0376-6748.

DIAGNOSTIC RADIOLOGY SERIES (NEW YORK, N.Y.). (DIAGNOSTIC RADIOLOGY SERIES). Vol. 1-. 0742-8383. Monographic Series. US. English. ir. Marcel Dekker Inc, 270 Madison Avenue, New York NY 10016. **Tel** (212)696-9000. Ed Louis Kreel and Morton A Meyer. **NLM** W1 DI258JR. This is an ongoing series. Each title has a different subject.

DIRECTORY OF LICENSEES - OREGON STATE BOARD OF RADIOLOGIC TECHNOLOGY. See Yearbooks, Almanacs, Directories.

DIRECTORY OF PERSONNEL RESPONSIBLE FOR RADIOLOGICAL HEALTH PROGRAMS. See Yearbooks, Almanacs, Directories.

ECHO-X. (ECHO-X : JOURNAL DE L'ORDRE DES TECHNICIENS EN RADIOLOGIE DU QUEBEC). 0820-6295. Periodical. CN. French. ir. Free. O.T.R.Q. 654 Est Boulevard Cremazie, Montreal Quebec H2P 1E9 Canada. **Tel** 376-0052. **DD** 616.0757060714. bk rev. adv acc. **Circ** 3,500.

ELECTRON MICROSCOPY AND X-RAY APPLICATIONS TO ENVIRONMENTAL AND OCCUPATIONAL HEALTH ANALYSIS. Vol. 1-. 0275-2204. US. English. an. $39.95. Ann Arbor Science Publishers Inc, 10 Tower Office Park, Woburn MA 01801. **Ind/Abst** Chem. Abstr. LC RA566.26. **DD** 628.50287. **NLM** W3 EL31H. **CODEN** EMXADA.

EUROPEAN JOURNAL OF RADIOLOGY. Vol. 1, No. 1 (Mar. 1981)-. 0720-048X. Periodical. US. English. qt. $93.00. Thieme Stratton Inc, 381 Park Avenue, New York NY 10016. **Tel** (212)683-5088. **Ind/Abst** Excerpta Med., Index Med., Chem. Abstr., Energy Res. Abstr. **NLM** W1 EU72ED. **CODEN** EJRADR.

EXCERPTA MEDICA. SECTION 14. RADIOLOGY. See Indexes/Abstracts.

EXCERPTA MEDICA. SECTION 23. NUCLEAR MEDICINE. See Indexes/Abstracts.

EXERCISES IN DENTAL RADIOLOGY. V. 1-. Monographic Series. US. English. ir. WB Saunders Co, West Washington Square, Philadelphia PA 19105. **Tel** (800)523-0713.

FEUILLETS DE RADIOLOGIE. V. 18- (103-. 0181-9801. Periodical. French. bm. Masson Publishing USA Inc, 211 East 43rd Street/Room 1306, New York NY 10017. **Tel** (212)370-1937. **Ind/Abst** Excerpta Med., Energy Res. Abstr. **NLM** W1 FE853. Feuillets d'Electroradiologie, 0015-0444.

FORTSCHRITTE AUF DEM GEBIETE DER ROENTGENSTRAHLEN. ERGANZUNGSBAND. German. ir. Thieme-Stratton, 381 Park Avenue South, New York NY 10016. **Tel** (212)683-5088.

FRONTIERS OF RADIATION THERAPY AND ONCOLOGY. V. 1-. 0071-9676. Monographic Series. US. English. ir. S Karger AG, PO Box 352, White Plains NY 10602. **Tel** 061-39 08 80. Ed J M Vaeth. **Ind/Abst** Index Med., Biol. Abstr., Chem. Abstr., Nuci. Sci. Abstr., Sci. Cit. Index, Abr. Ed. **NLM** W3 FR935. **CODEN** FRTOA7. Reports of extensive clinical studies that help define developments for medical and radiation oncologists.

GASTROINTESTINAL RADIOLOGY. V. 1- 1976-. 0364-2356. Periodical. US. English. qt. $66.00. Springer-Verlag, 175 Fifth Avenue, New York NY 10010. **Ind/Abst** Life Sci. Collect., Excerpta Med., Index Med., Energy Res. Abstr. **NLM** W1 GA459R.

GOLDEN'S DIAGNOSTIC RADIOLOGY. Section 1-. 0161-2824. Monographic Series. US. English. ir. Williams & Wilkins, PO Box 64025, Baltimore MD 21202. **Tel** (301)528-4000. **Ind/Abst** Chem. Abstr. **CODEN** GDRAD7.

HEALTH PHYSICS/RADIATION PROTECTION ENROLLMENTS AND DEGREES. VFOAT Health Physics, Radiation Protection Enrollments and Degrees. 0748-3333. US. English. an. National Technical Information Service, US Department of Commerce, Springfield VA 22161. LC RA569. **DD** 616.07570289.

ICRDB CANCERGRAM. CANCER DETECTION AND MANAGEMENT: DIAGNOSTIC RADIOLOGY. (ICRDB CANCERGRAM. SERIES CT14, CANCER DETECTION AND MANAGEMENT. DIAGNOSTIC RADIOLOGY). VFOAT Diagnostic Radiology. Began with Mar. 1978. 0164-1964. Periodical. US. English. mo. US Department of Commerce, National Technical Information Service, 5285 Port Royal Road, Springfield VA 22161. **NLM** ZQZ 241 I11C.

ICRDB CANCERGRAM. CLINICAL TREATMENT OF CANCER: RADIATION THERAPY. See Medicine - Neoplasma, Neoplastic.

ICRDB CANCERGRAM. RADIATION CARCINOGENESIS. See Medicine - Neoplasma, Neoplastic.

ICRP PUBLICATION. 1- 1959-. 0074-2740. Monographic Series. UK. English. ir. Pergamon Press, c/o Cashier, 395 Sawmill River Road, Elmsford NY 10523. **Ind/Abst** Chem. Abstr., Biol. Abstr. **CODEN** RDPTC4.

ICRU REPORT. VAT International Commission on Radiation Units and Measurements Report. 0579-5435. Monographic Series. US. English. ir. ICRU, 7910 Woodmont Avenue, Bethesda MD 20814. LC RA1231.R2. **DD** 612.01448. Report.

INDEX RADIOLOGIAE. See Indexes/Abstracts.

INDIAN JOURNAL OF RADIOLOGY. Vol. 37, No. 3. 0019-560X. Periodical. II. English. qt. Indian Radiological Association, 809 Harjivand Estate, Dr Ambed Road, Dadar Bombay 400014 India. **Ind/Abst** Excerpta Med., Biol. Abstr., Nuci. Sci. Abstr., Energy Res. Abstr. **NLM** W1 IN234. **CODEN** IJRAAY.

INNOVATIONS IN DIAGNOSTIC RADIOLOGY. 1981-. 0732-8931. US. English. an. Academic Press, 4805 Sand Lake Road, Orlando FL 32819. Ed Alexander R Margulis, Charles A Gooding. LC RC78.A1. **DD** 616.0757205. **NLM** W3 IN1038M. Diagnostic Radiology, 0146-2849.

INTERNATIONAL JOURNAL OF NUCLEAR MEDICINE & BIOLOGY. VAT International Journal of Nuclear Medicine and Biology. V. 1- Jan. 1973-. 0047-0740. Periodical. US. English, French, German or Russian. bm. Pergamon Press, 395 Sawmill River Road, Elmsford NY 10523. **Tel** (914)592-7700. **Ind/Abst** Electron. Commun. Abstr. J., ISMEC Bull., Pollut. Abstr. Indexes, Saf. Sci. Abstr., J., Life Sci. Collect., Excerpta Med., Index Med., Biol. Abstr., Comput. Control Abstr., Electr. Electron. Abstr., Sci. Abstr. Sect. A. Phys. Abstr., Nuci. Sci. Abstr., Bibliogr. Agric., Energy Res. Abstr., Sci. Cit. Index, Abr. Ed., Phys. Abstr. LC RC93.A1. **DD** 616.075705. **NLM** W1 IN77L. **CODEN** IJNMCI.

INVESTIGATIVE RADIOLOGY. V. 1- Jan./Feb. 1966-. 0020-9996. Periodical. US. English (summaries in interlingua). mo. $167.94. J B Lippincott Company, 2350 Virginia Avenue, Hagerstown MD 21740. **Ind/Abst** Life Sci. Collect., Pestdoc, Ringdoc, Vetdoc, Excerpta Med., Index Med., Int. Aerosp. Abstr., Chem. Abstr., Energy Res. Abstr., Hospit. Lit. Index. LC RC78. **DD** 616.075705. **NLM** W1 IN995E. **CODEN** INVRAV.

JAPANESE JOURNAL OF RADIOLOGICAL TECHNOLOGY. 1981, No. 1-. 0369-4305. English. ir. Maruzen Company Ltd, PO Box 5050, 100 31 Tokyo Japan. **NLM** W1 JA975H.

JOURNAL BELGE DE RADIOLOGIE. VFOAT Belgisch Tijdschrift Voor Radiologie. V. 13-1924-. 0021-7646. Periodical. BE. Dutch (English or French). bm. 5,500. Journal Belge de Radiologie, Dr J Ediers, SGB-GBM Redaction, Professor J Pringot, Avenue Hippocrate 10, 1200 Bruxelles Belgium. **Tel** 02/764 29 32. Ed J Pringot. **Ind/Abst** Life Sci. Collect., Excerpta Med., Index Med., CIS Abstr., Comput. Control Abstr., Electr. Electron. Abstr., Sci. Abstr. Sect. A. Phys. Abstr., Energy Res. Abstr., Phys. Abstr. **NLM** W1 JO234. **CODEN** JBRAAN. bk rev. adv acc. **Circ** 6,000. Publicates articles dealing with diagnostic radiology and related imaging techniques, therapeutic radiology, nuclear medicine and allied sciences. Journal de Radiologie, 0302-7449.

JOURNAL CANADIEN DE RADIOGRAPHIE RADIOTHERAPIE MEDECINE NUCLEAIRE. (LE JOURNAL CANADIEN DE RADIOGRAPHIE, RADIOTHERAPIE, MEDECINE NUCLEAIRE). V. 5, No. 5- Sept. 1974-. 0382-6333. Periodical. CN. French. qt. $9.28. Societe Canadienne des Techniciens en Radiologie, 280 Metcalfe Street/Suite 410, Ottawa Ontario K2R 1R7 Canada. **Tel** (613)234-0441. **DD** 616.075705. Journal Canadien de Radiographie, Radiotherapie, Nucleographie, 0382-6325.

JOURNAL DE RADIOLOGIE. V. 60- 1979-. 0221-0363. Periodical. French. ir. Masson Publishing USA Inc, 211 East 43rd Street/Room 1306, New York NY 10017. **Tel** (212)370-1937. **Ind/Abst** Life Sci. Collect., Excerpta Med., Index Med., Bull. Signal., Curr. Contents, Energy Res. Abstr. **NLM** W1 JO344C. Journal de Radiologie, d'Electrologie, et de Medecine Nucleaire, 0368-7964.

JOURNAL EUROPEEN DE RADIOTHERAPIE. VFOAT European Journal of Radiation Oncology. V. 1, No. 1-. 0243-1203. Periodical. English (articles in French). qt. **Ind/Abst** Excerpta Med., Energy Res. Abstr. **NLM** W1.

JOURNAL OF COMPUTER ASSISTED TOMOGRAPHY. V. 2- Jan. 1978-. 0363-8715. Periodical. US. English. bm. Raven Press, 1140 Avenue of the Americas, New York NY 10036. **Tel** (212)575-0335. **Ind/Abst** Life Sci. Collect., Excerpta Med., Comput. Control Abstr., Electr. Electron. Abstr., Sci. Abstr. Sect. A. Phys. Abstr., Index Med., Curr. Contents, Biol. Abstr., Energy Res. Abstr., Hospit. Lit. Index, Sci. Cit. Index, Abr. Ed., Phys. Abstr. **NLM** W1 JO595L. **CODEN** JCATD5. Journal of Computer Assisted Tomography, 0363-8715.

THE JOURNAL OF MORPHANALYSIS. VFOAT Morphanalysis. Vol. 1, No. 1 (June 1979)-. 0142-9981. Periodical. UK. English. sa. 9. International Center for Morphanalysis/Department of Anatomy/Medical School University, Manchester M13 9PT England. **Tel** 061-273-8241. Ed G P Rabey. **Ind/Abst** Excerpta Med. **NLM** W1 JO774J. bk rev. adv acc. **Circ** 300. Communication of clinical advances, research results, standards and systems in human morphanalysis.

JOURNAL OF NEURORADIOLOGY. VFOAT Journal de Neuroradiologie. V. 3- March 1976-. 0150-9861. Periodical. US. English (articles and summaries in French). qt. Masson Publications USA Inc, 211 East 43rd Street/Room 1306, New York NY 10017. **Tel** (212)370-1937. **Ind/Abst** Life Sci. Collect., Excerpta Med., Index Med., Biol. Abstr. **NLM** W1 JO795BK. **CODEN** JNEUD3. Journal de Neuroradiologie, 0335-0800.

THE JOURNAL OF NUCLEAR MEDICINE. V. 19- Jan. 1978-. 0161-5505. Periodical. US. English. mo. $100.00 Domestic, $110.00 Canada, $130.00 Foreign. Society of Nuclear Medicine, 136 Madison Avenue, New York NY 10016. **Tel** (212)889-0717. Ed Thomas P Hanie. **Ind/Abst** Life Sci. Collect., Excerpta Med., Index Med., Biol. Abstr., Comput. Control Abstr., Electr. Electron. Abstr., Sci. Abstr. Sect. A. Phys. Abstr., Chem. Abstr., Energy Res. Abstr. LC RM845. **DD** 616.075705. **NLM** W1 JO796D. **CODEN** JNMEAQ. bk rev. adv acc. **Circ** 13,700. Publishes original articles in the clinical and basic sciences of nuclear medicine, covering a broad range of subjects including diagnostic nuclear medicine, radiochemistry and radiopharmaceuticals, etc. JNM. Journal of Nuclear Medicine, 0097-9031.

JOURNAL OF THE CANADIAN ASSOCIATION OF RADIOLOGISTS. Main/Corp Canadian Association of Radiologists. VFOAT Journal de l'Association Canadienne des Radiologistes. V. 1- March 1950-. 0008-2902. Periodical. CN. English (French with summaries in both languages). qt. $25.15. Canadian Association of

Medicine—Radiology

Radiologists, 1440 St Catherine Street West/Suite 806, Montreal 107 Quebec Canada. **Tel** (514)866-2035. Ed Brian C Lentle. **Ind/Abst** Excerpta Med., Index Med., Life Sci. Collect., Biol. Abstr., Hospit. Lit. Index, Sci. Cit. Index, Abr. Ed. DD 616. NLM W1 JO915I. bk rev. adv acc. **Circ** 2,500. Advances the art and science of radiology.

K V P NEWS CEASED. V. 1-20, No. 2. 0022-7439. Periodical. CN. English. Manitoba Society of Radiological Technologists, 294 Duffield Street, Winnipeg Manitoba R3J 2J9 Canada.

KAKU IGAKU. VFOAT The Japanese Journal of Nuclear Medicine. Vol. 1- 1964-. 0022-7854. Periodical. JA. English (Japanese). bm. Japanese Society of Nuclear Medicine, 24-45 Hon-Komagome, 2-chome Bunkyo-ku, Tokyo Japan. **Ind/Abst** Excerpta Med., Index Med., Biol. Abstr., Chem. Abstr., Energy Res. Abstr. NLM W1 KA411H. **CODEN** KAIGBZ.

KLINISCH-RADIOLOGISCHES SEMINAR. 0342-443X. Monographic Series. GW. German. George Thieme Verlag, Postfach 732, Herdweg 63, D7000 Stuttgart 1 West Germany. **Ind/Abst** Chem. Abstr. NLM W3 KL63. **CODEN** KRSEDU.

LIEN - ORDRE DES TECHNICIENS EN RADIOLOGIE DU QUEBEC. (LE LIEN). V. 1, No 1 (Feb. 1980)-. 0713-7621. Periodical. CN. French. ir. Free to Members. Le Lien, c/o O T R Q, 654 East Boulevard Cremazie, Montreal Quebec H2P 1E9 Canada. DD 616.0757060714.

MAGYAR RADIOLOGIA. Began with V. 2, In 1950. 0025-0287. Periodical. HU. Hungarian (summaries in English, German, and Russian). bm. Akademiai Kiado, POB 24, 1363 Budapest Hungary. **Ind/Abst** Excerpta Med., Energy Res. Abstr. LC RM845. NLM W1 RA303. **CODEN** MARAAF. RADIOLOGIA HUNGARICA.

MEDICAL IMAGING. V. 1- 1976-. 0149-6727. Periodical. US. English. qt. $30.00. Barrington Publications, 825 South Barrington Avenue, Los Angeles CA 90040. NLM W1 ME341EI.

MEDICAL IMAGING. Series/Titl Karger Highlights. 1- 1979-. Periodical. English. ir. Ed H J Kaufmann. NLM W1 ME341E (P).

MEDICAL RADIOGRAPHY AND PHOTOGRAPHY. V. 23- 1947-. 0025-746X. Periodical. US. English. ir. Eastman Kodak Company, 343 State Street, Rochester NY 14650. **Ind/Abst** Excerpta Med., Index Med., CIS Abstr., Energy Res. Abstr. NLM W1 ME423. Radiography and Clinical Photography, 0093-2922.

MEDICINSKAJA RADIOLOGIJA. (MEDITSINSKAIA RADIOLOGIIA). V. 1- Jan./Feb. 1956-. 0025-8334. Periodical. UR. Russian (summaries in English). mo. Victor Kamkin Inc (70516), 12224 Parklawn Drive, Rockville MD 20852. Tel (301)881-5973. Ed $76.50. **Ind/Abst** Excerpta Med., Pestdoc, Ringdoc, Vetdoc, Index Med., Biol. Abstr., Comput. Control Abstr., Electr. Electron. Abstr., Sci. Abstr. Sect. A. Phys. Abstr., Chem. Abstr. LC RM845. NLM W1 ME801. **CODEN** MERAA9.

MEDICOR NEWS. 1971, No. 3-. Periodical. English. ir. **Ind/Abst** Comput. Control Abstr., Electr. Electron. Abstr., Sci. Abstr. Sect. A. Phys. Abstr., Energy Res. Abstr. **CODEN** MENED4.

MITGLIEDERVERZEICHNIS - GESELLSCHAFT FUR NUCLEARMEDIZIN. Main/Corp Society of Nuclear Medicine (1963-). VFOAT Membershiplist - Society of Nuclear Medicine. English (German with some French, and Spanish). ir. Gesellschaft fur Nuclearmedizin, D-8032 Grafelfing, West Germany. LC R895.A1.

MODERNE RONTGENFOTOGRAPHIE. 0138-2934. Periodical. German. ir. NLM W1.

MULTIPLE IMAGING PROCEDURES. V. 1-. 0195-9557. Monographic Series. US. English. ir. Grune & Stratton, 111 Fifth Avenue, New York NY 10033. Tel (212)614-3232. Ed L M Freeman and J H Shapiro. NLM W1 MU397I.

NEUE ASPEKTE RADIOLOGISCHER DIAGNOSTIK UND THERAPIE : JAHRBUCH . . . DER SCHWEIZERISCHEN GESELLSCHAFT FUR RADIOLOGIE UND NUKLEARMEDIZIN. See Yearbooks, Almanacs, Directories.

NEURORADIOLOGY. See Medicine - Neurology.

NEWSLETTER OF THE I.S.R. VAT Newsletter of the International Society of Radiology. V. 3- 1974-. 0390-5969. Periodical. SW. English. sa. $5.00. International Society of Radiology, PO Box 7449, S-103 91 Stockholm Sweden. NLM W1 NE998V. Newsletter of the I.C.R.E.

NM/MIRD PAMPHLET. Main/Corp Society of Nuclear Medicine. Medical Internal Radiation Dose Committee. VFOAT MIRD Pamphlets. VAT Nuclear Medicine/Medical Internal Radiation Dose Pamphlet, Medical Internal Radiation Dose Pamphlets. 0361-0497. Monographic Series. US. English. Society of Nuclear Medicine, 136 Madison Avenue, New York NY 10016. **Ind/Abst** Chem. Abstr. LC R895.A1. **CODEN** MIRPDH.

NUCLEAR MEDICINE COMMUNICATIONS. Vol. 1, No.1 (Mar. 1980)-. 0143-3636. Periodical. UK. English. mo. $180.00. Associated Book Publ, North Way Andover, Hampshire SP10 5BE England. Tel (0264) 62141. Ed K E Britton, P Ell, R F Jewkes and H Berger. **Ind/Abst** Electron. Commun. Abstr. J., ISMEC Bull., Pollut. Abstr. Indexes, Saf. Sci. Abstr. J., Life Sci. Collect., Excerpta Med., Biol. Abstr., Energy Res. Abstr., Chem. Abstr. NLM W1 NU124P. **CODEN** NMCODC. bk rev. adv acc. Rapid communications journal covering research and clinical work in nuclear medicine, of interest to those involved in radiopharmacy, radiochemistry, and nuclear magnetic resonance.

PEDIATRIC RADIOLOGY. See Medicine - Pediatrics.

PHYSICIANS' DESK REFERENCE FOR RADIOLOGY AND NUCLEAR MEDICINE. VFOAT PDR for Radiology and Nuclear Medicine. 1st- Ed. US. English. an. LC RM852. DD 616.0757. NLM QV 772 P577.

POLSKI PRZEGLAD RADIOLOGII I MEDYCYNY NUKLEARNEJ. Began with issue for Jan./Feb. 1961-. 0137-7183. Periodical. PL. Polish (summaries in English and Russian). bm. ARS Polona, Krakowskie Przedmiescie 7, 00-068 Warsaw Poland. **Ind/Abst** Index Med., Excerpta Med. NLM W1 PO2876. Polski Przeglad Radiologiczny.

POSTGRADUATE RADIOLOGY. Vol. 1, No. 1 (Jan. 1981)-. 0273-0278. Periodical. US. English. qt. $75.00 US, Canada and Mexico, $95.00 all other countries. PSG Publishing Company, 545 Great Road, Littleton MA 01460. Tel (617)486-8971. Ed Herbert L Abrams. **Ind/Abst** Excerpta Med. NLM W1 PO958F. bk rev. adv acc. A journal on continuing education offering authoritative up-to-date review articles, case histories, abstracts of literature and book reviews.

PROCEEDINGS OF THE ANNUAL MEETING OF THE NATIONAL COUNCIL ON RADIATION PROTECTION AND MEASUREMENTS. Main/Corp National Council on Radiation Protection and Measurements. Meeting. 15th (Mar. 14-15, 1979)-. 0195-7740. Periodical. US. English. an. National Council on Radiation Protection and Measurements, 7910 Woodmont Avenue/Suite 1016, Washington DC 20014. Tel (301)657-2652. Ed W Roger Ney. **Ind/Abst** GeoRef. Circ 1,000. Presentations on radiation protection and measurement matters at the annual meetings, a wide range of topics, medical, occupational, environmental standards and philosophy.

PROGRESS IN NUCLEAR MEDICINE. 0079-6573. Monographic Series. English. ir. S Karger Ag, PO Box, CH-4009 Basel Switzerland. Tel (061)390880. Ed A Donath and A N Serafini. **Ind/Abst** Index Med., Energy Res. Abstr., Chem. Abstr. NLM W1 PR675H. **CODEN** PGNMA4. Sophisticated developments in nuclear medicine interpreted in terms of their clinical utility.

PROGRESS IN PEDIATRIC RADIOLOGY. See Medicine - Pediatrics.

QUADERNI DI RADIOLOGIA. 0048-6086. Periodical. IT. Italian. bm. Instituto di Fisiologia Genera Universita, 35100 Padua Italy. **Ind/Abst** Energy Res. Abstr., Excerpta Med.

RADIATION CURING. Series/Titl Seminars in Print Series. 0146-4604. Periodical. US. English. qt. Technology Marketing Corporation, 17 Park Street, Norwalk CT 06851. Tel (203)846-2029. **Ind/Abst** Eng. Index Annu., Eng. Index Mon., Eng. Index, Eng. Index Bioeng., Eng. Index Energy Abstr., Int. Packag. Abstr., Print. Abstr., Chem. Abstr. **CODEN** RACUDO.

RADIATION CURING BUYER'S GUIDE. Began with issue for 1980. 0197-8039. US. English. an. $22.00. Technology Marketing Corp, 17 Park Street, Norwalk CT 06851. LC TP156.C8. DD 660.298. Buyer's Guide for Radiation Curing and Processing, 0146-5031.

RADIATION MEDICINE. Vol. 1, No. 1 (Jan/Mar 1983)-. 0288-2043. Periodical. US. English. qt. Igaku-Shoin Medical Publishers Inc, 1140 Avenue of the Americas, New York NY 10036. Tel (212)744-9540. NLM W1. A comprehensive journal dealing with new developments in the field of radiation medicine.

RADIATION REPORT CEASED. V. 11, No. 11- Jan./Feb. 1979-. 0195-9778. Periodical. US. English. bm. Trends Publishing Inc, National Press Building, Washington DC 20045. NLM W1 RA165. Radioisotope Report.

RADIOAKTIVE ISOTOPE IN KLINIK UND FORSCHUNG. Main/Conf Gasteiner Internationales Symposion. VFOAT Radioactive Isotopes in Clinical Medicine and Research. Began with V. 1, in 1954. 0252-9440. Periodical. German (articles in English or French). ir. Urban & Schwarzenberg Verlag, 7 East Redwood Street, Baltimore MD 21202. Tel 089/530181. **Ind/Abst** Chem. Abstr. NLM W1 ST759 BD.33 Etc. **CODEN** RIKFD7.

RADIOBIOLOGIA. RADIOTHERAPIA. Vol. 1- April/May 1960-. 0033-8184. Periodical. GE. German (English, French, and Russian; Vol. for 1960-62 in English and French). bm. $85.40. Kunst & Wissen Erich Bieber, Dufourstrasse 51, CH-8008 Zurich Switzerland. Tel (011)411694420. **Ind/Abst** Life Sci. Collect., Excerpta Med., Index Med., Biol. Abstr., Energy Res. Abstr., Chem. Abstr. LC RM845. NLM W1 RA196. **CODEN** RDBGAT.

RADIOBIOLOGIIA. VFOAT Radiobiology. Vol. 1- 1961-. 0033-8192. Periodical. UR. Russian (table of contents and summaries in English). bm. $50.00. Victor Kamkin Inc (70773), 12224 Parklawn Drive, Rockville MD 20852. Tel (301)881-5973. **Ind/Abst** Excerpta Med., Index Med., Life Sci. Collect., Int. Aerosp. Abstr., Biol. Abstr., Energy Res. Abstr., Chem. Abstr., Bibliogr. Agric. NLM W1 RA21. **CODEN** RADOA8.

RADIOGRAPHICS : A REVIEW PUBLICATION OF THE RADIOLOGICAL SOCIETY OF NORTH AMERICA, INC. VAT Radio Graphics. Vol. 1, No. 1 (Spring 1981)-. 0271-5333. Periodical. US. English. qt. $47.50. Radiological Society of North America, 20th and Northampton Streets, Easton PA 18042. Tel (215)829-5717. Ed William J Tuddenham. LC RC78.A1. DD 616.075705. bk rev. adv acc. Circ 17,000. (ctrl). A pictorial journal based on selected scientific exhibits and refresher courses presented at the annual meeting of the Radiological Society of North America.

RADIOGRAPHY. V. 1- 1935-. 0033-8281. Periodical. UK. English. mo. 36. College of Radiographers, 14 Upper Wimpole Street, London W1M 8BN England. Tel 01 935 5726. Ed Gwyneth Stokes. **Ind/Abst** Index Med., Cumul. Index Nurs. Allied Health Lit., Energy Res. Abstr., Hospit. Lit. Index. NLM W1 RA264. Index in last issue of volume - loose - separately paged. bk rev. adv acc. Circ 14,000. (ctrl). Journal for radiological technicians.

RADIOGRAPHY NEWS. Jan. 1979-. Periodical. UK. English. mo. College of Radiographers, 14 Upper Wimpole Street, London W1M 8BN England. NLM W1 RA264.

RADIOHIMIJA. (RADIOKHIMIIA). V. 1, No. 1-. 0033-8311. Periodical. UR. Russian. bm. $60.50. Victor Kamkin Inc (70777), 12224 Parklawn Drive, Rockville MD 20852. Tel (301)881-5973. **Ind/Abst** Energy Res. Abstr., Chem. Abstr. NLM W1 RA265K. **CODEN** RADKAU.

RADIOLOGE. (DER RADIOLOGE). Year. 1- April 1961-. 0033-832X. Periodical. WB. German. mo. Springer Verlag-New York Inc, 175-5th Avenue, New York NY 10010. Tel (212)460-1500. Ed F Heuck, E Loehr and W Wenz. **Ind/Abst** Excerpta Med., Energy Res. Abstr., Life Sci. Collect., Nucl. Sci. Abstr., Biol. Abstr., Index Med., Curr. Contents. NLM W1 RA266. **CODEN** RDLGBC. Diagnosis through radiology. Covers angiography, neuro-radiology, pediatric radiology, x-ray therapy, oncology, nuclear medicine for diagnosis and therapy, ultra-sound, biophysics and x-ray protection.

RADIOLOGIA DIAGNOSTICA. V. 1- 1960-. 0033-8354. Periodical. WB. German (text and summaries in French, English or Russian). bm. $82.43. Kunst & Wissen Erich Bieber, Dufourstrasse 51, CH-8008 Zurich Switzerland. **Tel** 011-41-1-69 44 20. **Ind/Abst** Excerpta Med., Index Med., Energy Res. Abstr., Chem. Abstr. **NLM** W1 RA294. **CODEN** RDGNA7.

RADIOLOGIA MEDICA. (RADIOLOGIA MEDICA, RIVISTA MENSILE). 0033-8362. Periodical. IT. Italian. mo. 120.00. Edizioni Minerva Medica, Corso Bramante 83, 10126 Torino Italy. **Tel** 67 82 82. **Ed** M Di Guglielmo. **Ind/Abst** Index Med., Energy Res. Abstr., Excerpta Med., Life Sci. Collect. **NLM** W1 RA314. bk rev. adv acc. Journal addressed to practitioners and specialists in radiology in Italy and abroad. It deals with topics radiology, scientific practice and research. *Minerva Radiologica, 0026-4962.*

THE RADIOLOGIC CLINICS OF NORTH AMERICA. Vol. 1, No. 1 (April 1963)-. 0033-8389. Periodical. US. English. qt. $60.00. W B Saunders Company, West Washington Square, Philadelphia PA 19105. **Tel** (215)574-3395. **Ed** Karen McFadden. **Ind/Abst** Life Sci. Collect., Excerpta Med., Index Med., Biol. Abstr., Energy Res. Abstr., Sci. Cit. Index, Abr. Ed., Hospit. Lit. Index. **LC** RM846. **DD** 616.075705. **NLM** W1 RA332. **CODEN** RCNAAU. (cum index). **Circ** 10,300. Practical updates for the clinician on the latest advances plus topics of current interest.

RADIOLOGIC TECHNOLOGY. V. 35- July 1963-. 0033-8397. Periodical. US. English. bm. $45.00. American Society of Radiologic Technology, 15000 Central Avenue, Albuquerque NM 87123. **Tel** (505)298-4500. **Ed** Pamela Wight. **Ind/Abst** Excerpta Med., Cumul. Index Nurs. Allied Health Lit., Hospit. Lit. Index, Energy Res. Abstr., Biol. Abstr., Index Med., Nucl. Sci. Abstr. **NLM** W1 RA332E. **CODEN** RATIB3. bk rev. adv acc. **Circ** 15,000. (ctrl). A scientific journal dedicated to the continuing education of radiologic technologists. *X-Ray Technician.*

RADIOLOGICA. **Series/Titl** Acta Universitatis Ouluensis, Series D Medica. No. 1-. 0358-4887. Monographic Series. FI. English (Finnish). ir. Professor Sakari Piha, University of Oulu, 90100 Oulu 10 Finland. **Tel** 358-81-332133. **Ed** Leo Hirvonen. **NLM** W1 AC954NM. adv acc. **Circ** 500. (ctrl). Monographs, reviews and dissertations in the field of diagnostic radiology.

RADIOLOGIE. (RADIOLOGIE : JOURNAL DU CEPUR). Vol. 1, No. 1 (March 1981)-. 0720-3322. Periodical. French. ir. Springer Verlag-New York Inc, Subs Department 175 5th Avenue, New York NY 10010. **Tel** (212)460-1500. **Ed** A Wackenheim. **Ind/Abst** Excerpta Med. **NLM** W1 RA339. All areas of diagnostic radiology, postgraduate studies in radiology on European and international level. Directed at hospital interns, assistants, experts in radiology and young doctors.

RADIOLOGY. V. 1- Sept. 1923-. 0033-8419. Periodical. US. English. mo. Radiological Society of North America, 20th & Northhampton Street, Easton PA 18042. **Tel** (215)258-9111. **Ind/Abst** Excerpta Med., Pestdoc, Ringdoc, Vetdoc, Comput. Control Abstr., Electr. Electron. Abstr., Sci. Abstr. Sect. A. Phys. Abstr., CIS Abstr., Life Sci. Collect., Energy Res. Abstr., Biol. Abstr., Chem. Abstr., Index Med., Int. Aerosp. Abstr., Nucl. Sci. Abstr., Hospit. Lit. Index, Sci. Cit. Index, Abr. Ed. **LC** RC78. **DD** 616.075705. **NLM** W1 RA354. **CODEN** RADLAX. (cum index).

RADIOLOGY & IMAGING LETTER. **VFOAT** Radiology and Imaging Letter. Vol. 4, No. 1 (Jan. 1, 1984)-. 0741-160X. Periodical. US. English. sm. $120.00. Quest Publishing Company, 1351 Titan Way, Brea CA 92621. **Tel** (714)738-6400. **Ed** Allan F Pacela and Lon Richardson. **NLM** W1. bk rev. adv acc. Written for hospitals radiology, diagnostic, imaging, and radiation therapy personnel. *Radiology Letter, 0273-4958.*

RADIOLOGY MANAGEMENT. V. 1- Jan. 1979-. 0198-7097. Periodical. US. English. qt. $30.00 Domestic, $35.00 Canada $40.00 Foreign. American Hospital Radiology, PO Box 334, Melrose MA 02167. **Tel** (617)443-7591. **Ed** Teresa V Cryan. **Ind/Abst** Hospit. Lit. Index. **NLM** W1 RA354F. bk rev. adv acc. **Circ** 2,6773. Information on management of the non-medical aspects of radiology operations.

RADIOTHERAPY AND ONCOLOGY : JOURNAL OF THE EUROPEAN SOCIETY FOR THERAPEUTIC RADIOLOGY AND ONCOLOGY. Vol. 1, No. 1 (Aug. 1983)-. 0167-8140. Periodical. English. bm. $250.50. Elsevier Science Publishers BV Biomedical Division, PO Box 1527, 1000 BM Amsterdam Netherlands. **Tel** (020)5803911. **Ed** E Van Der Schueren. **Ind/Abst** Life Sci. Collect., Excerpta Med. **NLM** W1. bk rev. adv acc. **Circ** 900. The journal publishes papers describing original research as well as review articles. It covers areas of interest relating to radiation oncology.

RADIOTSIONNYE ISSLEDOVANIIA. 1- 1974-. UR. Russian. **NLM** W1 RA373.

RECENT ADVANCES IN RADIOLOGY AND MEDICAL IMAGING. No. 6-. 0143-6961. Periodical. UK. English. **Ed** Sir T Lodge and R E Steiner. **NLM** W1 RE105YEK. *Recent Advances in Radiology.*

REVISTA INTERAMERICANA DE RADIOLOGIA. V. 1- July 1976-. 0034-9704. Periodical. US. Multilingual (English and Spanish). qt. $40.00. Interamerican College Radiology, 7421 Miller Road, Luis O Martinez, Miami FL 33155. **Tel** (305)674-2705. **Ed** Luis O Martinez. **Ind/Abst** Excerpta Med., Index Med. **LC** R895.A1. **DD** 616.075705. **NLM** W1 RE594L. bk rev. adv acc. **Circ** 1,500. (ctrl). Scientific papers on imageology and allied sciences.

RINSHO HOSHASEN. **VFOAT** Japanese Journal of Clinical Radiology. V. 1- 1956-. 0009-9252. Periodical. JA. Japanese (English). mo. Kamehara Shuppan Company, 31-34 2 Chome Yushima Buckyoku, Tokyo 113 Japan. **Ind/Abst** Excerpta Med., Index Med., Chem. Abstr., Energy Res. Abstr. **NLM** W1 RI2163K. **CODEN** RHOSAM.

RNM IMAGES (DOMESTIC ED.). (RNM IMAGES). **VFOAT** R.N.M. Images. Vol. 12, No. 1 (Feb. 82)-. 0744-9542. Periodical. US. English. bm. $30.00. Nickerson & Collins Company, 1800 Oakton Street, Des Plaines IL 60018. **NLM** W1 RN22. *Radiology/ Nuclear Medicine Magazine, 0161-7516.*

RONTGEN-BERICHTE. (RONTGEN-BERICHTE : ORGAN DER BAYERISCHEN RONTGENGESELLSCHAFT). **VFOAT** Rontgen Berichte. V. 1, No. 1 (Oct. 1972)-. 0302-7813. Periodical. German. **Ind/Abst** Energy Res. Abstr. **NLM** W1 RO255W.

RONTGENPRAXIS : ZEITSCHRIFT FUR RADIOLOGISCHE TECHNIK. **VFOAT** Zeitschrift fur Radiologische Technik. Vol. 16- Jan. 1963-. 0035-7820. Periodical. GW. German. mo. Hirzel S Verlag Stuttgart, Postfach 347, D7000 Stuttgart 1 West Germany. **Tel** (0711)2582 0. **Ind/Abst** Excerpta Med., Energy Res. Abstr., Index Med., Comput. Control Abstr., Electr. Electron. Abstr., Sci. Abstr. Sect. A. Phys. Abstr., Phys. Abstr. **NLM** W1 RO286T. **CODEN** RGPXB2. *Rontgen- und Laboratoriumspraxis.*

RSNA EDUCATIONAL MATERIALS QUARTERLY. **VFOAT** R.S.N.A. Educational Materials Quarterly. **VAT** Radiological Society of North America Educational Materials Quarterly. Vol. 2, No. 1 (Spring 1980)-. 0732-7021. Periodical. US. English. qt. Radiological Society of North America Inc, 1415 West 22nd Street/Suite 1150, Oak Brook IL 60521. **NLM** WR 18 R111. *Educational Materials Quarterly.*

SAUNDERS MONOGRAPHS IN CLINICAL RADIOLOGY. Vol. 1-. 0277-853X. Monographic Series. US. English. ir. WB Saunders Company, West Washington Square, Philadelphia PA 19105. **Tel** (800)523-0713. **LC** UNC. **NLM** W1 SA975B.

SEMINARS IN INTERVENTIONAL RADIOLOGY. Vol. 1, No. 1 (Mar. 1984)-. 0739-9529. Periodical. US. English. qt. $68.00. Thieme-Stratton Inc, 381 Park Avenue South/Suite 1501, New York NY 10016. **Tel** (212)683-5088. **Ed** Wilfrido Castaneda-Zuniga. **DD** 616. adv acc. **Circ** 1,400. Topic-oriented journal for the practitioner specializing in all phases of radiology.

SEMINARS IN ROENTGENOLOGY. **VFOAT** Roentgenology. V. 1- Jan. 1966-. 0037-198X. Periodical. US. English. qt. Grune & Stratton Inc, 111 Fifth Avenue, New York NY 10003. **Tel** (212)614-3110. **Ind/Abst** Life Sci. Collect., Excerpta Med., Energy Res. Abstr., Biol. Abstr., Chem. Abstr., Index Med., Nuci. Sci. Abstr., Sci. Cit. Index, Abr. Ed. **LC** RC78. **DD** 616.075705. **NLM** W1 SE489L. **CODEN** SEROAF.

SERIES IN RADIOLOGY. RADIOLOGICAL EXAMINATION OF THE GASTROINTESTINAL TRACT. **VFOAT** Radiological Examination of the Gastrointestinal Tract. V. 1-. 0167-465X. Monographic Series. English. ir. **NLM** W1 SE719.

SKELETAL RADIOLOGY. V. 1- 1976-. 0364-2348. Periodical. US. English. qt. $165.00. Springer Verlag-New York Inc, 175 5th Avenue, New York NY 10010. **Tel** (212)460-1500. **Ed** H G Jacobson, T E Keats and D J Stoker. **Ind/Abst** Life Sci. Collect., Excerpta Med., Index Med., Energy Res. Abstr. **NLM** W1 SK582. Serves as a forum for the dissemination of current knowledge and information dealing with disorders of the skeleton.

SPECIAL REPORT - BRITISH INSTITUTE OF RADIOLOGY. No. 9- 1976-. Monographic Series. UK. English. ir. British Institute of Radiology, 36 Portland Place, London WIN 3DG England. **NLM** W1 SP295I. *British Journal of Radiology. Special Report Series, 0306-2120.*

STRAHLENSCHUTZ IN FORSCHUNG UND PRAXIS. Vol. 1- 1961-. 0081-5888. Monographic Series. German. Georg Theime Verlag, Postfach 732, Herdweg 63, D7000 Stuttgart 1 West Germany. **Ind/Abst** Index Med., Energy Res. Abstr., Chem. Abstr. **NLM** W1 ST756. **CODEN** STFPAT.

STRAHLENTHERAPIE. V. 1- July 1912-. 0039-2073. Periodical. GW. German (summaries in English and French). mo. Urban and Vogel, Postfach 15 22 09, 8000 Munchen 15 West Germany. **Tel** (301)539-2550. **Ind/Abst** Excerpta Med., Index Med., Biol. Abstr., Energy Res. Abstr., Life Sci. Collect., Chem. Abstr., Hospit. Lit. Index, Sci. Cit. Index, Abr. Ed. **NLM** W1 ST758V. **CODEN** STRAAA.

TAEHAN PANGSASON HAKHOE CHI. **VFOAT** Journal of the Korean Radiological Society. No. 1 - 1964-. 0301-2867. Periodical. Korean (summaries also in English). ir. **NLM** W1 TA393P.

TEX-RAYS : OFFICIAL JOURNAL TEXAS SOCIETY OF RADIOLOGIC TECHNOLOGISTS, INC. Periodical. US. English. qt. $12.00. Texas Society of Radiologic Technologists, PO Box 1604, Nacogdoches TX 75961. **Tel** (409)569-9481. **Ed** Betty Shinn. bk rev. adv acc. **Circ** 1,200. (ctrl). State publication for the Texas Society of Radiologic Technologists.

UROLOGIC RADIOLOGY. *See* Medicine - Urology.

VESTNIK RENTGENOLOGII I RADIOLOGII. **VFOAT** Annales de Roentgenologie et de Radiologie. Vol. 1- 1920-. 0042-4676. Periodical. UR. Russian (summaries in German, 1929-33). bm. $31.50. Victor Kamkin Inc (70124), 12224 Parklawn Drive, Rockville MD 20852. **Tel** (301)881-5973. **Ind/Abst** Index Med. **NLM** W1 VE844.

VETERINARY RADIOLOGY. *See* Veterinary Medicine, Animal Culture.

WILEY SERIES IN DIAGNOSTIC AND THERAPEUTIC RADIOLOGY. 0277-2566. Monographic Series. US. English. ir. John Wiley & Sons Inc, 1 Wiley Drive, Somerset NJ 08873.

THE YEAR BOOK OF DIAGNOSTIC RADIOLOGY. *See* Yearbooks, Almanacs, Directories.

ZENTRALBLATT FUR DIE GESAMTE RADIOLOGIE *CEASED.* 0044-4146. Periodical. German. ir. **NLM** ZWN 100 Z56.

ZENTRALBLATT RADIOLOGIE. **VFOAT** Radiology. Vol. 125, No. 1-. 0722-3072. Periodical. English (abstracts in German). mo. Springer Verlag-New York Inc, 175 5th Avenue, New York NY 10010. **Tel** (212)460-1500. **Ed** B Chone, C Wieland and U Weischedel. **Ind/Abst** Energy Res. Abstr. **NLM** ZWN 100 Z56. Meeting reports, reviews, general radiology and specific radiology, ray biology, x-ray chemistry, immunology, side effects, x-ray protection, diagnosis, therapy, radioactive, isotopes and chemotherapy. *Zentralblatt fur die Gesamte Radiologie, 0044-4146.*

ZHONGHUA FANGSHE YIXUE YU FANGHU ZAZHI. (CHUNG-HUA FANG SHE I HSUEH YU FANG HU TSA CHIH). **VFOAT** Chinese Journal of Radiological Medicine and Protection. Vol. 1, 1981-. 0254-5098. Periodical. CC. Chinese. bm. $6.50. China Publication Centre, PO Box 2820, Beijing China. **Tel** 65-3031. **Ed** Lu-xin Wei. **Ind/Abst** Chem. Abstr. **NLM** W1 CH9816. **CODEN** ZFYZDY. **Circ** 6,000. Biological effect of ionizing radiation, clinical and experimental studies of radiation injury, radiotoxicology, radiation protection, dosimetry, environmental and personnel monitoring, management of radiation emergency, etc. *Fang Shi I Hsueh Yu Fang Hu.*

ZHONGHUA HEYIXUE ZAZHI. (CHUNG-HUA HO I HSUEH TSA CHIH). **VFOAT** Chinese Journal of Nuclear Medicine. 1981-. 0253-9780.

Periodical. CC. Chinese. qt. $3.60. China Publication Centre, PO Box 2820, Beijing China. **Ind/Abst** Spin, Chem. Abstr. **NLM** W1 CH9817D. **CODEN** CITCDE.

ZURNAL NEVROPATOLOGII I PSIHIATRII IM S.S. KORSAKOVA. (ZHURNAL NEVROPATOLOGII I PSIKHIATRII). **VFOAT** Zhurnal Nevropatologii I Psikhiatrii Imeni S.S. Korsakova. Began in 1952. 0044-4588. UR. Russian (summaries in English). ir. $47.50. Victor Kamkin Inc, 12224 Parklawn Drive, Rockville MD 20852. **Tel** (301)881-5973. **Ind/Abst** Life Sci. Collect., Excerpta Med., Pestdoc, Ringdoc, Vetdoc, Index Med., Biol. Abstr., Int. Aerosp. Abstr., Chem. Abstr., Psychol. Abstr., Sociol. Abstr., Lang. Lang. Behav. Abstr., Sci. Cit. Index, Abr. Ed. **NLM** W1 ZH422. **CODEN** ZNPIAP. *Nevropatologiia I Psikhiatriia.*

RESPIRATORY DISEASES

AAR TIMES. (AARTIMES : AN OFFICIAL PUBLICATION OF THE AMERICAN ASSOCIATION FOR RESPIRATORY THERAPY). **VFOAT** A.A.R. Times. **VAT** American Association for Respiratory Therapy Times. Vol. 1, No. 1 (July 1977)-. 0195-1777. Periodical. US. English. mo. $25.00. Daedalus Enterprises Inc, PO Box 35886, Dallas TX 75235. **Tel** (214)630-3540. **Ed** Sherry Milligan. **Ind/Abst** Cumul. Index Nurs. Allied Health Lit. **NLM** W1 AA116. adv acc. **Circ** 26,000. (ctrl). Provides updates on respiratory care trends across the country, legislative news, education topics, management and legal issues. Meetings are listed, as well as job opportunities.

ADVANCES IN ASTHMA ALLERGY & PULMONARY DISEASES. **VFOAT** Asthma Allergy & Pulmonary Diseases. **VAT** Advances in Asthma Allergy and Pulmonary Diseases. V. 4, No. 2- 1977-. 0164-7075. Periodical. US. English. qt. Arthur Retlaw & Associates Inc, 1603 Orrington Ave/Suite 2080, Evanston IL 60201. **NLM** W1 AD436BP. *Advances in Asthma & Allergy.*

ADVANCES IN ASTHMA & ALLERGY. **VAT** Advances in Asthma and Allergy. V. 1- July 1974-. 0163-1578. Periodical. US. English. ir. Fisons Corp, 2 Preston Court, Bedford MA 01730. **NLM** W1 AD436C.

ADVANCES IN TUBERCULOSIS RESEARCH. **VFOAT** Fortschritte der Tuberkuloseforschung, Progres l'Exploration de la Tuberculose. 18- 1972-. 0065-3500. Periodical. English. ir. S Karger Ag, PO Box 352, White Plains NY 10602. **Tel** 061-39 08 80. **Ed** W Fox, J Grosset and K Styblo. Recording the directions and changing concerns of tuberculosis research. *Bibliotheca Tuberculosea. Advances in Tuberculosis Research.*

AMERICAN HEART ASSOCIATION MONOGRAPH. 0065-8499. Monographic Series. US. English. ir. American Heart Association, 2005 Hightower Drive, Garland TX 75041. **Tel** (214)750-5466. **Ind/Abst** Biol. Abstr., Chem. Abstr. **LC** UNC. **NLM** W1 AM421H. **CODEN** AHMOAH.

THE AMERICAN REVIEW OF RESPIRATORY DISEASE. V. 80- July 1959-. 0003-0805. Periodical. US. English. mo. $90.00 US, Canada, and Mexico $100.00 all other countries. American Lung Association, 1740 Broadway, New York NY 10019. **Tel** (212)315-8700. **Ed** Reuben M Cherniack. **Ind/Abst** Coal Abstr., Excerpta Med., Energy Inf. Abstr., Environ. Abstr., Index Med., CIS Abstr., Biol. Abstr., Chem. Abstr., Energy Res. Abstr., Hospit. Lit. Index, Ringdoc, Sci. Cit. Index, Abr. Ed. **LC** RC306. **DD** 616.2005. **NLM** W1 AM7503. **CODEN** ARDSBL. adv acc. **Circ** 14,500. (ctrl). Features original articles in basic science, clinical problems and comprehensive reviews of state of art in respiratory topics. *American Review of Tuberculosis and Pulmonary Diseases, 0096-039X.*

ANNUAL REPORT - AMERICAN LUNG ASSOCIATION. **Main/Corp** American Lung Association. 1974/75-. 0364-6602. Monographic Series. US. English. an. American Lung Association, 1740 Broadway, New York NY 10019. **NLM** W1 AM5629.

ANNUAL REPORT - DIVISION OF TUBERCULOSIS CONTROL. (ANNUAL REPORT). Began with 1965. 0702-9306. CN. English. an. **LC** RA185.B7. **DD** 614.54209711. *Yearly Report of Ledgers.*

ANNUAL REPORT - KENYA TUBERCULOSIS AND RESPIRATORY DISEASES RESEARCH CENTRE. **Main/Corp** Kenya Tuberculosis and Respiratory Diseases Research Centre. English. an. Director Kenya Tuberculosis and Respiratory Diseases Research Centre, PO Box 47855, Nairobi Kenya.

ANNUAL REPORT - SINGAPORE ANTI-TUBERCULOSIS ASSOCIATION. **Main/Corp** Singapore Anti-Tuberculosis Association. **VFOAT** SATA Annual Report. 0129-6337. English. ir. **NLM** W1 SI519H.

ANNUAL REPORT - TUBERCULOSIS CONTROL SERVICES. (ANNUAL REPORT - TUBERCULOSIS CONTROL SERVICES, NOVA SCOTIA). 1st- 1957-. 0078-2505. Periodical. CN. English. ir. **NLM** W2 DC2.1 N9T9A.

ARCHIVIO MONALDI PER LA TISIOLOGIA E LE MALATTIE DELL'APPARATO RESPIRATORIO. *See* Genealogy and Heraldry - Archives.

ATEMWEGS- UND LUNGENKRANKHEITEN. Volume 1- 1975-. 0341-3055. Periodical. GW. German. bm. $97.00. Dustri Verlag, Dr Karl Feistle, Bahnofstrasse 9 Postfach 49, 8024 Deisenhofen West Germany. **Ind/Abst** Excerpta Med., Chem. Abstr., Life Sci. Collect., Sci. Cit. Index, Abr. Ed. **NLM** W1 AT212C. **CODEN** ATLUDF.

BASICS OF RD. V. 1- Oct. 1972-. 0162-9409. Periodical. US. English. qt. American Thoracic Society, 1740 Broadway, New York NY 10019. **NLM** W1 BA814T.

BRITISH JOURNAL OF DISEASES OF THE CHEST. V. 53- Jan. 1959-. 0007-0971. Periodical. UK. English. qt. 31.00. Bailliere Tindall, 1 St Annes Road, Eastbourne East Sussex BN21 3UN England. **Tel** (01)630-7887. **Ed** Duncan Empey. **Ind/Abst** Life Sci. Collect., Pestdoc, Ringdoc, Vetdoc, Excerpta Med., CIS Abstr., Nuci. Sci. Abstr., Biol. Abstr., Chem. Abstr., Index Med., Sci. Cit. Index, Abr. Ed. **NLM** W1 BR526F. **CODEN** BJDCAT. Each issue contains an index to its own contents - no vol index - loose. bk rev. adv acc. **Circ** 2,700. Original articles and reviews on clinical respiratory medicine. *British Journal of Tuberculosis and Diseases of the Chest.*

BRONCHO-PNEUMOLOGIE *CEASED.* V. 26-30. 0395-3904. Periodical. French (English). ir. **Ind/Abst** Chem. Abstr. **NLM** W1 BR817P. **CODEN** BRPNDB. *Bronches, 0007-2222.*

BUCHEREI DES PNEUMOLOGEN. Vol. 1- 1976-. 0342-4456. Monographic Series. GW. German. George Thieme Verlag, Postfach 732, Herdweg 63, D7000 Stuttgart 1 West Germany. **NLM** W1 BU157K. *Tuberkulose-Bucherei, 0344-6239.*

BULLETIN DE PHYSIO-PATHOLOGIE RESPIRATOIRE. V. 1-11. 0007-439X. Periodical. UK. articles in English or French with summaries in both languages or occasionally in English and German. bm. $140.00. European Society of Clinical Respiratory Physiology, Royal Hallamshire Hospital, Sheffield S10 2JF Endland. **Tel** (0742)26484. **Ed** P Howard. **Ind/Abst** Coal Abstr., Sci. Cit. Index, Abr. Ed. **NLM** W1 BU563K. bk rev. adv acc. **Circ** 1,500. To promote standardisation throughout Europe of respiratory function procedures. These are invaluable guides to all chest physicians, in particular, those in charge of respiratory function laboratories.

BULLETIN - INTERNATIONAL UNION AGAINST TUBERCULOSIS. **Main/Corp** International Union Against Tuberculosis. 1- 1924-. 0074-9249. Periodical. English. ir. 400 Domestic, $50.00 Foreign. International Union Against Tuberculosis, 3 rue Georges Ville, 75116 Paris France. **Tel** (1)45 01 70 73. **Ed** Annik Rouillon. **Ind/Abst** Life Sci. Collect., Excerpta Med., Index Med., Biol. Abstr. **NLM** W1 BU853X. **CODEN** UITBA2. bk rev. adv acc. **Circ** 6,000. Covers tuberculosis, respiratory diseases, public health, news of the International Union Against tuberculosis news of the World Health Organization.

BULLETIN SIGNALETIQUE 352 : MALADIES DE L'APPAREIL RESPIRATOIRE, DU COEUR ET DES VAISSEAUX. **VFOAT** Maladies de l'Appareil Respiratoire, du Coeur et des Vaisseaux. V. 34- 1973-. Periodical. FR. French. ir. Centre National de la Recherche Scientifique, Centre de Documentation, Humaines 54 Blvd Raspail, 75260 Paris Cedex 06 France. Index published separately - free - automatically sent. *Bulletin Signaletique 350: Pathologie Generale et Experimentale, 0007-5469.*

CLINICAL NOTES ON RESPIRATORY DISEASES *CEASED.* Began with V. 1- Summer 1962-. Ceased March 1983. 0009-9198. Periodical. US. English. qt. **NLM** W1 CL735. **CODEN** CNRCB.

CURRENT REVIEWS IN RESPIRATORY THERAPY. V. 1-. 0164-3126. Monographic Series. US. English. bw. Current Reviews in Respiratory, 7480 Fairway Drive/Suite 106, Miami Lakes FL 33014. **Tel** (305)822-1414. **Ind/Abst** Cumul. Index Nurs. Allied Health Lit. **NLM** W1 CU8093N.

DRUGS IN RESPIRATORY DISEASES. **Series/Titl** PRM : Physicians' Reference Manuals. No. 1 (1983)-. 0824-7099. CN. English. sm. 50.00. Drugs in Respiratory Diseases, c/o STA Communications 63 Place Frontenac, Pointe-Claire Quebec H9R 4Z7 Canada. **Tel** (514)695-6723. **Ed** Paul Brand. **DD** 615.72. adv acc. **Circ** 1,200. (ctrl). Drug reference manuals.

ERGEBNISSE DER GESAMTEN LUNGEN- UND TUBERKULOSEFORSCHUNG. Periodical. German. ir. Thieme-Stratton, 381 Park Avenue South, New York NY 10016. **Tel** (212)683-5088.

EUROPEAN JOURNAL OF RESPIRATORY DISEASES. V. 61- 1980-. 0106-4339. Periodical. DK. English (abstracts in French). ir. $122.39. Munksgaard Ltd, 35 Norre Sogade, DK-1370 Copenhagen K Denmark. **Tel** 1.12.70.30. **Ed** Erik Berglund. **Ind/Abst** Life Sci. Collect., Pestdoc, Ringdoc, Vetdoc, Excerpta Med., Cumul. Index Nurs. Allied Health Lit., Index Med., Biol. Abstr., Chem. Abstr., Curr. Contents, Energy Res. Abstr. **NLM** W1 EU72EG. **CODEN** EJRDD2. bk rev. adv acc. **Circ** 1,200. Diseases of the lung caused by infections, immunologic processes, air pollutions, pathophysiology and pharmacology of diseases included. *Scandinavian Journal of Respiratory Diseases, Acta Tuberculosea Et Pneumologica Belgica.*

EXPERIMENTAL LUNG RESEARCH. V. 1- Mar. 1980-. 0190-2148. Periodical. US. English. ir. $220.00. Hemisphere Publishing Corporation, 79 Madison Avenue/Suite 1110, New York NY 10016. **Tel** (202)783-3958. **Ed** Paul Nettesheim. **Ind/Abst** Life Sci. Collect., Chem. Abstr., Biol. Abstr., Curr. Contents, Excerpta Med., Index Med., Sci. Cit. Index, Abr. Ed. **LC** QP121.A1. **DD** 616.24. **NLM** W1 EX504U. **CODEN** EXLRDA. bk rev. adv acc. **Circ** 770. Experimental lung research emphasizing mechanisms of pulmonary biology and pathobiology conducted at the biochemical, subcellular, and cellular tissue levels.

GIORNALE ITALIANO DELLE MALATTIE DEL TORACE. V. 20- Jan./Feb. 1966-. 0017-0437. Periodical. IT. Italian. bm. 95.0. Giornale Italiano Delle, Via Luca Comercio 5, 20145 Milano Italy. **Tel** 02/3495026-795155. **Ed** Bottero Aldo. **Ind/Abst** Biol. Abstr., Chem. Abstr. **NLM** W1 GI761N. **CODEN** GIMTB4. bk rev. adv acc. **Circ** 2,000. Medical news from the world. Seven original works per issue about respiratory, cardiovascular, senological and allergic diseases of the chest; book reviews, notices, advertisings. *Giornale Italiano della Tubercolosi e delle Malattie del Torace.*

GYERHAIG MIC HOHUBGI JIROHAN. (KYORHAEK MIT HOHUPKI CHIRHWAN). **VFOAT** Tuberculosis and Respiratory Diseases. 0378-0066. Periodical. KO. English (Korean). qt. 121-150 Tangsan-Dong, Yongdungpo-Ku Seoul. **Ind/Abst** Excerpta Med., Chem. Abstr. **LC** RC306. **NLM** W1 KY973H. **CODEN** KHCHAM.

HJARTA, KARL, LUNGOR. V. 77, No. 1-. Periodical. SW. Swedish. qt. Svenska Nationalforeningen mot Hjart-Och Lungsjukdomar, Kungsgatan 54, 111 35 Stockholm Sweden. *Kvartalsskrift (Svenska Nationalforeningen mot Hjart-och Lungsjukdomar), 0373-2665.*

INDIAN JOURNAL OF CHEST DISEASES & ALLIED SCIENCES. *See* Medicine - Cardiovascular Diseases.

INDIAN JOURNAL OF TUBERCULOSIS. 0019-5707. Periodical. II. English. qt. $15.00. Tuberculosis Association of India, 3 Red Cross Road, New Delhi-110001 India. **Ind/Abst** Excerpta Med., Biol. Abstr., Chem. Abstr. **NLM** W1 IN239. **CODEN** IJTBAD.

IRCS MEDICAL SCIENCE. RESPIRATORY SYSTEM. (IRCS MEDICAL SCIENCE : RESPIRATORY SYSTEM). **VFOAT** Respiratory System. V. 3- Jan. 1975-. 0305-6937. Periodical. UK. English. qt. IRCS Medical Science, PO Box 500/St Leonards House, Lancaster LA1 1PF England. **Tel** (0524) 68116. **Ed** S Johnson. Publishes results of original research into all aspects of the respiratory system, both clinical and experimental, within weeks of completion. Papers fully refereed. *Research on the Respiratory System, 0305-2923.*

JAARVERSLAG - KONINKLIJKE NEDERLANDSE CENTRALE VERENIGING TOT BESTRIJDING DER TUBERCULOSE. **Main/Corp** Koninklijke Nederlandse Centrale Vereniging Tot Bestrijding der Tuberculose. 0167-4552. Dutch. ir. **NLM** W1 NE1094.

THE JOURNAL OF ASTHMA. Vol. 18, No. 1 (Jan. 1981)-. 0277-0903. Periodical. US. English. bm. $105.00. Marcel Dekker Inc, PO Box 11305/Church Street Station, New York NY 10249. **Tel** (212)696-9000. **Ed** Constantine John Falliers. **Ind/Abst** Excerpta Med., Life Sci. Collect., Index Med., Biol. Abstr., Chem. Abstr., Psychol. Abstr. **LC** RC591. **DD** 616.238005. **NLM** W1 JO544S. **CODEN** JOUADU. bk rev. adv acc. (ctrl). Each issue contains valuable guidelines for: the basic understanding of asthma, emergency as well as long term care, environmental counseling, and preventative measures. *Journal of Asthma Research, 0021-9134.*

THE JOURNAL OF ASTHMA RESEARCH *CEASED.* V. 1-17. 0021-9134. Periodical. US. English. qt. **Ind/Abst** Life Sci. Collect., Excerpta Med., Energy Res. Abstr. **LC** RC591. **NLM** W1 JO545. **CODEN** JOARAC.

THE JOURNAL OF RESPIRATORY DISEASES. V. 1- Oct. 1979-. 0194-259X. Periodical. US. English. mo. $28.00. Cliggott Publishing Company, 500 West Putnam Avenue/Box 4010, Greenwich CT 06830. **Tel** (203)661-0600. **LC** RC705. **DD** 616.2005. **NLM** W1 JO87D.

KEKKAKU. **VFOAT** Tuberculosis. 0022-9776. Periodical. JA. English. mo. 10.000. Japenese Society for Tuberculosis, c/o Research Institute for Tuberculosis, Malsyama 3-chome, Kiyose shi Tokyo 204 Japan. **Tel** 0424-91-2540. **Ed** Tadao Shimao. adv acc. **Circ** 3,000. Publishes original research works on tuberculosis and related diseases.

KYOBU GEKA. **VFOAT** Japanese Journal of Thoracic Surgery. Periodical. JA. English. ir. $117.51. Tokyo International, PO Box 5272, Tokyo Japan. **Tel** 03 811 7238. **Ind/Abst** Index Med. bk rev. adv acc. **Circ** 3,300. Only Japanese journal devoted to surgery of respiratory and cardiac system.

MONATSSCHRIFT FUR LUNGENKRANKHEITEN UND TUBERKULOSEBEKAMPFUNG *CEASED.* Year. 11-16. 0026-931X. Periodical. GE. German. mo. Deutscher Buch Export-Import, Leninstrasse 16, DDR-701 Leipzig East Germany. **Ind/Abst** Life Sci. Collect., CIS Abstr. **NLM** W1 MO359GN. *Monattschrfift fur Tuberkulosebekampfung, 0323-8393.*

NEWS-AMERICAN THORACIC SOCIETY. (NEWS - AMERICAN THORACIC SOCIETY). **VFOAT** ATS News. V. 1- Aug. 1975-. 0162-251X. Periodical. US. English. qt. **NLM** W1 NE993C. *ATS News.*

NEWS LETTER - NATIONAL TUBERCULOSIS INSTITUTE. V. 11, No. 3/4- Sept./Dec. 1974-. 0377-4937. Periodical. English. ir. **NLM** W1 NE996Y. *NTI News Letter, 0047-9136.*

PLUCNE BOLESTI : CASOPIS UDRUZENJA PNEUMOFTIZIOLOGA JUGOSLAVIJE. **VFOAT** Respiratory Diseases, The Journal of Yugoslav Association of Phthisiology and Pneumology. Vol. 36, No. 1-2 (Jan./June 1984)-. 0370-0380. Periodical. YU. Serbo-Croatian -R. qt. **Ind/Abst** Index Med. **NLM** W1. *Plucne Bolesti I Tuberkuloza.*

PLUCNEBOLESTI I TUBERKULOZA. (PLUCNE BOLESTI I TUBERKULOZA : CASOPSIS UDRUZENJA PNEUMOFTIZIOLOGA JUGOSLAVIJE). Vol. 21- Jan./March 1969-. 0300-8975. Periodical. YU. Croatian. qt. Jugoslovenska Knjica, PO Box 36, Beograd Yugoslavia. **Ind/Abst** Excerpta Med., Index Med. **NLM** W1 PL267. *Tuberkuloza.*

PNEUMONOLOGIA HUNGARICA. V. 29- Jan. 1976-. 0133-1728. Periodical. HU. Hungarian. mo. Akademiai Kiado, POB 24, 1363 Budapest Hungary. **Ind/Abst** Excerpta Med. **NLM** W1 PN299H. *Tuberkulozis es Tudobetegsegek, 0041-3887.*

PNEUMONOLOGIA POLSKA. V. 44- 1976-. 0376-4761. Periodical. PL. Polish (summaries in English and). mo. ARS Polona, Krakowskie Przedmiescie 7, 00-068 Warsaw Poland. **Ind/Abst** Excerpta Med., Index Med., Chem. Abstr. **NLM** W1 PN2991. **CODEN** PNPOD4. *Gruzlica I Choroby Puc.*

PNEVMOLOGIIA I FTIZIATRIIA. **VFOAT** Pneumologia I Ftiziatria. 0324-1491. Periodical. Bulgarian (summaries in Bulgarian and English). ir. $10.00. Hemus, 6 Boulevard Rusky, Sofia Bulgaria. **Ind/Abst** Chem. Abstr., Excerpta Med. **NLM** W1 PN41. **CODEN** PNFTD3. *Ftiziatrija, 0532-7709.*

POUMON *CEASED.* Periodical. FR. French. qt. Editions Techniques, 123 rue d'Alesia, 75678 Paris Cedex 14 France. **Tel** 45.39.22.91. **Circ** 11,500. (ctrl). Periodical restatement by movable installments renewed every ten years or more often. All installments gathered in bindings, constituting a treatise subscription reserved to owners of treaties.

POUMONS. V. 8, No 1- May/July 1974-. 0318-9236. Periodical. CN. French. qt. Societe du Timbre de Noel du Quebec, 264 rue Chenier, Quebec Quebec G1K 1R2 Canada. **DD** 616.2405. *Observation, Opinion, Orientation, 0029-7674.*

PRAXIS UND KLINIK DER PNEUMOLOGIE. V. 31, No. 4, April 1977-. 0342-7498. Periodical. GW. German (summaries in English). mo. $100.00. Thieme-Stratton Inc, 381 Park Avenue, New York NY 10016. **Tel** (212)683-5088/89. **Ind/Abst** Life Sci. Collect., Excerpta Med., Pestdoc, Ringdoc, Vetdoc, Index Med., Energy Res. Abstr., Chem. Abstr., Curr. Contents, Sci. Cit. Index, Abr. Ed. **NLM** W1 PR329N. **CODEN** PKPNDE. *Praxis der Pneumologie, 0032-7069.*

PROBLEMY TUBERKULEZA. 0032-9533. Periodical. UR. Russian. mo. $30.50. Victor Kamkin Inc (70731), 12224 Parklawn Drive, Rockville MD 20852. **Tel** (301)881-5973. **Ind/Abst** Chem. Abstr., Index Med. **CODEN** PRTUAX.

PROGRESS IN RESPIRATION RESEARCH. 0079-6751. English. ir. S Karger AG, PO Box, CH-4009 Basel Switzerland. **Tel** 061-39 08 80. **Ed** H Herzog. **Ind/Abst** Biol. Abstr., Chem. Abstr., Index Med. **NLM** W3 PR948. **CODEN** PGRRB6. Surveys of new knowledge on normal and impaired respiratory function. *Progress in Research in Emphysema and Chronic Bronchitis.*

RECENT ADVANCES IN RESPIRATORY MEDICINE. No. 1- 1976-. 0308-6623. Periodical. UK. English. ir. Churchill Livingstone Inc, 1560 Broadway, New York NY 10036. **Tel** (212)819-5400. **Ed** T B Stretton. **NLM** W1 RE105YG.

REFERENCE MANUAL - BUREAU OF DISEASE CONTROL, TUBERCULOSIS UNIT, NEW YORK STATE DEPARTMENT OF HEALTH. **VFOAT** Tuberculosis Control. 1974-. 0163-7002. Periodical. US. English. an. **NLM** W2 AN6 D35A. *Reference Manual - Bureau of Tuberculosis Control, New York State Department of Health.*

RESPIRATION. V. 25- 1968-. 0025-7931. Periodical. SZ. English (French and German). $194.00. S Karger AG, PO Box 352, White Plains NY 10602. **Tel** (061)39 08 80. **Ed** H Herzog. **Ind/Abst** Life Sci. Collect., Excerpta Med., Index Med., Biol. Abstr., CIS Abstr., Chem. Abstr., Curr. Contents, Sci. Cit. Index, Abr. Ed. **LC** RC705. **NLM** W1 RE248D. **CODEN** RESPBD. Index in last issue of volume - attached. adv acc. Features original papers concerning physiology, biochemistry, immunology, and morphology of respiration and respiratory organs. *Medicina Thoracalis.*

RESPIRATORY CARE. V. 25- 1980-. 0730-8418. Periodical. US. English. mo. $30.00. Daedalus Enterprises Inc, PO Box 35886, Dallas TX 75235. **Tel** (214)630-3540. **Ind/Abst** Life Sci. Collect., Excerpta Med., Cumul. Index Nurs. Allied Health Lit., Hospit. Lit. Index. **NLM** W1 RE248J. Index in last issue of volume - attached. *RC. Respiratory Care, 0098-9142.*

RESPIRATORY DISORDERS DIAGNOSIS & THERAPY. **VFOAT** Respiratory Disorders. Vol. 1, No. 1-. 0743-4332. Periodical. US. English. sa. Pharmaceutical Communications, 42-15 Crescent Street, Long Island City NY 11101. **DD** 616.

RESPIRATORY PHYSIOLOGY. V.1- 1974-. 0149-2950. UK. English. be.

RESPIRATORY TECHNOLOGY. **VFOAT** Technologie Respiratoire. V. 7, No. 2- June 1971-. 0319-1494. Periodical. CN. English (includes some text in French). ir. $9.28. Respiratory Technology, 406-504 Main Street, Winnipeg Manitoba R3B 1B8 Canada. **Tel** (204)942-6798. **Ed** Ted Yaehemetz. **Ind/Abst** Cumul. Index Nurs. Allied Health Lit. **DD** 615.836. **NLM** W1 RE248M. adv acc. **Circ** 2,000. (ctrl). Articles, ads, news related to the respiratory technologists membership publication. *Canadian Inhalation Therapy, 0008-3852.*

RESPIRATORY THERAPY. V. 1- July/Aug. 1971-. 0048-7392. Periodical. US. English. bm. $80.00. Brentwood Publishing Corporation, PO Box 49045, Los Angeles CA 90049. **Tel** (213)826-8388. **Ed** Esther Gross. **Ind/Abst** Hospit. Lit. Index, Cumul. Index Nurs. Allied Health Lit. **NLM** W1 RE248MR. bk rev. adv acc. **Circ** 19,678. (ctrl). On medical advances, department management, training, licensing equipment, new techniques, supplies and facilities report.

RESUSCITATION. V. 1- Mar. 1972-. 0300-9572. Periodical. UK. English. qt. Elsevier Scientific Publishers, Ireland Limited, PO Box 85, Limerick Ireland. **Ind/Abst** Excerpta Med., Biol. Abstr., Chem. Abstr., Curr. Contents, Life Sci. Collect., Index Med., Hospit. Lit. Index. **NLM** W1 RE2497K. **CODEN** RSUSBS.

REVUE DE PNEUMOLOGIE CLINIQUE : LE POUMON ET LE COEUR. **VFOAT** Pneumologie Clinique. V. 40, No 1 (Jan./Feb. 1984)-. Periodical. French. bm. Masson Publishing USA Inc, 1 Ames Court, Plainview NY 11803. **Ind/Abst** Index Med., Chem. Abstr., CIS Abstr., Excerpta Med. **NLM** W1. *Poumon et le Coeur.*

REVUE FRANCAISE DES MALADIES RESPIRATOIRES *CEASED.* Began in 1973. Ceased with Vol. 11, No. 6. 0301-0279. Periodical. FR. French. bm. Masson Publishing USA Inc, 211 East 43rd Street/Room 1306, New York NY 10017. **Tel** (212)370-1937. **Ind/Abst** Life Sci. Collect., Excerpta Med., Biol. Abstr., CIS Abstr., Chem. Abstr. **NLM** W1 RE849. **CODEN** RFMRAT. *Revue de la Tuberculose et de Pneumologie, 0035-1795.*

SELECTED PAPERS. **Main/Corp** Royal Netherlands Tuberculosis Association. **VFOAT** Selected Papers - Royal Netherlands Tuberculosis Association. V. 1- 1961-. 0485-5515. Periodical. English. ir. **Ind/Abst** Excerpta Med. **NLM** W1 SE32NP. *Proceedings of the Tuberculosis Research Council.*

SEMINARS IN RESPIRATORY MEDICINE. **VFOAT** Respiratory Medicine. V. 1- July 1979-. 0192-9755. Periodical. US. English. qt. $55.00. Thieme-Stratton Inc, 381 Park Avenue South/ Suite 1501, New York NY 10016. **Tel** (212)683-5088. **Ed** Thomas Petty and Reuben Cherniack. **Ind/Abst** Excerpta Med., Sci. Cit. Index, Abr. Ed. **NLM** W1 SE489I. adv acc. **Circ** 2,600. Topic-oriented journal designed for practitioners specializing in respiratory medicine and diseases.

STATE OF ALASKA TUBERCULOSIS REPORT. **Main/Corp** Alaska. Section of Communicable Disease Control. **VFOAT** Tuberculosis Annual Report. US. English. an. **LC** RA644.T7. **DD** 614.54209798.

TECHNOLOGY FOR RESPIRATORY THERAPY. 8756-8616. Periodical. US. English. mo. $70.00. ECRI, 5200 Butler Pike, Plymouth Meeting PA 19462. **Tel** (215)825-6000. **Ed** J Nobel. **DD** 616. bk rev. A newsletter for pulmonary specialists and respiratory therapists, summarizing health care technology issues, and reporting recalls, hazards, and problems with medical devices. *Health Devices Update. Respiratory Therapy.*

THORAX. *See* Medicine.

TUBERCLE. V. 1- Oct. 1919-. 0041-3879. Periodical. UK. English. qt. $80.00. Churchill Livingstone, PO Box 11318, Birmingham AL 35202. **Tel** (205)991-6920. **Ed** K P Goldman. **Ind/Abst** Life Sci. Collect., Excerpta Med., Pestdoc, Ringdoc, Vetdoc, Index Med., Biol. Abstr., Sci. Cit. Index, Abr. Ed., Hospit. Lit. Index. **NLM** W1 TU265J. **CODEN** TUBEAS. adv acc. An international forum for the exchange of knowledge on tuberculosis and other mycobacterial diseases. Addresses all aspects of respiratory maladies- clinical, bacterio-logical, and epidemiological. *BTTA Review, 0300-9602.*

TUBERCULOSE. **VFOAT** Tuberculosis. No. 32- Mar. 1974-. Periodical. French (English). ir. *Tuberculosis.*

TUBERCULOSIS BEDS IN HOSPITALS. 0095-1129. US. English. Tuberculosis Beds in Hospitals, Atlanta GA 30333. **LC** RC313. **DD** 362.19699500973. *Tuberculosis Beds in Hospitals and Sanatoria, 0732-5061.*

TUBERCULOSIS IN INDIANA. 0092-959X. US. English. an. Indiana State Board of Health, 1330 West Michigan Street, Indianapolis IN 46207. **LC** RC313.I6. **DD** 614.54209772.

Medicine—Surgery

TUBERCULOSIS IN TEXAS; ANNUAL REPORT. Main/Corp Texas. Bureau of Tuberculosis Services. 0192-5296. US. English. an. Department of Health Resources, Bureau of Tuberculosis Services, Austin TX 78756. LC RC313.T4. DD 614.54209764.

TUBERCULOSIS IN THE UNITED STATES. 0149-2616. US. English. an. Department of Health Education and Welfare, Tuberculosis Control Division, Atlanta GA 30333. LC RC313. DD 614.5420973. NLM W2 A C739T.

TUBERCULOSIS PROGRAMS. 1970-. 0090-9351. US. English. an. Center for Disease Control Tuberculosis Branch, Atlanta GA 30330. LC RC306. DD 312.39950973.

TUBERCULOSIS STATISTICS. See Statistics.

TUBERCULOSIS STATISTICS. MORBIDITY AND MORTALITY. See Statistics.

ZEITSCHRIFT FUR ERKRANKUNGEN DER ATMUNGSORGANE. Vol. 140- March 1974-. 0303-657X. Periodical. German. bm. $48.78. Kunst & Wissen Erich Bieber, Dufourstrasse 51, CH-8008 Zurich Switzerland. Tel 011-41-1-69 44 20. Ind/Abst Life Sci. Collect., Excerpta Med., Index Med., Biol. Abstr., Chem. Abstr. NLM W1 ZE321Q. CODEN ZEATAM. Zeitschrift fur Erkrankungen der Atmungsorgane Mit Folia Bronchologica, 0044-2631; Monatsschrift fur Lungenkrankheiten und Tuberkulosebekampfung, 0026-931X.

ZEITSCHRIFT FUR ERKRANKUNGEN DER ATMUNGSORGANE MIT FOLIA BRONCHOLOGICA. VFOAT Folia Bronchologica. Vol. 130-139. 0044-2631. Periodical. GE. German. bm. 58.10. Deutscher Buch Export-Import, Leninstrasse 16, DDR-701 Leipzig East Germany. Tel 70131. Ed W Schilling. Ind/Abst Chem. Abstr., Index Med. NLM W1 ZE321Q. bk rev. adv acc. Publishes new medical literature on all diseases of respiratory organs for practitioners, research workers and other specialists dealing with diagnostics, treatment, prevention and control of these diseases. Zeitschrift Fur Tuberkulose Und Erkrankungen der Thoraxorgane.

ZENTRALBLATT PNEUMONOLOGIE-TUBERKULOSE. Periodical. German. bm. Springer Verlag-New York Inc, 175 5th Avenue, New York NY 10010. Tel (212)460-1500.

SURGERY

5-YEAR CUMULATED BIBLIOGRAPHY OF ORTHOPAEDIC SURGERY. See Bibliographies.

AAOMS DIRECTORY. See Yearbooks, Almanacs, Directories.

ABMS DIRECTORY OF CERTIFIED COLON AND RECTAL SURGEONS. See Yearbooks, Almanacs, Directories.

ABMS DIRECTORY OF CERTIFIED NEUROLOGICAL SURGEONS. See Yearbooks, Almanacs, Directories.

ABMS DIRECTORY OF CERTIFIED ORTHOPAEDIC SURGEONS. See Yearbooks, Almanacs, Directories.

ABMS DIRECTORY OF CERTIFIED PLASTIC SURGEONS. See Yearbooks, Almanacs, Directories.

ABMS DIRECTORY OF CERTIFIED SURGEONS. See Yearbooks, Almanacs, Directories.

ABMS DIRECTORY OF CERTIFIED THORACIC SURGEONS. See Yearbooks, Almanacs, Directories.

ACTA CHIRURGIAE ORTHOPAEDICAE ET TRAUMATOLOGIAE CECHOSLOVACA. Vol. 17- 1950-. 0001-5415. Periodical. CS. Czech. bm. $57.80. Artia, Ve-Smeckach 30, Praha 1 Czechoslovakia. Ind/Abst Excerpta Med., Index Med., CIS Abstr. NLM W1 AC776N. Index in last issue of volume - attached. Sbornik Pro Chirurgii Pohyboveho Ustroji.

ACTA CHIRURGIAE PLASTICAE. 0001-5423. CS. English (articles in French, German or Russian with summaries in English, French, German, Russian and Spanish). qt. $77.00. Karger Libri AG, Petersgraben 31, CH-4009 Basel 11 Switzerland. Tel 061/390880. Ind/Abst Life Sci. Collect., Excerpta Med., Index Med., Sci. Cit. Index, Abr. Ed., Hospit. Lit. Index. NLM W1 AC7762.

ACTA CHIRURGICA ACADEMIAE SCIENTIARUM HUNGARICAE CEASED. VFOAT Acta Chirurgica. Vol. 1-23. 0001-5431. Periodical. HU. English (German, French or Russian). qt. $44.00 US. Akademiai Kiado, POB 24, 1363, Budapest Hungary. Tel 111-010. Ed A Babics. Ind/Abst Excerpta Med., Chem. Abstr., Index Med. NLM W1 AC7767. CODEN ACAHA3. Index in last issue of volume - attached. bk rev. adv acc. Circ 500.

ACTA CHIRURGICA AUSTRIACA. Yearly V. 1- 1969-. 0001-544X. Periodical. AU. German. bm. 680.00. Bruder Hollinek, Gallgasse 40 A, A 1130 Wien X111 Austria. Tel (0222)845346. Ind/Abst Life Sci. Collect., Excerpta Med. NLM W1 AC7768. bk rev. Austrian surgery.

ACTA CHIRURGICA BELGICA. V. 45-1946-. 0001-5458. Periodical. BE. French, English and Dutch. bm. $49.40. Association Societe, Scientifique Medica Belgica, 43 rue des Champs Elysees, B1050 Brussels Belgium. Tel 02 648 04 68. Ed Mendes da Costa. Ind/Abst Life Sci. Collect., Excerpta Med., CIS Abstr., Biol. Abstr., Chem. Abstr., Index Med., Hospit. Lit. Index. NLM W1 AC777. CODEN ACBEAX. bk rev. adv acc. Circ 1,050. (ctrl). General surgery periodical. All aspects of different clinical specialities and research accepted. Only original texts. Scientific review committee. Journal de Chirurgie et Annales de la Societe Belge de Chirurgie.

ACTA CHIRURGICA HUNGARICA. VFOAT Acta Chirurgica. Vol. 24, No. 1-. 0231-4614. Periodical. English. qt. Ind/Abst Index Med., Excerpta Med. NLM W1 AC7773. Acta Chirurgica Academiae Scientiarum Hungaricae, 0001-5431.

ACTA CHIRURGICA ITALICA. V. 10-1954-. 0001-5466. Periodical. IT. Italian. qt. 80.000. La Garangola, Via Montona 4, 35100 Padova Italy. Tel 049/20667. Ed La Garangola. Ind/Abst Excerpta Med., Biol. Abstr. NLM W1 AC7778. CODEN ACHIA7. bk rev. adv acc. Circ 1,200. Acta Chirurgica Patavina, 0390-6892.

ACTA CHIRURGICA IUGOSLAVICA. 0001-5474. YU. contributions in Serbo-Croatian. Mladost Export Import, POB 1028 Ilica 30, 41000 Zagreb Yugoslavia. Ind/Abst Index Med. NLM W1 AC7775. Acta Chirurgica.

ACTA CHIRURGICA SCANDINAVICA. V. 52- 1919/20-. 0001-5482. Periodical. SW. English (articles in French or German, with summaries in French, German and English, V. 52-95). bm. 770 Domestic, $100.00 Foreign. Almqvist & Wiksell Tryckeri AB, S-75181 Uppsala Sweden. Tel (013)121993. Ed Lars Thuren and S Lennquist. Ind/Abst Life Sci. Collect., Excerpta Med., Biol. Abstr., Chem. Abstr., Nuci. Sci. Abstr., Index Med., Energy Res. Abstr., Sci. Cit. Index, Abr. Ed., Hospit. Lit. Index. NLM W1 AC7812. CODEN ACHSA3. (cum index). bk rev. adv acc. Circ 2,500. (ctrl). Scientific publications within general surgery. Nordiskt Arkiv. Avd. 1. Arkiv for Kururgi.

ACTA NEUROCHIRURGICA. Vol. 1- Feb. 1950-. 0001-6268. Periodical. AU. English (articles and summaries in German, French, Italian or Spanish). ir. $400.00. Springer Verlag-New York Inc, 175 5th Avenue, New York NY 10010. Tel (212)460-1500. Ed F Loew. Ind/Abst Life Sci. Collect., Excerpta Med., Biol. Abstr., Chem. Abstr., Nuci. Sci. Abstr., Index Med., Sci. Cit. Index, Abr. Ed., Hospit. Lit. Index. NLM W1 AC866. CODEN ACNUA5. bk rev. Fields of interest: clinical neurosurgery-diagnosis and diagnostic techniques, operative surgery and results, postoperative treatment and research work in neurosciences.

ACTA NEUROCHIRURGICA. SUPPLEMENTUM. (ACTA NEUROCHIRURGICA : SUPPLEMENTUM). 0065-1419. Monographic Series. English. ir. Springer Verlag, 44 Hartz Way, Secaucus NJ 07094. Ind/Abst Life Sci. Collect., Index Med., Biol. Abstr., Nuci. Sci. Abstr. LC UNC. NLM W1 AC8661. CODEN ANCSBM.

ACTUALITES CHIRURGICALES. 1971-. 0376-6276. French. ir. Scientific & Medical Publ of France, 16 East 34th Street, New York NY 10016. Tel (212)683-4441. Ed C Olivier. NLM W3 AC192.

ADVANCES AND TECHNICAL STANDARDS IN NEUROSURGERY. V. 1- 1974-. 0095-4829. Periodical. US. English. ir. Springer Verlag, 44 Hartz Way, Secaucus NJ 07094. Tel (201)348-4033. Ed H Krayenbuehl. Ind/Abst Index Med. NLM W1 AD407. Circ 800. Publishes contributions from those fields of neurosurgery and related areas in which important recent advances have been made. Part of each volume is dedicated to detailed descriptions of standard operative procedures.

ADVANCES IN ANESTHESIA. Vol. 1 (1984)-. 0737-6146. US. English. an. Year Book Medical Publishers, 35 East Wacker Drive, Chicago IL 60601. Ed T James Gallagher. LC RD78.3. DD 617.9605. NLM W1.

ADVANCES IN NEUROSURGERY. 0302-2366. Monographic Series. US. English. ir. Springer Verlag-New York Inc, 175 5th Avenue, New York NY 10010. Tel (212)460-1584. Ind/Abst Chem. Abstr. LC UNC. NLM W1 AD684N. CODEN AVNSBV. Studies in neurosurgery.

ADVANCES IN OPHTHALMIC PLASTIC AND RECONSTRUCTIVE SURGERY. Vol. 1-. 0276-3508. Periodical. US. English. an. Pergamon Press, 395 Sawmill River Road, Elmsford NY 10523.

ADVANCES IN ORTHOPAEDIC SURGERY. V. 7, N. 1 (July/Aug. 1983)-. 0738-2278. Periodical. US. English. bm. $65.00. Williams & Wilkins, 428 East Preston Street, Baltimore MD 21202. Tel (301)528-4000. Ed Andrew F Brooker. LC RD701. DD 617.3005. NLM ZWE 168. adv acc. Circ 2,700. State-of-the-art orthopaedic journal includes in-depth condensations of important articles from the current literature plus review articles. Orthopaedic Survey, 0147-6793.

ADVANCES IN PLASTIC AND RECONSTRUCTIVE SURGERY. Vol. 1 (1984)-. 0748-5212. US. English. an. $60.00. Yearbook Medical Publishers, 35 East Wacker Drive, Chicago IL 60601. DD 617.

ADVANCES IN SURGERY. V. 1-. 0065-3411. US. English. an. Yearbook Medical Publishers, 35 East Wacker Drive, Chicago IL 60601. Ed C E Welch. Ind/Abst Index Med., Energy Res. Abstr. LC RD1. DD 617.007. NLM W1 AD877.

AESTHETIC PLASTIC SURGERY. V. 1-. 0364-216X. Periodical. US. English. qt. Springer Verlag-New York Inc, 175 5th Avenue, New York NY 10010. Tel (212)460-1500. Ed B O Rogers. Ind/Abst Life Sci. Collect., Excerpta Med., Index Med. LC RD119. DD 617.95005. NLM W1 AE957. The journal publishes original articles and case reports dealing with surgical techniques, complications and their treatment, psychosocial factors, and aesthetic reconstructive surgery.

AGGIORNAMENTI DI TECNICA CHIRURGICA. 1-. 0391-5565. Monographic Series. IT. Italian. ir. Edizioni Minerva Medica, Bramante 83-85, Torino 10126 Italy. Ed E Malan. NLM W1 AG334K.

AGGIORNAMENTI IN CHIRURGIA GENERALE. Monographic Series. IT. Italian. bm. Soc Edit Universo, via G B Morgagni 1, Roma 00161 Italy. NLM W1 AG336C.

AKTUELLE CHIRURGIE. 9- 1974-. 0001-785X. Periodical. German. bm. Thieme-Stratton Inc, 381 Park Avenue South, New York NY 10016. Tel (212)683-5088. Ind/Abst Life Sci. Collect., Excerpta Med. NLM W1 AK991C. (cum index). Actuelle Chirurgie.

THE AMERICAN JOURNAL OF COSMETIC SURGERY. (THE AMERICAN JOURNAL OF COSMETIC SURGERY : JOURNAL OF THE AMERICAN SOCIETY OF COSMETIC SURGEONS AND OFFICIAL PUBLICATION OF THE AMERICAN SOCIETY OF LIPO-SUCTION SURGERY). Vol. 1, No. 1 (Winter 1984)-. 0748-8068. Periodical. US. English. qt. $65.00. American Academy of Cosmetic Surgery Inc, 6333 Wilshire Boulevard/Suite 409, Los Angeles CA 90048. Tel (213)653-7700. Ed Richard Aronsohn. NLM W1. adv acc. Circ 5,000. (ctrl). Only medical journal devoted exclusively to cosmetic surgery.

THE AMERICAN JOURNAL OF SURGERY. V. 18, No. 9-V. 40. 0002-9610. Periodical. US. English. $67.00. Technical Publishing Company, 875 Third Avenue, New York NY 10022. Tel (212)605-9400. Ind/Abst Excerpta Med., Life Sci. Collect., Index Med., CIS Abstr., Chem. Abstr., Energy Res. Abstr., Sci. Cit. Index, Abr. Ed., Hospit. Lit. Index. LC RD1. DD 617. NLM W1 AM523. CODEN AJSUAB. (cum index). Available on microfilm. American Surgery and Gynecology, 0271-6402.

Medicine—Surgery

THE AMERICAN JOURNAL OF SURGICAL PATHOLOGY. V. 1- Mar. 1977-. 0147-5185. Periodical. US. English. mo. Raven Press, 1140 Avenue of the Americas, New York NY 10036. Tel (212)575-0335. **Ind/Abst** Life Sci. Collect., Excerpta Med., Index Med., Biol. Abstr., Energy Res. Abstr. LC RD57. DD 617.7105. **NLM** W1 AM523BJ. **CODEN** AJSPDX.

THE AMERICAN SURGEON. V. 17- Jan. 1951-. 0003-1348. Periodical. US. English. mo. $68.00. Lippincott/Harper, 2350 Virginia Avenue, Hagerstown MD 21740. **Ind/Abst** Excerpta Med., Life Sci. Collect., Index Med., Int. Aerosp. Abstr., Biol. Abstr., Energy Res. Abstr., Hospit. Lit. Index, Sci. Cit. Index, Abr. Ed. LC RD1. **NLM** W1 AM816. **CODEN** AMSUAW.
Southern Surgeon.

ANAESTHESIOLOGIA ES INTENSIV THERAPIA. 0133-5405. Periodical. HU. Hungarian. bm. Akademiai Kiado, POB 24, 1363 Budapest Hungary. **Ind/Abst** Chem. Abstr. **CODEN** AITHD7. Anaesthesiologia Es Reanimatio, 0324-4520.

ANAESTHESIOLOGIE UND INTENSIVMEDIZIN. VFOAT Anaesthesiology and Intensive Care Medicine. 109-. 0171-1814. Monographic Series. German (some articles in English). ir. **Ind/Abst** Excerpta Med., Biol. Abstr., Chem. Abstr. **NLM** W1 AN103YJ. **CODEN** ANIMD2. Anaesthesiologie und Wiederbelebung.

ANAESTHESIOLOGY. (ANAESTHESIOLOGY : SOUND RECORDING). No. 1 (1983)-. 0824-7412. Periodical. CN. English. ir. Medifacts Ltd, 471 Richmond Road, Ottawa Ontario K2A 0G3 Canada. DD 617.9605.

ANALES DE CIRUGIA. See Yearbooks, Almanacs, Directories.

ANESTEZIOLOGIJA I REANIMATOLOGIJA. (ANESTEZIOLOGIIA I REANIMATOLOGIIA). Jan./Feb. 1977-. 0201-7563. Periodical. UR. Russian (summaries in English). bm. $36.00. Victor Kamkin Inc (71102), 12224 Parklawn Drive, Rockville MD 20852. Tel (301)881-5973. **Ind/Abst** Excerpta Med., Index Med., Biol. Abstr., Chem. Abstr. **NLM** W1 AN217R. **CODEN** AREAD8.
Eksperimentalnaia Khirurgiia i Anesteziologiia.

ANESTHESIOLOGY NEWS. 0747-4679. Periodical. US. English. mo. $28.00. McMahon Publishing Company, 83 Peaceable Street, Georgetown CT 06829.

ANNALES CHIRURGIAE ET GYNAECOLOGIAE. V. 65- 1976-. 0355-9521. Periodical. FI. English. bm. $140.00. Finnish Medical Society Duodecim, Kalevankatu 11 A, 00100 Helsinki Finland. Tel 358-0-611050. Ed M Lempinen. **Ind/Abst** Life Sci. Collect., Excerpta Med., Index Med., Biol. Abstr., Chem. Abstr. **NLM** W1 AN3094. **CODEN** ACGYDJ. adv acc. **Circ** 2,000. Surgical research and closely related topics in operative gynecology and obstetrics as well as anesthesiology. Annales Chirurgiae et Gynaecologiae Fenniae, 0003-3855.

ANNALES DE CHIRURGIE. V. 3- 1950-. 0003-3944. Periodical. FR. French. mo. $234.15. Semaine des Hopitaux, 15 rue Saint Benoit, 75278 Paris Cedex 06 France. Tel 548-42-60. **Ind/Abst** Life Sci. Collect., Excerpta Med., Index Med. **NLM** W1 AN327L. Cahiers et Annales de Chirurgie.

ANNALES DE CHIRURGIE DE LA MAIN. Vol. 1, No. 1-. 0753-9053. Periodical. English (text also in French). qt. $99.00. **Ind/Abst** Excerpta Med. **NLM** W1.

ANNALES DE CHIRURGIE PLASTIQUE ET ESTHETIQUE. Vol. 28, No. 1-. 0003-3960. Periodical. French (with summaries in French and English). qt. Semaine des Hopitaux, 15 rue Saint Benoit, 75278 Paris Cedex 06 France. Tel 548-42-60. **Ind/Abst** Excerpta Med., Index Med. **NLM** W1. Annales de Chirurgie Plastique, 0003-3960.

ANNALES DE L'ANESTHESIOLOGIE FRANCAISE CEASED. Began in 1960? Ceased V. 22. 0003-4061. Periodical. FR. French (summaries in English, German, Italian, Russian and Spanish). mo. **Ind/Abst** Life Sci. Collect., Excerpta Med., CIS Abstr., Biol. Abstr., Chem. Abstr. LC UNC. DD 617.96. **NLM** W1 AN343S. **CODEN** AANFAE.

ANNALI ITALIANI DI CHIRURGIA. V. 1- Jan. 1922-. 0003-469X. Periodical. IT. Italian. bm. 40.00. Casa Editrice L Cappelli Spa, Via Marsili 9, 40124 Bologna Italy. Tel 330411. Ed G Marcozzi. **Ind/Abst** Excerpta Med., Index Med., Biol. Abstr. **NLM** W1 AN541. **CODEN** AICHAL. bk rev. adv acc. **Circ** 2,000. Covers general surgery.

ANNALS OF PLASTIC SURGERY. V. 1- Jan. 1978-. 0148-7043. Periodical. US. English. mo. $91.00. Little Brown & Company, 34 Beacon Street, Boston MA 02106. Tel (617)227-0730. Ed Lars M Vistnes. **Ind/Abst** Excerpta Med., Cumul. Index Nurs. Allied Health Lit., Index Med., Biol. Abstr., Energy Res. Abstr. LC RD118.AL. DD 617.95005. **NLM** W1 AN62L. **CODEN** APCSD4. bk rev. adv acc. **Circ** 4,000. Published specifically for the worldwide community of plastic surgery and related disciplines, original articles on clinical, plastic and reconstructive surgery.

ANNALS OF THE ROYAL COLLEGE OF SURGEONS OF ENGLAND. Main/Corp Royal College of Surgeons of England. V. 1- July 1947-. 0035-8843. Periodical. UK. English. bm. 60.00 Domestic, 69.00 Foreign. Royal College of Surgeons of England, 35-43 Lincoln's Fields, London WC2A 3PN England. Tel (01)407 3474. Ed R M Kirk. **Ind/Abst** Life Sci. Collect., Excerpta Med., Index Med., Biol. Abstr., Hospit. Lit. Index, Sci. Cit. Index, Abr. Ed. **NLM** W1 AN627E. **CODEN** ARCSAF. Index in last issue of volume - attached. (cum index). bk rev. adv acc. **Circ** 14,000. To report important clinical advances in all forms of surgery, dental surgery, and anaesthesia.

THE ANNALS OF THORACIC SURGERY. V. 1- Jan. 1965-. 0003-4975. Periodical. US. English. mo. $72.00. Little Brown & Company, 34 Beacon Street, Boston MA 02106. Tel (617)227-0730. Ed Thomas B Ferguson. **Ind/Abst** Life Sci. Collect., Excerpta Med., Cumul. Index Nurs. Allied Health Lit., Ref. Source, Biol. Abstr., Index Med., Nucl. Sci. Abstr., Energy Res. Abstr., Index Med., Sci. Cit. Index, Abr. Ed., Hospit. Lit. Index. LC RD536. DD 617.374005. **NLM** W1 AN627H. **CODEN** ATHSAK. bk rev. adv acc. **Circ** 7,600. Timely articles by outstanding cardiovascular and thoracic surgeons in the U.S. and abroad, including how to articles on surgical techniques.

ANNUAL BIBLIOGRAPHY OF ORTHOPAEDIC SURGERY. See Bibliographies.

ANNUAL BOOK OF ASTM STANDARDS. SECTION 13, MEDICAL DEVICES. Main/Corp American Society for Testing and Materials. VFOAT Medical Devices. Began with: 1983, Vol. 13.01. US. English. an. **NLM** W 26.

THE ANNUAL MEETING OF NORDISK NEUROKIRURGISK FORENING. Periodical. English. ir. **NLM** W1 AN754Q.

ANNUAL REPORT - BOARD OF REGISTRATION IN PODIATRY. Main/Corp Massachusetts. Board of Registration in Podiatry. US. English. an. Leverett Saltonstall Building Government Center, 100 Cambridge Street, Boston MA 02202. LC RD563. DD 353.97440084197585.

ARCHIV FUR JAPANISCHE CHIRURGIE. See Genealogy and Heraldry - Archives.

ARCHIVES OF ORTHOPAEDIC AND TRAUMATIC SURGERY. See Genealogy and Heraldry - Archives.

ARCHIVES OF SURGERY. See Genealogy and Heraldry - Archives.

ARCHIVIO PUTTI DI CHIRURGIA DEGLI ORGANI DI MOVIMENTO. See Genealogy and Heraldry - Archives.

ARCHIVIO SICILIANO DI MEDICINA E CHIRURGIA. See Genealogy and Heraldry - Archives.

ARTIFICIAL ORGANS. V. 1- Aug. 1977-. 0160-564X. Periodical. US. English. qt. Raven Press, 1140 Avenue of the Americas, New York NY 10036. Tel (212)575-0335. **Ind/Abst** Life Sci. Collect., Excerpta Med., Index Med., Biol. Abstr., Chem. Abstr. LC RD130. DD 617.95. **NLM** W1 AR956E. **CODEN** ARORD7.

ASIAN ARCHIVES OF ANAESTHESIOLOGY & RESUSCITATION. See Genealogy and Heraldry - Archives.

ATTUALITA IN CHIRURGIA. V. 1-. 0390-5527. Periodical. IT. Italian. qt. $45.00. Edizioni Luigi Pozzi, Via Panama 68, Rome Italy. **NLM** W1 AT8485.

AUDIO-DIGEST. SURGERY. V. 1- 19 -. 0571-8651. US. English. sm. $192.72. Audio Digest Foundation, 1577 Chevy Chase Drive, Glendale CA 91206. Tel (213)245-8505. Ed Claron L Oakley. A twice-monthly interactive system of audio cassette postgraduate medical education, with each one-hour program eligible for two Category I credit hours.

AUSTRALIAN AND NEW ZEALAND JOURNAL OF SURGERY. (THE AUSTRALIAN AND NEW ZEALAND JOURNAL OF SURGERY). V. 1- June 1931-. 0004-8682. Periodical. AT. English. mo. $75.00 Foreign, $110. US/Canada. Blackwell Scientific Publishers, 107 Barry Street, Carlton Victoria 3053 Australia. **Ind/Abst** Life Sci. Collect., Excerpta Med., Index Med., Int. Aerosp. Abstr., Biol. Abstr., Hospit. Lit. Index. **NLM** W1 AU499. **CODEN** ANZJA7. (cum index). Journal of the College of Surgeons of Australasia.

BEITRAGE ZUR NEUROCHIRURGIE CEASED. 1959-1970. 0067-5158. Periodical. German. ir. Deutscher Buch Export-Import, Leninstrasse 16, DDR-701 Leipzig East Germany.

BESSATSU SEIKEI GEKA. VFOAT Seikei Geka. No. 1-. Periodical. JA. Japanese. mo. $142.00. Japan Publishing Trading Company Ltd, PO Box 5030 Tokyo International, Tokyo 100-31, Japan. Tel 03 811 7238. **Ind/Abst** Biol. Abstr. **NLM** W1 BE954F. **CODEN** SEGEAW. bk rev. adv acc. **Circ** 9,000. The number one Japanese journal on orthopedic surgery.

BIBLIOGRAPHY OF SURGERY OF THE HAND. See Bibliographies.

BINOCULAR VISION. Vol. 1, No. 1-. 0749-386X. Periodical. US. English. qt. Binoculus, 2500 NW 23rd Terrace, Gainesville FL 32605. DD 617.

BOLETINES Y TRABAJOS - ACADEMIA ARGENTINA DE CIRUGIA. V. 53- 1969-. Periodical. Spanish. ir. **NLM** W1. Boletines y Trabajos - Sociedad de Cirugia de Buenos Aires.

BRISTOL MEDICO-CHIRURGICAL JOURNAL (1963). (BRISTOL MEDICO-CHIRURGICAL JOURNAL). Began with: Vol. 78, published in 1963. 0308-6356. Periodical. UK. English. qt. 12.00. Bristol Medico Chirurgical Society, Medical School Library, University Walk, Bristol 8 England. Tel 0272-682320. Ed M G Wilson. **Ind/Abst** Index Med. **NLM** W1 BR323. bk rev. adv acc. **Circ** 9,000. (ctrl). Scientific articles on medicine and surgery and comments on local medical affairs (West of England). Medical Journal of the South-West.

BRITISH JOURNAL OF ORAL & MAXILLOFACIAL SURGERY. (THE BRITISH JOURNAL OF ORAL & MAXILLOFACIAL SURGERY). VFOAT British Journal of Oral and Maxillofacial Surgery. Vol. 22, No. 1 (Feb. 1984)-. 0266-4356. Periodical. UK. English. bm. 42.00 ($80.00). Subscription Manager, Journal Department, Longman Group Ltd, Fouth Avenue, Harlow Essex CM19 5AA U K. **Ind/Abst** Index Med., Excerpta Med., Life Sci. Collect. **NLM** W1. British Journal of Oral Surgery, 0007-117X.

BRITISH JOURNAL OF ORAL SURGERY CEASED. Vol. 1-21. 0007-117X. Periodical. UK. English. qt. Longman Group Ltd, Fourth Avenue, Harlow Essex CM19 5AA England. **Ind/Abst** Life Sci. Collect., Excerpta Med., Biol. Abstr., Index Med., Nuci. Sci. Abstr. **NLM** W1. **CODEN** BJOSBV.

BRITISH JOURNAL OF PLASTIC SURGERY. Began with: Vol. 1 (Apr. 1948). 0007-1226. Periodical. UK. English. qt. $60.00. British Journal of Plastic Surgery, PO Box 11318, Brimingham AL 35202. Tel (205)991-6920. Ed Anthony C H Watson. **Ind/Abst** Life Sci. Collect., Excerpta Med., Biol. Abstr., Chem. Abstr., Nuci. Sci. Abstr., Sci. Cit. Index, Abr. Ed., Index Med. **NLM** W1 BR613. **CODEN** BJPSAZ. bk rev. adv acc. The official journal of the British Association of Plastic Surgeons. Presents significant findings from international contributors on latest techniques and procedures, profusely illustrated.

BRITISH JOURNAL OF SURGERY. Began with: 1, published in 1913. 0007-1323. Periodical. UK. English. mo. 52.50. Butterworths Scientific Ltd, Box 63, Westbury House/Bury Street, Guilford GU1 5BH England. Tel 0484-31261. Ed C W Jamieson. **Ind/Abst** Life Sci. Collect., Pestdoc, Ringdoc, Vetdoc, Excerpta Med., Biol. Abstr., Chem. Abstr., Nuci. Sci. Abstr., Index Med., Hospit. Lit. Index. **NLM** W1 BR638X. **CODEN** BJSUAM. (cum index). bk rev. adv acc. **Circ** 7,000. International journal of general surgery with particular emphasis on surgical research, includes case notes, reviews, original research and correspondence.

BULLETIN DE L'ACADEMIE DE CHIRURGIE DENTAIRE. Yearly V. 20- (No. 20-). 0339-9710. Periodical. FR. French. an. $9.32. Academie de Chirurgie Dentaire, 22 rue Emile-Menier, 75016 Paris France. **Ind/Abst** Index Dent. Lit. **NLM**

Medicine—Surgery

W1 BU5233. *Bulletin de l'Academie Dentaire, 0339-9729.*

BUTTERWORTHS INTERNATIONAL MEDICAL REVIEWS. SURGERY. VFOAT Surgery. 1-. 0260-0188. Monographic Series. UK. English. Ind/Abst Biol. Abstr. NLM W1 BU99M. CODEN SURGD4.

CADERNOS DE CIRURGIA. V. 1- Jan./Mar. 1974-. 0100-0462. Periodical. English (articles in Portuguese). ir. NLM W1 CA109D.

CANADIAN JOURNAL OF SURGERY. VFOAT Journal Canadien de Chirurgie. V. 1- Oct. 1957-. 0008-428X. Periodical. CN. Multilingual (includes some text in French, with summaries in English and French). bm. 30.00 US and Canada, 35.00 Foreign. Canadian Medical Association, CMA House, PO Box 8650, Ottawa Ontario K1G 0G8 Canada. Tel (613)731-9331. Ed L D MacLean and C B Mueller. Ind/Abst Life Sci. Collect., Excerpta Med., Nucl. Sci. Abstr., Biol. Abstr., Chem. Abstr., Index Med., Hospit. Lit. Index, Sci. Cit. Index, Abr. Ed. NLM W1 CA611. CODEN CJSUAX. bk rev. adv acc. Circ 9,000. Contributes to the effective continuing education of surgical specialists and provides Canadian surgeons with an effective vehicle for the dissemination of their observations in research.

CARDIAC/THORACIC SURGERY. Series/Titl Modern Technics in Surgery. VAT Cardiac Thoracic Surgery. 1-. 0163-7029. US. English. ir. Futura Publishing Co, 295 Main Street, Mt Kisco NY 10549.

CARDIOVASCULAR SURGERY. Began in 1962. 0069-0406. US. English. an. American Heart Association, 2005 Hightower Drive, Garland TX 75041. Tel (800)527-3308.

CENTRAL NERVOUS SYSTEM TRAUMA. (CENTRAL NERVOUS SYSTEM TRAUMA : JOURNAL OF THE AMERICAN PARALYSIS ASSOCIATION). Vol. 1, No. 1 (Fall 1984)-. 0737-5999. Periodical. US. English. qt. $65.00 1984, $90.00. Mary Ann Liebert Inc, 157 East 86th Street, New York NY 10028. DD 616. NLM W1.

CHILD'S NERVOUS SYSTEM : CHNS: OFFICIAL JOURNAL OF THE INTERNATIONAL SOCIETY FOR PEDIATRIC NEUROSURGERY. See Medicine - Pediatrics.

CHIRURGIA DEGLI ORGANI DI MOVIMENTO. Vol. 1 1917-. 0009-4749. Periodical. IT. Italian (some summaries in English, French and German). bm. 50.00. Casa Editrice L Cappelli Spa, Via Marsili 9, 40124 Bologna Italy. Tel 330411. Ed Mario Campanacci. Ind/Abst Index Med., Biol. Abstr. NLM W1 CH818V. CODEN CHOMA9. bk rev. adv acc. Circ 3,500. Bone and joint surgery.

CHIRURGIA E PATOLOGIA SPERIMENTALE. Began with V. 1, No. 7, Dec. 1953?. 0009-4757. Periodical. IT. Italian. 30.000. Clinica Chirurgica Uni Cattoic, Via Peneta Sacchetti 526, 0016 Rome Italy. Tel (06)33054437. Ind/Abst Excerpta Med., Index Med. NLM W1 CH8185. adv acc. Circ 300. (ctrl). *Patologia Sperimentale e Chirurgia.*

CHIRURGIA ITALIANA. V. 1- Jan./Feb. 1947-. 0009-4773. Periodical. IT. Italian (English). bm. 75.000. Chirurgia Italiana, Policliaico Burgo, Roma 37134 Verona Italy. Tel 045 933411. Ind/Abst Excerpta Med., Index Med. NLM W1 CH822. bk rev

CHIRURGIA NARZADOW RUCHY I ORTOPEDIA POLSKA. VFOAT Chirurgia Organum Motus et Orthopaedica Polonica, Acta Societatis Orthopaedicae Polonicae. Vol. 1- 1928-. 0009-479X. Periodical. PL. Polish (summaries in French, German, English, or Russian). bm. ARS Polona, Krakowskie Przedmiescie 7, 00-068 Warsaw Poland. Ind/Abst Excerpta Med., Index Med. NLM W1 CH8263.

CHIRURGIA PLASTICA. 1- 1971-. 0340-5664. Periodical. WB. German (English). qt. $76.00. Springer Verlag-New York Inc, 175 Fifth Avenue, New York NY 10010. Tel (212)460-1500. Ed F Finseth, G Friedlebold, G Hierholzer, J T Jackson, S T Jacobsson, E Kastenbauer, S Krupp, G E Matton, G Pfeifer and N Thompson. Ind/Abst Excerpta Med., Sci. Cit. Index, Abr. Ed. DD 617.95. NLM W1 CH827C. CODEN CHRPBY. Fields of interest: general plastic and reconstructive surgery, aesthetic-plastic, hand and craniofacial surgery, microsurgery and treatment of burns. *Chirurgia Plastica et Reconstructiva.*

CHIRURGIA TORACICA. (LA CHIRURGIA TORACICA). V. 1- Feb. 1948-. 0366-6298. Periodical. Italian. bm. Ind/Abst Excerpta Med. NLM W1 CH829.

CHIRURGIA TRIVENETA. V. 1- Jan./June 1961-. 0009-4811. Periodical. IT. Italian. qt. 15.000. Ospedale Civile Maggiore, 1 Div Chirurgica Ple Stefani 1, 37126 Verona Italy. Tel (045)932474. NLM W1 CH83. adv acc. Circ 900. (ctrl).

CHIRURGICA. Series/Titl Acta Universitatis Ouluensis. Series D, Medica. No. 1- 1972-. 0358-4917. Monographic Series. Fl. English (Finnish). ir. Professor Sakari Piha, University of Oulu, 90100 Oulu 10 Finland. Tel 358-81-332133. Ed Leo Hirvonen. NLM W1 AC954NM NO. 15 ETC. adv acc. Circ 500. (ctrl). Monographs, reviews, and dissertations in the field of surgery.

CHIRURGISCHE PRAXIS. 1957-. 0009-4846. Periodical. GW. German. bm. Hans Marseille Verlag, Buerkleinstrasse 12, D-8000 Munchen 22 West Germany. Tel 089/22 79 88. Ind/Abst Excerpta Med. NLM W1 CH835. Index published separately - free - automatically sent. (cum index).

CIRUGIA DEL URUGUAY. V. 4- 1970-. 0009-7381. Periodical. UY. Spanish. bm. Sociedad de Cirugia del Uruguay Hospital de Clinicas, Piso 4, Montevideo Uruguay. Ind/Abst Excerpta Med., Biol. Abstr. NLM W1 CI874T. CODEN CRGUAT. *Revista de Cirugia del Uruguay.*

CIRUGIA Y CIRUJANOS. Vol. 1 Aug 1933-. 0009-7411. Periodical. MX. Spanish (some summaries in English, French, and German). bm. $50.00. Cirugia y Cirujanos, Apartado Postal 7994, Mexico DF Mexico. Ind/Abst Excerpta Med. NLM W1 CI946.

THE CLEFT PALATE JOURNAL. V. 1- Jan. 1964-. 0009-8701. Periodical. US. English. qt. $60.00. American Cleft Palate Association, University of Pittsburgh, 331 Salk Hall, Pittsburgh PA 15261. Tel (412)681-9620. Ed Ralph Shelton Jr. Ind/Abst Life Sci. Collect., Excerpta Med., Index Med., Index Dent. Lit., Ref. Source. LC RD525. DD 617.5225043. NLM W1 CL145. CODEN CLPJA. bk rev. adv acc. Circ 3,000. (ctrl). Multidisciplinary, basic and applied research and clinical articles pertaining to cleft palate and craniofacial patients and their management. *Cleft Palate Bulletin, 0578-4840.*

CLINICAL ANESTHESIOLOGY. 0883-0282. Periodical. US. English. bw. $295.00. Nassau Publications, 11 Forest Street, New Canaan CT 06840. DD 617.

CLINICAL NEUROLOGY AND NEUROSURGERY. See Medicine - Neurology.

CLINICAL NEUROSURGERY. Main/Conf Congress of Neurological Surgeons. V. 1- 1953-. 0069-4827. US. English. ir. Williams & Wilkins, PO Box 64025, Baltimore MD 21202. Tel (301)528-4000. Ind/Abst Index Med., Chem. Abstr., Energy Res. Abstr., Hospit. Lit. Index, Sci. Cit. Index, Abr. Ed. LC RD593.A1. DD 617.48. NLM W1 CL732. CODEN CLNEA8. (cum index).

CLINICAL SURGERY INTERNATIONAL. Vol. 1-. 0263-4422. Monographic Series. UK. English. ir. Churchill Livingstone Inc, 19 West 44th Street, New York NY 10036. LC UNC. DD 617. NLM W1 CL795U.

CLINICS IN PLASTIC SURGERY. V. 1- Jan. 1974-. 0094-1298. Monographic Series. US. English. qt. $75.00. W B Saunders Co, West Washington Square, Philadelphia PA 19105. Tel (215)574-3395. Ed Nanette Bendynd. Ind/Abst Life Sci. Collect., Excerpta Med., Index Med., Energy Res. Abstr., Sci. Cit. Index, Abr. Ed. NLM W1 CL831D. Circ 3,000. Practical updates for the clinician on the latest advances plus topics of current interest to plastic surgeons.

COLLECTED LETTERS - CORRESPONDENCE SOCIETY OF SURGEONS. Main/Corp Correspondence Society of Surgeons. VFOAT Collected Letters in Surgery. 1977. 0162-6477. Periodical. US. English. mo. $59.00. Laux Co Inc, PO Box 700, Ayer MA 01432. Tel (617)772-4890. Ed Myraim Gaitan. bk rev. Circ 1,000.

COLO-PROCTOLOGY, INTERNATIONAL EDITION. (COLO-PROCTOLOGY). V. 2, No. 4 (July/Aug. 1980)-. 0174-2450. Periodical. English. ir. $72.00. NLM W1 CO242. *Protocology (English Ed.).*

COLPOSCOPY & GYNECOLOGIC LASER SURGERY. VFOAT Colposcopy and Gynecologic Laser Surgery. Vol. 1, No. 1-. 0741-6113. Periodical. US. English. qt $75.00. Mary Ann Liebert Inc Publishers, 157 East 86th Street, New York NY 10028. Tel (212)289-2300. Ed James Dorsey. DD 618. NLM W1. bk rev. adv acc. Circ 800. Papers on use of colposcope for diagnoses of gynecologic epitheleal diseases and CO_2 lasers as tools for the gynecology surgeon.

COMPREHENSIVE MANUALS OF SURGICAL SPECIALTIES. V. 1-. 0172-4827. Monographic Series. US. English. ir. Springer Verlag-New York Inc, 175 Fifth Avenue, New York NT 10010. Tel (212)460-1584. LC UNC. NLM W1 CO4526. Contains articles on plastic, cardiac, ambulatory, breast, burns, sports, urology and vascular surgery.

CONTEMPORARY NEUROSURGERY. Began with: 1, in 1979. 0163-2108. Periodical. US. English. ir. $205.00. Williams and Wilkins, 428 East Preston Street, Baltimore MD 21202. Tel (301)528-4000. Ed George T Tindall. NLM W1 CO769ND. adv acc. Circ 1,100. A twenty-seven lesson series features original articles on current topics in neurosurgery.

CONTEMPORARY SURGERY. V. 1- Jan./Feb. 1972-. 0045-8341. Periodical. US. English. $25.00. Bobit Publishing, 2500 Artesia Boulevard, Redondo Beach CA 90278. Tel (213)376-8788. Ind/Abst Hospit. Lit. Index. LC RD1. DD 617.005. NLM W1 CO769Y. CODEN CSGYA.

COSMETIC SURGERY CEASED. (COSMETIC SURGERY : THE OFFICIAL PUBLICATION OF THE AMERICAN ASSOCIATION OF COSMETIC SURGEONS). Vol. 1 (1981)-. 0276-0347. Periodical. US. English. an. EBSCO Industries, PO Box 1943, Birmingham AL 35201.

CURRENT PRACTICE IN ORTHOPAEDIC SURGERY. 1963-. 0070-203X. US. English. be. C V Mosby Company, 11830 Westline Industrial Drive, St Louis MO 63141. Ind/Abst Index Med., Energy Res. Abstr. LC RD701. DD 617.3. NLM W1 CU803D.

CURRENT PROBLEMS IN SURGERY. Jan. 1964-. 0011-3840. Periodical. US. English. mo. $65.00. Yearbook Medical Publishers Inc, 35 East Wacker Drive, Chicago IL 60601. Tel (312)726-9733. Ind/Abst Life Sci. Collect., Excerpta Med., Index Med., Energy Res. Abstr. DD 617. NLM W1 CU804S. CODEN CPSUA.

CURRENT REVIEWS IN CLINICAL ANESTHESIA. Periodical. US. English. bw. $165.00. NLM W1.

CURRENT SURGERY. V. 35- Jan./Feb. 1978-. 0149-7944. Periodical. US. English. bm $49.00. J B Lippincott Company, East Washington Square, Philadelphia PA 19105. Tel (215)238-4273. Ed Lloyd M Nyhus. Ind/Abst Index Med., Chem. Abstr., Energy Res. Abstr. LC RD1. DD 617.005. NLM ZWO 100 Q2. CODEN CUSUDB. bk rev. adv acc. Circ 2,474. Abstracts and reviews and editorial comment for the surgeon, resident, and intern who find it essential to keep abreast of progress and trends in surgery. *Review of Surgery, 0034-6780.*

CURRENT SURGICAL PRACTICE. V. 1- 1976-. 0141-3368. Periodical. UK. English. ir. Yearbook Publishing Company, 35 East Wacker Drive, Chicago IL 60601. NLM W1 CU813.

DETAILED DIAGNOSES AND SURGICAL PROCEDURES FOR PATIENTS DISCHARGED FROM SHORT-STAY HOSPITALS, UNITED STATES. Series/Titl DHHS Publication. US. English. an. Superintendent of Documents, US Government Printing Office, Washington DC 20402.

DEUTSCHE ZEITSCHRIFT FUR MUND-, KIEFER- UND GESICHTS-CHIRURGIE. V. 1-. 0343-3137. Periodical. GW. German (English and French summaries). bm. Carl Hanser Verlag, Postfach 860420/Kolbergerstr 22, 8 Muenchen 86 West Germany. Tel 089/9 26 94-0.

DIRECTORY OF DIPLOMATES. See Yearbooks, Almanacs, Directories.

DRUGS IN SURGERY. Series/Titl PRM : Physicians' Reference Manuals. No. 1 (1982)-. 0824-7021. Periodical. CN. English. sa. 50.00. Drugs in Surgery, c/o STA Communications 63 Place Frontenac, Pointe-Claire Quebec H9R 4Z7 Canada.

Medicine—Surgery

Tel (514)695-7623. Ed Paul Brand. **DD** 617.9. adv acc. **Circ** 2,000. (ctrl). Drug reference manuals.

EUROPEAN JOURNAL OF ANAESTHESIOLOGY. Vol. 1, No. 1 (Mar. 1984)-. 0265-0215. Periodical. UK. English. qt. **NLM** W1.

EUROPEAN SURGICAL RESEARCH. **VFOAT** Europaische Chirurgische Forschung, Recherches Chirurgicales Europeenes. V. 1- 1969-. 0014-312X. Periodical. SZ. English. bm. 336.-. S Karger AG, CH-4009 Basel Switzerland. **Tel** (061)39 08 80. Ed W Brendel and K Messmer. **Ind/Abst** Life Sci. Collect., Excerpta Med., Curr. Contents, Nucl. Sci. Abstr., Index Med., Biol. Abstr., Chem. Abstr., Sci. Cit. Index, Abr. Ed. **NLM** W1 EU733. **CODEN** EUSRBM. adv acc. Features original clinical and experimental papers and short technical notes. Coverage includes surgery, surgical pathophysiology, drug usage, and new surgical techniques.

EXCERPTA MEDICA. SECTION 9. SURGERY. See Indexes/Abstracts.

EXPERIMENTAL SURGERY AND ANESTHESIOLOGY. 0046-2934. Periodical. US. English (Russian). Cambridge Scientific Abstracts Inc, Suite 437/6611 Kenilworth Avenue, Riverdale MD 20840. **NLM** W1 EX513. **CODEN** ESANA.

FACIAL PLASTIC SURGERY. (FACIAL PLASTIC SURGERY : FPS). **VFOAT** FPS. Vol. 1, No. 1 (Fall 1983)-. 0736-6825. Monographic Series. US. English. qt. $64.00. Thieme Inc, 381 Park Avenue South/Suite 1501, New York NY 10016. **Tel** (212)683-5088. Ed M Eugen Tandy and Tony R Bull. **NLM** W1. adv acc. **Circ** 1,500. For the practitioner specializing in techniques and advances in facial plastic surgery.

FLORENCE J. OF SURGERY. **VFOAT** Firenze Chirurgica. Vol. 1, No. 1 (1983)-. Periodical. Italian and English. sa. $50.00. **NLM** W1.

FORSCHUNG UND FORTBILDUNG IN DER CHIRURGIE DES BEWEGUNGSAPPARATES. 1-. German. ir. **NLM** W1.

FORTSCHRITTE DER KIEFER- UND GESICHTS-CHIRURGIE. V. 1- 1955-. 0071-7916. Periodical. German. ir. Thieme-Stratton, 381 Park Avenue South, New York NY 10016. **Tel** (212)683-5088. **Ind/Abst** Index Med., Index Dent. Lit. **NLM** W1 FO855. (cum index).

GEKA CHIRY O. **VFOAT** Surgical Therapy. Vol. 1 Aug. 1950-. 0433-2644. Periodical. JA. Japanese. mo. Japan Publishing Trading Company Ltd, PO Box 5030, Tokyo International, Tokyo 110 Japan.

GEKA TO TAISHA, EIYO. (GEKA TO TAISHA, EIYO : NIHON GEKA TAISHA EIYO GAKKAI, KANZEN JOMYAKU EIYO KENKYUKAI KIKANSHI). **VFOAT** The Japanese Journal of Surgical Metabolism and Nutrition. Began in 1981. 0389-5564. Periodical. JA. Japanese. qt. Nihon Geka Taisha Eiyo Gakkai, 3-28-6 Mejirodai Bunkyo-ku, Tokyo 112 Japan. **Ind/Abst** Chem. Abstr. **CODEN** GTEIDA. Jutsugo Taisha Kenkyu Kaishi.

GENERAL SURGERY SPECIALIST PROGRAM. (GENERAL SURGERY SPECIALIST PROGRAM SOUND RECORDING). **VFOAT** General Surgery. **VAT** General Surgery (Ottawa). No. 1 (1983)-. 0824-7692. Periodical. CN. English. ir. Medifacts, 471 Richmond Road, Ottawa Ontario K2A 0G3 Canada. **DD** 617.005.

GRUDNAIA KHIRURGIIA. V. 1- Jan./Feb. 1959-. 0017-4866. Periodical. UR. Russian (summaries in English). bm. $41.00. Victor Kamkin Inc (70227), 12224 Parklawn Drive, Rockville MD 20852. **Tel** (301)881-5973. **Ind/Abst** Excerpta Med., Index Med. **NLM** W1 GR919.

HACETEPPE BULLETIN OF MEDICINE-SURGERY CEASED. (HACETEPPE BULLETIN OF MEDICINE/SURGERY). V. 1-15, No. 3/4. 0017-6451. Periodical. English. ir. $5.50. **Ind/Abst** Excerpta Med., Biol. Abstr. **NLM** W1. **CODEN** HBMSAU.

HAND CEASED. (THE HAND). V. 1-15, No. 3. 0072-968X. Periodical. UK. English. ty. **Ind/Abst** Life Sci. Collect., Excerpta Med. **NLM** W1 HA51. Index in last issue of volume - attached. (cum index).

HANDCHIRURGIE, MIKROCHIRURGIE, PLASTISCHE CHIRURGIE. (HANDCHIRURGIE, MIKROCHIRURGIE, PLASTISCHE CHIRURGIE : ORGAN DER DEUTSCHSPRACHIGEN ARBEITSGEMEINSCHAFT FUR HANDCHIRURGIE : ORGAN DER DEUTSCHSPRACHIGEN ARBEITSGEMEINSCHAFT FUR MIKROCHIRURGIE DER PERIPHEREN NERVEN UND GEFASSE : ORGAN DER VEREINIGUNG DER DEUTSCHEN VEREINIGUNG DER DEUTSCHEN PLASTISCHEN CHIRURGEN). 14 Year, Vol. 1-. 0722-1819. Periodical. German. qt. 219. Hippokrates & Verlag, Postfach 593, D-7000 Stuttgart 3 West Germany. **Tel** 0711/8931-0. Ed D Buck Gramcko, H Millesil, and P R Zellner. **Ind/Abst** Excerpta Med., Index Med., Biol. Abstr. **NLM** W1 HA52R. **CODEN** HMPCD9. bk rev. adv acc. **Circ** 1,650. This journal covers the field of hand surgery, microsurgery and plastic surgery. Its purpose is also addressed to general surgeons and orthopedists as well as to accident and reconstructive surgeons. Zeitschrift fur Plastische Chirurgie, 0342-29278; Handchirurgie.

HANDCHIRURGISCHE TASCHENBUCHER. V. 1-. 0171-9734. Monographic Series. German. ir. Perimed, Verlag Dr Med D Straube, D-8520 Erlangen West Germany. **NLM** W1 HA52T.

HEAD & NECK SURGERY. **VAT** Head and Neck Surgery (New York, N.Y.). V. 1- Sept./Oct. 1978-. 0148-6403. Periodical. US. English. bm. $88.00. Mack Printing Company, 20th and Northampton Streets, Easton PA 18042. **Tel** (800)526-5368. **Ind/Abst** Index Med., Biol. Abstr. LC RD523. **DD** 617.51005. **NLM** W1 HE12.

HEAD INJURY UPDATE. Vol. 1, No. 1 (Jan. 1986)-. 0887-1779. Periodical. US. English. mo. $75.00. Charles Haynes Publisher, 2600 South Gessner, Houston TX 77063. **DD** 617.

HEALTH INDUSTRY TODAY. 83/1-. 0745-4678. Periodical. US. English. mo. $8.50 Domestic, $10.00 Canada. Cassak Publications Inc, 454 Morris Avenue, Springfield NJ 07081. **Ind/Abst** Predicasts. **NLM** W1 HE351B. Surgical Business, 0039-6095.

HEART TRANSPLANTATION. Vol. 1, No. 1-. 0278-2723. Periodical. US. English. bm. $60.00. Heart Transplantation, 201 Lyons Avenue/Beth Israel Med, Newark NJ 07112. **Tel** (201)926-8007. Ed Jacques G Losman. **Ind/Abst** Excerpta Med. **NLM** W1 HE649D. adv acc. **Circ** 20,000. Performs as a forum for the exchange of ideas as well as an instrument to report to the medical community on the progress in research and improvement in survival of patients undergoing heart transplantation.

HIGHLIGHTS FROM INFECTIONS IN SURGERY. (HIGHLIGHTS FROM INFECTIONS IN SURGERY : A SERVICE TO THE SURGICAL PROFESSION FROM MSD, MERCK SHARP & DOHME). Vol. 1, No. 1 (June 1984!)-. 0743-9202. Periodical. US. English. ir. Infections in Surgery Associates, 256 Fifth Avenue, New York NY 10001. **DD** 617.

HIRURGIJA. (KHIRURGUIA). **VFOAT** Chirurgia. 0450-2167. Periodical. BU. Bulgarian. mo. $32.00. Victor Kamkin Inc (71045), 12224 Parklawn Drive, Rockville MD 20852. **Tel** (301)881-5973. **Ind/Abst** Excerpta Med., Index Med., Chem. Abstr. **NLM** W1 KH586. **CODEN** KHIGAF.

INDIAN JOURNAL OF PLASTIC SURGERY : OFFICIAL PUBLICATION OF THE ASSOCIATION OF PLASTIC SURGEONS OF INDIA. English. ir. $30.00. Prints India, 11 Darya Ganj, New Delhi 110002 India. **NLM** W1.

INDIAN JOURNAL OF SURGERY. V. 1- Mar. 1939-. 0019-5650. Periodical. II. English. mo. $35.00. Association of Surgeons of India, c/o Madurai Medical College, Madurah India. **Ind/Abst** Life Sci. Collect., Excerpta Med., Chem. Abstr., Biol. Abstr. **NLM** W1 IN235F. **CODEN** IJSUAV.

INFECTIONS IN SURGERY. Vol. 1, No. 1 (June 1982)-. 0277-7746. Periodical. US. English. mo. $37.89. Infections in Surgery, 134 West 29th Street, New York NY 10001. **Tel** (212)714-1740. **NLM** W1 IN406HK. Available on microfilm through University Microfilms International.

INJURY. (INJURY. THE BRITISH JOURNAL OF ACCIDENT SURGERY). V. 1- July 1969-. 0020-1383. Periodical. UK. English. bm. 39.00 Domestic, 47.00 Foreign. John Wright and Sons Ltd, 823-825 Bath Road, Bristol B54 5NW England. **Tel** (617)486-8971. Ed N Tubbs. **Ind/Abst** Excerpta Med., Biol. Abstr., Index Med., Hospit. Lit. Index. **NLM** W1 IN454. **CODEN** INJUBF. bk rev. adv acc. Offers wide-ranging coverage of all aspects of trauma, including injuries of the head, chest and abdomen, as well as fractures and soft tissue injuries.

INNOVATIONS IN SURGERY AT THE LAHEY CLINIC MEDICAL CENTER. **VFOAT** Innovations in Surgery. 0883-4954. Periodical. US. English. bm. $19.00. Medical Publishing Enterprises, One Bridge Plaza/Suite 270, Fort Lee NJ 07024. **DD** 617.

INSTRUCTIONAL COURSE LECTURES. **Main/Corp** American Academy of Orthopaedic Surgeons. **VFOAT** Instructional Course Lectures of the American Academy of Orthopaedic Surgeons. Vol. 1- 1943-. 0065-6895. US. English. an. C V Mosby Company, 11830 Westline Industrial Drive, St Louis MO 63141. **Tel** (800)325-4177. **Ind/Abst** Index Med. **DD** 617. **NLM** W1 IN627V.

INTER BLOC. Began with: No. 0 (Feb. 1979). 0242-3960. Periodical. French. qt. Masson Publishing USA Inc, 211 East 43rd Street/Room 1306, New York NY 10017. **Tel** (212)370-1937. **NLM** W1 IN653V.

INTERNATIONAL ADVANCES IN SURGICAL ONCOLOGY. V. 1- 1978-. 0190-1575. US. English. an. Alan R Liss, 150 5th Avenue, New York NY 10011. Ed G P Murphy. **Ind/Abst** Index Med., Biol. Abstr., Chem. Abstr. LC RD651. **DD** 616.99405905. **NLM** W1 IN701M. **CODEN** IASODL.

INTERNATIONAL ANESTHESIOLOGY CLINICS. **VFOAT** I.A.C. V. 1- Jan. 1962-. 0020-5907. Monographic Series. US. English. qt. $65.00. Little Brown & Company Inc, 34 Beacon Street, Boston MA 02106. **Tel** (617)227-0730. Ed Mary B Donchez. **Ind/Abst** Excerpta Med., Cumul. Index Nurs. Allied Health Lit., Biol. Abstr., Chem. Abstr., Index Med., Energy Res. Abstr., Sci. Cit. Index, Abr. Ed., Hospit. Lit. Index. LC RD81.A1. **DD** 617.9605. **NLM** W1 IN702. **CODEN** IACLAV. **Circ** 3,500. Features eminent guest editors and contributors who focus on one topic per issue that is of significant clinical importance in anesthesiology.

INTERNATIONAL ANGIOLOGY : A JOURNAL OF THE INTERNATIONAL UNION OF ANGIOLOGY. Vol. 1, No. 1 (June 1982)-. Periodical. English. qt. $60.00. Lippincott/Harper, 2350 Virginia Avenue, Hagerstown MD 21740. **Tel** (215)238-4295. Ed P Balas. **NLM** W1 IN703. Articles cover the broad field of angiology, including rare cases, historical notices, new surgical techniques, and letters to the editor.

INTERNATIONAL BIBLIOGRAPHY ON BURNS. SUPPLEMENT. See Bibliographies.

INTERNATIONAL HAIR ROUTE. **VAT** Hair Route (1981). Issue No. 6 (Feb. 1981)-. 0820-6880. Periodical. CN. English. ir. $16.00. Hair Route Publishing, PO Box 313/Port Credit Postal Station, Mississauga Ontario L5G 4L8 Canada. **DD** 617.47. Hair Route, 0820-6872.

INTERNATIONAL JOURNAL OF AESTHETIC SURGERY. Vol. 1, No. 1 (Aug. 1981)-. 0285-6506. Periodical. English. ir. **NLM** W1.

INTERNATIONAL SURGERY. V. 45- Jan. 1966-. 0020-8868. Periodical. IT. English (text in various European languages). bm. $60.00. Piccin Editore, Via Altinate 107, 35121 Padava Italy. **Tel** 049/655.566. Ed Pezzuoli. **Ind/Abst** Life Sci. Collect., Hospit. Lit. Index, Excerpta Med., Biol. Abstr., Chem. Abstr., Nuci. Sci. Abstr., Index Med., Energy Res. Abstr. **NLM** W1 IN865. **CODEN** INTSAO. adv acc. **Circ** 9,000. Original articles from research and clinical practice in the various surgical fields. Journal of the International College of Surgeons, 0096-557X; International Surgery Bulletin, 0097-5621.

INTERNATIONAL TRENDS IN THORACIC SURGERY. Vol. 1-. Monographic Series. US. English. **NLM** W1.

IRCS MEDICAL SCIENCE. SURGERY AND TRANSPLANTATION. (IRCS MEDICAL SCIENCE : SURGERY AND TRANSPLANTATION). **VFOAT** Surgery and Transplantation. V. 3- Jan. 1975-. 0305-6953. Periodical. UK. English. qt. $50.00. IRCS Medical Science, PO Box 500/St Leonards House, Lancaster LA1 1PF England. **Tel** (0524) 68116. Ed S Johnson. bk rev. Publishes results of original research into all aspects of surgery, both clinical and experimental, within weeks of completion. Papers fully refereed. Research on Surgery and Transplantation, 0305-294X.

THE ITALIAN JOURNAL OF SURGICAL SCIENCES. Began in 1981. 0392-3525. Periodical. US. English. qt. Masson Italia Periodici, Via Pinturicchio 1, 20133 Milano Italy. **Tel** 02/276268. **Ed** Vincenzo Speranza. **Ind/Abst** Excerpta Med., Index Med. **NLM** W1 IT36P. bk rev. adv acc. **Circ** 5,000. Offical organ of the Societa Italiana di Chirurgia. *Surgery in Italy, 0390-5640.*

JAPANESE JOURNAL OF SURGERY. V. 1- Mar. 1971-. 0047-1909. Periodical. JA. English. bm. Japan Publishing Trading Company, PO Box 5030, Tokyo International, Tokyo 100-31 Japan. **Ind/Abst** Life Sci. Collect., Excerpta Med., Biol. Abstr., Chem. Abstr., Index Med., Hospit. Lit. Index. **NLM** W1 JA975K. **CODEN** JJSGAY.

JOURNAL DE CHIRURGIE. 0021-7697. Periodical. FR. French. Masson Publishing USA Inc, 211 East 43rd Street/Room 1306, New York Ny 10017. **Tel** (212)370-1937. **Ind/Abst** Life Sci. Collect., Excerpta Med., CIS Abstr., Biol. Abstr., Nuci. Sci. Abstr., Bibliogr. Agric., Index Med. **NLM** W1 JO301. **CODEN** JOCHAQ. (cum index).

THE JOURNAL OF ARTHROPLASTY. 0883-5403. Periodical. US. English. qt. Churchill Livingstone Inc, 1560 Broadway, New York NY 10036. **Tel** (212)819-5400.

THE JOURNAL OF BLOODLESS MEDICINE AND SURGERY. *See* Medicine.

JOURNAL OF BONE AND JOINT SURGERY. AMERICAN VOLUME. (JOURNAL OF BONE AND JOINT SURGERY). V. 30A- Jan. 1948-. 0021-9355. Periodical. US. English. Journal of Bone and Joint Surgery, 10 Shattuck Street, Boston MA 02115. **Tel** (617)734-2835. **Ind/Abst** Life Sci. Collect., Cumul. Index Nurs. Allied Health Lit., Excerpta Med., Biol. Abstr., Chem. Abstr., Index Med., Energy Res. Abstr., Sci. Cit. Index, Abr. Ed., Hospit. Lit. Index. **DD** 617. **NLM** W1 JO57. **CODEN** JBJSA3. (cum index). Available on microfilm from University Microfilms. *Journal of Bone and Joint Surgery, 0375-9229.*

JOURNAL OF BONE AND JOINT SURGERY. BRITISH VOLUME. (JOURNAL OF BONE AND JOINT SURGERY). V. 30B- Feb. 1948-. 0301-620X. Periodical. UK. English. Journal of Bone and Joint Surgery, 10 Shattuck Street, Boston MA 02115. **Tel** (617)734-2839. **Ind/Abst** Excerpta Med., Life Sci. Collect., Index Med., Chem. Abstr., Hospit. Lit. Index, Sci. Cit. Index, Abr. Ed. **NLM** W1 JO57B. **CODEN** JBSUAK. *Journal of Bone and Joint Surgery, 0375-9229.*

JOURNAL OF BONE AND JOINT SURGERY. QUINQUENNIAL INDEX. *See* Indexes/Abstracts.

JOURNAL OF CARDIAC SURGERY. 0886-0440. Periodical. US. English. qt. $65.00. Futura Publishing Company Inc, 295 Main Street, Box 330, Mt Kisco NY 10549.

JOURNAL OF CARDIOVASCULAR SURGERY. *See* Medicine - Cardiovascular Diseases.

THE JOURNAL OF DERMATOLOGIC SURGERY AND ONCOLOGY. V. 3- Jan./ Feb. 1977-. 0148-0812. Periodical. US. English. mo. Journal of Dermatologic, 475 Park Avenue South, New York NY 10016. **Tel** (212)725-5157. **Ind/Abst** Life Sci. Collect., Excerpta Med., Index Med., Energy Res. Abstr. **LC** RD520. **DD** 617.477. **NLM** W1 JO619G. *Journal of Dermatologic Surgery, 0097-9716.*

THE JOURNAL OF FOOT SURGERY. 0449-2544. Periodical. US. English. bm. $55.00. Williams & Wilkins, 428 East Preston Street, Baltimore MD 21202. **Tel** (301)528-4000. **Ed** Richard Reinherz. **Ind/Abst** Excerpta Med., Index Med., Energy Res. Abstr. **NLM** W1 JO653. **CODEN** JFSUB. adv acc. Clinical advances in foot surgery present for podiatrists and orthopaedic foot surgeons. *American College of Foot Surgeons Journal, 0517-0591.*

THE JOURNAL OF HAND SURGERY. **VFOAT** Hand Surgery. V. 1- July 1976-. 0363-5023. Periodical. US. English. bm. $77.00. C V Mosby, c/o R K Kinnes, 11830 Westline Industrial Drive, St Louis MO 63146. **Tel** (314)872-8370. **Ed** Adrian E Flatt. **Ind/Abst** Excerpta Med., Index Med., Biol. Abstr. **LC** RD559. **DD** 617.575005. **NLM** W1 JO669R. **CODEN** JHSUDV. bk rev. adv acc. **Circ** 7,864. Devoted to the various aspects of surgery of the hand, including surgical techniques, diagnosis, and evaluation of the loss of function.

JOURNAL OF HAND SURGERY, BRITISH VOLUME. (THE JOURNAL OF HAND SURGERY : JOURNAL OF THE BRITISH SOCIETY FOR SURGERY OF THE HAND). British V. 9B, No. 1 (Feb. 1984)-. 0266-7681. Periodical. UK. English. ty. $59.00. **Ind/Abst** Excerpta Med., Index Med., Life Sci. Collect., Energy Res. Abstr. **NLM** W1. *Hand, 0072-978X.*

JOURNAL OF MAXILLOFACIAL SURGERY. V. 1- Mar. 1973-. 0301-0503. Periodical. US. English. qt. $88.00. Thieme-Stratton Inc, 381 Park Avenue South/Suite 1501, New York NY 10016. **Tel** (212)683-5088. **Ed** H P M Freihoffer. **Ind/Abst** Excerpta Med., Index Med., Index Dent. Lit., Energy Res. Abstr., Sci. Cit. Index, Abr. Ed. **NLM** W1 JO749M. **Circ** 2,100. Organ of the European Association for Maxillofacial Surgery.

THE JOURNAL OF NEUROLOGICAL AND ORTHOPAEDIC SURGERY. V. 1, No. 2- Apr. 1980-. 0271-1575. Periodical. US. English. qt. $30.00. American Academy of Neurologists, 2320 Rancho Drive/Suite 108, Las Vegas NV 89102. **Tel** (702)385-6886. **Ed** Michael R Rask. **LC** RD593. **DD** 618.48005. **NLM** W1 JO7876. bk rev. adv acc. **Circ** 1,200. (ctrl). A medical and surgical journal which deals with the medical science of neuromusculoskeletal medicine and surgery to improve patient care.

JOURNAL OF NEUROSURGICAL SCIENCES. **VFOAT** Minerva Neurochirurgica. V. 17- Jan./June 1973-. 0390-5616. Periodical. IT. English. qt. 60.00. Edizioni Minerva Medica, Corso Bramante 83, Torino Italy 10126. **Tel** 678282. **Ed** P E Maspes. **Ind/Abst** Excerpta Med., Index Med. **NLM** W1 JO795D. adv acc. Journal addressed to practitioners and specialists in neurosurgery in Italy and abroad. It deals with topics in scientific practice and research. *Minerva Neurochirurgica, 0026-4881.*

JOURNAL OF ORAL AND MAXILLOFACIAL SURGERY. (JOURNAL OF ORAL AND MAXILLOFACIAL SURGERY : OFFICIAL JOURNAL OF THE AMERICAN ASSOCIATION OF ORAL AND MAXILLOFACIAL SURGEONS). Vol. 40, No. 1 (Jan. 1982)-. 0278-2391. Periodical. US. English. mo. $55.00. Journal of Oral and Maxillofacial Surgery, Box 465, Hanover PA 17331. **Tel** (215)574-3395. **Ind/Abst** Life Sci. Collect., Excerpta Med., Index Med., Energy Res. Abstr. **LC** RK1. **NLM** W1 JO803SM. bk rev. adv acc. **Circ** 8,300. Scientific articles, case reports, and original articles covering oral and maxillofacial surgery. *Journal of Oral Surgery (American Dental Association : 1965), 0022-3255.*

JOURNAL OF ORAL SURGERY (AMERICAN DENTAL ASSOCIATION : 1965). (JOURNAL OF ORAL SURGERY). Vol. 23, No. 1 (Jan. 1965)-V. 39, No. 12 (Dec. 1981). 0022-3255. Periodical. US. English. mo. **Ind/Abst** Life Sci. Collect., Excerpta Med., Biol. Abstr., Chem. Abstr., Nuci. Sci. Abstr., Index Med., Energy Res. Abstr. **NLM** W1 JO804. **CODEN** JOSUA9. *Journal of Oral Surgery, Anesthesia, and Hospital Dental Service, 0095-9618.*

JOURNAL OF PEDIATRIC SURGERY. *See* Medicine - Pediatrics.

JOURNAL OF RECONSTRUCTIVE MICROSURGERY. Vol. 1, No. 1 (July 1984)-. 0743-684X. Periodical. US. English. qt. $64.00. Thieme-Stratton Inc, 381 Park Avenue South/Suite 1501, New York NY 10016. **Tel** (212)683-5088. **Ed** Berish Strauch. **Ind/Abst** Index Med. **DD** 617. **NLM** W1. adv acc. **Circ** 600. Topic-oriented journal for the practitioner specializing in microsurgical procedures.

JOURNAL OF REFRACTIVE SURGERY. (JOURNAL OF REFRACTIVE SURGERY : THE OFFICIAL JOURNAL OF THE INTERNATIONAL SOCIETY OF REFRACTIVE KERATOPLASTY). **VFOAT** Refractive Surgery. Vol. 1, No. 1 (Mar./Apr. 1985)-. 0883-0444. Periodical. US. English. bm. Slack Inc, 6900 Grove Road, Thorofare NJ 08086. **DD** 617.

JOURNAL OF SURGICAL ONCOLOGY. **VFOAT** Surgical Oncology. V. 1- 1969-. 0022-4790. Periodical. US. English. mo. Alan R Liss Inc, 41 East 11th Street, New York NY 10003. **Tel** (212)741-2515. **Ind/Abst** Life Sci. Collect., Excerpta Med., Biol. Abstr., Chem. Abstr., Nuci. Sci. Abstr., Index Med., Energy Res. Abstr., Sci. Cit. Index, Abr. Ed. **LC** RD651. **DD** 616.99406. **NLM** W1 JO905M. **CODEN** JSONAU.

THE JOURNAL OF SURGICAL RESEARCH. V. 1- May 1961-. 0022-4804. Periodical. US. English. mo. $240.00. Academic Press, 4805 Sand Lake Road, Orlando FL 32819. **Tel** (305)345-4100. **Ind/Abst** Life Sci. Collect., Excerpta Med., Biol. Abstr., Chem. Abstr., Nuci. Sci. Abstr., Index Med., Energy Res. Abstr., Hospit. Lit. Index, Sci. Cit. Index, Abr. Ed. **LC** RD1. **DD** 617. **NLM** W1 JO905Q. **CODEN** JSGRA2.

THE JOURNAL OF THE HOSPITAL FOR SPECIAL SURGERY. **Main/Corp** Hospital for Special Surgery. V. 1- Nov. 1975-. 0362-0727. US. English. New York Society for Relief of Ruptured and Crippled, 535 East 70th St, New York NY 10021. **LC** RD701. **DD** 617.3005. **NLM** W1 JO929.

THE JOURNAL OF THE LOUISIANA STATE MEDICAL SOCIETY *CEASED.* **Main/Corp** Louisiana State Medical Society. V. 105-134. 0024-6921. Periodical. US. English. mo. $12.00. Journal of Louisiana State Medical Society, 1700 Josephine Street, New Orleans LA 70113-1596. **Tel** (504)561-1033. **Ed** Mannie Paine. **Ind/Abst** Hospit. Lit. Index, Life Sci. Collect., CIS Abstr., Biol. Abstr., Chem. Abstr., Nuci. Sci. Abstr., Index Med., Energy Res. Abstr. **NLM** W1 JO936N. **CODEN** JLSMAW. bk rev. adv acc. **Circ** 5,800. Medical, organizational magazine featuring socioeconomic, educational articles and columns ie: EKG of the month, medical student section, auxiliary report and book review. *New Orleans Medical and Surgical Journal (New Orleans, La. : 1873), 0097-1790.*

JOURNAL OF THORACIC AND CARDIOVASCULAR SURGERY. V. 38- July 1959-. 0022-5223. Periodical. US. English. mo. $107.50. **Tel** (314)872-8370. **Ed** Dwight C McGoon. **Ind/Abst** Excerpta Med., CIS Abstr., Index Med., Life Sci. Collect., Biol. Abstr., Energy Res. Abstr., Chem. Abstr., Nuci. Sci. Abstr., Hospit. Lit. Index, Sci. Cit. Index, Abr. Ed. **LC** RD536. **NLM** W1 JO966I. **CODEN** JTCSAQ. adv acc. **Circ** 10,580. Published for surgeons specializing in diseases of the chest, heart, lungs, and great vessels where surgical intervention is indicated. *Journal of Thoracic Surgery.*

JOURNAL OF THORACIC IMAGING. Vol. 1, No. 1 (Dec. 1985)-. 0883-5993. Periodical. US. English. qt. $75.00. Journal of Thoracic Imaging, 16792 Oakmont Avenue, Gaithersburg MD 20877. **DD** 617.

THE JOURNAL OF TRAUMA. V. 1- Jan. 1961-. 0022-5282. Periodical. US. English. mo. $80.00. Williams & Wilkins Company, PO Box 64025, Baltimore MD 21264. **Tel** (301)528-4000. **Ed** John H Davis. **Ind/Abst** Life Sci. Collect., Excerpta Med., Cumul. Index Nurs. Allied Health Lit., CIS Abstr., Biol. Abstr., Chem. Abstr., Index Med., Nuci. Sci. Abstr., Energy Res. Abstr., Sci. Cit. Index, Abr. Ed., Hospit. Lit. Index. **LC** RD92. **NLM** W1 JO966P. **CODEN** JOTRA5. adv acc. **Circ** 6,350. Diagnosis, management, and recommendations for surgical approaches to traumatic injury for othopaedic, plastic, and general surgeons.

JOURNAL OF VASCULAR SURGERY. 0733-0839. Periodical. US. English. bm. C V Mosby Company, c/o C Leadbetter, 118 Westline Industrial Drive, St Louis MO 63141.

JOURNAL OF VASCULAR SURGERY. Vol. 1, No. 1 (Jan. 1984)-. 0741-5214. Periodical. US. English. bm. $93.00. C V Mosby Company, R K Kinnes, 11830 Westline Industrial Drive, St Louis MO 63146. **Tel** (314)872-8370. **Ed** Michael E DeBakey. **Ind/Abst** Index Med. **LC** RD598.5. **DD** 617.413005. **NLM** W1. bk rev. adv acc. **Circ** 5,244. Publishes original articles that emcompass various aspects of diseases and injuries of the arterial and venous systems and certain associated blood disturbances.

JOURNAL - ROYAL COLLEGE OF SURGEONS OF EDINBURGH. **Main/Corp** Royal College of Surgeons of Edinburgh. Periodical. UK. English. bm. 45.00. Royal College of Surgeons, Editorial Department, 18 Nicholson Street, Edinburgh EH8 9DW Scoutland. **Tel** (0272)290691. **Ed** B MacLeod. **Ind/Abst** Index Med., Hospit. Lit. Index. bk rev. adv acc. **Circ** 8,500. Journal containing a whole range of papers of interest to the practising surgeon.

KLINISCHE ANASTHESIOLOGIE UND INTENSIVTHERAPIE. Vol. 5-. 0341-5023. Monographic Series. German. ir. Springer Verlag-New York Inc, 175 5th Avenue, New York NY 10010. **Tel** (212)460-1584. **Ind/Abst** Index Med., Chem. Abstr. **NLM** W1 KL434. **CODEN** KAINDO. Numbered series.

LANGENBECKS ARCHIV FUR CHIRURGIE. *See* Genealogy and Heraldry - Archives.

Medicine—Surgery

LASERS IN SURGERY AND MEDICINE. Began with: Vol. 1, published in 1980. 0196-8092. Periodical. US. English. bm. Alan R Liss Inc, 41 East 11th Street, New York NY 10003. Tel (212)741-2515. Ind/Abst Excerpta Med., Index Med., Chem. Abstr. NLM W1 LA784. CODEN LSMEDI.

LILLE CHIRURGICAL. Yearly V. 1-. 0024-3493. Periodical. FR. French. qt. Societe Dechirugie Lille, 229 Boulevard de la Liberte, Lille France. Ind/Abst Excerpta Med. NLM W1 LI523.

LOMA LINDA UNIVERSITY SURGEON. Vol. 1, No. 1 (Sept. 1982)-. 0731-3063. Periodical. US. English. sa. $10.00. Loma Linda University Medical Center, Room 2563, Loma Linda CA 92534. Tel (714)824-4335. NLM W1 LO108J.

LYON CHIRURGICAL. V. 1- Nov. 1908-. 0024-7782. Periodical. French (summaries in English). bm. Masson Publ USA Inc, 211 East 43rd Street/Room 1306, New York NY 10017. Tel (212)370-1937. Ind/Abst Excerpta Med. NLM W1 LY53.

MAJOR PROBLEMS IN CLINICAL SURGERY. Vol. 1-. Monographic Series. US. English. ir. WB Saunders, West Washington Square, Philadelphia PA 19105. Tel (800)523-0713. Ind/Abst Energy Res. Abstr., Index Med. NLM W1 MA492R.

THE MALPRACTICE REPORTER. SURGEON'S. See Law.

MEDECINE & CHIRURGIE DIGESTIVES. See Medicine.

MEDICAL DIRECTORY. See Yearbooks, Almanacs, Directories.

MEDICAL ECONOMICS FOR SURGEONS. Vol. 1, No. 1 (Mar. 1982)-. 0744-4206. Periodical. US. English. mo. $36.00. Medical Economics Inc, 680 Kinderkamack Road, Oradell NJ 07649. LC RD27.42. DD 617.00681.

MICROSURGERY. Vol. 4, No. 1-. 0738-1085. Periodical. US. English. qt. $70.00. Alan R Liss Inc, 150 Fifth Avenue, New York NY 10011. Ind/Abst Excerpta Med., Curr. Contents, Index Med. LC RD33.6. DD 617.9. NLM W1 MI313L. *Journal of Microsurgery*, 0191-3239; *International Journal of Microsurgery*, 0222-5069.

MINERVA CHIRURGICA. V. 1- Mar. 1946-. 0026-4733. Periodical. IT. Italian. sm. 100.00. Edizioni Minerva Medica, Corso Bramante 83-85, Torino 10126 Italy. Tel 67 82 82. Ed P A Oludice. Ind/Abst Excerpta Med., Index Med. NLM W1 MI637. bk rev. adv acc. Journal addressed to practitioners and specialists in surgery in Italy and abroad. It deals with topics in scientific practice and research.

MODERN TECHNICS IN SURGERY. 0163-7045. US. English. ir. Futura Publishing Company, 295 Main Street, Mt Kisco NY 10549.

NETHERLANDS JOURNAL OF SURGERY. (THE NETHERLANDS JOURNAL OF SURGERY). V. 32- 1980-. 0167-2487. Periodical. NE. English (summaries in French, German and Dutch). qt. $84.00. Drukkerij Veenman BV, Postbus 7, 6700 AA Wageningen Netherlands. Tel 08370-19045. Ind/Abst Excerpta Med., Index Med., Biol. Abstr., Energy Res. Abstr. NLM W1 NE229S. CODEN NJSUDL. *Archivum Chirurgicum Neerlandicum*, 0004-0657.

NEURO-CHIRURGIE. V. 1- 1955-. 0028-3770. Periodical. FR. French (summaries in English). bm. Masson Publishing USA Inc, 211 East 43rd Street/Room 1306, New York NY 10017. Tel (212)370-1937. Ind/Abst Excerpta Med., Life Sci. Collect., Index Med., Biol. Abstr. NLM W1 NE326. CODEN NUREB9.

NEUROCHIRURGIA. V. 1- June 1958-. 0028-3819. Periodical. GW. English (French, and German, with summaries in Spanish). bm. $87.00. Thieme-Stratton Inc, 381 Park Avenue, New York NY 10016. Tel (212)683-5088. Ind/Abst Excerpta Med., Life Sci. Collect., Index Med., Biol. Abstr., Energy Res. Abstr., Sci. Cit. Index, Abr. Ed. NLM W1 NE324. CODEN NURABV.

NEUROSURGERY. V. 1- July/Aug. 1977-. 0148-396X. Periodical. US. English. mo. $115.00. Williams & Wilkins Company, 428 East Preston Street, Baltimore MD 21202. Tel (301)528-4000. Ed Clark Watts. Ind/Abst Excerpta Med., Life Sci. Collect., Index Med., Energy Res. Abstr. LC RD593. NLM W1 NE343U. adv acc. Circ 6,000. Practical, clinical information on neurosurgical techniques and devices plus pertinent research in neuroscience for the neurosurgeon.

NEUROSURGICAL REVIEW. V. 1-. 0344-5607. Periodical. English (summaries in German). qt. $95.00. Walter de Gruyter, 200 Saw Mill River Road, Hawthorne NY 10532. Tel (914)747-0110. Ed H W Pia and K Sano. Ind/Abst Excerpta Med., Index Med. NLM W1 NE344W. adv acc. An international forum in the field of neurosurgery. Presents scientific papers on the most recent developments in techniques and technology.

NOTIZIARIO CHIRURGICO. Vol. 1, N. 1 (Oct.-Dec. 1980)-. 0392-3584. Periodical. IT. Italian. qt. $37.32. Edizioni Minerva Medica, Corso Bramenta 83/85, Turin Italy 10126. Tel 67.82.82. Ind/Abst Excerpta Med. NLM W1 NO813I.

OCULAR REVIEW. 0748-2892. US. English. mo. Ocular Review c/o M Winnike, University of Illinois at Chicago, Eye & Eye Infirmary Library, PO Box 98, Chicago IL 60680. DD 617.

OCULAR SURGERY NEWS. Vol. 2, No. 17 (Sept. 1, 1984)-. 8750-3085. Periodical. US. English. bw. $55.00. Slack Inc, 6900 Grove Road, Thorofare NJ 08086-9435. Tel (609)848-1000. Ed Donald R Sanders. DD 617. bk rev. adv acc. Circ 17,000. (ctrl). News coverage of the latest developments affecting the practice of ophthalmology, together with special features of interest to the ophthalmic surgeon. *Iol & Ocular Surgery News*, 0745-709X.

OEKWA HAKHOE CHI. Main/Corp Taehan Oekwa Hakhoe. VFOAT Journal of the Korean Surgical Society. Periodical. KO. Korean (summaries in English). ir. Taehan Oekwa Hakhoe, 1 2-Ka Myong-Dong, Chung-Ku, Seoul South Korea. LC RD1.

OFFICIAL LIST : PHYSICIANS AND SURGEONS. Main/Corp New Mexico. State Board of Medical Examiners. 1948-. US. English. an. LC R712.A2. DD 614.24. NLM W 22 AN5 B6O.

ONGOING CURRENT BIBLIOGRAPHY OF PLASTIC AND RECONSTRUCTIVE SURGERY (CHICAGO, ILL.). See Bibliographies.

OPHTHALMIC SURGERY. Began in 1970. 0022-023X. Periodical. US. English. mo. Slack Inc, 6900 Grove Road, Thorofare NJ 08086. Tel (609)848-1000. Ind/Abst Life Sci. Collect., Excerpta Med., Index Med., Energy Res. Abstr., Biol. Abstr., Sci. Cit. Index, Abr. Ed. LC RE80. DD 617.71. NLM W1 OP25. CODEN OPSGAT. *Journal of Cryosurgery*.

ORAL AND MAXILLOFACIAL SURGERY DIRECTORY OF THE WORLD. See Yearbooks, Almanacs, Directories.

ORTHOPEDIC SURGERY. V. 11- Jan. 1966-. 0014-4371. Periodical. English. ir. 195.00. Elsevier Science Publishers, Biomedical Division, PO Box 1527, 1000 BM Amsterdam The Netherlands. Tel (020)5803911. LC RD701. NLM ZW 1 E978M. adv acc. Circ 350. Covering the entire area, this abstract journal begins with an introductory chapter on general orthopedics, subdivided on an anatomical basis. *Orthopedics and Traumatology*.

OSPEDALI D'ITALIA-CHIRURGIA. V. 1- Nov. 1959-. 0030-6266. Periodical. IT. Italian. bm. 100.00. Il Sedicesimo, Via Mannelli 29R, 50136 Firenze Italy. Tel 055/2476781. Ed Carlo Massimo. Ind/Abst Life Sci. Collect. NLM W1 OS542. bk rev. adv acc. Circ 1,000.

OSTOMY QUARTERLY. 1963. 0030-6517. Periodical. US. English. qt. $16.00. United Ostomy Association Inc, 2001 West Beverly Boulevard, Los Angeles CA 90057. Tel (213)413-5510. Ed Kathryn L Pape. NLM W1 OS96. bk rev. adv acc. Circ 50,000. (ctrl). Life following abdominal ostomy surgery; national association activities; new techniques in ostomy surgery; research briefs; rotating departments (seniors, penpals, clinical cases, etc.).

OTOLARYNGOLOGY AND HEAD AND NECK SURGERY. See Medicine - Otorhinolaryngology.

OUTPATIENT SURGERY. 0885-1166. Periodical. US. English. qt. Hanley & Belfus Inc, 210 South 13th Street, Philadelphia PA 19107.

PATIENT PLEASERS. Vol. 1, No. 1 (May 1985)-. 0882-6471. Periodical. US. English. mo. $87.00. Professional Communications Inc, 5799 Tall Oaks Road, Madison WI 53711. DD 617. *Impressions (Madison, Wis.)*, 0273-1592.

PATOLOGIA QUIRURGICA. CITOLOGIA EXFOLIATIVA. (PATOLOGIA QUIRURGICA, CITOLOGIA EXFOLIATIVA). V. 1- 1975-. 0185-0865. Periodical. Spanish (summaries in English). qt. NLM W1 PA977.

THE PELVIC SURGEON. V. 1- Apr. 1980-. 0198-5000. Periodical. US. English. mo. $75.00. Northern Chesapeake Publishers, PO Box 98, Riverwood MD 21139. NLM W1 PE269.

PERITONEAL DIALYSIS BULLETIN. VFOAT Bulletin. Vol. 1, No. 1 (June 1980)-. 0226-8787. Periodical. CN. English. qt. Free. c/o D Oreopoulos, Toronto Western Hospital, 299 Bathurst Street, Toronto Ontario M5T 2S8 Canada. Ind/Abst Excerpta Med. DD 617.461059. NLM W1 PE801.

PHILIPPINE JOURNAL OF SURGERY AND SURGICAL SPECIALTIES. Periodical. PH. English. qt. Philippine Journal of Surgery, PO Box 86, Manila Philippines.

PLASTIC AND RECONSTRUCTIVE SURGERY. V. 31- 1963-. 0032-1052. Periodical. US. English. mo. $90.00. Williams & Wilkins Company, 428 East Preston Street, Baltimore MD 21202. Tel (301)528-4000. Ed Robert M Goldwyn. Ind/Abst Life Sci. Collect., Excerpta Med., CIS Abstr., Energy Res. Abstr., Biol. Abstr., Chem. Abstr., Index Med., Nuci. Sci. Abstr. NLM W1 PL118. CODEN PRSUAS. adv acc. Circ 11,200. The leading journal in the field for every specialist using plastic and reconstructive surgery techniques. *Plastic and Reconstructive Surgery and the Transplantation Bulletin*, 0096-8501.

PLASTIC SURGEON. Vol. 1, No. 1 (Mar.-Apr. 1985)-. 0883-7848. Periodical. US. English. bm. $35.00 Members, $75.00 Non-Members. American Society of Plastic and Reconstructive Surgeons, 233 North Michigan Avenue/Suite 900, Chicago IL 60601. Tel (312)856-1818. Ed Susan Mack. DD 617. adv acc. Circ 3,000. (ctrl). Feature articles regarding members, activities, and meetings of organization. *Plastic Surgery News*, 0199-302X.

PLASTIC SURGERY. See Indexes/Abstracts.

PLASTIC SURGICAL NURSING. See Medicine - Nursing.

POLSKI PRZEGLAD CHIRURGICZNY. 0032-373X. Periodical. PL. Polish (contains English and Russian summaries, 1950-). mo. ARS Polona, Krakowskie Przedmiescie 7, 00-068 Warsaw Poland. Ind/Abst Index Med. NLM W1 PO284.

PRAKTISCHE ANAESTHESIE, WIEDERBELEBUNG UND INTENSIVTHERAPIE. Vol. 9-14. 0302-7600. Periodical. GW. German (summaries in English). bm. 198.-. Georg Thieme Verlag, Postfach 732 Herdweg 63, D7000 Stuttgart 1 West Germany. Tel (0711)8931240. Ed O H Just. Ind/Abst Excerpta Med., Curr. Contents, Phys. Chem. Earth Sci., Sci. Cit. Index, Abr. Ed., Index Med. NLM W1 PR253. Index in last issue of volume - attached. bk rev. adv acc. Circ 3,450. (ctrl). An important information source on anaesthesia giving competent information on clinical practice and research. *Zeitschrift fur Praktische Anaesthesie, Wiederbelebung und Intensivtherapie*.

PROBLEMS IN GENERAL SURGERY. Vol. 1, No. 1 (Jan. 1984)-. 0739-8328. Periodical. US. English. qt. $60.00 Domestic, $70.00 Foreign. J B Lippincott Company, 2350 Virginia Avenue, Hagerstown MD 21740. Tel (301)824-7300 Maryland, (800)638-3030 outside Maryland. NLM W1. Circ 2,500. Features a symposium on a specific topic in general surgery in each issue.

PROCEEDINGS - BELGIAN CONGRESS OF ANESTHESIOLOGY. Main/Conf Belgian Congress of Anesthesiology. Series/Titl Acta Anaesthesiologica Belgica; . V. 26, Suppl., Etc. English (with introductory material and summaries in English, French, and Dutch). ir. NLM W1 AC749.

PROCEEDINGS OF THE FORUM SESSIONS. Main/Conf Forum on Fundamental Surgical Problems. 1950-. English. ir. W B Saunders Company, 210 West Washington Square, Philadelphia PA 19105. LC RD11.

PROCEEDINGS OF THE RED DEER SURGICAL SOCIETY. Main/Corp Red Deer Surgical Society. 0711-4915. CN. English. An. Free to Physicians and Medical Libraries. Red Deer Surgical Society, 4914-46 Street, Red Deer Alberta T4N 1N3 Canada. DD 610.

PROGRESS IN NEUROLOGICAL SURGERY. V. 1- 1967-. 0079-6492. English. ir. S Karger AG, PO Box, CH-4009 Basel Switzerland. Tel 061-39 08 80. Ed A M Landolt. Ind/Abst Index Med. Theoretical and technical developments in neurological surgery expertly reviewed by international authorities.

PROGRESS IN SURGERY. VFOAT Progres en Chirurgie, Fortschritte der Chirurgie. Began with: Vol. 1, published in 1961. 0079-6824. Monographic

Series. SZ. articles in English, French, or German with summaries in the other two languages. ir. S Karger AG, PO Box 352, White Plains NY 10602. **Ed** E H Farthmann. **Ind/Abst** Life Sci. Collect., Biol. Abstr., Index Med., Sci. Cit. Index, Abr. Ed. **LC** RD11. **DD** 617.082. **NLM** W1 PR681M. **CODEN** PSURA2. Reference books that acquaint surgeons with new technical developments, procedures, and applications.

PROGRESS IN SURGICAL PATHOLOGY. V. 1- 1980-. 0271-2350. US. English. ir. Masson Distribution Inc, Box C-762, Brooklyn New York NY 11205. **LC** RD57. **DD** 617.07.

PROGRESSO MEDICO. (IL PROGRESSO MEDICO). V. 1- Aug. 1944-. 0370-1514. Periodical. IT. Italian. mo. 120.000. Lembardo Editore, Via Verona 22, 00161 Roma Italia. **Tel** (06)428905. **Ed** Vito Patrono. **Ind/Abst** Excerpta Med. **NLM** W1 PR706. **CODEN** PRMOAE. bk rev. adv acc. **Circ** 5,800. (ctrl). Editorials, reviews, original articles, case reports and clinical trials in the fields of internal medicine and surgery.

QUARTERLY JOURNAL OF SURGICAL SCIENCES. Periodical. II. English. qt. $10.00. Banaras Hindu University, Surgical Research Lab, College of Medical Science, Varanasi-5 India.

RAPPORT ANNUEL - L'ORDRE DES PODIATRES DU QUEBEC. **Main/Corp** Ordre des Podiatres du Quebec. 1.- 1974/75-. CN. French. an. Casier Postal 275, Succursale Postale Montreal-Nord, Montreal-Nord Quebec H1H 5L4 Canada. **LC** RD563. **DD** 617.5850062714.

RASSEGNA ITALIANA DI CHIRURGIA PEDIATRICA. V. 18- Jan./Mar. 1976-. 0390-0495. Periodical. IT. Italian. qt. Casa Editrice, Postale 295, 50100 Firenze Italy. **Ind/Abst** Excerpta Med. **NLM** W1 RA805P. *Rivista di Chirurgia Pediatrica, 0035-5801.*

RECENT ADVANCES IN PLASTIC SURGERY. No. 1- 1976-. 0309-2674. Periodical. UK. English. ir. Churchill Livingstone Inc, 1560 Broadway, New York NY 10036. **Tel** (212)819-5400. **Ed** J Calnan. **NLM** W1 RE105YC.

RECENT ADVANCES IN SURGERY. No. 1-. 0143-8395. Periodical. UK. English. ir. Churchill Livingstone, 1560 Broadway, New York NY 10036. **Tel** (212)819-5400. **Ed** W H Ogilvie. **NLM** W1 RE105YJL. Each issue contains an index to its own contents - no vol index - loose.

RECONSTRUCTION SURGERY AND TRAUMATOLOGY. Vol. 10-. 0080-0260. Monographic Series. English. ir. S Karger AG, PO Box, CH-4009 Basel Switzerland. **Tel** 061-39 08 80. **Ed** H Eberle. **Ind/Abst** Life Sci. Collect., Index Med. **NLM** W1 RE111I. New techniques and procedures described by the surgeons responsible for their development. *Wiederherstellungschirurgie und Traumatologie.*

REPORTS ON SURGERY OF THE HAND. Monographic Series. articles in English or Polish. ir. **NLM** W1 RE213C. *Biuletyn Informacyjny Sekcji Chirurgii Reki.*

RESEARCH IN EXPERIMENTAL MEDICINE. **VFOAT** Zeitschrift fur die Gesamte Experimentelle Medizin Einschliesslich Experimenteller Chirurgie. V. 157- 1972-. 0300-9130. Periodical. WB. English (German). ty. $203.00. Springer Verlag New York Inc, 175 5th Avenue, New York NY 10010. **Tel** (212)460-1500. **Ed** F -D Goebel. **Ind/Abst** Life Sci. Collect., Excerpta Med., Pestdoc, Ringdoc, Vetdoc, Index Med., Biol. Abstr., Energy Res. Abstr., Chem. Abstr., Sci. Cit. Index, Abr. Ed. **LC** R850.A1. **DD** 619.05. **NLM** W1 RE227FK. **CODEN** REXMAS. Publishes original papers pertinent to the development or application of new methods or devices in experimental medicine and surgery. *Zeitschrift fur die Gesamte Experimentelle Medizin Einschliesslich Experimenteller Chirurgie, 0044-2534.*

REVISTA BRASILEIRA DE ANESTESIOLOGIA. Year 1- April 1951-. 0034-7094. Periodical. BL. Portuguese (English and Spanish). bm. 720.00 Domestic, $200.00. Sociedade Brasileira de Aneste, rue das Marrecas 33, Apartado C-O, Rio de Janeiro Brazil. **Tel** (021)240-4578. **Ed** Massami Katayama. **Ind/Abst** Life Sci. Collect., Excerpta Med., Chem. Abstr., Biol. Abstr. **NLM** W1 RE304. **CODEN** RBANAV. bk rev. adv acc. **Circ** 4,500. (ctrl). Anesthesia reanimation.

REVISTA BRASILEIRA DE CIRURGIA. V. 1- 1932-. 0034-7124. Periodical. BL. Portuguese. bm. Rivista Brasileira de Cirurgia, PO Box 4357/Ave Nilo Pecanha, 38-60 Andar, Rio de Janeiro Brazil. **Ind/Abst** Biol. Abstr. **NLM** W1 RE311. **CODEN** RBCHAN.

REVISTA DE CHIRURGIE, ONCOLOGIE, RADIOLOGIE, O.R.L., OFTALMOLOGIE, STOMATOLOGIE. CHIRURGIA. (REVISTA DE CHIRURGIE, ONCOLOGIE, RADIOLOGIE, O. R. L., OFTALMOLOGIE, STOMATOLOGIE. CHIRURGIA). **VFOAT** Chirurgia. V. 23, No. 7- July/Aug. 1974-. 0377-5003. Periodical. RM. Romanian. bm. Ilexim Press Department, PO Box 1-136-1-137, Bucharest Romania. **Ind/Abst** Index Med., Biol. Abstr., Excerpta Med. **NLM** W1 RE378F. **CODEN** RCOCDA. *Chirurgia, 0009-4730.*

REVISTA DE LA SOCIEDAD MEDICO-QUIRURGICA DEL HOSPITAL DE EMERGENCIA PEREZ DE LEON. 0378-1852. Periodical. Spanish. ir. **NLM** W1 RE414P.

REVISTA MEDICO-CHIRURGICALA A SOCIETATII DE MEDICI SI NATURALISTI DIN IASI. **Main/Corp** Societatea de Medici Si Naturalisti Din Iasi. **VFOAT** Medical-Surgical Journal of the Society of Physicians and Naturalists IASI, Revue Medico-Chirurgicale de la Societe des Medecins et de Naturalistes, Zeitschrift fur Medezin und Chirurgie der Gesellschaft der Arzte und Naturforscher in Jassy, Mediko-Khirurgischeski Zhurnal Obshchestva Vrachei i Naturalisto V G Iassy. Vol. 60- Jan./Mar. 1956-. 0300-8738. Periodical. RM. Romanian (tables of contents and summaries in English, French, German and Russian). qt. Ilexim Press, PO Box 1-136-1-137, Bucharest Romania. **Ind/Abst** Excerpta Med., Index Med., Hospit. Lit. Index, Chem. Abstr. **NLM** W1 RE656. *Revue Medico-Chirurgicale.*

REVISTA QUIRURGICA ESPANOLA. (REVISTA QUIRURGICA ESPANOLA : RQE). **VFOAT** R.Q.E. 0210-2196. Periodical. SP. Spanish. bm. 2,500. Ediciones Doyma South Africa, Travesera de Gracia 17-21, 08021 Barcelona Spain. **Tel** 2000711. **Ed** Cristobal Pera. **NLM** W1 RE722. bk rev. adv acc. **Circ** 5,000. (ctrl). Editorials, originals, research in surgery, surgical techniques, experimental surgery, critical review, residents seminars, etc.

REVUE DE CHIRURGIE ORTHOPEDIQUE ET REPARATRICE DE L'APPAREIL MOTEUR. Vol. 37- Jan./Mar. 1951-. 0035-1040. Periodical. FR. French. Masson Publications USA Inc, 211 East 43rd Street/Room 1306, New York NY 10017. **Tel** (212)370-1937. **Ind/Abst** Life Sci. Collect., Excerpta Med., Index Med. **NLM** W1 RE777. Index published separately - free - automatically sent. (cum index). *Revue d'Orthopedie et de Chirurgie de l'Appareil Moteur.*

RIVISTA ITALIANA DI CHIRURGIA PLASTICA. V. 1-Jan./Apr. 1969-. 0391-2221. Periodical. IT. Italian. qt. 60.000. La Garangola, Via Montona 4, 35100 Padova Italy. **Tel** 049/20667. **Ind/Abst** Excerpta Med. **NLM** W1 RI767. bk rev. adv acc. **Circ** 1,500.

ROZHLEDY V CHIRURGII. Vol. 16- 1937/38. 0035-9351. Periodical. CS. Czech. mo. Artia, Ve Smeckach 30, PO Box 790, Praha 1 Czechoslovakia. **Ind/Abst** Index Med. **NLM** W1 RO981. *Rozhledy v Chirurgii a Gyneakologii.*

SAME-DAY SURGERY. **VFOAT** SDS. **VAT** Same Day Surgery. V. 1- Apr. 1977-. 0190-5066. Periodical. US. English. mo. American Health Consultants, 67 Peachtree Park Drive, Atlanta GA 30309. **Tel** (404)351-4523. **Ind/Abst** Cumul. Index Nurs. Allied Health Lit., Hospit. Lit. Index. **NLM** W1 SA448T.

SCANDINAVIAN JOURNAL OF PLASTIC AND RECONSTRUCTIVE SURGERY. V. 1, No. 1- 1967-. 0036-5556. Periodical. SW. English. ty. $59.00. Almqvist & Wiksell, 108 Drottninggatan, PO Box 45150, S-104 30 Stockholm Sweden. **Tel** 85413160. **Ind/Abst** Life Sci. Collect., Excerpta Med., Index Med., Biol. Abstr., Sci. Cit. Index, Abr. Ed. **NLM** W1 SC152. **CODEN** SJPRBG. Index in last issue of volume - attached.

SCANDINAVIAN JOURNAL OF THORACIC AND CARDIOVASCULAR SURGERY. V. 1-. 0036-5580. Periodical. SW. English. ir. $59.00. Almqvist & Wiksell, 108 Drottninggatan, PO Box 45150, S-104 30 Stockholm Sweden. **Tel** 85413160. **Ind/Abst** Life Sci. Collect., Excerpta Med., Index Med., Biol. Abstr., Energy Res. Abstr., Sci. Cit. Index, Abr. Ed. **LC** RD536. **DD** 617.54005. **NLM** W1 SC154C. **CODEN** SJTCAO.

SCHRIFTENREIHE INTENSIVMEDIZIN, NOTFALLMEDIZIN, ANASTHESIOLOGI. **VFOAT** Intensivmedizin, Notfallmedizin, Anasthesiologie. INA. V. 1-. 0342-4448. Monographic Series. GW. German. George Thieme Verlag, Postfach 732, Herdweg 63, D7000 Stuttgart 1 West Germany. **Ind/Abst** Chem. Abstr. **NLM** W3 SC427Z. **CODEN** SINADI.

SCIENCE AND PRACTICE OF SURGERY. 0731-1680. Monographic Series. US. English. ir. Marcel Dekker Inc, 270 Madison Avenue, New York NY 10016. **Tel** (212)696-9000. **Ed** Morris, Burke. **Ind/Abst** Chem. Abstr. **LC** UNC. **NLM** W1 SC679. **CODEN** SCSUDR. This in an ongoing series. Each title has a different subject.

SELECTED READINGS IN GENERAL SURGERY. Periodical. US. English. mo. $135.00. Department of Surgery, 5325 Harry Hines Boulevard, Dallas TX 75235. **Tel** (214)688-2756.

SEMINARS IN NEUROLOGICAL SURGERY. **VFOAT** Seminars in Neurological Surgery Series. 0160-2489. Monographic Series. US. English. ir. Raven Press, 1140 Avenue of the Americas, New York NY 10036. **Ind/Abst** Excerpta Med.

SEMINARS IN SURGICAL ONCOLOGY. 8756-0437. Periodical. US. English. qt. $65.00 Domestic, $76.00 Foreign. Alan R Liss, 41 East 11th Street, New York NY 10003. **DD** 616. *International Advances in Surgical Oncology, 0190-1575.*

SHONI GEKA. **VFOAT** Japanese Journal of Pediatric Surgery. Vol. 9- Jan. 1977-. 0385-6313. Periodical. JA. Japanese. ir. 31.000. Tokyo Igakusha Company, 3-35-4 Hongo Bunkyo-ku, Tokyo Japan. **Tel** 03-871-4119. **Ed** Keijiro Suruga. **Ind/Abst** Energy Res. Abstr. **NLM** W1 SH52G. bk rev. adv acc. **Circ** 5,000. (ctrl). Joint clinical conference, is an institution of interest on neonatal surgery for junior doctors and nurses. *Shoni Geka, Naika.*

SOCIO-ECONOMIC FACTBOOK FOR SURGERY. 1977-. 0193-3302. US. English. an. American College of Surgeons, 55 East Erie Street, Chicago IL 60611. **LC** RD27.42. **DD** 338.476170973. **NLM** W1 SO878M.

SOINS. (SOINS. CHIRURGIE). **VFOAT** Chirurgie. Began in 1982. Periodical. French. ir. **NLM** W1. *Soins. Chirurgie Generale et Specialisee.*

SOUTH AFRICAN JOURNAL OF SURGERY. **VFOAT** Suid-Afrikaanse Tydskrif vir Chirurgie. V. 1-. 0038-2361. Periodical. SA. English. qt. $12.39. Medical Association of South Africa, Medical House Central Square, Pinelands 7405 South Africa. **Tel** 53-3081. **Ed** C Brenner. **Ind/Abst** Life Sci. Collect., Excerpta Med., Index Med., Biol. Abstr., Index Dent. Lit., Hospit. Lit. Index. **NLM** W1 SO9057. **CODEN** SAJSBS. bk rev. adv acc. **Circ** 1,200. (ctrl). Original and review articles on surgical topics. Also case reports, abstracts, letters to the editor and book reviews.

SOUTHEAST ASIAN JOURNAL OF SURGERY. V. 1- July 1978-. Periodical. English. ir. **Ind/Abst** Excerpta Med. **NLM** W1 SO924N.

SOUTHERN MEDICAL JOURNAL. *See* Medicine.

SURGERY. V. 1- Jan. 1937-. 0039-6060. Periodical. US. English. mo. $88.00. C V Mosby, c/o R K Kinnes, 11830 Westline Industrial Drive, St Louis MO 63146. **Tel** (314)872-8370. **Ed** Walter F Ballinger and George D Zuidema. **Ind/Abst** Life Sci. Collect., Excerpta Med., Energy Res. Abstr., Biol. Abstr., Chem. Abstr., Index Med., Nuci. Sci. Abstr., Hospit. Lit. Index, Sci. Cit. Index, Abr. Ed. **LC** RD1. **DD** 617.05. **NLM** W1 SU746. **CODEN** SURGAZ. adv acc. **Circ** 10,555. Edited for practicing surgeons, including those of authority as department heads or professor in their hospitals and surgical community.

SURGERY ALERT. Vol. 1, No. 1 (July 1984)-. 0748-1942. Periodical. US. English. mo. $59.00. Surgery Alert, PO Box 1005, Oradell NJ 07649. **Tel** (404)351-4523. **Ed** William Silen and Michael Steer. **DD** 617. **Circ** 2,500. Abstracts and reviews of the medical literature specific surgery.

SURGERY ANNUAL. V. 1- 1969-. 0081-9638. US. English. an. $61.04. Appleton-Century Crofts, 25 Van Zant Street, East Norwalk CT 06855. **Tel** (203)838-4400. **Ed** Lloyd Nyhus. **Ind/Abst** Index Med., Biol. Abstr., Energy Res. Abstr., Chem. Abstr., Hospit. Lit. Index. **LC** RD9. **DD** 617.005. **NLM** W1 SU747.

Medicine—Surgery

CODEN SURABI. Collection of timely articles for the practicing surgeon.

SURGERY, GYNECOLOGY & OBSTETRICS CEASED. VFOAT SGO. VAT Surgery, Gynecology and Obstetrics. V. 1- July 1905-. 0039-6087. Periodical. US. English. mo. $20.00. Franklin H Martin Memorial Foundation, 55 East Erie Street, Chicago IL 60611. Ind/Abst Life Sci. Collect., Excerpta Med., Hospit. Lit. Index, Energy Res. Abstr., Biol. Abstr., Chem. Abstr., Index Med., Nucl. Sci. Abstr. LC RD1. DD 617.005. NLM W1 SU748. CODEN SGOBA9. (cum index).

SURGERY IN ITALY CEASED. Began in Mar. 1971. Ceased V. 10, No. 4, Dec. 1980. 0390-5640. Periodical. IT. English. qt. Ind/Abst Excerpta Med. NLM W1.

SURGERY (OXFORD, OXFORDSHIRE). (SURGERY). Vol. 1, No. 1 (June 1983)-. 0263-9319. Periodical. UK. English. mo. $91.95. Medicine Group, Pembroke House, 36/37 Pembroke Street, Oxford OX1 1BL England. Tel (0865)724631. Ed J S P Lumley and J L Craven. NLM W1. adv acc. (ctrl). Comprehensive text of modern surgical practice, including all aspects of general surgery and most specialties, surgical techniques and principles.

SURGICAL BUSINESS CEASED. V. 1-45. 0039-6095. Periodical. US. English. mo. NLM W1 SU763.

THE SURGICAL CLINICS OF NORTH AMERICA. Vol. 1, No. 1 (Feb. 1921)-. 0039-6109. Monographic Series. US. English. bm. $50.00. W B Saunders, West Washington Square, Philadelphia PA 19105. Tel (215)574-3395. Ed Nanette Bendyna. Ind/Abst Life Sci. Collect., Excerpta Med., Energy Res. Abstr., Biol. Abstr., Chem. Abstr., Index Med., Nucl. Sci. Abstr., Hospit. Lit. Index, Sci. Cit. Index, Abr. Ed. LC RD34. NLM W1 SU764L. CODEN SCNAA7. (cum index). Circ 14,000. Clinical updates on topics of current interest, including techniques and guidelines used by experts in the field. Surgical Clinics of Chicago, 0748-6650.

SURGICAL FORUM. Main/Corp American College of Surgeons. VFOAT Postgraduate Medicine and Surgery. V. 1- 1950-. 0071-8041. US. English. an. $12.00. American College of Surgeons, 55 East Erie Street, Chicago IL 60611. Tel (312)664-4050. Ind/Abst Excerpta Med., Energy Res. Abstr., Life Sci. Collect., Biol. Abstr., Chem. Abstr., Nucl. Sci. Abstr., Index Med. NLM W1 SU765F. CODEN SUFOAX.

SURGICAL FORUM. V. 1- Summer 1975-. 0147-4154. Periodical. US. English. ir. Surgical Forum Baptist Medical Center—Princeton, 701 Princeton Avenue, Birmingham AL 35211. NLM W1 SU765G.

SURGICAL NEUROLOGY. V. 1- Jan. 1973-. 0090-3019. Periodical. US. English. mo. $132.00. Elsevier Science Publishing Company Inc, PO Box 1663, Grand Central Station, New York NY 10163. Tel (212)370-5520. Ed Eben Alexander Jr. Ind/Abst Excerpta Med., Index Med., Biol. Abstr., Energy Res. Abstr., Sci. Cit. Index, Abr. Ed., Hospit. Lit. Index. LC RD593. DD 617.48005. NLM W1 SU767F. CODEN SGNRAI. bk rev. adv acc. Circ 4,400. Provides timely, comprehensive and international coverage of the many important advances being made in the field of neurosurgery, both in research and clinical applications.

SURGICAL PRACTICE NEWS. V. 9- 1980-. 0273-7655. Periodical. US. English. mo. $36.00. McMahon Publishing Company, 121 South Gertrude Avenue, Paramus NJ 07652. NLM W1 SU767H. Journal of Surgical Practice, 0161-9721.

SURGICAL PROCEDURES AND TREATMENTS. Main/Corp Statistics Canada. Hospital Morbidity Section. VFOAT Interventions Chirurgicales et Traitements. 1972-. 0317-3720. CN. text in English and French. an. $2.10. Statistics Canada, Publications Distribution, Ottawa Ontario K1A 0T6 Canada. NLM W2 DC2 D63S. Surgical Procedures and Treatments, 0317-3720.

SURGICAL PRODUCT NEWS. Vol. 1, No. 1 (Sept. 1981)-. 0279-4829. Periodical. US. English. bm. $12.00. Gordon Publications Inc, Box 1952 13 Emory Avenue, Dover NJ 07801-0952. Tel (201)361-9060. Ed Paul Gregory. adv acc. Circ 75,000. (ctrl). Providing surgeons, anesthesiologists, and hospital department heads with news on new medical/surgical products, equipment and services, and instruments used in the operating room, post-op and emergency departments.

SURGICAL ROUNDS. V. 1- Jan. 1978-. 0161-1372. Periodical. US. English. mo. Surgical Rounds Pub Company, 80 Shore Road, Port Washington NY 11050. Ind/Abst Cumul. Index Nurs. Allied Health Lit. LC RD1. DD 617.005. NLM W1 SU767LH.

SURGICAL TECHNIQUES ILLUSTRATED CEASED. V. 1-4. 0148-3471. Monographic Series. US. English. qt. $68.00. Little, Brown and Company, 34 Beacon Street, Boston MA 02106. LC RD41. DD 617.00222. NLM W1 SU767T.

THE SURGICAL TECHNOLOGIST. V. 11- Jan/Feb. 1979-. 0164-4238. Periodical. US. English. bm. $18.00. Association of Surgical Technologist, Caller No East, Littleton CO 80120. Tel (303)978-9010. Ind/Abst Cumul. Index Nurs. Allied Health Lit., Hospit. Lit. Index. NLM W1 SU768. Or Tech, 0275-4622.

TECHNOLOGY FOR SURGERY. Vol. 5, No. 7 (Jan. 1985)-. 8756-8624. Periodical. US. English. mo. $70.00. ECRI, 5200 Butler Pike, Plymouth Meeting PA 19462. Tel (215)825-6000. Ed J Nobel. DD 617. bk rev. A newsletter for surgeons and operating room supervisors, summarizing health care technology issues and reporting on product recalls, hazards, and problems. Health Devices Update. Surgery.

THAI JOURNAL OF SURGERY. (THAI JOURNAL OF SURGERY : OFFICIAL PUBLICATION OF THE ROYAL COLLEGE OF SURGEONS OF THAILAND). Vol. 1, No. 1 (Jan./Mar. 1980)-. 0125-6068. Periodical. TH. English. ir. $16.00. 3/3 Sukumvit 49, Sukumvit Road, Bangkok Thailand. Tel 258-7954. Ed Thongdee Shaipanich. Ind/Abst Biol. Abstr. NLM W1 TH116. CODEN TJSUDJ. adv acc. Circ 1,000. (ctrl). Original articles in the field of clinical and experimental surgery as well as surgical foundation.

THERAPEUTISCHE UMSCHAU. VFOAT TU, Revue Therapeutique. Vol. 17, No. 12- Dec. 1960-. 0040-5930. Periodical. SZ. German (French). mo. $30.60. Hogrefe International Inc, 12-14 Bruce Park Avenue, Toronto Ontario M4P 2S3 Canada. Tel (416)482-6339. Ed P Weidmann. Ind/Abst Life Sci. Collect., Excerpta Med., Index Med., CIS Abstr., Sci. Cit. Index, Abr. Ed. NLM W1 TH549H. bk rev adv acc. Circ 6,000. This journal includes all subjects in medicine and surgery. Therapeutische Umschau und Medizinizche Bibliographie.

THE THORACIC AND CARDIOVASCULAR SURGEON. V. 27- Feb. 1979-. 0171-6425. Periodical. English. bm. $130.00. Thieme-Stratton Inc, 381 Park Avenue South/Suite 1501, New York NY 10016. Tel (212)683-5088. Ed H G Borst. Ind/Abst Life Sci. Collect., Excerpta Med., Index Med., Chem. Abstr. NLM W1 TH895. CODEN TCSUD4. Circ 1,600. Thoraxchirurgie.

TOPICAL REVIEWS IN VASCULAR SURGERY. VFOAT Vascular Surgery. Vol. 1-. 0264-3014. UK. English. ir. Ed J G Pollock and A J McKay. NLM W1 TO533F.

TRANSACTIONS OF THE AMERICAN ASSOCIATION OF GENITO-URINARY SURGEONS. Main/Corp American Association of Genito-Urinary Suegeons. Vol. 1- 1906-. 0065-7204. US. English. an. Williams and Wilkins Company, 428 East Preston Street, Baltimore MD 21202. Ind/Abst Energy Res. Abstr. NLM W1 TR224J.

TRANSACTIONS OF THE MEETING OF THE AMERICAN SURGICAL ASSOCIATION. Main/Corp American Surgical Association. V. 1- 1880/1883-. 0066-0833. US. English. an. $20.00. Lippincott/Harper, 2350 Virginia Avenue, Hagerstown MD 21740. (cum index).

TRANSPLANTATION. V. 1- Jan. 1963-. 0041-1337. Periodical. US. English. mo. $130.00. Williams & Wilkins Company, 428 East Preston Street, Baltimore MD 21202. Tel (301)528-4000. Ed Anthony P Monaco. Ind/Abst Excerpta Med., Biol. Abstr., Chem. Abstr., Energy Res. Abstr., Nucl. Sci. Abstr. LC QP89. DD 617.95. NLM W1 TR234S. CODEN TRPLAU. adv acc. Circ 2,600. Available on microfilm. Original papers and abstracts from every pertinent specialty, including immunology, hematology, endocrinology, and embryology. Transplantation Bulletin.

TRANSPLANTATION AND IMMUNOLOGY LETTER. Vol. 1, No. 1 (Sept. 1984)-. 0748-1861. Periodical. US. English. qt. $24.00. World Medical Communications Organization, 5 Center Avenue, Little Falls NJ 07424. Tel (201)890-0500. Ed Barry D Kahan. DD 616. Circ 10,000,000. (ctrl). Up-to-date information on developments and techniques in the fields of transplantation and immunology, written by leaders in these fields, with tele-lecture presentation.

TRANSPLANTATION PROCEEDINGS. V. 1- Mar. 1969-. 0041-1345. Periodical. US. English. bm. Grune and Stratton Inc, 111 Fifth Avenue, New York NY 10003. Tel (212)614-3110. Ind/Abst Life Sci. Collect., Excerpta Med., Chem. Abstr., Biol. Abstr., Index Med., Nucl. Sci. Abstr., Energy Res. Abstr., Sci. Cit. Index, Abr. Ed. LC RD120.7. DD 617.95005. NLM W1 TR235K. CODEN TRPPA8.

TRANSPLANTATION TODAY. V. 1-. 0091-2719. Periodical. US. English. ir. Grune and Stratton, 111 Fifth Avenue, New York NY 10003. Tel (212)614-3110. LC RD120.7. DD 617.95. NLM W3 TR826N.

TRANSPLANTATION TODAY (DOWNSVIEW, ONT.). (TRANSPLANTATION TODAY). Vol. 1 (Aug. 1984)-. 0825-687X. Periodical. CN. English. qt. Transplantation Today, Suite 302/345 Wilson Avenue, Downsview Ontario M3H 5W1 Canada. DD 617.95005.

TRAUMA (PRINCETON, N.J.). (TRAUMA). 0883-0304. Periodical. US. English. bw. $305.00. Nassau Publications, 228 Alexander Street, PO Box 1291, Princeton NJ 08542. DD 617.

TRAUMA QUARTERLY. VFOAT Trauma. Vol. 1, No. 1 (Nov. 1984)-. 0743-6637. Periodical. US. English. qt. $45.95. Aspen Systems Corporation, 16792 Oakmont Avenue, Gaithersburg MD 20877. DD 617. NLM W1.

TRUDY INSTITUTA - NAUCNO-ISSLEDOVATELSKIJ INSTITUT KLINICESKOJ I EKSPERIMENTAL'NOJ HIRURGII M.Z. S.S.S.R. (TRUDY INSTITUTA - NAUCHNO-ISSLEDOVATEL'SKII INSTITUT KLINICHESKOI I EKSPERIMENTAL'NOI KHIRURGII MZ SSSR). Main/Corp Nauchno-Issledovatel'skii Institut Klinicheskoi I Eksperimental'noi Khirurgii. VFOAT Trudy Nauchnogo-Issledovatel'skogo Instituta Klinicheskoi I Eksperimental'noi Khirurgii MZ SSSR. 0302-8402. Periodical. UR. Russian. NLM W1 TR958P.

DER UNFALLCHIRURG. V. 88, No. 1, (Jan. 1985)-. 0177-5537. Periodical. US. German. mo. $104.00. Springer-Verlag, 175 Fifth Avenue, New York NY 10010. Unfallheilkunde.

UNFALLCHIRURGIE. VFOAT Accident Surgery. V. 1- 1975-. 0340-2649. Periodical. English (articles in German with summaries in both languages). qt. Urban & Vogel, Postfach 15 22 09, 8000 Munchen 15 West Germany. Tel (301)539-2550. Ind/Abst Excerpta Med., Index Med. NLM W1 UN1033.

UROLOGIC SURGERY. Series/Titl Modern Technics in Surgery. 0193-8568. US. English. sa. Futura Publishing Company, PO Box 330, Mt Kisco NY 10549.

VASCULAR SURGERY. V. 1- Apr. 1967-. 0042-2835. Periodical. US. English. bm. $60.00. Westminster Publications Ltd, 1044 Northern Boulevard, Roslyn NY 11576. Tel (516)484-6880. Ind/Abst Life Sci. Collect., Excerpta Med., Biol. Abstr., Energy Res. Abstr., Index Med. LC RD598. NLM W1 VA922. CODEN VASUA9. Index in last issue of volume - attached.

VOPROSY NEJROHIRURGII. (ZHURNAL' VOPROSY NEIROKHIRURGII IMENI N. N. BURDENKO). Vol. 1- Jan. 1977-. 0042-8817. Periodical. UR. Russian. Ind/Abst Excerpta Med., Index Med., Chem. Abstr. NLM W1 ZH4243. CODEN ZVNBDJ. Voprosy Neuirokhirurgii, 0042-8817.

WEST AFRICAN JOURNAL OF SURGERY. V. 1- Feb. 1976-. 0331-054X. Periodical. English. ty. 35.00. Professor J O Sodipo, c/o Department of Anaesthesia, PO Box 2601, Surulere Nigeria. Tel (01)837818. Ed Paul Omo-Dare. NLM W1 WE329S. bk rev. adv acc. Circ 2,000. (ctrl). Devoted to the publication on information on surgical practice and science in West African region.

WORLD DIRECTORY OF NEUROLOGICAL SURGEONS. PART 1, UNITED STATES OF AMERICA AND CANADA. See Yearbooks, Almanacs, Directories.

WORLD JOURNAL OF SURGERY. V. 1- Jan. 1977-. 0364-2313. Periodical. US. English (summaries in French). bm. $98.00. Springer Verlag-New York Inc, 175 5th Avenue, New York NY 10010. Tel (212)460-1500. Ed S A Wells Jr. Ind/Abst

Medicine—Toxicology

Excerpta Med., Index Med., Life Sci. Collect., Chem. Abstr., Energy Res. Abstr. **NLM** W1 WO88K. **CODEN** WJSUDI. bk rev. Presents invited contributions from recognized authorities and provides the latest information on major clinical problems in the field. *Bulletin de la Societe Internationale de Chirurgie.*

THE YEAR BOOK OF ANESTHESIA. See Yearbooks, Almanacs, Directories.

THE YEAR BOOK OF ORTHOPEDICS. See Yearbooks, Almanacs, Directories.

THE YEAR BOOK OF ORTHOPEDICS AND TRAUMATIC SURGERY. See Yearbooks, Almanacs, Directories.

THE YEAR BOOK OF PLASTIC AND RECONSTRUCTIVE SURGERY. See Yearbooks, Almanacs, Directories.

THE YEAR BOOK OF SURGERY. See Yearbooks, Almanacs, Directories.

ZEITSCHRIFT FUR EXPERIMENTELLE CHIRURGIE. Began with: Vol. 1, No. 2 (Feb. 2, 1976). Ceased in 1982. 0323-5580. Periodical. English and German, with summaries in Russian. bm. $66.59. Kunst & Wissen Erich Bieber, Dufourstrasse 51, CH-8008 Zurich Switzerland. Tel 011-41-1-69 44 20. **Ind/Abst** Excerpta Med., Chem. Abstr. **NLM** W1 ZE344. **CODEN** ZECHDX. *Zeitschrift fur Experimentelle Chirurgie und Chirurgische Forschung, 0044-2704.*

ZEITSCHRIFT FUR EXPERIMENTELLE CHIRURGIE, TRANSPLANTATION, UND KUNSTLICHE ORGANE : ORGAN DER SEKTION EXPERIMENTELLE CHIRURGIE DER GESELLSCHAFT FUR CHIRURGIE DER DDR. Vol. 16, No. 1-. Periodical. GE. German (summaries in English and Russian). bm. **Ind/Abst** Excerpta Med., Index Med., Chem. Abstr. **NLM** W1 ZE344D. *Zeitschrift fur Experimentelle Chirurgie.*

ZEITSCHRIFT FUR KINDERCHIRURGIE. (ZEITSCHRIFT FUR KINDERCHIRURGIE : ORGAN DER DEUTSCHEN, DER SCHWEIZERISCHEN UND DER OSTERREICHISCHEN GESELLSCHAFT FUR KINDERCHIRURGIE). **VFOAT** Surgery in Infancy and Childhood. Vol. 31, Issue 1 (Sept. 1980)-. 0174-3082. Periodical. German (English). bm. $188.00. Thieme-Stratton Inc, 381 Park Avenue South, New York NY 10016. Tel (212)683-5088. **Ind/Abst** Life Sci. Collect., Excerpta Med., Index Med., Biol. Abstr., Energy Res. Abstr. **NLM** W1 ZE43A. **CODEN** ZEKID8. *Zeitschrift fur Kinderchirurgie und Grenzgebiete.*

ZEITSCHRIFT FUR KINDERCHIRURGIE UND GRENZGEBIETE CEASED. Vol. 1-30, No. 4, 0044-2909. Periodical. German. ir.

ZEITSCHRIFT FUR PLASTISCHE CHIRURGIE CEASED. **VFOAT** Plastische Chirurgie. No. 1-5. 0342-7978. Periodical. GW. German. qt. Hippokrates & Verlag, Postfach 593, D-7000 Stuttgart West Germany. **Ind/Abst** Excerpta Med. **NLM** W1 ZE543.

ZENTRALBLATT FUR CHIRURGIE. Vol. 30- Jan. 3, 1903-. 0044-409X. Periodical. GE. German. wk. $59.57. Kunst & Wissen Erich Bieber, Dufourstrasse 51, CH-8008 Zurich Switzerland. Tel 011-41-1-69 44 20. **Ind/Abst** Life Sci. Collect., Excerpta Med., Index Med., Chem. Abstr., Sci. Cit. Index, Abr. Ed. **NLM** W1 ZE777H. **CODEN** ZECHAU. *Centralblatt fur Chirurgie.*

ZENTRALBLATT FUR CHIRURGIE. SONDERBAND. German. bm. 140.40. Deutscher Buch Export-Import, Leninstrasse 16, DDR-701 Leipzig East Germany. Tel 70131. Ed H Wolff. bk rev. adv acc. Readers are informed current, versatile and concise about practice, clinic, research and postgraduate training.

ZENTRALBLATT FUR NEUROCHIRURGIE. Vol. 1-. 0044-4251. Periodical. GE. German (summaries in Russian, English, or French). ir. $30.87. Kunst & Wissen Erich Bieber, Dufourstrasse 51, CH-8008 Zurich Switzerland. Tel 011-41-1-69 44 20. **Ind/Abst** Life Sci. Collect., Excerpta Med., Index Med. **NLM** W1 ZE78.

ZENTRALBLATT HALS-NASEN-OHRENHEILKUNDE, PLASTISCHE CHIRURGIE AN KOPF UND HALS. **VFOAT** Oto-Rhino-Laryngology, Plastic Surgery of Head and Neck. Vol. 128, No. 1-. German English. mo. Springer Verlag-New York Inc, 175 5th Avenue, New York NY 10010. Tel (212)460-1500. Ed H J Denecke, R Link, O Novotny and L Ruedi. **NLM** ZWV 100 Z56. Plastic surgery of head and neck, anesthesia, instruments, radiology, genetics, allergies, immunology, skull, head and facial structure, special problems of neck and and nose and chemotherapy.

ZENTRALORGAN CHIRURGIE. **VFOAT** Surgery. 226. Vol., No. 1-. 0722-6985. Periodical. German (English). mo. Springer Verlag-New York Inc, 175 5th Avenue, New York NY 10010. Tel (212)460-1500. Ed G Herber, F Linder, W Wachsmuth, D Zeidler, N Pfitzenmaier, J Hamer and H Buhr. **NLM** ZWO 100 Z56. General surgery, anesthesia, recovery, intensive care, pre and post-operative treatment, surgical pathophysiology, child surgery, burns, organ transplants, immunology, tumors, equipment and special surgeries. *Zentralorgan fur die Gesamte Chirurgie und Ihre Grenzgebiete.*

TOXICOLOGY

ACTA PHARMACOLOGICA ET TOXICOLOGICA. See Pharmacy.

ACTIVITIES - CHEMICAL INDUSTRY INSTITUTE OF TOXICOLOGY. (ACTIVITIES). **Main/Corp** Chemical Industry Institute of Toxicology. Vol. 1, No. 1 (June 1981)-. 8755-4259. US. English. mo. Free. Information Services of the Chemical Industry Institute of Toxicology, PO Box 12137, Research Triangle Park NC 27709. Tel (919)541-2070. Ed Willanna Griffin. LC RA1190. DD 615.9005. Circ 1,000. (ctrl) This newsletter reports on the research, testing, and training activities of CIIT, a not-for-profit toxicology laboratory engaged in the study of chemical safety.

ADVANCES IN ANALYTICAL TOXICOLOGY. Vol. 1-. 0749-7431. US. English. Biomedical Publications, PO Box 8209, Foster City CA 94404. Ed Randall Ca Baselt. LC RA1221. DD 615.90705. **NLM** W1.

ADVERSE DRUG REACTIONS AND ACUTE POISONING REVIEWS. Vol. 1, No. 1 (Spring 1982)-. 0260-647X. Periodical. UK. English. qt. $75.00. Oxford University Press, Journals Department, Walton Street, Oxford OX2 6DP England. Tel 0865 56767. Ed D M Davies and H de Glanville. **Ind/Abst** Excerpta Med., Chem. Abstr. **NLM** W1 AD92. **CODEN** ADRRDQ. bk rev. adv acc. Circ 83. Aimed at keeping the physician abreast of the extensive and scattered material in this growing subject providing critical and exhaustive reviews of current knowledge and developments.

AGENTS AND ACTIONS SUPPLEMENTS. (AGENTS AND ACTIONS. SUPPLEMENTS). **VFOAT** AAS. Agents and Actions Supplements. V. 1-. 0379-0363. Monographic Series. English. ir. Birkhauser Verlag GMBH, Postfach 133, CH-4010 Basel Switzerland. Tel 061/735300. **Ind/Abst** Life Sci. Collect., Index Med., Chem. Abstr. **NLM** W1 AG33A. **CODEN** AASUDJ. A book series accompanying the journal Agents and Actions.

ALTERNATIVE METHODS IN TOXICOLOGY. **VFOAT** Alternative Methods in Toxicology Series. Vol. 1-. 0737-402X. Periodical. US. English. $68.00 Vol. 1, $59.00 Vol. 2, $99.00 Vol. 3. Mary Ann Liebert Inc, 157 East 86th Street 2nd Floor, New York NY 10028. Tel (212)289-2300. Ed Alan M Goldberg. LC RA1199. DD 363.1964. Invitro toxicology will produce a reduction in animals used in testing while more effective methodologies will evolve to evaluate safety. To develop scientific knowledge that can lead to innovative method's for evaluation.

ANNALES DES FALSIFICATIONS, DE L'EXPERTISE CHIMIQUE ET TOXICOLOGIQUE. Yearly V. 72, No. 780 (Nov. 1979)-. 0242-6110. Periodical. FR. French. mo. 270. Commission Internationale des Industries Agricoles et Alimentaires, 35 rue du General-Foy, 75008 Paris France. **Ind/Abst** Chem. Abstr., Bibliogr. Agric. LC REVPAR. **NLM** W1 AN397AB. **CODEN** AFETDF. *Annales des Falsifications et de l'Experitse Chimique, 0003-4274.*

ANNUAL PLAN FOR FISCAL YEAR . . . - NATIONAL TOXICOLOGY PROGRAM (U.S.). **Main/Corp** National Toxicology Program (U.S.). **VFOAT** Annual Plan. 1980-. US. English. an. US Public Health Service, 200 Independence Avenue SW, Washington DC 20201. LC RA1199. DD 353.00841. **NLM** W2 A N42A. *Annual Plan, 0270-8213.*

ANNUAL REPORT OF THE INHALATION TOXICOLOGY RESEARCH INSTITUTE. **Main/Corp** Inhalation Toxicology Research Institute. **VFOAT** Inhalation Toxicology Research Institute Annual Report. 1972/73-. 0149-4392. US. English. an. $10.60. National Technical Information Service, 5285 Port Royal Road, Springfield VA 22161. LC RA1245. DD 615.91. **NLM** W1 AN76P. *Annual Report.*

ANNUAL REVIEW OF PHARMACOLOGY AND TOXICOLOGY. See Pharmacy.

API TOXICOLOGICAL REVIEWS. US. English. ir. American Petroleum Institute, 1220 L Street NW, Washington DC 20005. Tel (214)741-6791.

AQUATIC TOXICOLOGY (AMSTERDAM, NETHERLANDS). (AQUATIC TOXICOLOGY). Vol. 1, No. 1 (Apr. 1981)-. 0166-445X. Periodical. English. bm. Elsevier Science Publishers, PO Box 211, 1000 AE Amsterdam Netherlands. Tel (020)5803.911. **Ind/Abst** Life Sci. Collect., Can. Environ., Eng. Index Annu., Eng. Index Mon., Eng. Index Bioeng. Abstr., Eng. Index Energy Abstr., Sel. Water Resour. Abstr., Excerpta Med., Biol. Abstr., Chem. Abstr., Ringdoc, Pestdoc, Vetdoc, Energy Inf. Abstr., Environ. Abstr. LC QH545.W3. DD 574.5263. **NLM** W1. **CODEN** AQTODG.

AQUATIC TOXICOLOGY SERIES. Vol. 1-. 0734-1687. Monographic Series. US. English. ir. Raven Press, 1140 Avenue of the Americas, New York NY 10036. Tel (212)575-0335. Ed Lavern J Weber. **Ind/Abst** Biol. Abstr. **NLM** W1 AQ927. **CODEN** ATOXD5.

ARCHIVES OF ENVIRONMENTAL CONTAMINATION AND TOXICOLOGY. See Genealogy and Heraldry - Archives.

ARCHIVES OF TOXICOLOGY. See Genealogy and Heraldry - Archives.

ARCHIVES OF TOXICOLOGY. SUPPLEMENT. See Genealogy and Heraldry - Archives.

ARCHIVOS DE FARMACOLOGIA Y TOXICOLOGIA. See Genealogy and Heraldry - Archives.

BENCHMARK PAPERS IN TOXICOLOGY. Vol. 1-. 0739-4012. Periodical. US. English. ir. Princeton Scientific Publisher, PO Box 3159, Princeton NJ 08540. **NLM** W1.

BIBRA BULLETIN. Periodical. UK. English. mo. **NLM** W1.

BIORESEARCH TODAY. INDUSTRIAL HEALTH & TOXICOLOGY. See Industrial Health & Safety.

BROMATOLOGIA I CHEMIA TOKSYKOLOGICZNA. 0365-9445. Periodical. PL. Polish (tables of contents and summaries in English and Russian). qt. ARS Polona, Krakowskie Przedmiescie 7, 00-068 Warsaw Poland. **Ind/Abst** Life Sci. Collect., Excerpta Med., Chem. Abstr., Bibliogr. Agric. **NLM** W1 BR784. **CODEN** BCTKAG. *Zeszyty Naukowe Bromatologii i Chemii Toksykologicznej.*

BULLETIN - NATIONAL CLEARINGHOUSE FOR POISON CONTROL CENTERS CEASED. (BULLETIN). Ceased with V. 26, No. 2, April/June 1982. 0049-5484. Periodical. US. English. qt. US Department of Health and Human Services, Food & Drug Administration, Bureau of Drugs, Division of Poison Control, 5600 Fishers Lane/Room 1345, Rockville MD 20857. **Ind/Abst** Am. Stat. Index, Energy Res. Abstr. LC RA1190. DD 363.179. **NLM** W1 BU75T.

BULLETIN OF ENVIRONMENTAL CONTAMINATION AND TOXICOLOGY. V. 1- Jan./Feb. 1966-. 0007-4861. Periodical. US. English. mo. Springer Verlag New York Inc, 175 5th Avenue, New York NY 10010. Tel (212)460-1500. Ed H Nigg. **Ind/Abst** Eng. Index Annu., Eng. Index Mon., Eng. Index, Biol. Agric. Index, Life Sci. Collect., Ocean. Abstr., Can. Environ., Sel. Water Resour. Abstr., Pestdoc, Ringdoc, Vetdoc, Coal Abstr., Excerpta Med., Energy Inf. Abstr., Environ. Abstr., Index Med., Abstr. Bull. Inst. Paper Chem., Int. Aerosp. Abstr., Biol. Abstr., Curr. Contents, Chem. Abstr., Energy Res. Abstr., Biol. Agric. Index, Sci. Cit. Index, Abr. Ed., Ocean. Abstr., Pet. Abstr., Eng. Index. LC RA565.A1. DD 613.1. **NLM** W1 BU761C. **CODEN** BECTA6. Disseminates

Medicine—Toxicology

advances and discoveries in the areas of air, soil, water and food contamination and pollution. Provides a meeting ground for researchers to share in new discoveries as soon as they are made.

BULLETIN SIGNALETIQUE 330 : SCIENCES PHARMACOLOGIQUES, TOXICOLOGIE. See Pharmacy.

CLINICAL TOXICOLOGY CEASED. V. 1-18. 0009-9309. Periodical. US. English. mo. $302.00. Ind/Abst Life Sci. Collect., Pestdoc, Ringdoc, Vetdoc, Excerpta Med., Energy Inf. Abstr., Environ. Abstr., Biol. Abstr., CIS Abstr. LC RA1190. DD 615.9005. NLM W1. CODEN CTOXAO.

CLINICAL TOXICOLOGY CONSULTANT. 1979. 0196-3384. Periodical. US. English. sa. $17.50. Clinical Toxicology Consultant, 800 Madison, PO Box 63032, Memphis TN 38163. Tel (901)755-2193. Ed Vasilius A Skoutakis. Ind/Abst Chem. Abstr. LC RA1190. DD 615.9005. NLM W1 CL797E. CODEN CTCOD8. adv acc. Information and articles of toxicology nature and management of such cases.

COMPARATIVE BIOCHEMISTRY AND PHYSIOLOGY. COMPARATIVE PHARMACOLOGY AND TOXICOLOGY. See Pharmacy.

CONCEPTS IN TOXICOLOGY. Vol. 1-. Monographic Series. English. ir. Tel (061)39 08 80. Ed F Homburger. NLM W1. Body of knowledge undergoing extremely rapid change in a form which appeals to the beginner as well as to the advanced specialist who is curious about fields outside his own.

CRC CRITICAL REVIEWS IN TOXICOLOGY. Main/Corp Chemical Rubber Company. VFOAT Critical Reviews in Toxicology. V. 1, 1971-V.6, 1979. 0045-6446. Periodical. US. English. qt. CRC Press Inc, 2000 Corporate Boulevard NW, Boca Raton FL 33431. Tel (305)994-0555. Ind/Abst Chem. Abstr., Sci. Cit. Index, Abr. Ed., Pollut. Abstr. Indexes, Index Med. LC RA1190. DD 615.9005. NLM W1 C555N.

CURRENT ADVANCES IN PHARMACOLOGY & TOXICOLOGY. VFOAT Current Advances in Pharmacology and Toxicology. Vol. 1, No. 1 (Jan. 1984)-. 0741-1685. UK. English. mo. $375.00. Pergamon Press Inc, Maxwell House, Fairview Park, Elmsford NY 10523. Tel (914)592-7700. Ed H Smith. LC Z6665.A1, RM1. DD 016.6151. Circ 1,200. Gives listings of titles of pharmacological and toxicological papers published throughout the world. Classified into 114 major areas.

DEVELOPMENTS IN TOXICOLOGY AND ENVIRONMENTAL SCIENCE. V. 1-. 0165-2214. Monographic Series. English. ir. Elsevier Science Publications Inc Co, PO Box 1663 Grand Central Station, New York NY 10163. Tel (212)370-5520. Ind/Abst Index Med., Chem. Abstr. NLM W1 DE998T. CODEN DTESD7.

DIRECTORY OF TOXICOLOGY TESTING INSTITUTIONS IN THE UNITED STATES. See Yearbooks, Almanacs, Directories.

DRUG AND CHEMICAL TOXICOLOGY. V. 1- 1977/78-. 0148-0545. Periodical. US. English. bm. $139.00. Marcel Dekker Inc/Journals Department, PO Box 11305/Church Street Station, New York NY 10249. Tel (212)696-9000. Ed John G Keller. Ind/Abst Art Archaeol. Tech. Abstr., Biol. Abstr., Bull. Signal., Chem. Abstr., Curr. Aware. Bull., Curr. Contents, Life Sci. Collect., Environ. Period. Bibliogr., Excerpta Med., Index Med., Int. Pharm. Abstr., Sci. Cit. Index, Abr. Ed., Pestdoc, Ringdoc, Autom. Subj. Citation Alert. LC RA1190. DD 615.9005. NLM W1 DR513G. CODEN DCTODJ. bk rev. adv acc. (ctrl). Leading source in current scientific papers pertaining to: general animal toxicology, carcinogenesis, teratology, mutagenesis, metabolism and mechanism of action, and immunotoxicology.

DRUG METABOLISM AND DISPOSITION. (DRUG METABOLISM AND DISPOSITION : THE BIOLOGICAL FATE OF CHEMICALS). V. 1- Jan./Feb. 1973-. 0090-9556. Periodical. US. English. bm. $95.00. Williams & Wilkins Company, 428 East Preston Street, Baltimore MD 21202. Tel (301)528-4000. Ed Vincent G Zannoni. Ind/Abst Life Sci. Collect., Pestdoc, Ringdoc, Vetdoc, Excerpta Med., Index Med., Biol. Abstr., Chem. Abstr., Energy Res. Abstr., Sci. Cit. Index, Abr. Ed. LC RM301. DD 615.705. NLM W1 DR533M. CODEN DMDSAI. adv acc. Circ 1,075. Covers metabolism of pharmacologist agents or drugs and environmental chemicals, reactants, and preservatives for pharmacologists, toxicologists, and medicinal chemists.

DRUG METABOLISM REVIEWS CEASED. V. 1- 1972-. 0012-6594. Periodical. US. English. bm. $195.00. Marcel Dekker Inc, PO Box 11305, Church Street Station, New York NY 10249. Tel (212)696-9000. Ed Frederick J di Carlo. Ind/Abst Biol. Abstr., Chem. Abstr., Curr. Contents, Life Sci., Excerpta Med., Index Med., Life Sci. Collect., Pestdoc, Ringdoc, Sci. Cit. Index, Abr. Ed., Vetdoc, Energy Res. Abstr. LC RM301. DD 615.7. NLM W1 DR534. (cum index). bk rev. adv acc. (ctrl) Reviews of all aspects of drug metabolism research, ranging across established, new, and potential drugs as well as environmentally toxic chemicals.

EISHI JOHO. VFOAT NIHS Information. No. 1 (1981. 3)-. Periodical. JA. Japanese. ir. Kokuritsu Eisei Shikenjo Kagaku Busshitsu Johobu, 18-1 Kamiyoga 1, Setagaya-ku, Tokyo-To Japan. LC RA1190.

ESSAYS IN TOXICOLOGY. V. 1-. 0071-1446. US. English. Academic Press, Library Services, Orlando FL 32887. Tel (305)345-4500. Ed Wayland J Hayes Jr. Ind/Abst Energy Inf. Abstr., Environ. Abstr., Biol. Abstr., Chem. Abstr. LC RA1190. DD 615.9008. NLM W1 ES674TE. CODEN ETOXAC.

EXCERPTA MEDICA. SECTION 30. PHARMACOLOGY AND TOXICOLOGY. See Pharmacy.

EXCERPTA MEDICA. SECTION 52, TOXICOLOGY. VFOAT Toxicology. V. 1, Issue 1- - Abstracts No. 1-380-. 0167-8353. Periodical. English. ir. Elsevier Science Publishers, PO Box 211, 1000 AE Amsterdam The Netherlands. NLM ZW 1 E978WD. CODEN TXICDD. Excerpta Medica. Section 30, Pharmacology and Toxicology, Excerpta Medica. Section 30, Pharmacology and Toxicology.

FOOD AND CHEMICAL TOXICOLOGY. (FOOD AND CHEMICAL TOXICOLOGY : AN INTERNATIONAL JOURNAL PUBLISHED FOR THE BRITISH INDUSTRIAL BIOLOGICAL RESEARCH ASSOCIATION). V. 20, No. 1 (Feb. 1982)-. 0278-6915. Periodical. UK. English. mo. Pergamon Press, 395 Sawmill River Road, Elmsford NY 10523. Ind/Abst Electron. Commun. Abstr. J., ISMEC Bull., Pollut. Abstr. Indexes, Saf. Sci. Abstr. J., Life Sci. Collect., Pestdoc, Ringdoc, Vetdoc, Excerpta Med., Index Med., Biol. Abstr., Chem. Abstr., Agric., World Surf. Coat. Abstr. LC RA1190. DD 615.9005. NLM W1 FO403. CODEN FCTOD7. Food and Cosmetics Toxicology, 0015-6264.

FOOD AND COSMETICS TOXICOLOGY. V. 1-19. 0015-6264. Periodical. UK. English (French). bm. $100.00 Institutions, $25.00 Individuals. Maxwell House, Fairview Park, Elmsford NY 10523. Ind/Abst Excerpta Med., Energy Inf. Abstr., Environ. Abstr., Biol. Abstr., Chem. Abstr., Index Med., Nuci. Sci. Abstr., Sel. Water Resour. Abstr. LC RA1190. DD 614.3005. NLM W1 FO404. CODEN FCTXAV.

FUNDAMENTAL AND APPLIED TOXICOLOGY. (FUNDAMENTAL AND APPLIED TOXICOLOGY : OFFICIAL JOURNAL OF THE SOCIETY OF TOXICOLOGY). Vol. 1, No. 1 (Jan./Feb 1981)-. 0272-0590. Periodical. US. English. bm. $50.00 Domestic, $60.00 Foreign. Society of Toxicology, 475 Wolf Ledges Parkway, Akron OH 44311. Ind/Abst Electron. Commun. Abstr. J., ISMEC Bull., Pollut. Abstr. Indexes, Saf. Sci. Abstr. J., Life Sci. Collect., Excerpta Med., Coal Abstr., Index Med., Chem. Abstr. LC RA1190. DD 615.9005. NLM W1 FU538M. CODEN FAATDF.

HAZARDOUS AND TOXIC SUBSTANCES. V. 1-. 0163-9099. Monographic Series. US. English. ir. Marcel Dekker, 270 Madison Avenue, New York NY 10016. Ed S S Block. Ind/Abst Chem. Abstr. NLM W1 HA984M. CODEN HTSUDP.

HUMAN TOXICOLOGY. Vol. 1, No. 1-. 0144-5952. Periodical. UK. English. qt. $168.00. H Holt MacMillan Journals, Houndmills, Basingstoke Hants RG21 2XS United Kingdom. Tel (0256)29242. Ed Paul Turner. Ind/Abst Electron. Commun. Abstr. J., ISMEC Bull., Pollut. Abstr. Indexes, Saf. Sci. Abstr. J., Life Sci. Collect., Excerpta Med., Energy Inf. Abstr., Environ. Abstr., Index Med., Chem. Abstr., Energy Res. Abstr. NLM W1 HU465T. CODEN HUTODJ. bk rev. adv acc. Circ 800. Covers all aspects of human toxicology embracing both animal research with particular relevance to man and studies with humans.

INTERNATIONAL JOURNAL OF CLINICAL PHARMACOLOGY, THERAPY AND TOXICOLOGY (INTERNATIONAL SYMPOSIA ON CLINICAL PHARMACOLOGY : 1980). See Pharmacy.

JOURNAL DE TOXICOLOGIE MEDICALE. V. No. 1, (Jan./March 1981)-. 0249-6216. Periodical. US. French (English). bm. Masson Publishers USA Inc, 211 East 43rd Street/Room 1306, New York NY 10017. Tel (212)370-1937. Ind/Abst Life Sci. Collect., Excerpta Med., Chem. Abstr. NLM W1 JO363M. CODEN JTOMD3. Medecine Legale, Toxicologie, 0241-6751.

JOURNAL OF ANALYTICAL TOXICOLOGY. V. 1- Jan./Feb. 1977-. 0146-4760. Periodical. US. English. bm. $103.00. Journal of Analytical Toxicology, Niles IL 60648. Tel (312)965-0566. Ed Randall C Baselt. Ind/Abst Life Sci. Collect., Excerpta Med., Coal Abstr., Index Med., Biol. Abstr., Ref. Source, Chem. Abstr., Energy Res. Abstr., Sci. Cit. Index, Abr. Ed. LC RA1221. DD 615.90705. NLM W1 JO536CK. CODEN JATOD3. bk rev. adv acc. Circ 1,100. International journal publishing scientific communications relating to the isolation, identification and quantitation of potentially toxic substances and their biotransformation.

JOURNAL OF APPLIED TOXICOLOGY. (JOURNAL OF APPLIED TOXICOLOGY : JAT). VFOAT JAT. Vol. 1, No. 1 (Feb. 1981)-. 0260-437X. Periodical. US. English. bm. $143.00. Subscriptions Department of John Wiley & Sons, Baffins Lane, Chichester Sussex PO19 1UD England. Ind/Abst Electron. Commun. Abstr. J., ISMEC Bull., Pollut. Abstr. Indexes, Saf. Sci. Abstr. J., Life Sci. Collect., Excerpta Med., Coal Abstr., World Surf. Coat. Abstr., Index Med., Biol. Abstr., Chem. Abstr. LC RA1190. DD 615.9005. NLM W1 JO544KC. CODEN JJATDK. Issued also on microfilm or microfiche.

JOURNAL OF IN VITRO TOXICOLOGY. 0888-319X. Periodical. US. English. qt. Mary Ann Liebert Inc, 157 East 86th Street, New York NY 10028.

JOURNAL OF THE AMERICAN COLLEGE OF TOXICOLOGY. Vol. 1, No 1-. 0730-0913. Periodical. US. English. qt. $110.00. Mary Ann Liebert Inc, 157 East 86th Street, New York NY 10028. Tel (212)289-2300. Ed Mildred S Christian. Ind/Abst Electron. Commun. Abstr. J., ISMEC Bull., Pollut. Abstr. Indexes, Saf. Sci. Abstr. J., Life Sci. Collect., Chem. Abstr. LC RA1190. DD 615.9005. NLM W1. CODEN JACTDZ. bk rev. adv acc. Covers the entire field of toxicology, includes research in risk assessment, general toxicology, carcinogenesis, safety evaluation, reproductive and genetic toxicology, epidemiology and clinical toxicology, mechanisms of toxicity, etc.

JOURNAL OF TOXICOLOGICAL SCIENCES. (THE JOURNAL OF TOXICOLOGICAL SCIENCES). V. 1- Jan. 1976-. 0388-1350. Periodical. JA. Japanese (articles in Japanese). qt. $14.69. Japanese Society of Toxicol of Sciences, 4th Floor/Bakkai Building 4-16 Yayoi 2-Chme, Binkyo KY Tokyo 113 Japan. Ind/Abst Excerpta Med., Index Med., Biol. Abstr., Chem. Abstr. NLM W1 JO966J. CODEN JTSCDR.

JOURNAL OF TOXICOLOGY AND ENVIRONMENTAL HEALTH. V. 1- Sept. 1975-. 0098-4108. Periodical. US. English. $454.50. Hemisphere Publishing Corporation, 79 Madison Avenue #1110, New York NY 10016. Tel (202)783-3958. Ed G Zweig and R Kimbrough. Ind/Abst Excerpta Med., Can. Environ., Life Sci. Collect., Pestdoc, Ringdoc, Vetdoc, Coal Abstr., Energy Inf. Abstr., Environ. Abstr., Index Med., Biol. Abstr., Chem. Abstr., Bibliogr. Agric., Energy Res. Abstr., Sci. Cit. Index, Abr. Ed., Pollut. Abstr. Indexes. LC RA1190. DD 615.9005. NLM W1 JO966K. CODEN JTEHD6. bk rev. adv acc. Circ 1,100. Referred papers emphasizing the toxicological effects on humans of natural and anthropogenic environmental pollutants and their action on intact organisms as well as in-vitro systems.

JOURNAL OF TOXICOLOGY. CLINICAL TOXICOLOGY. VFOAT Clinical Toxicology. Vol. 19, No. 1 (Mar. 1982)-. 0731-3810. Periodical. US. English. bm. $285.00. Marcel Dekker Journals, PO Box 11305, Church Street Station, New York NY 10249. Ed Helmut M Redetzki. Ind/Abst CIS Abstr., Life Sci. Collect., Excerpta Med., Arch. Environ. Health, Biol. Dig., Chem. Abstr., Curr. Aware. Biol. Sci., Curr. Contents, Environ. Period. Bibliogr.,

Medicine—Toxicology

Int. Pharm. Abstr., Med. Abstr. Serv., Psychol. Abstr., Psychopharmacology Abstr., Sci. Cit. Index, Abr. Ed., Energy Res. Abstr., Biol. Abstr., Index Med. DD 615. NLM W1 JO966KC. CODEN JTCTDW. bk rev. adv acc. *Clinical Toxicology, 0009-9309.*

JOURNAL OF TOXICOLOGY. CUTANEOUS AND OCULAR TOXICOLOGY. VFOAT Cutaneous and Ocular Toxicology. Vol. 1, No. 1-. 0731-3829. Periodical. US. English. qt. $175.00. Marcel Dekker Inc, PO Box 11305 Church Street Station, New York NY 10249. Tel (212)696-9000. Ed Edward M Jackson. Ind/Abst Life Sci. Collect., Excerpta Med., Chem. Abstr. NLM W1. CODEN JTOTDO. bk rev. adv acc. (ctrl). Focuses three disciplines- toxicology, dermatology, and/or thalmology on interactions of the skin and eyes with tropical products and the environment.

JOURNAL OF TOXICOLOGY. TOXIN REVIEWS. VFOAT Toxin Reviews. Vol. 1, No. 1-. 0731-3837. Periodical. US. English. ir. $95.00. Marcel Dekker, PO Box 11308, Church Street Station, New York NY 10249. Tel (212)696-9000. Ed W T Shier. Ind/Abst Life Sci. Collect., Excerpta Med., Chem. Abstr. LC RA1190. DD 615.9005. NLM W1 JO966KD. CODEN JTTRD9. bk rev. adv acc. (ctrl). Gathers the latest interdisciplinary findings on toxins and toxin mechanisms, class, flying toxins by their mechanisms of action and on new, underutilized substances.

THE KETTERING ABSTRACTS OF AVAILABLE LITERATURE ON THE BIOLOGICAL AND RELATED ASPECTS OF LEAD AND ITS COMPOUNDS. See Indexes/Abstracts.

MODERN PHARMACOLOGY-TOXICOLOGY. See Pharmacy.

MONOGRAPHS IN TOXICOLOGY : ENVIRONMENTAL AND SAFETY ASPECTS. 0273-2939. Monographic Series. UK. English. ir. John Wiley & Sons, 605 Third Avenue, New York NY 10158.

MUTATION RESEARCH. GENETIC TOXICOLOGY TESTING. VFOAT Genetic Toxicology Testing. 0165-1218. Periodical. English. mo. Elsevier Science Publishers, PO Box 211, 1000 AE Amsterdam Netherlands. Tel (020)5803.911. Ind/Abst Bibliogr. Agric. NLM W1 MU973. CODEN MUREAV. *Mutation Research, 0027-5107.*

MUTATION RESEARCH. REVIEWS IN GENETIC TOXICOLOGY. VFOAT Reviews in Genetic Toxicology. 0165-1110. Periodical. English. bm. Elsevier Science Publishers, PO Box 211, 1000 AE Amsterdam Netherlands. Tel (020)5803.911. NLM W1 MU973. CODEN MUREAV. *Mutation Research, 0027-5107.*

NATIONAL FLUORIDATION NEWS. V. 1- Jan. 1955-. 0027-9269. Periodical. US. English. qt. $2.50 Domestic, $4.00 Foreign. The National Fluoridation News, PO Box 1611, San Anselmo CA 94960. Tel (415)453-0158. Ed Shirley Graves. bk rev. Circ 4,500. Articles on research as reported in medical and scientific journals on the toxicity of fluorides and fluoridation. Statements by professionals, legislation update, and news items.

NEUROBEHAVIORAL TOXICOLOGY AND TERATOLOGY. Vol. 3, No. 1 (Spring 1981)-. 0275-1380. Periodical. US. English. bm. $225.00. Ankho International Inc, PO Box 380227, San Antonio TX 78280. Tel (315)463-0182. Ed Zoltan Annau. Ind/Abst Excerpta Med., Life Sci. Collect., Index Med., Biol. Abstr., Chem. Abstr., Curr. Contents, Sci. Cit. Index, Abr. Ed., Psychol. Abstr. LC RA1224. DD 616.8. NLM W1 NE323FA. CODEN NTOTDY. adv acc. Publishes original reports of systematic studies in the areas of neural toxicology and teratology in which the primary emphasis and theoretical context are on the nervous system and behavior. *Neurobehavioral Toxicology, 0191-3581.*

NEUROTOXICOLOGY. VFOAT Neuro Toxicology. V. 1- 1979-. 0161-813X. Periodical. US. English. qt. Intox Press Inc, #1 Intox Drive, Redfield AR 72132. Tel (501)397-5209. Ed Joan M Cranmer. Ind/Abst Life Sci. Collect., Excerpta Med., Index Med., Biol. Abstr., Chem. Abstr., Sci. Cit. Index, Abr. Ed., Med. Abstr. Serv., Biol. Dig., Arch. Environ. Health, Curr. Contents. LC RC321. NLM W1 NE3494HB. CODEN NRTXDN. bk rev. adv acc. Circ 1,000. Covers all aspects of the effects of toxic substance on the nervous system of man and animals.

PROGRESS IN PESTICIDE BIOCHEMISTRY AND TOXICOLOGY. VFOAT Progress in Pesticide Biochemistry. Vol. 3 (1983)-. UK. English. Ed D H Hutson and T R Roberts.

LC QP801.P38. DD 632.95. *Progress in Pesticide Biochemistry, 0730-1898.*

PROGRESS IN TOXICOLOGY : SPECIAL TOPICS. V. 1- 1973-. Periodical. English. ir. Springer Verlag-New York Inc, 175 5th Avenue, New York NY 10010. Tel (212)460-1584.

REGISTRY OF TOXIC EFFECTS OF CHEMICAL SUBSTANCES. VFOAT Registry of Toxic Effects. Began with 1975. 0361-2546. US. English. an. Superintendent of Documents, US Government Printing Office, Washington DC 20402. LC RA1215. DD 615.9020212. NLM QV 605 T755. *Toxic Substances (Rockville, MD.).*

REGULATORY TOXICOLOGY AND PHARMACOLOGY. (REGULATORY TOXICOLOGY AND PHARMACOLOGY : RTP). VFOAT RTP. Vol. 1, No. 1 (June 1981)-. 0273-2300. Periodical. US. English. qt. $76.00. Academic Press, 4805 Sand Lake Road, Orlando FL 32819. Tel (305)345-4100. Ind/Abst Excerpta Med., Energy Inf. Abstr., Environ. Abstr., Index Med., Chem. Abstr. LC RA1190. DD 363.7384. NLM W1. CODEN RTOPDW.

REPRODUCTIVE TOXICOLOGY. Vol. 1, No. 1 (Apr. 5, 1982)-. 0736-5098. Periodical. US. English. bm. $80.00. Reproductive Toxicology, 2525 L Street NW, Washington DC 20037.

REVIEW OF CURRENT DHHS, DOE, AND EPA RESEARCH RELATED TO TOXICOLOGY. VFOAT Review of Current D.H.H.S., D.O.E., and E.P.A. Research Related to Toxicology. 0737-0547. US. English. an. Public Information Office, National Toxicology Program, PO Box 12233, Research Triangle Park NC 27709. LC RA1199. DD 615.90072073. *Review of Current DHEW Research Related to Toxicology, 0270-0573.*

REVIEWS IN BIOCHEMICAL TOXICOLOGY. 1-. 0163-7673. Periodical. US. English. ir. Elsevier Science Publishing, PO Box 1663/Grand Central Station, New York NY 10163. Tel (212)370-5520. Ind/Abst Chem. Abstr., Bibliogr. Agric. LC RA1190. DD 615.9005. NLM W1 RE257CEC. CODEN RBTODU.

REVIEWS IN ENVIRONMENTAL TOXICOLOGY. 1-. 0168-7255. NE. English. ir. Elsevier Science Publishing Company, 52 Vanderbilt Avenue, New York NY 10017. Ed Ernest Hodgson. Ind/Abst Chem. Abstr. LC QH545.A1. DD 574.522205. NLM W1. CODEN RETXEB.

RIVISTA DE TOSSICOLOGIA SPERIMENTALE E CLINICA. (RIVISTA DI TOSSICOLOGIA : SPERIMENTALE E CLINICA). Yearly V. 5- 1975-. 0390-6019. Periodical. IT. articles in Italian, English, or French. bm. Societa Editrece Universo, Via G B Morgagni 1, Roma Italy 00161. Ind/Abst Excerpta Med., Chem. Abstr. NLM W1 RI656D. CODEN RTSCDD. *Rivista de Clinica Tossicologica, 0390-6027.*

RUSSIAN PHARMACOLOGY AND TOXICOLOGY. See Pharmacy.

SUMMARY REPORT - FOOD PROTECTION AND TOXICOLOGY CENTER, UNIVERSITY OF CALIFORNIA, DAVIS. See Agriculture.

TOX-TIPS. (TOX-TIPS : TOXICOLOGY TESTING IN PROGRESS). VFOAT Toxicology Testing in Progress. Began with V. 1, No. 1, June 1976. 0146-1559. Periodical. US. English. mo. $50.00. National Technical Information Service, 5285 Port Royal Road, Springfield VA 22161. Tel (703)487-4630. NLM W1 T123.

TOXIC CONTROL. Vol. 4-. 0276-2242. Monographic Series. US. English. LC UNC. DD 363.179. NLM W3 TO7375. *Toxic Substances Control, 0275-5432.*

TOXIC SUBSTANCES JOURNAL. V. 1- Summer 1979-. 0199-3178. Periodical. US. English. qt. $95.00. Toxic Substances Journal, 26 Cavarly Hill Road, G Dominguez, Wilton CT 06897. Tel (203)762-7042. Ind/Abst Manage. Contents, Excerpta Med., Energy Inf. Abstr., Environ. Abstr., Chem. Abstr., Bibliogr. Agric. LC RA1190. DD 615.9005. CODEN TSUJDP.

TOXICITY ASSESSMENT BULLETIN. 0883-6345. Periodical. US. English. qt. John Wiley, 605 3rd Avenue, New York NY 10158.

TOXICOLOGIC PATHOLOGY. See Medicine - Pathology.

TOXICOLOGICAL AND ENVIRONMENTAL CHEMISTRY. Vol. 3, No. 3/4 (Mar. 1981)-. 0277-2248. Periodical. US. English. qt. 90.00. Gordon and Breach Science Publishers Inc, One Park Avenue, New York NY 10016. Ed Otto Hutzinger and Roland W Frei. Ind/Abst Life Sci. Collect., Biol. Abstr., Excerpta Med., Chem. Abstr. LC RA1190. NLM W1 TO892Z. CODEN TECSDY. bk rev. adv acc. *Toxicological and Environmental Chemistry Reviews, 0092-9867.*

TOXICOLOGICAL AND ENVIRONMENTAL CHEMISTRY REVIEWS. V. 1-3, No. 2. 0092-9867. US. English. ir. Gordon & Breach, PO Box 197, London WC2E 9PX England. Tel (01)8365125. Ind/Abst Energy Inf. Abstr., Environ. Abstr., Art Archaeol. Tech. Abstr., Chem. Abstr., Nuci. Sci. Abstr., Bibliogr. Agric. LC RA1190. DD 615.90205. NLM W1 TO893. CODEN TXECBP.

THE TOXICOLOGIST. (THE TOXICOLOGIST : AN OFFICIAL PUBLICATION OF THE SOCIETY OF TOXICOLOGY). Vol. 1, No. 1 (Mar. 1981)-. 0731-9193. Periodical. US. English. an. Society of Toxicology, 1133 15th Street NW #620, Washington DC 20005. Tel (202)293-5935. LC RA1190. DD 615.9005. Circ 4,000. Abstracts of papers presented during the Society of Toxicology annual meeting.

TOXICOLOGY. V. 1- Mar. 1973-. 0300-483X. Periodical. NE. English. mo. Elsevier Scientific Publishers, Irelands Limited, PO Box 85, Limerick Ireland. Ind/Abst Excerpta Med., Biol. Abstr., Chem. Abstr., Index Med., Life Sci. Collect., Pestdoc, Ringdoc, Vetdoc, Sci. Cit. Index, Abr. Ed., Ocean. Abstr., Pollut. Abstr. Indexes. LC RA1190. DD 615.9005. NLM W1 TO896. CODEN TXCYAC.

TOXICOLOGY ABSTRACTS. See Indexes/Abstracts.

TOXICOLOGY AND APPLIED PHARMACOLOGY. V. 1- Jan. 1959-. 0041-008X. Periodical. US. English. Academic Press, 4805 Sand Lake Road, Orlando FL 32819. Tel (305)345-4100. Ind/Abst Electron. Commun. Abstr. J., ISMEC Bull., Life Sci. Collect., Excerpta Med., Pestdoc, Ringdoc, Vetdoc, Energy Inf. Abstr., Environ. Abstr., Int. Aerosp. Abstr., CIS Abstr., Energy Res. Abstr., Bibliogr. Agric., Biol. Abstr., Chem. Abstr., Index Med., Nuci. Sci. Abstr., Sel. Water Resour. Abstr., Hospit. Lit. Index, Pollut. Abstr. Indexes, Sci. Cit. Index, Abr. Ed. LC RA1190. DD 615.05. NLM W1 TO95. CODEN TXAPA9.

TOXICOLOGY ANNUAL. 1974-. 0361-3410. US. English. ir. Dekker, 270 Madison Avenue, New York NY 10016. Ed C L Winek. Ind/Abst Chem. Abstr., Bibliogr. Agric. LC RA1190. DD 615.9005. NLM W1 TO95BE. CODEN TOANDB.

THE TOXICOLOGY FORUM ANNUAL MEETING. Main/Conf Toxicology Forum, Washington, D.C. 0198-9421. US. English. an. LC RA1191. DD 615.9005.

TOXICOLOGY IN VITRO. 0887-2333. Periodical. US. English. qt. $95.00. Pergamon Press, Maxwell House, Fairview Park, Elmsford NY 10523.

TOXICOLOGY LETTERS. V. 1- July 1977-. 0378-4274. Periodical. NE. English. bm. Elsevier Science Publishers, PO Box 211, 1000 AE Amsterdam Netherlands. Tel (020)5803.911. Ind/Abst Life Sci. Collect., Excerpta Med., Pestdoc, Ringdoc, Vetdoc, Energy Inf. Abstr., Environ. Abstr., Index Med., Biol. Abstr., Chem. Abstr., Bibliogr. Agric. NLM W1 TO95BL. CODEN TOLED5.

TOXICOLOGY RESEARCH PROJECTS DIRECTORY. See Yearbooks, Almanacs, Directories.

TOXICON. See Pharmacy.

TSCA STATUS REPORT FOR EXISTING CHEMICALS. VFOAT Toxic Substances. 0731-132X. Periodical. US. English. bm. US Environmental Protection Agency, Office of Pesticides & Toxic Substances Program Integration Division, Washington DC 20460. NLM W1 TS23. *Chemical Status Report.*

VETERINARY AND HUMAN TOXICOLOGY. V. 19- Feb. 1977-. 0145-6296. Periodical. US. English. bm. $30.00. Comparative Toxicology Lab, Kansas State University, Manhattan KA 66506. Tel (913)532-5679. Ed F W Oehme. Ind/Abst Electron. Commun. Abstr. J., ISMEC Bull., Pollut. Abstr. Indexes, Saf. Sci. Abstr., Life Sci. Collect., Excerpta Med., Energy Inf. Abstr., Environ. Abstr., Index Med., Cumul. Index Nurs. Allied Health Lit., Biol. Abstr., Chem. Abstr., Bibliogr. Agric., Hospit. Lit. Index, Sci. Cit. Index, Abr. Ed. LC SF757.5. DD 636.08959005. NLM W1 VE923. CODEN VHTODE. bk rev. adv acc. Circ 1,800. (ctrl). Scientific articles and reports on clinical toxicology problems in human beings and in animals, news from toxicology organizations, book reviews, job opportunities and news of forthcoming meetings of interest to toxicologists. *Veterinary Toxicology, 0091-5300.*

VOPROSY TRAVMATOLOGII, TOSIKOLOGII, SKOROPOSTIZHNOI SMERTI I DEONTOLOGII V EKSPERTNOI PRAKTIKE. UR. Russian. **NLM** W1 VO644Y. *Voprosy Travmatologii, Skoropostizh Skoropostizhnoi Smerti i Deontologii V Ekspertnoi Praktike.*

XENOBIOTICA. V. 1- Jan. 1971-. 0049-8254. Periodical. UK. English (French and German). mo. $370.00. Taylor & Francis Ltd, 242 Cherry Street, Philadelphia PA 19106. **Tel** (215)238-0939. **Ed** D V Parke. **Ind/Abst** Life Sci. Collect., Excerpta Med., Pestdoc, Ringdoc, Vetdoc, Index Med., Biol. Abstr., Chem. Abstr., Bibliogr. Agric., Sci. Cit. Index, Abr. Ed. **NLM** W1 XE17. **CODEN** XENOBH. Covers three main areas: general xenobiochemistry, molecular toxicology, and human metabolism and kinetics.

UROLOGY

ABMS DIRECTORY OF CERTIFIED UROLOGISTS. *See* Yearbooks, Almanacs, Directories.

ABSTRACTS - AMERICAN SOCIETY OF NEPHROLOGY. *See* Indexes/Abstracts.

ACTA DIABETOLOGICA LATINA. V. 1- Feb./Mar. 1964-. 0001-5563. Italian and English. qt. $100.00. Casa Editrice il Ponte, Piazzale Stefano Turr 5, 20149 Milano Italy. **Ind/Abst** Excerpta Med., Index Med., Biol. Abstr., Chem. Abstr., Sci. Cit. Index, Abr. Ed. **NLM** W1 AC793. **CODEN** ADILAS. (cum index).

ACTA UROLOGICA BELGICA. **Main/Corp** Societe Belge d'Urologie. V. 23- 1955-. 0001-7183. Periodical. BE. French (articles in English, Spanish, German or Italian, with summaries in French and English). qt. 2000. Assn Societe Scientifique Medica Belgica, 43 rue des Champs Elysees, B1050 Brussels Belgium. **Tel** 32-41-643677. **Ed** Christian Bouffioux. **Ind/Abst** Life Sci. Collect., Excerpta Med., Biol. Abstr., Chem. Abstr., Index Med., Nuci. Sci. Abstr. **NLM** W1 AC95524K. **CODEN** AUBEAN. Index in last issue of volume - attached. bk rev. adv acc. **Circ** 600. Clinical and investigative papers in urology.

ACTAS UROLOGICAS ESPANOLAS. Yearly V. 1 Jan/Feb 1977-. 0210-4806. Periodical. Spanish. ir. **Ind/Abst** Excerpta Med., Index Med. **NLM** W1 AC967H.

ACTUALITES NEPHROLOGIQUES DE L'HOPITAL NECKER. 1960-. 0567-8811. FR. French. an. $71.20. Flammarion & Cie, 106/110 rue Petit le Roy, 94150 Chevilly Larue France. **Ind/Abst** Excerpta Med., Chem. Abstr. **NLM** W1 AC9953. **CODEN** ANQNA8.

ADVANCES IN NEPHROLOGY FROM THE NECKER HOSPITAL. V. 1- 1971-. 0084-5957. US. English. an. Yearbook Medical Publishers, 35 East Wacker Drive, Chicago IL 60601. **Ind/Abst** Index Med., Chem. Abstr. **LC** RC902.A1. **DD** 616.61005. **NLM** W1 AD684. **CODEN** ANGYBQ.

AMERICAN JOURNAL OF KIDNEY DISEASES. (AMERICAN JOURNAL OF KIDNEY DISEASES : THE OFFICIAL JOURNAL OF THE NATIONAL KIDNEY FOUNDATION). Vol. 1, No. 1 (July 1981)-. 0272-6386. Periodical. US. English. mo. $150.00. Grune and Stratton Inc, 111 5th Avenue, New York NY 10003. **Tel** (212)614-3110. **Ind/Abst** Excerpta Med., Index Med. **NLM** W1 AM473.

AMERICAN JOURNAL OF NEPHROLOGY. 1/1 (Apr. 1981)-. 0250-8095. Periodical. English. bm. $181.00. S Karger AG, PO Box, CH-4009 Basel Switzerland. **Tel** (061)39 08 80. **Ed** S G Massry. **Ind/Abst** Life Sci. Collect., Excerpta Med., Index Med., Biol. Abstr., Chem. Abstr. **NLM** W1 AM494M. **CODEN** AJNED9. adv acc. Ranges from studies on the biochemistry and immunology of kidney diseases to new knowledge on such established clinical problems as dialysis, transplantation, and hypertension.

ANNALES D'UROLOGIE. *See* Yearbooks, Almanacs, Directories.

ANNUAL MEETING - AMERICAN UROLOGICAL ASSOCIATION INC. (ANNUAL MEETING - AMERICAN UROLOGICAL ASSOCIATION). **Main/Corp** American Urological Association. 0190-2393. Periodical. US. English. an. American Urological Association, 1120 North Charles Street, Baltimore MD 21201.

ARCHIVIO ITALIANO DI UROLOGIA E NEFROLOGIA. *See* Genealogy and Heraldry - Archives.

ARCHIVOS ESPANOLES DE UROLOGIA. *See* Genealogy and Heraldry - Archives.

AUA UPDATE SERIES. **VFOAT** A.U.A. Update Series. **VAT** American Urological Association Update Series. Vol. 1, Lesson 1-. 0740-7386. US. English. ir. $275.00. AUA Office of Education, PO Box 25147, Houston TX 77265. **Tel** (713)791-1470. **Ed** Thomas P Ball Jr. **NLM** W1 AU14D. **Circ** 2,000. (ctrl). Series of 40 original articles describing most recent techniques and changes in urology. Self-study program can be used for continuing medical education credits.

AUAA JOURNAL. (AUAA JOURNAL : OFFICIAL JOURNAL OF THE AMERICAN UROLOGICAL ASSOCIATION ALLIED). **VAT** American Urological Association Allied Journal. Began with: Vol. 1, No. 1 (July-Sept. 1980). 0882-9594. Periodical. US. English. qt. $15.00 Domestic, $17.00 Foreign. A U A A Office, 6845 Lake Shore Drive, PO Box 9397, Raytown MO 64133. **Ind/Abst** Cumul. Index Nurs. Allied Health Lit., Int. Nurs. Index. **DD** 616. **NLM** W1.

BEITRAGE ZUR UROLOGIE. Vol. 1-. 0250-3212. Monographic Series. SZ. German. ir. S Karger AG, CH-4009 Basel Switzerland. **Tel** (61)390880. **Ed** E Schmeidt and H W Bauer. **Ind/Abst** Biol. Abstr. **NLM** W1 BE461P. **CODEN** BEURDP. Experimental and applied urology. Monographic issues covering all aspects of urology, diagnosis and therapy of prostate cancer, and solving of kidney stones, for urologists, nephrologists, and oncologists.

BRITISH JOURNAL OF UROLOGY. (BRITISH JOURNAL OF UROLOGY : OFFICIAL JOURNAL OF THE BRITISH ASSOCIATION OF UROLOGICAL SURGEONS). 1929)-. 0007-1331. Periodical. UK. English. bm. $68.00. British Journal of Urology, PO Box 11318, Birmingham AL 35202. **Tel** (205)991-6920. **Ed** G D Chisholm. **Ind/Abst** Life Sci. Collect., Excerpta Med., Index Med., Biol. Abstr., Chem. Abstr., Nuci. Sci. Abstr., Sci. Cit. Index, Abr. Ed. **NLM** W1 BR646. **CODEN** BJURAN. (cum index). bk rev. adv acc. Features original articles on urological subjects including nephrology, from all over the world. Profusely illustrated with x-ray reproductions, diagrams and drawings.

BUTTERWORTHS INTERNATIONAL MEDICAL REVIEWS. UROLOGY. **VFOAT** Urology. 1-. 0260-0196. Monographic Series. UK. English. **NLM** W1.

CLINICAL NEPHROLOGY. V. 1- Jan./Feb. 1973-. 0301-0430. Periodical. GW. English. mo. $141.00. Dustri-Verlag, Dr Karl Feistle, Bahnofstrasse 9, Postfach 49, 8024 Deisenhofen West Germany. **Tel** 089-613 50 41. **Ind/Abst** Life Sci. Collect., Excerpta Med., Index Med., Biol. Abstr., Chem. Abstr., Energy Res. Abstr., Hospit. Lit. Index, Sci. Cit. Index, Abr. Ed. **NLM** W1 CL731N. **CODEN** CLNHBI.

CLINICAL TRENDS IN UROLOGY. V. 1- May 1972-. 0091-1682. Periodical. US. English. bm. Science & Medicine Publishing Co, 515 Madison Avenue, New York NY 10022. **NLM** W1 CL798N.

CONTEMPORARY ISSUES IN NEPHROLOGY. V. 1-. 0161-9934. Monographic Series. US. English. ir. Churchill Livingstone Inc, 1560 Broadway, New York NY 10036. **Tel** (212)819-5400. **Ed** B M Brenner and J H Stein. **Ind/Abst** Chem. Abstr. **DD** 616. **NLM** W1 CO769MR. **CODEN** CISND8.

CONTEMPORARY NEPHROLOGY. Vol. 1-. 0278-1700. Periodical. US. English. ir. Plenum Publishing Corp, 233 Spring Street, New York NY 10013. **Ed** Saulo Klahr and Shaul G Massry. **Ind/Abst** Chem. Abstr. **NLM** W1 CO769MX. **CODEN** CONHD7.

CONTRIBUTIONS TO NEPHROLOGY. V. 1- 1975-. 0302-5144. Monographic Series. SZ. English. ir. S Karger Ag, PO Box, CH-4009 Basel Switzerland. **Tel** (061)390880. **Ed** G M Berlyne and S Giovannetti. **Ind/Abst** Cumul. Index Nurs. Allied Health Lit., Index Med., Biol. Abstr., Chem. Abstr., Energy Res. Abstr., Sci. Cit. Index, Abr. Ed., Hospit. Lit. Index. **NLM** W1 CO778UN. **CODEN** CNEPDD. An exceptional series that explores problems of immediate importance for clinical nephrology.

CONTROVERSIES IN NEPHROLOGY. Vol. 1 (1979)-. 0270-2088. US. English. an. $40.00. Georgetown University Hospital, George Schreiner, Room 2212, Washington DC 20007. **Tel** (202)625-7253. **Ed** Schreiner, Winchester and Mendelson. **NLM** W3 CO978VP. **Circ** 1,500.

Nephrology and the various methods for treatment of disease.

COURIER. **VFOAT** Le Courrier. V. 1- Oct. 1969-. 0383-0330. Periodical. CN. text in English and French. qt. Kidney Foundation of Canada, Suite 200/5780 DeCelles Avenue, Montreal Quebec H3S 2C7 Canada. **DD** 616.61006271.

CURRENT LITERATURE IN NEPHROLOGY. 0743-8036. US. English. mo. $32.00. Current Literature Publications, 3149 Ellis Suite 301, Bellingham WA 98225. **DD** 616.

CURRENT NEPHROLOGY. V. 1- 1977-. 0148-4265. Periodical. US. English. an. Year Book Medical Publishers, 35 East Wacker Drive, Chicago IL 60601. **Ind/Abst** Chem. Abstr. **LC** RC902.A1. **DD** 616.61. **NLM** W1 CU799E. **CODEN** CUNED6.

CURRENT TRENDS IN UROLOGY. Vol. 1-. 0731-5910. US. English. ir. Williams and Wilkins, PO Box 64025, Balitmore MD 21264. **Tel** (301)528-4000. **Ed** Martin I Resnick. **NLM** W1 CU822T.

DEVELOPMENTS IN NEPHROLOGY. Vol. 1-. 0167-8205. Monographic Series. US. English. ir. Kluwer Boston Inc, 190 Old Derby Street, Hingham MA 02043. **Ind/Abst** Chem. Abstr. **DD** 616.61005. **NLM** W1. **CODEN** DNEPDO.

DIALOGUES IN PEDIATRIC UROLOGY. 0164-9507. Periodical. US. English. mo. $48.00. William J Miller Associates Inc, 45 Villa Road, Pearl River NY 10965. **Tel** (914)735-7853. **Ed** Richard M Ehrlich. **Circ** 550. Clinical publication for physicians and other medical personnel interested in the field of pediatric urology. Subscription publication.

END-STAGE RENAL DISEASE ANNUAL REPORT TO CONGRESS. **Main/Corp** U. S. Health Care Financing Administration. Office of Special Programs. 2d- 1979/80-. 0275-2298. US. English. an. **NLM** W2 A H615E. *End-Stage Renal Disease Program, Annual Report to Congress.*

EUROPEAN UROLOGY. V. 1- 1975-. 0302-2838. Periodical. SZ. English. bm. 396.-. S Karger AG, PO Box, CH-4009 Basel Switzerland. **Tel** (061)39 08 80. **Ed** C C Schulman. **Ind/Abst** Life Sci. Collect., Excerpta Med., Index Med., Biol. Abstr., Chem. Abstr., Sci. Cit. Index, Abr. Ed. **NLM** W1 EU735. **CODEN** EUURAV. adv acc. Articles offer useful information on such topics as oncology, andrology, infertility, endocrinology, lithiasis and infections.

EXCERPTA MEDICA. SECTION 28: UROLOGY AND NEPHROLOGY. *See* Indexes/Abstracts.

EXTRACTA UROLOGICA. V. 1-. 0344-5038. Periodical. German. ir. Acron Verlag Manfred Bolschakoff, Wittenbergplatz 1, 1000 Berlin 30 West Germany. **NLM** W1 EX752M.

GU, THE JOURNAL OF GENITOURINARY MEDICINE. **VFOAT** Journal of Genitourinary Medicine. V. 1- Jan. 1979-. 0164-4912. Periodical. US. English. mo. $35.00 Domestic, $40.00 Foreign. Medical Publishing, 50 Route 9, Morganville NJ 07751. **LC** RC870. **DD** 616.6005.

HINYOKIKA KIYO. **VFOAT** Acta Urologica Japonica. 0018-1994. Periodical. JA. Japanese (summaries in English). mo. $72.00. Japan Publishing Trading Company, PO Box 5030, Tokyo International, Tokyo 100-31 Japan. **Ind/Abst** Index Med., Excerpta Med., Nuci. Sci. Abstr., Chem. Abstr., Biol. Abstr. **NLM** W1 HI409. **CODEN** HIKYAJ.

ICRDB CANCERGRAM. ORGAN SITE CARCINOGENESIS. KIDNEY AND URINARY TRACT. *See* Medicine - Neoplasma, Neoplastic.

INFECTION CONTROL & UROLOGICAL CARE. **VAT** Infection Control and Urological Care. V. 2- Jan./Feb. 1977-. 0740-3615. Periodical. US. English. qt. $15.00 Domestic, $25.00 Canada. Infection Control and Urological Care, Suite 900/8 South Michigan Avenue, Chicago IL 60603. **Ind/Abst** Cumul. Index Nurs. Allied Health Lit., Int. Nurs. Index. **NLM** W1 IN406E. *Infection Control in Urological Care, 0740-3615.*

INNOVATIONS IN UROLOGY. **VFOAT** Urology. 0883-4962. Periodical. US. English. bm. $19.00. Medical Publishing Enterprises, One Bridge Plaza/Suite 270, Fort Lee NJ 07024. **DD** 616.

INTERNATIONAL JOURNAL OF ANDROLOGY. V. 1- Feb. 1978-. 0105-6263. Periodical. DK. English. bm. 570.00. Scriptor Publisher APS, Gasvaerksvej 15, DK-1565

Medicine—Urology

Copenhagen V Denmark. Tel (01) 22 92 01. Ind/Abst Life Sci. Collect., Excerpta Med., Index Med., Biol. Abstr., Chem. Abstr., Bibliogr. Agric. NLM W1 IN7653V. CODEN IJANDP. bk rev. adv acc.

THE INTERNATIONAL JOURNAL OF PEDIATRIC NEPHROLOGY. See Medicine - Pediatrics.

INTERNATIONAL PERSPECTIVES IN UROLOGY. VFOAT I.P.U. Vol. 1-. 0276-2315. Monographic Series. US. English. Williams and Wilkins, 428 East Preston Street, Baltimore MD 21202. LC UNC. NLM W1 IN827K.

INVESTIGATIVE UROLOGY CEASED. V. 1-19. 0021-0005. Periodical. US. English. bm. $30.00. Williams and Wilkins Company, 428 East Preston Street, Baltimore MD 21202. Ind/Abst Life Sci. Collect., Excerpta Med., Int. Aerosp. Abstr., Biol. Abstr., Chem. Abstr., Index Med., Nuci. Sci. Abstr., Energy Res. Abstr. LC RC870. DD 616.6005. NLM W1 IN995N.

IRCS MEDICAL SCIENCE. KIDNEYS AND URINARY SYSTEM. (IRCS MEDICAL SCIENCE : KIDNEYS AND URINARY SYSTEM). VFOAT Kidneys and Urinary System. V. 3- Jan. 1975-. 0305-6813. Periodical. UK. English. qt. $50.00. IRCS Medical Science, PO Box 500/St Leonards House, Lancaster LA1 1PF England. Tel (0524)68116. Ed S Johnson. bk rev. Publishes results of original research into all aspects of kidney and urinary system, both clinical and experimental, within weeks of completion. Papers fully refereed. *Research on the Kidneys and Urinary System, 0305-2796.*

JOURNAL OF DIALYSIS CEASED. V. 1- 1976/77-. 0362-8558. Periodical. US. English. qt. $120.00 Domestic, $130.00 Foreign. Marcel Dekker Journals, PO Box 11305 Church Street Station, New York NY 10249. Ind/Abst Life Sci. Collect., Excerpta Med. NLM W1 JO622. CODEN JDIADT.

THE JOURNAL OF THE AMERICAN ASSOCIATION OF NEPHROLOGY NURSES & TECHNICIANS CEASED. VFOAT AANNT, A.A.N.N.T. Began with V. 1-7. 0360-7615. Periodical. US. English. qt. NLM W1 JO908C.

THE JOURNAL OF UROLOGY. (THE JOURNAL OF UROLOGY : OFFICIAL JOURNAL OF THE AMERICAN UROLOGICAL ASSOCIATION, INC) V. 1- Feb. 1917-. 0022-5347. Periodical. US. English. mo. $120.00. Williams and Wilkins Company, 428 East Preston Street, Baltimore MD 21202. Tel (301)528-4000. Ed John T Grayhack. Ind/Abst Life Sci. Collect., Excerpta Med., Pestdoc, Ringdoc, Vetdoc, CIS Abstr., Art Archaeol. Tech. Abstr., Biol. Abstr., Chem. Abstr., Index Med., Nuci. Sci. Abstr., Energy Res. Abstr., Hospit. Lit. Index, Sci. Cit. Index, Abr. Ed. LC RC870. DD 616.605. NLM W1 JO968H. CODEN JOURAA. (cum index). adv acc. Circ 16,200. The premier journal in the field presents clinical papers, abstracts, commentary, research and innovative techniques for the urologist. *Investigative Urology, 0021-0005; Urological Survey, 0042-1146.*

THE KIDNEY. V. 1- 1967-. 0023-1304. Periodical. US. English. bm. $20.00. National Kidney Foundation, 2 Park Avenue, New York NY 10016. Tel (212)889-2210. Ind/Abst Excerpta Med. NLM W1 KI586N. CODEN KIDNA.

KIDNEY & URINARY TRACT DISEASES AND TREATMENT. Main/Corp National Institute of Arthritis, Metabolism, and Digestive Diseases. VFOAT NIAMDD Research Advances. VAT National Institute of Arthritis, Metabolism, and Digestive Diseases Research Advances, Kidney and Urinary Tract Diseases and Treatment. 1979-. US. English. an. National Institute of Arthritis Metabolism and Digestive Diseases, National Institutes of Health 9000 Rockville Pike, Bethesda MD 20014. NLM W1 KI586P.

KIDNEY DISEASE. V. 1-. 0270-062X. Monographic Series. US. English. ir. Marcel Dekker, 270 Madison Avenue, New York NY 10016. Ed Stewart Glassock and Van Ypersele. Ind/Abst Biol. Abstr., Chem. Abstr. LC UNC. NLM W1 KI586R. CODEN KIDID6. This is an ongoing series. Each title has a different subject.

KIDNEY DISEASE AND NEPHROLOGY INDEX. See Indexes/Abstracts.

KIDNEY INTERNATIONAL. V. 1- Jan. 1972-. 0085-2538. Periodical. US. English (summaries in French). mo. Springer Verlag-New York Inc, 175 5th Avenue, New York NY 10010. Tel (212)460-1500. Ed T E Andreoli. Ind/Abst Life Sci. Collect., Excerpta Med., Biol. Abstr., Chem. Abstr., Index Med., Sci. Cit. Index, Abr. Ed., Hospit. Lit. Index, Autom. Subj. Citation Alert. LC RC902.A1. DD 616.61005. NLM W1 KI586S. CODEN KDYIA5. Each issue of the journal covers recent laboratory and clinical research data on renal physiology, biochemistry, pathology, immunology, and morphology.

KLINISCHE UND EXPERIMENTELLE UROLOGIE. V. 1-. 0174-2512. Monographic Series. German. ir. Ind/Abst Chem. Abstr. NLM W1 KL575J. CODEN KEURDM.

MINERVA NEFROLOGICA. 0026-4873. Periodical. IT. Italian. qt. 60.00. Edizone Minerva Medica, Corso Bramante 83, Torino 10126 Italy. Tel 67 82 82. Ed P Stratta. Ind/Abst Excerpta Med., Chem. Abstr., Index Med. NLM W1 MI64805. CODEN MINEAT. bk rev. adv acc.

MINERVA UROLOGICA E NEFROLOGICA. VFOAT The Italian Journal of Urology and Nephrology. Vol. 36, 1/84 (Jan.-Mar. 1984)-. 0393-2249. Periodical. Italian. qt. 60.00. Tel 678282. Ed P Stratta. Ind/Abst Index Med. NLM W1. bk rev. adv acc. Journal addressed to specialists in urology and nephrology in Italy and abroad. It deals with topics in scientific practice and research. *Minerva Urologica, Minerva Nefrologica, 0026-4873.*

MONOGRAPHS IN UROLOGY. Vol. 1, No. 1 (Apr./May 1980)-. 0198-7577. Monographic Series. US. English. bm. Burroughs Wellcome Company, 3030 Cornwallis Drive, Triangle Park NC 27709. Tel (609)737-2250. LC UNC. DD 616.6. NLM W1 MO569M. *Urology Digest, 0197-7709.*

NEPHROLOGIE. (NEPHROLOGIE : JOURNAL TRIMESTRIEL PUBLIE PAR LA SOCIETE DE NEPHROLOGIE). Vol. 1, No 1-. 0250-4960. Periodical. SZ. French (summaries in English). qt. $31.00. Editions Medecine & Hygiene, Case Postale 229, CH-1211 Geneve 4 Switzerland. Tel (022) 46 93 55. Ind/Abst Excerpta Med., Biol. Abstr., Curr. Contents, Index Med. NLM W1 NE204D. CODEN NEPHDY.

NEPHROLOGY REVIEWS. 1980-. 0194-0090. US. English. an. John Wiley and Sons, 605 3rd Avenue, New York NY 10016. Ed L H Diamond and J E Balow. NLM ZWJ 300 N439.

NEUROUROL. URODYN. See Medicine - Neurology.

NEWSLETTER - EDMONTON EPILEPSY ASSOCIATION. (NEWSLETTER). 0824-4553. Periodical. CN. English. ir. Free. Edmonton Epilepsy Association, Suite 416, 10010-105 Street, Edmonton Alberta T5J 1C8 Canada. DD 616.853006071233. (ctrl).

NIAID CATALOG OF TISSUE TYPING ANTISERA. SUPPLEMENT. Main/Corp National Institute of Allergy and Infectious Diseases (U.S.). VFOAT N.I.A.I.D. Catalog of Tissue Typing Antisera. VAT National Institute of Allergy and Infectious Diseases Catalog of Tissue Typing Antisera. Supplement. 1978-. 0731-6585. US. English. an. Manager NIAID Serum Bank Genetics and Transplantation Biology Branch, Immunology Allergic and Immunological Diseases Program, National Institute of Allergy and Infectious Diseases, Westwood Building/Room 754, Bethesda MD 20205. NLM QW 26 N107A. *NIAID Research Resources Branch Catalog Supplement, 0277-5468.*

NUA. (NUA : INTERNATIONAL JOURNAL OF NEPHROLOGY, UROLOGY, ANDROLOGY). VFOAT International Journal of Nephrology, Urology, Andrology. Began in 1980. 0392-4629. Periodical. English. bm. Ind/Abst Excerpta Med., Biol. Abstr. NLM W1 NU106T. CODEN NIJADB.

PEDIATRIC NEPHROLOGY. See Medicine - Pediatrics.

PROCEEDINGS OF THE CLINICAL DIALYSIS AND TRANSPLANT FORUM. V. 1- 1971-. 0094-6044. Periodical. US. English. an. Dr George E Schreinter, ASAIO, PO Box 5028, Alexandria VA 22305. Ind/Abst Energy Res. Abstr., Chem. Abstr. NLM W1 PR585A. CODEN PCDFDA.

PROGRESS IN CLINICAL KIDNEY DISEASE AND HYPERTENSION. Vol. 1-. 0277-8564. Periodical. US. English. an. NLM W1 PR668GB.

PSYCHONEPHROLOGY. 1-. 0731-5899. Monographic Series. US. English. Plenum, 227 West 17th Street, New York NY 10011. Ed N B Levy. NLM W1 PS748F.

RAPPORT - REGISTRE CANADIEN DE L'INSUFFISANCE RENALE. (RAPPORT DE . . .). Main/Corp Registre Canadien de l'Insuffisance Renale. 1981-. 0821-7831. Periodical. CN. French. an. $2.50 Each Volume. Registre Canadien de l'Insuffisance Renale, c/o Fondation Canadienne des Maladies du Rein, Chapitre de l'Outaouais, 230-739B Ridgewood Avenue, Ottawa Ontario K1V 6M8 Canada. DD 616.61400971. *Report of the Canadian Renal Failure Registry, 0821-7823.*

RECENT ADVANCES IN RENAL DISEASE CEASED. No. 1- 1975-. 0309-2429. Periodical. UK. English. ir. Churchill Livingstone Inc, 1560 Broadway, New York NY 10036. Tel (212)819-5400. Ed N F Jones. Ind/Abst Chem. Abstr. NLM W1 RE105YF. CODEN RARDDE.

RECENT ADVANCES IN UROLOGY, ANDROLOGY. (RECENT ADVANCES IN UROLOGY/ANDROLOGY). No. 3-. 0261-8788. UK. English. ir. Churchill Livingstone Inc, 1560 Broadway, New York NY 10036. Tel (212)819-5400. Ed W F Hendry. NLM W1 RE105YP.

RENAL FAMILY. (THE RENAL FAMILY). 0714-8879. Periodical. CN. English. qt. The Renal Family, Suite 302/345 Wilson Avenue, Downsview Ontario M3H 5W Canada. DD 616.61005. NLM W1 RE198D.

RENAL FAMILY. (THE RENAL FAMILY). Vol. 4 (Mar. 1982)-. 0820-7283. Periodical. CN. French. qt. Fondation Canadienne des Maladies du Rein Siege Sociale Bureau 400, 1650 Ouest Boulevard de Maisonneuve, Montreal Quebec H3H 2P3 Canada. DD 616.61005.

RENAL PHYSIOLOGY. 0300-3434. UK. English. mo. $75.00. University of Sheffield, Biomedical Information Service, Sheffield S10 2TN England. Ind/Abst Sci. Cit. Index, Abr. Ed., Chem. Abstr. bk rev. Contains references on the physiology, biochemistry and pharmacology of the renal system. Also details of forthcoming events.

RENAL PHYSIOLOGY. V. 1- 1978-. 0378-5858. Periodical. SZ. English. bm. S Karger AG, PO Box, CH-4009 Basel Switzerland. Tel (061)39 08 80. Ed G M Berlyne and F Lang. Ind/Abst Life Sci. Collect., Excerpta Med., Index Med., Biol. Abstr., Chem. Abstr. NLM W1 RE198F. CODEN REPHDA. Index in last issue of volume - attached. adv acc. Original papers provide in-depth information on the anatomy, physiology, pharmacology, micropuncture and environment of the kidneys. Also reports on hemoperitoneum, dialysis and dietary therapy.

SCANDINAVIAN JOURNAL OF UROLOGY AND NEPHROLOGY. V. 1- 1967-. 0036-5599. Periodical. SW. English. ty. $80.00. Almqvist & Wiksell, 108 Drottninggatan, PO Box 45150, S-104 30 Stockholm Sweden. Tel 468166975. Ed Ake Fritjofsson. Ind/Abst Life Sci. Collect., Excerpta Med., Pestdoc, Ringdoc, Vetdoc, Index Med., Chem. Abstr., Hospit. Lit. Index, Sci. Cit. Index, Abr. Ed. NLM W1 SC154E. CODEN SJUNAS. Index in last issue of volume - attached. bk rev. adv acc. Circ 4,000. Publishes papers on urological and nephrological topics. The journal will foster basic and clinical research work.

SEMINARS IN NEPHROLOGY. Vol. 1, No. 1 (Mar. 1981)-. 0270-9295. Monographic Series. US. English. qt. $52.00. Grune & Stratton Inc, 111 5th Avenue, New York NY 10003. Tel (212)614-3110. Ind/Abst Chem. Abstr. NLM W1 SE489CM. CODEN SNEPDJ.

SEMINARS IN UROLOGY. Vol. 1, No. 1 (Feb. 1983)-. 0730-9147. Periodical. US. English. qt. $48.00. Grune and Stratton, 111 Fifth Avenue, New York NY 10003. Tel (212)614-3110. Ind/Abst Index Med. NLM W1.

TAEHAN PINYOGIKWA HAKHOE CHI. VFOAT Korean Journal of Urology. Periodical. Korean (summaries in English). ir. Taehan Pinyogikwa Hakhoe, c/o Department of Urology, Catholic Medical College, Seoul Korea. LC RC870.

DER UROLOGE. AUSG. A. Vol. 9-. 0340-2592. Periodical. WB. German. bm. Springer Verlag-New York Inc, 175-5th Avenue, New York NY 10010. Tel (212)460-1500. Ed W Knipper, J Sokeland and H R Winz. Ind/Abst Life Sci. Collect., Excerpta Med., Index Med., Biol. Abstr., Energy Res. Abstr., Curr. Contents, INIS Atomindex. NLM W1 UR624Q. CODEN URGABW. Covers all areas of urology and related areas including continued education for the urologist in the hospital and practice, also selected important subjects of general medicine and scientific articles on research. *Der Urologe.*

UROLOGE. AUSGABE B. (UROLOGE. B : ORGAN DES BERUFSVERBANDES DER DEUTSCHEN UROLOGEN). 0042-1111. Periodical. WB. German. bm. Springer Verlag-New York Inc, 715 5th Avenue, New York NY 10010. **Tel** (212)460-1500. **Ed** W Knipper, J Soekeland and H R Winz. **Ind/Abst** Excerpta Med., Life Sci. Collect., Index Med., Sci. Cit. Index, Abr. Ed. **NLM** W1 UR624R. Covers continued education for urologists including new experiences and research results in anesthesia, bacteriology, biomedical technology, surgery, dermato-venerology, gynecology and obstetrics, internal medicine and pediatrics. *Der Urologe.*

UROLOGIA. V. 1, Mar 1934-. 0042-112X. Periodical. IT. Italian (articles in English, French, German, or Spanish with summaries in Italian and English). bm. $100.00. Presso-Libreria Editrice Canova, Via Della Liberazione 40, 31030 Dosson Teviso Di Casier Italy. **Tel** (0422)547314. **Ed** Scrufari Vittorio. **Ind/Abst** Excerpta Med. **NLM** W1 UR627. bk rev. adv acc. **Circ** 700. (ctrl).

UROLOGIA INTERNATIONALIS. 0042-1138. Periodical. SZ. English. bm. 416.00. S Karger AG, PO Box 352, White Plains NY 10602. **Tel** (061)39 08 80. **Ed** G Mayor. **Ind/Abst** Chem. Abstr., Index Med., Excerpta Med. **NLM** W1 UR632. **CODEN** URINAC. adv acc. Reports of practice-oriented research into the etiology, pathophysiology and management of diseases of the urinary and urogenital tract.

UROLOGIC CLINICS OF NORTH AMERICA. (THE UROLOGIC CLINICS OF NORTH AMERICA). V. 1- Feb. 1974-. 0094-0143. Monographic Series. US. English. ty. $60.00. WB Saunders, West Washington Square, Philadelphia PA 19105. **Tel** (215)574-3395. **Ed** Livia Berardi. **Ind/Abst** Life Sci. Collect., Excerpta Med., Index Med., Biol. Abstr., Energy Res. Abstr., Hospit. Lit. Index, Sci. Cit. Index, Abr. Ed. **NLM** W1 UR638. **CODEN** UCNADW. **Circ** 13,000. Practical updates for the clinician on the latest advances plus topics of current interest to urologists.

UROLOGIC RADIOLOGY. V. 1- 1979-. 0171-1091. Periodical. US. English. qt. $82.00. Springer Verlag-New York Inc, 175 5th Avenue, New York NY 10010. **Tel** (212)460-1500. **Ed** J Becker, M A Bosniak, and Paul F G M Von Waes. **Ind/Abst** Life Sci. Collect., Excerpta Med., Index Med., Sci. Cit. Index, Abr. Ed. **NLM** W1 UR638R. Focuses on the study of the urinary tract utilizing radiography, angiography, ultrasonography, nuclear medicine, computed tomography, invasive techniques and associated modalities.

UROLOGIC SURGERY. *See* Medicine - Surgery.

UROLOGICAL RESEARCH. V. 1- Jan. 1973-. 0300-5623. Periodical. English. bm. $94.00. Springer Verlag New York Inc, 175 5th Avenue, New York NY 10010. **Tel** (212)460-1500. **Ed** L Andersson, G D Chisholm, D F Paulson, G Rutishauser, F Truss, and W Vahlensieck. **Ind/Abst** Life Sci. Collect., Excerpta Med., Index Med., Chem. Abstr., Sci. Cit. Index, Abr. Ed. **NLM** W1 UR639. **CODEN** URLRA5. Publishes original articles on research in the fields of clinical medicine, animal experimentation and laboratory techniques.

UROLOGICAL SURVEY *CEASED.* V. 1-31. 0042-1146. Periodical. US. English. bm. **Ind/Abst** Life Sci. Collect., Biol. Abstr. **LC** RC870. **DD** 616.6305. **NLM** ZWJ 100 U78. **CODEN** URSUAF.

UROLOGIJA I NEFROLOGIJA. (UROLOGIIA I NEFROLOGIIA). Vol. 30- Jan./Feb. 1965-. 0042-1154. Periodical. UR. Russian (summaries in English). bm. $21.00. Victor Kamkin Inc (71001), 12224 Parklawn Drive, Rockville MD 20852. **Tel** (301)881-5973. **Ind/Abst** Excerpta Med., Index Med., Biol. Abstr., Chem. Abstr. **NLM** W1 UR679A. **CODEN** URNEAA. *Urologiia.*

UROLOGY. V. 1- Jan. 1973-. 0090-4295. Periodical. US. English. mo. Professional Medical Services, PO Box 643, Ridgewood NJ 07451. **Tel** (201)444-8660. **Ind/Abst** Excerpta Med., Biol. Abstr., Energy Res. Abstr., Index Med., Life Sci. Collect., Hospit. Lit. Index. **LC** RC870. **DD** 616.6. **NLM** W1 UR679P. **CODEN** URGYA.

UROLOGY. **VFOAT** Audio-Digest. Urology Sound Recording. Periodical. US. English. mo. $96.36. Audio Digest Foundation, 1577 Chevy Chase Drive, Glendale CA 91206. **Tel** (213)240-7506. **Ed** Claron L Oakley. A system of audio cassette postgraduate medical education, with each one-hour program eligible for two Category I credit hours.

UROLOGY TIMES. V. 1- Nov. 1973-. 0093-9722. Periodical. US. English. mo. $60.00. Murray Communications, 95 Madison Avenue/Suite 1103, New York NY 10016. **Tel** (212)685-6767. **NLM** W1 UR68T.

VERHANDLUNGSBERICHT DER DEUTSCHEN GESELLSCHAFT FUR UROLOGIE. 1949-. 0070-413X. Periodical. German. ir. Springer Verlag-New York Inc, 175 5th Avenue, New York NY 10010. **Tel** (212)460-1584. **NLM** W1 VE4871D. Contains articles about urology. *Verhandlungsbericht der Urologentagung, 0372-8595.*

VESTNIK KHIRURGII IM. I.I. GREKOVA. 1935-. 0042-4625. Periodical. UR. Russian (summaries in English, 1956-). mo. $47.50. Victor Kamkin Inc (70128), 12224 Parklawn Drive, Rockville MD 20852. **Tel** (301)881-5973. **Ind/Abst** Excerpta Med., Index Med. **NLM** W1 VE836. *Vestnik Khirurgii I Porganichnykh Oblastei.*

WELLCOME TRENDS IN UROLOGY. **VFOAT** Trends in Urology. V. 1-V. 6, No. 2. Periodical. US. English. ir. Clinical Trends in Urology, 15 Park Row, New York NY 10038. *Clinical Trends in Urology, 0091-1682.*

WORLD JOURNAL OF UROLOGY. Vol. 1, No. 1 (Apr. 1983)-. 0724-4983. Periodical. WB. English. qt. $53.00. Springer-Verlag New York Inc, Journal Sales Department, 44 Hartz Way, Secaucus NJ 07094. **Ed** U Jonas and R J Krane. **Ind/Abst** Excerpta Med. **NLM** W1. adv acc. **Circ** 668. Available in microform from University Microfilms International. Practical and clinical relevance of new research in urology.

YEAR BOOK OF UROLOGY. *See* Yearbooks, Almanacs, Directories.

ZEITSCHRIFT FUR UROLOGIE UND NEPHROLOGIE. (ZEITSCHRIFT FUR UROLOGIE UND NEPHROLOGIE : ORGAN DER GESELLSCHAFT FUR UROLOGIE DER DDR UND DER GESELLSCHAFT FUR NEPHROLOGIE DER DDR). Began with: Vol. 57, published in 1964. 0044-3611. Periodical. SZ. German. mo. $68.37. Kunst & Wissen Erich Bieber, Dufourstrasse 51, CH-8008 Zurich Switzerland. **Tel** 011-41-1-69 44 20. **Ind/Abst** Excerpta Med., Index Med., Chem. Abstr., Sci. Cit. Index, Abr. Ed. **NLM** W1 ZE63L. **CODEN** ZURNAV. Index published separately - free - automatically sent. *Zeitschrift fur Urologie.*

METALS & METALLURGY

33 METAL PRODUCING. **VFOAT** Metal Producing. **VAT** Thirty-Three Metal Producing. Jan. 1977-. 0149-1210. Periodical. US. English. mo. $45.00. McGraw Hill Publications, Attn Cheryl Ross, PO Box 416, Hightstown NJ 08520. **Tel** (609)426-5000. **Ed** McGraw Hill. **Ind/Abst** Met. Abstr., World Alum. Abstr. **LC** TS300. **DD** 669.005. **CODEN** THMMAG. adv acc. (ctrl). *33, 0040-6155.*

ACCIAIO INOSSIDABILE. (L'ACCIAIO INOSSIDABILE). Yearly V. 1, Feb. 1933-. 0515-2291. Periodical. IT. Italian. qt. Avesta Spaacciaio Inosabi, Via Lancetti 36, Milan Italy. **Ind/Abst** Met. Abstr., World Alum. Abstr., Chem. Abstr. **LC** TA479.S7. **CODEN** ACCIAG.

ACERO Y ENERGIA. Yearly V. 1- 1944-. 0001-4850. Periodical. SP. Spanish. ir. Jose Antonio Primo de Riviera, 134-138 Esplugas de Llobregat, Barcelona Spain. **Ind/Abst** Chem. Abstr. **CODEN** ACEBA5.

ACTA METALLURGICA. V. 1- Jan. 1953-. 0001-6160. Periodical. US. English (French, or German). mo. $10.00 Member of Sponsoring Societies, $40.00 Member of Cooperating Societies. Pergamon Press, Maxwell House, Fairview Park, Elmsford NY 10523. **Ind/Abst** Eng. Index Mon., Eng. Index Bioeng. Abstr., Eng. Index Energy Abstr., Mintec, Min. Technol. Abstr., Minproc, GeoRef, Met. Abstr., World Alum. Abstr., Chem. Abstr., Eng. Index Annu., Eng. Index Mon., Int. Aerosp. Abstr., Nuci. Sci. Abstr., Energy Res. Abstr., Comput. Control Abstr., Electr. Electron. Abstr., Sci. Abstr. Sect. A. Phys. Abstr. **LC** TS200. **DD** 669.005. **CODEN** AMETAR. Available on microfilm from Microforms International Marketing Corp.

ADGEZIA RASPLAVOV I PAJHA MATERIALOV. (ADGEZIIA RASPLAVOV I PAIKA MATERIALOV). Vol. 1-. 0136-1732. Periodical. UR. Russian. 252601 Kiev-601 Gsp Ul Repina 3, Kiev Russian SFSR. **Ind/Abst** Int. Aerosp. Abstr., Chem. Abstr. **LC** TA401. **CODEN** ARPMDV.

ADVANCED MATERIALS & PROCESSES. **VFOAT** Advanced Materials and Processes. Vol. 1, No. 1 (Sept. 1985)-. 0882-7958. Periodical. US. English. mo. Free to Qualified Members and Individuals, $40.00 Others. American Society for Metals, Metals Park OH 44073. **DD** 671.

ADVANCES IN EXTRACTIVE METALLURGY. **VFOAT** Advances in Extractive Metallurgy and Refining. 1968-. UK. English. ir. Institution of Mining and Metallurgy, 44 Portland Place, London W1N 4BR England.

ALCAN NEWS *CEASED.* Began publication in June 1960. Ceased publication in 1982. 0002-4996. Periodical. CN. English. mo. Free. Alcan Canada Products Ltd, PO Box 269, Toronto Ontario M5K 1K1 Canada. **Ind/Abst** Met. Abstr., World Alum. Abstr. **DD** 338.476737220971. *Alcan Ingot, 0381-6427.*

ALERTA INFORMATIVA. SERIE C : CIENCIA Y TECNICA DE LOS METALES. Yearly V. 16-Jan. 1979-. SP. Spanish. ir. Instituto de Information y Documentacion en Ciencia y Tecnologia, C S I C, Joaquin Costa 22, Madrid-6 Spain. **LC** Z6678, TN665. *Resumenes de Articulos Cientificos y Tecnicos. Serie C: Ciencia y Tecnica de los Metales.*

ALLOY DIGEST. Sept. 1952-. 0002-614X. Periodical. US. English. mo. $100.00. Alloy Digest Inc, PO Box 823, Upper Montclair NJ 07043. **Tel** (201)761-1090. **Ed** Oscar O Miller. **Ind/Abst** Met. Abstr., World Alum. Abstr. **Circ** 1,000.

ALLOYS INDEX. *See* Indexes/Abstracts.

ALUMINIUM. March 1972-. Periodical. DK. Danish. ir. 48.00. Aluminium Branches Oplysingrad Forlags, Fredericiagade 16, 1310 Kbenhavn K Denmark. **LC** TA690.

ALUMINIUM. Began publication in 1919. 0002-6689. Periodical. GW. German (English). mo. 298. Aluminium Verlag GMBH, Konigsallee 30, 4000 Dusseldorf 1 West Germany. **Tel** 0211-320821. **Ind/Abst** Eng. Index Mon., Predicasts, Eng. Index Bioeng. Abstr., Eng. Index Energy Abstr., Excerpta Med., Int. Aerosp. Abstr., GeoRef, Chem. Abstr., Eng. Index Annu., Eng. Index Mon., Nuci. Sci. Abstr., Met. Abstr., World Alum. Abstr., Energy Res. Abstr. **CODEN** ALUMAB. bk rev. adv acc. **Circ** 3,000. International journal for science, technology and economics.

ALUMINUM INGOT AND MILL PRODUCTS. (CURRENT INDUSTRIAL REPORTS. M33-2, ALUMINUM INGOT AND MILL PRODUCTS). 0364-2739. Periodical. US. English. mo. $20.50. Data User Services Division, Customer Services Publication, Bureau of the Census, Washington DC 20233. **Tel** (301)763-4100. **Ind/Abst** Predicasts, Chem. Abstr., Am. Stat. Index. **LC** HD9539.A63. **DD** 380.1456737220973. **CODEN** CIAPDQ. Presents timely data on the production, inventories, and orders of approximately 5,000 products, which represents 40 percent of all US manufacturing.

ALUMINUM STATISTICAL REVIEW. *See* Statistics.

AMERICAN BLADE. *See* Manufacturing.

AMERICAN GOLD NEWS. *See* Engineering - Mining Engineering.

AMERICAN MACHINIST MANUFACTURING COST ESTIMATING GUIDE. *See* Manufacturing.

AMERICAN MACHINIST (NEW YORK, N.Y. : 1968). (AMERICAN MACHINIST). Vol, 112, No. 5 (Feb. 26, 1968)-. 0002-9858. Periodical. US. English. mo. $30.00. American Machinist, McGraw Hill Inc, c/o Cheryl Ross, PO Box 416, Hightstown NJ 1480361. **Tel** (609)426-5000. **Ind/Abst** Fluidex, Eng. Index Annu., Eng. Index Mon., Eng. Index Bioeng. Abstr., Eng. Index Energy Abstr., Predicasts, Excerpta Med., Int. Aerosp. Abstr., CIS Abstr., Met. Abstr., World Alum. Abstr., Appl. Sci. Technol. Index, ISMEC Bull., Eng. Index. **LC** TJ1. **DD** 621.805. **CODEN** AMMAAA. adv acc. (ctrl). Also available on microfilm. *American Machinist, Metalworking Manufacturing, 0096-5154.*

AMERICAN METAL MARKET. V. 1- 1882-. 0002-9998. Periodical. US. English. da. $150.00. Fairchild Publications, Capital Cities Media, 7 East 12th Street, New York NY 10003. **Ind/Abst** Trade Ind. Index, Predicasts, Met. Abstr., World Alum. Abstr., Chem. Abstr. **LC** HD9506.U6. **CODEN** AMMKA6. Available in microfilm from Fairchild Publishers. *Metalworking News.*

Metals & Metallurgy

AMERICAN TOOL, DIE & STAMPING NEWS. See Manufacturing.

I & SM CEASED. VFOAT Iron & Steelmaker. VAT I and SM. V. 1-7, No. 4. 0097-8388. Periodical. US. English. mo. Ind/Abst Coal Abstr., Chem. Abstr. LC TS300. DD 669.105. CODEN IRSMDW.

ANNUAL REPORT AND ACCOUNTS - NCHANGA CONSOLIDATED COPPER MINES LIMITED. Main/Corp Nchanga Consolidated Copper Mines Limited. English. ir. 74 Independence Avenue PO Box 48, Lusaka Zambia. LC TN447.Z3. DD 338.7622343.

ANNUAL REPORT - BNF METALS TECHNOLOGY CENTRE. See Technology (General).

ANNUAL REPORT - INTERNATIONAL TIN COUNCIL. Main/Corp International Tin Council. 1st- 1956/57-. 0074-9125. UK. English. an. International Tin Council, Haymarket House 1 Oxendon Street, London SW1Y 4EQ England. LC HD9539.T5.

ANNUAL REPORT - INTERNATIONAL TIN RESEARCH COUNCIL. (ANNUAL REPORT). Main/Corp International Tin Research Council. 0539-0826. UK. English. an. Tin Research Institute, 483 North 6th Avenue, Columbus OH 43201. LC TN793.A1. DD 669.605. *Report of the Tin Research Institute.*

ANNUAL REPORT - STEEL AUTHORITY OF INDIA LIMITED. Main/Corp Steel Authority of India Limited. English or Hindi. an. LC HD9526.I6.

ANNUAL RESEARCH REVIEW - INTERNATIONAL LEAD ZINC RESEARCH ORGANIZATION. Main/Corp International Lead Zinc Research Organization. US. English. an. International Lead Zinc Research Organization, 292 Madison Avenue, New York NY 10017. LC TN207. DD 669.4072.

ANNUAL SILVER REVIEW AND OUTLOOK. 0736-2455. US. English. an. J Aron & Company, 160 Water Street, New York NY 10038. LC HD9536.A1. DD 338.2742105.

ANNUAL STATISTICAL REPORT : AMERICAN IRON AND STEEL INSTITUTE. See Statistics.

ANUARIO BRASILEIRO DE ENTIDADES EM METALURGIA, MECANICA E AREAS CORRELATAS. See Yearbooks, Almanacs, Directories.

ANUARIO ESTATISTICO. See Yearbooks, Almanacs, Directories.

APPROVED WELDING ELECTRODE WIRE-FLUX AND WIRE-GAS COMBINATIONS. See Metals & Metallurgy - Welding.

ARCHITECTURAL METALS. V. 1- May 1955-. 0003-8563. US. English. bm. National Association of Architectural Metal Manufacturers, 100 South Marion Street, Oak Park IL 60302. Ind/Abst Met. Abstr., World Alum. Abstr. LC TH1651. DD 721.044705. *Architectural Metal.*

ARCHIV FUR DAS EISENHUTTENWESEN. See Genealogy and Heraldry - Archives.

ARCHIV FUR LAGERSTATTENFORSCHUNG DER GEOLOGISCHEN BUNDESANSTALT. See Genealogy and Heraldry - Archives.

ARCHIWUM HUTNICTWA. Vol. 1- 1956-. 0004-0770. Periodical. PL. Polish (table of contents and summaries in Russian and English). qt. ARS Polona, Krakowskie Przedmiescie 7, 00-068 Warsaw Poland. Ind/Abst Chem. Abstr., Eng. Index, Met. Abstr., World Alum. Abstr., Comput. Control Abstr., Electr. Electron. Abstr., Sci. Abstr. Sect. A. Phys. Abstr., Phys. Abstr. LC TN4.P57. CODEN AHUTA4. *Archiwum Gornictwa I Hutnictwa.*

AREA METALURGIA. Series/Titl Contributiones Cientificas Y Technologicas. VFOAT Metalurgia. Periodical. Spanish (summaries in English). ir. Direccion de Investigaciones Cientificas y Technologicas de la Universidad Tecnica del Estado etc, Avda Ecuador 3469, Santiago Chile. LC TN600.

ARSBERETNING - OLJEDIREKTORATET. See Engineering - Mining Engineering.

AS-SULB AL-ARABI. (AL-SULB AL-ARABI). VFOAT Acier Arabe. 0253-9659. Periodical. Arabic (French). mo. Al-Ittihad Al-Arabi Lil-Hadid Wa-Al-Sulb, PO Box 4 Al-Sharaqah, Al-Jazair Sudan. Ind/Abst Chem. Abstr. LC HD9528.A58. CODEN ACARD2.

ASM BIBLIOGRAPHY SERIES. See Bibliographies.

ATB METALLURGIE. V. 1-2. 0365-7302. Periodical. French (Flemish). qt. $16.20. Benelux Metallurgie, rue Ravenstein 3, B 1000 Brussels Belgium. Ind/Abst Met. Abstr., World Alum. Abstr., Chem. Abstr. CODEN ATBMA6.

AVTOMATIZACIJA METALLURGICESKOGO PROIZVODSTVA. (AVTOMATIZATSIIA METALLURGICHESKOGO PROIZVODSTVA). Began in 1973. 0320-0825. UR. Russian. ir. 1.49 Single Issue. Metallurgia, 119034 G-34 2-1 Obydenskii Per 14, Moskva USSR. Ind/Abst Chem. Abstr. LC TN675.5. CODEN AMPRDB.

BARRY FAIN'S PRIVATE BLUE BOOK OF GUN VALUES. See Manufacturing.

BAYERNMETALL. Periodical. GW. German. mo. Bayern Metall, Erhardtstrafe 6, 8 Munchen 5 West Germany. LC TS200.

BCIRA ABSTRACTS OF FOUNDRY LITERATURE. See Indexes/Abstracts.

BCIRA ABSTRACTS OF INTERNATIONAL FOUNDRY LITERATURE. See Indexes/Abstracts.

BERGSHISTORISKA SKRIFTSERIE. Main/Corp Jernkontoret, Stockholm. Swedish. ir. LC TN704.S9.

BIG BOOK OF METALWORKING MACHINERY. 0045-1983. US. English. an. $47.50. Zulch & Zulch Inc, PO Box 4427, Sylma CA 91342. LC TS215. DD 338.47671.

THE BLACKPOWDER REPORT. See Manufacturing.

BLECH, ROHRE, PROFILE. V. 17- 1970-. 0006-4688. Periodical. GW. German. mo. $57.62. Meisenbach KG, Postfach 2069, D-8600 Bamberg 1 West Germany. Tel 0951/861-0. Ind/Abst Eng. Index Annu., Eng. Index Mon., Eng. Index Bioeng. Abstr., Eng. Index Energy Abstr., Excerpta Med., Met. Abstr., World Alum. Abstr., Chem. Abstr., Energy Res. Abstr. CODEN BRPFBJ. *Blech.*

BNF NON-FERROUS METALS ABSTRACTS. See Indexes/Abstracts.

BOLETIN ESTADISTICO. Main/Corp Centro de Industriales Siderurgicos. Spanish. ir. LC HD9524.A9.

BRITISH CORROSION JOURNAL. See Engineering - Chemical Engineering.

BRITISH FOUNDRYMAN. (THE BRITISH FOUNDRYMAN). Vol. 50, Part 1 (Jan. 1957)-. 0007-0718. Periodical. UK. English. mo. $82.75. IBF Publs, Bridge House, 8th Floor, 121 Smallbrook, Queensway Birmingham B5 4JP England. Tel 44 21 643 4523. Ed Eric F Boultbee. Ind/Abst Eng. Index Annu., Eng. Index Mon., Eng. Index Bioeng. Abstr., Eng. Index Energy Abstr., Coal Abstr., Excerpta Med., CIS Abstr., Met. Abstr., World Alum. Abstr., Chem. Abstr., ISMEC Bull., Eng. Index. CODEN BRFOAT. bk rev. adv acc. Circ 3,718. Metalcasting, foundry technology, castings engineering. Also industry news, new products developments and special features. Professional news from the Institute of British Foundrymen.

BULETINUL INSTITUTULUI POLITEHNIC GHEORGHE GHEORGHIU-DEJ BUCURESTI. SERIA CHIMIE-METALURGIE. See Chemistry.

BULETINUL UNIVERSITATII DIN GALATI. FASICULA V, TEHNOLOGII IN CONSTRUCTIA DE MASINI, METALURGIE. (BULETINUL UNIVERSITATII DIN GALATI. FASCICULA V, TEHNOLOGII IN CONSTRUCTII SIC DE MASINI, METALURGIE). Vol. 1 (1978)-. 0254-5543. Periodical. English (French and German). an. Redactia Buletinului, 6200 Galati Str, Republicii Nr 47 Romania. Ind/Abst Met. Abstr.,

World Alum. Abstr., Chem. Abstr. LC TJ4. DD 669.005. CODEN BUGMDI.

BULLETIN DE LA CHAMBRE SYNDICALE DE LA SIDERURGIE FRANCAISE. SERIE BLEUE. See Statistics.

BULLETIN DE LA CHAMBRE SYNDICALE DE LA SIDERURGIE FRANCAISE. SERIE ROUGE. See Statistics.

BULLETIN DE LA CHAMBRE SYNDICALE DE LA SIDERURGIE FRANCAISE. SERIE VERTE, STATISTIQUES MENSUELLES. See Statistics.

BULLETIN DE LA CHAMBRE SYNDICALE DE LA SIDERURGIE. SERIE BLEUE, STATISTIQUES ANNUELLES, COMMERCE EXTERIEUR. See Statistics.

BULLETIN - INSTITUTION OF MINING AND METALLURGY. See Engineering - Mining Engineering.

BULLETIN OF ALLOY PHASE DIAGRAMS. See Engineering - Mining Engineering.

BULLETIN OF RESEARCH LABORATORY OF PRECISION MACHINERY AND ELECTRONICS, TOKYO INSTITUTE OF TECHNOLOGY. (BULLETIN OF RESEARCH LABORATORY OF PRECISION MACHINERY AND ELECTRONICS). Main/Corp Tokyo Kogyo Daigaku. Seimitsu Kogaku Kenkyujo. 0385-7832. Periodical. English. ir. Nagatsuta Midori-Ku, Tokyo Japan. Ind/Abst Math. Rev., Eng. Index Annu., Eng. Index Mon., Eng. Index Bioeng. Abstr., Eng. Index Energy Abstr., Fluidex, Int. Aerosp. Abstr., Comput. Control Abstr., Electr. Electron. Abstr., Sci. Abstr. Sect. A. Phys. Abstr., Met. Abstr., World Alum. Abstr. LC TS500. DD 681.05. CODEN BLPTDL.

BULLETIN SIGNALETIQUE 221 : GISEMENTS METALLIQUES ET NON METALLIQUES, ECONOMIE MINIERE. V. 37- 1976-. Periodical. FR. French. ir. $130.38. Editions du CNRS, 23 rue du Maroc, 75019 Paris France. *Bulletin Signaletique 221: Gitologie, Economie Miniere.*

BULLETIN SIGNALETIQUE. SECTION 740. METAUX, METALLURGIE. VFOAT Metaux, Metallurgie. V. 30- 1969-. 0007-5655. Periodical. FR. French. ir. $179.60. Editions du CNRS, 23 rue du Maroc, 75019 Paris France. *Bulletin Signaletique. Section 8: Chimie II. Chimie Appliquee, Metallurgie.*

BULLETIN - UNITED STATES DEPARTMENT OF THE INTERIOR, BUREAU OF MINES. See Engineering - Mining Engineering.

C I M REPORTER. See Engineering - Mining Engineering.

CADMIUM ABSTRACTS. See Indexes/Abstracts.

CANADIAN MACHINERY AND METALWORKING. See Engineering - Mechanical Engineering & Machinery.

CANADIAN METALLURGICAL QUARTERLY. VFOAT Metallurgical Society of CIM Annual Volume. V. 1-. 0008-4433. Periodical. CN. English. qt. Pergamon Press, 395 Sawmill River Road, Elmsford NY 10523. Ind/Abst Met. Abstr., World Alum. Abstr., Nucl. Sci. Abstr., Chem. Abstr., Eng. Index Annu., GeoRef, Sci. Cit. Index, Abr. Ed., Eng. Index. DD 669.005. CODEN CAMQAU.

THE CANNING HANDBOOK. 23rd Ed. (1982)-. UK. English. ir. E & F N Spon Ltd, 733 Third Avenue, New York NY 10017. LC TS653.A1. DD 671.705. *Canning Handbook on Electroplating.*

CASTEEL. 1-. Periodical. US. English. ty. Steel Founders Society of American Cast Metals, Federation Building, 555 State Street, Des Plaines IL 60016. Ind/Abst Met. Abstr., World Alum. Abstr.

DIE CASTING ENGINEER. See Manufacturing.

CASTINGS. V. 1- 1955-. 0008-7521. Periodical. AT. English. mo. 22.60. FW Publishers, GPO Box 2457, Sydney 2001 Australia. Tel (02)2671187. Ed Berry

Metals & Metallurgy

Smith. Ind/Abst CIS Abstr., Met. Abstr., World Alum. Abstr. LC TS200. bk rev. adv acc. Circ 1,350. Foundry casting industry, technical and up-to-date information.

CHARTING STEEL'S PROGRESS. Main/Corp American Iron and Steel Institute. 1954-. 0569-5910. US. English. an. American Iron & Steel Institute, 1000 16th Street Northwest, Washington DC 20036. LC HD9515. DD 338.2, 672.

CHILTON'S IAMI (METALWORKING EDITION). (CHILTON'S IAMI). VFOAT Chilton's I.A.M.I. 0195-2323. Periodical. US. English. mo. $60.00 Qualified Recipients. Chilton Co, Chilton Way, Radnor PA 19089. DD 671. Chilton's IAMI. Iron Age Metalworking International, 0163-030X.

CHILTON'S IRON AGE CEASED. VFOAT Iron Age. V. 219-226. 0164-5137. Periodical. US. English. sm. Free to Qualified Managers in US Metalworking Companies, $42.00 Others. Iron Age, PO Box 2040, Radnor PA 19089. Ind/Abst Appl. Sci. Technol. Index, Bus. Period. Index, Eng. Index Annu., Eng. Index Mon., Eng. Index Bioeng. Abstr., Eng. Index Energy Abstr., Excerpta Med. LC T1. DD 672.05. CODEN IRAGAN. Available in microform from University Microfilms International. Iron Age, 0021-1508.

CHILTON'S IRON AGE. METALS PRODUCER (INTERNATIONAL EDITION). (CHILTON'S IRON AGE. METALS PRODUCER). VFOAT Iron Age. Began with: V. 227, No. 2 (Jan. 2, 1984). 0749-1468. Periodical. US. English. mo. Iron Age, PO Box 2040, Radnor PA 19089. DD 671. Chilton's IAMI (Metal Producing Edition), 0749-6710.

CHIN SHU HSUEH PAO. VFOAT Acta Metallurgica and Sinica. Began with Mar. 1956 issue. 0412-1961. Periodical. CC. Chinese (with abstracts in English or Russian, (1978)). bm. Pei-Ching Pao Kan Fa Hsing, Chu Peking China. Ind/Abst Eng. Index Annu., Eng. Index Mon., Eng. Index Bioeng. Abstr., Eng. Index Energy Abstr., GeoRef, Chem. Abstr., Comput. Control Abstr., Electr. Electron. Abstr., Int. Aerosp. Abstr., Met. Abstr., Sci. Abstr. Sect. A. Phys. Abstr., World Alum. Abstr. LC TN4. DD 669.005. CODEN CHSPA4.

CHISHITSU KAISEKI IINKAI HOKOKUSHO. See Engineering - Mining Engineering.

CHITANIUMU, JIRUKONIUMU. VFOAT Titanium & Zirconium. Began in 1962. 0577-9391. Periodical. JA. Japanese. qt. 35.00. Maruzen Company Ltd, PO Box 5050, 100-31 Tokyo Japan. Ind/Abst Chem. Abstr. CODEN CHJIA6. Using examples of titanium, or monographs are reported. Chitaniumu.

CHOLGANG TONGGYE. See Statistics.

CHOLGANG TONGGYE YONBO. English (Korean). ir. Hanguk Cholgang Hyophoe, 51-8 Susong-Dong, Chongno-Ku Seoul Korea. LC HD926.K6.

CHOSA YONGU POGO. See Engineering - Mining Engineering.

CHUKEN HOKOKU. See Manufacturing.

CHUTANZO. See Engineering - Mining Engineering.

CIM BULLETIN. VFOAT Canadian Mining and Metallurgical Bulletin. Vol. 61, No. 669 (Jan. 1968)-. 0317-0926. Periodical. CN. English. mo. 90.00. Canadian Institute of Mining and Metallurgy, 1130 Sherbrooke Street West/Suite 400, Montreal Quebec H3A 2M8 Canada. Tel (514)842-3461. Ed P Michaud. Ind/Abst Phys. Abstr., CIS Abstr., Eng. Index Mon., Fluidex, Life Sci. Collect., Can. Environ., Coal Abstr., Energy Inf. Abstr., Environ. Abstr., Mintec, Min. Technol. Abstr., Minproc, GeoRef, Can. Bus. Index, ASTIS Bibliogr., ASTIS Curr. Aware. Bull., Electr. Electron., Sci. Abstr. Sect. A. Phys. Abstr., Chem. Abstr., Energy Res. Abstr., Excerpta Med., Met. Abstr., World Alum. Abstr., Sci. Cit. Index, Abr. Ed., Bibliogr. Index Geol., Appl. Sci. Technol. Index, Eng. Index. LC TN1. DD 669.00971. CODEN CIBUBA. adv acc. Circ 13,000. (ctrl). Publishes technical data and information relative to the Canadian minerals industry, and details the various activities of the Institute. Canadian Mining and Metallurgical Bulletin, 0008-4484.

CIS DOCUMENTACAO. VFOAT C.I.S. Documentacao. Periodical. Portuguese. mo. Ind/Abst Met. Abstr., World Alum. Abstr. LC Z6332, TN705.

CLOSURES FOR CONTAINERS. (CURRENT INDUSTRIAL REPORTS. M34H, CLOSURES FOR CONTAINERS). 0364-1902. Periodical. US. English. mo. $16.00. Data User Services Division, Customer Services Publication, Bureau of the Census, Washington DC 20233. Tel (301)763-4100. Ind/Abst Predicasts, Am. Stat. Index, Funk Scott Index Corp. Ind. Presents timely data on the production, inventories, and orders of approximately 5,000 products, which represents 40 percent of all US manufacturing.

COMMERCIAL STEEL FORGINGS CEASED. (CURRENT INDUSTRIAL REPORTS. MA-34C, COMMERCIAL STEEL FORGINGS). Ceased with 1980. 0744-2610. US. English. an. Bureau of the Census, Data User Services Division, Customer Services, Washington DC 20233. LC HD9529.S683. DD 338.476723320973.

CONSTRUCTION METALLIQUE. Began in 1964. 0045-8198. Periodical. FR. French. ty. Centre Technique Industrial de la Construction Metallique, Domain de Saint Paul, 78470 St Remy Chevreuse France. Tel (3) 052 92 00. Ind/Abst Eng. Index Mon., Eng. Index Bioeng. Abstr., Eng. Index Energy Abstr., Eng. Index Mon., Eng. Index Annu. CODEN COMQAQ.

CONTINENTALER STAHLMARKT CEASED. Periodical. GW. German. ir. 64.00. Monta und Wirtschaftsverlag, Lange Strasse 13, Frankfurt West Germany. LC HD9525.A2. Continentaler Eisenhandel.

CONTRIBUTIONS TO THE DATA ON THEORETICAL METALLURGY. US. English. ir. LC TN28. DD 669.

COPPER (BOR, SERBIA). (COPPER). English (summaries in Serbo-Croatian -R). qt. Copper Publications, 192 10 Bor Ure Akovica 14 PO Box 13, Yugoslavia. Ind/Abst Chem. Abstr. CODEN COPPD7.

COPPER CONTROLLED MATERIALS. (CURRENT INDUSTRIAL REPORTS. ITA-9008, COPPER CONTROLLED MATERIALS). 1st Quarter 1979-. 0197-8624. Periodical. US. English. qt. $11.00. Data User Services Division Customer Services Publication, Bureau of the Census, Washington DC 20233. Tel (301)763-4100. Ind/Abst Chem. Abstr., Am. Stat. Index, Predicasts. LC HD9539.C7. DD 338.476733320973. CODEN CIRTDL. Presents timely data on the production, inventories, and orders of approximately 5,000 products, which represents 40 percent of all US manufacturing. Current Industrial Reports, DIB-9008, Copper Controlled Materials.

COPPER INDUSTRY ANNUAL SUPPLEMENT. Series/Titl Mineral Industry Surveys. VFOAT Copper in . . . . US. English. an. US Department of the Interior, Bureau of Mines, Washington DC 20241.

COPPER STUDIES. V. 1- Apr. 6, 1973-. 0091-2204. Periodical. US. English. mo. $995.00. Copper Studies, 33 West 54th Street, New York NY 10019. Tel (212)765-9600. Ed R H Lesemann. Ind/Abst Met. Abstr., World Alum. Abstr. LC HD9539.C5. DD 338.4767330973. Circ 300. Articles on various aspects of the copper industry.

CORROSION. V. 1- March 1945-. 0010-9312. Periodical. US. English. mo. $75.00 Domestic, $85.00 Foreign. National Association of Corrosion Engineers, PO Box 218340, Houston TX 77218. Tel (713)492-0535. Ed Jesse Lumsden. Ind/Abst Sci. Cit. Index, Abr. Ed., Pet. Abstr., Phys. Abstr., Eng. Index Bioeng. Abstr., Eng. Index Energy Abstr., Fluidex, Abstr. Bull. Inst. Paper Chem., Art Archaeol. Tech. Abstr., Excerpta Med., Coal Abstr., Int. Aerosp. Abstr., Int. Packag. Abstr., Comput. Control Abstr., Electr. Electron. Abstr., Sci. Abstr. Sect. A. Phys. Abstr., Met. Abstr., Ship Abstr., World Alum. Abstr., World Surf. Coat. Abstr., Chem. Abstr., Appl. Sci. Technol. Index, Energy Res. Abstr., ISMEC Bull., Eng. Index. LC TA462. DD 620.1122. CODEN CORRAK. (cum index). adv acc. Circ 4,000. (ctrl). Available on microfiche. Permanent record of the progress in the science and technology of corrosion control. Focuses on research as it applies to corrosion science and engineering.

CORROSION ABSTRACTS. See Indexes/Abstracts.

CORROSION ABSTRACTS. See Indexes/Abstracts.

CORROSION & COATINGS, SOUTH AFRICA. (CORROSION & COATINGS SOUTH AFRICA). VAT Corrosion and Coatings South Africa. 0377-8711. Periodical. SA. English. bm. 52.00. George Warman Publ Pty Ltd, PO Box 3847/77 Hout Street, Capetown 8000 South Africa. Tel (021)245320. Ed Derek Lawley. Ind/Abst Coal Abstr., World Surf. Coat. Abstr., Met. Abstr., World Alum. Abstr., Chem. Abstr. LC TA418.74. DD 671.7305. CODEN CCSADT. adv acc. Circ 2,500. (ctrl). The only South African journal devoted entirely to corrosion prevention and surface coatings. It is the official journal of the South African Corrosion Institute.

CORROSION AUSTRALASIA. 0155-6002. Periodical. AT. English. bm. 35.00. Australasian Corrosion Association, c/o John Moresby PO Box 117, Glen Waverly Vic 3150 Australia. Tel (613) 555 0333. Ed John F Moresby. Ind/Abst World Surf. Coat. Abstr., Chem. Abstr. CODEN COAUDF. bk rev. adv acc. Circ 1,200. (ctrl). Publishes original papers in the fields of metallic corrosion surface treatments, coatings, linings, alloys, ceramics, plastics, preventatives water and fuel treatment, cathodic and anodic protection.

CORROSION PREVENTION-INHIBITION DIGEST. (CORROSION PREVENTION/INHIBITION DIGEST). 0364-3301. US. English. mo. $90.00. American Society for Metals, Metals Information, Metals Park OH 44073. Tel (216)338-5151. Ind/Abst Abstr. Bull. Inst. Paper Chem. LC TA462. DD 620.162305. This digest is 1 of 10 printed monthly. Each digest is a cost effective solution reproducing complete subject relevant abstracts as published in metals abstracts.

CORROSION SCIENCE. V. 1- Aug. 1961-. 0010-938X. Periodical. UK. English, French or German, with summaries in all three languages. mo. Pergamon Press, 395 Sawmill River Road, Elmsford NY 10523. Tel (914)592-7700. Ind/Abst Electron. Commun. Abstr. J., ISMEC Bull., Appl. Sci. Technol. Index, Appl. Mech. Rev., Chem. Abstr., Sci. Cit. Index, Abr. Ed., Phys. Abstr., Pet. Abstr., Life Sci. Collect., Coal Abstr., Ship Abstr., Excerpta Med., World Surf. Coat. Abstr., Energy Inf. Abstr., Environ. Abstr., Abstr. Bull. Inst. Paper Chem., Int. Aerosp. Abstr., Art Archaeol. Tech. Abstr., Comput. Control Abstr., Electr. Electron. Abstr., Sci. Abstr., Eng. Index, Met. Abstr., World Alum. Abstr. LC TA462. DD 620.16205. CODEN CRRSAA.

CURRENT INDUSTRIAL REPORTS. MA-34P, ALUMINUM FOIL CONVERTED CEASED. VFOAT Aluminum Foil Converted. 1981-. US. English. an. $1.25. Data User Services Division, Customer Services Publication, Bureau of the Census, Washington DC 20233. Tel (301)763-4100. LC HD9539.A63. DD 338.47673722823. Presents timely data on the production, inventories, and orders of approximately 5,000 products, which represents 40 percent of all US manufacturing. Current Industrial Reports. Series MA-34P, Aluminum Foil Converted.

CURRENT INDUSTRIAL REPORTS. MA33E, NONFERROUS CASTINGS. VFOAT Nonferrous Castings. US. English. mo. $21.00. Superintendent of Documents, Government Printing Office, Washington DC 20402. Tel (202)783-3238. Ind/Abst Am. Stat. Index.

CURRENT INDUSTRIAL REPORTS. SERIES MA-34P, ALUMINUM FOIL CONVERTED CEASED. VFOAT Aluminum Foil Converted. -1981. US. English. an. Data User Services Division, Customer Services, Washington DC 20402.

CUTTING TOOL ENGINEERING. 0011-4189. Periodical. US. English. bm. $20.00. CTE Publications Inc, 464 Central Avenue, Northfield IL 60093. Tel (312)441-7520. Ed Larry Teeman. Ind/Abst Electron. Commun. Abstr. J., ISMEC Bull., Pollut. Abstr. Indexes, Saf. Sci. Abstr. J., Eng. Index Mon., Eng. Index Bioeng. Abstr., Eng. Index Energy Abstr., Met. Abstr., World Alum. Abstr., Eng. Index Annu., Eng. Index. CODEN CTEGAP. bk rev. adv acc. Circ 40,000. (ctrl). Written and edited for decision makers in the metalworking field who use cutting tools, abrasives and accessories.

DAIHAN GUMSOG HAGHOI JI. (TAEHAN KUMSOK HAKHOE CHI). Main/Corp Taehan Kumsok Hakhoe. VFOAT Journal of the Korean Institute of Metals. 0253-3847. Periodical. KO. English (Korean). qt. Taehan Kumsok Hakhoe, San 76-561 Yoksam-Dong, Kangnam-Ku, Seoul South Korea. Ind/Abst Coal Abstr., Int. Aerosp. Abstr., Comput. Control Abstr., Electr. Electron. Abstr., Sci. Abstr. Sect. A. Phys. Abstr., Met. Abstr., World Alum. Abstr., Chem. Abstr. LC TN4. CODEN TKHCDJ.

Metals & Metallurgy

DEMONSTRATED RESERVE BASE OF COAL IN THE UNITED STATES. (DEMONSTRATED RESERVE BASE OF COAL IN THE UNITED STATES ON JANUARY 1, . . .). 1979-. 0731-3640. US. English. an. $4.75. Superintendent of Documents, Government Printing Office, Washington DC 20402. LC TN805.A3. DD 553.240973.

DENKI-SEIKO. Began 1925. 0011-8389. Periodical. JA. Japanese. qt. $35.00. Maruzen Company Ltd, PO Box 5050, 100-31 Tokyo Japan. **Ind/Abst** Met. Abstr., World Alum. Abstr., Chem. Abstr. **CODEN** DESEAT. (ctrl). Organ papers of study club about electrical furnace steel.

DESIGN IN STEEL. 1963-. 0418-7679. US. English. be. American Iron & Steel Institute, 1000-16th Street NW, Washington DC 20036. LC TA684. DD 672.

DESIGNFAX. V. 1- April 1979. 0163-6669. Periodical. US. English. mo. $20.00. Huebner Publications Inc, 6521 Davis Industrial Parkway, Salon OH 44139. **Tel** (216)248-1125. Ed David T Curry. adv acc. **Circ** 110,047. (ctrl). Serves the design engineering function in the original equipment market (OEM).

DIRECTORY - EUROPEAN COIL COATING ASSOCIATION. See Yearbooks, Almanacs, Directories.

DIRECTORY OF IRON AND STEEL WORKS OF THE UNITED STATES AND CANADA. See Yearbooks, Almanacs, Directories.

DIRECTORY OF THE LEADING FIRMS IN THE JOB PLATING AND ENAMELING INDUSTRY. See Yearbooks, Almanacs, Directories.

DOSSIER - INSTITUTE DE RECHERCHE EN EXPLORATION MINERALE. See Engineering - Mining Engineering.

DRAHT. 1950. 0012-5911. Periodical. GW. English. mo. Meisenbach KG, Postfach 2069, D-8600 Bamberg 1 West Germany. **Tel** (0951)861-0. Ed Klaus Ohlwein. **Ind/Abst** Eng. Index Mon., Eng. Index Bioeng. Abstr., Eng. Index Energy Abstr., Excerpta Med., Coal Abstr., Chem. Abstr., Eng. Index Annu., Eng. Index Mon., Nuci. Sci. Abstr., Energy Res. Abstr. **CODEN** DRAHA5. adv acc. **Circ** 4,855. (ctrl). Technical journal covering all aspects of wire and bar production and treatment.

DUCTILE IRON PIPE NEWS. Winter 1975/76-. Periodical. US. English. an. Ductile Iron Pipe Research Association, 1301 North 22nd Street/Suite 509, Oak Brook IL 60521. **Tel** (312)654-2945. Cast Iron Pipe News.

DUN'S INDUSTRIAL GUIDE, THE METALWORKING DIRECTORY. See Yearbooks, Almanacs, Directories.

EINKAUFSFUHRER UND ADRESSBUCH DER DEUTSCHEN UHREN-, SCHMUCKWAREN- U. METTALWAREN-INDUSTRIE. Periodical. German. ir. LC TS540. Adressbuch der Uhren-, Schmuckwaren- und Metallwaren-Industrie.

ENQUETE ANNUELLE D'ENTREPRISE : TRAVAIL DES METAUX. **Main/Corp** Centre d'Enquetes Statistiques de Caen. FR. French. ir. Documentation Francaise, 195 rue de Bercy Tour Gamma A, 75012 Paris France. LC HD9506.F7. DD 338.476710944.

EUROSTAT, BULLETIN TRIMESTRIEL DES STATISTIQUES SIDERURGIQUES. See Statistics.

EXTRACTIVE AND PROCESS METALLURGY. **VFOAT** Extractive & Process Metallurgy. 0273-3706. Periodical. US. English. ir. Gordon & Breach, 1 Bedford Street, London WC2E 9HD England. **Tel** 01 836 5125.

FABRICATED STRUCTURAL METAL INDUSTRY CEASED. **Main/Corp** Statistics Canada. Manufacturing and Primary Industries Division. **Series/Titl** Annual Census of Manufactures. **VFOAT** Fabrication d'Elements de Charpente Metallique. 1970-1980. 0527-5091. CN. English (French). an. 0.70.

FACHBERICHTE HUTTENPRAXIS METALLWEITERVERARBEITUNG. **VFOAT** Neue Fachberichte. Began with V. 3 (Oct. 1975). 0340-8043. Periodical. GW. German. mo. 292.-. Sprechsaal Verlag, PO Box 401, D-8630 Coburg West Germany. **Tel** 09561/7773. Ed Christoph Mueller. **Ind/Abst** Excerpta Med., Coal Abstr., Met. Abstr., World Alum. Abstr., Energy Res. Abstr., Chem. Abstr. **CODEN** FACHDN. bk rev. adv acc. **Circ** 7,700. International magazine dealing with iron and steel technologies, procedures and equipment raw material preparation, iron and steelmaking, refractories, continuous casting, rolling and finishing. Fachberichte fur Oberflachentechnik.

FACTS. **Main/Corp** Institute of Scrap Iron and Steel. 0163-3899. US. English. an. $5.00. Institute of Scrap Iron Steel, 1627 K Street NW, Washington DC 20006. **Tel** (202)466-4050. Ed Debra Levin. LC TS200. DD 338.476691. **Circ** 2,000. Statistical data on the iron and steel scrap processing industry. Historical data also included. Domestic and export tonage by grade of scrap, and scrap composite prices. Institute of Scrap Iron & Steel Yearbook, 0073-9685.

FEUERVERZINKEN. Periodical. German. ir. Verband Deutscher Feuerverzinkereien, Postfach 1020, 5800 Hagen West Germany. LC TS660. Verzinken.

IL FILO METALLICO. 0430-4578. Periodical. Italian (translated from the German). qt. Meisenbach KG, Postfach 2069, D-8600 Bamberg 1 West Germany. **Ind/Abst** Chem. Abstr. **CODEN** FIMEBG.

FINISHERS' MANAGEMENT. 1957. 0015-2358. Periodical. US. English. mo. $21.00. Publication Management Inc, 1800 Pickwick Avenue, Glenview IL 60025. **Tel** (312)699-1706. Ed Rex E Dimick. bk rev. adv acc. **Circ** 8,500. (ctrl). Management oriented "why to" editorial focused on improved management practices and more profitable operation of captive and job shops in metal finishing industry.

FINISHING INDUSTRIES. See Manufacturing.

FIZIKA METALLOV I METALLOVEDENIE. V. 1- 1955-. 0015-3230. Periodical. UR. Russian. mo. $117.00. Victor Kamkin Inc, 12224 Parklawn Drive, Rockville MD 20852. **Tel** (301)881-5973. **Ind/Abst** Int. Aerosp. Abstr., Comput. Control Abstr., Electr. Electron. Abstr., Sci. Abstr., Met. Abstr., World Alum. Abstr., Chem. Abstr., Energy Res. Abstr., Sci. Cit. Index, Abr. Ed., Phys. Abstr., GeoRef, Sci. Abstr. Sect. A. Phys. Abstr. LC TN690. **CODEN** FMMTAK.

FMA'S JOURNAL OF THE FABRICATOR. See Manufacturing.

FONDERIA. 0015-6078. Periodical. IT. Italian. mo. Corso Venezia 18, 20121 Milano Italy. **Ind/Abst** Chem. Abstr. LC TS200. DD 671.205. **CODEN** FNDAAR. Fonderia Italiana.

FONDERIA ITALIANA CEASED. Vol. 1- June 1951-. 0015-6086. Periodical. IT. Italian. bm. Tecnomedia, Via Sansovino 33, 20133 Milano Italy. **Ind/Abst** CIS Abstr., Met. Abstr., World Alum. Abstr., Chem. Abstr. adv acc. **Circ** 3,000. (ctrl).

FONDERIE. See Manufacturing.

FONDERIE BELGE. See Manufacturing.

FONDERIE, FONDEUR D'AUJOURD'HUI. New Series, 1 (Jan. 1981)-. 0249-3136. Periodical. FR. French (summaries in English or German). ir. $75.83. Editions Techniques Industries, 12 Ave Raphael, 75016 Paris France. **Tel** (1)45047250. **Ind/Abst** Art Archaeol. Tech. Abstr., Chem. Abstr., Comput. Control Abstr., Electr. Electron. Abstr., Met. Abstr., Sci. Abstr. Sect. A. Phys. Abstr., Energy Res. Abstr., World Alum. Abstr. LC TS200. DD 671.205. **CODEN** FFAUDJ. bk rev. adv acc. **Circ** 3,500. (ctrl). Science technology and information for foundries. Metallurgy (steel, castiron, non-ferrous alloys) moulding, risering, gating, coremaking, finishing equipment, health and safety inspection. Fonderie, 0015-6094; Fondeur Daujourdhui.

FORGING TOPICS. See Manufacturing.

FOUNDRY MANAGEMENT & TECHNOLOGY. **VFOAT** Foundry M&T. **VAT** Foundry Management and Technology. V. 102, No. 5- May 1974-. 0360-8999. Periodical. US. English. mo. Penton/IPC, PO Box 95759, Cleveland OH 44101. **Tel** (216)696-7000. **Ind/Abst** Trade Ind. Index, Eng. Index Mon., Eng. Index Bioeng. Abstr., Eng. Index Energy Abstr., Excerpta Med., Coal Abstr., Met. Abstr., World Alum. Abstr., Chem. Abstr., Eng. Index Annu., Eng. Index, Appl. Sci. Technol. Index, Predicasts. LC TS200. DD 671.205. **CODEN** FNMTBS. Available on microfilm from University Microfilms. Foundry, 0015-9034.

FOUNDRY OPERATIONS PLANBOOK. 0147-8796. US. English. $5.00 Single Issue. McGraw Hill, 1221 Avenue of the Americas, New York NY 10020. LC TS228.99. DD 671.205.

FOUNDRY TRADE JOURNAL. (THE FOUNDRY TRADE JOURNAL). 0015-9042. Periodical. UK. English. bw. $140.00. Fuel & Metallurgical Journals Ltd, Queensway House, 2 Queensway, Redhill Surrey RHI 105 England. **Ind/Abst** CIS Abstr., Art Archaeol. Tech. Abstr., Met. Abstr., World Alum. Abstr., Chem. Abstr., ISMEC Bull. LC TS200. **CODEN** FUTJAD. Iron and Steel Trades Journal, Foundry Trade Journal and Pattern Maker.

FOUNDRY TRADE JOURNAL INTERNATIONAL. Began in 1978. 0143-6902. Periodical. UK. English (tables of contents and occasional summaries in French, German, Italian, and Spanish). qt. 41.00 Domestic, 51.00 Foreign. Fuel & Metallurgical Journals Ltd, Queensway House 2 Queensway, Redhill Surrey RHI 105 England. **Tel** (0737)68611. Ed Cyril McCombe. **Ind/Abst** Eng. Index Annu., Eng. Index Mon., Eng. Index Bioeng. Abstr., Eng. Index Energy Abstr., Met. Abstr., World Alum. Abstr. **CODEN** FTJIDO. adv acc. (ctrl). Encompases the whole range of foundry technology: traditional sand-based foundry practices, investment casting, die-casting, etc.

FOUNDRY YEAR BOOK. See Yearbooks, Almanacs, Directories.

FUNTAI OYOBI FUMMATSU YAKIN. Began 1947. 0532-8799. Periodical. Japanese (includes English summaries). ir. Japan Publishing Trade Company Ltd, PO Box 5030, Tokyo International, Tokyo 100-31 Japan. **Ind/Abst** Eng. Index Annu., Eng. Index Mon., Eng. Index Bioeng. Abstr., Eng. Index Energy Abstr., Met. Abstr., World Alum. Abstr., Chem. Abstr. **CODEN** FOFUA2.

GALVANO-ORGANO CEASED. Vol. 41, No. 438-. 0302-6477. Periodical. FR. French (summaries in English and German). mo. $47.90. Galvano Organo, 79 Avenue des Champs Elysees, Paris 8E France. **Ind/Abst** Excerpta Med., Met. Abstr., World Alum. Abstr., Chem. Abstr., Energy Res. Abstr. LC TS200. DD 671.705. **CODEN** GVOGAV. Galvano.

GALVANOTECHNIK. See Engineering.

GEOLOGIA E METALURGIA; BOLETIM. Began with No. 1, Oct. 1945. 0100-4921. Periodical. Portuguese. ir. **Ind/Abst** GeoRef. LC TN239.B8. **CODEN** GMTBAC.

GEOPHYSICS: THE LEADING EDGE IN EXPLORATION. See Engineering - Mining Engineering.

GIESSEREI. (GIESSEREI : ZEITSCHRIFT FUR DAS GESAMTE GIESSEREIWESEN). Began 1951. Periodical. GW. German (table of contents in English and French). bw. Giesserei-Verlag GMBH, PO Box 3503, D-4 Duesseldorf West Germany. **Ind/Abst** Predicasts, Excerpta Med., CIS Abstr., Energy Res. Abstr. Die Neue Giesserei, 0369-3848.

GIESSEREI-RUNDSCHAU. (GIESSEREI RUNDSCHAU). Began in 1954?. 0016-979X. Periodical. German. mo. Verlag Loverz, Ebendorferstrasse 10, 1010 Vienna 1 Austria. **Ind/Abst** Chem. Abstr., Energy Res. Abstr. **CODEN** GIERBQ.

GIESSEREIFORSCHUNG. Vol. 19- 1967-. 0046-5933. Periodical. GW. German. qt. Giesserei-Verlag GMBH, PO Box 3503, D-4 Duesseldorf West Germany. **Ind/Abst** Eng. Index Annu., Eng. Index Mon., Eng. Index Bioeng. Abstr., Eng. Index Energy Abstr., Met. Abstr., World Alum. Abstr., Chem. Abstr., Energy Res. Abstr. **CODEN** GSFGBY. Die Giesserei. Technisch-Wissenschaftliche Beihefte. Metalkunde und Giesereiwesen.

GIJUTSU RENKAN CHOSA KENKYU HOKOKUSHO. See Manufacturing.

GJUTERIET. 0017-0682. Periodical. SW. English. mo. Tidskriften Gjuteriet, Wallingatan 44, S-11124 Stockholm Sweden. **Ind/Abst** Met. Abstr., World Alum. Abstr., Chem. Abstr., Eng. Index Mon., Eng. Index Annu., Eng. Index. **CODEN** GJUTAG.

GOLD & SILVER SURVEY. **VAT** Gold and Silver Survey. V. 1- Feb. 1980-. 0196-3546. Periodical. US. English. mo. $525.00. World Reports Ltd, 108 Horseferry Road, London SW1P 2EF England. **Tel** 01-222-3836.

GUIDE DU TRAVAIL DES METAUX. 0301-8539. French. ir. 65.00. Compagnie Francaise d'Editions, CCP 25 113 46, Paris France. **LC** TS203. **DD** 338.476817.

GUMSOG PYOMYEN CERI. (KUMSOK PYOMYON CHORI). **VFOAT** Journal of the Metal Finishing Society of Korea. 0253-3081. Periodical. KO. Korean. ir. Hanguk Kumsok Pyonyon Konghakhoe, 72-1 Sangsu-dong, Mapo-ku, Seoul South Korea. **Ind/Abst** Chem. Abstr. **LC** TS653.A1. **CODEN** KPCHDD.

HAN CHIEH HSUEH PAO. *See* Manufacturing.

HANGUK KUMHYONG KONGOP CHONGNAM. *See* Yearbooks, Almanacs, Directories.

HARTEREI-TECHNISCHE MITTEILUNGEN. 0017-6583. Periodical. GW. English. bm. Carl Hanser Verlag, Pstfch 860420, Kolbergerstr 22, 8 Muenchen 86 West Germany. **Ind/Abst** Eng. Index Mon., Eng. Index Bioeng. Abstr., Eng. Index Energy Abstr., Met. Abstr., World Alum. Abstr., Chem. Abstr., Nuci. Sci. Abstr., Eng. Index Annu., Eng. Index Mon., Energy Res. Abstr. **CODEN** HARTAH. *Harterei-Technik und Warmerehandlung.*

HEAT TREATING. 0017-9345. Periodical. US. English. mo. $35.00. Fairchild Publications, 7 East 12th Street, New York NY 10003. **Ind/Abst** Met. Abstr., World Alum. Abstr., Chem. Abstr. **LC** TN672. **DD** 671.3605. **CODEN** HETRDI.

HEAT TREATMENT OF METALS. V. 1-. 0305-4829. Periodical. UK. English. qt. $55.17. Wolfson Heat Treatment Centre, Univ Aston-Bham Gosta Green, Birmingham B4 7ET England. **Tel** (021)359-3611. **Ed** Alan J Hick. **Ind/Abst** Eng. Index Annu., Eng. Index Mon., Eng. Index, Eng. Index Bioeng. Abstr., Eng. Index Energy Abstr., Energy Inf. Abstr., Environ. Abstr., Comput. Control Abstr., Electr. Electron. Abstr., Sci. Abstr. Sect. A. Phys. Abstr., Chem. Abstr., Met. Abstr., World Alum. Abstr., Phys. Abstr. **LC** TN672. **DD** 671.3605. **CODEN** HTRMBS. bk rev. adv acc. **Circ** 1,000. The only regular British publication devoted exclusively to heat treatment practice and innovation.

HIGH TEMPERATURE TECHNOLOGY. *See* Engineering.

HSI YU CHIN SHU. **VFOAT** Rare Metals. Periodical. Chinese (abstracts in English). ir. Metallurgical Industry Press, 74 Dengshikuo, Beijing China. **Ind/Abst** Chem. Abstr., Met. Abstr., World Alum. Abstr. **LC** TN758. **DD** 673. **CODEN** XIJID9.

HUNTINGTON ALLOYS. 0191-7773. Monographic Series. US. English. Huntington Alloys, PO Box 1958, Huntington WV 25720. **Tel** (304)696-2150. **Ind/Abst** Chem. Abstr. **CODEN** HUALDH.

HUTNICKE LISTY. 0018-8069. Periodical. CS. mo. Artia, Smecky 30, PO Box 790, Prague 1 Czechoslovakia. **Ind/Abst** Eng. Index Annu., Eng. Index Mon., Eng. Index Bioeng. Abstr., Eng. Index Energy Abstr., Coal Abstr., CIS Abstr., Met. Abstr., World Alum. Abstr., Chem. Abstr., Eng. Index. **LC** TN4. **CODEN** HUTLA7.

HUTNIK: MIESIECZNIK ORGANIZCYJ HUTNICZYCH. V. 1- July 20, 1929-. 0018-8077. Periodical. PL. Polish. mo. ARS Polona, Krakowskie Przedmiescie 7, 00-068 Warsaw Poland. **Ind/Abst** Eng. Index Annu., Eng. Index Mon., Eng. Index Bioeng. Abstr., Eng. Index Energy Abstr., Coal Abstr., Met. Abstr., World Alum. Abstr., Chem. Abstr. **LC** TS200. **DD** 672.05. **CODEN** HUTNAD.

HYDROMETALLURGY. V. 1- Sept. 1975-. 0304-386X. Periodical. NE. English. qt. 470.00. Elsevier Science Publisher, PO Box 211, 1000 AE Amsterdam Netherlands. **Tel** (020)5803 911. **Ed** C M Ritcey and M J Slater. **Ind/Abst** Eng. Index Annu., Eng. Index Mon., Eng. Index Bioeng. Abstr., Eng. Index Energy Abstr., Coal Abstr., Minproc, GeoRef, Met. Abstr., World Alum. Abstr., Ref. Source, Chem. Abstr., Energy Res. Abstr., Sci. Cit. Index, Abr. Ed., Bibliogr. Index Geol., Eng. Index. **LC** TN688. **DD** 669.028305. **CODEN** HYDRDA. bk rev. adv acc. Aims to bring together studies on novel processes, process design, chemistry, modelling, control economics and interfaces between unit operations. Provides forum for discussions on case histories and operational difficulties.

N I M RESEARCH DIGEST. **Main/Corp** National Institute for Metallurgy. Periodical. SA. English. bm. Council for Mineral Technology, Private Bag X3015, Randburg 2125 South Africa.

IBA QUARTERLY REVIEW. V. 1-. Periodical. English (French). qt. $30.00. International Bauxite Association, 67 Knutsford Boulevard/PO Box 551, Kingston 5 Jamaica West Indies. **Ind/Abst** Bibliogr. Index Geol. **Circ** 300. Development in bauxite, alumina, aluminium industry and markets.

IBS REVISTA. **Main/Corp** Instituto Brasilerio de Siderurgia. **VAT** Instituto Brasileiro de Siderurgia Revista. Portuguese. ir. Editoria Grafica Barbero, Fernando Chinaglia Distribuidores, Rua Teodora da Silva 907, Rio de Janiero Brazil. **Ind/Abst** Met. Abstr., World Alum. Abstr. **LC** HD9524.B8.

IISS COMMENTARY : TECHNO-ECONOMIC REPORT. Vol. 1- 1972-. Periodical. US. English. mo. $400.00. Institute for Iron and Steel Studies, 1103 North Washington Avenue, Greenbrook NJ 08812. **Ind/Abst** Met. Abstr., World Alum. Abstr.

IMM ABSTRACTS. *See* Indexes/Abstracts.

IMM BULLETIN. No. 830- 1976-. 0308-9789. Periodical. UK. English. mo. 20.00. Institute of Mining and Metallurgy, 44 Portland Place, London W1N 4BR England. **Tel** 01-580-3802. **Ed** M J Jones. **Ind/Abst** Mintec, Min. Technol. Abstr., Minproc. bk rev. adv acc. **Circ** 5,500. News of members, announcements of conferences and courses worldwide, additions to the library, book reviews, conference reports, letters to the editor, etc. *Transactions. Section A. Mining Industry, 0371-7844; Transactions. Section B. Applied Earth Sciences, 0371-7453; Transactions. Section C. Mineral Processing & Extractive Metallurgy, 0371-9553.*

L'IMPRIMERIE NOUVELLE. *See* Engineering - Mining Engineering.

INDUSTRIAL HEATING. **VFOAT** Journal of Heat Technology. V. 1- Oct. 1934-. 0019-8374. Periodical. US. English. mo. $30.00. National Institute Publishing Company, 1000 Killarney Drive, Pittsburgh PA 15234. **Tel** (412)885-6550. **Ed** C T McClelland. **Ind/Abst** Eng. Index Mon., Eng. Index Bioeng. Abstr., Eng. Index Energy Abstr., Excerpta Med., Coal Abstr., Energy Inf. Abstr., Environ. Abstr., Met. Abstr., World Alum. Abstr., Chem. Abstr., Eng. Index Annu., Eng. Index Mon., Nuci. Sci. Abstr., ISMEC Bull., Eng. Index. **LC** TH7201. **DD** 697.05. **CODEN** INHTAZ. bk rev. adv acc. **Circ** 23,500. (ctrl). High temperature processing, technology interpreted for practical application by engineering managers in manufacturing and primary production. Primarily metallurgical and ceramics.

INDUSTRIAL PRODUCT IDEAS. *See* Manufacturing.

L'INDUSTRIE DES METAUX NON FERREUX. **Main/Corp** Organisation for Economic Co-Operation and Development. **VFOAT** The Non-Ferrous Metals Industry. Monographic Series. English (French). ir. OECD, 1750 Pennsylvania Avenue NW, Washington DC 20006. **Ind/Abst** Predicasts. **LC** HD9539.A1. **DD** 338.4.'7'673.

L'INDUSTRIE SIDERURGIQUE. *See* Economics - Economics: Industry & Production.

INFORME ANUAL - CARBOCOL. **Main/Corp** Carbocol. 1982-. Spanish. an. **LC** HD9554.C64. **DD** 354.8610082382. *Informe Anual de la Junta Directiva y de la Gerencia General.*

INFORME ESTATISTICO ANUAL, SETOR METALURGICO. *See* Statistics.

INFORME ESTATISTICO, SETOR METALURGICO. *See* Statistics.

INORGANIC MATERIALS. *See* Chemistry - Inorganic Chemistry.

INSTITUTE OF METALS MONOGRAPH AND REPORT SERIES. **VFOAT** Monograph and Report Series. 0073-9464. UK. English. ir. Institute of Metals, 1 Carlton House Terrace, London SW1Y 5DB England. **Tel** (01)839-4071. These books cover a broad spectrum of subjects from fundmental physical principles to process metallurgy and applications.

INSTRUMENTALNYE I PODSHIPNIKOVYE STALI. *See* Manufacturing.

INSTRUMENTATION IN THE MINING AND METALLURGY INDUSTRIES. *See* Engineering - Mining Engineering.

INSULATED WIRE AND CABLE. (CURRENT INDUSTRIAL REPORTS. MA-33L, INSULATED WIRE AND CABLE). 0278-9337. US. English. an. $1.75. Data User Services Division, Customer Services Publication, Bureau of the Census, Washington DC 20233. **Tel** (301)763-4100. Presents timely data on the production, inventories, and orders of approximately 5,000 products, which represents 40 percent of all US manufacturing.

INTERNATIONAL CAST METALS JOURNAL. **VFOAT** AFS International Cast Metals Journal. V. 1- Mar. 1976-. 0362-1723. Periodical. US. English. qt. $35.00 Member, $70.00 Non-Member. American Foundrymen's Society, Golf and Wolf Roads, Des Plaines IL 60016-2277. **Ind/Abst** Eng. Index Annu., Eng. Index Mon., Eng. Index Bioeng. Abstr., Eng. Index Energy Abstr., Excerpta Med., Chem. Abstr. **LC** TS228.99. **DD** 671.205. **CODEN** ICMJDO. Available on microfilm from University Microfilms. *Cast Metals Research Journal, 0008-7467.*

INTERNATIONAL COPPER INFORMATION BULLETIN. Began in 1976. 0309-2216. Periodical. UK. English. qt. Copper Development Association, Orchard House/Mutton Lane, Potters Bar Herts EN6 3AP England. **Ind/Abst** Met. Abstr., World Alum. Abstr. **LC** TN780. **DD** 669.305. *Selected Abstracts of Recent Literature on Copper and Copper Alloys, Kupfer-Mitteilungen.*

INTERNATIONAL GLASS-METAL CATALOG. *See* Glass and Ceramics.

THE INTERNATIONAL JOURNAL OF POWDER METALLURGY & POWDER TECHNOLOGY. **VFOAT** Powder Metallurgy & Powder Technology. **VAT** International Journal of Powder Metallurgy and Powder Technology. V. 10- Jan. 1974-. 0361-3488. Periodical. US. English. qt. American Powder Metallurgy Institute, 105 College Road East, Princeton NJ 08540. **Tel** (609)452-7700. **Ind/Abst** Eng. Index Annu., Eng. Index Mon., Eng. Index Bioeng. Abstr., Eng. Index Energy Abstr., Predicasts, Minproc, Int. Aerosp. Abstr., Met. Abstr., World Alum. Abstr., Ref. Source, Chem. Abstr., Appl. Sci. Technol. Index, Sci. Cit. Index, Abr. Ed., Int. Aerosp. Abstr., Eng. Index. **LC** TN695. **DD** 676.3705. **CODEN** IPMPCU. *International Journal of Powder Metallurgy, 0020-7535.*

INTERNATIONAL METALS REVIEWS. V. 21-. 0308-4590. Periodical. UK. English. bm. $138.90. American Society for Metals, Metals Information, Metals Park OH 44073. **Tel** (216)338-5151. **Ed** Trevor Hughes. **Ind/Abst** Eng. Index Annu., Eng. Index Mon., Eng. Index Bioeng. Abstr., Eng. Index Energy Abstr., Excerpta Med., Int. Aerosp. Abstr., Comput. Control Abstr., Electr. Electron. Abstr., Sci. Abstr. Sect. A. Phys. Abstr., Met. Abstr., World Alum. Abstr., Chem. Abstr., Phys. Abstr., Eng. Index. **LC** TN1. **DD** 669.005. **CODEN** IMERDA. **Circ** 450. In-depth treatment of specific topics from theory and practice of extraction, production, fabrication, properties and behavior of metals, to actual usage. *International Metallurgical Reviews, 0367-9020.*

INTERNATIONAL SERIES OF MONOGRAPHS ON METAL PHYSICS AND PHYSICAL METALLURGY. 0074-8218. Monographic Series. US. English. ir. Pergamon Press, c/o Cashier, 395 Sawmill River Road, Elmsford NY 10523.

INTERNATIONAL STEEL STATISTICS : SUMMARY TABLES. *See* Statistics.

INTERNATIONAL STEEL STATISTICS, UNITED KINGDOM. *See* Statistics.

INVENTORIES OF BRASS AND COPPER WIRE MILL SHAPES *CEASED.* (CURRENT INDUSTRIAL REPORTS. M33K, INVENTORIES OF BRASS AND COPPER WIRE MILL SHAPES). -Summary for 1983. 0364-1848. Periodical. US. English. mo. $1.75. Data User Services Division, Customer Services Publication, Bureau of the Census, Washington DC 20233. **Tel** (301)763-4100. **Ind/Abst** Predicasts, Am. Stat. Index. **LC** HD9539.B8. **DD** 338.4767338420973. Presents timely data on the production, inventories, and orders of approximately 5,000 products, which represents 40 percent of all US manufacturing.

INVENTORIES OF STEEL MILL SHAPES. (CURRENT INDUSTRIAL REPORTS. M33-3, INVENTORIES OF STEEL MILL SHAPES). 0145-5214. Periodical. US. English. mo. $16.00. Data User Services Division, Customer Services Publication, Bureau of the Census, Washington DC 20233. **Tel** (301)763-4100. **Ind/Abst** Predicasts, Am. Stat. Index. **LC** HD9511. **DD** 338.476691420973. Presents timely data on the production, inventories, and orders of approximately 5,000 products, which represents 40 percent of all US manufacturing.

Metals & Metallurgy

IRON AGE. V. 1- Apr. 1859-. 0021-1508. Periodical. US. English. mo. Chilton Company, Chilton Way, Radnor PA 19089. **Ind/Abst** Appl. Sci. Technol. Index, Bus. Period. Index, Chem. Abstr., Eng. Index, Nuci. Sci. Abstr. **DD** 605. *Hardware-Man's Newspaper and American Manufacturers' Circular.*

IRON AND STEEL CASTINGS. (CURRENT INDUSTRIAL REPORTS. M33A, IRON AND STEEL CASTINGS). **VFOAT** Iron and Steel Castings. 0145-5257. US. English. mo. $16.00. Data User Services Division, Customer Services Publication, Bureau of the Census, Washington DC 20233. **Tel** (301)763-4100. **Ind/Abst** Predicasts, Chem. Abstr., Am. Stat. Index, Funk Scott Index Corp. Ind. **CODEN** CISCD9. Presents timely data on the production, inventories, and orders of approximately 5,000 products, which represents 40 percent of all US manufacturing.

IRON AND STEEL FOUNDRIES AND STEEL INGOT PRODUCERS. *See* Manufacturing.

IRON AND STEEL INDUSTRY. **Main/Corp** British Steel Corporation. V. 15- Jan. 1970-. UK. English. mo. Iron and Steel Statistics Bureau, 12-16 Addiscombe Road, CR9 6BS Croydon England. **LC** HD9521.4. **DD** 338.476720942. *Iron and Steel.*

IRON AND STEEL INDUSTRY. ANNUAL STATISTICS FOR THE UNITED KINGDOM. *See* Statistics.

IRON AND STEEL INTERNATIONAL *CEASED.* V. 46, No. 3- June 1973-. 0308-9142. Periodical. UK. English (with some summaries in French, German, Italian and Spanish). bm. Industrial Newspapers, Queensway House, 2 Queensway, Redhill Surrey RH1 1QS England. **Ind/Abst** CIS Abstr., Eng. Index Annu., Eng. Index Mon., Eng. Index Bioeng. Abstr., Eng. Index Energy Abstr., Excerpta Med., Coal Abstr., Ship Abstr., Energy Inf. Abstr., Environ. Abstr., Comput. Control Abstr., Electr. Electron. Abstr., Sci. Abstr. Sect. A. Phys. Abstr., Met. Abstr., World Alum. Abstr., Ref. Source, Chem. Abstr. **LC** TS300. **DD** 672.05. **CODEN** ISINBO. *Iron and Steel.*

IRON AND STEEL MILLS. **Main/Corp** Canada. Statistics Canada. Manufacturing and Primary Industries Division. **Series/Titl** Annual Census of Manufactures. **VFOAT** Siderurgie. 1970-. 0575-884X. CN. English (text in French). an. .70. **Tel** (800)268-1151. *Iron and Steel Mills, 0575-884X.*

IRON AND STEEL WORKS OF THE WORLD. 1st- Ed. UK. English. ir. 60.00. Metal Bulletin PLC, Parkhouse Park Terr Worcester, Surrey KT4 7HV England. **Tel** 01-330-4311. **Ed** Richard Serjeantson, Raymond Cordero and Henry Cooke. adv acc. Detailed information on the world's major iron and steel producers. Over 1,900 entries given, where possible, head office address, capacity, work details, products, subsidiaries and management.

IRON & STEELMAKER. (IRON & STEELMAKER : A PUBLICATION OF THE IRON AND STEEL SOCIETY). **VFOAT** Iron and Steelmaker. Vol. 7, No. 5 (May 1980)-. 0275-8687. Periodical. US. English. mo. $90.00. Iron and Steel Society of AIME, 410 Commonweath Drive, PO Box 411, Warrendale PA 15086. **Tel** (412)776-1585. **Ind/Abst** Eng. Index Annu., Eng. Index Mon., Eng. Index Bioeng. Abstr., Eng. Index Energy Abstr., Met. Abstr., World Alum. Abstr., Chem. Abstr. **LC** TS300. **DD** 669.105. **CODEN** IRSTDJ. *I & SM, 0097-8388.*

IRON ORE. 1957-. 0075-0883. US. English. an. American Iron Ore Association, 1501 Euclid Avenue, 514 Bulkley Building, Cleveland OH 44115. **Ind/Abst** GeoRef. **LC** HD9512. **DD** 338.27305. **CODEN** IRORDR.

IRON ORE MANUAL. 19. English. 115.00 Australia; 120.00 Asia, North America, Canada; $125.00 Europe, Africa, South America. The Tex Report Ltd, 11-7 Kanda Nishikicho 2-Chome, Tokyo 101 Japan. **Tel** (03)233-0811. **Ed** H Sano. adv acc.

IRONCASTER. 0362-0425. Periodical. US. English. bm. $14.50. Iron Castings Society, 455 State Street, Des Plaines IL 60016. **Tel** (312)299-9160. **Ind/Abst** Met. Abstr., World Alum. Abstr. **LC** TS200. **DD** 672.205. *Gray and Ductile Iron News.*

IRONMAKING & STEELMAKING. V. 1- 1974-. 0301-9233. Periodical. UK. English (with summaries in French and German). bm. $150.00. Institute of Metals, 1 Carlton House Terrace, London SW1Y 5DB England. **Tel** (01)839 4071. **Ed** Trevor Hughes. **Ind/Abst** Eng. Index Annu., Eng. Index Mon., Eng. Index Bioeng. Abstr., Eng. Index Energy Abstr., Coal Abstr., Art Archaeol. Tech. Abstr., Met. Abstr., World Alum. Abstr., Chem. Abstr., Sci. Cit. Index, Abr. Ed., Eng. Index. **LC** TS300. **DD** 669.1405. **CODEN** IMKSB7. bk rev. adv acc. **Circ** 1,200. International coverage of all aspects of iron- and steelmaking up to and including the rolling of ferrous products.

ITOGI NAUKI I TEKHNIKI : DIAGRAMMY SOSTOIANIIA NEMETALLICHESKIKH SISTEM. OKISNYE SISTEMY. **VFOAT** Diagrammy Sostoianiia Nemetallischesikh Sistem. Okisnye Sistemy. V. 9-. UR. Russian. 0.60 Single Issue. Liubertsy, 10 Moskovskoi Obl, Oktiavrskii Props 403, Moskva USSR. **LC** TN690.

ITOGI NAUKI I TEKHNIKI : TEKHNOLOGIIA I OBORUDOVANIE KUZNECHNOGO-SHTAMPOVOCHNOGO PROIZVODSTVA. **VFOAT** Tekhnologiia I Oborudovanie Kuznechno-Shtampovochnogo Proizvodstva. V. 1-. Monographic Series. UR. Russian. wk. $115.80. Victor Kamkin Inc, 12224 Parklawn Drive, Rockville MD 20852. **Tel** (301)881-5973. **LC** TS225.

IZVESTIIA VYSSHIKH UCHEBNYKH ZAVEDENII CHERNAIA METALLURGIIA. Periodical. UR. English. bm. Victor Kamkin Inc, 12224 Parklawn Drive, Rockville MD 20852. **Tel** (301)881-5973. **Ind/Abst** Met. Abstr., World Alum. Abstr., Chem. Abstr., Eng. Index Annu., Eng. Index Mon., Eng. Index Bioeng. Abstr., Eng. Index Energy Abstr. **CODEN** IVUMAX.

IZVESTIJA AKADEMII NAUK SSSR, METALLY. (IZVESTIIA AKADEMII NAUK SSSR. METALLY). **VFOAT** Metally. 1965-. 0568-5303. Periodical. UR. Russian. bm. $60.00. Victor Kamkin Inc (70358), 12224 Parklawn Drive, Rockville MD 20852. **Tel** (301)881-5973. **Ind/Abst** Eng. Index Annu., Eng. Index Mon., Eng. Index Bioeng. Abstr., Eng. Index Energy Abstr., Int. Aerosp. Abstr., Comput. Control Abstr., Electr. Electron. Abstr., Sci. Abstr. Sect. A. Phys. Abstr., Met. Abstr., World Alum. Abstr., Chem. Abstr., Energy Res. Abstr. **CODEN** IZNMAQ. *Izvestiia. Metallurgiia I Gornoe Delo.*

JAHRBUCH OBERFLACHENTECHNIK. *See* Yearbooks, Almanacs, Directories.

JAPAN'S IRON & STEEL INDUSTRY. **VAT** Japan's Iron and Steel Industry. 1953/54-. 0075-3475. JA. English. $31.00. Kawata Publicity Inc, CPO Box 1157, Tokyo 100-91 Japan. **Ed** S Kawata. **LC** HD9526.J3.

JENAER RUNDSCHAU. *See* Manufacturing.

JERNINDUSTRI. Began publication in 1920. 0021-5899. Periodical. NO. Norwegian. mo. 200.00. Mekaniske Versteders Lands, Oscars Gate RK 20 Box 7072-H, Oslo 0306 Norway. **Tel** 02-465820. **Ed** H Lundgaard. **Ind/Abst** Ship Abstr., Met. Abstr., World Alum. Abstr. **LC** TS300. bk rev. adv acc. **Circ** 4,000. News (technology, research, contracts, trade prospects internationalisation, training, education) in Norwegian metalworking industry (offshore shipbuilding, machinery foundry construction).

JERNKONTORETS ANNALER. *See* Engineering - Mining Engineering.

JOSA NYENGU BOGO - JANWEN GAIBAR NYENGUSO. *See* Engineering - Mining Engineering.

JOURNAL DU FOUR ELECTRIQUE ET DES INDUSTRIES ELECTROCHIMIQUES. **VFOAT** Journal du Four Electrique. 0021-8189. Periodical. French. mo. PYC Edition, 254 rue de Vaugirard, 75740 Paris Cedex 15 France. **Ind/Abst** GeoRef, Coal Abstr., Bibliogr. Index Geol., Eng. Index. **LC** TN681. **DD** 669.028405.

JOURNAL - MINING AND METALLURGICAL INSTITUTE OF JAPAN. *See* Engineering - Mining Engineering.

JOURNAL OF APPLIED METALWORKING. *See* Engineering - Mining Engineering.

JOURNAL OF HEAT TREATING. V. 1- June 1979-. 0190-9177. Periodical. US. English. sa. $80.00. American Society for Metals, Periodical Publications, Metals Park OH 44073. **Tel** (216)338-51511. **Ed** Charles A Stickels. **Ind/Abst** Eng. Index, Met. Abstr., World Alum. Abstr., Chem. Abstr., Eng. Index Annu., Eng. Index Mon., Eng. Index Energy Abstr., Eng. Index Bioeng. Abstr. **LC** TN672. **DD** 671.3605. **CODEN** JHTRDR. bk rev. **Circ** 1,200. Latest developments in heat treating technology. Peer reviewed.

THE JOURNAL OF MATERIALS EDUCATION. *See* Engineering.

JOURNAL OF MATERIALS SCIENCE. V. 1- Feb. 1966-. 0022-2461. Periodical. UK. English. mo. Associated Book Publishers, North Way, Andover Hampshire SP10 5BE England. **Ed** W Bonfield. **Ind/Abst** Electron. Commun. Abstr. J., ISMEC Bull., Pollut. Abstr. Indexes, Saf. Sci. Abstr. J., Eng. Index Mon., Eng. Index Bioeng. Abstr., Eng. Index Energy Abstr., Excerpta Med., Energy Inf. Abstr., Environ. Abstr., GeoRef, Art Archaeol. Tech. Abstr., Met. Abstr., World Alum. Abstr., Chem. Abstr., Eng. Index Annu., Eng. Index Mon., Int. Aerosp. Abstr., Nuci. Sci. Abstr. **LC** TA401. **DD** 620.1105. **CODEN** JMTSAS. adv acc. Leading source of primary communications on the structure and properties of engineering materials.

JOURNAL OF MATERIALS SCIENCE LETTERS. Vol. 1, No. 1 (Jan. 1982)-. 0261-8028. Periodical. UK. English. mo. $795.00. Associated Book Publishers Ltd, North Way, Andover Hampshire SP10 5BE England. **Ed** W Bonfield. **Ind/Abst** Electron. Commun. Abstr. J., ISMEC Bull., Eng. Index Mon., Eng. Index Bioeng. Abstr., Eng. Index Energy Abstr., Coal Abstr., Int. Aerosp. Abstr., Comput. Control Abstr., Electr. Electron. Abstr., Chem. Abstr., Br. Technol. Index, Eng. Index Annu., Curr. Contents, World Alum. Abstr., Met. Abstr., Sci. Abstr. Sect. A. Phys. Abstr., Appl. Mech. Rev., Sci. Cit. Index, Abr. Ed., Energy Res. Abstr., Autom. Subj. Citation Alert. **LC** TA401. **DD** 620.1105. **CODEN** JMSLD5. adv acc. Leading source of primary communications on the structure and properties of engineering materials. *Journal of Materials Science, 0022-2461.*

JOURNAL OF METALS. V. 29, No. 1- Jan. 1977-. 0148-6608. Periodical. US. English. mo. Metallurgical Society, 420 Commonwealth Drive, Warrendale PA 15086. **Tel** (412)776-9000. **Ind/Abst** Eng. Index, Life Sci. Collect., Excerpta Med., Coal Abstr., Energy Inf. Abstr., Mintec, Min. Technol. Abstr., Environ. Abstr., Minproc, Comput. Control Abstr., Electr. Electron. Abstr., Met. Abstr., Eng. Index Annu., Phys. Abstr., World Alum. Abstr., Ref. Source, Chem. Abstr., Int. Aerosp. Abstr., Nuci. Sci. Abstr., Appl. Sci. Technol. Index, Sci. Cit. Index, Abr. Ed., Funk Scott Index Corp. Ind., Eng. Index Mon., Eng. Index Bioeng. Abstr., Eng. Index Energy Abstr., Predicasts, Sel. Water Resour. Abstr. **LC** TN1. **DD** 669.005. **CODEN** JOMTAA. *JOM, 0098-4558.*

JOURNAL OF MINES, METALS & FUELS : INCORPORATING INDIAN MINING JOURNAL & THE OFFICIAL ORGAN OF INDIAN MINE MANAGERS' ASSOCIATION. *See* Engineering - Mining Engineering.

JOURNAL OF THE HISTORICAL METALLURGY SOCIETY. **Main/Corp** Historical Metallurgy Society. **VFOAT** Historical Metallurgy. 0142-3304. Periodical. UK. English. sa. $18.00. Institute of Metals, 1 Carlton House Terrace, London SW1Y 5DB England. **Tel** 023 587 578. **Ed** R F Tylecote. **Ind/Abst** Met. Abstr., World Alum. Abstr., Chem. Abstr. bk rev. adv acc. **Circ** 800. History and prehistory of metallurgy. *Historical Metallurgy.*

JOURNAL OF THE INSTITUTION OF ENGINEERS. INDIA. PART MM: MINING AND METALLURGY DIVISION. *See* Engineering - Mining Engineering.

JOURNAL OF THE LESS-COMMON METALS. **VAT** Journal of the Less Common Metals. V. 1- Feb. 1959-. 0022-5088. Periodical. English (French or German). ir. $1137.95. Elsevier Sequoia SA, PO Box 851, 1001 Lausanne Switzerland. **Ind/Abst** Eng. Index Annu., Eng. Index Mon., Eng. Index Bioeng. Abstr., Eng. Index Energy Abstr., Minproc, GeoRef, Comput. Control Abstr., Electr. Electron. Abstr., Sci. Abstr. Sect. A. Phys. Abstr., Met. Abstr., World Alum. Abstr., Ref. Source, Chem. Abstr., Int. Aerosp. Abstr., Nuci. Sci. Abstr., Energy Res. Abstr., Sci. Cit. Index, Abr. Ed., Bibliogr. Index Geol., Phys. Abstr., Eng. Index. **LC** TN1. **DD** 669.705. **CODEN** JCOMAH.

JOURNAL OF THE SOUTH AFRICAN INSTITUTE OF MINING AND METALLURGY. (JOURNAL OF THE SOUTH AFRICAN INSTITUTE OF MINING & METALLURGY). **Main/Corp** South African Institute of Mining and Metallurgy. **VFOAT** Joernaal van die Suid-Afrikaanse

Metals & Metallurgy

Instituut vir Mynbon & Metallurgie. V. 57- 1956. 0038-223X. Periodical. SA. English. mo. 60.00. South African Institute of Mining, PO Box 61019 Marshalltown, 2107 Transvaal South Africa. **Tel** 832-2177. Ed H W Glen. **Ind/Abst** Eng. Index Mon., Eng. Index Bioeng. Abstr., Eng. Index Energy Abstr., Sel. Water Resour. Abstr., Coal Abstr., Mintec, Min. Technol. Abstr., Minproc, GeoRef, CIS Abstr., Met. Abstr., World Alum. Abstr., Chem. Abstr., Nuci. Sci. Abstr., Eng. Index Annu., Eng. Index Mon., Energy Res. Abstr., Energy Inf. Abstr., Environ. Abstr., Sci. Cit. Index, Abr. Ed., Appl. Mech. Rev., Eng. Index. **CODEN** JSAMAP. bk rev. adv acc. **Circ** 2,800. (ctrl). Major function is the publication of technical papers and notes related to research, development and practice in the mining and metallurgical industries. *Journal of the Chemical, Metallurgical and Mining Society of South Africa, 0368-1661.*

KANG TIEH PING LUN. 1 (July 1980)-. Periodical. CH. Chinese. ir. 0.60. Hsin Hua Shu Tien, Chung-Ching Fa Hsing So, Chung-Ching Shih China. LC TS300. DD 669.14205.

KEIKINZOKU. Began in 1951. 0451-5994. Periodical. Japanese (summaries in English). mo. Japan Publishers Trading Company Ltd, PO Box 5030, Tokyo International, Tokyo 100 31 Japan. **Ind/Abst** Eng. Index Annu., Eng. Index Mon., Eng. Index Bioeng. Abstr., Eng. Index Energy Abstr., Int. Aerosp. Abstr., Met. Abstr., World Alum. Abstr. **CODEN** KEIKA6.

KEIKINZOKU KOGYO TOKEI NEMPO. VFOAT Light Metal Statistics in Japan. JA. chiefly in Japanese. ir. 1000. Japan Light Metal Association, 2-2 Nihonbashi-Dori Chuo-Ku, Tokyo Japan. LC HD9539.A3.

KEYNOTES (ASSOCIATED LOCKSMITHS OF AMERICA). See Manufacturing.

KINZOKU ZAIRYO GIJUTSU KENKYUJO NEMPO. 1978-. JA. Japanese. an. Kagaku Gijutsucho Kinzoku Zairo Gijutsu Kenkyujo, 3-Ban 12-Go Naka Meguro, 2-Chome Meguro-Ku Tokyo 153 Japan. LC TN207.

KIT GUNS & HOBBY GUNSMITHING. See Manufacturing.

KNIVES. See Manufacturing.

KOGEPTERV KOZLEMENYEI. See Engineering - Mining Engineering.

KORROSJONS-NYTT. Periodical. NO. Norwegian. bm. Korrosjons-Nytt, Postbnoks 1041, 5001 Bergen Norway.

KOVOVE MATERIALY. VFOAT Mettalic Materials. 0023-432X. Periodical. CS. English (summaries in English, German, Russian). bm. 99.00. Kovove Materially, Slovak Academy of Sciences, Bratislava Czechoslovakia. **Tel** 375203. Ed Matej Bily. **Ind/Abst** Eng. Index Mon., Eng. Index Bioeng. Abstr., Eng. Index Energy Abstr., Comput. Control Abstr., Electr. Electron. Abstr., Sci. Sect. A. Phys. Abstr., Met. Abstr., World Alum. Abstr., Eng. Index, Eng. Index Annu., Int. Aerosp. Abstr., Chem. Abstr., Nuci. Sci. Abstr., Phys. Abstr. **CODEN** KOMAAW. bk rev. Fundamental research in material science, physical metallurgy and fracture mechanics, including experimental, theoretical and computational methods. *Zvaraesty Sbornik.*

KOY. KORROSION OCH YTSKYDD. VFOAT Korrosion Och Ytskydd. Periodical. Swedish (with some summaries in English). ir. 79.00. IPC Business Press, 205 East 42nd Street, New York NY 10017. LC TA418.74.

KOZAN. See Engineering - Mining Engineering.

KRZEPNIECIE METALI I STOPOW. Began in 1979. 0208-9386. Periodical. Polish. ir. 30.00. **Ind/Abst** Chem. Abstr. LC TS228.9. **CODEN** KMSTD6.

KUANGYE GONGCHENG. See Engineering - Mining Engineering.

KUZNECHNO-SHTAMPOVOCHNOE PROIZVODSTVO. Began in 1959. 0201-7296. Periodical. UR. Russian. mo $40.50. Victor Kamkin Inc (70451), 12224 Parklawn Drive, Rockville MD 20852. **Tel** (301)881-5973. **Ind/Abst** Met. Abstr., World Alum. Abstr., Chem. Abstr. **CODEN** KSPRAO. Index in last issue of volume - attached.

LAMIERA. 0391-5891. Periodical. IT. Italian. mo. $89.11. Tecniche Nouve SRL, Via Moscova 46-9, 20121 Milano Italy. **Tel** 02/ 6590351. **Ind/Abst** Chem. Abstr. **CODEN** LAMID6.

LEAD. V. 1- Nov. 1930-. 0023-9550. Periodical. US. English. bm. Lead Industries Association, 292 Madison Avenue, New York NY 10017. Ed Jerome F Smith. **Ind/Abst** Met. Abstr., World Alum. Abstr., Chem. Abstr. LC TA480.L4. DD 669.405. **Circ** 78,000.

LEAD ABSTRACTS (LONDON, ENGLAND : 1962). See Indexes/Abstracts.

LEAD AND ZINC INDUSTRY. Main/Corp Arizona. Dept. of Mineral Resources. 1960-. 0570-9369. US. English. an. Arizona Department of Mineral Resources, Mineral Building, Fairgrounds, Phoenix AZ 85029. LC HD9539.L38.

LEAD RESEARCH DIGEST. Main/Corp International Lead Zinc Research Organization. 0146-7980. Periodical. US. English. an. International Lead Zinc Research Organization, 292 Madison Avenue, New York NY 10017. **Ind/Abst** World Surf. Coat. Abstr., ISMEC Bull.

LIGHT METAL AGE. V. 1- May 1943-. 0024-3345. Periodical. US. English. bm. Light Metal Age, 693 Mission Street/Pent House, San Francisco CA 94105. **Tel** (415)781-1431. **Ind/Abst** Eng. Index Mon., Eng. Index Bioeng. Abstr., Eng. Index Energy Abstr., Predicasts, Coal Abstr., Met. Abstr., World Alum. Abstr., Chem. Abstr., Eng. Index Annu., Eng. Index Mon., Nuci. Sci. Abstr., Appl. Sci. Technol. Index, Funk Scott Index Corp. Ind., Eng. Index. LC TN1. DD 669.7. **CODEN** LMAGAL.

LIGHT METALS. Main/Corp American Institute of Mining, Metallurgical, and Petroleum Engineers. 0147-0809. US. English. an. $80.00. American Institute of Mining Metallurgical and Petroleum Engineers, PO Box 430, Warrendale PA 15086. **Tel** (412)776-9070. Ed H O Bohner. **Ind/Abst** Eng. Index, Chem. Abstr., Eng. Index Annu., Eng. Index Mon., Eng. Index Bioeng. Abstr., Eng. Index Energy Abstr. LC TN773. DD 669.72. **CODEN** LMPMDF.

LIMESTONE. (NLI LIMESTONE). Main/Corp National Limestone Institute, Washington, D.C. VAT National Limestone Institute Limestone. V. 1- July 1964-. 0547-0684. Periodical. US. English. qt. National Limestone Institute, 3251 Old Lee Highway, Suite 500, Fairfax VA 22030. **Tel** (703)273-8517. LC TN967.

LIST OF ELECTRODES CERTIFIED TO CSA W48 SERIES OF STANDARDS AND APPLICABLE AWS A5. SPECIFICATIONS. 0822-742X. CN. English. an. Canadian Welding Bureau, 254 Merton Street, Toronto Ontario M4S 1A9 Canada. DD 671.5212028.

LITEINCE PROIZVODSTVO, METALLOVEDENIE I OBRABOTKA METALLOV DAVLENIEM. Main/Corp Krasnoyarsk, Siberia. Institut Tsvetnykh Metallov. 0302-9069. UR. Russian. 0.47 Single Issue. Krasniarskoe Knizhnoe IZD-VO, Pro Mira 89, Krasnoiarsk Russian SFSR. LC TS200.

LITEJNOE PROIZVODSTVO. (LITEINOE PROIZVODSTVO). Main/Corp Kharkivskyi Politekhnichnyi Instytut Imeni V. I. Lenina. 0024-449X. UR. Russian. mo. $33.50. Victor Kamkin Inc (70491), 12224 Parklawn Drive, Rockville MD 20852. **Tel** (301)881-5973. **Ind/Abst** Met. Abstr., World Alum. Abstr., Chem. Abstr. LC T4, TS228.99. **CODEN** LIPRAX.

LITHIUM RESEARCH REVIEW SERIES. 0731-8065. Periodical. US. English. ir. Human Sciences Press, 72-5th Avenue, New York NY 10011.

LOCATOR. VFOAT MDNIS Locator. V. 1- Sept. 1969-. US. English. mo. $15.00. Machinery Dealers National Information System, 1110 Spring Street, Silver Springs MD 20910. **Tel** (301)585-9498. Ed Sheldon A Berman. LC TJ1040. DD 338.47621802573. adv acc. **Circ** 77,000. (ctrl). A publication listing classified ads of used metal working equipment available for sale from equipment dealers inventories.

LOCKSMITH LEDGER. See Household Hardware & Appliances.

I M M ABSTRACTS. See Indexes/Abstracts.

M P & P. METALWORKING PRODUCTION & PURCHASING. (M P & P, METAL-WORKING PRODUCTION & PURCHASING). VFOAT Metal-Working Production & Purchasing. V. 1- Oct. 1974-. 0383-090X. Periodical. CN. English. ir. $10.00. Action Communications Ltd, Suite 233/4 Lansing Square, Willowdale Ontario M2J 2T4 Canada. DD 671.

MACHINE OUTIL. Began in 1971. 0024-9149. Periodical. FR. French. mo $33.21. Sofetec, 3-5 rue Fernand Pelloutier, 92100 Boulogne France. **Tel** (14)825 50 30. **Ind/Abst** CIS Abstr. LC TJ1180. **DD** 621.90205. bk rev. adv acc. **Circ** 12,000. (ctrl). Manufacturing facts about metalworking. *Machine-Outil Francaise.*

MACHINERY AND PRODUCTION ENGINEERING. See Engineering - Mechanical Engineering & Machinery.

MAGNESIUM MILL PRODUCTS. (CURRENT INDUSTRIAL REPORTS. MA-33G, MAGNESIUM MILL PRODUCTS). 0735-8466. US. English. an. $1.00. Data User Services Division, Customer Services Publication, Bureau of the Census, Washington DC 20233. **Tel** (301)763-4100. LC HD9539.M27. DD 380.1456737230973. Presents timely data on the production, inventories, and orders of approximately 5,000 products, which represents 40 percent of all US manufacturing.

MAGYAR ALUMINUM. 0025-0058. Periodical. HU. Hungarian. mo. Akademiai Kiado, PO Box 24, 1363 Budapest Hungary. **Ind/Abst** Coal Abstr., Met. Abstr., World Alum. Abstr., Chem. Abstr. LC HD9539.A63. **CODEN** MAGABT.

MANUFACTURING SERIES C. NO. 7, BASIC METAL INDUSTRIES. Periodical. English. ir. Department of Statistics, Private Bag, Wellington New Zealand. LC HD9506.N45. DD 338.4767109931.

MATERIALS & DESIGN. See Engineering.

MATERIALS FORUM. 0883-2900. Periodical. US. English. qt. $115.00. Pergamon Press, Maxwell House, Fairview Park, Elmsford NY 10523. *Metals Forum, 0160-7952.*

MATERIALS-METALWORKING TECHNOLOGY SERIES. (MATERIALS/METALWORKING TECHNOLOGY SERIES). 0147-734X. US. English. ir. American Society of Metals, Metals Information, Metals Park OH 44073. **Ind/Abst** Chem. Abstr. **CODEN** MMTSDU.

MATERIALS PERFORMANCE. V. 13- Jan. 1974-. 0094-1492. Periodical. US. English. $50.00 Domestic $65.00 Others. National Association of Corrosion Engineers, PO Box 218340, Houston TX 77218. **Tel** (713)492-0535. Ed LC Rowe. **Ind/Abst** Eng. Index Mon., Eng. Index Bioeng. Abstr., Eng. Index Energy Abstr., Fluidex, Life Sci. Collect., Excerpta Med., Ship Abstr., Coal Abstr., World Surf. Coat. Abstr., Abstr. Bull. Inst. Paper Chem., Art Archaeol. Tech. Abstr., Met. Abstr., World Alum. Abstr., Ref. Source, Chem. Abstr., Eng. Index Annu., Eng. Index, Appl. Sci. Technol. Index, Pet. Abstr. LC TA462. DD 620.162305. **CODEN** MTPFBI. bk rev adv acc. **Circ** 15,500. (ctrl). Official monthly journal of NACW edited for the corrosion engineer, scientist, technician, and others involved in combating corrosion problems in practical situations. *Materials Protection and Performance, 0025-5378.*

MECHANICAL WORKING AND STEEL PROCESSING. 0147-7781. US. English. ir. Iron and Steel Society of AIME, PO Box 411, Warrendale PA 15086. **Ind/Abst** Chem. Abstr., Eng. Index. **CODEN** MWSPDI.

MEMBERSHIP DIRECTORY - METALLURGICAL SOCIETY OF AIME. See Yearbooks, Almanacs, Directories.

MEMOIRES ET ETUDES SCIENTIFIQUES DE LA REVUE DE METALLURGIE. (REVUE DE METALLURGIE. MEMOIRES ET ETUDES SCIENTIFIQUES). Began with May 1980 issue. 0245-8292. Periodical. FR. French. mo. La Revue de Metallurgie, 5 rue Paul Cezanne, 75008 Paris France. **Tel** 563 17 10. **Ind/Abst** Eng. Index Annu., Eng. Index Mon., Eng. Index Bioeng. Abstr., Eng. Index Energy Abstr., Excerpta Med., Int. Aerosp. Abstr., Comput. Control Abstr., Electr. Electron. Abstr., Sci. Abstr. Sect. A. Phys. Abstr., Energy Res. Abstr., Met. Abstr., World Alum. Abstr., Chem. Abstr. LC TN2. DD 669.005. **CODEN** MESMDJ. *Memoires Scientifiques de la Revue de Metallurgie.*

MEMOIRES SCIENTIFIQUES DE LA REVUE DE METALLURGIE CEASED. (LES MEMOIRES SCIENTIFIQUES DE LA REVUE DE METALLURGIE). Began with V. 56, No. 1 (June 1959)-. Ceased with Apr. 1980 issue. 0025-9128. Periodical. French. mo. **Ind/Abst** Coal Abstr., Excerpta Med. LC TN2. DD 669.05. **CODEN** MRMTAU. *Revue de Metallurgie.*

MEMORIA ANUAL - COMISION CHILENA DEL COBRE. Main/Corp Comision Chilena del Cobre. Spanish. an. Agustinas, 1161 40 Piso, Casilla 9493 Santiago Chile. LC HD9539.C7. DD 354.830082382.

Metals & Metallurgy

MEMORIA - EMPRESA NACIONAL DE FUNDICIONES. Main/Corp Empresa Nacional de Fundiciones (Bolivia). Periodical. BO. Spanish. ir. Empresa Nacional de Fundiciones, Av Villazon 1966, 7 Po S Piso Casilla 4301, La Paz Bolivia.

MEMORIA TECNICA - CONGRESO LATINAMERICANO DE SIDERURGIA. Main/Conf Congreso Latinamericano de Siderurgia. VFOAT Technical Proceedings - Latin American Iron and Steel Congress. Began in 1961. Spanish. ir. Instituto Latinamericano del Fierro y el Acero, Dario Urzua 1994 Casilla 16065, Santiago de Chile. Ind/Abst Chem. Abstr. LC HD9524.L3. CODEN CLSMBO.

MEMORIA Y CUENTA DE LA ASOCIACION DE INDUSTRIALES METALURGICOS Y DE MINERIA DE VENEZUELA. Main/Corp Asociacion de Industriales Metalurgicos y de Mineria de Venezuela. Spanish. ir. Edificio Camara de Industriales, Piso 9 - Esquina Puente Anauco, Caracas Venezuela. LC HD9506.V4.

METAALBEWERKING. Began in 1934. Periodical. NE. Dutch. sm. Tech Uitgeverij Veij Mestdagh, Markt 51, 4331 UK Middelburg Netherlands. Tel 01180-36320. Ed Ir D J de Korte. Ind/Abst CIS Abstr., Excerpta Med., Chem. Abstr. LC TS200. CODEN MBMEDC. bk rev. adv acc. Circ 3,500. Flexible automation and metalworking.

METAALBEWERKINGSMACHINE - INDUSTRIE EN MACHINEGEREEDSCHAPPENFABRIEKEN. See Engineering - Mechanical Engineering & Machinery.

METAL. 0377-7545. Spanish. ir. Fedemetal, Av Caracas No 37-15, Bogota Colombia. LC HD9743.C64.

METAL. V. 1- Jan. 1961-. 0539-4457. Periodical. Spanish. ir. International Metalworkers Federation, Plaza Ferrocarriles No 11 OF 32, Mexico 4 DF Mexico.

METAL BUILDING NEWS. See Building and Construction.

METAL BUILDING REVIEW. See Building and Construction.

METAL BULLETIN. V. 1- 1913-. 0026-0533. Periodical. UK. English. sw. $389.82. Metal Bulletin PLC, Parkhouse Park Terr Worcester, Surrey KT4 7HV England. Tel (01)330-4311. Ed J E Bailey and D S Gilbertson. Ind/Abst Predicasts, Coal Abstr., GeoRef, Chem. Abstr., Funk Scott Index Corp. Ind., Bibliogr. Index Geol. LC TN1. CODEN MTBLAX. bk rev. adv acc. Circ 9,865. Provides international news, views, market trends and almost 800 metal steel and scrap prices in each Tuesday and Friday issues.

METAL BULLETIN HANDBOOK. 1st- Ed. 0076-664X. UK. English. sa. $36.39. Metal Bulletin PLC, Parkhouse Park Terrace Worcester, KT4 7HV England. Tel (01)330-4311. Ed Ruby Packard. LC HD9506.4. DD 338.2, 669. adv acc. Detailed price changes and averages, statistics of production, import/exports for non-ferrous metals and steel products over a period of years.

METAL BULLETIN MONTHLY. VFOAT M B Monthly. Began with No. 1 (Jan. 1971). 0373-4064. Periodical. UK. English. mo. $209.15. Metal Bulletin PLC, Park House, Park Terrace, Worcester Surrey, KT4 7HV England. Tel (01)330-4311. Ed Richard Serjeantson. Ind/Abst Excerpta Med., Predicasts, GeoRef, Met. Abstr., World Alum. Abstr., Ref. Source, Funk Scott Index Corp. Ind., Bibliogr. Index Geol. LC TN1. DD 669.005. adv acc. Circ 12,361. Deals with all aspects of the steel, metals and scrap industries through global features and integrated supplements. Highlighting developments in processing equipment and machinery. Metal Bulletin, 0026-0533.

METAL CANS CEASED. Main/Corp United States. Bureau of the Census. Series/Titl Current Industrial Reports, Ser. M34D. Periodical. US. English. mo. $0.30 Single Copy. US Department of Commerce, Bureau of the Census, Washington DC 20233. Ind/Abst Predicasts.

METAL DISTRIBUTION. 1975-. 0098-2210. US. English. an. Metal/Center News, 7 East 12th Street, New York NY 10003. LC HD9506.U6. DD 381.456710973.

METAL FABRICATING NEWS. See Manufacturing.

THE METAL FABRICATOR. 0026-0568. Periodical. US. English. qt. $10.00. Walter B Frost & Company, 97 Columbia Street, Peace Dale RI 02883.

METAL FINISHING ABSTRACTS. See Indexes/Abstracts.

METAL FINISHING; PREPARATION, ELECTROPLATING, COATING. V. 38, No. 6- June 1940-. 0026-0576. Periodical. US. English. mo. $12.00. Metals and Plastics Publications, 1 University Plaza, Hackensack NJ 07601. Ind/Abst Eng. Index Annu., Eng. Index Mon., Eng. Index Bioeng. Abstr., Eng. Index Energy Abstr., Excerpta Med., Predicasts, World Surf. Coat. Abstr., Int. Aerosp. Abstr., Art Archaeol. Tech. Abstr., Met. Abstr., World Alum. Abstr., Ref. Source, Chem. Abstr., Nuci. Sci. Abstr., Appl. Sci. Technol. Index. CODEN MEFIA7. Available on microfilm from University Microfilms. Metal Industry, Organic Finishing.

METAL POWDER REPORT. V. 1- Sept. 1946-. 0026-0657. Periodical. UK. English. mo. $80.00. Powder Metallurgy Ltd, Old Banks Buildings, Bellstone/Shrewsbury, Shropshire SY1 1HU England. Tel (609)799-3300.

METAL PROGRESS. VFOAT Heat Treating Buyers Guide and Directory. V. 18, No. 3- Sept. 1930-. 0026-0665. Periodical. US. English. mo. $20.00. American Society for Metals, Metals Park OH 44073. Ind/Abst Art Archaeol. Tech. Abstr., Met. Abstr., World Alum. Abstr., Chem. Abstr., Eng. Index Annu., Eng. Index Mon., Nuci. Sci. Abstr., Int. Aerosp. Abstr., Appl. Sci. Technol. Index. LC TS200. DD 671.05. CODEN MEPOA7. (cum index). Transactions of the American Society for Steel Treating, 0096-476X.

METAL PROGRESS. HEAT TREATING BUYERS GUIDE AND DIRECTORY. See Yearbooks, Almanacs, Directories.

METAL PROGRESS WEST. 0362-935X. Periodical. US. English. qt. American Society for Metals, Metal Abstracts Trust, Metals Park OH 44073. LC TA459. DD 669.005.

METAL SCIENCE CEASED. V. 8, No. 1-V. 18. 0306-3453. Periodical. UK. English. mo. $43.00. Metals Society, 1 Carlton House Terrace, London SW1Y 5DB England. Ind/Abst Eng. Index Annu., Eng. Index Mon., Eng. Index Bioeng. Abstr., Eng. Index Energy Abstr., Int. Aerosp. Abstr., Comput. Control Abstr., Electr. Electron. Abstr., Sci. Abstr. Sect. A. Phys. Abstr., Met. Abstr., World Alum. Abstr., Chem. Abstr. LC TN1. DD 669.005. CODEN METSC7. Metal Science Journal, 0026-0681.

METAL STAMPING. 1967. 0026-069X. Periodical. US. English. mo. $75.00. Metal Stamping, 2720 Chardon Road, Richmond Heights OH 44143. Tel (216)585-8800. Ed H Daniels. Ind/Abst Excerpta Med., Energy Inf. Abstr., Environ. Abstr., Met. Abstr., World Alum. Abstr. LC TS200. Circ 30,000. (ctrl). Helpful information to the metal forming industry.

METAL STAMPING, PRESSING AND COATING INDUSTRY. Main/Corp Statistics Canada. Manufacturing and Primary Industries Division. Series/Titl Annual Census of Manufactures. VFOAT Industrie de l'Emboutissage, du Matricage et du Revetement des Metaux. VAT Industrie de l'Estampage, du Matricage et du Revetement des Metaux. 1970-. 0527-5687. CN. English (French). an. Receiver General for Canada, Statistics Canada Publications, Ottawa Ontario K1A 0T6 Canada. Metal Stamping, Pressing and Coating Industry, 0527-5687.

METAL STATISTICS. See Statistics.

METAL STATISTICS; THE PURCHASING GUIDE OF THE METAL INDUSTRIES. See Statistics.

METAL TRENDS. Issue No. 1 (Mar. 1983)-. 0824-7471. Periodical. CN. English. mo. $600.00. Metal Trends, Suite 1000/789 West Pinder Street, Vancouver British Columbia V6C 1H2 Canada. DD 338.205.

METALETTER. VAT Metal Letter. 0047-6870. Periodical. US. English. mo. American Federation of Labor, 815 16th Street NW, Washington DC 20006. Tel (202)347-7255.

METALL. V. 1- Sept. 1947-. 0026-0746. Periodical. GW. German. mo. $137.89. Alfred Huethig Verlag GMBH, Im Weiher 10 POB 10 28 69, 6900 Heidelberg 1 West Germany. Tel (06221)489-0. Ed Gerhard Elbing, Helmut Winkler, Dieter Kamphauser and Gustav Salffner. Ind/Abst Eng. Index Annu., Eng. Index Mon., Eng. Index Bioeng. Abstr., Eng. Index Energy Abstr., Excerpta Med., Int. Aerosp. Abstr., GeoRef, Energy Res. Abstr., Met. Abstr., World Alum. Abstr., Chem. Abstr. LC TN3. DD 338.27405. CODEN MTLLAF. bk rev. adv acc. International journal for trade and technology of metals and metal working.

METALL. VFOAT IGM Metall. 1- Oct. 10, 1949-. Periodical. GW. German. ir. Industriegewerkschaft Metall Wilhelm-Leuscher, Strasse 79-85 Postfach 3304, 6000 Frankfurt/Main 1 West Germany. LC HD6698.M5.

METALLE. See Business - Commerce.

I METALLI NON FERROSI IN ITALIA; STATISTICHE. See Statistics.

METALLOBERFLACHE. Began in 1947. 0026-0797. Periodical. GW. German. mo. Carl Hanser Verlag, Postfach 860420, Kolbergerstr 22, 8 Munchen 86 West Germany. Ind/Abst Eng. Index Annu., Eng. Index Mon., Eng. Index, Eng. Index Bioeng. Abstr., Eng. Index Energy Abstr., Excerpta Med., Energy Res. Abstr., Met. Abstr., World Alum. Abstr., Chem. Abstr. LC TS200. DD 671. CODEN MOFEAV.

METALLOFIZIKA. 0204-3580. Periodical. UR. Russian (summaries in English). bm. Izdatelstvo Naukova Dumka, 252601 Kiev Gsp, Ul. Repina 3, Kiev Ukrainian SSR. Ind/Abst Int. Aerosp. Abstr., Met. Abstr., World Alum. Abstr., Chem. Abstr. LC TN689. DD 669.905. CODEN MANFDD. Metallofizika.

METALLOFIZIKA. (PHYSICS OF METALS). Vol. 3, No. 1 (Nov. 1981)-. 0275-9144. Periodical. US. English (Russian). bm. $350.00 Per Vol. Gordon & Breach Science Publishers, One Park Avenue, New York NY 10016. Ed V N Gridnev. Ind/Abst Comput. Control Abstr., Electr. Electron. Abstr., Sci. Abstr. Sect. A. Phys. Abstr., Met. Abstr., World Alum. Abstr. LC TN689. DD 669.905. CODEN PMTSDT. bk rev. adv acc.

METALLOGRAPHIC REVIEW. (THE METALLOGRAPHIC REVIEW). V. 1- Sept. 1972-. 0090-2098. Periodical. US. English. qt. $20.00. International Microstructural Analysis Society, PO Box 2329, LaJolla CA 92037. Ind/Abst Eng. Index. LC TN689. DD 669.9505. CODEN MTGRB9.

METALLOGRAPHY. V. 1- Sept. 1968-. 0026-0800. Periodical. US. English. qt. Elsevier Science Publishing Company Inc, PO Box 1663 Grand Central Station, New York NY 10163. Tel (212)370-5520. Ind/Abst Eng. Index Mon., Eng. Index Bioeng. Abstr., Eng. Index Energy Abstr., Comput. Control Abstr., Electr. Electron. Abstr., Sci. Abstr. Sect. A. Phys. Abstr., Art Archaeol. Tech. Abstr., Energy Res. Abstr., Met. Abstr., World Alum. Abstr., Chem. Abstr., Eng. Index Annu., Eng. Index Mon., Nuci. Sci. Abstr., Sci. Cit. Index, Abr. Ed., Phys. Abstr., Eng. Index. LC TN690. DD 669.9505. CODEN MEIJAP.

METALLOVEDENIE I TERMICESKAJA OBRABOTKA. (METALLOVEDENIE I TERMICHESKAIA OBRABOTKA). V. 1-. 0026-0819. Periodical. UR. Russian. mo. $39.00. Victor Kamkin Inc (70534), 12224 Parklawn Drive, Rockville MD 20852. Tel (301)881-5973. Ind/Abst Energy Res. Abstr., Chem. Abstr. CODEN MTOBD3.

METALLOVEDENIE I TERMICHESKAYA OBRABOTKA METALLOV. (METAL SCIENCE AND HEAT TREATMENT). Vol. 5, No. 1 and 2 (Jan.-Feb. 1963)-. 0026-0673. Periodical. US. English (Russian). mo. $675.00 Domestic, $750.00 Foreign. Consultants Bureau Enterprises, 233 Spring Street, New York NY 10013. Tel (212)260-8000. Ed A Pgulyuaer. Ind/Abst Electron. Commun. Abstr. J., ISMEC Bull., Pollut. Abstr. Indexes, Eng. Index Mon., Eng. Index Bioeng. Abstr., Eng. Index Energy Abstr., Eng. Index Annu., Int. Aerosp. Abstr., Chem. Abstr., Curr. Contents, Met. Abstr., World Alum. Abstr., Sci. Cit. Index, Abr. Ed., Electr. Electron. Abstr., Phys. Abstr., Comput. Control Abstr., Eng. Index, Sci. Abstr. Sect. A. Phys. Abstr. LC TN4. DD 669.9405. CODEN MHTRAN. This journal is devoted to theoretical and practical aspects of metallurgy. The search for new alloys and the improvement of mechanical and other properties of alloys. Metallovedenie I Termicheskaya Obrabotka Metallov. English. Metal Science and Heat Treatment of Metals.

METALLURG. V. 1- 1956-. 0026-0827. Periodical. UR. Russian. mo. $25.50. Victor Kamkin Inc (70535), 12224 Parklawn Drive, Rockville MD 20852. Tel (301)881-5973. Ind/Abst Met. Abstr., World Alum. Abstr., Chem. Abstr., ISMEC Bull. LC TS300. CODEN METGA3.

METALLURGIA. V. 45- Jan. 1978-. 0141-8602. Periodical. UK. English. mo. $92.92. Fuel & Metallurgical Journals, 2 Queensway/Queensway House, Redhill Surrey RH1 1QS England. **Ind/Abst** Eng. Index Annu., Eng. Index Mon., Eng. Index, Eng. Index Bioeng. Abstr., Eng. Index Energy Abstr., Predicasts, Excerpta Med., Br. Technol. Index, Chem. Abstr., Eng. Index, Met. Abstr., World Alum. Abstr., Energy Inf. Abstr., Environ. Abstr., ISMEC Bull., Appl. Mech. Rev., Funk Scott Index Corp. Ind., Appl. Sci. Technol. Index. **LC** TN1. **DD** 669.005. **CODEN** MEMFAX. *Metallurgia and Metal Forming.*

METALLURGIA ITALIANA. (LA METALLURGIA ITALIANA). V. 1- Nov. 1909-. 0026-0843. Periodical. IT. Italian. mo. $47.52. Associazione Italiana Metallurgia, P le Rodolfo Morandi 2, 20121 Milano Italy. **Ind/Abst** Electron. Commun. Abstr. J., ISMEC Bull., Pollut. Abstr. Indexes, Saf. Sci. Abstr. J., Eng. Index Annu., Eng. Index Mon., Eng. Index, Eng. Index Bioeng. Abstr., Eng. Index Energy Abstr., Energy Inf. Abstr., Environ. Abstr., Met. Abstr., World Alum. Abstr., Chem. Abstr., Appl. Mech. Rev. **LC** TN4. **CODEN** MITLAC.

METALLURGICAL REPORTS. No. 8- 1966-. 0366-8037. Periodical. English (summaries in Flemish, French, and German). sa. Centre de Recherches Metallurgiques, 11 rue Solvay, Liege Belgium. **Ind/Abst** Eng. Index Annu., Eng. Index Mon., Eng. Index Bioeng. Abstr., Eng. Index Energy Abstr., Chem. Abstr. **LC** TN689. **DD** 669.005. **CODEN** MRCRB9. (cum index). *C.R.N.M. Centre National de Recherches Metallurgiques, 0577-1919.*

METALLURGICAL TRANSACTIONS A. (METALLURGICAL TRANSACTIONS. A. PHYSICAL METALLURGY AND MATERIALS SCIENCE). **VFOAT** Physical Metallurgy and Materials Science. V. 6A, No. 1- Jan. 1975-. 0360-2133. Periodical. US. English. mo. $175.50. American Society for Metals, Metals Information, Metals Park OH 44073. **Tel** (216)338-5151. **Ed** Anthony Thompson. **Ind/Abst** Eng. Index Annu., Eng. Index Mon., Eng. Index Bioeng. Abstr., Eng. Index Energy Abstr., Coal Abstr., Minproc, Int. Aerosp. Abstr., Comput. Control Abstr., Energy Inf. Abstr., Environ. Abstr., Electr. Electron. Abstr., Sci. Abstr. Sect. A. Phys. Abstr., Energy Res. Abstr., Met. Abstr., World Alum. Abstr., Chem. Abstr., Phys. Abstr., Eng. Index. **CODEN** MTTABN. **Circ** 3,000. Physical metallurgy-mechanical behavior, alloy phases/structure, transformations, environmental interactions, physical chemistry, transport phenomena; written to transfer basic research from lab to shop. *Metallurgical Transactions, 0026-086X.*

METALLURGICESKAJA TEPLOTHNIKA. (METALLURGICHESKAIA TEPLOTEKHNIKA). 0130-2884. Periodical. UR. Russian. sm. Victor Kamkin Inc (55256), 12224 Parklawn Drive, Rockville MD 20852. **Tel** (301)881-5973. **Ind/Abst** Energy Res. Abstr. **LC** TN600.

METALLURGIE. 0543-5757. Periodical. French. qt. $11.07. Universite Libre de Bruxelles, 50 Avenue F D Roosevelt, B-1050 Bruxelles Belgium. **Ind/Abst** Eng. Index. **LC** TN2. **CODEN** MTLGAY.

METALLURGIE. LEXIQUE. 0154-036X. FR. English (French). an. Informascience, Centre de Documentation Scientifique et Technique Service des Abonnements 26 rue Boyer, 75971 Paris Cedex 20 France. **LC** Z695.1.M55. **DD** 025.49669.

METALLURGIST. **VFOAT** Metallurg. Jan. 1957-. 0026-0894. Periodical. US. English (Russian). bm. $645.00 Domestic, $715.00 Foreign. Consultants Bureau, 227 West 17th Street, New York NY 10011. **Tel** (212)620-8000. **Ed** M A Pertser. **Ind/Abst** Excerpta Med., Coal Abstr., Chem. Abstr., Eng. Index, Eng. Index Mon., Nucl. Sci. Abstr., Curr. Contents, Met. Abstr., Met. Abstr., World Alum. Abstr. **LC** TS300. **DD** 669.05. **CODEN** MTLUA8. This journal reviews new techniques developed in international plants for improving the quantity and quality of production in the iron and steel industries.

METALLURGIST AND MATERIALS TECHNOLOGIST *CEASED.* (THE METALLURGIST AND MATERIALS TECHNOLOGIST). -V. 16. 0306-526X. Periodical. UK. English. mo. 30.00. Naylor, Aero Mill, Accrington BB5 4JS England. **Ind/Abst** Electron. Commun. Abstr. J., ISMEC Bull., Pollut. Abstr. Indexes, Saf. Sci. Abstr. J., Eng. Index Annu., Eng. Index Mon., Eng. Index Bioeng. Abstr., Eng. Index Energy Abstr., Excerpta Med., Coal Abstr., World Surf. Coat. Abstr., Met. Abstr., World Alum. Abstr., Ref. Source, Chem. Abstr. **LC** TN1. **DD** 669.005. **CODEN** MMTCAD. *Metallurgist.*

METALLURGY-MATERIALS EDUCATION YEARBOOK. *See* Yearbooks, Almanacs, Directories.

METALOZNAWSTWO I OBROBKA CIEPLNA. Jan./Feb. 1973-. 0137-3854. Periodical. PL. Polish (summaries in Russian, English, and German). bm. ARS Polona, Krakowskie Przedmiescie 7, 00-068 Warsaw Poland. **Ind/Abst** Met. Abstr., World Alum. Abstr., Chem. Abstr. **LC** TN689. **CODEN** MTOCA3.

METALS ABSTRACTS. *See* Indexes/Abstracts.

METALS ABSTRACTS INDEX. *See* Indexes/Abstracts.

METALS AND MATERIALS *CEASED.* **VFOAT** Metals & Materials and Metallurgical Reviews. **VAT** Metals & Materials. V. 1-8, Jan. 1967-Nov./Dec. 1974. 0026-0940. Periodical. UK. English. mo. **Ind/Abst** Excerpta Med., Coal Abstr., GeoRef, Ref. Source, Chem. Abstr. **CODEN** MEMTA7. *Metallurgist, Bulletin of the Institute of Metals.*

METALS & MINERALS INTERNATIONAL. **VFOAT** Metals and Minerals International. 1/ 1983 (Mar. 28, 1983)-. 0265-0983. Periodical. UK. English. qt. 34. London & Sheffield Publ Co Ltd, 5 Pond Street, Hampstead London NW3 England. **Tel** 794-0800. **Ed** J F S Russell. **Ind/Abst** Met. Abstr., World Alum. Abstr., Eng. Index Annu., Eng. Index Mon., Eng. Index Bioeng. Abstr., Eng. Index Energy Abstr. **LC** TN704.G7. **DD** 669.005. bk rev. adv acc. **Circ** 3,000. Containing plant write ups, technical articles on metals and their minerals, comment, conference and book reviews, contracts, personnel technology updates, etc. *British Steelmaker.*

METALS AND MINERALS REVIEW. 0026-0959. II. English. mo. $30.00. Pandeya Publications, Block F 105C New Alipore, Calcutta 700053 India. **Ind/Abst** Coal Abstr., GeoRef, Energy Res. Abstr., Chem. Abstr., Bibliogr. Index Geol. **LC** TN600. **DD** 669.005. **CODEN** MEMRAZ.

METALS FORUM. Vol. 1, No. 1 (Mar. 1978)-. 0160-7952. Periodical. AT. English. qt. Pergamon Press Australia, 19A Boundary Street, Rushcutters Bay New South Wales 2011 Australia. **Ind/Abst** Electron. Commun. Abstr. J., ISMEC Bull., Pollut. Abstr. Indexes, Saf. Sci. Abstr. J., Eng. Index Annu., Eng. Index Mon., Eng. Index Bioeng. Abstr., Eng. Index Energy Abstr., Int. Aerosp. Abstr., Comput. Control Abstr., Electr. Electron. Abstr., Sci. Abstr. Sect. A. Phys. Abstr., Met. Abstr., World Alum. Abstr., Chem. Abstr. **LC** TN1. **DD** 669.005. **CODEN** MEFODS. *Journal of the Australasian Institute of Metals.*

METALS TECHNOLOGY *CEASED.* Began with V. 1, Jan. 1974. Ceased with V. 11, Dec. 1984. 0307-1693. Periodical. UK. English. mo. 27.00. 1 Carlton House Terrace, London England. **Ind/Abst** Eng. Index Annu., Eng. Index Mon., Eng. Index Bioeng. Abstr., Eng. Index Energy Abstr., Int. Aerosp. Abstr., Met. Abstr., World Alum. Abstr., Ref. Source, Chem. Abstr., Appl. Sci. Technol. Index. **LC** TS200. **DD** 669.142. **CODEN** MTNYAU. *Journal of the Institute of Metals, 0020-2975; Journal of the Iron and Steel Institute, 0021-1567.*

METALS WEEK. V. 38- Jan. 1967-. Periodical. US. English. wk. $567.00. McGraw-Hill, Attn Bob Evans, 1221 Avenue of the Americas/43rd Floor, New York NY 10020. **Tel** (212)997-6126. **LC** Microfilm (O). *E & M J Metal and Mineral Markets.*

METALS WEEK PRICE HANDBOOK. 0363-1702. US. English. an. McGraw Hill Publishing Company, 1120 Vermont Avenue NW/Room 1200, Washington DC 20005. **Tel** (212)512-2823. **LC** HD9506.U6. **DD** 338.436710973.

METALURGIA. 0026-0983. BL. Portuguese. mo. $45.00. Assocuacao Brasileira de Metais, rua Antonio Comparato 218, 04605 Sao Paulo SP Brazil. **Tel** 011/ 531-5906 /543-3876/241-8. **Ind/Abst** Eng. Index Annu., Eng. Index Mon., Eng. Index Bioeng. Abstr., Eng. Index Energy Abstr., Art Archaeol. Tech. Abstr., Coal Abstr., Chem. Abstr., Met. Abstr., World Alum. Abstr. **LC** TN4. **CODEN** MABMA5.

METALURGIA Y ELECTRICIDAD. 0026-0991. Periodical. SP. Spanish. mo. Joaquin Garcia Morato, 39-41 Apartado 756, Madrid Spain. **Ind/Abst** Comput. Control Abstr., Electr. Electron. Abstr., Sci. Abstr. Sect. A. Phys. Abstr., Met. Abstr., World Alum. Abstr., Chem. Abstr., Phys. Abstr. **LC** T4. **DD** 669.05. **CODEN** MYELAF.

METALWORKING DIGEST. 0026-1009. Periodical. US. English. ir. Gordon Publications, 13 Emery Avenue, Box 1952, Randolph NJ 07801-0952. **Tel** (201)361-9060. *Industrial Digest.*

METALWORKING ENGINEERING AND MARKETING. Vol. 1, No. 1 (July 1979)-. Periodical. JA. English. bm. $15.00. News Digest Publ Company Ltd, 3-5-3 Uchiyama, Chikusa-ku Nagoya 464 Japan. **Ind/Abst** Electron. Commun. Abstr. J., ISMEC Bull., Pollut. Abstr. Indexes, Saf. Sci. Abstr. J.

METALWORKING MACHINERY. *See* Engineering - Mechanical Engineering & Machinery.

METALWORKING NEWS. V. 1- (No. 1-). 0026-1025. Periodical. US. English. wk. $32.00. Fairchild Publications, 7 East 12th Street, New York NY 10003. **Tel** (212)741-4000.

METALWORKING SALES LEADS. (METALWORKING SALES LEADS : MSL). **VFOAT** MSL. No. 43 (Mar. 26, 1981)-. 0275-6943. Periodical. US. English. sm. $397.00. McGraw Hill, 1221 Avenue of The Americas, New York NY 10020. **Tel** (212)512-2381. **Ed** Susan Kinirons-Rosso. **Circ** 100. Newsletter reporting new construction and expansions of metalworking plants throughout the United States. *Industry Mart's Metalworking Construction Report/MCR, 0193-3132.*

METAUX. CORROSION INDUSTRIE. (METAUX). V. 26- (No. 305-). 0026-1084. Periodical. FR. French. ir. 360.00. Editions Metaux, CC Postbus Paris 18.834-94, Saint-Germain-en-Laye France. **Ind/Abst** Eng. Index Annu., Eng. Index Mon., Eng. Index Bioeng. Abstr., Eng. Index Energy Abstr., Met. Abstr., World Alum. Abstr., Chem. Abstr. **LC** TA462. **DD** 620.11223. **CODEN** MTUXAS. *Metaux et Industries, Metaux & Corrosion.*

METAUX DEFORMATION. (TRAVAIL DES METAUX PAR DEFORMATION). No. 16- Jan./Feb. 1973-. 0153-9035. Periodical. FR. French. ir. 55.00. 254 rue Vaugirard, Paris France 75740. **Ind/Abst** Met. Abstr., World Alum. Abstr., Chem. Abstr. **LC** TS200. **DD** 671.05. **CODEN** TMDEDJ. *Formage des Materiaux.*

METLFAX. **VFOAT** Metlfax Magazine. 0026-1297. Periodical. US. English. mo. $20.00. Huebner Publications Inc, 6521 Davis Industrial Parkway, Solon OH 44139. **Tel** (216)248-1125. **Ed** Thomas H Dreher. bk rev. adv acc. **Circ** 107,000. (ctrl). Product news for the metalworking field.

METRIC STEEL. BULLETIN. (ACIER METRIQUE). **VFOAT** Metric Steel. **VAT** Bulletin. Acier Metrique. V. 1- Feb. 1974-. 0705-2081. Periodical. CN. English (French). ir. Free. Task Force for Metric Conversion in the Canadian Iron and Steel Industry, PO Box 4248 Station D, Hamilton Ont L8V 4L6 Canada. **DD** 672.8. (ctrl).

MICROSTRUCTURAL SCIENCE. **Main/Corp** International Metallographic Society. V. 1- 1972-. 0361-1213. US. English. ir. Elsevier Science Publishing Company Inc, PO Box 1663 Grand Central Station, New York NY 10163. **Tel** (212)370-5520. **Ind/Abst** Eng. Index Annu., Eng. Index Mon., Eng. Index Bioeng. Abstr., Eng. Index Energy Abstr., Coal Abstr., Chem. Abstr. **LC** TN689.2. **DD** 669.9505. **CODEN** MSSCDJ. *Proceedings: Annual Technical Meeting.*

MINERACAO METALURGIA. Vol. 47, No. 281 (May 1968)-. 0100-6908. Periodical. BL. Portuguese. mo. $45.00. rua do Catete 202 - Grupo 301, CEP 22220 Rio de Janeiro Brazil. **Tel** 205-0797. **Ind/Abst** Coal Abstr., Met. Abstr., World Alum. Abstr., Chem. Abstr. **CODEN** MINMAJ. bk rev. adv acc. **Circ** 10,000. Unpublished matters with technical subjects by well-known authors and professionals in the mining and metallurgical industry. *Engenharia, Mineracao, Metalurgia.*

MINERAL PROCESSING AND EXTRACTIVE METALLURGY REVIEW. *See* Engineering - Mining Engineering.

MINERAL PROCESSING AND TECHNOLOGY REVIEW. *See* Engineering - Mining Engineering.

MINERALS & METALLURGICAL PROCESSING. **VFOAT** Minerals and Metallurgical Processing. Vol. 1, No. 1 (May 1984)-. 0747-9182. Periodical. US. English. qt. $80.00. Society of Mining Engineers Inc, Caller No D, Littleton CO 80117. **Tel** (303)973-9550. **Ed** Burt C Mariacher. **Ind/Abst** Minproc. **DD** 669. **Circ** 600. Technical journal documents and disseminates new technological information dealing with the various methods for

Metals & Metallurgy

processing all types of minerals, metals, and energy materials.

MINERALS SCIENCE AND ENGINEERING CEASED. V. 1- Jan. 1969-. 0026-4660. Periodical. SA. English. qt. Ed E H Wainwright. **Ind/Abst** Eng. Index Annu., Eng. Index Mon., Eng. Index Bioeng. Abstr., Eng. Index Energy Abstr., Excerpta Med., Coal Abstr., GeoRef, Chem. Abstr., Mineral. Abstr. **LC** TN1. **DD** 669.005. **CODEN** MSENBE.

MISCELLANEOUS METAL FABRICATING INDUSTRIES. Main/Corp Statistics Canada. Manufacturing and Primary Industries Division. Series/Titi Annual Census of Manufactures. **VFOAT** Fabrication de Produit Metalliques Divers. **VAT** Industrie des Produits Metalliques Divers. 1970-. 0575-903X. **CN.** English (French). an. Receiver General for Canada, Statistics Canada Publications, Ottawa Ontario K1A 0T6 Canada. Miscellaneous Metal Fabricating Industries, 0575-903X.

MMR. MINERALS & METALS REVIEW. See Earth Sciences - Mineralogy.

MMTC NEWS. Main/Corp Minerals and Metals Trading Corporation of India Ltd. **VAT** Minerals and Metals Trading Corporation News. 0377-1482. Periodical. II. English. qt. Minerals & Metals Trading Corporation, 9 & 10 Bahadur Shah Zafar, New Delhi India. **LC** HD9506.14. **DD** 338.20954.

MODERN APPLICATIONS NEWS. (MODERN APPLICATIONS NEWS : MAN). **VFOAT** MAN. Vol. 13, No. 5 (Oct. 1979)-. 0277-9951. Periodical. US. English. bm. $24.00. A Verner Nelson, 2504 North Tamiami Trail, Nokomis FL 33555. **Tel** (813)966-3631. Ed A Verner Nelson. **DD** 669. bk rev. adv acc. **Circ** 60,000. (ctrl). Serves companies that design, develop and manufacture products in the metalworking field. SIC's covered included 3300, 3400, 3500, 3600, 3700, 3800, 3900, 7300 and other SIC's allied to the field. Modern Applications News for Design and Manufacturing, 0026-7473.

MODERN DEVELOPMENTS IN POWDER METALLURGY. Main/Conf International Powder Metallurgy Conference. V. 1- 1966-. 0097-2223. Monographic Series. US. English. ir. Plenum Press, Attn H Feldman, 233 Spring Street, New York NY 10013. **Tel** (212)620-8000. **Ind/Abst** Eng. Index Annu., Eng. Index Mon., Eng. Index Bioeng. Abstr., Eng. Index Energy Abstr., Chem. Abstr., Eng. Index. **CODEN** MDPDB2.

MODERN FINISHING METHODS. 1st- Ed. 0380-2299. **CN.** English. Canadian Paint and Finishing, 481 University Avenue, Toronto Ontario M5W 1A7 Canada. **Tel** (416)596-5714. Ed Nick Hancock. **DD** 667.905. adv acc. **Circ** 15,500. (ctrl). Covers machinery, machine tools, fabricating, foundries, stamping, mold-making, tool-and-die, CADICAM, metalworking in general, industrial surface finishing, and welding.

MODERN METALS. 0026-8127. Periodical. US. English. mo $45.00. Modern Metals, 211 East Chicago Avenue, Chicago IL 60611. **Tel** (312)337-0638. **Ind/Abst** Eng. Index Mon., Eng. Index Bioeng. Abstr., Eng. Index Energy Abstr., Excerpta Med., Energy Inf. Abstr., Energy Index, Int. Packag. Abstr., Met. Abstr., World Alum. Abstr., Chem. Abstr., Eng. Index Annu., Eng. Index Mon., Appl. Sci. Technol. Index. **LC** TS200. **DD** 671. **CODEN** MOMLAJ.

MOLYBDENUM MOSAIC. V. 1, No. 3- Spring 1976-. 0163-1888. Periodical. US. English. Climax Molybdenum Company, One Greenwich Plaza, Greenwich CT 06830. **Ind/Abst** Eng. Index Annu., Eng. Index Mon., Eng. Index Bioeng. Abstr., Eng. Index Energy Abstr., Met. Abstr., World Alum. Abstr., Chem. Abstr. **CODEN** MMOSD5. Mosiac, 0364-0639.

MONOGRAPH SERIES - AUSTRALIAN INSTITUTE OF MINING AND METALLURGY. See Engineering - Mining Engineering.

MONOGRAPHIES TECHNIQUES SUR L'UTILISATION DES ACIERS SPECIAUX. **VFOAT** Aciers Speciaux. 0544-8379. Monographic Series. FR. French. ir. Editions S E M A S, 12 rue de Madrid B P 58-08, 75362 Paris Cedex 08 France. **Ind/Abst** Chem. Abstr. **CODEN** MTUAAR.

MONTHLY REPORT OF THE IRON & STEEL STATISTICS. See Statistics.

MONTHLY STATISTICAL BULLETIN (INTERNATIONAL TIN COUNCIL). See Statistics.

NATIONAL LOCKSMITH. See Household Hardware & Appliances.

NATIONAL METALWORKING BLUE BOOK. (NATIONAL METAL WORKING BLUE BOOK). **VFOAT** Metal Working Blue Book. 0363-1737. US. English. National Blue Books Inc, 20929-3 Roscoe Boulevard, Canoga Park CA 91304. **LC** TS203. **DD** 338.47671302573.

NATIONAL POWDER METALLURGY CONFERENCE PROCEEDINGS. Series/Titi Progress in Powder Metallurgy. 0162-6299. US. English. ir. Metal Powder Industries Federation, 105 College Road East, Princeton NJ 08540. **LC** TN695. **DD** 671.37.

NAUCHNYE TRUDY (MOSKOVSKII INSTITUT STALI I SPLAVOV). (NAUCHNYE TRUDY - MOSKOVSKII INSTITUT STALI I SPLAVOV). No. 74- 1972-. 0131-5145. UR. Russian. 0.85 Single Issue. Metallurgiia, 2-1 Obydenskii Per 14, Moskva USSR. **Ind/Abst** Chem. Abstr. **LC** TN730. **CODEN** NTMSDL.

NAVY ARMS MUZZLELOADERS' JOURNAL. See Manufacturing.

NEFTJANOE HOZJAJSTVO. (NEFTIANOE KHOZIAISTVO). Began in 1945. 0028-2448. Periodical. UR. Russian (summaries in English). mo. $40.50. Victor Kamkin Inc (70619), 12224 Parklawn Drive, Rockville MD 20852. **Tel** (301)881-5973. **Ind/Abst** Eng. Index Annu., Eng. Index Mon., Eng. Index Bioeng. Abstr., Eng. Index Energy Abstr., GeoRef, Energy Res. Abstr. **LC** TN860. **CODEN** NEKHA6. Neftianaia Promyshlennost SSSR.

NEUE HUTTE. Vol. 1-. 0028-3207. Periodical. GE. German. mo $50.56. Kunst & Wissen Erich Bieber, Dufourstrasse 51, CH-8008 Zurich Switzerland. **Tel** 011-41-1-69 44 20. **Ind/Abst** Eng. Index Annu., Eng. Index, Eng. Index Mon., Eng. Index Bioeng. Abstr., Eng. Index Energy Abstr., Coal Abstr., CIS Abstr., Met. Abstr., World Alum. Abstr., Chem. Abstr. **LC** TN3. **CODEN** NEUHAM. Metallurgie.

NEW SILVER TECHNOLOGY. Jan. 1974-. 0095-9286. US. English. qt. $45.00. The Silver Institute, 1001 Connecticut Avenue NW/Suite 1138, Washington DC 20036. **Tel** (202)331-1485. Ed Robert Davies. **LC** QD181.A3. **DD** 669.23. (ctrl). A readable summary of the new technology showing where the work was done or reported and the patent designations for the technical publications carrying the texts of the reports.

NICKEL TOPICS (NEW YORK, N.Y. : 1966). (NICKEL TOPICS). Vol. 19, No. 1-. 0730-7764. Periodical. US. English. qt. Nickel Topics, International Nickel Company Inc, One New York New York Plaza, New York NY 10004. **Ind/Abst** Fluidex. **LC** TN757.N5. **DD** 673.733205. Info Nickel Topics.

NIHON KINZOKU GAKKAI KAIHO. **VFOAT** Bulletin of the Japan Institute of Metals. Began in 1962. 0369-4747. Periodical. JA. Japanese. mo. Japan Publishing Trading Company Ltd, PO Box 5030 Tokyo International, Tokyo 100-31 Japan. **Ind/Abst** Met. Abstr., World Alum. Abstr., Chem. Abstr. **CODEN** NKZKAU.

NIPPON KOKAN TECHNICAL REPORT. OVERSEAS. (TECHNICAL REPORT : OVERSEAS). Main/Corp Nippon Kokan Kabushiki Kaisha. No. 1- June 1963-. 0546-1731. English. an. **Ind/Abst** Eng. Index Annu., Eng. Index Mon., Eng. Index Bioeng. Abstr., Eng. Index Energy Abstr., Met. Abstr., World Alum. Abstr., Chem. Abstr. **LC** TS300. **CODEN** NKTRAL.

NML TECHNICAL JOURNAL. Main/Corp National Metallurgical Laboratory (India). **VAT** National Metallurgical Laboratory Technical Journal. V. 1- Feb. 1959-. 0027-6839. Periodical. II. English. qt. 15.00 Domestic, 2 Pounds, $4.50. National Metallurgical Laboratory, PO Burmamines, Jamshodput 7 India. **Tel** 26091. Ed M L Sharma. **Ind/Abst** Eng. Index Annu., Eng. Index Mon., Eng. Index Bioeng. Abstr., Eng. Index Energy Abstr., Met. Abstr., World Alum. Abstr., Chem. Abstr., Eng. Index. **LC** TN1. **DD** 669.005. **CODEN** NLMJA3. **Circ** 300. Topics on research development work pertaining to metallurgy and allied areas are published in this journal.

NON-FERROUS METAL DATA. 1974-. 0360-9553. US. English. an. $2.50 Domestic, $3.50 Foreign. American Bureau of Metal Statistics, 400 Plaza Drive, PO Box 1405, Secaucus NJ 07094. **Tel** (201)863-6900. **LC** HD9506.U6. **DD** 338.20973. **Circ** 3,000. It contains data for five comparative years and over 180 statistical tables for mine, smelter, and refined production, consumption, inventories, imports, exports, published prices, and other essential metal statistics. Year Book of the American Bureau of Metal Statistics.

NON-FERROUS METAL ROLLING, CASTING, AND EXTRUDING. See Economics - Economics: Industry & Production.

NON-FERROUS METAL WORKS OF THE WORLD. 0078-0987. EN. English. ir. 60.00. Metal Bulletin PLC, Parkhouse Park Terr Worcester, Surrey KT4 7HV England. **Tel** 01 330 4311. Ed Richard Serjeantson. adv acc. Detailed information on non-ferrous metal smelters, refinders, semi-fabricators and secondary info makers including head office address, management, ownership, processes, products, and raw materials used.

NON-FERROUS SCRAP METAL. Main/Corp Statistics Canada. **VFOAT** Metaux Non Ferreux de Recuperation. **CN.** English (French). an. $0.35. **LC** HD9539.A3. **DD** 338.47673. Non-Ferrous Scrap Metal, 0703-7279.

NONFERROUS CASTINGS. (CURRENT INDUSTRIAL REPORTS. M33E, NONFERROUS CASTINGS). 0146-5678. Periodical. US. English. mo. $16.00. Data User Services Division, Customer Services Publication, Bureau of the Census, Washington DC 20233. **Tel** (301)763-4100. **Ind/Abst** Predicasts, Chem. Abstr., Am. Stat. Index. **LC** HD9539.5.C383. **DD** 381.4567120973. **CODEN** CINCID. Presents timely data on the production, inventories, and orders of approximately 5,000 products, which represents 40 percent of all US manufacturing.

NORTH CAROLINA WORK INJURIES IN THE FABRICATED METAL PRODUCTS INDUSTRY. US. English. Research and Statistics Division, NC Department of Labor, 4 West Edenton Street, Raleigh NC 27601. **LC** HD7269.M52. **DD** 312.4309756.

NORTH CAROLINA WORK INJURIES IN THE PRIMARY METAL INDUSTRIES. US. English. Research and Statistics Division, NC Department of Labor, 4 West Edenton Street, Raleigh NC 27601. **LC** HD7269.M52. **DD** 312.4309756.

NOTES ON TIN. Main/Corp International Tin Council. No. 1- Mar. 1957-. 0535-3378. Periodical. UK. English. mo. $27.58. International Tin Council, Haymarket House, 1 Oxendon Street, London SW1Y 4EG England. Notes on Tin.

NOTIZIARIO DEL CENTRO ITALIANO SMALTI PORCELLANATI. **VFOAT** Notiziario Cisp. Vol. 23, No. 1 (Jan.-Mar. 1981)-. 0392-6648. Periodical. IT. Italian. sa. Free. Centro Italiano Smalti Porcellanati, Via Melchiorre Gioia 66, 21025 Milano Italy. **Tel** (02)6884565. **Ind/Abst** Chem. Abstr. **CODEN** NCIPD9. adv acc. **Circ** 2,400. Chemistry, physics, technology of Porcelain Enamel (PE), fields of application of PE properties, of PE articles, problems, related to steel cast iron and aluminum suitable for enamelling raw materials. Notiziario (Centro Italiano Smalti Porcellanati), 0577-3075.

NRIM CREEP DATA SHEET. **VFOAT** Kinzoku Zairyo Gijutsu Kenkyujo Kuripu Deta Shito. **VAT** National Research Institute for Metals Creep Data Sheet. Began in 1972. Monographic Series. English. ir. National Research Institute for Metals, 2-3-12 Nakameguro Meguro-Ku, Tokyo 153 Japan. **Ind/Abst** Met. Abstr., World Alum. Abstr., Chem. Abstr. **CODEN** NCDSDR.

OBERFLACHE. (OBERFLACHE + I.E. UND JOT). **VAT** Oberflache und Journal fur Oberflachen Technik. V. 17, No. 7- July 1977-. 0029-7488. Periodical. German. ir. 72.00. Bertelsmann Fachzeitschriften GMBH, Kreustr 14-16, 8000 Munchen West Germany. **Ind/Abst** Excerpta Med., Art Archaeol. Tech. Abstr., Energy Res. Abstr., Met. Abstr., World Alum. Abstr., Chem. Abstr., World Surf. Coat. Abstr. **LC** TS653.A1. **CODEN** OBJTDU. Oberflache, Jot.

OBROBKA PLASTYCZNA. Vol. 1- 1959-. 0472-4313. Periodical. Polish (Vols. 1-(4) have title and table of contents also in English, French, and other languages). ir. **Ind/Abst** Met. Abstr., World Alum. Abstr., Chem. Abstr. **LC** TS200. **CODEN** OBPLAX.

Metals & Metallurgy

OCHISTKA VODNOGO I VOZDUSHNOGO BASSEINOV NA PREDPRIIATIIAKH CHERNOI METALLURGII. UR. Russian. 1.12 Each Issue. Metallurgia, 119034 G-34 2-1 Obydenskii, Per D. 14, Moskva USSR. **Ind/Abst** Chem. Abstr. **LC** TD899.M43. **CODEN** OVVBA3.

THE OFFICIAL PRICE GUIDE TO AMERICAN SILVER AND SILVER PLATE. VFOAT American Silver and Silver Plate. 0743-9784. US. English. an. House of Collectibles Inc, Orlando Central Park, 1900 Premier Row, Orlando FL 32809. **LC** NK7112. **DD** 739.237730750973.

THE OFFICIAL PRICE GUIDE TO POCKET KNIVES. See Manufacturing.

OGNEUPORY. Vol. 1- 1933-. 0369-7290. Periodical. UR. Russian. mo. $38.00. Victor Kamkin Inc (70662), 12224 Parklawn Drive, Rockville MD 20852. **Tel** (301)881-5973. **Ind/Abst** GeoRef, Comput. Control Abstr., Electr. Electron. Abstr., Sci. Abstr. Sect. A. Phys. Abstr., Met. Abstr., World Alum. Abstr., Chem. Abstr., Phys. Abstr., Bibliogr. Index Geol. **LC** TN677. **CODEN** OGNPA2.

ORNAMENTAL AND ARCHITECTURAL METAL INDUSTRY. See Architecture.

OUTUKUMPU NEWS. See Engineering.

OXIDATION OF METALS. V. 1- Autumn 1969-. 0030-770X. Periodical. US. English. mo. $425.00 Domestic, $474.00 Foreign. Plenum Publishing Corp, 227 West 17th Street, New York NY 10011. **Tel** (212)620-8000. **Ed** D I Douglass. **Ind/Abst** Electron. Commun. Abstr. J., ISMEC Bull., Pollut. Abstr. Indexes, Saf. Sci. Abstr. J., Sci. Cit. Index, Abr. Ed., Phys. Abstr., Bibliogr. Index Geol., Eng. Index Energy Abstr., Coal Abstr., Energy Inf. Abstr., Environ. Abstr., GeoRef, Comput. Control Abstr., Electr. Electron. Abstr., Sci. Abstr. Sect. A. Phys. Abstr., Energy Res. Abstr., Met. Abstr., World Alum. Abstr., Chem. Abstr., Eng. Index Annu., Eng. Index Mon., Int. Aerosp. Abstr., Nuci. Sci. Abstr., Eng. Index, Sci. Cit. Index, Abr. Ed. **LC** QD171. **DD** 541.39. **CODEN** OXMEAF. bk rev. adv acc. A journal which provides a single forum for scientific contributions dealing with all aspects of gas-solid relations. It includes results of experimental and theoretical work.

P-M LITERATURE REFERENCE GUIDE. (P/M LITERATURE REFERENCE GUIDE). VAT Powder Metallurgy Literature Reference Guide. 1st- Ed.-. 0097-7241. US. English. American Powder Metallurgy Institute, PO Box 2054, Princeton NJ 08540. **LC** Z6679.P75, TS245. **DD** 016.67137.

PANORAMA MINERO. Periodical. Spanish. ir. Sucre 1333 (3. D), Buenos Aires Argentina. **LC** TN4.

PHYSICS OF METALS AND METALLOGRAPHY. (THE PHYSICS OF METALS AND METALLOGRAPHY). Vol. 4- 1957-. 0031-918X. Periodical. UK. English (Russian). mo. Pergamon Press, 395 Sawmill River Road, Elmsford NY 10523. **Tel** (914)592-7700. **Ind/Abst** Electron. Commun. Abstr. J., ISMEC Bull., Pollut. Abstr. Indexes, Saf. Sci. Abstr. J., Eng. Index Mon., Eng. Index Bioeng. Abstr., Eng. Index Energy Abstr., Int. Aerosp. Abstr., Comput. Control Abstr., Electr. Electron. Abstr., Sci. Abstr. Sect. A. Phys. Abstr., Met. Abstr., World Alum. Abstr., Chem. Abstr., Eng. Index Annu., Eng. Index Mon., Nuci. Sci. Abstr., Phys. Abstr. **LC** TN690. **DD** 669.905. **CODEN** PHMMA6.

PLANSEEBERICHTE FUR PULVERMETALLURGIE CEASED. Began with Oct. 1952 issue Ceased with V. 28, No 4, Dec. 1980. 0032-0765. Periodical. English (German). qt. **Ind/Abst** Energy Res. Abstr., Chem. Abstr., Nuci. Sci. Abstr., Int. Aerosp. Abstr., Eng. Index. **LC** TN695. **CODEN** PLPUA5. Powder Metallurgy Bulletin, 0096-8374.

PLATINUM-GROUP METALS. (PLATINUM-GROUP METALS IN . . .). Series/Titl Mineral Industry Surveys. US. English. an. US Department of the Interior, Bureau of Mines, Washington DC 20241.

PLENUM PRESS HANDBOOKS OF HIGH-TEMPERATURE MATERIALS. VFOAT Handbooks of High-Temperature Materials. No. 1-. 0079-2357. Monographic Series. US. English. ir. Plenum Press, c/o H Feldman, 233 Spring Street, New York NY 10013. **Tel** (212)620-8000. **LC** TN677.A1. **DD** 666.72.

P/M TECHNOLOGY NEWSLETTER. See Technology (General).

PMI. POWDER METALLURGY INTERNATIONAL. (POWDER METALLURGY INTERNATIONAL). VFOAT PMI, Powder Metallurgy International. V. 1- Sept 1969-. 0048-5012. Periodical. GW. English (summaries in French and German). bm. 205.00. Verlag Schmid GMBH, Postfach 1722, 7800 Freiburg 1 West Germany. **Tel** (07 61)44 20 30. **Ed** H H J Reh. **Ind/Abst** Electron. Commun. Abstr. J., ISMEC Bull., Pollut. Abstr. Indexes, Saf. Sci. Abstr. J., Eng. Index Mon., Eng. Index Bioeng. Abstr., Eng. Index Energy Abstr., Int. Aerosp. Abstr., Comput. Control Abstr., Electr. Electron. Abstr., Sci. Abstr. Sect. A. Phys. Abstr., Energy Res. Abstr., Met. Abstr., World Alum. Abstr., Ref. Source, Chem. Abstr., Nuci. Sci. Abstr., Eng. Index Annu., Eng. Index Mon., Sci. Cit. Index, Abr. Ed., Eng. Index, Phys. Abstr. **CODEN** PWMIBW. bk rev. adv acc.

POROSHKOVAIA METALLURGIIA. 1-. Periodical. UR. Russian (summaries in English and German). mo. $52.50. Victor Kamkin Inc (70700), 12224 Parklawn Drive, Rockville MD 20852. **Tel** (301)881-5973. **LC** TN695.

POROSHKOVAIA METALLURGIIA. (SOVIET POWDER METALLURGY AND METAL CERAMICS). Began with: 1962, No. 2. 0038-5735. Periodical. US. English (summaries in Russian). mo. $695.00 Domestic, $770.00 Foreign. Consultants Bureau, 233 Spring Street, New York NY 10013. **Tel** (212)620-8000. **Ed** I N Franksevich. **Ind/Abst** Eng. Index Mon., Eng. Index Bioeng. Abstr., Eng. Index Energy Abstr., Minproc, Int. Aerosp. Abstr., Comput. Control Abstr., Electr. Electron. Abstr., Sci. Abstr. Sect. A. Phys. Abstr., Appl. Mech. Rev., Chem. Abstr., Eng. Index Annu., Eng. Index Mon., Nuci. Sci. Abstr., Met. Abstr., World Alum. Abstr. **CODEN** SPMCAV. Index in last issue of volume - attached. This journal systematically presents theoretically and applied research in powder metallurgy and describes its application to various branches of industry. Poroshkovaiia Metallurgiia. English. Soviet Powder Metallurgy.

POROSKOVAJA METALLURGIJA. (POROSHKOVAIA METALLURGIIA). 0032-4795. Periodical. UR. Russian (summaries in English). bm. **Ind/Abst** Int. Aerosp. Abstr., Comput. Control Abstr., Electr. Electron. Abstr., Sci. Abstr. Sect. A. Phys. Abstr., Met. Abstr., World Alum. Abstr., Chem. Abstr. **LC** TN695. **CODEN** PMANAI.

POWDER COATING CONFERENCE. 0092-0479. US. English. Society of Manufacturing Engineers, 20501 Ford Road, Dearborn MI 48128. **LC** TS653.A1. **DD** 671.7308 S.

POWDER METALLURGY. No. 1/2- 1958-. 0032-5899. Periodical. UK. English. qt. **Ind/Abst** Eng. Index Mon., Eng. Index Bioeng. Abstr., Eng. Index Energy Abstr., Minproc, Comput. Control Abstr., Electr. Electron. Abstr., Sci. Abstr. Sect. A. Phys. Abstr., Met. Abstr., World Alum. Abstr., Nuci. Sci. Abstr., Eng. Index Mon., Eng. Index Annu. **LC** TN695. **CODEN** PWMTAU.

POWDER METALLURGY SCIENCE & TECHNOLOGY CEASED. VFOAT Powder Metallurgy Science and Technology. Began in 1968 with V. 1. 0048-5020. US. English. mo. Peters Technology Transfer Inc, 100 Park Avenue PO Box 216, Swarthmore PA 19081. **LC** TS245. **DD** 671.3705.

THE POWELL GOLD INDUSTRY GUIDE AND INTERNATIONAL MINING ANALYST. See Engineering - Mining Engineering.

PRACE INSTYTUTU METALURGII ZELAZA IM, ST. STASZICA. (PRACE INSTYTUTU METALURGII ZELAZA). **Main/Corp** Instytut Metalurgii Zelaza (Gliwice, Poland). V. 28, No 2-. 0137-9941. PL. Polish (summaries in English and Russian). qt. ARS Polona, Krakowskie Przedmiescie 7, 0068 Warszawa Poland. **Ind/Abst** Met. Abstr., World Alum. Abstr., Chem. Abstr. **LC** TN4. **CODEN** PIMZDL. Prace Intytutow Hutniczych.

PRACE - KRAKOW. AKADEMIA GORNICZO-HUTNICZA. INSTYTUT PODSTAW BUDOWY MASZY. See Engineering - Mining Engineering.

PRACE VYZKUMNEHO USTAVU GEOLOGICKEHO INZENYRSTVI. **Main/Corp** Vyzkumny Ustav Geologickeho Inzenyrstvi. SV. 32-. 0139-763X. Periodical. Czech (summaries in Russian and English or German). ir. Vyzumny Ustav Geologickeho Inzenyrstvi, Mozartova 1, Brno Czechoslovakia. **Ind/Abst** GeoRef, Chem. Abstr. **LC** TN860. **CODEN** PVUIDX. Prace Ustavu Geologickeho Inzenyrstvi, 0370-2421.

PRAKTISCHE METALLOGRAPHIE. VFOAT Practical Metallography. Vol. 1- 1964-. 0032-678X. Periodical. GW. English (German). mo. $66.55. Dr Riederer Verlag GMBH, Gutbrodstrasse 9, Postfach 447, D7000 Stuttgart 1 West Germany. **Tel** 0211/639797. **Ed** G Petzow. **Ind/Abst** Eng. Index Mon., Eng. Index Bioeng. Abstr., Eng. Index Energy Abstr., Coal Abstr., Comput. Control Abstr., Electr. Electron. Abstr., Sci. Abstr. Sect. A. Phys. Abstr., Energy Res. Abstr., Met. Abstr., World Alum. Abstr., Chem. Abstr., Nuci. Sci. Abstr., Eng. Index Annu., Eng. Index, Phys. Abstr. **LC** TN690. **CODEN** PMTLA5. bk rev. adv acc. **Circ** 2,000. Materials science.

LA PRATIQUE DU SOUDAGE. Periodical. French. ir. 300. Institut Belge de la Soudere, Rue des Drapiers 21, Bruxelles 1050 Belgium. **LC** TS227.A1.

PRECIOUS METALS. **Main/Corp** International Precious Metals Institute. Conference. 8756-0917. US. English. an. Pergamon Press, Maxwell House Fairview Park, Elmsford NY 10523. **DD** 669.

PRECIOUS METALS DIGEST. 1983-84-. 0740-4069. US. English. sa. $27.50. Malden House, PO Box 20005, Seattle WA 98102. **LC** HG258. **DD** 332.63.

PRECIOUS METALS MONTHLY REVIEW. Vol. 1, No. 1 (Oct. 1982)-. 0735-4770. Periodical. US. English. mo. $36.00. Precious Metals Monthly Review, PO Box 4754, Chicago IL 60680. **Tel** (312)566-4411.

PRECISION METAL. V. 25, No. 10- Oct. 1967-. 0032-714X. Periodical. US. English. mo. Penton-IPC, PO Box 95759, Cleveland OH 44101. **Ind/Abst** Met. Abstr., World Alum. Abstr., Chem. Abstr., Eng. Index Annu., Nuci. Sci. Abstr., ISMEC Bull. **CODEN** PCMEBG. Precision Metal Molding, 0096-9176.

PRIMARY IRON AND STEEL. **Main/Corp** Canada. Statistique Canada. Division des Industries Manufacturieres et Primaires. VFOAT Fer et Acier Primaire. V. 27- Jan. 1972-. 0380-7851. Periodical. CN. Multilingual (text in English and French). mo. $4.00. Statistics Canada, Publications Distribution, Ottawa Ontario K1A 0T6 Canada. Primary Iron and Steel.

PRO METAL. See Manufacturing.

PROBLEMY PROJEKTOWE. Vl. 31, No 1 (Jan./Mar. 1984)- 349-. 0999-2089. Periodical. PL. Polish. qt. RSW Prasa Ksiazka Ruch Centrala Kolportazu Prasy I, Wydawnictw Ul Towarowa 28, 00-958 Warszawa Poland. **LC** TN4. Problemy Projektowe Hutnictwa I Przemysu Maszynowego.

PROBLEMY PROJEKTOWE HUTNICTWA I PRZEMYSU MASZYNOWEGO. Periodical. PL. Polish. mo. ARS Polona, Krakowskie Przedmiescie 7, 00-068 Warsaw Poland. **LC** TN4.

PROCEEDINGS - AUSTRALASIAN INSTITUTE OF MINING AND METALLURGY. See Engineering - Mining Engineering.

PROCEEDINGS - COMMONWEALTH MINING AND METALLURGICAL CONGRESS. See Engineering - Mining Engineering.

PROCEEDINGS - ELECTRIC FURNACE CONFERENCE. See Technology (General).

PROCEEDINGS - IRONMAKING CONFERENCE. See Technology (General).

PROCEEDINGS OF METAL BULLETIN'S INTERNATIONAL FERRO-ALLOYS CONFERENCE. **Main/Conf** International Ferro-Alloy Conference. 1977-. UK. English. Metal Bulletin Ltd, Park House 3 Park Terrace, Worcester Park Surrey United Kingdom.

PROCEEDINGS OF THE ANNUAL CONVENTION OF THE WIRE ASSOCIATION INTERNATIONAL, INC. (PROCEEDINGS OF THE . . . ANNUAL CONVENTION OF THE WIRE ASSOCIATION INTERNATIONAL, INC). **Main/Conf** Wire Association International. Convention. VFOAT Conference Proceedings . . . Annual Convention. 0731-4191. US. English. an. Wire Association International, PO Box H, Guilford CT 06437. **Ind/Abst** Chem. Abstr. **LC** TS270.A1. **DD** 671.84205. **CODEN** PCWIDC.

Metals & Metallurgy

PROCEEDINGS OF THE ANNUAL MEETING OF THE CANADIAN HYDROMETALLURGISTS. Main/Corp Canadian Hydrometallurgists. 1st- 1971-. 0318-417X. Periodical. English. ir. DD 669.0283.

PROCEEDINGS OF THE ANNUAL MEETING OF THE CANADIAN MINERAL PROCESSORS. Main/Corp Canadian Mineral Processors. 1st- 1969-. 0590-5850. CN. English. an. $15.48. Canadian Mineral Processors, 552 Booth/Room 101, Ottawa Ontario K1A 0G1 Canada. Ind/Abst Minproc. *Proceedings of the Annual Meeting of the Canadian Gold Metallurgists, 0384-5931.*

PROCEEDINGS OF THE ANNUAL TECHNICAL CONFERENCE - SOCIETY OF VACUUM COATERS. See Manufacturing.

PROCEEDINGS OF THE CONFERENCE ON ELECTRON BEAM MELTING AND REFINING. Main/Conf Electron Beam Melting and Refining. VFOAT Proceedings of the Conference. Vol. 1 (1983)-. 0740-8706. US. English. an. $60.00 Domestic, $70.00 Foreign. Bakish Materials Corporation, PO Box 148, Englewood NJ 07631. Tel (201)567-5873. Ed R Bakish. DD 669. bk rev. Circ 500. Covers electron beam melting and refining technology, alloys, refractory and reactive metals and alloys.

PROCEEDINGS - STEELMAKING CONFERENCE. (PROCEEDINGS). Main/Conf Steelmaking Conference. VFOAT Steelmaking Proceedings. Vol. 64 (1981)-. 0731-7735. US. English. an. $60.00. Iron and Steel Society of AIME, 410 Commonwealth Drive, PO Box 411, Warrendale PA 15086. Tel (412)776-1585. Ed Lawrence Kuhn. Ind/Abst Chem. Abstr. CODEN STCPDH. Technology steelmaking. *Proceedings, 0097-2355.*

PRODUCTION. V. 32, No. 2- Aug. 1953- No. 2, Aug. 1953. 0032-9819. Periodical. US. English. mo. $35.00. Production Publishing Company, PO Box 101, Bloomfield Hills MI 48013. Tel (313)647-8400. Ed Robert F Huber. Ind/Abst ABI/Inform, Manage. Contents. LC TJ1180.A1. DD 621.905. CODEN PDTNAG. bk rev. adv acc. Circ 79,000. (ctrl) For key decisionmakers in the metalworking industries. Purpose is to help manufacturing managers and engineering executives interpret, evaluate and implement new technologies, methods and equipment into workable long-term manufacturing strategies. *Production Engineering & Management.*

PRODUCTION ENGINEER. See Manufacturing.

PRODUCTS FINISHING DIRECTORY. See Yearbooks, Almanacs, Directories.

PROGRESS IN EXTRACTIVE METALLURGY. V. 1- 1973-. 0091-6145. US. English. ir. Gordon & Breach, 50 West 23rd Street, New York NY 10010. Tel (212)206-8900. LC TN600. DD 669.05.

PROGRESS IN POWDER METALLURGY. 0079-6719. US. English. an. $42.00 General, $34.00 APMI Members, $30.00 MPIF Members. American Powder Metallurgy Institute, PO Box 2054, Princeton NJ 08540. Ind/Abst Eng. Index Annu., Eng. Index Mon., Eng. Index Bioeng. Abstr., Eng. Index Energy Abstr., Energy Res. Abstr., Chem. Abstr. CODEN PPWMAA. *Proceedings of the Annual Meeting.*

PROIZVODSTVO CHUGUNA. Began in 1975. 0320-0132. Periodical. UR. Russian. mo $74.00. Victor Kamkin Inc (56084), 12224 Parklawn Drive, Rockville MD 20852. Tel (301)881-5973. Ind/Abst Chem. Abstr. CODEN PRCHEF.

PROTECTION OF METALS. V. 1- Jan./Feb. 1965-. 0033-1732. Periodical. US. English (Russian). bm. $595.00 Domestic, $660.00 Foreign. Consultants Bureau, 233 Spring Street, New York NY 10013. Tel (212)620-8000. Ed Ya M Kolotyrkim. Ind/Abst Electron. Commun. Abstr. J., ISMEC Bull., Pollut. Abstr. Indexes, Saf. Sci. Abstr. J., Eng. Index Mon., Eng. Index Bioeng. Abstr., Eng. Index Energy Abstr., Life Sci. Collect., Excerpta Med., Int. Aerosp. Abstr., Art Archaeol. Tech. Abstr., Met. Abstr., World Alum. Abstr., Chem. Abstr., Eng. Index Annu., Eng. Index, Nucl. Sci. Abstr. LC TA462. CODEN PTNMAR. Covers theoretical and practical problems involved in thermodynamics, kinetics and mechanisms of metal detonation in corrosive environments.

PROTECTIVE COATINGS ON METALS. VFOAT Zashchitnye Pokrytiia na Metallakh. V. 1- 1969-. 0079-7030. Periodical. US. English. ir. Consultants Bureau, 233 Spring Street, New York NY 10013. LC TN752.S8. DD 671.

PRZEGLAD ODLEWNICTWA. See Manufacturing.

PRZEGLAD SPAWALNICTWA. See Computers and Computer Science.

QUARRY MANAGEMENT. Vol. 11, No. 1 (Jan. 1984)-. Periodical. UK. English. mo. 20.00. Quarry Managers' Journal Ltd, 7 Regent Street, Nottingham NG1 5BY England. Ind/Abst Eng. Index Annu., Eng. Index Bioeng. Abstr., Eng. Index Energy Abstr., Eng. Index Mon., Excerpta Med., Fluidex. LC TN950.A1. DD 622.31068. *Quarry Management and Products, 0305-9421.*

QUARTERLY BULLETIN OF STEEL STATISTICS FOR EUROPE. See Statistics.

QUARTERLY STATISTICAL BULLETIN (INTERNATIONAL TIN COUNCIL). See Statistics.

RAW MATERIALS REPORT. See Economics - International Economics.

DE RE METALLICA DE LA MINERIA Y LOS METALES : REVISTA DEL INSTITUTO GEOLOGICO, MINERO Y METALURGICO. See Earth Sciences - Geology.

REFERATIVNYI ZHURNAL : METALLURGIIA. 1956-. 0034-2491. Periodical. UR. Russian. mo. Victor Kamkin Inc, 12224 Parklawn Drive, Rockville MD 20852. Tel (301)881-5973. Ind/Abst Met. Abstr., World Alum. Abstr., Chem. Abstr. CODEN RZMTA5.

REFRACTORIES. V. 1- Jan./Feb. 1960-. 0034-3102. Periodical. US. English (Russian). $195.00 General, $55.00 Members of Societies of Acta Metallurgica. Consultants Bureau, 227 West 17th Street, New York NY 10011. Ind/Abst Eng. Index Mon., Eng. Index Bioeng. Abstr., Eng. Index Energy Abstr., Excerpta Med., Coal Abstr., GeoRef, Comput. Control Abstr., Electr. Electron. Abstr., Sci. Abstr. Sect. A. Phys. Abstr., Chem. Abstr., Eng. Index Annu., Eng. Index Mon., Nucl. Sci. Abstr., Phys. Abstr. LC TN677.A1. CODEN REFRAL.

REFRACTORIES JOURNAL. (THE REFRACTORIES JOURNAL). Began in 1925. 0034-3110. Periodical. UK. English. bm. 35.00. London Sheffield Publishing Company Ltd, 5 Pond Street Hampstead, London NW3 2PN England. Tel 01-794 0800. Ed J F S Russell. Ind/Abst Met. Abstr., World Alum. Abstr., Chem. Abstr., Eng. Index Mon., Eng. Index. LC TN677.A1. DD 669.8. CODEN REFJAV. (cum index). bk rev. adv acc. Circ 2,500. News, reviews, technical articles on all aspects of the refractories industry and related industries.

RELATORIO - CONSELHO DE NAO-FERROSOS E DE SIDERURGIA. Main/Corp Conselho de Nao-Ferrosos e de Siderurgia (Brazil). 1974-. BL. Portuguese. an. Esplanada dos Ministerios, Bloco 6, 5 Andar Brasilia Brazil. LC HD9524.B8. DD 338.476690981. *Relatorio - Conselho Nacional da Industria Siderurgica.*

REPERTORIO SIDERURGICO LATINOAMERICANO. See Economics - Economics: Industry & Production.

REPORT OF THE CASTINGS RESEARCH LABORATORY, WASEDA UNIVERSITY. (REPORT OF THE CASTINGS RESEARCH LABORATORY). Main/Corp Waseda Daigaku, Tokyo. Imono Kenkyujo. No. 1- 1950-. 0511-1927. English. ir. Ind/Abst Chem. Abstr., Eng. Index Annu., Eng. Index Bioeng. Abstr., Eng. Index Energy Abstr., Eng. Index Mon., GeoRef, Met. Abstr., World Alum. Abstr. CODEN RCRLAF.

REPORTE ANUAL. Main/Corp Southern Peru Copper Corporation. Sucursal del Peru. Spanish. ir. Avenue Caminos del Inco #171, Chacarilla del Estanque, Santiago de Surco Lima 33 Peru.

RESEARCH REPORT (STEEL FOUNDERS' SOCIETY OF AMERICA). (RESEARCH REPORT - STEEL FOUNDERS' SOCIETY OF AMERICA). US. English. 20611 Center Ridge Road, Cleveland OH 44116. LC TS200. DD 627.208. *Research Report.*

RESUMENES DE ARTICULOS CIENTIFICOS Y TECNICOS. SERIE C : CIENCIA Y TECNICA DE LOS METALES. Began with Oct. 1964 issue. SP. Spanish. ir. Instituto de Informacion y Documentacion en Ciencia y Tecnologia, C I S C, Joaquin Costa 22, Madrid 6 Spain. LC Z6678, TN665. *Indice de Revistas Cientificas y Tecnicas. Serie C: Ingenieria Mecanica y Tecnologia Varias.*

REVIEW OF METAL LITERATURE. CEASED. VFOAT A.S.M. Review of Metal Literature. V. 2-24. 0096-4808. Periodical. US. English. mo. LC TN1. DD 669.05. *American Society of Metals. A.S.M. Review of Metal Literature.*

REVIEWS ON COATINGS AND CORROSION. V. 1- 1972-. 0048-7538. Periodical. IS. English. qt. $25.00. Scientific Publications Division, Freund Publishing House, PO Box 35010, Tel-Aviv Israel. Ind/Abst Eng. Index Annu., Eng. Index Mon., Eng. Index Bioeng. Abstr., Eng. Index Energy Abstr., Excerpta Med., Met. Abstr., World Alum. Abstr., Chem. Abstr. LC TA418.76. DD 620.11223. CODEN RVCCBD.

REVIEWS ON POWDER METALLURGY AND PHYSICAL CERAMICS. V. 1- 1979-. 0379-0002. Periodical. UK. English. ir. $85.00. Freund Publishing House Ltd, PO Box 35010/61 Nachmani Street, Tel Aviv 61350 Israel. Ed M B Waldrond. Ind/Abst Met. Abstr., World Alum. Abstr., Chem. Abstr. CODEN RMPCDH. An international review journal reporting on overall research and development in powder metallurgy and physical ceramics, on topics of interest to the community of scientists, researchers and engineers.

REVIEWS ON SILICON, GERMANIUM, TIN, AND LEAD COMPOUNDS. V. 1- 1972-. 0048-7570. Periodical. IS. English. ir. $80.00. Freund Publishing House Ltd, PO Box 35010, Tel-Aviv Israel. Ed M Gielen. Ind/Abst Eng. Index Annu., Eng. Index Mon., Eng. Index Bioeng. Abstr., Eng. Index Energy Abstr., Met. Abstr., World Alum. Abstr., Chem. Abstr. LC QD410. DD 547.0568. CODEN RSGTAS. A quarterly review on the various aspects of the chemistry and technology of the Group IV elements: silicon, germanium, tin, and lead.

REVISTA DE METALURGIA. Began with Feb. 1965 issue. 0034-8570. Periodical. SP. Spanish. bm. $42.51. Centro National de Invest Metal, Ciudad Universitaria, Madrid 3 Spain. Tel (1)2538900. Ind/Abst Eng. Index Annu., Eng. Index Mon., Eng. Index Bioeng. Abstr., Eng. Index Energy Abstr., Met. Abstr., World Alum. Abstr., Chem. Abstr., Eng. Index. LC TN600. CODEN RMTGAC. bk rev. adv acc. Circ 2,500. Siderurgy, physical metallurgy corrosion, protection foundry mechanics, non ferrous metals, metallography, extractive metallurgy, minerals and preparation.

REVUE DE METALLURGIE. (REVUE DE METALLURGIE. CAHIERS D'INFORMATIONS TECHNIQUES). VFOAT Revue de Metallurgie - C.I.T., Techniques - Revue de Metallurgie. Yearly V. 77, No. 1 (Jan. 1980)-. 0035-1563. Periodical. FR. French (summaries in English). mo. La Revue de Metallurgie, 5 rue Paul Cezanne, 75008 Paris France. Tel 563 17 10. Ind/Abst Eng. Index Annu., Eng. Index Mon., Eng. Index Bioeng. Abstr., Eng. Index Energy Abstr., Energy Inf. Abstr., Environ. Abstr., Excerpta Med., Met. Abstr., World Alum. Abstr., Chem. Abstr., GeoRef, Energy Res. Abstr. LC TN2. DD 669.005. CODEN CITMDA. *Revue de Metallurgie, 0035-1563.*

RHEINSTAHL TECHNIK. German. ir. Rheinstahl Aktiengesellschaft, 43 Essen Am Rheinstahlhaus 1, Postfach 6980, Essen West Germany. LC TS300. DD 672.094355.

RUDARSKO-METALURSKI ZBORNIK. VFOAT Revue des Mines et de Metallurgie, Berg- und Huttenmannische Mitteilungen, Zhurnal Gornogo dela i Metallurgii, Mining and Metallurgy Quarterly. 1952-. 0035-9645. Periodical. YU. Slovak (summaries and table of contents in English and German). qt. Department of Mining and Metallurgy, Faculty of Natural Science and Technology, Ljubljana Yugoslavia. Ind/Abst Coal Abstr., Mintec, Min. Technol. Abstr., Minproc, GeoRef, Met. Abstr., World Alum. Abstr., Chem. Abstr., Bibliogr. Index Geol. LC TN4. CODEN RMZBAR. Index in last issue of volume - attached.

RUSSIAN METALLURGY. Jan./Feb.1962-. 0036-0295. Periodical. UK. English (Russian). bm. $600.00. Allerton Press Inc, 150 Fifth Avenue, New York NY 10011. Ind/Abst Sci. Cit. Index, Abr. Ed.,

Electr. Electron. Abstr., Phys. Abstr., Comput. Control Abstr. **LC** TN4.

RYLAND'S: THE DIRECTORY OF THE ENGINEERING INDUSTRY. *See* Yearbooks, Almanacs, Directories.

SBORNIK TRUDOV CHELIABINSKOGO ELEKTROMETALLURICHESKOGO KOMBINATA. **Main/Corp** Cheliabinskii Elektrometllurgicheskii Kombinat. Periodical. UR. Russian. 1.13 Single Issue. Metallurgia, G-34 2-OI Obydenskii Per D 14, Moskva Russian SFSR. **LC** TN681.

SCANDINAVIAN JOURNAL OF METALLURGY. 0371-0459. Periodical. English. bm. $100.00. Ehrenstromway 10, 00140 Helsinki Finland. **Tel** 358-0-174415. **Ed** Gerg Larinkari. **Ind/Abst** Eng. Index Annu., Eng. Index Mon., Eng. Index Bioeng. Abstr., Energy Res. Abstr., Eng. Index Energy Abstr., Chem. Abstr., Minproc, Met. Abstr., World Alum. Abstr., Comput. Control Abstr., Electr. Electron. Abstr., Sci. Abstr. Sect. A. Phys. Abstr., Sci. Cit. Index, Abr. Ed., Phys. Abstr. **CODEN** SJMLAG. bk rev. adv acc. **Circ** 1,100. Mining and metallurgy.

SCHWEIZER ALUMINIUM RUNDSCHAU. **VFOAT** Revue Suisse de l'Aluminium. Vol. 14, No. 1 (Jan. 1962)-. 0036-7257. Periodical. SZ. German (English and French). bm. $23.75. Schweizer Aluminium Rundschau, PO Box 978, 8034 Zurich Switzerland. **Tel** 01-47 24 10. **Ed** Roland Hauert and Rudolf Vogtlin. **Ind/Abst** Eng. Index Annu., Eng. Index Mon., Excerpta Med., Int. Packag. Abstr., Chem. Abstr., Met. Abstr., World Alum. Abstr., Eng. Index Bioeng. Abstr., Eng. Index Energy Abstr. **CODEN** SALRAY. bk rev. adv acc. **Circ** 6,000. Aluminium and it's applications. *Aluminium Suisse.*

SCIENCE OF SINTERING. V. 6- May 1974-. 0350-820X. Periodical. English (summaries in Russian). ir. 69.00. Jugoslovenska Knjica, PO Box 36, Beograd Yuguslavia. **Ind/Abst** Eng. Index Annu., Eng. Index Mon., Eng. Index Bioeng. Abstr., Eng. Index Energy Abstr., Comput. Control Abstr., Electr. Electron. Abstr., Sci. Abstr. Sect. A. Phys. Abstr., Chem. Abstr., Met. Abstr., World Alum. Abstr., Phys. Abstr., Eng. Index. **LC** TN695. **DD** 671.37. **CODEN** SCSNB4. Provides a suitable medium for the publication of papers on theoretical and experimental studies which can contribute to the better understanding of the behavior of powders and similar materials during consolidation processes. *Physics of Sintering.*

SCRAP AGE. 1944. 0036-9527. Periodical. US. English. mo. $18.00. Three Sons, 6311 Gross Point Road, Niles IL 60648. **Tel** (312)647-1000. **Ed** M D Oberman. **Ind/Abst** Energy Inf. Abstr., Environ. Abstr., Met. Abstr., World Alum. Abstr. bk rev. adv acc. **Circ** 4,500. (ctrl). Provides complete coverage of the ferrous and non-ferrous scrap metal recycling.

SCRIPTA METALLURGICA. V. 1- Oct. 1967-. 0036-9748. Periodical. US. English. mo. Pergamon Press, 395 Sawmill River Road, Elmsford NY 10523. **Tel** (914)592-7700. **Ind/Abst** Electron. Commun. Abstr. J., ISMEC Bull., Pollut. Abstr. Indexes, Saf. Sci. Abstr. J., Eng. Index Annu., Eng. Index Mon., Eng. Index Bioeng. Abstr., Eng. Index Energy Abstr., Int. Aerosp. Abstr., Comput. Control Abstr., Electr. Electron. Abstr., Sci. Abstr. Sect. A. Phys. Abstr., Energy Res. Abstr., Chem. Abstr., Met. Abstr., World Alum. Abstr., Sci. Cit. Index, Abr. Ed., Phys. Abstr. **LC** TN1. **CODEN** SCRMBU. Available on microfiche and microfilm from Microforms International Marketing Corporation.

SEAISI DIRECTORY. *See* Yearbooks, Almanacs, Directories.

SEAISI QUARTERLY. **Main/Corp** South East Asia Iron and Steel Institute. V. 1- Jan. 1972-. 0129-5721. Periodical. PH. English. qt. South East Asia Iron & Steel, PO Box 7759, Manila International Airport, Passay City Philippines. **Tel** 673-2161. **Ed** Masahi Kamakura. **Ind/Abst** Eng. Index Annu., Eng. Index Mon., Eng. Index Bioeng. Abstr., Eng. Index Energy Abstr., Coal Abstr., Chem. Abstr., Met. Abstr., World Alum. Abstr. **LC** TS300. **DD** 669.14205. **CODEN** SEQUDV. adv acc. (ctrl). The official journal of the Institute. Includes some technical papers from our annual conferences (March and September) plus other selected articles of international status which have relevance to South East Asia.

SHEET METAL INDUSTRIES. Began publication with Apr. 1927 issue. 0037-3435. Periodical. UK. English (issues for Jan. 1965- include abstracts of principal articles in French, German and Spanish). mo. $88.24. Fuel & Metallurgical Journals Ltd, Queensway House 2 Queensway, Redhill Surrey RHI 105 England. **Tel** (0737) 68611. **Ed** Jonathan Mitchell. **Ind/Abst** Electron. Commun. Abstr. J., ISMEC Bull., Pollut. Abstr. Indexes, Saf. Sci. Abstr. J., Eng. Index Annu., Eng. Index Mon., Eng. Index Bioeng. Abstr., Eng. Index Energy Abstr., Excerpta Med., CIS Abstr., Chem. Abstr., Met. Abstr., World Alum. Abstr., Eng. Index. **LC** TS250. **CODEN** SHMIAR. bk rev. adv acc. For 50 years it has acted as official organ to many important technical and trade bodies. Attracts editorial submissions from all over the world. *Metal Finishing, Press Tool Engineering.*

SHEET METAL INDUSTRIES YEARBOOK. *See* Yearbooks, Almanacs, Directories.

SHEET METAL WORKERS JOURNAL. V. 29, No. 9- Sept. 15, 1924-. 0037-3451. Periodical. US. English. mo. $3.00. Sheet Metal Workers International Association, 1750 New York Avenue NW, Washington DC 20006. **Tel** (202)296-5880. *Amalgamated Sheet Metal Workers Journal.*

SHIGEN TOKEI NEMPO. *See* Statistics.

SHINDO GIJUTSU KENKYUKAI SHI. **VFOAT** Journal of the Japan Copper and Brass Research Association. Began in 1962. 0370-985X. Periodical. Japanese (with summaries in English). an. 5200. Nihon Shingo Kyokai, 12-22 Tsukiji 1 Chuo-ku, Tokyo-t Japan. **Ind/Abst** Chem. Abstr. **CODEN** SGKEBX.

SHIPMENTS OF STEEL PRODUCTS : ALL GRADES INCLUDING CARBON, ALLOY AND STAINLESS. **Main/Corp** American Iron and Steel Institute. 1971-. Periodical. US. English. American Iron & Steel Institute, 1000 16th Street NW, Washington DC 20036.

SIDERURGIA. Year 1- Aug./Oct. 1974-. 0325-0520. Periodical. Spanish. ir. Instituto Argentino de Siderurgia, Bernardo de Irigoyen 308 9. Piso, Buenos Aires Argentina. **Ind/Abst** Comput. Control Abstr., Electr. Electron. Abstr., Sci. Abstr. Sect. A. Phys. Abstr., Chem. Abstr., Met. Abstr., World Alum. Abstr. **LC** TS300. **CODEN** SIDEDE.

LA SIDERURGIA ITALIANA IN CIFRE *CEASED.* **Main/Corp** Associazione Industrie Siderurgiche Italiane. IT. Italian. ir. Associazione Industrie Siderurgiche Italiane, Piazza Velasca 8, Milano 20122 Italy. **LC** HD9506.I8.

SIDERURGIA LATINOAMERICANA. No. 189- Jan. 1976-. 0379-7759. Periodical. CL. Spanish. mo. $56.00. Instituto Latinoamericano del Fierro el Acero, Casilla 16065, Santiago 9 Chile. **Ind/Abst** Coal Abstr., Chem. Abstr., Met. Abstr., World Alum. Abstr. **LC** TS300. **CODEN** SILAD8. *Revista Latinoamericana de Siderurgia.*

THE SILVER INSTITUTE LETTER. (SILVER INSTITUTE LETTER). 0730-8132. Periodical. US. English. The Silver Institute, 1001 Connecticut Avenue NW, Washington DC 20036.

SLEVARENSTVI. Began in 1953. 0037-6825. Periodical. Czech (summaries and table of contents in English, French, German, and Russian). mo. ARTIA, PO Box 790, Praha 1 Czechoslovakia. **Ind/Abst** CIS Abstr., Chem. Abstr., Met. Abstr., World Alum. Abstr. **CODEN** SLEVAK.

SMELTING AND REFINING. **Main/Corp** Statistics Canada. Manufacturing and Primary Industries Division. **Series/Titl** Annual Census of Manufactures : Preliminary Bulletin. **VFOAT** Fonte et Affinage. 0384-4927. Periodical. CN. English (French). an. 20.00 Domestic, 21.00 Foreign. Receiver General for Canada, Statistics Canada Publications, Ottawa Ontario K1A 0T6 Canada. **Tel** (800)268-1151.

SNIPS. *See* Heating, Plumbing, & Refrigeration.

SOETMUL. Periodical. KO. Korean. mo. Pohang Chonghap Chechol, Chusik Hoesa 5, Tongchon-Dong Pohang-Si Korea. **LC** TS304.K6.

SOURCE JOURNALS IN METALLURGY. *See* Bibliographies.

SOUTH CAROLINA METALWORKING DIRECTORY. *See* Yearbooks, Almanacs, Directories.

SOVIET NON-FERROUS METALS RESEARCH. **VFOAT** Izvestiia Vysshikh Uchebnykh Zavedenii. V. 1- 1973-. 0307-7349. Periodical. UK. English (translation of Lzvestiia Vysshikh Uchebnykh Zavedenii. Tsvetnaia Metallurgiia, V. 16-). bm. $350.00. Technicopy Ltd, 66 High Street, Stonehouse GL 10 2NA England. **Tel** (045)382-2444. **Ed** A W Brace. **Ind/Abst** Met. Abstr., World Alum. Abstr. Translation of Russian research papers on the extractive and physical metallurgy of non-ferrous metals.

SOVIET POWDER METALLURGY AND METAL CERAMICS. No. 7- Jan./Feb. 1962-. 0038-5735. Periodical. US. English (Russian). mo. $245.00. Consultants Bureau, 227 West 17th Street, New York NY 10011. **Ind/Abst** Fluidex, Appl. Mech. Rev., Chem. Abstr., Eng. Index, Eng. Index Mon., Nuci. Sci. Abstr. **LC** TN695. **CODEN** SPMCAV.

STAHL UND EISEN. Yearly Vol. 1-. 0340-479X. Periodical. GW. German. bw. 256.- Domestic, $100.00. Verlag Stahleisen MBH, Postfach 8229, D4000 Duesseldorf West Germany. **Tel** (0211)8894-0. **Ind/Abst** Electron. Commun. Abstr. J., ISMEC Bull., Eng. Index Annu., Eng. Index Mon., Eng. Index Bioeng. Abstr., Eng. Index Energy Abstr., Excerpta Med., Coal Abstr., Predicasts, Energy Inf. Abstr., Environ. Abstr., CIS Abstr., Energy Res. Abstr., Chem. Abstr., Met. Abstr., World Alum. Abstr., Sci. Cit. Index, Abr. Ed., Funk Scott Index Corp. Ind., Eng. Index. **LC** TS300. **DD** 669.105. **CODEN** STEIA3. (cum index). adv acc. **Circ** 1,000. (ctrl). Metallurgy and plant technology.

STAHLBAU RUNDSCHAU. AU. German. sa. $14.25. Bohmann Drick Und Verlag, Leberstrasse 122, A-1110 Wien Austria. **Tel** 0222/74 15 95. **Ed** Bohmann Druck U Verlag. **Ind/Abst** Energy Res. Abstr. **LC** TA684. adv acc. **Circ** 6,000. (ctrl).

STAINLESS STEEL AND ALLOY TOOL STEEL: U.S. IMPORTERS' PRICES, UNSHIPPED ORDERS, AND INVENTORIES, ANNUAL SURVEY. (STAINLESS STEEL AND ALLOY TOOL STEEL. U.S. IMPORTERS' PRICES, UNSHIPPED ORDERS, AND INVENTORIES, ANNUAL SURVEY : REPORT TO THE PRESIDENT ON INVESTIGATION NO. 332-94 UNDER SECTION 332 OF THE TARIFF ACT OF 1930). **Series/Titl** USITC Publication. 1978-. 0195-8747. US. English. an. Office of the Secretary, US International Trade Commission, 701 E Street NW, Washington DC 20436. **LC** HD9529.S623. **DD** 338.436720973. Vols. for 1978- distributed to depository libraries in microfiche.

STAINLESS STEEL AND ALLOY TOOL STEEL: U.S. PRODUCERS' PROFITS, UNSHIPPED ORDERS, INVENTORIES, CAPACITY, CAPITOL EXPENDITURES AND RESEARCH AND DEVELOPMENT EXPENDITURES ANNUAL SURVEY. (STAINLESS STEEL AND ALLOY TOOL STEEL. U.S. PRODUCERS' PROFITS, UNSHIPPED ORDERS, INVENTORIES, CAPACITY, CAPITAL EXPENDITURES, AND RESEARCH AND DEVELOPMENT EXPENDITURE ANNUAL SURVEY : REPORT TO THE PRESIDENT ON INVESTIGATION NO. 332-04 UNDER SECTION 332 OF THE TARIFF ACT OF 1980. TARIFF ACT OF 1980). **Series/Titl** USITC Publication. 0195-8992. US. English. an. Office of the Secretary, United States International Trade Commission, Washington DC 20436. **LC** HD9529.S623. **DD** 338.436720973.

STAINLESS STEEL INDUSTRY. 1973. 0306-2988. Periodical. UK. English. bm. 17.00. Modern Metals Publications Ltd, 14 Knoll Road Dorking, Surrey RH4 3EW England. **Tel** 0306 884079. **Ed** K T Rowland. **Ind/Abst** Art Archaeol. Tech. Abstr., Chem. Abstr., Met. Abstr., World Alum. Abstr. **CODEN** SSTID6. bk rev. adv acc. **Circ** 4,000. (ctrl). The only independent journal in the world dealing with commercial and technical developments relating to stainless steel.

STAINLESS STEELS DIGEST. 0730-8140. Periodical. US. English. mo. $90.00. Am Society for Metals, Metals Information, Metals Park OH 44073. **Tel** (216)338-5151. **Ind/Abst** Abstr. Bull. Inst. Paper Chem. Each digest is a cost effective solution reproducing complete subject relevant abstracts as published in metals abstracts.

STAL. Vol. 1- 1941-. 0038-920X. Periodical. UR. Russian. mo. $47.00. Victor Kamkin Inc (70877), 12224 Parklawn Drive, Rockville MD 20852. **Tel** (301)881-5973. **Ed** N I Korobov. **Ind/Abst** Coal Abstr., Chem. Abstr., Met. Abstr., World Alum. Abstr. **LC** TS300. **CODEN** STALAQ. *Metallurg, Rabochii Metallurg; Stal (Kharkov, R.S.S.F.R); Teoriia Praktika Metallurgii; Uralskaia Metallurgiia.*

STATISTICAL BULLETIN - CIPEC DOCUMENTATION CENTRE. *See* Statistics.

STATISTICAL BULLETIN (INTERNATIONAL TIN COUNCIL). *See* Statistics.

Metals & Metallurgy

STATISTICAL YEARBOOK. METALS FUTURES DATA. See Yearbooks, Almanacs, Directories.

STATISTICS OF WORLD TRADE IN STEEL (NEW YORK, N.Y. : 1976). See Statistics.

STEEL. 76/1- 1976-. 0730-8388. Periodical. US. English. bm. American Iron and Steel Institute, 1000 16th Street Northwest, Washington DC 20036. **Ind/Abst** Energy Inf. Abstr., Environ. Abstr. *Steel Facts, 0039-0917.*

STEEL FABRICATION JOURNAL. See Manufacturing.

STEEL FOUNDERS' RESEARCH JOURNAL. No. 1-. Periodical. US. English. qt. $100.00. Steel Founders Society of America Cast Metals, Federation Building, 455 State Street, Des Plaines IL 60016. **Tel** (312)299-9160. Ed John M Svoboda. **Ind/Abst** Met. Abstr., World Alum. Abstr. bk rev. adv acc. Steel foundry research.

STEEL IN THE U.S.S.R. (STEEL IN THE USSR). V. 1- Jan. 1971-. 0038-9218. Periodical. UK. English (Russian). mo. $293.00. Institute of Metals, 1 Carlton House Terrace, London SW1Y 5DB England. **Tel** (01)839-4071. Ed T L Hughes. **Ind/Abst** Eng. Index Annu., Eng. Index Mon., Eng. Index Bioeng. Abstr., Eng. Index Energy Abstr., Excerpta Med., Coal Abstr., Met. Abstr., World Alum. Abstr., Sci. Cit. Index, Abr. Ed., Eng. Index. **Circ** 400. Contains selected translated material from leading Soviet journals. Covers all aspects of ferrous metallurgy and relates technical developments in the Soviet steel industry. *Stal in English.*

THE STEEL INDUSTRY OF JAPAN. JA. English. an. The Japan Iron and Steel Federation Keidanren Kaikan, 9-4 1-Chrome Otemachi, Chiyoda-Ku 100, Tokyo Japan.

STEEL INDUSTRY REVIEW. V. 1- Winter 1978-. 0163-206X. Periodical. US. English. qt. Data Resources Inc, 29 Hartwell Avenue, Lexington MA 02173. **LC** HD9511. **DD** 338.476691420973.

THE STEEL MARKET IN . . . AND THE OUTLOOK FOR . . . . See Economics - Economics: Industry & Production.

STEEL MILL PRODUCTS. (CURRENT INDUSTRIAL REPORTS. MA-33B, STEEL MILL PRODUCTS). 0275-6862. US. English. an. $1.75. Data User Services Division, Customer Services Publication, Bureau of the Census, Washington DC 20233. **Tel** (301)763-4100. **LC** HD9514. **DD** 338.476720973. Presents timely data on the production, inventories, and orders of approximately 5,000 products, which represents 40 percent of all US manufacturing.

STEEL PRODUCTS MANUAL. 0275-2239. Periodical. US. English. ir. American Iron and Steel Institute, 1000 16th Street NW, Washington DC 20036. **Tel** (202)452-7100. **Ind/Abst** Eng. Index. **CODEN** SPMAAP.

STEEL SHIPPING DRUMS AND PAILS. **Main/Corp** United States. Bureau of the Census. **Series/Titl** Current Industrial Reports, Ser. M34K. 0145-4986. Periodical. US. English. qr. $7.50. Subscriber Services Section, Bureau of the Census, Washington DC 20233. **Tel** (301)763-7476. Ed Ed Coan. **LC** HD9529.B3. **DD** 338.47672. This report contains US manufacturers shipments of steel pails and drums on a quarterly basis. Both quantity and value date is available. Size data is also included.

STEEL TIMES. V. 188- Jan. 1964-. 0039-095X. Periodical. UK. English. mo. $118.00. Fuel & Metallurgical Journals Ltd, Queensway House 2, Queensway, Redhill Surrey RH1 105 England. **Ind/Abst** Eng. Index Annu., Eng. Index Mon., Eng. Index, Eng. Index Bioeng. Abstr., Eng. Index Energy Abstr., Excerpta Med., Coal Abstr., CIS Abstr., Art Archaeol. Tech. Abstr., Chem. Abstr., Met. Abstr., World Alum. Abstr. **CODEN** STLTA3. *Steel & Coal.*

STEEL TIMES ANNUAL REVIEW OF THE STEEL INDUSTRY. UK. English. an. Fuel & Metallurgical Journals Ltd, 17-19 John Adam Street, W2CN 6JH London England. **LC** HD9521.1. **DD** 338.476720942.

STEEL TODAY & TOMORROW : A PUBLICATION OF JAPAN IRON & STEEL EXPORTERS' ASSOCIATION. Periodical. JA. English. bm. Japan Iron & Steel Exporters, 3-2-10 Nihonbashi-Kayabacho, Chuo-Ku Tokyo Japan. **Tel** 03(669)4811. **Ind/Abst** Met. Abstr.,

World Alum. Abstr. **Circ** 15,500. (ctrl). It has been providing in-depth reporting of significant developments in the Japanese steel industry and furnishing extensive information about iron and steel products.

STEEL UPDATE. 0821-7351. Periodical. CN. English. ir. Canadian Steel Industries Construction Council, Suite 300/201, Consumers Road, Willowdale Ontario M2J 4G8 Canada. **Tel** (416)491-9898. **DD** 721.04471420971. Contains latest information on new steel buildings from owners, architects, and engineers' point of view.

STEELABOR. See Economics - Labor.

STEELS ALERT. Vol. 3, No. 1 (Jan. 1985)-. Periodical. US. English. mo. **Tel** (216)338-5151. Keeps abreast of developments all over the world to maintain your company's competitive position in this area. *Steels Supplement to Metals Abstracts.*

STEELWORKER 3&2. (STEELWORKER 3 & 2). **Main/Corp** Naval Education and Training Program Development Center. **Series/Titl** Rate Training Manual and Nonresident Career Course. **VAT** Steelworker Three and Two. 0193-9092. US. English. Superintendent of Documents, Government Printing Office, Washington DC 20402. **LC** VG593. **DD** 671.

STELCO TENDANCES. See Building and Construction.

SUMITOMO KEIKINZOKU GIHO. VFOAT Sumitomo Light Metal Technical Reports. Began in 1970. 0039-4963. Periodical. JA. Japanese. qt. $24.48. Sumitomo Light Metal Indus Ltd, 3-1-23 Chitose/Tech Res Lab, Minato-ku Nagoya 455 Japan. **Ind/Abst** Eng. Index Annu., Eng. Index Mon., Eng. Index Bioeng. Abstr., Eng. Index Energy Abstr., Chem. Abstr., Met. Abstr., World Alum. Abstr. **CODEN** SKEGA2.

SUMITOMO SEARCH. (THE SUMITOMO SEARCH). 1- May 1969-. 0585-9131. Periodical. US. English. sa. Sumitomo Metal America Inc, 420 Lexington Avenue, New York NY 10170. **Tel** (212)949-4760. **Ind/Abst** Eng. Index Annu., Eng. Index Mon. Eng. Index Bioeng. Abstr., Eng. Index Energy Abstr., Coal Abstr., Comput. Control Abstr., Electr. Electron. Abstr., Sci. Abstr. Sect. A. Phys. Abstr., Chem. Abstr., Met. Abstr., World Alum. Abstr., Phys. Abstr., Eng. Index. **LC** TS300.S8. **DD** 669.14205. **CODEN** SUSEAY.

SURFACE TECHNOLOGY. V. 4- Jan. 1976-. 0376-4583. Periodical. SZ. English. mo $356.23. Elsevier Sequoia SA, PO Box 851, 1001 Lausanne Switzerland. **Ind/Abst** Electron. Commun. Abstr. J., ISMEC Bull., Pollut. Abstr. Indexes, Saf. Sci. Abstr. J., Eng. Index, Excerpta Med., Comput. Abstr. Bull. Inst. Paper Chem., Minproc, Comput. Control Abstr., Electr. Electron. Abstr., Energy Res. Abstr., Art Archaeol. Tech. Abstr., Chem. Abstr., Eng. Index Annu., Met. Abstr., World Alum. Abstr., Phys. Abstr., Sci. Cit. Index, Abr. Ed., Eng. Index Mon., Eng. Index Sect. A. Phys. Abstr. **LC** TS670.A1. **DD** 671.705. **CODEN** SUTED8. *Electrodeposition and Surface Treatment.*

SURFACING JOURNAL. See Metals & Metallurgy - Welding.

SYNTHETIC METALS. V. 1- Oct. 1979-. 0379-6779. Periodical. SZ. English. mo. $212.77. Elsevier Sequoia SA, PO Box 851, 1001 Lausanne 1 Switzerland. **Ind/Abst** Electron. Commun. Abstr. J., ISMEC Bull., Pollut. Abstr. Indexes, Saf. Sci. Abstr. J., Eng. Index Annu., Eng. Index Mon., Eng. Index, Eng. Index Bioeng. Abstr., Eng. Index Energy Abstr., Comput. Control Abstr., Electr. Electron. Abstr., Sci. Abstr. Sect. A. Phys. Abstr., Energy Res. Abstr., Chem. Abstr., Met. Abstr., World Alum. Abstr., Phys. Abstr., Sci. Cit. Index, Abr. Ed. **LC** TN693.T7. **DD** 669.7. **CODEN** SYMEDZ.

TAIKABUTSU. VFOAT Refractories. V. 1, No. 1- June 1949-. 0039-8993. Periodical. JA. Japanese. mo. Technical Association of Refractories, 3-13 Ginza 7, Chome Chuo-ku, Tokyo 104 Japan. **Tel** (03)572-0705. **Ind/Abst** Coal Abstr., Chem. Abstr. **CODEN** TAKOAV. adv acc. **Circ** 2,100.

TECHNIQUES OF METALS RESEARCH. V. 1, Pt. 1-. 0082-2558. Monographic Series. US. English. ir. Interscience Publishers, 605 3rd Avenue, New York NY 10016. Ed R F Bunshah.

TECNICA METALURGICA. 0371-9537. Periodical. Spanish. mo. **Ind/Abst** Chem. Abstr., Met. Abstr., World Alum. Abstr. **LC** TN4. **CODEN** TMEBAC.

TIJDSCHRIFT VOOR OPPERVLAKTETECHNIEKEN VAN MATERIALEN. Vol. 25, No. 1 (Jan. 1981)-. 0167-5095. Periodical. NE. Dutch. mo. Tijl Tijdschriften BV, Postbus 9943, 1006 AP Amsterdam Netherlands. **Ind/Abst** CIS Abstr., Excerpta Med., Chem. Abstr. **CODEN** TOPMDF. *Belgisch-Nederlands Tijdschrift voor Oppervlaktetechnieken van Materialén, 0166-2686.*

TIN AND ITS USES. No. 1- Apr. 1939-. 0040-7941. Periodical. UK. English. qt. Tin Research Institute, 483 6th Avenue, Columbus OH 43201. **Ind/Abst** Electron. Commun. Abstr. J., ISMEC Bull., Pollut. Abstr. Indexes, Saf. Sci. Abstr. J., Fluidex, World Surf. Coat. Abstr., Chem. Abstr., Met. Abstr., Ship Abstr., World Alum. Abstr., Nuci. Abstr. **LC** TN793.A1. **DD** 669.6072. **CODEN** TIUSAD.

TIN INTERNATIONAL. See Engineering - Mining Engineering.

TIN NEWS. 0040-7968. Periodical. US. English. mo. Free. The Malaysian Tin Bureau, 1625 I Street NW/Room 913, Washington DC 20006. **Tel** (202)331-7550. Ed Muhamad Nor Muhamad. **Ind/Abst** Predicasts, Met. Abstr., World Alum. Abstr., Funk Scott Index Corp. Ind. **LC** HD9539.T5. adv acc. **Circ** 4,000. (ctrl). News and information including data on the world tin industry and matters related thereto.

TIN STATISTICS. See Statistics.

TIN TYPE. See Hobbies.

TITANIUM DEVELOPMENT ASSOCIATION BUYERS GUIDE. **VFOAT** Buyers Guide. 1985-. 8755-0016. US. English. an. $5.00. Titanium Development Association, PO Box 2307, Dayton OH 45401. **Tel** (513)223-8432. Ed Georgi Hockaday. **DD** 338. adv acc. **Circ** 2,000. Complete listing of companies in the titanium industry in North America. Includes product, service, geographical and personnel indices.

TITANIUM INGOT, MILL PRODUCTS, AND CASTINGS. (CURRENT INDUSTRIAL REPORTS. ITA-991, TITANIUM INGOT, MILL PRODUCTS, AND CASTINGS). Jan. 1979-. 0145-5109. US. English. ni. $16.00. Data User Services Division, Customer Services Publication, Bureau of the Census, Washington DC 20233. **Tel** (301)763-4100. **Ind/Abst** Predicasts, Am. Stat. Index, Chem. Abstr. **LC** HD9539.T73. **DD** 380.14567373220973. **CODEN** CIRIDM. Presents timely data on the production, inventories, and orders of approximately 5,000 products, which represents 40 percent of all US manufacturing. *Current Industrial Reports. DIB-991, Titanium Ingot, Mill Products, and Castings.*

TMS PAPER SELECTION. **Main/Corp** Metallurgical Society of AIME. **VAT** The Metallurgical Society Paper Selection. 0197-1689. Monographic Series. US. English. an. Metallurgical Society, PO Box 430, Warrendale PA 15086. **Ind/Abst** Chem. Abstr. **CODEN** TMPSAG.

TOOLING. See Manufacturing.

TRAITEMENT THERMIQUE. 0041-0950. Periodical. FR. French. ir. $77.83. PYC Edition, 254 rue de Vaugirard, 75740 Paris Cedex 15 France. **Ind/Abst** Energy Res. Abstr., Chem. Abstr., Met. Abstr., World Alum. Abstr. **LC** TN672. **CODEN** TRTHA4.

TRANSACTIONS. Main/Corp Canadian Institute of Mining and Metallurgy. V. 1- 1898-. Monographic Series. CN. English. an. **LC** TN1.

TRANSACTIONS OF POWDER METALLURGY ASSOCIATION OF INDIA. **VFOAT** Transactions of the P.M.A.I. 0377-9416. Periodical. II. English. an. $20.00. Powder Metallurgy Association of India, DMRL Kanchanbagh, Hyderabad 500258 Italy. **Ind/Abst** Met. Abstr., World Alum. Abstr., Chem. Abstr. **LC** TN695. **DD** 671.3705. **CODEN** TPMIDT.

TRANSACTIONS OF THE AMERICAN FOUNDRYMEN'S SOCIETY. (TRANSACTIONS). **Main/Corp** American Foundrymen's Society. 0065-8375. US. English. an. $144.00. American Foundrymens Society, Golf and Wolf Roads, Des Plaines IL 60016. **Ind/Abst** Chem. Abstr., Eng. Index Annu., Eng. Index, Nuci. Abstr., Eng. Index Mon. **CODEN** TAFOA6. (cum index).

TRANSACTIONS OF THE INDIAN INSTITUTE OF METALS. **Main/Corp** Indian Institute of Metals. V. 1- 1948-. 0019-493X. Periodical. II. English. bm. $60.00. Indian Institute of Metals, 2 Sambhunath Pandit Street, Calcutta 20

Metals & Metallurgy—Welding

India. **Ind/Abst** Eng. Index Mon., Eng. Index Bioeng. Abstr., Eng. Index Energy Abstr., Comput. Control Abstr., Electr. Electron. Abstr., Sci. Abstr. Sect. A. Phys. Abstr., Chem. Abstr., Eng. Index Annu., Phys. Abstr., Nuci. Sci. Abstr., Met. Abstr., World Alum. Abstr., Sci. Cit. Index, Abr. Ed. **LC** TN4. **DD** 669.005. **CODEN** TIIMA3. (cum index).

TRANSACTIONS OF THE INSTITUTE OF METAL FINISHING. **Main/Corp** Institute of Metal Finishing. V. 29-. 0020-2967. UK. English. ty. $73.56. Institute of Metal Finishing, Exeter House, 48 Holloway Head, Birmingham B1 1N1 England. **Tel** 021-622-7387. **Ed** D Pescod. **Ind/Abst** Eng. Index Annu., Eng. Index Mon., Eng. Index Bioeng. Abstr., Eng. Index Energy Abstr., Excerpta Med., World Surf. Coat. Abstr., Comput. Control Abstr., Electr. Electron. Abstr., Sci. Abstr. Sect. A. Phys. Abstr., CIS Abstr., Chem. Abstr., Met. Abstr., World Alum. Abstr. **CODEN** TIMFA2. bk rev. adv acc. **Circ** 2,000. (ctrl). Leading technical and scientific journal, well-known and highly respected throughout the world of surface finishing. *Journal of the Electrodepositors' Technical Society*.

TRANSACTIONS OF THE IRON AND STEEL INSTITUTE OF JAPAN. **Main/Corp** Nippon Tekko Kyokai. V. 1- June 1961-. 0021-1583. JA. English. mo. $160.00. Maruzen Company Ltd, PO Box 5050, 100-31 Tokyo Japan. **Tel** (03)279-6021. **Ind/Abst** Eng. Index, Sci. Cit. Index, Abr. Ed., Chem. Abstr. (cum index). **Circ** 5,500. (ctrl). A journal in order to inform the technique of iron and steel of Japan to abroad. *Tetsu-to-Hagane Abstracts*.

TRANSACTIONS OF THE IRON & STEEL SOCIETY OF AIME. **VFOAT** I.S.S. Transactions. Vol. 1 (Nov. 1982)-. 0737-0059. Periodical. US. English. Iron and Steel Society of AIME, 410 Commonwealth Drive, Warrendale PA 15086. **Ind/Abst** Chem. Abstr. **LC** TS300. **DD** 669.105. **CODEN** TISAEL.

TRANSACTIONS OF THE JAPAN INSTITUTE OF METALS. **Main/Corp** Nippon Kinzoku Gakkai. V. 1- July 1960-. 0021-4434. Periodical. JA. English (French or German). mo. $150.00. Maruzen Company Ltd, PO Box 5050, 100-31 Tokyo Japan. **Ind/Abst** Eng. Index Mon., Eng. Index Bioeng. Abstr., Eng. Index Energy Abstr., Energy Inf. Abstr., Environ. Abstr., Comput. Control Abstr., Electr. Electron. Abstr., Sci. Abstr. Sect. A. Phys. Abstr., Chem. Abstr., Eng. Index Annu., Nuci. Sci. Abstr., Int. Aerosp. Abstr., Met. Abstr., World Alum. Abstr., GeoRef, Sci. Cit. Index, Abr. Ed., Phys. Abstr., Bibliogr. Index Geol., Eng. Index. **LC** TN4. **DD** 669.005. **CODEN** TJIMAA. (ctrl). A journal of scientific research papers concerned with problems in the field of metals.

TRANSACTIONS OF THE NATIONAL RESEARCH INSTITUTE FOR METALS. **Main/Corp** Kinzoku Zairyo Gijutsu Kenkyujo (Japan). **VFOAT** Kinzoku Zairyo Gijutsu Kenkyujo Obun Hokuku. V. 1- 1959-. 0453-9222. Periodical. JA. English. bm. National Research Institute for Metals, 2 3 12 Nakameguro Meguro Ku, Tokyo 153 Japan. **Ind/Abst** Eng. Index Annu., Eng. Index Mon., Eng. Index Bioeng. Abstr., Eng. Index Energy Abstr., Minproc, Comput. Control Abstr., Electr. Electron. Abstr., Sci. Abstr. Sect. A. Phys. Abstr., Met. Abstr., World Alum. Abstr. **LC** TN4. **CODEN** TNRMAF.

TRANSITION METAL CHEMISTRY. V. 1- Oct. 1975-. 0340-4285. Periodical. US. English. mo. VCH Publishers Inc, 303 NW 12th Avenue, Deerfield Beach FL 33442. **Tel** (305)428-5566. **Ind/Abst** Eng. Index Annu., Eng. Index Mon., Eng. Index Bioeng. Abstr., Eng. Index Energy Abstr., Energy Res. Abstr., Chem. Abstr., Sci. Cit. Index, Abr. Ed. **CODEN** TMCHDN.

TREFILE. (LE TREFILE). 0374-2261. Periodical. GW. French. bm. Meisenbach KG, Postfach 2069, D-8600 Bamberg 1 West Germany. **Ind/Abst** Chem. Abstr., Met. Abstr., World Alum. Abstr. **CODEN** TREFDS.

TSVETNYE METALLY. **VFOAT** Soviet Journal of Non-Ferrous Metals. V. 1- Jan. 1960-. 0038-5484. Periodical. US. English (Russian). mo. $56.00. Victor Kamkin Inc, 12224 Parklawn Drive, Rockville MD 20852. **Tel** (301)881-5973. **Ind/Abst** Met. Abstr., World Alum. Abstr., Chem. Abstr., Eng. Index. **DD** 669.

TUNGSTEN NEWS. 0049-481X. Periodical. US. English. ir. Ind/Abst Met. Abstr., World Alum. Abstr.

TZ FUR METALLBEARBEITUNG. 0170-9577. Periodical. GW. German (summaries in English). mo. 129.60. Konradin-Verlag, Ptfch 100252 Ernst Mey Str 8, 7022 Leinfelden West Germany. **Tel** 0711/7594-0. **Ed** Konrad Kohlhammer. **Ind/Abst** Eng. Index, Chem. Abstr., ISMEC Bull., Eng. Index Annu., Eng. Index Mon., Eng. Index Bioeng. Abstr. **LC** TS200. **CODEN** TZMEDJ. bk rev. adv acc. **Circ** 10,200. Publication for metal working, manufacturing processes, machine tools, measuring and control systems, automation, numerics. *TZ Fur Praktische Metallbearbeitung*.

UHREN UND SCHMUCK. See Manufacturing.

UNESID : INFORMACION SIDERURGICA. See Economics - Economics: Industry & Production.

U.S. GLASS, METAL & GLAZING. See Glass and Ceramics.

URANIUM MILL TAILINGS MANAGEMENT. See Sanitation, Environmental Technology.

USSR SCIENTIFIC ABSTRACTS. MATERIALS SCIENCE AND METALLURGY. See Indexes/Abstracts.

VENEZUELA METALURGICA Y MINERA. Spanish. ir. Asociacion de Industriales Metalurgicos Y de Mineria, Av Principal Colinas de Bello Monte Ofic H, Caracas Venezuela. **LC** HD9506.V4. **DD** 338.20987.

VERWALTUNGSBERICHT DES BEZIRKS CLAUSTHAL-ZELLERFELD DER BERGBAU-BERUFSGENOSSENSCHAFT. See Engineering - Mining Engineering.

WAGA KUNI NO KOGOGYO : TEKKO HEN. **Main/Corp** Japan. Tsusho Sangyosho. Daijin Kambo. Chosa Tokeibu. JA. Japanese. ir. Daijin Kambo, 3-Ban 1-Go Kasumigaseki 1-Chome Chiyoda-Ku, Tokyo 100 Japan. **LC** HD9516.J3.

WERKZEUG MACHINEN FUR DIE METALLBEARBEITUNG, HANDBUCH. See Engineering - Mechanical Engineering & Machinery.

WESTERN MACHINERY & METALWORKING. See Engineering - Mechanical Engineering & Machinery.

WIRE AND WIRE PRODUCTS MANUFACTURERS. See Manufacturing.

WIRE INDUSTRY. 0043-6011. Periodical. UK. English. mo. Magnum Publications Ltd, 110-112 Station Road East, Oxted RH8 OQA Surrey England. **Tel** 8833-7755. **Ed** P A Clayton. **Ind/Abst** Eng. Index Annu., Eng. Index Mon., Eng. Index Bioeng. Abstr., Eng. Index Energy Abstr., Excerpta Med., Chem. Abstr., Nuci. Sci. Abstr., Eng. Index, Met. Abstr., World Alum. Abstr. **CODEN** WIRIAZ. bk rev. adv acc. **Circ** 5,600. News and technical papers on production of wire, power cables, telecom cables, wire products.

WIRE JOURNAL CEASED. V. 1-14 No. 3. 0043-602X. Periodical. US. English. mo. $30.00 Domestic, $35.00 Foreign. Wire Journal, 1570 Boston Post Road, Guilford CT 06437. **LC** TS270.A1. **DD** 671.84. Available on microfilm from University Microfilm. *Wire and Wire Products, 0043-6003*.

WIRE JOURNAL DIRECTORY-CATALOG. See Yearbooks, Almanacs, Directories.

WIRE JOURNAL INTERNATIONAL. See Manufacturing.

WIRE TECHNOLOGY. Vol 11, No. 1. 0361-4565. Periodical. US. English. bm. $25.00. Huebner Publications Inc, 6521 Davis Industrial Parkway, Solon OH 44139. **Tel** (216)248-1125. **Ind/Abst** Chem. Abstr., Phys. Abstr., Comput. Control Abstr., Electr. Electron. Abstr., Sci. Abstr. Sect. A. Phys. Abstr. **LC** TS270.A1. **DD** 671.84. **CODEN** WITED2.

WIRE TECHNOLOGY BUYER'S GUIDE. 0145-2886. US. English. $10.00. R J Callahan, PO Box 480, Stamford CT 06904. **LC** TS270.A1. **DD** 338.476718402573.

WORLD ALUMINUM ABSTRACTS. See Indexes/Abstracts.

WORLD CALENDAR OF FORTHCOMING MEETINGS : METALLURGICAL AND RELATED FIELDS. **VFOAT** World Calendar of Forthcoming Meetings :. Vol. 6, No. 1 (Jan.1981)-. UK. English. **Tel** (01)839-4071. Listing of the world's meetings and conferences in the field of metals and materials. *World Calendar of Forthcoming Meetings*.

WORLD CALENDAR OF FORTHCOMING MEETINGS: METALLURGICAL AND RELATED FIELDS CEASED. Ceased publication with 1973 No. 6, Nov./Dec. 1973. 0043-8294. UK. English. qt. Institute of Metals, 1 Carlton House Terrace, London SW1Y 5DB England. **Tel** (01)839-4071.

WORLD METAL STATISTICS. See Statistics.

WORLD STAINLESS STEEL STATISTICS. See Statistics.

WORLD STEEL EXPORTS : QUANTITY. **Main/Corp** International Iron & Steel Institute. English. ir. International Iron and Steel Institute, Avenue Hamoir 14, B-1180 Bruxelles Belgium. **LC** HD9510.4. **DD** 382.45669142.

WORLD STEEL EXPORTS : VALUE. **Main/Corp** International Iron & Steel Institute. English. ir. International Iron and Steel Institute, Avenue Hamoir 14, B-1180 Brussels Belgium. **LC** HD9510.4. **DD** 382.45669142.

YEH CHIN FEN HSI. **VFOAT** Metallurgical Analysis. Periodical. CC. Chinese. bm. 0.50. Hsin Hua Shu Tien, Pei-Ching fa Hsing So, Peking China. **LC** TN565. **DD** 669.905.

YONGUSO PO (POHANG CHONGHAP CHECHOL CHUSIK HOESA. KISUL YONG). (YONGUSO PO). Vol. 1-. Periodical. Korean (summaries in English). ir. **LC** TS305. **DD** 672.05.

YOUSE JINSHU. (YU SE CHIN SHU). **VFOAT** Journal of North-Eastern Forestry Institute. 0513-3424. Periodical. Chinese (added contents page in English). qt. $5.40. China Publication Centre, PO Box 2820, Beijing China. **Ind/Abst** Eng. Index Annu., Eng. Index Mon., Eng. Index Bioeng. Abstr., Eng. Index Energy Abstr., GeoRef, Met. Abstr., World Alum. Abstr., Chem. Abstr. **CODEN** YSCSAE.

ZASHCHITA METALLOV. **VFOAT** Metal's Protection, Protection of Metals. Vol. 1- Jan./Feb. 1965. 0044-1856. Periodical. UR. Russian. bm. $40.50. Victor Kamkin Inc (70335), 12224 Parklawn Drive, Rockville MD 20852. **Tel** (301)881-5973. **Ind/Abst** Int. Aerosp. Abstr., Chem. Abstr., Energy Res. Abstr., Met. Abstr., World Alum. Abstr., ISMEC Bull. **LC** TA467. **CODEN** ZAMEA9.

ZESZYTY NAUKOWE AKADEMII GORNICZO-HUTNICZEJ IM. STANISAWA STASZICA. See Engineering - Mining Engineering.

ZESZYTY NAUKOWE AKADEMII GORNICZO-HUTNICZEJ IM. STANISAWA STASZICA. METALURGIA I ODLEWNICTWO. **VFOAT** Metalurgia I Odlewnictwo. Vol. 1-. PL. English (Polish). qt. ARS Polona, Krakowskie Przedmiescie 7, 00-068 Warsaw Poland. **Ind/Abst** Chem. Abstr., Met. Abstr., World Alum. Abstr. **LC** TN600. **CODEN** MEODD6.

ZHONGNAN KUANGYE XUEYUAN XUEBAO. See Engineering - Mining Engineering.

ZINC. No.1- 1975-. 0319-6631. CN. text in English and French, each with special t.p. and separate paging. French text on inverted pages. Zinc Institute Inc, 8 King Street East, Toronto Ontario M5C 1B5 Canada. **DD** 669.5.

ZINC ABSTRACTS. See Indexes/Abstracts.

ZINC RESEARCH DIGEST. No. 28- Autumn 1971-. 0146-7999. Periodical. US. English. an. International Lead Zinc Research Organization, 292 Madison Avenue, New York NY 10017. **Ind/Abst** World Surf. Coat. Abstr., ISMEC Bull.

WELDING

ADGEZIA RASPLAVOV I PAJHA MATERIALOV. See Metals & Metallurgy.

APPROVED WELDING ELECTRODE WIRE-FLUX AND WIRE-GAS COMBINATIONS. **Main/Corp** American Bureau of Shipping. 0148-9380. US. English. an. $20.00. American Bureau of Shipping, 65 Broadway, New York NY 10006. **Tel** (212)440-0300. **LC** TK4660. **DD** 338.4767152025. **Circ** 3,000. Filler metals are listed by country and manufacturer according to welding process employed. Contains requirements and test schedules required for approval. An equivalency chart of AWS classifications to ABS grades.

AUSTRALIAN WELDING JOURNAL. V. 10, No. 3- Jan. 1967-. 0005-0431. Periodical. AT. English. qt. 20 Domestic, 25 Foreign. Associated Business Publ, PO Box 440, Broadway NSW 2007 Australia. **Tel** (02)212-2780. **Ed** Philip Wells. **Ind/Abst** Excerpta Med., Met. Abstr., World Alum. Abstr., Chem. Abstr. **CODEN** AUWJA7. bk rev. adv acc. **Circ** 10,000. (ctrl). To disseminate and promote knowledge of welding. Contains original articles written by leading industry authorities. *Welding Fabrication and Design.*

AUTOMATIC WELDING. Jan. 1959-. 0005-108X. Periodical. UK. English (Russian). mo. $413.76. Welding Institute, Abington Hall Abington, Cambridge CB1 6AL England. **Tel** 0223 891162. **Ind/Abst** CIS Abstr., Met. Abstr., World Alum. Abstr., Comput. Control Abstr., Electr. Electron. Abstr., Sci. Abstr. Sect. A. Phys. Abstr., Sci. Cit. Index, Abr. Ed., Phys. Abstr. **LC** TK4660.A1. **CODEN** AUWEAQ. Translation of Russian welding journal.

BULLETIN SIGNALETIQUE 745. SOUDAGE, BRASAGE ET TECHNIQUES CONNEXES. VFOAT Soudage, Brasage et Techniques Connexes. V. 33-1972-. 0301-3480. Periodical. FR. French. ir. $62.53. Editions du CNRS, 23 rue du Maroc, 75019 Paris France. **LC** Z7914.W4. **DD** 016.67152.

BULLETIN - WELDING RESEARCH COUNCIL (U.S.). (BULLETIN). VFOAT WRC Bulletin Series, WRC Bulletin. No. 70- July 1961-. 0043-2326. Monographic Series. US. English. Welding Research Council, 345 East 47th Street, New York NY 10017. **Ind/Abst** Eng. Index Annu., Eng. Index Mon., Eng. Index Bioeng. Abstr., Eng. Index Energy Abstr., Coal Abstr., Chem. Abstr., Int. Aerosp. Abstr., Met. Abstr. **LC** TS227. **DD** 671.5205. **CODEN** WRCBA2. *Welding Research Council Bulletin Series.*

CANADIAN WELDER & FABRICATOR. Began with V. 53, No. 6 (June 1962). 0008-5324. Periodical. CN. English. mo. 18.00 Domestic, 30.00 US, 36.00 Foreign. Sanford Evans Communications Ltd, Box 6900/1077 St James Street, Winnipeg Manitoba R3C 3B1 Canada. **Tel** (204)775-0201. **Ed** Tom Couture. **Ind/Abst** Met. Abstr., World Alum. Abstr. adv acc. **Circ** 6,800. (ctrl). Technical data and information for the welding and manufacturing industries. *Canadian Welder.*

CANADIAN WELDER AND FABRICATOR. DIRECTORY AND BUYERS' GUIDE. *See* Yearbooks, Almanacs, Directories.

FWP JOURNAL. VFOAT Founding, Welding, Production Engineering. Began in 1962?. 0015-9026. Periodical. US. English. mo. $25.00. Southern Media Management Inc, 1 Drayton Street, Savannah GA 31401. **Tel** (912)233-2270. **Ind/Abst** Electron. Commun. Abstr. J., ISMEC Bull., Pollut. Abstr. Indexes, Saf. Sci. Abstr. J., Eng. Index Annu., Eng. Index Mon., Eng. Index Bioeng. Abstr., Eng. Index Energy Abstr., Chem. Abstr., Excerpta Med., Met. Abstr., World Alum. Abstr. **CODEN** FWPJA7.

INDUSTRIAL WELDER. 0377-7391. Periodical. II. English. ir. Zita Villa, 212 Kalina Santa Cruz East, Bombay India. **LC** TS227.A1. **DD** 671.5205.

INTERNATIONAL METALS REVIEWS. *See* Metals & Metallurgy.

METAL CONSTRUCTION. V. 7- Jan. 1975-. 307-7896. Periodical. UK. English. mo. 49. Welding Institute, Abington Hall, Abington Cambridge CB1 6AL England. **Tel** 0223 891162. **Ed** R F Smith. **Ind/Abst** Electron. Commun. Abstr. J., ISMEC Bull., Pollut. Abstr. Indexes, Saf. Sci. Abstr. J., Eng. Index Annu., Eng. Index Mon., Eng. Index Bioeng. Abstr., Eng. Index Energy Abstr., Excerpta Med., Ship Abstr., CIS Abstr., Met. Abstr., World Alum. Abstr., Ref. Source, Chem. Abstr. **LC** TS227. **DD** 671.5205. **CODEN** MECODD. bk rev. adv acc. **Circ** 7,607. Fabricating and welding of metals, design, welding processes, metallurgical and mechanical properties of engineering materials, repair, quality and non-destructive testing. *Metal Construction and British Welding Journal.*

PHILIPS WELDING REPORTER. VFOAT Welding Reporter. 1965/1-. Periodical. NE. English. ir. Philips Industries, Welding Department, Building III-2, Eindhoven the Netherlands. **Ind/Abst** Eng. Index Annu., Eng. Index Mon., Eng. Index, Eng. Index Bioeng. Abstr., Eng. Index Energy Abstr. **CODEN** WEREDW. *Welding News.*

PRECISION METAL. *See* Metals & Metallurgy.

PROGRESS REPORTS - WELDING RESEARCH COUNCIL (U.S.). (PROGRESS REPORTS). Began with issue for Jan. 1977. 0743-1651. US. English. mo. Welding Research Council, United Engineering Center, 345 East 47th Street, New York NY 10017. **Ind/Abst** Met. Abstr., World Alum. Abstr. **LC** TS227.A1. **DD** 671.5205. *Reports of Progress of the Welding Research Council, 0161-1437.*

REVUE DE LA SOUDURE. VFOAT Lastijdschrift. Yearly V. 1-. 0035-127X. Periodical. BE. French (Dutch). qt. Institut Belge de la Soudure, rue des Drapiers 21, 1050 Brussels Beglium. **Ind/Abst** Eng. Index Annu., Eng. Index Mon., Eng. Index Bioeng. Abstr., Eng. Index Energy Abstr., Energy Res. Abstr., Met. Abstr., World Alum. Abstr., Chem. Abstr. **LC** TS227. **CODEN** RSOUA3.

RIVISTA ITALIANA DELLA SALDATURA. Began with Oct. 1949 issue. 0035-6794. Periodical. IT. Italian. bm. Ist Italiano della Saldatura, Viale Sauli 39, Genova I 16121 Italy. **Ind/Abst** Eng. Index Annu., Eng. Index Mon., Eng. Index Bioeng. Abstr., Eng. Index Energy Abstr., Energy Res. Abstr., Met. Abstr., World Alum. Abstr., Chem. Abstr. **LC** TS227. **CODEN** RISAAT.

SCHWEISSEN + SCHNEIDEN. (SCHWEISSEN UND SCHNEIDEN). Yearly V. 1-. 0036-7184. Periodical. GW. English. mo. $112.82. Deutschr Verlag Schweisstechnk, Postfach 2725, D 4 Dusseldorf 1 West Germany. **Tel** 211/15 40 40. **Ind/Abst** Eng. Index Mon., Eng. Index Bioeng. Abstr., Eng. Index Energy Abstr., Excerpta Med., Coal Abstr., Ship Abstr., CIS Abstr., Energy Res. Abstr., Eng. Index Annu., Eng. Index Mon., Chem. Abstr., Nuci. Sci. Abstr., Met. Abstr., World Alum. Abstr., Eng. Index. **LC** TS227. **CODEN** SCSCA4. bk rev. adv acc. **Circ** 11,000. (ctrl). Technical and scientific journal. Reports on welding, cutting, spraying, soldering, brazing, adhesive bonding, heat treatment, testing of materials, control and regulation.

SOUDAGE ET TECHNIQUES CONNEXES. V.9- 1955-. 0038-173X. Periodical. FR. French. bm. $58.04. Welding Institute of Canada, 75 Boulevard de Mortagne, Boucherville Quebec J4B6Y4 Canada. **Tel** (514)652-9002. **Ind/Abst** Eng. Index Annu., Eng. Index Mon., Eng. Index Bioeng. Abstr., Eng. Index Energy Abstr., Excerpta Med., Energy Res. Abstr., Chem. Abstr., Met. Abstr., World Alum. Abstr., Eng. Index. **CODEN** SOTCAP. *Soudure et Techniques Connexes.*

SOUDER. Periodical. FR. French. Publications Souder Autogene, 32 Boulevard de la Chapelle, 75880 Paris Cedex 18 France. **Tel** (331)203-94-05. **Ind/Abst** Comput. Control Abstr., Electr. Electron. Abstr., Sci. Abstr. Sect. A. Phys. Abstr., CIS Abstr., Chem. Abstr. **CODEN** SOUDAX.

SURFACING JOURNAL. 0307-7365. UK. English. qt. Welding Institute, Publishing Department, Abington Hall, Abington, Cambridge CB1 6AL England. **Tel** (0223)891. **Ind/Abst** Ship Abstr., Chem. Abstr., Met. Abstr., World Alum. Abstr., ISMEC Bull. **LC** TS227.A1. **DD** 667.9. **CODEN** SFCJAY.

SVAROCNOE PROIZVODSTVO. (SVAROCHNOE PROIZVODSTVO). Began in 1955. 0491-6441. Periodical. UR. Russian. mo. $33.50. Victor Kamkin Inc (70807), 12224 Parklawn Drive, Rockville MD 20852. **Tel** (301)881-5973. **Ind/Abst** Int. Aerosp. Abstr., Comput. Control Abstr., Chem. Abstr., Electr. Electron. Abstr., Sci. Abstr. Sect. A. Phys. Abstr., Energy Res. Abstr., Met. Abstr., World Alum. Abstr. **CODEN** SVAPAI. *Avtogennoe Delo.*

SVETSAREN, A WELDING REVIEW. 1973-. Periodical. SW. English. ty. Esab Fack, Herkulesgatan 72, 40270 Goteborg Sweden. **Ind/Abst** Electr. Electron. Abstr., Phys. Abstr., Comput. Control Abstr., Eng. Index. *Svetsaren. English Edition.*

SVETSEN. Began 1942. 0039-7091. Periodical. Swedish (summaries in English). bm. $13.31. Svetstekniska Foreningen Iva, Box 5073, Stockholm 5 Sweden. **Tel** 08-220780. **Ed** Gunnar B Tornguist. **Ind/Abst** Eng. Index Annu., Eng. Index Mon., Eng. Index Bioeng. Abstr., Eng. Index Energy Abstr., Ship Abstr., Energy Res. Abstr., Chem. Abstr., Met. Abstr., World Alum. Abstr. **CODEN** SVTNA5. bk rev. adv acc. **Circ** 4,000. (ctrl). Welding technology, welding metallurgy.

TECHNISCHE BERICHTE - THYSSEN. (THYSSEN TECHNISCHE BERICHTE). **Main/Corp** August Thyssen-Hutte. Vol. 6-. 0340-5060. Periodical. German (summaries in English and French). ir. Free. Thyssen Aktiengesellschaft, Postfach 11 05 61, 4100 Duisburg West Germany. **Tel** (0203)5224147. **Ind/Abst** Eng. Index Annu., Eng. Index Mon., Eng. Index Bioeng. Abstr., Eng. Index Energy Abstr., Excerpta Med., Int. Aerosp. Abstr., Energy Res. Abstr., Chem. Abstr., Met. Abstr., World Alum. Abstr. **LC** TN690. **CODEN** TBTHDV. **Circ** 8,000. Production, properties, further processing and utilization of steel; components and finished products made by manufacturing industry. *Thyssenforschung, Rheinstahl-Technik.*

TRANSACTIONS OF THE JAPAN WELDING SOCIETY. **Main/Corp** Yosetsu Gakkai. 0385-9282. JA. English. sa. 42.00. Maruzen Company Ltd, PO Box 5050, 100-31 Tokyo Japan. **Tel** 03-253-0488. **Ed** Keiji Tachiki. **Ind/Abst** Eng. Index Annu., Eng. Index Mon., Eng. Index Bioeng. Abstr., Eng. Index Energy Abstr., Chem. Abstr., Met. Abstr., World Alum. Abstr. **CODEN** TJWSAU. **Circ** 600. (ctrl). Introduces studies results of welding technology in Japan. An international forum for academic and a technological discussions to contribute to solutions of related problems.

WELDING & FABRICATING DATA BOOK. VFOAT Welding and Fabricating Data Book. 1980/81-. 0278-7067. US. English. be. Penton/IPC Inc, 614 Superior Avenue West, Cleveland OH 44113. **LC** TS227. **DD** 671.52. *Welding Data Book.*

WELDING & JOINING DIGEST. VAT Welding and Joining Digest. 0361-3747. US. English. mo. $90.00. American Society for Metals, Metals Information, Metals Park OH 44073. **Tel** (216)338-5151. **LC** TS227.A1. **DD** 671.5208. This digest is one of ten published monthly. Each is a cost effective solution that reproduces complete subject relevant abstracts as published in metals abstracts.

WELDING AND METAL FABRICATION. V. 19- Jan. 1951-. 0043-2245. Periodical. UK. English. bm. Industrial Newspapers, Queensway House, 2 Queensway, Redhill Surrey RH1 1QS England. **Tel** (0737) 68611. **Ed** Rodney Pitt. **Ind/Abst** Eng. Index, Ship Abstr., Comput. Control Abstr., Electr. Electron. Abstr., Sci. Abstr., CIS Abstr., Ref. Source, Chem. Abstr., Met. Abstr., World Alum. Abstr., Nuci. Sci. Abstr. **LC** TS227. **DD** 671.5205. **CODEN** WLMFAM. bk rev. adv acc. Over 50 years service to the industry, this is the major journal for all those involved with, or interested in the UK welding industry.

WELDING DATA BOOK. 1958/59-. 0511-4365. US. English. ir. $21.75. Penton-IPC, 1111 Chester Avenue, Cleveland OH 44114. **Tel** (216)696-7000. **Ed** Rosalie Brosilow. **LC** TS227. adv acc. **Circ** 24,000. (ctrl). Informs readers of new developments in design and manfacturing of welded products. Includes manfacturing techniques and equipment, up-to-date professional and management skills relating to welding engineering.

WELDING DESIGN & FABRICATION. VAT Welding Design and Fabrication. V. 1-6, No. 4, 1930-Oct. 1933. 0043-2253. Periodical. US. English. mo. $35.00. Penton/IPC, 1111 Chester Avenue, Cleveland OH 44114. **Tel** (216)696-7000. **Ed** Rosalie Browsilow. **LC** TS227. **DD** 671.5205. **CODEN** WDEFA. bk rev. adv acc. **Circ** 42,000. (ctrl). Information on new developments in design manufacturing, welded metal products, manufacturing techniques and equipment. New materials joining, forming, cutting processes inspection, testing, quality control. *Welding Engineer, 0043-227X.*

WELDING DISTRIBUTOR. V. 10- Jan./Feb. 1966. 0192-7671. Periodical. US. English. bm. $18.00. Penton/IPC, 1111 Chester Avenue, Cleveland OH 44114. **Tel** (216)696-7000. **Ed** Chuck Berka. bk rev. adv acc. **Circ** 8,000. (ctrl). A merchandising magazine for distributors of welding and cutting equipment, supplies, accessories, metal-working, tools and related safety items. *Welding Distributor and Safety Supplier.*

WELDING IN THE WORLD. VFOAT Soudage dans le Monde. V. 1- 1963-. 0043-2288. Periodical. UK. English. bm. $33.93. Publ de la Soudure Autogene, 32 Boulevard de la Chapelle, 75880 Paris Cedex 18 France. **Ind/Abst** Electron. Commun. Abstr. J., ISMEC Bull., Pollut. Abstr. Indexes, Saf. Sci. Abstr. J., Eng. Index Mon., Eng. Index Bioeng. Abstr., Eng. Index Energy Abstr., Excerpta Med., Ship Abstr., CIS Abstr., Chem. Abstr., Eng. Index Annu., Met. Abstr., World Alum. Abstr. **LC** TS227. **CODEN** WDWRAI.

WELDING JOURNAL. 0043-2296. Periodical. US. English. mo. $70.00. American Welding Society, PO Box 351040, Miami FL 33135. **Tel** (305)443-9353. **Ed** Jeff Weber. **Ind/Abst** Biogr. Index, Appl. Sci. Technol. Index, Eng. Index, Sci. Cit. Index, Abr. Ed.,

Metrology and Standardization

Int. Aerosp. Abstr., ISMEC Bull., Chem. Abstr., Appl. Mech. Rev. **LC** TS227. **CODEN** WEJUA3. bk rev. adv acc. **Circ** 35,000. Publication of the American Welding Society.

WELDING RESEARCH INTERNATIONAL. 0306-9427. Periodical. UK. English (summaries in French and German). qt. Abington Hall Abington, Cambridge CB1 6AL England. **Ind/Abst** Ship Abstr., Chem. Abstr., Eng. Index Mon., Eng. Index, Int. Aerosp. Abstr. **LC** TS227.A1. **DD** 671.5205. **CODEN** WASIAI. *Welding International, Research and Development.*

YOSETSU GAKKAI SHI. VFOAT Journal of the Japan Welding Society. Began in 1927. 0021-4787. Periodical. JA. Japanese (some summaries in English). 90.00. Maruzen Co Ltd, PO Box 5050, 100-31 Tokyo Japan. **Tel** 03-253-0488. **Ed** Keiji Tachiki. **Ind/Abst** Coal Abstr., Met. Abstr., World Alum. Abstr., Chem. Abstr. **LC** TS227.A1. **CODEN** YOGAAK. Index in last issue of volume - attached. **Circ** 5,500. (ctrl). Academic and technical journal concerned with welding. *Yosetsu Kyokai Shi.*

METROLOGY AND STANDARDIZATION

AL-TAQYIS : NASHRAT AL-MUNAZZAMAH AL-ARABIYAH LIL-MUWASAFAT WA-AL-MAQAYIS. **VFOAT** Standardization. Periodical. Arabic (English, anb French). mo. Almunazzamah Al-Arabiyah Lil-Muwasafat Wa-AL-Maqayis, Amman Al-Urdun, S.B. 926161, Amman Jordon. **LC** T59.A1.

AMERICAN METRIC JOURNAL. VFOAT AMJ SI Metropcac. V. 1, No. 1- 0094-3096. US. English. bm. AMJ Publishing Company, PO Box 3200, Carmarillo CA 93010. **Tel** (805)484-5787. **Ind/Abst** Curr. Index J. Educ., Appl. Sci. Technol. Index. **LC** QC92.U54. **DD** 389.152.

ANNUAL REPORT - AMERICAN NATIONAL METRIC COUNCIL. Main/Corp American National Metric Council. 0363-5260. US. English. an. American National Metric Council, 1625 Massachusetts Avenue Northwest, Washington DC 20036. **LC** QC90.8. **DD** 389.15205.

ANNUAL REPORT AND STATEMENT OF ACCOUNTS - MALAWI BUREAU OF STANDARDS. Main/Corp Malawi. Bureau of Standards. English. ir. Bureau of Standards, PO Box 946, Blantyre Malawi. **LC** QC100.M3. **DD** 354.689700821.

ANNUAL REPORT - AUSTRALIA. METRIC CONVERSION BOARD. Main/Corp Australia. Metric Conversion Board. AT. English. ir. $0.75. Commonwealth Government Printing Office, PO Box 84, Canberra ACT 2600 Australia. **LC** J905, QC92.A8. **DD** 328.9401 S, 354.9400821.

ANNUAL REPORT - BARBADOS METRICATION BOARD. Main/Corp Barbados. Metrication Board. 1st- 1974/75-. BB. English. ir. Ministry of Trade Industry and Commerce, Barbados Metrication Board, Reef Road, Bridgetown Barbados. **LC** QC92.B37. **DD** 389.1520972981.

ANNUAL REPORT - BUREAU INTERNATIONAL DE L'HEURE. Main/Corp Bureau International de l'Heure. English. ir. Bureau International de l'Heure, 61 Avenue de l'Observatoire, Paris France. **LC** QB209. **DD** 529.05.

ANNUAL REPORT - CENTER FOR MATERIALS SCIENCE (NATIONAL MEASUREMENT LABORATORY). (ANNUAL REPORT). **Main/Corp** Center for Materials Science (National Measurement Laboratory). **Series/Titl** NBSIR. Began with 1979. 0883-2862. US. English. an. Center for Materials Science, National Bureau of Standards, Washington DC 20234. Vols. for (1982-) distributed to depository libraries in microfiche.

ANNUAL REPORT - NATIONAL BUREAU OF STANDARDS. Main/Corp United States. National Bureau of Standards. **Series Corp** ITS Miscellaneous Publication - National Bureau of Standards. ITS Special Publication - National Bureau of Standards. **VFOAT** Research Highlights of the National Bureau of Standards. US. English. an. US Department of Commerce, National Bureau of Standards, Washington DC 20230. **LC** QC100. **DD** 389. *Annual Report of the Director - Bureau of Standards.*

ANNUAL REPORT - TANZANIA. BUREAU OF STANDARDS. Main/Corp Tanzania. Bureau of Standards. English. ir. Tanzania Bureau of Standards, PO Box 9524 S L P, Dar es Salaam Tanzania. *Director's Annual Report.*

ANNUAL REPORT, WEIGHTS AND MEASURES DIVISION (ARKANSAS). Main/Corp Arkansas. Division of Weights and Measures. **VFOAT** Weights and Measures Division Annual Report. US. English. an. Department of Commerce, Division of Weights and Measures, 4608 West 61st Street, Little Rock AR 72209. **LC** QC100.U6. **DD** 353.976700821.

ANNUAL REPORT - WEIGHTS AND MEASURES SECTION. Main/Corp Virginia. Weights and Measures Section. 0094-274X. US. English. an. 1 North 14th Street Room 032, Richmond VA 23219. **Tel** (212)460-1500. **LC** HF5714. **DD** 353.975500821.

ARSBERETNING - JUSTERVSENET. Main/Corp Denmark. Justervsenet. 1976/77-. DK. Danish. ir. Justervsenet, Amager Boulevard 115, 2300 Copenhagen S Denmark. **Tel** 45-1-540830. **Ed** Axel Vollertzen. **LC** QC100.D4. **Circ** 1,000. (ctrl). Technical testing within the fields of: (1) fire technology, (2) chemical technology, (3) civil engineering, (4) mechanical engineering and (5) metrology- legal and applied.

ASTM STANDARDIZATION NEWS. Main/Corp American Society for Testing and Materials. V. 1- Jan. 1973-. 0090-1210. Periodical. US. English. mo. $18.00. American Society Testing & Materials, 1916 Race Street, Philadelphia PA 19103. **Tel** (215)299-5585. **Ind/Abst** World Text Abstr., World Surf. Coat. Abstr., Ship Abstr., Excerpta Med., Coal Abstr., Energy Inf. Abstr., Environ. Abstr., Abstr. Bull. Inst. Paper Chem., Int. Aerosp. Abstr., GeoRef, Met. Abstr., World Alum. Abstr., Ref. Source, Bibliogr. Agric., Appl. Sci. Technol. Index, Comput. Control Abstr., Electr. Electron. Abstr., Sci. Abstr. Sect. A. Phys. Abstr., Phys. Abstr., Bibliogr. Index Geol. **LC** TA368. **DD** 620.004. **NLM** W1 A155J. **CODEN** STDNA. *Materials Research and Standards, 0025-5394.*

BECKMAN-REPORT. (BECKMAN REPORT). Began in 1959. 0005-755X. Periodical. GW. German. ir. Beckman Instruments GMBH, Abteilung Offentlichkeitsarbeit Frankfurter Ring 115, 8000 Munchen 40 West Germany. **Ind/Abst** Chem. Abstr., Energy Res. Abstr. **CODEN** BECRBZ.

BIBLIOGRAPHY ON ATOMIC TRANSITION PROBABILITIES. See Bibliographies.

BIULETYN POLSKIEGO KOMITETU NORMALIZACJI I MIAR. Main/Corp Poland. Komitet Normalizacji I Miar. July 1972-. 0324-8496. Periodical. PL. Polish. mo. ARS Polona, Krakowskie Przedmiescie 7, 00-068 Warsaw Poland. **LC** T59.2.P7. *Biuletyn.*

BOLETIM INFORMATIVO DO INPM. Main/Corp Instituto Nacional de Pesos e Medidas. Portuguese. ir. **LC** QC89.B8.

BRITISH STANDARDS YEARBOOK. See Yearbooks, Almanacs, Directories.

BSI CATALOGUE. VFOAT British Standards Institution Catalogue. 1984-. UK. English. an. $17.75. British Standards Institution, 2 Park Street, London WL2 2BS England. **LC** QC100, Z7914.A22. **DD** 016.60218. Index published separately - free - automatically sent. *British Standards Yearbook and Catalogue of Publications, 0068-2578.*

BULLETIN, CONVERSION AU SYSTEME METRIQUE. V. 1- March 29, 1978-. 0228-2690. Periodical. CN. French. ir. Free. Institut Canadien de la Construction en Acier, Bureau 300, 201 rue Consumer, Willowdale Ontario M2J 4G8 Canada. **DD** 338.4766910212.

BULLETIN DE METROLOGIE (BELGIUM). Main/Corp Belgium. Administration du Commerce. French. ir. 100. Administration du Commerce, Compte-Postale 191.69, GIE Service de la Metrologie, Bruxelles Belgium. **LC** QC89.B4.

BULLETIN D'INFORMATION-FRANCE. BUREAN NATIONAL DE METROLOGIE. Main/Corp France. Bureau National de Metrologie. V. 1- July 1970-. FR. French. ir. France Bureau National de Metrologie, 40 rue de Seine, Paris 6E 75 France. **LC** QC100.F7. **DD** 389.10944.

BULLETIN MENSUEL DE LA NORMALISATION FRANCAISE. See Engineering - Civil Engineering.

BULLETIN (SOUTH AFRICA. BUREAU OF STANDARDS). (BULLETIN). Vol. 4, No. 1 (Sept. 1974)- V. 11, No. 4 (Dec. 1981). Periodical. English (largely parallel text in Boers). mo. Free. South African Bureau of Standards, Private Bag X-191, Pretoria South Africa. **Tel** (012)-3411311. **Ed** J B Hoffeldt. **Circ** 4,000. (ctrl). Information on standardization. *SABS Bulletin.*

C. I. S. METRIC NEWSLETTER. Main/Corp Canadian Institute of Surveying. No. 1- Jan. 1973-. 0383-753X. Periodical. CN. English. ir. Free. Canadian Institute of Surveying, 512 Rochester Street/Suite 403, Ottawa Ontario K1S 4L9 Canada. **DD** 389.150971.

C S A INFORMATION UPDATE. Main/Corp Canadian Standards Association. No. 1- Oct. 1976-. 0702-7583. Periodical. CN. English. ir. $29.79. Canadian Standards Association, 178 Rexdale Boulevard, Rexdale Ontario M9W 1R3 Canada. **Tel** (416)747-2292. **Ed** Maria Fata. **DD** 016.620112. adv acc. **Circ** 1700. (ctrl). This subscription service gives a complete, concise rundown of CSA standards and certification activities, in CSA's nine program areas.

CALIBRATION AND RELATED MEASUREMENT SERVICES OF THE NATIONAL BUREAU OF STANDARDS. APPENDIX, FEES FOR SERVICES. Main/Corp United States. National Bureau of Standards. Office of Measurement Services. **Series/Titl** NBS Special Publication. Began with Oct. 1977. US. English. sa. Office of Measurement Services, National Bureau of Standards, Physics Building/Room B362, Washington DC 20234. Vols. for (June 1979-) distributed to depository libraries in microfiche. *Calibration and Test Services. Appendix, Fees for Services.*

CATALOG OF AMERICAN NATIONAL STANDARDS. Main/Corp American National Standards Institute. Periodical. US. English. an. $10.00. American National Standards Institution, 1430 Broadway, New York NY 10018.

COMITE INTERNATIONAL DES POIDS ET MESURES, COMITE CONSULTATIF D'ELECTRICITE. RAPPORT. VFOAT Rapport au Comite International des Poids et Mesures, Comite Consultatif d'Electricite. French. ir. Bureau International des Poids et Mesures, Pavillion de Breteuil, F-92310 Sevres France. **Tel** (1) 45 34 00 51. **LC** QC81. **DD** 537. **Circ** 350. Contains the proceedings of the meetings of the relevant committee, whose attendees are representatives of national laboratories engaged in standardization and related researches.

COMITE INTERNATIONAL DES POIDS ET MESURES, COMITE CONSULTATIF DES UNITES. RAPPORT. 1- Session. French. ir. Bureau International des Poids et Mesures, Pavillion de Breteuil, F-92310 Sevres France. **Tel** (1) 45 34 00 51. **LC** QC81. **DD** 389.1. **Circ** 350. Contains the proceedings of the meetings of the relevant committee, whose attendees are representatives of national laboratories engaged in standardization and related researches.

COMMERCIAL STANDARD. 1927-. 0083-1808. Monographic Series. US. English. ir. Superintendent of Documents, US Government Printing Office, Washington DC 20402. **LC** QC100. **DD** 389.

DIMENSIONS CEASED. (DIMENSIONS : THE MAGAZINE OF THE NATIONAL BUREAU OF STANDARDS, U.S. DEPARTMENT OF COMMERCE). **VFOAT** Dimensions/NBS. Began with V. 57, No. 8, Aug. 1973. Ceased V. 65, No. 8, (Oct. 1981). 0093-0458. Periodical. US. English. mo. **Ind/Abst** World Surf. Coat. Abstr., Coal Abstr., Energy Inf. Abstr., Environ. Abstr., GeoRef, Chem. Abstr., Predicasts, Index U.S. Gov. Period. **LC** T1. **DD** 605. **CODEN** NBSTAR. *Technical News Bulletin (United States. National Bureau of Standards), 0886-1218.*

DIRECTORY AND INDEX OF STANDARDS. SUPPLEMENT. See Yearbooks, Almanacs, Directories.

Metrology and Standardization

DIE GROSSWETTERLAGEN EUROPAS. V. 19, No. 13-. 0017-4645. Periodical. GW. German. mo. $22.73. Deutscher Wetterdienst, Frankfurterstr 135, 6050 Offenbach West Germany. Ed Deutscher Wetterdienst. LC QC880.4.A8. Report on the weather situation in Europe. *Grosswetterlagen Mitteleuropas.*

ISI BULLETIN. VFOAT I.S.I. Bulletin. VAT Indian Standards Institution Bulletin. Began in: 1949. 0019-0632. Periodical. II. English. mo. $18.00. Indian Standards Institution, 9 Bahadur Shah Zafar Marg, New Delhi 1 India. Ind/Abst CIS Abstr., Comput. Control Abstr., Electr. Electron. Abstr., Sci. Abstr. Sect. A. Phys. Abstr., Chem. Abstr., Phys. Abstr. LC TA368. DD 389.60954. CODEN ISTBA8.

ISO MEMENTO. Main/Corp International Organization for Standardization. VFOAT International Organization for Standardization Memento. 1961-. 0536-2067. English (French and Russian). ir.

JOURNAL OF RESEARCH OF THE NATIONAL BUREAU OF STANDARDS (WASHINGTON, D.C. : 1977). (JOURNAL OF RESEARCH OF THE NATIONAL BUREAU OF STANDARDS). Began with V. 82, No. 1, July/Aug. 1977. 0160-1741. Periodical. US. English. bm. US Government Printing Office, Superintendent of Documents, Washington DC 20402. Tel (202)783-3238. Ind/Abst Appl. Sci. Technol. Index, World Text Abstr., World Surf. Coat. Abstr., Abstr. Bull. Inst. Paper Chem., Int. Aerosp. Abstr., Comput. Control Abstr., Electr. Electron. Abstr., Eng. Index Annu., Eng. Index Mon., Sci. Abstr. Sect. A. Phys. Abstr., Chem. Abstr., Energy Res. Abstr., Index U.S. Gov. Period. LC QC100.U6. DD 505. NLM W1 JO87. CODEN JRNBAG. *Journal of Research of the National Bureau of Standards. Section A. Physics and Chemistry, 0022-4332; 0098-8979.*

KALENDAR ZNAMENATELNYKH I PAMIATNYKH DAT. 1957-. 0130-2051. Periodical. Russian. mo. $9.00. Victor Kamkin Inc (73206), 12224 Parklawn Drive, Rockville MD 20852. Tel (301)881-5973. LC D11.5.

KEY ABSTRACTS. PHYSICAL MEASUREMENTS AND INSTRUMENTATION. *See* Indexes/Abstracts.

LISTE DES MEMBRES. Main/Corp Institut Belge de Normalisation. VFOAT Ledenlijst. BE. Flemish and French. ir. Av de la Brabanconne 29, Bruxelles 1040 Belgium. LC T59.2.B4. DD 389.6061493.

MEASUREMENT : JOURNAL OF THE INTERNATIONAL MEASUREMENT CONFEDERATION. Vol. 1, No. 1 (Jan./March 1983)-. 0263-2241. Periodical. UK. English. qt. $76.63. Institute of Measurement and Control, 87 Gower Street, London WC1E 6AA England. Tel (01)387-4949.

MEET- EN REGELAPPARATEN- EN OVERIGE INSTRUMENTENINDUSTRIE. Series/Titl Produktiestatistieken Industrie. VFOAT Manufacture of Measuring and Controlling Units. 1980-1981-. NE. Dutch (summaries in English). be. 9.25. Centraal Bureau voor de Statistiek, Prinses Beatrixlaan 428 Postbus 959, 2270 AZ Voorburg Netherlands.

METERS AND MILES. Periodical. US. English. mo. Meters and Miles, 14283, Minneapolis MN 55414. Tel (612)835-3222.

METRIC BULLETIN. Main/Corp Keller (J. J.) & Associates. V. 2, No. 10- Aug. 1975-. 0363-2644. Periodical. US. English. mo. $5.00. J J Keller & Associates, 145 West Wisconsin Avenue, Neonah WI 54956. LC QC90.8. DD 389.15205. *Metric System Guide Bulletin, 0364-3336.*

METRIC CONVERSION BULLETIN. V. 1- Mar. 22, 1978-. 0228-2704. Periodical. CN. English. ir. Free. Canadian Institute of Steel Construction, Suite 300/201 Consumers Road, Willowdale Ontario M2J 4G8 Canada. DD 338.4766910212.

METRIC FACT SHEET. No. 1- Apr. 1975-. 0383-9184. Periodical. CN. English. ir. Canadian Metric Association, PO Box 35, Fonthill Ontario L0S 1E0 Canada. DD 389.1520971.

METRIC INFORMATION. (METRIC INFORMATION: BULLETIN). VFOAT Renseignements sur le Systeme Metrique : Bulletin. No. 1- Feb. 1979-. 0708-3548. Periodical. CN. English (French. Each language has its own title page). ir. Metric Commission of Canada, PO Box 4000, Ottawa Ontario K1S 5G8 Canada.

METRIC MESSAGE. VFOAT Message Metrique. V. 3, No. 2- June 1975-. 0318-6385. Periodical. CN. text in French and English. qt. 5.00. Canadian Metric Association, PO Box 35, Fonthill Ontario L0S 1E0 Canada. Tel (416)960-3288. Ed Joseph B Reid. DD 389.15206271. Circ 300. Metrication and related public education. *Newsletter, 0382-5647.*

METRIC MONITOR. VFOAT Moniteur Metrique. V. 1, No. 1- Mar. 1974-. 0700-2408. Periodical. CN. English (French). bm. Metric Commission of Canada, PO Box 4000, Ottawa Ontario K1S 5G8 Canada.

METRIC NEWS. 0093-3708. Periodical. US. English. bm. $5.00. Swani Pub Co, PO Box 248, Roscoe IL 61073. LC QC90.8. DD 389.15205.

METRIC NEWS CEASED. Began publication in 1974?. 0701-0036. Periodical. CN. English. bm. $9.00 Members, $15.00 Nonmembers. Canadian Manufacturers' Association, Yonge Street, Toronto Ontario M5E 1E5 Canada. DD 338.47670971.

METRIC YEARBOOK. *See* Yearbooks, Almanacs, Directories.

METROLOGIA. V. 1- Jan. 1965-. 0026-1394. Periodical. English (French, German or Spanish). qt. $79.00. Springer Verlag-New York Inc, 175 5th Avenue, New York NY 10010. Tel (212)460-1500. Ed R P Hudson. Ind/Abst Eng. Index Mon., Eng. Index Bioeng. Abstr., Eng. Index Energy Abstr., Energy Inf. Abstr., Environ. Abstr., Int. Aerosp. Abstr., Comput. Control Abstr., Electr. Electron. Abstr., Sci. Abstr. Sect. A. Phys. Abstr., Energy Res. Abstr., Chem. Abstr., Nuci. Sci. Abstr., Eng. Index Annu., Eng. Index, Eng. Index, Sci. Cit. Index, Abr. Ed., Phys. Abstr. LC QC81. CODEN MTRGAU. bk rev. Fields of interest: the improvement of basic measurements in physics, improved realizations of SI units, new values for the fundamental constants, international comparisons of standards, and innovative metrology in general.

METROLOGIA APLICATA. 0377-8134. Periodical. RM. Romany. qt. Ilexim Press Department, PO Box 1-136-1-137, Bucharest Romania. Ind/Abst Comput. Control Abstr., Electr. Electron. Abstr., Sci. Abstr. Sect. A. Phys. Abstr., Phys. Abstr., Eng. Index. CODEN MAPBA8. *Calitatea Produciei si Metrologie, 0377-8126.*

METROLOGISCHE ABHANDLUNGEN. 0232-3915. Periodical. German. ir. AMR fur Standardisierung Messwesen und Warenprufing, DDR 1162 Berlin, Furstenwalder Damm 388 East Germany. Ind/Abst Energy Res. Abstr. LC T50. DD 530.805.

MICROTECNIC. VFOAT Micro-News. Frb. 1947-. 0026-2854. Periodical. English (issues for 1947 are French ed. with section). qt. AGIFA Verlag AG, PO Box 257, CH-8033 Zurich Switzerland. Ind/Abst CIS Abstr., Eng. Index Mon., Eng. Index Bioeng. Abstr., Eng. Index Energy Abstr., Comput. Control Abstr., Electr. Electron. Abstr., Sci. Abstr. Sect. A. Phys. Abstr., Energy Res. Abstr., Chem. Abstr., Eng. Index Annu., Eng. Index Mon., Fluidex. LC QC81. DD 530.78. CODEN MITCAJ.

MONTHLY REVIEW (INSTITUTE OF TRADING STANDARDS ADMINISTATION (GREAT BRITIAN)). (THE MONTHLY REVIEW : THE JOURNAL OF THE INSTITUTE OF TRADING STANDARDS ADMINISTRATION). Vol. 80, No. 8 (Aug. 1972)-. Periodical. UK. English. mo. *Monthly Review (Institute of Weights and Measures Administration (Great Britain)).*

NATIONAL BUREAU OF STANDARDS. Main/Corp United States. National Bureau of Standards. Series/Titl NBS Special Publication. 0731-2067. US. English. Superintendent of Documents, US Government Printing Office, Washington DC 20402. LC QC100,QC100.U6. DD 602.18 S,607.2073.

NATIONAL BUREAU OF STANDARDS TECHNICAL NOTE. (NBS TECHNICAL NOTE). Began with No. 1. 0083-1913. Monographic Series. US. English. ir. Superintendent of Documents, US Government Printing Office, Washington DC 20402. Ind/Abst Comput. Control Abstr., Electr. Electron. Abstr., Sci. Abstr. Sect. A. Phys. Abstr., GeoRef, Chem. Abstr. LC QC100. DD 602.1. CODEN NBTNAE.

NATIONAL STANDARD REFERENCE DATA SERIES. Main/Corp United States. National Bureau of Standards. NSRDS-NBS 1-. Monographic Series. US. English. ir. US Department of Commerce, National Bureau of Standards, Washington DC 20230. Ind/Abst Eng. Index Annu., Eng. Index Mon., Eng. Index Bioeng. Abstr., Eng. Index Energy Abstr., Comput. Control Abstr., Electr. Electron. Abstr., Sci. Abstr. Sect. A. Phys. Abstr. LC QC100. DD 602.1. CODEN NSRDAP. (cum index).

NBS SERIAL HOLDINGS. Main/Corp United States. National Bureau of Standards. Library Division. Series/Titl NBSIR. VAT National Bureau of Standards Serial Holdings. Began with 1979. US. English. United States Department of Commerce, Library Division, National Bureau of Standards, Washington DC 20234. *New Serial Holdings.*

NCSL NEWSLETTER. Main/Corp National Conference of Standards Laboratories. VAT National Conference of Standards Laboratories Newsletter. 0194-5149. Periodical. US. English. qt. $10.00. Hewlett-Packard Company, 1501 Mill Page Road, Palo Alto CA 94304. Tel (303)497-3787.

NDE PUBLICATION. Series/Titl NBSIR. VFOAT N.D.E. Publication. VAT Nondestructive Evaluation Publications. Began with 1972-1977. US. English. an. Office of Nondestructive Evaluation, National Measurement Laboratory, National Bureau of Standards, Washington DC 20234. Vols. for 1981- distributed to depository libraries in microfiche.

PIAO CHUN HUA. VFOAT Standardization. Vol. 1 (Mar. 1983)-. Periodical. CH. Chinese. qt. 50.00. Chung-Hua Min Kuo Piao Chun, Hsieh Hui Box 540077, Taipei Taiwan. LC T59.2.T28. DD 389.60951249.

PIAO CHUN HUA TUNG HSUN. VFOAT Biaozhunhua Tongxun. Periodical. CH. Chinese. mo. 0.26. Post Office, Peking China. LC T59.A1. DD 389.605.

PROCEEDINGS - STANDARDS LABORATORY CONFERENCE. Main/Conf Standards Laboratory Conference. 1st- 1962-. US. English. be. LC QC100.

PUBLICATIONS OF THE NATIONAL BUREAU OF STANDARDS. CATALOG. (PUBLICATIONS OF THE NATIONAL BUREAU OF STANDARDS . . . CATALOG). Main/Corp United States. National Bureau of Standards. Series/Titl NBS Special Publication. Began with 1975. 0275-1348. US. English. an. Superintendent of Documents, US Government Printing Office, Washington DC 20402. LC QC100. DD 602.18 S, 016.6. *Publications of the National Bureau of Standards.*

QUALITY ASSURANCE. Began with Mar. 1975 Issue. 0306-2856. Periodical. UK. English. qt. 16 Domestic, $25.00 Foreign. Institute of Quality Assurance, 54 Princes Gate-Exhibition Road, London SW7 2PG England. Tel (01)584-9026. Ed J Goodes. Ind/Abst Eng. Index Annu., Eng. Index Mon., Eng. Index, Eng. Index Bioeng. Abstr., Eng. Index Energy Abstr., Ship Abstr., Comput. Control Abstr., Electr. Electron. Abstr., Sci. Abstr. Sect. A. Phys. Abstr., Energy Res. Abstr., Phys. Abstr., ISMEC Bull. LC TS156.A1. DD 658.562. CODEN QUASDZ. adv acc. Circ 8,100. Papers on all aspects of quality assurance including audits and assessments, inspection, metrology, statistical process control, standardization, and striving for excellence. *Quality Engineer, 0033-5215.*

RAPPORT AU COMITE INTERNATIONAL DES POIDS ET MESURES. Main/Corp Comite International des Poids et Mesures. Comite Consultatif de Photometrie et Radiometrie. 8.- Session. French. ir. Bureau International des Poids et Mesures, Pavillon de Breteuil, F-92310 Sevres France. Tel (1) 45 34 00 51. LC QC81. DD 535.22. Circ 350. Contains the proceedings of the meetings of the relevant committee whose attendees are representatives of national laboratories engaged in standardization and related researches. *Rapport au Comite International des Poids et Mesures.*

RAPPORT D'ACTIVITE - FRANCE. BUREAU NATIONAL DE METROLOGIE. Main/Corp France. Bureau National de Metrologie. 0750-7313. FR. French. an. 21 rue Casimir Perier, 75007 Paris France. LC QC100.F7. DD 354.4400821.

REFERATIVNYI ZHURNAL: METROLOGIIA I IZMERITELNAIA TEKHNIKA. VFOAT Metrologiia I Izmertelnaia Tekhnika. Ianv. 1963-. 0034-2505. Periodical. UR. Russian. mo. Victor Kamkin Inc (01872), 12224 Parklawn Drive, Rockville MD 20852. Tel

(301)881-5973. *Referativnyi Zhurnal: Izmeritelnaia Tekhnika.*

REPORT - METRIC COMMISSION CANADA. (REPORT). **Main/Corp** Metric Commission Canada. **VFOAT** Rapport. Began with V. for 1971/73. 0700-2394. Periodical. CN. English (French). an. Metric Commission of Canada, PO Box 4000, Ottawa Ontario K1S 5G8 Canada. **LC** QC92.C2. **DD** 345.7100821.

REPORT OF THE CHIEF INSPECTOR OF WEIGHTS & MEASURES, CITY OF BIRMINGHAM. **Main/Corp** Birmingham, Eng. Weights and Measures Dept. UK. English. an. Weights and Measures Department, 44 Board Street, Birmingham B1 2HP England. **LC** QC100.G7. **DD** 352.94210942496.

REPORT OF THE NATIONAL CONFERENCE ON WEIGHTS AND MEASURES. (REPORT OF THE . . . NATIONAL CONFERENCE ON WEIGHTS AND MEASURES). **Main/Conf** National Conference on Weights and Measures. **Series/Titl** NBS Special Publication. **VFOAT** Conference on Weights and Measures. Began with 20th, 1927. 0077-3964. US. English. an. Superintendent of Documents, US Government Printing Office, Washington DC 20402. **LC** QC89.U5. **DD** 389.1. (cum index). *Weights and Measures.*

A REPORT TO THE NATION ON THE MANAGEMENT OF METRIC IMPLEMENTATION. **Main/Corp** American National Metric Council. 0098-1443. US. English. $2.00 Single Issue. American National Metric Council, 1625 Massachusetts Avenue Northwest, Washington DC 20032. **LC** QC92.U54. **DD** 389.152.

REVUE DE METROLOGIE PRATIQUE ET LEGALE. Vol. 15, No. 7 (July 1937)- V. 17 (1939). 0035-158X. Periodical. FR. French. mo. $49.23. Revue de Metrologie Pratique, 102 rue de la Tour, Paris 16 France. **Ind/Abst** CIS Abstr. *Revue de Metrologie Pratique.*

SESSION - COMITE INTERNATIONAL DES POIDS ET MESURES. COMITE CONSULTATIF DE THERMOMETRIE. (SESSION). Began in 1962. Periodical. FR. French. ir. Bureau of International des Poids et Mesures, Pavillon de Breteuil F, 92310 Sevres France. **Ind/Abst** Chem. Abstr. **CODEN** CCTMCZ.

SINGAPORE STANDARDS YEARBOOK. See Yearbooks, Almanacs, Directories.

SPECIFICATIONS, TOLERANCES, AND OTHER TECHNICAL REQUIREMENTS FOR WEIGHING AND MEASURING DEVICES. **Main/Conf** National Conference on Weights and Measures. **Series/Titl** NBS Handbook. 1979-. 0271-4027. US. English. an. Superintendent of Documents, US Government Printing Office, Washington DC 20402. **LC** QC89.U5. **DD** 681.20218. *Specifications, Tolerances, and Other Technical Requirements for Commercial Weighing and Measuring Devices.*

STANDARDISIERUNG UND QUALITAT. Periodical. SZ. German. ir. $12.28. Kunst & Wissen Erich Bieber, Dufourstrasse 51, CH-8008 Zurich Switzerland. **LC** T59. *Standardisierung.*

STANDARDIZAREA ROMANA. Periodical. RM. Romanian. mo. Ilexim Press Department, PO Box 1-136-1-137, Bucharest Romania. **LC** TA368. *Standardizarea.*

STANDARDS ACTION. V. 1- 1970-. 0038-9633. Periodical. US. English. bw. ANSI, 1430 Broadway, New York NY 10018. *Magazine of Standards, 0097-2959.*

STANDARDS ENGINEERING. Began in 1949. 0038-9668. Periodical. US. English. bm. $20.00. Standards Engineering Society, 6700 Penn Avenue South, Minneapolis MN 55423. **Tel** (612)861-4990. **Ed** R E Monahan. **LC** T59. bk rev. adv acc. **Circ** 1,000. (ctrl). Contains articles directly or indirectly relating to the field of standardization but specializing in company, national, and international standards.

STANDARDS FORUM UPDATE. (STANDARDS FORUMUPDATE). Summer 1982-. 0824-4359. Periodical. CN. French. qt. Free. Acnor, 178 Boulevard Rexdale, Rexdale Ontario M9W 1R3 Canada. **DD** 389.60971.

STANDARDS FORUM UPDATE. (STANDARDS FORUMUPDATE). Spring 1982-. 0824-4340. Periodical. CN. English. qt. Free. CSA, 178 Rexdale Boulevard, Rexdale Ontario M9W 1R3 Canada. **DD** 389.60971.

STANDARDS (NEW ZEALAND). (STANDARDS : NEW ZEALAND STANDARDS BULLETIN). Vol. 24, No. 1 (1978)-. 0549-0561. Periodical. English. mo. Standards Association of New Zealand, Private Bag, Wellington New Zealand. *New Zealand Standards Bulletin.*

STANDARTY SEV I REKOMENDATSII SEV PO STANDARTIZATSII : UKAZATEL. See Indexes/Abstracts.

TECHNICAL HIGHLIGHTS - NATIONAL MEASUREMENT LABORATORY. **Main/Corp** National Measurement Laboratory (U.S.). 1979-. 0271-969X. US. English. an. $4.25. Superintendent of Documents, Government Printing Office, Washington DC 20402. **LC** QC100, QC39. **DD** 602.18 S, 530.8.

TMO UPDATE. **Main/Corp** Marley Organization. **VAT** The Marley Organization Update. 1977. 0270-0123. Periodical. US. English. sm. $130.00. The Marley Organization Inc, 11 Todds Road, Resources Information Service, Ridgefield CT 06877-9990. **Tel** (203)438-3801. **Ed** Charles W Hyer. bk rev. **Circ** 500. Reporting of and opinions concerning current issues in technical standardization and related product certification as they influence laboratory accreditation systems, both US and international.

U L C NEWS. **Main/Corp** Underwriters' Laboratories of Canada. No. 2- April 1974-. 0700-9623. Periodical. CN. French (No. 1 was printed only in English). Free. Underwriters' Laboratories of Canada, 7 rue Crouse, Scarborough Ontario M1R 3A9 Canada. **DD** 389.605.

UNE. **VFOAT** Boletin de la Normalizacion Espanola. Periodical. SP. Spanish. bm. 1500. Boletin de la Normalizacion Espanola, Zurbano 46, Madrid 10 Spain. **LC** T59.2.S646. **DD** 602.18. *Boletin de la Normalizacion Espanola UNE.*

U.S. METRIC BOARD ANNUAL REPORT. **Main/Corp** United States Metric Board. Began with 1979. 0270-4838. US. English. an. United States Metric Board, 1600 Wilson Boulevard, Arlington VA 22209. **LC** QC92.U54. **DD** 353.00821.

MILITARY SCIENCE

AAS MILAVNEWS. **Main/Corp** Aviation Advisory Services, Ltd. **VAT** Aviation Advisory Services Milavnews. Periodical. UK. English. mo. Aviation Advisory Services, Stapleford Airfield, Abridge Essex England. **LC** UG622. **DD** 358.40305.

ABSTRACTS OF MASTER OF MILITARY ART AND SCIENCE (MMAS) THESES AND SPECIAL STUDIES. See Indexes/Abstracts.

ABSTRACTS OF MILITARY BIBLIOGRAPHY. See Indexes/Abstracts.

ACCION CIVICA. Periodical. Spanish. ir. Guardia Nacionel de Nicaragua, Apartado de Correos 546, Primer Batallon Blindado Presidential, Managua Nicaragua. **LC** UA608.N54.

ACTIVITIES REPORT OF THE R & D ASSOCIATES. **Main/Corp** Research and Development Associates for Military Food and Packaging Systems. **VAT** Activities Report of the Research and Development Associates. 1947. 0198-0181. US. English. sa. $75.00. Research & Development Association, 103 Biltmore Drive/Suite 106, San Antonio TX 78213. **Tel** (512)344-5773. **Ed** Merton Singer. **Ind/Abst** Chem. Abstr., Eng. Index Annu., Eng. Index Bioeng. Abstr., Eng. Index Energy Abstr., Eng. Index Mon. **NLM** W1 AC98D. **CODEN** ARYTDT. bk rev. **Circ** 800. Benchwork in military food, packaging, feeding, and equipment. Keeps members current on research projects and requirements of armed forces and changes which affect industry. *Activities Report - Research and Development Associates for Military Food and Packaging Systems, Inc., 0099-6335.*

ADMINISTRATIVE DIRECTORY OF THE PROVISIONAL MILITARY GOVERNMENT OF SOCIALIST ETHIOPIA. See Yearbooks, Almanacs, Directories.

Military Science

ADVANCED MILITARY COMPUTING. See Computers and Computer Science.

ADVOCATE (FALLS CHURCH, VA.). See Law.

AERO ARMOR-SERIES. **VFOAT** Aero Armor Series. 0276-6760. US. English. ir. Aero Publ Inc, 329 West Aviation Road, Fallbrook CA 92028. **LC** UG446.5. **DD** 623.74750943.

AEROSPACE AND DEFENSE RESEARCH CONTRACTS ROSTER. **VFOAT** U.S. Government Research and Development Contracts in Aerospace and Defense. 1963/64-. US. English. an. **LC** U393. **DD** 353.00711.

AEROSPACE/DEFENSE MARKETS & TECHNOLOGY. (AEROSPACE & DEFENCE MARKETS & TECHNOLOGY). **VFOAT** Aerospace/Defense Markets and Technology. 0885-2286. Periodical. US. English. mo. Predicasts, 11001 Cedar Avenue, Cleveland OH 44106. *0738-0461.*

AFP ANNUAL REPORT. **Main/Corp** Philippines. Armed Forces. **VFOAT** A.F.P. Annual Report. English. an. Civil Relations Service, AFP Camp General Emilio, Aguinaldo Quezon City Philippines. **LC** UA853.P6. **DD** 355.009599.

AFRICAN DEFENCE JOURNAL. (AFRICAN DEFENCE JOURNAL : AFRICAN DEFENCE JOURNAL). **VFOAT** African Defence. No. 1 (Sept. 1980)-. 0244-0342. Periodical. English. mo. 11 rue de Teheran, 75008 Paris France. **Tel** 562 74 76 . **Ind/Abst** Predicasts. **LC** UA855. **DD** 355.0096. Magazine of military and strategical information.

AFRIQUE DEFENSE. No. 1 (Mar. 1978)-. 0182-2322. Periodical. FR. French. mo. 360.00. Societe S A P E F, 11 rue de Teheran, 75008 Paris France. **Tel** 562 74 76 . **Ed** Jacques de Lestapis. **LC** UA855. **DD** 355.03306. bk rev. adv acc. **Circ** 9,200. African geopolitical facts, reported by countries. Basic focus is on defence and security affairs.

AGENDA DES ARMEES. 1977-. French. ir. Limoges Lavauzelle, BP 8, Panazol NM 87350. **LC** U10.F7. **DD** 355.30944. *Agenda des Armees Terre, Air, 0376-6284.*

AIR DEFENSE ARTILLERY. Winter 1983-. 0740-803X. Periodical. US. English. qt. $13.50. Superintendent of Documents, US Government Printing Office, Washington DC 20402. **Tel** (202)783-3238. **Ind/Abst** Index U.S. Gov. Period., Predicasts. **LC** UG730. **DD** 358.41450973. *Air Defense Magazine, 0192-964X.*

THE AIR FORCE COMPTROLLER. Vol. 1, No. 1 (Oct. 1967)-. 0002-2365. Periodical. US. English. qt. Superintendent of Documents, US Government Printing Office, Washington DC 20402. **Tel** (202)783-3238. **Ind/Abst** Manage. Contents, Am. Stat. Index, Index U.S. Gov. Period. **LC** UG633. **CODEN** AFCTB3.

AIR FORCE ENGINEERING & SERVICES QUARTERLY CEASED. **VFOAT** Engineering & Services Quarterly. **VAT** Air Force Engineering and Services Quarterly. V. 16, No.3-V. 21, No. 1. 0362-188X. Periodical. US. English. qt. Superintendent of Documents, US Government Printing Office, Washington DC 20402. **Ind/Abst** Index U.S. Gov. Period. **LC** UG633.A1. **DD** 358.4. *Air Force Civil Engineer.*

AIR FORCE ENGINEERING & SERVICES QUARTERLY (TYNDALL AIR FORCE BASE (FLA.) : 1984). (AIR FORCE ENGINEERING & SERVICES QUARTERLY). **VFOAT** Air Force Engineering and Services Quarterly. AFRP 85-1, Vol. 25, No. 1 (Spring 1984)-. 0883-0193. Periodical. US. English. qt. Superintendent of Documents, US Government Printing Office, Washington DC 20402. **Ind/Abst** Predicasts. **DD** 358. *Quarterly (Air Force Engineering and Services Center (U.S.)).*

AIR FORCE JOURNAL OF LOGISTICS. Vol. 4, No. 1 (Winter 1980)-. 0270-403X. Periodical. US. English. qt. Superintendent of Documents, US Government Printing Office, Washington DC 20402. **Tel** (202)783-3238. **Ind/Abst** Predicasts, Index U.S. Gov. Period., Funk Scott Index Corp. Ind. **LC** UG1123. **DD** 358.4162120973. *Pipeline (Gunter Air Force Station (Ala.)), 0747-7651.*

AIR FORCE LAW REVIEW. See Law.

THE AIR FORCE LIST. **Main/Corp** Great Britain. Ministry of Defence. Periodical. UK. English. ir. Her Majestys Stationery Office, PO Box 276,

Military Science

London SW8 5DT England. **Tel** 01-622 3316. **LC** UG635.G7. **DD** 358.413310922. *Air Force List.*

AIR FORCE MAGAZINE. Vol. 54, No. 2 (Feb. 1971)-. 0730-6784. Periodical. US. English. mo. $13.00 US, $21.00 Canada and Mexico. Air Force Association, 1750 Pennsylvania Avenue NW/Suite 400, Washington DC 20006. **Tel** (202)633-3300. **Ind/Abst** Predicasts, Int. Aerosp. Abstr., Am. Hist. Life, Hist. Abstr. **LC** UG633. **DD** 358.400973. *Air Force and Space Digest, 0002-2349.*

THE AIR FORCE OFFICER'S GUIDE. Began with: 23rd Ed. 0739-635X. US. English. Stackpole Books, Cameron and Keller Streets, Harrisburg PA 17105. **Tel** (717)234-5041. **LC** UG633.A1. **DD** 358.400973. We publish books on guns, fishing and military outdoor skills. *Air Officer's Guide.*

AIR FORCE REPORT. (AIR FORCE REPORT TO THE . . . CONGRESS OF THE UNITED STATES OF AMERICA). **Main/Corp** United States. Dept. of the Air Force. 0273-4370. US. English. an. US Department of the Air Force, Washington DC 20330. **LC** UG633. **DD** 358.400973.

THE AIR RESERVIST. July 1952-. 0002-2535. Periodical. US. English. qt. Superintendent of Documents, US Government Printing Office, Washington DC 20402. **Tel** (202)783-3238. **Ind/Abst** Index U.S. Gov. Period. **LC** UG633. **DD** 358.405, 358. *Air Reserve Forces Review.*

AIR UNIVERSITY LIBRARY INDEX TO MILITARY PERIODICALS. *See* Indexes/Abstracts.

AIRLIFT OPERATIONS REVIEW. VFOAT A.O.R. Began with Oct. 1979 issue. 0732-7838. Periodical. US. English. qt. Military Airlift Command, HQ MAC AOS, Scott AFB IL 62225. **LC** UC333. **DD** 358.440973.

THE AIRMAN. (AIRMAN). Began with Aug. 1957. 0002-2756. Periodical. US. English. mo. Superintendent of Documents, US Government Printing Office, Washington DC 20402. **Ind/Abst** Index U.S. Gov. Period. **LC** UG 633.A1. **DD** 358.405.

AKABRI. VAT Akademi Angkatan Bersenjata Republik Indonesia. No. 1-. Indonesian. ir. Dinas Penerangan Akabri, Jl Gondangdia Lama No 1 B, Jakarta Indonesia. **LC** U660.I5.

AL-BAYRAQ. No. 1- May 1974-. Periodical. Arabic. ir. 3000. Qiyadat Quwat Dofa Al-Bahrayn, PO Box 245, Al-Bahrayn Bahrain. **LC** UA853.B34.

AL-DIFA AL-ARABI. VFOAT Arab Defence Journal. Periodical. in Arabic. ir. 150.00. Dar Al-Sayyad, PO Box 1038, Bayrut Lebanon. **Ind/Abst** Predicasts. **LC** U4.

AL-DIFA AL-ISLAMI. VFOAT Islamic World Defence. Periodical. UK. Arabic (English). qt. Islamic Press Agency, Crown Lane East Burnham NR Slough, Bucks SL2 3SG England. **LC** U4.

AL-DIFA WA-AL-AMN. VFOAT Addifa Wal-Amn. Periodical. Arabic. ir. $30.00. Intirkunir, 6 el Boursa el Guedida, Al-Qahirah United Arab Republic (Egypt). **LC** UF500.

AL-FIKR AL-ISTIRATIJI AL-ARABI. VFOAT Majallat Al-Inma Al-Arabi. V. 1, No. 1, (July 1981)-. Periodical. Arabic. ir. 40.00. Mahad Al-Inma Al-Arabi, Bayrut Al-Ramlah Al-Bayda, 77 Shari Alis Farid Al-Naqqash, SB 14/5300, Bayrut Lebanon. **LC** UA853.A6.

AL-QUWAH. Periodical. Arabic. ir. Al-Qiyadah Al-Ammah Li-Quwat Difa Al-Bahrayn Shubat Al-Alaqat Al-Ammah Wa-Al-Thaqafah, PO Box 245, Al-Manamah Bahrain. **LC** UA853.B34.

ALLGEMEINE SCHWEIZERISCHE MILITARZEITSCHRIFT. VFOAT ASMZ. Vol. 114, No.1 (Jan. 1948)-. Periodical. SZ. German. mo. 63.60. Huber & Company, CH-8500 Frauenfeld Switzerland. **Tel** (054)27 11 11. **LC** U3. **DD** 355.005. bk rev. adv acc. **Circ** 31,539. (ctrl). Official publication of the Swiss Officers Company. *Allgemeine Schweizerische Militarzeitung, Schweizerische Monatschrift fur Offiziere Aller Waffen.*

ALUMNI DIRECTORY - NEW YORK MILITARY ACADEMY. *See* Yearbooks, Almanacs, Directories.

AMERICAN DEFENSE ANNUAL. VFOAT American Defense. 1985-1986-. 0882-1038. Periodical. US. English. an. $26.00. Lexington Books, 125 Spring Street, Lexington MA 02173. **LC** UA23.A1. **DD** 355.033073.

AMERICAN INTELLIGENCE JOURNAL. Vol. 1, No. 1 (Fall 1977)-. 0883-072X. Periodical. US. English. qt. National Military Intelligence Association Inc, 1606 Laurel Lane, Annapolis MD 21401. **Ind/Abst** Predicasts. **DD** 355.

AMERICAN MILITARY INSTITUTE DIRECTORY OF MEMBERS. *See* Yearbooks, Almanacs, Directories.

AMI : ARMES, MILITARIA, INFORMATIONS, TIR. VFOAT Armes, Militaria, Informations, TIR. Periodical. French. mo. $4.00 Per Issue. Georges A Petersen, PO Box 805, Springfield VA 22150. **LC** TS532. **DD** 683.4005.

ANNUAL BULLETIN - UNITED STATES AIR FORCE ACADEMY. **Main/Corp** United States Air Force Academy. VFOAT Bulletin - United States Air Force Academy. US. English. an. United States Air Force Academy, Colorado Springs CO 80840.

ANNUAL CATALOG - UNITED STATES AIR FORCE ACADEMY CEASED. **Main/Corp** United States Air Force Academy. VFOAT United States Air Force Academy Catalog. Began with No. 5-25. US. English. an. 80840. *United States Air Force Academy.*

ANNUAL DIRECTORY AND REPORT - AMERICAN DEFENSE PREPAREDNESS ASSOCIATION. *See* Yearbooks, Almanacs, Directories.

ANNUAL MANAGEMENT REPORT OF THE DEFENSE LOGISTICS AGENCY. **Main/Corp** United States. Defense Logistics Agency. Began with 1976/77. 0190-6356. US. English. an. Department of Defense, Defense Logistics Agency, Cameron Station, Alexandria VA 22314. **LC** UC263. **DD** 355.6210973. *Annual Management Report of the Defense Supply Agency, 0360-0203.*

ANNUAL REPORT - ADMINISTRATOR OF VETERAN AFFAIRS. (ANNUAL REPORT). **Main/Corp** United States. Veterans Administration. 1958-. 0083-3533. US. English. an. Veterans Administration, Government Printing Office, Washington DC 20420. **LC** UB373. **DD** 353.8, 351.50973. **NLM** W2 A V49A. *Annual Report for Fiscal Year Ending . . .*

ANNUAL REPORT - ADVANCED ENGINEERING LABORATORY (AUSTRALIA). **Main/Corp** Advanced Engineering Laboratory (Australia). 1978-79-. AT. English. an. Advanced Engineering Laboratory of the Defence Research Centre in Salisbury, Box 2151 GPO, Adelaide South Australia 5001. **LC** UG485. **DD** 623.042072094.

ANNUAL REPORT - AIR FORCE HUMAN RESOURCES LABORATORY. **Main/Corp** Air Force Human Resources Laboratory. VFOAT AFHRL Annual Report. US. English. an. Department of the Air Force, Air Force Human Resources Laboratory, Brooks Air Force Base TX 78235.

ANNUAL REPORT - ALABAMA. DEPT. OF VETERANS AFFAIRS. **Main/Corp** Alabama. Dept. of Veterans Affairs. US. English. an. Department of Veterans Affairs, PO Box 1509, Montgomery AL 35192. **LC** UB358.A2. **DD** 353.976100812.

ANNUAL REPORT AND PROCEEDINGS OF THE ANNUAL ENCAMPMENT. (ANNUAL REPORT AND PROCEEDINGS OF THE ENCAMPMENT). **Main/Corp** United Spanish War Veterans. Dept. of Michigan. 0094-596X. US. English. an. 122 South Grand Avenue, Lansing MI 48913. **LC** E714.3. **DD** 369.18105. *Proceedings . . . Annual Encampment.*

ANNUAL REPORT - ARIZONA. NATIONAL GUARD. **Main/Corp** Arizona. National Guard. US. English. an. State of Arizona National Guard, Military Department, Phoenix AZ 85007. **LC** UA71. **DD** 355.35109791.

ANNUAL REPORT - ARSENALS CANADA. (ANNUAL REPORT). **Main/Corp** Arsenals Canada. VFOAT Rapport Annuel. VAT Rapport Annuel - Arsenaux Canada. 35th (Mar. 31, 1981)-. 0712-0567. CN. English (French). an. Arsenals Canada, 5 Montee des Arsenaux, Le Gardeur Quebec Canada. **LC** UF537.C3. **DD** 355.6220971. *Annual Report, 0384-2134.*

ANNUAL REPORT - CANADIAN ARSENALS LIMITED. (ANNUAL REPORT). **Main/Corp** Canadian Arsenals Limited. VFOAT Rapport Annuel. 28th (March 31, 1974)- 34th (March 31, 1980). 0384-2134. CN. English (French). an. **LC** UF537.C3. **DD** 355.6220971. *Annual Report of the Directors to the Honourable Minister of Supply and Services.*

ANNUAL REPORT - CIVIL AIR PATROL, ALASKA WING. **Main/Corp** United States. Civil Air Patrol. Alaska Wing. US. English. an. Civil Air Patrol, Box 1836, Anchorage AK 99501. **LC** UA928.A4. **DD** 358.4.

ANNUAL REPORT - COMMISSION FOR HIGHER EDUCATION, OFFICE OF VETERANS AFFAIRS. **Main/Corp** Connecticut. Office of Veterans Affairs for Education. 0149-8800. US. English. an. 340 Capitol Avenue, Hartford CT 06115. **LC** UB358.C8. **DD** 353.974600848.

ANNUAL REPORT - DEFENCE CONSTRUCTION (1951) LIMITED. **Main/Corp** Defence Construction (1951) Limited. VFOAT Rapport Annuel. 1968/69-. 0317-4077. CN. English (French). an. Free. Kenson Building, 225 Metcalfe Street, Ottawa Ontario K1A 0N3 Canada. **LC** UG460. **DD** 338.76230470971. *Annual Report to the Minister of National Defence, 0317-4077.*

ANNUAL REPORT - DEPARTMENT OF DEFENSE, STATE OF HAWAII. (ANNUAL REPORT - DEPARTMENT OF DEFENSE). **Main/Corp** Hawaii. Dept. of Defense. 1962-. 0147-5371. US. English. an. State of Hawaii, Department of Defense, Fort Ruger HI 96816. **LC** UA43.H3. **DD** 355.3709969. *Report of the Adjutant General.*

ANNUAL REPORT - DEPARTMENT OF MILITARY AFFAIRS (ALASKA). **Main/Corp** Alaska. Dept. of Military Affairs. US. English. an. Alaska Department of Military Affairs, 338 Denali Street, Anchorage AK 99501. **LC** UA43.

ANNUAL REPORT - DISTRICT OF COLUMBIA, NATIONAL GUARD (DISTRICT OF COLUMBIA). **Main/Corp** District of Columbia. National Guard. US. English. an. District of Columbia National Guard, 2001 East Capitol Street, Washington DC 20331. **LC** UA131. **DD** 355.3709753.

ANNUAL REPORT - DIVISION OF VETERAN'S AFFAIRS (FLORIDA). **Main/Corp** Florida. Division of Veterans Affairs. 1975/76-. US. English. an. Division of Veterans Affairs, PO Box 1437, St Petersburg FL 33731. **LC** UB358.F6. **DD** 353.975900848. *Report of the Department of Community Affairs, Division of Veterans Affairs to the Governor.*

ANNUAL REPORT - ELECTRONICS RESEARCH LABORATORY (AUSTRALIA). **Main/Corp** Electronics Research Laboratory (Australia). 1978-79-. AT. English. an. ERL Defence Research Centre, Salisbury Box 2151 GPO, Adelaide 5001 South Australia. **LC** U395.A8. **DD** 623.023072094.

ANNUAL REPORT - ILLINOIS DEPARTMENT OF VETERANS AFFAIRS. **Main/Corp** Illinois. Dept. of Veterans Affairs. US. English. an. Illinois Department of Veterans Affairs, 126 West Jefferson Street, Springfield IL 62705. **LC** UB358.I3. **DD** 353.977300848. *Annual Report.*

ANNUAL REPORT - MICHIGAN VETERANS TRUST FUND. BOARD OF TRUSTEES. **Main/Corp** Michigan Veterans Trust Fund. Board of Trustees. 16th (1946/1962)-. US. English. an. Michigan Veterans Trust Fund, Board of Trustees, Ottawa St Building, Corner of Ottawa & Pine, PO Box 30026, Lansing MI 48909. **LC** UB358.M5. **DD** 355.115109774.

ANNUAL REPORT - NATIONAL DEFENSE UNIVERSITY. (ANNUAL REPORT). **Main/Corp** National Defense University. Academic Year 1981-1982-. 0748-8718. US. English. an. National Defense University, Fort Lesley J McNair, 4th and P Street SW, Washington DC 20319. **LC** U412. **DD** 355.0071173. Vols. for 1981-82- distributed to depository libraries in microfiche. *National Defense University Report.*

ANNUAL REPORT - NEW JERSEY. DEPT. OF DEFENSE. **Main/Corp** New Jersey. Dept. of Defense. US. English. an. State of New Jersey, Department of Defense, Eggert Crossing Road, Box 979, Trenton NJ 08625. **LC** UA341. **DD** 355.3709749. *Report of Chief of Staff.*

ANNUAL REPORT - NEW YORK (STATE). DIVISION OF MILITARY AND NAVAL AFFAIRS. **Main/Corp** New York (State). Division of Military and Naval Affairs. Began with 1961. US. English. an. Division of Military

Military Science

and Naval Affairs, Public Security Building State Campus, Albany NY 12226. LC UA361. DD 355.3709747. *Annual Report of the Chief of Staff to the Governor.*

ANNUAL REPORT - NEW YORK (STATE). LEGISLATURE ASSEMBLY. STANDING COMMITTEE ON VETERANS' AFFAIRS. Main/Corp New York (State). Legislature Assembly. Standing Committee on Veterans' Affairs. VFOAT Annual Report of the Assembly Standing Committee on Veterans' Affairs. 1983-. US. English. an. The Assembly, State of New York, Standing Committee on Veterans Affairs, Albany NY 12248.

ANNUAL REPORT OF ACTIVITIES. (ANNUAL REPORT OF ACTIVITIES FOR CALENDAR YEAR . . .). Main/Corp United States. Veterans Administration. Merit Review Boards. 0730-8914. US. English. an. Veterans Administration, Washington DC 20420.

ANNUAL REPORT OF SOUTH CAROLINA DEPARTMENT OF VETERANS AFFAIRS. Main/Corp South Carolina. Dept. of Veterans Affairs. 0362-6229. US. English. an. Department of Veterans Affairs, 1205 Pendleton Street, Columbia SC 29201. LC UB358.S6. DD 353.975700848.

ANNUAL REPORT OF THE ADJUTANT GENERAL, DEPARTMENT OF MILITARY AFFAIRS, SOUTH DAKOTA. Main/Corp South Dakota. Dept. of Military and Veterans Affairs. VFOAT Annual Report, Department of Military and Veterans Affairs. 0272-1228. Periodical. US. English. an. Department of Military and Veterans Affairs/Office of the Adjutant General, PO Box 2150, Rapid City SD 57709. LC UA43.S8. DD 355.3709783.

ANNUAL REPORT OF THE ADJUTANT GENERAL (WEST VIRGINIA). Main/Corp West Virginia. Adjutant General's Office. US. English. an. State of West Virginia/Office of the Adjutant General, 1703 Coonskin Drive, Charleston WV 25311. LC UA43.W4. DD 355.3709754.

ANNUAL REPORT OF THE DEPARTMENT OF MILITARY AFFAIRS TO THE GOVERNOR OF MONTANA. (ANNUAL REPORT). Main/Corp Montana. Dept. of Military Affairs. 1971/72-. 0091-0368. US. English. an. Department of Military Affairs, 1100 North Main Street, Helena MT 59601. LC UA300. DD 353.978600895.

ANNUAL REPORT OF THE MISSISSIPPI EMERGENCY MANAGEMENT AGENCY. Main/Corp Mississippi Emergency Management Agency. July 1, 1979-June 30, 1980-. US. English. an. Mississippi Emergency Management Agency, PO Box 4501 Fondren Station, Jackson MS 39216. LC UA928.M7. DD 353.97620075405.

ANNUAL REPORT OF THE STATE OF WEST VIRGINIA, OFFICE OF EMERGENCY SERVICES. Main/Corp West Virginia. Office of Emergency Services. 0277-285X. US. English. an. Office of Emergency Services, State Capitol Building/Room EB-80, Charleston WV 25305. LC UA928.W4. DD 353.9754007505. *WVOES Annual Report, 0099-285X.*

ANNUAL REPORT - OFFICE OF THE ADJUTANT GENERAL, STATE OF MISSOURI. Main/Corp Missouri. Adjutant General's Office. US. English. an. Office of the Adjutant General, Jefferson City MO 65101. LC UA43.M86. DD 355.3709778.

ANNUAL REPORT ON ADMISSION POLICIES AND HEALTH CARE RESOURCES IN THE VA HOSPITAL SYSTEM. Main/Corp United States. Veterans Administration. 1975-. 0360-0947. US. English. an. Superintendent of Documents, US Government Printing Office, Washington DC 20402. LC UB369. DD 353.00848. NLM W2 A V49AE.

ANNUAL REPORT ON OUTSIDE ADVISORY MEDICAL OPINIONS. Main/Corp United States. Board of Veterans' Appeals. 0271-3322. US. English. an. Superintendent of Documents, US Government Printing Office, Washington DC 20402. LC UB369. DD 353.00812.

ANNUAL REPORT - SOUTH AFRICAN NATIONAL MUSEUM OF MILITARY HISTORY. See Museums.

ANNUAL REPORT - STATE OF ARIZONA, DEPARTMENT OF EMERGENCY & MILITARY AFFAIRS, DIVISION OF MILITARY AFFAIRS. Main/Corp Arizona. Division of Military Affairs. US. English. an. Division of Military Affairs, 5636 East McDowell Road, Phoenix AZ 85008. LC UA43.A6. DD 355.3709791.

ANNUAL REPORT - TEXAS VETERANS AGENT ORANGE ASSISTANCE PROGRAM. (ANNUAL REPORT). Main/Corp Texas Veterans Agent Orange Assistance Program. 0747-7864. US. English. an. Texas Department of Health, 1100 West 49th Street, Austin TX 78756. LC UB358.T5. DD 355.115609764.

ANNUAL REPORT, THE SURGEON GENERAL, UNITED STATES ARMY. Main/Corp United States. Dept. of the Army. Office of the Surgeon General. Fiscal year 1959-. 0278-6141. US. English. an. Office of the Surgeon General, Department of the Army, Washington DC 20315. LC UH223. DD 355.3450973. NLM W2 A2 S9R. *Annual Report of the Surgeon General, United States Army, 0278-6141.*

ANNUAL REPORT TO CONGRESS ON THE POST-VIETNAM ERA VETERANS' EDUCATIONAL ASSISTANCE PROGRAM. 6th (Feb. 24, 1984)-. 0747-6795. US. English. an. LC UB357. DD 355.11520973. Vols. for 1984- distributed to some depository libraries in microfiche.

ANNUAL REPORT TO THE GOVERNOR AND LEGISLATURE - KANSAS. STATE BOARD OF INDIGENTS' DEFENSE SERVICES. Main/Corp Kansas. State Board of Indigents' Defense Services. 1st-. US. English. an. State of Kansas Board of Indigents' Defense Services, 503 Kansas Avenue/Suite 536, Topeka KS 66603.

ANNUAL REPORT - UNITED STATES. FEDERAL EMERGENCY MANAGEMENT AGENCY. Main/Corp United States. Federal Emergency Management Agency. US. English. an. Federal Emergency Management Agency, Washington DC 20472. LC UA927. DD 353.00754. *A Report to the President on Comprehensive Emergency Management, 0276-6647.*

ANNUAL REPORT - UNITED STATES. NAVY. MILITARY SEALIFT COMMAND. Main/Corp United States. Navy. Military Sealift Command. US. English. an. Military Sealift Command, Atlantic Bayonne NJ 07002.

ANNUAL REPORT - UNITED STATES SOLDIERS' AND AIRMEN'S HOME. (ANNUAL REPORT). Main/Corp United States Soldiers' and Airmen's Home. Board of Commissioners. 1972/73-. 0360-6856. US. English. an. Superintendent of Documents, US Government Printing Office, Washington DC 20402. LC UB384.D5. DD 362.8. *Report of the Board of Commissioners.*

ANNUAL REPORT - VETERANS AFFAIRS. (ANNUAL REPORT). Main/Corp Rhode Island. Veterans Affairs Unit. 1st- 1970/71-. 0093-7185. US. English. an. Veterans Affairs Unit, 46 Aborn Street, Providence RI 02903. LC UB358.R4. DD 355.11509745.

ANNUAL REPORT - VIRGINIA. DEPT. OF MILITARY AFFAIRS. Main/Corp Virginia. Dept. of Military Affairs. Began with 1970. US. English. an. 401 East Main Street, Richmond VA 23219. LC UA43.V8. DD 355.3709755.

ANNUAL REPORT - WEAPONS SYSTEMS RESEARCH LABORATORY (AUSTRALIA). Main/Corp Weapons Systems Research Laboratory (Australia). 1978-79-. AT. English. an. Weapons Systems Research Laboratory, Defence Research Centre, Salisbury Box 2151 GPO, Adelaide South Australia 5001. LC U395.A8. DD 623.4072094.

ANNUAL REVIEW. CHIEF, NATIONAL GUARD BUREAU. (ANNUAL REVIEW). Main/Corp United States. National Guard Bureau. VFOAT Annual Review of the Chief, National Guard Bureau. Began with 1975/76. 0192-4559. US. English. an. National Guard Bureau, Attn: NGB-PAH, 5600 Columbia Pike, Falls Church VA 22041. Tel (703)756-1980. Ed Leonid Kondrativk. LC UA42. DD 355.370973. Circ 3,000. (ctrl). Official report to the secretaries of the Army and Air Force concerning the National Guard Bureau, Army and Air National Guard. *Annual Report, 0192-4761.*

ANNUAL REVIEW OF MILITARY RESEARCH AND DEVELOPMENT. 1982-. 0741-9090. US. English. an. Praeger Publishers, 521 Fifth Avenue, New York NY 10175. LC U393. DD 355.070973.

ANTICIPATED USE OF VETERANS G. O. BONDS REPORT PURSUANT TO AB 4354 CHAPTER 1477, 1974. Main/Corp California. Dept. of Veterans Affairs. Jan. 1, 1979-. US. English. an. 1227 O Street, Sacramento CA 95814. LC UB374.C2. DD 355.115. *Anticipated Use of Veterans Bonds Report Pursuant to AB 4354, Chapter 1477, 1974.*

AR. VFOAT A.R. Periodical. German. mo. Militarverlag Der DDR (Veb), Storkower Str 158 Postfach 46551, DDR-1055 Berlin West Germany. LC U3. *Armee-Rundschau.*

ARMADA INTERNATIONAL. V. 1- Feb. 1977-. 0252-9793. Periodical. US. English. ir. $180.00. Gene Selven and Associates, 10050 North Wolf Road SW, Suite 200, Cupertino CA 95014. Tel (408)996-7400. Ed Frank Lammas. Ind/Abst Funk Scott Index Corp. Ind. LC HD9743.A1. DD 338.47623405. adv acc. Circ 31,000. (ctrl).

ARMED FORCES. Jan. 1976-. Periodical. US. English. mo. 22,00. Strategic Publications, 4 Western House, 4 N Booysens Road, Booysens PO Box 23022 & Kosterst, Joubert Park 2044, Johannesburg South Africa. Tel (011)838-3373. Ed S J McIntosh. LC U1. DD 355.00968. bk rev. adv acc. Circ 9,000.

ARMED FORCES AND SOCIETY. VFOAT Armed Forces & Society. V. 1- Fall 1974-. 0095-327X. Periodical. US. English. qt. $35.00. Seven Locks Press, 7425 MacArthur Boulevard Box 37, Cabin John MD 20818. Tel (301)320-2130. Ed David R Segal. Ind/Abst Am. Hist. Life, Hist. Abstr., Part A, Mod. Hist. Abstr., Hist. Abst., Part B, Twent. Century Abstr., Sociol. Abstr., ABC Pol Sci, Writ. Am. Hist., Public Aff. Inf. Serv. Bull., Soc. Sci. Index, Soc. Sci. Citation Index, Lang. Lang. Behav. Abstr., Recent Publ. Artic., Hist. Abstr. LC U21.5. DD 301.59305. bk rev. adv acc. Circ 2,000. Features articles on military institutions, civil-military relations, arms control and peacekeeping.

THE ARMED FORCES COMPTROLLER. V. 1- July 1956-. 0004-2188. Periodical. US. English. qt. $7.00. American Society of Military Comptrollers, PO Box 91, Mount Vernon VA 22121. Tel (703)780-6164. Ed E W Edmonds Jr. Ind/Abst Manage. Contents, Account. Index. Suppl. LC UC20. bk rev. Circ 13,000. Comptrollership including budget, accounting and finance, resource management, auditing, data processing, banking, analysis, systems, and man power.

ARMED FORCES JOURNAL INTERNATIONAL. V. 110, No. 6- (No. 5619)-. 0196-3597. Periodical. US. English. mo. Army & Navy Journal Inc, 1414 22nd Street NW/Suite 603, Washington DC 20037. Tel (202)296-0450. Ind/Abst Predicasts. LC U1. DD 355.00973. *Armed Forces Journal, 0004-220X.*

ARMED FORCES PERSONNEL AND CIVILIANS IN DEFENCE ESTABLISHMENT BOOK ON SERVICE CONDITIONS. Main/Corp India. Ministry of Defence. II. English. an. Government of India, Ministry of Defence, New Delhi India. LC UB325.I4. DD 355.610954.

ARMED FORCES (ROYAL UNITED SERVICES INSTITUTE FOR DEFENCE STUDIES). (ARMED FORCES). Began with No. 1, 1978. 0142-4696. Periodical. UK. English. mo. $27.58. Ian Allan Ltd, Coombelands House, Weybridge KT15 1HV England. Tel 58511. Ed M Harris. Ind/Abst Predicasts. bk rev. adv acc. Circ 24,500. Worldwide news and reports of the activities and operations of naval, military and air forces with special reference to the armed services in NATO.

ARMEES D'AUJOURD'HUI. No. 1- July. 1975-. Periodical. FR. French. mo. Dawson France, Boite Postale 40, 91121 Palasieau Cedex France. LC U2. DD 355.005.

ARMOR. Vol. 59, No. 4 (July/Aug. 1950)-. 0004-2420. Periodical. US. English. US Armor Association, Post Office Box 607, Ft Knox KY 40121. Tel (504)942-8624. Ind/Abst Predicasts, Index U.S. Gov. Period., Funk Scott Index Corp. Ind. *Armored Cavalry Journal.*

ARMS AND ARMOR ANNUAL. V. 1- 1973-. 0093-6014. US. English. an. $9.95. Digest Books Inc, 540 Frontage Road, Northfield IL 60093. LC U799. DD 355.82.

Military Science

ARMS CONTROL CHRONICLE. No. 1 (Mar. 1984)-. 0825-1908. Periodical. CN. English. mo. Free to members. Canadian Centre for Arms Control and Disarmament, 5th Floor 275 Slater Street, Ottawa Ontario K1P 5H9 Canada. DD 327.17405.

ARMS CONTROL IMPACT STATEMENTS. (FISCAL YEAR . . . ARMS CONTROL IMPACT STATEMENTS : STATEMENTS SUBMITTED TO THE CONGRESS BY THE PRESIDENT PURSUANT TO SECTION 36 OF THE ARMS CONTROL AND DISARMAMENT ACT). **Main/Corp** United States. President. Began with 1976. 0195-4741. US. English. an. US Government Printing Office, Superintendent of Documents, Washington DC 20402. LC UF503. DD 355.80973. Vols. for (1983-) distributed to some depository libraries in microfiche.

ARMS CONTROL (LONDON, ENGLAND). (ARMS CONTROL). Vol. 1, No. 1 (May 1980)-. 0144-0381. UK. English. ty. 44.00. Frank Cass and Company Ltd, 11 Gainsborough Road, London E11 1RS England. Tel 01-530-4226. Ed Ian Bellany and Coit D Blacker. LC JX1974. DD 327.17405. bk rev. adv acc. Of interest to those whose study and research enables them to make a contribution to arms control and disarmament studies.

ARMS CONTROL TODAY. See Political Science - International Relations.

ARMS GAZETTE. 0197-2863. Periodical. US. English. mo. $15.00. Bienfeld Publishing Company, 12767 Saticoy Street, North Hollywood CA 91605.

ARMS, MEN, AND MILITARY BUDGETS. 1976/77-. 0162-038X. US. English. an. Crane Russak, 52 Vanderbilt, New York NY 16017. Tel (201)932-2280. LC UA23.A1. DD 355.033073.

ARMS RACE AND ARMS CONTROL. (THE ARMS RACE AND ARMS CONTROL). 0265-1807. UK. English. an. $10.00. Taylor & Francis Inc, 114 East 32nd Street, New York NY 10016. LC UF530. DD 355.8205.

ARMY. 0004-2455. Periodical. US. English. mo. Association of the U S Army, 2425 Wilson Boulevard, Arlington VA 22201. Tel (703)841-4300. Ind/Abst Predicasts, Ref. Source, Am. Hist. Life, Hist. Abstr., Funk Scott Index Corp. Ind. Army Combat Forces Journal, 0271-7336.

ARMY ADMINISTRATOR CEASED. Began with Dec. 1973 issue. 0361-7300. Periodical. US. English. bm. Atzi-Dcdrcd-Ad 46216. LC UB23. DD 355.60973.

ARMY AVIATION. VFOAT Army Aviation Magazine. 0004-248X. Periodical. US. English. ir. $14.00. Army Aviation Magazine, 1 Crestwood Road, Westport CT 06880. Tel (203)226-8184. Ed Dale Resten. adv acc. Circ 16,000. Pertains to Army aviation- military and industry.

ARMY CLUB SYSTEM ANNUAL REPORT. (ARMY CLUB SYSTEM ANNUAL REPORT, FISCAL YEAR . . .). **Main/Corp** United States. Adjutant-General's Office. Club and Community Activities Management Directorate. 1980-. 0270-9848. US. English. an. Club and Community Activities Management Directorate, Office of the Adjutant General, Headquarters Department of the Army, Washington DC 20402. LC U56. DD 355.341. Army Club System Annual Report, 0270-9848.

THE ARMY COMMUNICATOR. See Engineering - Electricity, Electrical Engineering, Electronics.

THE ARMY HISTORIAN. See History (General).

THE ARMY LAWYER. See Law.

ARMY LOGISTICIAN. Vol. 1, No. 1 (Sept./Oct. 1969)-. 0004-2528. Periodical. US. English. bm. $22.00. US Government Printing Office, Superintendent of Documents, Washington DC 20402. Tel (202)783-3238. Ind/Abst Predicasts, Index U.S. Gov. Period., Funk Scott Index Corp. Ind. LC U168.

ARMY MORALE, WELFARE, AND RECREATION. **Main/Corp** United States. Adjutant-General's Office. Nonappropriated Fund Financial Management Directorate. Fiscal Year 1982-. 0742-728X. US. English. an. Nonappropriated Fund Financial Management Directorate, Office of the Adjutant General Headquarters, Department of the Army, Alexandria VA 22331. LC UH810. DD 355.346. Army Morale Support Fund Annual Report.

ARMY MUSEUM NEWSLETTER. See Museums.

ARMY-NAVY STORE & OUTDOOR MERCHANDISER. (ARMY/NAVY STORE & OUTDOOR MERCHANDISER). VAT Army Navy Store and Outdoor Merchandiser. 0160-7278. Periodical. US. English. sa. $40.00. Howark Publishing Company, 567 Morris Avenue, Elizabeth NJ 07208.

THE ARMY OFFICER'S GUIDE. 39th- Ed. 0148-6799. US. English. $8.95. Stackpole Books, Cameron and Kelker Streets, Harrisburg PA 17105. LC U133.A6. DD 355.00973. Officer's Guide.

THE ARMY QUARTERLY AND DEFENCE JOURNAL. Periodical. UK. English. qt $48.00. Army Quarterly & Defence Journal, 1 West Street, Tavistock Devon England. Tel 0822-3577. Ed C H Stainforth. Ind/Abst Am. Hist. Life, Hist. Abstr., Part A, Mod. Hist. Abstr., Hist. Abst., Part B, Twent. Century Abstr., Predicasts, Public Aff. Inf. Serv. Bull., Funk Scott Index Corp. Ind., Hist. Abstr. LC U1. DD 355.005. bk rev. adv acc. Circ 20,000. (ctrl). International military journal covering defence policy and strategy weapons and equipment development, accounts of past battles and campaigns, defence diary, recent appointments, contracts and book reviews. Army Quarterly.

ARMY R, D & A. VFOAT R, D & A, Army Research Development & Acquisition Magazine. Publication began with V. 19, No. 2, Mar./Apr. 1978. 0162-7082. Periodical. US. English. bm. US Government Printing Office, Superintendent of Documents, Washington DC 20402. Ind/Abst Index U.S. Gov. Period., Predicasts. LC U393. DD 355.007.2073. Army Research and Development, 0004-2560.

ARMY RECREATION AND TRAVEL GUIDE. 0094-9736. US. English. LC UH810. DD 355.34602573.

ARMY RESERVE MAGAZINE. Began with Nov. 1954 issue. 0004-2579. Periodical. US. English. qt. Chief Army Reserve, DAAR-PA the Pentagon, Washington DC 20310. Tel (202)697-8619. Ind/Abst Index U.S. Gov. Period. LC UA23.A1. DD 355.370973. Army Reservist.

ARMY TRAINER. Vol. 1, No. 1 (Fall 1981)-. 0731-3144. Periodical. US. English. qt. $16.00. Superintendent of Documents, US Government Printing Office, Washington DC 20402. LC U408.3. DD 355.50973.

THE ARTILLERYMAN. Vol. 6, No. 3 (Summer 1985)-. 0884-4747. Periodical. US. English. qt. The Artilleryman, 4 Water Street, Boston MA 02174. DD 358. Muzzleloading Artilleryman, 0195-038X.

ASIAN COMMAND REVIEW. VFOAT ACR. Periodical. English. ir. 47C Jalan Ipoh, 02-12 Kuala Lumpur Malaysia. LC UA830. DD 355.0095.

ASIAN DEFENCE JOURNAL. VFOAT Asian Defence. 0126-6403. MY. English. mo. $55.00. Syed Hussain Publishers Sdn Bhd, PO Box 836, Kuala Lumpur Malaysia. Tel (03)636958. Ind/Abst Predicasts, Funk Scott Index Corp. Ind. LC UA830. DD 355.033059. The only journal in southeast Asian and Pacific region to focus on latest defense systems and weapon technology. Geo-political in the defense industry.

ASKAR. Year 1- (No. 1-). French. ir. Service d'Information des Forces Armees Tchadiennes etc, BP 171, Ndjamena Chad. LC UA859.3. DD 355.0096741.

ATOMIC VETERANS' NEWSLETTER. 0736-9255. Periodical. US. English. bm. National Association of Atomic Veterans, 1109 Franklin Street, Burlington IA 52601.

AUDIT REPORT. DEPARTMENT OF MILITARY. (AUDIT REPORT, DEPARTMENT OF MILITARY). **Main/Corp** Tennessee. Division of State Audit. 0148-3447. US. English. be. Tennessee Comptroller of the Treasury, Nashville TN 37202. LC UA461. DD 353.9768007232.

AURORA. (THE AURORA). Vol. 1, No. 1 (Nov. 19, 1980)-. 0821-5499. Periodical. CN. English. wk. $7.50 Canada, US and Europe, $10.00 Others. Canadian Forces Base Greenwood, PO Box 99, Greenwood Nova Scotia B0P 1N0 Canada. DD 355.10971634. Argus (Canada. Canadian Forces Base (Greenwood, N.S.)), 0821-5480.

AUTODEFESA. Portuguese. ir. Rua Cabral de Moncada 134 Caixa Postal 6071, Luanda Angola. LC UA929.A5.

BELLONA. KWARTALNIK WOJSKOWO-HISTORYCZNY. Began publication with Jan. 1918 Issue. Periodical. UK. Polish (summaries in English, French). ir. Polish Institut & Sikorski Mus, 20 Prince Gale, London SW 7 England. Ind/Abst Am. Hist. Life, Hist. Abstr. LC U4. (cum index).

BIENNIAL REPORT - ADJUTANT GENERAL'S DEPARTMENT, STATE OF NORTH DAKOTA. **Main/Corp** North Dakota. Adjutant General's Dept. US. English. be. Adjutant General's Department, Box 1817, Bismarck ND 58505. LC UA43. DD 355.37.09784. Report.

BIENNIAL REPORT OF THE DEPARTMENT OF EMERGENCY SERVICES. (BIENNIAL REPORT). **Main/Corp** Washington (State). Dept. of Emergency Services. 11th- 1971/72-. 0093-092X. US. English. be. LC UA928.W2. DD 353.97970075405.

BIENNIAL REPORT OF THE STATE OF NORTH DAKOTA DEPARTMENT OF VETERANS AFFAIRS TO THE GOVERNOR OF NORTH DAKOTA AND DEPARTMENT OF ACCOUNTS AND PURCHASES. **Main/Corp** North Dakota. Dept. of Veteran Affairs. 0160-4503. US. English. be. North Dakota Department of Veterans Affairs, PO Box 1287, Fargo ND 58102. LC UB358.N9. DD 353.978400848.

BIENNIAL REPORT - STATE OF MINNESOTA, DEPARTMENT OF MILITARY AFFAIRS. **Main/Corp** Minnesota. Dept. of Military Affairs. US. English. be. Department of Military Affairs, Veterans Service Building, State Capitol, St Paul MN 55101. LC UA271. DD 355.3709776.

BIENNIAL REPORT - STATE OF MINNESOTA, DEPARTMENT OF VETERANS AFFAIRS. **Main/Corp** Minnesota. Dept. of Veterans' Affairs. 1976/78-. US. English. be. State of Minnesota, Department of Veterans Affairs, St Paul MN 55101. LC UB358.M6. DD 353.977600848. Annual Report - Department of Veterans Affairs, State of Minnesota.

BIENNIAL REPORT - STATE OF WISCONSIN, DEPARTMENT OF VETERANS AFFAIRS. **Main/Corp** Wisconsin. Dept. of Veterans Affairs. 1975/77-. US. English. be. Department of Veteran Affairs, State of Wisconsin, 77 North Dickinson Street, Madison WI 53702. LC UB358.W6. DD 353.977500848.

BOARD OF CONTRACT APPEALS DECISIONS. **Main/Corp** United States. Armed Services Board of Contract Appeals. V. 56-2-. 0498-3637. US. English. an. Commerce Clearing House, 4025 West Peterson Avenue, Chicago IL 60646. Tel (312)583-8500. LC KF853.3.A2. DD 346.73023. Bound volumes of ASBCA, other Appeals Board decisions.

BOEI HANDOBUKKU. 1975-. JA. Japanese. ir. 450. Asakumo Shimbun Sha, 4 Shiba Sakaecho, Minato-ku 106 Tokyo Japan. LC UA845.

BOLETIN. **Main/Corp** Academia Cubana de la Lengua, Havana. V. 1-10, No.1/2. 0567-5685. Periodical. Spanish. ir. LC UB5.

BOLETIN OFICIAL DEL MINISTERIO DE DEFENSA : DIARIO OFICIAL DEL EJERCITO. **Main/Corp** Spain. Ejercito. Yearly V. 88- (No. 155-). Spanish. ir. Ejercito, Palacio de Buenavista Alcala, Madrid 51 Spain. LC UA781. Diaro Oficial.

BOLETIN OFICIAL DEL MINISTERIO DE DEFENSA : DIARIO OFICIAL DEL EJERCITO DEL AIRE. **Main/Corp** Spain. Ejercito del Aire. V. 37- (No. 81-). Periodical. Spanish. tw. 900. Ejercito del Aire, Princesa 88 Bajo, Madrid Spain. LC TL504. Boletin Oficial.

BRITISH DEFENCE EQUIPMENT CATALOGUE. VFOAT B.D.E.C. UK. English. ir. Combined Service Publications, PO Box 4, Farnborough Hampshire, Great Britain GU 14 7LR England. LC UC460. DD 355.8029441.

LE BUDGET DE LA DEFENSE POUR . . . . FR. French. ir. 6 rue Saint-Charles, 75015 Paris France. LC UA700. DD 355.6220944.

BUDGET DE PROGRAMMES. **Main/Corp** France. Service Central de l'Action Sociale des Armees. FR. French. an. Action Sociale des Armees,

Military Science

5 rue de Chazelles, 75017 Paris France. LC UH725.F7. **DD** 355.34.

BULLETIN OFFICIEL DES DECORATIONS, MEDAILLES ET RECOMPENSES (FRANCE). FR. French. ir. 54.00. 26 rue Desaix, 75727 Paris Cedex 15 France.

BULLETIN - STATE OF IDAHO, DEPARTMENT OF HEALTH AND WELFARE, DIVISION OF VETERANS AFFAIRS. (BULLETIN - STATE OF IDAHO, DIVISION OF VETERANS AFFAIRS). **Main/Corp** Idaho. Division of Veterans Affairs. No. 345- June 1975-. 0364-0310. Periodical. US. English. mo. Division of Veterans Affairs, PO Box 7765, Boise ID 83707. **LC** UB358.I2. **DD** 355.1509796.

BUNDESVERSORGUNGSBLATT. Periodical. German. ir. Verlag W Kohlhammer, Luxemburger Strasse 72, 5000 Koln 1 West Germany. **LC** UB359.G3. Bundesversongungsblatt im Bundesarbeitsblatt.

CANADA GUNSPORT. See Recreation, Leisure - Sports.

CANADIAN DEFENCE QUARTERLY (TORONTO, ONT.). (CANADIAN DEFENCE QUARTERLY). **VFOAT** Revue Canadienne de Defense. Vol. 1, No. 1 (Summer 1971)-. 0315-3495. Periodical. CN. English (includes some text in French). qt. 20.00. Canadian Defence Quarterly, 310 Dupont Street, Toronto Ontario M5R 1V9 Canada. **Tel** (416)968-7252. Ed John Gellner. **Ind/Abst** Predicasts. **LC** UA600. **DD** 355.033071. bk rev. adv acc. **Circ** 9,000. (ctrl). Our magazine carries articles on military and defence matters, military history and strategic studies, as well as book reviews on military or related subjects.

CANADIAN GUNNER. (THE CANADIAN GUNNER). Began with 1965 issue. 0068-8843. CN. English. an. $5.18. Royal Canadian Artillary, Canadian Forces Base Shilo, Shilo Manitoba R0K 2A0 Canada. **Tel** (204)765-2282. **DD** 358.10971. Gunner Bulletin, 0318-6350.

CANADIAN MILITARY JOURNAL. V. 11- 1944-. 0008-4468. Periodical. CN. includes some text in French. qt. $7.74. Canadian Military Journal, 3450 Durocher/Suite 8, Montreal Quebec H2X 2E1 Canada. Salute, 0382-7526.

CANADIAN MILITARY MEDALS & INSIGNIA JOURNAL. V. 7, No. 2-V. 17, No. 4. 0318-2436. Periodical. CN. English. qt. Canadian Society of Military Medals & Insignia, c/o R W Irwin, 14 Tamarack Place, Guelph Ontario Canada. Journal of the Canadian Society of Military Medals & Insignia, 0318-2444.

CATALOG - DEFENSE SYSTEMS MANAGEMENT COLLEGE. **Main/Corp** Defense Systems Management College. **VFOAT** D.S.M.C. . . . Catalog. US. English. an. Defense Systems Management College, Fort Belvoir VA 22060.

CCCO NEWS NOTES. **Main/Corp** Central Committee for Conscientious Objectors, Philadelphia. **VAT** Central Committee for Conscientious Objectors News Notes. 0008-5952. Periodical. US. English. CCCO, 2016 Walnut Street, Philadelphia PA 19103. **LC** UB342.U5. **DD** 355.2240973. News Notes.

THE CENTER FOR STRATEGIC AND INTERNATIONAL STUDIES, GEORGETOWN UNIVERSITY. (THE CENTER FOR STRATEGIC AND INTERNATIONAL STUDIES, GEORGETOWN UNIVERSITY. ANNUAL REPORT). **Main/Corp** Georgetown University. Center for Strategic and International Studies. 0272-2429. US. English. an. Center for Strategic and International Studies, 1800 K Street Northwest, Washington DC 20006. **LC** UA10.5. **DD** 327.0711753.

CFB GANDER GAZETTE. **VAT** Canadian Forces Base Gander Gazette. Vol. 3, No. 6 (April 1984)-. 0828-8046. Periodical. CN. English. mo. CFB Gander Gazette, PO Box 6000, Gander Newfoundland A1V 1X1 Canada. **DD** 355.109718. CFS Gander Gazette, 0823-7824.

CHUN SHIH CHIA. **VFOAT** Defense International. First published in 1984. Periodical. CH. Chinese. mo. $1,480.00. Lung Tien Chu Pan She, PO Box 111473, Taipei Taiwan.

CHUNG-HUA CHAN LUEH HSUEH KAN. Periodical. CH. Chinese. qt. $10.00. Chung-Hua Chan Lueh Hsueh Hui, 170 Hsin Sheng N Road, 3 Section, Tai-Pei Shih Taiwan. **LC** U162. **DD** 355.43005.

CINFAC BIBLIOGRAPHIC REVIEW. SUPPLEMENT. See Bibliographies.

CITIZEN AIRMEN : THE OFFICIAL MAGAZINE OF THE AIR NATIONAL GUARD AND AIR FORCE RESERVE. Periodical. US. English. ir. US Government Printing Office, Superintendent of Documents, Washington DC 20402. Air Reservist.

CIVIL & MILITARY LAW JOURNAL. See Law.

COMBAT CRAFT. See Naval Science, Navigation.

COMBAT CREW. Series/Titl SACRP. Began with Nov. 1950. 0010-213X. Periodical. US. English. mo. $34.00. US Government Printing Office, Superintendent of Documents, Washington DC 20402. **Tel** (202)783-3238. **Ind/Abst** Predicasts, Funk Scott Index Corp. Ind. **LC** UG633. **DD** 358.42. Professional Pilot.

COMBAT DATA SUBSCRIPTION SERVICE. **Main/Corp** Historical Evaluation and Research Organization. V. 1- Winter 1975-. 0098-7956. Periodical. US. English. qt. Historical Evaluation and Research Organization, Colonel John A C Andrews, PO Box 157, Dunn Loring VA 22027. **LC** U719. **DD** 355.405.

COMBAT ILLUSTRATED. 0199-1396. Periodical. US. English. bm. $7.50 Domestic, $8.50 Foreign. Challenge Publications Inc, 7950 Deering Avenue, Canoga Park CA 91304. **LC** UF530. **DD** 355.8205.

COMMAND. Began with V. 1 in 1956. 0010-2474. Periodical. US. English. qt. $12.00. Officers Christian Fellowship of the USA, PO Box 1177, Englewood CO 80150. **Tel** (303)761-1984. Ed Don Martin Jr. bk rev. **Circ** 6,000. To exalt the Lord Jesus Christ in the Armed Forces and to encourage Christians to live for him in our military society. Officers' Christian Union Bulletin, 0471-1505.

COMMANDERS CALL. **VFOAT** CDRS Call. Began in 1977. 0160-3744. Periodical. US. English. bm. US Army Ag Publications Center, Army Chief of Public Affairs, 2800 Eastern Boulevard, Baltimore MD 21220. **LC** UB1. **DD** 355.3305. CDRS Call, 0364-801X.

COMMERCIAL ACTIVITIES INVENTORY REPORT AND FIVE-YEAR REVIEW SCHEDULE. **Main/Corp** United States. Dept. of Defense. Fiscal Year 1981-. 0736-1807. US. English. an. Superintendent of Documents, US Government Printing Office, Washington DC 20402. **LC** UC263. **DD** 355.3410973. Commercial and Industrial-Type Activities Inventory Report and 5-Year Review Schedule.

COMMUNITY ACTIVITIES. (COMMUNITY ACTIVITIES - OREGON NATIONAL GUARD). **Main/Corp** Oregon. National Guard. 0145-353X. US. English. an. 2150 Fairgrounds Road NE, Salem OR 97303. **LC** UH723. **DD** 361.9795.

COMPARATIVE STRATEGY. See Political Science - International Relations.

CONGRESSIONAL PRESENTATION : SECURITY ASSISTANCE PROGRAM. **Main/Corp** United States. Defense Security Assistance Agency. US. English. **LC** UA12. **DD** 355.0320973.

CONSENSUS (CHICAGO, ILL.). (CONSENSUS). Vol. 1, No. 1 (Winter 1983)-. 0740-3461. Periodical. US. English. qt. Consensus, 1451 East 55th Street #1028, Chicago IL 60615. **LC** UA23. **DD** 355033073.

CONSOLIDATED INDEX OF ARMY PUBLICATIONS AND BLANK FORMS. See Indexes/Abstracts.

CONTRACT AUDIT MANUAL. **Main/Corp** United States. Defense Contract Audit Agency. **VFOAT** Defense Contract Audit Manual. 1979-. US. English. ir. US Department of Defense, Defense Contract Audit Agency, Washington DC 20402. Defense Contract Audit Manual.

CONTRACTING DMS INTELLIGENCE. See Aeronautics, Astronautics.

CONTRIBUTIONS IN MILITARY HISTORY. 0084-9251. Monographic Series. US. English. ir. Greenwood Press, 88 Post Road West, Box 5007, Westport CT 06881. **Tel** (203)226-3571. **LC** UNC. The history of the air, sea, and ground forces of the world is the focus of this monograph series.

AN COSANTOIR. Began with: Vol. 1, No. 1 (Dec. 27, 1940). Periodical. IE. English. mo. 7.50. Red House, Infirmary Road Parkgate, Dublin Ireland. **Tel**

779018. Ed Austin Pender. **LC** U1. **DD** 355.009417. bk rev. adv acc. **Circ** 5,000. Aims to provide a topical readable magazine on both internal and international military developments.

COUNTY VETERAN POPULATION. **Main/Corp** United States. Veterans Administration. Reports and Statistics Service. 0194-0511. US. English. **LC** UB357. **DD** 353.00848 S, 355.1150973.

CP3SI NEWS. **VFOAT** C Three I News. **VAT** Command, Control, Communications Intelligence News. Vol. 1, No. 1 (June 1984)-. 0749-4408. Periodical. US. English. mo. $120.00. Washington Defense Reports Inc, Box 34312, Bethesda MD 20817. **DD** 355.

CROSS & COCKADE JOURNAL. V. 1- Spring 1960-. 0011-1902. Periodical. US. English. qt. $15.00. Society of World War I Aero Historians, 10443 South Memphis Avenue, Whitter CA 90604. **Tel** (213)944-4003.

CRREL BENCHNOTES : U.S. ARMY CORPS OF ENGINEERS INFORMATION EXCHANGE BULLETIN. **VFOAT** USA Crrel Benchnotes. Publication began with May 1976. Periodical. US. English. ir. US Army Corps of Engineers Cold Regions, Cold Regions Research and Engineering Laboratory, Hanover NH 03755.

CUTTER RADAR PROJECT NEWSLETTER. Periodical. US. English. bm. Commandant (G-EEE-1/63), Attention: Cutter Radar Project, Washington DC 20590.

CW/PS SPECIAL STUDY. **VFOAT** CWPS Special Study. 0730-9058. Periodical. US. English. ir. $20.00. Center for War/Peace Studies, 218 East 18th Street, New York NY 10003.

DAI AL-WATAN. Periodical. Arabic. ir. **LC** UA853.A28.

DAN MIL. 1971-. Periodical. Danish (some summaries in English). ir. **LC** UG635.D4.

DATA ON VIETNAM ERA VETERANS. 0882-9837. US. English. an. Veterans Administration, Reports and Statistics Service, Office of Controller, 810 Vermont Avenue North West, Washington DC 20420.

DAV. (DAV : THE OFFICIAL VOICE OF THE DISABLED AMERICAN VETERANS AND DAV AUXILIARY). **VAT** Disabled American Veterans (Washington, D.C.). 0276-7465. Periodical. US. English. mo. $4.00. DAV National Headquarters, 3725 Alexander Pike, Cold Spring KY 41076. **LC** D570.A15. **DD** 355.1150973. DAV Magazine.

DCAS MANAGEMENT SYNOPSIS. EXECUTIVE SUMMARY. (DCAS MANAGEMENT SYNOPSIS EXECUTIVE SUMMARY). **Main/Corp** United States. Defense Supply Agency. **VAT** Defense Contract Administration Services Management Synopsis. Executive Summary. 0148-3293. US. English. an. Plans and Analysis Division, DCAS-JT Defense Supply Agency, Cameron Station, Alexandria VA 22314. **LC** UC267. **DD** 355.62110973.

DCAS MANUFACTURING COST CONTROL DIGEST. See Manufacturing.

DEFENCE. **Main/Corp** Canada. Dept. of National Defence. **VFOAT** Defence. 1971-. 0383-4638. Periodical. CN. English (French). an. $1.20. Department of National Defence, National Defence Headquarters, Ottawa Ontario K1A 0K2 Canada. **LC** UA600. **DD** 355.30971.

DEFENCE. **VFOAT** Defence Digest. V. 1- July 1970-. 0142-6184. Periodical. UK. English. mo. $55.00. Whitton Press, 50 High Street, Eton Berks England. **Ind/Abst** Predicasts. **LC** UF500. **DD** 355.8205.

DEFENCE FORCE JOURNAL. No. 1- Nov./Dec. 1976-. 0314-1039. Periodical. AT. English. ir. Building I/Room 1-32, Russell Offices, Canberra Australian Capital Territory 2600 North Melbourne Australia. **Ind/Abst** Predicasts. **LC** U1. **DD** 355.00994. Army Journal.

DEFENCE JOURNAL. V. 1- Feb. 1975-. Periodical. PK. English. mo. 8.00. Defence Journal, 16 B Central Street/Defence House Society, 46 Karachi Pakistan. **Tel** (541911)544969. Ed Brigadier A R Siddiqi. **LC** UA11. **DD** 355.005. bk rev. adv acc. **Circ** 3,000. (ctrl). A mirror and digest of geostrategic affairs.

DEFENCE MATERIEL. GREAT BRITAIN. (DEFENCE MATERIEL). 0308-5198. Periodical. UK. English. bm. 14.00. Eldon Publications Ltd, 30 Fleet Street, London EC4Y 1AH England. **Tel**

Military Science

01-353-9098. Ed William Prince. **Ind/Abst** Predicasts. LC UC465.G7. **DD** 355.80941. bk rev. adv acc. **Circ** 6,500. (ctrl). Journal examining developments through the Britain defence industry. *Defence Materiel, Great Britain.*

DEFENCE REVIEW. **Main/Corp** New Zealand. English. ir. Government Printer, Private Bag, Wellington New Zealand. LC UA874.3. **DD** 355.0330931.

DEFENCE TECHNOLOGY. Vol. 1, Issue 1 (Feb./Mar. 1982)-. Periodical. English. bm. Graphic Arts Pub Co, Sishane Mesrutiyet Cad, Yemenici Sok No 4, Beyoglu/Istanbul Turkey. LC UF500. **DD** 355.8205.

DEFENSE. **Main/Corp** Canada. Dept. of National Defence. CN. French. an. $0.50. Information Canada. LC UA600. **DD** 354.7100895.

DEFENSE ACQUISITION CIRCULAR. **Main/Corp** United States. Dept. of Defense. Publication began with No. 76-15, June 1978. US. English. ir. Superintendent of Documents, US Government Printing Office, Washington DC 20402. *Defense Procurement Circular, 0364-6734.*

DEFENSE & FOREIGN AFFAIRS. **VFOAT** Defense and Foreign Affairs. Vol. 7, No. 10 (10/1979)-. 0277-4933. Periodical. US. English. mo. $70.00. Copley and Associates, Lisa Neher, Administrative and Circulation Manager, 2030 M Street NW, Washington DC 20036. Ed Gregory R Copley. **Ind/Abst** Predicasts, Nexis. LC UA10. **DD** 355.0305. *Defense & Foreign Affairs Digest, 0740-2724.*

DEFENSE & FOREIGN AFFAIRS HANDBOOK. See Political Science.

DEFENSE (ARLINGTON, VA.). (DEFENSE). Jan. 1980-. 0737-1217. Periodical. US. English. mo. Superintendent of Documents, US Government Printing Office, Washington DC 20402. **Ind/Abst** Index U.S. Gov. Period., Predicasts. LC UA23.A1. **DD** 355.005. *Command Policy, 0270-9015.*

DEFENSE (BOCA RATON, FLA.). (DEFENSE). **Series/Titl** Social Issues Resources Series. V. 1, Article 1-. 0273-2491. Periodical. US. English. an. Social Issues Resources Series Inc, PO Box 2507, Boca Raton FL 33432. Ed Elecor C Goldstein. LC UA10. **DD** 355.03.

DEFENSE BUSINESS. Began with issue for Jan. 10, 1977. 0364-9008. US. English. wk. $240.00. Government Business Worldwide Reports, PO Box 4875, Washington DC 20008. LC UF530. *International Defense Business, 0360-8417.*

THE DEFENSE COMMUNICATION STUDY. 1984-85-. 0741-3602. US. English. an. $23.50. Corporate Communication Studies Inc, PO Box 9538, Daytona Beach FL 32020. LC U1. **DD** 355.005.

DEFENSE CONTRACT AUDIT MANUAL. **Main/Corp** United States. Dept. of Defense. July 1977-. US. English. ir. US Department of Defense, Washington DC 20402.

DEFENSE DAILY. Periodical. US. English. da. $850.00. Space Publishing Inc, 1341 G Street NW, Washington DC 20005.

DEFENSE INDUSTRY REPORT. 1970. 0275-0724. Periodical. US. English. sm. Industry News Service Inc, PO Box 457, Wilton CT 06897. Tel (203)762-3206. Ed Martha M Byrnes. Covers current developments in U.S. military weapon systems under development and in the early stages of production.

DEFENSE INTEGRATED DATA SYSTEMS DIDS PROCEDURES MANUAL. VOL. 4, ITEM IDENTIFICATION. **VFOAT** DIDS Procedures Manual. US. English. Defense Logistics Agency, Defense Logistics Services, Center Federal Center, Battle Creek MI 49016.

DEFENSE INTERGRATED DATA SYSTEM DIDS PROCEDURES MANUAL.VOL. 8, DOCUMENT IDENTIFIER CODE INPUT/OUTPUT FORMATS (FIXED LENGTH). **VFOAT** Defense Integrated Data System DIDS Procedures Manual. US. English. Defense Logistics Agency, Defense Logistics Services Center Federal Center, Battle Creek MI 49016.

DEFENSE LATIN AMERICA. 0261-233X. Periodical. UK. English. bm. Whitton Press Ltd, Park House Park Street, Maidenhead Berkshire LS5 1QS England. Tel 0628-30313. Ed Gregor Ferguson. **Ind/Abst** Predicasts. LC UF535.L29. **DD** 355.82098. bk rev. adv acc. Defense equipment, tactics and strategy, politico-military affairs, defense economics, news and information.

DEFENSE MAGAZINE. Periodical. French. ir. $3.00. Interconair (Eurafrique) SA, 96 Avenue de Tervueren, 1040 Bruxelles Belgium. LC U2. **DD** 355.005. *Defense.*

DEFENSE MANAGEMENT JOURNAL. Publication began with V. 3, No. 4, Fall 1967. 0011-7595. Periodical. US. English. qt. Superintendent of Documents, US Government Printing Office, Washington DC 20402. **Ind/Abst** Predicasts, Int. Aerosp. Abstr., Index U.S. Gov. Period., Public Aff. Inf. Serv. Bull., ABI/Inform. LC UC20. **DD** 353.605. **CODEN** DMJOB3. *Cost Reduction Journal, Defense Industry Bulletin, 0418-5021.*

DEFENSE MARKETS & TECHNOLOGY. **VFOAT** Defense Markets and Technology, D.M. & T., DM & T. Vol. 1, No. 1-3 (Jan/Mar. 1983)-. 0738-0461. US. English. mo. $750.00. Predicasts, 11001 Cedar Avenue, Cleveland OH 44106. LC UF530. **DD** 355.8205. (cum index).

THE DEFENSE MONITOR. V. 1- May 1972-. 0195-6450. Periodical. US. English. mo. $25.00. Center for Defense Information, 303 Capital Gallery West, 600 Maryland Avenue SW, Washington DC 20024. Tel (202)484-9490. LC UA23.A1. **DD** 355.033073. bk rev. **Circ** 80,000. Each issue focuses on one of the less-publicized, yet noteworthy aspects of the current status of the US military, with emphasis on nuclear programs and military spending.

DEFENSE NATIONALE. 29.- Yearly Vol. 0336-1489. Periodical. FR. French. ir. 295 Domestic, 396 Foreign. Defense Nationale, 1 Place Joffre, 75007 Paris France. Tel 15 (1) 45 55 92. **Ind/Abst** Am. Hist. Life, Hist. Abstr., Part A, Mod. Hist. Abstr., Hist. Abstr., Part B, Twent. Century Abstr., Predicasts, Foreign Lang. Index, Energy Res. Abstr., Funk Scott Index Corp. Ind., Hist. Abstr., PAIS Foreign Lang. Index. LC D410. bk rev. adv acc. **Circ** 8,000. (ctrl). *Revue de Defense Nationale.*

DEFENSE NEWS. 0884-139X. Periodical. US. English. wk. $50.00. Army Times Publishing Company, 6883 Commercial Drive, Springfield VA 22159.

DEFENSE PROCUREMENT BUDGET. **Main/Corp** Defense Marketing Services, Inc. 0160-5135. US. English. an. $100.00. DMS Inc, 100 Northfield Street, PO Box 4585, Greenwich CT 06830. Tel (203)661-7800. Ed F Dahm. LC UA23.A1. **DD** 355.62120973. **Circ** 5,000. Line item breakdown of the Department of Defense procurement budget.

DEFENSE R & D UPDATE. SPACE, AERONAUTICS & ELECTRONIC SYSTEMS. **VFOAT** Defense R and D Update. **VAT** Defense Research and Development Update. Space, Aeronautics, and Electronic Systems. Vol. 3, No. 4 (Apr. 1982)-. 0731-8030. Periodical. US. English. mo. Industry News Service Inc, PO Box 457, Wilton CT 06897. Tel (203)762-3206. Ed Martha M Byrnes. (cum index). Provides timely marketing information about military space, aeronautical and electronic systems in the early stages of development. *Defense R & D Update. Space & Aeronautics, 0272-0442; Defense R & D Update. Electronic Systems, 0272-0450.*

DEFENSE RDT&E BUDGET. **Main/Corp** Defense Marketing Services, Inc. **VAT** Defense Research, Development, Test and Evaluation Budget. 0149-9947. US. English. an. $100.00. DMS Inc, 100 Northfield Street, PO Box 4585, Greenwich CT 06830. Tel (203)661-7800. Ed F Dahm. LC U393.5. **DD** 355.070973. **Circ** 5,000. Line item breakdown of The Department of Defense Research, development, test and evaluation budget.

DEFENSE SCIENCE. **VFOAT** Defense Science 2000+ Plus. Vol. 1, No. 1 (May/June 1982). 0744-9704. Periodical. US. English. bm. Rush Franklin Publications Inc, 300 Orchard City Drive/Suite 134, Campbell CA 95008. Tel (408)370-3509. Ed Samuel J Greenberg. **Ind/Abst** Predicasts. adv acc. **Circ** 13,818. (ctrl). Addresses military systems development, strategic and tactical policies and posture, technology policy, alliances and treaties, aerospace 2002+, science and technology.

DEFENSE SCIENCE & ELECTRONICS. **VFOAT** Defence Science and Electronics. 1982. 0744-6241. Periodical. US. English. bm. $60.00. Rush Franklin Publ Inc, 300 Orchard City Drive/Suite 234, Campbell CA 95008. Tel (408)370-3509. Ed Jim Martin. **Ind/Abst** Predicasts. bk rev. adv acc. **Circ** 18,000. (ctrl). Aimed at engineering and management within DOD and the defense industry, and covers key technology and policy issues.

DEFENSE SCIENCE JOURNAL. 1- 1951-. 0011-748X. II. English. qt. $20.00. Director of Research and Development Organisation, Defence Scientific Information and Documentation Centre (DESIDOC), Metcalfe House, New Delhi-110054 India. **Ind/Abst** Eng. Index Annu., Eng. Index Mon., Eng. Index Bioeng. Abstr., Eng. Index Energy Abstr., Int. Aerosp. Abstr., Comput. Control Abstr., Electr. Electron. Abstr., Sci. Abstr. Sect. A. Phys. Abstr., Chem. Abstr., Math. Rev., Phys. Abstr., Eng. Index, Saf. Sci. Abstr. J., ISMEC Bull., Pollut. Abstr. Indexes. LC U395.I5. **CODEN** DSJOAA.

DEFENSE STANDARDIZATION AND SPECIFICATION PROGRAM, POLICIES, PROCEDURES, AND INSTRUCTIONS. **Main/Corp** United States. Office of the Under Secretary of Defense for Research and Engineering. **VFOAT** Defense Standardization Manual. 1978-. US. English. ir. Superintendent of Documents, Government Printing Office, Washington DC 20402. Tel (202)783-3238. *Standarization, Policies, Procedures and Instructions.*

DEFENSE SYSTEMS MANAGEMENT REVIEW CEASED. V. 1-3, No. 3. 0363-7727. Periodical. US. English. qt. National Technical Information Service, 5285 Port Royal Road, Springfield VA 22151. LC UF533. **DD** 355.820973. Available in microfiche.

DEFENSE TRANSPORTATION JOURNAL. See Transportation.

DEFENSE WEEK. 0273-3188. Periodical. US. English. wk. $1372.70. Llewellyn King Publications, 915-15th Street NW/Suite 400, Washington DC 20005. Tel (202)638-7430. Ed Jack Cushman. bk rev. **Circ** 1,500. A newsletter covering defense policy, strategic affairs, domestic and international. Includes coverage of industry, Congress, DOD, White House weapons development and acquisition.

DEFESA LATINA. Yearly V. 1, No. 11-. Periodical. Portuguese (Spanish). ir. $3500. Editora Aero Ltda, Av Joao Pedro Cardoso 225 Salas 3 E 5, Sao Paulo CEP 04355 Brazil. LC UA602.3. **DD** 355.0098. *Brasil Defesa.*

DELTION. **Main/Corp** Greece. Stratos. Geographike Hyperesia. Year 1- (No. 1-). Periodical. Greek and Modern. sa. LC UG470.

DEPARTMENT OF DEFENSE, 1947—... FACT BOOK. **VFOAT** Department of Defense Fact Book. US. English. an. US Organization Chart Service, PO Box 1335, La Jolla CA 92038. Tel (714)454-3711.

DEPARTMENT OF DEFENSE ATLAS/STATE DATA ABSTRACT FOR THE UNITED STATES. See Indexes/Abstracts.

DEPARTMENT OF DEFENSE ESTIMATED EXPENDITURES FOR STATES AND SELECTED AREAS. **Main/Corp** United States. Dept. of Defense. **VFOAT** Estimated Expenditures for States and Selected Areas. 0743-4480. US. English. an. Director, Washington Headquarters, Services Room 3E843/The Pentagon, Washington DC 20301. LC UA23. **DD** 355.6220973.

THE DEPARTMENT OF DEFENSE PROGRAM FOR RESEARCH, DEVELOPMENT AND ACQUISITION. (THE FY . . . DEPARTMENT OF DEFENSE PROGRAM FOR RESEARCH, DEVELOPMENT, AND ACQUISITION). **Main/Corp** United States. Office of the Under Secretary of Defense for Research and Engineering. **VFOAT** Fiscal Year . . . Department of Defense Program for Research, Development, and Acquisition. 0732-8451. US. English. Department of Defense, Office Assistant Secretary of Defense, Washington DC 20301. LC U393. **DD** 355.070973.

DEPARTMENT OF THE ARMY HISTORICAL SUMMARY. **Main/Corp** Center of Military History. **VFOAT** Historical Summary. Began with 1968/69. 0092-7880. US. English. an. US Department of the Army, The Pentagon, Washington DC 20310. LC UA23.A1. **DD** 353.62.

DESENVOLVIMENTO DO ORCAMENTO DA DESPESA FIXADA PARA O ANO ECONOMICO. **Main/Corp** Portugal. Ministerio do Exercito. PO. Portuguese. ir. Impr Nationale, Av Antonie Jose de al Eida, 1078 Lisboa Codex Portugal. LC UA762. **DD** 354.469066.

Military Science

DETAILED LISTING OF REAL PROPERTY OWNED BY THE UNITED STATES AND USED BY THE DEPARTMENT OF DEFENSE FOR MILITARY FUNCTIONS THROUGHOUT THE WORLD AS OF SEPTEMBER 30 .... US. English. an. General Services Administration, Washington DC 20405. LC UC403. DD 355.702573.

DFSC FUEL LINE. See Energy.

DHARMASENA. Dec. 1973-. Periodical. Indonesian. ir. Pusat Penerangan Hankam, Jln Merdeka Barat 13 - 14, Jakarta Indonesia. LC UA853.I5.

DICTIONARY OF THE DEFENSE INDUSTRY. VFOAT Directory of Aerospace and Military and Technology Abbreviations and Definitions. 1981-. 0734-1008. US. English. an. $175.00. US Organization Chart Service, PO Box 1335, La Jolla CA 92038. Tel (619)454-3711. LC U26. DD 355.00148. Exhaustive listing of virtually every abbreviation and definition used within the US and world defense, military, and technology industry, updated. *Directory of Aerospace and Military and Technology Abbreviations.*

DIGEST OF OPINIONS, THE JUDGE ADVOCATES GENERAL OF THE ARMED FORCES. V. 1- July 1, 1951-. Periodical. US. English.

THE DIRECTORY OF DEFENSE ELECTRONIC PRODUCTS AND SERVICES : UNITED STATES SUPPLIERS. See Yearbooks, Almanacs, Directories.

DIRECTORY OF SCHOOLS AND ESTABLISHMENTS APPROVED FOR VETERANS TRAINING. See Yearbooks, Almanacs, Directories.

DIRECTORY OF U.S.S.R. MINISTRY OF DEFENSE AND ARMED FORCES OFFICIALS. See Yearbooks, Almanacs, Directories.

DISARMAMENT TIMES. No. 1- Mar. 1, 1978. Periodical. US. English. ir. $10.00. Disarmament Information Bureau, 801 United Nations Plaza, New York NY 10017.

DISCOVERY. (DISCOVERY : FACULTY PUBLICATIONS AND PRESENTATIONS ... BY MEMBERS OF THE FACULTY, UNITED STATES AIR FORCE ACADEMY). Main/Corp United States Air Force Academy. 8755-7363. US. English. an. United States Air Force Academy, Colorado Springs CO 80840. LC UG638.5.F7. DD 358.40071173.

EL DJEICH; REVUE DE L'ARMEE NATIONALE POPULAIRE. VFOAT Revue de l'Armee Nationale Populaire. No. 1-. 0419-4799. Periodical. French. mo. $11.75. El Djeich, 3 Chemin de Gascogne, Algiers Algeria.

DM & S ADP PLAN. See Medicine.

D.M.A.A.C. TECHNICAL TRANSLATIONS LIST. (DMAAC TECHNICAL TRANSLATIONS LIST). Main/Corp Defense Mapping Agency. Aerospace Center. Technical Translation Branch. 0095-0742. US. English. Defense Mapping Agency, Areospace Center, St Louis MO 63118. LC Z6000. DD 016.526.

D.O.D. DIRECTORY OF CONTRACT ADMINISTRATION SERVICES COMPONENTS. See Yearbooks, Almanacs, Directories.

DOD STATISTICAL REPORT ON THE MILITARY RETIREMENT SYSTEM / OFFICE OF ACTUARY, DEFENSE MANPOWER DATA CENTER. See Statistics.

DOMESTIC BASE FACTORS REPORT. Main/Corp United States. Office of the Assistant Secretary of Defense (Manpower, Reserve Affairs, and Logistics). VFOAT Report on Domestic Base Factors. 0192-1150. US. English. an. Off of the Assistant Secretary of Defense Manpower Reserve Affairs & Logistics, Washington DC 20037. LC UA26. DD 355.70973.

DRAFT FACTS FOR GRADUATES AND GRADUATE STUDENTS. Main/Corp Scientific Manpower Commission. 0420-0942. US. English. $1.00. Scientific Manpower Commission, 2101 Constitution Avenue NW, Washington DC 20418. LC UB343. DD 355.2230973.

DRIS CATALOG OF SUPPORT SERVICES. VFOAT Catalog of Support Services. VAT Defense Retail Interservice Support Catalog of Support Services. 0883-0606. US. English. an. Defense Logistics Services Center, Federal Center, Battle Creek MI 49016. LC UC263. DD 355.6210973.

DWJ, DEUTSCHES WAFFEN-JOURNAL. VFOAT Deutsches Waffen-Journal. Periodical. German. ir. 43.00. Journal-Verlag Schwend, 717 Schwabisch Hall, Postfach 340, Schwabisch Hall West Germany. LC TS532.

EAST EUROPE REPORT. POLITICAL, SOCIOLOGICAL, AND MILITARY AFFAIRS. See Political Science.

EAWARUDO. VFOAT Air World. Periodical. JA. Japanese. mo. 835 Single issue. Kabushiki Kaisha Eawarudo, c/o Azabu Kuresuto Bldg, 8F 12-8 Roppongi 4 Minato-ku, Tokyo-to 106 Japan. LC UG622.

ELECTRONIC WARFARE (INTERAVIA DATA (FIRM)). See Engineering - Electricity, Electrical Engineering, Electronics.

EMPLOYMENT OF DISABLED AND VIETNAM ERA VETERANS IN THE FEDERAL GOVERNMENT. Main/Corp United States. Civil Service Commission. Jan./June 1975-. 0362-5788. Periodical. US. English. sa. $1.60. Civil Service Commission, 1900 East Street Room 5-F10, Washington DC 20415. LC UB357. DD 353.0013243.

ENGINEER (FORT BELVOIR, VA.). See Engineering.

ENGINEERING & SERVICES : AIR FORCE ENGINEERING AND SERVICES QUARTERLY. Vol. 21, No. 2 (May 1980)-. US. English. qt. US Government Printing Office, Superintendent of Documents, Washington DC 20402. Tel (202)783-3238. Ind/Abst Index U.S. Gov. Period. *Air Force Engineering & Services Quarterly, 0362-188X.*

ENLISTED TIMES. 0195-5349. Periodical. US. English. mo. $12.00. Military Studies Center, 2180 Bryant Street, San Francisco CA 94110.

ENSIGN (CORNWALLIS, N.S.). (ENSIGN). VFOAT Cornwallis Ensign. VAT Cornwallis Ensign (1983). Vol. 26, No. 34 (Aug. 29, 1983)-. 0822-9392. Periodical. CN. English. wk. Ensign, PO Box 280, Cornwallis Nova Scotia B0S 1H0 Canada. DD 355.10971633. *Cornwallis Ensign, 0822-9384.*

ESTIMATES. PART III, NATIONAL DEFENCE (CANADA). VFOAT Budget des Depenses. CN. English (in French). $9.00 Domestic, $10.80 Foreign. Canadian Government Publishing Centre, Supply and Services Canada, Ottawa Ontario K1A 0S9 Canada. LC UA600. DD 355.6220971.

ESTIMATES. PART III, VETERANS AFFAIRS CANADA. VFOAT Budget des Depenses. CN. English (in French). $12.00 Domestic, $14.40 Foreign. Canadian Government Publishing Centre, Supply and Services Canada, Ottawa Ontario K1A 0S9 Canada. LC UB359.C2. DD 354.7100812.

EXCHANGE & COMMISSARY NEWS. VAT Exchange and Commissary News. 0014-4452. Periodical. US. English. mo. $35.00. Executive Business Media, PO Box 1500, Westbury NY 11590. Tel (516)334-3030.

FEDERAL MEDICAL CENTERS, HOSPITALS, AND MEDICAL CLINICS WITH REPORTED MORBIDITY DATA. See Medicine - Medical Centers, Hospitals.

FEDERAL SUPPLY CLASSIFICATION LISTING OF DOD STANDARDIZATION DOCUMENTS. Main/Corp United States. Dept. of Defense. July 1963-. 0565-2669. US. English. ir. Superintendent of Documents, SSO GPO, Washington DC 20402. Tel (202)783-3238. LC UC263.

FIELD ARTILLERY JOURNAL. 0191-975X. Periodical. US. English. bm. $16.00. US Field Artillery Association, PO Box 33027, Fort Sill OK 73503. Tel (405)355-4677. Ed Roger A Rains. Ind/Abst Predicasts, Funk Scott Index Corp. Ind. LC UF1. DD 358.1205. Circ 13,000. (ctrl). Professional field artillery information, current and historical, forum for the professional artilleryman, both enlisted and officers. *Army.*

FINANCIAL PLANNING GUIDE FOR MILITARY PERSONNEL. 0146-7328. US. English. $1.95. AFTAC Enterprise, 4902 La Barranca, San Antonio TX 78223. LC U113. DD 332.024.

FINANCIAL REPORT - TEXAS. ADJUTANT-GENERAL'S DEPT. Main/Corp Texas. Adjutant-General's Dept. US. English. an. Adjutant General's Department, PO Box 5218, Austin TX 78763. LC UA43.T4. DD 353.9764007231.

FLYING SAFETY (WASHINGTON, D.C. : 1981). (FLYING SAFETY). Series/Titl Air Force Recurring Publication. Vol. 37, No. 1 (Jan. 1981)-. 0279-9308. Periodical. US. English. mo. Superintendent of Documents, US Government Printing Office, Washington DC 20402. Tel (202)783-3238. Ind/Abst Index U.S. Gov. Period. LC UG633. DD 358.400973. *Aerospace Safety, 0001-9429.*

FOR THE DEFENSE (MILWAUKEE, WIS.). (FOR THE DEFENSE). VFOAT F.T.D., FTD. Vol. 1, No. 1 (Mar. 1960)-. 0015-6884. Periodical. US. English. mo. Defense Research Institute Inc, 750 North Lake Shore Drive, Chicago IL 60611. LC KF8911.A3. DD 347.737, 347.3077. (cum index).

FORCES ARMEES FRANCAISES. No. 1- June 1972-. Periodical. FR. French. mo. Comite d'Etudes Aeronautiques Militaires, 5 Place Joffre, Paris VIIE France. LC U2. DD 355.00944. *Armee, Forces Aeriennes Francaises; Revue Maritime.*

LES FORCES ARMEES RWANDAISES. Periodical. RW. French (Kinyarwanda). bm. Ministere de la Defense, Nationale Service de Documentation, B P 23, Kigali Rwanda. LC UA869.R95. DD 355.00967571. *Forces de Securite au Service de la Nation.*

FOREIGN MILITARY SALES, FOREIGN MILITARY CONSTRUCTION SALES AND MILITARY ASSISTANCE FACTS. (FOREIGN MILITARY SALES, FOREIGN MILITARY CONSTRUCTION SALES AND MILITARY ASSISTANCE FACTS AS OF . . .). Sept. 1981-. 8756-5536. US. English. an. LC UA12. DD 355.0320973. *Foreign Military Sales and Military Assistance Facts, 0362-577X.*

FORSVAR. No. 1-. Periodical. DK. Danish. ir. 35.00. Skindergade 26, 1159 Kbenhavn K Denmark. LC UA690.

FORT. 1-. 0261-586X. Periodical. UK. English. an. Ind/Abst Archit. Period. Index, Avery Index Archit. Period., Repert. Int. Litt. Art.

FRONTIER MILITARY SERIES. See History (General) - History of North, South, and Central America.

FUERZA AEREA DE CHILE. Main/Corp Chile. Fuerza Aerea. VFOAT Revista de la Fuerza Aerea de Chile. CL. Spanish. ir. $15.00. Ministerio de Defensa Nacional, Plaza Bulnes, Santiago Chile. LC UG622. *Revista de la Fuerza Aerea.*

FUERZA AEREA (SANTIAGO, CHILE). (FUERZA AEREA). VFOAT Revista de la Fuerza Aerea de Chile. Periodical. CL. Spanish. ir. Revista de la Fuerza Aerea de Chile, Galvez 390 Depto A, Santiago Chile. LC UG635.C5. DD 358.400983. *Fuerza Aerea de Chile.*

FUERZAS ARMADAS. 1- 1965-. 0016-2485. Periodical. CK. Spanish. ir. Oficina de Relaciones Publicas, Ministerio de Guerra, Bagota Columbia. DD 359.

FUERZAS ARMADAS DE VENEZUELA (VENEZUELA. MINISTERIO DE LA DEFENSA : 1971). (FUERZAS ARMADAS DE VENEZUELA : ORGANO DEL MINISTERIO DE LA DEFENSA). No. 251, (1971)-. Periodical. VE. Spanish. ir. Ministerio de la Defensa, El Ministerio, Caracas Venezuela. DD 355. *Revista de la Fuerzas Armadas de Venezuela.*

FUSILIER. V. 1- Autumn 1973-. 0092-5322. Periodical. US. English. qt. $4.50. Baron Publishing Company, PO Box 293, LaPuente CA 91747. LC U790. DD 355.0075.

FY . . . US AIR FORCE PLAN FOR DEFENSE RESEARCH SCIENCES. VFOAT F.Y. . . . U.S. Air Force Plan for Defense Research Sciences. VAT Fiscal Year . . . United States Air Force Plan for Defense Research Sciences. 8756-5064. US. English. Air Force Office of Scientific Research, Bolling Air Force Base, Washington DC 20332. LC UG643. DD 358.4070973.

GAZETTE - CANADIAN FORCES BASE GAGETOWN. (GAZETTE). VFOAT Base Gagetown Gazette. VAT Base Gagetown Gazette (1981), Gagetown Gazette (1981). Vol. 21, No. 36 (Sept. 23, 1981)-. 0713-391X. Periodical. CN. English (includes some text in French). wk. Free. Gagetown Gazette, Building H-10/Room 114, CFB

Military Science

Gagetown, Oromocto New Brunswick E0G 2P0 Canada. **DD** 355.10971543. (ctrl). *Base Gagetown Gazette (1980),* 0712-919X.

GEKKAN ASAGUMO. VFOAT Asagumo. JA. Japanese. ir. 3300. Asagumo Shimbun Sha, c/o Korin Kaikan 3-6-23 Shiba Koen Minato-Ku, Tokyo 105 Japan. **LC** UA847.

GEOGRAPHIC DISTRIBUTION OF VA EXPENDITURES. VFOAT Geographic Distribution of V.A. Expenditures. VAT Geographic Distribution of Veterans Administration Expenditures. 0741-0611. US. English. Veterans Administration, Office of Reports and Statistics, Washington DC 20420. **LC** UB357. **DD** 353.00812.

GIORNALE DI MEDICINA MILITARE. See Medicine.

GLADIUS. V. 1- 1961-. 0436-029X. English, French or Spanish. ir. **LC** U800.A1.

GLEEN GOODMAN'S DEFENSE R&D WEEKLY. (GLENN GOODMAN'S DEFENSE R & D WEEKLY). VFOAT Glenn Goodman's Defense R and D Weekly. VAT Glenn Goodman's Defense Research and Development Weekly. 21 Nov. 1984-. 8756-0496. Periodical. US. English. wk. $225.00. Defense R & D Weekly, PO Box 12585, Arlington VA 22209. **Tel** (703)841-8924. Ed Glenn W Goodman Jr. **DD** 358. Circ 1,000. Newsletter providing information on military weapon system development programs, with easy to read short news summaries and an in-depth feature article on selected programs.

GLOBAL AUTOVON AUTOMATIC VOICE NETWORK, DEFENSE COMMUNICATIONS SYSTEM DIRECTORY. See Yearbooks, Almanacs, Directories.

GORGET ET SASH : JOURNAL OF THE EARLY MODERN WARFARE SOCIETY. See History (General).

GOVERNMENT LIFE INSURANCE PROGRAMS FOR VETERANS AND MEMBERS OF THE SERVICES, ANNUAL REPORT. See Insurance.

GUATEMALA (GUATEMALA, GUATEMALA : 1975). (GUATEMALA : REVISTA CULTURAL DEL EJERCITO). VFOAT Revista Cultural del Ejercito. Yearly V. 1, V. 1, June 30, 1975)-. Periodical. GT. Spanish. sa. Edificio del Instituto de Prevision Militar, 5A Avenida y Sexta Calle de la Zona 1 Ciudad de Guatemala, Guatemala.

GUIDE TO THE EVALUATION OF EDUCATIONAL EXPERIENCES IN THE ARMED SERVICES. See Education (General).

GULF WINGS. May 27, 1970-. 0319-2776. Periodical. CN. English. ir. 7.00. C F B Sumerside, 318 Water Street, Summerside Prince Edward Island Canada. **Tel** (902)436-2281. Ed J Clarkston. **DD** 355.1097171. bk rev. adv acc. **Circ** 2,000. (ctrl).

GUNG-HO (DERBY, CONN.). (GUNG-HO). VAT Gung Ho. 0279-4268. Periodical. US. English. mo. $30.00. Charlton Publications Inc, Charlton Building, Derby CT 06418. **Tel** (203)735-3381. **LC** U1. **DD** 355.005.

HANDLINGAR OCH TIDSKRIFT. Main/Corp Krigsvetenskapsakademien, Stockholm. SW. Swedish. bm. $6.66. Kungliga Krigsvetenskapsakademiens, Handlingar Och Tidskrift 5-100 45, Stockholm 90 Sweden. **LC** U4.

HANDLOADER'S DIGEST. See Recreation, Leisure - Sports.

HEALTH MANPOWER STATISTICS. See Statistics.

HERACLES. 0248-1642. Periodical. English. bm. $69.18. Publi Pyrenees, 127 rue de la Faisanderie, 75116 Paris France. **Tel** 1 504 18 24. **LC** UF500. **DD** 355.8205.

HERACLES. (HIRAQL). Periodical. Arabic. bm. **LC** UF500.

HISTORICAL REVIEW. Main/Corp U.S. Army Mobility Equipment Research & Development Command. 0739-8883. US. English. US Army Mobility Equipment, Research & Development, Command Belvoir VA 22060 22060. **LC** UC273. **DD** 355.830973.

HISTORY; ANNUAL SUPPLEMENT. Main/Corp United States Army Infantry Center. 0091-2271. US. English. an. United States Army Infantry Center, Ft Benning GA 31905. **LC** UA28. **DD** 356.10710758476.

HOGUK. Periodical. KO. Korean. mo. Kukkun Hongbo Kwalliso San, 2 Yongsan-dong Yongsan-ku, Seoul Korea. **LC** UA853.K6.

HSING HUO LIAO YUAN (SELECTIONS). (HSING HUO LIAO YUAN). Hsuan Pien Chih 1-. Periodical. CH. Chinese. sa. 2.10. Hsin Hua Shu Tien, Pei-Ching Fa Hsing So Peking China. **LC** UA837. **DD** 951.04.

IDSA JOURNAL. Main/Corp Institute for Defence Studies and Analyses. VFOAT Journal. V. 10- July/Sept. 1977-. Periodical. II. English. qt. $6.60. Institute of Defence Studies and Analyses, Sapru House/Barakhambra Road, New Delhi 110 001 India. **Tel** 387951. (cum index). *Journal.*

IFR— SUPPLEMENT, UNITED STATES. VFOAT DOD Flight Information Publication (Enroute). VAT Instrument Flight Rules Supplement, United States. Periodical. US. English. bm. Defense Mapping Agency, Aerospace Center, St Louis Air Force Station MO 63118.

IMPACT (UNITED STATES CIVIL DEFENSE COUNCIL). (IMPACT). Vol. 1, No. 1 (Fall 1982)-. 0740-3445. Periodical. US. English. qt. $12.00. United States Civil Defense Council, Box 6457, Great Falls MT 59406. **LC** UA927. **DD** 363.350973.

IMPLEMENTATION OF THE POST-VIETNAM ERA VETERANS' EDUCATIONAL ASSISTANCE ACT OF 1977. (IMPLEMENTATION OF THE POST-VIETNAM ERA VETERANS' EDUCATIONAL ASSISTANCE ACT OF 1977: AN ANNUAL JOINT REPORT PREPARED BY THE VETERANS ADMINISTRATION AND THE DEPARTMENT OF DEFENSE. . . SUBMITTED TO THE COMMITTEE ON VETERANS AFFAIRS, UNITED STATES SENATE). 0738-1166. US. English. an. **LC** UB357. **DD** 355.71520973.

INCOME TAX GUIDE FOR MILITARY PERSONNEL. 0098-1729. US. English. $1.95. AFTAC Enterprises, 4902 La Barranca, San Antonio TX 78233. **LC** KF6369.8.A67. **DD** 343.73052.

INDEX OF AIR FORCE-NAVY AERONAUTICAL DESIGN (AND) AND MILITARY (MS) STANDARDS. See Indexes/Abstracts.

INDEX OF BLANK FORMS. See Indexes/Abstracts.

INDEX OF SOVIET AND CHINESE MILITARY AFFAIRS IN ANNUAL US DEFENSE DEPARTMENT REPORTS. See Indexes/Abstracts.

INDEX OF STORAGE AND OUTLOADING DRAWINGS FOR AMMUNITION COMMODITIES. See Indexes/Abstracts.

INDIANA MILITARY HISTORY JOURNAL. See History (General) - History of North, South, and Central America.

INFANTRY. 1921. 0019-9532. Periodical. US. English. bm. $10.00. US Army Infantry School, Business Office/Box 2005, Ft Benning GA 31905-0605. **Tel** (404)545-2350. Ed Albert N Garland. **Ind/Abst** Index U.S. Gov. Period., Predicasts, Funk Scott Index Corp. Ind. bk rev. **Circ** 19,860. (ctrl). Current information on infantry organization, weapons, equipment, tactics and techniques. Serves as a forum for professional ideas. *Infantry School Quarterly.*

INFORMATIONSSCHRIFT - SOZIALWISSENSCHAFTLICHES INSTITUT DER BUNDESWEHR. Main/Corp Sozialwissenschaftliches Institut der Bundeswehr. **Series/Titl** Schriftenreihe Innererfuhrung: Reihe Aushildung und Bildung. 1-. German. ir. **LC** UA710.

INSCOM JOURNAL. VAT Intelligence and Security Command Journal. Publication began with V. 3, No. 2, Apr. 1980. 0270-8906. Periodical. US. English. mo. Editor The Journal, US Army Intelligence and Security Command, c/o IAPA, Arlington Hall Station VA 22212. **LC** UB251.U5. **DD** 355.34320973. *Journal of the U.S. Army Intelligence & Security Command,* 0194-9527.

INSTRUCTION AND CODE TABLE BOOKLET. Main/Corp United States. Veterans Administration. Health Professional Scholarship Program. US. English. ir. Publications Secret Order Department, PO Box 1015, North Highlands CA 95660. **Tel** (916)924-4800.

INTERNATIONAL ARMAMENTS MONTHLY. No. 1- Oct. 1972-. 0090-4813. Periodical. US. English. mo. $20.00. International Armaments Press, PO Box 40, Kailua HI 96734. **LC** UF520. **DD** 355.8205.

THE INTERNATIONAL COUNTERMEASURES HANDBOOK. 1st- Ed. 0145-2584. US. English. an. $42.50. E W Communications, 1170 East Meadow Drive, Palo Alto CA 94303. **Tel** (415)494-2800. **LC** UG485. **DD** 623.37. adv acc. **Circ** 8,000.

INTERNATIONAL DEFENSE BUSINESS. DEFENSE SURVEY. (INTERNATIONAL DEFENSE BUSINESS : DEFENSE SURVEY). No. 419- Jan. 1974-. 0161-0813. Periodical. US. English. wk. IMD/International, PO Box 4875, Washington DC 20008. **LC** UF530. **DD** 355.005. *International Defense Business. Survey,* 0160-9777.

INTERNATIONAL DEFENSE BUSINESS DEFENSE SURVEY. LOCATOR. (INTERNATIONAL DEFENSE BUSINESS DEFENCE SURVEY : LOCATOR). 0160-9785. Periodical. US. English. wk. IMD/International, PO Box 4875, Washington DC 20008. *International Defense Business : Locator.*

INTERNATIONAL DEFENSE BUSINESS. REPORT. (INTERNATIONAL DEFENSE BUSINESS : REPORT). 0161-0805. Periodical. US. English. wk. IMD/International, PO Box 4875, Washington DC 20008. **LC** UF530. **DD** 338.47355.

INTERNATIONAL DEFENSE BUSINESS. SUMMARY. (INTERNATIONAL DEFENSE BUSINESS : SUMMARY). 0161-0791. Periodical. US. English. mo. IMD/International, PO Box 4875, Washington DC 20008.

INTERNATIONAL DEFENSE REVIEW. V. 1- 1968-. 0020-6512. Periodical. SZ. English. mo. $204.00. Interavia, Avenue Louis-Casai 86, CH-1216 Geneva Switzerland. **Ind/Abst** Predicasts, Excerpta Med., Funk Scott Index Corp. Ind. **LC** U1.

INTERNATIONAL DEFENSE REVIEW. SPECIAL SERIES. VFOAT Special Series International Defense Review. Began in 1976. Periodical. English. ir. Interavia, Avenue Louis-Casai 86, CH-1216 Geneva Switzerland.

INTERSERVICE JOURNAL OF MILITARY & POLICE SCIENCE AND THE INTELLIGENCE PROFESSION. (THE INTERSERVICE JOURNAL OF MILITARY & POLICE SCIENCE AND THE INTELLIGENCE PROFESSION). VFOAT Interservice Journal of Military and Police Science and the Intelligence Profession. Vol. 1, No. 1 (Jan. 1982)-. 0734-3264. Periodical. US. English. qt. $34.95. Interservice Publishing Company, PO Box 5437, San Francisco CA 94101. **Tel** (415)221-9258. **LC** UB250. **DD** 355.34305.

IS. INTER SERVICE. See Business - Marketing.

ISKRA. No. 1- 1971-. Macedonian. ir. **LC** U4.

ISLAMIC DEFENCE REVIEW. Periodical. UK. English. qt. 10.00 Airmail. The Islamic Institute of Defence Technology, 16 Grosvenor Crescent, London SW1 England. **Ind/Abst** Predicasts. **LC** UA830. **DD** 355.033017671.

ISSUP STRATEGIC REVIEW. VFOAT I.S.S.U.P. Strategic Review, ISSUP Strategiese Oorsig. 0250-1961. Periodical. Afrikaans (English). ir. $20.00. Institute for Strategic Studies, University of Pretoria, Pretoria 0002 South Africa. **Tel** (012)4202693. **LC** UA10.5. **DD** 355.0305. **Circ** 2,000. (ctrl).

ISTRATIJYA. VFOAT Strategia. Periodical. Arabic. mo. $200.00. Al-Richeh Shams Building, PO Box 14-5158, Beirut Lebanon. **LC** UF530.

JAHRBUCH DER WEHRTECHNIK. See Yearbooks, Almanacs, Directories.

JAHRBUCH DES HEERES. See Yearbooks, Almanacs, Directories.

JANE'S ARMOUR AND ARTILLERY. Began with issue for 1979/80. 0143-9952. UK. English. an. $125.00. Janes Publishing Inc, 135 West 50th Street/50th Floor, New York NY 10020. **Tel** (212)586-7745. Ed Christopher F Foss. **LC** UG446.5. **DD** 358.1805. adv acc. Reference guide to armoured fighting vehicles and crewed guns in current service and production worldwide, including development, specifications, and deployment.

Military Science

JANE'S DEFENCE REVIEW. Began in 1980. 0144-0470. Periodical. UK. English. bm. $50.00 US. Jane's Publishers Company Ltd, 238 City Road, London EC1V 2PU England. Ind/Abst Predicasts, Ship Abstr. LC UF500. DD 355.8205.

JANE'S DEFENCE WEEKLY. VFOAT Defence Weekly. Vol. 1, No. 1 (14 Jan. 1984)-. 0265-3818. Periodical. UK. English. wk. $65.00. Janes Publishing Company, 286 Congress Street, Boston MA 02210. Tel (212)586-7745. Ed Derek Wood. Ind/Abst Predicasts. LC UF530. DD 355.8205. adv acc. (ctrl). Magazine covering world-wide defense and military developments and world affairs.

JANE'S INFANTRY WEAPONS. VFOAT Infantry Weapons. Began in 1975. US. English. an. $125.00. Janes Publishing Inc, 135 West 50th Street/12th Floor, New York NY 10020. Tel (212)586-7745. Ed Ian V Hogg. LC UD380. DD 623.4. adv acc. Reference guide to all portable weapons used worldwide. Includes weapon's development, operation, specifications and deployment.

JANE'S MILITARY COMMUNICATIONS. Began with 1st Ed. (1979-80) issue. 0144-0004. UK. English. an. $125.00. Janes Publications Inc, 135 West 50th Street/12th Floor, New York NY 10020. Tel (212)586-7745. Ed R J Raggett. LC UG590. DD 355.85. adv acc. Guide to communications equipment in service with naval, military and air forces worldwide, from satellite to underwater systems, major networks and handheld items.

JANE'S . . . MILITARY REVIEW. 2nd (1982-83)-. UK. English. an. $15.95. Jane's Publishing Company Ltd, 238 City Road, London EC1V 2PU England. Ed Ian V Hogg. LC UA15. DD 355.005. *Jane's . . . Military Annual.*

JANE'S WEAPON SYSTEMS. 1st- Ed. 0075-3068. US. English. an. $125.00. Janes Publications Inc, 135 West 50th Street/12th Floor, New York NY 10020. Tel (212)586-7745. Ed Ronald T Pretty. LC U104. DD 623.405. adv acc. Reference to the main non-infantry portable weapon systems of the world and defensive systems. Covers missiles, underwater and electronic warfare, radar and other detection equipment.

JOINT PERSPECTIVES. Vol. 1, No. 1 (Summer 1980)-. 0274-595X. Periodical. US. English. qt. Public Affairs Officer, Armed Forces Staff College, Norfolk VA 23511. LC U1. DD 355.005.

JOINT TRAVEL REGULATIONS. VOLUME 1. MEMBERS OF UNIFORMED SERVICES : ARMY, NAVY, MARINE CORPS, AIR FORCE, COAST GUARD, NATIONAL OCEANIC AND ATMOSPHERIC ADMINISTRATION CORPS, PUBLIC HEALTH SERVICE. Main/Corp United States. Dept. of Defense. VFOAT Members of Uniformed Services. Periodical. US. English. mo. Superintendent of Documents, US Government Printing Office, Washington DC 20402.

JOURNAL OF DEFENSE & DIPLOMACY. VFOAT Journal of Defense and Diplomacy. Vol. 1, No. 1 (Apr. 1983)-. 0736-5810. Periodical. US. English. mo. $36.00 Domestic, $48.00 Foreign. Defense and Diplomacy Inc, 6819 Elm Street, McLean VA 22101. Tel (703)448-1338. Ed Lois M Blake. LC UF530. DD 355.8205. bk rev. adv acc. Circ 18,000. (ctrl). Military, foreign affairs and economic issues presented succinctly for international policymakers. Monthly profile of a country.

JOURNAL OF ELECTRONIC DEFENSE. (JOURNAL OF ELECTRONIC DEFENSE : OFFICIAL PUBLICATION OF THE ASSOCIATION OF OLD CROWS). Vol. 1, No. 1 (July/Aug.- 1978)-. 0192-429X. Periodical. US. English. mo. $110.00. Horizon House, 610 Washington Street, Dedham MA 02026. Tel (617)326-8220. Ed Hal Gershanoff. Ind/Abst Predicasts, Funk Scott Index Corp. Ind. LC UG485. DD 623.04305. bk rev. adv acc. Circ 22,000. (ctrl). Articles, editorials, product and industry news and columns on military electronics and electronic warfare systems operation. Planning, technology and procurement for US/NATO forces and Soviet/Warsaw Pact.

JOURNAL OF STRATEGIC STUDIES. (THE JOURNAL OF STRATEGIC STUDIES). V. 1- May 1978-. 0140-2390. Periodical. UK. English. qt. 52.00. Frank Cass & Company Ltd, 11 Gainsborough Road, London E11 1RS England. Tel 01-530-4226. Ed Amos Perlmutter and John Gooch. Ind/Abst Am. Hist. Life, Hist. Abstr., Part A, Mod. Hist. Abstr., Hist. Abstr., Part B, Twent. Century Abstr., Soc. Sci. Citation Index, Recent Publ. Artic. LC U162. DD 355.005. bk rev. adv acc. Circ 500. The journal exists to bring the subject of strategy into sharp focuses and concentrate the abundant material that has hitherto been dispensed under other headings, and is to open to all related areas of stretegy and also devotes issues to specific topics.

THE JOURNAL OF THE ARMS & ARMOUR SOCIETY. VFOAT Journal of the Arms and Armour Society. Periodical. UK. English. sa. $16.00. Journal of the Arms & Armour, 121 Fawnbrake Avenue/Herne Hill, London SE24 0BG England. LC U799. DD 739.705.

JOURNAL OF THE CANADIAN SOCIETY OF MILITARY MEDALS AND INSIGNIA (198. (JOURNAL OF THE CANADIAN SOCIETY OF MILITARY MEDALS AND INSIGNIA). Vol. 18, No. 1 (Spring 1982)-. 0820-0572. Periodical. CN. English. qt. Free to Members. Journal of the Canadian Society of Military Medals and Insignia, PO Box 38, West Hill Ontario M1E 4R4 Canada. DD 355.134205. *Canadian Military Medals & Insignia Journal, 0318-2436.*

JOURNAL OF THE ROYAL ARMY MEDICAL CORPS. See Medicine.

THE JOURNAL OF THE ROYAL ARTILLERY. Began with: V. 32, No. 4 (July 1905). Periodical. UK. English. sa. Secretary Royal Artillery Institution, Woolwich SE 18, London SE18 4JJ England. bk rev. adv acc. (ctrl). Artillery matters. *Proceedings of the Royal Artillery Institution.*

JOURNAL OF THE ROYAL UNITED SERVICES INSTITUTE OF AUSTRALIA. Vol. 3, No. 2 (Nov. 1980)-. 0705-1514. Periodical. AT. English. sa $22.13. United Services Institute of Australia, PO Box 590, Canberra City Australian Capital Territory 2601 Australia. Tel (062)652763. Ed B W Cloughley. Ind/Abst APAIS, Aust. Public Aff. Inf. Serv. bk rev. adv acc. Circ 4,000. (ctrl). The aim of the journal is to advance the study of strategy, national defence and related matters (including military affairs in general). *Australian Journal of Defence Studies.*

JOURNAL OF THE UNITED SERVICE INSTITUTION OF INDIA. Main/Corp United Service Institution of India. VFOAT U.S.I. Journal. V. 1- (No. 1-). Periodical. II. English. qt. United Service Institution of India Kashmir House, King Georges' Avenue, New Delhi 110 11 India. LC U1. (cum index).

JUND UMAN. Periodical. Arabic. ir. PO Box 113, Masqat Muscat. LC UA853.O5.

KARYS. VFOAT The Warrior. 0022-9199. Periodical. US. Lithuanian. ir. Lithuanian Veterans Association, 341 Highland Avenue, Brooklyn NY 11207. LC U4.

KEPI BLANC. Began publication Apr. 30, 1947. Periodical. FR. French. ir. M le Chef du S I H L E, BP 78, 13673 Aubagne France. LC UA703.L5.

KETAHANAN NASIONAL. 0303-4992. Periodical. Indonesian. qt. Lembaga Pertahanan Nasional, Jalan Kebon Sirih 28, Jakarta Indonesia. LC UA853.I5. *Madjalah Ketahanan Nasional.*

KOKUBO MONDAI KENKYUKAI KOENROKUSHU. JA. Japanese. ir. Kokubo Mondai Kenkyukai, 7-11-502 Takatanobaba 2, Shinjuku-Ku Tokyo-To 160 Japan. LC UA845.

KRASNAIA ZVEZDA. 1925-. Periodical. UR. Russian. ir. $32.50. Victor Kamkin Inc (50058), 12224 Parklawn Drive, Rockville MD 20852. Tel (301)881-5973. LC U4.

LAPORAN KEGIATAN PUSWANKAMRA. Main/Corp Pusat Perlawanan dan Keamanan Rakyat (Indonesia). VAT Laporan Kegiatan Pusat Perlawanan dan Keamanan Rakyat. Periodical. Indonesian. sa. LC UA929.I45. *Laporan Puswankamra.*

LATEST EDITIONS OF U.S. AIR FORCE AERONAUTICAL CHARTS. Main/Corp National Ocean Survey. VAT Latest Editions of United States Air Force Aeronautical Charts. 0364-6793. Periodical. US. English. mo. US Department of Commerce, National Oceanic and Atmospheric Administration, National Ocean Survey Distribution Division C-44, Riverdale MD 20840.

LEATHERNECK. Began in 1917. 0023-981X. Periodical. US. English. mo. $7.00. Leatherneck Association, Box 1918, Quantico VA 22134. LC D501. DD 359.960973.

THE LEATHERNECK. 0023-981X. Periodical. US. English. mo $10.00. Marine Corps Association Inc, Box 1775, Quantico VA 22134. Tel (703)640-6161. Ed William V H White. bk rev. adv acc. Circ 91,000. Magazine with features and photographs of interest to Marines, past and present, as well as their families and persons interest in USMC activities, adventure, cartoons, historical, humor, satire, prose and poems. *Quantico Leatherneck.*

LEGION. V. 43, No. 8- Jan. 1969-. 0024-0435. Periodical. CN. English. mo. $3.09. Legion Magazine, Suite 504/359 Kent Street, Ottawa Ontario K2P 0N6 Canada. Tel (613)235-8741. Ed Jane Dewar. bk rev. adv acc. Circ 558,071. Veterans information and issues, military and defence articles of general interest to Canadians. *Legionary, 0380-4348.*

LEGISLATIVE CALENDAR - UNITED STATE HOUSE OF REPRESENTATIVES. COMMITTEE ON VETERANS' AFFAIRS. See Public Administration.

LIBER 25. VFOAT Liber Viginti Quinque. No. 1 (Mar.-April 1981)-. Periodical. Portuguese. bm. LC UA760. DD 355.009469.

LIST OF LOCAL BOARDS OF THE SELECTIVE SERVICE SYSTEM. Main/Corp United States. Selective Service System. 0094-4092. US. English. 1724 F Street NW, Washington DC 20435. LC UB343. DD 355.2236.

LIST OF MEMBERS - INTERNATIONAL INSTITUTE FOR STRATEGIC STUDIES. Main/Corp International Institute for Strategic Studies. 0306-8390. UK. English. an. International Institution of Strategic Studies, 18 Adam Street, London WC2 England. LC U1. DD 355.030601.

LISTE DER AUSLANDISCHEN MILITARATTACHES. German. ir. LC UB260. DD 355.3432.

LITERATURZUSAMMENSTELLUNGEN . . . DER TECHNISCHEN INFORMATIONS- UND DOKUMENTATIONSSTELLE DES BWB. Series/Titl Bwdok-Informationen. German. ir. LC U3. DD 355.005.

LUFTFAHRT INTERNATIONAL. Periodical. GW. German. mo. $55.52. Maximilian Verlagsgruppe, Postfach 2352, Steintorwall 17, 4900 Herford West Germany. Tel (0 52 21) 50001. LC UG1240. DD 623.74605.

THE LYLE OFFICIAL ARMS AND ARMOUR REVIEW. VFOAT Arms and Armour. Began with 1976 Vol. UK. English. an. $16.95. Quick Fox, 33 West 60th Street, New York NY 10023. LC U800. DD 739.70294.

THE MAC FLYER. Series/Titl MACRP. VAT Military Airlift Command Flyer. Began with V. 13, 1966. 0024-788X. Periodical. US. English. mo. Superintendent of Documents, US Government Printing Office, Washington DC 20402. Tel (202)783-3238. Ind/Abst Index U.S. Gov. Period. *Mats Flyer.*

THE MAGAZINE FOR EVERY US VETERAN. VFOAT U.S. Veteran. VAT The Magazine for Every United States Veteran. 0364-5169. Periodical. US. English. mo. $9.00. 115 Plaza Drive, Sunnyvale CA 94086. LC UB357. DD 355.1150973.

MAINTENANCE (WASHINGTON, D.C.). (MAINTENANCE). Began with Spring 1976. 0364-7145. Periodical. US. English. qt. $17.00. US Government Printing Office, Washington DC 20402. Tel (202)783-3238. Ind/Abst Index U.S. Gov. Period. LC UG1243. DD 623.746.

MAJALLAH AL-ASKARIYAH AL-FILASTINIYAH (TUNIS, TUNISIA). (AL-MAJALLAH AL-ASKARIYAH AL-FILASTINIYAH). VFOAT Revue Militaire Palestinienne. V. 1, No. 1, (Jan. 1, 1984)-. Periodical. Arabic. mo. $80.00. 57, rue Mouaouia Ibn Abi Soufian, El Menzah Vi Tunis Tunisie.

MAJALLAT AL-QUWAT AL-MUSALLAHAH AL-MALAKIYAH. Main/Corp Morocco. Al-Quwat Al-Musallahah Al-Malakiyah. VFOAT Revue des Forces Armees Royales. Periodical. Arabic or French. ir. 2.00 Single Issue. 45 Ave Moulay Ismail, Al-Rabat Morocco. LC U7. *Majallat Al-Quwat Al-Musallahah Al-Malakiyah.*

MAJALLAT KULLIYAT AL-MALIK KHALID AL-ASKARIYAH. VFOAT King Khalid Military Academy Quarterly. Periodical. Arabic (English). qt. 20 Riyals Individuals, 50 Riyals Institutions. PO Box 22140, Riyadh Saudi Arabia. LC U4.

MAN AT ARMS. Vol. 1, No. 1 (Jan./Feb. 1979)-. 0191-3522. Periodical. US. English. bm. $20.00. Andrew Mowbray Inc Publishers, PO Box 460, Lincoln

Military Science

RI 02865. **Tel** (401)726-8011. Ed Andrew Mowbray. **LC** NK6900. **DD** 355.824075. bk rev. adv acc. Colorful magazine on firearms, swords, militaria, security, field news, stolen arms alert, preservation, show calendar, bayonets, history, and expert question column.

MARINE CORPS GAZETTE. (THE MARINE CORPS GAZETTE). V. 1- March 1916-. 0025-3170. Periodical. US. English. mo. $10.00. Marine Corps Association, Box 1775, Quantico VA 22134. **Tel** (703)640-6161. Ed J E Greenwood. **Ind/Abst** Am. Hist. Life, Hist. Abstr., Part A, Mod. Hist. Abstr., Hist. Abst., Part B, Twent. Century Abstr., Predicasts, Air Univ. Libr. Index Mil. Period., Funk Scott Index Corp. Ind., Hist. Abstr. **LC** VE7. **DD** 359.9605. (cum index). bk rev. adv acc. **Circ** 34,000. (ctrl). A professional journal written for, and primarily by, US Marines focusing on marine corps operations and readiness and overall national security issues.

MARINES. Vol. 12, No. 7 (July 1983)-. Periodical. US. English. mo. US Government Printing Office, Superintendent of Documents, Washington DC 20402. HQMC Hotline.

MARITIME DEFENCE INTERNATIONAL. See Naval Science, Navigation.

MEDECINE ET ARMEES. Vol. 1- Jan. 1973-. 0397-8125. Periodical. FR. French. 150.80 Domestic, 200.00 Foreign. Medecine et Armees, Ministere Defense Nationale, Paris France. **Tel** (1)43291231. **Ind/Abst** CIS Abstr., Excerpta Med. **NLM** W1 ME139G. bk rev. adv acc. **Circ** 6,000. (ctrl). Review of military physicians and of military hospitals. Revue des Corps de Sante des Armees Terre, Mer, Air.

MEDICAL BULLETIN (UNITED STATES. ARMY. MEDICAL COMMAND, 7TH). See Medicine.

MEDICAL JOURNAL. ARMED FORCES INDIA. See Medicine.

MEMORIA Y CUENTA QUE EL MINISTERIO DE LA DEFENSA DE LA REPUBLICA DE VENEZUELA PRESENTA AL CONGRESO NACIONAL. Main/Corp Venezuela. Ministerio de la Defensa Nacional. VE. Spanish. ir. Ministerio Defensa Nacional, Caracas Republic Venezuela. **LC** UA643. **DD** 354.87066. Memoria Que el Encargado del Ministerio de la Defensa Nacional Presenta a la Asamblea Nacional Constituyente, Cuenta Que Presenta el Ministerio de la Defensa Nacional al Congreso de los Estados Unidos de Venezuela.

THE MIDDLE EAST MILITARY BALANCE. 1983-. English. an. $30.00. Jerusalem Post, 120 East 56th Street, New York NY 10022. **Tel** (212)355-4440.

DE MILITAIRE SPECTATOR. V. 1-16, 1832-48. Periodical. NE. Dutch. mo $14.38. ADM Militaire Spectator, Karel Doormanlaan 274, 2283 BB Rijswidjk Netherlands. **LC** U4.

MILITARIA AUCTION. Main/Corp Edward E. Denby & Associates. Sale No. 24 (Jan. 22, 1983)-. 0821-1930. Periodical. CN. English. ir. Edward E Denby & Associates, 1206 Yonge Street, Toronto Ontario M4T 1W1 Canada. **DD** 355.13420294. Auction of Military Medals & Militaria, 0226-9856.

MILITARTECHNIK. Began in 1961. Periodical. SZ. German. bm. $16.13. Kunst & Wissen Erich Bieber, Dufourstrasse 51, CH-8008 Zurich Switzerland. **LC** U3.

MILITARWISSENSCHAFTLICHE QUELLENKUNDE. See Bibliographies.

MILITARY AFFAIRS. (MILITARY AFFAIRS : JOURNAL OF THE AMERICAN MILITARY INSTITUTE). Vol. 5, No. 1 (Spring 1941)-. 0026-3931. Periodical. US. English. qt. $30.00. Kansas State University, Eisenhower Hall/Military Affairs History Department, Manhattan KS 66502. **Tel** (913)532-6733. Ed Robin Higham. **Ind/Abst** Writ. Am. Hist., Ref. Source, Hist. Abstr., Part A, Mod. Hist. Abstr., Hist. Abst., Part B, Twent. Century Abstr., Am. Hist. Life, Hist. Abstr. **LC** E181. **DD** 355.0973. Index in last issue of volume - loose - separately paged. (cum index). bk rev. adv acc. **Circ** 2,200. The international scholarly journal of military history with a concentration on military and naval areas and occasional pieces in the aviation field. Journal of the American Military Institute.

MILITARY ASSISTANCE PROGRAM ADDRESS DIRECTORY. See Yearbooks, Almanacs, Directories.

THE MILITARY BALANCE. 1963-1964-. 0459-7222. UK. English. an. $21.00. Marketing International Inc, 13 Park Avenue, Gaithersburg MD 20877. **Tel** (202)822-3197. **DD** 355.033205. Communist Bloc and the Western Alliances.

MILITARY BUSINESS REVIEW. See Business - Purchasing.

THE MILITARY CHAPLAIN. VFOAT Military Chaplain Newsletter. V. 19- July/Aug. 1948-. 0026-3958. Periodical. US. English. bm. $10.00. Military Chaplains Association, 7758 Wisconsin Avenue/Suite 401, Washington DC 20014. Army and Navy Chaplain.

MILITARY CHAPLAINS' REVIEW. Publication began with Jan. 1972. 0360-9693. Periodical. US. English. qt. US Army Chaplain Board, Watters Hall/Building 1207, Fort Monmmouth NJ 07703. **Ind/Abst** Index U.S. Gov. Period. **LC** UH23. **DD** 355.3470973. (cum index).

MILITARY CLUBS & RECREATION. V. 1- 1979-. 0192-2718. Periodical. US. English. mo. $10.00. Clubs & Recreation, PO Box 7088, Alexandria VA 22307. **Tel** (703)765-3388. adv acc. (ctrl) Club Executive, 0009-9554.

MILITARY COLLECTOR & HISTORIAN. VAT Military Collector and Historian. V. 1- Jan. 1949-. 0026-3966. Periodical. US. English. qt. Company of Military Historians, North Main Street, Westbrook CT 06498. **Tel** (203)399-9460. **Ind/Abst** Am. Hist. Life, Hist. Abstr., Part A, Mod. Hist. Abstr., Hist. Abst., Part B, Twent. Century Abstr., Writ. Am. Hist., Hist. Abstr. **LC** UC463. **DD** 355.00973. (cum index).

MILITARY DEALERS AND COLLECTORS DIRECTORY AND HANDBOOK. See Yearbooks, Almanacs, Directories.

THE MILITARY ENGINEER. See Engineering.

MILITARY ENGINEER. GEODESY, MAPPING, OCEANOGRAPHY. See Engineering.

MILITARY HISTORY OF TEXAS AND THE SOUTHWEST. Began with V. 9 in 1971. 0047-7389. Periodical. US. English. qt. $12.50. Military History Association Press, PO Box 5248, Austin TX 78763. **Ind/Abst** Am. Hist. Life, Hist. Abstr., Part A, Mod. Hist. Abstr., Hist. Abst., Part B, Twent. Century Abstr., Writ. Am. Hist., Recent Publ. Artic. **LC** F381. **DD** 976.4. Texas Military History.

MILITARY IMAGES MAGAZINE. V. 1- July/Aug. 1979-. 0193-9866. Periodical. US. English. bm. $16.00. Military Images Magazine, 205 West Miner Street, West Chester PA 19380. **Tel** (215)436-9763. Ed H Roach. **LC** UA23.A1. **DD** 355.00973. bk rev. adv acc. **Circ** 3,000. U S military history, 1839-1939, as seen in period photography.

MILITARY INTELLIGENCE. Publication began with Jan./March 1977. 0026-4024. Periodical. US. English. qt. US Government Printing Office, Superintendent of Documents, Washington DC 20402. **Tel** (202)783-3238. **Ind/Abst** Predicasts, Index U.S. Gov. Period. MI Magazine (Ft. Huachuca, Ariz.).

MILITARY LAW REPORTER. See Law.

MILITARY LAW REVIEW. See Law.

MILITARY LIFESTYLE (UNITED STATES EDITION). (MILITARY LIFESTYLE). 0885-8403. Periodical. US. English. mo. $10.00. Downey Communications Inc, 1732 Wisconsin Avenue NW, Washington DC 20007. **DD** 355. Ladycom, 0023-7183.

MILITARY LIVING AND CONSUMER GUIDE. V. 1-V. 9, No.4. 0580-6240. Periodical. US. English. ir. $11.00. Military Marketing Services, PO Box 4010, Arlington VA 22204. **Tel** (703)237-0203. Ed Ann Crawford. bk rev. adv acc. **Circ** 31,000. (ctrl). A general interest magazine for military families.

MILITARY MANPOWER STATISTICS. See Statistics.

MILITARY MARKET. See Business.

MILITARY MEDIA REVIEW. (MILITARY MEDIA REVIEW : MMR). VFOAT MMR. Began with 1974. 0095-635X. Periodical. US. English. qt. Department of the Army, Defense Information School, Fort Benjamin Harrison IN 46216. **Ind/Abst** Index U.S. Gov. Period. **LC** UH805. **DD** 355.005.

MILITARY MEDICINE. See Medicine.

MILITARY MODELER. 0195-1467. Periodical. US. English. mo. $26.50. Challange Publications Inc, 7950 Deering Avenue, Canoga Park CA 91304. **Tel** (213)887-0550.

MILITARY POLICE. V. 6, No. 3- Fall 1979-. 0199-7211. Periodical. US. English. qt. $16.00. Head Quarters USAMPS, Attn Magazine Branch, Fort McClellan AL 36205-5030. **Tel** (205)238-5405. Ed Lois C Perry. bk rev. **Circ** 8,000. Publication for the United States Army Military Police. Military Police Law Enforcement Journal, 0192-0138.

MILITARY POLICE JOURNAL (FORT MCCLELLAN, ALA.). (MILITARY POLICE JOURNAL). VFOAT Military Police. Vol. 9, No. 1 (Spring/Summer 1982)-. 0884-0024. Periodical. US. English. qt. $9.00. Military Police Journal, US Army Military Police School, Fort McClellan AL 36205. **Tel** (205)238-5405. Ed Lois C Perry. bk rev. **Circ** 9,250. The journal provides new doctrine and training concepts to the field. Other subjects of interest are: physical security, rear battle, and air-land battle. Military Police, 0199-7211.

MILITARY REVIEW. Vol. 24, No. 1 (Apr. 1944)-. Periodical. US. English. mo $12.60. Military Review, Funston Hall, Fort Leavensworth KS 66027-6910. **Tel** (913)684-5642. Ed Colonel Frederick W Timmerman. **LC** Z6723. (cum index). bk rev. **Circ** 20,000. Original articles on military related subjects contributing to the development of military professional, features on new equipment and technological developments and reviews of military books. Command and General Staff School Military Review.

MILITARY TECHNOLOGY AND ECONOMICS. (MILITARY TECHNOLOGY). VFOAT Miltech. Vol. 1, No. 1 (1977) -. 0344-6352. Periodical. English. bm. $36.00. **Tel** (703)790-5252. **Ind/Abst** Predicasts. adv acc. **Circ** 27,000. (ctrl). Executive overview of weapons systems and their technologies. Covers all military disciplines with a circulation emphasis on the Third World and developing countries of the world. Aerospace International.

MILSTRIP : MILITARY STANDARD REQUISITIONING & ISSUE PROCEDURES. VFOAT Military Standard Requisitioning & Issue Procedures. VAT Military Standard Requisitioning and Issue Procedures. US. English. ir. Department of Defense, Defense Supply Agency, Cameron Station, Alexandria VA 22314.

MILSTRIP. SUPPLEMENT NO. 1 : ROUTING IDENTIFIER CODES. VFOAT Routing Identifier Codes. VAT Military Standard Requisitioning and Issue Procedures. Periodical. US. English. ir. US Department of Defense, Defense Supply Agency, Washington Dc 20402.

MINERVA (ARLINGTON, VA.). (MINERVA). Vol. 1, No. 1 (Spring 1983)-. 0736-718X. Periodical. US. English. qt. $30.00. L de Pauw, 1101 South Arlington Ridge Road/ #210, Arlington VA 22202. **Tel** (703)892-4388. Ed Linda Grant DePauw. **LC** UB418.W65. **DD** 355.0088042. bk rev. **Circ** 400. The only periodical dealing exclusively and extensively with women and the military. Carries news, reviews, and commentary. Editorial policy emphasizes diversity.

MINIATURE WARFARE & MODEL SOLDIERS. Periodical. UK. English. mo. $10.50. Formstan Ltd, Stanhope House, Fairbridge Road, London N19 3HZ England. **LC** U310. **DD** 355. Miniature Warfare.

MONTANA DAV NEWS. VAT Montana Disabled American Veterans News. Periodical. US. English. mo. $2.00. Montana Disabled American, Box 7, Kalispell MT 59901.

MOUNTAINEER. (THE MOUNTAINEER). V. 1- April 2, 1975-. 0319-5562. CN. English. bw. $3. The Mountaineer, CFB Chilliwack, Vedder Crossing British Columbia V0X 1Z0 Canada. **DD** 355.10971133.

MOVES. 0146-8367. Periodical. US. English. bm. $8.00. Simulations Publications Inc, 44 East 23rd Street, New York NY 10010. **LC** U310. **DD** 793.9.

MUSEUM NOTES. See Museums.

THE MUTUAL SECURITY PROGRAM FOR FISCAL YEAR 1952-. Main/Corp United States. 0498-1367. Periodical. English. ir. **LC** UA12. **DD** 355.

NARODNA ARMIJA. V. 1- (No. 1-). Periodical. YU. Serbo-Croatian -C. wk. Jugoslovenska Knjica, PO Box 36, Beograd Yugoslavia. **LC** U4.

Military Science

NATIONAL DEFENSE. V. 58- (No. 320-). 0092-1491. Periodical. US. English. bm. $20.00. American Defense Preparedness Association, 1700 North Moore Boulevard/Suite 900, Arlington VA 22209. Tel (703)522-1820. Ed Deforrest Ballow. LC UF1. DD 355.8205. bk rev. adv acc. A source of respected and accurate ideas on military hardware, new defense technologies and strategic opinion, emphasizing the pursuing of a strong industrial base. Ordnance.

THE NATIONAL DEFENSE EXECUTIVE RESERVE ANNUAL REPORT TO THE PRESIDENT. (NATIONAL DEFENSE EXECUTIVE RESERVE . . . ANNUAL REPORT TO THE PRESIDENT). VFOAT Annual Report to the President. 0198-6120. US. English. an. Federal Emergency Management Agency, Office of Plans & Preparedness, Washington DC 20472. LC UA18.U5. DD 355.23.

NATIONAL GUARD. VFOAT National Guard Magazine. V. 32, No. 10- Nov. 1978-. 0163-3945. Periodical. US. English. mo. $10.00. National Guardsman, 1 Massachusetts Avenue NW, Washington DC 20001. Tel (202)789-0031. Ed Major Reid K Beveridge. LC UA42. DD 355.370973. adv acc. Circ 65,000. Military. Guardsman.

NATIONAL GUARD ALMANAC. See Yearbooks, Almanacs, Directories.

NATIONAL LEGAL BIBLIOGRAPHY. SUBJECT AREA LIST. MILITARY AND SECURITY LAW. See Bibliographies.

NATIONAL NEWS LETTER - FEDERATION OF MILITARY AND UNITED SERVICES INSTITUTES OF CANADA. (NATIONAL NEWS LETTER). Main/Corp Federation of Military and United Services Institutes of Canada. Vol. 1, No. 1 (Jan. 31,1974)-. 0713-0511. Periodical. CN. English. ir. Free. FMUSIC, 223 Sayward Building, 1207 Douglas Street, Victoria British Columbia V8W 2E7 Canada. DD 369.271.

THE NATIONAL SECURITY AFFAIRS FORUM. 0146-244X. Periodical. US. English. ty. National War College, Washington DC 20319. LC UA11. DD 355.033073. Forum (Washington, D.C.).

NATIONAL SECURITY MANAGEMENT PROGRAMS. ADMINISTRATIVE PROCEDURES. Main/Corp National Defense University. US. English. Department of the Defense, National Defense University, Washington DC 20319.

NATIONAL SECURITY RECORD. Began in Sept. 1978. 0162-3206. Periodical. US. English. mo $50.00. The Heritage Foundation, 214 Massachusetts Avenue NE, Washington DC 20002. Tel (202)546-4400. Ind/Abst Predicasts.

THE NATIONAL SECURITY REVIEW. V. 1- Mar. 1973-. Periodical. English. ir. National Defense College of the Philippines (The President), Fort Bonifaco Rizal/Atten National Security Review, Manila Philippines. LC HC451. DD 355.0330599.

NATIONAL VIETNAM VETERANS REVIEW. Periodical. US. English. mo. $15.00. National Vietnam Veterans, PO Box 35812, Fayetteville NC 28303. Tel (919)484-2343.

NATO'S SIXTEEN NATIONS. Vol. 28, No. 1 (Feb./Mar. 1983)-. Periodical. English. ir. 84.-. J Perel's Publishing Company, PO Box 914 35 Matterhorn, NL-1186, EB Amstelveen The Netherlands. Tel 20 454256. Ed Frederick Bonnart. Ind/Abst Predicasts. LC UA646. DD 355.03304. adv acc. An independent review of military, political and economic affairs and is obtainable only by subscriptions. NATO'S Fifteen Nations.

NEUE ZEITSCHRIFT FUR WEHRRECHT. See Law.

THE NEW PATRIOT. V. 1- Feb. 1974-. 0098-3314. US. English. Eangus Publications Committee, 1221 Baltimore, Kansas City MO 64105. LC UA42.A6. DD 355.370973.

NEWS REVIEW ON CHINA, MONGOLIA AND THE KOREAS. See Political Science - International Relations.

NEWS REVIEW ON JAPAN, SOUTH EAST ASIA, AND AUSTRALASIA. CEASED. Main/Corp Institute for Defence Studies and Analyses. -December 1983. Periodical. II. English. mo. $10.03. Institute for Defence Studies and Analyses, Sapru House Barakhambr Road, New Delhi 110 001 India. LC UA830. DD 355.03325.

NEWS REVIEW ON NORTH AMERICA & EUROPE. Main/Corp Institute for Defence Studies and Analyses. Feb. 1972-. II. English. mo. $10.03. Institute of Defence Studies and Analyses, Sapru House, Barakhamba Road, New Delhi 110 001 India. LC D839. DD 327.05. News Review on Science, Technology, and other Major Developments.

NEWSLETTER - DISASTER OPERATIONS OFFICE, STATE OF MISSOURI. Main/Corp Missouri. Disaster Planning and Operations Office, Civil Defense. V. 21, No. 5- Sept./Oct. 1974-. 0364-0337. Periodical. US. English. bm. Disaster Operations Office, 1717 Industrial Drive, Jefferson City MO 65102. LC UA928.M8. DD 363.3409778. Missouri Disaster Planning and Operations Newsletter.

NIKKAN KOKUBO KEIZAI TSUSHIN. THE KOKUBO KEIZAI TSUSHIN. VFOAT Kokubo Keizai Tsushin. JA. Japanese. ir. 90.000. c/o Korin Kaikan 9, Shiba Sakaecho, Minato-Ku Tokyo Japan. Tel 03-433-4878. Ed S Chikada. LC UA845. adv acc.

N.S.I. ADVISORY FOR THE DOD SECURITY EXECUTIVE. VFOAT NSI Advisory for the DOD Security Executive. 0882-9667. Periodical. US. English. mo. $195.00. National Security Institute, 2000 West Park Drive/POB 683, West Borough MA 01581. Tel (617)366-3642. Ed David A Marston. Circ 400. (ctrl). Designed to assist US defense contractors in administering their industrial security programs.

THE OBJECTOR. Vol. 2, No. 2 (March 31, 1981-). 0279-103X. Periodical. US. English. ir. $15.00. CCCO-Western Region, 1251 Second Avenue, San Francisco CA 94122. Tel (415)566-0500. Ed Ann Wrixon. bk rev. Circ 800. (ctrl). A journal for draft and military counselors. Up-to-date information concerning military and selective service laws and regulations. Published 8 times per year at six week intervals. Draft Counselors Newsletter, Newsletter on Military Law and Counseling.

OCCASIONAL BULLETIN (PACIFIC & ASIAN AMERICAN CENTER FOR THEOLOGY & STRATEGIES). (OCCASIONAL BULLETIN). VFOAT PACTS Occasional Bulletin. Periodical. US. English. qt. 1798 Scenis Avenue, Berkeley CA 94709.

THE OFFICER. V. 1- Jan. 1924-. 0030-0268. Periodical. US. English. mo. $12.00. Reserve Officer Association, 1 Constitution Avenue NE, Washington DC 20002. Tel (202)479-2200. LC UA23.A1. DD 355.3205.

OFFICER AND WARRANT OFFICER DIRECTORY. See Yearbooks, Almanacs, Directories.

OFFICER REVIEW. Began with Vol. 13, No. 5 (Jan./Feb. 1975). 0736-7317. Periodical. US. English. $2.50 Members, $3.00 Non-Members. Military Order of the World Wars, 1100 17th Street Northwest, Washington DC 20036. LC U56. DD 369.1860973. World Wars Officer Review, 0512-381X.

OFFICERSFORBUNDSBLADET. Began with 1932 issue. Periodical. SW. Swedish. ir. $6.93. Svenska Officersforbundet, Sturegatan 8 3 Tr, S 114 35 Stockholm Sweden. LC U4.

OFFICIAL ARMY NATIONAL GUARD REGISTER. Main/Corp United States. National Guard Bureau. VFOAT Army National Guard Register. Began with 1957. 0193-6557. US. English. an. National Guard Bureau, The Pentagon, Washington DC 20310. Official National Guard Register.

OFFICIAL DIRECTORY - UNITED STATES. ARMY. CORPS OF ENGINEERS. See Yearbooks, Almanacs, Directories.

THE OFFICIAL PRICE GUIDE TO COLLECTIBLES OF THE THIRD REICH. VFOAT Military. 1st Ed. (1985)-. 0748-8726. US. English. an. $9.95. House of Collectibles Inc, Orlando Central Park, 1900 Premier Row, Orlando FL 32809. Ed T E Hudgeons III. LC UC465.G3. DD 355.810943.

THE OFFICIAL PRICE GUIDE TO MILITARY COLLECTIBLES. VFOAT Military Collectibles. Began with vol. for 1982. 0747-5691. US. English. an. House of Collectibles Inc, Orlando Central Park, 1900 Premier Row, Orlando FL 32809. LC UC460. DD 355.14075.

ORBIS. See Political Science.

THE ORDNANCE MAGAZINE. V. 1, No. 1 (Spring 1983)-. 0746-2972. Periodical. US. English. qt. Free. The Ordnance Magazine, US Army Ordnance Center and School, Aberdeen Proving Ground MD 21005. LC UF23. DD 355.820973. (ctrl).

OSTERREICHISCHE MILITARISCHE ZEITSCHRIFT. V. 1-. 0048-1440. Periodical. AU. German. bm. $14.30. Carl Ueberreuter Druck Verlag, Alserstrasse 24, 1095 Vienna 9 Austria. Ind/Abst Writ. Am. Hist., Recent Publ. Artic. LC U3. Fur den Kommandanten, Reserveoffizier; LAndesverteidigung.

PACIFIC DEFENCE REPORTER. Began publication with 1974. 0311-385X. Periodical. English. ir. 45.00. Peter Isaacson Publishing Pty Ltd, 46-50 Porter Street/Box 172, Prahran Victoria 3121 Aoutralia. Tel (059)752111. Ed Denis Warner. Ind/Abst APAIS, Aust. Public Aff. Inf. Serv. bk rev. adv acc. Circ 6,000. Defence magazine covering the Asian pacific region and technological developments worldwide.

PAHLAWAN DALAM KENANGAN. Began with Vol. for 1967. Malay. ir. $1.00. Persatuan Bekas Perajurit Malaysia, Bilek 309/Bangunam Sing Hoe Motor 179 Jalan Ipoh, Kuala Lumpur Malaysia. LC UB359.M3.

PALLAS. Periodical. NE. Dutch (French). ir. 250. Association des Officers en Service Actif, Avenue Milcamps 77, 1040 Bruxelles Belgium. LC UA11.

PARAGLIDE. 0745-9688. Periodical. US. English. qt. Eighty-Second Airborne Division Association Inc, 2670 West Stansifer Court, Bloomington IN 47401. LC UA27.5 82D.

PARAMETERS. (PARAMETERS : JOURNAL OF THE US ARMY WAR COLLEGE). Publication began with 1971. 0031-1723. Periodical. US. English. qt. US Army War College, Carlisle Barracks PA 17013. Ind/Abst Predicasts, ABC Pol Sci, Recent Publ. Artic., Writ. Am. Hist., Am. Hist. Life, Hist. Abstr., Part A, Mod. Hist. Abstr., Hist. Abst., Part B, Twent. Century Abstr. LC U1. DD 355.005.

PARAPET. (THE PARAPET). V. 1- Jan. 14, 1971-. 0384-0417. Periodical. CN. text in English and French. mo. Canadian Forces Base Montreal, St Hubert Quebec J3Y 5T4 Canada.

PARATUS. 1949. Periodical. SA. Afrikaans (English). mo. 20.00. Department of Defense, Private Bag X158, Pretoria 0001 South Africa. Tel (012)211015. Ed A C J Collocott. LC U1. bk rev. adv acc. Circ 47,000. (ctrl). Military articles and news relating to the South African defence force. Kommando.

PATRICIA NEWS BULLETIN. Began with Dec. 1963 issue. 0316-5418. Periodical. CN. English. ir. Free to PPCLI Veterans of World War I and Libraries, $1. Per No. Others. Patricia Club News Service, PO Box 782 Station B, Ottawa Ontario K1P 5P8 Canada. DD 356.11.

PATRICIAN. (THE PATRICIAN). Began with 1948 issue?. 0316-4942. Periodical. CN. English. an. Editor/The Patrician, Princess Patricia's Canadian Light Infantry, c/o Regimental Adjutant, Currie Barracks, Calgary Alberta T3E 1T8 Canada. DD 356.110971.

PATRIOT. Periodical. BU. Bulgarian. ir. 4.201. G Dimitrov, Bul Khristo Botev 48, Sofiia 1000 Bulgaria. LC U4.

PEACE AND FREEDOM. 1920. 0015-9093. Periodical. US. English. ir. $10.00. Womens International League, 1213 Race Street, Philadelphia PA 19107. Tel (215)103-7110. Circ 15,000. Articles dealing with current issues for peace, jobs, freedom and to end racism, also issues on the Middle East, Central America and military spending.

PERIODICAL (COUNCIL ON AMERICA'S MILITARY PAST). (PERIODICAL). Vol. 11, No. 4 (Nov. 1981)- – No. 45 (Nov. 1981)-. Periodical. US. English. qt. Council on America's Military Past, PO Box 171, Arlington VA 22210. Periodical (Council on Abandoned Military Posts (U.S.)).

PETAWAWA POST. Vol. 30, No. 15 Feb. 11, 1981. 0712-9173. Periodical. CN. English (includes some text in French). wk. $10.00 Per Year. Petawawa Post, c/o Donald F Runge Ltd, 243 Pembroke Street West, Pembroke Ontario K8A 5N4 Canada. DD 355.10971381. Petawawa Base Post, 0316-4462.

PHALANX. See Computers and Computer Science.

PHILADELPHIA POLICY PAPERS. See Political Science.

PING CHI CHIH SHIH. VFOAT Bingqi Zhishi. Periodical. CC. Chinese. bm. Chung-Kuo Kuo Chi Shu Tien, PO Box 2820, Pei-Ching China. LC U799. DD 355.8205.

Military Science

PING KUNG HSUEH PAO. VFOAT Binggong Xuebao, Acta Armamentarii. Began in 1979. Periodical. CC. Chinese (abstracts in English). qt. 24.00. China Ordnance Society, PO Box 2431, Beijing China. **Tel** 89.2576. **Ed** Li Hong. **LC** UA10. **DD** 623.405. adv acc. **Circ** 6,000. Covers armoured vehicles, tanks, artillery, small arms, guided missles, rocketry, ammunitions, propellants, explosives, military optics, and electronics, as well as relevant basic and applied sciences.

THE PLOWSHARE. Periodical. US. English. qt. $25.00. Center Economic Conversion, 222 C View Street, Mountain View CA 94041. **Tel** (415)968-8798. bk rev. **Circ** 7,000. (ctrl) Covers news items, book reviews, and articles on issues of national interest, both theoretical and practical, with emphasis on current happenings in the economic conversion arena.

PORANTIM : EM DEFESA DA CAUSA INDIGENA. Periodical. Portuguese. mo. SDS Edifico Venancio III, Sala 310 CX Postal 11-1159, CEP 70.070 Brasilia D F Brazil.

PRIME CONTRACT AWARDS BY SERVICE CATEGORY AND FEDERAL SUPPLY CLASSIFICATION. US. English. an. Washington Headquarters Services, Directorate for Information Operations and Reports, The Pentagon, Washington DC 20301. *Military Prime Contract Awards by Service Category and Federal Supply Classification.*

PRIME CONTRACT AWARDS OVER $25,000 OUTSIDE THE UNITED STATES. VFOAT Prime Contract Awards over Twenty-Five Thousand Dollars Outside the United States. US. English. Directorate for Information Operations and Reports, the Pentagon, Washington DC 20301. **LC** UC267. **DD** 355.6211.

PROCEEDINGS - CANADIAN INSTITUTE OF STRATEGIC STUDIES. (PROCEEDINGS . . .). **Main/Corp** Canadian Institute of Strategic Studies. Seminar. VFOAT CISS Proceedings. 0824-2232. Periodical. CN. English. sa. Canadian Institite of Strategic Studies, 8 York Street, Toronto Ontario M5J 1R2 Canada. **DD** 355.033571. *Seminar (1980), 0711-4117.*

PROCEEDINGS OF THE SUBCOMMITTEE ON NATIONAL DEFENCE. **Main/Corp** Canada. Parliament. Senate. Subcommittee on National Defence. VFOAT Deliberations du Sous-Comite sur la Defense Nationale. CN. English (French). Canadian Government Publishing Centre, Supply and Services Canada, Hull Quebec KLA OS9 Canada. **LC** UA600. **DD** 355.033071.

PROCEEDINGS - SOCIETY OF LOGISTICS ENGINEERS. INTERNATIONAL SYMPOSIUM. (PROCEEDINGS). **Main/Corp** Society of Logistics Engineers. International Symposium. 0734-5461. US. English. an. $30.00 Domestic, $35.00 Foreign. Society of Logistics Engineers, 303 Williams Avenue/Park Plaza, Huntsville AL 35801. **Tel** (205)539-3800. **Ed** Elizabeth P Crowe. **LC** U168. **DD** 355.411. The papers presented delineate the broad extent and variable scope of the logistics profession, representing the contributive efforts of academicians, managers, and specialists.

PROFILE (NORFOLK, VA.). (PROFILE). Publication Began with V. 20 in Oct. 1976. 0145-112X. Periodical. US. English. mo. U S Department of Defense, High School News Service, Building X-18 Naval Station, Norfolk VA 23511. **Ind/Abst** Index Free Period., Index U.S. Gov. Period. **LC** UA23.A1. **DD** 355.00973. *Report (United States. Dept. of Defense. High School News Service).*

PROJET DE BUDGET DE PROGRAMMES. **Main/Corp** France. Service Central de l'Action Sociale des Armees. French. ir. Action Sociale des Armees, 5 rue de Chazelles, 75017 Paris France. **LC** UH769.F8. **DD** 354.44066.

PS (UNITED STATES. DEPT. OF THE ARMY). (PS). VFOAT PS Magazine. 0475-2953. Periodical. US. English. mo. US Government Printing Office, Superintendent of Documents, Washington DC 20420. **LC** UG503.

QUAD. 1- 1977-. 0706-8808. Periodical. CN. English. bm. 0.75 Each Number. Quad Magazine, Box 339, Paisley Ontario N0G 2N0 Canada. **DD** 355.10971.

QUADRENNIAL REPORT OF THE COMMANDING GENERAL CALIFORNIA MILITARY FORCES. **Main/Corp** California. Military Dept. 0098-4159. US. English. ir. California Military Department, 2829 Watt Avenue PO Box 214405, Sacramento CA 95821. **LC** UA91. **DD** 355.3709794.

QUADRENNIAL REVIEW OF MILITARY COMPENSATION. **Main/Corp** United States. Dept. of Defense. VFOAT QRMC. 0882-6935. US. English. ir. Department of Defense, The Pentagon, Washington DC 20301. **LC** UC74. **DD** 355.640973.

QUARTERLY DIGESTS OF UNPUBLISHED DECISIONS OF THE COMPTROLLER GENERAL OF THE UNITED STATES. PERSONNEL LAW, CIVILIAN PERSONNEL & MILITARY PERSONNEL. *See Law.*

QUARTERLY SUPPLEMENT TO THE . . . ANNUAL DEPARTMENT OF DEFENSE BIBLIOGRAPHY OF LOGISTICS STUDIES AND RELATED DOCUMENTS. *See Bibliographies.*

QUATRES-M'S CEASED. (LES QUATRE-M'S). VFOAT The Four-M's. V. 1-2, No. 1. 0318-0263. CN. English. Free to Members. Society of the Montreal Military and Maritime Museum, PO Box 1024 Station A, Montreal Quebec H3C 2W9 Canada. **DD** 355.0074011428.

THE RAIDERS PATCH. 8750-7021. Periodical. US. English. bm. United States Marine Raider Association, 3835 Lakeshore Boulevard, Lakeport CA 95453.

RAPPORT ANNUEL - BUREAU DE LA PROTECTION CIVILE DU QUEBEC. (RAPPORT ANNUEL). **Main/Corp** Bureau de la Protection Civile du Quebec. 1980-81-. 0714-7805. CN. French. an. **LC** UA929.Q3. **DD** 354.71400754. *Rapport d'Activites, 0229-849X.*

RECON. V. 1- June 1973-. 0093-5336. Periodical. US. English. mo. $10.00. Recon Publishing, PO Box 14602, Philadelphia PA 19134. **Ed** Chris Robinson. **LC** U1. **DD** 355.02130973. bk rev. adv acc. Keeps an eye on the Pentagon. Provides information to anti-military movements in U.S. and Third World. Nuclear freeze, arms sales, military spending, book reviews, etc.

REGISTER OF FORMER CADETS. SUPPLEMENT. 0743-1449. Periodical. US. English. ir. VMI Alumni Association, Virginia Military Institute, PO Box 932, Lexington VA 24450.

REGISTER OF GRADUATES AND FORMER CADETS OF THE UNITED STATES MILITARY ACADEMY. 1972-. 0090-2357. US. English. an. $16.00. Association of Graduates, United States Military Academy, West Point NY 10996. **Tel** (914)446-5800. **Ed** Paul W Child Jr. **LC** U410. **DD** 355.0071174731. adv acc. **Circ** 15,000. (ctrl). Provides a listing of all VSMA graduates from 1910-1985, with a short biographical section in each; a number of others lists of special interest to USMA graduates. *Register of Graduates and Former Cadets of the United States Military Academy.*

REGISTER PLANNED EMERGENCY PRODUCERS. (REGISTER OF PLANNED EMERGENCY PRODUCERS). Began with 1975. 0094-1905. US. English. an. Defense Logistics Agency, Attn DLA-XPD, Cameron Station, Alexandria VA 22314. **LC** UA18.U5. **DD** 355.2602573. *Register Planned Emergency Producers, 0094-1905.*

THE REPLICA WRAP-UP. Periodical. US. English. bm. $3.00. International Plastic Modlers Society, 6665 Green Valley Circle #218, Culver City CA 90230. **LC** U311. **DD** 745.5928205.

REPORT, BASIC FACTS ABOUT MILITARY SERVICE. **Main/Corp** United States. Dept. of Defense. High School News Service. VFOAT Basic Facts About Military Service. US. English. an. Dept of Defence/High School News Service, Great Lakes IL 60088. **LC** UB147. **DD** 355.00973. *Report - High School News Service.*

REPORT - LOUISIANA DEPT. OF VETERANS' AFFAIRS. *See Public Administration.*

REPORT - MASSACHUSETTS. COMMISSIONER OF VETERANS' SERVICES. **Main/Corp** Massachusetts. Commissioner of Veterans' Services. US. English. an. **LC** J87. **DD** 355.115.

REPORT - MISSISSIPPI. STATE VETERANS AFFAIRS BOARD. **Main/Corp** Mississippi. State Veterans Affairs Board. US. English. be. **LC** UB358.M7.

REPORT OF SECRETARY OF DEFENSE TO THE CONGRESS ON THE BUDGET, AUTHORIZATION REQUEST, AND DEFENSE PROGRAMS. (REPORT OF SECRETARY OF DEFENSE . . . TO THE CONGRESS ON THE FY . . . BUDGET, FY . . . AUTHORIZATION REQUEST, AND FY . . . DEFENSE PROGRAMS). **Main/Corp** United States. Dept. of Defense. VFOAT Department of Defense Annual Report. Began with 1979/80. 0191-6513. US. English. an. Superintendent of Documents, US Government Printing Office, Washington DC 20402. **LC** UA23.2. **DD** 353.605. Vols. for (1982-) distributed to depository libraries in microfiche. *Annual Report, 0082-9854.*

REPORT OF THE DIRECTOR OF DEFENCE SERVICE HOMES OF OPERATIONS OTHER THAN INSURANCE AND FINANCIAL STATEMENTS. **Main/Corp** Australia. Director of Defence Service Homes. VFOAT Defence Service Homes Annual Report. AT. English. ir. Australian Government Publishing Service, PO Box 84, Canberra Australian Capital Territory 2600 Australia. **LC** UB359.A8. **DD** 363.5.

REPORT OF THE FLORIDA CONFEDERATE PENSION BENEFITS. **Main/Corp** Florida. Division of Retirement. 0093-7975. US. English. Division of Retirement, The Capitol, Tallahassee FL 32304. **LC** UB374.F6. **DD** 355.115109759.

REPORT OF THE UTILIZATION OF CAL-VET FARM AND HOME PURCHASE FUNDS BY LOWER INCOME VETERANS. Jan. 1, 1979-. US. English. an. Department of Veterans Affairs, PO Box 1559, 1227 O Street, Sacramento CA 95814. **LC** UB358.C2. **DD** 355.115. *Report on the Utilization of Cal-Vet Farm and Home Purchase Funds by Lower Income Veterans.*

REPORT ON THE ACTIVITIES OF THE COMMITTEE ON ARMED SERVICES, UNITED STATES SENATE. *See Law.*

REPORT ON THE FEDERAL CATALOGING PROGRAM. **Main/Corp** United States. Dept. of Defense. US. English. an. Department of Defense, Washington DC 20301. **LC** UC263. **DD** 355.6210973. *Report, Department of Defense Cataloging and Standardization Programs.*

REPORT TO CONGRESS OF THE DEPARTMENT OF DEFENSE ON THE DEFENSE CATALOGING AND STANDARDIZATION ACT OF 1952. (SEMIANNUAL REPORT ON THE DEPARTMENT OF DEFENSE CATALOGING AND STANDARDIZATIONS PROGRAMS). **Main/Corp** United States. Office of the Assistant Secretary of Defense (Installations and Logistics). 0360-6961. US. English. sa. US Government Printing Office, Superintendent of Documents, Washington DC 20402. **LC** UC263. **DD** 355.6213.

REPORT - WEST VIRGINIA. DEPT. OF VETERAN'S AFFAIRS. **Main/Corp** West Virginia. Dept. of Veteran's Affairs. US. English. an. **LC** UB358.W4. **DD** 355.115.

THE REPORTER FOR CONSCIENCE' SAKE. 0034-4796. Periodical. US. English. mo. $2.50. National Interreligous Service Board for Conscientious Objectors, 550 Washington Building 15th Street & New York Avenue Northwest, Washington DC 20005. **LC** UB342.U5. **DD** 355.2240973. Vols. 1-30 Available from University Microfilm. *Reporter.*

RESEARCH AND DEVELOPMENT PROGRAMS GUIDE. (DEPARTMENT OF DEFENSE RESEARCH AND DEVELOPMENT PROGRAMS GUIDE). **Main/Corp** Information Group Inc. 0163-0202. US. English. an. $275.00. The Information Group, Box 39013, Washington DC 20016. **Tel** (301)681-5544. **Ed** Robert H Todd. **LC** U393. **DD** 355.820973. Guide to defense research and development, including funding, contractors, program details, future plans, and DOD management agency.

RESEARCH MONOGRAPH - CONNECTICUT OFFICE OF VETERANS AFFAIRS FOR EDUCATION. **Main/Corp** Connecticut. Office of Veterans Affairs for Education. No. 1- 1977-. Monographic Series. US. English. Board of

Military Science

Education, PO Box 1320, Hartford CT 06101. **LC** UB358.C8. **DD** 312.9.

RESERVE FORCES ALMANAC. See Yearbooks, Almanacs, Directories.

RESERVE FORCES MANPOWER CHARTS. 0193-1008. US. English. Deputy Assistant Secretary of Defense, 1777 T Street NW, Washington DC 20007. **LC** UA42. **DD** 355.22.

THE RESERVE MARINE. 0034-5547. Periodical. US. English. mo. Commandant of Marine Corps, Headquarters of Marine Corps, Washington DC 20380. **LC** UNC.

RESERVEOFFICEREN. Danish. ir. Reserveofficersforeningen I Danmark, Rosenvngets Sidealle 2 2100, Kbenhavn Denmark. **LC** UA697. Meddelelser.

RESISTANCE (VANCOUVER, B.C.). See Political Science.

RESOURCE MANAGEMENT JOURNAL. 1st Ed. 0274-5968. Periodical. US. English. qt. Resource Management Journal, Department of the Army DACA-RP, Washington DC 20310. **Ind/Abst** Index U.S. Gov. Period. **LC** UA25. **DD** 355.60973.

RETIRED MILITARY ALMANAC. See Yearbooks, Almanacs, Directories.

RETIRED OFFICER (ALEXANDRIA, VA.). (THE RETIRED OFFICER). Vol. 35, No. 1 (Jan. 1979)-. 0034-6160. Periodical. US. English. mo. $9.00 Nonmembers Domestic, $12.00 Nonmembers Foreign. Retired Officers Association, 201 North Washington Street, Alexandria VA 22314. **LC** UB413. **DD** 355.3705. Retired Officer Magazine, 0737-724X.

THE RETIRED OFFICER MAGAZINE. (THE RETIRED OFFICERS MAGAZINE). Began with issue for April 1945. 0737-724X. Periodical. US. English. mo. Retired Officers Association Inc, 201 North Washington Street, Alexandria VA 22314. **LC** UB413. **DD** 355.3705.

REVIEW OF DEFENCE POLICY. Main/Corp New Zealand. Ministry of Defence. English. ir. A R Shearer Government Print, Ministry of Defence/Private Bag, Wellington New Zealand. **LC** UA874.3. **DD** 355.0335931.

REVIEW OF THE SOVIET GROUND FORCES. Series/Titl Defense Intelligence Report. 1- Aug. 1977-. 0163-2353. Periodical. US. English. mo. Defense Intelligence Agency, Washington DC 20301. **LC** UA772. **DD** 355.00947.

REVIEW - ROYAL MILITARY COLLEGE OF CANADA CEASED. Main/Corp Royal Military College of Canada. VFOAT Centennial Review. Ceased with 1980. 0319-4418. Periodical. CN. English (includes some text in French).

REVISTA AERONAUTICA. Spanish. ir. Editorial Aeronautica Fab, Av Montes 734, la Paz Bolivia. **LC** UG635.B5.

REVISTA DE ARTILHARIA. Periodical. Portuguese. ir. **LC** UF1. **DD** 358.105.

REVISTA DE MARINA. Year 1- (No. 1-) 1885-. Periodical. CL. Spanish. bm. Armada de Chile, Correo Naval, Valparaiso Chile. **Ind/Abst** Am. Hist. Life, Hist. Abstr., Part A, Mod. Hist. Abstr., Hist. Abst., Part B, Twent. Century Abstr.

REVISTA DE SANIDAD MILITAR. See Medicine.

REVISTA DEL COLEGIO INTERAMERICANO DE DEFENSA. Main/Corp Washington, D.C. Inter-American Defense College. V. 1-. Periodical. US. Spanish (English or Portuguese). **LC** U407.

REVISTA DO EXERCITO BRASILEIRO. 0101-7284. Periodical. Portuguese. qt. **LC** U4. **DD** 355.005. Revista Militar Brasileira.

REVISTA MARITIMA BRASILEIRA. Began in 1881. 0034-9860. Periodical. BL. Portuguese. qt. $12.00. Servico Documentacao Mairnha, rua d'Mandel 15 Centro 20010, Rio de Janeiro RJ Brazil. **Tel** 221-7626. **LC** V5. bk review adv acc. **Circ** 3,200. (ctrl). Subjects connected to naval power and Brazilian Navy. Focuses on aspects of science and technology, history, navigation, strategy and maritime news, etc.

REVISTA MILITAR. Began in Jan. 1849. Periodical. PO. Portuguese. mo. $12.00. Empressa de Revista Militar, Largo da Anunciada 9, Lisbon Portugal. **LC** U4. Revista Militar, Revista do Exercito e da Armada; Revista da Administracao Militar; Portugal Militar.

REVISTA TRIMESTRAL - SERVICO DE ADMINISTRACAO MILITAR. Main/Corp Portugal. Servico de Adminstracao Militar. Portuguese. ir. Servico de Adminstracao Militar, rua Rodrigo da Fonseca No 180, Lisboa Portugal. **LC** UB83. **DD** 354.46906. Revista Bimestral - Servico de Administracao Militar.

REVUE AFRICAINE DE STRATEGIE. Jan./Mar. 1979-. Periodical. FR. French. mo. $13.04. CIBLE, 9 rue du Chateau d'Eau, F 75010 Paris France. **LC** UA855. **DD** 355.03306.

REVUE DE DROIT PENAL MILITAIRE ET DE DROIT DE LA GUERRE. See Law.

REVUE D'ETUDES ET D'INFORMATIONS (FRANCE. GENDARMERIE NATIONALE). (REVUE D'ETUDES ET D'INFORMATIONS). 0240-7892. Periodical. FR. French. qt. 60. Association pour le Developpement et la Diffusion de l'Information Militaire, 6 rue Saint-Charles, 75015 Paris France. **LC** UB825.F8. **DD** 355.13320944. Revue d'Etudes et d'Informations (France. Sous-Direction de la Gendarmerie).

REVUE HISTORIQUE DES ARMEES. 1.- Year. Periodical. FR. French. qt. $25.94. Revue Historique de Armees, Chateau de Vincennes, 94304 Vincennes Cedex France. **Tel** 374-11-55. **Ind/Abst** Am. Hist. Life, Hist. Abstr., Part A, Mod. Hist. Abstr., Hist. Abst., Part B, Twent. Century Abstr., Recent Publ. Artic., Hist. Abstr. **LC** UA700. **DD** 355.00944. Revue Historique de l'Armee.

REVUE INTERNATIONALE DES SERVICES DE SANTE DES ARMEES DE TERRE, DE MER ET DE L'AIR. See Medicine.

REVUE MILITAIRE SUISSE. FR. French. mo. $18.59. Dawson-France SA, BP 40, F-91 Palaiseau France. **LC** U2.

RIVISTA AERONAUTICA. See Aeronautics, Astronautics.

RIVISTA MILITARE. 0035-6980. Periodical. IT. Italian. bm. $10.70. SME-Sezione Administrativa, Via XX Settembre 123 A, Rome Italy. **Tel** 6794200. Ed Pier Giorgio Franzosi. **Ind/Abst** Am. Hist. Life, Hist. Abstr., Part A, Mod. Hist. Abstr., Hist. Abst., Part B, Twent. Century Abstr., Hist. Abstr. **LC** U4. bk rev. adv acc. **Circ** 30,000. Aim is to function as a vehicle for the dissemination of military thinking and as a forum of study and debate. Also serves as a means of informing the general public about the army. Rivista Militare Italiana.

ROBERT CAMPBELL'S SOUP TO NUTS. See Recreation, Leisure - Games & Amusements.

ROLLCALL. V. 1- Spring 1979-. 0227-8928. Periodical. CN. English. qt. Free to Ontario Cadets, $10.00 Per Year, Others. Rollcall, Army Cadet League of Canada, 1107 Avenue Road/ Suite 316A, Toronto Ontario M5N 2E4 Canada. **DD** 355.2232.

ROSTER OF CONFEDERATE PENSIONERS OF VIRGINIA. See Economics - Labor.

THE ROYAL AIR FORCE RETIRED LIST. Main/Corp Great Britain. Royal Air Force. VFOAT RAF Retired List. UK. English. an. 1.65. Royal Air Force, Adastral House/Room 610 Theobalds Roads, London WC1X BRU England. **LC** UB415.G7. **DD** 358.4111502541.

ROYAL CANADIAN MILITARY INSTITUTE YEARBOOK. See Yearbooks, Almanacs, Directories.

THE ROYAL ENGINEERS JOURNAL. See Engineering.

RUSI. Main/Corp Royal United Services Institute for Defence Studies. V. 117- (No. 665-)- March 1972-. 0307-1847. Periodical. UK. English. qt. 5.00. Royal United Services Institute for Defense Studies, Whitehall SWIA 2ET London England. **Ind/Abst** Am. Hist. Life, Hist. Abstr., Part A, Mod. Hist. Abstr., Hist. Abst., Part B, Twent. Century Abstr., Predicasts. **LC** U1. **DD** 355.005. Journal of the Royal United Services Institute for Defence Studies.

R.U.S.I. AND BRASSEY'S DEFENCE YEARBOOK. See Yearbooks, Almanacs, Directories.

RUSTUNGSBESCHRANKUNG UND SICHERHEIT. Vol. 1- 1961-. 0080-4800. GW. German. ir. Europa Union Verlag, Bachstrasse 32, D-5300 Bonn 1 West Germany.

SABRETACHE. Began publication with June 1958 issue. 0486-8013. Periodical. AT. English. qt. 20.00. Military Historical Society of Australia, PO Box 30, Garran Australian Capital Territory 2605 Australia. **Tel** (062)823261. Ed Alan Fraser. bk rev. adv acc. **Circ** 400. (ctrl). Australian military history 1788-present collecting military relics.

SAGAMORE ARMY MATERIALS RESEARCH CONFERENCE PROCEEDINGS. 21st (1974)-. 0197-2790. Monographic Series. US. English. ir. Plenum Press, 233 Spring Street, New York NY 10013. **Tel** (212)620-8000. **Ind/Abst** Comput. Control Abstr., Electr. Electron. Abstr., Sci. Abstr. Sect. A. Phys. Abstr., Chem. Abstr., Phys. Abstr. **CODEN** SAMPD2. Proceedings of the . . . Sagamore Army Materials Research Conference.

DER SCHWEIZER SOLDAT. Began in 1925. Periodical. SZ. German. mo. $23.25. Zeitschriften Verlag Stafa, 8712 Stafa AM Zurichsee, Zurich Switzerland. **Tel** 01/ 928 11 01. **LC** U3. **DD** 355.

SELECCIONES DE AIR UNIVERSITY REVIEW. V. 1- 1973-. 0362-8647. Periodical. US. Spanish. sa. Building 1211, Montgomery AL 36112.

SELECTED MANPOWER STATISTICS. See Statistics.

SELECTED MEDICAL CARE STATISTICS. See Statistics.

SELECTIVE SERVICE NEWS. V. 1- Aug. 1951-. 0361-2716. Periodical. US. English. mo. US Government Printing Office, Superintendent of Documents, Washington DC 20402.

SEMIANNUAL REPORT OF THE DIRECTOR OF SELECTIVE SERVICE. Main/Corp United States. Selective Service System. Began with July/Dec. 1967. Periodical. US. English. sa. Selective Service System, National Headquarters, Washington DC 20435. **LC** UB343. **DD** 355.223630973. Annual Report of the Director of Selective Service.

SENSOR TECHNOLOGY. 8756-4017. Periodical. US. English. mo. $237.00 Domestic, $273.00 Foreign. Technical Insights Inc, PO Box 1304, Fort Lee NJ 07024. **DD** 355.

SENTINEL. 1973/5- 1973-. 0037-2315. Periodical. CN. English. bm. 15.50 Domestic, 18.60 Foreign. Receiver General for Canada, Supply and Services, Ottawa Ontario K1A 0S9 Canada. **Tel** (819)997-2560. **Ind/Abst** Am. Hist. Life, Hist. Abstr. Canadian Forces Sentinel, 0008-3615.

SERGEANTS. 0360-7364. Periodical. US. English. mo. Air Force Sergeants Association, 4235 28th Avenue, Marlowe Heights MD 20031. **LC** UG633. **DD** 358.4005.

SERVICEMEN'S AND VETERANS GROUP LIFE INSURANCE PROGRAMS, ANNUAL REPORT (PHILADELPHIA, PA. : 1979). (SERVICEMEN'S AND VETERANS GROUP LIFE INSURANCE PROGRAMS, ANNUAL REPORT). 0732-104X. US. English. an. VA Center, Philadelphia PA 19101. **LC** UB373. **DD** 368.364. Vols. for (1983-) distributed to depository libraries in microfiche. Annual Report, Servicemen's and Veterans Group Life Insurance Program, 0161-3529.

SHIN BOEI RONSHU. VFOAT Journal of National Defense. V. 1-. Periodical. JA. Japanese. ir. 1920. Asakumo Shimbunsha, 9 Shiba Sakaecho Minato-Ku, Tokyo 105 Japan. **LC** UA845.

SHUKAN BOEI TOKUSHIN. Periodical. JA. Japanese. ir. c/o OMI Building, 1-18 Misakicho 3-Chome Chiyoda-ku, Tokyo 101 Japan. **LC** UA845.

SICHERHEITSPOLITIK HEUTE. Began in 1974. Periodical. German. ir. 60.00. Osang Verlag, Hauptstrasse 25A 534 1, Bad Honnef West Germnay. **LC** UA11.

THE SICILIAN DEFENCE. 1981-. 0732-3662. UK. English. an. Imprint Editions Inc, 1520 South College Avenue, Fort Collins CO 80525.

SIGNAL. Began with issue for Mar. 1951. 0037-4938. Periodical. US. English. mo. $25.75. Armed Forces Communications, 5641 Burke Centre Parkway, Burke VA 22015. **Tel** (703)425-8500. Ed Carolyn N Frazier. **Ind/Abst** Comput. Control Abstr., Electr. Electron. Abstr., Sci. Abstr. Sect. A. Phys.

Military Science

Abstr., Predicasts, Phys. Abstr. LC UG1. DD 358.24. CODEN SGNAAZ. bk rev. adv acc. Circ 31,500. The international journal for command, control communications and intelligence professionals. *Military Signals.*

SIGNAL. V. 1- Sept./Oct. 1946-. Periodical. US. English. bm. LC UG1. DD 623.7305.

SIGNUM. V. 1- Jan. 1974-. 0700-1525. Periodical. CN. English (French). ir. Dr Bryan Rollason, French Department, Royal Military College of Canada, Kingston Ontario Canada. Tel (613)545-7207.

SITREP. VFOAT SITRAP. V. 30, No. 8- Sept. 1973-. 0316-5620. Periodical. CN. English. Royal Canadian Military Institute, 426 University Avenue, Toronto Ontario M5G 1S9 Canada. DD 369.271. *Newsletter, 0316-5612.*

SMALL ARMS IN PROFILE. V. 1- 1973-. 0090-2276. US. English. Doubleday & Company, 501 Franklin Avenue, Garden City NY 11530. LC UD380. DD 623.442.

SOJA : A NEWS BULLETIN OF THE NIGERIAN ARMY. Periodical. English. mo. Army Public Relations Department, Bonny Camp, Victoria Island Lagos Nigeria.

SOLDAT UND TECHNIK. Vol. 1-. 0038-0989. Periodical. German. mo. $43.26. Umschau Verlag, Stuttgarter Str 18-24 Ptfh 10262, 6000 Frankfurt 1 West Germany. Tel 069-2600-1. Ed K H Meude. **Ind/Abst** Predicasts, Ship Abstr., Funk Scott Index Corp. Ind. LC U3. DD 355.005. bk rev. adv acc. **Circ** 31,000. (ctrl) Up-to-date aspects of the use of modern weapons systems in the armed forces of Germany and other world forces, particularly those of the Warsaw Pact.

SOLDIER. V. 1- Mar. 19, 1945-. Periodical. UK. English. ir. $23.83. Soldier, Ordnance Road Aldershot, Hants GU11 2DU England. Tel 0252-24431. Ed Peter Howard and Roland Thick. LC U1. bk rev. adv acc. Circ 29,000. Magazine of the British army, containing news and features on military matters of today and yesterday.

SOLDIER OF FORTUNE. V. 1- Summer 1975-. 0145-6784. Periodical. US. English. ir $26.00. Omega Group Ltd, Box 693, Boulder CO 80306. Tel (303)449-3750. **Ind/Abst** Pop. Mag. Rev. LC G539. DD 355.005.

SOLDIER SUPPORT JOURNAL. Began with Sept./Oct. 1980. 0274-9513. Periodical. US. English. bm. Editor of Soldier Support Journal, ATZI-PAO-SSJ, Fort Benjamin Harrison IN 46216. **Ind/Abst** Index U.S. Gov. Period. LC UB23. DD 355.610973. *Army Administrator, 0361-7300.*

SOLDIERS. Publication began with V. 26, No. 6, June 1971. 0093-8440. Periodical. US. English. mo. Superintendent of Documents, US Government Printing Office, Washington DC 20402. Tel (202)783-3238. **Ind/Abst** Index U.S. Gov. Period. LC UA23.A1. DD 355.00973. *Army Digest, 0004-2498.*

SOTILASAVUSTUS JA KOTIUTTAMISRAHA. Main/Corp Finland. Sosiaalihallitus. Suunnittelu- Ja Tilastotoimisto. VFOAT Militarunderstod och Hemporlovningspenning. Fl. Finnish (Swedish). ir. Valtion Painatuskeskus, Pl 516, 00101 Helsinki 10 Finland. LC UB365.F5. DD 355.1156094897.

SOVETSKOE VOENNOE OBOZRENIE. Began in 1965. Periodical. UR. Russian. mo. $27.00. Victor Kamkin Inc (70942), 12224 Parklawn Drive, Rockville MD 20852. Tel (301)881-5973. LC U4.

SOVIET ARMED FORCES REVIEW ANNUAL. V. 1- 1977-. 0148-0928. Periodical. US. English. an. $64.50. Academic International Press, Box 1111, Gulf Breeze FL 32561. Ed David R Jones. LC UA770. DD 355.00947. bk rev. adv acc. Since 1977, annually organizes all available data into articles on each Soviet service branch. Numerous special articles, figures, charts, tables, maps. Appears each fall.

SOVIET MILITARY POWER. 1981-. US. English. an. Superintendent of Documents, US Government Printing Office, Washington DC 20402.

SOVIET MILITARY REVIEW. Jan. 1965-. 0038-5220. Periodical. UR. English (Russian). mo. Soviet Military Review, #70893. **Ind/Abst** Predicasts, Am. Hist. Life, Hist. Abstr., Funk Scott Index Corp. Ind., Hist. Abstr., Part A, Mod. Hist. Abstr., Hist. Abst., Part B, Twent. Century Abstr. LC U1. DD 355.000947.

THE SPARTAN. 0147-3441. Periodical. US. English. qt $9.00. Spartan International Inc, Box 1017, Bellflower CA 90706. LC U310. DD 793.9.

SPECIAL REPORT ON VETERANS. Main/Corp Virginia Employment Commission. Labor Market Information Unit. 1978-. US. English. an. Labor Market Information Unit, Manpower Research, PO Box 1358, Richmond VA 23211. LC UB358.V8. DD 355.11509755.

STATE OF NEVADA CIVIL DEFENSE AND DISASTER AGENCY, AUDIT REPORT. Main/Corp Nevada. Legislative Auditor. US. English. Civil Defense and Disaster Agency, Capitol Complex, 2525 South Carson Street, Carson City NV 89710. LC UA928.N35. DD 353.97930075506.

STATE OF NEVADA, DEPARTMENT OF THE MILITARY, AUDIT REPORT. Main/Corp Nevada. Legislative Auditor. US. English. an. Legislative Auditor, Capitol Complex, Carson City NV 89710. LC UA321. DD 355.3709793.

STATEMENT OF SECRETARY OF DEFENSE BEFORE THE HOUSE ARMED SERVICES COMMITTEE ON THE DEFENSE BUDGET AND PROGRAM. Main/Corp United States. Dept. of Defense. VFOAT Annual Defense Department Report. 0091-6919. US. English. Superintendent of Documents, US Government Printing Office, Washington DC 20402. LC UA23.2. DD 355.033073.

STATISTIQUE MEDICALE DANS LES ARMEES. See Statistics.

STRATEGIC ANALYSIS. V. 1- Apr. 1977-. Periodical. II. English. mo $12.36. Institute Defence Studies & Analysis, Sapru House, Barakhamba Road, New Delhi 110 001 India. LC UA11. DD 355.0330047.

STRATEGIC DIGEST. Periodical. II. English. mo. $13.41. Institute of Defence Studies & Analysis, Sapru House, Barakhamba Road, New Delhi 110 001 India. LC UA840. DD 355.033254.

STRATEGIC REVIEW. V. 1- Spring 1973-. 0091-6846. Periodical. US. English. qt $42.00. US Strategic Institute, 265 Winter Street, Waltham MA 02154. Tel (617)890-5030. Ed Walter F Hahn. **Ind/Abst** Predicasts, Public Aff. Inf. Serv. Bull., Funk Scott Index Corp. Ind., Recent Publ. Artic. LC U162. DD 355.0330047. bk rev. Circ 3,500. Articles from defense policy experts on security issues affecting US and its allies, examining strategy in its broadest dimensions.

STRATEGIC STUDIES. V. 1- April/June 1977-. Periodical. English. ir. 50.00. Institute of Strategic Studies, PO Box 1173, Islamabad Pakistan. LC U162. DD 355.03305.

STRATEGIC SURVEY. See Political Science - International Relations.

STRATEGIE, AFRIQUE/MOYEN-ORIENT. VFOAT Strategie, Afrique Moyen-Orient. 0221-9670. Periodical. FR. French. qt. 130. 155 rue de Belleville, 75019 Paris France. LC UA855. DD 355.03306.

STRATEGIQUE. No 1- 1st Quarterly 1979-. Periodical. FR. French. ir. 250. Fondation Pour les Etudes de Defense Nationale, Hotel National des Invalides, 75007 Paris France. Tel 47051207. LC U162. DD 355.0205. Circ 1,200. Deals with stratetgical research and studies.

STRATEGY & DEFENCE. VFOAT Strategy and Defence. 0307-4420. Periodical. IE. English. mo. Mercadores Company Ltd, Quills and Stars House Ashgrove Dun Laoghire Company, Dublin Ireland. LC UF500. DD 355.005. *Aviation & Marine International, Ground Defence International; Asia & Africa Military Review.*

STRATEGY & TACTICS CEASED. VAT Strategy and Tactics. No. 1- 1967-. 0049-2310. Periodical. US. English. bm. $30.00. Dragon Publishing Company, PO Box, 110, Lake Geneva WI 53147. Tel (414)248-3625. Ed Charles R Ramsay. **Ind/Abst** Am. Hist. Life, Hist. Abstr. LC U310. bk rev. adv acc. Circ 12,000. Military historical hobby magazine with complete simulation game (counter and map) enclosed. Features historical articles, books, software and game reviews.

STRATEGY & TACTICS MAGAZINE. SPECIAL EDITION. (STRATEGY & TACTICS MAGAZINE). VFOAT Strategy and Tactics Magazine. Vol. 1, No. 1 (Spring 1983)-. 0736-654X. Periodical. US. English. sa. $24.00 Domestic, $32.40 Foreign. Dragon Publishing, Division of TSR Hobbies Inc, Box 110, Lake Geneva WI 53147. LC HD310. DD 355.4805.

STRATEGY FOR PEACE : US FOREIGN POLICY CONFERENCE. VFOAT US Foreign Policy Conference. 20th Anniversary (1979)-. 0081-5942. US. English. an. Stanley Foundation, 420 East 3rd Street, Muscatine IA 52761. *Strategy for Peace Conference Report.*

STUDIENMATERIAL - INSTITUT FUR MILITARISCHE GRUNDLAGENFORSCHUNG. Main/Corp Landesverteidigungsakedemie. Institut fur Militarische Grundlagenfouschung. German. ir. Institut fur Militarische Grundlagenforschung, Stiftgasse 2A Stift-Kaserne, Wien 1070 Austria. LC U3.

SUB-COMMITTEE OF THE STANDING COMMITTEE ON EXTERNAL AFFAIRS AND NATIONAL DEFENCE ON ARMED FORCES RESERVES. (SUB-COMMITTEE OF THE STANDING COMMITTEE ON EXTERNAL AFFAIRS AND NATIONAL DEFENCE ON ARMED FORCES RESERVES : MINUTES OF PROCEEDINGS AND EVIDENCE). Main/Corp Canada. Parliament. House of Commons. Sub-Committee of the Standing Committee on External Affairs and National Defense on Armed Forces Reserves. VFOAT Sous-Comite du Comite Permanent des Affairs Exterieures et de la Defense Nationale Charge d'Etudier les Forces Armees de Reserve. Issue No. 1 (May 14, 1981/June 16, 1981)-. 0713-7508. Periodical. CN. English (text in French in parallel columns). DD 355.220971. Canada. Parliament. House of Commons. Sub-Committee of the Standing Committee on External Affairs and National Defense on Armed Forces Reserves.

SUMMARIES OF CONCLUSIONS AND RECOMMENDATIONS ON DEPARTMENT OF DEFENSE OPERATIONS : REPORT TO THE HOUSE AND SENATE COMMITTEES ON APPROPRIATIONS BY THE COMPTROLLER GENERAL OF THE UNITED STATES. Main/Corp United States. General Accounting Office. US. English. an. US General Accounting Office, Information Handling and Support Facility, PO Box 6015, Gaithersburg MD 20877. LC UA23.2. DD 353.605. Vols. for (1985-) distributed to depository libraries in microfiche.

SUMMARY OF ACTIVITIES - COMMITTEE ON ARMED SERVICES, UNITED STATES SENATE. Main/Corp United States. Congress. Senate. Committee on Armed Services. 0148-0693. US. English. be. US Government Printing Office, Washington DC 20402. LC KF4987.A7. DD 343.7301.

SURVIVAL. V. 1- Mar./Apr. 1959-. 0039-6338. Periodical. UK. English. bm. $22.98. International Institute for Strategic Studies, 23 Tavistock Street, London 2C2E 7NQ England. Tel 01-379-7676. Ed Lynn Davis. **Ind/Abst** Predicasts, Am. Hist. Life, Hist. Abstr., Funk Scott Index Corp. Ind., Hist. Abstr., Part A, Mod. Hist. Abstr., Hist. Abst., Part B, Twent. Century Abstr. LC U162. bk rev. adv acc. Circ 7,000. Forum for debate and digest of important documents on whole range of strategic issues including East-West relations, military strategy, arms control, and regional security issues.

SVENARODNA OBRANA. Periodical. Serbo-Croatian(R). ir. LC U4.

TARJAMAT MUKHTARAH MIN AL-MAJALLAT AL-ASKARIYAH AL-ALAMIYAH. Periodical. Arabic. ir. LC U4.

TECHNICAL DATA DIGEST CEASED. VFOAT Air Technical Intelligence Technical Data Digest. V. 12, No. 1 (1 July 1947)-V. 17, (Nov. 1952). Periodical. US. English. sm.

TECHNICAL REPORT AFML-TR. Main/Corp United States. Air Force Materials Laboratory, Dayton, Ohio. VFOAT AFML-TR. VAT Technical Report Air Force Materials Laboratory Technical Report. 0099-8508. Monographic Series. US. English. ir. Air Force Materials Laboratory, Air Force Systems Command, Wright-Patterson Air Force Base OH 45433. **Ind/Abst** Chem. Abstr. LC UNC. CODEN XAMFAO.

TECHNISCHE MITTEILUNGEN FUR SAPPEURE, PONTONIERE, UND MINEURE. See Engineering - Civil Engineering.

TECNOLOGIA & DEFESA. VFOAT Tecnologia e Defesa. Periodical. English summaries. mo. 1100 Each Issue. Fonseca Livraria e Editora Ltda, rua Olavo Egidio 242 Santana Sao Paulo, Estado de Sao Paulo Brazil. LC UF500. DD 355.8205.

Military Science

TECNOLOGIA MILITAR. Began in 1959. 0722-2904. Periodical. Spanish. ir. $40.00. Moench Media Inc, 1350 Beverly Road/Suite 221, McLean VA 22101. Tel (703)790-5252. Ed Marvin Leibstone. LC UA10. DD 355.8205. adv acc. Circ 31,500. (ctrl). Importance of Spanish and Latin America countries as strategic and economic entities is emphasized.

TELEPHONE DIRECTORY - DEPARTMENT OF DEFENSE. See Yearbooks, Almanacs, Directories.

THANG-TIEN. Main/Corp Wisconsin. Resettlement Assistance Office. VFOAT Wisconsin Ways. V. 1, No. 1 Dec 1975-. Periodical. US. English (Vietnamese). mo. Department of Local Affairs and Development, Division of Emergency Government, 4802 Sheboygan Avenue/Room 99-A, Madison WI 53702.

TIDSKRIFT I FORTIFIKATION. 0040-6937. Periodical. SW. Swedish. qt. $3.33. Forsvarsstaben, Box 80001, 103 50 Stockholm Sweden. LC UG1.

TITLE 38, UNITED STATES CODE, VETERANS' BENEFITS. Main/Corp United States. VFOAT Veterans' Benefits. 1960-. US. English. ir. US Government Printing Office, Superintendent of Documents, Washington DC 20402. Tel (202)783-3238.

TREND DATA. 0740-1027. US. English. an. Veterans Administration Office of Reports and Statistics, Washington DC 20420. LC UB357. DD 355.1150973. Vols. for (1957-1981-) distributed to depository libraries in microfiche.

TRIDENT. VFOAT Marine Command Trident. V. 1- 19 Dec. 1966-. 0025-3413. Periodical. CN. English. sm. Ford Publishing Company Ltd, PO Box 3358, Halifax Nova Scotia Canada.

TRUPPENPRAXIS. Jan. 1957-. Periodical. GW. German. bm. $30.52. Maximilian Verlagsgruppe, Postfach 2352 Steintorwall 17, 4900 Herford West Germany. Tel 05221 50007. LC U3. bk rev. adv acc. Circ 32,400. (ctrl). Journal for all problems that officers are concerned with, especially education and military.

UNIFORMED SERVICES ALMANAC. See Yearbooks, Almanacs, Directories.

UNITED STATES AIR FORCE ACADEMY JOURNAL OF PROFESSIONAL MILITARY ETHICS. VFOAT U.S.A.F. Academy Journal of Professional Military Ethics. Vol. 1, No. 1 (Apr. 1980)-. 0731-2865. US. English. sa. Department of the Air Force Headquarters, United States Air Force Academy USAF Academy, Colorado Springs CO 80840. Tel (303)472-4070. Ed Charles W Hudlin. LC U22. DD 174.9355. bk rev. Circ 1,000. (ctrl). Articles on professional military ethics, morality and war, nuclear deterrence.

U.S. ARMS CONTROL AND DISARMAMENT AGENCY ANNUAL REPORT. Main/Corp United States. Arms Control and Disarmament Agency. 1st- 1961-. US. English. an.

UNITED STATES ARMY AVIATION DIGEST. Began with Feb. 1955 issue. 0004-2471. Periodical. US. English. mo. $15.70 Domestic, $19.65 Foreign. Superintendent of Documents, Government Printing Office, Washington DC 20402. Tel (202)783-3238. Ind/Abst Predicasts, Index U.S. Gov. Period. LC UG633. DD 358.400973. Army Aviation Digest.

U.S. ARMY RECRUITING AND CAREER COUNSELING JOURNAL. Main/Corp United States. Army Recruiting Command. VAT United States Army Recruiting and Career Counseling Journal. V. -31, No. 3. 0049-545X. Periodical. US. English. mo. US Army Recruiting Command, Building 48 C Usarcasp C, Ft Sheridan IL 60037. LC UB323. DD 355.2236. Recruiting & Career Counseling Journal.

UNITED STATES MILITARY POSTURE CEASED. (UNITED STATES MILITARY POSTURE FOR FY . . .). Main/Corp United States. Joint Chiefs of Staff. VFOAT Statement by Chairman, Joint Chiefs of Staff to the Congress on the Defense Posture of the United States. Ceased with FY 1982. 0148-060X. US. English. an. US Government Printing Office, Superintendent of Documents, Washington DC 20402. LC UA23.2. DD 355.033073.

UNTERRICHTSBLATTER FUR DIE BUNDESWEHRVERWALTUNG. Periodical. GW. German. mo. Dr Alfred Huethig Verlag GMBH, Postfach 102869, IM Weiher 10, D-69 Heidelberg 1 West Germany. LC UA710.

US MAGAZINE. 0362-4587. US. English. W B Bradbury Company, 6 East 43rd Street, New York NY 10017. LC U766. DD 355.129.

V DNI ZELENYKH SVIAT. VFOAT On Memorial Day. Vol. 1- 1955-. US. Ukrainian. ir. PO Box 708, Cooper Station, New York NY 10003. LC UB365.R8.

VA REPORT ON THE NATURE AND DISPOSITION OF ALL CASES IN WHICH AN INSTITUTION, APPROVED FOR VETERANS BENEFITS, UTILIZES ADVERTISING, SALES OR ENROLLMENT PRACTICES WHICH ARE ERRONEOUS, DECEPTIVE, OR MISLEADING. Main/Corp United States. Veterans Administration. US. English. Superintendent of Documents, Government Printing Office, Washington DC 20402. LC UB357. DD 355.11510973.

VART FORSVAR. SW. Swedish. ir. $7.98. Militarstaben, Ridd G 13, S 114 51 Stockholm Sweden. Tel 08/67-22-53. Ed Allmanna Forsvarsforeningen. LC U4. adv acc. Circ 6,000. Debate concerning security policy and defence problems in Northern Europe.

VERKSAMHETSBERATTELSE - CENTRALFORBUNDET FOR BEFALSUTBILDNING. Main/Corp Centralforbundet for Befalsutbildning. Swedish. ir. Centralforbundet for Befalsutbildning, Box 5034, 102 41 5 Stockholm Sweden. LC U4.

VEROFFENTLICHUNGEN AUS DEM INSTITUT FUR WEHRMEDIZIN UND HYGIENE, ERNST-RODENWALDT-INSTITUT. See Medicine.

VETERANOTES. V. 1- Aug. 1948-. 0278-7156. Periodical. US. English. bm. LC UB358.M5. DD 355.1150973.

VETERANS ADMINISTRATION PUBLICATIONS INDEX. See Indexes/Abstracts.

VETERANS BENEFITS UNDER CURRENT EDUCATIONAL PROGRAMS. US. English. ty. Veterans Administration, Department of Veterans Benefits, 810 Vermont Avenue NW, Washington DC 20420.

VETERANS BENEFITS UNDER CURRENT EDUCATIONAL PROGRAMS. INFORMATION BULLETIN. (VETERANS BENEFITS UNDER CURRENT EDUCATIONAL PROGRAMS). 0196-2655. Periodical. US. English. sa. Veterans Administration, Office of Controller, Statistical Review and Analysis Division, Washington DC 20420. LC LB2338, UB357. DD 355.11520973.

VETERANS IN NEBRASKA. US. English. an. Nebraska Department of Labor, Box 94600 Statehouse Station, Lincoln NE 68509. LC UB358.N2. DD 355.11509782.

VETERANS READJUSTMENT APPOINTMENTS IN THE FEDERAL GOVERNMENT. (VETERANS READJUSTMENT APPOINTMENTS IN THE FEDERAL GOVERNMENT : A REPORT PREPARED BY THE OFFICE OF PERSONNEL MANAGEMENT SUBMITTED TO THE COMMITTEE ON VETERANS' AFFAIRS, U.S. HOUSE OF REPRESENTATIVES). 0278-5803. US. English. sa. LC UB357. DD 353.001324305.

VETERANS RIGHTS NEWSLETTER. Vol. 1, No. 1 (May 1981)-. 0275-8350. Periodical. US. English. mo. $45.00. Veterans Education Project, PO Box 42130, Washington DC 20036. Tel (202)686-2599. Ed Keith Snyder. LC UB347. DD 355.115170973. bk rev. Circ 2,000. A legal reporting service that focuses on veterans' benefits and legal rights, tracks developments in courts, federal agencies and Congress of concern to veterans and their families. Discharge Upgrading Newsletter, 0161-3693.

VIKRANT. V. 1- Oct. 1970-. Periodical. II. English. ir. 25.00. 1 Todarmal Road, New Delhi 1 India. LC UA840. DD 355.00954.

VIRGINIA GUARDPOST. 0360-5876. Periodical. US. English. qt. Commonwealth of Virginia National Guard, 401 East Main Street, Richmond VA 23219. LC UA500. DD 355.3709755.

VOENNOISTORICHESKI SBORNIK. Began publication in 1927. US. English. Bulgarian (tables of contents also in Russian). ir. $28.00. Hemus, 6 Boulevard Rusky, Sofia Bulgaria.

VOENNYE ZNANIIA. See Civil Defense.

VOENNYJ VESTNIK. (VOENNYI VESTNIK : ORGAN MINISTERSTVA OBORONY SOIUZA SSR). Began in 1921. 0320-0752. Periodical. UR. Russian. mo. $26.00. Victor Kamkin Inc (70140), 12224 Parklawn Drive, Rockville MD 20852. Tel (301)881-5973. LC U4. Krasnaia Armiia I Shkola, Sputnik Politrabotnika; Vystrel.

WAR AND SOCIETY NEWSLETTER. 0344-3086. GW. English (German). ir. Karl Friedrichstrasse 14 18, D 7500 Kalsruhe West Germany. Ind/Abst Am. Hist. Life, Hist. Abstr., Part A, Mod. Hist. Abstr., Hist. Abst., Part B, Twent. Century Abstr. LC Z6724.H6, U27. DD 016.355.

WARRIOR. (THE WARRIOR). V. 4, No. 6- July 1978-. 0707-8056. Periodical. CN. English. The Shearwater Warrior, PO Box 190, Shearwater Nova Scotia B0J 3A0 Canada. DD 355.10971622. Shearwater Warrior, 0705-1980.

WEHRFORSCHUNG. Periodical. GW. German. ir. 24.00. Verlag Offene Worte, Bongasse 3, 53 Bonn West Germany. LC U3.

WEHRTECHNIK. Jan. 1969-. 0043-2172. Periodical. GW. German. mo. 76.50. Special Publication Service, Postfach 2060 Karl-Mand-Str 2, D-5400 Koblenz 1 West Germany. Tel 0261/803071. Ind/Abst Excerpta Med., Int. Aerosp. Abstr., Eng. Index, Energy Res. Abstr. LC U3. DD 355.005. CODEN WHTCAK. bk rev. adv acc. (ctrl). An up-to-date highly respected journal on defence economics and the military. Wehrtechnische Monatshefte, 0341-9991; Wehr Und Wirtschaft, 0043-2113.

WEISSBUCH . . . ZUR SICHERHEIT DER BUNDESREPUBLIK DEUTSCHLAND UND ZUR LAGE DER BUNDESWEHR. Main/Corp Germany (West). Bundesministerium der Verteidigung. Began in 1969. GW. German. ir. Presse- und Informationsamt der Bundesregierung, Welckerstr 11, 53 Bonn West Germany. LC UA710. DD 355.00943.

WEST POINT MUSEUM BULLETIN. See Museums.

WEST'S MILITARY JUSTICE REPORTER. See Law.

WHAT EVERY VETERAN SHOULD KNOW. 1937-. 0083-9108. US. English. an. $6.00. Veterans Information Service, PO Box 111, East Moline IL 61244.

WIEDZA OBRONNA : DWUMIESIECZNIK TOWARZYSTWA WIEDZY OBRONNEJ. 0209-0031. Periodical. Polish. bm. 240.00. Biuro Zarzadu Gownego Two, SKR Pocztowa 32, 00-911 Warszawa 62 Poland. LC U4.

WIFELINE. Began with Summer 1977. Periodical. US. English. qt. $15.00. Navy Internal Relations Activity, Distributor Branch, Room 2E329 Pentagon, Washington DC 20350. Tel (202)783-3238. Navy Wifeline.

WINGS OF GOLD (PENSACOLA, FLA.). (WINGS OF GOLD). Vol. 1, No. 1 (Apr. 1976)-. 0274-7405. Periodical. US. English. qt. $50.00. Association of Naval Aviation, 5205 Leesburg Pike/Suite 200, Falls Church VA 22041. Tel (703)998-7733. Ed M W Cagle. adv acc. Circ 10,000. (ctrl). Strategic considerations for USA, naval and aeronautical developments, tactical operations, training, manpower and logistic support, military pay and compensation.

WORLD MILITARY AND SOCIAL EXPENDITURES. See Business - Public Finance.

WORLD MILITARY EXPENDITURES AND ARMS TRANSFERS. See Law - International Law.

WORLD MISSILE FORECAST, RPV AND DRONE. (WORLD MISSILE FORECAST (RPV AND DRONE)). Main/Corp Forecast Associates. VFOAT World Missile Forecast. 0279-5094. Periodical. US. English. mo. $795.00. Forecast Associated Inc, 22 Commerce Road, Newtown CT 06470. Tel (203)426-0800. Complete reports on all missile, RPV, drone programs 10 year unit forecasts, special analysis of markets such as surface-to-air. Quirey service included.

WORLDWIDE U.S. ACTIVE DUTY MILITARY PERSONNEL CASUALTIES. VFOAT Worldwide US Active Duty Military Personnel Casualties. US. English. qt. Director, Washington Headquarters Services the Pentagon, Washington DC 20301.

THE YEAR IN BRIEF. (THE YEAR IN BRIEF, THE VA IN . . .). 0748-2086. US. English. an. Veterans Administration, Washington DC 20420. LC UB357. DD 353.00812.

Motion Picture

ZARUBEZHNOE VOENNOE OBOZRENIE. UR. Russian. mo. 0.50. LC U4.

ZEITSCHRIFT FUR HEERESKUNDE. Began in 1960. 0044-2852. Periodical. GW. German. bm. $24.35. W E Saarbach GMBH, Postfach 101610, D-5000 Koln 1 West Germany. Tel (8)881 067. **Ind/Abst** Am. Hist. Life, Hist. Abstr., Part A, Mod. Hist. Abstr., Hist. Abstr., Part B, Twent. Century Abstr. (cum index). *Zeitschrift fur Heeres- und Uniformkunde.*

ZNAMENOSETS. Vol. 14.- (No. 160-). Periodical. UR. Russian. mo. $14.50. Victor Kamkin Inc (70341), 12224 Parklawn Drive, Rockville MD 20852. Tel (301)881-5973. LC U4. *Starshina-Serzhant.*

MOTION PICTURE

4-H FILM CATALOGUE. Main/Corp University of Saskatchewan. Film Library. **VAT** Four-H Film Catalogue. 0822-4218. Periodical. CN. English. Film Library, University of Saskatchewan, Saskatoon Saskatchewan S7N 0W0 Canada. DD 017.137.

16 MM FILM CATALOGUE - LAKE ERIE REGIONAL LIBRARY SYSTEM. (16 MM FILM CATALOGUE). **Main/Corp** Lake Erie Regional Library System. **VAT** Sixteen Millimeter Film Catalogue - Lake Erie Regional Library System L.E.R.L.S. 16 MM Film Catalogue, Lake Erie Regional Library System Sixteen Millimeter Film Catalogue. Mar. 1981-. 0711-4540. CN. English. an. Lake Erie Regional Library System, 380 Saskatoon Street, London Ontario N5W 4R3 Canada. DD 018.137.

16 MM FILM CATALOGUE - RED RIVER COMMUNITY COLLEGE, LEARNING RESOURCES CENTRE. (16 MM FILM CATALOGUE). **Main/Corp** Red River Community College. Learning Resources Centre. VFOAT Film Catalogue. 1982-. 0820-9545. Periodical. CN. English. DD 017.537. *16 MM Films, 0228-9881.*

16 MM FILM CATALOGUE. SOUTHWESTERN LIBRARY SYSTEM. (16 MM FILM CATALOGUE - SOUTHWESTERN LIBRARY SYSTEM). **Main/Corp** Southwestern Regional Library System (Ontario). 1975-. 0380-7126. CN. English. Southwestern Regional Library System, 850 Ouellette Avenue, Windsor Ontario N9A 4M9 Canada. DD 010.

16 MM FILMS AVAILABLE FROM THE PUBLIC LIBRARIES OF METROPOLITAN TORONTO. (16MM FILMS AVAILABLE FROM THE PUBLIC LIBRARIES OF METROPOLITAN TORONTO). 1970-. 0315-7326. Periodical. CN. English. qt. Metropolitan Toronto Library Board, Business Office, 214 College Street, Toronto Ontario M5T 1R3 Canada. DD 018.1. *16MM Sound Films Available from the Public Libraries of Metropolitan Toronto, 0315-7326.*

16 MM. FILMS AVAILABLE THROUGH THE PUBLIC LIBRARIES IN CAMBRIDGE (GALT), GUELPH, HURON COUNTY (GODERICH), KITCHENER, STRATFORD AND WATERLOO. Main/Corp Midwestern Regional Library System (Ont.). 0227-5686. CN. English. be. $3.00. Midwestern Regional Library System, 637 Victoria Street North, Kitchener Ontario N2H 5G4 Canada. DD 018.137.

16MM FILM ADDENDUM - MIDWESTERN REGIONAL LIBRARY SYSTEM. (16 MM FILM ADDENDUM). **Main/Corp** Midwestern Regional Library System (Ont.). 1981-. 0821-1116. CN. English. Free. Midwestern Regional Library System, 637 Victoria Street North, Kitchener Ont N2H 5G4 Canada. DD 018.137. (ctrl).

24 IMAGES. VAT Vingt-Quatre Images. No. 1- Feb. 1979-. 0707-9389. Periodical. CN. French. qt. 11.61. 24 Images, 169 rue Labonte, Longueil Quebec J4H 3M6 Canada. Tel (514)651-3646. DD 791.4305. bk rev. adv acc. Circ 1,500. Interviews, films analysis, cinematographic theory, books, reviews, information about films and actuality (especially about Quebec production).

35/70: JOURNAL OF THE FEATURE FILM INDUSTRY. VFOAT Journal of the Feature Film Industry. Periodical. UK. English. LC PN1993.5.G7. DD 384.80941. *Wide-Screen.*

ADAM FILM WORLD GUIDE. ADAM FILM WORLD DIRECTORY OF ADULT FILMS. See Yearbooks, Almanacs, Directories.

ADULT CINEMA REVIEW. VFOAT Adult Cinema. Vol. 1, No. 1 (July 1981)-. 0277-2914. Periodical. US. English. mo. $33.00 US, $39.00 Foreign. Adult Review Magazine Subscription Department, 300 West 43rd Street, New York NY 10036.

ADULT VIDEO NEWS. 0883-7090. Periodical. US. English. mo. $27.00. Adult Video News Inc, P O Box 14306, Philadelphia PA 19115. Tel (215)752-3387. Ed Paul Fishbein. DD 791. adv acc. Circ 21,000. (ctrl). Complete coverage of the field of adult video reviews, of every video release, interviews, feature stories, profiles and industry news.

AFI EDUCATION NEWSLETTER. VAT American Film Institute Newsletter. V. 1- 1978-. 0883-6213. Periodical. US. English. bm. The American Film Institute Education Services, 2021 North Western Avenue P O Box 27999, Los Angeles CA 90027. **Ind/Abst** Film Lit. Index. DD 791.

AFTERIMAGE (LONDON, ENGLAND). (AFTERIMAGE). Began in 1970. 0261-4472. Periodical. UK. English. $20.00. Afterimage Publishing, 1 Birham Road, London N4 England. LC PN1993. DD 791.4305.

AL-SINIMA AL-ARABIYAH. Periodical. Arabic. qt. 0.50. Al-Sinima Al-Arabiyah, 218 Shari Al-Jaysh, Al-Qahirah United Arab Republic. LC PN1993.5.A65.

AL-SINIMA WA-AL-MASRAH. No. 1- Jan. 1974-. Periodical. Arabic. ir. 1.00. 9 Orabi Street, Al-Qahirah United Arab Republic (Egypt). LC PN1993.

AL-SINIMA WA-AL-NAS. VFOAT Cinema Wal Nas. V. 1- Jan. 1979-. Periodical. UA. Arabic. ir. 5.00. Majallat Al-Sinima Wa-Al-Nas Rais Al-Tahrir, PO Box 2742, Cairo Egypt. LC PN1993.5.A65.

AMAZING CINEMA. No. 1 (May 1981)-. Periodical. US. English. Cinema Enterprises, 12 Moray Court, Baltimore MD 21236.

AMERICAN CINEMATOGRAPHER. V. 1- 1920-. 0002-7928. Periodical. US. English. mo. $22.00. American Society of Cinematographers, Box 2230, Hollywood CA 90028. Tel (213)876-5080. Ed George Turner. **Ind/Abst** Film Lit. Index, Art Index. LC TR845. bk rev. adv acc. Circ 35,000. International journal of film and video production techniques.

AMERICAN CLASSIC SCREEN. Began with Vol. 1 (Sept./Oct. 1976) issue. 0195-8267. Periodical. US. English. bm $15.00. American Classic Screen, PO Box 7150, Overland Park KS 66207. **Ind/Abst** Film Lit. Index. LC PN1993. DD 791.4305.

AMERICAN FILM. V. 1- Oct. 1975-. 0361-4751. Periodical. US. English. mo. $15.00. American Film Institute, Johh F Kennedy Center, Washington DC 20566. **Ind/Abst** Mag. Index, Pop. Mag. Rev., Film Lit. Index, Book Rev. Index, Ref. Source, Index Book Rev. Humanit., Media Rev. Dig., Art Index, Humanit. Index. LC PN1993. DD 791.4305.

AMERICAN FILM FESTIVAL GUIDE. 1- 1959-. 0548-7129. Periodical. US. English. an. $12.00. Educational Film Library Association, 45 John Street/Suite 301, New York NY 10028. Tel (212)227-5599.

AMERICAN PREMIERE. VFOAT Premiere. Vol. 2, Issue 6 (20 May 1981)-. 0279-0041. Periodical. US. English. qt. $16.00. American Premiere, 8421 Wilshire Boulevard Penthouse, Beverly Hills CA 90211. Tel (213)852-0434. Ed Susan Royal. LC PN1993.5.U6. DD 384.80973. adv acc. Circ 17,500. Business magazine for film industry. Includes articles about film production, distribution, exhibition and finance with interviews with major filmmakers and industry leaders. *Premiere.*

ANDERE SINEMA. VFOAT Sinema. Periodical. BE. Dutch. ir. 380. De Ander Film V.Z.W., Gratiekapelstraat 7, 2000 Antwerpen Belgium. **Ind/Abst** Film Lit. Index.

ANIMATOR. 1972. Periodical. US. English. qt. $10.00. Northwest Film Study Center, 1219 Southwest Park, Portland OR 97205. Tel (503)221-1156. Ed Kathy Clark. bk rev. adv acc. Circ 2,000. A publication designed for film and video professionals which provide resource material and networking information in addition to feature articles on regional media professionals.

ANNUAIRE DU CINEMA ET TELEVISION. See Yearbooks, Almanacs, Directories.

ANNUAIRE DU CINEMA FRANCAIS ET DE L'AUDIOVISUEL. See Yearbooks, Almanacs, Directories.

ANNUAIRE DU FILM BELGE. See Yearbooks, Almanacs, Directories.

ANNUAL INDEX TO MOTION PICTURE CREDITS. See Indexes/Abstracts.

ANNUAL REPORT - CANADIAN FILM DEVELOPMENT CORPORATION. (ANNUAL REPORT). **Main/Corp** Canadian Film Development Corporation. 1st- 1968/69-. 0382-2273. CN. English (and French, each with special title page and separate paging with French text on inverted pages). an. Canadian Film Development Corporation, 800 Place Victoria, Montreal Quebec Canada.

ANNUAL REPORT - NATIONAL FILM BOARD OF CANADA. Main/Corp National Film Board of Canada. VFOAT Rapport Annuel. Began with 1939/40 issue. 0382-151X. CN. English (text also in French). an. National Film Board of Canada, Dir-Office Information, 150 Kent Street, Ottawa Ontario K1P 5P4 Canada. Tel (613)996-4861. LC PN1993. DD 354.7100854.

ANNUAL REPORT OF THE FILM CLASSIFICATION BRANCH - BRITISH COLUMBIA. (ANNUAL REPORT OF THE FILM CLASSIFICATION BRANCH FOR . . .). **Main/Corp** British Columbia. Film Classification Branch. VFOAT Annual Report of Film Classification for . . . . VAT Annual Report of Film Classification. 1978-. 0713-0643. CN. English. an. LC PN1994.A5. DD 302.23.

ANNUARIO DEL CINEMA ITALIANO. See Yearbooks, Almanacs, Directories.

ANUARIO DEL CINE. See Yearbooks, Almanacs, Directories.

ANUARIO IBEROAMERICANO DE CINE Y TELEVISION. See Yearbooks, Almanacs, Directories.

ART & CINEMA. See The Arts (General) - Art.

ARTIBUS ET HISTORIAE. No. Issue 1-. 0391-9064. Periodical. IT. English (French, German, and Italian). sa. 65.00. Licosa Libreria Comm Sansani, Via Lamarmora 45, 50121 Firenze Italy. Tel 579751. Ed Jozef Grabski. **Ind/Abst** Avery Index Archit. Period., Repert. Int. Litt. Art. LC NX1.A1. DD 705. Founded in 1980, an international journal for visual arts and cinema.

ASIFA. ASSOCIATION INTERNATIONALE DU FILM D'ANIMATION, CANADA. (ASIFA : BULLETIN DE L'ASSOCIATION INTERNATIONALE DU FILM D'ANIMATION, CANADA). **VAT** Association Internationale du Film d'Animation, Canada. 0828-7511. Periodical. CN. French (test also in English). ty. Free to Members. ASIFA-Canada, Bureau 3/10707 rue Grande-Allee, Montreal Quebec H3L 2M8 Canada. DD 778.5347.

ATTUALITA CINEMATOGRAFICHE. Began with Vol. for 1963. Italian. ir. 4000. Edizioni Letture, Piazza S Fedele 4, Milano 20121 Italy. Tel (02)804441. LC PN1993.3. bk rev. adv acc. Circ 6,200. (ctrl).

AUSTRALIAN FILMS. 1940/58-. 0045-0448. Periodical. AT. English. an. $5.87. National Film Sound Archives, McCoy Circuit, Action ACT Australia. LC PN1998.

A.V. GUIDE. See Education (General) - Theory, Practice of Education.

L'AVANT-SCENE. CINEMA. (L'AVANT-SCENE DU CINEMA). VFOAT Cinema, l'Avant-Scene. No. 1- Feb. 15 1961-. 0045-1150. Periodical. FR. French. 485.00. L'Avant-Scene Cinema, 1 rue Lord-Byron, 75008 Paris France. Tel 42 25 6520. **Ind/Abst** Point Repere, Film Lit. Index. LC PN1993. (cum index). bk rev. adv acc. Covers French scripts and photos, critics, etc.

BACK STAGE. Vol. 1 Dec.2, 1960-. 0005-3635. Periodical. US. English. wk. Back Stage Publications, 165 West 46th Street, New York NY 10036.

BACK STAGE. TV FILM & TAPE PRODUCTION DIRECTORY. See Yearbooks, Almanacs, Directories.

Motion Picture

BACK STAGE. TV FILM & TAPE SYNDICATION DIRECTORY. See Yearbooks, Almanacs, Directories.

BAM. See Music.

BEITRAGE ZUR FILM- UND FERNSEHWISSENSCHAFT : SCHRIFTENREIHE DER HOCHSCHULE FUR FILM UND FERNSEHEN DER DDR. VFOAT Schriftenreihe der Hochschule fur Film und Fernsehen der DDR. 82/1-. Periodical. German. ir. Hochschule fur Film und Fernsehen der DDR, Dokumentation/Publikation, 1502 Potsdam-Babelsberg, Rosa Luxemburg Str 24 Berlin East Germany. **LC** PN1993. **DD** 791.4305. *Filmwissenschaftliche Beitrage.*

BIBLIOGRAPHY. FIAF MEMBERS PUBLICATIONS. See Bibliographies.

THE BIG REEL. 0744-723X. Periodical. US. English. mo. $40.00. Big Reel, Route 3 Box 239A, Madison NC 27025. **Tel** (919)427-5850. Ed Donald Key. bk rev. adv acc. **Circ** 4,000. Monthly tabloid for persons that collect, buy, trade and sell movie memorabilia from the hobby aspect.

BILL-DALE MARCINKO'S AFTA. See Literary and Political Reviews.

BLACK VIDEO GUIDE. 0882-7532. Periodical. US. English. sa. $20.00. Video Publications Ltd, 140 8 N Kings Highway/Suite 105, St Louis MO 63113. **Tel** (314)534-8555. Ed William Dorsey. adv acc. **Circ** 100,000. The first definitive home reference directory to blacks appearing in films that are available on video whether informational, educational, or entertainment since the year 1900.

BOLETIM INFORMATIVO SIP. Main/Corp Instituto Nacional do Cienma. Setor do Ingresso Padronizado. VFOAT Informativo SIP. VAT Boletim Informativo Setor do Ingresso Padronizado. Portuguese. ir. Instituto Nacional do Cinema, Rua Mayrink Veiga 28-70 Andar, Rio de Janeiro Brazil. **LC** PN1993.5.B6.

BOXOFFICE. VAT Box Office. 0006-8527. Periodical. US. English. mo. $40.00. Boxoffice, 1020 South Wabash Avenue, Chicago IL 60605. **Tel** (312)922-9326. **Ind/Abst** Infobank. **DD** 791. *Boxoffice.*

BRITISH NATIONAL FILM & VIDEO CATALOGUE. VFOAT British National Film and Video Catalogue. Vol. 22, No. 1 (Spring 1984)-. UK. English. qt. British Film Institute, 127 Charing Cross Road, London WC2H 0EA England. **NLM** PN 1998.A1. *British National Film Catalog, 0007-1552.*

THE BRITISH NATIONAL FILM CATALOGUE CEASED. V. 1-21. 0007-1552. UK. English. qt. **LC** PN1998.A1. **NLM** PN 1998.A1 B862.

BULGARIAN FILMS. 1960-. 0007-3911. Periodical. BU. Bulgarian. ir. $13.00. Hemus, 6 Boulevard Rusky, Sofia Bulgaria. **Tel** 87-03-65. Ed CINEMATOGRAPHY COMMITTEE. **Ind/Abst** Film Lit. Index. adv acc. Publishes comments on films and artists. Propagandizes the Bulgarian films, illustrated.

BULLETIN, CALENDAR OF INTERNATIONAL FILM AND TELEVISION EVENTS. VFOAT Calendar of International Film and Television Events, Bulletin, Calendrier des Evenements Internationaux du Cinema et de la Television. English (French). ir. International Film & Television Council, Via Santa Susanna 17, Rome 00187 Italy. **LC** PN1998.A1. **DD** 791.4025.

BULLETIN KFT : MEDIA KARYAWAN FILM DAN TELEVISI INDONESIA. See Communication - Broadcasting.

CA : CINEMA. V. 1-. Periodical. FR. French. qt. 55.00. Editions Albatros, 14 rue de l'Armorique (XVE), Paris France. **LC** PN1993. **DD** 791.4305.

CAHIER DES FILMS VISES PAR CATEGORIES DE SPECTATEURS. (LISTE DES FILMS VISES PAR CATEGORIES DE SPECTATEURS). 0713-3529. Periodical. CN. French. mo. Gouvernement du Quebec, 600 St Amable 4E Etage, Quebec G1R 4Z1 Canada. **DD** 791.437505.

LES CAHIERS DE LA CINEMATHEQUE. No. 1-. FR. French. qt. $21.95. Les Cahiers de la Cinematheque, Palais des Congres, 66000 Perpignan France. **Ind/Abst** Film Lit. Index. **LC** UNC. (cum index).

CAHIERS DU CINEMA. No. 1- Apr. 1951-. 0008-011X. Periodical. French. mo. 255 Domestic, 320 Foreign. Cahiers du cinema, 9 Passage de la Boule Blanche, 75012 Paris France. **Tel** 43 43 92 20. **Ind/Abst** Film Lit. Index. **LC** PN1993. **DD** 791.4305. (cum index). bk rev. adv acc. **Circ** 35,000. Most prestigious journal on cinema in the world.

CAMERA OBSCURA. No. 1- Fall 1976-. 0270-5346. Periodical. US. English. ir. $27.00. Camera Obscura, PO Box 25899, Los Angeles CA 90025. **Tel** (213)825-7310. Ed Janet Bergstrom, Constance Penley, and Elisabeth Lyon. **Ind/Abst** Film Lit. Index, Altern. Press Index. bk rev. adv acc. **Circ** 3,000. (ctrl). Film theory and criticism focusing on feminism, psychoanalysis, semiotics, spectatorship, and issues of sexual differences.

CANADIAN FILM DIGEST YEARBOOK. See Yearbooks, Almanacs, Directories.

CANADIAN FILM DIGEST YEARBOOK. See Yearbooks, Almanacs, Directories.

CANADIAN FILM-MAKERS DISTRIBUTION CENTRE CATALOGUE. (CATALOGUE). Main/Corp Canadian Film-Makers Distribution Centre. 1972-. 0315-2715. CN. English (includes some text in French). an. Free. Canadian Filmmakers' Distribution Centre, Suite 430, 144 Front Street West, Toronto Ontario M5J 1G2 Canada. **DD** 011.

CANTRILL'S FILMNOTES. VFOAT Filmnotes. No. 1 (March 1971)-. 0158-4154. Periodical. AT. English. ir. $15.00. Arthur and Corinne Cantrill, Box 1295 L, GPO Melbourne Victoria 3001 Australia. Ed Arthur and Corinne Cantrill. **Ind/Abst** Film Lit. Index. **LC** PN1993. **DD** 791.4305.

IL CASTORO CINEMA. V. 1- 1974-). Periodical. IT. Italian. bm. $23.76. Nuova Italia Editrice, Via Ernesto Codignola, 50018 Scandicci Fl Italy.

CATALOG OF BRITANNICA FILMS. Main/Corp Encyclopaedia Britannica Educational Corporation. US. English. Encyclopaedia Britannica Educational Corporation, 425 North Michigan Avenue, Chicago IL 60611. **LC** LB1044.Z9. **DD** 011.

CATALOG OF CAPTIONED FILMS FOR THE DEAF. VFOAT Captioned Films for the Deaf. 0093-7215. US. English. an. Captioned Films for the Deaf, 5000 Park Street North, St Petersburg FL 33709. **Tel** (800)237-6213. **LC** HV2395. **DD** 011. **Circ** 20,000. (ctrl). Educational captioned films/videos, indexed by subject and audience level. New titles added to collection each year based on needs assessments from input of deaf educators and users.

CATALOGUE DE LA PRODUCTION CINEMATOGRAPHIQUE FRANCAISE. 1975-. 0224-7518. French. an. Service des Archives du Film du Centre National de la Cinematographie, 78390 Bois d'Arcy France. **LC** PN1998. **DD** 016.79143750944.

CATALOGUE DES DOCUMENTS AUDIOVISUELS. Main/Corp Quebec (Province). Cinematheque. CN. French. Ministere des Communications du Quebec, CP 1005, Quebec G1K 7B5 Canada. **LC** PN1998. **DD** 016.79143.

CATALOGUE - FUNNEL EXPERIMENTAL FILM THEATRE. Main/Corp Funnel Experimental Film Theatre. 1984-. 0826-2861. CN. English. an. $3.00. Funnel, 507 King Street East, Toronto Ontario M5A 1M3 Canada. **Tel** (416)364-7003. **DD** 018.137. adv acc. **Circ** 2,000.

CATALOGUE - NATIONAL FILM BOARD OF CANADA. Main/Corp National Film Board of Canada. 1978-. 0225-9141. CN. English (French). **DD** 011.37. *Film Catalogue, 0382-3369.*

CATALOGUE OF 16 MM. FILMS - NATIONAL LIBRARY OF AUSTRALIA. Main/Corp National Library of Australia. VFOAT Film Catalogue. English. ir. **LC** PN1998.A1. **DD** 371.335230838.

THE CFS REVIEW. VFOAT C.F.S. Review. II. English. an. Chennai Film Society, 6 Madley Road, Madras-17 India. **LC** PN1993.5.I8. **DD** 791.430954.

CHIA HO TIEN YING. VFOAT Golden Movie News. Periodical. chiefly Chinese. ir. $32.00. SSU Hai Chu Pan Shih Yeh Yu Hsien King SSU, 122B Argyle Street 1/F, Chiu-Lung China. **LC** PN1993.

CHITRABIKSHAN. V. 1-. English. ir. $4.00. 2 Chowringhee Road, Calcutta India. **LC** PN1993. **DD** 791.4305.

CHUNG-KUO TIEN YING NIEN CHIEN. 1981-. CH. Chinese. an. 9.00. Hsin Hua Shu Tien, Peking China. **LC** PN1993.5.C4. **DD** 791.430951.

CHUNG WAI YING HUA. VFOAT Movie News. Periodical. CH. Chinese. mo. $1.00. Development Publishers, 12 Jupiter Street/First Floor, Hong Kong. **LC** PN1993. **DD** 791.4305.

CINE AL DIA. Periodical. VE. Spanish. qt. Cine Al Dia, Apartado 50446, Sabana Grande, Caracas Venezuela. **Ind/Abst** Film Lit. Index.

CINE ARGENTINO. AG. Spanish. an. Ediciones Corregidor, Avda Corrientes 1583, Buenos Aires Argentina. **LC** PN1993.5.A7. **DD** 791.430982.

CINE BULLES. 0820-8921. Periodical. CN. French. ir. 10.00. Association des Cinemas Paralleles du Quebec, 4545 Pierre de Coubertin CP 1000 Succursale M, Montreal Quebec H1V 3R2 Canada. **Tel** (514)252-3021. **DD** 791.4309714. bk rev. adv acc. **Circ** 700. (ctrl). *Bulletin d'Information de l'A.C.P.Q.*

CINE CUBANO. V. 1 1960-. 0009-0946. Periodical. CU. Spanish. qt. $10.51. Empresa Ediciones Cubanas, Obispo 461, Apartado 605, Ciudad de la Habana Cuba. **Ind/Abst** Film Lit. Index.

CINE QUA NON. No. 1- Jan. 1972-. French. ir. **LC** PN1993. **DD** 791.4305.

CINE-TRACTS. V. 1- Spring 1977-. 0704-061X. Periodical. CN. English. qt. $8. Cine-Tracts, 4227 Explanade Avenue, Montreal Quebec H2W 1T1 Canada. **Ind/Abst** Film Lit. Index. **DD** 778.505.

CINEACTION . (CINEACTION : A MAGAZINE OF RADICAL FILM CRITICISM & THEORY). VFOAT Cine Action. No. 1 (Spring '85)-. 0826-9866. Periodical. CN. English. ty. $3.50 Per No., $10.00 for 4 issues. Cineaction Collective, 40 Alexander Street/Apt 705, Toronto Ontario M4Y 1B5 Canada. **DD** 791.4305.

CINEASTE. V. 1- Summer 1967-. 0009-7004. Periodical. US. English. qt. $13.00. Cineaste, PO Box 2242, New York NY 10009. **Tel** (212)982-1241. Ed Gary Crowdus, Dan Georgakas, Lenny Rubenstein, Susan Ohmer, Robert Sklar. **Ind/Abst** Film Lit. Index, Altern. Press Index, Media Rev. Dig. **LC** PN1993. bk rev. adv acc. **Circ** 6,000. America's leading magazine on the art and politics of the cinema including Hollywood, American independent cinema, European films, and emerging cinemas of the third world.

CINEFAN. No. 1- July 1974-. 0095-1447. Periodical. US. English. ir. $3.50. Fandom Unlimited Enterprises, PO Box 70868, Sunnyvale CA 94086. **Tel** (415)960-1151. Ed Randall D Larson. **LC** PN1995.9.F36. **DD** 791.43090915. bk rev adv acc. **Circ** 1,500. In-depth analysis and review of fantasy, horror and science fiction films, emphasizing independent, obscure and international films.

CINEFANTASTIQUE. 0145-6032. Periodical. US. English. ir. $24.00 Domestic, $28.00 Foreign. Cinefantastique, PO Box 270, Oak Park IL 60303. **Tel** (312)366-5566. Ed Frederick S Clarke. **Ind/Abst** Film Lit. Index, Media Rev. Dig. **LC** PN1995.9.H6. adv acc. **Circ** 20,000. (ctrl). The reviw of SF, fantasy, and horror films. Interviews with directors, producers, effects artists, in-depth articles, and behind the scenes insights.

CINEFEX. No. 1- March 1980-. 0198-1056. Periodical. US. English. qt. $15.00. Cinefex, PO Box 20027, Riverside CA 92516. **Tel** (714)242-9704. Ed Don Shay. **Ind/Abst** Film Lit. Index. **LC** TR858. **DD** 778.534505. **Circ** 15,000. Profusely illustrated journal on motion picture special effects-optical, physical, computer-generated and makeup.

CINEFORUM. Yearly V. 1- 19 -. 0009-7039. Periodical. IT. Italian. mo. Fed It Cineforum, CP 414, 30100 Venezia Italy. **Ind/Abst** Film Lit. Index. **LC** PN1993. **DD** 791.4305.

CINEGRAM. VFOAT Cinegram Magazine. V. 1- March/April 1976. 0145-3483. Periodical. US. English. qt. $4.00. Cinegram Magazine, 512 South Main, Ann Arbor MI 48103. **LC** PN1993. **DD** 791.4305.

CINEMA. No. 1- 1962-. 0009-7047. Periodical. US. English. ir. Spectator International Inc, 9667 Wilshire Boulevard, Beverly Hills CA 90212. **LC** PN1993. **DD** 791.4305.

CINEMA. Periodical. French (German). ir. 15.00. Arbeitsgemeinschaft Cinema, Postfach 1049, CH-8022 Zurich Switzerland. **Ind/Abst** Film Lit. Index. **LC** PN1993.

CINEMA AU QUEBEC, REPERTOIRE. (LE CINEMA AU QUEBEC, REPERTOIRE). 1979-. 0225-3151. CN. French. an. $15.00. Editions Cinema/

Motion Picture

Quebec, CP 309 Succursale Outremont, Montreal Quebec H2V 4N1 Canada. **DD** 791.4309714. *Cinema au Quebec, 0317-2333.*

CINEMA CANADA. No. 32-38, Sept./Oct. 1967-Sept./Oct. 1969. 0009-7071. Periodical. CN. English. bm. $35.60. Cinema Canada, Box 398 Outremont Station, Montreal Quebec H2V 9Z9 Canada. **Tel** (514)272-5354. Ed Connie Tadros. **Ind/Abst** Mag. Index, Can. Period. Index, Film Lit. Index, Media Rev. Dig. adv acc. *Canadian Cinematography, 0576-4823.*

CINEMA E CINEMA. Year 1- Oct./Dec. 1974-. Periodical. IT. Italian. qt. 45.000. Intrapresa, Via Caposile 2, 20137 Milano Italy. **Tel** (02)5451254. **LC** PN2995. **DD** 809.23. bk rev. adv acc. **Circ** 30,000. (ctrl). Essays on authors, trends, theory, and on the relationships of cinema/literature.

CINEMA FRANCAIS, PRODUCTION. FR. English (French). an. 25 rue de Berri, 75008 Paris France. **LC** PN1993.5.F7. **DD** 791.430944.

CINEMA JOURNAL. Began with Vol. for 1966/67. 0009-7101. Periodical. US. English. sa. $25.00. University of Illinois Press, 54 East Gregory Drive, Champaign IL 61820. **Tel** (217)333-0950. Ed Virginia Wright Wexman. **Ind/Abst** Writ. Am. Hist., Film Lit. Index, Art Index, Arts Humanit. Citation Index, Int. Index Film Period. **LC** PN1993. **DD** 791.4305. adv acc. **Circ** 1,050. Issued also in microform by University Microfilms International. Articles on film, movie history, television, film criticism, acting, production and film writing. *Journal.*

CINEMA NUOVO. Yearly V. 1 (N. 1-). 0009-711X. Periodical. IT. Italian. bm. 45.000. Edizioni Dedalo, Casella Postale 362, 70100 Bari Italy. **Tel** 080/371555. **Ind/Abst** Film Lit. Index. bk rev. adv acc. **Circ** 14,000.

CINEMA ONE. 1- 1967-. 0578-2988. Periodical. UK. English. qt. Secker & Warburg, University of London, Woburn Square, London WC14 0AB England.

CINEMA PAPERS. Began with Jan. 1974 issue. 0311-3639. Periodical. AT. English. bm. 23.00. MTV Publishing, 644 Victory Street, North Melbourn Victoria 3051 Australia. **Tel** (03)329 5983. Ed Nick Roddick. **Ind/Abst** Film Lit. Index, APAIS, Aust. Public Aff. Inf. Serv., Media Rev. Dig. **LC** PN1993.5.A8. **DD** 791.4305. bk rev. adv acc. **Circ** 15,000. (ctrl). Magazine containing film and book reviews. Also interviews with leading influential people within the motion picture industry. A reference to what is going on in the industry.

CINEMA (PORTO, PORTUGAL). (CINEMA). No. 1 (Sept. 82-). Periodical. Portuguese. qt. $100.00 Single Issue. Federacao Portuguesa de Cineclubes rua de Camoes, 777-4O DTO, 4000 Porto Portugal. **LC** PN1993. **DD** 791.4305.

CINEMA; REVISTA LUNARA DE CULTURA CINEMATIOGRAFICA. Year 1- 1963-. 0578-2910. Periodical. RM. Romanian. mo. Ilexim Press, PO Box 1-136-1-137, Bucharest Romania.

CINEMA TEXAS PROGRAM NOTES. (CINEMATEXAS PROGRAM NOTES). Began in 1972?. 0739-0378. Periodical. US. English. bm. University of Texas at Austin, CMA 6.118, Department of Radio/Television/Film, Austin TX 78712. **Tel** (512)471-1906. Ed Christopher Anderson. Critical introductions to nearly 100 films per year. An excellent reference source. Complete credits, detailed filmographies and suggestions for further reading.

CINEMA THE WORLD OVER. V. 1- July 1975-. Periodical. English. ir. 20.00. K S Hosain, 204-205 Hotel Metropole, Karachi Pakistan. **LC** PN1993. **DD** 791.4305.

CINEMA TV TODAY. Nov. 13, 1971-. Periodical. UK. English. wk. 142 Wardour St, London WIV 4BR England. *Today's Cinema.*

CINEMA VISION INDIA. V. 1- Jan. 1980-. Periodical. II. English. qt. Cinema Vision India, 1 Gentika SV Road Santacruz, West Bombay 400 054 India. **LC** PN1993.5.I8. **DD** 384.80954.

CINEMABOOK. V. 1- Spring 1976-. 0363-9665. Periodical. US. English. qt. $3.25. Cinemabook, 344 East 50th Street, New York NY 10022. **LC** PN1993. **DD** 791.4305.

CINEMACABRE. No.1- Winter/Spring 1978/79-. 0198-1064. Periodical. US. English. sa. $8.00. Geroge M Stover Jr, PO Box 10005, Baltimore MD 21204. **Tel** (301)828-0286. Ed George Stover. **Ind/Abst** Film Lit. Index, Media Rev. Dig. bk rev. adv acc. **Circ** 3,000. Feature articles, celebrity interviews, plus movie, book, and soundtrack reviews pertaining to the cinema of the fantastic. *Black Oracle.*

CINEMAG. No. 11- Oct. 1978-. 0709-5635. Periodical. CN. English. mo. $10. Domestic, $15.00 Foreign. **Ind/Abst** Film Lit. Index. **DD** 338.47791430971. *Trade News North, 0705-8799.*

CINEMAGIC (NEW YORK, N.Y.). (CINEMAGIC). Vol. 1, No. 1-. 0090-3000. Periodical. US. English. qt. Starlog Press Inc, 475 Park Avenue South, New York NY 10016. **Tel** (212)689-2830. Ed David Hutchison. **Ind/Abst** Film Lit. Index. **LC** TR858. **DD** 778.5345. adv acc. Guide to filmmaking. *Cinemagic, 0090-3000.*

CINEMAS. Series/Titl Business Monitor. UK. English. Librarian, Business Statistics Office, Cardiff Road, Newport Gwent NPT 1XG England. **LC** PN1993.5.G7. **DD** 38480941.

CINEMASCORE. Vol. 1, No. 1 (Jan. 1979)-. 0277-9803. Periodical. US. English. sa. $8.00. Fandom Unlimited Enterprises, PO Box 70868, Sunnyvale CA 94086. **Tel** (415)960-1151. Ed Randall D Larson. bk rev. adv acc. **Circ** 1,500. Reviews and analyses the art and technique of motion picture music, emphasizing interviews with film composers and retrospectives on specific film scores.

CINEMONKEY. 0162-0126. Periodical. US. English. qt. $7.00 Domestic, $9.50 Foreign. Cinemonkey, PO Box 8502, Portland OR 97207. **Ind/Abst** Film Lit. Index. **LC** PN1993. **DD** 791.4305. *Scintillation, 0147-5789.*

CINETHIQUE. No. 1- 1969-. Periodical. FR. French. ir. $26.61. Cinethique, PO Box 65, F-75722 Paris Cedex 15 France. **Ind/Abst** Film Lit. Index. adv acc. **Circ** 1,500. Work on any form of audiovisual pictures: movies, video TV including drawings, paintings and advertising.

CITRA FILM. Periodical. IO. Indonesian. mo. 750. Yayasan Pengembangan Perfilman Nasional, Menteng Raya No 62, Jakarta Indonesia. **LC** PN1993.

CLASSIC IMAGES. 0275-8423. Periodical. US. English. bm. $16.00. Classic Images, PO Box 809, Muscatine IA 52761. **Tel** (319)383-2377. **Ind/Abst** Film Lit. Index, Media Rev. Dig. **LC** PN1995.9.C54. **DD** 791.4305. bk rev. adv acc. **Circ** 3,000. Complete coverage: classic film field-film and video market, availability evaluation, historical articles. Biographies interviews, movie and book reviews, international, animation, technical. *Classic Film/Video Images, 0164-5560.*

CLOSE-UP. V. 1-. Periodical. English. ir. **LC** PN1993. **DD** 791.430954.

CNC STATISTIQUES. *See* Statistics.

COMMERCIAL PRICE LIST - N.F.B. PHOTOTHEQUE. (COMMERCIAL PRICE LIST). **Main/Corp** National Film Board of Canada. Phototheque. **VFOAT** Tarif Commercial. **VAT** Commerical Price List - National Film Board Phototheque, Tarif Commercial - O.N.F. Phototheque, Tarif Commercial - Office National du Film. Phototheque. 0709-678X. Periodical. CN. English (French). National Film Board of Canada Phototheque, Tunney's Pasture, Ottawa Ontario K1A 0M9 Canada. *Commercial Price List, 0706-1684.*

CONTINENTAL FILM & VIDEO REVIEW. **VFOAT** Continental Film and Video Review. Vol. 27, No. 10 (Aug. 1980)- – No. 334-. Periodical. UK. English. mo. $28.00. CFR Subscriptions, PO Box 1, Barking Essex IG11 8AZ England. *Continental Film Review.*

CONTRACAMPO. Yearly V. 1, No. 1, (April 1979)-. Periodical. SP. Spanish. ir. 3000. Contracampo, Apartado 17.048, Madrid Spain. **LC** PN1993. **DD** 791.4305.

COPIE ZERO. First issue in 1979. 0709-0471. Periodical. CN. French. qt. $11.61. La Cinematheque Quebecoise, 335 Boulevard de Maisonneuve Est, Montreal Quebec H2X K1K Canada. **Tel** (514)842-9763. Ed Pierre Jutras and Pierre Veronneau. **Ind/Abst** Point Repere, Film Lit. Index, Media Rev. Dig. **DD** 338.477914309714. adv acc. **Circ** 1,000. Information and reference magazine on the Quebecois cinema: dossiers on the filmakers, monographies, and yearly film listing. *Nouveau Cinema Canadien, 0550-1318.*

CRITIC. **VFOAT** Film Critic. V. 1- Sept./Oct. 1972-. 0090-9831. Periodical. US. English. wk. Film & Television Press Guild, 9 Compayne Gardens, London NW6 England. **Ind/Abst** Book Rev. Index, Book Rev. Digest. **LC** PN1993. **DD** 791.4305. *Film Society Review.*

CTVD, CINEMA, TV DIGEST. **VFOAT** Cinema, TV Digest. **VAT** Cinema Television Digest: Cinema, Television Digest. V. 1- Winter 1961/62-. 0007-9219. Periodical. US. English. ir. Hampton Books, Route 1 Box 202, Newberry SC 29108. **LC** P87. **DD** 791.437.

CULT MOVIE. Yearly V. 1, No. 1, (Dec. 1980)-. Periodical. Italian. bm. 2.000 Single Issue. Via del Sole, 10-50123 Firenze Italy. **LC** PN1993. **DD** 791.4305.

CULTURE STATISTICS. FILM INDUSTRY. *See* Statistics.

CURRENT RESEARCH IN FILM. Vol. 1-. 0748-8580. US. English. an. Ablex Publishing Corporation, 355 Chestnut Street, Norwood NJ 07648. **LC** PN1993. **DD** 384.805.

DAILY VARIETY. **VFOAT** Variety. 1933-. 0011-5509. Periodical. US. English. da. Variety Daily, 1400 North Cahuenga Boulevard, Hollywood CA 90028. **Tel** (213)469-1141. **Ind/Abst** Mag. Index, Infobank. **LC** PN1993.

DALIL AL-SINIMA AL-ARABIYAH. **VFOAT** Arab Cinema Guide. Arabic (English). an. 1.00. 218 Shari Al-Jaysh, Al-Qahirah Misr Egypt. Ed S Farid. **LC** PN1993.5.A65.

DANISH FILMS. English, French and German. ir. Danish Film Institute, Store Sndervoldstraede, DK-1419 Copenhagen Denmark. **LC** PN1993.3.

DIGEST. **Main/Corp** University Film Association. US. English. qt. $4.50. Southern Illinois University, Department of Cinema & Photography, Carbondale IL 62901. **LC** PN1993. **DD** 791.43062773994. *UFPA Digest.*

DIRECTORY - CANADIAN SOCIETY OF CINEMATOGRAPHERS. *See* Yearbooks, Almanacs, Directories.

DIRECTORY FOR MEMBERS - SOCIETY OF MOTION PICTURE AND TELEVISION ENGINEERS, INC. *See* Yearbooks, Almanacs, Directories.

DIRECTORY OF BLACK FILM/TV TECHNICIANS AND ARTISTS, WEST COAST. *See* Yearbooks, Almanacs, Directories.

DIRECTORY OF FILM LIBRARIES IN NORTH AMERICA. *See* Yearbooks, Almanacs, Directories.

DIRECTORY OF MEMBERS - DIRECTORS GUILD OF AMERICA. *See* Yearbooks, Almanacs, Directories.

DOCUMENTATION - BUREAU DE SURVEILLANCE DU CINEMA. (DOCUMENTATION). Ed. Feb. 5, 1981-. 0710-1252. Periodical. CN. English (French). wk. Gouvernement du Quebec, 600 St Amable 4E Etage, Quebec G1R 4Z1 Canada. **DD** 791.4305. *Revue de Presse, 0227-1958.*

DUTCH FILM. NE. English. ir. Government Printing Office, The Hague Netherlands. **LC** PN1993.3. **DD** 791.4309492.

ECRITS SUR LE CINEMA. 1982-. 0822-6350. CN. French. an. a/s Cinematheque Quebecoise Musee du Cinema, 335 Est Boul de Maisonneuve, Montreal Quebec H2X 1K1 Canada. **Tel** (514)842-9763. Ed Pierre Veronneau. **DD** 016.7914309714. **Circ** 1,000. A bibliography of publications on Quebec cinema from 1911 to 1981.

EDUCATORS GUIDE TO FREE FILMS. 1st- Ed. 0070-9395. Periodical. US. English. an. $29.00. Educators Progress Service, 214 Center Street, Randolph WI 53956. **Tel** (414)326-3126. Ed John C Diffor and Elaine N Diffor. **LC** LB1044. **DD** 371.335230838. **NLM** LB 1044 E24. A listing of free films available to educators on a free-loan basis.

EFLA EVALUATIONS. *See* Library and Information Science.

EIGA MOKUROKU. JA. Japanese. ir. Tokyo Toritsu Hibiya Toshokan, 1-Ban 1-Go Hibiya Koen, Chiyoda-Ku 100, Tokyo-To Japan. **LC** Z5784.M9, PN1993.5.J3.

EIGAKAN MEIBO. JA. Japanese. ir. 8 Kayabacho 3, Chuo-ku Tokyo Japan. **LC** PN1998.A1.

EIZO NENKAN. JA. Japanese. ir. 3500. Michi Shuppansha, 8-10 Sarugakucho 2 Chiyoda-Ku, Tokyo 101 Japan. **LC** PN1995.9.D6.

NA EKRANAKH MIRA. Vol. 1- 1966-. UR. Russian. 1.18 single issue. Iskusstvo, K-51 Tsvetnoi Bulvar 25, Moskva Russia. **LC** PN1993.

THE ESSENTIAL CINEMA. V. 1- 1975-. 0363-0900. US. English. ir. Anthology Film Archives, 80 Wooster, New York NY 10012. **LC** PN1993. **DD** 791.437.

ESTIMATES. PART III, NATIONAL FILM BOARD. **VFOAT** Budget des Depenses. CN. English (French). $6.00 Domestic, $7.20 Foreign. Canadian Government Publishing Centre, Supply and Services Canada, Ottawa Ontario K1A 0S9 Canada. **LC** PN1999.N26. **DD** 791.4306071.

ETUDES CINEMATOGRAPHIQUES. Vol. 1, No 1/2 (Spring 1960)-. 0014-1992. Periodical. FR. French. ir. $19.96. Lettres Modernes, 73 rue du Cardinal Lemoine, Paris 5E France.

FAMOUS MONSTERS. 0278-4203. Periodical. US. English. mo. $17.00 Domestic, $21.00 Canada. Warren Publishing Co., 145 East 32nd Street, New York NY 10016. **LC** PN1995.9.H6. **DD** 791.43090916. *Monster World.*

FAMOUS MONSTERS OF FILMLAND. **VFOAT** Famous Monsters. Began in 1958. 0014-7443. Periodical. US. English. mo. **LC** PN1995.9.H6.

FANTASTIC FILMS. 0273-7043. Periodical. US. English. bm. $15.00. Fantastic Films Magazine Incorporated, PO Box 1900, Evanston IL 60201.

FEATURE FILMS ON 8MM AND 16MM. 0071-4100. US. English. ir. $85.50. RR Bowker Company, PO Box 1807, Ann Arbor MI 48106.

FERNSEH- UND KINO-TECHNIK. 23.- Year. 0015-0142. Periodical. GW. German. mo. $56.73. Dr Alfred Huethig Verlag GMBH, Im Weiher 10, D-6900 Heidelberg 1 West Germany. **Tel** 6221/489-0. **Ed** Norbert Bolewski. **Ind/Abst** Comput. Control Abstr., Electr. Electron. Abstr., Sci. Abstr. Sect. A. Phys. Abstr., Phys. Abstr. **CODEN** FNKTAH. bk rev. adv acc. **Circ** 3,000. (ctrl). Official publication of the West German Society for TV and Film Technique and the Committee on Norms for Film and TV and the Association for Technical Industry for Film and Television. *Kino-Technik.*

DAS FERNSEHSPIEL IM ZDF. *See* Communication - Broadcasting.

FESTIVAL DES FILMS DU MONDE. (FESTIVAL DES FILMS DU MONDE : PROGRAMME). **VFOAT** World Film Festival : Program. 1978-. 0712-9548. CN. English (French). an. $4.00 Per No. World Film Festival, 1456 Maisonneuve Boulevard West, Montreal Quebec H3G 1M8 Canada. **DD** 791.43079. *Festival Canadien des Films du Monde (Program), 0712-953X.*

FESTIVAL INTERNATIONAL DU FILM DE LA CRITIQUE QUEBECOISE. 1977-. 0703-9824. Periodical. CN. French. $2.00 Per Number. Festival International du Film de la Critique Quebecoise, a/s G Charest, App 505 1855 rue du Havre, Montreal Quebec H2K 2K4 Canada. **DD** 010.

FILM. V. 1- 1973-. Periodical. PL. Polish. wk. ARS Polona, Krakowskie Przedmiescie 7, 00-068 Warsaw Poland.

FILM & HISTORY. **VAT** Film and History. Began in 1971. 0360-3695. Periodical. US. English. qt. $14.00. Historians Film Committee, New Jersey Institute of Technology (NJIT), Neward NJ 07102. **Tel** (201)596-3291. **Ed** John E O'Conner. **Ind/Abst** Am. Hist. Life, Hist. Abstr., Part A, Mod. Hist. Abstr., Hist. Abst., Part B, Twent. Century Abstr., Writ. Am. Hist., Recent Publ. Artic., Hist. Abstr. bk rev. adv acc. **Circ** 500. Study of film and television by historians and social scientists for their research, teaching, and scholarly output. *Newsletter - Historians Film Committee.*

FILM AND TELEVISION TECHNICIAN. V. 27, No. 196-V. 41, May 1961-1975. Periodical. UK. English. mo. 10.50. Association of Cinema Television and Technicians, 2 Soho Square, London W1 England. **Tel** 01 437 8506. **Ed** Peter Avis. bk rev. adv acc. **Circ** 22,000. Subjects of interest to our members. We are a trade union journal. *Film and TV Technician.*

FILM & TV WORLD. **VFOAT** Film and T.V. World. V. 4, No. 11 (Nov./Dec. 1981)-. 0712-5771. Periodical. CN. English. mo. $25.00 US/Canada, $32.00 Others. 535 Lake Shore Boulevard West, Toronto Ontario M5V 2V8 Canada. **LC** PN1993. **DD** 384.5540971, 384.80971. *Filmworld (Toronto, Ont.), 0708-0956.*

THE FILM AND VIDEO MAKERS DIRECTORY. *See* Yearbooks, Almanacs, Directories.

FILM & VIDEO NEWS. **VFOAT** Film and Video News. V. 38, No. 4 (Apr. 1984)-. 8750-068X. Periodical. US. English. qt. $12.00. 1058 Eighth Street, La Salle IL 61301. **LC** PN1993. **DD** 791.435305. *Film News (New York, N.Y. : 1960), 0195-1017.*

FILM (BRITISH FEDERATION OF FILM SOCIETIES). (FILM : THE BRITISH FEDERATION OF FILM SOCIETIES MONTHLY JOURNAL). No. 55 (Summer 1969)-. 0015-1025. Periodical. UK. English. ir. 13.80. Film, 20 Medwin Street, London SW4 7RS England. **Tel** (01)437-4355. **Ed** Peter Cargin. bk rev. adv acc. **Circ** 3,000. (ctrl). Covers film news, books, festival reports, and general information on all aspects of non-commercial cinema. *Film (Federation of Film Societies).*

FILM BULLETIN. V. 1- 1933-. 0015-1165. Periodical. US. English. mo. Wax Publications, 1239 Vine Street, Philadelphia PA 19107. **Ind/Abst** Film Lit. Index, Media Rev. Dig. **DD** 792.9305.

FILM CANADIANA. V. 1- Fall 1969-. 0015-1173. Periodical. CN. English (French). an. Canadian Film Institute, 303 Richmond Road, Ottawa Ontario K1Z 6X3 Canada.

FILM CATALOGUE - LAKE ONTARIO REGIONAL LIBRARY SYSTEM. (FILM CATALOGUE). **Main/Corp** Lake Ontario Regional Library System. **VFOAT** 16 MM Film Catalogue. **VAT** 16 MM Films Available from the Public Libraries of the Lake Ontario Regional Library System. 5th Ed. (1981)-. 0823-8227. CN. English. be. Lake Ontario Regional Library System, 38 Wright Crescent, Kingston Ontario K7L 4T9 Canada. **DD** 017.537. *Audio-Visual Catalogue, 0384-7608.*

FILM COMMENT. V. 1, No. 3-. 0015-119X. Periodical. US. English. bm. $12.00. Film Society of Lincoln Center, 140 West 65th Street, New York NY 10023. **Tel** (212)877-1800. **Ed** Richard Corliss and Harlan Jacobson. **Ind/Abst** Pop. Mag. Rev., Film Lit. Index, Book Rev. Index, Media Rev. Dig., Read. Guide Period. Lit., Art Index. **LC** PN1993. bk rev. adv acc. **Circ** 43,000. (ctrl). Available on microfilm from University Microfilms. Film journal containing articles directly related to the cinema. *Vision.*

FILM CRITICISM. V. 1- Spring 1976-. 0163-5069. Periodical. US. English. ty. $9.00. Film Criticism, Allegheny College, Meadville PA 16335. **Tel** (814)724-2351. **Ed** I Lloyd Michaels. **Ind/Abst** MLA Int. Bibliogr. Books Artic. Mod. Lang. Lit., Film Lit. Index. **LC** PN1993. **DD** 791.437505. bk rev. **Circ** 400. Scholarly writing on film.

FILM CULTURE. No. 1- Jan. 1955-. 0015-1211. Periodical. US. English. ir. $20.00 Domestic, $24.00 Foreign. Film Culture, US Government Printing Office, Box 1499, New York NY 10001. **Tel** (212)226-0578. **Ed** Jonas Mekas. **Ind/Abst** Film Lit. Index, Media Rev. Dig., Art Index. **LC** PN1993. **DD** 791.4305. (cum index). bk rev. adv acc. **Circ** 3,000. A journal devoted to Avantgarde Independent cinema. Writings by film-makers, interviews with film-makers and critical writing by scholars.

THE FILM DAILY YEAR BOOK. 10th-11th Ed. US. English. an. $12.95. Grove Press, 196 West Houston Street, New York NY 10014. *Film Year Book.*

FILM (DENVER, COLO.). (FILM). 1983-. 0740-1566. US. English. an. $12.95. Arden Press, PO Box 418, Denver CO 80201. **Tel** (303)837-8913. **Ed** Frederick Ramey. **LC** PN1995.9.E96. **DD** 791.43750973. **Circ** 15,000. Each volume treats the work of fifteen to twenty independent and experimental filmmakers informatively and critically and each has a different author.

FILM DIRECTIONS. V. 1-. Periodical. UK. English. qt. 4.50. Arts Council of Northern Ireland, 181A Stranmills Road, Belfast 9 Ireland. **Tel** (0232)667687. **Ed** Michael Open. **LC** PN1993.5.I85. **DD** 791.4305. bk rev. adv acc. **Circ** 3,000. Film reviews, general articles on cinema, video and other related matters.

FILM DIRECTORS. 1984-. 0740-2872. US. English. an. $39.95. Lone Eagle Publishers, 9903 Santa Monica Boulevard/Suite 204, Beverly Hills CA 90212-9942. **Tel** (213)471-8066. **Ed** Michael Singer. **LC** PN1998.A2. **DD** 791.43023305. adv acc. **Circ** 10,000. (ctrl). Most complete reference work on film directors: names, addresses, phone, credits, representatives. Cross-indexed by film and director. Includes interviews with six prominent directors and photos. *Directors (Beverly Hills, Calif.), 0732-4359.*

FILM DOPE. No. 1- Dec. 1972-. 0305-1706. Periodical. UK. English. ty. 6-00 Domestic, 13-00 Foreign. Film Dope, 45 Lupton Street, London NW5 2HS England. **Ed** Bob Baker and David Bidder. **Ind/Abst** Film Lit. Index. **Circ** 1,000. Complete and correct filmographies of the world's major film artists (directors, actors, photographers, composers, art directors, animators, etc.). Many stills.

THE FILM FILE. (THE FILM FILE . . .). 1981-1982-. 0731-5716. US. English. $45.00. Media Referral Service, PO Box 3586, Minneapolis MN 55403. **Tel** (612)933-2819. **Ed** Elizabeth L Burnam. **LC** PN1998. **DD** 011.37. **Circ** 5,000. Films and videocasettes available from 150 distributors. Subject area and alphabetical title sections updated annually.

LE FILM FRANCAIS. No. 1- 1944-. Periodical. FR. French. wk. Le Film Francais, 90 rue de Flandre, 75943 Paris Cedex 19 France. **Tel** 200 35 00. **LC** PN1993.

FILM HERITAGE *CEASED.* V. 1-V. 12, No. 3. 0015-1270. Periodical. US. English. qt. $3.00. Wright State University, College of Liberal Arts, Box 652, Dayton OH 45469. **Ind/Abst** Am. Hist. Life, Hist. Abstr., Part A, Mod. Hist. Abstr., Hist. Abst., Part B, Twent. Century Abstr. **LC** PN1993. **DD** 791.4305. Available on microfilm from University Microfilms.

FILM IN FINLAND (HELSINKI, FINLAND). (FILM IN FINLAND). Periodical. English. ir. Salomonkatu 17 B 6, SF-00100 Helsinki 10 Finland.

FILM INDEX. *See* Indexes/Abstracts.

THE FILM JOURNAL. V. 1- (Issue 1-). 0046-3787. Periodical. US. English. sm. $25.00. Pubsun Corporation, 224 West 49th Street/Suite 305, New York NY 10019. **Tel** (212)246-6460. **Ed** Robert H Sunshine. **Ind/Abst** Int. Index Film Period. **LC** PN1993. **DD** 791.4305. Index in last issue of volume - attached. bk rev. adv acc. **Circ** 11,500. (ctrl). Available on microfilm from University Microfilms. Coverage of the motion picture industry and ancillary markets, including video, concessions, and equipment, film reviews, interviews, etc.

FILM LIBRARY NEWS. *See* Education (General) - Theory, Practice of Education.

FILM LITERATURE : CURRENT. Vol. 1 (Jan. 1979)-. 0277-4003. Periodical. US. English. mo. $25.00 Institutions, $12.50 Individuals. Filmdex Part II Inc, Box 22477 Suny-A 1400 Washington Avenue, Albany NY 12222.

FILM LITERATURE INDEX. *See* Indexes/ Abstracts.

FILM MAKING *CEASED.* V. 8, No. 9-V. 18, No. 10. 0013-2543. Periodical. UK. English. mo. **Ind/Abst** Film Lit. Index.

FILM NEWS. **Main/Corp** Indonesia. Direktorat Film. No. 1/4-. Indonesian. ir. Mereka Barat 9, Jakarta Indonesia. **LC** PN1993. *Film News.*

FILM OG KINO. Began publication in: 1938. Norwegian. an. **LC** PN1993.3. **DD** 791.4305.

FILM QUARTERLY. V. 12- No. 1- 1958-. 0015-1386. Periodical. US. English. qt. $19.00. University of California Press, 2120 Berkeley Way, Berkeley CA 94720. **Tel** (415)642-6221. **Ed** Ernest Callenbach. **Ind/Abst** Mag. Index, Film Lit. Index, Biogr. Index, Art Index, Humanit. Index, Book Rev. Index, Media Rev. Dig., Access. **LC** PN1993. bk rev. adv acc. **Circ** 3,700. Available on microfilm. Articles on commercial, experimental and documentary of developments in film theory and criticism. *Quarterly of Film, Radio and Television.*

FILM READER. 1- 1975-. 0361-722X. Periodical. US. English. an. Film Reader, Northwestern University Speech Ann, Evanston IL 60201. **Tel** (312)492-7317. **Ed** Virginia Keller. **Ind/Abst** Film Lit. Index, Media Rev. Dig. **LC** PN1993. **DD** 791.4305. bk rev. adv acc. **Circ** 1,500. Film theory and criticism.

FILM REVIEW. Began publication in 1944?. US. English. an. A S Barnes & Company, 421 Canbury NY 08512. **Ed** F M Speed. **LC** PN1993. **DD** 791.4058.

FILM REVIEW. UK. English. mo. $13.42. EMI Cinemas Ltd, 30-31 Golden Square, London W1 England. **Tel** 01 937 4260.

Motion Picture

FILM REVIEW ANNUAL. 1981-. 0737-9080. US. English. an. $75.00. Jerome S Ozer Publishing Company, 340 Tenafly Road, Englewood NJ 07631. **Tel** (201)567-7040. **Ed** Jerome S Ozer. Reprints in full texts of reviews of feature length films released in the United States during the year. Gives cast and credits for each film and winners of major awards. *Film Review Digest Annual, 0146-1656.*

FILM REVIEW DIGEST. V. 1- Fall 1975-. 0098-0471. US. English. $45.00. Kraus-Thomson Organization, Route 100, Millwood NY 10546. **LC** PN1995. **DD** 791.437.

FILM STUDIES. **Main/Corp** Boston University. School of Public Relations and Communications. Communications Arts Division. **VFOAT** Boston University Film Studies. No. 1- 1964-. 0524-1324. Periodical. US. English. Boston University, 765 Commonwealth Avenue, Boston MA 02215.

FILM WORLD (BOMBAY, INDIA). (FILM WORLD). Began publication with vol. 1 in 1964?. 0015-1475. Periodical. II. English. mo. Film World International Private Ltd, 8 Horiman Circle/Botawala Building, Bombay India 400023. **LC** PN1993.

FILM YEAR BOOK. *See* Yearbooks, Almanacs, Directories.

FILMCRITICA. Began in Dec. 1950. Periodical. IT. Italian. mo $26.73. Licosa Libreria Comm Sansani, Via Lamarmora 45, 50121 Firenze Italy. **Tel** 055 579751. **Ed** Grifo-Montepuleiana. **Ind/Abst** Film Lit. Index.

FILMFAUST. Periodical. German. ir. 35.00. Filmfaust Verlag, D-6000 Frankfurt Am Main 1, Schumanstrasse 64, Frankfurt West Germany. **LC** PN1993.

FILMFORDERUNG . . . STATISTIK, FILMEINFUHR, STATISTIK. *See* Statistics.

FILM/HISTORIA. V. 1- May 1978-. Periodical. BO. Spanish. ir. $20.00. A G Dragon Film/Historia, Casilla 5828, La Paz Bolivia. **LC** PN1993.5.L3. **DD** 791.43098.

FILMKRITIK. Began with Jan. 1957 issue. 0015-1572. Periodical. GW. German. mo. $41.79. Filmkritker Kooperative, Kreittmayerstrasse 3, 8000 Munich 2 West Germany. **Ind/Abst** Film Lit. Index. **LC** PN1995.

FILMKRITIK. German. ir. Zweitausendeins, Postfach 710249, D 6000 Frankfurt/Main 71, Frankfurt West Germany. **LC** PN1995.

FILMKULTURA. (FILM KULTURA). 1969?-. 0015-1580. Periodical. HU. Hungarian. bm. Akadmeiai Kiado, POB 24, 1363 Budapest Hungary. **Ind/Abst** Film Lit. Index.

FILMKUNST. Number 1-. Periodical. AU. German. qt. 148,-. Rauhensteingasse 5, Postfach 253, A1015 Wien 1 Austria. **Tel** (0222)529936. **Ed** Ludwig Gesek. **Ind/Abst** Film Lit. Index. bk rev. adv acc. **Circ** 3,000. Motion picture and television as object of scientific research.

FILMROW. **VFOAT** Film Row. 1981-82-. 0195-7546. US. English. an. Filmrow Communications Group, 8272 Sunset Boulevard West, Hollywood CA 90046. **LC** PN1998.A1. **DD** 384.802573.

FILMRUTAN. Vol. 1- 1958-. 0015-1661. Periodical. Swedish. ql. **Ind/Abst** Film Lit. Index.

FILMS; A CATALOG OF THE FILM COLLECTION. **Main/Corp** New York. Public Library. Periodical. US. English. ir. Fifth Avenue & 42nd Street, New York NY 10018. **LC** PN1995.9.D6. **DD** 791.438.

FILMS A L'ECRAN. 0046-3825. Periodical. CN. French. sm. 24.00 Domestic, 35.00 Foreign. Office de Communications Socia, 4005 rue de Bellechasse, Montreal Que H1X 1J6 Canada. **Tel** (514)729-6391. **DD** 791.43705. Index for the evaluation of new films.

FILMS AND FILMING CEASED. V. 1-26 (No. 1-309). 0015-167X. Periodical. UK. English. mo. 16.50 Domestic, 21.00 Europe. Brevet Publishing, 43B Gloucester Road, Croydon CR0 2DH England. **Tel** (01)2224421. **Ed** John Russell Taylor. **Ind/Abst** Art Index. **LC** PN1993. **DD** 791.4305. bk rev. adv acc.

FILMS AND FILMING (CROYDON, LONDON, ENGLAND). (FILMS AND FILMING). Issue No. 345 (June 1983)-. 0015-167X. Periodical. UK. English. mo. Brevet Publishing Ltd, 445 Brighton Road, South Croydon Surrey CR2 6E England. **Ind/Abst** Film Lit. Index, Art Index. **LC** PN1993. **DD** 791.4305. *Films & Filming Incorporating Focus on Film.*

FILMS BY AND/OR ABOUT WOMEN. 0361-4581. US. English. ir. $5.50. Womens History Research, 2325 Oak Street, Berkeley CA 94708. **Tel** (415)548-1770.

FILMS - DARTMOUTH REGIONAL LIBRARY. (FILMS). **Main/Corp** Dartmouth Regional Library. 0711-6519. CN. English. te. Free. Films, c/o Reference Department, Dartmouth Regional Library, 100 Wyse Road, Dartmouth NS B3A 1M1 Canada. **DD** 018.137. *Films at the Dartmourth Regional Library.*

FILMS IN REVIEW. V. 1- Feb. 1950-. 0015-1688. Periodical. US. English. ir. National Board of Review of Motion Pictures, PO Box 589, New York NY 10021. **Tel** (212)628-1594. **Ed** Robin Little. **Ind/Abst** Film Lit. Index, Book Rev. Index, Ref. Source, Index Book Rev. Humanit., Media Rev. Dig., Art Index. **LC** PN1993. **DD** 791.437. (cum index). bk rev. adv acc. **Circ** 10,000. Every area of motion pictures investigated and written about by experts in the field. *New Movies.*

FILMS ON OFFER . . . . UK. English. an. 3.00. British Film Institute, 127 Charing Cross Road, London WC2H OEA England. **LC** PN1998. **DD** 011.37.

FILMS ON SCREEN AND VIDEO. Periodical. UK. English. mo. $14.00, $15.00 Overseas. Ocean Publications, 34 Buckingham Palace Road, London SW1W 9SA England. **LC** PN1993. **DD** 791.4305.

FILMSPIEGEL. Periodical. SZ. German. bw. Kunst & Wissen Erich Bieber, Dufourstrasse 51, Ch-8008 Zurich Switzerland.

FILMSSONEN, DANSK FILMFORTEGNELSE. **VFOAT** Dansk Filmfortegnelse. 79-80-. 0107-1033. Periodical. Danish. an. Bibliotekscentralen, Telegrafvej 5, 2750 Ballerup Denmark. **LC** PN1997.8.

FILMVIDEO-JOURNAL. GW. German. an. 6.80. GFW-Verlag, Poststrasse 21, Postfach 200 340, D-4000 Dusseldorf 1 West Germany. **LC** TR845. **DD** 778.505.

FISCHER FILM ALMANACH. *See* Yearbooks, Almanacs, Directories.

FOCUS. CHICAGO. (FOCUS : CHICAGO). 0362-0905. US. English. bm. Free to Members, $2.00 General. Facets Multimedia Inc, 755 West Buena Avenue, Chicago IL 60613. **LC** PN1993.F26. **DD** 791.4305.

FOCUS ON FILM CEASED. No. 1-37. 0015-5128. Periodical. UK. English. ty. $8.00. The Tantivy Press, 136-148 Tooley Street, London SE1 2TT England. **Ind/Abst** Film Lit. Index. **LC** PN1993. **DD** 791.4305. (cum index).

FOREMOST FILMS. (FOREMOST FILM OF . . .). 0145-3556. US. English. Gordon Press, PO Box 459 Bowling Green Station, New York NY 10004. **LC** PN1993.3. **DD** 791.430973.

FORMAT CINEMA. No. 1 June 1981. 0711-3315. Periodical. CN. French. bw. $25.00 Per Issue. Format Cinema, CP 397, Succursale Outremont, Outremont Quebec H2V 4N3 Canada. **DD** 338.477914309714.

FRAMEWORK. Began with issue No. 1 (1975). 0306-7661. Periodical. UK. English. $6.00 3 issues/Domestic, $16.00 3 issues/US. Framework, University of Arts Foundation, English and American Studies, University of East Anglia, Norwich NR4 7TJ England. **Ind/Abst** Film Lit. Index, Media Rev. Dig. **LC** PN1993. **DD** 791.4305.

FRAUEN UND FILM. Began with No. 1, published in 1974. Periodical. German. sa. 25.60. Stromfeld Buchversand, Holzhausenstr 4, D-6000 Frankfurt Am Main 1 West Germany. **Tel** 069-59 99 99. **Ed** Heide Schlupmann. **LC** PN1995.9.W6. **DD** 791.43088042. bk rev. adv acc. **Circ** 5,000. The only European feminist film journal, including film reviews, feature articles on women film productions, and related question of media reception.

FREE LOAN FILMS. **Main/Corp** Association-Sterling Films. **VFOAT** Free Loan 16 MM. Sound Motion Pictures. 0093-0881. US. English. Association-Sterling Films, 866 Third Avenue, New York NY 10022. **LC** PN1998. **DD** 011. *16 MM. Sound Free Loan Films, Sales and Rental Subjects.*

FUN FLICKS. **Main/Corp** Toronto Public Libraries. July 1975-. 0382-5388. Periodical. CN. English. Toronto Public Libraries, 40 Orchard View Boulevard, Toronto Ontario M4R 1B9 Canada. **DD** 028.52.

GOLDEN EAGLE FILM; AWARDS. 1957-. 0436-1377. Periodical. US. English. an. 1201 - 16th Street NW, Washington DC 20036. **LC** PN1999.4.

GREEN SHEET. 0533-2508. Periodical. US. English. ir. Motion Picture Association of America, 522 5th Avenue, New York NY 10036.

GROS PLAN (MONTREAL, QUEBEC). (GROS PLAN). Vol. 1, No. 1 (Oct. 81)-. 0712-6840. Periodical. CN. French (text in English). bm. Free. Association des Professionnels du Cinema du Quebec, Bureau 35 445 rue Saint-Francois-Xavier, Montreal Quebec H2Y 2T1 Canada. **DD** 791.43060714. (ctrl).

GUIDE TO COLLEGE COURSES IN FILM AND TELEVISION. *See* Education (General) - Higher Education.

GUIDE TO GOVERNMENT-LOAN FILMS. 1st- Ed. 0072-8462. US. English. **LC** PN1998. **DD** 791.438.

GUIDE TO LOCATION INFORMATION. 0148-8538. US. English. an. $15.00. Public Relations Department, Hollywood CA 90048. **LC** PN1998.A1. **DD** 791.430973.

HABLEMOS DE CINE. Periodical. PE. Spanish. ir. Hablemos de Cine, Libertadores 199 San Isidro, Lima 27 Peru. **Ind/Abst** Film Lit. Index.

HAN'GUK YONGHWA YON'GAM. 1977-. Yondopan. KO. Korean. ir. Yonghwe-Chinhung Kongsa, 34-5 Namsan-Dong 3-Ka, Chung-Ku, Seoul South Korea. **LC** PN1993.5.K6.

HERALDO DEL CINE. V. 37- (No. 1844/45). Periodical. Spanish. wk. $120.00. Heraldo Del Cine, Moreno 1215 1 Piso 1091, Capital Federal Argentina. *Heraldo Del Cinematografista.*

HITCH. Danish. ir. 6.00 Single Issue. Teglgardstrde 10 1452 K, V Hans Brsting, Kbenhavn Denmark. **LC** PN1993.

THE HOLLYWOOD REPORTER STUDIO BLU-BOOK DIRECTORY. *See* Yearbooks, Almanacs, Directories.

THE HOLLYWOOD REPORTER. TV SPECIAL. (THE HOLLYWOOD REPORTER TV SPECIAL). **VFOAT** TV Special. **VAT** Hollywood Reporter. Television Special. 1st- Summer 1979-. 0195-7481. Periodical. US. English. qt. $6.00. The Hollywood Reporter Inc, 6715 Sunset Boulevard, Hollywood CA 90028. **LC** PN1992. **DD** 791.450973. *Televisions.*

HOME VIDEO PUBLISHER. (HOME VIDEO PUBLISHER : HVP). **VFOAT** HVP. Vol. 1, No. 1 (July 16, 1984)-. 0748-0822. Periodical. US. English. wk. $225.00. Knowledge Industry Publications Inc, 701 Westchester Avenue, White Plains NY 10604. **Tel** (914)328-9157. **Ed** Leslie Grey. A newsletter which analyzes home video publishing opportunities for special interest programming as well as feature films.

HUNGAROFILM BULLETIN. 19 -. 0018-7798. Periodical. HU. English. ir. Hungarofilm, V Bathori U 10, Budapest PF 39 Hungary 1363. **Tel** 125-425. **Ind/Abst** Film Lit. Index. **Circ** 2,500. (ctrl). Information about Hungarian cinema: particular films (full-length and short films, TV-productions), directors, and other collaborators, all about the Hungarian cinema in general.

IFPA COMMUNICATOR. **Main/Corp** Information Film Producers of America. Jan. 1973-. 0099-1090. US. English. IFPA, PO Box 1470, Hollywood CA 90028. **LC** PN1993.I624. **DD** 791.43. *IFPA Newsletter.*

IKON. V. 12-27 (No. 40/41-103), Jan./July 1962-1977. 0019-1744. Periodical. IT. Italian. sa. $16.64. Franco Angeli Editore, Viale Monza 106, 20127 Milano Italy. **Tel** (02)28.27.651/2/3/. **Ind/Abst** Film Lit. Index. **LC** PN1795. *Revue Internationale de Filmologie.*

INDEPENDENT EYE. **VFOAT** Eye. **VAT** Eye (Toronto). Fall 1979-. 0225-9192. Periodical. CN. English. qt. 20.00. Canadian Filmmakers Distribution Centre, 67 A Portand Street, Toront Ontario M5V 2M9 Canada. **Tel** (416)593-1808. **Ed** Ross Turnbull. **DD** 791.430971. adv acc. **Circ** 450. A newsletter published for members giving updates on local events, films in progress, board/staff activities, job

Motion Picture

opportunities, meetings, festival information, screenings and general news.

INDEPENDENT (NEW YORK, N.Y. : 1978). (THE INDEPENDENT). Began in 1978. 0731-5198. Periodical. US. English. mo. Free to Members, $50.00 Institutions. Foundation for Independent Video and Film, 9th Floor/625 Broadway, New York NY 10012. LC PN1993. **DD** 791.430973.

INDEX OF 16MM & 35MM FEATURE LENGTH FILMS AVAILABLE IN CANADA. See Indexes/Abstracts.

INDEX TO 8MM MOTION CARTRIDGES. See Indexes/Abstracts.

INDIAN FILM CULTURE. VFOAT I.F.C. Periodical. English. qt. 5.00 Single Issue. Federation of Film Societies of India, C-7 Bharat Bhawan 3 Chittaranjan Avenue, Calcutta 700072 India. LC PN1993.5.I8. **DD** 791.430954.

INDIAN FILMS. 1972-. 0377-7359. English. an. 35.00. B V Dharap, Alaka Talkies, Poona-30 India. LC PN1998. **DD** 015.54.

INDIAN MOTION PICTURE ALMANAC. See Yearbooks, Almanacs, Directories.

INFORMACOES SOBRE A INDUSTRIA CINEMATOGRAFICA BRASILEIRA. BL. Portuguese. ir. Empresa Brasileira de Filmes, Departamento de Ingressos Padronizados, Rua Mayrink Veiga No 28 70 Andar, Rio de Janeiro Brazil. LC PN1993.3.

INFORMATIONS CNC. Main/Corp Centre National de la Cinematographie (France). VFOAT Bulletin d'Information du Centre National de la Cinematographie. VAT Informations Centre National de la Cinematographie. Periodical. French. ir. 15.00. Centre Nation de la Cinematographie, 12 rue de Lubeck, Paris 6E France. LC PN1993.5.F7. **DD** 338.47791430944. Bulletin d'Information.

INTERFILM REPORTS. English. ir. PO Box 515, Hilversum Netherlands. LC PN1993.3. **DD** 791.4305.

INTERNATIONAL FILM BUFF. VFOAT Film Buff. V. 1- Dec. 1975-. 0361-4131. Periodical. US. English. mo $9.00. International Film Buff Inc, 2309 Van Ness Avenue, San Francisco CA 94102. LC PN1993. **DD** 791.4305.

INTERNATIONAL FILM GUIDE. 1964-. 0074-6053. UK. English. an. $12.95. New York Zoetrope, 80 East 11th Street/Suite 516, New York NY 10003. **Tel** (212)420-0590. Ed Peter Cowie. LC PN1993.3. **DD** 791.43058. bk rev. adv acc. An indispensable guide to the who, what, where, and when of international cinema. Also a directory to festivals, archives, schools, bookstores, and non-theatrical films.

INTERNATIONAL INDEX TO FILM PERIODICALS. See Indexes/Abstracts.

IOWA FILMS. 1974/76-. Periodical. US. English. ir.

IPN CINE. VFOAT Cine. VAT Instituto Politecnico Nacional Cine. NP. Spanish. bm. Barranca Del Muerto, 208-304 San Jose Insurgentes, Mexico 19 DF Mexico.

ISKUSSTVO KINO. Began with: Vol. 6 in 1936. 0130-6405. Periodical. UR. Russian. mo. $58.50. Victor Kamkin Inc (70402), 12224 Parklawn Drive, Rockville MD 20852. **Tel** (301)881-5973. **Ind/Abst** Film Lit. Index. Sovetskoe Kino.

JEUNE CINEMA. No. 1- Sept./Oct. 1964-. Periodical. FR. French. ir. $14.63. Fedn Jean Vigo Cine Clubs, 8 rue Lamarche, Par le Film, Paris 18E France. **Ind/Abst** Film Lit. Index.

JOURNAL DU JEUNE CINEMA QUEBECOIS. (LE JOURNAL DU JEUNE CINEMA QUEBECOIS). V. 1- 7 June 1978-. 0705-5188. Periodical. CN. French. ir. $5.00. Journal du Jeune Cinema Quebecois, Bureau 3011/1600 Berri, Montreal Quebec H2L 4E4 Canada. **DD** 791.4309714.

JOURNAL OF FILM AND VIDEO. Vol. 36, No. 1 (Winter 1984)-. 0742-4671. Periodical. US. English. qt. $15.00 Domestic, $20.00 Foreign. Rosary College, Department of Communication Arts and Sciences, 7900 West Division Street, River Forest IL 60305. **Tel** (312)266-2490. Ed Patricia Ereus. **Ind/Abst** Int. Index Film Period., Film Lit. Index, Abstr. Pop. Cult., Arts Humanit. Citation Index. **DD** 778. bk rev

adv acc. **Circ** 1,200. Academic journal on film and video-television and pedagogy. Journal of the University Film and Video Association, 0734-919X.

JUMP CUT. V. 1- Jan. 1975-. Periodical. US. English. ir. $15.00 Domestic, $18.00 Foreign. Jump Cut/A Review of Cont Cine, PO Box 865, Berkeley CA 94701. **Tel** (415)658-4482. Ed John Hess, Chuck Kleinhaus and Julia Lesase. bk rev. adv acc. **Circ** 6,000. Building a vigorous Marxist theory and criticism of culture and aesthetics that recognizes the political and social critiques of people struggling for their liberation.

KATALOG FILM PRODUKSI P.F.N. Main/Corp Perusahaan Film Negara. Indonesian. ir. LC PN1998.

KEMPS INTERNATIONAL FILM & TELEVISION YEAR BOOK. See Yearbooks, Almanacs, Directories.

KINEMA JUMPO = KINEJUN : MOTION PICTURE TIMES. Japanese. ir. Kinema Jumpo Sha, c/o Park Building/3 Shiba Sakaecho 9 Minato-Ku (105), Tokyo Japan. LC PN1993.

KINO. 0023-1673. PL. Polish. mo. ARS Polona, Krakowskie Przedmiescie 7, 00-068 Warsaw Poland. **Ind/Abst** Film Lit. Index. LC PN1993.

KINO. CS. Czech. bw. Artia, PO Box 790, Praha 1 Czechoslovakia. LC PN1993.

KINO I VREMIA. Vol. 1-. Periodical. UR. Russian. 1.40 Single Issue. Izdatelstvo Iskusstvo, Tsvetnoi Bulvar 25, 103051 Moskva Russia. LC PN1993.

KINOBUCH. 1974/75-. German. ir. 10.00. Vertrieb: Stiftung Deutsche Kinemathek, Pommernalle 1, 19 Berlin 1 West Germany. LC PN1993.

KINOPANORAMA. Vol. 1-. Periodical. UR. Russian. 2.10. Iskusstvo, Sobinovskii Per 3, 103009 Moskva Russia. LC PN1993.5.R9.

KOSMORAMA. V. 1- No. 1-. 0023-4222. Periodical. DK. Danish. bm. 120.00. Danske Filmmuseum, St Sondervolistrade, Copenhagen K Denmark. Ed Kaare Schmidt. **Ind/Abst** Film Lit. Index. LC PN1993. bk rev. **Circ** 2,500. Available on microfilm from World Microfilms.

LANDERS FILM REVIEWS. Began in 1960?. 0023-785X. Periodical. US. English. qt. $45.00. Landers Associates, PO Box 27309, Escondido CA 92027. **Tel** (619)746-8923. Ed Bertha Landers and Steve Redding. **Ind/Abst** Media Rev. Dig. **DD** 791. Index published separately - free - automatically sent. Reviews and evaluations of nontheatrical films and videotapes on all subjects and for all age levels. Full bibliographical data provided. Bertha Landers Film Reviews.

LITERATURE FILM QUARTERLY. VFOAT Literature/Film Quarterly. V. 1- Winter 1973-. 0090-4260. Periodical. US. English. qt. $20.00. Salisbury State College, Salisbury MD 21801. **Tel** (301)543-6446. Ed James M Welsh and Thomas L Erskine. **Ind/Abst** Abstr. Engl. Stud., MLA Int. Bibliogr. Books Artic. Mod. Lang. Lit., Film Lit. Index, Media Rev. Dig., Humanit. Index, Years Work Eng. Stud. LC PN1995.3. **DD** 791.4305. bk rev. adv acc. **Circ** 600. Literature film adaptions; book reviews; interviews with directors, screenwriters, and critics.

MAADHYAM : BIMONTHLY ABOUT FILMS, FILMMAKERS & FILM SOCIETIES. Periodical. II. English. bm. 5.00. Maadhyam Publications, PB No 522, Dakar Bombay 400 014 India. LC PN1993. **DD** 791.4305.

MAGILL'S CINEMA ANNUAL. 1982-. 0739-2141. Periodical. US. English. an. Salem Press, Englewood Cliffs NJ 07632. Ed F N Magill. LC PN1993.3. **DD** 791.437505.

MARQUEE. V. 1- Apr./May 1976-. 0700-5008. Periodical. CN. English. ir. $12.00. Marquee Communications Inc, 277 Richmond Street West, Toronto Ontario M5V 1X1 Canada. **Tel** (416)593-7004. Ed David Haslam. LC PN1993. **DD** 791.4305. adv acc. **Circ** 510,000. (ctrl). Preview motion pictures four to six weeks prior to release.

MEDIA FILM INDONESIA. Periodical. IO. Indonesian. ir. Pusat Perfilman H Usmar, Ismail Jl Raya H R Rasuna, Said-Kuningan, Jakarta Indonesia. LC PN1993.5.I84.

MEDIA REVIEW. No. 1- Oct. 1974-. 0382-7771. Periodical. CN. English. ir. C Letovsky, PO Box 345 Snowdon Station, Montreal Quebec H3X 3T6 Canada. **DD** 791.430971.

MEDIA REVIEW DIGEST. See Education (General) - Theory, Practice of Education.

MEMBERSHIP DIRECTORY - UNIVERSITY FILM ASSOCIATION. See Yearbooks, Almanacs, Directories.

MMPI. VFOAT M.M.P.I. Periodical. Indonesian. ir. Pusat Perfilman H Usmar Ismail, Jl H Rasuna Said-Kuningan, Jakarta-Selatan Indonesia. LC PN1993.5.I84. Bulletin MMPI.

MODERN SCREEN. Began with Nov. 1930 issue. 0026-8429. Periodical. US. English. bm. $14.70. Sterlings Magazines, PO Box 1133, Dover NJ 07801. **Tel** (212)391-1400. LC PN1993.

MONOGRAPH (UNIVERSITY FILM ASSOCIATION). (MONOGRAPH). No. 2 (Summer 1979)-. Monographic Series. US. English. University Film Association University of Houston, School of Communication, Houston TX 77004. LC UNC. UFA Monograph.

MONTHLY FILM BULLETIN. V. 1- (No. 1-). 0027-0407. Periodical. UK. English. mo. 11-80. British Film Institute, 81 Dean Street, London W1V 6AA England. **Tel** 437-4355. Ed Richard Combs. **Ind/Abst** Film Lit. Index, Media Rev. Dig. LC LB1044. **DD** 371.335230838. adv acc. **Circ** 9,500. Reviews all new feature films in London plus articles, interviews, production histories, and documentation. Also selective coverage of videos short films and retrospectives of older films. Monthly Film Strip Review.

MOTION PICTURE PRODUCTION. Series/Titl D.B.S. Memorandum. VFOAT Production Cinematographique. 1952-. 0527-5768. CN. French (text only in English, 1951-1966). an. 20.00 Domestic, 21.00 Foreign. Receiver General for Canada, Statistics Canada Publications, Ottawa Ontario K1A 0T6 Canada. **Tel** (800)268-1151. **DD** 384.80971. Number of employees, salaries, gross revenues and an analysis of types of films produced.

MOTION PICTURE THEATRES AND FILM DISTRIBUTORS. VFOAT Cinemas et Distributeurs de Films. 1957-. 0380-6294. CN. French (text in English only, 1957-1966). an. Receiver General for Canada, Statistics Canada, Ottawa Ontario K1A 0T6 Canada. **DD** 384.830971. Motion Picture Theatres, Exhibitors and Distributors (1950), 0825-4133.

MOTION PICTURES. Main/Corp Florida. State University, Tallahassee. Media Services. US. English. LC LB1044.Z9. **DD** 011. Educational Films.

MOVIE. No. 1- June 1962-. 0027-268X. Periodical. UK. English. qt. Movie, 2A Roman Way, London N7 8XG England. **Ind/Abst** Film Lit. Index. LC PN1993.

MOVIE COLLECTOR'S WORLD. Issue No. 200 (Nov. 30, 1984)-. 8750-5401. Periodical. US. English. bw. $20.00. Krause Publications, 15767 Kingston, Fraser MI 48026-2312. **Tel** (313)294-6657. Ed Brian A Bukantis. **DD** 791. bk rev. adv acc. **Circ** 5,000. Video and film hobbyist publication for trading, buying and selling tapes, posters and other movie memorabilia. Movie & Film Collector's World, 0746-0325.

MOVIE MAKER. V. 1- Mar. 1967-. 0027-2701. Periodical. UK. English. mo. $44.45. Infonet Limited, 10-13 Times House Hemel, Hempstead Herts HP1 1BB England. **Tel** 01-437-0626. Ed Stuart Dollin. **Ind/Abst** Film Lit. Index. LC TR845. bk rev. adv acc. **Circ** 10,000. (ctrl). The complete magazine for the independent, student and amateur film-maker. Amateur Cine World, 8 MM. Movie Maker and Cine Camera; Film Making.

MOVIE MIRROR. 0027-271X. Periodical. US. English. bm. Sterlings Magazines Inc, PO Box 1133, Dover NJ 07801. **Tel** (212)391-1400. Photoplay combined with Movie Mirror, 0733-2734.

MOVIE WORKS WEEKLY. (THE MOVIE WORKS WEEKLY). Began publication in 1977. 0705-9175. Periodical. CN. English. wk. Movie Works Weekly, 112 1/2 Street, Toronto Ontario M5W 1H6 Canada. **DD** 338.47791430971.

MOVIE X. 0090-2039. Periodical. US. English. qt. $1.00 Single Issue. Magnum Royal Publications, 1560 Broadway, New York NY 10036. LC PN1995.9.S45. **DD** 791.4352.

Motion Picture

THE MOVIES. 0278-3797. Periodical. US. English. qt. Dave Almquist, 1301 Las Riendas #65, La Habra CA 90631.

MOVIES AND ENTERTAINMENT (SYOSSET, N. Y.). (MOVIES AND ENTERTAINMENT). **Series/Titl** The Video Tape/Disc Guide. 1980-. US. English.

MOVIES (NEW YORK, N.Y.). (THE MOVIES). Vol. 1, No. 1 (July 1983)-. 0742-4116. Periodical. US. English. mo. $18.00 Domestic, $23.00 Foreign. The Movies, PO Box 2724, Boulder CO 80322. **LC** PN1993. **DD** 791.4305.

MOVIES ON TV. **VAT** Movies on Television. 0160-4791. US. English. $2.95 Single Issue. Bantam Books, 666 Fifth Avenue, New York NY 10019. **LC** PN1992.8.F5. **DD** 791.4575. *TV Key Movie Guide.*

MOVIE/TV MARKETING. *See* Business - Marketing.

MULTICHANNEL NEWS. *See* Communication.

NEW YORK FILM ANNEX. (NEW YORK FILM ANNEX : CATALOG). 0884-2744. US. English. an. New York Film Annex, 163 Joralemon Street, Brooklyn Heights NY 11201. **LC** PN1998. **DD** 016.7914375.

THE NEW YORK TIMES DIRECTORY OF THE FILM. *See* Yearbooks, Almanacs, Directories.

THE NEW YORK TIMES FILM REVIEWS. 1913/68-. 0362-3688. Periodical. US. English. ir. Times Books, 130 Fifth Avenue, New York NY 10011. **Tel** (212)620-5900. **LC** PN1995. **DD** 791.437.

NEWS. Periodical. English. ir. Jugoslavija Film, Knez Mihailova 19 Cables, Beograd Yugoslavia. **LC** PN1993.

NEWSLETTER - ACADEMY OF CANADIAN CINEMA. (NEWSLETTER). **VAT** Newsletter - Academie du Cinema Canadien. Vol. 1, No. 1 (Nov. 1979)-. 0228-8087. Periodical. CN. English (includes some text in French). ir. Free to Members. Academy of Canadian Cinema, 2nd Floor 653 Yonge Street, Toronto Ontario M4Y 1Z9 Canada. **DD** 791.4306071.

NEWSLETTER - BRITISH COLUMBIA FILM INDUSTRY ASSOCIATION. (NEWSLETTER). Feb. 1980-. 0712-628X. Periodical. CN. English. ir. $5.00. BCFIA Newsletter, 1237 Richards Street, Vancouver British Columbia V6B 3G4 Canada. **DD** 791.4309711.

NEWSLETTER CALLED FRED. (A NEWSLETTER CALLED FRED). **VFOAT** Fred. Began with Spring 1971 issue. 0315-6923. Periodical. CN. English. bm. $34.83. Ontario Film Association Inc, Box 366 Station Q, Toronto Quebec M4T 2M5 Canada. **Tel** (416)925-5931. **Ed** Margaret Britt. bk rev. adv acc. **Circ** 400. Articles of interest to buyers and users of media, film and video reviews, filmographies, reports of media workshops and advertising.

NEWSLETTER - CANADIAN FEDERATION OF FILM SOCIETIES. **Main/Corp** Canadian Federation of Film Societies. Dec. 1977-. 0705-2162. Periodical. CN. English. ir. Canadian Federation of Film Societies, Apt 4, 897 Avenue Road, Toronto Ontario M5P 2K7 Canada. **DD** 791.4305. *C F F S Quarterly, 0705-2154.*

NEWSLETTER - CANADIAN SOCIETY OF CINEMATOGRAPHERS. (NEWSLETTER). **Main/Corp** Canadian Society of Cinematographers. **VAT** CSC Newsletter, Canadian Society of Cinematographers Newsletter. 0229-5989. Periodical. CN. English. ir. Canadian Society of Cinematographers, 22 Front Street West, Toronto Ontario M5J 1C4 Canada. **DD** 778.506071.

NEWSLETTER - FILM STUDIES ASSOCIATION OF CANADA. (NEWSLETTER). **Main/Corp** Film Studies Association of Canada. 0227-5015. Periodical. CN. English. qt. Free to Members. FSAC Newsletter, c/o Film Studies Association of Canada, R Hockey Sheridan College, 1430 Trafalgar Road, Oakville Ontario L6H 2L1 Canada. **DD** 791.4306071.

NEWSLETTER (INTERNATIONAL ASSOCIATION FOR AUDIO-VISUAL MEDIA IN HISTORICAL RESEARCH AND EDUCATION). (NEWSLETTER). Periodical. CK. English (French). qt. Iamhist Secretariat Copenhagen, Historisk Institut, Njalsgade 102, DK-2300 Copenhagen S Denmark. **LC** PN1995.2. **DD** 907.

NIHON NO YUSHU EIGA. **VFOAT** Outstanding Japanese Films. English (Japanese). ir. Nihon Eiga Kaigai Fukyu Kyokai, 9-13 Ginza 5 Chuo-Ku 104, Tokyo Japan. **LC** PN1993.5.J3.

NORTH AMERICAN FILM AND VIDEO DIRECTORY. *See* Yearbooks, Almanacs, Directories.

THE OFFICIAL PRICE GUIDE TO RADIO, TV & MOVIE MEMORABILIA. *See* Communication - Broadcasting.

ON LOCATION. 0149-7014. Periodical. US. English. mo. $40.00. On Location Publishing Inc, 6777 Hollywood Boulevard/Suite 600, Hollywood CA 90028. **Tel** (213)467-1268. **Ed** Steven Bernard. **LC** PN1993.5.U6. **DD** 791.430973. bk rev. adv acc. **Circ** 24,000. (ctrl). Covers all aspects of film, video, commercials, special effects, post-production, audio, music, video, and location production. Also covers equipment, facilities, mobile and new technologies used in production of all aspects of the entertainment industry.

ON LOCATION, THE NATIONAL FILM & VIDEOTAPE PRODUCTION DIRECTORY. *See* Yearbooks, Almanacs, Directories.

PANORAMA. Periodical. Czech (summaries in English, French, and Russian). ir. 32.00. Ons-Ued Odd Vyvozu Tisku Jindrisska 14, 125 05 Praha Czechoslovakia. **LC** PN1993.

PERSPECTIVES ON FILM. 0196-3007. Periodical. US. English. sa. Pennsylvania State University, 208 Special Services Building, University Park PA 16802. **LC** PN1995.9.D6. **DD** 791.4305.

PHOTOPLAY. V. 92, No. 6- July 1978-. 0162-5195. Periodical. US. English. mo. $9.95 Domestic, $11.95 Foreign. MacFadden Group, 215 Lexington Avenue, New York NY 10016. **Ind/Abst** Film Lit. Index. *Photoplay with TV Mirror, 0163-5115.*

PHOTOPLAY MOVIES & VIDEO. **VFOAT** Photoplay. **VAT** Photoplay Movies and Video. Periodical. UK. English. mo. $26.05. Infonet Limited, 10-13 Times Limited Hemel, Hempstead Herts HD1 1BB England. **Tel** 01 437 0626. **Ed** Lisa Dewson. bk rev. adv acc. **Circ** 26,500. Film reviews, star interviews, and video. Features new movies TV news and film gossip, picture previews and star profiles. *Films Illustrated.*

PHOTOPLAY STUDIES. V.1-6, No.30. Periodical. US. English. ir. Educational and Recreational Guides, 10 Brainerd Road, Summit NJ 07901. **LC** PN1993. **DD** 792.

PICTURE SHOW ANNUAL. Began publication in 1929. Periodical. UK. English. an. Amalgamated Press, 110 Peckham Rd, London SE 15 England. **LC** AP4. **DD** 791.4.

POLISH ANIMATED FILMS CATALOGUE. **Main/Corp** Film Polski. 1973-. English (French and German). ir. Film Polski, 6/8 Mazowiecka, 00-048 Warsaw Poland. **LC** NC1766.P6. **DD** 791.437. *Polish Animated Films.*

POLISH FILM. **VFOAT** Film Polonais. 1969-. 0015-136X. Periodical. PL. English (French). bm. ARS Polona, Krakowskie Przedmiescie 7, 00-068 Warsaw Poland. **Ind/Abst** Film Lit. Index. *Film Polski, 0428-366X.*

POSITI. **VFOAT** Revue de Cinema. 1- May 1952-. 0048-4911. Periodical. FR. French. mo. $51.88. Editions Opta, 1 Quai Conti, 75006 Paris France. **Tel** 4 354 40 96. **Ind/Abst** Point Repere, Film Lit. Index. (cum index). adv acc. **Circ** 15,000.

POST SCRIPT (JACKSONVILLE, FLA.). (POST SCRIPT). Vol. 1, No. 1 (Fall 1981)-. 0277-9897. Periodical. US. English. ty. $16.00. Jacksonville University, c/o Gerald Duchovnay, Jacksonville FL 32211. **Tel** (904)744-3950. **Ed** Gerald Duchovnay. **Ind/Abst** Book Rev. Index, MLA Int. Bibliogr. Books Artic. Mod. Lang. Lit., Index Book Rev. Humanit. **LC** PN1995. **DD** 791.437505. bk rev. adv acc. **Circ** 600. (ctrl). Film studies, directors, genres, cultural influences. Film and other art and humanities. Essays, interviews, book reviews, film studies bibliography.

EN PREMIERE. 23 Sept. 1976-. 0701-077X. Periodical. CN. French. En Premiere, CP 309 Succursale Outremont, Montreal Quebec H2V Canada. **DD** 791.4309714.

PREVIEW. V. 1- May 1979-. 0194-3847. Periodical. US. English. bm. American Film Institute, John F Kennedy Center, Washington DC 20566. **LC** PN1993. **DD** 791.4305.

PRIX GENIE. 1982-. 0714-5551. CN. English (French). an. Free. Genie Awards, c/o Academy of Canadian Cinema, 653 Yonge Street, Toronto Ontario M4Y 1Z9 Canada. **DD** 791.430971. *Genie Awards, 0714-5543.*

THE PRODUCER'S MASTERGUIDE. 1983-. 0732-6653. US. English. an. $74.90. New York Production Manual Inc, 611 Broadway/Suite 807, New York NY 10012-2608. **Tel** (212)777-4002. **Ed** Shmuel Bension. **LC** PN1993.5.U77. **DD** 384.550257. adv acc. **Circ** 20,000. International production manual for motion picture, broadcast-television, commercials, cable and videotape industries in the United States, Canada and the United Kingdom. *New York Production Manual, 0163-1276.*

PROFESSIONAL FILM PRODUCTION. V. 1- June 1975-. 0362-5974. Periodical. US. English. bm. $6.00. American Film Makers Magazine Inc, 250 Fulton Avenue, Hempstead NY 11550. **LC** PN1995.9.P7. **DD** 791.4302305.

QUADERNI DI CINEMA. Vol. 1, No. 1 (Apr. 1981)-. Periodical. Italian. ir.

QUADERNI DI DOCUMENTAZIONE DELLA CINETECA NAZIONALE. Monographic Series. IT. Italian. ir. Edizioni dell Ateno, Casella Postale 7216, 00100 Rome Italy.

QUARTERLY REVIEW OF FILM STUDIES. V. 1- Feb. 1976-. 0146-0013. Periodical. US. English. qt. Redgrave Publishing Company, 380 Adams Street, Bedford Hills NY 10507. **Tel** (914)241-7100. **Ind/Abst** Book Rev. Index, Film Lit. Index, Humanit. Index. **LC** PN1994. **DD** 791.4305.

QUEBEC FILM INDUSTRY HANDBOOK. 1979/80-. 0225-316X. CN. English. an. $15.00. Editions Cinema/Quebec, PO Box 309 Outremont Station, Montreal Quebec H2V 4N1 Canada. **DD** 791.4309714.

RECUEIL DES FILMS (MONTREAL). (RECUEIL DES FILMS DE . . .). 1- 1955/56-. 0085-543X. Periodical. CN. French. an. Office des Communications Sociales, 4635 Av de Lorimer, Montreal Quebec H3H 2B4 Canada. **DD** 010.

THE REEL DIRECTORY. *See* Yearbooks, Almanacs, Directories.

REEL WEST DIGEST. Vol. 3, No. 1 (1983)-. 0821-7947. CN. English. an. $7.95 Each Number. Reel West Productions, 212-811 Beach Avenue, Vancouver British Columbia V6Z 2B5 Canada. **DD** 991.430299. *Reel West Film and Video Digest, 0821-7939.*

RESUMEN CINEMATOGRAFICO. **VFOAT** Resumen Cinematografico de Los Estrenos en Los Cines de Madrid Durante el Ano. Spanish. ir. 4.000 Domestic, $50.00 Europe. Cine-Asesor, Plaza Marina Espanola 6 60.13, Madrid Spain. **Tel** 457-8851. **Ed** Sergio Alejandro Bellaba. **LC** PN1998.A1. bk rev adv acc. **Circ** 3,800. Releases in Spain, distribution, production, top grossing films in Spanish and European markets, TV news, video news, Latinamerican news.

REVUE BELGE DU CINEMA. No. 1- Sept. 1976-. Periodical. BE. French. ir. 550. J Debacker, Rue Lincoln 67, 1180 Bruxelles Belgium. **Ind/Abst** Film Lit. Index. **LC** PN1993.5.B4. **DD** 791.4309493.

REVUE DU CINEMA. (LA REVUE DU CINEMA). 0019-2635. Periodical. FR. French. ir. 140. 3 rue Recamier, 75341 Paris Cedex 07 France. **Ind/Abst** Point Repere, Film Lit. Index. **LC** PN1993. **DD** 791.4305. *Image et Son, Ecran.*

SAC MOVIE NEWS. **VAT** Society of Amateur Cinematographers Movie News. 0278-0410. Periodical. US. English. Society of Amateur Cinematographers (SAC), 2209 North Trinidad, Falls Church VA 22043. **LC** TR845. **DD** 778.534906073. *AC Movie News, 0537-8990.*

LA SAISON CINEMATOGRAPHIQUE. 1957-. 0558-2407. Periodical. FR. French. an. $6.91. Ligue Francasie Enseignement, Education de Permanente, rue recamier 3, 75341 Paris Cedex 07 France.

SCEN OCH SALONG. *See* Theater.

SCHWEIZER FILMINDEX. *See* Indexes/Abstracts.

SCIENCE FILM. *See* Science (General).

Motion Picture

SCREEN. V. 1- 1959-. 0036-9543. Periodical. UK. English. bm. $33.33. Society for Education in Film and Television, 29 Old Compton Street, London W1V 5PL England. **Tel** 01-734-5455/3211. adv acc. *Film Teacher.*

SCREEN ACTOR. V. 1- Aug. 1959-. 0036-956X. Periodical. US. English. qt. $7.00 Domestic, $10.00 Foreign. Screen Actors Guild, 7750 Sunset Boulevard, Hollywood CA 90046. **Tel** (213)867-3030. **Ed** Mark Locher. **LC** PN1993. **DD** 791.430973. bk rev. **Circ** 60,000. (ctrl). Official publication of the Screen Actors Guild. Covers craft and working conditions of performers in films, television and commerical.

SCREEN ACTOR NEWSLETTER. 0195-2684. Periodical. US. English. ir. $7.00. Screen Actors Guild, 7750 Sunset Boulevard, Hollywood CA 90046. **Tel** (213)876-3030. **Ed** Kim Fellner. bk rev. **Circ** 62,000. (ctrl). Screen Actors Guild official national publication; covers craft and conditions of professional motion picture performing arts, including film, TV and commercials.

SCREEN DIGEST. *See* Communication - Broadcasting.

SCREEN EDUCATION CEASED. No. 10/11 Spring/Summer 1974, No. 41 Winter/Spring 1982. 0306-0691. Periodical. UK. English. qt. $20.00. Society for Education in Film and Television, 29 Old Compton Street, London W1V 5PL England. **Ind/Abst** Film Lit. Index, Media Rev. Dig. **LC** PN1993.7. **DD** 791.4307. *Screen Education Notes.*

SCREEN INTERNATIONAL. Periodical. UK. English. wk. $99.00. King Publications Ltd, 6/7 Great Chapel Street, London W1V 4BR England. **LC** PN1993.5.G7. **DD** 338.47791430941. *Screen International & Cinema TV Today.*

SCREEN INTERNATIONAL FILM AND TV YEAR BOOK. *See* Yearbooks, Almanacs, Directories.

SCREEN STARS. V. 1- Apr. 1944-. Periodical. US. English. mo. Magazine Management Company, 575 Madison Avenue, New York NY 10022. **LC** PN1993. **DD** 791.405.

SCREEN WORLD. VFOAT John Willis' Screen World. V. 1- 1949-. 0080-8288. US. English. an. $19.95. Crown Publications Inc, 34 Engelhard Avenue, Avenel NJ 07001. **Tel** (212)532-9200. **Ed** D Blum. **LC** PN1993.3. **DD** 791.4305. bk rev. Pictorial and statistical annual of the current years box office hits. Contains vivid close-ups and portraits of all the stars.

SCRIPTWRITERS MARKET. 1983-. 0748-6456. US. English. sa. $21.95. Scriptwriters-Filmmakers Publishing, 8033 Sunset Boulevard/Suite 306, West Hollywood CA 90046. **Tel** (213)650-0060. **Ed** Gates and Buffum. adv acc. **Circ** 10,000. (ctrl). How and where to sell what you write for TV and film, and how to get an agent. *Screenplay Sales Directory, 0734-8592.*

SD. PACIFIC COAST STUDIO DIRECTORY. *See* Yearbooks, Almanacs, Directories.

SELECTED JAPANESE FEATURE FILMS. VFOAT Nihon No Gekieiga. JA. English (Japanese). ir. Unijapan Film Association for the Diffusion of Japanese Films Abroad inc, 9-13 Ginza 5 Chuo-ku, Tokyo 104 Japan. **LC** PN1993.5.J3. **DD** 791.43750952. *Nihon No Yushu Eiga.*

SEQUENCES. No. 1- 1955-. 0037-2412. Periodical. CN. French. qt. $13.93. Sequences/Canada, 4005 rue de Bellechasse, Montreal Quebec H1X 1J6 Canada. **Tel** (514)288-3764. **Ind/Abst** Film Lit. Index, Point Repere. adv acc. **Circ** 2,500. Magazine devoted to cinema articles, interviews, critics and chronicles.

SIGHT & SOUND. Ed. 1- Jan. 1976-. 0703-1408. Periodical. CN. English. Braun Electric Canada Ltd, Motion Picture Division, 3269 American Drive, Mississauga Ontario L4V 1B9 Canada. **DD** 778.5028. *ARRI News, 0703-1386; Sound & Light, 0703-1394.*

SIGHT AND SOUND. V. 1- Spring 1932-. Periodical. UK. English. qt. $10.73. British Film Institute, 81 Dean Street, London W1V 6AA England. **Tel** (01)437-4355. **LC** MICROFILM 06042PN, PN1993. Long-established and well-illustrated film and television quarterly published by the British Film Institute.

SIGHTLINES. V. 1- Sept./Oct. 1967-. 0037-4830. Periodical. US. English. ty. $16.00. Educational Film Library Association, 45 John Street/Suite 301, New York City NY 10038. **Tel** (202)227-5599. **Ed** Judith Trojan. **Ind/Abst** Film Lit. Index, Media Rev. Dig., Libr. Lit. **LC** LB1044.Z9. bk rev. adv acc. **Circ** 3,000. Articles focusing on the production, programming, and distribution of nontheatrical film and video. With special subject filmographies, interviews with film and video makers, etc. *Filmlist, Film Review Digest; EFLA Bulletin; FLQ, Film Library Quarterly.*

THE SILENT PICTURE. No. 1- Winter 1968/69-. 0037-5209. Periodical. US. English. qt. $4.00. First Media Press, 6 East 39th Street, New York NY 10016. **Ind/Abst** Am. Hist. Life, Hist. Abstr., Part A, Mod. Hist. Abstr., Hist. Abstr., Part B, Twent. Century Abstr. **LC** PN1993. **DD** 791.43. Available on microfilm from University Microfilms.

SILVER SCREEN. Publication began with: Vol. 1 (Nov. 1930). 0037-5365. Periodical. US. English. mo. **LC** PN1993. **DD** 791.4305.

SIMUI PAEKSO. KO. Korean. ir. Hanguk Kongyon Yulli Wiwonhoe 34-5 3-Ka Namsan-Dong Chung-Ku, Seoul Korea. **LC** PN1993.5.K6.

SINIMA. Periodical. Arabic. mo. **LC** PN1993.

SIPARIO. *See* Theater.

SMPTE JOURNAL. (SMPTE JOURNAL : PUBLICATION OF THE SOCIETY OF MOTION PICTURE AND TELEVISION ENGINEERS). VFOAT S.M.P.T.E. Journal. VAT Society of Motion Picture and Television Engineers Journal. Began with Jan. 1976. 0036-1682. Periodical. US. English. mo. $45.00 Domestic, $53.00 Foreign. SMPTE, 862 Scarsdale Avenue, Scarsdale NY 10583. **Ind/Abst** Eng. Index Annu., Eng. Index Mon., Eng. Index Bioeng. Abstr., Eng. Index Energy Abstr., Excerpta Med., Int. Aerosp. Abstr., Comput. Control Abstr., Electr. Electron. Abstr., Sci. Abstr. Sect. A. Phys. Abstr., Film Lit. Index, Ref. Source, Chem. Abstr., Appl. Sci. Technol. Index. **LC** TR845. **DD** 778.505. CODEN SMPJDF. (cum index). *Journal of the SMPTE, 0361-4573.*

SOVETSKIE KHUDOZHNIKI TEATRA I KINO. *See* Theater.

SOVIET FILM. 1- June 1957-. 0038-5395. Periodical. UR. English. mo. Soviet Film, English Edition. **Ind/Abst** Film Lit. Index. **LC** PN1993.5.R9. **DD** 791.430947.

SPIELFILME IM ERSTEN DEUTSCHEN FERNSEHEN. *See* Communication - Broadcasting.

SPOTLIGHT. Periodical. Danish. ir. 16.00. Rnnegarden 4, Nissum Seminarieby, 7620 Lemnig Denmark. **LC** PN1993.

THE STEVEN SPIELBERG FILM SOCIETY NEWSLETTER. VFOAT Newsletter. 0883-6094. Periodical. US. English. $10.00. Spielberg Film Society, c/o Judy Hubbard & Don Archer 4126 East 32nd Street, Tucson AZ 85711. **Ed** Judy Hubbard and Don Archer. **DD** 791. **Circ** 60. News and articles on the films of Steven Spielberg and others plus music of films in general and music of John Williams in particular.

STILLS. *See* Communication - Broadcasting.

SUKURIN (SEOUL, KOREA : 1984). (SUKURIN). VFOAT Screen. V. 1- (1984/3)-. Periodical. KO. Korean. mo. 30,000. Wolgan Sukurin, 188 Naesu-dong, Chongno-ku Seoul Korea. **LC** PN1993.

SUPER 8 FILMAKER CEASED. VAT Super Eight Filmaker. V. 1-9, No. 5. 0049-2574. Periodical. US. English. bm. $15.00 Domestic, $17.00 Canada. Super 8 Filmaker, Cinema Circle, Marion OH 43302. **Ind/Abst** Film Lit. Index. **LC** TR845. **DD** 778.53.

LE TECHNICIEN DU FILM ET DE LA VIDEO, LA TECHNIQUE, L'EXPLOITATION CINEMAGRAPHIQUE. No. 266 (Jan. 15,/Feb. 15, 1979)- – Vol. 25. Periodical. FR. French. ir. $41.90. Editions Dujarric, 33 Champs Elysees, 75008 Paris France. **Tel** 359-24-84. *Technicien du Film la Technique, l'Exploitation Cinematographique.*

TELEVISION NETWORK MOVIES. 0149-7359. Periodical. US. English. ir. $75.00. Television Index Inc, 40/29 27th Street/2nd Floor, Long Island City NY 11101. **Tel** (718)937-3990. **Ed** Jerry Leichter. **LC** PN1992. **DD** 791.437. Annual directory of theatrical movies, TV movies and dramas for TV, 90 minutes or longer, non-series, that were on TV during a current season.

TERROR FANTASTIC. VFOAT T.F. Yearly V. 1- (No. 1- Oct. 1971)-. Periodical. Spanish. ir. 50. PJE Pla 11-13, 10-B Barcelona Spain. **LC** PN1995.9.H6. **DD** 791.43090916.

TEXAS PRODUCTION MANUAL. Main/Corp Texas Film Commission. 1st- 1975-. US. English.

TEXTES DU CINEMA FRANCAIS. French. ir. 12 rue de Lubeck, 75784 Paris Cedex 16 France. **DD** 343.4407879143, 344. 4037879143. *Textes Reglementaires du Cinema Francais.*

TIEN YING TSO PIN. VFOAT Dian Ying Zuo Pin. Periodical. CH. Chinese. bm. 0.45. Cheng-Tu Shih Yu Cheng Chu, Cheng-Tu China. **LC** PN1993.5.C4. **DD** 791.430951.

TIEN YING WEN HUA. VFOAT Tien Ying Wen Hua Tsung Kan. Periodical. CH. Chinese. ir. 0.62. Hsin Hua Shu Tien Pei-Ching fa Hsing So Peking China. **LC** PN1993. **DD** 791.4305.

TIME & TIDE. 1952. 0040-7836. Periodical. II. English. mo. 16.00. Time & Tide Publications, 1 Ansari Road Darya Ganj, New Delhi 110002 India. **Tel** 272046 : 592383. **Ed** Devendra Kumar. **LC** PN1993. **DD** 791.4305. bk rev. adv acc. **Circ** 11,500. The visual scene including cinema, TV and video in relationship with society as well as a potential trade. A potential medium of communication dealing in various modes and aspects.

T.L.F. QUARTERLY. (TLF QUARTERLY). Main/Corp Time-Life Films. April/June 1973-. 0092-9263. US. English. qt. Time-Life Films, Room 33-43 Time-Life Building, New York NY 10020. **LC** PN1992.F5. **DD** 791.457.

TODAY'S FILM MAKER. VFOAT Film Maker. V. 1- Aug. 1971-. 0193-6085. Periodical. US. English. qt. $6.00 Domestic, $8.00 Foreign. American Film Makers Magazine, 250 Fulton Avenue, Hempstead NY 11550. **LC** TR845. **DD** 778.5305.

TORONTO FILMMAKERS' CO-OP. Sept. 1976-. 0704-5816. Periodical. CN. English. Toronto Filmmakers' Co-Operative, 67 Portland Street, Toronto Ontario M5V 2M9 Canada. **DD** 791.4307152.

TOUS LES FILMS. Periodical. FR. French. ir. Centurion, 17 rue de Babylone, 75007 Paris France. **LC** PN1997.8. **DD** 791.4305.

TRIBUTE GOES TO THE MOVIES. Vol. 1, Issue 1 (Feb. 1, 1984)-. 0826-1210. Periodical. CN. English. bm. $12.00. **DD** 791.4305.

TRIBUTE MAGAZINE. VFOAT Tribute. Vol. 1, Issue 1 (Winter 1981)-. 0823-678X. Periodical. CN. English. ir. $26.00 Domestic, $45.00 US, $55.00 Other Countries. Subscription Department, Tribute Publication Ltd, 184 Laird Drive, Toronto Ontario M4G 3V7 Canada. **DD** 791.4305.

TV AND MOVIE SCREEN. V. 1- Nov. 1953-. Periodical. US. English. bm. Sterlings Magazines Inc, PO Box 1133, Dover NJ 07801. **Tel** (212)391-1400.

UNDER WESTERN SKIES. 0279-6244. Periodical. US. English. mo. $9.60. The World of Yesterday, Rt 3 Box 263 H, Waynesville NC 28786. **Tel** (704)648-5647. **Ed** Linda S Downey. bk rev. adv acc. **Circ** 1,000. Magazine devoted to the western movies of the past and westerns on radio and TV.

VARIETY INTERNATIONAL MOTION PICTURE MARKETPLACE. VFOAT International Motion Picture Marketplace. Periodical. US. English. $50.00. Garland Publishing, 136 Madison Avenue, New York NY 10016. **Tel** (212)686-7492. **Ed** M Kaplan. Comprehensive reference guide to the international motion picture industry.

THE VELVET LIGHT TRAP. No. 1- June 1971-. 0149-1830. Periodical. US. English. qt. $20.00. Velvet Light Trap, c/o John Davis PO Box 9240, Madison WI 53715. **Tel** (608)263-3997. **Ed** Matthew Bernstein. **Ind/Abst** Film Lit. Index. **LC** PN1993. **DD** 791.4305. adv acc. **Circ** 600. Scholarly articles and interviews on the history of American movies, with essays on film theory and criticism.

VIDEO FEMMES. *See* Women.

VIDEO PRODUCT NEWS. V. 1- Oct./Dec. 1980-. 0271-5953. Periodical. US. English. bm. Steve Tolin, PO Box 2772, Palm Springs CA 92263. **Tel** (213)874-4331.

THE VIDEO PROGRAMS INDEX. *See* Indexes/Abstracts.

VIDEO SCENE. Vol. 1, No. 1 (Fall 1980)-. 0710-0876. Periodical. CN. English. bm. 10.00. Calder Publications Ltd, 542 Mt Pleasant Road/Suite 203,

Motorcycles

Toronto Ontario M4S 2M7 Canada. **Tel** (416)482-1696. **Ed** R E Calder. **DD** 778.59905. bk rev. adv acc. **Circ** 34,000. (ctrl). This magazine's role and purpose is to keep Canadians informed and up-to-date on the latest developments in the video field and new uses of the home television set.

THE VIDEO SOURCE BOOK. 1st. Ed.-. 0748-0881. US. English. National Video Clearinghouse Inc, 100 Lafayette Drive, Syosset NY 11791. **LC** PN1992.95. **DD** 011.37.

THE WAFL BOOK. Main/Corp Washington Area Filmmakers League. **VAT** Washington Area Filmmakers League. 1976-. 0160-872X. US. English. $5.45 Single Issue. The WAFL Book, PO Box 6475, Washington DC 20009. **LC** PN1993.5.U79. **DD** 384.8025753.

WARREN'S MOVIE POSTER PRICE GUIDE. (WARRENS MOVIE POSTER PRICE GUIDE). **VFOAT** Movie Poster Price Guide. 1st Ed.-. 0884-3791. Periodical. US. English. an. $12.95. Overstreet Publications Inc, 780 Hunt Cliff Drive NW, Cleveland TN 37311. **Tel** (615)742-4135. **Ed** J Warren. adv acc. Over 11,000 feature films listed from 1930-1959. Hundreds of rare posters illustrated, prices given for all types of movie paper, major stars index.

WIDE ANGLE. V. 1-. 0160-6840. Periodical. US. English. qt. $31.00. Johns Hopkins University Press, 701 West 40th Street/Suite 275, Baltimore MD 21211. **Tel** (301)338-6987. **Ed** Peter Lehman. **Ind/Abst** Film Lit. Index, Media Rev. Dig. **LC** PN1993. **DD** 791.4305. adv acc. **Circ** 1,378. The only film journal that is thematically organized around a single topic in each issue. All genres and historical periods are covered.

WORLD CATALOGUE OF VETERINARY FILMS/VIDEO TAPES AND FILMS/VIDEO TAPES OF VETERINARY INTEREST. See Veterinary Medicine, Animal Culture.

THE WORLD OF YESTERDAY. No. 1- Feb. 1976 -. 0273-5679. Periodical. US. English. ir. $7.20. The World of Yesterday, Route 3 Box 263H, Waynesville NC 28786. **Tel** (704)648-5647. **Ed** Linda S Downey. bk rev. adv acc. **Circ** 400. Magazine devoted to motion pictures of the past.

WRITING AWARDS : REMINDER LIST OF ELIGIBLE RELEASES. Main/Corp Academy of Motion Picture Arts and Sciences. **VFOAT** Annual Academy Awards for Achievements. Periodical. US. English. an. *Reminder List of Eligible Achievements.*

YIN MU CHU TSO. Periodical. CH. Chinese. bm. 0.50. Chuan Kuo Ko Ti Yu Chu China. **LC** PN1993.5.C4. **DD** 791.430951.

YING SHIH CHUN CHIU. Periodical. CC. Chinese. ir. 0.44. Hsin Hua Shu Tian, Shan-Tung Shen China. **LC** PN1993.5.C4. **DD** 791.430951.

YOUNG CINEMA & THEATRE. See Theater.

YOUNG VIEWERS. Began with Fall 1977 issue. Periodical. NO. English. qt. $20.00. Media Center for Children, 3 West 29th Street 11th Floor, New York NY 10001. **Tel** (212)689-0300. **Ed** Robert L Braun. **Ind/Abst** Film Lit. Index. bk rev. **Circ** 325. (ctrl). A review newsletter for adults who use, make, or distribute media for children ages three through twelve.

Z (OSLO, NORWAY). (Z). 0800-1464. Periodical. NO. Norwegian. ir. 100.00. Norsk Filmklubbforbund, Wesselsgt 4, Oslo 1 Norway. **LC** PN1993.

MOTORCYCLES

AMERICAN BICYCLIST AND MOTORCYCLIST. See Bicycles and Bicycling.

AMERICAN MOTORCYCLIST. V. 31, No. 8 I.E. 9 (Sept. 1977)-. 0277-9358. Periodical. US. English. mo. $10.00. American Motorcycle Association, PO Box 141, Westerville OH 43081. **Tel** (614)891-2425. **Ed** Greg Harrison. adv acc. **Circ** 119,000. (ctrl). Information for motorcycle enthusiasts who are AMA Members. It has reports on MC legislation, touring articles and competition information. *AMA News, 0003-0074.*

EL ANO DE LOMATO = ANNEE MOTO = MOTO YEAR. 1- 1975/76-. Spanish. ir. ISAAC, Peral 12, Madrid Spain. **LC** GV1060.

THE ANTIQUE MOTORCYCLE. 0364-6963. Periodical. US. English. qt. $8.50. 714 East Harwood Street, Apt 4, Orlando FL 32803. **LC** TL440. **DD** 629.2275075. *Quarterly Bulletin.*

ATV NEWS. VAT All Terrain Vehicle News. 0744-7809. Periodical. US. English. mo. $5.00. Cycle News Inc, 2201 Cheery Avenue, Long Beach CA 90806. **Tel** (213)595-4753. **Ed** John Ulrich. bk rev. adv acc. **Circ** 82,000. America's only monthly national newspaper edited exclusively for all terrain vehicle enthusiasts. Covers all aspects of ATV recreation and utility.

A B C DU MOTOCYCLISME. (L'A B C DU MOTOCYCLISME). 1975-. 0319-2857. CN. French. an. Brave Beaver Pressworks, 666 Boulevard St Croix, Montreal Quebec H4L 3Y2 Canada. **DD** 796.7505.

THE BEST OF DIRT BIKE TESTS. VFOAT Dirt Bike Tests. 0364-1562. US. English. an. $1.50. Hi-Torque Publications, PO Box 317, Encino CA 91316. **LC** TL440. **DD** 629.2275.

BRANHAM'S MOTORCYCLE AND SNOWMOBILE REFERENCE. US. English. an.

CANADIAN BIKER MAGAZINE. (THE CANADIAN BIKER MAGAZINE). Vol. 1, No. 15 (July 1982)-. 0820-8344. Periodical. CN. English. ir. $1.00 Per No. Canadian Biker Magazine, P O Box 4122 Station A, Victoria B C V8X 3X4 Canada. **DD** 796.750971. *Western Biker Magazine, 0229-6896.*

CANADIAN CYCLIST. VFOAT Cycliste Canadien. Began in 1973?. 0318-1669. CN. text in English and French. bm. $2. Canadian Cycling Association, 333 River Road, Vanier Ontario K1L 8B9 Canada. **DD** 796.605.

CANADIAN MOTORCYCLE BUSINESS. VFOAT CMB. Vol. 2, Issue 7 (Oct. '80 Ed.). 0227-602X. Periodical. CN. English. Canadian Motorcycle Dealer News, 2066 Queen Street East, Toronto Ont M4E 1C9 Canada. **DD** 338.4762922750971. *CMDN, Canadian Motorcycle Dealer News, 0225-3186.*

CANADIAN MOTORCYCLE RIDER. VAT CMR. Canadian Motorcycle Rider. No. 1, (1981)-. 0710-0590. Periodical. CN. English. $1.25 Per No. Canadian Motorcycle Rider, 2066 Queen Street East, Toronto Ont M4E 1C9 Canada. **DD** 796.750971.

CBS RIJWIEL- EN MOTORRIJWIELINDUSTRIE. See Bicycles and Bicycling.

CHILTON'S MOTORCYCLE REPAIR MANUAL. VFOAT Motorcycle Repair Manual. 0741-3246. Periodical. US. English. an. Chilton Book Co, Chilton Way, Radnor PA 19089. **LC** TL444. **DD** 629.2877505.

CMA CYCLE. Main/Corp Canadian Motorcycle Association. V. 29- Jan. 1972-. 0319-5872. Periodical. CN. English. mo. Canadian Motorcycle Association, 20 Jarvis Street, Hamilton Ontario L8R 1 Canada. *Canadian Motorcycling, 0008-4522.*

CUSTOM BIKE CHOPPERS. 0745-0567. Periodical. US. English. mo. *Choppers, 0195-069X; Custom Bike, 0363-8138.*

CYCLE. 0574-8135. 0574-8135. Periodical. US. English. mo. CBS Publications, 1515 Broadway, New York NY 10036, (subscription address: Neodata PO Box 2606 Boulder CO 80322). **Ind/Abst** Pop. Mag. Rev., Read. Guide Period. Lit., Consum. Index Prod. Eval. Inf. Source, Mag. Index.

CYCLE AGE CEASED. V. 1- Jan. 1974-. 0146-6526. Periodical. US. English. ir. $6.00. Babcox Publications, 11 South Forge Street, Akron OH 44304. **LC** TL440. **DD** 380.1456292275.

CYCLE CANADA. V. 1- Apr. 1971-. 0319-2822. Periodical. CN. English. mo. Brave Beaver Pressworks Ltd, 411 Richmond Street East/Suite 102, Toronto Ontario M5A 3S5 Canada. **Ed** John Cooper. adv acc. **Circ** 42,000. Authoritative Canadian motorcycle magazine with road tests, touring features, technical analyses and other special motorcycle features.

CYCLE GUIDE. See Bicycles and Bicycling.

CYCLE GUIDE ROAD TEST ANNUAL. 0590-4641. US. English. an. $1.25. Quinn Publications Etc, 1440 West Walnut Street, Compton CA 90220. **LC** TL440. **DD** 629.227505.

CYCLE GUIDE'S MOTORCYCLE ACCESSORIES GUIDE. VFOAT Motorcycle Accessories. 0090-4775. US. English. an. $1.00. Cycle Guide Publications Inc, PO Box 267, Mt Morris IL 61054. **LC** TL440. **DD** 629.227505.

CYCLE STREET AND TOURING GUIDE. VFOAT Street and Touring Guide. 0272-8923. Periodical. US. English. an. $4.95. Ziff-Davis Publishing Co Inc, One Park Avenue, New York NY 10016. **LC** TL440. **DD** 629.227505.

CYCLE WORLD. Began publication with V. 1, Jan. 1962. 0011-4286. Periodical. US. English. mo. CBS Publications, 1515 Broadway, New York NY 10036, (subscription address: Neodata PO Box 2606 Boulder CO 80322). **Tel** (800)243-8005. **Ind/Abst** Mag. Index, Consum. Index Prod. Eval. Inf. Source.

CYCLE WORLD TEST ANNUAL & BUYER'S GUIDE. Series/Titl CBS Leisure Transportation Series. **VFOAT** Test Annual & Buyer's Guide. **VAT** Cycle World Test Annual and Buyer's Guide. 0270-2746. Periodical. US. English. an. $2.95. CBS Publications, 1 Fawcett Place, Greenwich CT 06830. **LC** TL440. **DD** 629.227505.

DIRT BIKE. V. 1- June 1971-. 0364-1546. Periodical. US. English. mo. $14.98. Hi-Torque Publications, PO Box 9502, Mission Hills CA 91345. **Tel** (818)365-6831. **Ed** Tom Webb. **LC** TL440. **DD** 796.7. **Circ** 150,000. Directed to off-road motorcyclists of all ages, with equal emphasis on recreational and competitive cycling, plus do-it-yourself maintenance and riding tips.

DIRT BIKE & MOTORCROSS ACTION BUYER'S GUIDE. VFOAT Dirt Bike and Motorcross Action Buyer's Guide. US. English. $2.50. Daisey/Hi-Torque Publishing Company, 16200 Ventura Boulevard, Encino CA 91436. **LC** TL440. **DD** 62922750294. *Dirt Bike Buyer's Guide, 0090-8185.*

DIRT BIKE BUYER'S GUIDE. 0090-8185. US. English. $2.00. Hi-Torque Publications, 16200 Ventura Boulevard, Encino CA 91316. **LC** TL440. **DD** 629.227505.

DIRT RIDER. Issue 1 (Dec. 1982)-. 0735-4355. Periodical. US. English. mo. $11.94. Petersen Publishing Company, 6725 Sunset Boulevard, Los Angeles CA 90028. **Tel** (213)657-5100. **Ed** Charles Morey. adv acc. **Circ** 109,000. Updates on off-road motorcycles, trail rides, equipment, performance reports, personalities, races, and the rest.

EASYRIDERS. Began with June 1971 issue. 0046-0990. Periodical. US. English. mo. Easyriders Circulation Department, Box 711, Burbank CA 91502. **LC** GV1059.5. **DD** 796.7505.

ENDURO. 0092-6272. US. English. $1.25. Cycle Guide Publications, 1440 West Walnut Street, Compton CA 90220. **LC** GV1060. **DD** 796.7505.

FLT SERVICE MANUAL. Main/Corp Harley-Davidson Motor Company. **VFOAT** Service Manual, Tour Glide - FLT. 0275-5386. US. English. **LC** TL448.H3. **DD** 629.2877505.

FREEWHEELIN'. (FREEWHEELIN' : THE MAGAZINE FOR MOTORCYCLE PEOPLE). **VAT** Free Wheelin'. Vol. 1, No. 1 (Feb./Mar. 1980) -. 0228-6831. Periodical. CN. English. bm. $5.95. PO Box 938, Burlington Ontario L7R 3Y7 Canada. **DD** 629.22750971.

GUIDE DE LA MOTO. (LE GUIDE DE LA MOTO . . .). 84-. 0823-8499. CN. French. an. $12.95 Per No. Guide de la Moto, a/s Agence de Distribution Populaire, 955 rue Amherst, Montreal Quebec H2L 3K4 Canada. **DD** 629.2275.

INTERNATIONAL MOTOR CYCLE RACING BOOK. (INTERNATIONAL MOTOR-CYCLE RACING BOOK). 0306-5898. UK. English. Souvenir Press, 95 Mortimer Street, London W 1 England. **LC** GV1060. **DD** 796.75.

INTERNATIONAL MOTORCYCLE TRADE JOURNAL. VFOAT IMTJ. Began with Jan./Feb. 1979 issue. 0164-5463. Periodical. US. English (summaries in French, German, and Italian). bm. $12.00 US, $16.00 Mexico and Canada, $36.00 Europe and Asia. International Motorcycle Trade Journal, 393 7th Avenue, New York NY 10001. **LC** HD9710.5.A1. **DD** 629.22750688.

JAMMER'S HANDBOOK. Vol. 1-. 0147-9652. US. English. qt. $8.00. Jammer Cycle Products Inc, 801 South Main Street, Burbank CA 91506. **Tel** (800)432-2633. **LC** TL440. **DD** 629.227505.

LE LIVRE D'OR DE LA MOTO. 1976-. French. ir. LC GV1060. DD 796.75.

M D T. MOTORCYCLE DEALER & TRADE. (M D T, MOTORCYCLE DEALER & TRADE). VFOAT Motorcycle Dealer & Trade. 1st-Issue. 0705-2030. Periodical. CN. English. mo. Free. Brave Beaver Presworks, 290 Jarvis Street, Toronto Ontario M5B 2C5 Canada. DD 338.4762922750971.

MAGIC OF MOTORCYCLING. (THE MAGIC F MOTORCYCLING). 1975-. 0319-2849. CN. English. an. Brave Beaver Presworks, 413 Sherbourne Street, Toronto Ontario M4X 1K5 Canada. DD 796.7505.

MOPED AND ECONOMY MOTORCYCLE BUYER'S GUIDE. 0272-2275. English. an. $2.50 Domestic, $3.25 Canada. Petersen Publishing Company, 6725 Sunset Boulevard, Los Angeles CA 90028. LC TL440. DD 629.227505.

MOPED BIKING. 0160-1806. Periodical. US. English. bm. $8.00. Moped Publications, 370 Lexington Avenue, New York NY 10017.

MOPED DEALER. V. 1- June/July 1978-. 0161-4320. Periodical. US. English. bm. $9.00. Moped Publications, 370 Lexington Avenue, New York NY 10017. LC HD9710.6.U5. DD 658.896292272.

MOTO JOURNAL. V. 1- Spring 1972-. 0319-2865. Periodical. CN. French. mo. $18.58. Brave Beaver Presworks Ltd, 411 Richmond Street East/Suite 102, Toronto Ontario M5A 3S5 Canada. **Tel** (416)362-7966. Ed Jean Pierre Belmonte. adv acc. **Circ** 22,000. This is the authoritative motorcycle magazine with road tests, touring features, technical tips and more.

MOTOCOURSE. 1976/77-. 0148-687X. US. English. an. $21.95. Arco Publishing Company, 2119 Park Avenue South, New York NY 10003.

MOTOCROSS ACTION MAGAZINE. V. 1- July 1973-. 0146-3292. Periodical. US. English. mo. Hi-Torque Publications, PO Box 9502, Mission Hills CA 91345. **Tel** (818)365-6831. LC GV1060. DD 796.75.

MOTOR CYCLE AND CYCLE TRADER YEARBOOK. See Yearbooks, Almanacs, Directories.

MOTOR NEWS. 0194-8520. Periodical. US. English. mo. Chicago Motor Club, 66 East Water Street, Chicago IL 60637.

MOTORCYCLE BLUE BOOK. 0091-3774. US. English. $2.00. H Jones, PO Box 3068, San Francisco CA 94119. LC HD9710.5.U5. DD 380.145629227502573.

MOTORCYCLE BUYERS GUIDE. VFOAT C R V Motor Guide. 0317-6614. Periodical. CN. English. ir. CRV Publishing Company, 3414 Park Avenue/Suite 221, Montreal Quebec H2X 2H5 Canada. **Tel** (514)282-1091. Ed W E Taylor. DD 629.22'75. bk rev. adv acc. **Circ** 100,000. (ctrl). Advertising, editorial, listing of shows and accessories.

MOTORCYCLE DEALERNEWS. VFOAT Motorcycle Dealer News. 1965. 0192-0219. Periodical. US. English. ir. $24.00. Hester Communications Inc, Box 19531, Irvine CA 92713. **Tel** (714)549-4834. Ed John Brumm and Fred Clements. LC TL440. DD 629.22750688. adv acc. **Circ** 1. (ctrl). Product, merchandising, sales and business information pertinent to motorcycle dealers. *MDN. Motorcycle Dealer News.*

MOTORCYCLE DEALERNEWS MERCHANDISER. VFOAT MDN Merchandiser. 8755-4720. Periodical. US. English. mo. Hester Communications Inc, PO Box 19531, Irvine CA 92713. LC TL440. DD 629.22750688. *0192-0219.*

MOTORCYCLE DRAG RACING. 0883-7228. Periodical. US. English. mo. $18.00. Lenk Associates, 3936 Raceway Park Road, Mt Olive AL 35117-9790. **Tel** (205)849-7886. Ed Tony Lee. DD 796. bk rev. adv acc. **Circ** 5,000. (ctrl). National event coverage and schedules, technical information, rider interviews, what's happening, features, gossip of who is doing what on the national circuit. *Motorcycle Drag Racing Newspaper, 0199-8544.*

MOTORCYCLE DRAG RACING NEWSPAPER. VFOAT Motocycle Drag Racing. 0199-8544. Periodical. US. English. ir. $15.00. Motorcycle Drag Racing, 3936 Raceway Park Road, Mt Olive AL 35117. **Tel** (205)849-7886. Ed Tony Lee. adv acc. **Circ** 2,000. (ctrl). Drag racing motorcycle news. National race coverage, ET and MPH national records, product information, rider profiles, editorials, motorcycle products, services and schedule of events.

THE MOTORCYCLE INDUSTRY BUSINESS JOURNAL. Vol. 1, No. 1 (Apr./May 1982)-. 0731-3470. Periodical. US. English. ir. $32.00. Hancock-Brown Corporation, 3187 Airway Drive/Suite A-2, Costa Mesa CA 92626. **Tel** (714)957-1809.

MOTORCYCLE PRODUCT NEWS. 0164-8349. Periodical. US. English. mo. $18.00. Freed Crown Publishing Company, 6931 Van Nuys Boulevard, Van Nuys CA 91405. **Tel** (213)8731320. Ed Phil Kande. bk rev. adv acc. **Circ** 15,000. (ctrl). Edited for dealers, distributors, manufacturers, importers and exporters. Contains a variety of product information, industry news and special features.

MOTORCYCLE RIDER'S GUIDE. 0092-3095. Periodical. US. English. qt. $7.50. Hi-Torque Publications, 16200 Ventura Boulevard, Encino CA 91316. LC TL440. DD 629.227505. *Chopper Guide.*

MOTORCYCLE STATISTICAL ANNUAL. See Statistics.

MOTOSPORTS. V. 1- March 1975-. 0319-2229. Periodical. CN. French. ir. 0.75 Each Number. Motosports, Bureau 104 360 rue Levesque, Pont-Viau Laval Quebec H7G 4P4 Canada. DD 796.05.

N.A.D.A. MOTORCYCLE & MOPED APPRAISAL GUIDE. (N. A. D. A. MOTORCYCLE & MOPED APPRAISAL GUIDE). **Main/Corp** National Automobile Dealers Association. **VAT** National Automobile Dealers Association Motorcycle and Moped Appraisal Guide. 0197-1980. US. English. ty. $30.00. N A D A Appraisal Guides, PO Box 1407, Covina CA 91722. LC HD9710.5.A1. DD 381.4562922750973. *N.A.D.A. Motorcycle Appraisal Guide, 0095-6953.*

N.A.D.A. MOTORCYCLE APPRAISAL GUIDE. **Main/Corp** National Automobile Dealers Association. VFOAT Motorcycle Appraisal Guide. **VAT** National Automobile Dealers Association Motorcycle Appraisal Guide. 0095-6953. Periodical. US. English. ty. $45.00. National Automobile Dealers Association, PO Box 1407, Covina CA 91722. **Tel** (703)821-7192. LC HD9710.5.A1. DD 381.4562922750973.

NORTHEAST RIDING (MASS. EDITION). (NORTHEAST RIDING). 0742-2059. Periodical. US. English. mo. $1.50. Northeast Riding, 209 Whitney Street, Hartford CT 06105. **Tel** (203)236-6604. Ed P Fahy. For the touring motorcycle rider, in regional public northeast Hartford area.

OFF ROAD CYCLING. VFOAT Cycle Guide's Off Road Cycling. US. English. $1.25 Each Issue. Cycle Guide Publications, 1440 W Walnut Street, Compton CA 90220. LC GV1059.5. DD 796.75.

OREGON TRAFFIC ACCIDENTS. FOCUS ON MOTORCYCLES. See Transportation - Roads and Traffic.

PERFORMANCE DATA, NEW PASSENGER CARS AND MOTORCYCLES. See Transportation - Automobiles.

POPULAR CYCLING. See Bicycles and Bicycling.

RIDER. V. 1- Summer 1974-. 0095-1625. Periodical. US. English. mo. Trailer Life Publishing Company, 29901 Agoura Road, Agoura CA 91301, (subscription address: Neodata PO Box 2606, Boulder CO 80322). **Tel** (213)991-4980. LC GV1059.5. DD 796.7505.

RIDERANNUAL. 81-. 0278-596X. US. English. an. $3.00. Trailer Life Publishing Company Inc, 29901 Agoura Road, Agoura CA 91301. LC TL440. DD 629.2275.

ROAD RIDER. V. 1, No. 3- Dec. 1969/Jan. 1970-. 0035-7243. Periodical. US. English. mo. $15.97. Road Rider Magazine, PO Box 6040, Mission Viejo CA 92690. LC TL440.5. DD 796.7. *Road Rider News, 0161-4509.*

ROLLING EAST. Vol. 1, No. 4 (July 1984)-. 0828-5993. Periodical. CN. English. ir. $1.25 Per No. Rolling Thunder Publications, PO Box 213, Porter's Lake Nova Scotia B0J 2S0 Canada. DD 629.227509715. *Rolling Thunder (Porter's Lake, N.S.), 0828-5985.*

Museums

SANFORD EVANS GOLD BOOK OF MOTORCYCLE DATA AND USED PRICES. VFOAT Gold Book of Motorcycle Data and Used Prices. 0705-1840. CN. English. an. 9.95. Sanford Evans Communications Ltd, Box 6900/1077 St James Street, Winnipeg Manitoba R3C 3B1 Canada. **Tel** (204)775-0201. Ed G B Henry. DD 338.4362922750971. Contains registration data and realistic retail values for new and used motorcycles.

SOUTHERN MOTORACING. 0049-1616. Periodical. US. English. bw. $10.00. c/o Hank Schoolfield, 1049 Northwest Boulevard Box 500, Winston-Salem NC 27102. **Tel** (919)723-5227. Ed Hank Schoolfield. bk rev. adv acc. **Circ** 18,000. Aimed primarily at motor racing fans, with coverage emphasis on Southeastern US motor racing.

STREET & DIRT. VAT Street and Dirt. Vol. 1, No. 1 (Feb./Mar. 1983)-. 0820-7224. Periodical. CN. English. bm. $7.50. Street & Dirt, 23 Stafford Street, Toronto Ontario M5V 2S2 Canada. LC 629.22750971.

SUPER BMX. 0274-7243. Periodical. US. English. mo. $22.50. Challenge Publications Inc, 7950 Deering Avenue, Canoga Park CA 91304. **Tel** (213)887-0550. *Minicycle/BMX Action.*

SUPERCROSS ACTION (TORONTO). (SUPERCROSS ACTION). 1980-. 0825-0618. CN. English. an. $2.00 Each Volume. DD 796.750971.

SVENSKA TIDNINGSARTIKLAR. See Bicycles and Bicycling.

TRAFIKBLINKEN. See Transportation - Roads and Traffic.

TURBO. See Transportation - Automobiles.

WING WORLD. Vol. 6, Issue 12 (Dec. 1982)-. 0745-273X. Periodical. US. English. mo. $24.00 Domestic, $29.00 Foreign. Gold Wing Road Riders Association, 3662 West Lawrence Lane, Phoenix AZ 85021. *Wing News.*

MUSEUMS

AASTARAAMAT. See Anthropology.

ABHANDLUNGEN AUS DEM LANDESMUSEUM FUR NATURKUNDE ZU MUNSTER IN WESTFALEN. **Main/Corp** Munster. Landesmuseum fur Naturkunde. Vol. 1-. GW. Germany. ir. Abhandlungen aus dem Himmelreichallee, 50 Westfalen, 4400 Westmunster West Germany. *Jahresbericht des Westfalischen Provinzial-Vereins fur Wissenschaft und Kunst.*

ABHANDLUNGEN DES STAATLICHEN MUSEUMS FUR MINERALOGIE UND GEOLOGIE ZU DRESDEN. **Main/Corp** Dresden. Staatliches Museum fur Mineralogie und Geologie. V. 11-. 0070-7228. GE. German. ir. Deutscher Buch Export-Import, Leninstrasse 16, DDR-701 Leipzig East Germany. **Tel** 4 44 4 1. Ed G Mathe. **Ind/Abst** Chem. Abstr., GeoRef. LC QE351. DD 550.5. CODEN SMGAA8. **Circ** 600. Description and utilization of the paleontological and mineralogical collection of the museum, the stratigraphy of Saxony, the conservation of stone and the history of earth sciences. *Jahrbuch des Staatlichen Museums fur Mineralogie und Geologie zu Dresden.*

ABHANDLUNGEN UND BERICHTE DES NATURKUNDEMUSEUMS GORLITZ. **Main/Corp** Gorlitz. Naturkundemuseum. 1- Vol. Periodical. GE. German. ir. Deutscher Buch Export-Import, Leninstrasse 16, DDR-701 Leipzig East Germany. **Ind/Abst** GeoRef. LC QH5.

ABHANDLUNGEN UND BERICHTE DES STAATLICHEN MUSEUMS FUR VOLKERKUNDE, DRESDEN. **Main/Corp** Dresden. Staatliches Museum fur Volkerkunde. Vol. 21- 1962-. 9640-7295. GE. German (Vols. have table of contents also in English and Russian). ir. Deutscher Buch Export-Import, Leninstrasse 16, DDR-701 Leipzig East Germany. *Abhandlungen und Berichte.*

ABSTRACTS - INTERNATIONAL INSTITUTE FOR CONSERVATION OF HISTORIC AND ARTISTIC WORKS. See Indexes/Abstracts.

Museums

ACCESS. See Library and Information Science.

ACCESSIONS LIST - NATIONAL MUSEUMS OF CANADA. LIBRARY CEASED. (ACCESSIONS LIST). Main/Corp National Museums of Canada. Library. VFOAT Liste d'Acquisitions. VAT Library Accessions - National Museums of Canada (1975), Nouvelles Acquisitions - Musees Nationaux du Canada (1975). V. 19, No. 3-V. 26/4. 0708-4307. Periodical. CN. English (includes French publications). *Library Accessions, 0708-4315.*

ADLER MUSEUM BULLETIN. V. 5- Apr. 1979-. SA. English. ty. 12.00. Adler Museum History of Medicine, PO Box 1038, Johannesburg South Africa 2000. Tel 725-2846. Ed Rose Melzer. NLM W1 AD305. bk rev. Circ 1,500. (ctrl). All aspects of the history of medicine and the allied sciences as well as biographies and assessments of the great men and women of medicine and surgery. *Bulletin of The Adler Museum of the History of Medicine.*

ALBERTA MUSEUMS REVIEW. Began with Mar. 1974 issue. 0380-3279. Periodical. CN. English. sa. Alberta Museums Review, PO Box 545, Peace River Alberta Canada. DD 069.097123.

ALI-ABA COURSE OF STUDY. LEGAL ASPECTS OF MUSEUM OPERATIONS: MATERIALS. See Law.

ANALES DEL MUSEO DE HISTORIA NATURAL DE VALPARAISO. See Yearbooks, Almanacs, Directories.

ANALES Y BOLETIN DE LOS MUSEOS DE ARTE DE BARCELONA. See Yearbooks, Almanacs, Directories.

ANNALES HISTORICO-NATURALES MUSEI NATIONALIS HUNGARICI (BUDAPEST, HUNGARY : 1965). (ANNALES HISTORICO-NATURALES MUSEI NATIONALIS HUNGARICI). VFOAT Termeszettudomanyi Muzeum Enkonyve. V. 57- 1965-. 0521-4726. Periodical. HU. English (articles are in French, German, Hungarian, and Russian). an. Hungarian Natural History Museum, T M K Barros U-13, H-1088 Budapest Hungary. Ind/Abst GeoRef, Biol. Abstr., Bibliogr. Agric. CODEN AHMHAU. *Magyar Nemzeti Muzeum Termeszettudomanyi Muzeum Evokonyve.*

ANNALS OF THE CAPE PROVINCIAL MUSEUMS. HUMAN SCIENCES. VFOAT Human Sciences. V. 1, Pt. 1 (20th Mar. 1979)-. Periodical. English. ir. *Annals of the Cape Provincial Museums.*

ANNALS OF THE CAPE PROVINCIAL MUSEUMS. NATURAL HISTORY. VFOAT Natural History. Began in 1966. 0570-1880. English. ir. Ind/Abst Life Sci. Collect., GeoRef, Biol. Abstr., Bibliogr. Agric. CODEN ACPVAI. *Annals of the Cape Provincial Museums.*

ANNALS OF THE CARNEGIE MUSEUM. (ANNALS OF CARNEGIE MUSEUM). V. 45- Dec. 19, 1974-. 0097-4463. Periodical. US. English. bm. Carnegie Museum of Natural History, 4400 Forbes Avenue, Pittsburgh PA 15213. Tel (412)622-3284. Ed Hugh H Genoways. Ind/Abst GeoRef, Biol. Abstr., Zool. Rec., Bibliogr. Agric., Bibliogr. Index Geol. LC AS36. DD 500.9085. CODEN CIMUAU. Circ 500. Original scientific publications in zoology, ecology, systematics, mineralogy, invertebrate and vertebrate paleontology. *Annals of the Carnegie Museum, 0097-4463.*

ANNALS OF THE NATAL MUSEUM, PIETERMARITZBURG. (ANNALS OF THE NATAL MUSEUM). Main/Corp Natal Museum, Pietermaritzburg. VFOAT Annale van die Natalse Museum. V. 1- June 1906-. 0304-0798. SA. Afrikaans (English). ir. 65.00. Natal Museum, 237 Loop Street, Pietermartizburg 3201 South Africa. Tel 51404. Ed Jason Londt. Ind/Abst Life Sci. Collect., GeoRef, Biol. Abstr. LC Q85. DD 574.9605. CODEN ANMUA9. Index in last issue of volume - attached. (cum index). Circ 350. Scientific journal reporting research in systematic zoology, especially arachaeology, entomology, and malacology. Also in Southern African archaeology and ethnoarchaeology.

ANNALS OF THE SOUTH AFRICAN MUSEUM. Main/Corp South African Museum. VFOAT Annale van die Suid-Afrikaanse Museum. V. 1- June 1898-. 0303-2515. Monographic Series. SA. English. ir. South African Museum, PO Box 61, Cape Town South Africa 8000. Tel 24 3330. Ed A E Love. Ind/Abst Life Sci. Collect., Sel. Water Resour. Abstr., GeoRef, Biol. Abstr., Chem. Abstr., Bibliogr. Agric., Bibliogr. Index Geol., Abstr. Anthropol., Ocean. Abstr. LC QH1. CODEN ASAMAS. (cum index). Circ 360. (ctrl). Scientific journal covering ethnography, archaeology, palaentology, geology, marine biology, entomology, herpetology, ornithology and mammalogy.

ANNALS OF THE TRANSVAAL MUSEUM. VFOAT Annale van die Transvaal-Museum, Mededelingen van het Transvaal Museum. Vol. 1, No. 1 (Apr. 1908)-. 0041-1752. Periodical. SA. English. ir. Transvaal Museum, Postbus 413, 413, Pretoria South Africa 0001. Tel 287387. Ed N J Dippenaar. Ind/Abst GeoRef, Biol. Abstr., Bibliogr. Index Geol. LC QH1. DD 574. CODEN ATVMA4. Circ 400. Taxonomy, biology, ecology, paleontology of Southern African fauna.

ANNUAIRE DES MUSEES ROYAUX DES BEAUX-ARTS DE BELGIQUE. See Yearbooks, Almanacs, Directories.

ANNUAL - BALTIMORE MUSEUM OF ART. (ANNUAL). Main/Corp Baltimore Museum of Art. Vol. 1-. 0067-3080. US. English. an. Baltimore Museum of Art, Baltimore MD 21233. LC N515. DD 705.

ANNUAL REPORT - AKRON ART MUSEUM. (ANNUAL REPORT). Main/Corp Akron Art Museum. 1979/80-. 0277-4348. US. English. an. Akron Art Museum, 69 East Market Street, Akron OH 44308. LC N512.A4. DD 709.040074017136. *Biennial Report.*

ANNUAL REPORT AND BULLETIN - MUSEUMS OF MALAWI. Main/Corp Museums of Malawi. 1980-. English. an. The Museum, PO Box 30360, Chichiri, Blantyre 3 Malawi. LC AM91.M3. DD 069.096897. *Annual Report and Bulletin.*

ANNUAL REPORT - CITY OF JOHANNESBURG, AFRICANA MUSEUM. Main/Corp Africana Museum (Johannesburg, South Africa). VFOAT Annual Report of the Director for the Year, City of Johannesburg, Africana Museum. SA. English. ir. Free. Johannesburg South Africa. Tel 836-3787. Ed E B Nagelgast. LC AM101. DD 069.0968221. Circ 460. Reports on its branches are appended as well as details of exhibitions, publications, and staff.

ANNUAL REPORT - CORNING MUSEUM OF GLASS. (ANNUAL REPORT - THE CORNING MUSEUM OF GLASS). Main/Corp Corning Museum of Glass. 1976-. 0147-488X. US. English. an. Corning Museum of Glass, Corning NY 14831. Tel (607)937-5371. Ed John H Martin. LC NK5102.C65. DD 748.074014783. Circ 1,500. (ctrl). Outstanding acquisitions and gifts and a review of the special 1985 exhibition "Frederick Carder: Portrait of a Glassmaker" are part of the annual survey.

ANNUAL REPORT FOR FISCAL YEAR - VIRGIN ISLANDS BUREAU OF LIBRARIES, MUSEUMS, AND ARCHAEOLOGICAL SERVICES. See Library and Information Science.

ANNUAL REPORT - HENRY FRANCIS DU PONT WINTERTHUR MUSEUM. Main/Corp Henry Francis du Pont Winterthur Museum. 0440-6885. US. English. an. Henry Francis du Pont Winterthur Museum, Winterthur DE 19735. LC NK460.W5. DD 973.07401511.

ANNUAL REPORT - NEWARK MUSEUM. (ANNUAL REPORT. DELETE). Main/Corp Newark Museum. 1982-. 8755-1411. US. English. an. The Newark Museum, 49 Washington Street P O Box 540, Newark NJ 07101. *Newark Museum Quarterly.*

ANNUAL REPORT - NORTH CAROLINA STATE MUSEUM OF NATURAL HISTORY. Main/Corp North Carolina State Museum of Natural History. US. English. an. $15.00. North Carolina State Museum of Natural History, PO Box 27647, Raleigh NC 27647. Tel (919)733-7450. Ed Eloise F Potter. LC QH71.N68. DD 069.9508756. Circ 300. Taxonomy and systematics, ecology, zoogeography, evolution and behavior in the subdisciplines of invertebrate zoology, ichthyology, herpetology, mammalogy, ornithology and paleontology; southeast US. *Report.*

ANNUAL REPORT OF THE MUSEUM OF FINE ARTS BOSTON CEASED. Main/Corp Museum of Fine Arts, Boston. 1- 1876-. US. English. an. $5.00. Museum of Fine Arts, c/o P Jacoff, 465 Huntington Avenue, Boston MA 02115. LC N520.

ANNUAL REPORT OF THE PAPUA NEW GUINEA PUBLIC MUSEUM AND ART GALLERY. Main/Corp Papua New Guinea Museum. VFOAT Annual Report of the Trustees. PP. English. ir. Papua New Guinea Public Museum and Art Gallery, PO Box 635, Port Moresby Papua New Guinea. LC N3990.P6. DD 069.09953.

ANNUAL REPORT OF THE PHILADELPHIA MUSEUM OF ART CEASED. Main/Corp Philadelphia Museum of Art. US. English. an. Philadelphia Museum of Art, 26th and Parkway, Philadelphia PA 19101.

ANNUAL REPORT - ROYAL ONTARIO MUSEUM. Main/Corp Royal Ontario Museum. No. 1- 1949/50-. 0082-5115. Periodical. CN. English. an. 100 Queen Park, Toronto M5S 2C6 Ontario Canada. LC AM101. DD 069.0871.

ANNUAL REPORT - SANTA BARBARA MUSEUM OF ART. Main/Corp Santa Barbara Museum of Art. 1979-. US. English. an. Santa Barbara Musuem of Art, 1130 State Street, Santa Barbara CA 93101. LC N742.S15. DD 708.19493.

ANNUAL REPORT - SOUTH AFRICAN NATIONAL MUSEUM OF MILITARY HISTORY. Main/Corp South African National Museum of Military History. VFOAT Jaarverslag - Suid-Afrikaanse Nasionale Museum Vir Krygsgeskiedenis. 1974/75-. SA. Afrikaans and English. ir. South African National Museum of Military History, Erlswold Way Saxonwold, Johannesburg South Africa. LC D733. DD 355.0074096822. *Report.*

ANNUAL REPORT - THOMAS BURKE MEMORIAL WASHINGTON STATE MUSEUM. (ANNUAL REPORT). Main/Corp Washington (State). University. Museum. 0093-5670. US. English. an. Washington State Museum, Seattle WA 98121. LC AM101.S28. DD 069.0979777.

THE ANNUAL REPORTS OF THE SYNDICATE AND OF THE FRIENDS OF THE FITZWILLIAM. Main/Corp University of Cambridge. Fitzwilliam Museum. UK. English. an. University of Cambridge, Fitzwilliam Museum, Cambridge England. LC AM101.C157. DD 069.097444. *Annual Report.*

ANTIQUE PREVIEW. See Antiques.

ARBOK (NORDLAND FYLKESMUSEUM). See Yearbooks, Almanacs, Directories.

ARMY MUSEUM NEWSLETTER. No. 1- Sept. 1969-. 0004-2536. Periodical. US. English. ir. US Army, Center of Military History, Washington DC 20315. Tel (915)568-4133. LC U13.U6. DD 355.009730740153.

ARQUIVOS DO MUSEU NACIONAL. See Genealogy and Heraldry - Archives.

ART IN AMERICA. ANNUAL GUIDE TO GALLERIES, MUSEUMS, ARTISTS. See The Arts (General).

ARTS QUARTERLY (NEW ORLEANS MUSEUM OF ART). See The Arts (General).

ARTSCENE. See The Arts (General) - Art.

ASAHI GYARARI NENKAN. VFOAT Asahi Gallery Annual. 1978-. Periodical. JA. Japanese. ir. 3000. Kabushiki Kaisha Sampo Janaru, 10-17 Hamamatsucho 1 Minato-ku, Tokyo 105 Japan. LC N7358. *Asahi Geijutsu Nenkan.*

ATRIA. Main/Corp Royal Ontario Museum. Nov./Dec. 1982-. 0824-4251. CN. English. bm. Royal Ontario Museum, 100 Queen's Park, Toronto Ontario M5S 2C6 Canada. DD 069.109713541. *What's On at the ROM, 0824-4243.*

AU FIL DES COLLECTIONS. Aug.14/Nov.14 1982-. 0711-7086. Periodical. CN. French. qt. Free. Musee des Beaux-Arts de Montreal, 3400 Av du Musee, Montreal Quebec H3G 1K3 Canada. DD 069.970009714281. (ctrl).

AUDIT REPORT - STATE OF NEVADA. NEVADA STATE MUSEUM. (NEVADA STATE MUSEUM AUDIT REPORT). Main/Corp Nevada. Legislative Counsel Bureau. 0093-1586. US. English. an. Legislative Counsel Bureau, Legislative Building, Carson City NV 89701. LC AM101. DD 069.0979357.

Museums

BELSER KUNSTQUARTAL. VFOAT Belser Kunst Quartal. 1967-. Periodical. German. qt. Belser Verlag, Postfach 1002, 7 Stuttgart West Germany.

BERICHTE DES VEREINS NATUR UND HEIMAT UND DES NATURHISTORISCHEN MUSEUMS ZU LUBECK. Main/Corp Verein Natur und Heimat, Lubeck. No. 1- 1959-. 0505-2793. Periodical. GW. German. be. $10.15. Naturhistorisches Museum, Luebeck/Muhlendamm 1-3, D2400 Luebeck 1 West Germany. Circ 500. Biology and ecology of native biotopes. *Mitteilungen der Geographischen Gesellschaft Und des Naturhistorischen Museums in Lubeck.*

BERNICE P. BISHOP MUSEUM BULLETIN. VFOAT Bulletin. 1-. 0005-9439. Monographic Series. US. English. ir. Bishop Museum Press, PO Box 19000-A, Honolulu HI 96819.

BIBLIOGRAPHIE MUSEOLOGIQUE INTERNATIONALE. *See Bibliographies.*

THE BIBLIOGRAPHY OF MUSEUM AND ART GALLERY PUBLICATIONS AND AUDIO-VISUAL AIDS IN GREAT BRITAIN AND IRELAND. *See Bibliographies.*

BIBLIOTHEQUES ET MUSEES. Main/Corp Neuchatel (Switzerland). Conseil Communl. Section des Affaries Culturelles. VFOAT Bibliogtheques et Musees de la Ville de Neuchatel. French. an. LC Z837. DD 069.094943. *Bibliotheques et Musees.*

BIENNIAL EXHIBITION - WHITNEY MUSEUM OF AMERICAN ART. Main/Corp Whitney Museum of American Art. Began in 1973. US. English. be. Whitney Museum of American Art, 945 Madison Avenue, New York NY 10021. *Annual Exhibition of Contemporary American Painting.*

THE BIENNIAL REPORT, FIELD MUSEUM OF NATURAL HISTORY. (THE . . . BIENNIAL REPORT, FIELD MUSEUM OF NATURAL HISTORY). Main/Corp Field Museum of Natural History. 1979-1980-. 0730-2819. US. English. be. Field Museum of Natural History, Roosevelt Road at Lake Shore Drive, Chicago IL 60605. LC QH70.U62. DD 508.074017311. *Report.*

BILDERHEFTE. Main/Corp Berlin. Staatliche Museen (West Berlin). No. 1- 1967-. 0522-9790. Monographic Series. GW. German. ir. Gebrueder Mann Verlag, Lindenstrasse 76, D-1000 Berlin 61 West Germany. Tel 30-25913589. adv acc. Circ 1,000. Reports on partial holdings of the different departments of the National Museum sometimes due to special exhibits.

BIOME. Vol. 1:1-. 0712-9319. Periodical. CN. English. ir. National Museum of Canada, Information Center/Museum of Natural Science, Ottawa Ontario K1A 0M8 Canada. DD 505.

BLACK HISTORY MUSEUM NEWSLETTER. VFOAT UMUM: Unexplored Topics in Black History. V. 1, No. 1-4. Periodical. US. English. ir. $5.00. Black History Museum, PO Box 15057, Philadelphia PA 19130.

BOLETIN DEL MUSEO DE CIENCIAS NATURALES Y ANTROPOLOGICAS JUAN CORNELIO MOYANO. No. 1 (1980)-. 0326-1484. Periodical. AG. Spanish. an. Subsuelo Plaza Independencia, Mendoza Argentina. Ind/Abst GeoRef. *Revista del Museo de Historia Natural de Mendoza.*

BOLETIN DEL MUSEO DEL PRADO. Main/Corp Museo del Prado. V. 1, No. 1 (Jan.-April 1980)-. 0210-8143. SP. Spanish. ty. 850. El Museo, Museo del Prado, Madrid 14 Spain. Ind/Abst Art Archaeol. Tech. Abstr., Repert. Int. Litt. Art. LC AM101.M238. DD 069.094641.

BOLETIN DEL MUSEO NACIONAL DE HISTORIA NATURAL. (BOLETIN - MUSEO NACIONAL DE HISTORIA NATURAL). Main/Corp Museo Nacional de Historia Natural (Chile). V. 16-. 0027-3910. Monographic Series. CL. Spanish. ir. Museo Nacional Historia Natura, Casilla 787, Santiago Chile. Ind/Abst Life Sci. Collect., GeoRef, Bibliogr. Index Geol. LC QH7. Circ 1,000. Contains previously unpublished studies and contributions on the natural sciences disciplines and anthropology. *Boletin del Museo Nacional.*

BOLETIN (MUSEO DE ZARAGOZA). (BOLETIN). No. 1-. Spanish. ir. Apartado 848, Zaragoza Brazil. LC AM1. DD 069.0946553.

BOLLETTINO (CIVICI MUSEI VENEZIANI D'ARTE E DI STORIA). (BOLLETTINO). VFOAT Bollettino C. Musei Veneziani. N.S. 25, 1-4 (1980)-. Italian. an. San Marco 52, Venezia Italy. *Bollettino Dei Musei Civici Veneziani.*

BOLLETTINO DEI MUSEI CIVICI VENEZIANI. No. 1- 1956-. 0083-5447. Periodical. IT. Italian. ir. $4.00. Ca Giustinia 7, 30100 Venezia Italy. Ind/Abst Repert. Int. Litt. Art, Avery Index Archit. Period. Second Ed. Revis. Enlarged Suppl. (cum index).

BOLLETTINO DEL MUSEO CIVICO DI STORIA NATURALE DI VERONA. Main/Corp Verona. Museo Civico di Storia Naturale. V. 1- 1974-. 0392-0062. English, French, German or Italian. ir. Ind/Abst Life Sci. Collect., Biol. Abstr., GeoRef. LC QH7. CODEN BMCVD3.

BRASILIA. V. 1- 1942-. PO. Portuguese. ir. Universidade de Coimbra, 3049 Coimbra Codex, Coimbra Portugal. LC AS80. DD 068.81.

BRIEF DIRECTORY OF MUSEUMS IN INDIA. *See Yearbooks, Almanacs, Directories.*

BRUNEI MUSEUM JOURNAL. Main/Corp Muzium Brunei. V. 1- 1969-. Multilingual (English or Malay). bm. Brunei Museum, Bandar Seri Begawan, Brunei. LC DS646.35. DD 915.955005.

BULLETIN (ALABAMA MUSEUM OF NATURAL HISTORY). (BULLETIN - ALABAMA MUSEUM OF NATURAL HISTORY). No. 1-. 0196-1039. Monographic Series. US. English. ir. University of Alabama, Museum of Natural History, Box 5897, University City AL 35486. Tel (205)348-7550.

BULLETIN - ALLEN MEMORIAL ART MUSEUM. (BULLETIN - ALLEN MEMORIAL ART MUSEUM, OBERLIN COLLEGE). Main/Corp Oberlin College. Dudley Peter Allen Memorial Art Museum. VFOAT Allen Memorial Art Museum Bulletin. V. 1- June 1944-. 0002-5739. Periodical. US. English. sa. $10.00. Allen Memorial Art Museum, Oberlin College, Oberlin OH 44074. Tel (216)775-8665. Ind/Abst Art Index, Repert. Int. Litt. Art. LC N650. DD 708.171. (cum index). Circ 1,200. (ctrl). Available on microfilm from University Microfilms. Journal of museum exhibitions and activities with scholarly articles to illuminate the permanent collection published since 1944 and indexed.

BULLETIN - ART GALLERY OF YORK UNIVERSITY. (BULLETIN). 0822-7624. Periodical. CN. English. ir. Art Gallery of York University, 4700 Keele Street, Downsview Ontario M3J 2R7 Canada. DD 708.113541.

BULLETIN - ASSOCIATION DES ANATOMISTES. Main/Corp National Museum of Canada. Series Corp National Museum of Canada.** Folklore Series.** National Museum of Canada.** Biological Series.** National Museum of Canada.** Anthropological Series. No. 1- 1913-. Periodical. English. ir.

BULLETIN - CALIFORNIA MUSEUM OF PHOTOGRAPHY. (CMP BULLETIN). VFOAT C.M.P. Bulletin. VAT California Museum of Photography Bulletin. Vol. 1, No. 1-. 0731-2377. Periodical. US. English. bm. $25.00. California Museum of Photography, University of California, Riverside CA 92521. Tel (714)787-4787. Ed Charles Desmarais. bk rev. Circ 800. (ctrl). Reports on aspects of the museum's collections, exhibitions, and research. CMP collections comprise over 10,000 photographs, 350,000 stereographic negatives and prints; and 4,000 cameras.

BULLETIN DES MUSEES ET MONUMENTS LYONNAIS. V. 1- 1952-. 0521-7032. Periodical. FR. French. qt. Musee des Beaux-Arts, 20 Place des Terreaux, 69001 Lyon France.

BULLETIN DES MUSEES ROYAUX D'ART ET D'HISTOIRE (BELGIUM). Main/Corp Musees Royaux d'Art et d'Histoire (Belgium). V. 1-6, Oct. 1901-Sept. 1907. BE. Multilingual (English, and Flemish (Dutch)). ir. Partrimoine Musees Royaux Art Histoire, Parc Cinquantenaire 10, 1040 Bruxelles Belgium. Tel 02/733 96 10. Ind/Abst Avery Index Archit. Period., Repert. Int. Litt. Art. LC N1835. DD 708.9493. (cum index).

BULLETIN DU MUSEE HONGROIS DES BEAUX-ARTS. Main/Corp Szpmuveszeti Muzeum (Hungary). VFOAT Szepmuveszeti Muzeum Kozlemenyei. Vol. 1 1947-. HU. French and Hungarian. ir. Hungarian Museums, List Col Sli 41, Budapest 15 Hungary. Tel 429-759. Ind/Abst Repert. Int. Litt. Art. Circ 1,400. (ctrl). Classic archaeology, European art and history, chiefly Thirteenth to the Nineteenth Century.

BULLETIN DU MUSEE INGRES. Began publication in 1956. 0540-7575. Periodical. FR. French. sa. $8.00. Musee d'Ingres-Societe de Amis, 70 Avenue Gambetta, 82000 Montauban France. Tel (63) 03 48 43. Ind/Abst Repert. Int. Litt. Art. Life and work of the painter Dominique Ingres and his students.

BULLETIN DU MUSEE NATIONAL DE VARSOVIE. Main/Corp Muzeum Narodowe W Warszawie. V. 1- 1960-. 0027-3791. Periodical. PL. French or English. qt. ARS Polona, Krakowskie Prezedmiescie 7, 00-068 Warsaw Poland. Ind/Abst Repert. Int. Litt. Art.

BULLETIN DU MUSEUM NATIONAL D'HISTOIRE NATURELLE. Main/Corp Museum National d'Historie Naturelle (France). V. 1-34, 1895-1928. 0027-4070. Periodical. FR. French. ir. $167.63. Museum National d'Historie Naturelle, 38 rue Geoffroy-Saint-Hilaire, 75005 Paris France. Tel 331 71 24. Ind/Abst Bibliogr. Index Geol. CODEN BUNMAG.

BULLETIN DU MUSEUM NATIONAL D'HISTOIRE NATURELLE. SECTION A : ZOOLOGIE, BIOLOGIE ET ECOLOGIE ANIMALES. VFOAT Zoologie, Biologie et Ecologie Animales. 4. Ser. Vol. 1- Mar. 1979-. 0181-0626. Periodical. FR. French (English). ir. $103.77. Museum National d'Histoire Naturelle, 38 rue Geoffroy-Saint-Hilaire, 75005 Paris France. Tel 331 71 24. Ind/Abst Biol. Abstr., Bibliogr. Agric., Life Sci. Collect. CODEN BMNADT. Index published separately - free - automatically sent. *Bulletin du Museum National d'Histoire Naturelle. Zoologie, Bulletin du Museum National d'Histoire Naturelle. Ecologie Gener.*

BULLETIN DU MUSEUM NATIONAL D'HISTOIRE NATURELLE, SECTION C, SCIENCES DE LA TERRE, PALEONTOLOGIE, GEOLOGIE, MINERALOGIE. (BULLETIN DU MUSEUM NATIONAL D'HISTOIRE NATURELLE. SECTION C : SCIENCES DE LA TERRE : PALEONTOLOGIE, GEOLOGIE, MINERALOGIE). VFOAT Sciences de la Terre: Paleontologie, Geologie, Mineralogie. 4. Ser. Vol. 1- Mar. 1979-. 0181-0642. Periodical. FR. French (English). ir. $33.26. Museum National d'Histoire Naturelle, 38 rue Geoffroy-Saint-Hilaire, 75005 Paris France. Tel 331 71 24. Ind/Abst GeoRef, Life Sci. Collect., Biol. Abstr., Chem. Abstr., Bibliogr. Index Geol. CODEN BMNMDV. Index published separately - free - automatically sent. *Bulletin du Museum National d'Histoire Naturelle. Sciences de la Terre, Bulletin du Museum National d'Histoire Naturelle. Sciences Physico-Chimiques.*

BULLETIN DU MUSEUM NATIONAL D'HISTOIRE NATURELLE. SER.3. SCIENCES PHYSICO-CHIMIQUES. Main/Corp Museum National d'Histoire Naturelle (France). Periodical. FR. French. ir. Museum National d'Histoire Naturelle, 55 rue Buffon, 75005 Paris France. *Bulletin du Museum National d'Histoire Naturelle, 0027-4070.*

BULLETIN - GEORGIA MUSEUM OF ART, THE UNIVERSITY OF GEORGIA. (BULLETIN - GEORGIA MUSEUM OF ART). Main/Corp Georgia Museum of Art. VFOAT Georgia Museum of Art Bulletin. V. 1- Fall 1974-. 0147-1902. Periodical. US. English. qt. University of Georgia, Georgia Museum of Art, Administrative Office, Athens GA 30602. Ind/Abst Repert. Int. Litt. Art. LC N514.A8. DD 708.15818.

BULLETIN - INDIAN MUSEUM. Main/Corp Indian Museum, Calcutta. V. 1- Jan. 1966-. 0019-5987. Periodical. II. English. sa. Indian Museum Bulletin, 27 Jawaharal Nehru Road, Calcutta 13 India. LC AM101.

BULLETIN - LOS ANGELES COUNTY MUSEUM OF ART. (BULLETIN). V. 8- 1962-. 0024-6557. Periodical. US. English. ir. $6.00. Los Angeles County Museum of Art/Museum Shop, 5905 Wilshire Boulevard, Los Angeles CA 90036.

BULLETIN - METROPOLITAN MUSEUM OF ART. Main/Corp New York (City). Metropolitan Museum of Art. VFOAT Metropolitan Museum of Art Bulletin. V. 1-37, No. 6, Nov. 1905-June 1942. 0026-1521. Periodical. US. English. qt. $18.00. Metropolitan Museum of Art, Fifth Avenue and 82nd Street, New York NY 10028. Ed

Museums

Joan Holt. **Ind/Abst** Art Index, Avery Index Archit. Period., Am. Hist. Life, Hist. Abstr., Hist. Abstr., Part A, Mod. Hist. Abstr., Hist. Abst., Part B, Twent. Century Abstr. **LC** N610. **DD** 708. (cum index). Presents illustrated articles about objects in the collections and about the museum's activities.

BULLETIN - MONTCLAIR ART MUSEUM. Main/Corp Montclair, N.J. Art Museum. V. 1- Sept./Oct. 1929-. 0027-0059. Periodical. US. English. mo. **LC** N584. **DD** 708.14931.

BULLETIN - MUSEEN DER STADT KOLN. (BULLETIN). 1st No. 1 (July 1961)-. 0178-4218. Periodical. German. mo. Museen der Stadt Koln, Marspfortengasse 6, 5000 Koln 1 West Germany. **Ind/Abst** Repert. Int. Litt. Art. **LC** N2264.2. **DD** 708.355. *Museen in Koln, 0027-3813.*

BULLETIN - MUSEUM OF FINE ARTS, HOUSTON. (BULLETIN - THE MUSEUM OF FINE ARTS, HOUSTON). **Main/Corp** Museum of Fine Arts, Houston. V. 1- Feb. 1930-. 0018-6708. Periodical. US. English. qt. Museum of Fine Arts, PO Box 6826, Houston TX 77005. **Ind/Abst** Artbibliogr. Mod., Repert. Int. Litt. Art. **LC** N576.H7. **DD** 708.1641411.

BULLETIN - MUSEUM OF INDIAN ARCHAEOLOGY. UNIVERSITY OF WESTERN ONTARIO. (BULLETIN - MUSEUM OF INDIAN ARCHAEOLOGY). 0709-2628. Monographic Series. CN. English. ir. Museum of Indian Archaeology, Middlesex College/Room 28, University of Western Ontario, London Ontario N6A 5B7 Canada. **DD** 971.301.

BULLETIN - NATIONAL MUSEUM, NEW DELHI. Main/Corp Delhi. National Museum of India. No. 1- 1966-. 0418-5730. II. English. ir. National Museum of New Delhi, Janpath New Delhi 110011 India. **LC** DS401. **DD** 913.3403105.

BULLETIN - NEW YORK STATE MUSEUM. Main/Corp New York State Museum. No. 425- Feb. 1976-. 0278-3355. Monographic Series. US. English. ir. New York State Library, Gift and Exchange Section, Albany NY 12230. **Ind/Abst** GeoRef, Bibliogr. Agric. *Bulletin - New York State Museum and Science Service, 0097-028X.*

BULLETIN - NORTH CAROLINA MUSEUM OF ART. Main/Corp North Carolina. Museum of Art, Raleigh. V. 1- Spring 1957-. 0029-2567. Periodical. US. English. ir. c/o Gay M Hertzman, 107 East Morgan Street, Raleigh NC 27611. **Ind/Abst** Repert. Int. Litt. Art. **LC** N715.R2.

BULLETIN OF CARNEGIE MUSEUM OF NATURAL HISTORY. Main/Corp Carnegie Museum of Natural History. No. 1-. 0145-9058. Monographic Series. US. English. ir. Carnegie Museum of Natural History, 4400 Forbes Avenue, Pittsburgh PA 15213. **Tel** (412)622-3784. **Ed** Hugh H Genoways. **Ind/Abst** GeoRef, Biol. Abstr., Bibliogr. Index Geol. **CODEN** BCMHD9. **Circ** 500. Original scientific publications in zoology, anthropology, botany, ecology, systematics, mineralogy, invertebrate and vertebrate paleontology.

BULLETIN OF THE ALLYN MUSEUM. No. 1-. 0097-3211. Monographic Series. US. English. ir. Allyn Museum of Entomology, 3701 Bay Shore Road, Sarasota FL 33580. **Tel** (813)355-8475. **Ed** Lee D Miller. **Ind/Abst** Biol. Abstr., Bibliogr. Agric. **CODEN** BLAMBP. **Circ** 415. A reviewed journal devoted to the study of lepidoptera, especially rhopalocera. Publications to date include studies on life history, taxonomy, systematics, morphology, and ecology.

BULLETIN OF THE AMERICAN MUSEUM OF NATURAL HISTORY. Vol. 170-. 0003-0090. Monographic Series. US. English. ir. American Museum of Natural History, Central Park West at 79th Street, New York NY 10024. **Tel** (212)873-1300. **Ed** Brenda Jones. **Ind/Abst** Life Sci. Collect., Biol. Abstr., Zool. Rec. **CODEN** BUMNAE. **Circ** 1,500. Contains articles in the field of natural sciences relating to zoology, paleontology, geology and mineralogy. *Bulletin.*

BULLETIN OF THE ANCIENT ORIENT MUSEUM. VFOAT Kodai Oriento Hakubutsukan Kiy. Vol. 1 (1979)-. JA. English (Japanese). an. Ancient Orient Museum, 1-4 Higashi Ikebukuro 3-chome Toshima-ku, Tokyo 170 Japan. **LC** DS56. **DD** 935.005.

BULLETIN OF THE ART DIVISION OF THE LOS ANGELES COUNTY MUSEUM CEASED. **Main/Corp** Los Angeles County Museum. Art Division. Vol. 1, No. 1 (Spring 1947)-Vol. 1, No. 3 & 4 (Spring 1948). 0024-6557. Periodical. US. English. qt. **Ind/Abst** Art Index, Repert. Int. Litt. Art. **LC** N582.L7. (cum index).

BULLETIN OF THE BRITISH MUSEUM (NATURAL HISTORY) BOTANY. (BULLETIN OF THE BRITISH MUSEUM (NATURAL HISTORY). BOTANY SERIES). **VFOAT** Botany Series. Began with Vol. 6 (Sept. 28, 1978). 0068-2292. Monographic Series. UK. English. ir. British Museum of Natural History, Cromwell Road, London SW7 5BD England. **Ind/Abst** Bibliogr. Agric. **LC** QK1. **DD** 581. *Bulletin of the British Museum (Natural History) Botany.*

BULLETIN OF THE BRITISH MUSEUM (NATURAL HISTORY). GEOLOGY SERIES. VFOAT Geology Series. Vol. 29, No. 1 (Nov. 1977)-. 0007-1471. Periodical. UK. English. ir. British Museum Natural History, Cromwell Road, London SW7 5BD England. **Ind/Abst** GeoRef. **CODEN** BUBMAO. *Bulletin of the British Museum (Natural History). Geology.*

BULLETIN OF THE BRITISH MUSEUM (NATURAL HISTORY). HISTORICAL SERIES. Vol. 1, No. 1-. 0068-2306. Monographic Series. UK. English. ir. British Museum-Natural History, Cromwell Road, London SW7 5BD England. **Ind/Abst** GeoRef, Biol. Abstr., Am. Hist. Life, Hist. Abstr. **DD** 574. **CODEN** BBMHAX. (cum index).

THE BULLETIN OF THE CLEVELAND MUSEUM OF ART. Main/Corp Cleveland Museum of Art. Vol. 1 Apr. 1914-. 0009-8841. Periodical. US. English. ir. $25.00. Cleveland Museum of Art, 11150 East Boulevard, University Circle, Cleveland OH 44106. **Tel** (216)431-7340. **Ed** Jo Zuppan. **Ind/Abst** Avery Index Archit. Period., Repert. Int. Litt. Art, Art Archaeol. Tech. Abstr., Art Index, Am. Hist. Life, Hist. Abstr., Art Index. **LC** N552. **DD** 069. **Circ** 4,600. Available on microfilm from University Microfilms International. Articles about works of art in the Museum's collection which includes Ancient-Modern, Oriental-Western as well as Oceanic, African and American Indian objects. Includes annual report.

BULLETIN OF THE MUSEUM OF LIFE SCIENCES. No. 1-. Monographic Series. US. English. Museum of Life Sciences, Louisiana State University in Shreveport, 8515 Youree Drive, Shreveport LA 71115. **Tel** (318)226-7174. **Ed** Laurence M Hardy. **Ind/Abst** Biol. Abstr. **CODEN** BUSCDE. **Circ** 1,000. (ctrl). Any aspect of the natural history, systematics, or, ecology of the flora and fauna of the Southeastern United States.

BULLETIN OF THE PRINCE OF WALES MUSEUM OF WESTERN INDIA. Main/Corp Bombay. Prince of Wales Museum of Western India. No. 1- 1950/51-. 0523-9702. Periodical. II. English. ir. Hindustan Book Agency, 17 Ub Jawahar Nagar, Delhi 7 India.

BULLETIN OF THE WHITNEY MUSEUM OF AMERICAN ART. Main/Corp Whitney Museum of American Art. V. 1- Fall 1978-. US. English. an. $8.00. Whitney Museum of American Art, 945 Madison Avenue, New York NY 10021 945 madison. **Tel** (212)794-0600. **Ind/Abst** Repert. Int. Litt. Art. **LC** N618. **DD** 709.7307401471.

BULLETIN - PEABODY MUSEUM OF NATURAL HISTORY. Main/Corp Yale University. Peabody Museum of Natural History. No. 1-. 0079-032X. Monographic Series. US. English (summaries in German, Russian and Spanish). ir. Yale University, Peabody Museum of Natural History, 170 Whitney Avenue/PO Box 6666, New Haven CT 06511-8161. **Tel** (203)436-1131. **Ed** Karl M Waage. **Ind/Abst** Life Sci. Collect., GeoRef, Biol. Abstr. **LC** QH1. **DD** 500.905. **CODEN** YUPBA8. **Circ** 500. Scientific monographs of research in biology and geology. *Bulletin of the Bingham Oceanographic Collection.*

BULLETIN - ST. LOUIS ART MUSEUM. (BULLETIN - THE ST. LOUIS ART MUSEUM). **VFOAT** Bulletin of the St. Louis Art Museum. **VAT** Bulletin - Saint Louis Art Museum. New Ser., V. 7, No. 5- Jan./Feb. 1972-. 0009-7691. Periodical. US. English. sa. $5.00. Saint Louis Art Museum, Forest Park, St Louis MO 63110. **Tel** (314)721-0067. **Ed** Mary Ann Steiner. **Ind/Abst** Repert. Int. Litt. Art. **LC** N729. **DD** 708.17866. bk rev. adv acc. **Circ** 300. (ctrl). Complete information of the various collections of the St Louis Art Museum; detailed descriptions. *Bulletin (City Art Museum of St. Louis), 0364-8141.*

BULLETIN - UNIVERSITY OF IOWA, MUSEUM OF ART. Main/Corp Iowa. University. Museum of Art.V.1- Spring 1976-. 0364-4677. Periodical. US. English. sa. University of Iowa Museum of Art, Iowa City IA 52242. **Ind/Abst** Repert. Int. Litt. Art. **LC** N1. **DD** 705.

BULLETIN - UNIVERSITY OF MICHIGAN. MUSEUM OF ART. (BULLETIN). Vol. 1 (1978)-. 0076-8391. Periodical. US. English. ir. University of Michigan Museum, Alumni Memorial Hall, Ann Arbor MI 48109. **Tel** (313)764-0395. **Ed** Marvin Eisenberg and Lauren Arnold. **Ind/Abst** Avery Index Archit. Period., Repert. Int. Litt. Art. **LC** N513. **DD** 708.17435. **Circ** 1,750. Research on works of art in museums' collections. *Bulletin (University of Michigan. Museum of Art : 1966), 0076-8391.*

BULLETIN - UNIVERSITY OF NEW MEXICO. ART MUSEUM. (BULLETIN - THE UNIVERSITY OF NEW MEXICO ART MUSEUM). **Main/Corp** New Mexico. University. Art Museum. No. 1- Winter 1965/66-. 0077-8583. Periodical. US. English. ir. University of New Mexico, Art Museum, College of Fine Arts 1017, Albuquerque NM 87131. **Ind/Abst** Repert. Int. Litt. Art. **LC** N512.A5. **DD** 708.18961.

BULLETIN VAN HET RYKSMUSEUM. (BULLETIN VAN HET RIJKSMUSEUM). **Main/Corp** Rijksmuseum (Netherlands). NE. Dutch (summaries in English). qt. $8.64. Rijksmuseum, PB 50673, Amsterdam Netherlands. **Ind/Abst** Art Index, Avery Index Archit. Period., Repert. Int. Litt. Art. **Circ** 2,500. (ctrl). Articles on objects the museum owns: paintings, sculpture, applied arts, graphic arts and also, articles on objects illustrating the history of The Netherlands.

BULLETIN - VIRGINIA MUSEUM OF FINE ARTS. (BULLETIN - VIRGINIA MUSEUM). **Main/Corp** Virginia Museum of Fine Arts. **VFOAT** Virginia Museum Bulletin, Virginia Museum of Fine Arts Bulletin. 0363-3519. Periodical. US. English. bm. $5.00. Virginia Museum of Fine Arts, Boulevard and Grove Avenue, Richmond VA 23221. **Tel** (804)257-0534. **Ed** Monica M Hamm. **DD** 708. **Circ** 16,000. Calendar of museum events. *Members' Bulletin.*

BUNKAZAI NO HOZON. *See* History (General) - History of Asia.

CAHIERS DES ARTS VISUELS AU QUEBEC. *See* The Arts (General) - Art.

CAHIERS DU MUSEE NATIONAL D'ART MODERNE. Main/Corp Musee National d'Art Moderne (France). 1-. 0181-1525. Periodical. French. ir. Centre Georges Pompidou, Musee National d'Art Moderne, 7519 Paris Cedex 04 France. **Ind/Abst** Avery Index Archit. Period., Repert. Int. Litt. Art. **LC** N6490. **DD** 709.04.

CAIRN. (THE CAIRN). V. 1- Fall 1976-. 0701-0281. Periodical. CN. English. qt. 5.00. Peter Whyte Foundation, PO Box 160, Banff Alberta T0L 0C0 Canada. **Tel** 762-2291. **Ed** E J Hart. **DD** 708.11233. **Circ** 300. (ctrl). Museum members information, aquisitions, gallery shows, people who work within the foundation, basically all aspects of the museum.

CALENDAR - NORTH CAROLINA MUSEUM OF ART. Main/Corp North Carolina. Museum of Art. 0146-1680. Periodical. US. English. mo. $1.00. North Carolina Museum of Art, 107 East Morgan Street, Raleigh NC 27601. **LC** N715.R2. **DD** 708.15655. *Calendar of Art Events, 0149-6603.*

CALENDAR - UNIVERSITY OF CALIFORNIA, BERKELEY. UNIVERSITY ART MUSEUM. Main/Corp University of California, Berkeley. University Art Museum. **VFOAT** University Art Museum Berkeley. Periodical. US. English. mo. University Art Museum, 2625 Durant Avenue, Berkeley CA 94720.

CASOPIS MORAVSKEHO MUZEA. VEDY PRIRODNI. (CASOPIS MORAVSKEHO MUSEA V BRNE. VEDY PRIRODNI). **VFOAT** Acta Musei Moraviae, Scientiae Naturales. 37 (1952)-. 0521-2359. CS. Czech (summaries in English, German, and Russian). an. $29.40. Artia, PO Box 790, VE-Smeckach 30, Praha 1 Czechoslovakia. **Ind/Abst** GeoRef. **CODEN** CAMMAI. *Casopis Moravskeho Musea v Brne. 1, Folia Mendeliana, 0085-0748.*

CASOPIS NARODNIHO MUZEA V PRAZE. RADA HISTORICKA. VFOAT Rada Historicka. Vol. 146, Vol. 1-2-. Periodical. CS. Czech. qt. Artia, PO Box 790, Ve-Smeckach 30, Praha 1 Czechoslovakia. **LC** AM101. *Casopis Narodniho Muzea. Historicke Muzeum.*

CASOPIS SLEZSKEHO MUZEA. SERIE A : VEDY PRIRODNI. Main/Corp Opava, Czechoslovak Republic. Slezske Museum. **VFOAT** Acta Musei Silesiae. 13- 1964-. Periodical. CS.

Museums

Czech (some articles in German). ty. Artia, PO Box 790, Ve-Smeckach 30, Praha 1 Czechoslovakia.

CASOPIS SLEZSKEHO MUZEA. SERIE B, VEDY HISTORICKE. VFOAT Acta Musei Silesiae. 13, 1-. 0323-0678. Periodical. CS. Czech (summaries and tables of contents also in German and Russian). ty. Artia, PO Box 790 Ve-Smeckach 30, Praha 1 Czechoslovakia.

CCI JOURNAL. VFOAT C.C.I. Journal. Vol. 4 (1980)-. 0380-9854. CN. English (French). LC F1019. DD 069.530971. *CCI, The Journal of the Canadian Conservation Institute, 0380-9854.*

CERCETARI DE CONSERVARE SI RESTAURARE A PATRIMONIULUI MUZEAL. 1-. Periodical. Romanian (summaries in French). ir. Calea Victoriei 12, Bucuresti Romania. LC AM141.

CERCETARI ISTORICE. See History (General) - History of Europe.

THE CHRYSLER MUSEUM. V. 8, No. 10- Nov. 1979-. 0270-7926. Periodical. US. English. mo. Chrysler Museum, Olney Road and Mowbray Arch, Norfolk VA 23510. LC N626.5. DD 708.155521. *Chrysler Museum at Norfolk.*

THE CINCINNATI ART MUSEUM BULLETIN. Main/Corp Cinncinati Art Museum. VFOAT Bulletin. V. 1-. 0069-4061. Periodical. US. English. ir. Eden Park, Cincinnati OH 45202. Ind/Abst Repert. Int. Litt. Art. LC N550. DD 708. *Cincinnati Art Museum News.*

COLLECTORS' AUCTION. Main/Corp Harris Auction Galleries. 0093-1047. US. English. $4.00. Harris Auction Galleries, 873-875 North Howard Street, Baltimore MD 21201. LC Z999. DD 016.917303.

COMMUNICATIONS DIVISION ANNUAL REVIEW. (ANNUAL REVIEW). Main/Corp National Museum of Man. (Canada). Communications Division. VFOAT Revue Annuelle. VAT Annual Review - Communications Division, National Museum of Man, Revue Annuelle - Division des Communications, Musee National de l'Homme. 1972/73-. 0317-2716. CN. English (some text in French). an. National Museum of Manitoba, Education & Cultural Affairs Division, Ottawa Ontario K1A 0M8 Canada. LC AM101.O7. DD 069.9971.

COMUNICACIONES ANTROPOLOGICAS DEL MUSEO DE HISTORIA NATURAL DE MONTEVIDEO. Main/Corp Museo de Historia Natural (Uruguay). No. 1- 1956-. 0077-1244. UY. Spanish. ir. Museo de Historia Natural, Casilla de Correo 399, Montevideo Uruguay. LC WMLC L 83/771.

CONGRES ANNUEL. RESUMES - IIC. GC. (RESUMES). Main/Corp Institut International pour la Conservation des Oeuvres Historiques et Artistiques. Groupe Canadien. Congres. VAT Resumes - IIC. GC. 6th (July 4/6 1980)-. 0711-2610. CN. French. Institut International pour la Conservation Groupe Canadien, CP 9195, Ottawa Ontario K1G 3T9 Canada. DD 069.53. *Congres Annuel et Sessions de Formation, 0711-2599.*

CONTRIBUTIONS FROM THE MUSEUM OF PALEONTOLOGY, UNIVERSITY OF MICHIGAN. Vol. 3, No. 1 (Nov. 10, 1928)-. Periodical. US. English. ir. Contributions from the Museum of Paleontology, University of Michigan, Ann Arbor 48104. *Contributions from the Museum of Geology, University of Michigan.*

CORPUS VASORUM ANTIQUORUM. ITALIA. Vol. 1-. Monographic Series. IT. Latin. ir. 150.00. Lerma di Bretschneider SPA, Periodicals Department PO Box 6192, Via Cassi19-00193 Rome Italy. Tel 06 33.32.59. LC NK4640.C6. Circ 600. This publication is a corpus of all existing vases in different museums of Italy.

COUNCIL FOR MUSEUM ANTHROPOLOGY NEWSLETTER. See Anthropology.

CURATOR. V. 1- Jan. 1958-. 0011-3069. Periodical. US. English. qt. American Museum of Natural History, Central Park West at 79th Street, New York NY 10023. Ind/Abst Am. Hist. Life, Hist. Abstr., Part A, Mod. Hist. Abstr., Hist. Abstr., Part B, Twent. Century Abstr., GeoRef, Biol. Abstr., Art Archaeol. Tech. Abstr. LC QH70. DD 574.074. CODEN CRTRAH.

CURRENTLY. V. 1- Sept. 1977-. 0384-9627. Periodical. CN. English. bm. 9.00. Ontario Museum Association, 38 Charles St East, Toronto Ontario M4Y 1T1 Canada. Tel (416)923-3868. Ed Betty Ann Jordan. DD 069.09713. Circ 1,500. (ctrl). Provides current provincial, national, and international museum news.

DATELINE - ONTARIO ASSOCIATION OF ART GALLERIES. (DATELINE). Vol. 11 (Mar. 1982)-. 0824-6513. Periodical. CN. English. ir. Free to Members. Ontario Association of Art Galleries, 38 Charles Street East, Toronto Ontario M4T 1T1 Canada. DD 069.9709713. *Dateline O.A.A.G., 0828-6434.*

DIRECTORY OF CANADIAN MUSEUMS AND RELATED INSTITUTIONS = REPERTOIRE DES MUSEES CANADIENS ET INSTITUTIONS CONNEXES. See Yearbooks, Almanacs, Directories.

DIRECTORY OF MEMBERS & MUSEUMS. See Yearbooks, Almanacs, Directories.

DIRECTORY OF MUSEUMS, ARCHIVES & ART GALLERIES OF BRITISH COLUMBIA. See Yearbooks, Almanacs, Directories.

DIRECTORY OF MUSEUMS, ART GALLERIES, AND RELATED INSTITUTIONS. See Yearbooks, Almanacs, Directories.

DIRECTORY OF ONTARIO MUSEUMS. See Yearbooks, Almanacs, Directories.

DISCOVERY. (DISCOVERY : FRIENDS OF THE BRITISH COLUMBIA PROVINCIAL MUSEUM QUARTERLY REVIEW). VFOAT Friends of the British Columbia Provincial Museum Quarterly Review. 0822-5796. Periodical. CN. English. qt. Free to Members, Membership $5.00 per year. Friends of the British Columbia Provincial Museum, 675 Belleville Street, Victoria British Columbia V8V 1X4 Canada. DD 069.09711. *Newsletter (Friends of the British Columbia Provincial Museum).*

DOMODOMO : FIJI MUSEUM QUARTERLY. 1 (Mar. 1983)-. Periodical. English. qt $10.00. Fiji Museum, PO Box 2023, Suva Fiji. Tel 315-043. Ed Fergus Clunie. Circ 1,000. Factual, well-illustrated articles on Fijian history, culture and natural history.

EDUCATIONAL RESOURCES DIRECTORY. See Yearbooks, Almanacs, Directories.

EHIME KENRITSU HAKUBUTSUKAN KENKYU HOKOKU. VFOAT Bulletin of the Ehime Pref. Museum. No. 9-. JA. Japanese. ir. Ehime Kenritsu Hakuritsukan, Horinouchi, Matsuyama 790 Japan. LC QH188.

ENCOUNTERS. See Science (General).

ERWERBUNGEN, GESCHENKE UND LEIHGABEN. Main/Corp Germanisches Nationalmuseum Nurnberg. German. ir. Germanisches Nationalmuseum, Postfach 9580 Kartausergasse 1, 8500 Nurnberg 1 West Germany. LC N2350.

ESTIMATES. PART III, NATIONAL MUSEUMS OF CANADA. VFOAT Budget des Depenses. CN. English (French). $9.00 Domestic, $10.80 Foreign. Canadian Government Publishing Centre, Supply and Services Canada, Ottawa Ontario K1A 0S9 Canada. LC AM122. DD 069.9971.

FEDERATION MUSEUMS JOURNAL. V. 1/2- 1954/1955-. 0126-561X. Periodical. MY. English. ir. Muzium Negara, Jalan Damansara, Kuala Lumpur Malaysia. LC AM101. *Journal of the Federated Malay States Museums.*

FEDERATION NEWS - FEDERATION OF MUSEUMS, HERITAGE AND HISTORICAL SOCIETIES OF NOVA SCOTIA. (FEDERATION NEWS). VFOAT Fed. of M. H. & H. News. 0715-5190. Periodical. CN. English. qt. 12.00. Federation of Nova Scotian Heritage, 5516 Spring Garden Road/Suite 305, Halifax Nova Scotia B3J 1G6 Canada. Tel (902)423-4677. Ed Marina Nawrocki. DD 971.6006. bk rev. adv acc. Circ 250. Covers news (local, national and international), book reviews, special articles of interest to membership, representing museum, heritage and historical groups and other related groups around the province.

FELLOWS LECTURE. VFOAT Conference des Fellows. 1976-. 0384-7225. CN. English (French). an. $15.00 Each Number. Canadian Museums Association, Suite 400/331 Cooper Street, Ottawa Ontario K2P 0G5 Canada. DD 069.0971.

FEUILLES. No. 1 (May 1982)-. Periodical. FR. French. qt. 100.00. Musee-Galerie de la Seita, 12 rue Surcouf, 75007 Paris France.

FIELD MUSEUM OF NATURAL HISTORY BULLETIN. VFOAT Field Museum Bulletin, Bulletin. Vol. 43, No. 4 (Apr. 1972)-. 0741-2967. Periodical. US. English. mo. $3.00. Field Museum of Natural History, Roosevelt Road at Lake Shore Drive, Chicago IL 60605. *Bulletin (Field Museum of Natural History).*

FORSCHUNGEN UND BERICHTE - STAATLICHE MUSEEN BERLIN. (FORSCHUNGEN UND BERICHTE). Main/Corp Staatliche Museen Zu Berlin (Germany : East). Vol. 1 1957-. 0067-6004. GE. German. an. Akademie-Verlag, Adademie der Wissenschaften, Berlin East Germany. Tel 089/564722. Ind/Abst Repert. Int. Litt. Art. LC AM101. (cum index). Care and preservation of monuments.

GAKUSO - KYOTO KOKURITSU HAKUBUTSUKAN. Main/Corp Kyoto Kokuritsu Hakubutsukan. VFOAT Kyoto National Museum Bulletin. 1st Ed- 1979-. JA. Japanese (summaries in English). ir. Kyoto Kokuritsu Hakubutsukan, 527 Chayacho, Higashiyama-Ku, Kyoto Japan. LC AM101.K946.

GAZETTE - CANADIAN MUSEUMS ASSOCIATION. CEASED. Main/Corp Canadian Museums Association. V. 8-15, No. 4. 0317-6045. Periodical. CN. text in English and French. qt. Canadian Museums Association, PO Box 1328/Station B, Ottawa Ontario K1P 5R4 Canada. Ind/Abst Am. Hist. Life, Hist. Abstr., Part A, Mod. Hist. Abstr., Hist. Abstr., Part B, Twent. Century Abstr. DD 069.0971. *C M A Gazette, 0007-859X.*

THE GILCREASE MAGAZINE OF AMERICAN HISTORY AND ART. 1979. 0730-5036. Periodical. US. English. qt. $15.00. Gilcrease Museum, 1400 Gilcrease Museum Road, Tulsa OK 74127. Tel (913)582-7708. Ed Melanee McAfee. Ind/Abst Am. Hist. Life, Hist. Abstr., Part A, Mod. Hist. Abstr., Hist. Abstr., Part B, Twent. Century Abstr., Hist. Abstr. LC E151. DD 704.949978. bk rev. Circ 3,500. Articles on art, American history and the anthropology of the New World as related to paintings, sculpture, books, documents and artifacts in the Gilcrease collection. *American Scene, 0003-0929.*

GLENBOW. Mar./Apr. 1981-. 0710-3697. Periodical. CN. English. bm. Free to Members, $0.25 Nonmembers. Glenbow Museum, 130-9th Avenue South East, Calgary Alberta T2G 0P3 Canada. DD 708.11233.

GRANTS. Main/Corp Arkansas Museum Services. 1983/1985-. US. English. Arkansas Museum Services, Department of Parks & Tourism, One Capital Mall, Little Rock AR 72201. *Grants-in-Aid.*

GUMMA KENRITSU HAKUBUTSUKAN HO. Japanese. ir. Gumma Kenritsu Hakubutsukan, 1353 Ichinomiya (370-24), Tomioka Japan. LC AM101.T594.

HAKUBUTSUKAN KENKYU. VFOAT Museum Studies. JA. Japanese. ir. 150 Single Issue. Nihon Hakubutsukan Kyokai, c/o Uragami Tenjudo Daiichi Building 10-1 Nihonbashi Kayabacho Chuo-Ku, Tokyo 103 Japan. LC AM77.A1.

HAKUBUTSUKAN NYUSU. Began in 1966. JA. Japanese. ir. 150 Single Issue. Nihon Hakubutsukan Kyokai, c/o Uragami Tenjudo Daiichi Bld 10-1 Nihonbashi Kayabacho 1-Chome Chuo-Ku, Tokyo 103 Japan. LC AM77.A1.

HANDBOOK (BRITISH COLUMBIA PROVINCIAL MUSEUM). (HANDBOOK - BRITISH COLUMBIA PROVINCIAL MUSEUM). No. 1-. 0068-1628. Monographic Series. CN. English. ir. British Columbia Provincial Museum, 601 Belleville Street, Victoria British Columbia V8W 1A1 Canada.

HANDBOOK OF COLLECTIONS. Main/Corp Illinois State Museum. No. 1-. 0445-3387. Monographic Series. US. English. ir. Illinois State Museum, Spring and Edwards Street, Springfiled IL 62706. Tel (217)782-7836. Ed Nancy Wells. LC AM101. DD 069.0977356. Descriptive accounts based on museum collections.

HERITAGE. No. 1-. Periodical. SI. English. sa. $7.91. National Museum, Stamford Road, Singapore 0617 Republic of Singapore. LC AM1. DD 069.7095957.

HIGHLIGHTS OF THE COLLECTIONS. Aug.14/Nov.14 1982-. 0711-7078. Periodical. CN. English. qt. Free. Montreal Museum of Fine Arts, 3400

Museums

Avenue du Musee, Montreal Quebec H3G 1K3 Canada. **DD** 069.970009714281. (ctrl).

HOKKAIDO KAITAKU KINENKAN CHOSA HOKOKU. *See* History (General) - History of Asia.

HORIZONS (SAINT JOHN, N.B. : 1982). (HORIZONS). July 1982-. 0823-2393. Periodical. **CN.** English (text in French on inverted pages). bm. Free to Members, $25.00 Others. Association Museums of New Brunswick, 49 Canterbury Street, Saint John New Brunswick E2L 2C6 Canada. **DD** 069.09715. *Alerte (Association Museums New Brunswick : 1981). English & French, 0711-5393.*

ICMM NEWS. VAT International Congress of Maritime Museums News. 0883-1343. Periodical. **US.** English. sa. c/o Benjamin G Fuller, Editor Mystic Seaport Museum Inc, Mystic CT 06355. **DD** 387.

ICOM NEWS. (I C O M NEWS). **Main/Corp** International Council of Museums. **VFOAT** Nouvelles de l'I C O M. V. 1- Oct. 1, 1948-. 0018-8999. Periodical. FR. Beginning with February 1949, each issues is a combined English and French edition. qt. $7.00. International Council of Museums, 1 rue Miollis, 75015 Paris France. **Ind/Abst** Art Archaeol. Tech. Abstr.

INDIANA UNIVERSITY ART MUSEUM BULLETIN. V. 1- Fall 1977-. 0161-1003. Periodical. US. English. sa. $3.50. Indiana University Art Museum, Bloomington IN 47401. **Ind/Abst** Repert. Int. Litt. Art. **LC** N518.B4. **DD** 708.172255.

INFORMATIONEN FUR DIE MUSEEN DER DDR. Periodical. GW. German. ir. 1162 Berlin Muggelseedamm 200, Berlin East Germany. **LC** AM49.A1.

INSIDE SEMC. Main/Corp Southeastern Museums Conference. **VAT** Inside Southeastern Museums Conference. No. 1- June 1966-. 0195-833X. Periodical. US. English. bm. $10.00 Membership. Southeastern Museums Conference Inc, c/o William Bradshaw/Treasurer, Cumberland Museum and Science Center, 800 Ridley Avenue, Nashville TN 37203.

INTERNATIONAL JOURNAL OF MUSEUM MANAGEMENT AND CURATORSHIP. (THE INTERNATIONAL JOURNAL OF MUSEUM MANAGEMENT AND CURATORSHIP). **VFOAT** Journal of Museum Management and Curatorship. Vol. 1, No. 1 (Mar. 1982)-. 0260-4779. Periodical. UK. English. qt. $104.00. Magsub, Oakfield House/Perrymount Road, Haywards Heath RH16 3DH England. **LC** AM121. **DD** 069.905.

INVENTORY OF THE COLLECTIONS. No. 1-. 0095-2893. Monographic Series. US. English. ir. Illinois State Museum Society, Spring and Edwards Street, Springfield IL 62706. **LC** UNC.

THE J. PAUL GETTY MUSEUM JOURNAL. 1974-. 0362-1979. US. English. an. J Paul Getty Museum, PO Box 2112, Santa Monica CA 90406. **Ind/Abst** Repert. Int. Litt. Art. **LC** N582.M25. **DD** 708.19493.

JAHRBUCH DES MARKISCHEN MUSEUMS. *See* Yearbooks, Almanacs, Directories.

JAHRBUCH DES MUSEUMS FUR VOLKERKUNDE ZU LEIPZIG. *See* Yearbooks, Almanacs, Directories.

JAHRBUCH PREUSSISCHER KULTURBESITZ. *See* Yearbooks, Almanacs, Directories.

JOURNAL OF TAIWAN MUSEUM. VFOAT Tai-Wan Sheng Li Po Wu Kuan Pan Nien Kan. Vol. 36, No. 1 (June 1983)-. Periodical. English. sa. Taiwan Museum, No 2 Siangyang Road, Taiwan 100 Republic of China. **Ind/Abst** Life Sci. Collect. **LC** QH1. **DD** 574.951249. *Quarterly Journal of the Taiwan Museum, 0039-9116.*

THE JOURNAL OF THE ARTISTS' CHOICE MUSEUM. (THE JOURNAL OF THE ARTISTS' CHOICE MUSEUM : ACM). **VFOAT** ACM. 0882-8504. Periodical. US. English. sa. $10.00. The Artists' Choice Museum, 394 West Broadway, New York NY 10012. *ACM Newsletter.*

JOURNAL OF THE BARBADOS MUSEUM AND HISTORICAL SOCIETY. Main/Corp Barbados Museum and Historical Society. V. 1- Nov. 1933-. 0005-5891. BB. English. qt. $20.00. Barbados Museum and Historical Society, St Anns Garrison, Barbados West Indies. **Ind/Abst** Am. Hist. Life, Hist. Abstr., Part A, Mod. Hist. Abstr., Hist. Abst., Part B, Twent. Century Abstr. (cum index).

JOURNAL OF THE NEW BRUNSWICK MUSEUM. Main/Corp New Brunswick Museum. 1977-. 0703-0606. **CN.** English. an. Free to Members, $3.00 Per No. Others. 277 Douglas Avenue, St John New Brunswick E2K 1E5 Canada. **Ind/Abst** Am. Hist. Life, Hist. Abstr., Part A, Mod. Hist. Abstr., Hist. Abst., Part B, Twent. Century Abstr., GeoRef. **LC** F1042. **DD** 971.5005. *Museum Memo, 0027-4062.*

JOURNAL OF THE WALTERS ART GALLERY. Main/Corp Walters Art Gallery. V. 1- 1938-. 0083-7156. US. English. an. $15.00. Walters Art Gallery, 600 North Charles Street, Baltimore MD 21201. **Tel** (301)547-9000. Ed Joyce Duncan. **Ind/Abst** Repert. Int. Litt. Art, Art Index. **LC** N5220. **DD** 708.1. **Circ** 1,000. (ctrl). Scholarly publication of major fine art museum.

JOURNAL - WORCESTER ART MUSEUM. Main/Corp Worcester Art Museum. **VFOAT** Worcester Art Museum Journal. V. 1- 1977/78-. 0193-9564. US. English. an. $4.00. Worcester Art Museum, 55 Salisbury Street, Worcester MA 01608. **Tel** (617)799-4406. Ed Gaye L Brown. **Ind/Abst** Repert. Int. Litt. Art. **LC** N870. **DD** 708.1443. **Circ** 4,000. Articles relating to works of art in the museum collection; annual report. *Annual Report of the Trustees and Officers, Worcester Art Museum Bulletin, 0364-734X.*

KALORI. No. 1- Oct. 17, 1952-. 0047-312X. Periodical. AT. English. ir. Museums Association of Australia, The Australian Museum, 6-8 College Street, Sydney New South Wales 2000 Australia.

KANE MEMORIAL EXHIBITION. *See* The Arts (General) - Art.

KARNTNER MUSEUMSSCHRIFTEN. 1- 1954-. 0022-7587. Monographic Series. GW. German. ir. Dr Rudolf Habelt GMBH, Am Buchanheng 1, 5300 Bonn 1 West Germany. **LC** AM101.

KIMBELL ART MUSEUM PUBLICATION. 2-. Monographic Series. US. English. Kimball Art Museum, 1101 Will Rogers Road West/PO Box 9440, Ft Worth TX 76107. *Kimbell Publication.*

KLEINE SCHRIFTEN. Main/Corp Cologne. Wallraf-Richartz Museum. 1- 1964-. 0588-344X. Periodical. GW. German. ir. J B Metzler, Postfach 529, 7000 Stuttgart 1 West Germany.

KOKURITSU REKISHI MINZOKU HAKUBUTSUKAN KENKYU HOKOKU. VFOAT Bulletin of the National Museum of Japanese History. No. 1-. 0286-7400. Japanese (summaries in English). ir. Kokuritsu Rekishi Minzoku, Hakubutsukan 117 Jonai-Machi Sakura-Shi, Chiba-Ken 285 Japan. **LC** DS801.

KU KUNG HSUEH SHU CHI KAN. VFOAT National Palace Museum Research Quarterly. V. 1, (Autumn 1983)-. Periodical. CH. Chinese. qt. $720.00. Kuo Li Ku Kung Po Wu Yuan, Taipei Taiwan. *Ku Kung Chi Kan.*

KULTUR & TECHNIK. VFOAT Kultur und Technik. 1. Volume, Issue 1 (Sept. 1977)-. 0344-5690. Periodical. GW. German. qt. 16.00 Domestic, 20.00 Foreign. Verlag Karl Thiemig AG, Postfach 90 07 49, D-8000 Munchen 90 West Germany. **Tel** 089/ 62 48 0. **Ind/Abst** Coal Abstr., Artbibliogr. Mod.

LEGAL PROBLEMS OF MUSEUM ADMINISTRATION: MATERIALS. *See* Law.

LIAISON - SASKATCHEWAN MUSEUMS ASSOCIATION. (LIASON I.E. LIAISON : SASKATCHEWAN MUSEUMS ASSOCIATION NEWSLETTER). **VFOAT** Liaison. Issue 1, No. 1 (Mar./Apr. 1983)-. 0712-9246. Periodical. CN. English. qt. $7.74. Saskatchewan Museums Association, 1879 Lorne Street, Saskatchewan S4P 2L7 Canada. **Tel** (306)359-9797. Ed Maureen Murray. **DD** 069.0607124. bk rev. adv acc. **Circ** 2,000. (ctrl). Saskatchewan heritage issues including folklore, archaeology, architecture, conservation, preservation and other topics relating to Saskatchewan history and historic events.

THE LIBRARIES, MUSEUMS AND ART GALLERIES YEAR BOOK. *See* Yearbooks, Almanacs, Directories.

LIBRARY CATALOG OF THE METROPOLITAN MUSEUM OF ART. SUPPLEMENT. *See* Library and Information Science.

LIFE SCIENCES CONTRIBUTIONS. ROYAL ONTARIO MUSEUM. (LIFE SCIENCES CONTRIBUTIONS). No. 74-. 0384-8159. Monographic Series. CN. English. ir. Royal Ontario Museum, 100 Queens Park, Toronto 5 Ontario Canada. **Ind/Abst** GeoRef, Biol. Abstr. **LC** QL1. **DD** 590.5. **CODEN** ROMCAD. *Contribution (Royal Ontario Museum. Life Sciences Division), 0082-5085.*

THE LIVING MUSEUM. V. 1- May 1939-. 0024-5283. Periodical. US. English. bm. Free. Illinois State Museum Society, Spring and Edwards Street, Springfield IL 62706. **Tel** (217)782-5992. Ed Nancy M Wells. **Ind/Abst** Biol. Abstr. **LC** QH1. **DD** 069.09773. **CODEN** LIMUAR. (cum index). bk rev. **Circ** 15,000. Publication providing educational articles about natural history anthropology, and art as these topics relate to the Illinois State museum.

LORE. 0276-475X. Periodical. US. English. qt. Milwaukee Public Museum, 800 West Wells Street, Milwaukee WI 53233. **Tel** (414)278-2787. Ed Mary Garity. bk rev. **Circ** 5,500. (ctrl). Magazine published for friends of the museum. Articles on human and natural history; book and film/video reviews.

LOS ANGELES COUNTY MUSEUM OF ART REPORT. 1973/75-. 0197-5021. US. English. be. Los Angeles Museum of Art, 5905 Wilshire Boulevard, Los Angeles CA 90036. **LC** N582.L7. **DD** 708.19494.

LYMAN ENTOMOLOGICAL MUSEUM AND RESEARCH LABORATORY MEMOIR. Began publication in Oct. 1974. 0318-6784. Monographic Series. CN. English. Lyman Entomological Museum & Research Laboratory, Sainte Anne de Bellevue Province of Quebec Canada. **DD** 595.7008.

M BULLETIN (MUSEUM OF FINE ARTS, BOSTON). (M BULLETIN). **VAT** Museum Bulletin. Vol. 79 (1981)-. 0739-5736. US. English. an. $3.00 Domestic, $4.00 Foreign. Museum of Fine Arts, Boston MA 02115. **Ind/Abst** Repert. Int. Litt. Art. **LC** N520. **DD** 708.14461. *MFA Bulletin, 0732-2895.*

A MAGYAR OLAJIPARI MUZEUM EVKONYVE. V. 1-. Hungarian. ir. **LC** TN862.

MASCA JOURNAL. Main/Corp University of Pennsylvania. Museum Applied Science Center for Archaeology. **VAT** Museum Applied Science Center for Archaeology Journal. V. 1- Dec. 1978-. 0198-0106. Periodical. US. English. ty. $16.00. Museum Applied Science Center, University Museum 33 & Spruce Street Philadelphia PA 17104. **Tel** (215)898-4060. Ed Stewart Fleming. **Ind/Abst** Art Archaeol. Tech. Abstr., Chem. Abstr., GeoRef, Bibliogr. Index Geol. **LC** CC1. **DD** 930.105. **CODEN** MAJODK. bk rev. **Circ** 500. Specializing in science as applied to archaeology in seversl research areas including metals technology, pottery manufacture, floral and faunal analysis and paleopathology. *MASCA Newsletter.*

MEDDELANDEN FRAN LUNDS UNIVERSITETS HISTORISKA MUSEUM. Main/Corp Lund. Universitet. Historiska Museet Samt Mynt-Och Medaljkabinettet. **VFOAT** Memoires du Musee Historique de l'Universite de Lund. 1929/30-1973/74. SW. English (Swedish, French, or German). an. Memoires du Musee Historique, PO Box 1205, S-221 05 Lund Sweden. **LC** DL601.

MEMOIR - AUSTRALIAN MUSEUM *CEASED.* (MEMOIRS). **Main/Corp** Australian Museum. Vol. 18. 0067-1967. Monographic Series. English. ir. **Ind/Abst** Life Sci. Collect., GeoRef. **CODEN** AUNMA5.

MEMOIR - NEW YORK STATE MUSEUM AND SCIENCE SERVICE. (MEMOIR). 0548-8265. Monographic Series. US. English. ir. New York State Education Department, Gift & Exchange New York State Library, Albany NY 12230. **Ind/Abst** Chem. Abstr., GeoRef. **CODEN** NYOMAB. *Memoir (New York State Museum: 1903).*

MEMOIR - THE AUSTRALIAN MUSEUM, SYDNEY. Main/Corp Australian Museum. 1- 1851-. 0067-1967. Monographic Series. AT. English. ir. Australian Museum, PO Box A285, South Sydney, 2000 New South Wales Australia. **DD** 069.

MEMOIRES DU MUSEUM D'HISTOIRE NATURELLE (1815). (MEMOIRES DU MUSEUM D'HISTOIRE NATURELLE). V. 1-20. FR. French. ir. Museum National d'Histoire Naturelle, 38 rue Geoffroy-Saint-Hilaire, Paris 75009 France. **Tel** 331 71 24. *Annales du Museum d'Histoire Naturelle.*

Museums

MEMOIRS OF THE NATIONAL MUSEUM OF VICTORIA CEASED. (MEMOIRS OF THE NATIONAL MUSEUM OF VICTORIA, MELBOURNE). No. 14, Pt. 2-No. 44. 0083-5986. AT. English. an. $11.33. National Museum of Victoria, 285 Russell Street, Melbourne Victoria 3000 Australia. Tel 03/669-9888. Ed T A Darragh. Ind/Abst Life Sci. Collect., Biol. Abstr., Bibliogr. Agric., Chem. Abstr. CODEN MMVMAJ. Circ 700. Topics include zoology, geology, taxonomy, ecology. Memoirs of the National Museum, Melbourne, 0311-9548.

MEMOIRS OF THE PEABODY MUSEUM OF AMERICAN ARCHAEOLOGY AND ETHNOLOGY, HARVARD UNIVERSITY. Vol. 1, No. 1-. US. English. ir. HU Press, 79 Garden Street, Cambridge MA 02138.

MEMOIRS OF THE QUEENSLAND MUSEUM. Main/Corp Queensland Museum, Brisbane. V. 1-. 0079-8835. Periodical. AT. English. ir. Queensland Museum, Gregory Terrace, +Fortitude Valley, Queensland 4006 Australia. Tel 52 2716. Ed R Hamlyn-Harris. Ind/Abst Life Sci. Collect., Biol. Abstr., GeoRef, Bibliogr. Index Geol. LC QH1. CODEN MQUMA8. Annals of the Queensland Museum.

MEMORIAS DEL MUSEO DE HISTORIA NATURAL JAVIER PRADO. Main/Corp Museo de Historia Natural Javier Prado. No. 1-. 0457-9151. Monographic Series. PE. Spanish (summaries in English). ir. Universidad Nacional Mayor de San Marcos, Casilla 454, Lima 1 Peru. DD 574.

MEMORIE FUORI SERIE - MUSEO CIVICO DI STORIA NATURALE DI VERONA. Main/Corp Museo Civico di Storia Naturale de Verona. No. 1 1966-. 0507-5785. IT. Italian. ir. Atti Societa Italiana di, Corso Venezia 55, 20120 Milano Italy. Ind/Abst GeoRef. CODEN MCVMAH.

MESA VERDE RESEARCH SERIES. Paper No. 1-. Monographic Series. US. English. ir. Mesa Verde Museum Association Inc, Mesa Verde National Park CO 81330. LC UNC.

METROPOLITAN MUSEUM JOURNAL. Main/Corp New York (City). Metropolitan Museum of Art. V. 1- 1968-. 0077-8958. US. English. ir. Metropolitan Museum of Art, 5th Avenue & 82nd Street, New York NY 10028. Tel (212)879-5500. Ed M E D Laing. Ind/Abst Avery Index Archit. Period., Art Index, Repert. Int. Litt. Art. LC N610. DD 708.1471. Circ 600. Publishes original scholarly research focusing on the Metropolitan Museum's collections.

MFA BULLETIN. VFOAT MFA Bulletin of the Museum of Fine Arts, Boston. VAT Museum of Fine Arts Bulletin. Vol. 76 (1978)-V. 78 (1980). 0732-2895. Periodical. US. English. an. $3.00. Museum of Fine Arts, c/o P Jacoff, 465 Huntington Avenue, Boston MA 02115. Tel (617)267-9300. Ind/Abst Art Index, Am. Hist. Life, Hist. Abstr., Repert. Int. Litt. Art. LC N520. DD 708.14461. Boston Museum Bulletin, 0006-7997.

MISCELLANEOUS PAPERS (TEXAS MEMORIAL MUSEUM). (MISCELLANEOUS PAPERS - TEXAS MEMORIAL MUSEUM). No. 1-. 0082-3082. Monographic Series. US. English. ir. Texas Memorial Museum, 24th & Trinity Street, Austin TX 78705. Ind/Abst GeoRef. LC UNC. CODEN TMMMBI.

MISCELLANEOUS SERIES. Main/Corp University of Northern Colorado. Museum of Anthropology. No. 12?- 1970-. Periodical. US. English. ir. Museum of Anthropology, University Northern Colorado, George E Fay, Greenly CO 80639. Tel (303)351-2021. Miscellaneous Series.

MITTEILUNGEN AUS DEM HAMBURGISCHEN ZOOLOGISCHEN MUSEUM UND INSTITUT. Main/Corp Hamburg. Zoologisches Museum und Institut. V. 1- 1884-. 0072-9612. English summaries. ir. Zoologisches Museum und Institut, Martin-L-King Platz 3, Hamburg 13 Germany D-2000. LC QL1. (cum index).

MITTEILUNGEN AUS DEM ZOOLOGISCHEN MUSEUM IN BERLIN. Main/Corp Zoologisches Museum in Berlin. Began with: V. 2 in 1899. Periodical. SZ. English (German and/or French). ir. $56.79. Kunst & Wissen Erich Bieber, Dufourstrasse 51, Ch-8008 Zurich Switzerland. Tel 011-41-1-69 44 20. (cum index). Mitteilungen aus der Zoologischen Sammlung des Museums fur Naturkunde in Berlin.

MOTA. Main/Corp Museum of Temporary Art. VFOAT Museum of Temporary Art Magazine. 0149-4902. Periodical. US. English. ir. Museum of Temporary Art, 1206 G Street NW, Washington DC 20005. Tel (202)483-8039.

MUSE. No. 1-. 0077-2194. US. English. an. $8.00. Museum of Art & Archaeology, 1 Pickard Hall/ University of Mo-Col, Columbia MO 65211. Tel (314)882-3591. Ed Forrest McGill. Ind/Abst Repert. Int. Litt. Art, MLA Int. Bibliogr. Books Artic. Mod. Lang. Lit. LC N584.M5. DD 708.17829. Circ 2,000. Report of University of Missouri Museum of Art and Archaeology; articles on museum objects and museum sponsored archaeological excavations.

MUSE (OTTAWA, ONT.). (MUSE). Vol. 1, No. 1 (Spring 1983)-. 0820-0165. Periodical. CN. English (French). qt. $12.00. Canadian Museums Association, Suite 202/Metcalfe Street, Ottawa Ontario K2P 1R7 Canada. Ind/Abst Am. Hist. Life, Hist. Abstr., Part A, Mod. Hist. Abstr., Hist. Abst., Part B, Twent. Century Abstr. DD 069.0971. Gazette, 0317-6045.

MUSEES. V. 1- April 1978-. 0706-098X. Periodical. CN. French. qt. Free to Members, $5.00 Others. La Societe des Musees Quebecois, CP 8 Succursale Outremont, Montreal Quebec H2V 4M6 Canada. DD 069.09714.

MUSEES DE GENEVE. Years 1-16-. 0027-3821. Periodical. French. mo. Ind/Abst Am. Hist. Life, Hist. Abstr., Part A, Mod. Hist. Abstr., Hist. Abst., Part B, Twent. Century Abstr., GeoRef, Repert. Int. Litt. Art. LC AM68.G4. DD 069.094945. CODEN MSGVAD.

MUSEES ET COLLECTIONS PUBLIQUES DE FRANCE. No. 1- Oct./ Dec. 1954-. 0027-383X. Periodical. FR. French. qt. $9.32. Assn Desconservateurs de Coll, Palais du Louvre, 75041 Paris Cedex 01 France. Bulletin.

MUSEI E GALLERIE D'ITALIA. Began publication with Jan./June 1966 issue. 0027-3872. Periodical. IT. Italian. ir. de Luca Editore, Via di S Anna 16, Rome Italy. Ind/Abst Repert. Int. Litt. Art.

EL MUSEO CANARIO. 1- 19 -. Spanish. an. El Museo Canario, Dr Chile 25, Las Palmas de Gran Canary Isle. Ind/Abst Hist. Abstr., Part A, Mod. Hist. Abstr., Hist. Abst., Part B, Twent. Century Abstr., Am. Hist. Life.

MUSEOGRAMME. VFOAT Museogramme. V. 1- Apr. 1973-. 0380-4623. Periodical. CN. English (French). mo. $15.48. Canadian Museums Association, 280 Metcalfe Street/Suite 202, Ottawa Ontario K2P 1R7 Canada. Tel (613)233-5653. Ed Raymond Bendal and Denise Trauax. adv acc. Circ 2,300. Newsletter of the Canadian Museums Association.

MUSEOLOGIA. 1- 1972-. 0392-5528. IT. Italian. ir. 43.000. Centro du Studi per la Museologia, Via delle Forbici 24/26, 50133 Florence Italy. Tel 575372. Ed Carlo L Ragghianti. Ind/Abst Avery Index Archit. Period. Second Ed. Revis. Enlarged Suppl. LC AM1. DD 069.05. adv acc.

THE MUSEOLOGIST. V. 1- 1935-. 0027-397X. Periodical. US. English. qt. $20.00 Domestic, $22.50 Foreign. Mid-Atlantic Association Museums, PO Box 817, Newark DE 19715. Tel (814)863-3883. Ed Robert Ott. bk rev. adv acc. Circ 1,400. Articles relating to museum collections, education, registration, administration, etc. Advertising companies which serve museums; book reviews.

MUSEOLOGY. No. 1- Nov. 21, 1975-. 0196-0237. Monographic Series. US. English. ir. Museum Shop, The Museum, Texas Tech University, Lubbock TX 79409.

MUSEUM. V. 1- July 1948-. 0027-3996. Periodical. US. English (French). qt. $37.00. UNIPUB, PO Box 1222, Ann Arbor MI 48106. Tel (800)521-8110. Ind/ Abst Archit. Period. Index, Art Archaeol. Tech. Abstr., Art Index, Avery Index Archit. Period. LC AM1. DD 069.05. Serves as a survey of activities and means of research in the fields of museography. Mouseion (Paris, France).

MUSEUM. V.5, No.2- June 1973-. Periodical. US. English. mo. Ind/Abst GeoRef. Muse News.

MUSEUM AFRICUM. V. 1- 1972-. NR. English. an. University of Ibadan, Department of Classics, Oya State, Ibadan Nigeria West Africa. LC DE1. DD 913.0305. Nigeria and the Classics.

MUSEUM BRIEFS. No. 1- 1969-. 0580-6976. Monographic Series. US. English. ir. University of Missouri Columbia, 100 Swallow Hall, Columbia MO 65201. LC E151.

MUSEUM CRITICUM. VFOAT Quaderni Dell'Istituto di Filologia Classica dell'Universita di Bologna. 4 (1969)-. Periodical. IT. Italian. ir. Editrice Giardini, Via Santa Bibliana 28, 56100 Pisa Italy. Quaderni dell'Istituto di Filologia Greca.

MUSEUM (GEORG WESTERMANN VERLAG). (MUSEUM). Began in 1976. 0341-8634. Monographic Series. GW. German. mo. $39.97. Georg Westermann Verlag, Postfach 3220, D-33 Braunschweig West Germany. LC UNC.

THE MUSEUM JOURNAL. V. 1- 1957-. 0580-261X. US. English. an. West Texas Museum Association, PO Box 4499, Lubbock TX 79409. Tel (806)742-2443. LC AM1. DD 069.09764847.

MUSEUM MAGAZINE. V. 1- Mar./Apr. 1980-. 0199-5553. Periodical. US. English. bm. $15.00 Domestic, $18.00 Foreign. Museum Magazine, 260 Madison Avenue, New York NY 10016. Ind/Abst GeoRef. LC NX1. DD 700.5.

MUSEUM NEWS. V. 1- Jan. 1, 1924-. 0027-4089. Periodical. US. English. bm. $12.00 Members. American Association of Museums, 2233 Wisconsin Avenue Northwest, Washington DC 20007. Ind/Abst Art Archaeol. Tech. Abstr., Art Index, Avery Index Archit. Period. Second Ed. Revis. Enlarged Suppl., Book Rev. Index, Ref. Source. LC AM1. DD 069.0973. NLM W1 MU969. CODEN MUNSAJ. (cum index).

MUSEUM NEWS CEASED. Main/Corp Toledo Museum of Art. V. 1-3, No. 4, Nov. 1907-May 1910. 0049-4062. Periodical. US. English. ty. Ind/Abst Repert. Int. Litt. Art. LC N820.

MUSEUM NEWS - ASSOCIATION OF MANITOBA MUSEUMS. (MUSEUM NEWS). Feb. 1983-. 0822-9562. Periodical. CN. English. mo. Association of Manitoba Museums, 190 Rupert Avenue, Winnipeg Manitoba R3B 0N2 Canada. DD 069.097127.

MUSEUM NEWS - UKRAINIAN MUSEUM OF CANADA. (MUSEUM NEWS). VFOAT Muzeini Visti. VAT Muzejni Visti - Ukrajinskyj Muzej Kanada. Vol. 1, No. 1 (Spring 1979)-. 0710-1228. Periodical. CN. English (Issue for Spring 1979 has text in Ukrainian). sa. Free. Museum News, Ukrainian Museum of Canada, 910 Spadina Crescent East, Saskatoon Saskatchewan S7K 3G9 Canada. DD 305.891791071074011242. (ctrl).

MUSEUM NEWSLETTER - CANADIAN MUSEUM OF FLIGHT AND TRANSPORTATION. (MUSEUM NEWSLETTER). No. 14 (Nov. 1981)-. 0820-8336. Periodical. CN. English. ir. Free to Members. Canadian Museum of Flight and Transportation, 1040 Cambie Road, Richmond British Columbia V6X 1L2 Canada. DD 069.96291. CMFT Newsletter, 0823-6372.

MUSEUM NOTES. See Numismatics.

MUSEUM NOTES. (BULLETIN OF RHODE ISLAND SCHOOL OF DESIGN. MUSEUM NOTES). Main/Corp Rhode Island School of Design. Museum of Art. V. 1-29, No. 1/2. 1913-1941. 0027-4097. Periodical. US. English. an. $5.00. Rhode Island School of Design, 224 Benefit Street, Providence RI 02903. Tel (401)331-3511. Ed Janet Phillips. Ind/Abst Art Index. A comprehensive bulletin describing important new acquisitions, exhibitions, publications, lectures, loans and other activities for the past year.

MUSEUM NOTES. Main/Corp Massachusetts. 1st Corps of Cadets. US. English. 1st Corps of Cadets, 227 Commonwealth Avenue, Boston MA 02116. LC E470. DD 355.3.709744 S.

MUSEUM NOTES. 0228-2364. Periodical. CN. English. ir. Free. University of British Columbia, Museum of Anthropology, 2075 Westbrook Mall, Vancouver British Columbia V6T 1W5 Canada. DD 732.20971132074011133. (ctrl).

MUSEUM OF NORTHERN ARIZONA BULLETIN. No. 1-. 0361-9656. Monographic Series. US. English. ir. $10.00. Museum of Northern Arizona, Route 4 Box 720, Flagstaff AZ 86001. Tel (602)774-5211. Ed Diana Lubick. Ind/Abst GeoRef. LC F806. DD 979.1005. CODEN MNAZAS. Circ 1,000. Science on the Colorado plateau.

MUSEUM OF NORTHERN ARIZONA TECHNICAL SERIES. No. 1- 1953-. 0428-5395. Monographic Series. US. English. ir. Museum of Northern Arizona, Route 4 Box 720, Flagstaff AZ 86001.

MUSEUM OF THE GREAT PLAINS NEWSLETTER. No. 1- Spring 1977-. 0198-7763. US. English. ir. $7.50. Institute of the Great Plains, PO Box 68, Lawton OK 73502.

Museums

MUSEUM PICTORIAL. No. 1- 1951-. 0070-3745. Monographic Series. US. English. ir. Denver Museum of Natural History, City Park, Denver CO 80206. DD 500. CODEN MPMNAW.

MUSEUM PROGRAM GUIDELINES. Main/Corp National Council of the Arts. 0090-9890. US. English. National Council of Arts, National Endowment for the Arts, 2401 East Street NW, Washington DC 20506. LC AM11. DD 069.0973.

MUSEUM QUARTERLY. (MUSEUM QUARTERLY : THE JOURNAL OF THE ONTARIO MUSEUM ASSOCIATION). Vol. 12, No. 2 (May 1983)-. 0822-5931. Periodical. CN. English. qt. 35.00. Ontario Museum Association, 38 Charles Street East, Toronto Ontario M4Y 1T1 Canada. Tel (416)923-3868. Ed Betty Ann Jordan. DD 069.05. bk rev adv acc. Circ 1,600. (ctrl). Contains articles, book reviews, exhibit reviews, conservation and technical columns on museum matters. *Ontario Museum Quarterly, 0822-5923*.

MUSEUM ROUND-UP. No. 1- Jan. 1961-. 0045-3005. Periodical. CN. English. ir. $15.48. B C Museum Association, c/o Provincial Museum, Victoria British Columbia V8V 1X4 Canada. Tel (604)387-3315.

THE MUSEUM STUDIES JOURNAL. Vol. 1, No. 1- (Spring 1983)-. 0733-0960. Periodical. US. English. sa. $20.00. John F Kennedy University, 1717 Seventeenth Street, San Francisco CA 94103. Tel (415)626-1787. Ed Deborah Kirshman. LC AM1. DD 069.05. bk rev. adv acc. Circ 1,200. Full spectrum of information and commentary in the field of museum studies-articles on controversial issues, museum history, literature, research and methodology.

MUSEUM WASHINGTON. Began in 1985. 0884-1918. Periodical. US. English. mo. $18.00. JGT Communication, 1053 31st Street NW, Washington DC 20007. DD 069.

THE MUSEUM YEAR: ANNUAL REPORT OF THE MUSEUM OF FINE ARTS, BOSTON. Main/Corp Museum of Fine Arts, Boston. 90th- 1965-. 0740-0403. US. English. an. Free to Members. Museum of Fine Arts Boston, 465 Huntington Avenue, Boston MA 02115. *Annual Report of the Museum of Fine Arts Boston*.

MUSEUMLEVEN : TIJDSCHRIFT VAN DE NEDERLANDSTALIGE AFDELING VAN DE BELGISCHE MUSEUMVERENIGING. No. 1 (1974)-. BE. Dutch (some articles have summaries English). an. Besteladres: Gemeenschappelijk Fonds der Rijksmusea, Kortenberglaan 158, 1040 Brussel Belgium.

MUSEUMS AND ART GALLERIES IN GREAT BRITAIN AND IRELAND. VFOAT Museums and Galleries in Great Britain and Ireland. Began with 1974/75 Vol. 0141-6723. Periodical. UK. English. an. ABC Historic Publications, World Timetable Centre Church Street, Dunstable Bedfordshire LU5 4HB England. LC N1020. DD 069.02541. *Museums and Galleries in Great Britain and Ireland*.

MUSEUMS BULLETIN. V. 14- Apr. 1974-. 0307-2525. Periodical. UK. English. mo. $28.00. Museums Association, 34 Bloomsbury Way, London WC1A 2SF England. Tel 01-404-4767. Ed Gillian Bromley. LC AM1.M65. DD 069.0941. bk rev. adv acc. Circ 3,700. News, events, courses, letters, publications and other information for the museum professional, including job advertisements, and the interested lay person. *Monthly Bulletin - Museums Association, 0027-4151*.

MUSEUMS IN NOVA SCOTIA. 1975-. 0225-5235. CN. English. an. Nova Scotia Museum, 1747 Summer Street, Halifax Nova Scotia B3H 3A6 Canada. DD 061.16.

THE MUSEUMS JOURNAL. V. 1- July 1901-. 0027-416X. Periodical. UK. English. qt. $55.00. The Museums Association, 34 Bloomsbury Way, London WC1A 2SF England. Tel 01-404-4767. Ed Gillian Bromley. Ind/Abst Archit. Period. Index, Art Archaeol. Tech. Abstr., Art Index. LC AM1. DD 069.05. bk rev adv acc. Circ 3,100. Articles and book reviews on museums; relevant developments, achievements, discussions etc.

MUSEUMS - NATIONAL ENDOWMENT FOR THE ARTS. (MUSEUMS). 0737-7665. US. English. an. National Endowment for the Arts, 1100 Pennsylvania Avenue NW, Washington DC 20506. LC N8837. DD 700.79.

MUSEUMS YEARBOOK. *See* Yearbooks, Almanacs, Directories.

MUSEUMSKUNDE. Vol. 1-. 0027-4178. Periodical. GW. German. ir. 45,-. Museumskunde, Colmantstr 14-16, D 5300 Bonn 1 West Germany. Tel (0228)632158. Ind/Abst Repert. Int. Litt. Art. bk rev. Circ 1,600. Discusses conceptions of museums and exhibitions, educational and other problems concerning the museums' work.

MUSEUMSNYTT. Vol. 1-. 0027-4186. Periodical. Norwegian. ir.

MUWOP : MUSEOLOGICAL WORKING PAPERS. VFOAT Museological Working Papers. No. 1 (1980)-. Periodical. English (parallel text French). ir. Statens Historika Museum, Box 5405, S-114 84 Stockholm Sweden. LC AM1. DD 069.5.

MUZEEVEDENIE I OKHRANA PAMIATNIKOV. UR. Russian (Multilingual). mo. $15.30. Victor Kamkin Inc (64904), 12224 Parklawn Drive, Rockville MD 20852. Tel (301)881-5973. LC Z5052 AM1. *Novosti Nauchnoi Literatury, Muzeevedenie I Okhrana Pamiatnikov*.

MUZEI I PAMETNITSI NA KULTURATA. VFOAT MPK. Began in 1961. 0324-1793. Periodical. BU. Bulgarian. qt. $22.00. Hemus, 6 Boulevard Rusky, Sofia Bulgaria.

MUZEJNI A VLASTIVEDNA PRACE. Vol. 1. Periodical. CS. Czech (summaries also in English and Russian, 1966-1967). qt. Artia, PO Box 790, Praha 1 Czechoslovakia. LC DB191. *Casopis Spolecnosti Pratel Starozitnosti*.

MUZEUL NATIONAL. Main/Corp Muzeue de Istorie al Republicii Socialiste Romania. 1- 1974-. Romanian (summaries in French). ir. LC DR201.

NAHO. V. 5 No. 4-. 0027-7681. Periodical. US. English. qt. New York State Museum and Science Service, M Seffer 60 Commerce Way, Albany NY 12230. Tel (518)457-1715. Ed Miriam Soffer. Circ 10,000. (ctrl). History, natural science, and the arts in New York State. *Museum Education*.

NARA KOKURITSU HAKUBUTSUKAN NEMPO. VFOAT Annual Report of Nara National Museum. Japanese. ir. 50 Noboriojicho, Nara Japan. LC AM101.N26.

THE NATIONAL ART MUSEUM AND GALLERY GUIDE. CEASED. VFOAT Gallery Guide. 1969. 0735-2247. US. English. ir. $22.00. Art Now Inc, 320 Bonnie Burn Road/PO Box 219, Scotch Plains NJ 07076. Tel (201)322-8333. Ed Bernice Shor. DD 708. adv acc. Circ 3,500. (ctrl). Information on over 1,200 gallery and museum art exhibitions plus major gallery area maps.

NATIONAL INSTITUTE OF ARTS AND LETTERS, AMERICAN ACADEMY OF ARTS AND LETTERS. Periodical. US. English. ir. $12.00. National Institute of Arts and Letters, 633 West 155th Street, New York NY 10032. Tel (212)368-5900. LC AS36. DD 061. Circ 700. Speeches and citations by prominent persons in the arts at annual induction and award ceremony; commemorative tributes to artists, writers and composers by their colleagues. *American Academy of Arts and Letters*.

NATIONAL MUSEUM ACT: GUIDELINES FOR GRANT PROGRAMS. Main/Corp Smithsonian Institution. US. English. an. Smithsonian Institute, Washington DC 20560.

NATIONAL MUSEUMS OF CANADA GIFT CATALOGUE. VFOAT Musees Nationaux du Canada, Catalogue. 0225-5049. CN. English (French). an. National Museums of Canada, Ottawa Ontario Canada. DD 700.294.

NATIONAL PALACE MUSEUM BULLETIN. VFOAT Ku Kung Tung Hsun. Began in Mar. 1966. 0027-9846. Periodical. CH. English. bm. $5.00. National Palace Museum, Wai-Shvang-Hsi Shih-Lin, Taipei Taiwan China. LC N3750.T32.

NAUCHNYI REFERATIVNYI SBORNIK : MUZEEVEDENIE I OKHRANA PAMIATNIKOV. VFOAT Muzeevedenie I Okhrana Pamiatnikovov. Periodical. UR. Russian. ir. $7.50. Victor Kamkin Inc, 12224 Parklawn Drive, Rockville MD 20852. Tel (301)881-5973.

NEUE DENKSCHRIFTEN DES NATURHISTORISCHEN MUSEUMS IN WIEN. Main/Corp Naturhistorisches Mueseum (Austria). 1.- Vol. Monographic Series. AU. German (English). ir. Verlag Ferdinand Berger Eshone, Wienerstr 21-23, A-3580 Horn Austria. Tel 082/2317-0. Ind/Abst GeoRef. bk rev. *Denkschriften Des Naturhistorischen Museums in Wien*.

THE NEWARK MUSEUM QUARTERLY. V. 26- Winter 1975-. 0098-3373. Periodical. US. English. qt $7.00. Newark Museum, 43-49 Washington Street, Newark NJ 07101. Tel (201)733-6600. Ind/Abst Art Index, Am. Hist. Life, Hist. Abstr., Repert. Int. Litt. Art. LC AM1. DD 069.0974932. *Museum, 0027-4011*.

NEWS AND NOTES OF THE MARYLAND HISTORICAL SOCIETY. Main/Corp Maryland Historical Society. V. 1-6 No. 5. Periodical. US. English. bm. $4.00 Domestic, $5.25 Foreign. Maryland Historical Society, 201 West Mounment Street, Baltimore MD 21202. Tel (301)685-3750. Ed Ann Egerton. Circ 6,000. We relate to our members the activities of the museum, library, education, and special events departments of this institution. *Maryland History Notes*.

NEWS NOTES - NEWARK MUSEUM. (NEWS NOTES - THE NEWARK MUSEUM). Main/Corp Newark Museum Association, Newark, N.J. V. 1- Feb. 1944-. 0028-9256. Periodical. US. English. bm. Newark Museum, 43-49 Washington Street, Newark NJ 07101. Tel (201)733-6600. Ed Mary Chris Rospond. Circ 10,000. Lists exhibitions, talks, tours, workshops for children and adults, programs and new books published.

NEWSLETTER - FOGG ART MUSEUM. CEASED. Main/Corp Fogg Art Museum. V. 1-19, No. 2. 0440-3819. Periodical. US. English. LC N527.

NEWSLETTER - MARINE MUSEUM OF THE GREAT LAKES AT KINGSTON. (NEWSLETTER). Vol. 1, No. 1 (Mar. 1983)-. 0823-5317. Periodical. CN. English. qt. Free. Marine Museum of the Great Lakes at Kingston, 55 Ontario Street, Kingston Ontario K7L 2Y2 Canada. DD 069.9387209713. (ctrl).

NEWSLETTER - MARITIME MUSEUM OF BRITISH COLUMBIA. (NEWSLETTER). Main/Corp Maritime Museum of British Columbia. Fall 1982-. 0826-0435. Periodical. CN. English. ir. Free to Members. Maritime Museum of British Columbia, 28 Bastion Square, Victoria British Columbia V8W 1H9 Canada. DD 069.9387209711. *Bulletin (Maritime Museum of British Columbia), 0710-6114*.

NEWSLETTER - MUSEUM OF INDIAN ARCHAEOLOGY. UNIVERSITY OF WESTERN ONTARIO. (NEWSLETTER - MUSEUM OF INDIAN ARCHAEOLOGY). Main/Corp Museum of Indian Archaeology. V. 1- Feb. 1979-. 0709-2261. Periodical. CN. English. qt. $5. Museum of Indian Archaeology, Room 28 Middlesex College, University of Western Ontario, London Ontario N6A 3K7 Canada. DD 971.301.

NEWSLETTER - NATIONAL PALACE MUSEUM = KU KUNG CHAN LAN TUNG HSUN. Main/Corp Kuo Li Ku Kung Po Wu Yuan. V. 1- Nov. 1968-. CH. English. mo. National Palace Museum, Wai-Shuang-Hsi Shin-Lin, Taipei Taiwan China. LC N3750.T32. DD 708.951249.

NEWSLETTER - PRINCE EDWARD ISLAND MUSEUM AND HERITAGE FOUNDATION. (NEWSLETTER). 0823-8324. Periodical. CN. English. Free to members. Prince Edward Island Museum and Heritage Foundation, 2 Kent Street, Charlottetown Prince Edward Island C1A 1M6 Canada. DD 971.7005. *Newsletter (Prince Edward Island Heritage Foundation), 0823-8316*.

NEWSLETTER - THUNDER BAY HISTORICAL MUSEUM SOCIETY. CEASED. Main/Corp Thunder Bay Historical Museum Society. 0317-9427. CN. English. ir. Free to Members. Thunder Bay Historical Museum Society, 219 South May Street, Thunder Bay Ontario P7E 1B5 Canada. DD 971.3120074.

NEWSLETTER - WESTERN REGIONAL CONFERENCE, AMERICAN ASSOCIATION OF MUSEUMS. Main/Corp American Association of Museums. Western Regional Conference. Periodical. US. English. qt. $15.00. Western Regional Conference, PO Box 7887, San Francisco CA 94120.

NIHON NO HAKUBUTSUKAN SORAN. 1970- Vol. JA. Japanese. ir. 900. c/o Tokyo Kokuritsu Habubutsukan, Nihon Hakubutsukan Kyokai, 13.9 Ueno Koen Taito-Ku, Tokyo 110 Japan. LC AM77.A1.

NOTABLE ACQUISITIONS. Main/Corp Metropolitan Museum of Art (New York, N.Y.). 1975/79-. 0192-6950. US. English. an. Metropolitan

Museums

Museum of Art, 5th Avenue & 82nd Street, New York NY 10028. **LC** N610. **DD** 708.1471.

NOVA SCOTIA MUSEUM PROGRAM OF EVENTS. **VAT** Nova Scotia Museum Programme of Events. 0225-5006. Periodical. CN. English. bm. Nova Scotia Museum, 1747 Summer Street, Halifax Nova Scotia B3H 3A6 Canada. **DD** 069.10971622.

NOVAIA SOVETSKAIA LITERATURA PO KULTURE I ISKUSSTVU : MUZEEVEDENIE I OKHRANA PAMIATNIKOV. Nov./Dec. 1974-. UR. Multilingual (Russian). mo. Prospekt Kalinina 3, Moskva 101000 Russia. **LC** Z5052, AM5.

OBJETS ET MONDES. (OBJETS ET MONDES : LA REVUE DU MUSEE DE L'HOMME, MUSEUM NATIONAL D'HISTOIRE NATURELLE). Began in Spring 1961. 0029-7615. Periodical. FR. French. qt. $15.96. Musee de l'Homme, Palais Chaillot Place Trocader, 75116 Paris France. **Ind/Abst** MLA Int. Bibliogr. Books Artic. Mod. Lang. Lit., Recent Publ. Artic. **LC** GN1. **DD** 306.05.

OBZORNAIA INFORMATSIIA : RESTAVRATSIIA, ISSLEDOVANIE I KHRANENIE MUZEINYKH KHUDOZHESTVENNYKH TSENNOSTEI. **VFOAT** Restavratsiia, Issledovanie I Khranenie Muzeinykh Khudozhestvennykh Tsennostei. Periodical. UR. Russian. sa. $4.80. Victor Kamkin Inc, 12224 Parklawn Drive, Rockville MD 20852. **Tel** (301)881-5973.

OCCASIONAL PAPERS - BOWDOIN COLLEGE. MUSEUM OF ART. **Main/Corp** Bowdoin College. Museum of Art. No. 1 (1972)-. US. English. ir. Bowdoin College, Museum of Fine Arts, Brunswick ME 04011. **Tel** (207)725-8731. **Ind/Abst** Repert. Int. Litt. Art.

OCCASIONAL PAPERS - MUSEUM OF SOUTHWESTERN BIOLOGY. (OCCASIONAL PAPERS). No. 1 (17 June 1983)-. 0749-2421. Monographic Series. US. English. ir. The Director, The Museum of Southwestern Biology Department of Biology, University of New Mexico, Albuquerque NM 87131. **DD** 574.

OCCASIONAL PAPERS - MUSEUM, TEXAS TECH UNIVERSITY. (OCCASIONAL PAPERS - THE MUSEUM, TEXAS TECH UNIVERSITY). No. 1-. 0149-175X. Monographic Series. US. English. ir. $6.00. Exchange Librarian, Texas Tech University Library, Lubbock TX 79409. **Ind/Abst** GeoRef. **LC** UNC. **CODEN** OPTMDL.

OCCASIONAL PAPERS - NEVADA STATE MUSEUM. **Main/Corp** Nevada. State Museum, Carson City. **VFOAT** Nevada State Museum Occasional Papers. No. 1-. 0077-7919. Monographic Series. US. English. ir. Nevada State Museum, Capitol Complex, Carson City NV 89710. **LC** UNC.

OCCASIONAL PAPERS OF BERNICE P. BISHOP MUSEUM. **Main/Corp** Bernice Pauahi Bishop Museum. **VFOAT** Occasional Papers of the Bernice Pauahi Bishop Museum of Polynesian Ethnology and Natural History. V. 1- 1898-. 0005-9439. Monographic Series. US. English. ir. Bishop Museum Press, PO Box 19000-A, Honolulu HI 96819. **Tel** (800)847-3511. **Ind/Abst** GeoRef, Biol. Abstr. **DD** 570. **CODEN** OPBMAU.

OCCASIONAL PAPERS OF THE BRITISH COLUMBIA PROVINCIAL MUSEUM. **Main/Corp** British Columbia Provincial Museum. Began publication 1939?. 0068-1636. Monographic Series. CN. English. ir. British Columbia Provincial, 601 Belleville Street, Victoria British Columbia V8W 1A1 Canada.

OCCASIONAL PAPERS OF THE IDAHO MUSEUM OF NATURAL HISTORY. 0196-7703. Monographic Series. US. English. be. Idaho Museum of Natural History, Campus Box 8096, Idaho State University, Pocatello ID 83201. **Tel** (208)236-3882. **LC** E78.I18. **DD** 970 S. Circ 2,00. A series of papers dealing with aspects of archaeological research in the intermountain west. *Occasional Papers of the Idaho State University Museum, 0073-4551.*

OCCASIONAL PAPERS OF THE MUSEUM OF NATURAL HISTORY. (OCCASIONAL PAPERS OF THE MUSEUM OF NATURAL HISTORY, THE UNIVERSITY OF KANSAS). **VFOAT** Occasional Papers of the Museum of Natural History, University of Kansas (No. 87). No. 1-. 0091-7958. Monographic Series. US. English. ir. University of Kansas, Museum of Natural History, Lawrence KS 66045. **Tel** (913)864-4540. **Ed** Joseph T Collins. **Ind/Abst** GeoRef, Biol. Abstr. **LC** QH1. **DD** 574.05. **CODEN** OPMNAK. Circ 1,500. Scientific information from research. *University of Kansas Publications, Museum of Natural History, 0075-5036.*

OCCASIONAL PAPERS OF THE MUSEUM OF ZOOLOGY. **Main/Corp** Louisiana State University, Baton Rouge. Museum of Zoology. 0097-0425. Monographic Series. US. English. Louisiana State University, Baton Rouge LA 70803. **Ind/Abst** Biol. Abstr. **LC** QL3. **DD** 591.08. **CODEN** LMZOAY. *Occasional Papers.*

OCCASIONAL PAPERS OF THE MUSEUM OF ZOOLOGY, UNIVERSITY OF MICHIGAN. No. 1-. 0076-8413. Monographic Series. US. English. ir. University of Michigan, Museum of Zoology, Ann Arbor MI 48109. **Ind/Abst** Life Sci. Collect., Biol. Abstr., Bibliogr. Agric. **LC** QL1. **DD** 591. **CODEN** MUZOAX.

OCCASIONAL PAPERS - UNIVERSITY OF ARKANSAS MUSEUM. **Main/Corp** University of Arkansas Museum. 0148-0960. Periodical. US. English. ir. University of Arkansas Museum, Fayetteville AR 72701. **Ind/Abst** Chem. Abstr. **CODEN** UAMOAI.

THE OFFICIAL DIRECTORY OF CANADIAN MUSEUMS AND RELATED INSTITUTIONS. *See* Yearbooks, Almanacs, Directories.

OFFICIAL MUSEUM DIRECTORY. *See* Yearbooks, Almanacs, Directories.

THE OFFICIAL MUSEUM PRODUCTS AND SERVICES DIRECTORY. *See* Yearbooks, Almanacs, Directories.

OKINAWA KENRITSU HAKUBUTSUKAN DAYORI. No. 1- 1977. JA. Japanese. ir. Okinawa Kenritsu Hakubutsukan, 1-1 Shuri Onakacho, Naha 903 Japan. **LC** AM101.N256.

OKINAWA KENRITSU HAKUBUTSUKAN NEMPO. No. 8- 1975-. Japanese. an. Free. Okinawa Kenritsu Hakubutsukan, 1 Shuri Onakacho 1, Naha 903 Japan. **Tel** 0988-84-2243. **LC** AM101.N256. Report of operation of the Okinawa Prefectural Museum. *Okinawa Kenritsu Hakubutsukan Kampo.*

OLD STURBRIDGE VISITOR. Vol. 22, No. 1 (Spring 1982)-. 0744-3781. Periodical. US. English. qt. Old Sturbridge Inc, Sturbridge MA 01566. **Tel** (617)347-3362. **Ind/Abst** Am. Hist. Life, Hist. Abstr., Part A, Mod. Hist. Abstr., Hist. Abst., Part B, Twent. Century Abstr. Circ 13,000. (ctrl). Relating to exhibits and interpretation at museum of early-19th century rural life - working farms, historical crafts, furnished houses in village setting. *Rural Visitor, 0485-6724.*

OPENBAAR KUNSTBEZIT. 1. Vol. (1957)-. Periodical. NE. Dutch. qt. Administratie, Postbus 5555, Amsterdam The Netherlands. **Ind/Abst** Repert. Int. Litt. Art.

OSTERREICHISCHE ZEITSCHRIFT FUR KUNST UND DENKMALPFLEGE. *See* The Arts (General) - Art.

PAPERS AND RECORDS - THUNDER BAY HISTORICAL MUSEUM SOCIETY. **Main/Corp** Thunder Bay Historical Museum Society. V. 1- 1973-. 0703-7058. Periodical. CN. English. an. Thunder Bay Historical Museum Society Inc, 219 South May Street, Thunder Bay Ontario P7E 1B5 Canada. *Annual Reports.*

PAPERS OF THE PEABODY MUSEUM OF ARCHAEOLOGY AND ETHNOLOGY, HARVARD UNIVERSITY. 1955-. US. English. ir. Harvard University Press, 79 Garden Street, Cambridge MA 02138. **LC** E51.

THE PEARCE-SELLARDS SERIES. **Main/Corp** Texas. Memorial Museum. No. 1- June 1963-. 0079-0354. US. English. ir. Texas Memorial Museum, 24th & Trinity Street, Austin TX 78705. **Ind/Abst** GeoRef, Biol. Abstr., Bibliogr. Index Geol. **CODEN** PSSEAL.

PEI-CHING TZU JAN PO WU KUAN YEN CHIU PAO KAO. **VFOAT** Memoirs of Beijing Natural History Museum. Began in 1979. Monographic Series. CC. Chinese (summaries in English). ir. Peking Natural History Museum, 126 Tien Chiao Street, Peking 2 China Mainland.

PERCEPTIONS. (PERCEPTIONS : AN ANNUAL PUBLICATION OF THE INDIANAPOLIS MUSEUM OF ART). Vol. 1 (1981)-. 0730-5435. Periodical. US. English. an. Free to Members. Indianapolis Museum of Art, 1200 West 38th Street, Indianapolis IN 46208. **Ind/Abst** Repert. Int. Litt. Art. **LC** N577. **DD** 708.17252.

THE POLISH MUSEUM OF AMERICA QUARTERLY. **Main/Corp** Chicago. Polish Museum of America. 0149-9653. Periodical. US. English. qt. Polish Museum of America, 984 North Milwaukee Avenue, Chicago IL 60622. **LC** E184.P7. **DD** 973.049185.

POPULAR SERIES - NEVADA STATE MUSEUM. (POPULAR SERIES). No. 1 (Jan. 1965)-. 0077-7927. Monographic Series. US. English. ir. Nevada State Museum, Department of Anthropology, Capitol Complex, Carson City NV 89710. **LC** AM101. **DD** 069.0979357.

PROCEEDINGS OF ASPAC MUSEUM CONFERENCE. **Main/Conf** ASPAC Museum Conference. **VAT** Proceedings of Asian and Pacific Council Museum Conference. 0377-2896. English. ir. Cultural and Social Centre for the Asian and Pacific Region, CPO Box 3129, Seoul Korea. **LC** AM71.A2. **DD** 069.095.

PROVENANCE. (PROVENANCE : NEWSLETTER OF THE LONDON HISTORICAL MUSEUMS AND LONDON HISTORICAL MUSEUMS ASSOCIATION). Vol. 1, No. 1 (Sept./Oct. 1983 1983)-. 0826-1164. Periodical. CN. English. bm. Free. Provenance c/o London Historical Museums, 1017 Western Road, London Ontario N6G 1G5 Canada. **DD** 069.9971326.

PUBLICACIONES DEL MUSEO ARQUEOLOGICO DE LA SERENA; BOLETIN. *See* Archaeology.

PUBLICACIONES DEL MUSEO MUNICIPAL DE CIENCIAS NATURALES LORENZO SCAGLIA. **Main/Corp** Museo Municipal de Ciencias Naturales de Mar del Plata Lorenzo Scaglia. V. 2, No. 3, August 1976-. Periodical. Spanish (English). ir. CC 1207 Correo Central, 7600 Mar del Plata Argentina. **Ind/Abst** GeoRef. **CODEN** MPMMBU. *Publicaciones del Museo Municipal de Ciencias Naturales de Mar del Plata.*

PUBLICATIONS - VIRGINIA MUSEUM OF FINE ARTS, RICHMOND. **Main/Corp** Virginia Museum of Fine Arts. Vol. 1 1936/38-. US. English. ir. Virginia Museum of Fine Arts, Boulevard and Grove Avenue, Richmond VA 23221. **LC** N716.V45. **DD** 708.1.

PURABHILEKH-PURATATVA : JOURNAL OF THE DIRECTORATE OF ARCHIVES, ARCHAEOLOGY AND MUSEUM, PANAJI-GOA. *See* Genealogy and Heraldry - Archives.

QUADERNI DEL MUSEO DI STORIA NATURALE DI LIVORNO (1982). (QUADERNI DEL MUSEO DI STORIA NATURALE DI LIVORNO). Vol. 3 (1982)-. Italian (summaries in English). an. Provinc Livorno, Via Orma 234, 57100 Livorno Italy. *Quaderni di Storia Naturale.*

QUARTERLY BULLETIN - ROSWELL MUSEUM AND ART CENTER. (QUARTERLY BULLETIN). **Main/Corp** Roswell Museum and Art Center. Began with V. 5, No. 4 in 1957. 0557-3645. US. English. ty. $15.00. Roswell Museum & Art Center, 11th and Main Streets, Roswell NM 88201. **Tel** (505)624-6744. Circ 1,300. (ctrl). Museum catalog of past and future exhibits and museum activities. *Bulletin, 0483-3945.*

QUARTERLY JOURNAL OF THE TAIWAN MUSEUM *CEASED.* Vol. 1, No. 3 (July 1948)-Vol. 35, No. 3 & 4 Dec. 1982). 0039-9116. Periodical. English (Chinese). qt. **Ind/Abst** Life Sci. Collect., GeoRef, Biol. Abstr. **LC** QH1. **DD** 574.951. **CODEN** QJTMAW. *Tai-Wan Sheng Po Wu Kuan Chi Kan.*

QUARTERLY - MUSEUM OF THE FUR TRADE. *See* History (General) - History of North, South, and Central America.

QUARTERLY - ONTARIO MUSEUM ASSOCIATION. **Main/Corp** Ontario Museum Association. V. 8, No. 2-V. 10, No. 4. 0709-3543. Periodical. CN. English. qt. $19.35. Ontario Museum Association, 38 Charles Street East, Toronto Ontario M4Y 1T1 Canada. **Tel** (416)923-3868. **Ed** Betty Ann Jordon. **DD** 069.05. bk rev. adv acc. (ctrl). A compendium of articles, how-to columns, book, museum, and exhibition reviews. Museum ethics, research, education, management, collecting, architecture, and funding are regular topics. *Newsletter, 0384-9619.*

Museums

RAPPORT - INSTITUT OF MUSEES NATIONAUX. Main/Corp Institut des Musees Nationaux. French. ir. LC AM91.Z28. DD 069.096751.

RAPPORT (JONKOPINGS LANS MUSEUM). (RAPPORT). No. 1-. 0349-7887. Periodical. Swedish. ir.

RECORD OF THE ART MUSEUM, PRINCETON UNIVERSITY. Main/Corp Princeton University. Art Museum. V. 1- Spring 1942-. 0032-843X. US. English. sa. $8.40. Princeton University, Art Museum, Princeton NJ 08544. Tel (609)452-4341. Ed Bitite Vinklers. Ind/Abst Art Index. Circ 2,000. (ctrl). Contains scholarly articles about art objects in the museum's collection. Includes annual listing of new acquistions of the museum; illustrated.

RECORDS OF THE AUSTRALIAN MUSEUM. Main/Corp Australian Museum. V. 1- Mar. 1890-. 0067-1975. AT. English. ir. 100.00. Australian Museum, Bolton Anthropologists Department, PO Box A285, Sydney New South Wales 2000 Australia. Tel 3398111. Ed Jim Lowry. Ind/Abst Life Sci. Collect., GeoRef, Biol. Abstr., Bibliogr. Index Geol. LC QH1. CODEN RAUMAJ. Circ 800. (ctrl).

RECORDS OF THE PAPUA NEW GUINEA PUBLIC MUSEUM AND ART GALLERY. Main/Corp Papua New Guinea Museum. No. 5- 1975-. English. be. National Museum & Art Gallery, PO Box 5560, Boroko Papua New Guinea. LC GN671.N5. DD 995. Records of the Papua New Guineas Museum, 0304-1816.

RECORDS OF THE SOUTH AUSTRALIAN MUSEUM. Main/Corp South Australian Museum, Adelaide. V. 1- May 1918-. 0376-2750. Periodical. AT. English. ir. 20.00. South Australian Museum, North Terrace, Adelaide South Australia 5000 Australia. Tel (08)2238 8. Ed C Anderson, H Aslin, A Pring and D Lee. Ind/Abst Life Sci. Collect., Biol. Abstr. CODEN RAMUA3. Circ 400. Publishes original papers in zoology, anthropology and earth sciences, with a strong taxonomic orientation.

RECORDS OF THE WESTERN AUSTRALIAN MUSEUM. Main/Corp Western Australian Museum. V. 3- 1974-. 0312-3162. AT. English. ir. Western Australian Museum, Francis Street, Perth WA 6000 Australia. Ind/Abst Biol. Abstr. LC QH1. DD 500.9941. CODEN REMUDY.

THE REGISTER OF THE SPENCER MUSEUM OF ART. Main/Corp Helen Foresman Spencer Museum of Art. Vol. 5, No. 5 (1978)-. 0733-866X. Periodical. US. English. sa. University of Kansas, Spencer Museum Bookstore, Lawrence KS 66045. Tel (913)864-4710. Ed Carol Shankel. Ind/Abst Repert. Int. Litt. Art. Circ 1,000. Scholarly journal with articles on art objects in the Spencer Museum collection, and a museum report. Register of the Museum of Art, 0041-9672.

REPORT OF THE DIRECTOR - PEABODY MUSEUM OF SALEM. Main/Corp Peabody Museum of Salem, Salem, Mass. 1950-. 0190-7905. US. English. an. Free to Fellows and Friends. Peabody Museum of Salem, East India Square, Salem MA 01970. LC AM101. DD 069.097445.

REPORT ON THE BRITISH MUSEUM (NATURAL HISTORY). Main/Corp British Museum (Natural History) Trustees. 1963-65-. 0524-6474. Periodical. UK. English. ir. British Museum Natural History, Cromwell Road, London SW7 5BD England.

RESEARCH NOTES (LIVINGSTONE MUSEUM). (RESEARCH NOTES). No. 1 (Oct. 1979)-. ZA. English. ir. Livingstone Museum, PO Box 60498, Livingstone Zambia.

REVIEW OF THE YEARS . . . . Main/Corp Victoria and Albert Museum. 1974-1978-. UK. English. Her Majesty's Stationery Office, PO Box 276, London SW8 5DT England. LC N1150. DD 708.2134.

REVISITA DE ARCHIVOS BIBLIOTECAS Y MUSEOS (MADRID, SPAIN : 1897). See Genealogy and Heraldry - Archives.

REVISTA DEL MUSEO DE LA PLATA. SECCION ZOOLIGIA. V. 1-. 0372-4638. Periodical. Spanish. ir. Ind/Abst GeoRef. LC QL1. DD 590.5. CODEN LURZAF. Notas del Museo de la Plata. Zoologia, 0372-4549; Revista del Museo de la Plata, 0375-1147.

REVISTA DEL MUSEO HISTORICO REGIONAL. Main/Corp Museo Historico Regional. Yearly V. 5- (No. 3/4/5-). Periodical. Spanish. ir. Casa de la Cultura del Peru, Cana Inca Garcilaso, Calle Heladeros, Cuzco Peru. Revista del Museo Virreynal.

REVISTA DO MUSEU PAULISTA. 0303-9846. BL. Portuguese (with some articles in French and in English). an. Museu Paulista da Univ de Sao, Caixa Postal 42503, 04263 Sao Paulo Brasil. Ind/Abst Am. Hist. Life, Hist. Abstr., Part A, Mod. Hist. Abstr., Hist. Abst., Part B, Twent. Century Abstr., Hist. Abstr. LC Q33. NLM W1 RE521S. (cum index).

REVISTA MUZEELOR SI MONUMENTELOR : MUZEE. 0035-0206. Periodical. RM. Romanian (summaries in French). mo. Ilexim Press Department, PO Box 1-136-1-137, Bucharest Romania. LC AM69.R8. DD 06909498.

LA REVUE DU LOUVRE ET DES MUSEES DE FRANCE. V. 11- (No. 1-). 0035-2608. Periodical. FR. French. bm. Inter Presse Service, 12 rue Paul Lelong, 75095 Paris Cedex 02 France. Ind/Abst Artbibliogr. Mod., Avery Index Archit. Period. Second Ed. Revis. Enlarged Suppl., Art Index, Repert. Int. Litt. Art. Revue des Arts. Musees de France.

RHEINISCHES MUSEUM FUR PHILOLOGIE. VFOAT Museum fur Philologie. Vol. 1- (1833) Vol. 6- (1839). 0035-449X. Periodical. GW. German (articles in English, French, Greek and Latin). qt. 174.00. J D Sauerlaenders Verlag, Finkenhofstrasse 21, D6000 Frankfurt 1 West Germany. Tel 069/55 52 17. Ed Carl Werner Mueller. Ind/Abst MLA Int. Bibliogr. Books Artic. Mod. Lang. Lit., Recent Publ. Artic. LC PA3. DD 938.005. Index published separately - free - automatically sent. (cum index). Greek/Latin literature, codicology, ancient philosophy, classical archeology, ancient cultural and political history, ancient history of science, history of classical scholarship and textual criticism enclosed. Rheinisches Museum fur Philologie, Geschichte und Griechische Philosophie.

THE RINGLING MUSEUM OF ART JOURNAL. 1983-. 0738-9353. Periodical. US. English. an. John and Mable Ringling Museum of Art, PO Box 1838, Sarasota FL 33578. Ind/Abst Repert. Int. Litt. Art. LC N742.S5. DD 705.

RINGLING MUSEUMS. 0731-7956. Periodical. US. English. Ringling Museums, PO Box 1838, Sarasota FL 33578. LC N742.S5. DD 708.15961. Ringling Museums Newsletter, 0035-5461.

S & L MUSEUM NEWSLETTER. Main/Corp Sydney & Louisburg Railway Historical Society. VAT Sydney and Louisburg Railway Historical Society Museum Newsletter. 0715-5034. Periodical. CN. English. bm. Free to members - membership, $3.00 per year. Sydney & Louisburg Railway Historical Society, Membership Committee, P O Box 225, Louisburg Nova Scotia B0A 1M0 Canada. DD 385.0607169.

SAGA KENRITSU HAKUBUTSUKAN NEMPO. Began with the report for 1970. JA. Japanese. ir. 15-23 Jonai 1-Chome, Saga Japan. LC AM101.S138.

SAITAMA KENRITSU HAKUBUTSUKAN KIYO. JA. Japanese. ir. 219 Takahanacho 4 Chome, Omiya 330 Japan. LC AM101.O44.

SAMAB. V. 1- Sept. 1936-. 0370-8314. SA. Afrikaans (English). qt. $6.20. South African Musuems Association, PO Box 61, Cape Town 8000 South Africa. Tel 45-1628. Ed E Bigalke. LC AM89.A1. DD 069.0968. bk rev. adv acc. Circ 600. All matters relating to the study of museums, the activities of museums and the Museums Association of Southern Africa.

SAN BERNARDINO COUNTY MUSEUM ASSOCIATION CEASED. (SAN BERNARDINO COUNTY MUSEUM ASSOCIATION QUARTERLY). Began in 1953. 0581-4871. Monographic Series. US. English. qt. $10.00. Association Publishers, 2024 Orange Tree Lane, PO Box 2258, Redlands CA 92373. Tel (714)793-6345. Ed Gerald A Smith. Ind/Abst Abstr. Anthropol. Circ 1,300. (ctrl). Reports on anthropological research or excavation and history and natural history.

SAN DIEGO MUSEUM PAPERS. No. 4-. Monographic Series. US. English. ir. San Diego Museum of Man, 1350 El Prado Balboa Park, San Diego CA 92101. Tel (619)239-2001. Archaeology.

SASKATCHEWAN MUSEUMS QUARTERLY CEASED. Began with Spring 1975 issue Ceased V. 7, No. 4 1981/82. 0381-1042. Periodical. CN. English. qt. Free to members of the Association, $5.00 Per Year Others. Saskatchewan Museums Association, 1915 South Railway Street, Regina Saskatchewan S4P 0B1 Canada. DD 069.0627124.

SBORNIK NARODNIHO MUZEA V PRAZE. RADA C, LITERARNI HISTORIE. VFOAT Literarni Historie., Acta Musei Nationalis Pragae. Series C, Historia Litterarum. V. 1- 1956-. 0036-5351. Periodical. CS. Czech (Russian or German). qt. Artia, PO Box 790, Praha 1 Czechoslovakia. Ind/Abst Am. Hist. Life, Hist. Abstr., Part A, Mod. Hist. Abstr., Hist. Abst., Part B, Twent. Century Abstr., Hist. Abstr.

SCHOOL BROADSHEET - ROM. (THE SCHOOL BROADSHEET). VAT School Broadsheet - Royal Ontario Museum. No. 1-. 0229-4133. Periodical. CN. English. ir. Free to Public Schools and High Schools in Ontario. School Broadsheet, c/o Royal Ontario Museum, 100 Queen's Park, Toronto Ontario M5S 2C6 Canada. DD 069.109713.

SCHULE UND MUSEUM. Periodical. GW. German. ty. Moritz Diesterweg, Postfach 110651, D-6 Frankfurt 11 West Germany.

SCIENTIFIC PAPERS - ILLINOIS STATE MUSEUM. (SCIENTIFIC PAPERS). Series/Titl MCJA Special Paper. V. 1 (1940)-. 0445-3395. Monographic Series. US. English. ir. Illinois State Museum Society, Spring and Edwards Street, Springfield IL 62706. Ind/Abst GeoRef.

SEATTLE ART MUSEUM. Nov. 1978-. Periodical. US. English. mo. Seattle Art Museum, Volunteer Park, Seattle WA 98112. Seattle Art Museum Newsletter, 0197-5242.

SEMC NOTES. Main/Conf Southeastern Museums Conference. US. English. qt.

SEMINARIOS DO MUSEU DA CASA BRASILEIRA : BOLETIM. Main/Corp Museu da Casa Brasileira. No. 1- 1974-. PE. Portuguese. ir. Av Brigadeiro Farria, Lima 774 Peru. LC F2631.

THE SEROLOGICAL MUSEUM BULLETIN. No. 1- Oct. 1948-. Periodical. US. English. sa. Serological Museum, Rutgers University, Bureau of Biological Research, New Brunswick NJ 08903.

SHIZENSHI KENKYU = OCCASIONAL PAPERS FROM THE OSAKA MUSEUM OF NATURAL HISTORY. Main/Corp Osaka Shiritsu Shizen Kagaku Hakubutsukan. V. 1- 1968-. Periodical. JA. Japanese. ir. Osaka Museum of Natural History, Nagi Park, Higashi-Sumiyoshi-ku Osaka 546 Japan.

SMITHSONIAN. V. 1- Apr. 1970-. 0037-7333. Periodical. US. English. mo. $18.00. Smithsonian Associates, 900 Jefferson Drive, Washington DC 20560, (subscription address: Neodata PO Box 2606 Boulder CO 80322). Tel (212)490-1840. Ed Don Moser. Ind/Abst Am. Hist. Life, Hist. Abstr., Part A, Mod. Hist. Abstr., Hist. Abst., Part B, Twent. Century Abstr., Mag. Index, Energy Inf. Abstr., Environ. Abstr., Int. Aerosp. Abstr., GeoRef, Artbibliogr. Mod., Art Archaeol. Tech. Abstr., Ref. Source, Read. Guide Period. Lit., Ocean. Abstr., Pollut. Abstr. Indexes, Soc. Sci. Citation Index, Bibliogr. Agric., Abr. Read. Guide, Book Rev. Index, Hist. Abstr., Pop. Mag. Rev. LC AS30. DD 505. CODEN SMSNA5. bk rev. adv acc. Circ 2,000,000. Available on microfilm from Xerox University Microfilms. A beautifully illustrated, colorful magazine exploring the world of man and nature - past, present, and future.

SONORENSIS. VFOAT ASDM Sonorensis. V. 1- Summer/Fall 1978-. 0277-4887. Periodical. US. English. qt. Arizona-Sonora Desert Museum, Route 9 Box 900, Tucson AZ 85704. ASDM Newsletter.

THE SOUTH DAKOTA MUSEUM. V. 1, No. 1-. 0885-9140. Periodical. US. English. sa. W H Over Dakota Museum, University of South Dakota, Vermillion SD 57069. Ind/Abst Am. Hist. Life, Hist. Abstr., Part A, Mod. Hist. Abstr., Hist. Abst., Part B, Twent. Century Abstr. DD 069. Museum News.

SOUTHWEST MUSEUM PAPERS. VFOAT Papers / Southwest Museum. No. 1 (Apr. 1928)-. 0076-0994. US. English. ir. Southwest Museum, Box 128, Los Angeles CA 90042. Tel (213)221-2164. Ed Steven A LeBlanc. These occasional papers focus on the anthropology and archaeology of the Americas.

SOVETSKII MUZEI (1984). (SOVETSKII MUZEI). VFOAT Soviet Museum. 1 (Jan.-Feb. 1984)- - 75-. 0208-2403. Periodical. UR. Russian. bm. LC AM1. SOVETSKII MUZEI (1931).

SPECIAL PUBLICATIONS - BERNICE PAUAHI BISHOP MUSEUM. Main/Corp Bernice Pauahi Bishop Museum. No. 1-. 0067-6179. Monographic Series. US. English. ir. Bishop Museum Press, PO Box 19000-A, Honolulu HI 96819. **Tel** (808)847-3511. **Ed** Henry Bennett. bk rev. adv acc.

SPECIAL PUBLICATIONS IN BIOLOGY AND GEOLOGY. (MILWAUKEE PUBLIC MUSEUM SPECIAL PUBLICATIONS IN BIOLOGY AND GEOLOGY). No. 2- Nov. 1977-. 0160-5208. Monographic Series. US. English. ir. Milwaukee Public Museum, 800 West Wells Street, Milwaukee MI 53233. **Tel** (414)278-2787. **Ed** Mary Garity. **Ind/Abst** GeoRef. **DD** 505. Monograph-length original work in the natural sciences, published occasionally. Titles range from general field guides to systematics and taxonomy. Written for general use. *Special Publications in Biology and Geology, 0160-5208.*

SPECIAL PUBLICATIONS. THE MUSEUM, TEXAS TECH UNIVERSITY. (SPECIAL PUBLICATIONS - THE MUSEUM, TEXAS TECH UNIVERSITY). Main/Corp Texas Tech University. Museum. No. 1- Dec. 1972-. 0149-1768. Monographic Series. US. English. ir. Exchange Librarian, Texas Tech University Library, Lubbock TX 79409. **Ind/Abst** GeoRef. **DD** 500.

SPECTRUM. V. 1- May/June 1978-. Periodical. US. English. qt. Science Museum of Virginia, 2500 West Broad Street, Richmond VA 23220. *Newsletter - Science Museum of Virginia.*

STEAM PASSENGER SERVICE DIRECTORY. See Yearbooks, Almanacs, Directories.

STUDIES IN MUSEOLOGY. V. 1- 1965-. 0081-8259. II. English. ir. Indian Books & Periodical, 3341 Christian Colony-Pyarey Lal Road, New Delhi 110005 India. **LC** AM1.

SYLLOGEUS - NATIONAL MUSEUM OF NATURAL SCIENCES. VAT Syllogeus - Musee National des Sciences Naturelles. No. 1-. 0704-576X. Monographic Series. CN. English (French). ir. McClelland and Stewart Ltd, 25 Hollinger Road, Toronto Ontario M4B 3G2 Canada. **Ind/Abst** ASTIS Bibliogr., ASTIS Curr. Aware. Bull., Biol. Abstr., Can. Environ., GeoRef, Bibliogr. Index Geol. **DD** 509.71. **CODEN** SYLGBY.

SYMBOLS : A PUBLICATION OF THE PEABODY MUSEUM AND THE DEPARTMENT OF ANTHROPOLOGY, HARVARD UNIVERSITY. See Anthropology.

TALES OF THE TWELVE. (TALES OF THE TWELVE : NEWSLETTER OF THE ST. CATHARINES HISTORICAL MUSEUM). VFOAT Newsletter. Vol. 1, Issue 1 (Spring 1982)-. 0713-3901. Periodical. CN. English. qt. Free to Members, 4.00 Others. St Catharines Historical Museum, 343 Merritt Street, St Catharines Ontario L2T 1K7 Canada. **Tel** (416)227-2962. **DD** 069.9971351. bk rev. **Circ** 650. Articles about the activities, programmes, and events of the St. Catharines Historical Museum. *Newsletter, 0706-7461.*

TANZANIA NOTES AND RECORDS. No. 65 (Mar. 1966)-. 0039-9485. Periodical. TZ. English. ir. Tanzania Society, National Museum, PO Box 511, Dar es Salaam Tanzania. **Ind/Abst** Am. Hist. Life, Hist. Abstr., Part A, Mod. Hist. Abstr., Hist. Abst., Part B, Twent. Century Abstr., Hist. Abstr. **NLM** W1 TA56. *Tanganyika Notes and Records.*

TECHNICAL HANDBOOKS FOR MUSEUMS AND MONUMENTS. Series/ Titl Protection of the Cultural Heritage. 1-. Monographic Series. English. ir. United Nations Educational Scientific and Cultural Organization, 7 Place de Fontenoy, 75700 Paris France. **LC** UNC. **DD** 069.53.

TECHNICAL REPORTS (UNIVERSITY OF MICHIGAN. MUSEUM OF ANTHROPOLOGY). (TECHNICAL REPORTS - MUSEUM OF ANTHROPOLOGY, UNIVERSITY OF MICHIGAN). No. 1-. 0196-8297. Monographic Series. US. English. ir. University of Michigan, Museum of Anthropology, Ann Arbor MI 48109. **LC** UNC.

TEXTILE MUSEUM JOURNAL. V. 1- Nov. 1962-. 0083-7407. Periodical. US. English. ir. Textile Museum, 2320 S Street NW, Washington DC 20008. **Tel** (202)667-0442. **Ed** Patricia Fiske. **Ind/Abst** World Text Abstr., Art Archaeol. Tech. Abstr., Art Index, Avery Index Archit. Period. **LC** NK8802.W3. **DD** 069.9746. (ctrl). Traditional motif evaluation/symbolism; ethnographic relationship between design, technique, and raw materials; new insights as a result of current scholarship and research. *Workshop Notes.*

TOKYO DAIGAKU SOGO KENKYU SHIRYOKAN YORAN. JA. Japanese. ir. 3-1 Hongo 7-Chome Bunkyo-Ku (113), Tokyo Japan. **LC** AM101.T555.

TORRENS. Series/Titl Publicacio de l'Arxiu, Biblioteca i Museu de l'Ajuntament de Torrent. 1 (1982)-. Periodical. Spanish. an. Arxiu Municipal de Torrent, c/o Ramon y Cajal Num 7 Torrent, Valencia Spain.

TUVA. VFOAT Inyo County Museums Department Bulletin. 0196-1071. Periodical. US. English. mo. $3.00. Eastern California Museum, 155 Grant Street, PO Box 206, Independence CA 93526.

ULSTER MUSEUM SERIES. Monographic Series. UK. English. Blackstaff Press, 255A Upper Newtownards Road, Belfast BT4 3JF Northern Ireland. **LC** AM101.U56. **DD** 069.09416. *Publication.*

THE UNIVERSITY MUSEUM, THE UNIVERSITY OF TOKYO. Main/Corp Tokyo Daigaku. Sogo Kenkyu Shiryokan. JA. English. ir. University of Tokyo, 2 21 1 Oosawa, 113 Tokyo Japan. **LC** AM101.T555. **DD** 069.0952135.

UNIVERSITY OF ALASKA MUSEUM ANNUAL REPORT. (ANNUAL REPORT - UNIVERSITY OF ALASKA MUSEUM). Main/Corp Alaska. University. Museum. 0093-7436. US. English. an. University of Alaska Museum, Fairbanks AK 99701. **LC** AM101.F3. **DD** 069.097986.

UPDATE. Main/Corp Smithsonian Institution. Traveling Exhibition Service. 0272-0345. US. English. an. Smithsonian Institution, Traveling Exhibition Service, Washington DC 20560. **Tel** (202)357-3168. **Ed** Andrea Stevens. **LC** Q11. **DD** 069.509753. **Circ** 8,000. Catalog of traveling exhibitions from the Smithsonian. More than 100 different topics covered. Rental fee charged to exhibitors as low as $500.00 for weeks. *Catalogue.*

UPDATE - UKRAINIAN MUSEUM OF CANADA. (UPDATE). VFOAT Novynky. Vol. 1, No. 1 (Fall 1979)-. 0821-5235. Periodical. CN. English (Ukrainian on inverted pages). ir. Free. Update, Ukrainian Museum of Canada, 910 Spadina Cresc East, Saskatoon Saskatchewan S7K 3H5 Canada. **DD** 305.891791071074011242. (ctrl).

VERSLAG VAN DE HOOFDCONSULENT VOOR DE MUSEA. Main/Corp Netheralands(Kingdom, 1815-). Ministerie van Cultuur, Recreatie en Maatschappelijk Werk. Dutch. ir. **LC** AM57.

VERSLAG VAN DIE DIREKTEUR MUSEUMDIENS. Main/Corp Orange Free State (Province). Afdeling Provinsiale Museumdiens. VFOAT Jaarverslag van die Afdeling Provinsiale Museumdiens. Afrikaans. ir. **LC** AM89.A1.

VINCULOS. V. 1- 1975-. 0304-3703. CR. English or Spanish. sa. $25.00. Museo Nacional, Apartado 749, San Jose Costa Rica. **Tel** 210295. **Ind/Abst** Avery Index Archit. Period. **LC** F1545. bk rev. **Circ** 1,000. Covers anthropology, archaeology, ethnology, prehistory, Mesoamerican, and intermediate area techniques.

WAKAYAMA KENRITSU HAKUBUTSUKAN NEMPO. Japanese. an. Wakayama Kenritsu Hakubutsukan, 1 Ichibancho, Wakayama-shi Japan. **LC** AM101.W1937.

WEST POINT MUSEUM BULLETIN. 0147-281X. Periodical. US. English. qt. Free to agencies or individuals with letterhead. West Point Museum, US Military Academy, West Point NY 10996. **LC** U13.U62. **DD** 355.0074014731.

WESTERN ANNUAL. Main/Corp Denver Art Museum. US. English. an. **LC** N6525. **DD** 709.75074018883.

WHITNEY REVIEW. 1960/61-. 0511-8824. US. English. an. Whitney Museum of American Art, 945 Madison Avenue and 75th, New York NY 10021. **LC** N618. **DD** 708.1471.

WORLD MUSEUM PUBLICATIONS. See Yearbooks, Almanacs, Directories.

YAMAGUCHI KENRITSU YAMAGUCHI HAKUBUTSUKAN KANPO. Japanese. an. Yamaguchi Kenritsu Yamaguchi Hakubutsukan, 8-2 Kasugacho, Yamaguchi-Shi 753 Japan. **LC** AM101.Y2858.

YEAR BOOK - ULSTER FOLK AND TRANSPORT MUSEUM. See Yearbooks, Almanacs, Directories.

YEARBOOK - SWAZILAND NATIONAL MUSEUM. See Yearbooks, Almanacs, Directories.

YOKOSUKA-SHI HAKUBUTSUKAN SHIRYOSHU. VFOAT Miscellaneous Report of the Yokosuka City Museum. Vol. 1-. 0386-4286. JA. Japanese (summaries in English). ir. Yokosuka-Shi Hakubutsukan, Yokosuka 238 Japan. **LC** AM101.Y58.

MUSIC

1. I.E. ERSTE OSTERREICHISCHER MUSIK-EXPRESS. VFOAT Musik-Express. German. ir. $7.00. 2542 Kottingbrunn Waldgasse 5, Kottingbrunn Austria. **LC** ML5. **DD** 784.05.

1/1. (1/1 : THE QUARTERLY JOURNAL OF THE JUST INTONATION NETWORK). VFOAT One/One. Vol. 1, No. 1 (Winter 1985)-. 8756-7717. Periodical. US. English. qt. $15.00 Domestic, $17.50 Foreign. Just Intonation Network, 535 Stevenson Street, San Francisco CA 94103. **Tel** (415)864-8213. **Ed** David B Doty. **DD** 781. bk rev. adv acc. **Circ** 300. Journal covering developments in just intonation, including instrument design, scores, book and record reviews, musical analyses, tutorials, interviews, and occasional fun.

19TH CENTURY MUSIC. VAT Nineteenth Century Music. V. 1- July 1977-. 0148-2076. Periodical. US. English. ty. $25.00. University of California Press, 2120 Berkeley Way, Berkeley CA 94720. **Tel** (415)642-4191. **Ed** D Kern Holoman. **Ind/Abst** Music Index, Humanit. Index, Index Book Rev. Humanit., Humanit. Index, RILM Abstr. **LC** ML1. **DD** 780.9034. bk rev. adv acc. **Circ** 1,100. Interdisciplinary studies, history and research on 19th century music.

1810 OVERTURE. VAT Eighteen Hundred and Ten Overture. 0093-0288. Periodical. US. English. 1810 Hinman Avenue, Evanston IL 60201. **LC** ML1. **DD** 016.78.

AAMOA REPORTS. Main/Corp Afro-American Music Opportunities Association, Inc. 0360-7178. Periodical. US. English. bm. Aamoa Reports, Box 662, Minneapolis MN 55440.

ABOUT THE HOUSE. V. 1- Nov. 1962-. Periodical. UK. English. ty. $9.20. Friends of Covent Garden Ltd, Royal Opera House/45 Flora Street, London WC 2 England. **Ind/Abst** Music Index, RILM Abstr. **LC** ML5. **DD** 782.105. Available on microfilm from University Microfilms.

ABSTRACTS OF PAPERS READ AT THE ANNUAL MEETING OF THE AMERICAN MUSICOLOGICAL SOCIETY. See Indexes/Abstracts.

ACADEMY NEWS. Main/Corp Vancouver Academy of Music. Vol. 1, No. 1 (Dec. 1980)-. 0711-3471. Periodical. CN. English. ir. Vancouver Academy of Music, 1270 Chestnut Street, Vancouver British Columbia V6J 4R9 Canada. **DD** 780.72971133.

ACCENT ON MUSIC. VFOAT Accent. 0730-8906. Periodical. US. English. bm. $5.50 Domestic, $6.25 Foreign. Accent Publishing Company, 1418 Lake Street, Evanston IL 60204. **LC** ML1. **DD** 780.5. *Accent (Evanston, Ill.), 0362-6059.*

ACCENTS (NEW BRUNSWICK TEACHERS' ASSOCIATION. MUSIC EDUCATION COUNCIL). (ACCENTS : THE NEWSLETTER OF THE MUSIC EDUCATION COUNCIL OF THE NEW BRUNSWICK TEACHERS' ASSOCIATION). Vol. 1, No. 1 (Feb. 1975)-. 0710-6335. Periodical. CN. English. ir. Music Education Council of the New Brunswick Teachers' Association, PO Box 752, Fredericton NB E3B 5R6 Canada. **Ind/Abst** Can. Educ. Index. **DD** 780.7.

ACCORD. Periodical. US. English. $12.00. Ernest Deffner Publishing Inc, P O Box 608 Department S, Mineola NY 11501. **LC** ML990.A4. **DD** 786.97.

ACOUSTIC MUSIC. 0143-568X. Periodical. UK. English. bm. Karl Dallas Editorial Office, 28 Gordon Mansions Torrington Place, London WC1E 7HF England. **LC** ML5. **DD** 780.741. *Folk News.*

ACQUISITIONS - METROPOLITAN TORONTO LIBRARY, MUSIC DEPARTMENT. (ACQUISITIONS - METROPOLITAN TORONTO LIBRARY. MUSIC DEPT). Main/Corp Metropolitan Toronto Library. Music Dept. Vol. 1, No. 1 (Mar. 1980)-. 0226-2541.

Music

Periodical. CN. English. Metropolitan Toronto Library Board, 789 Yonge Street, Toronto Ontario M4W 2G8 Canada. DD 016.78. *Selected List of Acquisitions, 0227-7492.*

ACTA MOZARTIANA. Year 1- 1954-. 0001-6233. Periodical. GW. German. qt. 45.00. Deutsche Mozart Gesellshaft, Karlstrasse 6, 8900 Augsburg West Germany. **Tel** 0821/518588. Ed V Augsburg. **Ind/Abst** Music Index, RILM Abstr. (cum index). Publication of the German Mozart Society.

ACTA MUSICOLOGICA. V. 3- 1931-. 0001-6241. Periodical. GW. English (French, German, Italian). sa. 705.60. Barenreiter Verlag, Postfach 10 03 29, D-3500 Kassel West Germany. **Tel** 0567/30077-17. Ed Hellmut Fislerhofer. **Ind/Abst** Music Index. **LC** ML5. (cum index). adv acc. **Circ** 7,500. (ctrl). The periodical furthers the aims of the IMS: it encompasses music researchers from all nations, administrations, international projects and various reciprocal research. *Mitteilungen der Internationalen Gesellschaft fur Musikwissenschaft.*

ADEM. 19 -. Periodical. BE. ir. $19.15. Adem, Herestraat 53, B-3000 Leuven Belgium. **Tel** 16/23 39 67. Ed J Joris. **Ind/Abst** Music Index, RILM Abstr. bk rev. adv acc. **Circ** 5. Church music, choir, organ, music education, instrumental and vocal music education, history of music, anthology of about 120 music reviews, discography, bibliography.

AFRICAN MUSIC. V. 1- 1954-. 0065-4019. SA. English (French). an. International Library of African Music, c/o ISER, PO Box 94, 6140 Grahamstown South Africa. **Ind/Abst** RILM Abstr., Music Index. **LC** ML5. **DD** 780.96. *African Music Society Newsletter.*

AFRICAN MUSICOLOGY. Vol. 1, No. 1 (Sept. 1983)-. Periodical. KE. English (and French). ir. 30.00. Scientific Publications Division Eleza Services Ltd, PO Box 14925, Nairobi Kenya. **LC** ML5. **DD** 781.7296.

THE AGO TIMES. Main/Corp American Guild of Organists. New York City Chapter. **VAT** American Guild of Organists Times. 0362-5907. Periodical. US. English. qt. American Guild of Organists, 456 West 23rd Street, New York NY 10011. **LC** ML1. **DD** 786.505.

AL-MAJALLAH AL-MUSIQIYAH. Began in 1936. Periodical. Arabic. ir. 0.10. Al-Tawzi Dar Al-Ahram, 9 Harat Imad Aldin, Al-Qahirah UA Egypt. **LC** ML5.

ALBUM DE ORO. Vol. 1 No. 1-. Periodical. US. Spanish. qt. Angel L Marquez Publications, Box 691 Madison Square Station, New York NY 10010. **Tel** (718)339-8398. Ed Angel L Marquez. **LC** ML3486.P8. **DD** 780.42097295. adv acc. **Circ** 15,500. Biography of well known composer and singers from Latin America, internationally known in the hispanic community.

THE ALBUM NETWORK. 0739-1641. Periodical. US. English. wk. $245.00. Album Network, 8265 Sunset Boulevard, Hollywood CA 90046. **Tel** (213)656-9910. Ed Stephen R Smith. adv acc. **Circ** 5,000. (ctrl). The #1 source for contemporary music research services.

ALLA BREVE. Vol. 1, No. 1 (May 1984)-. 0825-1754. Periodical. CN. French. qt. $4.00. Instiut Kodaly du Canada Filiale de Montreal, C P 649 Succursale N D G, Montreal Quebec H4H 3R1 Canada. **DD** 780.7.

ALLEGRO. 1921. 0002-5704. Periodical. US. English. mo. $10.00. Association of Musicians of Greater New York, 330 West 2nd Street 2nd Floor, New York NY 10036. **Tel** (212)757-7722. Ed Tim Ledwith. **LC** ML1. **DD** 331.881178. adv acc. **Circ** 20,000. (ctrl).

ALMANACCO MUSICA. *See* Yearbooks, Almanacs, Directories.

AMC NEWSLETTER. V. 19- Sept. 1976-. Periodical. US. English. qt. $10.00. American Music Center Inc, 250 West 54th Street Room 300, New York NY 10019. **Tel** (212)247-3121. bk rev. adv acc. **Circ** 1,600. Information on new music as far as first performances, new recordings, publications, and news in the new music field. *American Music Center Newsletter.*

AMERICAN CHORAL REVIEW. V. 4, No. 1- Oct. 1961-. 0002-7898. Periodical. US. English. qt. $20.00. Association of Professional Vocal Ensembles, 251 South 18th Street, Philadelphia, PA 19103. **Tel** (201)273-8489. Ed Alfred Mann. **Ind/Abst** Music Index, RILM Abstr. (cum index). adv acc. **Circ** 1,500. A musicological periodical dealing with the choral repertoire from all eras.

AMERICAN FOLK MUSIC AND FOLKLORE RECORDINGS. *See* Folklore.

THE AMERICAN HARP JOURNAL. Began with Spring 1967 issue. 0002-869X. Periodical. US. English. sa. $15.00. American Harp Journal, c/o C Jensen, 187 West Palisade Avenue, Englewood NJ 07631. **Tel** (201)569-4674. **Ind/Abst** Music Index. **LC** ML1. **DD** 787. bk rev. adv acc. **Circ** 3,100. (ctrl). Chronicle of the harp and its history; articles on distinguished harpists past and present; bibliographies of music, new publications, etc. *Harp News.*

AMERICAN MUSIC EXPORT BUYERS GUIDE. **VFOAT** American Music - For - Export Buyers Guide. 1982-. 0737-8874. US. English. an. Maher Publications, 22 West Adams Street, Chicago IL 60606. *Annual American Music Export Buyers Guide, 0277-6626.*

AMERICAN MUSIC (SONNECK SOCIETY). (AMERICAN MUSIC). Vol. 1, No. 1 (Spring 1983)-. 0734-4392. Periodical. US. English. qt. $28.50 Domestic, $31.00 Foreign. University of Illinois Press, 54 East Gregory Drive, Champaign IL 61820. **Tel** (217)333-0950. Ed John Graziano. **Ind/Abst** Music Index. **LC** ML1. **DD** 781.77305. bk rev. adv acc. **Circ** 1,300. Articles on all aspects of American music and music in America, on composers, performers, publishers. and the music industry.

THE AMERICAN MUSIC TEACHER. V. 1- Sept./Oct. 1951-. 0003-0112. Periodical. US. English. bm. $10.00. Music Teachers National Association, 2113 Carew Tower, Cincinnati OH 45202. **Tel** (513)421-1420. Ed Homer Ulrich. **Ind/Abst** Book Rev. Index, Educ. Index, Music Artic. Guide, Music Index. **LC** ML1. **DD** 780.7. bk rev. adv acc. **Circ** 23,257. Features articles on keyboard, major instruments, theory and history which are geared to assist private, studio, secondary and college or university teachers.

AMERICAN OLD TIME FIDDLERS' NEWS. V. 1- 1964-. 0003-0228. Periodical. US. English. qt. American Old Time Fiddler Association, 6141 Morrill Avenue, Lincoln NE 68507. **LC** ML1. **DD** 787.105.

THE AMERICAN ORGANIST. V. 13- Jan. 1979-. 0164-3150. Periodical. US. English. mo. $25.00. American Guild of Organists, 815 Second Avenue Suite 318, New York NY 10017. **Tel** (291)687-9188. Ed Anthony Baglivi. **Ind/Abst** Ref. Source, Music Index. **LC** ML1. **DD** 786.505. bk rev. adv acc. (ctrl). Official journal American Guild of Organists is for organists, and choral conductors. Includes news, reviews, books, records, music, articles, calendar positions available, new organs, and advertising. *Music, 0027-4208.*

AMERICAN RECORD GUIDE. *See* Sound Recordings and Systems.

THE AMERICAN RECORDER. Began with Vol. 1 (Winter 1960). 0003-0724. Periodical. US. English. qt. $18.00. American Recorder Society, 596 Broadway 902, New York NY 10012-3234. **Tel** (212)966-1246. Ed Sigrid Nagle. **Ind/Abst** Music Index, RILM Abstr., Ref. Source. bk rev. adv acc. **Circ** 4,500. Articles on early music and recorder. Book, music, record reviews. Reports on events in early music. Serves the hobbiest and professional alike.

AMERICAN STRING TEACHER. V. 1- Jan. 1951-. 0003-1313. Periodical. US. English. qt. $25.00. American String Teachers Association, Georgia University, Box 2066, Athens GA 30612-0066. **Tel** (404)542-5254. Ed Jody Atwood. **Ind/Abst** Music Index. **LC** ML27.U5. **DD** 787.07. bk rev. adv acc. **Circ** 5,500. (ctrl). A quarterly journal containing pertinent articles, book and music reviews, as well as advertisements of interest to string students, teachers, and performers.

ANACRUSIS. Vol. 3, No. 2 (Winter 1983)-. 0826-7464. Periodical. CN. English. qt. 20.00. Association of Canadian Choral Conductors, PO Box 6000, Fredericton New Brunswick E3B 5H1 Canada. **Tel** (506)453-5892. Ed Carolyn Nielsen. **DD** 784.96306071. bk rev. adv acc. **Circ** 600. (ctrl). Contains relevant articles, special features, interviews, music and audio reviews, notes on national and international choral events. *ACCC, 0711-0448.*

ANALECTA MUSICOLOGICA. V. 1-. 0569-9827. Monographic Series. GW. German. an. Laaber Verlag & Muller-Buscher, Regensburger Strasse 19, D-8411 Laaber West Germany. **Tel** 9498-758. Ed Peter Cahn, Hermann Danuser, Renate Groth and Gislher Schubert. **Ind/Abst** RILM Abstr. Three to five essays on musical theory per issue. Texts from the history of music theory will be reproduced and discussed. Yearly bibliography and list of events also included.

ANALOG SOUNDS. No. 1- Oct. 1974-. 0097-6482. Periodical. US. English. qt. $16.00. Analog Sounds, 12 West 17th Street, New York NY 10011. **Ind/Abst** RILM Abstr. **LC** ML1. **DD** 789.9.

ANCIENT TIMES. (THE ANCIENT TIMES). V. 1- March 1973-. 0091-7176. Periodical. US. English. qt. $1.00. H Lawrence Carlson, Company of Fibers & Drummers Inc, 14 Winter Avenue, Deep River CT 06417. **LC** ML1. **DD** 785.0671.

ANNALES PADEREWSKI. No. 1 (Oct. 1979)-. Periodical. SZ. French. ir. Societe Paderewski, CH 1110 Morges Switzerland. **LC** ML410.P114. **DD** 786.10924, B.

L'ANNEE DU ROCK. 1 (82-83)-. Periodical. French. an. **LC** ML3533.8.

ANNUAIRE - SOCIETE DE MUSIQUE DES UNIVERSITES CANADIENNES. *See* Yearbooks, Almanacs, Directories.

ANNUAIRE SUISSE DU FOLK : MUSICIENS. *See* Yearbooks, Almanacs, Directories.

ANNUAIRE SUISSE DU FOLK : ORGANISATEURS. *See* Yearbooks, Almanacs, Directories.

ANNUAIRE SUISSE FOLK & CHANSON CHANSON. MUSICIENS, ORGANISATFURS. *See* Yearbooks, Almanacs, Directories.

ANNUAL INDEX TO POPULAR MUSIC RECORD REVIEWS. *See* Indexes/Abstracts.

ANNUAL REPORT AND ACCOUNTS FOR . . . - ROYAL MUSICAL ASSOCIATION. Main/Corp Royal Musical Association. UK. English. an. British Library, Great Russel Street, London WG 1B 3DG England. **LC** ML27.G7. **DD** 780.6041.

ANNUAL REPORT (METROPOLITAN OPERA (NEW YORK, N. Y.)). (ANNUAL REPORT. METROPOLITAN OPERA ASSOCIATION). 1966/67-. US. English. an.

ANNUAL REVIEW OF JAZZ STUDIES. 1-. 0731-0641. Periodical. US. English. an. Transaction Books & Periodical, Rutgers University, New Brunswick NJ 08903. **Tel** (201)932-2280. **Ind/Abst** Am. Hist. Life, Hist. Abstr., Part A, Mod. Hist. Abstr., Hist. Abst., Part B, Twent. Century Abstr., Jazz Index, Music Index. **LC** ML3505.8. **DD** 785.4205. *Journal of Jazz Studies, 0093-3686.*

ANNUAL WINNIPEG FOLK FESTIVAL. (ANNUAL WINNIPEG FOLK FESTIVAL : SOUVENIR PROGRAM). 76-. 0229-1843. CN. English. an. Winnipeg Folk Festival, 171 Lilac Street, Winnipeg Manitoba R3M 1S1 Canada. **DD** 780.7971274. *Winnipeg Folk Festival : Souvenir Program, 0229-1835.*

ANSCHLAGE. Periodical. German. ir. 72.00. Archiv fur Populare Musik, Ostertorsteinweg 3, 2800 Bremen 1 West Germany. **LC** ML3469. **DD** 786.4205.

ANUARIO INTERAMERICANO DE DE INVESTIGACION MUSICAL. *See* Yearbooks, Almanacs, Directories.

ANUARIO MUSICAL. *See* Yearbooks, Almanacs, Directories.

APC NEWSLETTER : JOURNAL OF THE ASSOCIATION OF PROFESSIONAL COMPOSERS. **VFOAT** A.P.C. Newsletter. Periodical. UK. English. APC Administration, 81A Priory Road, London NW6 3NL England.

ARABESQUE. V. 1- May/June 1975-. 0148-5865. Periodical. US. English. bm. $16.00. Arabesque, 1 Sherman Square #22F, New York NY 10023. **Tel** (212)595-1677. Ed Ibrahim Farrah. **LC** GV1703.N36. adv acc. **Circ** 6,000. Focus on ethnic music and dance, primarily from the Middle and Near East but many articles on Spanish, Indian, and other ethnic forms.

ARCHIV FUR MUSIKWISSENSCHAFT. *See* Genealogy and Heraldry - Archives.

Music

ARCHIV FUR MUSIKWISSENSCHAFT. BEIHEFTE. See Genealogy and Heraldry - Archives.

ARIA. V. 2, No 1- March 1979-. 0709-5694. Periodical. CN. French. qt. $7.74. Aria, 5800 Ave des Chenes, Montreal Province of Quebec H1T 2R2 Canada. Tel (514)254-5132. DD 782.109714. bk rev. adv acc. Circ 4,000. An opera magazine covering all forms of classical vocal concerts, oratorios, recitals, etc. Bulletin, 0709-5716.

ARIZONA MUSIC NEWS. VFOAT AMN. Began in 1957?. 0518-6129. Periodical. US. English. ty. $5.00. Arizona Music News c/o R Teare, 8637 East Hubbell Street, Scottsdale AZ 85257. Tel (602)945-4919. Ed Ronald C Teare. bk rev. adv acc. Circ 1,000. (ctrl). Ideas for innovative school and college music programs; "Think Pieces" on arts, education.

ARMONIA DI VOCI. VFOAT Armonia de Voci Corali. Periodical. Italian. bm. 22.000. Editrice Elle di ci Corso, Francia 214, 10096 Leumann Torino Italy. Tel (011)9591091. LC M1. DD 783.02605. adv acc. Circ 1,200. (ctrl). Musical proposals for Christian communities. Each issue is monographical presenting several items for the choir and the congregation mostly with organ accompaniments.

ARS NOVA. V. 1- 1969-. Periodical. SA. Afrikaans (English). an. 7.00. University of South Africa, PO Box 392, Department of Publisher Services, Pretoria 00001 South Africa. Tel (012)440-1603. Ed B van der Linde. LC ML5. DD 780.5. bk rev. Circ 500. (ctrl). Articles on composers and compositions bibliographical data, contributions from students and musicologists on music.

ARS ORGANI. Issue 1- 1953-. 0004-2919. Periodical. GW. German. qt $12.98. W E Saarbach GMBH, Postfach 101610, D-5000 Koln 1 West Germany. Ind/Abst Music Index, RILM Abstr.

ARTI MUSICES. 1- 1969-. 0587-5455. YU. Serbo-Croatian (Croatian, with summaries in English). sa. $15.00. Institute of Musicology, Music Academy in Zagreb, Gunduliceva 6 Zagreb Yugoslavia. Tel (041)420-277. Ind/Abst Music Index, RILM Abstr. LC ML5. bk rev. adv acc. Sociology of music and aesthetics of music and articles on musicological research in Croatia (Yugoslavia) together with articles on history of music.

DER ARTIST. Began in 1883. Periodical. GW. German. w. in Droste Verlag GMBH, Presse Martin Luther Platz, 4 Duesseldorf 1 West Germany. LC ML5.

ARTSPACE. See The Arts (General) - Art.

ASCAP IN ACTION. Main/Corp American Society of Composers, Authors and Publishers. VAT American Society of Composers, Authors and Publishers in Action. Fall 1979-. 0197-7849. Periodical. US. English. American Society of Composers Authors and Publishers, Building One, Lincoln Plaza, New York NY 10023. Ind/Abst Music Index. LC ML27.U5. DD 338.47780973. ASCAP Today.

ASIAN MUSIC. 1- Winter 1968/69-. 0044-9202. Periodical. US. English (German). sa. $25.00. Society for Asian Music, 50 Washington Square South, New York NY 10012. Tel (212)663-0584. Ed Mark Slobin and Martin Hatch. Ind/Abst MLA Int. Bibliogr. Books Artic. Mod. Lang. Lit., Music Index, RILM Abstr. LC ML1. DD 780.95. bk rev. Circ 500. Scholarly articles on all aspects of the performing arts of Asia.

ASTERISK. (ASTERISK : A JOURNAL OF NEW MUSIC). V. 1- Dec. 1974-. 0097-8116. Periodical. US. English. sa. $6.00. 1215 Kuchnle Avenue, Ann Arbor MI 48103. LC ML1. DD 780.5.

ASUC JOURNAL OF MUSIC SCORES. Main/Corp American Society of University Composers. VFOAT Journal of Music Scores. VAT American Society of University Composers Journal of Music Scores. V. 1-. 0196-1438. Periodical. US. English. ir. $9.50 Per Vol. European American Music Distributors Corporation, 195 Allwood Road, Clifton NJ 07012. LC M1.

AUFSATZE UND JAHRESBERICHT - KARL-MARX-UNIVERSITAT MUSIKINSTRUMENTEN-MUSEUM. Main/Corp Leipzig. Universitat. Musikinstrumenten-Museum. German. ir. 1.00. Musikinstrumenten-Museum der Karl-Marx-Universitat, 701 Leipzig Taubchenweg 2 C, Leipzig East Germany. LC ML5. DD 780.5.

AUSTRALIAN JOURNAL OF MUSIC EDUCATION. Began in 1967. 0004-9484. AT. English. ir. Ind/Abst Music Index. LC ML5. DD 780.7.

AUSTRALIAN MUSIC DIRECTORY. See Yearbooks, Almanacs, Directories.

AUTOHARP. No. 1- Apr. 7, 1961-. 0091-8687. Periodical. US. English. University of Illinois, 361 Lincoln Hall, Urbana IL 61801. LC ML1. DD 784.4005.

THE AUTOHARPOHOLIC. Spring 1980-. 0736-3796. Periodical. US. English. qt. $10.00 Domestic, $12.50 Canada. I.A.D. Publications, PO Box 504, Brisbane CA 94005. LC ML1015.A9. DD 787.8.

AUTOMATIC MUSICAL INSTRUMENTS PRICING GUIDE. 0148-818X. US. English. $20.00. WH Edgerton, Box 88, Darien CT 06820. LC ML155. DD 789.7075.

L'AVANT SCENE OPERA. No. 1-44. Periodical. FR. French. mo. $82.88. L'Avant-Scene, 1 rue Lord-Bryon, 75008 Paris France. Tel 1/ 225 65 20.

AWC NEWS. Main/Corp American Women Composers. 0193-0850. Periodical. US. English. qt. $15.00. American Women Composers Inc, 7315 Hooking Road, McLean VA 22101. Tel (703)821-6769. Ed Helene Dunn Bodman. bk rev. adv acc. Circ 500. Articles about American women composers; lists of scores available through our music library, review of books, records, listing of all activities of AWC, and information about copyrights.

AWC NEWS/FORUM. VFOAT A.W.C. News Forum. Vol. 4, No. 1 & 2 (Feb./May 1983)-. Periodical. US. English. qt. $15.00. American Women Composers Inc, 7315 Hooking Road McLean Station, McLean VA 22101. Tel (703)821-6769. Ed Helene Dunn Bodman. bk rev. adv acc. Circ 500. Coverage of composers (with bios and bibliography/discography), reviews of record books, listing of new music in AWC Music Library, news on competitions, news on AWC chapter programs and activities. AWC News, 0193-0850.

AXES. (AXES : BULLETIN D'INFORMATION DU CENTRE DE RECHERCHE G.I.M. INC) Vol. 1, No. 1-. 0828-7465. Periodical. CN. French. bm. Centre de Recherche G.I.M. Inc, 167 St Louis Local 451, Rimouski Quebec G5L 5R2 Canada. DD 784.5005.

T A B C NEWS. (TABC NEWS). VAT Toronto Area Bluegrass Committee News. 0821-2449. Periodical. CN. English. mo. Toronto Area Bluegrass Committee, 39 MacPherson Avenue, Toronto Ontario M5R 1W7 Canada. DD 784.52.

BACH. V. 1- Winter 1970-. 0005-3600. Periodical. US. English. qt. Ind/Abst Music Index, RILM Abstr. LC ML410.B4. DD 780.924.

BACH-JAHRBUCH. Vol. 1 1904-. 0084-7682. GE. German. an. 16. Evangelische Verlagsanstalt, Krautstrasse 52, 1017 Berlin East Germany. Tel 2 700 521. Ind/Abst RILM Abstr. LC ML410.B1. (cum index). Circ 5,000. Sources and documents enlarging the knowledge of Bach, instructions for acute treatises and issues, expositions promoting the discussion on all subjects of international Bach research.

BAGINA. V. 1- July/Sept. 2030- 1973/74-. Periodical. Nepali. ir. 2.00. Narayan Gopal Narsingh Kyap, Thamel Nepal. LC ML5.

BAM. 0194-5793. Periodical. US. English. sm. $18.00. Bam, 5951 Canning Street, Oakland CA 94609. Tel (415)652-3810. Ed Bill Forman. bk rev. adv acc. Circ 120,000. (ctrl). Interviews with famous rock stars, record reviews, musical instruments, product reviews, coming events and happenings in California.

BAND & FESTIVAL GUIDE. VFOAT Band and Festival Guide. 0735-4711. US. English. an. $8.00. Tri-State Bluegrass Association, Rural Route 1, Kohoka MO 63445. Ed Erma Spray. LC ML19. DD 784.52002573. adv acc. Circ 5,000. (ctrl). Bluegrass band pictures and information. Bluegrass festival listings and information music related businesses and agencies.

BANDMASTERS REPORT. (THE BANDMASTERS REPORT). V. 1- June 1973-. 0092-8019. Periodical. US. English. qt. $5.00. PO Box 33, Folcroft PA 19032. LC ML1. DD 785.1205.

BANJO NEWSLETTER. V. 1- Nov. 1973-. 0190-1559. Periodical. US. English. mo. $16.00. Banjo Newsletter, PO Box 364, Greensboro MD 21639. Tel (301)482-6278. Ed Hub Nitchie. LC ML1. DD 787.705. bk rev. adv acc. Circ 7,500. A monthly magazine devoted to the 5-string banjo in all its musical styles, articles, reviews, history, collecting, repairing.

BANJO SOUNDSHEET. 0748-2728. Periodical. US. English. bm. $30.00. R Sacks, 25-40 31st Avenue Apartment 6H, Long Island City NY 11106. LC ML1015.B3. DD 787.705.

BASLER JAHRBUCH FUR HISTORISCHE MUSIKPRAXIS : EINE VEROFFENTLICHUNG DER SCHOLA CANTORUM BASILIENSIS AN DER MUSIK-AKADEMIE DER STADT BASEL. See Yearbooks, Almanacs, Directories.

BASS PLAYER QUARTERLY. Began with Feb. 1980 issue. 0734-0206. Periodical. US. English. qt. Bass Player Quarterly, 333 Gross Street, Pittsburgh PA 15224. LC ML920.

BBC MUSIC GUIDES. 1-. 0084-8018. Monographic Series. US. English. ir. University of Washington Press, Seattle WA 98105. Ed Gerald Abraham.

B.C. MUSIC EDUCATOR. (THE B. C. MUSIC EDUCATOR). V. 20, No. 2- Oct. 1977-. 0705-9019. Periodical. CN. English. ir. British Columbia Music Educators' Association, 22259 48th Avenue, Langley British Columbia V3A 3A7 Canada. Ind/Abst Can. Educ. Index. DD 780.7. Newsletter, 0382-8182; British Columbia Music Educator, 0007-0564.

BEETHOVEN STUDIES. 1-. 0737-5832. Periodical. US. English. ir. Press Syndicate of the University of Cambridge, 32 East 57th Street, New York NY 10022. Ed A Tyson.

BEITRAGE ZUR JAZZFORSCHUNG. VFOAT Studies in Jazz Research. 1- 1969-. AU. German (or English). International Society for Jazz Research, Leonhardstrake 15, A8010 Graz Austria. LC ML55. DD 785.4208.

BEITRAGE ZUR MITTELRHEINISCHEN MUSIKGESCHICHTE. Number 1-1962-. 0522-6937. Periodical. GW. German. ir. B Schotts Soehne, Postfach 3640, D-6500 Mainz West Germany. Tel 06131/246-0. Ed B Schotts Soehne.

BEITRAGE ZUR MUSIKWISSENSCHAFT. SONDERREIHE : BIBLIOGRAPHIEN. See Bibliographies.

BELL TOWER. (THE BELL TOWER) 0092-8666. Periodical. US. English. ir. American Bell Association, Box 286, Road #1, Natrona Heights PA 15065. Tel (412)296-9623. LC ML1.

BERICHT UBER DIE MUSIKWISSENSCHAFTLICHEN ARBEITEN IN DER DEUTSCHEN DEMOKRATISCHEN REPUBLIK CEASED. GE. German. an. Deutscher Buch Export-Import, Leninstrasse 16, DDR-701 Leipzig East Germany. LC ML5. DD 780.0105.

BIBLIOGRAPHIC GUIDE TO MUSIC. See Bibliographies.

BIBLIOGRAPHIE DE LA FRANCE. SUPPLEMENT 3. MUSIQUE. See Bibliographies.

BIBLIOGRAPHIE DES MUSIKSCHRIFTTUMS. See Bibliographies.

BIBLIOGRAPHIES IN AMERICAN MUSIC. See Bibliographies.

BIBLIOTHECA MUSICA. V. 1- 1972-. in Czech. ir. LC ML113.

BIBLIOTHECA MUSICAE, COLLANA DI CATALOGHI E BIBLIOGRAFIE. V. 1- 1962-. Italian. ir. Each issue contains an index to its own contents - no vol index - loose.

BIG APPLE JAZZ. Winter 1977-. 0147-6645. Periodical. US. English. $2.00 Per Issue. F F O Graphics, 888 7th Avenue, New York NY 10019. LC ML1. DD 785.42097471.

THE BIG BANDS. Nov. 1977-. 0738-7067. Periodical. US. English. mo. $15.00 US, $20.00 Foreign. Studio City Advertising/ Publishing, 4914 Lankershim Boulevard Suite 1, North Hollywood CA 91601.

BIG BEAT. 0302-1254. Periodical. FR. in French. qt. 17.00. Federation des Amateurs de Rock n Roll et de Country n Western, 40 rue de Lesperance, 42100 CCP Lyon 4584 44 France. LC ML5. DD 784.

BIG TIME MUSIC MAGAZINE. (THE BIG TIME MUSIC MAGAZINE). No. 1-. 0825-8422. Periodical. CN. English. qt. $4.00 Per No. Big Time Music Magazine, P O Box 3746, Courtenay B C V9N 7P1 Canada. DD 784.50605.

BILLBOARD. Jan. 5, 1963-. 0006-2510. Periodical. US. English. wk. $148.00. Billboard Publishers Inc, 1515 Broadway, New York NY 10036. Tel (212)764-4559. Ed Adam White. Ind/Abst Trade Ind.

Index, Music Index, Infobank. **LC** PN2000. bk rev. adv acc. **Circ** 48,000. Available on microfilm from KTO Microfilm, or Xerox University Microfilms. *Billboard Music Week.*

BILLBOARD COUNTRY MUSIC SOURCEBOOK. (BILLBOARD. COUNTRY MUSIC SOURCEBOOK). 0273-1428. US. English. an. $17.00. Billboard Publishers Inc, 1515 Broadway, New York NY 10036. **Tel** (212)764-4559. **LC** ML18. **DD** 784.52002573. Information on radio stations, performing artist, booking agents, personal managers, record companies and more. *Billboard's Country Music Source Book.*

BILLBOARD EN ESPANOL. July 1980-. 0731-9460. Periodical. US. Spanish. mo. $65.00. 1515 Broadway, New York NY 10036. **LC** ML3486.5. **DD** 789.91245098.

BILLBOARD INTERNATIONAL BUYER'S GUIDE. VFOAT International Buyer's Guide. 1970/71-. US. English. an. $38.00. Billboard Publishers Inc, 1515 Broadway, New York NY 10036. **Tel** (212)764-4559. adv acc. Listings include name, address, phone number and marketing information of record companies, music publishers, distributors, accessory manufacturers and suppliers. *Billboard . . . International Music-Record-Tape Buyers Guide.*

BILLBOARD INTERNATIONAL TALENT & TOURING DIRECTORY. *See* Yearbooks, Almanacs, Directories.

BILLBOARD'S ON TOUR. VFOAT On Tour. 0361-5383. US. English. $5.00. Billboard Publications, 9000 Sunset Boulevard, Los Angeles CA 90069. **LC** ML18. **DD** 338.477802573.

BING. Periodical. UK. English. qt. $3.00. 7 Greenmeadow Close, Monmouthshire NP4 3NR England. **LC** ML420.C93. **DD** 784.0924.

BIO-BIBLIOGRAPHIES IN MUSIC. VFOAT Biobibliographies in Music. No. 1-. 0742-6968. US. English. ir. Greenwood Press, 88 Post Road West/PO Box 5007, Westport CT 06881. **DD** 016.

BIOS JOURNAL. VFOAT B.I.O.S. Journal. Vol. 1 (1977)-. 0005-3155. UK. English. an. 18.00. Positif Press, 130 Southfield Road, Oxford OX4 1PA England. **Tel** (0865)243220. **LC** ML549.8. **DD** 786.505. bk rev. adv acc. **Circ** 700. Scholarly articles on historic and new organs, composers, organbuilders, tuning and temperament.

BLACK MUSIC & JAZZ REVIEW (LONDON, ENGLAND). (BLACK MUSIC & JAZZ REVIEW : BM). **VFOAT** Black Music and Jazz Review. V. 3, Issue 11 (Mar. 1981)-. Periodical. UK. English. mo. $52.00. Napfield Ltd, 153 Praed St, London W2 England. **LC** ML3469. **DD** 781.7296. *Black Music and Jazz Review.*

BLACK MUSIC RESEARCH JOURNAL. VFOAT B.M.R. Journal. 1980-. 0276-3605. Periodical. US. English. an. $6.00. Center Black Music Research, 600 South Michigan Avenue/ Columbia College, Chicago IL 60605. **Tel** (312)663-9462. **Ed** Samuel A Floyd Jr. **Ind/Abst** Jazz Index. **LC** ML3556. **DD** 781.729607305. adv acc. **Circ** 150. Articles devoted to philosophy, aesthetics and criticism of black music research.

BLACK MUSIC RESEARCH NEWSLETTER. VFOAT BMR Newsletter. V. 1- Summer 1977-. 0271-3799. Periodical. US. English. sa. $2.00. Center Black Music Research, 600 South Michigan Avenue/ Columbia College, Chicago IL 60605. **Tel** (312)663-9462. **Ed** Samuel A Floyd, Jr. **Circ** 150. Communications among scholars in the field of black music research and in other disciplines.

BLACK PERSPECTIVE IN MUSIC. (THE BLACK PERSPECTIVE IN MUSIC). V. 1- Spring 1973-. 0090-7790. Periodical. US. English. sa. $16.00. Foundation for Research in the Afro-American Creative Arts, PO Drawer I, Cambia Heights NY 11411. **Ed** Eileen Southern. **Ind/Abst** Jazz Index, Music Index, RILM Abstr. **LC** ML3556. **DD** 781.7296. (cum index). bk rev. **Circ** 1,000. (ctrl). This scholarly journal focuses on the history of black music, current events, bibliography and discography.

BLACK WAX MAGAZINE. Periodical. UK. English. mo. 15/1/75. Flat 3 108 Greyhound Lane, SW16 London England. **LC** ML5. **DD** 784.

DIE BLASMUSIK. Began publication in 1950. 0344-8231. Periodical. German. ir. **LC** ML5. **DD** 788.005.

BLGARSKA MUZIKA. (BULGARSKA MUZIKA). Began publication in 1953. 0323-9314. Periodical. Bulgarian. ir. $24.00. Hemus, 6 Boulevard Rusky, Sofia Bulgaria. **Ind/Abst** Music Index, RILM Abstr. *Muzika (Sofia, Bulgaria).*

BLOCK. No. 1- Mar./April 1975-. Periodical. Dutch. ir. 7.50. Persbureau Bossa Nova, Postbus 244, 7600 Ae Almeo Netherlands. **Ind/Abst** Jazz Index. **LC** ML5. **DD** 784.

BLOSSOM MUSIC CENTER. (BLOSSOM MUSIC CENTER : FESTIVAL BOOK). 0748-6294. US. English. an. Blossom Music Center, 1145 West Steels Corners Road, Cuyahoga Falls OH 44223.

BLUEGRASS. 0149-919X. US. English. $15.00. Bluegrass Unlimited Inc, Box 111, Broad Run VA 22014. **Tel** (703)361-8992. **Ed** Peter V Kuykendall. **LC** ML1. **DD** 784. bk rev. adv acc. **Circ** 19,000. (ctrl). A magazine serving the bluegrass, old-time and traditional country music community. Includes monthly appearance calendar, annual artist directory and annual festival calendar. Also includes news and personality profiles.

THE BLUEGRASS DIRECTORY. *See* Yearbooks, Almanacs, Directories.

BLUEGRASS MUSIC NEWS. 1950. 0199-8625. Periodical. US. English. ir. $8.00. Bluegrass Music News, Box 353 Route 5, Russellville KY 42276. **Tel** (502)726-6427. **Ed** Hazel O Carver. bk rev. adv acc. **Circ** 2,000. Official magazine for the Kentucky Music Educators Association. Articles, news items dealing with all areas of school music at Kentucky University. Includes mucic education trade items.

BLUEGRASS REFLECTIONS. 0361-5774. Periodical. US. English. mo. $1.00 Per Issue. Southwest Bluegrass Club, 2704 Haley Avenue, Ft Worth TX 76117. **LC** ML1. **DD** 784.

THE BLUEGRASS STAR. Periodical. US. English. mo. $5.00. 1206 Bell Grimes Lane, Nashville TN 37207. **LC** ML1. **DD** 780.42.

BLUEGRASS UNLIMITED. V. 1- July 1966-. 0006-5137. Periodical. US. English. mo. $15.00. Bluegrass Unlimited, Box 111, Broad Run VA 22014. **Tel** (703)361-8992. **Ed** Peter V Kuykendall. **Ind/Abst** Music Index, MLA Int. Bibliogr. Books Artic. Mod. Lang. Lit. **LC** ML1. **DD** 784. bk rev. adv acc. **Circ** 18,172. (ctrl). The original publication serving the bluegrass and old time country music community. Festival listings, artist profiles, questions, answers, songbook, letters, personal appearance listings, rare photos.

BLUES. V. 1- Feb. 1970-. Periodical. BE. in French. ir. $3.00. 39 rue Chambery, 1040 Bruxelles Belgium. **LC** ML5. **DD** 784.

BLUES & SOUL. VFOAT Blues and Soul. No. 412 (July 31-Aug. 13, 1984)-. Periodical. UK. English. bw. 22.90. Napfield Ltd, 153 Praed Street, London W2 England. **Tel** 723-1362. **Ed** Bob Kilbourn. adv acc. **Circ** 42,000. Covers news, reviews, and charts of the soul music scene. *Black Music & Jazz Review (London, England).*

BLUES AND SWING MAGAZINE. No. 1- 1971-. Periodical. French. ir. $5.00. Parc Ste Anne 10 42 Bd de la Fabrique, 13009 Marseille France. **LC** ML5. **DD** 784.

BLUES LIFE. 78/1-. 0250-4421. Periodical. in German. qt. $15.00. c/o F & F Svacina, Kegelgasse 40, A1030 Vienna Austria. **Tel** (0222)723765. **Ed** Fritz Svacina. **Ind/Abst** Jazz Index. **LC** ML3521. **DD** 784.53005. bk rev. adv acc. **Circ** 2,000. Covers articles, reviews, discographies, photos, instruments, and videos on blues and related music.

BLUES-LINK. (BLUES LINK). No. 1- Aug./Sept. 1973-. 0307-7241. Periodical. UK. English. bm. 1.50. 94 Puller Road, Herts EN5 4HD UK England. **LC** ML5. **DD** 784.

BLUES MAGAZINE *CEASED*. V. 1-5, No. 2. 0702-911X. Periodical. CN. English. bm. $5.00. Blues Magazine, PO Box 585 Station P, Toronto Ontario M5S 2T1 Canada. **LC** ML5. **DD** 784.

BLUES NOTES. V. 1- Sept. 1969-. Periodical. AU. in German. ir. 50.00. Bischofstrasse 9, A-4020 Linz Austria. **LC** ML5. **DD** 784.

BLUES UNLIMITED. No. 1- 1963-. 0006-5153. Periodical. UK. English. qt. $14.00. Blues Unlimited, 36 Belmont Park Lewisham, London SE13 5DB England. **Ed** B W Turner and M J Rowe. **Ind/Abst** MLA Int. Bibliogr. Books Artic. Mod. Lang. Lit., Jazz Index. **LC** ML5. bk rev. adv acc. **Circ** 4,500. Articles, reviews, and photographs on all areas of black American blues.

BMG. BANJO, MANDOLIN, GUITAR. (BMG : BANJO, MANDOLIN, GUITAR). **VFOAT** Banjo, Mandolin, Guitar. Nov. 1973-. 0005-321X. Periodical. UK. English. mo. $7.50. D K Keogh, 20 Earlham Street, London WC2H 9LR England. **LC** ML5. **DD** 787.6105. *Guitarist.*

BMI ORCHESTRAL PROGRAM SURVEY. Main/Corp Broadcast Music, Inc. **VFOAT** Orchestral Program Survey. **VAT** Broadcast Music Incorporated Orchestral Program Survey. 0521-9604. US. English. ir. Broadcast Music Inc, 40 West 57th Street, New York NY 10019. **LC** ML1. **DD** 785.06610973.

BN. VFOAT Blues News. Periodical. FI. Finnish. ir. 95.-. Finnish Blues Society RY, Pl 257, 00531 Helsinki 53 Finland. **Tel** 90-760755. **Ed** Pertti Nurmi. **LC** ML3556. **DD** 781.7296073. bk rev. adv acc. **Circ** 1,400. Covers blues, rhythm and blues, soul, rock and roll (old), funk, gospel, dooop, reggae, etc.

BOLETIM INFORMATIVO. Main/Corp Liga dos Amigos do Canto Gregoriano. PO. Portuguese. ir. Campo dos Martires DA, Datria 96, 2 Lisboa Portugal. **LC** ML28.L63. **DD** 783.505.

BOLETIN DE MUSICA Y DANZA. No. 1- April 1978-. Periodical. Spanish. ir. Jr Ancash 390, Lima 1 Peru.

BOLLETINO DEL CENTRO ROSSINIANO DI STUDI. 1955-. 0411-5384. Periodical. IT. Italian. qt. $14.85. Fondazione G Rossini, Piazza Olivieri 5, 61100 Pesaro Italy. **Tel** 0721 30053. **LC** ML5.

BOOMBAH HERALD. Vol. 1, No. 1 (Dec. 1973)-. 8755-5832. Periodical. US. English. sa. $6.00. Loren D Geiger, 15 Park Boulevard, Lancaster NY 14086. **Ed** Loren D Geiger. **DD** 785. bk rev. adv acc. **Circ** 100. Articles on concert and marching band music, biographical sketches of composers, music for band or solo instrument included in each issue.

BORGO. (LE BORGO). No. 1 (June 1979)-. 0712-645X. Periodical. CN. French. ir. Alliance Chorale Nouveau-Brunswick, 236 rue St Georges, Moncton New Brunswick E1C 1W1 Canada. **DD** 784.10060715.

THE BOSTON ORGAN CLUB NEWSLETTER. (BOSTON ORGAN CLUB NEWSLETTER). 0524-1170. Periodical. US. English. ir. $5.00. Boston Organ Club, PO Box 104, Harrisville NH 03450. **Tel** (603)827-3055. bk rev. **Circ** 200. Musical and historical study of pipe organ building, especially in New England.

BRAILLE SCORES CATALOG. INSTRUMENTAL. (BRAILLE SCORES CATALOG—INSTRUMENTAL). **Main/Corp** Library of Congress. National Library Service for the Blind and Physically Handicapped. **Series/Titl** Music & Musicians. 0145-3165. US. English. Music Section/ National Library Service for the Blind and Physically Handicapped, Library of Congress, Washington DC 20542. **LC** ML136.U52. **DD** 016.7808. Available also in Braille.

BRASS BULLETIN. No 1- Oct. 1971-. 0303-3848. SZ. English, French and German. qt. $20.00. Brass Bulletin, rue du Moleson 14, CH-1630 Bulle Switzerland. **Tel** (0041)29-24422. **Ed** Jean-Pierre Mathez. **Ind/Abst** Music Index. **LC** ML5. **DD** 788.0104. bk rev. adv acc. **Circ** 5,000. International magazine for brass players with articles (history, inquiries, techniques, biographies), illustrations, correspondence, new publications with reviews (scores, records, books, instruments etc.) Promotes international contacts in 80 countries.

BRASS RESEARCH SERIES. 0363-454X. Monographic Series. US. English. 136 Eighth Avenue North, Nashville TN 37203-3798. **Tel** (615)254-8969. **Ed** Stephen L Glover. **LC** UNC. **Circ** 700. Historical and bibliographical texts about the trumpet, horn, trombone, and tuba.

BREAK-THROUGH (HARTNEY, MAN.). (BREAK-THROUGH). Issue 1 (Oct./Nov. 83)-. 0824-6653. Periodical. CN. English. bm. 3.00. Break-Through, P O Box 160, Hartney Man R0M 0X0 Canada. **DD** 784.0924.

BRIO. V. 1- Spring 1964-. 0007-0173. Periodical. UK. English. sa. International Association of Music Libraries, Sutton Coldfield Music Library, Lower Parade, Sutton Coldfield, Birmingham B72 1XX

England. **Tel** 021 472 1301. **Ed** Ian Ledsham. **Ind/Abst** Music Index, Libr. Inf. Sci. Abstr., RILM Abstr. bk rev. adv acc. **Circ** 400. Journal of the United Kingdom branch of the International Association of Music libraries, archives and documentation centres.

BRISTOL FOLK NEWS. **VFOAT** Folk News. Periodical. UK. English. John Maher, Shambee Claremont Avenue/Bishopston 7, Bristol England. **LC** ML5. **DD** 781.70942.

BRITISH BANDSMAN. Began 1899. Periodical. UK. English. wk. 18.75. British Bandsman Ltd, The Old House-London End, Beaconsfield Bucks England. **Tel** 049 46 4411. **Ed** Peter Wilson. bk rev. adv acc. News and views of the world of bands. *British Musician.*

THE BRITISH CATALOGUE OF MUSIC. Jan./Mar. 1957-. 0068-1407. UK. English. ir. 44.45. British Library, Bibliographic Services Division, 2 Sheraton Street, London W1V 4BH England. **Tel** 01-636 1544. **LC** ML120.G7. **DD** 781.971.

BRITISH COUNTRY MUSIC ASSOCIATION YEARBOOK. *See* Yearbooks, Almanacs, Directories.

BRITISH JOURNAL OF MUSIC THERAPY. **VFOAT** BJMT. V. 1- Autumn 1968-. 0308-244X. Periodical. UK. English. ty. 16.00. British Society for Music Therapy, 69 Avondale Avenue, East Barnet Herts EN4 8NB England. **Tel** (01)368-8879. **Ed** Margaret Campbell. **LC** ML5. **DD** 615.83705. **NLM** W1 BR58. bk rev. **Circ** 400. (ctrl). Articles on all aspects of music therapy and activities of the British Society for Music Therapy.

BRITISH MUSIC SOCIETY JOURNAL. **VFOAT** Journal of the British Music Society. Periodical. UK. English. **LC** ML5. **DD** 781.74105.

BROADSIDE. No. 1- 1962-. 0740-7955. Periodical. US. English. mo. $25.00. Broadside Ltd, PO Box 1464, New York NY 10023. **Tel** (212)873-2100. **Ed** Jeff Ritter. **DD** 784. bk rev. adv acc. **Circ** 1,000. Current topical folksongs with words and music by today's most important writers and performers such as Pete Seeger, Arlo Guthrie, Tom Paxton, and Holly Near. Topics include, Mideast, nuclear energy and Central America.

THE BRUSSELS MUSEUM OF MUSICAL INSTRUMENTS BULLETIN. **Main/Corp** Musee Royal Instrumental de Musique a Bruxelles. V. 1- 1971-. Periodical. NE. Dutch, English, French, German, Russia, or Spanish. ir. Fritz Knuf Publishers, PO Box 20, 2707 Buren Netherlands. **Ind/Abst** Music Index, RILM Abstr. **LC** ML459. **DD** 781.9105. Describes different instruments written by different authors.

BUDDY. 0192-9097. Periodical. US. English. mo. Buddy Inc, 501 N Good Latimer Expressway, Dallas TX 75204. **Tel** (214)826-8742.

BULGARSKO MUZIKOZNANIE. Began in 1971. Periodical. BU. Bulgarian (summaries in English and French). ir. $39.00. IZD-VO na Bulgarskata Akademiia na Naukite, UL Dimitur Polianov 21, 1504 Sofia Bulgaria. **Ind/Abst** MLA Int. Bibliogr. Books Artic. Mod. Lang. Lit. **LC** ML5.

BULGARSKO MUZIKOZNANIE (SOFIA , BULGARIA : 1979). (BULGARSKO MUZIKOZNANIE). Began in 1979. 0204-823X. Periodical. BU. Bulgarian. ir. 2.00. Izd-Vo Na Bulgarskata Akademiia na Naukite, Institut za Muzikoznanie, Ul Dimitur Poliznov 21, 1504 Sofiia Bulgaria. **LC** ML5. *Muzikoznanie.*

BULGARSKOTO MUZIKALNO IZPULNITELSTVO PO SVETA. 1976-. Bulgarian. ir. **LC** ML5.

BULLETIN - CANADIAN FOLK MUSIC SOCIETY. (BULLETIN). **Main/Corp** Societe Canadienne de Musique Folklorique. Vol. 15, No. 1 (Spring 1981)-. 0820-0742. Periodical. CN. French (English). qt. Societe Canadienne de Musique Folklorique, 809 Chemin Woodland, Vancouver British Columbia V5L 3R5 Canada. **DD** 781.706071.

BULLETIN - CENTRE D'ETUDES DE MUSIQUE ORIENTALE. **Main/Corp** Centre d'Etudes de Musique Orientale. Began with Dec. 1967 issue. FR. French. ir. 30.00. Centre d'Etudes de Musique Orientale, CCP 14.856-78, Paris France. **LC** ML5 B .C273.

BULLETIN - DOLMETSCH FOUNDATION, HASLEMERE, ENGLAND. **Main/Corp** Dolmetsch Foundation, Haslemere, England. No. 1- April 1962-. 0419-618X. Periodical. UK. English. sa. 10.60. Dolmetsch Foundation, Derwen Star Hill Churt, Surrey GU10 2HS England. **Tel** 0428-713410. **Ed** S Godwin. **Ind/Abst** Music Index. bk rev. adv acc. **Circ** 750. (ctrl). Development of early instruments, music and dance, methods of playing, musicology and manuscripts.

BULLETIN - GERMANY (EAST). MUSIKRAT. **Main/Corp** Germany (East). Musikrat. Began with: Vol. 1, in 1964. 0433-678X. Periodical. German. ir. Leipziger Strasse 26, 108 Berlin West Germany.

BULLETIN - HOT CLUB DE FRANCE. **Main/Corp** Hot Club de France. Began in 1950. Periodical. French. ir. 32. Hot Club de France, CCP: Toulouse 390-45, Montauban France. **Ind/Abst** Jazz Index. **LC** ML5. **DD** 789.913654205.

BULLETIN - KODALY MUSICAL TRAINING INSTITUTE INC. (BULLETIN). **Main/Corp** Kodaly Musical Training Institute. 0094-3258. US. English. Kadaly Musical Training Institute, 525 Worcester Street, Wellesley MA 02181. **LC** MT4.W365. **DD** 780.7297447.

BULLETIN (MIDWEST KODALY MUSIC EDUCATORS OF AMERICA). (BULLETIN). **VFOAT** M.K.M.E.A. Bulletin. Vol. 10, No. 1 (Sept. 1981)-. Periodical. US. English. qt. $7.50 Membership. Lynee Ransom, MKMEA Editor, Department of Music, Iowa State University, Ames IA 50011. **LC** MT1. **DD** 780.72977. *Official Magazine (Midwest Kodaly Music Educators of America).*

BULLETIN - MORAVIAN MUSIC FOUNDATION *CEASED.* (BULLETIN - THE MORAVIAN MUSIC FOUNDATION). **Main/Corp** Moravian Music Foundation. **VFOAT** Moravian Music Foundation Bulletin. V. 9-25. 0027-1020. Periodical. US. English. sa. Drawer Z Salem Station, Winston-Salem NC 27108. **LC** ML1. **DD** 780.5. *News Bulletin of the Moravian Music Foundation, 0545-0322.*

BULLETIN - NATIONAL MUSIC COUNCIL *CEASED.* **Main/Corp** National Music Council. V. 1-39, No. 2. 0027-9749. Periodical. US. English. sa. National Music Council, 250 West 57th Street/Suite 626, New York NY 10019. **Ind/Abst** Music Index. **LC** ML27.U5. **DD** 780.6273.

BULLETIN - NATIONAL SHEVCHENKO MUSICAL ENSEMBLE GUILD OF CANADA. **Main/Corp** National Shevchenko Musical Ensemble Guild of Canada. No. 2- Nov. 1972-. 0703-9999. Periodical. CN. English. ir. Free. National Shevchenko Musical Ensemble Guild of Canada, 626 Bathurst Street, Toronto Ontario M5S 2R1 Canada. **DD** 785.06271. (ctrl). *Shevchenko Ensemble Bulletin, 0703-9980.*

THE BULLETIN OF HISTORICAL RESEARCH IN MUSIC EDUCATION. 0739-5639. Periodical. US. English. sa. $10.00. University of Kansas, Department of Art and Music Education and Music Therapy, 311 Bailey Hall, Lawrence KS 66045.

BULLETIN OF RESEARCH IN MUSIC EDUCATION. **VFOAT** PMEA Bulletin of Research in Music Education. Periodical. US. English. ir. Indiana University of Pennsylvania, Cogswell Hall, Dr Calvin Weber, Indiana PA 15701. **LC** ML1. **DD** 780.7.

BULLETIN OF THE COUNCIL FOR RESEARH IN MUSIC EDUCATION. (BULLETIN - COUNCIL FOR RESEARCH IN MUSIC EDUCATION). **Main/Corp** Council for Research in Music Education. **VFOAT** Bulletin of the Council for Research in Music Education. 0010-9894. Periodical. US. English. qt. $15.00. University of Illinois, 2136 Music Building, 1114 West Nevada, Urbana IL 61801. **Tel** (217)333-1027. **Ed** Richard Colwell. **Ind/Abst** Music Index, RILM Abstr., Educ. Index, Psychol. Abstr. **LC** UNC. **DD** 780. bk rev. The bulletin of the council for research publishes research-related articles of interest to music educators and critiques of research studies in the field of music education.

BULLETIN OF THE INTERNATIONAL COUNCIL FOR TRADITIONAL MUSIC. **Main/Corp** International Council for Traditional Music. No. 59 (Oct. 1981)-. 0739-1390. Periodical. US. English. sa. Free. Columbia University, Department of Music, New York NY 10027. **Tel** (212)678-0332. **Ed** Dieter Christensen. **LC** ML26. **DD** 781.70601. **Circ** 1,100. Reports from national committees and liaison office of ICTM about events related to music and dance in their respective country.

BULLETIN - SVENSKT MUSIKHISTORISKT ARKIV. **Main/Corp** Svenskt Musikhistoriskt Arkiv. No. 1- 1966-. 0586-0709. Swedish. ir. **Ind/Abst** RILM Abstr.

CADENCE. **VFOAT** Cadence Magazine. Began with Jan. 1976 issue. 0162-6973. Periodical. US. English. mo. $25.00. Cadence Jazz & Blues Review, Route 1 Box 345, Redwood NY 13679. **Tel** (315)287-2852. **Ed** Robert Rusch. **Ind/Abst** Jazz Index, Music Index. **LC** ML3505.8. **DD** 781.5705. bk rev. adv acc. The most complete coverage of the worldwide jazz and blues scene of any magazine. Thousands of reviews plus interviews, oral histories, news, etc.

CADENZA. 1942-. 0007-9405. Periodical. US. English. ty. $5.00 Domestic, $10.00 Foreign. Joseph A Mussulman, Thayer Road, Mill Creek, Lolo MT 59847. **Tel** (406)273-2112. **Ed** Joseph A Mussulman. adv acc. **Circ** 1,000. (ctrl). Montana Music Educatiors Association Newsletter.

CADENZA. Opus 12, No. 2 (Jan. 1977)-. 0703-8380. Periodical. CN. English. ir. $15.00 Membership. B Nicholls, 208-4313 Rae Street, Regina Saskatchewan S4S 3A6 Canada. **Ind/Abst** Can. Educ. Index. **DD** 780.705. *Journal, 0317-5073; Newsletter, 0381-9051.*

CADERNO DE MUSICA. No. 1 (Sept. 1980)-. Periodical. Portuguese. ir. $700 (6 issues). Federacao Paulista de Conjuntos Corais, Rua Domingos de Morias 2452, 04036 Sao Paulo SP Brazil. **LC** ML1499. **DD** 784.100981.

CAHIERS CANADIENS DE MUSIQUE. (LES CAHIERS CANADIENS DE MUSIQUE). **VFOAT** Canada Music Book. 1- Spring/Summer 1970-. 0007-9634. Periodical. CN. English (French). sa. Canadian Music Council, c/o Periodica, 7045 Avenue du Parc, Montreal Quebec H3N 1X8 Canada. **Ind/Abst** Music Index, RILM Abstr. **LC** ML5. **DD** 780.971.

CAHIERS DEBUSSY. No. 1-3, 1974-76. 0395-1200. FR. French. ir. Centre de Documentation Claude Debussy, 11 rue d'Alsace, Saint-Germain-En-Laye France. **Ind/Abst** RILM Abstr. **LC** ML410.D28. **DD** 780.924, B.

CAHIERS D'INFORMATION SUR LA RECHERCHE EN EDUCATION MUSICALE. No. 1 (Sept. 1982)-. 0821-5456. Periodical. CN. French. ir. $3.00 Per Number. Ecole de Musique, Universite Laval, Quebec Quebec G1K 7P4 Canada. **DD** 780.7.

CAHIRS DE L'ARMUQ. (LES CAHIERS DE L'ARMUQ). **VFOAT** Cahier. **VAT** Cahiers de l'Association pour l'Avancement de la Recherche en Musique du Quebec. No. 1, (April 1983)-. 0821-1817. Periodical. CN. French. ir. ARMUQ, C P 695 Tour de la Bourse, Montreal Quebec H4Z 1J9 Canada. **DD** 781.7714072.

CALGARY FOLK CLUB. (CALGARY FOLK CLUB : BROCHURE). 0821-2791. CN. English. an. **DD** 781.706071233.

CALYPSO. Periodical. English. ir. $2.75. Unique Services, 17 Cassia Avenue, Pleasantville Trinidad. **LC** ML5. **DD** 784.7696072983.

CANADIAN BLUEGRASS REVIEW. V. 1- May 1978-. 0706-7623. Periodical. CN. English. bm. $8.51. Canadian Bluegrass Review, PO Box 143, Waterdown Ontario L0R 2H0 Canada. **Tel** (416)689-5861. **Ed** Pat Buttenham. **LC** ML3519. **DD** 784.5200971. bk rev. adv acc. **Circ** 1,800. (ctrl). Dedicated to the promotion of bluegrass and old-time country music in Canada.

THE CANADIAN COMPOSER. **VFOAT** Le Compositeur Canadien. No. 1- May 1965-. 0008-3259. Periodical. CN. English (French). mo. Canadian Composer, 1407 Yonge Street/Suite 501, Toronto Ontario M4T 1Y7 Canada. **Ind/Abst** Mag. Index, Can. Period. Index, Music Index, Point Repere, RILM Abstr. **DD** 780.971. Available on microfiche from Micromedia Limited Available also on microfilm: Canadian Composer, Toronto, Micromedia, 1976-.

CANADIAN FOLK MUSIC BULLETIN. **VFOAT** Bulletin de Musique Folklorique Canadienne. Vol. 16, No. 2 (April 1982)-. Periodical. CN. English (French). qt. 20.00. Canadian Folk Music Society, Box 4232 Station C, Calgary Alberta T2T 5N1 Canada. **Tel** (403)244-2804. **Ed** T B Rogers. **LC** ML3563. **DD** 781.77105. bk rev. adv acc. **Circ** 1,000. (ctrl). Articles, features, songs, news, and reviews on the subject of Canadian folk music. *Bulletin, 0820-0742.*

CANADIAN FOLK MUSIC JOURNAL. V. 1- 1973-. 0318-2568. CN. English (French). an. $10.00 or free to members. E Fowke, 5 Notley Place, Toronto Ontario M4B 2M7 Canada. **Tel** (403)244-2804. **Ind/Abst** MLA Int. Bibliogr. Books Artic. Mod. Lang. Lit., Music Index. **LC** ML5. **DD** 781.771.

CANADIAN MUSIC EDUCATOR. (THE CANADIAN MUSIC EDUCATOR). V. 1- June 1959-. 0008-4549. Periodical. CN. English. qt. Canadian

Music

Music Educators' Association, 34 Cameron Street, St Catherines Ontario L2P 3E2 Canada. **Ind/Abst** Can. Educ. Index.

CANADIAN MUSIC INDUSTRY DIRECTORY. See Yearbooks, Almanacs, Directories.

CANADIAN MUSIC THERAPY JOURNAL. V. 1, No. 3- Dec. 1973-. 0319-6283. Periodical. CN. English. sa. $1. Oxford Mental Health Centre, PO Box 310, Woodstock Ontario N4S 7X9 Canada. **DD** 615.83705. Canadian Music Therapy Bulletin, 0319-6275.

CANADIAN MUSICIAN. Began with Vol. 1, No. 1 (March/April 1979). 0708-9635. Periodical. CN. English. bm. $22.44. Canadian Musician, 832 Mount Pleasant Road, Toronto Ont M4P 2L3 Canada. **Tel** (416)485-8284. **Ed** Ted Burles. **Ind/Abst** Jazz Index, Music Index. **LC** ML3848. **DD** 780.5. bk rev. adv acc. Exposure of Canadian music-to aid in the development of Canadian music and Canadian music trade.

CANADIAN OPERA COMPANY. See Yearbooks, Almanacs, Directories.

CANADIAN RECORD CATALOGUE. 1-. 0714-8070. CN. English (French). ir. $203.79. CIRPA ADISQ Foundation, Suite 300/144 Front Street West, Toronto Ontario M5J 2L7 Canada. **Tel** (416)593-4545. **DD** 016.7899120971. Available in microform.

CANADIAN UNIVERSITY MUSIC REVIEW. VFOAT Revue de Musique des Universites Canadiennes. 1 (1980)-. 0710-0353. Periodical. CN. English (French). an. 15. Carleton University, Alan Gillmor, Department of Music, Ottawa Ontario K1S 5B6 Canada. **Tel** (613)564-3633. **Ed** Alan Gillmor. **Ind/Abst** Music Index. **LC** ML5. **DD** 780.5. bk rev. **Circ** 400. Juried collection of scholarly articles covering all aspects of music education, historical, performance, sociological and theoretical. Journal (Canadian Association of University Schools of Music), 0315-3541.

CANTIO SACRA. 1955-. Monographic Series. German. ir.

CARAS NEWS. VAT Canadian Academy of Recording Arts and Sciences News. July 1979-. 0712-6255. Periodical. CN. English. bm. Free to CARAS Members. CARAS News, Canadian Academy of Recording Arts and Sciences, 89 Bloor Street East, Toronto Ontario M4W 1A9 Canada. **DD** 789.912079. (ctrl). Canadian Academy of Recording Arts and Sciences (Newsletter), 0712-6347.

CARILLON NEWS. (CARILLON NEWS : NEWSLETTER OF THE GUILD OF CARILLONNEURS IN NORTH AMERICA). 0730-5001. Periodical. US. English. sa. The Guild of Carillonneurs in North America, 3115 Ocean Drive, Corpus Christi TX 78404. **LC** ML1039. **DD** 789.505.

CARNET MUSICAL. No. 1- June 1971-. 0315-3916. Periodical. CN. French. qt. $3.00. Ensemble Claude Gervaise, CP 91, Chambly Quebec Canada. **Ind/Abst** Music Index. **LC** ML5. **DD** 780.5. (cum index).

LA CARTELLINA. No. 1-. Italian. ir. **LC** ML5.

CASH BOX. See Sound Recordings and Systems.

CASSETTES & CARTRIDGES CEASED. No. 1- April 1973-. Periodical. UK. English. mo. $9.00. 177-179 Kenton Road, Harrow Middlexes HA3 0HA England. **LC** ML5. **DD** 384.

CATALOG OF PUBLICATIONS - THE JAPAN FEDERATION OF COMPOSERS. **Main/Corp** Nihon Sakkyokuka Kyogikai. 1970/71-. English and Japanese. ir. c/o Ominato Building, 14 Sufacho, Shinjuku-ku, 160 Tokyo Japan. **LC** ML120.J3.

CATALOGUE DISQUES. **Main/Corp** Centre Regional de Documentation Pedagogique de Besancon. FR. French. ir. CRDP, 16-17 rue Ernest Renan, Besancon France. **LC** ML156.2. **DD** 016.789912.

CATALOGUE OF PRINTED MUSIC IN THE BRITISH LIBRARY : ACCESSIONS. **Main/Corp** British Library. UK. English. **LC** ML136.L8. **DD** 016.78.

CATALOGUS MUSICUS. Vol. 1-. 0069-116X. Monographic Series. GW. German. ir. Baerenreiter Music Corporation, 224 King Street, Englewood NJ 07631. **Tel** 561-30011. **LC** ML113. An irregularly appearing series of important music bibliographies. Catalogues and inventories of the sixteenth century.

CAYO PUBLICATION. **Main/Corp** Canadian Association of Youth Orchestras. VFOAT Publication AOJC. VAT Canadian Assocaition of Youth Orchestras Publication, Publication Association des Orchestres de Jeunes du Canada. 0712-3272. Periodical. CN. English (includes some text in French). ty. Canadian Association of Youth Orchestras, Box 1020, Banff Alberta T0L 0C0 Canada. **DD** 78506271. C A Y O News and Views, 0709-6739.

CBC CLASSICAL CATALOGUE. (CBC CLASSICAL RECORD CATALOGUE). **Main/Corp** Canadian Broadcasting Corporation. Merchandising. VAT Canadian Broadcasting Corporation Classical Record Catalogue. 0713-1283. CN. English (includes some text in French). an. Free. Canadian Broadcasting Corporation, Box 500, Terminal A, Toronto 1 Ontario Canada. **DD** 016.789912. (ctrl).

CBC CLASSICAL RECORD REFERENCE BOOK. (THE WORLD'S LARGEST PUBLIC BROADCASTING SERVICE PRESENTS THE . . . CBC CLASSICAL RECORD REFERENCE BOOK). **Main/Corp** Canadian Broadcasting Corporation. VAT Manuel de Reference de Disques Classiques, Canadian Broadcasting Corporation Classical Record Reference Book. Premiere Ed. (1980/81)-. 0711-9828. CN. English (French). an. **DD** 016.789912.

CBC JAZZ AND POPULAR RECORD CATALOGUE. **Main/Corp** Canadian Broadcasting Corporation. Merchandising. VAT Canadian Broadcasting Corporation Jazz and Popular Record Catalogue. 0713-1291. CN. English (includes some text in French). an. Free. Canadian Broadcasting Corporation, Box 500, Terminal A, Toronto 1 Ontario Canada. **DD** 016.789912. (ctrl).

CBDA JOURNAL. (C B D A JOURNAL). **Main/Corp** Canadian Band Directors' Association. VAT Canadian Band Directors' Association Journal. V. 1- Sept. 1976-. 0703-9077. Periodical. CN. English. qt. K Mann, PO Box 75, Penhold Alberta Canada. **DD** 785.06710971.

C.B.M.S. NEWSLETTER. (CBMS NEWSLETTER). **Main/Corp** Colorado Bluegrass Music Society. VAT Colorado Bluegrass Music Society Newsletter. No. 1- Sept. 1972-. 0092-5063. Periodical. US. English. mo. $5.00. Colorado Bluegrass Music Society, 2307 Spruce Street, Boulder CO 80302. **LC** M127.U5. **DD** 780.42.

CBS MAIN ALPHABETICAL & NUMERICAL CATALOGUE. **Main/Corp** Columbia Broadcasting System, Inc. CBS Records Division. VFOAT CBS Catalogue. VAT Columbia Broadcasting System Main Alphabetical & Numerical Catalogue. UK. English. $10.00. CBS Records, 28 Theobalds Road, London WCLX 8PB England. **LC** ML156. **DD** 016.789912.

CENTRAL OPERA SERVICE BULLETIN. VFOAT Bulletin. Began in 1959. 0008-9508. Periodical. US. English. qt. $15.00 Domestic, $25.00 Foreign. Central Opera Service, Metropolitan Opera Lincoln Center, New York NY 10023. **Tel** (212)957-9871. **Ed** Maria F Rich. **Ind/Abst** Music Index. **LC** ML27.U5. **DD** 782.105. bk rev. **Circ** 2,000. All aspects of opera and music theater, current performances, available sets, translations, competitions, conferences, support new auditoriums and theaters.

CENTRE NOTES. V. 1, No. 1 (July/Aug. 1983)-. 0822-9635. Periodical. CN. English. ir. Free. Canadian Music Centre/Ontario Region, 1263 Bay Street, Toronto Ontario M5R 2C1 Canada. **DD** 780.9713.

CENTREGRAMME. (CENTREGRAMME : THE NEWSLETTER OF THE B.C. REGIONAL BRANCH OF THE CANADIAN MUSIC CENTRE). Feb. 1981-. 0227-3233. Periodical. CN. English. Canadian Music Centre, #3-2007 West 4th Avenue, Vancouver British Columbia V6J 1N3 Canada. **DD** 780.971. Newsletter, 0225-7688.

CEOL. No. 1- Summer 1963-. 0009-0174. Periodical. IE. English. ir. Breandan Breathnach, 47 Frascati Park, Blackroot Dublin Ireland. **Ind/Abst** MLA Int. Bibliogr. Books Artic. Mod. Lang. Lit., Music Index, RILM Abstr. **DD** 780.

CESKE HUDEBNINY A GRAMOFONOVE DESKY. 0323-1569. Periodical. CS. Czech. qt. Artia, PO Box 790, Ve-Semckach 30, Praha 1 Czechoslovakia. Ceske a Slovenske Hudebniny.

CHAMBER MUSIC MAGAZINE. Vol. 1, No. 1 (Spring 1984)-. 8755-0725. Periodical. US. English. qt. $25.00. Chamber Music of America, 215 Park Avenue South, New York NY 10003. **Tel** (212)460-9030. **Ed** Barbara L Sand. **LC** ML1. **DD** 785.7005. bk rev. adv acc. **Circ** 7,000. (ctrl). Aimed at professional musicians, interested amateur players, concert managments and music educators. Serves as a "trade journal" by including articles of practical information for chamber musicians and concert managers. American Ensemble, 0197-3134.

THE CHAMPLAIN VALLEY FIDDLERS CLUB, INC. NEWS LETTER. V. 1- April 1972-. Periodical. US. English. mo. Champlain Valley Fiddlers Club Inc, Box 501, Middlebury VT 05753. **LC** ML1. **DD** 781.773.

CHANSONS D'AUJOURD'HUI. V. 1, No. 1, Record 1 (Nov. 1977)-. 0227-5023. Periodical. CN. French. ir. 10.00 Domestic, 15.00 Foreign. Office des Communications Sociales, 4005 rue de Bellechasse, Montreal Quebec H1X 1J6 Canada. **Tel** (514)729-6391. **DD** 784.5009714. Evaluation of songs written in French.

CHAPTER NEWSLETTER - BIG BAND SOCIETY. (CHAPTER NEWSLETTER). VFOAT Newsletter, Big Band Society, Washington D.C. Metro Area, Ed Walker Chapter, Inc. 0731-4051. Periodical. US. English. mo. Big Band Society, Ed Walker Chapter, POB 6103, Silver Spring MD 20906.

CHEER. June 1979-. 0229-1509. Periodical. CN. English. $15.00. Cheer Productions, 24 Ryerson Avenue, Toronto Ontario M5T 2P3 Canada. **DD** 780.4205.

CHI E - DOV' E. See Sound Recordings and Systems.

CHINESE MUSIC. V. 2, No. 2- June 1979-. 0192-3749. Periodical. US. English. qt. $22.00. Chinese Music Society of North America, 2329 Charmingare, Woodbridge IL 60515. **Tel** (312)985-1606. **Ed** Sin-yan Shen. **Ind/Abst** RILM Abstr. **LC** ML336. **DD** 781.751. bk rev. **Circ** 500. Covers all phases of research and performance activities in Chinese music. It also contains news items, book and record reviews. The first and only journal published in the United States devoted wholly to Chinese music. Chinese Music General Newsletter, 0190-4086.

CHOIRS ONTARIO. (CHOIRS ONTARIO : THE NEWSLETTER OF THE ONTARIO CHORAL FEDERATION). V. 12, No. 2 (Dec. 1982/Jan. 1983)-. 0822-4749. Periodical. CN. English. bm. Ontario Choral Federation, Suite 303, 208 Bloor Street West, Toronto Ontario M5S 1T8 Canada. **DD** 784.10060713. Newsletter, 0317-0497.

THE CHORAL JOURNAL. V. 1- May 1959-. 0009-5028. Periodical. US. English. mo. $12.00. American Choral Directors Association, PO Box 6310, Lawton OK 73506. **Tel** (405)355-8161. **Ed** Wesley Coffman. **Ind/Abst** Music Index, RILM Abstr. **LC** ML1. **DD** 784.1005. bk rev. adv acc. **Circ** 12,000. (ctrl). Manuscripts related to the historical, the practical, or the informative aspects of choral music. Reviews of choral music and books, and general information about the American Choral Directors Association.

CHORAL MUSIC IN PRINT. Series/Titl Music-in-Print Series. 1st- Ed. US. English. 18 West Chelten Avenue, Philadelphia PA 19144. **Ed** T R Nardone, J H Nye and M Resnick.

CHORAL OVERTONES. V. 1- Oct./Dec. 1970-. 0360-2443. Periodical. US. English. qt. $2.25. 127 Ninth Avenue North, Nashville TN 37234. **LC** ML1. **DD** 783.

CHORAL PRAISE. V. 1- Oct./Dec. 1974-. 0362-0409. Periodical. US. English. qt. $2.25. Sunday School Board of the Southern Baptist Convention, 127 Ninth Avenue North, Nashville TN 37234. **LC** ML1. **DD** 783.405.

CHORAL TONES. V. 1- Oct./Dec. 1970-. 0360-2524. Periodical. US. English. qt. $2.25. 127 Ninth Avenue North, Nashville TN 37234. **LC** ML1. **DD** 783.

CHORALE. V. 1. No. 1 (July/Aug. 1980)-. Periodical. UK. English. bm. Chorale Publications, 12 Bass Mead, Cookham Berkshire England. **LC** ML1499. **DD** 784.1005.

CHORD AND DISCORD. V. 1- Feb. 1932-. 0069-3758. Periodical. US. English. ir. Brucker Society of America, Box 2570, Iowa City IA 52240. **Tel** (319)338-0313. **LC** ML1. **DD** 780.5. Articles dealing with the composers Mahler and Bruckner and their works.

CHORISTERS GUILD LETTERS. **Main/Corp** Choristers' Guild. VFOAT Letters. V. 1- 1949-. 0412-2801. Periodical. US. English. mo. $30.00.

Choristers Guild, 2834 West Kingsley Road, Garland TX 75041. **Tel** (214)271-1521. **Ed** Donald Jensen. **LC** ML1. bk rev. adv acc. **Circ** 9,000. (ctrl). A journal for directors of childrens and youth choirs with supplements of music and materials.

DER CHORSANGER. Periodical. German. ir. Mitteldeutscher Sangerband, Ulmestrasse 16, 35 Kassel W Germany. **LC** M127.G3.

CHORUS. (CHORUS : NOVA SCOTIA CHORAL FEDERATION NEWSLETTER). Vol. 6, No. 1-. 0821-1108. Periodical. CN. English. bm. 35.00. Nova Scotia Choral Federation, Suite 304, 5516 Spring Garden Road, Halifax Nova Scotia B3J 1G6 Canada. **Tel** 423-4688. **Ed** E Batstone. **DD** 784.96060716. **Circ** 300. (ctrl). Aimed towards members with news of Nova Scotia Choral Federation programs, member news and articles of interest. *NSCF News, 0712-6352.*

DE CHRISTELIJKE MUZIEKBODE. Began Publication in 1932. 0009-5176. Periodical. NE. Dutch. W J Timmer, PO Box 204, Winterswijk Netherlands.

CHURCH MUSIC *CEASED.* 1966-1980. 0009-6458. Periodical. US. English. an. $4.50. Concordia Publishing House, 3558 South Jefferson Avenue, St Louis MO 63118. **Ind/Abst** Music Index, Relig. Index One, Period. **LC** ML1.

CHURCH MUSIC DIGEST. V. 1, No. 1 (Sept./Oct. 1984)-. 8756-0461. Periodical. US. English. bm. $12.95 Domestic, $26.00 Foreign. Church Music Digest, PO Box 43247, Cincinnati OH 45243. **LC** ML2999. **DD** 016.78302605.

CHURCH MUSIC QUARTERLY. 1970. Periodical. UK. English. qt. $7.66. Royal School of Church Music, Addington Palace, Croydon CR9 5AD England. **Tel** 01-654 7676. **Ed** John Ottley. **LC** ML5. **DD** 783.026305. bk rev. adv acc. **Circ** 16,500. (ctrl). Of general interest to all concerned with church music: topical articles, information on new publications, reviews of new music and records.

THE CHURCH MUSICIAN. V. 1- Oct. 1950-. 0009-6466. Periodical. US. English. mo. $16.25. Materials Services Department, 127 Ninth Avenue North, Nashville TN 37234. **Tel** (615)251-2961. **Ed** William M Anderson. **Ind/Abst** Christ. Period. Index. **LC** ML1. **DD** 783.8. **Circ** 19,000. Magazine for church music leaders in a local baptist church. Human interest, and success stories about ministering through music are popular.

CINEMA ORGAN. Periodical. English. ir. Cinema Organ Society, 3 Coombe Cottages Witley Road, Milford Heath, Godalming Surrey England. **LC** ML5. **DD** 786.605.

CINEMASCORE. *See* Motion Picture.

CIRCUS (NEW YORK, N.Y. : 1979). (CIRCUS). Oct. 1979-. 0009-7365. Periodical. US. English. mo. $19.00. Circus Enterprise Corp, PO Box 265, Mount Morris IL 61054. **Tel** (212)685-5050. **LC** ML3533.8. **DD** 784.54005. *Circus Weekly, 0164-9248.*

CIRCUS ROCK IMMORTALS. No. 1-. 0740-7858. Periodical. US. English. Circus Enterprises Corp, 115 East 57th Street, New York NY 10022. **LC** ML3533.8. **DD** 784.5400922.

CITY OPERA SPOTLIGHT. (CITY OPERA SPOTLIGHT : THE MAGAZINE OF THE NEW YORK CITY OPERA GUILD). **VFOAT** Spotlight. 0737-8009. Periodical. US. English. qt. New York City Opera Guide, New York State Theater, Lincoln Center, New York NY 10023. **Tel** (212)870-5640. **Ed** June Wolfberg. **LC** ML1699. **DD** 782.1097471. adv acc. **Circ** 5,000. (ctrl). Opera topics related to performances of New York City Opera.

CIVILITA VENEZIANA. FONTI E TESTI. SERIE TERZA : LETTERE, MUSICA E TEATRO. V. 1- 1962-. 0578-4034. Periodical. IT. Italian. ir. Cosella Postale, PO Box 66, 50100 Firenze Italy.

THE CLARINET. Began with Oct. 1973 issue. 0361-5553. Periodical. US. English. qt. $20.00 US, Canada, & Mexico, $30.00 all other countries. International Clarinet Society, c/o N Heim, 7492 Wells Boulevard, Hyattsville MD 20783. **Tel** (301)422-9006. **Ed** James Gillespie. **Ind/Abst** Music Index. **LC** ML1. **DD** 788.6205. bk rev. adv acc. **Circ** 2,000. Articles about the clarinet, music, book, concert reviews.

CLARINET AND SAXOPHONE. Vol. 5, No. 3 (July 1980)-. Periodical. UK. English. qt. Clarinet & Saxophone Society of Great Britain, 26 Monks Orchard, Wilmington Kent England. **LC** ML929. **DD** 788.605.

CLARINETWORK. V. 1, No. 1 (Feb./March 1982)-. 0733-3544. US. English. $20.00 General Membership, $10.00 Students. Jean A Hite/Editor, 830 South Ashburton Road, Columbus OH 43227. **LC** ML929. **DD** 788.6205.

CLASSICAL MUSIC. Began with June 16, 1979. Periodical. UK. English. bm. $61.30. Classical Music Magazine, 52 Floral Street, London WC2E 9DA England. **Tel** (01) 836 2536. **Ed** Robert Maycock. **LC** ML5. **DD** 780.5. bk rev. adv acc. **Circ** 20,000. (ctrl). The fornightly news magazine for music, opera and dance, serving Britain and worldwide. *Classical Music & Album Reviews.*

CLAVIER. V. 1- March/April 1962-. 0009-854X. Periodical. US. English. mo. $15.00. Instrumentalist Company, 200 Northfield, Northfield IL 60093. **Tel** (312)446-5000. **Ed** Barbara Kreader. **Ind/Abst** Educ. Index, Ref. Source, Music Index, Music Artic. Guide, RILM Abstr. **LC** ML1. **DD** 786.05. bk rev. adv acc. **Circ** 21,000. (ctrl). Available on microfilm from University Microfilms. A magazine for pianists and organists, it has an international circulation and is noted for its interviews with famous performers, its master classes and its practical teaching articles. *Piano Teacher.*

CLAVIER'S PIANO EXPLORER. **VFOAT** Piano Explorer. 0279-0858. Periodical. US. English. mo. The Instrumentalist Company, 1418 Lake Street, Evanston IL 60204. **LC** ML3930.A2. **DD** 786.105.

CLEM. CONTACT LIST OF ELECTRONIC MUSIC. (CLEM : CONTACT LIST OF ELECTRONIC MUSIC). **VFOAT** Contact List of Electronic Music. **VAT** Contact List of Electronic Music. 0820-7356. Periodical. CN. English. qt. 12.00 Domestic, 18.00 Foreign. CLEM, PO Box 86010, North Vancouver British Columbia V7L 4J5 Canada. **Tel** (604)985-5996. **Ed** Alex Douglas. **DD** 789.99025. bk rev. **Circ** 1,500. A listing of all aspects of the underground world of electronic and independent music, world wide.

CLES POUR LA MUSIQUE. Began with Jan. 1969 issue. Periodical. BE. French. ir. Cles Pour la Musique Arts Spec, 10 rue Royale-Palais Beaux-Art, 1000 Brussels Belgium. **LC** ML5. **DD** 780.5.

CMEA NEWS. **Main/Corp** California Music Educators Association. **VAT** California Music Educators Association News. Began publication with V. 1, Feb. 1948. 0007-8638. Periodical. US. English. ir. $8.00. California Music Educators, 3924 Cottonwood Drive, Concord CA 94519. **Tel** (415)685-3237. **Ed** Jerri Burke. bk rev. adv acc. **Circ** 2,700. (ctrl). Information applicable to public school music teachers in grades one to twelve plus college.

CMJ, PROGRESSIVE MEDIA. **VFOAT** C.M.J., Progressive Media. 0731-5708. Periodical. US. English. mo. $95.00. PO Box 258, Roslyn NY 11576. **LC** ML3477. **DD** 784.5005. *CMJ, College Media Journal, 0195-7430.*

COAST TO COAST COUNTRY. Vol. 2, Issue 1 (Feb. 1984)-. 0826-3140. Periodical. CN. English. bm. $1.50 Per No. Coast to Coast Country, Suite 300, 11821-1123 Street, Edmonton Alberta T5L 0G7 Canada. **DD** 784.5200971. *Alberta Country, 0826-3132.*

COC NEWS. **VAT** Canadian Opera Company News. Vol. 1, Issue 1 (Winter)-. 0822-8922. Periodical. CN. English. qt. COC News, 417 Queen's Quay West, Toronto Ontario M4V 1A2 Canada. **DD** 782.106071. *Overtures (Toronto, Ont.), 0382-778X.*

CODA *CEASED.* V. 1- May 1958-. 0010-017X. Periodical. CN. English. bm. $15.00. Coda Publications, Box 87 Station J, Toronto Ontario M4J 4X8 Canada. **Tel** (416)593-7230. **Ed** William E Smith. **Ind/Abst** Music Index. bk rev. adv acc. **Circ** 3,500. Comprehensive coverage of the international jazz scene. Articles, reviews, commentary, essential research material.

CODA MAGAZINE. **VFOAT** CODA. **VAT** CODA (1981). Issue No. 177 (1981)-. 0820-926X. Periodical. CN. English. bm. $12.00 Canada and US, $15.00 Others except UK. CODA Magazine, PO Box 87/ Station J, Toronto Ontario M4J 4X8 Canada. **Ind/Abst** Jazz Index, Music Index, Can. Period. Index. **DD** 785.4205. Issued also in microfilm. *CODA, 0010-017X.*

COLLANA DI STUDI PALESTRINIANI. 1- 1960-. 0069-5211. Periodical. IT. Italian. ir. Via Gioanni Pascoli 55, 20133 Milano Italy.

COLLEGE BAND DIRECTORS NATIONAL ASSOCIATION JOURNAL. **VFOAT** C.B.D.N.A. Journal. Vol. 1, No. 1 (Spring 1984)-. 0742-8480. Periodical. US. English. sa. $10.00. College Band Directors National Association, 1866 College Road, Columbus OH 43210. **DD** 785.

COLLEGE MUSIC SYMPOSIUM. V. 1- 1961-. 0069-5696. Periodical. US. English. an. $12.50. College Music Society, 1444 15th Street, Boulder CO 80303. **Tel** (303)449-1611. **Ind/Abst** Music Index, RILM Abstr. **LC** ML1. **DD** 780.5.

COLLEGE NEWSLETTER - ROYAL CANADIAN COLLEGE OF ORGANISTS. (THE COLLEGE NEWSLETTER). 0826-2950. Periodical. CN. English. Royal Canadian College of Organists, Suite 300A 212 King Street West, Toronto Ontario M5H 1K5 Canada. **DD** 786.506071. *Stretto, 0710-6440.*

THE COMPLETE GUIDE TO GOSPEL MUSIC. *See* Yearbooks, Almanacs, Directories.

THE COMPOSER *CEASED.* **VFOAT** Composer Magazine. V. 1-12. 0010-4345. Periodical. US. English. an. $4.00. PO Box 671, Hamilton OH 45012. **LC** ML1. **DD** 780.5.

COMPOSER. No. 1-. 0010-4337. Periodical. UK. English. ty. 3.75 Domestic, $10.00 Foreign. Composers Guild of Great Britain, 10 Stratford Place, London W1N 9AE England. **Tel** 01-499-4795. **Ed** Francis Routh. **Ind/Abst** Music Index. (cum index). bk rev. adv acc. **Circ** 1,000. Modern British classical music (20th Century.). *Bulletin - Composers' Guild of Great Britain.*

COMPOSERS. Began with 1980-81. 0196-1985. US. English. an. National Endowment for the Arts, Music Program, 2401 E Street NW, Washington DC 20506. **LC** ML62. **DD** 780.7973. *Composer/Librettist Fellowships, 0193-5461.*

COMPOSERS WEST. V. 2, No. 3- Sept. 1979-. 0709-8219. Periodical. CN. English. qt. Alberta Composers' Association, c/o Department of Music, University of Calgary, Suite 2920, 24 Avenue Northwest, Calgary Alberta T2N 1N4 Canada. **DD** 780.97123. *A C A Newsletter, 0705-1557.*

COMPUTATIONAL MUSICOLOGY NEWSLETTER. V. 1- (No. 1-). 0093-0253. Periodical. US. English. J Wenker, 11 Carlton Club Drive, Piscataway NJ 08854. **LC** ML1. **DD** 780.0102854.

COMPUTER MUSIC JOURNAL. V. 1- Feb. 1977-. 0148-9267. Periodical. US. English. qt. $53.00. MIT Press Journals, 28 Carleton Street, Cambridge MA 02142. **Tel** (617)253-2889. **Ed** Curtis Roads. **Ind/Abst** Electron. Commun. Abstr. J., ISMEC Bull., Pollut. Abstr. Indexes, Saf. Sci. Abstr. J., Music Index, Comput. Control Abstr., Electr. Electron. Abstr., Sci. Abstr., RILM Abstr. **LC** ML1. **DD** 789.9. **CODEN** CMUJDY. bk rev. adv acc. **Circ** 2,400. Concentrates on skills, technologies, and promises of computer-processed and digital sound. Includes new product reviews, interviews, illustrated reports, coverage of new developments in field, etc.

CON BRIO. V. 1- Nov. 1977-. 0707-5103. Periodical. CN. English (French). sa. Free. National Arts Centre, Orchestrea Association, Ottawa Ontario Canada. **DD** 785.0661. (ctrl).

CONCERT MAGAZINE. V. 1, No. 1 (March/April '81)-. 0277-9560. Periodical. US. English. bm. Free. New Sound Concerts, 545 High Street, Walpole MA 02081. **LC** ML3533.8. **DD** 784.54005.

CONCERT NOTES; CARL FISCHER NEWSLETTER. V. 1- Winter 1972-. Periodical. US. English. Carl Fischer, 62 Cooper Square, New York NY 10003. **LC** ML1. **DD** 780.65.

CONCERTINA. Vol. 1, No. 1 (Winter 1983)-. 0740-0993. Periodical. US. English. qt. $10.00. Concertina Magazine, PO Box 68, Gloucester Point VA 23062. **LC** ML1083. **DD** 786.97.

CONCERTO : DAS MAGAZIN FUR ALTE MUSIK. **VFOAT** Magazin fur Alte Musik. V. 1 (Nov. 1983)-. Periodical. GW. German. bm. Gitarre & Laute Verlagsges, Leserservice Concerto, Postfach 410408, 5000 Koln 41 West Germany.

CONNECTICUT ASSESSMENT OF EDUCATIONAL PROGRESS. ART AND MUSIC. *See* The Arts (General) - Art.

CONNOTES. V. 1- May 1980-. 0227-8693. Periodical. CN. English. ir. 6.00. Royal Conservatory of Music, 273 Bloor Street West, Toronto Ontario M5S 1W2 Canada. **Tel** 978-3771. **Ed** Mary Ann Ross. **DD** 780.729713541. **Circ** 2,400. The Bulletin of the Royal Conservatory of Music, Toronto, Canada. Used primarily by music teachers and students, to assist in their academic endeavours. *Bulletin, 0495-8977.*

CONSORT (HALIFAX, N.S.). (CONSORT). Vol. 4, No. 1 (Sept. 1983)-. 0823-8278. Periodical. CN. English. ir. Early Music Society of Nova Scotia, c/o Department of Music, Dalhousie University, Halifax Nova Scotia B3H 3J5 Canada. **DD** 780.902. *Early Music Society of Nova Scotia Newsletter.*

Music

CONTACT (LONDON, ENGLAND). (CONTACT). Began with Spring 1971 issue. 0308-5066. Periodical. UK. English. sa. $9.20. Philip Martin Music Books, 22 Huntington Road, York Y03 7RL England. **Tel** 0904 36111. **Ed** Keith Potter and Hilary Bracefield. **LC** ML197. **DD** 780.904. bk rev. adv acc. **Circ** 600. Covers the work of contemporary composers worldwide, new books, important performances, festivals, and developments in electronic and computer music, with open debate on controversial topics.

CONTACT (RICHMOND, B.C.). (CONTACT). 1st Ed. (June 1980)-. 0229-1266. Periodical. CN. English. ir. Contact c/o Entercom Media Services, 1730 Burrard Street, Vancouver British Columbia V6J 3G4 Canada. **Tel** (604)738-2232. **Ed** J Austair Palmer. **DD** 338.477809711. adv acc. **Circ** 230,000. (ctrl). Entercom media services is the exclusive publisher of the expo 86 world festival program involving 5 issues from May to October 1986. The festival includes dance and music.

CONTEMPORARY KEYBOARD CEASED. V. 1-7. 0361-5820. Periodical. US. English. mo. $18.00. **Ind/Abst** RILM Abstr. **LC** ML1. **DD** 786.105.

CONTEMPORARY MUSIC ALMANAC. See Yearbooks, Almanacs, Directories.

CONTEMPORARY MUSIC REVIEW. 0749-4467. Periodical. US. English. Harwood Academic Publishers, PO Box 786 Cooper Station, New York NY 10276. **Ed** Neil Osborne. bk rev. adv acc.

CONTEMPORARY SHOWCASE. SYLLABUS. (SYLLABUS - CONTEMPORARY SHOWCASE). 1970-. 0316-893X. Periodical. CN. English. be. Free. Contemporary Music Showcase Association, 3296 Cindy Crescent, Mississauga Ontario L4Y 3J6 Canada. **DD** 780.79713541.

CONTINUO. V. 1, No. 7- April 1978-. 0705-6656. Periodical. CN. English. mo. $22.00. Continuo, 6 Dartnell Avenue, Toronto Ontario M5R 3A4 Canada. **Tel** (416)964-0819. **Ed** Douglas Valleau. **DD** 780.5. bk rev. adv acc. **Circ** 1,000. An early music magazine covering the renaissance, baroque and early classical periods. Articles, interviews, concert listings, etc. For amateur and professional musicians alike. Early Music Directory, 0705-6648.

CONTRIBUTIONS TO MUSIC EDUCATION. No. 1- 1972-. 0190-4922. US. English. an. Kent State University, School of Music, c/o Terry Kuhn, Kent OH 44242. **Tel** (216)672-2220. **Ed** Terry Lee Kuhn. **Ind/Abst** Music Index. **LC** ML1. **DD** 780.72. bk rev. **Circ** 500. (ctrl). Contributions to music education. Publishes research reports pertinent to instruction in music.

CONTRIBUTIONS TO THE STUDY OF MUSIC AND DANCE. No. 1-. 0193-9041. Monographic Series. US. English. ir. Greenwood Press, 88 Post Road West Box 5007, Westport CT 06881. **Tel** (203)226-3571. This series is devoted to an examination of music and dance throughout the world. Historical as well as contemporary concerns are treated.

CORPUS OF EARLY KEYBOARD MUSIC. 1-. 0070-0371. GW. English. ir. Hanssler Verlag, Bismarckstrasse 4, Postfach 1220, D-7303 Stuttgart West Germany. **Tel** (7158)1770. **Ed** John Caldwell. Early music for keyboards.

COUNTERPOINT CLASSICAL RECORD REVIEW. No. 1- June 1979-. 0709-7166. Periodical. CN. English. ir. $1. Per No. Counterpoint Publishing Co, PO Box 186 Station Z, Toronto Ontario M5N 2Z Canada. **DD** 789.913105.

COUNTERPOINT'S BASIC CLASSICAL RECORD LIBRARY GUIDE. 1st- Ed. 0709-7158. CN. English. be. $3.25 Per No. Counterpoint Publ Co, PO Box 186, Station Z, Toronto Ontario M5N 2Z4 Canada. **DD** 789.913105.

COUNTRY CORNER. Erscheint Regelmassig Seit 1965. Periodical. GW. German. ir. $2.50. H Paul, 28 Bremen 2 Einsteinstrasse 3A, Bremen Western Germany. **LC** ML5. **DD** 784.

COUNTRY HERITAGE. Vol. 8, No. 10 (May 1982)-. 0733-8759. Periodical. US. English. mo. $6.50. Beverly King, Rural Route 1 Box 320, Madixx OK 73446. **Ed** Beverly King. **LC** ML459 .D6. **DD** 784.52005. adv acc. **Circ** 400. (ctrl). Traditional country music, plus resonator guitar (Dobro). Interviews, photos, news, songs, Dobro instructional material (tablatures, etc.), aps, etc. related to Dobro and/or traditional music. Resophonic Echoes, 0273-3242.

COUNTRY MUSIC. Began in 1972. 0090-4007. Periodical. US. English. bm. Country Music Association, PO Box 2004, Rock Island IL 61207, (subscription address: Fulfillment Corporation of America 205 West Center Street Marion OH 43302). **Tel** (214)889-4600. **LC** ML1. **DD** 784.

COUNTRY MUSIC BOOKING GUIDE. 0360-8131. US. English. $0.75. 1717 West End Avenue, Nashville TN 37203. **LC** ML19. **DD** 338.47784.

COUNTRY MUSIC EXPLORER. 0360-8697. Periodical. US. English. mo. $5.00. International Association of Country Music, PO Box 147, Hamilton OH 45012. **LC** ML1. **DD** 784.

COUNTRY MUSIC NEWS. 0098-9037. Periodical. US. English. mo. $5.00. PMA Publishing Co, Rtes 54 and Old 147, Turbotville PA 17772. **LC** ML1. **DD** 784.0973.

COUNTRY MUSIC NEWS (OTTAWA, ONT.). (COUNTRY MUSIC NEWS). Vol. 2, No. 10 (Jan. 1982)-. 0714-8356. Periodical. CN. English. mo. $10.00. Country Music News, Box 7323 Vanier Terminal, Ottawa Ontario K1L 8E4 Canada. **DD** 784.5200971. Capital Country News, 0228-0191.

COUNTRY MUSIC NEWS (THORNHILL, ONT.). (COUNTRY MUSIC NEWS). Vol. 1, Issue No. 1 (Dec. 1979)-. 0225-5863. Periodical. CN. English. ir. Country Music News, PO Box 574, Thornhill Ontario L3T 4A2 Canada. **DD** 780.4206. What's News, 0709-5422.

THE COUNTRY MUSIC NEWSLETTER. No. L- Jan. 1970-. Periodical. English. ir. $0.30. Earl Heywood Fan Club, PO Box 186, 2484 New South Wales Australia. **LC** ML5.G725. **DD** 784.

COUNTRY MUSIC PEOPLE. 1970. 0591-2237. Periodical. UK. English. mo. $19.92. Country Music People, 17 Broomwood Road, St Paul's Cray, Orpington Kent BR5 2JH England. **Tel** 0689 70433. **Ed** Bob Powel. **LC** ML5. **DD** 784. bk rev. adv acc. **Circ** 13,000. Covers all areas of country music from country rock to country gospel.

COUNTRY MUSIC REVIEW. VFOAT CMR. Periodical. UK. English. mo. Swift Fleet Ltd, 19 Westbourne Road, London N78 AN England. **LC** ML5. **DD** 784.

COUNTRY MUSIC TIMES. Periodical. AT. English. ir. PO Box 35, North Quay, Queensland Australia 4000. **LC** ML5. **DD** 784.

COUNTRY MUSIC WORLD. V. 1- July/Aug. 1972-. 0094-1344. Periodical. US. English. $5.95. Dodson Pub Co, Box 3693, Arlington VA 22203. **LC** ML1. **DD** 784.

COUNTRY RAMBLINGS. Vol. 1, Issue 1 (Feb. 1983)-. 0823-714X. Periodical. CN. English. mo. $10.00. Country Ramblings, 556 Maple Street West, Moose Jaw Saskatchewan S6H 4X1 Canada. **DD** 784.5200971.

COUNTRY RECORDING VOICE. 0092-4059. Periodical. US. English. mo. 0.50. PO Box 1393, Nashville TN 37202. **LC** ML1. **DD** 784.

COUNTRY RHYTHMS. 1981. 0732-5614. Periodical. US. English. mo. Starlog Press Inc, 475 Park Avenue South, New York NY 10016. **Ed** Dan Fields. **DD** 780. adv acc. **Circ** 250,000. Country lifestyle and music including interviews with country music stars.

COUNTRY SONG ROUNDUP. Began publication with first issue in 1950. 0011-0248. Periodical. US. English. mo. Charlton Publ, Charlton Building, Derby CT 06418. **Tel** (203)735-3381.

COUNTRY SONG ROUNDUP. SPECIAL. 0277-3554. US. English. an. $2.00. Charlton Publications Inc, Charlton Building, Derby CT 06418. **LC** M1630.18.

COUNTRY SONG ROUNDUP YEARBOOK. See Yearbooks, Almanacs, Directories.

COUNTRY SOUNDS OF THE SOUTHWEST. Mar. 1973-. 0147-5738. Periodical. US. English. mo. Country Sounds of the Southwest Circulation Department, 5326 West Bellfort, Suite 215, Houston TX 77035. **LC** ML1. **DD** 784.

COUNTRY SQUIRE. 0092-0991. Periodical. US. English. PO Box 4551, Rochester NY 14513. **LC** ML1. **DD** 784.

COUNTRY STYLE MONTHLY. (COUNTRY STYLE). 0364-0078. Periodical. US. English. mo. $7.00. Country Style Publications Co, 11058 West Addison Street, Franklin Park IL 60131. **LC** ML1. **DD** 780.42.

COUNTRY TIMES (THORNHILL, ONT.). (COUNTRY TIMES). Issue 1983 # 1 (Dec. 1982)-. 0821-7971. Periodical. CN. English. ir. 25.00. Academy of Country Music Entertainment, PO Box 574, Thornhill Ontario L3T 4A2 Canada. **Ed** Mary Quartarone. **DD** 780.4206. bk rev. **Circ** 1,000. (ctrl). News on the activities of academy members — artists, record company and broadcasting personnel. Updates on the business of the academy. Country Music News (Thornhill, Ont.), 0225-5863.

COUNTRYSIDE. 0098-4566. Periodical. US. English. mo. $5.50. Box 677, Minneapolis MN 55440. **LC** ML1. **DD** 784. Country & Western News Scene.

COUNTRYWIDE ANNUAL YEARBOOK. See Yearbooks, Almanacs, Directories.

COURANT (ANN ARBOR, MICH.). (THE COURANT). Began with: Vol. 1, No. 1 (Jan. 1983). Periodical. US. English. qt. $15.00. Academy of Early Music, School of Music, 2221 Moore Building University of Michigan, Ann Arbor MI 48109.

LE COURRIER MUSICAL DE FRANCE CEASED. Began with No. 1, 1963. Ceased with No. 71/72. 0011-0620. Periodical. French. qt. **Ind/Abst** Music Index, RILM Abstr. (cum index).

CREATIVE GUITAR INTERNATIONAL. V. 1- Fall 1973-. 0092-8887. Periodical. US. English. ty. $5.00. Mockingbird Press, Box 1275, Edinburg TX 78539. **Ind/Abst** Music Index. **LC** ML1. **DD** 787.6105.

CREATIVE WORLD. 0360-7135. US. English. $4.00. S Kenton, PO Box 35216, Los Angeles CA 90035. **LC** ML1. **DD** 785.0672.

CREEM. 0011-1147. Periodical. US. English. mo. $32.00. Creem, 120 Brighton Avenue, Clifton NJ 07012. **Tel** (313)642-8833. **Ind/Abst** Music Index, Media Rev. Dig., Access. **LC** ML1. **DD** 784.54005.

CREEM CLOSE-UP. 0737-1918. Periodical. US. English. bm. $4.45 Per Copy. Creem Magazine Inc, PO Box 1064, Birmingham MI 48012. **LC** ML3533.8. **DD** 784.54005.

CRESCENDO. (CRESCENDO : JOURNAL OF THE PRINCE EDWARD ISLAND MUSIC EDUCATORS' ASSOCIATION). VFOAT Newsletter. 0225-9370. Periodical. CN. English. ir. Free to Members. Prince Edward Island Music Educators' Association, c/o P Campbell, Apt 2, 44 Mount Edward Road, Parkdale Prince Edward Island C1A 5S3 Canada. **DD** 780.7.

CRESCENDO INTERNATIONAL. Began in May 1967. 0011-118X. Periodical. UK. English. mo. 15.00 Domestic, $25.00 Foreign. Crescendo Publications Ltd, 888-8th Avenue, New York NY 10019. **Tel** (01)729-5800. **Ed** Dennis H Matthews. **Ind/Abst** Jazz Index, Music Index. **LC** ML3505.8. **DD** 785.4205. bk rev. adv acc. **Circ** 5,000. (ctrl). Interviews with jazz and film musicians news on music events and technical articles on music and instruments in the jazz and light music fields. Crescendo (London, England).

CUE TRACK. (CUE TRACK : THE CANADIAN RECORD & TAPE GUIDE). 1st Ed. (1980)- . -. 0229-1533. Periodical. CN. English (includes some text in French). qt. Cue Track, PO Box 2309, Winnipeg Manitoba R3C 4A6 Canada. **DD** 016.789912.

CULTURE MUSICALI : SEMESTRALE DELLA SOCIETA ITALIANA DI ETNOMUSICOLOGIA. Yearly V. 1, No. 1, (Jan./June 1982)-. Periodical. Italian (summaries in English). sa. 20.000. 14 Via dei Liburni, 00185 Roma Italy.

CUM NOTIS VARIORUM. (CUM NOTIS VARIORUM : THE NEWSLETTER OF THE MUSIC LIBRARY, UNIVERSITY OF CALIFORNIA, BERKELEY). VFOAT C.N.V. 0161-1186. Periodical. US. English. mo. Editor CNV, University of California, Music Library, 240 Morrison Hall, Berkeley CA 94720. **Tel** (415)642-6232. **Ed** Ann Basart. **LC** ML1. **DD** 780.5. bk rev. adv acc. **Circ** 550. Newsletter of the Music Library, University of California, Berkeley.

CURRENT ISSUES IN MUSIC EDUCATION. V. 1- 1963-. US. English. ir. $6.00. Ohio State University, School of Music, 105B Hughes Hall/1899 College, Columbus OH 43210. **Tel** (614)422-7940. **Ed** James Major. **Circ** 300. (ctrl). A summary of the Current Issues Symposia held

Music

annually on announced topic. The series began in the late 1960's and continues today.

CURRENT MUSICOLOGY. No. 1-. 0011-3735. Periodical. US. English. sa. $20.00. Columbia University, Department of Music, New York NY 10027. **Tel** (212)280-3826. **Ed** Murray Dineen. **Ind/Abst** Music Index, Humanit. Index, RILM Abstr. **LC** ML1. **DD** 780.0105. (cum index). bk rev. adv acc. **Circ** 1,000. (ctrl). Musicology and musical research; reviews of recent literature reports from major musicological institutions.

THE DALLAS OPERA MAGAZINE. Vol. 4, No. 1-. 0731-8529. Periodical. US. English. qt. $1.00 Single Issue. Dallas Opera Office, 3000 Turtle Creek Plaza, Dallas TX 75219. **LC** ML699. **DD** 782.1097642812. *Dallas Civic Opera Magazine, 0277-0113*.

DANCE MUSIC REPORT. 0883-1122. Periodical. US. English. bw. $35.00 US, $40.00 Canada. Dance Music Report, 1747 First Avenue, New York NY 10128. **DD** 784.

DANSK AMATRMUSIK. Periodical. DK. Danish. ir. 30.00. Holbaekvej 34 4571, Gravienge Denmark. **LC** ML5.

DANSK MUSIKFORTEGNELSE. VFOAT Danish National Bibliography, Music. 1931-32-33-. Danish (English). an. **LC** ML120.D3. **DD** 016.7817489.

DANSK ORGELAARBOG. VFOAT Danish Organ Yearbook. V. 1 (1981-82)-. 0107-4857. Danish (text and summaries in English and German). an. Dansk Orgelaarbok, Rolighedsvej 6, DK-3400 Hillerd Denmark. **LC** ML549.8. **DD** 786.6248905.

DARMSTADTER BEITRAGE ZUR NEUEN MUSIK. Vol. 1- 1958-. 0418-3878. GW. German. an. B Schotts Soehne, Postfach 3640, D-6500 Mainz West Germany. **Tel** 06131/246-0. **Ed** Ernst Thomas. **Ind/Abst** RILM Abstr. **LC** ML5.

DEE JAY AND RADIO MONTHLY. See Communication - Broadcasting.

DELIUS SOCIETY JOURNAL. (THE DELIUS SOCIETY JOURNAL). No. 43- April 1974-. UK. English. qt. $17.00. Delius Society, 85A Farley Hill, Luton Luiseg Bedford England. **Ed** S Lloyd. **Ind/Abst** Music Index. **LC** ML410.D35. **DD** 780.924. bk rev. **Circ** 450. (ctrl). Life and works of Frederick Delius, including book and record reviews and reports on functions of Delius Society and related events.

DELTIO KRITIKES DISKOGRAPHIAS. No. 1-. Greek, Modern. ir. 150.00. Lesche Tou Diskou, Stoa Sine Opera Akademias 57, Athenai Greece. **LC** ML156.9.

DENKMALER RHEINISCHER MUSIK. 1- 1951-. 0416-9816. Periodical. German. ir. CF Peters, 373 Park Avenue South, New York NY 10016. **Tel** (212)686-4147. **Ed** Waldstein, Neefe, Miles and De Castro. **Circ** 10. A series of critical editions dealing with early music from the Rhineland.

DER KIRCHENMUSIKER. (DER KIRCHENMUSIKER : MITTEILUNGEN DER ZENTRALSTELLE FUR EVANGELISCHE KIRCHENMUSIK). VFOAT Kirchen Musiker. 1st Year, 1st Issue (Mar./Apr. 1950)-. 0023-1819. Periodical. GW. German. Grossohaus Wegner Company, PO Box 10 25 40, D-2000 Hamburg 1 West Germany. **Ind/Abst** Music Index, RILM Abstr.

DETROIT MONOGRAPHS IN MUSICOLOGY. No. 1-. Monographic Series. US. English. ir. Information Coordinators Inc, 1435-37 Randolph Street, Detroit MI 48226. **Tel** (313)962-9720.

DETROIT STUDIES IN MUSIC BIBLIOGRAPHY. See Bibliographies.

DEUTSCHE BIBLIOGRAPHIE : MUSIKALIEN-VERZEICHNIS. See Bibliographies.

DEUTSCHE BIBLIOGRAPHIE : SCHALLPLATTEN-VERZEICHNIS. See Bibliographies.

DEUTSCHE MUSIKBIBLIOGRAPHIE. Began publication in 1829. 0012-0502. Periodical. German. mo. $37.71. Kunst & Wissen Erich Bieber, Dufourstrasse 51, CH-8008 Zurich Switzerland. **Tel** 01/69 44 20. **LC** ML113. *Handbuch der Musikalischen Literatur*.

DEVIL'S BOX. (THE DEVIL'S BOX). No. 8- March 1969-. 0092-0789. Periodical. US. English. qt. $2.00. Route 11, 16 Bond Street, Clarksville TN 37040. **Ind/**Abst MLA Int. Bibliogr. Books Artic. Mod. Lang. Lit. **LC** ML1. **DD** 787.105.

DEVOTEE. V. 1- Spring 1979-. 0197-7784. Periodical. US. English. qt. $9.00 US, $12.00 Foreign. Devotee, 28-24th Street, New York NY 12180. **Ind/Abst** Music Index. **LC** ML1100. **DD** 785.7005.

DIALOGUE IN INSTRUMENTAL MUSIC EDUCATION. V. 1- Winter 1977-. 0147-7544. Periodical. US. English. sa. $6.00. School of Music, Humanities Building, University of Wisconsin, Madison WI 53706. **Tel** (608)263-1902. **Ed** David Nelson. **Ind/Abst** Music Index. **LC** ML1. **DD** 780.7. bk rev. **Circ** 300. (ctrl). The purpose of DIME is to provide a medium that will aid in improving instruction and the preparation of music teachers.

THE DIAPASON. 1st Year- (No. 10-). 0012-2378. Periodical. US. English. mo. $7.50. Scranton Gillette Communications Inc, 380 Northwest Highway, Des Plaines IL 60016. **Ind/Abst** Music Index, Music Artic. Guide, RILM Abstr. **LC** ML1. **DD** 786.505. Available on microfilm from University Microfilms International.

DIAPASON (BOULOGNE, FRANCE). (DIAPASON). Periodical. FR. French. ir. 170,00. Impr Diapason, 6 rue Jules Simon, 92100 Boulogne France. **LC** ML5. **DD** 780.5. *Diapason Microsillon*.

DIAPASON : CATALOGUE GENERAL. VFOAT Catalogue Disques et Cassettes Diapason. FR. French. ir. 43.00. 6 rue Jules Simon, 92100 Boulogne France. **LC** ML156.2. **DD** 016.789912. *Catalogue General de Musique Classique et de Diction*.

DICK DAMRON COUNTRY MUSIC NEWSLETTER (1980). (DICK DAMRON COUNTRY MUSIC NEWSLETTER). No. 7 (July 1980)-. 0710-0981. Periodical. CN. English. ir. Dick Damron International Fan Club, Box 123, Petawawa Ontario K8H 2X2 Canada. **DD** 784.5200924. *Newsletter (Dick Damron International Fan Club), 0710-1198*.

DICTIONARIUM MUSICUM. Began with 1, 1965. 4459-1129. Monographic Series. NE. English. ir. Fritz Knuf, 2707 Buren Postbox 20, Hilversum Netherlands.

DICTIONARY CATALOG OF THE MUSIC COLLECTION : SUPPLEMENT - BOSTON PUBLIC LIBRARY. See Encyclopedias & General Reference Books.

DIGEST - ROYAL CANADIAN COLLEGE OF ORGANISTS. (DIGEST). No. 24 (June 1980)-. 0228-9768. CN. English. an. Royal Canadian College of Organists, Suite 300A/212 King Street West, Toronto Ontario M5H 1K5 Canada. **DD** 786.605. *Royal Canadian College of Organists Quarterly, 0380-8424*.

DIRECTORIO MUSICAL VENEZOLANO. See Yearbooks, Almanacs, Directories.

DIRECTORY - AMERICAN BELL ASSOCIATION. See Yearbooks, Almanacs, Directories.

DIRECTORY - CANADIAN BAND DIRECTORS' ASSOCIATION, ALBERTA CHAPTER. See Yearbooks, Almanacs, Directories.

DIRECTORY - NATIONAL ASSOCIATION OF SCHOOLS OF MUSIC. See Yearbooks, Almanacs, Directories.

DIRECTORY - NATIONAL BAND ASSOCIATION. See Yearbooks, Almanacs, Directories.

DIRECTORY OF AUSTRALIAN MUSIC ORGANIZATIONS. See Yearbooks, Almanacs, Directories.

DIRECTORY OF BRITISH BRASS BANDS. See Yearbooks, Almanacs, Directories.

DIRECTORY OF CANADIAN ORCHESTRAS AND YOUTH ORCHESTRAS. See Yearbooks, Almanacs, Directories.

DIRECTORY OF FEMALE JAZZ PERFORMERS. See Yearbooks, Almanacs, Directories.

DIRECTORY OF MEMBERS AND FRIENDS. See Yearbooks, Almanacs, Directories.

DIRECTORY OF MEMBERS & MUSEUMS. See Yearbooks, Almanacs, Directories.

DIRECTORY OF MEMBERS AND SUBSCRIBERS - AMERICAN MUSICOLOGICAL SOCIETY. See Yearbooks, Almanacs, Directories.

DIRECTORY OF MUSIC FACULTIES IN COLLEGES AND UNIVERSITIES, U.S. AND CANADA. See Yearbooks, Almanacs, Directories.

DIRECTORY OF NEW MUSIC. See Yearbooks, Almanacs, Directories.

A DIRECTORY OF SUMMER CHAMBER MUSIC WORKSHOPS, SCHOOLS & FESTIVALS. See Yearbooks, Almanacs, Directories.

DIRECTORY OF THE CANADIAN ASSOCIATION OF UNIVERSITY SCHOOLS OF MUSIC. See Yearbooks, Almanacs, Directories.

DISC AND THAT. V. 1- July/Aug. 1973-. 0092-0436. Periodical. US. English. mo. Pruitt/Scott Publications, PO Box 228 Kingsbridge Station, New York NY 10463. **LC** ML1. **DD** 338.477899105.

DISC COLLECTOR (CHESWOLD, DEL. : 1981). (DISC COLLECTOR). No. 100 (Jan. 1981)-. 0731-843X. Periodical. US. English. mo. $3.00. Disc Collector Publishing, POB 315, Cheswold DE 19936. **Tel** (302)674-3149. **Ed** Lou Deneumoustier. **LC** ML1. **DD** 016.789912. bk rev. adv acc. **Circ** 950. (ctrl). Reviews and sales of old time country, bluegrass, cowboy and Western music records, tapes, and books. *Disc Collector Newsletter, 0360-8700*.

DISC COLLECTOR NEWS LETTER CEASED. (DISC COLLECTOR NEWSLETTER). No. 1- Jan. 1964-. 0360-8700. Periodical. US. English. ir. **LC** ML1. **DD** 616.789912.

DISCO 45. Periodical. UK. English. -/-/5 Single Issue. Wells Gardner Barton & Company, Faygate Hoosham, Sussex England. **LC** ML1. **DD** 789.912.

DISCO FEVER. 1978-. 0706-7763. CN. English (French). an. Canadian Association of Professional D J's, Suite 1/7149 Sainte Laurent Boulevard, Montreal Quebec H2S 3E2 Canada. **DD** 780.4205. *Disco, 0703-7740*.

DISCOGRAPHIES. V. 1-. 0192-334X. Monographic Series. US. English. ir. Greenwood Press, 88 Post Road West/PO Box 5007, Westport CT 06881. **Tel** (203)226-3571. **Ed** Michael Gray. **LC** UNC.

DISCOTECA HI-FI. See Sound Recordings and Systems.

DIVISIONS. 0192-6128. Periodical. US. English. qt. $9.50. Divisions, PO Box 18647, Cleveland Heights OH 44118. **LC** ML1. **DD** 780.5.

DOBLINGER'S NEWS LETTER. 1973-. 0377-7073. English. ir. Verlag Doblinger, Dorotheergasse 10, 1010 Wien Austria. **LC** ML5. **DD** 780.5.

DOCUMENTA MUSICOLOGICA. 1. REIHE. DRUCKSCHRIFTEN-FAKSIMILES. 0419-5205. Periodical. GW. German. ir. Baerenreiter Music Corporation, 224 King Street, Englewood NJ 07631. **Tel** 561-30011. **Ed** Int Vereinigugn Musikbibliotheken and Int Ges F Musikwissenschaft. Facsimile editions of important sources in musicology, music theory and performance practice from the renaissance to the 18th century. *Documenta Musicologica*.

DOCUMENTA MUSICOLOGICA. 2. REIHE: HANDSCHRIFTEN-FAKSIMILES. Vol. 1 1955-. 0417-805X. GW. German. ir. Barenreiter-Verlag, Postfach 10 03 29, D3500 Kassel West Germany.

DONIZETTI SOCIETY JOURNAL. (JOURNAL - DONIZETTI SOCIETY). VFOAT Journal of the Donizetti Soceity. No. 1- 1974-. 0307-1448. Periodical. UK. English. an. $6.00. Donizetti Society, 56 Harbut Road, London SW11 2RB England. **LC** ML410.D7. **DD** 782.10924.

DOUBLE PLATINUM CIRCUS. 0198-8654. Periodical. US. English. 115 East 57 Street, New York NY 10022. **LC** ML3533.8. **DD** 784.54005.

THE DOUBLE REED. Vol. 1, No. 1 (Mar. 1978)-. 0741-7659. Periodical. US. English. ty. Michigan State University, Department of Music, East

Music

Lansing MI 48823. *To the World's Oboists,* 0091-9683; *To the World's Bassoonists,* 0828-1475.

DOWN BEAT. V. 1- July 1934-. 0012-5768. Periodical. US. English. mo. $18.00. Maher Publishers, 180 West Park Avenue, Elmhurst IL 60126. **Tel** (312)941-2030. **Ed** Art Lange. **Ind/Abst** Music Index, Mag. Index, Read. Guide Period. Lit., Book Rev. Index. bk rev. adv acc. **Circ** 91,000. Available on microfilm from University Microfilms. Published for contemporary musicians.

DOWN HOME. VFOAT Downhome. V. 1- Sept. 1976-. 0703-458X. Periodical. CN. English. bm. $1. Per No. J Hustler, Downhome, 66 Carlton Drive, Orangeville Ontario L9W 2X9 Canada. **DD** 780.4205.

DRIVING WHEEL. V. 1- Dec. 1973-. 0095-3717. US. English. 82 Clematis Avenue, Waltham MA 02154. **LC** ML1. **DD** 780.5.

DRUM CORPS NEWS. 0012-6748. Periodical. US. English. ir. $22.50. Drum Corps News, Box 146, Revere MA 02151. **Tel** (617)289-8571.

DRUM CORPS REVIEW. 0094-3649. US. English. $0.50. Government Printing Office, Box 495, Brooklyn NY 11201. **LC** ML1. **DD** 785.0671. *Eastern Review.*

DRUM CORPS WORLD. 1971. 0164-3223. Periodical. US. English. ir. $25.00. Drum Corps World/Second Class, PO Box 8052, Madison WI 53708. **Tel** (608)241-2292. **Ed** Steve Vickers. **LC** ML1306. **DD** 785.067105. adv acc. **Circ** 6,000. The most complete coverage of drum and bugle corps and color guard activities available today.

THE DULCIMER PLAYERS NEWS. V. 1- Jan. 1975-. 0098-3527. Periodical. US. English. qt. $10.00. Dulcimer Player News, PO Box 2164, Winchester VA 22601. **Tel** (703)668-6152. **Ed** Madeline MacNeil. **LC** ML1. **DD** 787.9. bk rev. adv acc. **Circ** 2,200. Information on hammer and fretted dulcimers for builders and players. Events calendar, reviews, interviews, and musical arrangements.

EAR MAGAZINE (1983). (EAR MAGAZINE). 0734-2128. Periodical. US. English. ir. $20.00. New Wilderness Foundation, 325 Spring Street Room 208, New York NY 10013. **Tel** (212)807-7944. **Ed** Carol E Tuynman. bk rev. adv acc. **Circ** 6,000. Interdisciplinary approach to new music, articles, scores, interviews by and about composers and performers. *Ear Magazine East.*

EARLY CHILDHOOD MUSIC NEWSLETTER. VFOAT Early Childhood Music. Vol. 1, No. 2 (Sept. 1984)-. 0747-5446. Periodical. US. English. bm. $15.00. Early Childhood Music, 10001 El Monte, Overland Park KS 66207. **DD** 372.

EARLY ENGLISH CHURCH MUSIC. No. 1- 1963-. 0424-0359. Monographic Series. UK. English. sa. Stainer & Bell, 82 High Road, London N2 9PN England. **Ed** Frank L Harrison.

EARLY KEYBOARD STUDIES NEWSLETTER. (EARLY KEYBOARD STUDIES NEWSLETTER : A PUBLICATION OF THE WESTFIELD CENTER FOR EARLY KEYBOARD STUDIES, INC). Vol. 1, No. 1 (Dec. 1984)-. 0882-0201. Periodical. US. English. qt. $20.00, Free to Members. Westfield Center for Early Keyboard Studies Inc, 1 Cottage Street, Easthampton MA 01027. **DD** 786.

EARLY MUSIC. V. 1- Jan. 1973-. 0306-1078. Periodical. UK. English. qt. $40.00. Oxford University Press, PO Box 11806, Birmingham AL 35202. **Tel** (205)991-6925. **Ed** Nicholas Kenyon. **Ind/Abst** Am. Hist. Life, Hist. Abstr., Music Index, RILM Abstr., Art Archaeol. Tech. Abstr., Ref. Source, Hist. Abstr., Part A, Mod. Hist. Abstr., Hist. Abst., Part B, Twent. Century Abstr. **LC** ML5. **DD** 780.5. bk rev. adv acc. Offers a comprehensive fully illustrated guide to every aspect of medieval, renaissance, baroque, and classical music. Covers reviews of books, music and recordings, correspondence and saleroom reports.

EARLY MUSIC HISTORY. 1-. 0261-1279. Periodical. UK. English. an. $54.00. Cambridge University Press, 510 North Avenue, New Rochelle NY 10801. **Ed** Iain Fenlon. **LC** ML169.8. **DD** 780.90205. Journal devoted to studies of Western music from its origins to c 1700. Encourages traditional approaches to historical writing emphasizing interdisciplinary work and studies pursuing new methodological ideas.

EARLY MUSIC JOURNAL. V. 1- June 1978-. Periodical. English. ir. 3.00. PO Box 10264, Wellington New Zealand. **LC** ML169.8. **DD** 780.902.

EARLY MUSIC NEWS. No. 1- Aug. 1977-. Periodical. UK. English. mo. 27 Lanhill Road, London W9 2BS England. **LC** ML5. **DD** 780.5.

EASTMAN NOTES. **Main/Corp** Eastman School of Music. 0147-345X. US. English. qt. University Rochester, Eastman School Music 26 Gibbs Street, Rochester NY 14604. **Tel** (716)275-3031. **Ed** Albert Rodenald. **LC** MT4.R6. **DD** 780.72974789. bk rev. **Circ** 8,000. (ctrl). Information and articles of interest to Eastman School alumni and friends.

EASY LISTENING. No. 1- Jan. 1973-. Periodical. UK. English. mo. 0.30 Single Issue. Cardfont Publishers, 7 Carnaby Street, London W1V 1PG London England. **LC** ML5. **DD** 780.4205.

ECHO JEUNESSE. No 2 (May 1983)-. 0826-4236. Periodical. CN. French. ir. Free. Echo Jeunesse, 236 rue Saint-Georges Local 22, Moncton New Brunswick E1C 1W1 Canada. **DD** 784.10060715. (ctrl). *Ton Journal,* 0823-6771.

EDISON PHONOGRAPH MONTHLY. V. 1- March 1903-. Periodical. English. ir. **LC** ML155.59. **DD** 789.9105.

L'EDUCATION MUSICALE. Began 1945. 0013-1415. Periodical. FR. French. mo. $21.29. L'Education Musicale, 23 rue Benard, 75014 Paris France. **Ed** Charles Negiar. **Ind/Abst** RILM Abstr. adv acc. **Circ** 7,000. (ctrl). Review centers on musical subjects: history, musicology, psychology, pedagogy, techniques and instruments.

EGLISE QUI CHANTE. No. 1- 1957-. 0013-2357. Periodical. FR. French. bm. $12.64. Association of St Ambroise, 85 rue de Paris, 03000 Moulins France. Chants for Liturgical Assemblies.

EIGSE CHEOL TIRE. (IRISH FOLK MUSIC STUDIES). V. 1- 1972/73-. 0332-198X. IE. English or Irish. an. Folk Music Society of Ireland, c/o Hugh Shields, 3 Syderham Road/Dundrum, Dublin 14 Ireland. **Tel** (01)744447. **Ed** Hugh Shields. **Ind/Abst** RILM Abstr. **LC** ML3654. **DD** 781.7415. bk rev. adv acc. **Circ** 1,000. Studies, reviews, current bibliography and discography of Irish folk music.

EISERNE LERCHE. Periodical. GW. German. ir. 8.00. Verlag Plane, Postfach 827, 4600 Dortmund 1 West Germany. **LC** ML5. **DD** 784.68.

ELECTRONIC MUSIC & MUSICAL ACOUSTICS. *See* Engineering - Electricity, Electrical Engineering, Electronics.

ELECTRONOTES. V. 5- (No. 33-). 0160-1148. Periodical. US. English. mo. $18.00. Electronotes, 1 Pheasant Lane, Ithaca NY 14850. **Tel** (607)273-8030. **Ind/Abst** RILM Abstr. *Electronotes Newsletter.*

ENGLISH CHURCH MUSIC (ROYAL SCHOOL OF CHURCH MUSIC, CROYDON, SURREY : 1963) CEASED. (ENGLISH CHURCH MUSIC). 1963-1980. 0071-0555. UK. English. an. 2.24. Royal School of Church Music, Addington Palace, Croydon CR9 5AD England. **Ind/Abst** RILM Abstr. **DD** 783.0263.

ENGLISH DANCE AND SONG. V. 1- Sept. 1936-. 0013-8231. Periodical. UK. English. ty. English Folk Dance and Song Society, Cecil Sharp House, 2 Regents Park, London NW1 7AY England. **Ed** Dave Arthur. **Ind/Abst** MLA Int. Bibliogr. Books Artic. Mod. Lang. Lit., Music Index, RILM Abstr. **LC** ML5. **DD** 793.3105. bk rev. adv acc. **Circ** 11,000. (ctrl). All aspects of English folk song, dance, and drama plus related aspects of popular culture. *E.F.D.S. News.*

THE ENGLISH HARPSICHORD MAGAZINE. Periodical. UK. English. sa. $4.50. E Hunt, Rose Cottage/Bois Lane, Chesham Bois, Amersham England. **LC** ML5. **DD** 786.22105. *Harpsichord Magazine.*

ENSEIGNEMENT MUSICAL. Periodical. FR. French. ir. 120.00. E G P, S A 9 rue Coetlogon, 75006 Paris France. **LC** ML5. **DD** 780.5.

ENTRE NOUS (MONTREAL, QUEBEC : 1981). (ENTRE NOUS : C.I.O.F.F. BULLETIN). VFOAT Entre Nous. CN. English (text in French and on inverted pages). an. Canadian Folk Arts Council, Suite 200/1499 de Bleury, Montreal Quebec H3A 2H5 Canada. **DD** 791.6.

DAS ERBE DEUTSCHER MUSIK. SONDERREIHE. VFOAT Sonderreihe. V. 1-. 0425-1695. GW. German. ir. Baerenrieter Music Corporation, 224 King Street, Englewood NJ 07631. **Tel** 561-30011. A series of music monuments divided among several publishers. Baereneiter's divisions: chamber music, middle ages, oratorio and cantata.

L'ESCARGOT. Periodical. French. ir. 40.00. Folk Song International 202 rue du Chateaudes Rentiers, Paris France 75013. **LC** ML5. **DD** 784.4005.

L'ESCARGOT FOLK?. No. 43- May 1977-. Periodical. FR. French. ir. 60.00. Folk Song International, 43 rue Leon Frot, Paris France 75011. **LC** ML5. **DD** 784.4005. *L'Escargot.*

ETHNOMUSICOLOGY. Vol. 1, No. 9 (Jan. 1957)-. 0014-1836. Periodical. US. English. ir. $35.00. Society of Ethnomusicology, PO Box 2984, Ann Arbor MI 48106. **Tel** (313)665-9400. **Ed** Peter Etzkorn. **Ind/Abst** MLA Int. Bibliogr. Books Artic. Mod. Lang. Lit., Music Index, RILM Abstr., Ref. Source, Index Book Rev. Humanit., Music Artic. Guide, Humanit. Index. **LC** ML1. Index in last issue of volume - attached. (cum index). bk rev. adv acc. **Circ** 2,000. (ctrl). Available on microfilm. Advancement of research and study in all cultural contexts. *Ethno-Musicology,* 0014-1836.

ETHNOMUSICOLOGY AT UCLA. (ETHNOMUSICOLOGY AT UCLA : NEWSLETTER OF THE PROGRAM IN ETHNOMUSICOLOGY, UCLA DEPARTMENT OF MUSIC). VFOAT Ethnomusicology At U.C.L.A. **VAT** Ethnomusicology at University of California, Los Angeles. Vol. 1, No. 1-. 0749-4033. Periodical. US. English. Free. Ethnomusicology at UCLA, UCLA Department of Music, Los Angeles CA 90024. **Tel** (213)825-5947. **Ed** Roger Weight. **DD** 781. **Circ** 2,000. Reports on the activities and research conducted by the program in enthomusicology at UCLA.

EX TEMPORE. (EX TEMPORE : ANALYTICAL AND THEORETICAL PAPERS FROM THE DEPARTMENT OF MUSIC, THE UNIVERSITY OF CALIFORNIA AT SAN DIEGO). Vol. 1 (Jan. 1981)-. 0276-6795. Periodical. US. English. ty. $10.00. University of California at San Diego, Department of Music B-026, La Jolla CA 92093. **Tel** (619)453-1632. **Ed** John W MacKay. **LC** ML1. **DD** 780.5. bk rev. adv acc. **Circ** 50. Theoretical and analytical research in contemporary music and contemporary music theory.

EXPLORATIONS IN MUSIC LIBRARIANSHIP. *See* Library and Information Science.

FACES ROCKS. VFOAT Faces. Vol. 1, No. 1 (Nov. 1983)-. 0882-2921. Periodical. US. English. mo. $19.00 Domestic, $25.00 Foreign. Faces, 211 East 43rd Street/Suite 1205, New York NY 10017. **LC** ML3533.8. **DD** 784.54005.

FACSIMILIA MUSICA NEERLANDICA. Vol. 1-. Monographic Series. NE. English (Latin). ir. Vereniging voor Nederlandse Muziekgeschiedenis, PO Box 720, 4116 ZJ Burean The Netherlands. **LC** M2.

FALLEN LEAF MUSIC REFERENCE BOOKS. *See* Encyclopedias & General Reference Books.

FALLEN LEAF PUBLICATIONS IN CONTEMPORARY MUSIC. 8755-2698. Monographic Series. US. English. ir. Fallen Leaf Press, PO Box 10034, Berkeley CA 94709. **Tel** (415)848-7805. **Ed** Ann Basart. Monographic series of musical scores by contemporary American composers.

FANFARE. V. 1- Sept. 1977-. 0148-9364. Periodical. US. English. bm. $24.00. Fanfare, PO Box 720, Tenafly NJ 07670. **Tel** (201)567-3908. **Ed** Joel Flegler. **Ind/Abst** Music Index. **LC** ML156.9. bk rev. adv acc. **Circ** 20,000. Largest record review magazine in the world concentrating mostly on classical reviews. Equipment and book reviews also.

FAST FOLK MUSICAL MAGAZINE. Vol. 1, No. 1 (Jan. 1984)-. 8755-9137. Periodical. US. English. ir. $50.00. Fast Folk Musical Magazine Incorporated, 178 West Houston Street/Suite 9, New York NY 10014. **Tel** (212)989-7088. **Ed** Jack Hardy. **LC** ML3551. **DD** 781.77305. adv acc. **Circ** 1,500. (ctrl). A unique full-length album/magazine. Each issue containing 12 recorded songs with accompanying magazine listing lyrics and related written articles.

FEEDBACK PAPERS. 1.- March 1971-. Periodical. GW. German. ir. Feedback Studio Koln Johannes Fritsch, Genter Strasse 23, 5000 Koln 1 West Germany. **LC** ML197. **DD** 780.904.

FESTIVAL OF FRIENDS. (FESTIVAL OF FRIENDS : PROGRAM). **Main/Conf** Festival of Friends (Hamilton, Ont.). 0822-4978. Periodical. CN. English. ir. Festival of Friends, 21 Augusta Street, Hamilton Ont L8N 1P6 Canada. **DD** 780.7971352.

Music

FICTA. V. 1- Nov./Dec. 1976-. Periodical. AG. Spanish. ir. Mexico 1208, Buenos Aires 1097 Argentina. **LC** ML5. **DD** 780.5.

FIDDLE & A BOW. VAT Fiddle and A Bow. 0160-0850. Periodical. US. English. mo. $2.00. 1008 N Monterey Street, Alhambra CA 91801. **LC** ML1. **DD** 780.42.

FIGA. Main/Corp Fretted Instrument Guild of America. **VAT** Fretted Instrument Guild of America. May/June 1978-. 0196-187X. Periodical. US. English. bm. $12.50 Domestic, $15.00 Foreign. Fretted Instrument Guild of America, 2344 South Oakly Avenue, Chicago IL 60608. **Tel** (312)376-1143. **Ed** Glen Lemmer. **LC** MLl. **DD** 787.005. adv acc. Music news on banjo, mandolin guitar and kindred instuments. International, knowledgeable information and music for these instruments and their artists. *FIGA Review, 0196-1861.*

FIND CATALOG. V. 1- Oct. 1971-. 0091-7591. US. English. $14.00. Find Service International, PO Box 775, Terre Haute IN 47808. **LC** ML156.2. **DD** 381.45789912.

THE FIRST PRIZES. Main/Corp Federation of International Music Competitions. English (French). an. Federation des Concours Internationaux de Musique, Secretariat 12 rue de l'Hotel de Ville, CH-1204 Geneve Suisse Switzerland. **LC** ML385. **DD** 780.922, B.

FLAG; THE MUSIC SCENE. V. 2- (No. 8/9-). 0090-7308. Periodical. US. English. mo. $6.00. F P B Enterprises, 310 Evesham Road, Glendora NJ 08029. **LC** ML1. **DD** 784. *Freedoms Country Flag.*

FLORIDA MUSIC DIRECTOR. V. 23- Aug. 1969-. 0046-4155. US. English. ir. $8.00. National Music Magazine, PO Box 17657, Tampa FL 33682-7657. **Ed** Al Chiaramonte. **LC** ML1. **DD** 780.729759. bk rev. adv acc. **Circ** 4,800. (ctrl). Carries articles and news of interest to music educators, music teachers, and music students in Florida, including reviews of band, orchestra, piano, and choral music. *Music Director.*

FLUTE TALK. Vol. 1, No. 1 (Sept. 1981)-. 0744-6918. Periodical. US. English. ir. $7.00. Instrumentalist Co, 200 Northfield Road, Northfield IL 60093. **Tel** (312)446-5000. **Ed** Polly Hansen. **LC** ML929. **DD** 788.5105. bk rev. adv acc. **Circ** 10,000. (ctrl). The art of flute playing including interviews with classical and jazz flutists; performance guides on standard pieces in flute repertoire; other flute related topics.

THE FLUTE WORKER. 0737-8459. Periodical. US. English. sa. The Flute Works Etc, 1146 Biltmore Drive NE, Atlanta GA 30329. **LC** ML929. **DD** 788.5105.

THE FLUTIST QUARTERLY. (THE FLUTIST QUARTERLY : THE OFFICIAL MAGAZINE OF THE NATIONAL FLUTE ASSOCIATION). Vol. 9, No. 3 (Spring 1984)-. 8756-8667. Periodical. US. English. qt. $15.00. The Flutist Quarterly, PO Box 1038, Royal Oak MI 48068. **Tel** (817)387-9472. **Ed** Glennis M Stout. **DD** 788. adv acc. **Circ** 3,500. (ctrl). Articles and information on flutes and flutist: history, teaching, performing, music, competitions, classes, conventions, flute making and design. Biographies and interviews. *Newsletter (National Flute Association).*

FOLIO-DEX VOCAL, PIANO AND ORGAN FINDING LIST. 1963. US. English. bm. $225.00. Folio Dex, 4728 King Road, Loomis CA 95650. **Tel** (916)652-6976. **Ed** Darlene Poole. **Circ** 1,100. Music reference book, includes song titles, composers, copyright owners and publishers. All types of music. Updated monthly.

FOLK HARP JOURNAL. V. 1- June 1973-. 0094-8934. Periodical. US. English. qt. $12.00. Folk Harp Journal, PO Box 161, Mt Laguna CA 92048. **Tel** (619)473-8556. **Ed** R L Robinson. **Ind/Abst** Music Index. **LC** ML1. **DD** 787.505. bk rev. adv acc. **Circ** 1,000. Concerns all aspects of the harp including folk harp history, current events, music, plans for building, book and record reviews, technical aspects of interest to harpists and harp makers.

THE FOLK LETTER. V. 1- Mar. 1971-. 0145-3734. US. English. mo. $6.00. Folk Song Society of Greater Boston, c/o 11 Sunset Road, Newton MA 02158. **LC** ML1. **DD** 781.705.

FOLK MAGAZIN. Periodical. GW. German. ir. 3.00 Single Issue. Verlag Edition Venceremos, Heinrichstrasse 15, 6090 Rüsselsheim West Germany. **LC** ML3630. **DD** 784.4943.

FOLK MUSIC MAGAZINE. V. 1- Sept. 1978-. 0190-6577. Periodical. US. English. bm. $10.00. Folk Music Magazine Inc, 6730 East McDowell #117, Scottsdale AZ 85257. **LC** ML1. **DD** 781.705.

FOLK MUSIC MINISTRY. Vol. 1, No. 1 (July 1981)-. 0276-6655. Periodical. US. English. bm. $24.00. Folk Music Ministry, PO Box 3443, Annapolis MD 21403. **Tel** (301)263-4030. **LC** ML2999. **DD** 783.7.

FOLK NEWS. No. 1- Jan. 1971-. Periodical. UK. English. bm. British Federation of Folk Clubs, Cecil Sharp House 2 Regents Park Road, London NW1 7AY England. **LC** ML5. **DD** 781.742.

FOLK REVIEW. Began Publication with issue for Mar. 1972?. Periodical. UK. English. mo. Folk Review, Austin House Hospital Street, Nantwich/Cheshire England. *Folk & Country.*

THE FOLKNIK. V. 1- Oct. 1964-. 0146-9169. Periodical. US. English. bm. San Francisco Folk Music Club, 885 Clayton Street, San Francisco CA 94117. **LC** ML1. **DD** 781.705.

FONO FORUM. Began publication with Vol. for 1956. 0015-6140. Periodical. GW. German. mo. $24.35. PC Moderner Verlags GMBH, Herzogenstrasse 64, D-8000 Munchen 40 West German. **Ind/Abst** RILM Abstr. **LC** ML5.

FONTES ARTIS MUSICAE. Vol. 1 1954-. 0015-6191. Periodical. SZ. English (French and German). qt. **Ind/Abst** Music Index, Ref. Source, Libr. Inf. Sci. Abstr., Libr. Lit., RILM Abstr. **LC** ML5.

FOOTNOTE. V. 1- Oct. 1969-. 0308-1990. Periodical. UK. English. bm. $12.50. Foot Note, 66 High Street, Attn Terry Dash, Melbourn Royston, Herts SG8 6AJ England. **Tel** (0763)60823. **Ed** Terry Dash. **Ind/Abst** Jazz Index, Music Index. **LC** ML5. **DD** 784. bk rev. adv acc. **Circ** 1,500. (ctrl). Covers the field of New Orleans and traditional jazz including ragtime. We run articles on past and present musicians. Our review section covers books, records and the latest information.

FORCES FOLK. Periodical. English. ir. 0.50 Single Issue. Christine Lewis-Jones c/o PS2 Sub-Sect Sy Wing, Int & Sy Gp Germany Bfpo 33, Hannover West Germany. **LC** ML5. **DD** 784.4005.

FORSCHUNGSBEITRAGE ZUR MUSIKWISSENSCHAFT. Vol. 1- 1954?-. 0532-226X. Monographic Series. GW. German. ir. Gustav Bosse Verlag, Postfach 417, 8400 Regensburg West Germany.

FRANKIE CROCKER'S MUSIC TRACK. VFOAT Music Track. 0883-0223. Periodical. US. English. $30.00. Music Track, PO Box 6570, New York NY 10150. **LC** ML1. **DD** 784.

FREE MUSIC MAGAZINE. VFOAT Free Music. Vol. 1, No. 1 (Nov. 1983)-. 0826-5984. Periodical. CN. English. ir. Free. Free Music Magazine, 4 Walmsley Boulevard, Toronto Ontario M4V 1X5 Canada. **DD** 784.5400971.

FRETS. V. 1- Mar. 1979-. 0162-0401. Periodical. US. English. mo. $16.95. GPI Publications, 20605 Lazaneo, Cupertino CA 95014. **Tel** (408)446-1105. **Ind/Abst** Jazz Index, Music Index. **LC** ML1. **DD** 787.005. *Pickin', 0098-1761.*

IL FRONIMO. Vol. 1- Oct. 1972-. Periodical. IT. Italian. qt. 30.000. Edizioni Suvini Zerboni, Via MF Quintiliano 40, 20138 Milan Italy. **Tel** 02 5084365. **Ind/Abst** RILM Abstr. **LC** ML5. **DD** 787.6105. bk rev adv acc. **Circ** 3,000. Devoted to the guitar and the lute and to their literature. It handles problems of these instruments. It contains book and scores reviews.

FUGUE. V. 1- Sept. 1976-. 0702-8393. Periodical. CN. English. ir. $10.00. Watts and Johnson Publications Ltd, 69 Sherbourne Street/Suite 315, Toronto Ontario M5A 3X7 Canada. **Ind/Abst** Music Index. **DD** 780.5.

FULL BLAST. V. 1- Winter 1979-. 0191-1953. US. English. $2.00. Full Blast Enterprises, 1800 Austin, Oklahoma City OK 73127. **LC** ML1. **DD** 784.

GA PLAINSONG NOTES. (GA PLAINSONG NOTES : NEWSLETTER OF THE GREGORIAN ASSOCIATION OF CANADA). **VFOAT** G.A. Newsletter. **VAT** Gregorian Association of Canada Plainsong Notes, Gregorian Association of Canada Newsletter, Plainsong Notes. Aug. 1982-. 0821-509X. Periodical. CN. English. ir. Free. Gregorian Association of Canada, 2221 Yonge Street/Suite 250, Toronto Ontario M4S 2B4 Canada. **DD** 783.506071.

GEMEINSCHAFTSKATALOG. 1st Ed.-. GW. German. ir. Josef Keller Verlag, Postfach 1440, D8130 Starnberg West Germany. **LC** ML156.2. **DD** 016.789912.

GENERAL MUSIC JOURNAL. 8755-5905. Periodical. US. English. ty. $15.00. Martha J Waters, PO Box 181 Oxford OH 45056. **Tel** (513)523-6508. **Ed** Martha J Waters. **DD** 372. bk rev. **Circ** 650. (ctrl). Mix of scholarly pieces and how-to articles for teachers of classroom music. Forum for instructional problems, research findings.

GEORGIA MUSIC NEWS. 0046-5798. Periodical. US. English. qt. $4.00. Georgia Music News, PO Box 422, Marietta GA 30061. **LC** ML1.

GERMAN BLUES GUIDE. GW. English (German). ir. German Blues Circle, Postfach 180212, D-6000 Frankfurt 18 West Germany. **LC** ML2. **DD** 784.530025.

GILBERT & SULLIVAN JOURNAL *CEASED.* (THE GILBERT & SULLIVAN JOURNAL). Began in 1925. Ceased with Autumn 1981 issue. 0016-9951. UK. English. Gilbert & Sullivan Society, 34 Pont Street, London SW1 England. **Ind/Abst** Music Index. **LC** ML410.S95. **DD** 782.810924.

GITARRE + LAUTE. VAT Gitarre und Laute. V. 1-. 0172-9683. Periodical. GW. German. bm. 39.00. Gitarre + Laute, Verlagsgesselschaft MBH, Sielsdorfer Strasse la Postfach 410408, 5000 Koln 41 West Germany.

GLORY SONGS. VFOAT Easy Choir Music. 0731-0781. Periodical. US. English. qt. $5.25. Materials Services Department, 127 9th Avenue North, Nashville TN 37234. **Tel** (615)251-2000.

GOLDMINE *CEASED.* 0271-2520. Periodical. US. English. bw. $35.00. Kraus Publications, 700 East State Street, Iola WI 54990. **Tel** (715)445-2214. **Ed** Trey Forester. bk rev. adv acc. **Circ** 12,000. Magazine for record collectors, articles and advertising covering all types of music from all eras. Rock, country, blues, soul, soundtrack, thousands of records for sale in each issue.

GOSPEL CHOIR. V. 1- Oct./Dec. 1974-. 0362-0417. Periodical. US. English. qt. $5.75. Materials Services Department, 127 9th Avenue North, Nashville TN 37234. **Tel** (615)251-2000. **LC** ML1. **DD** 783.705.

GOSPEL MUSIC ASSOCIATION ANNUAL DIRECTORY & YEARBOOK. See Yearbooks, Almanacs, Directories.

GOSPEL MUSIC OFFICIAL DIRECTORY. See Yearbooks, Almanacs, Directories.

GOSPEL WORLD. Vol. 1, No. 1 (April 1980)-. 0278-3436. Periodical. US. English. mo. $12.00 Domestic, $14.00 Foreign. Gospel World, PO Box T, Cambria Heights NY 11411. **LC** ML3186.8. **DD** 783.7.

GRAMOPHONE *CEASED.* V. 1- April 1923-. 0017-310X. Periodical. UK. English. mo. 20.60. General Gramophone Publishing, 177-179 Kenton Road, Harrow Middlesex HA3 0HA England. **Tel** 01 907 4476. **Ed** Anthony C Polland. **Ind/Abst** Music Index. **LC** ML5. bk rev. adv acc. **Circ** 60,000. Reviews of the major UK classical CD, LP and tape releases, latest audio equipment and developments in the world of recorded sound. *Vox, Radio Critic; Broadcast Review.*

GRAMOPHONE CLASSICAL CATALOGUE. No. 88- March 1975-. 0309-4367. UK. English. qt. 15.60. Gramophone, 177-179 Kenton Road, Harrow HA3 0HA England. **Tel** 01 907 4476. **Ed** Malcolm Walker. **LC** ML156.2. **DD** 016.789912. adv acc. **Circ** 10,000. Listing of UK classical releases on LP and tape. *Gramophone Classical Record Catalogue.*

THE GRAMOPHONE NEWS. 0147-8494. Periodical. US. English. $6.00. 1163 Cherry Avenue, San Jose CA 95125. **LC** ML1. **DD** 621.3893305.

GRAMOPHONE POPULAR CATALOGUE. 0309-4359. UK. English. qt. $6.00. General Gramophone Publications Ltd, 177-179 Kenton Road, Harrow HA3 0HA England. **LC** ML156.2. **DD** 016.789912. *Gramophone Popular Record Catalogue.*

GRAPEVINE. (THE GRAPEVINE). V. 1- Nov. 1972-. 0092-0592. Periodical. US. English. $3.20 5 Issues. L Ransil, 19801 Braemar Drive, Saratoga CA 95070. **LC** ML1. **DD** 784.

Music

THE GREENWOOD ENCYCLOPEDIA OF BLACK MUSIC. See Encyclopedias & General Reference Books.

GREGORIUSBLAD. 1.- Vol. Jan. 1876-. Periodical. NE. Dutch. qt. 38.50 Domestic, 45.- Foreign. Nederlandse Sint-Gregoriusver, A V Ostadenl 2, 3583 AJ Utrecht Netherlands. **Tel** (030)5137 39. **LC** ML5. bk rev. adv acc. Liturgy and liturgial music.

DIE GROSSEN DARSTELLUNGEN DER MUSIKGESCHICHTE IN BAROCK UND AUFKLARUNG. 1964-. 0533-3067. German. ir. Akademische Druck-U Verlagsanstalt, Neufeldweg 75 POB 598, A 8011 Graz Australia. Ed Von Othmar Wessely.

GUILD GAZETTE. (THE GUILD GAZETTE : A MEMBERSHIP NEWSLETTER OF REGINA GUILD OF FOLK ARTS). 0823-7875. Periodical. CN. English. bm. Free to Members. Regina Guild of Folk Arts, PO Box 1203, Regina Saskatchewan S4P 3B4 Canada. **DD** 781.706071244.

GUILD NEWS. Main/Corp Canadian Opera Guild. V. 1- Fall 1968-. 0045-5229. Periodical. CN. English. ty. Canadian Opera Guild, 35-39 Front Street East, Toronto Ontario M5E 1B3 Canada.

GUITAR. Periodical. UK. English. mo. $24.52. Musical News Services Ltd, 3 Bimport Shaftesbury, Dorset England. **Tel** (0747) 3427. Ed George Clinton. **LC** ML5. **DD** 787.6105. bk rev. adv acc. With its international readership and contributors, Guitar International is the most highly respected and influential magazine. The English language for classical guitarists.

GUITAR & LUTE. VFOAT Guitar & Lute Magazine. VAT Guitar and Lute. No. 1- April/June 1974-. 0199-9117. Periodical. US. English. bm. Guitar & Lute, 1229 Waimanu Street, Honolulu HI 96814. **Tel** (808)537-2774. **Ind/Abst** Music Index.

GUITAR & MANDOLIN. VAT Guitar and Mandolin. V. 2, No. 2- March 1980-. 0270-9325. Periodical. US. English. bm. $9.00. Guitar & Mandolin, 1600 Billman Lane, Silver Springs MD 20902. **LC** ML1. **DD** 787.6105. Mandolin Notebook, 0148-5482.

GUITAR NEWS. Vol. 1 1951-. 0434-9342. UK. English. ir. International Classic Guitar Association, Cheltenham GLO 50 3RA England.

GUITAR PLAYER. VFOAT Guitar Player Magazine. V. 1- 1967-. 0017-5463. Periodical. US. English. mo. $23.95. GPI Publications, 20605 Lazaneo, Cupertino CA 95014. **Tel** (408)446-1105. **Ind/Abst** Mag. Index, Jazz Index, Pop. Mag. Rev., Music Index.

GUITAR (PORT CHESTER, N.Y.). (GUITAR). Vol. 1, No. 1 (Nov. 1983)-. 0738-937X. Periodical. US. English. mo. $27.95. Cherry Lane Music Company, 110 Midland Avenue, Port Chester NY 10573.

GUITAR REVIEW. (THE GUITAR REVIEW). VFOAT GR. Began with: No. 1 (Oct./Nov. 1946)-. 0017-5471. Periodical. US. English. qt. $26.00. Guitar Review, 40 West 25th Street, New York NY 10010. **Tel** (212)924-4651. Ed Rose Augustine. **Ind/Abst** Music Index, RILM Abstr. **LC** ML1. **DD** 787.6105. bk rev. adv acc. Circ 4,000. International magazine devoted to the classic guitar. Contains in-depth articles, interviews with prominent artists, book, music, and concert reviews, and rare music supplements.

GUITAR TORONTO. (GUITAR TORONTO : THE BULLETIN OF THE GUITAR SOCIETY OF TORONTO). VFOAT Bulletin of the Guitar Society of Toronto. V. 1, No. 1 (Dec. 81/Jan. 82)-. 0820-6392. Periodical. CN. English. ir. Free to Members. Guitar Toronto, 19 Berkeley Street, Toronto Ontario M5R 1T9 Canada. **DD** 787.6109713541.

GUITAR TRADER'S VINTAGE GUITAR BULLETIN. VFOAT Vintage Guitar Bulletin. 0734-9173. US. English. mo. $15.00. Guitar Trader, 12 Broad Street, Red Bank NJ 07701. **LC** ML1015.G9. **DD** 787.612029473.

GUITARRA MAGAZINE. VFOAT Guitarra. Began with issue for Mar./Apr. 1963. 0434-9350. Periodical. US. English. bm. $15.50 Domestic, $21.50 Foreign. Guitarra Magazine, 3145 West 63rd Street, Chicago IL 60629. **Ind/Abst** Music Index. In depth interviews with performing guitarists, publicaton (music), reviews, record reviews, calendar of events, where and when artists are performing, technique and history.

HALLE YEARBOOK. See Yearbooks, Almanacs, Directories.

HANDBOOK - NATIONAL ASSOCIATION OF SCHOOLS OF MUSIC. Main/Corp National Association of Schools of Music. VFOAT NASM Handbook. 1974-. 0164-2847. US. English. be. $7.00. National Association of the School of Music, 11250 Roger Bacon Drive/Suite 5, Reston VA 22090. **Tel** (703)437-0700. Ed Michael Yaffe. **LC** MT27.U5. **DD** 780.72973. Circ 1,500. NASM standards for music curricular at nondegree granting junior college and baccalaureate level as well as the associations constitution, bylaws, rules of practice and procedure and code of ethics.

HANDBOOK TO THE SEASON - CINCINNATI SYMPHONY ORCHESTRA. (HANDBOOK TO THE SEASON). Main/Corp Cincinnati Symphony Orchestra. 1981-1982-. 0732-2321. US. English. an. $3.00. Cincinnati Symphony Orchestra, 1241 Elm Street, Cincinnati OH 45210. **Tel** (513)621-1919. Ed Elizabeth Smart Runyon. **LC** MT125. **DD** 785.073977178. adv acc. Circ 7,000. (ctrl) Complete program notes for the 1985-86 season of the Cincinnati Symphony Orchestra.

HARMONIE-OPERA HI-FI CONSEIL. VFOAT Hi-Fi Conseil. New Series, Yearly V. 17, No. 15, (Dec. 1981)-. 0248-9651. Periodical. FR. French. mo. $24.61. Nouvel Office d'Edition, 216 Boulevard Saint Germain, 75007 Paris France. **Tel** 544 38 23. **Ind/Abst** Music Index. Harmonie Hi-Fi Conseil.

HARMONIE-QUEBEC. (HARMONIE-QUEBEC : BULLETIN OFFICIEL, FEDERATION DES HARMONIES DU QUEBEC). 0713-8059. Periodical. CN. French. ir. $6.00. Harmonie-Quebec, c/o Federation des Harmonies du Quebec, 1415 East rue Jarry, Montreal Quebec H2E 2Z7 Canada. **DD** 785.067.

HARMONIKA-REVUE. Periodical. German. ir. 10.00. Postfach 160, Trossingen West Germany. **LC** ML5. **DD** 786.9705.

THE HARMONIZER. 0017-7849. Periodical. US. English. bm. $6.00. Soc Pres Barber Shop Quartet, 6315 3rd Avenue, Kenosha WI 53140-5199. **Tel** (414)654-9111. Ed Lynne Soto. **DD** 784.06273. adv acc. Circ 40,000. (ctrl) Vocal music education through barbershop harmony; quartet and choral singing; vocal technique; news and information pertaining to association. Barber Shop Re-Chordings.

HARMONY. V. 1- May 1975-. 0099-0604. Periodical. US. English. mo. $5.00. Acts 29, RR 2 Box 218, Harmony PA 16037. **LC** ML1. **DD** 783.7.

HARVARD PUBLICATIONS IN MUSIC. 1- 1967-. 0073-0629. Monographic Series. US. English. ir. Harvard University Press, 79 Garden Street, Cambridge MA 02138. **Tel** (617)661-3761.

HEAVY METAL TIMES. 0739-4306. Periodical. US. English. qt. $8.50 U.S., $12.50 Countries outside of U.S. 216 Vernon Castle, Benbrook TX 76126. **LC** ML3533.8. **DD** 784.54005.

HETEROFONIA. No. 1- (No. 1-). 0018-1137. Periodical. MX. Spanish. qt. $22.00. Conservatorio Nacional de Musica, Mazaryk 582, 11560 Mexico DF Mexico. **Tel** 5234810-520-1013. **Ind/Abst** Music Index, RILM Abstr. **LC** ML5. **DD** 780.5. bk rev. Circ 1,000. (ctrl). We fight for a real musical understanding between all the countries of America. Also encourage research into the little known Colonial music of Mexico.

HIFI STEREO. See Sound Recordings and Systems.

HIGH FIDELITY. MUSICAL AMERICA EDITION. (HIGH FIDELITY). VFOAT High Fidelity/Musical America. Vol. 30, No. 8 (Aug. 1980)-. 0735-777X. Periodical. US. English. mo. ABC Leisure Magazine Inc, 825 7th Avenue, New York NY 10019, (subscription address: Communication Data Services 112 Tenth Street Des Moines IA 50309). **Ind/Abst** Abr. Read. Guide, Music Index, Film Lit. Index, Pop. Mag. Rev., Read. Guide Period. Lit. High Fidelity & Musical America, 0735-9268.

HISTOIRE DU ROCK. No. 1- 1973-. Periodical. CN. French. wk. Messageries Dynamiques Inc, 775 Boulevard Lebeau, Montreal Quebec H4N 1S5 Canada. **DD** 780.4209.

HITMEN. V. 1, No. 1-. 0737-7959. Periodical. US. English. $12.95. S Y Bradley, 5909 Wilkinson Avenue, North Hollywood CA 91607. **LC** MT662. **DD** 789.1.

HOGAKU (NEW YORK, N.Y.). (HOGAKU). Vol. 1, No. 1 (Spring 1983)-. Periodical. US. English. sa. 33 West 42nd Street, New York NY 10036. Ed H Burnett. **Ind/Abst** Music Index. **LC** ML340. **DD** 781.75205.

HOME ORGANIST AND LEISURE MUSIC. Aug./Sept. 1977-. Periodical. UK. English. mo. Cover Publications Ltd, Sales Agents, 1500 Broadway/19th Floor, New York NY 10036. **LC** ML597. **DD** 786.9205.

THE HORN CALL. V. 1- Feb. 1971-. 0046-7928. Periodical. US. English. sa. $40.00. International Horn Society, SE Oklahoma State University of Music, Durant OK 74401. **Tel** (405)924-0121. Ed Paul Mansur. **LC** ML1. bk rev. adv acc. Circ 2,400. (ctrl). Historical and technical research reports, music and record reviews, reprints, horn pedagogy, biographical sketches of noted hornists, humor, etc. in regard to the horn.

HORTUS MUSICUS. 1- 1950-. Monographic Series. GW. ir. Baerenreiter Music Corporation, 224 King Street, Englewood NJ 07631. **Tel** 561-30011. A series of interesting and important works for string and wind instruments with various instrumentation - solo instruments, chamber music, orchestral works, of the renaissance to the early classical period.

HOT BUTTERED SOUL. 0302-0762. Periodical. UK. English. mo. 1.80. C Savory, 36 Scrapsgate Road, Minster Sheppey England. **LC** ML5. **DD** 784.

HOT WACKS. VFOAT Hot Wax. 1-. 0714-864X. Periodical. CN. English. sa. Hot Wacks, Blue Flake Productions, Box 2666/Station B, Kitchener Ontario N2H 6N2 Canada. **DD** 016.789912.

HOT WACKS QUARTERLY. V. 1- Winter 1979-. 0709-8928. Periodical. CN. English. qt. $7.00 Per Year US and Canada, $9.00 Others. Blue Flake Productions, PO Box 2666/Station B, Kitchener Ontario N2H 6N2 Canada. **DD** 016.789912.

HOT WIRE. Vol. 1, No. 1 (Nov. 1984)-. 0747-8887. Periodical. US. English. ty. $14.00. Not Just A Stage, 1321 West Rosedale, Chicago Il 60660. **DD** 780.

HUDEBNI NASTROJE. Periodical. CS. Czech (summaries in English, German, and Russian). bm. Artia, PO Box 790, Praha 1 Czechoslovakia. **Ind/Abst** RILM Abstr. **LC** ML5.

HUDEBNI ROZHLEDY. 0018-6996. Periodical. CS. Czech. mo. Artia, PO Box 790, Praha 1 Czechoslovakia. **Ind/Abst** Music Index, RILM Abstr.

HUDEBNI VEDA. 0018-7003. Periodical. GW. Czech (summaries in Russian and German). qt. Kubon and Sagner, Postfach 34 01 08, D-8000 Munchen 34 West Germany. **Tel** (089)52 20 27. **Ind/Abst** Music Index, RILM Abstr. A journal of scientific studies of music. Deals with a great variety of branches of musicology, such as the history of music, aesthetics and theory of musical art, theory of musical composition and structure, the sociology of music and popular music.

HUDOBNY ARCHIV. 1- 1974-. Slovak (summaries in German and Russian). ir. 22.00. **LC** ML247.1.

HUGH LE CAINE PROJECT NEWSLETTER. (THE HUGH LE CAINE PROJECT NEWSLETTER). Issue No. 1 (June 1979)-. 0229-6659. Periodical. CN. English. qt. Free. Hugh le Caine Project, 27 Davies Avenue, Toronto Ontario M4M 2A9 Canada. **DD** 789.990924.

HUNGARIAN MUSICAL GUIDE CEASED. Publication ceases in 1984. English. ir. 5 POB, 80 Vorosmarty Ter 1. **LC** ML21. **DD** 780.9439.

HURDY GURDY. 0191-6785. Periodical. US. English. bm. $16.50. Armateur Organist Association, 7720 Morgan Avenue, Minneapolis MN 55423. **Tel** (612)866-3421.

THE HYMN. V. 1- Oct. 1949-. 0018-8271. Periodical. US. English. qt. $25.00. The Hymn Society of America, National Headquarters, Texas Christian University, Fort Worth TX 76129. **Tel** (817)921-7608. Ed Paul Westermeyer. **Ind/Abst** Music Index, Relig. Index One, Period., Relig. Theol. Abstr. **LC** ML1. **DD** 783.905. bk rev. adv acc. Circ 3,500. (ctrl). Journal of congregational song for church musicians, clergy and institutional libraries containing practical and scholarly articles reflecting diverse cultural and theological identities and providing exemplary hymn texts and tunes in various styles.

THE HYMN SOCIETY OF GREAT BRITAIN AND IRELAND BULLETIN. Main/Corp Hymn Society of Great Britain and Ireland. Began publication in 1937. 0018-828X. Periodical. UK. English. ty. Hymn Society of Great Britain and Ireland,

30 East Meads, c/o John Wilson Guildford, Surrey GU2 5SP England. **Ed** B S Massey. **Ind/Abst** Music Index. **LC** ML5. **DD** 783.905. (cum index). adv acc. **Circ** 500. Articles, book and record reviews concerning words and music of hymns and related items such as their origins, selection and use, their authors and composers.

HYMNOLOGISKE MEDDELELSER. 0106-4940. Periodical. DK. Danish (text in Norwegian and Swedish). qt. Salmehistorisk Selskab Kbenhavns Universitet, Institut fur Kirkehistorie Kbmagergade 44-46, DK-1150 Kbenhavn K Denmark. **Ind/Abst** MLA Int. Bibliogr. Books Artic. Mod. Lang. Lit. **LC** ML3142.

HYPE. 0097-6539. US. English. $2.75 Four Issues. PO Box 14001, Washington DC 20044. **LC** ML1. **DD** 784.

IAJRC JOURNAL. **Main/Corp** International Association of Jazz Record Collectors. **VAT** International Association of Jazz Record Collectors Journal. 0098-9487. Periodical. US. English. qt. $6.25. International Association of Jazz Record Collectors, Bozy White, PO Box 10208, Oakland CA 94610. **Ind/Abst** Jazz Index, Music Index. **LC** ML156.9. **DD** 785.067205.

IHWA UMAK. **VFOAT** Journal of Music, EWHA Women's University. V. 1- 1972-. Periodical. Korean. an. **LC** ML5.

IJS JAZZ REGISTER. **Main/Corp** Rutgers University. Institute of Jazz Studies. June 1979-. US. English. qt. $25.00. Transaction Books and Periodical, Rutgers University, New Brunswick NJ 08903. **Tel** (201)932-2280. Each issue contains an index to its own contents - no vol index - loose. (cum index).

ILLINOIS MUSIC COUNTRY MAGAZINE. 0098-3535. Periodical. US. English. qt. $4.50. Illinois Country Opry Inc, PO Box 313, Petersburg IL 62675. **LC** ML1. **DD** 784.

THE ILLINOIS MUSIC EDUCATOR. 0019-2147. Periodical. US. English. ir. $5.00. Illinois Music Educators Association, 2 Harriet Lane, Springfield IL 62702.

ILWC NEWSLETTER. **Main/Corp** International League of Women Composers. Periodical. US. English. qt. ILWC Newsletter, PO Box 3463, Arlington VA 22203.

IMAGINE. 0162-6450. Periodical. US. English. bm. $9.00 12 Issues. Gorman Bechard, Box 2715, Waterbury CT 06720. **LC** ML3476.8. **DD** 780.4205.

IMPROMPTU. (IMPROMPTU : A PUBLICATION OF THE MUSIC DIVISION OF THE LIBRARY OF CONGRESS). Vol. 1, No. 1 (Fall 1982)-. 0737-5190. Periodical. US. English. Free. Library of Congress, Research Services/Music Division, Washington DC 20540. **Tel** (202)287-5503. **Ed** Paula Forrest. **LC** ML110. **DD** 026.7809753. **Circ** 3,500. Activities of the Music Division in the Library of Congress. Includes scholarly articles, news of acquisitions, and chamber music performances at the library.

IN STEP. (IN STEP : SOUTHERN CALIFORNIA'S GUIDE TO MARCHING ACTIVITIES). Vol. 1, No. 1 (Oct. 1982)-. 0735-8431. Periodical. US. English. mo. $11.95. In Step, 787b East Washington Boulevard #4, Pasadena CA 91104.

IN THEORY ONLY. Vol. 1- Apr. 1975-. 0360-4365. Periodical. US. English. ir. $15.00. In Theory Only, University of Michigan School of Music, Ann Arbor MI 48109. **Tel** (313)764-0583. **Ed** Dave Headlam. **Ind/Abst** Music Index. **LC** ML1. **DD** 781.05. bk rev. **Circ** 400. Papers, articles, comments on any theory-related topics.

INDIANA MUSICATOR. (THE INDIANA MUSICATOR). V. 1- Mar. 1946-. 0273-9933. Periodical. US. English. qt. $8.00. Indiana Music Education Association, Director of Music Ball/State University, Muncie IN 47306. **Tel** (317)288-5496. **Ed** Marilyn Vincent. **LC** ML1. adv acc. **Circ** 1,500. (ctrl). Presents timely articles dealing with music education. Also presents information dealing with the work of the Music Educators National Conference and the Indiana Musicator.

INDIANA THEORY REVIEW. V. 1- Sept. 1977-. 0271-8022. Periodical. US. English. ty. $10.00. Indiana Theory Review, Indiana University/School of Music, Sycamore Hall/Room 041, Bloomington IN 47401. **Tel** (812)336-5716. **Ed** Rudy T Marcozzi. **Ind/Abst** Music Index, RILM Abstr. **LC** MT6. **DD** 781.05. bk rev. **Circ** 200. Contains information on: music-theoretical analyses, current issues in the field of music theory including analysis, perception, and history and pedagogy.

INDIANAPOLIS SYMPHONY ORCHESTRA : PROGRAMS. Began in 1930. US. English. an. Indianapolis Symphony, 45 Monument Circle, Indianapolis IN 46204-2901. **Tel** (317)924-6321.

INFO-COMPTOIR MUSICAL. **Main/Corp** Alliance Chorale Alberta. Vol. 1, No. 1 (Nov. 1981)-. 0822-8167. Periodical. CN. French. ir. Free. Alliance Chorale Alberta, 101-8925 82 Av, Edmonton Alberta T6C 0Z2 Canada. **Ed** Yes. **DD** 016.784106.

INFO (GERMAN BLUES CIRCLE). **Main/Corp** German Blues Circle. No. 1 (Aug. 1976)-. Periodical. GW. chiefly in German. mo. German Blues Circle, Postfach 180212, 6000 Frankfurt 18 West Germany. **Ind/Abst** Jazz Index.

THE INSTRUMENTALIST. 0020-4331. Periodical. US. English. mo. $18.00. Instrumentalist Company, 200 Northfield Road, Northfield IL 60093. **Tel** (318)446-5000. **Ed** Anne Driscoll. **Ind/Abst** Educ. Index, Music Index. **DD** 780. bk rev. adv acc. **Circ** 22,000. Contains practical professional information for school band and orchestra directors and other music educators.

THE INSTRUMENTALIST. Periodical. US. English. mo. Instrumentalist, 200 Northfield, Northfield IL 60093. **Tel** (312)446-5000.

INSTRUMENTENBAU. Periodical. German (summaries in English, French, and Italian). ir. 51.00. Verlag F Schmitt, Kaiserstr 99-101, 5200 Siegburg, Postfach 243, Siegburg West Germany. **LC** ML5. **DD** 781.9105. *Instrumentenbau Zeitschrift.*

INSTRUMENTENBAU - ZEITSCHRIFT *CEASED.* (INSTRUMENTENBAU ZEITSCHRIFT). Vols. 1-28. 0020-4390. Periodical. GW. German. mo. 64,00. Verlag Franz Schmitt, Kaiserstrasse 99-101, 5200 Siegburg West Germany. **Tel** 02241/640 30. **Ed** H G Hamm. **Ind/Abst** RILM Abstr. **LC** ML5. **DD** 781.9105.

INTER-AMERICAN MUSIC REVIEW. V. 1- Fall 1978-. 0195-6655. Periodical. US. English (Portuguese and Spanish). ir. $13.00. Theodore Front Musical Literature, 16122 Cohasset Street, Van Nuys CA 91406. **Tel** (818)994-1902. **Ed** Robert Stevenson. **Ind/Abst** Music Index, RILM Abstr. **LC** ML1. **DD** 780.5. bk rev. Articles on aspects of music in the Americas. Emphasis on the scholarly subject.

INTERFACE. V. 1- Apr. 1972-. 0303-3902. Periodical. NE. English. qt. 80.-. Swets & Zeitlinger BV, 347 Heereweg, 2161 Ca Lisse The Netherlands. **Tel** 02521-19113. **Ed** Jan L Broecks. **Ind/Abst** Music Index, RILM Abstr., Comput. Control Abstr., Electr. Electron. Abstr., Sci. Abstr., Phys. Abstr., Sci. Abstr. Sect. A. Phys. Abstr. **LC** ML5. **DD** 780.5. **CODEN** IFCEBC. bk rev. adv acc. **Circ** 600. A journal devoted to discussions of all questions which fall into the borderline areas between music on one hand, and the physical and human sciences on the other. *Electronic Music Reports, Jaarboek.*

THE INTERNATIONAL CONGRESS ON WOMEN IN MUSIC NEWSLETTER. **VFOAT** Women in Music Newsletter. Vol. 1, No. 1 (Jan. 1983)-. Periodical. US. English. qt. International Congress on Women in Music, PO Box 366, Loyola Boulevard at West 80th, Los Angeles CA 90045.

INTERNATIONAL INVENTORY OF MUSICAL SOURCES. No. 1- 1960-. 0538-8007. US. Introductory matter in English, French, and German. ir. European American Music, PO Box 850, Valley Forge PA 19482. **Tel** (215)648-0506. **LC** ML113.

INTERNATIONAL JOURNAL OF MUSIC EDUCATION. **VFOAT** Music Education. No. 1 (May 1983)-. Periodical. AT. English. sa. University Western Australia, Department of Music, Nedlands Western Australia. **Tel** (09)3802051. **Ed** Gary McPherson. bk rev. adv acc. **Circ** 3,000. (ctrl). Publishes articles of interest to musicians around the world, also reviews books, sheet music and teacher aids in the comprehensive review section of the journal.

INTERNATIONAL LEAGUE OF WOMEN COMPOSERS NEWSLETTER. **VFOAT** Newsletter. Dec. 1981-. 0748-5735. Periodical. US. English. qt. International League of Women Composers, PO Box 3463, Arlington VA 22203. *Newsletter (International League of Women Composers).*

INTERNATIONAL MUSIC EDUCATION. *See* Yearbooks, Almanacs, Directories.

INTERNATIONAL MUSIC GUIDE. 1977-. UK. English. an. $12.95. New York Zeotrope, 80 East 11th Street/Suite 516, New York NY 10003. **Tel** (212)420-0590. **Ed** Jane Dudman. **LC** ML5. **DD** 780.5. bk rev. adv acc. Featuring reports from concert halls, recording studios, and music festivals worldwide. Also includes new record releases, books, magazines, music in print, early music, schools, etc.

THE INTERNATIONAL MUSIC REVIEW. **VFOAT** Music Review. Vol. 1, No. 1 (July 1982)-. 0734-5054. Periodical. US. English (Spanish). mo. $45.00 US and Canada $60.00 Air Mail. International Music Review Inc, 3120 West 8th Avenue, Hialeah FL 33012. **LC** ML1. **DD** 784.5005.

INTERNATIONAL MUSICIAN. 1- 1901-. 0020-8051. Newspaper. US. English. mo. $15.00. American Federation of Musicians, 1500 Broadway, New York NY 10036. **Tel** (212)869-1330. **Ind/Abst** Pop. Mag. Rev., Music Index.

INTERNATIONAL MUSICIAN AND RECORDING WORLD. UK. English. $1.25 Single Issue. Independent Magazine Ltd, 181 Queen Victoria Street, London England. **LC** ML5. **DD** 780.4205.

INTERNATIONAL MUSICIAN AND RECORDING WORLD. V. 1- Mar. 1979-. 0273-673X. Periodical. US. English. mo. $21.00. International Musician and Recording World, 12 West 32nd Street, New York NY 10001. **Tel** (212)947-6740. **LC** ML3469. **DD** 780.4205.

THE INTERNATIONAL PIPER. V. 1- May 1978-. Periodical. UK. English. ir. $23.00 US Airmail. International Piper Ltd, Seaton Works, Edinburgh Road, Cockenzie East Lothian EH32 CHQ Scotland. **LC** ML980. **DD** 788.9205.

INTERNATIONAL TROMBONE ASSOCIATION SERIES. 0363-5708. Monographic Series. US. English. 136 Eighth Avenue North, Nashville TN 37203-3798. **Tel** (615)254-8969. **Ed** Stephen L Glover. **Circ** 600. Trombone music series.

INTERVAL. V. 1- May 1978-. 0276-3052. Periodical. US. English. ir. $18.00. Interval, PO Box 8027, San Diego CA 92102. **Tel** (619)295-9023. **Ed** Jonathan Glasier. **Ind/Abst** Music Index. bk rev. adv acc. **Circ** 350. New music research in new instruments, scales, computers. Works by Dartch, Harrison, Darreg Ben Johnston and microtonal composers and theorists from US and abroad.

INTERVALLE. Feb./Mar. 1969-. Periodical. GW. German. qt. 6.00. Arbeitskreis fur Musik in der Jugend, Hoffmann-Von-Fallersleben-Str 8 Postfach 14 60, 3340 Wolfenbuttel West Germany. **LC** ML5. **DD** 780.5.

IOWA JOURNAL OF RESEARCH IN MUSIC EDUCATION. **VFOAT** Journal of Research in Music Education. No. 1- 1976-. 0270-7098. Periodical. US. English. an. $1.50. University of Iowa, School of Music, Iowa City IA 52242. **Tel** (319)353-3715.

I.S.A.M. MONOGRAPHS. **Main/Corp** Brooklyn College. Institute for Studies in American Music. No. 1-. Monographic Series. US. English. ir. Institute for Studies in American Music, Brooklyn College/Department of Music, Brooklyn NY 11210. **Tel** (718)780-5655. **Ed** H Wiley Hitchcock. A series of bibliographies, discographies, extended essays, and reference works covering all aspects of American music.

ISRAEL STUDIES IN MUSICOLOGY. **VFOAT** Mehkarim Be-Musikologyah. V. 1- 1978-. Periodical. IS. English. an. Hebrew University, PO Box 503, Jerusalem Israel. **LC** ML5. **DD** 780.5.

ITG JOURNAL. **Main/Corp** International Trumpet Guild. **VFOAT** Journal of the International Trumpet Guild. **VAT** International Trumpet Guild Journal. V. 1- Oct. 1976-. 0363-2849. US. English. qt. $20.00. Gordon Mathie, Crane School of Music SUC, Potsdam NY 13676. **Tel** (315)265-9635. **Ed** Anne F Hardin. **Ind/Abst** Music Index. **LC** ML1. **DD** 788.105. bk rev. adv acc. **Circ** 3,500. (ctrl). Trumpet performance and teaching. *ITG Newsletter, 0363-2857.*

ITG NEWSLETTER *CEASED.* **Main/Corp** International Trumpet Guild. **VAT** International Trumpet Guild Newsletter. -V. 8, No. 3. 0363-2857. Periodical. US. English. ty. $10.00. **LC** ML1. **DD** 788.105.

IYUNIM BE-MUSIKAH. **VFOAT** Musical Prose. Periodical. IS. Hebrew. ir. Israel Composers' League, Nordau Boulevard 73/POB 11180, Tel-Aviv Israel. **LC** ML5. **DD** 780.95694.

J & F RECORD SPECIAL. **VAT** J and F Record Special. V. 1- Apr./May 1976-. 0363-8367. Periodical. US. English. bm. J & F Southern Record

Music

Sales, 44 North Lake, Pasadena CA 91101. **LC** ML156.9. **DD** 789.913105.

JAHRBUCH. See Yearbooks, Almanacs, Directories.

JAHRBUCH DER DEUTSCHEN MUSIKORGANISATION. See Yearbooks, Almanacs, Directories.

JAHRBUCH DER MUSIKBIBLIOTHEK PETERS. See Yearbooks, Almanacs, Directories.

JAHRBUCH FUR LITURGIK UND HYMNOLOGIE. See Yearbooks, Almanacs, Directories.

JAHRBUCH PETERS / HERAUSGEGEBEN VON EBERHARDT KLEMM. See Yearbooks, Almanacs, Directories.

JAHRESVERZEICHNIS DER MUSIKALIEN UND MUSIKSCHRIFTEN. V. 118-. 0323-3693. German. sa. Alexander Broude Inc, 575 Eighth Avenue, New York NY 10018. **Tel** (212)586-1674. *Jahresverzeichnis der Deutschen Musikalien und Musikschriften, 0075-2959.*

JAMBOREE COUNTRY MUSIC MAGAZINE. VFOAT Jamboree. Vol. 1, No. 7 (Oct. 1980)-. 0229-2203. Periodical. CN. English. mo. $4.00. Jamboree Country Music Magazine, PO Box 452, St Catharine Ontario L2R 6V9 Canada. **DD** 784.52005. *Fan Fair Country Music Magazine, 0229-219X.*

JAZZ CEASED. VFOAT Jazz Magazine. V. 1-4, No. 2. 0145-2843. Periodical. US. English. qt. $10.00. Stites-Oakey Inc, PO Box 212, Northport NY 11768. **Ind/Abst** Music Index. **LC** ML1. **DD** 781.5705.

JAZZ. Vol. 1- Feb. 1956-. 0021-5600. Periodical. PL. Polish. qt. ARS Polona, Krakowskie Prxedmiescie 7, 00-068 Warsaw Poland. **Ind/Abst** RILM Abstr. **LC** ML5.

JAZZ DIGEST. 0092-0525. Periodical. US. English. mo. $5.00. E Steane, 1973 Kennedy Drive, McLean VA 22101. **LC** ML1. **DD** 789.913654205. *HIP.*

JAZZ EDUCATORS JOURNAL. (JAZZ EDUCATORS JOURNAL : OFFICIAL MAGAZINE OF THE NATIONAL ASSOCIATION OF JAZZ EDUCATORS). Vol. 13, No. 2 (Dec. 1980/Jan. 1981)-. 0730-9791. Periodical. US. English. qt. $12.00. National Association of Jazz Educators, Box 724, Manhattan KS 66502. **Tel** (913)776-8744. Ed John Kuzmich Jr. **Ind/Abst** Jazz Index, Music Index. **LC** ML1. **DD** 785.4205. bk rev. adv acc. **Circ** 6,500. (ctrl). Educational and historical articles, sources for up-to-date teaching and performing material, graded music lists, and other necessary aids for jazz education. *Naje Educator.*

JAZZ FESTIVALS INTERNATIONAL DIRECTORY. See Yearbooks, Almanacs, Directories.

JAZZ FORUM. Began with Vol. for 1967. 0021-5635. Periodical. US. English. bm. Jazz World Society, PO Box 777, Times Square Station, New York NY 10108. Ed Jan A Byrczek. **Ind/Abst** Jazz Index, Music Index. **LC** ML3505.8. **DD** 785.4205. bk rev. adv acc. **Circ** 6,000. Market place for jazz industry offering opportunities for communication and cooperation worldwide.

JAZZ-INDEX. See Indexes/Abstracts.

JAZZ JOURNAL INTERNATIONAL. V. 30, No. 5- May 1977-. 0140-2285. Periodical. UK. English. mo. $35.00. Jazz Journal Ltd, 35 Great Russell Street, London WC1B 3PP England. **Tel** 01 580 6976. Ed Eddie Cook. **Ind/Abst** Jazz Index, Music Index, Ref. Source. bk rev. adv acc. **Circ** 12,000. Jazz music: records, musicians, books, films, profiles, interviews, previews, and reviews. *Jazz Journal.*

THE JAZZ LINE. 0732-5797. Periodical. US. English. mo. College Media, 47 Reed Drive, Rosslyn NY 11576. **LC** ML3505.8. **DD** 785.4205.

JAZZ OTTAWA. V. 1- Mar. 1975-. 0383-9206. Periodical. CN. English. Jazz Ottawa, 1702-500 Laurier Avenue West, Ottawa K1R 5E1 Canada. **DD** 785.420971384.

JAZZ PODIUM. V. 1- 1952-. 0021-5686. Periodical. GW. German. ir. 42. Jazz Podium, Vogelsangstrasse 32, Stuttgart 1 West Germany. **Tel** (0711)631530. Ed Dieter Zimmerle. **Ind/Abst** Jazz Index, Music Index, RILM Abstr. **LC** ML5. bk rev. adv acc. **Circ** 10,500. All about jazz music: radio and club programs, concerts, news, portraits, reports, interviews, etc.

JAZZ RAG. 0270-4048. Periodical. US. English. mo. $3.00. Jazz Rag, PO Box 1124, Berkeley CA 94701. **LC** ML156.9. **DD** 016.7889912542.

JAZZ SPOTLITE NEWS. Periodical. US. English. qt. $15.00. Jazz Spotlite Productions, 701 7th Avenue/Suite 9W New York NY 10036. **Ind/Abst** Jazz Index.

JAZZ TIMES. June 1980-. 0272-572X. Periodical. US. English. mo. $12.00. Jazz Times, 8055 13th Street/Suite 301, Silver Springs MD 20910. **Tel** (301)588-41149. Ed M Joyce. **Ind/Abst** Jazz Index, Music Index. **LC** ML1. **DD** 785.4205. bk rev. adv acc. **Circ** 50,000. We review and promote jazz in all its varieties, concerts, books, recordings, and musicians. *Radio Free Jazz, 0145-5125.*

JAZZ (WASHINGTON, D.C.). (JAZZ). Began with 1979/80. US. English. an. National Endowment for the Arts, 2401 East Street NW, Washington DC 20506. *Jazz/Folk Music.*

JAZZ WORLD INDEX. See Indexes/Abstracts.

JAZZ WORLD (NEW YORK, N.Y. : 1984). (JAZZ WORLD). Vol. 14, No. 59-. 0749-4564. Periodical. US. English. bm. $25.00. Jazz World Society, PO Box 777, Times Square Station, New York NY 10108. **Tel** (201)939-0836. Ed Jan A Byrczek. **Ind/Abst** Jazz Index. **LC** ML3505.8. **DD** 785.4205. bk rev. **Circ** 6,000. As an organ of the Jazz World Society it serves as a market place for the whole jazz industry offering worldwide opportunities for communication and cooperation. *Jazz World Index, 0886-1927.*

JAZZBAND. V. 1- March/April 1972-. Periodical. AG. Spanish. ir. $2.00 Single Issue. Yerbal No 2291, Dpto 62, Buenos Aires Argentina. **LC** ML5. **DD** 785.4205.

DER JAZZFREUND. Began with No. 1, 1959?. 0021-5724. Periodical. German. ir. 2.00. Gerhard Conrad, Von-Stauffenburg Str 24, D-5750 Menden West Germany. **Ind/Abst** Jazz Index. **LC** ML5.

JAZZIZ. Vol. 1, No. 1 (Jan./Feb. 1984)-. 0741-5885. Periodical. US. English. bm. $4.00. The Jazziz Magazine Inc, PO Box 8309, Gainesville FL 32605-8309.

JAZZNYTT. (JAZZ-NYTT). 0332-7248. Periodical. Swedish. ir. Svenska Jazzriksforbundet, Box 570 101 27 1, Stockholm Sweden. **Ind/Abst** Jazz Index. **LC** ML5.

THE JAZZOLOGIST. 0198-6805. US. English. ir. $26.75. New Orleans Jazz Club of California, PO Box 1225, Kerrville TX 78028.

JEFFERSON. 0345-5653. Periodical. Swedish. ir. 30.00. Hans Andreasson, Eskadervagen 32 III, S-183 54 Taby Sweden. **Ind/Abst** Jazz Index. **LC** ML5. **DD** 784.

JEMF QUARTERLY. Main/Corp John Edwards Memorial Foundation. VAT John Edwards Memorial Foundation Quarterly. 0021-3632. Periodical. US. English. qt. $14.00. John Edwards Memorial Foundation, University of California/Folklore and Myth Center, Los Angeles CA 90024. Ed Linda Painter. **Ind/Abst** Am. Hist. Life, Hist. Abstr., MLA Int. Bibliogr. Books Artic. Mod. Lang. Lit., Music Index, RILM Abstr., Ref. Source, Hist. Abstr., Part A, Mod. Hist. Abstr., Hist. Abst., Part B, Twent. Century Abstr. **LC** ML1. **DD** 784.4008. bk rev. **Circ** 1,000. American traditional music: researches, interviews, or memories of performers. *JEMF Newsletter.*

JEUNESSE ET ORGUE. No. 1, April/May 1970-. Periodical. French. qt. 32.00. Residence Ophelia, Christiane Trieu-Colleney, Pessac 33600 France. **Ind/Abst** Music Index. **LC** ML5. **DD** 786.505.

JMC BULLETIN. Main/Corp Jeunesses Musicales of Canada. V. 1- Jan. 1974-. 0317-0489. Periodical. CN. English. ir. Jeunesses Musicales of Canada, 462 Cote Ste-Catherine Road, Montreal Quebec H2V 2B4 Canada. **DD** 785.06271.

JOEL WHITBURN'S TOP COUNTRY SINGLES & LPS. VFOAT Top Country Singles & LPs. VAT Joel Whitburn's Top Country Singles and LPs. 1978-. 0195-4083. US. English. an. Record Research Inc, PO Box 200, Menomonee Falls WI 53051. **Tel** (414)251-5408. Ed Bill Hathaway. **LC** ML156.4.P6. **DD** 016.789912452. Top country and western 1949-1971 supplements available for 1972-1982. Book lists every record to hit billboards top 100 on their country chart for the given years. *Joel Whitburn's Top Country & Western Records.*

JOEL WHITBURN'S TOP EASY LISTENING SINGLES. VFOAT Top Easy Listening Singles. 1978-. 0195-4067. US. English. an. Record Research Inc, PO Box 200, Menomonee Falls WI 53051. **Tel** (414)251-5408. Ed Bill Hathaway. Easy listening 1961-1974 supplements available for 1975 to 1982. Lists every artist and their records to make the billboard easy listening chart. *Joel Whitburn's Top Easy Listening Records.*

JOEL WHITBURN'S TOP LPS. VFOAT Top LPs. Began with 1973 issue. 0195-4075. US. English. an. Free. Record Research Inc, PO Box 200, Menomonee Falls WI 53051. **Tel** (414)251-5408. Ed Bill Hathaway. **LC** ML156.4.P6. Top Pop albums 1955-1985, lists every artist and their Top 200 Albums chart.

JOEL WHITBURN'S TOP SOUL SINGLES & LPS. VFOAT Top Soul Singles & LPs. VAT Joel Whitburn's Top Soul Singles and LPs. 0195-4059. US. English. an. Record Research Inc, PO Box 200, Menomonee Falls WI 53051. **Tel** (414)251-5408. Ed Bill Hathaway. **LC** ML156.4.S6. **DD** 016.789912455. Top rhythem and blues 1949-1971. Supplements are available for 1972-1982. List every record to make the black hot 100 chart.

JOSLIN'S JAZZ JOURNAL. Vol. 1, No. 1 (Feb. 1982)-. 0735-1585. Periodical. US. English. qt. $5.00 US, $8.00 Overseas. Joslins Jazz Journal, Box 213, Parsons KS 67357. **Ind/Abst** Jazz Index. **LC** ML156.4.J3. **DD** 789.91254205.

JOURNAL - ASSOCIATION FOR RECORDED SOUND COLLECTIONS. See Sound Recordings and Systems.

JOURNAL - CANADIAN ASSOCIATION FOR MUSIC THERAPY. (THE JOURNAL - CANADIAN ASSOCIATION FOR MUSIC THERAPY). Main/Corp Canadian Association for Music Therapy. VFOAT Journal. Began publication in 1977?. 0708-9643. CN. English (French text on inverted pages). an. $3. Canadian Association for Music Therapy, 205-7600 Earle Road, Montreal Quebec H4W 1N9 Canada. **DD** 615.83705. *Journal, 0381-6850.*

JOURNAL - GALPIN SOCIETY. (THE GALPIN SOCIETY JOURNAL). Main/Corp Galpin Society. No. 1- March 1948-. 0072-0127. UK. English. an. $22.98. Bruce Young, 11 Eton Place, London NW3 2BT England. **Tel** 01-723-5148. Ed M Byrne. **Ind/Abst** Music Index, RILM Abstr. **LC** ML1. **DD** 781.9105. (cum index). bk rev. adv acc. **Circ** 1,500. (ctrl). Musical instrument research.

JOURNAL - INTERNATIONAL TROMBONE ASSOCIATION. Main/Corp International Trombone Association. 0145-3513. US. English. qt. $22.00. North Texas State University, School of Music, c/o Vern Kagarice, Denton TX 76203. **Ind/Abst** Music Index. **LC** ML1. **DD** 788.205.

JOURNAL OF BAND RESEARCH. VFOAT ABA Journal of Band Research. V. 1- Autumn 1964-. 0021-9207. Periodical. US. English. sa. Journal of Band Research, Troy State University Press, Troy AL 36082. **Tel** (205)566-3000. Ed Jon R Piersol. **Ind/Abst** Music Index, RILM Abstr., Account. Index. Suppl. **LC** UNC. (cum index). bk rev. **Circ** 1,200. A scholarly journal encompassing the whole spectrum of band/wind ensemble research, serves as a stimulus and outlet for valid scholarly research.

JOURNAL OF CHURCH MUSIC. V. 1- Jan. 1959-. 0021-9703. Periodical. US. English. mo. $7.00. Fortress Press, 2900 Queen Lane, Philadelphia PA 19129. **Ind/Abst** RILM Abstr., Ref. Source, Music Index, Music Artic. Guide. **LC** ML1. Available on microfilm from University Microfilms.

JOURNAL OF COUNTRY MUSIC. (THE JOURNAL OF COUNTRY MUSIC). V. 2, No. 4- Winter 1971-. 0092-0517. Periodical. US. English. ty. $15.00 Domestic, $25.00 Foreign. Country Music Foundation, 4 Music Square East, Nashville TN 37203. **Tel** (615)256-1639. Ed Paul Kingsbury. **Ind/Abst** MLA Int. Bibliogr. Books Artic. Mod. Lang. Lit., Ref. Source, RILM Abstr. **LC** ML1. bk rev. **Circ** 1,000. (ctrl). Articles and reviews by leading scholars and pertaining to country music.

JOURNAL OF GUITAR ACOUSTICS. Began publication with Vol. 1, No. 1, Dec. 1980. 0735-4371. Periodical. US. English. qt. $38.00. Journal of Guitar Acoustics, 11000 Seymour Road, Grass Lake MI 49240. **Tel** (313)665-7808. Index in last issue of volume - attached.

JOURNAL OF JAZZ DISCOGRAPHY. *See* Bibliographies.

JOURNAL OF JEWISH MUSIC AND LITURGY. Vol. 1, No. 1 (June 1976)-. 0197-0100. Periodical. US. English (Hebrew). an. Yeshiva University/Cantorial Council of America, 500 West 186th Street, New York NY 10033. **Tel** (212)960-5359. **Ed** Macy Nulman. **LC** ML3195. **DD** 783.029605. adv acc. **Circ** 500. An analytical study of Jewish music and the liturgy of the synagogue services. Related articles concerning the cantorial profession.

THE JOURNAL OF MUSIC THERAPY. (JOURNAL OF MUSIC THERAPY). V. 1- Mar. 1964-. 0022-2917. Periodical. US. English. qt. $20.00. National Association for Music Therapy Inc, 505 11th Street SW, Washington DC 20003. **Tel** (202)543-6864. **Ed** Richard Graham. **Ind/Abst** Hospit. Lit. Index, Music Index, Educ. Index, Except. Child Educ. Resour., Psychol. Abstr., RILM Abstr., Soc. Sci. Citation Index. **LC** ML1. **DD** 615.83705. **NLM** W1 JO776. **CODEN** JMUTA2. bk rev. **Circ** 4,500. Research studies are presented on the use of music in a therapeutic environment and the influence it may have on an individual. *Bulletin of NAMT.*

THE JOURNAL OF MUSICOLOGICAL RESEARCH. V. 3- Oct. 1979-. 0141-1896. Periodical. US. English. ir. $110.00. Gordon & Breach, PO Box 197, London WC2E 9PX England. **Ed** F J Smith. **LC** ML5. **DD** 780.5. bk rev. adv acc. *Music & Man, 0306-2082.*

THE JOURNAL OF MUSICOLOGY. (THE JOURNAL OF MUSICOLOGY : JM). **VFOAT** JM. Vol. 1, No. 1 (Jan. 1982)-. 0277-9269. Periodical. US. English. qt. $24.00 Domestic, $28.00 Foreign. Journal of Musicology, PO Box 4516, Louisville KY 40204. **Tel** (502)459-5222. **Ed** Marian Green. **LC** ML1. **DD** 780.5. bk rev. adv acc. **Circ** 1,500. (ctrl). Music history, criticism, analysis, performance practice.

JOURNAL OF RESEARCH IN MUSIC EDUCATION. Periodical. US. English. qt. $17.00 Domestic, $19.00 Canada, $21.00 Others. Music Education National Conference, 1901 Association Drive, Reston VA 22091. **Tel** (703)860-4000. **Ed** Jack Taylor. **Ind/Abst** Educ. Index, Music Artic. Guide, Music Index, Psychol. Abstr., Bibliogr. Index, Curr. Index J. Educ. **Circ** 5,200. (ctrl). Publishes reports of research studies in the field of music and music education.

JOURNAL OF RESEARCH IN SINGING. V. 1- July 1977-. 0272-6440. Periodical. US. English. sa. $25.00 Foreign. International Association of Research in Singing, c/o Dr John Large, Box 13771/NT Station, Denton TX 76203. **Tel** (817)382-4537. **Ed** John W Large. **Ind/Abst** Music Index. bk rev. adv acc. **Circ** 1,000. Research reports and pedagogical articles in voice function, literature, pedagogy, therapy, psychology, and performance. Association news. Checklist of recent research.

JOURNAL OF SYNAGOGUE MUSIC. V. 1- Feb. 1967-. 0449-5128. Periodical. US. English, German, Hebrew, or Spanish. sa. $12.50. Cantors Assmebly, 150 5th Avenue, New York NY 10011. **Tel** (212)691-8020. **Ed** Hazzan Samuel Rosenbaum. **LC** ML1. **DD** 783.029605. bk rev. **Circ** 650. (ctrl). The only journal in the world devoted exclusively to Jewish liturgical music.

JOURNAL OF THE AMERICAN LISZT SOCIETY. **Main/Corp** American Liszt Society. V. 1- June 1977-. 0147-4413. Periodical. US. English. sa. $17.00. American Liszt Society, c/o Maurice Hinson, Box 1828/SBTS 2825 Lexington, Louisville KY 40280. **Tel** (502)897-4421. **Ed** Maurice Hinson. **Ind/Abst** Music Index, RILM Abstr. **LC** ML410.L7. **DD** 780.924. bk rev. **Circ** 500. Covers the life, music and contributions of Franz Liszt. Includes areas such as piano, composition, conducting, criticism, teaching and literary writing.

JOURNAL OF THE AMERICAN MUSICAL INSTRUMENT SOCIETY. **Main/Corp** American Musical Instrument Society. V. 1- 1975-. 0362-3300. US. English. an. $20.00. American Musical Instrument Society, c/o The Shrine to Music Museum, 414 East Clark Street, University of South Dakota, Vermillion SD 57069. **Tel** (605)677-5306. **Ed** Martha Maas. **Ind/Abst** Music Index, RILM Abstr. **LC** ML1. **DD** 780.5. bk rev. adv acc. **Circ** 600. (ctrl). Scholarly articles concerning musical instruments in all cultures and from all periods, their design, use, and history.

JOURNAL OF THE AMERICAN MUSICOLOGICAL SOCIETY. **Main/Corp** American Musicological Society. V. 1- Spring 1948-. 0003-0139. Periodical. US. English. ty. $20.00. American Musicological Society Inc, 201 South 34th Street, Philadelphia PA 19104. **Ind/Abst** Music Index, Index Book Rev. Humanit., Humanit. Index, RILM Abstr. **LC** ML27.U5. **DD** 780.5.

JOURNAL OF THE ARNOLD SCHOENBERG INSTITUTE. **Main/Corp** Arnold Schoenberg Institute. V. 1- Oct. 1976-. 0146-5856. US. English. sa. $20.00. Arnold Schoenburg Institute University of Southern California, University Park MC 1011, Los Angeles CA 90089. **Tel** (213)743-5362. **Ed** Leonard Stein. **Ind/Abst** Music Index, Ref. Source, RILM Abstr. **LC** ML410.S283. **DD** 780.924, B. adv acc. **Circ** 800. (ctrl). The journal brings to light the multi-faceted genius of Arnold Schoenberg through the publication of newly discovered and translated materials from his archives. *Bulletin - Arnold Schoenberg Institute.*

JOURNAL OF THE CATGUT ACOUSTICAL SOCIETY. No. 42 (Nov. 1984)-. 0882-2212. Periodical. US. English. sa. Catgut Acoustical Society, 112 Essex Avenue, Montclair NJ 07042. *Catgut Acoustical Society Newsletter, 0576-9280.*

JOURNAL OF THE CONDUCTORS' GUILD. Vol. 1, No. 1 (Winter 1980)-. 0734-1032. Periodical. US. English. qt. $20.00. American Symphony Orchestra League, 633 East Street NW, Washington DC 20004. **Tel** (202)628-0099. **Ed** J Voois. **LC** ML457. **DD** 781.63505. bk rev. adv acc. **Circ** 500. (ctrl). Scholarly articles of interest to conductors and musicologists.

JOURNAL OF THE INDIAN MUSICOLOGICAL SOCIETY. **Main/Corp** Indian Musicological Society. V. 2- Jan./Mar. 1971-. 0251-012X. Periodical. II. English. sa. $10.00. Indian Musicological Society, Jambu Bet-Dandia Bazar, Baroda India. **Ind/Abst** Music Index, RILM Abstr. **LC** ML5. **DD** 781.75405. *Sangeet Kala Vihar. English Supplement.*

THE JOURNAL OF THE MUSIC ACADEMY, MADRAS. **Main/Corp** Music Academy (Madras, India). V. 1- Jan. 1930-. II. English. an. $10.00. Journal of the Music Academy, 306 T T K Road, Madras 14 India. **Ed** T S Parthasarathy. **LC** ML5. bk rev. **Circ** 400. Concerns music and dance.

JOURNAL OF THE PLAINSONG & MEDIAEVAL MUSIC SOCIETY. **Main/Corp** Plainsong and Mediaeval Music Society. V. 1- 1978-. Periodical. UK. English. an. Free to Members, $1.50 Nonmembers. The Treasurer, Plainsong and Mediaeval Music Society, 46 Bond Street, Englefield Greenfield Green, Surrey TW 20 0PY England. **LC** ML169.8. **DD** 780.902.

JOURNAL OF THE VIOLA DA GAMBA SOCIETY OF AMERICA. **Main/Corp** Viola da Gamba Society of America. V. 1- 1964-. 0507-0252. US. English. an. John Whisler, 2493 Knox Road/ Route 4, Beaverton MI 48612. **Ind/Abst** Music Index, RILM Abstr. **LC** ML1.

JOURNAL OF THE VIOLIN SOCIETY OF AMERICA. **Main/Corp** Violin Society of America. V. 2, No. 2- Spring 1976-. 0148-6845. Periodical. US. English. qt. $25.00. Journal of the Violin Society of America, c/o Ms Gloria Burton, 1372 Broadway/14th Floor, New York NY 10018. **Ind/Abst** Music Index, RILM Abstr. **LC** ML1. **DD** 787.105. *News Bulletin - The Violin Society of America, 0193-6352.*

JOURNAL (SANGEET RESEARCH ACADEMY (CALCUTTA, INDIA)). (JOURNAL). **VFOAT** Sangeet Research Academy Journal. Vol. 1, No. 1 (July 1980)-. Periodical. Bengali (text in English and Hindi). ir. Free. Sangeet Research Academy, 1 Netaji Subhas Chandra Bose Road, Calcutta 700040 India. **LC** MT3.I48. **DD** 781.75405.

JUNIOR RIDERS. **VFOAT** Junior Riders Magazine. Vol. 1, No. 1 (Nov.-Dec. 1984)-. 0748-9226. Periodical. US. English. bm. $12.00 Domestic, $28.00 Foreign. Junior Riders, PO Box 50382, St Louis MO 63105. **DD** 789.

K-BAR-T COUNTRY ROUNDUP. 0091-908X. Periodical. US. English. $5.00. 2730 Baltimore Avenue, Pueblo CO 81003. **LC** ML1. **DD** 784.

KANSAI ONGAKU BUNKA SHIRYO *CEASED.* 1972-. JA. Japanese. ir. 300. Osaka College of Music, 1-4-1 Meishinguchi Toyonaka, Osaka 561 Japan. **LC** ML21.

KANSAS MUSIC REVIEW. 0022-8702. Periodical. US. English. ir. $1.00. Kansas Music Education Association, School of Music/Wichita State University, Wichita KS 67208. **LC** ML1. **DD** 780.72781.

KATALOG DER FILMSAMMLUNG. **Main/Corp** Kassel. Deutsches Musikgeschichtliches Arhciv. V. 1, No. 1- Spring 1955-. GW. German. ir. Baerenreiter Music Corporation, 224 King Street, Englweood NJ 07631. **Tel** 561-30011. **Ed** Harald Heckmann and Guergen Kindermann. **LC** ML120.G3. **DD** 781.97. A general catalogue on the known sources of German music history. Prints and manuscripts for Musica Practica and Musica Theoretica.

KEEPING UP WITH KODALY CONCEPTS IN MUSIC EDUCATION. V. 1- Sept./Oct. 1974-. 0098-0668. Periodical. US. English. bm. $10.00. Keeping Up With Music Education, 1220 Ridge Road, Municie IN 47304. **LC** ML1. **DD** 780.7.

KEEPING UP WITH ORFF-SCHULWERK IN THE CLASSROOM. V. 1- Sept. 1973-. 0092-797X. Periodical. US. English. bm. $10.00. Keeping up with Music Education, 1220 Ridge Road, Muncie IN 47304. **LC** ML1. **DD** 780.77.

KEMPS INTERNATIONAL MUSIC & RECORDING INDUSTRY YEAR BOOK. **VFOAT** International Music & Recording Industry Year Book. 1980-. UK. English. an. UNIPUB, PO Box 1222, Ann Arbor MI 48106. **Tel** (800)521-8110. **LC** ML12. **DD** 338.4778025.

KEMP'S MUSIC & RECORDING INDUSTRY YEARBOOK. *See* Yearbooks, Almanacs, Directories.

KEMP'S MUSIC & RECORDING INDUSTRY YEARBOOK INTERNATIONAL. *See* Yearbooks, Almanacs, Directories.

KENKYU KIYO - KUNITACHI ONGAKU DAIGAKU. **Main/Corp** Kunitachi Ongaku Daigaku. **VFOAT** Memoirs of Kunitachi Music College. Began in 1966. Japanese. ir. Kunitachi Ongaku Daigaku, 12-19 Nishi 2-Chome, Kunitachi 186 Japan. **LC** ML5.

THE KERAULOPHON. 0735-8660. Periodical. US. English. qt. $5.00. Greater New York City Chapter of OHS Inc, Post Office Box 104, Harrisville NH 03450. **Tel** (603)827-3055. **Ed** John K Ogasapian. bk rev. **Circ** 60. Musical and historical study of pipe organ building, especially in New York City and environments.

KEY NOTES. Began with issue for June 1975. Periodical. English. sa. .10. Donemus, Jacob Obrechtstraat 51, Amsterdam Netherlands. **Ind/Abst** Music Index, RILM Abstr. **LC** ML5. **DD** 780.9492. *Sonorum Speculum.*

KEY VIVE. Periodical. AT. English. qt. $3.69. Australian Society for Keyboard Music, 64/8-12 Sutherland Road, Chatswood New South Wales 2067 Australia. **Tel** 02/406-5131.

KEYBOARD. Periodical. UK. English. bm. $5.00. Music Industry Publications, 10A High Street, Tunbridge Wells Kent England. **LC** ML5. **DD** 786.05.

KEYBOARD ARTS. V. 1- Winter 1972-. 0090-3361. Periodical. US. English. ty. $6.00 Domestic, $8.00 Foreign. Keyboard Arts Magazine, 10636 Lindbrook Drive, Los Angeles CA 90024. **Tel** (213)474-8966. **Ed** Thomas McBeth. **LC** ML1. **DD** 780.5. adv acc. **Circ** 1,000. (ctrl). Relates to research and practical, down to earth help for progressive piano teaching methods and materials.

KEYBOARD CLASSICS & VIRTUOSO. **VFOAT** Keyboard Classics and Virtuoso. Began in Sept. 1981. 0744-3218. Periodical. US. English. bm. $9.97. Keyboard Classics Magazine, 351 Evelyn Street, Paramus NJ 07652. **Tel** (914)232-8108. **Ed** Stuart Isacoff. **Ind/Abst** Music Index. bk rev. adv acc. **Circ** 55,000. Composed of folios of classical selections as well as features of special intrumentalist. *Virtuoso & Keyboard Classics, 0273-9909; Sheet Music Magazine's Keyboard Classics, 0273-9526.*

KEYBOARD (CUPERTINO, CALIF.). (KEYBOARD). Vol. 7, No. 7 (July 1981)-. 0730-0158. Periodical. US. English. mo. $18.95. GPI Publications, 20605 Lazaneo, Cupertino CA 95014. **Tel** (408)446-1105. **Ind/Abst** Music Index, Jazz Index. **LC** ML1. **DD** 786.105. *Contemporary Keyboard, 0361-5820.*

KEYBOARD WORLD. V. 1- Jan. 1972-. 0199-3313. Periodical. US. English. mo. $8.00. Keyboard World Inc, PO Box 4399/8066 Telegraph Road, Downey CA 90241. **LC** ML549. **DD** 786.05. *Organist Magazine.*

Music

KEYBOARDS, COMPUTERS & SOFTWARE. VFOAT Keyboards, Computers, and Software. Vol. 1, No. 1 (Feb. 1986)-. 0886-6228. Periodical. US. English. bm. $15.00 US, $19.00 Foreign. Computers & Software Inc, PO Box 615, East Northport NY 11731. DD 789.

KEYNOTE. Began in 1966?. 0317-5855. CN. English. ir. Free. Keynote, c/o Ms C Moon, Registar of Junior Symphony Society of Vancouver, 557 West 12th Avenue, Vancouver British Columbia V5Z 3X7 Canada. DD 780.971133.

THE KILT AND HARP. (THE KILT AND HARP : JOURNAL OF THE SCOTTISH HARP SOCIETY OF AMERICA). 0882-6811. Periodical. US. English. $15.00 Membership. Scottish Harp Society of America, c/o Christina Tourin, R D 2, Waterbury VT 05676. DD 782.

THE KING'S LETTER. 0147-1384. US. English. $15.00. Department 1276 Rural Free Delivery #1, Winstead CT 06098. LC ML1. DD 786.605.

KIRCHENMUSIKALISCHES JAHRBUCH. See Yearbooks, Almanacs, Directories.

KLACTO JAZZ MAGAZINE. June-July 1981-. Periodical. US. English. sa. Mike Bloom, 916 McCully Street, Honolulu HI 96826. Ind/Abst Jazz Index. *Klacto (Honolulu, Hawaii).*

KODALY ENVOY. US. English. $20.00. Organization of American Kodaly Educators, University of Wisconsin, Whitewater WI 53190. Ed Floice Lund. LC ML1. DD 780.7. bk rev. adv acc. Circ 1,000. (ctrl). Information regarding the Kodaly concert in music education.

KOLNER BEITRAGE ZUR MUSIKFORSCHUNG. V. 1- 1938-. Periodical. GW. German. ir. Gustav Bosse Verlag, Postfach 417, 8400 Regensburg West Germany.

KOUNTRY KORRAL MAGAZINE. Periodical. SW. Swedish. ir. 22.00. Box 8014, 720 08 Vasteras 8 Sweden. LC ML5. DD 784. bk rev. adv acc. Circ 2,500.

KRITIKA I MUZYKOZNANIE. Began in 1975. Periodical. UR. Russian. 1.50. Izdatelstvo Muzyka Leningradskoe Otdelenie, Inzhenernaia Ul 9, 191011 Leningrad Russia. LC ML3880.

KURT WEILL NEWSLETTER. Fall 1983-. Periodical. US. English. The Kurt Weill Foundation for Music, Lincoln Towers/L42 West End Avenue/Suite 1-R, New York NY 10023.

THE LATIN MUSIC YEARBOOK. See Yearbooks, Almanacs, Directories.

LEBLANC WORLD OF MUSIC. Fall 1975-. 0361-5758. US. English. G Leblanc Corporation, 7019 30th Avenue, Kenosha WI 53141. LC ML1. DD 785.0670973. *World of Music.*

A L'ECOUTE. V. 1- Sept. 1976-. 0700-3900. Periodical. CN. French. mo. Free. Alliance des Chorales du Quebec, 1415 Est rue Jarry, Montreal Quebec H2E 2Z7 Canada. DD 784.96.

LIBRARY BULLETIN. See Library and Information Science.

LIKEMBE; REVUE ZAIROISE DE MUSIQUE. Periodical. CG. French. ir. 46 rue de Lubaki, Kin-Bumbu BP 9624, Kinshasa 1 Zaire. LC ML5. DD 781.76751.

LING NAN YIN YUEH. VFOAT Lingnanyinyue. Periodical. Chinese. mo. 0.10. Post Office Canton. LC ML5. DD 780.95127.

LIRICA NEL MONDO. Yearly V. 1- Dec. 1971-. Periodical. IT. Italian. mo $22.60. Lirica Nel Mondo, CP 7246, Rome Italy. LC ML5. DD 782.105.

A LIST OF DOCTORAL DISSERTATIONS IN MUSICOLOGY AND ALLIED FIELDS. Ed. 1, 1951. Periodical. US. English. ir. American Musicological Society, 201 South 34th Street, Philadelphia PA 19104. Ed H David.

LISTENERS' GUIDE - WGMS. (LISTENERS' GUIDE). V. 1- March 1977-. 0147-0388. Periodical. US. English. mo. $15.00. WGMS, 11300 Rockville Pike, Rockville MD 20852. LC ML1. DD 780.5.

LISTENING POST. Began in 1970. 0148-3544. Periodical. US. English. mo. $12.50. Bro-Dart, 1236 South Hatcher Street, City of Industry CA 91749. LC ML156.9. DD 789.9131.

LISZT SAECULUM. No. 23- 1978-. Periodical. UK. English (German). sa. Editor Liszt Saeculum/ILC Music Department 35, Stanhope Road, Deal Kient CT14 6AD England. Ed L Rabes. LC ML410.L7. DD 780.924. *I.L.C. Quarterly.*

THE LISZT SOCIETY JOURNAL. Periodical. UK. English. Liszt Society, 32 Chivelston, 78 Wimbledon Park Side, London SW19 5LH England. LC M1410.L7. DD 780.924. *Newsletter (Liszt Society, London, England : 1971).*

LITERATURE, MUSIC, FINE ARTS. See Literature.

LITURGICAL CHANT NEWSLETTER. No. 1 (Winter 1985)-. 0887-3879. Periodical. US. English. sa. $5.00. University of Delaware, Music Department, Newark DE 19716.

LIVE (LAVAL, QUEBEC). (LIVE). Vol. 1, No. 1 10/24 May 1980. 0713-4991. Periodical. CN. French. ir. $14.00. Live, CP 281, Laval-des-Rapides, Laval Quebec H7N 4Z9 Canada. DD 784.54005.

LIVING BLUES. No. 1- Spring 1970-. 0024-5232. Periodical. US. English. bm. $50.00. University of Mississippi, Center for the Study of Southern Culture, University MS 38677. Tel (601)232-5993. Ed Frank Children. Ind/Abst Jazz Index, Music Index, MLA Int. Bibliogr. Books Artic. Mod. Lang. Lit., RILM Abstr. LC ML1. DD 784. bk rev. adv acc. Circ 3,000. Available on microfilm from University Microfilms. Journal of Black American Blues Tradition. Interviews, feature articles, record and book reviews, obituaries, photographs, festival dates and club dates.

LIVING MUSIC. Vol. 1, No. 1 (Fall 1983)-. 8755-092X. Periodical. US. English. qt. $8.00. Minuscule University Press, 66358 Buena Vista Avenue, Desert Hot Springs CA 92240. Tel (619)329-8463. Ed Dwight Winenger. DD 780. adv acc. Circ 550. (ctrl). Original articles and news of interest to composers and performers of "New Music", biographical information and publicity. Make music, not war.

LLOYD'S CANADIAN MUSIC DIRECTORY. See Yearbooks, Almanacs, Directories.

LOISIRS FOLKLORIQUES. Vol. 1, No. 2 (Jan./Feb.)-. 0822-9295. Periodical. CN. French. bm. Free to Members. Association des Violoneux du Quebec, 1415 Est rue Jarry, Montreal Quebec H2E 2Z9 Canada. DD 781.771406. *Association des Violoneux du Quebec (Journal), 0822-9287.*

A L'UNISSON (AQUARELLES DE BLAINVILLE INC.). (A L'UNISSON). V. 1, No. 1, (Fall 1980)-. 0228-5959. Periodical. CN. French. ir. Free. Acquarelles de Blainville Inc, 103 rue Alain, Blainville Quebec J7C 2V2 Canada. DD 784.96. (ctrl).

LUTE SOCIETY JOURNAL CEASED. (JOURNAL). 0460-007X. UK. English. an. Ind/Abst RILM Abstr. LC ML5.

LUTRIN. (LE LUTRIN). V. 1- Sept. 1979-. 0226-868X. Periodical. CN. French. qt. Free. Orchestre Symphonique de Quebec, 116 Cote de la Montagne, Quebec Quebec G1K 4E5 Canada. DD 785.062714471.

LYD & I.E. OG BILDE. No. 1-. NO. Norwegian. ir. 10.00. Forlaget Pem-Inform, Postboks 3073, Elisenberg 2, Oslo 2 Norway. LC ML5.

LYONS TEACHER-NEWS. 0093-0164. Periodical. US. English. ty. Lyons Band, 430 Wrighwood Avenue, Elmhurst IL 60126. LC ML1. DD 780.7.

LYRIC OPERA NEWS. 0024-7839. Periodical. US. English. sa. Lyric Opera of Chicago, 20 North Wacker Drive, Chicago IL 60606.

TA MA KO YU CHIH SHENG. VFOAT Sound of Malaysian's Musician. V. 1-. Periodical. Chinese. ir. $0.30 Each Issue. Ta Ma Ko Yu Pan She, 18 Dato Koyah Road, Penang Malaysia. LC ML5.

MADAMINA. V. 1, No. 1 (Fall 1980)-. 0740-5812. Periodical. US. English. sa. Music Associates of America, 224 King Street, Englewood NJ 07631. Tel (201)569-2898. Ed George Sturm. adv acc. Circ 5,000. (ctrl). Includes news, interviews with personalities in the arts, articles of general interest on music-related themes.

THE MAESTRO. V. 1- Jan./July 1969-. 0541-8771. Periodical. US. English. ir. $35.00. Arturo Toscaninini Society, 812 Dumas Avenue, Dumas TX 79029. LC ML422.T67. DD 785.0924, B.

MAGAZINE RENE ET NATHALIE. V. 1, No. 1 (Summer 1983)-. 0824-6289. Periodical. CN. French. qt. $1,99 le no. Fan Club International Rene et Nathalie, Bureau 1 2306 Est rue Sherbrooke, Montreal Quebec H2K 1E5 Canada. DD 784.0922.

MAGAZYN MUZYCZNY : MM. VFOAT MM, M.M. 0021-5600. Periodical. PL. Polish. mo. 600.00. Krajowe Wydawn Czaspism RSW Prasa-Ksi Azka-Ruch, Noakowskiego 14, 00-666 Warszawa Poland. LC ML5. DD 780.4205. *Jazz.*

MAGYAR NEMZETI BIBLIOGRAFIA : ZENEMUVEK BIBLIOGRAFIAJA. See Bibliographies.

MAGYAR ZENE. Began in 1960. 0025-0384. Periodical. HU. Hungarian. qt. Akademiai Kiado, POB 24, 1363 Budapest Hungary. Ind/Abst Music Index, RILM Abstr. LC ML5.

MAIN TITLE. 0360-1935. Periodical. US. English. qt. Entr' Acte Recording Society, PO Box 2319, Chicago IL 60690. LC ML1. DD 782.85.

MANCHESTER FOLK DIRECTORY. See Yearbooks, Almanacs, Directories.

MANITOBA COMPOSERS' ASSOCIATION. (MANITOBA COMPOSERS' ASSOCIATION : NEWSLETTER). Vol. 1, No. 1 (Summer 1984)-. 0824-7358. Periodical. CN. English. qt. Free. Manitoba Composers' Association, 3rd Floor/374 Donald Street, Winnipeg Manitoba R3B 2J2 Canada. DD 780.922.

MANUSCRIPTS FOR TUBA SERIES. 0363-6585. Monographic Series. US. English. ir. 136 Eighth Avenue North, Nashville TN 37203-3798. Tel (615)254-8969. Ed Stephen L Glover. Circ 400. Tuba music series.

MAPA MUNDI. VFOAT Spanish Church Music. No. 1- 1978-. UK. English (scores in Latin). Bruno Turner, 72 Brewery Road, King's Cross, London N79NE England.

MARBURGER BEITRAGE ZUR MUSIKFORSCHUNG. V. 1- 1967-. 0542-6502. Monographic Series. GW. German. ir. Baerenreiter Music Corporation, 224 King Street, Englewood NJ 07631. Tel 561-30011. Ed Heinrich Hueschen. An irregularly appearing series of dissertations of the Musicological Institute of the University of Marburg.

MARCHING BANDS & CORPS. VFOAT Marching Bands and Corps. 0736-4814. Periodical. US. English. mo. River City Publications Inc, PO Box 8341, Jacksonville FL 32211. LC ML1300. DD 785.067105.

THE MARQUEE. 0364-815X. Periodical. US. English. mo. $6.00. World Wide Publishing Company, PO Box 509 Norwalk CA 90650. LC ML1. DD 780.4205.

MARYLAND MUSIC EDUCATOR. Periodical. US. English. qt. $7.50. Maryland Music Educator, J Avampato, 501 Giles Street, Bel Air MD 21014. LC UNC.

MASSACHUSETTS MUSIC NEWS. V. 22- Fall 1973-. 0147-2550. Periodical. US. English. qt. $6.00. Mass Music Educators Association, PO Box 532, West Springfield MA 01090. Tel (413)739-9065. Ed J Anthony Di Giore. bk rev. adv acc. Circ 1,600. (ctrl). A publication on documenting the progress of music education in Massachusetts. *MMEA Music News.*

MASTER LIST OF KNOWN CANADIAN MUSIC EDUCATORS. Began publication with 1969 issue. 0317-5863. Periodical. CN. English. ir. C M E A National Resource Centre, Box 1461, St Catherines Ontario L2R 7J8 Canada. DD 780.72971.

MASTERS AND MONUMENTS OF THE RENAISSANCE. Vol. 1-. 8756-0828. Monographic Series. US. English. ir. Broude Brothers Ltd, 141 White Oaks Road, Williamstown MA 01267. Tel (413)458-8131. DD 780.

MATRIKEL. Main/Corp Musikaliska Akademien, Stockholm. Swedish. ir. Valhatlavagen 103-109, 115 31 Stockholm Sweden. LC MT5.S88.

THE MATTHAY NEWS. 0360-8484. Periodical. US. English. ty. $5.00. American Matthay Association, 63 West Water Street, Gettysburg PA 17325. LC ML423.M42. DD 786.2106273.

MAXIMUM ROCKNROLL. VFOAT Maximum Rock and Roll. Began in 1982. 0743-3530. Periodical. US. English. ir. $8.00 Six Issues. Maximum Rock 'n' Roll, PO Box 288, Berkeley CA 94701.

Music

MBS NEWS BULLETIN. VFOAT M.B.S. News Bulletin. 0732-7897. Periodical. US. English. bm. c/o Mrs C W Fabel, Route 3 Box 202, Morgantown IN 46160. LC ML26. DD 789.805.

MD; MUZIEK EN DANS IN ONDERWIJS EN PRAKTIJK. VAT Muziek en Dans. Vol. 1-. Periodical. Dutch. ir. 45.00. Stichting Muzisch Tijdschrift, Van Miereveldstrat 13, Amsterdam Netherlands. **Ind/Abst** Excerpta Med. LC ML5. DD 780.5.

MEAN MOUNTAIN MUSIC. 0195-6191. Periodical. US. English. bm. $12.00. Mean Mountain Music, Milwaukee WI 04352. LC ML156. DD 016.789912454.

MECCA. V. 1- Jan. 1974-. 0094-0321. Periodical. US. English. mo. $12.00. Mecca, 611 Gravier Street/Room 913, New Orleans LA 70130. LC ML1. DD 785.4205.

THE MEH BULLETIN. See Physically Impaired.

MEISTERWERKE DER MUSIK. No. 1-. Monographic Series. GW. German. ir. Wilhelm Fink Verlag KG, Ohmstrasse 5, D8000 Muenchen West Germany. **Tel** (809)34 80 17.

MELODIE. Periodical. German. mo. Artia, PO Box 790, Praha 1 Czechoslovakia. LC ML156.9. Schallplattenring Illustrierte.

MELODIE UND RHYTHMUS. Began in 1957. 0025-9004. Periodical. German. mo. Kunst and Wissen Erich Bieber, Dufourstrasse 51, CH-8008 Zurich Switzerland. **Ind/Abst** RILM Abstr.

MELODY MAKER. Began in 1926. 0025-9012. UK. English. wk. $80.00. Business Press International, Perrymount Road/Haywards Heath, West Sussex RH163BR England. **Ind/Abst** Jazz Index, Music Index. LC ML5. DD 780.5. Rhythm.

MEMBERS - INTERNATIONAL FOLK MUSIC COUNCIL. Main/Corp International Folk Music Council. Began publication in 1970?. CN. English. ir. International Folk Music Council, Department of Music, Queen's University, Kingston Ontario K7L 3N6 Canada. DD 784.40601.

MEMBERSHIP DIRECTORY - CHAMBER MUSIC AMERICA. See Yearbooks, Almanacs, Directories.

MEMBERSHIP DIRECTORY - INTERNATIONAL COUNCIL FOR TRADITIONAL MUSIC. See Yearbooks, Almanacs, Directories.

MEMBERSHIP DIRECTORY - INTERNATIONAL TRUMPET GUILD. See Yearbooks, Almanacs, Directories.

MEMBERSHIP DIRECTORY - NATIONAL ASSOCIATION FOR MUSIC THERAPY. See Yearbooks, Almanacs, Directories.

MEMBERSHIP LIST - CANADIAN ASSOCIATION OF MUSIC LIBRARIES. See Library and Information Science.

MEMBERSHIP LIST - CAPAC. (MEMBERSHIP LIST). Main/Corp Composers, Authors and Publishers Association of Canada. VFOAT Liste des Membres. VAT Membership List - Composers, Authors and Publishers Association of Canada. 1983-. 0823-955X. CN. English (text in French). an. Composers Authors and Publishers Association of Canada, 1240 Bay Street, Toronto Ontario M5R 2C2 Canada. DD 780.6071. Membres de la C A P A C, 0319-4035.

MEMBERSHIP LIST - THE GALPIN SOCIETY. Main/Corp Galpin Society. UK. English. Galpin Society, Attn Bruce Young, 11 Eton Place, London NW3 2BT England. LC ML27.E8. DD 781.910621.

MEMBERSHIP ROSTER - AMERICAN MUSICAL INSTRUMENT SOCIETY. Main/Corp American Musical Instrument Society. US. English. $20.00. AMIS Membership Office, c/o Shrine to Music Museum, 414 East Clark Street, Vermillion SD 57069. **Tel** (605)677-5306. **Circ** 600. (ctrl). Alphabetical and geographical list of AMIS membership.

MEMORY LANE (LEIGH-ON-SEA, ESSEX). (MEMORY LANE). Periodical. UK. English. **Ind/Abst** Jazz Index.

THE MEMPHIS MUSIC DIRECTORY. See Yearbooks, Almanacs, Directories.

MENDELSSOHN STUDIEN. V. 1- 1972-. GW. English or German. ir. Duncker & Humblot, Dietrich Schaferweg 9 Postfach 410329, D1000 Berlin 41 West Germany. LC ML410.M5. DD 780.924, B.

MENS EN MELODIE. Vol. 3, No. 1 (Jan. 1948)-. Periodical. NE. Dutch. mo. 54.- Domestic, 88.- Foreign. Uitgeverij Frits Knuf Bv, Postbus 720, Gelderland 4116, ZJ Buren Netherlands. **Tel** 03447-1691. Ed John Kasander. **Ind/Abst** Music Index, RILM Abstr., Recent Publ. Artic. bk rev. adv acc. **Circ** 4,000. (ctrl). Articles about classical music: performances, composers, analyses and. Mensch en Melodie.

METAL K.O. Vol. 1, No 1 (Jan. 1984)-. 0824-7056. Periodical. CN. French. mo. $6,00 for Six Months. Metal K O, CP 237, Succursale Delorimer, Montreal Quebec H2H 2N6 Canada. DD 784.54.

METALLION. Vol. 1, No. 1 (Sept. 84)-. 0825-7590. Periodical. CN. English. bm. 12.50. Rock Express Communications, 37 Madison Avenue, Toronto Ontario M5R 2S2 Canada. **Tel** (416)964-6624. Ed Lenny Stoute. DD 784.54. adv acc. **Circ** 35,000. (ctrl). Heavy rock music with interviews of Canadian and international rock musicians concert and record reviews.

METROPOLITAN OPERA BOX. No. 1-. 0736-4229. Monographic Series. US. English. ir. $28.00. Education at the Met, 1865 Broadway at 61st Street, New York NY 10023. LC UNC.

MICHIGAN MUSIC. V. 2, No. 3- Dec. 1977-. 0160-9483. Periodical. US. English. mo. $6.00. Box 724, Detroit MI 48232. LC ML1. DD 780.9774. Michigan Musician.

MICHIGAN MUSIC EDUCATOR. Began publication with issue for Oct. 1954. 0026-234X. Periodical. US. English. ir. $5.00. Mary D Teal, Department of Music, Eastern Michigan University, Ypsilanti MI 48197. **Tel** (313)487-1044. Ed Mary D Teal. bk rev. adv acc. **Circ** 1,600. (ctrl). Focus is on topics of interest to music educators-general, vocal, instrumental-grades K-university level.

MINNESOTA BLUEGRASS & OLD-TIME MUSIC ASS'N. (MINNESOTA BLUEGRASS OLD-TIME MUSIC ASS'N. : NEWSLETTER). VAT Minnesota Bluegrass and Old-Time Music Association. 0737-0857. Periodical. US. English. mo. $12.00. Music Association Newsletter, MBOTMA, PO Box 9782, Minneapolis MN 55440. **Tel** (612)374-3391. Ed Larry Jones. bk rev. adv acc. **Circ** 1,000. (ctrl). Music magazine, specifically bluegrass and associated styles of American music. Newsletter - Minnesota Bluegrass and Old Time Music Association.

MISCELLANEA MUSICOLOGICA. VFOAT Adelaide Studies in Musicology. Vol. 1- March 1966-. 0076-9355. AT. English. ir. University of Adelaide, Prof McCreedie, Music Department, Adelaide 5000 South Australia. **Tel** 228-5333. Ed Andrew D McCredie. **Ind/Abst** Music Index, APAIS, Aust. Public Aff. Inf. Serv., RILM Abstr. **Circ** 200. (ctrl). A periodic publication of musicological essays covering a variety of topics with each volume centered around a defined theme.

THE MISSISSIPPI RAG. No. 1- Nov. 1973-. 0742-4612. Periodical. US. English. mo. $37.50. Mississippi Rag, PO Box 19068, Minneapolis MN 55419. **Tel** (612)920-0312. Ed Leslie Johnson. **Ind/Abst** Jazz Index. bk rev. adv acc. **Circ** 2,200. Articles traditional jazz and ragtime topics and performers, historical features festival coverage, book and record reviews, photo features, current jazz and ragtime news.

MISSOURI JOURNAL OF RESEARCH IN MUSIC EDUCATION. Vol. 1, No. 1 (Autumn 1962)-. 0085-350X. Periodical. US. English. an. $2.00. University of Missouri/Kansas City, Consvr Music, 4420 Warwick Boulevard, Kansas City MO 64111. **Tel** (816)363-4300. Ed Jack R Stephenson. **Ind/Abst** Music Index.

MITTEILUNGEN DER ARBEITSGEMEINSCHAFT FUR MITTELRHEINISCHE MUSIKGESCHICHTE. Main/Corp Arbeitsgemeinschaft fur Mittelrheinische Musikgeschichte. No. 1- Aug. 1961-. Periodical. GW. German. ir. Arbeitsgemeinschaft fur Mittelrheinische Musikgeschichte, Postfach 3980, 65 Mainz West Germany. LC ML275.7.R5. DD 780.9434.

MITTEILUNGEN DER DEUTSCHEN GESELLSCHAFT FUR MUSIK DES ORIENTS. (MITTEILUNGEN). Main/Corp Deutsche Gesellschaft fur Musik des Orients. Began in 1962. 0417-2051. Multilingual (English, German). ir. Brummerstrasse 48 1 33, Berlin W Germany. **Ind/Abst** RILM Abstr. LC ML5. DD 780.95.

MITTEILUNGEN DER OSTERREICHISCHEN GESELLSCHAFT FUR MUSIKWISSENSCHAFT. Main/Corp Osterreichische Gesellschaft fur Musikwissenschaft. V. 1- Nov. 1973-. German. ir. Postfach 1461, A-1011 Wien Austria. **Ind/Abst** RILM Abstr. LC ML27.A9.

MITTEILUNGEN - TONKUNSTLER-VERBAND COBURG. Main/Corp Tonkunstler-Verband Coburg. German. ir. Tonkunstler-Verband, Steinweg 17, Coburg W GErmany. LC ML28.C625.

MITTEILUNGSBLATT. Main/Corp Schweizerische Musikforschende Gesellschaft. No. 1-53. German. an. **Ind/Abst** RILM Abstr. Mitteilungen der Schweizerischen Musikforschenden Gesellschaft.

DE MIXTUUR. No. 1 (Nov. 1970)-. Periodical. Dutch. ir. 9.00 for 3 Numbers. De Mixtuur, Vincent Van Goghlaan 29, Schagen Netherlands. LC ML549.8.

MLA INDEX SERIES. See Indexes/Abstracts.

MM. Periodical. DK. Danish. ir. 148.-. Gothersgade 21 1 TV, DK-1123 Copenhagen K Denmark. **Tel** (01)323331. Ed Torben Bille. **Ind/Abst** Jazz Index. LC ML5. bk rev. adv acc. **Circ** 15,000.

MODERN DRUMMER. (MODERN DRUMMER : MD). VFOAT MD. Began with Jan. 1977 issue. 0194-4533. Periodical. US. English. mo. $39.95. Modern Drummer Publications, 1000 Clifton Avenue, Clifton NJ 07013. **Tel** (800)221-1988. Ed Ronald Spagrardi. **Ind/Abst** Jazz Index, Music Index. LC ML1035. DD 789.105. bk rev. adv acc. **Circ** 47,000. A publication for drummers and percussionists.

MODERN HI-FI AND MUSIC. 0097-2533. Periodical. US. English. mo. $1.00 Each Issue. Maco Publishing Company, 699 Madison Avenue, New York NY 10021. LC ML1. DD 780. Modern Hi-Fi & Stereo Guide.

MODERN RECORDING & MUSIC. VFOAT Modern Recording and Music. Vol. 5, No. 10 (July 1980)-. 0273-8511. Periodical. US. English. mo. $18.00. Modern Recording & Music, 1120 Old Country Road, Plainview NY 11803. **Tel** (516)433-6530. Ed Larry Zide and Jeff Tamarkin. **Ind/Abst** Pop. Mag. Rev. LC ML1. DD 621.3893. adv acc. **Circ** 25,000. (ctrl). Published for the small recording studio operator and musician. Features focus on audio equipment and it's usage. Artist producer profiles; test reports; new product listings. Modern Recording, 0361-0004.

MODERN RECORDING & MUSIC'S BUYER'S GUIDE. (MODERN RECORDING & MUSIC'S . . . BUYER'S GUIDE). VAT Modern Recording and Music's Buyer's Guide. 1981-. 0276-9239. US. English. an. $2.95. 14 Vanderventer Avenue, Port Washington NY 11050. LC TK7881.4. DD 381.4562138930973. Modern Recording's Buyer's Guide, 0161-1496.

MOLE. (THE MOLE). 1 (Mar. 1984)-. 0827-2387. Periodical. CN. English. ir. Mole, c/o B Mowat 169 Locke Street North, Hamilton Ontario L8P 4B2 Canada. **Tel** (416)525-7966. Ed B F Mowat. DD 784.54005. adv acc. **Circ** 1,000. (ctrl). Rock-and-roll music.

MONDE DU ROCK. (LE MONDE DU ROCK). 0823-0498. Periodical. CN. French. mo. 9.75. Monde du Rock, 558 6E rue, Quebec Quebec G1J 2S4 Canada. **Tel** (418)524-2731. Ed Michel Jacques. DD 784.54005. bk rev. adv acc. **Circ** 20,000. (ctrl). Covers the rock music scene of Eastern Canada, especially in the Quebec Province. We work in French and try to promote local talents.

MONOGRAPH SERIES IN ETHNOMUSICOLOGY. VFOAT UCLA Monograph Series In Ethnomusicology. No. 1-. Monographic Series. US. English. Program in Enthnomusicology, Department of Music, University of California, Los Angeles CA 90024. **Tel** (213)825-5947. Ed Roger Wright. LC UNC. **Circ** 600. In-depth scholarly studies in the field of ethnomusicology.

MONOGRAPHS ON MUSIC IN HIGHER EDUCATION. No. 1- 1973-. 0093-6642. US. English. National Association of Schools of Music, 1 Dupont Circle Northwest/Suite 650, Washington DC 20036. LC MT1. DD 780.72.

MONOLITH. Began with Nov. 1976/Feb. 1977 issue. 0147-6653. Periodical. US. English. bm. $1.00 Each Issue. Monolith Publications Inc, 1411 Bellevue Avenue, Seattle WA 98122. LC ML1. DD 780.4209795.

Music

MONSALVAT. No. 1- Dec. 1973-. 0210-4083. Spanish. ir. 50. Pza Gala Placidia 1, Edificio Autopistas, Barcelona Spain. **Ind/Abst** Music Index, RILM Abstr. LC ML5.

THE MONTHLY GUIDE TO RECORDED MUSIC. Periodical. UK. English. mo. Sir Thomas Beecham Trust Ltd, 43 Frognal, London NW36YA England.

MONUMENTA MONODICA MEDII AEVI. 1- 1956-. 0544-9987. Monographic Series. GW. Latin. ir. Baerenreiter Music Corporation, 224 King Street, Englewood NJ 07631. **Tel** 561-30011. LC M2. The irregularly appearing volume of this series present the repertoire of monodic music from antiquity to the end of the middle ages.

MONUMENTA MUSICAE SACRAE. 1- 1952-. 0545-0004. Monographic Series. FR. Latin. ir. Protat Freres Imprimerie, 1 rue de la Barre, F-71000 Macon France. LC M2.

MONUMENTA MUSICAE SVECICAE. 1-. 0077-1473. Monographic Series. English (German). ir. Edition Reimers AB, Fack 30, S-16 115 Broma-Stockholm Sweden. **Tel** 08 26 45 01. **Circ** 500. A philological and practical documentation of old Swedish music.

MONUMENTOS DE LA MUSICA ESPANOLA. 1-. Monographic Series. SP. Spanish. ir. Consejo Super Invest Cientific, Vitruvio 8, Apartado 14 458, 28006 Madrid Spain.

MONUMENTS OF RENAISSANCE MUSIC. 0077-1503. Periodical. US. English. ir. University of Chicago Press, PO Box 37005, Chicago IL 60637.

MORAVIAN MUSIC JOURNAL. Vol. 26, No. 1 (Spring 1981)-. 0278-0763. Periodical. US. English. qt. $10.00. Moravian Music Foundation, 20 Cascade Avenue, Winston Salem NC 27107. **Tel** (919)725-0651. Ed Richard Starbuck. **Ind/Abst** Music Index. LC ML1. DD 780.5. bk rev. **Circ** 2,200. (ctrl). Articles and information on research and composers of Moravian music, book and music reviews, and inquiries for research. *Bulletin (Moravian Music Foundation)*, 0027-1020.

MOTIF. V. 1- Aug. 1979-. 0273-2114. Periodical. US. English. qt. $6.00. Motif, 1445 Boonville, Springfield MO 65802. **Tel** (417)862-2781. Ed Lawrence B Larsen. LC ML3000. DD 783.02605. **Circ** 999. (ctrl). Primarily an inspirational and informational quarterly publication to the ministers of music in the General Council of the Assemblies of God denomination.

MOUNTAIN MUSIC AND WHERE TO FIND IT. V. 1- 1971-. 0149-8096. Periodical. US. English. PO Box 98, Mineral Bluff GA 30559. LC ML1. DD 784.

MOUTHPIECE. (THE MOUTHPIECE). V. 1- Feb. 1970-. 0380-0601. Periodical. CN. English. qt. Music Department, Canadian National Institute for the Blind, 1929 Bayview Avenue, Toronto Ontario M4G 3E8 Canada.

MOZART-JAHRBUCH. 0077-1805. GW. German. Baerenreiter Music Corporation, 224 King Street, Englewood NJ 07631. **Tel** 561-30011. Ed Int Stiftung Mozarteum Salzburg. Index published separately - free - upon request. Essays on the music, life, environment, and performance practice of Mozart's works and bibliographies on the writings.

IL MUCCHIO SELVAGGIO. No. 1- Oct. 1977-. Periodical. IT. Italian. ir. 1000 Single Issue. Lakota, Via Val Trompia 140, 00141 Roma Italy. LC ML3533.8.

MUGENDAI. Periodical. JA. Japanese. ir. Nihon Ai Bi Emu Kabushiki Kaisha, 2-12 Roppongi 3 Minato-Ku, Tokyo-To 106 Japan. LC ML5.

MUGWUMPS. V. 1- Jan. 1972-. 0149-8517. Periodical. US. English. bm. $12.00. MIH Publications, 15 Arnold Place, New Bedford MA 02740. **Tel** (617)993-0156. **Ind/Abst** Music Index. LC ML1. DD 781.91.

MUNCHNER VEROFFENTLICHUNGEN ZUR MUSIKGESCHICHTE. Vol. 1-. GW. German. ir Musikverlag Hans Schneider, Mozartstrasse 6, D-8132 Tutzing West Germany.

MUSELETTER (WASHINGTON, D.C.). (MUSELETTER). 0736-6949. Periodical. US. English. W A P S, 425 13th Street NW/Suite 712, Washington DC 20004. LC ML28.W2. DD 790.209753. *WPAS Museletter*, 0092-4113.

MUSI-STAFF. Periodical. English. ir. LC ML5. DD 780.5.

MUSIC ALIVE. Periodical. US. English. mo. $120.00. Cherry Lane Music Company Inc, PO Box 430, Port Chester NY 10573. **Tel** (914)937-8601.

MUSIC ANALYSIS. Vol. 1, No. 1 (Mar. 1982)-. Periodical. UK. English. ty. $75.00 Domestic, $86.00 Foreign. Basil Blackwell Publisher, 108 Cowley Road, Oxford OX4 4JF England.

MUSIC & AUTOMATA. VFOAT Music and Automata. Vol. 1, No. 1 (Mar. 1983)-. 0262-8260. Periodical. UK. English. sa. Arthur W J G Ord-Hume, 14 Elmwood Road, London W4 3DY England.

MUSIC AND COMMUNICATION. Monographic Series. English. ir. Casa Editrice Leo S Olschki, Casella Postale PO Box 66, 50100 Firenze Italy.

MUSIC & LETTERS. VAT Music and Letters. V. 1- Jan. 1920-. 0027-4224. Periodical. UK. English. qt. $42.00. Oxford University Press, PO Box 11806, Birmingham AL 35202. **Tel** (205)991-6925. Ed Edward Olleson and Nigel Fortune. **Ind/Abst** Abstr. Engl. Stud., MLA Int. Bibliogr. Books Artic. Mod. Lang. Lit., Music Index, RILM Abstr., Annu. Bibliogr. Engl. Lang. Lit., Humanit. Index, Abstr. Engl. Stud., Years Work Eng. Stud., Recent Publ. Artic. LC ML5. (cum index). bk rev. adv acc. Journal for musicologists, educators, students, and all classical music lovers. Each issue contains comprehensive, diverse, and interpretative articles with book reviews, biographies and complete indexes.

MUSIC AND LITURGY. V. 1- Autumn 1974-. 0305-4438. UK. English. ty. $20.00. Society of Saint Gregory, Olkham Road, North West Horsley Surrey England. **Ind/Abst** Cathol. Period. Lit. Index. LC ML5. DD 783.026205. *Life and Worship, Church Music*.

MUSIC AND MUSICIANS. (MUSIC & MUSICIANS). Sept. 1981-. 0027-4232. Periodical. UK. English. mo. 35.14. Brevet Publishing Ltd, 43B Goucester Road, Croydon CR0 2DH England. **Tel** (01)689-4116. Ed Robert Matthew-Walker. **Ind/Abst** Ref. Source. LC ML5. DD 780.5. bk rev. adv acc. Features concert and opera reviews, book and record reviews, music societies, music guide. *Music and Musicians*, 0027-4232; *Records & Recording*.

MUSIC & MUSICIANS. BRAILLE SCORES CATALOG. ORGAN. (MUSIC & MUSICIANS. BRAILLE SCORES CATALOG ORGAN). **Main/Corp** Library of Congress. National Library Service for the Blind and Physically Handicapped. VFOAT Braille Scores Catalog Organ. VAT Music and Musicians. Braille Scores Catalog. Organ. 1978-. 0145-3149. US. English. Music Section of the National Library Service for the Blind and Physically Handicapped, Library of Congress, Washington DC 20540. LC ML136.U52. DD 016.7868.

MUSIC & MUSICIANS. BRAILLE SCORES CATALOG, VOICE. **Main/Corp** Library of Congress. National Library Service for the Blind and Physically Handicapped. VFOAT Braille Scores Catalog, Voice. VAT Music and Musicians. Braille Scores Catalog, Voice. 1979-. 0145-3157. US. English. Free. Library of Congress, Music Section, Washington DC 20542. LC ML136.U52. DD 016.784.

MUSIC & MUSICIANS. INSTRUCTIONAL CASSETTE RECORDINGS CATALOG. (MUSIC & MUSICIANS : INSTRUCTIONAL CASSETTE RECORDINGS CATALOG). **Main/Corp** Library of Congress. National Library Service for the Blind and Physically Handicapped. VFOAT Instructional Cassette Recordings Catalog. VAT Music and Musicians. Instructional Cassette Recording Catalog. 0145-2525. US. English. an. Free. National Library Service for the Blind and Physically Handicapped, Music Section Library of Congress, Washington DC 20542. LC ML156.2. DD 016.789912.

MUSIC & MUSICIANS. INSTRUCTIONAL DISC RECORDINGS CATALOG. **Main/Corp** Library of Congress. National Library Service for the Blind and Physically Handicapped. VFOAT Instructional Disc Recordings Catalog. VAT Music and Musicians. Instructional Disc Recordings Catalog. 0145-2517. US. English. an. National Library Service for the Blind and Physically Handicapped, Library of Congress, Washington DC 20542. LC ML156.2. DD 016.78991207. *Music & Musicians. Instructional Disc Recordings Catalog*, 0145-2517.

MUSIC & MUSICIANS. LARGE-PRINT SCORES AND BOOKS CATALOG. **Main/Corp** Library of Congress. National Library Service for the Blind and Physically Handicapped. VFOAT Large-Print Scores and Books Catalog. VAT Music and Musicians. Large-Print Scores and Books Catalog. 1978-. 0363-8472. US. English. National Library Service for the Blind and Physically Handicapped, Library of Congress, Washington DC 20542. LC ML136.U52. DD 016.7808. *Music & Musicians. Large-Print Scores and Books Catalog*, 0363-8472.

MUSIC AND RECORDINGS. 1955-. US. English. an. Ed F V Grunfeld. LC ML1. DD 780.973.

MUSIC & SOUND BUYER'S GUIDE. VFOAT Music and Sound Buyer's Guide. 1982-. US. English. an. $3.00. Output International Publications Inc, 220 Westbury Avenue, Carle Place NY 11514. LC ML459. DD 789.00294.

THE MUSIC & SOUND ELECTRONICS RETAILER. VFOAT Music and Sound Electronics Retailer. Dec. 1983-. 0746-8067. Periodical. US. English. mo. $15.00. Sound Arts Merchandising Inc, 220 Westbury Avenue, Carle Place NY 11514. **Tel** (516)334-7880. Ed Elliot Luber. LC ML1092. DD 621.389305. adv acc. **Circ** 8,500. (ctrl). News tabloid for music and sound dealers relating the latest news and product developments of instruments and sound gear. *Sound Arts Merchandising Journal*, 0161-1720.

MUSIC ARTICLE GUIDE. V. 1- Winter 1966-. 0027-4240. Periodical. US. English. qt. $35.00. Music Article Guide, PO Box 27066, Philadelphia PA 19118. **Tel** (215)848-3540. Ed Morris Henken. LC ML1. The nation's only annotated guide to signed feature articles in American music to the special needs of school and college music educators.

MUSIC AT YALE. **Main/Corp** Yale University. Music Executive Committee. V. 1- Fall/Winter 1971/72-. 0146-096X. Periodical. US. English. qt. $5.00. Yale University Music Executive Committee, School of Music 96 Wall Street, New Haven CT 06520. LC ML1. DD 780.97468.

MUSIC BOOK GUIDE. Series/Titl Computext Book Guide Series. 0360-1943. US. English. an. $ G K Hall, 70 Lincoln Street, Boston MA 02111. LC ML113. DD 016.78.

MUSIC, BOOKS ON MUSIC, AND SOUND RECORDINGS. Series/Titl Library of Congress Catalogs. VFOAT Music. Began with Jan./June 1973. 0092-2838. US. English. ir. $105.00. Library of Congress, Navy Yard/Annex Building 159, Washington DC 20541. **Tel** (202)287-5000. LC Z881.A1. DD 016.78. NLM Z 881 L697. *Library of Congress Catalog. Music and Phonorecords*, 0041-7793.

THE MUSIC BOX. Began with issue for Winter 1962. Periodical. UK. English. qt. Musical Box Society of Great Britain, Bylands Crockham Hill, Kent England. LC ML5. DD 789.705.

MUSIC BUSINESS DIRECTORY. See Yearbooks, Almanacs, Directories.

MUSIC CAPITOL NEWS. COUNTRYWIDE. VFOAT Countrywide. V. 1- Summer 1971-. 0092-1041. Periodical. US. English. $5.00. PO Box 186, Fairfax VA 22030. LC ML1. DD 784.

MUSIC CATALOGING BULLETIN. 0027-4283. Periodical. US. English. mo. $12.00. Music Library Association, PO Box 487, Canton MA 02021. **Tel** (617)828-8450. LC ML111. DD 025.348.

MUSIC CIRCULAR. No. 1 (Dec. 1980)-. 0278-9051. US. English. National Library Service for the Blind and Physically Handicapped, Library of Congress, Washington DC 20542. LC Z663.119. DD 780.

MUSIC CITY NEWS. 0027-4291. Periodical. US. English. mo. $15.00. Music City News Inc, PO Box 22975, Nashville TN 37202. **Tel** (615)329-2200.

MUSIC CLUBS MAGAZINE. V. 43, No. 2- Dec. 1963- 1964-. 0161-2654. Periodical. US. English. qt. National Federation of Music Clubs, 1336 North Delaware Street, Indianapolis IN 46202. **Tel** (317)638-4003. **Ind/Abst** Music Index. LC ML1. DD 780.973. *Showcase (Mount Morris, Ill.)*.

MUSIC COMPETITION FESTIVALS. **Main/Corp** Canada. Statistics Canada. Cultural Information Section. VFOAT Festivals de Concours de Musique. 1st- 1971-. CN. English and French. .50.

Music

Information Canada, Receiver General for Canada Statistics Canada Publication, Ottawa Ontario K1A 0T6 Canada. LC ML76. DD 780.7971.

MUSIC DIRECTORY CANADA. See Yearbooks, Almanacs, Directories.

MUSIC EDUCATION NEWS. V. 1- 1977-. UK. English. an. Chappell, 50 New Bond Street, London W1 England. DD 780.72.

MUSIC EDUCATORS JOURNAL. 0027-4321. Periodical. US. English. mo. Music Educators National Conference, 1902 Association Drive, Reston VA 22091. Tel (703)860-4000. Ed Rebecca Grier Taylor. Ind/Abst Pop. Mag. Rev., Book Rev. Index, Except. Child Educ. Resour., Educ. Index, Music Artic. Guide, Music Index, Curr. index J. Educ., Ref. Source, RILM Abstr. LC ML1. bk rev. adv acc. Circ 56,600. (ctrl). Publishes articles about all aspects of the teaching of music, preschool through college level. *Music Supervisors' Journal.*

MUSIC EXPRESS (WILLOWDALE, ONT.). (MUSIC EXPRESS). 1976. 0710-6076. Periodical. CN. English. mo. 12.00. Rock Express Communications, 37 Madison Avenue, Toronto Ontario M5R 2S2 Canada. Tel (416)964-6624. Ed Keith Sharp. DD 780.420971. bk rev. adv acc. Circ 106,000. (ctrl). Contemporary pop, rock music: interviews with regional and international pop stars, record reviews, concert reviews, musical and stereo information. *Alberta Music Express.*

MUSIC FOR CHILDREN. CARL ORFF CANADA. (MUSIC FOR CHILDREN : CARL ORFF CANADA). VFOAT Carl Orff Canada. March 1975-. 0382-0777. Periodical. CN. English. ir. Urff-Schulwerk Association of Canada, Front Campus, Toronto Ontario M5S 7A6 Canada. DD 372.87042.

MUSIC HALL. No. 9- Oct. 1979-. Periodical. UK. English. bm. 5.95. Tony Barker, 50 Reporton Road, London SW6 England. LC PN1968.G7. DD 792.70941. *Music Hall Records.*

MUSIC HALL RECORDS. No. 1-8. UK. English. bm. $7.35. Music Hall Records, 50 Reporton Road, London SW6 England. LC PN1968.G7. DD 792.70941.

MUSIC IN HIGHER EDUCATION. 1st- 1967-. 0077-2410. US. English. an. National Association of Schools of Music, 11250 Roger Bacon Drive No 5, Reston VA 22090. LC ML27.U5. DD 780.72.

MUSIC IN LONDON. Vol. 1, No. 1 (Nov. 1967)-. 0710-1937. Periodical. CN. English. mo. DD 780.971326.

MUSIC IN PRINT ANNUAL SUPPLEMENT. 1979-. 0192-4729. US. English. an. $216.00. Musicdata Inc, PO Box 48010, Philadelphia PA 19144. Tel (215)842-0555. LC ML118. DD 016.78. adv acc. Circ 800. Reference list cataloging music in print worldwide. Updates annually each category of music in the music-in-print series.

MUSIC-IN-PRINT SERIES. V. 1-. 0146-7883. Monographic Series. US. English. ir. Musicdata Inc, PO Box 48010, Philadelphia PA 19144. Tel (214)842-0555. adv acc. Reference catalog listing various categories of printed music published worldwide.

MUSIC IN WORSHIP. No. 1 (Sept. 1977)-. Periodical. UK. English. 78 Trevellance Way, Garston Hertfordshire WD2 6LZ England. LC ML3001. DD 783.02605.

THE MUSIC INDEX. See Indexes/Abstracts.

MUSIC INDUSTRY BULLETIN. V. 1- June 1980-. 0270-3203. Periodical. US. English. qt. National Association of Pastoral Musicians, 225 Sheridan Street Northwest, Washington DC 20011.

MUSIC INDUSTRY DIRECTORY. See Yearbooks, Almanacs, Directories.

MUSIC JOURNAL (NEW YORK, N.Y.). (MUSIC JOURNAL). V. 4, No. 5- Sept./Oct. 1946-. 0027-4364. Periodical. US. English. mo. Elemo Publishing, 149 Hampton Road, Southampton NY 11968. Ind/Abst Music Index, Educ. Index, Music Artic. Guide, Music Index, RILM Abstr. LC ML1. *Music Publishers Journal, Educational Music Magazine; Music & Artists, 0027-4216.*

THE MUSIC LEADER. V. 1- Oct./Dec. 1970-. 0027-4372. Periodical. US. English. ir. $18.50. Southern Baptist, 127 Ninth Avenue North, Nashville TN 37234. Tel (615)251-2966. Ed Derrell Billingsley. LC ML1. DD 783. Circ 50,000. (ctrl). For church music leaders of boys and girls ages four through eleven. Contents include guidance materials, training aids, and enrichment for leaders of children and preschoolers.

MUSIC LIBRARY ASSOCIATION TECHNICAL REPORTS. VFOAT MLA Technical Reports. 0094-5099. Monographic Series. US. English. ir. Music Library Association, PO Box 487, Canton MA 02021. Tel (215)569-3948.

MUSIC MCGILL. No. 1- Summer 1976-. 0702-9012. Periodical. CN. English. sa. Faculty of Music McGill University, 555 Sherbrooke Street West, Montreal Quebec H3A 1E3 Canada. DD 780.729714281.

MUSIC MAGAZINE. V. 1- Jan./Feb. 1978-. 0705-4009. Periodical. CN. English. ir. $10.83. Music Magazine, 56 The Esplanada/Suite 202, Toronto Ontario M5E 1A7 Canada. Tel (416)364-5938. Ed Ulla Colgrass. Ind/Abst Music Index. LC ML5. DD 780.5. bk rev. adv acc. Circ 12,000. Presents the lively world of classical music. Interviews, articles, photo features, audio news and reviews of books and records in glossy, beautiful format.

MUSIC MAKERS. V. 1- Oct./Dec. 1970-. 0162-4377. Periodical. US. English. qt. $3.75. Materials Services Department, 127 9th Avenue North, Nashville TN 37234. Tel (615)251-2000. LC ML1.

MUSIC NEWS FROM PRAGUE. Periodical. CS. English. Music Information Center, Czechoslovakia Music Federation Besedni 3, 11800 Prague 1 Czechoslovakia. Tel 539 720. Ed Jan Ledec. Ind/Abst Music Index. LC ML5. DD 780.943712. Circ 10. Contemporary Czech music culture.

MUSIC NOW. 0027-4437. Periodical. US. English. ty. $3.00. Appalachian State University, Scott Meister Music Department, Boone NC 28608. Tel (704)262-3020.

MUSIC PERCEPTION. Vol. 1, No. 1 (Fall 1983)-. 0730-7829. Periodical. US. English. qt. $60.00. University of California Press, 2120 Berkeley Way, Berkeley CA 94720. Tel (415)642-4191. Ed Diana Deutsch. LC ML1. DD 780.5. bk rev. adv acc. Circ 600. Approaches by scientists and musicians to the study of musical phenomena.

THE MUSIC REFERENCE COLLECTION. No. 1-. 0736-7740. Monographic Series. US. English. ir. Greenwood Press, PO Box 5007 88 Post Road West, Westport CT 06881. LC UNC.

THE MUSIC RESEARCHER'S EXCHANGE. V. 1- May 1974-. 0271-5163. Periodical. US. English. ir. $5.00. Columbia University Teachers College, Box 139 Music & Arts Education, New York NY 10027. Tel (212)678-3283. Ed Harold F Abeles. bk rev. Circ 724. A newsletter for active researches in music education, psychology of music and acoustics.

MUSIC REVELATION. 0882-8229. Periodical. US. English. mo. $21.60. Music Revelation, 7 Elmwood Court, Rockville MD 20850. Tel (301)424-2956. Ed C Harry Causey. DD 783. bk rev. Circ 1,000. Variety of articles by a variety of writers on worship and the music ministry of the local church. Designed to equip, inform, motivate, and inspire.

MUSIC REVIEW. (THE MUSIC REVIEW). V. 1- Feb. 1940-. 0027-4445. Periodical. UK. English. qt. 39.00 Domestic, $70.00 Foreign. W Heffer & Sons Ltd, Kings Hedges Road, Cambridge CB4 2PQ England. Tel 351571. Ed A E Leighton-Thomas. Ind/Abst Music Index, RILM Abstr., Ref. Source, Index Book Rev. Humanit., Humanit. LC ML5. DD 780.5. (cum index). adv acc. Circ 1,500.

MUSIC SCENE (DIETIKON, SWITZERLAND). (MUSIC SCENE). Beginning in 1982, numbering begins with No. 1. Periodical. French (German). ir. 62.00. MSM Music Sales & Management AG, Gjuchtstrasse 15, 8953 Dietikon Switzerland. Tel 740 94 44. LC ML3469. DD 784.5005.

MUSIC SCORE CATALOGUE - CARLETON UNIVERSITY. (MUSIC SCORE CLASSED CATALOGUE MICROFORM). Main/Corp Carleton University. Library. 0823-1338. Periodical. CN. English. ir. 3.00. Carleton University Library, Ottawa Ontario K1S 5B6 Canada. DD 016.7808. Catalogue of all music scores in Carleton University Library's collection, organized by subject headings.

MUSIC, SOUND OUTPUT. VFOAT Music & Sound Output. Began with Nov./Dec. 1980 issue. 0273-8902. Periodical. US. English. bm. $18.00. Output International Publications Inc, 200 Westbury Avenue, Carle Place NY 11514. Tel (516)334-78800. Ed Chris Clark. LC ML3469. DD 780.4205. adv acc. Circ 80,000. The magazine for performers of music, engineers, and sound engineers.

MUSIC TEACHER (LONDON, ENGLAND : 1968). (MUSIC TEACHER). Vol. 47, No. 1 (Jan. 1968)-. 0027-4461. Periodical. UK. English. mo. 13.20. Rhinegold Publishing Ltd, 239-241 Shaftesbury Avenue, London SC2H 8EH England. Tel 01 836 2534. Ed Marianne Barton. Ind/Abst Music Index. bk rev. adv acc. Circ 6,000. Also available on microfilm from University Microfilms International. Magazine for primary and secondary school music teachers. New music, examination set works, teaching notes, and book reviews. *Music Teacher and Piano Student.*

MUSIC THEORY SPECTRUM. VFOAT Spectrum. V. 1- 1979-. 0195-6167. US. English. an. $25.00. Society Music Theory, Indiana University School of Music c/o Prof Wennerstrom, Bloomington IN 47405. Tel (812)335-7346. Ed John Clough. Ind/Abst Music Index, RILM Abstr. LC MT6. DD 781.05. bk rev. adv acc. Circ 1,000. (ctrl). Articles and book reviews on all aspects of music theory (analytical, historical, pedagogical).

MUSIC THEORY TRANSLATION SERIES. 1- 1963-. 0541-4024. Monographic Series. US. English. ir. Yale University Press, 92A Yale Station, New Haven CT 06520. Tel (203)436-7583.

MUSIC THERAPY. (MUSIC THERAPY : THE JOURNAL OF THE AMERICAN ASSOCIATION FOR MUSIC THERAPY). Vol. 1, No. 1 (Summer 1981)-. 0734-7367. Periodical. US. English. an. $26.25. American Association for Music Therapy, 66 Morris Avenue, Springfield IL 07081. Tel (201)379-1100. Ed Susan Munro. LC ML3920. DD 615.8515405. Circ 600. A publication which examines the therapeutic use of music in a variety of educational and clinical settings. Written for students and professionals in the field.

MUSIC THERAPY PERSPECTIVES. Vol. 1, No. 1 (Spring/Summer 1982)-. 0734-6875. US. English. National Association for Music Therapy, 1001 Connecticut Avenue Northwest/Suite 800, Washington DC 20036. LC ML3920. DD 615.8515405.

MUSIC TRADES. V. 1- 1890-. 0027-4488. Periodical. US. English. mo $10.00. Music Trades Corporation, PO Box 432, 80 West Street, Englewood NJ 07631. Ind/Abst Predicasts, Music Index. LC ML1.

MUSIC TRADES INTERNATIONAL. V. 60- (No. 708-). Periodical. UK. English. mo. Trade Papers, 157 Hagden Lane, Watford Herts WD1 8LW England. LC ML5. DD 380.14578191. *Piano World and Music Trades Review.*

MUSIC TRADES INTERNATIONAL DIRECTORY. See Yearbooks, Almanacs, Directories.

MUSIC TRADES INTERNATIONAL YEARBOOK. See Yearbooks, Almanacs, Directories.

MUSIC USA. VAT Music United States of America. 0197-4173. US. English. an. $25.00. American Music Conference, 1000 Skokie Boulevard, Wilmette IL 60091. LC ML3795. DD 338.47780973.

MUSIC VIDEO RETAILER. (MUSIC/VIDEO RETAILER). Vol. 10, No. 2 (Aug. 1981)-. 8750-569X. Periodical. US. English. mo. Music Video Retailer, 210 Boylston Street, Chestnut Hill MA 02167. *Music Retailer, 0192-818X.*

MUSIC WEEK INDUSTRY YEAR BOOK. See Yearbooks, Almanacs, Directories.

MUSIC WORKS. No. 1- Apr. 1976-. 0193-5127. Periodical. US. English. sa. $5.00. D S Rapaport and D T Wills, 83 McAllister Street/Room 403, San Francisco CA 94102. Ed E Sergeant and D T Wills. LC ML1. DD 338.47780973.

MUSIC WORLD (LONDON, ENGLAND). (MUSIC WORLD). Periodical. UK. English. mo. 33.20. Circulation Department, 4 Local Board Road, Watford Herts WD1 2JS England. LC ML5. DD 381.4568180941. *Music Trades International.*

MUSIC WORLD MAGAZINE. V. 1- Nov. 1972-. 0090-3663. Periodical. US. English. mo. $5.00. 6472 Santa Monica Boulevard, Hollywood CA 90038. LC ML1. DD 780.5.

MUSIC WORLD YEAR BOOK. See Yearbooks, Almanacs, Directories.

MUSICA. Vol. 1-. 0027-4518. Periodical. GW. German. bm. $21.67. Barenreiter Verlag, Postfach 10 03 29, D-3500 Kassel West Germany. Ed Clemens

Kuhn. **Ind/Abst** Music Index, RILM Abstr. **LC** ML5. **DD** 780.5. adv acc. **Circ** 6,500. (ctrl). Issues bring the multiplicity of contemporary musical life into focus and lend perspective.

MUSICA. Yearly Vol. 1- May/June 1977-. Periodical. IT. Italian. qt. 45.000. Trimestrale Info Musicale Disc, Via Ampere 60, 20131 Milano Italy. **Tel** (02)23.67.615. **Ed** Umberto Masini. **LC** ML5. **DD** 780.5. bk rev. adv acc. **Circ** 35,000. (ctrl). Most important Italian magazine entirely devoted to classical music-every issue. Includes records, reviews as well as book reviews, and various articles about musicians and performers.

MUSICA BRITANNICA. Began with: V. 1, in 1951. UK. English. ir. Stainer & Bell, 82 High Road East Finchley, London N2 9PW England.

MUSICA (CASA DE LAS AMERICAS: 1980). (MUSICA). **VFOAT** Boletin de Musica. Periodical. CU. Spanish. ir. Casa de las Americas, 3RA Y G Vedado, La Habana Cuba. **LC** ML5. **DD** 780.5. *Boletin de Musica.*

MUSICA DISCIPLINA. V. 2- 1948-. 0077-2461. GW. English. an. Hanssler Verlag, Bismarckstrasse 4 Postfach 1220, D-7303 Stuttgart West Germany. **Ed** A Carapetyan. **Ind/Abst** Music Index, RILM Abstr. (cum index). *Journal of Renaissance and Baroque Music.*

DE MUSICA DISPUTATIONES PRAGENSES. 1- 1972-. German. ir. 85.00. **LC** ML5. **DD** 780.5.

MUSICA DOMANI : ORGANO DELLA SOCIETA ITALIANA PER L'EDUCAZIONE MUSICALE. 0391-4380. Periodical. IT. Italian. qt. 20.000. G Ricordi & Company SPA, Via Berchet 2, 20121 Milano Italy. **Tel** (02)8881208. **LC** MT3.I8. **DD** 780.7245. bk rev. adv acc. **Circ** 3,500. (ctrl). An instrument of information and connection for all those working in every order and degree in the sector of the musical education, including the teachers of the primary and secondary school.

MUSICA (HILVERSUM, NETHERLANDS). (MUSICA). Periodical. NE. Dutch. mo. Tijdschriftenfonds JJ Lispet, Postbus 338, Bussum Netherlands.

MUSICA HISPANA. SER. C : MUSICA DE CAMARA. **VFOAT** Musica de Camara. 1-. Periodical. Spanish. ir.

MUSICA JUDAICA. V. 1-. 0147-7536. Periodical. US. English, French, German, or Hebrew. bm. American Society of Jewish Music, 155 Fifth Avenue, New York NY 10010. **Ind/Abst** Music Index, RILM Abstr. **LC** ML1. **DD** 781.7292405.

MUSICA MEDII AEVI. Began with: 1, Pub. 1965. 0077-247X. PL. Polish. ir. ARS Polona, Krakowskie Przedmiescie 7, 00-068 Warsaw Poland. **Ed** J Morawski. **Ind/Abst** RILM Abstr. **LC** ML170. **DD** 780.9022 19.

LA MUSICA POPOLARE. Yearly V. 1- Summer 1975-. Periodical. Italian. ir. $12.00. Amicizia Musicale Italiana, Conto Corrente Postale 3/20838, Intestato a la Musica Popolare, Via Giulini 5, Milano 20123 Italy. **LC** ML5.

MUSICAE SACRAE MINISTERIUM (ROME). (MUSICAE SACRAE MINISTERIUM). 1964. Periodical. IT. German (English and French). ir. 10.00. Consociatio Internationalis, Rudolf Pohl, Katschhof 2, D-5200 Aachen West Germany. **Tel** (02652)1329. **Ed** Rudolf Pohl. **Ind/Abst** RILM Abstr. bk rev. **Circ** 600. Church music and liturgy, bulletin of information for members of Consociatio Internationalis Musicae Sacrae.

THE MUSICAL BOX SOCIETY INTERNATIONAL. (BULLETIN). 0027-4577. Periodical. US. English. ty. $10.00. Musical Box Society International, Box 202 Route 3, Morgantown IN 46160. **Tel** (812)988-7545. **Ed** Martin Roenigk. **Ind/Abst** Music Index. **LC** ML1. **DD** 789.805. bk rev. adv acc. **Circ** 2,800. (ctrl). For people interested in collecting and preserving antique musical mechanical instruments. *Bulletin (Musical Box Society).*

MUSICAL CULTURE MONTREAL. No. 1 (Sept./Oct. 1983)-. 0715-8262. Periodical. CN. English. bm. 12.00 Domestic, 15.00 Foreign. Musical Culture Montreal, 1800 Docteur Penfield Suite 305, Montreal Quebec H3H 1B4 Canada. **DD** 780.9714281.

MUSICAL DENMARK. No. 1- Mar. 1952-. 0027-4585. DK. English. an. $12.50. Danish Institute, 2 Kultorvet, 1175 Copenhagen Denmark. **Tel** (45-1) 13 54 48. **Ed** Knud Ketting. **Ind/Abst** Music Index. **LC** UNC. adv acc. **Circ** 3,000. Articles about Danish music and musicians. Bibliographies listing first performances, Danish music on disc/tape, published music, books/periodicals.

MUSICAL EXPRESS. V. 1- Dec. 1978-. 0709-3381. Periodical. CN. English. ty. Free. Bel Air Records, PO Box 2111, Bramalea Ontario L6T 3X4 Canada. **DD** 784.520971. (ctrl).

MUSICAL HERITAGE REVIEW. V.1, No. 13- Oct. 17, 1977-. 0192-8627. Periodical. US. English. ir. $48.00. Musical Heritage Society, 14 Park Road, Tinton Falls NJ 07724. **Tel** (201)544-8441. *0160-3876.*

THE MUSICAL MAINSTREAM. Began with V. 1, Jan./Feb. 1977. 0364-7501. Periodical. US. English. bm. National Library Service for the Blind and Physically Handicapped, Library of Congress, Washington DC 20542. **LC** ML1. **DD** 780.5. Available in braille and cassette formats. *New Braille Musician, 0093-2817.*

MUSICAL MERCHANDISE REVIEW. **VFOAT** MMR. V. 117- Jan. 1958-. 0027-4615. Periodical. US. English. mo. Larkin Publishing Company, 210 Boylston Street, Chestnut Hill MA 02167. **Tel** (617)964-5100. **LC** ML1. *Musical Merchandise Magazine, Piano & Organ Review.*

MUSICAL NEWS. No. 1- Apr. 1979-. 0709-7174. Periodical. CN. English. ir. .75. Counterpoint Publishing Company, PO Box 186 Station Z, Toronto Ontario M5N 2Z4 Canada. **DD** 780.5.

MUSICAL NEWS. (THE MUSICAL NEWS). **VFOAT** MN. 1934. 0748-9293. Periodical. US. English. mo. $15.00. Musicians Union Local #6 of the American Federation of Musicians, 230 Jones Street, San Francisco CA 94102. **Tel** (415)775-8118. **Ed** Don Menary. **LC** ML1. **DD** 331.881178. adv acc. **Circ** 4,000. (ctrl). Local 6 union and other labor related information.

MUSICAL OPINION. **VFOAT** Musical Opinion and Trade Review. V. 51- (No. 601-). Periodical. UK. English. mo. 13.50 Domestic, $29.00 US. Musical Opinion Ltd, 3-11 Spring Road, Bournemouth Dorset England. **Tel** (0202)23397. **Ed** Charles Myers. bk rev. adv acc. **Circ** 3,000. Classical music opera and organ music. *Musical Opinion and Music Trade Review.*

THE MUSICAL QUARTERLY. V. 1- Jan. 1915-. 0027-4631. Periodical. US. English. qt. $28.00. G Schirmer Inc, 866 Third Avenue, New York NY 10022. **Tel** (212)702-5500. **Ed** Eric Salzman. **Ind/Abst** Mag. Index, Annu. Bibliogr. Engl. Lang. Lit., RILM Abstr., Book Rev. Index, Index Book Rev. Humanit., Music Artic. Guide, Music Index, Read. Guide Period. Lit., Humanit. Index, Book Rev. Digest, Recent Publ. Artic. **LC** ML1. (cum index). bk rev. adv acc. **Circ** 4,000. (ctrl). Musicological and general essays on all subjects pertaining to music. Book reviews usually in essay format.

THE MUSICAL SALVATIONIST. Periodical. UK. English. qt. Salvationist Publisher & Supplier Ltd, 117-121 Judd Street, Kings Cross WC1H 9NN England. **LC** M2198.

MUSICAL TIMES (LONDON, ENGLAND : 1957). (THE MUSICAL TIMES). V. 98- (No. 1367-). 0027-4666. Periodical. UK. English. mo. $30.00. Novello and Company Ltd, Borough Green Sevenoak, Kent TN15 8DT England. **Tel** 01-734-8080. **Ed** Stanley Sadie. **Ind/Abst** Index Book Rev. Humanit., Music Index, Ref. Source, RILM Abstr., Recent Publ. Artic. **LC** ML5. bk rev. adv acc. **Circ** 6,600. For the serious musician, covering all aspects of music in UK and abroad. *Musical Times & Singing Class Circular (London, England : 1910).*

MUSICAL TRADITIONS. No. 1 (Mid 1983)-. 0265-5063. UK. English. 3.00. Keith Summers Editor, Flat 9 Westwood Lodge Rayleigh Road, Thundersley Essex United Kingdom.

THE MUSICAL WOMAN. 1983-. 0737-0032. US. English. an. Greenwood Press, PO Box 5007, Westport CT 06881. **LC** ML82. **DD** 780.88042.

MUSICANADA (CANADIAN MUSIC COUNCIL : 1976). (MUSICANADA). **VFOAT** Music Canada. No. 30 (Nov. 1976)-. 0700-4745. Periodical. CN. English (French). qt. 6.00 Domestic, 7.00 Foreign. Canadian Music Council, 36 Elgin, Ottawa Ontario K1P 5K5 Canada. **Tel** (613)238-5893. **Ed** Guy Huot. **Ind/Abst** Music Index, Art Archaeol. Tech. Abstr. **LC** ML5. **DD** 780.971. bk rev. adv acc. **Circ** 4,000. News and views about Canadian music and musicians.

MUSICA / REALTA. Vol. 1, N. 1 (Apr. 1980)-. Periodical. Italian. ty. 15.000. Edizioni Unicopli, Via Ruggero Bonghi 4, 21041 Milano Italy. **LC** ML5. **DD** 780.5.

MUSICIAN (GLOUCESTER, MASS.). (MUSICIAN). No. 42 (Apr. 1982)-. 0733-5253. Periodical. US. English. mo. $18.00 Domestic, $24.00 Canada and other countries. Musician, Box 1923, Marion OH 43305. **Ind/Abst** Jazz Index. **LC** ML1. **DD** 780.4205. *Musician, Player, and Listener, 0161-9543.*

MUSICIAN OF THE SALVATION ARMY IN AUSTRALIA. Periodical. AT. English. sm. Salvation Army Auxillary Co Australia, 69 Bourke Street, Melbourne Victoria Australia.

THE MUSICIAN OF THE SALVATION ARMY IN THE U.S.A. **Main/Corp** Salvation Army. **VAT** Musician of the Salvation Army of the United States of America. V. 1- Oct. 1978-. 0195-041X. Periodical. US. English. mo. $3.25. The Musician Salvation Army, 799 Bloomfiled Avenue, Verona NJ 07044. **LC** ML1. **DD** 780.5.

THE MUSICIAN'S GUIDE *CEASED.* 1st-6th Ed. 0580-3160. US. English. ir. **LC** ML13.

MUSICIAN'S GUIDE. V. 2, No. 8- Aug. 1975-. 0362-2959. Periodical. US. English. mo. $5.00. New England Musician's Guild, 739 Boylston Street, Boston MA 02116. **LC** ML1. **DD** 780.5. *New England Musician's Guide.*

MUSICIEN AMATEUR. (LE MUSICIEN AMATEUR : LE JOURNAL DE CAMMAC). **VFOAT** The Amateur Musician : Cammac Journal. Feb. 1980-. 0227-4310. Periodical. CN. English (text in French). ir. Cammac Office, PO Box 353, Westmount Quebec H3Z 2T5 Canada. **DD** 780.6071. *Cammunique, 0045-4095.*

MUSICIEN QUEBECOIS. (LE MUSICIEN QUEBECOIS). V. 1- April/May 1974-. 0380-870X. Periodical. CN. French. bm. Le Musicien Quebecois, 867 Place Champlain, Charny Quebec G6W 4R1 Canada. **DD** 780.9714.

MUSICK. V. 1- Summer 1979-. 0226-8620. Periodical. CN. English. qt. $7.00. Vancouver Society for Early Music, 1542 West 7th Avenue, Vancouver British Columbia V6H 1B7 Canada. **Tel** (604)732-1610. **Ed** Gregory Johnston. **DD** 780.971133. bk rev. adv acc. **Circ** 4,500. Journal with articles on all aspects of early music, instruments and performance practice, book and record reviews. Vancouver Society for Early Music Newsletter outlining society activities, concerts, etc.

MUSICLINE. **VFOAT** Music Line. Vol. 1, No. 1 (May 1983)-. 0746-7656. Periodical. US. English. mo. $34.50. CCM Publishing Inc, 25831 Paseo de Alicia/ Suite 201 PO Box 6300, Laguna Hills CA 92653. **Tel** (714)951-9106. **Ed** John W Styll. bk rev. adv acc. **Circ** 5,500. The most immediate printed news source about gospel music available anywhere in the world. It is a must for anyone who is serious about the gospel music industry.

MUSICOLOGICA AUSTRIACA. 1- 1977-. German. ir. **LC** ML5. **DD** 750.5.

MUSICOLOGICAL STUDIES AND DOCUMENTS. No. 2-. 0077-2496. Monographic Series. English. ir. Hanssler Verlag, Bismarckstrasse 4, Postfach 1220, D-7303 Stuttgart West Germany. **Tel** 071581770. **Ed** Armen Carapetyan. Translations, reproductions, facsimile and critical editions of musicological documents of 13th century. *Studies and Documents.*

MUSICOLOGY. V. 1- 1964-. 0077-250X. AT. English. ir. $20.00. Musicological Society of Australia, University of New South Wales PO Box 1 Union Box 67, Kensington New South Wales 2033 Australia. **Ed** Stephen Wild. **Ind/Abst** Music Index, APAIS, Aust. Public Aff. Inf. Serv., RILM Abstr. **LC** ML5. **DD** 780.5. bk rev. **Circ** 500. (ctrl). Concentrates on musicology in all its aspects.

MUSICOLOGY SERIES. **VFOAT** Monographs on Musicology. Vol. 1-. 0275-5866. Monographic Series. US. English. ir. Gordon and Breach Science Publishers, One Park Avenue, New York NY 10016. **DD** 780.

MUSICOM. Began publication with Dec. 1972 issue. 0383-9419. Periodical. CN. English. ir. Musican, PO Box 1151, Stony Plain Alta T0E 2G0 Canada. **DD** 785.067097123. *C B D A Newsletter.*

MUSICUS. Periodical. SA. Afrikaans (English). ir. 12.00. Universiteit van Suid-Afrika, PO Box 392, Pretoria 0001 South Africa. **Tel** (012)440-1603. **Ed**

Music

Hennie Joubert. LC ML5. DD 780.5. adv acc. Circ 1,500. (ctrl). Aspects of music teaching and performance, South African musicians and composers, church music, articles for examination candidates and analyses of prescribed work.

MUSICWORKS. VFOAT Music Works. 1- Mar. 1978-. 0225-686X. Periodical. CN. English. qt. $9.28. Musicworks, 1087 Queen Street West, Toronto Ontario M6J 1H3 Canada. Tel (416)533-0192. Ed Tina Pearson. DD 780.971. adv acc. Circ 1,000. A journal with casette publication from Canada. Serves as a resource of information on innovations in new and possible musics, human and otherwise.

MUSIIKKI. 1.- Year. Periodical. FI. Finnish (some issues have summaries in English). ir. 50.00. Musiikki, Vironkatu 1 C 17, 00170 Helsinki 17 Finland. LC ML5. DD 780.5.

MUSIK & I.E. OG FORSKNING. Main/Corp Copenhagen. Universitet. Det Musikvidenskabelige Institut. Danish or English. ir. Ind/Abst RILM Abstr. LC ML5. DD 780.5.

MUSIK & I.E. OG TEATER. 1- Vol. Periodical. Danish. bm. Bagsvaerd Hovedgade 99 14 E, 2880 Bagsvaerd, Kbenhavn Denmark. LC PN1566.

MUSIK & THEATER (SAINT GALL, SWITZERLAND). (MUSIK & THEATER). VFOAT Musik und Theater. Periodical. German. mo. 6.00 (single issue). Verlag Musik & Theater, Postfach 926, 9001 St Gallen Switzerland. LC ML5. DD 782.05.

MUSIK DES OSTENS. 1-. GW. German. ir. Baerenreiter Music Corporation, 224 King Street, Englewood NJ 07631. Tel 561-30011. Ed Fritz Feldmann and Hubert Unverricht. Ind/Abst RILM Abstr. Collected essays on music in Eastern Europe and Byzantium.

MUSIK EXPRESS. Periodical. German. ir. 2.50 (single issue). Christian Krummer Verlag GMBH, Winterhuder Weg 29, 2 Hamburg 76 West Germany. LC ML5. DD 784.

MUSIK IN BAYERN. Periodical. German. ir. Verlag Hans Schneider, Mozartstrasse 6, D-8132 Tutzing Germany.

MUSIK INFO. Periodical. GW. German. mo. Sigert-Verlag GMBH, Ekbertstrasse 14, 3300 Braunschweig West Germany. *Musik-Informationen*.

MUSIK-INFORMATION; BIBLIOGRAPHISCHE TITELUBERSICHT. See Bibliographies.

MUSIK INTERNATIONAL. Began with issue for Jan. 1980. 0720-0439. Periodical. German (summaries in English, French, and Italian). mo. 56.00. Verlag F Schmitt, Kaiserstr 99-101 Postfach 243, 5200 Siegburg West Germany. Ind/Abst Music Index. LC ML5. DD 781.9105. *Instrumentenbau*.

MUSIK REPORT. 1- 1971-. German. ir. 19.80. Ulmenstr 8, 48 Bielefeld West Germany. Ed I Harden. LC ML5. DD 789.9136.

MUSIK UND BILDUNG. Vol. 1-. 0027-4747. Periodical. German. ir. B Schotts Sohne, Weihergarten 1-9 Postfach 36 40, 65 Mainz West Germany. Ind/Abst Music Index, RILM Abstr. LC ML5. DD 780.72. *Musik im Unterricht*.

MUSIK UND GESELLSCHAFT. 1.- Year. 0027-4755. Periodical. SZ. German. mo. $19.40. Kunst & Wissen Erich Bieber, Dufourstrasse 51, CH-8008 Zurich Switzerland. Tel 011-41-1-69 44 20. Ind/Abst Music Index, RILM Abstr., Humanit. Index. LC ML5.

MUSIK UND GOTTESDIENST. 1st Year-. Periodical. SZ. German. bm. 50.-. Gotthelf Verlag, Badenstrasse 69, CH-8026 Zinrich Switzerland. Tel (01)242-8155. Ind/Abst Music Index, RILM Abstr. LC ML5. DD 783.05. bk rev. adv acc. Circ 3,600. Organ of organist and church choir of Switzerland.

MUSIK UND KIRCHE. Vol. 1-. 0027-4771. Periodical. GW. German. bm. $17.21. Barenreiter Verlag, Postfach 10 03 29, D-3500 Kassel West Germany. Tel 0567/30011-17. Ed Walker Blankenburg, Renate Glinger and Gerhard Schuhmucher. Ind/Abst Music Index, RILM Abstr. LC ML5. DD 783.05. bk rev. adv acc. Circ 22,000. (ctrl). Discusses church music within the framework of ecumenical questions-including liturgy and organ playing. *Zeitschrift fur Evangelische Kirchenmusik*.

MUSIKALIER I DANSKE BIBLIOTEKER. VFOAT Music in Danish Libraries. 1970-. Periodical. Danish. an. Bibliotekscentralen, Telegrafvej 5, DK 2750 Ballerup Denmark. Tel 02 97 40 00. This catalogue lists Danish and foreign printed music acquired by Danish public libraries and Danish research libraries during a years period.

MUSIKALISCHE DENKMALER. Vol. 1-. 0077-2526. Monographic Series. GW. German. ir. Verlag B Schotts Sonne, Postfach 3640, D-65 Mainz West Germany. Tel 06131/246-0.

MUSIKBIBLIOGRAPHISCHER DIENST CEASED. 1.-13. Vol. GW. German. bm. Deutsches Bibliotheksinstitut, Bundesallee 184/185, D-1000 Berlin 31 West Germany. LC ML113. DD 016.78.

MUSIKBRANCHENS ARBOG. See Yearbooks, Almanacs, Directories.

MUSIKERZIEHUNG. Vol. 1-. Periodical. AU. German. ir. Osterreichischer Bundesverlag, Schwarzenbergstrasse 5 Postfach 79, A-1015 Wien 1 Austria. Ind/Abst RILM Abstr., Music Index. LC ML5. DD 780.729436.

MUSIKETHNOLOGISCHE SAMMELBANDE. Periodical. AU. German. Akademische Druck U Verlag, Auerspergasse 12, A-8010 Graz Austria. Ed Wolfgang Suppan. A monographic series on European folk music, historical research, rhythm and metrics in the European folk songs and folk dances.

DIE MUSIKFORSCHUNG. Vol. 1-. 0027-4801. Periodical. GW. German. qt. 90.-. Barenreiter Verlag, Postfach 10 03 29, D-3500 Kassel West Germany. Tel (0561)30011. Ind/Abst Music Index, RILM Abstr. LC ML5. DD 780.5. bk rev. adv acc. Circ 2,500. (ctrl). Articles on musicological themes; reviews of musicological books and music. *Mitteilung*.

MUSIKFORUM. 16.- Year. Periodical. SZ. German. bm. Kunst & Wissen Erich Bieber, Dufourstrasse 51, CH-8008 Zurich Switzerland. Ind/Abst Music Index, RILM Abstr. LC ML5. DD 780.5. *Volksmusik*, 0042-8558.

MUSIKHANDEL. 1st Year-. Periodical. GW. Germany. ir. 36.- Foreign. Av Musikhandel Verlag, Friedrich Wilhelm Strasse 31, 5300 Bonn West Germany. Tel (0228)238565. Ind/Abst Music Index, RILM Abstr. LC ML5. bk rev. adv acc. Circ 2,400. The official journal for the German music publishers and the German music dealers.

DAS MUSIKINSTRUMENT. 1- Yearly. 0027-4828. Periodical. GW. German. mo. 93,50. Verlag das Musikinstrument, Gr Eschenheimer Str 16, D-6000 Frankfurt West Germany. Tel 069/295091. Ed Erwin Kohl and Joachim Muller. Ind/Abst RILM Abstr. LC ML5. bk rev. adv acc. Circ 6,000. (ctrl). International magazine specialized in manufacturing, trade, handicraft and research in the sections of musical instruments and musical electronics.

DER MUSIKMARKT. Periodical. GW. German. sm. $61.35. Josef Keller Verlag, Postfach 1440, D-8130 Stranberg West Germany. LC ML5. DD 780.5.

MUSIKREVY. 1946. 0027-4844. Periodical. SW. Swedish. ir. $145.00. Musikrevy, Box 14 147, S-104 41 Stockholm Sweden. Tel 08-61 02 42. Ed Bengt Pleijel. Ind/Abst Music Index. bk rev. adv acc.

MUSIKTEXTE. No. 1 (Oct. 1983)-. Periodical. German. ir. 40.00. Verlag Musiktexte G B R, Postfach 30 04 80, D-5000 Koln 30 West Germany.

MUSIKTHEATER. See The Arts (General) - Performing Arts.

MUSIKTHERAPEUTISCHE UMSCHAU. 0172-5505. Periodical. GW. German (summaries in English). qt. 76.-. Gustav Fischer Verlag, Wollgrasweg 49, D7000 Stuttgart 72 West Germany. Tel 0711-455038. Ed Volker Bernius. Ind/Abst Excerpta Med. LC ML3920. DD 615.8515405. bk rev. Circ 1,500. (ctrl). Leading German journal in the growing field of music therapy and official journal of the German Society of the Music Therapy.

MUSIKTIDNINGEN. Periodical. Swedish. ir. 40.00. Forlags AB Musiktidnigen, Radarvagen 7 183 61, Taby Sweden. LC ML5.

MUSIKWISSENSCHAFTLICHE STUDIENBIBLIOTHEK. Periodical. GW. German. ir. Hanssler Verlag, Bismarckstrasse 4 Postfach 1220, D-7303 Stuttgart West Germany.

MUSIQUE ET INSTRUMENTS. Sept./Oct. 1964-. Periodical. FR. French. bm. $15.96. EGP, 9 rue Coetlogon, 75006 Paris France. LC ML5. *Musique et Radio*.

MUSIQUE PERIODIQUE. (LA MUSIQUE PERIODIQUE). V. 1- Nov. 1976-. 0702-9160. Periodical. CN. French. mo. $15. Editions Rogemo, CP 301, Succursale Beaconsfield Quebec H9W 5T7 Canada. DD 780.9714.

MUZICA. V. 1- Aug. 1950-. Periodical. RM. Roman (summaries in Russian, English, French and German). mo. Ilexim Press, PO Box 1-136/1-137, Bucharest Romania. Ind/Abst RILM Abstr. (cum index).

MUZIEK & I.E. EN DANS. Periodical. NE. Dutch. ir. 58.-. Openbaar Kunstbezit, PO Box 5294, 1380 GG Weesp The Netherlands. Tel 02940-16266. Ed Sytze Smit. LC ML5. DD 780.5. bk rev. adv acc. Circ 5,000. Dutch magazine issued ten times a year with articles on music and dance.

MUZIEK EN THEATER. Main/Corp Netherlands. Centraal Bureau voor de Statistiek. Dutch. ir. 6.75. Central Bureau Voor de Statistiek, Stattsuitgeverij, S-Gravenhage Netherlands. LC ML21. DD 780.9492. *Statistiek Van Het Concert-, Opera/Operette- en Balletbezoek, Statistiek van het Gesubsidieerde Toneel*.

MUZIKOLOSKI ZBORNIK. VFOAT Musicological Annual. Back issue 1 1965-. 0580-373X. YU. Slovenian (summaries in English). ir. Jugoslovenska Knjica, PO Box 36, Beograd Yuguslavia. Ind/Abst Music Index, RILM Abstr.

MUZSIKA. V. 1-. 0027-5336. Periodical. HU. Hungarian. mo. Akademiai Kiado, POB 24, 1363 Budapest Hungary. Ind/Abst Music Index, RILM Abstr.

MUZYKA. Periodical. UR. Russian. mo. .35 Each Issue. Tsentr Prospekt Kalinina, 3 Gos Biblioteka SSSR Im V I Lenina, Informatsionnyi Tsentr PO Problemam Kultury I Iskusstva, Sektor Redpodogotovkii Rasprostraneniia Izdanii, Moskva Russian SFSR. LC ML5. *Novosti Nauchnoi Literatury: Muzyka*.

MUZYKA I ZIZN. (MUZYKA I ZHIZN). 0303-5689. UR. Russian. 1.24 Single Issue. Izd-Vo Sovetskii Kompozitor, D-65 Nevskii Pr 11, Leningrad Russia. LC ML300.5.

MUZYKALNAIA FOLKLORISTIKA. Vol. 1- 1973-. UR. Russian (summaries in English and German). 0.79 Single Issue. Sovetskii Kompozitor, Naberzhnaia Morisa Toreza, Moskva 30 Russia. Ind/Abst MLA Int. Bibliogr. Books Artic. Mod. Lang. Lit. LC ML3547.1.

MUZYKALNAIA ZHIZN. V. 1- 1958-. 0131-2383. Periodical. UR. Russian. sm. $29.00. Victor Kamkin Inc (70551), 12224 Parklawn Drive, Rockville MD 20852. Tel (301)881-5973.

MUZYKALNOE VOSPITANIE Y SHKOLE. UR. Russian. .57 Each Issue. Izd-Vo Muzyku, Neglinnaia 14, Moskva Russia. LC MT3.R8.

MUZYKALNYI SOVREMENNIK. Began in 1973. Periodical. UR. Russian. 1.89. Sovetskii Kompozitor, K-6 Sadovaia-Triumfalnaia Ul 14-12, Moskva Russian SFSR. LC ML300.5.

NAAM. Main/Corp National Association of Awareness in Music. VAT National Association of Awareness in Music. V. 1- Jan. 1977-. 0147-4618. Periodical. US. English. mo. $24.00. National Association of Awareness in Music, 11441 California Avenue, Lynwood CA 90262. LC ML1. DD 786.605.

N.A.C.W.P.I. JOURNAL. (NACWPI JOURNAL). Main/Corp National Association of College Wind and Percussion Instructors. 1951. 0027-576X. Periodical. US. English. qt. $20.00. Northeast Missouri State University, Division of Fine Arts, Kirksville MO 63501. Tel (816)785-4442. Ed Richard Weerts. Ind/Abst Music Index, RILM Abstr. LC ML27.U5. DD 788.006273. bk rev. adv acc. Circ 6,000. (ctrl). A forum for communication within the profession of applied music on the college and university campus.

NAGELS MUSIK-ARCHIV. Number 1- 1927-. Monographic Series. GW. German. ir. Baerenreiter Music Corporation, 224 King Street, Englewood NJ 07631. Tel 561-30011. LC M2. A series of interesting instrumental music for solo instruments, chamber music and orchestral works of the Renaissance to the 18th Century.

NAJE EDUCATOR CEASED. Main/Corp National Association of Jazz Educators. V. 2, No. 2-V. 13, No. 1. Periodical. US. English. qt. LC ML1. DD 785.4205.

Music

NAMIT JOURNAL. Main/Corp National Association of Musical Instrument Technicians. VAT National Association of Musical Instrument Technicians Journal. V. 1- Jan. 1977-. 0163-612X. US. English. mo. $4.00. NAMIT Publications Inc, PO Box 1824, South Bend IN 46634. LC ML1. DD 781.91028.

NASHVILLE WEST. V. 1- Sept. 1975-. Periodical. US. English. mo. $0.50 Single Issue. Nashville West Enterprises, PO Box 14722, Austin TX 78761. LC ML1. DD 784.

THE NATIONAL BLUEGRASS MUSIC NEWS. V. 1- April 1977-. 0147-9938. Periodical. US. English. mo. $5.00. Route 3 Box 364, Claremone OK 74017. LC ML1. DD 784. *National Bluegrass News, 0099-0035.*

NATIONAL MUSIC COUNCIL NEWS. Vol. 1, No. 1 (Jul. 1984)-. 0882-1801. Periodical. US. English. Free to Members, $10.00 Other. National Music Council, 10 Columbus Circle/13th Floor, New York NY 10019. DD 780.

THE NATS BULLETIN. VAT National Association of Teachers of Singing Bulletin. V. 1- 1945-. 0027-6073. Periodical. US. English. qt. $6.00 Domestic, $6.50 Canada. National Association of Teachers of Singing, 20832 Sparta Lane, Olympia Field IL 60461. **Ind/Abst** Music Artic. Guide, Music Index, RILM Abstr.

THE NATS JOURNAL. VAT National Association of Teachers of Singing Journal. Vol. 42, No. 1 (Sept./Oct. 1985)-. 0884-8106. Periodical. US. English. bm. National Association of Teachers of Singing, 2800 University Boulevard/JU Station, Jacksonville FL 32211. **Ind/Abst** Music Index, RILM Abstr., Music Artic. Guide. DD 784. *NATS Bulletin, 0027-6073.*

THE NEBRASKA MUSIC EDUCATOR. 0732-1503. Periodical. US. English. qt. $5.00. Nebraska Music Educators Association, 2620 S 40th, Lincoln NE 68506. Tel (402)488-7792. Ed H Arthur Schrepel. LC UNC. adv acc. Circ 1,900. News of the association, officer columns, convention news, major news happenings in state, music reviews, college calendars and advertising. Also articles on music.

NENKAN SHUSHO MOKUROKU. See Bibliographies.

NEUE MUSIK IN DER BUNDESREPUBLIK DEUTSCHLAND. (NEUE MUSIK IN DER BUNDESREPUBLIK DEUTSCHLAND. DOKUMENTATION). 1957/58-. 0548-2879. German. be. LC ML275.5.

NEULAND. Vol. 1-. GW. German. ir. Neuland Musikverlag Herb Hinch, Fussfallstrasse 60, 5000 Koln 91 West Germany. LC ML5. DD 780.5.

THE NEW CONSENSUS AND REVIEW OF THE LATEST ISSUES OF RECORDED CLASSICAL MUSIC. Periodical. UK. English. mo. Henry Stave & Company, Record Specialties, 9 Dean Street, London W1 England. LC ML156.9. DD 789.9131. *Consensus and Review of the Latest issues of Recorded Classical Music.*

THE NEW ENGLAND FOLK DIRECTORY. See Yearbooks, Almanacs, Directories.

THE NEW ENGLAND MUSICIAN'S GUIDE. 0098-3381. Periodical. US. English. mo. $1.00. New England Musician's Guild, 739 Boylston Street, Boston MA 02115. LC ML1. DD 780.5.

NEW GOSPEL TREASURE SELECT-A-SONG. 1st- Ed. 0362-7357. US. English. an. $9.95. 201 Grizzard R-12, Nashville TN 37207. LC ML128.V7. DD 016.783675.

NEW HAMPSHIRE QUARTER NOTES. 0028-5315. US. English. Hazen Print Co, Concord NH 03301. LC ML1. DD 780.729742.

NEW MUSIC. (THE NEW MUSIC). V. 1- Aug. 1978-. 0706-7984. Periodical. CN. English. mo. Free. New Music, PO Box 430 Station A, Toronto Ontario M5W 1C2 Canada. DD 780.4205.

NEW MUSIC NEWS. V. 1- Nov. 1979-. 0197-5994. Periodical. US. English. mo. Composers Forum, Box 501 Canal Street Station, New York NY 10013. LC ML197. DD 780.904.

NEW MUSIC PERFORMANCE AND CHAMBER MUSIC. Main/Corp National Endowment for the Arts. VFOAT New Music Performance and Chamber Music Application Guidelines. 1979/80-80/81-. US. English. be. National Endowment for the Arts, 2401 East Street North West, Washington DC 20506.

NEW ON THE CHARTS. See Sound Recordings and Systems.

THE NEW RECORDS. V. 1- 1933-. 0028-6559. Periodical. US. English. mo. $10.50. H Royer Smith Co, 2019 Walnut Street, Philadelphia PA 19103. Tel (215)567-1676. Ed E J Hamilton. LC ML1. DD 789.91205. Circ 10,000. Reviews of recordings of permanent interest (classical).

NEW WORKS ACCEPTED INTO THE LIBRARY OF THE CANADIAN MUSIC CENTRE FROM . . . . Main/Corp Canadian Music Centre. VFOAT Nouvelles Oeuvres Acceptees a la Musicotheque du Centre de Musique Canadienne du . . . . 0822-8264. CN. English. an. Free. Canadian Music Centre, 1263 Bay Street, Toronto Ontario M5R 2C1 Canada. DD 016.781771.

NEW YORK ROCKER. Periodical. US. English. bm. New York Rocker, PO Box 253, Elmhurst NY 11373. Ed A Betrock.

NEWSBRIEF - AMERICAN CONSERVATORY OF MUSIC. (NEWSBRIEF). Main/Corp American Conservatory of Music. Oct. 1981-. 0735-7079. Periodical. US. English. ir. American Conservatory of Music, 116 South Michigan Avenue, Chicago IL 60603.

NEWSETTER - AMERICAN BRAHMS SOCIETY. (NEWSLETTER). VFOAT American Brahms Society Newsletter. Vol. 1, No. 1 (Spring 1983)-. 8756-8357. Periodical. US. English. sa. $20.00. The American Brahms Society School of Music, DN-10, University of Washington, Seattle WA 98195. Tel (206)543-1200. Ed Virginia Hancock. DD 785. bk rev. Circ 1,500. A newsletter with feature articles and reviews, as well as announcements of current research on Brahms.

NEWSLETTER - AMERICAN RECORDER SOCIETY. Main/Corp American Recorder Society. No. 1- Jan. 20, 1950-. Periodical. US. English. qt. American Recorder Society, 596 Broadway #902, New York NY 10012. LC ML27.U5. DD 788.5306273.

NEWSLETTER - ASSOCIATION OF CANADIAN WOMEN COMPOSERS. (NEWSLETTER). VFOAT ACWC Newsletter. Spring 82-. 0823-6755. Periodical. CN. English. ir. Free to Members, $3.00 per year to Non-members. Association of Canadian Women Composers Secretary, 1263 Bay Street, Toronto Ontario M5R 2C1 Canada. DD 780.6071.

NEWSLETTER - BLUEGRASS CLUB OF NEW YORK. Main/Corp Bluegrass Club of New York. 0098-3632. US. English. $4.00. Bluegrass Club of New York, PO Box 1B, 417 East 89 Street, New York NY 10028. LC ML28. DD 780.42.

NEWSLETTER - BOOSEY AND HAWKES INC. Main/Corp Boosey and Hawkes, Inc., New York. V. 1- Fall 1965-. 0006-7598. Periodical. US. English. ir. Boosey & Hawkes Inc, 200 Smith Street/CS6, Farmingdale NY 11735. Tel (516)752-1122.

NEWSLETTER - BOSTON AREA FRIENDS OF BLUEGRASS & OLD-TIME COUNTRY MUSIC. Main/Corp Boston Area Friends of Bluegrass & Old-Time Country Music. Periodical. US. English. mo. 238 Putman Avenue, Cambridge MA 02139. LC ML28.C18. DD 784.06274461.

NEWSLETTER - BRITISH COLUMBIA CHORAL FEDERATION. (NEWSLETTER). VAT B.C.C.F. Newsletter, BCCF Newsletter, British Columbia Choral Federation Newsletter. 0822-8175. Periodical. CN. English. ir. British Columbia Choral Federation, 205-1380 Jervis Street, Vancouver British Columbia V6B 2E5 Canada. DD 784.10060711.

NEWSLETTER - BRITISH COLUMBIA MUSIC EDUCATOR'S ASSOCIATION OF THE BRITISH COLUMBIA TEACHERS' FEDERATION. (NEWSLETTER). Summer 1981-. 0714-7384. Periodical. CN. English. qt. Free to Members. BCMEA Newsletter, c/o British Columbia Teachers' Federation, 2235 Burrard Street, Vancouver British Columbia V6J 3H9 Canada. DD 780.7. *B.C. Music Educator, 0705-9019.*

NEWSLETTER - CANADIAN ASSOCIATION OF MUSIC LIBRARIES. (NEWSLETTER). VFOAT Nouvelles. VAT CAML Newsletter (1978), ACBM Nouvelles (1978). Vol. 7, No. 1 (Feb. 1978)-. 0383-1299. Periodical. CN. English (includes some test in French). qt. 10.00. Canadian Association of Music Libraries, University of Western Ontario, London Ontario N6A 3K7 Canada. Tel (416)978-6920. Ed Kathleen McMorrow. DD 026.7806071. bk rev. adv acc. Circ 150. Articles regarding Canadian music, cataloging practices, bibliographic projects, and information of interest to music libraries. *C A M L Newsletter, 0825-3730.*

NEWSLETTER - CANADIAN BAND DIRECTORS ASSOCIATION. Main/Corp Canadian Band Directors Association. Feb. 1971-. 0381-9159. Periodical. CN. English. bm. Canadian Band Directors Association, 21 Tecumshe Street, Brantford Ontario N3S 2B3 Canada. DD 785.06710971.

NEWSLETTER - CANADIAN FOLK MUSIC SOCIETY. Main/Corp Societe Canadienne de Musique Folklorique. VFOAT Bulletin - Societe Canadienne de Musique Folklorique. V. 1-15, No 4 I.E. V. 14, No. 4. 0576-5234. Periodical. CN. English French. qt. 20.00. Canadian Folk Music Society, Box 4232 Station C, Calgary Alberta T2T 5N1 Canada. Tel 244-2804. Ed Tim Rogers. bk rev. adv acc. Circ 1,000. Articles, songs, reviews, columns, features on Canadian folk music from traditional to contemporary.

NEWSLETTER - CANADIAN MUSIC EDUCATORS' ASSOCIATION. Main/Corp Canadian Music Educators' Association. No. 1- Apr. 1968-. 0045-5172. Periodical. CN. English. Canadian Music Educators' Association, 34 Cameron Road, St Catherines Ontario L2P 3E2 Canada.

NEWSLETTER : CONCERT RECORDINGS. Main/Corp Symposium at Guerneville. VFOAT Concert Recordings. V. 1- Sept. 1973-. US. English. mo. $7.50. Box 465, Guerneville CA 95446. LC ML156.9. DD 789.9131.

NEWSLETTER - FESTIVAL SINGERS OF CANADA. Main/Corp Festival Singers of Canada. V. 1- June 1973-. 0318-1464. CN. English. ir. Free. Festival Singers of Canada, Suite 455-151 Bloor Street West, Toronto Ontario M5S 1S4 Canada. DD 784.06271.

NEWSLETTER - FLORIDA FRIENDS OF BLUEGRASS SOCIETY. (NEWSLETTER - THE FLORIDA FRIENDS OF BLUEGRASS SOCIETY). Main/Corp Florida Friends of Bluegrass Society. 0160-5119. Periodical. US. English. bm. 7318 Sequaia Drive, Tampa FL 33617. LC ML1. DD 784.

NEWSLETTER - FOLKLORE SOCIETY OF GREATER WASHINGTON. Main/Corp Folklore Society of Greater Washington. V. 1- Oct. 23, 1964-. Periodical. US. English. $5.00. Folklore Society of Greater Washington, PO Box 19303 20th Street Station, Washington DC 20036. LC ML1. DD 784.40062754.

NEWSLETTER - HUNTSVILLE ASSOCIATION OF FOLK MUSICIANS. (NEWSLETTER). Main/Corp Huntsville Association of Folk Musicians. No. 1- July 1968-. 0091-9764. US. English. Huntsville Association of Folk Musicians, PO Box 1444, Huntsville AL 35807. LC ML28.H9. DD 781.706276197.

NEWSLETTER - INSTITUTE FOR STUDIES IN AMERICAN MUSIC. Main/Corp Brooklyn College. Institute for Studies in American Music. VFOAT I.S.A.M. Newsletter. VAT Institute for Studies in American Music Newsletter. V. 1- Nov. 1971-. 0145-8396. Periodical. US. English. sa. Free. Institute Studies in American Music, Brooklyn College Department of Music, Brooklyn NY 11210. Tel (718)780-5655. Ed H Wiley Hitchcock. LC ML28.B81. DD 781.773. bk rev. adv acc. Circ 3,500. Includes essays, book and record reviews, research reports, and information on all aspects of American music.

NEWSLETTER (INTERNATIONAL SOCIETY OF BASSISTS : 1979). (NEWSLETTER). VFOAT Bass World. Vol. 5, No. 2 (Spring 1979)-. Periodical. US. English. qt. International Society of Bassists, University of Cincinnati, College-Conservatory of Music, Cincinnati OH 45221. **Ind/Abst** Music Index. *International Society of Bassists Newsletter, 0885-3509.*

NEWSLETTER - INTERNATIONAL TROMBONE ASSOCIATION CEASED. (NEWSLETTER). VFOAT I.T.A. Newsletter. Ceased with V. 8, No. 4, 1981. 0094-6141. Periodical. US. English. qt. $10.00 Students, $15.00 Regular Membership and Libraries. Stan Adams I T A Treasurer, Music Department, University of Arizona,

Music

Tucson AZ 85721. **Ind/Abst** Music Index. **LC** ML1. **DD** 788.205.

NEWSLETTER - MANITOBA CHORAL ASSOCIATION. (NEWSLETTER). June 1984-. 0827-2972. Periodical. CN. English. qt. Free to Members. Manitoba Choral Association, Suite 3/374 Donald Street, Winnipeg Manitoba R3B 2J2 Canada. **DD** 784.100607127. *Manitoba Choral Association (Newsletter), 0827-2980.*

NEWSLETTER - MUSIC OCLC USERS GROUP. **Main/Corp** Music OCLC Users Group. No. 1- 1977-. 0161-1704. Periodical. US. English. ir. $10.00. c/o Judy Weidow, PO Box 8272, Austin TX 7813-8272. **Tel** (512)471-5879. **Ed** Sue Stancu. **Circ** 500. Organizational information, names of contact people, surveys, statistics, news from interpretation and use of the formats.

NEWSLETTER - MUSICOLOGICAL SOCIETY OF AUSTRALIA. **Main/Corp** Musicological Society of Australia. V. 1- Dec. 1977-. 0155-0543. Periodical. AT. English. sa. 5.00. University of New South Wales, Union Box 67, PO Box 1, Kensington New South Wales 2033 Australia. **Ed** Jennifer Marshall. **Circ** 500. (ctrl). Contains information about musicological events within Australia and overseas to its members and subscribers.

NEWSLETTER OF THE AMERICAN MUSICAL INSTRUMENT SOCIETY. (NEWSLETTER - AMERICAN MUSICAL INSTRUMENT SOCIETY). **Main/Corp** American Musical Instrument Society. V. 1- Nov. 1971-. 0160-2365. Periodical. US. English. ty. 17 Lincoln Avenue, Massapequa NY 11762. **Ind/Abst** Music Index. **LC** ML1. **DD** 781.9106273.

NEWSLETTER - ONTARIO CHORAL FEDERATION CEASED. **Main/Corp** Ontario Choral Federation. Began publication in 1970. Ceased with V. 12, No. 1, Oct./Nov. 1982. 0317-0497. Periodical. CN. English. ir. Ontario Choral Federation, Room 503/151 Bloor Street, West Toronto Ontario M5S 1T6 Canada. **DD** 784.96.

NEWSLETTER - OPERA ORCHESTRA OF NEW YORK. (NEWSLETTER). VFOAT Opera Orchestra Newsletter. Vol. 1, No. 1 (Spring 1982)-. 0736-6876. Periodical. US. English. qt. OONY, 211 West 56th Street, New York NY 10019. **LC** ML1699. **DD** 782.1097471.

NEWSLETTER - ROYAL SCHOOL OF CHURCH MUSIC (WARREN, CONN.). (NEWSLETTER). 0748-0148. Periodical. US. English. Royal School of Church Music in America, PO Box 176, Warren CT 06754.

NEWSLETTER - SALT LAKE CITY SONG MINERS TRADITIONAL FOLK MUSIC CLUB OF CENTRAL NEW YORK. (NEWSLETTER - THE SALT CITY SONG MINERS TRADITIONAL FOLK MUSIC CLUB OF CENTRAL NEW YORK). **Main/Corp** Salt City Song Miners Traditional Folk Music Club of Central New York. 0191-1791. Periodical. US. English. mo. Editors: John and Wobus, 723 Broad Street, Syracuse NY 13210. **LC** ML1. **DD** 781.773.

NEWSLETTER - SASKATCHEWAN CHORAL FEDERATION. See The Arts (General) - Performing Arts.

NEWSLETTER - TEXAS BLUEGRASS ASSOCIATION. **Main/Corp** Texas Bluegrass Association. Periodical. US. English. mo. Texas Bluegrass Association, 6544 Balcer Boulevard, Ft Worth TX 76118. **LC** ML27.U5. **DD** 780.42.

NEWSLETTER - UNIVERSITY OF SOUTHERN CALIFORNIA. ARMENIAN MUSICAL STUDIES. (NEWSLETTER). **Main/Corp** University of Southern California. Aemenian Musical Studies. Vol. 1, No. 1 (Summer 1980)-. 0732-8966. US. English. sa. Armenian Musical Studies, University of Southern California, 950 West Jefferson Boulevard/Room 253, Los Angeles CA 90007. **LC** MT4. **DD** 781.7292206079494.

NEWSLETTER - WESTERN PENNSYLVANIA BLUEGRASS COMMITTEE. **Main/Corp** Western Pennsylvania Bluegrass Committee. Periodical. US. English. mo. $5.00. Western Pennsylvania Bluegrass Committee, PO Box 10223, Pittsburgh PA 15232. **LC** ML1. **DD** 784.

NIGHTMOVES. Issue 1-. 0824-6718. Periodical. CN. English. Nightmoves, 66 Ashburn Drive, Nepean Ontario K2E 6N3 Canada. **DD** 784.5400971384.

NIGHTOUT. V. 1- Jan. 26/Feb. 15, 1976-. 0384-5842. Periodical. CN. English. bm. 25. per issue. Nightout, 75 Sherbourne Street, Toronto Ontario M5A 2P9 Canada. **DD** 780.9713541.

NIHON ONGAKU BUNKEN YOSHI MOKUROKU. 1- 1973-. JA. Multilingual (Japanese, English, French, and German). ir. Rilon Kokunai Iinkai c/o Nanki Ongaku Bunko/Nihon Kindai Bungakukan, 4-3-55 Komabu Meguro-Ku, Tokyo (153) Japan. **LC** ML113.

NIHON SHIYO KYOKUSHU. Japanese (text with vocal score and piano accompaniment). an. 2500. Tokyo Gakufu Shuppansha, 5-22-Obinata 1 Bunkyo-Ku, Tokyo-To 11 Japan. **LC** M1812.

NO CAUSE FOR CONCERN?. 0828-6590. Periodical. CN. English. ir. $0.75 per issue. No Cause for Concern, c/o Janine Frenken, 559 Laurier Avenue West, Ottawa Ontario K1R 5C9 Canada. **DD** 784.54.

NOA NEWSLETTER. (NOA NEWSLETTER : OFFICIAL ORGAN, NATIONAL OPERA ASSOCIATION). VFOAT N.O.A. Newsletter. **VAT** National Opera Association Newsletter. 0749-9345. Periodical. US. English. **DD** 782.

NORSK MUSIKERBLAD. Began in 1914. 0029-2044. Periodical. NO. English. ir. Norsk Musikerforbund, Youngs Gate 11, 0181 Oslo 1 Norway. **Tel** 02/ 40 10 50. **Ind/Abst** Music Index.

NORSK MUSIKKGRANSKNING. Norwegian. ir. **LC** ML312.

NORSK MUSIKKTIDSSKRIFT. VFOAT Norsk Musikk Tidsskrift. Began in 1964. 0332-5482. Periodical. Norwegian. qt. 50. Ostre Strandgt 7A, N-4600 Kristiansand Norway. **Tel** 42-25989. **Ed** Jorg Johnsen. **Ind/Abst** RILM Abstr. bk rev. adv acc. **Circ** 1,600. Publication for music teachers and musicians normally published four times each year. Subscribers are music teachers, musicians, composers and libraries.

NORTH & CENTRAL AMERICAN DIRECTORY. See Yearbooks, Almanacs, Directories.

NORTH DAKOTA MUSIC EDUCATOR. 0029-2753. Periodical. US. English. qt. $6.00. Minot State College, c/o James Croonquist, Division of Music, Minot ND 58701. **Tel** (701)857-3185. **Ed** James Croonquist. adv acc. **Circ** 800. (ctrl). Official state music magazine of MENC in North Dakota.

NORTH STAR. 0092-2021. Periodical. US. English. 270 Fort Washington Avenue, New York NY 10032. **LC** ML1. **DD** 784.

NORTHERN LIGHTS FESTIVAL. VFOAT Festival Boreal. 75-. 0827-3995. CN. English (French). an. Northern Lights Festival, 3rd Floor/136 Larch Street, Sudbury Ontario P3E 1C2 Canada. **DD** 784.40079713133. *Northern Lights, 0827-3987.*

NOTES - CANADIAN STRING TEACHERS' ASSOCIATION. **Main/Corp** Canadian String Teachers' Association. V. 1- Winter 1977-. 0707-5677. Periodical. CN. English. ty. Free to Members, Membership: $8. Canadian String Teachers' Association, c/o P Burroughs Department of Fine Arts-Music Faculty of Education at the University of Western Ontario, London Ontario N6G 1G7 Canada. **DD** 787.010712.

NOTES - KODALY INSTITUTE OF CANADA. **Main/Corp** Kodaly Institute of Canada. V. 1- Feb. 1976-. 0700-3269. Periodical. CN. English (includes some text in French). qt. 10. Kodaly Institute of Canada, Margery Littley Registrar/4053 Angeleah Place, Victoria British Columbia V8Z 6T1 Canada. **Tel** (604)479-8831. **Ed** Connie More. **DD** 372.87042. bk rev. **Circ** 500. (ctrl). Contains articles, book, and music reviews, regional news, internal business reports, and events calendar relating to adaption of Hungarian music education system.

NOTES - MUSIC LIBRARY ASSOCIATION. **Main/Corp** Music Library Association. No. 1-15, July 1934-Dec. 1942. 0027-4380. Periodical. US. English. qt. $31.00 Domestic, $35.00 Foreign. Academic Services, 115 Marion Street, Brookline MA 02146. **Ind/Abst** Libr. Inf. Sci. Abstr., Book Rev. Index, Ref. Source, Int. Index, Libr. Lit., Access Index, Humanit. Index, RILM Abstr. **LC** ML27.U5. **DD** 026.78. (cum index).

NOTES. SUPPLEMENT FOR MEMBERS. **Main/Corp** Music Library Association. No. 1- Sept. 1947-. Periodical. US. English. ir. **LC** ML27.U5.

NOTEWORTHY. 0736-9484. Periodical. US. English. KJOS West, 4382 Jutland Drive, San Diego CA 92117. **LC** MT220. **DD** 786.304105.

NOUVELLES DE CAMMAC MONTREAL. **Main/Corp** Cammac Montreal. VFOAT CAMMAC Montreal News. V. 15, No. 4, (April 1984)-. 0828-6035. Periodical. CN. English (text in French). ir. Cammac Montreal, Apt 214/300 rue St-Georges, St-Lambert Quebec J4P 3P9 Canada. **DD** 780.60714281. *Cammac Montreal Bulletin, 0708-7853.*

NOVA BULGARSKA MUZIKA. Bulgarian. ir. **LC** ML390.

NOVAIA SOVETSKAIA I INOSTRANNAIA LITERATURA PO KULTURA I ISKUSSTVU : MUZYKA. Periodical. UR. Multilingual (Russian). mo. 101000 Tsentr, Prospekt Kalinina 3. **LC** ML5.

NOVINKY HUDEBNI LITERATURY. Multilingual (Czech). ir. Mestska Knihovna, Nam Dr V Vack C 1, V Praze Czechoslovakia. **LC** ML113. **DD** 016.78.

NSMEA NOTES. VFOAT N.S.M.E.A. Newsletter. **VAT** Nova Scotia Music Educators' Association Notes, Nova Scotia Music Educators' Association Newsletter. 0821-3283. Periodical. CN. English. ir. NSMEA Notes, c/o Terrance E Hill, Head of Department of Music, Breton Education, New Waterford Nova Scotia B1H 3T4 Canada. **DD** 780.729716. *Newsletter, 0382-0785.*

NSOA BULLETIN. **Main/Corp** National School Orchestra Association. **VAT** National School Orchestra Association Bulletin. 1960. 0146-9975. Periodical. US. English. qt. $8.00. National School Orchestra Association, 330 Bellevue Drive, Bowling Green KY 42101. **Tel** (303)351-2092. **Ed** Donald Hamann. **Ind/Abst** Music Index. **LC** ML1. **DD** 785.066. **Circ** 1,500. (ctrl). Pertinent information of public school orchestra field including articles on pedagogy, music reviews, and professional information on orchestra events.

NUMERICAL LISTING OF SUPRAPHON LP RECORDS. **Main/Corp** Supraphon. US. English. ir. Qualiton Imports Ltd, 39-28 Crescent Street, Long Island City NY 11101. **LC** ML156.S9. **DD** 016.789912.

NUOVA RIVISTA MUSICALE ITALIANA. 0029-6228. Periodical. IT. Italian. qt. 32.000 Domestic, 40.000 Foreign. Eri-Edizioni Rai Radiotu Ital, Via Arsenale 41, Torino Italy. **Tel** 3686/2286. **Ind/Abst** Music Index, RILM Abstr. **LC** ML5. **DD** 780.94. bk rev. adv acc. **Circ** 4,000. (ctrl). Historical and musicological studies on music history, criticism, actuality, book music, record reviews, musical events, calendar and obituary. *Rivista Musicale Italiana.*

NUTIDA MUSIK. Vol. 1- 1957/58-. 0029-6597. Periodical. SW. Swedish. qt. $7.98. Sveriges Radio, 105 10 Stockholm Sweden. **Tel** (8)784-1819. **Ind/Abst** Music Index, RILM Abstr. **LC** ML5. **DD** 780.904.

OAK MUSIC REPORT. Vol. 1, No. 4 (Spring 1981)-. 8755-1837. Periodical. US. English. qt. Oak Publications, Department EP Bellvale Road, Chester NY 10918. **Ind/Abst** Music Index. **DD** 780. *Oak Report, 0737-8343.*

OAXACA CULTURAL : SU MUSICA. V. 1- Jan. 1978-. MX. Spanish. ir. $20.00 Each Issue. Ediciones Culturales, 5 de Febrero No 115, Oaxaca Mexico. **LC** M1682. **DD** 780.9727.

OCSM NEWSLETTER. **VAT** Organization of Canadian Symphony Musicians Newsletter (1980), O.C.S.M. Newsletter (1980). 0823-8162. Periodical. CN. English (includes some text in French). ir. Free. OCSM Newsletter, c/o Murray Ginsberg, Apt 216/4000 Yonge Street, Toronto Ontario M4N 2N9 Canada. **DD** 785.06071. (ctrl). *Newsletter (Organization of Canadian Symphony Musicians), 0229-2211.*

OFFICIAL MUSIC & RECORD DIRECTORY. See Yearbooks, Almanacs, Directories.

THE OFFICIAL PRICE GUIDE TO COLLECTIBLE RECORDS. VFOAT Collectible Records. 1st Ed. (1983)-. 8756-4955. US. English. House of Collectibles Inc, Orlando Central Park, 1900 Premier Row, Orlando FL 32809. **Ed** T E Hudgeons. **DD** 789.

OFFICIAL PRICE GUIDE TO MUSIC COLLECTIBLES (ORLANDO, FLA. : 1984). (THE OFFICIAL PRICE GUIDE TO MUSIC COLLECTIBLES). VFOAT Music Collectibles. 3rd Ed. (1984)-. 0748-111X. US. English. an. House of Collectibles Inc, Orlando Central Park, 1900 Premier Row, Orlando FL 32809. **LC** ML152. **DD** 780.750973. *Official Price Guide to Music Machines & Instruments.*

Music

THE OFFICIAL PRICE GUIDE TO RECORDS. VFOAT Records. 4th Ed. (1983)-. 0747-7392. US. English. an. House of Collectibles Inc, Orlando Central Park, 1900 Premier Row, Orlando FL 32809. **LC** ML156.4.P6. **DD** 789.912450750973. *Official Price Guide to Collectible Rock Records.*

THE OFFICIAL SOUVENIR PROGRAM OF SPOLETO FESTIVAL U.S.A. Main/Corp Spoleto Festival U.S.A. VAT Official Souvenir Program of Spoleto Festival United States of America. 1977-. 0147-5991. US. English. an. David L Rawle Associates, PO Box 157, Charleston SC 29402. **LC** ML38.C52. **DD** 780.79757915.

OLD TIME MUSIC. 1- Summer 1971-. 0048-1653. Periodical. UK. English. qt. $10.00. Old Time Music, 22 Upper Tollington Park, London N4 3EL England. **Ed** Tony Russell. **Ind/Abst** Music Index, MLA Int. Bibliogr. Books Artic. Mod. Lang. Lit. bk rev. adv acc. **Circ** 1,200. American traditional and country music: features, interviews, news, record and book reviews, research and discography, reprints, photographs, and correspondence.

OLD TIME SONGS & POEMS. VAT Old Time Songs and Poems (Seabrook). V. 1- Summer 1976-. 0363-8960. Periodical. US. English. qt. $3.50. House of White Birches, Box 428, Seabrook NH 03974. **LC** ML1. **DD** 784.30605.

ON KEY. No. 1 (Sept. 1982)-. 0734-0281. Periodical. US. English. mo. JDL Publications, PO Box 1213, Montclair NJ 07042. **Tel** (201)746-8967.

ONE SPOT NEW RELEASE REPORTER. VFOAT New Release Reporter. 0748-0415. US. English. wk. $6.00 Monthly. One-Spot Publishing Division, Trade Service Publication, 1000 West Central Road, Mt Prospect IL 60056. **LC** ML156.4.P6. **DD** 016.789912.

ONGAKU GEIJUTSU. 0030-2600. Periodical. JA. English. mo. Japan Publs Trading Company Ltd, PO Box 5030 Tokyo International, Tokyo 100-31 Japan.

ONGAKUGAKU = JOURNAL OF THE JAPANESE MUSICOLOGICAL SOCIETY. Began in 1954. Periodical. JA. Japanese (with summaries in English, French or German). ir. 64.00. Maruzen Company Ltd, PO Box 5050, 100-31 Tokyo Japan. **Ind/Abst** RILM Abstr. **LC** ML5. Organ paper of Tokyo Artistic University.

OOR. Vol. 14, No. 6 (24 March 1984)-. Periodical. Dutch. bw. 93.50. Oor Abonnementen, Postbus 1881, 1000 BW Amsterdam Netherlands. **LC** ML5. **DD** 784.5009492. *Muziekkrant Oor.*

OP. CIT. (MEXICO CITY, MEXICO). (OP. CIT). **VAT** Opere Citato. Yearly V. 1, No. 1, (Jan 6-19 1981)-. Periodical. MX. Spanish. bw. Yucalpeten No. 2 Manzana 166, Col. Padierna Tlalpan, Mexico 20 DF. **Ed** Jamie A Mendoza.

OPER. 1 - 1966-. GW. German. ir. Friedrich Verlag, Velber Bei, Hannover Germany. **LC** ML5. **DD** 782.105.

OPER HEUTE. Began with vol. for 1978. German. an. **LC** ML1699. **DD** 782.10904. *Musikbuhne.*

OPER UND BALLETT IM FILM. VFOAT Opera and Ballet on Film. English, French or German. ir. Gesellschaft fur Musiktheater, Briete Gasse 12, A-1070 Wien Austria. **LC** ML2075. **DD** 016.7821073.

OPER UND KONZERT. 1963. Periodical. GW. German. mo. $30.44. Industrie und Handelswerbung, Ungerer Str 191 Vi App 601, D8000 Munich 40 West Germany. **Ed** A Hannschile. **Ind/Abst** Music Index. **LC** ML5. bk rev. adv acc. **Circ** 4,150. Opera reviews of Germany (West) and abroad, book and disk reviews, information of the opera-scene, interviews, etc.

OPERA. V. 1- Feb. 1950-. 0030-3526. Periodical. UK. English. mo. $35.25. Data Services Bureau, 18A The Broadway/Wickford, Essex SS11 7AA England. **Ind/Abst** Humanit. Index, Music Index, RILM Abstr. **LC** ML5. **DD** 782.105.

OPERA CANADA *CEASED.* (OPERA IN CANADA). V. 1-4, No. 2. 0030-3577. Periodical. CN. English. qt. $19.35. Canadian Opera Association, 35-39 Front Streat East, Toronto M5A 3B1 Canada. **Tel** (416)363-0395. **Ed** Ruby Mercer. **Ind/Abst** Music Index. **LC** ML5. bk rev. adv acc. **Circ** 7,000. Articles, reviews of performances, books, and records, calendar listings, artist profiles and interviews about opera in Canada and around the world.

OPERA INTERNATIONAL. No. 1 (Oct. 1977)-. Periodical. FR. French. mo. 210.- Domestic, 270.- Foreign. Opera International, 122 Avenue des Champs Elysees, 75008 Paris France. **Tel** 43.59.27.71. *Opera.*

OPERA JOURNAAL. Periodical. Dutch. mo. 8.50. Nederlandse Operastichting, Stadsschouwburg Marnixstraat 427, Amsterdam Netherlands. **Ind/Abst** Music Index. **LC** ML5. **DD** 782.105.

OPERA-MUSICAL THEATER. *See* Theater.

OPERA NEWS. Began with Dec. 1936 issue. 0030-3607. Periodical. US. English. ir. $30.00. Metropolitan Opera Guild Inc, 1865 Broadway at 61st Street, New York NY 10023. **Tel** (212)582-7500. **Ed** Robert Jacobson. **Ind/Abst** Mag. Index, Humanit. Index, Book Rev. Index, Music Artic. Guide, Music Index, Read. Guide Period. Lit., Humanit. Index, RILM Abstr., Pop. Mag. Rev. **LC** ML1. **DD** 782. bk rev. adv acc. **Circ** 120,000. Issued also on microfilm by University Microfilms and Bell & Howell. The world's leading opera publication. Regular features singers and related aspects of the field, reviews from around the world and TV and radio operatic coverage.

THE OPERA QUARTERLY. Vol. 1, No. 1 (Spring 1983)-. 0736-0053. Periodical. US. English. qt. $24.00. University of North Carolina Press, PO Box 2288, Chapel Hil NC 27514. **Tel** (919)966-3561. **Ind/Abst** Music Index. **LC** ML1699. **DD** 782.105.

OPERA REVIEW. V. 1- June/July 1977-. 0146-6062. Periodical. US. English. bm. $28.00. Opera Review, c/o Craver Mathews Smith and Company, Suite 1004/1501 Wilson Boulevard, Arlington VA 22209. **LC** ML1. **DD** 782.105.

OPERA WORLD. V. 1- 1952/53-1953/54-. US. English.

OPERNWELT. Vol. 1- Oct. 1960-. 0030-3690. Periodical. German. mo. $49.03. W E Saarbach GMBH, Postfach 101610, D-5000 Koeln 1 West Germany. **Tel** 02 21-23 46 31. **Ind/Abst** Music Index. **LC** ML5.

OPTION (LOS ANGELES, CALIF.). (OPTION). **VFOAT** Option Magazine. Began in 1985. 0882-178X. Periodical. US. English. bm. $12.00 Domestic, $18.00 Canada and Mexico. Sonic Options Network, PO Box 491034, Los Angeles CA 90049. **DD** 780. *OP, 0276-8747.*

OPUS. 0700-5318. Periodical. CN. English. Opus, c/o Faculty of Music, University of Western Ontario, London Ontario N6A 3K7 Canada. **DD** 780.72971326.

OPUS. Began publication in 197-?. 0225-6355. eriodical. CN. English. ir. Free to Members. Music Council, Newfoundland Teachers' Association, 3 Kenmount Road, St John's Newfoundland A1B 1W1 Canada. **DD** 780.7.

OPUS (COPENHAGEN, DENMARK). (OPUS). V. 1, No. 1, (March 1981)-. 0107-2919. Periodical. DK. Danish. ir. 110.00. Opus DMPF, St Kongensgade 65 B, 1264 Kbenhavn K Denmark. **LC** MT3.D4.

OPUS (HARRISBURG, PA.). (OPUS). Vol. 1, No. 1 (Nov./Dec. 1984)-. 8750-488X. Periodical. US. English. bm. $18.00. Historical Times Inc, 2245 Kohn Road, PO Box 8200, Harrisburg PA 17105. **Tel** (717)657-9555. **Ed** James R Oestreich. bk rev. adv acc. **Circ** 50,000. Articles and reviews of classical music on recordings, radio and television.

OPUS MUSICUM. Vol. 1- 1969-. Periodical. CS. Czech. ir. Artia, PO Box 790, Praha 1 Czechoslovakia. **Ind/Abst** Music Index, RILM Abstr. **LC** ML5.

OPUS TWO. V. 1- Oct./Dec. 1970-. 0147-1597. Periodical. US. English. qt. $2.50. Southern Baptist Convention, Sunday School Board, 127 9th Avenue North, Nashville TN 37234. **LC** ML1. **DD** 783.705.

ORBIS MUSICAE. VFOAT Assaph: Studies in Arts. V. 1- Aug. 1971-. 0303-3937. Periodical. IS. English (French or German). sa. $8.00. Tel-Aviv University, Section A Department of Musicology, Ramat-Aviv Israel 69978. **Tel** 420332. **Ind/Abst** Music Index. **LC** ML5. bk rev. **Circ** 600. (ctrl). Scholarly essays in the history and theory of music, ethnomusicology and musicology. the Middle East.

DAS ORCHESTER. Vol. 1-. 0030-4468. Periodical. German. ir. B Schotts Soehne, Postfach 3640, Weihergarte 1-11, D-6500 Mainz West Germany. **Tel** 06131/246-0. **Ind/Abst** Music Index. **LC** ML5. **DD** 785.05. Index in last issue of volume - loose - separately paged.

ORCHESTRA CANADA. VFOAT Orchestres Canada. V. 1- Oct. 1973-. 0380-1799. Periodical. CN. English (text in French). ir. $3.86. Association of Canadian Orchestras, 56 Esplanade/Suite 311, Toronto Ontario M5E 1A7 Canada. **Tel** (416)366-8834. **Ed** Jack Edds. adv acc. **Circ** 1,500. Topics include government communications, fund raising ideas, workshops, conferences, summer programs and orchestra news. Includes the following columns: Musical Chairs, Artists' Corner, From the Board Room. *Orchestra Letter, 0380-1780.*

ORCHESTRA RESOURCE GUIDE. 0824-3654. CN. English. an. Ontario Federation of Symphony Orchestras, Suite 311/56 The Esplanade, Toronto Ontario M5E 1A7 Canada. **DD** 785.0661.

OREGON MUSIC EDUCATOR. V. 1- Nov. 1949-. Periodical. US. English. ty. $2.00. Oregon Music Educator, 337 West Riverside Drive, Roseburg OR 97470.

ORFF ECHO. (THE ORFF ECHO). 0095-2613. US. English. qt. $35.00. American Orff Schulwerk Association, PO Box 391089, Cleveland OH 44139. **Tel** (216)543-5366. **Ed** Mary E Shamrock. **LC** ML1. **DD** 780.7. bk rev. adv acc. **Circ** 3,300. (ctrl). Orff-schalwerk, its use in music education, music therapy, church music and practical applications.

THE ORGAN. V. 1- 1921-. 0030-4883. Periodical. UK. English. qt. 7.60. Musical Opinion Limited, 3-11 Spring Road, Bounemouth Dorset BH1 4QA England. **Tel** (0202)23397. **Ed** Douglas Carrington. **Ind/Abst** Music Index, RILM Abstr. bk rev. adv acc. **Circ** 3,000. Classical music and organ journal.

ORGAN HANDBOOK. Main/Corp Organ Historical Society. National Convention. 28th (1983)-. 0882-2085. US. English. an. Organ Historical Society, Box 26811, Richmond VA 23261. **LC** ML549.8. **DD** 786.605. *Annual National Convention of the Organ Historical Society, 0148-3099.*

THE ORGAN YEARBOOK. *See* Yearbooks, Almanacs, Directories.

ORGANA AUSTRIACA. V. 1-. AU. German. ir. W- Braumuller Universitat- Verlagsbuchhandlung, A-1092 Wien Austria. **LC** ML5.

THE ORGANIST'S COMPANION. Began in Dec. 1978. 0749-3533. Periodical. US. English. bm. $12.95. Belwin Mills Publishing Corporation, 25 Deshon Drive, Melville NY 11747. **LC** M7. **DD** 786.

L'ORGANO. Began in 1960. Periodical. IT. Italian. ir. $23.76. Patron Editore SRL, Via Badini 12, 40127 Bologna Italy. **LC** ML5.

ORGEL (AMERSFOORT, NETHERLANDS). (HET ORGEL). Periodical. NE. Dutch. ir. 70. Nederlandse Organistenvereniging, Juliettestraat 41, 3816 RB Amersfoort Netherlands. **Tel** 033-723814. **LC** ML549.8. **DD** 786.505. bk rev. adv acc. **Circ** 2,100. (ctrl). Information on organ building and restoration, articles on organ-playing, repertoire and church music, musicological articles, reviews of music and books, news of new gramophone recordings.

ORGLET. V. 1- Oct. 1971-. Danish. ir. Ole Olesen Sigerslevvester, 3600 Frederikssund, Kbenhaven Denmark. **LC** ML5.

ORKESTER JOURNALEN. Began in 1933. 0030-5642. Periodical. SW. Swedish. mo. 275.0. Orkester Journalen AB, Box 16252, 103 25 Stockholm Sweden. **Tel** 08-109976. **Ed** Lars Westin and Bo Scherman. **Ind/Abst** Music Index, Jazz Index. **LC** ML5. bk rev. adv acc. **Circ** 5,000. (ctrl). Jazz; live and recorded, articles, reviews, interviews, pictures. Covers both the Swedish and the international scene.

OSTERREICHISCHE MUSIKZEITSCHRIFT. Vol. 1- Jan. 1946-. 0029-9316. Periodical. AU. German. mo. 46. Bauer-Verlag, Postsparkassenkonto Wien 7502.571, Wien Austria. **Ind/Abst** Music Index, RILM Abstr. **LC** ML5. **DD** 780.9436.

OVATION. V. 1- Feb. 1980-. 0196-433X. Periodical. US. English. mo. $15.00 Domestic, $17.00 Canada, $20.00 Foreign. Ovation, PO Box 924, Farmingdale NY 11737. **Ind/Abst** Music Index. **LC** ML1. **DD** 780.5.

OVERTONES. Periodical. US. English. qt. **LC** ML1.

OVERTURE. 1924. 0030-7556. Periodical. US. English (Spanish). mo. $24.00. Musicians Union, Local 47 AF of M 817 Vine Street, Los Angeles CA 90038. **Tel** (213)462-2161. **Ed** Serena Kay Williams. **LC** ML1. **DD** 331.881178. adv acc. **Circ** 17,000. (ctrl). News for members of Musicians' Union Local 47 of Los Angeles.

Music

OVERTURES. (C O C OVERTURES). Main/Corp Canadian Opera Company. V. 1-V. 3, No. 3. 0382-778X. Periodical. CN. English. qt. $19.35. Canadian Opera Guild, 417 Queens Quay West, Toronto Ontario M5V 1A2 Canada. DD 782.106571.

PACIFIC REVIEW OF ENTHNOMUSICOLOGY. Vol. 1 (1984)-. Periodical. US. English. an. University of California, Ethnomusicology, Department of Music, Schoenberg Hall, Los Angeles CA 90024.

PAID MY DUES. V. 1- 1974-. 0097-8035. Periodical. US. English. qt. $1.00 Single Issue. Woman's Soul Publishing, PO Box 5476, Milwaukee WI 53211. LC ML1. DD 780.5.

PALMARES LA QUEBECOISE. V. 1- June 23, 1975-. 0319-8421. Periodical. CN. French. bw. Association Quebecoise des Producteurs des Disques Inc, 7033 Route Trans-Canadienne, Ville St-Laurent Quebec H4T 1S2 Canada. DD 016.789912.

PANORAMA DE LA MUSIQUE ET DES INSTRUMENTS. 0336-2574. Periodical. FR. French. ir. 100.00. Panorama de la Musique, 20 Avenue Kleber, Paris France 75116. Ind/Abst RILM Abstr. LC ML5. DD 780.5.

PANORAMA MUSIQUES. Periodical. FR. French. bm. $12.64. Panorama Musiques, 20 Av Kleber, 75116 Paris France. LC ML5. DD 780.5.

PAR SI PAR LA. Vol. 1, No. 1 Spring 1980. 0712-290X. Periodical. CN. French. ty. Free. Par Si Par La, Alliance Chorale Alberta 102, 9942-82 Avenue, Edmonton Alberta T6E 1Y9 Canada. DD 784.960607123.

PARLANDO. Periodical. Hungarian. ir. 36.00. VI Gorkij Fasor 38, Budapest Hungary. Ind/Abst RILM Abstr. LC ML5.

PASSING TONES. 0712-5062. Periodical. CN. English. mo. Free to Members. Passing Tones, c/o Winnipeg Jazz Society, 911 Valour Road, Winnipeg Manitoba R3G 3B6 Canada. DD 785.420971274.

PASSKAZY O'MUZYKE. Vol. 1- 1968-. UR. Russian. 0.50 Single Issue. Muzkya, Neglinnaia 14, Moskva USSR. LC ML63.

PASTORAL MUSIC. V. 1- Oct./Nov. 1976-. 0363-6569. Periodical. US. English. bm. $30.00. National Association Pastoral Musicians, 225 Sheridan Street NW, Washington DC 20011. Tel (202)723-5800. Ed Dan Connors. Ind/Abst Music Index, Cathol. Period. Lit. Index. LC ML1. DD 783.026205. bk rev. adv acc. Circ 7,200. (ctrl). Newsletter for members. Includes report on Association and Chapter activities, job referral notices, music and book reviews, spotlight on members, and general educational articles. Musart, 0027-3724.

PASTORAL MUSIC NOTEBOOK. (PASTORAL MUSIC NOTEBOOK : A PUBLICATION OF THE NATIONAL ASSOCIATION OF PASTORAL MUSICIANS). VFOAT Pastoral Musicians Notebook. Vol. 1, No. 1 (May 1977)-. 0145-6636. Periodical. US. English. bm. $18.00. National Association of Pastoral Musicians, 225 Sheridan Street NW, Washington DC 20011. Tel (202)723-5800. Ed Dan Connors. LC ML2999. DD 783.02605. bk rev. adv acc. Circ 8,500. (ctrl). One central theme per issue dealing with music, the arts, and worship. Includes music and book reviews, calendar of events and job referrals.

PAUL'S RECORD MAGAZINE. 0360-2109. Periodical. US. English. mo. $5.00. P E Bezanker, 105 Preston Street, Hartford CT 06114. LC ML156.9. DD 789.912.

PAUTA. Vol. 1, No. 1 (Jan/March 1982)-. Periodical. MX. Spanish. qt. $20.00. Seccion de Publicationes/Uam-Iztapalapa, AV Michoacan y Purisima, 09340 Mexico DF Mexico. Tel 686-03-22. bk rev. Circ 4,000. Musical articles, critics about musical events, classic and contemporary, as well as literary news.

PEDALPOINT. Vol. 1, No. 1 (Oct. Nov. Dec. 1981)-. 0272-9199. Periodical. US. English. qt. $28.00. Materials Services Department, 127 9th Avenue North, Nashville TN 37234. LC ML2999. DD 783.1.

THE PENN STATE MUSIC SERIES. No. 1-27. 0553-5042. Monographic Series. US. English.

PERCUSSIVE NOTES. Began in 1962. 0553-6502. Periodical. US. English. bm. $25.00. Percussive Arts Society, 214 West Main Street/Box 697, Urbana IL 61801-0697. Tel (312)367-4098. Ed Robert Schietroma and Jean Charles Francois. Ind/Abst Music Index. LC ML1. DD 789.0105. bk rev adv acc. Circ 6,000. (ctrl). Includes information on symphonic jazz, drum set, corps, timpani, mallet-keyboard, publications, new products, recordings, personalities and research in the percussion field.

PERCUSSIVE NOTES. RESEARCH EDITION. Vol. 19, No. 3 (Fall 1982)-. 0749-1344. Periodical. US. English. sa. $15.00 (Membership, Professional, Music Educator, Library, U.S.), $10.00 (Membership, Student, U.S.), $18.00 (Membership, Professional, Music Educator, Library, Canada/Mexico), $13.00 (Membership, Student, Canada/Mexico). Percussive Arts Society, 214 West Main Street, Box 697, Urbana IL 61801-0697. Ind/Abst Music Index. LC ML1. DD 789.0105. Percussive Notes. Research Edition: Percussionist, 0749-1336.

PERFORM. Periodical. UK. English. Free to Members. Perform, 10 Chapelfield Place Thorpe Hesley Rotherham, S Yorkshire S61 2TN U K. LC ML3650. DD 781.74205.

PERFORMING RIGHT NEWS. 1-. UK. English. Performing Right Society, 29/33 Berners Street, London W1P 4AA England. LC ML5. DD 790.20941. Performing Right.

THE PERFORMING RIGHT YEARBOOK. See Yearbooks, Almanacs, Directories.

THE PERFORMING WOMAN. V. 1- June 1978-. 0191-1554. US. English. sa. $5.00. The Performing Woman, Subscription Department, Grand View Avenue, Hayward CA 94542. LC ML1. DD 780.2573.

PERIODICA MUSICA. (PERIODICA MUSICA : NEWSLETTER OF THE REPERTOIRE INTERNATIONAL DE LA PRESSE MUSICALE DU XIXE SIECLE, CENTRES INTERNATIONAUX DE RECHERCHE SUR LA PRESSE MUSICALE). VAT Ripmxix Newsletter Repertoire International de la Presse Musicale de Xixe Siecle Newsletter. Vol. 1, No. 1 (Spring 1983)-. 0822-7594. Periodical. CN. English (includes some text in Italian). an. $10.00 US. Centre for Studies in Nineteenth Century Music, University of British Columbia, 6361 Memorial Road, Vancouver British Columbia V6T 1W5 Canada. Tel (416)228-3578. Ed H Robert Cohen, Peter Loeffler and Zolton Roman. DD 780.5. bk rev. Circ 250. Periodical dealing with research into the musical press of the nineteenth century.

PERSPECTIVES OF NEW MUSIC. V. 1- Fall 1962-. 0031-6016. Periodical. US. English. sa. $76.00. Perspectives of New Music Inc, School Music DN-10 University of Washington, Seattle WA 98195. Tel (206)543-0196. Ed John Rahn. Ind/Abst RILM Abstr., Index Book Rev. Humanit., Music Index. LC ML1. DD 780.5. bk rev. adv acc. Circ 2,000. An internationally known, scholarly journal concentrating on atonal, serial, electronic, and computer music by living composers, and abstract or speculative matters relevant thereto.

PESQUISA BRASILEIRA DO DISCO. Periodical. Portuguese. ir. $50.00. Editora Pesquisa Brasileira do Disco, Rua Timbiras 502 30 Conj 307, Sao Paulo Brazil. LC ML5. DD 789.91205.

PESQUISA NACIONAL DO SUCESSO. Periodical. Portuguese. ir. $15.00. Pesquisa Nacional do Sucesso, Sociedade Civil Ltda, Rua Timbiras No 502 30., Andar c/307-310, Sao Paulo Brazil. LC ML5. DD 780.4205.

PETERS NOTES. V. 1- Fall-Winter 1976/77-. 0364-5487. Periodical. US. English. sa. C F Peters Corporation, 373 Park Avenue South, New York NY 10016. LC ML1. DD 780.5. Peters Notes, 0364-5487.

PHONO. V. 1- Fall 1954-. Periodical. German. bm. LC ML5.

PHONO PRESS. German. ir. Bundesverband der Phonographischen Wirschaft, 2000 Hamburg 11, Katharinenstrasse 11, Hamburg West Germany. LC ML5. DD 789.912.

PHONOLOG REPORTER. Began publication in 1948. Periodical. US. English. wk. $306.00. Trade Service Publishing Inc, 10996 Torreyana Road PO Box 85007, San Diego CA 92121. Tel (619)457-5920. Ed Mario Negranza. This 6,000 page loose-leaf publication contains over 1,000,000 current listings of pop titles, pop artists, pop albums, classical titles, classical artists and composers.

PIANO GUILD NOTES. Began in 1945. 0031-9546. Periodical. US. English. bm. $10.00. National Guild of Piano Teachers, PO Box 1807, Austin TX 78767. Tel (512)478-5775. Ed Barbara Stooksberry. LC UNC. bk rev. adv acc. Circ 14,000. Publishing work of piano teacher members and their students. A common bond between organization teachers and their students.

PIANO-JAHRBUCH. VFOAT Piano Jahrbuch. 1980-. 0173-8607. Periodical. GW. German. an. Piano-Verlag, Kornerplatz 8, D-4350 Recklinghausen West Germany. LC ML650. DD 786.105.

THE PIANO QUARTERLY. No. 25- Fall 1958-. 0031-9554. Periodical. US. English. qt. $14.00. Piano Quarterly, PO Box 815, Wilmington VT 05363. Tel (802)464-5149. Ed Robert Joseph Silverman. Ind/Abst Music Index, RILM Abstr. LC ML1. DD 786.105. bk rev. adv acc. Circ 13,000. Interviews with great pianists and composers. First publication of diaries of pianists of the past. Articles, reviews of new music, books, records and much more. Piano Quarterly Newsletter, 0735-7125.

PIANO TECHNICIAN'S JOURNAL. See Technology (General).

PIERCE PIANO ATLAS. VFOAT Piano Atlas. 1946. 0733-429X. US. English. ir. $15.95. Pierce Piano Atlas, 1880 Termino, Long Beach CA 90815. Tel (213)597-7535. Ed Bob Pierce. adv acc. The bible of piano business worldwide used by dealers, toners, manufacturers and libraries. Michel's Piano Atlas.

PIG PAPER. (THE PIG PAPER). VFOAT Schweine Zeitung = Swine Newspaper. 0710-3034. Periodical. US. English. ir. Pig Productions, PO Box 2700, Huntington Beach CA 92647. DD 780.4205.

PIONERSKII MUZYKALNYI KLUB. Vol. 1-. Periodical. UR. Russian. LC ML5.

PIPE BAND. Periodical. UK. English. bm. Royal Scottish Pipe Band Association, 45 Washington Street, Glasgow G3 9AZ Scotland.

THE PITCH PIPE. 0882-214X. Periodical. US. English. qt. Free Members, $4.00 Includes Subscription to the Rechorder. Sweet Adelines Inc, 5334 East 46th Street, Tulsa OK 74135. LC ML1. DD 781.

PITTSBURGH MUSICIAN. V. 1- May 1949-. Periodical. US. English. mo. LC ML1.

PITTSBURGH SYMPHONY ORCHESTRA PROGRAM MAGAZINE. Periodical. US. English. ir. $25.00. Pittsburgh Symphony Society, 600 Penn Avenue Heinz Hall, Pittsburg PA 15222. Tel (412)392-4870. Ed Denise Wagner. LC MT125.P58. adv acc. (ctrl). Concert programs.

PLAYBOARD. See The Arts (General) - Performing Arts.

PMEA NEWS. Main/Corp Pennsylvania Music Educators Association. VAT Pennsylvania Music Educators Association News. 0030-8102. Periodical. US. English. qt. $8.00. Pennsylvania Music Educators Association, 823 Old Westtown Road, West Chester PA 19382. Tel (215)436-9281. Ed Richard C Merrell. LC UNC. bk rev acc. adv acc. Circ 5,000. (ctrl). Music education in the schools of Pennsylvania.

THE PODIUM. (THE PODIUM : MAGAZINE OF THE FRITZ REINER SOCIETY). Vol. 1, No. 1 (1976)-. Periodical. US. English. sa. 1525 Lunt Avenue, Chicago IL 60626. Ind/Abst Music Index. LC ML422.R38. DD 785.0924.

POEM I TANTSUEM. Periodical. UR. Russian. LC M1757.18.

POLISH MUSIC. VFOAT Polnische Musik. 0032-2946. Periodical. PL. English. qt. ARS Polona, Krakowskie Przedmiescie 7, 00-068 Warsaw Poland. Ind/Abst Music Index. LC ML5. DD 780.9438.

POLYPHONIC MUSIC OF THE FOURTEENTH CENTURY. Vol. 1 1956-. 0477-5139. Monographic Series. English. ir. Editions l'Oiseau-Lyre, Les Remparts, Monaco. Tel (93)30 09 44. adv acc. Describes polyphonic music of the fourteenth century with 24 volumes plus one supplementary volume; subscription only for the whole series.

POLYPHONY. 0163-4534. Periodical. US. English. bm. $12.00. Polyphony Publishing Company, 1020 West Wilshire Boulevard, Oklahoma City OK 73116. Tel (405)842-5480. Ind/Abst Music Index.

POP DIRECTORY. See Yearbooks, Almanacs, Directories.

Music

POP, JAZZ & SHOW CHOIR MAGAZINE. VFOAT Pop, Jazz and Show Choir Magazine. VAT Pop Jazz Show Choir Mag. 8755-9994. Periodical. US. English. qt. $8.00. Scott Fredrickson, Box 2435, Greeley CO 80632. Ed Scott Fredrickson. DD 784. bk rev. adv acc. Circ 6,000. (ctrl). Education and entertainment for choral music directors who direct pop, jazz and show choir groups.

POP ROCK. 0713-8121. Periodical. CN. French. ir. $15.00. Pop Rock, c/o Editions de l'Ultra Monde, 408 St-Gabriel, Montreal Quebec H2Y 2Z9 Canada. DD 784.54005.

POPSWOP. Periodical. UK. English. wk. Spotlight Publications, 1 Bernwell Road, N7 7AX London England. LC ML1. DD 784.

POPULAR MUSIC AND SOCIETY. V. 1- Fall 1971-. 0300-7766. Periodical. US. English. qt. $20.00. Bowling Green University, Journals Department, Popular Cultural Building, Bowling Green OH 43202. Tel (419)372-2981. Ind/Abst Music Index, RILM Abstr., Index Book Rev. Humanit., Book Rev. Index. LC ML1. DD 780.42.

POPULAR MUSIC (CAMBRIDGE UNIVERSITY PRESS). (POPULAR MUSIC). 1-. 0261-1430. UK. English. an. $52.00. Cambridge University Press, 510 North Avenue, New Rochelle NY 10801. Ed Richard Middleton and David Horn. Ind/Abst Jazz Index. LC ML3469. DD 780.4205. bk rev. Each issue contains some ten to fifteen authoritative essays on a specific theme, written in an accessible style.

POPULAR MUSIC MAGAZINE. V. 7- Dec./Jan. 1979-. Periodical. US. English. bm. $7.90. The Heritage Music Press, 501 East Third Street, PO Box 802, Dayton OH 45401. LC M1630.18. *Best of Popular Music Magazine: Piano, Vocal, Guitar, Best of Popular Music Magazine: Organ, Vocal.*

POPULAR MUSIC NEWS. 0092-4741. Periodical. US. English. Eastend Music & Art Workshop, 842 West Avenue, Miami Beach FL 33139. LC ML1. DD 780.5.

POPULAR MUSIC PERIODICALS INDEX. See Indexes/Abstracts.

PORADNIK MUZYCZNY. 0551-5351. Periodical. PL. Polish. mo. ARS Polona, Krakowskie Przedmiescie 7, 00-068 Warsaw Poland. Ind/Abst RILM Abstr. LC ML5.

POURQUOI CHANTER? V. 1- March 1977-. 0705-8780. Periodical. CN. French. ir. .50 Each Number. Association Action-Chanson du Quebec, C P 205 Succursale G, Montreal Quebec H2W 2M9 Canada. DD 780.5.

PRAIRIE SOUNDS. (PRAIRIE SOUNDS : NEWSLETTER OF THE CANADIAN MUSIC CENTRE, PRAIRIE REGION). Vol. 1, No. 2 (Oct. 1980)-. 0822-7500. Periodical. CN. English. ir. Canadian Music Centre, Prairie Region, 911 Library Tower, 2500 University Drive NW, Calgary Alberta T2N 1N4 Canada. DD 780.9712. *Canadian Music Centre (Newsletter), 0822-7497.*

PRELUDE. V. 1- Fall 1975-. 0381-890X. Periodical. CN. English. ty. Calgary Philharmonic Society, 210 320-9th Avenue Southwest, Calgary Alberta T2P 1K6 Canada. DD 785.06271233. *Bravura, 0381-8918.*

PRELUDIUM. VFOAT Concertgebouw-Nieuws. Periodical. Dutch. ir. LC ML5.

PRENONS NOTRE MUSIQUE EN MAIN. No. 1- Feb. 1979-. 0228-0868. Periodical. CN. French. mo. Free to Members. Syndicat de la Musique du Quebec, 938 Est Rachel, Montreal Quebec H2J 2J1 Canada. DD 780.60714.

PRICE GUIDE FOR SOUND TRACK RECORDS. 0882-6889. US. English. an. $9.95. Sound Track Album Retailer, PO Box 7, Quarryville PA 17566. Tel (717)284-2573. Ed James W Reed. (ctrl). An alphabetical listing of sound track music on record showing title, label and number, composer, market value and price we pay for each.

PRINCETON STUDIES IN MUSIC. No. 1-. 0079-5259. Monographic Series. US. English. ir. Princeton University Press, Box A, 3175 Princeton Pike, Lawrenceville NJ 08648. Tel (609)896-2111.

PRO MUSICA. 0164-7490. Periodical. US. English. mo. $24.00 Domestic, $32.00 Canada. Service Communications, 50 Rockefeller Plaza/Suite 921, New York NY 10020.

PRO MUSICA MAGAZINE. V. 1- Jan./Feb. 1976-. 0363-5244. Periodical. US. English. bm. $6.00. K Lignell, 861 Arlington Boulevard, El Cerrito CA 94530. LC ML1. DD 780.902. *Westcoast Early Music Magazine.*

PRO MUSICA SANA. 0361-9559. Periodical. US. English. qt. Miklos Rozsa Society, 303 East 8th Street, Apt. 12, Bloomington IN 47401. LC ML1. DD 782.8505.

PROBLEMY MUZYKALNOI NAUKI. Vol. 1.- 1972-. UR. Russian. 1.97. LC MT6.

PROCEEDINGS OF THE ANNUAL CONFERENCE - AMERICAN SOCIETY OF UNIVERSITY COMPOSERS. (PROCEEDINGS OF THE ANNUAL CONFERENCE). Main/Corp American Society of University Composers. 0066-0701. US. English. an. $5.00. American Society of University Composers, 2109 Broadway, Suite 15-79, New York NY 10023. LC ML1. DD 780.

PROCEEDINGS OF THE ANNUAL MEETING - NATIONAL ASSOCIATION OF SCHOOLS OF MUSIC. Main/Corp National Association of Schools of Music. 0190-6615. US. English. an. $9.00. National Association Schools of Music, 11250 Roger Bacon Drive #5, Reston VA 22090. Tel (703)437-0700. Ed Michael Yaffe. Ind/Abst Music Index. Circ 1,500. Proceedings includes papers, addresses and committee reports presented at annual meetings. *Annual Meeting.*

PROGRAM - CHICAGO SYMPHONY ORCHESTRA. Main/Corp Chicago Symphony Orchestra. 58th Season, 1st Program (Oct. 7 & 8, 1948)-. US. English. an. Chicago Symphony Orchestra, 220 South Michigan Avenue, Chicago IL 60604. Tel (312)435-8122. *Program Notes, 0740-6290.*

PROGRAM - CLEVELAND ORCHESTRA. Main/Corp Cleveland Orchestra. 24th Program, 64th Season (1981-1982). US. English. bw. $10.00. Musical Arts Association, 11001 Euclid, Cleveland OH 44106. Tel (231)231-7300. Ed Klaus G Roy. LC MT125. DD 785.062771. adv acc. Circ 100. Program notes for Cleveland Orchestra Concerts at Severance Hall and the Blossom Music Center.

PROGRAMS - ST. LOUIS SYMPHONY ORCHESTRA. Main/Corp St. Louis Symphony Orchestra. Periodical. US. English. an. St Louis Symphony Orchestra, Symphony Hall, 718 North Grand Boulevard, St Louis MO 63103. Tel (314)533-2500.

PROPAGANDA (NEW HYDE PARK, N.Y.). (PROPAGANDA). Issue 1 (Winter 1982)-. 0737-0776. Periodical. US. Enlgish. ir. PO Box 296, New Hyde Park NY 11040. Ed Fred Berger. LC ML3533.8. DD 784.54. adv acc. Circ 4,500. Punk avant-garde underground music, fashion, personalities, clubs, movies. Lots of top quality unusual photos, and fast lively text. Large format glossy paper, and slick layout.

PSALLITE. Periodical. AG. Spanish. qt. Parroquia San Roque, Calle 40 N 577, La Plata Argentina. Ind/Abst RILM Abstr. LC ML5. DD 783.05.

PSG NEWSLETTER. VFOAT P.S.G. Newsletter. Began publication in 1967. 0031-9627. Periodical. US. English. $8.00. c/o Carol Moseley, 24 Brookline Avenue, Albany NY 12203.

PSYCHOLOGY OF MUSIC. V. 1- Jan. 1973-. 0305-7356. Periodical. UK. English. sa. $16.85. Society for Research in Psychology of Music and Music Education, c/o Dr D Hargreaves, The University/ Department of Psychology, Leicester LE1 7RH England. Ind/Abst RILM Abstr., Psychol. Abstr. LC ML5. DD 781.15.

PUBLICATIONS - NORTH CAROLINA, UNIVERSITY. Main/Corp North Carolina. University. Library. Hanes Foundation for the Study of the Origin and Development of the Book. US. English. ir. $28.00 US, $32.00 Foreign and Canada. University of North Carolina Press, Box 2288, Chapel Hill NC 27514. Tel (919)966-3561. Ed Irene and Sherwin Sloan. bk rev. adv acc. Circ 4,500. Presents 6-10 original articles in each issue on all aspects of opera. Reviews books, recordings and videotapes. Autumn issue is commemorative editions, focused on one topic. Back issues available.

QUADERNI. Main/Corp Siena. Accademia Musicale Chigiana. No. 1-. 0065-0714. Monographic Series. Italian. ir. LC ML5.

QUADERNI DELLA RASSEGNA MUSICALE. VFOAT Rassegna Musicale. Quaderni. 1- 1964-. 0486-0365. IT. Italian. ir. Guilio Einaudi, Via Umberto Bianlamano, Torino Italia. *Rassegna Musicale.*

QUADERNI VIVALDIANI. 1-. Monographic Series. IT. Italian. ir. L S Olschki, Casella Postale PO Box 66, 50100 Firenze Italy. LC ML410.V82. DD 780.924.

QUALITY ROCK READER. No. 1- Sept. 1975-. 0360-4071. Periodical. US. English. qt. $5.00. K Seebacher, GPO Box 1201, New York NY 10001. LC ML1. DD 784.

QUARTER NOTES. VFOAT Youth and Music. Vol. 1, No. 1 (Summer 1981)-. 0711-0170. Periodical. CN. English. ir. Free. Quarter Notes, Youth and Music Canada, 57 Adelaide Street East, Toronto Ontario M5C 1K6 Canada. DD 780.6071.

QUARTERLY - GUILD OF AMERICAN LUTHIERS. (QUARTERLY - THE GUILD OF AMERICAN LUTHIERS). Main/Corp Guild of American Luthiers. 0273-4389. Periodical. US. English. qt. Guild of American Luthiers, 8222 S Park, Tocoma WA 98408. LC ML755. DD 787.005.

QUARTERLY JOURNAL - NATIONAL CENTRE FOR THE PERFORMING ARTS. See The Arts (General) - Performing Arts.

QUEBEC ROCK. V. 1- April 1977-. 0226-7187. Periodical. CN. French. mo. $21.67. Quebec Rock, CP 70, Succursale Longueuil, Longueuil Quebec J4K 4Y3 Canada. Tel (514)525-2531. DD 780.4205.

QUELLENKATALOGE ZUR MUSIKGESCHICHTE. 1-. 0079-905X. Monographic Series. German. ir. C F Peters Corporation, 373 Park Avenue South, New York NY 10016. Tel (212)686-4147. Ed Richard Schaal. Circ 10. A series of source catalogues for music history, cloth-bound.

QUIRES. Vol. 11, No. 1 (Mar. 1, 1983)-. 0826-4996. Periodical. CN. English. ir. Alberta Choral Federation, 9510 158th Street, Edmonton Alberta T5P 2W7 Canada. DD 784.96. *Newsletter (Alberta Choral Federation), 0821-7076.*

R AND B MAGAZINE. No. 1- Jan./Feb. 1970-. Periodical. US. English. bm. $3.00. Pea Vine Music Company, 18612 Nordhoff Street, Northridge CA 91324. LC ML1. DD 784.05.

R P M WEEKLY. V. 9- Mar. 2, 1968-. 0033-7064. Periodical. CN. English. wk. R P M Music Weekly, 6 Brentcliff Road, Toronto Ontario M4G 3Y2 Canada. Tel (416)425-0257. Ed Walter Girealis. bk rev adv acc. Music industry (CDN) news; singles and LP charts; classified section. *R P M Music Weekly, 0315-6001.*

RACKETT. (THE RACKETT : A JOURNAL OF EARLY MUSIC NEWS AND INFORMATION). Vol. 1, No. 1 (Summer 1978)-. 0229-9844. Periodical. CN. English. qt. $4.00. Rackett, c/o Towne Waytes Society, 1921 West 4th Avenue, Vancouver British Columbia V6J 1M7 Canada. DD 780.9031.

RADIO ACTIVITE INC. See Communication - Broadcasting.

RADIO & RECORDS. (RADIO & RECORDS : R & R). VFOAT Radio and Records. 0277-4860. Periodical. US. English. wk. $215.00. Radio & Records Inc, 1930 Century Park West, Los Angeles CA 90067. Tel (213)553-4330. LC PN1991.67.P67. DD 384.540973. adv acc. Trade newspaper for the radio and record industries containing national airplay charts, FCC and industry news and editorial for music, sales, management and programming.

RADIO GUIDE. (RADIO GUIDE : THE GUIDE TO CBC RADIO AND CBC STEREO). No. 1 (May 9-22, 1981). 0711-642X. Periodical. CN. English. mo. $11.61. CBC Radio Guide, 70 Bond Street/Lower Level, Toronto Ontario M5B 2J3 Canada. Tel (416)365-1148. Ed David Scott. DD 791.440971. bk rev. adv acc. Circ 32,000. (ctrl). Enterprise's magazine which features detailed listings and articles for CBS radio and stereo programs. *CBC Radio Program Guide, 0707-896X.*

RAG TIMES. 0090-4570. Periodical. US. English. bm. $7.00. Maple Leaf Club, 5560 West 62nd Street, Los Angeles CA 90056. Ed Dick Zimmerman. LC ML1. DD 785.42. bk rev. adv acc. Circ 550. (ctrl). All the latest news about all areas of ragtime-past and present.

Music

RAGTIMER. (THE RAGTIMER). Apr. 1967-. 0033-8672. Periodical. CN. English. bm. $7.74. The Ragtime Society, PO Box 520 Station A, Weston Ontario M9N 3N3 Canada. **Ind/Abst** Music Index. **LC** ML5. **DD** 786.21. **Circ** 450. (ctrl). Dedicated to the preservation of classical ragtime. *Ragtime Society Dedicated to the Preservation of Classic Ragtime.*

RANDSCHRIFTEN. 0092-4105. Periodical. US. English. University of California, Music Department, Riverside CA 92502. **LC** ML1. **DD** 789.505.

RASSEGNA MUSICALE CURCI. Year 1- 1948-. 0033-9806. Periodical. IT. Italian. ir. Edizioni Curci SRL, Galleria del Corso 4, 20122 Milano Italy. **Tel** 79-47-46. **Ind/Abst** Music Index.

RECENT RESEARCHES IN AMERICAN MUSIC. 0147-0078. Monographic Series. US. English. qt. $12.95 Each Volume. A-R Editions Inc, 315 West Gorham Street, Madison WI 53703. **LC** UNC.

RECENT RESEARCHES IN THE MUSIC OF THE BAROQUE ERA. V. 1-. 0484-0828. Monographic Series. US. English. qt. $12.95. A-R Editions Inc, 315 West Gorham Street, Madison WI 53703. **LC** M2.

RECENT RESEARCHES IN THE MUSIC OF THE CLASSICAL ERA. **VFOAT** Recent Researches in the Music of the Pre-Classical, Classical, and Early Romantic Eras. V. 1-. 0147-0086. Monographic Series. US. English. qt. $12.95 Each Volume. A-R Editions Inc, 513 West Gorham Street, Madison WI 53703. **LC** M2.

RECENT RESEARCHES IN THE MUSIC OF THE MIDDLE AGES AND EARLY RENAISSANCE. V. 1- 1975-. 0362-3572. US. English. qt. $12.95 Each Volume. A-R Editions Inc, 315 West Gorham Street, Madison WI 53603. **LC** M2. **DD** 780.9.

RECENT RESEARCHES IN THE MUSIC OF THE NINETEENTH AND EARLY TWENTIETH CENTURIES. V. 1-. 0193-5364. Monographic Series. US. English. qt. $15.95. A-R Editions 315 West Gorham Street, Madison WI 53703. **LC** M2. **DD** 780.904.

RECENT RESEARCHES IN THE MUSIC OF THE RENAISSANCE. V. 1-. 0486-123X. Monographic Series. US. English. qt. $12.95 Each Volume. A-R Editions Inc, 315 West Gorham Street, Madison WI 53703. **LC** M2.

RECORD. (THE RECORD). Vol. 1, No. 1 (Nov. 1981)-. 0745-2594. Periodical. US. English. mo. $12.00. Straight Arrow, 745 5th Avenue, New York NY 10151. **Tel** (212)350-1298. **Ed** Jon Bowermaster. bk rev. adv acc. **Circ** 140,000. Offers definitive answers to questions regarding the most influential artists. Coverage of top established artists and promising newcomers, special sections devoted to music video, audio, consumer electronics, and musical instruments.

RECORD. (THE RECORD). 0712-8290. Periodical. CN. English. wk. $75.00 Domestic, $80.00 US. The Record, c/o Dave Farrell, Box 201/Station M, Toronto Ontario M6S Canada. **DD** 380.145789912.

THE RECORD COLLECTOR. 0034-155X. Periodical. UK. English. bm. $24.00. Record Collector, 18 Penhydd Street/Pontrhydyfen/Port Talbot, West Glamorgan SA12 9SB Wales Great Britain. **Tel** Port Talbot 896392. **Ed** Clifford Williams. **LC** ML156.9. bk rev. **Circ** 700. Biography discography and appreciation of gramophone records of a particular operatic singer, plus articles and reviews of interest to collectors of recorded operatic singing.

RECORD COLLECTOR'S MONTHLY. **VFOAT** RCM. 8755-6154. Periodical. US. English. mo. $12.00. Record Collector's Monthly, PO Box 75, Mendham NJ 07945. **Tel** (201)543-9520. **Ed** Don Mennie. **DD** 789. bk rev. adv acc. **Circ** 5,000. Covers collectible disc recordings from 1950 to 1965. Rock and roll, rhythm and blues, doo-wop, rockabilly. Feature articles on recording artists, record labels, and up-to-date convention listings.

RECORD RESEARCH. V. 1- Feb. 1955-. 0034-1592. Periodical. US. English. 8m $4.00 10 Issues. Record Research, 65 Grand Avenue, Brooklyn NY 11205. **Ind/Abst** Jazz Index, Music Index. **LC** ML1. **DD** 789.91205.

RECORD REVIEW (LOS ANGELES, CALIF.). *See* Sound Recordings and Systems.

RECORD WORLD. 0034-1622. Periodical. US. English. wk. Record World, 1697 Broadway, New York NY 10019.

THE RECORD YEAR. 1-. UK. English. an. 42.00. Gerald Duckworth & Company Ltd, The Old Piano Factory 43 Gloucester Crescent, London NW1 England. **LC** ML156.2. **DD** 016.78.

RECORDER. (THE RECORDER). Began with Sept. 1958 issue. 0704-7231. Periodical. CN. English. qt. $23.21. Ontario Music Educators Association, 7 Riviera Drive, Scarborough Ontario M1N 1J9 Canada. **DD** 780.7.

RECORDER & MUSIC. **VFOAT** Recorder and Music. Began with Dec. 1973 issue. 0306-4409. Periodical. UK. English. qt. $11.70. Magnamusic Distributors Inc, Sharon CT 06069. **Tel** (203)364-5431. **Ed** Edgar Hunt. **Ind/Abst** Music Index. **LC** ML5. **DD** 788.53. bk rev. adv acc. **Circ** 150. (ctrl). Music and book (music) reviews, articles concerning musical performances and courses offered in England, interviews with well-known performers and composers. *Recorder and Music Magazine.*

RECORDS IN REVIEW. *See* Sound Recordings and Systems.

RED SHOES. Vol. 1., No. 1 (Jan. 1980)-. 0710-0817. Periodical. CN. English. mo. $0.60 Each Number. Red Shoes Magazine, 685 Cherrywood Drive, Burlington Ontario L7T 3W9 Canada. **DD** 784.5400971.

REFERATE UND INFORMATIONEN. **Main/Corp** Deutscher Musikrat. 0538-8791. Periodical. German. ty. Deutscher Musikrat, AM Michaelshof 4 A, Postfach 200367, 5300 Bonn 2 West Germany. *Referate Informationen.*

REFORMED LITURGY AND MUSIC. *See* Religion, Mythology, Rationalism - Theology.

REGGAE QUARTERLY. Vol. 1, No. 1 (July 13, 1982)-. 0714-4369. Periodical. CN. English. qt. 3.00. Reggae Quarterly, #1501 10 Walmer Road, Toronto Ontario M5R 2W4 Canada. **Tel** (416)924-8519. **Ed** Beth Lesser. **DD** 784.5. adv acc. **Circ** 3,000. Reggae music and Jamaican music culture, interviews, articles on new upcoming stars, history of the music, best picks for new releases; covers the dance hall scene especially.

RELIX. 0146-3489. Periodical. US. English. bm. $11.00. Relix Magazine, 1734 Coney Island Avenue, Brooklyn NY 11230. **Tel** (718)645-0818. **Ed** Toni A Brown. bk rev. adv acc. **Circ** 20,000. San Francisco and sixties related music is our specialty especially Grateful Dead. *Dead Relix.*

REMINISCING. (REMINISCING : THE OFFICIAL JOURNAL OF THE BUDDY HOLLY MEMORIAL SOCIETY). 0738-7717. Periodical. US. English. qt. $18.00. The Buddy Holly Memorial Society, PO Box 6123, Lubbock TX 79413. **Tel** (806)799-4299. **Ed** William F Griggs. adv acc. **Circ** 4,800. Devoted to music and memory of Buddy Holly and related people, with interviews, articles, and reviews of pertinent items, and up-to-date news relating to Buddy Holly. Licensed by Holly Estate.

RENAISSANCE MANUSCRIPT STUDIES. 0196-7037. Monographic Series. US. English. ir. Hanssler Verlag, Bismarckstrasse 4, Postfach 1220, D-7303 Stuttgart West Germany. **LC** ML169.8. **DD** 780.9031.

RENASENCE. V. 1- Aug. 1945-. Periodical. US. English. bm. **LC** ML1. **DD** 780.5.

REPLAY MAGAZINE. V. 1- Oct. 1975-. 0360-7348. Periodical. US. English. wk. Replay Publishing Inc, PO Box 2550, Woodland Hills CA 91365. **Tel** (213)347-3820. **LC** ML1. **DD** 784.

RESOUND : A QUARTERLY OF THE ARCHIVES OF TRADITIONAL MUSIC. Vol. 1, No. 1 (Jan. 1982)-. 0749-2472. Periodical. US. English. qt. $15.00. Archives of Traditional Music, Maxwell Hall 057, Indiana University, Bloomington IN 47405. **Tel** (812)335-8632. **Ed** Marilyn Graf. **DD** 781. **Circ** 500. Includes articles about collections of sound recording recently added to the archives (written by the collectors), and articles about some of the more interesting older collections. The publication primarily is of interest to sound archivests, ethnomusicologists, and anthropologists.

RETAIL MUSIC PRODUCTS INDUSTRY REPORT. 1981 Ed-. US. English. an. NAMM, 500 North Michigan Avenue, Chicago IL 60611. *Merchandising & Operating Experiences (1979),* 0197-324X.

REVISTA BRASILEIRA DE MUSICA. V. 1- March 1934-. 0486-6398. Periodical. BL. Portuguese. ir. Universidade do Brasil, Avenida Vancelan Braz 95, Rio de Janeiro Brazil. **LC** ML5. **DD** 780.5. *Revista.*

REVISTA DE MUSICA LATINOAMERICANA. **VFOAT** Latin American Music Review. V. 1- Spring/Summer 1980-. 0163-0350. Periodical. US. English (Portuguese or Spanish). sa. $25.00. University of Texas Press, Box 7819, Austin TX 78712. **Tel** (512)471-4531. **Ed** Gerard Behague. **Ind/Abst** MLA Int. Bibliogr. Books Artic. Mod. Lang. Lit., Music Index. **LC** ML199. **DD** 781.78105. bk rev. adv acc. **Circ** 450. (ctrl). Devoted exclusively to the study of the oral and written musical traditions of Latin America, from folk to art music.

REVISTA DE MUSICOLOGIA. Vol. 1, No. 1-2-. Periodical. SP. Spanish. sa. $20.00. Ferysa, Ordonez 1, Madrid 29 Spain. **LC** ML5. **DD** 780.5.

REVISTA DO MUSICO. Yearly V. 1- Sept. 1974-. Periodical. Portuguese. ir. Irmanaultson Realizacoes, Av 13 de Maio 47/S 1713, Rio de Janeiro Brazil. **LC** ML5.

REVISTA INIDEF. **Main/Corp** Instituto Interamericano de Etnomusicologia y Folklore. **VAT** Revista Instituto Interamericano de Etnomusicologia y Folklore. No. 1-. Periodical. Spanish. ir. Instituto Nacional de Cultura y Bellas Artes, Apartado 6238, Caracus Venezuela. **LC** ML5. **DD** 781.705.

REVISTA MUSICAL CHILENA. Vol. 1- (No. 1-). 0035-0192. Periodical. CL. Spanish. sa. $30.00. Facultad de Artes, University Chile Casilla 2100 Compania, 1264 Santiago Chile. **Tel** 6965767. **Ind/Abst** Music Index, RILM Abstr. **LC** ML5. bk rev. adv acc. **Circ** 700. Our publication is specially dedicated to the study of Chilean and Latin American music from colonial epoch to 20th century music.

REVUE BELGE DE MUSICOLOGIE. **VFOAT** Belgisch Tijdschrift voor Muziekwetenschap. V. 1- 1946/47-. BE. French, Flemish, English, German or Italian. ir. Societe Belge de Musicologie, 30 rue de la Regence, Brussels Belgium. **Ind/Abst** Music Index, RILM Abstr.

REVUE DE MUSICOLOGIE. **Main/Corp** Societe Francaise de Musicologie. **VFOAT** Bulletin de la Societe Francaise de Musicologie. V. 1 (1917/19)- – Nos. 1/5-. FR. French. sa. 180. Edit Musicale Transatlantiques, 50 rue Joseph de Maistre, 75018 Paris France. **Tel** 228 21 40. bk rev. Musical articles.

REVUE DE MUSICOLOGIE. (REVUE DE MUSICOLOGIE : PUBLIEE PAR LA SOCIETE FRANCAISE DE MUSICOLOGIE). New Series, Vol. 6, No. 1 (Mar. 1922)-. 0035-1601. Periodical. FR. French. sa. Inter Presse Service, 12 rue Paul Lelong, 75095 Paris Cedex 02 France. **Ind/Abst** Music Index, RILM Abstr. *Bulletin de la Societe Francaise de Musicologie.*

REVUE INTERNATIONALE DE MUSIQUE FRANCAISE : ORGANE DE LA SOCIETE INTERNATIONALE DE MUSIQUE FRANCAISE. **VFOAT** RIMF. Yearly V. 1, No. 1, (Feb. 1980)-. Periodical. FR. French. ty. 80. Editions Slatkine-France, BP 12, 01170 Gex France. **LC** ML270. **DD** 781.74405.

LA REVUE MUSICALE. V. 1-25, 1920-1951. 0035-3736. Periodical. FR. French. ir. 675. Editions Richard-Masse, 7 Place Saint-Sulpice, Paris vie France. **Tel** 43262836. **Ed** Richard Masse. **Ind/Abst** Music Index. **LC** ML5. bk rev. adv acc. Music reviews. Varese, Berio Victor Hugo- and the mMsic-Bach and Divine Music.

REVUE MUSICALE DE SUISSE ROMANDE. Began with: 16. V. (Mar. 1963). Periodical. French. qt. 36.-. Revue Musicale de Suisse, Case Postale 157, 1401 Yverdon Switzerland. **Tel** (024)212327. **Ind/Abst** Music Index, RILM Abstr. **LC** ML5. adv acc. **Circ** 4,000. (ctrl). Includes articles on music and certain musicians and information concerning recordings and musical manifestations. *Feuilles Musicales.*

RHYTHM (SASKATOON, SASK.). (RHYTHM). Jan./Feb. 1982-. 0820-9626. Periodical. CN. English. bm $1.95 Per No. Rhythm, PO Box 7950, Saskatoon Saskatchewan S7K 6C7 Canada. **DD** 784.5005.

RIDIM-RCMI NEWSLETTER. (RIDIM/RCMI NEWSLETTER). **Main/Corp** International Repertory of Musical Iconography (Organization). **VAT** Repertoire Internationale d'Iconographie Musicale/Research

Music

Center for Musical Iconography Newsletter. V. 1- Aug. 1975-. 0360-8727. Periodical. US. English. sa. $15.00. Research Center for Musical Iconogra, 33 West 42nd Street/ Room 1001, New York NY 10036. **Tel** (212)790-4282. Ed Terrence Ford. LC ML26. **DD** 780.08. **Circ** 300. (ctrl). Organ of the Repertoire International d'Iconographie Musicale Research Center for Musical Iconography. Articles and news on musical iconography.

RIGHT ON POSTER BOOK. VFOAT Right on Annual Poster Book. 0747-5977. Periodical. US. English. an. $2.95. D S Magazines Inc, 105 Union Avenue, Cresskill NJ 07626. **Tel** (201)569-5055. Ed Cynthia Horner. bk rev. adv acc. Huge 16x22 inch posters with information of favorite TV and music stars. A must for every teenage dreamer's bedroom walls.

RILM ABSTRACTS. See Indexes/Abstracts.

THE RING. 0098-1788. US. English. The Ring, 1629 K Street NW/ Suite 5089, Washington DC 20006. LC ML1. **DD** 782.105.

RISVEGLIO MUSICALE : RM. VFOAT RM. Yearly V. 1, (Feb. 1, 1982)-. Periodical. Italian. bm. 30.000. Via Marianna Dionigi, 43-00193 Roma Italy. LC ML5. **DD** 780.5. Risveglio Bandistico.

RITMO (MEXICO CITY, MEXICO). (RITMO). Yearly V. 1, No. 1, (April 21, 1982)-. Periodical. Spanish. sm. Oficina Internacional de Publicidad, 605 Third Avenue/ Room 1620, New York City NY 10158. LC ML3485. **DD** 784.500972.

RIVER CITY. 0360-4381. Periodical. US. English. qt. Old Flatiron Building, 2148 North Broadway, Wichita KS 67214. LC ML1, M1630.18, ML54.6. **DD** 784.

RIVISTA INTERNAZIONALE DI MUSICA SACRA. VFOAT The International Church Music Review. No. 1 (Jan./Mar. 1980)-. Periodical. IT. English (French and Italian). qt. $31.00. Viale Gorizia 5, 20144-Milano Italy. **Ind/Abst** RILM Abstr. LC ML2999. **DD** 783.02605.

RIVISTA ITALIANA DI MUSICOLOGIA. V. 1-. 0035-6867. Periodical. IT. Italian. sa. $29.11. Casa Editrice Leo S Olschki, Casella Postale/PO Box 66, 50100 Firenze Italy. **Ind/Abst** Music Index, RILM Abstr. LC ML5.

ROCK. 0092-0401. Periodical. US. English. qt. $8.00. Rev Peter P S Ching, 144-25 Roosevelt Avenue, Flushing NY 11354. LC ML1. **DD** 784.

ROCK & ROLL INTERNATIONAL MAGAZINE. Periodical. NE. Dutch and English. ir. 35.00. Rock & Roll International Magazine, PO Box 712, Hengelo 7700 Netherlands. LC ML5. **DD** 784.

ROCK & SOUL. VFOAT Rock and Soul. 8756-3487. Periodical. US. English. bm. $17.00. Dilo Inc, PO Box 355, Hewlett NY 11557. **DD** 784. Rock & Soul Songs, 0035-743X.

ROCK MAGAZINE. 0739-408X. Periodical. US. English. bm. $9.00 Domestic, $12.00 Canada. Jolson Publications, 1112 La Cienega Boulevard, Los Angeles CA 90069. LC ML3533.8. **DD** 784.5400973.

ROCK POSTER MAGAZINE. 8755-8661. Periodical. US. English. qt. $3.00 Per Vol., Domestic; $3.50 Per Vol., Canada. Rock Poster Magazine, 475 Park Avenue South, New York NY 10016. **DD** 784.

ROCK SCENE. V. 1- Mar. 1973-. 0090-3353. Periodical. US. English. bm. $4.00. Four Seasons Publications, Fairwood Road, Bethany CT 06520. LC ML1. **DD** 784.

ROCK STAR BAZAAR. 0735-8326. US. English. Rock Star Bazaar, 114 West Bayaud, Denver CO 80223. LC ML3533.8. **DD** 784.54005.

THE ROCKAMERICA GUIDE TO VIDEO/MUSIC. VFOAT Rockamerica Guide to Video, Music. 1984/1985-. 0883-6469. US. English. Rockamerica Inc, 27 East 21st Street, New York NY 10010. **DD** 338.

ROCKERS (KINGSTON, JAMAICA). (ROCKERS). Periodical. English. bm. Rockers Productions, PO Box 46/Hagley Park PO, Kingston 11 Jamaica West Indies. LC ML3533.8. **DD** 784.540097292.

ROCKINGCHAIR. V. 1- Apr. 1977-. 0146-1885. Periodical. US. English. mo. $20.85 Librarians, $24.95 Non-Librarians. Cupola Productions, PO Box 27, Philadelphia PA 19105.

ROCKLINE. VFOAT Rock Line. 0749-5048. Periodical. US. English. mo. $18.00 Domestic, $21.00 Foreign. Kia-Ora Publications Inc, 157 West 57th Street, New York NY 10019. **DD** 784.

ROCKVILLE INTERNATIONAL. Periodical. Dutch or English. ir. $9.00. Middelburg, Postbus 3, Holland The Netherlands. LC ML5. **DD** 784.

ROCKY MOUNTAIN FOLK CLUB RECORDER. (THE ROCKY MOUNTAIN FOLK CLUB RECORDER). VFOAT Recorder. VAT Recorder (Calgary). Vol. 5, No. 2 (Nov./Dec. 1981)-. Periodical. CN. English. ir. $1.00 Per No. Rocky Mountain Folk Club, 1623 Bowness Road NW, Calgary Alberta T2N 3K1 Canada. **DD** 780.971233. Rocky Mountain Folk Club Newsletter.

ROCKY MOUNTAIN MUSICAL EXPRESS. 0148-7493. Periodical. US. English. mo. Rocky Mountain Musical Express, PO Box B, Boulder CO 80306. **Tel** (303)443-2061. **DD** 780.420978.

ROLLING STONE. No. 1- Nov. 9, 1967-. 0035-791X. Periodical. US. English. bw. $15.95. Straight Arrow Publishers, 745 Fifth Avenue, New York NY 10022. **Ind/Abst** Pop. Mag. Rev., Music Index, Film Lit. Index, Book Rev. Index, Media Rev. Dig., Read. Guide Period. Lit., Abr. Read. Guide. LC AP2. **DD** 784.

ROYAL COLLEGE OF MUSIC MAGAZINE. VFOAT RCM Magazine. V. 1- 1904-. Periodical. UK. English. ir. 2.00. Royal College of Music Union, Prince Consort Road, London SW7 England. **Tel** (01)589-3643. Ed John Cruft. **Ind/Abst** Music Index. bk rev. Circ 2,000. (ctrl). For students, past students and staff of the Royal College of Music.

RUCH MUZYCZNY. Began publication with May 1957 issue. 0035-9610. Periodical. PL. Polish. bw. ARS Polona, Krakowskie Przedmiescie 7, 00-068 Warsaw Poland. **Ind/Abst** Music Index, RILM Abstr.

RYTMY. Periodical. PL. Polish. ir. 10.00 Single Issue. Polksie Wydawn Muzyczne, Senatorska 13/15, Warszawa Poland. LC ML5.

SABIN'S RADIO FREE JAZZ U.S.A. (SABIN'S RADIO FREE JAZZ USA). VFOAT Radio Free Jazz USA. 0093-0490. Periodical. US. English. mo. $6.00. Sabins Discount Records, 3212 Pennsylvania Avenue Southeast, Washington DC 20020. LC ML1. **DD** 785.4205.

SACRED MUSIC. V. 92- Spring 1965-. 0036-2255. Periodical. US. English. qt. $10.00. Church Music Association of America, 3800 Crystal Lake Boulevard, Minneapolis MN 55422. **Tel** (612)293-1710. Ed Richard J Schuler. **Ind/Abst** Ref. Source, Cathol. Period. Lit. Index, Music Artic. Guide, Music Index. bk rev. adv acc. Circ 1,000. Sacred music for the Catholic Church in accord with directives of the Vatican Council, in theory and practice. Catholic Choirmaster, 0197-551X; Caecilia.

THE SACRED ORGAN JOURNAL. 0036-2263. Periodical. US. English. bm. $10.95. Lorenz Publishing Company, 501 East 3rd Street, Dayton OH 45401. **Tel** (513)228-6118.

SAINT JOHN FOLK CLUB RAG. (THE SAINT JOHN FOLK CLUB RAG). 0715-4976. Periodical. CN. English. bm. Free. Saint John Folk Club, 176 Germain Street, Saint John New Brunswick E2L 2G3 Canada. **DD** 781.771532.

SAITENSPIEL. German. ir. 12.00. Deutscher Zithermusik-Bund, Schriftleitung: 8 Munchen-Solln, Brunbauerstrasse 20, Nurnberg West Germany. LC ML5. **DD** 787.805.

SAMMELBANDE DER ROBERT-SCHUMANN-GESELLSCHAFT. Main/Corp Robert-Schumann-Gesellschaft. 1.- 1961-. 0557-1634. GE. German. ir. 13,50 Domestic. Deutscher Buch Export-Import, Leninstrasse 16, DDR-701 Leipzig East Germany. **Tel** 2636. LC ML410.S4. Circ 500. Gives the Robert-Schumann-Gesellschaft, Zwickau/DDR a scientific congress for the life and work of Robert Schumann. The participation is international.

SAMMELBANDE ZUR MUSIKGESCHICHTE DER DEUTSCHEN DEMOKRATISCHEN REPUBLIK. V. 1- 1969-. US. German. ir. Alexander Broude Inc, 575 Eighth Avenue, New York NY 10018. **Tel** (212)586-1674. LC ML275.5. **DD** 780.9431.

THE SAN DIEGO SOUND POST. 0036-407X. Periodical. US. English. mo. American Federation of Musicia Musicians, 1717 Morena Boulevard, San Diego CA 92110.

SAN FRANCISCO SYMPHONY MAGAZINE. Periodical. US. English. mo. San Francisco Symphony Orchestra Association, 107 War Memorial Veterans Building, San Francisco CA 94102. **Tel** (415)861-6240.

SANGEET NATAK. See The Arts (General) - Performing Arts.

SANGER UND MUSIKANTENZEITUNG. 0036-2328. Periodical. German. ir. 15.00. Blv Verlagsgesllschaft, 8 Munchen 40, Lothstrasse 29, Postfach 400 320, Munchen West Germany. **Ind/Abst** RILM Abstr. LC ML5.

SBORNIK. UMENI. Main/Corp Plzen. Pedagogicka Fakulta. 3.-. Czech (summaries in Russian and German). ir. LC ML247. Sbornik. Umeni.

DAS SCHALLPLATTEN ABC. SINGLE SCHALLPLATTEN, GESAMTVERZEICHNIS. VFOAT Schallplatten A.B.C. German. ty. Helmut Sander Verlag, Hohenfriedbergweg 1, 4950 Minden West Germany. LC ML156.4.P6. **DD** 016.7899124500943.

SCHALLPLATTEN ZUM AUSLEIHEN, NEUERWERBUNGEN. See Bibliographies.

THE SCHOOL MUSIC NEWS. VFOAT New York State School Music News. 0036-6668. Periodical. US. English. ir. $8.00. School Music News, PO Box 9620, Schenectady NY 12309. **Tel** (518)372-8349. Ed Robert Campbell. LC ML1. **DD** 780.7205. bk rev. adv acc. Circ 60,000. (ctrl). Articles, reviews of music, education oriented materials, listing of NYSSMA sponsored activities.

THE SCHOOL MUSICIAN DIRECTOR & TEACHER. (THE SCHOOL MUSICIAN DIRECTOR AND TEACHER). V. 36, No. 4- Dec. 1964-. 0036-6676. Periodical. US. English. mo. $12.00. School Musician Director and Teacher, 4049 West Peterson Avenue Sibel, Chicago IL 60646. **Tel** (312)463-7484. **Ind/Abst** Educ. Index, Music Index. School Musician, 0886-2184.

SCHRIFTEN ZUR VOLKSMUSIK. Periodical. AU. German. ir. Verlag Dr A Schendl MBH, Postfach 29 Karlsgasse 15, A-1041 Wien Austria.

SCHUTZ-JAHRBUCH. 1.-Yearly volume. GW. German (summaries in English, French, and Swedish). ir. Baerenreiter Music Corporation, 224 King Street, Englewood NJ 07631. **Tel** 561-30011. Ed Int Heinrich Schuetz-Ges Werner Breig. **Ind/Abst** Music Index. LC ML410.S35. **DD** 780.924, B. Essays on the music, life, environment, and performance practice of Schuet's works and bibliographies on the writings.

SCHWANN ARTIST ISSUE CEASED. 0582-1487. US. English. $3.95. Schwann Artist Issue, 137 Newbury Street, Boston MA 01266. **Tel** (212)265-8360. LC ML156.2. **DD** 016.789912. adv acc. Circ 25,000. A directory listing artists and their recordings. Schwann Artist Listing Long Playing Record Catalog.

SCHWEIZER BEITRAGE ZUR MUSIKWISSENSCHAFT CEASED. V. 1-4. SZ. German. ir. LC ML5. **DD** 780.

SCHWEIZER MUSIK AUF SCHALLPLATTEN. VFOAT Musique Suisse sur Disques, Swiss Music on Records. Began with 1975/76 issue. Periodical. French (German). ir. Schweizerisches Musik-Archiv, Bellariastrasse 82, CH-8038 Zurich Switzerland. LC ML156.2. **DD** 016.789912.

SCHWEIZERISCHE BLASMUSIKZEITUNG. VFOAT Revue des Musiques Suisses, Rivista Bandistica Svizzera. Periodical. SZ. Multilingual (German, French, and Italian). ir. $9.89. Zollikofer & Company AG, Buch und Offsetdruck, 9001 St Gallen Switzerland. **Tel** 071/ 29 22 22.

SCIMITAR AND SONG ANTHOLOGY. 1st- 1976-. US. English. an. Scimitar and Song, PO Box 151, Edgewater MD 21037. Each issue contains an index to its own contents - no vol index - loose.

SCOTTISH FOLK DIRECTORY. See Yearbooks, Almanacs, Directories.

SEE THE MUSIC. VFOAT Live Music Talent Directory. No. 1 - 0826-5216. Periodical. CN. English. be. Free. Toronto Musicians' Association, 101

Music

Thorncliffe Park Drive, Toronto Ontario M4H 1M2 Canada. **Tel** (416)421-1020. **Ed** Hazel Walker. **DD** 780.25713541. adv acc. **Circ** 15,000. (ctrl). A live music catalog. This talent directory consists of ads from musicians who play miscelaneous engagements, weddings, parties, etc.

SELECTED REPORTS IN ETHNOMUSICOLOGY. 0361-6622. US. English. ir. UCLA, Department of Music, Los Angeles CA 90024. **Tel** (213)825-5947. **Ed** Roger Wright. **Ind/Abst** MLA Int. Bibliogr. Books Artic. Mod. Lang. Lit., Music Index, RILM Abstr. **LC** ML3799. **DD** 781.705. **Circ** 300. Progress reports of depth and breadth on ethnomusicological theory, methods, world areas and comparative analyses.

S.E.M. NEWSLETTER CEASED. Main/Corp Society for Ethnomusicology. **VAT** Society for Ethnomusicology Newsletter. V. 1-14. 0036-1291. Periodical. US. English. ty. **LC** ML27.U5. Membership List - Society for Ethnomusicology, 0731-1583.

SENZA SORDINO. V.1- 1963-. Periodical. US. English. bm. $6.00. Senza Sordino, c/o Tom Hall 2800 Lake Shore Drive 4001, Chicago IL 60657. **Tel** (312)327-6939. **Ed** Tom Hall. **Circ** 6,000. (ctrl). Official publication of the International Conference of Symphony and Opera Musicians (ICSOM).

SERIES A. (MASTERWORKS OF YESTERDAY). Main/Corp Colorado College Music Press. 1- 1955-. 0588-490X. Periodical. US. English. Colorado College, Colorado Springs CO 80903.

SHADES. Began with Feb. 1978 issue. 0228-3115. Periodical. CN. English. mo. $11.14. Shady Publications, Box 310 Station B, Toronto Ontario M5T 2W2 Canada. **Tel** (416)929-9493. **Ed** Sheila Wawanash. **DD** 784.54009713541. bk rev. adv acc. **Circ** 7,000. An attempt to analyze and articulate, by demonstration, the leading tips of our culture and thought.

SHEET MUSIC MAGAZINE. EASY ORGAN. Vol.4, No. 6 Aug./Sept. 1980-. 0197-3487. Periodical. US. English. mo. $13.97 Domestic, $15.97 Foreign. Sheet Music Magazine, Subscription and Customer Service Office, 352 Evelyn Street, Paramus NJ 07652. **LC** M1630.18. **DD** 784.50605. Sheet Music Magazine. Standard/Easy Organ, 0197-3509.

SHEET MUSIC MAGAZINE. EASY PIANO/GUITAR. VFOAT Easy Piano/Guitar. VAT Sheet Music Magazine. Easy Piano Guitar. Began in Oct. 1980. 0273-6470. Periodical. US. English. mo. $2.00. Shacor Inc, 352 Evelyn Street, Paramus NJ 07652. **LC** M1630.18. **DD** 784.50605. Sheet Music Magazine. Easy Piano, 0197-3517.

SHEET MUSIC MAGAZINE. STANDARD ORGAN. Vol. 4, No. 6 Aug./Sept. 1980-. 0197-3495. Periodical. US. English. mo. $13.97 Domestic, $15.97 Foreign. Sheet Music Magazine, Subscription and Customer Service Office, 352 Evelyn Street, Paramus NJ 07652. **LC** M1630.18. **DD** 784.50605. Sheet Music Magazine. Standard/Easy Organ, 0197-3509.

SHEET MUSIC MAGAZINE. STANDARD PIANO/GUITAR. VFOAT Standard Piano Guitar. VAT Sheet Music Magazine. Standard Piano Guitar. 0273-6462. Periodical. US. English. ir. $13.97. Sheet Music Magazine, 352 Evelyn Street, Paramus NJ 07652. **Tel** (201)967-9495. **LC** ML1. **DD** 784.50605. Sheet Music Magazine. Standard Piano, 0197-3525.

SHINDIG IN THE BARN. (THE SHINDIG IN THE BARN). 0093-1950. US. English. 434 Strasburge Pike, Lancaster PA 17602. **LC** ML1. **DD** 784.

SHOW MUSIC. 8755-9560. Periodical. US. English. qt. $10.00 US, $12.00 England/Europe, $13.00 Pacific. Max O Preeo, 5800 Pebble Beach Boulevard, Las Vegas NV 89108. **Tel** (702)647-3533. **Ed** Max O Preeo. **DD** 782. bk rev. adv acc. **Circ** 3,000. (ctrl). Reviews new original cast albums and related interest records and books from USA and around the world.

SHOWCASE. (SHOWCASE : MAGAZINE OF THE MINNESOTA ORCHESTRA). VFOAT Show Case. 0196-1586. Periodical. US. English. mo. $18.00. Minnesota Orchestra Hall, 1111 Nicollet Mall, Minneapolis MN 55403. **Tel** (612)371-5639. **Ed** Karen Koepp. **LC** MT125.M5. **DD** 785.06776579. adv acc. **Circ** 30,000. (ctrl). Contains music features, news items, as well as program listings and full program notes. Symphony.

SINFONIAN (EVANSVILLE, IND. : 1980). (THE SINFONIAN). VFOAT Sinfonian Magazine. Vol. 30, No. 1 (Sept. 1980)-. 8750-5347. Periodical. US. English. qt. $5.00. Phi Mu Alpha Sinfonia, Fraternity of America, 10600 Old State Road, Evansville IN 47711. **Tel** (812)867-2433. **Ed** Jonathan Krutz. **DD** 780. **Circ** 20,000. (ctrl). Contains musical and fraternal articles, and news of the national, chapter, and alumni activities of the nation's largest music fraternity. Sinfonian Newsletter.

THE SINFONIAN NEWSLETTER. VFOAT The Sinfonian. 0037-5594. Periodical. US. English. ir. $7.50. Phi Mu Alpha Sinfonia Fraternity, 10600 Old State Road, Evansville IN 47711. **Tel** (812)867-2433. **Ed** Jonathan Krutz. **DD** 780. **Circ** 20,000. The educational and communication vehicle of Phi Mu Alpha Sinfonia National Music Fraternity and its affiliates the Sinfonia Foundation.

SING OUT. V. 1- May 1950-. 0037-5624. Periodical. US. English. qt. $15.00. Sing Out Inc, Box 1071, Easton PA 18044. **Tel** (215)253-8105. **Ed** Mark D Moss. **Ind/Abst** Mag. Index, MLA Int. Bibliogr. Books Artic. Mod. Lang. Lit., Altern. Press Index, Music Index, Access, New Period. Index. **LC** ML1. **DD** 784.05. bk rev. adv acc. **Circ** 5,000. Features, columns, reviews, and news covering folk music in its broadest possible definitions. Also includes at least 20 songs and instruction in "teach-in" format.

THE SING OUT BULLETIN. Aug. 1982-. 0737-1705. Periodical. US. English. mo. $2.00 Each Copy. Sing Out Bulletin, Box 1480, New York NY 10023. **LC** ML1. **DD** 780.973.

SINGENDE KIRCHE. Began with issue for Sept. 1953. Periodical. AU. German. qt. $8.55. Zeitschrift Diozesancomm-Kirch, Stock IM Eisen Platz 3, A-1010 Wien Austria. **Tel** 0222/53 25 61. **Ind/Abst** Music Index, RILM Abstr. **LC** ML5. bk rev. adv acc. **Circ** 4,000. (ctrl). Spiritual leading articles, interesting facts on the history of church music, worth-knowing-about organ builders and organs, new built organs and restoration, review of performances, new editions, etc.

SLOVAK MUSIC. 1969-. Periodical. English. ir. Slovak Music Foundation, Music Information Centre, Fucikova 29, Bratislava Czechoslovakia. **Ind/Abst** Music Index. **LC** ML5. **DD** 781.7437305.

SMASH HITS. 0740-1655. Periodical. US. English. bm. Charlton Publications Inc, Charlton Building, Derby CT 06418. **LC** ML54.6. **DD** 784.50505.

SOCIETY FOR ETHNOMUSICOLOGY SPECIAL SERIES. 0270-1766. Monographic Series. US. English. ir. The Society for Ethnomusicology Inc, Room 513, 201 South Main Street, Ann Arbor MI 48108.

SOCIETY NEWS (BROOMALL, PA.). (SOCIETY NEWS). VFOAT Society News Magazine. 8756-8861. Periodical. US. English. Contemporary Record Society, 724 Winchester Road, Broomall PA 19008. **Tel** (215)544-5920. **Ed** Caroline Hunt. **DD** 780. bk rev. adv acc. **Circ** 100,000. Assists in developing various funding for the support of performances, phonograph recordings, lectures and composer commissions for recordings. Generating public interest and international appreciation of the performers and composers. Society Newsletter, 0748-5867.

SOL MAYOR : REVISTA DE MUSICA. No. 1 (July 1981)-. Periodical. PE. Spanish. ir. Sol Mayor, Huascar 1908, Jesus Maria, Lima Peru.

SOLSTICE NEWS. Issue 38 (Aug. 1982)-. 0821-4743. Periodical. CN. English. mo. $0.50 Each Number. Summer Solstice Festival, 14 210 South Algoma Street, Thunder Bay Ontario P7A 5A1 Canada. **DD** 780.7971312. Solstice News & Program, 0821-4743.

SON MAGAZINE. Began with Nov. 1969 issue. Periodical. FR. French. mo. $27.94. Editions Frequences, 1 Bld Ney, 75018 Paris France. **Tel** 256-72-72. **LC** ML5. **DD** 621.389305.

SONANCES. Vol. 1, No. 1 (Oct. 1981). 0712-2438. Periodical. CN. French. qt. $13.16. Sonances, 857 Avenue du Chanoine Martin, Sainte Foy Quebec Canada G1V 3P6. **Tel** (418)651-1967. **Ed** Jean Michel Boulay. **DD** 780.5. bk rev. adv acc. **Circ** 900. An information quarterly for musicians and music lovers alike which contains leading articles and commentaries on musical events and reviews.

SONG HITS MAGAZINE. (SONG HITS). 0038-1365. Periodical. US. English. mo. Charlton Publications Corporation, Charlton Building/Division Street, Derby CT 06418. **Tel** (203)735-3381.

SONGWRITER'S MARKET. 1979-. 0161-5971. US. English. an. Writers Digest, 9933 Alliance Road, Cincinnati OH 45242. **Tel** (513)984-0717. **Ed** Rand Ruggeberg. **LC** MT67. **DD** 338.47784. 2,000 listings of song buyers; contact name/address, pay rates, submission requirements, types of songs wanted, and business tips.

SONIDO (NEW YORK, N.Y.). (SONIDO). Vol. 1, No. 1 (May 1981)-. 0734-2896. Periodical. US. English. qt. Boys Harbor Inc, 1 East 104th Street, New York NY 10029. **LC** ML3475. **DD** 780.42098.

THE SONNECK SOCIETY NEWSLETTER. VFOAT Newsletter - Sonneck Society. V. 1- Summer 1975-. 0196-7967. Periodical. US. English. ty. $30.00. Sonneck Society c/o K Keller Treas, 410 Fox Chapel Lane, Radnor PA 19087. **Tel** (215)688-6989. **Ed** John Graziano. bk rev. adv acc. **Circ** 1,500. American music and music in American life.

SONUS. Vol. 1, No. 1 (Fall 1980)-. 0739-229X. Periodical. US. English. sa. $15.00. Sonus 24 Avon Hill, Cambridge MA 02140. **Tel** (617)868-0215. **Ed** Pozzi Escot and Robert Cogan. **LC** ML1. **DD** 780.5. adv acc. **Circ** 250. A journal of investigations into global and interdisciplinary musical possibilities.

SORT IT OUT. No. 1-. 0229-6640. Periodical. CN. English. ir. $0.80 Each Number. Sort It Out, c/o D Meyer, 11 Virgil Road, Ottawa Ontario K2H 6B2 Canada. **DD** 784.54005.

THE SOUL & JAZZ RECORD. (THE SOUL AND JAZZ RECORD). 0361-2619. Periodical. US. English. mo. The Soul and Jazz Record, 1680 Vine Street, Suite 1017, Hollywood CA 90028. **LC** ML1. **DD** 784.

SOUL IN REVIEW. V. 1- Feb. 1975-. 0098-0730. US. English. $1.00 Each Issue. Soul in Review Publication, 572 West 125 Street, New York NY 10016. **LC** ML1. **DD** 784.

SOUND IMAGE. 1975- No. 1-. 0362-3955. Periodical. US. English. sa. $20.00. Sound Image Inc, County Road, Deerfield MA 01002. **LC** ML1. **DD** 700.5.

SOUND POST (GRANITE FALLS, MINN.). (SOUND POST). Vol. 1, No. 1 (Jan. 1984)-. 0749-0755. Periodical. US. English. qt. $10.00. Hardanger Fiddle Association of America, Granite Falls MN 56241. **Tel** (612)564-3408. **Ed** Carland Amy Narvestad. bk rev. adv acc. **Circ** 250. (ctrl). Music and sagas of Norwegian 8-stringed hardanger fiddle, other Scandinavian folk instruments, old dances, news of current performers, work shops, reviews, learning aids.

SOUNDBOARD. VFOAT Guitar Foundation of America Soundboard, GFA Soundboard. V. 1- Feb. 1974-. 0145-6237. Periodical. US. English. qt. $20.00. Guitar Foundation of America, PO Box 5311, Garden Grove CA 92645. **Ed** Jim Forrest. **Ind/Abst** Music Index. bk rev. adv acc. **Circ** 2,000. (ctrl). Classical guitar information including technique, performance, pedagogy, music, records, events, calendar, construction and reviews.

SOUNDINGS. No. 1- Autumn 1970-. 0081-2080. UK. English. sa. 11. Cardiff Press, PO Box 78/Cathys Park, Cardiff CF1 1XL United Kingdom. **Tel** 0222-44211. **Ed** Stephen Walsh. **Ind/Abst** Music Index. **LC** ML5. **DD** 780.5. bk rev. adv acc. **Circ** 300. Musicological research with a bias toward 20th century classical music.

SOUTH AFRICAN JOURNAL OF MUSICOLOGY. VFOAT Suid-Afrikaanse Tydskrif Vir Musiekwetenskap. Vol. 1 (1981)-. Periodical. Afrikaans (English). an. 20.-. Musicology Society of South Africa, Box 29958 Sunnyside, 0132 Pretoria South Africa. **Ed** R Walton. bk rev. **Circ** 200. Any articles on musicology and ethnomusicology with preference to those on subjects relevant to Southern Africa.

SOUTH AFRICAN MUSIC TEACHER. (THE SOUTH AFRICAN MUSIC TEACHER). VFOAT Die Suid-Afrikaanse Musiekonderwyser. 0038-2493. Periodical. SA. English. sa. 5.00. South African Society of Music Teachers, 20 Erica Place, Bergvliet 7945 South Africa. **Tel** (021)72-4682. **Ed** M Whiteman. **Ind/Abst** Music Index. **LC** ML5. bk rev. adv acc. **Circ** 1,800. (ctrl). Informative articles on music teaching in general and activities of the South African Society of Music Teachers; also list of members twice yearly.

SOUTH DAKOTA MUSICIAN. V.1- Oct. 1966-. 0038-3341. Periodical. US. English. ty. Northern State College, Aberdeen SD 57401. South Dakota Music Educator, South Dakota Bandmasters Journal.

Music

SOUTHERN CALIFORNIA EARLY MUSIC SOCIETY NEWSLETTER. 0749-4106. Periodical. US. English. mo. Southern California Early Music Society, 6000 Sunset Boulevard, Suite 209, Los Angeles CA 90028. DD 780. *Southern California Early Music Society.*

THE SOUTHWESTERN MUSICIAN COMBINED WITH THE TEXAS MUSIC EDUCATOR. Began publication with Dec. 1934 issue. Periodical. US. English. mo. Texas Music Educators Association, PO Box 49469, Austin TX 78765. Ed Bill Cormack. LC ML1. adv acc. Circ 5,500. (ctrl). Means of communication between our members, promote the field of music education throughout the state. *Texas Music Educator, Southwestern Musicale.*

SOVETSKAIA MUZYKA. UR. Russian. mo. $42.50. Victor Kamkin Inc (70840), 12224 Parklawn Drive, Rockville MD 20852. Tel (301)881-5973. Ind/Abst Music Index. LC ML300.

SOZIALISTISCHES MUSIKSCHAFFEN DER DEUTSCHEN DEMOKRATISCHEN REPUBLIK. GW. German. an. 25.-. Sachsisches Landesbibliothek, Marienallee 1, DDR-806 Dresden West Germany. Tel 5 26 77. Ed Ludwig Muller. LC ML120.G3. DD 016.7809431. Circ 750. (ctrl). Index of first performances.

SPELEMANNSBLADET. 0333-0370. Periodical. NO. Norwegian. ir. Ola Grsland, Stavanergt 25, Oslo 4 Norway. LC ML3704. DD 781.748105.

SPIN. Began in 1961. 0038-7533. Periodical. UK. English. qt. LC ML5. DD 784.4005.

SPIRIT CANADA. May 1979-. 0229-7930. Periodical. CN. English. mo. $3.00 for 10 issues. Spirit Canada, PO Box 6812 Station A, Toronto Ontario M5W 1X6 Canada. DD 784.5400971.

SPRECHPLATTEN KATALOG. Multilingual (in German). ir. 4.50. Bielefelder Verlagsanstalt, Ulmenstrasse 8, Bielefeld West Germany. LC ML156.2. DD 011.

STAFF NOTES. 0146-5791. Periodical. US. English. ir. $3.00. University Society, 25 Cottage Street, Milland Park NJ 07432. *International Library of Music Staff Notes.*

STANYAN NEWS. 0092-0398. Periodical. US. English. Cheval/Stanyan Company, PO Box 2783, Hollywood CA 90028. LC ML1. DD 784.05.

STAR FILE ANNUAL. UK. English. an. 1.50. The Hamlyn Publishing Group, Astronaut House, Feltham, Middlesex England. LC ML156.4.R6. DD 016.78991245400941.

STEEDE REPORT CEASED. (THE STEEDE REPORT). VFOAT Steede Report to the Music Industry. V. 3, No. 1- Jan. 8, V. 3, No. 1, Jan. 8, 1977. Ceased with V. 5, No. 8. 0702-7699. Periodical. CN. English (includes some text in French). bw. $60.00. Steede Sound Ideas Reg'd, 3455 Redpath Street/Suite 405, Montreal Quebec H3G 2G7 Canada. DD 780.4205. *Steede Report to the Music Industry, 0318-7616.*

STEINWAY NEWS. Periodical. US. English. qt. Steinway & Sons, Steinway Place, Long Island City NY 11105. LC ML1. DD 786.205.

STEREO. Periodical. GW. German. mo. PC Moderner Verlag GMBH, Herzogstrasse 64 8 Munchen 40 West Germany. LC ML5. DD 780.5.

STORYVILLE. V. 1- (No. 1- Oct. 1965-. Periodical. UK. English. bm. $19.92. Storyville Publication Company, 66 Fairview Drive, Chigwell Essex IG7 6HS England. Tel (01)500-6098. Ed Laurie Wright. Ind/Abst Jazz Index. LC ML5. DD 785.4205. bk rev. adv acc. Circ 2,500. Covers the earlier forms of jazz and blues with interviews, articles, record and book reviews and discographical research featured. Always includes rare photographs from its period.

STRAD. (THE STRAD). V. 1- (No. 1-). 0039-2049. Periodical. UK. English. mo. $29.00. Novello & Company Ltd, Borough Green Sevenoaks, Kent TN15 8DT England. Tel (0732)883261. Ed Anne Inglis. Ind/Abst Music Index. LC ML5. DD 787.0105. bk rev. adv acc. Circ 9,300. For those interested in the stringed instrument field, player, manufacturer, collector, student, and teacher.

STRING EXPLORER. Began in 1983. 0746-8318. Periodical. US. English. ir. $10.00 (1 set of 8). Accent Publishing Company, 1418 Lake Street, Evanston IL 60201. Tel (312)446-5000. Ed Moria Brady. For beginning string students.

STRINGYBARK & GREENHIDE. VFOAT Stringybark and Greenhide. Vol. 1, No. 1-. 0157-7832. Periodical. English. qt. S & G, PO Box 424, Newcastle New South Wales 2300 Australia. LC ML3544. DD 781.79405.

STUDENT MUSICOLOGISTS AT MINNESOTA. V. 1- July 1966-. 0585-4598. US. English. ir. University of Minneapolis, College of Liberal Arts, Department of Music, Minneapolis MN 55455. LC ML1. DD 780.072.

STUDI MUSICALI. Vol. 1- 1972-. Periodical. IT. Multilingual (English, French, German, Italian). sa. $16.51. Casa Editrice, Leo S Olschki, Casella Postale PO Box 66, 50100 Firenze Italy. Ind/Abst RILM Abstr.

STUDI VERDIANI. 1-. Periodical. English (text in French, German, Italian, and Spanish). ir. 15.000. EDT Musica, Via Alfieri, 19 10121 Torino Italy. LC ML410.V4. DD 782.10924.

STUDIA MUSICOLOGICA. ACADEMIAE SCIENTIARUM HUNGARICA. (STUDIA MUSICOLOGICA). Vol. 1-. 0039-3266. HU. English (French, German, Italian or Russian). an. $44.00. Akademiai Kiado, POB 24, 1363 Budapest Hungary. Ind/Abst MLA Int. Bibliogr. Books Artic. Mod. Lang. Lit., Music Index, RILM Abstr.

STUDIA MUSICOLOGICA NORVEGICA. Began with V. 1, 1968. 0332-5024. NO. Norwegian (English). an. 19.00. Universitetsforlaget, PO Box 2959-Toyen, Oslo 6 Norway. Tel (45)2-27 60 60. Ed Owain Edwards Kjell Oversand and Arvid O Vollsness. Ind/Abst Music Index, RILM Abstr. Circ 150. Contains articles on music studies, both general and Norwegian.

STUDIEN ZUR ITALIENISCH-DEUTSCHEN MUSIKGESCHICHTE CEASED. Series/Titl Analecta Musicologica. Began in 1963. 0585-6086. Monographic Series. GW. German (Italian or English). ir. Ed P Kast. LC ML160.

STUDIEN ZUR MUSIKGESCHICHTE DES 19. JAHRHUNDERTS. Vol.1- 1965-. 0081-7341. Monographic Series. GW. German. ir. Gustav Bosse Verlag, Postfach 417, D-8400 Regensburg West Germany.

STUDIEN ZUR MUSIKWISSENSCHAFT. 1-Vol. 0081-3222. GW. German. ir. B Schotts Soehne, Postfach 3640, D-6500 Mainz West Germany. Tel 06131/246-0. Ed B Schotts Soehne. LC ML55.

STUDIEN ZUR TRADITIONELLEN MUSIK JAPANS. Vol. 1-. Monographic Series. GW. German. ir. Baerenreiter Music Corporation, 224 King Street, Englewood NJ 07631. Tel 561-30011. Ed Robert Guenter. Publications are issued irregularly and examine special themes of Japanese music traditions which have rapidly fallen into oblivion.

STUDIEN ZUR WERTUNGSFORSCHUNG. No. 1. Monographic Series. AU. German. ir. Institut fur Wertungsforschung, Akademie fur Musik und Darstellende Kunst, Graz Austria. LC ML55. DD 780.

STUDIES AND DOCUMENTS. Main/Corp American Musicological Society. No. 1- 1947-. Monographic Series. US. English. ir. Galaxy Music Corporation, c/o E C Schirmer, 138 Ipswich Street, Boston MA 02215. Tel (617)236-1935. Monographs and historical editions in an irregular series.

STUDIES IN MUSIC. No. 1- 1967-. 0081-8267. AT. English. ir. $8.85. University of Western Australia, University Bookshop, Nedlands WA 6009 Australia. Tel (213)994-1902. Ed Frank Carraway, D Tunley, and D Symons. Ind/Abst Music Index, RILM Abstr., APAIS, Aust. Public Aff. Inf. Serv. LC ML5. DD 780.5. Report of the results of musicological studies in Australia and New Zealand, with contributions from scholars in other countries, for all facets of musical thought.

STUDIES IN MUSIC FROM THE UNIVERSITY OF WESTERN ONTARIO. Main/Corp University of Western Ontario. Dept. of Music History. 1- 1976-. 0703-3052. CN. English. Free. Dr T Bailey, Department of Music History Faculty of Music Talbot College, London Ontario N6A 3K7 Canada. LC ML5. DD 780.5. (ctrl).

STUDIES IN THE HISTORY OF MUSIC. VFOAT S.H.M. Vol. 1-. 0743-9822. Periodical. US. English. LC ML1. DD 780.9.

STUDIES IN THE PSYCHOLOGY OF MUSIC. Main/Corp University of Iowa. V. 1- 1932-. 0090-2888. Periodical. US. English. ir. University of Iowa, 17 West College Street, Iowa City IA 52242. NLM W1 ST937F.

SUMLEN. 0346-8119. German (summaries in Swedish and in English). ir. 70. Svenskt Visarkiv Hagagatan, 23 A11, S-113 47 Stockholm Sweden. Tel 340935. Ed Bengt R Jonsson. Ind/Abst MLA Int. Bibliogr. Books Artic. Mod. Lang. Lit., RILM Abstr. LC ML3545. DD 781.705. bk rev. Circ 1,000. (ctrl). Vocal and instrumental folk music, folk and medieval poetry in Scandinavia.

SUMMA MUSICAE MEDII AEVI. 0585-9158. Monographic Series. GW. German. ir. Hanssler Verlag, Bismarckstrasse 4, Postfach 1220, D-7303 Stuttgart West Germany.

SUOMALAISTEN AANILEVYJEN LUETTELO. Series/Titl Suomen Aanitearkiston Julkaisu. VFOAT Catalogue of Finnish Records. 1902/45-. Fl. Finnish (English, German, or Swedish). ir. 30. Suomen Aanitearkisto R Y, Pietarinkatu 12A21, 00140 Helsinki 14 Finland. LC ML156.4.N3. DD 016.78991209471.

SUSSEX FOLK DIARY. No. 20- Mar./Apr. 1973-. Periodical. UK. English. bm. Vic Smith, 7 Stanmer Villas, BN7 7HQ Sussex England. LC ML5. DD 781.70254225. *Brighton Folk Diary.*

SUZUKI WORLD. Vol. 1, No. 1 (Jan./Feb. 1982)-. 0731-1532. Periodical. US. English. bm. $20.00. Suzuki World, Box 4260, Athens OH 45701-4260. Tel (614)592-3547. Ed Lorraine Fink. bk rev. adv acc. Circ 4,000. (ctrl). Covers all aspects of music education by the Suzuki method. Features for parents, teachers and children plus book reviews, psychology and instrument columns.

SVENSK TIDSKRIFT FOR MUSIKFORSKNING. VFOAT Swedish Journal of Musicology. V. 1, 1919-. 0081-9816. SW. Swedish. an. 128.-. Swedish Society for Musicology, Box 16326, 103 26 Stockholm Sweden. Tel (08)119252. Ed Erik Kjellberg. Ind/Abst Music Index. bk rev. Circ 500. Articles covering various fields of musicology; reports of unpublished theses research projects, congresses, etc. Review section, listings of Swedish music literature and recent Swedish music.

SWEET POTATO. 1976. 0147-5282. Periodical. US. English. bw. $9.00. Sweet Potato Inc, Box 385, Portland ME 04112. Tel (207)775-5991. Ed Bennie Green. LC ML1. DD 784. bk rev. adv acc. Circ 75,000. (ctrl). A music and entertainment magazine for Southern Maine. Also available are Massachusetts and New Hampshire editions. Includes club listings, calendar of events, and local coverage of events.

SYMPHONY GOLD BOOK. 0275-9381. US. English. an. $10.00. American Symphony Orchestra League, Box 669, Vienna VA 22180. LC ML27.U5. DD 785.06273.

SYMPHONY MAGAZINE. V. 31, No. 3- June/July 1980-. 0271-2687. Periodical. US. English. bm. $25.00. American Symphony Orchestra League, 633 East Street NW, Washington DC 20004. Tel (202)628-0099. Ed Robin Perry Allen. Ind/Abst Music Index. LC ML1. DD 785.05. bk rev. adv acc. Circ 15,000. (ctrl). Articles and information about symphony orchestra activities and personnel, internal affairs of parent organization (American Symphony Orchestra League), issues in orchestra management. *Symphony News, 0090-5380.*

SYMPHONY NEWS CEASED. V. 22, No. 5-V. 31, No. 2. 0090-5380. Periodical. US. English. bm. $0.50 Each Copy. American Symphony Orchestra League, PO Box 66, Vienna VA 22180. LC ML1. DD 785.05.

THE SYMPHONY USER'S JOURNAL. 8750-9415. Periodical. US. English. mo. $60.00. The Symphony User's Journal, 301 North Hurstbourne Lane/Suite 115, Louisville KY 40222. Tel (502)425-7756. Ed Steven S Cobb. Circ 2,500. (ctrl). Tips for symphony users.

SYNAPSE. 0145-5435. Periodical. US. English. bm. $6.00. Schill and Schill Pub, PO Box 359, North Hollywood CA 91603. LC ML1. DD 789.9.

TALENT & BOOK'S DISCO. (TALENT & BOOKING'S DISCO, THE BOOK). VFOAT Disco, the Book. VAT Talent and Booking's Disco. 0194-1771. US. English. an. $20.00. Talent & Booking Publications Company, 7033 Sunset Boulevard/Suite 222, Los Angeles CA 90028. LC ML3526. DD 785.41.

Music

TALK TALK. Began with issue for Fall 1979. Periodical. US. English. $6.00 for Six Issues. Talk Talk Publications, PO Box 36, Lawrence KS 66044. LC ML3533.8. DD 784.54005.

TALKIN' UNION. Began in 1981. 0738-7911. Periodical. US. English. ty. $12.00. Talkin' Union Box 5349, Takoma Park MD 20912. Tel (301)587-0349. Ed Saul Schniderman. Circ 700. Labor song, history and folklore, cultural news and happenings in unions.

TAPES BY MAIL CATALOGUE. Main/Corp Northwestern Regional Library System (Ont.). 0822-9783. Periodical. CN. English. ir. Northwestern Regional Library System, 910 Victoria Avenue, Thunder Bay Ontario P7C 1B4 Canada. DD 016.78.

THE TARAKAN MUSIC LETTER. 0272-9520. Periodical. US. English. bm. Sound Advice Enterprises, 40 Holly Lane, Roslyn Heights NY 11577. Tel (516)621-2445.

TEILTON. Monographic Series. GW. German. ir. Baerenreiter Music Corporation, 224 King Street, Englewood NJ 07631. Tel 561-30011. Ed Heinrich Strobel-Stiftung Baden. This irregularly appearing series studies questions about music and frequency technique, electric/electronic music experiments, in the dimension of music and radio.

TEMPO. No. 1-15, Jan. 1939-June 1946. 0040-2982. Periodical. UK. English. qt. $12.00. Boosey & Hawkes, 200 Smith Street CS 6, Farmingdale New York 11735. Tel (516)752-1122. Ed Calum MacDonald. Ind/Abst Music Index, RILM Abstr., Index Book Rev. Humanit. LC ML5. DD 780.5. (cum index). bk rev. A quarterly review of modern music.

TEXAS COUNTRY WESTERN MAGAZINE. Periodical. US. English. mo. $10.00. Ransehc Pub, PO Box 77411, Alief TX 77411. LC ML1. DD 784.

THE TEXAS FIDDLER. Main/Corp Texas Old Time Fiddlers Association. V. 1, No. 2- May 1973-. 0148-270X. Periodical. US. English. mo. Texas Old Time Fiddlers Association, Route 2 Box 726, Burleson TX 76028. LC ML27.U5. DD 787.1062764. *Texas Fiddler, 0148-270X.*

THE ROCK YEAR BOOK. See Yearbooks, Almanacs, Directories.

THEORY AND PRACTICE. (THEORY AND PRACTICE : NEWSLETTER-JOURNAL OF THE MUSIC THEORY SOCIETY OF NEW YORK STATE). V. 1- June 1975-. 0741-6156. Periodical. US. English. sa. Music Theory Society of New York State School of Music, Ithaca College, Mary Arlin Secretary, Ithaca NY 14850. Ind/Abst RILM Abstr.

TIBIA. 1976-. Periodical. GW. German. ty. $15.05. Moeck Verlag, Postfach 143, D 31 Celle West Germany. Ind/Abst Music Index. LC ML929. DD 788.005.

TIC-TOC-CHOC. (LE TIC-TOC-CHOC : JOURNAL DU STUDIO DE MUSIQUE ANCIENNE DE MONTREAL). Vol. 1, No.1 (Nov. 1979)-. 0227-4299. Periodical. CN. French. qt. 10.00. Studio Musique Ancienne Montre, 3894 rue St-Hubert, Montreal Quebec H2L 4A5 Canada. Tel (514)845-2707. DD 780.5. bk rev. adv acc. Circ 500. To familiarize music lovers with music before 1800: articles, book and record review; historical and practical aspects of early music.

TIJDSCHRIFT VAN DE VERENIGING VOOR NEDERLANDSE MUZIEKGESCHIEDENIS. V. 19, Nos. 1,2 (1960-61)-. 0042-3874. Periodical. NE. Dutch. ir. 25.00 US. Vereniging voor Netherlands, Muziekgeschiedenis/Drift 21, 3512 BR Utrecht Netherlands. Tel (030)392320. Ed Willem Elders. Ind/Abst Music Index, RILM Abstr. Dutch music history. *Tijdschrift voor Muziekwetenschap.*

TIMBRE. (TIMBRE : EVERGREEN DISTRICT BULLETIN OF THE SOCIETY FOR THE PRESERVATION AND ENCOURAGEMENT OF BARBER SHOP QUARTET SINGING IN AMERICA, INC). 8750-782X. Periodical. US. English. bm. $2.00. S P E B S Q S A Inc, 6315 3rd Avenue, Kenosha WI 53140-5199.

TIME BARRIER EXPRESS. 0099-0396. Periodical. US. English. bm. $9.00. Time Barrier Express, PO Box 206, Yonkers NY 10710. LC ML1. DD 784.

TOCHER; TALES, SONGS, TRADITION. No. 1- Spring 1971-. Periodical. UK. English (and/or Gaelic). ir. School of Scottish Studies, 27 George Square, Edinburgh EH8 9LD England. Tel (031)667-1011. Ed A Bruford. LC ML5. DD 784.4941. bk rev. Circ 1,500. Tales and legends and personal memories of ordinary and extraordinary Scots, recalling customs and superstitions, clan feuds, Scots, and Gaelic folksong and ballad.

TONIC (ROBERT SIMPSON SOCIETY). (TONIC : THE JOURNAL OF THE ROBERT SIMPSON SOCIETY). 0260-7425. Periodical. UK. English. qt. 7.50. Robert Simpson Society/John and Sylvia Brooks, 3 Engel Park, London NW7 2HE England. LC ML410.S587. DD 780.924.

TOP 10'S AND TRIVIA OF ROCK & ROLL AND RHYTHM & BLUES. VFOAT Top 10's & Trivia of Rock & Roll and Rhythm & Blues. VAT Top Tens and Trivia of Rock & Roll and Rhythm & Blues. US. English. ir. $6.00. Blueberry Hill Publishing Company, Box 24170, St Louis MO 63130. Tel (314)727-0880. Ed Joe Edwards. Finding every artists and song that made Billboard's weekly top 10 singles and top 5 albums (artist, record, title, label and serial number, the year(s) each record made the top 10 and if it made #1 are all included.).

TOP MUSIQUE. Periodical. French. ir. 2.00 Each Issue. 45 rue Richer, Paris France 75009. LC ML5.

TORONTO MUSIC GUIDE. June 1971-. 0049-4208. Periodical. CN. English. mo. $3.00. Toronto Music Guide Magazine Subscription Department, 130 Glenforest Road, Toronto Ontario M4N 1Z9 Canada. DD 780.9713541.

TORONTO SYMPHONY PROGRAMME MAGAZINE CEASED. Sept./Oct. 1983-May/Aug. 1984. 0822-9090. Periodical. CN. English. bm. Toronto Symphony Orchestra, Advertising and Business Office, 7 Labatt Avenue, Toronto Ontario M5A 3P2 Canada. DD 785.062713541. *Toronto Symphony (Newsletter), 0822-4870.*

TOYO ONGAKU KENKYU. VFOAT Studies on Oriental Music. V. 1, No. 1- Nov. 1937-. 0039-3851. JA. Japanese. ir. Japan Publishing Trading Company Ltd, PO Box 5030, Tokyo International, Tokyo 100-31 Japan. Ind/Abst RILM Abstr.

THE TRACKER. 1956. 0041-0330. Periodical. US. English. qt. $22.00. Organ Historical Society Inc, PO Box 26811, Richmond VA 23261. Tel (804)353-9226. Ed Susan D Friesen. LC ML1. bk rev. adv acc. Circ 2,000. Musical and historical study of pipe organ building in North America.

TRANSLATIONS. Main/Corp Colorado College Music Press. No. 1- 1967-. 0588-4926. Periodical. US. English. ir. Colorado College Music Press, Colorado College, Colorado Springs CO 80903.

TREOIR. 0790-004X. Periodical. US. English (Irish). bm. $10.00. Treoir, 70 Westminister Drive, West Hartford CT 06107. LC ML5. DD 781.7415.

TRIAD - OHIO MUSIC EDUCATION ASSOCIATION. (TRIAD : OFFICIAL PUBLICATION OF THE OHIO MUSIC EDUCATION ASSOCIATION). Began in 1933. 0041-2511. Periodical. US. English. bm. $10.00. c/o Marcus L Neiman, 946 West Abbey Drive, Medina OH 44256. Tel (216)723-6393. Ed Marcus L Neiman. LC ML1. DD 780.729771. bk rev. adv acc. Circ 4,500. (ctrl). The official publication of the Ohio Music Education Association and addresses issues concerning music education.

THE TRIANGLE OF MU PHI EPSILON. Main/Corp Mu Phi Epsilon. V. 1- 1905-. 0041-2600. Periodical. US. English. qt. $6.00. Mu Phi Epsilon National Executive Office, 833 Laurel Avenue, c/o Mimi Altman, Highland Park IL 60035. Tel (503)246-4764. Ed Jean Compton. Ind/Abst Music Index. LC ML1. DD 780.6273. Circ 10,000. (ctrl). International professional music fraternity magazine.

TROUBADOUR. (THE TROUBADOUR). 0713-8113. Periodical. CN. English. ir. Free. Troubadour, New Brunswick Choral Federation, Department of Education, PO Box 6000, Kings Place, Fredericton New Brunswick E3B 5H1 Canada. DD 784.9060715. (ctrl).

TROUSER PRESS. 0164-1883. Periodical. US. English. ir. $12.00. Trans-Oceanic Trouser Press, 212 5th Avenue, New York NY 10010. Ind/Abst Music Index. LC ML3533.8. DD 784.54005. *Trans-Oceanic Trouser Press.*

TSLYL. (TATSLIL). VFOAT Tatzlil, Chord. 1960-. 0082-2132. IS. Hebrew (summaries in English). an. Ind/Abst Music Index. LC ML5.

T.U.B.A. JOURNAL. Main/Corp Tubists Universal Brotherhood Association. VAT Tubists Universal Brotherhood Association Journal. V. 4- Fall 1976-. 0363-4787. Periodical. US. English. qt. $15.00. TUBA Journal, c/o Dr David Randolph, Georgia University Station, Box 2555, Athens GA 30602. Tel (404)542-3737. LC ML1. DD 788.4805. *T.U.B.A. Newsletter, 0363-4779.*

T.U.B.A. MEMBERSHIP ROSTER. Main/Corp Tubists Universal Brotherhood Association. VAT Tubists Universal Brotherhood Association Membership Roster. 0163-5360. US. English. Donald C Little, School of Music, North Texas State University, Denton TX 76203. LC ML26. DD 788.48.

TUNE UP. 0161-3081. Periodical. US. English. ir. $6.00. Philadelphia Folksong Society, PO Box 215, Philadelphia PA. LC ML1. DD 781.705.

THE TUNING BOARD. V. 1- Sept. 1974-. 0362-6091. Periodical. US. English. mo. $2.00. V Barker Enterprises, 2300 Fairview Road, Costa Mesa CA 92626. LC ML1. DD 781.773.

TVORCHESTVO; VESTNIK KOMPOZITORA. V. 1- 1973-. UR. Russian. 0.63 Each Issue. Izd-Vo Sovetskii Kompozitor, Naberezhnaia Morisa Toreza 30, Moskva Russia. LC ML300.5.

THE TWIN FIDDLE TREASURY. Began with Jan. 1978. 0731-4469. Periodical. US. English. mo. Twin Fiddle Treasury, PO Box 3776, Santa Rosa CA 95402. Ed Tim Rued. LC ML3544. DD 787.15205.

TWIST & SHOUT. VFOAT T&S. Vol. 1, Issue 1-. 0710-3476. Periodical. CN. English. DD 784.54005.

UDVALGSLISTE OVER ORKESTERMATERIALE. Main/Corp Copenhagen. Kongelige Bibliotek. Danish. ir. LC ML136.C78.

UKRAINIAN MUZYKA CEASED. Vol. 1, No. 1 (Fall 1982)-. 0715-8637. Periodical. CN. English. ir. 6.00. Ukrainian Muzyka, PO Box 125, Station St Michel, Montreal Quebec H2A 3L9 Canada. DD 781.729179105.

UKRAINSKE MUZYKOZNAVSTVO. 1-1964-. 0566-6155. UR. Ukrainian (Vol. 1 in Russian). an. LC ML308.U4.

UKULELE YES . (UKLELE YES). V. 1- June 1976-. 0703-184X. Periodical. CN. English. sa. $3.00 Each Number. Ukulele Yes, Doane Musical Enterprises, PO Box 125, Armdale Halifax Nova Scotia B3L 4J9 Canada. Ed J C Doane. DD 787.920971.

UMAK SEGYE. VFOAT Music World. Periodical. Korean. mo. 30,000. LC ML3469.

UMAK TONGA. VFOAT The Eumak Dong-A. V. 1-(1984, 4)-. Periodical. KO. Korean. mo. Tong Ilbosa, 139 Sejongno Chongno-ku, Seoul 110 Korea. LC ML5.

UMAK YONGU. VFOAT Hanguk Umak Hakhoe Nonmunjip. V. 1- Series (Feb. 1982)-. Periodical. Korean (summaries in English). ir. Hanguk Umak Hakhoe, 432-32 Sogye-Dong, Yongsan-Ku, Seoul South Korea. LC ML5.

UNIVERSITY FOLK. Periodical. UK. English. University Union, Oxford Road, M13 9PR Manchester England. LC ML28.M19. DD 784.400624272.

UPDATE. Vol. 1, No. 1 (May 1982)-. Periodical. US. English. ty. $8.00. Update/University of South Carolina, Department of Music, Columbia SC 29208. Tel (803)777-7154. Ed Charles A Elliott. bk rev adv acc. (ctrl). The applications of research in the teaching of public school music.

UPDATE : THE APPLICATIONS OF RESEARCH IN MUSIC EDUCATION. Periodical. US. English. ty. Department of Music, University of South Carolina, Columbia SC 29208.

UPDATE - UNIVERSITY OF SOUTH CAROLINA. DEPT. OF MUSIC. (UPDATE). Vol. 1, No. 1 (May 1982)-. 8755-1233. Periodical. US. English. ty. $8.00. Update, Department of Music University of South Carolina, Columbia SC 29208. Tel (803)777-7154. Ed Charles A Elliott. DD 781. bk rev. adv acc. Circ 500. The applications of research in public school music instruction. Research findings presented in a jargon-free manner.

UPPER MIDWEST COUNTRY & WESTERN NEWS-SCENE. V. 1- May 1973-. Periodical. US. English. mo. $0.60 Each Issue. 2017 E Hennipin Avenue/Room 325, Minneapolis MN 55413. LC ML1. DD 784.

Music

UTAH MUSIC EDUCATOR. 0502-871X. Periodical. US. English. ir. $5.00. Utah Music Educator Association, Alvin Wardle, 844 North 14th East, Logan UT 84321.

UTAH SYMPHONY. (UTAH SYMPHONY. PROGRAM). 0191-1635. Periodical. US. English. Utah Symphony Orchestra, 55 West 1st South, Salt Lake City UT 84101. **Tel** 533-5626. **Ed** Gilbert W Scharffs. **LC** MT125. **DD** 785.015. adv acc. **Circ** 4,500. (ctrl). Notes on program, intermission notes, player profile, meet the board.

UTRECHTSE BIJDRAGEN TOT DE MUZIEKWETENSCHAP. Main/Corp Utrecht. Rijksuniversiteit. Instituut voor Miziekwetenschap. Vol. 1 1958. 0566-4632. Dutch. ir. Creyghton, Postbox 38, Bilthoven The Netherlands.

VANCOUVER OPERA JOURNAL. V. 1- Spring 1977-. 0704-738X. Periodical. CN. English. qt. Free to Members. Vancouver Opera Association, 111 Dunsmuir Street, Vancouver British Columbia V6B 1W8 Canada. **DD** 782.106271133.

VANCOUVER SYMPHONY. 0826-0109. Periodical. CN. English. Vancouver Symphony Society, c/o Cornwall Publishers, #17-1035 Richards Street, Vancouver British Columbia V6B 3E4 Canada. **DD** 785.06271133. *V S O, Vancouver Symphony Orchestra*, 0704-0504.

VARIATIONS. V. 1- Sept./Oct. 1977-. 0705-1832. Periodical. CN. English (French). ir. $1.00 Each Number. Montreal Symphony Orchestra, Place des Arts, 200 Maisonneuve West, Montreal Quebec H2X 1Y9 Canada. **DD** 780.5.

VEDETTE ROCK. **VAT** Rock (Montreal). V. 1- May 1978-. 0705-2839. Periodical. CN. French. $1.25 Each Number. Bert-Hold Inc, 9393 Av Edison, Montreal Quebec H1J 1E6 Canada. **DD** 784.05.

VERDI NEWSLETTER. No. 3- June 1977-. 0160-2667. Periodical. US. English (Italian). an. $15.00. American Institute for Verdi Studies, New York University, Department of Music, 24 Waverly Place/Room 268, New York NY 10003. **Tel** (212)598-3433. **Ed** Martin Chusid and Andrew Porter. **Ind/Abst** RILM Abstr. **LC** ML410.V4. **DD** 782.10924, B. bk rev. adv acc. **Circ** 500. Articles, reviews, and other information relating to the music and life of Giuseppe Verdi, composer of operas. *Aivsnewsletter*, 0148-0383.

VERMONT MUSIC NEWS. V. 1- 1959?-. 0042-4188. Periodical. US. English. ir. Vermont Music News, Harwood Union High School, Moutown Vermont 05401.

VEROFFENTLICHUNG - GESELLSCHAFT DER ORGELFREUNDE. Main/Corp Gesellschaft der Orgelfreunde. Vol. 1 1952-. 0435-8112. English. ir. Verlag Merseburger Berlin GMBH, Postfach 10 38 80 Motzstrase 13, D3500 Kassel West Germany.

VEROFFENTLICHUNGEN DES INSTITUTS FUR NEUE MUSIK UND MUSIKERZIEHUNG DARMSTADT. V. 1-. 0418-3827. Monographic Series. GW. German. ir. D Schotts Soehne, Postfach 3640 Weihergarte 1 11, D6500 Mainz West Germany.

VIBES. V. 1- Mar. 1978-. 0270-6350. Periodical. US. English. bm. $1.00 Single Issue. Ideal Publishing Corporation, 2 Park Avenue, New York 10016. **LC** ML3469. **DD** 784.5005.

VIBRATIONS. V. 1- June 1977-. 0703-9883. Periodical. CN. English (French, June 1977-Dec. 1977). mo. 0.50 Each Number. Starfish Publishing, Suite 108/5871 Victoria Avenue, Montreal Quebec A3W 2R7 Canada. **DD** 780.4205.

VIE MUSICALE EN FRANCE SOUS LES ROIS BOURBONS. ETUDES. Vol. 1-. 0083-6109. Monographic Series. FR. French. ir. A & J Picard, 82 rue Bonaparte, Paris 75006 France. **Tel** (1)43294489. **Ed** A J Picard.

THE VINYL EDITION. Vol. 1, No. 1 (Mar. 1978)-. 0278-5455. US. English. mo. **LC** ML3476.8. **DD** 784.54005.

VIOL CEASED. V. 1- Nov. 1975-. 0363-762X. Periodical. US. English. qt. $4.00. 115 Clairmont Avenue, Decatur GA 30030. **Ind/Abst** Music Index. **LC** ML1. **DD** 787.0105.

VIVALDI INFORMATIONS. V. 2- 1973-. French (German and English). ir. Societe Intl Antonio Vivaldi, c/o Instituto Ital Cultura, Gjoerlingsvejii Hellerup Denmark.

V.M.E.A. NOTES. Main/Corp Virginia Music Educators Association. **VFOAT** VMEA Notes. **VAT** Virginia Music Educators Association Notes. V. 1- Jan./Feb. 1949-. 0733-8562. Periodical. US. English. ir. Virginia Music Education Education, 14 Martell Road, Newark DE 19713. **LC** ML27.U5. **DD** 780.729755.

VOCIES OF THE PAST. 1956-. Periodical. UK. English. Oakwood Press, 50 York Road, Leeds 9 England. **LC** ML156.4 .V7. **DD** 789.913.

VOICE OF WASHINGTON MUSIC EDUCATORS. V.17- Sept. 1971-. 0147-4367. US. English. qt. $3.00. Washington Music Educator Association, 913 East 8th Avenue, Ellensburg WA 98926. **Tel** (509)925-3609. **Ed** Coyne G Burnett Sr. **LC** ML1. **DD** 780.729797. adv acc. **Circ** 1,600. (ctrl). A journal for music educators, with emphasis upon trends in methodology, governmental relations and trade news. *Washington Music Educator*.

DIE VOLKSMUSIK. V. 1-. Periodical. German. mo. **LC** ML5.

VOPROSY MUZYKALNOI FORMY. Vol. 1-. 0507-3723. UR. Russian. **Ed** VI Protopopov. **LC** ML448.

WAGNER. New Ser. Vol. 1, No. 1 (Nov. 1980)-. Periodical. UK. English. qt. **LC** ML410.W1. **DD** 782.10924. bk rev. adv acc. **Circ** 1,000. (ctrl). Articles on the music life thought and reception of Richard Wagner.

WAGNER NEWS (LONDON, ENGLAND). (WAGNER NEWS). 0261-3468. Periodical. UK. English. 15.00. Penny Scantleburg Editor, 63 Brunswick Road, London MW5 1AQ England. **Ed** Penny Scantelbury. **LC** ML410.W1. **DD** 782.10924. bk rev. adv acc. **Circ** 1,000. (ctrl). News and reviews of Wagner performances recordings books.

THE WASHINGTON OPERA MAGAZINE. 0196-3236. Periodical. US. English. $20.00. Washington Opera Guild, PO Box 4157, Washington DC 20015. **LC** ML1699. **DD** 782.109753.

WAVELENGTH (NEW ORLEANS, LA.). (WAVELENGTH). **VFOAT** Wave Length. Vol. 1, No. 1 (Nov. 1980)-. 0741-2460. Periodical. US. English. mo. $12.00. Wavelength, PO Box 15667, New Orleans LA 70175. **Tel** (504)895-2342. **Ed** Connie Atkinson. bk rev. adv acc. **Circ** 30,000. (ctrl). New Orleans music magazine, devoted to all types of music from rock to early rhythm; blues reviews, articles, calendar, etc.

WCLV GUIDE. Nov./Dec. 1977-. 0274-7278. Periodical. US. English. mo $10.00. Northern Ohio Live, 11310 Juniper Road, Cleveland OH 44106.

WEB. (THE WEB). **VFOAT** Workshop Exchange Bulletin. 0093-6170. Periodical. US. English. mo. Musician's Workshop, 82 Clematis Avenue, Waltham MA 02154. **LC** ML28.W185. **DD** 338.47780974461.

THE WELLESLEY EDITION. No. 1-. 0083-7881. US. English. ir. Yesterday Service Inc, 1430 Massachusetts Avenue, Cambridge MA 02138. **Ed** Jan la Rue. **LC** M2.

WER SPIELTE WAS?. *See* Theater.

WESTCOAST MUSIC. Vol. 4, No. 1 (Sept. 1980)-. 0228-8168. Periodical. CN. English. mo. $1.00 Each Number. Westcoast Music Magazine, 1870 West First Avenue, Vancouver British Columbia V6J 1G5 Canada. **DD** 780.4209711. *Open Door West Coast Music*, 0228-8176.

WESTERN BULLETIN. Periodical. DK. English or Danish. ir. Box 1218, 2300 Copenhagen S Denmark. **LC** ML5. **DD** 784.

WESTERN ROUNDUP COUNTRY MUSIC TRADE DIRECTORY & NEWS REPORT. *See* Yearbooks, Almanacs, Directories.

WESTERN ROUNDUP : WESTERN NEW YORK'S COUNTRY MUSIC GUIDE. **VFOAT** Western New York's Country Music Guide. Periodical. US. English. qt. $3.00. Western Roundup Country Music Guide, 7168 Rapids Road, Lockport NY 14094. **LC** ML1. **DD** 784.

THE WHEEL OF DELTA OMICRON. Main/Corp Delta Omicron International Music Fraternity. 0043-4752. Periodical. US. English. qt. $3.00. Delta Omicron, 1352 Redwood Court, Columbus OH 43229. **Tel** (614)888-2640. **Ed** Patricia Almon. **LC** ML27.U5. **Circ** 5,500. (ctrl). Organization news.

WHISKEY, WOMEN, AND . . . . No. 1- 1971-. 0091-7664. Periodical. US. English. ir. $12.50. Whiskey, Women & . . . , P O Box 1245, Haverhill MA 01831-1645. **Tel** (617)372-0101. **Ed** Daniel P Kocharkian. **Ind/Abst** Jazz Index. **LC** ML1. **DD** 784. bk rev. adv acc. **Circ** 1,000. Explores the recordings and artists of black american blues, jazz, gospel and vocal group history. Geared to the collector, artist and label photos abound.

WHO PUT THE BOMP. 0039-7873. Periodical. US. English. qt. $8.00. G Shaw, PO Box 7112, Burbank CA 91510. **LC** ML1. **DD** 784.

WIENER MUSIKWISSENSCHAFTLICHE BEITRAGE. Vol. 1- 1955-. 0511-9294. Monographic Series. AU. German. ir. Hermann Boehlaus Nachfolger, Postfach 200, A-1014 Wien Austria.

WINDSTORM. **VFOAT** Wind Storm. June 1983-. 0737-7789. Periodical. US. English. mo. $14.00 Domestic, $18.00 Canada. Windstorm Inc, 15160 West 8 Mile Road Suite 309, Oak Park MI 48237. **LC** ML3186.8. **DD** 783.705.

WINEK INFO. Main/Corp Werkgroep Integratie Nederlandstalige Kerkmuziek. **VAT** Werkgroep Integratie Nederlandstalige Kerkmuziek-Info. No. 1- Jan. 1977-. Periodical. Dutch. ir. 25.00. Werkgroep Integratie Nederlandstalige Kerkmuziek, Biltstraat 51 Bis, Utrecht Netherlands. **LC** ML5.

WINNIPEG FOLK FESTIVAL NEWSLETTER. (THE WINNIPEG FOLK FESTIVAL NEWSLETTER). V. 1- April/May 1976-. 0700-3129. Periodical. CN. English. Winnipeg Folk Festival, 253 Hugo Street North, Winnipeg Manitoba R3M 2N2 Canada. **DD** 781.705.

THE WISCONSIN SCHOOL MUSICIAN. V. 1- Feb. 1930-. 0043-6658. Periodical. US. English. qt. $6.00. The Wisconsin School Musician, 515 North Whitney Way, Madison WI 57305. **Tel** (608)273-2222. **Ed** Richard G Gaarder. **LC** ML1. **DD** 780.72. adv acc. **Circ** 4,200. (ctrl). Articles and informational material regarding all facets of music education for pre-school through adult and continuing education.

WOLGAN UMAK. **VFOAT** Weolgan Eumag. Periodical. KO. Korean. ir. 7,000. Wolgan Umak Sa, 60-1 4-Ka Chungmu-Ro, Chung-Ku, Seoul South Korea. **LC** ML5.

WOODWIND/BRASS & PERCUSSION. **VFOAT** Woodwind/Brass and Percussion. **VAT** Woodwind Brass and Percussion. Vol. 20, No. 4 (Sept. 1981)-. 0279-3431. Periodical. US. English. mo. Evans Publications, 25 Court Street, Deposit NY 13754. **Tel** (607)467-3000. **LC** ML1. **DD** 788.005. *Woodwind World-Brass & Percussion*, 0098-4574.

WORLD JAZZ CALENDAR OF FESTIVALS & EVENTS. **VFOAT** World Jazz Calendar of Festivals and Events. Vol. 1, No. 1 (June-Dec. 1980)-. 0275-973X. Periodical. US. English. be. $10.00. International Jazz Federation Inc, PO Box 777 Times Square Street, New York NY 10108. **LC** ML3505.8. **DD** 785.42079.

THE WORLD OF CHURCH MUSIC. 1981-. Periodical. UK. English. an. Royal School of Church Music, Addington Palace, Croydon CR9 5AD England. **Tel** 01-654-7676. **Ed** Lionel Dakers. **LC** ML5. **DD** 783.026305. bk rev. **Circ** 1,200. Symposium of essays on aspects of church music and its place in workshop. Contributors from throughout the Christian world. *English Church Music (Royal School of Church Music, Croydon, Surrey : 1963)*, 0071-0555.

THE WORLD OF COUNTRY MUSIC. 1st- Ed. 1963/64-. Periodical. English. ir.

WORLD OF MUSIC. (THE WORLD OF MUSIC). Began with: V. 1 (June 1957). 0043-8774. Periodical. GW. English. ty. $14.00. Heinrichsofens Verlag, PO Box 620, Liebigstr 16, D294 Wilhelmshaven West Germany. **Tel** (04421)202004. **Ed** Joan Vandor. **Ind/Abst** Music Index, RILM Abstr. **LC** ML5. bk rev. adv acc. **Circ** 1,500. (ctrl).

THE WORLD OF OPERA CEASED. V. 1-. 0160-8673. Periodical. US. English. sm. $54.00 Domestic, $62.10 Foreign. Marcel Dekker Journals, PO Box 11305 Church Street Station, New York NY 10249. **LC** ML1. **DD** 782.105.

WORLD-WIDE OFFICIAL ORGAN BLUE BOOK. **VFOAT** Official Organ Blue Book. **VAT** World Wide Official Organ Blue Book. 0277-4135. US. English (text in Dutch, and German).

Z Billings, 600 Larry Court, Waukesha WI 53187. **LC** ML597. **DD** 786.92075.

WWIM. WHO'S WHERE IN MUSIC. (WHO'S WHERE IN MUSIC : WWIM). **VFOAT** WWIM. V. 1- Dec. 1976/Feb. 1977-. 0146-1966. Periodical. US. English. qt. $4.50. Who's Where in Music Corp, 5410 Wilshire Boulevard/Suite 905, Los Angeles CA 90036. **LC** ML1. **DD** 784. *0360-4411*.

XENHARMONIKON. V. 1- (No. 1-). 0098-3330. US. English. sa. John H Chalmers Jr, 10819 Shannon Hills Drive, Houston TX 77099. **LC** ML1. **DD** 780.904.

YEAR BOOK & REGISTER OF MEMBERS. See Yearbooks, Almanacs, Directories.

YEARBOOK & REGISTER MEMBERS. See Yearbooks, Almanacs, Directories.

YEARBOOK FOR TRADITIONAL MUSIC. See Yearbooks, Almanacs, Directories.

YEARBOOK OF THE INTERNATIONAL FOLK MUSIC COUNCIL. See Yearbooks, Almanacs, Directories.

YEARBOOK - ROYAL CANADIAN COLLEGE OF ORGANISTS. See Yearbooks, Almanacs, Directories.

THE YEAR'S WORK IN MUSIC. 1947/48-. UK. English. an. Trade Department of the Pinnacles, Harlow Essex England. **LC** ML5. **DD** 780.58.

YESTERDAY'S MEMORIES. V. 1- 1975-. 0098-1796. US. English. $3.50. Freebizak Inc, PO Box 1825 FDR Station, New York NY 10022. **LC** ML1. **DD** 784.

YIN YUEH HSUEH TSUNG KAN. Vol. 1- (1981 Year Aug. 8, 1981)-. Periodical. CH. Chinese. ir. 0.75. Hsin Hua Shu Tien Pei-Ching Fa Hsing So, Peking China. **LC** ML5. **DD** 780.5.

YIN YUEH SHENG HUO. **VFOAT** Hifi Musical Life. Began with July 1962 issue. Periodical. Chinese. ir. $18.00. Chung Kuang Yu Hsien Kung SSU, 907 Takshing House Des Voeux Road, Hong Kong China. **LC** ML5.

YIN YUEH YU YIN HSIANG. **VFOAT** Music & Audiophile. Vol. 1-. CH. Chinese. ir. **LC** ML5.

YOUNG MUSICIANS. 0044-0841. Periodical. US. English. qt $5.50. Materials Services Department, 127 9th Avenue North, Nashville TN 37234. **Tel** (615)251-2000. **LC** ML1. **DD** 783.02605.

YUBAL GOBES MEHQARIM SEL HA-MERKAZ LE-JEQER HA-MUSIQAH HA-YHUDIT. (YUVAL). 1-. 0084-439X. IS. English (summaries in French and Hebrew). ir. Magnes Press, The Hebrew University, Jerusalem Israel. **Ind/Abst** RILM Abstr. **LC** ML3776.

Z DZIEJOW MUZYKI POLSKIEJ. Began in 1960. Periodical. Polish. ir. **LC** ML5.

ZEITGENOSSISCHES MUSIKSCHAFFEN IN DER DEUTSCHEN DEMOKRATISCHEN REPUBLIK. 1982-. 0232-9387. German. an. 18.00. Sachsische Landesbibliothek Musikabteilung, Marienallee 12, DDR 8060 Dresden West Germany. **LC** ML120.G3. **DD** 016.7809431.

ZEITSCHRIFT FUR SPIELMUSIK. Periodical. German. mo. Magnamusic Distrubutors, Sharon CT 06069. **Tel** (203)364-54311. **Ed** Alia P Mix. **Circ** 50. (cntl). Recorder music some with percussion or continuo. *Zeitschrift fur Spielmusik Auf Allerlei INstrumenten*.

ZEITSCHRIFTENDIENST. See Bibliographies.

ZEITSCHRIFTENDIENST MUSIK. **VFOAT** ZD Musik. GW. German. mo 105.-. Deutsches Bibliotheksinstitut Bundesallee 184/185, D1 Berlin 31 West Germany. **Tel** (030)85050. **LC** ML118. **DD** 780.5. **Circ** 200.

ZFMP, ZEITSCHRIFT FUR MUSIKPADAGOGIK. **VFOAT** Zeitschrift Fur Musikpadagogik. Periodical. GW. German. qt. 29.50. Gustav Bosse Verlag, Postfach 417, 8400 Esslingen West Germany. **Tel** 0941/55455. **Ed** Gustav Bosse Verlag. **LC** ML5. **DD** 780.72943. bk rev. adv acc. **Circ** 2,300. Contains information on music and musical education.

ZFMTH. ZEITSCHRIFT FUR MUSIKTHEORIE. (ZEITSCHRIFT FUR MUSIKTHEORIE). **VFOAT** ZFMTH. Vol. 1-. 0342-3395. Periodical. GW. German. ir. Rohrdorfer Musikverlag, Friedhofstrasse 47, 7271 Rohrdorf West Germany. **Ind/Abst** Music Index, RILM Abstr.

ZIGZAG. Periodical. UK. English. mo. 0.25 Each issue. Spicebox Books Ltd, 37 Soho Square, London W1 England. **LC** ML5. **DD** 784.

ZOUNDS. V. 1- Mar. 1975-. 0703-4709. Periodical. CN. English. mo. Free. Fancon Productions, Box 214 Station A, MIssissauga Ontario L5A 2Z7 Canada. **DD** 780.4205.

ZUPFMUSIK, GITARRE. 0722-0545. Periodical. GW. German. qt. 12.00. Bund Deutscher Zupfmusiker E V, 6382 Friedrichsdorf 4 West Germany. **LC** ML5. **DD** 787.6105. *Zupfmusik*.

ZVUK: JUGOSLOVENSKA MUZICKA REVIJA. 0044-555X. Periodical. Serbo-Croatian - R. ir. **Ind/Abst** Music Index, RILM Abstr. **LC** ML5.

NATURAL HISTORY

ABHANDLUNGEN AUS DEM LANDESMUSEUM FUR NATURKUNDE ZU MUNSTER IN WESTFALEN. See Museums.

ABHANDLUNGEN DER SENCKENBERGISCHEN NATURFORSCHENDEN GESELLSCHAFT. Essay 428-. 0365-7000. Monographic Series. German. ir. **Ind/Abst** GeoRef, Biol. Abstr. **CODEN** ASNGA7.

ABHANDLUNGEN UND BERICHTE DES NATURKUNDEMUSEUMS GORLITZ. See Museums.

ACTA SOCIETATIS PRO FAUNA ET FLORA FENNICA CEASED. (ACTA SOC. PRO FAUNA ET FLORA FENNICA). **Main/Corp** Societas Pro Fauna et Flora Fennica. V. 1-82. 0373-6660. Monographic Series. Fl. English (Finnish, German, Norwegian or Swedish). ir. **LC** QH7. **DD** 574.94897. **CODEN** AFFFA9. (cum index).

AL-BIAH. V. 1, No. 1, (Jan. 1980)-. Periodical. Arabic. qt. Amanat Al-Lajnah Al-Qawmiyah Lil-Biiah, Al-Majlis Al-Qawmi Lil-Buhuth S B 2404, Al-Khartum Sudan. **LC** QH195.S9.

ALBERTA NATURALIST. **VFOAT** Newsletter. Began publication in 1971. 0318-5540. Periodical. CN. English. qt. 10.00. Federation Alberta Naturalists, Box 1472, Edmonton Alta T5J 2N5 Canada. **Tel** 428-3033. **Ed** Derek Johnson. **DD** 500.97123. bk rev. adv acc. **Circ** 500. (cntl). Articles on descriptive and experimental natural history of Alberta; items on environmental conservation, book reviews and bibliography, organizational notes and news.

ALBERTA NATURALIST. SPECIAL ISSUE. No. 1 (July 1981)-. 0714-8372. Periodical. CN. English. ir. 10.00. Alberta Naturalist, c/o Fan, Box 1472, Edmonton Alberta T5J 2N5 Canada. **Tel** (403)428-3033. **Ed** Derek Johnson. **DD** 508.7123. bk rev. adv acc. **Circ** 800. (cntl). Articles concerning natural history in Alberta. Coverage and announcements of meetings field trips and events of interest to Alberta naturalists and conservationists.

ALOUETTE. SUPPLEMENT. (L'ALOUETTE. SUPPLEMENT). No. 1 (1976)-. 0704-626X. Periodical. CN. French. ir. L'Alouette, a/s L Fortin, 9 rue St-Thomas, Levis Quebec G6V 2M6 Canada. **DD** 509.714.

THE AMERICAN MIDLAND NATURALIST. V. 1, No. 5- Dec. 1909-. 0003-0031. Periodical. US. English. qt. $45.00. American Midland Naturalist, University of Notre Dame, Notre Dame IN 46556. **Tel** (219)239-7481. **Ed** R P McIntosh. **Ind/Abst** Can. Environ., Life Sci. Collect., Sel. Water Resour. Abstr., GeoRef, Biol. Abstr., Curr. Contents, Chem. Abstr., Bibliogr. Agric., Energy Res. Abstr., Gen. Sci. Index, Biol. Agric. Index, Curr. Contents, Agric. Biol. Environ. Sci., Environ. Period. Bibliogr., Bibliogr. Index, Bibliogr. Index Geol., Sci. Cit. Index, Abr. Ed. **LC** QH1. **CODEN** AMNAAF. **Circ** 1,500. Available on microfilm and microfiche from University Microfilms, Vols. 1-63 available on microcard from J. S. Canner. General biological journal. *Midland Naturalist, 0271-6844*.

THE AMERICAN NATURALIST. V. 1- Mar. 1867-. 0003-0147. Periodical. US. English. mo. University of Chicago Press, PO Box 37005, Chicago IL 60637. **Tel** (312)753-3347. **Ind/Abst** GeoRef, Math. Rev., Can. Environ., Sel. Water Resour. Abstr., Energy Inf. Abstr., Environ. Abstr., Biol. Abstr., Chem. Abstr., Bibliogr. Agric., Energy Res. Abstr., Biol. Agric. Index, Life Sci. Collect., Gen. Sci. Index, Sci. Cit. Index, Abr. Ed., Bibliogr. Index Geol. **LC** QH1. **DD** 574.05. **NLM** W1 AM66. **CODEN** AMNTA4. Available on microfilm from University Microfilms.

ANALES DEL MUSEO DE HISTORIA NATURAL DE VALPARAISO. See Yearbooks, Almanacs, Directories.

ANALES - MUSEO NACIONAL DE HISTORIA NATURAL (URUGUAY). See Yearbooks, Almanacs, Directories.

ANNALES HISTORICO-NATURALES MUSEI NATIONALIS HUNGARICI (BUDAPEST, HUNGARY : 1965). See Museums.

ANNALS OF THE CAPE PROVINCIAL MUSEUMS. NATURAL HISTORY. See Museums.

ANNALS OF THE CARNEGIE MUSEUM. See Museums.

ANNALS OF THE TRANSVAAL MUSEUM. See Museums.

ANNUAIRE DU MUSEUM NATIONAL D'HISTOIRE NATURELLE POUR L'ANNEE. See Yearbooks, Almanacs, Directories.

ANNUAL - NEPAL NATURE CONSERVATION SOCIETY. **Main/Corp** Nepal Nature Conservation Society. 1977-. English. ir. **LC** QH193.N4. **DD** 333.95095496.

ANNUAL REPORT - ARKANSAS NATURAL HERITAGE COMMISSION. See Public Administration.

ANNUAL REPORT - CHESAPEAKE BAY FOUNDATION. (ANNUAL REPORT). **Main/Corp** Chesapeake Bay Foundation. 0742-5066. US. English. an. Chesapeake Bay Foundation, 162 Prince George Street, Annapolis MD 21401. **LC** QH104.5.C45. **DD** 333.9181606075518.

ANNUAL REPORT FOR . . . ON THE ALASKA COASTAL MANAGEMENT PROGRAM. **Main/Corp** Alaska Coastal Policy Council. US. English. an. **LC** QH76.5.A4. **DD** 333.91709798.

ANNUAL REPORT FOR THE YEAR ENDED 30TH JUNE - NORTHERN TERRITORY. TERRITORY PARKS AND WILDLIFE COMMISSION. **Main/Corp** Northern Territory. Territory Parks and Wildlife Commission. 1st (1978)-. AT. English. an. Territory Parks and Wildlife Commission, PO Box 1046, Alice Springs Northern Territory 5750 Australia. **LC** QH197. **DD** 354.942900863.

ANNUAL REPORT - INSTITUTE OF TERRESTRIAL ECOLOGY. **Main/Corp** Institute of Terrestrial Ecology. 1974-. UK. English. an. 4.00. Her Majestys Stationery Office, 49 High Holborn, London WC1 V6HB England. **LC** QH540. **DD** 574.526405.

ANNUAL REPORT OF THE SADO MARINE BIOLOGICAL STATION, NIIGATA UNIVERSITY. **Main/Corp** Niigata Daigaku. Rigakubu. Sado Rinkai Jikkenjo. **VFOAT** Sado Rinkai Jikkenjo Kenkyu Nempo. No. 1- 1971-. JA. English. ir. Niigata University, Faculty of Science, Niigata Japan. **Ind/Abst** Biol. Abstr. **LC** QH91.A1. **DD** 574.9205. **CODEN** SRJKAK.

ARCHIVES OF NATURAL HISTORY. See Genealogy and Heraldry - Archives.

ARCHIVOS DEL INSTITUTO DE ACLIMATACION. See Genealogy and Heraldry - Archives.

ARNOLDIA CEASED. (ARNOLDIA (RHODESIA)). V. 1, No. 17 (Oct. 29, 1964)-V. 8, No. 38 (Nov. 7, 1978). 0066-7781. Periodical. RH. English. ir. National Museums of Southern Rhodesia, Salisbury Rhodesia. **Ind/Abst** Life Sci. Collect. **LC** QH1. **DD** 508.6. **CODEN** ARNPBS. *Arnoldia (Harare, Zimbabwe)*.

ARNOLDIA ZIMBABWE. (ARNOLDIA ZIMBABWE : SERIES OF MISCELLANEOUS PUBLICATIONS BY THE NATIONAL MUSEUM AND MONUMENTS). V. 8, No. 39 (Apr. 30, 1980)-. 0250-6386. Monographic Series. English. ir. **Tel** 60045. **Ind/Abst** GeoRef, Biol. Abstr. **LC** QH1. **DD** 508.6. **CODEN** AZIMDI. **Circ** 400. (cntl). Short papers

Natural History

recording the results of scientific investigations in the natural science disciplines in Southern Africa. *Arnoldia, Zimbabwe Rhodesia, 0066-7781.*

ARQUIPELAGO. SERIE CIENCIAS DA NATUREZA : REVISTA DO INSTITUTO UNIVERSITARIO DOS ACORES. VFOAT Serie Ciencias da Natureza. No. 1 (July 1980)-. Periodical. Portuguese. an. LC QH132.A9. DD 508.4699.

ATTI DELLA SOCIETA ITALIANA DI SCIENZE NATURALI E DEL MUSEO CIVICO DI STORIA NATURALE DI MILANO. 0037-8844. Periodical. IT. Italian (English). qt. Atti Societa Italiana di Corso, Venezia 55, 20121 Milano Italy. **Ind/Abst** Life Sci. Collect., GeoRef, Biol. Abstr., Chem. Abstr. **NLM** W1 AT782Q. **CODEN** ASIMAY. *Atti della Societa Italiana di Scienze Naturali.*

AUSTRALIAN NATURAL HISTORY. V. 14- Mar. 1962-. 0004-9840. Periodical. AT. English. qt. $11.07. Australian Museum, PO Box A285, South Sydney 2000 NSW Australia. **Tel** 339 8234. **Ed** Fiona Doig. **Ind/Abst** GeoRef, Biol. Abstr., Art Archaeol. Tech. Abstr., Bibliogr. Index Geol., Funk Scott Index Corp. Ind. **LC** QH1. **CODEN** AUNHAO. Index published separately - free - automatically sent. bk rev. adv acc. **Circ** 19,000. A magazine covering all aspects of natural history- animals, plants, anthropology and geology, accredited scientifically. *Australian Museum Magazine.*

BEITRAGE ZUR NATURKUNDE NIEDERSACHSENS. 1.- Yearly V. 0340-4277. Periodical. German. ir. **Ind/Abst** Bibliogr. Agric. **LC** QH5.

BERICHT AUS DEM HAUS DER NATUR IN SALZBURG. Main/Corp Salzburg. Haus der Natur. 0302-9654. German. ir. Haus der Natur, Museumsplatz 5, A-5020 Salzburg Austria. **Ind/Abst** GeoRef. **LC** QH5.

BERICHTE DES VEREINS NATUR UND HEIMAT UND DES NATURHISTORISCHEN MUSEUMS ZU LUBECK. See Museums.

BIBLIOTECA DELLA RIVISTA DI STORIA DELLE SCIENZE MEDICHE E NATURALI. 1- 1947-. Periodical. IT. Italian. ir. Casa Editrice Leo S Olschki, Casella Postale PO Box 66, 50100 Firenze Italy.

THE BIENNIAL REPORT, FIELD MUSEUM OF NATURAL HISTORY. See Museums.

BIENNIAL REPORT - IOWA PRESERVES BOARD. Main/Corp Iowa Preserves Board. Began with Vol. for 1975/76. US. English. be. Iowa Preserves Board, Des Moines IA 50319. LC QH105.I8. DD 353.9777008232.

BIOLOGIE-ECOLOGIE MEDITERRANEENNE. Series/Titl Annales de L'Universite de Provence. VFOAT Revue de Biologie-Ecologie Mediterraneenne. V. 6, No. 1-. 0397-2836. Periodical. English (and French with summary in the other language). ir. 100. MLLE C Vignal, Laboratoire de Botanique Centre St-Charles, Place Victor Hugo, 13331-Marseille Cedex France. **Ind/Abst** Bibliogr. Agric. **LC** QH150. DD 574.909822. *Biologie et Ecologie Mediterranneenne.*

BLUE JAY. V. 1- 1942/43-. 0006-5099. Periodical. CN. English. qt. Saskatchewan Natural History Society, PO Box 1321, Regina Saskatchewan Canada. **Tel** (306)746-4544. **Ind/Abst** Can. Environ. **CODEN** BLJYA3. bk rev. adv acc. **Circ** 2,000. (ctrl). Articles pertaining to the flora and fauna of the prairie provinces of Canada.

BLUE JAY NEWS. Issue No. 63 (May 1983)-. 0822-9988. Periodical. CN. English. qt. Free. Saskatchewan Natural History Society, PO Box 1784, Saskatoon Saskatchewan S7K 3S1 Canada. **DD** 508.712405. (ctrl). *Newsletter, 0581-8443.*

BOLETIM DO INSTITUTO OCEANOGRAFICO. See Earth Sciences - Oceanography.

BOLETIN DE DIVULGACIONES. Main/Corp Dominican Republic. Direccion General de Estadistica. No. 1-. 0417-9455. Periodical. MX. Spanish. ir. Publ Sociedad Mexicana Hist Nat, Av Dr Vertiz No 724, Mexico 12 DF Mexico.

BOLETIN DEL MUSEO NACIONAL DE HISTORIA NATURAL. See Museums.

BOLETIN - INSTITUTO DEL MAR DEL PERU. (BOLETIN). Began with: Vol. 1 in 1964. 0378-7699. Monographic Series. PE. Spanish (summaries in English). ir. Instituto del Mar del Peru, Lima Peru. LC QH95.52. DD 574.9205.

BOLLETTINO DEL MUSEO CIVICO DI STORIA NATURALE DI VENEZIA. Main/Corp Museo Civico di Storia Naturale di Venezia. V. 7- 1954-. 0505-205X. Periodical. IT. Italian. ir. Museo Civico di Storia Natural, Corso Venezia 55, 20121 Milano Italy. **Ind/Abst** Life Sci. Collect. **LC** QH7. **DD** 574. *Bollettino del Societa Veneziana di Storia Naturale E Museo Civico de Storia Naturale di Venezia.*

BOLLETTINO DEL MUSEO CIVICO DI STORIA NATURALE DI VERONA. See Museums.

BRAUNSCHWEIGER NATURKUNDLICHE SCHRIFTEN. Vol. 1, No. 1 (Nov. 1980)-. 0174-3384. Periodical. German (English summaries). ir. Staatliches Naturhistorisches, Museum Pockelsstrasse 10A D-3300 Braunschwieg, Bundesrepublik Deutschland.

BULLETIN (ALABAMA MUSEUM OF NATURAL HISTORY). See Museums.

BULLETIN - BRITISH ANTARCTIC SURVEY. Main/Corp British Antarctic Survey. No. 1- June 1963-. 0007-0262. Periodical. UK. English. qt. $64.36. British Antarctic Survey, Blackhorse Road/Letchworth, Herts SG6 1HN England. **Ind/Abst** GeoRef, Biol. Abstr., Chem. Abstr., Bibliogr. Index Geol. LC QH84.2. **CODEN** BANBAD.

BULLETIN DE LA SOCIETE D'HISTOIRE NATURELLE DE L'AFRIQUE DU NORD. Main/Corp Societe d'Histoire Naturelle de l'Afrique du Nord, Algiers. Vol. 1- Nov. 1909-. 0374-0994. Periodical. AE. English (French). qt. Universite d'Algiers, Societe d'Histoire Naturelle de l'Afrique du Nord, 2 rue Didouche Mourad, Algiers Algeria. **Ind/Abst** GeoRef, Biol. Abstr., Bibliogr. Agric. LC QH3. **CODEN** BHNAAP. (cum index).

BULLETIN DE L'ASSOCIATION DES NATURALISTES DU MALI. Main/Corp Association des Naturlistes du Mali. French. ir. Association des Naturalistes du Mali, B P 1746, Bamako Mali. LC QH195.M475. DD 500.96623.

BULLETIN DE L'INSTITUT NATIONAL SCIENTIFIQUE ET TECHNIQUE D'OCEANOGRAPHIE ET DE PECHE. Main/Corp Al-Mahad Al-Qawmi Al-Ilmi Wa-Al-Fanni Lil-Uqyanus Wa-Al-Sayd. VFOAT Nashrat Al-Mahad Al-Qawmi Al-Ilmi Wa-Al-Fanni Lil-Uqyanus Wa-Al-Sayd Bi-Salambu. V. 1-. 0579-7926. French (English, with summaries also in Arabic). ir. **Ind/Abst** GeoRef. LC QH90.A1. DD 551.46005. *Bulletin - Station Oceanographique de Salammbo.*

BULLETIN DU MUSEUM NATIONAL D'HISTOIRE NATURELLE. See Museums.

BULLETIN DU MUSEUM NATIONAL D'HISTOIRE NATURELLE. SECTION A : ZOOLOGIE, BIOLOGIE ET ECOLOGIE ANIMALES. See Museums.

BULLETIN DU MUSEUM NATIONAL D'HISTOIRE NATURELLE, SECTION C, SCIENCES DE LA TERRE, PALEONTOLOGIE, GEOLOGIE, MINERALOGIE. See Museums.

BULLETIN DU MUSEUM NATIONAL D'HISTOIRE NATURELLE. SER.3. SCIENCES PHYSICO-CHIMIQUES. See Museums.

BULLETIN - MANITOBA NATURALISTS SOCIETY. (BULLETIN). Vol. 1, No. 1 (Sept. 1977)-. 0823-2911. Periodical. CN. English. mo. 25.00. Manitoba Naturalists Society, 302-128 James Avenue, Winnipeg Manitoba R3B 0N8 Canada. **Tel** (204)943-9029. **Ed** Susan Griffiths. DD 574.90607127. bk rev. adv acc. **Circ** 1,400. (ctrl). For members, items of CanadaF2 11976nitoba's environmental concerns, natural history and book reviews, listings of society activities including trips, workshops, and meetings.

BULLETIN OF CARNEGIE MUSEUM OF NATURAL HISTORY. See Museums.

BULLETIN OF THE ALLYN MUSEUM. See Museums.

BULLETIN OF THE AMERICAN MUSEUM OF NATURAL HISTORY. See Museums.

BULLETIN OF THE BIOLOGICAL SOCIETY OF WASHINGTON. No. 1-. 0097-0298. Monographic Series. US. English. ir. Biological Society of Washington, National Museum of Natural History/Treasurer, Washington DC 20560. **Ind/Abst** GeoRef. LC QH105.D6. DD 574.05. **CODEN** BBSWA6.

BULLETIN OF THE BRITISH MUSEUM (NATURAL HISTORY) BOTANY. See Museums.

BULLETIN OF THE BRITISH MUSEUM (NATURAL HISTORY). ENTOMOLOGY CEASED. VFOAT Entomology. Vol. 1, No. 1 (June 1950)-. 0524-6431. Monographic Series. UK. English. ir. 133. British Museum of Natural History, Cromwell Road, London SW7 5BD England. **Tel** 01 589 6323. **Ed** L A Mound. **Ind/Abst** Life Sci. Collect., Biol. Abstr. LC QL461. DD 595.7. **Circ** 600. Insect systematics and taxonomy.

BULLETIN OF THE BRITISH MUSEUM (NATURAL HISTORY). GEOLOGY SERIES. See Museums.

BULLETIN OF THE BRITISH MUSEUM (NATURAL HISTORY). HISTORICAL SERIES. See Museums.

BULLETIN OF THE MUSEUM OF LIFE SCIENCES. See Museums.

BULLETIN - PEABODY MUSEUM OF NATURAL HISTORY. See Museums.

BULLETIN - STATE GEOLOGICAL AND NATURAL HISTORY SURVEY OF CONNECTICUT. Main/Corp State Geological and Natural History Survey of Connecticut. No. 1-. 0095-8638. Monographic Series. US. English. ir. Connecticut State Library, 231 Capitol Avenue, Hartford CT 06115. **Tel** (203)566-5354. **Ind/Abst** GeoRef. LC QH105.C8. DD 508.746. **CODEN** CNGBAC.

CAHIERS DE L'INDO-PACIFIQUE. V. 1- Jan. 1979-. 0180-9954. Periodical. FR. French (summaries in English). ir. Fondation Singer-Polingnac, 43 Avenue, Georges Mandel 75016, Paris France. LC QH198.A1. DD 574.9257. *Cahiers du Pacifique.*

CAMP ITINERANT SOUS TERRE ET EN MONTAGNE. Main/Corp Camp Rolland-Germain. 1973-. 0700-3005. CN. French. an. Camp Rolland-Germain, Frelighsburg Que J0J 1C0 Canada. DD 500.9714.

CASOPIS MORAVSKEHO MUZEA. VEDY PRIRODNI. See Museums.

CASOPIS NARODNIHO MUZEA : ODDIL PRIRODOVEDNY. Main/Corp Prague. Narodni Muzeum. Vol. 117- 1948-. 0008-7351. Periodical. CS. Czech. ir. Artia, PO Box 790, Ve Smeckach 30, Praha 1 Czechoslovakia. **Ind/Abst** GeoRef, Biol. Abstr., Chem. Abstr., Bibliogr. Agric. LC QH7. DD 574.9437. **CODEN** CMOPAJ. *Casopis Narodniho Musea. Oddil Prirodovendy.*

CATALOGUE OF FORAMINIFERA. SUPPL. (CATALOGUE OF FORAMINIFERA. SUPPLEMENT). Began with 1943. 0885-7083. Periodical. US. English. an. $225.00. American Museum of Natural History, Central Park West and 79th Street, New York NY 10024. **Tel** (212)873-1405. **Ed** J A Van Couvering. DD 560. **Circ** 300. Extracts and verifies type descriptions of all new species and genus names since 1800- now 35,000 names and increasing 700 per year in the foraminifera - main use oil exploration.

CAZA FOTOGRAFICA. No. 1- Oct. 1973-. Periodical. Spanish (summaries in English). ir. 1,500. Castello 59, Madrid 1 Spain. LC QH7. DD 910.5.

CIMBEBASIA. SERIS A. NATUURWETENSKAPPE. (CIMBEBASIA. SER. A. NATUURWETENSKAPPE. NATURAL HISTORY). VFOAT Naatuurwetenskappe. Natural History. V. 1- 1967-. 0590-6342. Periodical. English (Afrikaans, or German). ir. Staatsmuseum, Box 1303, Windhoek Africa. **Tel** (061)29391. **Ed** H Rust. **Ind/Abst** Biol. Abstr. **CODEN** CBANB3. **Circ** 400. (ctrl). Articles by specialists on cultural history and natural history preferably of South West Africa/Namibia. *Cimbebasia.*

Natural History

CIRCULAR - ILLINOIS NATURAL HISTORY SURVEY. Main/Corp Illinois. Natural History Survey Division. 46- April 1961-. 0073-4926. Monographic Series. US. English. ir. Illinois Natural History, Survey Division, 196 Natural Resources Building, Urbana IL 61801. **Ind/Abst** Biol. Abstr., Chem. Abstr., Sel. Water Resour. Abstr. **DD** 574. **CODEN** INHCAI. *Circular - Natural History Survey Division.*

COLLECTIONS. V. 56, No. 1/2- Oct. 1976-. 0160-0664. Periodical. US. English. qt. $3.50. Buffalo Museum of Science, Humboldt Parkway, Buffalo NY 14211. **Ind/Abst** GeoRef. **LC** QH1. **DD** 500.905. *Science on the March, 0036-8474.*

COMUNICACIONES ANTROPOLOGICAS DEL MUSEO DE HISTORIA NATURAL DE MONTEVIDEO. *See* Museums.

CONTRIBUTIONS IN SCIENCE (LOS ANGELES, CALIF.). (CONTRIBUTIONS IN SCIENCE). No. 1 (Jan. 23, 1957)-. 0459-8113. Monographic Series. US. English. ir. Natural History Museum of Los Angeles County, 900 Exposition Boulevard, Los Angeles CA 90007. Ed Daniel M Cohen. **Ind/Abst** GeoRef, Biol. Abstr. **LC** Q11. **DD** 508. **CODEN** LANHA5. (cum index). **Circ** 1,000. (ctrl). Original research in earth and life sciences. *Science Bulletin, 0076-0935.*

CURATOR. *See* Museums.

CURLEW. (THE CURLEW). 0011-3093. Periodical. CN. English. mo. Willow Field Naturalist Club, 578 Lakeshore Road, Cobourg Ontario Canada.

CURRENT ADVANCES IN ECOLOGICAL SCIENCES. V. 1- Jan. 1975-. 0306-3291. UK. English. mo. Pergamon Press, Attn Cashier, 395 Sawmill River Road, Elmsford NY 10523. **LC** QH540. **DD** 016.5745. **NLM** Z 5322.E2 C976.

DIRASAT : NATURAL SCIENCES. VFOAT Dirasat: Al-Ulum Al-Tabiyah. V. 1- Dec. 1974-. Periodical. English. ir. **LC** QH1. **DD** 505.

DISCOVERY. V. 1- Fall 1965-. 0012-3625. Periodical. US. English. sa. $6.00. Peabody Museum of Natural History, Yale University, 170 Whitney Avenue, PO Box 6666, New Haven CT 06511. **Tel** (203)436-1131. Ed Zelda Edelson. **Ind/Abst** GeoRef. **LC** QH1. **CODEN** DISCAH. bk rev. Circ 1,000. The award-winning magazine of the Yale Peabody Museum features lively authoritative, and well-illustrated articles for the general reader on dinosaurs, human origins, raccoons and other scientific subjects.

DURBAN MUSEUM NOVITATES. V. 1- June 1914-. 0012-723X. SA. English. ir. Durban Museum, PO Box 4085, Durban 4000 South Africa. **LC** QH1.

E.A.N.H.S. BULLETIN. Main/Corp East Africa Natural History Society. VFOAT East Africa Natural History Society Bulletin. Jan. 1971-. Periodical. English. ir. Easr Africa Natural History Society, PO Box 44486, Nairobi Kenya. **Ind/Abst** Bibliogr. Agric. **LC** QH195.A23. **DD** 574.96705. *EANHS Newsletter.*

EHIME KENRITSU HAKUBUTSUKAN KENKYU HOKOKU. *See* Museums.

EKOLOGIA POLSKA. VFOAT Polish Journal of Ecology. V. 22-. 0420-9036. Periodical. PL. English (summaries in Polish). qt. ARS Polona, Krakowskie Przemiescie 7, 00-068 Warsaw Poland. **Ind/Abst** Life Sci. Collect., Sel. Water Resour. Abstr., Excerpta Med., GeoRef, Biol. Abstr., Chem. Abstr., Bibliogr. Agric. **LC** QH162. **DD** 574.505. **NLM** W1 EK27D. **CODEN** ELPLBS. *Ekologia Polska. Seria A.*

EKOLOGIJA. (EKOLOGIIA). 1970-. 0367-0597. Periodical. UR. Russian. bm. $42.50. Victor Kamkin Inc (71116), 12224 Parklawn Drive, Rockville MD 20852. **Tel** (301)881-5973. **Ind/Abst** Biol. Abstr., Chem. Abstr., Index Med., Ocean. Abstr., Pollut. Abstr. Indexes. **LC** QH540. **DD** 574.505. **NLM** W1 EK27H. **CODEN** EKIAAK.

EKOLOGIJA. VFOAT Acta Biologica Iugoslavica. V. 1- 1966-. 0531-9110. Periodical. Serbo-Croatian with some English, German, French, and Russian. sa. **LC** QH540.

ENVIRONMENTAL ASSESSMENT OF THE ALASKAN CONTINENTAL SHELF. (ENVIRONMENTAL ASSESSMENT OF THE ALASKAN CONTINENTAL SHELF. QUARTERLY REPORTS OF PRINCIPAL INVESTIGATORS FOR . . .). VFOAT Alaskan OCS Principal Investigators' Reports. Began with July/Sept. 1975. 0160-2861. Periodical. US. English. qt. Outer Continental Shelf Environmental Assessment Program, US Department of Commerce, Boulder CO 80303. **LC** QH105.A4. **DD** 500.9798.

ENVIRONMENTAL MUTAGENESIS. *See* Sanitation, Environmental Technology.

EPETERIS MOUSEIOU GOULANDRE. Main/Corp Mouseion Goulandre Physikes Historias. VFOAT Annales Musei Goulandris. 1- 1973-. 0302-1033. English, French, German, or Latin. ir. Mouseiou Goulandre Physikes Historias, Levidhou 13, Greece. **Ind/Abst** GeoRef, Biol. Abstr., Bibliogr. Agric. **LC** QH151. **DD** 500.9495. **CODEN** AMUGAY.

THE EXPLORER. V. 1- Nov. 1922-. 0014-5009. Periodical. US. English. ir. Cleveland Museum of Natural History, Wade Oval University Circle, Cleveland OH 44106. **Ind/Abst** Biol. Abstr. **LC** QH71.C6.

FIELD MUSEUM OF NATURAL HISTORY BULLETIN. *See* Museums.

FIELD STUDIES. Began in 1959. 0428-304X. UK. English. ir. $13.80. E W Classex Ltd, Park Road Faringdon, Oxon SN7 7DR England. **Ind/Abst** Life Sci. Collect., GeoRef, Biol. Abstr., Bibliogr. Index Geol. **LC** QH137. **CODEN** FSTUBX.

FOREST AND BIRD. No. 31- 1933-. Periodical. NZ. English. qt. 220.00. Royal Forest & Bird Protection Society, PO Box 631, Wellington New Zealand. **Tel** (04)728-154. Ed G Hutching. adv acc. **Circ** 22,000. (ctrl). An independently published magazine combining colour illustrated articles on natural history and the politics of conservation.

FRONTIERS. V. 1- 1979-. 0016-2159. Periodical. US. English. an. The Academy of Natural Sciences Nineteenth and the Parkway, Philadelphia PA 19103. **Ind/Abst** GeoRef. **LC** QH1. **DD** 574.05. **CODEN** FRBGAT. *Frontiers.*

THE GREAT BASIN NATURALIST. V. 1- July 25, 1939-. 0017-3614. Periodical. US. English. qt. $24.00. Great Basin Naturalist, 290 MLBM, Brigham Young University, Provo UT 84602. **Tel** (801)378-2226. Ed Stephen L Wood. **Ind/Abst** Life Sci. Collect., Excerpta Med., Coal Abstr., GeoRef, Chem. Abstr., Biol. Abstr., Nuci. Sci. Abstr., Bibliogr. Agric., Sel. Water Resour. Abstr., Energy Res. Abstr., Bibliogr. Index Geol. **LC** QH1. **DD** 574.978. **CODEN** GRBNAR. **Circ** 500. Biological natural history of Western North America.

GREAT BASIN NATURALIST MEMOIRS. No. 1-. 0160-239X. Monographic Series. US. English. ir. $24.00. Great Basin Naturalist, 290 MLBM Brigham Young University, Provo UT 84602. **Tel** (901)378-5053. Ed Stephen L Wood. **Ind/Abst** Chem. Abstr. **CODEN** GBNMD9. **Circ** 500. Biological natural history of Western North America.

GROSSE NATURFORSCHER. V. 1, 1947-. 0072-7741. Monographic Series. GW. German. ir. Wissenschaftliche Verlagsge- Sellschaft MBH/ Postfach 40, D7000 Stuttgart 1 West Germany.

HALIFAX FIELD NATURALISTS NEWSLETTER. No. 1 (Nov. 1975)-. 0715-3627. Periodical. CN. English. bm. Free to Members. Halifax Field Naturalists c/o Nova Scotia Museum, 1747 Summer Street, Halifax Nova Scotia B3H 3A6 Canada. **DD** 574.906071622.

HANDBOOK - NATIONAL MUSEUM OF VICTORIA. Main/Conf National Museum of Victoria. No. 1- 1950-. 0505-4362. Monographic Series. AT. English. ir. National Museum of Victoria, 285 Russell Street, Melbourne Victoria 3000 Australia. **LC** AM101.

HISTOIRE ET NATURE. VFOAT Cahiers de l'Association pour l'Historie des Sciences de la Nature. No 3- Sept. 1973-. 0396-9681. Periodical. FR. French (summaries in English). sa. $14.00. Museum National d'Histoire Naturelle, 55 rue Buffon, 75005 Paris France. **Ind/Abst** GeoRef, Bibliogr. Index Geol. **NLM** W1 HI76N. *Histoire et Biologie, 0441-6732.*

HISTORIA NATURAL Y PRO NATURA. Began in Sept. 1964. 0018-2346. GT. Spanish. qt. Historia Natural y Pro Natura, Apartado Postal 987, Guatemala Guatemala.

HUNTER NATURAL HISTORY. (V. 8, No. 1 (29))-. 0046-8312. Periodical. AT. English. qt. Newcastle Flora & Fauna Protection Society, 114 Victoria Street, New Lambton New South Wales 2305 Australia. **Ind/Abst** Bibliogr. Agric.

INFO-NATURE : ILE DE LA REUNION. No. 1/4-12. French. ir. 14.00. Museum d'Histoire Naturelle, B P 1012, Saint-Denis Reunion. **LC** QH196.R4. **DD** 333.95096981.

IRISH NATURALISTS' JOURNAL. (THE IRISH NATURALISTS' JOURNAL). V. 1- Sept. 1925-. 0021-1311. Periodical. UK. English. qt. $20.00. Irish Naturalists Journal, Department of Zoology, Queens University, Belfast BT9 5ED England. **Ind/Abst** Life Sci. Collect., GeoRef, Ref. Source, Biol. Abstr., Chem. Abstr. **CODEN** INAJA4. (cum index).

JAHRBUCH DER SCHWEIZERISCHEN NATURFORSCHENDEU GESELLSCHAFT. *See* Yearbooks, Almanacs, Directories.

JAPANESE JOURNAL OF ECOLOGY. VFOAT Nihon Seitai Gakkai Shi. Began in 1983. 0021-5007. Periodical. English (Japanese). qt. $56.00. Kyowa Book Company Inc, 1-38 Kanda Jinbo-Cho, Chiyoda-Ku 101 Tokyo Japan. **Tel** 293-0727. **Ind/Abst** Life Sci. Collect., GeoRef, Chem. Abstr., Biol. Abstr. **CODEN** JJECDN. *Nihon Seitai Gakkai Shi.*

JOURNAL CHICOBI. SECTION SCIENTIFIQUE. Main/Corp Camp-Ecole Chicobi. First issue in Nov. 1972. 0318-420X. Periodical. CN. French. qt. $1. Camp-Ecole Chicobi Guyenne, Abitibi-Ouest, Quebec J0Y 1L0 Canada. **DD** 500.1.

JOURNAL OF NATURAL HISTORY. Periodical. UK. English. bm. $380.00. Taylor & Francis Ltd, 242 Cherry Street, Philadelphia PA 19106. **Tel** (215)238-0939. Ed A A Fincham and D Hollis. **Ind/Abst** Bibliogr. Index Geol., Sci. Cit. Index, Abr. Ed. Publishes original research and reviews in systematics, evolutionary and general biology.

JOURNAL OF NATURAL HISTORY. V. 1- Jan./Mar. 1967-. 0022-2933. Periodical. UK. English (French or German). bm. Taylor & Francis Ltd, 4 John Street, London WC1N 2ET England. **Tel** 468011. Ed Kincham and Wollis. **Ind/Abst** Life Sci. Collect., Energy Inf. Abstr., Environ. Abstr., GeoRef, Ref. Source, Sel. Water Resour. Abstr., Biol. Abstr., Bibliogr. Agric. **LC** QH1. **DD** 574.05. **CODEN** JNAHA9. Index in last issue of volume - attached. bk rev. adv acc. **Circ** 600. Original research and reviews in evolutionary and general biology; entomology, zoology, taxonomy, parasitology, behaviour, and ecology. *Annals & Magazine of Natural History.*

JOURNAL OF TAIWAN MUSEUM. *See* Museums.

JOURNAL OF THE BOMBAY NATURAL HISTORY SOCIETY. Main/Corp Bombay Natural History Society. V. 1- Jan. 1886-. 0006-6982. Periodical. II. English. ty. $50.00. Bombay Natural History Society, Hornbill House/ Shahid Bhagat, Bombay 1 Br India. **Ind/Abst** Life Sci. Collect., Excerpta Med., Biol. Abstr., GeoRef, Bibliogr. Agric., Energy Res. Abstr. **CODEN** JBOMAA. (cum index).

KANAGAWA SHIZENSHI SHIRYO. VFOAT Natural History Report of Kanagawa. Began in 1979. Periodical. JA. Japanese. ir. Kanagawa Kenritsu Hakubutsukan, 5-60 Minami Nakadori, Naka-ku 231, Yokohama-shi Japan. **LC** QH188.

KAO CHA YU YEN CHIU. VFOAT Investigatio et Studium Naturae. V. 1, 1983-. Periodical. CH. Chinese. ir. 0.35. Shang-Hai Tzu Jan Po Wu Kuan, Shanghai China. **LC** QH7. **DD** 508.51.

LAMMERGEYER. (THE LAMMERGEYER). V. 1-3, 1960-65. 0075-7780. Periodical. English. ir. National Parks Game and Fish Preservation, PO Box 662, Pitermaritzburg Natal South Africa. **Tel** PMB 51221. Ed D N Johnson. **Ind/Abst** Sel. Water Resour. Abstr., Chem. Abstr. **LC** QH195.N3. **DD** 500.9. **CODEN** LMGYA3. **Circ** 400. (ctrl). Nature conservation research in Natal.

LAPORAN TAHUNAN DIREKTORAT PERLINDUNGAN DAN PENGAWETAN ALAM. Main/Corp Indonesia. Direktorat Perlindungan dan Pedgawetan Alam. Indonesian. ir. Direktorat Perlingungan dan Pengawetan Alam, Jalan Ir H Juanda No 9, Bogor Indonesia. **LC** QH186.

LINNEEN. (LE LINNEEN). Published since Fall 1976?. 0227-2377. Periodical. CN. French. sa. Free to Members, $1.00 Per No. a/s Societe Linneenne de Quebec Aquarium de Quebec, 1675 Av du Parc, Sainte-Foy Quebec G1W 4S3 Canada. **DD** 509.714.

Natural History

THE LIVING WILDERNESS CEASED. V. 1-46 (No. 1-157). 0024-5305. Periodical. US. English. qt. Ed R S Yard. Ind/Abst Coal Abstr., Energy Inf. Abstr., Environ. Abstr., Book Rev. Index, Biol. Abstr., Read. Guide Period. LC QH1. DD 574.973. CODEN LIWIA7. (cum index).

LUONNON TUTKIJA. Began publication in 1897. 0024-7383. Fl. Finnish. ir. 70.-. Akakeeminen-Kirjakuppa, PO Box 128, 00101 Helsinki Finland. Tel (90)651 122. Ind/Abst Life Sci. Collect., Biol. Abstr., GeoRef, Bibliogr. Agric. LC QH7. CODEN LUTUAA.

MALAYAN NATURALIST. V. 33, No. 1-. Periodical. English. qt. LC QH185. DD 333.951609595.

MARGAULX. (LE MARGAULX). V. 1- July/Aug. 1976-. 0705-050X. Periodical. CN. French (English). wk. Free to visitors to the Perce region. Centre d'Histoire Naturelle de Perce, CP 190, Perce Quebec G0C 2L0 Canada. DD 500.971479.

MEMOIR - SAN DIEGO SOCIETY OF NATURAL HISTORY. (MEMOIRS - SAN DIEGO SOCIETY OF NATURAL HISTORY). Main/Corp San Diego Society of Natural History. VFOAT San Diego Society of Natural History Memoir. V. 1-. 0080-5920. Monographic Series. US. English. ir. San Diego Society of Natural History, Balboa Park, Box 1390, San Diego Ca 92112. Tel (619)232-3821. Ed G Pregill. Ind/Abst Biol. Abstr., GeoRef, Bibliogr. Index Geol. LC QH1. CODEN SDNMAG. Original research in botany, paleontology, mammology, ornithology, herpetology, marine inverts, and entomology.

MEMOIRES. DEUXIEME SERIE. Main/Corp Brussels. Institut Royal des Sciences Naturelles de Belgique. VFOAT Verhandelingen. Tweede Reeks. Issue 2, Ser. 1949-. Monographic Series. BE. text chiefly in French. ir. Institut Royal des Sciences, Naturelles de Belgique, 31 rue Bautier, Bruxelles Belgium B1040. LC QH3. Memoires. Deuxieme Serie.

MEMOIRES DU MUSEUM D'HISTOIRE NATURELLE (1815). See Museums.

MEMOIRES - INSTITUT ROYAL DES SCIENCES NATURELLES DE BELGIQUE. Main/Corp Brussels. Institut Royal des Sciences Naturlles de Belgique. VFOAT Verhandelingen - Koninklijk Belgisch Instituut voor Natuurwetenschappen. No. 111- 1949-. Monographic Series. BE. articles chiefly in French. ir. Patrimoine Institut of Royal Science Nature, 31 rue Vautier, B 1040 Bruxelles Belgium. LC QH3. Memories du Musee Royal d'Histoire de Belgique.

MEMOIRS OF THE NATURAL HISTORY FOUNDATION OF ORANGE COUNTY. Vol. 1-. 0749-1743. Monographic Series. US. English. ir. Natural History Foundation of Orange County, PO Box 7038, Newport Beach CA 92660. Ind/Abst Chem. Abstr.

MEMOIRS OF THE QUEENSLAND MUSEUM. See Museums.

MEMORIAS DEL MUSEO DE HISTORIA NATURAL JAVIER PRADO. See Museums.

MEMORIE DEL MUSEO TRIDENTINO DI SCIENZE NATURALI CEASED. Main/Corp Museo Tridentino di Scienze Naturali. 0392-6729. Italian (German or with summaries in English). ir. 3.500. Museo Tridentino di Scienze Naturali, Conto Corrente Postale N 14/2189 Via Rosmini 19, Trento Italy. Ind/Abst GeoRef, Chem. Abstr. LC QH7.T7. DD 500.905. CODEN MTNMBT. Memorie del Museo di Storia Naturale Della Venezia Tridentina.

MEMOURIA. (NEMOURIA : OCCASIONAL PAPERS OF THE DELAWARE MUSEUM OF NATURAL HISTORY). VFOAT Occasional Papers of the Delaware Museum of Natural History. Began in 1970. 0085-3887. Monographic Series. US. English. ir. Delaware Museum of Natural History, PO Box 3937, Greenville DE 19807. Ind/Abst Biol. Abstr. LC QL1. DD 590.5. CODEN NOPHD2.

THE MICHIGAN AUDUBON NEWSLETTER. V. 6, No. 4-V. 25, No. 5. 0543-9736. Periodical. US. English. qt. $7.50. Michigan Audubon Society, 409 West E Avenue, Kalamazoo MI 49007. Tel (616)344-8648. Ed Maria Schneiderman. bk rev. adv acc. Circ 6,000. (ctrl). Statewide conservation and natural history articles and material also environmental education and meetings and 40 local chapter activities. Michigan Audubon News.

MICRONESICA. V. 1- June 1964-. 0026-279X. Periodical. GU. English. sa. 56.00. University of Guam, UOG Station, Mangilao Guam 96923. Tel (671)734-3676. Ed James A Marsh, Jr. Ind/Abst Life Sci. Collect., GeoRef, Biol. Abstr., Bibliogr. Agric., Nuci. Sci. Abstr., Bibliogr. Index Geol. LC QH198.M48. DD 574.9965. CODEN MCNSBU. bk rev. Circ 600. Journal of the University of Guam devoted to the natural sciences of Guam, Micronesia, and related areas.

MISCELANEA - FUNDACION MIGUEL LILLO. Main/Corp Fundacion Miguel Lillo. No. 42- 1972-. 0074-025X. Monographic Series. AG. Spanish. ir. Ind/Abst Bibliogr. Agric. Miscelanea - Universidad Nacional de Tucuman, Fundacion e Instituto Miguel Lillo.

MITTEILUNGEN AUS DEM LUDWIG BOLTZMANN-INSTITUT FUR UMWELTWISSENSCHAFTEN UND NATURSCHUTZ. Main/Corp Ludwig Boltzmann-Instutut fur Umweltwissenschaften und Naturschutz. 1975-. German. ir. Peinrichstrasse 5/III, 8010 Graz Austria. LC QH75.A1. DD 333.9505.

MONOGRAPH SERIES - DELAWARE MUSEUM OF NATURAL HISTORY. (MONOGRAPH SERIES). No. 1-. 0084-9650. Monographic Series. US. English. ir. Delaware Museum of Natural History, PO Box 3937, Greenville DE 19807. LC UNC. CODEN MDMHDZ.

MUSEOLOGIA. Oct. 1973-. 0301-6463. Dutch or English, with summaries in the other language. sa. 24.59. Quadriga-Drukwerken, Amstel 21 C, Amsterdam Netherlands. Ind/Abst GeoRef. LC QH7. DD 500.905. CODEN MSLGCT.

MUSEUM PICTORIAL. See Museums.

NARRAGANSETT NATURALIST. (THE NARRAGANSETT NATURALIST). 0027-805X. Periodical. US. English. qt. $3.00. Audubon Society of Rhode Island, 40 Bowen Street, Providence RI 02903. LC QH76.5.N45. DD 500.974.

NATTURUFRINGURINN. 1.- Vol. 0369-5921. Periodical. IC. Icelandic. qt. Free to members. H Islenska Natturufrifelag, Stefan Stefansson, Storholti 12 Postholf 836, Reykjavik Iceland. Ind/Abst GeoRef, Bibliogr. Agric. LC QH166. CODEN NTFDA6. (cum index).

NATUR UND HEIMAT. V. 1- 1934-. 0028-0593. Periodical. GW. German. qt. Museum fur Naturkunde, Himmelreichallee 50, 44 Munster-Wstfln West Germany. Ind/Abst Biol. Abstr. LC QH5. CODEN NTRHAA.

NATUR UND LANDSCHAFT. Periodical. GW. German. mo. W Kohlhammer Verlag GMBH, Hessbruhlstrasse 69 PF 800430, 7000 Stuttgart 80- West Germany. Ind/Abst Coal Abstr., GeoRef, Pollut. Abstr. Indexes, Ocean. Abstr. LC QH77.G3.

NATURA. V. 1- Nov. 1909-. 0369-6243. Periodical. IT. Italian. qt. Societa Italiana di Scienze Naturali, Palazzo del Museo Civico di Storia Naturale Corso Venezia 55, 20121 Milano Italy. Ind/Abst GeoRef, Life Sci. Collect. LC QH7. DD 574.05. CODEN NTRMAP. Index published separately - free - automatically sent.

NATURA. 1st.- Year. 0028-0631. Periodical. NE. Dutch. mo. K N N V Bureau, Hoogenboomlaan 24, Noogwoud Netherlands.

NATURA BRESCIANA. IT. Italian. ir. Museo Civico di Storia Naturale, Corso Venezia 55, 20121 Milano Italy. LC QH152. DD 500.9094526.

NATURAL HISTORY. V. 19- Jan. 1919-. 0028-0712. Periodical. US. English. mo. $10.00 Domestic, $12.00 Domestic. American Museum of Natural History, Central Park West at 79th Street, New York NY 10024, (subscription address: Communication Data Services 112 Tenth Street Des Moines IA 50309). Tel (201)384-4466. Ind/Abst Life Sci. Collect., Energy Inf. Abstr., Environ. Abstr., Int. Aerosp. Abstr., GeoRef, ASTIS Bibliogr., ASTIS Curr. Aware. Bull., Writ. Am. Hist., Book Rev. Digest, Bibliogr. Agric., Biogr. Index, Biol. Abstr., Nuci. Sci. Abstr., Read. Guide Period. Lit., Abr. Read. Guide, Gen. Sci. Index, Book Rev. Index, Sci. Cit. Index, Abr. Ed., Mag. Index, Bibliogr. Index Geol., Abr. Read. Guide, Abstr. Anthropol., Pop. Mag. Rev. LC QH1. NLM W1 NA804N. CODEN NAHIAX. American Museum Journal, Nature Magazine.

NATURAL HISTORY BOOK REVIEWS. V. 1- Jan. 1976-. UK. English. ir. A B Academic Publishers, Box 97, Berkhamsted Herts HP4 2PX England. Tel 01-876-1091. Ed Frank Brightman. LC QH1. DD 016.5009. bk rev. adv acc. A critical international bibliographic review journal invaluable to all those involved in buying books in all fields of natural history.

NATURAL HISTORY BULLETIN. Main/Corp Siam Society. V. 1- Feb. 1914-. 0080-9462. Periodical. TH. English. sa. $25.00. Siam Society, PO Box 65, Bangkok Thailand. Tel 258-3491. Ed Tem Smitinand. Ind/Abst Am. Hist. Life, Hist. Abstr. Circ 1,500. (ctrl). The study of the natural history in Thailand and neighbouring countries.

NATURAL HISTORY HANDBOOK SERIES. No. 1- 1954-. 0499-9975. Monographic Series. US. English. ir. Superintendent of Documents, US Government Printing Office, Washington DC 20402. DD 574.

NATURAL HISTORY MISCELLANEA. No. 1-. 0096-9109. Monographic Series. US. English. ir. Chicago Academy of Sciences, Lincoln Park 2001 North Clark Street, Chicago IL 60614. Ind/Abst GeoRef, Biol. Abstr. LC QH1. DD 500.905. CODEN NHMIA6.

NATURAL HISTORY THEME STUDIES. No. 1-. Monographic Series. US. English.

NATURALEZA. 0369-6251. Periodical. MX. Spanish. bm. $20.00. Asociacion para la Divulgacion Cientifica, H A Lorentz, Comercio y Administracion 26, Mexico 20 Mexico 04460. Tel 548-8435. Ind/Abst Chem. Abstr. LC QH7. CODEN NTRZAU.

NATURALIA. V. 1- 1975-. 0101-1944. Periodical. English (Portuguese). an. Rua Cristovao Colombo, 2265 CEP 15.100, Sao Paulo Brazil. Ind/Abst Math. Rev., Life Sci. Collect., GeoRef, Chem. Abstr. LC QH7. DD 505. CODEN NTRLDP.

NATURALIST. V. 8, No. 3- 1957-. 0547-9649. Periodical. US. English. qt. $12.00. Natural History Society, 725 Medical Arts Building, Minneapolis MN 55402. Tel (612)333-7887. Minnesota Naturalist.

NATURALIST (CASCADE, TRINIDAD AND TOBAGO). See Conservation & Natural Resources.

NATURALISTE CANADIEN. See Biology.

NATURALISTES BELGES. (LES NATURALISTES BELGES). Began with Jan. 1930. 0028-0801. Periodical. French. mo. Ind/Abst Biol. Abstr., Bibliogr. Agric. LC QH3. CODEN NTUBA7. Bulletin Mensuel.

THE NATURALISTS' NEWS. Periodical. US. English. Quarry Hill Nature Center, 701 Silver Creek Road NE, Rochester MN 55901.

NATURE AND SYSTEM. V. 1- Mar. 1979-. 0191-2941. Periodical. US. English. qt. $14.50 Domestic, $15.50 Foreign. Nature and Systems Inc, PO Box 3368, Tucson AZ 85722. Ind/Abst Philos. Index. LC QH1. DD 500.901.

NATURE MALAYSIANA. V. 1-. 0126-5318. Periodical. English. ir. Tropical Press SDN, 64-A Jim Bukut Bintang, Kuala Lumpur Malaysia. Ind/Abst Bibliogr. Agric. LC QH185. DD 500.9595105.

NATURE WALKABOUT. Periodical. AT. English. sa. $1.25. Education Supplies Branch, Department of Education, 23 Miles Road, Kewdale West Australia 6105 Australia. Tel 09/458 5033. LC QH197.

NATUURHISTORISCHE REEKS. VFOAT Natural History Series. No. 1-. Monographic Series. NE. Dutch (English). ir. Secretariat of the Foundation for Scientific Research in Surinam and the Netherlands Antilles, c/o Zoological Laboratory Plompetorengracht 9, Utrecht Holland. Tel (0)30-392478. Ed P Wagenaar Hummelinck, L J v d Steen. LC QH7. Circ 1,000. (ctrl). Publications on natural sciences (in widest sense) of Caribbean region, especially Netherlands Antilles and Surinam.

N.B. NATURALIST. (N. B. NATURALIST). V. 1- Jan. 1970-. 0047-9551. Periodical. CN. English. qt. 10. New Brunswick Federation of Naturalists, 277 Douglas Avenue, St John New Brunswick E2K 1E5 Canada. Tel (506)658-1842. Ed Mary Majka and David Christie. bk rev. adv acc. Circ 500. (ctrl). Natural history of New Brunswick.

NEW ZEALAND JOURNAL OF ECOLOGY. See Biology.

NEWS LETTER OF THE THUNDER BAY FIELD NATURALISTS. Main/Corp Thunder Bay Field Naturalists. Began with Jan. 27, 1947 issue. 0317-3356. CN. English. qt. 10.00.

Natural History

Thunder Bay Field Naturalists, Box 1073, Thunder Bay F Ontario P7C 4X8 Canada. **Tel** (807)577-3297. Ed Bill Addison. **DD** 500.971312. bk rev. **Circ** 250. (ctrl). Newsletter focuses on the natural history of Northwestern Ontario and the protection of the local environment.

NEWSLETTER - ASSOCIATION OF SYSTEMATICS COLLECTIONS. **Main/Corp** Association of Systematics Collections. **VFOAT** ASC Newsletter. V. 1- Summer 1973-. 0147-7889. US. English. bm. $30.00. University of Kansas, Museum of Natural History, Lawrence KS 66045. **Tel** (913)864-5686. Ed George Pisani. bk rev. adv acc. **Circ** 1,700. Covers needs of biological collections including grants, computerization, book reviews, awards, positions available, curatorial methods, pest control, collection research and management.

NEWSLETTER - NEW ZEALAND. NATURE CONSERVATION COUNCIL. **Main/Corp** New Zealand. Nature Conservation Council. No. 1- Oct. 1972-. English. ir. New Zealand Nature Conservation Council, PO Box 5014, Wellington New Zealand. **LC** QH77.N45. **DD** 333.7209931.

NEWSLETTER - PRINCE EDWARD ISLAND NATURAL HISTORY SOCIETY. (NEWSLETTER). No. 18 (Nov. 1976)-. 0713-7559. Periodical. CN. English. mo. Free to Members. Natural History Society of Prince Edward Island, PO Box 2346, Charlottetown Prince Edward Island C1A 7N8 Canada. **DD** 508.717. *Natural History Society of Prince Edward Island Newsletter, 0713-7540.*

NEWSLETTER - SASKATCHEWAN NATURAL HISTORY SOCIETY. **Main/Corp** Saskatchewan Natural History Society. No. 1-62. 0581-8443. Periodical. CN. English. qt. PO Box 1321, S4P 3B8.

NIGERIAN FIELD. (THE NIGERIAN FIELD). V. 1- July 1931-. 0029-0076. Periodical. UK. English. qt. 12. Nigerian Field Society, Mrs H Fell, Limestone House Alma Road, Tideswell Buxton, Derbyshire SK17 8ND England. **Tel** 0298 871 462. **Ind/Abst** MLA Int. Bibliogr. Books Artic. Mod. Lang. Lit., Bibliogr. Index Geol. **LC** QH195.N5. **DD** 574.966. **CODEN** NIFIAC. (cum index). bk rev. adv acc. (ctrl). All topics concerned with Flora, Fauna, topography and culture of Nigeria.

NIHON BENTOSU KENKYUKAI SHI. **VFOAT** Bulletin of Japanese Association of Benthology. No. 21/22- (Aug. 1981)-. Japanese (with summaries in English). sa. $15.00 US Membership. Nihon Bentosu Kenkyukai c/o Kyudai Rinkai Jikkenjo Tomioka Reihoku-Machi Amakusa-Gun, Kumanoto-Ken 863-25 Japan. **LC** QH90.8.B46. *Bentosu Kenkyukai Renrakushi.*

NORTH QUEENSLAND NATURALIST. (THE NORTH QUEENSLAND NATURALIST). V. 1- Oct. 1932-. Periodical. AT. English. ir. $3.69. North Queensland Naturalist, Box 991, PO Cairns, 4870 Queenslands Australia. **Ind/Abst** Bibliogr. Agric.

NORTHERN RESEARCH SURVEY CEASED. Began publication in 1970. Ceased in June 1977. 0319-6682. Periodical. CN. English. qt. $15.00. Arctic Institute of North America, 1020 Pine Avenue West, Montreal Quebec H3A 1A2 Canada. **LC** QH84.1. **DD** 016.9198005.

NORTHWEST DISCOVERY. V. 1- June 1980-. 0272-1570. Periodical. US. English. ir. Northwest Press, 1439 East Prospect Street, Seattle WA 98112. **Ind/Abst** Writ. Am. Hist., GeoRef. **LC** F851. **DD** 979.5005. A scholarly and scientific journal on the history and natural history of Northwest America; includes prime source materials and bibliographic reference citations.

NYMPHAEA. **Main/Corp** Muzeul Tarii Crisurilor. 1- 1973-. 0253-4649. Romanian (with summaries in English, French, or German). ir. Comitetul de Cultura si Educatie Socialista al Judetuliu, Str Stadionului Nr 2, Bihor Romania. **Ind/Abst** GeoRef, Bibliogr. Agric. **LC** QH178.R8.

OBJETS ET MONDES. See Museums.

OCCASIONAL PAPERS - BELL MUSEUM OF NATURAL HISTORY, UNIVERSITY OF MINNESOTA. (OCCASIONAL PAPERS). **Main/Corp** Bell Museum of Natural History. No. 10-. 0097-1677. Monographic Series. US. English. ir. Bell Museum of Natural History, University of Minnesota, Minneapolis MN 55455. **Tel** (612)373-3192. Ed Donald E Gilbertson.

CODEN OPBMB. **Circ** 2,000. Studies on the natural history of animals and plants. *Occasional Papers (University of Minnesota (Minneapolis - St. Paul Campus). Museum of Natural History), 0097-0409.*

OCCASIONAL PAPERS OF BERNICE P. BISHOP MUSEUM. See Museums.

OCCASIONAL PAPERS OF THE BRITISH COLUMBIA PROVINCIAL MUSEUM. See Museums.

OCCASIONAL PAPERS OF THE IDAHO MUSEUM OF NATURAL HISTORY. See Museums.

OCCASIONAL PAPERS OF THE MUSEUM OF NATURAL HISTORY. See Museums.

OCHRONA PRZYRODY. No. 1- 1920-. 0078-3250. Monographic Series. Polish. ir. **Ind/Abst** Biol. Abstr. **LC** QH75. **CODEN** OCPZAE.

OCROTIREA NATURII SI A MEDIULUI INCONJURATOR. **VFOAT** Ocrotirea Mediului Inconjurator, Natura, Terra. V. 19-. Periodical. RM. Romanian (summaries in English, French, or German). sa. Ilexim Press Department, PO Box 1-136-1-137, Bucharest Romania. **Ind/Abst** GeoRef. **LC** QH7. *Ocrotirea Naturii.*

OSPREY. (THE OSPREY). 0710-4847. Periodical. CN. English. ir. Free to Members. Newfoundland Natural History Society, PO Box 1013, Saint John's Newfoundland A1C 5M3 Canada. **DD** 574.09718.

OTTAR. No. 1- June 1954-. 0030-6703. Monographic Series. NO. Norwegian (with some text in Lappish). ir. 10.00. Tromso Museum, Tromso Norway. **Tel** 083/86080. Ed Ivar Bjolklund and Arne C Milssen. **Ind/Abst** GeoRef. **LC** DL401. **CODEN** OTTADD. adv acc. (ctrl). Popular science on cultural and natural history of Northern Norway.

PACIFIC DISCOVERY. V. 1- Jan./Feb. 1948-. 0030-8641. Periodical. US. English. qt. $11.00. California Academy of Science, Golden Gate Park, San Francisco CA 94118. **Tel** (415)668-7379. Ed Sheridan Warrick. **Ind/Abst** Life Sci. Collect., GeoRef, Biol. Abstr., Bibliogr. Agric., Bibliogr. Index Geol. **LC** Q1. **DD** 505. **CODEN** PADIAZ. Discoveries and new understandings in natural history and science research. Mainly in the pacific region.

PAMIATKY, PRIRODA : PP. **VFOAT** PP. Periodical. Slovak. bm. 6.00 Single Issue. Vydavatel Stvo Obzor, 815 85 Bratislava UL CS, Armandy 35 Czechoslovakia.

PEI-CHING TZU JAN PO WU KUAN YEN CHIU PAO KAO. See Museums.

THE PENNSYLVANIA NATURALIST. V. 1- Oct./Nov. 1978-. 0164-7822. Periodical. US. English. bm. $6.50. TPN, Box 47 Huntingdon PA 16652.

PERIPLO. Periodical. SP. Spanish. ir. $26.00. Instituto de la Caza Fotografica y Ciencias de la Naturaleza, Castello 59, Madrid-1 Spain. **LC** QH7.

PICA. V. 1- Fall 1979-. 0225-7114. Periodical. CN. English. qt. Free to Members (Membership, $7.50). Calgary Field Naturalists' Society, PO Box 981, Calgary Alberta T2P 2K4 Canada. **DD** 509.7123. *Calgary Field Naturalist, 0318-8434.*

POSTILLA. No. 1 (Mar. 10, 1950)-. 0079-4295. Monographic Series. US. English. ir. Peabody Museum of Natural History, Yale University, New Haven CT 06520. **Ind/Abst** Life Sci. Collect., GeoRef, Biol. Abstr. **LC** QH1. **DD** 574.05. **CODEN** PSTLAD. (cum index).

PRACE. SERIA B. **Main/Corp** Bydgoskie Towarzystwo Naukowe. Wydzial Nauk Przyrodniczych. 1- 1961-. 0572-5844. Periodical. PL. Polish. ir. ARS Polona, Seria B, Krakowskie Przedmiescie 7, 0068 Warsaw Poland.

PRAIRIE NATURALIST. (THE PRAIRIE NATURALIST). V. 1- March 1968-. 0091-0376. Periodical. US. English. ir. $15.00 Domestic, $18.00 Foreign. North Dakota Natural Science Society, PO Box 8238 University Station, Grand Forks ND 58202-8238. **Tel** (701)777-2199. Ed Paul B Kannowski. **Ind/Abst** Biol. Abstr. **LC** QH540. **DD** 574.9784. **CODEN** PRNTBZ. bk rev. **Circ** 360. (ctrl). Communication of research on grasslands in general and the natural history of the Great Plains region in particular.

PRIRODA I CHELOVEK. Began in 1981. 0203-4867. Periodical. UR. Russian. mo. 0.70 Single Issue. Moskovskoe Otd-Nie Gidrometeoizdata, 107061 Moskva, Buzheninovskaia Ul D 42/1, Moskva Russian SFSR. **LC** QH45.5.

PROCEEDINGS - DORSET NATURAL HISTORY AND ARCHAEOLOGICAL SOCIETY. **Main/Corp** Dorset Natural History and Archaeological Society. V. 1- 1877-. 0070-7112. UK. English. an. **LC** DA670.D69. (cum index).

PROCEEDINGS - ISLE OF MAN NATURAL HISTORY AND ANTIQUARIAN SOCIETY. **Main/Corp** Isle of Man Natural History and Antiquarian Society. V. 1- Aug. 23, 1906-. UK. English. be.

PROCEEDINGS OF THE ACADEMY OF NATURAL SCIENCES OF PHILADELPHIA. **Main/Corp** Academy of Natural Sciences of Philadelphia. V. 1- 1841-. 0097-3157. US. English. an. $26.00. Scientific Publications, Academy of Natural Sciences of Philadelphia, 19th and The Parkway, Philadelphia PA 19103. **Tel** (215)299-1050. Ed K Elaine Hoagland. **Ind/Abst** Life Sci. Collect., GeoRef, Bibliogr. Agric., Biol. Abstr., Chem. Abstr., Nuci. Sci. Abstr., Sel. Water Resour. Abstr. **LC** QH1. **CODEN** PANPA5. (cum index). **Circ** 1,200. Original research articles on evolution, systematics, ecology, biogeography, and natural history.

PROCEEDINGS OF THE LINNEAN SOCIETY OF NEW SOUTH WALES. **Main/Corp** Linnean Society of New South Wales. V. 1- 1875-. 0370-047X. AT. English. qt. 45.00. Linnean Society of New South Wales, 6/24 Cliff Street, PO Box 457, Milsons Point New South Wales 2061 Australia. **Tel** 929 0253. Ed T G Vallance. **Ind/Abst** Life Sci. Collect., Coal Abstr., GeoRef, Biol. Abstr., Chem. Abstr., WRC Inf., Bibliogr. Agric. **CODEN** PLSWAQ. (cum index). Original research in natural history.

PROCEEDINGS OF THE PEORIA ACADEMY OF SCIENCE. Began in 1968. 0079-0745. Periodical. US. English. an. Lakeview Center for the Arts and Sciences, 1125 West Lake Avenue, Peoria IL 61614. **LC** QH105.I3. **DD** 508. **CODEN** PPASDN.

PROCEEDINGS. SECTION B, BIOLOGICAL SCIENCES. **VFOAT** Biological Sciences. Vol. 76, Pts. 1/3-. 0308-2113. Periodical. UK. English. $55.00. Royal Society of Edinburgh, 22 George Street, Edinburgh EH2 2PQ Scotland. **Tel** 225-6057. **Ind/Abst** Life Sci. Collect., Excerpta Med., GeoRef, Biol. Abstr., Chem. Abstr. **LC** Q41. **DD** 574.05. **NLM** W1 PR587PS. **CODEN** PRSSDP. *Proceedings. Section B, Natural Environment, 0308-2113.*

PROCEEDINGS - WILDERNESS CONFERENCE. **Main/Conf** Wilderness Conference. 0511-9456. Monographic Series. US. English. ir. Sierra Club, 530 Bush Street, San Francisco CA 74108. **LC** QH75. **DD** 333.7.

PROGRESS REPORT - ARKANSAS NATURAL HERITAGE COMMISSION. **Main/Corp** Arkansas Natural Heritage Commission. US. English. Arkansas Natural Heritage Commission, Suite 500/Continental Building, Main & Markham, Little Rock AR 72201. **LC** QH76.5.A6. **DD** 333.78209767.

PROTEUS. Letnik 1- 1934-. Periodical. Serbo-Croatian -R. ir. Ed Pavel Groselj. **LC** QH7.

PRZYRODA POLSKA. Began in 1957. 0552-430X. Periodical. PL. Polish (some issues have summaries in English or French). mo. ARS Polona, Krakowskie Przedmiescie 7, 00-068 Warsaw Poland. **Ind/Abst** Energy Res. Abstr. **LC** QH7.

PUBBLICAZIONI. **Main/Corp** Ferrara. Civico Museo di Storia Naturale. 1- 1952-). 0428-2396. Periodical. IT. Italian. ir. Cicico Museo de Storia Naturale, Ferrara Italy 50122.

PUBLICACION EXTRA. **Main/Corp** Museo Argentino de Ciencias Naturales Bernardino Rivadavia. No. 1- 1925-. Periodical. Spanish. ir.

PUBLICATION - NATURAL HISTORY RESEARCH CENTER. **Main/Corp** Jamiat Baghdad. Markaz Buhuth Al-Tarikh Al-Tabii. **VFOAT** Nashrah - Markaz Buhuth Al-Tarikh Al-Tabii. English (Arabic, German, and Latin). ir. **LC** QH1. **DD** 500.908. *Publication.*

QUADERNI DEL MUSEO DI STORIA NATURALE DI LIVORNO (1982). See Museums.

Natural History

QUARTERLY JOURNAL OF THE TAIWAN MUSEUM. See Museums.

QUEENSLAND NATURALIST. V. 1- Mar. 31, 1908-. 0079-8843. Periodical. AT. English. ir. Queensland Naturalists Club, c/o Librarian, GPO Box 1220, Brisbane Queensland 4001 Australia. Ed J Cribb. Ind/Abst GeoRef, Biol. Abstr., Bibliogr. Agric. CODEN QLNAAE. Circ 450. Reports on the activities of the Queensland Naturalists Club and the scientific findings of these natural history activities.

RANGER RICK. Vol. 17, No. 1 (Jan. 1983)-. 0738-6656. Periodical. US. English. mo. $10.50 Domestic, $14.50 Foreign. National Wildlife Federation, 8925 Leesburg Pike, Vienna VA 22184. Ind/Abst Child. Mag. Guide. LC QH48. DD 591.05. Ranger Rick's Nature Magazine, 0033-9229.

RANGER RICK'S NATURE MAGAZINE. V. 1- Jan. 1967-. 0033-9229. Periodical. US. English. mo. National Wildlife Federation, 1412 16th Street Northwest, Washington DC 20036. Tel (202)797-6850. Ind/Abst Child. Mag. Guide. LC QH48. DD 508.

RECENT PUBLICATIONS IN NATURAL HISTORY. VFOAT R.P.I.N.H. Vol. 1, No. 1 (Mar. 1983)-. 0738-0925. Periodical. US. English. qt. $10.00 US and Canada, $13.00 Foreign. American Museum of Natural History, Central Park West at 79th Street, New York NY 10024. Tel (212)873-1300. Ed Bryan R Johnson. bk rev. Circ 500. Bibliographies and reviews of recent books in the natural sciences (including astronomy and anthropology), classified into 25 subject headings with cross-reference. Curator, 0011-3069.

RECORDS OF THE WESTERN AUSTRALIAN MUSEUM. See Museums.

RELATORIO - FUNDACAO ZOOBOTANICA DO RIO GRANDE DO SUL. Main/Corp Fundacao Zoobotanica do Rio Grande do Sul. Portuguese. ir. Rua Cel Vicente 281 - 60. Andar 90.000, Porto Alegre Brazil. LC QH117.

REPORT ON THE BRITISH MUSEUM (NATURAL HISTORY). See Museums.

RESEARCH REPORT (UNIVERSITY OF NORTH DAKOTA. INSTITUTE FOR ECOLOGICAL STUDIES). (RESEARCH REPORT). Monographic Series. US. English.

REVISTA DE LA SOCIEDAD BOLIVIANA DE HISTORIA NATURAL. Main/Corp Sociedad Boliviana de Historia Natural. Yearly V. 1- Feb. 1974-. Spanish (some summaries in English). ir. Sociedad Boliviana de Historia Natural, Casilla de Correo 538, Cochabamba Bolivia. LC QH115.

SALIT. 1- January 1973-. Periodical. IS. Hebrew. ir. 100.00. Hevrah La-Haganat Ha-Teva Rehov Ha-Shefelah 4, Tel-Aviv Israel. LC QH77.I7.

SANCTUARY. V. 20- Aug./Sept. 1980-. 0272-8966. Periodical. US. English. mo. $20.00 Family, $15.00 Individual. Massachusetts Audubon Society, Lincoln MA 01773. LC QH76.5.N45. DD 333.73005.

SAVON LUONTO. Periodical. Finnish (summaries in English, German). ir. 15. Kupion Luonnun Ystavain Yhdistys, Kupion Museo Luonnontiereen Osato, Kauppak 23, 70100 Kuopio 10 Finland. LC QH178.F5.

SBORNIK NARODNIHO MUZEA V PRAZE. RADA B. PRIRODNI VEDY. (SBORNIK NARODNIHO MUZEA V PRAZE. RADA B : PRIRODOVEDECKA). Main/Corp Narodni Muzeum v Praze. VFOAT Acta Musei Nationalis Pragae. Ser. B : Historia Naturalis. V. 1- 1938-. 0036-5343. Periodical. CS. Czech (English, German, Latin, or Russian). ir. Artia, PO Box 790, Praha 1 Czechoslovakia. Ind/Abst Bibliogr. Agric., Biol. Abstr. LC QH7. DD 574.05. CODEN SNMPAM.

SCHRIFTENREIHE. BEIHEFT - INSTITUT FUR NATURSCHUTZ. Main/Corp Institut fur Naturschutz. Monographic Series. German. ir.

SCIENCE SERIES. No. 1- Apr. 1930-. 0076-0943. Periodical. US. English. ir. Natural History Museum, 900 Exposition Boulevard, Los Angeles CA 90007. Ind/Abst GeoRef.

SCIENTIFIC REVIEWS ON ARID ZONE RESEARCH. Vol. 1 (1982)-. II. English. an. $60.00. Scientific Publishers, Maan Bhawan Ratanada Road, Jodhpur 342 001 India. LC QH541.5.A74. DD 551.4.

SEASONS. V. 20, No. 1- Spring 1980-. 0227-793X. Periodical. CN. English. qt. $17.00 Per Year Membership for Individuals and Libraries. Federation of Ontario Naturalists, 355 Lesmill Road, Don Mills Ontario M3B 2W8 Canada. Ind/Abst Can. Environ., Can. Period. Index, Energy Inf. Abstr., Environ. Abstr. DD 574.9713. Ontario Naturalist, 0030-3046.

SENCKENBERGIANA BIOLOGICA. See Biology.

SHIZENSHI KENKYU = OCCASIONAL PAPERS FROM THE OSAKA MUSEUM OF NATURAL HISTORY. See Museums.

SITZUNGS-BERICHTE DER GESELLSCHAFT NATURFORSCHENDER FREUNDE ZU BERLIN. Main/Corp Gesellschaft Naturforschender Gesellschaft Naturforschender Freunde (Berlin, Germany) Freunde. 1839-1942. 0433-8731. Periodical. GW. German. sa. Duncker and Humblot, Dietrich Schaeffer Weg 9, 1 Berlin 41 West Germany. LC QH5.

SKENECTADA. V. 1 (1979)-. 0270-2614. Periodical. US. English. sa. $50.00. Skenectada, PO Box 22820, 1400 Washington A, Albany NY 12222. Tel (518)869-1969. Ind/Abst Biol. Abstr. LC QH105.N7. DD 508.74742. CODEN SKNCD4.

SMITHERSIA. No. 1 (Feb. 1983)-. 0250-300X. Periodical. English. ir. Tel 60045. Ind/Abst Life Sci. Collect. Circ 400. (ctrl). Long papers (theses, surveys, etc.), discussing scientific research in the natural science disciplines in Southern Africa. Occasional Papers of the National Museums and Monuments. Series B. Natural Sciences, 0253-1070.

SNOOP. VFOAT Snoop Teacher's Guide. 0712-5410. Periodical. CN. English. ir. Free in Saskatchewan, $14.60 Other Provinces. Snoop, c/o L A Weigl Educational Associates, 2114 College Avenue, Regina Saskatchewan S4P 1C5 Canada. DD 505.

SNOWY EGRET. V. 15- Spring 1941-. 0037-7473. Periodical. US. English. sa. $5.00. Snowy Egret, 205 South 9th Street, Williamsburg KY 40769. Tel (606)549-0850. Ed Humphrey A Olsen. bk rev. Circ 400. Explores literary, artistic, history, philosophic aspects of natural history. Fresh nature essays, poetry, fiction and reviews. Unique outdoor flavor. Animal World.

SOUTH AUSTRALIAN NATURALIST. 1919. 0038-2965. Periodical. AT. English. qt. $7.38. Field Naturalist Society of South Australia Inc, Box 1594 M, Government Printing Office, Adelaide South Australia. Ed Russell Cook. Ind/Abst Biol. Abstr., Bibliogr. Agric. LC QH1. CODEN SANAAR. Circ 500. Natural history.

SOUTH YORKSHIRE. 1- 1974-. UK. English. Doncaster Museum and Art Gallery, Curator, Doncaster England. LC DA670.Y59. DD 914.274008.

THE SOUTHWESTERN NATURALIST. V. 1- Jan. 1956-. 0038-4909. Periodical. US. English (Spanish). qt. $30.00. Texas A & M University, Department of Wildlife, c/o D Fred Hendricks, College Station TX 77843. Tel (409)845-5704. Ed Francis Rose. Ind/Abst Life Sci. Collect., GeoRef, Ref. Source, Biol. Abstr., Nuci. Sci. Abstr., Sel. Water Resour. Abstr., Bibliogr. Agric., Sci. Cit. Index, Abr. Ed., Bibliogr. Index Geol., Biol. Abstr. LC QH1. CODEN SWNAAB. (cum index). bk rev. Circ 1,400. (ctrl). Field studies of plants and animals, living and fossil, in the Southwestern United States, Mexico and Central America.

SPECIAL PUBLICATION (CARNEGIE MUSEUM OF NATURAL HISTORY). (SPECIAL PUBLICATION - CARNEGIE MUSEUM OF NATURAL HISTORY). No. 1-. 0145-9031. Monographic Series. US. English. Carnegie Museum of Natural History, 4400 Forbes Avenue, Pittsburgh PA 15213. Ind/Abst Biol. Abstr. LC UNC. CODEN SPCHDX.

SPECIAL PUBLICATION - SASKATCHEWAN NATURAL HISTORY SOCIETY. Main/Corp Saskatchewan Natural History Society. V. 1- 1958-. 0080-6552. Monographic Series. CN. English. ir. Saskatchewan Natural History Society, PO Box 1784, Saskatoon Saskatchewan S7K 351 Canada. DD 574, 574.9.

STUDIES IN NATURAL SCIENCES. V. 1-. 0097-4412. Monographic Series. US. English. ir. Eastern New Mexico University, Museum of Natural Science, Portales NM 88130. Ind/Abst Biol. Abstr., Chem. Abstr. LC QH1. DD 500.905. CODEN SNTSBX.

TANE. Began in 1950. 0496-8026. English. ir. 13.00. Auckland University Field Club, c/o Botany Department, University of Auckland, Private Bag, Auckland New Zealand. Tel 544-136. Ed Michael C Morris. Ind/Abst Life Sci. Collect., GeoRef. LC QH197.5. DD 500.9931. Circ 500. Natural history of Northern New Zealand expecially offshore islands.

TEBIWA (1982). (TEBIWA). Vol. 19 (1982)-. 0040-0823. US. English. an. $6.00. Idaho Museum of Natural History, Campus Box 8096, Idaho State University, Pocatello ID 83209. Tel (208)236-3882. Ed Barry Keller. bk rev. adv acc. Circ 1,000. An intermountain natural history journal. Tebiwa (1976).

TECHNICAL REPORT - STANFORD UNIVERSITY, NATURAL HISTORY MUSEUM. Main/Corp Stanford University. Natural History Museum. Monographic Series. US. English. ir.

TERRA. V. 9, No. 2- Fall 1970-. Periodical. US. English. bm. $12.00. Natural History Museum, 900 Exposition Boulevard, Los Angeles CA 90007. Tel (213)744-3330. Ed Robin A Simpson. Ind/Abst GeoRef, Bibliogr. Index Geol., Abstr. Anthropol. CODEN TRRAB8. bk rev. adv acc. Circ 14,000. (ctrl). Articles on natural history, anthropology, and history for a general audience. Sent as a benefit of membership in Natural History Museum of Los Angeles County. Quarterly.

TEXAS NATURAL HISTORY. Vol. 1, No. 1 (Spring 1985)-. 0882-5335. Periodical. US. English. qt. $12.74 Domestic, $16.98 Foreign. Texas Natural History, PO Box 226585, Dallas TX 75222-6585. DD 508.

TRAIL & LANDSCAPE. V. 1- Mar./Apr. 1967-. 0041-0748. Periodical. CN. English. ir. $13.16. Ottawa Field Naturalists Club, Box 3264 Postal Station C, Ottawa Ontario K1Y 4J5 Canada. Tel (613)996-1665. Ed J Reddoch. Circ 1,200. (ctrl). Local Ottawa natural history.

TRANSACTIONS OF THE NATURAL HISTORY SOCIETY OF NORTHUMBRIA. V. 42, No. 2- Nov. 1974-. 0144-221X. UK. English. ir. Natural History Society of Northumbria, Hancock Museum Newcastle on Tune New England. Ind/Abst Life Sci. Collect., Biol. Abstr., GeoRef, Chem. Abstr. CODEN TNHND5. Transactions.

TRANSACTIONS OF THE SAN DIEGO SOCIETY OF NATURAL HISTORY. VFOAT Transactions of San Diego Society of Natural History. Vol. 1, No. 1-. 0080-5947. Monographic Series. US. English. ir. San Diego Society Natural History, Box 1390, San Diego CA 92112. Tel (619)232-3821. Ed Gregory Pregill. Ind/Abst GeoRef, Bibliogr. Agric., Biol. Abstr. LC QH1. DD 574.05. CODEN TSDSAW. Circ 3,500. Original research in taxonomy and systematics; in paleontology, malacology, ornithology, mammalogy, entomology, botany and herpetology.

TRAVAUX DES CAMPEUSES D'ETE AU CAMP ROLLAND-GERMAIN. (TRAVAUX DES CAMPEUSES DE L'ETE AU CAMP ROLLAND-GERMAIN). Main/Corp Camp Rolland-Germain. 1976-. 0704-1993. CN. French. an. Camp Rolland-Germain, Frelighsburg Quebec J0J 1C0 Canada. DD 500.9'714'62. Rapports des Campeuses, 0704-1977.

TRAVAUX SCIENTIFIQUES DU PARC NATIONAL DE LA VANOISE. Main/Corp France. Directin Generale de la Protection de la Nature. Series/Titl Cahiers du Parc National de la Vanoise. Vol. 1- 1970-. 0180-961X. French (summaries in English, German and Italian). ir. Director Generale de la Protection de la Nature, 15 rue du Docteur-Juliand, Chambery France 73000. Ind/Abst Life Sci. Collect. LC QH147. DD 500.94448.

VERHANDLUNGEN DES NATURWISSENSCHAFTLICHEN VEREINS IN HAMBURG (1979). (VERHANDLUNGEN DES NATURWISSENSCHAFTLICHEN VEREINS IN HAMBURG). No. 23 (1979)-. 0173-749X. GE. German (summaries in English). ir. Verlag Paul Parey, Spitalerstrasse 12, D-2000 Hamburg 1 West Germany. Abhandlungen und Verhandlungen des Naturwissenschaftlichen Verins in Hamburg, 0301-2697.

VERMONT NATURAL HISTORY. June 1973-. 0270-5982. US. English. an. Vermont Institute of Natural Science, Woodstock VT 05091.

VICTORIA NATURALIST. (THE VICTORIA NATURALIST). V. 1- 1944-. 0049-612X. Periodical. CN. English. bm. Victoria Natural History Society, PO

Naval Science, Navigation

Box 1747, Victoria British Columbia V8W 2Y1 Canada. Ed Roy Prior. bk rev. Circ 500. (ctrl). Newsletter for members. Articles on local plants, birds and field trips. Lists of first sightings of birds for seasons in the area. Also lists of field trips in the area. Includes reports and special articles.

VICTORIAN NATURALIST. (THE VICTORIAN NATURALIST). V. 1- Jan. 1884-. 0042-5184. Periodical. AT. English. bm. 25.00. Field Naturalist Club of Victoria National Herbarium/S Yarra, 3141 Victoria Australia. Ind/Abst MLA Int. Bibliogr. Books Artic. Mod. Lang. Lit., GeoRef, Bibliogr. Agric., Bibliogr. Index Geol. LC QH1. DD 508.94. CODEN VICNAW. Circ 900. Club news and scientific articles on natural history.

VIDENSKABELIGE MEDDELELSER FRA DANSK NATURHISTORISK FORENING. Main/Corp Dansk Naturhistorisk Forening. Vol. 130- 1967-. 0373-3874. DK. English, French, and German (introduction in Danish). an. 350. Dansk Naturhistorisk Forening, Universitetsparken 15, DK 2100 Copenhagen 0 Denmark. Tel 45-0135411. Ed Ole Tendal. Ind/Abst Biol. Abstr., Bibliogr. Agric., Life Sci. Collect. CODEN VMDFA7. Circ 1,000. All aspects of zoology. Videnskabelige Meddelelser Fra Dansk Naturhistorisk Forening I Kbenhavn.

VIVA ORIGINO. Periodical. Japanese (with some abstracts in English). ir. Seimei No Kigen Oyobi Shinka Gakkai c/o Kyoto Daigaku Genshiro Jikkenjo Noda, Kumatori-cho Sennan-Gun, Osaka-fu 590-04 Japan. LC QH325. DD 577.05.

VOPROSY GEOGRAFII TURKMENISTANA. VFOAT Turkmenistanyng Geografiiasyng Meseleleri. Periodical. UR. Russian. 1.15 Single Issue. Izd-Bo Ylym, Ul Engelsa 6, Ashkhabad Russian SFSR. LC QH191.

WILTSHIRE ARCHAEOLOGICAL AND NATURAL HISTORY MAGAZINE (1982). See Archaeology.

YELLOWSTONE INTERPRETIVE SERIES. No. 1- 1976-. 0512-7696. Monographic Series. US. English. LC F722. DD 574.

ZAPOVEDNIKI BELORUSSII. Began in 1977. 0136-7595. Periodical. UR. Russian. 0.80. LC QH77.S626. DD 914.765.

ZBORNIK VYCHODOSLOVENSKEHO MUZEA V KOSICIACH. PRIRODNE VEDY. VFOAT Prirodne Vedy, Acta Musei Slovaciae Regionis Orientalis Kosice. 20 (1979)-. Periodical. Slovak (with summaries in German and Russian). an. 15.00. LC QH178.C8. DD 508.437305. Zbornik Vychodoslovenskeho Muzea V Kosiciach. Seria AB, Prirodne Vedy.

ZESZYTY NAUKOWE WYDZIAU BIOLOGII I NAUK O ZIEMI. BIOLOGIA. Main/Corp Uniwersytet Gdanski. Wydzia Biologii I Nauk O Ziemi. No. 1-. Periodical. English (Polish or Russian). ir. 20.00. LC QH301. DD 574.

NAVAL SCIENCE, NAVIGATION

100 A1. VAT One Hundred A One. No. 1- June 1958-. 0266-8971. Periodical. UK. English. qt. Lloyd's Register of Shipping, 71 Fenchurch Street, London EC3M 4BS England. Ind/Abst Met. Abstr., World Alum. Abstr. LC VM1.

ACCESS (WASHINGTON, D.C. : 1978. (ACCESS : THE NAVY DATA AUTOMATION REVIEW). Vol. 1, No. 1 (Sept/Oct 1978)-. Periodical. US. English. bm. Naval Data Automation Command Building, 166 Washington Navy Yard, Washington DC 20374.

ACTES - COLLOQUE INTERNATIONAL D'HISTOIRE MARITIME. Main/Conf Colloque International d'Histoire Maritime. VFOAT Navire et l'Economie Maritime. 1st- 1956-. 0531-0067. Periodical. FR. French. ir. 1 rue des Fosses St Jacques, 75005 Paris France.

ADMIRALTY LIST OF RADIO SIGNALS DIAGRAMS RELATING TO RADIOBEACONS. English. an. LC VK397. DD 623.8932.

ADMIRALTY SCIENCE PUBLICATION. Main/Corp Great Britain. Hydrographic Dept. (1-1963)-. 0436-4309. UK. English. ir. Her Majestys Stationery Office, PO Box 276, London SW8 5DT England.

AIDS TO NAVIGATION BULLETIN. Periodical. US. English. qt. US Coast Guard Headquarters, Washington DC 20593.

ALL HANDS. Publication began in 1922?. 0002-5577. Periodical. US. English. mo. $19.00 Domestic, $23.75 Foreign. Navy Internal Relations, c/o Activity Office of the Chief of Information, District Branch/Room 2E329 Pentagon, Washington DC 20350. LC VA52. DD 359.

ALLE HENS. 0002-5674. NE. Dutch. mo. 18.50 Domestic, 28.50 Foreign. Alle Hens, Lange Voorhout 7, The Hague Netherlands. Tel (070)721876. Ed J L van Zwet. Ind/Abst Ship Abstr. LC VA530. bk rev. adv acc. Circ 28,000. Material and personnel matters in relation with the Royal Netherlands Navy and naval allies and developments in the widest sense in this field.

THE ALMANAC OF SEAPOWER. See Yearbooks, Almanacs, Directories.

ALMANACCO NAVALE. See Yearbooks, Almanacs, Directories.

THE AMERICAN MARINE ENGINEER. V. 1- Jan. 1906-. 0002-9866. Periodical. US. English. mo. LC VM1. DD 387.5.

THE AMERICAN MARITIME LIBRARY. See Library and Information Science.

THE AMERICAN NEPTUNE. V. 1- Jan. 1941-. 0003-0155. Periodical. US. English. qt. $32.00. Peabody Museum, East India Marine Hall, Salem MA 01970. Tel (617)745-7119. Ed Archibald Lewis. Ind/Abst Twent. Century Lit., Hist. Abstr., Recent Publ. Artic., Writ. Am. Hist., Am. Hist. Life, Hist. Abstr., Part A, Mod. Hist. Abstr., Hist. Abstr., Part B, Twent. Century Abstr. LC V1. DD 387.05. (cum index). bk rev. adv acc. Circ 900. Maritime history and marine art.

ANAIS HIDROGRAFICOS. Main/Corp Brazil. Diretoria de Hidrografia e Navegacao. BL. Portuguese. ir. Diretoria de Hidrografia, e Navegacao, Ilha Fiscal Rio de Janeiro Brazil. LC VK597.B8. Circ 1,300. (ctrl). Evolution of the techniques and preservation of the directorate's memory. Anais Hidrograficos.

ANCIENT INTERFACE. (THE ANCIENT INTERFACE). Main/Conf AIAA Symposium on the Aero/Hydronautics of Sailing. VFOAT Sailing Hydronautics. 1- 1969-. 0097-8442. US. English. an. Western Periodicals, 13000 Raymer Street, North Hollywood CA 91605. Tel (213)875-0555. LC VM351. DD 623.822. Boat design-aerodynamics of sailing vessels.

ANGELIAI TOIS NAUTILLOMENOIS. Greek, Modern. ir. Archigeion Nautikou Hydrographike Hyperesia Bst 902, Athenai Greece. LC VK866.

ANNAPOLIS, THE UNITED STATES NAVAL ACADEMY CATALOG CEASED. Main/Corp United States Naval Academy. VFOAT United States Naval Academy Catalog. Ceased with 1983-1984. US. English. an. United States Naval Academy, Annapolis MD 21402. United States Naval Academy Catalog.

ANNUAIRE DES MAREES. See Yearbooks, Almanacs, Directories.

ANNUAL EDITION : NOTICES TO MARINERS. Main/Corp Canada. Coast Guard. Aids and Waterways Branch. VFOAT Notices to Mariners. 1977-. CN. English. an. Minister of Supply & Services Canada, 88 Metcalfe Street/5th Floor, Ottawa Ontario K1A 0S9 Canada. LC VK798. DD 387.1. Annual Edition: Notices to Mariners.

ANNUAL OF THE CHINESE SOCIETY OF NAVAL ARCHITECTURE AND MARINE ENGINEERING. Main/Corp Chung-Kuo Tsao Chuan Kung Cheng Hsueh Hui (China). Vol. 1 (1982)-. English. an. China Academic Publishers, 137 Chaonei Street, Bejing China. LC VM1. DD 623.805.

ANNUAL REPORT - GEORGETOWN SHIPYARD INC. (ANNUAL REPORT). Main/Corp Georgetown Shipyard Inc. (P.E.I.). 0704-8343. CN. English. an. P E I Georgetown Shipyard Inc, Post Office Box 220, Georgetown Prince Edward Island Canada. LC VM301.G44. DD 338.762383097177.

ANNUAL REPORT - MYSTIC SEAPORT MUSEUM. Main/Corp Mystic Seaport Museum. US. English. an. Mystic Seaport Museum Inc, Mystic CT 06355. LC V13.U6. DD 623.807401465.

ANNUAL REPORT - ROYAL INSTITUTE OF NAVIGATION (GREAT BRITAIN). Main/Corp Royal Institute of Navigation (Great Britain). UK. English. an. c/o Royal Geographical Society, 1 Kensington Gore, London SW7 2AT England. LC VK555. DD 629.04506041.

ANNUAL SUMMARY OF AUSTRALIAN NOTICES TO MARINERS. Main/Corp Australia. Dept. of the Navy. 0312-6056. AT. English. ir. Royal Australian Navy, PO Box 706, Darlinghurst 2010 Australia. LC VK927. DD 623.8905.

ANNUAL SUMMARY OF AUSTRALIAN NOTICES TO MARINERS IN FORCE ON 1ST JANUARY . . . . Main/Corp Australia. Hydrographic Service. 0727-2405. English. an. LC VK927. DD 523.8905.

ANNUAL SUMMARY OF NOTICES TO MARINERS. Main/Corp Israel. Agaf Ha-Sapanut Veha-Nemalim. 0304-8462. IS. English. ir. Ministry of Transport, PO Box 1860, Haifa Israel. LC VK798. DD 354.5694008775.

EL ANO DE LA NAUTICA. No. 1- 1976/77-. Spanish. ir. 1.500. Edisport, Issac Peral 12, Madrid Spain. LC VK4.

ANUARIO MARITIMO ESPANOL. See Yearbooks, Almanacs, Directories.

APPROACH (NORFOLK, VA.). (APPROACH). Vol. 1, No. 1 (July 1955)-. 0570-4979. Periodical. US. English. mo. Superintendent of Documents, US Government Printing Office, Washington DC 20402. Tel (202)783-3238. Ind/Abst Int. Aerosp. Abstr., Index U.S. Gov. Period. LC VG93. DD 629.13255, 629.126. United States Naval Aviation Safety Bulletin.

ARCTIC PILOT. Main/Corp Great Britain. Hydrographic Dept. Monographic Series. UK. English. LC VK807. DD 656, 623.892.

ASTROLABE (NAVY LEAGUE OF CANADA). (ASTROLABE). 0229-4451. Periodical. CN. English. qt. Free. Astrolabe, Navy League of Canada, 4 Queen Elizabeth Drive, Ottawa Ontario K2P 2H9 Canada. DD 359.2232. (ctrl).

ATTI DELL'ISTITUTO ITALIANO DI NAVIGAZIONE. Main/Corp Istituto Italiano di Navigazione. Periodical. IT. Italian. ir. Istituto Italiano di Navigazione, Piazza Cavour 25, Roma 00193 Italy. Ind/Abst Int. Aerosp. Abstr. LC VK4.

AUDIT REPORT. FLEET ADMIRAL CHESTER W. NIMITZ MEMORIAL NAVAL MUSEUM COMMISSION. VFOAT Fleet Admiral Chester W. Nimitz Memorial Naval Museum Commission. US. English. State Auditor/John H Reagan State Office Building, PO Box 12067, Austin TX 78711. LC V13.U6. DD 359.0074016465.

AVIS AUX NAVIGATEURS. Main/Corp France. Service Hydrographique et Oceanographique de la Marine. 10 July. 1971-. Periodical. French. ir. 13 rue de l'Universite, 7E Arr Paris France. LC VK798. DD 623.89205. Avis Aux Navigateurs.

AVIS AUX NAVIGATEURS. Main/Corp Canada. Garde Cotiere. Direction des Aides et des Voies Navigables. V. 1- Jan. 2, 1976-. 0700-1827. Periodical. CN. French. wk. Receiver General for Canada, Supply & Services, Ottawa Ontario K1A 0S9 Canada. Avis aux Navigateurs, 0700-1835.

AVISO AOS NAVEGANTES. RELACAO DAS CARTAS NAUTICAS COM AS CORRECOES. Main/Corp Brazil. Diretoria de Hidrografia E Navegacao. Portuguese. ir. LC Z6026.H9, GA351.

AVISOS A LOS NAVEGANTES. Main/Corp Uruguay. Servicio de Oceanografia e Hidrografia. April 1974-. Spanish. ir. Servicio de Oceanografia E Hidrografia, Capurro 980, Casilla de Correo No 1381, Montevideo Uruguay. LC VK798. Avisos a Los Navegantes.

AVISOS A LOS NAVEGANTES. Main/Corp Uruguay. Servicio de Oceanografia, Hidrografia y Meteorologia. Periodical. Spanish. ir. Capurro 980, Montevideo Uruguay. LC VK798. Avisos a los Navegantes.

THE BLUEJACKETS' MANUAL. 1st- Ed., 1902-. US. English. ir. Naval Institute Press, Annalpolis MD 21402. Tel (301)268-6110. LC V113. DD 359.

BOLETIN DEL CENTRO NAVAL. Main/Corp Argentine Republic. Ministerio de Marina. 1-1882-. Periodical. AG. Spanish. qt. Centro Naval

Naval Science, Navigation

Florida, 801 Av Cordoba 354, 1054 Buenos Aires Argentina.

BULLETIN DE L'ASSOCIATION TECHNIQUE MARITIME ET AERONAUTIQUE. Began with V. 25, 1914. 0066-9814. FR. French. an. 480. Association Technique Maritime Aeronautique, 47 rue du Monceau, 75008 Paris France. Tel (1)45 61 99 11. Ind/Abst Eng. Index Annu., Eng. Index Mon., Eng. Index Bioeng. Abstr., Eng. Index Energy Abstr., Int. Aerosp. Abstr. CODEN BATMA8. Circ 500. Publishes technical papers and corresponding discussions of the members annual meetings. *Bulletin.*

BULLETIN (INTERNATIONAL ASSOCIATION OF LIGHTHOUSE AUTHORITIES). (BULLETIN). VFOAT Bulletin de l'AISM. 1958. 0379-2811. FR. English (French). qt. Association Internationale Signalisation Maritime, 13 rue y Villarceau, 75116 Paris France. Tel 33(1)500 38 60. Ed Strahan Soames. Ind/Abst Ship Abstr. LC VK1000. DD 387.155. bk rev. Circ 600. (ctrl) Various techniques related to aids to marine navigation (visual, audible, radio), their powering and maintenance. *AISM-IALA.*

BULLETIN OFFICIEL DES ARMEES : EDITION CHRONOLOGIQUE. MARINE NATIONALE : PARTIE TECHNIQUE. Main/Corp France. Ministere de la Defense. Periodical. FR. French. ir. Ministere de la Defense, Impr Nationale, Paris France. LC V2. DD 623.805. *Bulletin Officiel des Armees: Edition Chronologique. Marine Nationale: Partie Technique.*

THE BULLETIN - U.S. COAST GUARD ACADEMY ALUMNI ASSOCIATION. (BULLETIN - U.S. COAST GUARD ACADEMY ALUMNI ASSOCIATION). Main/Corp United States. Coast Guard Academy, New London, Conn. Alumni Association. VAT Bulletin - United States Coast Guard Academy Alumni Association. 0191-9814. Periodical. US. English. bm. $181.00. U S Coast Guard Academy, Alumni Association, PO Box 31A-A, New London CT 06320. LC V437. DD 359.9707117456. *Alumni Bulletin, 0094-744X.*

BUNDESMARINE. Periodical. German. ir. 24.00. Bundesministerium der Verteidigung, 1 Postfach 161, 53 Bonn 1 West Germany. LC V3.

CAMPUS (PENSACOLA, FLA.) CEASED. (CAMPUS). Ceased with Jan. 1983 issue?. 0096-1361. Periodical. US. English. mo. Superintendent of Documents, US Government Printing Office, Washington DC 20402. LC V411. DD 359.50973.

CANADIAN TIDE AND CURRENT TABLES. ATLANTIC COAST. VFOAT Tables des Marees et Courants du Canada. Cote Atlantique. 0576-2103. CN. English (text also in French). an. LC VK785. DD 623.89490971.

CANADIAN TIDE AND CURRENT TABLES. PACIFIC COAST. VFOAT Tables des Marees et Courants du Canada. 0576-2243. CN. English. $2.10. Canadian Government Publishing Centre, Supply and Services Canada, Hull Quebec K1A 0S9 Canada. LC VK745. DD 623.894909711.

CARGOWORLD. 0172-9314. Periodical. English. mo $67.75. Broecker Verlag, Celsiusweg 15, Postfach 1347, D2000 Hamburg 50 Altona West Germany. Ind/Abst Ship Abstr. LC VM1. DD 623.82405. *New Ships.*

CATALOGUE : PUBLICATIONS OF THE INTERNATIONAL MARITIME ORGANIZATION. Main/Corp International Maritime Organization. UK. English. Secretariat of The International Maritime Organization, Publications Section, 101-194 Piccadilly London W1V 0AE England. LC Z6839.S2, VK200. DD 016.6238884.

CHART-KIT. REGION 1. PORTSMOUTH, N.H. TO CANADIAN BORDER. (CHART-KIT. REGION 1 : PORTSMOUTH, N.H. TO CANADIAN BORDER). Main/Corp Better Boating Association. VAT Chart-Kit. Region One. Portsmouth, New Hampshire to Canadian Border. 0147-6319. US. English. an. $14.95. Better Boating Association, Box 407, Needham MA 02192.

CHART-KIT. REGION 2. BLOCK ISLAND, R.I. TO PORTSMOUTH, N.H. (CHART-KIT. REGION 2 : BLOCK ISLAND, R. I. TO PORTSMOUTH, N.H). 0147-6327. US. English. an. $14.95. Better Boating Association, Box 407, Needham MA 02192. LC G1211.P5. DD 623.892.

CHART-KIT. REGION 7 : FLORIDA, EAST COAST AND THE KEYS. Main/Corp Better Boating Association. VAT Chart-Kit. Region Seven: Florida, East Coast and the Keys. V. 1- 1978-. 0162-9204. US. English. an. $16.95. Better Boating Association, Box 407, Needham MA 02192. LC G1356.P5. DD 623.89209759.

CHART KIT. VIRGIN ISLANDS. (CHART KIT, THE VIRGIN ISLANDS). Main/Corp Better Boating Association. 0271-5066. US. English. Better Boating Association, Box 407, Needham MA 02192. LC G1641.P5. DD 623.8920972972.

CHOSA KENKYU JIHO - KOKAI KUNRENJO. Main/Corp Kokai Kunrenjo. VFOAT Journal of the Institute for Sea Training. Periodical. JA. Japanese (some summaries in English). ir. Kokai Kunrenjo, 1-3 Kasumigaseki 2-Chome Chiyoda-ku, Tokyo 100 Japan. LC VK4.

CHOSON CHARYOJIP. VFOAT Shipbuilding Data Bank. English (Korean). ir. Hanguk Choson Kongop Hyophoe, 15-5 Chong-Dong, Chung-Ku Seoul Korea. LC VM299.7.K6.

CHOSON KONGOP HYOPHOE PO. VFOAT Shipbuilding News Service. Periodical. KO. Korean. mo. Hanguk Choson Kongop Hyophoe, 15-5 Chong-Dong, Chung-Ku Seoul Korea. LC VM298.5.

CHUAN PO KUNG CHENG. VFOAT Chuanbo Gongcheng. Periodical. CH. Chinese. bm. Chung-Kuo Kuo Chi Shu Tien, PO Box 2820, Peking China. Tel 281030. Ed Zhu Song. Ind/Abst Ship Abstr. LC VM4. DD 623.805. adv acc. Circ 11,000. The official journal of the Chinese Society of Naval Architecture and Marine Engineering.

CHUNG CHUAN CHI KAN. CH. Chinese. qt. Chung Chuan Chi Kan She, 20 Pa Te Road 3 Section, Taipei Taiwan. LC VM4. *Tai Chuan Chi Kan.*

CIS NEWSLETTER. (C I S NEWSLETTER). Main/Corp Canadian Institute of Surveying. VAT Canadian Institute of Surveying Newsletter. V. 1- Feb. 1977-. 0703-5853. Periodical. CN. English (includes some text in French). ir. Canadian Institute of Surveying, Box 5378 Station F, Ottawa Ontario K2C 3C1 Canada. DD 526.906271.

THE COAST GUARD RESERVIST. CEASED. -Nov.-Dec. 1981. 0364-104X. Periodical. US. English. bm. Commandant, US Coast Guard Headquarters, G-R-1, Washington DC 20593.

COASTGUARD. Periodical. UK. English. ir. Department of Transport, Room 513, 17A-2 Marsman Street, London SW7P 3EB England. Tel 01-212 8077. Ed Geoffrey Pallet. bk rev. adv acc. Circ 15,000. (ctrl) Sea safety and marine.

CODE OF FEDERAL REGULATIONS. 33, NAVIGATION AND NAVIGABLE WATERS. VFOAT Navigation and Navigable Waters. US. English. an. Superintendent of Documents, US Government Printing Office, Washington DC 20402. Vols. for (1984-) distributed to some depository libraries in microfiche.

COLS BLEUS. FR. French. ir. 105.00. Addim, 6 rue Saint Charles, 75015 Paris France. LC VA500. DD 359.00944.

COMBAT CRAFT. Vol. 1, No. 1 (Jan. 1983)-. 0264-4649. Periodical. UK. English. bm. 50.00. Capstan Publishing Company Ltd, PO Box 8, Tadworth Surrey KT20 5QR England. Tel 073781-3063. Ed Robin Burnett. Ind/Abst Electron. Commun. Abstr. J., ISMEC Bull., Pollut. Abstr. Indexes, Saf. Sci. Abstr. J., Ship Abstr. LC V750. DD 359.3258. bk rev. adv acc. Circ 3,000. The international journal for design, arming and operation of offshore patrol and coastal defence craft.

COMBAT FLEETS OF THE WORLD. 1976/77-. 0364-3263. Periodical. US. English (French). $49.50. United States Naval Institute, Annapolis MD 21402. LC VA40. DD 623.8259094.

COMMAND HISTORICAL REPORT. *See* History (General).

COMMAND HISTORY - UNITED STATES. NAVAL FACILITIES ENGINEERING COMMAND. (COMMAND HISTORY). Main/Corp United States. Naval Facilities Engineering Command. VFOAT Naval Facilities Engineering Command History. 0740-6029. US. English. an. Naval Facilities Engineering Command, 200 Stovall Street, Alexandria VA 22332. LC VG593. DD 359.4170973.

COMMISSARYMAN 1 & C. Main/Corp United States. Naval Training Publications Detachment. VAT Rate Training Manual. VAT Commissary Man First Class and Chief Commissary Man. 0097-9910. US. English. Naval Training Command, Betty Sponaugle Code Elex 08TA, Washington DC 20363. LC VC353. DD 359.341. *Commisaryman 1 & C, 0097-9910.*

CONNAISSANCE DES TEMPS. 0181-3048. FR. French. an. Bureau des Longitudes, 77 Avenue Denfert Rochereau, 75014 Paris France. LC QB8. DD 528.05. *Connaissance des Temps ou Mouvements Celestes a l'Usage des Astronomes et des Navigateurs.*

LA CONSTRUCTION NAVALE. Main/Corp Chambre Syndicale des Constructeurs de Navires et de Machines Marine. French. ir. 47 rue de Monceau, Paris France 75008. LC VM298.5. DD 354.44008775.

CONSTRUCTIONMAN. Main/Corp United States. Naval Education and Training Command. Series/Titl Rate Training Manual and Nonresident Career Course. US. English. Naval Education and Training Command, US Government Printing Office, Washington DC 20402. LC VG593. DD 359.9820973.

CRYPTOLOG. 0740-7602. Periodical. US. English. qt. Association National Office, 3065 Olive Street, Denver CO 80207. LC VB255. DD 359.3432. *Naval Cryptologic Veterans Association Newsletter.*

DANSKE FYRLISTE. Main/Corp Denmark. Farvandsdirektoratet. Danish. ir. LC VK1163.

DEUTSCHE HYDROGRAPHISCHE ZEITSCHRIFT. VFOAT German Hydrographic Journal. Vol. 1- Jan. 1948-. 0012-0308. Periodical. GW. German (individual numbers in V. 1 have cover title also in English). bm. 120.-. Hydrographisches Institut, Bernhard Nochtstrasse 78, 2000 Hamburg 4 West Germany. Tel 040 3190-1. Ind/Abst Int. Aerosp. Abstr., Energy Res. Abstr., Ocean. Abstr., Fluidex, Sel. Water Resour. Abstr., Excerpta Med. LC VK588. DD 526.99. CODEN DHYZA7. (cum index). bk rev. Circ 650. Scientific articles and short communications: deep-sea and coastal surveying, nautical science, navigation, time service, geomagnetism, ship's magnetism, nautical techniques, tides, physical and chemical oceanography. *Annalen der Hydrographie und Maritimen Meteorologie.*

DEUTSCHER KUSTEN-ALMANACH. *See* Yearbooks, Almanacs, Directories.

DIRECTORY - U. S. COAST GUARD ACADEMY ALUMNI ASOCIATION. *See* Yearbooks, Almanacs, Directories.

DOCUMENTATION - INTERNATIONAL MARITIME COMMITTEE. Main/Corp International Maritime Committee. 1969-. 0538-8643. English (French). ir. International Maritime Committee, c/o Messrs Henry Voet-Genicto, 17 Borzestraat, Antwerp B2000 Belgium. Conference.

THE DOG WATCH. No. 28- 1971-. AT. English. ir. $3.00. Editor Shiplovers' Society of Victoria, Box 1169K G P O, Melbourne 3001 Australia. LC V1. DD 623.805. *Annual Dog Watch.*

EDITION ANNUELLE : AVIS AUX NAVIGATEURS. Main/Corp Canada. Coast Guard. Aids and Waterways Branch. CN. French. an. Free. Coast Guard, Aids and Waterways Branch, Ottawa Ontario K1A 0N7 Canada. Tel 990-3021. LC VK780. DD 623.892. adv acc. Circ 18,000. Issued to mariners, contains information, notices to help mariners navigate safely in our waters.

EFTERRETNINGER FOR SFARENDE. Main/Corp Denmark. Frakvandsdirektoratet. 94.- Volume. Periodical. DK. Danish. ir. 231.80. Farvandsdirektoratet, Nautisk Afdeling, Esplanaden 19, 1263 Kbenhavn Denmark. Tel (01)135175. LC VK802. Circ 1,300. (ctrl). Notices to mariners, navigational warning, corrections to Danish charts and nautical publications. *Efterretninger for Sfarende.*

ELECTRO-NAV. VFOAT Safety at Sea. 0142-0666. Periodical. UK. English. mo. 31.50. Industrial Marine Publications Ltd, Queensway House 2 Queensway, Redhill Surrey RH1 1QS England. LC VK200. DD 623.893.

EPITHEORESIS NAUTILIAKOU DIKAIOU. *See* Law.

ESCALE. (L'ESCALE). Published since spring 1983. 0822-4056. Periodical. CN. French. qt. $10,00 Domestic, $20,00 Foreign. L'Escale, CP 232 Station B, Quebec Quebec G1K 7A6 Canada. DD 623.8809714.

Naval Science, Navigation

EXPERIMENTAL YACHT SOCIETY JOURNAL. Sept. 1977-. 0149-239X. Periodical. US. English. qt. 591 Island Avenue, Tarpon Springs FL 33589. LC VM320. DD 623.82205.

FACEPLATE. Began with 1971. 0190-3306. Periodical. US. English. qt. Superintendent of Documents, US Government Printing Office, Washington DC 20402. Tel (202)783-3238. Ind/Abst Index U.S. Gov. Period. LC VM975. DD 359.984.

FACT BOOK - NAVAL RESEARCH LABORATORY (U.S.). (FACT BOOK). Main/Corp Naval Research Laboratory (U.S.). VFOAT N.R.L. Fact Book. 0739-3229. US. English. Naval Research Laboratory, Washington DC 20375. LC U394.W3. DD 359.07073.

FATHOM (NORFOLK, VA.). (FATHOM). Began with 1969. 0014-4822. Periodical. US. English. qt. Superintendent of Documents, US Government Printing Office, Washington DC 20402. Tel (202)783-3238. Ind/Abst Ship Abstr., Index U.S. Gov. Period. LC V383.

FEUX ET SIGNAUX DE BRUME. Main/Corp France. Service Hydrographique et Oceanographique de la Marine. French. ir. Etablissement Principal du Service Hydrographique et Oceanographique de la Marine, 29283 Brest, Paris France. LC VK1150. DD 387.155. *Feux et Signaux de Brume.*

FISCAL YEAR REPORT TO THE CONGRESS - UNITED STATES. NAVY DEPT. (FISCAL YEAR ... REPORT TO THE CONGRESS). Main/Corp United States. Navy Dept. 1984-. 0748-1039. US. English. an. Navy Internal Relations Activity, Print Media Division, Hoffman Number 2, 200 Stovall Street, Alexandria VA 22332. LC VA52. DD 359.00973. *Secnav/CNO Report.*

FOCUS ON FOUR. Main/Corp United States. Naval Mobile Construction Battalion Four. VFOAT Deployment. US. English. Department of The Navy, US Naval Mobile Construction, Battalion Four FPO San Francisco CA 96601. Vols. for 1980/81- distributed to depository libraries in microfiche.

FORCES SOUS-MARINES. VFOAT Forces Sous Marines. No. 1, (Dec. 1977)-. Periodical. English (French, No. 5-(8)). qt. 295.00. BP 80 08, 75362 Paris Cedex 08 France. LC V859.F7. DD 623.8205.

FORTITUDINE. (FORTITUDINE : NEWSLETTER OF THE MARINE CORPS HISTORICAL PROGRAM). 0362-9910. Periodical. US. English. qt. US Marine Corps, History & Museum Division Headquarters, Washington DC 20380. Tel (202)433-3841. Ind/Abst Index U.S. Gov. Period. LC VE23.A1. DD 359.960973.

FRENCH BOATING EXPORT. VFOAT Construction Nautique Francaise. 1976-. English, French, and Spanish. ir. 35.00. Intreval Editions, 3 rue Fortia, 13001 Marseille France. LC VM320. DD 623.82020944.

GEARTEST. 0308-6437. Periodical. UK. English. 8.00. K M Publications, 13-14 Homewell Havant, Hampshire PO9 1EF England. LC VM320. DD 623.8605.

GEGEVENS BETREFFENDE HET NAUTISCH ONDERWIJS. Main/Corp Netherlands. Ministerie van Onderwijs en Wetenschappen. Dutch. an. Ministerie Van Onderwijs en Wetenschappen, Staatsuitgeverij, 'S-Gravenhage Netherlands. LC VK477.

GREAT CIRCLE. (THE GREAT CIRCLE : JOURNAL OF THE AUSTRALIAN ASSOCIATION FOR MARITIME HISTORY). Vol. 1, No. 1 (Apr. 1979)-. 0156-8698. Periodical. English. sa. 35.00. Frank Broeze Litt D, Editor Department of History, University of Western Australia, Nedlands WA 6009 Australia. Tel (02)419-4698. Ed Vaughan Evans. Ind/Abst Am. Hist. Life, Hist. Abstr., Part A, Mod. Hist. Abstr., Hist. Abst., Part B, Twent. Century Abstr. LC VK15. DD 623.8905. bk rev. adv acc. Circ 450. History of seafaring, shipping, navies, ports, fishing, whaling, and overseas trade. Covers the whole world, but special emphasis is on Australia, Indian Ocean and Pacific Ocean.

GUIDE DU NAVIGATEUR. Main/Corp France. Service Hydrographique et Oceanographique de la Marine. No. 1-. FR. French. ir. Service Hydrographique et Oceanographique de la Marine, BP 426, 29275 Brest Cedex France. LC VK2. DD 623.89. *Renseignements Relatifs aux Documets Nautiques et a la Navigation.*

GUIDE FOR THE SELECTION OF TANKERS. 1983-. 0882-2913. US. English. an. Tanker Advisory Center Inc, 10 East End Avenue, New York NY 10021. LC VM455. DD 623.8245.

GYOMU YORAN - KYUSHU KAIUNKYOKU. Main/Corp Japan. Kyushu Kaiunkyoku. Japanese. ir. LC HE891.

HAEGI. VFOAT Monthly Hae Gi. Periodical. KO. Korean. mo. Hanguk Haegisa Hyophoe, 1212-7 Choryang-Dong Tong-Ku, Pusan Korea. LC VM595.

HANDBOOK OF THE HOSPITAL CORPS, UNITED STATES NAVY. Main/Corp United States. Bureau of Medicine and Surgery. No. 1- 1914-. US. English. ir. US Government Printing Office, Superintendent of Documents, Washington DC 20402. LC VG463. DD 359.34, 610.2.

HANDBOOK OF TIDE TABLES, PARTICULARS OF DOCKS, & C. Main/Corp Port of London Authority. 1951-. UK. English. an. LC VK638.5. DD 525.6942.

HANSA. 1863-. Periodical. Greek, Modern. bm. $107.94. Schroedter & Company, PO Box 11039/Stubbenhuk 10, D-2000 Hamburg 11 West Germany. Tel 040 36 49 87. Ed Hans Maack. Ind/Abst Met. Abstr., World Alum. Abstr. LC VK3. bk rev. adv acc. Circ 6,500. (ctrl). Serves German and international maritime quarters with latest information, topical news, detailed articles on shipping, shipbuilding, marine engineering, port matters, and cargo handling.

HIROSHIMA SHOSEN KOTO SEMMON GAKKO KIYO. VFOAT The Bulletin of Hiroshima Mercantile Marine College. No. 1-. JA. Japanese. ir. Hiroshima Shosen Koto, Semmon Gakko 4272-1 Higashinocho Toyota-Gun Hiroshima-Ken Japan. LC V5.

HOKKYOKUSEI HOIKAKU HYO. See Yearbooks, Almanacs, Directories.

HOLLAND SHIPBUILDING. V. 14, No. 11- Jan. 1966-. 0018-3571. Periodical. NE. English. mo. 130.-. C E Radius & P Gruppelaar, 5 Grote Kerksolein, Dordrecht Netherlands. Tel (078)131598. Ed K Glas. Ind/Abst Electron. Commun. Abstr. J., ISMEC Bull., Pollut. Abstr. Indexes, Saf. Sci. Abstr. J., Eng. Index Annu., Eng. Index Mon., Eng. Index Bioeng. Abstr., Eng. Index Energy Abstr., Fluidex, Life Sci. Collect., Ship Abstr. LC VM77. DD 338762382009492. CODEN HOSHAG. bk rev. adv acc. Circ 6,000. (ctrl). International maritime. *Holland Shipbuilding—Marine Engineering and Shipping Herald.*

HOOK (BONITA, CALIF.). (THE HOOK). 0736-9220. Periodical. US. English. qt. $20.00. Tailhook Association, PO Box 40, Bonita CA 92002. Tel (619)566-6019. Ed Robert L Lawson. bk rev. adv acc. Circ 11,000. Tells story of US navy carrier aviation, past and present, issues contain a carrier and squadron histories along with news from current naval operations.

I CEASED. VFOAT A C U C I. Began publication in 1974/1975. 0700-3706. Periodical. CN. English (includes some text in French). ir. Free. Association of Canadian Underwater Councils, 333 River Road, Vanier Ontario K1L 8B9 Canada. DD 797.230971. (ctrl).

INDEX OF CURRENT REGULATIONS OF THE MARITIME ADMINISTRATION, MARITIME SUBSIDY BOARD, NATIONAL SHIPPING AUTHORITY. See Indexes/Abstracts.

INDEX OF SELECTED PUBLICATIONS. See Indexes/Abstracts.

INTERCONAIR AVIAZIONE E MARINA INTERNAZIONALE. VFOAT Aviazione e Marina Internazionale. Periodical. Italian. mo. $37.50. Skybooks International Inc, 48 East 50th Street, New York NY 10022. LC VG90. DD 358.4005. *Interconair Aviazione E Marina.*

INTERNATIONAL DREDGING REVIEW. See Engineering.

INTERNATIONAL MARINE SAFETY DIRECTORY. See Yearbooks, Almanacs, Directories.

INTERNATIONAL NAUTICAL INDEX. See Indexes/Abstracts.

INTERNATIONAL SHIPBORNE BARGE REGISTER. 0273-2106. US. English. an. US Department of Transportation, Maritime Administration, Washington DC 20590. LC VM466.B3. DD 623.829. *Listing of Barges Specially Designed to be Carried Aboard Another Vessel.*

INTERNATIONAL SHIPBUILDING PROGRESS. V. 1- 1954-. 0020-868X. Periodical. English. mo. International Shipbuilding, 193 Heemraadssingel, 3023 CB Rotterdam Holland. Tel (010)773325. Ind/Abst Electron. Commun. Abstr. J., ISMEC Bull., Pollut. Abstr. Indexes, Saf. Sci. Abstr. J., Eng. Index Mon., Eng. Index Bioeng. Abstr., Eng. Index Energy Abstr., Life Sci. Collect., Fluidex, Excerpta Med., Ship Abstr., Eng. Index Annu., Eng. Index Mon., Nuci. Sci. Abstr., Appl. Mech. Rev., Ocean. Abstr., Eng. Index. CODEN ISBPAS.

JACHTFUNKDIENST MITTELMEER FUR NICHTAUSRUSTUNGSPFLICHTIGE SCHIFFE. Main/Corp Deutsches Hudrographisches Institut. 1st Edition. GW. German. ir. Deutsches Hydrographisches Institut, Bernhard-Nocht-Strasse 78, 2000 Hamburg 4 West Germany. LC VK397.

JACHTFUNKDIENST NORD- UND OSTSEE FUR NICHTAUSRUSTUNGSPFLICHTIGE SCHIFFE. Main/Corp Deutsches Hydrographisches Institut. German. ir. Deutsches Hydropgraphisches Institut, 2000 Hamburg 4, Bernhard-Nocht-Strasse 78, Hamburg West Germany. LC VK1151. DD 623.8932094.

THE JAG JOURNAL. See Law.

JAHRBUCH DER MARINE. See Yearbooks, Almanacs, Directories.

JAHRBUCH DER SCHIFFBAUTECHNISCHEN GESELLSCHAFT. See Yearbooks, Almanacs, Directories.

JANE'S FIGHTING SHIPS. 0075-3025. US. English. an. $125.00. Janes Publishing Inc, 135 West 50th Street/12th Floor, New York NY 10020. Tel (212)586-7745. Ed John Moore. adv acc. Current information on the world's naval fleets, alphabetically by country, including history, specifications, armament and crew of individual ships, with illustrations. *All the World's Fighting Ships.*

JANE'S MERCHANT SHIPS. See Transportation - Ships & Shipping.

JANE'S ... NAVAL ANNUAL CEASED. 1981-82. UK. English. an. $14.95. Jane's Publishing Inc, 730 Fifth Avenue, New York NY 10019. Ed John Moore. LC VA40. DD 359.005.

JANE'S NAVAL REVIEW. 1982/83-. UK. English. an. $14.95. Jane's Publishing, 286 Congress Street, Boston MA 02210. Tel (212)586-7745. Ed John Moore. Collection of approximately 30 articles on world's current naval dispositions and potential points of friction. *Jane's Naval Annual.*

JAPAN SHIPBUILDING & MARINE ENGINEERING. VAT Japan Shipbuilding and Marine Engineering. V. 1-. 0021-4647. Periodical. JA. English. qt. $34.00. Japan Association for Technical Information, 4-7-107 Yamazaki-Cho Machida-City Tokyo 194-01 Japan. Ind/Abst Life Sci. Collect. LC VM105. CODEN JSMEBS.

JITSUYO KAIJI ROPPO. Main/Corp Japan. Japanese. ir. 2500. Seizendo Shoten, 4-51 Minami Motomachi Shinjuku-ku, Tokyo 160 Japan.

JOURNAL DE LA NAVIGATION FLUVIALE & I.E. ET MARITIME. Began in 1903. US. French. ir. LC Mirofilm 01355HE, HE668.

JOURNAL OF NAVIGATION. (THE JOURNAL OF NAVIGATION). V. 25- Jan. 1972-. 0373-4633. Periodical. UK. English. ty. $95.00. Cambridge University Press, 510 North Avenue, New Rochelle NY 10801. Ed M W Richey. Ind/Abst Fluidex, Life Sci. Collect., Excerpta Med., Ship Abstr., Int. Aerosp. Abstr., Comput. Control Abstr., Electr. Electron. Abstr., Sci. Abstr. Sect. A. Phys. Abstr., Sci. Cit. Index, Abr. Ed., Ocean. Abstr. LC VK1. DD 629.04505. CODEN JONVAL. bk rev. Contains original papers on every aspect of navigation- air, sea and space; and of every type- scientific, historical and narrative. *Journal of the Institute of Navigation,* 0020-3009.

Naval Science, Navigation

JOURNAL OF SHIP RESEARCH. Periodical. US. English. qt. Society of Naval Architecture and Marine Engineering, One World Trade Center/Suite 1369, New York NY 10048. **Tel** (212)432-0310. **Ind/Abst** Appl. Mech. Rev., Sci. Cit. Index, Abr. Ed., Ocean. Abstr., Eng. Index.

KAIJI ROPPO. *See* Law.

KAINAN TOKEI NEMPO. Main/Corp Japan. Unyusho. Daijin Kambo. Joho Kanribu. JA. Japanese. ir. Saiban No Dokuritsu O Mamoru Kai, c/o Seni Boeki Kaikan, 16-9 Uchi Kanda 2-chome, Chiyoda-ku Tokyo Japan. **LC** VK1288.J3. *Kainan Tokei Nempo.*

KATALOG OVER NORSKE SJKART OG NAUTISKE PUBLIKASJONER. *See* Bibliographies.

KEEPER'S LOG. Vol. 1, No. 1 (Fall 1984)-. 0883-0061. Periodical. US. English. qt. $15.00 Keeper, $25.00 Family Memberships, $50.00 District Inspector, $100.00 Members of the Commissioner's Circle. US Lighthouse Society, 130 St Elmo Way, San Francisco CA 94127. **LC** VK1000. **DD** 387.155.

KIYO - YUGE SHOSEN KOTO SEMMON GAKKO. Main/Corp Yuge Shosen Koto Semmon Gakko. 1979 Edition. JA. English or Japanese. ir. Yuge Shosen Koto Semmon Gakko, Himoyuge Yugemachi, Ochi-Gun 794-25, Ehime-Ken Japan. **LC** VK4.

KLASINGS BOOTSMARKT INTERNATIONAL. Began in 1968. GW. German. ir. Verlag Delius Klasing, Siekerwall 21, 48 Bielefeld 1 West Germany. **LC** VM361. **DD** 623.82230294.

KOBE SHOSEN DAIGAKU KIYO. DAI 2-RUI, SHOSEN, RIKOGAKU HEN. VFOAT Review of Kobe University of Mercantile Marine. Part II, Maritime Studies, and Science and Engineering. 0450-609X. English (Japanese). ir. Kobe Shosen Daigaku, 1-1 Fukae Minami-Machi 5-chome Higashinada-ku, Kobe-Shi Japan. **Ind/Abst** Chem. Abstr., Life Sci. Collect. **LC** VK4. **CODEN** KDKRDX. *Kobe Shosen Kaigaku Kiyo. Dai 2-rue, Kokai-Kikan-Genshi Koryoku-Rigaku Hen.*

KONGOP KISUL. VFOAT Industrial Technology for Machinery & Shipbuilding. Periodical. Korean. mo. Hanguk Kigye Yonguso, 66 Sangnam-dong Changwon-si, Kyongnam Korea. **LC** T4.

LIGHT LIST. Main/Corp United States. Coast Guard. Periodical. US. English. an. US Department of Transportation, Coast Guard, Washington DC G-NSR-3 20953. **Tel** (202)426-9566. **Ed** Frank Parker. **Circ** 70,000. A listing of federal and privately maintained aids to navigation that are found on the waters of the US and its territories.

LIST OF LIGHTS AND FOG SIGNALS. BRITISH ISLES, ENGLISH CHANNEL, AND NORTH SEA. VFOAT British Isles, English Channel, and North Sea. US. English. an. Defense Mapping Agency, Office of Distribution Services, Washington DC 20315.

LIST OF LIGHTS, BUOYS AND FOG SIGNALS. ATLANTIC COAST. (LIST OF LIGHTS, BUOYS AND FOG SIGNALS). **Main/Corp** Canada. Coast Guard. **VFOAT** Atlantic Coast, List of Lights, Bouys and Fog Signals. **VAT** Atlantic Coast. List of Lights, Buoys and Fog Signals. 1976-. 0590-9384. CN. English. an. $11.88. Receiver General for Canada, Supply and Services, Ottawa Ontario K1A 0S9 Canada. **Tel** (819)997-2560. *List of Lights, Buoys and Fog Signals.*

LIST OF LIGHTS, BUOYS AND FOG SIGNALS, ATLANTIC COAST INCLUDING THE GULF AND RIVER ST. LAWRENCE TO MONTREAL. Main/Corp Canada. Coast Guard. Aids and Waterways Branch. **VFOAT** Atlantic Coast. 1977-. CN. English. an. $6.00. Transport Canada, Canadian Coast Guard, Ottawa Ontario K1A 0S9 Canada. **LC** VK1026. **DD** 623.89440971. *List of Lights, Buoys and Fog Signals, Atlantic Coast including the Gulf and River St. Lawrence to Montreal.*

LIST OF LIGHTS, BUOYS AND FOG SIGNALS. PACIFIC COAST. (LIST OF LIGHTS, BUOYS AND FOG SIGNALS, PACIFIC COAST, AND THE RIVERS AND LAKES OF BRITISH COLUMBIA). **Main/Corp** Canada. Coast Guard. **VFOAT** Pavific Coast. **VAT** Pacific Coast. List of Lights, Buoys and Fog Signals. 1976-. 0382-1080. CN. English. an. Receiver General for Canada, Supply & Services, Ottawa Ontario K1A 0S9 Canada. **LC** VK1027.P3. **DD** 623.89409711. *List of Lights, Buoys and Fog Signals.*

LIST OF MEMBERS - SOCIETY FOR NAUTICAL RESEARCH. (LIST OF MEMBERS - THE SOCIETY FOR NAUTICAL RESEARCH). **Main/Corp** Society for Nautical Research, London. 0306-9850. UK. English. an. The Hon Secretary c/o National Maritime Museum, Greenwich SE10 9NF England. **LC** V1.S58. **DD** 623.806242.

LIST OF NAUTICAL CHARTS AND ITS CORRECTIONS BY NOTICES TO MARINERS : PERMANENT, PRELIMINARY AND TEMPORARY. *See* Bibliographies.

LISTS OF LIGHTS, BUOYS AND FOG SIGNALS. INLAND WATERS. (LIST OF LIGHTS, BUOYS AND FOG SIGNALS). **Main/Corp** Canada. Coast Guard. **VFOAT** Inland Waters. **VAT** Inland Waters. Lists of Lights, Buoys, Fog Signals. 1976-. 0381-3401. CN. English. an. $4.20. **LC** VK1245. **DD** 623.892971. *List of Lights, Buoys and Fog Signals.*

LIVRE DES FEUX, DES BOUEES ET DES SIGNAUX DE BRUME : COTE DE L'ATLANTIQUE Y COMPRIS LE GOLFE ET LE FLEUVE SAINT-LAURENT JUSQU'A MONTREAL. Main/Corp Canada. Coast Guard. 1976-. CN. French. $5.40. **LC** VK1245. **DD** 623.892971. *Livre des Feux, des Bouees et des Signaux de Brume: Cote de l'Atlantique y Compris le Golfe et le Fleuve Saint-Laurent Jusqu'a Montreal.*

LIVRE DES FEUX, DES BOUEES ET DES SIGNAUX DE BRUME. EAUX INTERIEURES. (LIVRE DES FEUX, DES BOUEES ET DES SIGNAUX DE BRUME). **Main/Corp** Canada. Garde Cotiere. **VFOAT** Eaux Interieures: Livre des Feux, des Bouees et des Signaux de Brume. 1976-. 0381-3398. CN. French. an. Transport Canada, Coast Guard, Ottawa Ontario Canada. **Tel** 990-3021. adv acc. Contains list of all fixed lighted aids in Canada and contiguous waters.

LIVRE DES FEUX, DES BOUEES ET DES SIGNAUX DE BRUME : EAUX INTERIEURES (A L'OUEST DE MONTREAL ET A L'EST DE LA COLOMBIE-BRITANNIQUE). Main/Corp Canada. Coast Guard. CN. French. an. Receiver General for Canada, Supply & Services, Ottawa Ontario K1A 0S9 Canada. **LC** VK1245. **DD** 016.623892971.

LIVRE DES FEUX, DES BOUEES ET DES SIGNAUX DE BRUME, TERRE-NEUVE, Y COMPRIS LES EAUX COTIERES DU LABRADOR. Main/Corp Canada. Coast Guard. Aids and Waterways Branch. **VFOAT** Terre-Neuve. CN. French. Receiver General for Canada, Supply & Services, Ottawa Ontario K1A 0S9 Canada. **LC** VK1027.N4. **DD** 623.894409718.

LIVRE DES FEUX, DES BOUEES ET DES SIGNAUX DE BRUME. COTE DU PACIFIQUE. (LIVRE DES FEUX, DES BOUEES ET DES SIGNAUX DE BRUME : COTE DU PACIFIQUE ET LES RIVIERES ET LACS DE LA COLOMBIE-BRITANNIQUE). **Main/Corp** Canada. Coast Guard. Aids and Waterways Branch. **VFOAT** Cote du Pacifique : Livre des Feux, des Bouees et des Signaux de Brume. **VAT** Cote du Pacifique. Livres des Feux, des Bouees et des Signaux de Brume. 1977-. 0704-5417. CN. French. an. $3.00. Coast Guards, Aids and Waterways Branch, Ottawa Ontario K1A 0S9 Canada. **LC** VK1027.P3. **DD** 623.89409711.

LLOYD'S MARINE EQUIPMENT GUIDE. VFOAT Marine Equipment Guide. 1982-3-. English. an. **LC** VM781. **DD** 623.860294. *International Shipping and Shipbuilding Directory.*

LLOYD'S NAUTICAL YEAR BOOK. *See* Yearbooks, Almanacs, Directories.

LLOYD'S SHIPBUILDING REVIEW. UK. English. 30. Lloyd's of London Press Ltd, Circulation Office/Lloyd's Lime Street, London EC3M 7HA England. **LC** VM57. **DD** 623.805.

MAJALLAT AL-AKADIMIYAH AL-ARABIYAH LIL-NAQL AL-BAHARI. Main/Corp Al-Akadimiyah Al-Arabiyah Lil-Naql Al-Bahari (Egypt). **VFOAT** Journal of Arab Maritime Transport Academy. Periodical. Arabic (or English). ir. $12.00. PO Box 1029, Al-Iskandariyah Uruguay. **Ind/Abst** Ship Abstr. **LC** VK4.

MALACCA AND SINGAPORE STRAITS TIDE TABLES. VFOAT Tide Tables, Malacca and Singapore Straits. English. ir. **LC** VK710. **DD** 623.89490916565.

MANAGEMENT DATA LIST (ML) BASIC NAVY MICROFORM. VFOAT Navy Management Data List. US. English. mo. Commander Attn DLSC-APPP, Federal Center, Battle Creek MI 49016.

MARINE. Periodical. German. ir. 24.00. Verlag Redaktion Bundesmarine, Postfach 161, 53 Bonn 1 West Germany. **LC** VA510.

MARINE ACCIDENT REPORTS. SUMMARY FORMAT. Issue No. 1 (Jan. through June 1978)-. US. English. $65.00. National Technical Information Service, 5285 Port Royal Road, Springfield VA 22161. **Tel** (703)487-4630. Vols. for (1983-) distributed to depository libraries in microfiche.

MARINE ENGINEERING/LOG (BRISTOL, CONN. : 1979). (MARINE ENGINEERING/LOG). **VFOAT** Marine Engineering Log. V. 84, No. 1 (Jan. 1979)-. 0732-5460. Periodical. US. English. mo. Simmons-Boardman Publishing Corporation, PO Box 530, Bristol CT 06010. **Ind/Abst** Electron. Commun. Abstr. J., ISMEC Bull., Life Sci. Collect., Pollut. Abstr. Indexes, Saf. Sci. Abstr. J., Predicasts, Excerpta Med., Coal Abstr., Ship Abstr., Energy Inf. Abstr., Environ. Abstr., Appl. Sci. Technol. Index. **LC** VM1. **DD** 623.805. Available on microfilm from University Microfilms International. *Marine Engineering/Log International,* 0885-4912.

MARINE EQUIPMENT CATALOG. 1984-. 0882-1984. US. English. an. $65.00. Maritime Activity Reports Inc, 107 East 31st Street, New York NY 10016. **DD** 623.

MARINE POLICY REPORTS. VFOAT Reports of the Center for the Study of Marine Policy. Vol. 1, No. 1 (Jan. 1977)-. 0735-5912. Periodical. US. English. $12.00 US/Canada, $15.00 Foreign. University of Delaware, College of Marine Studies, Center for the Study of Marine Policy Studies, Newark DE 19711. **Tel** (302)451-8086. **Ed** Gerard J Mangone. bk rev. **Circ** 2,500. Succinct and cogent analyses of contemporary policy issues on the uses of the oceans, the seabed and the coastal zone.

MARINE-RUNDSCHAU. 1.- Yearly Vol. 0025-3294. Periodical. GW. German. bm. $29.22. Special Publication Service, Postfach 2060 Karl-Mand-Str 2, D-5400 Koblenz 1 West Germany. **Tel** (0261)803071. **Ed** Bernard S Graefe. **Ind/Abst** Am. Hist. Life, Hist. Abstr., Part A, Mod. Hist. Abstr., Hist. Abstr., Part B, Twent. Century Abstr., Ship Abstr., Writ. Am. Hist., Recent Publ. Artic., Hist. Abstr. **LC** V3. bk rev. adv acc. (ctrl). Journal of naval and maritime affairs.

MARINE TECHNOLOGY. V. 1- Oct. 1964-. 0025-3316. Periodical. US. English. qt. $40.00. Society of Naval Architects & Marine Engineers, One World Trade Center/Suite 1369, New York NY 10048. **Tel** (212)432-0310. **Ind/Abst** Life Sci. Collect., Eng. Index Mon., Eng. Index Bioeng. Abstr., Eng. Index Energy Abstr., Excerpta Med., Ship Abstr., Chem. Abstr., Eng. Index Annu., Eng. Index, Appl. Sci. Technol. Index, Energy Inf. Abstr., Environ. Abstr., Sci. Cit. Index, Abr. Ed., Ocean. Abstr. **LC** VM1. **DD** 623.8. **CODEN** MARTA4. Marine engineering, naval architecture, and related fields.

MARINE WEEK CEASED. Began with V. 1, Apr. 5, 1974-. Ceased June 6, 1980. 0306-347X. Periodical. UK. English. wk. $55.00. IPC Industrial Press, 40 Bowling Green Lane, London EC1R 0NE England. **Ind/Abst** Eng. Index Annu., Eng. Index Mon., Eng. Index Bioeng. Abstr., Eng. Index Energy Abstr. **LC** VM1. **DD** 623.805. **CODEN** MRWKAJ. *Shipbuilding and Shipping Record.*

MARINE WEEK MARINE DESIGN INTERNATIONAL. VFOAT Marine Design International. 1974-. UK. English. an. IPC Industrial Press, PO Box 147, 40 Bowling Green Lane, London EC1R 0NE England. **LC** VM1. **DD** 623.805. *S & SR Marine Design International.*

MARINEBLAD. Vol. 1-. Periodical. NE. Dutch. mo. $29.29. Koninklijke Drukkerij Uitgeverij de Boer, PO Box 507, Hilversum Netherlands. **Tel** 035-1 30 51. **Ind/Abst** Excerpta Med. **LC** V5.

MARINERS'. V. 1- 1972/73-. 0303-4445. English. ir. Singapore Polytechnic Marine Engineering Society, 9 Prince Edward Road, Singapore Singapore. **LC** VM595. **DD** 623.805.

THE MARINER'S CATALOG. V. 1- 1973-. 0198-9618. US. English. an. $7.95. International Marine Publishing Company, 21 Elm Street, Camden ME 04843. **LC** VM320. **DD** 623.82023029473. Each issue contains an index to its own contents - no vol index - loose.

MARINER'S MIRROR. (THE MARINER'S MIRROR). V. 1- Jan. 1911-. 0025-3359. Periodical. UK. English. qt. 40.00. Society for Nautical Research, c/o Department Water Transporation, Science Museum, London SW7 2DD England. **Ed** B H Dolley. **Ind/Abst** Am. Hist. Life, Hist. Abstr., Part A, Mod. Hist. Abstr., Hist. Abst., Part B, Twent. Century Abstr., Ship Abstr., Writ. Am. Hist., Hist. Abstr., Recent Publ. Artic. **LC** VK1. **DD** 623.805. (cum index). bk rev. adv acc. **Circ** 2,500. (ctrl). Nautical history, archaeology and all aspects of maritime activity through the centuries.

MARINERS WEATHER LOG. *See* Earth Sciences - Meteorology.

MARINNYTT. No. 1- 1953-. 0025-3375. Periodical. SW. Swedish. ir. 6.00. Marinstaben, Marinnytt, Fack, 104 50 Stockholn Sweden. **LC** V5.

MARITIM KONTAKT. 1-. 0106-7818. Periodical. Danish. ir. Kontaktudvalget for Dansk Maritim Historie-OG Samfundsforskning, Hellerupvej 51 E, 2900 Hellerup Denmark.

MARITIME DEFENCE. Vol. 4, No. 10 (Oct. 1979)-. 0308-5201. Periodical. UK. English. mo. Eldon Publications Ltd, 30 Fleet Street, London EC4Y 1AH United Kingdom. **Tel** (01)353-9098. **Ed** Geoffrey Wood. **Ind/Abst** Life Sci. Collect. **LC** V1. **DD** 359.005. bk rev. adv acc. **Circ** 3,277. (ctrl). Journal of International Naval Technology embracing all naval hulls, weapons, electronics, aircraft (fixed and rotary wing). *Maritime Defence International.*

MARITIME DEFENCE INTERNATIONAL. **VFOAT** Maritime Defence. Began with Aug. 1976 issue. 0308-5201. Periodical. UK. English. mo. Eldon Publications Ltd, 30 Fleet Street, London EC4Y 1AH England. **Ind/Abst** Life Sci. Collect., Predicasts, Ship Abstr. **LC** V1. **DD** 359.005.

MARITIME GUIDE. 1984-. 0264-6420. UK. English. an. Lloyd's Register of Shipping, 71 Fenchurch Street, London EC3M 4BS England. *Appendix (Lloyd's Register of Ships).*

MARITIME SURVEY. Began with vol. for 1973. UK. English. an. .60 Domestic, 2.00 Foreign. Navy League, Broadway House, The Broadway, Wimbledon London SW19 1RL England. **LC** VK8. **DD** 387.0941. *Navy Year Book and Diary.*

MECH. Began in 1968. 0025-6471. Periodical. US. English. bm. Government Printing Office, Washington DC 20402. **Tel** (202)783-3238. **Ind/Abst** Index U.S. Gov. Period. **LC** VG93. *Aircraft Mishaps Involving Maintenance and Servicing.*

MEDDELELSER FRA SJFARTSDIREKTORATET. **Main/Corp** Norway. Sjfartsdirektoratet. Periodical. Norwegian. ir. **LC** VK4.

MER. MARINE ENGINEERS REVIEW. *See* Engineering.

MRIS ABSTRACTS. *See* Indexes/Abstracts.

NAAMBOEK VAN OFFICIEREN DER KONINKLIJKE MARINE. **Main/Corp** Netherlands (Kingdom, 1815-). Departement van Defensie. NE. Dutch. ir. Ministerie van Defensie, Lange Voorhout 7, S-Gravenhage Netherlands. **LC** VB315.N4.

NAUTICAL CHART CATALOG 2. UNITED STATES PACIFIC COAST, INCLUDING HAWAII, GUAM AND SAMOA ISLANDS. **VFOAT** United States Pacific Coast, Including Hawaii, Guam and Samoa Islands. US. English. an. Distribution Division, National Oceanic and Atmospheric Administration, Riverdale MD 20840.

NAUTICAL CHART CATALOG 3. UNITED STATES, ALASKA, INCLUDING THE ALEUTIAN ISLANDS. **VFOAT** United States, Alaska, Including the Aleutian Islands. US. English. an. Distribution Division, National Oceanic and Atmospheric Administration, Riverdale MD 20840.

THE NAUTICAL MAGAZINE : A JOURNAL OF PAPERS ON SUBJECTS CONNECTED WITH MARITIME AFFAIRS. Vol. 1, No. 1 (Mar. 1832)-. Periodical. UK. English. mo. 17.16. Brown Son & Ferguson Ltd, 4/10 Darnley Street, Glasgow G4A 2SD Scotland. **Tel** 429-1234. **Ed** L Ingram-Brown. bk rev. adv acc. **Circ** 2,000. Merchant navy and those interested in the sea.

NAUTICAL RESEARCH JOURNAL. Began with Jan. 1949 issue. 0738-7245. Periodical. US. English. qt. $13.00. Nautical Research Guild, 6413 Dahlonega Road, Bethesda MD 20816. **Tel** (301)229-0473. **Ed** Merritt A Edson Jr. **Ind/Abst** Am. Hist. Life, Hist. Abstr., Part A, Mod. Hist. Abstr., Hist. Abst., Part B, Twent. Century Abstr., Writ. Am. Hist. **LC** V1. bk rev. adv acc. **Circ** 2,000. (ctrl). Historical data on maritime materials useful for modelers historians and collectors.

NAUTICAL REVIEW. V. 1- Mar./Apr. 1977-. 0309-6254. Periodical. UK. English. Lloyd's of London Press, 3/4 Lime Street, London EC3M 7HA England. **Ind/Abst** Life Sci. Collect. **LC** VK1. **DD** 387.05.

NAUTOLOGIA. V. 1- 1966-. 0548-0523. Periodical. PL. Polish. qt. ARS Polona, Krakowskie Przedmiescie 7, 00-068 Warsaw Poland. **LC** VK4.

NAVAL ABSTRACTS. *See* Indexes/Abstracts.

NAVAL AFFAIRS. Began in 1921. 0028-1409. Periodical. US. English. mo. $6.00. Fleet Reserve Association, 1303 New Hampshire Avenue, Washington DC 20036. **LC** VA49. **DD** 359.

NAVAL ARCHITECT. (THE NAVAL ARCHITECT). Began with April 1971. 0306-0209. Periodical. UK. English. mo. $68.96. Royal Institute of Naval Architects, 10 Upper Belgrave Street, London SW1X 8BQ England. **Tel** 01-235-4622. **Ed** Michael Wake. **Ind/Abst** Eng. Index Annu., Eng. Index Mon., Eng. Index Bioeng. Abstr., Eng. Index Energy Abstr., Life Sci. Collect., Ship Abstr., Energy Inf. Abstr., Environ. Abstr., Energy Res. Abstr. **CODEN** NVARA3. bk rev. adv acc. **Circ** 8,024. Covers the world of marine design from small craft to ships and offshore structures. High technical content, including at least one technical paper per issue. *Transactions, 0035-8967.*

NAVAL ARCHITECTURE AND OCEAN ENGINEERING. V. 15- 1977-. 0387-5504. Periodical. English. ir. Society of Naval Architects of Japan, 15-16 Toranomon 1 Chome, Minato-Ku Tokyo Japan. **Ind/Abst** Eng. Index Annu., Eng. Index Mon., Eng. Index Bioeng. Abstr., Eng. Index Energy Abstr. **LC** VM4. **DD** 623.8108.

NAVAL AVIATION NEWS. Began publication Oct. 1, 1919. 0028-1417. Periodical. US. English. bm. Superintendent of Documents, US Goverment Printing Office, Washington DC 20402. **Tel** (202)783-3238. **Ind/Abst** Funk Scott Index Corp. Ind., Index U.S. Gov. Period. **LC** VG93. **DD** 629.1. Index in last issue of volume - attached.

NAVAL ENGINEERS JOURNAL. *See* Engineering.

NAVAL FORCES. Vol. 1, No. 1-. Periodical. UK. English. qt. **Tel** (703)790-5252. **Ind/Abst** Predicasts. **LC** V1. **DD** 359.005. adv acc. **Circ** 18,450. (ctrl). A forum for discussion and focuses attention on the importance of naval forces worldwide. Provides information on hardware, weapons systems, strategy, and modern technology in world's navies.

NAVAL RESEARCH LOGISTICS QUARTERLY. Began with 1954. 0028-1441. Periodical. US. English. qt. $80.00. John Wiley & Sons, 605 Third Avenue, New York NY 10158. **Tel** (800)526-5368. **Ind/Abst** Math. Rev., Eng. Index Annu., Eng. Index Mon., Eng. Index Bioeng. Abstr., Eng. Index Energy Abstr., Int. Aerosp. Abstr., Comput. Control Abstr., Electr. Electron. Abstr., Sci. Abstr. Sect. A. Phys. Abstr., Ship Abstr., Index U.S. Gov. Period., Sci. Cit. Index, Abr. Ed., Phys. Abstr., Comput. Rev., Eng. Index. **LC** V179. **DD** 359.410973. **CODEN** NRLQAR. Issued also in microform.

NAVAL RESEARCH REVIEWS. **Series/Titl** Navso P. 0028-145X. Periodical. US. English. qt. Superintendent of Documents, US Government Printing Office, Washington DC 20402. **Ind/Abst** Life Sci. Collect., Predicasts, Ship Abstr., Comput. Control Abstr., Electr. Electron. Abstr., Sci. Abstr. Sect. A. Phys. Abstr., GeoRef, Index U.S. Gov. Period., Chem. Abstr., Biol. Abstr., Nuci. Sci. Abstr., Int. Aerosp. Abstr. **NLM** W1 UN6983. **CODEN** NARRA9. *Research Reviews, 0193-1334.*

NAVIGATION. 0077-6262. AT. English. an. $3.69. Australian Institute of Navigation, GPO Box 2250, Sydney New South Wales 2001 Australia. **Ind/Abst** Int. Aerosp. Abstr. **LC** V1. **DD** 623.8905.

NAVIGATION. V. 1- Mar. 1946-. 0028-1522. Periodical. US. English. qt. $24.00. Institute of Navigation, 815 15th Street NW/Suite 832, Washington DC 20005. **Tel** (202)783-4121. **Ed** Stephen W Gilbert. **Ind/Abst** Eng. Index Mon., Eng. Index Bioeng. Abstr., Eng. Index Energy Abstr., Life Sci. Collect., Ship Abstr., Comput. Control Abstr., Electr. Electron. Abstr., Sci. Abstr. Sect. A. Phys. Abstr., Ref. Source, Eng. Index Annu., Eng. Index Mon., Int. Aerosp. Abstr., Phys. Abstr., Ocean. Abstr., Eng. Index. **LC** VK1. **DD** 527.05. **CODEN** NAVIB3. bk rev. adv acc. **Circ** 3,000. (ctrl). Covers development and application of navigation systems for aerospace, nautical and land use.

NAVIGATION. V. 1- (No. 1-). 0028-1530. Periodical. FR. French. qt. 250. Institut Francais de Navigation, 3 Avenue Octave, Greard 75007 Paris France. **Tel** (1)42603330. **Ind/Abst** Int. Aerosp. Abstr., Comput. Control Abstr., Electr. Electron. Abstr., Sci. Abstr. Sect. A. Phys. Abstr. **LC** VK2. **CODEN** NVGNAL. bk rev. adv acc. **Circ** 1,500. (ctrl). Technical review of maritime air and space navigation.

NAVIGATOR. 0100-1248. Portuguese. ir. $6.00. Servico de Documentacao Geral da Marinha, rua d Monoel No 15 Praca 15 de Novembro, Rio de Janeiro Brazil. **Tel** 221-7626. **LC** F2522. **Circ** 2,500. Naval history, naval science and navigation.

NAVIGATOR (WASHINGTON, D.C.). (THE NAVIGATOR). 0028-1557. Periodical. US. English. qt. US Government Printing Office, Washington DC 20402. **Tel** (202)783-3238. **Ind/Abst** Index U.S. Gov. Period. *Aircraft Observer.*

NAVIRES, PORTS ET CHANTIERS. (NAVIRES, PORTS & CHANTIERS). 1.- Year. 0028-159X. Periodical. FR. French. mo. Navires Ports and Chantiers, 190 Boulevard Hussmann, Paris 75008 France. **Ind/Abst** Ship Abstr., CIS Abstr., Energy Res. Abstr. **LC** VM2.

NAVORD OD. **Main/Corp** United States. Naval Ordnance Systems Command. Periodical. US. English. Department of the Navy, Washington DC 20362. *Navord Report.*

NAVSEA JOURNAL. **Main/Corp** United States. Naval Sea Systems Command. **VAT** Naval Sea Systems Command Journal. 0161-9411. Periodical. US. English. mo. Naval Sea Systems Command, Sea Ood2 Department of the Navy, Washignton DC 20362. **LC** V1. **DD** 623.805.

NAVY CHAPLAINS BULLETIN. 0028-1654. Periodical. US. English. qt. Chief of Chaplains, Office of the Chief of Naval Operations Navy Department, Washington DC 20370. **LC** VG23. **DD** 359.3470973. *Items of Interest.*

NAVY CONTRACTING DIRECTIVES. **Main/Corp** United States. Navy Dept. US. English. ir. US Department of Defense, Navy Department, Chief of Navy Material, Washington DC 20402. *Navy Procurement Directives.*

NAVY INTERNATIONAL. V. 77-Jan. 1972-. 0144-3194. Periodical. UK. English. mo. $47.06. Maritime World Ltd, 72 High Street, Haslemere Surrey GU2 72LA England. **Tel** 0306-77-442. **Ed** Anthony J Watts. **Ind/Abst** Predicasts, Ship Abstr., Funk Scott Index Corp. Ind. **LC** V1. **DD** 359.005. bk rev. adv acc. **Circ** 4,100. International coverage in detail, studying all aspects of maritime defense and its importance for maintaining the freedom of the seas.

NAVY LIFELINE. **VFOAT** Lifeline. Began with Sept./Oct. 1972. Ceased with V. 13, No. 5, Sept.-Oct. 1984. 0192-6748. Periodical. US. English. bm. Superintendent of Documents, US Government Printing Office, Washington DC 20402. **Ind/Abst** CIS Abstr., Index U.S. Gov. Period. **LC** VM1. **DD** 614.852. *Safety Review, Bioenvironmental Safety.*

THE NAVY LIST. **Main/Corp** Great Britain. Ministry of Defence. UK. English. 8.00. Ministry of Defence, Old Admiral Building Spring Gardens, London SW1 A 2BE England. **LC** V11.G7. **DD** 359.30941. *Navy List.*

NAVY TECHNICAL DISCLOSURE BULLETIN. 0364-3646. Periodical. US. English. mo. Office of Naval Research, Department of the Navy, Arlington VA 22217. **LC** V1. **DD** 623.805.

NAVY TIMES. Began publication In 1951. 0028-1697. Periodical. US. English. wk. $42.00. Army Times Publishing Company, 6883 Commercial Drive, Springfield VA 22159. **Tel** (703)750-8612. **Ed** Tom Philpott. **LC** V1. bk rev. adv acc. Contains current government information for Navy personnel. It is also an independent forum for analysis of military policy. *Armed Force.*

NEPTUNIA. No. 1- 1946-. Periodical. FR. French. qt. 200. ASSPC Amis Musees la Marine, Palais Chaillot Place Tracader, Paris XVI France. **Tel** 553 31

Naval Science, Navigation

70. LC V2. The three main subjects are maritime, history modelism specialized in models 17th and 18th century and underwater archeology, museums. *Bulletin Trimestriel, Triton.*

NEPTUNUS. 66/1 (March 1966)-. Periodical. BE. Dutch (French). bm. 300 Domestic, 500 Foreign, and $10.00 US. Neptunus, Postbus 17, B-8400 Oostende Belgium. **Tel** 59-803999. **LC** VA480. **DD** 359.009493. bk rev. adv acc. **Circ** 3,500. (ctrl). Covers naval history, ship building, ports, military navy book reviews, bibliographies, fishery, naval vocabulary, and sailing.

NEWSLETTER - NAVY SUPPLY CORPS. (NEWSLETTER). 0360-716X. Periodical. US. English. bm. Navy Supply Corps Newsletter, Supply Systems Command 091, Navy Department, Washington DC 20376. **LC** VC35. **DD** 355.621. *Monthly Newsletter (United States. Navy Dept. Bureau of Supplies and Accounts).*

NEWSLETTER OF THE AUSTRALIAN ASSOCIATION FOR MARITIME HISTORY. 0158-5312. English. ir. **LC** VK121. **DD** 387.50994.

NIHON HAKUYO KIKAN GAKKAI SHI. VFOAT Journal of the Marine Engineering Society in Japan. Periodical. JA. Japanese (summaries in English). ir. Nihon Hakuyo Kikan Gakkai, c/o Osaoa Building, 2-gokan Chiyoda-ku 2-2 Uchisatwaicho 1, Tokyo Japan. **Ind/Abst** Coal Abstr., Ship Abstr., Chem. Abstr. **LC** VM595. **CODEN** NHGADN.

NIHON SHOSEN SEMPUKU TOKEI. Saku 47-Nen 11-Gatsu . . . Dai 1-Go O Hakkan. JA. Japanese. ir. c/o Kaiun Building, 6-4 Hirakawacho 2 Chiyoda-Ku, Tokyo 102 Japan. **LC** VK105.

NIHON ZOSEN GAKKAI RONBUNSHU. VFOAT Journal of the Society of Naval Architects of Japan. 0514-8499. Periodical. JA. Japanese. sa. $122.00. Japan Publishing Trading Company Ltd, PO Box 5030, Tokyo International Tokyo 100-31 Japan. **Ind/Abst** Life Sci. Collect., Met. Abstr., Ship Abstr., Chem. Abstr., World Alum. Abstr. **CODEN** NZGRDU.

NOMENCLATURE DES STATIONS DE NAVIRE. Main/Corp International Telecommunication Union. General Secretariat. 1-Ed. French (cover title also in English and Spanish, Dec. 1960-). ir. **LC** VK397.

NORSK TIDSSKRIFT FOR SJOVESEN. 0029-2222. Periodical. NO. Norwegian. bm. $12.00. Norsk Tidskrift for Sjovesen, PO Box 3370, N-5033 Varden Norway. **Ind/Abst** Ship Abstr. **LC** V5.

THE NORTH RIVER NAVIGATOR. Periodical. US. English. mo. $20.00. Hudson River Sloop Restora Inc, 112 Market Street, Poughkeepsie NY 12601.

NORWEGIAN MARITIME RESEARCH. 0304-1743. Periodical. English. qt. Selvigs Forlag, c/o PO Box 9070 Vaterland, Oslo 1 Norway. **Ind/Abst** Electron. Commun. Abstr. J., ISMEC Bull., Pollut. Abstr. Indexes, Saf. Sci. Abstr. J., Eng. Index Annu., Eng. Index Mon., Eng. Index Bioeng. Abstr., Eng. Index Energy Abstr., Life Sci. Collect., Excerpta Med., Ship Abstr., Energy Res. Abstr., Appl. Mech. Rev., Ocean. Abstr., Chem. Abstr., Funk Scott Index Corp. Ind., Eng. Index. **LC** VM1. **DD** 623.805. **CODEN** NWMRB3.

NOTICE TO MARINERS. Publication began with Sept. 23, 1978. 0092-1262. US. English. wk. US Naval Oceanographic Office, Washington Naval Yard, Code 6421/B 203, Washington DC 20373. **Tel** (202)433-3660. **LC** VK798. **DD** 623.89205. *Notice to Mariners, 0092-1262.*

NOTICES TO MARINERS. ANNUAL EDITION. (NOTICES TO MARINERS). **Main/Corp** Canada. Coast Guard. Aids and Waterways Branch. 1977-. 0700-1789. CN. English. wk. Receiver General for Canada, Supply & Services, Ottawa Ontario K1A 0S9 Canada. *Notices to Mariners, 0700-1789.*

NOUVEAUTES TECHNIQUES MARITIMES. Periodical. FR. French. ir. Nouveautes Techniques, 190 Bd Haussmann, Paris 75008 France. **Tel** 563-1155. **LC** VM2.

ON SCENE. Began with Jan. 1972. 0093-2124. Periodical. US. English. qt. US Department of Transportation, US Coast Guard, Washington DC 20590. **LC** VK1323. **DD** 363.34. *National Maritime SAR Review, 0047-8946.*

PERSONNELMAN 1 & C. Main/Corp Naval Education and Training Program Development Center. **Series/Titl** Rate Training Manual. **VAT** Personnelman One and C. 0565-0313. US. English. Superintendent of Documents, US Government Printing Office, Washington DC 20402. **LC** VB258. **DD** 359.60973. *Personnelman 1 & C, 0565-0313.*

PERSPEKTIVA ANGKATAN LAUT. Periodical. Indonesian. ir. Dinas Penerangan Tni-Al, Jln Gunungsahari No 66, Jakarta Indonesia. **LC** V5.

PILOTING, SEAMANSHIP AND SMALL BOAT HANDLING. 1922-. US. English. $11.95. Motor Boating & Sailing, 224 West 57th Street, New York NY 10019. **LC** VM341. **DD** 623.882.3105.

PORT OF TOLEDO NEWS. Began with: Jan./Feb. 1967. 0032-4868. Periodical. US. English. ir. Free. Toledo-Lucas County Port Authority, One Maritime Plaza/7th Floor, Toledo OH 43604-1866. **Tel** (419)243-8251. **Ed** Jeffery A Bryant. **Circ** 3,200. (ctrl). Details activities of Toledo-Lucas County Port Authority's three main divisions: seaport, aviation and economic development. Editorial copy and layout is for general audience (no technical copy). *Port of Toledo Newsletter.*

PORTOS E NAVIOS. 0101-5664. Periodical. BL. Portuguese. mo. Rue Leandro Martins, 1 901 02 OX Postal 2791, Rio de Janeiro Brazil. **Ind/Abst** Ship Abstr. **LC** VM41.

PORTS OF THE WORLD (LONDON, ENGLAND) CEASED. (PORTS OF THE WORLD). Began with 1st Ed. Ceased with with 34th Ed. 1981. 0079-4066. UK. English. an. **Ed** Archibald Hurd. **DD** 387.1058, 382. *Shipping World Year Book & Who's Who.*

PROCEEDINGS OF THE ANNUAL MEETING - INTERNATIONAL OMEGA ASSOCIATION. (PROCEEDINGS OF THE . . . ANNUAL MEETING). **Main/Corp** International Omega Association., Meeting. **VFOAT** Annual Meeting, International Omega Association, Inc. 0278-9396. US. English. an. $80.00. International Omega Association Inc, PO Box 2324, Arlington VA 22202. **LC** VK560. **DD** 623.893205.

PROCEEDINGS OF THE MARINE SAFETY COUNCIL. Began with V. 28, No. 5, May 1971. 0364-0981. Periodical. US. English. mo. US Coast Guard, Commandant G-CMC, Washington DC 20590. **Ind/Abst** Ship Abstr., Energy Inf. Abstr., Environ. Abstr., Index U.S. Gov. Period. **LC** VK23. **DD** 614.86405. *Proceedings (United States. Merchant Marine Council).*

PROCEEDINGS OF THE NATIONAL OCEAN SURVEY HYDROGRAPHIC SURVEY CONFERENCE, ANNUAL MEETING. (PROCEEDINGS OF THE NATIONAL OCEAN SURVEY HYDROGRAPHIC SURVEY CONFERENCE, . . . ANNUAL MEETING). **Main/Conf** National Ocean Survey Hydrographic Survey Conference. 0276-4849. US. English. an. Environmental Science Information Center and the Environmental Data & Information Service of the NOAA, 6009 Executive Boulevard, Rockville MD 20852. **LC** VK589. **DD** 526.99.

PROCEEDINGS OF THE NORTH AMERICAN SOCIETY FOR OCEANIC HISTORY. Main/Corp North American Society of Oceanic History. **VFOAT** Proceedings for the North American Society of Oceanic History. 1977-. 0198-7194. Periodical. US. English. an. North American Society for Oceanic History, US Naval Academy History Department, Annapolis MD 21402. **LC** VK15. **DD** 387.509.

PROCEEDINGS - SHIP TECHNOLOGY AND RESEARCH (STAR) SYMPOSIUM. Main/Conf Ship Technology and Research (Star) Symposium. **VFOAT** Star Proceedings. 1st- 1975-. Periodical. US. English. an. **Ind/Abst** Eng. Index Annu., Eng. Index Mon., Eng. Index Bioeng. Abstr., Eng. Index Energy Abstr. **CODEN** PTRSDY.

PROCEEDINGS - UNITED STATES NAVAL INSTITUTE. Main/Corp United States Naval Institute. **VFOAT** Record. 1873. 0041-798X. US. English. mo. $38.00. US Naval Institute, Annapolis MD 21402. **Tel** (301)268-6110. **Ed** Fred H Rainbow. **Ind/Abst** Am. Hist. Life, Hist. Abstr., Part A, Mod. Hist. Abstr., Hist. Abst., Part B, Twent. Century Abstr., Int. Aerosp. Abstr., Predicasts, Ship Abstr., Recent Publ. Artic., Hist. Abstr. **LC** V1. **DD** 359.00973. (cum index). bk rev. adv acc. **Circ** 105,000. (ctrl). Historical essays, pictorals, opinion forum, book reviews, professional notes, "insider" news articles. *Papers and Proceedings, Naval Review, 0077-6238.*

PRZEGLAD MORSKI. Began in 1928. Periodical. PL. Polish. mo. ARS Polona, Krakowskie Przedmiescie 7, 00-068 Warsaw Poland. **LC** V5.

RADIO NAVIGATION AIDS INCLUDING DETAILS OF DIRECTION-FINDER STATIONS, RADIOBEACONS, NAVIGATIONAL WARNINGS, TIME SIGNALS, ETC. Main/Corp United States. Hydrographic Office. Periodical. US. English. Superintendent of Documents, Government Printing Office, Washington DC 20402. **LC** VK397. **DD** 551.5.

RADIO NAVIGATIONAL AIDS. ATLANTIC AND MEDITERRANEAN AREA. (RADIO NAVIGATIONAL AIDS : ATLANTIC AND MEDITERRANEAN AREA). **Main/Corp** United States. Defense Mapping Agency. Hydrographic Center. **VFOAT** Radio Aids. 0363-5597. US. English. $4.00. **LC** VK397. **DD** 623.89320251821.

RADIONAVIGATION JOURNAL. Main/Corp Wild Goose Association. 0161-3715. US. English. an. Wild Goose Association, Lloyd Higginbottom, 4 Townsend Road, Acton MA 01720. **LC** VK560. **DD** 623.8932.

RAPPORT ANNUEL - BELGIUM. OFFICE DE LA NAVIGATION. Main/Corp Belgium. Office de la Navigation. **VFOAT** Rapport sur le Fontionnement de l'office de la Navigation. French. an. **LC** HE673. **DD** 386.09493.

REGISTER OF COMMISSIONED AND WARRANT OFFICERS OF THE UNITED STATES NAVY AND MARINE CORPS. Main/Corp United States. Bureau of Naval Personnel. 1814-. US. English. ir. **LC** V11.

REGISTER OF COMMISSIONED AND WARRANT OFFICERS OF THE UNITED STATES NAVY AND RESERVE OFFICERS ON ACTIVE DUTY. Main/Corp United States. Navy. **VFOAT** Register of Navy Officers on Active Duty. Began with 1971. 0193-8665. US. English. an. Superintendent of Documents, US Government Printing Office, Washington DC 20402. **LC** V11.U7. **DD** 359.3320973. *Register of Commissioned and Warrant Officers of the United States Navy and Marine Corps and Reserve Officers on Active Duty.*

REGISTER OF OFFICERS - COAST GUARD. (REGISTER OF OFFICERS). **Main/Corp** United States. Coast Guard. **Series/Titl** Comdtinst. Began with 1 July 1976. 0364-8753. US. English. an. US Coast Guard, G-PO-3, Washington DC 20593. **LC** VG53. **DD** 359.97. *Register of Officers and Cadets, 0095-2818.*

REGISTER OF RESERVE OFFICERS. Main/Corp United States. Coast Guard. **Series/Titl** Comdtinst. **VFOAT** USCG Reserve Register. 0147-8982. US. English. an. US Coast Guard (G-RA-3), Washington DC 20593. **LC** VG53. **DD** 359.970973. Vols. for 1981- distributed to depository libraries in microfiche. *Register of Commissioned and Warranted Officers of the Coast Guard Reserve.*

RELATORIO - DEPARTAMENTO NACIONAL DE PORTOS E VIAS NAVEGAVEIS. Main/Corp Brazil. Departamento Nacional de Portos e Vias Navegaveis. Portuguese. ir. **LC** HE555.B8. **DD** 354.810087705. *Relatorio - Departamento Nacional de Portos, Rios e Canais.*

REPORT ON THE WORK OF THE BUREAU SINCE THE PREVIOUS CONFERENCE. Main/Corp International Hydrographic Bureau. English. ir. Intl Hydrographic Bureau, BP 345 7 Ave Pres JF Kennedy, MC98000 Monaco. **LC** VK596. **DD** 341.44.

A REPORT TO CONGRESS, ACTIVITIES RELATING TO THE PORT AND TANKER SAFETY ACT OF 1978. Main/Corp United States. Coast Guard. **VFOAT** Activities Relating to the Port and Tanker Safety Act of 1978. **VAT** A Report to Congress, Activities Relating to the Port and Tanker Safety Act of Nineteen Hundred and Seventy-Eight. July 1980-. 0276-7236. US. English. an. US Department of Transportation, US Coast Guard, Washington DC 20590. **LC** KF2558.T2. **DD** 343.730965, 347.303965. *Activities Relating to Title II Ports and Waterways Safety Act of 1972, 0147-4448.*

REPRESENTATION NAVALE. Main/Corp Bureau Veritas. FR. French. ir. Bureau Veritas, 31 rue Henri-Rochefort, 75321 Paris Cedex 17 France. **LC** HE565.A3. **DD** 387.2025.

Naval Science, Navigation

REVIEW - NAVAL RESEARCH LABORATORY (U.S.). (REVIEW). 1981-. 0736-4849. US. English. an. Naval Research Laboratory, Washington DC 20375. LC V394.W2. DD 623.80724. Vols. for 1981- distributed to depository libraries in microfiche. *NRL Review, 0732-7609.*

REVISTA DA ADISMAR. Main/Corp Fundacao Estudos do Mar. Associacao dos Diplomados. Portuguese. ir. Associacao dos Diplomados da Fundaco Estudos do Mar, Rua Marques de Olinda 18 ZC-02, Rio de Janeiro Brazil. LC VK4.

REVISTA DE HISTORIA NAVAL. Yearly V. 1, No. 1-. Periodical. Spanish. ty. $2.00 Single Issue. Museo Naval, Montalban, 2 Madrid-14 Espana Spain. LC D215.

RIVER CURRENTS (ST. LOUIS, MO. : 1981). (RIVER CURRENTS). Vol. 1, No. 1 (Apr./May 1981)-. 0145-0689. Periodical. US. English. bm. Second Coast Guard District, 1430 Olive Street, St Louis MO 63103. LC VG53. DD 359.970973. *River Currents, 0145-0689.*

RIVISTA MARITTIMA. Yearly V. 1- 1868-. 0035-6964. IT. Italian. mo. $10.70. Direzione di Commissariato MM, Via Domenico Albzrto Azuni 2, 00196 Rome Italy. **Ind/Abst** Am. Hist. Life, Hist. Abstr., Part A, Mod. Hist. Abstr., Hist. Abst., Part B, Twent. Century Abstr., Int. Aerosp. Abstr., Recent Publ. Artic. LC V4.

ROTEIRO : COSTA NORTE. Main/Corp Brazil. Diretoria de Hidrografia e Navegacao. Portuguese. ir. LC VK967.

SAFETY AT SEA. Began with Jan. 1978 issue. 0142-0666. Periodical. UK. English. mo. 32.50. Fuel & Metallurgical Journals Ltd, Queensway House, 2 Queensway Redhill, Surrey RH1 1QS England. **Ind/Abst** Electron. Commun. Abstr. J., ISMEC Bull., Pollut. Abstr. Indexes, Saf. Sci. Abstr. J., Life Sci. Collect. LC VK200. DD 623.88805. *Safety at Sea International.*

SAIL ASSISTANCE NEWS. Began with: Vol. 1, No. 1 (May 1982). 0882-5238. Periodical. US. English. qt. $100.00. Saila, 1553 Bayville Street, Norfolk VA 23503. **Tel** (804)588-6022. Ed Kathryn Hill. DD 797. bk rev. Circ 400. (ctrl) Illustrated digest of news and information, events and publications in the field of wind propulsion for commercial vessels of all kinds around the world.

SAILING DIRECTIONS, GREAT LAKES. VOL. I. 7th Ed. (1976)-. 0823-4329. CN. English. ir. LC VK983. DD 623.8922977. *Great Lakes Pilot. Vol. I.*

SCHIFF & HAFEN. (SCHIFF UND HAFEN). Began in April 1949. 0036-603X. Periodical. GW. German. mo. 247.20. Seehafen Verlag/Blumenfeld MBH, Postfach 105605/Wandalenweg 1, D-2000 Hamburg 1 West Germany. **Tel** 23714-02. Ed Hans Jurgen Witthoft. **Ind/Abst** Excerpta Med., Ship Abstr., CIS Abstr., Energy Res. Abstr., Fluidex, Met. Abstr., World Alum. Abstr. LC VM3. **CODEN** SCHHAW. bk rev. adv acc. Circ 6,011. (ctrl).

SCHIFF UND ZEIT. Yearly V. 1-. German. ir. Koehlers Verlagsgesellschaft, Postfach 310245, 4 Dusseldorf-Kaiserswerth West Germany. LC V3. DD 387.205.

SCHIFFBAUFORSCHUNG. (SCHIFFBAUFORSCHUNG : WISSENSCHAFTLICH-TECHNISCHE MITTEILUNGEN). 1. Yearly. (1962)-. 0036-6056. Periodical. GE. German. qt. BEB Kombinat Schiffbau, Doberaner Strobe 110/111, 2500 Rostock 6 West Germany. **Tel** 368 246. **Ind/Abst** Ship Abstr. bk rev. Research and development in shipbuilding, hydrodynamics model testing, vibrational behaviour and strength of ship structures, marine propulsion plants, behaviour of materials, corrosion.

SCHIP EN WERF. Began in 1934. Periodical. NE. Dutch. bw. Wyt & Zonen BV, Postbus 268/3000 AG, Rotterdam The Netherlands. **Ind/Abst** Excerpta Med., Ship Abstr., CIS Abstr. LC VM4.

SEA CLASSICS. 0048-9867. Periodical. US. English. $13.50. Challenge Publications, 7950 Deering Avenue, Canoga Park CA 91304. **Tel** (213)887-0550. **Ind/Abst** Am. Hist. Life, Hist. Abstr., Part A, Mod. Hist. Abstr., Hist. Abst., Part B, Twent. Century Abstr. LC VM1. DD 387.205. *Sea Combat, 0199-087X.*

SEA HISTORY. No. 1- Apr. 1972-. 0146-9312. Periodical. US. English. qt. $10.00 Includes Membership, $5.00 Students and Retired. National Maritime Historical Society, 2 Fulton Street, Brooklyn NY 11238. **Ind/Abst** Am. Hist. Life, Hist. Abstr., Part A, Mod. Hist. Abstr., Hist. Abst., Part B, Twent. Century Abstr., Artbibliogr. Mod. LC VK23. DD 387.00973.

THE SEAFARER. No. 1- Jan. 1934-. UK. English. qt. $8.43. Marine Society, 202 Lambeth Road, London SE1 7JW England. **Tel** 01 261 9535. Ed R Hope. **Ind/Abst** Ship Abstr. LC VK1. DD 656. bk rev. adv acc.

SEARCH. See Archaeology.

SELECTED EDUCATIONAL OPPORTUNITIES. Main/Corp Naval Research Laboratory. V. 30- 1974/75-. 0098-4256. US. English. Naval Research Laboratory, Washington DC 20375. LC V394.W2. DD 359.00720753. *Science Education Program, 0565-8616.*

SENIN ROPPO. Main/Corp Japan. Japanese. ir. 6500. Seizando Shoten, 4-51 Minami-Motocho, Shinjuku-ku 160 Tokyo Japan.

SENPAKU KAIYO KOGAKU GIJUTSU BUNKEN SOKUHO. See Indexes/Abstracts.

SHIP & BOAT INTERNATIONAL. ANNUAL GUIDE. VFOAT Ship and Boat International. 1983-. UK. English. an. Whitehall Press Ltd, Earl House/27 Earl Street, Maidstone Kent ME14 England. **Ind/Abst** Ship Abstr. LC VM320. DD 623.82005.

SHIPBUILDING AND BOATBUILDING. VFOAT Construction de Navires et d'Embarcations. 1981-. 0319-8987. CN. English (French). an. $5.00 Domestic, $6.00 Foreign. Publication Sales and Services, Statistics Canada, Ottawa Ontario K1A 0T6 Canada. DD 338.47623830971. *Boatbuilding and Repair (Final), 0527-4834; Shipbuilding and Repair (Final), 0527-6144.*

SHIPMATE. Began with May 1938 issue. 0488-6720. Periodical. US. English. mo. $20.00. US Naval Academy Alumni Association, Annapolis MD 21402. **Tel** (301)263-4448. Ed James W Hammond Jr. LC VA49. DD 359.05. bk rev. adv acc. Circ 26,000. Alumni magazine for United States naval academy- includes news of alumni, obituaries, chapters, general articles, both historical and current, concerning United States navy and naval academy.

SHIPPING CASUALTIES AND DEATH, VESSLES REGISTERED IN THE UNITED KINGDOM. Main/Corp Great Britain. Dept. of Trade and Industry. UK. English. an. 0.26. HMSO, Department of Trade and Industry, 49 High Holborn, London WC1V 6BH England. LC VK1282.G7. DD 387.5. *Shipping Casualties and Deaths, Vessels Registered in the United Kingdom.*

SJFARTSHISTORISK ARBOK. See Yearbooks, Almanacs, Directories.

SKIBSTILSYNETS MEDDELELSER. Main/Corp Denmark. Direktoratet for Statens Skibstilsyn. DK. Danish. ir. 40.00. Direktoratet for Statens, Skibstilsyn Snorresgade 19, 2300 Kbenhavn S Denmark. *Meddelelser.*

SOBO. Main/Corp Hanguk Sonbak Yonguso. VFOAT Bulletin of Kris. Vol. 1- No. Periodical. English (Korean). ir. Hanguk Sonbak Yonguso, PO Box 315, Taejon Korea. LC VM4. DD 623.82005.

SOUTH AFRICAN TIDE TABLES. VFOAT Suid—Afrikaanse Getytafels. SA. Afrikaans and English. ir. $0.75. Maritime Headquarters, Hydrographic Office, Youngsfield South Africa. LC VK687.1.

SOUTHERN CALIFORNIA CHART KIT. Main/Corp Better Boating Association. VFOAT Chart Kit. V. 1- 1979/80-. 0197-7407. US. English. $24.95. Better Boating Association, Box 407, Needham MA 02192. LC G1526.P5. DD 623.892097949.

SOVIET SHIPBUILDING. 0094-9892. US. English. Naval Intelligence Support Center, Translation Division, 4301 Suitland Road, Suitland MD 20390. LC VM4. DD 623.82005.

STATISTICS OF NAVY MEDICINE. See Statistics.

STOREKEEPER 3 & 2. Main/Corp Naval Education and Training Program Development Center. **Series/Titl** Rate Training Manual and Nonresident Career Course. VAT Storekeeper Three and Two. 0192-5350. US. English. Superintendent of Documents, Government Printing Office, Washington DC 20402. LC VC263. DD 658.7. *Storekeeper 3 & 2, 0192-5350.*

SUBMARIN. Periodical. German. ir. 3.00 Each Issue. Heering-Verlag, Ortrlerstrasse 8 8 70, Munchen West Germany. LC VM975.

SUIKO. Periodical. JA. Japanese. mo. Suikokai, 5-3 Jingumae 1, Shibuya-Ku 150, Tokyo-To Japan. LC V69.J3.

SUIROBU GIHO. VFOAT Technical Bulletin of Hydrography. Vol. 1- (March 1983)-. Periodical. JA. Japanese. ir. Kaijo Hoancho Suirobu, 3-ban 1-go Tsukiji 5-chome Chuo-ku, Tokyo-to 104 Japan. LC VK588.

SUOMEN RANNIKON LOISTOT. Main/Corp Finland. Merenkulkuhallitus. VFOAT Fyrar vid Finlands Kuster, List of Lights of Finland. 1978-. FI. Finnish (Swedish, with summaries in English). ir. Valtion Painatuskeskus, Lokero 158 Vuorimiehenkatu 1A, Helsinki 14 Finland. LC VK1185.F5. *Suomen Rannikon Loistot.*

SUPPLEMENT TO MERCHANT VESSELS OF THE UNITED STATES CEASED. -1 Jan. 1981. 0364-0957. Periodical. US. English. mo. Department of Transportation, U S Coast Guard, Washington DC 20593.

SUPPLEMENTAL TIDAL PREDICTIONS, ANCHORAGE, NIKISHKA, SELDOVIA, AND VALDEZ, ALASKA. 0270-8876. US. English. National Ocean Service, Rockville MD 20852. LC VK743. DD 623.894909798.

SUPPLEMENTARY PAPERS - ROYAL INSTITUTION OF NAVAL ARCHITECTS. Main/Corp Royal Institution of Naval Architects. 0373-529X. UK. English. Royal Institution of Naval Architects, 10 Upper Belgrave Street, London SW1X 8BQ England. **Ind/Abst** Life Sci. Collect. LC VM1. DD 623.8108.

SURFACE WARFARE. VFOAT Surface Warfare Magazine. Began with Sept. 1975. 0145-1073. Periodical. US. English. bm. $20.00. Superintendent of Documents, US Government Printing Office, Washington DC 20402. **Tel** (202)783-3238. LC V1. DD 359.005.

SURVEY OF CONTRACTING STATISTICS. See Statistics.

SVERIGES FLOTTA. Publication began in 1905. Periodical. Swedish. sm. LC V5.

SYMPOSIUM ON NAVAL HYDRODYNAMICS. PROCEEDINGS. VFOAT Naval Hydrodynamics. 1st- 1956-. 0082-0849. US. English. ir. LC V393. DD 532.5082.

TABLAS DE PREDICCION DE MAREAS : PUERTOS DEL OCEANO PACIFICO. Main/Corp Servicio Mareografico Nacional (Mexico). MX. Spanish. ir. Universidad Nacional Autonoma de Mexico, Instituto de Geofisica, Mexico 20 DF Mexico. LC VK749. DD 623.89490972. *Tablas de Prediccion de Mareas: Puertos del Oceano Pacifico.*

TABLICE MORSKIH MIJENA : JADRANSKO MORE, ISTOCNA OBALA. 1974-. Serbo-Croatian(R). ir. 40.00. LC VK664.

TABUAS DAS MARES : COSTA DO BRASIL E PORTOS ESTRANGEIROS. Portuguese. ir. LC VK767. DD 623.89490981. *Tabuas das Mares: Costa do Brasil.*

TARJAMAT MUKHTARAH MIN AL-MAJALLAT AL-ASKARIYAH AL-ALAMIYAH. See Military Science.

TELESCOPE. Began in June 1952. 0040-2702. Periodical. US. English. ir. $7.50 Domestic, $8.50 Foreign. Great Lakes Maritime Institute, Belle Isle, Detroit MI 48207. LC VK23.7. DD 386.50977.

TEXAS CRUISING GUIDE. 1980-. 0197-4114. US. English. an. Texas Cruising Guide, 2708 Sackett, Houston TX 77098. LC VK975. DD 623.8929764.

TIDAL CURRENT TABLES. ATLANTIC COAST OF NORTH AMERICA. VFOAT Atlantic Coast of North America. 1958-. 0501-8234. US. English. an. National Ocean Survey, US Department of Commerce, Coast and Geodetic Survey, Rockville MD 20852. LC VK781. DD 623.8949091634. *Current Tables. Atlantic Coast, North America for the Year . . ., 0743-7064.*

TIDAL CURRENT TABLES, PACIFIC COAST OF NORTH AMERICAN AND ASIA. (TIDAL CURRENT TABLES. PACIFIC COAST OF NORTH AMERICA AND ASIA FOR THE YEAR . . .). VFOAT Pacific Coast of North America and Asia. 1958-. US. English. an. National Ocean Service, US Department of Commerce, Coast and

Naval Science, Navigation

Geodetic Survey, Rockville MD 20852. LC VK747. DD 623.894909164. Vol. for 1984 distributed to depository libraries in microfiches. *Current Tables. Pacific Coast, North America and Asia for the Year . . . .*

TIDE, DISTANCE AND SPEED TABLES. 1951-. UK. English. an. Brown Son & Ferguson, 4 10 Darnley Street, Glasgow G41 2SD Scotland. LC VK627. DD 525.69.

TIDE TABLES, HIGH AND LOW WATER PREDICTIONS, EUROPE AND WEST COAST OF AFRICA, INCLUDING THE MEDITERRANEAN SEA. (TIDE TABLES . . . HIGH AND LOW WATER PREDICTIONS, EUROPE AND WEST COAST OF AFRICA, INCLUDING THE MEDITERRANEAN SEA). VFOAT Europe and West Coast of Africa, Including the Mediterranean Sea. Began with 1958. 0748-1047. US. English. an. National Ocean Service, Rockville MD 20852. LC VK610. DD 623.894909163. *Tide Tables, High and Low Water Predictions, Europe and West Coast of Africa (including Mediterranean Sea).*

TIDE TABLES, HIGH AND LOW WATER PREDICTIONS, WEST COAST OF NORTH AND SOUTH AMERICA, INCLUDING THE HAWAIIAN ISLANDS. (TIDE TABLES . . . HIGH AND LOW WATER PREDICTIONS, WEST COAST OF NORTH AND SOUTH AMERICA, INCLUDING THE HAWAIIAN ISLANDS). VFOAT West Coast of North and South America, Including the Hawaiian Island. Began with 1958. US. English. an. National Ocean Service, Rockville MD 20852. LC VK741. DD 623.8949091642. *Tide Tables, West Coast, North and SouthAmerica, (including the Hawaiian Islands).*

TIDE TABLES, MALAYSIA AND SINGAPORE. 1982-. English. ir. LC VK710. DD 623.894909595.

TIDEVANDSTABELLER FOR DANMARK. Main/Corp Denmark. Farvandsdirektoratet. Nautisk Afdeling. DK. Danish (English). ir. Farvandsdirektoratet Nautisk Afdeling Esplanaden 19, 1263 Kbenhavn K Denmark. LC VK623.

TIDEVANDSTABELLER FOR FRERNE. Main/Corp Denmark. Farvandsdirektoratet. Nautisk Afdeling. Vol. 1-. DK. Danish (English). ir. Farvandsdirektoratet Nautisk Afdeling Esplanaden 19, 1263 Kbenhavn K Denmark. LC VK614.F2.

TIDEVANDSTABELLER FOR GRNLAND. Began in 1966. 0107-0398. DK. Danish (English). an. Farvandsdirektoratet Nautisk Afdeling, Esplanaden 19, 1263 Kbenhavn K Denmark. LC VK614.G7. DD 623.894809982.

TIDSSKRIFT FOR SVSEN. 0040-7186. Periodical. Danish. mo. Ind/Abst Ship Abstr. LC V5.

TOYAMA SHOSEN KOTO SEMMON GAKKO KENKYU SHUROKU. No. 1-. JA. some articles in English. ir. 1-2 Ebie Neriai Shimminato, Toyama Japan. LC VK4.

TRANSACTIONS. Main/Conf International Buoy Technology Symposium. VFOAT Buoy Technology. 1964-. Periodical. US. English.

TRANSACTIONS OF THE INSTITUTION OF ENGINEERS AND SHIPBUILDERS IN SCOTLAND. Main/Corp Institution of Engineers and Shipbuilders in Scotland, Glasgow. V. 1- 1857/58-. 0020-3289. UK. English. Institution of Engineers & Charing Cross, Tower/10 Elmbank, Glasgow G2 4HT Scotland.

TRANSACTIONS - SOCIETY OF NAVAL ARCHITECTS AND MARINE ENGINEERS. (TRANSACTIONS - THE SOCIETY OF NAVAL ARCHITECTS AND MARINE ENGINEERS). Main/Corp Society of Naval Architects and Marine Engineers, New York. V. 1- 1893-. 0081-1661. US. English. an. $45.00. Society of Naval Architects and Marine Engineers, One World Trade Center/Suite 1369, New York NY 10048. Tel (212)432-0310. Ind/Abst Eng. Index Annu., Eng. Index Mon., Eng. Index Energy Abstr., Eng. Index, Eng. Index Bioeng. Abstr. LC VM1. DD 623.8105. CODEN SNAMAL. (cum index). Circ 7,000. (ctrl). A record of the Society's annual meeting papers for that year.

UNITED STATES COAST PILOT 1 : ATLANTIC COAST. EASTPORT TO CAPE COD. Main/Corp National Ocean Survey. 8th Edition-. Periodical. US. English. an. LC VK981. *United States Coast Pilot 1: Atlantic Coast. Eastport to Cape Cod.*

UNITED STATES COAST PILOT. 2, ATLANTIC COAST. CAPE COD TO SANDY HOOK. VFOAT Atlantic Coast. VAT United States Coast Pilot. Two, Atlantic Coast. Cape Cod to Sandy Hook. 6th Ed. (1960)-. 0363-695X. US. English. an. National Ocean Service, Rockville MD 20852. LC VK981. DD 623.892974. Vols. for 17th Ed., Jan. 1982-18th Ed., Jan. 1983 Distributed to depository libraries in microfiche. *United States Coast Pilot. Atlantic Coast. Section B, Cape Cod to Sandy Hook, 8755-2345.*

UNITED STATES COAST PILOT. 3, ATLANTIC COAST. SANDY HOOK TO CAPE HENRY. VFOAT Atlantic Coast. 6th Ed. (1953)-. 0363-3217. US. English. an. National Ocean Service, Rockville MD 20852. LC VK982.M53. DD 623.892974. Vol. for (19th Ed., July 1981)-20th Ed., July 1982 distributed to depository libraries in microfiche. *United States Coast Pilot. Atlantic Coast. Section C, Sandy Hook to Cape Henry, 8756-1581.*

UNITED STATES COAST PILOT. 4, ATLANTIC COAST. CAPE HENRY TO KEY WEST. VFOAT Atlantic Coast. VAT United States Coast Pilot. Four, Atlantic Coast. Cape Henry to Key West. 6th Ed. (1955)-. 0362-7713. US. English. an. National Ocean Service, Rockville MD 20852. LC VK982.S68. DD 623.892976. Vol. for (19th Ed., July 1981)-20th Ed., July 1982 distributed to depository libraries in microfiche. *United States Coast Pilot. Atlantic Coast. Section D, Cape Henry to Key West, 8755-142X.*

UNITED STATES COAST PILOT. 5, ATLANTIC COAST. GULF OF MEXICO, PUERTO RICO, AND VIRGIN ISLANDS. VFOAT Atlantic Coast. 6th Ed. (1967)-. 0360-0149. US. English. an. US Department of Commerce, National Oceanic & Atmospheric Administration, Washington DC 20230. LC VK975. DD 623.892976. *United States Coast Pilot. 5, Gulf Coast, Puerto Rico, and Virgin Islands, 8755-1446.*

UNITED STATES COAST PILOT. 6, GREAT LAKES, LAKES ONTARIO, ERIE, HURON, MICHIGAN, AND SUPERIOR AND ST. LAWRENCE RIVER. VFOAT Great Lakes, Lakes Ontario, Erie, Huron, Michigan, and Superior and St. Lawrence River. VAT United States Coast Pilot. Six, Great Lakes, Lakes Ontario, Eric, Huron, Michigan, and Superior and Saint Lawrence River. Began with 1978. 0161-4444. US. English. an. National Ocean Service NOAA, Rockville MD 20852. LC VK983. DD 628.892977. *United States Great Lakes Pilot. Lakes Ontario, Erie, Huron, Michigan, and Superior, and St. Lawrence River, 0362-8329.*

UNITED STATES COAST PILOT. 8, PACIFIC COAST. ALASKA: DIXON ENTRANCE TO CAPE SPENCER. (UNITED STATES COAST PILOT. 8, PACIFIC COAST. ALASKA, DIXON ENTRANCE TO CAPE SPENCER). VFOAT Pacific Coast. VAT United States Coast Pilot. Eight, Pacific Coast. Alaska: Dixon Entrance to Cape Spencer. 0163-9471. US. English. be. National Ocean Survey, Rockville MD 20852. LC VK943.U7. DD 623.8929798. Vol. for 1982 was distributed to depository libraries in microfiche. *United States Coast Pilot. Southeast Alaska, Dixon Entrance to Yakutat Bay.*

UNITED STATES COAST PILOT 9, PACIFIC AND ARTIC COASTS. ALASKA: CAPE SPENCER TO BEAUFORT SEA. (UNITED STATES COAST PILOT. 9, PACIFIC AND ARCTIC COASTS. ALASKA, CAPE SPENCER TO BEAUFORT SEA). VFOAT Pacific and Arctic coasts. Began with 7th ed. in 1964. 0278-0089. US. English. be. US Department of Commerce, National Oceanic & Atmospheric Administration, National Ocean Survey C44, Riverside MD 20840. LC VK943.U7. DD 623.8929798. Vol. for 11th Ed., Jan. 1983 Distributed to depository libraries in microfiche. *United States Coast Pilot. 9, Alaska. Cape Spencer to Arctic Ocean.*

U.S. MARITIME MONTHLY. (U.S. MARITIME MONTHLY : NATIONAL NEWSPAPER OF THE U.S. MARITIME INDUSTRIES). VFOAT US Maritime Monthly. VAT United States Maritime Monthly. 0744-8651. Periodical. US. English. mo. $3.00. Banner News Service, 622 6th Avenue West, Seattle WA 98119. Tel (206)284-6176.

UTILITIESMAN 3 & 2. Main/Corp United States. Naval Training Command. Series/Titl Rate Training Manual. 0095-7410. US. English. LC VC417.5. DD 623.75.

UTILIZATION OF SHIPBUILDING AND REPAIR FACILITIES SERIES. Series Corp United Nations. Document. No. 1- 1972-. US. English. United Nations Industrial Development Organization, Sales Section/Room A3315, New York NY 10017. LC JX1977. DD 623.82008 S.

VERKEERSGEGEVENS. Series/Titl Nota DVK. NE. Dutch. an. Rijkswaterstaat Onderafdeling Permanente, Inwinning en Uitvoer, Postbus 20906, 2500 Ex's-Gravenhage Netherlands. LC HE674.

VESSEL SAFETY REVIEW. 0145-1146. Periodical. US. English. mo. Washington Department of Transportation/Coast Guard, Commondant G CSP/61, Washington DC 20590. LC VK200. DD 623.8905. *Vessel Safety Newsletter.*

VIKINGEN. Began with Vol. for 1924. Periodical. Danish. ir. 4.65 Single Issue. Christiansborggade 1, 1558 Kbenhavin Denmark. LC VM4.

WARSHIP. Jan. 1977-. 0142-6222. Periodical. UK. English. qt. 14.00 Domestic, $26.00. Conway Maritime Press, 24 Bridge Lane/Fleet Street, London EC4Y 8DR England. Tel (01)483-2412. Ed Andrew Lambert. LC V765. DD 359.83. bk rev. adv acc. Circ 4,000. Design, development, and service history of warships. Emphasis on accuracy and high quality illustration.

WARSHIP INTERNATIONAL. V. 1-. 0043-0374. Periodical. US. English. qt. $18.00. International Naval Research Organization, 1729 Lois Court, Toledo OH 43613. Tel (419)472-1331. Ed Christorpher C Wright. Ind/Abst Am. Hist. Life, Hist. Abstr., Part A, Mod. Hist. Abstr., Hist. Abst., Part B, Twent. Century Abstr., Writ. Am. Hist., Hist. Abstr., Recent Publ. Artic. LC V750. DD 359.83. bk rev. Circ 4,500. Naval history of ships all over the world.

WATER LEVELS. TIDAL HIGHS AND LOWS. (WATER LEVELS : TIDAL HIGHS AND LOWS). Main/Corp Tides, Currents and Water Levels (Canada). VFOAT Niveaux d'Eau : Hauteurs de Pleine et Basse Mer. VAT Niveaux d'Eau. Hauteurs de Pleine et Basse Mer. 1975-. 0706-2346. CN. English (French). an. $4.00 Domestic, $4.80 Foreign. Printing and Publishing, Supply and Services Canada, Ottawa Ontario K1A 0S9 Canada. LC V794. DD 623.89490971. *Water Levels, 0068-7669.*

WATERWAY GUIDE. NORTHERN EDITION. (WATERWAY GUIDE). 0090-712X. Periodical. US. English. an. Waterway Guide Inc, 850 Third Avenue, New York NY 10022. Tel (212)715-2600. Ed Queene Hooper. adv acc. Circ 75,000. Navigational advice for the waters of the East Coast and the Gulf Coast, the ICW and the Great Lakes. *Inland Waterway Guide. Northern Edition.*

WEYER'S FLOTTENASCHENBUCH. (WEYER'S WARSHIPS OF THE WORLD). 1968-. 0741-000X. US. English. an. $49.95. Nautical & Aviation Publishing Company of America, 8 Randall Street, Annapolis MD 21401. Ed A Bredt. LC V10. DD 623.82505.

WEYERS FLOTTENTASCHENBUCH. Began publication with 1900 issue. Vols. for 1977/78- in German and English. ir. Ed B Weyer and A Bredt. LC V10.

THE WORK BOAT. 1- 1944-. 0043-8014. Periodical. US. English. mo. $20.00. H L Peace Publications, PO Box 2400, Covington LA 70434. Tel (504)893-2930. Ed Rick Stouffer. Ind/Abst Ocean. Abstr. LC VK1. DD 386.205. adv acc. Circ 12,000. (ctrl). The publication strives to analyze national and international developments of vital interest to those in the work boat industry of the US.

WORLD WARSHIPS FORECAST. 1984-. 0882-5610. US. English. an. Defense Marketing Services, 100 Northfield Street, Greenwich CT 06830. LC V750. DD 623.825025.

YEARBOOK. *See* Yearbooks, Almanacs, Directories.

YOKYUJO KAINAN TOKEI. Began with 1970 issue. JA. Japanese. ir. Kaijo Hoancho Keibi Kyunanbu, Koko Anzen Kikakika, 1-3 Kasumigaseki 2-chome Chiyoda-ku, Tokyo Japan. LC VK1288.J3.

ZEEMANSGIDS VOOR DE NEDERLANDSE KUST. Main/Corp Netherlands (Kingdom, 1815-). Hydrografisch Bureau. Dutch. ir. Hydrografische Bureau, Staatsdrukkerij, 'S-Gravenhage Netherlands. LC V825. *Zeemansgids voor de Nederlandsche Kust.*

NEWSPAPERS

2 RIVES. (LES 2 RIVES). **VAT** Deux Rives. Vol. 1, No. 1 12 Sept 1978-. 0710-5541. Newspaper. CN. French. wk. $15.00. Publ S P G, Les 2 Rives, 57 rue Georges, Sorel Quebec J3P 1B9 Canada. **DD** 071.1451.

7 15. LE JOURNAL DES JEUNES. (7/15, LE JOURNAL DES JEUNES). No. 1- May 1976-. 0700-303X. Periodical. CN. French. $5. Journal 7/15, CP 457 Succursale Beaubien, Montreal Quebec H2B 3E2 Canada. **DD** 070.483205.

20 DE MAYO. **VAT** Veinte de Mayo. 1969. 0164-5234. Newspaper. US. Spanish. sw. $28.00. 20 de Mayo, 1824 Sunset Boulevard Suite 202, Los Angeles CA 90026. **Tel** (213)483-8511. **Ed** Abel Perez. adv acc. **Circ** 25,000. A Spanish newspaper with a variety of subjects ranging from politics, sports and social events among many others. Oriented to the Hispanic community of Southern California.

1441. **VFOAT** Fourteen Forty-One. **VAT** Fourteen Forty-One, Quatorze Quarante et Un. Vol. 1, No. 1 (Apr. 1979)-. 0824-4561. Newspaper. CN. English (text also in French). mo. YMCA Montreal Dowtown Branch, 1441 Drummond Street, Montreal Quebec H3G 1W5 Canada. **DD** 071.14281.

ABC FACTBOOK CEASED. (A B C FACTBOOK). **Main/Corp** Audit Bureau of Circulations. 1971/72-1979/1980. 0098-2520. US. English. an.

ACHIMOWIN. V. 3, No. 25- Aug. 25, 1975-. 0705-839X. Periodical. CN. English. wk. Achimowin Program, c/o A Guiboche Editor, 1 Public Road, Thompson Manitaba R8N 0M3 Canada. **DD** 071.1272. Achimowin Weekly, 0705-839X.

ACTION. (L'ACTION). V. 1, No. 4- 18 Sept 1974-. 0318-0336. CN. French. $12.00. L'Action, CP 1118, Rawdon Quebec Canada. **DD** 071.14415. L'Action de Montcalm, 0318-0328.

ADEL NEWS TRIBUNE. Vol. 95, No. 1, (July 6, 1983)-. 0746-0716. Monographic Series. US. English. wk. Cook Publishing Co Inc, 131 South Hutchinson Avenue, Adel GA 31620. Adel News, Cook County Tribune.

ADVANCE. (THE ADVANCE). 0824-6610. Newspaper. CN. English. wk $10.00. The Advance, P O Box 190, Zurich Ont N0M 2T0 Canada. **DD** 071.1322.

THE ADVANCE REPORTER. Began in Jan. 1976?. 0747-3338. Newspaper. US. English. wk $8.00 Williams & adjoining Ohio counties, $10.00 Others. The Advance Reporter, Box 626, Stryker OH 43557. West Unity Reporter, Stryker Advance.

ADVERTISER (MONTGOMERY, ALA.). (THE ADVERTISER). 155th Year, No. 232 (Nov. 22, 1982)-. 4435-3221. Newspaper. US. English. da. $105.56. Montgomery Advertiser, PO Box 1000-C, Montgomery AL 36192. **Tel** (205)262-1611. Available on microfilm. Montgomery Advertiser.

ADVOCATE (STAMFORD, CONN.). (THE ADVOCATE). 0279-5167. Newspaper. US. English. da. $163.80. Stamford Advocate, 75 Tressor Boulevard P O Box 9307, Stamford CT 06904. **Tel** (203)964-2359.

THE AFRICAN NEWSPAPER INDEX. See Indexes/Abstracts.

AFRO-AMERICAN (BALTIMORE, MD. : 1965) CEASED. (THE AFRO-AMERICAN). **VFOAT** Afro American. 74th year, No. 18 Nov. 20, 1965-77th year, No. 24 (Dec. 28, 1968). Newspaper. US. English. wk. Afro-American Newspapers, PO Box 1857, Baltimore MD 21203. **Tel** (301)728-8200. Philadelphia Afro-American.

L'AGENDA. 0279-8212. Periodical. US. English. sm. $10.00. Italian American News, 26 Court Street, Brooklyn NY 11242. **Tel** (212)875-0580. Available in microfilm.

AGRI NEWS. 0745-3450. Newspaper. US. English. wk. Post Bulletin Company, 18 First Avenue SE, Rochester MN 55901. **Tel** (507)285-7600.

AL AHRAM. Newspaper. Arabic. da. 80.00. Al Ahram, Al Galaa Street, Cario UAR Egypt. **Tel** 755500.

AIRDRIE & DISTRICT ECHO. V. 1- Nov. 26, 1975-. 0383-1248. Newspaper. CN. English. wk. $5. Airdrie & District Echo, PO Box 568, Airdrie Alberta T0M 0B0 Canada. **DD** 071.1233.

AIRNEWS. V. 1, No. 1 (Sept. 15, 1981)-. 0711-7221. Newspaper. CN. English. da. Free. Airnews Southam Inc, 321 Bloor Street East, Toronto Ontario M4W 1H3 Canada. **DD** 071.1. (ctrl).

AIRS, INDEX TO THE DAILY GLEANER OF JAMAICA. See Indexes/Abstracts.

AKROPOLIS. (E ACROPOLIS). **VFOAT** Acropolis Newspaper. **VAT** Acropolis (Vancouver). 15 July 1977-. 0713-8539. Newspaper. CN. Greek and Modern. mo. Akropolis, Suite 215/222 Ash Street, New Westminister Brithish Columbia V3M 3M4 Canada. **DD** 071.1133.

AL-THAWRAH AL-USBUI. **VFOAT** Ath-Thawra Weekly. Periodical. Arabic. wk. .02 Single Issue. Dar Al-Thawrah Lil-Sihafah Wa-Al-Nashr Sahat Aqabat IBN Nafi Tariq Muaskar Al-Rashid, S B 2009, Baghdad Iraq.

AL-UMMAH AL-ISLAMIYAH. V. 1, No. 1, Al-Jumah Ghurrat Dhu Al-Qadah 1402 AGH. Newspaper. UA. Arabic. mo. 0.10 Single Issue. S B 38 Al-Azhar, Al-Qahirah Egypt.

THE ALABAMA JOURNAL. (ALABAMA JOURNAL). Began in 1888. 0745-323X. Newspaper. US. English. da. $105.56. Alabama Journal, PO Box 1000, Montgomery AL 36192. **Tel** (205)262-1611. **LC** NEWSPAPER.

ALBERT LEA TRIBUNE. Newspaper. US. English. $60.00. Albert Lea Tribune, PO Box 16, Albert Lea MN 56007. **Tel** (507)373-1411.

ALBERTAN'S NORTH SIDE MIRROR. (THE ALBERTAN'S NORTH SIDE MIRROR). **VFOAT** North Side Mirror. Began with March 18, 1975 issue. 0319-5414. Newspaper. CN. English. wk. The Albertan, 830-10th Avenue Southwest, Calgary Alberta T2R 0B1 Canada. **DD** 071.1233.

THE ALBION RECORDER. 8750-9008. Newspaper. US. English. da. The Albion Recorder, 111 West Center, Albion MI 49224. Ablion Evening Recorder.

ALBUQUERQUE JOURNAL. **VFOAT** Sunday Journal. V. 189, No. 81 (June 20, 1926)-. Newspaper. US. English. da. 717 Silver Avenue Southwest, Albuquerque NM 87103. **LC** NEWSPAPER 8813. Albuquerque Morning Journal (Albuquerque, N. Mex. : 1903).

THE ALBUQUERQUE TRIBUNE. Began with Feb. 20, 1933 issue. Newspaper. US. English. da. 717 Silver Avenue Southwest, Albuquerque NM 87103. **LC** NEWSPAPER. New Mexico State Tribune.

ALEXANDRIA DAILY TOWN TALK. **VFOAT** Daily Town Talk. Mar. 17, 1883-. Newspaper. US. English. da. $84.00. Alexandria Daily Town Talk, PO Box 7558, Alexandria LA 71306. **Tel** (318)487-6421. **Ed** Jim Butler. bk rev. adv acc. **Circ** 40,000. Newspaper.

THE ALEXANDRIA JOURNAL. 0162-2064. Newspaper. US. English. da. $39.00. Journal Newspaper Group, 6885 Commercial Drive, Springfield VA 22151. **Tel** (703)551-3014.

ALEXANDRIA LAKE REGION PRESS. Newspaper. US. English. wk. $27.00. Alexandria Newspaper, PO Box 549, Alexandria MN 56308. **Tel** (612)763-3133.

THE ALEXANDRIA TIMES-TRIBUNE. **VAT** Alexandria Times Tribune. 0746-1542. Newspaper. US. English. wk. Elwood Publishing Company, 317 South Anderson Street, Elwood IN 46036.

ALFABETA. Yearly V. 1, No. 1 (May 1979)-. Periodical. IT. Italian. mo. $23.76. Cooperativa Intraprese, Via Caposile 2, 20137 Milano Italy. bk rev. adv acc. **Circ** 30,000. (ctrl). Local and international news of literature and other cultural arts.

ALLIANCE UPDATE. 0273-8023. Periodical. US. English. ir. American Alliance for Health, Physical Education, Recreation and Dance, 1900 Association Drive/Business Office, Reston VA 22091. **Tel** (703)476-3400. Aahperd Update, 0199-932X.

ALTON TELEGRAPH (ALTON, ILL : 1852 : DAILY). (ALTON TELEGRAPH). Began in 1852. Newspaper. US. English. da. $93.00. Alton Telegraph, 111 East Broadway, Alton IL 62002. **Tel** (618)463-2511. **LC** Newspaper 7574-X.

Newspapers

THE AMADOR PROGRESS NEWS AND THE IONE VALLEY ECHO. (THE ... AMADOR PROGRESS NEWS AND THE IONE VALLEY ECHO). **VFOAT** Ione Valley Echo. 8750-5002. Newspaper. US. English. ir. $15.00 In County, $21.00 Out of County. The Amador Progress-News, PO Box 606, Ione CA 95640.

THE AMERICAN. 1885-1898. Newspaper. US. English. da. $84.00. Lake Charles American, 327 Broad Street P O Box 2893, Lake Charles LA 70602. **Tel** (318)439-2781. **Ed** Jim Bean and Buddy Threatt. bk rev. adv acc. **Circ** 40,000. Complete news and sports coverage in Southwest Louisiana with over 70% home delivered penetration.

AMERICKE LISTY. V. 1, No. 28 (Dec. 16, 1962)-. Newspaper. US. Czech (some advertisements in English). wk. 283 Oak Street, Perth Amboy NJ 08861. **LC** Newspaper 8908B. Available on microfilm from the Library of Congress Photo Duplication Service. New Yorske Listy (New York, N.Y.).

AMERIKAN UUTISET. V. 29, No. 96 (Aug. 16, 1960)-. 0745-9971. Newspaper. US. Finnish. $23.00. Amerikan Uutiset Inc, 337 South Third Street, Lantana FL 33462. **LC** Newspaper. Minnesota Uutiset.

AMERISKA DOMOVINA. **VFOAT** American Home. V. 22, No. 24 (Feb. 26, 1919)-. 0164-680X. Newspaper. US. Slovenian (English). ir. Ameriska Domovini, 6117 St Clair Avenue, Cleveland OH 44103. Clevelandska Amerika.

ANCHORAGE DAILY NEWS. Began in 1946. 0194-6870. Newspaper. US. English. da. Anchorage Daily News, Pouch 6616, Anchorage AK 99502. **Tel** (907)786-4375. **Ed** Gerald Grilly. **LC** NEWSPAPER. adv acc. **Circ** 51,180. (ctrl). Daily news for national, international, Alaska state wide and Anchorage area.

ANCHORAGE DAILY TIMES. Began in 1916. Newspaper. US. English. da. $96.00. Anchorage Times Publishing Co, PO Box 40, Anchorage AK 99510. **Tel** (907)263-9009. **Ed** Tony Durr. **LC** NEWSPAPER. bk rev. adv acc. **Circ** 50,000. (ctrl). Alaska's leading newspaper.

ANDERSON HERALD (ANDERSON, IND. : DAILY). (THE ANDERSON HERALD). **VFOAT** Anderson Sunday Herald. Newspaper. US. English. ir. Anderson Newspapers Inc, Old Mansfield Road, Anderson IN 46015. **Tel** (216)264-6666.

THE ANN ARBOR NEWS. Newspaper. US. English. da. 340 East Huron Street, Ann Arbor MI 48106. **LC** NEWSPAPER. Ann Arbor Times News.

ANNUAIRE DE LA PRESSE ET DE LA PUBLICITE. See Yearbooks, Almanacs, Directories.

THE ANOKA COUNTY UNION. **VFOAT** Anoka Weekly Union. Began in 1869. Newspaper. US. English. wk. $10.00. Anoka County Union, PO Box 99, Anoka MN 55303. **Tel** (612)421-4444. **LC** Newspaper 8447. Anoka Weekly Union.

ANTELOPE VALLEY LEDGER-GAZETTE. **VFOAT** Antelope Valley Ledger Gazette. Began in 1886. Newspaper. US. English. da. Daily Ledger Gazette, PO Box 4048, Lancaster CA 93534. **Tel** (805)948-4701. Antelope Valley Gazette, Antelope Valley Ledger.

ANTELOPE VALLEY PRESS. **VFOAT** Valley Press. 1915. 0744-5830. Newspaper. US. English. ir. $55.00. Antelope Valley Newspapers, PO Box 880/708 East Avenue Q-9, Palmdale CA 93550. **Tel** (805)273-2700. **Ed** Vern Lawson. bk rev. adv acc. **Circ** 46,000. (ctrl). General news and features at local, state and national levels with emphasis on local and sports features.

ANTIGONISH SPECTATOR. (THE ANTIGONISH SPECTATOR). Vol. 1, No. 1 (Dec. 8, 1976)-. 0229-799X. Newspaper. CN. English. bw. $0.25 Per No. Antigonish Spectator, PO Box 1542, Antigonish NS B2G 2L8 Canada. **DD** 071.1614.

ANZA VALLEY OUTLOOK. 0883-6124. Newspaper. US. English. wk. Anza Valley Outlook, PO Box 1050, Anza CA 92306.

APACHE COUNTY INDEPENDENT-NEWS. Began in 1883. Periodical. US. English. ir. White Mountain Publishing Company, Box 639, St Johns AZ 85936.

APNA WATAN (MONTREAL, QUEBEC). (APNA WATAN). **VFOAT** APNA Watan. 0824-5568. Newspaper. CN. English (text also in Urdu). mo. Free. APNA Watan, Suite 16 1675 Grenet Street, Saint-Laurent, Quebec H4L 2R6 Canada. **DD** 954.005.

2051

Newspapers

APPEAL-DEMOCRAT. VFOAT Appeal Democrat. Began with Sept. 1, 1927 issue. Newspaper. US. English. da. Marysville Appeal Democrat, 319 G Street, Marysville CA 95901. **Tel** (916)741-2345. *Marysville Appeal, Marysville Democrat.*

AQUI Y AHORA LA JUVENTUD. Yearly V. 1, No. 1 (16 Al 29 De Sept., 1982). Periodical. Spanish. sm. Casilla de Correo 674, 1000 Correo Central Buenos Aires Argentina.

ARAB NEWS. V. 1-. 0254-833X. Newspaper. SU. English. da. $200.00. Saudi Research & Marketing Inc, 1331 Pennsylvania Avenue NW #920, Washington DC 20004. **Tel** (202)638-7183. bk rev. adv acc. **Circ** 40,000. Saudi Arabia's foremost English-language daily newspaper, provides firsthand information about Saudi business activities, local and international news and social activities.

ARAB NEWS. VAT Akhbar Al-Arab Fi Toronto. V. 1- May 1978-. 0707-3372. Newspaper. CN. English (text also in Arabic). Arab News, PO Box 378 Station A, Ottawa Ontario K1N 8V4 Canada. **DD** 071.13541.

ARC. May 20, 1980-. 0274-5704. Periodical. US. English. mo. ARC, The Softball Magazine of Texas, 3537 Wayland, Fort Worth TX 76013.

ARCADE HERALD. 0746-102X. Newspaper. US. English. wk. Arcade Herald Inc, 290 Main Street, Arcade NY 14009.

ARCADIAN RECORDER. (THE ARCADIAN RECORDER). VFOAT Recorder. VAT Recorder (Halifax). 0710-1120. Newspaper. CN. English. $6.50. PO Box 2437 Station M, Halifax NS B3J 3E4 Canada. **DD** 071.1622.

THE ARGUS. VFOAT Cape Argus. Jan. 3, 1857-. Newspaper. SA. English. da. $158.38. The Argus/South Africa, PO Box 56, Cape Town 8000 South Africa. **Tel** (021)231163. Ed Andrew Drysaacc. bk rev. adv acc. **Circ** 90,000. Largest English daily, Monday through Saturday, published in Cape Town.

THE ARGUS-CHAMPION. VFOAT Argus Champion. Began in 1927. Newspaper. US. English. wk. $18.00. Argus-Champion, 18A West Street, PO Box 509, Newport NH 03773. **Tel** (603)863-1776. Ed Peggy Grossman. adv acc. **Circ** 6,000. (ctrl). Community newspaper offering news of local interest. *New Hampshire Argus and Spectator Republican Champion.*

THE ARGUS-TIMES. VAT Argus Times. Vol. 80, No. 5 (Aug. 4, 1983)-. 0746-1623. Newspaper. US. English. wk. Argus-Times Newspaper, 111 South 2nd, Texhoma OK 73949. *Argus (Texhoma, Okla.), Texhoma Times.*

ARIZONA DAILY STAR. Newspaper. US. English. da. $260.00. Tucson Citizen, PO Box 26807, Tucson AZ 85726. **Tel** (602)573-4511.

THE ARIZONA REPUBLIC. Began with May 19, 1890 issue. Newspaper. US. English. da. $377.00. Phoenix Newspapers Inc, PO Box 1950, 120 East Van Buren Street, Phoenix AZ 85001. **Tel** (602)271-8503. LC Newspaper.

ARIZONA SILVER BELT. Began with May 2, 1878 issue. Newspaper. US. English. wk. $9.00. Copper Belt Printing & Publishing Company, PO Box 31, Globe AZ 85501. **Tel** (602)425-7121.

ARIZONA WILDLIFE VIEWS : THE NEWSPAPER OF THE ARIZONA GAME AND FISH DEPARTMENT. VFOAT Wildlife Views. 0882-5572. Periodical. US. English. mo. $3.00. Arizona Game and Fish Department, 2222 West Greenway Road, Phoenix AZ 85023. *Wildlife Views, 0043-5538.*

ARKANSAS DEMOCRAT (LITTLE ROCK, ARK. : 1878.). (ARKANSAS DEMOCRAT). Began in 1878. Newspaper. US. English. da. $132.00. Arkansas Democrat, PO Box 2221, Little Rock AR 72203. **Tel** (501)378-3400. Ed John R Starr. bk rev. adv acc. (ctrl). Metropolitan Daily and Sunday newspaper covering the entire state of Arkansas circulation wise. *Evening Star (Little Rock, Ark.).*

ARKANSAS GAZETTE INDEX. See Indexes/Abstracts.

ARKANSAS TIMES. 0164-6273. Periodical. US. English. mo. $10.00. Arkansas Writers' Project Inc, Union Station Square, Little Rock AR 72201. *Union Station Times.*

THE ARLINGTON JOURNAL. 0273-6381. Newspaper. US. English. da. $39.00. Journal Newspaper Group, 6883 Commercial Drive, Springfield VA 22159. **Tel** (703)751-3014. *Arlington Journal and Globe, 0199-0551.*

THE ARMENIAN MIRROR-SPECTATOR. VAT Armenian Mirror Spectator. 0004-234X. Newspaper. US. English. wk. $30.00. Baikar Association Inc, 755 Mt Auburn Street, Watertown MA 02172. **Tel** (617)924-4420. Ed Ara Kalaydjian. bk rev. adv acc. **Circ** 3,300. (ctrl). We cover the North American Armenian community news of cultural, social, political and religious activities. *Armenian Mirror.*

ARMENIAN OBSERVER. 0044-894X. Newspaper. US. English. wk. $25.00. Armenian Observer, 6646 Hollywood Boulevard Suite 207, Los Angeles CA 90028. **Tel** (213)467-6767.

THE ARMENIAN REPORTER. 0004-2358. Newspaper. US. English. wk. $35.00. Armenian Reporter, PO Box 600, Fresh Meadow NY 11365. **Tel** (718)380-3636. Ed Edward K Bogosian. bk rev. adv acc. **Circ** 5,000. Covers and reports all the news pertaining to the Armenian community and people.

THE ARMENIAN WEEKLY. Began in 1969. 0004-2374. Periodical. US. English. wk. $25.00. Hairenik Association, 212 Stuart Street, Boston MA 02116. **Tel** (617)542-3650.

THE ARMOUR CHRONICLE. VFOAT Armour, S.D. Chronicle. 8750-2488. Newspaper. US. English. wk. $10.00 Douglas & Charles Mix Counties, $12.00 Elsewhere in State, $14.00 Out of State. The Armour Chronicle, Box 1287, Armour SD 57313-0128. *Chronicle (Armour, S.D.).*

ARROWSMITH STAR. (THE ARROWSMITH STAR). V. 1- March 4, 1975-. 0319-5589. Newspaper. CN. English. wk. Free. The Arrowsmith Star, PO Box 1300, Parksville British Columbia V0R 2S0 Canada. **DD** 071.1134.

ARTHUR ADVANCE-TIMES. (THE ARTHUR ADVANCE-TIMES). VFOAT Advance-Times. V. 1- Aug. 1, 1979-. 0226-6652. Newspaper. CN. English. wk. $9.50 Canadian, $13.50 Foreign. Fergus-Elora News Express, PO Box 338, Arthur Ontario N0G 1A0 Canada. **DD** 071.1342.

ASAHI EVENING NEWS. 0025-2816. Newspaper. JA. English. da. 74,160. Oversea Courier Service, No 9 Shibaura 2-Chome, Minato-Ku Japan. **Tel** 03-543-3321. adv acc. **Circ** 30,280. English edition of Asahi newspaper with articles on current events.

ASAHI SHINBUN. Newspaper. JA. Japanese. da. $492.50. Japan Publications Trading Company Limited, PO Box 5030, Tokyo International, Tokyo 100-31 Japan.

ASBURY PARK EVENING PRESS. VFOAT Asbury Park Evening Press and Evening News. Began June 22, 1903 issue. Newspaper. US. English. da. $168.00. 3601 Highway 66 Box 1550, Neptune NJ 07754. **Tel** (201)922-6000. Ed E Donald Lass. bk rev. adv acc. **Circ** 130,672. Newspaper serving Monmouth and Ocean counties with general news and advertising. *Asbury Park Daily Press.*

ASHARQ AL-AWSAT. VFOAT Asharq Al Awsat. 0265-5772. Newspaper. UK. Arabic. da. $200.00. Asharq Al-Awsat, 2100 West Loop South #1000, Houston TX 77027.

ASHEVILLE CITIZEN (ASHEVILLE, N.C. : 1885). (THE ASHEVILLE CITIZEN). VFOAT Asheville Citizen and Asheville Times. Began in 1885. Newspaper. US. English. da. 14 O Henry Avenue, Asheville NC 28802. LC Newspaper 9137-X.

THE ASHEVILLE TIMES. VFOAT Asheville Citizen and Asheville Times. Vol. 21, No. 6 (Feb. 21, 1916)-. Newspaper. US. English. da. 14 O Henry Avenue, Asheville NC 28802. LC Newspaper 7002. *Asheville Gazette-News.*

ASIAN TRIBUNE. (THE ASIAN TRIBUNE). V. 1- June 1978-. 0707-3380. Periodical. CN. English. mo. 30 Per No. The Asian Tribune, 853 Gladstone Avenue, Toronto Ontario M6H 3J7 Canada. **DD** 954.005.

ASIANWEEK. VFOAT Asian Week. Began in 1979. 0195-2056. Newspaper. US. English. wk. $15.00. Asian Week, 811 Sacramento Street, San Francisco CA 94108. **Tel** (415)397-0220. Ed Patrick Andersen. bk rev. adv acc. **Circ** 30,000. (ctrl). News concerning Asian Americans.

ASPAREZ. VFOAT Asbarez Daily Newspaper, Asbarez. Began Aug. 14, 1908. 0004-4229. Newspaper. US. English. da. $50.00. Asbarez, 108 North Brand Boulevard, Glendale CA 91203.

THE ASPERMONT NEWS. 8750-6092. Newspaper. US. English. wk. $6.00 (In County), $10.00 (Elsewhere). The Aspermont News, Aspermont TX 79502.

ATHENAI. VFOAT Detroit Athens. Began in 1928. Newspaper. US. Greek, Modern. wk. 520 Monroe Avenue, Detroit MI 48226. LC NEWSPAPER.

ATLANTA CONSTITUTION (ATLANTA, GA. : 1897). (THE ATLANTA CONSTITUTION). (April 1, 1897)-. Newspaper. US. English. da. Atlanta Constitution, Box 4689, Atlanta GA 30302. **Tel** (404)526-5024. LC Newspaper. Available on microform from Microfilm Corporation of America. *Evening Constitution.*

ATLANTA DAILY WORLD. Began in August 1928. Newspaper. US. English. wk. $11.00. Atlanta Daily World, 145 Auburn Avenue NE, Atlanta GA 30303. **Tel** (404)659-1110. *Atlanta World.*

THE ATLANTA JOURNAL. Began with Feb. 24, 1883 issue. Newspaper. US. English. da. Atlanta Journal, Box 4689, Atlanta GA 30302. **Tel** (404)526-5024.

THE ATLANTA JOURNAL, THE ATLANTA CONSTITUTION INDEX. See Indexes/Abstracts.

ATLANTIC LIFE BUSINESS. Began publication in 1979 with V. 1, No. 8 or 9. 0225-7629. Periodical. CN. English. mo. $7.20 for 24 issues. Atlantic Life Business, PO Box 12, Fredericton New Brunswick E3B 4Y2 Canada. **DD** 071.15. *Atlantic Life, 0225-7629.*

ATLANTIS. 0700-9119. Periodical. CN. Greek, Modern. Atlantis, 5178 Park Avenue, Montreal Quebec H2V 4G6 Canada. **DD** 071.14281.

ATLIN NUGGET. (THE ATLIN NUGGET). V. 1- Nov. 1978-. 0226-6296. Newspaper. CN. English. mo. $6.00 Domestic, $12.00 U.S., $15.00 Others. D Sack, The Atlin Nugget, PO Box 227, Atlin BC V0W 1A0 Canada. **DD** 071.111.

ATLIN RAG TIMES. 0710-0035. Newspaper. CN. English. mo. $12.00. PO Box 14, Atlin British Columbia V0W 1A0 Canada. **DD** 071.111.

THE ATMORE ADVANCE. 0746-1968. Newspaper. US. English. wk. Atmore Newspapers Inc, 301 South Main Street, Atmore AL 36504.

ATSIMOOWIN. VFOAT Atchimouwin. Vol. 1, Issue 1-. 0714-9395. Newspaper. CN. English. ir. $6.00. Atsimoowin Newsletter, PO Box 208, Ile a la Crosse Saskatchewan S0M 1C0 Canada. **DD** 071.1241.

ATUAQNIK. V. 1- Jan. 1979-. 0708-5990. Newspaper. CN. English (text in Inuktitut). mo. $35.00 2 Years. Taqralik-Atuaqnik, PO Box 59, Fort Chime Quebec J0M 1C0 Canada. **DD** 071.1417.

AUFBAU. (AUFBAU : NACHRICHTENBLATT DES GERMAN-JEWISH CLUB, INC., NEW YORK, N. Y). VFOAT Reconstruction. Vol. 1, No. 1 (1. Dec. 1934)-. 0004-7813. Newspaper. US. German (English). bw. $38.00. New World Club Inc, 2121 Broadway, New York NY 10023. **Tel** (212)873-7400. Available on microfilm.

AUGUSTA AREA TIMES. 1874-. 0749-7083. Newspaper. US. English. wk. $10.00 Wisconsin. Michael D Jensen, 156 West Lincoln, Augusta WI 54722.

AUGUSTA CHRONICLE (AUGUSTA, GA. : 1885). (THE AUGUSTA CHRONICLE). VFOAT Augusta Chronicle Augusta Herald. Began in 1885. 0747-1343. Newspaper. US. English. da. $126.00. Augusta Chronicle, PO Box 1928, Augusta GA 30913. *Daily Chronicle & Constitutionalist.*

AUGUSTA HERALD (1890). (THE AUGUSTA HERALD). Began in 1890. 0746-942X. Newspaper. US. English. da. Augusta Herald, PO Box 1928, Augusta GA 30913.

AUSTIN AMERICAN-STATESMAN. VFOAT Sunday American-Statesman. Began publication in 1914. 0199-8560. Newspaper. US. English. da. $170.90. American Statesman, 308 Guadalupe/PO Box 670, Austin TX 78767. **Tel** (512)445-3500.

Newspapers

THE AUSTIN CHRONICLE. Periodical. US. English. bw. Austin Chronicle Corp, PO Box 49066, Austin TX 78765.

AUSTIN HERALD. Newspaper. US. English. da. $69.00. Austin Daily Herald, 310 NE Second Street, Austin MN 55912. **Tel** (507)433-8851.

THE AUSTIN LIGHT. Newspaper. US. English. wk. $12.50. Austin Light, 713 6th Street, Austin TX 78701. **Tel** (512)477-5853.

AVA-YI IRAN. **VFOAT** The Voice of Iran. Sal 1, Shamarah 1 (20 Favriyah, 1981)-. 0711-3900. Newspaper. CN. Persian, Modern. mo. $8.00 Canada, $12.00 Others. Voice of Iran, PO Box 129, Station B, Ottawa Ontario K1P 6C3 Canada. **DD** 955.05405.

AVENIR DU NORD. (L'AVENIR DU NORD). V. 1, No. 1, (Aug. 26, 1981)-. 0714-427X. Newspaper. CN. French. wk. Free. L'Avenir du Nord, 335 rue Labelle, CP 21, Sainte-Jerome Quebec J7Z 5T7 Canada. **DD** 071.1424.

AVIRON. (L'AVIRON). 15 Dec. 1982-. 0821-1477. Newspaper. CN. French. wk. 22.00 Canada, $34.00 USA. L'Aviron, CP 129, New Richmond Quebec G0C 2B0 Canada. **Tel** (418)392-5083. **Ed** Guy Lavoie. **DD** 071.1478. adv acc. **Circ** 14,535. (ctrl) General information in our community, sports, etc.

AWAZ (TORONTO, ONT.). (AWAZ). Vol. 1, No. 1 (April 1980)-. 0715-4135. Newspaper. CN. Urdu. mo. 15.00 Domestic, 20.00 US. Awaz, PO Box 2114/Station B, Scarborough Ontario M1N 2E5 Canada. **Tel** (416)283-7255. **Ed** Sohail Akhtar. **DD** 071.13541. bk rev. adv acc. **Circ** 3,000.

AYLMER BULLETIN. No. 1, 1st Year (May 21, 1981)-. 0710-5401. Newspaper. CN. English. wk. $10.00. Aylmer Bulletin, 478 de Bruyne Crescent, Aylmer Quebec J9H 5N7 Canada. **DD** 071.14221.

AZALEA CITY NEWS & REVIEW. **VFOAT** Azalea City News and Review. 0744-5318. Newspaper. US. English. wk. $10.00. William Beckner, PO Box 91354, Mobile AL 36691-1354. **Tel** (205)666-9115. **Ed** Patricia McArthur. bk rev. adv acc. **Circ** 7,500. An alternative to the local daily, the ACN & R provides in-depth news coverage, and features, sports, a food page, extensive arts coverage OP/ED and comics.

BABILLARD DE R.D.P. (LE BABILLARD DE R.D.P.). **VAT** Babillard de Riviere des Prairies. Vol. 1, No. 1 (1 Sept. 1982)-. 0714-9107. Newspaper. CN. French. mo. Free to Residents. Babillard de R.D.P., 12755 42E Avenue, Montreal Quebec H1E 2G2 Canada. **DD** 071.14281.

BACON'S NEWSPAPER DIRECTORY. U. S. EDITION. See Yearbooks, Almanacs, Directories.

BAGATELLE. (LA BAGATELLE). V. 1- Feb. 1972-. 0319-4841. Newspaper. CN. French. ir. $3. La Bagatelle, MME A Grenier, Landirenne Quebec J0Y 1V0 Canada. **DD** 071.1413.

BAGLEY FARMERS INDEPENDENT. Newspaper. US. English. ir.

THE BAKERSFIELD CALIFORNIAN. 0276-5837. Newspaper. US. English. da. $78.00. Bakersfield Californian, PO Box 440, Bakersfield CA 93302. **Tel** (805)395-7330.

BALITA. V. 1, No. 11- Jan. 16/31, 1979-. 0709-0358. Newspaper. CN. English (includes some text in Tagalog). sm. 4.00. Kalayaan Media Balita, PO Box 392 Station A, Toronto Ontario M5W 1C2 Canada. **DD** 071.13541. Balita Natin, 0709-034X.

BALLSTON JOURNAL (BALLSTON SPA, N.Y. : 1952). (BALLSTON JOURNAL). Vol. 14, No. 131 (Apr. 3, 1952)-. Newspaper. US. English. wk. Ballston Spa Journal.

BANAR. Began publication with Nov. 1967 issue. 0225-6193. Periodical. CN. English. mo. Free. Blackburn Community Association, L Driscoll, 97 Bearbrook Road, Ottawa Ont K1B 3H5 Canada. **DD** 071.1383. (ctrl).

THE BANGKOK POST. 1946. Newspaper. TH. English. da. $332.60. Allied Newspapers Ltd, 968 Rama IV Road, Bangkok 2 Thailand. **Tel** 233-8030. **Ed** Michael J Gorman. adv acc. **Circ** 40,000. (ctrl).

BANGKOK WORLD. (1-1957)-. Newspaper. English. da. Allied Newspaper Ltd, 968 Rama IV Road, Bangkok Thailand.

THE BANGLADESH OBSERVER. 1949. Newspaper. BG. English. da. $252.00. Bangladesh Observer, Observer House, Notijheel Dacca 2 Bangladesh. **Tel** 235105-9. **Ed** Obaidul Huq. bk rev. adv acc. **Circ** 80,000. Entire area of publications including editorials. Contains ideal thoughts, continental developments, current topics, population control home and abroad.

BANGOR DAILY NEWS. Began with June 18, 1889 issue. Newspaper. US. English. ir. $84.00. Bangor Daily News, 491 Main Street, Bangor ME 04401. **Tel** (207)942-4881. **Ed** V Paul Reynolds. **LC** Newspaper. adv acc. **Circ** 76,782. (ctrl). Sections include international, national, state, and local news, sports, home improvements, editorial, financial, obituaries, TV radio schedule, classified ads, and amusements. Bangor Daily Whig and Courier.

BANK OF BRITISH COLUMBIA'S PIONEER NEWS. **VFOAT** Pioneer News. 0712-5321. Periodical. CN. English. bm. Free to Pioneer Service Plan Members. Pioneer News, c/o Bank of British Columbia, 1725-555 Burrard Street, Vancouver British Columbia V7X 1K1 Canada. **DD** 071.1133.

BANKUBA SHINPO. **VFOAT** Vancouver Shimpo. 0710-1236. Newspaper. CN. Japanese. wk. Vancouver Shimpo, PO Box 69780 Station K, Vancouver BC V5K 4 Canada. **DD** 071.1133.

BANNER-HERALD/THE DAILY NEWS. **VFOAT** Daily News. 0745-9904. Newspaper. US. English. wk. Athens Newspapers, PO Box 912, Athens GA 30613.

BANNER TIMES. V. 1, No. 1 (Mar. 11 1985)-. 8750-8419. Newspaper. US. English. wk. $8.00 Local, $9.00 Others. North Country Publications Inc, 7590 Jefferson Street, Pulaski NY 13142. Pulaski Democrat.

THE BARNSTABLE PATRIOT. (BARNSTABLE PATRIOT). **VFOAT** Barnstable Patriot and Commercial Advertiser. 0744-7221. Newspaper. US. English. wk. Barnstable Patriot, 24 Pleasant Street, Hyannis MA 02601. Barnstable Patriot, and Commercial Advertiser.

BAROMETER. V. 1- Jan. 5, 1978-. 0705-3746. Periodical. CN. English. wk. 25 Per No. Barometer Publishing Ltd, PO Box 9, Halifax Nova Scotia B3J 2L4 Canada. **DD** 071.1622.

BARRE GAZETTE (BARRE, MASS. : 1839). (BARRE GAZETTE). Began in 1839. Newspaper. US. English. wk. $11.00. Exchange Street, Barre MA 01005. **Tel** (617)355-4000. **Ed** Linda Leppanen. bk rev. adv acc. **Circ** 1,850. (ctrl). Covering local as well as items of interest to families, young and old alike editorials welcome as well as news, photos and illustrations. Barre Weekly Gazette.

BARRIERE BULLETIN. Vol. 1, No. 1 (July 24, 1974)-. 0715-5336. Newspaper. CN. English. bw. Barriere Bulletin, P O Box 281, Barriere B C V0E 1E0 Canada. **DD** 071.112.

BARRIO (WASHINGTON, D.C.). (EL BARRIO). Vol. 1, No. 1 (Aug. 1981)-. 0276-7902. Periodical. US. Spanish. mo. $5.00. El Barrio Centro de Juventud Latinoamericana, 3045 15th Street NW, Washington DC 20009.

THE BATES COUNTY NEWS-HEADLINER. 0746-1569. Newspaper. US. English. wk. Bates County News-Headliner, 611 West Ft Scott, Butler MO 64730.

BATTLEFORD TELEGRAPH. **VFOAT** Telegraph. **VAT** Telegraph (Battleford). V. 1- Apr. 20, 1978-. 0226-6377. Newspaper. CN. English. wk. $15. W R Warwick, Battleford Telegraph, 102-23rd Street East, Battleford Sask S0M 0E0 Canada. **DD** 071.1242.

THE BAY STATE BANNER. **VFOAT** Banner. Began with V. 1, Sept. 25, 1965. Newspaper. US. English. wk. $15.00. Banner Publishing Company, 925 Washington Street, Dorchester MA 02124. **Tel** (617)288-4900. **Ed** M B Miller.

BEACON. (THE BEACON). **VFOAT** Parry Sound Beacon. Vol. 1, No. 1 (May 15, 1980)-. 0229-6802. Newspaper. CN. English. wk. $13.16. Parry Sound Beacon, 32 Seguin Street, Parry Sound Ontario P2A 1B1 Canada. **Tel** (705)746-4228. **DD** 071.1315.

THE BEACON. 0744-7930. Newspaper. US. English. wk. Beacon Minute Man Publishing, PO Box 217, Acton MA 01720. **Tel** (617)263-3761. Assabet Valley Beacon.

BEACON. (THE BEACON). 0712-4988. Periodical. CN. English. wk. Free. The Beacon, c/o Citizen Publishing, 17 Prince Street, Sydney Nova Scotia B1P Australia. **DD** 071.1695.

BEACON TIMES. (THE BEACON TIMES). V. 1- Dec. 4, 1975-. 0703-2102. Newspaper. CN. English. wk. H Wyonch, Beacon Times, Box 580, Port Elgin Ontario N0H 2C0 Canada. **DD** 071.1321. Port Elgin Times, Beacon News, 0703-2110.

BEACONSFIELD REPORTER. Vol. 1, No. 1 (Oct. 1969)-. 0712-3027. Newspaper. CN. English (French). ir. Free. Reporter, 303 Beaconsfield Boulevard, Beaconsfield Quebec H9W 4A7 Canada. **DD** 352.071428.

BEAUCE MEDIA. Vol. 1, No. 1 (Aug. 19 1980)-. 0711-3420. Newspaper. CN. French. wk. $27.09. Beauce Media, 164 Notre Dame South Street, Marie Bea Beauceville Quebec G0S 2Y0 Canada. **Tel** (418)387-8000. **DD** 071.1471.

BEAUMONT JOURNAL. Began in 1889. 0744-1207. Newspaper. US. English. da. Beaumont Journal, PO Box 2991, Beaumont TX 77704.

BEAVER VALLEY NEWS. (THE BEAVER VALLEY NEWS). V. 1- Oct. 1, 1976-. 0703-1572. Newspaper. CN. English. wk. 25. Per No. Ourtowne Publications, PO Box 1198, Rossland British Columbia V0G 1Y0 Canada. **DD** 071.1144.

BELFAST TELEGRAPH. MICROFORM. Newspaper. US. English. da. $254.87. Belfast Telegraph Newspapers Ltd, 124-144 Royal Ave, Belfast BT1 1EB N Ireland. **Tel** 224800. **Ed** Roy Lilley. bk rev. adv acc. **Circ** 152,000. Ireland's leading evening newspaper.

BELL & HOWELL NEWSPAPER INDEX TO THE BOSTON GLOBE. See Indexes/Abstracts.

BELL & HOWELL NEWSPAPER INDEX TO THE CHICAGO SUN-TIMES. See Indexes/Abstracts.

BELL & HOWELL NEWSPAPER INDEX TO THE CHRISTIAN SCIENCE MONITOR. See Indexes/Abstracts.

BELL & HOWELL NEWSPAPER INDEX TO THE HOUSTON POST. See Indexes/Abstracts.

BELL & HOWELL NEWSPAPER INDEX TO THE LOS ANGELES TIMES. See Indexes/Abstracts.

BELL & HOWELL NEWSPAPER INDEX TO THE ST. LOUIS POST-DISPATCH. See Indexes/Abstracts.

BELL & HOWELL'S NEWSPAPER INDEX TO THE DETROIT NEWS. See Indexes/Abstracts.

BELL & HOWELL'S NEWSPAPER INDEX TO THE HOUSTON POST. See Indexes/Abstracts.

BELL & HOWELL'S NEWSPAPER INDEX TO THE LOS ANGELES TIMES. See Indexes/Abstracts.

BELL & HOWELL'S NEWSPAPER INDEX TO THE SAN FRANCISCO CHRONICLE. See Indexes/Abstracts.

BELLEVILLE DAILY NEWS-DEMOCRAT. Newspaper. US. English. da. $101.40. Belleville News Democrat Daily, 120 South Illinois Street, Belleville IL 62220.

BELMONT CITIZEN. Began with Mar. 29, 1919 issue. Newspaper. US. English. wk. 72 Trapelo Road, Belmont MA 92178.

BEMIDJI PIONEER. Newspaper. US. English. da. $80.00. Nielson and Pioneer Street, PO Box 554, Bemidji MN 56601. **Tel** (218)751-3740.

BENITO STANDARD. V. 1- Dec. 21, 1973-. 0316-0270. Newspaper. CN. English. $2. within 40 miles of Benito area, $3. elsewhere in Canada. Benito Standard, PO Box 424, Benito Man R0L 0C0 Canada. **DD** 0711272.

BENN'S PRESS DIRECTORY. INTERNATIONAL. See Yearbooks, Almanacs, Directories.

BERKELEY BARB CEASED. Began with 1-1965. Ceased July 4, 1980. 0005-9161. Periodical. US. English. bm.

BERLINGSKE TIDENDE. Newspaper. Danish. da. $284.43. A S Berlingske Tidende, Pilestraded 34, 1147 Copenhagen K Denmark. **Tel** 451-15 75 57. **Ed** Hans Dam. adv acc. **Circ** 130,000. (ctrl). Daily morning paper.

Newspapers

BETTER LIVING. V. 1- Jan. 1981-. 0273-6160. Periodical. US. English. qt. $5.00. Better Living, 1775 Broadway, New York NY 10019. **Tel** (212)581-2000. **Ind/Abst** Pop. Mag. Rev.

BI-STATE REPORTER. **VFOAT** Lakeland Newspapers. 0745-4813. Newspaper. US. English. wk. $9.50. Bi-State Reporter, 952 Main Street, Antioch IL 60002.

BIG COUNTRY VOICE. (THE BIG COUNTRY VOICE). V. 1- Oct. 2, 1975-. 0382-7577. Newspaper. CN. English. wk. $8. Big Country Voice, PO Box 70, Hafford Saskatchewan S0J 1A0 Canada. **DD** 071.1242.

BIG MUDDY ROUND UP. V. 1- Sept. 4, 1975-. 0380-6588. Newspaper. CN. English. wk. $5. Domestic, $6. Foreign. Big Muddy Round Up, PO Box 370, Radville Saskatchewan S0C 2G0 Canada. **DD** 071.1244.

BILALIAN NEWS CEASED. V. 1- 1975-. 0161-8644. Periodical. US. English. wk. Bilalian News Inc, 7801 South Cottage Grove Avenue, Chicago IL 60619. *Muhammad Speaks*.

BILLINGS GAZETTE (BILLINGS, MONT. : DAILY : 1914). (THE BILLINGS GAZETTE). V. 13, No. 50 (Jan. 1, 1914)-. Newspaper. US. English. da. The Billings Gazette, PO Box 2507, Billings MT 59101. **Tel** (406)657-1200. **Ed** Richard Wesnick. **LC** Newspaper. adv acc. **Circ** 62,000. Also available on microfilm from Micro Photo Division, Bell and Howell. General interest daily and Sunday newspaper. *Billings Daily Gazette*.

THE BIRMINGHAM TIMES. Began with Vol. 1, No. 1 (Feb. 1964)?. Periodical. US. English. wk. The Birmingham Times, PO Box 10503, Birmingham AL 35202.

BIULLETEN INOSTRANNOI KOMMERCHESKOI INFORMATSII. 1948-. Periodical. UR. Russian. ir. $306.00. Victor Kamkin Inc, 12224 Parklawn Drive, Rockville MD 20852. **Tel** (301)881-5973.

BIWABIK TIMES. Newspaper. US. English. wk. Mesaba Range Publishing Company, Biwarik MN 55708.

BLACK PRESS INFORMATION HANDBOOK. 1974/75-. 0147-2828. US. English. $5.00 Per Issue. National Newspapers Publishers Association, 770 National Press Building, Washington DC 20004. **LC** PN4882.5. **DD** 071.3.

THE BLACKSHEAR TIMES. Began in 1876. 0746-9330. Newspaper. US. English. sw. Blackshear Times, PO Box 410, Blackshear GA 31516.

BLACKWELL JOURNAL-TRIBUNE. **VFOAT** Blackwell Journal Tribune. Began in 1940?. Newspaper. US. English. da. Blackwell Journal Tribune, Box 760, Blackwell OK 74631. Also available on microfilm from Microfilm Center Inc., and Oklahoma Historical Society. *Blackwell Journal, Blackwell Morning Tribune*.

BLITZ. Newspaper. II. English. wk. $15.84. Blitz Publication Private Ltd, Canada Building Dr DN Road, Bombay 4000 001 India. **Tel** 267022.

BLITZ WEEKLY. V. 1- Oct. 14, 1978-. 0707-7335. Newspaper. CN. English. wk. 25 Domestic, $10.00 Canada, $15.00 US. Blitz Weekly, Suite 102 8286 St George Street, Vancouver BC V5X 3S5 Canada. **DD** 971.13300491411.

BLOOR WEST VILLAGER. **VAT** Villager (Toronto). Began publication in May 1971. 0703-1912. Newspaper. CN. English. mo. $3.50. Village Publications, Box 185 Station M, Toronto Ont M6S 4T3 Canada. **DD** 071.13541.

BLUE & GOLD ILLUSTRATED. **VFOAT** Blue and Gold Illustrated. V. 3, Issue 1 (Aug. 29, 1983)-. 0746-2557. Periodical. US. English. wk. Blue & Gold Illustrated, PO Box 477, Notre Dame IN 46556. *Go Irish, 0744-950X*.

BONJOUR CHEZ-NOUS. No. 1- March 1976-. 0383-7866. Newspaper. CN. French. wk. $11.61. Bonjour Chex Nous, 2-2-1 Laurier CP 1149, Rockland Ont Canada. **Tel** (613)446-5196. **Ed** Pierre Cremer. **DD** 071.1385. bk rev. adv acc. **Circ** 2,600. Community news and information.

BORDERLAND REPORTER. Vol. 1, No. 1 (July 22, 1982)-. 0821-6177. Newspaper. CN. English. wk. Borderland Reporter, PO Box 569, Coronach Saskatchewan S0H 0B0 Canada. **DD** 071.1244.

BOSTON GLOBE. Mar. 4, 1872-. Newspaper. US. English. da. $469.00. Globe Newspaper Company, 135 Morrissey Boulevard, Boston MA 02107. **Tel** (617)929-2000.

THE BOSTON GLOBE INDEX. See Indexes/Abstracts.

BOSTON HERALD AMERICAN BOSTON, MASS. : 1973) CEASED. (BOSTON HERALD AMERICAN) Vol. 1, No. 170 (Jan. 1, 1973)- V.12, No. 354 (Dec. 20, 1982). Newspaper. US. English. da. Available on microfilm from Micro Photo Division, Bell & Howell Company. *Boston Herald Traveler and Record American*.

THE BOSTON PHOENIX. **VFOAT** Phoenix. Began in 1972. 0163-3015. Periodical. US. English. wk. $41.50. The Boston Phoenix, Attn Stephen M Mindich, 100 Massachusetts Avenue, Boston MA 02115. **Tel** (617)536-5390. **Ed** Richard Gaines. bk rev. adv acc. **Circ** 134,000. Newspaper covering politics, arts, lifestyle topics, and special interest areas.

BOUEILLE. (LA BOUEILLE). Published since July 1975?. 0226-8663. Newspaper. CN. French. wk. $10.00. Editions du Sud, CP 329, Cap-Pele New Brunswick E0A 1J0 Canada. **DD** 071.15.

BOUNDARY CREEK TIMES. (THE BOUNDARY CREEK TIMES). Apr. 15, 1983-. 0822-8671. Newspaper. CN. English. wk. Boundary Creek Times, 318 Cooper Street, Greenwood City B C V0H 1J0 Canada. **DD** 071.1142.

BOUNDARY ROAD. (THE BOUNDARY ROAD). V. 1, No. 9- Jan. 26, 1979-. 0225-5464. Newspaper. CN. English. wk. Free. Preview Publications Ltd, PO Box 80598, South Barnaby British Columbia V5H 3X9 Canada. **DD** 071.1133. (ctrl). *Burnaby Leisure Guide*.

BOW VALLEY VIEWS. V. 1, No. 3- Oct. 11, 1974-. 0316-697X. CN. English. Bow Valley Views, PO Box 831, Canmore Alberta T0L 0M0 Canada. **DD** 071.1233. *Valley Views, 0316-6961*.

BOWDEN EYE OPENER. (THE BOWDEN EYE OPENER). Vol. 1 No. 1 (Oct. 6, 1976)-. 0704-0490. Newspaper. CN. English. wk. Bowden Printers, Box 70, Bowden Alta T0M 0K0 Canada. **DD** 071.1233.

THE BOWLING GREEN TIMES. 0162-6701. Newspaper. US. English. wk. 106 W Main Street, Bowling Green MO 63334.

BRAINERD DISPATCH. Newspaper. US. English. ir. $65.00. Brainerd Daily Dispatch, 215 South 6th Street, Brainerd MN 56401. **Tel** (218)829-4705.

BRANDON VALLEY CHALLENGER. **VFOAT** Challenger. Began in 1983. 0746-8261. Newspaper. US. English. wk. Brandon Valley Challenger, 1300 Rushmore, Brandon Minnehaha SD 57005.

BRANT NEWS. V. 1- Feb. 1, 1978-. 0707-7998. Newspaper. CN. English. wk. $21.67. The Brant News, PO Box 2079, Brantford Ontario N3T 5Y6 Canada. **Tel** (519)759-5550. **DD** 071.1347. *Brant Shopping News*.

BRAZIL HERALD. Periodical. BL. English. da. The Brazil Herald, Rua do Resende 65 ZC06, Rio de Janeiro Brazil.

BREWSTER TRIBUNE. Newspaper. US. English. wk. $5.00. Heron Lake News, Box 227, Heron Lake MN 56137. **Tel** (507)793-2327.

THE BRIDEGPORT TELEGRAM. V. 86, No. -247. Newspaper. US. English. da. $90.00. The Post Publishing Company, 410 State Street, Bridgeport CT 06604. **Tel** (203)333-0161. **Ed** Donald Casciato. **LC** Newspaper. bk rev. adv acc. **Circ** 20,000.

BRISTOL HERALD COURIER, BRISTOL VIRGINIA-TENNESSEAN. **VFOAT** Bristol Herald Courier. 8750-6505. Newspaper. US. English. da. Bristol Newspapers, 320 Morrison Boulevard, Bristol VA 24201.

BRONX TIMES REPORTER. 8750-4499. Newspaper. US. English. bw. $2.50. ABC Newspapers, 2887 Miles Avenue, Bronx NY 10465.

BROOKLYN CENTER POST. Newspaper. US. English. wk. $15.50. Post Publications, 8801 Bass Lake Road, Minneapolis MN 55428. **Tel** (612)537-8484.

BROOKLYN COURIER. 0744-7728. Newspaper. US. English. wk. $105.00. Courier Life Inc, 1733 Sheepshead Bay Road, Brooklyn NY 11235. **Tel** (718)769-4400.

BROSSARD ECLAIR. **VFOAT** Eclair. **VAT** Eclair (Brossard). Vol. 1, No 1 (21 Oct. 1980)-. 0713-620X. Periodical. CN. French. wk. Brossard Eclair, 2860 Croissant de la Marquise, Brossard Quebec J4Y 1P4 Canada. **DD** 071.1434.

BROUGHTON BULLETIN. (THE BROUGHTON BULLETIN). V. 1- Feb. 18, 1976-. 0383-8013. Newspaper. CN. English. wk. The Broughton Bulletin, PO Box 632, Port McNeill British Columbia V0N 2R0 Canada. **DD** 071.1134.

THE BROWNSTOWN BANNER. Began in Apr. 1869. Newspaper. US. English. sw. $13.00 in County, $16.50 Elsewhere Indiana, $19.50 Out of State. PO Box 6, 116 East Cross Street, Brownstown IN 47220. **Tel** (812)358-2111. **Ed** John Pesta. **LC** Newspaper 7002. bk rev. adv acc. **Circ** 5,600. The community newspaper features Jackson County news, sports, and feature stories. Farming and light industry.

DE BRUG. Mar. 1978-. Periodical. NE. Dutch. wk. 39.- Domestic, 78.- Foreign. Abdij Van Berne, Abdijstraat 53, NL 5473 AC Heeswijk-Dinther Netherland. **Tel** 04139-1394. **Ed** N van Beijnen. bk rev. adv acc. **Circ** 50. (ctrl). A newspaper for nearly ten villages in a radius of 25 KM.

BUFFALO WEEKLY CHALLENGER. BUFFALO ROCHESTER EDITION. (BUFFALO WEEKLY CHALLENGER). 0278-3320. Periodical. US. English. wk. $12.00. 1301 Fillmore Avenue, Buffalo NY 14211. *Buffalo, New York Challenger News Weekly*.

BULL GATOR. 0745-1083. Periodical. US. English. wk. Bull Gator News Inc, PO Box 13512, Gainesville FL 32604.

BULLETIN TODAY. V. 1- Nov. 22, 1972-. Newspaper. English. da. $152.08. Bulletin Publishing Company, PO Box 769, Manila Philippines.

BULLSEYE. **VFOAT** Nellis Bullseye. 0193-5178. Periodical. US. English. wk. Bullseye, PO Box 3936, North Las Vegas NV 89030.

BURLINGTON NEWSPAPER INDEX. See Indexes/Abstracts.

BURNABY TODAY. Oct. 23, 1979-. 0229-6780. Newspaper. CN. English. wk. $15.00. Burnaby Today, 7774 Royal Oak Avenue, Burnaby British Columbia Canada. **DD** 071.1133.

THE BURNSVILLE CURRENT. 0193-3000. Newspaper. US. English. wk. $25.00. Current Newspaper Inc, 1209 East Cliff Road, Burnsville MN 55337.

BUTLER EAGLE. 0744-401X. Newspaper. US. English. da. $48.00. Eagle Printing Company Inc, 114 West Diamond Street, Butler PA 16001.

BYRON ADVOCATE. (THE BYRON ADVOCATE). Issue 1- Oct. 24, 1976-. 0703-1696. Newspaper. CN. English. bw. $5. T P Smith, The Byron Advocate, 1105 Baseline Road West, London Ontario N6K 2C7 Canada. **DD** 071.1326.

C D N P A-C M E C NEWSLETTER. **Main/Corp** Canadian Daily Newspaper Publishers Association. V. 4, No. 2 (Feb. 1976)-. 0381-1220. Periodical. CN. English. mo. Canadian Daily Newspaper Publishers Association, 250 Bloor Street East, Toronto Ontario M4W 1E7 Canada. **DD** 071.

CALDWELL INFORMER. 0883-1645. Newspaper. US. English. wk. Caldwell Informer, 8 South Main Street, Granite Falls NC 28630.

CALEDON CITIZEN. 0823-9681. Newspaper. CN. English. wk. $10.00. Caledon Citizen, PO Box 878, Bolton Ontario L0P 1A0 Canada. **DD** 071.13535.

CALENDAR. (THE CALENDAR). Vol. 1 I.E. 28, No. 1 (Oct. 1, 1979)-. 0715-5778. Newspaper. CN. English. wk. The Calendar, PO Box 54, Winfield British Columbia V0H 2C0 Canada. **DD** 071.1142. *Winfield Calendar*.

THE CALIFORNIA ADVOCATE. V.8, No.9, V.9 No.14-. Periodical. US. English. sm. $15.00. California Advocate, PO Box 11826, Fresno CA 93775. **Tel** (209)268-0941.

CALIFORNIA COUNTRY. V. 1- Jan. 1979-. 0194-5165. Periodical. US. English. mo. $1.00 Members, $2.00 Nonmembers. California Country, 1601 Exposition Boulevard, Sacramento CA 94705.

CALIFORNIA VOICE (OAKLAND, CALIF. : 1919). (CALIFORNIA VOICE). Began in 1919. Newspaper. US. English. wk. California Voice, 814 27th Street, Oakland CA 94607. **Ed** J L Gilmer and K Maddox-Abdegeo.

Newspapers

THE CALIFORNIAN AND THE VALLEY PRESS. 0199-8439. Newspaper. US. English. wk. PO Box 970, Tenecula CA 92390.

CALL AND POST. VFOAT Cleveland Call & Post. Feb. 22, 1921-. 0045-4036. Newspaper. US. English. wk. Cleveland Call and Post, PO Box 6237, Cleveland OH 45201. **Tel** (216)791-7600.

CALMAR SUN. (THE CALMAR SUN). VFOAT Sun. Vol. 1, No. 1 (April 7, 1982)-. 0823-6623. Newspaper. CN. English. $0.25 Per No. The Calmar Sun, PO Box 720, Devon Alta T0C 1E0 Canada. **DD** 071.1233.

CAMERON CHRONICLE. 8750-202X. Newspaper. US. English. wk. Cameron Chronicle, 114 Fannin, Cameron TX 76530. **DD** 071.

CAMPBELL RIVER UPPER ISLANDER. (THE CAMPBELL RIVER UPPER ISLANDER). Began publication in 1967?. 0318-9538. Newspaper. CN. English. wk. $7.50. The Campbell River Upper Islander, Box 159, Campbell River British Columbia V9W 5A7 Canada. **DD** 071.1134.

CANADA HERALD. April 1980-. 0711-6888. Newspaper. CN. German. mo. $4.00 Domestic, $5.00 Foreign. Canada Herald, Box 1330, Almonte Ontario K0A 1A0 Canada. **DD** 071.1384. *Ottawa Herald, 0317-0195.*

CANADA NEWS CEASED. (THE CANADA NEWS). No. 1-527. 0319-2962. Newspaper. CN. Korean. ir. $5.20. Korea Times, 230 Parliament Street, Toronto Ontario M5A 3A4 Canada. **DD** 071.13541.

CANADIAN DAILY/WEEKLY NEWSPAPER CIRCULATION FACTBOOK. (ABC CANADIAN DAILY/WEEKLY NEWSPAPER CIRCULATION FACTBOOK). VAT Canadian Daily Weekly Newspaper Circulation Factbook, Audit Bureau of Circulations Canadian Daily Weekly Newspaper Circulation Factbook. 1980/1981-. US. English. an. Audit Bureau of Circulation, 900 North Meacham Road, Schaumberg IL 60195. **Tel** (312)885-0910. **DD** 071.1. adv acc. **Circ** 600. Circulations of Canadian daily and weekly newspapers by census divisions and metropolitan areas. Includes ranking tables. *A B C Factbook, 0098-2520.*

CANADIAN ILLUSTRATED NEWS. INDEX TO ILLUSTRATIONS. See Indexes/Abstracts.

CANADIAN NEWS INDEX. See Indexes/Abstracts.

CANINE CHRONICLE. 0746-1410. Periodical. US. English. sw. $25.00. Routledge Publications, PO Box 115, Montpelier IN 47359.

CANMORE LEADER. 0824-3646. Newspaper. CN. English. wk. $25.00 Domestic, 50.00 US. Canmore Leader, PO Box 1320, Canmore Alberta T0L 0M0 Canada. **Tel** 678-2365. Ed Jim McCurdy. **DD** 071.1233. adv acc. **Circ** 6,400. (ctrl) Community newspaper that also publishes two tourist guide publications, and printing of all types.

CANNON FALLS BEACON. Newspaper. US. English. wk. Cannon Falls Beacon, Cannon Falls MN 55099.

THE CANTON EAGLE. 0192-6446. Newspaper. US. English. wk. Associated Newspapers Inc, 35540 Michigan Avenue West, Wayne MI 48184. **Tel** (313)729-4000.

CANTONS. (LES CANTONS). VFOAT Journal les Cantons. Vol. 1, No. 1 June 15 1981-. 0713-0139. Newspaper. CN. French. mo. Journal les Cantons, c/o Progres de Magog, 287 Ouest rue Principale, Magog Quebec J1X 2A8 Canada. **DD** 917.146044.

THE CANYON COURIER WEEKENDER. VFOAT Weekender. 0192-0197. Newspaper. US. English. wk. $10.00. Canyon Courier, PO Box 430, Evergreen CO 80439. **Tel** (303)674-5534.

CANYON CRIER NEWS. VFOAT Canyon Crier. 0746-9926. Newspaper. US. English. wk. Canyon Crier News, 10215 Riverside Drive, Toluca Lake CA 91602.

CANYON ECHO. 0164-7024. Periodical. US. English. mo. $5.00. Canyon Echo, 3052 North Fontana, Tucson AZ 85705. **Tel** (602)624-7152.

CAPE COD TIMES. 0747-1467. Newspaper. US. English. da. Cape Cod Times, 319 Main Street, Hyannis MA 02601.

CAPE TIMES. Established 1876. Newspaper. SA. English. da. $45.10. Cape Times Cape Town, PO Box 492, Salt River 7925 South Africa.

THE CAPITAL. June 22, 1981-. Newspaper. US. English. da. The Capital, 213 West Street, Annapolis MD 21401. *Evening Capital.*

THE CAPITAL TIMES. Vol. 1, No. 1 (Dec. 13, 1917)-. 0749-4068. Newspaper. US. English. da. $142.60. Madison Newspaper Inc, PO Box 8056, Madison WI 53708. **Tel** (608)252-6400. Ed David Zweifel. bk rev. adv acc. **Circ** 30,000. Local, national and international news and columnists.

THE CAPITOL REVIEW. Vol 1, No. 1 (Sept. 6, 1983)-. 0746-3294. Newspaper. US. English. wk. $10.00 Domestic, $15.00 Foreign. Capitol Review, PO Box 750, Wheeler TX 79096.

CARDSTON CHRONICLE. (THE CARDSTON CHRONICLE). V. 1- Jan. 15, 1980-. 0227-1192. Newspaper. CN. English. wk. $38.69. Cardston Chronicle, Box 8, Cardston Alta T0K 0K0 Canada. **Tel** (403)653-3607. **DD** 071.1234. *Westwind News, 0319-1664.*

CARIBOU. (LE CARIBOU). V. 1- March 28, 1977-. 0704-0792. Newspaper. CN. French. wk. Free. Le Caribou, 131 rue d'Auteuil, Thetford-Mines Quebec G6B 2N3 Canada. **DD** 071.14575.

THE CARILLON. 1962-. 0008-6576. Newspaper. CN. English. wk. $11.61. University of Regina, Students Union Regina Campus, Regina Saskatchewan Canada. **Tel** (304)586-8811.

CARLETON COUNTY CLAPTRAP. (THE CARLETON COUNTY CLAPTRAP). No. 1- Sept. 19, 1974-. 0381-100X. Periodical. CN. English. Canadian University Press, Ottawa Ontario K1S 5B6 Canada. **DD** 070.59405.

CAROLINIAN (RALEIGH, N.C. : 1940). (THE CAROLINIAN). Began with Apr. 6, 1940 issue?. 0045-5873. Newspaper. US. English. sw. $25.00. The Carolinian, 518 East Martin Street, Raleigh NC 27601. **Tel** (919)834-5558.

CARPENTERSVILLE COUNTRYSIDE. VFOAT Countryside. 0744-5261. Newspaper. US. English. wk. Barrington Press, 200 James Street, Barrington IL 60010. *Fox Valley Countryside, 0194-1232.*

CARROLL COUNTY TIMES. 0746-7494. Newspaper. US. English. da. Carroll County Times, PO Box 346, Westminister MD 21157-0346. *Times (Westminster, MD.).*

CARSON GROVE NEWS. Began with Sept. 7, 1976 issue. 0701-1040. Newspaper. CN. English. bw. Free to Carson Grove residents. V Baker, 1332 Lotus Street, Ottawa Ontario K1J 8A8 Canada. **DD** 071.1383. *Grove News, 0701-1032.*

CARSTAIRS COURIER. (THE CARSTAIRS COURIER). V. 1, No. 1 (Nov. 30, 1982)-. 0823-7557. Newspaper. CN. English. wk. Free to residents. Carstairs Courier, PO Box 40, Irricana Alberta T0M 0B0 Canada. **DD** 071.1233.

CASHIERS CROSSROADS CHRONICLE. VFOAT Crossroads Chronicle. V. 1, No. 1 (May 2, 1984)-. 0747-332X. Newspaper. US. English. wk. $8.00 Within area, $12.00 Outside area. Cashiers Crossroads Chronicle, PO Box 1040, Cashiers NC 28717. *Cashiers Chronicle.*

CASTOR REVIEW. V. 1- Oct. 1977-. 0707-4956. Newspaper. CN. English. mo. $3.00. Castor Review, PO Box 359, Russell Ontario K0A 3B0 Canada. **DD** 071.1385.

CATHEDRAL CITY POST. VFOAT Post. Vol. 6, No. 18 (July 31, 1985)-. 0884-6189. Newspaper. US. English. wk. Cathedral City Post, 68-625 Perez Road/12B, Cathedral City CA 92234. *Cathedral Citizen, 0745-5496.*

THE CEDAR FALLS CITIZEN. Dec. 8, 1984-. 8750-5665. Newspaper. US. English. wk. Cedar Falls Citizen, PO Box 726, 222 Main Street, Cedar Falls IA 50613. *Cedar Falls Sun, 0747-2323.*

CEDAR RAPIDS GAZETTE. Began with Jan. 10, 1883 issue. Newspaper. US. English. da. $110.00. Cedar Rapids Gazette, PO Box 511, Cedar Rapids IA 52406. **Tel** (319)398-8333. **LC** Newspaper 7002.

CELTA SOCIAL. Began publication in 1976 or 1977. 0705-9124. Newspaper. CN. Spanish. $10. Centro Gellego de Toronto, 973 College Street, Toronto Ontario M6H 1A6 Canada. **DD** 071.13541. *Celta, 0705-9116.*

CENTRAL BUTTE STAR. (THE CENTRAL BUTTE STAR). V. 1- Oct. 20, 1976-. 0701-0842. Periodical. CN. English. wk. $5. The Central Butte Star, Box 460, Central Butte Saskatchewan S0H 0T0 Canada. **DD** 071.1243.

CENTRAL CITY PEOPLE. Vol. 1, Ed. 1 (Sept. 4, 1980-). 0821-0063. Newspaper. CN. English. bw. **DD** 071.1274.

CENTRAL DAILY NEWS. 1929-. Newspaper. CH. English. da. $76.00. Central Daily News, 83 Chung Hiao Road West, Lane 1 Taipei Taiwan.

CENTRAL FONTENAC TIMES. (THE TIME). VAT Times (Verona). Aug. 12, 1981-. 0715-4585. Newspaper. CN. English. wk. $10.00. Central Frontenac Times, PO Box 400, Verona Ontario K0H 2W0 Canada. **DD** 071.1371.

THE CENTRAL IDAHO STAR-NEWS. VFOAT Central Idaho Star News. 0747-248X. Newspaper. US. English. wk. $18.72 Idaho, $23.00 Out of State. The Central Idaho Star-News, PO Box 985, 1000 First Street, McCall ID 83638. **Tel** (208)634-2123. Ed Tom Grote. adv acc. **Circ** 3,500.

CENTRE DAILY TIMES. Vol. 37, No. 1 (Apr. 2, 1934)-. 0745-483X. Newspaper. US. English. da. Centre Daily Times, PO Box 89, State College PA 16801. *State College Times.*

THE CENTRE DEMOCRAT. (CENTRE DEMOCRAT). 0747-0118. Newspaper. US. English. wk. $12.00. Centre Democrat, PO Box 746, Bellefonte PA 16823-0746. **Tel** (814)355-4881. Ed Michael B Sullivan. bk rev. adv acc. **Circ** 2,700. General circulation weekly newspaper covering central Pennsylvania.

THE CENTREVILLE PRESS. Newspaper. US. English. wk. Centreville Press, Central Alabama Publishing Company Inc, 119 Court Square West, Centreville AL 35042. *County Press.*

CHAHTA ANUMPA (THE CHOCTAW TIMES). VFOAT Choctaw Times. 1- 1968-. 0577-5043. Periodical. US. English. mo. Chata Anumpa/The Choctaw Times, Box 12392, Nashville TN 37212.

CHAMPLIN DAYTON PRESS. Newspaper. US. English. wk. $7.50. Larson Publications, 200 Central Avenue, Osseo MN 55369. **Tel** (612)425-3323.

CHAPTERS. No. 1- June 1980-. 0270-8035. Periodical. US. English. mo. $10.00. Chapters, 4 Brattle Street Room 304, Cambridge MA 02138.

CHARLESTON NEWSPAPER INDEX. See Indexes/Abstracts.

CHARLOTTE NEWS (CHARLOTTE, N.C. : 1916). (THE CHARLOTTE NEWS). Began in 1916?. 0744-429X. Newspaper. US. English. da. The Charlotte News, PO Box 65103, Charlotte NC 28265.

CHARLOTTE OBSERVER (CHARLOTTE, N.C. : 1916). (THE CHARLOTTE OBSERVER). VFOAT Charlotte Sunday Observer. April 3, 1916-. Newspaper. US. English. da. $238.40. 600 South Tryon Street, Charlotte NC 28202. **Tel** (704)379-6300. **LC** NEWSPAPER. *Charlotte Daily Observer, Charlotte Daily Observer (Charlotte, N.C. : 1897).*

CHARLOTTESVILLE ALBEMARLE OBSERVER. VFOAT Charlottesville/Albemarle Observer. 0882-9322. Newspaper. US. English. wk. Charlottesville, Albemarle Observer Inc, PO Box 617, Charlottesville VA 22901. *Charlottesville Observer.*

CHATSWORTH RECORD AND THE QUEEN'S BUSH QUILL. (THE CHATSWORTH RECORD AND THE QUEEN'S BUSH QUILL). Began publication in 1974. 0702-7982. Newspaper. CN. English. The Chatsworth Record, Box 128, Chatsworth Ontario N0H 1G0 Canada. **DD** 071.1318.

THE CHAUTAUQUAN DAILY. 0746-0414. Periodical. US. English. wk. $18.70. Chautauqua Daily, Chautauque Institution, Chautaque NY 14722. *Chautauqua Assembly Herald.*

CHELSEY OVERVIEW. VFOAT Overview. V. 1- June 1979-. 0225-7017. Newspaper. CN. English. wk. $7. The Chesley Overview, PO Box 560, Chesley Ontario N0G 1L0 Canada. **DD** 071.1318.

CHEROKEE ADVOCATE (TAHLEQUAH, OKLA. : 1977). (CHEROKEE ADVOCATE). V. 1- Feb. 1977-. Newspaper. US. English. sa. $10.00. Cherokee Advocate, PO Box 948, Tahleqoh OK 74465. **Tel** (918)456-0671. Ed Lynn Howard. bk rev. adv acc. **Circ** 5,000. Cherokee nation tribal newspaper news of services, programs, government and issues affecting

Newspapers

Cherokees as the second largest tribe in the US. *Cherokee Nation News, Cherokee Voices.*

CHEROKEE DAILY TIMES. VFOAT Daily Times. 0747-4776. Newspaper. US. English. da. $56.50 Local, $66.50 Others. Cherokee Daily Times, PO Box 281, Cherokee IA 51012. *Cherokee Times (Cherokee, Iowa : 1870).*

CHEROKEE NATION NEWS. 1- Mar. 15, 1968-. 0009-322X. Periodical. US. English. $10.00. Cherokee Nation News, Box 119 Cherokee Indian Site Muskogee, Tallequal OK 74464. **Tel** (918)456-0671. Ed Lynn M Howard. bk rev. adv acc. **Circ** 4,500. Newspaper of 68,000-member Indian tribe and government. News about programs, services and enterprises of Cherokee Nation and administration.

THE CHEVRON. Newspaper. CN. English. ir. University of Waterloo, Federation of Students, Waterloo Ontario Canada.

CHIA CHING HUA PAO. VFOAT National Capital Chinese Community Newsletter. VAT Capital Chinese News. V. 1- July 1977-. 0711-6705. Newspaper. CN. Chinese. NCCC Newsletter, PO Box 5461, Station C, Ottawa Ontario K2C 3M1 Canada. **DD** 071.1384.

CHICAGO DAILY DEFENDER. Newspaper. US. English. da. $266.40. Chicago Daily Defender, 2400 Michigan Avenue, Chicago IL 60616. **Tel** (312)225-2400.

CHICAGO TRIBUNE (CHICAGO, ILL. : 1963). (CHICAGO TRIBUNE). 116th year, No. 48 (Feb. 17, 1963)-. Newspaper. US. English. da. $164.50. Chicago Tribune, 435 North Michigan Avenue/Room 300 FC, Chicago IL 60611. **Tel** (312)222-2242. Ed James Squires. **Ind/Abst** Infobank. Index available. bk rev. adv acc. **Circ** 800,000. (ctrl). Available on microfilm from Microphoto, Inc., Cleveland, Ohio. *Chicago Daily Tribune (1872).*

CHICAGO TRIBUNE INDEX. *See* Indexes/Abstracts.

EL CHICANO (COLTON, CALIF.). (EL CHICANO). Vol. 1, No. 1 (1967)-. Newspaper. US. English (Spanish). wk. $22.00. El Chicano, PO Box 827, Colton CA 92324. **Tel** (714)325-0964. Ed Gloria Macias. bk rev. adv acc. **Circ** 10,000. Available on microfilm from University Microfilms. Mexican Americans in the US and local community news.

CHICO ENTERPRISE (CHICO, CALIF. : 1872). (CHICO ENTERPRISE). Began in June 1872. Ceased in 1885?. Newspaper. US. English. da. $78.00. Enterprise Publishing Company, Box 9, Chico CA 95927. **Tel** (916)891-1234. Ed Jack Winning. adv acc. **Circ** 26,500. (ctrl)

THE CHIEF. VFOAT Chief-Leader. Began in 1897. 0009-3807. Newspaper. US. English. wk. $16.00. The Chief, 150 Nassau Street, New York NY 10038. **Tel** (212)962-2690. Ed Frank J Prial III. adv acc. **Circ** 65,000. (ctrl) Oldest newspaper concentrating in the civil service field. Read by thousands of city, state, and federal civil servants as well as prospective civil servants.

CHIEFTAIN. (THE CHIEFTAIN). Vol. 1, No. 1 (June 9, 1982)-. 0821-7696. Newspaper. CN. English. wk. Limited Free Local Distribution, $12.00 Others. The Chieftain, PO Box 253 Shopping Plaza, Iroquois Ontario K0E 1K0 Canada. **DD** 071.1375. *Iroquois Post.*

CHINA DAILY. 1983. Newspaper. CC. English. da. $99.00. China Daily Distribution Corp, 15 Mercer Street, Suite 401, New York NY 10013. **Tel** (212)219-0130. Ed Feng Xiliang. adv acc. **Circ** 5,000. The only English language newspaper published in the Peoples Republic of China, providing a fast, accurate and impartial coverage of Chinese and international events.

CHINA NEWS ANALYSIS. No. 1 (Aug. 25, 1953)-. 0009-4404. Periodical. HK. English. bw. $140.00. China News Analysis, Government Printing Office, Box 3225, Honk Kong China. **Tel** 5-488-125. **LC** DS777.55. **DD** 951.05. (cum index). Analysis of People's Republic of China media on current or background political, economic and social questions. One topic in each issue.

CHINA POST. 1972. Newspaper. US. English. da. $65.00. China Post, 133 Canal Street, New York NY 10002-5033. **Tel** (212)431-3897. Ed Hanson Chan. bk rev. adv acc. **Circ** 23,000. Intended to explain America to its Chinese readers, keep open the avenues of communications among America's multi-ethnic societies, articulate the needs and problems of the Chinese communities.

CHINOOK REPORTER. V. 1- March 20, 1978-. 0707-3860. Newspaper. CN. English. wk. Lethbridge Herald, Room 122 McFarland Building, Lethbridge Alberta Canada. **DD** 071.1234.

CHISAGO COUNTY PRESS. Newspaper. US. English. wk. $10.00. Chisago County Press, Lindstrom MN 55045. **Tel** (612)257-5115. Ed John A Silver. adv acc. **Circ** 4,000. (ctrl). Coverage of area news and events, published as a newspaper.

THE CHOWAN HERALD. 0739-0246. Newspaper. US. English. wk. $10.40 in NC, $11.00 Elsewhere. Chowan Herald, PO Box 207, Edenton NC 27932.

CHRISTIAN SCIENCE MONITOR (BOSTON, MASS. : 1983). (THE CHRISTIAN SCIENCE MONITOR). Vol. 75, No. 218 (Oct. 3, 1983)-. 0882-7729. Newspaper. US. English. da. $99.00. The Christian Science Monitor, One Norway Street, Boston MA 02115. **Tel** (617)262-2300. Ed Katherine Fanning. **Ind/Abst** Art Archaeol. Tech. Abstr., Book Rev. Index, Infobank, Music Index, Nexis. **DD** 071. bk rev. adv acc. **Circ** 160,000. Pulitzer prize-winning daily newspaper reporting on global issues. Correspondents worldwide write on political, cultural, social, economic, religious trends and topics. *Christian Science Monitor (Eastern Edition); Christian Science Monitor (Central Edition); Christian Science Monitor (New England Edition); Christian Science Monitor (Pacific Edition).*

CHRONIQUE. (LA CHRONIQUE). Vol. 1, No. 1 (Sept. 1980)-. 0712-7464. Newspaper. CN. French. mo. $2.00. La Municipalite de Beauport la Chronique, c/o La Mairie, CP 159, 5 Chemin la Tour du Lac, Lac Beauport Quebec G0A 2C0 Canada. **DD** 071.1447. *Passe-Montagne.*

CHUGAN KWANGGO. VFOAT Korean Street Journal. 0279-9758. Newspaper. US. Korean. wk. The Korean Street Journal, 2836 West 8th Street, Los Angeles CA 90005.

CHUNG-KUO SHAO NIEN PAO. VFOAT Zhongguo Shaonian Bao. Periodical. CC. Chinese. da. $5.76. China Publication Centre, PO Box 2820, Beijing China.

CHUNG PAO YUEH KAN. VFOAT Chung Pao Monthly. Began with Feb. 1980 issue. Periodical. HK. Chinese. mo. $1.25 US. Chung Newspapers Ltd, 171-172 Gloucester Road, Wanchai Hong Kong. **LC** AP95.C4. **DD** 059.951.

CHUTO TSUHO. VFOAT Middle East News. Periodical. JA. Japanese. ir. 3600. Middle East Institute of Japan, Jutaku Kodan Building, 10-21 Akasaka 5-Chome Minato-Ku, Tokyo Japan. **LC** DS41.

CINCINNATI ENQUIRER (CINCINNATI, OHIO : 1872). (THE CINCINNATI ENQUIRER). Vol. 36, No. 47 (Feb. 18, 1872)-. Newspaper. US. English. da. Cincinnati Enquirer, 617 Vine Street, Cincinnati OH 45201. **Tel** (513)721-2700. **LC** Newspaper 9240. bk rev. adv acc. **Circ** 300,000. Available on microfilm from Microphoto Division Bell & Howell Co. A general circulation daily newspaper. *Cincinnati Daily Enquirer (Cincinnati, Ohio : 1852); Commercial Tribune (Cincinnati, Ohio).*

CIRCLEVILLE HERALD (1883 : DAILY). (THE CIRCLEVILLE HERALD). Began with June 4, 1883 issue. Newspaper. US. English. da.

CISILUTE. (LA CISILUTE). No. 1 May 1973-. 0704-7282. Newspaper. CN. Italian (text in Friulian Dialect). ir. Free to Friulans Across Canada. La Cisilute, PO Box 427, Rexdale Ontario M9W 5L4 Canada. **DD** 071.1.

CITES NOUVELLES. V. 1- 7 March 1974-. 0319-5198. Newspaper. CN. French. wk. Cites Nouvelles, 112 Promenade Leacock, Pointe Claire Quebec Canada. **DD** 071.1428.

THE CITIZEN. 0009-7543. Periodical. US. English. mo. $7.50. Citizen, 1390 Logan Street, Denver CO 80203.

CITIZEN. (THE CITIZEN). 0229-0405. Newspaper. CN. English. wk. Free. The Citizen, 1005 Ottawa Street North, Kitchener Ontario N2A 1H2 Canada. **DD** 071.1345. (ctrl).

CITIZEN. (THE CITIZEN). 0710-5436. Newspaper. CN. English. wk. $0.25 Per Number. The Citizen, PO Box 1480, Sydney Nova Scotia B1P 5T4 Canada. **DD** 071.1696.

CITIZEN (AUBURN, N.Y.). (THE CITIZEN). 0738-7520. Newspaper. US. English. da. Auburn Publishers Inc, 25 Dill Street, Auburn NY 13021.

CITIZEN. CAPITAL IDEAS. (THE CITIZEN. CAPITAL IDEAS). VFOAT Capital Ideas. No. 1 (June 7, 1978)-. 0712-1075. Newspaper. CN. English. da. $131.56. Citizen, 1101 Baxter Road, Box 5020, Ottawa Ontario K2C 3M4 Canada. **Tel** (613)829-9100. **DD** 071.1384.

CITIZEN (FROSTBURG, MD.). (THE CITIZEN). 0746-5424. Newspaper. US. English. wk. $4.50. The Citizen, Route 2 Box 584, Frostburg MD 21532.

THE CITIZEN GEORGIAN. VFOAT Citizen and Georgian. 0883-7007. Newspaper. US. English. wk. The Citizen & Georgian, PO Box 387, Montezuma GA 31063. *Macon County Citizen.*

CITIZEN (JAY, OKLA.). (THE CITIZEN). Began in 1983. 0745-7561. Newspaper. US. English. wk. $6.18 Delaware, McDonals, Benton, Mayes & Cherokee Counties, $7.21 Elsewhere in Oklahoma, $9.00 Elsewhere in US. The Citizen, PO Box 660, Jay OK 74346. *Jay Citizen.*

CITOYEN. (LE CITOYEN : JOURNAL INTERMUNICIPAL, SECTEUR NORD). 0229-3943. Newspaper. CN. French. mo. $0,25 Per No. Le Citoyen, CP 368, Normetal Quebec J02 3A0 Canada. **DD** 071.1417.

CITOYEN. (LE CITOYEN). 0822-8957. Newspaper. CN. French. wk. Free. Citoyen a/s Editions Charles Gagnon, 107 rue Albert, Cowansville Quebec J2K 2W4 Canada. **DD** 071.1462.

CITY PAPER. 0195-0843. Newspaper. US. English. wk. $20.00. City Paper, 2612 North Charles Street, Baltimore MD 21218. **Tel** (301)889-6600. Ed Russ Smith. bk rev. adv acc. **Circ** 70,000. (ctrl). Baltimore's largest weekly. Circulates Metro Area, targets young adult readers with an emphasis on news, art, and entertainment.

CLAREMORE DAILY PROGRESS. Began in 1909. Newspaper. US. English. da. 315 West Will Rogers, Claremore OK 74017. **LC** NEWSPAPER 9347-X. Also available on microfilm from Bell and Howell, Microphoto Division, and Oklahoma Historical Society.

CLARIDAD. Yearly V. 1- (No. 1-). 0279-313X. Periodical. US. Spanish. wk. $30.00. Editorial Claridad, Av Ponce de Leon 1866, PD26 1/2, Santurce Puerto Rico 00909. **Tel** (212)674-5440. **Ind/Abst** Index Am. Period. Verse.

CLARION. (THE CLARION). V. 1- April 23, 1975-. 0319-5554. Newspaper. CN. English. wk. 15. Per No. The Clarion, PO Box 28, Prince George British Columbia V2L 4R9 Canada. **DD** 071.112.

CLARION. (THE CLARION). Began publication June 15, 1972. 0316-0211. Newspaper. CN. English. wk. 15. Per No. The Clarion, PO Box 1027, Capreol Ontario P0M 1H0 Canada. **DD** 07113133.

THE CLARION-LEDGER. (CLARION-LEDGER). VFOAT Clarion Ledger. May 8, 1841-. 0744-9526. Newspaper. US. English. da. $148.00. Mississippi Publishing Company, PO Box 40, 311 East Pearl Street, Jackson MS 39205. **Tel** (601)961-7000. **LC** Newspaper. *Daily Clarion-Ledger.*

CLERMONT COURIER. 0745-2772. Newspaper. US. English. wk. $9.00. Clermont Newspaper Inc, 1329 Arlington Street, Cincinnati OH 45225. **Tel** (513)542-8833. Ed Douglas E Sandhage. adv acc. **Circ** 6,000. Community news with special features like cooking and hunting plus all the court/legal news that is fit to print.

CLEVELAND ADVOCATE (CLEVELAND, TEX.). (THE CLEVELAND ADVOCATE). 0746-7125. Newspaper. US. English. wk. Cleveland Advocate, PO Box 1628, Cleveland TX 77327.

CLOQUET PINE KNOT-BILLBOARD. VFOAT Pine Knot-Billboard. VAT Cloquet Pine Knot Billboard. 0744-8597. Newspaper. US. English. sw. $20.00. Cloquet Pine Knot Billboard, PO Box 236, Cloquet MN 55720. **Tel** (218)879-6761. *Cloquet Pine Knot, Cloquet Billboard.*

COASTAL COURIER. (THE COASTAL COURIER). V. 1- Sept. 14, 1977-. 0707-6916. Newspaper. CN. English. wk. $23.21. Bay Publishing Company, PO Box 369, Grace Bay Nova Scotia B1A 5V5 Canada. **Tel** (902)849-1830. **DD** 071.1695.

Newspapers

COASTER. (THE COASTER). V. 1- Sept. 9, 1978-. 0707-2325. Newspaper. CN. English. bw. $20.00 Domestic, $30.00 Foreign. Bebb Publishing, Box 623, Grand Falls Newfoundland 2A2 2K2 Canada. **DD** 071.18.

COCHRANE TIMES. V. 1- May 15, 1974-. 0319-745X. Newspaper. CN. English. wk. Cochrane Times, PO Box 776, Cochrane Alberta Canada. **Tel** (403)932-2055. Ed M Maxie. **DD** 071.1233. bk rev. adv acc. **Circ** 2,300. (ctrl). Weekly community newspaper. Covers all general news in area surrounding Cochrane Alberta.

THE COEUR D'ALENE PRESS. Began with Feb. 17, 1891 issue. Newspaper. US. English. da. $72.00. Coeur d'Alene Press, Second and Lakeside, Coeur d'Alene ID 83814. LC Newspaper 7564.

COFFEY COUNTY TODAY. VFOAT Today. Vol. 1, No. 1 (May 2, 1983)-. 0745-838X. Newspaper. US. English. tw. Coffey County Today, 324 Hudson Street, Burlington KS 66839. *Daily Republican (Burlington, Kan.).*

COIN DE RUE. V. 1- July 12, 1977-. 0702-6919. Newspaper. CN. French. mo. Coin de rue, 255 Ste-Ursule, l'Assomption Quebec J0A 1G0 Canada. **DD** 071.14416.

COLDWATER DAILY REPORTER. 0745-6794. Newspaper. US. English. da. Coldwater Daily Reporter, 15 West Pearl Street, Coldwater MI 49036.

COLDWATER JOURNAL. (THE COLDWATER JOURNAL). Vol. 1, No. 1 (July 18, 1979)-. 0711-2181. Newspaper. CN. English. wk. Free. The Coldwater Journal, Box 280, Coldwater Ontario L0K 1E0 Canada. **DD** 071.1317.

THE COLLIER COUNTY STAR NEWS. 0191-7323. Newspaper. US. English. da. $109.00. Naples Daily News, 1075 Central Avenue, Naples FL 33941. **Tel** (813)262 3161.

COLLINGWOOD TIMES. (THE COLLINGWOOD TIMES). VFOAT Times. VAT Times (Collingwood). 0710-0078. Newspaper. CN. English. wk. $8.51. Collingwood Times, Box 339, Elmvale Ontario L0L 1PQ Canada. **Tel** (705)322-1871. **DD** 071.1317.

THE COLLINSVILLE HERALD. Began with Sept. 15, 1879 issue. 0883-6574. Newspaper. US. English. wk. Madison County Publications Inc, 113 East Clay Street, PO Box 389, Collinsville IL 62234.

COLORADO SPRINGS GAZETTE-TELEGRAPH. VFOAT Colorado Springs Gazette Telegraph. Began with Feb. 5, 1946 issue. Newspaper. US. English. da. $54.00. Colorado Springs Gazette, 30 South Prospect Street, PO Box 1779, Colorado Springs CO 80901. **Tel** (303)636-0304. LC Newspaper. *Colorado Springs Gazette, Colorado Springs Evening Telegraph.*

THE COLORADOAN. 0273-8260. Newspaper. US. English. da. Fort Collins Newspapers, PO Box 1577, Fort Collins CO 80522. **Tel** (303)493-6397. *Fort Collins Coloradan, 0164-9167.*

COLUMBIA FLIER. 1969. 0192-7841. Newspaper. US. English. wk. Patuxent Publishing Corp, 10750 Little Patuxent Parkway, Columbia MD 21044. **Tel** (301)730-3620. Ed Jean F Moon. adv acc. **Circ** 25,500. Concerns opinion, news, education, health, religion, community service, business, marketplace, villages, people, teen music; homelife, recreation, sports, theater, real estate, classifieds.

COLUMBIA MISSOURIAN. Began with 15th year, No. 236 (June 1, 1923)?. 0747-1874. Newspaper. US. English. da. Missourian Publishing Association, 311 South Ninth Street, Columbia MO 65205. *Columbia Evening Missourian.*

COLUMBUS DAILY ENQUIRER. VFOAT Daily Columbus Enquirer. Began in 1858. Newspaper. US. English. da. $114.00. Columbus Enquirer, PO Box 711, Columbus GA 31994. Ed Bill Brown. LC Newspaper 7488-X. adv acc. **Circ** 57,209. (ctrl). Daily newspaper.

THE COLUMBUS LEDGER. VFOAT Saturday Enquirer and Ledger. Began in 1886. Newspaper. US. English. da. $114.00. Columbus Ledger, PO Box 711, Columbus GA 31994. Ed Bill Brown. LC Newspaper. adv acc. **Circ** 57,209. (ctrl). Daily newspaper.

THE COMMERCIAL APPEAL. July 1, 1894-. Newspaper. US. English. da. Memphis Publishing Company, 495 Union Avenue, Memphis TN 38101. **Tel** (901)529-2666. Ed Joseph Williams. adv acc. *Memphis Commercial, Appeal; Avalanche.*

THE COMMERCIAL DISPATCH. Began with March 12, 1922 issue. Newspaper. US. English. da. $7.00 month. Commercial Dispatch, 516 Main Street, Columbus MS 39701. **Tel** (601)328-2424. Ed Birney Imes. LC Newspaper 7002. *Columbus Commercial, Columbus Dispatch.*

THE COMMERCIAL-NEWS. VAT Commercial News. 0742-8286. Newspaper. US. English. da. $148.00. Commercial-News, 17 West North Street, Danville IL 61832. LC Newspaper. *Danville Commercial-News.*

COMMUNITY COURIER (CHESTERFIELD, IND.). (COMMUNITY COURIER). 0745-7308. Newspaper. US. English. wk. $4.00. Newsprint Productions Inc, 406 East Main Street, Chesterfield IN 46017.

COMMUNITY HERALD (MONONA, WIS.). (THE COMMUNITY HERALD). V. 15, No. 32 (March 9, 1983)-. 0745-6646. Newspaper. US. English. wk. Community Herald, 6041 Monona Drive, Monona WI 53716. Ed J Freitag. Available on microfilm from the State Historical Society of Wisconsin. *Monona Community Herald.*

COMMUNITY REFLECTION. 0710-0086. Newspaper. CN. English. wk. $10.40. Community Reflections, 299 Lawrence Avenue, Kitchener Ontario N2M 1Y5 Canada. **DD** 071.1345.

COMUNIDADE. Yearly V. 1- Jan. 1974-. 0382-8794. Periodical. CN. Portuguese. 25 Per No. Comunidade, 140 Wright Street, Hull Quebec J8X 2G9 Canada. **DD** 071.1383.

COMUNIDADE. Began publication in 1975. 0703-9255. Newspaper. CN. Portuguese. mo. $5. Movimento Comunitario, Portugues 931 College Street, Toronto Ontario M6A 1A1 Canada. **DD** 071.13541.

CONCORD MONITOR (CONCORD, N.H. : 1970). (CONCORD MONITOR). No. 192 (Aug. 18, 1970)-. Newspaper. US. English. da. Monitor Publishing Co, 3 North State Street, Concord NH 03301. LC NEWSPAPER. *Concord Daily Monitor (Concord, N.H. : 1946).*

CONFLUENCE. V. 1- March 1977-. 0228-0515. Newspaper. CN. English. wk. 25. Per No. MacKenzie News, Confluence, PO Box 346, Fort Simpson Northwest Territories X03 0N0 Canada. **DD** 071.193.

CONSERVATIVE NEWSLINE. Sept. 1982. Periodical. UK. English. mo. $7.66. Conservative Central Office, c/o D K Britto, 32 Smith Square, London SW1 P3HH England. **Tel** 01-222-9000. Ed Joseph Tobin. bk rev. adv acc. **Circ** 100,000. This is the newspaper of the conservative party and is bought by members of the party-in power in the UK. For six years articles by government ministers. *Conservative News.*

CONSUMER GUIDES. (THE CONSUMER GUIDES). V. 1- Nov. 10, 1971-. 0317-381X. Newspaper. CN. English. wk. Free. King's Printing and Stationery Ltd, 9-11 O'Brien Avenue, Kapuskasing Ontario P5N 1X4 Canada. **DD** 071.13132.

CONTACT LAVAL. 0228-9008. Newspaper. CN. French. wk. Free. Contact Laval, 680 Boulevard Labelle, Laval Quebec H7V 2T9 Canada. **DD** 071.14271. (ctrl). *Journal Contact Laval, 0228-8990.*

CONTACT (TEMISCAMING, QUEBEC). (CONTACT). 0821-2341. Periodical. CN. English (French). wk. Free. Association Communautaire de Temiscaming, PO Box 757, Temiscaming Quebec J0Z 3R0 Canada. **DD** 071.14212. (ctrl).

CONTACT WEST ISLAND. Vol. 1, Ed. 1 (Nov. 21, 1979)-. 0226-9074. Newspaper. CN. English (French). wk. Free. Contact West Island, 88 Donegani, Pointe Claire Quebec H9R 2V4 Canada. **DD** 071.1428.

THE COOK COUNTY NEWS-HERALD. VFOAT Cook County News Herald. Began in 1911. Newspaper. US. English. wk. $18.00. Grand Marais New Herald, PO Box 157, Grand Marais MN 55604. LC Newspaper 8468. *Cook County Herald, Grand Marais News.*

CORNELL CHRONICLE. Began in 1970. 0747-4628. Periodical. US. English. wk. Cornell Chronicle, Editorial Office, 110 Day Hall, Ithaca NY 14853.

IL CORRIERE DELLA SERA. VFOAT Nuovo Corriere Della Sera. Newspaper. IT. Italian. ir. $255.00. Editoriale del Corriere Della, Via Solferino 28, 20100 Milano Italy. **Tel** 02/6339. Ed Del Corriere Della Sera. adv acc. **Circ** 700,000. (ctrl). Largest Italian newspaper covering news, politics, and economics.

CORSICANA DAILY SUN. 8750-2518. Newspaper. US. English. da. Corsicana Daily Sun, 405 East Collin Street, Corsicana TX 75110.

COSTA MESA NEWS. 0195-0126. Newspaper. US. English. wk. $42.35. Costa Mesa News, 1609 Babcock Avenue, Newport Beach CA 92663. **Tel** (714)631-8120.

THE COUNCILOR. (COUNCILOR). Began with V. 1, 1963. 0010-9991. Periodical. US. English. mo. The Councilor, 1827 Texas Avenue, Shreveport LA 71102.

THE COUNTRY ALMANAC. 1966. 0192-0111. Newspaper. US. English. wk. $15.00. Country Almanac, PO Box 4033, Woodside CA 94062. **Tel** (415)851-0200. Ed Elaine Levine. bk rev. adv acc. **Circ** 13,000. (ctrl). Community interest is the theme for this weekly newspaper.

COUNTRY NEWS. 0746-3251. Periodical. US. English. mo. $10.00 US, $13.50 Foreign. Country News, PO Box 674, Mt Juliet TN 37122. *Country Hotline News, 0199-6444.*

COUNTRY PRESS. 0745-9920. Newspaper. US. English. wk. Country Press, 113 South 6th Street, Brownfield TX 79316.

THE COUNTRY TODAY. 0192-9658. Newspaper. US. English. wk. $6.00. The Country Today, 401 Seaver Street, PO Box 570, Eau Claire WI 54701. **Tel** (715)834-3471.

COUNTY COURIER. 0274-7189. Newspaper. US. English. wk. $30.00. Damascus Weekly Courier, PO Box 300, Damascus MD 20750. **Tel** (301)253-6161.

COUNTY LINE COURIER. V. 1- Sept. 4 1974-. 0316-0335. Newspaper. CN. English. $6.00. County Line Courier, PO Box 337, Kensington PEI C0B 1M0 Canada. **DD** 071.171.

COUNTY NEIGHBOURS. (THE COUNTY NEIGHBOURS). 0715-545X. Newspaper. CN. English. wk. Free. County Neighbours, c/o Beacon Herald, 108 Ontario Street, Stratford Ontario N5A 6T6 Canada. **DD** 071.1323.

COUP D'OEIL (NAPIERVILLE, QUEBEC). (COUP D'OEIL). V. 1, No. 1 25 Oct. 1978-. 0710-3786. Newspaper. CN. French. wk. Free. Journal Coup d'Oeil, 412 Saint Jacques, Napierville Quebec J0J 1L0 Canada. **DD** 071.1438.

COURIER. (THE COURIER). V. 10- Jan. 1972-. 0318-0220. Periodical. English (includes some text in French). ir. *Newsletter, 0318-0212.*

COURIER. (THE COURIER). Issue 1- July, 30, 1975-. 0319-7026. Newspaper. CN. English. wk. 6.50. The Courier, 4 Elgin Street, St Thomas Ontario N5R 3L6 Canada. **DD** 071.1335.

COURIER - CANADIAN FORCES BASE COLD LAKE. (COURIER). VFOAT Canadian Forces Base Cold Lake Courier. 0045-8872. Newspaper. CN. English. bw. Free. Courier, PO Box 2350, Medley Alberta T0A 2M0 Canada. **DD** 358.4170971233.

COURIER DEMOCRAT. 0745-6956. Newspaper. US. English. da. Arkansas Newspapers Inc, 201 East 2nd Street, Russellville AR 72801. *Daily Courier Democrat.*

COURIER EXPRESS DE VAUDREUIL-SOULANGES. (LE COURRIER EXPRESS DE VAUDREUIL-SOULANGES). VFOAT Courrier Express. VAT Courrier Express (Dorion). V. 1, No. 1, (June 11, 1980)-. 0710-9938. Newspaper. CN. French. wk. Free. Le Courrier Express, CP 37, Dorion Quebec J7V 5V8 Canada. **DD** 071.1426.

THE COURIER-JOURNAL. Mar. 7, 1869-. Newspaper. US. English. da. Louisville Courier Journal, 525 West Broadway, Louisville KY 40202. **Tel** (800)626-6315. LC MICROFILM (N. *Louisville Courier-Journal.*

COURIER (ORLEANS). (THE COURIER). V. 1- Nov. 16, 1973-. 0316-0262. Newspaper. CN. English. mo. Wynmur Publications Ltd, PO Box 515, Orleans Ontario K1C 1S9 Canada. **DD** 071.1383.

Newspapers

COURIER WEEKEND. V. 1- Mar. 4, 1978-. 0707-4905. Newspaper. CN. wk. $23.21. St Croix Printing & Publishing Company, PO Box 250, St Stephen New Brunswick E3L 2X2 Canada. **Tel** (506)466-3220. Ed Marianne Janowicz. **DD** 071.1533. adv acc. **Circ** 8,800. A community newspaper covering local national and international issues.

COURRIER DE GRAND'MERE. (LE COURRIER DE GRAND'MERE). **VFOAT** Courrier. 0228-6645. Newspaper. CN. French. wk. $6,00. Le Courrier, 578 8E rue Grand-Mere, Quebec G9T 4K5 Canada. **DD** 071.14465. *Metropolitain.*

COURRIER DE LOTBINIERE. (LE COURRIER DE LOTBINIERE). 13 June 1978-. 0226-9139. Newspaper. CN. French. wk. Free. Le Courrier de Lotbiniere, 1000 rue St-Joseph, Laurier-Station, Quebec G0S 1N0 Canada. **DD** 017.1458. (ctrl).

COURRIER DE PORTNEUF. (LE COURRIER DE PORTNEUF). **VFOAT** Courrier. **VAT** Courrier (Connacona). Vol. 1, No. 1 (8 Nov., 1977)-. 0228-6297. Newspaper. CN. French. wk. Le Courrier de Portneuf, CP 1030, Donnacona Quebec G0A 1T0 Canada. **DD** 071.14466.

COURRIER DU SURVENANT. (LE COURRIER DU SURVENANT). Vol. 1, No. 1 (Sept. 21 1981)-. 0710-4561. Newspaper. CN. French. wk. Free. Courrier du Survenant, 645 Route Marie-Victorin, Tracy Quebec J3R 1K9 Canada. **DD** 071.1451.

COURRIER FRONTENAC. **VFOAT** Courrier de Frontenac. 21 Mar. 1977-. 0704-0474. Newspaper. CN. French. $110.00. Courrier de Frontenac, Box 789, Thetfd Mns Quebec G8G 5V3 Canada. **Tel** (418)338-5181. **DD** 071.457. adv acc. **Circ** 19,153. (ctrl). Regional news (in general).

COURRIER SAINT-HUBERT. Vol. 1, No. 1 (24 Mar. '82)-. 0712-6794. Newspaper. CN. French. wk. Free. Courrier Saint-Hubert, 1136 rue Victoria, Ville Lemoyne Quebec Canada. **DD** 071.1437.

COWICHAN NEWS. Began publication in 1976. 0703-9220. Newspaper. CN. English. wk. Free. Cowichan Valley News, 101A-225 Canada Avenue, Duncan British Columbia V9L 1T6 Canada. **DD** 071.1434.

CRANBROOK'S RESPONSE. V. 1- July 4, 1978-. 0708-0239. Newspaper. CN. English. sw. $10.00. Cranbrook's Response, 915 Baker Street, Cranbrook British Columbia V1C 1A4 Canada. **DD** 071.1145.

CREATIVE LOAFING. V. 6, Issue 47- Apr. 29, 1978-. Newspaper. US. English. wk. $10.00. Creative Loafing News Atlanta, 1011 West Peachtree Street, Atlanta GA 30309. **Tel** (404)873-1053. *Atlantan/Creative Loafing.*

CRIEE. (LA CRIEE : JOURNAL LOCAL DE SAINTE-SOPHIE DE LEVRARD). V. 1, No. 1 (June 1981)-. 0227-0803. Periodical. CN. French. mo. Free. La Criee, c/o N Gerard, 163 rue St-Antoine, Sainte-Sophie-de-Levrard Quebec G0X 3C0 Canada. **DD** 071.1455.

CRITICA. Began publication with Nov. 7, 1977 issue?. 0709-0382. Newspaper. CN. Spanish. wk. $15.00. O Modolo, Critica, 2063 Dundas Street West, Toronto Ontario M6R 1W8 Canada. **DD** 071.13551.

CROATIA PRESS. V. 1- 1947-. 0011-1627. Periodical. US. English (Croatian). qt. $10.00. Croatia Press, PO Box 1767 Grand Central Station, New York NY 10017. **Ind/Abst** Public Aff. Inf. Serv. Bull. **LC** DR301. **DD** 079.4972.

THE CROCKETT CO. SENTINEL, TRI-CO. NEWS, CROCKETT TIMES. **VFOAT** Crockett Co. Sentinel. 0746-0309. Newspaper. US. English. wk. Crockett Times, 128 West Main Street, Alamo TN 38001.

CROOKSTON TIMES. Newspaper. US. English. da. Crookston Times Printing Co, Crookston MN 56716. **Tel** (218)281-2730.

LA CROSSE TRIBUNE. **VFOAT** La Crosse Tribune. 0745-9793. Newspaper. US. English. da. $120.00. La Crosse Tribune, 402 North 3rd Street, La Crosse WI 54601. **Tel** (608)782-9710. adv acc. **Circ** 36,000.

CROSSFIELD CHRONICLE. May 18, 1982-. 0822-8299. Newspaper. CN. English. wk. Airdrie & District Echo Publ Company, PO Box 580, Airdrie Alberta T0M 0B0 Canada. **DD** 071.1233.

CROSSROADS (SHOAL LAKE, MAN.). (CROSSROADS). Vol. 1, NO. 1 (Apr. 22, 1982)-. Newspaper. CN. English. mo. $12.50. Crossroads, P O Box 160, Shoal Lake Manitoba R0J 1Z0 Canada. **Tel** (204)759-2644. Ed Gregory Nesbitt. **DD** 071.1273. bk rev. adv acc. **Circ** 7,000. (ctrl). General news, sports and advertising.

CULTURE STATISTICS, NEWSPAPERS AND PERIODICALS. See Statistics.

CUMBERLAND EVENING TIMES. **VFOAT** Cumberland Sunday Times. Began with Sept. 25, 1916 issue. Newspaper. US. English. da. Times and Alleganian Co, 7-9 South Mechanic Street, Cumberland MD 21502. **LC** Newspaper. *Evening Times.*

CUMHURIYET. 1974-. TU. Turkish. da. 150. Cumhuriyet/Surface Mail, Turkocagi Cad No 39-41, Cagaloglu Istanbul Turkey. **Tel** 15261000. Ed Hajan Cemal. bk rev. adv acc. **Circ** 150,000. (ctrl).

CUU QUOC. 0574-8070. Newspaper. VM. Vietnamese. ir. Xunhasaba, 32 Hai Ba Trung, Hanoi DRV North Vietnam.

DAGENS NYHETER. Newspaper. SW. Swedish. da. Premurationsavdelningen, S-10110 Stockholm Sweden.

DAILY AMERICAN (SOMERSET, PA.). (THE DAILY AMERICAN). 8750-247X. Newspaper. US. English. da. Somerset Newspapers, 334 West Main Street, Somerset PA 15501.

THE DAILY ARDMOREITE. **VFOAT** Sunday Ardmoreite-Press. Began with Oct. 28, 1893 issue. Newspaper. US. English. da. PO Box 1328, Ardmore OK 73401. **LC** NEWSPAPER 7002. Also available on microfilm from Microfilm Center Inc., and Oklahoma Historical Society.

DAILY BRITISH WHIG. (THE DAILY BRITISH WHIG MICROFORM). 0824-2968. Newspaper. CN. English. Preston Microfilm Services, 2215 Queen Street East, Toronto Ontario M4E 1E8 Canada. **DD** 071.1372.

DAILY CITIZEN (BEAVER DAM, WIS.). (DAILY CITIZEN). 0749-1379. Periodical. US. English. da. Daily Citizen, 805 Park Avenue, Beaver Dam WI 53916. *Beaver Dam Daily Citizen.*

THE DAILY COMMERCIAL RECORDER. **VFOAT** Commercial Recorder. 8750-734X. Periodical. US. English. da. The Daily Commercial Recorder, 414 Dolorosa Street, San Antonio TX 78204.

DAILY CRITIC (WASHINGTON, D.C. : 1872). (DAILY CRITIC). Vol. 5 No. 1,296, (Oct. 17, 1872)-V. 13, No. 3,938 (June 11, 1881). Newspaper. US. English. ir. $42.50. Atlanta Daily World, 145 Auburn Avenue NE, Atlanta GA 30303. **Tel** (404)659-1110. **LC** Newspaper 7331. *Critic.*

DAILY DEMOCRAT. DAVIS EDITION. Began publication in 1966?. Periodical. US. English. da. Daily Democrat, 702 Court Street, Woodland CA 95695.

DAILY EXPRESS. Periodical. UK. English. da. $239.06. Express Newspapers PIC, 121 Fleet Street, London EC4P 4JT England. **Tel** 01-353 8000.

THE DAILY GLEANER. Newspaper. JM. English. da. Gleaner Company Limited, 7 North Street, PO Box 40, Kingston Jamaica WI. **Tel** 932-3400.

DAILY GLOBE NEWS. 0744-740X. Newspaper. US. English. da. Daily Globe News, 236 Main Street, Auburn WA 98002.

THE DAILY HERALD. **VFOAT** Sun-Herald. Began with June 14? 1910 issue. Newspaper. US. English. da. Daily Herald, PO Box 4567, Biloxi MI 39531. **LC** Newspaper. *Biloxi Daily Herald, Gulfport Daily Herald.*

THE DAILY INDEPENDENT. 0744-6837. Newspaper. US. English. ir. $72.45. Bell & Howell Micro Photo Division, Box 311, Wooster OH 44691. **Tel** (606)324-2136. *Ashland Daily Independent, Catlettsburg Daily Press; Ashland Daily Commercial.*

THE DAILY JOURNAL. 0277-4941. Newspaper. US. English. da. $840.00. Daily Journal, 101 University/Suite 260, Denver CO 80206. **Tel** (303)393-8100. Ed Claude Powe. adv acc. **Circ** 3,905. (ctrl). Construction trend newspaper of legal notices for city and state offices. Covers construction of commercial and industrial buildings in Colorado and Wyoming.

DAILY JOURNAL (ELIZABETH, N.J.). (THE DAILY JOURNAL). Issue No. 28,283 (June 1, 1960)-Issue No. 5,172 (Sept. 27, 1972). Newspaper. US. English. da. Daily Journal, 295 North Broad Street, Elizabeth NJ 07207. also issued on microfilm by Micro Photo Div., Bell & Howell Co. *Elizabeth Daily Journal.*

DAILY LOCAL NEWS (WEST CHESTER). (DAILY LOCAL NEWS). **VFOAT** West Chester Local News. Vol. 1, No. 1 (Nov. 19, 1872)-. 0163-3082. Newspaper. US. English. da. $40.00. Daily Local News, 250 North Bradford Avenue, Box 517, West Chester PA 19380.

DAILY MAIL. May 4, 1896-. Newspaper. UK. English. da. 225.84. Associated Newspapers Group, Carmelite House, London EC4Y OJA England. **Tel** 01 353 6000. Ed David English. bk rev. adv acc. **Circ** 1,800,000. International and national news, features and sports coverage.

DAILY MARKET RECORD. Newspaper. US. English. da. Minneapolis Daily Market, 320 South 4th Street, Minneapolis MN 55415.

DAILY MESSENGER (CANANDAIGUA, N.Y.). (THE DAILY MESSENGER). Newspaper. US. English. da. $61.00. Cananaigua Daily Messenger, PO Box 344, Canandaigua NY 14424. Available on microfilm from Microphoto Division, Bell and Howell Co.

DAILY MESSENGER (UNION CITY, TENN.). (DAILY MESSENGER). **VFOAT** Union City Daily Messenger. 0745-5534. Newspaper. US. English. da. $36.00 in County, $52.00 Elsewhere. Union City Daily Messenger Inc, 613 Jackson Street, Union City TN 38261.

DAILY MIDWAY DRILLER. 0745-5364. Newspaper. US. English. da. $45.00. Daily Midway Driller, 800 Center Street, Taft CA 92806. *Taft Daily Midway Driller.*

DAILY MIRROR. Periodical. UK. English. wk. Mirror Group Newspapers Ltd, Holborn Circus, London EC1P 1DQ England.

DAILY NEWS. Periodical. VI. English. da. Virgin Islands Daily News, PO Box 7638, St Thomas Virgin Islands 00801.

DAILY NEWS. Newspaper. US. English. wk. $35.00. Wahpeton Breckenridge Daily, 601 Dakota Avenue, Wahpeton ND 58075. **Tel** (701)642-8585.

DAILY NEWS. Vol. 70, No. 231 (Mar. 1, 1981)-. 0279-8026. Newspaper. US. English. da. $182.00. Van Nuys Publ Co, PO Box 855, Van Nuys CA 91408. **Tel** (213)997-4259. Ed Ali Sar. bk rev. adv acc. **Circ** 175,000. (ctrl). Daily newspaper. *Valley Views, 0192-7264.*

DAILY NEWS HALIFAX-DARTMOUTH EDITION. (THE DAILY NEWS). 0715-4321. Newspaper. CN. English. da. 76.00. 1533 Barrington Street, Halifax Nova Scotia B3J 2M5. **Tel** (902)425-8170. Ed Lyndon Watkins. **DD** 071.1622. bk rev. adv acc. **Circ** 22,000. (ctrl). General interest pertaining to Halifax, Dartmouth, Nova Scotia, Canada.

DAILY NEWS JOURNAL. 0744-7337. Newspaper. US. English. da. Daily News Journal, 600 South Washington Street, Kent WA 98031.

DAILY NEWS JOURNAL (MURFREESBORO, TENN.). (THE DAILY NEWS JOURNAL). 0745-2683. Newspaper. US. English. da. $72.00. Murfreesboro Daily News, PO Box 68, Murfreesboro TN 37130.

DAILY NEWS (MCKEESPORT, PA.). (DAILY NEWS). Began with July 1, 1884 issue. Newspaper. US. English. ir. Daily News Publ Co, PO Box 128, McKeesport PA 15134.

DAILY NEWS (NEW YORK, N.Y. : 1920). (DAILY NEWS). **VFOAT** Sunday News. Vol. 2 No. 87 (Oct. 5, 1920) V. 61, No. 289 (May 28, 1980). Newspaper. US. English. da. New York News Inc, 220 East 42nd Street, New York NY 10017. **LC** Newspaper. Available on Microfilm. *News, Sunday News (New York, N.Y.).*

DAILY NEWS (RHINELANDER, WIS.). (THE DAILY NEWS). 0746-5866. Newspaper. US. English. da. Northern Lakes Publishing Company, 314 Courtney Street, Rhinelander WI 54501.

Newspapers

DAILY NEWS (WHITTIER, CALIF.). (THE DAILY NEWS). 0746-6188. Newspaper. US. English. da. $130.00. San Gabriel Valley Tribune, PO Box 1135, Covina CA 91722.

DAILY PRESS (ESCANABA, MICH.). (THE DAILY PRESS). Began in 1977. Newspaper. US. English. da. 600 Ludington Street, Escanaba MI 49829. LC Newspaper. *Escanaba Daily Press.*

DAILY PRESS (UTICA, N.Y.). (THE DAILY PRESS). Began in 1882. Periodical. US. English. da. $115.00. Utica Daily Press, 221 Oriskany Plaza, Utica NY 13503. Tel (315)792-5000.

DAILY PROGRESS (CHARLOTTESVILLE, VA.). (THE DAILY PROGRESS). 0746-0430. Newspaper. US. English. da. $120.00. Charlottesville Daily Progress, Box 1287, Charlottesville VA 22902. Tel (804)295-0856.

DAILY RECORDED (SACRAMENTO, CALIF.). (THE DAILY RECORDER). Began in 1911. 0197-8055. Periodical. US. English. da. $60.00. Sacramento Daily Recorder, PO Box 1048, Sacramento CA 95805. *Sacramento Press-Journal.*

THE DAILY REPORTER. V. 1- 1899-. 0749-7113. Newspaper. US. English. da. $75.00. Daily Reporter/Wisconsin, 704 West Wisconsin Avenue, Milwaukee WI 53233. Tel (414)276-0273. Ed Webster Woodmansee. adv acc. Circ 2,100. Daily newspaper of general circulation devoted to commerce, construction, purchasing, real estate and law.

DAILY ROCKY MOUNTAIN NEWS (DENVER, COLO. : 1860). (DAILY ROCKY MOUNTAIN NEWS). VFOAT Rocky Mountain News. -July 3, 1879. Newspaper. US. English. da. $156.00. Rocky Mountain News, PO Box 719, Denver CO 80201. LC Newspaper 7220. *Daily Denver Mountaineer, Daily Commonwealth (Denver, Colo.).*

DAILY SENTINEL (WOODSTOCK, ILL.). (THE DAILY SENTINEL). 0747-3702. Newspaper. US. English. da. Daily Sentinel, 109 South Jefferson, Woodstock IL 60098.

DAILY STAR (ONEONTA, N.Y.). (THE DAILY STAR). Vol. 83, No. 285 (May 28, 1974)-. Newspaper. US. English. da. $82.00. Daily Star, 102 Chestnut Street, Oneonta NY 13820. Tel (607)432-1000. Ed Gary Grossman. adv acc. Circ 19,000. Available on microfilm from Microphoto Division, Bell and Howell, Co. (-May 1977). A newspaper focusing on local news of Otsego, Delaware, Chemango and Schorie counties of upstate New York. *Oneonta Star.*

DAILY TELEGRAPH. VFOAT London Daily Telegraph. No. 35608-. Newspaper. US. English. da. 120.12. Daily Telegraph Ltd, 135 Fleet Street, London EC4P 4BL England. Tel (212)582-2626. (cum index). *Daily Telegraph and Morning Post.*

DAILY TIMES. Jan. 3, 1949-. Newspaper. NR. English. da. $1362.34. Daily Times of Nigeria Ltd, PO Box 1198 Surulere, Lagos Nigeria West Africa. Tel 900850-900859. Ed Farouk Umar Muhemmed. bk rev. adv acc. Circ 250,000. (ctrl). An independent newspaper: fearless and vocal. The choice of readers. With up to date information on economic, social and government activities. *Nigerian Daily Times.*

DAILY TIMES (DAVENPORT, IOWA : 1887). (THE DAILY TIMES). Newspaper. US. English. Daily Times-Iowa, Davenport IA 52802. LC Newspaper 7002.

DAILY TIMES (SALISBURY, MD.). (THE DAILY TIMES). VFOAT Sunday Times. Began with Dec. 12, 1964 issue. Newspaper. US. English. da. Daily Times, PO Box 1937, Salisbury MD 21801. LC Newspaper. *Salisbury Times.*

DAILY WORLD. July 16, 1968-. 0011-5533. Newspaper. US. English. da. Long View Publishing Co, PO Box 544 Old Chelsea Station, New York NY 10011. Tel (212)924-2523. *The Worker.*

DAKOTA COUNTY TRIBUNE. VFOAT Tribune. 1884. 8750-2895. Newspaper. US. English. wk. $24.00. Dakota County Tribune, PO Box 1439, Burnsville MN 55337. Tel (612)894-1111. Ed Donna Gilson. bk rev. adv acc. Circ 6,000. All general news, feature articles.

THE DAKOTA SUN. 0194-9691. Newspaper. US. English. wk. $10.00. Standing Rock Community College, Box 483, Fort Yates ND 58538. Tel (701)854-3425. Ed Rinissa Fitzpatrick. bk rev. adv acc. Circ 1,400. News pertinent to the Lakota, Dakota people on the standing rock reservation. Also news pertinent to persons of Sioux County, North Dakota.

DALLAS MORNING NEWS. Began April 11, 1842. Newspaper. US. English. da. $96.00. Dallas Morning News, PO Box 225237, Dallas TX 75265. Tel (214)745-8321.

THE DALLAS POST TRIBUNE. 0746-7303. Newspaper. US. English. wk. Post Tribune, PO Box 24727, Dallas TX 75224. *Post Tribune.*

THE DALLAS TIMES HERALD. No. 104 (May 12, 1954)-. Newspaper. US. English. da. $180.00. Dallas Times Herald, 1101 Pacific Avenue, Dallas TX 75202. Tel (214)744-6111. *Daily Times Herald.*

DALMENY REVIEW. V. 1- Sept. 15, 1977-. 0225-7025. Newspaper. CN. English. bw. $4. Saskatchewan, $5. Canada, and $6. other countries. G Grimsdale, Dalmeny Review, PO Box 249, Dalmeny Saskatchewan S0K 1E0 Canada. DD 071.1242.

DANICA. VFOAT Morning Star. Periodical. US. Serbo-Croatian(R). wk. 30.00. Danica, 4851 Drexel Boulevard, Chicago IL 60615. Ed Castimir Majie. bk rev. adv acc. Circ 2,500.

DEN DANSKE PIONEER. VFOAT Dansk Pioneer. Began with Aug. 1, 1872 issue. 0747-3869. Newspaper. US. Danish (English). bw. $20.00. Bertelsen Publishing Company, 1582 Glen Lake Road, Hoffman Estates IL 60421. Ed H Miller. LC Newspaper.

DANVILLE ADVOCATE-MESSENGER. VFOAT Danville Advocate Messenger. Newspaper. US. English. da. $68.25. The Advocate Messenger, Box 149, Danville KY. Tel (606)236-2551. LC Newspaper 7885-X. *Kentucky Advocate, Danville Daily Messenger.*

THE DANVILLE REGISTER. 1848. 0744-3242. Newspaper. US. English. da. $82.80. Register Publishing Co Inc, Circulation Department, Danville VA 24541. Tel (804)793-2311. Ed Jim McNair. adv acc. Circ 28,000. (ctrl). A daily newspaper featuring local and national news and ads.

DARIEN NEWS-REVIEW. VAT Darien News Review. V. 10, No. 9 (March 4, 1982)-. 0744-3862. Newspaper. US. English. wk. $12.00. Darien News Corp, 24 Old Kings Highway South, Darien CT 06820. Tel (203)655-7476. *Darien News, 0192-0154; Darien Review.*

DAWN. VFOAT Dawn Overseas Weekly. Periodical. English. ir. 725 Domestic, $50.00 US. Pakistan Herald Publishing Limited, Haroon Hse/Dr Ziauddin Ahmed, Karachi 1 Pakistan. Tel 516761. Ed Ahmed Ali Khan. bk rev. adv acc. Circ 90,000. General newspaper directed at the upper strata of public. Read by leading businessmen, civil servants and those who make or influence decisions.

D.C. GAZETTE. VAT District of Columbia Gazette. V. 1- Dec. 1969-. 0071-7153. Periodical. US. English. bw. Capital East Gazette, 1739 Connecticut Avenue NW, Washington DC 20009. LC F191. DD 071.53.

DEATH VALLEY GATEWAY GAZETTE. VFOAT Gateway Gazette. 0746-7419. Newspaper. US. English. wk. Gateway Gazette, PO Box 217, Beatty NV 89003.

DEFENSOR CHIEFTAIN. 0011-7633. Newspaper. US. English. sw. $14.00. Tres Verdes Inc, PO Box Q, Socorro NM 87801. Tel (505)835-0520. Ed Valerie Smallridge. bk rev. adv acc. Circ 2,750. Newspaper serving high tech and college community; explosives, mining technology and radioastronomy.

DELAWARE COUNTY TIMES. Vol. 139, No. 39 (Oct. 5, 1978)-. 0745-0206. Newspaper. US. English. wk. $10.00. Delaware County Times, 4 Court Street, Delhi NY 13753. *Delaware Republican-Express.*

DELAWARE STATE NEWS. Began in 1901. US. English. da. $73.00. Delaware State News, PO Box 737, Dover DE 19901. Tel (302)674-3600. LC Newspaper. Circ 25,000 Daily 33,000 Sunday.

DELTA DEMOCRAT-TIMES. VFOAT Democrat-Times. Sept. 1, 1938-. Periodical. US. English. da. $72.00. Greenville Delta Democrat, PO Box 1618, Greenville MS 38701. Tel (601)335-1155. *Delta Star, Daily Democrat-Times.*

DELTA OPTIMIST. (THE DELTA OPTIMIST). 0710-1422. Newspaper. CN. English. Ernest Bexley Publisher, PO Box 40, Delta British Columbia V4K 3N5 Canada. DD 071.1133.

DELTA WEEKLY. 0746-0538. Newspaper. US. English. wk. Delta Democrat-Pub. Co, 988 North Broadway, Greenville MS 38702-1618.

DEMING HEADLIGHT. 0738-8349. Newspaper. US. English. da. $48.00. Deming Newspaper Inc, 219 East Maple Street, Deming NM 88030. Tel (505)546-2611. Ed Rich Van Cleef. bk rev. adv acc. Circ 3,450. (ctrl). News. *Deming Graphic.*

THE DEMOCRAT-LEADER (FAYETTE, MO.). (THE DEMOCRAT-LEADER). VFOAT Democrat Leader. 0746-9934. Newspaper. US. English. wk. The Democrat-Leader, 202 East Morrison, Fayette MO 65248.

DEMPA SHIMBUN. Newspaper. JA. Japanese. ir. Dempa Shimbun Sha, 11-15 Higashi Gotanda 1 Shinagawa-ku, Tokyo 141 Japan. LC Newspaper.

DENNI HLASATEL. VFOAT Nedelni Hlasatel. Vol. 1, No. 1 (4 April 1891)-. 0744-6586. Newspaper. US. Czech. da. $72.00 daily, $35.00 Sunday. 6426 West Cermak Road, Berwyn IL 60402. Tel (312)749-1891. Ed Josef Kucera. LC Newspaper. adv acc. Circ 9,000. Preserves Czechoslovak heritage, calling attention to the situation in Czechoslovakia.

THE DENVER POST. Began with Oct. 28, 1895 issue. Newspaper. US. English. da. $324.00. Denver Post, 650-15th Street, Denver CO 80202. LC Microfilm N.

THE DES MOINES REGISTER. VFOAT Des Moines Sunday Register. Vol. 68, No. 93 (Oct. 1, 1916)-. Newspaper. US. English. da. Des Moines Register, PO Box 957, Des Moines IA 50304. Tel (515)284-8236. LC Newspaper. Available on microfilm. *Des Moines Register and Leader.*

DES PLAINES TIMES. VFOAT Times. 0745-8681. Newspaper. US. English. wk. $15.50. Des Plainer Publishing Co, 1000 Executive Way, Des Plaines IL 60018. Tel (312)824-1111. Ed Herman Baumann. adv acc. Circ 10,388. Community news, features, photos and advertising. *Des Plaines Subsurban Times.*

THE DESERT TRAIL. 0746-5599. Newspaper. US. English. wk. $12.00 San Bernardino County, $17.00 Outside County, $22.00 Out of State. Desert Trail, PO Box 159, Twentynine Palms CA 92277.

DETROIT FREE PRESS (DETROIT, MICH. : 1858). (DETROIT FREE PRESS). Vol. 22, No. 60 (Aug. 18, 1858)-. Newspaper. US. English. da. Detroit Free Press Inc, 321 West Lafayette, Detroit MI 48231. LC NEWSPAPER 8415. *Detroit Daily Free Press (Detroit, Mich. : 1851).*

DETROIT NEWS. 1876. Newspaper. US. English. da. $303.00. Evening News Association, 615 Lafayette Boulevard, Detroit MI 48231. Tel (313)222-2380. Ed Lionel Linder. bk rev. adv acc. Circ 680,000 Daily 850,000 Sunday. International, national, and local news plus features and editorial comment. Michigan's largest newspaper.

DEUTSCH KANADISCHER POSTILLION. Vol. 1 (Apr. 1983)-. 0824-538X. Newspaper. CN. English (German). $9.00. Deutsch-Kanadischer Postillion, 1675 Ottawa Street, Windsor Ontario N8Y 1 Canada. DD 971.3320043105.

DEUTSCHE ZEITUNG. V. 1-. Periodical. GW. German. wk. $39.93. W E Saarbach GMBH, Postfach 101610, D-5000 Koeln 1 West Germany. Tel 02 21-23 46 31.

DEUTSCHES ALLGEMEINES SONNTAGSBLATT. VAT Deutsches Allgemeines Sonntags Blatt. V. 20, No. 40, Oct. 1, 1967-. Newspaper. GW. German. wk. Hansisches Druck, Verlagshaus 2, Hamburg 13 West Germany. *Sonntagsblatt.*

DEVON DISPATCH. (THE DEVON DISPATCH). Vol. 1, No. 1 May 27th, 1976. 0710-5495. Newspaper. CN. English. wk. Devon Printing and Publishing, The Devon Dispatch, Box 720, Devon Alberta T0C 1E0 Canada. DD 071.1233.

DIARIO. (EL DIARIO). Yearly V. 2, No. 9, (March 1983)-. 0824-3182. Newspaper. CN. Spanish. mo. Free. Diario, 8322-166 Street, Edmonton Alberta T5R 2S8 Canada. DD 071.1233. (ctrl). *Diario Hispano, 0824-3174.*

DIARIO LAS AMERICAS. Began with issue for July 4, 1953. 0744-3234. Newspaper. US. Spanish. da. $84.00. The Americas Publishing Company, 2900 Northwest 39th Street, Miami FL 33142. Tel (305)633-3341. Ed Horacio Aguirre. bk rev. adv acc. Circ 63,732. (ctrl). Spanish-language daily newspaper with complete news coverage and features such as

Newspapers

food section, travel, business, sports, lifestyle, social, real estate, editorials, movie reviews, etc.

THE DICKENSON STAR. 0746-584X. Newspaper. US. English. wk. $10.00. Dickenson County Publishing Co, PO Box 398, Clinchco VA 24226. Tel (703)835-8625. Ed Howard C Owen. adv acc. Circ 3,600. (ctrl). County newspaper.

DICKEY COUNTY LEADER. Newspaper. US. English. wk. $9.00. Dickey County Leader, 216 Main, Ellendale ND 58436. Tel (701)349-3222.

DICKINSON PRESS. 1883. Newspaper. US. English. da. $75.00. Mariana Publishing Inc, Box 1367, Dickinson ND 58601. Tel (701)225-8111. Ed Jay Ulku. adv acc. Circ 9,450. (ctrl)

DIDSBURY BOOSTER AND MOUNTAIN VIEW COUNTY NEWS. V. 13, No. 2- Jan. 8, 1974-. 0316-683X. Newspaper. CN. English. wk. $3.00. McCoy Publishing Ltd, 2013 19th Avenue, Didsbury Alberta Canada. DD 071.1233. *Didsbury Booster, 0316-6848; Didsbury Pioneer; Mountain View County News.*

DINUBA SENTINEL. 0745-6654. Newspaper. US. English. wk. Dinuba Sentinel, POB 247, Dinuba CA 93618.

THE DIRECTORS ENCYCLOPEDIA OF NEWSPAPERS. *See* Encyclopedias & General Reference Books.

THE DISPATCH. 0163-3090. Newspaper. US. English. da. $60.00. The Dispatch Co, PO Box 908, Lexington NC 27292. Tel (704)249-3981.

DODGE COUNTY INDEPENDENT. Newspaper. US. English. wk. $12.00. Kasson Dodge County, 105 First Avenue NW, Kasson MN 55944. Tel (507)634-7503.

EL DORADO GAZETTE, GEORGETOWN GAZETTE & TOWN CRIER. VFOAT El Dorado Gazette. VAT El Dorado Gazette, Georgetown Gazette and Town Crier. 8750-6289. Newspaper. US. English. wk. $15.00 El Dorado County, $20. Elsewhere. El Dorado Gazette, Gazette Building, PO Box 156, Georgetown CA 95634. *Georgetown Gazette & Town Crier.*

DOUGLAS DAILY DISPATCH. Began in Apr. 1903. Newspaper. US. English. da. Douglas Daily Dispatch, PO Box H, Douglas AZ 85607. Tel (602)364-3424. Ed Gary Dillard. LC Newspaper 7071. bk rev. adv acc. Circ 3,500. *Douglas Dispatch.*

DOWNTOWNER. (THE DOWNTOWNER). Vol. 1, No. 1 (Nov. 7, 1979)-. 0710-1619. Newspaper. CN. English. wk. Free. The Downtowner, 33 Britain Street, Toronto Ontario M5A 3Z3 Canada. DD 071.13541. (ctrl).

THE DRIPPING SPRINGS DISPATCH. 0746-603X. Newspaper. US. English. wk. Dripping Springs Dispatch, Star Route 1A/Box 51B, Dripping Springs TX 78620.

DROVER'S JOURNAL. V. 89- Jan. 4, 1961-. 0012-6454. Periodical. US. English. ir. $20.00. Drovers Journal, 7950 College Boulevard/PO Box 2939, Shawnee Mission KS 66201. Tel (913)451-2200. *Chicago Daily Drovers Journal, Drovers Telegram; Stockman's Journal; Livestock Reporter.*

DRUMHELLER SUN. (THE DRUMHELLER SUN). V. 12, No. 16- Aug. 16, 1978-. 0709-0595. Newspaper. CN. English. wk. $7.00 Domestic, $8.00 Foreign. The Drumheller Sun, PO Box 1480, Drumheller Alberta T0J 0Y0 Canada. DD 071.1233. *Big Country News.*

DU QUOIN EVENING CALL. Began in 1895. Newspaper. US. English. da.

DULUTH BUDGETEER. Newspaper. US. English. da. $10.00. Duluth Budgeteer, 5807 Grand Avenue, Duluth MN 55807. Tel (215)624-3665. Ed Richard F Palmer. adv acc. Circ 47,000.

DULUTH HERALD (DULUTH, MINN.: 1910). (DULUTH HERALD). Began in 1910. Ceased Aug. 1, 1982. Newspaper. US. English. da. LC Newspaper 7002. *Duluth Evening Herald.*

THE DULUTH NEWS-TRIBUNE CEASED. VFOAT Duluth News Tribune. Began with V. 7, No. 148, Oct. 6, 1892. Ceased V. 113, No. 98, Aug. 1, 1982. Newspaper. US. English. da. LC Newspaper 7002. *Duluth Daily News, Duluth Daily Tribune.*

DURHAM MORNING HERALD. VFOAT Sunday Herald-Sun. Began with Oct. 5, 1919 issue. Newspaper. US. English. da. 115 Market Street, Durham NC 27702. LC Newspaper 7002. *Morning Herald (Durham, N.C.).*

THE DURHAM SUN. Began in 1911. Newspaper. US. English. da. 115 Market Street, Durham NC 27702. LC Newspaper 7002. *Durham Daily Sun.*

DZIENNIK POLSKI. VFOAT Polish Daily News. Began with Mar. 4, 1904 issue. 0279-5019. Newspaper. US. Polish. ir. $20.00. Polish Daily News Inc, 19600 Van Dyke, Detroit MI 48234. Tel (313)366-4900. Ed Stanley Krajenski. LC Newspaper. bk rev. adv acc. Circ 17,000. (ctrl).

EAGAN CHRONICLE. 0273-8651. Newspaper. US. English. wk. $25.00. Current Newspapers, 1209 East Cliff Road, Burnsville MN 55337.

EAGLE II. VFOAT Eagle 2. 8756-1824. Newspaper. US. English. wk. Eagle Printing Co, 114-116 West Diamond Street, Butler PA 16001.

EAGLEVIEW POST. (THE EAGLEVIEW POST). Vol. 1, No. 1 (Sept. 15, 1981)-. 0821-2171. Newspaper. CN. English. bw. Free. The Eagleview Post, P O Box 771, Turner Valley Alberta T0L 2A0 Canada. DD 071.2122. (ctrl).

EAR FALLS ECHO. (THE EAR FALLS ECHO). Began publication in July 1975. 0702-9020. Newspaper. CN. English. wk. 20 per No. Ear Falls Echo, Box 54, Ear Falls Ontario P0V 1T0 Canada. DD 071.13112.

EAST AFRICAN STANDARD. 1902-. Newspaper. KE. English. da. $191.93. The Standard Limited, PO Box 30080, Nairobi Kenya.

EAST LONDON NEWS. Issue 1- Oct. 2, 1974-. 0316-6511. Newspaper. CN. English. wk. Free. East London News, PO Box 811 Station B, London Ontario N6A 4X3 Canada. DD 071.1326.

EAST ROCKAWAY LYNNBROOK OBSERVER. 0746-2093. Newspaper. US. English. wk. OB Publications, POB 567, Oceanside NY 11572.

EASTERN SHORE ECHO. V. 1- Feb. 1977-. 0707-6908. Newspaper. CN. English. sm. $.25. Eastern Marine Arts Technology and Crafts Heritage Society, PO Box 186, Sheet Harbour Nova Scotia B0J 3B0 Canada. DD 071.1622.

EAU CLAIRE LEADER-TELEGRAM CEASED. Ceased with V. 9, No. 102 (Oct. 6, 1978). Newspaper. US. English. da. $50.00. Leader Telegram, 701 South Farwell, Eau Claire WI 45701. Tel (715)834-3471. LC AN.W5.

ECHO. (L'ECHO). VFOAT Echo du K R T. V. 1- Nov. 4, 1975-. 0381-1034. Newspaper. CN. French. wk. $9.50. L'Echo, CP 1026, Riviere-du-Loup Quebec G5R 4C3 Canada. DD 071.1476.

ECHO. (THE ECHO). 0823-826X. Newspaper. CN. English. mo. The Echo, Suite 36/120 Norfinch Drive, Downsview Ontario M3N 1X3 Canada. DD 071.13541. *Jane Echo, 0823-8251.*

ECHO DES FRONTIERES. (L'ECHO DES FRONTIERES). Vol. 1, No. 1 (24 May 1983)-. 0823-5503. CN. French. wk. Free to Citizens. L'Echo des Frontieres, 420 2E Avenue, Iberbille Quebec J2X 2X8 Canada. DD 071.1461.

ECLAIREUR PROGRES. First issue in 1957. 0319-5546. Newspaper. CN. French. wk. 15- L Eclaireur Progres, 12625 1st Avenue, Ville St-Georges Canada. Tel (418)228-8858. DD 071.1471. adv acc. Circ 12,000. (ctrl). General news of the region with a special place for economy, arts, agriculture, sports and politics. *L'Eclaireur.*

ECLUSE. (L'ECLUSE). VFOAT Journal l'Ecluse. Vol. 1, No. 1 (28 Jan. 1981)-. 0710-1708. Newspaper. CN. French. wk. $20.00. Journal l'Ecluse, 810 rue East Main, Welland Ontario L3B 3Y5 Canada. DD 071.1338.

EDGEWATER TRIBUNE. 0745-774X. Newspaper. US. English. wk. $18.00. Edgewater Tribune, 5838 West 25th Avenue, Edgewater CO 80214.

EDINA SUN. Newspaper. US. English. wk. $25.00. Minnesota Suburban Newspapers, 7401 Bush Lake Road, Edina MN 55435. Tel (612)831-1200.

EDITION SPECIALE. V. 1- 14 Jan. 1976-. 0383-803X. Newspaper. CN. French. bm. 1495 rue Roberval Bureau 1, Saint-Bruno Quebec J3V 3P8 Canada. DD 071.1436.

EDITOR & PUBLISHER. VFOAT E & P. VAT Editor and Publisher. V. 1-14, No. 40, June 29, 1901-Mar. 13, 1915. 0013-094X. Periodical. US. English. wk. $40.00. Editor & Publisher, 11 West 19th Street, New York NY 10011. Tel (212)675-4380. Ed Robert U Brown. Ind/Abst Trade Ind. Index, Bus. Period. Index, Infobank, Print. Abstr., ABI/Inform. LC PN4700. DD 070.4. adv acc. Circ 30,000. Newsmagazine reporting to the newspaper industry, its suppliers, advertisers and advertising agencies. *Journalist, Advertising; Fourth Estate.*

EDITOR & PUBLISHER. SYNDICATE DIRECTORY. *See* Yearbooks, Almanacs, Directories.

THE EDMONTON JOURNAL, MICROFORM. Newspaper. CN. English. da. $220.00. Edmonton Journal, PO Box 2421 Circulation Department, Edmonton T5J 2S6 Alberta Canada. Tel 468-4010. Ed Steve Hume. adv acc. Circ 163,000. (ctrl).

EDMONTON SUN. (THE EDMONTON SUN). No. 1- Nov. 12, 1977-. 0705-405X. Newspaper. CN. English. da. Edmonton Sun/Daily, 9300-47th Street, Edmonton Alberta T6B 2P6 Canada. Tel (403)468-5121. DD 071.1233.

EDMORE HERALD. 8750-5444. Newspaper. US. English. wk. Ness Press, Box 157, Fordville ND 58231.

THE EDWARD WILLIAMS WEEKLY. Vol. 159. No. 15 Mar. 16, 1984)- – N.S. V.1, No. 1-. 0747-170X. Newspaper. US. English. wk. The Edward Williams Weekly, 249 Main Street, Vegennes VT 04591. *Vergennes Citizen, 0745-9440.*

THE EGYPTIAN GAZETTE. VFOAT Egyptian Mail. No. 1- 1880-. Newspaper. UA. English. da. $105.00. United Distributing Co, 21 Kasr El Nil Street, Cairo Egypt.

EHNWHEOT NATIVE NEWS. 0225-154X. Newspaper. CN. English. Ehnwheot Native Communications, 68 Xavier Street, Sudbury Ontario P3C 2B9 Canada. DD 971.00497.

THE EL PASO TIMES. 0746-3588. Newspaper. US. English. da. The El Paso Times, PO Box 20, El Paso TX 79999.

THE ELBERTON STAR. 8750-6734. Newspaper. US. English. ir. The Elberton Star - The Elberton Beacon Inc, 10 Oliver Street, Elberton GA 30635.

THE ELK CITY DAILY NEWS. Began in 1901. Newspaper. US. English. da. 200-206 West Broadway, Elk City OK 73644. LC Newspaper 9347-X. Also available on microfilm from Microfilm Center Inc. *Elk City News-Democrat.*

ELK ISLAND TRIANGLE. (THE ELK ISLAND TRIANGLE). V. 1- Aug. 17, 1971-. 0704-0229. Newspaper. CN. English. wk. Elk Island Triangle, Box 208, Andrew Alberta T0B 0C0 Canada. Tel (403)365-3939. DD 071.1233.

ELK POINT LAKELAND REVIEW. VAT Lakeland Review (1984). 0828-7759. Newspaper. CN. English. wk. $0.25 Per No. Elk Point Lakeland Review, PO Box 309, Elk Point Alberta T0A 1A0 Canada. DD 071.1233. *Lakeland Review, 0828-7740.*

ELK POINT REFLECTIONS. V. 1- Apr. 10, 1979-. 0226-6350. Newspaper. CN. English. wk. $5.00 Domestic, $10.00 Foreign. Mannville Reflections, Elk Point Reflections, PO Box 668, Elk Point Alberta T0A 1A0 Canada. DD 071.1233.

ELK POINT SENTINEL. VFOAT Sentinel. VAT Sentinel (Elk Point). V. 1- Sept. 26, 1979-. 0226-6369. Newspaper. CN. English. wk. Elk Point Sentinel, PO Box 608, Elk Point Alberta T0A 1A0 Canada. DD 071.1233.

THE ELK VALLEY TIMES OBSERVER AND NEWS. VFOAT Elk Valley Times. 0747-3761. Newspaper. US. English. wk. Lakewood Publishers, 418 North Elk Avenue, Fayetteville TN 37334.

THE ELKHART TRUTH. Began in 1889. 0746-7516. Newspaper. US. English. ir. $91.20. Elkhart Truth, c/o Circulation, PO Box 487, Elkhart IN 46515. Tel (219)294-1661. Ed John F Dillie. LC Newspaper 7002. adv acc.

O ELLEN AGGELIAPHOROS. VFOAT Greek Messenger. Vol. 1, No. 1 (Mar. 1976)-. 0229-7892. Newspaper. CN. Greek, Modern. sm. $0.35 Each No. O Ellen Aggeliaphoros, 457 Ontario Street, London Ontario N5W 3X1 Canada. DD 071.1326.

Newspapers

ELLENIKA NEA. (TA ELLENIKA NEA). VFOAT The Hellenic News. 0821-7270. CN. Greek, Modern. mo. $10.00. Ta Ellenika Nea c/o G Drossos, 43 Agincourt Gardens, London Ontario N5Z 4E5 Canada. **Tel** (519)681-5450. **Ed** G N Drossos. **DD** 071.1326. bk rev. adv acc. **Circ** 1,000. A review magazine with news and articles on education, finance, art, literary news, philosophy, science, travel, classified, etc.

ELLENO-KANADIKA CHRONIKA. VFOAT Chronika. 20 May 1981-. 0820-7801. Newspaper. CN. Greek, Modern. wk. Chronicles, Suite 220/370 Danforth Avenue, Toronto Ontario M4K 1N8 Canada. **DD** 071.13541.

ELLENOKANADIKON VEMA. VFOAT Greek Canadian Tribune. Began in 1963?. 0046-6387. Newspaper. CN. Greek, Modern. ir. Ellinokanadika Vima, 5619 Park Avenue, Montreal Quebec 152 Canada. **Tel** (514)272-6873. **DD** 071.14281.

ELMIRA STAR-GAZETTE. Ceased with Dec. 31, 1963. Newspaper. US. English. da. $89.00. Star Gazette, 201 Baldwin Street, Elmira NY 14902. Available on microfilm. *Gazette and Free Press; Elmira Evening Star; Elmira Evening News.*

ELMORE EYE. Newspaper. US. English. wk. Elmore Eye, Elmore MN 56027.

ELY ECHO. 0746-7087. Newspaper. US. English. wk. Ely Echo, 2 East Sheridan Street, Ely MN 55731.

EMIGRANTE. (O EMIGRANTE). Yearly V. 1- May 20, 1977-. 0704-190X. Newspaper. CN. Portuguese. wk. Sociedade de Publicacoes de Montreal, O Emigrant, 59 Duluth Street East, Montreal Quebec H2W 1G9 Canada. **DD** 071.14281.

ENCONTRO. V. 1- Mar. 8, 1974-. 0317-0624. Newspaper. CN. Portuguese. sm. Encontro, c/o Rev Jose Ponti, 1423 East 13Av, Vancouver BC V5N 2B5 Canada. **Tel** (604)879-6261. **DD** 071.1133.

THE ENID MORNING NEWS. VFOAT News. Began with Feb. 1923 issue. Newspaper. US. English. da. 227 West Broadway, Enid OK 73701. LC Newspaper 7002. Also available on microfilm from Microfilm Center Inc., and Bell and Howell, Microphoto Division. *Enid Daily News.*

THE ENNIS DAILY NEWS. 8755-9056. Newspaper. US. English. da. United Publishing Company, 213 North Dallas Street, Ennis TX 75119.

ENTERPRISE (BOARDMAN, OR.). (THE ENTERPRISE). 0747-4067. Newspaper. US. English. wk. The Enterprise, PO Box 21, Boardman OR 97818-0021.

EPIK KAKOUNA CEASED. VFOAT Epik. V. 1-6, No. 1. 0319-3918. Newspaper. CN. French. ir. $2. Service d'Information de Cacouna, CP 152 Cacouna Cte, Riviere-du-Loup Quebec G5R 3Y8 Canada. **DD** 071.1476.

EPIMORPHOTIKA NEA. VFOAT Cultural News. Began with Apr. 28, 1977? issue. 0705-1301. Newspaper. CN. Greek, Modern. Cultural News, 1305-7th Avenue, New Westminister British Columbia V3M 2J9 Canada. **DD** 071.1133.

ERSKINE ECHO. Newspaper. US. English. wk. $8.00. Erskine Echo, Erskine MN 56535. **Tel** (218)687-3775.

ERU PRESS INDEX. *See* Indexes/Abstracts.

ESQUIMALT STAR. (THE ESQUIMALT STAR). 0821-0403. Newspaper. CN. English. Free to Residents. The Esquimalt Star, 1534 Monterey Avenue, Victoria British Columbia V8R 5V4 Canada. **DD** 071.1134.

ESQUIMALT SUN. V. 1- Dec. 4, 1974-. 0380-3902. Newspaper. CN. English. Community News, 506 David Street, Victoria British Columbia V8T 2C8 Canada. **DD** 071.1134.

ESSEX JOURNAL. Series/Titl Early American Newspapers in Microprint. 1773-1777. Newspaper. English. ir.

ESTADO DE SO PAULO. Newspaper. BL. Portuguese. mo. Av Eng Caetano Alvares 55, Cep 02550 Caixa Postal 8005, Sao Paulo Brazil.

ETCHEMIN DE ST-ROMUALD. (L'ETCHEMIN DE ST-ROMUALD). Vol. 1, No. 1 (Nov. 1980)-. 0711-4761. Newspaper. CN. French. mo. Free to Citizens of St-Romuald. Etchemin de St-Romuald, CP 2180, St-Romuald Quebec G6W 5V5 Canada. **DD** 071.1459.

ETHELBERT ECHO. 0712-2624. Newspaper. CN. English. Ethelbert Echo, Box 102, Pine River Manitoba R0L 1M6 Canada. **DD** 071.1272.

ETOILE DE L'OUTAOUAIS-ST-LAURENT. (L'ETOILE DE L'OUTAOUAIS-ST-LAURENT). V. 1- 16 Sept. 1968-. 0319-4124. Newspaper. CN. French. wk. L'Etoile de l'Outaouais-St-Laurent, 111 rue Dumont, Doroin Quebec J7V 1W9 Canada. **DD** 071.1426.

ETTELAAT. Newspaper. Persian, Modern. ir. 1260.00. Ettala At, Teheran Iran. **Tel** 3281. **Ed** J Rafee. bk rev. adv acc. **Circ** 200,000. One of their two main newspapers in Iran, covering foreign news and international news in the fields of politics economics, sports etc.

THE EVANSTON POST. 0746-5947. Newspaper. US. English. wk. $1.00. Alexander Ragtime, 800 Main Street Box 181, Evanston WY 82930.

THE EVANSVILLE PRESS. Began in 1906. Newspaper. US. English. da. $119.40. Evansville Printing Corporation, PO Box 450, Evansville IN 47703-0454. **Tel** (812)464-7601. **Ed** Tom Tuley. LC Newspaper 7002. bk rev. adv acc. **Circ** 42,000. (ctrl). General-circulation evening and Sunday newspapers.

EVEIL. (L'EVEIL). First issue in 1972?. 0384-7845. Newspaper. CN. French. wk. Editions Deux-Montagnes, CP 23, 53 rue Saint-Eustache, Saint-Eustache Quebec J7R 4K5 Canada. **DD** 071.1425.

EVENING EXPRESS (PORTLAND, ME. : 1882). (EVENING EXPRESS). VFOAT Portland Evening Express. Began Oct. 12, 1882. Newspaper. US. English. da. Guy Gannett Publishing Company, PO Box 1460, Portland ME 04104. LC Newspaper 7002.

THE EVENING INDEPENDENT. VFOAT Independent. Began with Nov. 4, 1907 issue. Newspaper. US. English. da. $122.20. St Petersburg Times & Indep, PO Box 1121, St Petersburg FL 33731. **Tel** (813)893-8166. LC Newspaper 7002.

EVENING JOURNAL (LUBBOCK, TEX.). (EVENING JOURNAL). Began in 1983. 0745-547X. Newspaper. US. English. da. $186.00. Avalanche-Journal Publishing Company, 710 Avenue J, Lubbock TX 79408. **Tel** (806)762-8844. **Ed** Thomas Jay Harris. bk rev. adv acc. **Circ** 70,926. (ctrl). *Lubbock Avalanche-Journal.*

EVENING NEWS (BEACON, N.Y.). (THE EVENING NEWS). V. 1, No. 1 (Feb. 10, 1961)-. Newspaper. US. English. da. Beacon Evening News, 264 Main Street, Beacon NY 12508. **Tel** (914)831-0400. **Ed** M D Herbert. Available on microfilm from Microphoto Division, Bell and Howell Co. *Newburgh-Beacon News (Newburgh, N.Y. : Beacon Ed.)*

EVENING SUN (BALTIMORE, MD.). (THE EVENING SUN). Vol. 1, No. 1 (April 18, 1910)-. Newspaper. US. English. da. A S Abell Company, 501 North Calvert Street, Baltimore MD 21203. LC Newspaper.

EVENING TIMES (SAYRE, PA.). (THE EVENING TIMES). 0746-4843. Newspaper. US. English. da. $56.00. The Evening Times, 201 North Lehigh Avenue, Sayre PA 18840.

EVERYMAN'S. VFOAT Everyman's Weekly. V. 1- July 7, 1973-. English. ir. R K Misra etc, Bahadurshsh Zafar Marg, New Delhi-1 India. LC DS401. **DD** 079.54.

EXAMINER. (THE EXAMINER). 0710-1155. Newspaper. CN. English. wk. $8.00. Mailman Publishing Co, PO Box 250, Bridgetown Nova Scotia B0S 1C0 Canada. **DD** 071.1633.

EXAMINER. NORTH EDMONTON EDITION. (THE EXAMINER). VAT North Edmonton Examiner (1979). V. 1, No. 32- Apr. 11, 1979-. 0226-7136. Newspaper. CN. English. wk. Free. Grove Publishers Ltd, 13512-97 Street, Edmonton Alberta T5E 4E2 Canada. **DD** 071.1233. (ctrl). *North Edmonton Examiner, 0708-0301.*

EXETER INDEPENDENT NEWS. (THE EXETER INDEPENDENT NEWS). VFOAT Independent News. Began publication in 1974 or 1975. 0382-800X. Newspaper. CN. English. wk. **DD** 071.1322.

EXETER NEWS-LETTER (EXETER, N. H. : 1867). (THE EXETER NEWS-LETTER). VFOAT Exeter News Letter. Vol. 36, No. 44 (Jan. 14, 1867)-. Newspaper. US. English. wk. Exeter News-Letter, PO Box 250, 255 Water Street, Exeter NH 03833-0250. LC Newspaper 8731. *Exeter News-Letter and Rockingham Advertiser.*

EXPRESS. (L'EXPRESS). May 73-. 0713-5483. Newspaper. CN. French. wk. Free. L'Express, 393 rue Heriot, Drummondville Quebec J2B 2B1 Canada. **DD** 071.14563.

EXPRESS (BANGOR, MICH.). (THE EXPRESS). Vol. 1, No. 48 (Tuesday, Mar. 13, 1984)-. 0747-4113. Newspaper. US. English. wk. The Express, 404 West Monroe Street, Bangor MI 49103. *Bangor Trust Express, 0745-9521.*

EXPRESS DE TORONTO. (L'EXPRESS DE TORONTO). 0823-163X. Newspaper. CN. French. wk. Express de Toronto, 135 Av Broadview, Toronto Ontario M4M 2E9 Canada. **DD** 071.13541. *Express, 0823-163X.*

EXPRESS-NEWS (SAN ANTONIO, TEX.). (EXPRESS-NEWS). VFOAT Express News. 8750-3115. Newspaper. US. English. da. Express-News, PO Box 2171, San Antonio TX 78297.

EYE OPENER. (THE EYE OPENER). 0229-5520. Newspaper. CN. English. wk. Free. Eye Opener, PO Box 520, Yorkton Saskatchewan S3N 2W4 Canada. **DD** 071.242.

FAIRBANKS DAILY NEWS-MINER. VFOAT Fairbanks Daily News Miner. Began in 1908?. 8750-5495. Newspaper. US. English. da. $177.75. Fairbanks Publishing Company, PO Box 710, Fairbanks AK 97707. **Tel** (907)456-6661. **Ed** Kent Sturgis. LC Newspaper 7044. DD 183900. adv acc. **Circ** 19,034. *Fairbanks Daily News, Tanana Miner; Tanana Tribune.*

THE FAIRFAX JOURNAL. 0273-6403. Newspaper. US. English. da. $39.00. Journal Newspaper Group, 6885 Commercial Drive, Springfield VA 22151. **Tel** (703)751-3014. *Fairfax Journal and Globe, 0199-0543.*

FAIRMONT SENTINEL. Newspaper. US. English. da. $46.95. Fairmont Sentinel, PO Box 681, Fairmont MN 56031. **Tel** (218)235-3303.

FAIRMOUNT NEWS. 8750-4545. Newspaper. US. English. wk. $9.00 within 50 mile radius, $11.00 elsewhere. Richland Publishing Company, 107 Mian, Hankinson ND 58041.

FALCON FLYER. (THE FALCON FLYER). Began with Jan. 1973 issue. 0316-5639. Newspaper. CN. English. mo. $0.30 Per No., $3.60 Per Year. Garry Lacey, PO Box 217, Falconbridge Ontario P0M 1S0 Canada. **DD** 071.13133.

FARIBAULT DAILY NEWS. Began with Dec. 1, 1914 issue. Newspaper. US. English. da. Faribault News, 514 Central Avenue, Faribault MN 55021. LC Newspaper 7002.

FARMWEEK. VAT Farm Week. 0197-6680. Periodical. US. English. wk. $2.00, Included in membership fee. Farmweek, PO Box 2901, Bloomington IL 61701.

FARO. (EL FARO). First issue in 1974?. 0318-1855. Newspaper. CN. Spanish (text in Espangnol). 20. Per No. El Faro, 98 Chemin Winona, Toronto Ontario M6G 3S7 Canada. **DD** 071.13541.

FATEH. Newspaper. English. sm. Fateh, PO Box 5427, Beirut Lebonon.

FAYETTEVILLE OBSERVER (FAYETTEVILLE, N.C. : 1896). (THE FAYETTEVILLE OBSERVER). VFOAT Fayetteville Observer Fayetteville Times. Began in 1896. Newspaper. US. English. da. 458 Whitfield Street, Fayetteville NC 28306. LC Newspaper 9155.

FERGUS-ELORA PHOENIX. VFOAT Phoenix. Vol. 1, Issue 1 May 13, 1981. 0714-8135. Newspaper. CN. English. wk. $8.00 Per Year. Fergus-Elora Phoenix, 122 Street Andrew Street West, Fergus Ontario N1M 1N5 Canada. **DD** 071.1342.

FERTILE JOURNAL. Newspaper. US. English. wk. $13.00. Fertile Journal, Fertile MN 56540. **Tel** (218)945-6843.

FIEJ BULLETIN. Yearly V. 18- (No. 67-). 0046-3531. Periodical. French. qt. International Federation of Newspaper Publishing, 6 rue du Faubourg-Poissonniere, 75010 Paris France. **Tel** 523/3888. Ind/Abst Print. Abstr.

THE FIJI TIMES. Began publication in 1869. Newspaper. FJ. English. da. Fiji Times & Herald Ltd, 20-Gordon Street, GPO Box 1167, Suva Fiji. *Western Pacific Herald, Suva Times.*

Newspapers

FILIPINO FORUM. (THE FILIPINO FORUM). V. 1- April 1977-. 0705-4068. Newspaper. CN. English. mo. 25 Per No. The Filipino Forum, 6687 Chester Avenue, Montreal Quebec H4V 1K1 Canada. DD 071.14281.

FINANCIAL TIMES. New Series, No. 1- Feb. 13, 1888-. Newspaper. UK. English. da. $365.00. Financial Times, 14 East 60th Street, The Penthouse, New York NY 10022. Tel (212)752-4500. Ind/Abst Chem. Abstr., Funk Scott Index Corp. Ind., Infobank. *London Financial Guide.*

FINGER LAKES TIMES. 83rd Year, No. 29 (July 1, 1977)-. Newspaper. US. English. da. $80.00. Finger Lakes Times Circulating, 218 Genesee Street, PO Box 393, Geneva NY 14456. Tel (315)536-6776. Also available on microfilm from the Microphoto Division, Bell & Howell. *Geneva Times (Geneva, N.Y.).*

FLAMBOROUGH NEWS. Vol. 1, No. 1 (Apr. 29, 1981)-. 0710-5339. Newspaper. CN. English. wk. $0.10 Per No. Flamborough News, 928 Queenston Road, Stoney Creek Ontario L8G 3X7 Canada. DD 071.1352.

FLINT JOURNAL (1935). (THE FLINT JOURNAL). VFOAT Saturday A.M. Flint Journal. Began with June 2, 1935 Issue. Newspaper. US. English. da. 200 East First Street, Flint MI 48502. LC Newspaper 7002. *Flint Daily Journal.*

THE FLORIDA FLAMBEAU. 1914-. US. English. ir. The Florida Flambeau Foundation, PO Box U 7001, Tallahassee FL 32306. Tel (904)681-6692.

FLORIDA TIMES-UNION (JACKSONVILLE, FLA. : 1910). (THE FLORIDA TIMES-UNION). VFOAT Florida Times Union. Jan. 20, 1903-. 0740-2325. Newspaper. US. English. da. $70.20. Florida Publishing Company, 1 Riverside Avenue, Jacksonville FL 32202. *Semi-Weekly Times-Union.*

FLORIDA'S HORSE COUNTRY. VFOAT Horse Country. V. 1- Oct. 1979-. 0195-296X. Periodical. US. English. mo. $6.00. Horse Country, PO Box 17721, Orlando FL 32860. Tel (305)298-6405.

FOGHORN. (THE FOGHORN). V. 1- Jan. 31, 1975-. 0380-2922. Newspaper. CN. English. bw. $5.00. The Foghorn, PO Box 10, Harbour Breton Newfoundland A0H 1P0 Canada. DD 071.18.

THE FOND DU LAC CLARION. VFOAT Clarion. 0747-4415. US. English. mo. The Fond du Lac Clarion, 39 North Sophia Street, Fond du Lac WI 54935. *Diocese of Fond du Lac.*

FOREST HILL VILLAGER. VFOAT Forest Hill Village. Vol. 1, No. 1 (May 26, 1981)-. 0715-464X. Newspaper. CN. English. mo. Free. c/o Town Crier Inc, 3 Massey Square, Toronto Ontario M4C 5L5 Canada. DD 071.13541. (ctrl).

FOREST LAKE TIMES. Began in 1906. Newspaper. US. English. wk. Forest Lake Times, PO Box 250, 120 North Lake Street, Forest Lake MN 55025. Tel (612)464-4601.

FORT COLLINS REVIEW. VFOAT Fort Collins Triangle Review. 0744-3870. Newspaper. US. English. wk. PO Box 2063, Fort Collins CO 80522. *Review,* 0164-419X.

FORT LANGLEY SENTINEL. (THE FORT LANGLEY SENTINEL). Began with June 23, 1975, V. 1, No. 33-. 0381-5803. Newspaper. CN. English. Fort Langley Sentinel, Box 78, Fort Langley British Columbia V0X 1J0 Canada. DD 071.1133. *Fort Langley Advertiser,* 0381-5811.

FORT LAUDERDALE NEWS. 0744-8147. Newspaper. US. English. da. $226.20. News Sun and Sentinel Company, Box 14488, Fort Lauderdale FL 33302. Tel (305)761-4702.

FORT MCMURRAY EXPRESS. Vol. 1, No. 1 (June 21, 1979)-. 0715-4925. Newspaper. CN. English. $0.50 Per Number. Fort McMurray Express Northstar Communications, 8323 Fraser Avenue, Fort McMurray Alberta T9H 1W9 Canada. DD 071.1232.

FORT MCMURRAY TODAY. V. 1- Oct. 8, 1974-. 0316-7542. CN. English. ir. $92.86. Fort McMurray Today, 9701 Franklin Avenue, Fort McMurray Alberta Canada. DD 071.1232.

FORT MYERS NEWS-PRESS. US. English. da. $159.00. Ft Myers News Press, PO Box 10 Fort Myers FL 33902. Tel (813)334-2351.

THE FORT RILEY POST. VFOAT Post. Vol. 1, No. 1 (Nov. 6, 1959)-. Newspaper. US. English. wk. *Fort Riley Traveler.*

FORT SIMPSON JOURNAL. V. 1- Nov. 16, 1976-. 0701-0850. Newspaper. CN. English. 0.20 Per Number. DD 071.193.

FORT SMITH JOURNAL. Began publication in 1978?. 0228-0329. Newspaper. CN. English. 0.25 Per Number. Fort Smith Journal, Fort Smith, District of MacKenzie Northwest Territories Canada. DD 071.193.

FORT SMITH NEWS. No. 1- Aug. 3, 1978-. 0707-2317. Newspaper. CN. English. wk. $12.00 Domestic, $20.00 Foreign. Fort Smith News, Box 990, Fort Smith Northwest Territories X0E 0P0 Canada. DD 071.193.

FORT WORTH NEWS-TRIBUNE. VAT Fort Worth News Tribune. 0744-8619. Newspaper. US. English. wk. $20.00. Fort Worth News Tribune, PO Box 1116, Fort Worth TX 76101. Tel (817)338-1055. Ed Mack H Williams. bk rev. adv acc. Circ 21,450. Coverage of Fort Worth and Texas News. *News-Tribune.*

FORUM (FARGO, N.D.). (THE FORUM). VFOAT Sunday Forum. V. 88, No. 99 (Apr. 1, 1966)-. Newspaper. US. English. da. The Forum, PO Box 2020, Fargo ND 58107. Available on microfilm from Microphoto. *Fargo Forum Daily Republican and Moorhead Daily News.*

THE FORUM INDEX. *See* Indexes/Abstracts.

FORVERTS (NEW YORK, N.Y.). (FORVERTS). VFOAT Forward. Began Apr. 22, 1897. 0746-7869. Newspaper. US. Yiddish. wk. The Forward Association Inc, 45 East 33rd Street, New York NY 10016. *Forverts (Chicago, Ill.).*

FORWARD TIMES. V. 1- Jan. 30, 1960-. Newspaper. US. English. wk. $13.50. Forward Times, PO Box 2962, Houston TX 77004. Tel (913)026-4727.

FOUR-TOWN JOURNAL. (THE FOUR-TOWN JOURNAL). Vol. 1, No. 1 (Oct.7, 1981)-. 0712-6387. Newspaper. CN. English. wk. $12.00 Domestic, 26.00 Foreign. Four-Town Journal, PO Box 68, Langenburg Saskatchewan S0A 2A0 Canada. Tel (306)743-2617. Ed William Johnston. DD 071.1244. adv acc. Circ 2,040. (ctrl). An award winning newspaper covering news events in east-central Saskatchewan.

FRANCE-ACTUALITE. V. 1- 1978-. 0705-4645. CN. French. an. $286.32. Microfor Inc, 800 Place d'Youville/Suite 1805, Quebec Quebec G1R 3P4 Canada. Tel (418)692-4369. DD 054.1.

FRANCE-AMERIQUE. VAT France Amerique. 0747-2757. Newspaper. US. French. wk. $32.00. France-Amerique, POB 415, New York NY 10028. Tel (916)633-0106. Ed Henri Morny and Jean-Louis Turlin. LC AP21. bk rev. adv acc. Circ 30,000. French newspaper.

FRANCESVILLE TRIBUNE. 0747-1793. Newspaper. US. English. wk. Francesville Tribune, PO Box 458, Francesville IN 47946.

FRANCISCAN HERALD. 0015-9816. Periodical. US. English. mo. Franciscan Herald, 1434 West 51st Street, Chicago IL 60609.

FRANCO-TEM. V. 1- Jan. 24, 1978-. 0226-6334. Newspaper. CN. French. wk. $15.00 Domestic, $20.00 Foreign. Franco-Tem, CP 2199, New Liskeard Ontario P0J 1P0 Canada. DD 071.13144.

FRANKFURTER ALLGEMEINE. 0174-4909. Newspaper. German. da. $345.00. German Language Publishing Inc, 560 Sylvan Avenue, Englewood Cliffs NJ 07632. Tel (212)736-7455. Ind/Abst Energy Res. Abstr.

FRANKFURTER RUNDSCHAU. 1945-. Newspaper. German. da. $249.00. German Language Publishing Inc, 560 Sylvan Avenue, Englewood Cliffs NJ 07632. Tel (212)736-7455. Also available on microfilm from Mikrofilmarchiv der Deutschsprachigen Presse E. V.

FRANKLIN PARK HERALD-JOURNAL WITH NEWS OF NORTHLAKE. VFOAT Franklin Park Herald-Journal. VAT Franklin Park Herald Journal with News of Northlake. 0745-3752. Newspaper. US. English. wk. $10.75. Pioneer Press Inc, 1232 Central, Wilmette IL 60091. Tel (312)251-4300. *Franklin Park Herald.*

FRASER LAKE BUGLE. (THE FRASER LAKE BUGLE). V. 1- Oct. 18, 1978-. 0706-7038. Newspaper. CN. English. wk. Omineca Advertiser Ltd, PO Box 1007, Vanderhoof British Columbia V0J 3A0 Canada. DD 071.112.

FRAZEE FORUM. 1960. Newspaper. US. English. wk. $9.50. Frazee Forum, PO Box 187, Frazee MN 56544. Tel (218)334-3566. Ed Jerold J Brenk. adv acc. Circ 1,625. Local area happenings.

THE FREDERICK POST. Began in 1912?. Newspaper. US. English. da. Great Southern Ptg and Mfg Company, 200 East Patrick Street, Frederick MD 21701. LC Newspaper. *Evening Post.*

FREDERICKSBURG STANDARD RADIO POST. VFOAT Fredericksburg Standard/Radio Post. 8755-9331. Newspaper. US. English. wk. Fredericksburg Publishing Company, PO Box 473, 108 East Main Street, Fredericksburg TX 78624. *Fredericksburg Standard.*

FREE PRESS. (THE FREE PRESS). Vol. 1, No. 1 (Nov. 13, 1981)-. 0715-5131. Newspaper. CN. English. sw. 42.00. Free Press, c/o Fernie Free Press, 342 Second Avenue, Box 1320, Fernie British Columbia V0B 1M0 Canada. Tel (604)423-4666. Ed W Johnson. DD 071.114. adv acc. Circ 4,000. (ctrl).

FREE VENICE BEACHHEAD. Series/Titl Bell and Howell Underground Press Collection. No. 1- Dec. 1, 1968-. Newspaper. US. English. mo. $5.00. Free Venice Beachhead, PO Box 504, Venice CA 90291. Tel (213)823-5092.

FREELANCER. (THE FREELANCER). V. 1- Apr. 5, 1978-. 0706-7224. Newspaper. CN. English. wk. $7.74. Lynard Publishing Ltd, PO Box 785, Mayerthorpe Alberta T0E 1N0 Canada. Tel (403)786-2602. DD 071.1233.

THE FRESNO BEE. Newspaper. US. English. da. $165.00. Fresno Bee, 1626 East Street, Fresno CA 93786. Tel (209)441-6111.

FRIDAY CITIZEN. (THE FRIDAY CITIZEN). 0711-4451. Newspaper. CN. English. wk. Free. The Friday Citizen, PO Box 609, Miland Ontario L4R 4L3 Canada. DD 071.1317. (ctrl).

FRIDAY TIMES. (THE FRIDAY TIMES). V. 1- May 4, 1977-. 0707-543X. Newspaper. CN. English. wk. Free. Markle Community Newspapers, 521 Bay Street, Box 609, Midland Ontario Canada. DD 071.1317. (ctrl).

FRIDLEY SUN. Newspaper. US. English. wk. Sun Newspaper, 7401 Bush Lake Road, Edina MN 55435. Tel (612)831-1200.

THE FROSTPROOF NEWS. 1915-. Periodical. US. English. wk. $13.00. Frostproof News, Box 67, Frostproof FL 33843. Tel (813)635-2171.

FT. GARRY PIONEER. V. 1- Aug. 18, 1976-. 0700-9410. Periodical. CN. English. wk. Reliance Press, 1397 Erin Street, Winnipeg Manitoba R3E 2S9 Canada. DD 071.1274.

THE FULTON SUN. 8750-6696. Newspaper. US. English. da. Waters Publications Inc, 5th and Ravine Streets, Fulton MO 65251. *Kingdom Daily Sun-Gazette.*

LA GACETA DE CUBA CEASED. No. 1-187. 0435-0251. Periodical. CU. Spanish. ir.

GAINESVILLE SUN. June 24, 1963-. Newspaper. US. English. da. $90.00. Gainesville Sun, PO Drawer A, Gainesville FL 32602. *Gainesville Daily Sun.*

THE GAITHERSBURG GAZETTE. 0195-2447. Newspaper. US. English. wk. Gaithersburg Gazette, PO Box 606, Gaithersburg MD 20877. Tel (301)948-3120. bk rev. adv acc.

THE GALVA NEWS. Began in Oct. 1879. 0747-282X. Newspaper. US. English. wk. Galva News, 210 Exchange Street, Galva IL 61434.

THE GARDEN ISLAND. 0744-4028. Newspaper. US. English. ir. Kaua'i Publishing Company, 3137 Kuhio Hwy, Lihue HA 96766.

GASETA MUNICIPAL. Main/Corp Barcelona (Spain). Catalan. tm. 1.500. Placa de Sant Jaume 3A Planta, Barcelona Spain. *Gaseta Municipal de Barcelona.*

GASKIYA TA FI KWABO. Began in Jan. 1939. Newspaper. NR. Hausa. wk. New Nigerian Newspaper Ltd, PO Box 254, Kaduna Nigeria. Tel 062 214389. Ed Muhammad Sabanzara Hassan. bk rev. adv acc. Circ 66,000. The paper publishes news both, local and foreign. It also covers other areas like religion, agriculture, sports, health and features on various topics.

Newspapers

THE GAYLORD HUB. VFOAT Hub. 0742-1591. Newspaper. US. English. wk. $11.00. Gaylord Hub, 234 4th Street, Gaylord MN 55334. **Tel** (612)237-2476.

GAZETTE. (LA GAZETTE). VFOAT The Gazette. 0228-9164. Newspaper. CN. English (French). wk. 0.25 Per Number. The Gazette, 165 Broadway, Grand Falls New Brunswick E0J 1M0 Canada. **DD** 071.1553.

GAZETTE DE MALARTIC. (LA GAZETTE DE MALARTIC). V. 1- May 1975-. 0703-7198. Newspaper. CN. French. mo. 25 Per No. Gazette de Malartic, CP 1092, Malartic Quebec J0Y 1Z0 Canada. **DD** 071.14212.

GAZETTE DU C.L.S.C. (LA GAZETTE DU C. L. S. C). **Main/Corp** Centre Local de Services Communautaires Saint-Hubert. **VAT** Gazette du Centre Local de Services Communautaires St-Hubert. V. 1- July 1977-. 0227-1206. Periodical. CN. French. ir. Free. Centre Local de Services Communautaires Saint-Huber, Bureau 225, 5245 Boulvard Cousineau, St-Huber Quebec J3Y 6J8 Canada. **DD** 071.1437. (ctrl).

GENESIS 2. VAT Genesis Two. 0016-6669. Periodical. US. English. ir. $15.00. Genesis 2, 99 Bishop Allen Drive, Cambridge MA 02139. **Tel** (617)491-0138. Also available from University Microfilms.

GEORGIAN. (THE GEORGIAN). Began with Nov. 5, 1970 issue. 0381-9566. Newspaper. CN. English (includes some text in French). wk. $21.67. Robinson-Blackmore Publishing Ltd, PO Box 129, Grand Falls Newfoundland A2A 2J4 Canada. **Tel** (709)489-2162. **DD** 071.18.

GIGMANAG. V. 1- Mar. 1976-. 0226-6202. Newspaper. CN. English. mo. Free to Members, $3.00 Nonmembers. Prince Edward Island Association of Metis and Non-Status Indians, PO Box 2170, Charlottetown Prince Edward Island C1A 8B9 Canada. **DD** 971.700497.

GIORNALE DI SICILIA, EDIZIONE SETTIMANALE PER IL CANADA. (GIORNALE DI SICILIA : EDIZIONE SETTIMANALE PER IL CANADA). 0710-0108. Newspaper. CN. Italian. wk. $29.00. Giornale di Sicilia, 1165 A Saint Clair Avenue, Toronto Ont M6E 1B2 Canada. **DD** 971.35410045105.

GLEBE REPORT. V. 1- June, 1973-. 0702-7796. Newspaper. CN. English. mo. Free to residents of Glebe area. Pike, 276 Second Avenue, Ottawa Ontario K1S 2H8 Canada. **DD** 071.1384. *Glebe News, 0702-780X.*

GLENCOE ENTERPRISE. Began in 1880. Newspaper. US. English. wk. Glencoe Enterprise, Glencoe MN 55336.

GLOBAL NEWS. V. 1- June 17, 1977-. 0704-0202. Newspaper. CN. English. wk. $21. Domestic, $21. US. Global News, 70 Snidercroft Road Concord, Toronto Ontario L4K 1B1 Canada. **DD** 071.13541.

GLOBE AND MAIL. (THE GLOBE AND MAIL). Nov. 23, 1936-. 0319-0714. Newspaper. CN. English. da. $130.78. The Globe and Mail, 444 Front Street West, Toronto Ontario M5V 2S9 Canada. **Tel** (416)585-5250. **Ind/Abst** Can. Bus. Index, Can. News. Index. *Globe, Mail and Empire.*

GLOS LUDOWY. VFOAT The People's Voice. Newspaper. US. Polish (English). wk. 5854 Chene Street, Detroit MI 48211. **LC** Newspaper 8416B.

GLOUCESTER COUNTY TIMES. Began in 1975?. Newspaper. US. English. da. 309 South Broad Street, Woodbury NJ 08096. **LC** NEWSPAPER. *Woodbury Daily Times.*

GOLDEN GAZETTE. 0229-7167. Newspaper. CN. English. wk. $5.00. Golden Gazette, PO Box 273, Golden British Columbia V0A 1H0 Canada. **DD** 071.1145.

GOLDEN VALLEY SUN. Newspaper. US. English. Golden Valley Sun, 7401 Bush Lake Road, Minneapolis MN 55435.

GOLDSTREAM GAZETTE. V. 1- Mar. 17, 1976-. 0383-1213. Newspaper. CN. English. wk. Goldstream Gazette, No 9-721 Station Road, Langford British Columbia V9B 2S1 Canada. **DD** 71.1134.

GOOD MORNING. V. 1, Issue 5- Oct. 1976-. 0702-8946. Newspaper. CN. English. bw. T R Hawkins, PO Box 999, Shelburne Nova Scotia B0T 1W0 Canada. **DD** 071.1625. *Good Morning in Shelburne County.*

GOOD TIMES. 0191-4995. Periodical. US. English. bw. $15.00. Good Times, 230 Arlington Circle, East Hills NY 11548. **Tel** (516)484-4477.

THE GOSHEN NEWS. 8750-3867. Newspaper. US. English. da. Goshen News, PO Box 569, Goshen IN 46526-0569.

GOULBOURN MIRROR. V. 3, No. 1- Sept. 5, 1974-. 0316-6635. Newspaper. CN. English. wk. $3.50 Within 40 Miles of Goulbourn Township, $4.50 Others. Goulbourn Mirror, PO Box 400, Stittsville Ontario K0A 3G0 Canada. **DD** 071.1383. *Stittsville Review, 0316-6651; Richmond Review, 0316-6643.*

THE GRANBURY TABLET. 0746-2131. Newspaper. US. English. wk. Granbury Tablet, 108 West Pearl, Granbury TX 76048.

GRAND BEND SUN. (THE GRAND BEND SUN). V. 6, No. 26- June 28, 1979-. 0227-3470. Newspaper. CN. English. wk. $6.19. Leader Publication Ltd, Box 490, Dresden Ontario N0T 1M0 Canada. **Tel** (519)683-4485. **DD** 071.1327. *North Lambton Sun, 0319-5430.*

GRAND FORKS HERALD. VFOAT Daily Herald, Grand Forks Daily Herald. Vol. 35, No. 210 (July 1, 1916)-. 0745-9661. Newspaper. US. English. da. $105.04. Grand Forks Herald, 120 North 4th Street, Grand Forks ND 58201. **LC** Newspaper. Also available on microfilm from Micro Photo Division, Bell and Howell Co., and Recordak.

GRAND ISLAND DAILY INDEPENDENT (MAIL EDITION). (THE GRAND ISLAND DAILY INDEPENDENT). VFOAT Grand Island (Neb.) Daily Independent. 0748-5379. Newspaper. US. English. da. Grand Island Daily Independent, 1st and Cedar Streets, Grand Island NE 68802.

THE GRAND RAPIDS PRESS. Began with Nov. 1, 1913 issue. Newspaper. US. English. da. 155 Michigan Street NW, Grand Rapids MI 49503. **LC** Newspaper 7002. *Grand Rapids Evening Press.*

GRAND TRUNK POPLAR PRESS. (THE GRAND TRUNK POPLAR PRESS). VFOAT Poplar Press. V. 1- Aug. 22, 1979-. 0226-6415. Newspaper. CN. English. bw. Free. W E Publishers, Grand Trunk Poplar Press, PO Box 359, Wildwood Alberta T0E 2M0 Canada. **DD** 071.1233. (ctrl).

GRANTSVILLE GAZETTE. VFOAT Gazette. 8750-7684. Newspaper. US. English. wk. $18.00. Grantsville Gazette, PO Box 800, Grantsville UT 84029. **Tel** (801)884-6224. Ed Mary S Thornton. **adv acc.** Circ 1,000. Covers community news.

GRAPEVINE GAZETTE. 8750-7412. Periodical. US. English. mo. Grapevine Gazette, 4023 East Grant Road/Suite C, Tucson AZ 85712.

THE GRAPEVINE SUN. VFOAT Sun & News-Advertiser. Began in 1895. Newspaper. US. English. sw. Grapevine Sun, PO Box 400, Grapevine TX 76051. **LC** Newspaper 7002.

GRASSLAND GAZETTE. 8750-5320. Newspaper. US. English. wk. News Chronicle Publishing Co, 117 East 5th Street, Scott City KS 67871.

GRAVELBOURG GAZETTE. Vol. 1, No. 1 (Sept. 30, 1981)-. 0715-4488. Newspaper. CN. English. wk. 12.00. Gravelbourg Gazette, PO Box 863, Gravelbourg Saskatchewan S0H 1X0 Canada. **DD** 071.1243.

GRAVENHURST LEADER. (THE GRAVENHURST LEADER). VFOAT Leader. V. 1, No: 1 (Jan. 28, 1981)-. 0710-1082. Newspaper. CN. English. wk. $10.00 Within 40 Miles of Gravenhurst, $12.00 Elsewhere in Canada. Gravenhurst Leader, 160 Muskoka Road South, Gravenhurst Ontario P0C 1G0 Canada. **DD** 071.1316.

THE GREAT BEND DAILY TRIBUNE. VFOAT Great Bend Tribune. Vol. 9, No. 99 (Dec. 7, 1908)-. Newspaper. US. English. da. $62.40. Great Bend Tribune, PO Box 228, Great Bend KS 67530. **LC** Newspaper 7814. *Great Bend Item-Rustler, Great Bemd Morning News; Great Bend Tribune (1909); Barton County Democrat (1915); Western Kansas Press.*

GREAT LAKER. (THE GREAT LAKER). No. 1- Sept. 1959-. 0317-1078. CN. English. mo. Free to Employees. Great Lakes Paper Company, PO Box 430, Thunder Bay Ontario P7C 4W3 Canada. **DD** 071.1312.

GREENFIELD PARK JOURNAL. VFOAT Greenfield Park Bulletin. V. 1, No. 1 (Sept. 23, 1982)-. 0821-3038. Newspaper. CN. English (text also in French). sm. Free to Residents of Greenfield Park. Greenfield Park Journal, PO Box 333, St-Lambert Quebec J4P 3P8 Canada. **DD** 071.1437.

GREENSBORO NEWS & RECORD. VFOAT Greensboro News and Record. V. 94, No. 79 (March 19, 1984). 0747-1858. Newspaper. US. English. da. Greensboro News & Record Inc, 200 East Market Street, Greensboro NC 27401. **LC** Newspaper. *Greensboro Daily News, 0746-0740; Greensboro Record.*

GREENWICH NEWS. Began in 1983?. 0746-8539. Newspaper. US. English. wk. Greenwich News Inc, 33 East Elm, Greenwich CT 06830.

GRIFFON. (LE GRIFFON). No. 1 Oct 1978-. 0710-5649. Newspaper. CN. French. ir. $0.50 Per No. Le Griffon, CP 892, Drummondville Quebec J2B 6X1 Canada. **DD** 071.14563.

GRIT. 0017-4289. Newspaper. US. English. wk. $26.96. Grit Publishing Co, 208 West Third Street, Williamsport PA 17701. **Tel** (717)326-1771.

GROVE EXAMINER. (THE GROVE EXAMINER). V. 1- April 2, 1974-. 0318-1650. Newspaper. CN. English. wk. $11.61. Grove Publishing Ltd, Box 2190, Spruce Grove Alberta T0E 2C0 Canada. **Tel** (403)962-4257. **DD** 071.1233.

GUADALUPE COUNTY COMMUNICATOR. (GUADALUPE COMMUNITY COMMUNICATOR). VFOAT Communicator. 0746-1399. Newspaper. US. English. wk. $12.50 In-County, $15.00 Elsewhere. Silver Enterprises, 241 4th Street, Santa Rosa NM 88435.

THE GUARDIAN. May 5, 1821-. Newspaper. UK. English. da. $292.69. The Guardian, 164 Deansgate, Manchester M60 2RR England. **Tel** (061)832 7200. **Ind/Abst** Infobank.

GUARDIAN (LONDON). (THE GUARDIAN). Began with Aug. 24, 1959 issue. 0261-3077. Newspaper. UK. English. da. $91.63. Jones Yarrel Co Ltd, 227-239 Tooley Street, London SE1 2PA England. **Ind/Abst** Infobank. Issued also in microfilm. *Manchester Guardian.*

GUARDIAN WEEKLY (MANCHESTER, GREATER MANCHESTER) CEASED. (THE GUARDIAN WEEKLY). V. 99, N. 8 (Aug. 23, 1968)-V. 119, N. 24 (Dec. 10, 1978). Newspaper. US. English. wk. The Guardian Weekly, 20 East 53rd Street, New York NY 10022. *Manchester Guardian Weekly, Monde.*

GUELPH EXAMINER. (THE GUELPH EXAMINER). VFOAT Examiner. VAT Examiner (Guelph). V. 1, Issue 1 (Oct. 3, 1979)-. 0229-6799. Newspaper. CN. English. wk. $0.25 Per No. No. 69 Wyndham Street North, Guelph Ontario N1H 4E7 Canada. **DD** 071.1343.

GUELPH LIFE. Began publication in 1975?. 0704-6901. Newspaper. CN. English. wk. 15. Per No. G Turner, Guelph Life, 93 Regal Road, Guelph Ontario N1H 6R1 Canada. **DD** 071.1343. *Saturday Life.*

GUFFEY'S EXECUTIVE JOURNAL. VFOAT Guffey's Journal. 0744-6977. Newspaper. US. English. wk. $15.00. Guffeys Executive Journal, 1100 Classen Drive/Room 205, Oklahoma City OK 73103. **Tel** (918)587-4734.

GUIDA. (LA GUIDA). Began publication in 1978?. 0228-2208. Newspaper. CN. Italian. La Guida, PO Box 1674, Guelph Ontario N1H 6R7 Canada. **DD** 071.1343.

GUIDE. (LE GUIDE). VFOAT The Guide. V. 1- Jan. 29, 1974-. 0316-6880. Newspaper. CN. English (text in French). wk. Free. The Guide, 245 Principale Street, Cowansville Quebec J2K 1J4 Canada. **DD** 071.1462.

GUIDE. (LE GUIDE). VFOAT The Guide. V. 1, Publ. 1 (Sept. 20, 1977). 0227-5368. Newspaper. CN. French (English). wk. Free. Le Guide, CP 569, Hawkesbury Ontario K6A 2Y2 Canada. **DD** 071.1385.

GUIDE DE L'EST. (LE GUIDE DE L'EST). V. 1- 4 July 1974-. 0380-4151. Newspaper. CN. French. Le Guide de l'Est, CP 3187, Ste-Anne-Des-Monts Quebec G0E 2G0 Canada. **DD** 071.14775.

GUIDE TO PERIODICALS AND NEWSPAPERS - MIDWESTERN REGIONAL LIBRARY SYSTEM. See Bibliographies.

Newspapers

GUJARAT VARTMAN. (GUJARAT VARTMAN : INDO-CANADIAN CULTURAL AND NEWS MONTHLY). **VFOAT** Gujarat Varthmana. 0229-7868. Newspaper. CN. Gujarati. mo. $5.00. G Vartman, 86 Pilkey Crescent, Scarborough Ontario M1B 2A9 Canada. **DD** 071.13541.

GULF COAST FISH CHEER. Vol. 1, No. 1- Feb. 1971-. Newspaper. US. English. *Fish Cheer.*

GUOJI RIBAO. (KUO CHI JIH PAO). **VFOAT** International Daily News. 0741-126X. Newspaper. US. Chinese. da. $90.00. International Daily News, 870 Monterey Pass Road, Monterey Park CA 91754. **Tel** (213)265-1317. Ed Anthony Yuen. adv acc. **Circ** 100,000. Articles on: sports, local news, community services, international news, entertainment section, etc.

HA'ARETZ. Newspaper. Hebrew. da. $230.00. Israel Communications Inc, 350 5th Avenue/Room 1912, New York NY 10118. **Tel** (212)695-2998.

HALIFAX LOYALIST. (THE HALIFAX LOYALIST). V. 1- July 16, 1977-. 0703-2161. Newspaper. CN. English. wk. 25. Per No. Metro Publishers, The Halifax Loyalist, PO Box 9, 1823 Hollis Street, Halifax Nova Scotia B3J 2L4 Canada. **DD** 071.1622.

HALSTAD VALLEY JOURNAL. 1884. Newspaper. US. English. wk $16.50. Valley Journal, Box 267, Halstad MN 56548. **Tel** (218)456-2133. Ed Harold V Nelson. bk rev. adv acc. **Circ** 3,500. Our newspaper is a general interest publication featuring people, organizations and things in the Red River Valley of northwestern Minnesota and eastern North Dakota.

THE HAMILTON COUNTY NEWS. Newspaper. US. English. wk. Also available on microfilm from New York State Library.

HAMILTON EXPRESS. (LE HAMILTON EXPRESS). V. 1- Nov. 1976-. 0705-081X. Newspaper. CN. French. wk. Le Hamilton Express, PO Box 127 Station F, Toronto Ontario M4Y 2L4 Canada. **DD** 071.1352.

THE HAMMOND VINDICATOR. Newspaper. US. English. wk. Hammond Vindicator, 107 South Cate Avenue, Hammond LA 70401. **LC** Newspaper 7946-X. *Southern Vindicator.*

HAMPSTEAD JOURNAL. Vol. 1, No. 1 (July 2, 1981)-. 0714-8844. Newspaper. CN. English. qt. Free to Hampstead Residents, $9.00 Others. Hampstead Journal, 1928 Centre Street, Montreal Quebec H3K 1H9 Canada. **DD** 071.1428.

THE HAMPTON UNION. **VFOAT** Hampton Union and Rockingham County Gazette. Began with Jan. 1, 1898 issue. Newspaper. US. English. wk. Hampton Union, Depot Square, Hampton NH 03842. **LC** Newspaper 7002.

HANGUK ILBO (HOUSTON, TEX.). (HANGUK ILBO). **VFOAT** Minju Hanguk, The Korea Times. 0744-5520. Newspaper. US. Korean. sw. Minju Hanguk, 1222 Antoine Drive, Houston TX 77055.

HANGUK ILBO, SAEN PURANSISUKO. **VFOAT** The Korea Times San Francisco Edition. 0747-8356. Newspaper. US. Korean. da. $7.50 Per Month. Korea Daily News Inc, 274 Shotwell Street, San Francisco CA 94110.

HANGUK ILBO, SIAETUL. **VFOAT** The Korea Times Seattle Edition. 8750-6564. Newspaper. US. Korean. wk. $12.00. Korea Times Seattle Bureau, 1121 Dexter Avenue North, Seattle WA 98109.

HANGUK ILBO, WOSINGTON. **VFOAT** The Miju Hankook Ilbo. 0883-6647. Newspaper. US. Korean. da. Korea Times, 4817 Georgia Avenue Northwest, Washington DC 20011.

THE HARDWICK GAZETTE. 0744-5512. Newspaper. US. English. wk. Hardwick Gazette, Hardwick VT 05843. *Green Mountain Gazette.*

HARRISBURG BULLETIN. 8750-4820. Newspaper. US. English. wk. Warren D Giles, 172 Smith Street, PO Box 267, Harrisburg OR 97446.

THE HARTFORD COURANT. Vol. 50, No. 161 July 9, 1887. Newspaper. US. English. da. $127.40. Hartford Courant, 285 Broad Street, Hartford CT 06101. **Tel** (203)241-6574. **LC** Newspaper 7234. *Hartford Daily Courant.*

THE HARTVILLE NEWS. 0746-8016. Newspaper. US. English. wk. Knowles Press Inc, 316 East Maple Street, Hartville OH 44632.

THE HARVARD POST. 0747-3036. Newspaper. US. English. wk. Harvard Post the Common, Elm Street, Harvard MA 01451-0308.

HAUPPAGE NEWS. 8750-1023. Newspaper. US. English. wk. Graphic Square Corporation, PO Box 108-P, One East Man Street, Bay Shore NY 11706.

HAVELOCK CITIZEN. Began with July 9, 1975 issue. 0382-0017. Newspaper. CN. English. wk. Havelock Citizen, Box 250, Marmora Ontario K0K 2M0 Canada. **DD** 071.1367.

HAVRE. (LE HAVRE). V. 1- 12 Oct. 1977-. 0226-6407. Newspaper. CN. French. wk. $12.50 Domestic, $15.60 Foreign. Le Havre, C P 910, Chandler Quebec G0C 1K0 Canada. **DD** 071.1479.

HAWAII FILIPINO NEWS. V. 1- Mar. 1, 1977-. 0732-9970. Periodical. US. English. sm. $10.00. Hawaii Filipino News Corp, 275 Puuhale Road, Honolulu HI 96819. **Tel** (808)841-1886. Ed Pepi Nieva and Juan C Dionicio. bk rev. adv acc. **Circ** 12,000. A local newspaper containing news and notes of the Filipino-American population in Hawaii and the United States.

HAWAII HERALD (HONOLULU, HAWAII : 1980). (THE HAWAII HERALD). V. 1, No. 1 (May 16, 1980)-. 8750-913X. Newspaper. US. English. sm. The Hawaii Herald, PO Box 17429, Honolulu HI 96817. *Hawaii Herald (Honolulu, Hawaii : 1969), 8750-913X.*

HAWAIIAN FALCON. Newspaper. US. English. wk. Laissez Faire Group Inc, 1290 Maunakea Street/Suite 309, Honolulu HI 96817.

HAWKESBURY EXPRESS. **VAT** Express (Hawkesbury). V. 1- March 2, 1979-. 0226-6318. Newspaper. CN. English (French). wk. Free. Hawkesbury Express, 228 James Street, Hawkesbury Ontario K6A 1S8 Canada. **DD** 071.1385.

HAWLEY HERALD. Newspaper. US. English. wk. $24.00. Hawley Herald, Hawley MN 56549. **Tel** (218)483-3306.

THE HAZARD TIMES. Began in 1985. 0883-752X. Newspaper. US. English. wk. $10.50. The Hazard Times, PO Box 1239, Hazard KY 41701. **Tel** (606)439-5189. Ed Billy Kilburn. bk rev. adv acc. **Circ** 9763. A publication enhancing the life in Appalachian while keeping the residents up on current events.

HE PROINE. (PROINE). **VFOAT** Proini. 0749-3126. Newspaper. US. Greek, Modern (with some English). da. Petallides Publishing, 9-11 East 37th Street, New York NY 10016. **DD** 071.

HEALDSBURG TRIBUNE, ENTERPRISE AND SCIMITAR. (HEALDSBURG TRIBUNE-ENTERPRISE AND SCIMITAR). 0017-8810. Periodical. US. English. Healdsburg Tribune, PO Box 517, Healdsburg CA 95448.

HEARST TRIBUNE. (THE HEARST TRIBUNE). Began with Nov. 14, 1973 issue. 0319-860X. Newspaper. CN. English (includes some text in French). wk. 10. Per No. Northern Times Ltd, PO Box 8, Kapuskasing Ontario P5N 2Y1 Canada. **DD** 071.13142.

HEBDO DE BELLECHASSE, DORCHESTER. (L'HEBDO DE BELLECHASSE (DORCHESTER). Vol. 1, No. 1 (1 Sept. 1981)-. 0714-4784. Newspaper. CN. French. wk. Free. Hebdo de Bellechasse, 164 Sud rue Notre-Dame, Ste-Marie Beauce Quebec G0S 2X0 Canada. **DD** 071.14733.

HEBDO DE LA ROUGE. (L'HEBDO DE LA ROUGE). V. 1, No. 1, (Feb. 3, 1981)-. 0711-8074. Newspaper. CN. French. wk. $0.35 Per Issue. Publilaur Inc, CP 365, 248 rue Isabelle, l'Annonciation Quebec J0T 1T0 Canada. **DD** 071.14225.

HEBDO DE LAVAL. (L'HEBDO DE LAVAL). Vol. 1, No. 1 (23 Mar. 1983)-. 0822-7535. Newspaper. CN. French. wk. Free. Hebdo de Laval, 245 Boulevard des Laurentides, Laval Quebec H7G 2T7 Canada. **DD** 071.14271.

HEBDO JOURNAL. No. 1-. 0229-9887. Newspaper. CN. French. wk. $1.00 Per No. Publications Domaine Ltee, CP 368 Succursale Ndg, Montreal Quebec H3P 3P7 Canada. **DD** 971.404.

HEBDO VEDETTES. Published since Oct. 1975?. 0228-0272. Periodical. CN. French. wk. Editions Pop-Jeunesse, 9922 Saint-Laurent, Montreal Quebec H3L 2N7 Canada. **DD** 054.1.

HELLENOKANADIKI HEBDOMADA. **VFOAT** Greek Canadian Weekly. Began with Oct. 15, 1976 issue. 0705-1336. Newspaper. CN. Greek, Modern. wk. 50 Per No. Greek Canadian Weekly, 59 Cambridge Avenue, Toronto Ontario M4K 2L2 Canada. **DD** 071.13541.

HELSINGIN SANOMAT. Newspaper. Fl. Finnish. ir. 3480.-. Helsingin Sanomat, Box 240, 00101 Helsinki 10 Finland. **Tel** 358 0 1221. Ed Heikki Tikkanen, Keijo Kulha, Simopekka Nortamo and Seppo Kievari. adv acc. **Circ** 427,335. (ctrl). General daily newspaper.

HENDERSON HOME NEWS. Began in 1951. Newspaper. US. English. sw. Henderson Home News, 22 Water Street, Henderson NV 89015. **LC** NEWSPAPER 8694.

THE HERALD. Began in 1909. 0744-7302. Newspaper. US. English. da. $78.00. Sharon Herald, PO Box 51, Sharon PA 16146.

HERALD. (THE HERALD). **VFOAT** Visnyk. V. 1- Jan./Feb. 1971-. 0700-8244. Periodical. CN. English. ir. $9.28. Reliance Press, 1397 Erin St, Winnipeg Man T3C 2S9 Canada. **Tel** 694-0173. Ed The Herald. adv acc. **Circ** 29,000. (ctrl). Snap, crackle, pop.

THE HERALD. 1880. Newspaper. US. English. da. $78.00. Herald Publishing Company, 1 Herald Square, PO Box 2050, New Britian CT 06050. **Tel** (203)225-4601. Ed Judith W Brown. **LC** Newspaper. adv acc. **Circ** 41,000. (ctrl). Central Connecticut and greater Hartford's largest afternoon daily for local, national, and world news. *New Britain Herald.*

HERALD-CITIZEN (COOKEVILLE, TENN.). (HERALD-CITIZEN). **VFOAT** Herald Citizen. 8750-5541. Newspaper. US. English. da. Herald-Citizen 124 S Dixie, PO Box 2729, Cookeville TN 38502.

HERALD (CRYSTAL LAKE, ILL.). (THE HERALD). 8750-0396. Newspaper. US. English. ir. Robert A Shaw, 7803 Pyott Road Box 250, Crystal Lake IL 60014.

THE HERALD (EVERETT, WASH.). (THE HERALD). April 6, 1981-. Newspaper. US. English. da. $102.00. The Herald, WA/Mail, Box 930, Everett WA 98206. **Tel** (206)339-3200. *Everett Herald.*

HERALD (MACKENZIE). (THE HERALD). V. 1- April 24, 1974-. 0318-1863. Newspaper. CN. English. wk. The Herald, PO Box 609, MacKenzie British Columbia V0J 2C0 Canada. **DD** 071.111.

HERALD-NEWS (PASSAIC, N.J.). (THE HERALD-NEWS). **VFOAT** Herald News. Began Apr. 4, 1932. Newspaper. US. English. da. 988 Main Avenue, Passaic NJ 07055. **LC** NEWSPAPER 7002. Also issued on microfilm by the Microphoto Div., Bell & Howell Co. *Daily Herald (Passaic, N.J.), Daily News (Passaic, N.J.).*

THE HERALD-TELEPHONE. V. 101, No. 1 (May 12, 1977-). 0745-7936. Newspaper. US. English. da. Herald-Telephone, Box 909, Bloomington IN 47401. **Tel** (812)332-4401. *Daily Herald-Telephone.*

THE HESSTON RECORD. Vol. 1, No. 1 (Dec. 8, 1932)-. Newspaper. US. English. wk.

HI-DESERT STAR. **VFOAT** Hi Desert Star. 0746-2301. Newspaper. US. English. sw. $12.00 in County, $17.00 California, $22.00 Others. Hi-Desert Star, Hi-Desert Star Building, /7333 Apache Tr, Yucca Valley CA 92284.

HIBBING TRIBUNE. 1901. Newspaper. US. English. da. $52.00. Hibbing Daily Tribune, 2142 1st Avenue, Hibbing MN 55746. **Tel** (218)262-1011. Ed Alan Zoon. adv acc. **Circ** 11,600. A daily newspaper published Monday through Friday and Sunday.

HIGH PRAIRIE REPORTER. V. 1- Feb. 27, 1974-. 0316-7534. CN. English. wk. $45.50 Per Year. High Prairie Reporter, PO Box 1194, High Prairie Alberta T0G 1E0 Canada. **DD** 071.1231.

HIGH SPRINGS HERALD. **VFOAT** Herald. 0746-1046. Newspaper. US. English. wk. $7.00 Within County, $9.00 Others. High Springs Herald, PO Box 745, High Springs FL 32643. *Herald (High Springs, Fla.).*

HIGHLAND PARK LIFE. 0191-5460. Newspaper. US. English. wk. Learner Newspaper, 7519 North Ashland, Chicago IL 60625. **Tel** (312)761-7200.

HIGHLANDER (SYDNEY, N.S.). (HIGHLANDER). Vol. 1, No. 1 (Nov. 12, 1980)-. 0710-1171. Newspaper. CN. English. wk. $18.00

Newspapers

Domestic, $26.00 Foreign. Stott Publishing Corporation Ltd, PO Box 608, Nova Scotia B1P 6H7 Canada. **DD** 071.1696.

HIGHWAY 12 WEEKENDER. VFOAT Stettler Independent. Vol. 1, No. 1 (Oct. 16, 1981)-. 0821-4824. Newspaper. CN. English. wk. Stettler Independent, PO Box 310, Stettler Alberta T0C 2L0 Canada. **DD** 071.1233.

HIGHWAY 43 LEADER. VFOAT Leader. VAT Highway Forty Three Leader. Aug. 23, 1977-. 0704-0458. Newspaper. CN. English. wk. Free to Rate Payers of Lac Ste Anne County. Barrhead Printers and Stationers, Highway 43 Leader, Box 10, Barrhead Alberta T0G 0E0 Canada. **DD** 071.1233.

HIGHWAY 43 TRIBUNE. (THE HIGHWAY 43 TRIBUNE). VFOAT Highway Forty-Three Tribune. VAT Tribune (Whitecourt). Began publication in July 1978. 0226-630X. Newspaper. CN. English. bw. Free. The Highway 43 Tribune, PO Box 630, Whitecourt Alberta T0E 2L0 Canada. **DD** 071.1233.

THE HILO TIMES. VFOAT Hiro Taimusu. Began in 1955?. Newspaper. US. Japanese. sm. Hilo Times, 639 Kilauea Avenue, Hilo HI 96720.

HINDU. Newspaper. US. English. wk. Mr N Ravi Irene, 4701 Willard Avenue, Chevy Case MD 20015.

HINDUSTAN TIMES. Newspaper. II. English. da. $114.00. Hindustan Times, 18-20 Kasturba Gandhi Marg, New Delhi India 11001.

EL HISPANO. Jun. 1966-. Newspaper. US. Spanish. wk. 7.00. El Hispano/New Mexico, 900 Park Avenue SW/PO Box 986, Albuquerque NM 87102. **Tel** (505)243-6161. Ed A B Collado. bk rev. adv acc. **Circ** 10,000. (ctrl). Spanish weekly newspaper El Hispano.

EL HISPANO. 1968. Periodical. US. Spanish (text in English). wk. $12.00. El Hispano, PO Box 2856, Sacramento CA 95812. **Tel** (916)442-0267. Ed Pedrp Chavez. bk rev. adv acc. **Circ** 5,000. Different weekly newspaper subjects. Hispanoamericano.

HLASATEL. Began with June 1, 1892 issue. Newspaper. US. Czech. ir. $28.00. Denni-Hlastel Print and Publishing Company, 1545 West 18th Street, Chicago IL 60608. **Tel** (312)863-5315. **LC** Newspaper 7602-A.

HOKUBEI HOCHI. VFOAT The North American Post. 8756-6451. Newspaper. US. Japanese. tw. North American Post Inc, PO Box 14100, Seattle WA 98104. **DD** 071.

HOLLAND REPORTER. (THE HOLLAND REPORTER). 0300-8800. Newspaper. US. Multilingual (Dutch and English). ir. Holland Reporter, 3680 Division Street, Los Angeles CA 90065.

HOMESTEAD (KENTVILLE, N.S.). (HOMESTEAD). 0712-6476. Newspaper. CN. English. sm. Free. Homestead, PO Box 430, Kentville Nova Scotia B4N 3X2 Canada. **DD** 071.1633. (ctrl).

THE HONEOYE FALLS TIMES. Began in 1882. Newspaper. US. English. wk. Brador Publications, 10 Ontario Street, Honeoye Falls NY 14472.

THE HONOLULU ADVERTISER. VFOAT Sunday Star-Bulletin & Advertiser. Vol. 64, No. 12,249 (Mar. 31, 1921)-. Newspaper. US. English. da. Hawaii Newspaper Agency Inc, PO Box 3350, Honolulu HI 96801. **LC** Newspaper. (cum index). Pacific Commerical Advertiser (Honolulu, Hawaii : 1885).

HONOLULU STAR BULLETIN. Newspaper. US. English. da. $256.75. Hawaii Newspaper Agency Inc, PO Box 3350, Honolulu HI 96801.

HOODOOS HIGHLANDER. (THE HOODOOS HIGHLANDER). 0229-768X. Newspaper. CN. English. wk. $6.50. The Hoodoos Highlander, PO Box 657, Canmore Alberta T0L 0M0 Canada. **DD** 071.1233.

HOPKINS SUN. Newspaper. US. English. wk. Sun Newspaper, 7401 Bush Lake Road, Edina MN 55435. **Tel** (612)831-1200.

HORIZON. V. 1- May 28, 1979-. 0708-580X. Periodical. CN. Armenian. wk. 20.00. Horizon, 3401 Olivar-Asselin, Montreal Quebec H4J 1L5 Canada. **DD** 071.14281.

HOTLINE - NEWSLETTER ASSOCIATION OF AMERICA. (HOTLINE). 0749-1255. Periodical. US. English. bw. NAA, 1341 G Street NW/Suite 603, Washington DC 20005. **DD** 070.

HOUMA DAILY COURIER AND THE TERREBONNE PRESS. Began in 1878. Newspaper. US. English (French). da. $84.00. Houma Courier and Terrebonne Press, 312 School Street, Houma LA 70360. **Tel** (504)879-1557. **LC** Newspaper 7946-X.

THE HOUSTON CHRONICLE. VFOAT Houston Chronicle and Herald. Began with Oct. 14, 1901. Newspaper. US. English. da. $270.00. Houston Chronicle, 801 Texas Avenue, Houston TX 77002. **Tel** (713)220-7171. Ind/Abst Infobank.

HOUSTON INFORMER. May 24, 1919-. Newspaper. US. English. wk. Freedmens Publishing Company, 1609 Binz/PO Box 3086, Houston TX 77001.

HOUSTON POST (1932). (THE HOUSTON POST). Vol. 47, No. 303 (Feb. 1, 1932)-. Newspaper. US. English. da. $222.00. The Houston Post, Mail Subscription Department, 4747 SW Freeway, Houston TX 77001. **Tel** (713)840 5000. Houston Post-Dispatch.

HSUEH PAO (SSU-CHUAN TA HSUEH). (HSUEH PAO). VFOAT Ssu-Chuan Ta Hsueh Hsueh Pao, Sichuandaxue Xuebao. Periodical. CC. Chinese. qt. 0.40. SSU-Chuan Jen Min Chu Pan She, Post Office, Cheng-Tu Shih China. **LC** AS452.C462. **DD** 089.951.

HUAFU YOUBAO. (HUA FUYU PAO). VFOAT Washington China Post. No. 1 (1983 Nien, 4 Yueh, 5 Jih)-. 0739-831X. Periodical. US. Chinese. wk. $10.00. Washington China Post, PO Box 5905, Bethesda MD 20814.

THE HUGOTON HERMES. Began with Aug. 4, 1887 issue. Newspaper. US. English. wk. $13.00. Hugoton Hermes, PO Box 849, Hugoton KS 67951. **Tel** (316) 544-4321. **LC** Newspaper 7817.

THE HUMBOLDT BEACON AND FORTUNA ADVANCE. VFOAT Humboldt Beacon. 0746-777X. Newspaper. US. English. sw. $15.00. Humboldt Beacon Inc, 928 Main Street, Fortuna CA 95540.

HUNTER SAFETY INSTRUCTOR. (HUNTER SAFETY INSTRUCTOR : THE OFFICIAL PUBLICATION OF THE NORTH AMERICAN ASSOCIATION OF HUNTER SAFETY COORDINATORS). Vol. 2, No. 3 (June/July 1983)-. 0737-6227. Periodical. US. English. mo. $12.00. Hunter Safety Instructor, PO Box C-19000, Seattle WA 98109. Hunter Safety News (Seattle, Wash.).

HUNTERDON COUNTY DEMOCRAT. Began in 1847. 0018-7844. Newspaper. US. English. $70.00. Hunterdon County Democrat, PO Box 32, Flemington NJ 08822. **Tel** (201)782-4747. **LC** Newspaper 8768-X. Hunterdon Democrat, Democrat-Advertiser.

HUNTINGTON BEACH INDEPENDENT. 0194-6021. Newspaper. US. English. da. $85.00. West Orange Publishing Company, 13261 Century Boulevard, Garden Grove CA 92643. **Tel** (714)537-7510.

HUNTSVILLE TIMES. Began with Mar. 23, 1910 issue. Newspaper. US. English. da. $72.00. Huntsville Times, PO Box 1487/West Station, Huntsville AL 35807. **Tel** (205)532-4000. Ed Patrick McCaulley. **LC** Newspaper. bk rev. adv acc. **Circ** 60,000.

HUTCHINSON LEADER. Began with July 17, 1880 issue. Newspaper. US. English. bw. $27.00. The Hutchinson Leader, 36 Washington Avenue West, Hutchinson MN 55350. **Tel** (612)587-5000. Ed Cathy Nevanen. **LC** Newspaper 7002. adv acc. **Circ** 6,000. (ctrl). A 6,000 circulation rural newspaper.

THE HUTCHINSON NEWS. Began with July 4, 1885 issue. Newspaper. US. English. da. $76.09. The Hutchinson News, 300 West Second Street, Hutchinson KS 67501. **Tel** (316)662-3311. Ed Jim Hitch. **LC** Newspaper. adv acc. **Circ** 43,000 Daily, 46,000 Sunday. General daily news.

HYDE PARK TRIBUNE, THE MATTAPAN TRIBUNE. VFOAT Hyde Park Tribune/Mattapan Tribune. VAT Hyde Park Tribune, Mattapan Tribune. 0745-9262. Newspaper. US. English. wk. Tribune Publishing Company, 1205 Hyde Park Avenue, Hyde Park MA 02136. Hyde Park Tribune.

IDAHO MOUNTAIN EXPRESS. VFOAT Mountain Express. 1974. 0279-8964. Newspaper. US. English. wk. $22.00. Ketchum Mountain Express, PO Box 1013, Ketchum ID 83340. **Tel** (208)726-8060. Ed Pam Morris. adv acc. **Circ** 10,000. Local news and features for the Sun Valley and Wood River Valley areas of Idaho.

IDAHO STATE JOURNAL. Began in 1922. Newspaper. US. English. da. $90.00. Tribune Journal Publishing Company, Box 431, Pocatello ID 83204. **Tel** (208)232-4161. Ed Lylr Olson. **LC** Newpaperr 7570. bk rev. adv acc. **Circ** 20,200. Daily newspaper.

IDAHO STATESMAN. Newspaper. US. English. da. $139.00. Idaho Statesman Daily and Sunday, Box 40/1200 North Curtis Road, Boise ID 83707. **Tel** (208)377-6200.

IGNACE COURIER. VAT Ignace Courier Weekly News. 0715-5352. Newspaper. CN. English. wk. $5.00 Per Year. Ignace Courier, PO Box 510, Ignace Ontario P0T 1T0 Canada. **DD** 071.13112.

IGNACE DRIFTWOOD. 0710-2046. Newspaper. CN. English. wk. $0.35 Per No./$20.00 Per Year for Out of Town Residents. Ignace Driftwood, PO Box 989, Ignace Ontario P0T 1T0 Canada. **DD** 071.13112.

THE ILLINOIS INFORMER. Periodical. US. English. ir. Illinois Informer, 910 South Michigan/18th Floor, Chicago IL 60605. **Tel** (312)793-3800.

ILLINOIS RUNNER. Began wtih issue for Oct. 1983?. 0747-4911. Periodical. US. English. mo. $10.00. Illinois Runner, PO Box 244, Normal IL 61761.

ILLINOIS TIMES. 1975. 0199-7823. Periodical. US. English. wk. $52.00. Illinois Times, PO Box 3524, Springfield IL 62708. **Tel** (217)753-2226. Ed Fletcher F Farrar Jr. bk rev. adv acc. **Circ** 23,000. Ideas in the area of downstate Illinois.

IMAGE DE LA RIVE SUD. (L'IMAGE DE LA RIVE SUD). VFOAT South Shore Image. Vol. 1, No. 1 (8 March 1978)-. 0227-5430. Newspaper. CN. French (English). wk. $0.15 each No. L'Image de la Rive Sud, 460 Ouest rue St-Charles, Longueuil Quebec J4H 1G4 Canada. **DD** 071.1437.

IMPACT. (L'IMPACT). Vol. 1, No. 1-. 0824-4286. Periodical. CN. French. bm. Revue de Ville de Val-Belair, 1105 Nord Avenue de l'Eglise, Val-Belair Quebec G0A 1G0 Canada. **DD** 071.1447.

EL IMPARCIAL. 0536-5708. Newspaper. Spanish. da. $54.00. El Imparcial, 7A Calle 10-54 Zona 1, Guatemala Central America.

IMRUZ. VFOAT Imroze. 0715-3899. Newspaper. CN. Persian, Modern. sm. Impoze, 89 John Tabor Trail, Scarborough Ontario M1B 2P5 Canada. **DD** 071.13541.

THE IMS AYER DIRECTORY OF PUBLICATIONS. See Yearbooks, Almanacs, Directories.

IN THE CREASE. 0744-5172. Periodical. US. English. ir. $31.00. In the Crease/The Lacrosse, PO Box 281, Riderwood MD 21139. **Tel** (301)433-0743.

IND-EX (DURHAM, N.C. : ANNUAL). See Indexes/Abstracts.

INDEKS BERITA DAN ARTIKEL SURAT KABAR BIDANG ILMU-ILMU SOSIAL DAN KEMANUSIAAN. See Indexes/Abstracts.

INDEPENDENT. (THE INDEPENDENT). April 10, 1975-. 0319-1400. Newspaper. CN. English. wk. $5. The Independent, PO Box 3000, Kincardine Ontario N0G 2G0 Canada. **DD** 071.1321.

INDEPENDENT. (THE INDEPENDENT). VFOAT Port Hope Independent. Vol. 1, Issue 1 (May 6, 1981)-. 0712-4953. Periodical. CN. English. wk. Free. Port Hope Independent, 8 Queen Street, Port Hope Ontario L1A 2Y7 Canada. **DD** 071.1356.

INDEPENDENT (LITTLETON, COLO.). (THE INDEPENDENT). Vol. 95, No. 39 (Fri., Dec. 3, 1982)-. 0745-3280. Newspaper. US. English. sw. Littleton Independent, POB 811, Littleton CO 80160. Littleton Independent.

INDEX TO BLACK NEWSPAPERS. See Indexes/Abstracts.

INDEX TO ST. LOUIS NEWSPAPERS. See Indexes/Abstracts.

THE INDEX TO THE LONG ISLANDER. See Indexes/Abstracts.

INDEX TO THE ST. PAUL DISPATCH & ST. PAUL PIONEER PRESS NEWSPAPERS. See Indexes/Abstracts.

INDEX TO THE TIMES OF INDIA. See Indexes/Abstracts.

Newspapers

INDIA ABROAD. 0046-8932. Newspaper. US. English. wk. $20.00. India Abroad, 43 West 24th Street/7th Floor, New York NY 10010. **Tel** (212)929-1727.

INDIAN EXPRESS. Newspaper. English. da. $65.99. Indian Express Newspapers Ltd, Express Towers, PB No 867, Nariman Point Bombay 1. **Tel** 294838-8.

INDIAN EXPRESS INTERNATIONAL WEEKLY. USA-CANADA EDITION. (INDIAN EXPRESS INTERNATIONAL). **VAT** Indian Express International (Montreal). 0715-5832. Periodical. CN. English. wk. $15.00. Indian Express International, PO Box 906/Station B, Montreal Quebec H3B 3K5 Canada. **DD** 954.0005.

INDIANA HERALD. Began publication in 1953?. 0019-6630. Newspaper. US. English. wk. $9.50. Ol Tandy, 723 North West Street, Indianapolis IN 46202. **Tel** (317)634-8117.

INDIANA NEWSPAPER DIRECTORY AND RATE BOOK. *See* Yearbooks, Almanacs, Directories.

THE INDIANA TIMES. VFOAT Louisville Times/Indiana. Newspaper. US. English. da. 525 West Broadway, Louisville KY 40202.

INDIANAPOLIS NEWS (INDIANAPOLIS, IND. : 1876). (THE INDIANAPOLIS NEWS). **VFOAT** Indianapolis Daily News. Whole No. 2001 (May 9, 1876)-. Newspaper. US. English. da. $95.00. Indianapolis Newspapers Inc, PO Box 145, Indianapolis IN 46206. LC Newspaper. *Evening News (Indianapolis, Ind.)*.

THE INDIANAPOLIS RECORDER. Vol. 13, No. 28 Jan. 15, 1910. Newspaper. US. English. wk. $12.00. Indianapolis Recorder, 2901 Norrth Tacoma Avenue, Indianapolis IN 46218. Ed M Stewart. LC Newspaper 7002. *Recorder*.

THE INDIANAPOLIS STAR. VFOAT Indianapolis Sunday Star. Vol. 4, No. 364 (June 4, 1907)-. Newspaper. US. English. da. $159.00. Indianapolis Newspapers Inc, PO Box 145, Indianapolis IN 46206. LC Newspaper. *Indianapolis Morning Star.*

INDO CANADIAN TIMES. V. 1- Mar. 24, 1978-. 0708-949X. Newspaper. CN. Panjabi. wk. 30.00. T S Hayer, Indo Canadian Times, PO Box 118, Surrey British Columbia V3T 4W4 Canada. **Tel** (604)584-6480. Ed Tara Singh Hayer. **DD** 071.1133. bk rev. adv acc. **Circ** 13,000. (ctrl). Covers news, political essays, short stories, poems, sports, letters, and editorial.

INDONESIAN OBSERVER. Newspaper. English. da. $65.00. Indonesian Observer Ltd, Djalan M Sangadji, Djakarta Indonesia.

INFORMACION SISTEMATICA. 0185-2973. Periodical. MX. Spanish. mo. $110.00. Informacion Sistematica, Valencia 84 Apt Postal 19-308, Mexico 19 D F Mexico. **Tel** 598-6043. Ed Bernardo Aualos. adv acc. **Circ** 2,000. (ctrl). 3,000 abstracts a month of 13 major Mexican newspapers included in publication permit access to 15,000 clippings systematically structured. Published each month since 1976.

INFORMATION. (L'INFORMATION). V. 1- 20 Nov. 1975-. 0700-9062. Newspaper. CN. French. ir. Information, Ste-Julie et St-Amable Ltee, CP 359, Sainte-Julie Quebec J0L 2C0 Canada. **DD** 071.436.

INFORMATION BELLECOMBE. 0823-6879. Periodical. CN. French. mo. Free to Citizens. Information Bellecombe, Ste-Agnes-de-Bellecombe, Quebec J0Z 1K0 Canada. **DD** 071.14212.

INFORMER. (THE INFORMER). Began publication in Oct. 1977?. 0227-7999. Newspaper. CN. English. bw. $5.00. The Informer, PO Box 204, Tiverton Ontario N0G 1T0 Canada. **DD** 071.1321.

INNISFIL SCOPE. (THE INNISFIL SCOPE). Began publication in Aug. 1978. 0225-1604. Newspaper. CN. English. wk. 12.00. Innisfil Scope Inc, PO Box 310, Beeton Ontario L0G 1A0 Canada. **Tel** (416)729-2287. Ed Bruce R Haire. **DD** 071.1317. bk rev. adv acc. General and community news.

INNIU. Newspaper. IE. Irish. wk. $24.81. Inniu, 29 Lower O'Connell Street, Dublin Ireland.

INTER-CITY EXPRESS. 0274-7464. Periodical. US. English. da. Inter City Express, 614 Madison Street, Oakland CA 94607.

INTERIOR JOURNAL (1984). (THE INTERIOR JOURNAL). Vol. 125, No. 40 (Nov. 1, 1984)-. Newspaper. US. English. wk. $9.75 Kentucky, $14.75 Elsewhere. The Interior Journal, PO Box 196, Stanford KY 40484. *Interior Journal & Lincoln County Post, 8750-1554.*

INTERLAKE'S REGIONAL NEWS. (THE INTERLAKE'S REGIONAL NEWS). Vol. 1, Issue 1 (July 26, 1978)-. 0824-149X. Newspaper. CN. English. bw. Interlakes' Regional News, 322 Manitoba Avenue, Selkirk Manitoba R1A 0Y7 Canada. **DD** 071.1272.

INTERNATIONAL FALLS JOURNAL. Newspaper. US. English. ir. $101.80. North Star Publishing Company, PO Box 951, International Falls MN 56649.

INTERNATIONAL MEDIA GUIDE. NEWSPAPERS WORLDWIDE. VFOAT Newspapers, Worldwide. 1983-. Periodical. US. English. an. 150 Fifth Avenue/Suite 610, New York NY 10011. *0093-9447.*

IRISH TIMES ANNUAL REVIEW. 1966-. IE. English. an. Irish Times Ltd, PO Box 74/11-15 d'Oliver Street, Dublin 2 Ireland. **Tel** 722022. *Irish Review and Annual.*

THE IRVINE WORLD NEWS. 0195-4822. Newspaper. US. English. wk. $24.00. Irvine World News, PO Box C 19512, Irvine CA 92513. **Tel** (714)833-1950.

IRVING DAILY NEWS. 8750-7870. Newspaper. US. English. da. Irving Daily News, 1622 West Irving Boulevard, Irving TX 75060.

ISANTI COUNTY NEWS. VFOAT American-News. 8750-2267. Newspaper. US. English. wk. $10.00 Residents of Minnesota, $7.00 for Senior Citizens, $15.00 Others. The Isanti News, PO Box 160, Isanti MN 55040. *Isanti News.*

ISLAND STAR. V. 1, No. 49- Oct. 9, 1974-. 0318-207X. Newspaper. CN. English. wk. $6.00. Island Star Press, 863 Eighth Street, Courtenay British Columbia V9N 1N9 Canada. **DD** 071.1134. *Comox Valley Star, 0318-2061.*

ISRAEL TODAY (ENCINO, CALIF.). (ISRAEL TODAY). Newspaper. US. English. da. $80.00. Israel Toady, CA/1661 Ventura Boulevard, Encino CA 91436. **Tel** (213)786-4000.

ITALIAN TRIBUNE (NEWARK, N.J.). (ITALIAN TRIBUNE). Began with July 29, 1931 issue. 0740-2597. Newspaper. US. English (Italian). wk. Free. The Italian Tribune, 427 Bloomfield Avenue, Newark NJ 07107. **Tel** (201)485-6000. Ed Joan Alagna. LC Newspaper. bk rev. adv acc. **Circ** 25,000. General news pertaining to the Italian American community. Printed entirely in English for 55 years.

ITHACA TIMES. V. 1- June 22/28, 1978-. 0277-1187. Periodical. US. English. wk. $18.00. Ithaca Times, Box 27, Ithaca NY 14850. **Tel** (607)273-6092. Ed Sandra List. bk rev. adv acc. **Circ** 19,050. (ctrl) *Good Times Gazette, Ithaca New Times.*

JACKSON ADVOCATE. Began 1939. 0047-1704. Newspaper. US. English. wk. $20.00. The Jackson Advocate, PO Box 3708, Jackson MS 39207.

THE JACKSON CITIZEN PATRIOT. VFOAT Sunday Citizen Patriot. Newspaper. US. English. da. 214 South Jackson Street, Jackson MI 49204. LC Newspaper 8431. *Jackson Citizen Press, Daily Patriot.*

THE JACKSONVILLE ADVOCATE. VFOAT Advocate. 0882-6560. Newspaper. US. English. wk. $16.00. Florida Advocate Publishing Company, PO Box 12563, Jacksonville FL 32209.

JACKSONVILLE DAILY JOURNAL. 1831. Newspaper. US. English. da. Jacksonville Journal Courier Company, 235 West State Street, Jacksonville IL 62651. **Tel** (217)245-6121. Ed John R Power. bk rev. adv acc. **Circ** 16,000. National, international, state and local news. *Jacksonville Journal (Jacksonville, Ill. : 1878 : Daily).*

JACKSONVILLE JOURNAL. Vol. 35, No. 290 (June 6, 1922 1922)-. 0743-0914. Newspaper. US. English. da. $52.00. Florida Publishing Company, 1 Riverside Avenue, Jacksonville FL 32201. **Tel** (904)359-4111. *Florida Metropolis.*

JAMESTOWN POST-JOURNAL. VFOAT Jamestown Post-Journal. V. 1, No. 1 (Oct. 1, 1941)-. Newspaper. US. English. da. $69.20. Post Journal, 11021 Second Street, Jamestown NY 14701. **Tel** (716)487-1111. Ed J A Hall. Available on microfilm from New York State Library and Bell and Howell. *Jamestown Post, Jamestown Journal.*

JANE CORRIDOR. (THE JANE CORRIDOR). V. 1- Apr. 1974-. 0701-1083. Periodical. CN. English (includes some text in Italian). mo. Free to the Area Residents. The Jane Corridor, PO Box 2331 Station C, Downsview Ontario M3N 2V8 Canada. **DD** 071.1354.

JANG. Newspaper. Urdu. da. Daily Jang of Karachi, PO Box 52, Off LL Chundrigar, Karachi 1 Pakistan.

THE JAPAN TIMES. Began in 1956. Newspaper. English. da. Japan Publishing Trading Company, PO Box 5030/Tokyo International, Tokyo 100-31 Japan. *Nippon Times.*

THE JAPAN TIMES WEEKLY. INTERNATIONAL EDITION. (THE JAPAN TIMES WEEKLY). V. 1- 1961-. 0447-5763. Newspaper. JA. English. wk. $68.00. Japan Publishing Trading Company Ltd, PO Box 5030/Tokyo International, Tokyo 100-31 Japan.

THE JAPANESE PRESS. Began in 1950?. English. an. $20.00. Nihon Shinbun Kyokai, 2-1 Uchisaiwaicho 2-Chome, Chiyoda-Ku Tokyo 100 Japan. **Tel** (03)591-4401. Ed Osamu Asano. adv acc. **Circ** 3,000. A year-book describing trends and giving statistical facts on the newspaper industry in Japan. Also lists Japanese newspaper, Japanese correspondents overseans, etc. *Japanese Press, Past and Present.*

JASPER JOURNAL. 0744-3110. Newspaper. US. English. wk. Pipestone Publishing Company, 101 2nd Street NE/Box 470, Pipestone MN 56164.

THE JEANNETTE SPIRIT. 0746-5971. Newspaper. US. English. wk. Jeannette Spirit, 310 Clay Avenue, Jeannette PA 15644.

JEFFREY CITY NEWS. 0745-0176. Newspaper. US. English. wk. $12.00. Jeffrey City News, PO Box J, Lander WY 82520. **Tel** (307)544-2525.

JEN MIN JIH PAO SO YIN. Periodical. CC. Chinese. $36.00. China National Publishing Company, 380 Bei Su Zhou Lu, Shanghai China. bk rev. adv acc. (ctrl). This publication is a microprinted collection of People's Daily, which is the most authoritative news paper in China belonged to the Central Committee of Communist Party.

JEN MIN JIH PAO SO YIN HO TING PEN. VFOAT Renmin Ribao. 1981.1-. Newspaper. CC. Chinese. $43.20. China National Publishing Company, 380 Bei Su Zhou Lu Shanghai China. *Jen Min Jih Pao Ho Ting Pen.*

THE JERUSALEM POST. 0021-597X. Newspaper. IS. English. da. $250.00. Jerusalem Post, PO Box 81, Jerusalem 9100 Israel. **Tel** (02)551616. Ed Ari Rath and Erwin Frenkel. bk rev. adv acc. **Circ** 25,000. Covers events in Israel and the Middle East as well as the Jewish world; provides in-depth analysis and commentary endeavouring to reflect a wide gamut of opinion.

JEWISH JOURNAL. Began 1971. 0745-0818. Newspaper. US. English. wk. $15.00. Brooklyn Jewish Journal, 8721 3rd Avenue, Brooklyn NY 11209.

JEWISH NEWS (SOUTHFIELD, MICH. : 1942) CEASED. (THE JEWISH NEWS). Vol. 1, No. 1 (Mar. 27, 1942). Ceased in 1969. Newspaper. US. English. wk. The Jewish News, 17515 West Nine Mile Road/Suite 865, Southfield MI 48075. *Detroit Jewish Chronicle.*

JEWISH TIMES (PHILADELPHIA, PA. : 1973). (THE JEWISH TIMES). Vol. 43, No. 27 (July 5, 1973)-. Newspaper. US. English. wk. Jewish Times Corp, 2417 Welch Road/Suite 23, Philadelphia PA 19114. *Philadelphia Jewish Times (Philadelphia, PA. : 1947).*

JEWISH WEEKLY NEWS. 0021-6860. Periodical. English. wk. $9.00. Jewish Weekly News, c/o Leslie B Kahn, PO Box 1569, Springfield MA 01101. **Tel** (413)739-4771. Ed Leslie B Kahn. bk rev. adv acc. **Circ** 2,500. Anglo-Jewish weekly newspaper of western Massachusetts.

JIM PETERSON'S OUTDOOR NEWS. 1969. Newspaper. US. English. wk. $14.00. Outdoor News Inc, PO Box 27145, Golden Valley MN 55427. **Tel** 546-4251. Ed Jim Peterson. adv acc. **Circ** 23,000. (ctrl). Hunting and fishing weekly news.

Newspapers

JORNAL ACOREANO. V. 1- July 1975-. 0319-6801. Newspaper. CN. Portuguese. $6.00. Jornal Acoreano, C P 288 Succursale C, Toronto Ontario M6J 3P4 Canada. **Tel** 071.13541.

JORNAL DO BRASIL. Began publication in 1890. Newspaper. BL. Portuguese. $1,100.00. Journal do Brasil, Av Brasil 500, 20000 Rio de Janeiro Brazil. adv acc. (ctrl). Daily paper, various matters: economics, financing, world, country, and city politics, opinions, sports, culture, pleasure, etc.

JORNAL NOVO. Newspaper. PO. Portuguese. ir. 400 Single Issue. Novimprensa, Distribuidora Dig, Rua das Chagas, 2 Lisboa Portugal. LC Newspaper.

JORNAL PORTUGUES (ALAMEDA, CALIF.). (JORNAL PORTUGUES). VFOAT Portuguese Journal. V. 1, No. 1 (July 1, 1932)-. 8756-2200. Newspaper. US. Portuguese (English). wk. $15.00. Portuguese Journal, 1912 Church Lane, San Pablo CA 94806. **Tel** (415)237-0888. DD 071. *Jornal de Noticias, Colonia Portuguesa; Imparcial.*

JOUR. (LE JOUR.) V. 1- Feb. 4, 1977-. 0703-699X. Newspaper. CN. French. wk. $50.00 Domestic, $60.00 Foreign. Journal le Jour Inc, Bureau 801/1435 rue de Bleury, Montreal Quebec H3A 2H7 Canada. DD 071.14.

JOURNAL. V. 1- 20 Sept. 1978-. 0227-1249. Newspaper. CN. English (French). wk. Free. A Vigeant, The Journal, PO Box 564/387 Principale Street, Lachute Quebec J8H 1Y1 Canada. DD 071.1423. (ctrl).

THE JOURNAL. 0744-3285. Newspaper. US. English. wk. Editorial Associates Inc, PO Box 2048, Camp Verde AZ 86322.

JOURNAL. (THE JOURNAL). VFOAT Logan Lake Leader. 0824-6394. Newspaper. CN. English. wk. $0.25 Per No. Journal Publishing, PO Box 190, Ashcroft British Columbia V0K 1A0 Canada. DD 071.1141.

JOURNAL A R C ARABE. VFOAT A R C Arabic Journal. V. 1- (No. 8-). 0700-9771. Periodical. CN. English (text in Arabic and French). mo. $3.75. Journal A R C Arabe, PO Box 516/Station B, Montreal Quebec H3B 3K3 Canada. DD 071.14281. *A R C Journal,* 0700-9763.

JOURNAL ACTON REGIONAL. VAT Journal Acton. Vol. 1, No 1 (10 Oct. 1979)-. 0228-6289. Newspaper. CN. French. wk. $12.00. Journal Acton Regional, C P 1138, Acton Vale Quebec J0H 1A0 Canada. DD 071.14525.

JOURNAL AND GUIDE. Apr. 3 1977-. Newspaper. US. English. wk. $15.60. Journal and Guide, Box 209/RCH Street, Norfolk VA 23501. **Tel** (804)625-3686. *New Journal and Guide.*

JOURNAL CHALEUR. (LE JOURNAL CHALEUR). VFOAT Chaleur. V. 1- 19 March 1975-. 0318-2134. Newspaper. CN. French. wk. $8.50. Le Journal Chaleur, CP 550 Place Richmond, New Richmond Quebec Canada. DD 071.1478.

JOURNAL COTE-DES-NEIGES. Vol. 1, No. 1 (May 83)-. 0822-0794. Periodical. CN. English (French). mo. Free. Journal Cote-des-Neiges, Suite 204/3600 Van Horne, Montreal Quebec H3S 1R6 Canada. **Tel** (514)731-0346. DD 071.14281. adv acc. **Circ** 15,000. It is a community newspaper interested in local activities and local actuality. Principal subjects: youth, community groups, education, ethics, crime prevention, housing, etc.

JOURNAL DE CORNWALL. (LE JOURNAL DE CORNWALL). V. 1- 26 Aug. 1977-. 0704-0660. Newspaper. CN. French. wk. 10.00. Le Journal de Cornwall, 113 Chemin Montreal, Cornwall Ontario K6H 1B2 Canada. **Tel** (613)938-1433. Ed Roger Duplantie. DD 071.1376. adv acc. **Circ** 1,300. Local newspaper (French). Municipal coverage, school boards, other activities. *Francor,* 0712-9270.

JOURNAL DE LA COTE. VFOAT Cote. Published since 1976. 0227-2911. Newspaper. CN. French. bw. Publications Bernard Cleary, 2873 Chemin Ste-Foy, CP 9694, Sainte-Foy Quebec G1V 4C2 Canada. DD 071.1448.

JOURNAL DE VILLERAY. (LE JOURNAL DE VILLERAY). Vol. 1, No. 1 (8 Sept 1982)-. 0821-5081. Newspaper. CN. French. wk. Free to Citizens. Journal de Villeray, 1008 Est rue Fleury, Montreal Quebec H2C 1P7 Canada. DD 071.14281.

JOURNAL DES RIVIERES. 1st- V. 0319-5074. Newspaper. CN. French. Journal des Rivieres, C P 368, Place Estrie, Bedford Quebec Canada. DD 071.1462.

JOURNAL D'OUTREMONT. (LE JOURNAL D'OUTREMONT). Vol. 1, No. 1 (May 1983)-. 0824-1317. Periodical. CN. French. mo. Free. Journal d'Outremont, CP 727, Montreal Quebec H2V 4N9 Canada. DD 071.14281. (ctrl).

JOURNAL DU NORD-OUEST. (LE JOURNAL DU NORD-OUEST). V. 1- Oct. 7, 1974-. 0380-2051. Newspaper. CN. French. da. $1.50 Per Week. La Frontiere, 167 Dallaire, CP 490, Rouyn Quebec J9X 4T3 Canada. DD 071.1413.

JOURNAL DU SAMEDI. (LE JOURNAL DU SAMEDI). V. 2, No. 1 (April 5-11 1981)-. 0229-981X. Newspaper. CN. French. wk. $37.00 Domestic, $50.00 Foreign. Publications Quebecor, 225 rue Roy, Montreal Quebec H2W 2N6 Canada. DD 071.14.

JOURNAL-EVERY EVENING. Began in 1886. Newspaper. US. English. da. $89.00. The News Journal Company, 831 Orange Street, Wilmington DE 19899. LC Newspaper.

JOURNAL-GAZETTE (FORT WAYNE, IND.). (THE JOURNAL-GAZETTE). VFOAT Journal Gazette. Nov. 10, 1944-. 0734-3701. Newspaper. US. English. da. $106.40. Fort Wayne Journal Gazette, D & S, 600 Main Street, Fort Wayne IN 46802. Ed Craig Klugman. adv acc. **Circ** 60,219 Daily 123,575 Sunday. (ctrl). Daily newspaper based in Fort Wayne Indiana. *Fort Wayne Journal-Gazette.*

JOURNAL INDEX TO THE ALBUQUERQUE JOURNAL. See Indexes/Abstracts.

JOURNAL (KING GEORGE, VA.). (THE JOURNAL). Vol. 2, No. 35 (Aug. 9, 1984)-. 8750-2275. Newspaper. US. English. wk. $8.50. The Journal, PO Box 408, King George VA 22485. *King George Journal.*

JOURNAL LA MITIS. VFOAT Mitis. V. 1, No. 1- Oct. 4, 1978-. 0228-2569. Newspaper. CN. French. wk. $15.60 Canada, $20.00 Others. Journal la Mitis, CP 10, 1600 Boul Jacques Cartier, Mont-Joli Quebec G5H 3K8 Canada. DD 071.14771.

JOURNAL LA REPUBLIQUE. VFOAT Republique. VAT Republique (Edmunston). V. 1, No. 1- Aug. 30, 1978. 0226-3580. Newspaper. CN. French. wk. $15.60 Canada, $20.00 Others. Journal la Republique, CP 606, 173 rue Victoria, Edmunston New Brunswick E3V 3L2 Canada. DD 071.1554.

JOURNAL LE NORD. VFOAT Nord. VAT Le Nord (Annonciation). Published since March 1977?. 0228-278X. Newspaper. CN. French. wk. $8. Journal le Nord, CP 820, L Annonciation Quebec Canada. DD 071.14225.

JOURNAL LE ST-FRANCOIS. VFOAT Le St-Francois. V. 1- Dec. 7, 1977-. 0227-1222. Newspaper. CN. French. Les Editions Gerard Cadieux, 211 rue Victoria, Valleyfield Quebec J6T 1A8 Canada. DD 071.1432.

JOURNAL L'INFORMATION DU NORD. VFOAT Information du Nord. Vol. 1, No 1 Nov. 2, 1981-. 0713-6420. Newspaper. CN. French. wk. Free. Journal l'Information du Nord, CP 1480, St-Jovite Quebec J0T 2H0 Canada. DD 071.1424.

JOURNAL MASKOUTAIN. (LE JOURNAL MASKOUTAIN). Vol. 1, No. 1 Mar. 18 1981-. 0711-4745. Newspaper. CN. French. wk. Free to Citizens of St-Hyacinthe. J G Asselin, Journal Maskoutain, CP 700, St-Hyacinthe Quebec J2S 7C2 Canada. DD 071.14523.

THE JOURNAL MESSENGER. 0745-6859. Newspaper. US. English. da. Prince William Publishing Company, 9009 Church Street, PO Drawer 431, Manassas VA 22110.

JOURNAL OF NEWSPAPER AND PERIODICAL HISTORY. Vol. 1, No. 1 (Winter 1984)-. 0265-5942. Periodical. UK. English. ty. World Microfilms Publications, 62 Queens Grove, London NW8 6ER England.

JOURNAL PONTI-ART. VFOAT Ponti-Art Newspaper. Began with Aug. 9, 1974 issue. 0384-6229. Newspaper. CN. English (French). bw. $3. Editor, PO Box 730, Fort-Coulonge Quebec J0X 1V0 Canada. DD 071.14215.

JOURNAL REGIONAL. (LE JOURNAL REGIONAL). V. 1- Aug. 29, 1978-. 0706-3318. Newspaper. CN. French. wk. $20.00 Domestic, $25.00 Foreign. Le Journal Regional, 1310 rue Principale, Saint-Roch de l Achigan Quebec J0K 3H0 Canada. DD 071.14416.

JOURNAL REGIONAL. (LE JOURNAL REGIONAL). VFOAT Regional. VAT Regional (Saint-Jean). 0821-414X. Newspaper. CN. French. Le Journal Regional, 169 Boulevard du Seminaire, St-Jean Quebec J3B 5J4 Canada. DD 071.1438.

THE JOURNAL STAR. Vol. 117, No. 94 (Oct. 2, 1971). Newspaper. US. English. da. $176.80. 1 News Plaza, Peoria IL 61643. **Tel** (309)686-3000. Ed Thomas Driscoll. LC Newspaper. adv acc. **Circ** 100,000. Available on microfilm. Daily and Sunday newspaper. *Peoria Journal Star.*

JOURNAL WEST (DUNDAS, ONT.). (JOURNAL WEST). Vol. 2, No. 1 (Sept. 16, 1976)-. 0229-7611. Newspaper. CN. English. wk. $7.50. Journal West, 36 King Street East, Dundas Ontario L9H 1B8 Canada. DD 071.1352.

JOURS DE FRANCE. V. 1- 1954-. 0022-5681. Periodical. FR. French. wk. $71.83. Societe de Presse Jours de France 7 Rond-Point-D-Champs- Elysees, 75383 Paris Cedex 08 France. **Tel** 359 53 19. **Circ** 52.

THE JUNCTION CITY UNION. Feb. 15, 1909-July 13, 1974. Newspaper. US. English. da. $72.00. Junction City Union, 814 North Washington Street, Junction City KS 66441. **Tel** (913)762-5000. Ed John G Montgomery. LC Newspaper 7821. bk rev. adv acc. **Circ** 9,000. General daily newspaper printed daily and Sunday. *Daily Union (Junction City, Kan. : 1896).*

JUNEAU EMPIRE. Feb. 11, 1980-. Newspaper. US. English. da. $300.00. Juneau Empire, 235 2nd Street, Juneau AK 99801. *Southeast Alaska Empire.*

JUNG TORONTO. 0821-6789. Newspaper. CN. English (text in Urdu). sm. Jung Toronto, 741 Broadview Avenue/Suite 306, Toronto Ontario M4K 3Y3 Canada. DD 071.13541.

KALAMAZOO GAZETTE (1916). (THE KALAMAZOO GAZETTE). Began in November 1916. Newspaper. US. English. da. 401 South Rudick Street, Kalamazoo MI 49003. LC Newspaper 7002. *Gazette-Telegraph.*

KAMI SAMACAR. VFOAT Quomi Samachar. V. 1, No. 1-. 0712-3507. Newspaper. CN. Panjabi (text in Gurmukhi script). sm. $20.00 Canada and US. Quomi Samachar, 7171 Stride Avenue, Burnaby British Columbia V3N 1T8 Canada. DD 071.1133.

KAMOURASKA. (LE KAMOURASKA). 1st- Year. 0707-7157. Newspaper. CN. French. wk. $12.50. L'Echo du Bas St-Laurent, 192 Est rue Saint-Germain, Rimouski Quebec G5L 1A8 Canada. DD 071.1475.

KANADA KURIER. ALBERTA AUSGABE. (KANADA KURIER). V. 91, No. 38 (18 Sept 1980)-. 0712-8878. Newspaper. CN. German. wk. $0.60 Per No. Kanada Kurier Alberta Ausgabe, c/o Courier Press, 955 Alexander Avenue, Winnipeg Manitoba R3C 2X8 Canada. DD 071.123. *Alberta Courier der Nordwesten.*

KANADA KURIER. AUSGABE FUR BRITISH COLUMBIA. (KANADA KURIER). VFOAT Ausg. fur British Columbia. -. 0712-8886. Newspaper. CN. German. wk. $0.60 Per No. Kanada Kurier B C Ausgabe, c/o Courier Press, 955 Alexander Avenue, Winnipeg Manitoba R3C 2X8 Canada. DD 071.11. *British Columbia Courier.*

KANADA KURIER. MANITOBA AUSGABE. (KANADA KURIER). V. 91, No. 38 (18 Sept 1980)-. 0712-8894. Newspaper. CN. German. wk. $29.02. Courier Press Ltd, PO Box 1054, Winnipeg Manitoba Canada R3C 2X8 Canada. **Tel** (204)774-1883. Ed E Priebe. DD 071.127. bk rev. adv acc. **Circ** 22,000. National and international news, fashions, travel and sports. *Manitoba Courier der Nordwesten.*

KANADA KURIER. MONTREAL AUSGABE. (KANADA KURIER). V. 91, No. 38 (Sept. 18, 1980)-. 0712-8908. Newspaper. CN. German. wk. $0.60 Per No. Kanada Kurier, Montreal Ausgabe, c/o Courier Press, 955 Alexander Avenue, Winnipeg Manitoba R3C 2X8 Canada. DD 071.14281. *Montreal Courier.*

KANADA KURIER. ONTARIO AUSGABE. (KANADA KURIER). V. 91, No 38 (18 Sept 1980)-. 0712-8916. Newspaper. CN. German. wk. $0.60 Per No. Kanada Kurier Ontario Ausgabe, c/o Courier Press, 955 Alexander Avenue, Winnipeg Manitoba R3C 2X8 Canada. DD 071.13. *Ontario Courier.*

KANADA KURIER. OTTAWA AUSGABE. (KANADA KURIER). V. 91, No. 38 (18 Sept 1980)-. 0712-8924. Newspaper. CN. German. wk. $0.60 Per No. Kanada Kurier Ottawa Ausgabe, c/o Courier Press, 955 Alexander Avenue, Winnipeg Manitoba R3C 2X8 Canada. DD 071.1384. *Ottawa Courier,* 0227-2563.

Newspapers

KANADA KURIER. SASKATCHEWAN AUSGABE. (KANADA KURIER). V. 91, No. 38 (18 Sept. 1980)-. 0712-8932. Newspaper. CN. German. wk. $0.60 Per No. Kanada Kurier, Saskatchewan Ausgabe, c/o Courier Press, 955 Alexander Avenue, Winnipeg Manitoba R3C 2X8 Canada. DD 071.124. *Saskatchewan Courier der Nordwesten.*

KANADA KURIER. TORONTO AUSGABE. (KANADA KURIER). V. 91, No. 38 (18 Sept. 1980)-. 0712-8940. Newspaper. CN. German. wk. $0.60 Per No. Kanada Kurier Toronto Ausgabe, c/o Courier Press, 955 Alexander Avenue, Winnipeg Manitoba R3C 2X8 Canada. DD 071.13541. *Toronto Courier.*

KANADA KURIER. VANCOUVER AUSGABE. (KANADA KURIER). V. 91, No. 38 (18 Sept. 1980)-. 0712-8959. Newspaper. CN. German. wk. $0.60 Per No. Kanada Kurier, Vancouver Ausgabe, c/o Courier Press, 955 Alexander Avenue, Winnipeg Manitoba 3C 2X8 Canada. DD 071.1133. *Vancouver Courier der Nordwesten.*

KANADIER. (DER KANADIER : THE NEWSPAPER OF THE CANADIAN FORCES IN EUROPE). VFOAT L'Hebdomadaire des Forces Canadiennes en Europe. 0175-6346. Newspaper. GW. English (French). wk. Free. Canadian Armed Forces, CFPO 5000, 7630 Lahr Federal Republic of Germany. DD 355.10971. (ctrl).

KANADSKE LISTY. V. 7- Jan. 1973-. 0449-7368. CN. Czech (Slovak). mo. Kanadske Listy Canadian News, Box 520/Station D, Toronto Ontario M6P 3K1 Canada. Tel (416)2784116. LC F1035.C9. DD 971.0049186. *HLAS Novych.*

THE KANSAS CITY JEWISH CHRONICLE. 0022-8524. Newspaper. US. English. wk. $21.00. Kansas City Jewish Chronicle, 7373 West 107th Street, Overland Park KS 66212. Tel (913)648-4620.

THE KANSAS CITY KANSAN. Began with Apr. 3, 1916 issue. Newspaper. US. English. da. $65.00. The Kansas City Kansan, 901 North 8th Street, Kansas City KS 66101. Tel (913)371-4300. LC Newspaper.

KANSAS CITY STAR (KANSAS CITY, MO. : 1885). (THE KANSAS CITY STAR). Began in Sept., 1885. 0745-1067. Newspaper. US. English. Kansas City Star, 1729 Grand Avenue, Kansas City MO 64108. LC Newspaper 7002. *Kansas City Evening Star.*

KANSAS REGISTER. Vol. 1, No. 1 (Jan. 7, 1982)-. 0744-2254. Periodical. US. English. wk. $47.50. Secretary of State, Kansas State Capitol, Topeka KS 66612. Tel (913)296-3489. Ed Nancy R Clark. LC KFK36. DD 348.78101, 347.81081. Index published separately - free - automatically sent. (cum index). Circ 1,500. Official state paper, contains legal notices; contracts for bid; state agency meeting, hearing and public notices; new state laws; legislative bills; administration regulations; attorney general opinions, etc.

KASARA JATA. VFOAT Kesri Jot. V. 1- Aug. 15, 1979-. 0225-2244. Newspaper. CN. Panjabi (includes some text in English). sm. $11.00. Kesri Jot, PO Box 1250/Station B, Mississauga Ontario L4Y 3W5 Canada. DD 071.13535.

KASLO UPDATE. Issue No. 1 (July 1983)-. 0824-5819. Newspaper. CN. English. mo. $0.40 Per No. Kaslo Update, PO Box 1074, Kaslo British Columbia V0G 1M0 Canada. DD 071.1143.

KAUKAUNA TIMES. Vol. 1, No. 1 (Sept. 16, 1880)-. Newspaper. US. English. sw. *Kaukauna Sun.*

KAWARTHA CANADIAN. V. 1- Jan. 14, 1975-. 0318-1847. Newspaper. CN. English. wk. $5. Kawartha Canadian, Rural Route #3, Lakefield Ontario K01 2H0 Canada. DD 071.1367.

KAYHAN INTERNATIONAL. 1967-. 0885-8160. Newspaper. US. English. wk. Kayhan Inc, PO Box 7729, Silver Spring MD 20907. DD 071.

KEENE EVENING SENTINEL. VFOAT New Hampshire Sentinel. Began with Oct. 20, 1890 issue. Newspaper. US. English. da. Keene Evening Sentinel, 60 West Street, Keene NH 03431. LC Newspaper 7002.

KELOWNA TODAY. V. 1- Aug. 26, 1976-. 0227-3489. Newspaper. CN. English. wk. 20 Per No. Kelowna Today, 561 Lawrence Avenue, Kelowna British Columbia V1Y 6L8 Canada. DD 071.1142.

KENNEBECASIS VALLEY POST. VFOAT Valley Post. Vol. 1, No. 1 (Dec. 12, 1979)-. 0228-7897. Newspaper. CN. English. wk. Kennebecasis Valley Post, PO Box 250, Rothesay New Brunswick E0G 2W0 Canada. DD 071.1541.

THE KENTUCKY NEWS. VFOAT KY. News. Vol. 17, No. 4 (Apr. 11, 1984)-. Newspaper. US. English. wk. *Shopper News (Paducah, KY. : 1980).*

THE KENTUCKY PRESS. Began in 1929. 0023-0324. Periodical. US. English. mo. Kentucky Press, 63 Fountain Place, Frankfort KY 40601. LC UNC. DD 071.69.

THE KENTUCKY STANDARD. 8750-0760. Newspaper. US. English. sw. Standard Publishing Company, 110 West Stephan Foster Avenue, Bardstown KY 40004.

KETCHIKAN DAILY NEWS. (THE KETCHIKAN DAILY NEWS). Began with Aug. 1, 1947 issue. 0274-581X. Newspaper. US. English. da. $80.00. Ketchikan Daily News, Box 7900, Ketchikan AK 99901. Tel (907)225-3157. Ed Heidi Ekstrund. LC Newspaper. bk rev. adv acc. Circ 4,600. Local, national and international news. *Ketchikan Daily Alaska Fishing News.*

KETTLE RIVER ECHO. (THE KETTLE RIVER ECHO). 0715-5360. Newspaper. CN. English. bw. $4.50. Kettle River Echo, Box 65/Rock Creek, British Columbia V0H 1Y0 Canada. DD 071.1141.

THE KEY WEST CITIZEN. Began in 1879. Newspaper. US. English. ir. $80.60. Key West Citizen, PO Box 1120, Key West FL 33041. Tel (305)294-6641. LC Newspaper 7448-X.

KING TOWNSHIP WEEKLY. (THE KING TOWNSHIP WEEKLY). V. 1, No. 25- Nov. 20, 1974. 0380-3686. Newspaper. CN. English. wk. The King Township Weekly, PO Box 331, Woodbridge Ontario L4L 1B2 Canada. DD 071.1354. *King Township & Nobleton Advertiser, 0380-3678.*

KINGSTON REPORTER. Vol. 1, No. 1 (Feb. 9, 1984)-. 0747-2692. Newspaper. US. English. wk. The Kingston Reporter, PO Box 959, Plymouth MA 02360. *Silver Lake News, 0746-6064.*

KINGSTON THIS WEEK. 0712-9068. Newspaper. CN. English. wk. Free. Kingston This Week, 677 Gardiners Road, Kingston Ontario K7M 3Y4 Canada. DD 071.1372. (ctrl). *Kingston Shoppers News, 0228-0507.*

KITCHENER-WATERLOO RECORD. (KITCHENER-WATERLOO RECORD MICROFORM). VFOAT Kitchener-Waterloo. Jan. 1948-. 0824-5150. Newspaper. CN. English. DD 071.1345. *Kitchener Daily Record.*

THE KNICKERBOCKER NEWS. V. 1, No. 1- 197-. Periodical. US. English. da. $135.00. Capitol Newspaper Group, Box 15-627/Mail Subscription Department, Albany NY 12212. Tel (518)454-5704.

THE KNICKERBOCKER NEWS, UNION-STAR. VFOAT Knickerbocker News. Vol. 32, No. 251 (Apr. 28, 1969)-V. 40, No. 82 (Oct. 6, 1975). Newspaper. US. English. ir. Bell & Howell, Micro Photo Division, Old Mansfield Road, Wooster OH 44691. Tel (216)264-6666. Ed R G Fichenberg. LC Newspaper. Available on microfilm from Microphoto Division, Bell and Howell Co. *Knickerbocker News (Albany, N.Y. : 1937), Union-Star.*

KNOXVILLE GAZETTE. V. 1- 197 -. Periodical. US. English. bm. PO Box 3071, Knoxville TN 37917.

KNOXVILLE JOURNAL (KNOXVILLE, IOWA). (KNOXVILLE JOURNAL). Began with June 11, 1874 issue. Newspaper. US. English. wk. Marion County Publishing Company, PO Boz 458, Knoxville IA 50138. Tel (515)842-2155. LC Newspaper. *Iowa Voter, Melcher Union.*

KOKOMO TRIBUNE. (THE KOKOMO TRIBUNE). Began in 1850. 0746-2034. Newspaper. US. English. da. Kokomo Tribune, 300 North Union Street, Kokomo IN 46901. LC Newspaper 7701-X.

THE KOKOMO TRIBUNE (1929). (THE KOKOMO TRIBUNE). Vol. 46, No. 257 (July 24, 1929)-. Newspaper. US. English. da. $98.80. The Kokomo Tribune, 300 North Union Street, Kokomo IN 46901. Tel (317)459-3121.

KOMSOMOL'SKAIA PRAVDA. Began publication in May 1925. Newspaper. UR. Russian. da. $32.50. Victor Kamkin Inc, 12224 Parklawn Drive, Rockville MD 20852. Tel (301)881-5973.

KOOTENAY GRAPEVINE. (THE KOOTENAY GRAPEVINE). Vol. 1, No. 1 (Jan. 13, 1981)-. 0715-4593. Newspaper. CN. English. wk. Free. Kootenay Grapevine, 501D Vernon Street, Nelson British Columbia V1L 3E9 Canada. DD 071.1144.

THE KOREA HERALD. Newspaper. English. da. $52.00. Korea Herald, 250 West 54th Street/7th Floor, New York NY 10019. Tel (212)582-5205. Ed Kyu Jang Choi. bk rev. adv acc. Circ 5,000. Only English newspaper published daily covering developments in Korea. Edited in New York for the American reader, presenting the latest news of business, culture, or politics in Korea.

KOREA TIMES. TORONTO EDITION. (THE KOREA TIMES). VFOAT Hankookilbo (Toronto), Hankulibo (Toronto). No. 528 (June 1, 1981)-. 0712-1733. Newspaper. CN. Korean. da. $90.00. Korea Times, 1025 Dupont Street, Toronto Ontario M6H 1Z7 Canada. DD 071.13541. *Canada News, 0319-2962.*

KOREAN JOURNAL. (THE KOREAN JOURNAL). V. 1- Nov. 26, 1972-. 0700-3226. Periodical. CN. Korean. Y R Ryu, 257 Olive Avenue, Willowdale Ontario M2N 4P5 Canada. DD 071.13541.

KUANG MING RIBAO. Newspaper. CC. Chinese. da. China Publication Centre, PO Box 2820, Beijing China.

KURISUCHYON HEROLDU. VFOAT Christian Herald. Began in 1977. 0749-0143. Newspaper. US. Korean. wk. $40.00. Christian Herald, 801 South Wilton Place, Los Angeles CA 90005. DD 071.

KURYER ZJEDNOCZENIA. (KURYER ZJEDNOCZENIA : OFFICAL ORGAN OF THE UNION OF POLES IN AMERICA). VFOAT Polish Courier. Began in 1939. 0744-8910. Newspaper. US. Polish (English). mo. $4.00. Kuryer Publishers Company, 6805 Lansing Avenue, Cleveland OH 44105. *Kuryer, Zjednoczeniec.*

A LA PAGE (STE-MARIE (BEAUCE, QUEBEC). (A LA PAGE). Vol. 1, No, 1 (27 April 1984)-. 0824-1481. Newspaper. CN. French. wk. A la Page, c/o M Pierre Gregoire C P 1195 55 Nord rue Notre-Dame, St-Marie Beauce Quebec G6E 3C3 Canada. DD 071.1471.

THE LA PORTE HERALD-ARGUS. Began in 1888. Newspaper. US. English. da. Herald-Argus, 701 State Street, La Porte IN 46350. Tel (219)362-2161. LC Newspaper 7002.

LABRADORIAN. (THE LABRADORIAN). 0715-4941. Newspaper. CN. English. $0.25 Per Number. The Labradorian, Happy Valley-Goose Bay, PO Box 484, Labrador Newfoundland A0P 1C0 Canada. DD 071.182.

LACON HOME JOURNAL. Began with June 27, 1866 issue. Newspaper. US. English. wk. $14.00. Home Journal, 204 South Washington Street, Lacon IL 61540. Tel (309)246-2865. LC Newspaper 7663. *Illinois Gazette.*

LAIKS (BROOKLYN, N.Y. : 1949). (LAIKS). VFOAT Time. Began in 1949. Newspaper. US. Latvian. sw. Laiks, 7307 Third Avenue, Brooklyn NY 11209.

LAISVE. VFOAT Liberty. Began with Apr. 5, 1911 issue. 0044-703X. Newspaper. US. Lithuanian (some advertisements in English). sm. $12.00 US, $15.00 Canada. Laisve, 102-02 Liberty Avenue, Ozone Park NY 11417. DD 071.

LAKE CHARLES AMERICAN PRESS. 0739-1196. Newspaper. US. English. da. $84.00. Lake Charles American Press, 327 Broad Street, Lake Charles LA 70601. Tel (318)439-2781. Ed Jim Bean. bk rev. adv acc. Circ 42,000. Daily newspaper.

LAKE ELSINORE VALLEY SUN-TRIBUNE. VAT Lake Elsinore Valley Sun Tribune. 0745-1350. Newspaper. US. English. wk. $12.00. Lake Elsinore Valley Sun, PO Box 86, Lake Elsinore CA 92330. Tel (714)674-1535.

LAKE FORESTER. 0744-7973. Newspaper. US. English. wk. $20.75. Pioneer Press, 1232 Central Avenue, Wilmette IL 60091. Tel (312)251-4300.

THE LAKE NEWS. 8750-3689. Newspaper. US. English. wk. $7.50. Lake News, PO Box 498, Calvert City KY 42029. Tel (502)395-5858. Ed Loyd W Ford. bk rev. adv acc. Circ 4,500. General interest newspaper located in a top tourist and resort area adjacent to the largest developed man-made lake in the world.

Newspapers

LAKE PARK JOURNAL. Newspaper. US. English. wk. $8.00. Lake Park Journal, Lake Park MN 56554. Tel (218)238-5828. Ed Gerald W Schlueter. adv acc. **Circ** 1,000.

THE LAKE WORTH HERALD. Began in 1912. Newspaper. US. English. wk. $10.00. Lake Worth Herald, 130 South H Street, Lake Worth FL 33460. Tel (305)585-9387. LC Newspaper 7002.

LAKEFIELD, THE CHRONICLE. VFOAT Lakefield Chronicle. Vol. 1, No. 1 (Oct. 6, 1982)-. 3241-4816. Newspaper. CN. English. wk. $10.00 Domestic, $25.00 Foreign. Lakefield Chronicle, PO Box 250, Marmora Ontario K0K 2M0 Canada. **DD** 071.1367.

THE LAKER. Newspaper. US. English. wk. $12.00. The Laker, PO Box 82, Mound MN 55364. Tel (612)472-1140.

LAKESIDE LEADER. 0821-3372. Newspaper. CN. English. wk. $9.00. Lakeside Leader, PO Box 1700, Slave Lake Alberta T0G 2A0 Canada. **DD** 071.1231. *Northland Free Press, 0821-3380.*

LAKEWOOD SENTINEL. VFOAT Sentinel. 0747-2013. Newspaper. US. English. wk. $16.25. Sentinal Publications Co, PO Box 15457, Lakewood CO 80215.

LAMBTON COUNTY GAZETTE. (THE LAMBTON COUNTY GAZETTE). V. 1- April 1, 1976-. 0383-8080. Newspaper. CN. English. wk. Free. Sarnia Gazette Publishing Company Ltd, 287 Front Street North, PO Box 99, Sarnia Ontario N7T 5S6 Canada. **DD** 071.1327.

LANAIAN (LANAI CITY, HAWAII : 1978). (THE LANAIAN). Newspaper. US. English. mo. Lanai Community Services Council, PO Box 327, Lanai City HI 96763.

LANCASTER INDEPENDENT PRESS. V. 1- 1969-. Newspaper. US. English. wk. Lancaster Independent Press, PO Box 275, Lancaster PA 17604. Available on microfilm (in underground newspaper collection).

THE LAND. Periodical. AT. English. wk. $330.55. Land Newspaper Ltd, PO Box 299, Windsor New South Wales 2756 Australia.

LAND O LAKES MIRROR. VFOAT Land O'Lakes Mirror, Mirror. V. 1- 1971-. 0196-5840. Periodical. US. English. qt. $2.50 Domestic, $4.50 Foreign, $1.00 Members. Land O'Lakes Mirror, 4001 North Lexington Avenue, St Paul MN 55112. *Land O'Langes News, Felco Mirror.*

LANGFORD TO COLWOOD TELEGRAM. VFOAT Telegram. V. 1- Jan. 29, 1975-. 0380-4607. Newspaper. CN. English. wk. Community News, 506 David Street, Victoria British Columbia V8T 2C8 Canada. **DD** 071.1134.

LANGLEY LOCAL NEWS. V. 1- May 10, 1978-. 0228-0582. Newspaper. CN. English. wk. Free. Langley Local News Ltd, 20216 Fraser Highway, Langley British Columbia V3A 4E7 Canada. **DD** 071.1133. (ctrl).

LANGLEY TIMES. Vol. 1, No. 1 (Feb. 18, 1981)-. 0711-7450. Newspaper. CN. English. wk. Free. Langley Times Publishing Company, 102-20560-56th Avenue, Langley British Columbia V3A 4S1 Canada. **DD** 071.1133. (ctrl).

THE LANSING STAR. Series/Titl Bell and Howell Underground Press Collection. Newspaper. US. English. mo.

LANSING STATE JOURNAL. Vol. 126, No.120 (August 25, 1980)-. 0274-9742. Newspaper. US. English. da. $135.50. Gannet Corp, 120 East Lenawee Street, Lansing MI 48919. Also available on microfilm from Bell & Howell. *State Journal (Lansing, Mi. : 1911).*

LANTZVILLE LOG. (THE LANTZVILLE LOG). 0710-5487. Newspaper. CN. English. mo. Free to Residents, $4.00 Per Year Others. Box 114, Lantzville British Columbia V0R 2H0 Canada. **DD** 071.1134. *Lantzville Newsletter.*

LAS VEGAS VOICE. Began in 1963?. 0023-8546. Newspaper. US. English. wk. Las Vegas Voice, POB 4686, Las Vegas NV 89106. Ed D Baker. Available on microfilm from Microphoto Division, Bell & Howell, Wooster, Ohio.

LATINO. Edicion Numero 38- 29 Oct./4 Nov. 1979-. 0226-0611. Newspaper. CN. Spanish. wk. $12.00. Latino, Suite 501/344 Bloor Street West, Toronto Ontario M5S 1W9 Canada. **DD** 071.13541. *Toronto Latino, 0226-062X.*

THE LAUREL LEADER-CALL. VFOAT Laurel Leader Call. Began with Feb. 3, 1930 issue. Newspaper. US. English. da. Laurel Leader-Call, 130 Beacon Street, Laurel MS 39440. Ed J W West. LC Newspaper 7002. *Laurel Daily Leader, Morning Call (Laurel, Miss.).*

LAVORO ITALIANO. Yearly V. 1- May 27, 1949-. Periodical. IT. Italian. wk. $14.26. Lavoro Italiano, Via Lucullo 6, 00187 Roma Italy.

LAWRENCE DAILY JOURNAL-WORLD. VFOAT Lawrence Daily Journal World. Journal V. 55, No. 43 (Feb. 20, 1911)-V. 55, No. 65 (Mar. 16, 1911). Newspaper. US. English. da. $56.76. Lawrence Daily Journal World, Box 888, Lawrence KS 66044. Tel (913)843-1000. Ed Dolph C Simons Jr. LC Newspapers 7002. adv acc. **Circ** 19,059. Daily, general circulation news paper with news emphasis on Lawrence, Kansas and area communities and the University of Kansas. *Lawrence Daily World, Lawrence Daily Journal.*

LE MONDE. REIMPRESSION EN MINIFORMAT. (LE MONDE). Dec. 19, 1944-. 0153-789X. Newspaper. FR. French. da. $126.91. Le Monde Service Abonnements, BP 50709, 75422 Paris Cedex 09 France. Tel 246-72-23. **Ind/Abst** Funk Scott Index Corp. Ind.

LEADER. (THE LEADER). VFOAT Le Leader. Vol. 1, No. 1 (Sept. 1981)-. 0713-7761. Periodical. CN. English (French). bm. Free. Leader, PO Box 8333, Ottawa Ontario K1G 3V5 Canada. **DD** 071.1383.

LEADER. ENNISMORE, SMITH TWP. (THE LEADER, ENNISMORE, SMITH TWP). Began Publication in Oct. or Nov. 1976. 0706-8840. Newspaper. CN. English. wk. Free to Residents, $5.00 Others. The Leader Press, Box 610, Lakefield Ontario K0L 2H0 Canada. **DD** 071.1367. *Leader, Ennismore, Bridgenorth and Smith, 0706-8832.*

LEADER (GARFIELD HEIGHTS, OHIO). (THE LEADER). 8750-8095. Newspaper. US. English. wk. The Leader, 4818 Turney Road, Garfield Heights OH 44125. *Garfield Heights Leader.*

LEADER (POINT PLEASANT BEACH, N.J.). (THE LEADER). 0745-6816. Newspaper. US. English. wk. The Leader, PO Box 1771, Point Pleasant Beach NJ 08742.

LEADING STAR. VFOAT Ledstjarnan. 0744-7485. Periodical. US. English. mo. Leading Star, 515 Union Street, Seattle WA 98101.

LEASIDE VILLAGER. (THE LEASIDE VILLAGER). Vol. 1, No. 1 (Sept. 16, 1981)-. 0715-4631. Newspaper. CN. English. mo. Free. c/o Town Crier Inc, 3 Massey Square, Toronto Ontario M4C 5L5 Canada. **DD** 071.13541. (ctrl).

THE LEAVEN. V. 1- July 6, 1979-. 0194-9799. Periodical. US. English. wk. $8.00. The Leaven, 2220 Central, Box 2329, Kansas City KS 66110. Tel (913)621-4131. *Eastern Kansas Register, 0012-883X.*

THE LEDGER. 0163-0288. Periodical. US. English. da. $140.40. Lakeland Ledger, PO Box 408, Lakeland FL 33802.

THE LEESVILLE LEADER. Began in 1898?. 0747-1998. Newspaper. US. English. da. The Leesville Leader, PO Box 619, Leesville LA 71446.

LEMONT METROPOLITAN. VFOAT MET. 8750-6998. Newspaper. US. English. wk. Lemont Metropolitan, PO Box 1399, Bolingbrook IL 60439.

THE LETHBRIDGE HERALD MICROFORM. Newspaper. CN. English. Commonwealth Microfilm Limited, 760 Gordon Baker Road, Willowdale Ontario M2H 3B4 Canada. **DD** 071.1233.

LETOPIS' GAZETNYKH STATEI. Began in 1936. 0024-1172. UR. Russian. wk. $94.00. Victor Kamkin Inc (57602), 12224 Parklawn Drive, Rockville MD 20852. Tel (301)881-5973. LC Al15. NLM ZAI 15 L646.

LEWISTON JOURNAL. Oct. 15, 1979-. Newspaper. US. English. da. Lewiston Journal, 104 Park Street, Lewiston ME 02420. LC Newspaper. *Lewiston Evening Journal.*

LEWISTON MORNING TRIBUNE. Began with Sept. 1, 1892 issue. Newspaper. US. English. da. $97.20. Tribune Publishing Company, PO Box 957, Lewiston ID 83501. Tel (208)743-9411. LC Newspaper 7002.

THE LEXINGTON ADVERTISER. Began with Jan. 4, 1907 issue. Newspaper. US. English. wk. *Times-Advertiser.*

THE LEXINGTON HERALD. VFOAT Saturday Herald-Leader. Began in 1905. Newspaper. US. English. da. Tel (606)231-3100. bk rev. adv acc. **Circ** 114,203. *Morning Herald.*

LIAISON ST-LOUIS. VFOAT Liais-o-n-St-Louis. V. 1- Mar. 1977-. 0704-6723. Newspaper. CN. French (text in English, Spanish, and Greek). ir. Free. Journal Liaison St-Louis Inc, 3950 Avenue de l'Hotel-de-Ville, Montreal Quebec H2T 1C5 Canada. **DD** 071.14281.

LIBAN AU CANADA. Vol. 1-. 0705-7970. Newspaper. CN. French (text in English and Arabic). wk. 0.50 Per No. Publications Y H, Liban au Canada, 7619 rue St-Hubert, Montreal Quebec H2R 2N7 Canada. **DD** 071.14281.

LIBERTYVILLE REVIEW. 0744-852X. Newspaper. US. English. wk. $9.50. Pioneer Press, 1232 Central Avenue, Wilmette IL 60091. Tel (312)251-4300.

LIGHT II. VFOAT Light 2. Sept. 13, 1984-. 8750-2755. Newspaper. US. English. wk. $16.00 San Diego Co., $24.50 50 elsewhere in US. Light II, PO Box 1927, La Jolla CA 92038.

LIGHTHOUSE LOG. (THE LIGHTHOUSE LOG). 0824-6068. Newspaper. CN. English. wk. $0.20 Per No. Lighthouse Log c/o Lighthouse Publishing, 353 York Street, Bridgewater Nova Scotia B4V 3K1 Canada. **DD** 071.1623.

THE LINCOLN DAILY STAR. Began with Oct. 2, 1902 issue. Newspaper. US. English. da. Journal Star Printing Company, 926 P Street, Lincoln NE 68508. LC Newspaper 8663-X.

LINCOLN JOURNAL. Apr. 11, 1977-. Newspaper. US. English. da. Journal Star Printing Company, 926 P Street, Lincoln NE 68508. LC Newspaper. *Lincoln Evening Journal (Lincoln, Neb. : 1973).*

LINDSAY THIS WEEK. V. 1- Sept. 13, 1978-. 0228-0566. Newspaper. CN. English. wk. 20. Per No. Lindsay This Week Ltd, 64 Lindsay Street South, Lindsay Ontario K9V 2V2 Canada. **DD** 071.1364.

THE LITCHFIELD COUNTY TIMES. 0744-6705. Newspaper. US. English. wk. $21.00. Litchfield County Times, 32 Main Street, New Milford CT 06776. Tel (203)355-4141. Ed John Sicher. bk rev. adv acc. **Circ** 10,100. An upscale weekly newspaper covering major news stories in Litchfield County, Connecticut. Includes a feature/life section and business/real estate/classified section.

LITTLE BEND. V. 1- Sept., 1974-. 0316-6902. Newspaper. CN. English. bm. 15. Per No. Westco Enterprises Limited, PO Box 250, Petitcodiac New Brunswick E0A 2H0 Canada. **DD** 071.1523.

LITTLETON INDEPENDENT. 0744-7949. Newspaper. US. English. wk. Beacon Minute Man Corporation, PO Box 217, Acton MA 07120. Tel (617)263-3761. *Independent.*

LOCAL EXCHANGE. (THE LOCAL EXCHANGE). V. 1- Sept. 7, 1977-. 0706-7046. Periodical. CN. English. wk. $8. The Local Exchange, PO Box 1400, Fort Quappelle Saskatchewan S0G 1S0 Canada. **DD** 071.1244.

LONDON TRIBUNE. Vol. 1, No. 1 (Sept. 4, 1980)-. 0710-281X. Newspaper. CN. English. wk. $0.25 Per Number. London Tribune, 364 Richmond Street, London Ontario N6A 3C3 Canada. **DD** 071.1326.

LONG ISLAND JEWISH WORLD. 0199-2899. Periodical. US. English. ir. $15.00. Long Island Jewish World, PO Box 948, Farmingdale NY 11737. Tel (516)829-4000. *Jewish World.*

LOOKOUT. (THE LOOKOUT). V. 1- Sept. 1, 1976-. 0383-8102. Periodical. CN. English. wk. $12. The Lookout, PO Box 1359, Sioux Lookout Ontario P0V 2T0 Canada. **DD** 071.13112.

LOS ANGELES HERALD EXAMINER. V. 107, No. 44 (May 13, 1977)-. Newspaper. US. English. da. Los Angeles Herald-Examiner, Box 2416/Terminal Annex, Los Angeles CA 90051. Tel (213)744-8311. LC Newspaper. Available on Microfilm. *Los Angeles Evening and Sunday Herald Examiner.*

LOS ANGELES SENTINEL. 1933?-. Newspaper. US. English. wk. $25.00. Los Angeles Sentinel, 1112 East 43rd Street, Los Angeles CA

Newspapers

90011. Tel (213)232-3261. Ed Ruth Washington. bk rev. adv acc. **Circ** 39,800. (ctrl).

THE LOS ANGELES TIMES. VFOAT Los Angeles Daily Times. V. 10, No. 119 (Oct. 23, 1886)-. 0458-3035. Newspaper. US. English. da. $234.00. Los Angeles Times, Times Mirror Square, Los Angeles CA 90053. Tel (213)972-4959. **Ind/Abst** Infobank. LC Newspaper 7114-X. Also available on microfilm from the Micro Photo Div., Bell & Howell Co. and the Los Angeles Times Microfilm Services. *Los Angeles Daily Times.*

THE LOUISBURG HERALD. VFOAT Herald. Began with July 4, 1876 issue. 8750-6378. Newspaper. US. English. wk. The Louisburg Herald, Box 99 Louisburg KS 66053. LC Newspaper 7845.

THE LOUISVILLE MESSENGER. 0746-0961. Newspaper. US. English. wk. $11.00 Cass County, $13.00 elsewhere. Louisville Messenger, PO Box 235, Louisville NE 68037.

LOUISVILLE TIMES (1885). (THE LOUISVILLE TIMES). Began in 1885. Newspaper. US. English. da. Louisville Courier Journal, 525 West Broadway, Louisville KY 40202. Tel (800)626-6315. LC Newspaper 7885-X. *Evening Times.*

LOVELAND HERALD. 0745-2756. Newspaper. US. English. wk. $11.00. Cincinnati Suburan Press, 1329 Arlington Street, Cincinnati OH 45225. Tel (513)542-9474.

LUCAN TOWNE CRIER. (THE LUCAN TOWNE CRIER). Dec. 1983-. 0826-3159. Periodical. CN. English. mo. Free. Lucan Towne Crier, R R 3, Lucan Ontario N0M 2J0 Canada. DD 071.1325.

LUMBY REVIEW. Vol. 1, No. 1 (Mar. 26, 1981)-. 0715-4569. Newspaper. CN. English. wk. $0.15 Per No. Lumby Review, Box 160, Lumby British Columbia Canada. DD 071.1142.

LUSITANO. (O LUSITANO). No. 1- July 21, 1978-. 0707-5324. Newspaper. CN. Portuguese. bw. $4.00. O Lusitano, 1236 Valentine Drive, Cambridge Ontario N3H 2N8 Canada. DD 071.1344.

LUSO AMERICANO. Began in 1928. Newspaper. US. Portuguese (English). wk. 88 Ferry Street, Newark NJ 07105. LC Newspaper.

MAARIV. Newspaper. IS. Hebrew. da. $180.00. Maariv Promotions Ltd, PO Box 20010, Tel Aviv Isreal. Tel (212)679-5767.

THE MABUHAY REPUBLIC. Newspaper. US. English. $2.00. Mabuhay Republic, 833 Market Street/Suite 502, San Francisco CA 94103. Tel 392-1261. *Mabuhay.*

MCCURTAIN GAZETTE. Began in 1905. Newspaper. US. English. sw. 109 South Central Street, Idabel OK 74745. LC Newspaper 7002. Also available on microfilm from Oklahoma Historical Society. *Signal.*

MCINTOSH TIMES. 1888. Newspaper. US. English. wk. $31.00. McIntosh Times, McIntosh MN 56556. Tel (218)563-3585. Ed Richard Richards. bk rev. adv acc. **Circ** 1,700. (ctrl). Small town newspaper servicing our merchants and advertisers. Interesting to our readers.

MACKENZIE DRIFT. V. 1- Apr. 3, 1979-. 0228-0558. Newspaper. CN. English. bw. 10.00 NWT and Yukon, 12.50 Southern Canada, 18.00 all other countries. Rosmar Publications, PO Box 2600, Inuvik NWT X0E 0T0 Canada. DD 071.196.

MACKLIN MIRROR. V. 1- Nov. 10, 1977-. 0706-7240. Newspaper. CN. English. bw. $5. Canada, $7 Foreign. Holmes Publishing Company, Box 100, Macklin Sask S0L 2C0 Canada. DD 071.1242.

MACON BEACON. Began in 1862?. Newspaper. US. English. wk. Beacon, PO Box 32, Macon MS 39341. LC Newspaper 8525-X. *Union Beacon.*

MACON COUNTY TIMES. 0745-5976. Newspaper. US. English. wk. Macon County Times, PO Box 69, Lafayette TN 37083.

MADOC NEWS. (THE MADOC NEWS). V. 1- Apr. 5, 1978-. 0706-7011. Newspaper. CN. English. The Madoc News, Box 655, Madoc Ont K0K 2K0 Canada. DD 071.13585.

MADOC REVIEW. 0712-4910. Periodical. CN. English. wk. $8.00 Canada, $20.00 Others. Madoc Review, 21 Street Lawrence Street, Madoc Ontario L0K 2K0 Canada. DD 071.13585. *North Hastings Review.*

THE MAGNA TIMES. 0748-7363. Newspaper. US. English. wk. $8.00. Magna Times, 9124 West 2700 S, Magna UT 84044.

THE MAINE PAPER. 0199-154X. Newspaper. US. English. wk. Maine Paper, PO Box 71, Hallowell ME 04347. Tel (207)622-4783.

MAINE TIMES. Began Oct. 4, 1968. 0025-0783. Newspaper. US. English. wk. $18.00. Maine Times, 41 Main Street, Topsham ME 04086. Tel (207)729-0126. Ed Peter Cox. bk rev. adv acc. **Circ** 20,000. (ctrl). Newspaper focusing on current issues and news of Maine with particular emphasis on environment, regional industries, coastal development and cultural affairs.

MAINICHI DAILY NEWS. No. 1- April 12, 1922-. Newspaper. US. English. da. Overseas Courier Service, 27-08 42nd Road, Long Island NY 11101. Tel (718)392-2070.

MAIZE THIS WEEK. VFOAT Maize This Week Colwich News. 0745-9947. Newspaper. US. English. wk. Maize This Week, 521 East Murdock, Wichita KS 67214.

MAKEDONSKA TRIBUNA. VFOAT Macedonian Tribune. 0024-9009. Periodical. US. Bulgarian (with some English). wk. $12.00 Domestic, $15.00 Foreign. Macedonian Patriotic Organization, 124 W Wayne, Fort Wayne IN 46802-2505. Tel (219)422-5900. Ed Dorie Atzeff. bk rev. adv acc. **Circ** 2,500. Bi-weekly newspaper published by the Central Committee of the Macedonian Patriotic Organization.

THE MALIBU SURFSIDE NEWS. 0191-7307. Newspaper. US. English. wk. $10.00. Malibu Surfside News, PO Box 903, Malibu CA 90265. Tel (213)457-2112.

MALTON PILOT. (THE MALTON PILOT). 0700-8082. Newspaper. CN. English. wk. Offset Publications, 7205 Goreway Drive, Mississauga Ontario L4T 2T9 Canada. DD 071.13535.

MANCHESTER GUARDIAN WEEKLY WITH LE MONDE, ENGLISH SECTION. 0025-200X. Newspaper. UK. English. wk. $98.00. Manchester Guardian, Eve NWS 20 East 53rd Street, New York NY 10022. Tel (212)688-1330. **Ind/Abst** Infobank.

MANITOBA CHINESE POST. V. 1- Nov. 1978-. 0708-9457. Newspaper. CN. Chinese. mo. Free. Manitoba Chinese Post, PO Box 58, Winnipeg Manitoba R3C 3K3 Canada. DD 071.1274.

MANKATO FREE PRESS (MANKATO, MINN. : 1887). (MANKATO FREE PRESS). Began with Apr. 7, 1887 issue. Newspaper. US. English. da. $71.95. Mankato Free Press, 418 South 2nd Street, Mankato MN 56001. Tel (507)625-4451. Ed Ken Berg. LC Newspaper 7002. adv acc. **Circ** 27,500. Daily newspaper.

MANNVILLE REFLECTIONS. V. 1- July 18, 1978-. 0228-054X. Newspaper. CN. English. wk. $5.00 Local, $7.00 Other Parts of Canada, $10.00 Other Countries. Mannville Reflections Ltd, PO Box 444, Mannville Alberta T0B 2W0 Canada. DD 071.1233.

MANOTICK NEWS. (THE MANOTICK NEWS). 0700-8058. Periodical. CN. English. wk. $6.00. J Curry, PO Box 610, Stittsville Ontario K0A 3G0 Canada. DD 071.1383.

MAPLEWOOD REVIEW. Newspaper. US. English. wk. T R Lillie, 2515 East 7th Avenue North, St Paul MN 55109.

MAQUIGNON DE LEVRARD. (LE MAQUIGNON DE LEVRARD). 0228-2763. Periodical. CN. French. mo. Le Maquignon de l'Evrard, 614 rue Saint-Antoine, Sainte-Sophie-de-l'Evrard Quebec G0X 3C0 Canada. DD 071.1455.

MARCO POLO. (IL MARCO POLO). Vol. 1- Oct. 1974-. 0319-1699. Newspaper. CN. text in Italian and English. ir. 25 Per No. Il Marco Polo, PO Box 204/Station A, Vancouver British Columbia V6B 2M3 Canada. DD 071.1133.

MARSHALLTOWN TIMES-REPUBLICAN (1923 : DAILY). (MARSHALLTOWN TIMES-REPUBLICAN). VFOAT Times-Republican. Vol. 49, No. 216 (Sept. 11, 1923)-V. 100, No. 29 (Feb. 2, 1974). Newspaper. US. English. ir. $57.20. Times-Republican, Marshalltown IA 50158. LC Newspaper 7002. *Evening Times-Republican.*

THE MARTIN COUNTY MERCURY. VFOAT Mercury. 0883-3745. Newspaper. US. English. wk. $19.00. Martin County Publishing Company, PO Box 246, Inez KY 41224. Tel (606)298-3711. Ed Sandance K Howard. adv acc. **Circ** 3,500. (ctrl). Newspaper covering Martin, County, Kentucky, Mingo and Wayne counties in West Virginia sepcifically and Lawerence, Pike, and Johnson counties in Kentucky.

MASON CITY GLOBE-GAZETTE. VFOAT Mason City Globe Gazette. Began in 1893. Newspaper. US. English. da. $100.00. Globe Gazette, Box 271, Mason City IA 50401. Tel (515)423-4270. LC Newspaper 7800.

MATCHEDASH MIRROR. Began with Jan. 1, 1978 Issue. 0707-5421. Newspaper. CN. English. sm. $5.50 Domestic, $6.00 US, $7.00 Other Countries. Matchedash Mirror, Box 291, Washago Ontario L0K 2B0 Canada. DD 071.1317.

THE MAUI NEWS. VFOAT Semi-Weekly Maui News. Vol. 1, No. 1 (Feb. 17, 1900)-. 8750-457X. Newspaper. US. English. da. Maui Publishing Company, PO Box 550, Wailuku Maui HI 96793-0550. LC Newspaper.

THE MAYVILLE NEWS. 0749-7105. Newspaper. US. English. wk. $8.00 In-State, $10.00 Out-of-State. Mayville News Inc, 126 Bridge Street PO Box 271, Mayville WI 53050.

MEAFORD CENTENNIAL. (THE MEAFORD CENTENNIAL). V. 1- June 6, 1974-. 0319-1672. Newspaper. CN. English. wk. $4.00 Senior Citizens, $6.00 Others Domestic, $8.00 Foreign. The Meaford Centennial, PO Box 1509, 39 Sykes Street, Meaford Ontario N0H 1Y0 Canada. DD 071.1318.

MEIE ELU. Newspaper. CN. Estonian. wk. Estonian Publ Company Toronto Ltd, 958 Broadview Avenue, Toronto Ontario M4K 2R6 Canada. Tel (416)466-0951.

MELROSE PARK HERALD WITH NEWS OF STONE PARK. VFOAT Melrose Park Herald. 0745-3744. Newspaper. US. English. wk. Pioneer Press Inc, 1232 Central, Wilmette IL 60091. *Herald.*

MEMBERSHIP DIRECTORY - SUBURBAN NEWSPAPERS OF AMERICA. See Yearbooks, Almanacs, Directories.

MENARD TIME. V. 1-. US. English. mo. $3.00. Menard Time, Menard Correctional Center, Menard IL 62239. LC Microfilm 05482 HV, HV9475.I32.

MENSUEL DE LACHUTE. (LE MENSUEL DE LACHUTE). VFOAT Journal le Mensuel de Lachute Enr. V. 1, No. 1, (Dec. 1983)-. 0824-9040. Newspaper. CN. French. mo. Free to citizens of Lachute and its surroundings. Journal le Mensuel de Lachute, Enr 1117 rue Gilles Vigneault, Blainville Quebec J7C 2X8 Canada. DD 071.1423.

MENSUEL DE STE-DOROTHEE. (LE MENSUEL DE STE-DOROTHEE). 0823-6941. Newspaper. CN. French. mo. Free to Citizens. Mensuel de Ste-Dorothee, C P 123 Succursale Ste-Dorothee, Laval Quebec H7X 2T5 Canada. DD 071.14271.

MERCREDI SOIR. (LE MERCREDI SOIR). 0710-3794. Newspaper. CN. French. wk. Free. Mercredi Soir, Les Editions le Mercredi Soir, CP 4070, Val-Belair Quebec G0A 1G0 Canada. DD 071.1447.

MERDEKA. Oct. 1, 1945-. Newspaper. English. da. Merdeka Press, JI M Sangadji 11, Jakarta Indonesia.

THE MEREDITH NEWS. Began in July 1880. Newspaper. US. English. wk. Meredith News, 5 Water Street, Meredith NH 03253. LC Newspaper 8701-X.

THE MERIDIAN STAR. Began in 1911?. Newspaper. US. English. da. Meridian Star, 814 Twenty-Second Avenue Box 1591, Meridian MS 39301. LC Newspaper. *Evening Star.*

MERIDIANO. (IL MERIDIANO). V. 1- Oct. 1979-. 0225-6878. Newspaper. CN. Italian (English). DD 971.14400451.

LA MESA COURIER. 0744-8759. Newspaper. US. English. wk. $12.00. La Mesa Courier, PO Box 216, La Mes CA 92041. Tel (714)461-1021.

MESSAGER DE LA MINGANIE. (LE MESSAGER DE LA MINGANIE). Vol. 1, No. 1 (3 Sept. 1980)-. 0713-6862. Newspaper. CN. French. wk. Free. Le Messager de la Minganie, 74 rue Lemaire, Sept-Iles Quebec G4S 1A3 Canada. DD 071.1417.

MESSAGER DORVAL. (LE MESSAGER DORVAL). 0821-4174. Newspaper. CN. English (French). bw. $20.00. Dorval Messenger, 1015 Notre-Dame, Lachine Quebec H8S 2C3 Canada. DD 071.1428.

Newspapers

MESSAGER REGIONAL. 0713-326X. Newspaper. CN. French. wk. $15.00. Messager Regional, CP 1119, St-Jovite Quebec Canada. DD 071.144. *Messager (St-Jovite, Quebec), 0713-3251.*

MESSAGGERO DI OTTAWA. (IL MESSAGGERO DI OTTAWA). V. 1, No. 1, (Oct. 3, 1981)-. 0715-3287. Newspaper. CN. Italian. bw. Free. IL Messaggero di Ottawa, 1176 Emperor Avenue, Ottawa Ontario K1Z 8C2 Canada. DD 071.1384.

THE MESSENGER. 0191-6211. Newspaper. US. English. wk. The Messenger, 2108 North Charles Street, Baltimore MD 21218.

THE MESSENGER. Periodical. US. English. wk. $20.00. Onon Town Publ Company, Box 108, Baldwinsville NY 13027. **Tel** (315)635-3921. Ed C Alan Baker. adv acc. **Circ** 7,000. (ctrl).

MESSENGER (BRANDENBURG, KY.). (THE MESSENGER). 0746-8113. Newspaper. US. English. wk. The Messenger, PO Box 612, Brandenburg KY 40108. *Meade County Messenger.*

MESSENGER (CENTRAL CITY, KY.). (THE MESSENGER). Began in 1932. Newspaper. US. English. wk. The Messenger, PO Box 268, Covington KY 41012. **LC** Newspaper 7885-X.

MESSENGER (FORT DODGE, IOWA). (THE MESSENGER). 0740-6991. Newspaper. US. English. da. The Messenger, 713 Central Avenue, Fort Dodge IA 50501.

METIS NEWSPAPER. (THE METIS NEWSPAPER). July 22, 1980-. 0710-6262. Newspaper. CN. English. bw. $7.00. Metis Newspaper, 38/1st Avenue North West, Dauphin Manitoba R7N 1G7 Canada. DD 971.272. *Dauphin Metis Newspaper, 0710-6270.*

METRO MATIN. V. 1, No. 44 (Jan. 15, 1979)-. 0709-4663. Newspaper. CN. French. da. 0.25 Each Number. Les Publications P G M, 8401 Boulevard Ray-Lawson, Ville d'Anjou Quebec H1J 1K6 Canada. DD 071.1427. *Metro P.M., 0709-4655.*

METRO-SUD. First issue in 1966. 0381-5080. Newspaper. CN. French. wk. Metro-Sud, 937 Boul Taschereau, Longueil Quebec J4K 2X2 Canada. DD 071.1437.

METRO TIMES. Vol. 1, No 1 (Apr. 2, 1980)-. 0229-687X. Newspaper. CN. English. bw. Free. Metro Times, Suite 14673/108th Avenue, Surrey British Columbia Canada. DD 071.1133. (ctrl).

METRO TIMES (DETROIT, MICH.). (THE METRO TIMES). 0746-4045. Periodical. US. English. wk. $18.00. Metro Times, Palms Building, 2111 Woodward, Detroit MI 48201. *Detroit Metro Times, 0279-2370.*

METUCHEN, EDISON REIVEW. VFOAT Metuchen/Edison Review. 0747-2390. Newspaper. US. English. wk. $9.50. The Metuchen, Edison Review, PO Box 804, Edison NJ 08818-0804.

MIAMI DAILY NEWS CEASED. Began in April 1924. Newspaper. US. English. da. $182.00. Miami Daily News Daily, 1 Herald Plaza, Miami FL 33101. **LC** Newspaper 7002. *Miami News-Metropolis.*

MIAMI HERALD (MIAMI, FLA.). (THE MIAMI HERALD). Began in 1910. Newspaper. US. English. da. Miami Herald Publishing Company, 1 Herald Plaza, Miami FL 33101. **Tel** (305)376-3325. **Ind/Abst** Energy Inf. Abstr., Environ. Abstr., Infobank. Available on microfilm from the Micro Photo Div., Bell & Howell. *Morning News-Record.*

MIAMI NEWSPAPERS INDEX. *See* Indexes/Abstracts.

MICHIGAN CHRONICLE. 1936-. Newspaper. US. English. wk. $16.00. Michigan Detroit Chronicle, 479 Ledyard Street, Detroit MI 48201. **Tel** (313)963-5522. **LC** Newspaper. Available on microfilm.

MICHIGAN FREE PRESS. No. 1- Jan. 9, 1974-. 0147-7110. Periodical. US. English. wk. Michigan Free Press, 204 South Fourth Street, Ann Arbor MI 48108.

MID-ISLAND TIMES & LEVITTOWN TIMES. VFOAT Mid-Island Times and Levittown Times. 0747-4741. Newspaper. US. English. wk. $5.50. Mid-Island Times & Levittown Times, 81 East Barclay Street, Hicksville NY 11801. *Mid-Island Times.*

MID-NORTH MONITOR. (THE MID-NORTH MONITOR). VFOAT Monitor. V. 1- Oct. 11, 1978-. 0227-3853. Newspaper. CN. English. wk. $10.83. Mid North Monitor, Box 1126, Espanola Ontario P0P 1C0 Canada. DD 071.13133. *Mid-North Weekly, 0228-0000.*

MID-TOWN/MT. PLEASANT REVUE. (REVUE, MID-TOWN/MT.PLEASANT). 0710-5363. Newspaper. CN. English. $0.10 Per No. The Revue, 5171 Victoria Drive, Vancouver British Columbia V5P 3V1 Canada. DD 071.1133.

MID-WEEK NEWS MAGAZINE. VFOAT Midweek News Magazine. 0745-6867. Newspaper. US. English. wk. $15.00. Mid-Week News Magazine, PO Box 695, Morgantown WV 26505.

MIDDLESBORO DAILY NEWS. Began in 1909. Newspaper. US. English. ir. $53.00. Middlesboro Daily News, PO Box 579, c/o Louis Derosett, Middlesboro KY 40965. **Tel** (606)248-1010. **LC** Newspaper 7932.

MILE ZERO NEWS. (THE MILE ZERO NEWS). V. 1- 31 Jan. 1979-. 0228-037X. Newspaper. CN. English. wk. 5.00 Domestic, 15.00 Canada. MacKenzie Highway News/Mile Zero News, PO Box 1010, Grimshaw Alberta T0H 1W0 Canada. DD 071.1231.

MILES CITY DAILY STAR. Began with May 23, 1911 issue. Newspaper. US. English. mo. $65.00. Miles City Star, PO Box 1216, Miles City MT 59301. **Tel** (406)232-0450. Ed Gerlad Anglum and D Scanland. bk rev. adv acc. **Circ** 4,500. (ctrl). National, state and local news; special interest stories for eastern Montana.

THE MILLCREEK SUN. 0747-2943. Newspaper. US. English. wk. 106 Vine Street, Girard PA 16417.

MILTON WEEKLY TRIBUNE. V. 1- Sept. 20, 1978-. 0706-683X. Newspaper. CN. English. wk. 0.20 Each Number. L Fairbanks, Milton Weekly Tribune, 158 Main Street East, MIlton Ontario L9T 1N6 Canada. DD 071.13533. *Milton Month, 0707-4921.*

THE MILWAUKEE COURIER. (MILWAUKEE COURIER). Vol. 1, No. 1 (June 27, 1964)-. 0026-4350. Newspaper. US. English. wk. $25.00. Milwaukee Courier, 2431 West Hopkins Street, Milwaukee WI 53206. **Tel** (414)445-2031.

MILWAUKEE-HEROLD (1939) CEASED. (MILWAUKEE-HEROLD). VFOAT Milwaukee Herold. V. 78, No 47 (April 12, 1939)-. Newspaper. US. German. wk. *Milwaukee-Herold-Sonntagspost.*

THE MILWAUKEE JOURNAL. Began with June 8, 1980 issue. Newspaper. US. English. da. $109.20. Newspapers Inc, 333 West State Street, Milwaukee WI 53201. **Tel** (414)224-2000. Ed Sig Gissler. adv acc. **Circ** 828,900. Daily and Sunday newspapers. *Milwaukee Daily Journal.*

MILWAUKEE SENTINEL. Dec. 4, 1844-. Newspaper. US. English. da. $71.65. Newspapers Inc, PO Box 661, Milwaukee WI 53201. **Tel** (414)224-2000. Ed Robert Wills. adv acc. **Circ** 185,000. Daily newspapers.

MINCHUNG SINMUN. VFOAT Minjoong Shinmoon. No. 1- Feb. 23, 1979-. 0225-1205. Newspaper. CN. Korean. wk. Minjoong-Shinmoon Ltd, Suite 306/741 Broadview Avenue, Toronto Ontario M4K 2P6 Canada. DD 071.13541.

MINNEAPOLIS STAR AND TRIBUNE. VFOAT Minneapolis Tribune. Vol. 1, No. 1 (April 5, 1982)-. 0744-5458. Newspaper. US. English. da. $163.80. Minneapolis Tribune, 425 Portland Avenue, Minneapolis MN 55415. **Tel** (612)372-3985. **LC** Newspaper. Available on microfilm. *Minneapolis Star (Minneapolis, Minn. : 1947), Minneapolis Tribune (Minneapolis, Minn. : 1964).*

MINNEAPOLIS STAR AND TRIBUNE INDEX. *See* Indexes/Abstracts.

THE MINOT DAILY NEWS. VFOAT Daily Optic Reporter, Ward County Independent. 1884. 0885-3053. Newspaper. US. English. Minot Daily News, PO Box 1150, Minot ND 58702. **Tel** (701)852-3341. Ed Raymond C Dobson. bk rev. adv acc. **Circ** 29,736. Daily newspaper. *Minot Daily News and Daily Optic-Reporter, Ward County Independent.*

MIRABEL. (LE MIRABEL). V. 1- 22 May 1974-. 0316-9103. CN. French. wk. Le Mirabel, C P 365, Sainte-Theresa Quebec J73 4J4 Canada. DD 071.1424.

MIRABEL. (LE MIRABEL). VFOAT Journal le Mirabel. V. 1, No. 1, (March 3, 1981)-. 0711-3781. Newspaper. CN. French. wk. Free. Le Mirabel, CP 274, 15 rue Saint-Eustache, Saint-Eustache Quebec J7R 2L1 Canada. DD 071.1425. (ctrl).

LA MIRADA LAMPLIGHTER. 0192-0324. Newspaper. US. English. sw. West Orange Publishers Company, 13261 Century Boulevard, Garden Grove CA 92643. **Tel** (714)537-7510.

MIRROR. VFOAT Ching Pao. V. 1- June 10, 1977-. 0704-0482. Newspaper. CN. Chinese (English). wk. 0.20 Per Number. Strathcona Community News Service, Mirror, 820 Jackson Street, Vancouver British Columbia V6A 3G1 Canada. DD 071.1133. (ctrl).

MIRROR. (THE MIRROR). VFOAT Dawson Creek Mirror. Vol. 1, No. 1 (May 8, 1980)-. 0712-1105. Newspaper. CN. English. wk. Free. The Mirror, 1707 Alaska Avenue/Dawson Creek, British Columbia V1G 1P5 Canada. DD 071.111.

MIRROR. (THE MIRROR). Vol. 1, No. 1 Sept. 15, 1981. 0714-5071. Newspaper. CN. English. wk. Free. Mirror, c/o Winnipeg Sun, 100-290 Garry Street, Winnipeg Manitoba R3C 1H3 Canada. DD 071.1274.

THE MISHAWAKA ENTERPRISE RECORD. VFOAT Mishawaka Enterprise-Record. Newspaper. US. English. wk. Enterprise Record, 126 LWE, PO Box 188, Mishawaka IN 46544. *Mishawaka Enterprise (1854).*

MN INFORMATION. MICROFORM. MOSCOW NEWS. VFOAT M.N. Information. No. 1 (July 25, 1978)-. Newspaper. UR. English. sw. Izvestia Press, 1612 Gorky Street, Moscow USSR.

THE MOBILE BEACON & ALABAMA CITIZEN. VFOAT Mobile Beacon and Alabama Citizen. Began in 1944. Newspaper. US. English. wk. $14.00. Beacon & Alabama Citizen, PO Box 1407, Mobile AL 36633. **LC** Newspaper.

THE MOBILE PRESS REGISTER. Feb. 21, 1932-. Newspaper. US. English. da. $360.00. Mobile Press Register, PO Box 2488, Mobile AL 36630. **Tel** (205)433-1551. **LC** Newspaper.

THE MOBILE REGISTER. VFOAT Mobile Sunday Register. Vol. 83, No. 100 (May 26, 1903)-. Newspaper. US. English. da. The Mobile Press Register, PO Box 2488, Mobile AL 36630. **LC** Newspaper.

MOLINE DAILY DISPATCH. Began with July 31, 1878 issue. Newspaper. US. English. da. $109.20. Moline Dispatch Publishing Company, 1720 5th Avenue, Moline IL 61265. **Tel** (309)797-0345. Ed Len R Small. **LC** Newspaper. adv acc. **Circ** 36,000 Daily, 39,000 Sunday. (ctrl). Daily newspaper published in Moline IL, Covering west and Central IL. and eastern Iowa.

MON JOURNAL LAURIER DES LAURENTIDES. V. 1- Aug. 1979-. 0225-0969. Newspaper. CN. French. bm. Free to Laurentides. Mon Journal Laurier des Laurentides, 390 Chemin Gauthier, La Plaine Quebec J0N 1B0 Canada. DD 071.144. *Mon Journal des Laurentides, 0225-0950.*

LE MONDE. Vol. 1, No. 1 (Dec. 19, 1944)-. 0395-2037. Newspaper. FR. French. ir. 5 rue des Italiens, 75427 Paris France. **Ind/Abst** Infobank, Predicasts. Available on microfilm from Research Publications. *Temps (Paris, France : 1861).*

LE MONDE DIPLOMATIQUE. May 1954-. 0026-9395. Newspaper. FR. French. mo. $25.41. Le Monde Service Abonnements, BP 50709, 75422 Paris Cedex 09 France. **Tel** 246-72-23. **Ind/Abst** Bibliogr. Index Geol.

MONDE. SELECTION HEBDOMADAIRE. (LE MONDE. SELECTION HEBDOMADAIRE). VFOAT Selection Hebdomadaire du Journal le Monde. Began in 1948. Newspaper. FR. French. wk. $34.20. Monde, 5 rue des Italiens, 75427 Paris Cedex 09 France.

IL MONDO. Vol. 1- 19, 1949-. Periodical. IT. Italian. wk. $92.00. Rizzoli Editore, Via A Rizzoli 2, 20132 Milano Italy. **Tel** 02/2588. **LC** AP37. (cum index).

MONITOR. Began publication in 1975. 0703-1513. Newspaper. CN. English. wk. $7.50. Monitor, 102A Queen Street, Charlottetown Prince Edward Island C1N 3N8 Canada. DD 071.175.

MONITOR. (THE MONITOR). Vol. 1, Issue 1 (Oct. 30, 1982)-. 0823-7549. Newspaper. CN. English. wk. Free to Residents. Monitor, PO Box 3099, Salmon Arm British Columbia V0E 2T0 Canada. DD 071.1141.

MONROVIA DAILY NEWS-POST. Began in 1929. Newspaper. US. English. wk. Monrovia News Post, 10 North 1st Avenue, Arcadia CA 91006. **LC** Newspaper 7114-X. *Monrovia Daily News, Monrovia Post.*

Newspapers

THE MONTGOMERY ADVERTISER. *CEASED.* Ceased in November 1982. Newspaper. US. English. da. LC Newspaper. *Montgomery Daily Advertiser.*

MONTHLY AANCHAL. Began publication in Aug. 1977?. 0709-5090. Newspaper. CN. Urdu. mo. $8.00. Monthly Aanchal, PO Box 42, Malton Ontario L4T 3B5 Canada. DD 071.13541.

MONTICELLO TIMES. Newspaper. US. English. wk. $16.00. Monticello Times, PO Box 548, Monticello MN 55362. **Tel** (612)295-3131.

MORINVILLE MIRROR. Vol. 1, No. 1 Sept. 26, 1979. 0711-3811. Newspaper. CN. English. wk. $0.25 Per Issue. Morinville Mirror, PO Box 1649, Morinville Alberta T0G 1P0 Canada. DD 071.1233.

MORNING CHRONICLE (HALIFAX, N.S.). (THE MORNING CHRONICLE). Newspaper. UK. English. British Library, 7 Rathbone Street, London W1P 2AL England. DD 071.1622.

THE MORNING NEWS OF SOUTHEASTERN IDAHO. VFOAT Morning News. 0745-712X. Newspaper. US. English. da. Bulletin Publishing Company, 27 NW Main Street, Blackfoot ID 83221. *Blackfoot News.*

MORNING NEWS (WILMINGTON, DEL.). (THE MORNING NEWS). Began Mar. 1, 1880. Newspaper. US. English. da. $78.00. News Journal Company, 831 Orange Street, Wilmington DE 19899. **Tel** (302)573-2000. LC Newspaper 7269-X. *Morning Herald (Wilmington, Del.).*

THE MORNING RECORD AND JOURNAL. Newspaper. US. English. ir. $116.00. Meriden Record Journal, Crown Street Square, Meriden CT CT 06450. **Tel** (203)235-1661. LC Newspaper. *Meriden Record, Meriden Daily Journal.*

THE MORNING STAR. V. 1- Jan. 1894-. Periodical. UK. English. da. 152.88. Morning Star Co-Op Society Ltd, 75 Farringdon Road, London EC1M 3JX England. **Tel** 01 405 9242. Ed Tony Chater. Index in last issue of volume - attached. bk rev. adv acc. **Circ** 28,500. Newspaper of the left owned by its readers in co-operative society. *Excellent Things.*

THE MORNING SUN. Newspaper. US. English. da. $56.04. Morning Sun, PO Drawer H, Pittsburg KS 66762. LC Newspaper. *Pittsburg Sun.*

MORRIS TRIBUNE. Newspaper. US. English. ir. Morris Tribune, Box 470, Morris MN 56267. **Tel** (612)589-2525.

MORTON GROVE CHAMPION. 0193-7251. Periodical. US. English. wk. $8.75. Pioneer Press, 1232 Central Avenue, Wilmette IL 60091. **Tel** (312)251-4300.

MOSCOW NEWS. 0027-1306. Newspaper. UR. English. wk. Moscow News, Mezhdunarod Naja Kniga USSR, Moscow USSR.

MOTHEROOT JOURNAL. V. 1- Spring 1979-. 0739-5272. Periodical. US. English. qt. Motheroot Publications, PO Box 8306, Pittsburgh PA 15218. **Tel** (412)241-0628. **Ind/Abst** Altern. Press Index, Sociol. Abstr., Lang. Lang. Behav. Abstr.

MOUNT BRYDGES BULLETIN. (THE MOUNT BRYDGES BULLETIN). Began publication in Aug. 1973?. 0316-0254. Newspaper. CN. English. wk. $4.00 Domestic, $5.00 US. Neighborly News Publishing, 17 Adelaide Street South, Mount Brydges Ontario N0L Canada. DD 071.1325.

THE MOUNT OLIVE HERALD. 0747-458X. Newspaper. US. English. wk. Mt Olive Herald, 305 East Maine Street, Mt Olive IL 62069.

MOUNT PROSPECT TIMES. VFOAT Mt. Prospect Times. Began in 1984?. 0747-2595. Newspaper. US. English. mo. $15.50. Circulation Department, Mount Prospect Times, 1000 Executive Way, Des Plaines IL 60018. **Tel** (312)824-111. Ed Herman Baumann. adv acc. **Circ** 5,149. (ctrl). Community newspaper. *Suburban (Mt. Prospect, Ill.),* 0279-7887.

MOUNTAIN DEMOCRAT AND EL DORADO NEWS. VFOAT Mountain Democrat. 0745-7677. Newspaper. US. English. tw. Mother Lode Printing and Publishing Company, 447 Main Street, Placerville CA 95667. *Mountain Democrat and Placerville Times.*

MOUNTAIN DEMOCRAT (PLACERVILLE, CALIF.). (THE MOUNTAIN DEMOCRAT). Ceased in 1938?. Newspaper. US. English. ir. $36.00. Mountain Democrat, Box 1088, Placerville CA 95667. LC Newspaper 7114-X. *Weekly Mountain Democrat.*

THE MOUNTAIN EAGLE. Began in 1907. Newspaper. US. English. wk. $11.00. Tom Gish, PO Box 808, Whitesburg KY 41858. **Tel** (606)633-2252. Ed T E Gish.

MOUNTAIN MESSENGER (GIBSONVILLE, CALIF.). (THE MOUNTAIN MESSENGER). VFOAT California Mountain Messenger. Began in 1855. 0278-4394. Newspaper. US. English. wk. $12.00. Mountain Messenger, PO Box 691, Nevada City CA 95929. **Tel** (916)289-3262. Ed J A Vaughn. *Gibonsville Trumpet.*

THE MOUNTAIN STATESMAN. 0745-1334. Newspaper. US. English. da. The Mountain Statesman Inc, 914 West Main Street, Grafton WV 26354.

MOUNTAINEER POSTMASTER. 0194-536X. Periodical. US. English. bm. Mountaineer Postmaster, 416 Mansion Street, Hamlin WV 25523.

THE MUNDAY COURIER. 8750-6750. Newspaper. US. English. wk. The Munday Courier, PO Box 130, Munday TX 76371.

MUNDELEIN REVIEW. 0744-8538. Newspaper. US. English. wk. $9.50. Pioneer Press, 1232 Central Avenue, Wilmette IL 60091. **Tel** (312)251-4300.

THE MUSKEGON CHRONICLE. VFOAT Sunday Chronicle. Began in March 1913. Newspaper. US. English. da. 981 Third Street, Muskegon MI 49443. LC Newspaper 7002. *Muskegon News Chronicle.*

MUSKOGEE DAILY PHOENIX AND TIMES-DEMOCRAT. VFOAT Muskogee Daily Phoenix and Times Democrat. Vol. 70, No. 130 (May 31, 1971)-. Newspaper. US. English. da. PO Box 1968 214 Wall Street, Muskogee OK 74401. LC Newspaper. *Muskogee Daily Phoenix.*

MUSKOGEE TIMES-DEMOCRAT. VFOAT Muskogee Times Democrat. Began in Mar. 1906. Newspaper. US. English. da. PO Box 1968 214 Wall Street, Muskogee OK 74410. LC Newspaper 7002. Also available on microfilm from Oklahoma Dept. of Libraries, and Oklahoma Historical Society. *Muskogee Evening Times, Muskogee Democrat.*

MUSKOKA FREE PRESS. V. 1- June 30, 1976-. 0701-1199. Periodical. CN. English. wk. 8.00. F T Botham Publications, 53 Main Street, Huntsville Ontario P0A 1K0 Canada. DD 071.1316.

MYSTERY NEWS. Vol. 1, No. 1 (Nov. 1981)-. 0734-9076. Periodical. US. English. bm. $11.95. Mystery News, PO Box 2637, Rohnert Park CA 94928. **Tel** (707)584-4843.

N. W. AYER & SON'S DIRECTORY, NEWSPAPERS AND PERIODICALS. MID-YEAR SUPPLEMENT. *See* Yearbooks, Almanacs, Directories.

LA NACION. V. 1- 1964-. Periodical. AG. Spanish. wk. $696.00. S A la Nacion, Casilla de Correo 773, 1000 Buenos Aires Argentina. **Tel** 313-1003. adv acc. **Circ** 250,000. (ctrl).

NACIONAL (CARACAS, VENEZUELA). (EL NACIONAL). Began with Aug. 3, 1943 issue. Newspaper. US. Spanish. da. Press Agencias SA, Apartado 2763, Caracas Venezuela.

NAPA COUNTY RECORD AND NAPA VALLEY NEWS. VFOAT Napa County Record. 0744-6942. Newspaper. US. English. wk. The Napa County Record, 520 3rd Street, Napa CA 94558.

THE NAPLES SUN. Vol. 1, No. 1 (Jan. 12, 1984)-. 0746-9977. Newspaper. US. English. wk. Reynolds Enterprises, 1315 5th Avenue South, Naples FL 33940.

NASHUA DAILY TELEGRAPH. Began with Mar. 1, 1869 issue. Newspaper. US. English. da. Telegraph, 60 Main Street, Nashua NH 03061. LC Newspaper 8701-X.

NATCHEZ DAILY DEMOCRAT (NATCHEZ, MISS. : 1916). (NATCHEZ DAILY DEMOCRAT). Vol. 51, N.S. No. 1 (Aug. 1, 1916)-. Newspaper. US. English. da. Natchez Daily Democrat, North Canal Street PO Box 1447, Natchez MS 39120. LC Newspaper. *Natchez News-Democrat.*

NATCHEZ WEEKLY DEMOCRAT. Began in 1865. Newspaper. US. English. wk. $112.00. Natchez Democrat, PO Box 1447, Natchez MS 39120. **Tel** (601)442-9101. Ed John Mathew. LC Newspaper 8525-X. adv acc. **Circ** 15,000. General news.

THE NATCHITOCHES TIMES. Began with Mar. 13, 1903 issue. Newspaper. US. English. sw. $38.40. The Natchitoches Times, PO Box 448/904 Highway I South, Natchitoches LA 71457. **Tel** (318)352-3618. LC Newspaper 7962.

NATIONAL DIRECTORY OF WEEKLY NEWSPAPERS, INCLUDING SEMI-WEEKLY AND TRI-WEEKLY NEWSPAPERS. *See* Yearbooks, Almanacs, Directories.

NATIONAL JESUIT NEWS. VFOAT NJ. 0199-0284. Periodical. US. English. mo. National Jesuit News, St Joseph's University, 5600 City Avenue, Philadelphia PA 19131. DD 255.

NATIONAL JOB MARKET. 0747-4296. Periodical. US. English. wk. $125.00. N J M Inc, PO Box 286, Kensington MD 20895. **Tel** (301)946-8910. Ed Walter McGivney. DD 331. adv acc. The most complete and the lowest priced national job newspaper in the US. The only job publication that features private, federal and international jobs.

NATIONAL NEWSPAPER ASSOCIATION DIRECTORY. *See* Yearbooks, Almanacs, Directories.

NATIONAL NEWSPAPER INDEX (ANNUAL). *See* Indexes/Abstracts.

THE NATIONAL OBSERVER. NEWSPAPER INDEX. *See* Indexes/Abstracts.

NATIONAL RIGHT TO LIFE NEWS. VFOAT NRL News, N.R.L. News. 1973. 0164-7415. Periodical. US. English. sm. $10.00. National Right to Life News, 419 7th Street/Suite 402, Washington DC 20004. **Tel** (202)626-8800. Ed Dave Andrusko. bk rev. adv acc. **Circ** 100,000. (ctrl). Publishes current information on biomedical issues such as abortions, euthanasia and infanticide, currently in the 13th year of publication.

NATION'S CITIES WEEKLY. V. 1, No. 44- Dec. 4, 1978-. 0164-5935. Periodical. US. English. wk. National League of Cities, 1301 Pennsylvania Avenue NW, Washington DC 20004. DD 352. *Nation's Cities,* 0028-0488; *City Weekly,* 0164-5595.

NAUJIENOS. VFOAT Lithuanian Daily News. Began Feb. 9, 1914. 0745-5445. Newspaper. US. Lithuanian. da. Lithuanian News Publishing Company, 1739 South Halsted Street, Chicago IL 60608.

NAVAJO TIMES (WINDOW ROCK, ARIZ. : 1960). (NAVAJO TIMES). Vol. 1, Issue 1 (Aug. 4, 1960). 0470-5106. Newspaper. US. English. da. $50.00. Navajo Times Today, PO Box 310, Window Rock AZ 86515. **Tel** (602)871-6641. Ed Mark Trahant. adv acc. **Circ** 8,000. General interest daily newspaper published on the Navajo Indian reservation. *Navajo Times (Window Rock, Ariz. : 1959).*

NEA PATRIDA. No. 1- Oct. 15, 1978-. 0225-0594. Newspaper. CN. Greek, Modern (text includes some text in English). bw. 50. Per Issue. Nea Patrida Publications, 1089 West Broadway, Vancouver British Columbia V6H 1E5 Canada. DD 071.1133.

NEA TOY HAMILTON. No. 1 (July 1980)-. 0715-4410. Newspaper. CN. Greek, Modern. mo. $5.00. Nea Toy Hamilton, 23 Myrtle Avenue, Hamilton Ontario L8M 2E8 Canada. DD 071.1352.

NEAR NORTH NEWS. 0028-1778. Newspaper. US. English. wk. $20.00. Near North News Inc, 26 East Huron, Chicago IL 60611. **Tel** (312)787-2677. Ed Arnie Matanky. bk rev. adv acc. **Circ** 7,500. Community newspaper of Chicago's most important neighborhood, with emphasis on arts, politics, entertainment and business.

NEDJELJNA DALMACIJA. Periodical. Serbo-Croatian(R). ir. Slobodna Dalmacija, Splitskog Odreda 4, Split Yugoslavia. LC AP56.

NEOS KOSMOS. VFOAT Nouveau Monde. VAT Nouveau Monde (Montreal). 1977. V. 1- 8 Dec. 1977-. 0704-1527. Newspaper. CN. Greek, Modern. bw. $132.81. Ethnic Publications, 235A Russell Street, Melbourne Victoria 3000 Australia. **Tel** 03 663 4822. DD 071.14281.

NEUER WEG *CEASED.* V. 1- 1 -. Newspaper. RM. German. da. $50.00. Ilexim Press Department, PO Box 1-136-1-137, Bucharest Romania.

NEVADA APPEAL (CARSON CITY, NEV. : 1968). (NEVADA APPEAL). Vol. 104, No. 220 (Sept. 1, 1968)-. Newspaper. US. English. da. Nevada Appeal, 200 Batch Street, Carson City NV 89701. LC NEWSPAPER. *Carson City Nevada Appeal.*

Newspapers

THE NEVADA COUNTY INDEPENDENT MESSENGER. VFOAT Independent Messenger. 8750-8729. Newspaper. US. English. wk. The Independent Messenger, 417 Broad Street/Suite C, Nevada City CA 95959.

NEW AMERICAN : OFFICIAL PUBLICATION FOR THE COMMITTEE FOR THE ABSORPTION OF SOVIET EMIGREES. 0274-998X. Newspaper. US. Russian. wk. $40.00. New American Press, 80 Grand Street, Jersey City NJ 07302. Tel (201)332-7962. *Novyi Amerikanets.*

NEW BRIGHTON BULLETIN. 1956. Newspaper. US. English. wk. $38.00. Theodore Lille, 909 7th Avenue NW, Brighton MN 55112. Tel (612)777-8800. Ed Gene Skiba. bk rev. adv acc. Circ 27,800. Local newspaper serving the northern suburbs of St. Paul Minnesota.

NEW BRUNSWICK COURIER. (NEW BRUNSWICK COURIER MICROFORM). VAT Courier (Saint John). 0823-3934. Newspaper. CN. English. Canadian Library Association, 151 Sparks Street, Ottawa Ontario, K1P 5E3 Canada. DD 071.15.

THE NEW CRUSADER. V. 41, No. 31 (Dec. 26, 1981). Newspaper. US. English. wk. $10.00. Jefferson-Leavell Publ Company Inc, 6428 South Park Avenue, Chicago IL 60637. LC Newspaper 7574-X. Available on microfilm from Bell & Howell.

NEW EDINBURGH NEWS. Began publication in 1976. 0703-9042. Newspaper. CN. English. Free. E Dunn, 34 Dufferin Road, Ottawa Ontario K1M 2A8 Canada. DD 071.1384.

NEW ERA. (THE NEW ERA). V. 1- Nov. 15, 1979-. 0227-8030. Newspaper. CN. English. wk. $12.00. New Era/Canada, 106 Main Street, Melita Manitoba R0M 1L0 Canada. Tel (204)522-3491. Ed A W Lenz. DD 071.1382. adv acc. Circ 2,500.

NEW HAMPSHIRE SUNDAY NEWS. Began 1946. Newspaper. US. English. wk. The Union Leader, 35 Amherst Street, Manchester NH 03105. LC Newspaper.

NEW HAMPSHIRE TIMES. 1971. 0163-3066. Newspaper. US. English. wk. $24.95. New Hampshire Times, PO Box 35, Concord NH 03301. Tel (603)224-9100. Ed Jeff Blake. Ind/Abst Energy Inf. Abstr., Environ. Abstr. bk rev. adv acc. Circ 15,000. (ctrl). Is the state's only statewide newspaper, a consistent source of provocative and entertaining features on the issues, events, and people that make New Hampshire unique.

THE NEW HAVEN REGISTER. Jan. 1, 1961-. Newspaper. US. English. da. $127.40. The Jackson Newspapers, 40 Sargent Drive, New Haven CT 06511. Tel (203)562-1121. *New Haven Evening Register.*

NEW MEXICAN (SANTA FE, N. MEX. : 1951). (THE NEW MEXICAN). VFOAT Sante Fe New Mexican. Nov. 1, 1951-. Newspaper. US. English. da. PO Box 2048, Santa Fe NM 87501. LC Newspaper. *The Santa Fe New Mexican.*

THE NEW MEXICO INDEPENDENT. 0193-5356. Newspaper. US. English. wk. $50.00. Independent Publishing Company, PO Box 429-325 Fifth Street SW, Albuquerque NM 87103. Tel (505)843-6440.

NEW NIGERIAN. Began publication in 1966?. Newspaper. NR. English. da. New Nigerian Newspaper Ltd, PO Box 254, Kaduna Nigeria. Tel 243386-8.

NEW ORLEANS TIMES-PICAYUNE. 1836. US. English. da. $138.00. Times Picayune Publ Corp, 3800 Howard Avenue, New Orleans LA 70140. Tel (504)586-3400.

NEW PITTSBURGH COURIER (CITY ED.). (NEW PITTSBURGH COURIER). VFOAT Pittsburgh Courier. Began in 1966?. Newspaper. US. English. wk. New Pittsburgh Courier, 315 East Carson Street, Pittsburgh PA 15219. *Pittsburgh Courier (City ED. : 1955).*

NEW SOLIDARITY. 0028-6737. Periodical. US. English. sw. $50.00. Campaigner Publications Inc, PO Box 17726, Washington DC 20041-0726. Tel (703)777-9401. Ed Nancy Spannaus. bk rev. adv acc. Circ 63,000. Nonpartisan national newspaper of the American system. *Solidarity.*

NEW SUNDAY TIMES, MALAYSIA. Newspaper. English. da. $131.31. New Straits Times Press Berhad, 31 Jalan Riong, Kuala Lumpur 22-03 Malaysia. *Sunday Times, Malaysia.*

NEW SURREY NEWS. V. 1- Dec. 3, 1975-. 0383-1183. Newspaper. CN. English. bw. New Surrey News, 8028 Enterprise Street, Burnaby BC British Columbia V5A 1V7 Canada. DD 071.1133.

NEW TIMES (PHOENIX, ARIZ. : 1981). (NEW TIMES). 0279-3962. Periodical. US. English. wk. New Times, PO Box 2510, Phoenix AZ 85002. Tel (602)271-0040. *New Times Weekly, 0273-9836.*

NEW ULM JOURNAL. Newspaper. US. English. ir. $55.25. The Journal New ULM MN, Markstrasse North 303, New Ulm MN 56073. Tel (507)359-2911. adv acc. Circ 11,000. Daily newspaper.

NEW UNITY. Series/Titl Bell and Howell Underground Press Collection. Began publication in 1971. 0047-9950. Newspaper. US. English. ir. New Unity, Box 891, Springfield MA 01101.

NEW YORK CITY TRIBUNE. 8750-5282. Newspaper. US. English. da. News World Communications, 401-5th Avenue, New York NY 10016. *New York Tribune (1983), 0745-8010.*

NEW YORK POST. Began with Mar. 29, 1934 issue. Newspaper. US. English. da. $165.00. Kingston Newspaper Mailing Company, C P O Box 1517, Kingston NY 12401. Tel (914)331-1865 (800)331-6052. LC Newspaper 7115. *New York Evening Post.*

THE NEW YORK TIMES. Sept. 18, 1851-. 0362-4331. Newspaper. US. English. da. New York Times, PO Box 5792, New York NY 10242. Tel (800)631-2500. Ind/Abst Infobank, Chem. Abstr., Funk Scott Index Corp. Ind. Microfilm available from University Microfilm.

NEW YORK TIMES SCHOOL MICROFILM COLLECTION INDEX BY REELS. See Indexes/Abstracts.

NEW YORK VOICE. VFOAT Jamaica Queen's Voice. Began Publication in 1959. 0042-8051. Newspaper. US. English. wk. $20.00. New York Voice, 78-36 Parsons Boulevard, Flushing NY 11366.

NEW YORKER STAATS-ZEITUNG UND HEROLD (1976). (NEW YORKER STAATS-ZEITUNG UND HEROLD). VFOAT New Yorker Staats Zeitung und Herold. V. 141 No. 40 (Nov. 6/7 1976)-. Newspaper. US. German. wk. 36-30 37th Street, Long Island City NY 11101. *Sonntagsblett Staats-Zeitung und Herold.*

NEW ZEALAND NEWS CEASED. 1927. 0028-8500. Periodical. UK. English. wk. 17. New Zealand News, PO Box 10, Berwick-Upon-Tweed Northumberland England. Tel 0289 306677. Ed Wayne Butler. LC DU400. bk rev. adv acc. Circ 13,500. The closest link to home for thousands of New Zealanders either travelling or living overseas.

NEW ZEALAND NEWS UK. VFOAT New Zealand News U.K. Began in 1927. Periodical. UK. English. wk. 17.-. New Zealand News UK, PO Box 10, Berwick-Upon-Tweed Northumberland England. Tel 0289 306677. Ed Wayne Butler. LC DU400. DD 993.1005. bk rev. adv acc. Circ 13,500. The closest link to home for thousands of New Zealanders either travelling or living overseas.

NEWCASTLE INDEPENDENT. (THE NEWCASTLE INDEPENDENT). VFOAT Newcastle Independent. 0710-0116. Newspaper. CN. English. wk. Free to Residents of Newcastle. Newcastle Independent, 62-66 King Street West, Bowmanville Ontario L1M 3K9 Canada. DD 071.1356.

NEWFOUNDLAND HERALD. (THE NEWFOUNDLAND HERALD). VAT Herald (St. John's). 0824-3581. Periodical. CN. English. wk. Newfoundland Herald, PO Box 2015, St John's Newfoundland A1C 5R7 Canada. DD 051. *Sunday Herald.*

NEWFOUNDLAND SIGNAL. (THE NEWFOUNDLAND SIGNAL). V. 1- Nov. 6, 1974-. 0317-2309. Newspaper. CN. English. wk. Newfoundland Signal, 396 Avenue Road, Apartment 214, Toronto Ontario M4V 2H Canada. DD 971.8005.

NEWINGTON TOWN CRIER. 0745-0796. Newspaper. US. English. wk. Imprint Publications Inc, 20 Isham Road, West Hartford CT 06107. Tel (203)236-5884.

NEWS. (THE NEWS : THE VOICE OF THE NORTH FRASER VALLEY). Vol. 2, No. 21 (Oct. 10, 1979)-. 0227-2598. Newspaper. CN. English. wk. $0.15 Per No. Janor Publications, 22757 Selkirk Avenue, Maple Ridge British Columbia V2X 2Y1 Canada. DD 071.1133. *Meadow Ridge News.*

NEWS. (THE NEWS). VFOAT Les Nouvelles. 0710-5592. Newspaper. CN. English (French). wk. $0.20 Per No. Miller Publishing Company, 6526 Somerland, Montreal Quebec Canada. DD 071.1428.

NEWS ADVERTISER. (THE NEWS ADVERTISER). Began with Nov. 7, 1972 issue. 0316-0238. Newspaper. CN. English. Free distribution in Kitimat, Terrace, Thornhill. Northern Sentinel Press, 626 Enterprise Avenue, Kitimat British Columbia V8C 2E4 Canada. DD 071.1132.

THE NEWS AMERICAN. Jan. 13, 1964-. Newspaper. US. English. da. The News American, 301 East Lombard Street, PO Box 1795, Baltimore MD 21203. LC NEWSPAPER. *Baltimore American, Baltimore News-Post.*

NEWS AND COURIER (CHARLESTON, S.C. : DAILY). (NEWS AND COURIER). VFOAT Saturday, The News and Courier, The Evening Post, Sunday News, Sunday, The News and Courier, The Charleston Post, Sunday, The News and Courier, The Evening Post. V. 10, No. 2256 (1873)-. Newspaper. US. English. da. $111.80. Charleston News, PO Box 758, Charleston SC 29402. Also available on microfilm from Microphoto Div., Bell & Howell Company. *Charleston Daily News, Charleston Daily Courier.*

NEWS & OBSERVER (RALEIGH, N.C. : 1894). (THE NEWS & OBSERVER). VFOAT News and Observer. Vol. 37, No. 19 (Aug. 12, 1984)-. Newspaper. US. English. da. 215 South McDowell Street, Raleigh NC 27601. LC NEWSPAPER 7002. *News-Observer-Chronicle.*

NEWS BURLINGTON. V. 1, No. 35- Aug. 30, 1973-. 0317-9885. Newspaper. CN. English. wk. Box 807, Burlington Ontario Canada. DD 071.13533. *Sports Burlington, 0317-9877.*

NEWS FROM NEASDEN. 0307-2304. Periodical. UK. English. ty. News from Neasden, 22 Fleet Road, London England.

NEWS-GAZETTE (SAINT CLOUD, FLA.). (NEWS-GAZETTE). VFOAT News Gazette. 92nd Year, 33rd Ed. (Oct. 18, 1984)-. 8750-5029. Newspaper. US. English. wk. News-Gazette, PO Box 1060, Kissimmee FL 32741. *Kissimmee Gazette.*

NEWS HERALD (SARALAND, ALA.). (THE NEWS HERALD). 0747-4512. Newspaper. US. English. wk. Mobile County Publications, PO Box 5809, Saraland AL 56571.

NEWS-LEADER. 0163-4011. Newspaper. US. English. da. $57.20. News Leader, 15 NE 1st Road, Homestead FL 33030.

NEWS (PATERSON, N.J.). (THE NEWS). Began in 1981?. Newspaper. US. English. da. 1 News Plaza, Paterson NJ 07509. LC NEWSPAPER. *Paterson Evening News.*

NEWS-PILOT. VFOAT News Pilot. 0747-4180. Newspaper. US. English. da. News-Pilot, 5215 Torrance Boulevard, Torrance CA 90509.

THE NEWS REPORTER. Began in 1895. Newspaper. US. English. sw. PO Box 707, Whiteville NC 28472. LC NEWSPAPER 7002.

NEWS (ROBLIN (MAN. : TOWN)). (THE NEWS). Vol. 1, No. 1 (Mar. 16, 1977)-. 0229-7752. Newspaper. CN. English. wk. Hal-Man Publications, Box 299, 182 Main Street, Roblin R0L 1P0 Canada. DD 071.1272.

NEWS, SOUTHERN AFRICA. V. 1- June 1978-. 0709-6119. Periodical. CN. English. Manitoba Anti-Apartheid Coalition, Box 55 Station C, Winnipeg Manitoba R3M 3S3 Canada. DD 968.005. *South Africa Newsclippings, 0381-5420.*

NEWS TRANSCRIPT. 0191-5908. Newspaper. US. English. wk. $22.00. Monmouth News Inc, Route 9, PO Box 679, Freehold NJ 07728. Tel (201)462-0292. *Colonial News Transcript.*

NEWS-TRIBUNE & HERALD. VFOAT News Tribune and Herald. V. 1, No. 1 (Aug. 2, 1982)-. Newspaper. US. English. da. $136.76. 424 West First Street, Duluth MN 55802. Tel (218)723-5281. Ed Larry Fortner. LC NEWSPAPER. bk rev. adv acc. Circ 393,320. (ctrl). *Duluth News-Tribune, Duluth Herald (Duluth, Minn. : 1910).*

THE NEWS-VIRGINIAN. VFOAT News Virginian. 8750-7862. Newspaper. US. English. da. $42.00. The News-Virginian, Box 1027, Waynesboro VA 22980.

NEWSDAY. V. 1-. Newspaper. US. English. da. $223.00. Newsday Inc, Atten: Mail Subscriptions, Long Island NY 11747. Tel (516)454-2150.

Newspapers

NEWSFILE (TORONTO, ONT.). (NEWSFILE). Vol. 1, Issue 1 (Sept. 1981)-. 0711-1762. Periodical. CN. English. sm. $35.00. Newsfile, c/o Moore & Moore Design, 284 Avenue Road, Toronto Ontario M4V 2G7 Canada. DD 016.07.

NEWS/NORTH. VFOAT News of the North, News North. June 20, 1980-. 0828-1521. Newspaper. CN. English. wk. $38.69. Northern News Services Ltd, PO Box 2820, Yellowknife Northwest Territories 1XA 2R1 Canada. Tel (403)873-4033. *News of the North.*

NEWSPAPER. (THE NEWSPAPER). V. 1- Sept. 6, 1978-. 0227-7409. Newspaper. CN. English. wk. Free, University of Toronto Campus. $15.00 Others. Planet Publications, The Newspaper, Room 121, 10 Saint George Street, University of Toronto, Toronto Ontario M5S 1A1 Canada. DD 071.13541.

NEWSPAPER GEOG. LIST - CARLETON UNIVERSITY. (NEWSPAPER GEOG. LIST MICROFORM). Main/Corp Carleton University. Library. VFOAT Newspaper Index. 0823-132X. Periodical. CN. English. ir. 1.00. Carleton University Library, Ottawa Ontario K1S 5B6 Canada. Tel (613)564-6647. DD 018.135. Catalogue of all newspapers in Carleton University library, organized by country, and provincial breakdown for Canadian items.

THE NEWSPAPER GUILD, AFL-CIO, CLC CONSTITUTION. VFOAT Constitution of the Newspaper Guild. As amended by the 1971-Convention. 0270-2223. US. English. an. $.75. The Newspaper Guild, 1125-15th Street NW, Washington DC 20005. LC PN4841. DD 331.8811070172. *Constitution of the American Newspaper Guild, AFL-CIO, CLC.*

NEWSPAPER RATES AND DATA. See Business - Advertising & Public Relations.

NEWSPAPER RESEARCH JOURNAL. V. 1- Nov. 1979-. 0739-5329. Periodical. US. English. qt. $20.00. Newspaper Research Journal, Memphis State University, Journalism Department, Memphis TN 38152. Tel (901)454-2854. Ed Gerald C Stone. bk rev. adv acc. Circ 1,200. (ctrl). Practical research of interest to the newspaper industry on topics including advertising, circulation, management, ownership, reporting, legal and writing.

NEWSPAPERS AND JOURNALS ON MICROFILM HELD IN PERIODICALS ROOM, DOUGLAS LIBRARY, QUEEN'S UNIVERSITY AT KINGSTON. Main/Corp Douglas Library. Sept. 1980-. 0711-3951. CN. English. te. Newspapers and Journals on Microfilm, c/o Periodicals Room/Douglas Library, Queen's University, Kingston Ontario Canada. DD 018.136. *Newspapers and Journals on Microform Held in Periodicals Room, Douglas Library, Queen's University at Kingston, 0380-5662.*

NEWSPAPERS AND PERIODICALS CURRENTLY RECEIVED BY THE LIBRARY OF PARLIAMENT INCLUDING THE READING ROOM OF THE HOUSE OF COMMONS. Main/Corp Canada. Library of Parliament. VFOAT Journaux et Revues Recus par la Bibliotheque du Parlement y Compris la Salle de Lectures de la Chambre des Communes. 0708-1596. Periodical. CN. English (French publications). Library of Parliament, Ottawa Ontario Canada. DD 016.05.

NEWSPAPERS IN MICROFORM. FOREIGN COUNTRIES. Main/Corp Library of Congress. Catalog Management and Publication Division. Series/Titl Library of Congress Catalogs. US. English. Library of Congress, Catalog Management and Publication Division, Madison Building, Washington DC 20540. *0192-1231.*

NEWSPAPERS IN MICROFORM. UNITED STATES. Main/Corp Library of Congress. Catalog Management and Publication Division. Series/Titl Library of Congress Catalogs. US. English. Library of Congress, Catalog Management and Publication Division, Madison Building, Washington DC 20540. *Newspapers in Microform: United States, 0192-124X.*

NEWSPAPERS RECEIVED CURRENTLY IN THE LIBRARY OF CONGRESS. (NEWSPAPERS RECEIVED CURRENTLY IN THE LIBRARY OF CONGRESS). Main/Corp Library of Congress. Serial & Government Publications Division. 7th Ed.-. 0093-6464. US. English. be. Superintendent of Documents, US Government Printing Office, Washington DC 20402. LC Z6945.U5, PN4731. DD 016.07. *Newspapers Received Currently in the Library of Congress, 0093-6464.*

NEWSTIME (LONDON, ENGLAND). (NEWSTIME). Periodical. UK. English. mo. 10. Newspaper Society, 6 Carmelite Street, London EC4Y 0BL England. LC PN4701. DD 070.05.

NEWTON KANSAN (NEWTON, KAN. : 1952). (THE NEWTON KANSAN). Vol. 68, No. 19 (Mar. 1, 1952)-. Newspaper. US. English. da. *Evening Kansan-Republican, Newton Journal (NEWTON, KAN. : 1904); Harvey County News (Newton, Kan. : 1932).*

NEWTON PRESS-MENTOR. VFOAT Press-Mentor. 0745-788X. Newspaper. US. English. sw. Newton Press-Mentor, 101 South Jackson Street, Newton IL 62448.

NICHI BEI TIMES. VFOAT Japanese American Daily, Nichi Bei Jiji. May 23, 1946-. 0739-2443. Periodical. US. English (Japanese). da. $51.00. Nichi Bei Times, PO Box 3098, San Francisco CA 94119.

NICOLA INDIAN. Began publication in Oct.? 1978. 0228-2194. Newspaper. CN. English. mo. $5. Nicola Valley Indian Administration, PO Box 188, Merritt British Columbia V0K 2B0 Canada. DD 971.141.

THE NIGERIAN NEWS. Vol. 1, No. 1 (Feb. 15, 1984)-. 0749-5145. Periodical. US. English. sm. $12.00. PO Box 5663, Providence RI 02903. DD 071.

NIHON SHINBUN ZASSHI BENRAN. Began in 1962. Japanese. an. LC Z3303. Each issue contains an index to its own contents - no vol index - loose.

NIKKA TAIMUSU. VFOAT The Nikka Times. V. 1- Oct. 17, 1979-. 0226-2002. Newspaper. CN. Japanese. wk. $12.00. N Iromoto, The Nikka Times, Suite 2/761 Jane Street, Toronto Ontario M6N 4B4 Canada. DD 071.13451.

NOBLES COUNTY REVIEW. Newspaper. US. English. wk. $9.00. Nobles County Review, PO Box 536, Ray Bohn, Adriana MN 56110. Tel (507)483-2213.

THE NOME NUGGET. Began with May 18, 1901 issue. Newspaper. US. English. wk. $40.00. Nome Nugget, PO Box 610, Nome AK 99672. Tel (907)443-5235. Ed Nancy L McQuire. LC NEWSPAPER. adv acc. Circ 3,000. (ctrl). Alaska news, local and statewide. Concentrates on Nome area news.

NOR OR. Began in 1923. Newspaper. US. Armenian. sw. Nor Or Publishing Company, 7466 Beverly Boulevard/Suite 101, Los Angeles CA 90036. LC Newspaper 7002.

LE NORD. V. 1- March 24, 1976-. 0382-8883. Newspaper. CN. French. wk. $17.02. Le Nord, Hearst Ontario P0L 1N0 Canada. Tel (705)362-8464. DD 071.13142.

NORDEN : FINSKA AMERIKANAREN : FOLKTIDING FOR FINLANDSSVENSKARNA I AMERIKA. V. 39, No. 18, (May 2, 1935)-. Newspaper. US. Swedish (some advertisements in English). wk. $20.00. Norden News Inc, 8104-5th Avenue, New York NY 11209. Tel (718)238-4433. Ed Erik R Hermans. bk rev. adv acc. Circ 1,000. (ctrl). Current news from Finland. *Finska Amerikanaren.*

NORDIC. (LE NORDIC). VFOAT Nordic Week-End. 0712-7189. Newspaper. CN. text in French and English on inverted pages with separate pagination. wk. $30.95. Les Editions Nordique, 375 Laure Avenue, Sept-iles G4R 1X2 Canada. Tel (418)962-9441. DD 071.1417.

NORDISK TIDENDE. VFOAT Norske Nyheder. V. 93, No. 50, (Dec. 29 1983). Newspaper. US. Norwegian (English). wk. $35.00. Nordisk Tidende, 8104 Fifth Avenue, Brooklyn NY 11209. Tel (212)238-1100. LC NEWSPAPER.

NORFOLK GAZETTE. (THE NORFOLK GAZETTE). V. 1- Jan. 19, 1977-. 0704-0245. Newspaper. CN. English. wk. The Norfolk Gazette, Ad-Rite Associates Ltd, PO Box 418, Cayuga Ontario N0A 1E0 Canada. DD 071.1336.

NORMAN COUNTY INDEX. See Indexes/Abstracts.

NORSK UKEBLAD. 0029-2257. Newspaper. NO. Norwegian. wk. $98.75. c/o Nor Data, Postboks 2233, 7001 Trondheim Norway.

NORTH BAY LIVING. V. 1- May 14, 1975-. 0383-0764. Newspaper. CN. English. ir. DD 071.13147.

THE NORTH CADDO COUNTY NEWS. 8750-3719. Newspaper. US. English. wk. North Caddo County News, 108 East Main, Hinton OK 73047.

NORTH COUNTRY GAZETTE. VFOAT Gazette. 0745-628X. Newspaper. US. English. wk. $10.00. North Country Gazette, Route 9 Box 408, Chestertown NY 12817.

NORTH DELTA SENTINEL. Began with Nov. 1973 issue. 0316-0203. Newspaper. CN. English. mo. Delta Publications, 9345-120th Street, North Delta British Columbia Canada. DD 071.1133.

NORTH-EAST REGION COMMUNITY BOOSTER. (THE NORTH-EAST REGION COMMUNITY BOOSTER). V. 1- Mar. 1972-. 0703-9034. Newspaper. CN. English. ir. 25. Per No. Community Printers Ltd, Box 2014, Nipawin Saskatchewan S0E 1E0 Canada. DD 071.1242.

NORTH FRONTENAC NEWS. Began publication with Dec. 1970 issue. 0700-950X. Newspaper. CN. English. bm. $3. North Frontenac News, PO Box 250, Sharbot Lake Ontario K0H 2P0 Canada. DD 071.1371.

NORTH HAVEN POST. 0191-5541. Newspaper. US. English. wk. Wallingford Post, PO Box 100, Wallingford CT 06492.

NORTH HENNEPIN POST. Began in 1950. Newspaper. US. English. wk. $14.50. Post Publications, 8801 Bass Lake Road, Minneapolis MN 55428. LC NEWSPAPER 8496. *Robbinsdale Post.*

NORTH IDAHO PRESS. Began in 1912. Newspaper. US. English. da. $57.00. North Idaho Press, 506 Sixth Street, Wallace ID 83877. Tel (206)556-1561. LC Newspaper 7573.

NORTH KAWARTHA TIMES. No. 1 (Mar. 2, 1983)-. 0823-7387. Newspaper. CN. English. wk. North Kawartha Times, 7 Francis Street, Fenelon Falls Ontario K0M 1N0 Canada. DD 071.1364.

NORTH LAKE TAHOE BONANZA. (NORTH LAKE TAHOE BONANZA). 0192-3129. Periodical. US. English. sw.

NORTH LANCE. 0821-2376. Newspaper. CN. English. wk. North Lance, 620 Dakota Street, Winnipeg Manitoba R2M 3K2 Canada. DD 071.1274.

NORTH PEACE PICTORIAL. Oct. 30, 1973-. 0700-3420. Periodical. CN. English. Free - distribution limited to residents of North Peace area. North Peace Pictorial, PO Box 1266, Peace River Alberta T0H 2X0 Canada. DD 071.1231.

NORTH SHORE NEWS. 0712-5348. Newspaper. CN. English. wk. North Shore News, 202/1139 Lonsdale Avenue, North Vancouver British Columbia V7M 2H4 Canada. DD 071.1133. (ctrl).

NORTH SHORE TIMES. (THE NORTH SHORE TIMES). V. 1- Nov. 3, 1976-. 0701-0761. Periodical. CN. English. Les Editions, JMC 15 rue de I Eglise, Ste-Therese Quebec J7E 3K Canada. DD 071.1424.

NORTH THOMPSON JOURNAL. 0823-7425. Periodical. CN. English. wk. North Thompson Journal, Box 720, Barriere British Columbia V0E 1E0 Canada. DD 071.1141. *North Thompson Review and Bulletin, 0823-7417.*

NORTHBROOK LIFE. 0191-6300. Newspaper. US. English. wk. Life Newspaper, 1908 Sheridan Department, Highland Park IL 60035. Tel (312)142-9090.

NORTHBROOK STAR. 0744-9550. Newspaper. US. English. wk. $20.75. Pioneer Press, 1232 Central Avenue, Wilmette IL 60091. Tel (312)251-4300.

NORTHEAST MISSISSIPPI DAILY JOURNAL. 1934. 0744-5431. Newspaper. US. English. bm. The Tupelo Daily Journal, PO Box 909, Tupelo MS 38802. Tel (601)842-2611. Ed Tom Pittman. bk rev. adv acc. Circ 35,000. (ctrl). Contains local features, world briefs, and obituaries. Other articles/information concerns sports, music, movies, people, and business.

NORTHEASTER. 1978. Periodical. US. English. sm. $10.00. Minneapolis Northeaster, 1909 Central Avenue NE, Minneapolis MN 55418. Tel (612)788-9003. Ed Amy Clements. adv acc. Circ 30,000. Community newspapers for Northeast Minneapolis, St Anthony, and Columbia Heights Minnesota area. Distiguished in investigative reporting, and aggressive local advertising.

Newspapers

NORTHERN JOURNAL. (THE NORTHERN JOURNAL). Vol. 1, No. 1 (July 8, 1981)-. 0715-514X. Newspaper. CN. English. wk. $0.30 per issue. Northern Journal/Whisky Jack Enterprises, PO Box 1829, La Ronge Saskatchewan S0J 1L0 Canada. DD 071.1241.

NORTHERN LIFE. V. 1- Apr. 11, 1973-. 0700-527X. Periodical. CN. English. wk. $24.76. Laurentian Publishing Co, 158 Elgin Street South, Sudbury Ontario P3E 3N5 Canada. DD 071.13133.

NORTHERN MOSAIC. V. 1- Aug. 1975-. 0384-0840. Periodical. CN. English. qt. $3.86. Thunder Bay Multicultural Association, PO Box 2334, 278 Bay Street, Thunder Bay Ontario P7B 5EB Canada. Tel (807)345-0551. Ed Frank Obljubek. DD 971.312004. bk rev. adv acc. Circ 2,000. A newspaper promoting and publicizing the concept of multiculturalism to create an awareness and appreciation of the cultural diversity of our area.

NORTHERN PEN. (THE NORTHERN PEN). 1980. 0229-0391. Newspaper. CN. English. wk. $46.43. The Northern Pen, c/o Bern Bromley, St Anthony Newfoundland Canada. Tel (709)454-2191. Ed Bernard Bromley. DD 017.18. adv acc. Circ 4,500. (ctrl). News and sports from the local area, TV listings and features on local people.

NORTHERN PIONEER. (THE NORTHERN PIONEER). V. 1- Feb. 5, 1976-. 0383-1221. Newspaper. CN. English. wk. The Northern Pioneer, PO Box 1018, High Level Alberta T0H 1Z0 Canada. DD 071.1231.

NORTHERN TIMES. Began with Nov. 6, 1975 issue. 0383-8137. Newspaper. CN. English. sm. Northern Times NB, Box 880, Terrace British Columbia V8G 4R1 Canada. DD 071.1132.

NORTHERN TIMES. (THE NORTHERN TIMES). V. 1- July 24, 1978-. 0227-2512. Newspaper. CN. English. ir. Yukon News, Northern Times, PO Box 5149, Whitehorse Yukon 4S3 Canada. DD 071.191.

NORTHFIELD NEWS. 1876. Newspaper. US. English. wk. $27.00. Northfield News, PO Box 58, Northfield MN 55057. Tel (507)645-5615. Ed Margaret Lee. bk rev. adv acc. Circ 5,800. Local, state and regional news; culture; education; sports; government; politics and people.

NORTHUMBERLAND NEWS. V. 1- May 30, 1979-. 0228-0531. Newspaper. CN. English. wk. $12.38. Northumberland News, PO Box 517, Chatham New Brunswick E1N 3A8 Canada. Tel (506)773-9431. Ed Lois F Martin. DD 071.1521. adv acc. Circ 5,500. (ctrl). A newspaper which covers highlights of events which occur in Northumberland county as well as opinions, sports and features on people, past and present.

NORTHWEST EXPLORER. VFOAT Explorer. VAT Explorer (Sioux Lookout). Vol. 1, No. 1 (Oct. 17, 1979)-. 0712-5089. Newspaper. CN. English. wk. $6.50. Northwest Explorer, c/o F Smith, PO Box 989, Sioux Lookout Ontario P0V 2T0 Canada. DD 071.13112.

NORTHWEST PASSAGE. 1969. 0029-3415. Newspaper. US. English. mo. Northwest Passage, 1017 East Pike, Seattle WA 98122. Tel (206)323-0354. Ed Kris Fulsaas and Erin Moore. Ind/Abst Altern. Press Index. bk rev. adv acc. Circ 3,000. Includes independent alternative news, local and regional, some national and international; feminism, prisoners, environment, anti- militarism, opinion, reviews, and poetry.

NORWALK WEEKLY TRADER. 0191-9091. Periodical. US. English. wk. $4.00. Norwalk News, 136 Main Street, Westport CT 06880.

NORWICH BULLETIN. Newspaper. US. English. da. $138.00. Norwich Bulletin, 66 Franklin Street, Norwich CT 06360. Tel (203)887-9211. LC Newspaper 7002. *Norwich Morning Bulletin.*

NORWOOD TIMES. 1963. Newspaper. US. English. ir. $20.00. Norwood Times, 601 Washington Street, Norwood MA 02062. Tel 769-1725. Ed John J Cook. adv acc. Circ 4,250. (ctrl). General news, stories, births, deaths and real estate transfers.

NOTTAWASAGA/SUNNIDALE NEWS. (THE NOTTAWASAGA/SUNNIDALE NEWS). VFOAT News. VAT News (Nottawasaga/Sunnidale). Vol. 1, No 1 (Jan. 28, 1981)-. 0710-1740. Newspaper. CN. English. wk. DD 071.1317.

NOUVEAU JOURNAL DE ST-MICHEL. (LE NOUVEAU JOURNAL DE ST-MICHEL). VFOAT Journal de St-Michel. Vol. 1, No. 1 (17 OCT. 1979)-. 0712-2489. Newspaper. CN. French. wk. Free. Le Nouveau Journal de St-Michel/Suite 1, Montreal Quebec H1Z 3E1 Canada. DD 071.14281. (ctrl).

NOUVEL-EST. 30 Sept. 1980-. 0821-7378. Newspaper. CN. French. wk. $15.00. Nouvel-Est, 148 rue de la Cathedrale, Rimouski Quebec G5L 5H8 Canada. DD 071.147.

NOUVELLE. (LA NOUVELLE : BEAUMONT). Vol. 1, No. 1 (Jan. 9, 1984)-. 0827-2085. Newspaper. CN. English. bw. 10.00. La Nouvelle, PO Box 91, Beaumont Alberta T0C 0H0 Canada. Tel 929-5552. Ed Barbara Willis. DD 071.1233. adv acc. Circ 1,300. We are a community newspaper for the town of Beaumont and area.

NOUVELLE DU HAUST ST-FRANCOIS. (LA NOUVELLE DU HAUT ST-FRANCOIS). V. 3, No. 6- 6 Oct. 1976-. 0701-113X. Periodical. CN. French. wk. 7.00. Imprimerie Cormier Inc, 178 St-Pierre, East Angus Quebec J0B 1R0 Canada. DD 071.1468. *Nouvelle, 0382-0858.*

NOUVELLES D'OUTREMENT. VFOAT Outrement News. V. 1- Apr. 25, 1979-. 0227-8472. Newspaper. CN. English (text in French). wk. A M Advertising, Suite 20/2425 Grand Boulevard, Montreal Quebec H4B 2X Canada. DD 071.14281.

NOVA. V. 1- Apr. 9, 1974-. 0316-019X. Newspaper. CN. English. wk. 5.00 Annapolis & Kings Counties, 6.50 Elsewhere in Canada, 8.00 Foreign. Nova, PO Box 1027, Middleton Nova Scotia B0S 1P0 Canada. DD 0711633.

NOVAIA GAZETA = NEW GAZETTE. VFOAT New Gazette. Began with issue for May 9-15, 1980. Newspaper. US. Russian. wk. $38.00. Novia Gazeta, 209 East 14th Street, New York NY 10003.

NOVO MUNDO (TORONTO, ONT.). (NOVO MUNDO). Yearly V. 3, No. 128 (August 24, 1983)-. 0822-8035. Newspaper. CN. Portuguese. wk. $.50 per No. Novo Mundo, 946 College Street, Toronto Ontario M6G 1A5 Canada. DD 071.13541. *Mundo (Toronto, Ont.), 0229-1118.*

NOVYJ AMERIKANEC. (NOVYI AMERIKANETS). VFOAT New American. 0274-998X. Periodical. US. Russian. wk. $28.00 Domestic, $40.00 Foreign. Novy Amerikanetz, 80 Grand, Street, Jersey City NJ 07302.

NUEVA GACETA (HAVANA, CUBA). (LA NUEVA GACETA). No. 1 (August 1980)-. Periodical. CU. Spanish. mo. $21.01. Ediciones Cubanas, Obispo No 461, Apartado 605, Ciudad de la Habana Cuba. *Gaceta de Cuba.*

NUNATSIAQ NEWS. VFOAT Nunatsiark. V. 4, No. 23- July 7, 1976-. 0702-7915. Newspaper. CN. English (Inuit). wk. 11.61. Frobisher Press Ltd, Box 8 Frobisher Bay, Northwest Territories X0A 0H0 Canada. Tel (819)979-5357. Ed Monica Connelly. DD 071.195. bk rev adv acc. Circ 3,000. Newspaper. *Inuksuk, 0702-7923.*

NUOVO CIARLATANO. (IL NUOVO CIARLATANO). Began publication in 1975?. 0705-8756. Periodical. CN. Italian. mo. F Coscarella, Il Nuovo Ciarlatano, PO Box 1274/Station B, Oshawa Ontario L1J 5Z1 Canada. DD 071.1356.

NUOVO MONDO. (IL NUOVO MONDO : L'UNICO GIORNALE ITALIANO DELL' ALBERTA). 0821-6525. Newspaper. CN. Italian. mo. $5.00 Canada, $6.00 Alberta Residents, IL Nuovo Mondo 4545-118 Avenue, Edmonton Alberta T5W 1A8 Canada. DD 071.1233.

OAK BAY STAR. Began publication in 1974?. 0380-4542. Newspaper. CN. English. Community News, 506 David Street, Victoria British Columbia V8T 2C8 Canada. DD 071.1134.

OAK LAKE TOWN AND COUNTRY NEWS. 0702-763X. Newspaper. CN. English. sm. $5.00. Oak Lake Town & Country, Newspaper Board, Oak Lake Manitoba R0M 1P0 Canada. DD 071.1273.

OAK LEAVES. Newspaper. US. English. wk. Pioneer Press, 1232 Central Avenue, Wilmette IL 60091. Tel (312)251-4300. LC Newspaper 7672. *Vindicator.*

OAKDALE BEACON. 0746-5920. Newspaper. US. English. wk. Oakdale Beacon, PO Box 725, Oakdale LA 71463.

OAKLAND TRIBUNE. Ceased with Oct. 25, 1982 issue. Newspaper. US. English. da. $174.00. Oakland Tribune, PO Box 24304, Oakland CA 94623. Tel (415)645-2601. LC Newspaper 7002. *Oakland Daily Evening Tribune.*

OBITUARIES FROM THE TIMES. 1961/70-. US. English. ir. Meckler Books, 11 Ferry Lane West, Westport CT 06880. Ed Frank C Roberts.

OBSERVER. Newspaper. US. English. mo. $15.00. Observer Press Inc, Box 85, Bard College, Annadaleon Hudson NY 12504. Tel (617)431-1993.

THE OBSERVER-DISPATCH. Sept. 29, 1969-. Newspaper. US. English. da. $180.00. Utica Observer Dispatch, 221 Oriskany Plaza, Utica NY 13503. Tel (315)792-5000. Ed M C Taylor. Also available on microfilm from the Microphoto Division, Bell and Howell. *Utica Observer-Dispatch.*

OCALA STAR-BANNER. 0163-3201. Newspaper. US. English. da. $102.00. Ocala Star Banner, 819 SE 1st Terrace, Ocala FL 32670. Tel (904)629-0011.

OELWEIN DAILY REGISTER. Began in 1906. Newspaper. US. English. da. $48.00. Oelwein Daily Register, 16-20 East Charles Street, Oelwein IA 50662. Tel (319)283-2144. LC Newspaper 7002.

THE OFFICIAL WASHINGTON POST INDEX. See Indexes/Abstracts.

OGGI CANADA. VAT Canada Today (Downsview). First Year, No. 1 (14/20 March 1980)-. 0712-4929. Newspaper. CN. Italian. wk. $0.50 Each Number. OGGI Canada Pub, Unite 13 101 di Toro Road, Downsview Ontario M3J 2Z1 Canada. DD 071.13541.

OKANAGAN FALLS VIEWPOINT. 0715-5441. Newspaper. CN. English. wk. $6.00. Okanagan Falls Viewpoint, PO Box 448, Okanagan Falls British Columbia V0H 1R0 Canada. DD 071.1142. *Okanagan Falls News, 0715-5433.*

THE OKARCHE CHIEFTAIN. VAT Oklahoma Arapacho Cheyenne Chieftain. 8750-393X. Newspaper. US. English. wk. Okarchie Chieftain, PO Box 468, Okarche OK 73762.

OLIVIA TIMES-JOURNAL. Newspaper. US. English. wk. $13.00. Olivia Times Journal, 816 E Lincoln, Olivia MN 56277. Tel (612)523-2032.

OMAHA WORLD-HERALD (OMAHA, NEB. : 1954 : SUNRISE ED.). (OMAHA WORLD-HERALD). VFOAT Omaha World Herald. Vol. 90, No. 1 (Oct. 2, 1954)-. Newspaper. US. English. da. $174.20. Omaha World Herald, 14th and Dodge, Omaha NE 68102. Tel (402)444-1000. Ed G Woodson Howe. LC newspaper. bk rev. adv acc. Circ 224,000. (ctrl). Available on microfilm. Complete daily and Sunday. *Morning World-Herald (Omaha, Neb. : 1937).*

OMINECA ADVERTISER. (THE OMINECA ADVERTISER). V. 1- June 7, 1978-. 0708-000X. Newspaper. CN. English. wk. Free. Omineca Advertiser, PO Box 1007, Vanderhoof British Columbis V0J 3A0 Canada. DD 071.112. (ctrl).

ONOWAY TRIBUNE. (THE ONOWAY TRIBUNE). 0823-7131. Newspaper. CN. English. wk. $0.25 Each Number. The Onoway Tribune, PO Box 570, Onoway Alberta T0E 1V0 Canada. DD 071.1233. *Tribune (Onoway, Alta.).*

OPASQUIA TIMES. V. 1- Mar. 17, 1978-. 0707-5448. Newspaper. CN. English. ir. $15.48. Opasquia Times, Box 750, The Pas Manitoba R9A 1K8 Canada. Ed Murray Harvey. DD 071.1272. adv acc. Circ 3,252. (ctrl). Includes community and provincial news, sports, crafts, home improvement, law, politics, health, medicine, education, family care, entertainment.

OR BLANC. (L'OR BLANC). V. 1- Aug. 12, 1975-. 0383-1949. Newspaper. CN. French. wk. 25. Per No. Editions de l'Amiante, 131 d'Auteuil, CP 516, Thetford Mines Quebec G6G 2N3 Canada. DD 071.1714575.

ORANGE COUNTY NEWS. 0192-0421. Newspaper. US. English. wk. $85.00. West Orange Publishing Company, 13261 Century Boulevard, Garden Grove CA 92640. Tel (714)537-7510.

ORANGEVILLE CITIZEN. (THE ORANGEVILLE CITIZEN). V. 1- Sept. 18, 1974-. 0319-180X. Newspaper. CN. English. wk. The Orangeville Citizen, 81 Broadway, Orangeville Ontario L9W 1K1 Canada. DD 071.1341.

OREGONIAN. Newspaper. US. English. da. $160.00. Oregonian Publishing Company, 1320 SW Broadway, Portland OR 97201. Tel (503)221-5704.

ORILLIA SUN. Oct. 27, 1982-. 0823-6763. Newspaper. CN. English. wk. DD 071.1317.

Newspapers

THE ORLANDO SENTINEL. 106th year, No. 116 (April 26, 1982)-. 0744-6055. Newspaper. US. English. da. $87.10. Sentinel Communications Co, PO Box 2833, Orlando FL 32802. **Tel** (305)420-5305. *Sentinel Star.*

OROMOCTO POST. (THE OROMOCTO POST). 0710-5460. Newspaper. CN. English. wk. $15.00. Oromocto Post, 101 Hersey Street, Oromocto New Brunswick Canada. **Tel** (506)357-9813. Ed Al Rogers. DD 071.1543. bk rev. adv acc. **Circ** 4,800. (ctrl). A weekly community newspaper.

OROVILLE MERCURY. Vol. 1, No 1 (July 17, 1873)-. Newspaper. US. English. da. $63.00. Oroville Mercury Register, PO Box 651, Oroville CA 95965. **Tel** (916)533-3131. Ed Donald Shaffer. LC NEWSPAPER 7131. bk rev. adv acc. **Circ** 10,500. Daily newspaper of Oroville in Butte County California. Covers local, state, national and international news.

OSCAR. OTTAWA SOUTH COMMUNITY ASSOCIATION REVIEW. (OSCAR : OTTAWA SOUTH COMMUNITY ASSOCIATION REVIEW). VFOAT Ottawa South Community Association Review. 0715-5476. Newspaper. CN. English. mo. Free to Ottawa South Homes and Business. Ottawa South Community Association, 260 Sunnyside Avenue, Ottawa Ont K1S 0R7 Canada. DD 071.1384.

OSHAWA THIS WEEKEND. 0229-7744. Newspaper. CN. English. wk. Inland Publishing Co, 54 Main Street, Stouffville Ontario Canada. DD 071.1356.

OSTERREICHER. (DER OSTERREICHER). VFOAT Austrian. 0712-6395. Newspaper. CN. German. wk. $19.00. Austrian Publications, PO Box 355 Postal Station Z, Toronto Ontario M5N 2Z5 Canada. DD 071.13541.

OTTAWA COURIER. V. 73/91 No. 12- 20 March 1980-. 0227-2563. Newspaper. CN. German. wk. $15. Courier Press, 955 Alexander Avenue, Winnipeg Manitoba R3C 2X8 Canada. DD 071.1384.

OTTAWA HEROLD CEASED. Aug. 1970-March 1980. 0317-0195. Newspaper. CN. German (includes some text in English). mo. Ottawa Herold, 965 Richmond Road, Ottawa Ontario Canada. **Tel** (613)224-7467. DD 071.1384. *Mitteilungsblatt dew Deutschsprachigen Vereinigungen Ottawa's und Umgebung, 0712-8843.*

OTTAWA JOURNAL. July 1979-. 0226-1081. Periodical. CN. English. mo. $600. Commonwealth Microfilm Library, 3395 American Drive, Unit 11, Mississauga Ontario L4V 1T5 Canada. DD 071.1384.

OTTAWA REPORTER. (THE OTTAWA REPORTER). Vol. 1, No. 1 (Apr. 15, 1981)-. 0715-3325. Newspaper. CN. English. mo. Ottawa Reporter, 403 Catherine Street, Ottawa Ontario K1R 5T6 Canada. DD 071.1384.

OTTAWA SUNDAY HERALD. VFOAT Herald. VAT Sunday Herald (Ottawa). V. 1, No 1 (Mar. 27, 1983)-. 0823-633X. Newspaper. CN. English. wk. $20.00. DD 071.1384.

OUR CANADA. V. 1, No. 7- July 1978-. 0708-1359. Newspaper. CN. English. mo $13.93. Our Canada Publications, PO Box 843 Station F, Toronto Ontario M4Y 2N7 Canada. **Tel** (416)922-1936. DD 071.13541. *World Peace and Freedom Monthly, 0708-1340.*

OUTDOORS TODAY. 0199-3666. Periodical. US. English. wk. $15.00. Outdoors Today, PO Box 6852, St Louis MO 63144.

THE OVERSEAS HINDUSTAN TIMES. Began publication in 1950. 0048-2536. US. English. wk. $60.00. Hindustan Times Ltd, 18-20 Kasturba Gandhi Marg, New Delhi 110-001 India.

OWEN SOUND LIFE. V. 1- Feb. 23, 1977-. 0704-0237. Newspaper. CN. English. wk. Free. Wednesday Publications, Owen Sound Life, Box 218, Owen Sound Ontario N4K 5P3 Canada. DD 071.1318.

PACIFIC DAILY NEWS. 0196-2485. Newspaper. English. da. $220.50. Pacific Media Inc, PO Box DN, Agana Guam 96910.

THE PADUCAH SUN. Newspaper. US. English. ir. $78.00. The Paducah Sun, PO Box 2300, Paducah KY 42002. **Tel** (502)443 1771. LC NEWSPAPER. *Sun-Democrat (Paducah, Ky. : 1962).*

EL PAIS. Yearly V. 1- (No. 1-). Newspaper. SP. Spanish. da. $126.90. P.R.I.S.A., Miguel Yuste 40, Madrid 17 Spain. **Tel** (91)754 38 00. bk rev. adv acc. **Circ** 52. (ctrl). A resumee of the most relevant news published along the week daily.

PAIS (MADRID, SPAIN : EDICION INTERNACIONAL). (EL PAIS). Yearly V. 1, No. 1, (May 30, 1983)-. Newspaper. SP. Spanish. wk. EL Pais, Miguel Yuste, 40 Madrid-17 Spain.

PAKISTAN TIMES MICROFORM. V. 1 (1947)-. Newspaper. English. da. $222.38. Progressive Papers Ltd, Opp Mayo Hospital, Lahore Pakistan.

PALACHUV HLASATEL. VFOAT The Palach Herald. 0317-7033. Periodical. CN. Czech. ir. Palach Herald, 245 Dunn Avenue/Apartment 910, Toronto Ontario M6K 1S6 Canada.

PALMYRA ENTERPRISE. 8755-0539. Newspaper. US. English. wk. $5.00 In Advance, $8.00 Out of State. Poe Printers and Publishers, Mains Street, Palmyra WI 53156.

PANHANDLE PRESS (CHESTER, W. VA.). (PANHANDLE PRESS). VFOAT The Chester-Newell. Vol. 1, No.1 (July 23, 1969)-. Newspaper. US. English. wk. Marlen Publications, Chester WV 26034. Ed Shirley Allen.

PANJABI ESHEEA TAEEMZ. March 1975-. 0715-4801. Periodical. CN. Panjabi. sm. $0.60 Per No. Panjabi Asia Times, 1433 Bloor Street West, Toronto Ontario M6P 3L6 Canada. DD 954.005. *Panjabi Asia Times, 0319-8707.*

PAPER CLIP. (THE PAPER CLIP). Vol. 1, No. 1 (June 15, 1979)-. 0229-6764. Newspaper. CN. English. The Paper Clip, Ingomar Nova Scotia B0T 1H0 Canada. DD 071.1625.

PARK RAPIDS ENTERPRISE. Newspaper. US. English. sw. $20.00. Park Rapids Enterprise, PO Box 111, Park Rapids MN 56470. **Tel** (218)732-3364.

PARK RIDGE ADVOCATE. 0744-5385. Newspaper. US. English. wk. Pioneer Press, 1232 Central Avenue, Wilmette IL 60091.

THE PARKERSBURG NEWS. 8750-3956. Newspaper. US. English. da. Parkersburg News, 519 Juliana Street, Parkersburg WV 26101.

PARKSVILLE-QUALICUM NEWS ADVERTISER. (THE PARKSVILLE-QUALICUM NEWS ADVERTISER). VFOAT Advertiser. 0821-0055. Newspaper. CN. English. wk. Free. Parksville Qualicum News Advertiser, PO Box 2579, Parksville British Columbia V0R 2S0 Canada. DD 071.1134. (ctrl). *Parksville-Qualicum Weekly Advertiser, 0821-0047.*

PAROIKIAKA NEA. Began publication in 1973?. 0700-947X. Newspaper. CN. Greek, Modern. 25. Per No. Paroikiaka Nea 7, Cote St Catherine Road, Montreal Quebec H2V 1Z9 Canada. DD 071.14281.

PARSONS ADVOCATE. 0747-3303. Newspaper. US. English. wk. $12.00 W. Va., $14.00 Elsewhere. The Parsons Advocate, 212 Main Street, Parsons WV 26287.

PAS GRAPHIC. (THE PAS GRAPHIC). V. 1, No. 1 (Wed., Aug. 15, 1979)-. 0229-4702. Newspaper. CN. English. wk. $6.00. Nor-Man Graphics, PO Box 1738, The Pas Manitoba R9A 1L5 Canada. DD 071.1272.

PASS PROMOTER. (THE PASS PROMOTER). V. 1- Feb. 14, 1973-. 0380-4135. Newspaper. CN. English. wk. The Pass Promoter, Box 1019, Blairmore Alberta T0L 0E0 Canada. **Tel** (403)562-2672. DD 071.1234.

PATRIS (VANCOUVER, B.C.). (PATRIS). VFOAT Fatherland. No. 1 (Nov. 26, 1976)-. 0715-5913. Newspaper. CN. Greek, Modern. wk. $.35. Patris, 2856 West Broadway, Vancouver British Columbia V6K 2G7 Canada. DD 071.1133.

PAYNESVILLE PRESS. Newspaper. US. English. wk. Paynesville Press, Box 54, Paynesville MN. **Tel** (612)243-3772.

PAZIFISCHE RUNDSCHAU. VAT Pacific Review (Vancouver). V. 6, No. 67 (Jan. 10, 1970)-. 0048-3095. Newspaper. CN. German. $0.15 Per No. Pazifische Rundschau, PO Box 2033, Vancouver British Columbia V5G 3R6 Canada. DD 071.1133. *Dies und Das, 0715-5239.*

PEACE ARCH NEWS. (THE PEACE ARCH NEWS). V. 1- Feb. 10, 1976-. 0700-9003. Newspaper. CN. English. sm. Free. Peace Arch Publications Ltd, PO Box 131, White Rock British Columbia V4B 4Z7 Canada. DD 071.1133. (ctrl).

PEACE ARCH NEWS WEEKENDER. (THE PEACE ARCH NEWS WEEKENDER). Vol. 1, No. 1 (Sept. 12, 1982)-. 0821-5251. Newspaper. CN. English. wk. Free. The Peace Arch News Weekender, PO Box 131, White Rock British Columbia V4B 4Z7 Canada. DD 071.1133. (ctrl).

PEKIN DAILY TIMES. 0745-7863. Newspaper. US. English. da. The Pekin Daily Times, 20 South 4th, PO Box 430, Pekin IL 61554.

PENINSULA FREE PRESS. Vol. 1, No. 1 (Nov.7, 1979)-. 0710-0787. Newspaper. CN. English. wk. $0.15 Per Number. Peninsula Free Press Ltd, 9803 Third Street, Sidney British Columbia V0S 1M0 Canada. DD 071.1134.

THE PENNY PRESS REVIEW. 0276-573X. Periodical. US. English. sa. $7.00. The Penny Press Review, PO Box 703, Palo Alto CA 94302.

PENSE PROGRESS. 0715-5735. Newspaper. CN. English. mo. Pense Progress, Box 236, Pense Sask S0G 3W0 Canada. **Tel** (306)345-2235. Ed Linda Kushniryk. DD 071.1244. adv acc. **Circ** 250. (ctrl). Local news and interests announcements and reports. *Pense Paper.*

PERDESI PANJAB. V. 1- Mar. 10, 1977-. 0708-9503. Newspaper. CN. Panjabi. sm. $35.00. Pardesi Panjab, 2749 Dundas St West, Toronto Ont M6P 141 Canada. **Tel** 767-2726. Ed Gurdip Chauhan. DD 071.13541. adv acc. **Circ** 5,000.

DE PERE JOURNAL. New Vol. 48, No. 11 (June 16, 1966)-. 0748-6219. Newspaper. US. English. wk. $8.00 in-county, $9.00 elsewhere. Journal Publishing Company, 126 South Broadway, De Pere WI 54115. Available on microfilm from the State Historical Society of Wisconsin. *De Pere Journal-Democrat.*

PERFORMANCE NEWSPAPER. VFOAT Performance. 0746-9772. Periodical. US. English. wk. $89.00. Performance, 1020 Currie Street, Ft Worth TX 76107.

PERIODICALS & NEWSPAPERS - CALGARY PUBLIC LIBRARY. (PERIODICALS & NEWSPAPERS). Main/Corp Calgary Public Library. VAT Periodicals, Newspapers - Calgary Public Library. 0714-3591. CN. English. Calgary Public Library, 616 MacLeod Trail South East, Calgary Alberta T2G 2M2 Canada. DD 018.134.

PERIODICALS AND NEWSPAPERS - SOUTH CENTRAL REGIONAL LIBRARY SYSTEM. Main/Corp South Central Regional Library System (Ontario). 1976-. 0384-0018. Periodical. CN. English. ir. South Central Regional Library System, 220 Dundurn Street South, Hamilton Ont L8P 4K7 Canada. DD 016.05.

PETERBOROUGH COMMON PRESS. V. 1- June 10, 1975-. 0382-6104. Newspaper. CN. English. wk. 15. Per No. Peterborough Common Press, 262 Rubidge Street, Peterborough Ontario K9J 3P2 Canada. DD 071.1368.

PETERBOROUGH EXAMINER (DAILY). (PETERBOROUGH EXAMINER). Newspaper. CN. English. Preston Microfilming Services, 2215 Queen Street East, Toronto Ont M4E 1E8 Canada. DD 071.1368.

PETIT PROMENEUR. (LE PETIT PROMENEUR). No. 2- April 30, 1979-. 0225-2066. Newspaper. CN. French. ir. $3.00 for 15 No. Journal le Petit Promeneur, CP 493, Ste-Marthe-sue-le-Lac Quebec J0N 1P0 Canada. DD 071.1425. *Promeneur-Matin, 2225-2058.*

PETITE NATION. (LA PETITE NATION). 0228-9954. Newspaper. CN. French. wk. $8.00. La Petite Nation, CP 240, Saint-Andre-Avellin Quebec J0V 1W0 Canada. DD 071.14227. *Vallee de la Petite Nation.*

PETROLIA-ENNISKILLEN GAZETTE. (THE PETROLIA-ENNISKILLEN GAZETTE). VFOAT Gazette. Vol. 1, No. 1 (Mar. 15, 1979)-. 0229-7701. Newspaper. CN. English. wk. The Petrolia-Enniskillen Gazette, PO Box 99, Sarnia Ontario N7T 7H8 Canada. DD 071.1327.

PEUPLE DE LA CHAUDIERE. (LE PEUPLE DE LA CHAUDIERE : L'HEBDO DES CHUTES). Vol. 1, No. 1 (3 Sept. 1980)- . -. 0228-703X. Newspaper. CN. French. wk. $15.00. Le Peuple de la Chaudiere, Centre Normandie Local 27 845 Marie-Victorin St-Nicolas Est, Quebec G0S 3L0 Canada. DD 071.1459.

PEUPLE. HEBDO DE LOTBINIERE. (LE PEUPLE : HEBDO DE LOTBINIERE). VFOAT Peuple de Lotbiniere. Vol. 1, No 1 (21 June 1978)-. 0228-5703. Newspaper. CN. French. wk. $17.02. Peuple Hebdo de Lotbiniere, PO Box 130/167 Boul

Newspapers

Laurier, Laurier Station G0S 1N0 Canada. DD 071.1458.

PEUPLE-TRIBUNE. V. 1- Aug. 6, 1975-. 0383-7572. Newspaper. CN. French. wk. 69.64. Publications Le Peuple, 2 Route Trans-Canada #48, Levis Quebec G6V 6W8 CN. Tel (418)833-9398. DD 071.147. adv acc. Circ 37,900. (ctrl). General news, local and surrounding areas, sports news, local and regional.

PEUPLE/COURRIER DE LA COTE-DU-SUD. Ser. D, V. 1, No. 1 Jan. 4/11, 1973-. 0713-679X. Newspaper. CN. French. Peuple/Courrier de la Cote-du-Sud, 55 Avenue de la Fabrique, Montmagny Quebec G5V 2J3 Canada. DD 071.1473.

PHENIX (ST-FULGENCE). (LE PHENIX). First issue in 1973. 0318-9317. CN. French. Le Phenix, Hotel de Ville St-Fulgence, St-Fulgence Quebec Canada. DD 071.1416.

PHILADELPHIA CITY PAPER. VFOAT City Paper. 0733-6349. Periodical. US. English. mo. $6.00. Philadelphia City Paper, 6381 Germantown Avenue, Philadelphia PA 19144.

THE PHILADELPHIA INQUIRER MICROFILM. Began with April 2, 1860 issue. Newspaper. US. English. *Pennsylvania Inquirer and National Gazette*.

PHILADELPHIA INQUIRER STATE/REGIONAL NEWS INDEX. See Indexes/Abstracts.

PHILADELPHIA TRIBUNE. Began publication with Nov. 2, 1884 issue?. 0048-3702. Newspaper. US. English. sw. $23.35. Philadelphia Tribune, 520 S 16th Street, Philadelphia PA 19146. Tel (215)893-4050.

PHILIPPINES GAZETTE. (THE PHILIPPINES GAZETTE). 0710-3603. Newspaper. CN. English. Free to Members (Membership $3 .00). Filipino Gazette, PO Box 1311 Station H, Montreal Quebec Canada. DD 971.42810049921.

PHILIPPINES TODAY (WASHINGTON, D.C. : 1983). (PHILIPPINES TODAY). Vol. 1, No. 1 (Aug. 23, 1983)-. Newspaper. US. English. bw. Editorial Offices, 1617 Massachusetts Avenue NW, Washington DC 20036.

PHOENIX. Series/Titl Bell and Howell Undergound Press Collection. Began Publication in 1972?. Newspaper. US. English. wk. San Francisco State University, Journalism Department, 1600 Holloway Avenue, San Francisco CA 94132. Tel (415)469-1689.

PHOENIX GAZETTE. Newspaper. US. English. da. $52.00. Phoenix Newspapers Inc, PO Box 1950, 120 E Van Buren Street, Phoenix AZ 85001. Tel (602)271-8503.

PIASUARUSIRMI PIVATLIAYAT MITIMATALIKMI. No. 1- Jan. 21, 1972-. 0384-076X. Newspaper. CN. Eskimo (text in Inuit and English). Simon Awa, c/o Adult Education Center, Pond Inlet NWT X0A 0S0 Canada. DD 071.195.

PIATT COUNTY JOURNAL. Newspaper. US. English. wk. $11.00. Piatt County Journal Republican, 224 East Livingston, Montecello IL 61856. Tel (217)762-2511. LC Newspaper 7669. *Monticello Bulletin*.

PICKENS COUNTY HERALD AND WEST ALABAMIAN. VFOAT Pickens County Herald. 0746-0473. Newspaper. US. English. wk. $8.52 County, $14.91 Out of County. Pickens County Herald, PO Box 447, Aliceville AL 35442.

PIERCE COUNTY HERALD. 0192-1401. Newspaper. US. English. ir. $40.00. Pierce County Herald, PO Box 517, Puyallup WA 98371. Tel (206)848-4565.

PIERRE-BRILLANT. (LE PIERRE-BRILLANT). Vol. 1, No. 1 (18 June 1980)-. 0711-4753. Newspaper. CN. French. mo $5.00. Pierre-Brillant, c/o Journal de Val-Brillant, 9A St-Pierre Ouest, Val-Brillant Quebec G0J 3L0 Canada. DD 071.14775.

PINAWA PRESS. Vol. 1, No. 1 (Nov. 11, 1981)-. 0712-4937. Periodical. CN. English. wk. $8.00 Per Year. Pinawa Press, Box 572, Pinawa Manitoba R0E 1L0 Canada. DD 071.1274.

PIONEER. (THE PIONEER). V. 1- Dec. 6, 1979-. 0228-0523. Newspaper. CN. English. wk. 12.00 Domestic, 20.00 Foreign. T W Wilson, PO Box 600, Chetwynd British Columbia V0C 1J0 Canada. DD 071.111.

PIONEER. (THE PIONEER). Vol. 1, No. 1 (Sept. 3, 1980)-. 0710-5428. Newspaper. CN. English. sm. Free. Pioneer, PO Box 776, Cochrane Alta T0L 0W0 Canada. DD 071.1234.

PIPESTONE COUNTY STAR. Newspaper. US. English. wk. $18.00. Pipestone County Star, PO Box 470, Pipestone MN 56164. Tel (507)825-3333.

THE PLACER HERALD. Began with Sept. 11, 1852 issue. Newspaper. US. English. wk. $6.00. Placer Herald, c/o Auburn Journal, PO Box 1488, Auburn CA 95603. Tel (916)885-2471. LC Newspaper 7114-X.

PLACOTEUX. (LE PLACOTEUX). Vol. 1, No. 1 (12 Sept. 1978)-. 0708-207X. Periodical. CN. French. wk. Le Placoteux, CP 181, St-Pascal Quebec G0L 3Y0 Canada. DD 071.1475.

PLAIN DEALER. (THE PLAIN DEALER). V. 1- June 4, 1976-. 0701-0877. Newspaper. CN. English. da. $137.80. Plain Dealer, PO Box 70014 T, Cleveland OH 44190. Tel (216)344-4500. DD 071.1551.

PLAYGROUND DAILY NEWS. VFOAT Fort Walton Beach Playground News. Sept.3, 1962-. Newspaper. US. English. da. $78.00. Playground News, PO Box 2949, Fort Wlaton Beach FL 32549. *Playground News*.

PLEIN-JOUR SUR CHARLEVOIX. VFOAT Plein-Jour. V. 1- 24 July. 1974-. 0317-0683. CN. French. wk. 15. Per No. Plein-Jour sur Charlevoix, CP 760, Forestville Quebec G0T 1E0 Canada. DD 071.1449.

POINT. (LE POINT). V. 1- Aug. 27, 1975-. 0319-5805. Newspaper. CN. text in French and English. wk. Free to citizens of LaSalle and St-Pie, $10.00 Others. Journal le Point Inc, 2107 Lapierre Street, Lasalle Quebec Canada. DD 071.1428.

POINT. (LE POINT). V. 1- 19 Nov. 1975-. 0382-6309. Newspaper. CN. French. wk. Les Publications Dolbeau Inc, 1945 Provencher, Bolbeau Quebec Canada. DD 071.1414.

POINT. (LE POINT). Yearly V. 1, April 12, 1978- 1978-. 0227-2288. Newspaper. CN. French. wk. $9.28. Bathurst le Point, PO Box W, Bathurst New Brunswick Canada. Tel 506/548-8924. DD 071.1512.

POINT. (LE POINT). V. 1, No. 1, (Aug. 5, 1980)-. 0228-9199. Newspaper. CN. French. wk. $0,25 Per No. Le Point, a/s Guy Levac, 126 rue Principale, Alexandria Ontario, K0C 1A Canada. DD 071.1377.

POINT DE VUE. (LE POINT DE VUE). 0229-3277. Periodical. CN. French. mo. $0,40 Le No. Imprimerie Senneterre, CP 1830, Senneterre Quebec J0Y 2M0 Canada. DD 071.1413. *Senneterre, 0229-3269*.

POINT EDWARD GAZETTE. 0229-7612. Newspaper. CN. English. wk. $0.15 Per Number. Point Edward Gazette, PO Box 99, Sarnia Ontario N7T 7H8 Canada. DD 071.1327.

POL-AM JOURNAL (CHICAGO EDITION). (POL-AM JOURNAL). VFOAT Polish American Journal. 0749-0445. Newspaper. US. English. mo. $7.50. Panagraphics, 761 Fillmore Avenue/Suite 201, Buffalo NY 14212. Tel (716)852-8211. Ed David Franczyk. bk rev. adv acc. Circ 20,000. (ctrl). News of Polish Americans: business, religion, music, politics, science, women, etc.

PONT. (LE PONT). Yearly V. 1, June 20, 1979-. 0227-2296. Newspaper. CN. French. wk. $10.00 Domestic, $15.00 Foreign. Le Pont, CP 55, Grand-Mere Quebec G9T 5K7 Canada. DD 071.14465.

PONTE. (IL PONTE). Vol. 1 Mar. 2, 1978-. 0707-4239. Periodical. CN. Italian. wk. $10. Publication et Imprimerie Mimosa, Suite 207/2125 Jean Talon Street East, Montreal Quebec H2E 1V4 Canada. DD 071.14281.

POPULAR. (O POPULAR). Yearly V. 1- Dec. 1975-. 0382-9308. Periodical. CN. Portuguese. DD 071.13541.

PORT STANLEY BEACON. (THE PORT STANLEY BEACON). VFOAT Beacon. VAT Beacon (Port Stanley). 0229-656X. Newspaper. CN. English. sm. Free. The Beacon, PO Box 459, Port Stanley Ontario N0L 2A0 Canada. DD 071.1334. (ctrl).

PORTAGE. (LE PORTAGE). 0228-6262. Newspaper. CN. French. wk. $19.35. Le Portage, 336 rue la Fontaine, Rivier Loop Quebec G5R 4C3 Canada. Tel (418)867-1465. DD 071.1476.

PORTAGE JOURNAL. Vol. 1, No. 1 (June 16, 1983)-. 0746-8776. Newspaper. US. English. wk. Portage Journal, PO Box 370, Portage IN 46368. Tel (219)762-9564. Ed Deborah Krieter.

THE PORTAGE LAKES HERALD. VFOAT Herald. 0746-6021. Newspaper. US. English. wk. Herald Publishing Company, PO Box 831, 70 Fourth Street NW, Barberton OH 44203.

PORTAL. (THE PORTAL). V. 1- Jan. 21, 1976-. 0383-1094. Newspaper. CN. English. wk. $10.00. The Portal, 100 Deer Park Avenue, Kimberley British Columbia V1A 2J4 Canada. DD 071.1145.

PORTLAND OBSERVER. Vol. 1, No. 1 (Oct. 1, 1970)-. Newspaper. US. English. wk. $10.00. Portland Observer, PO Box 3137, Portland OR 97208. Tel (503)283-2487. Ed Carol Ann Barnett. bk rev. adv acc. Circ 22,000. (ctrl). Anything on multi ethnic groups in the country.

THE PORTSMOUTH HERALD. Began in 1936?. 0746-6218. Newspaper. US. English. da. $78.00. The Portsmouth Herald, PO Box 119, Portsmouth NH 03801. Tel (603)436-1800. Ed G Robinson. LC Newspaper 7002. bk rev. adv acc. Circ 15,000. (ctrl). Daily and Sunday newspaper. *Portsmouth Herald and Times, New Hampshire Gazette*.

PORTUGUESE TIMES. 1st Ed. 1982-. 0821-4727. Newspaper. CN. Portuguese (includes some text in English). $0.30. Portuguese Times, #201 14 George Street North, Brampton Ontario L6X 1R2 Canada. DD 071.13535.

PORTUGUESE TIMES (NEW BEDFORD, MASS). (PORTUGUESE TIMES). 1971. 0746-3928. Newspaper. US. Portuguese. wk. $50.00. Portuguese Times, Box N-1288 1709 Acushnet Avenue, New Bedford MA 02746. Tel (617)997-3118. Ed Manuel Ferreira. adv acc. Circ 16,000. (ctrl). Foreign language news.

POST EAGLE. Began publication in 1962. 1630-6786. Newspaper. US. English. wk. Post Eagle, PO Box 2127, Clifton NJ 07013. Tel (201)473-5414.

POSTILLON DE CHAMPLAIN. (LE POSTILLON DE CHAMPLAIN : AU FIL DU CHEMIN DU ROY). V. 1, No. 1, (Dec. 1980)-. 0229-320X. Newspaper. CN. French. ty. Le Postillon, a/s Gaetain Duchaine Inc, 2830 Ave St-Charles, Point-du-Lac Quebec G0X 1Z0 Canada. DD 971.4465.

POTTSBORO PRESS. Began in 1984. 0747-4253. Newspaper. US. English. wk. $16.00. Pottsboro Press, 110 Franklin Street, Pottsboro TX 75076. Tel (214)786-4051. Ed John Crawford. adv acc. Circ 1,500. Local news and advertising.

POWELL RIVER PROGRESS. (THE POWELL RIVER PROGRESS). V. 1- Feb. 25, 1976-. 0382-7518. Newspaper. CN. English. wk. 15.00 Each Number. Powell River Progress, 5831 Ash Avenue, Powell River British Columbia V8A 4R5 Canada. DD 071.1133.

THE PRAIRIE STATER. 0195-2854. Periodical. US. English. mo. Free to Members, $20.00 Others. Prairie Stater, 2720 East Lincoln Street, Bloomington IL 61701.

PRAVDA. V. 1.- Chyslo 1/2-. 0316-781X. Periodical. CN. Ukrainian. qt. $6.00. c/o Alexander Moch, 6 Churchill Avenue, Toronto Ontario M6J 2B4 Canada. Tel (301)881-5973. LC AP58.U5.

PRAVDA (PRAGUE, CZECHOSLOVAKIA). (PRAVDA). Periodical. CS. Czech. da. $7.95. Pravda Czech, Sturova 6, Bratislava Czechoslovakia.

PREGONERO (WASHINGTON, D.C.). (EL PREGONERO). 8750-9326. Newspaper. US. English. wk. $4.50 Domestic, $6.00 Foreign. El Pregonero, PO Box 4464, Washington DC 20017.

LA PRENSA. Newspaper. AG. Spanish. da. La Prensa/Argentina, 568 Avenue de Mayo, 1319 Buenos Aires Argentina.

LA PRENSA (LIMA, PERU). (LA PRENSA). Newspaper. US. Spanish. da. $420.00. La Prensa of Peru, Baquijano 745/765 Apartado 1993, Lima Peru.

PRESCOTT'S WEEKLY. 0194-9748. Newspaper. US. English. wk. $11.00. Prescotts Weekly, 129 North Cortez, Prescott AZ 86301. Tel (602)778-3100.

PRESENT. (LE PRESENT). Vol. 1, No. 1 Sept 8 1981-. 0712-2640. Newspaper. CN. French. wk. Free. Le Present, 195 du Phare O, CP 244, Matane Quebec G4W 1V8 Canada. DD 071.14775.

Newspapers

PRESS. (THE PRESS). 0823-7611. Periodical. CN. English. wk. DD 071.1133. *Shopper Press.*

THE PRESS ADVERTISER. 0192-6519. Newspaper. US. English. da. $145.44. Oakland Press, 48 West Huron Street, Pontiac MI 48056. **Tel** (313)858-2600.

THE PRESS DEMOCRAT. 0747-220X. Newspaper. US. English. da. The Press Democrat, 427 Mendocino Avenue, Santa Rosa CA 95401.

PRESS-INDEX BIDANG ILMU-ILMU SOSIAL DAN KEMANUSIAAN. *See* Indexes/Abstracts.

DIE PRESSE. Began with 1, 1946. Periodical. AU. German. da. $196.62. Morawa & Co Buchhandlung & Zeitungsburo, Wollzeile 11, 1011 Wien Austria.

PRESSE-LIBRE. No. 1 (March 1981)-. 0711-2963. Periodical. CN. French. mo. $1.00 Each Number, $10.00 Each Issue. Presse-Libre, 356 East rue Ontario, Montreal Quebec H2X 1H8 Canada. DD 071.14.

PRINCE ALBERT SUN. VFOAT Sun. VAT Sun (Prince Albert). 0714-8534. Newspaper. CN. English. wk. $16.70. Prince Albert Sun, 135 River Street West, Prince Albert Saskatchewan S6V 3K6 Canada. DD 071.1242.

PRINCETON TIMES-REPUBLIC. VFOAT Princeton Times Republic. 8755-397X. Newspaper. US. English. wk. $8.00 In-County, $12.00 Elsewhere In-State, $30.00 all Others. Princeton Times-Republic, PO Box 10, Berlin WI 54923. Available on microfilm from the State Historical Society of Wisconsin. *Princeton Times, Princeton Republic.*

PRINSBURG NEWS. VFOAT Raymond-Prinsburg News. 8750-0698. Newspaper. US. English. wk. $10.00. Prinsburg News, Prinsburg MN 56281. **Tel** (612)967-4244. Ed Bill Paterson. bk rev. adv acc. **Circ** 1,100. (ctrl). Weekly newspaper in west central Minnesota.

PROCTOR JOURNAL. Began with June 23, 1906 Issue. Newspaper. US. English. wk. Proctor Journal, 215 5th Street, Proctor MN 55810. **Tel** (218)624-3344. LC Newspaper 8495.

PROGRES DU NORD, AHUNTSIC. VAT Progres du Nord (1981). No. 29, (Aug. 4, 1981)-. 0822-563X. Newspaper. CN. French. wk. DD 071.1428. *Progres du Nord.*

PROGRESS. (THE PROGRESS). Began publication in 1976. 0703-1718. Newspaper. CN. English. ir. Free. RMP Publishing Company, PO Box 70, Maple Ridge British Columbia Y2X 7E9 Canada. DD 071.1133.

PROMOTION & PROFITS. VAT Promotion et Profits, Journal Promotion & Profits. V. 1- Nov. 1978-. 0226-8671. Newspaper. CN. French. mo. J G Bourbonnais et Associes Inc, 1435 Boul St Martin/Suite 60, Chomedy Laval Quebec H7S 2C6 Canada. **Tel** (514)669-3513. DD 658.8005.

PROVIDENCE DAILY JOURNAL. 1863. Newspaper. US. English. da. $209.04. Providence Journal Company, 75 Fountain Street, Providence RI 02902. **Tel** (401)277-7000. Ed Charles Hauser. adv acc. **Circ** 134,123.

PRUDHOE BAY JOURNAL. 0743-8303. Newspaper. US. English. bw. $17.50. Prudhoe Bay Publishing Inc, P O Box 80969, Fairbanks AK 99708.

PUBLIC SERVANT (ST. PAUL, MINN.). (PUBLIC SERVANT). 8750-7447. Periodical. US. English. wk. $24.00. Public Servant, 1264 Dayton Avenue, St Paul MN 55104.

PUBLISHERS' AUXILIARY. 1865. 0048-5942. Periodical. US. English. bw. $25.00. National Newspaper Association, 1627 K Street NW/Suite 400, Washington DC 20006. **Tel** (202)466-7200. Ed Chuck Holahan. LC PN4700. bk rev. adv acc. **Circ** 12,000. The newspaper industry's oldest newspaper. Covers news and features of interest to publishers, editors and other key employees.

THE PUEBLO CHIEFTAIN. VFOAT Daily Colorado Chieftain. Began with Apr. 28, 1872 issue. 0747-3559. Newspaper. US. English. da. $91.00. Star-Journal Publishing Company, Pueblo CO 81002. **Tel** (303)544-3520. LC Newspaper 7002.

PUEBLO STAR-JOURNAL AND SUNDAY CHIEFTAIN. VAT Pueblo Star Journal and Sunday Chieftain. Began in 1933. Newspaper. US. English. da. Star Journal Publishing Company, Pueblo CO 81002. **Tel** (303)544-3520. LC Newspaper.

PUTNAM COUNTY COURIER (CARMEL, N.Y. : 1852). (PUTNAM COUNTY COURIER). VFOAT Putnam Courier. Began with Jan. 10, 1852 issue. Newspaper. US. English. wk. $17.00 Out-Of-State. Putnam County Courier, Box 220 45 Gleneida Ave, Carmel NY 10512. **Tel** (914)225-3633. Ed Howard O Burr. LC Newspaper 8829-X. adv acc. **Circ** 9,000. *Democratic Courier.*

QUAD-CITY TIMES. Newspaper. US. English. da. $197.60. Quad City Times, PO Box 3828, Davenport IA 52808. **Tel** (319)383-2250. LC Newspaper. *Times Democrat.*

QUEBEC DIMANCHE. V. 1 (Dec. 12, 1982)-. 0820-7216. Newspaper. CN. French. wk. $0.75 Per Issue. Quebec Dimanche, 157 Ouest rue des Chenes, Quebec Quebec G1L 1G8 Canada. DD 071.14.

QUEBEC SUD-OUEST. V. 1- 17 Aug. 1977-. 0707-7572. Newspaper. CN. French. wk. Les Productions Sud-Ouest, 18B Montee du Lac, Ste-Barbe Quebec J0S 1P0 Canada. DD 0711431.

QUEBECOIS LIBRE D'OUTREMONT. (LE QUEBECOIS LIBRE D'OUTREMONT). Vol. 1, No. 1 Oct. 1973-. 0710-5797. Newspaper. CN. French. Quebecois Libre, 700 Avenue McEachran, Outremont Quebec H2V 3C7 Canada. DD 971.404.

QUEENSWEEK. VFOAT Queens Week. 0747-086X. Newspaper. US. English. wk. $8.00. Queensweek, PO Box 29, Middle Village NY 11379.

QUINCENARIO HISPANO. Began publication in 1971 or 1972. 0704-6820. Newspaper. CN. Spanish. sm. Quincenario Hispano, PO Box 6884 Station S, Vancouver British Columbia V5R 5T3 Canada. DD 071.1133.

'QUOTE UNQUOTE''. (QUOTE UNQUOTE). Vol. 1, Issue 1 (Oct. 1978)-. 0229-978X. Periodical. CN. English. ir. Quote Unquote, Room 264, University Centre, University of Guelph, Guelph Ontario N1G 2W1 Canada. DD 071.1343.

RACONTEUR. (LE RACONTEUR). 0712-2810. Newspaper. CN. French. wk. $13.00 Timmins and Iroquois Falls, $15.00 Others. Raconteur, 70 Avenue 6 East, Timmins Ontario P4N 5L9 Canada. DD 071.13142.

RADWASTE NEWS. 0737-6960. Periodical. US. English. sm. Radwaste News, PO Box 7166, Alexandria VA 22307.

RAG. Newspaper. US. English. ir. Rag, 2330 Guadalupe, Austin TX 78705.

RA'ID AL-ARABI. (AL-RAID AL-ARABI : SAHIFAH ARABIYYAH USBUIYYAH). VFOAT Al-Raid Al-Arabi. 0715-5018. Newspaper. CN. Arabic. wk. $0.25 Per No. Al-Raid Al-Arabi, Suite 1205 20 Graydon Hall Drive, Don Mills Ont M3A 3A1 Canada. DD 071.13541.

RAINY LAKE CHRONICLE. Newspaper. US. English. wk. $16.50. Rainy Lake Chronicle, PO Box 9, Rainer MN 56668. **Tel** (218)286-3378.

THE RALEIGH COUNTY GULF TIMES. 0746-8598. Newspaper. US. English. wk. The Raleigh County Gulf Times, Box 1190, Sophia WV 25921. *Gulf Times.*

RANCHO MIRAGE POST. VFOAT Post. Vol. 9, No. 18 (Wednesday, July 31, 1985)-. 0884-6170. Newspaper. US. English. wk. Desert Community Newspapers, 71-537 Highway 111/Suite B, Rancho Mirage CA 92270. *Rancho Mirage Chronicle, 0745-5577.*

RANDALLSTOWN NEWS. 0883-7104. Newspaper. US. English. wk. Randallstown News, PO Box 346, Westminster MD 21157.

RANDOM HARVEST WEEKLY. VFOAT Random Harvest. 8750-0930. Newspaper. US. English. wk. Odyssey Publications, Box N, Trumansburg NY 14886.

RANJIT. 0715-3910. Newspaper. CN. Panjabi. ir. Ranjeet, PO Box 67516 Station O, Vancouver British Columbia V5W 3T9 Canada. DD 071.1133.

RAPID CITY JOURNAL. Newspaper. US. English. da. $84.00. Rapid City Journal, PO Box 450-507 Main Street, Rapid City SD 57701. **Tel** (605)342-0280.

RAYNE ACADIAN TRIBUNE. 195?-. Newspaper. US. English. sw. Acadian Tribune Inc, South Adams Street, Rayne LA 70578. **Tel** (318)334-3186.

THE RECORD. (THE RECORD : LOUISVILLE ARCHDIOCESAN NEWSPAPER). Began publication in Feb. 1879. 0746-8474. Periodical. US. English. wk. $9.00. The Record, 400 Civil Plaza Building, 701 West Jefferson Street, Louisville KY 40202.

RECORD (HACKENSACK, N.J.). (THE RECORD). VFOAT Sunday Record. Began with Sept. 14, 1960 issue. Newspaper. US. English. da. 150 River Street, Hackensack NJ 07602. LC Newspaper. *Bergen Evening Record.*

THE RECORDER. V. 1- Jan. 1978-. 0709-0315. Newspaper. CN. English. mo. 6.00. Katipunan Publishers The Recorder, PO Box 697 Station A, Toronto Ontario M5W 1G2 Canada. DD 071.13541.

RECORDER (NIWOT, COLO.). (THE RECORDER). Began in 1984. 8750-1597. Newspaper. US. English. wk. $10.00 Boulder County, $20.00 Elsewhere. Recorder, PO Box 206, Niwot CO 80544. *Niwot Recorder, 0747-4709.*

RED WING REPUBLICAN EAGLE. Began in 1971?. Newspaper. US. English. da. 433 West Third Street, Red Wing MN 55066. LC Newspaper.

REDCLIFF REVIEW. V. 1- Oct. 6, 1976-. 0701-0079. Newspaper. CN. English. wk. $6.00. Redcliff Publications, 120 Broadway East, Redcliff Alberta T0J 2P0 Canada. DD 071.1234.

REFLECTOR. Newspaper. US. English. wk. $20.00. Mississippi State University, Box X, Mississippi State MS 39762. **Tel** (601)325-2374.

REFLET D'AMOS. (LE REFLET D'AMOS). V. 1- 5 July. 1978-. 0707-5529. Newspaper. CN. French. wk. $10.00. Le Reflet d'Amos, 25 1ere Avenue Est, Amos Quebec J9T 1H2 Canada. DD 071.1413.

REFLET DE MON MILIEU. Vol. 1 (Oct. 1976)-. 0229-3560. Newspaper. CN. French. mo. Free. Reflet de Mon Milieu, 809 Boulevard des Chutes, Beauport Quebec Canada. DD 071.1447. (ctrl).

REFLET DE TADOUSSAC. (LE REFLET : JOURNAL COMMUNAUTAIRE DE TADOUSSAC). 0821-1728. Periodical. CN. French. bw. $0.50 Each Number. Reflet, C P 41, Tadoussac Quebec G0T 2A0 Canada. DD 071.1417. *Reflet de Tadoussac, 0821-1728.*

REGENT PARK COMMUNITY NEWS. Began publication with Feb. 1972 issue. 0704-7053. Newspaper. CN. English. mo. Free. Regent Park Community Improvement Association, 44 Blevins Place, Toronto Ontario M5A 3M4 Canada. DD 071.13541. (ctrl).

REGIONAL. (THE REGIONAL). Vol. 1, Issue No. 1 (Oct. 26, 1983)-. 0827-2611. Periodical. CN. English. wk. $0.25 Each Number. Regional, c/o Kenora Daily Miner & News PO Box 1620 33 Main Street South, Kenora Ontario P9N 3X7 Canada. DD 071.13112.

REGIONAL DE DRUMMONDVILLE. (LE REGIONAL DE DRUMMONDVILLE : CAHIER AGRICOLE). Sept. 16, 1980-. 0711-4834. Newspaper. CN. French. wk. Free. La Parole, 1159 Boulevard St-Joseph, Drummondville Quebec J2C 2C8 Canada. DD 071.14563. (ctrl).

REGIONAL ECHO. (THE REGIONAL ECHO). Began publication in 1973?. 0319-1656. Newspaper. CN. English. T Wyatt, PO Box 38, Makefing Manitoba R0L 1B0 Canada. DD 071.1272.

REGIONAL NEWS. (THE REGIONAL NEWS). V. 1- Nov. 10, 1976-. 0704-0261. Newspaper. CN. English. wk. Free to Householders and Businesses in the Haldimand Region, $7.50 Others in Canada and US, $10.00 Other Countries. The Regional News, PO Box 418, Cayuga Ontario N0A 1E0 Canada. DD 071.1337.

REGIONAL NEWSPAPER. (THE REGIONAL NEWSPAPER). May 12, 1981-. 0712-1083. Newspaper. CN. English. sm. $7.00. Regional Newspaper, 38-1st Avenue North West, Dauphin Manitoba R7N 1G7 Canada. DD 071.1272.

REGIONAL TELEGRAPH. (THE REGIONAL TELEGRAPH). Began with Jan. 15, 1975 issue. 0317-5847. CN. English. wk. $2.50 Domestic, $4.00 Foreign. The Regional Telegraph, PO Box 340, Cayuga Ontario N0A 1E0 Canada. DD 071.1337.

Newspapers

REGISTER (SANTA ANA, CALIF.). (THE REGISTER). 0746-8628. Newspaper. US. English. da. The Register, PO Drawer 11626, Santa Ana CA 92711. **Tel** (714)835-1234.

RENFRO VALLEY BUGLE. 0034-4451. Periodical. US. English. mo. $6.00. Renfro Valley Folks Inc, Renfro Valley KY 40473. **Tel** (606)256-2664.

RENO GAZETTE-JOURNAL. VFOAT Reno Gazette Journal. Oct. 1, 1983-. 0745-1415. Newspaper. US. English. da. Reno Newspapers Inc, PO Box 280, Reno NV 89504. *Nevada State Journal (Reno, Nev. : 1907), Reno Evening Gazette, 0745-1431.*

REPORTER. (THE REPORTER). Began with Aug. 21, 1974 issue. 0380-0032. Newspaper. CN. English. wk. The Reporter, PO Box 610, Port McNeill British Columbia V0N 2R0 Canada. **DD** 071.1134.

REPORTER. (THE REPORTER). V. 1- Oct. 1, 1975-. 0380-8874. Newspaper. CN. English. wk. $8. The Reporter, PO Box 1079, Port Elgin Ontario N0H 2C0 Canada. **DD** 071.1321.

REPORTER. (THE REPORTER). 0710-0949. Newspaper. CN. English. wk. $0.20 Each Number. Reporter, PO Box 998, Alliston Ontario L0M 1A0 Canada. **DD** 071.1317. *Alliston & Cookstown Reporter, 0707-5502.*

REPORTER. (THE REPORTER). 0828-6248. Newspaper. CN. English. bw. Free. Reporter c/o A MacFarlane School of Journalism, Middlesex College/University of Western Ontario, London Ontario N6H 5B7 Canada. **DD** 071.1326.

REPORTER (LONG BEACH, CALIF.). (THE REPORTER). 0746-5688. Periodical. US. English. sw. $25.00. Pfanstiel Publishers & Printers, 3010 East Anaheim Street, Long Beach CA 90804. *Long Beach Reporter.*

REPUBLICAN JOURNAL (BELFAST, ME.). (THE REPUBLICAN JOURNAL). Feb. 6, 1829-. 0034-5075. Newspaper. US. English. wk. Norumbega Publishing, PO Box 327, Belfast ME 04915. **Tel** (207)338-3333. **Ed** B Griffin. **LC** Newspaper. *Waldo Democrat.*

REVEIL A CHICOUTIMI. (LE REVEIL A CHICOUTIMI). VAT Reveil (Chicoutimi). 16 May 1978-. 0228-6653. Newspaper. CN. French. wk. $17.50. Editions du Reveil, CP 520, Jonquiere Quebec G7X 7X9 Canada. **DD** 071.1416.

REVEIL A JONQUIERE. (LE REVEIL A JONQUIERE). VAT Reveil (Jonquiere). 0228-636X. Newspaper. CN. French. wk. $17.50. Editions du Reveil, 73 rue du Vieux Pont, Jonquiere Quebec G7X 3M7 Canada. **DD** 071.1416. *Reveil.*

REVEIL A LA BAIE. (LE REVEIL A LA BAIE). VAT Reveil (Ville de la Baie). 0228-6661. Newspaper. CN. French. wk. $15.00. Le Reveil a la Baie, 1222 6E Av Secteur Port-Alfred Ville de la Baie, Quebec G7B 1R4 Canada. **DD** 071.1416.

REVEIL DU PONTIAC. (LE REVEIL DU PONTIAC). 0229-0936. Newspaper. CN. French (text in English). mo. $0.25 Per Number. Le Reveil du Pontiac, CP 766, Fort-Coulonge Quebec J0X 1V0 Canada. **DD** 071.14215.

REVISTA RIO BRAVO. Vol. 1, No. 1 (Winter 1981)-. Periodical. US. English (Spanish). qt. $10.00 Domestic, $15.00 Foreign. Revista Rio Bravo, PO Box 3086, Laredo TX 78040.

REVOLUTIONARY WORKER. 0193-3485. Newspaper. US. English. wk. $40.00. RCP Publications, PO Box 3486, Merchandise Mart, Chicago IL 60654. **Tel** (312)663-5920.

REVUE DE PAPINEAU. (LA REVUE DE PAPINEAU). 0226-9945. Newspaper. CN. French. wk. La Revue de Papineau, 761 Boulevard Maloney, Gaineau Quebec J8P 1E5 Canada. **DD** 071.14227.

REXDALE TIMES REVIEW. VFOAT Times Review. Began publication Aug. 29, 1974. 0316-5442. Newspaper. CN. English. wk. .10 Per No. Times Review, PO Box 2053 Station B, Rexdale Ontario M9V 2G2 Canada. **DD** 071.13541.

REZZ. (THE REZZ). 0715-4429. Newspaper. CN. English. $0.35 Per No.; $9.10 for 26 Nos. Local Delivery. L'Benedict, Cornwall Island, Cornwall Ontario K6H 5R7 Canada. **DD** 071.1431.

THE RICHFIELD REAPER. 0746-6730. Newspaper. US. English. sw. $10.00 in Utah, $14.00 Elsewhere. The Richfield Reaper, 43 South Main Street, Richfield UT 84701.

RICHFIELD SUN. Newspaper. US. English. wk. Sun Newspapers, 7401 Buch Lake Road, Edina MN 55435. **Tel** (612)831-1200.

THE RINGGOLD RECORD. 0164-9116. Newspaper. US. English. wk. $10.00. Ringgold Record, PO Box 563, Ringgold LA 71068.

RIVER GROVE MESSENGER. 0744-5369. Newspaper. US. English. wk. $8.75. Pioneer Press, 1232 Central Avenue, Wilmette IL 60091. **Tel** (312)251-4300.

RIVER REVIEW. V. 1- Aug. 18, 1976-. 0700-9208. Newspaper. CN. English. wk. Reliance Press, 1397 Erin Street, Winnipeg Manitoba R3E 2S9 Canada. **DD** 071.1274.

RIVERVIEW GAZETTE. (THE RIVERVIEW GAZETTE). Vol. 1, No. 1 (Feb. 1, 1983)-. 0823-7573. Newspaper. CN. English. wk. $20.00. Riverview Gazette, PO Box 354, Amherst Nova Scotia, B4H 3Z5 Canada. **DD** 071.1611.

RIVERVIEW THIS WEEK. Vol. 1, No. 1 (Nov. 1983)-. 0827-2689. Newspaper. CN. English. wk. 17.50. This Week Publications, 567 Cloverdale Road/Coverdale Square, Riverdale New Brunswick E1B 3K7 Canada. **Tel** (506)387-3006. **Ed** Elizabeth Malone. **DD** 971.1531. bk rev. adv acc. **Circ** 8,500. Weekly community newspaper serving an area with a population base of 30,000 people in Southeast New Brunswick. Includes columns and special features.

ROBLIN NEWS. (THE ROBLIN NEWS). 0229-7760. Newspaper. CN. English. wk. Hal-Man Publications, Box 299, 182 Main Street, Roblin R0L 1P0 Canada. **DD** 071.1272. *News (Roblin (Man. : Town)), 0229-7752.*

ROCHESTER ECCENTRIC. 0194-1917. Newspaper. US. English. sw. Rochester Eccentric, 410 Main Street, Rochester MI 48063. **Tel** (313)651-7575.

ROCHESTER POST-BULLETIN. VFOAT Rochester Post Bulletin. Began in 1925. Newspaper. US. English. da. Rochester Post Bulletin, 18 First Avenue SE, Rochester MN 55901. **Tel** (507)285-7676 OR 285-7682. **Ed** William Boyne. **LC** Newspaper 7002. bk rev. adv acc. **Circ** 40,000. (ctrl). *Rochester Daily Post and Record, Rochester Daily Bulletin.*

ROCK FLUFF. Began with June 1968 issue. 0381-6613. Newspaper. CN. English. ir. Box 2703 Whitehrse, Yukon Y1A 2C6 Canada. **DD** 071.191.

ROCKFORD REGISTER STAR. VFOAT Sunday Register Star. Jan. 2, 1979-. Newspaper. US. English. da. 97 East State Street, Rockford IL 61105. **LC** Newspaper.

ROCKVILLE CENTRE'S THE LONG ISLAND NEWS AND THE OWL. Vol. 49, No. 35 (Aug. 28, 1964)-. Newspaper. US. English. wk. *Long Island News and the Owl.*

ROCKY VIEW FIVE VILLAGE WEEKLY. 0821-7262. Newspaper. CN. English. wk. Free Locally. Rocky View Five Village Weekly, PO Box 40, Irricana Alberta T0M 1B0 Canada. **DD** 071.1233.

ROCKY VIEW TIMES. (THE ROCKY VIEW TIMES). 0715-4992. Newspaper. CN. English. wk. $0.20 Per No. Rocky View Times, PO Box 580, Airdrie Alberta T0M 0B0 Canada. **DD** 071.1233.

ROSEBUD COUNTY PRESS. 8750-2097. Newspaper. US. English. wk. Rosebud County Press, PO Box 734, Colstrip MT 59323-0734.

ROSEMONT PROGRESS. 0744-5407. Newspaper. US. English. wk. $8.75. Pioneer Press, 1232 Central Avenue, Wilmette IL 60091. **Tel** (312)251-4300.

ROSSLAND AND DISTRICT WEEKLY. (THE ROSSLAND AND DISTRICT WEEKLY). V. 1- March 24, 1976-. 0383-8153. Newspaper. CN. English. wk. $9.90. Ourtowne Publications, PO Box 1198, Rossland British Columbia V0G 1Y0 Canada. **DD** 071.1144.

ROUGH PATCH. 1st Ed. (Dec. 1983)-. 0824-1953. Periodical. CN. English. mo. $0.50 Per No. Rough Patch, PO Box 74, Nakina Ontario P0T 2H0 Canada. **DD** 071.1312.

RURAL ROUTE (WALLACEBURG, ONT.). (RURAL ROUTE). 0715-5271. Newspaper. CN. English. wk. Free. Wallaceburg News, 222 Wellington Street, Wallaceburg Ontario N8A 4L5 Canada. **DD** 338.109713. (ctrl).

RUSSKAJA ZIZN. (RUSSKAIA ZHIZN). Began in 1922. Newspaper. US. Russian (English). ir. $75.00. Russian Life Inc, 2458 Sutter Street, San Francisco CA 94115. **Tel** (415)921-5380. **LC** Newspaper 7187.

SAANICH COURIER. V. 1- Aug. 28, 1974-. 0380-4577. Newspaper. CN. English. wk. Community News, 506 David Street, Victoria British Columbia V8T 2C8 Canada. **DD** 071.1134.

SAANICH TRIBUNE. Vol. 1, No. 1 (Dec. 10, 1980)-. 0712-2098. Newspaper. CN. English. wk. $10.00. Saanich Tribune, 111-3347 Oak Street, Victoria British Columbia V8X 1R2 Canada. **DD** 071.1134.

THE SABINE INDEX. See Indexes/Abstracts.

SABRAS. VFOAT Subras. 0821-5189. Newspaper. CN. Gujarati. mo. $10.00. Mihir Publications, 4226 Torino Cres, Mississauga Ontario L4W 3T5 Canada. **DD** 059.91471.

THE SACRAMENTO BEE. Began in 1908. Newspaper. US. English. da. $114.00. Delivery by Mail Department, 21st and Q Streets, PO Box 15779, Sacramento CA 95813. **Tel** (916)446-9404. **Ed** C K McClatchy. **LC** Newspaper 7135. bk rev. adv acc. **Circ** 224,589 Daily, 259,069 Sunday. Available on microfilm from Bay Microfilm, Inc. *Evening Bee.*

THE SACRAMENTO OBSERVER. Began in 1962. 0036-2212. Newspaper. US. English. wk. $20.00. Observer Publishing Company, PO Box 209, Sacramento CA 95801. **Tel** (916)452-4781.

SAGINAW NEWS (1929). (THE SAGINAW NEWS). Began with Jan. 1, 1929 issue. Newspaper. US. English. da. 203 South Washington Avenue, Saginaw MI 48605. **LC** Newspaper 7002. *Saginaw Daily News.*

THE ST. AUGUSTINE RECORD. VFOAT Saint Augustine Record. Began in 1894. Newspaper. US. English. da. $109.20. St Augustine Record, PO Drawer 1630, St Augustine FL 32084. **Tel** (904)829-6586. **Ed** Steve Cottier. **LC** Newspaper 7488-X. bk rev. adv acc. **Circ** 11,500. (ctrl). Local newspaper which includes national news.

ST. BONIFACE JOURNAL. V. 1- Aug. 18, 1976-. 0700-9402. Newspaper. CN. English. wk. Reliance Press, 1397 Erlin Street, Winnipeg Manitoba R3E 2S9 Canada. **DD** 071.1274.

ST. CATHARINES REPORT. Vol. 1, No. 1 (Mar. 1979)-. 0229-2777. Periodical. CN. English. ir. Saint Catharines Downtown Association, PO Box 813, Suite 417/80 King Street, Saint Catharines Ontario L2R 6Y3 Canada. **DD** 071.1338.

ST. CROIX AVIS. VFOAT Avis. V. 1, No. 1, (Jan. 1, 1844)-. Newspaper. English (Danish (1844-Dec.31, 1904)). ir. St Croix Avis, Brodhurst Printery, St Croix Virgin Islands. *Dansk Vestindisk Regierings Avis (Saint Croix, V.I. : 1815).*

ST. JOSEPH GAZETTE (SAINT JOSEPH, MO. : 1902). (ST. JOSEPH GAZETTE). VFOAT Saint Joseph Gazette. Began in 1902. Newspaper. US. English. da. St Joseph Gazette, Ninth and Edmonds Streets, St Joseph MO 64502. **LC** Newspaper. *Saint Joseph Gazette-Herald.*

ST. JOSEPH NEWS-PRESS. VFOAT Saint Joseph News Press. Began with Mar. 1, 1905 issue. Newspaper. US. English. da. Ninth and Edmonds Streets, Saint Joseph MO 64502. **LC** Newspaper 7002. *St. Joseph News and Press.*

ST. LAMBERT JOURNAL. VFOAT Journal St-Lambert. 0826-4295. Newspaper. CN. English (French). ir. Free to residents of St. Lambert. St Lambert Journal, PO Box 333, St Lambert Quebec J4P 3P8 Canada. **DD** 071.1437.

ST. LOUIS ARGUS. Began publication in 1912?. Newspaper. US. English. wk. $10.00. Argus, 4595 Dr Martin Luther King Drive, St Louis MO 63113.

ST. LOUIS GLOBE-DEMOCRAT. VFOAT Saint Louis Globe Democrat. New Ser. Vol. 1, No. 1 (May 20, 1975)-. Newspaper. US. English. da. $99.00. 710 North Tucker Boulevard, St Louis MO 63101. **Tel** (314)342-1212. **Ed** William Fevstel. bk rev. adv acc. **Circ** 200,000. (ctrl). Metropolitan newspaper published in St. Louis Missouri with circulation throughout Eastern Missouri and Southern Illinois. *St. Louis Daily Globe, St. Louis Democrat (Saint Louis, Mo. : 1873); St. Louis Republic.*

SAINT LOUIS PARK SUN. Newspaper. US. English. wk. Edina St Louis Park Sun, 7401 Bush Lake Road, Edina MN 55435. **Tel** (612)831-1200.

Newspapers

ST. LOUIS POST-DISPATCH. VFOAT Saint Louis Post Dispatch. VAT Saint Louis Post-Dispatch. Began in March 1879. Newspaper. US. English. da. $214.00. Saint Louis Post-Dispatch, Mail Subscription Division, St Louis MO 63101. Tel (314)342-6030. Ed David Lipman. bk rev. adv acc. Available on microfilm. One of nation's leading newspapers. Pulitzer Publishing Company. *St. Louis Post and Dispatch.*

ST. LOUIS SENTINEL. Began publication in 1968?. Newspaper. US. English. wk. Woods Publications Inc, 3338 Olive/Suite 206, St Louis MO 63103.

ST. MARY'S BEACON. Vol. 4, No. 46 (Sept. 5, 1867)-. 0745-0680. Newspaper. US. English. wk. Ralph Hostetter, 22 Courthouse Drive, Leonardtown MD 20650. Tel (301)475-8078. *St. Mary's Gazette.*

ST. PAUL DISPATCH. VFOAT Saint Paul Dispatch. Vol. 1, No. 1 (Feb. 29, 1868)-. 0746-7028. Newspaper. US. English. da. $146.12. St Paul Dispatch-Pioneer Press, 345 Cedar Street, St Paul MN 55101. Tel (612)222-5039. LC Newspaper 7002.

ST. PAUL PIONEER PRESS (SAINT PAUL, MINN. : 1909). (ST. PAUL PIONEER PRESS). VFOAT Saint Paul Pioneer Press. Vol. 56, No. 356 (Dec. 22, 1909)-. 0746-701X. Newspaper. US. English. da. St Paul Pioneer Press, 55-63 East Fourth Street, St Paul MN 55101. LC Newspaper 7002. *Daily Pioneer Press.*

ST. PAUL RECORDER. VFOAT Saint Paul Recorder. Began with Aug. 10, 1934 issue. Newspaper. US. English. wk. $9.00. St Paul Recorder, 3744 4th Avenue South, Minneapolis MN 55409. Tel (612)224-4846. Ed Launa Q Newman. LC Newspaper 8506. adv acc. Circ 10,000. Includes news, opinion, features, sports, entertainment, of, by and for the black community. Display, classified and legal advertising.

ST. PETERSBURG TIMES (1892). (ST. PETERSBURG TIMES). VFOAT Saint Petersburg Times. Began in October 1982. Newspaper. US. English. da. $156.00. St Petersburg Times, PO Box 1121, St Petersburg FL 33731. Tel (813)893-8166. LC Newspaper 7002.

ST. VITAL LEADER. V. 1- Aug. 18, 1976-. 0700-9518. Newspaper. CN. English. wk. Reliance Press, 1397 Erin Street, Winnipeg Manitoba R3E 2S9 Canada. DD 071.1274.

SALAMANCA PRESS. 115th Year, No. 108 (Sept. 1, 1981)-. 8755-9110. Newspaper. US. English. da. *Salamanca Republican Press.*

THE SALINA JOURNAL. Began in 1871. 0745-127X. Newspaper. US. English. da. $48.00. Salina Journal Inc, Box 779, Salina KS 67401. Tel (913)8236363. LC Newspaper 7857.

SALMON RIVER NEWS. 0193-0311. Newspaper. US. English. Oswego County Weeklies, North Jefferson Street, Box 1, Mexico NY 13114.

SAN DIEGO UNION (SAN DIEGO, CALIF. : DAILY) CEASED. (THE SAN DIEGO UNION). Ceased in Dec. 1888. Newspaper. US. English. da. $420.00. San Diego Union, PO Box 191, San Diego CA 92112. Tel (619)299-4141. Ed Gerald Warren. LC Newspaper. bk rev. adv acc. *San Diego Daily Union.*

THE SAN FRANCISCO BAY GUARDIAN. VFOAT Bay Guardian. 1966. 0036-4096. Periodical. US. English. wk. $24.00. San Francisco Bay Guardian, 2700 19th Street, San Francisco CA 94110. Ed Bruce B Brugmann. bk rev. adv acc. Circ 61,000. Alternative journalism: investigative reporting, consumer news and reports, political news and endorsements, entertainment news and reviews.

SAN FRANCISCO CHRONICLE. Vol. 10, No. 27 Aug. 15, 1869. Newspaper. US. English. da. $218.00. San Francisco Newspaper Agency, PO Box 7259, San Francisco CA 94120. Tel (415)777-7559. Ind/Abst Infobank. LC Newspaper. *Daily Morning Chronicle (San Francisco, Calif.).*

THE SAN FRANCISCO EXAMINER. VFOAT San Francisco Sunday Examiner and Chronicle. Vol. 76, No. 87 (Mar. 28, 1902)-. Newspaper. US. English. da. $218.00. San Francisco Newspaper Agency, PO Box 7259, San Francisco CA 94120. Tel (415)777-7559. Ind/Abst Energy Inf. Abstr., Environ. Abstr. LC Newspaper. *Examiner.*

THE SAN FRANCISCO JOURNAL. V.1- 1976-. Newspaper. US. English. wk. $10.00. 927 Kearny Street, San Francisco CA 94133. LC X.

THE SAN FRANCISCO JOURNAL. CHINESE EDITION. (SHIH TAI PAO). VFOAT The San Francisco Journal. Began in 1972. 0199-462X. Newspaper. US. Chinese. da. $60.00. San Francisco Journal, 1600 Armstrong Avenue, San Francisco CA 94124. Tel (415)822-1155. adv acc. Circ 6,000. Chinese language daily newspaper representing the Chinese-American community. News coverage includes national and international news, sports, and entertainment.

THE SAN FRANCISCO PROGRESS. 0191-8192. Newspaper. US. English. ir. $65.00. San Francisco Progress, 851 Howard Street, San Francisco CA 94103. Tel (415)982-8022. Ed Lynette Evans. adv acc. Circ 222,200. (ctrl). General interest newspaper concentrating on Bay area and San Francisco news, sports and entertainment. Legal advertising vehicle for city and county of San Francisco.

SAN JOSE MERCURY (SAN JOSE, CALIF. : 1885). (SAN JOSE MERCURY). VFOAT San Jose Mercury-News. -Aug. 28, 1983. Newspaper. US. English. da. $180.00. San Jose Mercury News, Mail Subscription, 750 Ridder Park Drive, San Jose CA 95190. Tel (408)920-5609. LC Newspaper 7200. *Daily Mercury and Times.*

THE SAN JUAN STAR. Nov. 2, 1959-. 8750-6122. Newspaper. PR. English. wk. The San Juan Star, GPO Box 4187, San Juan PR 00936.

SAN MARCOS COURIER. 0273-9259. Newspaper. US. English. wk. $35.00. Press Courier-Circulation, PO Box 2188, Vista CA 92083. Tel (619)724-7161. Newspaper.

SANDARA. (SANDARA. THE LEAGUE). VFOAT League. Began 1913. 8750-2348. Newspaper. US. Lithuanian. bw. $10.00. Sandara, 840 West 33rd Street, Chicago IL 60608. DD 071.

SANDESH. Began publication in Jan. 1976?. 0380-2949. Monographic Series. CN. English (Lahnda). bw. .50 Per No. Sandesh, 714 Campbell Street, Winnipeg Manitoba R3N 1C3 Canada. DD 071.1274.

THE SANDHILL CITIZEN AND NEWS OUTLOOK. 0746-6137. Newspaper. US. English. sw. $6.00 Moore and adjoining counties, $7.00 Others. The Sandhill Citizen and News Outlook, PO Box 336, Aberdeen NC 28315. *Sandhill Citizen.*

SANDOVAL COUNTY TIMES-INDEPENDENT. 0193-5348. Periodical. US. English. wk. Independent Newspapers, PO Box 429, Albuquerque NM 87103.

SANGCHO NYUSU. VFOAT The Sangcho News. Began publication in 196-?. 0226-8647. Newspaper. CN. Korean. .25 Per No. Korean Society of Vancouver, 200-96 East Broadway, Vancouver British Columbia V5T 1V6 Canada. DD 971.133.

SANJH SAVERA. V. 1- Oct. 1977-. 0708-9449. Newspaper. CN. Panjabi. bw. .60 Per No. Sanjh Savera, PO Box 652, Brampton Ontario L6V 2L6 Canada. DD 071.13535.

SANTA BARBARA NEWS & REVIEW. Series/Titl Bell and Howell Underground Press Collection. V.1- Feb. 11, 1972-. Newspaper. US. English. wk. $9.75. Santa Barbara News & Review, 1930 de la Vina Street, Santa Barbara CA 93101. Tel (805)966-3928.

SANTA BARBARA NEWS-PRESS (1932). (SANTA BARBARA NEWS-PRESS). VFOAT Santa Barbara News Press. Began in 1932. Newspaper. US. English. da. $72.00. Santa Barbara News Press, Drawer NN, Santa Barbara CA 93102. Tel (803)966-3911. LC Newspaper 7205. *Morning Press, Santa Barbara Daily News.*

SARATOGA NEWS. 0745-6255. Newspaper. US. English. wk. $288.00. Roy Boody, 12378 Saratoga-Sunnyvale Road/Suite 8, Saratoga CA 95070. Tel (408)255-7500. Ed Iver Davidson. adv acc. Circ 7,796. (ctrl). One of eleven community newspapers in the Meredith newspaper chain reaching over 189,000 households in the San Jose Ca PMSA.

SATURDAY. 0746-0929. Newspaper. US. English. wk. 134 Columbus Street, Charleston SC 29402.

SATURDAY EVENING POST (PHILADELPHIA, PA. : 1839). (THE SATURDAY EVENING POST). VFOAT United States Saturday Post. Vol. 18, No. 954 (Nov. 9 1839)-. 0048-9239. Periodical. US. English. mo. Benjamin Franklin Literary & Medical Society, 1100 Waterway Boulevard, PO Box 567, Indianapolis IN 46202. Ind/Abst Pop. Mag. Rev., GeoRef, Read. Guide Period. Lit., Abr. Read. Guide. LC AP2. DD 051. CODEN SAEPAR. *Atkinson's Evening Post and Philadelphia Saturday News, Country Gentleman,* 0147-4928.

SAVANNAH DAILY MORNING NEWS. Newspaper. US. English. da. $114.00. Savannah Evening Press, PO Box 1088, Savannah GA 31402. Tel (912)236-9511. LC Newspaper 7488-X.

SAVANNAH EVENING PRESS. Began with Nov. 19, 1891 issue. 8750-4685. Newspaper. US. English. da. $84.00. Savannah Evening Press, PO Box 1088, Savannah GA 31402. Tel (912)236-9511. Ed Wallace M Davis Jr. LC Newspaper 7002. bk rev. adv acc. Circ 22,000. Publishes two daily and a Sunday newspaper.

SAVANNAH MORNING NEWS, SAVANNAH EVENING PRESS (COASTAL EMPIRE EDITION). (SAVANNAH MORNING NEWS, SAVANNAH EVENING PRESS). VFOAT Savannah Evening Press. 8750-8273. Newspaper. US. English. wk. $36.00 Georgia & South Carolina, $114.00 Other States. Savannah Morning News, Savannah Evening Press, 5 Whitaker Street, Savannah GA 31401.

THE SAVANNAH TRIBUNE. Vol. 1, No. 35 (July 29, 1876)-. Newspaper. US. English. wk. $12.00. Savannah Tribune, 916 Montgomery Street, Savannah GA 31401. Tel (912)233-6128. LC Newspaper. bk rev. adv acc. Circ 6,000. Also available in microfilm. National and local news of community interest, especially targeted to black readers. *Colored Tribune.*

SAWT AL- URUBAH (TORONTO, ONT.). (SAWT AL- URUBAH). VFOAT Arabs' Voice. VAT Arabs' Voice (Toronto), Arab Voice (Toronto). V. 1, No. 1 (November 1981)-. 0821-6428. Newspaper. CN. Arabic. mo. $12.00. Sawt Al- Urubah, Toronto Ontario Canada. DD 071.13541.

SCHILLER PARK INDEPENDENT. 0744-5377. Newspaper. US. English. wk. Pioneer Press, 1232 Central Avenue, Wilmette IL 60091. Tel (312)251-4300.

SCHOLASTIC NEWS (CITIZEN EDITION). (SCHOLASTIC NEWS). V. 51, No. 1 (Sept. 10, 1982)-. 0736-0614. Periodical. US. English. wk. $3.70 Student, $14.00 Teachers Edition. Scholastic Inc, 50 West 44th Street, New York NY 10036. DD 051. Available on microfilm from Xerox University Microfilms. *Scholastic News Citizen,* 0091-2484.

SCHOMBERG-NOBLETON NEWS. VFOAT News. Vol. 1, No. 1 (Oct. 3, 1979)-. 0229-6071. Newspaper. CN. English. wk. $9.50. PBK Publishers, 9 Mill Street East, PO Box 70, Tottenham Ontario Canada. DD 071.13547.

SCHWEIZER ILLUSTRIERTE ZEITUNG. 0036-7362. Periodical. SZ. German. wk. Ringier & Company AG, CH-4800 Zofingen Switzerland. Tel 062-50 31 11.

SCOTT COUNTY VIRGINIA STAR. VFOAT Star. Vol. 80, No. 45 (Oct. 17, 1984)-. 8750-3832. Newspaper. US. English. wk. Scott County Virginia Star, PO Box 218, Gate City VA 24251. *Scott County Herald Virginian, Scott County Press.*

SCRATCHING RIVER POST. (THE SCRATCHING RIVER POST). V. 1- Jan. 16, 1978-. 0707-2333. Newspaper. CN. English. wk. $10.00. The Scratching River Post, Box 160, Morris Manitoba R0G 1K0 Canada. DD 071.1274.

SEATTLE DAILY TIMES. 1896. Newspaper. US. English. da. $508.00. Seattle Times, PO Box 70, Seattle WA 98111. Tel (206)464-2175. Ed W J Pennington. Ind/Abst Infobank. adv acc. Circ 419,000. (ctrl). Metropolitan daily newspapers.

SEATTLE POST-INTELLIGENCER (1921). (SEATTLE POST-INTELLIGENCER). VFOAT Seattle Post Intelligencer. V. 79, No. 155-. Newspaper. US. English. da. 521 Wall Street, Seattle WA 98121. Available on microfilm. *Post-Intelligencer.*

THE SEBRING NEWS. 0163-3988. Newspaper. US. English. wk. $9.00. The Sebring News, Richard Hitt, PO Drawer D, Sebring FL 33870.

Newspapers

SELSKAIA ZHIZN. Apr. 17, 1960-. Newspaper. UR. Russian. da. $37.00. Victor Kamkin Inc, 12224 Parklawn Drive, Rockville MD 20852. **Tel** (301)881-5973. *Selskoe Khoziaistvo.*

SEMAINE. (LA SEMAINE). First edition March 31, 1976. 0705-2073. Newspaper. CN. French. wk. Free. Les Publications Charlesbourg, 4256 Boulevard Henri Bourassa, Charlesbourg Quebec G1H 3A5 Canada. **DD** 071.1447.

SEMAINE. (LA SEMAINE). V. 1- 6 Dec. 1977-. 0707-3984. Newspaper. CN. French. wk. Les Editions le Gardeur, Bureau 4/642 rue Notre-Dam, Repentigny Quebec J6A 2V8 Canada. **DD** 071.14416.

SEMAINE. (LA SEMAINE). Vol. 1, No. 1 (Sept. 3 1983)-. 0823-5422. CN. French. $1.00 Per No. Semaine, Bureau 310/230 Est rue Henri-Bourassa, Montreal Quebec H3L 1B8 Canada. **DD** 054.1.

THE SENTINEL MONTGOMERY COUNTY. Began with Aug. 15, 1974 issue. Newspaper. US. English. wk. Montgomery County Sentinel, PO Box 1272, Rockville MD 20850. LC Newspaper. *Montgomery County Sentinel.*

SENTINEL (SHILLINGTON, PA.). (THE SENTINEL). Began in 1984. 0747-1610. Newspaper. US. English. wk. Berks-Mont Newspapers Inc, 310 West Broad Street, Shillington PA 19601.

SENTINEL-STANDARD. **VAT** Sentinel Standard. 0745-2128. Newspaper. US. English. da. $46.80. Ionia Sentinel Standard, 114 North Depot Street, Ionia MI 48846. **Tel** (616)527-2100. *Ionia Sentinel-Standard.*

SERIAL ARTICLES PUBLISHED IN NEWSPAPERS. US. English. mo. State Library of Pennsylvania Library Services Division, Newspaper Section/Room 120, Forum Building, Harrisburg PA 17105. **LC** Al3. **DD** 071.48.

SERICHON. **VFOAT** Sereechon Newspaper, Sereechon. 0747-3990. Newspaper. US. Thai. tw. $25.00. Sereechon Enterprises, 1901 West 8th Street/Suite 109, Los Angeles CA 90057. **DD** 071.

SETTIMANA. (LA SETTIMANA). Began publication in 1975. 0701-0141. Newspaper. CN. Italian. wk. 0.25 Per No. La Settimana, 183 Sherman Avenue North, Hamilton Ontario L8L 6M8 Canada. **DD** 071.1352.

SETTIMANALE. (IL SETTIMANALE). Yearly V. 5, No. 7-. 0229-5687. Newspaper. CN. Italian. Il Settimanale, 70 Wilson Avenue, Downsview Ontario M3K 1E1 Canada. **DD** 055.1. *Settimanale TV (Toronto, Ont.), 0229-5695.*

SETTIMANALE DI MONTREAL. (IL SETTIMANALE DI MONTREAL). Began publication in 1976. 0701-015X. Newspaper. CN. Italian. wk. $18.00. Il Settimanale di Montreal, 6615 Jarry Street East, Montreal Quebec H1P 1W5 Canada. **DD** 071.14281.

SEVERN-WASHAGO MIRROR. V. 1, No. 17- Aug. 1, 1977-. 0704-0431. Newspaper. CN. English. bw. 5.50. Severn-Washago Mirror, Box 291, Washago Ontario L0K 2B0 Canada. **DD** 071.1316. *Severn-Washago Newspaper.*

SEXTANT. (LE SEXTANT). **VFOAT** Journal le Sextant, The Sextant. 0711-0774. Newspaper. CN. English (text in French with parallel columns). mo. Free. The Sextant, c/o D Mauger, Chevery Quebec G0G 1G0 Canada. **DD** 379.15310971417.

SHAKOPEE VALLEY NEWS. Newspaper. US. English. wk. $17.50. Shakopee Valley News, 1257 Marschall Road, Shakopee MN 55379. **Tel** (612)445-3333.

SHAONIEN ZHONGGUO. (SHAO NIEN CHUNG-KUO). **VFOAT** The Young China. Entered as second class matter August 19, 1910 at the Post Office A. 0749-7679. Newspaper. US. Chinese (also text in English in 1926 only). da. $68.00. Young China Daily, 49-51 Hang AH Street, San Francisco CA 94108. **DD** 071.

SHARE. V. 1- Apr. 8, 1978-. 0709-4647. Newspaper. CN. English. wk. Free. Share Communications of Toronto, 1500 Eglington Avenue West/Suite 402, Toronto Ontario M6E 2G5 Canada. **DD** 971.354100496.

SHAWNEE NEWS-STAR. **VFOAT** Shawnee News Star. Began in 1944?. Newspaper. US. English. da. PO Box 1688, Shwanee OK 748801. LC Newspaper 7002. Also available on microfilm from Oklahoma Historical Society. *Shawnee Morning News, Shawnee Evening Star.*

THE SHELBY DAILY STAR. Began in 1936. Newspaper. US. English. da. 315 East Graham Street, Shelby NC 28150. LC Newspaper 7002. *Cleveland Star.*

SHELF LISTING - MIDWESTERN REGIONAL LIBRARY SYSTEM. (SHELF LISTING MICROFORM). **Main/Corp** Midwestern Regional Library System (Ont.). **VFOAT** Shelf Listing of Adult Books. 0710-6564. CN. English. an. Midwestern Regional Library System, 637 Victoria Street, Kitchener Ontario N2H 5G4 Canada. **DD** 017.13.

SHIBAO ZHOU KAN. (SHIH PAO CHOU KAN). **VFOAT** China Times Weekly. Began in 1985. 0883-6655. Newspaper. US. Chinese. wk. China Times Inc, 1040 National Press Building, Washington DC 20045. **DD** 071. *Chung-Kuo Shih Pao, 0733-2270.*

SHIJIE RIBAO. (SHIH CHEIH JIH PAO). **VFOAT** World Journal. Began in 1891-. 0747-5071. Newspaper. US. Chinese. Shih Chieh Jih Pao She, 210 Mississippi Street, San Francisco CA 94107. *Hsien Cheng Pao, Wen Hsing Jih Pao.*

SHINING MOUNTAIN SENTINEL. 0192-687X. Periodical. US. English. mo. Shining Mountain Sentinel, PO Box 15, Brady MT 59416.

THE SHO-BAN NEWS. V. 1- Dec. 11, 1976-. 0197-7954. Periodical. US. English. wk. $10.00. Fort Hall Business Council, PO Box 306, Fort Hall ID 83203. **Tel** (208)238-3888. Ed Laverne Sheppard. adv acc. **Circ** 2,400. Local news, Indian national news.

SHOESTRING PRESS. June 1975-. 0383-8161. Newspaper. CN. English (includes some text in French and Italian). mo. Free. Shoestring Press, 787 1/2 Somerset Street West, Ottawa K1R 6R3 Canada. **DD** 071.1384.

SHUKAN ASAHI. Began in April 1922. Periodical. JA. Japanese. ir. 26,000. Oversea Courier Service Co Ltd, 9 Shibaura 2-Chome Minato-ku, Tokyo 108 Japan. **Tel** 03-454-0131. Ed Ahahi Shinbunsha Shuppankyoku. adv acc. **Circ** 47,000. Asahi newspaper coverage centering on current topics for weekly magazine. *Junkan Asahi.*

SHUKAN TOCHO. **VFOAT** Tocho. Newspaper. JA. Japanese. wk. 190. Tokyo-to Tomin Shiryoshitsu, 5-1 Marunouchi 3 Chiyoda-ku, Tokyo 100 Japan.

SICILIA. (LA SICILIA). Vol. 1- 22 June 1978-. 0709-6399. Newspaper. CN. Italian. bw. La Sicilia Publishing Co, 1739 Eglinton Avenue West, Toronto Ontario M6E 2H4 Canada. **DD** 071.13541.

THE SIDNEY HERALD. 0738-8454. Newspaper. US. English. sw. $17.00 Local Counties, $20.00 Elsewhere in Montana, $23.00 Out of State. Sidney Herald, 121 North Central Avenue, Sidney MT 59270.

SIDNEY REVIEW. (THE SIDNEY REVIEW). Began with Jan. 1, 1970 issue. 0700-8228. Newspaper. CN. English. wk. $6.00. Review Publications, 9831 Third Street, Sidney British Columbia V8L 3A6 Canada. **DD** 071.1134.

SIGNAL. (THE SIGNAL). **VFOAT** Central Peace Signal. Vol. 1, No. 1 (May 14, 1980)-. 0712-1296. Newspaper. CN. English. wk. $6.00. Schierbeck Printing and Publishing, PO Box 250, Rycroft Alberta T0H 3A0 Canada. **DD** 071.1231.

SILANGAN. Vol. 1, No. 1 (Feb. 1977)-. 0704-0547. Newspaper. CN. Tagalog (English). mo. Silangan, 696 Buckingham Road, Winnipeg Manitoba R3R 1C2 Canada. **DD** 071.1274.

SILENT NEWS. 1969. 0049-0490. Newspaper. US. English. mo. $10.00. The Silent News Inc, PO Box 584, Paramus NJ 07652. **Tel** (201)265-0288. Ed Walter Schulman. bk rev. adv acc. **Circ** 6,000. (ctrl). National newspaper for the deaf reports on all legislative, technological, medical, social, and sports news, plus regular feature columns.

SIMCOE MIRROR. (THE SIMCOE MIRROR). Vol. 1, No. 1 (Oct. 27, 1981)-. 0712-5569. Newspaper. CN. English. wk. Free. Simcoe Mirror, PO Box 1024, Simcoe Ontario N3Y 5B3 Canada. **DD** 071.1336. (ctrl).

SINAR HARAPAN. Newspaper. IO. Indonesian. ir. Sinar Harapin, Pintu Besar Selatan 80, Jakarta Kota Indonesia.

SIOUX FALLS ARGUS-LEADER. **VFOAT** Sioux Falls Argus Leader. -V. 92, No. 315. Newspaper. US. English. da. $143.00. Sioux Falls Argus-Leader, 200 South Minnesota Avenue, Sioux Falls SD 57102. **Tel** (605)331-2200. Available on microfilm.

SKANNER. Vol. 1, No. 1 (Oct. 9, 1975)-. Newspaper. US. English. wk. $15.00. IMM Publications, Box 5455, Portland OR 97228. **Tel** (503)287-3562. Available in microform.

SLAVE RIVER JOURNAL. V. 1- June 2, 1977-. 0707-4964. Newspaper. CN. English. wk. $15.48. Slave River Journal, PO Box 990, Fort Smith North West Territories X0E 0PO Canada. **Tel** (403)872-2784. Ed Don Jaque. **DD** 071.193. bk rev. adv acc. **Circ** 1,800. (ctrl). A newspaper serving the community and the area from Ft. Chipewyan to Ft. Resolution with a view to the current issues in the South Mackenzie, Northwest Territories.

SLOVAK V AMERIKE. **VFOAT** Daily Slovak American, Dennik Slovak v Amerike, Slovak American. Began with Dec. 21, 1889 issue. 0199-6819. Newspaper. US. Slovak (English). mo. Michael J Krajsa, Box 150, Middletown PA 17057. **Tel** (717)944-0461.

SMITHS FALLS STAR. V. 1- July 15, 1975-. 0381-8365. Newspaper. CN. English. wk. $5.00. Smiths Falls Star, PO Box 784, Smiths Falls Ontario K7A 4W6 Canada. **DD** 071.1382.

SMOKY LAKE SIGNAL. 0229-7949. Newspaper. CN. English. wk. $5.00. Smoky Lake Signal, PO Box 328, Smoky Lake Alberta T0A 3C0 Canada. **DD** 071.1233.

SMOKY RIVER NEWS. (THE SMOKY RIVER NEWS). **VFOAT** Falher Courier and Smoky River News. Vol. 1, No. 38 (June 1, 1953)-. 0227-9304. Newspaper. CN. English. wk. $2.00. Sun Publishing, 10815 Whyte Avenue, Edmonton Alberta Canada. **DD** 071.1231. *Courier (Edmonton, Alta. : 1952), 0227-9290.*

THE SMYRNA TIMES. Began with July 5, 1854 issue. Newspaper. US. English. wk.

SNOW LAKE NEWS. Vol. 1, No. 1 (Mar. 10, 1983)-. 0826-2241. Newspaper. CN. English. wk. $0.25 Each Number. Snow Lake News, P O Box 550, Snow Lake Manitoba R0B 1M0 Canada. **DD** 071.1272.

THE SOLON TIMES. 0194-3677. Periodical. US. English. wk. $12.50. Chagrin Solon Times, PO Box 408, Chagrin Falls OH 44022.

SOMERSET HERALD (PRINCESS ANNE, MD. : 1985). (SOMERSET HERALD). **VFOAT** Marylander & Herald. 8756-6397. Newspaper. US. English. wk. Somerset Herald, 120 South Somerset Avenue, Princess Anne MD 21853. *Marylander and Herald.*

THE SOPERTON NEWS. Began in 1914. Newspaper. US. English. wk. $15.60. Soperton News, PO Box 537/106 First Street, Soperton GA. **Tel** (912)529-6624. Ed James T Windsor. adv acc. **Circ** 3,500.

THE SOUND OF PRINCE WILLIAM. Vol. 1, No. 1 (May 23, 1984)-. 0743-8370. Newspaper. US. English. wk. $25.00. The Sound of Prince William, PO Box 729, Whittier AK 99693.

THE SOURCE. **VFOAT** Mawrid. Newspaper. CN. English and Arabic. bw. $10.00. PO Box 992, Edmonton Alberta Canada. LC NEWSPAPER.

SOUTH ALABAMIAN. V. 1- June 8, 1839-. Newspaper. US. English. da. $10.70. South Alabamian, Box 68 1064 Coffeeville Road, Jackson AL 36545. **Tel** (205)246-4494. Ed Marilyn Barrett. LC NEWSPAPER. adv acc. **Circ** 4,000. Clarke and Washington counties' progressive newspaper. Publishers, printing, office, office supplies.

SOUTH BEND TRIBUNE. Began with May 28, 1873 issue. Newspaper. US. English. da. $70.50. F D Schurz, South Bend IN 46626. **Tel** (219)233-6161. Ed Jack McGann. LC Newspaper. bk rev. adv acc. **Circ** Daily 106,000 Sunday 125,000. (ctrl). *South-Bend Daily Tribune.*

SOUTH CENTRAL BANNER. V. 1- Jan. 17, 1978-. 0707-2295. Newspaper. CN. English. wk. $5.00. Crystal City Banner, Box 143, Crystal City Manitoba R0K 0N0 Canada. **DD** 071.1274.

SOUTH EAST LANCE. V. 1- May 19, 1976-. 0384-7934. Newspaper. CN. English. wk. Lance Publishing Company, 620 Dakota Street, Winnipeg Manitoba R2M 3K2 Canada. **DD** 071.1274. *St. Boniface Courier, 0384-7926; St. Vital Lance, 0383-7254.*

SOUTH SAINT PAUL SUN. Newspaper. US. English. wk. Sun Newspaper, 7401 Bush Lake Road, Edina MN 55435. **Tel** (612)831-1200.

Newspapers

SOUTH SHORE NEWS. Vol. 1, No. 1 (June 4, 1980)-. 0710-0213. Newspaper. CN. English. wk. Free. 120 Dufferin Street, Bridgewater Nova Scotia B4V 2G5 Canada. DD 071.1623. (ctrl).

SOUTH VANCOUVER REVIEW. V. 2, No. 2- Mar. 1975-. 0319-7344. Newspaper. CN. English. mo. $2.00. Fraserview-Killarney Area Council, 1950 Argyle Drive, Vancouver British Columbia V5P 2A8 Canada. DD 071.1133. *South Van Review, 0319-7352.*

SOUTH VOICE. (THE SOUTH VOICE). 0824-6726. Newspaper. CN. English. wk. Free to Citizens of Fort Carry, St Norbert, River Heights, and Tuxedo Manitoba, $18.00 Others. South Voice, 105-1383 Pembina Highway, Winnipeg Manitoba R3T 2B9 Canada. DD 071.1274.

SOUTHEAST MISSOURIAN. Began with Mar. 8, 1918 issue. 0746-4452. Newspaper. US. English. da. Southeast Missourian, 301 Broadway, Cape Girardeau MO 63701. LC NEWSPAPER.

SOUTHERN DUTCHESS NEWS. 0192-9631. Newspaper. US. English. wk. $10.00. Southern Dutchess News, 84 East Main Street, Wappingers Falls NY 12590. Tel (914)297-3723. Ed H Osten and B Osten. *Wappingers and Southern Dutchess News.*

SOUTHERN GAZETTE. V. 1- May 29, 1975-. 0319-6224. Newspaper. CN. English. wk. $21.67. Robinson-Blackmore Publ Ltd, PO Box 129, Grand Falls Newfoundland A2A 2J4 Canada. Tel 489-2162. DD 071.18.

THE SOUTHERN IDAHO MAGAZINE & WEEKLY NEWS. VFOAT Southern Idaho Magazine and Weekly News. 8750-4944. Newspaper. US. English. wk. Southern Idaho Magazine & Weekly News, PO Box 146, Malad ID 83252.

THE SOUTHERN POST. 0744-1118. Newspaper. US. English. wk. The Southern Post Inc, PO Box 85, Coinjock NC 27923-0085.

SOUTHERN UTE DRUM. 0587-0674. Periodical. US. English. bw. $4.00. Southern Ute Drum, Tribal Affairs Building, PO Box 737, Ignacio CO 81137. Tel (303)563-4525. Ed James M Jefferson. adv acc. (ctrl).

SOUTHSIDE MIRROR. (THE SOUTHSIDE MIRROR). V. 3, No. 5- May 1, 1976-. 0701-1423. Periodical. CN. English. bw. The Southside Mirror, Suite 1/8431 Granville Street, Vancouver British Columbia V6P 4Z9 Canada. DD 071.1133. *Magpie.*

SPEC (NEW CARLISLE, QUEBEC). (SPEC). 0226-9120. Newspaper. CN. English. wk. $10.00. Spec, PO Box 99, New Carlisle Quebec G0C 1Z0 Canada. DD 071.1477.

SPECTRUM (OTTAWA, ONT.). (SPECTRUM). Vol. 1, No. 1-. 0706-4519. Newspaper. CN. English. mo. $3.00. Spectrum, PO Box 143, Station B, Ottawa Ontario K1P 6C3 Canada. DD 071.1384.

SPRINGFIELD DAILY NEWS. VFOAT Daily News. 0191-2828. Newspaper. US. English. da. $200.20. Springfield Newspapers Inc, 651 Boonville, Springfield MO 65801. Tel (417)836-1100.

SQUOL-QUOL LUMMI INDIAN NEWS. VFOAT Lummi Squol-Quol. Vol. 3, No. 23 (June 21, 1975)-. Periodical. US. English. mo. $10.00. The Lumni Squol Quol, 2616 Kwinna Road, Bellingham WA 98225. Tel (206)734-8180.

STANDARD. Began publication between July-Oct. 1976. 0702-7893. Newspaper. CN. English. $2.00. Standard, PO Box 1629, Swan River Manitoba R0L 1Z0 Canada. DD 071.1272. *Parkland Standard, 0702-7907.*

STANDARD-TIMES (NEW BEDFORD, MASS.). (THE STANDARD-TIMES). VAT Standard Times (New Bedford, Mass.). 0745-3574. Newspaper. US. English. ir. Standard Times Publishing Company Inc, 555 Pleasant Street, New Bedford MA 02742.

STAR. (THE STAR). VFOAT City-Wide Star. Vol. 1, No. 1 (Aug. 31, 1983)-. 0824-7501. Newspaper. CN. English. wk. Free. The Star, 1157 Newport Avenue, Victoria British Columbia V8S 5E6 Canada. DD 071.1134. (ctrl).

STAR-EXPONENT. VFOAT Star Exponent. 0746-7923. Newspaper. US. English. da. Star-Exponent, Carter Glass Newspapers Inc, PO Box 111, Culpeper VA 22701.

STAR (FRANKFORT, ILL.). (THE STAR). 0746-5742. Newspaper. US. English. sw. Williams Press Inc, 20 South Route 45, Frankfort IL 60423. *Frankfort-Mokena Star.*

STAR (HARVEY-MARKHAM AREA ED.). (THE STAR). 0746-5173. Newspaper. US. English. sw. The Star Williams Press Inc, 154th and Broadway, Suite 201, Harvey IL 60426. *Harvey Star-Tribune, Markham Star-Tribune.*

STAR (JOHANNESBURG, SOUTH AFRICA). (THE STAR). VFOAT Johannesburg Star. Newspaper. SA. English. $12.03. S A Associated Newspapers Ltd, PO Box 1138, Johannesburg 2000 South Africa.

STAR (NEW YORK, N.Y.). (THE STAR). 0745-8509. Periodical. US. English. mo. District 1-B'Nai B'Rith, 823 United Nations Plaza, New York NY 10017. *Metropolitan Star, 0026-1580.*

THE STATE JOURNAL. Began with June 20, 1912 issue. Newspaper. US. English. da. $87.15. The State Journal, 321 West Main, Frankfort KY 40601. Tel (502)227-4556. Ed Carl West. bk rev. adv acc. Circ 11,500. *Frankfort News-Journal.*

THE STATE JOURNAL-REGISTER. June 29, 1974-. Newspaper. US. English. da. $215.00. Copley Newspapers, PO Box 219, Springfield IL 62705. Tel (217)544-5711. LC Newspaper. *Illinois State Journal, Illinois State Register.*

STATESMAN. Newspaper. English. wk. Statesman Ltd, 4 Chowringhee Square, Calcutta 700 001 India. Tel 23-5361-5369.

STEVENS POINT JOURNAL. 0748-6332. Newspaper. US. English. da. $43.00 Selected Counties, $56.00 Others in State, $65.00 Elsewhere. Journal Printing Company, Box 7, Stevens Point WI 54481.

THE STEWART TRIBUNE CEASED. Began in 1896. 0746-3200. Newspaper. US. English. wk. The Stewart Tribune, 743 Hall Street, Stewart MN 55385. *Messenger.*

STEWARTVILLE STAR. Newspaper. US. English. wk. Stewartville Star, Stewartville Publishing Company, PO Box 365, Stewartville MN 55976. Tel (218)533-4271.

STOCKTON DAILY EVENING RECORD. Began with March 2, 1904?. Newspaper. US. English. da. $168.00. Stockton Record, 530 East Market, Stockton CA 95202. Tel (209)948-1702.

STOUFFVILLE SUN. Vol. 1, No. 1 (Oct. 27, 1982)-. 0821-0225. Newspaper. CN. English. wk. $20.00 Domestic, $45.00 Foreign. Stouffville Sun, 11 Main Street West, Stouffville Ontario L0H 1L0 Canada. DD 071.1354.

THE STRAITS ECHO. Est. 1903. Newspaper. English. ir. $55.00. K S Choong, 8 Leith Street, Georgetown Penang Malaysia. Tel (04)367853. Ed K S Choong. bk rev. adv acc. Circ 15,000. Newspaper publisher.

THE STRAITS TIMES. Est. 1845. Newspaper. Sl. English. da. $146.20. Straits Times, Circulation Department, 390 Kim Seng Road, Singapore 0923 Singapore. Tel 7370011. Ed Peter Lim. bk rev. adv acc. Circ 260,000.

STRATHCLAIR & DISTRICT REVIEW. Vol. 1, Issue 1 (Jan. 12, 1978)-. 0229-6519. Newspaper. CN. English. wk. $6.00. Strathclair & District Review, PO Box 244, Strathclair Manitoba R0J 2C0 Canada. DD 071.1273.

SUBURBAN. COTE ST. LUC EDITION. (THE SUBURBAN). 0226-9686. Newspaper. CN. English (includes some text in French). wk. Free. Michael Publishers, 8170 Wavell Street, Cote-Saint-Luc Quebec H4W 1M3 Canada. DD 071.1428. (ctrl).

SUBURBAN. DOLLARD DES ORMEAUX EDITION. (THE SUBURBAN). 0229-298X. Newspaper. CN. English (includes some text in French). wk. Free. Michael Publishers, 8170 Wavell Street, Cote-Saint-Luc Quebec H4W 1M3 Canada. DD 071.1428. (ctrl).

SUBURBAN. LAVAL EDITION. (THE SUBURBAN). 0229-3048. Periodical. CN. English (includes some text in French). wk. Free. Michael Publishers, 8170 Wavell Street, Cote-Saint-Luc Quebec H4W 1M3 Canada. DD 071.14271. (ctrl).

SUBURBAN MIRROR. (THE SUBURBAN MIRROR). VAT Mirror (St. John's). V. 1- Nov. 2, 1977-. 0704-7363. Newspaper. CN. English. wk. $17.00 Domestic, $20.00 Foreign. The Suburban Mirror, 18 O'Leary Avenue, St John's Newfoundland A1B 2C7 Canada. DD 071.18.

SUBURBAN. NEW BORDEAUX, CARTIERVILLE EDITION. (THE SUBURBAN). 0229-3013. Newspaper. CN. English (includes some text in French). wk. Free. Michael Publications, 8170 Wavell Street, Cote-Saint-Luc Quebec H4W 1M3 Canada. DD 071.14281. (ctrl). *Suburban (Nouveau-Bordeaux Edition), 0712-7316.*

SUBURBAN NEWS (FRANKLIN LAKES, N.J. : 1981). (SUBURBAN NEWS). Began in 1981?. 0746-052X. Newspaper. US. English. wk. Pennysaver Inc, 795 Susguehanna Avenue, Franklin Lakes NJ 07417. *United Suburban News, 0274-6646.*

SUBURBAN. NOTRE DAME DE GRACE EDITION. (THE SUBURBAN). 0229-2971. Newspaper. CN. English (includes some text in French). wk. Free. Michael Publishers, 8170 Wavell Street, Cote-Saint-Luc Quebec H4W 1M3 Canada. DD 071.14281. (ctrl).

SUBURBAN. ST. LAURENT EDITION. (THE SUBURBAN). 0229-303X. Newspaper. CN. English (includes some text in French). wk. Free. Michael Publishers, 8160 Wavell Street, Cote-Saint-Luc Quebec H4W 1M3 Canada. DD 071.1428. (ctrl).

SUBURBAN. TOWN OF MOUNT ROYAL EDITION. (THE SUBURBAN). 0229-3021. Newspaper. CN. English (includes some text in French). wk. Free. Michael Publishers, 8170 Wavell Street, Cote-Saint-Luc Quebec H4W 1M3 Canada. DD 071.14281. (ctrl).

SUBURBAN. WESTMOUNT EDITION. (THE SUBURBAN). 0229-3005. Newspaper. CN. English (includes some text in French). wk. Free. Michael Publisher, 8170 Wavell Street, Cote-Saint-Luc Quebec H4W 1M3 Canada. DD 071.14281. (ctrl).

LE SUEUR HERALD. Newspaper. US. English. wk. $10.00. Eastwood House of Printing, 111 North Main Street, Le Sueur MN 56058.

THE SUFFOLK SOURCE. VFOAT Source. 8750-0922. Newspaper. US. English. mo. $2.99. Suffolk Source, 136 Carman Street, Patchogue NY 11772.

THE SUMTER JOURNAL. 0747-0304. Newspaper. US. English. sw. $10.00 In Florida, $15.00 Elsewhere. The Sumter Journal, PO Box 546, Lake Panaskoffkee FL 33538.

THE SUN. Newspaper. US. English. da. $216.00. A S Abell Company, 501 North Calvert, Baltimore MD 21203.

SUN. (THE SUN). V. 1- Aug. 13, 1975-. 0380-8912. Monographic Series. CN. English. wk. $5.20. Sunparlour Publishing Company, 33 John Street, Leamington Ontario N8H 1H3 Canada. DD 071.1331.

SUN. (THE SUN). V. 1- Feb. 1, 1978-. 0705-4033. Newspaper. CN. English (includes some text in French). wk. $8.00. The Sun Publishing Ltd, 524 King Street, Fredericton New Brunswick E3B 1E6 Canada. DD 071.1551.

SUN (BALTIMORE, MD. : 1837). (THE SUN). VFOAT Baltimore Sun. Vol. 1, No. 1 (May 17, 1837)-. Newspaper. US. English. da. A S Abell Company, 501 North Calvert Street, Baltimore MD 21203. LC Newspaper.

SUN-FLYER. VAT Sun Flyer. Began in 1984?. Newspaper. US. English. wk. Free. RFD Publications Inc, 46-016 Alaloa Street, Kaneohe HI 96744.

SUN (GRAND CENTRE, ALTA.). (SUN). VFOAT Grand Centre-Cold Lake Sun. 0710-0019. Newspaper. CN. English. wk. $11.61. Grand Center Cold Lake, Box 268, Grande Center Alberta T0A 1T0 Canada. Tel (403)594-5881. Ed Jim Bentein. DD 071.1233. adv acc. Circ 6,742. Weekly community newspaper.

SUN (LAGRANGE, ILL.). (THE SUN). 8750-2003. Newspaper. US. English. wk. $13.50. Sun Newspapers Inc, 500 East Avenue, Lagrange IL 60525. DD 071.18.

SUN-SENTINEL. VAT Sun Sentinel. 0744-8139. Newspaper. US. English. da. $226.20. News and Sun Sentinel Company, Box 14488, Fort Lauderdale FL 33302. Tel (305)761-4702.

Newspapers

THE SUN TIMES SENTINEL. 8750-6483. Newspaper. US. English. wk. 811 Pear Road, Brunswick OH 44212. *Brunswick Sun Times.*

SUNDAY (CHARLESTON, S.C.). (SUNDAY). 7386-0937. Newspaper. US. English. wk. Sunday, 134 Columbus Street, Charleston SC 29402.

SUNDAY GAZETTE. VFOAT Sunday Gazette/Herald. 0711-2149. Newspaper. CN. English. wk. $.15 Each Number. Maple Ridge Gazette, 22610 Dewdney Trunk Road, Maple Ridge British Columbia V2X Canada. DD 071.1133.

THE SUNDAY INDEPENDENT. 0744-883X. Newspaper. US. English. wk. Independent Newspapers Ltd, 90 Middle Abbey Street, Dublin 1 Ireland.

SUNDAY SUN (BALTIMORE, MD.). (THE SUNDAY SUN). Vol. 14, No. 46 (Nov. 15, 1914)-. Newspaper. US. English. wk. A S Abell Company, 501 North Calvert Street, Baltimore MD 21203. LC NEWSPAPER. *Sun (Baltimore, Md. : 1914).*

SUNDAY SUN-JOURNAL. VFOAT Sunday. Vol. 1, No. 1 (Oct. 2, 1983)-. 0747-1432. Newspaper. US. English. wk. Sunday, 104 Park Street, Lewiston ME 04240.

SUNDAY TIMES. March 4, 1906-. Newspaper. SA. English. $30.07. S A Associated Newspapers Ltd, PO Box 1138, Johannesburg 2000 South Africa.

SUNDAY WORLD-HERALD (OMAHA, NEB. : 1937). (SUNDAY WORLD-HERALD). VFOAT Sunday World Herald. Vol. 52, No. 50 (Aug. 29, 1937)-. Newspaper. US. English. wk. World-Herald Square, Omaha NE 68102. LC Newspaper. Available on microfilm. *Omaha World-Herald (Omaha, Neb. : 1928 : Sunday Ed.).*

SUNSHINE NEWS. (THE SUNSHINE NEWS). V. 1- Feb. 1979-. 0709-5651. Periodical. CN. English. mo. $2.00. Canadian Sunshine Publications Ltd, 465 King Street East, Toronto Ontario M5A 1L Canada. DD 051.

SURBURBAN. COTE DES NEIGES EDITION. (THE SUBURBAN). 0229-2998. Newspaper. CN. English (includes some text in French). wk. Free. Michael Publishers, 8170 Wavell Street, Cote-Saint-Luc Quebec H4W 1M3 Canada. DD 071.14281. (ctrl).

SURREY TIMES. (THE SURREY TIMES). Vol. 1, No. 1 (Feb. 28, 1979)-. 0229-6861. Newspaper. CN. English. wk. $0.20 Each Number. The Surrey Times, Office D, Suite 14673/108th Avenue, Surrey British Columbia Canada. DD 071.1133.

SURREY/NORTH DELTA TODAY. (SURREY/N.DELTA TODAY). VFOAT Surrey, North Delta Today. Vol. 1, No. 1 (Sept. 15, 1980)-. 0712-1113. Newspaper. CN. English. wk. Free. Surrey/N Delta Today #2, 13634 104th Avenue, Surrey British Columbia V3T 1W2 Canada. DD 071.1133.

SUSSEX-SURRY DISPATCH. VAT Sussex, Surry Dispatch. 0745-9467. Newspaper. US. English. wk. Sussex-Surry Dispatch, PO Box 370, Wakefield VA 23888.

SUVAGUQ. No. 1- Feb. 1974-. 0384-0778. Newspaper. CN. Eskimo (text in Inuit and English). mo. Editor of Suvaquq, Pond Inlet North West Territories X0A 0S0 Canada. DD 071.195. *Piasuarusirmi Pivatliyat Mitimatalikmi, 0384-076X.*

SVETLINA. VFOAT Light. 0700-9615. Newspaper. CN. Bulgarian. bw. .25 Each Number. Svetlina, PO Box 477 Station J, Toronto Ontario M4J 4Z2 Canada. DD 071.13541.

SVOBODA (JERSEY CITY, N.J.). (SVOBODA). VFOAT Liberty. Began in 1893. 0274-6964. Newspaper. US. Ukrainian (Sunday edition in English). ir. $40.00. Ukrainian National Association, PO Box 76-30, Montgomery Avenue, Jersey City NJ 07303. Tel (201)434-0237. Ed Zenon Znylyk. Ind/Abst MLA Int. Bibliogr. Books Artic. Mod. Lang. Lit. LC Newspaper 8777. bk rev. adv acc. Circ 14,000. (ctrl).

SWIFT COUNTY MONITOR. Newspaper. US. English. wk. $18.00. Swift County Monitor News, PO Box 227, Benson MN 56215. Tel (612)842-4101.

THE SWORD OF THE LORD. Began in 1934?. 0039-7547. Periodical. US. English. bw. The Sword of the Lord, 224 Bridge Avenue, PO Box 1099, Murfreesboro TN 37130.

THE SYDNEY MORNING HERALD. Vol. 14, No. 1623 (Aug. 1, 1842)-. Newspaper. AT. English. da. $187.41. John Fairfax & Sons Ltd, Box 506 Government Printing Office, Sydney New South Wales 2001 Australia. *Sydney Herald, Australian Free Press.*

TA-KUNG-PAO. 0039-8675. Newspaper. HK. Chinese. wk. $14.89. Fei Yi Ming, 342 Hennessy Road, Hong Kong. Tel 5-741173.

TAHSIS INLET OUTLET. (THE TAHSIS INLET OUTLET). V. 1- July 11, 1974-. 0383-7343. Newspaper. CN. English. bw. $5.00. C la Flam, PO Box 380, Tahsis British Columbia V0P 1X0 Canada. DD 071.1134.

TAI-PEI SHIH CHU PAN SHIH YEH CHI KOU I LAN. Chinese. ir. LC Z464.T3586.

TAIWAN GONGLUNBAO. (TAI-WAN KUNG LUN PAO). VFOAT Tai Wan Kung Lun Pao, Taiwan Tribune. No. 1 (July 24, 1981)-. 0743-5355. Newspaper. US. Chinese. sw. $60.00 Domestic, $70.00 Canada. Taiwan Tribune, PO Box 1527, Long Island City NY 11101.

TALLAHASSEE DEMOCRAT. Began in 1914. 0738-5153. Newspaper. US. English. da. Tallahassee Democrat, 277 North Magnolia, Box 990, Tallahassee FL 32301.

TAOS NEWS. Began with July 30, 1959 issue. Newspaper. US. English. wk. 11 Guadalupe Plaza, Taos NM 87571. LC NEWSPAPER. *El Crepusculo de la Libertad.*

TELEGRAPH-HERALD. VFOAT Telegraph Herald. Began with May 7, 1935 issue. Newspaper. US. English. da. $119.60. Dubuque Telegraph-Herald, Dubuque IA 52001. LC Newspaper. *Telegraph-Herald and Times-Journal.*

TELLER. Newspaper. US. English. wk. $10.00. The Teller, Richard Bradbury, Box 308, Milnor ND 58060. Tel (701)427-9472.

TEMISCAMIEN. (LE TEMISCAMIEN). 0382-0653. Newspaper. CN. French. wk. $16.00 Residents, $20.00 Others. Le Temiscamien, C P 219, Ville-Marie Quebec J0Z 3W0 Canada. DD 071.14212. *Journal Temiscamien, 0821-3178.*

TEMPO. Newspaper. Portuguese. ir. 680.00. Imprenova, Travessa das Chagas 4 - 1, Lisboa Portugal. LC NEWSPAPER.

TEMPO DI MONTREAL. (IL TEMPO DI MONTREAL). Vol. 1. Jan 1974-. 0382-8670. Newspaper. CN. Italian. bw. $. Il Tempo di Montreal, 8739 rue Hochelaga, Montreal Quebec H1L 2M7 Canada. DD 071.14281.

THE TENNESSEAN. June 6, 1972-. Newspaper. US. English. da. Newspaper Printing Corporation, 1100 Broadway, Nashville TN 37202. Tel (615)259-8300. Also available on microfilm from Microfilming Corporation of America. *Nashville Tennessean.*

THE TENTMAKER'S JOURNAL. 0272-6939. Periodical. US. English. bm. Tentmaker's Publishing Group Inc, PO Box 23129, Lexington KY 40523. Tel (606)276-2390.

TERESIEN. (LE TERESIEN). Vol. 1, No. 1-. 0229-205X. Periodical. CN. French. Free. Ville de Saint-Therese, a/s J Bertrand, 34-Ouest rue Blainville, Saint-Therese Quebec J7E 4H7 Canada. DD 071.1424.

THE TERRE HAUTE GAZETTE. Vol. 1, No. 1 (Oct. 31, 1984)-. 8755-934X. Newspaper. US. English. wk. Terre Haute Gazette, 1313 Wabash Avenue, Terre Haute IN 47807. *Macksville Gazette, 0747-0584.*

THE TERRE HAUTE STAR. Began in 1903. Newspaper. US. English. da. $95.00. The Terre Haute Star, Terre Haute IN 47808. LC Newspaper 7002. *Terre Haute Morning Star.*

TEVERE. (IL TEVERE). Vol. 1- Dec. 30, 1972-. 0382-8786. Periodical. CN. Italian. bw. $6. Il Tevere 1951, Avenue Eglinton Toronto Ontario Canada. DD 071.13541.

TEXAS PRESS MESSENGER. V. 7, No. 7-V. 54, No. 5. 0040-4624. Periodical. US. English. mo. $6.00. Texas Press Messenger, 718 West 5th Avenue, Austin TX 78701. Tel (512)477-6755. Ed Lyndell Williams. bk rev. adv acc. Circ 900. News of and about newspaper publishers, staff members, newspaper industry, education and profession.

THAMES VALLEY TIMES. Vol. 1, No. 1 (1979)-. 0229-6594. Newspaper. CN. English. mo. Natural Dynamics, PO Box 640, Jarvis Ontario N0A 1J0 Canada. DD 640.

THAMESFORD TOWN CRIER. VFOAT Town Crier. VAT Town Crier (Thamesford). V. 1- Nov. 24, 1977-. 0707-4794. Newspaper. CN. English. wk. $7.50. Thamesford Town Crier, Box 399, Thamesford Ontario N0M 2M0 Canada. DD 071.1346.

THE ROCK COUNTY STAR-HERALD. VFOAT Rock County Star Herald. Began in 1942. Newspaper. US. English. wk. $15.00. Tollefson Publishing, PO Box 327, Luverne MN 56156. Tel (507)283-2333. LC Newspaper 8475. *Rock County Star, Rock County Herald.*

THIEF RIVER FALLS TIMES. 8750-3883. Newspaper. US. English. sw. $13.00. Thief River Falls Times, 325 North Main Avenue, Thief River Falls MN 56701. Tel (218)681-1450.

THIRTEEN TOWNS. Newspaper. US. English. wk. $10.00. Thirteen Towns, Box 505, Fosston MN 56542. Tel (218)435-1313.

THIS WEEK. (THIS WEEK : HARROW AND COLCHESTER SOUTH). VFOAT Harrow and Colchester South. 0821-2333. Newspaper. CN. English. wk. $0.15 Each Number. c/o T Hunter, Harrow Ontario N0R 1G0 Canada. DD 071.1331.

THIS WEEK IN REVELSTOKE. VAT Revelstoke This Week. 0715-5255. Newspaper. CN. English. wk. DD 071.1145.

THOMASVILLE TIMES-ENTERPRISE. VFOAT Thomasville Times Enterprise. 0746-4894. Newspaper. US. English. da. $83.40. Thomasville Times Enterprise, PO Box 650, Thomasville GA 31792. Tel (912)226-2400.

THORNHILL MONTH. 0229-7248. Periodical. CN. English. mo. $12.00. Thornhill Month, PO Box 250, Thornhill Ontario L3T 3N3 Canada. DD 071.13547.

THE THREE VILLAGE HERALD. Newspaper. US. English. ir. $12.00. Three Village Herald, Box 703, East Setauket NY 11733. Tel (517)751-1550. Ed Kevin Ireland. adv acc. Circ 9,500. Also available on microfilm from Berhan Industries Ltd. Covers news and features on this community and its people. Also focuses on how state, county, and federal events affect us.

THUNDERBIRD. (THE THUNDERBIRD). V. 1- Oct. 3, 1978-. 0225-8293. Newspaper. CN. English. wk. $21.00. Cariboo Press Ltd, The Thunderbird, PO Box 390, Bella Coola British Columbia V0T 1C0 Canada. DD 071.1132.

TIDE. (THE TIDE). Vol. 1, No. 1 (Apr. 12/25)-. 0713-0562. Newspaper. CN. English. wk. $0.20 Each Number. The Tide, 166 Main Street, Lewisburg Newfoundland A0G 3A0 Canada. DD 071.18.

THE TIDEWATER ADVANTAGE. NEWPORT NEWS EDITION. (THE TIDEWATER ADVANTAGE). 0744-7116. Newspaper. US. English. wk. Advantage Publications, POB 731, Surry VA 23883.

EL TIEMPO. Periodical. CK. Spanish. da. $470.00. El Tiempo, Avenida Jimenez No 6-77, Bogota Colombia.

THE TIMES. Newspaper. UK. English. da. 286.87. Quadrant, Oakfield House, Perrymount Road, Haywards Heath Sussex England. Tel 011 444 444 59188. Ind/Abst Infobank, Funk Scott Index Corp. Ind.

TIMES. (THE TIMES). Vol. 1, No. 1 (Oct. 22, 1980)-. 0821-2473. Newspaper. CN. English. wk. $7.00 Domestic, $8.00 US. Reliance Press Community Newspapers, 1397 Erin Street, Winnipeg Manitoba R3E 2S9 Canada. DD 071.1274.

TIMES-ARGUS (CENTRAL CITY, KY). (THE TIMES-ARGUS). VFOAT Times Argus. Began in 1906. Newspaper. US. English. wk. Central City Publishing Corporation, PO Box 31, 204 West Broad Street, Central City KY 42330.

THE TIMES-BULLETIN. VFOAT Times Bulletin. 8750-1503. Newspaper. US. English. da. $54.00 County, $56.00 Ohio State, $60.00 Elsewhere. Times-Bulletin, PO Box 271, Van Wert OH 45891. *Van West Times Bulletin.*

THE TIMES INDEX. See Indexes/Abstracts.

Newspapers

TIMES OF DOWNTOWN LONDON. (THE TIMES OF DOWNTOWN LONDON). **VAT** Times (London, Ont.). Vol. 1, No. 1 (Aug. 1981)-. 0715-450X. Periodical. CN. English. mo. Free. Times of Downtown London, Suite # 1/110 Dundas Street, London Ontario N6A 1G1 Canada. **DD** 071.1326.

TIMES OF INDIA. Newspaper. English. da. $146.00. Bennett Coleman & Company Ltd, 26 Station Approach, Sudbury Wembley Middx England.

TIMES OF NORTH AND WEST VANCOUVER. (THE TIMES OF NORTH AND WEST VANCOUVER). Began with Dec. 30, 1971 issue. 0380-4569. Newspaper. CN. English. wk. 0.15 Each Copy. The Times of North and West Vancouver, 1442 Pemberton Avenue North, Vancouver British Columbia V7P 2R8 Canada. **DD** 071.1133. *Lions Gate Times.*

TIMES OF THE AMERICAS. (THE TIMES OF THE AMERICAS). Began in 1966. 0040-7917. Periodical. US. English (Spanish). bw. $25.00. Times of the Americas, 910 17th Street NW/Suite 632, Washington DC 20006. **Tel** (202)293-2849. Ed Carl E Moore. **LC** F1401. **DD** 980.005. bk rev. adv acc. **Circ** 2,500. The only English-language newspaper that reports on social, political, developmental and economic news of Latin America. *Times of Havana.*

TIMES OF TI. 0746-0392. Newspaper. US. English. wk. Times of Ti, Denton Publications, PO Box 338, Elizabethtown NY 12932.

THE TIMES OF ZAMBIA. 1964?-. Newspaper. English. da. $118.94. Kingstons (Zambia) Ltd, President Avenue, PO Box 139, Ndola Zambia.

THE TIMES-PICAYUNE CEASED. **VFOAT** Times Picayune. Began with V. 51, No. 42, (May 12, 1914). Ceased with V. 144, No. 129, (June 1, 1980). Newspaper. US. English. da. **LC** NEWSPAPER. *Times-Democrat and the Daily Picayune.*

TIMES-PICAYUNE, THE STATES-ITEM. **VFOAT** Times-Picayune. Vol. 144, No. 130 (June 2, 1980)-. Newspaper. US. English. da. Times-Picayune, 3800 Howard Avenue, New Orleans LA 70140. **LC** NEWSPAPER. Available on microfilm from Microphoto Division, Bell and Howell Co. *Times-Picayune, States-Item.*

TIMES-POST. **VAT** Times Post. 0746-3901. Newspaper. US. English. wk. $12.00. Times Post, PO Box 269, Houston MS 38851. **Tel** (601)456-3771.

TIMES RECORD (TROY, N.Y.). (THE TIMES RECORD). Newspaper. US. English. da. $120.00. Times Record, 501 Broadway, Troy NY 12181. **Tel** (518)272-2000. Ed D Marvin. Available on microfilm from Microphoto, Inc., Cleveland, Ohio.

TIMES (TRENTON, N.J. : PRINCETON-METRO EDITION). (THE TIMES). 8750-9083. Newspaper. US. English. da. The Times, PO Box 847, Trenton NJ 08605. *Trenton Times (Trenton, N.J. : 1976).*

TIMES-UNION. (THE TIMES-UNION). **VFOAT** Times Union. V. 46, No. 170- Sept. 30, 1963-. 0744-1851. Newspaper. US. English. da. $119.00. Rochester Times Union, 55 Exchange Street, Rochester NY 14614. **Tel** (716)232-7100. *Rochester Times-Union.*

THE TIMES-UNION. Began with Nov. 17? 1891 issue. Newspaper. US. English. da. Times-Union, News Plaza Box 1500, Albany NY 12212. **LC** Newspaper.

TIMESDAILY (SHOALS EDITION). (TIMESDAILY). **VFOAT** Times Daily. Began with: Vol. 114, No. 226 (Aug. 14, 1983). 0743-1511. Newspaper. US. English. da. $78.00. T S P Newspapers Inc, 219 West Tennessee Street, Florence AL 35630. *Times Tri-Cities Daily.*

TIMMINS PORCUPINE NEWS. V. 1- Nov. 6, 1974-. 0316-6872. Newspaper. CN. English. wk. 10.50 Domestic, 12.50 Foreign. Timmins Porcupine News, 815 Pine Street South, Timmins Ontario P4N 2M2 Canada. **DD** 071.14142.

TIPTON COUNTY TRIBUNE. **VFOAT** Tipton Tribune. 0746-0619. Newspaper. US. English. da. Tipton County Tribune, 317 South Anderson Street, Elwood IN 46036.

TLS. TIMES LITERARY SUPPLEMENT. (TLS, THE TIMES LITERARY SUPPLEMENT). 0307-661X. UK. English. wk. 12 Each Issue. Times Newspapers Limited, PO Box 7, 200 Gray's Inn Road, London WC1X 8EZ England. **Ind/Abst** Annu. Bibliogr. Engl. Lang. Lit., Book Rev. Index, Humanit. Index, Index Book Rev. Humanit., Ref. Source. **LC** AP4. **DD** 072.1. *Times Literary Supplement, 0040-7895.*

TODD COUNTY TRIBUNE. Newspaper. US. English. wk. $17.00. Figert Printing Inc, Mission SD 57555.

THE TOMBALL SUN. 8750-619X. Newspaper. US. English. wk. Free. The Tomball Sun, 314 Commerce Street, Tomball TX 77375.

THE TOMBSTONE EPITAPH. Began with May 1, 1880 issue. Newspaper. US. English. mo. Tombstone Epitaph, PO Box 1880, Tombstone AZ 85638. **Tel** (602)457-2211. **LC** NEWSPAPER.

TONGPANG NYUS. **VFOAT** Dong-Bang Nyus. 0715-4666. Newspaper. CN. Korean. Korean Dong-Baung News, 22 Rundlehorn Crescent, North East Calgary T1Y 1C6 Canada. **DD** 071.1233.

TOPEKA CAPITAL-JOURNAL (TOPEKA, KAN. : MORNING ED.). (THE TOPEKA CAPITAL-JOURNAL). **VFOAT** Topeka Capital Journal. Vol. 106, No. 307 (Sept. 2, 1980)-. Newspaper. US. English. da. $119.00. Topeka Capital Journal, 6th and Jefferson, Topeka KS 66607. **Tel** (913)295-1111. *Topeka Daily Capital, Topeka State Journal (Topeka, Kan. : Daily).*

THE TORCH. (THE TORCH : A MONTHLY NEWSPAPER FOR THE SMITHSONIAN INSTITUTION). No. 80-7 (July 1980)-. 0730-2231. Periodical. US. English. mo. Free. Office of Public Affairs, Room 2410, Arts and Industries Building, Washington DC 20560. **Tel** (202)357-2627. Ed Kathryn Lindeman. **Ind/Abst** Index U.S. Gov. Period. **LC** Q11.S8. **DD** 069.09753. **Circ** 8,200. (ctrl). Smithsonian-related articles and columns of interest to SI employees. *Smithsonian Torch, 0037-7341.*

TORONTO CLARION. **VFOAT** Clarion. Vol. 1, No. 1 (Oct. 15, 1976)-. 0229-3196. Newspaper. CN. English. mo. $23.21. Western Gap Communication Cooperative, 73 Bathurst Street, Toronto Ontario M5V 2P6 Canada. **Tel** (416)363-4404. **DD** 071.13541.

TORONTO EXPRESS. (LE TORONTO EXPRESS). V. 1- 1 Mar. 1976-. 0705-1069. Newspaper. CN. French. wk. 24. Domestic, 48.00 Foreign. Le Toronto Express Inc, 135 Broadview Avenue, Toronto Ont M4M 2E9 Canada. **Tel** (416)465-2107. Ed Jean Mazare. **DD** 071.13541. bk rev. adv acc. **Circ** 20,000. (ctrl). Containing general news and features.

TORONTO STAR. 0319-0781. Newspaper. CN. English. da. $425.61. Toronto Star Ltd., 1 Yonge Street, Toronto Ontario M5E 1E6 Canada. **Tel** (416)367-2138. **Ind/Abst** Can. News. Index. *Toronto Daily Star.*

TOULADI. (LE TOULADI). Vol. 1, No. 1 Oct. 3-. 0712-3299. Newspaper. CN. French. wk. Free. Le Touladi, Publications Temiscouataines, 117-B Commerciale, Cabano Quebec G0L 1E0 Canada. **DD** 071.1476.

TOWN CRIER. (THE TOWN CRIER). Vol. 1, No. 1 (Oct. 8, 1980)-. 0710-541X. Newspaper. CN. English. Free. Cochrane Times, Town Crier, Box 776, Cochrane Alberta T0L 0W0 Canada. **DD** 071.1233.

TOWN OF VAUGHAN VANGUARD. (THE TOWN OF VAUGHAN VANGUARD). **VFOAT** Vaughan Vanguard. Began with Aug. 26, 1976 issue. 0701-0869. Periodical. CN. English. wk. 0.10 Each Number. Vaughan Vanguard, Suite 4/7784 Martin Grove Road, Woodbridge Ontario L4L 1B1 Canada. **DD** 071.1354.

TOWN OF VAUGHAN WEEKLY. (THE TOWN OF VAUGHAN WEEKLY). V. 1- June 6, 1974-. 0380-3694. Newspaper. CN. English. wk. The Town of Vaughan Weekly, PO Box 331, Woodbridge Ontario L4L 1B2 Canada. **DD** 071.1354.

TOWNSHIPS SUN. (THE TOWNSHIPS SUN). Began publication in 197-. 0316-022X. Newspaper. CN. English. Free to English Households in Administrative Region 5, Sherbrooke. The Townships Sun, 105 Gordon Street, Sherbrooke Quebec Canada. **DD** 071146.

TRAIT D'UNION. (LE TRAIT D'UNION). V. 1, No. 1, (Sept. 1976)-. 0227-5562. Newspaper. CN. French. wk. Le Trait d'Union, CP 116, Mascouche Quebec J0N 1C0 Canada. **DD** 071.14416.

TRENTON TIMES (TRENTON, N.J. : 1976). (TRENTON TIMES). **VFOAT** Saturday Times. Vol. 94, No. 290 (Sept. 13, 1976)-. Newspaper. US. English. da. 500 Perry Street, Trenton NJ 08605. **LC** NEWSPAPER. *Evening Times (Trenton, N.J.).*

TRI-COUNTY NEWS (OSSEO, WIS. : 1965). (THE TRI-COUNTY NEWS). **VFOAT** Tricounty News. 1890-. 0749-7040. Newspaper. US. English. wk. $11.00 Wisconsin. Michael D Jensen, 1721 Omaha Street, Osseo WI 54758. *Tri-County News (Eleva, Wis. : Eleva Ed.), Tri-County News (Osseo, Wis. : Osseo, Ed.); Tri-County News (Strum, Wis. : Strum, Ed.).*

TRI-LAKE RECORDER. (THE TRI-LAKE RECORDER). **VFOAT** Recorder. **VAT** Recorder (Penticton). Vol. 1, No. 1 (Jan. 29, 1979)-. 0710-0221. Newspaper. CN. English. wk. Free in Penticton. The Recorder, 2375 Government Street, Penticton British Columbia V2A 6J7 Canada. **DD** 071.1142.

THE TRI-VALLEY HERALD. **VFOAT** Herald. 8750-9946. Newspaper. US. English. da. The Herald, PO Box 3000, Dublin CA 94568-0300.

LA TRIBUNA DE NORTH JERSEY. **VFOAT** Tribuna. Began in June? 1978. Newspaper. US. Spanish. sm. 70 Kossuth Street, PO Box 902, Newark NJ 07101. **LC** Newspaper. *La Tribuna de New Jersey.*

TRIBUNA ITALIANA. (LA TRIBUNA ITALIANA). Yearly V. 1- Oct. 15, 1963-. 0049-464X. Periodical. CN. Italian. mo. La Tribuna Italiana, 257 Dante Street, Montreal Quebec 327 Canada.

TRIBUNE. No. 1- Jan. 1937-. 0041-2821. Periodical. UK. English. wk. 21. Tribune Publishing Company, 308 Gray's Inn Road, London WC1X 8DS England. **Tel** (01)278-0911. Ed Nigel Williamson. bk rev. adv acc. Newspaper covering political and current affairs.

TRIBUNE-TIMES. **VFOAT** Tribune Times. 0747-1165. Newspaper. US. English. wk. $20.00. Tribune-Times, PO Box 789, Mauldin SC 29662. **Tel** (803)963-8934. Ed Teri Hammond. bk rev. adv acc. **Circ** 5,000. General interest weekly serving Greenville county, South Carolina.

TRINIDAD & TOBAGO REVIEW. **VFOAT** Trinidad and Tobacco Review. Began Publication in 1977?. Periodical. TR. English. sm. $321.00. Trinidad Expr Newspapers Ltd, 35 Independence Square, Port of Spain W1 Trinidad. **Tel** 62 31711/8. *TAPIA.*

TRIUMPH (LOS ANGELES, CALIF.). (THE TRIUMPH). V. 1, No. 1 (Sept. 1984)-. 8750-2542. Periodical. US. English. bm. The Triumph, 741 Gayley Avenue, Los Angeles CA 90024.

TROISIEME AGE. (LE TROISIEME AGE). First issue Dec. 1970-. 0702-1100. CN. French. mo. $6.19. Troisieme Age, 8162 St Denis Street, Montreal Quebec H2P 2G6 Canada.

THE TROY MESSENGER. 0746-3278. Newspaper. US. English. da. Tillotson Publications, 113 North Market Street, Troy AL 36081.

TRUE CITIZEN (LOCAL EDITION). (THE TRUE CITIZEN). 8750-6297. Newspaper. US. English. wk. $10.40 Burke and Neighboring Counties, $25.00 Elsewhere. The True Citizen, 610 Academy Avenue, Waynesboro GA 30830.

TRUE NORTH. V. 1- Oct. 1974-. 0319-7956. Newspaper. CN. English. mo. $4.50. True North, Box 4 Site 36 R R 2, Sudbury Ontario P3E 4N3 Canada. **DD** 071.13133.

THE TRYON DAILY BULLETIN. Began with Jan. 31, 1928 issue. Newspaper. US. English. da. Tryon Daily Bulletin Inc, Box 790, Tryon NC 28782.

TUCSON DAILY CITIZEN. Began with Dec. 15, 1901 issue. Newspaper. US. English. da. $156.00. Tucson Citizen, PO Box 26767, Tucson AZ 85726. **Tel** (602)573-4511. **LC** NEWSPAPER. *Arizona Daily Citizen.*

TUCSON'S MOUNTAIN NEWSREAL MICROFORM. Vol. 4, No. 5 (Jan. 1977)-. Newspaper. US. English. mo.

TULSA WORLD (TULSA, OKLA.). (TULSA WORLD). V. 72, No. 266 (June 9, 1977)-. 8750-5959. Newspaper. US. English. da. World Publishing Company, PO Box 1770, 315 South Boulder, Tulsa OK 74102. **LC** Newspaper. Also available on microfilm from Bell and Howell, Microphoto Division. *Tulsa Daily World (Tulsa, Okla. : 1927).*

TUNDRA TIMES. Began with Oct. 1, 1962 issue. 0049-4801. Newspaper. US. English. wk. $50.00. Eskimo Indian Aleut Publ Company, PO Box 104480, Anchorage AK 99510-4480. **Tel** (907)274-2512. Ed Bill E Hess. **LC** NEWSPAPER. bk rev. adv acc. **Circ** 5,000. Issues that relate to Alaska natives and issues that relate to rural Alaskans.

Newspapers

TUPPER LAKE FREE PRESS AND TUPPER LAKE HERALD. 1895. Newspaper. US. English. wk. $16.00. Tupper Lake Free Press, 136 Park Street, Tupper Lake NY 12986. **Tel** (518)359-2166. **Ed** M Dan McClelland. adv acc. **Circ** 3,700. (ctrl). Also available on microfilm from Capitol Microfilm Services, Inc. (Schenectady, N.Y.). Weekly hometown newspaper.

TURTLE MOUNTAIN STAR. Newspaper. US. English. ir. PO Box 849, Rolla ND 58367.

TWIN CITIES COURIER. Began publication in 1966. 0300-6603. Newspaper. US. English. wk. $8.50. Twin Cities Courier, 84 South 6th Street/Suite 501, Minneapolis MN 55402. **Tel** (612)332-3211. **Ed** Mary J Kyle. bk rev. adv acc. **Circ** 16,396. Newspaper emphasizing black news, and news of other ethnic minorities.

TWIN CITIES READER. 0193-2802. Periodical. US. English. wk. $18.00. Minneapolis Twin Cities Reader, 100 North 7th Street, Minneapolis MN. **Tel** (612)338-2900.

TWO MOUNTAINS JOURNAL. VFOAT Journal Deux-Montagnes. Vol. 1, No. 1-. 0229-7957. Newspaper. CN. English (includes some text in French). bm. Two Mountains Journal, PO Box 67, Deux-Montagnes Quebec J7R 4K1 Canada. **DD** 071.1425.

UCHITELSKAIA GAZETA. Oct. 1924-. Newspaper. UR. Russian. ir. $24.50. Victor Kamkin Inc, 12224 Parklawn Drive, Rockville MD 20852. **Tel** (301)881-5973.

UKENS NYTT / AFTENPOSTEN. Newspaper. NO. Norwegian. ir. $39.72. CHR Schibsteds Forlag, Kristian IV Sgt 1, Oslo 1 Norway.

UKRAINIAN TIMES. (THE UKRAINIAN TIMES). Began publication in 1974 or 1975. 0382-6686. Newspaper. CN. English (includes some text in Ukrainian). $3.00. The Ukrainian Times, 676 Manitoba Avenue, Winnipeg Manitoba R2W 2H4 Canada. **DD** 971.00491791.

ULEN UNION. Newspaper. US. English. wk. $10.00. Ulen Union, Box 98, Ulen MN 56585.

ULSTER COUNTY GAZETTE (KINGSTON, N.Y. : 1798) CEASED. (ULSTER COUNTY GAZETTE). VFOAT Ulster and Delaware Gazette. Began May 5, 1798? Ceased in 1803. US. English. wk. $10.50. Kingston Ulster County, PO Box 3507, Kingston NY 12401. **Tel** (914)338-1111. *Rising Sun (Kingston, N.Y.)*.

THE ULYSSES NEWS. Vol. 46, No. 27 (Oct. 7, 1937)-. Newspaper. US. English. wk. $20.00. Ulysses News, PO Box 706, Ulysses KS 67880. **Tel** (316)356-1201. *Grant County Republican*.

UMPQUA FREE PRESS. 0745-7588. Newspaper. US. English. wk. Umpqua Free Press Inc, 425 NW Second Avenue, PO Box 729, Myrtle Creek OR 97457. *Mail (Myrtle Creek, OR.)*.

THE UNDERWOOD NEWS. 8750-7285. Newspaper. US. English. wk. The Underwood News, Borlang Publishing Company, 216 Lincoln Avenue, Underwood ND 58576.

UNICORN TIMES. 0192-0375. Periodical. US. English. mo. $8.00. Unicorn Times, 920 F Street/Suite 511 NW, Washington DC 20004. **Tel** (202)783-6363.

UNION LEADER. 0161-9292. Periodical. US. English. wk. $14.00. Suburban Publishing Corporation, 1291 Stuyvesant Avenue, Union NJ 07083. **Tel** (201)686-7700. **Ed** Tim Owens and Phil Gimson. bk rev. adv acc. **Circ** 8,500. Local news.

THE UNION LEADER (MANCHESTER, N.H. : STATE EDITION). (THE UNION LEADER). VFOAT Manchester (N.H.) Union Leader. 118th Year, No. 153 (Sept. 24, 1980)-. Newspaper. US. English. da. The Union Leader, 35 Amherst Street, Manchester NH 03105. LC Newspaper. *Manchester New Hampshire Union Leader*.

UNION LIST OF PERIODICALS AND NEWSPAPERS IN U.S. VIRGIN ISLANDS LIBRARIES. Began in 1977. 0737-3414. US. English. an. LC Z6945, PN4832. **DD** 011.34.

UNION-SUN JOURNAL. VFOAT Union Sun and Journal. 0747-3788. Newspaper. US. English. da. Lockport Union Sun & Journal Inc, 459-491 South Transit Street, Lockport NY 14094.

UNITE. (L'UNITE). VFOAT Journal l'Unite. V. 1- 2 Mar. 1978-. 0705-9043. Newspaper. CN. French. $2.80. L'Unite, Suite 307/764 Sainte-Joseph East, Quebec G1K 3C4 Canada. **DD** 071.14.

UNITE. ENGLISH/SPANISH ED. (UNITY). VFOAT Unidad. V. L- Sept. 1978-. 0740-4603. Periodical. US. English (Spanish). sm. $15.00. Unity Newspaper, PO Box 127, Oakland CA 94604. **Tel** (415)652-4327. *Getting Together, Revolutionary Cause*.

UNITED DAILY NEWS. Newspaper. CH. Chinese. ir. $66.00. United Daily News, 555 Chunghsiao East Road Section 4, Taipei 105 Taiwan Republic of China. **Tel** 7681234-2232-2530.

U.S. PRESS. VFOAT US Press. VAT United States Press. Began in 1984?. 8755-2663. Newspaper. US. English. wk. $26.00. Circulation US Press, PO Box 3275, Silver Spring MD 20901. **DD** 071.

U.S. PUBLICITY DIRECTORY. NEWSPAPERS. *See* Yearbooks, Almanacs, Directories.

UNITY; UNIDAD. VFOAT T'Uan Chieh Pao. V. 1- Sept. 1978-. Periodical. US. English (Chinese). bw. Getting Together Publications, 850 Kearny Street, San Francisco CA 94126. *Getting Together, Revolutionary Cause*.

EL UNIVERSAL, EL GRAN DIARO DE MEXICO. Newspaper. MX. Spanish. da. $11.72. Cia Periodistica Nacional, PO Box 909, Bucareli 8 Mexico DF Mexico.

UPDATE (WHITE ROCK, B.C.). (UPDATE). Vol. 1, No. 1 (Sept. 1979)-. 0229-6837. Newspaper. CN. English. mo. **DD** 071.1133.

UPSURGE. No. 1- Sept. 1975-. Periodical. US. English. mo. Upsurge, PO Box 18213, Cleveland OH 44118.

UPTOWNER. Vol. 1, No. 1 (13 Apr. 1983)-. 0822-630X. Periodical. CN. English. Free in Uptown Toronto Area, $20.00 Others. Uptowner c/o Uptowner Publications, Suite 3/11 Mowat Avenue, Toronto Ontario M6K 3E3 Canada. **DD** 071.13541.

USA POLONIA; POLISH AMERICAN WEEKLY. VFOAT Polish American Weekly. VAT United States of America Polonia. 0199-6886. Newspaper. US. Polish (English). mo. $17.00. Tytan, 896 Manhattan Avenue, Brooklyn NY 11222. *Tydzien*.

USA TODAY (ARLINGTON, VA.). (USA TODAY). VFOAT U.S.A. Today. VAT United States of America Today (Arlington, Va.). Vol. 1, No. 1 Sept. 15, 1982 -. 0734-7456. Newspaper. US. English. da. $59.65. Data Entry Department, PO Box 7856, Washington DC 20044. **Tel** (800)872-0001.

VACAVILLE REPORTER. Began in 1883. Newspaper. US. English. ir. $45.00. Vacaville Reporter, PO Box 1509, Vacaville CA 95688. **Tel** (707)448-6401. LC Newspaper 7114-X.

VAL LORETTE. (LE VAL LORETTE). V. 1- June 1, 1974-. 0382-0076. Newspaper. CN. French. 20. Per No. Le Val Lorette, 1961 Boul Hamel, Ancienne Lorette Quebec Canada. **DD** 071.1447.

THE VALLEY-FOOTHILLS NEWS. VFOAT Valley & Foothills News. 0745-5321. Newspaper. US. English. wk. Valley-Foothills News, 11351 Foothills Boulevard, Yuam AZ 85365. **Tel** (602)342-1332. **Ed** Michael R Bush. adv acc. **Circ** 10,000. Free-distribution newspaper covering the east Yuma, Arizona, Mesa and eastern Yuma county. *Valley and Foothills News*.

VALLEY REPORTER. 0715-321X. Newspaper. CN. English. Valley Reporter, PO Box 129, Salmo British Columbia V0G 1Z0 Canada. **DD** 071.1144.

VALLEY REVIEW (PEMBROKE, ONT.). (VALLEY REVIEW). 0711-4427. Newspaper. CN. English. wk. .15 Per No. Vallley Review, PO Box 983, Pembroke Ontario K8A 7M5 Canada. **DD** 071.1381.

THE VALLEY SUN. 0192-8589. Newspaper. US. English. wk. Valley Publications Inc, PO Box 1780, Wasilla AK 99687. **Tel** (907)376-5225.

VANCOUVER EXPRESS. V. 1- Feb. 21, 1970-. 0227-3772. Periodical. CN. English. ir. $78.47. Vancouver Express, 554 East 15th Avenue, Vancouver British Columbia V5T 2R5 Canada. **DD** 071.1133.

VANCOUVER NEWS. (THE VANCOUVER NEWS). 0715-4895. Newspaper. CN. English. sm. Free to residents of East Vancouver. Vancouver News, c/o Foremost Publishing Company, 3 East Broadway/Suite 2033, Vancouver British Columbia V5T 1V5 Canada. **DD** 071.1133.

THE VANCOUVER SUN. Newspaper. CN. English. da. $78.94. Division of Pacific Press Ltd, 2250 Granville Street, Vancouver British Columbia V6H 3G2 Canada. **Tel** (604)732-2534.

LA VANGUARDIA ESPANOLA. Newspaper. SP. Spanish. da. La Vanguardia Espanola, Departmento de Sus Pelayo 28, Barcelona 1 Spain.

VARSITY. (THE VARSITY). Began publication in 1880?. 0042-2789. Periodical. CN. English. ir. $35.00. The Varsity, 91 St George Street, Toronto Ontario M5G 2E8 Canada. **Tel** (416)979-2831. **Ed** Margaret Webb. bk rev. adv acc. **Circ** 25,000. We are the official undergraduate paper of the University of Toronto. We provide news, reviews, entertainment and opinions. We are the largest student paper in Canada.

VAUGHAN COURIER. (THE VAUGHAN COURIER). VFOAT Courier. 0710-0191. Newspaper. CN. English. wk. $0.10 Per No. Vaughan Courier, PO Box 462, Kleinburg Ontario Canada. **DD** 071.13547.

VAUXHALL ADVANCE. (THE VAUXHALL ADVANCE). VFOAT Advance. VAT Advance (Vauxhall). V. 1- Oct. 26, 1978-. 0706-7550. Newspaper. CN. English. wk. $8. Domestic, $28. Foreign. Vauxhall Advance, Vauxhall Alberta Canada. **DD** 071.1234.

VERDIGRIS MAGAZINE. 0826-113X. Periodical. CN. English. mo. Free. Verdigris Magazine, 12 Forsythe Avenue, Kingston Ontario K7M 2L8 Canada. **DD** 051.

VERO BEACH PRESS JOURNAL. 1919-. US. English. da. $51.00. Vero Beach Press Journal, PO Box 1268, Vero Beach FL 32960. **Tel** (305)562-2315.

VERSUS. Periodical. Portuguese. mo. Versus Ltda, Av Liberdade 704, Sao Paulo Brazil.

VICTORIA COUNTY RECORD. V. 1- Oct. 1976-. 0703-8747. Newspaper. CN. English. mo. $4.95 Domestic, $5.95 Foreign. The Victoria County Record, PO Box 928, Perth-Andover New Brunswick E0J 1V0 Canada. **DD** 071.1553.

VICTORIA TIMES. (THE VICTORIA TIMES). May 17, 1979-. 0229-7310. Newspaper. CN. English. wk. $10.00. The Victoria Times, PO Box 599, Port Hawkesbury Nova Scotia B0E 2V0 Canada. **DD** 071.1693.

VILLAGEOIS. (LE VILLAGEOIS). Vol. 1, No 1 (July, 1979)-. 0711-3439. Newspaper. CN. French. mo. $5.00 Per Issue. Le Villageois, CP 269, St-Jean-Baptiste Quebec J0L 2B0 Canada. **DD** 071.1453.

VILLAGER. (THE VILLAGER). V. 1- Apr. 1980-. 0226-5907. Newspaper. CN. English. mo. $3.86. Villager, 2520 Bloor Street West, Toronto Ontario M6S 1N8 Canada. **Tel** (416)767-3644. **DD** 071.13535.

THE VINCENNES SUN. Began in Feb. 1879. Newspaper. US. English. da. Vincennes Sun Commercial, 702 Main Street, Vincennes IN 47591. LC Newspaper 7701-X.

VINDICATOR (LIBERTY, TEX.). (THE VINDICATOR). 0746-6838. Newspaper. US. English. sw. $18.00 Liberty and surrounding counties, $24.00 elsewhere in the US. The Vindicator, PO Box 1041, Liberty TX 77575. *Liberty Vindicator*.

THE VINTON MESSENGER. 8750-7919. Newspaper. US. English. wk. $10.00 Vinton and Roanoke Counties, $14.00 Elsewhere. The Vinton Messenger, PO Box 508, Vinton VA 24179.

LAS VIRGENES ENTERPRISE. 0193-9904. Newspaper. US. English. wk. $7.50. Las Virgenes Enterprise, Box 27, Calabasas CA 91302.

VIRGIN ISLANDS NEWSPAPERS, SUBSTANTIVE INDEX. *See* Indexes/Abstracts.

VIRGINIA GAZETTE (WILLIAMSBURG, VA. : 1930). (VIRGINIA GAZETTE). V. 1- Jan. 10, 1930-. 0049-6480. US. English. wk. $13.00. Virginia Gazette, PO Box 419, Williamsburg VA 23185. **Tel** (804)220-1736.

VISALIA TIMES-DELTA. Began with Mar. 1, 1928 issue. Newspaper. US. English. da. $110.00. Visalia Times Delta, PO Box 31, Visalia CA 03279. **Tel** (209)734-5821. **Ed** Robert Conley. LC Newspaper 7210. adv acc. **Circ** 19,000. *Visalia Morning Delta, Visalia Daily Times*.

Newspapers

VISHVA BHARTI. 0712-1814. Newspaper. CN. Hindi. bw. $12.00. Vishva Bharti, c/o 867 Pape Avenue, Toronto Ontario M4K 3T7 Canada. **DD** 071.13541.

VISITANDIN. (LE VISITANDIN). Vol. 1, No. 1 (31 Mar. 1981)-. 0714-3230. Newspaper. CN. French. ir. $5.00. Le Visitandin, 116 rue St-Joseph, La Visitation Quebec J0G 1C0 Canada. **DD** 071.1454.

EL VISITANTE DOMINICAL. 0194-9160. Periodical. US. Spanish. wk. $36.00. El Visitante, PO Box 1130, San Antonio TX 78294. **Tel** (512)736-1916.

VOCE CANADESE. (LA VOCE CANADESE). Yearly V. 1- Feb. 8, 1975-. 0317-3771. CN. Italian. La Voce Canadese, 790 Ouest rue Dundas, Toronto Ontario M6J 1V1 Canada. **DD** 071.13541.

VOICE (SAN FRANCISCO, CALIF. : 1979). (THE VOICE). 0273-5814. Periodical. US. English. wk. $60.00. Voice, 1782 Pacific Avenue, San Francisco CA 94109. **Tel** (415)441-0560.

VOICES. 0193-1474. Newspaper. US. English. wk. $30.00. Voices, PO Box 383, Southbury CT 06488. **Tel** (203)263-2116. Ed Mary Jane Musgaf. adv acc. **Circ** 16,000. (ctrl). Specializes in total local news for a market of 57,000 population.

VOILIER. (LE VOILIER). No. 1- Aug. 1965-. 0383-6444. Newspaper. CN. French. wk. $11.61. Le Voilier, Box 878, Caraquer New Brunswick E0B 1K0 Canada. **Tel** (506)727-2923. **DD** 071.1512.

VOZ (DENVER, COLO.). (LA VOZ). 0746-0988. Newspaper. US. English (Spanish). wk. $12.50. Hispano Publications, PO Box 9650, c/o JG Montoya, Denver CO 80209. **Tel** (303)623-4814.

VOZ DO IMIGRANTE. (A VOZ DO IMIGRANTE). First issue in 1975. 0318-9899. CN. Portuguese. A Voz Do Imigrante, CP 336 Station N, Montreal Quebec H2X 3M4 Canada. **DD** 071.14281.

WAKONDA TIMES OBSERVER. VFOAT Wakonda Times-Observer. 0747-3257. Newspaper. US. English. wk. Wakonda Times Observer, Box 207, Gayville SD 57301. *Wakonda Times.*

THE WALL STREET FINAL. 0270-9910. Periodical. US. English. da. $250.00. The Wall Street Final, 66 Greene Street, New York NY 10012.

WALL STREET IRREGULAR. 1973-. Periodical. US. English. ir. National Corporate Sciences, 485 Lexington Avenue, New York NY 10017. **Tel** (212)249-1964.

WALL STREET JOURNAL. MIDWEST EDITION. (THE WALL STREET JOURNAL). V. 31, No. - Jan. 2, 1951-. Newspaper. US. English. da. $45.00. Dow Jones & Company, 200 Burnett Road, Chicopee MA 01021. **Ind/Abst** Wall Street J. Index. Available on microfilm from Microphoto Division, Bell & Howell. *Chicago Journal of Commerce and La Salle Street Journal.*

THE WALL STREET TRANSCRIPT. Began in 1963. 0043-0102. Periodical. US. English. wk. $2420.00. Wall Street Transcript, 99 Wall Street, New York NY 10005. **Tel** (212)747-9500. **Ind/Abst** Predicasts. LC UNC.

WALLKILL VALLEY TIMES. 0746-0333. Newspaper. US. English. wk. Wallkill Valley Times, POB 446, Walden NY 12586.

WANGAR. Vol. 1, No. 1 Oct./Nov. 1976. 0712-1865. Newspaper. CN. Sanskarit (text in Devanagai Sanscrit). bm. $5.00. Wangar, PO Box 69646/Station K, Vancouver British Columbia V5K 4W7 Canada. **DD** 071.1133.

WARD 9 COMMUNITY NEWS. V. 1- Mar. 1, 1972-. 0228-068X. Newspaper. CN. English. sm. Free. Ward 9 Community News, 907 Kingston Road, Toronto Ontario M4H 1S4 Canada. **DD** 071.13541. (ctrl).

WARREN SHEAF. Newspaper. US. English. Warren Sheaf, Box 45, Warren MN 56762.

WASAGA BEACH NEWS. V. 2- May 1979-. 0704-4895. Newspaper. CN. English. wk. 0.15 Each Number. Wasaga Publications, PO Box 254, Wasaga Beach Ontario L0L 2P0 Canada. **DD** 071.1317. *Wasaga Beach News Magazine, 0704-4887.*

WASAGA BEACH TIMES. 0712-4945. Periodical. CN. English. wk. $12.00. Wasaga Beach Times, Box 187 25 Second Street, Collingwood Ontario L9Y 3Z5 Canada. **DD** 071.1317.

WASCANA WITNESS. V. 1- July 17, 1975-. 0382-8379. Newspaper. CN. English. wk. Wascana Witness, Box 3053, Regina Saskatchewan S4P 3G7 Canada. **DD** 071.1244.

WASHBURN COUNTY REGISTER. 8755-0520. Newspaper. US. English. wk. $8.50 Local, $10.00 Elsewhere Domestic, $18.00 Foreign. Washburn County Register, Box E, Shell Lake WI 54871.

WASHINGTON COUNTY BULLETIN. Newspaper. US. English. wk. $12.50. Bulletin Publishing Corporation, 7162 80th Street South, Cottage Grove MN 55106. **Tel** (612)459-3434.

WASHINGTON COUNTY NEWS. 0279-795X. Newspaper. US. English. sw.

WASHINGTON COUNTY POST (SALEM, N.Y. : 1837). (WASHINGTON COUNTY POST). Began in 1837. Newspaper. US. English. wk. Washington County Post, 32 East Maine Street, Cambridge NY 12816. **LC** Newspaper 8829-X. *County Post and North Star.*

WASHINGTON JEWISH WEEK. *See* Religion, Mythology, Rationalism - Judaism.

THE WASHINGTON POST INDEX. *See* Indexes/Abstracts.

WASHINGTON POST (WASHINGTON, D.C. : 1974). (THE WASHINGTON POST). 97th year, No. 27 (Jan. 1, 1974)-. 0190-8286. Newspaper. US. English. da. PO Box 925, Farmingdale NY 11737. **Tel** (202)334-4278. Ed Ben Bradlee. **Ind/Abst** Nexis, Predicasts, Energy Inf. Abstr., Environ. Abstr., Infobank, Funk Scott Index Corp. Ind. bk rev. adv acc. **Circ** 50,000. Available on microfilm from Research Publications, Inc. and Micro Photo Division, Bell and Howell. *Washington Post, Times Herald.*

THE WASHINGTON TIMES. Vol. 1, No. 1 (May 17, 1982)-. 0732-8494. Newspaper. US. English. da. $52.00. Washington Times Daily, 3400 New York Avenue NE, Washington DC 20002. **Tel** (202)636-3000.

WATAUGA DEMOCRAT. 0745-1903. Newspaper. US. English. tw. Watauga Democrat, POB 353, Boone NC 28607.

WATERBURY REPUBLICAN. Began with Jan. 2, 1884 issue. Newspaper. US. English. da. $78.00. Waterbury Republican Daily, Waterbury CT 06720. **Tel** (203)574-3636.

WATERLOO COURIER CEDAR FALLS. VFOAT Courier. 8750-0868. Newspaper. US. English. da. Waterloo Courier Inc, Cedar Falls Record, Box 540, Waterloo IA 50701. *Waterloo Courier, the Cedar Falls Record, 0746-181X.*

WATERLOO DAILY COURIER. Began with Dec. 13, 1890 issue. Newspaper. US. English. da. $87.95. WH Hartman Company, PO Box 540, Waterloo IA 50704. **Tel** (319)291-1400.

WEB; NEWSPAPER AND MAGAZINE PRODUCTION. V. 7, No. 10- Oct. 1978-. 0191-4634. Periodical. US. English. qt. $6.00. Ohio State University, 29 West Woodruff, 200 Ramseyer Hall, Columbus OH 43224. **Tel** (614)422-0711. Ed Charlotte Huck and Janet Hickman. LC Z119. **DD** 658.809070571. bk rev. **Circ** 2,100. *Newspaper Production for North and South America, 0148-964X.*

WEEK-END NATIONAL. (LE WEEK-END NATIONAL). V. 1, No. 1, (March/1, April 1983)-. 0823-6011. Periodical. CN. French. wk. $1.00 Per No. Le Week-End National, Bureau 200/2121 Est rue Sherbrooke, Montreal Quebec H2K 1C3 Canada. **DD** 054.1.

WEEKEND DESERT POST. VFOAT Desert Post. 8750-4316. Newspaper. US. English. wk. Desert Post, PO Box 459, Palm Desert CA 92261.

WEEKEND JOURNAL (HUDSON, QUEBEC). (WEEKEND JOURNAL). Vol. 1, No. 1 (Oct. 26, 1977)-. 0227-4574. Newspaper. CN. English (text in French). wk. Free. Editions Weekend Ltee, PO Box 694, Hudson Quebec J0P 1H0 Canada. **DD** 071.14263.

WEEKEND MAGAZINE INDEX CARDS. *See* Indexes/Abstracts.

WEEKLY INDIA TRIBUNE. VFOAT India Tribune. 0744-4524. Newspaper. US. English. ir. $6.00. India Tribune Publishers Inc, 3955 West Lawrence Avenue, Chicago IL 60625. **Tel** 583-6150. Ed Prashant Shah. bk rev. adv acc. **Circ** 15,000. (ctrl).

WEEKLY NEWS (MARKSVILLE, LA.). (THE WEEKLY NEWS). 0739-7534. Newspaper. US. English. wk. $15.00. The Weekly News, PO Box 209, Marksville LA 71351.

WEEKLY RECORD. (THE WEEKLY RECORD). Vol. 1, No. 1 (May 16, 1979)-. 0710-0183. Newspaper. CN. English. wk. $12.00. Weekly Record, PO Box 946, Truro Nova Scotia B2N 5G7 Canada. **DD** 071.1612.

WEEKLY REVIEW. (THE WEEKLY REVIEW). Vol. 1, No. 1 (Feb. 14, 1978)-. 0710-0175. Newspaper. CN. English. wk. $7.74. The Weekly Review, Box 240, Viking Alberta T0B 4N0 Canada. **DD** 071.1233.

WEEKLY WORLD NEWS. V. 1- Oct. 16, 1979-. 0199-574X. Newspaper. US. English. wk. $12.95. Weekly World News, 600 South East Coast Avenue, Lantana FL 33642. **Tel** (305)586-0201.

WELLAND GUARDIAN EXPRESS. VFOAT Guardian Express. Vol. 1 (Nov. 3, 1982)-. 0823-7565. Newspaper. CN. English. wk. Free. Welland Guardian Express, 60 Main Street East, Welland Ontario L4B 3W3 Canada. **DD** 071.1338. (ctrl).

WELLAND NEWS MAGAZINE. VAT Welland Consumer News (1981). Vol. 3, No. 16 (4/21/81)-. 0712-1806. Newspaper. CN. English. wk. $0.25 Each Number. Consumer News, PO Box 458, Welland Ontario L3B 5R2 Canada. **DD** 071.1338. *Welland Consumer News, 0712-1792.*

WELLINGTON FREE PRESS. (THE WELLINGTON FREE PRESS). 0710-0205. Newspaper. CN. English. Wellington Free Press, PO Box 239, Wellington Ontario K0K 3L0 Canada. **DD** 071.13587.

DIE WELT. Newspaper. German. da. German Language Publ Inc, 560 Sylvan Avenue, Englewood Cliffs NJ 07632. **Tel** (212)736-7455.

WELT AM SONNTAG. Periodical. German. wk. $130.00. German Language Publications Inc, 560 Sylvan Avenue, Englewood Cliffs NJ 07632. **Tel** (212)736-7455.

WEST CARLETON BANNER. VFOAT Banner. VAT Banner (Carp). Vol. 1, No. 1 (Apr. 10, 1979)-. 0229-6713. Newspaper. CN. English. wk. $10.00 Carp, $14.00 Elsewhere in Canada, $25.00 Others. West Carelton Banner, PO Box 279, Carp Ontario K0A 1L0 Canada. **DD** 071.1383.

WEST COAST PEDDLER. 0199-3356. Periodical. US. English. bw. West Coast Peddler, PO Box 4489, Downey CA 90241.

WEST COUNTY TIMES. 0746-6323. Newspaper. US. English. da. $42.00. Lesher Communications Inc, 2640 Shadelands Drive, Walnut Creek CA 94598.

WEST EDMONTON EXAMINER. VFOAT Examiner. VAT Examiner (West Edmonton). V. 1- Nov. 9, 1977-. 0707-509X. Newspaper. CN. English. wk. Free. Grove Publishing, 9509—156 Street, Edmonton Alberta T5P 4J5 Canada. **DD** 071.1233. (ctrl).

WEST ENDER. Vol. 1, No. 1 (July 12, 1979)-. 0229-6012. Newspaper. CN. English. wk. $40.24. Westender, 1035 Davie Street, Vancouver British Columbia V6E 1M5 Canada. **Tel** (604)682-0686. **DD** 071.1133.

WEST LONDON NEWS. VFOAT London News. Began with Sept. 12, 1973 (No. 48). 0381-8489. Newspaper. CN. English. ir. West London News, PO Box 811 Station B, London Ontario N6A 4Z3 Canada. **DD** 071.1326. *Westmount News.*

WEST PRINCE GRAPHIC. Vol. 1, No. 1 (Oct. 22, 1980)-. 0710-6416. Newspaper. CN. English. wk. $50.30. The West Prince Graphic, PO Box 339, Alberton Prince Edward Island C0B 1B0 Canada. **Tel** (902)853-3320. **DD** 071.171.

WEST SAINT PAUL SUN. Newspaper. US. English. wk. Edina West St Paul Sun, 7401 Bush Lake Road, Edina MN 55435. **Tel** (612)831-1200.

WEST TOLEDOHERALD. VFOAT Herald. 8750-1872. Newspaper. US. English. wk. Herald Newspapers Inc, 4444 West Alexis Road, Toledo OH 43623.

WEST TORONTO NEWS-EXPRESS. (THE WEST TORONTO NEWS-EXPRESS). 0821-5197. Newspaper. CN. English. mo. Free. The West Toronto News-Express, 1264 College Street, Toronto Ontario M6H 1R4 Canada. **DD** 071.13541. (ctrl). *Enviro-News Express.*

Newspapers

WEST VIRGINIA HILLBILLY. Hillbilly. 1956-. Newspaper. US. English. wk. c/o Harry D Lynch Editor, PO Box 279, Summersville WV 26651. **Tel** (304)846-4067.

WESTCOAST READER. (THE WESTCOAST READER). 0822-7225. Periodical. CN. English. mo. Free. Westcoast Reader, c/o Capilano College, 2055 Purcell Way, North Vancouver British Columbia V7J 3H5 Canada. **DD** 071.11. (ctrl). *Westcoaster, 0826-0257.*

WESTERN BEACON MONTHLY NEWSPAPER MAGAZINE. VFOAT Western Beacon. Vol. 1, No. 1 (June 15 1979)-. 0229-7922. Newspaper. CN. English. mo. $3.00 Yarmouth and Shelbourne Counties, $7.00 Elsewhere in Canada. Western Beacon Publication Company, PO Box 402, Yarmouth Nova Scotia B5A 4B3 Canada. **DD** 071.1631.

WESTERN VIKING. 1889. Periodical. US. Multilingual (English and Norwegian). wk. $20.00. Western Viking, 2040 NW Market Street, PO Box 70408, Seattle WA 98107. **Tel** (206)784-4617. Ed Henning C Boe. bk rev. adv acc. **Circ** 5,000. A Norwegian and English language weekly with nationwide circulation. Now in its 96th year of uninterrupted publication.

WESTERN WHEEL. (THE WESTERN WHEEL). V. 1- Aug. 3, 1976-. 0701-1571. Periodical. CN. English. wk. $30.00. Western Wheel, Box 238, Okotoks Alberta T0L 1T0 Canada. **Tel** (403)938-6397. Ed Judi Weaver. **DD** 071.1234. adv acc. **Circ** 7,800. (ctrl). Local news for towns and rural areas in municipal district of foothills.

WESTON TIMES REVIEW. VFOAT Times Review. Began publication Aug. 29, 1974. 0316-5434. Periodical. CN. English. wk. .10 Per No. Times Review, PO Box 2053 Station B, Rexdale Ontario M9V 2G3 Canada. **DD** 071.13541.

WHEAT RIDGE SENTINEL. 0747-2021. Newspaper. US. English. wk. $16.25. Sentinel Publications Company, PO Box 15457, Lakewood CO 80215.

WHIPPING POST / STARSHIP. Series/ Titl Bell and Howell Underground Press Collection. Began publication in 1972. Newspaper. English. ir.

WHISTLER QUESTION. (THE WHISTLER QUESTION). V. 1- April 14, 1976-. 0383-820X. Newspaper. CN. English. wk. .15 Each Number. Burrows Enterprises, PO Box 126, Whistler British Columbia V0N 1B0 Canada. **DD** 071.1133.

WHITE BEAR PRESS. Began in 1914. Newspaper. US. English. wk. $11.00. Press Publications, 409 Bloom Avenue, White Bear Lake MN 55110. **Tel** (612)429-7781. **LC** Newspaper 7002. *White Bear Life.*

WHITE BLUFF CHRONICLE. 0738-6125. Newspaper. US. English. wk. $10.40. White Bluff Chronicle, 211 North Strawberry Avenue, PO Drawer 939, Demopolis AL 36732.

THE WHITE CASTLE TIMES. 0744-575X. Newspaper. US. English. wk. $12.00. White Castle Times, PO Box 589, Plaquemine LA 70764. **Tel** (504)545-3941. Ed Ellie Hebert. bk rev. adv acc. **Circ** 1,500. General news, society, and sports.

WHITECOURT FREE PRESS. (THE WHITECOURT FREE PRESS). Vol. 1, No. 1 (Oct. 13, 1982)-. 0821-5553. Newspaper. CN. English. wk. $0.25 Each Number. The Whitecourt Free Press, PO Box 336, Whitecourt Alberta T0E 2L0 Canada. **DD** 071.1233.

THE WHITEHALL TIMES. Began in 1860. Newspaper. US. English. wk. $14.00. Whitehall Times Inc, Printers & Publishers, Whitehall NY 12887. **Tel** (518)499-1500. *American Sentinel (Whitehall, N.Y.).*

WILD ROSE CHRONICLE. V. 1- Jan. 1978-. 0706-5094. Newspaper. CN. English. mo. $7.00. Wild Rose Chronicle Ltd, PO Box 1654, Vermilion Alberta T0B 4M0 Canada. **DD** 071.1233.

THE WILKES-BARRE TIMES LEADER. VFOAT Times Leader. 1879. 0199-0519. Newspaper. US. English. da. $90.00. Times Leader, 15 North Main Street, Wilkes Barre PA 18711. **Tel** (717)829-7140. Ed Dale Duncan. adv acc. **Circ** 50,000 Daily. Daily newspaper except Sunday.

WILLIAMS NEWS. Began in 1890. Newspaper. US. English. wk.

WILLISTON DAILY HERALD. Newspaper. US. English. da. $55.00. Williston Herald Attn: Gene Springer, Box 1447, Williston ND 58801.

WILLMAR WEST CENTRAL DAILY TRIBUNE. 1895. Newspaper. US. English. ir. $49.00. West Central Tribune, PO Box 839, Willmar MN 56201. **Tel** (612)235-1150. Ed Forrest Peterson. bk rev. adv acc. **Circ** 16,500. (ctrl). Daily newspaper covering 7 counties in West Central Minnesota.

WILMETTE LIFE. 0745-0044. Newspaper. US. English. wk. $20.75. Pioneer Pressing, 1232 Central Avenue, Wilmette IL 60091. **Tel** (312)251-4300.

WILMINGTON MORNING STAR. VFOAT Sunday Star-News. Vol. 108, No. 81 (Nov. 27, 1921)-. 0163-402X. Newspaper. US. English. da. Star-News Newspapers Company, 1003 South 17th Street, Wilmington NC 28401. *Morning News (Wilmington, N.C.).*

WILSHIRE CENTER'S LARCHMONT CHRONICLE. VFOAT Larchmont Chronicle. 1964. 0192-1932. Newspaper. US. English. mo. $7.50. Larchmont Chronicle, 542 1/2 North Larchmont Boulevard, Los Angeles CA 90004. **Tel** (213)462-2241. Ed Jane Gilman. adv acc. **Circ** 20,000. (ctrl). Local newspaper covering residents and issues relevant to Hancock Park area of Los Angeles and immediate surroundings.

WINDMILL HERALD. (THE WINDMILL HERALD : GOED NIEUWS). VAT Goed Nieuws (1972). Vol. 14, No. 189 (Jan. 21, 1972)-. 0712-6417. Newspaper. CN. Dutch (English). sm. $0.15 Each No. Windmill Herald, PO Box 533, New Westminister British Columbia V3L 4Y8 Canada. **DD** 071.1133. *Goed Nieuws, 0712-6409.*

THE WINDSOR STAR. Reel 694 (Feb. 10/27, 1960)-. Newspaper. CN. English. Preston Microfilm Services, 2115 Queen Street East, Toronto Ontario M4E 1E8 Canada. **DD** 071.1332. *Windsor Daily Star.*

WINNIPEG FREE PRESS. Jan. 1932-. 0828-1785. Newspaper. CN. English. da. $1227.30. Winnipeg Free Press Company Ltd, 300 Carlton Street, Winnipeg Manitoba R3C 3C1 Canada. **Tel** (204)943-9331. Ed M Burt. Ind/Abst Can. News. Index. adv acc. **Circ** 179,000. Local and international news coverage. *Manitoba Free Press.*

WINNIPEG GUIDE. (THE WINNIPEG GUIDE). Began publication in 197-. 0703-5292. Newspaper. CN. English. bw. Central Manitoba Publishing, Suite 1-590 Roseberry Street, Winnipeg Man R3H 0T1 Canada. **DD** 071.1274.

WINNIPEG SUN. (THE WINNIPEG SUN). Vol. 1, No. 1 (Nov. 5, 1980)-. 0711-3773. Newspaper. CN. English. da. $120.72. Winnipeg Sun, 1670 Church Avenue, Winnipeg Man RX2 2W9 Canada. **Tel** 633-7781. **DD** 071.1274.

WINONA COURIER. Newspaper. US. English. bw. $5.00. Diocese of Winona, PO Box 53, Winona MN 55987. **Tel** (507)454-4369.

WINONA DAILY NEWS. Vol. 1, No. 1 (Sept. 14, 1916)-. 0273-9941. Newspaper. US. English. da. $115.00. Winona Daily News, PO Box 147, Winona MN 55987. **Tel** (507)454-6804. **LC** Newspaper 8520. *Winona Republican-Herald.*

WINONA TIMES. Newspaper. US. English. wk. $13.00. Winona Times, PO Box 151, Winona MS 38967. **Tel** (601)283-1131.

WINSTED JOURNAL. Newspaper. US. English. ir. Winsted MN 55395.

WINSTON-SALEM CHRONICLE. VFOAT Winston Salem Chronicle. Vol. 1, No. 1 (Sept. 5, 1974)-. Newspaper. US. English. wk. $13.52 Domestic, $18.52 Foreign. 617 North Liberty Street, Winston-Salem NC 27102. **Tel** (919)722-8624. Ed Allen H Johnson III. **LC** NEWSPAPER. bk rev. adv acc. **Circ** 6,000. (ctrl). Newspaper focusing on community news directly affecting black community. Also contains monthly supplement, black college sports review covering CIAA, MEAC, SIAC, and SWAC.

WINSTON-SALEM JOURNAL. VFOAT Winston Salem Journal. Began with Apr. 3, 1897 issue. Newspaper. US. English. da. 416-420 North Marshall Street, Winston Salem NC 27102. **LC** Newspaper 7002.

WINTER PARK SUN HERALD. US. English. wk. $20.00. Winter Park Sun Herald, PO Box 416, Winter Park FL 32790. **Tel** (305)647-1217.

WINTERS EXPRESS. Began in 1883. Newspaper. US. English. wk. $6.50. Winters Express, 312 Railroad Avenue, Winters CA 95694. **Tel** (916)795-4551. **LC** Newspaper 7002.

WISCONSIN STATE JOURNAL. VFOAT Sunday State Journal. 0749-405X. Newspaper. US. English. da. Madison Newspaper Inc, PO Box 8056, Madison WI 53708.

WOODSTOCK DAILY SENTINEL. Began with Dec. 24, 1930 issue. Newspaper. US. English. da. $49.00. Woodstock Publishing Company, 109 South Jefferson, PO Box 709, Woodstock IL 60098. **Tel** (815)338-1300. **LC** Newspaper 7700. *Woodstock Sentinel and American.*

THE WORKING PEOPLE'S DAILY. Newspaper. English. da. $92.00. Working Peoples Daily, PO Box 43, 212 Theinbyu Street, Rangoon Burma.

WORLD ISLAMIC TIMES. Vol. 1, No. 1 (Jan. 12-18, 1983)-. Periodical. English. wk. $100.00. World Islamic Times, Municipal Road G-6/2, Islamabad Pakistan.

WORTHINGTON GLOBE. 1873. Newspaper. US. English. da. $115.00. Worthington Daily Globe Inc, Box 631, Worthington MN 56187. **Tel** (507)376-9711. Ed Ray Crippen. adv acc. **Circ** 16,500. (ctrl). News and sports from Southwest Minnesota and Northwest Iowa, the nation and the world.

WOTANIN WOWAPI. Began in 1974 or 1975. Periodical. US. English. sm. $15.00. Wotanin Wowapi, Box 493, Poplar MT 59255. **Tel** (406)768-5241. Ed Bonnie C Red Elk. bk rev. adv acc. **Circ** 8,000. Available in microform. Newspaper of tribal government news for Assiniboine and Sioux tribal members of the Fort Peck Indian Reservation, Montana. *Wotanin.*

WRANGELL SENTINEL. Began May 20, 1909. Newspaper. US. English. wk. $22.00. Wrangell Sentinel, PO Box 798, Wrangell AK 99929. **Tel** (901)874-2301. Available in microform.

WRIGHT COUNTY JOURNAL PRESS. Newspaper. US. English. wk. $10.00. Buffalo Wright County Journal, 108 Central Avenue, Buffalo NY 55313. **Tel** (612)681-1221.

WYOMING STATE TRIBUNE. US. English. da. $63.00. Cheyenne Newspapers Inc, 110 East 17th Street, Cheyenne WY 82001. **Tel** (307)634-3361.

THE Y WEEKLY. VFOAT Yweekly. 0883-3133. Newspaper. US. English. wk. The Y Weekly, 6110 US Highway/ 290 West, Austin TX 78735.

YORK REGIONAL TOPIC. (THE YORK REGIONAL TOPIC). VAT Topic (Bradford). 0710-2011. Newspaper. CN. English. wk. $30.95. Bradford Paper Group, PO Box 1090, Bradford Ont LOG 1CO Canada. **DD** 071.13547.

YORKTON THIS WEEK. V. 1- Sept. 10, 1975-. 0380-2833. Newspaper. CN. English. wk. $7.80. Yorkton This Week, PO Box 1300, Yorkton Saskatchewan S3N 2X3 Canada. **DD** 071.1242.

YOUNGSTOWN VINDICATOR (YOUNGSTOWN, OHIO : 1960). (YOUNGSTOWN VINDICATOR). VFOAT Youngstown Daily Vindicator. Vol. 71, No. 247 (May 4, 1960)-. Newspaper. US. English. da. $74.50. Vindicator Square, Youngstown OH 44501. Available on microfilm from Bell & Howell Microphoto Division. *Youngstown Vindicator and the Youngstown Telegram.*

YUKON NEWS. Began with July 21, 1972 issue. 0318-1952. Newspaper. CN. English. ir. 100.00. Yukon Press Limited, 211 Wood Street, Whitehorse Yukon Y1A 2EA Canada. **Tel** (403)667-6286. Ed Patricia Living. **DD** 071.191. bk rev. adv acc. **Circ** 8,600. Community newspaper covering all of Yukon, Canada's Northwest Territory. *Yukon Daily News.*

ZAMBIA DAILY MAIL. Aug. 13, 1965-. Newspaper. English. da. Zambia Publishing Company, Box 1421, Lusaka Zambia.

ZASSHI SHIMBUN SOKATAROGU. VFOAT Periodicals in Print. No. 1-. JA. Japanese. ir. Media Risachi Senta, c/o Sky Building, 10-1 Shinjuku 5 Shinjuku-ku, Tokyo 160 Japan. **LC** Z6958.J3, PN5407.P4.

ZEITUNGS-INDEX. See Indexes/Abstracts.

ZENKOKU SHIMBUN MAIKUROFIRUMU SEISAKU SHOZO ICHIRAN. VFOAT List of Japanese Newspapers on Microfilm in Japan. 1970-. JA. Japanese. ir. Kohuritsu Kokkai Toshokan, 1-10-1 Nagatacho Chiyoda-Ku, Tokyo Japan. **LC** Z6958.J3.

Numismatics

NUMISMATICS

AL-MASKUKAT. Journal 1- July 1969-. Periodical. IQ. Arabic (summaries in English). be. Directorate of Antiquities, Ministry Culture & Information, Baghdad Iraq. LC CJ3770.

ANNUAL CONVENTION - CANADIAN NUMISMATIC ASSOCIATION. Main/Corp Canadian Numismatic Association. Began with 1970? issue. 0318-4951. Periodical. CN. English. Charlton Numismatics Ltd, 299 Queen Street West, Toronto Ontario M5V 1Z9 Canada. DD 737.4971. *Convention Sale Catalogue, 0318-496X.*

ANNUAL EVALUATION OF U. S. GOLD COIN PRICES. 0092-3303. US. English. an. D Mason and Associates Investment Consultants, PO Box 21023, Long Beach CA 90801. LC CJ1834. DD 737.4973.

ANNUAL REPORT OF THE AMERICAN NUMISMATIC SOCIETY. Main/Corp American Numismatic Society. 1962-. 0569-6720. US. English. an. American Numismatic Society, Broadway Between 155th and 156th Streets, New York NY 10032. Tel (212)234-3130. Ed M M Martin. LC CJ15. DD 737.06273. Circ 2,000. Report of the American Numismatic Society. *Proceedings of the American Numismatic Society, Annual Meeting, 0743-877X.*

ANTIKE MUNZEN UND GESCHNITTENE STEINE. V. 1- 1969-. 0420-025X. Monographic Series. US. German. ir. Walter de Gruyter Inc, 200 Saw Mill River Road, Hawthorne NY 10532. Tel (914)747-0110.

ATLANTIC NUMISMATIST. (THE ATLANTIC NUMISMATIST). V. 15, No. 6- June 1979-. 0708-3181. Periodical. CN. English. mo. Atlantic Provinces Numismatic Association, PO Box 243, Armdale Post Office, Halifax Nova Scotia B3L 4K1 Canada. DD 737.062715. *A. P. N. A. Newsletter, 0044-9903.*

AUCTION PRICES REALIZED. U.S. COINS. VFOAT Auction Prices Realized. US Coins. 1982-. 0737-6634. US. English. an. Auction Prices Realized, Krause Publications, 700 East State Street, Iola WI 54990. Ed Bob Wilhite. LC CJ1826. DD 737.4973. *Rome's Prices Realized for U.S. Coins, 0277-6510.*

AUSTRALIAN NUMISMATIC JOURNAL. Periodical. English. qt. Numismatic Society of South Australia, Box 80 GPO, Adelaide 5001 South Australia. LC CJ1. DD 737.099423. *South Australian Numismatic Journal.*

BANK NOTE REPORTER. 0164-0828. Periodical. US. English. mo. $14.50. Krause Publications, 700 East State Street, Iola WI 54990. Tel (715)445-2214. Ed Courtney Coffing. bk rev. adv acc. Circ 5,000. (ctrl). News on collecting of bank notes; stories on what's new, finds, etc.

DE BEELDENAAR. Periodical. Dutch. ir. 40.00. Genootschap voor Hunt-en Penningkunde, Postbus 420, Zeist Netherlands. LC CJ9. *Geuzenpenning, De Florijn.*

BLATT FUR SORTENWESEN. 0300-4627. Periodical. German. mo. $19.47. Alfred Strother Verlag, Postfach 5847/Osterstrasse 32, D-3000 Hannover 1 West Germany.

BULLETIN DE LA SOCIETE FRANCAISE DE NUMISMATIQUE. Main/Corp Societe Francaise de Mumismatique. 3.- Year. 0037-9344. Periodical. FR. French. mo. 150. Bibliotheque Nationale, 58 rue de Richelieu, 75084 Paris Cedex 02 France. Tel (1)261 82 83. Ed Societe Francaise de Numismatique. (cum index). Circ 800. Ancient medieval and modern numismatics. *Proces-Verbal de la Seance du . . . .*

CANADIAN COIN NEWS. V. 14, No. 2- June 21/July 5, 1976-. 0702-3162. Periodical. CN. English. bw. $19.00. McLaren Publications Ltd, PO Box 12000, Bracebridge Ont P0B 1C0 Canada. Tel (705)687-6691. Ed Diane Ujfalussy. DD 737.05. bk rev. adv acc. Circ 20,000. Canadian coin news brings the world of Canadian and world numismatics to the collector/dealer. It offers regular, informed columnists, feature articles and a very useful trends section. *Coin, Stamp, Antique News, 0010-0439.*

CANADIAN NUMISMATIC JOURNAL. (THE CANADIAN NUMISMATIC JOURNAL). V. 1- Jan. 1956-. 0008-4573. Periodical. CN. English. mo. 23.21. Canadian Numismatic Association, PO Box 226, Barrie Ontario L4M 4T2 Canada. Tel (705)737-0845. Ed Robert C Wiley. bk rev. adv acc. Circ 2,000. Current and historical information on numismatics and the study of same. General information on dealers and advertisements regarding current items. Useful to both beginner and experienced collector. *The C.N.A. Bulletin, 0315-4882.*

CHARLTON CANADIAN TRADE DOLLAR GUIDE. (THE CHARLTON CANADIAN TRADE DOLLAR GUIDE). 1st- Ed. 0228-152X. CN. English. an. $7.95 Per No. Charlton Press, 299 Queen Street West, Toronto Ontario M5V 1Z9 Canada. DD 737.4971.

CHARLTON NUMISMATIC BULLETIN. (THE CHARLTON NUMISMATIC BULLETIN). V. 1, No. 5- Fall 1976-. 0703-5837. Periodical. CN. English. Charlton International Pulications Ltd, Mail Order Department MOC/TB, 299 Queen Street West, Toronto Ontario M5V 1Z9 Canada. DD 737.4971. *Charlton Bulletin, 0381-677X.*

CHARLTON STANDARD CATALOGUE OF CANADIAN COINS. (THE CHARLTON STANDARD CATALOGUE OF CANADIAN COINS). 31st Ed. (Winter 1981)-. 0714-6701. Periodical. CN. English. sa. $3.50 Per No. Charlton Press, 299 Queen Street West, Toronto Ontario M5V 1Z9 Canada. DD 737.4971. *Charlton's Standard Catalogue of Canadian Coins, 0706-0424.*

CHARLTON STANDARD CATALOGUE OF CANADIAN PAPER MONEY. (THE CHARLTON STANDARD CATALOGUE OF CANADIAN PAPER MONEY). 1st- Ed. 0706-0432. CN. English. an. $18.96. The Charlton Press, 290 Queen Street West, Toronto Ontario M5V 1Z9 Canada. DD 769.55971. *Standard Catalogue of Canadian Coins, Tokens and Paper Money, 0585-038X.*

COIN ADDENDUM TO THE STANDARD CATALOGUE OF CANADIAN COINS TOKENS & PAPER MONEY. (COIN ADDENDUM TO THE STANDARD CATALOGUE OF CANADIAN COINS, TOKENS AND PAPER MONEY). 1st- Ed. 0381-6672. CN. English. an. $1. Per No. Charlton International Publishing Inc, 299 Queen Street West #2, Toronto Ontario M5V 1Z9 Canada. DD 737.4971.

COIN & MEDAL NEWS. Vol. 19, No. 1 (Dec. 1981)-. 0261-7072. Periodical. UK. English. mo. Epic Publishing Ltd, PO Box 3DE, London W1A 3DE England. LC CJ1. DD 737.05. *Coins and Medals (1974).*

COIN HOARDS. Main/Corp Royal Numismatic Society, London. V.1-. UK. English. ir. Department of Coins & Medals, British Museum, London WC1 England. Tel 01-636-1555. Ed M J Price. LC CJ153.A2. DD 737.4. Circ 1,200. (ctrl).

COIN PRICES. 0010-0412. Periodical. US. English. bm. $25.50. Krause Publications Inc, 700 East State Street, Iola WI 54945. Tel (715)445-2214.

COIN WORLD. 1960. 0010-0447. Periodical. US. English. wk. $23.95. Amos Press Inc, PO Box 482, Sidney OH 45367. Tel (513)498-0800. Ed Beth Deisher. bk rev. adv acc. Circ 75,000. The leading weekly publication for coin collectors, investors and hobbyists. The most comprehensive news coverage and price trends available hobbywide.

COIN WORLD ALMANAC. See Yearbooks, Almanacs, Directories.

COIN YEAR BOOK. See Yearbooks, Almanacs, Directories.

COINAGE. V. 1- Winter 1964-. 0010-0455. Periodical. US. English. mo. Miller Magazines Inc, 2660 East Main Street, Ventura CA 93003. Tel (805)643-3664. LC CJ1. DD 737.405.

COINAGE MAGAZINE'S GOLD & SILVER. VFOAT Gold & Silver. VAT Coinage Magazine's Gold and Silver. 0270-4625. Periodical. US. English. Behn-Miller Publishers Inc, 17337 Ventura Boulevard, Encino CA 91316. LC CJ113. DD 737.4.

COINS. 0010-0471. Periodical. US. English. mo. $43.00. Krause Publications, 700 East State Street, Iola WI 54990. Tel (715)445-2214. Ed Arlyn G Sieber. adv acc. Circ 70,000. (ctrl). Basic information and news on all aspects of US and world coin collecting.

COINS (IOLA, WIS.). (COINS). Began with V. 9 in 1962. 0010-0471. Periodical. US. English. mo. Coins Magazine, Iola WI 54990. Tel (715)445-2214. bk rev. adv acc. Circ 80,000. Also available in microfilm from University Microfilms. All about coin and paper money collecting for someone in the hobby. *Coin Press Magazine.*

COINS MARKET VALUES. UK. English. an. Link House Magazines Ltd, Link House, Dingwall Avenue, Croydon CR9 2TA England. LC CJ2476. DD 737.4941.

COLLECTORS' JOURNAL OF ANCIENT ART. See The Arts (General) - Art.

THE COLONIAL NEWSLETTER. V. 1- Oct. 1960-. 0010-1443. Periodical. US. English. qt. (cum index).

THE COPPERHEAD COURIER. V. 11, No. 3- Fall 1977-. Periodical. US. English. qt $5.00. Grellman, 6733 Post Oak Lane, Montgomery AL 36117-2423. Tel (205)277-1529. Ed Will Mumford. bk rev. adv acc. Circ 850. (ctrl). Published to promote the study of Civil War tokens along with historic, educational, and scientific lines. *Journal.*

CORNUCOPIAE. VFOAT Ancient Coin Society Cornucopiae. Aug. 1972-. 0319-1184. Periodical. CN. English. an. $10. Secretary of the Ancient Coin Society of Canada, PO Box 794 Station F, Toronto Ontario M4Y 2N7 Canada. DD 737.40901.

CTD POCKET GUIDE. (THE CTD POCKET GUIDE). VAT Canadian Trade Dollars Pocket Guide. 1st Ed. (1981 I.E. 1981)-. 0713-813X. CN. English. an. $2.50 Per Volume. J G Cote, 12 Lyon Heights Road, Scharborough Ontario M1P 3V7 Canada. DD 737.4971.

CURRENT COINS OF THE WORLD. 1st- ed. 0070-1882. US. English. Western Publ Co, PO Box 700, Racine WI 53401. Tel (201)471-1441. Ed A Friedberg and I Friedberg. LC CJ1755. DD 737.4. adv acc. Comprehensive listing with photos and prices of all coins made in the world as of 1955 to date.

DEUTSCHES MUNZPREIS-JAHRBUCH. German. ir. 90.00. Battenberg, Ernst Battenberg Verlag, Munchen West Germany. LC CJ2706. DD 737.4943.

EDMUND'S UNITED STATES COIN PRICES. Main/Corp Edmund Publications Corporation (West Hempstead, N.Y.). VFOAT United States Coin Prices. V. 1- Oct. 1980-. 0270-8949. US. English. qt. $12.00. Edmunds Publications Corp, 515 Hempstead Turnpike, West Hempstead NY 11552. Tel (516)292-0044. LC CJ1826. DD 737.4973.

FELL'S INTERNATIONAL COIN BOOK. 1st-. 0430-2958. US. English. $12.95. Frederick Fell Publishers, 386 Park Avenue South, New York NY 10016. Ed Charles J Andrews. LC CJ1. DD 737.4.

GARY NORTH'S INVESTMENT COIN REVIEW. VFOAT Investment Coin Review. Vol. 1, No. 1 (Aug. 10, 1984)-. 8750-4502. Periodical. US. English. mo. $67.00. PO Box 8204, Fort Worth TX 76124. Tel (817)595-2691. Ed Gary North. DD 332. adv acc. Circ 6,000. Introduces the hard money investor to the profitable rare coin markets. The ICR sells information not coins.

GUIDE NUMISMATIQUE CHARLTON. 18th- Ed. 0706-0467. CN. French. an. Charlton International Publishers, 15 Birch Avenue, Toronto Ontario M4V 1E1 Canada. DD 737.4971. *Guide Numismatique Avec Liste des Primes pour les Pieces de Monnaies et Billets de Banque Canadiens et Americains Ainst que les Pieces de Monnaie de Grande-Bretagne, 0319-3764.*

GUIDEBOOK OF FRANKLIN MINT ISSUES. VFOAT Franklin Mint Issues. 1974-. 0163-7231. US. English. an. $8.50. Ed V Culver and C L Krause. LC CJ1826. DD 737.0973.

HAMILTON'S COIN AND MEDAL DESPATCH. VFOAT Coin and Medal Despatch. V. 1-. UK. English. ir. 4.00 UK and Europe. A D Hamilton & Co Ltd, 7 St Vincent Place, Glasgow GL 2DW Scotland. LC CJ1. DD 737.05.

HANDBOOK OF UNITED STATES COINS, WITH PREMIUM LIST. 1st- Ed. 0072-9949. US. English. Ed R S Yeoman, L F Hewitt, and C E Green. LC CJ1826.

HANGUK HWAPYE KAGYOK TOROK. KO. Korean. an. 3,500. Kumhwa Chulpansa, 18 Kwanhundong Chongno-Ku, Seoul Korea. LC CJ3730.

Numismatics

HAY DRAMAGITAKAN HANDES. VFOAT Armenian Numismatic Journal. Vol. 1, No. 1 (Mar. 1975)-. Periodical. US. Armenian (English). qt. $6.00. 8511 Beverly Park Place, Pico Rivera CA 90660. **Tel** (213)695-0380. **Ed** Y T Nercessian. bk rev. **Circ** 150. (ctrl). Covers unpublished Armenian coins, banknotes, and medals. The latest Armenian numismatic literature is abstracted (in English) in every issue.

INDEX OF SCULPTORS. See Indexes/Abstracts.

INSTANT (TORONTO). (THE INSTANT). **Main/Corp** Israel Numismatic Society of Toronto. VFOAT Instant. V. 1- Jan. 1973-. 0316-9138. Periodical. CN. English. Israel Numismatic Society of Toronto, PO Box 395, Willowdale Ontario M2N 5T1 Canada. **DD** 737.095694.

INTERNATIONAL NUMISMATIC DIRECTORY. See Yearbooks, Almanacs, Directories.

ISRAEL NUMISMATIC JOURNAL. Began with V. 1 in 1963. 0021-2288. Periodical. IS. English. ir. $17.60. Shraga Qedar, PO Box 520, 91004 Jerusalem. **Tel** 02-630302. **Ed** Dan Barag. **Ind/Abst** New Testam. Abstr. bk rev. adv acc. **Circ** 400. (ctrl). The sole periodical of the Israel Numismatic Society, publishing research about the coins of the Eastern Mediterranean.

THE JOURNAL OF THE NUMISMATIC SOCIETY OF INDIA. **Main/Corp** Numismatic Society of India. V. 1- 1939-. 0029-6066. Periodical. II. English. sa. Numismatic Society of India, PO Hindu University, Varanasi 5 India. **LC** CJ3530. **DD** 737.06254. (cum index).

MEDAL (LONDON, ENGLAND). (THE MEDAL). 0263-7707. Periodical. UK. English. **LC** CJ5501. **DD** 737.2205.

MEDALS YEARBOOK. See Yearbooks, Almanacs, Directories.

MILITARIA AUCTION - TOREX. (MILITARIA AUCTION). **Main/Corp** Torex. 0822-4943. Periodical. CN. English. ir. $2.50 Each Number. Charlton Auctions, 299 Queen Street West, Toronto Onatrio M5V 1Z9 Canada. **DD** 737.2230294713541.

MINKUS STAMP & COIN JOURNAL. See Philately.

MODERN GOLD COINAGE. 1976-. 0149-4279. US. English. an. $10.00. Gold Institute, 1001 Connecticut Avenue, Washington DC 20036. **LC** CJ113. **DD** 737.405.

MODERN SILVER COINAGE. Began with vol. for 1969/72. 0149-7707. US. English. an. $5.00. Silver Institute, 1001 Connecticut Avenue, Washington DC 20036. **LC** CJ1546. **DD** 737.4.

MONEDAS. Began with Jan. 1959 issue. Periodical. MX. Spanish. ir. Apartado Sociedad Numismatica de Puebla, Postal 329, Puebla Pue Mexico. **LC** CJ9.

MUNZEN REVUE. Periodical. German. mo. 54.00. Verlag Munzen Revue AG, Birmanngasse 39/Postfact 405, CH-4009 Base West Germany. **LC** CJ3240. **DD** 737.4943.

DER MUNZENSAMMLER MIT DEM MUNZENMARKT. Began with issue for Dec. 1973. Periodical. German. ir. 48.00. DMV Verlag fur Munzliteratur GMBH, Eimermacherweg 30, D-4400 Munster West Germany. **LC** CJ5. **DD** 737.075.

MUSEUM NOTES. Vol. 1-. 0145-1413. US. English. an. $30.00. American Numismatic Society, Broadway at 155th Street, New York NY 10032. **Tel** (212)234-3130. **Ed** Leslie A Elam. **LC** CJ1. **DD** 737.06273. **Circ** 2,400. Scholarly journal covering all fields with emphasis on ancient Greek, Roman, and Islamic medieval.

NEWS SUPPLEMENT - ANCIENT COIN SOCIETY OF CANADA. (NEWS SUPPLEMENT). 0229-4125. Periodical. CN. English. qt. Free to Members. News Supplement, Ancient Coin Society of Canada, PO Box 794 Station F, Toronto Ontario M4Y 2N7 Canada. **DD** 737.40901. Supplement (Ancient Coin Society of Canada : 1972), 0229-4117.

NOMISMATIKA CHRONIKA. No. 1-. Greek, Modern (summaries in English). ir. $3.00. Tes Hellenikes Nomismatikes Hetaereias, Megaron Palaias Voules Hodos Stadiou T T 124, Athens Greece. **LC** CJ9.

NORDISK NUMISMATISK ARSSKRIFT ARSSKRIFT. SCANDINAVIAN NUMISMATIC JOURNAL. 0078-107X. Periodical. No. Multilingual. an. Universitetsforlaget, PO Box 2959-Toyen, Oslo 6 Norway.

NUMISMATE. (LE NUMISMATE). First issue in 1977?. 0704-7010. Periodical. CN. French. mo. Free to Members. Association Numismatique de Quebec, R Boily, 71 rue Saint-Pierre CP 397, Quebec Quebec G1R 4R2 Canada. **DD** 737.0971.

NUMISMATIC AUCTION - CHARLTON AUCTIONS. (NUMISMATIC AUCTION). **Main/Corp** Charlton Auctions. 0822-4900. Periodical. CN. English. ir. $2.50 Per No. Charlton Auctions, 299 Queen Street West, Toronto Ontario M5V 1Z9 Canada. **DD** 737.49710294713541. Unreserved Public Mini Auction, 0822-7713.

NUMISMATIC AUCTION - TOREX. (NUMISMATIC AUCTION). **Main/Corp** Torex. 0822-4951. Periodical. CN. English. ir. $2.50 Per No. Charlton Auctions, 299 Queen Street West, Toronto Ontario M5V 1Z9 Canada. **DD** 737.40294713541.

THE NUMISMATIC CIRCULAR. **Main/Corp** Spink & Son, Ltd., London. V. 1- Dec. 1892-. Periodical. UK. English. ir. $30.65. Spink & Son Ltd, 5-7 King Street, St James London SW1 England.

NUMISMATIC LITERATURE. No. 1- Oct. 1947-. 0029-6031. US. English. sa. $10.00. American Numismatic Society, Broadway at 155th Street, New York NY 10032. **Tel** (212)234-3130. **Ed** Rebecca Akers. **LC** Z6866. **DD** 016.737. **Circ** 2,700.

NUMISMATIC NEWS. US. English. $23.00. Krause Publications, 700 East State Street, Iola WI 54990. **Tel** (715)445-2214. **Ed** Dave Harper. **LC** MICROFILM 05652 CJ, CJ1. bk rev. adv acc. **Circ** 53,000. (ctrl). Newspaper covering all aspects of the numismatic hobby. Numismatic News Weekly.

NUMISMATIC NOTES AND MONOGRAPHS. 0078-2718. Monographic Series. US. English. ir. American Numismatic Society, Broadway and 155th Street, New York NY 10032. **LC** UNC.

NUMISMATIC STUDIES. 0517-404X. Monographic Series. US. English. ir. American Numismatic Society, Broadway at 155th Street, New York NY 10321.

NUMISMATICA GIUSEPPE DE FALCO. **Main/Corp** Giuseppe de Falco (Firm). VFOAT Numismatica. Periodical. IT. Italian. ir. Giuseppe de Falco, 24 Corso Umberto I, 80138 Napoli Italy.

NUMISMATICKY SBORNIK. 1- 1953-. 0546-9414. Czech (summaries in Russian and French). ir. Ceskoslovenske Akademie Ved, PO Box 3713, The Hague Holland. **Ed** Jiri Sejbal. **LC** CJ9. **DD** 737.405. **Circ** 1,000. Contains scientific studies on numismatics and reports on founds of coins in Czechoslovakia.

THE NUMISMATIST. Began publication in 1888. 0029-6090. Periodical. US. English. mo. $28.00. American Numismatic Association, 818 North Cascade Avenue, Colorado Springs CO 80903-3279. **Tel** (303)632-2646. **Ed** N Neil Harris. **LC** CJ1. **DD** 737.05. (cum index). bk rev. adv acc. **Circ** 35,000. (ctrl). For collectors of coins, medals, tokens and paper money. Devoted to the science of numismatics, the journal publishes carefully documented, illustrated articles on US and world numismatics.

NUMIZMATIKA I SFRAGISTIKA. 1- 1963-. 0550-371X. UR. Russian. **LC** CJ23.

NUMIZMATIKAI KOZLONY. Began in 1902. Hungarian (summaries in English or German). ir. Akademiai Road, 1085 Budapest Csepreghy U 4, Budapest Hungary. **LC** CJ2640.

NUMMUS. 2. SERIE. VFOAT Nvmmvs. Vol. I-. Portuguese. ir. Each issue contains an index to its own contents - no vol index - loose. Nummus, 0085-364X.

THE OFFICIAL BLACKBOOK PRICE GUIDE OF UNITED STATES COINS. (OFFICIAL BLACKBOOK PRICE GUIDE OF UNITED STATES COINS). 16th- ed. 0193-9610. US. English. an. $1.95. House of Collectibles, 771 Kirkman Road/Suite 100, Orlando FL 32811. **LC** CJ1830. **DD** 737.4973. Official Black Book of United States Coins.

THE OFFICIAL GUIDE TO COIN COLLECTING. VFOAT Coin Collecting. 0747-5683. US. English. an. House of Collectibles Inc, Orlando Central Park, 1900 Premier Row, Orlando FL 32809. **LC** CJ81. **DD** 737.4973075.

THE OFFICIAL HEWITT-DONLON PRICE GUIDE TO UNITED STATES PAPER MONEY. VFOAT Official Hewitt Donlon Price Guide to United States Paper Money. 8756-1646. US. English. an. $4.95. House of Collectibles Inc, Orlando Park, 1900 Premier Row, Orlando FL 32809. **Ed** M Hudgeons. **LC** HG591. **DD** 769.559730750973.

THE OFFICIAL INVESTORS GUIDE, BUYING, SELLING SILVER COINS. See Business - Investments.

THE OFFICIAL PRICE GUIDE TO MINT ERRORS AND VARIETIES. VFOAT Mint Errors and Varieties. 2nd Ed-. 0748-2108. US. English. House of Collectibles Inc, Orlando Central Park, 1900 Premier Row, Orlando FL 32809. **LC** CJ125. **DD** 737.4973. Official Guide to Mint Errors, 0748-2094.

ONTARIO NUMISMATIST. (THE ONTARIO NUMISMATIST). V. 1- Nov. 1961-. 0048-1815. Periodical. CN. English. mo. Ontario Numismatic Association, PO Box 33, Waterloo Ontario Canada.

PAPER MONEY. V. 1- 1962-. 0031-1162. Periodical. US. English. bm. Society of Paper Money Collectors, PO Box 186, c/o Roger Durand, Rehoboth MA 02769. **LC** HG353.

PROCEEDINGS OF GOLD AND MONEY SESSION AND GOLD TECHNICAL SESSION. **Main/Conf** Pacific Northwest Metals and Minerals Conference. VFOAT Gold and Money Session and Gold Technical Session. 0271-1257. US. English. ir. State Department of Geology and Mineral Industries, 1069 State Office Building, Portland OR 97201. **Tel** (503)229-5580. **Ind/Abst** GeoRef.

RARE COIN REVIEW. 0095-263X. US. English. Bowers and Ruddy Galleries, 6922 Hollywood Boulevard, Los Angeles CA 90028. **LC** CJ1. **DD** 737.405.

RARE COINS & MEDALS. **Main/Corp** Galerie des Monnaies of Geneva, Ltd. VAT Rare Coins and Medals. Vol. 1- Winter/Spring 1978-. Periodical. US. English. Galerie des Monnaies of Geneva Ltd, 970 Madison Avenue, New York NY 10021.

REVUE NUMISMATIQUE. V. 1-20, 1836-1855. 0484-8942. FR. French. ir. $34.59. Societe Edition Belles Lettres, 95 Boulevard Raspail, 75006 75006 Paris France. (cum index).

SAID MALTA COIN, BANKNOTE, AND MEDAL CATALOGUE. VFOAT Malta Coin, Banknote, and Medal Catalogue. 1st Ed. (1982)-. English. ir. Emmanuel Said Publishers, 32 Melita Street, PO Box 345, Valletta Malta. **LC** CJ3199.5. **DD** 737.094585.

SAID S.M.O.M. STAMP AND COIN CATALOGUE. See Philately.

SEABY'S COIN AND MEDAL BULLETIN. No. 1- 19 -. Periodical. UK. English. ir. B A Seaby Ltd, Audley House, 11 Margaret Street, London W1N 8AT England. **Tel** 01 580 3677. **Ed** Peter A Clayton. bk rev. **Circ** 5,000. (ctrl). Articles on numismatics and lists of numismatic materials and antiquities for sale.

SHORE LINE. (THE SHORE LINE). V. 1- Jan. 1976-. 0380-8866. Periodical. CN. English. mo. North Shore Numismatic Society, PO Box 86241, North Vancouver British Columbia V7L 4J8 Canada. **DD** 737.06271133. North Shore Numismatic Society.

STANDARD CATALOGUE OF BRITISH COINS. VFOAT Seaby Standard Catalogue of British Coins. UK. English. an. $15.24. B A Seaby Limited, Audley House, 11 Margaret Street, London W1N 8AT England. **LC** CJ2476. **DD** 737.4941. Seaby's Standard Catalogue of British Coins.

STANDARD CATALOGUE OF MALAYSIA-SINGAPORE-BRUNEI COINS AND PAPER MONEY. 3rd Ed. (1981)-. 0126-9682. English. an. 19.00. International Stamp & Coin Agency, 2.4 & 2.5 Pertama Shopping Complex 2nd Floor Jalan Tuanku Abdul Rahman, Kuala Lumpur Malaysia. **Tel** 03-2926373. **Ed** Steven Tan. **LC** CJ3624. **DD** 737.09595. **Circ** 3,000. (ctrl). Complete listing of Malaysia, Singapore, and Brunei coins and paper money including J I M tokens, etc. Coin & Paper Money Catalogue of Malaysia, Singapore & Brunei.

STANDARD U.S. COIN CATALOGUE. (STANDARD . . . U.S. COIN CATALOGUE). **Main/Corp** Scott Publishing Co. VFOAT Standard . . . US

Nutrition and Dietetics

Coin Catalogue. 0741-9236. US. English. $2.95. Scott Publishing Company, 530 Fifth Avenue, New York NY 10036. LC CJ1826. DD 737.4973.

STUDII SI CERCETARI DE NUMISMATICA. Main/Corp Academia de Stiinte Sociale si Politice a Repbulicii Socialiste Romania. Institutul de Arheologie. V. 5- 1971-. English, French, German, Romanian or Russian. ir. LC CJ3330. *Studii Si Cercetari de Numismatica.*

SYLLOGE NUMMORUM GRAECORUM. (SYLLOGE NUMMORUM GRAECORUM (NEW YORK)). 0271-3993. US. English. ir. American Numismatic Society, Broadway at 155th Street, New York NY 10032.

TAMS JOURNAL. Main/Corp Token and Medal Society. VFOAT Journal. VAT Token and Medal Society Journal. 1- 1961?-. 0039-8233. Periodical. US. English. bm. TAMS Journal, Box One, Tecumseh MI 49286.

TOREX. 0711-2920. CN. English. an. Torex, 299 Queen Street West, Toronto Ontario M5V 1Z9 Canada. DD 737.40294713541.

TRESORS MONETAIRES. 1- 1979-. 0223-4300. FR. French. ir. Bibliotheque National, 58 rue de Richelieu, 75084 Paris Cedex 02 France. LC CJ3. DD 737.4944.

TRIDENT (WASHINGTON, D.C.). See Philately.

UKRAINSKYI FILATELIST (SOIUZ UKRAINSKYKH FILATELISTIV I NUMIZMATYKIV). See Philately.

U.S. COINS, CURRENCY & STAMPS. Series/Titl The Official Collector's Price Report. VFOAT US Coins, Currency & Stamps. VAT United States Coins, Currency & Stamps. 1st Ed.-. 0743-9350. US. English. an. $3.50. The House of Collectibles Inc, Orlando Central Park, 1900 Premier Row, Orlando FL 32809. LC CJ1826. DD 737.4973.

U.S. COINS OF VALUE. VAT United States Coins of Value. 1965-. 0271-3969. US. English. an. $2.25. Dell Publishing Company, 245 East 47th Street, New York NY 10017. LC CJ1826. DD 737.4973.

UNITED STATES MINT COINAGE EXECUTED DURING . . . . Periodical. US. English. mo. Bureau of the Mint, Washington DC 20220. *Domestic Coinage Executed During . . . .*

THE VIRGINIA NUMISMATIST. V. 1- 1959-. Periodical. US. English. bm. $7.00. The Virginia Numismatist, PO Box 353, Hampton VA 23669. Ed Donald Roberts. bk rev. adv acc. Circ 500. (ctrl). Places emphasis on the interests of the numismatic hobbiest.

WORLD COIN NEWS. 0145-9090. Periodical. US. English. wk. $54.00. Krause Publications Inc, 700 East State Street, Iola WI 54990. Tel (715)445-2214. Ed Arlyn Sieber. adv acc. Circ 8,500. (ctrl). Magazine covering all aspects of foreign collecting in numismatics.

WORLD COINS. 0043-8359. Periodical. US. English. mo. $5.00. PO Box 150, Sidney OH 45365. LC CJ1. DD 380.1457374.

NUTRITION AND DIETETICS

ACCESS TO NUTRITIONAL DATA. 0740-4484. Periodical. US. English. mo. $150.00. PO Box 52, Ashby MA 01431.

ACTA VITAMINOLOGICA ET ENZYMOLOGICA. VFOAT Rivista Internazionale di Vitaminologia e di Enzimologia. V. 21- 1967-. 0300-8924. Periodical. IT. Italian (with English summaries and some articles in English, French, or German). qt. $35.00. Cedrim Srl, Via MD Aviano 2/5, 20131 Milano Italy. Ind/Abst Pestdoc, Ringdoc, Vetdoc, Life Sci. Collect., Excerpta Med., Biol. Abstr., Chem. Abstr., Nuci. Sci. Abstr., Index Med., Bibliogr. Agric. LC QP801.V5. DD 741.5973. NLM W1 AC9564. bk rev. Circ 3,200. Vitaminology in the fields of nutrition and therapy. *Acta Vitaminologica.*

ADA REPORT FOR EDUCATORS. See Education (General) - Special Aspects of Education.

ADVANCES IN FOOD RESEARCH. V. 1-. 0065-2628. US. English. ir. Academic Press, 4805 Sand Lake Road, Orlando FL 32887. Tel (305)345-4100. Ed E M Mrak and George F Stenart. Ind/Abst Life Sci. Collect., Energy Inf. Abstr., Environ. Abstr., Index Med., Chem. Abstr., Bibliogr. Agric., Energy Res. Abstr., Biol. Agric. Index. LC TX537. DD 641.1072. NLM W1 AD602. CODEN AFREAW. (cum index).

ADVANCES IN MODERN NUTRITION. V. 1-. 0145-3718. Monographic Series. US. English. ir. Hemisphere Publishing Corp, 1010 Vermont Avenue NW/Suite 612, Washington DC 20005. Tel (212)725-1999. Ed M A Mehlman. Ind/Abst Chem. Abstr. LC UNC. NLM W1 AD682M. CODEN AMNUDA.

ADVANCES IN NUTRITIONAL RESEARCH. V. 1-. 0149-9483. US. English. ir. Plenum Press, Attn H Feldman, 233 Spring Street, New York NY 10013. Tel (212)620-8000. Ind/Abst Index Med., Chem. Abstr. LC QP141.A1. DD 613.205. NLM W1 AD685N. CODEN ANURD9.

AKTUELLE ERNAHRUNGSMEDIZIN. VFOAT Aktuelle Ernahrungsmedizin in Klinik und Praxis. V. 1- Sept./Oct. 1976-. 0341-0501. Periodical. German. bm. $67.00. Thieme-Stratton Inc, 381 Park Avenue, New York NY 10016. Tel (212)683-5088. Ind/Abst Life Sci. Collect., Excerpta Med., Chem. Abstr. NLM W1 AK992B. CODEN AEKPDQ.

ALIMENTA. See Food & Drink.

ALIMENTAZIONE, NUTRIZIONE, METABOLISMO. V. 1- Oct./Dec. 1979-. 0392-7512. Periodical. IT. Italian. bm. Free. Societa Editrice Universo, Via G B Morgagni, Roma 00161 Italy. Tel (06)862835. Ed Michelangelo Cairella. Ind/Abst Biol. Abstr., Chem. Abstr. NLM W1 AL378NB. CODEN ANMTD9. bk rev. adv acc. Circ 3,000. Clinical dietetics in disorders of metabolism. *Alimentazione, Nutrizione, Metabolismo, 0392-8071.*

ALIVE. V. 1- May 1978-. Periodical. UK. English. mo. 25 Per Copy. Parkdale Dunham Road, Altrincham Cheshire WA14 4QG England. LC TX392. DD 613.262. *New Vegetarian.*

ALIVE (VANCOUVER, B.C.). (ALIVE). No. 1 (4-75)-. 0228-586X. Periodical. CN. English. ir. 10.83. Canadian Health Reform Prod Lt, Box 67333, Vancouver BC V5X 3Y3 Canada. Tel (604)438-1919. Ed Rebecca Clarkes. DD 641.1. bk rev. adv acc. Circ 115,000,000. (ctrl). Health related topics, information and product knowledge.

AMERICAN JOURNAL OF CLINICAL NUTRITION. V. 1- Sept./Oct. 1952-. 0002-9165. Periodical. US. English. mo. American Society for Clinical Nutrition, 9650 Rockville Park, Bethesda MD 20014. Tel (301)530-7027. Ind/Abst Biol. Agric. Index, Index Med., Sci. Cit. Index, Abr. Ed., Women Stud. Abstr., Hospit. Lit. Index, Chem. Abstr. LC RC584.

ANNALES DE LA NUTRITION ET DE L'ALIMENTATION CEASED. V. 1-34. 0003-4037. Periodical. French (summaries in English). bm. Ind/Abst Biol. Abstr., Chem. Abstr., Nuci. Sci. Abstr., Index Med., Bibliogr. Agric. CODEN ANAIAF.

ANNALS OF NUTRITION AND METABOLISM. (ANNALS OF NUTRITION & METABOLISM). Vol. 25, No. 1 (Jan/Feb 1981)-. 0250-6807. Periodical. SZ. English (French and German). bm. $124.00. S Karger AG, PO Box, CH-4009 Basel Switzerland. Tel (061)39 08 80. Ed N Zollnor. Ind/Abst Life Sci. Collect., Pestdoc, Ringdoc, Vetdoc, Excerpta Med., Index Med., Biol. Abstr., Chem. Abstr., Bibliogr. Agric., Chem. Abstr. NLM W1 AN616M. CODEN ANUMDS. adv acc. Original findings dealing with: consequences of specific diets and dietary supplements, nutritional factors in the etiology of metabolic and gastrointestinal disorders, and the epidemiological association between dietary habits and disease incidence, etc. *Nutrition and Metabolism, 0029-6678; Annales de la Nutrition et de l'Alimentation, 0003-4037.*

ANNUAL REPORT - CALIFORNIA STATE CHILD NUTRITION ADVISORY COUNCIL. Main/Corp California State Child Nutrition Advisory Council. US. English. an. LC TX361.C5. DD 363.8088054.

ANNUAL REPORT - HUMAN NUTRITION RESEARCH CENTER. Main/Corp Prairie View A & M University. Human Nutrition Research Center. (1974/75-). Periodical. US. English. an.

ANNUAL REPORT - NATIONAL ADVISORY COUNCIL ON CHILD NUTRITION. (ANNUAL REPORT). Main/Corp United States. National Advisory Council on Child Nutrition. 1971-. 0091-598X. US. English. an. Superintendent of Documents, US Government Printing Office, Washington DC 20402. LC TX361.C5. DD 362. NLM W2 A N142A.

ANNUAL REPORT OF THE NATIONAL INSTITUTES OF HEALTH. PROGRAM BEHAVIORAL NUTRITION RESEARCH AND TRAINING. Main/Corp National Institutes of Health (U.S.). Nutrition Coordinating Committee. Series/Titl NIH Publication. Began With: 1977. 0732-7013. US. English. an. N.I.H. Nutrition Coordinating Committee, Building 31 Room 4B59 National Institutes of Health, Bethesda MD 20205. LC QP141.A1. DD 613.2072073. NLM W2 A N203A.

ANNUAL REPORT OF THE NATIONAL INSTITUTES OF HEALTH PROGRAM IN BIOMEDICAL AND BEHAVIORAL NUTRITION RESEARCH AND TRAINING. Main/Corp National Institutes of Health (U.S.). Nutrition Coordination Committee. VFOAT Program in Medical and Behavioral Nutrition Research and Training. US. English. an. Nutrition Coordinating Committee, Building 31/Room 4B59, National Institutes of Health, Bethesda MD 20205. Vols. for 1982- distributed to depository libraries in microfiche.

ANNUAL REPORT ON NUTRITION ACTIVITIES CARRIED OUT IN THE STATES & UNION TERRITORIES. VFOAT Annual Report on Nutrition Activities Carried Out in the States and Union Territories. 1968-. 0253-7680. Periodical. English. an. NLM W1 AN764. *Report on Nutrition Work Done in States.*

ANNUAL REPORT - ZAMBIA. NATIONAL FOOD AND NUTRITION COMMISSION. Main/Corp Zambia. National Food and Nutrition Commission. 1967/68-. English. ir. Public Relations Unit of the National Food and Nutrition Commission, PO Box 2699, Lusaka Zambia. Tel 211724/211515. LC TX341. DD 354.68940077. Circ 800. (ctrl). Materials for nutrition education.

ANNUAL REVIEW OF NUTRITION. Vol. 1 (1981)-. 0199-9885. US. English. an. $31.00 Domestic, $34.00 Foreign. Annual Reviews, 4139 El Camino Way, Palo Alto CA 94306. Tel (415)493-4400. Ed Robert E Olsen. Ind/Abst Life Sci. Collect., Index Med., Biol. Abstr., Chem. Abstr. LC QP141.A1. DD 613.205. NLM W1 AN778D. CODEN ARNTD8. Comprehensive, thorough coverage of latest advances in nutrition, written by acknowledged experts in the field. Extensive literature citations included.

APPETITE. Vol. 1, No. 1 (Mar. 1980)-. 0195-6663. Periodical. UK. English. qt. $117.00. Academic Press, 4805 Sand Lake Road, Orlando FL 32819. Tel (305)345-4100. Ind/Abst Life Sci. Collect., Excerpta Med., Index Med., Chem. Abstr., Psychol. Abstr., Sci. Cit. Index, Abr. Ed. LC QP136. DD 599.013. NLM W1 AP49H. CODEN APPTD4.

ARCHIVOS LATINOAMERICANOS DE NUTRICION. See Genealogy and Heraldry - Archives.

BALTIMORE VEGETARIANS. 0883-1165. Periodical. US. English. mo. $12.00 Members. Baltimore Vegetarians, PO Box 1463, Baltimore MD 21203. Tel (301)753-8348. bk rev. adv acc. Circ 1,000. Vegetarianism and veganism including ecology, animal rights, world hunger, health. Contains essays, recipes, poetry, cartoons, restaurant reviews, food hints, raising vegetarian children, etc.

BARODA JOURNAL OF NUTRITION. (THE BARODA JOURNAL OF NUTRITION). V. 1- Feb. 1974-. 0301-8210. Periodical. II. English. an. $20.00. Baroda University, Biochemistry Department, Baroda India. Ind/Abst Life Sci. Collect., Chem. Abstr. LC QP141.A1. DD 613.205. NLM W1 BA777. CODEN BRJNBD.

BESTWAYS. V. 1- May 1973-. 0362-4250. Periodical. US. English. mo. $12.00. Bestways Magazine, PO Box 2028, Carson City NV 89702. Tel (702)883-7311. Ed Barbara Bassett. LC RA784. DD 613.05. bk rev. adv acc. Circ 300,000. Your health diet and nutrition.

BIBLIOTHECA NUTRITIO ET DIETA. VFOAT Nutritio et Dieta. Supplement. Vol. 1- 1960-. 0067-8198. Periodical. SZ. German (English). ir. S

Nutrition and Dietetics

Karger AG, PO Box 352, White Plains NY 10602. **Tel** 061-39 08 80. Ed J C Somogyi. **Ind/Abst** Life Sci. Collect., Biol. Abstr., Chem. Abstr., Nuci. Sci. Abstr., Bibliogr. Agric., Index Med., Hospit. Lit. Index. **NLM** W1 BI422. **CODEN** BNDSA3. A body of literature reflecting the wide-reaching importance of nutrition in health and society.

BIOLOGY OF CARBOHYDRATES. Vol. 1-. 0730-7918. Periodical. US. English. ir. John Wiley and Sons, 1 Wiley Drive, Somerset NJ 08873. **Tel** (212)850-6000. Ed Victor Ginsburg and Phillips Robbins. **Ind/Abst** Chem. Abstr. **NLM** W1 BI852M. **CODEN** BICADE.

BNF NUTRITION BULLETIN. (NUTRITION BULLETIN). **Main/Corp** British Nutrition Foundation. **VAT** British Nutrition Foundation Bulletin. No. 19- 1977-. 0141-9684. Periodical. UK. English. ty. $13.80. British Nutrition Foundation, 15 Belgrave Square, London SW1X 8PS England. **Tel** 01 235 4904. Ed Mrs Janice Ryley. **Ind/Abst** Excerpta Med., Chem. Abstr. **CODEN** BNUBD6. bk rev. **Circ** 1,500. All aspects of human nutrition. BNF Bulletin, 0307-3548.

BOLETIM DA ASSOCIACAO BRASILEIRA DE NUTRICIONISTAS. **Main/Corp** Associacao Brasileira de Nutricionistas. 0571-4931. Portuguese. ir. **NLM** W1 BO15W.

BOLETIM DA SOCIEDADE BRASILEIRA DE CIENCIA E TECNOLOGIA DE ALIMENTOS. See Food & Drink.

BOLETIN DEL CENTRL NACIONAL DE ALIMENTACION Y NUTRICION. (BOLETIN DEL CENTRO NACIONAL DE ALIMENTACION Y NUTRICION (C.E.N.A.N.)). 0211-1128. Periodical. SP. Spanish. qt. Servicio de Publicaciones de Publicaciones del Ministerio de Sanidad y Seguridad Social, Paseo del Prado 18, Madrid 14 Spain. **Ind/Abst** Chem. Abstr. **CODEN** BCNSDD.

BOX 6190. (BOX 6190 : LIFELINE). **VAT** Box Six Thousand One Hundred and Ninety. 0273-5741. Periodical. US. English. mo. $8.50. Overeaters Anonymous, 2190 190th Street, Torrance CA 90504. Lifeline.

BRITISH JOURNAL OF NUTRITION. (THE BRITISH JOURNAL OF NUTRITION). V. 1- Sept. 1947-. 0007-1145. Periodical. UK. English. bm. $280.00. Cambridge University Press, 510 North Avenue, New Rochelle NY 10801. **Tel** (914)235-0300. Ed R H Smith. **Ind/Abst** Life Sci. Collect., Pestdoc, Ringdoc, Vetdoc, Excerpta Med., Energy Inf. Abstr., Environ. Abstr., Biol. Abstr., Chem. Abstr., Index Med., Bibliogr. Agric., Biol. Agric. Index, Nuci. Sci. Abstr., Sci. Cit. Index, Abr. Ed. **LC** TX501. **DD** 641.06242. **NLM** W1 BR584. **CODEN** BJNUAV. Original work in all branches of nutrition, including clinical and human nutrition, experimental nutrition and the nutrition of farm animals.

BULLETIN - CORPORATION PROFESSIONNELLE DES DIETETISTES DU QUEBEC. **Main/Corp** Corporation Professionnelle des Dietetistes du Quebec. First issued in 1973. 0319-7808. Periodical. CN. French (English). Free to members. Corporation Professionnelle des Dietetistes du Quebec, Bureau 130/934 Est rue Ste-Catherine, Montreal Quebec H2L 2E9 Canada.

CAHIERS DE NUTRITION ET DE DIETETIQUE. V. 1- 1966-. 0007-9960. French. bm. $60.54. SEPAIC, 42 rue du Louvre, 75001 Paris France. **Tel** 233-16-32. **Ind/Abst** Sci. Cit. Index, Abr. Ed., Chem. Abstr.

CAJANUS. No. 1- Feb. 1968-. 0376-7655. Periodical. JM. English. qt. $12.00 Developed Nations, $16.00 Developing Nations, Free to Latin America and Carribbean. Caribean Food & Nutrition Institute, Box 140, Mona Kingston 7 Jamaica. **Tel** (809)78338. Ed B A Okwesa. **Ind/Abst** Bibliogr. Agric. **NLM** W1 CA162M. bk rev. **Circ** 2,500. (ctrl). Highlights food and nutrition concerns in the English speaking Caribbean. Includes reports, research, articles, topics, and comments.

CATALOG. SUPPLEMENT - FOOD AND NUTRITION INFORMATION AND EDUCATIONAL MATERIALS CENTER. See Bibliographies.

CENTER FOR DISEASE CONTROL NUTRITION SURVEILLANCE. (NUTRITION SURVEILLANCE). Began with Sept. 1975. 0193-1377. US. English. ir. Center for Disease Control, Nutrition Division, Atlanta GA 30333. **Ind/Abst** Am. Stat. Index. **LC** TX360.U6. **DD** 362.19639. **NLM** W2 A C15N.

THE CHRONICLE. See Public Health and Safety.

CLINICA DIETOLOGICA. See Medicine - Allergic, Metabolic, Nutritional Diseases.

CLINICAL DISORDERS IN PEDIATRIC NUTRITION. 1-. 0733-933X. Monographic Series. US. English. ir. Marcel Dekker Inc, 270 Madison Avenue, New York NY 10016. **Tel** (212)696-9000. Ed Fima Lifshitz. **Ind/Abst** Chem. Abstr. **LC** UNC. **DD** 618.9239. **NLM** W1 CL694I. **CODEN** CDPNDQ. This is an ongoing series. Each titles has a different subject.

CLINICAL NUTRITION. (CLINICAL NUTRITION : OFFICIAL JOURNAL OF THE EUROPEAN SOCIETY OF PARENTERAL AND ENTERAL NUTRITION). Vol. 1, No. 1 (Mar. 1982)-. 0261-5614. Periodical. UK. English. qt. 56.00 Domestic, 110.00 Foreign. Churchill Livingstone Inc, Longman Group Ltd, Fourth Avenue Harrlow, Edinburgh Essex CM19 5AA England. **Tel** (031)336-6291. Ed H F Woods. **Ind/Abst** Chem. Abstr. **NLM** W1 CL739F. **CODEN** CLNUDP. bk rev. adv acc. Original articles and review papers on all the factors in disease which have metabolic and nutritional significance.

CLINICAL NUTRITION (PLEASANTVILLE, N.J.). (CLINICAL NUTRITION). Vol. 1, No. 1 (Sept./Oct. 1982)-. 0733-2327. Periodical. US. English. bm. $39.00. C V Mosby Company, 11830 Westline Industrial Drive, St Louis MO 63146. **Tel** (314)872-8370. Ed David M Paige. **NLM** W1. **Circ** 3,127. In-depth reviews of important topics in human nutrition prepared by recognized experts in the field. Unique continuing education quiz.

CNI WEEKLY REPORT CEASED. **Main/Corp** Community Nutrition Institute. **VAT** Community Nutrition Institute Weekly Report. 0191-0833. Periodical. US. English. wk. $35.00. Community Nutrition Institute, 1146 19th Street NW, Washington DC 20036. **NLM** W1 C488.

COMMUNIQUE - CDA. (COMMUNIQUE). **VAT** Communique - ACD, Communique - Canadian Dietetic Association, Communique - Association Canadienne des Dietetistes. 0711-8112. Periodical. CN. English. ir. Free. Canadian Dietetic Association, 7 Pleasant Boulevard, Toronto Ontario M4T Canada. **DD** 641.02371. (ctrl).

CONSUMER HEALTH & NUTRITION INDEX. See Indexes/Abstracts.

CONTEMPORARY ISSUES IN CLINICAL NUTRITION. Vol. 1-. 0736-4369. Monographic Series. US. English. ir. Alan R Liss Inc, 41 East 11th Street, New York NY 10003. **Tel** (212)475-7700. Ed Richard S Rivlin. **LC** UNC. **NLM** W1 CO769MQH. Nutrition-clinical.

CORNELL INTERNATIONAL NUTRITION MONOGRAPH SERIES. No. 1-. 0198-9510. Monographic Series. US. English. ir. Cornell University, Division Nutritional Science, Ithaca NY 14853. **LC** UNC. **NLM** W1 CO8596M.

CRC CRITICAL REVIEWS IN FOOD SCIENCE AND NUTRITION CEASED. **Main/Corp** Chemical Rubber Company. **VFOAT** Critical Reviews in Food Science and Nutrition. **VAT** Chemical Rubber Company Critical Reviews in Food Science and Nutrition. V. 6- June 1975-. 0099-0248. US. English. ir. $116.00. Chemical Rubber Company Press Inc, 2000 Corporate Boulevard NW, Boca Raton FL 33431. **Tel** (305)994-0555. **Ind/Abst** Life Sci. Collect., Excerpta Med., Energy Inf. Abstr., Environ. Abstr., Index Med., Biol. Abstr., Chem. Abstr., Bibliogr. Agric., Energy Res. Abstr., Sci. Cit. Index, Abr. Ed. **LC** TP368. **DD** 664.005. **NLM** W1 C555F. **CODEN** CRFND6. Presents critical viewpoints of food technology food science, and nutrition. CRC Critical Reviews in Food Technology, 0007-9006.

CRC HANDBOOK SERIES IN NUTRITION AND FOOD. SECTION G : DIETS, CULTURE MEDIA, FOOD SUPPLEMENTS. **VFOAT** Diets, Culture Media, Food Supplements. V. 1- 1977-. 0191-1368. Periodical. US. English. Ed M Rechcigl Jr. **NLM** W1 C58D.

CURRENT CONCEPTS IN NUTRITION. V. 1-. 0090-0443. Periodical. US. English. ir. John Wiley & Sons Inc, 1 Wiley Drive, Somerset NJ 08873. **Ind/Abst** Index Med., Chem. Abstr., Bibliogr. Agric., Energy Res. Abstr. **NLM** W1 CU788AS. **CODEN** CCNTBP.

CURRENT TOPICS IN NUTRITION AND DISEASE. See Medicine - Allergic, Metabolic, Nutritional Diseases.

CURRENT TOPICS IN NUTRITIONAL SCIENCES. V. 1- 1974-. 0340-1960. Monographic Series. volumes in English or German. ir. Dr Dietrich Steinkopff Verlag, PO Box 1008, Saalbaustrasse 12, 6100 Darmstadt 11 West Germany. **Tel** 06151-26538. Ed K Lang. **NLM** W1 CU82T. A book serial about current topics in nutritional sciences. Beitrage zur Ernahrungswissenschaft, 0067-4982.

CURRENTS. (CURRENTS : THE JOURNAL OF FOOD, NUTRITION & HEALTH). Vol. 1, No. 1 (Winter Quarter, 1985)-. 0882-7915. Periodical. US. English. qt. $17.00. Currents, Institute of Nutrition of the University of North Carolina, 311 Pittsboro Street, 256-H, Chapel Hill NC 27514. **Tel** (919)929-3846. Ed John Timothy Hesla. **DD** 613. adv acc. **Circ** 2,000. This publication provides a forum for a variety of observations on the many and ever-changing issues which affect food, nutrition and health in contemporary society.

DAIRY COUNCIL DIGEST. See Agriculture - Dairy & Related Technologies.

DEVELOPMENTS IN FOOD CARBOHYDRATE. Series/Titl Developments Series. 1-. 0260-4345. UK. English. ir. Elsevier Applied Science Publishing, Crown House Linton Road, Barking Essex IG11 8JU England. **Tel** 01 594 7272. **Ind/Abst** Chem. Abstr. **LC** TX553.C28. **DD** 641.1305. **NLM** W1 DE997VX. **CODEN** DFCADF.

DEVELOPMENTS IN NUTRITION AND METABOLISM. V. 1-. 0167-6504. Monographic Series. English. ir. **Ind/Abst** Chem. Abstr., Bibliogr. Agric. **LC** UNC. **NLM** W1 DE998L. **CODEN** DNMEDV.

DIET & EXERCISE. Series/Titl Better Homes and Gardens Creative Ideas. **VFOAT** Diet and Exercise. 0163-0334. Periodical. US. English. an. $2.25. Special Interest Publications, Publishing Group of Meredith Corp, 1716 Locust Street, Des Moines IA 50336. **LC** RA784. **DD** 613.2505.

DIETARY ASPECTS OF CARCINOGENESIS. **Main/Corp** International Cancer Research Data Bank. Series/Titl ICRDB Cancergram. Periodical. US. English. Department of Health Education and Welfare, Public Health Service, National Institutes of Health, National Cancer Institute, Springfield VA 22161.

DIETETIQUE. V. 1- June 1976-. 0701-1350. Periodical. CN. French. 40.00. Corporation Professionnelle des Dietetistes du Quebec, 934 East rue Sainte-Catherine Bureau 130, Montreal Quebec H2L 2E9 Canada. **Tel** (514)842-7923. Ed Gisele Fournier. **DD** 613.2062714. bk rev. adv acc. **Circ** 1,700. Professional information - news of the health and food industries - information on the corporation's activities - and so on.

DIRECTORY OF DIETETIC PROGRAMS : ACCREDITED AND APPROVED. See Yearbooks, Almanacs, Directories.

ECOLOGY OF FOOD AND NUTRITION. V. 1-. 0367-0244. Periodical. US. English. qt. $322.00. Gordon & Breach, PO Box 197, London WC2E 9PX England. **Tel** (01)836-5125. Ed J R K Robson. **Ind/Abst** Life Sci. Collect., Energy Inf. Abstr., Environ. Abstr., Biol. Abstr., Chem. Abstr., Bibliogr. Agric., Sci. Cit. Index, Abr. Ed. **LC** TX341. **DD** 641.105. **NLM** W1 EC917. **CODEN** ECFNBN. bk rev. adv acc.

EDRO RESEARCH REPORTS. **Main/Corp** United States. Food and Drug Administration. Executive Director of Regional Operations. **VFOAT** EDRO Research Progress Report. **VAT** Executive Director of Regional Operations Research Progress Report. Periodical. US. English. sa. Food and Drug Administration, Field Research and Technical Support Branch, Division of Field Science and Technology, Executive Director of Regional Operations, 5600 Fishers Lane, Rockville MD 20857. **LC** TX341. **DD** 664.07.

EIYO TO SHOKURYO CEASED. **VFOAT** Journal of Japanese Society of Food and Nutrition. Ceased in 1982. 0021-5376. Periodical. Japanese. ir. **Ind/Abst** Chem. Abstr. **NLM** W1 EI675. **CODEN** EISOAU. Eiyo Shokuryo Gakkaishi, 0367-0554.

Nutrition and Dietetics

EN-TROPHY INSTITUTE REVIEW. VAT En-Trophy Review. V. 2, No. 1-. 0707-2406. Periodical. CN. English. bm. $19.50. En-Trophy Institute, 20 Hilton Street, Hamilton Ontario L8P 3K2 Canada. DD 641.1'05. *En-Trophy Institute for Advanced Study, 0707-2716.*

ENVIRONMENTAL NUTRITION NEWSLETTER. VFOAT Environmental Nutrition. 1977. 0195-4024. Periodical. US. English. mo. $75.00. Environmental Nutrition, 52 Riverside Drive/Suite 15-A, New York NY 10024. Tel (212)362-0424. Ed Susan Male Smith. bk rev. Circ 4,500. Written for the health professional, researched articles on nutrition and its relationship to health. Topics include caffeine, sodium, exercise, cancer, additives. Independent. Fully referenced.

ERNAHRUNGSBERICHT. Main/Corp Deutsche Gesellschaft fur Ernahrung. German. ni. Deutsche Gesellschaft fur Ernahrung, 6000 Frankfurt A M, Feldbergstrasse 28, Frankfurt West Germany. LC TX341. DD 613.205.

ERNAHRUNGSFORSCHUNG. Vol. 19- 1974-. 0071-1179. Periodical. German. ir. $34.43. Kunst & Wissen Erich Bieber, Dufourstrasse 51, CH-8008 Zurich Switzerland. Tel 011-41-1-69 44 20. Ind/Abst Life Sci. Collect., Chem. Abstr., Bibliogr. Agric., Excerpta Med. NLM W1 ER6922. CODEN ERNFA7. *Ernahrungsforschung. Berichte und Mitteilungen.*

ETUDE FAO : ALIMENTATION ET NUTRITION. Monographic Series. French. ir.

FAO NUTRITION MEETINGS REPORT SERIES. Main/Corp Food and Agriculture Organization of the United Nations. VAT Food and Agriculture Organization Nutrition Meetings Report Series. No. 1- 1948-. 0071-707X. Monographic Series. some No. are in French. ir. FAO, Via Delle Terme di Caracalla, 00100 Rome Italy. Ind/Abst Chem. Abstr. LC S401. DD 612, 613. NLM W1 F197. CODEN FAONAU.

FETT IN DER PARENTERALEN ERNAHRUNG. Main/Conf Symposium in Rottach-Egern. 1 (March 10, 1979)-. 0720-8731. Periodical. German. ir. Ed J Eckart and G Wolfram. NLM W3 SY34F.

FNP NEWSLETTER. FOOD, NUTRITION AND HEALTH. (FNP NEWSLETTER : FOOD, NUTRITION AND HEALTH). VFOAT Food, Nutrition and Health. VAT Food and Nutrition Press Newsletter. Food, Nutrition and Health. V.1- Apr. 1977-. 0160-8053. Periodical. US. English. mo. $55.00. Food & Nutrition Press Inc, 155 Post Road East, PO Box 71, Westport CT 06881. Ed Paul A Lachance and Michele C Fisher. Ind/Abst Bibliogr. Agric. NLM W1 F384. bk rev. Doctors Lachance and Fisher draw on their unique backgrounds in nutrition-food science to make clear distinctions between food, nutrition and health research, education and policy issues.

FNS NOTICE. Main/Corp United States. Food and Nutrition Service. Periodical. US. English.

FOOD AND NUTRITION. V. 1- 1975-. 0304-8942. Periodical. US. English. sa. $7.00. UNIPUB, PO Box 1222, Ann Arbor MI 48106. Tel (800)521-8110. Ind/Abst Index Med., Bibliogr. Agric., Mag. Index, Hospit. Lit. Index, Index U.S. Gov. Period. LC TX341. DD 641.105. NLM W1 FO428C. Review of world development in nutrition. *Nutrition Newsletter, 0428-9447.*

FOOD AND NUTRITION BOARD. Main/Corp National Research Council. Food and Nutrition Board. 1973-. 0197-0925. US. English. an. NLM QU 22 AA1 N2D. *Directory - Food and Nutrition Board, 0470-245X.*

FOOD AND NUTRITION BULLETIN. Vol. 1, No. 1 (Oct. 1978)- Oct. 1978. 0379-5721. Periodical. JA. English. qt. U N University, 29th floor, Toho Seimei Building, 15-1 Shibuya 2-Chome, Shibuya-Ku Tokyo 150 Japan. Tel (03)499-2811. Ed Nevin S Scrimshaw. Ind/Abst Bibliogr. Agric. LC TX341. DD 641.305. NLM W1 FO428M. bk rev. Circ 6,000. Food and nutrition problems of developing countries. Food and nutrition policy, nutrition education and training, food science and technology for developing countries, and and applied nutrition. *PAG Bulletin, 0377-760X.*

FOOD AND NUTRITION IN AFRICA. See Food & Drink.

FOOD AND NUTRITION NOTES AND REVIEWS. See Food & Drink.

FOOD FOR THOUGHT. 1978. 0198-0246. Periodical. US. English. bm. $5.00. Medical College of Georgia, Georgia Institute for Human Nutrition, Augusta GA 30912. Tel (404)828-4861. Ed Diana K Smith. Circ 1,500. (ctrl). Summary of ongoing nutritional events and review of contemporary nutritional information.

FOOD SCIENCE AND TECHNOLOGY ABSTRACTS. See Indexes/Abstracts.

FOOD VALUES OF PORTIONS COMMONLY USED. VFOAT Bowes' and Church's Food Values of Portions Commonly Used. 2nd Ed.-. US. English. ir. Lippincott/Harper, 2350 Virginia Avenue, Hagerstown MD 21740. Ed C F Church and H N Church. *Food Values of Portions Commonly Served.*

GOOD HEALTH (AGINCOURT, ONT.). See Consumer Interests.

THE HEALTH FOODS COMMUNICATOR. See Food & Drink.

HEALTH FOODS RETAILING. 0017-8977. Periodical. US. English. $28.00. Communication Channels Inc, 390 Fifth Avenue, New York NY 10018. Tel (212)613-9700. Ed D J Caulfield. LC HD9321.1. DD 641.3020688. bk rev. adv acc. Circ 11,000. (ctrl). The leading business publication serving the health and natural food, fitness and nutrition market.

HEALTH NEWS (UNIVERSITY OF TORONTO. FACULTY OF MEDICINE). See Medicine.

HEALTH SCIENCE (TAMPA, FLA. : 1985). (HEALTH SCIENCE). Vol. 8, No. 3 (May/June 1985)-. 0883-8216. Periodical. US. English. bm. $20.00 Membership. American Natural Hygiene Society, 12816 Race Track Road, Tampa FL 33625. DD 613. *Vegetarian Health Science, 8750-1643.*

HEALTHY HORIZONS. See Food & Drink.

HEARTLINE. Script No. 1- Jan. 7, 1974-. 0381-3886. Periodical. CN. English. wk. Alberta Agriculture, Nutrition and Food Marketing Section 208 Chinook Centre 6455 MacLeod Trail Southwest, Calgary Alberta T2H 0K8 Canada. DD 616.120654.

HOCHSCHULSAMMLUNG MEDIZIN. ERNAHRUNGSWISSENSCHAFT. VFOAT Ernhrungswissenschaft. V. 1-. 0720-5619. Monographic Series. German. ir. NLM W1 HO459B.

HUMAN NUTRITION. (HUMAN NUTRITION : A COMPREHENSIVE TREATISE). V. 1- 1979-. Monographic Series. US. English. Ed Rosyln B Alfin, Slater and David Kritchev. Ind/Abst Bibliogr. Agric. NLM QU 145 H9183.

HUMAN NUTRITION. APPLIED NUTRITION. VFOAT Applied Nutrition. Vol. 36A, No. 1 (Feb. 1982)-. 0263-8495. Periodical. UK. English. bm. $2.00 Per Issue. John Libbey & Company Ltd, 80-84 Bondway, London SW8 1SF England. Ind/Abst Excerpta Med., Index Med., Chem. Abstr. LC QP141.A1. DD 613.205. NLM W1 HU448V. CODEN HNAND8. *Journal of Human Nutrition, 0308-4329.*

HUMAN NUTRITION. CLINICAL NUTRITION. VFOAT Clinical Nutrition. Vol. 36C, No. 1-. 0263-8290. Periodical. UK. English. bm. $86.00. John Libbey & Company Ltd, 80-84 Bondway, London SW8 1SF England. Ind/Abst Excerpta Med., Index Med., Chem. Abstr. LC QP141. DD 613.205. NLM W1 HU448VC. CODEN HNCNDI. *Journal of Human Nutrition, 0308-4329.*

ICRDB CANCERGRAM. DIETARY ASPECTS OF CARCINOGENESIS. See Medicine - Neoplasma, Neoplastic.

IFMA SCIENTIFIC SYMPOSIA. 0378-3324. Monographic Series. English. ir. NLM W3 I328.

INDIAN JOURNAL OF NUTRITION AND DIETETICS. (THE INDIAN JOURNAL OF NUTRITION AND DIETETICS). V. 7- Jan. 1970-. 0022-3174. Periodical. II. English. mo. $30.00. SRI Avinashilingam Home Science, College for Women, Coimbatore 11 India. Tel 33211. Ed Rajammal P Devadas, M Swaminathan and Usha Chandrasekhar. Ind/Abst Life Sci. Collect., Int. Aerosp. Abstr., Biol. Abstr., Chem. Abstr., Nuci. Sci. Abstr., Bibliogr. Agric. LC TX341. DD 641.105. NLM W1 IN221K. CODEN IJNDAN. bk rev. adv acc. Circ 700. Original and review papers, book reviews, news, views, announcements, and current literature supplement. *Journal of Nutrition and Dietetics.*

INSIDE NUTRITION. Issue 1 (Jan. 9, 1984)-. 0742-3799. Periodical. US. English. bw. Clayman Enterprises Inc, 5560 Woodbridge Drive, Columbus OH 43212. LC TX341. DD 613.205.

INTERNATIONAL CLINICAL NUTRITION REVIEW. Began with: Vol. 3, No. 1 (Jan. 1983). 0725-7090. Periodical. English. qt. NLM W1. *Orthomolecular Review.*

THE INTERNATIONAL JOURNAL FOR BIOSOCIAL RESEARCH. VFOAT International Journal of Biosocial Research. Vol. 3, No. 2-. 0731-9169. Periodical. US. English. sa. $22.00. Biosocial Publishing, PO Box 1174, Tacoma WA 98401. Tel (206)272-0530. Ed Alexander G Schauss. Ind/Abst Life Sci. Collect., Sociol. Abstr., Psychol. Abstr. LC BF1. DD 301.05. NLM W1. bk rev. Circ 800. Current research on nutrition and behavior toxic substances and behavior, color/light research and behavior, biomedical research. Human behavior. *Journal of Behavioral Ecology, Biosocial, 0275-8989.*

INTERNATIONAL JOURNAL FOR VITAMIN AND NUTRITION RESEARCH. (BEIHEFT ZUR INTERNATIONALE ZEITSCHRIFT FUR VITAMIN- UND ERNAHRUNGSFORSCHUNG). No. 12 -. 0300-9831. Periodical. SZ. English (text in German or French). qt. $75.70. Verlag Hans Huber AG, Laenggassstrasse 76 POB, CH-3000 Bern 9 Switzerland. Tel 031 24 25 33. Ed G Ritzer. Ind/Abst Index Med., Chem. Abstr. NLM W1 IN7652R. bk rev. Circ 1,000. (ctrl). Vitamin and nutrition research. *Internationale Zeitschrift fur Vitaminforschung. Beiheft.*

INTERNATIONAL NUTRITION POLICY SERIES. 2-. 0190-8480. Monographic Series. US. English. MIT Press, 29 Carleton Street, Cambridge MA 02142. LC UNC. NLM W1 IN827B. *Cornell/MIT International Nutrition Policy Series.*

JEWISH VEGETARIANS OF NORTH AMERICA. (JEWISH VEGETARIANS OF NORTH AMERICA : NEWSLETTER). VFOAT Jewish Vegetarians. Began with issue for Fall 1984. 0883-1904. Periodical. US. English. qt. $12.00. J V N A, PO Box 1463, Baltimore MD 21203. Tel (301)752-8348. Ed Debra Wasserman and Charles Stahler. DD 296. bk rev. adv acc. Circ 500. Relationship between Judaism and vegetarianism including kindness to animals, world hunger, ecology, ethics, recipes, health, issues, animal rights, restaurants, and local Jewish vegetarian contacts. *Jewish Vegetarians.*

JOURNAL DU RESO COOPERATIF D'ALIMENTATION SAINE DU KEBEC. See Economics - Cooperatives.

JOURNAL-NEW ZEALAND DIETETIC ASSOCIATION. Main/Corp New Zealand Dietetic Association. Periodical. English. ir. Ind/Abst Bibliogr. Agric.

JOURNAL OF APPLIED NUTRITION. (THE JOURNAL OF APPLIED NUTRITION). V. 6- 1953-. 0021-8960. Periodical. US. English. sa. $16.00. International College of Applied Nutrition, Box 386, La Habra CA 90631. Tel (213)697-4576. Ed M Taher Fouad. Ind/Abst Excerpta Med., Chem. Abstr., Biol. Abstr., Bibliogr. Agric., Biol. Agric. Index. NLM W1 JO541R. CODEN JNAPAX. (cum index). bk rev. Circ 1,500. Information which stresses the practical application of nutritional knowledge. *Journal of the American Academy of Applied Nutrition, 0095-9839.*

JOURNAL OF FOOD & NUTRITION. VFOAT Journal of Food and Nutrition. Vol. 38, No. 1 (1981)-. 0728-4713. Periodical. AT. English. ir. Australian Government Publishing Service, PO Box 84, Canberra Australian Capital Territory 2600 Australia. Tel (062) 95 4411. Ind/Abst Electron. Commun. Abstr. J., ISMEC Bull., Pollut. Abstr. Indexes, Saf. Sci. Abstr. J., Life Sci. Collect., Bibliogr. Agric. LC TX341. DD 612.305. NLM W1 JO65PM. *Food and Nutrition Notes and Reviews, 0015-6329.*

JOURNAL OF FOOD BIOCHEMISTRY. VFOAT FNP Journal of Food Biochemistry. VAT Food and Nutrition Press Journal of Food Biochemistry. V. 1- Jan. 1977-. 0145-8884. Periodical. US. English. qt. $80.00. Food & Nutrition Press Inc, 155 Post Road East/PO Box 71, Westport CT 06881. Tel (203)227-6596. Ed Herb Hultin, N F Hoard and J R Whitaker. Ind/Abst Life Sci. Collect., Ref. Source, Chem. Abstr., Bibliogr. Agric., Sci. Cit. Index, Abr. Ed. LC TX545. DD 664.001574192. NLM W1 JO65Q. CODEN JFBIDW. bk rev. adv acc. Now established as the leading journal for all disciplines that bear on the problems of food biochemistry.

Nutrition and Dietetics

JOURNAL OF FOOD SCIENCE AND TECHNOLOGY. V. 1- Apr. 1964-. 0022-1155. Periodical. II. English. bm. $40.00. Association of Food Technologists, CFTRI Campus, Mysore 13 India. Ind/Abst Life Sci. Collect., Excerpta Med., Int. Packag. Abstr., Biol. Abstr., Chem. Abstr., Nucl. Sci. Abstr., Bibliogr. Agric. LC TX341. NLM W1 JO651S. CODEN JFSTAB. bk rev. adv acc. Food science and technology.

JOURNAL OF HUMAN NUTRITION CEASED. V. 30-35. 0308-4329. Periodical. UK. English. bm. Newman Publishing Ltd, 48 Portland Street, London W1V 4PP England. Ind/Abst Excerpta Med., Ref. Source, Chem. Abstr., Bibliogr. Agric. LC QP141.A1. DD 613.2.05. NLM W1 JO673VS. CODEN JHNUD6. *Nutrition.*

JOURNAL OF MICRONUTRIENT ANALYSIS. 0266-349X. UK. English. qt. Covers all methods for the detection and determination of micronutrients and their metabolites at all stages within the food chain.

JOURNAL OF NUTRITION EDUCATION. V. 1- Summer 1969-. 0022-3182. Periodical. US. English. bm. $30.00. George F Stickley Company, 210 West Washington Square, Philadelphia PA 19106. Tel (215)922-7126. Ed Barbara Shannon. Ind/Abst Life Sci. Collect., Educ. Index, Bibliogr. Agric., Curr. Index J. Educ., Gen. Sci. Index. LC QP141.A1. DD 613.205. NLM W1 JO798G. bk rev. adv acc. Circ 8,000. Designed to stimulate interest and research in applied nutritional sciences, with reports, articles, letters, and book reviews.

JOURNAL OF NUTRITION FOR THE ELDERLY. V. 1- Spring 1980-. 0163-9366. Periodical. US. English. qt. Haworth Press, 28 East 22nd Street, New York NY 10010. Tel (212)228-2800. Ed Annette B Natow, and Jo-Ann Heslin. Ind/Abst Excerpta Med., Nutr. Abstr. Rev., Ser. A, Hum. Exp. LC TX361.A3. DD 613.2. NLM W1 JO798H. CODEN JNELDA. bk rev. adv acc. Circ 1,778. Covers all essential aspects of nutrition and publishes research papers from a variety of fields in the biological and social sciences.

JOURNAL OF OBESITY AND WEIGHT REGULATION. VFOAT Obesity and Weight Regulation. Vol. 2, No. 1 & 2 (Spring/Summer 1982/1983)-. 0731-4361. Periodical. US. English. qt. $66.00. Human Sciences Press, 72 Fifth Avenue, New York NY 11102. Ind/Abst Excerpta Med., Psychol. Abstr. LC RC628. DD 616.398005. NLM W1. *Obesity and Metabolism, 0190-2318.*

JOURNAL OF PEDIATRIC GASTROENTEROLOGY AND NUTRITION. See Medicine - Pediatrics.

JOURNAL OF PLANT FOODS. V. 3-. 0142-968X. Periodical. UK. English. ir. $90.00. John Libbey & Company Ltd, 80/84 Bondway Vauxhall, London SW8 1SF England. Tel 01 582 5266. Ed J W T Dickerson and A R Leeds. Ind/Abst Excerpta Med., Chem. Abstr. NLM W1 JO837B. CODEN JPFOD4. bk rev. adv acc. Concerned with the physiological effects of plant foods and with the production, preservation and presentation of potential foods from plants. *Plant Foods for Man, 0306-2686.*

JOURNAL OF THE AMERICAN COLLEGE OF NUTRITION. Vol. 1, No. 1-. 0731-5724. Periodical. US. English. bm. Alan R Liss, 41 East 11th Street, New York NY 10003. Tel (212)741-2515. Ind/Abst Life Sci. Collect., Excerpta Med., Index Med., Chem. Abstr. LC RC620.A1. DD 613.205. NLM W1 JO908TR. CODEN JONUDL.

JOURNAL OF THE AMERICAN DIETETIC ASSOCIATION. Main/Corp American Dietetic Association. V. 1- June 1925-. 0002-8223. Periodical. US. English. mo. $50.00. American Dietetic Association, PO Box 10959, Chicago IL 60611. Tel (312)280-5000. Ed Elaine R Monsen. Ind/Abst Biol. Abstr., Chem. Abstr., Nucl. Sci. Abstr., Index Med., Bibliogr. Agric., Gen. Sci. Index, Biol. Agric. Index. bk rev. adv acc. Circ 55,000. The journal publishes reports of original research and other papers covering all aspects of dietetics including nutrition and diet therapy, community nutrition, education and administration. *Bulletin of the American Dietetic Association.*

JOURNAL OF THE ASSOCIATION OF PUBLIC ANALYSTS. Main/Corp Association of Public Analysts (Great Britain). VFOAT J.A.P.A. V. 1- 1st Quarter 1963-. 0004-5780. Periodical. UK. English. qt. $57.80. Academic Press, 4805 Sand Lake Road, Orlando FL 32819. Tel (305)345-4100. Ind/Abst Life Sci. Collect., Energy Inf. Abstr., Environ. Abstr., Nucl. Sci. Abstr., Chem. Abstr., Bibliogr. Agric., Sci. Cit. Index, Abr. Ed. LC TX501. NLM W1 JO912P. CODEN JPANA7.

JOURNAL OF THE CANADIAN DIETETIC ASSOCIATION. Main/Corp Canadian Dietetic Association. 0008-3399. Periodical. CN. some text in French. qt. $21.67. Canadian Dietetic Association, 385 Yonge Street/Suite #304, Toronto Ontario M5B 1S1 Canada. Tel (416)596-0857. Ed Louise Bell. Ind/Abst Hospit. Lit. Index, Ref. Source, Chem. Abstr., Bibliogr. Agric. NLM W1 JO915P. CODEN JCDTAH. bk rev. adv acc. Circ 4,300. (ctrl) Original research in nutrition, dietetics, food administration and management as well subjects of related interest.

JOURNAL OF THE NUTRITIONAL ACADEMY. VFOAT International Journal of the Nutritional Academy. V. 1- Mar. 1978-. 0197-0666. Periodical. US. English. NLM W1 JO943W.

JPEN. JOURNAL OF PARENTERAL AND ENTERAL NUTRITION. (JPEN, JOURNAL OF PARENTERAL AND ENTERAL NUTRITION). VFOAT Journal of Parenteral and Enteral Nutrition. V. 1- 1977-. 0148-6071. Periodical. US. English. bm. C B Slack Inc, 6900 Grove Road, Thorofare NJ 08086. Ind/Abst Life Sci. Collect., Excerpta Med., Index Med., Cumul. Index Nurs. Allied Health Lit., Chem. Abstr., Bibliogr. Agric., Energy Res. Abstr. LC RM224. DD 615.8. NLM W1 J514C. CODEN JPENDU.

KEEPING ABREAST, JOURNAL OF HUMAN NURTURING. 0164-7083. Periodical. US. English. qt. $10.00 Members, $19.50 Nonmembers. RHNI, 3885 Forest Street, PO Box 6861, Denver CO 80206. Ind/Abst Cumul. Index Nurs. Allied Health Lit. NLM W1 KE2615C. *Keeping Abreast Journal, 0146-7638.*

KOKURITSU EIYO KENKYUJO KENKYU HOKOKU. 1950-. 0368-5209. JA. Japanese (English, (1950-71, Japanese only)). an. Toyamacho Shinjuku-Ku, Tokyo Japan. LC TX341. *Annual Report of the National Institute of Nutrition.*

KONSERVNAIA I OVOSHCHESUSHILNAIA PROMYSHLENNOST. Began publication in 1957. 0023-3587. Periodical. UR. Russian. mo. Ind/Abst Chem. Abstr., Bibliogr. Agric. LC TX599. CODEN KOPRAU. *Konservnaia I Plodoovoshchnaia Promyshlennost.*

LET'S LIVE. See Medicine.

LETTRE - CORPORATION PROFESSIONNELLE DES DIETETISTES DU QUEBEC. (LA LETTRE - CORPORATION PROFESSIONNELLE DES DIETETISTES DU QUEBEC). Main/Corp Corporation Professionnelle des Dietetistes du Quebec. No. 1 Oct. 1976-. 0701-1660. Periodical. CN. French. mo. Corporation Professionnelle des Dietetistes du Quebec, Bureau 130, 934 East rue Sainte-Catherine, Montreal Quebec H2L 2E9 Canada. DD 613.209714.

MAIGRIR MEDECINE BEAUTE. VFOAT Maigrir. VAT Maigrir (1982). No. 37-. 0714-3761. CN. French. mo. $1.95 Per No. Maigrir, 3280 Boulevard Ste-Rose, Laval Quebec H7P 5B9 Canada. DD 613.2505. *Maigrir et Rester Belle (Laval, Quebec : 1980), 0710-4472.*

MARKETING, NUTRITION AND ENGINEERING SCIENCES. See Business - Marketing.

MEMBERSHIP DIRECTORY - SOCIETY FOR NUTRITION EDUCATION. See Yearbooks, Almanacs, Directories.

MILCHWISSENSCHAFT. See Agriculture - Dairy & Related Technologies.

MINNESOTA NUTRITION CONFERENCE. See Veterinary Medicine, Animal Culture.

MISSOURI NUTRITION EDUCATION & TRAINING PROGRAM. VFOAT Missouri Nutrition Education and Training Program. Fiscal Year 1981-. US. English. an. Missouri Department of Social Services Division of Health, Broadway State Office Building, PO Box 570, Jefferson City MO 65102. LC TX364. DD 641.10710778.

MONOGRAPHS OF THE AMERICAN COLLEGE OF NUTRITION. V. 1-. 0164-0585. Monographic Series. US. English. ir. Spectrum Publications Inc, 175-20 Wexford Terrace, Jamaica NY 11432. Tel (212)658-0888. Ind/Abst Chem. Abstr. NLM W1 MO569QP. CODEN MACNDG.

MONTHLY SUPPLY LETTER. See Restaurants.

NAHRUNG. (DIE NAHRUNG). Vol. 1-. 0027-769X. Periodical. GE. German (summaries in English and Russian). $112.80. Kunst & Wissen Erich Bieber, Dufourstrasse 51, CH-8008 Zurich Switzerland. Tel 011-41-1-69 44 20. Ind/Abst Life Sci. Collect., Excerpta Med., Index Med., Biol. Abstr., Chem. Abstr., Bibliogr. Agric., Sci. Cit. Index, Abr. Ed. LC TX341. NLM W1 NA116. CODEN NAHRAR. Index published separately - free - automatically sent.

NARINGSFORSKNING. Vol. 1- Feb. 1957-. 0465-7675. Periodical. English (Swedish). ir.

NAUCHNAIA SESSIIA - GOSUDARSTVENNYI NAUCHNO-ISSLEDOVATEL'SKII INSTITUT VITAMINOLOGII. UR. Russian. NLM W1 NA941.

NESTLE NUTRITION WORKSHOP SERIES. 0742-2806. Monographic Series. US. English. ir. Raven Press, 1140 Avenue of the Americas, New York NY 10036. Ind/Abst Chem. Abstr. NLM W1. CODEN NNWSDT.

NIGERIAN JOURNAL OF NUTRITIONAL SCIENCES. (NIGERIAN JOURNAL OF NUTRITIONAL SCIENCES : OFFICIAL ORGAN OF THE NUTRITION SOCIETY OF NIGERIA). Began with V. 1, No. 1 (Jan./June 1980). 0189-0913. Periodical. NR. English. sa. Business Manager, Nigerian Journal of Nutritional Sciences, Department of Human Nutrition, University of Ibadan, Ibadan Nigeria. Ind/Abst Chem. Abstr. CODEN NJNSEP.

NUTRIGUIDE. V. 1- Winter 1976/77-. 0701-1997. Periodical. CN. French. ir. $1.50 Per Number. Copunat Inc, Bureau 119/305 East Boulevard Saint-Joseph, Montreal Quebec H2T 1J3 Canada. DD 641.105.

NUTRISYON. (NUTRISYON : A PUBLICATION OF THE PHILIPPINE SOCIETY OF DIETITIANS AND NUTRITIONISTS, INC. (PSDN)). 0115-4516. Periodical. PH. English. ty. 50.00. University of Philippines, College of Home Economics, Diliman Quezon City Philippine. Tel 816-41-97. Ed Rachel A Arboleda. NLM W1 NU855. Circ 1,000. (ctrl) New trends in nutrition, and results of research studies. *Nutrilite.*

NUTRITION ABSTRACTS AND REVIEWS. See Indexes/Abstracts.

NUTRITION ABSTRACTS AND REVIEWS. SERIES A. HUMAN AND EXPERIMENTAL. See Indexes/Abstracts.

NUTRITION ACTION. V. 1- Jan. 1974-. 0199-5510. Periodical. US. English. mo. Center for Science & Public Interest, 1501-16th Street NW, Washington DC 20036. Tel (202)332-9110. Ind/Abst Altern. Press Index, Bibliogr. Agric. NLM W1 NU862D.

NUTRITION-ACTUALITE. Vol. 1, No. 1 (1977)-. 0229-0863. Periodical. CN. French. qt. Bureau Laitier du Canada, Bureau 1703, 1010 Ouest rue Sherbrooke, Montreal Quebec H3A 2R7 Canada. DD 641.105.

NUTRITION AND BEHAVIOR. Vol. 1, No. 1 (1982)-. 0733-4575. Periodical. US. English. qt. $70.00 US, $78.00 Canada. Alan R Liss Inc, 150-5th Avenue, New York NY 10011. Ind/Abst Life Sci. Collect., Chem. Abstr., Psychol. Abstr. LC QP141.A1. DD 599.013. NLM W1 NU862M. CODEN NUBEDX.

NUTRITION AND CANCER. V. 1- Fall 1978-. 0163-5581. Periodical. US. English. qt. The Franklin Inst Press, Box 2266, Philadelphia PA 19103. Tel (215)448-1239. Ed Gio B Gori. Ind/Abst Excerpta Med., Index Med., Biol. Abstr., Chem. Abstr., Bibliogr. Agric. NLM W1 NU879. CODEN NUCADQ. bk rev. adv acc. Circ 500. Reports and reviews current findings on the effects of nutrition on the etiology, therapy, and prevention of cancer.

NUTRITION AND CLINICAL NUTRITION. V. 1-. 0360-7259. Monographic Series. US. English. ir. Marcel Dekker, Continuation Department, 270 Madison Avenue, New York NY 10016. Ed R Olson. LC UNC. NLM W1 NU863D. This is an ongoing series. Each title has a different subject.

THE NUTRITION & DIETARY CONSULTANT. VFOAT Nutrition and Dietary Consultant. 8750-8370. Periodical. US. English. mo. $15.96. The Nutrition & Dietary Consultant, 2375 East

Tropicana/Suite 270, Las Vegas NV 89109. **Tel** (702)454-1665. **Ed** Myra E Holcomb. **DD** 613. adv acc. **Circ** 46,000. A professional journal dedicated to the practice of nutritional consulting with emphasis on private practice and articles written for the professional. *Your Nutritional Consultant, 8750-3395.*

NUTRITION & FOOD SCIENCE. (NUTRITION AND FOOD SCIENCE). No. 22- Jan. 1971-. 0034-6659. Periodical. UK. English. bm. $30.00. Forbes Publications, 120 Bayswater Road, London W2 3JH England. **Tel** (1)229 9322. **Ed** Dilys Wells. **Ind/Abst** Chem. Abstr., Bibliogr. Agric. **CODEN** NFSCD7. bk rev. adv acc. **Circ** 3,500. Developments in the subject areas are presented in a readable form to provide a link between education and the food science world. *Review of Nutrition and Food Science.*

NUTRITION AND HEALTH. V. 1-. 0270-658X. Periodical. US. English. bm. $38.50. Nutrition & Health, 701 West 168th Street, Mrs S Silver, New York NY 10032. **Tel** (212)694-6991. **Ed** Myron Winick. **NLM** W1 NU863J. **Circ** 5,000. Current and informative information on health topics such as heart disease, obesity diabetes, cancer, high blood pressure, etc.

NUTRITION AND HEALTH (BERKHAMSTED, HERTFORDSHIRE). (NUTRITION AND HEALTH). Vol. 1, No. 1-. 0260-1060. Periodical. UK. English. qt. A B Academic Publishers, Box 97 Berkhamsted, Herts HP4 2PX England. **Ed** Kenneth Barlow. **Ind/Abst** Sociol. Abstr., Chem. Abstr., Index Med. **CODEN** NUHEDT. bk rev. adv acc. Research and reviews of recent advances on aspects of nutrition with special relevance to health and prevention of disease. Includes book reviews.

NUTRITION AND METABOLISM *CEASED.* V. 12-24. 0029-6678. Periodical. SZ. articles in English, French or German. bm. $100.00. S Karger AG, Arnold-Bocklin-Strasse 25, CH-4011 Basel Switzerland. **Ind/Abst** Excerpta Med., Biol. Abstr., Bibliogr. Agric., Chem. Abstr., Index Med., Nuci. Sci. Abstr. **NLM** W1 NU863N. **CODEN** NUMEBI. *Nutritio et Dieta.*

NUTRITION AND THE BRAIN. V. 1- 1977-. 0149-2667. Monographic Series. US. English. ir. Raven Press, 1140 Avenue of the Americas, New York NY 10036. **Tel** (212)575-0335. **Ed** R J Wurtman and J J Wurtman. **Ind/Abst** Chem. Abstr., Bibliogr. Agric. **NLM** W1 NU8632. **CODEN** NUBRD4.

NUTRITION & THE M.D. **VFOAT** Nutrition and the M.D. V. 1- 1974-. 0732-0167. Periodical. US. English. mo. $65.00. PM Incorporated, Po Box 2160, Van Nuys CA 91404. **Tel** (213)873-4399. **Ed** Gerald McKee. **Ind/Abst** Bibliogr. Agric. bk rev. **Circ** 10,000. (ctrl). Clinical nutrition information for those involved in professional health care ie: registered dietitian, physicians, food service managers, etc.

NUTRITION CLINICS. 0888-3483. Periodical. US. English. bm. $24.00. George F Stickley Co, 210 West Washington Square, Philadelphia PA 19106.

NUTRITION FORUM. Vol. 1, No. 1 (Oct. 1984)-. 0748-8165. Periodical. US. English. mo. $30.00. George F Stickley Co, 210 West Washington Square, Philadelphia PA 19106. **DD** 613.

NUTRITION HEALTH REVIEW. 1976. 0164-7202. US. English. qt. $12.00. Frank R Rifkin, 143 Madison, New York City NY 10016. **Tel** (212)679-3590. **Ed** Frank Ray Rifkin. bk rev. **Circ** 16,800. Nutrition and health information gleaned from medical and psychiatric publications plus original manuscripts.

NUTRITION IN HEALTH AND DISEASE (NEW YORK, N.Y. : 1979). (NUTRITION IN HEALTH AND DISEASE). Vol. 1-. 0160-2470. Monographic Series. US. English. Raven Press, 1140 Avenue of the Americas, New York NY 10036. **Ind/Abst** Chem. Abstr. **NLM** W1 NU888. **CODEN** NHDIDW.

NUTRITION LEGISLATION NEWS. *See* Law.

NUTRITION NEWS. V. 1- Oct. 1937-. 0369-6464. Periodical. US. English. qt. $3.00. National Dairy Council, 6300 North River Road, Rosemont IL 60018. **Tel** (312)696-1020. **LC** TX501. **DD** 641.105. **NLM** W1 NU908. bk rev. **Circ** 75,000. (ctrl). Nutrition research, developments and teaching techniques with emphasis on dairy foods.

NUTRITION NEWS (POMONA, CALIF.). (NUTRITION NEWS). 8756-5919. Periodical. US. English. mo. $18.00. Nutrition News, PO Box J, Pomona CA 91769. **Tel** (714)629-1557. **Ed** Siri Khalsa. **DD** 613. **Circ** 80,000. We publish a four-page newsletter on a particular health topic or on a vitamin or mineral supplement.

NUTRITION NOTES. Periodical. US. English. qt. American Institute of Nutrition, 9650 Cockville Pike, Bethesda MD 20014. **LC** TX341. **DD** 641.1.

NUTRITION PLANNING. V. 1- Feb. 1978-. 0149-6743. Periodical. US. English. qt. $75.00. Oelgeschlager Gunn & Hain Inc, 131 Claredon Street, Boston MA 02116. **Tel** (617)437-9620. **Ed** Joanne P Nestor Tighe. **LC** TX359. **DD** 362.5. **NLM** ZQU 145.3 N976. bk rev. adv acc. **Circ** 2,500. An international journal of abstracts about food and nutrition policy, planning, and programs.

NUTRITION QUARTERLY. 0710-166X. Periodical. CN. English. qt. Free. Dairy Bureau of Canada, Nutrition Division, 20 Holly Street, Toronto Ontario M4S 2E6 Canada. **DD** 641.105. (ctrl).

NUTRITION REPORTS INTERNATIONAL. V. 1- Jan. 1970-. 0029-6635. Periodical. US. English. mo. $140.00. Geron-X Inc, Box 1108, Los Altos CA 94023. **Ed** Anthony Albanese. **Ind/Abst** Life Sci. Collect., Excerpta Med., Energy Inf. Abstr., Environ. Abstr., Bibliogr. Agric., Biol. Abstr., Chem. Abstr., Sci. Cit. Index, Abr. Ed. **LC** QP141.A1. **DD** 574.13. **NLM** W1 NU94. **CODEN** NURIBL. adv acc. **Circ** 550. Concise reports of original research in the area of clinical and experimental nutrition. Communicates advances and more recent knowledge of nutrition, nutritional biochemistry and food science.

NUTRITION RESEARCH CONCENTRATES FOR HEALTH PROFESSIONALS. **VFOAT** Nutrition Research. Began in 1983. 0739-4454. Periodical. US. English. bm. $96.00. Nutrition Research Publications, PO Box 218113, Houston TX 77218. **DD** 616. **CODEN** NRCPDG.

NUTRITION RESEARCH (NEW YORK, N.Y.). (NUTRITION RESEARCH). Vol. 1., No. 1 (1981)-. 0271-5317. Periodical. US. English. mo. $175.00. Pergamon Press, Attn: Cashier, 395 Sawmill River Road, Elmsford NY 10523. **Tel** (914)592-7700. **Ind/Abst** Life Sci. Collect., Chem. Abstr. **LC** QP141.A1. **DD** 616.39. **CODEN** NTRSDC. Also available in microform from the publisher.

NUTRITION RESEARCH NEWSLETTER. 1982. 0736-0037. Periodical. US. English. mo. $96.00. Nutrition Research Newsletter, PO Box 700, Palisades NY 10964. **Tel** (914)359-8282. **Ed** Lillian Langseth. **Circ** 75,000. (ctrl). A literature survey service for professionals (covering over 300 biomedical journals) reporting latest research news in nutrition and health related sciences.

NUTRITION REVIEWS. V. 1- Nov. 1942-. 0029-6643. Periodical. US. English. mo. $72.00. Nutrition Reviews, 888 Seventeenth Street NW, Washington DC 20006. **Tel** (202)872-0778. **Ind/Abst** Life Sci. Collect., Excerpta Med., Energy Inf. Abstr., Environ. Abstr., Energy Res. Abstr., Bibliogr. Agric., Biol. Agric. Index, Chem. Abstr., Index Med., Nuci. Sci. Abstr., Gen. Sci. Index, Sci. Cit. Index, Abr. Ed. **LC** TX341. **DD** 641.105. **NLM** W1 NU945. **CODEN** NUREA8. (cum index).

NUTRITION (SPRINGFIELD, ILL.). (NUTRITION). Jan. 1980-. Periodical. US. English. ir. Free. Illinois State Council on Nutrition, 524 South Second Street, Springfield IL 62706.

NUTRITION SURVEILLANCE. ANNUAL SUMMARY. US. English. an. US Department of Health and Human Services, Public Service Centers for Disease Control, Atlanta GA 30333.

NUTRITION TODAY. V. 1- Mar. 1966-. 0029-666X. Periodical. US. English. bm. $24.75. Williams & Wilkins, 428 East Preston Street, Balitmore MD 21202. **Tel** (301)528-4000. **Ed** Cortez Enloe. **Ind/Abst** Bibliogr. Agric., Appl. Sci. Technol. Index, Gen. Sci. Index. **LC** RA784. **DD** 613.2. **NLM** W1 NU958. adv acc. **Circ** 15,000. Informative and entertaining articles on new developments in nutrition for dietitians, nutritionists, and physicians.

NUTRITION UPDATE. Vol. 1-. 0735-4762. Periodical. US. English. ir. John Wiley & Sons, 1 Wiley Drive, Continuation Department, Somerset NJ 08873. **Tel** (212)850-6000. **Ed** Jean Weininger and George M Briggs. **DD** 613. **NLM** W1.

NUTRITION WEEK. Vol. 13, No. 1 (Jan. 6, 1983)-. 0736-0096. Periodical. US. English. ir. $60.00. Community Nutrition Institute, 2001 S Street Northwest/Suite 530, Washington DC 20009. **Tel** (202)462-4700. **Ed** Rodney E Leonard. **NLM** W1. **Circ** 3,100. *CNI Weekly Report, 0191-0833.*

NUTRITIONAL BIOCHEMICALS. **VFOAT** ICN Nutritional Biochemicals Catalog. US. English. ICN Nutritional Biochemicals, PO Box 28050, Cleveland OH 44128.

NUTRITIONAL PERSPECTIVES. Vol. 1, No. 1 (Jan. 1978)-. 0160-3922. Periodical. US. English. qt. $20.00. Nutritional Perspectives, 318 North Royal Avenue/Dr Carl Miller, Front Royal VA 22630. **Tel** (703)635-8844. **Ed** Gordon Lawson. bk rev. adv acc. (ctrl). Technical articles on nutrition.

NUTRITIONAL SUPPORT SERVICES. **VFOAT** N.S.S. Vol. 1, No. 1 (Apr. 1981)-. 0279-9480. Periodical. US. English. mo. $90.00. Creative Age Publications, 7628 Densmore Avenue, Van Nuys CA 91406. **Tel** (818)782-7328. **Ed** Joan Hart. **Ind/Abst** Life Sci. Collect., Chem. Abstr. **NLM** W1 NU974. **CODEN** NSUSDK. bk rev. adv acc. **Circ** 22,500. (ctrl). The journal of practical application in clinical nutrition, contains interdisciplinary articles on the development and application of clinical parenteral and enteral nutritional support techniques.

NUTRITIONAL UPDATE. V. 1- June 1973-. 0091-4045. Periodical. US. English. qt. Keats Publishing Inc, 212 Elm Street, New Canaan CT 06902. **LC** TX341. **DD** 641.105.

O.N.E. NEWSLETTER. **VAT** Organization for Nutrition Education Newsletter. Vol. 1, No. 1 -. 0229-1428. Periodical. CN. English. qt. Free to Members. O N E Newsletter, Organization for Nutrition Education, PO Box 818, Guelph Ontario N1H 6L8 Canda. **DD** 641.105.

OUTPOST EXCHANGE. *See* Food & Drink.

PETITS PROPOS CULINAIRES. UK. English. ty. $18.00. Barbara Beaumont-PPC, 12 Pascack Road, Park Ridge NJ 07656. **Tel** (201)391-1258. **LC** TX341. **DD** 641.05.

PHILIPPINE JOURNAL OF NUTRITION. V. 15, No. 3- July/Sept. 1962-. 0031-7640. Periodical. PH. English. qt. Nutrition Foundation of Philippines, 107 E Rodriguez Sr Boulevard, Quezon City Philippines. **Tel** 59-51-13. **Ed** Velona A Corpus. **Ind/Abst** Excerpta Med., Biol. Abstr., Chem. Abstr. **NLM** W1 PH569D. **CODEN** PJNUAF. bk rev. **Circ** 1,500. Researches on foods and nutrition and other commentaries related to the subject. *Nutrition News.*

THE PHILIPPINE NUTRITION PROGRAM 5 YEAR ACCOMPLISHMENT REPORT. **Main/Corp** National Nutrition Council (Philippines). 1974/79-. Periodical. English. ni. **NLM** W2 LP5 N5A. *PNP Annual Report, 0115-5490.*

PROBLEMI NA HRANENETO. (PROBLEMI NA KHRANENETO). Vol. 1- 1979-. 0205-003X. Bulgarian. ir. **Ind/Abst** Chem. Abstr. **NLM** W1 PR572ER. **CODEN** PRKHEL.

PROCEEDINGS OF THE NUTRITION SOCIETY. (THE PROCEEDINGS OF THE NUTRITION SOCIETY). **Main/Corp** Nutrition Society. V. 1-5, 1944-47. 0029-6651. UK. English. ty. $140.00. Cambridge University Press, 32 East 57th Street, New York NY 10022. **Ed** R H Smith, J W T Dickerson, R F Grimble and N F Suttle. **Ind/Abst** Life Sci. Collect., Pestdoc, Ringdoc, Vetdoc, Energy Inf. Abstr., Environ. Abstr., Bibliogr. Agric., Biol. Abstr., Chem. Abstr., Index Med., Nuci. Sci. Abstr., Biol. Agric. Index, Sci. Cit. Index, Abr. Ed. **LC** TX501. **DD** 641.06242. **NLM** W1 PR586HN. **CODEN** PNUSA4. Complete records of invited papers read at the symposia of the Society and Abstracts of Communications which are summaries of papers read by members at the society's scientific meetings.

PROCEEDINGS OF THE NUTRITION SOCIETY OF AUSTRALIA. **Main/Corp** Nutrition Society of Australia. Conference. 1st (Aug. 1976)-. 0314-1004. AT. English. an. $7.38. Nutrition Society of Australia, Division of Animal Production, c/o CSIRO, Private Bag PO, Wembley Western Australia 6013 Australia. **Tel** (09)387 0313. **Ed** A Sinclair. **Ind/Abst** Chem. Abstr., Bibliogr. Agric., Biol. Abstr. **NLM** W1. **CODEN** PNSADB. **Circ** 1,000. Proceedings of the Annual Scientific Conference of the Nutrition Society of Australia.

PROCEEDINGS OF THE NUTRITION SOCIETY OF INDIA. **Main/Corp** Nutrition Society of India. No. 1-. 0253-7567. Monographic Series. English. ir. **NLM** W3 PR945SL.

PROCEEDINGS - WESTERN HEMISPHERE NUTRITION CONGRESS. Main/Conf Western Hemisphere Nutrition Congress. 1st- 1965-. 0163-6847. US. English. LC TX345. DD 338.191812. NLM W3 WE521.

THE PROFESSIONAL NUTRITIONIST. Began in Nov./Dec. 1969. 0033-0159. Periodical. US. English. qt. Professional Nutritionist Editorial Offices, 2226 Clay Street, San Francisco CA 94115. Ind/Abst Chem. Abstr., Bibliogr. Agric. NLM W1 PR599. CODEN PRNUD6.

PROGRAM PLAN - UNITED STATES. FOOD SAFETY AND INSPECTION SERVICE. (PROGRAM PLAN). Main/Corp United States. Food Safety and Inspection Service. VFOAT Food Safety and Inspection Service Program Plan. Fiscal Year 1982-. 0735-2395. US. English. an. United States Department of Agriculture, Food Safety and Inspection Service, Washington DC 20250. LC TX501. DD 353.007782.

PROGRESS IN FOOD AND NUTRITION SCIENCE. (PROGRESS IN FOOD & NUTRITION SCIENCE). V. 1- 1975-. 0306-0632. Periodical. UK. English. mo. Pergamon Press, 395 Sawmill River Road, Elmsford NY 10523. Ind/Abst Life Sci. Collect., Energy Inf. Abstr., Environ. Abstr., Index Med., Biol. Abstr., Chem. Abstr., Bibliogr. Agric., Hospit. Lit. Index, Sci. Cit. Index, Abr. Ed. LC QP141.A1. DD 612.3. NLM W1 PR668V. CODEN PFNSDI.

QUADERNI DELLA NUTRIZIONE. 0033-488X. Periodical. IT. Italian. qt. Ist Nazion Della Nutriz, Citta Universitaria, Rome Italy. Ind/Abst Index Med.

RAPPORT DES ACTIVITES DU BUREAU DE NUTRITION. Main/Corp Haiti (Republic). Bureau de Nutrition. HT. French. ir. Departement de la Sante Publique et de la Population, Bureau de Nutrition, Port-Au-Prince Haiti. LC TX360.H2. DD 354.729400841.

RECENT ADVANCES IN CLINICAL NUTRITION. (RECENT ADVANCES IN CLINICAL NUTRITION : PROCEEDINGS OF THE . . . INTERNATIONAL SYMPOSIUM ON CLINICAL NUTRITION). Main/Conf International Symposium on Clinical Nutrition. 1st (9-11 July 1980)-. 0260-8170. Periodical. UK. English. Ed A N Howard and I M Baird. Ind/Abst Chem. Abstr. NLM W3 IN916VM. CODEN RENUD5.

RECENT ADVANCES IN OBESITY RESEARCH. 1- 1974-. 0306-7548. Periodical. UK. English. ir. 30.00. Newman Publishing Ltd, 48 Poland Street, London W1V 4PP United Kingdom. Tel 01-582 5266. Ed Alan Howard. Ind/Abst Chem. Abstr. NLM W3 RE353. CODEN RAORD7. Covers proceedings of the International Congress on Obesity held approximately every two to three years.

REPERTOIRE DES MEMBRES - CORPORATION PROFESSIONNELLE DES DIETETISTES DU QUEBEC. Main/Corp Corporation Professionnelle des Dietetistes du Quebec. 1978/79-. 0226-2649. CN. French. be. Corporation Professionnelle des Dietetistes du Quebec, Bureau 130, 934 East rue Sainte-Catherine, Montreal Quebec H2L 2E9 Canada. DD 613.2060714. Membres, 0318-8175.

REPORT BY THE SUB-COMMITTEE ON NUTRITIONAL SURVEILLANCE. Main/Corp Great Britain. Committee on Medical Aspects of Food Policy. Subcommittee on Nutritional Surveillance. Series/Titl Reports on Health and Social Subjects. VFOAT Report. 1st (1973)-. 0301-4924. UK. English. ir. NLM W1 RE212VM NO. 6 etc.

REPORT OF THE NUTRITION CENTER OF THE PHILIPPINES. Main/Corp Nutrition Center of the Philippines. 1974/75-. English. ir. Nutrition Center of the Philippines, South Superhighway Rizal, Makati Philippines. LC TX367. DD 363.

RESEARCH PROGRAMS OF THE NATIONAL INSTITUTE OF CHILD HEALTH AND HUMAN DEVELOPMENT. NUTRITION AND ENDOCRINOLOGY. Main/Corp Center for Research for Mothers and Children (U.S.). Nutrition and Endocrinology Section. VFOAT Nutrition and Endocrinology. US. English. be. National Institute of Child Health and Human Development, Center for Research for Mothers and Children, Nutrition and Endocrinology Section, 9000 Rockville Pike, Bethesda MD 20205.

REVISTA CENTROAMERICANA DE NUTRICION Y CIENCIAS DE ALIMENTOS. V. 1- Jan./March 1976-. 0304-4033. Periodical. Spanish. ir. Instituto de Nutricion de Centro America y Panama, Apartado 1188, Carretera Roosevelt Zona 11, Guatemala Guatemala. LC TX367. NLM W1 RE3464.

RIVISTA ITALIANA DELLE SOSTANZE GRASSE. See Chemistry.

SIK-RAPPORT. 0436-2071. Monographic Series. SW. Swedish. ir. Sik Fack, S-4000 23 Goteborg Sweden. Ind/Abst Bibliogr. Agric., Chem. Abstr. LC TX341. CODEN SIKRDK. Sik-Rapport.

SIK SAENGHWAL. VFOAT Wolgan Sik Saenghwal. V. 1- (1984, 9)-. Periodical. KO. Korean. mo. 10,000. Sik Saenghwal Kaeson Pom Kungmin Undong Ponbu, 731 Socho-Dong Kangman-Ku, Seoul Korea. LC TX724.5.K65.

SIKPUM KWA YONGYANG. VFOAT Food and Nutrition. Periodical. KO. Korean. qt. Nongchon Yongyang Kaeson Yonsuwon, 88-2 Sodun-dong, Suwoni-si Korea 170. LC TX360.K6.

SNE COMMUNICATOR. (SNE COMMUNICATOR : NEWSLETTER OF THE SOCIETY FOR NUTRITION EDUCATION). VFOAT S.N.E. Communicator. VAT Society for Nutrition Education Communicator. 0744-2343. Periodical. US. English. qt. $12.00. Society for Nutrition Education, 1736 Franklin Street, Suite 900, Oakland CA 94612. Tel (415)444-7133.

SOURCEBOOK ON FOOD AND NUTRITION. 1st- Ed. English. ir. $49.50. Marquis Whos Who Inc, 200 East Ohio Street, Chicago IL 60611. Tel (800)621-9669. NLM QU 145.3 S724. Volume presents 400 selected articles on nutritional subjects.

SOYFOODS. Vol. 1, No. 3 (Summer 1980)-. 8755-9188. Periodical. US. English. qt. $15.00. Soycrafters Association of North America, Soyfoods Sunrise Farm Heath Road, Colrain MA 01340. LC TX558.S7. DD 641.35655. Soycraft.

SPECIAL PAPER - JOINT FAO-WHO-OAU. REGIONAL FOOD AND NUTRITION COMMISSION FOR AFRICA. (SPECIAL PAPER - JOINT FAO/WHO/OAU REGIONAL FOOD AND NUTRITION COMMISSION FOR AFRICA). VAT Special Paper - Joint Food and Agriculture Organization-World Health Organization-Organization for African Unity Regional Food and Nutrition Commission for Africa. No. 1- 1967-. 0378-2239. Monographic Series. English. ir. NLM W1 SP295DJ.

STRENGTH & HEALTH. See Physical Training.

STUDIES IN MEDICAL GEOGRAPHY. See Medicine.

SUBJECT INDEX TO NUTRITION LITERATURE. See Indexes/Abstracts.

SYMPOSIA OF THE SWEDISH NUTRITION FOUNDATION. V. 1-. 0082-0415. Monographic Series. English. ir. Almqvist & Wiksell, 108 Drottninggatan, PO Box 45150, S-104 30 Stockholm Sweden. Tel Telex #85413160. Ind/Abst Chem. Abstr. NLM W1 SY432M. CODEN SSNFAW.

TECHNICAL REPORT (U.S. ARMY NATICK RESEARCH AND DEVELOPMENT LABORATORIES. FOOD ENGINEERING LABORATORY). (TECHNICAL REPORT). Monographic Series. US. English. Technical Report (United States. Army Natick Research and Development Command. Food Engineering Laboratory.

TIAOWEI FUSHIPIN KEJI. (TIAO WEI FU SHIH PIN KO CHI). VFOAT Tiaoweifushipinkeji. 0253-6080. Periodical. CC. Chinese. mo. 0.30. Tiao Wei Fu Shih Pin Ko Chi Tsa Chih Tai Hao 14-13, Post Office, Harbin China. Ind/Abst Chem. Abstr. LC TX553.A3. DD 664.0605. CODEN TFKED5.

TOPICS IN CLINICAL NUTRITION. 0883-5691. Periodical. US. English. qt. $46.50. Aspen Systems Corporation, 16792 Oakmont Avenue, Gaithersburg MD 20877.

TUFTS UNIVERSITY DIET & NUTRITION LETTER. V. 1, No. 1 (March 1983)-. Periodical. US. English. mo.

ULTRANUTRITION DIGEST. V. 1- July 1980-. 0270-7918. Periodical. US. English. bm. $15.00. Ultranutrition Institute, 1825 NE 149 Street, Miami FL 33161.

VEGETARIAN (ALTRINCHAM, CHESHIRE : 1980). See Food & Drink.

VEGETARIAN TIMES. 0164-8497. Periodical. US. English. mo. $19.95. Vegetarian Times, Suite 921/41 East 42nd Street, New York NY 10017. Tel (212)490-3999. Ed Paul Obis. Ind/Abst Bibliogr. Agric. LC TX392. DD 613.26205. bk rev. adv acc. Contains information on: health, nutrition, natural foods, recipes, exercise, holistic living; features, people profiles, book reviews and news. Well-Being, 0146-7824.

VITAMIN E ABSTRACTS. See Indexes/Abstracts.

VOEDING. V. 1. Apr. 1939-. 0042-7926. Periodical. NE. Dutch (most summaries in French and English). mo. 60.-. Tijdschrift Voeding, Postbus 95945, 2509 CX Den Haag The Netherlands. Tel 701471441. Ed W Bosman. Ind/Abst Life Sci. Collect., Chem. Abstr., Bibliogr. Agric. LC TX341. DD 641.05. NLM W1 VO201. CODEN VOEDAK. bk rev. adv acc. Circ 4,500. (ctrl). Scientific journal on nutrition, food and health.

VOPROSY PITANIIA. V. 1-32, 1932-1973. 0042-8833. Periodical. UR. Russian (some English summaries). bm. $19.50. Victor Kamkin Inc (70153), 12224 Parklawn Drive, Rockville MD 20852. Tel (301)881-5973. Ind/Abst Life Sci. Collect., Index Med., Biol. Abstr., Int. Aerosp. Abstr., Chem. Abstr., Bibliogr. Agric. NLM W1 VO6414. CODEN VPITAR.

WEIGHT WATCHERS. VFOAT Weight Watchers Magazine. V. 1- Feb. 1968-. 0043-2180. Periodical. US. English. mo. Weight Watchers Magazine, 360 Lexington Avenue/11th Floor, New York NY 10017, (subscription address: Neodata PO Box 2606 Boulder CO 80322). Tel (212)888-9166. Ind/Abst Bibliogr. Agric., Mag. Index. LC RM222.2.

WHOLE FOODS. 1976. 0193-1504. Periodical. US. English. mo. $18.00. Whole Foods Communications Inc, 195 Main Street, Metchen NJ 08840. Tel (201)494-2889. Ed Marsha Cox. DD 338. bk rev. adv acc. Circ 13,000. (ctrl). Trade publication which covers the natural foods industry, with news, statistics, articles on trends, plus new product coverage.

WHOLE LIFE TIMES. 1979. 0279-5604. Periodical. US. English. ir. Whole Life Times, 18 Shepard Street, Department S, Brighton MA 02135. Tel (617)783-8030. Ed Shelly Kellman. bk rev. adv acc. Circ 140,000. (ctrl). Natural lifestyle magazine with articles on health, diet, exercise, nutrition and the environment.

WIC COMMUNIQUE : ISSUES OF THE SPECIAL SUPPLEMENTAL FOOD PROGRAM FOR WOMEN. Publication began with Aug. 1978. Periodical. US. English. qt. US Department of Agriculture Food and Nutrition Service, Washington DC 20250.

WORLD REVIEW OF NUTRITION AND DIETETICS. V. 1-. 0084-2230. English. ir. S Karger Ag, PO Box, CH-4009 Basel Switzerland. Tel (061)390880. Ed G H Bourne. Ind/Abst Index Med., Biol. Abstr., Chem. Abstr., Bibliogr. Agric., Hospit. Lit. Index. LC QP141.A1. DD 612.3082. NLM W1 W0898. CODEN WRNDAT. Volumes in this series consist of exceptionally thorough reviews on topics selected as fundamental to improved understanding of nutrition.

ZEITSCHRIFT FUR ERNAEHRUNGSWISSENSCHAFT. VFOAT Journal of Nutritional Sciences, Journal des Sciences de la Nutrition. Supplementum. Vol. 1 1961-. 0084-5337. Monographic Series. German (English and French). qt. $83.00. Springer Verlag-New York Inc, 175 Fifth Avenue, New York NY 10010. Tel (212)460-1500. Ed K H Bassler and A Fricker. Ind/Abst Index Med., Sci. Cit. Index, Abr. Ed. Features original articles on aspects of nutritional science and related fields.

ZYWIENIE CZOWIEKA. Vol. 1- 1974-. 0303-7851. Periodical. PL. Polish (table of contents in English, German, or Russian). Panstwowy Zaklad Wydawnictw Lekarskich Ul Duga 38/40, 00-238 Warszawa Poland. Ind/Abst Biol. Abstr., Chem. Abstr. NLM W1 ZY99. CODEN ZYCZDN.

OCCUPATIONS AND CAREERS

AIRLINE GUIDE TO STEWARDESS AND STEWARD CAREERS CEASED. 1968-1979/80. 0065-4914. US. English. an.

Occupations and Careers

AMERICAN NUCLEAR SOCIETY CAREER GUIDE. VFOAT Career Guide. 1982 Ed.-. 0738-1042. US. English. $30.00. American Nuclear Society, 555 North Kensington Avenue, La Grange Park IL 60525.

ANNUAL CAREERS GUIDE : OPPORTUNITIES IN THE PROFESSIONS, INDUSTRY, COMMERCE AND THE PUBLIC SERVICE. VFOAT Opportunities in the Professions, Industry, Commerce and the Public Service. Began in 1950. UK. English. an. 1/30/-. Her Majestys Stationery Office, PO Box 276, London SW8 5DT England. **LC** HF5382.5.G7. **DD** 331.7020941.

ANNUAL REPORT ON STATE OCCUPATIONAL REQUIREMENTS FOR VOCATIONAL EDUCATION (CONNECTICUT). Main/Corp Connecticut. Employment Security Division. US. English. an. **LC** HD5725.C8. **DD** 331.1209746.

ARTSEARCH. See The Arts (General) - Performing Arts.

AVENIRS. No. 1- Jan. 1947-. 0005-1969. Periodical. FR. French. ir. Onisep Diffusions, 46-52 rue Albert, 75635 Paris Cedex 13 France. **Tel** 583-32-21. **Ind/Abst** Int. Labour Doc., Foreign Lang. Index. **LC** HF5382.

BAC OU PAS BAC, QUE FAIRE APRES. FR. French. an. 32. Onisep, 75225 Paris Cedex 05 France.

BETWEEN US (WINDSOR, ONT.). See Education (General) - Higher Education.

BUSINESSWEEK'S GUIDE TO CAREERS. VFOAT Guide to Careers. Began in Mar. 1983. 8756-9116. Periodical. US. English. bm. $12.00. MacGraw-Hill Inc, 1221 Avenue of the Americas, New York NY 10020. Ed J Robert Connor. bk rev. adv acc. (ctrl). This magazine offers young adults, 20-25 years old, up-to-date information about jobs, where they are, how to get them and how to manage a career.

CANADIAN SECRETARY. Sept. 1976-. 0709-5236. Periodical. CN. English. qt. $13.93. MacLean Hunter, Circulation/Accounting Department, PO Box 100 Station A, Toronto Ontario M5W 1A7 Canada. **DD** 651.37410971.

CAREER CANDIDATES - CARLETON UNIVERSITY. SCHOOL OF PUBLIC ADMINISTRATION. Main/Corp Carleton University. School of Public Administration. 1975/1976-. 0703-5314. CN. English. an. Carleton University, School of Public Administration, Colonel by Drive, Ottawa Ontario K1S 5B6 Canada. **DD** 350.00071171384.

CAREER CURRENTS. Main/Corp Wisconsin Career Information Systems. Periodical. US. English. Wisconsin Vocational Studies Center, University of Wisconsin-Madison, 1025 West Johnson Street, 1078 Educational Science Building, Madison WI 53706.

THE CAREER DEVELOPMENT BULLETIN. Vol. 1, No. 1 (Winter 1979)-. 0738-7075. Periodical. US. English. qt. $28.00. Editorial Office, 814 Uris Columbus University, New York NY 10027. **Tel** (212)280-2830. Ed Elizabeth Warren. **LC** HF5381.A1. **DD** 650.1405. bk rev. **Circ** 2,000. (ctrl). Serves as a clearing house for important new information and research in the fields of career development and human resource management.

CAREER DEVELOPMENT, DROPOUT PREVENTION PROGRAM, EXPERIMENTAL PROGRAMS, TEACHER LEADERSHIP PROGRAM, REGIONAL SERVICE UNITS. See Education (General).

CAREER DIRECTIONS. Periodical. US. English. qt. Alumni Hall, University of Tennessee, Knoxville TN 37916. Resources for Student Vocational Pursuits.

CAREER EDUCATION NEWS : CENTRAL NEWS SERVICE FOR THE WORLDS OF WORK AND LEARNING. Periodical. US. English. ir $110.00. Diversified Learning, 72-300 Vallat Road, Rancho Mirage CA 92270. **Tel** (619)346-3336.

CAREER EDUCATION PLANS AND PROGRAMS OF THE STATES. 0145-8051. US. English. Chronicle Guidance Publications Inc, Aurora Street, Moravia NY 13118.

CAREER EDUCATION PROGRAM. PROGRAM PLAN. (CAREER EDUCATION PROGRAM : PROGRAM PLAN). Main/Corp National Institute of Education. 0361-1507. US. English. National Institute of Education, 1200 19th Street Northwest, Washington DC 20208. **LC** LC1041. **DD** 370.1130973.

CAREER EDUCATION PROJECTS FUNDED UNDER SECTIONS 402 AND 406 OF PUBLIC LAW 93-380 : YEARLY PROGRAM. See Education (General) - Special Aspects of Education.

CAREER INSIGHTS. 1982/83-. 0278-8934. Periodical. US. English. an. $7.50. Career Insights, Box 1951, Brown University, Providence RI 02912. **LC** WMLC L 83/154.

CAREER NEWS. V. 1- Sept. 1978-. 0709-0366. Periodical. CN. English. qt. Career Information Centre, University of Waterloo, Waterloo Ont N2L 3G1 Canada. **DD** 331.7020971. Centrepages, 0702-7230.

CAREER OPPORTUNITY INDEX (PROFESSIONAL EDITION : 1985). See Indexes/Abstracts.

CAREER OUTLOOK, UNIVERSITY AND COMMUNITY COLLEGE : ADMINISTRATION/SOCIAL SCIENCES AND SERVICES. VFOAT Perspectives de Carrieres, Universites et Colleges. CN. English and French. Manpower and Immigration, 222 NePean Street, Ottawa Ontario K1A 0J5 Canada. **LC** HF5382.5.C2. **DD** 331.7020971.

CAREER PLANNING. Periodical. US. English. mo. $18.00. Susan Cohn, 245 South Robertson Boulevard, Beverly Hills CA 90211.

CAREER PLANNING AND ADULT DEVELOPMENT JOURNAL. (CAREER PLANNING AND ADULT DEVELOPMENT JOURNAL : A QUARTERLY PUBLICATION OF THE CAREER PLANNING AND ADULT DEVELOPMENT NETWORK). Vol. 1, No. 1 (Spring 1983)-. 0736-1920. Periodical. US. English. qt. Free to Members, $15.00 Nonmembers. Career Planning and Adult Development Network, 1190 South Bascom Avenue/Suite 211, San Jose CA 95128. **LC** HF5381.A1. **DD** 331.70205.

CAREER PLANNING ANNUAL - UNIVERSITY AND COLLEGE PLACEMENT ASSOCIATION. (CAREER PLANNING ANNUAL). 1980/81-. 0229-4346. CN. English. an. Free. University and College Placement Association, 10th Floor 43/Eglinton Avenue East, Toronto Ont M4P 1A2 Canada. **DD** 331.70202571. (ctrl). University & College Career Planning Annual, 0705-775X.

CAREER TRAINING. 0882-6439. Periodical. US. English. qt. $5.00. NATTS, 2251 Wisconsin Avenue Northwest Suite 200, Washington DC 20007. **DD** 373.

CAREER WORLD (HIGHLAND PARK, ILL.). (CAREER WORLD). Began with issue for Sept. 1981. 0744-1002. Periodical. US. English. mo. $4.50. Curriculum Innovations Inc, 3500 Western Avenue, Highland Park IL 60035. Ind/Abst Child. Mag. Guide. **LC** HF5381.A1. **DD** 331.170205. Career World 1, 0198-7615; Career World 2, 0198-7623.

CAREERISM NEWSLETTER : ZEROING IN ON CAREER AND JOB OPPORTUNITIES. Began in 1976. Periodical. US. English. bm. $75.00. WWWWW/Information Services Inc, Box 10046, Rochester NY 14610.

CAREERS. 1st- Ed. 0094-6087. US. English. $1.95. Graphic Arts Center, 2000 NW Wilson Street, Portland OR 97209. **LC** HF5382.5.U6. **DD** 331.702.

CAREERS. 1979-. 0193-1873. US. English. an. $5.00. Vitality Associates, PO Box 164, Saratoga CA 95070. **LC** Z7164.V6, HF5382.5.U5. **DD** 331.702.

CAREERS CANADA. Main/Corp Canada. Employment and Immigration Canada (Commission). Occupational and Career Analysis and Development. 0707-3038. Monographic Series. CN. English. ir. Receiver General for Canada, Supply & Services Canada, Ottawa Ontario K1A 0S9 Canada. Careers Canada, 0707-3038.

CAREERS (EDMONTON, ALTA.). (CAREERS). Vol. 3, Issue 1-. 0229-379X. Periodical. CN. English. ir. $17.00. Reed Vocational Resource Library, Suite 800, 4445 Calgary Trail South, Edmonton Alta T6H 5C3 Canada. **DD** 331.702. Reed Career Magazine, 0706-716X.

CAREERS FOR GRADUATES. VFOAT Carrieres pour Diplomes. 1974-. 0318-6229. Periodical. CN. English and French. Free to Graduating Students. Development Publications, POB 84 Succursale A, Willowdale Ontario M2N 5S7 Canada. **Tel** (416)636-2230. Ed H Kane. **DD** 331.70202571. adv acc. **Circ** 13,000. (ctrl). Mailed to placement offices in universities across Canada for free distribution to graduating students.

CAREERS GUIDE. English. ir. Careers Publications, PO Box 374, Salisbury Zimbabwe. **LC** HF5382.5.Z55. **DD** 331.702096891.

CAREERS IN BUSINESS. 1954-. 0576-7334. Periodical. US. English. an. Careers Inc, 1165 Fifth Avenue, New York NY 10029.

CAREERS IN THE UNITED STATES DEPARTMENT OF THE INTERIOR. Main/Corp United States. Dept. of the Interior. Series/Titl Personnel Management Publication. 0502-0166. US. English. ir. US Department of the Interior, 2401 E Street NW, Washington DC 20241. **LC** JK864. **DD** 353.3.

CAREERS TOMORROW. Periodical. US. English. bm. $6.00 Members, $9.00 Others & Libraries. 4916 St Elmo Avenue, Bethesda MA 20814.

CATALYST MEDIA REVIEW. VFOAT Media Review. 1981. 0736-0274. US. English. qt. Catalyst Media Review, 14 East 60th Street, New York NY 10022. **Tel** (212)759-9700. Ed Kathleen Weir. **Circ** 500. An annotated mediagraphy on career and family issues.

CHAINLETTER. (CHAINLETTER : BI-MONTHLY NEWSLETTER OF THE CAREER INFORMATION RESOURCE ADVISORY GROUP). Vol. 1, No. 1 (Jan. 1976)-. 0714-2005. Periodical. CN. English. ty. $15.00. Career Information Resource Advisory Group c/o Susan Reid, Ryerson Placement Centre, Ryerson Polytechnical Institute, 50 Gould Street, Toronto Ontario M5B 1E8 Canada. Ed Ellen Shenk. **DD** 371.42509713. bk review. **Circ** 44. Contents include articles on career and education topics, book reviews, news and notes from member institutions and other information of interest to subscribers.

CHRONICLE CAREER INDEX. See Indexes/Abstracts.

CLASSIFICATION CANADIENNE DESCRIPTIVE DES PROFESSIONS. CN. French. an. Emploi et Immigration Canada, Approvisionnements et Services Canada, Ottawa Ontario K1A 0S9 Canada. **Tel** (819)994-2973. **LC** HB2619. **DD** 331.700971. **Circ** 25,000. Formed from the basis of the CCDO and provides a systematic classification structure in which the working population could be categorized.

COLLEGE & CAREER DIRECTORY. MARYLAND, DELAWARE. See Yearbooks, Almanacs, Directories.

COLLEGE & CAREER DIRECTORY. PENNSYLVANIA. See Yearbooks, Almanacs, Directories.

COLLEGE PLACEMENT ANNUAL CEASED. 19587-1983. 0069-5734. US. English. an. $29.95. College Placement Council Inc, 62 Highland Avenue, Bethlehem PA 18017. **Tel** (215)868-1421. Ed Joan M Bowser. **LC** HF5382.5.U5. **DD** 371.425. adv acc. **Circ** 1,000,000. (ctrl). Three-volume occupational directory for college graduates. Volume 1 offers advice on the job search. Other two volumes include information on job opportunities.

COLLEGIATE WOMAN'S CAREER MAGAZINE. See Women.

THE CPC ANNUAL. VFOAT C.P.C. Annual. 1984-. 0749-7474. US. English. an. College Placement Council, 62 Highland Avenue, Bethlehem PA 18017. **Tel** (215)868-1421. **DD** 331. **Circ** 1,000,000. Three-volume occupational directory for college graduates. Volume one offers advice on the job search. Other volumes include information on job opportunities. College Placement Annual, 0069-5734.

CRIMINAL JUSTICE CAREER DIGEST. Vol. 1, No. 1 (Oct. 1981)-. 0278-5277. Periodical. US. English. mo. $30.00. Checkpoint Inc, PO Box 565, Phoenix AZ 85001.

CURRENT CAREER AND OCCUPATIONAL LITERATURE. 1973/77-. 0161-0562. US. English. be. H W Wilson, Book Order Department, 950 University Avenue, Bronx NY 10452. **LC** Z7164.V6, HF5381.A1. **DD** 016.3317020973.

Occupations and Careers

DIRECTORIO NACIONAL DE PROFESIONALES. See Yearbooks, Almanacs, Directories.

DIRECTORY OF OPPORTUNITIES FOR GRADUATES. See Yearbooks, Almanacs, Directories.

DUDE RANCHER. 0012-6969. Periodical. US. English. an. $10.00. Dude Ranchers Association, South Laramie, Tie Siding WY 82084.

EDUCATION AND CAREERS IN SOUTH AFRICA. See Education (General).

EDUCATION FOR ALLIED HEALTH CAREERS. Began with 1976 Vol. 0198-6244. US. English. be. Single Copies Free. American Medical Association, Department of Allied Health Education and Accreditation, 535 North Dearborn Street, Chicago IL 60610. LC R847.5. DD 610.737071173.

EDUCATIONAL CONSIDERATIONS. See Education (General) - Special Aspects of Education.

EMPLOYER PROFILES. (EMPLOYER PROFILES : A GUIDE TO CAREERS AND EMPLOYMENT IN CANADA). 1981-. 0228-4936. Periodical. CN. English. sa. $15.00/issue - Members, #30.00 per issue - Nonmembers. Employer Profiles, University and College Placement Association, 10th Floor, 43 Eglinton Avenue East, Toronto Ontario M4P 1A2 Canada. DD 331.1240971.

THE EXECUTIVE. V.L- Spring 1973-. Periodical. US. English. ty. University of Alabama, Box J, University AL 35486.

FEDERAL CAREER DIRECTORY; A GUIDE FOR COLLEGE STUDENTS. See Yearbooks, Almanacs, Directories.

FEDERAL CAREER INSIGHTS. VFOAT Insights. Vol. 1, No. 1 (Apr. 1985)-. 0882-5637. Periodical. US. English. mo. $67.00. Federal Research Service, PO Box 1059, Vienna VA 22180. Tel (703)281-0200. Ed Suzanne Montgomery. DD 331. bk rev. (ctrl) Reports to federal workers on pay issues, fringe benefits, retirement, professional development, career advancement, new management tools, problem solving techniques; developments in federal policy and procedures.

FEDERAL GOVERNMENT LEGAL CAREER OPPORTUNITIES. US. English. ir. American Bar Association, Law Student Division, 750 North Lake Shore Drive, Chicago IL 60611. DD 331.7.

GUIDE TO A SUCCESSFUL LIFE INSURANCE CAREER. (A GUIDE TO A SUCCESSFUL LIFE INSURANCE CAREER). VAT Improve Your Lifestyle, Lifestyle (Don Mills). 0381-6532. CN. English. an. Life Underwriters Association of Canada, 41 Lesmill Road, Don Mills Ontario M3B 2T3 Canada. DD 368.3200715.

GUIDE TO FEDERAL CAREER LITERATURE. 0097-8701. US. English. Superintendent of Documents, US Government Printing Office, Washington DC 20402. LC JK639. DD 353.0010023.

HEALTH CAREER OPPORTUNITY GRANTS FOR THE DISADVANTAGED. Series/Titl OHRO Digest. DHEW Publication. Began with: 1978. 0197-8705. US. English. an. Department of Health Education and Welfare, Public Health Service, Health Resources Administration, Office of Health Resources Opportunity, Hyattsville MD 20782. NLM W 22 AA1 H43.

HEALTH CAREERS NEWS. Winter 1976-. 0701-1210. Periodical. CN. English. Ontario Hospital Association, Hospital Careers Department, 150 Ferrand Drive, Don Mills Ontario M3C 1H6 Canada. DD 610.69. *Hospital Careers News, 0701-1202.*

ILLINOIS OCCUPATIONAL INFORMATION QUARTERLY. VFOAT Occupational Information Quarterly. US. English. qt. Research and Analysis Division, Bureau of Employment Security/910 South Michigan Avenue, Chicago Il 60605.

INDICE DE PROFESIONALES DEL URUGUAY. See Indexes/Abstracts.

INTERNSHIPS. 1981-. 0272-5460. US. English. an. Writers Digest, 9933 Alliance Road, Cincinnati OH 45242. Tel (513)984-0717. Ed Lisa A Hulse. LC L901. DD 331.25922. bk rev. Most comprehensive, current information on training opportunities in fields ranging from business to science to theater.

INTERP CENTRAL CLEARINGHOUSE NEWSLETTER. 1978. Periodical. US. English. bm. $40.00 Domestic, $45.00 Foreign. Interp Central Inc, PO Box 28, Chelsea MI 48118. Tel (313)475-7070. Ed Gabriel J Cherem. Circ 150. Literature updates, training opportunities, news bulletins, employment opportunities, want ads, and product listings for public contact personnel and interpretive professionals.

THE JOB CATALOG. 1st Ed. (1979)-. 0278-5706. US. English. an. $9.00. Mail Order USA, PO Box 19083, Washington DC 20036. Tel (202)686-9521. Ed Dorothy O'Callaghan. LC HF5382.75.U6. DD 650.14025753. Circ 6,000. Where to find creative jobs in Washington DC and Baltimore: book, magazine and newspaper publishers; fast news media, public relations, performing arts, conventions; professional organizations to join.

JOB CLASSIFICATION REFERENCE MANUAL. VAT Stevenson and Kellogg Salary Survey. Job Classification Specifications. 1982-. 0826-0311. CN. English. an. $520.00. Thorne Stevenson and Kellogg, 1600 Board of Trade Tower/1177 West Hastings Street, Vancouver British Columbia V6E 2K3 Canada. DD 658.30605. *S & K Salary Survey. Job Classification Specifications, 0706-6953.*

JOB INFORMATION LETTER. VFOAT JIL. 8756-1670. Periodical. US. English. bm. $50.00. National Association of Government Communicators, 80 South Early Street, Alexandria VA 22304. Tel (703)823-4821. Ed Deborah M Trocchi. DD 331. (ctrl). A report on communication jobs available in federal, state, local government and private industries.

JOB OPENINGS FOR ECONOMISTS. VFOAT JOE. 1974-. 0196-1551. Periodical. US. English. bm. American Economic Association, 1313 21st Avenue, Nashville TN 37212.

JOB SEARCH. A GUIDE FOR UNIVERSITY OF VERMONT STUDENTS. 0742-9223. US. English. an. Free. College Placement Council Inc, 62 Highland Avenue, Bethlehem PA 18001.

JOBS CANADA. Vol. 1, No. 1 (Winter 1984)-. 0823-9878. CN. English. an. $2.00 Per No. Jobs Canada, c/o Bridging the Gap, 155 College Street, Toronto Ontario M5T 1P6 Canada. DD 331.7020971. *Jobs for Your Future, 0823-986X.*

JOBS-IN-PRINT. VFOAT Jobs in Print. 0742-7042. Periodical. US. English. sm. $8.00. Rutgers University School of Communication, Information and Library Studies, 4 Huntington Street, New Brunswick NJ 08903. Tel (201)932-7127. Ed Mary Ross. Circ 300. Job placement listings.

JOBS, THIS SUMMER. 1983-. 0822-5753. CN. English. an. 5.50. Guidance Centre Faculty of Education, University of Toronto, Toronto Ontario M5S 2Y3 Canada. Tel (416)978-3206. Ed Carl L Bedal. DD 650.140971. Handbook for technical institute, CEGEP, community college, and university students looking for summer jobs.

JOURNAL OF CAREER PLANNING & EMPLOYMENT. VFOAT Journal of Career Planning and Employment. Vol. 46, No. 1 (Fall 1985)-. 0884-5352. Periodical. US. English. qt. $20.00. College Placement Council Inc, 62 Highland Avenue, Bethelem PA 18017. Tel (215)868-1421. Ind/Abst Educ. Index, Account. Index. Suppl., Curr. Index J. Educ., Ref. Source. DD 378. bk rev. adv acc. Circ 4,000. Articles on new ideas, techniques, and current issues, book reviews, how-to and readers views departments. *Journal of College Placement, 0021-9770.*

JOURNAL OF EMPLOYMENT COUNSELING. 0022-0787. Periodical. US. English. qt $11.00. American Association of Counseling Development, 5999 Stevenson Avenue, Alexandria VA 22304. Tel (703)823-9800. Ed Robert Drummond. Ind/Abst Manage. Contents, Curr. Index J. Educ., Soc. Sci. Citation Index, Psychol. Abstr. LC HF5382.5.U5. DD 331.7020973. CODEN JECODE. adv acc. Circ 597. (ctrl). Available on microfilm from University Microfilms. Articles on research techniques, concerns and all issues related to employment counseling.

JOURNAL OF STUDIES IN TECHNICAL CAREERS. V. 1- Fall 1978-. 0163-3252. Periodical. US. English. qt. $15.00. Southern Illinois University, School Technical Careers/SIU, Carbondale IL 62901. Tel (618)536-6682. Ed Vivienne Lucas Hertz. Ind/Abst Curr. Index J. Educ. LC TL1. DD 607.1. bk rev. adv acc. Circ 1,000. Scholarly journal publishing articles of research, practices, and concerns related to technical and vocational education. Has an international perspective.

KAIHATSU TO KENSHU. Periodical. JA. Japanese. ir. Tokyo-to Sogo Gino, Kaihatsu Kenshujo 1-5, Uchi Kanda 1 Tokyo Japan. LC HD5715.5.J3.

LOVEJOY'S CAREER AND VOCATIONAL SCHOOL GUIDE. See Education (General) - Special Aspects of Education.

MCGRAW-HILL'S COMPUTER CAREERS. VFOAT Computer Careers. V. 1, No. 1 (May 1985)-. 0882-3979. Periodical. US. English. qt. $16.00. McGraw-Hill's Computer Careers, 1221 Avenue of the Americas, New York NY 10124. DD 001.

MICHIGAN LICENSED OCCUPATIONS. 0093-6421. US. English. 7310 Woodward Avenue, Detroit MI 48202. LC HD3630.U7. DD 344.774017.

MIDDLE EAST EDUCATION & TRAINING. See Education (General).

MISSOURI OCCUPATIONAL STAFFING PATTERNS OF SELECTED NON-MANUFACTURING INDUSTRIES SURVEYED. (MISSOURI OCCUPATIONAL STAFFING PATTERNS OF SELECTED NON-MANUFACTURING INDUSTRIES). Main/Corp Missouri. Division of Employment Security. VFOAT Occupational Employment Statistics: Nonmanufacturing Staffing Patterns. 0148-1851. US. English. Division of Employment Security, PO Box 59, Jefferson City MO 65101. LC HD5725.M8. DD 331.1109778.

MLA JOB INFORMATION LIST. ENGLISH ED. VFOAT MLA Job Information List. VAT Modern Language Association of America Job Information List. Periodical. US. English. qt. $30.00. Modern Language Association of America, 62 Fifth Avenue, New York NY 10011. Tel (212)741-5593. Ed Roy Chustek. bk rev. adv acc. Circ 6,000. Information on teaching positions in English and foreign languages at the college level.

NATIONAL EMPLOYMENT LISTING SERVICE FOR THE CRIMINAL JUSTICE SYSTEM. SPECIAL EDITION : EDUCATIONAL OPPORTUNITIES. Main/Corp Sam Houston State University. National Employment Listing Service for the Criminal Justice System. VFOAT Special Edition: Educational Opportunities. 0194-0805. US. English. an. $65.00. National Employment Listing Service, Texas Criminal Justic Center, Sam Houston State University, Huntsville TX 77341. Tel (409)294-1692. Ed Laure Pegoda. LC HV8143. DD 364.071173. adv acc. Circ 2,500. Publication of current various criminal justice fields.

NATIONAL NEWSLETTER - ASSOCIATION OF PART-TIME PROFESSIONALS (U.S.). (NATIONAL NEWSLETTER). VFOAT APTP National Newsletter. Began with issue for spring 1981?. 0739-2931. Periodical. US. English. mo. $15.00. Association of Part Time, 7655 Old Springhouse Road, McLean VA 22101. Tel (703)734-7975. Ed Diane Rothberg. bk rev. Circ 1,500. (ctrl). Trends in part-time employment, profiles of successful part-time professionals, employer use, family and work issues, and older workers.

NEVADA STATE PLAN FOR CAREER EDUCATION. Main/Corp Nevada. State Board for Vocational Education. 0091-5106. US. English. an. Nevada State Board of Vocational Education, 151 E Park Street, Carson City NV 89701. LC LC1046.N3. DD 379.155.

NEW JERSEY JOB GUIDE. No. 1- 1962-. US. English. LC HF5382. DD 331.70209749.

NEWS AND CAREERS. V. 1- Jan. 28, 1977-. 0226-0956. Periodical. CN. English. bw. Free. Canadian Hospital Association, 410 Laurier Avenue West, Ottawa Ontario K1R 7T6 Canada. DD 362.110971. (ctrl).

NEWSLETTER ABOUT LIFE/WORK PLANNING. Oct. 1974-. 0738-9205. Periodical. US. English. ir. $10.00. National Career Development Project, PO Box 379, Walnut Creek CA 94596. Tel (415)935-1865. Ed Richard N Bolles.

OCCUPATIONAL BRIEF. VFOAT Chronicle Occupational Briefs. No. 1- 19. US. English. ir. $89.37. Chronicle Guidance Publications Inc, PO Box 271,

Occupations and Careers

Moravia NY 13118. Tel (315)497-0330. Ed Paul A Downes. Circ 12,000. Information on work performed, working conditions, hours and earnings, education and training, licenses, unions, entry methods, advancement, related occupations, and other sources of information. Coded by D.O.T., 4th edition.

OCCUPATIONAL DEVELOPMENTS MAGAZINE. V. 1- Summer 1979-. 0271-5589. Periodical. US. English. qt. Indiana Office of Occupational Development, 150 West Market Street/ 7th Floor, Indianapolis IN 46204. *Manpower Developments, 0271-5570.*

OCCUPATIONAL OPPORTUNITIES INFORMATION FOR WISCONSIN CEASED. 0512-6355. US. English. qt. Department of Industry Labor and Human Relations, Box 7944, Madison WI 53707. LC HD5725.W5. DD 331.12409775.

OCCUPATIONAL OUTLOOK AND DEVELOPMENT. Main/Corp Indiana. Employment Security Division. US. English. Research and Statistics Section, Indiana Employment Security Division, 10 North Senate Avenue, Indianapolis IN 46204. LC HD5725.I6. DD 331.1109772.

OCCUPATIONAL OUTLOOK FOR MANITOBA. 1981 Ed.-. 0710-8508. CN. English. an. LC HD5729.M3. DD 331.124097127. *Outlook of Job Opportunities by Major Occupational Group, 0710-8532.*

OCCUPATIONAL OUTLOOK HANDBOOK. Began with 1949 Ed. US. English. ir. Superintendent of Documents, Government Printing Office, Washington DC 20402. Tel (202)783-3238. NLM W1 OC588.

OCCUPATIONAL OUTLOOK INFORMATION REPORT, STATE OF ILLINOIS. 1974-1985-. US. English. be. LC HD5725.I3. DD 331.12409773.

OCCUPATIONAL OUTLOOK QUARTERLY. VFOAT O.O.Q., OOQ, Vol. 2, No. 3 (Sept. 1958)-. 0199-4786. Periodical. US. English. qt. Superintendent of Documents, US Government Printing Office, Washington DC 20402. Ind/Abst ABI/ Inform, Am. Stat. Index, Curr. Index J. Educ., Hospit. Lit. Index, Index U.S. Gov. Period., Mag. Index, Public Aff. Inf. Serv. Bull. LC HF5382.5 .U5. DD 331.120973. CODEN OOQUAK. *Occupational Outlook.*

OCCUPATIONAL PATTERNS OF SELECTED NONMANUFACTURING INDUSTRIES IN UTAH. Main/Corp Utah. Dept. of Employment Security. Research and Analysis Section. US. English. an. Utah Department of Employment Security, 174 Social Hall Avenue, Box 11249, Salt Lake City UT 84147. LC HD5725.U8. DD 331.12509792.

OCCUPATIONAL PENSION SCHEMES. Main/Corp Great Britain. Government Actuary. 1st- 1958-. UK. English. -/-/47. Her Majesty's Stationery Office, PO Box 276, London SW8 5DT England. LC HD7106.G8. DD 331.2520942.

THE OCCUPATIONAL PREFERENCES OF HIGH SCHOOL SENIORS IN TEN COUNTIES IN IDAHO. US. English. be. Idaho Department of Employment, Bureau of Research & Analysis, Boise ID. LC HF5382.5.U6. DD 331.7023.

OCCUPATIONAL PROFILES OF OREGON'S MANUFACTURING INDUSTRIES. Main/Corp Oregon. Employment Division. Research and Statistics Section. 1971-. 0147-1333. US. English. Oregon Department of Human Resources Development, 155 Cottage Street NE, Salem OR 97310. LC HD5725.O7. DD 3311109795.

OCCUPATIONAL PROFILES OF SELECTED NON-MANUFACTURING INDUSTRIES IN OREGON. Main/Corp Oregon. Employment Division. Research and Statistics Section. 1973-. 0148-2890. US. English. Oregon Department of Human Resources, Salem OR 97310. LC HD5725.O7. DD 331.1109795.

OCCUPATIONAL PROGRAMS IN CALIFORNIA PUBLIC COMMUNITY COLLEGES. 0731-8650. US. English. qt. Leo A Meyer Associates Inc, 23850 Clawiter Road, Hayward CA 94545. Tel (415)785-1091. Circ 1,600. Directory of occupational programs in California community colleges. Includes general information for each and indexes programs three ways.

OCCUPATIONAL PROJECTIONS AND TRAINING DATA. 0273-382X. US. English. Superintendent of Documents, US Government Printing Office, Washington DC 20402. LC HD5723. DD 331.120973.

OCCUPATIONAL STARTING WAGES IN THE STATE OF UTAH AND UTAH PLANNING DISTRICTS. US. English. Utah Department of Employment Security, 174 Social Hall Avenue, PO Box 11249, Salt Lake City UT 84147. LC HD4976.U8. DD 331.20792.

OCCUPATIONAL STRESS. V. 1- Jan. 1980-. 0143-7666. Periodical. UK. English. mo. $62.00. University of Sheffield, Biomedical Information Service, Sheffield S10 2TN England.

OCCUPATIONAL SUPPLY AND DEMAND. Began July 1978. US. English. an. Alaska Department of Labor, PO Box 1149, Juneau AK 99811. LC HD5725.A4. DD 331.1209798.

OCCUPATIONAL VACANCY SURVEY. Main/Corp New Zealand. Dept. of Labour (1954-). Research and Planning Division. English. ir. LC HD5850.4. DD 331.7009931.

OCCUPATIONAL WAGE INFORMATION IN MICHIGAN AND FLINT SMSA. See Statistics.

OCCUPATIONS OF FEDERAL BLUE-COLLAR WORKERS. Main/Corp United States. Civil Service Commission. Work Force Analysis and Statistics Division. VFOAT Federal Civilians Workforce Statistics. 1976. 0146-2490. Periodical. US. English. wk. $15.00. New York Construction News Inc, 1 East 42nd Street, New York NY 10017. *Occupations of Federal Blue-Collar Workers, 0146-2490.*

OCCUPATIONS OF FEDERAL WHITE-COLLAR AND BLUE-COLLAR WORKERS. Oct. 31, 1981-. 0739-1404. US. English. be. US Office of Personnel Management, Compliance and Investigations, Group Office of Workforce Information, 1900 E Street NW, Washington DC 20415. LC JK639, JK671. DD 353.001, 331.7950973. Volumes for 1981 distributed to depository libraries in microfiche. *Occupations of Federal White-Collar Workers, 0146-4906; Occupations of Federal Blue-Collar Workers, 0146-2490.*

THE OFFICIAL GUIDE TO MBA PROGRAMS, ADMISSIONS, & CAREERS. See Education (General) - Higher Education.

THE OFFICIAL GUIDE TO STEWARDESS AND STEWARD CAREERS. VFOAT Stewardess and Steward Careers. 13th Ed. (1980/81)-. US. English. an. $7.95. International Publishers, 665 LaVilla Drive, Miami Springs FL 33166. Tel (305)887-1701. Ed Veronica M Denis and Steven G Gulka. Directory of airlines, how to apply base locations, training schools, the interview, age and height requirements, how to use the guide. *Airline Guide to Stewardess and Steward Careers.*

THE OFFICIAL GUIDE TO TRAVEL AGENT & TRAVEL CAREERS. (THE OFFICIAL ... GUIDE TO TRAVEL AGENT & TRAVEL CAREERS). VFOAT Travel Agent and Travel Careers. 1st ed. (1980-1981)-. 8755-0458. US. English. be. $8.95. Passenger & Inflight Service, 655 Lavilla Drive, Miami Springs FL 33166. Tel (305)887-1701. Ed Veronica Dennis. DD 387. adv acc. Travel agent jobs, training and education, starting your own agency.

OOQ, OCCUPATIONAL OUTLOOK QUARTERLY. VFOAT Occupational Outlook Quarterly. V. 1- Feb. 1957-. 0029-7968. Periodical. US. English. ir. Superintendent of Documents, US Government Printing Office. Tel (202)783-3238. Ind/ Abst Public Aff. Inf. Serv. Bull., Index U.S. Gov. Period., Am. Stat. Index, Mag. Index. LC HF5382.5.U5. *Occupational Outlook Review.*

OPPORTUNITIES. Periodical. US. English. bm. $20.00. Natural Si for Youth Found, 763 Silvermine Road, New Canaan CT 06840. Tel (203)966-5643. Ed Mildred DeScherer. Circ 300. (ctrl). Employment opportunities available in natural science field-nature centers, museums, etc.

OPPORTUNITIES FOR GRADUATES. VFOAT Opportunities for Graduates in Southern Africa. SA. English (Afrikaans). ir. Management Development Publishers, PO Box 10061, Johannesburg South Africa 2000.

OPPORTUNITIES FOR MATRICULANTS AND SCHOOL LEAVERS. VFOAT Opportunities for Matriculants and School Leavers in Southern Africa. English. ir. MSL Publications, PO Box 47433, Parklands 2121 South Africa. Tel 0903-011-788 4605. adv acc. Circ 35,000. Aimed to act as a guide to matriculants and schoolleavers to further study their interests and requirements needed for positions that are available to them.

PCEC. PRIVATE CAREER EDUCATION COUNCIL. (P C E C). Main/ Corp Private Career Education Council. VFOAT Membership Directory of Private Career Schools, Ontario. VAT Private Career Education Council. Began publication in 197-. 0705-3126. CN. English. an. Free. Private Career Education Council, Suite 205/1530 Albion Road, Rexdale Ontario M9V 1B4 Canada. DD 374'.013'025713.

PLACEMENT NEWS. V. 1- Sept. 1980-. Periodical. US. English. ir. $15.00. Women's Caucus Religious Studies, 210 Herrick Road, Newton Centre MA 02159. Tel (617)625-2956. *Doctoral Placement Service.*

THE POLICE CAREER INFORMATION DIGEST. See Law Enforcement.

PRACE PSYCHOLOGICZNE. See Psychology.

PROCEEDINGS, ANNUAL CONFERENCE OF GUIDANCE PERSONNEL IN OCCUPATIONAL EDUCATION. Main/Corp Conference of Guidance Personnel in Occupational Education. 4th- 1970-. 0277-6332. US. English. ir. University of the State of New York, State Education Department, Bureau of Guidance, Albany NY 12224. LC HF5381.A1. DD 371.425.

PROFESSIONAL SCHOOLS FACTSHEETS. See Education (General) - Higher Education.

REPORT OF SOUTH DAKOTA'S PROFESSIONAL AND OCCUPATIONAL LICENSING BOARDS AND COMMISSIONS. See Public Administration.

REPORT ON SHORTAGE OCCUPATIONS. Main/Corp Himachal Pradesh, India. State Employment Market Information Unit. II. English. ir. State Employment Market Information Unit/Himachal Pradesh, Simla India. LC HD5820.H5. DD 331.126.

THE RHODES REPORT; CAREER OPPORTUNITIES IN EDUCATION. VFOAT Career Opportunities in Education. Began in 1965?. 0048-8224. Periodical. US. English. mo. $25.00. EFR Corporation, PO Box 649, Luray VA 22835. Tel (703)743-6861. Ed Eric F Rhodes. adv acc. Circ 1,000. Placement information and current positions available for public school and college administrators and teachers.

SITUATIONS WANTED; JOBS WANTED. 0739-2222. Periodical. US. English. sa. Center for Self Sufficiency, Box 7234, Houston TX 77248.

THE SOUTH AFRICAN CAREERS GUIDE. SA. English. ir. 2.00. Management Development Publishers, PO Box 10061, Johannesburg 2000 South Africa. LC HF5382.5.S6. DD 331.7020968.

SPOTLIGHT ON CAREER PLANNING, PLACEMENT AND RECRUITMENT. V. 1- Sept. 1978-. 0162-1068. Periodical. US. English. bm. College Placement Council, 62 Highland Avenue, Bethlehem PA 18017. Tel (215)868-1421.

SUCCESS (CHICAGO, ILL.). (SUCCESS). Vol. 28, No. 3 (Mar. 1981)-. 0745-2489. Periodical. US. English. mo. $24.00. Hal Publications, 342 Madison Avenue, New York NY 10173, (subscription address: Communication Data Services PO Box 4966 Des Moines IA 50340). Tel (303)442-4282. *Success Unlimited, 0039-4424.*

SUCCESSFUL WOMAN. See Women.

TODAY'S PROFESSIONALS. 0163-299X. Periodical. US. English. $12.00 Domestic, $14.00 Foreign. Todays Professionals Inc, 3030 West 6th Street, Los Angeles CA 90020.

Office Equipment & Services

UTAH JOB OUTLOOK FOR VOCATIONAL-TECHNICAL OCCUPATIONS, STATEWIDE AND PLANNING DISTRICTS. US. English. an. Utah Department of Employment Security, 174 Social Hall Avenue, PO Box 11249, Salt Lake City UT 84147. LC HD5725.U8. DD 331.1209792.

VICA. (VICA : OFFICIAL JOURNAL OF THE VOCATIONAL INDUSTRIAL CLUBS OF AMERICA). **VAT** Vocational Industrial Clubs of America. 1966. 0042-1839. Periodical. US. English. qt. Vocational Industrial Clubs of America, PO Box 3000, Leesburg VA 22075. **Tel** (703)777-8810. **Ed** Larry W Johnson. bk rev. adv acc. **Circ** 272,000. Articles deal with organization programs and projects, leadership, development how-to's, career interests achievements, and hobbies. Includes club and national news.

THE VOCATIONAL GUIDANCE QUARTERLY. V. 1- Autumn 1952-. 0042-7764. Periodical. US. English. qt. $14.00. American Association of Counseling Development, 5999 Stevenson Avenue, Alexandria VA 22304. **Tel** (703)823-9800. **Ed** David Jepsen. **Ind/Abst** Soc. Work Res. Abstr., Educ. Index, Psychol. Abstr., Sociol. Educ. Abstr., Curr. Index J. Educ., Soc. Sci. Citation Index, Abstr. Soc. Work. LC HF5381.A1. DD 373.24. CODEN VOGOAT. adv acc. **Circ** 2,028. (ctrl) Available on microfilm from University Microfilms. Articles on theory, research, and practical applications of career counseling.

WHAT COLOR IS YOUR PARACHUTE? 1971-. 8755-4658. Periodical. US. English. an. $8.95. Ten Speed Press, PO Box 7123, Berkeley CA 94705. **Tel** (415)845-8414. LC HF5382.7. DD 650.1405. The best selling career book ever. A practical manual for job-hunters and career changers.

WORK AND OCCUPATIONS. Vol. 9, No. 1 (Feb. 1982)-. 0730-8884. Periodical. US. English. qt. Sage Publications Inc, 275 South Beverly Drive, Beverly Hills CA 90212. **Tel** (213)274-8003. **Ind/Abst** Manage. Contents, Int. Labour Doc., Sociol. Abstr., ABI/Inform, Curr. Index J. Educ., Psychol. Abstr. LC HT675. DD 306.3605. *Sociology of Work and Occupations, 0093-9285.*

WORKPLACE EDUCATION. See Education (General) - Special Aspects of Education.

YOUR COMPUTER CAREER. Vol. 1, No. 1 (Sept. 1985)-. 0884-4615. Periodical. US. English. qt. $9.95 Domestic, $18.00 Foreign. Data Processing Management Association, 505 Busse Highway, Park Ridge IL 60068-3191. DD 004.

ZDRAVOTNICKA PRACOVNICE. Began with: Vol. 1, 1951. 0049-8572. Periodical. CS. Czech. mo. Artia, Ve Smeckach 30, PO Box 790, Praha 1 Czechoslovakia. NLM W1 ZD855.

OFFICE EQUIPMENT & SERVICES

ACM TRANSACTIONS ON OFFICE INFORMATION SYSTEMS. See Computers and Computer Science.

ADMINISTRATIVE DIGEST. V. 1- Nov. 1967-. 0001-835X. Periodical. CN. English. mo. Southam Communications Ltd, 1450 Don Mills Road, Don Mills Ontario M3B 1X2 Canada. **Tel** (403)260-3161. *Office Administration.*

AUTOMATED OFFICE SYSTEMS. (AUTOMATED OFFICE SYSTEMS : AOS). **VFOAT** AOS. Began with V. 1 in Jan. 1981. 0739-8743. Periodical. US. English. mo. $125.00. Office Systems Consulting Group Inc, PO Box 352, Cambridge MA 02134.

BLI REPORTS ON OFFICE PRODUCTS. US. English. bm. $525.00. Buyers Laboratory Inc, 20 Railroad Avenue, Hackensack NJ 07601. **Tel** (201)488-0404. **Ed** Burt Merrow. **Circ** 4,000. Issue evaluations of office equipment, furniture, software and supplies, based on tests.

THE BLUE BOOK. 1977-. 0148-9402. US. English. $19.95. PO Box 2315, Boca Raton FL 33432. LC HD9999.O43. DD 381.45651202573.

BRAND RECOGNITION STUDY. OFFICE EQUIPMENT & METHODS. (BRAND RECOGNITION STUDY : OFFICE EQUIPMENT & METHODS). **Main/Corp** MacLean-Hunter Research Bureau. **VFOAT** Recognition Study. No. 8- 1975-. 0380-9463. Periodical. CN. English. be. MacLean-Hunter, PO Box 100 Station A, Toronto Ontario M5W 1A7 Canada. DD 658.83865120971. *Recognition Study: Office Equipment, 0316-9340.*

BUROMASCHINEN TECHNIK. **VFOAT** Buromaschinen-Technik. 0302-0991. Periodical. German. ir. 69.50. Schwab-Intercontact, Postfach 1448, 6702 Bad Durckheim West Germany. LC HF5548. *Buromaschinen Mechaniker.*

BUSINESS SYSTEMS UPDATE. See Computers and Computer Science.

CANADIAN OFFICE. See Business - General Management.

CANADIAN OFFICE PRODUCTS & STATIONERY. V. 1- Sept./Oct. 1967-. 0008-462X. Periodical. CN. English. bm. Southam Communications Ltd, 1450 Don Mills Road, Don Mills Ont M3B 1X2 Canada. **Tel** (416)445-6641.

CENTURY 21 REPORTER. Periodical. US. English. ir. South-Western Publishing Co, 5101 Madison Road, College University Department, Cincinnati OH 45227. *Typewriting News.*

COMMUNIQUE - NATIONAL BOARD. ASSOCIATION OF ADMINISTRATIVE ASSISTANTS. (COMMUNIQUE). Vol. 20, No. 3 (Spring 1977)-. 0384-9066. Periodical. CN. English. Association of Administrative Assistants, Box 5107 Station A, Toronto Ontario M5W 1N4 Canada. DD 651.3. *Communique, 0380-4895.*

COMPUTERS AND OFFICE AND ACCOUNTING MACHINES. (CURRENT INDUSTRIAL REPORTS. MA-35R, COMPUTERS AND OFFICE AND ACCOUNTING MACHINES). Began with 1978. 0744-0170. US. English. an. $1.25. Data User Services Division Customer Services Publication, Bureau of the Census, Washington DC 20233. **Tel** (301)763-4100. LC HD9801.U54. DD 380.145621381950973. Presents timely data on the production, inventories, and orders of approximately 5,000 products, which represents 40 percent of all US manufacturing. *Office, Computing, and Accounting Machines.*

CURRENT INDUSTRIAL REPORTS. MA-26B, SELECTED OFFICE SUPPLIES AND ACCESSORIES. **VFOAT** Selected Office Supplies and Accessories. 1981-. US. English. an. $1.00. Data User Services Division, Customer Services Publication, Bureau of the Census, Washington DC 20233. **Tel** (301)763-4100. LC HD9800.U5. DD 381.456816. Presents timely data on the production, inventories, and orders of approximately 5,000 products, which represents 40 percent of all US manufacturing.

CURRENT INDUSTRIAL REPORTS. MA-27A, BUSINESS FORMS, BINDERS, CARBON PAPER, AND INKED RIBBONS. See Business.

DATAPRO OFFICE COPIER NEWS. **VFOAT** Office Copier News. 0730-7438. Periodical. US. English. mo. $119.60. Datapro Research Corp, 1805 Underwood Boulevard, Delran NJ 08075. **Tel** (609)764-0100.

DATAPRO REPORTS ON COPIERS & DUPLICATORS. **VFOAT** Copiers & Duplicators. 0730-8825. Periodical. US. English. mo. $660.16. Datapro Research Corp, 1805 Underwood Boulevard, Delran NJ 08075. **Tel** (609)764-0100.

DATAPRO REPORTS ON OFFICE SYSTEMS. See Computers and Computer Science.

FACILITY MANAGEMENT ISSUES. Vol. 1, No. 1 (July 1984)-. 0748-0652. Periodical. US. English. qt. Facility Management Institute, 3971 South Research Park Drive, Ann Arbor MI 48104. DD 651.

GEYERS DEALER TOPICS CEASED. Began with V. 117-, Jan. 1955. Ceased in 1983. 0016-948X. Periodical. US. English. mo. $14.00. Geyer-McAllister Publications, 51 Madison Avenue, New York NY 10010. **Ind/Abst** Predicasts. CODEN GYDTA2. *Geyer's Topics.*

GEYER'S OFFICE DEALER. **VFOAT** Office Dealer. Vol. 149, No. 1 (Jan. 1984)-. 8336-8997. Periodical. US. English. mo. $16.00. Geyer's Office Dealer, Box 1129, Dover NJ 07801. **Ind/Abst** Predicasts. LC TS1228. DD 680. *Geyers Dealer Topics, 0016-948X.*

IBM SYSTEMS JOURNAL. See Computers and Computer Science.

INFORMATION & RECORDS MANAGEMENT CEASED. **VFOAT** IRM, I.R.M. Began with V. 8, No. 1 Dec. 1. 1973/Jan. 1974. Ceased with V. 16, No. 12 Dec. 1982. 0019-9966. Periodical. US. English. mo. $10.00. Information and Records Management Inc, 250 Fulton Avenue, Hempstead NY 11550. **Ind/Abst** Predicasts, Abstr. Bull. Inst. Paper Chem., Libr. Inf. Sci. Abstr. LC HF5736. DD 651.505. NLM W1 I2696. Also available on microfilm from University Microfilms International. *Information and Records Management, 0019-9966.*

INFORMATION INDUSTRY REVIEW. See Computers and Computer Science.

INFORMATION MEDIA & TECHNOLOGY : THE JOURNAL OF NRCD. See Library and Information Science.

INFOSYSTEMS. V. 19, No. 7- July 1972-. 0364-5533. Periodical. US. English. mo. Hitchcock Publication Company, Hitchcock Building, Wheaton IL 60188. **Tel** (312)665-1000. **Ind/Abst** ABI/Inform, Bus. Period. Index, Predicasts, Comput. Control Abstr., Electr. Electron. Abstr., Electron. Pub. Abstr., Sci. Abstr. Sect. A. Phys. Abstr., Public Aff. Inf. Serv. Bull., Account. Index. Suppl., Comput. Rev., Funk Scott Index Corp. Ind., Phys. Abstr. LC HF5548.2. DD 658.05405. CODEN IFSYAF. *Business Automation, 0007-6546.*

INVENTORY OF AUTOMATIC DATA PROCESSING EQUIPMENT IN THE FEDERAL GOVERNMENT. 1961-. 0565-0798. Periodical. US. English. ir. Superintendent of Documents, US Government Printing Office, Washington DC 20402. LC JK468.A8. DD 651.

ISS MATCHBOOK. **VFOAT** ISS Matchbook. Vol. 1 (1983)-. 0738-3819. English. ir. LC HF5548. DD 681.

JAPANESE BUSINESS MACHINES. **Main/Corp** Nihon Jimu Kikai Kogyokai. JA. English. ir. Kikai Shinko Building 21-1-5, Shiba-Koen Minato-Ku, Tokyo 105 Japan. LC HF5548. DD 338.47681.

KAVIM. Hebrew. ir. LC HF5548.

KOMPYUTOPIA. See Computers and Computer Science.

LETTERHEADS. 1- 1977-. US. English. an. Letterheads, PO Box 591, Ashland KY 41101. LC HF5733.L4. DD 651.75.

MANAGEMENT WORLD. See Business - General Management.

MINNELLA'S POCKET-GUIDE TO COPIERS. **VFOAT** Minnella's Pocket Guide to Copiers, Pocket Guide to Copiers. 0883-4377. US. English. be. Minnella Enterprises, PO Box 137, Little Falls NJ 07424. LC HF5548. DD 681.650294.

MODERN OFFICE TECHNOLOGY. Vol. 28, No. 10 (Oct. 1983)-. 0746-3839. Periodical. US. English. mo. $30.00 Domestic, $50.00 Foreign. Penton/IPC, 1111 Chester Avenue, Cleveland OH 44114. **Ind/Abst** Manage. Contents, Trade Ind. Index, Mag. Index, ABI/Inform, Comput. Control Abstr., Consum. Index Prod. Eval. Inf. Source, Electr. Electron. Abstr., Sci. Abstr. Sect. A. Phys. Abstr., Electron. Pub. Abstr., Bus. Period. Index. LC HF5547.A2. DD 651.05. CODEN MDOPAW. *Modern Office Procedures, 0026-8208.*

NOPA DEALER OPERATING RESULTS. **VFOAT** N.O.P.A. Dealer Operating Results. US. English. an. NOPA, 301 North Fairfax Street, Alexandria VA 22314. LC HD9800.U5. DD 381.4568.

NOPA MANUFACTURER SELLING COSTS SURVEY. **VFOAT** N.O.P.A. Manufacutrer Selling Costs Survey. **VAT** National Office Products Association Manufacturer Selling Costs Survey. 1975-. 0741-3238. US. English. an. National Office Products Association, 301 North Fairfax Street, Alexandria VA 22314. **Tel** (703)549-9040. LC HF5439.O4. DD 338.4368. A survey on six classifications of selling costs, subdivided into seven sales volume categories, supplies and furniture product lines.

NORTH AMERICAN COPIER CATALOG. **VFOAT** Copier Catalog. Issue 1 (Summer-Fall 1984)-. 8755-1071. Periodical. US. English. sa. $59.90. Info-Market, Box 25166, Rochester NY 14625. LC HF5548. DD 686.44.

Optometry

OA JOHO. VFOAT O.A. Joho, Office Automation Info. Periodical. JA. Japanese. qt. 1800 Each Issue. Denpa Shinbunsha, 11-15 Higashi Gotanda 1 Shinagawa-ku, Tokyo-to Japan. LC HF5548.125.

OE&M. OFFICE EQUIPMENT & METHODS. (O E & M, OFFICE EQUIPMENT & METHODS). VAT OE&M. Office Equipment and Methods (1979), Office Equipment & Methods (1979). V. 25- Jan./Feb. 1979-. 0709-5228. Periodical. CN. English. ir. $30.18. MacLean Hunter, PO Box 100 Station A, Toronto Ontario M5W 1A7 Canada. DD 651.05. *Office Equipment & Methods, 0030-0179.*

OEP : OFFICE EQUIPMENT & PRODUCTS. VFOAT Office Equipment & Products. Periodical. US. English. mo. $158.00. Dempa Publications, 400 Madison Avenue, New York NY 10017. Tel (212)752-3003. Ed Tetsuo Hirayama. Ind/Abst ABI/Inform, Comput. Control Abstr., Electr. Electron. Abstr., Sci. Abstr. Sect. A. Phys. Abstr. CODEN OEPRA4. adv acc. Circ 82,500. Report on new products, market trends and industry issues relating to office and work place automation.

THE OFFICE. Began in 1936. 0030-0128. Periodical. US. English. mo. $30.00. Office Publications Incorporated, PO Box 1231, Stamford CT 06904. Tel (203)327-9670. Ed William R Schulhof. Ind/Abst ABI/Inform, Comput. Control Abstr., Electr. Electron. Abstr., Sci. Abstr. Sect. A. Phys. Abstr., Consum. Index Prod. Eval. Inf. Source, Electron. Pub. Abstr., Bus. Period. Index, Phys. Abstr. LC HF5001. DD 651.205. CODEN OFISAD. bk rev. adv acc. Circ 160,000. Magazine for the office, administrative, EDP, MIS, systems, executives. Extensive editorial coverage of office related subjects. Introduces over 1,000 new products annually. *Office Economics.*

OFFICE ADMINISTRATION AND AUTOMATION. See Business - General Management.

OFFICE AND STORE MACHINERY MANUFACTURERS. VFOAT Fabricants de Machines pour le Bureau et le Commerce. 1970-. 0527-589X. CN. English (text in French, 1968-). an. 20.00 Domestic, 21.00 Foreign. Receiver General for Canada, Statistics Canada Publications, Ottawa Ontario K1A 0T6 Canada. Tel (800)268-1151.

OFFICE AUTOMATION. 1955-. 0472-6049. Periodical. US. English. Larry Lawier, Administrative Management, 1123 Broadway, Suite 1107, New York NY 10010. Tel (212)924-8989. Ed Don Johnson. LC HF5548. DD 651.26. bk rev. adv acc. Circ 300,000. (ctrl). The administration, management and automation of offices and businesses.

OFFICE AUTOMATION CONFERENCE DIGEST. See Computers and Computer Science.

OFFICE AUTOMATION NEWS. (OFFICE AUTOMATION NEWS : THE PUBLICATION OF THE OFFICE AUTOMATION SOCIETY INTERNATIONAL). 0882-0198. Periodical. US. English. qt. $30.00 Each Publication. Office Automation Society International, 2108-C Gallows Road, Vienna VA 22180. DD 001.

THE OFFICE AUTOMATION REPORT. Vol. 28, No. 1 (Jan. 1, 1985)-. 0886-6767. Periodical. US. English. sm. The Automated Office Ltd, 1123 Broadway, New York NY 10010. DD 651. *Information & Word Processing Report, 0276-587X.*

OFFICE AUTOMATION REPORTING SERVICE. VFOAT Office Automation. Began with issue for Dec. 1979?. 0742-6453. Periodical. US. English. mo. $395.00. International Data Corporation, 5 Speen Street, PO Box 955, Framingham MA 01701. Tel (617)872-8200. Covers office automation technology markets for executives. Includes industry analysis, market trends and case histories.

OFFICE CONNECTIONS. Apr./May 1983-. 0824-4073. Periodical. CN. English. bm. Paul Talbot & Associates, PO Box 2275, Vancouver British Columbia V6B 3W5 Canada. DD 650.1305. *PTA Report, 0822-4234.*

OFFICE DATA NETWORKS REPORT. Vol. 1, No. 1 (Sept. 28, 1984)-. 8755-349X. Periodical. US. English. bw. $377.00. RND Ventures Division, Capitol Publications, Suite 1600/1300 North 17th Street, Arlington VA 22209. DD 651.

OFFICE EQUIPMENT AND SUPPLIES MARKET IN CANADA. (THE OFFICE EQUIPMENT AND SUPPLIES MARKET IN CANADA). VFOAT The Office Equipment & Supplies Market in Canada. VAT Market and Media Report. The Office and Equipment and Supplies Market in Canada. 1977/78-. 0705-5153. CN. English. an. $40.00.

MacLean-Hunter Research Bureau, 481 University Avenue, Toronto Ontario M5W 1A7 Canada. DD 381.456512. *Office Equipment Market in Canada, 0315-9787.*

OFFICE FURNITURE. (CURRENT INDUSTRIAL REPORTS. MA-25H, OFFICE FURNITURE). Began with 1976. 0732-8400. US. English. an. $1.25. Data User Services Division, Customer Services Publication, Bureau of the Census, Washington DC 20233. Tel (301)763-4100. LC HD9803.U6. DD 380.1456841. Presents timely data on the production, inventories, and orders of approximately 5,000 products, which represents 40 percent of all US manufacturing. *Current Industrial Reports. MA-25H, Manufacturers' Shipments of Office Furniture.*

OFFICE GUIDE TO ORLANDO. Vol. 1, No. 1 (Spring 1982)-. 0733-1266. Periodical. US. English. qt. $30.00. Zinc Publishing Inc, 1009 Maitland Center Common 206, Maitland FL 32751-7205. Tel (305)660-5775. Ed Carey A Jasa. adv acc. Circ 12,093. (ctrl). A complete guide to office space, products and services for the greater Orlando area.

THE OFFICE PRODUCTS ANALYST. (THE OFFICE PRODUCTS ANALYST : OPA). VFOAT OPA. Vol. 1, No.1 (Feb. 1977)-. 0197-4602. Periodical. US. English. mo. $220.00. Office Products Analyst, 150 Broadway/Suite 1606, New York NY 10038. Tel (212)406-5200. Ed Robert S Anderson. LC HF5548. DD 680. Circ 1,000. Unbiased source of analysis for users of office equipment such as copier duplicators, mini-computer office systems, electronic typewriters, PBX, cans, and facsimile equipment.

OFFICE PRODUCTS DEALER. V. 107, No. 10- Oct. 1979-. 0199-1329. Periodical. US. English. mo. Hitchcock Publication Company, Hitchcock Building, Wheaton IL 60188. Tel (312)665-1000. LC HF5541.T9. DD 684.100688. *Office Products, 0030-0144.*

OFFICE PRODUCTS, MASTER CATALOG & BUYING GUIDE. VAT Office Products, Master Catalog and Buying Guide. 0163-9935. US. English. mo. $47.55. Reliable Information Publishing Company, PO Box 52, 6354 Vitznau Switzerland. LC HF5548. DD 381.456512002573.

OFFICE SYSTEMS. (OFFICE SYSTEMS : THE MAGAZINE FOR SMALL AND MEDIUM OFFICES). Vol. 1, No. 1 (July-Aug. 1984)-. 8750-3441. Periodical. US. English. mo. $36.00. Office Systems Magazine Corporation, PO Box 150, Georgetown CT 06829. Tel (203)544-9526. Ed William M Hogan. DD 651. bk rev. adv acc. Circ 95,000. (ctrl). Serves the small and midsize office industry for those with 50-500 employees.

OFFICE TECHNOLOGY MANAGEMENT. VFOAT Office Technology. Vol. 1, No. 1 (June 1982)-. 0733-5164. Periodical. US. English. mo. $59.00. Office Technology Management, 10076 Boca Entrada Boulevard, Boca Raton FL 33433.

OFFICE TOPICS. 0746-5122. Periodical. US. English. bw. $55.00. Economics Press Inc, 12 Daniel Road, Fairfield NJ 07004. Tel (201)227-1224. Ed Bob Guder. Circ 18,500. (ctrl). Booklets that improve job performance of office support staff.

OFFICE WORLD NEWS. VFOAT Office World News Own. 0164-5951. Periodical. US. English. mo. $28.00. Office World News, 645 Stewart Avenue, Garden City NY 11530. Ind/Abst Predicasts, Funk Scott Index Corp. Ind.

OFFICEMATION PRODUCT REPORTS. 1977. 0733-2564. Periodical. US. English. mo. Management Information Corporation, 140 Barclay Center, Cherry Hill NJ 08034. Tel (608)428-1020. Ed David Peterson. bk rev. Objective evaluations of office automation products. *Officemation Reports, 0161-8768.*

THE OPTICAL MEMORY REPORT. See Computers and Computer Science.

PACIFIC STATIONER AND OFFICE OUTFITTER. 0191-8389. Periodical. US. English. mo. Allen-Pacific Publications, 41 Sutter Street, San Francisco CA 94104. Tel (415)986-4323.

PLATFORM. (PLATFORM, THE FORMS MANAGEMENT QUARTERLY). Vol. 1, No. 1 (Oct. 1982)-. 0714-3567. Periodical. CN. English. qt. Canadian Association for Business Forms Management, PO Box 5338 Station A, Toronto

Ontario M5W 1N6 Canada. DD 651.2905. *Platform (Toronto, Ont.).*

PURCHASING PREFERENCE SURVEY. OFFICE EQUIPMENT & SUPPLIES. See Business - Purchasing.

REPERTOIRE DES ENTREPRISES CANADIENNES DE SERVICES INFORMATIQUES. See Computers and Computer Science.

SECRETARIAL SERVICES TODAY. Vol. 1, No. 1 (Dec. 1984)-. 8755-4038. Periodical. US. English. mo. $18.00. Secretarial Services Today, PO Box 29203, Shreveport LA 71149-9203. DD 651.

SERVICES. (SERVICES : THE MAGAZINE OF THE BUILDING SERVICE CONTRACTORS ASSOCIATION INTERNATIONAL). Vol. 1, No. 1 (Jan. 1981)-. 0279-0548. Periodical. US. English. mo. $30.00 Domestic, $60.00 Foreign. Building Service Contractors Association International, 8315 Lee Highway/Suite 301, Fairfax VA 22031. Tel (703)698-8810. Ed Robert E Simanski. LC TX955. DD 648.05. adv acc. Circ 11,500. (ctrl). Management and technical articles for providers and purchasers of contract cleaning services such as office cleaning, carpet and floor care, window cleaning, and exterior maintenance.

THE SIZZLE SHEET. See Business - Marketing.

SMALL SYSTEMS WORLD. See Computers and Computer Science.

SOUTHERN OFFICE. 0584-455X. Periodical. US. English. mo. Market/Show Publications, St 701 Mony Building, 1655 Peachtree, Atlanta GA 30309. LC HF5548. DD 658.809651200973.

SOUTHERN STATIONER AND OFFICE OUFITTER. 0038-4593. Periodical. US. English. mo. Ernest H Abernathy Publishing Company, 75 3rd Street NW, Atlanta GA 30308.

SPECCHECK (SAN JOSE, CALIF.). (SPECCHECK). Vol. 1, No. 1 (Aug. 1985)-. Periodical. US. English. sa. $46.90. LC HF5548. DD 681.65.

STATE OF THE ART REVIEWS. OFFICE PROCEDURES. VFOAT Office Procedures. Vol. 1, No. 1 (Jan.-Mar. 1986)-. 0885-1131. Periodical. US. English. qt. $48.00 Domestic, $68.00 Foreign. Hanley & Belfus Inc, 210 South 13th Street, Philadelphia PA 19107. DD 651.

TODAY'S OFFICE (GARDEN CITY, N.Y.). (TODAY'S OFFICE). 0744-2815. Periodical. US. English. mo. $30.00. Hearst Business Communications, 645 Stewart Avenue, Garden City NY 11530. Tel (516)222-2500. Ind/Abst Predicasts, ABI/Inform. LC HF5547.A2. DD 651.305. *Office Products News, 0030-0241.*

VENDING MACHINE OPERATORS. VFOAT Exploitants de Distributeurs Automatiques. 1970-. 0527-6411. Periodical. CN. English (French, 1967-). ir. Receiver General for Canada, Statistics Canada Publications, Ottawa Ontario K1A 0T6 Canada.

WAPURO NENKAN. JA. Japanese. an. 2000. Shin Kigensha 1-9 Shinjuku 4 Shinjuku-ku, Tokyo-to 160 Japan. LC Z52.4.

WILEY SEARCH UPDATE USER NETWORK. See Computers and Computer Science.

WILEY WORD PROCESSING SERIES. 0277-268X. Monographic Series. US. English. ir. John Wiley & Sons, 605 Third Avenue, New York NY 10158.

WORD PROCESSING. 0196-8114. Periodical. US. English. Office Products Division, International Business Machines Corp, 400 Parson's Pond Drive, Franklin Lakes NJ 07417.

WORDS. See Computers and Computer Science.

THE WORLD'S FAIR. No. 1- 1904-. Periodical. UK. English. wk. Worlds Fair Ltd, PO Box 52, 2 Daltry St Shaw Road, Oldham Lancs OL1 4BB England.

OPTOMETRY

20/20. VFOAT Twenty/Twenty. 0192-1304. Periodical. US. English. mo. $15.00. Jobson Publishing Company, 325 Park Avenue South, New

Optometry

York NY 10010. **Tel** (212)685-4848. **Ed** Jody Stone. **adv acc**. **Circ** 34,000. (ctrl) Eyecare products and marketing trends for optical retailers.

THE AMERICAN JOURNAL OF OPTOMETRIC MEDICINE. Vol. 1, No. 1 (Mar. 1981)-. Periodical. US. English. qt. $20.00. American College of Optometric Physicians, P O Box 41774, Memphis TN 38104. **Tel** (901)725-5569.

AMERICAN JOURNAL OF OPTOMETRY AND PHYSIOLOGICAL OPTICS. V. 51, No. 1- Jan. 1974-. 0093-7002. Periodical. US. English. mo. $65.00. Williams & Wilkins, 428 East Preston Street, Baltimore MD 21202. **Tel** (301)528-4000. **Ed** W M Lyle. **Ind/Abst** Excerpta Med., Life Sci. Collect., Index Med., Int. Aerosp. Abstr., CIS Abstr., Biol. Abstr., Energy Res. Abstr., Comput. Control Abstr., Electr. Electron. Abstr., Sci. Abstr. Sect. A. Phys. Abstr., Phys. Abstr., Hospit. Lit. Index. **LC** RE1. **DD** 617.7505. **NLM** W1 AM497G. **CODEN** AOPOCF. adv acc. **Circ** 3,950. Articles, document research and clinical findings in optometry, plus case reports and instrument and technique reviews. *American Journal of Optometry and Archives of American Academy of Optometry, 0002-9408.*

AMERICAN OPTOMETRIC ASSOCIATION NEWS. V. 11- Jan. 1972-. 0094-9620. Periodical. US. English. sm. $7.00. American Optometric Association, 243 North Lindbergh, St Louis MO 63141. **Tel** (314)991-4100. **Ed** Suzy Farren. **NLM** W1 AM67H. adv acc. **Circ** 25,000. General news of interest to all optometrists, including feature stories, legislation, etc. *AOA News, 0095-0440.*

ARCHIVOS DE LA SOCIEDAD AMERICANA DE OFTALMOLOGIA Y OPTOMETRIA. *See* Genealogy and Heraldry - Archives.

ARKANSAS HEALTH MANPOWER STATISTICS. OPTOMETRISTS. *See* Statistics.

AUGENOPTIK. 0004-7910. Periodical. SZ. German. bm. Kunst & Wissen Erich Bieber, Dufourstrasse 51, CH-8008 Zurich, Switzerland. **Tel** 01/69 44 20. **NLM** W1 AU206P.

DER AUGENOPTIKER. *See* Medicine - Ophthalmology.

THE AUSTRALIAN JOURNAL OF OPTOMETRY. V. 42, No. 4/5- Apr./May 1959-. 0045-0642. Periodical. AT. English. bm. $29.52. Australian Journal of Optometry, 204 Drummond Street, Carlton Victoria 3053 Australia. **Tel** 03 347 0833. **Ed** A W Johnston. bk rev. adv acc. **Circ** 1,500. Scientific and clinical research into optometry. *Australasian Journal of Optometry.*

THE BLUE BOOK OF OPTOMETRISTS. 1- 1912-. US. English. be. **LC** RE940.

BRITISH JOURNAL OF PHYSIOLOGICAL OPTICS CEASED. Began with New Ser., V. 7. Ceased with V. 34, 1980. 0007-1218. Periodical. UK. English. qt. **Ind/Abst** Excerpta Med., Int. Aerosp. Abstr., Biol. Abstr., Index Med. **NLM** W1 BR603D. **CODEN** BJPOAN. *Dioptric Review and the British Journal of Physiological Optics.*

CALIFORNIA OPTOMETRY. V. 6- 1980-. 0273-804X. Periodical. US. English. mo. $20.00. California Optometric Association, 921 11th Street, PO Box 2591, Sacramento CA 95812. **Tel** (916)441-3990. **NLM** W1 CA403CA. *California Optometrist.*

CANADIAN JOURNAL OF OPTOMETRY. VFOAT Revue Canadienne d'Optometrie. Began with May 1939 issue. 0045-5075. Periodical. CN. English. qt. $18.58. Editorial & Publication Office, 77 Metcalfe Street/Suite 207, Ottawa Ont K1P 5L6 Canada. **Tel** (613)238-2006. **Ed** G Maurice Belanger. **NLM** W1 CA598C. bk rev. adv acc. **Circ** 3,000. (ctrl) Official in-house publication of the Canadian Association of Optometrists: original research, book reviews, association and professional historical news.

CANADIAN OPTICIAN. VFOAT Canadian Optician Magazine. 0826-5623. Periodical. CN. English. Free. Canadian Optician, Suite 1406/ 100 Adelaide Street West, Toronto Ontario M5H 1S3 Canada. **DD** 617.75205. (ctrl). *Ontario Optician, 0710-5533.*

CHILTON'S REVIEW OF OPTOMETRY. VFOAT Review of Optometry, OJRO. V. 114, No. 5- May 1977-. 0147-7633. Periodical. US. English. mo.

Chilton Company, PO Box 1412, Riverton NJ 08077. **Tel** (215)964-4370. **Ed** Richard L Guerrein. **LC** RE1. **DD** 617.75. **NLM** W1 CH739. adv acc. **Circ** 26,050. Serves the practice and patient care needs of optometrists, vision care professionals who are the major dispensers of ophthalmic materials. *Optical Journal and Review of Optometry, 0030-3925.*

CONTACT AND INTRAOCULAR LENS MEDICAL JOURNAL CEASED. V. 1-8, No. 4. 0360-1358. Periodical. US. English. qt. $18.00. Jack Hartstein MD, Editor in Chief, MD Medical Center, 8631 Delmar Boulevard, St Louis MO 63124. **Ind/Abst** Excerpta Med. **LC** RE977.C6. **DD** 617.752305. **NLM** W1 CO764. **CODEN** CILJD. *Contact Lens Medical Bulletin, 0010-728X.*

CONTACT LENS SPECTRUM. 0885-9175. Periodical. US. English. mo. $24.00. Viscom Publications Inc, 50 Washington Street, Norwalk CT 06854.

DIE CONTACT-LINSE. Began with 1, 1967. Periodical. GW. German. ir. 86.40. Verlag Willy Schrickel GMBH, Ernest Mey St 8 Pstfch 10 02 52, 7022 Leinfelden West Germany. **Tel** 0711/7594-0. **Ed** Konrad Kohlhammer. bk rev. adv acc. **Circ** 3,200. Journal for the contact lens specialist.

CONTACTOLOGIA-BUCHEREI. VFOAT Contactologia Bucherei. V. 1-. 0724-6226. German. ir. **Ed** Wulf Ehrich and Robert Heitz. **NLM** W1.

DIRECTORY OF THE AMERICAN OPTOMETRIC ASSOCIATION. *See* Yearbooks, Almanacs, Directories.

DIE FACHVORTRAGE DES WVAO-JAHRESKONGRESSES. **Main/Corp** Wissenschaftliche Vereinigung fur Augenoptik und Optometrie (Ger.). 1977-. German. an. Wissenschaftliche Vereinigung fur Augenoptik und Optometrie Mainz, Adam-Karrillon-Strasse 32, Mainz West Germany. **Tel** (06131)613061. **LC** RE951. adv acc. **Circ** 10,000. The essays of the annual congresses. *Eroffnungsvortrage des Wvao-Jahreskongresses.*

INDEX OF CANADIAN OPTOMETRISTS CEASED. VFOAT Repertoire de l'Optometrie du Canada. 1977-1982. 0703-9379. CN. English (text in French). Index of Canadian Optometrists 210 Gladstone Avenue/Suite 2001, Ottawa Ontario K2P 0Y6 Canada. **DD** 617.7506271.

INSIGHT (ARMONK, N.Y.). (INSIGHT). Began with Jan. 1985 issue. 0883-9026. Periodical. US. English. mo. $40.00 Domestic, $50.00 Canada. Advisory Enterprises Inc, Circulation Offices, 880 Main Street, Stamford CT 06902. *Optical Management, 0090-0834; Eye Talk 0164-3487.*

INTERNATIONAL CONTACT LENS CLINIC CEASED. V. 1- Spring 1974-. 0094-1840. Periodical. US. English. qt. Professional Press Inc, 5615 West Cermak Road, Cicero IL 60560. **Tel** (212)741-4000. **LC** RE977.C6. **DD** 617.752305. **NLM** W1 IN736L. Merged with Optometric Monthly to form International Eyecare.

JOURNAL - AMERICAN OPTOMETRIC ASSOCIATION. **Main/Corp** American Optometric Association. 2- 1930-. Periodical. US. English. mo. American Optometric Association, 243 North Lindbergh, St Louis MO 63141. **Tel** (314)991-4100. **Ed** Milton J Eger. (cum index). bk rev. adv acc. **Circ** 25,000. (ctrl). Technical articles of interest to optometrists, etc. *A.O.A. Organizer.*

JOURNAL OF OPTOMETRIC EDUCATION. V. 1- Winter 1975-. 0098-6917. Periodical. US. English. qt. $15.00. Association of Schools and Colleges of Optometry, 600 Maryland Avenue SW/Suite 410, Washington DC 20024. **Tel** (202)484-9406. **Ed** John Potter. **Ind/Abst** Curr. Index J. Educ. **LC** RE956. **DD** 617.750711. **NLM** W1 JO803RH. bk rev. adv acc. **Circ** 3,000. Publishes reports, papers and other material relative to optometric education.

JOURNAL OF OPTOMETRIC VISION DEVELOPMENT. V. 7, No. 3- Sept 1976-. 0149-886X. Periodical. US. English. qt. $25.00. C O V P Publications, PO Box 373, Worthington MN 56187. **Ed** Martin Kane. **NLM** W1 JO803RN. bk rev. adv acc. **Circ** 1,000. *Journal of Optometric Vision Therapy, 0149-8940.*

JOURNAL OF THE AMERICAN OPTOMETRIC ASSOCIATION. **Main/Corp** American Optometric Association. Began in 1929. 0003-0244. Periodical. US. English. mo. American Optometric Association, 243 North Lindbergh, St Louis MO 63141. **Ind/Abst** Excerpta Med., Index Med., Biol. Abstr., Chem. Abstr., Psychol. Abstr., Energy Res. Abstr., Cumul. Index Nurs. Allied Health Lit. **LC** RE1. **DD** 617.706273. **NLM** W1 JO909Y. **CODEN** JAOPBD. Part of title on microfilm.

JOURNAL OF THE ILLINOIS OPTOMETRIC ASSOCIATION. 0279-6422. Periodical. US. English. bm. Illinois Optometric Association, 1301 West 22nd Street/Suite 308, Oak Brook IL 60521. **Tel** (312)325-8012. **NLM** W1 JO93E.

JOURNAL OF THE INDIAN OPTOMETRIC ASSOCIATION. (THE JOURNAL OF THE INDIAN OPTOMETRIC ASSOCIATION). June 1969-. 0378-8164. Periodical. English. sa. **NLM** W1 JO931D. *Indian Journal of Optometry.*

MICROGRAPHICS AND OPTICAL STORAGE EQUIPMENT REVIEW. 0882-3294. US. English. an. Meckler Publishing, 11 Ferry Lane West, Westport CT 06880. *Micrographics Equipment Review, 0362-1006.*

NEBRASKA HEALTH MANPOWER REPORTS. OPTOMETRISTS. (NEBRASKA HEALTH MANPOWER REPORTS : OPTOMETRISTS). **Main/Corp** Nebraska. Division of Health Data and Statistical Research. 0149-9599. US. English. 301 Centinnial Mall South, PO Box 95007, Lincoln NE 68509. **LC** RE943.N2. **DD** 331.11.

NEW ENGLAND JOURNAL OF OPTOMETRY. 0028-4807. Periodical. US. English. mo. $5.00. New England Council of Optometrists, 101 Tremont Street/Suite 614, Boston MA 02108.

NEW YORK STATE OPTOMETRY. 0199-5731. Periodical. US. English. qt. $8.00. New York State Optometric Association, 90 South Swan Street, Albany NY 12210. **NLM** W1 NE894Q. *New York State Journal of Optometry, 0361-932X.*

NEWSLETTER - OPTOMETRIC HISTORICAL SOCIETY. **Main/Corp** Optometric Historical Society. V. 1- Jan. 1970-. Periodical. US. English. qt. Optometric Historical Society, 243 North Lindbergh Boulevard, St Louis MO 63141. **LC** RE951. **DD** 617.7509.

OPHTHALMIC & PHYSIOLOGICAL OPTICS. (OPHTHALMIC & PHYSIOLOGICAL OPTICS : THE JOURNAL OF THE BRITISH COLLEGE OF OPHTHALMIC OPTICIANS (OPTOMETRISTS)). VFOAT Ophthalmic and Physiological Optics. Vol. 1, No. 1-. 0275-5408. Periodical. UK. English. qt. $102.00. Pergamon Press, 395 Sawmill River Road, Elmsford NY 10523. **Ind/Abst** Life Sci. Collect., Excerpta Med., Index Med., Biol. Abstr., Comput. Control Abstr., Electr. Electron. Abstr., Sci. Abstr. Sect. A. Phys. Abstr., Psychol. Abstr. **NLM** W1 OP216. **CODEN** OPOPD5. *British Journal of Physiological Optics, 0007-1218.*

OPHTHALMIC OPTICIAN. (THE OPHTHALMIC OPTICIAN). Vol. 1, No. 1 (Jan. 14, 1961)-. 0030-3739. Periodical. UK. English. fr. $53.63. Ophthalmic Optician, 233-234 Blackfriars Road, London SEI 8NW England. **Ed** Gerald Ward. **Ind/Abst** CIS Abstr. **NLM** W1 OP235. bk rev. adv acc. **Circ** 6,500. (ctrl). Official journal of Association of Optical Practitioners. Scientific and clinical articles on optometry, new product developments, contact lens, reviews, reports on conferences and exhibitions. *A.O.P. News, Dioptric News.*

OPTICAL INDEX. *See* Indexes/Abstracts.

OPTICAL MANAGEMENT CEASED. V. 1- Oct. 1972-Ceased with Nov./Dec. 1984 issue. 0090-0834. Periodical. US. English. mo. $18.00 Domestic, $24.00 Foreign. Optical Management, One Holland Avenue, White Plains NY 10603. **LC** RE72. **DD** 658.916177005.

OPTICAL PRISM. No. 1 (Apr. 1983)-. 0824-3441. Periodical. CN. English. bm. 24.00. Prism Publishing Company, 31 Hastings Drive, Unionville Ontario L3R 4Y5 Canada. **Tel** (416)475-9343. **Ed** Allan K Vezina. **DD** 617.0068. bk rev. adv acc. **Circ** 7,000. (ctrl). Independent optical magazine mailed to all opthalmologists, optometrists, opticians, suppliers and manufacturers across Canada. Emphasizes product news, new developments, contact lenses, clinical studies, management.

OPTICAL SCIENCES CENTER NEWSLETTER. **Main/Corp** Arizona. University. Optical Sciences Center. 0066-7609. Periodical. US. English. University of Arizona, Optical Sciences Center, Tucson AZ 85721. **Ind/Abst** Int. Aerosp. Abstr., Chem. Abstr. **CODEN** OSCADN.

Packaging

THE OPTICIAN. Vol. 84, No. 2163 (Sept. 9, 1932)-. 0030-3968. Periodical. UK. English. wk. $65.00. IPC Consumer Industries Ltd, Quadrant House/The Quadrant, Sutton Surrey, London SM2 5AS England. NLM W1 OP861. *Optician and Scientific Instrument Maker.*

OPTO PRESSE. Vol. 1, No 1 (Sept./Oct. 1976)-. 0227-0730. Periodical. CN. French. ir. Free to Members. Ordre des Optometristes du Quebec, 1080 Boul. Rosemont, Montreal Quebec H2S 2A1 Canada. DD 617.75060714.

OPTOMETRIC MANAGEMENT. V. 1- Jan. 1965-. 0030-4085. Periodical. US. English. mo. Advisory Enterprises Inc, 5 North Greenwich Road, Armonk NY 10504. Tel (914)273-6666. DD 338. NLM W1 OP92.

OPTOMETRIC MONTHLY CEASED. V. 69, No. 5- Feb. 1978-. 0160-9254. Periodical. US. English. mo. $40.00. Professional Press Inc, 5615 West Cermak Road, Cicero IL 60560. Tel (212)741-4000. LC RE1. DD 617.7505. NLM W1 OP92H. Merged with International Contact Lens Clinic to form International Eyecare. *Optometric Weekly, 0030-4093.*

OPTOMETRIC OBSERVER & CONTACT LENS NEWS. V. 1-. Periodical. US. English. bm. Optometric Observer & Contact Lens News, 1414 Avenue of the Americas, New York NY 10019.

OPTOMETRIC WORLD. 0030-4107. Periodical. US. English. mo. $6.00. Occidental Publishing Company, 1411 Kenweth Road, Glendale CA 91201. Tel (213)240-3244. NLM W1 OP9253.

OPTOMETRISTE. (L'OPTOMETRISTE). V. 1- April 1979-. 0708-3173. Periodical. CN. French. qt. $15.00. Association Professionnelle des Optometristes du Quebec, Bureau 302 614 Ouest rue Saint-Jacques, Montreal Quebec H3C 1E2 Canada. DD 617.7505.

OPTOMETRY TODAY. 1970. Periodical. II. English. qt. $30.00. Dr Narendra Kumar, Post Box 2812 Ganga Ram Hospital, New Delhi 110060 India. Tel 5727662. Ed Narendra Kumar. bk rev. adv acc. Circ 1,200. (ctrl). Articles, news, reviews, advertisements, on ophthalmic optical products and services.

OREGON OPTOMETRY. V. 47- Spring 1980-. 0274-6549. Periodical. US. English. qt. $9.00. Oregon Optometric Association, PO Box 298, McMinnville OR 97128. Tel (503)472-2413. Ed William J Baker. adv acc. Circ 2,000. (ctrl). News of professional associations and articles relating to the art and science of vision care. *Oregon Optometrist, 0030-476X.*

DER SCHWEIZER OPTIKER. VFOAT L'Opticien Suisse, L'Ottico Svizzero. Periodical. SZ. German (some material in French). ir. Keller Ltd, Printers & Editors, 6002 Lucerne Switzerland.

SCOTTISH OPHTHALMIC PRACTITIONER. July 1976-. 0308-7670. Periodical. UK. English. mo. $82.75. Scottish National Committee on Ophthalmic Opticians, 179 West Georgia Street, St Glasgow G2 2LQ Scotland. *Scottish Optician, Optics.*

THE SILENT PARTNER. 0361-3291. Periodical. US. English. mo. Ed D.A. Frantz. NLM W1 SI459.

THE SOUTH AFRICAN OPTOMETRIST. VFOAT Suid-Afrikaanse Oogkundige. 1932. 0378-9411. Periodical. SA. English. qt. Mims Pty Ltd, PO Box 2059, Pretoria 0001 South Africa. Tel 471101. Ed Dave Reynolds. bk rev. adv acc. Circ 1,400. (ctrl). The journal is the official organ of the South African Optometric Association, and carries articles of interest to optometrists in practice in the Republic.

SOUTHEASTERN OPTICIAN. 0163-9285. Periodical. US. English. mo. Optical Media Inc, 105 Sanford Street, Box 5054, Hamden CT 06518.

SOUTHERN JOURNAL OF OPTOMETRY CEASED. V. 1- Jan./Feb. 1959. Ceased in 1982. 0038-4275. Periodical. US. English. mo. Southern Council of Optometrists, 4661 North Shallowford Road, Atlanta GA 30338. Tel (404)451-8206. DD 617. NLM W1 SO954. *Journal of the Florida Optometric Association.*

PACKAGING

ADVANCING CONVERTING AND PACKAGING TECHNOLOGIES. 0882-5777. Periodical. US. English. qt. Technical Association of the Pulp & Paper Industry, 1 Dunwoody Park, Atlanta GA 30341.

AEROSOL. VFOAT Aerosol Market Report. US. English. an.

AEROSOL AGE. V. 1- May 1956-. 0001-9291. Periodical. US. English. mo. $14.00. Industry Publications Inc, 10 Canfield Road, Cedar Grove NJ 07009. Tel (201)239-5800. Ed Michael L Sangiovanni. Ind/Abst Pestdoc, Ringdoc, Vetdoc, Predicasts, Energy Inf. Abstr., Environ. Abstr., Int. Packag. Abstr., Funk Scott Index Corp. Ind. LC TS198.P7. DD 688.8. bk rev. adv acc. Circ 7,000. (ctrl). For manufacturers of aerosol and pump packaging and for marketers, distributors, fillers and research people in the aerosol industry.

AEROSOL RELEASE AND TRANSPORT PROGRAM QUARTERLY PROGRESS REPORT. Oct.-Dec. 1981-. Periodical. US. English. qt. GPO Sales Program/Division of Technical Information and Document Control, U S Nuclear Regulatory Commission, Washington DC 20555. Vols. for (Jan.-Mar. 1983-) distributed to depository libraries in microfiche.

AEROSOL-REPORT. (AEROSOL REPORT). 0001-9313. Periodical. GW. English. mo. $110.29. Dr Alfred Huethig Verlag GMBH, Postfach 102869/IM Weiher 10, D-69 Heidelberg 1 West Germany. Ind/Abst Excerpta Med., Int. Packag. Abstr., Met. Abstr., World Alum. Abstr., Chem. Abstr., Eng. Index. CODEN AERRBV.

AEROSOL REVIEW. 1966-. 0568-062X. UK. English. an. Morgan Grampian, Royal Sovereign House, 40 Beresford, London SE18 6BQ England. Tel 01 854 2200. *Manufacturing Chemist and Aerosol News.*

AEROSOL SCIENCE AND TECHNOLOGY. See Chemistry.

ANNUAL CONFERENCE PROCEEDINGS - AMERICAN PRODUCTION AND INVENTORY CONTROL SOCIETY CEASED. Main/Corp American Production and Inventory Control Society. Conference. VFOAT APICS Conference Proceedings, Conference Proceedings. 19th-23. 0191-1783. US. English. an. American Production and Inventory Control Society, International Headquarters Watergate Office Building/Suite 504, 2600 Virginia Avenue NW, Washington DC 20037. Ind/Abst Eng. Index Mon., Eng. Index Bioeng. Abstr., Eng. Index Energy Abstr., Eng. Index Annu. LC TS157.A1. DD 658.5005. CODEN APASDS. *International Technical Conference Proceedings, 0190-8340.*

ANNUAL REPORT AND ACCOUNTS - INSTITUTION OF PRODUCTION ENGINEERS. Main/Corp Institution of Production Engineers, London. 0308-5643. UK. English. an. Institution of Production Engineers, 146 Cromwell Road, Kensington, London SW7 4EF England. LC TS176. DD 658.5006241.

THE AUSTRALIAN LITHOGRAPHER, PRINTER AND PACKAGER. See Printing.

AUSTRALIAN PACKAGING. Periodical. AT. English. mo. Business Press Intl Australia, 162 Gouldburn Street, Darlinghurst 2012 Australia. Ind/Abst Abstr. Bull. Inst. Paper Chem., Int. Packag. Abstr., Art Archaeol. Tech. Abstr.

L'AUXILIAIRE DES FABRICANTS DE CARTONNAGES. See Paper & Pulp Industry.

THE BEST IN PACKAGING. Series/Titl The Print Casebooks. 1975-. 0360-8689. US. English. be. $13.95. R C Publications, 6400 Goldsboro Road Northwest, Washington DC 20034. LC TS195.A1. DD 688.805.

DER BETRIEBSLEITER. Periodical. German. ir. 6.00 Single Issue. Verlag fur Technik und Wirtschaft Meynen, 62 Weisbaden Postfach 5769, Kaiser-Friedrich-Ring 49, Weisbaden West Germany. LC TS155.A1. *Betriebs-Management Service.*

BIOS. See Food & Drink.

BULK, SOLIDS, STORAGE, MOVEMENT, AND CONTROL. Periodical. UK. English. bm. 25.80. Turret Press Ltd, 886 High Road, Finchley London N12 9SB England. Ind/Abst Coal Abstr. LC TS180.8.B8. DD 621.86. *Bulk, Storage, Movement, Control.*

BULK, STORAGE, MOVEMENT, CONTROL CEASED. V. 1-7, No. 2. Periodical. UK. English. bm. 12.00. 886 High Road, Finchley N12 9SB England. Ind/Abst Coal Abstr. LC TS180.8.B8. DD 621.86.

BULLETIN DES DESSINS ET MODELES INTERNATIONAUX : PUBLICATION MENSUELLE DU BUREAU INTERNATIONAL DE L'ORGANISATION MONDIALE DE LA PROPRIETE INTELLECTUELLE. INTERNATIONAL BUREAU OF THE WORLD INTELLECTUAL PROPERTY ORGANIZATION. VFOAT International Designs Bulletin. 0250-7730. English (French). mo. 135.00. Bureau International de l'Organisation Mondiale de la Propriete Intellectuelle, 34 Chemin des Colombettes Case Postale 18, 1211 Geneve 20 Suisse Switzerland. LC TS171.A1. DD 745.2027.

CANADA'S PACKAGING MARKET. VFOAT Statistical Report on Canada's Packaging Market. Began with 1968/69 issue. 0317-042X. CN. English. an. MacLean-Hunter Research Bureau, 481 University Avenue, Toronto Ontario M5G 1W8 Canada. Ind/Abst Predicasts. DD 380.145621757.

CANADIAN PACKAGING. Began publication in 1948. 0008-4654. Periodical. CN. English. ir. $31.72. MacLean Hunter, PO Box 100, Station A, Toronto Ont M5W 1A7 Canada. Ind/Abst Predicasts, Abstr. Bull. Inst. Paper Chem., Can. Bus. Index, Int. Packag. Abstr., Art Archaeol. Tech. Abstr., Funk Scott Index Corp. Ind.

CANADIAN PACKAGING. BUYERS GUIDE. Began with 1963/64 issue. CN. English. an. $10. Domestic, $12. US and United Kingdom. MacLean-Hunter Ltd, 481 University Avenue, Toronto Ontario M5G 1W8 Canada. DD 338.4762175702571.

CANNED FOOD PACK STATISTICS. See Statistics.

CHARACTERISTICS OF PACKAGED FLUID MILK SALES IN PENNSYLVANIA. See Business - Marketing.

CONFERENCE TRANSACTIONS - QUALITY CONTROL CONFERENCE. (CONFERENCE TRANSACTIONS). Main/Conf Quality Control Conference. VFOAT Transactions. 0732-4278. US. English. an. American Society for Quality Control, 161 West Wisconsin Avenue, Milwaukee WI 53203. Ind/Abst Energy Res. Abstr. LC TS156.A1. DD 658.562. *R.S.Q.C. Conference Transactions.*

CONSUMPTION OF CONTAINERS AND OTHER PACKAGING SUPPLIES BY THE MANUFACTURING INDUSTRIES. VFOAT Consommation de Contenants et Autres Matieres d'Emballage, par Industrie Manufacturiere. 1962-. 0576-0186. CN. English. an. 0.70. Statistics Canada, Publication Distribution, Ottawa Ontario K1A 0T6 Canada. LC HD9839.P33. DD 381.4567630971. *Consumption of Containers and Other Packaging Supplies by the Manufacturing Industries, 0576-0186.*

CONTAINERS AND PACKAGING. Main/Corp United States. Business and Defense Services Administration. Containers and Packaging Division. Periodical. US. English. ir. Superintendent of Documents, US Government Printing Office, Washington DC 20402. LC HD9999.C743. DD 658.78844.

CONTAINERS AND PACKAGING. Main/Corp United States. Industry and Trade Administration. Forest Products Packaging and Printing Division. V. 30, No. 4- Winter 1977/78-. 0090-578X. Periodical. US. English. qt. $3.00. US Government Printing Office, Superintendent of Documents, Washington DC 20402. Ind/Abst Predicasts, Public Aff. Inf. Serv. Bull. LC HD9999.C743. DD 338.4768. *Containers and Packaging, 0090-578X.*

CONTROL CIBERNETICA Y AUTOMATIZACION. Periodical. CU. Spanish. qt. $12.61. Empresa Ediciones Cubanas, Sub-Direccion Exportacion, Oreilly 407 Ciudad Havana Cuba. LC TS156.8. CODEN CCAZAB.

Packaging

CONVERTED FLEXIBLE PACKAGING PRODUCTS. (CURRENT INDUSTRIAL REPORTS. MQ-26F, CONVERTED FLEXIBLE PACKAGING PRODUCTS). 0364-1783. US. English. an. $1.00. Data User Services Division, Customer Services Publication, Bureau of the Census, Washington DC 20233. Tel (301)763-4100. **Ind/Abst** Predicasts. LC HD9999.C743. DD 381.45.68880973. Presents timely data on the production, inventories, and orders of approximately 5,000 products, which represents 40 percent of all US manufacturing.

DAIRY PACKAGING NEWSLETTER. See Agriculture - Dairy & Related Technologies.

DESIGN NEWS. VFOAT Dezain Joho. 0385-3462. Periodical. JA. Japanese. ir. Nihon Sangyo Dezain Shinkokai, c/o Sekai Boeki Senta Bldg., 4-1 Hamamatsucho 2, Minato-Ku 105, Tokyo Japan. LC TS171.A1.

DEUTSCHE AUSWAHL. Main/Corp Design Center Stuttgart. 1980-. GW. German. an. Design Center Stuttgart des Landesgewerbeamts Baden-Wurttemberg, Kienesstrasse 18, 7000 Stuttgart 1 West Germany. LC TS171.A1. *Jahresauswahl.*

DEVELOPMENTS IN FOOD PACKAGING. 1-. 0263-3752. UK. English. ir. Elsevier Applied Science Publishers, Crown House, Linton Road, Barking Essex 1G11 8JU England. Tel 01 594 7272. **Ind/Abst** Chem. Abstr. CODEN DFPADC.

EMBALAGEM. 0013-6530. Periodical. Portuguese. ir. $6.00. Editora Metodos, CX Postal 15085, 20 000 Rio de Janeiro Brazil. LC HF5770.A1. DD 658.56405.

EMBALLAGES. (EMBALLAGES MAGAZINE). 0013-6553. Periodical. French. Tel 622 13 62. **Ind/Abst** Predicasts, Abstr. Bull. Inst. Paper Chem., Int. Packag. Abstr., Met. Abstr., World Alum. Abstr. LC TS158.

EMBOUTEILLAGE, CONDITIONNEMENT. VFOAT Revue Mensuelle de l'Embouteillage et des Industries du Conditionnement. No. 164- Oct. 1976-. 0397-8079. Periodical. French. ir. *Revue de l'Embouteillage et des Industries du Conditionnement: Traitement, Distribution, Transport.*

EUROPEAN PACKAGING NEWSLETTER. 1961. Periodical. FR. English. mo. $240.00. European Packaging Newsletter, 80 South Early Street, Alexandria VA 22304. Tel (703)823-6966. Ed Pierre J Louis. (ctrl) Serves the packaging industry as a clearinghouse for the latest information on innovative techniques, new machinery, and processes.

FIBRE BOX HANDBOOK. 0196-7215. US. English. Fibre Box Association, 5725 East River Road, Chicago IL 60631. Tel (312)693-9600. Ed Thomas J Muldoon. LC HF5770.A1. Circ 67,000. (ctrl). A compendium of the regulations on the construction of corrugated boxes plus information on their proper usage.

FNP NEWSLETTER. FOOD PACKAGING AND LABELING. (FNP NEWSLETTER : FOOD PACKAGING AND LABELING). VAT Food and Nutrition Press Newsletter. Food Packaging and Labeling. V.1, No.1- Jan. 1977-. 0194-2980. Periodical. US. English. mo. $55.00. Food & Nutrition Press, 155 Post Road East, PO Box 71, Westport CT 06881. Tel (203)227-6596. Ed Stanley Sacharow. bk rev. Stan Sacharow, a recognized expert in food packaging, aids and informs readers on the latest trends, emerging, markets, and legislation in food packaging and labeling.

FOLDING CARTON AND SET-UP BOX MANUFACTURERS (FINAL) CEASED. (FOLDING CARTON AND SET-UP BOX MANUFACTURERS). VFOAT Fabricants de Cartons Pliants et de Boites Montees. 1970-1980. 0384-4676. CN. English (French). an. DD 338.47676320971. *Manufacturers of Folding Cartons and Set-Up Boxes, 0575-8920.*

FOLDING CARTON INDUSTRY. 0306-168X. UK. English. qt. $35.00. Binsted Publications, Walton HSE/90 London Road/Hook, Hampshire RG27 9LF England. Tel Hook 025672 4176/7. **Ind/Abst** Abstr. Bull. Inst. Paper Chem., Int. Packag. Abstr. LC TS1200.A1. DD 676.32.

FOOD & DRUG PACKAGING. (FOOD AND DRUG PACKAGING). V. 1- Nov. 12, 1959-. 0015-6272. Periodical. US. English. mo. Food & Drug Packaging, 1 East 1st Street, Duluth MN 55806. Tel (218)723-9200. Ed Ben Miyares. **Ind/Abst** Predicasts, Int. Packag. Abstr., Funk Scott Index Corp. Ind. adv acc. (ctrl).

GOOD PACKAGING. 0017-2170. Periodical. US. English. mo. $30.00. Good Packaging, 1313 East Julian Street, San Jose CA 95116. **Ind/Abst** Energy Inf. Abstr., Environ. Abstr., Int. Packag. Abstr.

GORDIAN (1948). (GORDIAN). 1895. 0017-2243. Periodical. GW. German. mo. $41.79. A Gordian Gmbh & Co, Bellevue 24, Postfach 60 51 28, D-2 Hamburg 60 West Germany. Ed P Pries. **Ind/Abst** Int. Packag. Abstr., Chem. Abstr., Bibliogr. Agric., Energy Res. Abstr. CODEN GORDAM. bk rev. adv acc. Topics include raw material, quality control, products development, packaging and storage, microbiology, sanitation, modern production plants, etc.

HANDBOOK, CORRUGATED AND SOLID FIBREBOARD BOXES AND PRODUCTS. Main/Corp Fibre Box Association. VFOAT Corrugated and Solid Fibreboard Boxes and Products. US. English. ir. Fibre Box Association, 5725 East River Road, Chicago IL 60631. LC TS1200.

IDENTIFICATION JOURNAL. See Manufacturing.

INDUSTRY WAGE SURVEY. CORRUGATED AND SOLID FIBER BOXES. See Economics - Labor.

THE INTERNATIONAL BOTTLER AND PACKER. Periodical. UK. English. mo. 16.00. Binsted House, Walton House/90 London Road, Hook Hampshire RG27 9LF England. Tel 025672 4176. Ed Edward Binsted. **Ind/Abst** Int. Packag. Abstr. bk rev. adv acc. Circ 6,178. (ctrl). Reports world-wide bottling and packaging developments. Read by top management, technical and production directors, etc. in brewing soft drinks, cider, milk and bottling industries.

INTERNATIONAL PACKAGING ABSTRACTS. See Indexes/Abstracts.

JAPAN PACKAGE DESIGN. 0882-1097. Periodical. US. English. an. Kodansha International, 10 East 53rd Street, New York NY 10022.

JOURNAL OF AEROSOL SCIENCE. Periodical. US. English (French and German). bm. Pergamon Press, 395 Sawmill River Road, Elmsford NY 10523. Tel (914)592-7700. **Ind/Abst** Appl. Mech. Rev., Eng. Index, Electr. Electron. Abstr., Phys. Abstr., Comput. Control Abstr., Sci. Cit. Index, Abr. Ed., Chem. Abstr.

JOURNAL OF OPERATIONS MANAGEMENT. Vol. 1, No. 1 (Aug. 1980)-. 0272-6963. Periodical. US. English. qt. $10.00 Members, $15.00 Nonmembers. American Production and Inventory Control Society, 500 West Annandale Road, Falls Church VA 22046. **Ind/Abst** Manage. Contents, ABI/Inform. LC TS155.A1. DD 658.5005.

LAGERN UND FORDERN. German. ir. 180.00. Bohmann Verlag, Canovagasse 5, 1010 Wien Austria. LC TS180. *Lagern-Fodern-Transportieren.*

MANUFACTURERS OF CORRUGATED BOXES. See Manufacturing.

MANUTENTION-EMBALLAGES. VFOAT Behandeling-Verpakkingen. Dutch (French). ir. Institut Belge de l Emballage, Editeur-Proprietaire, S A Imprimerie et Publicite du Marais N V, rue de Flandre 169, 1000 Bruxelles Belgium. LC TS180.

MHBG, MATERIALS HANDLING BUYER'S GUIDE. VFOAT Materials Handling Buyers' Guide. UK. English. an. Turret Press, 886 High Road Finchley, London N129SB England. LC TS180. DD 338.476218602541.

MM. MINOSEG ES MEGBIZHATOSAG. 0580-4485. Periodical. HU. Hungarian. bm. Akadmeiai Kiado, POB 24, 1363 Budapest Hungary. **Ind/Abst** Energy Res. Abstr., Comput. Control Abstr., Electr. Electron. Abstr., Sci. Abstr. Sect. A. Phys. Abstr. LC TS156.A1.

MODERN PACKAGING ENCYCLOPEDIA ISSUE. Periodical. English. ir.

NADEZHNOST I KONTROL KACHESTVA. Periodical. UR. Russian. mo. $76.50. Victor Kamkin Inc, 12224 Parklawn Drive, Rockville MD 20852. Tel (301)881-5973. **Ind/Abst** Math. Rev. LC TS173.

NV; NEUE VERPACKUNG. VFOAT Neue Verpackung. 0341-0390. Periodical. GW. German. ir. 98.80. Verlag fur Fachliteratur, Bismarchplatz 1, 1000 Berlin 1 West Germany. **Ind/Abst** Abstr. Bull. Inst. Paper Chem., Int. Packag. Abstr., Energy Res. Abstr., Met. Abstr., World Alum. Abstr. LC TS195.A1.

PACK & PRINT. VFOAT Pack and Print. Periodical. SA. English. mo. $17.35. Thomson Publications South Africa Pty Ltd, PO Box 8308, Johannesburg 2000 South Africa.

PACKAGE DEVELOPMENT & SYSTEMS CEASED. VAT Package Development and Systems. Sept./Oct. 1976-. 0145-5273. Periodical. US. English. bm. $20.00. 381/2 Wolden Road, Building D-A, Ossining NY 10562. **Ind/Abst** Chem. Abstr. LC TS195.A1. DD 621.75705. CODEN PDSYDD. Available on microfilm from Xerox University Microfilms. *Package Development.*

PACKAGE ENGINEERING. BUYERS GUIDE & DIRECTORY. See Yearbooks, Almanacs, Directories.

PACKAGE PRINTING. V. 25, No 3- March 1978-. 0163-9234. Periodical. US. English. mo. Package Printing, North American Building, 401 North Broad Street, Philadelphia PA 19108. **Ind/Abst** Abstr. Bull. Inst. Paper Chem., Int. Packag. Abstr., Print. Abstr. LC TS196.7. DD 621.757. Available on microfilm from University Microfilms. *Package Printing and Diecutting, 0098-7778.*

PACKAGING. V. 1- April 1930-. 0030-9060. Periodical. UK. English. bm. Turret Wheatland Ltd, PO Box 64, Rickmansworth Herts WD3 1SN England. **Ind/Abst** Funk Scott Index Corp. Ind. LC TS158. *European Packaging Continental Packaging PCB. Plastics Packaging Paper Converters Bulletin.*

PACKAGING. (PACKAGING ENCYCLOPEDIA & YEARBOOK). VFOAT Packaging Encyclopedia and Yearbook. 0883-5411. US. English. an. Packaging Encyclopedia & Yearbook, PO Box 5594, Denver CO 80217.

PACKAGING ABSTRACTS. See Indexes/Abstracts.

PACKAGING (BOSTON, MASS.). (PACKAGING). Vol. 28, No. 10 (Sept. 1983)-. 0746-3820. Periodical. US. English. mo. Cahners Publishing Company, 221 Columbus Avenue, Boston MA 02116. **Ind/Abst** Abstr. Bull. Inst. Paper Chem., Life Sci. Collect., Predicasts, Appl. Sci. Technol. Index. LC TS195.A1. DD 688.805. *Package Engineering Including Modern Packaging, 0747-9999.*

PACKAGING DESIGN. 0030-9109. Periodical. US. English. an. $45.00. Art Directions Book Company, 10 East 39th Street/16th Floor, New York NY 10016. Tel (212)889-6500.

PACKAGING DIGEST. V. 1- 1963-. 0030-9117. Periodical. US. English. mo. $65.00. Delta Publications, 400 North Michigan Avenue, Chicago IL 60611. Tel (312)222-2000. **Ind/Abst** Trade Ind. Index, Int. Packag. Abstr.

PACKAGING DIRECTORY. See Yearbooks, Almanacs, Directories.

THE PACKAGING ENCYCLOPEDIA. 1981-. 0736-0908. US. English. an. Cahners Publishing Company Inc, 221 Columbus Avenue, Boston MA 02116. LC TS195.A1. DD 688.805. *Modern Packaging Encyclopedia and Buyers Guide.*

PACKAGING MARKETPLACE. 1978-. US. English. ir. $120.00. Gale Research Co, Book Tower, Detroit MI 48226. Ed J F Hanlon. A directory of over 4,000 manufacturers, distributors, and wholesalers covering sources of packaging information, services, materials and equipment.

PACKAGING NEWS. Began in 1954. 0030-9133. Periodical. UK. English. mo. 30.00. MacLean Hunter Ltd, 76 Oxford Street, London W1N 9FD England. Tel 01-434 2233. Ed Rosemary Mason. **Ind/Abst** Abstr. Bull. Inst. Paper Chem., Int. Packag. Abstr. bk rev. adv acc. Circ 18,634. (ctrl). The leading packaging publication in Europe. Offers a complete news service for buyers of packaging materials, equipment and services.

PACKAGING STRATEGIES. Began in 1983. 8755-6189. Periodical. US. English. sm. $157.00. Packaging Strategies, 641B Lancaster Pike Suite B-277, Malvern PA 19355. DD 658.

PACKAGING TECHNOLOGY. V. 10, No. 3- May/June 1980-. 0274-4996. Periodical. US. English. bm. $35.00 Domestic, $55.00 Foreign. Business

Paints and Painting

Publications Inc, 70 Oak Street, Norwood NJ 07648. **Tel** (201)767-6800. Ed Glenn Melvin. **Ind/Abst** Eng. Index Annu., Eng. Index Mon., Eng. Index Bioeng. Abstr., Eng. Index Energy Abstr., Abstr. Bull. Inst. Paper Chem., Chem. Abstr., Int. Packag. Abstr. **LC** TS195.A1. **DD** 688.805. **CODEN** PTHJDP. adv acc. **Circ** 22,000. (ctrl). Available on microfilm from University Microfilms. Technically oriented magazine on all aspects of packaging products, innovations, technological developments in the field. *Package Development & Systems, 0145-5273.*

PACKUNG & TRANSPORT. See Transportation.

PAL. PACKAGING AND LABELING. REGULATORY SUPPLEMENT. (PAL, PACKAGING AND LABELING. FEDERAL LEGISLATIVE AND REGULATORY SUPPLEMENT). **VFOAT** Packaging and Labeling. **VAT** Packaging and Labeling, Packaging and Labeling. Federal Legislative and Regulatory Supplement. 0145-434X. US. English. Federal State Reports Inc, PO Box 986, Courthouse Station, Arlington VA 22216. **LC** KF1619.A3692. **DD** 343.73082.

PAPER & PACKAGING BULLETIN. 0142-5307. Periodical. UK. English. qt. $295.00. Economist Intelligence Unit, 40 Duke Street, London W1M 5DG England. **Tel** 01-493-6711. Ed Mark Hudson. **Ind/Abst** Int. Packag. Abstr., Pap. Board Abstr. Analysis and forecasts of trends in packaging, paper and raw materials.

PAPER, FILM & FOIL CONVERTER. (PAPER, FILM AND FOIL CONVERTER). V. 27, No. 9- Sept. 1953-. 0031-1138. Periodical. US. English. mo. $40.00. MacLean-Hunter Publications, 300 West Adams Street, Chicago IL 60606. **Tel** (312)726-2802. Ed James R Martin. **Ind/Abst** Predicasts, Abstr. Bull. Inst. Paper Chem., Int. Packag. Abstr., Funk Scott Index Corp. Ind. adv acc. **Circ** 32,000. (ctrl). Serves the field which fabricates paper, paperboard, plastic films and resins, and foil materials into packaging products. *American Paper Converter, 0096-090X.*

PAPERBOARD PACKAGING'S INTERNATIONAL CONTAINER DIRECTORY. See Yearbooks, Almanacs, Directories.

PAPERBOARD PACKAGING'S OFFICIAL CONTAINER DIRECTORY. See Yearbooks, Almanacs, Directories.

PERFORMANCE. Periodical. US. English. bm. $12.00. Charger Productions, PO Box HH, Capistrano Beach CA 92624. **LC** TS168. **DD** 658.56.

POWDER/BULK SOLIDS. **VFOAT** Powder Bulk Solids. 8750-6653. Periodical. US. English. bm. $20.00 US and Canada, $42.00 all other countries. Machalek Publishing Company, 15 South Ninth Street, Minneapolis MN 55402. **Tel** (612)370-0413. Ed Dale Thompson. adv acc. **Circ** 26,000. (ctrl). A product news publication directed to over 20 industries involved with processing, handling, packaging and storing dry particulates and bulk solids.

PROBLEMY JAKOSCI. PL. Polish. bm. ARS Polona, Krakowskei Przedmiescie 7, 00-068 Warsaw Poland. **LC** TS156.A1.

PROCEEDINGS. ANNUAL RELIABILITY AND MAINTAINABILITY SYMPOSIUM. (PROCEEDINGS : ANNUAL RELIABILITY AND MAINTAINABILITY SYMPOSIUM). **Main/Conf** Reliability and Maintainability Symposium. **VFOAT** Annals of Assurance Sciences. 1972-. 0149-144X. US. English. an. $24.00. Institute of Electrical and Electronics Engineers, 445 Hoes Lane, Piscataway NJ 08854. **Tel** (201)981-0060. **Ind/Abst** Index IEEE Publ., Coal Abstr., Energy Res. Abstr. **LC** TS173. **DD** 003. *Proceedings.*

PROCEEDINGS PLP. PRODUCT LIABILITY PREVENTION CONVENTION. (PROCEEDINGS PLP). **Main/Conf** Product Liability Prevention Conference. **VAT** Proceedings, Product Liability Prevention. Product Liability Prevention Conference. 1st- 1970-. 0162-2919. US. English. an. $15.00. New Jersey Institute of Technology, 323 High Street, Newark NJ 07102. **Ind/Abst** Eng. Index. **LC** TS175. **DD** 658.56.

PROCEEDINGS PLP. PRODUCT LIABILITY PREVENTION SEMINAR. (PROCEEDINGS PLP). **Main/Conf** Product Liability Prevention Seminar. **VAT** Proceedings Product Liability Prevention. Product Liability Prevention Seminar. 1st- 1977-. 0162-279X. US. English. $10.00. New Jersey Institute of Technology, 323 High Street, Newark NJ 07102. **LC** TS175. **DD** 658.56.

PRODUCTION & INVENTORY MANAGEMENT REVIEW & APICS NEWS. **VFOAT** Production and Inventory Management Review and APICS News. **VAT** Production and Inventory Management Review and American Production and Inventory Control Society News. Vol. 1, No. 1 (Jan. 1981)-. 0274-9874. Periodical. US. English. mo. Free to Society Members, $36.00 Others Domestic, $45.00 Others Foreign. T D A Publications, 1617 South 21st Avenue, Hollywood FL 33020. **LC** TS156.A1. **DD** 658.5005. *APICS News, Production and Inventory Management, 0032-9843.*

PUMJIL KWALLI HAKHOE CHI. **VFOAT** Journal of the Korean Society for Quality Control. Periodical. KO. Korean (summaries in English). ir. Hanguk Pumjil Kwalli Hakhoe, 105-153 Kongdok-dong, Mapo-ku 121, Seoul South Korea. **LC** TS155.A1.

REGISTER OF QUALITY ASSESSED UNITED KINGDOM MANUFACTURERS. See Manufacturing.

RULES FOR CERTIFICATION OF CARGO CONTAINERS. **Main/Corp** American Bureau of Shipping. **VFOAT** Certification of Cargo Containers. 0740-7297. US. English. American Bureau of Shipping, 45 Eisenhower Drive, Paramus NJ 07652. **Tel** (201)386-9100. Ed Donald Monroe. **LC** TS195.6. **DD** 688.8. **Circ** 200. Design, certification, quality and assurance of cargo containers. Also, testing and materials.

SANOP TIJAIN. **VFOAT** Industrial Design. 68-. Periodical. KO. Korean. bm. 8.000. Hanguk Tijain Pojang Sento, 128-8 Yongon-dong Chongno-ku, Seoul Korea. **LC** TS171.A1. *Tijain, Pojang.*

SCHWEIZER VERPACKUNGSKATALOG. **VFOAT** Catalogue Suisse de l'Emballage. German. an. Verlag Max Binkert & Company, Laufenburg Switzerland. **LC** TS158. **DD** 688.805. *Schweizer Verpackungs- und Transportkatalog.*

STATISTICAL REVIEW. See Statistics.

VERPACKUNG. (DIE VERPACKUNG). Began in 1960. 0042-4269. Periodical. SZ. German (some articles have summaries in English and Russian). bm. 65.00. Kunst & Wissen Erich Bieber, Dufourstrasse 51, CH-8008 Zurich Switzerland. **Tel** 1-9108022. Ed Const Gabbi. **Ind/Abst** Int. Packag. Abstr. **LC** TS158. **DD** 658.56405. (cum index). adv acc. Package design and marketing, packaging and canning, packaging materials and machinery, product information, and industry information.

VERPACKUNGS RUNDSCHAU. 1954, No. 1- Jan. 1954-. 0042-4307. Periodical. GW. German. mo. $102.13. P Keppler KG, Industriestrasse 2, 6056 Heusenstamm West Germany. **Tel** 06104/6060. Ed E Thomas. **Ind/Abst** Life Sci. Collect., Energy Inf. Abstr., Environ. Abstr., Abstr. Bull. Inst. Paper Chem., Int. Packag. Abstr., Energy Res. Abstr., Met. Abstr., World Alum. Abstr. bk rev. adv acc. **Circ** 10,000. (ctrl). News reporting on essential segments of the packaging market. Covering the sectors of packaging techniques and market economy.

VERPAKKING. Vol. 1-. Periodical. Dutch. mo. **LC** HF5770.A1.

WOLGAN POJANG SANOP. **VFOAT** Monthly Packaging Industry. Periodical. KO. Korean. mo. 20,000. Pojang Sanop, 297-4 Toksan-dong Kuro-ku, Seoul Korea. **LC** TS195.A1.

PAINTS AND PAINTING

AMERICAN PAINT AND COATINGS JOURNAL. 1916. 0098-5430. Periodical. US. English. wk. $25.00. American Paint & Coatings, 2911 Washington, St Louis MO 63103. **Tel** (314)534-0301. Ed Chuck Reitter. **Ind/Abst** Trade Ind. Index, World Surf. Coat. Abstr., Predicasts, Art Archaeol. Tech. Abstr., Chem. Abstr., Funk Scott Index Corp. Ind. **LC** TP934. **DD** 338.4766790973. **CODEN** APCJDB. bk rev. adv acc. **Circ** 7,000. News, technical, business, marketing, regulatory, production statistics, company features of interest ot the paint manufacturing industry.

AMERICAN PAINT & COATINGS JOURNAL. CONVENTION DAILY. V. 59- 1974-. 0097-4749. US. English. da. $25.00. American Paint Journal Company, 2911 Washington Avenue, St Louis MO 63103. **Tel** (314)534-0301. Ed Chuck Reitter. **LC** TP934. **DD** 667.906273. adv acc. **Circ** 8,000. News technical marketing raw material prices and trades of interest to the paint and resin manufacturing industry. *American Paint Journal. Convention Daily.*

AMERICAN PAINTING CONTRACTOR. V. 40, No. 6- June 1963-. 0003-0325. Periodical. US. English. mo. $24.00. American Paint Journal Company, 2911 Washington Avenue, St Louis MO 63103. **Tel** (314)534-0301. Ed Rick Hirsch. **Ind/Abst** Art Archaeol. Tech. Abstr. adv acc. **Circ** 25,000. How to, general management, health and safety, industrial maintenance, educational and construction subjects pertinent to the paint contracting and paint maintenance markets. *American Painter and Decorator, 0096-0918.*

ANNUAL REPORT - NATIONAL PAINT & COATINGS ASSOCIATION. **Main/Corp** National Paint and Coatings Association. 0095-2729. US. English. an. National Paint & Coatings Association, 1500 Rhode Island Avenue Northwest, Washington DC 20005. **LC** TP934. **DD** 667.906273.

ANUARIO BRASILEIRO DE TINTAS & I.E. E VERNIZES. See Yearbooks, Almanacs, Directories.

APPLICATIONS OF POLYMER EMULSIONS. 0143-716X. Periodical. UK. English. bm. 118 Domestic, 250 Foreign. Solihull Chemical Services, 284 Warwich Road, West Midlands B9S 7AF England. **Ind/Abst** Chem. Abstr. **CODEN** APEMDU. **Circ** 65. A survey issued 6 times per annum of recent developments. Totals at least 60 pages with comments by editor based on his own experience, i.e. not merely a list of abstracts.

CA SELECTS. COATINGS, INKS, & RELATED PRODUCTS. **VFOAT** Chemical Abstracts Selects. 0275-7036. US. English. bw. $110.00. Chemical Abstracts Service, PO Box 3012, Columbus OH 43210. **Tel** (614)421-3600. Ed David W Weisgerber. **Ind/Abst** Chem. Abstr. **CODEN** CCIPDO. Covers chemistry, chemical and physical properties, and analysis of decorative and protective coatings: paints, lacquers, varnishes, organic enamels, ink vehicles, drying oils, pigments and other components.

CA SELECTS. PAINT ADDITIVES. **VFOAT** Paint Additives. **VAT** Chemical Abstracts Selects. Paint Additives. 0734-8762. US. English. bw. $110.00. Chemical Abstracts Service, PO Box 3012, Columbus OH 43210. **Tel** (614)421-3600. Ed David W Weisgerber. **CODEN** CAPADY. Covers materials added to paints (pigmented coatings) other than the basic polymeric binder, solvents and pigments.

COATINGS. V. 1- Sept. 1979-. 0225-6363. Periodical. CN. English. bm. $12.38. Coatings Magazine, 86 Wilson Street, Suite A, Oakville Ontario L6K 365 Canada. **Tel** (416)844-9773. Ed G Barry Kay. **Ind/Abst** Met. Abstr., World Alum. Abstr. **DD** 667.905. adv acc. **Circ** 7,300. (ctrl). Edited for management in paint, coatings manufacturing, and industrial finishing.

COATINGS IN CANADA. V. 52, No. 10- Sept./Oct. 1978-. 0706-5124. Periodical. CN. English. mo. MacLean-Hunter, PO Box 100, Station A, Toronto Ontario M5W 1A7 Canada. **DD** 338.4766760971. *Canadian Paint and Finishing, 0008-4662.*

COATINGS TECHNOLOGY ANNUAL. 1978-. 0161-6145. Periodical. US. English. an. Noyes Data Corporation, Mill Road at Grand Avenue, Park Ridge NJ 07656. **LC** TP156.C57. **DD** 667.90272.

CORROSION Y PROTECCION. 0045-8678. Periodical. SP. Spanish. bm. 45.00. Editorial Garsi, Londres 17, Madrid 28 Spain. **Tel** 2556800. Ed Miguel Angel Guillen. **Ind/Abst** Met. Abstr., World Alum. Abstr., Chem. Abstr. **CODEN** CPTNAP. bk rev adv acc. **Circ** 1,000. Corrosion, naval, industrial, paints anodizing treatments.

CURRENT INDUSTRIAL REPORTS. MA28F, PAINT AND ALLIED PRODUCTS. **VFOAT** Paint and Allied Products. 1981-. US. English. an. $16.00. Data User Services Division, Customer Services Publication, Bureau of the Census, Washington DC 20233. **Tel**

(301)763-4100. **LC** HD9660.P253. **DD** 381.4566760981. Presents timely data on the production, inventories, and orders of approximately 5,000 products, which represents 40 percent of all US manufacturing.

DECORATIVE PRODUCTS WORLD. *See* Interior Design.

DEFAZET. DEUTSCHE FARBEN-ZEITSCHRIFT. (DEFAZET, DEUTSCHE FARBEN-ZEITSCHRIFT). **VFOAT** Deutsche Farben-Zeitschrift. 0012-009X. Periodical. GW. German. mo. $29.63. Editio Lack und Chemie, Karl Benz Strasse 11, Postfach 1168, D-7024 Filderstadl 1 West Germany. **Ind/Abst** CIS Abstr., Chem. Abstr., Predicasts, Energy Res. Abstr., Excerpta Med. **CODEN** DFZTBF. *Defazet-Aktuell.*

DAS DEUTSCHE MALERBLATT. 0012-0448. Periodical. German. mo. 111.60. Deutsche Verlags-Anstalt, Postfach 209, 7000 Stuttgart West Germany. **LC** TT300. **DD** 667.9.

A DIRECTORY AND LISTING OF PAINTINGS AS SHOWN IN THE MAGAZINE ANTIQUES. *See* Yearbooks, Almanacs, Directories.

DOUBLE LIAISON-CHIMIE DES PEINTURES. 0012-5709. Periodical. FR. French. mo. 55.87. 68 rue Jena Jaures, 92800 Puteaux France. **Tel** (01)47730123. **Ind/Abst** Funk Scott Index Corp. Ind., Chem. Abstr. bk rev. adv acc. **Circ** 5,000. The sole French review about paints, inks, and adhesives.

DYES AND PIGMENTS. (DYES AND PIGMENTS : AN INTERNATIONAL JOURNAL). Vol. 1, No. 1 (July-Sept 1980). 0143-7208. Periodical. UK. English. bm. 127 Domestic, 114 United Kingdom. Elsevier Applied Science Publishing, Crown House Linton Road, Barking Essex IG11 8JU England. **Ed** A T Peters. **Ind/Abst** Eng. Index Annu., Eng. Index Mon., Eng. Index Bioeng. Abstr., Eng. Index Energy Abstr., Life Sci. Collect., Art Archaeol. Tech. Abstr., Chem. Abstr. **LC** TP890. **DD** 667.205. **CODEN** DYPIDX. bk rev. adv acc. Publishers research papers on all aspects of the chemistry of dyes and pigments.

FARBE + I.E. UND LACK ADRESSBUCH MIT BEZUGSQUELLENNACHWEIS. German. ir. Curt R Vincentz Verlag, 3000 Hannover 1, Schiffgraben 41-43, Hannover West Germany. **LC** TP934.5.

FARBE + LACK. (FARBE UND LACK). 0014-7699. Periodical. GW. German. mo. 76.20. Curt R Vincentz Verlag, Postfach 62 47, D3000 Hannover 1 West Germany. **Tel** (0511)24 999 12. **Ed** Lother Vincentz and Erlwine Dewald. **Ind/Abst** Predicasts, Excerpta Med., Coal Abstr., Ship Abstr., World Surf. Coat. Abstr., Int. Packag. Abstr., Art Archaeol. Tech. Abstr., Nuci. Sci. Abstr., Chem. Abstr., Energy Res. Abstr., Funk Scott Index Corp. Ind. **CODEN** FALAAA. bk rev. adv acc. **Circ** 5,100. Formulation, production and distribution of coatings plus related research.

FINISHING. Vol. 6, No. 6 (June 1982)-. 0264-2506. Periodical. UK. English. mo. $49.00. Turret-Wheatland Ltd, Penn House, Penn Place, Rickmansworth Herts WD3 1SN England. **Tel** 0923 777000. **Ed** Peter De Lacey. **Ind/Abst** Chem. Abstr., World Alum. Abstr., World Surf. Coat. Abstr., Comput. Control Abstr., Electr. Electron. Abstr., Sci. Abstr. Sect. A. Phys. Abstr., Predicasts, Met. Abstr. **LC** TS670.A1. **DD** 671.705. **CODEN** FINIE2. bk rev. adv acc. **Circ** 4,200. (ctrl). All aspects of surface finishing, including electroplating, powder coating and paint finishes, plus associated pretreatments and application equipment. *Finishing Industries, 0309-3018.*

FORMULARY OF PAINTS AND OTHER COATINGS. V. 1-. Periodical. US. English.

INDUSTRIAL FINISHING. **VFOAT** Finishing, Industrial. V. 1- Nov. 1924-. 0019-8323. Periodical. US. English. mo. $50.00. Hitchcock Publication Company, Hitchcock Building, Wheaton IL 60188. **Tel** (312)665-1000. **Ed** Steve Suslik. **Ind/Abst** Trade Ind. Index, Eng. Index Mon., Eng. Index Bioeng. Abstr., Eng. Index Energy Abstr., Excerpta Med., Met. Abstr., World Alum. Abstr., Chem. Abstr., Eng. Index Annu., Eng. Index Mon., Sel. Water Resour. Abstr., Appl. Sci. Technol. Index, Energy Inf. Abstr., Environ. Abstr., Eng. Index. **LC** TT325.A1. **DD** 667.905. **CODEN** IFIIAJ. bk rev. adv acc. **Circ** 36,000. (ctrl). Technical information on the manufacture and application of paints and coatings.

INDUSTRIAL FINISHING. BUYERS' GUIDE. **VFOAT** Buyers' Guide. '84-'85-. US. English. an. $30.00 US, $40.00 Canada and Mexico. Hitchcock Publishing Company, 25 West 550 Geneava Road, Wheaton IL 60188.

INTERNATIONAL FINISHING INDUSTRIES MANUAL. 1st- Ed. UK. English (summaries in French and German). Wheatland Journals Ltd, 157 Hagden Lane, Watford WD1 8LW England. **LC** TT300. **DD** 667.905. *Industrial Finishing Year Book.*

JCT, JOURNAL OF COATINGS TECHNOLOGY. **VFOAT** Journal of Coatings Technology. V. 48- (No. 612-). 0361-8773. Periodical. US. English. mo. Federation of Society Coatings Technology, 1315 Walnut Street/Suite 830, Philadelphia PA 19107. **Tel** (215)545-1507. **Ind/Abst** Electron. Commun. Abstr. J., Excerpta Med., ISMEC Bull., Pollut. Abstr. Indexes, Saf. Sci. Abstr. J., Predicasts, Ship Abstr., World Surf. Coat. Abstr., Int. Aerosp. Abstr., Int. Packag. Abstr., Art Archaeol. Tech. Abstr., Met. Abstr., World Alum. Abstr., Ref. Source, Chem. Abstr., Print. Abstr., Appl. Sci. Technol. Index, Funk Scott Index Corp. Ind., Sci. Cit. Index, Abr. Ed., Eng. Index, Eng. Index Annu., Eng. Index Mon., Eng. Index Energy Abstr., Eng. Index Bioeng. Abstr. **LC** TP934. **DD** 667.905. **CODEN** JCTEDL. *Journal of Paint Technology, 0022-3352.*

JOURNAL OF WATER BORNE COATINGS. V. 1- Feb. 1978-. 0163-4526. Periodical. US. English. qt. $72.00 Domestic, $83.00 Foreign. Tehnology Marketing Corporation, 17 Park Street, Norwalk CT 06851. **Tel** (203)846-2029. **Ed** John Fitzwater. **Ind/Abst** Eng. Index Annu., Eng. Index Mon., Eng. Index Bioeng. Abstr., Eng. Index Energy Abstr., Chem. Abstr. **CODEN** JWBCDV. bk rev. adv acc. **Circ** 1,000. Features the latest developments and applications of water borne coatings.

LAKARTIDNINGEN. V. 62- 1965-. 0023-7205. Periodical. SW. Swedish. wk. $49.90. Update AB, Box 53120, S-400 15 Goteborg Sweden. **Ind/Abst** Excerpta Med., Index Med., CIS Abstr., Energy Res. Abstr. **NLM** W1 LA256L. *Svenska Lakartidningen.*

MODERN PAINT AND COATINGS. V. 65- Jan. 1975-. 0098-7786. Periodical. US. English. mo. $27.00. Communication Channels Inc, 6255 Barfield Road, Atlanta GA 30328. **Tel** (404)256-9800. **Ind/Abst** Excerpta Med., Predicasts, World Surf. Coat. Abstr., Art Archaeol. Tech. Abstr., Chem. Abstr., Appl. Sci. Technol. Index, Funk Scott Index Corp. Ind. **LC** TP934. **DD** 667.905. **CODEN** MPCODM. *PVP. Paint and Varnish Production, 0190-9533.*

NAVAL STORES *CEASED.* **Main/Corp** United States. Crop Reporting Board. 0091-5351. US. English. mo.

NAVAL STORES REVIEW (NEW ORLEANS, LA. : 1979). (NAVAL STORES REVIEW). Began with Jan./Feb. 1979 issue. 0164-4580. Periodical. US. English. bm. Naval Stores Review, PO Box 2406, New Orleans LA 70176. **Tel** (504)524-2119. **Ind/Abst** Public Aff. Inf. Serv. Bull. **LC** TP977. **DD** 668.37205. *Naval Stores Review & Terpene Chemicals, 0028-1468.*

OBERFLACHE. **VFOAT** Surface. 9. Year, Issue 1 (Jan. 1968)-. 0048-1270. Periodical. French (German). mo. 60.00. Forster-Verlag AG, Alte Landstrasse 43 Postfach, CH-8700 Kuesnacht Switzerland. **Tel** 1-9108022. **Ed** J Leudolph. **Ind/Abst** Eng. Index Annu., Eng. Index Mon., Eng. Index Bioeng. Abstr., Eng. Index Energy Abstr., Excerpta Med., Met. Abstr., World Alum. Abstr., Chem. Abstr. **CODEN** OBSUA7. bk rev. adv acc. **Circ** 4,000. *Galvanotechnik + Oberflachenschutz.*

PAINT & COATINGS INDUSTRY. **VFOAT** Paint and Coatings Industry. Vol. 1, No. 1 (Jan./Feb. 1985)-. 0884-3848. Periodical. US. English. bm. $12.00 Domestic, $20.00 Foreign. Paint & Coatings Industry, 7335 Topanga Canyon Boulevard/Suite 209, Canoga Park CA 91303-9990. **Tel** (818)710-1066. **DD** 667. bk rev. adv acc. **Circ** 12,000. (ctrl). Edited for administrative, production, research and development, engineering, purchasing and marketing, personnel in the following fields: manufacturer of paints, coatings, adhesives, sealants and printing inks. *Western Paint & Decorating, 0274-8703.*

PAINT & RESIN. **VFOAT** Paint and Resin. V. 51, No. 2 (March/April 1981)-. 0261-5746. Periodical. UK. English. bm. $72.03. Turret Wheatland Ltd, PO Box 64, Rickmansworth Herts WD3 1SN England. **Tel** 0923 777 000. **Ed** Nick Dellow. **Ind/Abst** Excerpta Med., Predicasts, World Surf. Coat. Abstr., Chem. Abstr. **LC** TP934. **DD** 667.605. **CODEN** PTRNDJ. bk rev. adv acc. **Circ** 2,000. Details of developments in raw materials and equipment for the paint, ink and varnish industries, marketing developments, company news, etc. *Paint Manufacture incorporating Resin News.*

PAINT AND VARNISH MANUFACTURERS. *See* Manufacturing.

PAINT RED BOOK. 1st- Ed. 0090-5402. US. English. an. $35.50. Communication Channels Inc, 6255 Barfield Road, Atlanta GA 30328. **Tel** (404)256-9800. **LC** TP934.5. **DD** 338.4766760257.

PAINT, VARNISH, AND LACQUER. (CURRENT INDUSTRIAL REPORTS. M28F, PAINT, VARNISH, AND LACQUER). 0145-5230. Periodical. US. English. mo. $16.00. Data User Services Division, Customer Services Publication, Bureau of the Census, Washington DC 20233. **Tel** (301)763-4100. **Ind/Abst** Predicasts, Chem. Abstr., Am. Stat. Index. **CODEN** CIRVAO. Presents timely data on the production, inventories, and orders of approximately 5,000 products, which represents 40 percent of all US manufacturing.

PAINTINDIA. ANNUAL. (PAINTINDIA). **VAT** Paint India. Annual. Began in 1968. 0030-9540. English. mo. 50.00. Colour Publications Pvt Ltd, 126A Dhuruwadi Off Dr Nariman, Bombay 40025 India. **Tel** 430 9610/9318/6319. **Ed** R V Raghavan. **Ind/Abst** Art Archaeol. Tech. Abstr., Chem. Abstr., World Surf. Coat. Abstr. **LC** TP934. **DD** 338.4766760954. **CODEN** PIDABZ. bk rev. adv acc. **Circ** 4,876. Technical articles, special columns and news reports pertaining to the paint and printing ink manufacturing industries. *Paintindia.*

PAINTING & DECORATING JOURNAL. UK. English. mo. 2.75. J Yates Publications, Old Colony House South King Street, Manchester M2 2DA England. **Ind/Abst** CIS Abstr. **LC** NK1160. **DD** 698.05. *International Painting & Decorating Journal.*

PAINTING & WALLCOVERING CONTRACTOR. (PAINTING & WALLCOVERING CONTRACTOR : MAGAZINE OF THE PAINTING & DECORATING CONTRACTORS OF AMERICA). **VFOAT** Painting and Wallcovering Contractor. Vol. 45, No. 2 (Feb. 1983)-. 0735-9713. Periodical. US. English. mo. $36.00. Painting and Decorating Contractor of America, 7223 Lee Highway, Falls Church VA 22046. **Tel** (703)534-1201. **LC** TT300. **DD** 698.105. *Professional Decorating & Coating Action, 0099-0310.*

PIGMENT & RESIN TECHNOLOGY. **VFOAT** Pigment and Resin Technology. V. 1- Jan. 1972-. 0369-9420. Periodical. UK. English. mo. $49.50. Sawell Publications Ltd, 127 Stanstead Road Forest Hill, London SE23 1JE England. **Tel** 01-699 6792. **Ed** J E Bean. **Ind/Abst** Excerpta Med., Predicasts, World Surf. Coat. Abstr., Art Archaeol. Tech. Abstr., Chem. Abstr., Print. Abstr., Funk Scott Index Corp. Ind. **LC** TP934. **DD** 667.62305. **CODEN** PGRTBC. bk rev. adv acc. **Circ** 1,550. A publication dealing with the formulation and manufacture of paints, printing, inks, and adhesives. *Paint Technology.*

PINTURAS Y ACABADOS INDUSTRIALES. 0031-9953. Periodical. SP. Spanish. ir. 40.00. Cedel, PO Box 5326, Barcelona Spain. **Tel** (93)215-6088. **Ed** Oriol Avila. **Ind/Abst** World Surf. Coat. Abstr., Art Archaeol. Tech. Abstr., Chem. Abstr. **LC** TT300. **CODEN** PACIDY. bk rev. adv acc. **Circ** 4,000. Metal and industrial finishing. Painting and electroplating.

PLATING AND SURFACE FINISHING. V. 62, No. 4- Apr. 1975-. 0360-3164. Periodical. US. English. mo. $35.00 US/Canada, $45.00 Others. American Electroplaters Society, 12644 Research Parkway, Orlando FL 32826-3225. **Tel** (305)281-6441. **Ed** Steve Isham. **Ind/Abst** Appl. Sci. Technol. Index, Eng. Index Mon., Eng. Index Bioeng. Abstr., Eng. Index Energy Abstr., Excerpta Med., Energy Inf. Abstr., Environ. Abstr., Comput. Control Abstr., Electr. Electron. Abstr., Sci. Abstr. Sect. A. Phys. Abstr., Chem. Abstr., Eng. Index Annu., Met. Abstr., World Alum. Abstr., Nuci. Sci. Abstr., Sel. Water Resour. Abstr., Tech. Data Dig., Sci. Cit. Index, Abr. Ed., Phys. Abstr., Eng. Index. **LC** TS670. **DD** 671.7305. **CODEN** PSFMDH. bk rev. adv acc. **Circ** 11,000. (ctrl). For professionals in the surface finishing industry. Editorial content includes articles and technical papers on electronics, pollution control, electroplating painting and other finishing operations. *Plating, AES Research Report, 0361-0411.*

POLYMERS, PAINT AND COLOUR JOURNAL. (POLYMERS PAINT COLOUR JOURNAL). Vol. 160, No. 3801 (Sept. 17, 1971)-. 0370-1158. Periodical. UK. English. bw. $164.00. Fuel & Metallurgical Journals Limited, Queensway House, 2 Queensway, Redhill Surrey RH1 105 England. **Ind/Abst** Excerpta Med., Predicasts, Coal Abstr., Ship Abstr., World Surf. Coat. Abstr., Print. Abstr., Chem. Abstr. **CODEN** PPCJA3. *Paint, Oil & Colour Journal.*

POLYMERS PAINT COLOUR YEAR BOOK. *See* Yearbooks, Almanacs, Directories.

Paleontology

POWDER COATINGS. V. 1- Mar. 1978-. 0163-4542. Periodical. US. English. sa. Technology Marketing Corporation, 17 Park Street, Norwalk CT 06851. **Tel** (203)846-2029. **Ind/Abst** Eng. Index Annu., Eng. Index Mon., Eng. Index Bioeng. Abstr., Eng. Index Energy Abstr., Chem. Abstr. **CODEN** PCOADG. bk rev. adv acc. **Circ** 1,000. Concentrates on practical applications, markets, and research and development news as reported by the International Powder Coatings Community.

POWDER COATINGS BULLETIN. VFOAT Powder Coatings. Began publication in 1978. 0140-8445. Periodical. UK. English. mo. $150.00. St Harris (PCC) Ltd, Old Rectory/Nether Whitcare, West Midlands B46 2DU England. **Tel** 0675 81452. **Ed** S T Harris. bk review. **Circ** 300. Up-to-date technical and market developments in powder coatings technology.

PROGRESS IN ORGANIC COATINGS. V. 1- Mar. 1972-. 0300-9440. Periodical. SZ. English. qt. $133.59. Elsevier Sequoia SA, PO Box 851, 1001 Lausanne Switzerland. **Ind/Abst** Eng. Index Mon., Eng. Index Bioeng. Abstr., Eng. Index Energy Abstr., World Surf. Coat. Abstr., Art Archaeol. Tech. Abstr., Energy Res. Abstr., Chem. Abstr., Eng. Index Annu., Eng. Index Mon., Met. Abstr., World Alum. Abstr., Eng. Index. **CODEN** POGCAT.

THE RAUCH GUIDE TO THE U.S. PAINT INDUSTRY. VFOAT Rauch Guide to the US Paint Industry. VAT Rauch Guide to the United States Paint Industry. 1983, 1984-. 8755-0261. US. English. be. $137.00. Rauch Associates, PO Box 6802, Bridgewater NJ 08807. **Ed** James A Rauch. Contains industry data on productions, uses and supplies.

SALES OF PAINTS, VARNISHES AND LACQUERS CEASED. **Main/Corp** Statistics Canada. Manufacturing and Primary Industries Division. VFOAT Ventes de Peintures, Vernis et Laques. V. 27-35, No. 2. 0380-7924. Periodical. CN. English (French). mo. $1.50. Sales of Paints, Varnishes and Lacquers, 0380-7924.

SKANDINAVISK TIDSKRIFT FOR FARG OCH LACK. VFOAT Farg Och Lack. Began 1955. 0037-6094. Periodical. DK. Swedish. mo. 275.-. Stoke Kongensgade 40H, DK 1264 Copenhagen Denmark. **Tel** 1-328500. **Ed** Helge Meyer. **Ind/Abst** Art Archaeol. Tech. Abstr., Ship Abstr., World Surf. Coat. Abstr. **LC** TP934. **CODEN** STFLAH. adv acc. **Circ** 2,000. (ctrl). The objective is to inform engineers and technicians about research results within the paint and varnish industry.

TORYO WA TOJANG. VFOAT The Paint & Finish. Periodical. Korean. bm. 20,000. Hanguk Toryo Tojang Yonguso, PO Box 7152, Chungang Ucheguk, Seoul 100 Korea. **LC** TP934.

TU LIAO KUNG YEH. VFOAT Tuliao Gongye, Paint & Coatings Industry. 0253-4312. Periodical. CH. Chinese (added contents page in English). bm. 6.00. China Publication Centre, PO Box 2820, Beijing China. **Tel** 22997. **Ind/Abst** Chem. Abstr. **CODEN** TLKYD5. adv acc. **Circ** 13,000. Deals with the research, technology and advance of coatings, pigments and additives in China and outside. Application of coatings also is introduced.

WORLD SURFACE COATINGS ABSTRACTS. See Indexes/Abstracts.

PALEONTOLOGY

ACTA PALAEONTOLOGICA POLONICA. V. 1-. 0567-7920. Periodical. PL. Polish (tables of contents also in English, Russian, or French). qt. ARS Polona, Krakowskie Przedmiescie 7, 00-068 Warsaw Poland. **Ind/Abst** Life Sci. Collect., GeoRef, Biol. Abstr., Bibliogr. Index Geol. **LC** QE755.P7. **CODEN** APGPAC.

ADDRESS DIRECTORY - SOCIETY OF VERTEBRATE PALEONTOLOGY. See Yearbooks, Almanacs, Directories.

ALCHERINGA. V. 1-. 0311-5518. Periodical. AT. English. sa. 18.45. Geological Society of Australia, 10 Martin Place, Sydney New South Wales 2000 Australia. **Tel** (02)231-4696. **Ed** J Pickett. **Ind/Abst** GeoRef, Bibliogr. Index Geol., Pet. Abstr., MLA Int. Bibliogr. Books Artic. Mod. Lang. Lit., Sci. Cit. Index, Abr. Ed. **LC** QE758.A1. **DD** 560.99. **CODEN** ALCHDB. **Circ** 700. Journal of Australasian paleontology.

AMEGHINIANA. Vol. 1- Jan. 1957-. 0002-7014. AG. Spanish (Summaries in English and Portuguese). $35.00. Asociacion Paleontologica Argentina, Maipu 645 Piso 1 5047, 1006 Buenos Aires Argentina. **Tel** 392-2820. **Ind/Abst** GeoRef, Biol. Abstr., Bibliogr. Index Geol. **LC** QE752.A7. **CODEN** AMGHB2. (cum index). adv acc. **Circ** 700. (ctrl). Writings on paleontology of Argentina and South America.

AMERICAN MUSEUM NOVITATES. See Zoology-Vertebrate and Invertebrate.

ANNALES DE PALEONTOLOGIE. INVERTEBRES CEASED. VFOAT Invertebres. V. 50-67. 0570-1619. Periodical. French. qt. **Ind/Abst** Life Sci. Collect., GeoRef, Biol. Abstr. **DD** 562. **CODEN** APIUA6. Annales de Paleontologie, 0003-4142.

ANNALES DE PALEONTOLOGIE (PARIS, FRANCE : 1982). (ANNALES DE PALEONTOLOGIE). Vol. 68, No. 1-. French. qt. $180.00. Masson Publishing USA Inc, 211 East 43rd Street/Room 1306, New York NY 10017. **Tel** (212)370-1937. **Ind/Abst** Biol. Abstr., Life Sci. Collect. Annales de Paleontologie. Invertebres, 0570-1619; Annales de Paleontologie. Vertebres, 0570-1627.

ANNALES DE PALEONTOLOGIE. VERTEBRES CEASED. VFOAT Vertebres. V. 50-67. 0570-1627. Periodical. French. qt. **Ind/Abst** Life Sci. Collect., GeoRef, Biol. Abstr. **DD** 562. **CODEN** APVEAK. Annales de Paleontologie, 0003-4142.

ANNALES - SOCIETE GEOLOGIQUE DU NORD. See Earth Sciences - Geology.

ANNUAL REPORT - PALEONTOGRAPHICAL SOCIETY, LONDON. **Main/Corp** Paleontographical Society, London. UK. English. an. Paleontographical Society, Johnson Reprint Co Ltd, 24-28 Oval Road, London NW1 7DX England.

ARBEITEN AUS DEM INSTITUT FUR GEOLOGIE UND PALAONTOLOGIE AN DER UNIVERSITAT STUTTGART. See Earth Sciences - Geology.

ARGUMENTA PALAEOBOTANICA. Year 1- 1966-. 0587-5404. GW. English (German). ir. R A Remy Verlag, Postfach 6622, D-44 Munster West Germany. **Ind/Abst** GeoRef, Bibliogr. Index Geol. **LC** QE901. **CODEN** ARPBCV.

BEITRAGE ZUR PALAONTOLOGIE VON OSTERREICH. No. 1-. GW. German. ir. Otto Koeltz Science Publishers, PO Box 1380, D-624 Koenigstein West Germany. **Ind/Abst** GeoRef, Biol. Abstr. **LC** QE755.A8. **CODEN** BPOEDX.

BIBLIOGRAPHY AND INDEX OF MICROPALEONTOLOGY. See Indexes/Abstracts.

BOLLETTINO DELLA SOCIETA PALEONTOLOGICA ITALIANA. **Main/Corp** Societa Paleontologica Italiana. V. 1-. 0375-7633. Periodical. IT. Italian (articles preceded by English abstracts). sa. $30.00. Soc Paleontologica Italiana, Corso Venezia 55, Milano Italy. **Tel** 02/62085405. **Ind/Abst** GeoRef, Biol. Abstr. **LC** QE755.I8. **CODEN** BSPIAY. Index in last issue of volume - attached. (cum index). bk review. **Circ** 800. Paleontology.

BULLETIN - GEOLOGICAL SURVEY OF SOUTH AUSTRALIA. See Earth Sciences - Geology.

BULLETIN OF THE SOUTHERN CALIFORNIA PALEONTOLOGICAL SOCIETY. **Main/Corp** Southern California Paleontological Society. 1960. 0160-4937. Periodical. US. English. bm. $14.00. Southern California Paleontological Society, 3510 East Hilhaven Drive, West Covina CA 91791. **Tel** (818)332-8649. **Ed** June Maxwell. **Ind/Abst** GeoRef. bk review. **Circ** 120. (ctrl). Original articles and reports of society activities and also reprints sometimes of articles from other professional and amateur publications.

BULLETIN SIGNALETIQUE. 227 : PALEONTOLOGIE. VFOAT Paleontologie. V. 33-42. 0300-9335. Periodical. FR. French. ir. $82.48. Editions du CNRS, 23 rue du Maroc, 75019 Paris France. **LC** QE701. **DD** 016.56. Bulletin Signaletique. 216: Geologie, Paleontologie, Bibliograpie des Sciences de la Terre. Cahier H: Paleontologie.

BULLETINS OF AMERICAN PALEONTOLOGY. V. 1- (No. 1-). 0007-5779. Monographic Series. US. English. ir. $50.00. Paleontological Research Institute, 1259 Trumansburg Road, Ithaca NY 14850. **Tel** (607)273-6623. **Ed** Peter R Hoover. **Ind/Abst** Int. Aerosp. Abstr., GeoRef, Pet. Abstr., Bibliogr. Index Geol. **CODEN** BAPLAJ. **Circ** 500. (ctrl). A publication outlet for longer manuscripts that use fossils as the data base or that provide neontological information for application in paleontological studies.

CAHIERS DE MICROPALEONTOLOGIE. Began in 1965. 0068-5054. Monographic Series. FR. French (summaries in English). ir. Editions du CNRS, 15 Quai Anatole France, F-75700 Paris France. **Tel** (212)683-4441. **Ind/Abst** GeoRef, Bibliogr. Index Geol. Original articles on all areas of micropaleontology.

CATALOGUE OF CONODONTS. GW. English. ir. E Schweizerbartsche Verlag, Johannesstrasse 3-A, D7000 Stuttgart 1 West Germany. **Tel** 0711/625001. **Ed** Willi Ziegler. Contains information about paleontology.

CONTRIBUTIONS FROM THE MUSEUM OF PALEONTOLOGY, UNIVERSITY OF MICHIGAN. See Museums.

CRETACEOUS RESEARCH. Vol. 1, No. 1 (March 1980)-. 0195-6671. Periodical. UK. English (French). qt. $125.00. Academic Press, 4805 Sand Lake Road, Orlando FL 32819. **Tel** (305)345-4100. **Ind/Abst** GeoRef, Chem. Abstr., Pet. Abstr., Bibliogr. Index Geol. **CODEN** CRRSDD.

DEVELOPMENTS IN PALEONTOLOGY AND STRATIGRAPHY. 1-. Monographic Series. English. ir. Elsevier Science Publishing Company Inc, PO Box 1663 Grand Central Station, New York NY 10163.

ETUDES QUATERNAIRES LANGUEDOCIENNES. Issue No. 1 (1st Semester 1981)-. Periodical. FR. French. sa. Etudes Quaternaires Languedociennes Laboratoire de Prehistoire, de Vauvert 4 Avenue Robert Gourdon, F-30600 Vauvert France. **Tel** 66.88.46.80. **LC** UNC. **DD** 560.178. bk review. **Circ** 300. (ctrl). Covering geology, palaeoclimatology, and prehistoric life studies.

EVOLUTIONARY THEORY. See Biology.

EZHEGODNIK. **Main/Corp** Vsesoiuznoe Paleontologicheskoe Obshchestvo. V. 1-. 0201-9280. Russian (title also in French, V. 1-). ir. **Ind/Abst** GeoRef. **LC** QE701. **CODEN** EVPOA4.

EZHEGODNIK VSESOIUZNOGO PALEONTOLOGICHESKOGO OBSHCHESTVA. V. 16 (1955-1956)-. UR. Russian. ir. **LC** QE701. **DD** 560.5. Ezhegodnik Vserossiskogo Paleontologicheskogo Obshchestva.

FACIES. Began in 1979. 0172-9179. Periodical. GW. German (with English summaries). sa. 100 Domestic. Institut fur Palaontologie, Loewenichstrasse 28, D8520 Erlangen West Germany. **Tel** 09131-852622. **Ed** Prof Erik Flugel and Dr Erentraud Flugel. **Ind/Abst** GeoRef. **LC** QE640. **DD** 551.7. **Circ** 300. Papers dealing with facies analysis, paleoecology, sedimentology, and basin analysis.

FOSSILS QUARTERLY. Vol. 1, No. 1 (Spring 1982)-. 0734-5909. Periodical. US. English. qt. $9.00. Geotech Archives Ltd, 3616 Garden Club Lane, Charlotte NC 28210. **Ind/Abst** GeoRef. **LC** QE701. **DD** 560.5.

FREIBERGER FORSCHUNGSHEFTE. REIHE C. See Earth Sciences.

GEOBIOS (LYON, FRANCE). (GEOBIOS). No. 1-. 0016-6995. Periodical. FR. French. qt. $78.00. Geobios, Universite Claude Bernard, Departement des Sciences de la Terre, 43 Boulevard du 11 Novembre, 69622 Villeurbanne France. **Tel** 78898124. **Ed** L David. **Ind/Abst** GeoRef, Biol. Abstr., Pet. Abstr. **CODEN** GEBSAJ. bk review. (ctrl). An important journal of paleontology in all its aspects, paleoecology, biostratigraphy, biogeography. It publishes informations, bibliographical reviews and so on.

GEOLOGICA ET PALEONTOLOGICA. See Earth Sciences - Geology.

GEOLOGICA HUNGARICA. SERIES PALAEONTOLOGICA. VFOAT Series Palaeontologica. Issue 1. 0374-1893. HU. English, French, and German Hungarian and Russian. ir. Collets Holdings Ltd, Denington Estate,

Paleontology

Wellingborough England. **Ind/Abst** Biol. Abstr., GeoRef. **LC** QE755.H9. **CODEN** GHPADH. *Palaeontologia Hungarica.*

GOTTINGER ARBEITEN ZUR GEOLOGIE UND PALAONTOLOGIE. See Earth Sciences - Geology.

INA NEWSLETTER. See Bibliographies.

INTERNATIONAL QUARTERLY OF ENTOMOLOGY. See Zoology-Vertebrate and Invertebrate.

JAHRESBERICHTE UND MITTEILUNGEN DES OBERRHEINISCHEN GEOLOGISCHEN VEREINES. See Earth Sciences - Geology.

JOURNAL OF PALEONTOLOGY. V. 1- July 1927-. 0022-3360. Periodical. US. English. bm. $78.00. Society of Economic Paleontologists and Mineralogists, PO Box 4756, Tulsa OK 74104. **Tel** (607)273-6623. Ed Richard Hoare. **Ind/Abst** Life Sci. Collect., Coal Abstr., Int. Aerosp. Abstr., GeoRef, Nuci. Sci. Abstr., Biol. Abstr., Chem. Abstr. **LC** QE701. **CODEN** JPALAZ. (cum index). **Circ** 2,500. Contributions in any field of paleontology including invertebrates, vertebrates, micropaleontology, and paleobotany. Contributions may emphasize taxonomic, biostratigraphic, paleoecological, paleoclimatological, or paleobiogeographic aspects.

JOURNAL OF THE PALAEONTOLOGICAL SOCIETY OF INDIA. Main/Corp Paleontological Society of India. V. 1- 1956-. 0552-9360. Periodical. II. English. an. $70.00. Indian Books and Periodicals Syndicate, B-5/62 Dev Nagar PO Road Karol Bagh, New Delhi 110005 India. **Tel** 472-5444. **Ind/Abst** GeoRef, Bibliogr. Index Geol. **LC** QE756.I4. **CODEN** PLSIBJ. bk rev. **Circ** 1,000.

JOURNAL OF VERTEBRATE PALEONTOLOGY. Vol. 1, No. 1 (June 1981)-. 0272-4634. Periodical. US. English. qt. $70.00. Society of Vertebrate Paleontology, 900 Exposition Boulevard, Natural History Museum of Los Angeles County, Los Angeles CA 90007. **Tel** (213)744-3445. Ed Richard Estes. **Ind/Abst** Biol. Abstr., GeoRef. **LC** QE841. **CODEN** JVPADK. **Circ** 1,200. The journal covers all theoretical and applied aspects of paleontology of the chordates including their origins, evolution, anatomy, taxonomy, biostratigraphy, paleoecology, paleogeography, and paleoanthropology.

KASEKI. VFOAT Fossils. Began Publication in 1960. 0022-9202. Periodical. Japanese (includes abstracts in English). ir. Nihon Koseibutsu Gakkai, c/o Nihon Gakkai Jimu Senta 4-16, Yayoi 2 Bunkyo-ku Tokyo-to Japan. **Ind/Abst** GeoRef. **LC** QE701. **CODEN** KASKAS.

LETHAIA. V. 1- Jan. 1968-. 0024-1164. Periodical. NO. English (French or German). qt. 77.-. Universitetsforlaget, PO Box 2959/Toyen, Oslo 6 Norway. **Tel** (45)-2-27 60 60. Ed Anita Lofgren. **Ind/Abst** Life Sci. Collect., Coal Abstr., Biol. Abstr., GeoRef, Pet. Abstr., Bibliogr. Index Geol., Sci. Cit. Index, Abr. Ed., Pet. Abstr. **LC** QE701. **CODEN** LETHAT. adv acc. **Circ** 1,400. Publishes articles of international interest in the fields of palaeontology and stratigraphy.

MARINE MICROPALEONTOLOGY. V. 1- July 1976-. 0377-8398. Periodical. NE. English. qt. Elsevier Science Publishers, PO Box 211, 1000 AE Amsterdam Netherlands. **Tel** (020)5803.911. **Ind/Abst** Can. Environ., Life Sci. Collect., Biol. Abstr., GeoRef, Energy Res. Abstr., Sci. Cit. Index, Abr. Ed., Pet. Abstr., Bibliogr. Index Geol. **LC** QE719. **DD** 560. **CODEN** MAMIDH.

MEDEDELINGEN VAN DE WERKGROEP VOOR TERTIAIRE EN KWARTAIRE GEOLOGIE. See Earth Sciences - Geology.

MEMOIR (PALEONTOLOGICAL SOCIETY). (MEMOIR). 1-. 0078-8597. Monographic Series. US. English. ir. **Ind/Abst** Biol. Abstr., GeoRef. **CODEN** PSMECR.

MICROPALEONTOLOGY. V. 1- Jan. 1955-. 0026-2803. Periodical. US. English. qt. $90.00. Micropaleontology, PO Box 368, Lawrence KS 66044. **Tel** (913)843-1234. Ed John Van Couvering. **Ind/Abst** Coal Abstr., GeoRef, Biol. Abstr., Chem. Abstr., Int. Aerosp. Abstr., Life Sci. Collect., Pet. Abstr., Bibliogr. Index Geol. **LC** QE701. **CODEN** MCPLAI. **Circ** 1,400. (ctrl). The leading journal in its field, containing international research on stratigraphy, systematics, morphology, paleobiology, and paleoecology of all microorganisms with fossilized hard parts. *Micropaleontologist.*

MICROPALEONTOLOGY SPECIAL PUBLICATION. No. 1-. 0160-2071. Monographic Series. US. English. ir. $80.00. Micropaleontology Press, American Museum of Natural History, Central Park West at 79th Street, New York NY 10024. **Tel** (212)873-1405. Ed S A van Couvering. **Ind/Abst** GeoRef. **LC** UNC. **CODEN** MSPUDO. Research monographs and symposia on micropaleontology.

MITTEILUNGEN DER ABTEILUNG FUR GEOLOGIE, PALAONTOLOGIE UND BERGBAU AM LANDESMUSEUM JOANNEUM. See Earth Sciences - Geology.

MITTEILUNGEN DER BAYERISCHE STAATSSAMMLUNG FUR PALAONTOLOGIE UND HISTOR. GEOLOGIE. (MITTEILUNGEN - BAYERISCHE STAATSSAMMLUNG FUR PALAONTOLOGIE UND HISTORISCHE GEOLOGIE). Main/Corp Bayerische Staatssammlung fur Palaontologie und Historische Geologie. No. 1- 1961-. 0077-2070. German. ir. 2 Richard-Wagner-Strasse 10, Munchen West Germany. **Ind/Abst** GeoRef, Biol. Abstr. **LC** QE701. **CODEN** BSPGBT.

MIZUNAMI-SHI KASEKI HAKUBUTSUKAN KENKYU HOKOKU. VFOAT Bulletin of the Mizunami Fossil Museum. No. 1- 1974-. 0385-0900. English (Japanese). ir. Mizunami-Shi Kaseki Hakubutsukan, Yamanouchi Akiyocho, Mizunami 509-61 Japan. **Ind/Abst** GeoRef. **LC** QE756.J29.

MODERN QUATERNARY RESEARCH IN SOUTHEAST ASIA. Periodical. NE. English. an. 35.00. A A Balkema, Box 1675, 3000 BR Rotterdam Netherlands. **Tel** (3110)4145822. Ed G G Bartstra and W A Casparie. **Ind/Abst** GeoRef. **LC** QE696. **DD** 551.7905. **Circ** 500. Information on research projects and results. *Modern Quaternary Research in Southeast Asia.*

THE MOSASAUR. (THE MOSASAUR : THE JOURNAL OF THE DELAWARE VALLEY PALEONTOLOGICAL SOCIETY). Vol. 1 (Jan. 1983)-. 0736-3907. Periodical. US. English. ir. $12.00. Department of Geology, University of Pennsylvania, B-4 240 South 33rd Street, Philadelphia PA 19104. **Ind/Abst** GeoRef. **LC** QE701.M68. **DD** 560.5.

NATUURHISTORISCH MAANBLAD : ORGAAN VAN HET NATUURHISTORISCH GENOOTSCHAP IN LIMBURG. See Biology.

NEUES JAHRBUCH FUR GEOLOGIE UND PALAONTOLOGIE. ABHANDLUNGEN. See Yearbooks, Almanacs, Directories.

NEUES JAHRBUCH FUR GEOLOGIE UND PALAONTOLOGIE. MONATSHEFTE. See Yearbooks, Almanacs, Directories.

NEWS BULLETIN (AUSTIN, TEX.). (NEWS BULLETIN - SOCIETY OF VERTEBRATE PALEONTOLOGY). No. 1- Mar. 20, 1941-. 0096-9117. Periodical. US. English. ty. $12.00. Society of Vertebrate Paleontology, 900 Exposition Boulevard, Los Angeles CA 90007. **Tel** (213)744-3445. Ed John M Harris and Judy Bell. **Ind/Abst** GeoRef, Bibliogr. Index Geol. **LC** QE701. **DD** 566.05. **CODEN** SVPNAJ. **Circ** 1,200. Contains activity reports from vertebrate paleontologists in museums, colleges and universities, announcements of special meetings, publications, job opportunities, and new fossil preparation techniques.

NEWSLETTERS ON STRATIGRAPHY. See Earth Sciences - Geology.

NOTES DU LABORATOIRE DE PALEONTOLOGIE DE L'UNIVERSITE DE GENEVE. (NOTES DU LABORATOIRE DE PALEONTOLOGIE). Main/Corp Geneva. Universite. Laboratoire de Paleontologie. No. 1- 1977-. 0253-3251. Periodical. SZ. French. ir. Universite de Geneve, 13 rue des Manaichers, 1211 Geneve 4 Switzerland. **Ind/Abst** GeoRef.

NOTES - NEW YORK PALEONTOLOGICAL SOCIETY. Main/Corp New York Paleontological Society. US. English. $0.25 per copy. New York Paleontological Society, PO Box 287, Planetarium Station 127 West 83rd Street, New York NY 10024. **LC** QE701. **DD** 560.5.

OCEANIC MICROPALAEONTOLOGY. V. 1- 1977-. Periodical. US. English.

OSLENYTANI VITAK. Hungarian. ir. **Ind/Abst** GeoRef.

PALAEOGEOGRAPHY, PALAEOCLIMATOLOGY, PALAEOECOLOGY. V. 1- Mar. 1965-. 0031-0182. Periodical. English (French or German). ir. Elsevier Science Publishers, PO Box 211, 1000 AE Amsterdam Netherlands. **Tel** (020)5803.911. **Ind/Abst** Life Sci. Collect., Coal Abstr., GeoRef, ASTIS Bibliogr., ASTIS Curr. Aware. Bull., Biol. Abstr., Chem. Abstr., Nuci. Sci. Abstr., Curr. Contents, Bull. Signal., Bibliogr. Index Geol., Sci. Cit. Index, Abr. Ed., Pet. Abstr. **LC** QE500. **CODEN** PPPYAB. (cum index).

PALAEONTOGRAPHICA. ABTEILUNG B : PALAOPHYTOLOGIE. V.78- 1933-. 0375-0299. GW. English (German). ir. E Schweizerbartsche Verlag, Johannesstrasse 3-A, D7000 Stuttgart 1 West Germany. **Tel** 0711/625001. Ed H J Schweitzer. **Ind/Abst** Coal Abstr., Biol. Abstr., GeoRef. **CODEN** PABPAD. adv acc. Contains information on paleophytology. *Palaeontographica.*

PALAEONTOGRAPHICA AMERICANA. V. 1- 1916-. 0078-8546. US. English. ir. Paleontological Research Institute, 1259 Trumansburg Road, Ithaca NY 14850. Ed Peter R Hoover. **Ind/Abst** GeoRef, Biol. Abstr. **CODEN** PALAAI. **Circ** 400. (ctrl). A publication outlet for longer manuscripts that use fossils as the data base, or that provide neontological information for application in paleontological studies.

PALAEONTOGRAPHICAL SOCIETY MONOGRAPHS. (MONOGRAPHS - PALAEONTOGRAPHICAL SOCIETY (GREAT BRITAIN)). Main/Corp Palaeontographical Society (Great Britain). Volume I- Issued for 1847-. 0376-2734. Monographic Series. UK. English. ir. **Ind/Abst** Biol. Abstr., GeoRef. **CODEN** PLTSAJ.

PALAEONTOLOGIA AFRICANA. V. 1- 1953-. 0078-8554. Periodical. SA. English. ir. Bernard Price Institute for Palaeontological, Research of Witwatersrand University, 1 Jan Smuts Avenue, Johannesburg 2001 South Africa. **Tel** (011)716-2727. Ed M A Raath. **Ind/Abst** GeoRef, Art Archaeol. Tech. Abstr., Biol. Abstr., Bibliogr. Index Geol. **CODEN** PBPRAS. **Circ** 600. All aspects of paleontology: vertebrate, invertebrate, plant, taphonomy, biostratigraphy, phylogeny, systematics.

PALAEONTOLOGIA JUGOSLAVICA. V. 1- 1958-. 0552-9352. Periodical. YU. Serbo-Croatian - C. qt. 30.00. Jugoslavenska Akademija Zansti, Razred za Prirodne Znanosti, 41000 Zagreb Yugoslavia. **Tel** (041)449-093. Ed Mirko Malez. **Ind/Abst** Biol. Abstr., GeoRef, Bibliogr. Index Geol. **LC** QE701. **CODEN** PLJUA9. (ctrl). Covers micropaleontology, nanofossils, biostratigraphy, and vertebrate paleontology.

PALAEONTOLOGIA POLONICA. No. 1-. 0078-8562. Monographic Series. PL. English. ir. ARS Polona, Krakowskie Przedmiescie 7, 00-068 Warsaw Poland. **Ind/Abst** Biol. Abstr., GeoRef. **CODEN** PLPOAL.

PALAEONTOLOGICAL BULLETIN (NEW ZEALAND GEOLOGICAL SURVEY). (PALAEONTOLOGICAL BULLETIN). Began with: No. 1, published in 1913. Monographic Series. NZ. English. ir. Science Information Publishing Center, Box 9741, Wellington New Zealand. **Tel** 858 939. Ed Ian MacKenzie. **Ind/Abst** Bibliogr. Index Geol. **Circ** 800. Taxonomy and chronology of New Zealand fossil groups.

PALAEONTOLOGY. V. 1- Nov. 1957-. 0031-0239. Periodical. UK. English. qt. 86.00. Marston Book Services, PO Box 87, Oxford OX4 1LB England. **Tel** 0865 722146. Ed D E G Briggs. **Ind/Abst** Life Sci. Collect., Coal Abstr., GeoRef, Biol. Abstr., Pet. Abstr., Bibliogr. Index Geol. **CODEN** PONTAD. (cum index). **Circ** 500. Publishes papers on all aspects of paleontology and stratigraphic paleontology. Review articles and short papers are also included and each issue is illustrated.

PALAEOVERTEBRATA. V. 1- June 1967-. 0031-0247. Periodical. French (with some articles in English or German). ir. Universite Montpellier, Place Eugene Bataillon, 34060 Montpellier Cedex France. **Ind/Abst** GeoRef, Bibliogr. Index Geol. **NLM** W1 PA361U. **CODEN** PLVTAW.

PALAIOS. 0883-1351. Periodical. US. English. bm. $32.00 Members; $50.00 Nonmembers. Society of Economic Paleontologists and Mineralogists, PO Box 4756, Tulsa OK 74159-0756.

PALEOBIOLOGY. V. 1- Winter 1975-. 0094-8373. Periodical. US. English. qt. $35.00. Paleobiology Subscriptions, PO Box 115, Jacksonville NY 14854. Tel (607)273-6623. Ed J J Sepkoski. **Ind/Abst** Life Sci. Collect., Biol. Abstr., GeoRef, Bibliogr. Index Geol., Pet. Abstr., Sci. Cit. Index, Abr. Ed., Abstr. Anthropol. LC QE701. DD 560.5. **CODEN** PALBBM. bk rev. adv acc. Circ 2,250. (ctrl). Publishes original contributions dealing with any aspect of biological paleontology. Emphasis is place upon biological or paleobiological processes and patterns.

PALEOBIOS. VFOAT Paleo Bios. Began in 1967. 0031-0298. Monographic Series. US. English. ir. $3.00. Museum of Paleontology, University of California, Berkeley CA 97420. Tel (415)642-1821. Ed Michael G Kellogg. **Ind/Abst** GeoRef. LC QE701. DD 560.5. **CODEN** PLBIA. Circ 1,000. All aspects of paleontology and other studies having clear paleontological implications.

PALEOCLIMAS. No. 1- 1971-. 0100-5472. Periodical. Portuguese (summaries in English). ir. **Ind/Abst** GeoRef. **CODEN** PLCLDI.

PALEONTOLOGIA MEXICANA. Main/Corp Universidad Nacional Autonoma de Mexico. Instituto de Geologia. No. 1- 1954-. 0543-7652. Monographic Series. MX. Spanish. ir. Institute Geologia University Nacional, Ciudad Universitaria, 04510 Mexico DF Mexico. **Ind/Abst** GeoRef, Bibliogr. Index Geol. LC QE749. **CODEN** MUGPA9.

PALEONTOLOGICAL JOURNAL. V. 1- 1967-. 0031-0301. Periodical. US. English (Russian). qt. John Wiley & Sons Inc, 605 Third Avenue, New York NY 10158. Tel (800)526-5368. **Ind/Abst** GeoRef, Bibliogr. Index Geol. LC QE701. DD 560.5. **CODEN** PJOUA.

PALEONTOLOGICHESKII ZHURNAL. VFOAT Paleontological Journal. 1959-. 0031-031X. Periodical. UR. Russian (tables of contents also in English). qt. $40.50. Victor Kamkin Inc (70690), 12224 Parklawn Drive, Rockville MD 20852. Tel (301)881-5973. **Ind/Abst** Biol. Abstr., GeoRef, Bibliogr. Index Geol. LC QE701. DD 560.5. **CODEN** PAZHA7.

PALEONTOLOGY AND GEOLOGY OF THE BADWATER CREEK AREA, CENTRAL WYOMING. Series/Titl Annals of Carnegie Museum. US. English. Carnegie Museum, 4400 Forbes Avenue, Pittsburgh PA 15213. LC AS36. DD 500.908 S.

PALYNOS. See Biology - Botany.

PAPERS ON PALEONTOLOGY. No. 1-. 0148-3838. Monographic Series. US. English. ir. University of Michigan, Museum of Paleontology, Ann Arbor MI 48109. **Ind/Abst** GeoRef. LC QE701. DD 560.5. **CODEN** PPUMD3.

THE PLASTER JACKET. No. 1- Sept. 1966-. 0554-288X. US. English. ir. Florida State Museum, Florida University, Gainesville FL 32711. **Ind/Abst** GeoRef. LC QE841. DD 566.09759. **CODEN** PLJABI.

PRAPARATOR. See Earth Sciences.

QUATERNARY RESEARCH. V. 1- Sept. 1970-. 0033-5894. Periodical. US. English. bm. Academic Press, 4805 Sand Lake Road, Orlando FL 32819. Tel (305)345-4100. **Ind/Abst** Can. Environ., Int. Aerosp. Abstr., Life Sci. Collect., GeoRef, Comput. Control Abstr., Electr. Electron. Abstr., Sci. Abstr. Sect. A. Phys. Abstr., ASTIS Bibliogr., ASTIS Curr. Aware. Bull., Biol. Abstr., Chem. Abstr., Sel. Water Resour. Abstr., Bibliogr. Agric., Sci. Cit. Index, Abr. Ed., Bibliogr. Index Geol., Phys. Abstr. LC QE696. **CODEN** QRESAV.

REVIEW OF PALAEOBOTANY AND PALYNOLOGY. V. 1- Mar. 1967-. 0034-6667. Periodical. English (with some articles in French and German). ir. Elsevier Science Publishers, PO Box 211, 1000 AE Amsterdam The Netherlands. Tel (020)5803.911. **Ind/Abst** Life Sci. Collect., Coal Abstr., GeoRef, ASTIS Bibliogr., ASTIS Curr. Aware. Bull., Biol. Abstr., Curr. Contents, Bull. Signal., Bibliogr. Agric., Sci. Cit. Index, Abr. Ed., Pet. Abstr., Bibliogr. Index Geol. LC QE993. DD 561.05 **CODEN** RPPYAX. (cum index).

REVISTA ESPANOLA DE MICROPALEONTOLOGIA. V. 1- 1969-. 0556-655X. Periodical. SP. Spanish. ty. $67.49. Revista Espanola de Micropal, Serrano 116, Madrid 6 Spain. **Ind/Abst** GeoRef, Biol. Abstr., Bibliogr. Index Geol. **CODEN** RTEMB5.

REVUE DE MICROPALEONTOLOGIE. Yearly V. 1-. 0035-1598. Periodical. FR. French. qt. $45.23. Reuve de Micropaleontologie, Maison D Geologie BP 11-705, 75224 Paris Cedex 05 France. Ed M M Neumann. **Ind/Abst** GeoRef, Bibliogr. Index Geol. **CODEN** RMCPAM. (cum index). bk rev. adv acc. Contains information about micropaleontology, microfossils, stratigraphy, ecology, palaeoecology, biogeography, systematic, evolution.

REVUE DE PALEOBIOLOGIE. Vol. 1, No. 1 (June 1982)-. Periodical. French (English). sa. Museum d'Histoire Naturelle, 1 Route de Malagnou, 1211 Geneve 6 Suisse Switzerland. LC QE701. DD 560.5.

RIVISTA ITALIANA DI PALEONTOLOGIA E STRATIGRAFIA. V. 1- 1895-. 0035-6883. Periodical. IT. English (Italian). qt. 59.500. Dipartimento di Scienze Terra, Univ Milano, Via Mangiagalli 34, Milan Italy. Tel 292813. **Ind/Abst** GeoRef, Biol. Abstr., Pet. Abstr., Bibliogr. Index Geol. LC QE701. DD 560.5. **CODEN** RPLSAT. bk rev. adv acc. Circ 450. Covers macropaleontology, micropaleontology, stratigraphy, paleogeography, paleoecology, taxonomy, and morphology. Rivista Italiana di Paleontologia.

RIVISTA ITALIANA DI PALEONTOLOGIA E STRATIGRAFIA. MEMORIA. 0375-9784. Monographic Series. IT. Italian (summaries in English). ir. Dipartimento di Scienze Terra, University Milanovia, Mangialalli 34, Milano Italy. **Ind/Abst** GeoRef, Bibliogr. Index Geol. **CODEN** RVPMA5.

SBORNIK GEOLOGICKYCH VED. PALEONTOLOGIE. VFOAT Svornik Geologickych Ved. Vol. 1-. 0036-5297. CS. Czech, English, and German with summaries in Russian and Czech. ir. $7.75. Artia, PO 790 VE Smeckach, Praha 1 Czechoslovakia. **Ind/Abst** GeoRef. LC QE755.C95. **CODEN** SGPABC. Sbornik Ustredniho Ustavu Geologickeho.

SCHWEIZERISCHE PALAEONTOLOGISCHE ABHANDLUNGEN. VFOAT Memoires Suisses de Paleontologie. V. 1- 1874-. 0080-7389. Monographic Series. US. German (French). ir. Birkhauser Boston Inc, 380 Greeen Street, PO Box 3005, Cambridge MA 02139. Tel (617)576-6638. **Ind/Abst** Bibliogr. Index Geol. **CODEN** SPAAAX.

SENCKENBERGIANA LETHAEA. Vol. 35-. 0037-2110. Periodical. GW. German (text in French or English). bm. 66.50. Verlag Dr Waldemar Kramer, Bornheimer Landwher 57A, 6000 Frankfurt 60 West Germany. Tel 069-449046. Ed Wolfgang Struve. **Ind/Abst** Life Sci. Collect., GeoRef, Biol. Abstr., Chem. Abstr., Bibliogr. Index Geol. LC QE701. DD 560.5. **CODEN** SLETAE. Index in last issue of volume - attached. Papers on paleontology (paleozoology and paleobotany) with reference to actuogeology and biochronology are published. Senckenbergiana.

SEPM SHORT COURSE. Main/Corp Society of Economic Paleontologists and Mineralogists. VFOAT S.E.P.M. Short Course. VAT Society of Economic Paleontologists and Mineralogists Short Course. No. 1-. 0160-0966. US. English. ir. Society of Economic Paleontologists and Mineralogists, PO Box 4756, Tulsa OK 74159. Tel (918)743-9765. **Ind/Abst** Chem. Abstr., GeoRef. **CODEN** SEPMD2.

SMITHSONIAN CONTRIBUTIONS TO PALEOBIOLOGY. No. 1-. 0081-0266. Monographic Series. US. English. Smithsonian Institute Press, PO Box 1579, Washington DC 20013. **Ind/Abst** Life Sci. Collect., GeoRef, Biol. Abstr. LC QE701. DD 560.8 S. **CODEN** SPBYA8.

SPECIAL PAPERS IN PALEONTOLOGY. No. 1-. 0038-6804. Monographic Series. UK. English. qt. 86.00. Marston Book Services, 108 Conley Road, Oxford OX4 1JF England. Tel (0865)722146. Ed D E G Briggs. **Ind/Abst** Biol. Abstr., GeoRef, Bibliogr. Index Geol. **CODEN** SPPAB7. Circ 500. Publishes papers on all aspects of paleontology. Reviews and short papers are included as well as high quality photographs.

TOHOKU DAIGAKU RIGAKUBU CHISHITSUGAKU KOSEIBUTSUGAKU KYOSHITSU KENKYU HOBUN HOKOKU. See Earth Sciences - Geology.

TULANE STUDIES IN GEOLOGY AND PALEONTOLOGY. See Earth Sciences - Geology.

UNIVERSITY OF KANSAS PALEONTOLOGICAL CONTRIBUTIONS. ARTICLE. Main/Corp Kansas. University. VFOAT Paleontological Contributions. 1-. 0075-5044. Monographic Series. US. English. ir. Exchange and Gifts Department, University of Kansas Libraries, Lawrence KS 66045. Tel (913)864-3338. Ed Richard A Robison. **Ind/Abst** GeoRef, Biol. Abstr. LC QE701. DD 560.82. **CODEN** KUPABM. Circ 700. Principally systematic invertebrate paleontology.

UNIVERSITY OF KANSAS PALEONTOLOGICAL CONTRIBUTIONS. MONOGRAPH. (UNIVERSITY OF KANSAS PALEONTOLOGICAL CONTRIBUTIONS. MONOGRAPHS). 1-. 0278-9744. Monographic Series. US. English. ir. Paleontological Institute, University of Kansas Library Sales Office, Lawrence KS 66045. Tel (913)864-3338. Ed Richard A Robison. **Ind/Abst** GeoRef. Circ 700. (ctrl). Systematic paleontology, usually dealing with invertebrates, often with geological implications.

UNIVERSITY OF KANSAS PALEONTOLOGICAL CONTRIBUTIONS. PAPERS. (UNIVERSITY OF KANSAS PALEONTOLOGICAL CONTRIBUTIONS. PAPER). VFOAT Paleontological Contributions. Began in 1965. 0075-5052. Monographic Series. US. English. ir. University of Kansas Libraries, Exchange and Gifts Department, Library Sales Office, Lawrence KS 66045. **Ind/Abst** GeoRef, Biol. Abstr. LC QE701. DD 560.5. **CODEN** KCPCA3.

UNIVERSITY OF LOUISVILLE STUDIES IN PALEONTOLOGY AND STRATIGRAPHY. Main/Corp Louisville. University. No. 1- 1973-. 0275-5513. Monographic Series. US. English. ir. University of Louisville, c/o J Ballard, Campus Store, Louisville KY 40292. **Ind/Abst** GeoRef, Bibliogr. Index Geol.

UTRECHT MICROPALEONTOLOGICAL BULLETINS. 1-. 0083-4963. Monographic Series. NE. English. ir. T Van Schalk, Singel 105, Okijk Netherlands. Ed T Van Schaik. **Ind/Abst** GeoRef, Bibliogr. Index Geol. LC QE719. DD 560.5. **CODEN** UTMBAA.

UTRECHT MICROPALEONTOLOGICAL BULLETINS. SPECIAL PUBLICATION. No. 1-. 0165-2753. Monographic Series. NE. English. ir. Sales Office, UMB Singel 105, Odijk the Netherlands. **Ind/Abst** GeoRef. **CODEN** UMBPDJ.

VOPROSY MIKRO-PALEONTOLOGII. 1-. 0507-3693. UR. Russian. Victor Kamkin Inc, 12224 Parklawn Drive, Rockville MD 20852. Tel (301)881-5973. **Ind/Abst** GeoRef. LC QE719. **CODEN** VMIKAD.

PAPER & PULP INDUSTRY

ABITIBI-PRICE. Began publications in 197-. 0705-7490. Newspaper. CN. English. Abitibi Paper Company, Public Relations Department Toronto-Dominion Centre, Toronto Ontario M5K 1B3 Canada. DD 338.76349.

ABSTRACT BULLETIN OF THE INSTITUTE OF PAPER CHEMISTRY. See Indexes/Abstracts.

ALKALINE PULPING CONFERENCE. Main/Corp Technical Association of the Pulp and Paper Industry. VFOAT Tappi Alkaline Pulping Conference Preprint. 0364-2763. US. English. an. Technical Association of the Pulp and Paper Industry, Ond Dunwoody Park, Atlanta GA 30341. **Ind/Abst** Chem. Abstr. **CODEN** TAPCDN.

L'ANNUAIRE DU PAPIER. See Yearbooks, Almanacs, Directories.

ANNUAL NEWSPRINT SUPPLEMENT. CANADIAN PULP AND PAPER ASSOCIATION. (ANNUAL NEWSPRINT SUPPLEMENT - CANADIAN PULP AND PAPER ASSOCIATION). Main/Corp Canadian Pulp and Paper Association. 1971-. 0316-4241. CN. English (text also in French). an. 2300 Sun Life Building, Montreal

Paper & Pulp Industry

Quebec H3B 2X9 Canada. **LC** HD9839.N4. **DD** 338.476762860971. *Annual Newsprint Supplement.*

ANNUAL REPORT - INTERNATIONAL PAPER COMPANY. **Main/Corp** International Paper Company. 0190-6461. US. English. an. **LC** HD9829. **DD** 338.76762.

ANNUAL REPORT - PULP AND PAPER RESEARCH INSTITUTE OF CANADA. **Main/Corp** Pulp and Paper Research Institute of Canada. 0079-7960. Periodical. CN. English. an. Pulp and Paper Institute of Canada, 570 St John's Boulevard/Pointe Claire, Quebec H9R 3J9 Canada. **LC** TS1080. **DD** 676.072071.

ANNUAL STATISTICAL SUMMARY - AMERICAN PAPER INSTITUTE. *See* Statistics.

ARBERETNING OG REGNSKAP - UNION. **Main/Corp** Union A/S. (1972-). Periodical. Norwegian. ir.

ATCP. **Main/Corp** Associaion Mexicana de Tecnicos de las Industrias de la Celulosa y del Papel. Began with May 1961 issue. Periodical. MX. Spanish. bm. $61.00. AV Insurgentes #3493, Poseidon 504, 14020 Mexico DF Mexico. **Tel** 573-14-44. Ed Octavio Tirado. **LC** TS1080. bk rev. adv acc. **Circ** 1,500. (ctrl). Local and international technical papers and news, statistics, etc. International commercial advertisement. Materials are written or translated into Spanish making available to Spanish-speaking countries.

ATIP. ASSOCIATION TECHNIQUE DE L'INDUSTRIE PAPETIERE. (ATIP). **Main/Corp** Association Technique de l'Industrie Papetiere. **VFOAT** Revue ATIP. V. 20- 1966-. 0004-5896. Periodical. French. ir. Association Technique de l'Industrie Papetiere, 154 Boulevard Haussmann, 75008 Paris France. **Ind/Abst** Abstr. Bull. Inst. Paper Chem., Chem. Abstr. **CODEN** ATIPBH. *Techniques et Recherches Papetieres, Bulletin.*

L'AUXILIAIRE DES FABRICANTS DE CARTONNAGES. Periodical. FR. French. ir. 50.00. 31 Place St Ferdinand, Paris 75017 France. **LC** TS185.A1. **DD** 676.305. *Auxiliaire: Cartonnages & i.e. et Complexes.*

BARR'S POST CARD NEWS. 1973. 0744-4540. Periodical. US. English. wk. $15.00. Barr's Post Card News, 70 South Sixth Street, Lansing IA 52151. **Tel** (319)538-4500. Ed Bill Cote. bk rev adv acc. **Circ** 4,000. All the facts about post cards and other american paper. Includes post card news, articles, mail auctions, calendar of events, classified advertising, sales, etc.

BIBLIOGRAPHIC SERIES - INSTITUTE OF PAPER CHEMISTRY. *See* Bibliographies.

BOXBOARD CONTAINERS. 0006-8497. Periodical. US. English. mo. MacLean-Hunter Publishing Corporation, 300 Adams Street, Chicago IL 60606. **Tel** (312)726-2802. **Ind/Abst** Predicasts, Abstr. Bull. Inst. Paper Chem., Int. Packag. Abstr., Print. Abstr., Funk Scott Index Corp. Ind. **LC** TS1200.A1. **DD** 338.4767628805. *Shears.*

BUMAZNAJA PROMYSLENMOST'. (BUMAZHNAIA PROMYSHLENMOST'). 1- July 1922-. 0007-5817. Periodical. UR. Russian. mo $39.50. Victor Kamkin Inc (70090), 12224 Parklawn Drive, Rockville MD 20852. **Tel** (301)881-5973. **Ind/Abst** Sel. Water Resour. Abstr., Abstr. Bull. Inst. Paper Chem., Pap. Board Abstr., Chem. Abstr. **CODEN** BUMPAK.

BUSINESS MONITOR. REPORT ON THE CENSUS OF PRODUCTION. PAPER AND BOARD. *See* Business.

CANADIAN PAPER ANALYST. V. 1- Feb. 1978-. 0705-6710. Periodical. CN. English. ir. $135.42. JDR Publications, PO Box 300 Victoria Station, Westmount Que H3Z 2V5 Canada. **Tel** (514)933-8749. Ed Jim Rowland. **DD** 338.476760971. Analysis in marketing, prices, costs etc. on Canadian pulp, paper and paperboard industry.

CANADIAN PULP AND PAPER ASSOCIATION. NEWSPRINT DATA. (NEWSPRINT DATA - CANADIAN PULP AND PAPER ASSOCIATION). 32nd- 1970-. 0068-9491. Periodical. CN. English. ir. Canadian Pulp and Paper Association, 2300 Sun Life Building, Montreal Quebec H3B 2X9 Canada. **DD** 338.47676286. *Newsprint Data, 0317-4506.*

CANADIAN PULP AND PAPER CAPACITY. **VFOAT** Capacite Canadienne de Production de Pates et Papiers. 0823-2873. CN. English. an. Canadian Pulp And Paper Association, Sun Life Building 23rd Floor/1155 Metcalfe Street, Montreal Que H3B 2X9 Canada. **DD** 338.476760971. *Canadian Pulp and Paper Industry, 0823-2865.*

CANADIAN PULP AND PAPER INDUSTRY. (CANADIAN PULP AND PAPER INDUSTRY MICROFORM). 0008-4867. Periodical. US. English. University Microfilms International, Customer Service, 300 North Zeeb Road, Ann Arbor MI 48106. **DD** 676.0971. *Western Pulp and Paper, 0701-8320.*

CANADIAN PULP AND PAPER PRODUCTS. **Main/Corp** Canadian Pulp and Paper Association. Economic and Statistical Service. **VFOAT** Produits des Pates et Papiers du Canada, Exports and Imports. 1973/1974-. 0708-8426. CN. English (French). an. Canadian Pulp and Paper Association, Suite 2300/1155 Metcalfe Street, Montreal Quebec H3B 2X9 Canada. **DD** 382.456760971. *Canadian Pulp and Paper Products. Exports, 0708-8418.*

CARACTERE. *See* Printing.

THE COMPETITIVE GRADE FINDER FOR THE PAPER INDUSTRY. US. English. an. $12.50. Grade Finders Inc, PO Box 444, Bala-Cynwyd PA 19004. **LC** TS1088. **DD** 338.47676202573.

CONVERTER. (THE CONVERTER). Began with Jan. 1964?. 0010-8189. Periodical. UK. English. mo. Quadrant Subscription Services Ltd, Oakfield House, Perrymount Road, Haywards Heath Sussex England. **Ind/Abst** Abstr. Bull. Inst. Paper Chem., Int. Packag. Abstr., Pap. Board Abstr.

DIRECTORY - TECHNICAL ASSOCIATION OF THE PULP AND PAPER INDUSTRY. *See* Yearbooks, Almanacs, Directories.

DISPOSABLES AND NONWOVENS. **VFOAT** Disposables & Nonwovens. Vol. 1-5, July 1970-1974. 0012-3811. Periodical. UK. English. ir. 12 Domestic 14 Foreign. Chandler Publications Ltd, 2 South Street, Totnes Devon England. **Tel** (0803) 864668. Ed S R D Heming. **Ind/Abst** World Text Abstr. **LC** TS1828. bk rev. adv acc. **Circ** 4,000. A newssheet for the wood-based disposable market covering manufacture, formulation, conversion and industrial news.

ENGINEERING CONFERENCE. 0271-9959. US. English. an. One Dunwoody Park, Atlanta GA 30338. **Ind/Abst** Eng. Index Annu., Eng. Index Mon., Eng. Index Bioeng. Abstr., Eng. Index Energy Abstr., Chem. Abstr. **LC** TS1080. **DD** 676.2. **CODEN** ECOPD8.

EUROPA BIRKNER. **VFOAT** Papier, Papiererzeugnisse, Zellstoff. English (French), German, Italian, Portuguese, and Spanish). an. Birkner Co, Postfach 520660 Wichmannstrasse 4, D-2000 Hamburg 52 West Germany. **LC** HD9835.A1. **DD** 338.767620254.

FIBRE BOX HANDBOOK. *See* Packaging.

FINE PAPER DIRECTORY. *See* Yearbooks, Almanacs, Directories.

FINNISH PAPER AND TIMBER. V. 1-31. 0015-2455. Periodical. Fl. English. bm. Finnish Paper and Timber Journal Company, PO Box 176, SF-00100 Helsinki 14 Finland. **Ind/Abst** Predicasts. *Suomen Paperi- Ja Puutavaralehti.*

FORET ET PAPIER. No. 1- Jan. 1975-. 0319-762X. CN. French. bm. $33.27. MacLean Hunter, PO Box 100, Station A, Toronto Ontario M5W 1A7 Canada. **DD** 338.476760971.

GADGET COMPETITION. **VFOAT** Concours de Gadgets. 1980-. 0229-7078. CN. English (includes some text in French). an. Canadian Pulp and Paper Association, Technical Section, 2300 Sun Life Building, Montreal Quebec H3B 2X9 Canada. **DD** 676.079. *Gadget Competition Entries, 0382-6244.*

GADGET COMPETITION ENTRIES. **Main/Corp** Canadian Pulp and Paper Association. Technical Section. -1979. 0382-6244. CN. English (French). an. 4.00 Members, 5.00 Nonmembers. Canadian Pulp and Paper Association, 2300 Sun Life Building, Montreal Quebec H3B 2X9 Canada. **Tel** (514)866-6621. **DD** 676.079. **Circ** 300. Includes all entries made by Canadian pulp, paper or board mill workers of innovative gadgets which have been proved to be of value to the industry.

GIDROLIZNAIA I LESOKHIMICHESKAIA PROMYSHLENNOST. (HYDROLYSIS AND WOOD CHEMISTRY USSR). **VFOAT** Hydrolysis and Wood Chemistry U.S.S.R. 1977, No. 1-. 0730-8124. Periodical. US. English (Russian). ir. Allerton Press Inc, 150 Fifth Avenue, New York NY 10011. **Tel** (212)924-3950. **Ind/Abst** Excerpta Med., Bibliogr. Agric. **LC** TS1171. **DD** 676.12.

GOLFKARTON- EN KARTONNAGE-INDUSTRIE PRODUKTIESTATISTIEKEN. **Main/Corp** Netherlands (Kingdom, 1815-). Centraal Bureau voor de Statistiek. Hoofdafdeling Statistieken van Industrie en Bouwnijverheid. **VFOAT** Corrugated Board and Folding Carton Converting Production Statistics. Dutch (summaries in English). ir. 8.75. Centraal Bureau voor de Statistiek, Hoofdafdeling Statistieken van Industrie en Bouwnijverheid, Staatsuitgeverij, S-Gravenhage Netherlands. **LC** HD9839.P33.

IEEE CONFERENCE RECORD OF ANNUAL PULP AND PAPER INDUSTRY TECHNICAL CONFERENCE. **Main/Conf** Pulp and Paper Industry Technical Conference. **VAT** Institute of Electrical and Electronics Engineers Conference Record of Annual Pulp and Paper Industry Technical Conference. 1971-. 0190-2172. US. English. ir. IEEE, 445 Hoes Lane, Piscataway NJ 08854. **Ind/Abst** Eng. Index, Index IEEE Publ. **LC** TS1109. **DD** 675. **CODEN** CRCFDZ. *Pulp and Paper Industry Technical Conference.*

INDIAN PRINT AND PAPER. **VFOAT** Indian Print & Paper. Periodical. English. ir. Indian Print and Paper, Chartered Bank Building, Calcutta India.

INDIAN PULP & PAPER. (INDIAN PULP AND PAPER). Began publication with July 1946 issue. 0019-6231. Periodical. II. English. bm. $9.00. Indian Pulp and Paper, 15 India Exchange Place, 3rd Floor, Calcutta 700 001 India. **Tel** 22-3411. Ed R K Dam. **Ind/Abst** Abstr. Bull. Inst. Paper Chem., Pap. Board Abstr., Chem. Abstr., Bibliogr. Agric. **CODEN** IPPAAW. bk rev. adv acc. **Circ** 3,000. Promotion of Indian pulp and paper industry.

INDICATORE CARTARIO : RASSEGNA BIBLIOGRAFICA MENSILE. Began in 1980. 0392-9108. Periodical. Italian. mo. **Ind/Abst** Abstr. Bull. Inst. Paper Chem.

INDICE DE TECNICOS PAPELEROS ESPANOLES. *See* Indexes/Abstracts.

INDUSTRIA DELLA CARTA. 1st Year, Jan. 1963-. 0019-7548. Periodical. IT. Italian. mo. $35.64. Industria Della Carta, c/o Italia N6, 20122 Milano Italy. **Ind/Abst** Abstr. Bull. Inst. Paper Chem., Pap. Board Abstr., Chem. Abstr. **CODEN** ICAMA4.

INDUSTRIE DES PATES ET PAPIERS. (L'INDUSTRIE DES PATES ET PAPIERS DANS LES PAYS MEMBRES DE L'OCDE). **VFOAT** Pulp and Paper Industry in the OECD Member Countries, The Pulp and Paper Industry in the OECD Member Countries. 1968/69-. French (English). an. OECD, 1750 Pennsylvania Avenue NW, Washington DC 20006. **LC** HD9769.W5. **DD** 338.476760212. *Industrie des Pates et Papiers dans les Pays Membres de l'OECD la Finlande.*

INFORMATION - SWEDISH PULP AND PAPER ASSOCIATION. **Main/Corp** Svenska Cellulosa- Och Pappersbruksforeningen. Periodical. SW. English. mo. Swedish Pulp and Paper Association, Villagatan 1, S-114 32 Stockholm Sweden. **Tel** 46 8 789 28 00. **Ind/Abst** Pap. Board Abstr.

INSTRUMENTATION IN THE PULP AND PAPER INDUSTRY. 0361-4719. Periodical. US. English. an. Instrument Society of America, PO Box 3561, Durham NC 27702. **Tel** (412)281-3171. **Ind/Abst** Eng. Index, Eng. Index Annu., Eng. Index Mon. **CODEN** IPPICO.

INTERNATIONAL PAPER BOARD INDUSTRY. Began publication with Vol. 1, 1958. 0020-8191. Periodical. UK. English. mo. $26.05. Binsted Publications, Walton House/90 London Road/Hook, Hampshire RG27 9LF England. **Tel** 025672 4176/7. **Ind/Abst** Abstr. Bull. Inst. Paper Chem., Int. Packag. Abstr., Pap. Board Abstr. **LC** TS1135.

INTERNATIONAL PULP & PAPER DIRECTORY. *See* Yearbooks, Almanacs, Directories.

JAPAN PULP AND PAPER. **VFOAT** Japan Pulp & Paper. Began in 1963. 0285-726X. Periodical. JA. English. qt. Japan Publishing Trading Company Ltd, PO Box 5030, Tokyo International, Tokyo 100-31 Japan. **Ind/Abst** Abstr. Bull. Inst. Paper Chem., Pap. Board Abstr., Chem. Abstr., Bibliogr. Agric. **CODEN** JPUPAB.

Paper & Pulp Industry

JOURNAL OF PULP AND PAPER SCIENCE. (JOURNAL OF PULP AND PAPER SCIENCE : TRANSACTIONS OF THE TECHNICAL SECTION). **VFOAT** JPPS. Vol. 9, No. 1 (Mar. 1983)-. 0826-6220. Periodical. CN. English (abstracts also in French). bm. $50.30 US and Canada 75.00 Others. Canadian Pulp and Paper Association, 2300 Sun Life Building, Montreal Province of Quebec H3B 2X9 Canada. **Tel** (514)866-6621. **Ed** Derek Page. **Ind/Abst** Abstr. Bull. Inst. Paper Chem., Comput. Control Abstr., Electr. Electron. Abstr., Eng. Index Annu., Eng. Index Bioeng. Abstr., Eng. Index Energy Abstr., Eng. Index Mon., Sci. Abstr. Sect. A. Phys. Abstr. **DD** 676.05. **CODEN** JPUSDN. **Circ** 6,000. Scientific research papers on pulp and paper science. *Transactions of the Technical Section, 0317-882X.*

KAMI PARUPU KOGYO SETSUBI CHOSA HOKOKUSHO. **Main/Corp** Japan. Tsusho Sangyosho Daijin Kambo. Chosa Tokeibu. JA. Japanese. ir. Nihon Seishi Rengokai, 9-11 Ginza 3, c/o Kami Parupu Building, Chuo-ku 104 Tokyo Japan. **LC** TS1117.

KAMI PARUPU SEIZO SETSUBI CHOSA HOKOKUSHO. JA. Japanese. ir. Nihon Seishi Rengokai, c/o Kami Parupu Kaikan, 9-11 Ginza, 3 Chuo-Ku Tokyo 104 Japan. **LC** TS1117. *Kami Parupu Kogyo Setsubi Shosa Hokokusho.*

LISTES - ASSOCIATION CANADIENNE DES PRODUCTEURS DE PATES ET PAPIERS, SECTION TECHNIQUE. (LISTES : LISTES DE PAPIERS TECHNIQUES DE LA SECTION TECHNIQUE DE L'ACCP PUBLIES AU COURS DE . . .). **VFOAT** Indices : Indices to Technical Papers of the Technical Section, CPPA, Published During . . . . **VAT** Indices - Canadian Pulp and Paper Association, Technical Section (English and French Ed.). 1981-. 0822-4811. CN. English (includes some text in French). an. Free. Canadian Pulp and Paper Association, 23rd Floor/Sun Life Building, 1155 Metcalfe Street, Montreal Quebec H3B 2X9 Canada. **DD** 676.05. *Indices (Canadian Pulp and Paper Association. Technical Section), 0227-616X.*

LOCKWOOD'S DIRECTORY OF THE PAPER AND ALLIED TRADES. *See* Yearbooks, Almanacs, Directories.

MEMBERSHIP DIRECTORY - TECHNICAL SECTION, CANADIAN PULP AND PAPER ASSOCIATION. *See* Yearbooks, Almanacs, Directories.

MISCELLANEOUS PAPER CONVERTERS. **VFOAT** Transformations Diverses du Papier. 1970-. 0384-4773. Periodical. CN. English (French). an. Receiver General for Canada, Statistics Canada Publications, Ottawa Ontario K1A 0T6 Canada.

MISCELLANEOUS PAPER CONVERTERS INCLUDING ASPHALT ROOFING MANUFACTURERS. **VFOAT** Transformations Diverses du Papier, y Compris la Fabrication de Papier de Couverture Asphalte. 1981-. 0319-8936. CN. English (French). an. $4.75 Domestic, $5.70 Foreign. Publication Sales and Services, Statistics Canada, Ottawa Ontario K1A 0V7 Canada. **DD** 338.4767620971. *Asphalt Roofing Manufacturers (Statistics Canada : Final), 0384-2746; Miscellaneous Paper Converters (Final), 0527-5727.*

MONTHLY NEWSPRINT STATISTICS. CANADIAN PULP AND PAPER ASSOCIATION. *See* Statistics.

MONTHLY STATISTICSL SUMMARY - AMERICAN PAPER INSTITUTE. *See* Statistics.

NCASI TECHNICAL REVIEW : BULLETIN. **Main/Corp** National Council of the Paper Industry for Air and Stream Improvement. No. 3-. Periodical. US. English. ir. $315.00. National Council of the Paper Industry for Air and Stream Improvement, 260 Madison Avenue, New York NY 10016. **Tel** (212)532-9000. *National Council Technical Review : Bulletin.*

NORSK SKOGBRUK. *See* Forestry.

NORSK SKOGINDUSTRI. Began with Jan. 1947 issue. 0029-2095. Periodical. NO. Norwegian. ir. Selvig Publishing, c/o PO Box 9070 Vaterland, 0134 Oslo 1 Norway. **Tel** (02)42 58 67. **Ed** Karl Jorgen Gurandsrud. **Ind/Abst** Abstr. Bull. Inst. Paper Chem., Bibliogr. Agric., Chem. Abstr., Pap. Board Abstr., Predicasts, Sel. Water Resour. Abstr. **LC** TS800. **CODEN** NOSKAN. adv acc. A journal for paper, cartons cellulose, wood pulp, timber, fibre boards and particle boards, published 11 times annually. *Papir-Journalen.*

NORTHERN ONTARIO BUSINESS. *See* Business.

OFFICIAL BOARD MARKETS. **VFOAT** Yellow Sheet. 0030-0284. Periodical. US. English. wk. Official Board Markets, 1 East First Street, Duluth MN 55802. **Tel** (218)723-9555. **Ed** Fred Sharring. **Ind/Abst** Abstr. Bull. Inst. Paper Chem. Paper pricer.

I P H INFORMATION. Nos. 1-6, N.F. V. 1-. Periodical. German (English and French). ir. **Ind/Abst** Abstr. Bull. Inst. Paper Chem.

PALPU, CHONGI KISUL. **VFOAT** Journal of the Technical Association of Pulp and Paper Industry of Korea. 0253-3200. Periodical. English (Korean). ir. **Ind/Abst** Abstr. Bull. Inst. Paper Chem., Chem. Abstr., Pap. Board Abstr. **LC** TS1080. **CODEN** PCGIDY.

PAPEL. (O PAPEL). Began in 1939. 0031-1057. Periodical. BL. Portuguese. mo. 60.00 US. Editora Orientador Ltd, Caixa Postal 1430, Sao Paulo Brazil. **Tel** 223-5478. **Ed** Paulo Engelberg. **Ind/Abst** Abstr. Bull. Inst. Paper Chem., Art Archaeol. Tech. Abstr., Pap. Board Abstr., Chem. Abstr. **LC** TS1080. **CODEN** PAPLA3. adv acc. **Circ** 2,700. (ctrl). Everything concerning the pulp and paper industry and forestry.

PAPER. Began with June 1972 issue. 0306-8234. Periodical. UK. English. ir. 39.00 Domestic, 49.00 Foreign. Benn Publications Limited, Sovereign Way, Tonbridge Kent TN9 1RW England. **Tel** (44)732-364422. **Ed** Martin Bayliss. **Ind/Abst** Abstr. Bull. Inst. Paper Chem., Chem. Abstr., Excerpta Med., Pap. Board Abstr., Predicasts, Funk Scott Index Corp. Ind., Chem. Abstr. **LC** TS1080. **DD** 676.205. **CODEN** PAPRCN. bk rev. adv acc. **Circ** 8,600. International coverage of commercial and technical developments in pulp and paper. The world's leading news magazine for the industry, including annual statistical review. *Paper Maker, World's Paper Trade Review; Disposables International.*

PAPER AGE. 0031-1081. Periodical. US. English. mo. $35.00. Business Press, 70 Oak Street, Norwood NJ 07648. **Tel** (201)767-6800. **Ed** Kenneth A Johnson. **Ind/Abst** Abstr. Bull. Inst. Paper Chem., Int. Packag. Abstr., Pap. Board Abstr. bk rev. adv acc. **Circ** 18,100. (ctrl).

PAPER & BOARD ABSTRACTS. *See* Indexes/Abstracts.

PAPER & PACKAGING BULLETIN. *See* Packaging.

PAPER & TWINE JOURNAL. **VFOAT** Paper and Twine Journal. 0031-1103. Periodical. US. English. mo. Paper & Twine Journal, 1860 Broadway, New York NY 10025. **Ind/Abst** Abstr. Bull. Inst. Paper Chem. **LC** TS1080. **DD** 676.

PAPER CONSERVATOR. (THE PAPER CONSERVATOR : JOURNAL OF THE INSTITUTE OF PAPER CONSERVATION). Began with 1976. 0309-4227. Periodical. UK. English. an. 52,00. The Secretary, Institute of Paper Conservation, Leigh Lodge Leigh, Worlester WR6 5LB England. **Ed** Jane Mcausland. **Ind/Abst** Art Archaeol. Tech. Abstr. **LC** TS1109. **DD** 676.2820288. bk rev. adv acc. **Circ** 1,000. (ctrl). The Institute exists to diseminate information on conservation of art on paper, archives and books. Members are all those interested in the subject.

PAPER, PAPERBOARD & WOOD PULP. Vol. 59, No. 9 (Sept. 1981)-. Periodical. US. English. mo. American Paper Institute, 260 Madison Avenue, New York NY 10016. *Monthly Statistical Summary, 0003-0341.*

PAPER REVIEW OF THE YEAR. 0302-4180. UK. English. Benn Brothers Ltd, Lyon Tower 125 High Street Colliers Wood, SW19 2JN London England. **LC** HD9820.1. **DD** 338.476762.

PAPER SALES. 0031-1170. Periodical. US. English. mo. Paper Sales, 1 East First Street, Duluth MN 55802. **Tel** (218)723-9200. **LC** TS1080. **DD** 658.89676. *Paper Specialties.*

PAPER TECHNOLOGY AND INDUSTRY. V. 16- Feb. 1975-. 0306-252X. Periodical. UK. English. mo. 38.00. Piva House, Randalls Road, Leatherhead Surrey KT22 7RU England. **Tel** 372-376161. **Ed** D Attwood. **Ind/Abst** Eng. Index Annu., Eng. Index Mon., Eng. Index Bioeng. Abstr., Eng. Index Energy Abstr., Excerpta Med., Energy Inf. Abstr., Environ. Abstr., Abstr. Bull. Inst. Paper Chem., Pap. Board Abstr., Chem. Abstr., Eng. Index. **LC** TS1080.B73. **DD** 676.205. **CODEN** PTIND8. bk rev. adv acc. **Circ** 3,000. Pulp paper board and convertions technology plus news of PIRA UK Technology Centre for Paper Industry and activities of PITA/Paper Industry Technical Association of UK. *Paper Technology, 0031-1189.*

PAPER TRADE JOURNAL. Began with issue for May 27, 1872. 0031-1197. Periodical. US. English. mo. $19.00. Vance Publishing Corp, PO Box 400, Prairie View IL 60069. **Tel** (312)634-2600. **Ed** Peter Wuerl. **Ind/Abst** Trade Ind. Index, Predicasts, Sel. Water Resour. Abstr., Coal Abstr., Energy Inf. Abstr., Environ. Abstr., Abstr. Bull. Inst. Paper Chem., Pap. Board Abstr., Chem. Abstr., Bus. Period. Index, Funk Scott Index Corp. Ind. **LC** TS1080. **CODEN** PTJOAD. bk rev. adv acc. **Circ** 26,600. (ctrl). Feature stories covering new and improved methods, facilities, equipment and processes; and personnel news affecting the industry and its suppliers.

THE PAPER YEAR BOOK. *See* Yearbooks, Almanacs, Directories.

PAPERI JA PUU. **VFOAT** Papper Och Tra, Paper and Timber. V. 32-. 0031-1243. Periodical. FI. English (Finnish and Swedish). mo. $49.00. Fin Paper & Timber, PO Box 176, SF 00141 Helsinki 14 Finland. **Tel** 358 0 664 166. **Ed** Anneli Hattari. **Ind/Abst** Predicasts, Sel. Water Resour. Abstr., Energy Inf. Abstr., Environ. Abstr., Abstr. Bull. Inst. Paper Chem., CIS Abstr., Energy Res. Abstr., Pap. Board Abstr., Chem. Abstr., Bibliogr. Agric., Sci. Cit. Index, Abr. Ed., Funk Scott Index Corp. Ind. **LC** HD9765.F4. **DD** 338.476740094897. **CODEN** PAPUAU. bk rev. adv acc. **Circ** 3,500. (ctrl). Scientific-technical publication of the Mechanical and Chemical Forest Industry in Finland. *Suomen Paperi- Ja Puutavaralehti.*

PAPERS PRESENTED AT A TAPPI ANNUAL MEETING. **Main/Corp** Technical Association of the Pulp and Paper Industry. Meeting. US. English. an. One Dunwoody Park, Atlanta GA 30341. **LC** TS1080. **DD** 676.205.

PAPETIER. (LE PAPETIER). V. 1- Jan. 1964-. 0048-2889. Periodical. CN. French. Conseil des Producteurs de Pates et Papiers du Quebec, 500 Est Grande-Allee, Quebec Quebec G1R 2J7 Canada.

DAS PAPIER. Vol. 1-. 0031-1340. Periodical. GW. German. mo. 154.50. Ed Roether Verlag, PO Box 4101, Berliner Allee 56, D6100 Darmstadt West Germany. **Tel** 06151/33 2 55. **Ed** Edward Roether. **Ind/Abst** World Text Abstr., Excerpta Med., Predicasts, Energy Inf. Abstr., Environ. Abstr., Abstr. Bull. Inst. Paper Chem., Pap. Board Abstr., Chem. Abstr., Bibliogr. Agric., Funk Scott Index Corp. Ind., Chem. Abstr. **LC** TS1080. **DD** 676. **CODEN** PAERAY. bk rev. adv acc. **Circ** 4,000. Periodical for the production of wood pulp, cellulose, paper and board; chemical technology of cellulose; joint organ of the German Pulp and Paper Trade Associations.

PAPIER AUS OSTERREICH. No. 1 (July 1984)-. Periodical. German. mo. $430.00. Haus der Osterreichischen Papierindustrie, Gumpendorfer Strasse 6, 1061 Wien 6 Austria. **Ind/Abst** Abstr. Bull. Inst. Paper Chem. *Osterreichische Papier.*

PAPIER, CARTON ET CELLULOSE. Began with March/April 1952. 0031-1367. Periodical. French (with summaries in English, German and Spanish). mo. 255.00 Domestic, 307.00 Foreign. CEP Information Industrie, 23 rue Laugier, 75017 Paris France. **Tel** 622.13.62. **Ind/Abst** Excerpta Med., Abstr. Bull. Inst. Paper Chem., Art Archaeol. Tech. Abstr., Pap. Board Abstr., Chem. Abstr. **CODEN** PCCLAK.

PAPIER UND DRUCK. *See* Printing.

PAPIER-ZEITUNG. V. 84, No. 3 (Mar. 1978)-. Periodical. German. ir. *Osterreichische Papier-Zeitung.*

PAPIR A CELULOSA. 0031-1421. Periodical. UR. Latvian (tables of contents also in Russian, German, and English). mo. Artia, PO Box 790, Praha 1 Czechoslovakia. **Ind/Abst** Sel. Water Resour. Abstr., Abstr. Bull. Inst. Paper Chem., CIS Abstr., Pap. Board Abstr., Chem. Abstr. **LC** TS1080. **CODEN** PCELAU.

PAPIRIPAR ES MAGYAR GRAFIKA. 1-1957-. Periodical. Hungarian. ir. **LC** TS1080. *Papir- es Nyomdatechnika.*

PHILLIPS PAPER TRADE DIRECTORY. *See* Yearbooks, Almanacs, Directories.

PIMA. **Main/Corp** Paper Industry Management Association. **VFOAT** PIMA Magazine. V. 60, No. 2- Feb. 1978-. 0161-1364. Periodical. US. English. mo.

Paper & Pulp Industry

Paper Industry Management Association, 2400 East Oakton Street, Arlington Heights IL 60005. **Tel** (312)956-0250. Ed James Linn. **Ind/Abst** Eng. Index Annu., Eng. Index Mon., Eng. Index Bioeng. Abstr., Eng. Index Energy Abstr., Abstr. Bull. Inst. Paper Chem., Predicasts, Energy Inf. Abstr., Environ. Abstr., Pap. Board Abstr., Appl. Sci. Technol. Index. LC TS1080. DD 338.47.6760973. CODEN PMAGDY. adv acc. **Circ** 12,000. (ctrl) A magazine for papermaking professionals. *Paper Industry, 0197-3991.*

PIMA CATALOG. VFOAT P.I.M.A Catalog. 0739-2133. US. English. an. $25.00. PIMA, 2400 East Oakton Street, Arlington Heights IL 60005. **Tel** (312)956-0250. Ed William D Hall. LC TS1088. DD 338.47676202573. adv acc. **Circ** 5,000. (ctrl) Information for equipment, materials and services required by pulp and paper manufacturers. Also engineering data and state-of-the-art reports on papermaking processes and production. *Pulp and Paper Mill Catalog and Engineering Handbook.*

PLYWOOD & PANEL WORLD. See Forestry.

PREHL'AD LESNICKEJ, DREVARSKEJ, CELULOZOVEJ A PAPIERENSKEJ LITERATURY. See Indexes/Abstracts.

PREPRINTS A - TECHNICAL SECTION, CANADIAN PULP & PAPER ASSOCIATION. (PREPRINTS A). **Main/Corp** Canadian Pulp and Paper Association. Technical Section. Meeting. VFOAT Pretires A. 68th Annual Meeting (Jan. 26/27, 1982)-. 0822-5206. CN. English (summaries in French). an. Canadian Pulp and Paper Association, Technical Section, 1155 Metcalfe Street/Suite 2300, Montreal Quebec H3B 2X9 Canada. **Ind/Abst** Eng. Index Annu., Eng. Index Bioeng. Abstr., Eng. Index Energy Abstr., Eng. Index Mon. DD 676.05. *Preprints of Papers to be Presented at the Annual Meeting, 0316-6732.*

PREPRINTS B - TECHNICAL SECTION, CANADIAN PULP AND PAPER ASSOCIATION. (PREPRINTS B). **Main/Corp** Canadian Pulp and Paper Association. Technical Section. Meeting. VFOAT Pretires B. 68th Annual Meeting (Jan. 28/29, 1982)-. 0822-5214. CN. English. an. Canadian Pulp and Paper Association, Technical Section, 1155 Metcalfe Street/Suite 2300, Montreal Quebec H3B 2X9 Canada. **Ind/Abst** Eng. Index Annu., Eng. Index Bioeng. Abstr., Eng. Index Energy Abstr., Eng. Index Mon. DD 676.05. *Preprints of Papers to be Presented at the Annual Meeting, 0316-6732.*

PREPRINTS OF PAPERS TO BE PRESENTED AT THE ANNUAL MEETING CEASED. **Main/Corp** Canadian Pulp and Paper Association. Technical Section. Ceased with 1981 issue. 0316-6732. CN. English. an. Canadian Pulp and Paper Association, Technical Section, 2300 Sun Life Building, Montreal Quebec H3B 2X9 Canada. **Ind/Abst** Eng. Index Annu. DD 676.05.

PRETIRES - CONFERENCE TECHNOLOGIQUE ESTIVALE. (PRETIRES, CONFERENCE TECHNOLOGIQUE ESTIVALE). **Main/Corp** Association Canadienne des Producteurs de Pates et Papiers. Section Technique. 1978-. 0707-8951. CN. French. Association Canadienne des Producteurs de Pates et Pariers Section Technique, 2300 Edifice Sun Life, Montreal Que H3B 2X9 Canada. DD 676.0971.

PROCEEDINGS - EXECUTIVES' CONFERENCE, INSTITUTE OF PAPER CHEMISTRY. **Main/Conf** Executives' Conference, Institute of Paper Chemistry, Appleton, Wisconsin. Began publication with No. 5, 1940. US. English. an.

PROCEEDINGS OF THE TECHNICAL ASSOCIATION OF THE PULP AND PAPER INDUSTRY. **Main/Corp** Technical Association of the Pulp and Paper Industry. 0272-7269. US. English. ir. $404.55. Technical Association of Pulp & Paper Industry, Tech Park, Box 105113, Atlanta GA 30348. **Ind/Abst** Eng. Index Annu., Eng. Index Mon., Eng. Index Bioeng. Abstr., Eng. Index Energy Abstr. CODEN PSYPDJ. *Conference Proceedings.*

PROJECT REPORT - PULP AND PAPER POLLUTION ABATEMENT. See Sanitation, Environmental Technology.

PROJECTED PULP AND PAPER MILLS IN THE WORLD. English. an. Free. Food & Agriculture Organization of the United Nations, via Delle Terme di Caracalla, 00100 Rome Italy. **Tel** 57974132. LC HD9820.1. DD 338.4767605. List of pulp and paper mills planned to be established, expanded or closed down in next ten year period.

PRZEGLAD PAPIERNICZY. VFOAT Polish Papers Review. Began publication in 1945. 0033-2291. Periodical. PL. Polish (table of contents also in Russian and English). mo. ARS Polona, Krakowskie Przedmiescie 7, 00-068 Warsaw Poland. **Ind/Abst** Abstr. Bull. Inst. Paper Chem., Art Archaeol. Tech. Abstr., Pap. Board Abstr., Chem. Abstr. LC TS1080. CODEN PRZPAE.

PULP & PAPER. VAT Pulp and Paper. 0033-4081. Periodical. US. English. Miller Freeman Publishing, 500 Howard Street, San Francisco CA 94105. **Ind/Abst** Can. Environ., Excerpta Med., Predicasts, Abstr. Bull. Inst. Paper Chem., Pap. Board Abstr., Chem. Abstr., Bus. Period. Index, Sel. Water Resour. Abstr., Funk Scott Index Corp. Ind., Pollut. Abstr. Indexes. LC TS1080. DD 338.47676. CODEN PUPAA8. *Pulp & Paper Industry, 0096-4816; Paper Mill News, 0096-1892.*

PULP AND PAPER. **Main/Corp** Organization for Economic Co-operation and Development. VFOAT Pates et Papiers. 1974-. Periodical. English and French. ir. **Ind/Abst** Predicasts, Abstr. Bull. Inst. Paper Chem., Pap. Board Abstr.

PULP & PAPER BULLETIN. VAT Pulp and Paper Bulletin. 0197-1069. Periodical. US. English. 29 Hartwell Avenue, Data Resources Inc, Lexington MA 02173. LC HD9820.4. DD 338.476760973.

PULP & PAPER BUYERS GUIDE. See Business - Purchasing.

PULP & PAPER CANADA. VAT Pulp and Paper Canada. V. 75, No. 9- Sept. 1974-. 0316-4004. Periodical. CN. English. mo. 12.00 Domestic, $30.00 Foreign. National Business Publications Ltd, 310 Victoria Avenue, Westmount Quebec H3Z 2M9 Canada. **Ind/Abst** Energy Inf. Abstr., Environ. Abstr., Excerpta Med., Abstr. Bull. Inst. Paper Chem., Comput. Control Abstr., Electr. Electron. Abstr., Sci. Abstr. Sect. A. Phys. Abstr., Can. Bus. Index, Chem. Abstr., Bibliogr. Agric., Pap. Board Abstr., Sel. Water Resour. Abstr. LC TS1080. DD 338.476760971. CODEN PPCAAA. *Pulp & Paper Magazine of Canada, 0033-4103.*

PULP & PAPER CANADA ANNUAL AND DIRECTORY. See Yearbooks, Almanacs, Directories.

PULP & PAPER INTERNATIONAL. (PULP AND PAPER INTERNATIONAL). 0033-409X. Periodical. US. English. mo. $60.00. Miller Freeman Publications, 500 Howard Street, San Francisco CA 94105. **Tel** 538-60-40. Ed John Kalish. **Ind/Abst** Abstr. Bull. Inst. Paper Chem., Pap. Board Abstr. DD 338. adv acc. **Circ** 8,972. (ctrl) Serves worldwide pulp and paper, paperboard, paper converting and pulpwood industries.

PULP & PAPER JOURNAL. Vol. 35, No. 1 (Jan. 1982)-. 0713-5807. Periodical. CN. English. ir. $25.00. Pulp & Paper Journal, c/o MacLean Hunter, 481 University Avenue, Toronto Ontario M5W 1A7 Canada. **Ind/Abst** Can. Environ., Predicasts, Abstr. Bull. Inst. Paper Chem., Can. Bus. Index, Sel. Water Resour. Abstr. LC TS1080. DD 676.05. *Canadian Pulp & Paper Industry, 0008-4867.*

PULP AND PAPER MILLS. **Main/Corp** Statistics Canada. Manufacturing and Primary Industries Division. VFOAT Usines de Pates et Papiers. VAT Usines de Pates et Papiers (Ed Provisoire). Began with issue for 1970. 0384-4625. CN. English (French). an. 20.00 Domestic, 21.00 Foreign. Receiver General for Canada, Statistics Canada Publications, Ottawa Ontario K1A 0T6 Canada. **Tel** (800)268-1151.

PULP & PAPER NORTH AMERICA INDUSTRY FACTBOOK. VAT Pulp and Paper North America Industry Factbook. 0273-3781. US. English. Miller Freeman Publications, 500 Howard Street, San Francisco CA 94105. LC HD9821. DD 338.476760973.

PULP & PAPER PROJECT REPORT. VFOAT Pulp and Paper Project Report. 0748-1608. Periodical. US. English. mo. Miller Freeman Publications, 500 Howard Street, San Francisco CA 94105. DD 676.

PULP AND PAPER REPORT. Began publication in 1969. 0068-9505. Periodical. CN. English. an. Canadian Pulp & Paper, 1155 Metcalfe Street/23rd Floor, Montreal Quebec H3B 2X9 Canada. **Tel** (514)866-6621. **Ind/Abst** MLA Int. Bibliogr. Books Artic. Mod. Lang. Lit., Am. Hist. Life, Hist. Abstr. DD 338.476760971.

PULP & PAPER REVIEW. **Main/Corp** Data Resources, Inc. VFOAT Data Resources Pulp and Paper Review. VAT Pulp and Paper Review. V. 1- Dec. 1977-. 0161-7079. US. English. Data Resources Inc, 29 Hartwell Avenue, Lexington MA 02173. LC HD9821. DD 338.476760973.

PULP & PAPER STATISTICS. See Statistics.

PULP & PAPER WEEK PRICE/EXPORT-IMPORT DATABOOK. VFOAT Price/Export-Import Databook. VAT Pulp and Paper Week Price Export Import Databook. 1980-. 0277-0156. US. English. wk. $427.00. Miller Freeman Publications, 500 Howard Street, San Francisco CA 94105. **Tel** (415)397-1881. Ed Will E Mies. LC HD9821. DD 338.436760973. **Circ** 1,300. (ctrl) Newsletter of markets and prices for the pulp and paper industry.

PULP, PAPER, AND BOARD. (CURRENT INDUSTRIAL REPORTS. M26A, PULP, PAPER, AND BOARD). 0146-3527. US. English. an. Data User Services Division, Bureau of the Census, Washington DC 20233. **Ind/Abst** Predicasts, Abstr. Bull. Inst. Paper Chem., Am. Stat. Index.

PULPWOOD HIGHLIGHTS. V. 1- May 1979-. 0748-142X. Periodical. US. English. mo. American Pulpwood Association, 1619 Massachusetts Avenue NW, Washington DC 20036. **Ind/Abst** Bull. Inst. Paper Chem. DD 676. *Pulpwood Highlights, 0748-142X.*

PULPWOOD PRODUCTION IN THE NORTH CENTRAL REGION BY COUNTY. Series/Titl Resource Bulletin NC. Began with 1965. US. English. an. North Central Forest Experiment Station, Forest Service, US Department of Agriculture, 1992 Folwell Avenue, St Paul MN 55108. LC SD11, HD9757. A3. DD 333.750977 S, 338. 1749830977. Vols. for (1979-) distributed to depository libraries in microfiche.

REBEL. See Economics - Labor.

REFERENCE TABLES - CANADIAN PULP AND PAPER ASSOCIATION. **Main/Corp** Canadian Pulp and Paper Association. Began publication in 1948. 0317-0934. Periodical. CN. English. an. Canadian Pulp & Paper Association, 1155 Metcalfe Street, 23rd Floor, Montreal Quebec H3B 2X9 Canada. **Tel** (514)866-6621. DD 338.476760971.

RELATORIO ESTATISTICO. Portuguese. ir. LC HD9834.B8. DD 338.4767620981.

REPORT - PULP AND PAPER FOUNDATION. (REPORT). **Main/Corp** Pulp and Paper Foundation. 0882-8954. US. English. an. North Carolina State University, Pulp and Paper Foundation Inc, Robertson Wing Biltmore Hall, PO Box 5288, Raleigh NC 27650.

REPRODUCTION BULLETIN. No. 69 (Apr. 1971)-. 0736-1238. Periodical. US. English. qt. Andrews Paper & Chemical Company, 1 Channel Drive, Box 509, Port Washington NY 10050. **Ind/Abst** Abstr. Bull. Inst. Paper Chem. *Reproduction Paper News Bulletin.*

REVIEW - CANADIAN PULP AND PAPER ASSOCIATION. ENVIRONMENTAL SERVICES OFFICE. (REVIEW - CANADIAN PULP AND PAPER ASSOCIATION, ENVIRONMENTAL SERVICES OFFICE). **Main/Corp** Canadian Pulp and Paper Association. Environmental Services Office. No. 11- Feb. 1971-. 0319-6399. Periodical. CN. English. ir. Canadian Pulp and Paper Association, Environmental Service Office, 2300 Sun Life Building, Montreal Quebec H3B 2x9 Canada.

REVIEW OF THE LITERATURE ON PULP AND PAPER EFFLUENT MANAGEMENT. Series/Titl Stream Improvement Technical Bulletin. US. English. an. National Council of the Paper Industry for Air & Stream Improvement, 260 Madison Avenue, New York NY 10016. LC TD899.P3. DD 676.

REVISTA PADURILOR-INDUSTRIA LEMNULUI, CELULOZA SI HIRTIE. CELULOZA SI HIRTIE. VFOAT Celuloza Si Hirtie. Vol. 23, No. 3- July/Sept. 1974-. Periodical. Romanian (summaries in English, French, German and Russian). qt. 20.00. Rompresfilatelia Ser Export-Import Presa, Cal Grivitei NR 64-66, POB 2001, Bucuresti Romania. **Ind/Abst** Bull. Inst. Paper Chem., Chem. Abstr., Pap. Board Abstr. LC TS1080. CODEN RPLHDX. *Celuloza si Hirtie, 0008-879X.*

Parapsychology and the Occult Sciences

RIUNIONE ANNUALE - ATICELCA. Main/Corp Associazione Tecnica Italiana per la Cellulosa e la Carta. IT. Italian. ir. Aticelca Via Botticelli 19, 20133 Milano Italy. LC TS1080.

SOUTHERN LOGGIN' TIMES. See Forestry.

SOUTHERN PULP & PAPER. (SOUTHERN PULP AND PAPER). Vol. 43, No. 3 I.E. 4 (Apr. 1980)-. 0270-5222. Periodical. US. English. mo. $18.00. Southern Pulp and Paper, 75 Third Street NW, Atlanta GA 30308. Tel (404)881-6442. Ind/Abst Abstr. Bull. Inst. Paper Chem., Pap. Board Abstr. LC TS1080. DD 676.05. CODEN SOPPDD. *Southern Pulp and Paper Manufacturer, 0038-4488.*

STATISTICS OF PAPER, PAPERBOARD AND WOOD PULP. See Statistics.

STATISTIQUES DE L'INDUSTRIE FRANCAISE DES PATES, PAPIERS ET CARTONS. See Statistics.

STUDIA PAPYROLOGICA CEASED. Vol. 1-22. 0039-3290. Periodical. Spanish (contributions in English, French, German and Italian). sa.

SVENSK PAPPERSTIDNING. VFOAT Swedish Paper Journal. 0039-6680. Periodical. SW. Multilingual (Swedish and English). ir. Svensk Papperstidning, Villagatan 1, 114 32 Stockholm Sweden. Tel 46 8 789 28 00. Ed Anders Forsstrom. Ind/Abst Chem. Abstr., Sci. Cit. Index, Abr. Ed., Funk Scott Index Corp. Ind. CODEN SVPAAE. bk rev. adv acc. Circ 4,025. Industrial information about technology and research in Sweden and abroad in the pulp and paper field.

TAPPI-CPPA CONFERENCE PAPERS. (TAPPI/CPPA CONFERENCE PAPERS). Main/Corp Paper Finishing & Converting Conference. VAT Technical Association of the Pulp and Paper Industry-Canadian Pulp and Paper Association Conference Papers. 0161-2271. US. English. One Dunwoody Park, Atlanta GA 30338. LC TS1118.F5. DD 676.234.

TAPPI JOURNAL. VFOAT T.A.P.P.I. Journal. Vol. 65, No. 9 (Sept. 1982)-. 0734-1415. US. English. mo. Technical Association of the Pulp and Paper Industry, 15 Technology Park South, Norcross GA 30092. Ind/Abst Abstr. Bull. Inst. Paper Chem., Art Archaeol. Tech. Abstr., Bibliogr. Agric., Can. Environ., Chem. Abstr., Eng. Index Annu., Eng. Index Bioeng. Abstr., Eng. Index Energy Abstr., Eng. Index Mon., Excerpta Med., Fluidex, Int. Packag. Abstr., Pap. Board Abstr., Predicasts, Print. Abstr., Sel. Water Resour. Abstr., World Surf. Coat. Abstr., World Text Abstr., Appl. Sci. Technol. Index. LC TS1080. DD 676.05. CODEN TAJODT. Issued also in microform by Princeton Microfilm Corp. *TAPPI, 0039-8241.*

TAPPI MONOGRAPH SERIES. Main/Corp Technical Association of the Pulp and Paper Industry. VAT Technical Association of the Pulp and Paper Industry Monograph Series. No. 1-. 0097-2169. Monographic Series. US. English. ir. Ind/Abst Chem. Abstr. DD 676.05. CODEN TPMSAM.

TECHNICAL SECTION PROCEEDINGS. Main/Corp Canadian Pulp and Paper Association. Technical Section. Began publication in 1915. 0068-9521. CN. English. an. $30.00 Members, $40.00 Non-members. Canadian Pulp and Paper Association Technical Section, 2300 Sun Life Building, Montreal Quebec H3B 2X9 Canada. Tel (514)866-6621. Ed Catharine Findley. Ind/Abst Abstr. Bull. Inst. Paper Chem. LC TS1080. DD 676.05. Circ 75. Branch, committee and section annual reports, award winners, all papers published by the section during the year in Pulp and Paper Canada or Journal of Pulp and Paper Science.

TIMBER HARVESTING. See Forestry - Lumber & Wood.

TRANSACTIONS OF THE TECHNICAL SECTION CEASED. Main/Corp Canadian Pulp and Paper Association. Technical Section. VFOAT Journal of Pulp and Paper Science. Began with V. 1-8, No. 3, I.E. No. 4. 0317-882X. CN. English (and abstracts in French, June 1976-Dec. 1982). qt. Free to Members, $30.00 Nonmembers, $2.00 Libraries. Technical Section, Canadian Pulp and Paper Association, 2300 Sun Life Building, Montreal Quebec H3B 2X9 Canada. Ind/Abst Eng. Index Annu., Eng. Index Mon., Eng. Index Bioeng. Abstr., Eng. Index Energy Abstr., Chem. Abstr. DD 676.05. CODEN TSCPDL. 0317-8811.

TREND. No. 1- Autumn 1963-. 0041-2295. Periodical. CN. English. Pulp and Paper Research Institute of Canada, 570 St Johns's Boulevard, Pointe Claire Quebec H9R 3J9 Canada. Ind/Abst Can. Environ., Abstr. Bull. Inst. Paper Chem., Bibliogr. Agric., Pap. Board Abstr. LC TS1171. CODEN TRNDAU.

U.S. SECONDARY FIBRE STUDY. Series/Titl DRI Forest Products Special Study Series. VFOAT US Secondary Fibre Study. VAT United States Secondary Fibre Study. 0741-823X. US. English. an. Data Resources Inc, 24 Harwell Avenue, Lexington MA 02173. LC HD9839.W33. DD 338.476761420973.

WAGA KUNI NO KOKOGYO : KAMI PARUPU KOGYO HEN. Main/Corp Japan. Tsusho Sangyosho. Daijin Kambo. Chosa Tokeibu. JA. Japanese. ir. Daijin Kambo, 3-Ban 1-Go Kasumigaseki 1-Chome Chiyoda-Ku, Tokyo 100 Japan. LC HD9836.J3.

WALDEN'S ABC GUIDE AND PAPER PRODUCTION YEARBOOK. See Yearbooks, Almanacs, Directories.

WOCHENBLATT FUR PAPIERFABRIKATION. Began in 1870. 0043-7131. Periodical. GW. German. ir. $43.02. Guentter Staib Verlag, PO Box 14 52, D-7950 Biberach 1 West Germany. Tel 07351/6969. Ed Ulrich Kirchner. Ind/Abst Excerpta Med., Predicasts, Sel. Water Resour. Abstr., Abstr. Bull. Inst. Paper Chem., Pap. Board Abstr., Chem. Abstr. LC TS1080. CODEN WBPFAZ. bk rev. adv acc. Circ 3,000. Pulp and paper production from wood to finishing.

WOOD PULP AND FIBER STATISTICS. See Statistics.

ZELLSTOFF UND PAPIER. 0044-3867. Periodical. SZ. English. bm. $16.13. Kunst & Wissen Erich Bieber, Dufourstrasse 51, CH-8008 Zurich Switzerland. Tel 011-41-1-69 44-20. Ind/Abst Excerpta Med., Abstr. Bull. Inst. Paper Chem., Pap. Board Abstr., Chem. Abstr., Sci. Cit. Index, Abr. Ed. LC TS1080. CODEN ZLPAAL. *Papier und Druck.*

ZHONGGUO ZAOZHI. See Engineering - Chemical Engineering.

PARAPSYCHOLOGY AND THE OCCULT SCIENCES

ACTION. V. 1- 1975-. 0700-5067. Periodical. CN. English. Church of Scientology, Mission of Windsor, 437 Ouelette Avenue, Windsor Ontario N9A 4J2 Canada. DD 131.3505.

ADVANCES IN PARAPSYCHOLOGICAL RESEARCH. V. 1- 1977-. 0195-9867. Monographic Series. US. English. ir. Plenum Press, 233 Spring Street, New York NY 10013. Tel (212)620-8000. NLM W1 AD709.

AMERICAN DOWSER. (THE AMERICAN DOWSER). V. 9, No. 3- Aug. 1969-. 0093-099X. Periodical. US. English. qt. American Society of Dowsers Inc, Danville VT 05828. LC BF1628. DD 133.32305. *Quarterly Digest - American Society of Dowsers, 0569-8154.*

ANCIENT MYSTERIES. 0308-5406. Periodical. UK. English. Institute of Geomantic Research, 142 Pheasant Rise, Bar Hill Cambridge CB3 8SD England.

ANUARIO ALLAN KARDEC. See Yearbooks, Almanacs, Directories.

ASPR NEWSLETTER. VFOAT American Society for Psychical Research Newsletter. 1969-. Periodical. US. English. qt. $10.00. American Society of Psychical Research, 5 West 73rd Street, New York NY 10023. Tel (212)799-5050. NLM W1 A154K.

ASTRES. No. 1-. Periodical. French. mo. 30.00 (Single Issue). Nouvelle Edition Veritas, Arcades Jaulim Route Royale, Rose-Hill Ile Maurice Mauritius. LC BF1002. DD 133.05.

BULLETIN D'INFORMATION UFOLOGIQUE. See Folklore.

BULLETIN PSILOG. (LE BULLETIN PSILOG). Vol. 1, No. 1 1981-. 0706-120X. Periodical. CN. French. ir. $11.00. Le Bulletin Psilog, St-Francois-du-Lac Quebec J0G 1M0 Canada. DD 133.05.

CAHIERS DE COURS DE L'HOLANTHROPE. (LES CAHIERS DE COURS DE L'HOLANTHROPE). V. 1- Oct. 1975-. 0318-7349. Periodical. CN. French. qt. $2.00 Per No. Cosmos-Express, CP 3, Jonquiere Quebec G7X 7V8 Canada. Ed C G Sarrazin. DD 133.05.

CRITIQUE (SANTA ROSA, CALIF.). (CRITIQUE). Began with 1 (Autumn 1980). 0735-6501. Periodical. US. English. sa. $14.00. Critique Journal of Conspiracy, PO Box 11451, Santa Rosa CA 95406. Tel (707)525-9401. Ed Bob Banner. bk rev. adv acc. Circ 3,000. A journal exploring unusual, esoteric, disturbing, and mysterious realities. Publishe Publishes all the stuff that most of the media doesn't touch.

ENCYCLOPEDIA OF OCCULTISM & PARAPSYCHOLOGY. 0731-7840. US. English. ir. Gale Research Company, Book Tower, Detroit MI 48226. Ed Leslie A Shepard. Containing over 6,000 entries, it is a completely revised, updated, and reset reference guide to occult phenomena and personalities.

ERE ATLANTEENNE. (L'ERE ATLANTEENNE). V. 1, No. 1, (Dec. 1979)-. 0225-543X. Periodical. CN. French. wk. $18.00. L'Ere Atlanteenne, CP 1223, Belleville Ontario K8N 5E9 Canada. DD 133.05.

FANGORIA. 0164-2111. Periodical. US. English. ir. $16.98. Starlog Press Incorporated, 475 Park Avenue South, New York NY 10016. Tel (212)689-2830.

FATE (CHICAGO, ILL.). (FATE). 0014-8776. Periodical. US. English. mo. $12.00. Fate Magazine, 170 Future Way, Marion OH 43302. Ind/Abst Mag. Index, Access. LC BF1995. DD 133.05.

GNOSTICA. No. 22- May 1974-. 0145-885X. Periodical. US. English. bm. $7.50 Domestic, $10.00 Foreign. Llewellyn Publications, Box 3383, St Paul MN 55165. LC BF1001. DD 133.05. Available in microform from University Microfilms. *Gnostica News, 0362-8922.*

GNOSTICA NEWS AND VIEWS. No. 53-. Periodical. English. *Gnostica.*

HOMEM, MITO & I.E. E MAGIA. V. 1- 1973-. Periodical. BL. Portuguese. ir. $180.00. Editoria Tres, Avenue Paulista 2 006, 15 E 16 Andares Caixa Postal 1481, Sao Paulo Brazil. LC BF1005.

INNER LIFE CEASED. Began with No. 15 (Sept. 1974). 0318-0697. CN. English. ir. $.015 Per No. Inner Life, 214 Glengarry Avenue, Toronto Ontario M5M 1E4 Canada. DD 133.09713541. *Newsletter.*

THE INTERNATIONAL DIRECTORY OF ASTROLOGERS & PSYCHICS. See Astrology.

INTERNATIONAL GUIDE TO PSI PERIODICALS AND ORGANIZATIONS. See Bibliographies.

THE INTERNATIONAL PSYCHIC REGISTER. V. 1- 1977-. 0147-782X. US. English. an. Ornion Press, Box 1816, Erie PA 16507. Tel (814)459-7730. LC BF1024.5. DD 131.302517421.

JOURNAL OF AUTOMATIC WRITING. (THE JOURNAL OF AUTOMATIC WRITING). V. 1- June 1974-. 0315-5412. Periodical. CN. English. mo. The Spiritual Press, PO Box 464, Don Mills Ontario M3C 2T3 Canada.

JOURNAL OF PARAPSYCHOLOGY. (THE JOURNAL OF PARAPSYCHOLOGY). V. 1- March 1947-. 0022-3387. Periodical. US. English. qt. $25.00. Parapsychology Press, Box 6847/College Station, Durham NC 27708. Tel (919)688-8241. Ed K R Rao. Ind/Abst Biol. Abstr., Ref. Source, Psychol. Abstr., Soc. Sci. Index, Soc. Sci. Citation Index. LC BF1001. DD 133.072 159.961. NLM W1 JO827D. CODEN JPRPAU. (cum index). bk rev. Circ 1,000. (ctrl). The journal publishes articles on parapsychology, surveys of literature, book reviews, correspondence, and abstracts of reports from unpublished material and other journals.

THE JOURNAL OF RELIGION AND PSYCHICAL RESEARCH. Vol. 4, No. 1 (Jan. 1981)-. 0731-2148. Periodical. US. English. qt. $8.00. Academy of Religion and Psychical Research, PO Box 614, Bloomfield CT 06002. Tel (203)242-4593. Ed Mary Carman Rose. Ind/Abst Relig. Index One, Period. DD 133. bk rev. Circ 301. (ctrl). A scholarly journal dealing with the area in which religion and psychical research interface. *Journal of the Academy of Religion and Psychical Research, 0272-7188.*

Parapsychology and the Occult Sciences

JOURNAL OF RESEARCH IN PSI PHENOMENA. (THE JOURNAL OF RESEARCH IN PSI PHENOMENA). V. 1- May 1976-. 0384-5001. Periodical. CN. English. Queen's University, J Bigu, Kingston Ontario K7L 3N6 Canada. DD 133.05.

JOURNAL OF THE SOCIETY FOR PSYCHICAL RESEARCH. Main/Corp Society for Psychical Research (London, England). V. 1- (No. 1-). 0037-9751. Periodical. UK. English. qt. 18 Domestic, 35 Foreign. Society for Psychical Research, 1 Adam and Eve Mews Kensington, London W, 6UG England. Tel 01-937-8984. Ed John Beloff. Ind/Abst Psychol. Abstr. LC BF1011. DD 133.805. NLM W1 JO954P. bk rev. Circ 1,000. (ctrl). To examine without prejudice or prepossession, and in a scientific spirit those faculties of man, real or supposed, which appear to be inexplicable in terms of any generally recognized hypotheses.

KABALARIAN COURIER. Began publication in 1969?. 0319-1648. Periodical. CN. English. bm. Kabalarian Courier, 908 West 7th Avenue, Vancouver British Columbia V5Z 1C3 Canada. DD 135.405.

LUNG TSAI TIEN. Began with June 1980 issue. Periodical. CH. Chinese. bm. $20.00 US. Lung Tsai Tien Tsa Chih She, 34 Lane 66 Tung Ming Chieh, Chung-Li Shih Taiwan. LC BF1773.2.C5. DD 133.305.

THE MAGICK CIRCLE DIRECTORY OF OCCULT GOODS AND SERVICES. See Yearbooks, Almanacs, Directories.

MAIN. VAT Mark-Age Inform-Nations. 0147-1201. Periodical. US. English. bm $15.00 US, $20.00 Foreign. Mark Age, PO Box 290368, Ft Lauderdale FL 33329. Tel (305)587-5555. Ed Nada-Yolanda. bk rev. Circ 1,000. (ctrl). Publishes news, information, education and guidelines for linking of light workers and groups as a preparation for second coming and new age of aquarius.

METALUNE. Vol. 1, No. 1 Nov. 1981-. 0711-6004. Periodical. CN. French. mo. $0.60 Per No. Students $0.75 Per No. $1.10 Canada. Metalune, 2833 rue le Royer, Sherbrooke Quebec J1K 2X3 Canada. DD 133.05.

MING HSIANG. V. 1-. Periodical. CH. Chinese. mo. 36.00. Li Yuan Shu Pao She, Chiu-Lung Hong Kong. LC BF1868.C5. DD 133.305.

MYSTICS QUARTERLY (IOWA CITY, IOWA). See Religion, Mythology, Rationalism.

NEW AGE JOURNAL (BRIGHTON, MASS.). (NEW AGE JOURNAL). Oct. 1983-. 0746-3618. Periodical. US. English. mo. $18.00. New Age Journal, 342 Western Avenue, Brighton MA 02135. Ind/Abst Altern. Press Index. New Age, 0164-3967.

NEW ATLANTEAN JOURNAL. 0147-6548. Periodical. US. English. qt. New Atlantean Research Society, 5963 32nd Avenue North, St Petersburg FL 33710. Tel (813)347-1213.

NEW ENGLAND JOURNAL OF PARAPSYCHOLOGY. V. 1-. 0147-3395. Periodical. US. English. ir. Franklin Pierce College, SUNY Albany, Albany NY 12222. Tel (603)899-5111. LC BF1001. DD 133.805.

NEW HORIZONS. V. 1- Summer 1972-. 0225-8536. CN. English. an. New Horizons Research Foundation, PO Box 427 Station F, Toronto Ontario M4Y 2L8 Canada. DD 133.05.

NEW REALITIES. V. 1- 0147-7625. Periodical. US. English. bm. $12.97. New Realities, PO Box 26289, San Francisco CA 94126. Tel (415)776-2600. LC BF1001. Psychic, 0033-2798.

NOSTRADAMUS. EDITION QUEBECOISE. (NOSTRADAMUS). Yearly V. 2, No. 58- 13/20 Aug. 1973-. 0380-4127. Periodical. CN. French. wk. 35 Per No. Distributions Eclair, 8320 Place de Lorraine, Montreal Quebec H1J 1E6 Canada. DD 001.9405.

OCCULT. V. 1- Jan. 1970-. Periodical. US. English. qt. LC BF1001. DD 133.05.

PARAPSYCHOLOGICAL MONOGRAPHS. No. 1-. 0078-9437. Monographic Series. US. English (summaries in French, German, Italian and Spanish). Parapsychology Foundation, 29 West 57th Street, New York NY 10019. NLM W1 PA633M.

PARAPSYCHOLOGY ABSTRACTS INTERNATIONAL. See Indexes/Abstracts.

PARAPSYCHOLOGY (CANADIAN INSTITUTE OF PARAPSYCHOLOGY). (PARAPSYCHOLOGY). Autumn 1978-. 0227-6119. Periodical. CN. English. qt. $3.00. Canadian Institute of Parapsychology, PO Box 6147/Station J, Ottawa Ontario K2A 1T2 Canada. DD 133.072.

PARAPSYCHOLOGY IN THE USSR. VFOAT Parapsychology in the U.S.S.R. Pt. 1-. 0748-0156. Periodical. US. English. Washington Research Center, 3101 Washington Street, San Francisco CA 95115. LC BF1001. DD 133.80947.

PARAPSYCHOLOGY REVIEW. V. 1- Mar./Apr. 1970-. 0031-1804. Periodical. US. English. bm. $9.00. Parapsychology Foundation Inc, 228 East 71st Street, New York NY 10021. Tel (212)628-1550. Ed Betty Shapin. Ind/Abst Psychol. Abstr. LC BF1001. DD 133.05. NLM W1 PA635S. CODEN PAREDT. bk rev. Circ 1,500. Contains articles covering a wide range of studies by leading authorities from all the sciences, book reviews, reports on conferences, educational notes, and others. Newsletter of the Parapsychology Foundation, Inc.

PHENOMENA. V. 1- Jan. 1977-. 0701-4945. Periodical. CN. English. mo. $10.00, $7.50 for groups of 10 or more. Phenomena Publications, Box 6228, Toronto A Ontario Canada. DD 133.505.

PROCEEDINGS OF THE PARAPSYCHOLOGICAL ASSOCIATION CEASED. Main/Corp Parapsychological Association. 1st-8th. 0090-5399. US. English. an. Scarecrow Press, 52 Liberty Street, PO Box 656, Metuchen NJ 08840. Ed W G Roll and J G Pratt. LC BF1021. NLM W1 PR586Q.

PROCEEDINGS OF THE SOCIETY FOR PSYCHICAL RESEARCH. Vol. 1 (1882/83)-. UK. English. ir. Society for Psychical Research, 1 Adam & Eve News, London W8 England. Tel (01)937-8984. Ed John Beloff. bk rev. Circ 1,000. (ctrl). The proceedings, published in parts as and when suitable material becomes available, are devoted to major pieces of research, Presidential Addresses and papers of a theoretical or analytical nature.

PSI-M. 5317-2138. Periodical. US. English. mo. $7.00 Members of American MENSA, $9.00 Associate Members. PSI-M, The Psychic Science Special Interest Group Inc, 7514 Belleplaine Drive, Dayton OH 45424.

PSI RESEARCH. Vol. 1, No. 1 (Mar. 1982)-. 0749-2898. Periodical. US. English. qt. $28.00. PSI Research, 3101 Washington Street, San Francisco CA 95115. Tel (415)563-7780. Ed Larissa Vilenskaya. Ind/Abst Psychol. Abstr. DD 133. bk rev. adv acc. Circ 300. (ctrl). International quarterly on parapsychology and related studies, with emphasis on research in the USSR, Eastern Europe and China.

PSYCHIC OBSERVER. 0048-573X. Periodical. US. English. ir. ESP Press Inc, PO Box 55482, Washington DC 20011. Tel (202)723-4578. Ed Henry J Nagorka. bk rev. adv acc. A broadly eclectic journal of spiritual science well respected since 1938, specializing in metaphysics, inner development, psychic phenomena, new age concepts and psychotronics.

PSYCHOTRONIK. V. 1-. 0379-7449. Periodical. German. ir. NLM W1 PS89.

PU SHIH HSING HSIANG. V. 1-. Periodical. Chinese. ir. $24.00. Wai Chi Lee, 294 King's Road 6th Floor, Hsiang-Kang Hong Kong. Ed Chien-Li. LC BF1868.C5.

QUESTION DE SPIRITUALITE, TRADITION, LITTERATURES. VFOAT Question de. No. 1- 4th Quarterly 1973-. Periodical. French. bm. $23.68. Retz, Bolte Postale 49/59930, la Chapelle d'Armentieres France.

RAYS FROM THE ROSE CROSS. VFOAT Rosicrucian Fellowship Magazine. V. 66, No. 12- Dec. 1974-. 0744-432X. Periodical. US. English. bm. Rosicrucian Fellowship, PO Box 713, Oceanside CA 92054. Rosicrucian Fellowship Magazine.

REALITE. V. 1- April 1975-. 0384-6016. Periodical. CN. French. mo. Eglise de Scientologie de Quebec, 781 Est Boulevard Charest, Quebec Quebec G1K 3J6 Canada. DD 131.3505. Connection Francaise.

REFORMADOR. Periodical. Portuguese. ir. LC BF1005. DD 133.905.

RESEARCH IN PARAPSYCHOLOGY. Main/Corp Parapsychological Association. 1972-. 0093-4798. US. English. ir. Scarecrow Press Incorporated, PO Box 656, Metuchen NJ 08840. LC BF1021. DD 133. NLM W1 RE227JK. Proceedings of the Parapsychological Association, 0090-5399.

ROSES EN EVEIL. Vol. 1, No 1 (Sept./Oct. 1978)-. 0227-4566. Periodical. CN. French. bm. 1.00 Per Number. Fraternite Rosicrucienne de Max Heindel, CP 310, Succursale Bourassa, Montreal Quebec H2C 3G2 Canada. DD 135.4305.

ROSICRUCIAN DIGEST. 1932. 0035-8339. Periodical. US. English. mo. $12.00. Rosicrucian Park, San Jose CA 95114. Ed Robin Thompson. LC BF1623.R7. Mystic Triangle.

SCIENZA E IGNOTO. Vol. 1- Sept. 1972-. Periodical. Italian. ir. 6,500. I'Talamonti Faenza Editrice, Via Conte di Vetry 6 Ca Post 68, 48018 Faenza Roma Italy. LC BF1004.

THE SEEKER NEWSLETTER CEASED. 0145-8361. Periodical. US. English. qt. $15.00. Seeker Magazine, PO Box 7601, San Diego CA 92107. Tel (619)225-0133. Ed Diane K Pike. Circ 750. (ctrl). Membership publication focused on personal and spiritual growth, consciousness expansion and the ancient wisdom. Special focus on Heart Center Love, using the love project principles.

THE SKEPTICAL INQUIRER. V. 2, No. 2- Spring/Summer 1978-. 0194-6730. Periodical. US. English. qt $18.00. Skeptical Inquirer, Box 229 Central Park Station, Buffalo NY 14215. Tel (716)834-3222. Ed Kendrick Frazier. Ind/Abst Sociol. Abstr. LC BF1001. DD 001.9. NLM W1 SK583. bk rev. adv acc. Circ 25,000. (ctrl). Offers scientific evidence in the debunking of paranormal claims. Zetetic, 0148-1096.

SORCERER'S APPRENTICE (SCOTTSDALE, ARIZ.). (SORCERER'S APPRENTICE). 0276-3575. Periodical. US. English. qt. Sorcerer's Apprentice, PO Box 1467, Scottsdale AZ 85252. Tel (602)966-4727.

SOUL SEARCHER. V. 1- Spring/Summer 1977-. 0275-6501. Periodical. US. English. qt. Free to Members, $6.00 Nonmembers. Foundation for Christian Psychic Research Inc, 351 Main Street, Ridgefield CT 06877.

SPIRITUAL PRESS. (THE SPIRITUAL PRESS). V. 1, No. 14- Nov. 1975-. 0381-6621. Periodical. CN. English. Spiritual Press, PO Box 464, Don Mills Ontario M3C 2T3 Canada. DD 133.93.

THETA. No. 1- Apr. 1963-. 0040-6066. Periodical. US. English. qt. $14.00. Psychical Research Foundation, Box 3356, Chapel Hill NC 27514. Tel (919)968-4956. Ed Rhea White and W G Roll. LC BF1001. DD 133.901305. bk rev. Circ 1,000. Focuses on the question of whether personality and consciousness extend beyond bodily existence.

TIJDSCHRIFT VOOR PARAPSYCHOLOGIE. Periodical. NE. Dutch. qt. 40.-. Studievereniging voor Pyschical Research, Postbus 786, NL-35 AT Utrecht Netherlands. Tel (020)255469. LC BF1008.D8. NLM W1 TI715. bk rev. adv acc. Philosophical, anthropological and psychological articles on parapsychology including experiments cases and book reviews.

TORONTO DIMENSIONS. No. 1 (May 21, 1983)-. 0822-8000. Periodical. CN. English. ir. 6.00. Toronto Dimensions, 214 Glengarry Avenue, Toronto Ontario M5M 1E4 Canada. Tel (416)787-3395. Ed Ero Talvila. DD 133.09713541. bk rev. adv acc. Circ 6,700. A 12-page Toronto-centered tabloid of calendar news and articles focusing on self-development: nutrition, alternative therapies and occult, psychic and spiritual concerns. Inner Life Newsletter, 0822-7993.

AS UFONOTAS. See Science (General).

VITAL SIGNS (STORRS, CONN.). (VITAL SIGNS). 0749-856X. Periodical. US. English. qt. $25.00 Domestic, $30.00 Foreign. International Association for Near-Death Studies, Box U-20 Psych #258 406 Cross Campus Road, Storrs CT 06268. Tel (203)486-4170. Ed Nancy Evans Bush. DD 133. bk rev. Circ 800. (ctrl). Personal accounts and general discussion of near-death and related experiences, including book reviews, news and notes, etc.

THE WHITE LIGHT. 0742-8820. Periodical. US. English. qt. $5.00 Domestic, $8.00 Foreign. Temple of Truth, PO Box 93124, Pasadena CA 91109. Tel (818)794-6013. Ed Nelson H White. DD 133.4305. bk rev. adv acc. Circ 200. Ceremonial magic and related areas: Qaballah, etc., occultism.

Petroleum and Natural Gas

ZEITSCHRIFT FUR PARAPSYCHOLOGIE UND GRENZGEBIETE DER PSYCHOLOGIE. Vol. 1-. 0514-2725. Periodical. GW. German (summaries in English, French). ir. 36.-. Aurum Verlag, Postfach 5204D-7800, Freiburg 1 Br West Germany. Tel (0761)36409. Ed Autum Verlg and Gunther Berkau. Ind/Abst Excerpta Med. LC BF1003. DD 133.05. NLM W1 ZE531T. bk rev. Parapsychology.

ZETETIC SCHOLAR. Vol. 1, No. 1-. 0741-6229. Periodical. US. English. sa. $18.00. Eastern Michigan University, Department Sociology, Marcello Trvzzi Ypsilanti MI 48971. Tel (616)487-0012. Ed Marcello Trvzzi. Ind/Abst Sociol. Abstr. LC BF1001. DD 133.05. bk rev. Circ 600. Scientific exchanges on anomalies and the paranormal between critics and proponents plus reviews and bibliogrophies.

PETROLEUM AND NATURAL GAS

AAPG CONTINUING EDUCATION COURSE NOTE SERIES. See Earth Sciences - Geology.

AAPG EXPLORER. See Earth Sciences - Geology.

AAPG REPRINT SERIES. See Earth Sciences - Geology.

ACTIVITE DE L'INDUSTRIE PETROLIERE (PARIS, FRANCE : 1982). (ACTIVITE DE L'INDUSTRIE PETROLIERE). French. ir. LC HD9572.2. DD 338.27280944. Activite de l'Industrie du Petrole et du Gaz Naturel.

ACTUACIONES. Main/Corp Frente Nacional Pro-Defensa del Petroleo Venezolano. Yearly V. 1- 1970-. Spanish. ir. LC HD9574.V4.

ADVANCES IN PETROLEUM GEOCHEMISTRY. Vol. 1-. 0739-8352. UK. English. an. Academic Press Inc, 4905 Sand Lake Road, Orlando FL 32819. LC TN860. DD 553.28. CODEN APGEEH.

AFRICA-MIDDLE EAST PETROLEUM DIRECTORY. See Yearbooks, Almanacs, Directories.

AGA MONTHLY. VAT American Gas Association Monthly. Vol. 66, No. 10 (Oct. 1984)-. 0885-2413. Periodical. US. English. mo. $30.00. American Gas Association, 1515 Wilson Boulevard, Arlington VA 22209. Ind/Abst Environ. Period. Bibliogr., Gas Abstr., Sci. Cit. Index, Abr. Ed. LC TP700. DD 363.630973. American Gas Association Monthly, 0002-8584.

AKHBAR AL-BATRUL WA-AL-SINAAH. Arabic. ir. PO Box 9, Abu Zaby United Arab Emirates. LC HD9576.U5.

AL-NAFT WA-AL-ALAM. VFOAT Al Naft Wal Aalam. Periodical. Arabic (English). ir. .5. Wizarat Al-Naft, PO Box 6118, Mansour Iraq. LC HD9576.I7.

AL-NAFT WA-AL-TANMIYAH. VFOAT Oil and Development Magazine. Periodical. Arabic. ir. $30.00. Dar Al-Thawrah Lil-Sihafah Wa-Al-Nashr, PO Box 6124, Baghdad Iraq. LC HD9560.1.

AL-TAQRIR AL-IHSAI AL-SANAWI - MUNAZZAMAT AL-AQTAR AL-ARABIYAH AL-MURSADDIRAH LIL-BITRUL, AL-IDARAH AL-IQTISADIYAH. Main/Corp Organization of Arab Petroleum Exporting Countries. Economic Dept. VFOAT Annual Statistical Report - Organization of Arab Petroleum Exporting Countries (OAPEC), Economic Department. Arabic (English). ir. LC HD9578.A55. Taqrir Al-Ihsai Al-Sanawi - Munazzamat Al-Aqtar Al-Arabiyah Al-Musaddirah Lil-Bitrul, Al-Idarah Al-IQtisadiyah, Qism.

AL-WATANIYAH. Periodical. Arabic. mo. Malallat Al-Wataniyah, S B 70, Al-Safah Al-Kuwayt. LC HD9578.A55.

ALAM AL-NAFT. Periodical. Arabic. ir. 200.00. PO Box 115079, Beirut Lebanon. LC HD9560.1.

ALASKA CONSTRUCTION & OIL. VAT Alaska Construction and Oil. 0002-4473. Periodical. US. English. mo. $18.00. Vernon Publications Inc, 109 West Mercer Street, Seattle WA 98119. Tel (206)285-2050. Ind/Abst Coal Abstr., Energy Inf. Abstr., Environ. Abstr., ASTIS Bibliogr., ASTIS Curr. Aware. Bull., Energy Res. Abstr., Pet. Abstr. LC HC107.A45. DD 338.09798. Alaska Construction.

ALASKA PETROLEUM & INDUSTRIAL DIRECTORY. See Yearbooks, Almanacs, Directories.

ALBERTA DRILLING PROGRESS AND PIPELINE RECEIPTS WEEKLY REPORT. 0227-3357. Periodical. CN. English. wk. 170.00. Energy Resources Conservation Board, 604 5th Avenue Southwest, Calgary Alberta T2P 3G4 Canada. Tel (403)297-8311. DD 622.3382097123. Summary of oil pipeline gathering operations in Alberta and details of drilling activity.

ALBERTA OIL AND GAS CONSERVATION SCHEMES. Main/Corp Alberta. Energy Resources Conservation Board. 1978-. 0709-5902. CN. English. an. Energy Resources Conservation Board, 603 6th Avenue SW, Calgary Alberta T2P 0T4 Canada. Tel (403)297-8311. Summary of data on fluid injection and conservation projects by field and pool for Alberta. Oil Conservation Projects and Gas Conservation Schemes, Province of Alberta, 0380-433X.

ALBERTA OIL AND GAS INDUSTRY : ANNUAL STATISTICS. See Statistics.

ALBERTA PETROLEUM STATISTICS. See Statistics.

ALBERTA POOL PRODUCTION AND INJECTION MONTHLY SUPPLEMENT. Main/Corp Alberta. Energy Resources Conservation Board. 0702-3286. Periodical. CN. English. mo. 35.00. Energy Resource Conservation Board, 640 5th Avenue Southwest, Calgary Alta T2P 3G4 Canada. Tel (403)297-8311. Production and injection totals for oil and gas by field and pool for province of Alberta.

ALBERTA'S RESERVES OF CRUDE OIL, GAS, NATURAL GAS LIQUIDS AND SULPHUR CEASED. (ALBERTA'S RESERVES OF CRUDE OIL, GAS, NATURAL GAS LIQUIDS, AND SULPHUR AT 31 DECEMBER . . .). VFOAT Reserves. VAT Reserves (Calgary). 16th Ed. (1976)-. 0706-3199. CN. English. an. Energy Resources Conservation Board, 640 5th Avenue Southwest, Calgary Alberta T2P 3G4 Canada. LC TN873.C22. DD 553.28097123. Reserves of Crude Oil, Gas, Natural Gas Liquids, and Sulphur, Province of Alberta, 0380-4453.

ALBERTA'S RESERVES OF CRUDE OIL, OIL SANDS, GAS, NATURAL GAS LIQUIDS, AND SULPHUR AT DECEMBER 31 . . . . Series/Titl ERCB ST. VFOAT Alberta's Reserves. CN. English. an. 50.00. Energy Resources Conservation Board, 640 Fifth Avenue Southwest, Calgary Alberta T2P 3G4 Canada. Tel (403)297-8311. LC TN873.C22. DD 553.28097123. Alberta's Reserves of Crude Oil, Gas, Natural Gas Liquids, and Sulphur at 31 December . . ., 0706-3199.

ALBERTA'S RESERVES OF GAS. (ALBERTA'S RESERVES OF GAS, COMPLETE LISTING AT 31 DECEMBER . . .). Series/Titl ERCB. 1978-. 0229-8546. CN. English. an. $100.00. Energy Resources Conservation Board, 640 Fifth Avenue South West, Calgary Alta T2P 3G4 Canada. LC TN873.C22. DD 553.285097123.

ALI-ABA COURSE OF STUDY : OIL SPILLS AND THE LAW : MATERIALS. See Law.

ALPHABETIC SUBJECT INDEX TO PETROLEUM ABSTRACTS. See Indexes/Abstracts.

AMERICAN GAS ASSOCIATION MONTHLY CEASED. VFOAT A.G.A. Monthly. V. 1- Jan. 1919-. 0002-8584. Periodical. US. English. mo. American Gas Association, 1515 Wilson Boulevard, Arlington VA 22209. Tel (703)841-8400. Ind/Abst Life Sci. Collect., Eng. Index Annu., Eng. Index Mon., Eng. Index Bioeng. Abstr., Eng. Index Energy Abstr., Predicasts, Coal Abstr., Energy Inf. Abstr., Environ. Abstr., Int. Aerosp. Abstr., Environ. Period. Bibliogr., Gas Abstr., Sci. Cit. Index, Abr. Ed., Energy Res. Abstr., Pet. Abstr., Funk Scott Index Corp. Ind., Eng. Index. LC TP700. DD 333.823305. CODEN AGAMAC. Gas Institute News.

THE AMERICAN OIL & GAS REPORTER. VFOAT American Oil and Gas Reporter. 0145-9198. Periodical. US. English. mo. Domestic Petroleum Publishers, 1069 Parklane, Wichita KS 67218-3287. Tel (316)681-3560. Ind/Abst Pet. Abstr. LC TN872. DD 553.280973.

ANALYSES OF NATURAL GASES. Began with 1961. US. English. an. US Bureau of Mines, Pittsburgh PA 15213.

ANEP. ANNUAIRE EUROPEEN DE PETROLE. See Yearbooks, Almanacs, Directories.

ANNUAL BULLETIN OF GAS STATISTICS FOR EUROPE. See Statistics.

ANNUAL CONFERENCE - ONTARIO PETROLEUM INSTITUTE. (THE ONTARIO PETROLEUM INSTITUTE, . . . ANNUAL CONFERENCE : PROCEEDINGS). VFOAT Annual Conference. 1st (1962)-. 0078-5040. Periodical. CN. English. an. Ontario Petroleum Institute, PO Box 396, Chatham Ontario Canada. Tel (519)862-1473. adv acc. (ctrl). The papers enclosed in our bound volume are the technical papers that are presented at the annual conference, held in October 1985.

ANNUAL MEETING - INTERNATIONAL OIL SCOUTS ASSOCIATION. (ANNUAL MEETING). Main/Corp International Oil Scouts Association. 0731-9800. US. English. an. International Oil Scouts Association, PO Box 2121, Austin TX 78767. Ind/Abst GeoRef. LC TN860. DD 622.338205.

ANNUAL MEETING PAPERS - DIVISION OF PRODUCTION (AMERICAN PETROLEUM INSTITUTE). Main/Corp American Petroleum Institute. Division of Production. 1971-1975. 0196-9978. US. English. an. $15.00. American Petroleum Institute, 1220 L Street Northwest, Washington DC 20005. Tel (214)741-6791. Ind/Abst GeoRef, Pollut. Abstr. Indexes.

ANNUAL OIL AND GAS REPORT - ARKANSAS. OIL AND GAS COMMISSION. Main/Corp Arkansas. Oil and Gas Commission. US. English. an. The Commission, 314 East Oak, El Dorado AR 71730. LC TN872.A85.

ANNUAL OIL AND GAS STATISTICS. See Statistics.

ANNUAL OIL MARKET REPORT. VAT Oil Market Report. English. an. OECD Publications, 2 rue Andre-Pascal, 75775 Paris Cedex 16 France. LC HD9560.1. DD 338.2728205.

ANNUAL PETROLEUM REVIEW. 0747-5594. US. English. an. California Energy Commission Publications Unit, 1111 Howe Avenue Room 613, Sacramento CA 95825. LC TN872.C2. DD 665.509794.

ANNUAL PRODUCTION BY ACTIVE FIELDS, OIL AND GAS DIVISION. Main/Corp Texas. Railroad Commission. Oil and Gas Division. VFOAT Oil and Gas Annual Production by Active Fields. 0098-4043. US. English. an. Railroad Commission of Texas, Capital Station, PO Drawer 20545, Austin TX 78711. LC TN872.T4. DD 338.272809764.

ANNUAL PROGRESS REPORT, TRACT C-A. See Technology (General).

ANNUAL REPORT - ALBERTA PETROLEUM MARKETING COMMISSION. Main/Corp Alberta. Petroleum Marketing Commission. 1st- 1974-. 0703-2358. CN. English. an. Alberta Petroleum Marketing Commission, 1000 Bow Valley Square 11, 205-5th Avenue South West, Box 9084, Edmonton Alberta Canada. LC HD9574.C23. DD 354.7123008238.

ANNUAL REPORT AND FINANCIAL STATEMENTS - PETROBRAS QUIMICA. Main/Corp Petrobras Quimica. English. an. Cidade Universite Quadra, 7 Postal 809, 21910 Rio de Janeiro Brazil. LC HD9579.C34. DD 338.76618040981.

ANNUAL REPORT AND STATEMENT OF ACCOUNTS FOR THE YEAR ENDED 31ST DECEMBER . . . - AGIP (TANZANIA) LTD. Main/Corp AGIP (Tanzania) Ltd. English. an. AGIP (Tanzania) Ltd, PO Box 9540, Dar es Salaam Tanzania. LC HD9577.T344. DD 338.7622338209678.

ANNUAL REPORT - BRITISH COLUMBIA. MINISTRY OF ENERGY, MINES AND PETROLEUM RESOURCES. See Engineering - Mining Engineering.

ANNUAL REPORT - BRITISH COLUMBIA PETROLEUM CORPORATION. Main/Corp British Columbia Petroleum Corporation. CN. English. an. British Columbia Petroleum Corporation, 1199 West Hastings

Petroleum and Natural Gas

Street/6th Floor, Vancouver BC V6E 3C2 Canada. **LC** HD9574.C24. **DD** 354.71100826228506.

ANNUAL REPORT - DELEK, THE ISRAEL FUEL CORPORATION. Main/Corp Delek, Hevrat Ha-Delek Ha-Yisreelit. English. ir. The Israel Fuel Corporation, 6 Ahuzat Bayit Street, Tel-Aviv Israel. **LC** HD9576.I82. **DD** 338.762233282095694.

ANNUAL REPORT FOR THE YEAR - FIJI. MINERAL RESOURCES DIVISION. See Earth Sciences - Geology.

ANNUAL REPORT - INDIAN OIL CORPORATION LIMITED. Main/Corp Indian Oil Corporation Limited. English. an. **LC** HD9576.I44. **DD** 338.762233820954.

ANNUAL REPORT - KUWAIT OIL COMPANY (K. S. C.). Main/Corp Sharkat Naft Al-Kuwayt. English. ir. Kuwait Oil Company (K S C), Kuwait Investment Co Building, Kuwait Kuwait. **LC** HD9576.K84. **DD** 33876223382095367. *Annual Review of the Operations.*

ANNUAL REPORT - KUWAIT PETROLEUM CORPORATION. Main/Corp Kuwait Petroleum Corporation. 1st (1980-1981)-. English. ir. Kuwait Petroleum Corporation, PO Box 26565, Safat Kuwait. **LC** HD9576.K84. **DD** 354.5367008238806.

ANNUAL REPORT - LIQUEFIED PETROLEUM GAS DIVISION OF THE RAILROAD COMMISSION OF TEXAS. Main/Corp Texas. Railroad Commission. Liquefied Petroleum Gas Division. **VFOAT** Annual Report - Railroad Commission of Texas, Liquefied Petroleum Gas Division. 0492-8717. Periodical. US. English. ir. Liquefied Petroleum Gas Division of the Railroad Commission of Texas, Austin TX 78711. **DD** 338.2.

ANNUAL REPORT OF THE OIL AND GAS DIVISION (AUSTIN). (ANNUAL REPORT OF THE OIL AND GAS DIVISION; TO THE GOVERNOR). Main/Corp Texas. Railroad Commission. Oil and Gas Division. **VFOAT** Oil and Gas Annual. Periodical. US. English. an. $10.00. Railroad Commission of Texas, Capitol Station, PO Drawer 12967, Austin TX 78711. **Tel** (512)475-2439. **LC** HD9567.T3.

ANNUAL REPORT OF THE RAILROAD COMMISSION OF TEXAS, GAS UTILITIES DIVISION. Main/Corp Railroad Commission of Texas. Gas Utilities Division. 1922/23-. US. English. an. **LC** TN880.

ANNUAL REPORT OF THE STATE OIL AND GAS SUPERVISOR (CALIFORNIA). Main/Corp California. Division of Oil and Gas. 0362-1243. US. English. an. Department of Conservation Oil & Gas, 1416 9th Street, Sacramento CA 95814. **Tel** (916)445-9686. Ed Susan F Hodgson. **LC** TN872.C2. **DD** 354.9794008238805. **CODEN** CDOOAL. **Circ** 2,500. California oil, gas, and geothermal production and injection statistics.

ANNUAL REPORT ON PIPELINE SAFETY. Main/Corp United States. Materials Transportation Bureau. Calendar year 1979-. 0277-3287. US. English. an. US Department of Transportation, Research and Special Programs Administration, Materials Transportation Bureau, Washington DC 20590. **LC** TN880.5. **DD** 363.12. Vols. for (1983-) distributed to depository libraries in microfiche. *Annual Report of Pipeline Safety, 0277-3287.*

ANNUAL REPORT - ORGANIZATION OF THE PETROLEUM EXPORTING COUNTRIES. Main/Corp Organization of Petroleum Exporting Countries. **VFOAT** OPEC Annual Report. 1977-. English. ir. Public Relations Department, Organization of Petroleum Exporting Countries, Obere Donaustrasse 93, A-1020 Vienna Austria. **LC** HD9560.1. **DD** 341.75472282.

ANNUAL REPORT. OUTER CONTINENTAL SHELF OIL AND GAS LEASING AND PRODUCTION PROGRAM. Main/Corp United States. Minerals Management Service. **Series/Titl** OCS Report. 8755-2884. US. English. an. Office of Offshore Information Services, Minerals Management Service MS, 640 Main Interior Building, Washington DC 20240. **LC** HD242.5. **DD** 353.0082308. *Outer Continental Shelf Oil and Gas Leasing and Production Program Annual Report.*

ANNUAL REPORT - STATE OF MINNESOTA, DEPARTMENT OF REVENUE, PETROLEUM DIVISION. Main/Corp Minnesota. Dept. of Revenue. Petroleum Division. 1973-. 0095-3024. US. English. an. Centennial Office Building, St Paul MN 55145. **LC** HD9579.G5. **DD** 353.977600724. *Annual Report - State of Minnesota, Dept. of Taxation, Petroleum Division.*

ANNUAL REPORT - UNIAO DE INDUSTRIAS PETROQUIMICAS. English. ir. Uniao de Industrias Petroquimicas, Rua Araujo Porto Alegre 36/4. Andar, Rio de Janeiro Brazil. **LC** HD9579.C34 U547.

ANNUAL REPORT, YEAR TO 31ST MARCH . . . (BRITISH-BORNEO PETROLEUM SYNDICATE). Main/Corp British-Borneo Petroleum Syndicate. UK. English. an. British-Borneo Petroleum Syndicate P L C, Registered Office/Pembroke House, 40 City Road, London EC1Y 2AD England. **LC** HD9576.B64. **DD** 338.887. *Annual Report.*

ANNUAL REVIEW FOR THE YEAR RELATING TO OIL AND GAS (MONTANA). Main/Corp Montana. Oil and Gas Conservation Division. **VFOAT** Annual Review for the Year. V. 15- 1971-. 0190-3926. US. English. an. **LC** HD9567.M9. **DD** 338.272809786. *Annual Review for the Year Relating to Oil and Gas, 0190-3926.*

ANNUAL REVIEW OF CALIFORNIA OIL AND GAS PRODUCTION. **VFOAT** California Oil and Gas Production. 1965-. 0197-5641. US. English. an. $50.00. Conservation Committee of California, 417 South Hill Street Suite 930, Los Angeles CA 90013. **Tel** (213)625-7731. Ed Craig Bowman. **Circ** 500. Over 500 pages of annual and cumulative statistical data on California's oil and gas industry includes breakdowns by company and by field and pool. *Annual Review of California Crude Oil Production.*

ANNUAL SUMMARY OF OPERATIONS - PETROLEUM RESOURCES BRANCH. BRITISH COLUMBIA DEPARTMENT OF MINES AND PETROLEUM RESOURCES CEASED. (ANNUAL SUMMARY OF OPERATIONS - PETROLEUM RESOURCES BRANCH). Main/Corp British Columbia. Petroleum Resources Branch. Ceased publication with 1980 issue. 0382-3067. CN. English. an. **LC** HD9574.C2. **DD** 354.7110082327.

ANNUAL SUMMARY REPORT - LOUSIANA STATE UNIVERSITY. PETROLEUM ENGINEERING DEPT. Main/Corp Louisiana State University, Baton Rouge. Petroleum Engineering Dept. **VFOAT** Annual Report. US. English. an. Petroleum Engineering Department, Louisiana State University, Baton Rouge LA 70803.

ANNUAL SURVEY OF OIL AND GAS. (CURRENT INDUSTRIAL REPORTS. MA-13K, ANNUAL SURVEY OF OIL AND GAS). 1973-. 0193-2403. US. English. an. $1.00. Data User Services Division Customer Services Publication, Bureau of the Census, Washington DC 20233. **Tel** (301)763-4100. **LC** HD9564. **DD** 338.27280973. Includes final statistics covering oil and gas field exploration, development, and production activity for the year, with some comparative figures for previous years.

AOCS MONOGRAPH. See Chemistry.

AOSTRA JOURNAL OF RESEARCH. Vol. 1, No. 1 (Sept. 1984)-. 0822-2509. Periodical. CN. English. qt. 60.00 Canada/US, 77.00 Foreign. Alberta Scientific Publishing Group, Department of Chemistry University of Alberta, Edmonton Alberta T6G 2G2 Canada. **Tel** (403)432-3641. Ed D S Montgomery. **DD** 622.33705. **Circ** 250. Research and development technology related to bituminous sands, heavy oils, oil source rocks and territory recovery of conventional petroleum.

APEA JOURNAL. (THE APEA JOURNAL). Main/Corp Australian Petroleum Exploration Association. **VAT** The Australian Petroleum Exploration Association Journal. V. 1- 1961-. 0084-7534. AT. English. sa. $80.00. Australian Petroleum Exploration Association, Box 3974 GPO, Sydney New South Wales 1002 Australia. **Ind/Abst** Eng. Index Annu., Eng. Index Mon., Eng. Index Bioeng. Abstr., Eng. Index Energy Abstr., Coal Abstr., Energy Inf. Abstr., Environ. Abstr., GeoRef, Chem. Abstr., Energy Res. Abstr. **LC** TN271.P4. **DD** 622.1828205. **CODEN** APXJAB. adv acc. Contains the technical papers presented at the APEA Conference in Australia as well as other important information on exploration. Very useful to companies and and people involved in the oil exploration and production industry.

API INDEXES. INDEX TERM USE STATISTICS. See Indexes/Abstracts.

API MONTHLY REPORT COVERING INVENTORIES OF NATURAL GAS LIQUIDS AND LIQUEFIED REFINERY GASES. Apr. 1985-Feb. 1986. Periodical. US. English. mo. American Petroleum Institute, 156 William Street, New York NY 10038. *Liquefied Petroleum Gas Report.*

A.P.O.A. REVIEW. (A. P. O. A. REVIEW). Main/Corp Arctic Petroleum Operators' Association. **VAT** Arctic Petroleum Operators' Association Review (English Edition). V. 1- Feb. 1978-. 0709-5686. Periodical. CN. English. ir. Free. A P O A Information Service, PO Box 1281, Station M, Calgary Alberta T2P 2L2 Canada. **Ind/Abst** ASTIS Bibliogr., ASTIS Curr. Aware. Bull. **DD** 338.27282097199.

ARAB OIL AND ECONOMIC REVIEW. V. 2- Jan. 1979-. Periodical. UK. English. mo. Arab Oil & Economic Review, 3 Dunraven Street, London W1Y 3FG England. **LC** HC498.A1. **DD** 338.2728209174927. *Arab Oil.*

ARAB OIL & GAS DIRECTORY. See Yearbooks, Almanacs, Directories.

ARAB OIL (ARAB OIL PUB. CO. : 1980.). (ARAB OIL). Periodical. UK. English. mo. Arab Oil, 3 Dunraven Street, London W1Y 3FG England. **Ind/Abst** Ship Abstr., Excerpta Med. **LC** HC498.A1. **DD** 338.2728209174927. *Arab Oil and Economic Review.*

ARCTIC GAS. BIOLOGICAL REPORT SERIES. See Biology.

ARKANSAS OIL AND GAS STATISTICAL BULLETIN. See Statistics.

ARMSTRONG OIL DIRECTORIES, EASTERN UNITED STATES. See Yearbooks, Almanacs, Directories.

ARMSTRONG OIL DIRECTORIES. LOUISIANA, TEXAS GULF COAST, EAST TEXAS, ARK. AND MISS. See Yearbooks, Almanacs, Directories.

ARMSTRONG OIL DIRECTORIES. ROCKY MOUNTAIN AND CENTRAL UNITED STATES. See Yearbooks, Almanacs, Directories.

ARMSTRONG OIL DIRECTORIES, TEXAS AND SOUTHEASTERN NEW MEXICO. See Yearbooks, Almanacs, Directories.

ASCOPE DIRECTORY. See Yearbooks, Almanacs, Directories.

ASIA & AUSTRALASIA. BASIC OIL LAWS AND CONCESSION CONTRACTS, ORIGINAL TEXTS. SUPPLEMENT. (ASIA & AUSTRALASIA : BASIC OIL LAWS AND CONCESSION CONTRACTS. ORIGINAL TEXTS (SUPPLEMENT)). Main/Corp Petroleum Legislation, New York. No. 1- 1960-. 0094-6559. US. English. qt. $4,500.00. Barrows Company Inc, 116 East 66th Street, New York NY 10023. **DD** 346.504682.

ASIA-PACIFIC PETROLEUM DIRECTORY. See Yearbooks, Almanacs, Directories.

ATUALIDADES. Main/Corp Conselho Nacional de Petroleo (Brazil). BL. Portuguese. ir. Assessoria de Relacoes Publicas, Av 13 de Maio 13 260 Andar, Rio de Janeiro Brazil. **LC** TN873.B8. **DD** 338.272820981.

AUSSENHANDEL. REIHE 4 : GENERALHANDEL. EIN- UND AUSFUHR VON MINERALOL. Main/Corp Germany (West). Statistisches Bundesamt. **VFOAT** Aussenhandel. Jan. 1962-. 0072-1670. German. mo. **LC** HD9573.1.

AUSSENHANDEL. REIHE 4.1 : EIN- UND AUSFUHR VON MINERALOL, GENERALHANDEL. Main/Corp Germany (West). Statistisches Bundesamt. **VAT** Aussenhandel. Reihe Vier. Eins: Ein- Und Ausfuhr Von Mineralol, Generalhandel. Jan. 1977-. Periodical. GW. German. mo. $42.24. Kohlhammer Verlag/ABT Veroef Fentl Stat Bundesamt, Postfach 421120, D6500 Mainz 42 West Germany. **Tel** 0 61 31/ 5 90 94/95. **LC**

Petroleum and Natural Gas

HD9573.1. Aussenhandel. Reihe 4: Generalhandel. Ein-und Ausfuhr Von Mineralol.

AUSTRALIAN GAS INDUSTRY DIRECTORY. See Yearbooks, Almanacs, Directories.

AUSTRALIAN GAS JOURNAL. (THE AUSTRALIAN GAS JOURNAL). V. 27, No. 6-. 0004-9166. Periodical. AT. English. qt. $14.75. Australian Gas Association, PO Box 323, Canberra Australian Capital Territory 2061 Australia. Tel (062)473955. Ed Anne-Maree T Low. Ind/Abst Coal Abstr., GeoRef, Bibliogr. Index Geol. LC TP700. adv acc. Circ 2,000. (ctrl). Reports on the latest in domestic and technical marketing and overseas news affecting the gas industry. Australian Gas Bulletin.

AUSTRALIAN MINING AND PETROLEUM LAW ASSOCIATION YEARBOOK. See Yearbooks, Almanacs, Directories.

AUSTRALIAN PETROLEUM STATISTICS. See Statistics.

AUTOMOTIVE FUEL ECONOMY PROGRAM. ANNUAL REPORT TO THE CONGRESS. (AUTOMOTIVE FUEL ECONOMY PROGRAM). VFOAT Annual Automotive Fuel Economy Program Report to the Congress. Began with 1st, 1977. 0146-5236. US. English. an. US Department of Transportation, National Highway Traffic Safety Administration, Washington DC 20590. LC HD9561. DD 353.008242. Vols. for 1982- distributed to depository libraries in microfiche.

AZERBAIDZHANSKII KHIMICHESKII ZHURNAL. See Chemistry.

B P STATISTICAL REVIEW OF THE WORLD OIL INDUSTRY. See Statistics.

BAHAN BAHAN INFORMASI MINYAK DAN GAS BUMI INDONESIA. Indonesian. ir. LC HD9576.I5.

BASIC PETROLEUM DATA BOOK (WASHINGTON, D.C. : 1981). (BASIC PETROLEUM DATA BOOK). Vol. 1, No. 1-. 0730-5621. Periodical. US. English. ty. $45.00. American Petroleum Institute, 1220 L Street Northwest, Washington DC 20005. Tel (202)682-8378. Ind/Abst Predicasts. (ctrl). Continuing source of information, 1947 to current on domestic and world statistical information. Chapters on energy, reserves, exploration and drilling, production, demand, prices, and refining. Basic Petroleum Data Book, 0730-5621.

BEAUFORT. (BEAUFORT). Vol. 1, No. 1 (Aug. 1981)-. 0714-4741. Periodical. CN. English. qt. Free. Beaufort, CP 200, Calgary Alberta T2P 2H8 Canada. DD 333.823150916327.

BENZENE ANNUAL. 0091-3529. US. English. wk. Dewitt & Company Inc, 3650 Dresser TWR/601 Jefferson, Houston TX 77002. Tel (713)652-0576. LC HD9560.4. DD 338.27282.

BERITA MIGAS. Main/Corp Indonesia. Direktorat Jenderal Minyak Dan Gas Bumi. VAT Berita Minyak Dan Gas Bumi. V. 6, No. 3- Mar. 1973-. Periodical. Indonesian. ir. Direktorat Jenderal Minyak Dangas Bumi, Merdeka Selatan 18, Jakarta Indonesia. LC HD9576.I5. Berita Migas.

BILANCIO CONSOLIDATO. Main/Corp Ente Nazionale Idrocarburi. Italian. ir. LC HD9575.I84.

BIP. BULLETIN DE L'INDUSTRIE PETROLIERE. VFOAT Bulletin de l'Industrie Petroliere. 1964. 0300-4554. Periodical. FR. French. da. 7552. Bureau Info Professionnelles, 142 rue Montmartre, 75002 Paris France. Tel 42 61 83 21. Ed Jacques Marie. Ind/Abst Coal Abstr. bk rev. Circ 800. News and comments on oil and gas in the world.

BOLETIM TECNICO DA PETROBRAS. V. 1- Oct. 1957-. 0006-6117. Periodical. BL. Portuguese. qt. Centro Pesquisas Desenvolvimen Cidade, Univ-Quadra 7-Pstl 809, 21910 Rio de Janeiro RF Brazil. Tel 280-4547. Ind/Abst GeoRef, Chem. Abstr., Pet. Abstr. CODEN BTPEAT. Circ 2,100. (ctrl). Studies and researches of a technical and scientific approach, from Brazil and other countries, concerning petroleum and derivates, exploration and the oil industry in general.

BOLETIN DE PETROLEOS. See Economics - Companies: Industry & Production.

BOLETIN TECNICO - ARPEL. (BOLETIN TECNICO). Main/Corp Asistencia Reciproca Petrolera Estatal Latinoamericana. VAT Boltin Tecnico - Asistencia Reciproca Petrolera Estatal Latinoamericana. V. 1- (No.1-). 0253-6005. Periodical. Spanish (some articles in Portuguese). ir.

BOYCOTT REPORT. VFOAT Developments and Trends Affecting the Arab Boycott. V. 1- Mar. 1977-. 0738-5161. Periodical. US. English. ir. $30.00. American Jewish Congress, 15 East 84th Street, New York NY 10028. Tel (212)879-4500. Ed Will Maslow. Circ 5,000. Developments and trends affecting the Arab Boycott of Israel and Arab influence in the USA.

BP SHIELD INTERNATIONAL. VFOAT B.P. Shield International. 0045-1274. Periodical. UK. English. mo. British Petroleum Company Ltd, Britanic House Moor Lane, London EC2 England. Ind/Abst Coal Abstr., Energy Res. Abstr., Fluidex.

BP STATISTICAL REVIEW OF THE WORLD OIL INDUSTRY. See Statistics.

BROWN'S DIRECTORY OF NORTH AMERICAN AND INTERNATIONAL GAS COMPANIES. See Yearbooks, Almanacs, Directories.

BULETINUL INSTITUTULUI DE PETROL, GAZE SI GEOLOGIE. V. 6 (1960)-V. 20 (1973). 0485-6414. Periodical. Romanian (summaries in English and Russian). ir. Ind/Abst GeoRef. CODEN BIPGAQ.

BULETINUL INSTITUTULUI DE PETROL SI GAZE. Began in 1974. 0376-4516. Periodical. RM. Romanian (English). ir. Institutului de Petrol si Gaze, Biblioteca Centrala PO Box 22, 2000 Ploiesti Romania. Ind/Abst GeoRef, Chem. Abstr., Energy Res. Abstr. LC TN860. CODEN BIPGDT. Buletinul Institutului de Petrol, Gaze Si Geologie.

BULLETIN DES CENTRES DE RECHERCHES EXPLORATION-PRODUCTION ELF-AQUITAINE. Main/Corp Elf-Aquitaine (Company). Vol. 1- June 1977-. 0396-2687. Periodical. FR. English or French with summary in the other language. sa. 140. Sneap Edition, Centre Micoulau, 64018 Pau Cedex France. Tel (59) 836237. Ed H J Oertli. Ind/Abst Coal Abstr., GeoRef, Chem. Abstr. LC QE1. DD 550.5. CODEN BCREDP. Circ 2,000. Results of general interest arising from research undertaken by Elf Aquitaine or by scientists working in collaboration with Elf Aquitaine. Bulletin du Centre de Recherche de Pau, 0008-9672.

BULLETIN MENSUEL D'INFORMATION (FRANCE. SERVICE DE CONSERVATION DES GISEMENTS). (BULLETIN MENSUEL D'INFORMATION). 0290-0556. French. mo. Le Service, 366 Avenue Napoleon Bonaparte, 92501 Rueil-Malmaison France. LC TN874.F8. DD 338.27280944.

BULLETIN OF CANADIAN PETROLEUM GEOLOGY. V. 11- Mar. 1963-. 0007-4802. Periodical. CN. English. qt. 45.00. Canadian Society of Petroleum, 206 7th Avenue Southwest/Room 505, Calgary Alberta T2P 0W7 Canada. Ind/Abst Eng. Index Mon., Eng. Index Bioeng. Abstr., Eng. Index Energy Abstr., Can. Environ., Coal Abstr., GeoRef, ASTIS Bibliogr., ASTIS Curr. Aware. Bull., Biol. Abstr., Chem. Abstr., Eng. Index, Eng. Index Annu., Energy Res. Abstr., Pet. Abstr., Bibliogr. Index Geol. CODEN BCPGAI. Covers sedimentary, petroleum geology, stratigraphy, structural geology and related topics. Journal of the Alberta Society of Petroleum Geologists, 0317-4107.

BULLETIN OF THE OIL AND NATURAL GAS COMMISSION. (BULLETIN). Main/Corp India (Republic). Oil and Natural Gas Commission. V. 1- Dec. 1964-. 0537-0094. Periodical. English. ir. Oil and Natural Gas Commission, 9 Kaulagarh Road, Dehra Dun UP 248195 India. Ind/Abst GeoRef. LC TN876.I5.

BULLETIN PERTAMINA. Main/Corp Pertamina (Organization). Periodical. IO. Indonesian. Indonesian State Owned Oil and Gas, Merdeka Timur No 1, Jakarta Indonesia. Tel 347615. Ed Yus Soekidjo and A Sidick N. LC HD9576.I54. bk rev. Circ 7,500. (ctrl). Spreads out the policy on oil and gas business in Indonesia.

BULLETIN - STANDARD OIL COMPANY OF CALIFORNIA. Main/Corp Standard Oil Company of California. V. 1-53, May 1913-1976. Periodical. US. English. qt. Standard Oil Company of California, 225 Bush Street, San Francisco CA 94104. LC HD9569.S82. DD 665.5065.

BULLETIN - STATE OF ALASKA, ALASKA OIL AND GAS CONSERVATION COMMISSION. Main/Corp Alaska Oil and Gas Conservation Commission. 1979-. Periodical. US. English. mo. Alaska Oil & Gas Conservation Commission, 3001 Porcupine Drive, Anchorage AK 99501. Tel (907)279-1433. Bulletin - State of Alaska, Division of Oil and Gas Conservation.

BURMASS' TEX-OK-KAN OIL DIRECTORY. See Yearbooks, Almanacs, Directories.

BUTANE-PROPANE NEWS. VAT Butane Propane News. V. 1- Sept. 1969-. 0007-7259. Periodical. US. English. mo. $11.90. Butane Propane News, Box 419, Arcadia CA 91006. Tel (818)357-2168. Ed Natalie Peal. LC TP761.B8. DD 665.773. adv acc. Circ 17,500. (ctrl). Comprehensive and analytical coverage of the LP-gas field. Safety together with regular legislative issues. Subjects on carburetion load building, fuel sales, supply, demand and prices. Butane-Propane News, 0007-7259.

CALIFORNIA - ALASKA OIL AND GAS REVIEW. 1969-. Periodical. US. English. an. $40.00. Munger Oil Information Service, 9800 South Sepulveda Boulevard/Suite 723, Los Angeles CA 90045. Tel (213)776-3990. California Oil and Gas Exploration, 0527-2890.

CANADA A-Z. See Yearbooks, Almanacs, Directories.

CANADA OFFSHORE BUYERS GUIDE. VFOAT Offshore Canada. VAT Oilweek. Canada Offshore Buyers Guide. 1983/84-. 0822-8698. CN. English. an. 10.00. Canada Offshore Buyers Guide, Suite 200/1015 Centre Street North, Calgary Alberta T2E 1P8 Canada. Tel (403)276-7881. Ed Vic Humphreys. DD 622.2902571. adv acc. Circ 6,000. (ctrl). Listings of suppliers to the offshore oil and gas industry.

CANADA OIL & GAS DATA CHART. PROPANE AND BUTANES. SUPPLY AND DISPOSITON. CANADA. (CANADA OIL & GAS DATA/CHART). VFOAT Canada L P G Data/Chart. V. 1- Nov. 1973-. 0701-8398. Periodical. CN. English. mo. $100. Cancrude Consultants Ltd, PO Box 6210 Station D, Calgary Alberta T2P 2C8 Canada. DD 338.47665773.

CANADA OIL & GAS DATA/CHART. NATIONAL STATISTICS ON CRUDE OIL, NATURAL GAS, SULPHUR, PROPANE AND BUTANES. (CANADA OIL & GAS DATA/CHART). VFOAT Data/Chart. V. 1- Jan. 1971-. 0701-8428. Periodical. CN. English. mo. 90. Cancrude Consultants Ltd, PO Box 6210/Postal Station D, Calgary Alberta T2P 268 Canada. Tel (403)264-4310. Ed Gordon A Littke. DD 338.27280971. Circ 160. Statistical summary of Canada's hydrocabon energy industry, production, domestic use and exports of crude oil, natural gas, propane, butanes, sulphur and coal.

CANADIAN GAS FACTS. 1st- Ed. 0316-3547. CN. English. an. Canadian Gas Association, Statistical Department, 55 Scarsdale Road, Don Mills Ont M3B 2R3 Canada. LC HD9581.C3. DD 333.82.

CANADIAN OIL AND GAS. 1955-. 0384-8965. CN. English. sm. Butterworth & Company Ltd, 2265 Midland Avenue, Scarborough Ontario M1P 4S1 Canada.

CANADIAN OIL & GAS HANDBOOK. VFOAT Canadian Oil and Gas Handbook. 1980-1981-. 0710-622X. CN. English. an. $20.12. Northern Miner Press Ltd, 7 Labatt Avenue, Toronto Ont M5A 3P2 Canada. Tel (416)368-3481. Ed C D Gardiner. LC HD9574.C2. DD 338.27280971. bk rev. adv acc. Directory of oil and gas companies in Canada.

CANADIAN OIL INDUSTRY DIRECTORY. See Yearbooks, Almanacs, Directories.

CANADIAN OIL REGISTER. VFOAT Nickle's Canadian Oil Register. 1961/62-. 0068-9394. Periodical. CN. English. an. 100.00. Canadian Oil Register, 300 999-8th Street Southwest, Calgary Alberta T2R 1N7 Canada. Tel (403)244-6111. Ed Doreen McArthur. DD 338.272802571. adv acc. Circ 5,000. (ctrl). Directory of comprehensive information on companies in Canada's oil and gas and related industries. Canadian Oil and Gas Directory, 0315-4866.

CAPITAL INVESTMENTS OF THE WORLD PETROLEUM INDUSTRY. 0577-571X. US. English. an. Chase Manhattan Bank, Energy Division, Chase Manhattan Plaza, New York

Petroleum and Natural Gas

NY 10081. **LC** HD9560.1. **DD** 338.43. *Capital Investments by the World Petroleum Industry.*

CASE HISTORIES OF OIL AND GAS FIELDS IN ASIA AND THE FAR EAST. **Main/Corp** United Nations. Economic Commission for Asia and the Far East. **Series Corp** Its Mineral Resources Development Series. 1st- Series. US. English. United Nations Economic Commission, Sales Section Room A3315, New York NY 10017. **LC** JX1977. **DD** 300.8 S, 622.338095.

CATALOGUE : BRITISH SUPPLIERS TO THE OIL, GAS, PETROCHEMICAL, AND PROCESS INDUSTRIES. **Main/Corp** Energy Industries Council (Great Britain). 1982-. UK. English. be. Energy Industries Council, 178-202 Great Portland Street, London W1N 6 England. *CBMPE Catalogue.*

CHEMICAL AND PETROLEUM ENGINEERING. *See* Engineering - Chemical Engineering.

CHEMICAL REVIEW. *See* Chemistry.

CHEMISTRY AND TECHNOLOGY OF FUELS AND OILS. *See* Chemistry.

CHEMSPHERE. *See* Chemistry.

CHEVRON FOCUS. Vol. 46, No. 5 (Aug. 1984)-. 0748-6367. Periodical. US. English. ir. Chevron Corporation, Publication Office, 225 Bush Street, Room 1172, San Francisco CA 94104. **DD** 338. *Standard Oiler, 0738-2846.*

CHEVRON WORLD. V. 54- Winter 1977-. [148-3102. Periodical. US. English. ir. Chevron Corporation, 225 Bush Street, San Francisco CA 94104. **Tel** (415)894-3498. **Ed** Charles Michals. **Ind/Abst** Coal Abstr., Energy Res. Abstr., Predicasts. **LC** HD9569.S82. **DD** 338.7665509794. **Circ** 321. Covers domestic and world-wide company operations from exploration, refining, research, transportation, and marketing. Basically, a stockholder and employee's publication. *Bulletin (Standard Oil Company of California).*

CIRCULAR - WEST VIRGINIA GEOLOGICAL AND ECONOMIC SURVEY. *See* Earth Sciences - Geology.

COASTAL ZONE MANAGEMENT. 1- Nov. 1970-. 0045-723X. Periodical. US. English. ir. $295.00. Nautilus Press, 1201 National Press Building, Washington DC 20045. **Tel** (202)347-6643. **Ed** John R Botzum. **DD** 333.9170973. Specializes in reporting federal-state relationships in the US exclusive economic zone, and the outer continental shelf, with special emphasis on offshore oil and gas development. *World Ecology Report and Environmental Monitor.*

COLLECTION DES DICTIONNAIRES TECHNIQUES. No. 1- 1963-. 0530-7678. Periodical. FR. French. ir. 670.00. Societe des Editions Technip, 27 rue Ginoux, 75737 Paris Cedex 15 France. **Tel** 1 45 77 11 08. Includes the sum of vocabularies in geology, geochemistry, geophysics, drilling, production, well-logging, reservoir engineering, enhanced recovery, offshore technology, refining, petrochemistry etc.

COMPAGNIE FRANCAISE DES PETROLES AND THE TOTAL GROUP. English. an. Compagnie Francaise des Petroles, 5 rue Miehel Ange, 75781 Paris Cedex 16 France. **LC** HD9572.9.C58. **DD** 338.887. *Annual Report.*

COMPENDIUM - DEUTSCHE GESELLSCHAFT FUR MINERALOLWISSENSCHAFT UND KOHLECHEMIE E.V. **Main/Corp** Deutsche Gesellschaft fur Mineralolwissenschaft und Kohlechemie. 0341-6852. German. an. **Ind/Abst** Coal Abstr., Chem. Abstr. **LC** TN863. **CODEN** CDGKD6.

CONOCO. **Main/Corp** Continental Oil Company. **VAT** Continental Oil Company. V. 1-. 0884-7045. Periodical. US. English. qt. Conoco, 1007 Market Street, Wilmington DE 19898. **Tel** (302)594-3409. **Ind/Abst** Index Free Period., Energy Inf. Abstr., Environ. Abstr. **LC** HD9569.C65. **DD** 665.

THE CPC EAST COAST REPORT. **VAT** Computer Petroleum Corporation East Coast Report. 8750-5568. Periodical. US. English. wk. CPC Publications, 6949 Valley Creek Road, St Paul MN 55125. **Tel** (612)738-1088. **Ed** Douglas E Hartman. Suppliers posted terminal prices at over 250 locations throughout the US customized for an individual company's needs.

CPC PETRONEWS. **VAT** Computer Petroleum Corporation Petronews. 8750-5584. Periodical. US. English. wk. CPC Publications, 6949 Valley Creek Road, St Paul MN 55125. **Tel** (612)738-1088. **Ed** Douglas E Hartman. Trends, forecasts, of petroleum prices along with general information concerning news events in the petroleum industry.

CPDP BULLETIN MENSUEL. **Main/Corp** Comite Professionel du Petrole, Paris. FR. French. mo. Comite Professionnel Petrole, 51 Boulevard de Courcelles, 75008 Paris France. **Tel** 4766 0382. **LC** HD9572.1. **DD** 338.272805. Statistical data on French and foreign petroleum industry.

CRUDE-OIL AND REFINED- PRODUCTS PIPELINE MILEAGE IN THE UNITED STATES. (CRUDE-OIL AND REFINED PRODUCTS PIPE-LINE MILEAGE IN THE UNITED STATES). 1977-. 0498-7772. US. English. te. US Department of Energy, Energy Information Administration, Office of Energy Data and Interpretation, Washington DC 20461. **LC** HD9580.U4. **DD** 388.5.

CRUDE PETROLEUM AND NATURAL GAS INDUSTRY. (THE CRUDE PETROLEUM AND NATURAL GAS INDUSTRY). **Main/Corp** Statistics Canada. Manufacturing and Primary Industries Division. **VFOAT** L'Industrie du Petrole Brut et du Gaz Naturel. 1970-. 0068-7103. Periodical. CN. English (French). an. Receiver General for Canada, Statistics Canada Publications, Ottawa Ontario K1A 0T6 Canada. *The Crude Petroleum and Natural Gas Industry, 0068-7103.*

CRUDE PETROLEUM AND NATURAL GAS PRODUCTION. **VFOAT** Production de Petrole Brut et de Gaz Naturel. V. 24- Jan. 1972-. 0702-6846. Periodical. CN. English (French). mo. Receiver General for Canada, Statistics Canada Publications, Ottawa Ontario K1A 0T6 Canada. *Crude Petroleum, Natural Gas, and Manufactured Gas.*

CURRENT INDUSTRIAL REPORTS. MA-28C, INDUSTRIAL GASES. **VFOAT** Industrial Gases. Began with 1978. US. English. an. $16.00. Data User Services Division Customer Services Publication, Bureau of the Census, Washington DC 20233. **Tel** (301)763-4100. **LC** HD9581.U49. **DD** 338.476670973. Presents timely data on the production, inventories, and orders of approximately 5,000 products, which represents 40 percent of all US manufacturing.

DAFTAR PERBANDINGAN KONTROLE PENGOLAHAN KELAPA SAWIT. **Main/Corp** Sumatra Planters Association. Research Institute. Indonesian. ir. **LC** TP684.P3.

DAILY MUNGER OILOGRAM. **VFOAT** Munger Oilogram. 0276-5934. Periodical. US. English. da. Munger Oil Information Service, 9800 South Sepulveda Boulevard/Suite 723, Los Angeles CA 90045. **Tel** (213)776-3990.

DATA BANKS. **Main/Corp** Wharton Econometric Forecasting Associates. Middle East Economic Service. **VFOAT** Middle East Economic Service Data Banks. 8756-5439. US. English. Wharton Econometric Forecasting Associates, 3624 Science Center, Philadelphia PA 19104. **LC** HD9560.1. **DD** 338.2728202854.

DATOS BASICOS SOBRE LA INDUSTRIA PETROLERA Y LA ECONOMIA VENEZOLANA. Spanish. ir. **LC** HD9574.V4. **DD** 338.272820987021.

DEALER'S VOICE. 0192-4451. Periodical. US. English. mo. Dealers Voice, Box 182-38 Central Square East, Boston MA 02128.

DENVER OIL & GAS INDUSTRY SURVEY. **VFOAT** Denver Oil and Gas Industry Survey. US. English. Mountain States Employers Council Inc, PO Box 539, Denver CO 80201.

DEVELOPMENT OF THE OIL AND GAS RESOURCES OF THE UNITED KINGDOM. **Main/Corp** Great Britain. Dept. of Energy. 1973-. UK. English. an. 2.75. H M Stationery Office, Department of Energy, Government Bookshops, 49 High Holborn, London WC1V 6HB England. **LC** HD9571.1. **DD** 333.823150941.

DEVELOPMENTS IN PETROLEUM GEOLOGY. 1-. 0260-4248. Periodical. UK. English. ir. Elsevier Applied Science Publishers, Crown House Linton Road, Barking Essex IG11 8JU England. **Ind/Abst** Chem. Abstr. **CODEN** DPEGDB.

DEVELOPMENTS IN PETROLEUM SCIENCE. 1- 1975-. 0376-7361. Monographic Series. US. English. ir. Elsevier Science Publishing Co Inc, PO Box 1663 Grand Central Station, New York NY 10163. **Ind/Abst** Eng. Index Annu., Eng. Index Mon., Eng. Index Bioeng. Abstr., Eng. Index Energy Abstr., Chem. Abstr. **CODEN** DPSCDZ.

DIESEL AND NATURAL GAS ENGINE SALES SURVEY. **Main/Corp** Statistics Canada. Merchandising and Services Division. **VFOAT** Enquete sur les Ventes de Moteurs Diesel et a Gaz Naturel. 1972-. 0317-753X. CN. English (French). an. $0.50. Statistics Canada, Merchandising & Services Division, Publication Distribution, Ottawa Ontario K1A 0T6 Canada. **LC** HD9705.C2. **DD** 381.4562925060971.

DIESEL FUEL DIRECTORY. *See* Yearbooks, Almanacs, Directories.

DIRECTORY - COUNCIL OF PETROLEUM ACCOUNTANTS SOCIETIES (U.S.). *See* Yearbooks, Almanacs, Directories.

DIRECTORY OF CERTIFIED PETROLEUM GEOLOGISTS. *See* Yearbooks, Almanacs, Directories.

DIRECTORY OF CHEMICAL ABSTRACTS REGISTRY NUMBERS AND EPA NUMBERS FOR COMMON PETROLEUM CHEMICALS. *See* Yearbooks, Almanacs, Directories.

DIRECTORY OF LIMITED MEMBERS - COUNCIL OF PETROLEUM ACCOUNTANTS SOCIETIES (U.S.). *See* Yearbooks, Almanacs, Directories.

DIRECTORY OF TENNESSEE MINING, OIL, AND GAS OPERATIONS. *See* Yearbooks, Almanacs, Directories.

DIYARUNA WA-AL-ALAM. *See* Economics - Economics: Industry & Production.

DRILLING. **VFOAT** Drilling-DCW. Began Nov. 1939. 0012-6241. Periodical. US. English. mo. Free to qualified subscribers, $34.50 all others. Drilling Associated Publishers, PO Box 7000, Dallas TX 75209. **Ind/Abst** Energy Inf. Abstr., Environ. Abstr., Excerpta Med., GeoRef. **LC** TN860.

DRILLING CONTRACTOR. (THE DRILLING CONTRACTOR). 1- 1944-. 0046-0702. Periodical. US. English. mo. $30.00. International Association of Drilling Contractors, PO Box 4287, Houston TX 77084. **Tel** (713)578-7171. **Ed** Alvaro Franco. **Ind/Abst** Pet. Abstr. **LC** TN860. **DD** 622.33805. bk rev. adv acc. **Circ** 21,000. Covers the drilling and production industry.

DRILLING REVIEW. **VFOAT** Data Resources Drilling Review. V. 1- Oct. 1979-. 0197-2413. Periodical. US. English. 29 Hartwell Avenue, Lexington MA 02173. **LC** HD9561. **DD** 338.272820973.

DRILLSITE. Vol. 1, No. 1 (Jan. 7, 1980). 0228-7587. Periodical. CN. English. ir. $26.32. MacLean Hunter Ltd, 102/ 11504-170 Street, Edmonton Alberta T5S 1J7 Canada. **Tel** (403)276-7881. **Ed** Val Christensen. **DD** 622.33820971. adv acc. **Circ** 8,900. (ctrl). Western Canadian magazine servicing the petroleum drilling, servicing and production sectors.

EAST COAST OFFSHORE. **VFOAT** Offshore. 0823-1788. Periodical. CN. English. ir. $2.00 Per No. East Coast Offshore, c/o Anchor Films Ltd, PO Box 9433, St John's Newfoundland A1A 2Y3 Canada. **DD** 38.2728209715. *Newfoundland Offshore, 0822-6121.*

EASTERN HEMISPHERE PETROLEUM DIRECTORY. *See* Yearbooks, Almanacs, Directories.

EASTERN OFFSHORE NEWS. Vol. 1, No. 1 (Feb. 1979)-. 0710-5142. Periodical. CN. English. qt. Free. Eastern Offshore News, c/o Petroleum Industry Office for East Coast Offshore 173 Water Street, St John's Newfoundland A1C 1B1 England. **Ind/Abst** GeoRef. **DD** 338.2728209715.

ECOLIBRIUM. Began publication in 1972. 0149-8398. Periodical. US. English. qt. Shell Oil Company, 1522 One Shell Plaza, Houston TX 77002. **Ind/Abst** Energy Inf. Abstr., Environ. Abstr., Chem. Abstr. **LC** TD195.P4. **DD** 333.7. **CODEN** ECOLDU.

ECONOMICS OF THE PETROCHEMICAL INDUSTRY. THE EPI SOURCEBOOK. *See* Economics.

ENERGY FROM BIOMASS AND WASTES. **VFOAT** Energy from Biomass & Wastes. 3 (1978)-. 0277-7851. US. English. ir. $100.00. Institute of Gas Technology, 3424 South State Street, Chicago IL 60616. **Ind/Abst** Eng. Index Annu., Eng.

Petroleum and Natural Gas

Index Mon., Eng. Index Bioeng. Abstr., Eng. Index Energy Abstr., Chem. Abstr. LC TP360. DD 662.8. CODEN EBWADU. *Clean Fuels from Biomass and Wastes, 0743-7374.*

ENERUGI TOKEI GEPPO. Main/Corp Japan. Tsusho Sangyosho. Daijin Kambo. Chosa Tokeibu. VFOAT Tsusho Sangyosho Enerugi Tokei Geppo. Japanese. ir. 12000. Tsusho Sangyo Chosakai, 15-2 Ginza 6-chome chuo-ku, Tokyo Japan. LC HD9502.J3.

ENERUGI TOKEI NEMPO. *See* Statistics.

ENHANCED OIL-RECOVERY FIELD REPORTS. V. 3, No. 2- 1977-. 2430-337X. Periodical. US. English. qt. $35.00. Society of Petroleum Engineers of AIME, 6200 North Central Expressway, Dallas TX 75206. Tel (214)669-3377. Ind/Abst Energy Res. Abstr. *Improved Oil-Recovery Field Reports, 0147-7897.*

ENVIRONMENT PROTECTION BOARD GAS PIPELINE NEWSLETTER. *See* Sanitation, Environmental Technology.

ENVIRONMENTAL DEVELOPMENT PLAN (EDP). ENHANCED GAS RECOVERY. Main/Corp United States. Dept. of Energy. Office of Energy Technology. VFOAT Enhanced Gas Recovery. 1977-. US. English. an. US Department of Energy, Office of Energy Technology, Springfield VA 22161.

ERCB ST. VFOAT E.R.C.B. S.T., Reserve Report Series E.R.C.B., Reserve Report Series ERCB. Monograph Series. CN. English. Energy Resources Conservation Board, 640 Fifth Avenue Southwest, Calgary Alberta T2P 3G4 Canada. *ERCB, 0701-8711.*

ERDOEL ERDGAS ZEITSCHRIFT. VFOAT Oil and Gas Monthly. 81 Yearly Volume, Issue 3-98. 0014-004X. Periodical. German. mo. Urban-Verlag Hamburg/Wien GMBH, PO Box 701606, D2000 Hamburg 70 West Germany. Tel 49(40)656-70-71-73. Ed Thomas Vieth. Ind/Abst Eng. Index Mon., Eng. Index Bioeng. Abstr., Eng. Index Energy Abstr., Coal Abstr., Energy Inf. Abstr., Environ. Abstr., GeoRef, Chem. Abstr., Nucl. Sci. Abstr., Eng. Index Annu. CODEN EEZSAF. bk rev. adv acc. Circ 3,400. Scientific/technical monthly on exploration (geology/geophysics), drilling and production on and offshore, gas technology, pipeline and plant engineering, underground storage, treatment and processing. *Erdoel Erdgas.*

ERDOL & KOHLE, ERDGAS, PETROCHEMIE. VAT Erdol und Kohle, Erdgas, Petrochemie. Vol. 13, Issue 8- Aug. 1960-. 0014-0058. Periodical. GW. German (English). mo. Industrieverlag Hernhaussen, Postfach 100252, Enbst Mey Str 8, 7022 Leinfelden West Germany. Tel 0711/79 08 0. Ind/Abst Electron. Commun. Abstr. J., ISMEC Bull., Pollut. Abstr. Indexes, Saf. Sci. Abstr. J., Fluidex, Life Sci. Collect., Excerpta Med., Coal Abstr., GeoRef, CIS Abstr., Chem. Abstr., Energy Res. Abstr., Predicasts, Sci. Cit. Index, Abr. Ed., Int. Aerosp. Abstr., Pet. Abstr., Funk Scott Index Corp. Ind., Bibliogr. Index Geol. CODEN EKEPAB. *Erdol und Kohle, 0367-1305; Brennstoff-Chemie.*

ESSO NORTH. Vol. 1, No. 1 (Winter 1982)-. 0823-7751. Periodical. CN. English. qt. ESSO Resources Canada, 237-4th Avenue SW, Calgary Alberta T2P 0H6 Canada. DD 338.27280607193.

ESTIMATED OIL AND GAS RESERVES, SOUTHERN CALIFORNIA OUTER CONTINENTAL SHELF. Began with Jan. 1, 1977. US. English. an. US Department of the Interior, Geological Survey, Reston VA 22092.

EUROPE. BASIC OIL LAWS AND CONCESSION CONTRACTS. ORIGINAL TEXTS. SUPPLEMENT. *See* Law.

EUROPEAN PETROLEUM DIRECTORY. *See* Yearbooks, Almanacs, Directories.

EXPLORATION AND ECONOMICS OF THE PETROLEUM INDUSTRY. Main/Conf Institute on Petroleum Exploration and Economics. VFOAT Exploration & Economics of the Petroleum Industry. Began with Vol. 10. 0537-9741. US. English. an. Matthew Bender, 235 East 45th Street, New York NY 10017. Ind/Abst Coal Abstr., GeoRef, Eng. Index. LC HD9561. DD 338.272820973. CODEN EEPIA3.

EXXON USA. VAT Exxon United States of America. V. 12- Jan./Mar 1973-. 0749-1115. Periodical. US. English. qt. Exxon Company USA/Public Affairs Department, PO Box 2180, Houston TX 77001. Ind/Abst Energy Inf. Abstr., Environ. Abstr., Index Free Period., GeoRef, Public Aff. Inf. Serv. Bull. CODEN EXUSDO. *Humble Way.*

FEDERAL POWER COMMISSION NEWS RELEASE. MONTHLY FUEL COST AND QUALITY INFORMATION, FPC ISSUES REPORT ON FUEL COST. Main/Corp United States. Federal Power Commission. VFOAT Monthly Fuel Cost and Quality Information, FPC Issues Report on Fuel Cost. Periodical. US. English. mo. Federal Power Commission, Office of Public Information, Washington DC 20426. *Staff Report on Monthly Report of Cost and Quality of Fuels for Steam-Electric Plants.*

FEDERAL TAXATION OF OIL AND GAS TRANSACTIONS. *See* Business - Public Finance.

FINANCIAL TIMES OIL AND GAS INTERNATIONAL YEAR BOOK. *See* Yearbooks, Almanacs, Directories.

FINANZEN UND STEUERN. REIHE 9. 3 : MINERALOLSTEUER. Main/Corp Germany (West). Statistisches Bundesamt. VAT Finanzen Und Steuern. Reihe Neun. Drei: Mineralolsteuer. 1976-. German. ir. 3.20. LC HD9573.4. *Finanzen Und Steuern. Reihe 8: Verbrauchsteuern. III. Mineralolsteuer.*

FIRST BREAK. Vol. 1, No. 1 (Jan. 1983)-. 0263-5046. Periodical. UK. English. mo. $145.00 US and Canada. Blackwell Scientific Publications Ltd, PO Box 88, Oxford England. Tel 0865-240201. Ed N R Goulty. bk rev. adv acc. Circ 4,000. (ctrl). Aimed at the practising applied geophysicist, it provides short authoritative articles on seismic, gravitational and electromagnetic geophysical techniques with current news about the industry.

FLAMBEE. (LA FLAMBEE). V. 3, No. 4- May/June 1965-. 0705-1751. Periodical. CN. French. bm. Free. Association des Marchands d'Huile a Chauffage du Quebec, 294 Boulevard Desmarchais, Montreal Quebec H4H 1S4 Canada. DD 338.47665538409714. (ctrl). *Bulletin, 0705-1743.*

FOSTER BULLETIN ON DEREGULATED GAS. 0749-7377. Periodical. US. English. mo. Foster Associates Inc, 1101 17th Street NW, Washington DC 20036. LC HD9581.U49. DD 338.23.

FOSTER NATURAL GAS REPORT FROM WASHINGTON. Main/Corp Foster Associates (Washington, D.C.). 0095-1587. Periodical. US. English. wk. 1101 17th Street NW, Washington DC 20036. LC KF1870.A15. DD 338.2728505. *Report from Washington to Producers of Natural Gas.*

FOSTER OIL PIPELINE REPORT FROM WASHINGTON. Main/Corp Foster Associates (Washington, D.C.). No. 1- Jan. 1978-. 0270-3718. Periodical. US. English. mo. $320.00. Foster Associates Inc, 1101 17th Street NW/Suite 500, Washington DC 20036. Tel (202)296-2380. Ed M W Rockefeller. LC KF2398.A15. DD 343.7309305.

FUEL. 0016-2361. Periodical. UK. English. mo. Butterworth Scientific Limited, PO Box 63 Westbury House Bury House, Guildford GU2 5BH England. Ind/Abst Coal Abstr., Eng. Index Annu., Eng. Index Mon., Eng. Index Bioeng. Abstr., Eng. Index Energy Abstr., Excerpta Med., GeoRef, Int. Aerosp. Abstr., Chem. Abstr., Energy Res. Abstr., Energy Inf. Abstr., Environ. Abstr. CODEN FUELAC. Index published separately - free - automatically sent. *Fuel in Science and Practice.*

FUEL ABSTRACTS AND CURRENT TITLES. *See* Indexes/Abstracts.

FUEL ALCOHOL U.S.A. VFOAT Fuel Alcohol USA. VAT Fuel Alcohol United States of America. Vol. 3, No. 12 (Dec. 1981)-. 0744-0421. Periodical. US. English. bm. $16.00 Domestic, $19.00 Foreign. Circulation Department Fuel Alcohol USA, PO BOx 9547, Kansas City MO 64133-0347. Ind/Abst Energy Res. Abstr., Coal Abstr. LC TP358. DD 662.669. *Gasahol U.S.A., 0194-9136.*

FUEL ECONOMY NEWS : THE NEWSLETTER OF THE VOLUNTARY TRUCK AND BUS FUEL ECONOMY PROGRAM. Periodical. US. English. qt. Voluntary Truck and Bus Fuel Economy Program, US Department of Energy, Washington DC 20461.

FUEL OIL NEWS. 0016-2396. Periodical. US. English. mo. $34.90. Hunter Publishing Company, PO Box 280, Colonia NJ 07067. Tel (201)381-7279. Ed George Schultz. adv acc. Circ 17,000. (ctrl). Directed to the oil heating retailer to provide assistance in business operation. Report on competitive conditions, products, industry news, management techniques and technical data.

FUEL OIL WEEK. 0162-2730. Periodical. US. English. wk. $77.00. Capitol Publications, 2430 Pennsylvania Avenue NW/Suite G-12, Washington DC 20037.

FUEL OILS BY SULFUR CONTENT CEASED. Series/Titl Mineral Industry Surveys. Energy Information Reports. Energy Data Reports. VFOAT Availability of Heavy Fuel Oils by Sulfur Levels. 1972-Mar. 1980. 0193-001X. Periodical. US. English. mo. US Department of Energy, Washington DC 20585. Ind/Abst Chem. Abstr., Predicasts.

FUEL SCIENCE AND TECHNOLOGY. Vol. 1, No. 1 (July 1982)-. 0254-3567. Periodical. English. qt. $18.00. Central Fuel Research Institute, PO F R I 828108, Dhanbad Bihar India. Ind/Abst Chem. Abstr., Coal Abstr. LC TP315. DD 662.605. CODEN FSTEDL. *FRI News.*

FUELOIL & OIL HEAT AND SOLAR SYSTEMS. VAT Fueloil and Oil Heat and Solar Systems, Fueloil, Oil Heat and Solar Systems SYSTEMS. V. 36, No. 8- Aug. 1977-. 0148-9801. Periodical. US. English. mo. $22.00. Industry Publications Inc, 10 Canfield Road, Cedar Grove NJ 07009. Tel (201)239-5800. Ind/Abst Trade Ind. Index, Bus. Period. Index, Energy Res. Abstr. LC TP690.A1. DD 697.04405. *Fueloil & Oil Heat, 0016-2418.*

GAS. V. 1- May 1925-. Periodical. English. ir. LC TP700. *Oil & Gas Equipment Review.*

GAS. 0343-2092. Periodical. German. ir. 82.00. R Oldenbourg Verlag GMBH, Postfach 801360, 8000 Munchen 80 West Germany. Ind/Abst Coal Abstr. LC TN880.A1.

GAS ABSTRACTS. *See* Indexes/Abstracts.

GAS APPLIANCE MERCHANDISING. 0016-4879. Periodical. US. English. bm. $10.00. Harcourt Brace Jovanovich Publications, 757 Third Avenue, New York NY 10017. LC TP758.A1. DD 658.8096838. *Heating & Gas Appliance Merchandising.*

GAS (BARCELONA, SPAIN). (GAS : DOCUMENTACION ANUAL DE SEDIGAS). Periodical. SP. Spanish. an. Ediciones Doyma SA, Trevesera de Gracia 17-21, Barcelona 21 Spain. LC HD9581.S7. DD 338.272850946.

GAS DATA BOOK: BRIEF EXCERPTS FROM GAS FACTS. 1st- Ed. 0433-194X. US. English. sa. American Gas Association, Bureau of Statistics, 1515 Wilson Boulevard, Arlington VA 22209. DD 338.2.

GAS DIGEST. 0161-4851. Periodical. US. English. mo. Gas Digest, PO Box 35819, Houston TX 77235. Tel (713)723-7456. Ind/Abst Coal Abstr., Energy Res. Abstr. LC TP700. DD 338.47665705.

GAS DIRECTORY AND WHO'S WHO. *See* Yearbooks, Almanacs, Directories.

GAS ENERGY REVIEW. Vol. 7, No. 4 (Jan. 1979)-. 8756-5471. Periodical. US. English. mo. American Gas Association, 1515 Wilson Boulevard, Arlington VA 22209. Tel (703)841-8512. DD 333. *Gas Supply Review, 0270-6423.*

GAS ENGINEERING AND MANAGEMENT. V. 14- Jan. 1974-. 0306-6444. Periodical. UK. English. mo. $45.98. Institution of Gas Engineers, 17 Grosvenor Crescent, London SW1 7ES England. Ind/Abst Coal Abstr., Energy Inf. Abstr., Energy Res. Abstr., Eng. Index Annu., Eng. Index Bioeng. Abstr., Eng. Index Energy Abstr., Eng. Index Mon., Environ. Abstr., Excerpta Med., Life Sci. Collect., Met. Abstr., Ref. Source, World Alum. Abstr., Eng. Index. LC TP700. DD 665.705. CODEN GEMABL.

GAS FACTS. Main/Corp American Gas Association. Dept. of Statistics. 1967-. 0361-4298. US. English. an. American Gas Association, 1515 Wilson Boulevard, Arlington VA 22209. Tel (703)841-8490. Ed Patrick J Curley. LC TP722. DD 338.476657097. Circ 3,500. A statistical yearbook of the natural gas industry. A must for anyone researching or studying the natural gas industry. *Gas Facts, Assistance Act, 1948/49.*

Petroleum and Natural Gas

GAS INDUSTRIES. 0194-2468. Periodical. US. English. mo. $15.00. Gas Industries E & A News Inc, O'Hare East, PO Box 558, Park Ridge IL 60068. **Tel** (312)693-3682. Ed Paul Lasy and Gene Masters. **Ind/Abst** Coal Abstr., Energy Inf. Abstr., Environ. Abstr. bk rev. adv acc. **Circ** 12,000. (ctrl). Contains gas pipeline, transmission and utility, distribution operations, engineering and marketing.

THE GAS SUPPLIES OF INTERSTATE NATURAL GAS PIPELINE COMPANIES. US. English. ir. National Energy Information Center, 100 Independence Avenue SW/EI-22, Washington DC 20585. **Tel** (202)275-4006.

THE GAS SUPPLIES OF INTERSTATE NATURAL GAS PIPELINE COMPANIES. 0565-0127. US. English. an. US Government Printing Office, Superintendent of Documents, Washington DC 20402. LC HD9581.U49. DD 553.2850973.

GAS UTILITIES. Main/Corp Canada. Statistique Canada. Division des Industries Manufacturieres et Primaires. VFOAT Services de Gaz. V. 14- Jan. 1972-. 0380-2329. Periodical. CN. text in English and French. mo. 100.00 Domestic, 110.00 Foreign. Receiver General for Canada, Statistics Canada Publications, Ottawa Ontario K1A 0T6 Canada. **Tel** (800)268-1151. Receipts and disposition of natural gas by province, month; commodity distance, sales, revenues, customers by rate structrue, imports and exports. Gas Utilities.

GAS WARME INTERNATIONAL. Vol. 16-. 0020-9384. Periodical. German (summaries in English and French). mo. 212.-. Vulkan Verlag, Dr W Classen, Postfach 103962, Hollerstrasse 1G, D-4300 Essen 1 West Germany. **Tel** 0201/ 22 18 51. Ed Beckervordersandfort, Hering, T Holle, J Kentmann, H P Niepenberg, H Simon, Skunca and J Stephanek. **Ind/Abst** Eng. Index Annu., Eng. Index Mon., Eng. Index Bioeng. Abstr., Eng. Index Energy Abstr., Coal Abstr., Energy Inf. Abstr., Environ. Abstr., Int. Aerosp. Abstr., Chem. Abstr., Energy Res. Abstr. **CODEN** GWINAT. bk rev. adv acc. **Circ** 3,550. Journal of gas utilization and gas furnace engineering. Internationale Zeitschrift Fur Gaswarme.

GAS, WASSER, WAERME. (GAS, WASSER, WARME). VFOAT GWW. V. 1- 1947-. 0016-5018. Periodical. AU. German. mo. $64.75. Osterreich Gas u Wasserfach, Schubertring 14, A-1010 Vienna Austria. **Ind/Abst** Eng. Index Annu., Eng. Index Mon., Eng. Index Bioeng. Abstr., Eng. Index Energy Abstr., Coal Abstr., Excerpta Med., GeoRef, Chem. Abstr. **CODEN** GAWWA6. Gas und Wasser.

GAS WORLD (1978). (GAS WORLD). V. 179- Jan. 1978-. 0308-7654. Periodical. UK. English. mo. $73.56. Benn Publications Limited, Sovereign Way, Tornbridge Kent TN9 1RW England. **Tel** 0732 364422. Ed Roger Pechey. **Ind/Abst** Predicasts, Energy Res. Abstr., Energy Inf. Abstr., Environ. Abstr., Coal Abstr. bk rev. adv acc. **Circ** 3,000. For engineering management in the transmission distribution and utilization sectors of the gas industry. Gas World and Gas Journal.

GASAVERS NEWS. VAT Gas Savers News. V. 1- 1980-. 0271-082X. Periodical. US. English. mo. $24.00. Fuel Expanders Inc, 173 East Paularino, Costa Mesa CA 92626. **Tel** (714)641-0833.

GASSTATISTIK FUR DIE BUNDESREPUBLIK DEUTSCHLAND. See Statistics.

GASVERWENDUNG. 0016-5182. Periodical. GW. German. ir. 42.20. ZFGW-Verlag GMBH, D-6000 Frankfurt Am Main 90 West Germany. **Ind/Abst** Chem. Abstr. **CODEN** GASVDK.

GAZ ACTUALITES. French. ir. Societe pour le Developpment de l'Industrie du Gaz, 13 Bis Boulevard Berthier, 75823 Paris France. LC TP733.F8. DD 338.4766570944.

GAZ D'AUJOURD'HUI. 91- 1967-. 0016-5328. Periodical. FR. French. mo. $79.82. Gaz d'Aujourd'Hui, 62 rue de Courcelles, Paris 8E France. **Ind/Abst** CIS Abstr., Energy Res. Abstr. Journal des Industries du Gaz.

GAZOVAIA PROMYSHLENNOST. 1956-. 0016-5581. Periodical. UR. Russian. mo. $33.50. Victor Kamkin Inc (70210), 12224 Parklawn Drive, Rockville MD 20852. **Tel** (301)881-5973. **Ind/Abst** Appl. Mech. Rev., Chem. Abstr.

GAZOVAIA PROMYSHLENNOST. SERIIA EKONOMIKA, ORGANIZATSIIA I UPRAVLENIE V GAZOVOI PROMYSHLENNOSTI. VFOAT Seriia Edonomika, Organizatsiia I Upravlenie V Gazovoi Promyshlennosti. Began in 1970. Periodical. UR. Russian. mo. LC TP733.S57.

GEOLOGIJA I NEFTEGAZONOSNOST TURKMENISTANA. (GEOLOGIIA I NEFTEGAZONOSNOST TURKMENISTANA). Began in 1976?. 0135-1605. Periodical. UR. Russian. 0.80. YLYM, 744000 Ashkahabad, UI Engelsa 6, Ashkhabad Turkmen SSR. **Ind/Abst** Chem. Abstr. LC TN875. **CODEN** GNTUDB.

GEOLOGY OF PETROLEUM. 0275-3960. Monographic Series. US. English. ir. John Wiley & Sons Inc, 1 Wiley Drive, Somerset NJ 08873.

GLOBAL DIRECTORY OF GAS COMPANIES. See Yearbooks, Almanacs, Directories.

GRID. VFOAT Gas Research Institute Digest. Periodical. US. English. Gas Research Institute Digest, 10 West 35th Street, Chicago IL 60616. **Ind/Abst** Energy Inf. Abstr., Environ. Abstr. Gridigest.

GUIDE DU PETROLE, GAZ-PETROCHIMIE. French. ir. 252 rue de Faubourg Saint Honore, Paris France 75008. LC HD9572.2. DD 338.27280944. Guide du Petrole et de la Chimie.

GUIDE TO AMERICAN OFFSHORE FLEETS. OFFSHORE SERVICE VESSELS. See Transportation - Ships & Shipping.

GUIDE TO PETROLEUM STATISTICAL INFORMATION. See Statistics.

GUIDE TO STATIONARY PHASES FOR GAS CHROMATOGRAPHY. VFOAT Analabs Guide to Stationary Phases for Gas Chromatography. 0533-9855. US. English. be. Analabs Inc, 80 Republic Drive, North Haven CT 06473.

GULF COAST OIL DIRECTORY. See Yearbooks, Almanacs, Directories.

GULF COAST OIL REPORTER. 0744-9070. Periodical. US. English. mo. $24.00. Hart Publications, PO Box 1917, Denver CO 80201. **Tel** (303)837-1917. Ed Michael Crowder. LC HD9567.A13. DD 338.476223380976. adv acc. Regional publication covering the petroleum industry in the gulf coast region.

GULF DEALER. VAT Gulf Canada Dealer News (1976). V. 34- Mar./April 1979-. 0704-5980. Periodical. CN. English. mo. Gulf Oil Canada, Public Relations Department, 800 Bay Street, Toronto Ontario M5S 1Y8 Canada. DD 381.45665538270971. Gulf Canada Dealer News, 0380-3457.

GULF STATES OIL AND GAS DIRECTORY. See Yearbooks, Almanacs, Directories.

HADSHOT HA-NEFT VEHA-ENERGYAH. No. 155/156- December 1974-. Periodical. Hebrew. ir. 26 Ha-Universita Street, Ramat Aviv Israel. LC HD9576.I78. Hadshot Ha-Neft.

HENRY L. DOHERTY SERIES. V. 1-. 0149-6409. Monographic Series. US. English. ir. Society of Petroleum Engineers, 6200 North Central Expressway, Dallas TX 75206. **Ind/Abst** GeoRef. LC UNC.

HOSE & NOZZLE. See Business - Marketing.

HOUSTON OIL DIRECTORY. See Yearbooks, Almanacs, Directories.

HYDROCARBON PROCESSING CATALOG. 0271-5724. US. English. an. $10.00 US, $12.00 Foreign. Hydrocarbon Processing, PO Box 2608, Houston TX 77001. LC TP690.A1. DD 665.505.

ILLINOIS PETROLEUM. No. 1- 0073-5108. Monographic Series. US. English. ir. State Geological Survey, Natural Resource Building, Urbana IL 61802. **Ind/Abst** GeoRef, Chem. Abstr. LC TN872.I3. DD 553.2809773. **CODEN** ILGPA4.

ILLINOIS PETROLEUM MONITOR. Jan. 1981-. Periodical. US. English. mo. Illinois Institute of Natural Resources, 325 West Adams Street/Room 300, Springfield IL 62706. Illinois Petroleum Monitor: Motor Gasoline.

INACTIVE OIL AND GAS FIELDS. Main/Corp Texas. Railroad Commission. Oil and Gas Division. 0360-6236. US. English. ir. R R Commission, Oil and Gas Division, Capital Street, PO Drawer 12967, Austin TX 78711. LC TN867. DD 622.33809764.

INDO-BURMA PETROLEUM COMPANY LIMITED ANNUAL REPORT. (ANNUAL REPORT). 0376-9968. II. English. an. Indo-Burma Petroleum Company, Gillander House Netaji Subhas Road, Calcutta-1 India. LC HD9576.I54. DD 338.76650954.

INDONESIA PETROLEUM REPORT. IO. English. ir. 3 Jalan Meniens Raya, Jarkata Indonesia. LC HD9576.I5. DD 338.2728209598.

INDUSTRIAL ENERGY. V. 3- May/June 1973-. 0094-1646. Periodical. US. English. bm. 10.00. Gas Industries Equipment and Appliance News, 3 North Michigan Avenue, Chicago IL 60601. LC TP345.A1. DD 665.705. Gas in Industry.

INFORMASA. See Business.

INFORMATION ABOUT THE OIL INDUSTRY, FOR THE OIL INDUSTRY. Periodical. UK. English. Associated Octel Company Limited, PO Box 17/Oil Sites Road, Ellesmere Port South Wirral L65 4HF England.

INFORMATION (GAZ DE FRANCE). (INFORMATION). FR. French. ir. Gaz de France, 23 rue Philibert-Delorme, 75840 Paris Cedex 17 France. LC HD9581.F7. DD 338.272850944. Information.

INFORME ANUAL - PETROLEOS DE VENEZUELA, S.A. Main/Corp Petroleos de Venezuela, S.A. 1959-. Spanish. ir. LC HD9574.V44. DD 354.870082388.

INFORME PETROLERAS. Main/Corp Bolivia. Direccion General de Hidrocarburos. Vol. 1- January 1973-. Periodical. Spanish. ir. Direction General de Hidrocarburos Ave Mariscal Santa Cruz No 1322-5, Piso Casilla 4819 La Paz Bolivia. LC HD9576.B6.

INJURIES IN OIL AND GAS DRILLING AND SERVICES. See Industrial Health & Safety.

INSIDE F.E.R.C. See Energy.

INSIDE GAS MARKETS. VFOAT IGM. 8750-1945. Periodical. US. English. wk. Spencer Publishing Company, 6699 Port West #120, Houston TX 77024. DD 338. Inside Oil & Gas, 0742-3055.

INTERNATIONAL CONFERENCE ON THE FUTURE OF HEAVY CRUDE AND TAR SANDS. 1st (1979)-. US. English. Mining Informational Services, McGraw Hill Inc, 1221 Avenue of the Americas, New York NY 10020. **Tel** (212)512-6158. Ed M Unitar. Information provided by unitar conferences.

INTERNATIONAL GAS TECHNOLOGY HIGHLIGHTS. V. 1- APR. 26, 1971-. 0276-4040. Periodical. US. English. bw. Institute of Gas Technology, 3424 State Street, Chicago IL 60616. **Tel** (312)567-3970. **Ind/Abst** Coal Abstr. **Circ** 2,500. Brief news articles about the natural gas industry producers pipelines, utilities, research and government—aimed primarily at management.

INTERNATIONAL OIL AND GAS DEVELOPMENT. VFOAT Yearbook. V. 30- 1959-. 0535-1634. US. English. sa. International Oil Scouts Association, 5000 East Ben White Boulevard/Suite 301, Austin TX 78741. **Tel** (512)448-4088. Ed Barbara Lockstedt. **Ind/Abst** GeoRef. **Circ** 600. Petroleum statistics in yearbook format; part exploration and part production, published since 1930. Oil and Gas Field Development in the United States and Canada, Statistics of Oil and Gas Development and Production.

INTERNATIONAL OIL NEWS. 0043-8855. Periodical. US. English. wk. International Oil News, PO Box 1421, Stamford CT 06904-1421.

INTERNATIONAL OIL SCOUTS ASSOCIATION. (INTERNATIONAL OIL SCOUTS ASSOCIATION : OFFICIAL PUBLICATION). VFOAT Official Publication. Vol. 1, No. 1 (Dec., 1959)-. 0277-6812. Periodical. US. English. qt. $10.00. International Oil Scouts Association, 5000 East Ben White Boulevard/Suite 310, Austin TX 78741. **Tel** (512)448-4088. Ed Barbara Lockstedt. adv acc. **Circ** 1,200. (ctrl). Newsletter with information on the association's publications and activities.

INTERNATIONAL PETROCHEMICAL DEVELOPMENT. 1980. 0270-1138. Periodical. US. English. sm. $395.00 US, Canada, Mexico, $450.00 Foreign. Rickian Ind, 56 Roundtree Route 9W, Piermont NY 10968. **Tel** (914)359-4643. Ed H L List. **Circ** 100. A review of products and processes in the international petrochemical industry.

THE INTERNATIONAL PETROCHEMICAL REPORT. Vol. 1, No. 1 (May 18, 1982)-. 0733-009X. Periodical. US. English. wk. $427.00. McGraw Hill Publishing, c/o G Higgins, 1221 Avenue of the Americas, New York NY 10021. **Tel** (212)997-4462.

INTERNATIONAL PETROLEUM ABSTRACTS. See Indexes/Abstracts.

Petroleum and Natural Gas

INTERNATIONAL PETROLEUM ENCYCLOPEDIA. 1968-. 0148-0375. US. English. an. $78.50. Pennwell Publishing Company, PO Box 1260, Tulsa OK 74101. Tel (918)835-3161. Ed John C McCaslin. LC HD9560.1. DD 338.272805. adv acc.

INTERNATIONAL PETROLEUM FINANCE. Main/Corp Petroleum Analysis, Ltd. 1978. 0193-9270. US. English. sm. $515.00. Petroleum Analysis Ltd, 20 East 53rd Street, New York NY 10022. Tel (212)755-7484. Ed Carol M Epstein. Analysis of management strategies, earnings and finances of oil companies and of key oil industry. Developments arount the world.

THE INTERSTATE OIL COMPACT COMMISSION COMMITTEE BULLETIN. Main/Corp Interstate Oil Compact Commission. V. 1- June 1959-. 0020-9732. Periodical. US. English. sa. Interstate Oil Compact Commission, 900 NE 23rd Street, Oklahoma OK 73105. Ind/Abst Coal Abstr., Energy Inf. Abstr., Environ. Abstr., GeoRef, Energy Res. Abstr., Bibliogr. Index Geol., Pet. Abstr. LC TN860. CODEN IOCBAV.

IPI DATA SERVICE. EUROPE. VFOAT International Petroleum Industry. Europe Supplement. 197 -. Periodical. US. English. mo. $1150.00. Intl Petroleum Industry, 116 East 66th Street, New York NY 10021.

IPI DATA SERVICE. MIDDLE EAST. VFOAT International Petroleum Industry. Middle East Supplement. 197 -. Periodical. US. English. mo. $1150.00. International Petroleum Industry, 116 East 66th Street, New York NY 10021.

IPI DATA SERVICE. NORTH AMERICA. CONSOLIDATED TABLE OF CONTENTS. 1979-. Periodical. US. English. ir. Barrows Company Inc, 116 East 66th Street, New York NY 10023. DD 338.27280973.

IPI DATA SERVICE. WORLD. CONSOLIDATED TABLE OF CONTENTS. 1979-. Periodical. US. English. ir. Barrows Company Inc, 116 East 66th Street, New York NY 10023. DD 338.27280212.

IRAQ OIL NEWS BULLETIN. Periodical. English. ir. Ministry of Oil, Information and Public Relations Division, PO Box 6118, Al-Mansoui, Baghdad Iraq. LC HD9576.I7. DD 338.2728209567. *Iraq Oil News.*

ITOGI, SUMMARIES OF SCIENTIFIC PROGRESS. DEVELOPMENT OF OIL AND GAS DEPOSITS. (ITOGI, SUMMARIES OF SCIENTIFIC PROGRESS : DEVELOPMENT OF OIL AND GAS DEPOSITS). VFOAT Development of Oil and Gas Deposits. Monographic Series. US. English (Russian). G K Hall, 70 Lincoln Street, Boston MA 02111. LC TN860. DD 622.338.

IUPW VIEWS. See Economics - Labor.

IZVESTIIA VYSHIKH UCHEBNYKH ZAVEDENII. NEFT I GAZ. V. 1- 1958. 0445-0108. Periodical. Russian. mo. Victor Kamkin Inc (70371), 12224 Parklawn Drive, Rockville MD 20852. Tel (301)881-5973. Ind/Abst Eng. Index Annu., Eng. Index Mon., Eng. Index Bioeng. Abstr., Eng. Index Energy Abstr., Coal Abstr., Chem. Abstr., Energy Res. Abstr. CODEN IVUNA2.

JAPAN PETROLEUM & ENERGY WEEKLY. VFOAT Japan Petroleum and Energy Weekly. 1966. 0386-6165. Periodical. JA. English. wk. $850.00. Japan Petroleum Energy Consultants, PO Box 1185/Tokyo Central, Tokyo Japan. Tel (03)359-8145. Ed K Kurokawa. Ind/Abst Predicasts. Circ 500. The only English-language weekly carrying up-to-date news on the petroleum and energy industries in Japan. Contains articles on the government's energy policies and the activities of Japanese energy and oil companies. *Japan Petroleum Weekly.*

JAPAN PETROLEUM & ENERGY WEEKLY. MONTHLY STATISTICAL SUPPLEMENT. See Statistics.

JAPAN PETROLEUM & ENERGY YEARBOOK. See Yearbooks, Almanacs, Directories.

JAPAN PETROLEUM INDUSTRY YEARBOOK. See Yearbooks, Almanacs, Directories.

JIS HANDOBUKKU : SEKIYU. Began with Vol. for 1967. Japanese. ir. 2200. Nihon Kikaku Kyokai, 1-24 Akasaka 4-Chome Minato-Ku, Japanese Standards Association, Tokyo Japan. LC TP691.

JOURNAL OF CANADIAN PETROLEUM TECHNOLOGY. (THE JOURNAL OF CANADIAN PETROLEUM TECHNOLOGY). V. 1- Spring 1962-. 0021-9487. Periodical. CN. English. bm. 32.00 Domestic, 42.00 US, 52.00 Foreign. Petroleum Society of C I M, 906 Drummondville Building, 1117 Ste Catherine Street West, Montreal Quebec H3B 1J3 Canada. Tel (514)842-3461. Ed P Michaud. Ind/Abst Eng. Index Mon., Eng. Index Bioeng. Abstr., Eng. Index Energy Abstr., Can. Environ., Life Sci. Collect., Coal Abstr., Energy Inf. Abstr., Environ. Abstr., Mintec, Min. Technol. Abstr., GeoRef, ASTIS Bibliogr., ASTIS Curr. Aware. Bull., Chem. Abstr., Eng. Index Mon., Eng. Index Annu., Energy Res. Abstr. CODEN JCPMAM. bk rev. adv acc. Circ 6,400. (ctrl). Magazine focusing on activities and technology within the petroleum and natural gas industry.

JOURNAL OF MINES, METALS & FUELS : INCORPORATING INDIAN MINING JOURNAL & THE OFFICIAL ORGAN OF INDIAN MINE MANAGERS' ASSOCIATION. See Engineering - Mining Engineering.

JOURNAL OF PETROLEUM ACCOUNTING. Vol. 4, No. 1 (Spring 1985) -. Periodical. US. English. ty. *Journal of Extractice Industries Accounting,* 0885-3452.

JOURNAL OF PETROLEUM GEOLOGY. V. 1- July 1978-. 0141-6421. Periodical. UK. English. qt. $130.00 US. Scientific Press Ltd, PO Box 21 Beaconsfield, Bucks HP9 1NS England. Tel 04946-5139. Ed E N Tiratsoo. Ind/Abst Eng. Index Annu., Eng. Index Mon., Eng. Index, Eng. Index Bioeng. Abstr., Eng. Index Energy Abstr., Life Sci. Collect., Coal Abstr., GeoRef, Chem. Abstr., Energy Res. Abstr., Pet. Abstr., Bibliogr. Index Geol. LC TN870.5. DD 553.2805. CODEN JPEGD9. bk rev. adv acc.

JOURNAL OF PETROLEUM TECHNOLOGY. Began 1949. Periodical. US. English. mo. Tel (214)669-3377. bk rev. adv acc. Circ 57,500. Journal reporting advances in engineering technology of drilling, exploration, and production of oil and gas, including project management and economics.

KULBRINTER. Main/Corp Statistical Office of the European Communities. VFOAT Kohlenwasserstoffe. 1977-. English (French and German). ir. $16.50. European Community Information Service, 2100 M Street NW/Suite 707, Washington DC 20037. LC HD9575.E97. DD 338.2728094. *Kvartalsbulletin Energistatistik.*

THE LAMP. 0023-7418. Periodical. US. English. qt. Exxon Corporation, 1251 Avenue of the Americas, New York NY 10020. Tel (212)398-3072. Ind/Abst Index Free Period., GeoRef, Public Aff. Inf. Serv. Bull., Predicasts, Cumul. Index Nurs. Allied Health Lit., Funk Scott Index Corp. Ind. LC HD9560.1. DD 338.2728205.

LAND DRILLING & OILWELL SERVICING CONTRACTORS. VFOAT Land Drilling and Oilwell Servicing Contractors. 0748-139X. US. English. an. $75.00 US/Canada, $93.50 Others. Petroleum Publishing Company, Directory Division, PO Box 1260, Tulsa OK 74101. Tel (918)835-3161. Ed William R Leek Jr. LC TN867. DD 338.27282. adv acc. Circ 1,800. *Land Drilling and Oilwell Servicing Contractors Directory,* 0277-0954.

LATIN AMERICA PETROLEUM DIRECTORY. See Yearbooks, Almanacs, Directories.

LAW OF OIL AND GAS LEASES. US. English. ir. Matthew Bender & Company Inc, 1275 Broadway, Albany NY 12201. Tel (800)833-9844.

LIQUEFIED GAS DIRECTORY OF AMERICA INC. WESTERN REGION. See Yearbooks, Almanacs, Directories.

LIQUEFIED NATURAL GAS CEASED. Discontinued with No. 80-04 (Oct.-Dec. 1980). 0024-4228. Periodical. US. English. qt. US Department of Commerce, National Bureau of Standards, Cryogenic Data Center, 325 Broadway Boulder CO 80303. LC TP761.L5.

LIQUEFIED PETROLEUM GAS REPORT. Main/Corp American Petroleum Institute. 1956. 0024-421X. Periodical. US. English. mo. $10.00. American Petroleum Institute, 1220 L Street NW, Washington DC 20005. Tel (202)682-8378. Includes inventories of liquified petroleum and liquified refinery gases located at plants and refineries, in underground storage/area/product.

LIQUID FOSSIL FUEL TECHNOLOGY, QUARTERLY TECHNICAL PROGRESS REPORT. Periodical. US. English. qt. Bartlesville Energy Technology Center, PO Box 1398, Bartlesville OK 74003. Ind/Abst Energy Inf. Abstr., Environ. Abstr.

LIQUID GAS CARRIER REGISTER. 0305-1803. UK. English. ir. $145.00. International Publishing Service, Taylor & Francis Inc, 242 Cherry Street, Philadelphia PA 19106. Tel (800)821-8312. LC HE566.T3. DD 387.245.

LNG DIGEST. (LNG DIGEST : THE LIQUEFIED NATURAL GAS NEWSLETTER OF ENERGY RESEARCH ASSOCIATES). VAT Liquified Natural Gas Digest. 1975. 0276-5918. Periodical. US. English. mo. $1125.00. Energy Research Associates, PO Box 1516 Wall Street Station, New York NY 10005. Tel (212)338-5384. Ed J L Birnbaum. Analysis of LNG industry.

THE LOG ANALYST. See Energy.

LONDON OIL REPORTS. V. 1- Jan. 15, 1979-. 0143-0111. Periodical. UK. English. wk. $1900.00. Lor Guernsey Ltd, la Tour Gand House, Pollet Guernsey Channel Isle England.

LOUISIANA ANNUAL OIL AND GAS REPORT. 1976-. 0735-0716. US. English. sm. R W Byram and Company, Box 44262 Capitol Station, Baton Rouge LA 70804. Tel (504)344-1679. Ind/Abst GeoRef. LC TN872.L8. DD 338.272809763. *Annual Oil and Gas Report,* 0459-8393.

LP GAS REVIEW. V. 1- Jan. 1977-. Periodical. UK. English. qt. 26. British Continental Trade Press Ltd, High Street, Canbrook Kent TN17 3DR England. Tel 0580 714044. Ed Garry Parker. LC TP359.L5. adv acc. Circ 4,800. (ctrl). Covers every aspect of liquified petroleum gas from bulk, containerisation and transport for domestic automotive, industrial and commercial marketing.

L.P.G. LANDMAN'S PETROLEUM GAZETTE. (L. P. G). Main/Corp Landman's Petroleum Gazette Ltd. VAT Landman's Petroleum Gazette. V. 1- Aug. 23, 1979-. 0709-9029. Periodical. CN. English. sm. $170. Landman's Petroleum Gazette Ltd, Box 48/Site 2 S S#3, Calgary Alberta T3C 3N9 Canada. DD 338.27282097123.

LP/GAS. (LP-GAS). 0024-7103. Periodical. US. English. mo. LP-Gas Magazine, 1 East First Street, Duluth MN 55802. Tel (218)723-9200.

LUNDBERG LETTER. 0195-4563. US. English. wk. $231.00. Tele-Drop Inc, 12041 Strathern Street/ PO Box 3996, North Hollywood CA 91609. Tel (818)768-5111. Ed Trilby Lundberg. Covers the US fuels marketing trends, analysis and statistics.

MARATHON WORLD. V.1-. 0025-2743. Periodical. US. English. qt. Marathon Oil Company, 539 South Main Street, Findlay OH 45840. Ind/Abst Index Free Period., Energy Res. Abstr. DD 051.

MARINE AND PETROLEUM GEOLOGY. See Earth Sciences - Geology.

MEMBERSHIP AND STATISTICAL DIRECTORY - NEW ENGLAND GAS ASSOCIATION. See Yearbooks, Almanacs, Directories.

MEMBERSHIP DIRECTORY - AMERICAN ASSOCIATION OF PETROLEUM LANDMEN. See Yearbooks, Almanacs, Directories.

MEMBERSHIP DIRECTORY - INDONESIAN PETROLEUM ASSOCIATION. PROFESSIONAL DIVISION. See Yearbooks, Almanacs, Directories.

MEMOIR - CANADIAN SOCIETY OF PETROLEUM GEOLOGISTS. See Earth Sciences - Geology.

MEMORIA DE LABORES - PETROLEOS MEXICANOS. Main/Corp Petroleos Mexicanos. Spanish. ir. LC HD9574.M62.

MEMORIA Y BALANCE. Main/Corp Empresa Nacional del Petroleo (Chile). VFOAT Memoria y Balances. 1974-. Spanish. an. LC HD9574.C44. DD 338.762233820983. *Memoria.*

MICHIGAN'S OIL AND GAS FIELDS. 1963-. 0543-8470. US. English. an. LC TN872.M5. DD 333.82309774. *Summary of Operations, Oil and Gas Fields.*

MICHIGAN'S OIL & GAS NEWS. VFOAT Michigan's Oil and Gas News. Vol. 89, No. 1 (Jan. 7, 1983)-. 0746-5769. Periodical. US. English. wk.

Petroleum and Natural Gas

$50.00. Michigan's Oil and Gas News, PO Box 250, Mt Pleasant MI 48858. *Oil & Gas News (Mt. Pleasant, Mich.), 0739-2249.*

MIDCONTINENT OIL WORLD. 0883-7325. Periodical. US. English. mo. $24.00 Industry, $58.00 to Non-Industry. Hart Publications Inc, PO Box 1917, 1900 Grant Street/Suite 400, Denver CO 80201-1917. DD 665.

MIDDLE EAST ECONOMIC SURVEY. VFOAT MEES. V. 1- Nov. 19, 1957-. 0544-0424. Periodical. CY. English. wk. $995.00. PO Box 4940, Nicosia Cyprus. Tel 357-2-445431. Ed Fuad W Itayim. LC HD9576.N36. bk rev. Review of petroleum, finance and banking, and political developments in the Middle East and North Africa.

MINE, PETROL, GAZE. See Engineering - Mining Engineering.

MINERIA Y PETROLEO. See Earth Sciences - Mineralogy.

MINING MONTHLY. See Engineering - Mining Engineering.

MINUTES OF PROCEEDINGS AND EVIDENCE OF THE SPECIAL COMMITTEE ON A NORTHERN GAS PIPELINE. Main/Corp Canada. Parliament. House of Commons. Special Committee on a Northern Gas Pipeline. VFOAT Proces-Verbaux et Temoignages du Comite Special sur un Pipe-Line pour le Gaz du Nord. VAT Pip-Line pour le Gaz du Nord, Northern Gas Pipeline. Feb. 23, 1978-. 0707-3216. Periodical. CN. English (with French in parallel columns). Queens Printer, c/o Receiver General of Canada, Ottawa Ontario K1A 0S9 Canada. LC TN880.5. DD 388.5.

MINUTES OF PROCEEDINGS AND EVIDENCE OF THE STANDING COMMITTEE ON NORTHERN PIPELINES. Main/Corp Canada. Parliament. House of Commons. Standing Committee on Northern Pipelines. VFOAT Proces-Verbaux et Temoignages du Comite Permanent sur les Pipe-Lines du Nord. VAT Northern Pipelines, Pipe-Lines du Nord. Oct. 31, 1978-. 0707-8978. Periodical. CN. English (text in French in parallel Columns). Queens Printer, c/o Receiver General of Canada, Ottawa Ontario K1A 0S9 Canada. LC TN880.5. DD 388.5.

MISCELLANEOUS ASTM STANDARDS FOR PETROLEUM PRODUCTS. Main/Corp American Society for Testing and Materials. Committee D-2 on Petroleum Products and Lubricants. VAT Miscellaneous America Society for Testing and Materials Standards for Petroleum Products. 0569-7743. US. English. an. *ASTM Standards Relating to Petroleum Products and Lubricants.*

MISCELLANEOUS PUBLICATION. See Earth Sciences - Geology.

MISSISSIPPI OIL & GAS PRODUCTION REPORT. VAT Mississippi Oil and Gas Production Report. 0274-6980. Periodical. US. English. mo. $60.00. State Oil and Gas Board, PO Box 1332, Jackson MS 39205. *Mississippi State Oil & Gas Board Bulletin.*

MOBIL WORLD. V. 26- Mar./Apr. 1960-. Periodical. US. English. mo. Mobil Oil Corporation, 150 East 42 Street, New York NY 10017. Ind/Abst Energy Res. Abstr. *Flying Red Horse.*

THE MONOGRAM. Periodical. US. English. ir. American Petroleum Institute, 1220 L Street NW, Washington DC 20005. Tel (214)741-6791.

MONTANA OIL JOURNAL. (MONTANA OIL JOURNAL WITH NEWS IN THE WILLISTON BASIN AREA. MONTANA-NORTH DAKOTA). 0047-794X. Periodical. US. English. wk. $25.00. Montana Oil Journal, PO Box 20255, Billings MT 59104. Tel (406)656-0886. Ed Roy Boles. adv acc. Circ 5,200. (ctrl). Oil and gas activity in Montana, North and South Dakota.

MONTHLY GAS UTILITY STATISTICAL REPORT. See Statistics.

MONTHLY MOTOR FUEL REPORTED BY STATES. Jan. 1985-. US. English. ir. US Department of Transportation, Federal Highway Administration, 400 7th Street SW, Washington DC 20590.

MONTHLY OIL AND GAS PRODUCTION AND INJECTION REPORT. Jan. 1982-. 0742-4086. US. English. mo. LC HD9567.C2. DD 338.272809794. *Monthly Oil and Gas Production Report.*

MONTHLY OIL AND GAS PRODUCTION REPORT. Nov. 1978-. 0228-5622. Periodical. CN. English. mo. $77.38. Department of Mineral Resources, 1914 Hamilton Street, Regina Saskatchewan S4P 4V4 Canada. Tel (306)565-2528. LC HD9574.C23. DD 338.2728097124. *Monthly Oil and Gas Report, 0702-9926.*

MONTHLY PETROLEUM INFORMATION. Main/Corp Nigerian National Petroleum Corporation. Economic Research and Intelligence Dept. 0549-2513. Periodical. NR. English. mo. Nigerian National Petroleum Corp, P M B 12701, Lagos Nigeria. LC HD9577.N5. DD 338.2728209669. *Monthly Petroleum Information, 0549-2513.*

MONTHLY PETROLEUM STATISTICS REPORT. See Statistics.

MONTHLY REPORT - CANADIAN PETROLEUM ASSOCIATION. Main/Corp Canadian Petroleum Association. 0383-1671. Periodical. CN. English. an. Canadian Petroleum Association, 1500 633 Sixth Avenue SW, Calgary Alberta T2P 2Y5 Canada. Tel (403)269-6721.

MONTHLY REPORT OF HEATING OIL AND OTHER MIDDLE DISTILLATES SALES BY STATES. Main/Corp Ethyl Corporation. Petroleum Chemicals Division. VFOAT Heating Oil and Other Middle Distillates Sales by States. 0277-7479. Periodical. US. English. mo. $16.00. American Petroleum Institute, 1220 L Street NW, Washington DC 20005. Tel (214)741-6791.

MONTHLY STATISTICAL REPORT. See Statistics.

MUJTAMA AL-BATRUL. VFOAT Petroleum Community. Periodical. Arabic (English). mo. Sharikat Batrul Abuzaby Al-Wataniyah, S B 898 Aruzaby, Idarat Al-Alaqat Al-Ammah.

NAFT AL-ARAB. Periodical. Arabic. ir. 10.00. Maktab Abd Allah Al-Tariqi Lil-Istishaharat Al-Naftiyah, PO Box 22699 Safat-Kuwait, Al-Kuwayt Kuwait. LC HD9578.A55.

NAFTA. V. 1- 1945-. 0027-7541. PL. Polish (tables of contents also in Russian and English). mo. ARS Polona, Krakowskie Przedmiescie 7, 00-068 Warsaw Poland. Ind/Abst Coal Abstr., Energy Inf. Abstr., Environ. Abstr., Chem. Abstr. LC TN860. CODEN NAFPAB.

NATIONAL EMISSIONS DATA SYSTEM (NEDS). VFOAT NEDS Fuel Use Report. US. English. an. National Technical Information Service, 5285 Port Royal Road, Springfield VA 22161. Vols. for 1974-1975 distributed to depository libraries in microfiche.

NATIONAL PETROLEUM COUNCIL. (NATIONAL PETROLEUM COUNCIL NEWS). VFOAT News. 0741-1464. Periodical. US. English. ir. National Petroleum Council, 1625 K Street NW/Suite 601, Washington DC 20006.

NATURAL GAS ANNUAL. 1980-. 0736-9808. US. English. an. Superintendent of Documents, US Government Printing Office, Washington DC 20402. LC HD9581.U49. DD 338.272850973. *Natural Gas Production and Consumption, 0732-6629.*

NATURAL GAS FOR INDUSTRY AND COMMERCE. 0140-3222. Periodical. UK. English. bm. 4.00. Benn Brothers Ltd, 125 High Street Colliers Wood, London SW19 2JN England. Ind/Abst World Surf. Coat. Abstr. LC TN880.A1. DD 665.705. *Natural Gas for Industry, 0305-2028; Natural Gas for Commerce.*

NATURAL GAS FROM CALIFORNIA FIELDS. 0272-4863. US. English. an. Conservation Committee of California Oil Producers, 417 South Hill Street/Suite 930, Los Angeles CA 90013. LC TN881.C2. DD 553.28509794.

NATURAL GAS HANDBOOK. 0744-6500. Periodical. US. English. ir. $295.00. Federal Programs Advisory Services, 1725 K Street NW/Suite 200, Washington DC 20037. Tel (202)872-1766. LC KF1870.A15. DD 343.73092605, 347.30392605.

NATURAL GAS INTELLIGENCE. (NATURAL GAS INTELLIGENCE : A WEEKLY NEWSLETTER). Vol. 1, No. 1 (June 15, 1981)-. 0739-1811. Periodical. US. English. wk. $475.00. Intelligence Press, PO Box 24078, Washington DC 20024. Tel (703)759-4711. Ed Ellen Beswick. Natural gas market report including news and prices from Texas, Oklahoma, Louisiana, Appalachia, The Rockies and Calgary. Also political, and financial reports.

NATURAL GAS MONTHLY. Oct. 1982-. 0737-1713. Periodical. US. English. mo. $55.00. Superintendent of Documents, US Government Printing Office, Washington DC 20402. Ind/Abst Chem. Abstr., Am. Stat. Index, Predicasts. DD 333. CODEN NGMODK. *Natural Gas Monthly Report, 0731-9479; Underground Natural Gas Storage in the United States, 0275-9535; US Imports and Exports of Natural Gas; Main Line Sales of Natural Gas to Industrial Users.*

NATURAL GAS PROCESSING PLANTS IN CANADA. Series/Titl Operators List. 1960-. 0077-6041. CN. English. an. 75. Energy Policy Sector, IC, Ottawa Ontario Canada.

NATURAL GAS PRODUCER PRICES (APPALACHIAN EDITION). (NATURAL GAS PRODUCER PRICES). Vol. 1, No. 1 (June 1984)-. 0747-6272. US. English. mo. $295.00. Thompson Publishing Group, Suite 200, 1725 K Street NW, Washington DC 20006. DD 333.

NATURAL GAS PRODUCER PRICES (GULF COAST EDITION). (NATURAL GAS PRODUCER PRICES). Vol. 1, No. 1 (June 1984)-. 0747-6280. US. English. mo. $295.00. Thompson Publishing Group, 1725 K Street NW/Suite 200, Washington DC 20006. DD 333.

NATURAL GAS PRODUCER PRICES (WESTERN EDITION). (NATURAL GAS PRODUCER PRICES). Vol. 1, No. 1 (June 1984)-. 0747-6299. US. English. mo. $295.00. Thompson Publishing Group, Suite 200/1725 K Street NW, Washington DC 20006. DD 333.

NATURAL GAS TODAY. V. 1- Apr. 1962-. 0547-9568. Periodical. CN. English. bm. Trans Canada Pipe Lines, PO Box 54, Commerce Court West, Toronto Ontario M5L 1C2 Canada. Tel (416)869-2111.

NATURAL GAS WEEK. 8756-3037. Periodical. US. English. wk. The Oil Daily Inc, 1401 New York Avenue NW/Suite 500, Washington DC 20005. Tel (800)621-0050. The newsletter that provides you with unique, current and cumulative natural gas price information and news about developments that affect prices.

NAVAL PETROLEUM AND OIL SHALE RESERVES ANNUAL REPORT OF OPERATIONS. (NAVAL PETROLEUM AND OIL SHALE RESERVES ANNUAL REPORT OF OPERATION). Fiscal Year 1981-. 0883-1521. US. English. an. National Technical Information Service, US Department of Commerce, Springfield VA 22161. LC TN872. DD 359.83. *Annual Report of Operations (United States. Office of Naval Petroleum and Oil Shale Reserves), 0193-4899.*

NEFT I GAZ. Periodical. UR. Russian. 0.95. Victor Kamkin Inc, 12224 Parklawn Drive, Rockville MD 20852. LC TN860.

NEFTEGAZONOSNYE I PERSPEKTIVNYE KOMPLEKSY TSENTRALNYKH I VOSTOCHNYKH OBLASTEI RUSSKOI PLATFORMY. UR. Russian. 1.65 Single Issue. Nedra, K-12 Tretiakovskii Proezd, D 1/19 Moskva Russian SFSR. LC TN860.

NEFTEKHIMIIA. V. 1-. 0028-2421. Periodical. UR. Russian (Vols. 1-(2) have tables of contents also in English). bm. $50.00. Victor Kamkin Inc (70617), 12224 Parklawn Drive, Rockville MD 20852. Tel (301)881-5973. Ind/Abst Energy Res. Abstr., Chem. Abstr., Curr. Abstr. Chem. Index Chem. LC TP690.A1. CODEN NEFTAH.

NEFTEPERERABOTKA, NEFTEHIMIJA I SLANCEPERERABOTKA. (NEFTEPERERABOTKA, NEFTEKHIMIIA, SLANTSEPERERABOTKA). No. 1- 2. 0131-1670. UR. Russian. 0.50. M-35 Ul T Makarovoi, Moskva 12 Russia. Ind/Abst Chem. Abstr. LC TP690.A1. CODEN NNNSAF. *Neftepererabotka i Neftekhimiia (Moscow, R.S. F.S.R. : 1963).*

NEFTIANAIA PROMYSHLENNOST. SERIIA NEFTEPROMYSLOVOE STROITELSTVO. VFOAT Neftepromyslovoe Stroitelstvo. Periodical. UR. Russian. bw. $21.60. Victor Kamkin Inc, 12224 Parklawn Drive, Rockville MD 20852. Tel (301)881-5973. Ind/Abst Chem. Abstr. CODEN NPNSDW. *Nefteprpmyslovoe Stroitelstvo, 0321-2580.*

NEFTIANIK. Began with Jan. 1956 issue. 0028-243X. Periodical. UR. Russian. mo. $24.50. Victor Kamkin Inc (70618), 12224 Parklawn Drive, Rockville MD 20852. Tel (301)881-5973. Ind/Abst Energy Res. Abstr., Chem. Abstr. LC TN860. CODEN NFTYA7.

NENRYO KYOKAISHI. Began in 1922. 0369-3775. Periodical. Japanese (summaries in English). mo. 100.00. Maruzen Company Ltd, PO Box

Petroleum and Natural Gas

5050, 100-31 Tokyo Japan. **Tel** 03-834-6456. **Ind/Abst** Eng. Index Annu., Eng. Index Mon., Eng. Index Bioeng. Abstr., Eng. Index Energy Abstr., Coal Abstr., Met. Abstr., World Alum. Abstr., Chem. Abstr. **CODEN** NENKAU. Index in last issue of volume - attached. adv acc. (ctrl). Contains information about administration and use of fuel.

NEWS & VIEWS - INDEPENDENT PETROLEUM ASSOCIATION OF CANADA. (NEWS & VIEWS). Oct. 19, 1981-. 0820-0874. Periodical. CN. English. Free. News & Views, c/o I.P.A.C., 700-707-7th Avenue SW, Calgary Alberta T2P 0Z2 Canada. **DD** 338.272820971. *Fact Sheet (Independent Petroleum Association of Canada), 0820-0866.*

NEWS BULLETIN - ORGANIZATION OF ARAB PETROLEUM EXPORTING COUNTRIES *CEASED.* **Main/Corp** Organization of Arab Petroleum Exporting Countries. **VFOAT** OAPEC Bulletin. V. 1-5, No. 1. Periodical. KU. English. mo. $48.00. Organization of Arab Petroleum Exporting Center, PO Box 20501, Safat Kuwait. **Tel** 2448200. **LC** HD9578.A55. **DD** 382.422820601.

NOROIL. **VFOAT** Norsk Oljetidskrift. V. 1- 1973-. 0332-544X. Periodical. Norwegian (English in parallel columns). mo. $165.00. Noroil Publishing Hse Ltd, c/o Kings House 10 Haymarket, London SW1Y 4BP England. **Tel** (01)930-9456. Ed O J Kvinnsland. **Ind/Abst** Life Sci. Collect., Predicasts, Ship Abstr., Energy Inf. Abstr., Environ. Abstr., GeoRef, Energy Res. Abstr., Funk Scott Index Corp. Ind., Pet. Abstr., Bibliogr. Index Geol. bk rev. adv acc. **Circ** 15,500. (ctrl). Top selling European offshore oil and gas magazine. Covers exploration, engineering, construction, field development, latest news and politics plus latest offshore technology.

NORTH SEA OIL & GAS DIRECTORY. See Yearbooks, Almanacs, Directories.

NORTHEAST OIL REPORTER. Vol. 1, No. 1 (Feb. 1981)-. 0279-7798. Periodical. US. English. mo. $24.00. Hart Publications Inc, PO Box 1917, Denver CO 80201. **Tel** (303)837-1917. Ed Lynn Maslowski. **Ind/Abst** GeoRef. **LC** TN860. **DD** 681.76. adv acc.

NORWEGIAN OFFSHORE INDEX. See Indexes/Abstracts.

NOTES ET MEMOIRES. **Main/Corp** Compagnie Francaise des Petroles. No. 1- May 1962-. 0588-8700. French. ir. Compagnie Francaise des Petroles, 5 rue Michel-Ange, Paris France.

NOUVELLES GULF CANADA. **Main/Corp** Gulf Oil Canada. V. 27-33. 0380-3465. Periodical. CN. French. Gulf Oil Canada, Public Affairs, 130 Adelaide Street West, Toronto Ontario M5H 3R6 Canada. **DD** 338.766550971. *Nouvelles B A, 0380-3481.*

NPN. (NPN. NATIONAL PETROLEUM NEWS). V. 51, No. 5- May 1959-. Periodical. US. English. mo. $22.00. Hunter Publishing Co, 950 Lee Street, Des Plaines IL 60016. **Tel** (312)296-0770. Ed Marvin Reid. **Ind/Abst** Bus. Period. Index, Funk Scott Index Corp. Ind. adv acc. **Circ** 18,000. Serves petroleum marketers with news background on the industry, analysis of emerging trends and events of importance. *National Petroleum News.*

OAPEC, ORGANIZATION OF ARAB PETROLEUM EXPORTING COUNTRIES. **Main/Corp** Organization of Arab Petroleum Exporting Countries. **VFOAT** OAPEC Bulletin. V. 5, No. 2- Feb. 1979-. Periodical. English. ir. $16.00. Organization of Arab Petroleum Exporting Countries, Box 20501, Kuwait Kuwait. **LC** HD9578.A55. **DD** 382.422820601. *News Bulletin - Organization of Arab Petroleum Exporting Countries.*

OCEAN CONSTRUCTION LOCATOR. See Building and Construction.

OCEAN CONSTRUCTION REPORT. See Building and Construction.

OCEAN OIL WEEKLY REPORT. Periodical. US. English. wk. $215.00 US, Canada, Mexico, $245.00 Others. Pennwell Publishing Company, PO Box 1260, Tulsa OK 74101. **Tel** (918)832-9246. Ed Ann S Cohen. Worldwide activities of the offshore petroleum and supporting marine service industries. Includes oil and gas discoveries and rig construction reports.

OFFSHORE. V. 1- Sept. 1954-. 0030-0608. Periodical. US. English. ir. $45.00. Pennwell Publishers, PO Box 1260, Tulsa OK 74101. **Tel** (918)835-3161. Ed Robert G Burke. **Ind/Abst** Bibliogr. Index Geol., Pet. Abstr., Appl. Sci. Technol. Index, Ocean. Abstr. **LC** TN871.3. **CODEN** OFSHAU. bk rev. adv acc. **Circ** 36,000. (ctrl).

OFFSHORE ABSTRACTS. See Indexes/Abstracts.

OFFSHORE CONTRACTORS AND EQUIPMENT DIRECTORY. See Yearbooks, Almanacs, Directories.

OFFSHORE INDUSTRIAL DIRECTORY. See Yearbooks, Almanacs, Directories.

OFFSHORE MICROFORM. V. 2, No. 3 (May 1955)-. 0030-0608. US. English. an.

OFFSHORE OIL AND GAS LANDS. Oct. 1st 1978-. 0228-4979. Periodical. CN. English. sa. Department of Energy Mines and Resources, 580 Booth Street, Ottawa Ontario K1A 0E4 Canada. **DD** 354.710082388046. *Offshore Oil and Gas Permits, 0228-4960.*

OFFSHORE OIL & GAS YEARBOOK. See Yearbooks, Almanacs, Directories.

OFFSHORE PETROLEUM INDUSTRY. Periodical. US. English. ir. $1,100.00. Barrows Company Inc, 116 East 66th Street, New York NY 10021. Analysis of offshore operations by country.

OFFSHORE RESOURCES. Vol. 1, No. 1 (Spring 1983)-. 0820-0858. Periodical. CN. English. qt. $15.00. Offshore Resources, PO Box 91760, West Vancouver British Columbia V7V 4S1 Canada. **DD** 622.290971.

OFFSHORE RIG LOCATION REPORT. (THE OFFSHORE RIG LOCATION REPORT). 0733-0928. Periodical. US. English. mo. $285.00. Offshore Rig Data Services Inc, PO Box 19909, Houston TX 77224.

THE OFFSHORE RIG NEWSLETTER. V. 1- Feb. 1974-. 0147-1481. Periodical. US. English. mo. $175.00. Offshore Data Services Inc, PO Box 19909, Houston TX 77224. **Tel** (713)781-2713. Ed Jerry Greenberg. **Circ** 1,500. Reports on the offshore drilling rig market.

OFFSHORE TECHNOLOGY YEARBOOK. See Yearbooks, Almanacs, Directories.

OIL AND AUSTRALIA - THE FIGURES BEHIND THE FACTS. (OIL AND AUSTRALIA). 1958-. 0472-7584. Periodical. AT. English. an. Free. Australian Institute of Petroleum Ltd, 227 Collins Street, Melbourne Victoria 3000 Australia. **Tel** (03)654-1411. Ed Douglas Rose. **Ind/Abst** GeoRef. **LC** HD9578.A8. **DD** 338.2. **CODEN** OIAUAY. **Circ** 38,000. (ctrl). Statistical information concerning oil and gas industries in Australia.

OIL & ENERGY TRENDS. **Main/Corp** Energy Economics Research Ltd. UK. English. an. Energy Economics Research Ltd, 7-9 Queen Victoria Street, Reading Berkshire RG1 1SY United Kingdom. **Tel** 0734-589689. **Ind/Abst** Ship Abstr. **LC** HD9560.4. **DD** 338.20212.

THE OIL AND GAS COMPACT BULLETIN. (THE OIL AND GAS COMPACT BULLETIN : OFFICIAL PUBLICATION OF THE INTERSTATE OIL COMPACT COMMISSION). Vol. 14, No. 1 (June 1955)-. 0196-7177. Periodical. US. English. sa. Interstate Oil Compact Commission, PO Box 53127, Oklahoma City OK 73105. **Ind/Abst** Energy Inf. Abstr., Environ. Abstr., GeoRef, Energy Res. Abstr., Public Aff. Inf. Serv. Bull., Pet. Abstr., Bibliogr. Index Geol. **LC** TN872.A5. *Interstate Oil Compact Quarterly Bulletin.*

OIL AND GAS DEVELOPMENTS IN PENNSYLVANIA. **Main/Corp** Pennsylvania. Bureau of Topographic and Geologic Survey. 1950-. US. English. an. Bureau of Topographical and Geologic Survey, PO Box 2357, Harrisburg PA 17120. **LC** QE157. **DD** 553.28.

THE OIL AND GAS DIRECTORY. See Yearbooks, Almanacs, Directories.

OIL AND GAS FEDERAL INCOME TAX MANUAL. 0474-0076. Periodical. US. English. ir. Arthur Andersen & Company, 69 West Washington Street, Chicago IL 60602.

OIL AND GAS FIELD CODE MASTER LIST. See Engineering - Mining Engineering.

OIL AND GAS FIELD STUDIES. Began with: No. 1, published in 1972. 0161-0961. US. English. **Tel** (801)581-6831. **Ind/Abst** GeoRef. **CODEN** OSUSDV. bk rev. **Circ** 500. (ctrl). Descriptions of oil and gas fields with history, production, and geologic structure.

OIL AND GAS FORUM. (OIL AND GAS FORUM : CONVERSATIONS WITH CANADIANS). Vol. 1, No. 1 (Fall 1979)-. 0229-608X. Periodical. CN. English. ir. Petroleum Resources Communication Foundation, PO Box 6746 Station D, Calgary Alberta T2P 2E6 Canada. **Tel** (403)264-6064. **DD** 338.27280971.

OIL & GAS INVESTOR. See Business - Investments.

OIL & GAS JOURNAL. **VFOAT** Oil and Gas Journal. V. 9- 1910-. 0030-1388. Periodical. US. English. wk. $17.00 Domestic, Affiliated with Petroleum Industry, $19.00 Foreign, Affiliated with Petroleum Industry, $65.00 Non-Industry Rate. Petroleum Publishing Company, Subscriber Service Manager, PO Box 1260, Tulsa OK 74101. **Ind/Abst** Eng. Index Mon., Eng. Index Bioeng. Abstr., Fluidex, Life Sci. Collect., Excerpta Med., Predicasts, Coal Abstr., Ship Abstr., Energy Inf. Abstr., Environ. Abstr., Int. Aerosp. Abstr., GeoRef, CIS Abstr., ASTIS Bibliogr., ASTIS Curr. Aware. Bull., Energy Res. Abstr., Met. Abstr., World Alum. Abstr., Chem. Abstr., Eng. Index Annu., Eng. Index Energy Abstr., Nuci. Sci. Abstr., Sel. Water Resour. Abstr., Nexis, Appl. Sci. Technol. Index, Infobank, Bus. Period. Index. **LC** TN860. **CODEN** OIGJAV. Available on microfilm from University Microfilms. *Oil Investors Journal.*

OIL AND GAS LAW. See Law.

OIL & GAS (OXFORD, OXFORDSHIRE). See Law.

OIL AND GAS PRICE REGULATION ANALYST. V. 1- Jan. 1979-. 0199-3410. Periodical. US. English. mo. Executive Enterprise, 33 West 60th Street, New York NY 10023. **Tel** (212)489-2670. **LC** KF1860.A15. **DD** 343.7308522805.

THE OIL & GAS PRODUCING INDUSTRY IN YOUR STATE. Series/Titl Petroleum Independent. **VFOAT** Oil and Gas Producing Industry in Your State. 1984-. US. English. an. $12.00. Petroleum Independent Publishers Inc, 1101 16th Street Northwest, Washington DC 20036. **Tel** (202)857-4775. Ed Joseph Taylor. adv acc. **Circ** 12,000. Petro-gas production stats for US petro industry by state and other petro industry data i.e. labor, capital expended, invested. *Oil Producing Industry in Your State, 0191-0396.*

OIL AND GAS PRODUCTION IN KANSAS. 0273-3811. US. English. an. Kansas Geological Survey, University of Kansas, 1930 Avenue A, Campus West, Lawrence KS 66044. **LC** TN872.K2. **DD** 338.272809781.

OIL AND GAS PRODUCTION REPORT. 0702-8202. Periodical. CN. English. mo. $30.95. Minister of Finance, Ministry of Mines & Petroleum Research, Victoria British Columbia Canada. **Tel** (604)387-3188.

OIL AND GAS PRODUCTION REPORT. NORTHERN ROCKIES. 0270-5400. US. English. an. Petroleum Information Corporation, PO Box 2612, Denver CO 80201. **LC** HD9567.A17. **DD** 338.27280978.

OIL AND GAS PRODUCTION REPORT. SOUTHERN ROCKIES. 0270-5419. US. English. an. Petroleum Information Corporation, PO Box 2612, Denver CO 80201. **LC** HD9567.A165. **DD** 338.27280978.

OIL AND GAS PRODUCTION STATISTICS. See Statistics.

OIL & GAS REPORT. **VFOAT** Florida Petroleum Report. **VAT** Oil and Gas Report (Tallahassee, Fla.). Vol. 3, No. 7 (Aug. 18, 1972)-. 0735-7583. Periodical. US. English. wk. $84.00. Oil & Gas Report, PO Box 10151, Tallahassee FL 32302. **Tel** (904)222-0228. *News.*

OIL AND GAS REPORTER. V. 1- 1952-. 0472-7630. Periodical. US. English. mo. $115.00. Matthew Bender & Company Inc, 1275 Broadway, Albany NY 12201. **Tel** (800)833-9844.

OIL AND GAS STATISTICS. See Statistics.

OIL & GAS STOCKS HANDBOOK. See Business - Investments.

OIL & GAS TAX ALERT. See Business - Public Finance.

Petroleum and Natural Gas

OIL & GAS TAX QUARTERLY. VAT Oil and Gas Tax Quarterly. V. 1- Oct. 1951-. 0030-1396. Periodical. US. English. qt. $125.00. Matthew Bender & Company Inc, 1275 Broadway, Albany NY 12201. Tel (800)833-9844. Ind/Abst Leg. Resour. Index, Index Leg. Period., Coal Abstr., Energy Res. Abstr., Curr. Law Index. LC K15. DD 336.2786655. (cum index).

OIL & GAS TAXES NATURAL RESOURCES. VFOAT Oil and Gas Taxes—Natural Resources Report. Periodical. US. English. mo. Prentice-Hall, Sylvan Avenue, Englewood Cliffs NJ 07632.

OIL & GAS TECHNOLOGY. VFOAT Oil and Gas Technology. Vol. 7, No. 9 (Oct. 1984)-. 8750-4804. Periodical. US. English. bm. $6.00. Gordon Publications, 13 Emery Avenue, Randolph NJ 07801-0952. DD 338. *Petrochemical Equipment News, 0192-8554.*

OIL & PETROCHEMICAL POLLUTION. VFOAT Oil and Petrochemical Pollution. Vol. 1, No. 1-. 0143-7127. Periodical. UK. English. qt. 44.00 Domestic, 47.00 Foreign. Elsevier Applied Science Publishers, Crown House Linton Road, Barking Essex IG11 8JU England. Ed J Wardley Smith. Ind/Abst Electron. Commun. Abstr. J., ISMEC Bull., Pollut. Abstr. Indexes, Saf. Sci. Abstr. J., Excerpta Med., Ship Abstr., Energy Res. Abstr., Chem. Abstr. LC TD196.P4. DD 363.738205. CODEN OPPOD7. The principal aim is to publish up-to-date material of high quality in all areas of oil and petrochemical pollution.

OIL CONSERVATION PROJECTS AND GAS CONSERVATION. PROVINCE OF ALBERTA. (OIL CONSERVATION PROJECTS AND GAS CONSERVATION SCHEMES, PROVINCE OF ALBERTA). Main/Corp Alberta. Energy Resources Conservation Board. 1970-1977. 0380-433X. CN. English. an. Energy Resources Conservation Board, 640 5th Avenue Southwest, Calgary Alberta T2P 3G4 Canada. *Oil Conservation Projects and Gas Conservation Schemes, Province of Alberta, 0380-433X.*

THE OIL DAILY. No. 1- 1951-. 0030-1434. US. English. $347.00. Attn Barbara Davis, 1401 New York Avenue Northwest/Suite 500, Washington DC 20005. Tel (800)621-0050. Ed Devan Shumway. Ind/Abst Trade Ind. Index, Infobank. LC HD9561. DD 338.27282. adv acc. The daily newspaper of the petroleum industry reports on politics and energy; corporate events, product prices; oil finance and economics; exploration updates and environmental issues.

OIL DEVELOPMENT AND PRODUCTION IN INDIANA DURING . . . . 1954-. US. English. an. Indiana Department of Conservation, Geological Survey, Bloomington IN. DD 338.2.

OIL DIRECTORY OF ALASKA. See Yearbooks, Almanacs, Directories.

OIL DIRECTORY OF LOUISIANA AND PRODUCTION SURVEY. See Yearbooks, Almanacs, Directories.

OIL DIRECTORY OF TEXAS. See Yearbooks, Almanacs, Directories.

OIL EXPRESS. 0195-0576. Periodical. US. English. wk. $178.00. United Communications Group, 4550 Montgomery Avenue/Suite 700 North, Bethesda MD 20814. Tel (301)656-6666.

OIL, GAS. (OIL GAS : EUROPEAN MAGAZINE). 0342-5622. Periodical. English. sa. Urban Verlag-Hamburg Wien GMBH, PO Box 701606, D2000 Hamburg 70 West Germany. Ind/Abst Life Sci. Collect., Coal Abstr., Ship Abstr., Energy Inf. Abstr., Environ. Abstr., Energy Res. Abstr. LC TN860. DD 553.2805.

OIL, GAS & PETROCHEM EQUIPMENT. VAT Oil, Gas and Petrochem Equipment. V. 15, No. 9- July 1969-. 0030-1353. Periodical. US. English. mo. $20.00. Pennwell Publishing Company, PO Box 1260, Tulsa OK 74101. Tel (918)835-3161. Ind/Abst Pet. Abstr. LC TN871.5. DD 622.338028.

OIL, GAS, MARINE DIRECTORY OF THE GULF SOUTH/ATLANTIC COAST. See Yearbooks, Almanacs, Directories.

OIL IN CALIFORNIA. 0279-6325. Periodical. US. English. mo. $264.00. Petroleum Information Corporation, PO Box 2612, Denver CO 80201.

OIL IN THE ROCKIES. 0276-5985. Periodical. US. English. mo. $264.00. Petroleum Information Corporation, PO Box 2612, Denver CO 80201.

OIL INDUSTRY COMPARATIVE APPRAISALS. 0276-5993. Periodical. US. English. mo. $425.00. John S Herold Inc, 35 Mason Street, Greenwich CT 06830. Tel (203)869-2585.

OIL INDUSTRY GAZETTE. V. 1- May 1975-. 0360-8026. US. English. Bitting & Company, 111 South Bemiston Avenue, St Louis MO 63105. LC HD9564. DD 338.272820973.

OIL INDUSTRY NEWS. VFOAT OIN. 0743-6289. Periodical. US. English. mo. $12.00 Domestic, $30.00 Foreign. Oil Industry News, 1610 28th Street, Bakersfield CA 93301.

OIL INDUSTRY OUTLOOK FOR THE UNITED STATES. 1st Ed.- 0741-3343. US. English. an. $150.00 US and Canada, $187.50 all other countries. Pennwell Directories, Box 1260, Tulsa OK 74101. Tel (918)835-3161. Ed Robert J Beck. LC HD9561. DD 338.272820973. Circ 1,000. Assembles all the elements in the petroleum industry picture to help you plan strategies and reduce prices.

OIL INDUSTRY U.S.A. VAT Oil Industry United States of America. 0364-6831. US. English. LC HD9561. DD 338.272820973. *Oil Industry U.S.A., 0364-6831.*

THE OIL LETTER. 0196-8246. Periodical. US. English. wk. $97.00. Observer Publishing Company, 3635 Ordway Street Northwest, Washington DC 20016.

OIL, LIFESTREAM OF PROGRESS. VFOAT Oil Progress. V. 1- July 1951-. 0030-1310. Periodical. US. English. qt. Caltex Petroleum Corporation, PO Box 619500, Dallas TX 75261. Tel (214)830-1000. Ind/Abst Index Free Period. LC HD9560.1. DD 338.2728.

OIL PATCH. V. 1- July/Aug. 1977-. 0164-887X. Periodical. US. English. bm. 20.00. Resource Publications Inc, 3210 Marquart, Houston TX 77027. Tel (713)961-4191. Ed John W Wilson. DD 553. adv acc. Circ 15,500. (ctrl). Covers drilling and production in Texas, Louisiana, Oklahoma, Alabama, Mississippi, Arkansas, and Florida. Features include surveys on fluids, bits, steel and filtration.

OIL PATCH (EDMONTON, ALTA.). (OIL PATCH). 0821-5162. Periodical. CN. English. ir. Free. Oil Patch, 10070-151 Street, Edmonton Alberta T5P 1T3 Canada. DD 338.272820971.

OIL PATCH HOTLINE. 0279-6333. Periodical. US. English. bw. $45.00. Hotline, Box 208, Williston ND 58801. Tel (701)774-8757. Ed Dennis M Blank. bk rev. adv acc. Circ 2,700. Regional, national, oil, gas, coal news, rig locations, land sale results, North Dakota, South Dakota, Montana, drilling permits issued, well completions, stock quotes, and climate.

OIL PIPE LINE TRANSPORT. Main/Corp Statistics Canada. Manufacturing and Primary Industries Division. VFOAT Transport du Petrole par Pipe-Lines. 1969-. 0410-5591. Periodical. CN. English (French). an. 10.00 Domestic, 11.00 Foreign. Receiver General for Canada, Statistics Canada Publications, Ottawa Ontario K1A 0T6 Canada. Tel (800)268-1151. Cubic metres of oil carried by gathering and trunk lines by province, by month; receipts and deliveries, cubic-metre kilometres, pipe line distance; balance sheet, property account revenues, revenues, expenses, income, employees, salaries and wages. *Oil Pipe Line Transport, 0410-5591.*

OIL PIPE LINE TRANSPORT. Main/Corp Canada. Statistique Canada. Division des Industries Manufacturieres et Primaires. VFOAT Transport du Petrole par Pipe-Lines. V. 22- Jan. 1972-. 0380-4615. CN. text in English and French. mo. 80.00 Domestic, 90.00 Foreign. Receiver General for Canada, Statistics Canada Publications, Ottawa Ontario K1A 0T6 Canada. Tel (800)268-1151. Receipts and deliveries by source and by movement of crude oil and refined petroleum products by gathering and trunk lines by provinces; barrel-miles, operating revenues. *Oil Pipe Line Transport, 0380-4615.*

OIL PRICE DATABOOK. VFOAT Oil Buyers' Guide Oil Price Databook. 0193-4171. US. English. $125.00. PO Box 998, Lakewood NJ 08701. LC HD9564. DD 338.4366550973.

OIL PRICE INFORMATION SERVICE. Vol. 1, No. 1 (Jan. 12, 1981)-. 0279-7801. Periodical. US. English. wk. $890.00. United Communications Group, 4550 Montgomery Avenue/Suite 700 N, Bethesda MD 20814. Tel (301)656-6666.

OIL PRICING, THE OIL WEAPON AND THE ARMS RACE IN THE MIDDLE EAST. 0160-5879. US. English. an. Harvard Square, Box 92, Cambridge MA 02138. LC HD9576.N36. DD 338.23.

THE OIL PRODUCING INDUSTRY IN YOUR STATE. Main/Corp Independent Petroleum Association of America. US. English. an. $23.50 for 2 years. I P A A National Headquarters, 1101 16th Street Northwest, Washington DC 20036. Tel (202)587-4760. Ed Deborah Rowell. LC HD9564. DD 338.2728. adv acc. Circ 20,000. Statistical profile of the 33 oil and gas producing states - including maps, tables and graphs covering drilling prices, production, reserves, etc. Also summarizes total US data in tables.

OIL SCOUTS DIRECTORY. See Yearbooks, Almanacs, Directories.

OIL SPILL INTELLIGENCE REPORT. V. 1- Oct. 1978-. 0195-3524. Periodical. US. English. wk. $487.00. Cahners Publishing Company, PO Box 716, Back Bay Annex, Boston MA 02117. Tel (617)536-7780.

OIL WORLD STATISTICS. See Statistics.

OILFIELD SERVICE, SUPPLY AND MANUFACTURERS WORLDWIDE DIRECTORY. See Yearbooks, Almanacs, Directories.

OILMAN. (THE OILMAN). Oct. 1982-. 0264-0759. Periodical. UK. English. Ind/Abst Fluidex, Life Sci. Collect., Comput. Control Abstr., Electr. Electron. Abstr., Sci. Abstr. Sect. A. Phys. Abstr., Energy Res. Abstr., Ship Abstr. LC TN871. DD 338.27280941. CODEN OLMNAQ. *Offshore Services and Technology.*

THE OKLAHOMA OIL REPORTER. 0745-2268. Periodical. US. English. da. $540.00. Oklahoma Business News Company, 605 NW 13th-Suite C, PO Box 1177, Oklahoma City OK 73101. Tel (405)521-1405. Ed Leroy A Ritter. (ctrl). Oil industry; Insurance filings; liquor licenses and laws; legislation; and energy and environment.

OLIPHANT WASHINGTON SERVICE. DIGEST AND CALENDAR OF ACTIVITIES OF POSSIBLE INTEREST. (OLIPHANT WASHINGTON SERVICE. DIGEST AND CALENDAR OF ACTIVITIES OF THE. . .CONGRESS . . . SESSION OF POSSIBLE INTEREST). 0733-0227. Periodical. US. English. wk. $250.00. Oliphant Washington Service, 1729 H Street NW, Washington DC 20006. Tel (202)298-7690.

OLJEMARKNADEN. No. 1 (Quarterly 1976)-. 0349-537X. SW. Swedish. qt. 200. Statens Pris Och Kartellnamnd Box 1115, S-111 81 Stockholm Sweden. Tel (08)142080 National, (468)142080 International. LC HD9575.S85. Circ 600. Descriptions of the Swedish and the international oil markets.

OLJYPOSTI. Finnish. ir. Free. Nest Oy, Keilaniemi, 02150 Espoo Finland. Tel 358-0-4501. Ed Helena Haapalinna. LC TP315. adv acc. Circ 35,000. Covers oil, refining, plastics, energy, exploration, petroleum, natural gas, shipping, environment, new technology, research.

ONGC BULLETIN. VFOAT Bulletin of Oil & Natural Gas Commission. Vol. 13, No. 1-2 (June & Dec. 1976)-. Periodical. II. English. sa. $10.00. Research & Training Institute Oil & Natural Gas Commission Kalagur, PO Box 40, Dehran Dum India. *Bulletin of the Oil & Natural Gas Commission, 0537-0094.*

OPEC BULLETIN. 0474-6279. Periodical. English. Ind/Abst Coal Abstr., Public Aff. Inf. Serv. Bull., Recent Publ. Artic. LC HD9560.1. DD 341.754722820601.

OPEC REVIEW. VFOAT O.P.E.C. Review. VAT Organization of Petroleum Exporting Countries Review. Began with Oct. 1976 issue. 0277-0180. Periodical. English. qt. $48.00. Pergamon Press, Maxwell House, Fairview Park, Elmsford NY 10523. Tel 265511. Ind/Abst Energy Inf. Abstr., Environ. Abstr., Energy Res. Abstr., Chem. Abstr., Public Aff. Inf. Serv. Bull. LC HD9560.1. DD 338.2728205. CODEN OPECDI.

OPERATING SECTION PROCEEDINGS. Main/Corp American Gas Association. Operating Section. VFOAT Proceedings. 0362-4994. US. English. an. American Gas

Petroleum and Natural Gas

Association, 1515 Wilson Boulevard, Arlington VA 22209. **Ind/Abst** Coal Abstr., Chem. Abstr., Energy Res. Abstr. **LC** TN880.A1. **DD** 665.705. **CODEN** POAGAB.

OUTER CONTINENTAL SHELF STANDARD. GSS-OSC. No. 1- 1976-. Periodical. US. English. ir.

OXY TODAY. Began publication with: No. 1 (Winter 1973). Periodical. US. English. qt. Occidental Petroleum Corporation, 10889 Wilshire Boulevard, Los Angeles CA 90024. **Tel** (213)879-1700.

PACIFIC OIL WORLD. V. 64- 1971-. 0008-1329. Periodical. US. English. mo. Pacific Oil World, PO Box 129, 222 South Brea Boulevard, Brea CA 92621. **Tel** (213)691-1419. Ed H Bob Roberts. **Ind/Abst** Energy Inf. Abstr., Environ. Abstr., GeoRef, Pet. Abstr., Bibliogr. Index Geol. **LC** TN860. **DD** 553.2820979. adv acc. **Circ** 3,000. *California Oil World, 0161-9950.*

PAPERS AND DISCUSSIONS - ARAB PETROLEUM CONGRESS. Main/Conf Arab Petroleum Congress. 1st- 1959-. 0570-5274. English. ir. **LC** TN863.

PCH. VFOAT Petroleum Concession Handbook. 0275-6129. US. English. qt. Barrows, PO Box 1591 Grand Central Station, New York NY 10017. **LC** HD9560.65. **DD** 333.339.

PEO. (PEO : PETROLEUM EQUIPMENT OUTLOOK). VFOAT P.E.O. 1984. 0744-9534. Periodical. US. English. wk. $247.00. Inside Gas Markets, 1101 Post Oak/Suite 306, Houston TX 77056. **Tel** (713)627-7128. Ed Geo Spencer. **Circ** 1,500. Report on gas markets from the oil and gas capital.

PERSPEKTIVANALYSEN. Norwegian. an. Oljedirektoratet, Lagardsv 80, 4000 Stavanger Norway.

PETROBRAS. Main/Corp Petroleo Brasileiro, S. A. Periodical. Portuguese. bm. Petroleo Brasileiro, Caixa Postal 809 ZC-00, Rio de Janeiro Brazil. **LC** HD9574.B84.

PETROBRAS. PETROBRAS NEWS. VFOAT Petrobras News. 0031-6334. Periodical. BL. English. mo. free. Petroleo Brasileiro SA, Forgn Reltns Div Av Chile 65 #20 Andar, 20035 Rio de Janeiro Brazil. **Tel** 21204477. Ed Cesar Francisco Alves. **Ind/Abst** Bibliogr. Index Geol. **Circ** 6,000. (ctrl). Newsletter on oil operations in Brazil as well as abroad, exports, petrochemicals, non oil mining, marketing, fertilizers, energy, alternatives.

PETROCHEMICAL NEWS. Began in 1963. 0031-6342. Periodical. US. English. wk. $350.00. William F Bland, PO Box 1421, Stamford CT 06904. **Tel** (203)359-1125. Ed Susan Bland Zaro. A report of current news about the worldwide petrochemical business.

PETROL SI GAZE. V. 1-25, No. 6. Periodical. Romanian (table of contents in Russian, French, German and English). mo. CNIT, St Ion Gaica 3, Bucharest Rumania. **Ind/Abst** CIS Abstr.

PETROLE. ELEMENTS STATISTIQUES (1968). See Statistics.

PETROLE ET ENTERPRISE. (OIL & ENTERPRISE). **VAT** Oil and Enterprise. No. 1 (Aug. 1983)-. 0755-7981. Periodical. French. mo. **Ind/Abst** Fluidex. **LC** TN860.P364. **DD** 338.2728205. *Industrie du Petrole. Gaz-Chimie.*

PETROLE ET TECHNIQUES. No 241- Feb. 1977-. 0152-5425. Periodical. FR. French. mo. Assn Francaise Tech du Petrole, 14 Avenue de la Grande Armee, Paris France 75017. **Ind/Abst** Coal Abstr., GeoRef, Energy Res. Abstr., Chem. Abstr. **LC** TN860. **DD** 665.505. **CODEN** PETEDX. *Revue de l'Association Francaise des Techniciens du Petrole.*

PETROLE INFORMATIONS. (PETROLE INFORMATIONS INTERNATIONAL). No 1583 (Jan. 15 1983). 0150-6463. Periodical. FR. French (English). bm. $123.05. Bureau d'Info Professionalles, 142 rue Montmartre, 75002 Paris France. **Tel** 42 61 83 21. Ed Elisabeth Liegeois. **Ind/Abst** Energy Res. Abstr. bk rev. adv acc. **Circ** 5,600. (ctrl). Comprehensive analysis of developments in the international industry. *Petrole Informations.*

EL PETROLEO. Main/Corp Petroleos Mexicanos. Spanish. ir. Petroleos Mexicanos, Marina Nacional No 329, Edificio 1810-1 Piso, Mexico City Mexico. **LC** TN873.M6.

PETROLEO E GAS. Main/Corp Shell Brasil, S. A. (Petroleo). Portuguese. ir. Shell Brazil, Av Rio Branco, 109-10 Andar, Rio de Janeiro Brazil. **LC** HD9560.1.

PETROLEO E PETROQUIMICA. No. 1- Oct. 1972-. Periodical. Portuguese. ir. 60.00. Engetec, Rua Nestor Pestana 125 50-CJ 54, Sao Paulo Brazil. **LC** HD9574.B8.

PETROLEO INTERNACIONAL. 0093-7851. Periodical. US. Spanish. bm. $12.00. Pennwell Publishing Company, PO Box 1260, Tulsa OK 74101. **Tel** (800)331-4463. **Ind/Abst** Predicasts, Chem. Abstr., GeoRef, Pet. Abstr., Funk Scott Index Corp. Ind. **LC** TN860. **CODEN** PTRIB2. *Petroleo y Petroquimica Internacional.*

PETROLEO Y OTROS DATOS ESTADISTICOS. See Statistics.

PETROLEUM ABSTRACTS INFORMATION SYSTEM DESCRIPTOR FREQUENCY LIST. See Indexes/Abstracts.

PETROLEUM ABSTRACTS (TULSA, OKLA.). See Indexes/Abstracts.

PETROLEUM ACTIVITY REPORT. Main/Corp Louisiana. Office of Conservation. Engineering Division. 0360-974X. Periodical. US. English. mo. **LC** TN872.L8. **DD** 353.9763008232. *Petroleum Activity Report, 0360-974X.*

PETROLEUM & NATURAL GAS INDUSTRY OF INDONESIA. English. ir. Direktorat Jenderal Minyak dan Gas Bumi, Jl M H Thamrin No 1, Jakarta Indonesia. **LC** HD9576.I5. **DD** 338.272809598.

PETROLEUM AND NATURAL GAS PRICE AND INCENTIVES HEARING. Main/Corp British Columbia. Energy Commission. CN. English. an. British Columbia Energy Commission, 1177 West Hastings Street, Vancouver British Columbia Canada. **LC** HD9574.C23. **DD** 338.23.

PETROLEUM ASIA JOURNAL. V. 1- Dec. 1978-. Periodical. II. English. qt. $250.00. Himachal Times Building, 57-B Rajpur Road, Dehra Dun India. **Ind/Abst** Life Sci. Collect. **LC** TP690.2.A78. **DD** 622.338095.

PETROLEUM ECONOMIST. (THE PETROLEUM ECONOMIST). V. 41- Jan. 1974-. 0306-395X. Periodical. UK. English. mo. $134.00. Petroleum Economist, 107 Charterhouse Street Box 105, London EC1M 6AY England. **Tel** 251-2501. Ed Bryan Cooper. **Ind/Abst** Trade Ind. Index, Predicasts, Coal Abstr., Ship Abstr., Energy Inf. Abstr., Environ. Abstr., GeoRef, Public Aff. Inf. Serv. Bull., Bus. Period. Index, Funk Scott Index Corp. Ind. **LC** HD9560.1. **DD** 338.272805. **CODEN** PEECDK. bk rev. adv acc. **Circ** 6,000. Worldwide coverage of the economic and financial implications of energy development, particularly oil, but including coal, gas, nuclear, etc. *Petroleum Press Service.*

PETROLEUM-ENERGY BUSINESS NEWS INDEX. See Indexes/Abstracts.

PETROLEUM ENGINEER INTERNATIONAL. V. 39, No. 6- June 1967-. 0164-8322. Periodical. US. English. ir. $38.00. Petroleum Engineering International, Energy Publishing Division of HBJ, PO Box 1589, Dallas TX 75221. **Tel** (214)691-3911. Ed W B Bleakley. **Ind/Abst** Energy Inf. Abstr., Environ. Abstr., Eng. Index Mon., Eng. Index Bioeng. Abstr., Eng. Index Energy Abstr., Life Sci. Collect., Excerpta Med., Ship Abstr., Energy Res. Abstr., Ref. Source, GeoRef, Eng. Index Annu., Appl. Sci. Technol. Index, Pet. Abstr., ISMEC Bull., Bibliogr. Index Geol., Eng. Index. **DD** 622. **CODEN** PENGA6. bk rev. adv acc. **Circ** 37,000. (ctrl). Issued also in microfilm by University Microfilms International. Edited for engineering, operating, contractor, management specialists active in international exploration, drilling, production for oil and gas.

PETROLEUM EXPLORATION MAP. 0277-6650. US. English. an. Indiana Geological Survey, 611 North Walnut Grove, Bloomington IN 47405. **Tel** (812)337-7636. **Ind/Abst** GeoRef.

PETROLEUM FRONTIERS. Vol. 1, No. 1-. 0740-1817. Periodical. US. English. qt. $100.00. Petroleum Information Corp, PO Box 2612, Denver CO 80201. **Ind/Abst** GeoRef. **LC** TN872. **DD** 553.280973.

PETROLEUM GAZETTE. 1952. 0048-3591. Periodical. AT. English. qt. Free. Australian Institute of Petroleum, 227 Collins Street, Melbourne Victoria 3000 Australia. **Tel** (03)654 1411. Ed Douglas Rose. **Ind/Abst** GeoRef. **LC** TN860. **Circ** 38,000. (ctrl). An aid to public understanding of the oil industry.

PETROLEUM GEOLOGY. V. 2- 1958-. Periodical. US. English. sm. Petroleum Geology, Box 171, McLean VA 22101. **Ind/Abst** Pet. Abstr., Bibliogr. Index Geol. **LC** TN860. **DD** 553.280947. Digest of soviet geological literature on oil and gas.

PETROLEUM INDEPENDENT. Vol. 41, No. 11 (Mar.-Apr. 1971)-. 0747-2528. Periodical. US. English. ir. $12.00. Independent Petroleum Association of America, 1101 16th Street Northwest, Washington DC 20036. **Tel** (201)857-4775. Ed Joseph Taylor. **Ind/Abst** Predicasts, Pet. Abstr., Funk Scott Index Corp. Ind. **LC** HD9561. **DD** 338.272820973. adv acc. **Circ** 12,000. Covers domestic petroleum industry, US independent producers, particular emphasis plus political developments in taxes, safety, that bear on industry. *Independent Petroleum Monthly.*

THE PETROLEUM INDUSTRY IN KOREA. English. ir. Korea Petroleum Association, Samil Boulevard, 22nd Floor 10, Kwanchul-dong Seoul Korea. **LC** HD9576.K6. **DD** 338.27282095195.

PETROLEUM INFORMATION INTERNATIONAL. VFOAT PII. Vol. 1, No. 1 (Oct. 5, 1981)-. 0730-7632. Periodical. US. English. wk. $276.00. Petroleum Information Corp, PO Box 1702, Houston TX 77251. **Tel** (713)961-5660. Ed James C Tanner. bk rev. Daily briefing on world oil and gas exploration.

PETROLEUM INFORMATION'S NATIONAL WILDCAT MONTHLY. (NATIONAL WILDCAT MONTHLY : AN ANALYSIS OF NEW FIELD EXPLORATION IN THE U.S). 0744-8007. Periodical. US. English. mo. National Wildcat Monthly, PO Box 2612, Denver CO 80201.

PETROLEUM INTELLIGENCE WEEKLY. Began in 1962. 0480-2160. US. English. wk. $1045.00. Petroleum Intelligence Weekly, One Times Square Plaza, New York NY 10036. **Tel** (212)575-1242. **LC** HD9560.1. **DD** 338.2728205.

PETROLEUM LAND JOURNAL. V. 1- (Mar. 22, 1968)-. 0315-8411. Periodical. CN. English. bw. Petroleum Land Journal, 737 8th Avenue SW, Calgary Alberta T2P 1H5 Canada.

PETROLEUM MARKET DATA. VFOAT Market Data. Periodical. US. English. wk. $192.00. Petroleum Market Data, 962 University Avenue, St Paul MN 55014. **Tel** (612)645-2913.

PETROLEUM MARKETER. 1933. 0362-7799. Periodical. US. English. bm. McKeand Publishing Inc, 636 First Avenue, West Haven CT 06516. Ed Jon Swebilius. **LC** HD9561. **DD** 338.272820973. adv acc. **Circ** 10,000. (ctrl). *Petroleum & TBA Marketer.*

PETROLEUM MARKETERS' HANDBOOK. 0747-5721. US. English. an. Petroleum Publications, PO Box 998, Lakewood NJ 08701. **LC** HD9563. **DD** 338.7622338202573.

PETROLEUM MARKETING MONTHLY. See Business - Marketing.

PETROLEUM NEWS. Began with vol. for Dec. 1978. 0253-0775. Periodical. HK. English. mo. Petroleum News Southeast Asia Ltd, 10th Floor, 146 Prince Edward Road, West Kowloon Hong Kong. **Ind/Abst** GeoRef. **LC** HD9576.S65. **DD** 338.272820959. *Petroleum News, Southeast Asia.*

PETROLEUM NEWS, SOUTHEAST ASIA. 1969. Periodical. HK. English. mo. $150.00. Petroleum News Southeast Asia, 146 Prince Edward Road West, Kowloon Hong Kong. **Tel** (03)805294. Ed Don Speakman and Hannah Moore. **Ind/Abst** Pet. Abstr., Bibliogr. Index Geol. **LC** HD9576.S65. **DD** 338.272820959. bk rev. adv acc. **Circ** 7,000. (ctrl). An energy magazine that covers Asia's whole oil scene.

PETROLEUM NEWSLETTER. (THE PETROLEUM NEWSLETTER). 0312-9837. Periodical. AT. English. qt. Free. Bureau of Mineral Resources, PO Box 378, Canberra Australian Capital Territory 2601 Australia. **Tel** (062)499111. **Ind/Abst** GeoRef. **LC** TN878.A1. **DD** 338.27280994. **CODEN** PNGGD3. **Circ** 1,000. (ctrl). Covers petroleum exploration and development in Australia includes seismic surveys, rigs, well names and status, wells and meters drilled.

Petroleum and Natural Gas

PETROLEUM OPERATIONS OF FARMER COOPERATIVES. See Economics - Cooperatives.

PETROLEUM OUTLOOK. V. 1- 1948-. 0031-6490. Periodical. US. English. mo. $65.00. Petroleum Outlook, 35 Mason Street, Greenwich CT 06830. Ind/Abst Energy Res. Abstr.

PETROLEUM PRODUCTION REVENUE FORECAST. Dec. 1978-. US. English. qt. Petroleum Revenue Division, Department of Revenue, 201 East 9th Avenue, Anchorage AK 99501. LC HJ4186.M56. DD 353.979800726.

PETROLEUM REFINERIES CEASED. Series/Titl Annual Census of Manufacturers. VFOAT Raffineries de Petrole. 1960-1980. 0068-7162. Periodical. CN. English (French). an. 20.00 Domestic, 21.00 Foreign. Receiver General for Canada, Statistics Canada Publications, Ottawa Ontario K1A 0T6 Canada. Tel (800)268-1151. DD 338.476655380971. Petroleum Products Industry, 0700-0200.

PETROLEUM REVIEW. Began with V. 22, No. 253, Jan 1968. 0020-3076. Periodical. UK. English. mo. $64.90. Institute of Petroleum, 61 New Cavendish Street, London W1M 8AP England. Tel 01 636 1004. Ed Geoffrey Mayhen. Ind/Abst Eng. Index, Eng. Index Bioeng. Abstr., Eng. Index Energy Abstr., Fluidex, Excerpta Med., Coal Abstr., Ship Abstr., GeoRef, Energy Res. Abstr., Ref. Source, Chem. Abstr., Eng. Index Mon., Eng. Index Annu., Energy Inf. Abstr., Environ. Abstr., Pet. Abstr. LC TP690.A1. DD 665.505. CODEN PETRB2. bk rev. adv acc. Circ 9,100. (ctrl). Magazine of the Institute of Petroleum containing news, features and other technical articles about oil, gas and petrochemicals, internationally. Review (Institute of Petroleum (Great Britain)), 0367-9810.

PETROLEUM SOFTWARE WORLDWIDE DIRECTORY. See Yearbooks, Almanacs, Directories.

PETROLEUM STATISTICS. See Statistics.

PETROLEUM SUPPLY ANNUAL. 1981-. US. English. an. Superintendent of Documents, US Government Printing Office, Washington DC 20402. LC HD9561. DD 338.4766550973. Crude Petroleum, Petroleum Products, and Natural Gas Liquids, 0162-623X; Petroleum Refineries in the United States and U.S. Territories, 0197-3711; Sales of Liquefied Petroleum Gases and Ethane in . . ., 0162-900X; Deliveries of Fuel Oil and Kerosene in . . ., 0744-0510.

PETROLEUM SUPPLY MONTHLY. Mar. 1982-. 0733-0553. Periodical. US. English. mo. $51.00. Superintendent of Documents, US Government Printing Office, Washington DC 20402. Tel (202)783-3238. Ind/Abst Predicasts, Chem. Abstr. LC HD9561. DD 338.272820973. CODEN PSMODO. Monthly Petroleum Statement, 0731-0188; Availability of Heavy Fuel Oils by Sulfur Levelby Sulfur Level; Monthly Petroleum Statistics Report, 0364-0205.

PETROLEUM TAXATION, PETROLEUM LEGISLATION REPORT. VFOAT World Petroleum Taxation and Legislation Report. No. 1- 1972-. 0733-6241. Periodical. US. English. bm. $800.00. Barrows Company Inc, 116 East 66th Street, New York NY 10021. Tel (212)772-1199. Letter on oil and law changes. Petroleum Taxation Report, Petroleum Legislation Report.

PETROLEUM TIMES (LONDON, ENGLAND : 1981). (PETROLEUM TIMES). Vol. 85, No. 2138 (Apr. 15, 1981)-. 0263-3590. Periodical. UK. English. mo. Business Press International Limited, Perrymount Road, Haywards Heath, W Sussex RH163BR England. Ind/Abst Fluidex, Predicasts, Coal Abstr., Energy Res. Abstr. LC HD9560. DD 333.82305. Microform. International Petroleum Times, 0141-4437.

PETROLEUM TODAY. V. 1- Autumn 1959-. 0031-6555. Periodical. US. English. qt. Committee on Public Affairs, American Petroleum Institute, 1220 L Street NW, Washington DC 20005. Ind/Abst Coal Abstr., GeoRef, Public Aff. Inf. Serv. Bull. LC TN860. DD 338.272820973. CODEN PTTDAU.

PETROLIERI INTERNATIONAL. VFOAT Petrolieri d'Italia. 0391-9919. Periodical. English or Italian. ir. 10.000. Via A Doria 3, Milano 20124 Italy. Ind/Abst Chem. Abstr. LC TN860. CODEN PTITDQ.

PETROMIN ASIA DIRECTORY. See Yearbooks, Almanacs, Directories.

PHILLIPS SHIELD. Oct. 1976-. 0161-2697. Periodical. US. English. qt. Ind/Abst Coal Abstr. LC HD9569.P53. DD 338.762233805.

PIPELINE. V. 46, No. 6- June 1974-. 0148-4443. Periodical. US. English. $17.00. Pipeline News, PO Box 22267, Houston TX 77207. Tel (713)662-0676. Ed Oliver Klinger. Ind/Abst Energy Res. Abstr., Met. Abstr., World Alum. Abstr., Chem. Abstr., Predicasts. LC HD9581.U5. DD 388.50973. CODEN PPLNAQ. bk rev. adv acc. Circ 13,000. (ctrl). Management, operations, engineering, and construction coverage of oil and gas pipeline industry. Pipeline News, 0032-0153.

PIPELINE & GAS JOURNAL. VAT Pipeline and Gas Journal. V. 197, No. 6- May 1970-. 0032-0188. Periodical. US. English. mo. Pipeline & Gas Journal, PO Box 1589, Dallas TX 75221. Tel (218)723-9200. Ind/Abst Trade Ind. Index, Eng. Index Mon., Eng. Index Bioeng. Abstr., Eng. Index Energy Abstr., Fluidex, Life Sci. Collect., Predicasts, Coal Abstr., Energy Inf. Abstr., Environ. Abstr., Int. Aerosp. Abstr., GeoRef, Energy Res. Abstr., Met. Abstr., World Alum. Abstr., Ref. Source, Eng. Index Mon., Eng. Index Annu., Appl. Sci. Technol. Index, Pet. Abstr., Funk Scott Index Corp. Ind., Bibliogr. Index Geol., Eng. Index. DD 338. CODEN PLGJAT. American Gas Journal, 0096-4409; Pipeline Engineer, 0096-8293.

PIPELINE DIGEST. 1963. 0197-1506. Periodical. US. English. sm. $65.00. Universal News Incorporated, Box 55225, Houston TX 77255. Tel (713)468-2626. Ed Thelma Marlowe. Ind/Abst Fluidex. LC TJ930. DD 621.867205. bk rev. adv acc. Circ 9,000. Twice monthly covers design, construction and operation of pipelines and related facilities, worldwide. Includes details of proposed projects, contracts awarded, and industry news.

PIPELINE UPDATE. No. 1- Apr. 26, 1976-. 0383-8145. Periodical. CN. English. bw. Canadian Wildlife Federation, 1673 Carling Avenue, Ottawa K2A 1C4 Canada. DD 333.82.

PL, PETROLEUM LEGISLATION. VFOAT Petroleum Legislation. 1970-. Periodical. US. English. mo. $2,950.00. Barrows Company Inc, 116 East 66th Street, New York NY 10021. Worldwide analysis by country.

PLATT'S OHA DIGEST. VFOAT OHA Digest. VAT Platt's Office of Hearings and Appeals Digest. V. 1- Nov. 5, 1979-. 0196-1454. Periodical. US. English. wk. $397.00. Platts Oilgram Service, PO Box 412, Highstown NJ 08520. Tel (212)997-3016. LC KF2120.A59. DD 346.730467902636, 347.306467902636.

PLATT'S OIL MARKETING BULLETIN. See Business - Marketing.

PLATT'S OIL POLICY AND REGULATION REPORT. VFOAT Platt's Oil Policy. 0278-2278. Periodical. US. English. wk. $357.00. Platts Oilgram Services, PO Box 412, Hightstown NJ 08520. Platt's Oil Regulation Report, 0190-4124.

PLATT'S OIL PRICE HANDBOOK AND OILMANAC. VFOAT Oil Price Handbook and Oilmanac. 29th- Ed. 0160-4457. US. English. an. $95.00. Platts Oilgrams/McGraw Hill, 1120 Vermont Avenue/Suite 1200, Washington DC 20005. Tel (212)997-3016. LC HD9564.A1. DD 338.23. Platt's Oil Price Handbook.

PLATT'S OILGRAM NEWS. VFOAT Oilgram News. 0163-1284. Periodical. US. English. da. Platts Oilgram News Service, 1221 Avenue of the Americas, New York NY 10020. Ind/Abst Nexis.

PLATT'S OILGRAM NEWS SERVICE. VFOAT Oilgram News Service. 0032-1427. Periodical. US. English. da. $507.00. McGraw-Hill Inc, 1221 Avenue of the Americas, New York NY 10020. LC HD9561. DD 338.2728.

PLATT'S OILGRAM PRICE REPORT. VFOAT Oilgram Price Report. 0163-1292. Periodical. US. English. da. $747.00. McGraw-Hill Inc, 1221 Avenue of the Americas, New York NY 10020. LC HD9561. DD 338.23. Platt's Oilgram Price Service, 0149-581X.

PREPRINTS - AMERICAN CHEMICAL SOCIETY. DIVISION OF PETROLEUM CHEMISTRY. See Chemistry.

PREPRINTS OF PAPERS PRESENTED - AMERICAN CHEMICAL SOCIETY. DIVISION OF FUEL CHEMISTRY. See Chemistry.

PRINCIPAL FINDINGS OF THE U.S. CRUDE OIL, NATURAL GAS, AND NATURAL GAS LIQUIDS RESERVES ANNUAL REPORT. (PRINCIPAL FINDINGS OF THE U.S. CRUDE OIL, NATURAL GAS, AND NATURAL GAS LIQUIDS RESERVES . . . ANNUAL REPORT). VFOAT Principal Findings of the US Crude Oil, Natural Gas, and Natural Gas Liquids Reserves . . . Annual Report. VAT Principal Findings of the United States Crude Oil, Natural Gas, and Natural Gas Liquids Reserves Annual Report. 0734-6697. US. English. an. US Department of Energy, Energy Information Administration, National Energy Information Center EI-20/Forrestal Building, Washington DC 20585. LC TN872. DD 553.280973.

PRINCIPLES & PRESENTATION. OIL AND GAS. VFOAT Principles and Presentation. 0736-6779. US. English. an. Peat Marwick Mitchell & Company, 345 Park Avenue, New York NY 10154. LC HF5686.P3. DD 657.862.

PROCEEDINGS - JOINT SPE/DOE SYMPOSIUM ON ENHANCED OIL RECOVERY. (PROCEEDINGS). Main/Conf Joint SPE/DOE Symposium on Enhanced Oil Recovery. VFOAT SPE/DOE Symposium on Enhanced Oil Recovery. VAT Proceedings - Joint Society of Petroleum Engineers/Department of Energy Symposium on Enhanced Oil Recovery, Proceedings - Joint SPE, DOE Symposium on Enhanced Oil Recovery. 1st-. 0278-3711. US. English. Ind/Abst GeoRef.

PROCEEDINGS OF SYNTHETIC PIPELINE GAS SYMPOSIUM. (PROCEEDINGS OF . . . SYNTHETIC PIPELINE GAS SYMPOSIUM). Main/Conf Synthetic Pipeline Gas Symposium. 0146-6267. US. English. ir. American Gas Association, 1515 Wilson Boulevard, Arlington VA 22209. Tel 703 524-2000. Ind/Abst Chem. Abstr. LC TP345.A1. DD 665.7705. CODEN PSGSD6.

PROCEEDINGS OF THE ANNUAL APPALACHIAN GAS MEASUREMENT SHORT COURSE. Main/Conf Appalachian Gas Measurement Short Course. VFOAT Proceedings of the Annual Gas Measurement Short Course. 28th- 1968-. US. English. an. Proceedings of the Annual Appalachian Gas Measurement Short Course.

PROCEEDINGS OF THE ANNUAL CONVENTION - INDONESIAN PETROLEUM ASSOCIATION. Main/Corp Indonesian Petroleum Association. Began with Vol. for 1972. 0126-1126. IO. English. ir. Indonesian Petroleum Association, 3 Jalan Menteng Raya, Jakarta Indonesia. Ind/Abst GeoRef, Chem. Abstr., Bibliogr. Index Geol. LC TN863. DD 553.2809598. CODEN PCIADK.

PROCEEDINGS OF THE ANNUAL INSTITUTE - EASTERN MINERAL LAW FOUNDATION (U.S.). ANNUAL INSTITUTE. See Law.

PROCEEDINGS OF THE . . . ANNUAL INSTITUTE OF OIL AND GAS LAW AND TAXATION. See Law.

PROCEEDINGS OF THE . . . ANNUAL INSTITUTE ON OIL AND GAS LAW AND TAXATION AS IT AFFECTS THE OIL AND GAS INDUSTRY CEASED. Main/Conf Institute on Oil and Gas Law and Taxation. VFOAT Institute on Oil and Gas Law and Taxation as it Affects the Oil and Gas Industry. 1st-10th. US. English. an. Matthew Bender & Company Inc, 1275 Broadway, Albany NY 12201. Tel (800)833-9844. Each issue contains an index to its own contents - no vol index - loose. (cum index).

PROCEEDINGS OF THE ANNUAL SOUTHWESTERN PETROLEUM SHORT COURSE. Main/Conf Southwestern Petroleum Short Course. 1953. 0361-5987. Periodical. US. English. an. $25.00. Texas Tech University, PO Box 4099 Tech Station, Lubbock TX 79409. Tel (806)742-3573. Ed D A Crawford. Ind/Abst Chem. Abstr., Eng. Index Annu., Eng. Index Mon., Eng. Index Bioeng. Abstr., Eng. Index Energy Abstr. CODEN PSPCD3. Circ 500. State-of-the-art technical papers on petroleum drilling, production reservoir operations and surface facilities with emphasis on artificial lift. Proceedings.

PROCEEDINGS OF THE CANADIAN GAS ASSOCIATION GAS MEASUREMENT SCHOOL. Main/Corp Canadian Gas Association. Gas Measurement School. Began with 1962? issue. 0705-0135. CN. English. an.

Petroleum and Natural Gas

Canadian Gas Association, 55 Scarsdale Road, Don Mills Ontario M3B 2R3 Canada. **DD** 665.74.

PROCEEDINGS OF THE GAS CONDITIONING CONFERENCE. **Main/Conf** Gas Conditionong Conference. 0474-067X. US. English. an. **Ind/Abst** Eng. Index Annu., Eng. Index Mon., Eng. Index Bioeng. Abstr., Eng. Index Energy Abstr., Coal Abstr., Energy Res. Abstr., Chem. Abstr. **CODEN** PGCCAL.

PROCEEDINGS OF THE NATIONAL INSTITUTE FOR PETROLEUM LANDMEN. **Main/Corp** National Institute for Petroleum Landmen. **VFOAT** National Institute for Petroleum Landmen. No.1- 1959. 0547-7441. Periodical. US. English. ir. M Bender, 1275 Broadway, Albany NY 12201. **LC** HD9561.

PROCEEDINGS OF THE SPECIAL COMMITTEE OF THE SENATE ON A NORTHERN GAS PIPELINE. **Main/Corp** Canada. Parliament. Senate. Special Committee on a Northern Gas Pipeline. **VFOAT** Deliberations du Comite Special du Senat sur un Pipe-Line pour la Gaz du Nord. **VAT** Nothern Gas Pipeline (Senate of Canada), Pipe-Line pour le Gaz du Nord (Senat du Canada). Mar. 21, 1978-. 0707-8994. Periodical. CN. English (text in French paralle columns). Queens Printer, c/o Receiver General of Canada, Ottawa Ontario K1A 0S9 Canada. **LC** TN880.5. **DD** 388.5.

PROCEEDINGS OF THE SPECIAL COMMITTEE OF THE SENATE ON THE NORTHERN PIPELINE. **Main/Corp** Canada. Parliament. Senate. Special Committee on the Northern Pipeline. **VFOAT** Deliberations du Comite Special du Senat sur le Pipe-Line du Nord. **VAT** Northern Pipeline, Pipe-Line du Nord. Nov. 15, 1978-. 0707-9001. CN. English (text in French in parallel columns). Queens Printer, c/o Receiver General of Canada, Ottawa Ontario K1A 0S9 Canada. **LC** TN880.5. **DD** 388.5.

PROCEEDINGS OF THE TECHNICAL SESSION : ANNUAL MEETING - KENTUCKY OIL AND GAS ASSOCIATION. **Main/Corp** Kentucky Oil and Gas Association. 1953-. US. English. an. **LC** QE115. **DD** 553.28062769.

PROCEEDINGS - REFINING DEPARTMENT. **Main/Corp** American Petroleum Institute. Division of Refining. V. 56- 1977-. 0163-495X. US. English. an. American Petroleum Institute, 1220 L Street NW, Washington DC 20005. **Tel** (214)741-6791. **Ind/Abst** Energy Res. Abstr., Chem. Abstr. **LC** TP690.A1. **DD** 665.53. Proceedings - American Petroleum Institute, Refining Department, 0364-4030.

PRODUCTION STATISTICS AND ACTIVITY REPORT. See Statistics.

PROPANE CANADA. Began with V. 61, No. 1 (Summer 1968). 0033-1260. Periodical. CN. English. bm. 12.00. Sanford Evans Communications Ltd, Box 6900, 1077 St James Street, Winnipeg Manitoba R3C 3B1 Canada. **Tel** (403)265-4750. Ed Scott Jeffrey. bk rev. adv acc. **Circ** 5,600. (ctrl). Edited for the Canadian LP Gas industry, devoting its energies to the promotion and well-being of the oil and gas marketplace. Canadian Gas Journal, 0366-5925.

QUARTERLY ECONOMIC REVIEW OF OIL IN LATIN AMERICA AND THE CARIBBEAN CEASED. 1976, 4th Quarter-1980. 0142-4327. Periodical. UK. English. qt. $66.00. Spencer House, 27 St James's Place, London SW1A 1NT England. **LC** HD9574.L28. **DD** 338.27282098. QER: Oil in Latin America and the Caribbean, 0306-4808.

QUARTERLY ECONOMIC REVIEW OF OIL IN THE FAR EAST AND AUSTRALASIA. See Economics - Economic History, Conditions.

QUARTERLY ECONOMIC REVIEW OF OIL IN THE MIDDLE EAST CEASED. 4th Quarter 1976-4th Quarter 1980. 0142-4335. Periodical. UK. English. qt. $66.00. Spencer House, 27 St James's Place, London SW1A 1NT England. **LC** HD9576.N36. **DD** 338.272820956. QER: Oil in the Middle East.

QUARTERLY ECONOMIC REVIEW OF OIL IN WESTERN EUROPE. 1976, 4th Quarter-. Periodical. UK. English. qt. $66.00. London Economist Intelligence Unit Ltd, Spencer House, 27 St-James's Place, London SW1A 1NT England. **LC** HD9575.A1. **DD** 338.27282094. QER: Oil in Western Europe, 0306-2066.

QUARTERLY ENERGY REVIEW. AFRICA. See Energy.

QUARTERLY OIL AND GAS STATISTICS. See Statistics.

QUARTERLY OIL STATISTICS. See Statistics.

QUARTERLY REPORT OF GAS INDUSTRY OPERATIONS. **VFOAT** Gas Industry Operations. 0197-503X. Periodical. US. English. qt. American Gas Association, 1515 Wilson Boulevard, Arlington VA 22209. **Tel** (703)524-2000.

QUARTERLY REVIEW OF DRILLING STATISTICS FOR THE UNITED STATES. See Statistics.

O R G A NEWS. **Main/Corp** Ontario Retail Gasoline and Automotive Service Association. Began publication in Nov. 1975?. 0383-9028. Periodical. CN. English. ir. Free to Members. Ontario Retail Gasoline and Automotive Service Association, 312 Dolomite Drive/Suite 210, Downsview Ontario M3J 2N2 Canada. **DD** 338.476292860971. Voice of the Ontario Gasoline Retailer, 0380-7142.

RAPPORT ANNUEL - COMITE DE CONCERTATION ET DE CONTROLE DU PETROLE. **Main/Corp** Belgium. Comite de Concertation et de Controle du Petrole. English. an. Ministere des Affaires Economiques Comite de Concertation et du Controle du Petrole, Rue de Mot, 30-1040 Bruxelles Belgium. **LC** HD9575.B4. **DD** 354.493008238806.

REFINED PETROLEUM PRODUCTS. **Main/Corp** Statistics Canada. Manufacturing and Primary Industries Division. **VFOAT** Produits Petroliers Raffines. V. 27- Jan. 1972-. 0380-8629. Periodical. CN. text in English and French. mo. $4.00. Statistics Canada, Publications Distribution, Ottawa Ontario K1A 0T6 Canada. Refined Petroleum Products, 0380-8629.

REFINED PETROLEUM PRODUCTS. VOLUME 2. CONSUMPTION OF PETROLEUM PRODUCTS. (REFINED PETROLEUM PRODUCTS : CONSUMPTION OF PETROLEUM PRODUCTS). **Main/Corp** Statistics Canada. Manufacturing and Primary Industries Division. **VFOAT** Produits Petroliers Raffines : Consommation des Produits Petroliers. 1970-. 0575-9587. CN. English (French). mo. Receiver General for Canada, Statistics Canada Publications, Ottawa Ontario K1A 0T6 Canada. **LC** HD9574.C2. **DD** 338.9766550971. Refined Petroleum Products.

REFINING, PETROCHEMICAL & GAS PROCESSING WORLDWIDE DIRECTORY. See Yearbooks, Almanacs, Directories.

RELATORIO DAS ATIVIDADES DE ... E PROGRAMACAO PARA . . . . **Main/Corp** Instituto Brasileiro de Petroleo. **VFOAT** Relatorio das Atividades de . . . . Portuguese. an. Instituto Brasileiro de Petroleo, Av rio Branco 156-10O Andar-Gr 1035, 20043 Rio de Janeiro RJ Brazil. **LC** HD9574.B8. Relatorio das Atividades em . . . .

REPORT - CALIFORNIA DIVISION OF OIL & GAS. (REPORT; TR TECHNICAL REPORT). **Main/Corp** California. Division of Oil and Gas. **VAT** Report - California Division of Oil and Gas. No. 1-. 0271-6984. Monographic Series. US. English. **Ind/Abst** GeoRef.

REPORT - COMMITTEE FOR THE STUDY OF THE INFLUENCE OF NATURAL GAS ON VEGETATION. See Biology - Botany.

REPORT - INDIA. DEPT. OF PETROLEUM. **Main/Corp** India. Dept. of Petroleum. 1982-83-. English. an. **LC** HD9576.I4. **DD** 354.54008238806. Annual Report (1980-81).

RESEARCH AND DEVELOPMENT - AMERICAN GAS ASSOCIATION. (RESEARCH AND DEVELOPMENT). **Main/Corp** American Gas Association. 0091-2786. US. English. American Gas Association, 1515 Wilson Boulevard, Arlington VA 22209. **LC** TP723. **DD** 665.7072073.

RESEARCH AND DEVELOPMENT PROGRAM FOR OUTER CONTINENTAL SHELF OIL AND GAS OPERATIONS, TECHNICAL REPORT. **Main/Corp** United States. Geological Survey. US. English. an. US Department of the Interior, Geological Survey, Reston Va 22092.

RESERVOIR ANNUAL. (RESERVOIR ANNUAL). **VFOAT** Saskatchewan Reservoir Annual. Began with 1977. 0707-2562. CN. English. an. **Ind/Abst** GeoRef. **LC** TN873.C22. **DD** 553.28097124. Petroleum & Natural Gas Reservoir Annual, 0704-5743.

RESPONSE. 0276-6043. Periodical. US. English. wk. American Petroleum Institute, 1220 Street Northwest, Washington DC 20005. **Tel** (214)741-6791.

RESUMOS INDICATIVOS DA INDUSTRIA DO PETROLEO. Began 1963. Portuguese. ir.

REVIEW - IMPERIAL OIL LIMITED. (THE REVIEW - IMPERIAL OIL LIMITED). **Main/Corp** Imperial Oil Limited. V. 60, No. 5 (Issue No. 331)- 1976-. 0700-5156. Periodical. CN. English. mo. Imperial Oil Ltd, 111 Sainte Clair Avenue West, Toronto Ontario M4W 1M5 Canada. **Ind/Abst** Can. Period. Index, Public Aff. Inf. Serv. Bull. **DD** 338.272820971. Imperial Oil Review, 0380-903X.

REVISTA DEL INSTITUTO MEXICANO DEL PETROLEO. **Main/Corp** Instituto Mexicano del Petroleo. Began with: Vol. 1, No. 1 (Jan. 1969). 0538-1428. Periodical. MX. Spanish (summaries in English). qt. $40.00. Instituto Mexicano del Petrole, Av de los/Cien Metros No 152, Mexico 14 DF Mexico. Ed Armando Comaduran D. **Ind/Abst** Eng. Index Annu., Eng. Index Mon., Eng. Index Bioeng. Abstr., Eng. Index Energy Abstr., GeoRef, Chem. Abstr., Eng. Index. **LC** TN873.M6. **CODEN** RVMPAX. (ctrl). Petroleum science and technology.

REVISTA DO GAS. Periodical. Portuguese. ir. Associgas, Av Paulista 1009 - 16, Sao Paulo Brazil. **LC** TP700. GLP.

REVISTA TECNICA INTEVEP. **VFOAT** Revista Tecnica de INTEVEP, Revista Tecnica I.N.T.E.V.E.P. Vol. 1, No. 1 (Jan. 1981)-. 0251-4478. Periodical. VE. English (Spanish). sm. Free. Revista Tecnica INTEVEP, Centro de Informacion Tecnica, Apartado Postal 76343, Caracas 1070A Venezuela. **Tel** (02)908-6643. **Ind/Abst** Eng. Index Annu., Eng. Index Mon., Eng. Index Bioeng. Abstr., Eng. Index Energy Abstr., Chem. Abstr. **CODEN** RTEIDT. **Circ** 5,000. (ctrl). A multidisciplinary journal that covers original research and development developed within the Venezuelan petroleum industry.

REVUE - COMPAGNIE PETROLIERE IMPERIALE. (LA REVUE - COMPAGNIE PETROLIERE IMPERIALE). **Main/Corp** Compagnie Petroliere Imperiale. V. 60, No. 4- (Issue No. 329-) 1976-. 0700-5148. Periodical. CN. French. Compagnie Petroliere Imperiale Ltee, CP 310, Montreal Quebec Canada. **Ind/Abst** Point Repere, Can. Period. Index. **DD** 054.1. Revue Imperial Oil, 0380-9048.

REVUE DE L'INSTITUT FRANCAIS DU PETROLE. **Main/Corp** Rueil-Malmaison, France. Institut Francais du Petrole. V. 29, No. 1- Jan./Feb. 1974-. 0373-532X. Periodical. FR. French (summaries in English and Spanish). bm. 920. Societe des Editions Technip, 27 rue Ginoux, 75737 Paris Cedex 15 France. **Tel** (1)45771108. Ed Jacqueline Funck. **Ind/Abst** Eng. Index Annu., Eng. Index Mon., Eng. Index Bioeng. Abstr., Eng. Index Energy Abstr., Excerpta Med., Coal Abstr., Energy Inf. Abstr., Environ. Abstr., GeoRef, Int. Aerosp. Abstr., Energy Res. Abstr., Chem. Abstr., Appl. Mech. Rev., Bibliogr. Index Geol., Sci. Cit. Index, Abr. Ed., Eng. Index. **LC** TP690.A1. **DD** 665.5. **CODEN** RFPTBH. **Circ** 1,700. Includes studies in fields linked to prospection, processing and use of hydrocarbons, oil, natural gas and their derivatives or alternative products. Revue de l'Institut Francais du Petrole et Annales des Combustibles Liquides, 0020-2274.

RIO BLANCO OIL SHALE COMPANY; ANNUAL PROGRESS REPORT, TRACT C-A. **VFOAT** Annual Progress Report Tract C-A. US. English. an. Rio Blanco Oil Shale Company, 2851 South Parker Road, Aurora CO 80014.

RISALAT AL-BATRUL AL-ARABI. **Main/Corp** Muassasat Risalat Al-Batrul Al-Arabi. Periodical. Arabic. ir. Muassasat Risalat Al-Batrul Al-Arabi, PO Box 6732, 3 Bayrut Lebanon. **LC** HD9578.A55.

ROCKY MOUNTAIN PETROLEUM DIRECTORY. See Yearbooks, Almanacs, Directories.

ROPA A UHLIE. Began in 1959-. 0035-8231. Periodical. Slovak (table of contents also in English, French, German, and Russian). mo. Slovart Foreign Trade Company Ltd, Gottwaldova Nam 6, 817 64 Bratislv Czechoslovakia. **Tel** 48841-49. **Ind/Abst** Met.

Petroleum and Natural Gas

Abstr., World Alum. Abstr., Chem. Abstr. **CODEN** ROUHAY.

SALES OF LUBRICATING AND INDUSTRIAL OILS AND GREASES *CEASED.* **Series/Titl** Current Industrial Reports. US. English. an. Commerce Department, Bureau of the Census, Washington DC 20233.

SCHEDULE OF WELLS DRILLED FOR OIL AND GAS. PROVINCE OF ALBERTA. (SCHEDULE OF WELLS DRILLED FOR OIL AND GAS, PROVINCE OF ALBERTA). **Main/Corp** Alberta. Energy Resources Conservation Board. **VAT** Schedule of Wells Drilled for Oil and Gas. 1971-1978. 0380-4305. **CN.** English. an. 500.00. Energy Resources Conservation Board, 640 5th Avenue SW, Calgary Alberta T2P 3G4 Canada. **Tel** (403)297-8311. **LC** HD873.C22. **DD** 338.27280257123. *Data on wells in Alberta. Schedule of Wells Drilled for Oil and Gas. Province of Alberta, 0380-4305.*

SCHEDULE OF WELLS DRILLED FOR OIL AND NATURAL GAS IN BRITISH COLUMBIA. **Main/Corp** Biritsh Columbia. Petroleum Resources Branch. **VFOAT** Schedule of Wells. **VAT** Schedule of Wells (Victoria). V. 3A- 1976-. 0524-5508. **CN.** English. an. Minister of Finance, Publications Section, Parliament Building, Victoria British Columbia V8V 1X4 Canada. **LC** TN873.C22. **DD** 553.2809711. *Schedule of Wells Drilled for Oil and Natural Gas in British Columbia, 0524-5508.*

SECRETARY GENERAL'S ANNUAL REPORT. **Main/Corp** Organization of Arab Petroleum Exporting Countries. General Secretariat. **VFOAT** Organisation of Arab Petroleum Exporting Countries Secretary General's Annual Report Presented to the . . . Ordinary Meeting of the Council of Ministers. 1st- 1974-. English. ir. Organization of Arab Petroleum Exporting Countries, PO Box 20501, Safat Kuwait. **LC** HD9578.A55. **DD** 341.7547282.

SEKIYU SHUNJU. Periodical. JA. Japanese. mo. 12000. Sekiyu Shunjusha 8-10 Toranomon 1 Minato-ku, Tokyo-to Japan. **LC** HD9576.J3.

SEKIYU TO SHOHI DOTAI TOKEI NENPO, SHO-KO- KOGYO. See Yearbooks, Almanacs, Directories.

SELECTED DOCUMENTS OF THE INTERNATIONAL PETROLEUM INDUSTRY. 1967-. US. English. ir. Information Department of the Organization of the Petroleum Exporting Countries, Obere Donaustrasse 93, 1020 Vienna Austria. **Tel** 26 55 110. **LC** Microfilm 05084 HD, HD9560.1. **DD** 341.75472282.

SERVICE STATION MANAGEMENT. See Transportation - Automobiles.

SHELL NEWS. 0275-3243. Periodical. US. English. bm. Shell Oil Company, 1 Shell Plaza, PO Box 2463, Houston TX 77001. **Ind/Abst** GeoRef. **LC** TP690.A1. **DD** 665.5065.

SHIH YU KAN TAN YU KAI FA. **VFOAT** Petroleum Exploration and Development. Began in 1974. Periodical. **CC.** Chinese (English). bm. $10.80. China Publication Centre, PO Box 2820, Beijing China. **Ind/Abst** GeoRef. **LC** TN870.5. **DD** 553.28205.

SHIYOU XUEBAO. (SHIH YU HSUEH PAO). **VFOAT** Acta Petrolei Sinica. Vol. 1, No. 1 (Jan. 1980)-. 0253-2697. Periodical. **CC.** Chinese (table of contents and abstracts in English). qt. China Publication Centre, PO Box 2820, Beijing China. **Ind/Abst** Fluidex, GeoRef, Energy Res. Abstr., Chem. Abstr. **CODEN** SYHPD9.

SOCIETY OF PETROLEUM ENGINEERS JOURNAL. **VFOAT** SPE Journal, SPEJ. Vol. 1, No. 1 (Mar. 1961)-. 0197-7520. Periodical. US. English. bm. $7.50 SPE-AIME Members, Engineering School Libraries, $15.00 Nonmembers. Society of Petroleum Engineers of the American Institute of Mechanical Engineers, 6200 North Central Expressway, Dallas TX 75206. **Ind/Abst** Eng. Index Mon., Eng. Index Bioeng. Abstr., Eng. Index Energy Abstr., Life Sci. Collect., Fluidex, Excerpta Med., Coal Abstr., Energy Inf. Abstr., Environ. Abstr., Appl. Sci. Technol. Index, Energy Res. Abstr., Chem. Abstr., Eng. Index Annu., Eng. Index Mon., Nuci. Sci. Abstr., Sel. Water Resour. Abstr., GeoRef. **LC** TN860.S66. **DD** 665.505. **CODEN** SPTJAJ.

SOGYU. **VFOAT** Petroleum. Periodical. KO. Korean. qt. Free. Hanguk Sogyu Kaebal Kongsa, 45 Mugyo-dong, Chung-ku, Seoul South Korea. **LC** HD9560.1.

SOGYU HYOPHOE PO. Began with Mar. 1981 issue. Periodical. KO. Korean. mo. Taehan Sogyu Hyophoe, 10 Kwanchol-Dong, Chongno-Ku, Seoul South Korea. **LC** HD9560.1.

SOGYU YONBO. 1982-. English (Korean). ir. Taehan Sogyu Hyophoe, 10 Kwanchol-Dong, Chongno-Ku, Seoul South Korea. **LC** HD9576.K6.

SOHIO. Vol. 52, No. 3 (Winter 1980/81)-. Periodical. US. English. qt. Government and Public Affairs, Department of Standard Oil Company, 1775 Guild Hall Building, Cleveland OH 44115. **Ind/Abst** Predicasts, Energy Inf. Abstr., Environ. Abstr., Energy Res. Abstr. *Sohioan.*

SOHIO NEWS. 0273-1843. Periodical. US. English. mo. The Standard Oil Company Ohio, 1762 Guildhall Building, J Eppink, Cleveland OH 44115. **Tel** (216)575-5568. **Ind/Abst** Funk Scott Index Corp. Ind.

SOUTH EAST ASIA OIL DIRECTORY, SINGAPORE. See Yearbooks, Almanacs, Directories.

SPEARS REPORT: PRODUCTION. (SPEARS REPORT, PRODUCTION). **Main/Corp** Spears and Associates. 0193-2438. US. English. Spears and Associates Inc, 5525 East 51st Street, Tulsa OK 74135. **LC** HD9569.S67. **DD** 338.4768176650973.

STANDARD OILER. **Main/Corp** Standard Oil Company of California. **VFOAT** Standard Oiler. Ceased with Vol. 46, No. 4 (June/July, 1984). 0738-2847. Periodical. US. English. ir. Standard Oil Company of California, 225 Bush Street, San Francisco CA 94104. **Ind/Abst** GeoRef. **DD** 338.

STANGER'S DRILLING FUND YEARBOOK. See Yearbooks, Almanacs, Directories.

STANVAC INDONESIA. Periodical. IO. Indonesian. qt. P T Stanvac Indonesia, JI H O S Cokroaminoto 85, Jakarta Pusat Indonesia. **LC** HD9576.I54.

STATE ACTION REPORTER, NATURAL GAS AND ELECTRIC POWER. ABSTRACTS/INDEX. See Indexes/Abstracts.

STATISTICAL REPORT - STATE OF ALASKA, ALASKA OIL AND GAS CONSERVATION COMMISSION. See Statistics.

STATISTICAL REPORT (WEST VIRGINIA. OFFICE OF OIL AND GAS). See Statistics.

STATISTICAL SUMMARY - CANADIAN GAS ASSOCIATION. See Statistics.

STATISTICAL YEAR BOOK - THE AUSTRALIAN GAS INDUSTRY. See Yearbooks, Almanacs, Directories.

STATISTICS OF INTERSTATE NATURAL GAS PIPELINE COMPANIES. See Statistics.

STATISTIQUES F. O. A. : DISTRIBUTION DES FUELS-OILS. See Statistics.

STATUS OF THE CONSUMER PRICE EQUALIZATION FUND . . . . PH. English. ir. Ministry of Energy, 7901 Makati Avenue, Makati Metro Manila Philippines. **LC** HD9576.P6. **DD** 354.599007247.

STATUTS, LISTE DES MEMBRES - INSTITUT BELGE DU PETROLE. **Main/Corp** Institut Belge du Petrole. **VFOAT** Statuten, Ledenlijst - Belgisch Petroleum Instituut. BE. Flemish and French. ir. Institut Belge du Petrole, Rue de la Science 4, 1040 Bruxelles Belgium. **LC** HD9575.B42. **DD** 338.2272062493.

STRATEGIC PETROLEUM RESERVE ANNUAL REPORT. Began with 1980. 0199-9613. US. English. an. National Technical Information Service, 5285 Port Royal Road, Springfield VA 22161. **LC** TP692.5. **DD** 333.8232110973. *Annual Strategic Petroleum Reserve Report, 0162-9891.*

STROITELSTVO TRUBOPROVODOV. Vol. 1- March 1956-. Periodical. UR. Russian. mo. $33.50. Victor Kamkin Inc (70888), 12224 Parklawn Drive, Rockville MD 20852. **Tel** (301)881-5973. **LC** TN879.5.

SUMMARY OF NATURAL GAS STATISTICS. See Statistics.

SUMMARY OF OIL FIELDS WELL CHANGES. (SUMMARY OF . . . OIL FIELDS WELL CHANGES). 0276-8453. US. English. Conservation Committee of California Oil Producers, 417 South Hill Street, Room 868, Los Angeles CA 90013.

SUMMARY OF RATE SCHEDULES OF NATURAL GAS PIPELINE COMPANIES AS FILED WITH THE FEDERAL ENERGY REGULATORY COMMISSION AND THE NATURAL ENERGY BOARD OF CANADA. (SUMMARY OF RATE SCHEDULES OF NATURAL GAS PIPELINE COMPANIES AS FILED WITH THE FEDERAL ENERGY REGULATORY COMMISSION AND THE NATIONAL ENERGY BOARD OF CANADA). **Main/Corp** H. Zinder & Associates. 0190-2997. US. English. sa. $150.00. H Zinder & Associates Inc, 1828 L Street NW, Washington DC 20036. **Tel** (202)862-3446. **LC** HD9581.U53. **DD** 338.43. *Summary of Rate Schedules of Natural Gas Pipeline Companies as Filed with Federal Power Commission, 0146-1907.*

SUPPLY, DISPOSITION, AND STOCKS OF ALL OILS BY P.A.D. DISTRICTS AND IMPORTS INTO THE UNITED STATES, BY COUNTRY. **Main/Corp** United States. Energy Information Administration. Office of Oil and Gas Statistics. **Series/Titl** Energy Data Reports. US. English. an. US Department of Energy, Energy Information Administration, Washington DC 20461.

A SURVEY OF FINANCIAL REPORTING AND ACCOUNTING DEVELOPMENTS IN THE PETROLEUM INDUSTRY. See Business - Accounting.

A SURVEY OF SECONDARY AND ENHANCED RECOVERY OPERATIONS IN TEXAS. **Main/Corp** Texas. Railroad Commission. Oil and Gas Division. Engineering Research and Inspection. 1976-. 0161-5920. US. English. be. $32.00. Railroad Commission of Texas, Capitol Station/PO Drawer 12967, Austin TX 78711. **Tel** (512)475-2439. **LC** TN864, TN872. **DD** 665.509764 S, 622. 338209764. *Survey of Enhanced Recovery Operations in Texas.*

SYMPOSIUM ON PETROLEUM ECONOMICS AND EVALUATION. US. English. ir. Society of Petroleum of Engineers, PO Box 833836, Richardson TX 75083. **Tel** (214)669-3377.

SYNERGY (EDMONTON, ALTA.). (SYNERGY). Vol. 1, No. 1 (Fall 1981)-. 0714-2307. Periodical. **CN.** English. qt. Free. Synergy, c/o Syncrude Canada, 10030-107 Street, Edmonton Alberta T5J 3E5 Canada. **DD** 338.7622338097123.

SYNFUELS HANDBOOK. **VAT** Synfuels Hand Book. 1980-. 0732-1120. US. English. an. $67.00. Coal Week, McGraw-Hill Publications Company, 457 National Press Building, Washington DC 20045. **LC** TP360. **DD** 662.6605.

SYNTHETIC FUELS UPDATE. SFU-81/1 (Jan. 1981)-. 0273-2971. US. English. mo. $45.00 Domestic, $90.00 Foreign. US Department of Energy, Technical Information Center, National Technical Information Service, 5285 Port Royal Road, Springfield VA 22161. **LC** TP360. **DD** 662.6605.

TAI-WAN CHU CHAN YEH NIEN PAO. **VFOAT** Shih yu hua Hsueh Kung Je Kan. Chinese. an. **LC** HD9579.C33. **DD** 338.476618040951249.

TAR PAPER. (THE TAR PAPER). Issue 1- May 1978-. 0704-9811. Periodical. **CN.** English. Free. Oil Sands Research Department, 6th Floor Highfield Place 10010-106 Street, Edmonton Alberta T5J 3L8 Canada. **Tel** (403)427-8382. **Ed** H Radvanyi-Starr. **Ind/Abst** Mintec, Min. Technol. Abstr., Minproc. **Circ** 2,000. (ctrl) *Information on and about oil sand, heavy oil and enhanced recovery processes. Contains listing of relevant meetings, courses, etc.*

TECHNICAL PAPERS. **Main/Corp** Institute of Petroleum (Great Britain). 1974-. Periodical. UK. English. mo. Institute of Petroleum, 61 New Cavendish Street, London W1M 8AR England. **Tel** (01)636-1004. **Ind/Abst** Eng. Index. (cum index). **Circ** 500. (ctrl) *Various matters dealing with petroleum. Journal.*

TECNICO COMERCIAL. Spanish. ir. Departamento de Difusion y Ceremonial, Esmeralda 255 Piso 8, Buenos Aires Argentina. **LC** TP690.2.A7.

TENTATIVE OIL AND GAS UNIT OF PRODUCTION VALUES. (TENTATIVE . . . OIL AND GAS UNIT OF PRODUCTION VALUES). 0883-7449. US. English. an. New York State Board of Equalization and Assessment Agency, Building #4, Governor Nelson A Rockefeller, Empire State Plaza, Albany NY 12223.

Petroleum and Natural Gas

TEXAS EXPLORATION AND PRODUCTION. VFOAT Texas Year Book. Vol. 1 (1973)-. 0092-7996. US. English. an. $35.00. International Oil Scouts Association, PO Box 2121, Austin TX 78767. Ind/Abst GeoRef. LC TN872.T4. DD 338.272809764. CODEN IOSRAN.

TEXAS NATURAL RESOURCES REPORTER. V. 1- Jan. 1977-. 0197-2340. Periodical. US. English. mo. $400.00. RPC Services Inc, 500 SW Tower, Austin TX 78701. Tel (512)472-7765. Ed Bonnie Sonnek. Circ 200. The publication covers seven state agencies that regulate natural resources, and includes 2 volumes of rules for the agencies.

TEXAS OIL REGISTER. 0272-8915. US. English. qt. $270.00. Howell Publ Company, PO Box 27561, Houston TX 77027. LC HD9567.T3. DD 338.7622338025764.

TIPRO REPORTER. Main/Corp Texas Independent Producers and Royalty Owners Association. VAT Texas Independent Producers and Royalty Owners Association Reporter. 0039-8403. Periodical. US. English. qt. $25.00. Texas Independent Producers Royalty Owners, 1770 Austin National Bank Tower, Austin TX 78701. Ind/Abst Energy Res. Abstr. LC HD9567.T3.

TOTAL GROUP FINANCIAL AND ECONOMIC STATEMENTS. Main/Corp Compagnie Francaise des Petroles. English. ir. Compagnie Francaise des Petroles, 5 rue Michel-Ange, Paris France. LC HD9572.9.C58. DD 338.887.

TP, TECHNIQUES PETROMONDE. VFOAT Techniques Petromonde. New Series, No. 1- 8 Sept. 1977-. Periodical. French. ir. 350. 99 Avenue du Roule, Nenilly-Sur-Seine 92200 France. LC TP690.A1. DD 338.47665505. Techniques du Petrole, Petromonde.

TRANSACTIONS OF THE SOCIETY OF PETROLEUM ENGINEERS. VFOAT Transactions. Vol. 267 (1979)-. 8756-8152. Periodical. US. English. an. Society of Petroleum Engineers, PO Box 64706, Dallas TX 75206. LC TN1. DD 665.505. Transactions of the Society of Petroleum Engineers of the American Institute of Mining, Metallurgical, and Petroleum Engineers, Inc., 0081-1696.

TRANSACTIONS OF THE SPWLA ANNUAL LOGGING SYMPOSIUM. Main/Corp Society of Professional Well Log Analysts. VFOAT Annual Logging Symposium Transactions. VAT Transactions of the Society of Professional Well Log Analysts Annual Logging Symposium. 1960. 0081-1718. US. English. an. Society of Professional Well Log Analysts, 66001 Gulf Freeway/Suite C129, Houston TX 77023. Tel (713)928-8925. Ind/Abst GeoRef, Chem. Abstr. CODEN SPWLA6. Circ 3,000. Technical articles dealing with formation evaluation.

TRENDS IN REFINERY CAPACITY AND UTILIZATION. See Engineering - Chemical Engineering.

TRUDY - VSESOIUZNYI NAUCHNO-ISSLEDOVATELSKII INSTITUT PO PERERABOTKE NEFTI. Main/Corp Vsesoiuznyi Nauchno-Issledovatelskii Institut Po Pererabotke Nefti. Monographic Series. UR. Russian. LC TP690.A1. Trudy.

TWENTIETH CENTURY PETROLEUM STATISTICS. See Statistics.

U. K. PETROLEUM INDUSTRY STATISTICS RELATING TO CONSUMPTION AND REFINERY PRODUCTION. See Statistics.

UAE OIL STATISTICAL REVIEW. See Statistics.

UK OFFSORE OIL & GAS DIRECTORY. See Yearbooks, Almanacs, Directories.

U.K. PETROLEUM INDUSTRY STATISTICS. CONSUMPTION AND REFINERY PRODUCTION. See Statistics.

UNDERGROUND STORAGE OF NATURAL GAS BY INTERSTATE PIPELINE COMPANIES. (UNDERGROUND STORAGE OF NATURAL GAS BY INTERSTATE PIPELINE COMPANIES FOR . . .). 0193-5658. US. English. an. Superintendent of Documents, US Government Printing Office, Washington DC 20402. LC TP756. DD 665.7420973.

UNIFORM SYSTEM OF ACCOUNTS PRESCRIBED FOR NATURAL GAS COMPANIES. Jan. 1, 1940-. US. English. ir. $12.60 Domestic, $15.65 Foreign. Federal Power Commission, Office of Public Information, Washington DC 20426.

U.S. CRUDE OIL DISTILLATION REFINING CAPACITY SURVEY. (U.S. CRUDE OIL DISTILLATION REFINING CAPACITY SURVEY FOR . . .). VFOAT US Crude Oil Distillation Refining Capacity Survey for . . . . VAT United States Crude Oil Distillation Refining Capacity Survey. 0740-9966. US. English. American Petroleum Institute, 2101 L Street NW, Washington DC 20037. LC TP690.3. DD 338.47665530973.

U.S. CRUDE OIL, NATURAL GAS, AND NATURAL GAS LIQUIDS RESERVES, ANNUAL REPORT. (U.S. CRUDE OIL, NATURAL GAS, AND NATURAL GAS LIQUIDS RESERVES . . . ANNUAL REPORT). VFOAT US Crude Oil, Natural Gas, and Natural Gas Liquids Reserves, Annual Report. 1979-. 0731-924X. US. English. an. US Government Printing Office, Superintendent of Documents, Washington DC 20402. LC TN872.A5. DD 553.280973. U.S. Crude Oil and Natural Gas Reserves, 0272-3670.

UNITED STATES FOREIGN TRADE. BUNDER FUELS. (UNITED STATES FOREIGN TRADE. FT810, BUNKER FUELS). Began with Jan. 1977. 0735-1828. US. English. mo. $19.00 Domestic, $23.75 Foreign. Superintendent of Documents, US Government Printing Office, Washington DC 20402. Ind/Abst Am. Stat. Index. LC HD9561. DD 382.4566550973. Bunker Fuels, 0363-6798.

U.S. OIL WEEK. VFOAT Oil Week. VAT United States Oil Week. 0502-9767. Periodical. US. English. wk. $199.00. Capitol Publications Inc, 1300 North 17th Street, Arlington VA 22209. Tel (703)528-5400. Ed Tom Guay. For oil marketers: regulations, litigation, alcohol fuels, storage tanks, major oil companies, fuel oil, refiners' gas and heating oil terminal prices and price changes, convenience store marketing.

UPPER TEXAS COAST REPORT. V. 1- July 26, 1977-. 0148-2157. Periodical. US. English. wk. $432.00. Petroleum Information Corporation, 375 Delaware Street, Denver CO 80223.

U.S.A. OIL INDUSTRY DIRECTORY. See Yearbooks, Almanacs, Directories.

THE VALUE OF OIL PRODUCERS. 0276-6027. Periodical. US. English. mo. $280.00. Buxton Incorporated, PO Box 7052, Reno NV 89510. Tel (702)825-5593. Ed W John Buxton. Circ 500.

WAGA KUNI SEKIYU KAIHATSU NO GENJO. Main/Corp Sekiyu Kogyo Remmei. Kikaku Chosabu. Japanese. ir. Jekiyu Kogyo Remmei Kikaku Chosabu, c/o Keidanren Kaikan Building, 9-4 Otemachi 1, Chiyoda-Ku 100 Tokyo Japan. LC HD9576.J3.

WEEKLY BPN PROPANE NEWSLETTER. VFOAT Weekly Propane Newsletter. VAT Weekly Butane Propane News Newsletter. 0193-4724. US. English. wk. $95.00. Butane-Propane News Inc, Box 419, Arcadia CA 91006. Tel (818)357-2168. Ed William Clark. Circ 2,100.

WEEKLY PETROLEUM STATUS REPORT. June 19, 1981-. US. English. wk. Superintendent of Documents, US Government Printing Office, Washington DC 20402. Tel (202)783-3238. Ind/Abst Am. Stat. Index. Energy Information Administration Weekly Petroleum Status Report.

WEEKLY PRODUCTION AND DRILLING STATISTICS, ALBERTA OIL AND GAS INDUSTRY. See Statistics.

WEEKLY STATISTICAL BULLETIN - AMERICAN PETROLEUM INSTITUTE, STATISTICS DEPARTMENT. See Statistics.

WELL SERVICING. V. 1- Jan./Feb. 1961-. 0043-2393. Periodical. US. English. bm. Associated Oil Well Servicing Center, 6060 North Central Expsy/Suite 538, Dallas TX 75206. Ind/Abst Pet. Abstr. LC TN860.

WESTERN CANADA OIL & GAS DIRECTORY. See Yearbooks, Almanacs, Directories.

WESTERN OIL REPORTER. 0043-3985. US. English. $3.00. A Bell, 2400 Curtis Street, Denver CO 80205. LC TN872. DD 338.27280978. Pacific States and Rocky Mountain Oil Reporter.

WESTERN PETROLEUM REGISTER. 33d- Ed. 0273-1762. US. English. an. $40.00. Frank M Chapman Publications Services, PO Box 4185, Glendale CA 91202. Tel (818)241-6856. Ed Frank Chapman. adv acc. Circ 1,000. Directory of Western oil, gas and energy industries, including companies, refineries, plants, personnel, associations, governmental agencies, contractors, manufacturers, distributors, services companies plus buyers guide. California Petroleum Register, 0198-7526.

THE WHOLE WORLD OIL DIRECTORY. See Yearbooks, Almanacs, Directories.

WORLD CRUDE OIL PRODUCTION. Series/Titl Energy Data Reports. VFOAT Petroleum Production, Annual. US. English. ir. Department of Energy, Consumer Affairs, Room 73054, Washington DC 20585.

WORLD NATURAL GAS. Series/Titl Energy Data Reports. Began with 1976. 0195-6965. US. English. an. Superintendent of Documents, US Government Printing Office, Washington DC 20402. LC HD9581.A1. DD 333.823305. World Natural Gas, Annual.

WORLD OIL. V. 126, No. 6- July 1947-. 0043-8790. Periodical. US. English. mo. Robert C Slick Circulation Manager, PO Box 2608, Houston TX 77001. Tel (713)529-4301. Ed T R Wright. Ind/Abst Eng. Index Annu., Eng. Index Mon., Eng. Index Bioeng. Abstr., Eng. Index Energy Abstr., Excerpta Med., Energy Inf. Abstr., Environ. Abstr., Predicasts, Sel. Water Resour. Abstr., Ship Abstr., Mintec, Min. Technol. Abstr., GeoRef, Chem. Abstr., Bus. Period. Index, Environ. Period. Bibliogr., Public Aff. Inf. Serv. Bull., Energy Res. Abstr., Appl. Sci. Technol. Index. LC TN860. DD 665.505. CODEN WOOIAS. adv acc. Circ 40,000. (ctrl). Available on microfilm from University Microfilms. Covers the exploration, drilling and production of oil and gas for management and technical personnel. World Weekly.

WORLD OIL MARKET ANALYSIS. June 1983-. 0824-5533. Periodical. CN. English. ty. Canadian Energy Research Institute, 3512-33 Street NW, Calgary Alberta T2L 2A6 Canada. DD 338.27282.

WORLD SOLID FUELS, ELECTRICITY, GAS, IRON AND STEEL AND PETROLEUM STATISTICS. See Statistics.

WORLD TRADE IN LIQUEFIED PETROLEUM GASES. US. English. Poten & Partners Inc, 711 3rd Avenue, New York NY 10017. LC HD9579.P4. DD 382.45665773.

WORLDWIDE PETROCHEMICAL DIRECTORY. See Yearbooks, Almanacs, Directories.

WORLDWIDE PIPELINE AND CONTRACTORS DIRECTORY. See Yearbooks, Almanacs, Directories.

WORLDWIDE PIPELINES AND CONTRACTORS DIRECTORY. See Yearbooks, Almanacs, Directories.

WORLDWIDE REFINING AND GAS PROCESSING DIRECTORY (TULSA, OKLA. : 1978). See Yearbooks, Almanacs, Directories.

WYOMING OIL AND GAS STATISTICS. See Statistics.

YANKEE OILMAN. 0044-0205. Periodical. US. English. mo. $10.00. New England Fuel Institute, Box A, Swampscott MA 01907. Tel (612)593-0177. Ed Lee Yaft. adv acc. Circ 4,500. (ctrl). Feature copy is primarily devoted to New England and oil heating and the related heating contracting industry.

YEAR BOOK FOR NORWEGIAN PETROLEUM SOCIETY. See Yearbooks, Almanacs, Directories.

YOUR ANNUAL MAP REVIEW OF CANADIAN OIL AND NATURAL GAS DEVELOPMENTS. Main/Corp Canadian Imperial Bank of Commerce. Petroleum and Natural Gas Dept. VAT Canadian Oil and Natural Gas Developments. Began publication in 1951. 0707-6231. CN. English. an. Free. Petroleum and Natural Gas Department of the Canadian Imperial Bank of

Commerce, PO Box 2585, Calgary Alberta T2P 2P2 Canada. DD 338.27280971.

YU TIEN KAI FA LUN WEN CHI. VFOAT Symposium on Oil Field Development. Vol. 1- (March 1982)-. Periodical. Chinese (abstracts in English). ir. 1.10. Shih Yu Kung Yeh Chu Pan She, Peking China. LC TN870. DD 622.338.

ZUMAQUE. Periodical. Spanish. ir. Sociedad Venezolana de Ingenieros de Petroleo, Los Caobos Apartado 20006, Caracas Venezuela. LC TN860. DD 338.27280987.

PETS

ACFA BULLETIN. (ACFA BULLETIN : OFFICIAL PUBLICATION OF THE AMERICAN CAT FANCIERS ASSOCIATION). VFOAT A.C.F.A. Bulletin. VAT American Cat Fanciers Association Bulletin. 0744-9631. Periodical. US. English. mo. American Cat Fanciers Association, PO Box 203, Point Lookout MO 65726.

AEGYON UI OL. Periodical. KO. Korean. ir. Taehan Kunyonggyon Hyophoe, 108-1 4-Ka Chungmu-Ro, Chung-Ku Seoul Korea. LC SF421.

THE AFGHAN HOUND REVIEW. 8750-9776. Periodical. US. English. bm. $28.00. The Afghan Hound Review, PO Box 30430, Santa Barbara CA 93130. Tel (805)682-1771. Ed Bo N Bengtson. DD 636. bk rev. adv acc. Circ 2,000. Specialist publication for Afghan Hound fanciers - show, racing, obedience, grooming, care, etc.

AKITA TAYORI. Began publication in 197-. 0381-7393. Periodical. CN. English. bm. L Gauthier, Editor, 2230 Somerset Road, Kelowna BC V1Z 2K8 Canada. DD 636.75.

AKVARIUM, TERARIUM. Periodical. Czech. ir. 30.00. PNS-Ustredni Expedice A, Dovoz Tisku Kafkova 19, 160 00 Praha 6 Czechoslovakia. LC SF456. DD 639.3405. *Akvarium a Terarium.*

THE AMERICAN BULLMASTIFF. 0002-774X. Periodical. US. English. qt. $2.00. The Greeleys, Box 13201, Syracuse NY 13261. LC SF429.B86. DD 636.73.

THE AMERICAN CHOW CHOW INC. 0194-5173. Periodical. US. English. qt. American Chow Chow, 3524 Linda Drive, Dallas TX 75220.

THE AMERICAN KENNEL CLUB SHOW, OBEDIENCE AND FIELD TRIAL AWARDS. VFOAT Show, Obedience and Field Trial Awards. Vol. 1, No. 1 (Jan. 1981)-. 0272-4383. US. English. mo. $18.00. American Kennel Club, 51 Madison Avenue, New York NY 10010. Tel (212)696-8226. adv acc. Circ 19,500. *Pure-Bred Dogs, American Kennel Gazette, 0033-4561.*

AMERICAN KENNEL CLUB STUD BOOK REGISTER. V. 1- 1879-. 0162-2013. Periodical. US. English. mo. $30.00. American Kennel Club, 51 Madison Ave, New York NY 10010. **Tel** (212)696-8226. LC SF423. Circ 500.

ANIMAG. V. 1- June 1978-. 0709-4116. Periodical. CN. French. ty. 35. Animag, CP 2024, Succursale Jacques Cartier, Sherbrooke Quebec J1J 3Y1 Canada. DD 636.088705.

ANIMAL CARE AND CONTROL. Vol 1 (Summer/Fall 1983)-. 0826-2306. Periodical. CN. English. sa. Free. Animal Control Centre, London England. DD 636.083.

ANIMAL MAGAZINE. (L'ANIMAL MAGAZINE). V. 1, No. 1 March, 1981. 0710-9148. Periodical. CN. French. bm. $10.00. L'Animal Magazine, CP 399 Succursale A, Longueuil Quebec J4H 3Z2 Canada. DD 636.088705.

ANIMAL ORGANIZATIONS & SERVICES DIRECTORY. See Yearbooks, Almanacs, Directories.

ANIMAL WELFARE. LIST OF REGISTERED CARRIERS AND INTERMEDIATE HANDLERS. VFOAT List of Registered Carriers and Intermediate Handlers. 0747-5136. US. English. an. USDA Animal and Plant Health Inspection Service, Veterinary Services, Washington DC 20250. LC SF415.5. DD 380.524.

ANIMALS CANADA. V. 7, No. 2- 1977-. 0706-8042. Periodical. CN. English. 10.00. Canadian Federation of Humane Societies, 101 Champagne Avenue, Ottawa Ontario K1S 4P3 Canada. Tel (613)728-2516. DD 179.306271. bk rev. adv acc. Circ 10,000. (ctrl). Addresses animal welfare issues, and promotes animal rights, humane education and responsible pet ownership, through articles and features by experts in those fields. *Newsletter, 0317-1116.*

ANIMALS' VOICE. See Veterinary Medicine, Animal Culture.

ANNUAL MEMBERSHIP ROSTER - SIMIAN SOCIETY OF AMERICA. Main/Corp Simian Society of America. US. English. an. Simian Society of America, Box 343, Wakefield MA 01880. LC SF459.P7. DD 636.98.

AQUARAMA. Periodical. French. ir. 24.00. Association pour la Vulguristion de l'Aquariophilie et Terrariophilie, 1 rue du Rocher 75008 Paris France. LC SF456. DD 639.3405.

BASENJI. (THE BASENJI). 0094-9744. Periodical. US. English. mo $12.00. The Basenji, 789 Linton Hill Road, Newtown PA 18940. Tel (215)860-8254. Ed Susan Coe. LC SF429.B15. DD 636.753. bk rev. adv acc. Circ 1,250. Publication for Basenji (dog) breeders, fanciers and pet owners. Sharing information.

BLOODLINES : DOG AND PET STOCK JOURNAL. 1913. Periodical. US. English. bm. $12.00. United Kennel Club Inc, 100 East Kilgore Road, Kalamazoo MI 49001. Tel (616)343-9020. Ed John J Miller. bk rev. adv acc. Circ 5,000. Devoted principally to working and show dogs, obedience training and trials. Includes information on health and care, training and events.

BOARDING KENNEL PROPRIETOR. 0190-0226. Periodical. US. English. mo. $12.50. Boarding Kennel Proprietor, 2785 North Speer Boulevard, Denver CO 80211. LC SF428. DD 646.708.

CANADIAN CANINE REVIEW. Vol. 1, No. 1 (May 1978)-. 0229-5555. Periodical. CN. English. mo. $10.00. Canine Review, 7534 Filley Drive, Delta BC V4C 6W5 Canada. DD 636.7009711.

CARING FOR ANIMALS (OTTAWA, ONT.). See Veterinary Medicine, Animal Culture.

CAT FANCIERS' NEWS. 1984. 0069-1003. Periodical. US. English. an. $21.95. Cat Fancier's Association, 1309 Allaire Avenue, Ocean NJ 07712. Tel (201)531-2390. Ed Marna Fogarty. adv acc. Circ 2,000. Articles on cats and cat shows.

CAT FANCY. VFOAT International Cat Fancy Magazine. 0008-7602. Periodical. US. English. mo. $32.00. Fancy Publications Inc, PO Box 2606, Boulder CO 80322. Tel (714)240-6001.

CAT WORLD. 0163-1926. Periodical. US. English. bm. $7.95 Domestic, $8.95 Foreign. Cat World, PO Box 35635, Phoenix AZ 85069.

CATS MAGAZINE. VFOAT Cats. 0008-8544. Periodical. US. English. mo. $18.50. Cats Magazine, PO Box 83048, Lincoln NE 68501. Tel (904)788-2770. Ed Linda J Walton. bk rev. adv acc. Circ 140,000. Regular edition provides general articles, care and health information, poems, photos, columns for all cat people. Exhibitor edition has 48-page insert for cat breeders and exhibitors.

CHILDREN & ANIMALS. See Education (General) - Theory, Practice of Education.

COLLIE CUES. 0279-0777. Periodical. US. English. mo. Collie Cues, 6200 Bay View Avenue, Richmond Heights CA 94806.

COLLIE REVIEW. 0744-0731. Periodical. US. English. mo. $25.00. Drucker Publications, 8760 Appian Way, Los Angeles CA 90046. Tel (213)553-9277. Ed M D Drucker. bk rev. adv acc. Circ 5,000. *Collie & Shetland Sheepdog Review.*

DOG FANCIER. (THE DOG FANCIER). May 1981-. 0711-5865. Periodical. CN. English. mo $18.00 Canada and US, $25.00 Others. The Dog Fancier, PO Box 160, Williamston Ontario K0C 2J0 Canada. DD 636.700971. *Canadian Dog Fancier, 0709-8154.*

DOG FANCY. VFOAT Dog Fancy Magazine, International Dog Fancy Magazine. V. 1- Sept./Oct. 1970-. 0012-4834. Periodical. US. English. mo. $15.97. Fancy Publications Inc, PO Box 4030, San Clemente CA 92672, (subscription address: Neodata PO Box 2606 Boulder CO 80322). Tel (714)498-1600.

DOG WORLD: THE COMPLETE ALL-BREED MAGAZINE. Began with V. 1, Jan. 1916. 0012-4893. Periodical. US. English. mo. $11.00. MacLean Hunter Publishing Corporation, 300 West Adams Street, Chicago IL 60606. Tel (312)726-2802. Ed Enid S Bergstrom. bk rev. adv acc. Circ 63,000. Everyone interested in purebred dogs.

DOGS IN CANADA. V. 28, No. 6- Mar. 1940-. 0012-4915. Periodical. CN. English. mo $35.60. Apex Publications & Publishing Ltd, 43 Railside Road, Don Mills Ontario M3A 3L9 Canada. Tel (416)441-3228. *Kennel and Bench, Dogs Annual, 0317-1485.*

FRESHWATER AND MARINE AQUARIUM. V. 1- Jan. 1978-. 0160-4317. Periodical. US. English. mo. $22.00. Freshwater and Marine Aquarium, PO Box 487, Sierra Madre CA 91024. Tel (818)355-1476. LC SF456. DD 639.3405.

GREYHOUND BREEDER'S JOURNAL. V. 1- 1977-. 0191-7633. US. English. Greyhound Breeder's Journal, 604 NW 3rd, Abilene KS 67410. LC SF429.G8.

GROOM & BOARD. VFOAT Groom and Board. V. 1, No. 1 (Jan./Feb. 1980)-. 0199-8366. Periodical. US. English. bm. $25.00. H H Backer Associates Inc, 207 South Wabash Avenue, Chicago IL 60604. LC SF427.5. DD 636.708305.

HODOWCA GOEBI POCZTOWYCH. V. 50, No. 1- Jan. 1976-. Periodical. PL. Polish. mo. ARS Polona, Krakowskie Przedmieschie 7, 00-608 Warsaw Poland.

HOUNDS AND HUNTING. 1903. 0018-6384. Periodical. US. English. mo. $10.00. Hounds and Hunting, Box 372-554 Derrick Road, Bradford PA 16701. Tel (814)368-6154. Ed R F Slike. bk rev. adv acc. Circ 12,000. The largest single breed magazine in the world devoted to field trial beagling and gun-dog trials and the beagle hound.

THE JOURNAL OF SMALL ANIMAL PRACTICE. See Veterinary Medicine, Animal Culture.

THE KENNEL GAZETTE : A MONTHLY JOURNAL PUBLISHED BY THE KENNEL CLUB. Periodical. UK. English. mo. $30.65. Kennel Club, 1-5 Charles Strasse/Piccadilly, London W1Y 8AB England. Tel 01 493 6651.

KENNEL REVIEW. Began with Jan. 1898 issued. 0164-4289. Periodical. US. English. ir. $18.00. B & E Publications, 828 North La Brea Avenue, Hollywood CA 90038. LC SF425.15. DD 636.7081105. *Collie, Dogology.*

KTQ CEASED. VFOAT Kitty Torture Quarterly. 0270-1162. Periodical. US. English. qt. $4.00. Skrabanek & Souby, 1907 West 42nd Street, Austin TX 78753. Tel (512)451-4884. Ailurophobia, cat disdain.

MAINSTREAM (ANIMAL PROTECTION INSTITUTE OF AMERICA). (MAINSTREAM). Periodical. US. English. qt. $7.50. Animal Protection Institute of America, PO Box 22505, Sacramento CA 95822. Tel (916)422-1921. Ed Cathy Smith. bk rev. adv acc. Circ 80,000. (ctrl). To inform and educate readers about major animal welfare problems of the day and current events in the humane movement.

MY PET. V. 1- Winter 1979-. 0707-4360. Periodical. CN. English. qt. 8.49 (for 2 years). My Pet Magazine, Suite 302/160 Eglinton Avenue East, Toronto Ontario M4P 1G3 Canada. DD 636.088705.

NEWSLETTER - SIBERIAN HUSKY CLUB OF AMERICA. (NEWSLETTER). Main/Corp Siberian Husky Club of America. 0583-1776. Periodical. US. English. bm. Newsletter, c/o G Cingel, 118 Mott Hill Road, East Hampton CT 06424. LC SF429.S65. DD 636.73.

NOS ANIMAUX. Vol. 1, No 1 (June-July.)-. 0229-6926. Periodical. CN. French. bm. $7.74. Nos Animaux, 4930 Cote des Neiges, Montreal Quebec H3V 1H2 Canada. Tel (514)733-9461. Ed Francois Lubrina. Ind/Abst Point Repere. DD 636.088705. adv acc. Circ 25,000. (ctrl). For pet owners, wildlife defenders, veterinarians, and veterinary students. Covers animal health, practical advices, pet grooming, breeding, wildlife, current news and events, cruelty, and new available products.

OFF-LEAD. VAT Off Lead. 1971. 0094-0186. Periodical. US. English. mo. $18.00. Arner Publications, PO Drawer A 13 Clinton Street, Clark Mills NY 13321-0500. Tel (315)853-8375. Ed Lorenz D Arner. LC SF431. DD 636.7083. bk rev. adv acc. Circ

Pharmacy

5,000. Includes more than 10,000 dog owners actively engaged in dog care and training, including professional trainers, dog training clubs, sportsmen, government agencies, individual competitors, and house pet owners.

PET AGE. V. 1- July 1971-. 0098-5406. Periodical. US. English. mo. $25.00. H H Backer Associates Inc, 207 South Wabash Avenue, Chicago IL 60604. **Tel** (312)663-4040. LC SF414.7. DD 381.416088705.

THE PET ANIMAL HEALTH LETTER. Vol. 1, No. 1 (Feb. 1982)-. 0731-468X. Periodical. US. English. mo. $24.00. The Pet Animal Health Letter, PO Box 450521, Atlanta GA 30345.

PET BUSINESS. 0191-4766. Periodical. US. English. mo. $24.00. Pet Business Inc, 7330 NW 66th Street, Miami FL 33166. **Tel** (916)872-1200. *Aquarium Industry.*

PET DEALER. V. 1- Feb. 1927-. 0553-8572. Periodical. US. English. mo. $40.00. Howark Publishing Company, 567 Morris Avenue, Elizabeth NJ 07208. **Tel** (201)353-7373. Ed Alan Richman. LC SF411. DD 658.896366. bk rev. adv acc. **Circ** 13,000. (ctrl). Geared to the pet shop retailer/buyer of supplies and/or livestock.

PET LOVERS' GAZETTE. VFOAT Pet Lovers'. 0742-9746. Periodical. US. English. mo. $10.00. Pet Lovers' Gazette, 31 West Main Street, Marlton NJ 08053.

PET MASS MARKETING. See Business - Marketing.

PETFOOD INDUSTRY. V. 1- 1959-. 0031-6245. Periodical. US. English. bm. Watt Publishing Company, Sandstone Boulevard, 122 South Wesly, Mt Morris IL 61054.

PETS SUPPLIES MARKETING. See Business - Marketing.

PETS (TORONTO, ONT.). (PETS). VAT Pets Magazine (Sept./Oct. 1983)-. Vol. 1, No. 2 (Sept./Oct. 1983). 0715-8947. Periodical. CN. English. bm. 15.00. Moorshead Publications Ltd, 1300 Don Mills Road, Don Mills Ontario M3B 3M8 Canada. **Tel** 445-5600. Ed Halvor Moorshead. DD 636.088705. adv acc. **Circ** 76,000. Aimed at the pet-owning family. Distributed through veterinarians, pet stores and newsstands and by subscription. *Pets Magazine, 0822-8892.*

POMERANIAN REVIEW. VFOAT Pomeranian Review of the American Pomeranian Club, Inc. 0744-8546. Periodical. US. English. qt. American Pomeranian Club, PO Box 31927, Tucson AZ 85751.

THE POODLE REVIEW. 0477-5449. Periodical. US. English. bm. Poodle Review, PO Box 3067, Urbana IL 61801. LC SF429.P85. DD 636.72.

POODLE VARIETY. 0882-2816. Periodical. US. English. mo. $24.00. Poodle Variety, PO Box 30430, Santa Barbara CA 93130. **Tel** (805)682-1771. Ed Bo N Bengtson. DD 636. bk rev. adv acc. **Circ** 1,800. Specialist interest magazine for poodle fanciers interested in breeding, showing, obedience, etc.

POPULAR DOGS. V. 1- Jan. 6, 1928-. Periodical. US. English. wk. LC SF421.

PURE-BRED DOGS, AMERICAN KENNEL GAZETTE. VAT Pure Bred Dogs, American Kennel Gazette. 0033-4561. Periodical. US. English. mo. $18.00. American Kennel Club, 51 Madison Avenue, New York NY 10010. **Tel** (212)696-8260. Ed Patricia Beresford. LC SF421. DD 636.70973. bk rev. adv acc. **Circ** 50,000. Contains a wide range of articles to interest to the pure-bred dog fancier. Reports vital information in all areas of pure-bred dog breeding and showing. *American Kennel Gazette, Pure-Bred Dogs, 0737-8807.*

PURRRRR. Vol. 1, No. 1 (Apr. 1982)-. 0731-0366. Periodical. US. English. mo. $18.00. Meow Company, 118 Massachusetts Avenue/Suite 187, Boston MA 02115.

QUARTERLY - CANADIAN CAT ASSOCIATION. (THE QUARTERLY). VAT CCA Quarterly (1984), Canadian Cat Association Quarterly (1984). Vol. 21, No. 1 (Winter 1984)-. 0828-4865. Periodical. CN. French (English). qt. $12.00. Canadian Cat Association, R R 4, 12580 Chemin Heritage, Georgetown Ontario L7G 4S7 Canada. DD 636.8006071. *CCA Quarterly, 0711-074X.*

THE SAMOYED QUARTERLY. 0161-0651. Periodical. US. English. qt. $28.00. Samoyed Quarterly, 6917 West 83rd Way, Arvada CO 80003. LC SF429.S35. DD 636.73.

THE SETTER MAGAZINE. 0164-372X. Periodical. US. English. bm. $12.50. The Setter Magazine, 2254 Wyandotte Street, Mountain View CA 94043.

SHELTIE INTERNATIONAL. 0745-2012. Periodical. US. English. bm. Sheltie International, 2140 Vuelta Court, Carlsbad CA 92008.

SHELTIE PACESETTER. 0744-6608. Periodical. US. English. bm. $30.00. Sheltie Pacesetter, 28614 Quail Hill Drive, Rancho Palos Verdes CA 90274. **Tel** (213)541-7820.

SHOW RING. July/Aug. 1976-. 0701-0001. Periodical. CN. English. bm. $15.00. Show Ring Publications, PO Box 2077, New Westminster British Columbia 5A3 Canada. DD 636.70888.

THE SIBERIAN QUARTERLY. V. 1- Summer 1980-. 0274-7286. Periodical. US. English. qt. $24.00. Hoflin Publishing, 5766 Old Wadsworth Boulevard, Arvada CO 80002.

SIGHTHOUND REVIEW. Vol. 1, No. 1 (May–June 1984)-. 8750-1953. Periodical. US. English. bm. $24.00. Sighthound Review, 3145 Calle Frenso, Santa Barbara CA 93105. **Tel** (805)682-1771. Ed Bo N Bengtson. DD 636. bk rev. adv acc. **Circ** 2,000. Average 100+ pages Sighthound/Greyhound type breed fanciers: showing, racing, coursing, obedience, care, training, etc. *Sighthound, 0744-3323.*

SOUTHERN DOG LOVERS DIGEST. V. 1- Fall 1964-. 0561-1245. Periodical. US. English. qt. $2.00. PO Box 9270, Shreveport LA 71139. LC SF421. DD 636.7005.

STABLE & KENNEL NEWS OF THE SOUTH. See Horses and Horsemanship.

SV-ZEITUNG. VFOAT SV Zeitung. VAT Schaferhund Verein Zeitung. Periodical. German. mo. *Zeitung des Vereins fur Deutsche Schaferhunde.*

TROPICAL FISH HOBBYIST. V. 1- 1952/53-. 0041-3259. Periodical. US. English. mo. $15.00. T F H Publications, 211 West Sylvania Avenue, Neptune City NJ 07753. **Tel** (201)988-8400. Ed John Quinn. bk rev. adv acc. **Circ** 50,000. (ctrl). World's leading tropical fish magazine, features timely articles about rare and popular fish.

YORKSHIRE JOURNAL. 0044-0612. Periodical. US. English. mo. $10.00. American Yorkshire Club Inc, 1769 US 52 North Box 2417, West Lafayette IN 47906. **Tel** (317)436-3593. Ed Glenn E Conaster. **Circ** 4,000. Provides information for Yorkshire breeders to help breed and improve the Yorkshire breed.

THE YORKSHIRE TERRIER QUARTERLY. V. 1- May 1968-. Periodical. US. English. ir. Yorkshire Terrier Quarterly, Box 256, Times Square Station, New York NY 10036. LC SF429.Y6. DD 636.755.

YOUR FAMILY PET. Series/Titl Better Homes and Gardens Creative Ideas. VFOAT Family Pet. 0278-744X. Periodical. US. English. an. $2.25. Special Interest Publications, 1716 Locust Street, Des Moines IA 50336. LC SF411. DD 636.088705.

PHARMACY

483 VALIDATION MONITOR FOR STERILE, NON-STERILE AND MEDICAL DEVICES. See Medicine.

ABSTRACTS ON MANAGEMENT & ADMINISTRATION OF PHARMACY. See Indexes/Abstracts.

ACADEMY REPORTER. V. 1-17, No. 1. 0515-2089. Periodical. US. English. bm. $15.00. American Pharmaceutical Association, 2215 Constitution Avenue NW, Washington DC 20037. **Tel** (202)628-4410.

ACTA FARMACEUTIOA BONAERENSE : PUBLICACION DEL COLEGIO DE FARMACEUTICOS DE LA PROVINCIA DE BUENOS AIRES (ARGENTINA). Vol. 1, No. 1-. 0326-2383. Periodical. Spanish (summaries in English). sa. Calle 5 #966, La Plata 1900 Argentina. **Ind**/Abst Biol. Abstr., Chem. Abstr. CODEN AFBODJ. *Revista del Colegio de Farmaceutucis de la Provincia de Buenos Aires.*

ACTA PHARMACEUTICA FENNICA. V. 86- 1977-. 0356-3456. Periodical. articles mainly in English with some in Finnish. qt. Farmasian Laitos, Fabianinkatu 35, SF-00170 Helsinki 17 Finland. **Tel** 90-191 2766. Ed T Harmia. **Ind**/Abst Pestdoc, Ringdoc, Vetdoc, Excerpta Med., Chem. Abstr. NLM W1 AC917D. CODEN APHFDO. bk rev. adv acc. Publishes original papers, review articles and short communications in various branches of pharmacy with the understanding that they are subject to editorial revision. *Farmaseuttinen Aikakauslehti, 0367-259X.*

ACTA PHARMACEUTICA HUNGARICA. V. 23- 1953-. 0001-6659. Periodical. Hungarian. ir. **Ind**/Abst Pestdoc, Ringdoc, Vetdoc, Excerpta Med., Index Med., Chem. Abstr. NLM W1 AC917H. CODEN APHGAO. *Ertesitoje.*

ACTA PHARMACEUTICA SUECICA. 0001-6675. Periodical. SW. English (French and German). bm. $37.00. Swedish Academy of Pharmaceutical Sciences, Box 1136 S-111, 81 Stockholm Sweden. **Ind**/Abst Life Sci. Collect., Pestdoc, Ringdoc, Vetdoc, Excerpta Med., Biol. Abstr., Chem. Abstr., Nuci. Sci. Abstr., Index Med., Sci. Cit. Index, Abr. Ed. NLM W1 AC9177. CODEN APSXAS.

ACTA PHARMACEUTICA TECHNOLOGICA. VFOAT APV-Informationsdienst. VAT Arbeitsgemeinschaft fur Pharmazeutische Verfahrenstechnik Informationsdienst. 21-. 0340-3157. Periodical. English (German). qt. 116,-. Wissenschaftliche Verlagsgesellschaft, Postfach 40, D7000 Stuttgart 1 West Germany. **Tel** (0711)2582-0. **Ind**/Abst Pestdoc, Ringdoc, Vetdoc, Excerpta Med., Chem. Abstr. NLM W1 AC9177J. CODEN APTEDD. bk rev. adv acc. **Circ** 2,500. (ctrl). *Informationsdienst - Arbeitsgemeinschaft fur Pharmazeutische Verfahrenstechnik E. V. APV Mainz, 0001-2254.*

ACTA PHARMACEUTICA TURCICA. Vol. 26, Sayi 1 (1984)-. Periodical. Turkish. **Ind**/Abst Chem. Abstr., Life Sci. Collect. CODEN APTUES. *Eczacilik Bulteni.*

ACTA PHARMACOLOGICA ET TOXICOLOGICA. V. 1- 1945-. 0001-6683. Periodical. DK. English (articles in French or German). $114.43. Munksgaard International Publishers Limited, 35 Norre Sogade, DK-1370 Copenhagen K Denmark. **Tel** 1.12.70.30. Ed Jeus Schou. **Ind**/Abst Life Sci. Collect., Pestdoc, Ringdoc, Vetdoc, Excerpta Med., CIS Abstr., Biol. Abstr., Chem. Abstr., Psychol. Abstr., Nuci. Sci. Abstr., Index Med., Sel. Water Resour. Abstr., Energy Res. Abstr., Sci. Cit. Index, Abr. Ed. NLM W1 AC9182. CODEN APTOA6. adv acc. **Circ** 1,000. Forensic medicine, pharmacology and toxicology.

ACTA PHYSIOLOGICA ET PHARMACOLOGICA BULGARICA. See Biology - Physiology.

ACTA POLONIAE PHARMACEUTICA. Began in 1937. 0001-6837. Periodical. PL. Polish. bm. ARS Polona, Krakowskie Przedmiescie 7, 00-068 Warsaw Poland. **Ind**/Abst Chem. Abstr., Excerpta Med., Index Med., Pestdoc, Ringdoc, Vetdoc, Index Dent. Lit. NLM W1 AC927. CODEN APPHAX.

ACTA THERAPEUTICA. V. 1- 1975-. 0378-0619. Periodical. BE. articles in Dutch, English, or French. qt. $39.52. Acta Therapeutica, Place de Bastogne 8, B-1080 Brussels Belgium. **Tel** 32/2/759 40 45. Ed L Van Keer. **Ind**/Abst Pestdoc, Ringdoc, Vetdoc, Excerpta Med., Chem. Abstr. NLM W1 AC95K. CODEN ACTTDZ. **Circ** 4,000. Journal of pharmaceutical medicine for the publication of papers relating to the preclinical and clinical development of drugs for human use.

ACTUALITES DE CHIMIE ANALYTIQUE, ORGANIQUE, PHARMACEUTIQUE ET BROMATOLOGIQUE. See Chemistry.

ACTUALITES PHARMACOLOGIQUES. V. 1- 1949-. 0567-8854. Periodical. French. ir. Scientific & Medical Publishers of France, 16 East 34th Street, New York NY 10016. **Tel** (212)683-4441. Ed R Hazard. **Ind**/Abst Pestdoc, Ringdoc, Vetdoc, Chem. Abstr., Index Med. NLM W1 AC997D. CODEN ACPMAP. *Pharmaco, 0395-966X.*

ADVANCES IN BIOCHEMICAL PSYCHOPHARMACOLOGY. See Medicine - Neurology.

Pharmacy

ADVANCES IN CYTOPHARMACOLOGY. See Biology - Cytology and Histology.

ADVANCES IN DRUG RESEARCH. V. 1- 1964-. 0065-2490. UK. English. ir. Ed N J Harper and A B Simmonds. **Ind/Abst** Life Sci. Collect., Pestdoc, Ringdoc, Vetdoc. **LC** RS1. **DD** 615.1072. **NLM** W1 AD549R.

ADVANCES IN PHARMACEUTICAL SCIENCES. V. 1- 1964-. 0065-3136. UK. English. ir. Academic Press, 4805 Sand Lake Road, Orlando FL 32887. **Tel** (305)345-4100. Ed H S Bean, A H Beckett and J E Carless. **Ind/Abst** Pestdoc, Ringdoc, Vetdoc, Index Med. **LC** RS1. **NLM** W1 AD774.

ADVANCES IN PHARMACOLOGY AND CHEMOTHERAPY. V. 7- 1969-. 0065-3144. US. English. ir. $45.00. Academic Press, c/o Library Services, Orlando FL 32887. **Tel** (305)345-2000. Ed Silvio Garattini, Abraham Goldin Frank Hawking and Irwin J Kopin. **Ind/Abst** Life Sci. Collect., Pestdoc, Ringdoc, Vetdoc, Excerpta Med., Index Med., Chem. Abstr., Energy Res. Abstr., Sci. Cit. Index, Abr. Ed. **LC** RM30. **DD** 615.05. **NLM** W1 AD78K. **CODEN** AVPCAQ. *Advances in Pharmacology, Advances in Chemotherapy.*

ADVANCES IN PHARMACOTHERAPY. Vol. 1-. 0253-2093. Monographic Series. English. ir. S Karger AG, PO Box, CH-4009 Basel Switzerland. **Tel** 061-39 08 80. Ed G Stille, W Wagner and W M Herrmann. **Ind/Abst** Biol. Abstr., Chem. Abstr. **NLM** W1 AD78N. **CODEN** ADPHDK. Guidance for physicians who want their patients to benefit from the newest developments in clinical pharmacology.

ADVANCES IN STEROID BIOCHEMISTRY AND PHARMACOLOGY. See Biology - Biochemistry.

ADVERSE DRUG REACTION BULLETIN. Began in 1966. 0044-6394. Periodical. UK. English. bm. $7.00. A D R Bulletin Editorial Office, Shotley Bridge, General Hospital, Durham DH8 0NB England. **Tel** (0207)503456. Ed D M Davies. **Ind/Abst** Life Sci. Collect., Excerpta Med., Biol. Abstr. **NLM** W1 AD93. **CODEN** ADRBBA. **Circ** 100,000. Includes brief authoritative reviews on adverse drug reactions.

ADVERSE DRUG REACTIONS. (ADVERSE DRUG REACTIONS MICROFORM). Began with: 1975/78. 0739-8832. Periodical. US. English. qt. **NLM** QV 772 A344.

ADVERSE DRUG REACTIONS AND ACUTE POISONING REVIEWS. See Medicine - Toxicology.

AGENTS AND ACTIONS. V. 1- July 1969-. 0065-4299. SZ. English. ir. 470. Birkhauser Verlag, PO Box 133 Elisabethen Strasse 19, CH 4010 Basel Switzerland. **Tel** 73 53 00. Ed V Brune. **Ind/Abst** Life Sci. Collect., Pestdoc, Ringdoc, Vetdoc, Excerpta Med., Index Med., Curr. Contents, Biol. Abstr., Chem. Abstr., Nuci. Sci. Abstr. **LC** RM1. **DD** 615. **NLM** W1 AG33. **CODEN** AGACBH. adv acc. **Circ** 900. Official journal of the European workshop on inflammation by the European Histamine Research Society.

DAS AKTUELLE SCHAUFENSTER. 1- 1951-. Periodical. GW. German. ir. Deutscher Apotheker Verlag, Postfach 40, Birkenwaldstr 44, D7000 Stuttgart 1 West Germany. Ed Peter Ditzel. bk rev. adv acc. **Circ** 22,000. (ctrl).

AMERICAN DRUG INDEX. See Indexes/Abstracts.

AMERICAN DRUGGIST BLUE BOOK. Began publication in 1928. 0364-7471. US. English. an. $25.00. American Druggist Blue Book Annual, 224 West 57th Street, New York NY 10019. **Tel** (212)399-3084. **LC** HD9666.4. **DD** 338.436151. **NLM** QV 772 A512.

AMERICAN DRUGGIST BLUE BOOK. OCTOBER UP-DATED EDITION. (1975-). Periodical. US. English. an.

AMERICAN DRUGGIST (HEARST CORPORATION : 1974). (AMERICAN DRUGGIST). Began Jan. 1974. 0190-5279. Periodical. US. English. $24.00. Hearst Agency Desk, Box 771, New York NY 10019. **Tel** (516)294-7820. **Ind/Abst** Predicasts, Excerpta Med., Funk Scott Index Corp. **Ind. LC** RS1. **DD** 338.47615405. **NLM** W1 AM393. *American Druggist Merchandising, 0090-6638.*

AMERICAN HOSPITAL FORMULARY SERVICE DRUG INFORMATION. VFOAT AHFSI DI. 84-. 8756-6028. US. English. an. The Society, 4630 Montgomery Avenue, Bethesda MD 20814. **DD** 615. **NLM** QV 740. *American Hospital Formulary Service.*

AMERICAN JOURNAL OF HOSPITAL PHARMACY. V. 15- Jan. 1958-. 0002-9289. Periodical. US. English. mo. $170.00. American Society of Hospital Pharmacists, 4630 Montgomery Avenue, Bethesda MD 20814. **Tel** (301)657-3000. **Ind/Abst** Life Sci. Collect., Hospit. Lit. Index, Pestdoc, Ringdoc, Vetdoc, Cumul. Index Nurs. Allied Health Lit., Excerpta Med., Index Med., Chem. Abstr., Sci. Cit. Index, Abr. Ed. **NLM** W1 AM456. **CODEN** AJHPA9. *Bulletin.*

AMERICAN JOURNAL OF PHARMACEUTICAL EDUCATION. (THE AMERICAN JOURNAL OF PHARMACEUTICAL EDUCATION). V. 1- Jan. 1937-. 0002-9459. Periodical. US. English. qt. American Association of Colleges of Pharmacy, 4630 Montgomery Avenue, Suite 201, Bethesda MD 20014. **Ind/Abst** Life Sci. Collect., Biol. Abstr., Chem. Abstr., Curr. Contents Educ., Curr. Contents. Life Sci., Excerpta Med., Hospit. Lit. Index, Int. Pharm. Abstr., Iowa Drug Inf. Serv., Curr. Index J. Educ. **LC** RS110. **DD** 615.071173. **NLM** W1 AM498C. **CODEN** AJPDAD.

AMERICAN JOURNAL OF PHARMACY AND THE SCIENCES SUPPORTING PUBLIC HEALTH. VFOAT American Journal of Pharmacy. V. 153/No. 1 (Oct.-Dec. 1981)-. 0730-7780. Periodical. US. English. qt $12.00. American Journal of Pharmacy, 43rd Street Kingsessing and Woodland Avenues, Philadelphia PA 19104. **Ind/Abst** Biol. Abstr., Chem. Abstr., Excerpta Med., Ref. Source. **NLM** W1 AM498H. **CODEN** APSHDH. *PM. Pharmacy Management, 0163-464X.*

AMERICAN PHARMACY. New Ser., V. 18- Jan. 1978-. 0160-3450. Periodical. US. English. mo. $40.00. American Pharmaceutical Association, 2215 Constitution Avenue NW, Washington DC 20037. **Tel** (202)628-4410. **Ind/Abst** Life Sci. Collect., Ref. Source, Biol. Abstr., Chem. Abstr., Curr. Contents, Life Sci. Collect., Excerpta Med., FDA Clin. Exp. Abstr., Hospit. Lit. Index, Index Med., Int. Pharm. Abstr., Iowa Drug Inf. Serv., Med. Socioecon. Res. Source, Energy Res. Abstr. **LC** RS1. **DD** 362.1. **NLM** W1 AM699K. **CODEN** AMPHDF. *Journal of the American Pharmaceutical Association, 0003-0465.*

ANAIS DA FACULDADE NACIONAL DE FARMACIA. V. 1-8. 0100-7440. Periodical. Portuguese. ir. **NLM** W1 AN1093C.

ANALES - ACADEMIA DE FARMACIA, MADRID. See Yearbooks, Almanacs, Directories.

ANALYTICAL PROFILES OF DRUG SUBSTANCES. See Chemistry - Physical and Theoretical Chemistry.

ANNALES PHARMACEUTIQUES FRANCAISES. V. 1- Jan. 1943-. 0003-4509. Periodical. FR. French. bm. Masson Publishing USA Inc, 211 East 43rd Street/Room 1306, New York NY 10017. **Tel** (212)838-8510. **Ind/Abst** Life Sci. Collect., Pestdoc, Ringdoc, Vetdoc, Excerpta Med., CIS Abstr., Biol. Abstr., Chem. Abstr., Nuci. Sci. Abstr., Index Med., Bibliogr. Agric., Energy Res. Abstr. **NLM** W1 AN465. **CODEN** APFRAD. *Journal de Pharmacie et de Chimie, Bulletin des Sciences Pharmacologiques.*

ANNALES SCIENTIFIQUES DE L'UNIVERSITE DE FRANCHE-COMTE -BESANCON. (ANNALES SCIENTIFIQUES DE L'UNIVERSITE DE FRANCHE-COMTE-BESANCON. MEDECINE ET PHARMACIE). Issue No. 1-. 0224-5264. Monographic Series. French. ir. **Ind/Abst** Chem. Abstr. **NLM** W1 AN47KL. **CODEN** AUFPDB.

ANNALS OF THE INSTITUTE FOR ORGONOMIC SCIENCE. Vol. 1, No. 1 (Sept. 1984)-. 8755-3252. Periodical. US. English. an. $15.00 Domestic, $17.00 Foreign. Institute for Orgonomic Science, PO Box 304, Gwynedd Valley PA 19436. **DD** 615.

ANNUAL ADMINISTRATION REPORT OF THE FOOD AND DRUG ADMINISTRATION, MAHARASHTRA STATE. See Public Administration.

ANNUAL REPORT - NORTH DAKOTA STATE BOARD OF PHARMACY. Main/Corp North Dakota. State Board of Pharmacy. US. English. an. State Board of Pharmacy, PO Box 1354, Bismark ND 58501.

ANNUAL REPORT OF THE MARYLAND BOARD OF PHARMACY. Main/Corp Maryland. Board of Pharmacy. 0098-0099. US. English. an. **LC** RS67.U7. **DD** 615.409752.

ANNUAL REPORT - OFFICE OF OKLAHOMA STATE BOARD OF PHARMACY. Main/Corp Office of Oklahoma State Board of Pharmacy. US. English. an. Joe Schwemin Secretary, Suite 112/North Terrace, Lincoln Plaza Office Center, 4545 Lincoln Boulevard, Oklanoma City OK 73105. **LC** R55. **DD** 353.766007784. *Report.*

ANNUAL REPORTS IN FERMENTATION PROCESSES. See Engineering - Chemical Engineering.

ANNUAL REPORTS IN MEDICINAL CHEMISTRY. 1965-. 0065-7743. US. English. ir. Academic Press, 4805 Sand Lake Road, Orlando FL 32887. **Tel** (305)345-4100. Ed Cornelius K Cain. **Ind/Abst** Sci. Cit. Index, Abr. Ed. **LC** RS402. **DD** 615.08. **NLM** W1 AN769G.

ANNUAL REVIEW OF CHRONOPHARMACOLOGY. VFOAT Chronopharmacology. Vol. 1-. 0743-9539. UK. English. an. Pergamon Press, Maxwell House Fairview Park, Elmsford NY 10523. **LC** RS201.C64. **DD** 615.7.

ANNUAL REVIEW OF PHARMACOLOGY AND TOXICOLOGY. V. 16- 1976-. 0362-1642. US. English. an. $31.00 Domestic, $34.00 Foreign. Annual Reviews Inc, 4139 El Camino Way, Palo Alto CA 94306. **Tel** (414)493-4400. Ed Robert George and Ronald Okun. **Ind/Abst** Life Sci. Collect., Pestdoc, Ringdoc, Vetdoc, Excerpta Med., Index Med., Biol. Abstr., Chem. Abstr., Psychol. Abstr., Energy Res. Abstr., Sci. Cit. Index, Abr. Ed., Hospit. Lit. Index. **LC** RM16. **DD** 615.05. **NLM** W1 AN778K. **CODEN** ARPTDI. Comprehensive, thorough coverage of latest advances in pharmacology and toxicology, written by acknowledged experts in the field. Extensive literature citations included. *Annual Review of Pharmacology, 0066-4251.*

APHARMACY WEEKLY. V. 14, No. 2- Jan. 11, 1975-. 0098-2814. Periodical. US. English. wk. American Pharmaceutical Association, 2215 Constitution Avenue NW, Washington DC 20037. **Tel** (202)628-4410. **NLM** W1 AP15. *APHA Newsletter, 0567-409X.*

THE APOTHECARY. 0003-6560. Periodical. US. English. mo. $18.00. The Apothecary, PO Box AP, Los Altos CA 94022. **Tel** (415)941-3955. Ed Jerold K Karabensh. **NLM** W1 AP236F. **Circ** 63,000. (ctrl). Available on microfilm from University Microfilm. Topics of interest to the pharmacist as a business person including management, merchandising, records, processing, patient service and interaction, and community involvement in health education. *Apothecary and New England Druggist.*

DIE APOTHEKENHELFERIN. V. 1- July 1953-. Periodical. GW. German. bm. Deutscher Apotheker Verlag, Postfach 40, Birkenwaldstr 44, D7000 Stuttgart 1 West Germany. Ed Renate Weber. bk rev acc. **Circ** 22,000. (ctrl).

APOTHEKER-JAHRBUCH. 0066-5347. GW. German. an. Wissenschaftliche Verlagsgesellschaft MBH, Postfach 40, D7000 Stuttgart 1 West Germany. **Tel** (0777)2582-0. adv acc. **Circ** 4,000. (ctrl).

APOTHEKER UND KUNST. 1-. 0341-0110. Periodical. GW. German. ir. Deutscher Apotheker Verlag, Postfach 40 Birkenwaldstr 44, D7000 Stuttgart 1 West Germany. **NLM** W1 AP261.

APPROVED PRESCRIPTION DRUG PRODUCTS WITH THERAPEUTIC EQUIVALENCE EVALUATIONS *CEASED.* 1980-5th Ed., 1984. 0733-4036. US. English. ir. US Government Printing Office, Superintendent of Documents, Washington DC 20402. **Tel** (202)783-3238. **LC** RM301.45. **DD** 615.1. **NLM** QV 772 U582A. *Approved RX Drug Products.*

ARCHIV DER PHARMAZIE. See Genealogy and Heraldry - Archives.

ARCHIV FOR PHARMACI OG CHEMI. See Genealogy and Heraldry - Archives.

ARCHIV FOR PHARMACI OG CHEMI. See Genealogy and Heraldry - Archives.

ARCHIVES INTERNATIONALES DE PHARMACODYNAMIE. See Genealogy and Heraldry - Archives.

ARCHIVES INTERNATIONALES DE PHARMACODYNAMIE ET DE THERAPIE. See Genealogy and Heraldry - Archives.

Pharmacy

ARCHIVOS DE FARMACOLOGIA Y TOXICOLOGIA. See Genealogy and Heraldry - Archives.

THE ARIZONA PHARMACIST. 0004-1602. Periodical. US. English. bm. $15.00. Arizona Pharmacist, 2202 North 7th Street, Phoenix AZ 85006. Ed Warren Ellison. NLM W1 AR801. adv acc. Circ 1,400. (ctrl). Current Arizona news and continuing education.

ARKANSAS HEALTH MANPOWER STATISTICS. PHARMACISTS. See Statistics.

ARQUIVOS. Main/Corp Coimbra. Universidade. Instituto de Farmacologia e Terapeutica Experimental. 1- 1931-. 0412-8877. Periodical. PO. Portuguese. ir. 5 rua de d Francasico Manelme, Lisbon 1 Portugal.

ARS PHARMACEUTICA. 0004-2927. SP. Spanish. qt. $6.55. Universidad de Granada, Facultad de Farmacia, Granada Spain. Ind/Abst Chem. Abstr., Excerpta Med., Life Sci. Collect. NLM W1 AR941. CODEN APHRAN.

THE ART OF MEDICATION. Vol. 1, No. 1 (Sept. 1980)-. 0731-3047. US. English. The Art of Medication, 120 Brighton Road, Clifton NJ 07012. NLM W1 AR948G.

ARZNEIMITTEL-FORSCHUNG. VFOAT Drug Research. V. 1- April 1951-. 0004-4172. Periodical. GW. German (English). mo. 315.00. Editio Cantor, Postfach 12 55, D-7960 Aulendorf West Germany. Tel 07525/4 31. Ed Hans Georg Classen. Ind/Abst Life Sci. Collect., Pestdoc, Ringdoc, Vetdoc, Excerpta Med., Biol. Abstr., Chem. Abstr., Nuci. Sci. Abstr., Index Med., Sci. Cit. Index, Abr. Ed. NLM W1 AR966. CODEN ARZNAD. bk rev. adv acc. Circ 5,100. The scientific journal with an international reputation in all fields of drug research and testing. *Pharmazie*.

ARZNEIMITTELTHERAPIE. Year 1, No. 1 (Jan./Feb. 1983)-. 0723-6913. Periodical. German. ir. NLM W1 AR969G.

ASHP NEWSLETTER. Main/Corp American Society of Hospital Pharmacists. VAT American Society of Hospital Pharmacists Newsletter. 0001-2483. Periodical. US. English. ir. $80.00. American Society of Hospital Pharmacists, 4630 Montgomery Avenue, Bethesda MD 20814. Tel (202)657-3000.

ASHP SIGNAL. VFOAT A.S.H.P. Signal. VAT American Society of Hospital Pharmacists Signal. 0278-2685. Periodical. US. English. bm. $15.00 (members, included in dues). American Society of Hospital Pharmacists, 4630 Montgomery Avenue, Bethesda MD 20814.

ASIAN JOURNAL OF PHARMACEUTICAL SCIENCES. V. 1- June 1979-. 0129-4172. Periodical. Sl. English. qt. Medical Book Center, Asian Journal of Pharmaceutical Sciences, Crawford PO Box 666, Singapore 9119 Singapore. Ind/Abst Chem. Abstr. NLM W1 AS139V. CODEN AJSCDS.

ASIAN JOURNAL OF PHARMACY. V. 1- 1967-. 0066-8419. Periodical. PH. English. ir. Federation of Asian Pharmaceutical Associations, 29 Queen Boulevard, Quezon City Philippines. Ind/Abst Chem. Abstr. NLM W1 AS1391. CODEN ASJPCG.

AUSTRALIAN JOURNAL OF HOSPITAL PHARMACY. V. 1- 1971-. 0310-6810. Periodical. AT. English. qt. 40. Society Hospital Pharmacists Australian, PO Box 72, Abbotsford 3067 Australia. Tel (613)488-2366. Ed Michael J Ryan. Ind/Abst Electron. Commun. Abstr. J., ISMEC Bull., Pollut. Abstr. Indexes, Saf. Sci. Abstr. J., Pestdoc, Ringdoc, Vetdoc, Excerpta Med., Biol. Abstr., Chem. Abstr. NLM W1 AU612. CODEN AUHPAI. bk rev. adv acc. Circ 2,100. Contains practical and original information submitted by and tailored for practising hospital pharmacists and pharmacists employed in education and research.

AUSTRALIAN JOURNAL OF PHARMACEUTICAL SCIENCES CEASED. -V. 10, No. 4. 0310-7116. Periodical. AT. English. ir. Ind/Abst Ringdoc, Pestdoc, Vetdoc, Excerpta Med. NLM W1 AU613P.

AUSTRALIAN JOURNAL OF PHARMACY. (AJP. THE AUSTRALIAN JOURNAL OF PHARMACY). V. 58- (No. 683)-. 0705-8454. Periodical. AT. English. mo. 44.00. Australia Pharmaceutical Publishing Company, 35 Walsh Street, West Melbourne Victoria 3003 Australia. Tel 329-5799. Ed S Dickson. Ind/Abst Excerpta Med.

NLM W1 A117GN. adv acc. Circ 8,500. Latest drugs on the market. *Australian Journal of Pharmacy*, 0311-8002.

BASIC DRUG LIST. Main/Corp United Mine Workers of America Health and Retirement Funds. 1975-. 0361-8900. US. English. $2.50. United Mine Workers of America Health and Retirement Funds, 2021 K Street Northwest, Washington DC 20006. LC RS1. DD 615.105.

BERLINER SEMINAR. 1-. 0172-6897. Monographic Series. German. ir. NLM W3 BE679S.

BIO LINES. (BIO LINES : HEALTH COMMUNICATION FROM CONNAUGHT). VFOAT Biolines. 0715-4615. Periodical. CN. English. ir. Connaught Laboratories Ltd, 1755 Steeles Avenue, West Willowdale Ontario M2N 5T8 Canada. DD 615.10720713541.

BIOCHEMICAL PHARMACOLOGY. V. 1- July 1958-. 0006-2952. Periodical. UK. English. sm. Pergamon Press, 395 Sawmill River Road, Elmsford NY 10532. Tel (914)592-7700. Ind/Abst Life Sci. Collect., Pestdoc, Ringdoc, Vetdoc, Excerpta Med., Int. Aerosp. Abstr., CIS Abstr., Biol. Abstr., Chem. Abstr., Psychol. Abstr., Nuci. Sci. Abstr., Index Med., Sel. Water Resour. Abstr., Bibliogr. Agric., Sci. Cit. Index, Abr. Ed. LC QP901. DD 615.7. NLM W1 BI622. CODEN BCPCA6. (cum index).

BIOENERGETIC ANALYSIS. (BIOENERGETIC ANALYSIS : THE CLINICAL JOURNAL OF THE INTERNATIONAL INSTITUTE FOR BIOENERGETIC ANALYSIS). Vol. 1., No. 1 (Spring 1984)-. 0743-4804. Periodical. US. English. sa. $8.00 Members, $15.00 Non-Members, $28.00 Institutions. Bioenergetic Analysis, Hog Hill Road, Pepperell MA 01463. DD 615.

BIOMEDICINE & PHARMACOTHERAPY. See Medicine.

BIOMETRIE IN DER CHEMISCH-PHARMAZEUTISCHEN INDUSTRIE. 1-. German. ir. NLM W1 BI859P.

BIOPHARMACEUTICS & DRUG DISPOSITION. VAT Biopharmaceutics and Drug Disposition. V. 1- July/Sept. 1979-. 0142-2782. Periodical. UK. English. qt. John Wiley & Sons, Baffins Lane Chichester, Sussex PO19 1UD England. Tel (0243) 784531. Ind/Abst Life Sci. Collect., Pestdoc, Ringdoc, Vetdoc, Excerpta Med., Index Med., Chem. Abstr., Sci. Cit. Index, Abr. Ed. DD 615. NLM W1 BI876MF. CODEN BDDID8.

BIOSIS/CAS SELECTS. FOOD & DRUG LEGISLATION. See Food & Drink.

THE BLUE SHEET. V. 19, No. 29- July 21, 1976-. 0162-3605. Periodical. US. English. wk. F D C Reports Inc, 5550 Friendship Boulevard Suite 1, Chevy Chase MD 20815. Tel (301)657-9830. Ind/Abst Pharm. News Index. NLM W1 BL925. CODEN DRRSAL. *Drug Research Reports*.

BOKIN BOBAI : NIHON BOKIN BOBAI GAKKAI SHI. VFOAT Journal of Antibacterial and Antifungal Agents, Japan. 0385-5201. Japanese (with summaries in English). mo. 6500 Membership. Nihon Bokin Bobai Gakkai, c/o Taikei Building, 9-16 Nishi Hon-Machi Machi 1-Chome Nishi-Ku, Osaka-Chi 550 Japan. Ind/Abst Chem. Abstr. LC RM409. CODEN BOBODP.

BOLETIN DE LA SOCIEDAD ESPANOLA DE HISTORIA DE LA FARMACIA. Main/Corp Sociedad Espanola de Historia de la Farmacia. Yearly V. 1- (No. 1-). 0583-7472. Periodical. SP. Spanish. $15.00. Soc Espanola Historia Farmacia, Farmacia 11, Madrid 4 Spain. Ind/Abst Am. Hist. Life, Hist. Abstr., Part A, Mod. Hist. Abstr., Hist. Abstr., Part B, Twent. Century Abstr., Hist. Abstr. NLM W1 BO249.

BOLLETTINO CHIMICO FARMACEUTICA. Began in 1892. 0006-6648. Periodical. IT. Italian. mo $86.67. Societa Edite Pharmaceutica, Via Ausonio 12, 20132 Milano Italy. Ind/Abst Pestdoc, Ringdoc, Vetdoc, Excerpta Med., Index Med., Chem. Abstr., Bibliogr. Agric. NLM W1 BO46. CODEN BCFAAI. *Bolletino Farmaceutica*.

BRITISH JOURNAL OF CLINICAL PHARMACOLOGY. V. 1- Feb. 1974-. 0306-5251. Periodical. UK. English. mo. 117 Domestic, 250 Foreign. Blackwell Scientific, PO Box 88 Osney Mead, Oxford OX2 0EL England. Tel 0865 240201. Ed C F George. Ind/Abst Life Sci. Collect., Pestdoc, Ringdoc, Vetdoc, Excerpta Med., Index Med., Biol. Abstr., Chem. Abstr., Sci. Cit. Index, Abr.

Ed., Hospit. Lit. Index. NLM W1 BR519RI. CODEN BCPHBM. adv acc. Circ 2,000. Contains papers on all aspects of drug action in man, invited reviews, original papers, short communications and correspondence.

BRITISH JOURNAL OF CLINICAL PRACTICE. SYMPOSIUM SUPPLEMENT. VFOAT B.J.C.P. Supplement. 0262-8767. Monographic Series. UK. English. ir. Ind/Abst Index Med. NLM W1 BR519S.

BRITISH JOURNAL OF PHARMACEUTICAL PRACTICE. VFOAT Pharmaceutical Practice. V. 1- 1979-. 0144-8803. Periodical. UK. English. 18 Domestic, 36 Europe, 40 outside Europe. Medical News Tribune, Tower House Southampton Street, London WC2E 7LS England. Tel (01)379-6005. Ed Ian Harrison. Ind/Abst Pestdoc, Ringdoc, Vetdoc. NLM W1 BR597. bk rev. adv acc. Circ 4,500. (ctrl). Original Papers, comment, news, features on hospital pharmacy and clinical pharmacy in the community.

BRITISH JOURNAL OF PHARMACOLOGY. V. 34- Sept. 1968-. 0007-1188. Periodical. UK. English. mo. $390.00. H Holt MacMillan Journals, Houndmills, Basingstoke Hants RG21 2XS United Kingdom. Tel (0256)29242. Ed Gordon Lees. Ind/Abst Life Sci. Collect., Pestdoc, Ringdoc, Vetdoc, Excerpta Med., Index Med., Int. Aerosp. Abstr., Biol. Abstr., CIS Abstr., Chem. Abstr., Sci. Cit. Index, Abr. Ed. NLM W1 BR601. CODEN BJPCBM. adv acc. Circ 3,000. Publishes up-to-date articles from all parts of the world on all aspects of pharmacology. *British Journal of Pharmacology and Chemotherapy*.

BRITISH NATIONAL FORMULARY. UK. English. $14.00. British Medical Journal, Tavistock Square, London WC1H 9JR England.

BRITISH PHARMACOPIA. UK. English. ir. Her Majestys Stationery Office, PO Box 276, London SW8 5DT England. Tel 01-622 3316. LC RS141.3. DD 615.11.

BULLETIN - AUSTRALIAN DRUG AND MEDICAL INFORMATION GROUP. (BULLETIN - THE AUSTRALIAN DRUG & MEDICAL INFORMATION GROUP). No. 1- Oct. 1976-. 0314-0059. Periodical. AT. English. ir. NLM W1 BU934FM.

BULLETIN DES TRAVAUX DE LA SOCIETE DE PHARMACIE DE LYON. V. 1- 1957-. 0037-9107. Periodical. FR. French. mo. Societe de Pharmacie de Lyon, 11 rue d'Algerie, 69009 Lyon France. Tel 28-82-25. Ind/Abst Chem. Abstr. NLM W1 BU621. CODEN BTSLAV.

BULLETIN D'INFORMATION - ASSOCIATION INTERNATIONALE DE STANDARDISATION BIOLOGIQUE. Main/Corp International Association of Biological Standardization. VFOAT Newsletter - International Association of Biological Standardization. No. 15- Jan. 1973-. English (French). ir. International Association of Biological Standardization, 1211 Geneva 4 Switzerland. LC RS189. DD 610.28.

BULLETIN D'INFORMATION OFFICIEL DE L'ASSOCIATION DES PHARMACIENS DES ETABLISSEMENTS DE SANTE DU QUEBEC. Main/Corp Association des Pharmaciens des Etablissements de Sante du Quebec. Vol. 6, No. 6 (Sept. 1973)-. 0713-5033. Periodical. CN. French. Association des Pharmaciens des Etablissements de Sante du Quebec, CP 176 Succursale E, Montreal Quebec H2T 3A7 Canada. DD 615.4060714. *Bulletin d'Information Officiel de la Societe Professionnelle des Pharmaciens d'Hopitaux*, 0381-7091.

THE BULLETIN OF JAPANESE SOCIETY OF PHYCOLOGY. Main/Corp Japanese Society of Phycology. Vol. 1, No. 1 (Mar. 1953)-. Periodical. Japanese. ir. Japanese Society of Pharmacology, c/o Faculty of Pharmaceutical, Kyoto University, Kyoto 606 Japan.

BULLETIN SIGNALETIQUE 330 : SCIENCES PHARMACOLOGIQUES, TOXICOLOGIE. VFOAT Sciences Pharmacologiques, Toxicologie. V. 22- 1961-. 0007-5442. Periodical. FR. French. ir. Centre National de la Recherche Scientifique, 14 Quai Anatole, Paris 75700 France. *Bulletin Signaletique*.

Pharmacy

BUTTERWORTHS INTERNATIONAL MEDICAL REVIEWS. CLINICAL PHARMACOLOGY AND THERAPEUTICS. VFOAT Clinical Pharmacology and Therapeutics. 1-. 0260-0099. Monographic Series. UK. English. ir. **Ind/Abst** Biol. Abstr., Chem. Abstr. **NLM** W1 BU98N. **CODEN** CPTHDA.

BYOIN YAKUGAKU. VFOAT Japanese Journal of Hospital Pharmacy, Journal of the Nippon Hospital Pharmacists Association. Began in 1975. 0389-9098. Periodical. JA. Japanese. bm. Yakuji Nipposha, 1-11 Izumi-cho Kanda Chiyoda-ku, Tokyo 101 Japan. **Ind/Abst** Chem. Abstr., Excerpta Med. **CODEN** BYYADW.

THE CALENDAR OF THE PHARMACEUTICAL SOCIETY OF GREAT BRITAIN. Main/Corp Pharmaceutical Society of Great Britain, London. 1866-. UK. English. an. Pharmaceutical Press, 1 Lambeth High Street, London SE1 7JN England. **LC** RS1. **NLM** W1 PH176.

CALIFORNIA PHARMACIST. (CALIFORNIA PHARMACIST : OFFICIAL PUBLICATION OF THE CALIFORNIA PHARMACISTS ASSOCIATION). 1952. 0739-0483. Periodical. US. English. mo. $10.00. California Pharmacist, 1112 I Street, Sacramento CA 95814. **Tel** (916)444-7811. Ed Hal Silliman. **NLM** W1 CA408C. adv acc. **Circ** 7,200. (ctrl). Pharmacy news, new drug information, clinical, management news for the community, chain, hospital and long-term care pharmacist in California.

CALIFORNIA PHARMACY LAWS, WITH RULES AND REGULATIONS. See Law.

CANADIAN DRUG IDENTIFICATION CODE. VFOAT Code Canadien d'Identification des Drogues. 0824-2666. Monographic Series. text in English and French in parallel columns. ir. **DD** 615.1029471.

CANADIAN JOURNAL OF HOSPITAL PHARMACY. V. 21- Jan./Feb. 1969-. 0008-4123. Periodical. CN. English (includes some text in French). bm. $23.21. 123 Edward Street/Suite 303, Toronto Ontario M5G 1E2 Canada. **Tel** (416)979-2049. Ed B Jane Gilliespie. **Ind/Abst** Hospit. Lit. Index, Pestdoc, Ringdoc, Vetdoc, Excerpta Med., Biol. Abstr. **NLM** W1 CA59. **CODEN** CJHPAV. bk rev. adv acc. **Circ** 3,000. (ctrl). Original articles on hospital pharmacy practice, drugs and therapeutics. Also, reports of society business and meetings. Hospital Pharmacist, 0317-4050.

CANADIAN JOURNAL OF PHYSIOLOGY AND PHARMACOLOGY. See Biology - Physiology.

CANADIAN PHARMACEUTICAL JOURNAL. Began publication in 1868. 0317-199X. Periodical. CN. English. mo. 37.50. Canadian Pharmaceutical Association, 104-1815 Alta Vista Drive, Ottawa Ontario K1G 3Y6 Canada. **Tel** (613)523-7877. Ed Jean-Guy Cyr. **Ind/Abst** Hospit. Lit. Index, Pestdoc, Ringdoc, Vetdoc, Excerpta Med., Can. Bus. Index, Chem. Abstr. **NLM** W1 CA636. **CODEN** CPJOAC. bk rev. adv acc. **Circ** 12,500. Pharmacy, medicine, therapeutics, small business profiles, new product announcements, book reviews, continuing education articles.

THE CAROLINA JOURNAL OF PHARMACY. V. 1- 1915-. 0528-1725. Periodical. US. English. $12.00. North Carolina Pharmaceutical Association, Chapel Hill NC 27514. **NLM** W1 CA876.

CESKOSLOVENSKA FARMACIE. V. 1- 1952-. 0009-0530. Periodical. CS. Czech (articles have summaries in Russian and English). ir. Artia, VE Smeckach 30, PO Box 790, Praha 1 Czechoslovakia. **Ind/Abst** Pestdoc, Ringdoc, Vetdoc, Excerpta Med., Index Med., CIS Abstr., Chem. Abstr. **NLM** W1 CE881. **CODEN** CKFRAY.

CHEMICAL & PHARMACEUTICAL BULLETIN. See Chemistry.

CHEMIST & DRUGGIST DIRECTORY AND TABLET & CAPSULE IDENTIFICATION GUIDE. See Yearbooks, Almanacs, Directories.

CHEMISTRY AND PHARMACOLOGY OF DRUGS. See Chemistry.

CHEYAK KISUL CHONGBO. VFOAT Technical Information for Pharmaceutical Industry. Periodical. Korean. mo. **LC** RM1.

CHONG. Periodical. KO. Korean. mo. Ilsong Sinyak Chusik Hoesa, 44-7 Wonhyo-Ro Yongsan-Ku, Seoul Korea. **LC** RS1.

CLINICAL AND EXPERIMENTAL PHARMACOLOGY & PHYSIOLOGY. VAT Clinical and Experimental Pharmacology and Physiology. V. 1- Jan./Feb. 1974-. 0305-1870. Periodical. UK. English. bm. $220.00. Blackwell Scientific Publ Ltd, PO Box 88, Oxford OX2 OEL England. **Ind/Abst** Life Sci. Collect., Pestdoc, Ringdoc, Vetdoc, Excerpta Med., Index Med., Chem. Abstr., Sci. Cit. Index, Abr. Ed. **NLM** W1 CL664E. **CODEN** CEXPB9. Proceedings of the Australian Society for Medical Research, 0067-2130.

CLINICAL NEUROPHARMACOLOGY. V. 1-. 0362-5664. Periodical. US. English. qt. $70.00. Raven Press, 1140 Avenue of the Americas, New York NY 10036. **Tel** (212)575-0335. **Ind/Abst** Life Sci. Collect., Excerpta Med., Index Med., Chem. Abstr., Sci. Cit. Index, Abr. Ed. **LC** RM315. **DD** 616.8046105. **NLM** W1. **CODEN** CLNEDB.

CLINICAL PHARMACOKINETICS. V. 1- 1976-. 0312-5963. Periodical. US. English. bm. $160.00. Adis Press, 401 South State Street, Newton PA 18940. **Tel** (212)860-2000. **Ind/Abst** Life Sci. Collect., Pestdoc, Ringdoc, Vetdoc, Excerpta Med., Index Med., Biol. Abstr., Chem. Abstr., Energy Res. Abstr., Sci. Cit. Index, Abr. Ed. **NLM** W1 CL764. **CODEN** CPKNDH. **Circ** 1,500. (ctrl). In-depth analytical reviews and original research articles on the pharmacokinetics of drugs during actual clinical use.

CLINICAL PHARMACOLOGY. Vol. 1-. Monographic Series. US. English. ir. Marcel Dekker Inc, 270 Madison Avenue, New York NY 10016. **Tel** (212)696-9000. Ed Murray Weiner. **NLM** W1. This is an ongoing series. Each title has a different subject.

CLINICAL PHARMACOLOGY AND DRUG EPIDEMIOLOGY. 1-. 0165-1285. Monographic Series. English. ir. Elsevier Science Publishers, PO Box 211, 1000 AE Amsterdam Netherlands. **Ind/Abst** Chem. Abstr. **NLM** W1 CL764P. **CODEN** CPDEDN.

CLINICAL PHARMACOLOGY AND THERAPEUTICS. V. 1- Jan./Feb. 1960-. 0009-9236. Periodical. US. English. mo. $103.00. C V Mosby, c/o R K Kinnes, 11830 Westline Industrial Drive, St Louis MO 63416. Ed Marcus Reidenberg. **Ind/Abst** Life Sci. Collect., Pestdoc, Ringdoc, Vetdoc, Excerpta Med., Index Med., Biol. Abstr., Chem. Abstr., Energy Res. Abstr., Sci. Cit. Index, Abr. Ed., Hospit. Lit. Index. **LC** RM1. **NLM** W1 CL765. **CODEN** CLPTAT. adv acc. **Circ** 5,835. Devoted to the clinical study of the nature, action, efficacy and total evaluation of drugs, both new and established, as they are used in man.

CLINICAL PHARMACY. V. 1, No. 1 (Jan./Feb. 1982)-. 0278-2677. Periodical. US. English. bm. $35.00 Institutions & Non-Member Domestic, $40.00 Institutions & Non-Member Foreign. American Society of Hospital Pharmacists, 4630 Montgomery Avenue, Bethesda MD 20814. **Ind/Abst** Pestdoc, Ringdoc, Vetdoc, Excerpta Med., Index Med., Biol. Abstr., Chem. Abstr. **NLM** W1 CL764K. **CODEN** CPHADV.

CLINICAL RESEARCH PRACTICES AND DRUG REGULATORY AFFAIRS. Vol. 1, No. 1-. 0735-7915. Periodical. US. English. qt. $155.00. Marcel Dekker Inc, PO Box 11305/Church Street Station, New York NY 10249. **Tel** (212)696-9000. Ed Gary M Matoren. **Ind/Abst** Excerpta Med. **LC** RS122. **DD** 615.1072. **CODEN** CRPADH. bk rev adv acc. (ctrl). The only publication devoted exclusively to documenting clinical research in the pharmaceutical industry.

CLINICALLY IMPORTANT ADVERSE DRUG INTERACTIONS. Vol. 1-. 0167-4080. Monographic Series. US. English. ir. Elsevier Science Publishing Co Inc, PO Box 1663 Grand Central Station, New York NY 10163. **Tel** (212)370-5520. Ed J C Petrie and L E Cluff. **Ind/Abst** Chem. Abstr. **LC** UNC. **DD** 615.704. **NLM** W1 CL802. **CODEN** CLAIDQ.

CODE OF FEDERAL REGULATIONS. 21, FOOD AND DRUGS. See Law.

COLLEGES AND SCHOOLS OF PHARMACY. See Education (General) - Higher Education.

THE COLORADO JOURNAL OF PHARMACY. VFOAT CJP. V. 1- Feb. 1958-. 0010-163X. Periodical. US. English. ir. $5.00. University of Colorado, School of Pharmacy, Boulder CO 80309. **Tel** (303)492-5594. Ed F C Hammerness. **NLM** W1 CO249. Pharmaceutical sciences.

COMMON USAGE DRUG SCHEDULE. VFOAT Liste des Produits de Prescription Courante. V. 1- Oct./Dec. 1975-. 0707-1035. Periodical. CN. French (English). sa. Ministere de la Sante Plan de Medicaments sur Ordonnance, CP 690, Moncton New Brunswick E1C 8M7 Canada.

COMMUNICATIONS IN PSYCHOPHARMACOLOGY. V. 1-. 0145-5699. Periodical. UK. English. bm. $55.00. Subscription Fulfillment, Manager Headington Hill Hall, Oxford OX3OBW England. **Ind/Abst** Excerpta Med., Chem. Abstr., Energy Res. Abstr. **NLM** W1 CO4279. **CODEN** CPSZDP.

COMMUNITY PHARMACY. (COMMUNITY PHARMACY . . . . ANNUAL SURVEY). VFOAT Canadian Community Pharmacy in . . . . VAT Canadian Community Pharmacy (1975). 34th (1975)-. 0228-5533. CN. English. an. $15.00 Per No. Canadian Pharmaceutical Association, 1815 Alta Vista Drive, Ottawa Ontario K1G 3Y6 Canada. **DD** 381.4561540971. Annual Survey of Community Pharmacy, 0710-5525.

COMPARATIVE BIOCHEMISTRY AND PHYSIOLOGY. COMPARATIVE PHARMACOLOGY AND TOXICOLOGY. (COMPARATIVE BIOCHEMISTRY AND PHYSIOLOGY. C, COMPARATIVE PHARMACOLOGY AND TOXICOLOGY). VFOAT Comparative Pharmacology and Toxicology. Vol. 74C, No. 1-. 0742-8413. Periodical. UK. English. bm. $300.00. Pergamon Press Incorporated, Maxwell House, Fairview Park, Elmsford NY 10523. **Ind/Abst** Can. Environ., Excerpta Med., Index Med., Life Sci. Collect. **NLM** W1 CO435CD. Issued also in microform. Comparative Biochemistry and Physiology. C: Comparative Pharmacology, 0306-4492.

COMPENDIUM OF PHARMACEUTICALS AND SPECIALTIES. VFOAT CPS. VAT CPS (1974). 9th Ed. (1974)-. 0715-3066. CN. English. an. 62.00. Canadian Pharmaceutical Association, 1815 Alta Vista Drive, Ottawa Ontario K1G 3Y6 Canada. **DD** 615.1171. adv acc. **Circ** 78,000. Compiled and produced by the staff of the Canadian Pharmaceutical Association for the benefit of health professionals. Compendium of Pharmaceuticals and Specialties (Canada), 0069-7966.

COMPTES RENDUS DE THERAPEUTIQUE ET DE PHARMACOLOGIE CLINIQUE. V. 1, No. 1 (Sept. 1982)-. 0293-9908. Periodical. French. ir. **Ind/Abst** Excerpta Med., Chem. Abstr. **NLM** W1 CO455D. **CODEN** CRTCD9.

COMPUTERTALK FOR THE PHYSICIAN. VFOAT Computer Talk for the Physician. 0736-3885. Periodical. US. English. mo. $40.00. Computertalk Associates, 1750 Walton Road, Blue Bell PA 19422. **Tel** (215)825-7686. Ed Neil R Bauman. adv acc. (ctrl). Practical advice on buying and using computers in retail pharmacy; new product introductions, legal advice, interviews, industry, news, etc.

CONSILIUM CEDIP PRACTICUM. VFOAT Memento Consilium Cedip Practicum. 13. Deutsche Aufl. (84/85)-. German. an. **NLM** WB 39. Consilium Cedip.

CONTEMPORARY PHARMACY PRACTICE CEASED. VFOAT Pharmacy Practice. V. 1 Summer 1978. Ceased with Vol. 5. 0162-3761. Periodical. US. English. qt. $7.00 Members, $12.00 Non-Members. American Pharmaceutical Association, 2215 Constitution Avenue NW, Washington DC 20037. **Ind/Abst** Excerpta Med. **LC** RS122.5. **DD** 615.105. **NLM** W1 CO769NT.

CONTEMPORARY WRITINGS ON LONG TERM CARE PHARMACY. Began with: Vol. 1, published 1978. US. English. ir. American Society of Consultant Pharmacists, 2300 9th Street South, Arlington VA 22204. **NLM** W1.

CONTINUING EDUCATION. Main/Corp University of Toronto. Faculty of Pharmacy. 1975-. 0318-5141. Monographic Series. CN. English. Ontario College of Pharmacy, 483 Huron Street, Toronto Ontario M5R 2R4 Canada. **DD** 615.405. Continuing Education Programme, 0318-515X.

CONTROLLED DRUG BIOAVAILABILITY. Vol. 1-. Monographic Series. US. English. **NLM** W1.

Pharmacy

CONTROLLED FLUID ADMINISTRATION. Began in 1984. 8756-9957. Periodical. US. English. mo. $150.00. Peters Technology Transfer, PO Box 216, Swarthmore PA 19081. **DD** 615.

COPNIP LIST. Began with 1, Sept. 1953. 0007-8816. US. English. qt. Committee of Pharmaceutical, Nonserial Industrial Publications, 235 Park Avenue South, New York NY 10003.

CPJ. CANADIAN PHARMACEUTICAL JOURNAL. (CPJ : CANADIAN PHARMACEUTICAL JOURNAL). **VFOAT** RPC : La Revue Pharmaceutique Canadienne. **VAT** Canadian Pharmaceutical Journal (1984), RCP. Revue Pharmaceutique Canadienne, Revue Pharmaceutique Canadienne (1984). Vol. 117, No. 5 (May 1984)-. 0828-6914. Periodical. CN. English (French). mo. Free to Members, $35.00 Others. Canadian Pharmaceutical Association, 101-1815 Alta Vista Drive, Ottawa Ontario K1G 3Y6 Canada. **DD** 615.05. *Canadian Pharmaceutical Journal, 0317-199X.*

CRIB : CHEMOTHERAPY RESEARCH BULLETIN. **VAT** Chemotherapy Research Institute Bulletin. 0577-6392. Periodical. US. English. mo. **LC** RM260. *Chemotherapy Research Bulletin.*

CURRENT CONCEPTS IN HOSPITAL PHARMACY MANAGEMENT. Began with: V. 1 (1978). 0164-7857. Periodical. US. English. qt. MacMillan Professional Journal, 640 North LaSalle Street/Suite 380, Chicago IL 60610. Tel (312)944-5888. **Ind/Abst** Hospit. Lit. Index. **NLM** W1 CU7876C.

CURRENT DEVELOPMENTS IN PSYCHOPHARMACOLOGY. V. 1- 1975-. 0097-8361. US. English. an. Halsted Press, 605 Third Avenue, New York NY 10016. Tel (212)479-9360. Ed W B Essman and L Valzelli. **Ind/Abst** Index Med., Chem. Abstr. **LC** RM315. **DD** 615.7805. **NLM** W1 CU788BP. **CODEN** CDPSD7.

CURRENT DRUG HANDBOOK (PHILADELPHIA, PA. : 1982). (CURRENT DRUG HANDBOOK). 1982-1984-. 0738-6249. US. English. be. WB Saunders Co, Fulfillment Department, West Washington Square, Philadelphia PA 19105. Tel (800)523-0713. Ed H Robert Patterson, Edward A Gustafson and Eleanor Sheri. **NLM** QV 772 C976C. *Falconer's Current Drug Handbook, 0272-197X.*

CURRENT PRESCRIBING. V. 1- Mar. 1975-. 0097-8620. Periodical. US. English. mo. $16.00 US, $20.00 Foreign. Current Prescribing, PO Box 536, Oradell NJ 07649. **LC** RM1. **DD** 615.5805. **NLM** W1 CU8033.

CURRENT STATUS OF MODERN THERAPY. V. 1-. 0192-7736. Monographic Series. US. English. ir. University Park Press, 300 North Charles Street, Baltimore MD 21201. Tel (800)638-7511. **Ind/Abst** Chem. Abstr. **NLM** W1 CU81S.

CURRENT THERAPEUTIC RESEARCH. V. 1- Sept. 1959-. 0011-393X. Periodical. US. English. mo. Therapeutic Research Press, PO Box 514, Tenafly NJ 07670. Tel (201)568-3774. **Ind/Abst** Life Sci. Collect., Pestdoc, Ringdoc, Vetdoc, Excerpta Med., Chem. Abstr., Psychol. Abstr., Index Med., Sci. Cit. Index, Abr. Ed. **NLM** W1 CU815. **CODEN** CTCEA9.

CURRENT THERAPEUTICS. 1972-. 0311-905X. Periodical. AT. English. mo. Adis Press Pty Ltd, 404 Sydney Road/PO Box 132, Balgowlah NSW New South Wales 2093 Australia. **Ind/Abst** Excerpta Med. **NLM** W1 CU815T. *New Ethicals, 0028-5064.*

CURRENT THERAPY. 1949-. 0070-2102. US. English. an. $45.00. WB Saunders Co, Fulfillment Department, West Washington Square, Philadelphia PA 19105. Tel (800)523-0713. **LC** RM101. **DD** 616.058. **NLM** W1 CU817.

D-LIST. **VFOAT** Facts and Comparisons. **VAT** Discontinued List. 1979-. 0196-4143. US. English. an. $3.95. Facts and Comparisons Inc, 111 West Port Plaza/Suite 423, St Louis MO 63141. *Discontinued Drug Products, 0270-0549.*

DAIHAN YANGRIHAG JABJI. (TAEHAN YANGNIHAK CHAPCHI). **VFOAT** Korean Journal of Pharmacology. Vol. 1-. 0377-9459. Periodical. KO. Korean (summaries in English). ir. $12.00. c/o Department of Pharmacology, College of Medicine, Seoul National University, Seoul Korea. Tel (02)7601-3391. Ed Chan Woong Park. **Ind/Abst** Excerpta Med., Chem. Abstr. **LC** RM1. **NLM** W1 TA397. **CODEN** TYCPAQ. Circ 600. Interactions of chemicals with biological systems such as pharmacology in general, toxicology, chemotherapy, biochemical neurology and pharmacokinetics.

DER DEUTSCHE APOTHEKER. 0366-8622. Periodical. German. ir. **Ind/Abst** Biol. Abstr., Chem. Abstr. **NLM** W1 DE592. **CODEN** DAPOAG.

DEUTSCHE DROGISTEN ZEITUNG. Periodical. GW. German. sm. Verlag Luitpold Lang, Theresienhohe 10, 8 Munich 12 West Germany.

DEVELOPMENTAL PHARMACOLOGY AND THERAPEUTICS. Vol. 1, No. 1-. 0379-8305. Periodical. SZ. English. bm. $119.00. S Karger AG, PO Box, CH-4009 Basel Switzerland. Tel (061)39 08 80. Ed J V Aranda. **Ind/Abst** Life Sci. Collect., Pestdoc, Ringdoc, Vetdoc, Excerpta Med., Index Med., Biol. Abstr., Chem. Abstr. **NLM** W1 DE997UNE. **CODEN** DPTHDL. adv acc. Publishes outstanding papers on the effects of drugs in the perinatal-pediatric population.

DICTIONNAIRE VIDAL. 1961-. 0419-1153. FR. French. an. $59.87. Off Vulgarisation Pharmaceutiq, 11 rue Quentin Bauchart, 75384 Paris Cedex 08 France. Tel 1 723 90 91. *Dictionnaire de Specialites Pharmaceutiques.*

DIMS, DRUG INDEX FOR MALAYSIA & SINGAPORE. See Indexes/Abstracts.

DIRECTORY - AMERICAN SOCIETY FOR CLINICAL PHARMACOLOGY AND THERAPEUTICS. See Yearbooks, Almanacs, Directories.

DIRECTORY OF DRUG STORE & HBA CHAINS INCLUDES DRUG WHOLESALERS. See Yearbooks, Almanacs, Directories.

DIRECTORY OF REGISTERED PHARMACISTS AND PHARMACIES. See Yearbooks, Almanacs, Directories.

DISCOVERIES IN PHARMACOLOGY. Vol. 1-. Monographic Series. US. English. ir. Elsevier Science Pub Co, 52 Vanderbilt Avenue, New York NY 10017. **Ind/Abst** Chem. Abstr. **NLM** W1. **CODEN** DIPHDK.

DRAGOCO REPORT. Vol. 1 1954-. 0012-5881. Periodical. US. English. ir. Dragoco Inc, PO Box 261, Totowa NJ 07511. **Ind/Abst** Life Sci. Collect., Chem. Abstr. **DD** 615. **CODEN** DRFSDW.

DROGUES. **VFOAT** Revue Drogues. 0753-5449. Periodical. FR. French. bm. 7A rue Des Mineurs, 67000 Strasbourg France.

DRUG & COSMETIC . . . CATALOG. **VFOAT** Drug and Cosmetic . . . Catalog. 12th Ed. (1967-57)-. Periodical. US. English. an. $15.00 US and Canada, $20.00 Foreign. Harcourt Brace Jovanovich Publications, 737 Third Avenue, New York NY 10017. **LC** TP200. *Drug and Cosmetic Review, 0735-5408.*

DRUG & COSMETIC INDUSTRY. **VFOAT** D&CI. **VAT** Drug and Cosmetic Industry. V. 30, No. 2- Feb. 1932-. 0012-6527. Periodical. US. English. mo. Drug & Cosmetic Industry, 1 East First Street, Duluth MN 55802. Tel (218)723-9200. **Ind/Abst** Trade Ind. Index, Life Sci. Collect., Predicasts, Pestdoc, Ringdoc, Vetdoc, Excerpta Med., Energy Inf. Abstr., Environ. Abstr., Int. Packag. Abstr., Ref. Source, Chem. Abstr., Bus. Period. Index, Sci. Cit. Index, Abr. Ed., Funk Scott Index Corp. Ind. **LC** RS1. **NLM** W1 DR514. **CODEN** DCINAQ. *Drug Markets.*

DRUG AND DEVICE RECALL BULLETIN. Jan. 1985-. 8756-5935. Periodical. US. English. mo. $40.00. RX-Data-Pac Service, Box 42020, Cincinnati OH 45242. Tel (513)489-0943. Ed I H Goodman. **DD** 363. Circ 5,000. (ctrl). Complete data about drug and device recalls including generic recalls. Compiled from FDA enforcement report. Helps satisfy JCAH recall activity documentation.

DRUG AND THERAPEUTICS BULLETIN. V. 1- May 3, 1963-. 0012-6543. Periodical. UK. English. bw. $32.94. Consumers Association, 1 Caxton Hill, Hertford Herts SG13 7LZ England. Ed Andrew Herxheimer. **Ind/Abst** Excerpta Med., Index Med., Hospit. Lit. Index. **NLM** W1 DR518. An impartial pharmaceutical fact sheet. *Medical Letter.*

DRUG DESIGN AND DELIVERY. 0884-2884. US. English. an. Harwood Academic Publishers, c/o STBS, 1 Bedford Street, London WC2E 9PP England.

DRUG DEVELOPMENT AND EVALUATION. 1-. 0343-4842. Monographic Series. English (articles in French or German). ir. VCH Publishers Inc, 303 North West 12th Avenue, Deerfield Beach FL 33442. **Ind/Abst** Chem. Abstr. **NLM** W1 DR521BH. **CODEN** DDEVD6.

DRUG DEVELOPMENT AND INDUSTRIAL PHARMACY. V. 3-. 0363-9045. Periodical. US. English. ir. $275.00. Marcel Dekker Inc, PO Box 11305 Church Street Station, New York NY 10249. Tel (212)696-9000. Ed Christopher T Rhodes. **Ind/Abst** Life Sci. Collect., Pestdoc, Ringdoc, Vetdoc, Biol. Abstr., Chem. Abstr., Curr. Contents. Life Sci., Excerpta Med., Int. Pharm. Abstr., Sci. Cit. Index, Abr. Ed., Kokunai Igaku Zasshi Kiji Sakuin, Sci. Cit. Index, Abr. Ed. **LC** RS402. **DD** 615.105. **NLM** W1 DR521BL. **CODEN** DDIPD8. bk rev. adv acc. (ctrl). Keeps you informed on all aspects of pharmaceutical formulation, pharmaceutical production, pharmacokinetics, biopharmaceuticals, drug regulatory affairs and quality control. *Drug Development Communications, 0095-5183.*

DRUG DEVELOPMENT RESEARCH. Vol. 1, No. 1-. 0272-4391. Periodical. US. English. ir. Alan R Liss Inc, 41 East 11th Street, New York NY 10003. Tel (212)741-2515. **Ind/Abst** Life Sci. Collect., Pestdoc, Ringdoc, Vetdoc, Excerpta Med., Energy Inf. Abstr., Environ. Abstr., Biol. Abstr., Chem. Abstr. **NLM** W1 DR521CM. **CODEN** DDREDK.

DRUG FACTS AND COMPARISONS. **VFOAT** Facts and Comparisons. 1982 Ed.-. 0277-9714. US. English. an. $59.50. Facts and Comparisons Division, J B Lippincott Co, 111 West Port Plaza/Suite 423, St Louis MO 63141. **LC** RM300. **DD** 615.1. **NLM** QV 772 D7924. *Facts and Comparisons (Annual Edition), 0162-1491.*

DRUG FATE AND METABOLISM. **VFOAT** Drug Fate & Metabolism. Vol. 1-. 0160-6697. Periodical. US. English. Marcel Dekker, 270 Madison Avenue, New York NY 10016. Ed Edward R Garrett and Jean L Hirtz. **Ind/Abst** Chem. Abstr. **LC** RS189. **DD** 615.705. **NLM** QV 38 D792. **CODEN** DFMED9.

DRUG INDEX. See Indexes/Abstracts.

DRUG INTELLIGENCE & CLINICAL PHARMACY. **VFOAT** Drug Intelligence and Clinical Pharmacy. Began with June 1969 issue. 0012-6578. Periodical. US. English. mo. $35.00 Domestic, $37.00 Canada. Drug Intelligence and Clinical Pharmacy Inc, PO Box 42435, Cincinnati OH 45242. **Ind/Abst** Life Sci. Collect., Pestdoc, Ringdoc, Vetdoc, Excerpta Med., Index Med., Chem. Abstr., Biol. Abstr., Curr. Contents Clin. Pract., Hospit. Lit. Index, Index Sci. Rev., Med. Care Rev., Excerpta Med., Int. Pharm. Abstr., Abstr. Health Care Manage. Stud., Cumul. Index Nurs. Allied Health Lit., Iowa Drug Inf. Serv. **LC** RM300. **DD** 615.105. **NLM** W1 DR524. **CODEN** DICPBB. *Drug Intelligence.*

DRUG INTERACTIONS NEWSLETTER. Vol. 1, No. 1-. 0271-8707. Periodical. US. English. mo. $27.00. Applied Therapeutics Inc, PO Box 1903, Spokane WA 99210. Tel (509)534-5713. Ed Philip D Hansten and John R Horn. **NLM** W1 DR525. Circ 1,500. (ctrl). Provides current information for those who need to know the clinical implications of drug interactions. Analyzes reported interactions and assesses their significance.

DRUG INTERACTIONS UPDATE. 1982-. US. English. an. **NLM** ZQV 38.

DRUG MERCHANDISING. V. 6- 1925-. 0012-6586. Periodical. CN. English. mo. $30.18. MacLean Hunter, PO Box 100 Station A, Toronto Ontario M5W 1A7 Canada. **Ind/Abst** Can. Bus. Index. **NLM** W1 DR533. *Druggists' Weekly.*

DRUG METABOLISM NEWSLETTER. 0199-7912. Periodical. US. English. qt. American Society of Pharmaceutical and Experimental Therapy, Atten: A Condatore, 9650 Rockville Pike, Bethesda MD 20014.

DRUG METABOLISM REVIEWS. V. 1-. 0360-2532. US. English. $215.00. Marcel Dekker Journals, Box 11305/Church Street Station, New York NY 10249. Ed Frederick Jo Di Carlo. **Ind/Abst** Pestdoc, Ringdoc, Vetdoc, Energy Res. Abstr., Life Sci. Collect., Biol. Abstr., Chem. Abstr., Curr. Contents. Life Sci., Excerpta Med., Index Med., Int. Pharm. Abstr., Index Sci. Rev., Curr. Aware. Biol. Sci., Bull. Signal., Autom. Subj. Citation Alert. **DD** 615. **CODEN** DMTRAR.

DRUG NEWSLETTER. **VFOAT** Facts and Comparisons Drug Newsletter. Vol. 1, No. 1 (Apr. 1982)-. 0731-5163. Periodical. US. English. mo.

$36.00. JB Lippincott Co, 111 West Port Plaza/Suite 423 F & C Division, St Louis MO 63141. **Tel** (314)878-2515. Summarizes information on new findings and recent developments in drug therapy, new drugs and drug products, OTC drug products, etc.

DRUG-NUTRIENT INTERACTIONS. Vol. 1, No. 1-. 0272-3530. Periodical. US. English. qt. Alan R Liss Inc, 41 East 11th Street, New York NY 10003. **Tel** (212)741-2515. **Ind/Abst** Life Sci. Collect., Excerpta Med., Index Med., Biol. Abstr., Chem. Abstr. **LC** RM302.4. **DD** 615.7045. **CODEN** DNIND4.

DRUG STORE NEWS. V. 1- Jan. 8, 1979-. 0191-7587. Periodical. US. English. bw. $12.00 Domestic, $13.00 Foreign. Lebhar-Friedman, 425 Park Avenue, New York NY 10022. **Ind/Abst** Infobank. **LC** HD9666.1. **DD** 381.4561510973.

DRUG STORE NEWS. REFERENCE FOR PHARMACY PRACTICE. **VFOAT** Reference for Pharmacy Practice. 1979-. US. English. bw. $14.00. Lebhar Friedman Publ Co, 99 Park Avenue, New York NY 10016. **Tel** (212)371-9400.

DRUG THERAPEUTICS. 1979-. 0163-1705. US. English. an. Elsevier-North Holland Inc, 52 Vanderbilt Avenue, New York NY 10017. **Ind/Abst** Index Med. **LC** RM260. **DD** 615.5805. **NLM** W1 DR609.

DRUG THERAPY. **VFOAT** Drug Therapy (Hosp). V. 1- 1976-. 0160-9459. Periodical. US. English. mo. Biomedical Information Corporation, 919 Third Avenue, New York NY 10022. **Tel** (212)599-3400. **NLM** W1 DR61H.

DRUG THERAPY TOPICS. 0882-6684. Periodical. US. English. mo. Drug Information Service University of Washington, 1959 NE Pacific Street SB-55, Seattle WA 98195. **Tel** (206)543-9487. **Ed** Patrick M Malone. **DD** 615. **Circ** 1,000. Newsletter containing information on the use of medications and the treatment of disease. Also, contains news items regarding the University of Washington Pharmacy and P & T Committee.

DRUG TOPICS. V. 1-56, No. 52, 1883-Dec. 23, 1940. 0012-6616. Periodical. US. English. sm. $34.00. Medical Economics Inc, 680 Kinderkamack Road, Oradell NJ 07649. **Tel** (201)262-3030. **Ed** Val Cardinale. **Ind/Abst** Trade Ind. Index, Predicasts, ABI/Inform, Funk Scott Index Corp. Ind. **NLM** W1 DR611. **CODEN** DGTNA7. adv acc. **Circ** 80,000. (ctrl). Available on microfilm. News for retail pharmacy.

DRUG TOPICS HEALTH & BEAUTY AIDS DIRECTORY. *See* Yearbooks, Almanacs, Directories.

DRUG TOPICS RED BOOK. 48th- 1944/45-. US. English. an. $21.00. Medical Economics, Box 553, Oradell NJ 07649. *Drug Topics Price Book.*

DRUG TOPICS REDBOOK UPDATE. **VFOAT** Redbook Update. Vol. 1, No. 1 (Dec. 1981)-. 0731-8596. US. English. mo. $75.00. Redbook Update, Box 5538, Oradell NJ 07649.

DRUG UPDATE. 0192-9496. Periodical. US. English. ir. Biomedical Information Corp, 800 Second Avenue, New York NY 10017.

DRUGS. V. 1- 1971-. 0012-6667. Periodical. NZ. English. mo. $320.00. Adis Press International Ltd, PO Box 34-030, Auckland 10 New Zealand. **Tel** (212)860-2000. **Ind/Abst** Excerpta Med., Biol. Abstr., Chem. Abstr., Index Med., Life Sci. Collect., Pestdoc, Ringdoc, Vetdoc, Sci. Cit. Index, Abr. Ed., Hospit. Lit. Index. **DD** 615. **NLM** W1 DR892G. **CODEN** DRUGAY. **Circ** 2,500. (ctrl). A key reference journal for libraries: evaluations on new drugs, review articles, practical therapeutics, selected summaries, guide charts, and tables on efficiency, properties, and hazards of drugs.

DRUGS & DEVICES. **VFOAT** Drogues & Dispositifs. Vol. 1, No. 1 (May 1983)-. 0823-7786. Periodical. CN. English (text in French with French text on inverted pages). qt. Continuing Medical Education Programme, 70 Bond Street Suite 200, Toronto Ontario M5B 1X3 Canada. **DD** 615.105.

DRUGS AND THE PHARMACEUTICAL SCIENCES. V. 1- 1975-. 0360-2583. Monographic Series. US. English. ir. Marcel Dekker, 270 Madison Avenue, New York NY 10016. **Ed** J Swarbrick. **Ind/Abst** Chem. Abstr. **NLM** W1 DR893B. **CODEN** DPHSDS.

DRUGS AND THERAPEUTICS FOR MARITIME PRACTITIONERS. V. 1- Jan. 1978-. 0705-291X. Periodical. CN. English. bm. $12.50. Dalhousie University, Department of Pharmacology, Halifax Nova Scotia B3H2H7 Canada. **Tel** (902)424-3435. **Ed** J D Gray and C B Tuttle. **DD** 615.705. **Circ** 5,100. (ctrl). Reviews of the properties and clinical uses of drugs; their side effects and toxicities, reviews and guidelines for the approach to drug management of various disease states.

DRUGS BULLETIN. Periodical. English. ir. **NLM** W1.

DRUGS IN CARDIOLOGY (POINTE-CLAIRE, QUEBEC). (DRUGS IN CARDIOLOGY). **Series/Titl** PRM : Physicians' Reference Manuals. No. 1 (1982)-. 0824-7110. Periodical. CN. English. sm. 50.00. Drugs in Cardiology, c/o STA Communications 63 Place Frontenac, Pointe-Claire Quebec H9R 4Z7 Canada. **Tel** (514)695-7623. **Ed** Paul Brand. **DD** 615.71. adv acc. **Circ** 800. (ctrl). Drug reference manuals.

DRUGS IN CURRENT USE AND NEW DRUGS. 15- 1969-. 0070-7392. US. English. an. Springer Publ Co, 536 Broadway, New York NY 10012. **Tel** (212)431-4370. **Ed** W Modell. **LC** RS79. **DD** 615.105. **NLM** QV 740 AA1 D75. *Drugs in Current Use.*

DRUGS IN FAMILY MEDICINE. 3rd Ed. (1983/84)-. 0826-3094. CN. English. an. 50.00. STA Communications, 63 Place Frontenanc, Pointe-Claire Quebec H9R 4Z7 Canada. **Tel** (514)695-7623. **Ed** Paul Brand. **DD** 615.1. adv acc. **Circ** 20,000. (ctrl). Drug reference manuals. *Canadian Encyclopedia of Drug Therapy, 0710-233X.*

DRUGS IN HEALTH CARE. V. 1- Summer 1974-. 0095-2346. Periodical. US. English. qt. $15.00. American Society of Hospital Pharmacists Research and Education Foundation, 4630 Montgomery Avenue, Washington DC 20014. **LC** HD9665.1. **DD** 338.4761510973. **NLM** W1 DR893P.

DRUGS IN OBSTETRICS/ GYNECOLOGY. *See* Medicine - Gynecology & Obstetrics.

DRUGS IN RESEARCH. (DRUGS IN RESEARCH MICROFORM). 0739-8824. Periodical. US. English. bm. **NLM** QV 772 D3215. *De Haen Frugs in Research.*

DRUGS IN RHEUMATOLOGY. **Series/Titl** PRM : Physicians' Reference Manuals. No. 1 (1982)-. 0826-3167. Periodical. CN. English. sa. 50.00. STA Communications, 63 Place Frontenac, Pointe-Claire Quebec H9R 4Z7 Canada. **Tel** (514)695-7623. **Ed** Paul Brand. **DD** 616.723061. adv acc. **Circ** 1,200. (ctrl). Drug reference manuals.

DRUGS MADE IN GERMANY. V. 1- 1958-. 0012-6683. Periodical. English. qt. 30.00. Editio Cantor, Postfach 12 55, D-7060 Aulendorf West Germany. **Tel** 07525/431. **Ed** Rolf Halt and Viktor Schramm. **Ind/Abst** Pestdoc, Ringdoc, Vetdoc, Excerpta Med., Biol. Abstr., Chem. Abstr. **LC** RS1. **NLM** W1 DR894. **CODEN** DRMGAS. bk rev. adv acc. **Circ** 5,500. International exchange of information on the development, manufacture, distribution and therapeutic use of qualifield drugs.

DRUGS OF CHOICE. 1958/59-. 0070-7406. US. English. be. $54.95. C V Mosby Company, 11830 Westline Industrial Drive, St Louis MO 63141. **Ed** W Modell. **Ind/Abst** Chem. Abstr. **LC** RM101. **NLM** W1 DR895. **CODEN** DRCHAF.

DRUGS OF THE FUTURE. V. 1- Jan. 1976-. 0377-8282. Periodical. SP. English. mo. 380.00 Domestic. J R Prous International Publishers, Apartado de Correos 540, Barcelona Spain. **Tel** (343)258-5250. **Ed** J R Prous. **Ind/Abst** Excerpta Med., Biol. Abstr. **LC** RM1. **DD** 615.105. **NLM** W1 DR897. **CODEN** DRFUD4. adv acc. **Circ** 3,000. (ctrl). A survey of new drugs and potential pharmacological tools in comprehensive monograph form.

DRUGS UNDER EXPERIMENTAL AND CLINICAL RESEARCH. V. 1- Apr. 1977-. 0378-6501. Monographic Series. English (articles and summaries in French). mo. Bioscience Ediprint Inc, Rue Winkelried 8, C P 307, 1211 Geneva 1 Switzerland. **Tel** 022/ 31 62 92. **Ind/Abst** Life Sci. Collect., Pestdoc, Ringdoc, Vetdoc, Excerpta Med., Chem. Abstr. **LC** UNC. **NLM** W1 DR897N. **CODEN** DECRDP.

DUC HOC. Periodical. VM. Vietnamese. mo. Bo Y Te, 7 Trinh Hoai Duc, Ha-Noi Vietnam. **LC** RM1.

THE EAST AFRICAN PHARMACEUTICAL JOURNAL. 0046-094X. Periodical. English. qt. **LC** RM1. **DD** 615.109676. **NLM** W1 EA824D.

EASTERN PHARMACIST. 0012-8872. Periodical. English. mo. $40.00. Eastern Pharmacist, 507 Ashok Bhawan 93 Nehru Place, New Delhi 110 024 India. **Tel** 6433315. **Ed** Mohan C Bazaz. **Ind/Abst** Chem. Abstr. bk rev. adv acc. **Circ** 5,000. Pharmaceutical subjects and medical information.

ECHO (OTTAWA, ONT. : 1977). (ECHO). 0821-7785. Periodical. CN. English (French text on inverted pages). ir. Ottawa Valley Regional Drug Information Service, 43 Bruyere, Ottawa Ontario K1N 5C8 Canada. **DD** 615.5805.

EDMUND'S PRESCRIPTION DRUG PRICES. **VFOAT** Prescription Drug Prices. Vol. 1, No. 1 (1981)-. 0730-0794. US. English. an. $2.50. **LC** HD9666.1. **DD** 615.1029473.

EGYPTIAN JOURNAL OF PHARMACEUTICAL SCIENCES. **VFOAT** Majallah Al-Misriyah Lil-Ulum Al-Saydaliyah. V. 13- 1972-. 0301-5068. Periodical. English (summaries in Arabic). ir. $16.50. National Information and Documentation Centre, Shari Al-Tahrir, Cairo Egypt. **Ind/Abst** Life Sci. Collect., Chem. Abstr. **LC** RS1. **DD** 615.105. **NLM** W1 EG914J. **CODEN** EJPSBZ. *United Arab Republic Journal of Pharmaceutical Sciences, 0301-5076.*

ESSAYS IN NEUROCHEMISTRY AND NEUROPHARMACOLOGY. *See* Medicine - Neurology.

ETHICAL TABLET & CAPSULE HANDBOOK. **VFOAT** Ethical Tablet and Capsule Handbook. 1st Ed. (1980)-. 0157-9509. English. an. Ed R A Wailes. **NLM** QV 772 E86.

EUROPEAN JOURNAL OF CLINICAL PHARMACOLOGY. V. 3- 1970-. 0031-6970. Periodical. GW. English. mo. $364.00. Springer Verlag-New York Inc, 175-5th Avenue, New York NY 10010. **Tel** (212)460-1500. **Ed** J K Aronson, H J Dengler, L Dettli and F Follath. **Ind/Abst** Life Sci. Collect., Pestdoc, Ringdoc, Vetdoc, Excerpta Med., CIS Abstr., Nuci. Sci. Abstr., Biol. Abstr., Chem. Abstr., Index Med., Energy Res. Abstr., Hospit. Lit. Index, Sci. Cit. Index, Abr. Ed. **NLM** W1 EU72D. **CODEN** EJCPAS. bk rev. Coverage of studies on therapeutic trials, reports on adverse reactions, drug metabolism, pharmacokinetics, and drug interactions. *Pharmacologia Clinica.*

EUROPEAN JOURNAL OF DRUG METABOLISM AND PHARMACOKINETICS. V. 1- Jan./Mar. 1976-. 0398-7639. Periodical. FR. English. qt. 165.00 Domestic, $90.00 Foreign. Editions Medecine & Hygiene, Case Postale 229, CH-1211 Geneve 4 Switzerland. **Tel** (022) 46 93 55. **Ind/Abst** Pestdoc, Ringdoc, Vetdoc, Excerpta Med., Index Med., Biol. Abstr., Chem. Abstr., Energy Res. Abstr., Life Sci. Collect., Sci. Cit. Index, Abr. Ed. **LC** RM301. **DD** 615.705. **NLM** W1 EU72DD. **CODEN** EJDPD2.

EUROPEAN JOURNAL OF PHARMACOLOGY. V. 1- Jan. 1967-. 0014-2999. Periodical. NE. English (summaries in French, German and Spanish). sm. $1057.93. Elsevier Science Publishers, PO Box 211, 1000 AE Amsterdam Netherlands. **Tel** (020)5803.911. **Ind/Abst** Life Sci. Collect., Pestdoc, Ringdoc, Vetdoc, Excerpta Med., Bibliogr. Agric., Biol. Abstr., Chem. Abstr., Index Med., Nuci. Sci. Abstr., Psychol. Abstr., Sci. Cit. Index, Abr. Ed. **NLM** W1 EU72E. **CODEN** EJPHAZ. (cum index). *Acta Physiologica et Pharmalogica Neerlandica.*

EVALUATIONS OF DRUG INTERACTIONS. **Main/Corp** American Pharmaceutical Association. 1st- Ed. 0090-6654. US. English. ir. 2388 Schuetz Road, St Louis MO 63146. **Tel** (202)628-4410. **Ed** Arthur F Shinn. **LC** RM302. **DD** 615.704. **NLM** W1 EV13M. 459 Monographs covering drug interactions, including discussions of their mechanism and recommendations for alternative therapy or management.

EVALUATIONS OF DRUG INTERACTIONS. SUPPLEMENT. **Main/Corp** American Pharmaceutical Association. 0094-8640. US. English. $2.00. American Pharmaceutical Association, 2215 Constitution Avenue Northwest, Washington DC 20037. **LC** RM302. **DD** 615.704.

EXCERPTA MEDICA. SECTION 30, PHARMACOLOGY. **VFOAT** Pharmacology. V. 57, Issue 1- Abstracts No. 1-380-. 0014-4347. Periodical. English. ir. Elsevier Science Publishers, PO Box 211, 1000 AE Amsterdam Netherlands. **NLM** ZW 1 E978JC. **CODEN** PTOXAV. *Excerpta Medica. Section 30, Pharmacology and Toxicology, Excerpta Medica. Section 30, Pharmacology and Toxicology.*

Pharmacy

EXCERPTA MEDICA. SECTION 30. PHARMACOLOGY AND TOXICOLOGY *CEASED.* VFOAT Pharmacology and Toxicology. VAT Excerpta Medica. Section Thirty. Pharmacology and Toxicology. V. 22-56. 0014-4347. Periodical. NE. English. sm. **Ind/Abst** Chem. Abstr. **NLM** ZW 1 E978J. **CODEN** PTOXAV. *Excerpta Medica. Section 2C. Pharmacology and Toxicology.*

EXCERPTA MEDICA. SECTION 37, DRUG LITERATURE INDEX. *See* Indexes/Abstracts.

EXECUTIVE DIRECTORY OF THE U. S. PHARMACEUTICAL INDUSTRY. *See* Yearbooks, Almanacs, Directories.

THE EXTRA PHARMACOPOEIA. UK. English. ir. Rittenhouse Book Distributors, 511 Feheley Drive, King of Prussia PA 19406. **Tel** (215)277-1414.

FACTS AND COMPARISONS. Main/Corp Facts and Comparisons, Inc., Saint Louis. 0014-6617. US. English. mo. $99.50. Facts & Comparisons, 111 West Post Plaza/Suite 423, St Louis MO 63141. **Tel** (314)878-2515. Ed Erwin K Kastrup.

FALCONER'S THE DRUG, THE NURSE, THE PATIENT. VFOAT Drug, The Nurse, The Patient. 7th Ed.-. 0735-5602. US. English. ir. **LC** RM125. **DD** 615.105. *Drug, The Nurse, The Patient.*

THE FAMILY PHARMACY NEWSLETTER. V. 1- Aug. 1977-. 0190-5406. Periodical. US. English. mo. $6.00. The Family Pharmacy Newsletter, 3311 West 2400 South, Salt Lake City UT 84119. **NLM** W1 FA4507.

THE FAMILY PHYSICIAN'S COMPENDIUM OF DRUG THERAPY. VFOAT Compendium of Drug Therapy. 1980/81-. 0276-4318. US. English. an. Biomedical Information Corporation, 800 Second Avenue, New York NY 10017. **LC** RM300. **DD** 615.5805.

FARMACEUTICKY OBZOR. VFOAT Casopis pre Farmaceuticku Vedu a Prax. Began in 1961. 0014-8172. Periodical. CS. Slovak (summaries and table of contents in English, German and Russian). mo. **Ind/Abst** Excerpta Med., Biol. Abstr., Bibliogr. Agric. **NLM** W1 FA6904. **CODEN** FAOBAS.

FARMACEVTISK REVY. 0014-8210. Periodical. SW. Swedish. mo. $21.29. Sveriges Farmeceutforbund, Box 613, 101 28 Stockholm Sweden. **Tel** 08/140840. Ed Lindfors. **Ind/Abst** Bibliogr. Agric. **NLM** W1 FA683. bk rev. adv acc. **Circ** 6,500. (ctrl). Pharmacy and union policy in the same field.

FARMACO. (IL FARMACO). Began with V. 8, in 1953. 0430-0920. Periodical. Italian. mo. Editoriale Il Farmaco, PO Box 227, 27100 Pavia Italy. **Ind/Abst** Bibliogr. Agric., Life Sci. Collect., Pestdoc, Ringdoc, Vetdoc, Excerpta Med., Index Med., Chem. Abstr. **NLM** W1 FA826. **CODEN** FRPSAX. *Farmaco.*

FARMAKOTERAPEUTICKE ZPRAVY SPOFA. SUPPLEMENTUM. 0533-0300. Monographic Series. Czech. ir. **Ind/Abst** Chem. Abstr. **NLM** W1 FA877A. **CODEN** FTZSAT.

FARMATSIIA. 0367-3014. Periodical. UR. Russian. bm. $18.00. Victor Kamkin Incorporated (71038), 12224 Parklawn Drive, Rockville MD 20852. **Tel** (301)881-5973. **NLM** W1 FA892DE.

THE FATE OF DRUGS IN THE ORGANISM; A BIBLIOGRAPHIC SURVEY. *See* Bibliographies.

FDC REPORTS. PRESCRIPTION AND OTC PHARMACEUTICALS. VFOAT Prescription and OTC Pharmaceuticals. Vol. 44, No 3 Jan. 18, 1982. 0734-6514. Periodical. US. English. wk. $350.00. F D C Reports Inc, Suite One/5550 Friendship Boulevard, Chevy Chase MD 20815. **Ind/Abst** Pharm. News Index. **NLM** W1 FD411. *FDC Reports. Ethical and OTC Pharmaceuticals, 0272-913X.*

FDC REPORTS. PRESCRIPTION AND OTC PHARMACEUTICALS. MID-WEEK REPORT. VFOAT Prescription and OTC Pharmaceuticals. Vol. 1, No. 1 (Jan. 13, 1982)-. 0734-6506. Periodical. US. English. wk. $150.00. FDC Reports, 5550 Friendship Boulevard/Suite 1, Chevy Chase MD 20815. **Tel** (301)657-9830. **Ind/Abst** Pharm. News Index. **NLM** W1 FD411C. Specialized in-depth review of pharmaceutical industry, regulatory overview by Congress, FDA, FTC: new developments and products, mergers, financial news, sales and earnings performances.

FEDERAL PHARMACIST. 0428-1179. US. English. ir. Federal Wholesale Druggists Association, PO Box 238, Alexandria VA 22313. **DD** 615.

FLORIDA PHARMACY JOURNAL. V. 42, No. 5- May 1978-. 0161-746X. Periodical. US. English. mo. $20.00. Florida Pharmaceutical Association, 610 North Adams Street, Tallahassee FL 32301. **Tel** (904)222-2400. Ed James B Powers. **NLM** W1 FL852J. bk rev. adv acc. **Circ** 3,000. Editorials, continuing education, legislative issues, news releases. *Florida Pharmaceutical Journal, 0015-4202.*

FOLIA PHARMACOLOGICA JAPONICA. V. 1- 1925-. 0015-5691. Periodical. JA. text in Japanese, English or German. mo. Kyowa Book Company Inc, 1-38 Kanda Jinbocho/Chiyoda-ku, Tokyo 101 Japan. **Tel** 293-0727. **Ind/Abst** Chem. Abstr., Index Med., Sci. Cit. Index, Abr. Ed. **CODEN** NYKZAU.

THE FOOD & DRUG LETTER. *See* Food & Drink.

FOOD-DRUGS FROM THE SEA; PROCEEDINGS. 2nd- 1969-. Periodical. US. English. *Drugs from the Sea.*

A GAZETA DA FARMACIA *CEASED.* V. 1- (No. 1-) 1932-. Periodical. BL. Spanish. mo. Antonio Nunes Lago, Caixa Postal 528, Rio de Janeiro ZC00 Brazil.

GENERAL PHARMACOLOGY. Began with Mar. 1975. 0306-3623. Periodical. UK. English. bm. Pergamon Press, 395 Sawmill River Road, Elmsford NY 10523. **Ind/Abst** Life Sci. Collect., Index Med., Excerpta Med., Chem. Abstr., Pestdoc, Ringdoc, Vetdoc, Biol. Abstr., Sci. Cit. Index, Abr. Ed. **LC** RM1. **DD** 615.105. **NLM** W1 GE255. **CODEN** GEPHDP. *Comparative and General Pharmacology, 0010-4035.*

GENERICS MAGAZINE. VFOAT Generics. Vol. 1, Issue 1 (Spring 1984)-. 0742-308X. Periodical. US. English. qt. $12.50. Generics Magazine, 541 North Fairbanks Court, Chicago IL 60611. **DD** 615.

GESUNDHEITSPOLITISCHE UMSCHAU. (GESUNDHEITSPOLITISCHE UMSCHAN. GU). VFOAT GU. Vol. 23-. 0016-9307. Periodical. German. ir. **NLM** W1 GE916B. *Gesundheitspolitische Umschau.*

GYOGYSZERTERAPIAS DOKUMENTACIOS SZEMLE. V. 16-. Periodical. HU. Hungarian. ir. Orszagos Gyogyszereszeti Intezet, Uzsoki U 36/A, 1145 Budapest XIV Hungary. **LC** Z6675.P5, RM300. **NLM** ZQV 4 G997. *Gyogyszersezeti es Gyogyszerterapias Dokumentacios Szemle.*

DE HAEN DRUG INTERACTIONS. Main/Corp Paul de Haen Inc. VFOAT Drug Interactions. 1972-. 0091-2689. Monographic Series. US. English. ir. Lea & Febiger, 600 Washington Square, Philadelphia PA 19106. **Tel** (215)922-1330. **NLM** ZQV 38 D322.

DE HAEN NEW DRUG ANALYSIS, EUROPE & JAPAN. VFOAT New Drug Analysis, Europe and Japan. VAT De Haen New Drug Analysis, Europe and Japan. Began with: Vol. 8 (1974-1978). 0740-9273. US. English. an. $275.00. Paul De Haen International Inc, 2750 South Shoshone, Englewood CO 80110. **Tel** (800)438-0296. Ed Harold L Bober. **NLM** QV 772 D278. **Circ** 200. (ctrl). Statistical and marketing analysis of drugs introduced in Europe and Japan during the past ten years. *De Haen New Drug Analysis, Europe.*

DE HAEN NEW DRUG ANALYSIS, U.S.A. VFOAT De Haen New Drug Analysis, USA. VAT De Haen New Drug Analysis, United States of America. 1964. 0730-9236. US. English. an. $225.00. Paul De Haen International Inc, 2750 South Shoshone, Englewood CO 80110. **Tel** (800)438-0296. Ed Harold L Bober. **Circ** 200. (ctrl). Statistical and marketing analysis of drugs introduced in USA during the past ten years.

DE HAEN NONPROPRIETARY NAME INDEX. *See* Indexes/Abstracts.

HANDBOOK OF EXPERIMENTAL PHARMACOLOGY. V. 50-. 0171-2004. Monographic Series. English. ir. Ed G V R Born and others. **Ind/Abst** Life Sci. Collect., Chem. Abstr. **NLM** W1 HA51L. **CODEN** HEPHD2. *Handbuch der Experimentellen Pharmakologie. New Series, 0073-0033.*

HANDBOOK OF NONPRESCRIPTION DRUGS. 1st- Ed. US. English. ir. American Pharmaceutical Association, 2215 Constitution Avenue NW, Washington DC 20037. **Tel** (202)628-4410.

HANDBUCH DER EXPERIMENTELLEN PHARMAKOLOGIE. 0073-0033. German. ir. Springer Verlag, 44 Hartz Way, Secaucus NJ 07094. **Tel** (201)348-4033. Ed G V R Born. **Ind/Abst** Chem. Abstr. **Circ** 300. Provides critical and comprehensive discussions of the most significant areas of pharmacological research, written by leading international authorities. It is an unrivaled reference source.

HAYES DRUGGIST DIRECTORY. *See* Yearbooks, Almanacs, Directories.

HINDUSTAN ANTIBIOTICS BULLETIN. Began with Aug. 1958 issue. 0018-1935. Periodical. II. English. qt. $15.00. Hindustan Antibiotics Ltd, Pimpri Library, Pune 411 018 India. Ed P S Borkar. **Ind/Abst** Life Sci. Collect., Excerpta Med., Biol. Abstr., Chem. Abstr., Index Med., Nuci. Sci. Abstr., Bibliogr. Agric. **LC** RM265. **DD** 615.32905. **NLM** W1 HI407. **CODEN** HINAAU. bk rev. adv acc. **Circ** 350. Biotechnology-fermentation process, pharmacology and clinical trials of new drugs, reviews and bibliography on antibiotics.

HOSPITAL FORMULARY. V. 10, No. 6- June 1975-. 0098-6909. Periodical. US. English. mo. Hospital Formulary, 1 East First Street, Duluth MN 55802. **Tel** (218)723-9200. **Ind/Abst** Hospit. Lit. Index, Pestdoc, Ringdoc, Vetdoc, Cumul. Index Nurs. Allied Health Lit., Biol. Abstr. **NLM** W1 HO779. **CODEN** HOFODY. *Hospital Formulary Management, 0018-5655.*

HOSPITAL PHARMACY. VFOAT Lippincott's Hospital Pharmacy. 0018-5787. Periodical. US. English. mo $43.00. J B Lippincott Company, East Washington Square, Philadelphia PA 19105. **Tel** (215)238-4273. Ed Neil M Davis. **Ind/Abst** Hospit. Lit. Index, Excerpta Med., Biol. Abstr. **NLM** W1 HO869B. **CODEN** HOPHAZ. adv acc. **Circ** 27,800. Deals with all areas of interest to pharmacists serving hospital inpatients and outpatients.

HOSPITAL PHARMACY SERVICE INSTANT UP-DATE. VFOAT Instant Update. 0739-9561. Periodical. US. English. mo. $25.00. RX-Data-Pac, 7702 Stonehedge Drive, Cincinnati OH 45242.

I.I.M.S. INDONESIA INDEX OF MEDICAL SPECIALITIES. *See* Indexes/Abstracts.

ILLINOIS PHARMACIST. Vol. 41- Sept. 1979-. 0195-2099. Periodical. US. English. mo. $10.00. Illinois Pharmaceutical Association, 222 West Adams Street, Chicago IL 60606. **NLM** W1 IL433B. *Illinois Journal of Pharmacy, 0147-8222.*

INDEX NOMINUM. *See* Indexes/Abstracts.

INDIAN JOURNAL OF HOSPITAL PHARMACY. 1964. 0019-526X. Periodical. II. English. bm. 15.00. Indian Hospital Pharmacist Association, R-566 New Rajinder, New Delhi 60 India. **Tel** 583331. Ed B D Miglani. **Ind/Abst** Chem. Abstr., Excerpta Med., Biol. Abstr. **NLM** W1 IN209J. **CODEN** IJHPBU. bk rev. adv acc. **Circ** 3,000. Ideas in the areas on pharmaceutical services in hospitals. Continued education, programmed for pharmacists, drug information and phamaceutical research.

INDIAN JOURNAL OF PHARMACEUTICAL EDUCATION. (INDIAN JOURNAL OF PHARMACEUTICAL EDUCATION : OFFICIAL PUBLICATION OF ASSOCIATION OF PHARMACEUTICAL TEACHERS OF INDIA). Vol. 1, No. 1 (Jan.-June 1967)-. 0019-5464. Periodical. II. English. sa. $20.00. Association of Pharmaceutical Teachers of India, Nagpur University, Nagpur 44001 India. **Tel** 24324. **Ind/Abst** Chem. Abstr. **LC** RS119.I5. **DD** 615.071154. **NLM** W1 IN224P. **CODEN** IJPEB3. **Circ** 400. Covers pharmaceutical education only.

INDIAN JOURNAL OF PHARMACEUTICAL SCIENCES. V. 40, No. 2- Mar./Apr. 1978-. 0250-474X. Periodical. II. English. bm. $25.00. Indian Pharmaceutical Association, Kalina/Santa Cruz East, Bombay 29 India. **Ind/Abst** Pestdoc, Ringdoc, Vetdoc, Excerpta Med., Biol. Abstr., Chem. Abstr., Bibliogr. Agric. **NLM** W1 IN224V. **CODEN** IJSIDW. *Indian Journal of Pharmacy, 0019-5472.*

INDIAN JOURNAL OF PHARMACOLOGY. 0253-7613. Periodical. II. English. qt. $40.00. Department of Pharmacology and Therapeutics, Government Medical College, Jammu Tawi 180001 India. **Tel** 46824. **Ed** R K Raina. **Ind/Abst** Excerpta Med., Chem. Abstr. **NLM** W1 IN2251. **CODEN** INJPD2. adv acc. **Circ** 1,000. Pharmacology, medicinal chemistry, chemotherapy, clinical toxicology, drugs, drug development, drug kinetics, pharmacodynamics and clinical trials.

INDIAN JOURNAL OF PHARMACY. 0019-5472. Periodical. II. English. mo. $8.80. Indian Pharmaceutical Association, Kalina Santacruz East, Bombay 29 AS India. **Ind/Abst** Nuci. Sci. Abstr., Bibliogr. Agric., Biol. Abstr., Chem. Abstr. **NLM** W1 IN2252. **CODEN** IJPAAO.

INDIAN JOURNAL OF PHYSIOLOGY AND PHARMACOLOGY. *See* Biology - Physiology.

INDUSTRIAL PHARMACOLOGY. V. 1-. 0093-3589. Monographic Series. US. English. ir. Futura Publishing Company Inc, 295 Main Street, PO Box 298, Mount Kisco NY 10549. **Tel** (914)666-3505. **Ind/Abst** Chem. Abstr. **NLM** W1 IN391R. **CODEN** IDPYAK.

INFORMATION LETTER - UNITED NATIONS, DIVISION OF NARCOTIC DRUGS. (INFORMATION LETTER). Began in 1971. 0378-2220. Periodical. AU. English. bm. United Nations Division of Narcotic Drugs, Vienna International Center, PO Box 500, A-1400 Vienna Austria. **NLM** W1.

L'INFORMATORE FARMACEUTICO. **VFOAT** Italian Directory of Drugs and Manufacturers. 1968-. 0073-7984. IT. Italian. ir. 196.00. Org Edit Medico Farmaceutica, Via Edolo 42 PO Box 10434, 20125 Milano Italy. **Tel** 02-600.376. **Ed** Lucio Marini. bk rev. adv acc. **Circ** 25,000. Italian list of 25,000 drugs, 6,000 pharmaceutical raw materials and more than 2,000 manufacturer's addresses, updated every 2 months. *Informatore Farmaceutico Italiano.*

INFORMED. BLUE BANNER EDITION. (INFORMED). **VAT** Infor Med. Blue Banner Edition. 0730-6628. Periodical. US. English. wk. $395.00. MDT Publishing, 2915 Bissonnet, Houston TX 77005.

INHALO-SCOPE. (L'INHALO-SCOPE : PUBLICATION OFFICIELLE DE LA CORPORATION DES INHALOTHERAPEUTES DU QUEBEC). Vol. 1, No. 1 (Oct. 1983)-. 0824-8281. Periodical. CN. French. qt. Free to Members. Corporation des Inhalotherapeutes du Quebec, Suite 2004/666 Ouest rue Sherbrooke, Montreal Quebec H3A 1E7 Canada. **DD** 615.836. *Bulletin, 0712-9610.*

INPHARMA. **VFOAT** Adis Inpharma. No. 1- Aug. 15, 1975-. 0377-0095. Periodical. US. English. ir. Adis Press, 401 South State Street, Newtown PA 18940. **Tel** (215)860-2000. **NLM** W1 IN456. adv acc. **Circ** 1,300. A bulletin that brings up-to-date information on international coverage of drugs and drug treatment in easy to read reports and summaries.

INTERNATIONAL DRUG REVIEW. Vol. 1, No. 1 (Apr. 1982)- Issue 1-. 0734-9084. Periodical. US. English. ir. $640.00. Paregian Associates, 250 Davenport Avenue, New Rochelle NY 10805. **Tel** (914)235-8035. **Ed** Philip Paregian. Covers new drugs under development in Europe, Japan, USSR, and India giving stage of progress, description, chemistry, clinical evaluations, markets, patents, licensees, etc.

INTERNATIONAL DRUG THERAPY NEWSLETTER. Began in 1966. 0020-6571. Periodical. US. English. ir. $32.00. Ayd Medical Communications, 1130 East Cold Spring Lane, Baltimore MD 21239. **Tel** (301)433-9220. **Ed** Frank J Ayd Jr. **NLM** W1 IN747. bk rev. adv acc. **Circ** 7,000. An authoritiative source of valuable information on psychopharmacotherapy. Realistic, balanced information on psychoactive drug therapy and use.

INTERNATIONAL ENCYCLOPEDIA OF PHARMACOLOGY AND THERAPEUTICS. *See* Encyclopedias & General Reference Books.

INTERNATIONAL JOURNAL OF CLINICAL PHARMACOLOGY RESEARCH. **VFOAT** Clinical Pharmacology Research. Began with Vol. 1 in 1981. 0251-1649. Periodical. English. qt. **Ind/Abst** Life Sci. Collect., Excerpta Med., Index Med., Chem. Abstr. **NLM** W1 IN766DKH. **CODEN** CPHRDE.

INTERNATIONAL JOURNAL OF CLINICAL PHARMACOLOGY, THERAPY AND TOXICOLOGY (INTERNATIONAL SYMPOSIA ON CLINICAL PHARMACOLOGY : 1980). (INTERNATIONAL JOURNAL OF CLINICAL PHARMACOLOGY, THERAPY AND TOXICOLOGY). Vol. 18, No. 1 (Jan. 1980)-. 0174-4879. Periodical. GW. English. mo. $138.50. Dustri-Verlag, Dr Karl Feistle Bahnhofstrasse 9 Postfach 49, 8024 Deisenhofen West Germany. **Ind/Abst** Life Sci. Collect., Pestdoc, Ringdoc, Vetdoc, Excerpta Med., Index Med., Chem. Abstr., Psychol. Abstr., Hospit. Lit. Index. **NLM** W1 IN766DL. Index in last issue of volume - attached. *International Journal of Clinical Pharmacology and Biopharmacy, 0340-0026.*

INTERNATIONAL JOURNAL OF CRUDE DRUG RESEARCH *CEASED.* Vol. 20, No. 1 (Feb. 1982)-Vol. 21, No. 2 (Aug. 1983). 0167-7314. Periodical. NE. English (French, German, and Spanish). qt. 80.00. Swets & Zeitlinger BV, 347 Heereweg, 2161 Ca Lisse The Netherlands. **Tel** 02521-19113. **Ed** John A Beutler. **Ind/Abst** Pestdoc, Ringdoc, Vetdoc, Biol. Abstr., Chem. Abstr. **CODEN** IJCREE. bk rev. adv acc. **Circ** 600. Devoted to the recording of the history, taxonomy, ecology, geographical distribution, morphology, histology, chemistry, methods of determination of plant and animal crude drugs. *Quarterly Journal of Crude Drug Research, 0033-5525.*

INTERNATIONAL JOURNAL OF IMMUNOPHARMACOLOGY. V. 1-. 0192-0561. Periodical. UK. English. ir. Pergamon Press, 395 Sawmill River Road, Elmsford NY 10523. **Ind/Abst** Life Sci. Collect., Pestdoc, Ringdoc, Vetdoc, Excerpta Med., Index Med., Biol. Abstr., Chem. Abstr., Sci. Cit. Index, Abr. Ed. **NLM** W1 IN768K. **CODEN** IJIMDS.

INTERNATIONAL JOURNAL OF PHARMACEUTICAL TECHNOLOGY & PRODUCT MANUFACTURE. **VFOAT** International Journal of Pharmaceutical Technology and Product Manufacture. Vol. 1, No. 1 (Autumn 1979)-. 0260-6267. Periodical. UK. English. ir. $105.00. Childwall University Press Ltd, PO Box 78, London NW11 OPG England. **Tel** (UK01)455-0011. **Ed** A S Goldberg. **Ind/Abst** Pestdoc, Ringdoc, Vetdoc, Excerpta Med., Biol. Abstr., Chem. Abstr. **NLM** W1 IN771S. **CODEN** IPTMDN. bk rev. adv acc. **Circ** 1,500. Pharmaceutical technology and manufacturing, including analysis, manufacture, process, stability, etc.

INTERNATIONAL JOURNAL OF PHARMACEUTICS. V. 1- Jan./Feb. 1978-. 0378-5173. Periodical. English. ir. Elsevier Science Publishers, PO Box 211, 1000 AE Amsterdam Netherlands. **Tel** 9020 5803.911. **Ind/Abst** Life Sci. Collect., Pestdoc, Ringdoc, Vetdoc, Excerpta Med., Biol. Abstr., Chem. Abstr., Bibliogr. Agric. **NLM** W1 IN771T. **CODEN** IJPHDE.

INTERNATIONAL NONPROPRIETARY NAMES (INN) FOR PHARMACEUTICAL SUBSTANCES. **Main/Corp** World Health Organization. **VFOAT** Denominations Communes Internationales (DCI) pour les Substances Pharmaceutiques. Monographic Series. US. Multilingual. Who Publications Centre, PO Box 5584 Church Street Station, New York NY 10249. **Tel** (518)436-9686. *Cumulative List of Proposed International Non-Proprietary Names for Pharmaceutical Preparations.*

INTERNATIONAL PHARMACEUTICAL ABSTRACTS. *See* Indexes/Abstracts.

INTERNATIONAL PHARMACEUTICAL TECHNOLOGY & PRODUCT MANUFACTURE ABSTRACTS. *See* Indexes/Abstracts.

THE INTERNIST'S COMPENDIUM OF DRUG THERAPY. **VFOAT** Compendium of Drug Therapy. 1980/81-. 0276-4342. US. English. an. Biomedical Information Corporation, 800 2nd Avenue, New York NY 10017. **LC** RM300. **DD** 615.58.

IOWA DRUG INFORMATION SERVICE. Periodical. US. English. ir.

IOWA PHARMACIST. V. 1- Nov. 1946-. Periodical. US. English. mo. $15.00. Iowa Pharmacists Association, 8515 Douglas Street/Suite 24, Des Moines IA 50322. **Tel** (515)270-0713.

IRCS MEDICAL SCIENCE. CLINICAL PHARMACOLOGY AND THERAPEUTICS. (IRCS MEDICAL SCIENCE : CLINICAL PHARMACOLOGY AND THERAPEUTICS). **VFOAT** Clinical Pharmacology and Therapeutics. V. 3- Jan. 1975-. 0305-6759. Periodical. UK. English. bm. $70.00. IRCS Medical Science, PO Box 500, St Leonards House, Lancaster LA1 1PF England. **Tel** (0524)68116. **Ed** S Johnson. **Ind/Abst** Pestdoc, Ringdoc, Vetdoc. bk rev. Publishes results of original research into the effects of drugs in man including clinical trials, reports of side effects and clinical pharmacology studies within weeks of completion. Papers fully refereed. *Research on Clinical Pharmacology and Therapeutics, 0305-2664.*

IRCS MEDICAL SCIENCE. PHARMACOLOGY. (IRCS MEDICAL SCIENCE : PHARMACOLOGY). **VFOAT** Pharmacology. V. 3- Jan. 1975-. 0305-6872. Periodical. UK. English. mo. $170.00. IRCS Medical Science, PO Box 500/St Leonards House, Lancaster LA1 1PF England. **Tel** (0524)68116. **Ed** S Johnson. **Ind/Abst** Pestdoc, Ringdoc, Vetdoc. bk rev. Results of original research into the effects of drugs on whole organisms, tissues and purified preparations within weeks of completion. Papers fully refereed. *Research on Basic Pharmacology, 0305-2869.*

IRISH PHARMACY JOURNAL. Began with Jan. 1972 issue. Periodical. English. ir. 4.00. 18 Mary's Abbey 7, Dublin Ireland. **LC** RS1. **DD** 615.105. **NLM** W1 IR458. *Irish Chemist & Druggist.*

IRYANG. Periodical. KO. Korean. bm. Iryang Yakpum Kongop Chusik Hoesa, 24-5 Hawolgok-Dong Stongbuk-Ku, Seoul 132 Korea. **LC** RM1.

ITOGI NAUKI : FARMAKOLOGIIA, KHIMIOTERAPEVTICHESKIE SREDSTVA, TOKSIKOLOGIIA, PROBLEMY FARMAKOLOGII. **VFOAT** Farmakologiia, Khimioterapevticheskie Sredstva, Toksikologiia, Problemy Farmakologii. Began in 1969. UR. Russian. 1.09 Single Issue. **LC** RM30.

JANSSEN RESEARCH FOUNDATION SERIES. V. 1-. 0165-8352. Monographic Series. English. ir. Elsevier/North Holland Inc, 52 Vanderbilt Avenue, New York NY 10017. **Ind/Abst** Life Sci. Collect., Chem. Abstr. **NLM** W1 JA82. **CODEN** JRFSDU.

JANSSEN RESEARCH NEWS. **VFOAT** Research News. Periodical. US. English. bm. Janssen Pharmaceutica, 501 George Street, New Brunswick NJ 08903.

JAPANESE JOURNAL OF ANTIBIOTICS. (THE JAPANESE JOURNAL OF ANTIBIOTICS). V. 21- Feb. 1968-. 0368-2781. Periodical. JA. Japanese (summaries in English). mo. $50.00. Japan Antibiotics Research Association, 2-20-8 Kamiosaki Shinagawa-Ku, Tokyo 141 Japan. **Tel** 03 491-0181. **Ind/Abst** Life Sci. Collect., Excerpta Med., Pestdoc, Ringdoc, Vetdoc, Index Med., Chem. Abstr. **NLM** W1 JA95N. **CODEN** JJANAX. *Journal of Antibiotics. Series B.*

JAPANESE JOURNAL OF PHARMACOLOGY. (THE JAPANESE JOURNAL OF PHARMACOLOGY). V. 1- Sept. 1951-. 0021-5198. Periodical. JA. English. mo. $100.00. Japan Publishing Trading Company Ltd, PO Box 5030, Tokyo International, 100-31 Tokyo Japan. **Ind/Abst** Life Sci. Collect., Excerpta Med., Pestdoc, Ringdoc, Vetdoc, Nuci. Sci. Abstr., Psychol. Abstr., Biol. Abstr., Chem. Abstr., Index Med., Sci. Cit. Index, Abr. Ed. **LC** QP901. **DD** 615.05. **NLM** W1 JA971. **CODEN** JJPAAZ. *Japanese Journal of Medical Sciences. Section 4. Pharmacology, 0368-3745.*

JAPTA LIST; JAPANESE DRUG DIRECTORY. *See* Yearbooks, Almanacs, Directories.

JOURNAL DE PHARMACIE CLINIQUE. **VFOAT** International Journal of Clinical Pharmacy. 1 (1)-. 0291-1981. Periodical. French (with summaries in English). qt. Lavoisier Abonnements, 11 rue Lavoisier, F75384 Paris France. **Tel** 12.65.71.67. **Ind/Abst** Excerpta Med., Chem. Abstr. **CODEN** JPCLDE. bk rev. adv acc. **Circ** 1,250. (ctrl). Publishes papers on all aspects of pharmaceutical sciences applied to man such as biopharmacy, analytical chemistry, pharmacokinetics, adverse drug reactions and toxicology, therapeutics and clinical pharmacology.

JOURNAL DE PHARMACIE DE BELGIQUE. Began publication with 1919. 0047-2166. Periodical. French. bm. Masson Publishing USA Inc, 211 East 43rd Street/Room 1306, New York NY 10017. **Tel** (212)370-1937. **Ind/Abst** Life Sci. Collect., Excerpta Med., Pestdoc, Ringdoc, Vetdoc, Bibliogr. Agric., Biol. Abstr., Chem. Abstr., Index Med., Nuci. Sci. Abstr. **CODEN** JPBEAJ. *Journal de Pharmacie, 0368-3613.*

JOURNAL DE PHARMACOLOGIE. V. 1- Jan. 1970-. 0021-793X. Periodical. US. French (summaries in English). qt. Masson Publishing USA

Inc, 211 East 43rd Street/Room 1306, New York NY 10017. **Tel** (212)370-1937. **Ind/Abst** Life Sci. Collect., Excerpta Med., Pestdoc, Ringdoc, Vetdoc, Index Med., Chem. Abstr., Biol. Abstr., Energy Res. Abstr. **LC** RM1. **NLM** W1 JO328U. **CODEN** JNPHAG.

JOURNAL DE PHARMACOLOGIE CLINIQUE. **VFOAT** Human Pharmacology and Drug Research. V. 1- Jan./Mar. 1973-. 0301-4762. Periodical. FR. English. ir. Edifor, 49 rue Saint-Andre-Des -Arts, 75006 Paris France. **Ind/Abst** Chem. Abstr. **NLM** W1 JO328UK. **CODEN** JPCCBJ.

JOURNAL - NATIONAL PHARMACEUTICAL ASSOCIATION. **Main/Corp** National Pharmaceutical Association. **VFOAT** NPHA Journal. 0027-9897. Periodical. US. English. qt. Howrad University, PO Box 934, National Pharmaceutical Association, Washington DC 20059. **Tel** (202)636-7491. **NLM** W1 JO941P.

JOURNAL OF ANTIBIOTICS. V. 6- Feb. 1953-. Periodical. JA. English. mo. $120.00. Japan Antibiotic Research Association, 2-20-8 Kamiosaki Shihagawaku, Tokyo Japan. **Tel** 03/491-0181. **NLM** W 1 JO537. *Journal of Antibiotics. Ser. A.*

JOURNAL OF AUTONOMIC PHARMACOLOGY. Vol. 1, No. 1 (Nov. 1980)-. 0144-1795. Periodical. UK. English. qt. $80.00. Galen Press, 18 North Bar Within Beverley, North Humberside Hl17 8AX England. **Tel** (0482)868922. **Ed** M D Day. **Ind/Abst** Life Sci. Collect., Excerpta Med., Index Med., Biol. Abstr., Chem. Abstr. **NLM** W1 JO547P. **CODEN** JAPHDU. bk rev. **Circ** 650. Effect of drugs and related substances on the structure and functioning of the mammalian autonomic nervous system including man.

JOURNAL OF BIOLOGICAL RESPONSE MODIFIERS. Vol. 1, No. 1-. 0732-6580. Periodical. US. Englsih. bm. $105.00. Raven Press, 1140 Avenue of the Americas, New York NY 10036. **Tel** (212)575-0335. **Ind/Abst** Life Sci. Collect., Excerpta Med., Index Med., Chem. Abstr. **LC** RM270. **DD** 615.37. **NLM** W1 JO564EM. **CODEN** JBRMDS.

JOURNAL OF CHRONIC DISEASES AND THERAPEUTICS RESEARCH. V. 1- 1977-. 0141-3317. Periodical. UK. English. qt. International Society for the Prevention of Stress, 9 Suffold Drive, Laidon Essex SS15 6PL England. **NLM** W1 JO585T.

JOURNAL OF CLINICAL AND HOSPITAL PHARMACY. V. 5- Mar. 1980-. 0143-3180. Periodical. UK. English. qt. $117.00. Blackwell Scientific Publishing Ltd, PO Box 88, Oxford OX2 0EL England. **Tel** 0865 260201. **Ed** A Linan Po. **Ind/Abst** Life Sci. Collect., Pestdoc, Ringdoc, Vetdoc, Excerpta Med., Index Med., Biol. Abstr., Chem. Abstr. **NLM** W1 JO587AC. **CODEN** JCHPDS. bk rev. adv acc. **Circ** 412. Concerns with the manufacture quality control and formulation of medicine, drug information services, pharmacokinetics, radiopharmacy and drug distribution systems. *Journal of Clinical Pharmacy, 0308-6593.*

JOURNAL OF CLINICAL PHARMACOLOGY. (THE JOURNAL OF CLINICAL PHARMACOLOGY). V. 13. No. 5/6- May/June 1973-. 0091-2700. Periodical. US. English. $65.00. Le Jacq Publishing Inc, 53 Park Place, New York NY 10007. **Tel** (212)766-4300. **Ind/Abst** Electron. Commun. Abstr. J., ISMEC Bull., Pollut. Abstr. Indexes, Saf. Sci. Abstr. J., Life Sci. Collect., Pestdoc, Ringdoc, Vetdoc, Excerpta Med., Index Med., Biol. Abstr., Chem. Abstr., Psychol. Abstr., Energy Res. Abstr., Sci. Cit. Index, Abr. Ed. **DD** 615. **NLM** W1 JO5899. **CODEN** JCPCBR. *Journal of Clinical Pharmacology and New Drugs, 0021-9754.*

THE JOURNAL OF CONTINUING EDUCATION IN HOSPITAL & CLINICAL PHARMACY. **VFOAT** J.C.E. Hospital & Clinical Pharmacy. **VAT** Journal of Continuing Education in Hospital and Clinical Pharmacy. V. 1- Jan./Mar. 1979. 0163-481X. Periodical. US. English. qt. $10.00. Journal of Continuing, Education in Hospital and Clinical Pharmacy, 445 Central Avenue, Northfield IL 60093.

JOURNAL OF ETHNOPHARMACOLOGY. **VFOAT** Ethnopharmacology. V. 1- Jan. 1979-. 0378-8741. Periodical. English. ir. Elsevier Scientific Publishers Irelands Ltd, PO Box 85, Limerick Ireland. **Ind/Abst** Life Sci. Collect., Excerpta Med., Index Med., Biol. Abstr., Ref. Source, Chem. Abstr., Sci. Cit. Index, Abr. Ed. **NLM** W1 JO644CH. **CODEN** JOETD7.

JOURNAL OF MEDICINAL CHEMISTRY. Vol. 6, No. 1 (Jan. 1963)-. 0022-2623. Periodical. US. English. mo. $182.00. American Chemical Society, PO Box 57136/West End Station, Washington DC 20037. **Tel** (202)872-4600. **Ed** Philip S Portoghese. **Ind/Abst** Life Sci. Collect., Excerpta Med., Pestdoc, Ringdoc, Vetdoc, Energy Inf. Abstr., Environ. Abstr., Ref. Source, Biol. Abstr., Chem. Abstr., Index Med., Nuci. Sci. Abstr., Energy Res. Abstr., Sci. Cit. Index, Abr. Ed., Curr. Abstr. Chem. Index Chem. **LC** RS402. **NLM** W1 JO757G. **CODEN** JMCMAR. bk rev. adv acc. **Circ** 4,257. Publishes approximately 300 papers yearly with the relationship of chemistry to biological activity, and features rapid communication of major advances in drug design and development. *Journal of Medicinal and Pharmaceutical Chemistry, 0095-9065.*

JOURNAL OF MICROENCAPSULATION. **VFOAT** J. Microencapsulation. Vol. 1, No. 1 (Jan.-Mar. 1984)-. 0265-2048. Periodical. UK. English. qt. $58.00. Taylor & Francis Inc, 242 Cherry Street, Philadelphia PA 19106. **NLM** W1.

JOURNAL OF OCULAR PHARMACOLOGY. *See* Medicine - Ophthalmology.

JOURNAL OF PARENTERAL SCIENCE AND TECHNOLOGY. Vol. 35, No. 1 (Jan./Feb. 1981)-. 0279-7976. Periodical. US. English. bm. $45.00 Domestic, $60.00 Foreign. Parenteral Drug Association Inc, Broad and Chestnut Streets/W S B Building, Philadelphia PA 19107. **Tel** (215)735-9752. **Ed** Joseph R Robinson. **Ind/Abst** Excerpta Med., Pestdoc, Ringdoc, Vetdoc, Index Med., Biol. Abstr., Chem. Abstr., Energy Res. Abstr. **NLM** W1 JO827Q. **CODEN** JPATDS. adv acc. (ctrl). Vehicle for publication of scientific/technical papers recognized as significant contributions to field of parenteral science and technology. *Journal of the Parenteral Drug Association, 0161-1933.*

JOURNAL OF PHARMACEUTICAL AND BIOMEDICAL ANALYSIS. **VFOAT** Journal of Pharmaceutical & Biomedical Analysis. Vol. 1, No. 1-. 0731-7085. Periodical. UK. English. bm. $100.00. Pergamon Press, c/o Cashier, 395 Sawmill River Road, Elmsford NY 10523. **Ind/Abst** Life Sci. Collect., Excerpta Med. **NLM** W1. Available on microfiche simultaneously with the paper edition and on microfilm at the end of the subscription year.

JOURNAL OF PHARMACEUTICAL SCIENCES. V. 50- Jan. 1961-. 0022-3549. Periodical. US. English. mo. $75.00. American Pharmaceutical Association, 2215 Constitution Avenue Northwest, Washington DC 20037. **Tel** (202)628-4410. **Ed** Sharon G Boots. **Ind/Abst** Life Sci. Collect., Excerpta Med., Pestdoc, Ringdoc, Vetdoc, Int. Aerosp. Abstr., Int. Packag. Abstr., Bibliogr. Agric., Biol. Abstr., Chem. Abstr., Psychol. Abstr., Nuci. Sci. Abstr., Index Med., Energy Res. Abstr., Sci. Cit. Index, Abr. Ed., Curr. Abstr. Chem. Index Chem., Hospit. Lit. Index. **NLM** W1 JO829. **CODEN** JPMSAE. bk rev. adv acc. **Circ** 7,500. (ctrl). Devoted to covering the latest developments in pharmaceutical research, including biopharmaceutics, pharmacokinetics, medicinal chemistry, novel analytical methods, etc. *Journal of the American Pharmaceutical Association. Scientific Edition, 0095-9553; Drug Standards, 0096-0225.*

JOURNAL OF PHARMACOBIO-DYNAMICS. V. 1- Mar. 1978-. 0386-846X. Periodical. JA. English. mo. 125.00. Maruzen Company Ltd, PO Box 5050, 100-31 Tokyo Japan. **Tel** 03-406-3321. **Ed** Yutaka Kasuya. **Ind/Abst** Electron. Commun. Abstr. J., ISMEC Bull., Pollut. Abstr. Indexes, Saf. Sci. Abstr. J., Life Sci. Collect., Excerpta Med., Pestdoc, Ringdoc, Vetdoc, Index Med., Biol. Abstr., Chem. Abstr., Sci. Cit. Index, Abr. Ed. **NLM** W1 JO829N. **CODEN** JOPHDQ. **Circ** 2,000. (ctrl). Monographs about dynamic mutual effect of medicine and organism, and the main point of a public performance, concerned with related field of this journal.

JOURNAL OF PHARMACOKINETICS AND BIOPHARMACEUTICS. V. 1- Feb. 1973-. 0090-466X. Periodical. US. English. bm. $190.00 Domestic, $212.00 Foreign. Plenum Publishing Corporation, 233 Spring Street, New York NY 10013. **Tel** (212)620-8000. **Ed** Sidney Riegelman. **Ind/Abst** Index Med., Sci. Cit. Index, Abr. Ed., Chem. Abstr., Pestdoc, Ringdoc, Vetdoc, Biol. Abstr., Excerpta Med., Curr. Contents, Int. Pharm. Abstr., Energy Res. Abstr. **LC** RM1. **DD** 615.105. **NLM** W1 JO829P. **CODEN** JPBPBJ. adv acc. A journal devoted to illustrating the importance of pharmacokinetics and biopharmaceutical applications in the understanding of.

JOURNAL OF PHARMACOLOGICAL METHODS. **VFOAT** Pharmacological Methods. V. 1- June 1978-. 0160-5402. Periodical. US. English. $218.00. Elsevier Science Publishing Company, Inc, 52 Vanderbilt Avenue, New York NY 10017. **Tel** (212)370-5520. **Ed** P S J Spenser and J H McNeill. **Ind/Abst** Life Sci. Collect., Excerpta Med., Pestdoc, Ringdoc, Vetdoc, Index Med., Biol. Abstr., Chem. Abstr. **LC** QP901. **DD** 615.1028. **NLM** W1 JO829PS. **CODEN** JPMED9. adv acc. Covers current methods of investigation used in pharmacology and toxicology.

THE JOURNAL OF PHARMACOLOGY AND EXPERIMENTAL THERAPEUTICS. V. 1- June 1909-. 0022-3565. Periodical. US. English. mo. $220.00. Williams & Wilkins Company, 428 East Preston Street, Baltimore MD 21202. **Tel** (301)528-4000. **Ed** Eva K Killam. **Ind/Abst** Life Sci. Collect., Excerpta Med., Pestdoc, Ringdoc, Vetdoc, Int. Aerosp. Abstr., Biol. Abstr., Chem. Abstr., Nuci. Sci. Abstr., Index Med., Bibliogr. Agric., Energy Res. Abstr. **LC** RS1. **DD** 615.705. **NLM** W1 JO83. **CODEN** JPETAB. (cum index). adv acc. **Circ** 2,900. Available on microfilm. Broad coverage of all aspects of the interactions of chemicals with biological systems for pharmacologists, toxicologists, and biochemists.

JOURNAL OF PHARMACOTHERAPY. V. 1- Aug. 1977-. 0140-7317. UK. English. ir. House of Pearse, 325 Staines Road, Twickenham TW2 5AX England. **Ind/Abst** Excerpta Med., Pestdoc, Ringdoc, Vetdoc. **NLM** W1 JO83M.

JOURNAL OF PHARMACY AND PHARMACOLOGY. V. 1- Jan. 1949-. 0022-3573. Periodical. UK. English. mo. $105.00. Pharmaceutical Press, 1 Lambeth High Street, London SE1 7JN England. **Tel** 01 735 9141. **Ed** John R Fowler. **Ind/Abst** Life Sci. Collect., Excerpta Med., Pestdoc, Ringdoc, Vetdoc, Bibliogr. Agric., Biol. Abstr., Chem. Abstr., Nuci. Sci. Abstr., Index Med., Curr. Abstr. Chem. Index Chem., Index Med., Sci. Cit. Index, Abr. Ed., Hospit. Lit. Index. **NLM** W1 JO831. **CODEN** JPPMAB. adv acc. Reviews, paper, communications on research in the sciences contributing to the development and evaluation of medicinal substances. Toxicology. *Quarterly Journal of Pharmacy and Pharmacology, 0370-2979.*

THE JOURNAL OF POSTGRADUATE PHARMACY. COMMUNITY EDITION. (THE JOURNAL OF POSTGRADUATE PHARMACY). V. 1- Jan./Feb. 1979-. 0163-3759. Periodical. US. English. bm. $48.00 Including Registration and Certification of Continuing Education Credits by the Council of Ohio Colleges of Pharmacy. Circulation Department, Journal of Postgraduate Pharmacy, 110 Hillside Avenue, Springfield NJ 07081. **NLM** W1 JO839.

THE JOURNAL OF POSTGRADUATE PHARMACY. HOSPITAL EDITION. (THE JOURNAL OF POSTGRADUATE PHARMACY). V. 1- Jan./Feb. 1979-. 0163-3910. Periodical. US. English. bm. $48.00 Including Registration and Certification of Continuing Education Credits by the Council of Ohio Colleges of Pharmacy. Circulation Department, Journal of Postgraduate of Pharmacy, 110 Hillside Avenue, Springfield NJ 07081. **LC** RS1. **DD** 615.105. **NLM** W1 JO839C.

JOURNAL OF SOCIAL AND ADMINISTRATIVE PHARMACY : JSAP. **VFOAT** JSAP. Vol. 1, No. 1-. 0281-0662. Periodical. English. qt. 150. JSAP PO Box 1136, S 111 81 Stockholm Sweden. **NLM** W1.

JOURNAL OF TEXTURE STUDIES. *See* Food & Drink.

JOURNAL OF THE PHARMACEUTICAL ASSOCIATION OF THAILAND. V. 1- Oct. 1947-. Periodical. TH. Thai. ir. **NLM** W1.

KANGSHENGSU. (KANG SHENG SU). Began in 1979. 0254-6116. Periodical. Chinese (abstracts in English). bm. 0.40. Editorial Office C J A, Shan-Ban-Qiao Chengdu, Sichuan China. **Ind/Abst** Life Sci. Collect., Excerpta Med., Chem. Abstr. **LC** RM265. **DD** 612.0157605. **CODEN** KANGDS. *Kang Chun Su.*

THE KENTUCKY PHARMACIST. 0194-567X. Periodical. US. English. mo. $15.00. Kentucky Pharmacist Association, PO Box 715,

Pharmacy

Frankfort KY 40602. Tel (502)227-2303. Ed Paul F Davis. NLM W1 KE722. bk rev. adv acc. Circ 1,800. (ctrl). News, educational articles and laws-regulations affecting the practice of pharmacy in Kentucky.

KRANKENHAUSPHARMAZIE. V. 1, 1 (July, Aug., Sept. 1980)-. 0173-7597. Periodical. GW. German. qt. $41.44. Deutscher Apotheker Verlag, Postfach 40 Birkenwaldstr 44, D7000 Stuttgart 1 West Germany. Tel (0711)25820. Ed Susanne Heinzel. Ind/Abst Pestdoc, Ringdoc, Vetdoc, Chem. Abstr. CODEN KRANDZ. bk rev. adv acc. Circ 2,500. (ctrl). The whole field of hospital pharmacy and of pharmacotherapy in the clinic. Krankenhaus-Apotheke.

LEGAL ASPECTS OF PHARMACY PRACTICE. See Law.

LILLY DIGEST. Main/Corp Lilly (Eli) and Company. Pharmaceutical Division. 1955-. 0193-5097. US. English. an. Eli Lilly and Company, General Offices and Principal Laboratories, Indianapolis IN 46206. Lilly Digest of Retail Drug-Store Income and Expense Statements.

LIQUID SCINTILLATION COUNTING. Main/Conf Symposium on Liquid Scintillation Counting. V. 1- 1970-. UK. English. ir. Heyden and Son Ltd, Spectrum House/Hillview Gardens, London NW4 2JQ England. Tel (305)345-4100. Ed Chin-Tzu Peng, Donald L Hurrocks and Edward L Alpen. NLM W3 LI454.

LE LIVRE BLANC. Publication began in 1931. FR. French. ir. Henri Perrier, 7 rue la Boule Kouge, Paris 9E France. LC RS125. DD 615.13. NLM QV 740 GF7 L7.

LLOYD'S CANADIAN CHEMICAL, PHARMACEUTICAL AND PRODUCT DIRECTORY. See Yearbooks, Almanacs, Directories.

THE LOUISIANA PHARMACIST. 0192-3838. Periodical. US. English. mo. LA State Pharmaceutical Association, 2337 St Claude Avenue, New Orleans LA 70117. NLM W1 LO915F.

LYON PHARMACEUTIQUE. Began 1923. 0024-7804. Periodical. French. bm. Medipharly, 12 rue de la Barre, 69002 Lyon France. Ind/Abst Chem. Abstr., Pestdoc, Ringdoc, Vetdoc. NLM W1 LY538. CODEN LYPHAD.

MANUFACTURERS OF PHARMACEUTICALS AND MEDICINES (FINAL) CEASED. (MANUFACTURERS OF PHARMACEUTICALS AND MEDICINES). Series/Titl Annual Census of Manufactures. VFOAT Manufacturiers de Produits Medicinaux et Pharmaceutiques. 1960-1980. 0701-7340. Periodical. CN. English. an. DD 338.476151910971. Medicinal and Pharmaceutical Preparations Industry, 0701-7359.

THE MARYLAND PHARMACIST. VFOAT MP. The Maryland Pharmacist. 0025-4347. Periodical. US. English. mo. Maryland Pharmacist, 650 West Lombard Street, Baltimore MD 21201. NLM W1 MA766.

MATERIA MEDICA POLONA. VFOAT Polish Journal of Medicine and Pharmacy. V. 1- Jan./June 1969-. 0025-5246. Periodical. English. qt. 48.00. Foreign Trade Publicity Publ Ent, POB 726 Marszalkowska 124, 00 950 Warsaw Poland. Tel 26 92 21. Ind/Abst Excerpta Med., Life Sci. Collect., Index Med., Biol. Abstr., Chem. Abstr. NLM W1 MA937N. CODEN MMDPA6. bk rev. adv acc. Circ 3,000. (ctrl). Clinical medicine, pharmacy, physiology, pathology, pharmacology, public health, history of medicine and medical education.

MEDICAL ADVISORY COUNCIL (SERIES). (MEDICAL ADVISORY COUNCIL : MEDAC). VFOAT MEDAC. Began with: 1980. Monographic Series. US. English. ir. Raven Press, 1140 Avenue of the Americas, New York NY 10036. Tel (212)575-0335. NLM W1.

THE MEDICAL LETTER ON DRUGS AND THERAPEUTICS. V. 1-(Issue 1-). 0025-732X. Periodical. US. English. bw. $50.00. Medical Letter, 56 Harrison Street, New Rochelle New York NY 10801. Tel (343)258-5250. Ed J R Prous. Ind/Abst Life Sci. Collect., Excerpta Med., Index Med., Energy Res. Abstr., Sci. Cit. Index, Abr. Ed., Hospit. Lit. Index. NLM W1 ME366. Circ 3,000. (ctrl). Spanish edition of original U.S. edition of the medical letter on drugs and therapeutics.

MEDICAL ONCOLOGY AND TUMOR PHARMACOTHERAPY. See Medicine - Neoplasma, Neoplastic.

MEDICAL SCIENCES BULLETIN. Began in 1979. 0199-4905. Periodical. US. English. mo. $19.00. Pharmaceutical Information Association Ltd, PO Box 186, Collegeville PA 19426. Ed Lawrence E Liberti. Circ 2,500. Provides accounts of new developments in the fields of pharmacology and therapeutics.

MEDICAMENTOS DE ACTUALIDAD. VFOAT Drugs of Today. Began publication with V. 8, Jan. 1965. 0025-7656. Periodical. SP. English (Spanish). mo. 135. J R Prous International Publ, Apartado de Correos 540, Barcelona Spain. Tel (343)258-5250. Ed J R Prous. Ind/Abst Excerpta Med., Biol. Abstr., Chem. Abstr. NLM W1 ME55. CODEN MDACAP. bk rev. adv acc. Circ 2,500. (ctrl). Describes in monograph form, drugs recently launched on international market. Features review articles on specific drug groups and treatment of particular diseases.

MEDICAMENTS D'AUJOURD'HUI. V. 1- Sept. 1976-. 0702-8970. Periodical. CN. French. mo. $15.00. Medicaments Daujourdhui, 5115 rue Saint-Denis, Montreal Quebec H2J 2M1 Canada. DD 615.105.

MEDICINAL CHEMISTRY. V. 1- 1963-. 0076-6054. Monographic Series. US. English. ir. Academic Press, 4805 Sand Lake Road, Orlando FL 32887. Tel (305)345-4100. Ed Peter P Mager. Ind/Abst Biol. Abstr., Chem. Abstr. LC UNC. NLM W1 ME64. CODEN MDCHAG.

MEDICINAL RESEARCH REVIEWS. Vol. 1, No. 1 (Spring 1981)-. 0198-6325. US. English. qt. John Wiley & Sons, 605 Third Avenue, New York NY 10158. Tel (800)526-5368. Ind/Abst Excerpta Med., Pestdoc, Ringdoc, Vetdoc, Index Med., Chem. Abstr. LC RM300. DD 615.105. NLM W1 ME64J. CODEN MRREDD.

MEDIZINISCHE MONATSSCHRIFT FUR PHARMAZEUTEN. 1.- Yearly V. 0342-9601. Periodical. GW. German. mo. 99.-. Wissenschaftliche Verlagsge- Sellschaft MBH, Postfach 40, D7000 Stuttgart 1 West Germany. Tel (0711)25820. Ed Susanne Heinzl. Ind/Abst Life Sci. Collect., Excerpta Med., Pestdoc, Ringdoc, Vetdoc, Index Med., Chem. Abstr. NLM W1 ME8286. CODEN MMPHDB. bk rev. adv acc. Circ 13,000. (ctrl). Drug therapy reviews, educational articles, and reports from medical literature and national and international meetings.

MEMBERSHIP DIRECTORY - AMERICAN SOCIETY OF HOSPITAL PHARMACISTS. See Yearbooks, Almanacs, Directories.

METHODS AND FINDINGS IN EXPERIMENTAL AND CLINICAL PHARMACOLOGY. V. 1- Apr. 1979-. 0379-0355. Periodical. SP. English. mo. $135.00. J R Prous International Publication, Apartado de Correos 540, Barcelona Spain. Tel (343)258-5250. Ed J R Prous. Ind/Abst Life Sci. Collect., Excerpta Med., Pestdoc, Ringdoc, Vetdoc, Index Med., Biol. Abstr., Chem. Abstr., Sci. Cit. Index, Abr. Ed. NLM W1 ME9613G. CODEN MFEPDX. bk rev. adv acc. Circ 3,000. (ctrl). A forum for presentation of methodologies used and results obtained in assessment of drugs in animals and man.

METHODS IN PHARMACOLOGY. V. 1-. 0091-3030. US. English. Plenum Press, 227 West 17th Street, New York NY 10011. Ind/Abst Biol. Abstr., Chem. Abstr. LC QP905. DD 615.7. NLM W1 ME9616N. CODEN MTPHBO.

MILL'S PHARMACY STATE BOARD REVIEW. 29th Ed.-. 0163-8084. US. English. Medical Examination Publishing Company Inc, 3003 New Hyde Park Road, New Hyde Park NY 11040. Ed J A Romano and M B Wiener. LC RS97. DD 615.1076. NLM QV 18 P538. Pharmacy State Board Questions and Answers and Review, 0163-8106.

MIMS AFRICA. V. 16- 1976-. 0140-4415. Periodical. UK. English. bm. A E Morgan Publications Ltd, Stanley House, 9 West Street, Epsom Surrey KT187RL England. NLM QV 772 M105. African Mims.

MIMS ANNUAL, AUSTRALIAN EDITION. (THE MIMS ANNUAL). 1st- Ed. 0725-4709. AT. English. an. $30.99. IMS Publishing, PO Box 977, Crows Nest New South Wales 2065 Australia. Ed Chris Wills. NLM QV 772 M662. adv acc. Listing of drugs available in Australia giving full prescribing information. Indexes for products by manufacturer, indications and actions, and proprietry and generic names. Australian Drug Compendium.

MISES AU POINT DE BIOCHIMIE PHARMACOLOGIQUE. VFOAT Advances in Biochemical Pharmacology. 1- Series. Periodical. articles in English or French. ir. Ed G Siest and C Heusghem. Ind/Abst Life Sci. Collect., Chem. Abstr. NLM W1 MI791QP. CODEN MPBPDK.

MISSISSIPPI PHARMACIST. 0161-3189. Periodical. US. English. bm. University of Mississippi Press, Oxford MS 38655.

MISSOURI PHARMACISTS. 1974-. 0026-6663. Periodical. US. English. mo. NLM W2 AM8 C4M.

MODERN METHODS IN PHARMACOLOGY. Vol. 1-. 0732-7218. Periodical. US. English. ir. Alan R Liss, 41 East 11th Street, New York NY 10003. Tel (212)475-7700. Ed Sydney Spector and Nathan Back. Ind/Abst Biol. Abstr., Chem. Abstr. LC RM301. DD 615.1072. NLM W1 MO166M. CODEN MMEPDE. A book series concerning modern methods used in pharmacology.

MODERN PHARMACOLOGY-TOXICOLOGY. V. 2-. 0098-6925. Monographic Series. US. English. ir. Marcel Dekker, 270 Madison Avenue, New York NY 10016. Tel (212)696-9000. Ed Bousquet and Palmer. Ind/Abst Life Sci. Collect., Chem. Abstr. LC UNC. NLM W1 MO167T. CODEN MPTOD5. This is an ongoing series. Each title has a different subject. Modern Pharmacology, 0092-0150.

MODERNE ARZNEIMITTEL-THERAPIE. V. 1- April 1976-. 0340-630X. Periodical. GW. German. ir. 80. Urban & Schwarzemberg, Pettenkoferstrasse 18, D-8000 Munchen 2 West Germany. Ind/Abst Chem. Abstr. NLM W1 MO178. CODEN MARTD7.

MOLECULAR PHARMACOLOGY. V. 1- July 1965-. 0026-8952. Periodical. US. English. mo. $165.00. Williams & Wilkins Company, 428 East Preston Street, Baltimore MD 21202. Tel (301)528-4000. Ed Joel Hardman. Ind/Abst Excerpta Med., Pestdoc, Ringdoc, Vetdoc, Energy Res. Abstr., Bibliogr. Agric., Biol. Abstr., Chem. Abstr., Index Med., Life Sci. Collect., Nuci. Sci. Abstr., Sci. Cit. Index, Abr. Ed. LC QP901. DD 615.705. NLM W1 MO197. CODEN MOPMA3. adv acc. Circ 1,450. Covers research on drug action and selective toxicity at the molecular level for pharmacologists and biochemists.

MONOGRAPHS IN CLINICAL PHARMACOLOGY. V. 1-. 0190-5120. Monographic Series. US. English. ir. Churchill Livingstone Inc, 1560 Broadway, New York NY 10036. Tel (212)819-5400. Ed D L Azarnoff. LC UNC. NLM W1 MO567KP.

MONOGRAPHS IN PHARMACOLOGY AND PHYSIOLOGY. V. 1-. 0364-2569. Monographic Series. US. English. ir. Spectrum Publications Inc, 175-20 Wexford Terrace, Jamaica NY 11432. Tel (212)479-9360. Ind/Abst Chem. Abstr. LC UNC. NLM W1 MO568J. CODEN MPPHDW.

MONOGRAPHS OF THE MARIO NEGRI INSTITUTE FOR PHARMACOLOGICAL RESEARCH. Main/Corp Istituto di Richerche Farmacologiche Mario Negri. 0085-3100. Monographic Series. US. English. ir. Raven Press, 1140 Avenue of the Americas, New York NY 10036.

NABP NEWSLETTER. VAT Newsletter - National Association of Boards of Pharmacy, National Association of Boards of Pharmacy Newsletter. V. 1- Oct. L971-. 8756-4483. Periodical. US. English. mo. $15.00. National Association Boards of Pharmacy, 1 East Wacker Drive/Suite 2210, Chicago IL 60601. Tel (312)467-6220. DD 615. NABP Quarterly, 0027-5700.

N.A.C.D.S.-LILLY DIGEST. See Business.

NAN-CHING YAO HSUEH YUAN HSUEH PAO. 0254-5055. Periodical. Chinese (abstract in English). qt. $40.00. Nanjing College of Pharmacy Teaching, Material Division, 24 Tongjia Xiang Nianjing, Jiangsu PRC China. Tel 31611-260. Ed Peng Sixun. Ind/Abst Chem. Abstr. CODEN NYXUDF. bk rev. adv acc. Consists of original research paper, research notes, reviews, communications and scientific news.

NARD NEWSLETTER. Main/Corp National Association of Retail Druggists (U.S.). VAT National Association of Retail Druggists Newsletter. V. 100- Aug. 1977-. 0162-1602. Periodical. US. English. mo. $35.00. National Association of Retail Druggists, 205 Daingerfield Road, Alexandria VA 22314. LC

Pharmacy

HD9666.1. **DD** 381.4561510973. *NARD Journal, 0027-5972.*

NASE LIECIVE RASTLINY. **VFOAT** Liecive Rastliny. Periodical. CS. Czech. bm. Slovart Foreign Trade Company Ltd, Gottwaldovo Nam 6, 817 64 Bratislava Czechoslavakia. **Tel** 48841-49. **LC** RS164. **NLM** W1 NA181H.

THE NATIONAL CAPITAL PHARMACIST. V. 1- Sept. 1939-. 0027-8890. Periodical. US. English. bm. $20.00. District of Columbia Pharmaceutical Association, 6400 Georgia Avenue NW/Suite 6, Washington DC 20015. **Tel** (202)829-1515. Ed Cari W Pao. **LC** HD9666.8.W3. **DD** 658.916154. **NLM** W1 NA347. adv acc. **Circ** 300. (ctrl). Publication for the pharmacists of Washington, DC and the metropolitan area.

NATIONAL PRESCRIPTION AUDIT. THERAPEUTIC CATEGORY REPORT. (NATIONAL PRESCRIPTION AUDIT : THERAPEUTIC CATEGORY REPORT). **Main/Corp** IMS America Ltd. 0145-5451. US. English. mo. IMS America Ltd, Butler Pike & Maple Avenue, Ambler PA 19002. **LC** HD9666.1. **DD** 381.4561510973.

NAUNYN-SCHMIEDEBERG'S ARCHIVES OF PHARMACOLOGY. *See* Genealogy and Heraldry - Archives.

NCI INVESTIGATIONAL DRUGS. (NCI INVESTIGATIONAL DRUGS, PHARMACEUTICAL DATA). **VFOAT** N.C.I. Investigational Drugs, Pharmaceutical Data. **VAT** National Cancer Institute Investigational Drugs, Pharmaceutical Data. Began with 1980. 0271-3292. US. English. an. National Institutes of Health, National Cancer Institute, 9000 Rockville Pike, Bethesda MD 20205. **LC** RS1. **DD** 615.105. **NLM** QV 772 N104.

NEBRASKA HEALTH MANPOWER REPORTS. PHARMACISTS. *See* Economics - Labor.

NEBRASKA MORTAR & PESTLE. **VAT** Nebraska Mortar and Pestle. 0028-1891. Periodical. US. English. mo. Nebraska Mortar & Pestle, 1001 Anderson Building, Lincoln NE 68508.

NEUE ARZNEIMITTEL. (NEUE ARZNEIMITTEL : BEILAGE DER DEUTSCHEN APOTHEKER ZEITUNG). Vol. 27, 1/2 (Jan./Feb. 1982)-. 0724-567X. GW. German. ir. 1.80. Deutscher Apotheker Verlag, Postfach 40, 7000 Stuttgart 1 West Germany. **NLM** W1 NE239G.

NEUROPHARMACOLOGY. V. 9- Jan. 1970-. 0028-3908. Periodical. UK. English. mo. Pergamon Press, 395 Sawmill River Road, Elmsford NY 10523. **Tel** (914)592-7700. **Ind/Abst** Excerpta Med., Life Sci. Collect., Pestdoc, Ringdoc, Vetdoc, Chem. Abstr., Biol. Abstr., Psychol. Abstr., Index Med., Nuci. Sci. Abstr., Sci. Cit. Index, Abr. Ed. **LC** RM315. **DD** 615.7805. **NLM** W1 NE337T. **CODEN** NEPHBW. *International Journal of Neuropharmacology.*

NEW DRUG COMMENTARY. 0734-1989. Periodical. US. English. mo. $540.00. Paregian Associates, 250 Davenport Avenue, New Rochelle NY 10805. **Tel** (914)235-8035. Ed Philip Paregian. Covers new drugs under development in the US giving stage of progress description, chemistry, clinical evaluations, markets and patents.

NEW ETHICALS. **VFOAT** New Ethicals and Medical Progress. V. 13, No. 10- Oct. 1976-. Periodical. English. mo. **NLM** W1 NE395K. *New Ethicals and Medical Progress.*

NEW ETHICALS CATALOGUE. 1962. Periodical. NZ. English. ty. 60. Adis Press, Private Bag Mairangi Bay, Auckland 10 New Zealand. **Tel** 419-1040. Ed J Sutherland. **NLM** QV 772 N531. adv acc. **Circ** 9,000. (ctrl). Listing of all prescription medicine drugs available in New Zealand by brand with all prescribing data, adverse reactions etc. Extensive cross references to medical journal articles. *New Ethicals and Medical Progress.*

THE NEW JERSEY JOURNAL OF PHARMACY. V. 1- Jan. 1928-. 0028-5773. Periodical. US. English. mo. N J Pharmaceutical Association, 118 West State Street, Trenton NJ 08608. **Tel** (609)394-5596. **LC** RS1. **DD** 615.05. **NLM** W1 NE446L.

NEW PRICE REPORT. (NEW PRICE REPORT : NPR). **VFOAT** Blue Book New Price Report. Vol. 1, No. 1 (Aug. 1982)-. 0744-9461. Periodical. US. English. mo. Hearst Corporation, 224 West 57th Street, New York NY 10019.

THE NEW YORK STATE JOURNAL OF PHARMACY. (THE NEW YORK STATE JOURNAL OF PHARMACY : OFFICIAL JOURNAL OF THE NEW YORK STATE COUNCIL OF HOSPITAL PHARMACISTS). Vol. 1, No. 1 (Feb. 1981)-. 0279-8778. Periodical. US. English. bm. New York State Council of Hospital Pharmacists, 211 East 43rd Street, New York NY 10017. **DD** 615. *Newsletter - New York State Council of Hospital Pharmacists, 0199-6169.*

NEW YORK STATE PHARMACIST, CENTURY II. **VFOAT** NY State Pharmacist-Century II. Vol. 57, No. 1 (Fall 1982)-. 0739-7062. Periodical. US. English. qt. Free to members, $5.00 to nonmembers. Pharmaceutical Society of the State of New York, 1975 Linden Boulevard, Elmont NY 11003. **NLM** W1 NE898F. *NY State Pharmacist, 0163-1586.*

NIGERIAN JOURNAL OF PHARMACY. (THE NIGERIAN JOURNAL OF PHARMACY : THE OFFICIAL ORGAN OF THE PHARMACEUTICAL SOCIETY OF NIGERIA). 0331-670X. Periodical. English. bm. $48.00. **Ind/Abst** Chem. Abstr. **NLM** W1. **CODEN** NJPHDZ. *Journal of Pharmacy (Yaba, Nigeria).*

NORVEGICA PHARMACEUTICA ACTA : MEDDELELSER FRA NORSK FARMACEUTISK SELSKAP. 45, No. 1-. 0800-2606. Periodical. English (articles in Norwegian). ir. **Ind/Abst** Excerpta Med. **NLM** W1. *Meddelelser Fra Norsk Farmaceutisk Selskap, 0029-1927.*

NURSING DRUG HANDBOOK. *See* Medicine - Nursing.

NY STATE PHARMACIST. V. 52, No. 6- June 1977-. 0163-1586. Periodical. US. English. bm. Pharmaceutical Society of New York State, 1975 Linden Boulevard, Elmont NY 11003. **Tel** (516)285-8822. Ed Charles F Bell. **NLM** W1 N88D. adv acc. **Circ** 2,500. (ctrl). News and articles of professional and practical interest to all types of pharmacy practitioners. *New York State Pharmacist, 0028-7660.*

OAZ. OSTERREICHISCHE APOTHEKER-ZEITUNG. (OAZ, OSTERREICHISCHE APOTHEKER-ZEITUNG). **VFOAT** Osterreichische Apotheker-Zeitung. 25.- Vol. 0253-5238. Periodical. AU. German. wk. $55.97. Oesterr Apothekerverlag GMBH, Spitalgasse 31, A-1094 Wien Austria. **Tel** 42 35 88. Ed Mag Pharm G Zimmermann. **Ind/Abst** Chem. Abstr., Pestdoc, Ringdoc, Vetdoc. **NLM** W1 O23S. **CODEN** OAZEAL. bk rev. adv acc. Journal of the Austrian Pharmacists, dealing with pharmaceutical sciences, drug related problems in every aspect, politics of the profession, health authorities, communication platform. *Osterreichishe Apotheker Zeitung.*

THE OBSTETRICIAN'S & GYNECOLOGIST'S COMPENDIUM OF DRUG THERAPY. *See* Medicine - Gynecology & Obstetrics.

OPERATING RESULTS. *See* Business.

ORDONNANCE. (ORDONNANCE : BULLETIN DE L'ORDRE DES PHARMACIENS DU QUEBEC). 1 (Sept. 1976)-. 0710-6122. Periodical. CN. French. ir. Free to Members. Ordre des Pharmaciens du Quebec, Bureau 160, 1253 Avenue/McGill College, Montreal Quebec H3B 2Y5 Canada. **DD** 615.4060714.

ORDONNANCE/DOSSIER. (ORDONNANCE. DOSSIER). **VFOAT** Dossier. 1 (Sept. 1976)-. 0710-6130. Periodical. CN. French. ir. Ordre des Pharmaciens du Quebec, Bureau 160, 1253 Avenue/McGill College, Montreal Quebec H3B 2Y5 Canada. **DD** 615.409714.

THE OSTEOPATHIC PHYSICIAN'S COMPENDIUM OF DRUG THERAPY. **VFOAT** Compendium of Drug Therapy. 1980/81-. 0272-7064. US. English. an. Biomedical Information Corporation, 800 2nd Avenue, New York NY 10017. **LC** 300. **DD** 615.1.

OYO YAKURI. **VFOAT** Pharmacometrics. Vol. 1- Sept. 1967-. 0300-8533. Periodical. JA. Japanese (with some text in English). mo. $70.00. Oyo Yakuri Kenkyukai, CPO Box 180, Sendai 980-91 Japan. **Tel** 0222-67-3810. Ed Hikaru Ozawa. **Ind/Abst** Excerpta Med., Chem. Abstr. **NLM** W1 OY65. **CODEN** OYYAA2. adv acc. **Circ** 1,150. (ctrl). Topics on pharmacology, pharmacodynamics, pharmacokinetics, toxicology, drug screening test.

I P S F NEWS BULLETIN. 0019-039X. Periodical. CN. English. qt. International Pharmaceutical Students' Federation, Vancouver British Columbia Canada.

PACIFIC INFORMATION SERVICE ON STREET-DRUGS. 0148-5733. Periodical. US. English. bm. $3.00. John K Brown, c/o School of Pharmacy, University of the Pacific, Stockton CA 95211. (cum index).

PAGIDEX. *See* Beauty & Cosmetics.

PEDIATRIC PHARMACOLOGY (NEW YORK, N.Y.). *See* Medicine - Pediatrics.

PENNSYLVANIA PHARMACIST. 0031-4633. Periodical. US. English. mo. Pennsylvania Pharmacist, 508 North Third Street, Harrisburg PA 17101.

PERSPECTIVES IN CLINICAL PHARMACOLOGY. Vol. 1, No. 1 (July 1983)-. 0737-2914. Periodical. US. English. mo. $60.00. Elsevier Science Publishing Co, 52 Vanderbilt Street, New York NY 10017. **Tel** (212)370-5520. Ed Milo Gibaldi. **Ind/Abst** Life Sci. Collect. **NLM** W1. **CODEN** PCPHE9. Reports the most recent advances in drug research and clinical practice, offering a broad perspective that stresses basic underlying pharmacokinetic principles.

PHARMA-DIALOG. (PHARMA DIALOG). 1-. 0172-0104. Monographic Series. German. ir. Bundesverband der Pharmazeutischen Industrie, Karlstrasse 21, Frankfurt Am Main West Germany. **LC** UNC. **NLM** W1 PH105T.

PHARMA INTERNATIONAL. Began in 1968. 0301-1356. Periodical. English. bm. $66.79. Verlag Coating Thomas & Company, Bankgasse 8, CH-9001 St Gallen Switzerland. **Tel** 071/22 32 39. **LC** HD9665.1. **NLM** W1 PH106H. *Cosmo Pharma International.*

PHARMACA. 0031-6857. Periodical. Serbo-Croatian. ir. $50.00 (Includes Bilten Pharmaca Subscription). Zajednica Zdravstvenih Organizacija Sr Hrvatska, P P 913, Yugoslavia. **Ind/Abst** Chem. Abstr. **CODEN** PHAMBF. *Lijekove.*

PHARMACEUTICA ACTA HELVETIAE. V. 1- 1926-. 0031-6865. Periodical. SZ. German. mo. $54.42. Schweuzer Apothekerverein, Postfach 3006, Marktgasse 52, 3000 Bern 7 Switzerland. **Tel** 031/22 04 54. **Ind/Abst** Life Sci. Collect., Excerpta Med., Pestdoc, Ringdoc, Vetdoc, Index Med., Chem. Abstr. **NLM** W1 PH127. **CODEN** PAHEAA.

PHARMACEUTICAL CHEMISTRY JOURNAL. No. 1- Jan. 1967-. 0091-150X. Periodical. US. English (Russian). mo. $575.00 Domestic, $640.00 Foreign. Consultants Bureau, 233 Spring Street, New York NY 10013. **Tel** (212)620-8000. Ed D Kh Skalaban. **Ind/Abst** Biol. Abstr., Chem. Abstr., Chem. Titles, Ind. Med., Biol. Sci. **LC** RS402. **DD** 615.19005. **NLM** W1 PH161D. **CODEN** PCJOAU. Presents latest research concerned in pharmaceutical chemistry by scientists in USSR.

THE PHARMACEUTICAL CODEX. 11th-Ed. UK. English. Each issue contains an index to its own contents - no vol index - loose. *British Pharmaceutical Codex.*

PHARMACEUTICAL ENGINEERING. V. 1- Nov. 1980/Jan. 1981-. 0273-8139. Periodical. US. English. bm. $30.00. International Society of Pharmaceutical Engineers, 8910 North Dale Narby/Suite 27, Tampa FL 33614. **Tel** (813)932-6069. Ed C David Boyer. bk rev. adv acc. **Circ** 8,700. (ctrl). Application and specification editorials for the construction, supervision and maintenance of process equipment, plant systems, instrumentation and facilities in health care manufacturing.

PHARMACEUTICAL EXECUTIVE. Vol. 1, No. 1 (Jan. 1981)-. 0279-6570. Periodical. US. English. mo. Aster Publishing Corp, 320 North A Street, PO Box 50, Springfield OR 97477. **Tel** (503)726-1200. Ed Judee Shuler. **LC** RS1. **DD** 338.4761510973. adv acc. **Circ** 9,000. (ctrl). A business and marketing magazine for executives in the pharmaceutical industry, featuring case histories, how-to articles, trends, issues, columns and monthly profile cover story.

PHARMACEUTICAL JOURNAL. V. 131- July 1, 1933-. 0031-6873. Periodical. UK. English. wk. $71.26. Pharmaceutical Press, 1 Lambeth High Street, London SE1 7JN England. *Pharmaceutical Journal and Pharmacist, 0301-5432.*

PHARMACEUTICAL JOURNAL OF KENYA. 0378-228X. Periodical. English. ir. Pharmaceutical Society of Kenya, PO Box 44290, Nairobi Kenya. **NLM** W1 PH163K.

PHARMACEUTICAL MEDICINE. Vol. 1, No. 1 (Dec. 1984)-. 0265-0673. Periodical. UK. English. qt. $99.00. MacMillan Press Ltd, Houndmills,

Basingstoke Hampshire RG21 2XS England. **Tel** 0256 29242. **Ed** Robert N Smith. bk rev. adv acc. **Circ** 600. This international journal includes papers on the validation of new and established methods of testing drugs in man, written by investigators both inside and outside the pharmaceutical industry.

PHARMACEUTICAL NEWS INDEX. *See* Indexes/Abstracts.

PHARMACEUTICAL PREPARATIONS, EXCEPT BIOLOGICALS. (CURRENT INDUSTRIAL REPORTS. MA-28G, PHARMACEUTICAL PREPARATIONS, EXCEPT BIOLOGICALS). 0732-8419. US. English. an. $1.25. Data User Services Division, Customer Services Publication, Bureau of the Census, Washington DC 20233. **Tel** (301)763-4100. **LC** HD9666.1. **DD** 380.14561510973. Presents timely data on the production, inventories, and orders of approximately 5,000 products, which represents 40 percent of all US manufacturing.

PHARMACEUTICAL RESEARCH. 1984, No. 1 (Jan. 1984)-. 0724-8741. Periodical. US. English. bm. $79.00. Thieme Stratton Inc, 381 Park Avenue South/Suite 1501, New York NY 10016. **Tel** (212)683-5088. **Ed** Wolfgang Sadee. **NLM** W1. **Circ** 2,000. Original and review articles in pharmacology and medicinal chemistry.

PHARMACEUTICAL TECHNOLOGY. V. 1- June 1977-. 0147-8087. Periodical. US. English. mo. Pharmaceutical Technology Inc, 320 North A Street, Springfield OR 97477. **Tel** (503)726-1200. **Ed** Sally McPherson. **Ind/Abst** Excerpta Med., Pestdoc, Ringdoc, Vetdoc, Chem. Abstr. **LC** RS1. **DD** 615.19005. **NLM** W1 PH178J. **CODEN** PTECDN. bk rev. adv acc. **Circ** 23,000. (ctrl). The premier forum for industrial pharmacy technology in the US, covering production and manufacturing, QA/QC, research and development packaging, engineering, and regulatory issues.

PHARMACEUTICALS, CLEANING COMPOUNDS, AND TOILET PREPARATIONS. **VFOAT** Produits Pharmaceutiques, Produits de Nettoyage et Produits de Toilette. 1981-. 0319-9061. CN. English (French). an. Publication Sales and Services, Statistics Canada, Ottawa Ontario K1A 0T6 Canada. **DD** 338.4766. *Manufactureres of Toilet Preparations (Final), 0384-3882; Manufacturers of Soap and Cleaning Compounds (Final), 0384-3912; Manufacturers of Pharmaceuticals and Medicine (Final), 0701-7340; Sales of Toilet Preparations in Canada, 0575-9633.*

PHARMACEUTISCH TIJDSCHRIFT VOOR BELGIE. Vol. 1.-47. 0369-9714. Periodical. BE. Dutch (some summaries in French). bm. $65.00. Association Pharmaceutique, rue Archimede 11, 1040 Brussel Belgium. **Tel** 02/733.98.20. **NLM** W1 PH179.

PHARMACEUTISCH WEEKBLAD. Began Nov. 1955. 0031-6911. Periodical. Dutch. wk. Pharmaceutisch Weekblad, Postbus 23, Deventer The Netherlands. **Ind/Abst** CIS Abstr., Excerpta Med., Pestdoc, Ringdoc, Vetdoc. *Pharmaceutisch Weekblad voor Nederland.*

PHARMACIE MONDIALE. No. 87- Oct. 1976-. Periodical. FR. French. ir. $11.97. Production Mondiale, 70 rue de l'Aqueduc, 75010 Paris France. **NLM** W1 PH268EC. *Pharmacie Mondiale, Pharmascopie.*

PHARMACIEN. (LE PHARMACIEN). V. 1- 1930-. 0031-692X. CN. French. mo. MacLean Hunter, PO Box 100 Station A, Toronto Ontario M5W 1A7 Canada. **NLM** W1 PH2683.

PHARMACISTS DIRECTORY. *See* Yearbooks, Almanacs, Directories.

PHARMACOCHEMISTRY LIBRARY. *See* Library and Information Science.

PHARMACOGNOSY TITLES. Periodical. US. English. ir.

PHARMACOLOGICA ET PHYSIOLOGICA. No. 1-. 0358-4828. Monographic Series. FI. English (Finnish). ir. Professor Sakari Piha, University of Oulu, 901000 Oulu 10 Finland. **Tel** 358-81-332133. **Ed** Leo Hirvonen. **NLM** W1 AC954NM NO.20 ETC. adv acc. **Circ** 500. (ctrl). Monographs, reviews, and dissertations in the fields of physiology and pharmacology.

PHARMACOLOGICAL AND BIOCHEMICAL PROPERTIES OF DRUG SUBSTANCES. V. 1-. 0161-2603. Monographic Series. US. English. sm. American Pharmaceutical Association, 2215 Constitution Avenue NW, Washington DC 20037. **Ed** Morton E Goldberg. **Ind/Abst** Chem. Abstr. **NLM** W1 PH275S. **CODEN** PBPSDY.

PHARMACOLOGICAL RESEARCH COMMUNICATIONS. V. 1- Mar. 1969-. 0031-6989. Periodical. UK. English. mo. Academic Press, 4805 Sand Lake Road, Orlando FL 32819. **Tel** (305)345-4100. **Ind/Abst** Life Sci. Collect., Excerpta Med., Pestdoc, Ringdoc, Vetdoc, Index Med., Biol. Abstr., Chem. Abstr., Sci. Cit. Index, Abr. Ed. **LC** RS122. **DD** 615.05. **NLM** W1 PH276. **CODEN** PLRCAT. *Archivio Italiano di Farmacologia.*

PHARMACOLOGICAL REVIEWS. V. 1- Apr. 1949-. 0031-6997. Periodical. US. English. qt. $70.00. Williams & Wilkins Company, 428 East Preston Street, Baltimore MD 21202. **Tel** (301)528-4000. **Ed** James A Bain. **Ind/Abst** Life Sci. Collect., Excerpta Med., Pestdoc, Ringdoc, Vetdoc, Energy Inf. Abstr., Environ. Abstr., Int. Aerosp. Abstr., Energy Res. Abstr., Biol. Abstr., Chem. Abstr., Index Med., Nuci. Sci. Abstr., Sci. Cit. Index, Abr. Ed. **LC** RS1. **NLM** W1 PH277. **CODEN** PAREAQ. adv acc. **Circ** 2,200. Important review articles on topics of high current interest for pharmacologists, toxicologists, and biochemists.

PHARMACOLOGIE PRATIQUE. V. 1- 1969/70-. 0316-7526. Periodical. CN. French. Hotel-Dieu 5 rue Quesnel, Arthabaska Quebec Canada. **DD** 615.105.

THE PHARMACOLOGIST. V. 1- Spring 1959-. 0031-7004. Periodical. US. English. qt. American Society for Pharmacology and Experimental Therapy, 9650 Rockville Pike, Bethesda MD 20014. **Tel** (301)530-7060. **Ind/Abst** Excerpta Med., Pestdoc, Ringdoc, Vetdoc, Biol. Abstr., Chem. Abstr. **LC** RM1. **DD** 615.105. **NLM** W1 PH281. **CODEN** PHMCAA. Available on microfilm from University Microfilms International.

PHARMACOLOGY. V. 1-. 0031-7012. Periodical. SZ. English. mo. 314.-. S Karger AG, PO Box, CH-4009 Basel Switzerland. **Tel** (061)39 08 80. **Ed** K Lederis, K F Sewing and E S Vesell. **Ind/Abst** Life Sci. Collect., Excerpta Med., Pestdoc, Ringdoc, Vetdoc, Biol. Abstr., Chem. Abstr., Index Med., Nuci. Sci. Abstr., Sci. Cit. Index, Abr. Ed. **LC** RM1. **DD** 615.105. **NLM** W1 PH283. **CODEN** PHMGBN. adv acc. Covers biochemical pharmacology, molecular pharmacology, drug metabolism, pharmacokinetics, and clinical pharmacology. *Medicina et Pharmacologia Experimentalis.*

PHARMACOLOGY & THERAPEUTICS. **VFOAT** Pharmacology and Therapeutics. V. 4-. 0163-7258. Periodical. UK. English. ir. Pergamon Press, 395 Sawmill River Road, Elmsford NY 10523. **Ind/Abst** Excerpta Med., Life Sci. Collect., Pestdoc, Ringdoc, Vetdoc, Index Med., Biol. Abstr., Chem. Abstr., Sci. Cit. Index, Abr. Ed. **LC** RM1. **DD** 615.105. **NLM** W1 PH283S. **CODEN** PHTHDT. *Pharmacology and Therapeutics. Part A. Chemotherapy, Toxicology and Metabolic Inhibitors, 0362-5478; Pharmacology and Therapeutics. Part B, 0306-039X; Pharmacology and Therapeutics. Part C. Clinical Pharmacology and Therapeutics, 0362-5486.*

PHARMACOLOGY, BIOCHEMISTRY AND BEHAVIOR. **VFOAT** Pharmacology, Biochemistry & Behavior. V. 1- Jan./Feb. 1973-. 0091-3057. Periodical. US. English. mo. $495.00. Ankho International Inc, PO Box 380227, San Antonio TX 78280. **Tel** (315)463-0182. **Ed** Matthew J Wayner. **Ind/Abst** Life Sci. Collect., Excerpta Med., Pestdoc, Ringdoc, Vetdoc, Index Med., Energy Res. Abstr., Biol. Abstr., Chem. Abstr., Psychol. Abstr., Sci. Cit. Index, Abr. Ed. **LC** QP901. **DD** 615.78. **NLM** W1 PH284F. **CODEN** PBBHAU. bk rev. adv acc. Publishes original reports of systematic studies in pharmacology, biochemistry, toxicology and behavior in which the primary emphasis and theoretical context are behavioral.

PHARMACOLOGY BIOCHEMISTRY & BEHAVIOR. SUPPLEMENT. **VAT** Pharmacology Biochemistry and Behavior. Supplement. V. 1-. Monographic Series. US. English. Ankho International Inc, PO Box 380227, San Antonio TX 78280.

PHARMACOLOGY IN NURSING. *See* Medicine - Nursing.

PHARMACOLOGY RESEARCH ASSOCIATE PROGRAM OF THE NATIONAL INSTITUTE OF GENERAL MEDICAL SCIENCES, NATIONAL INSTITUTES OF HEALTH. US. English. an. Pharmacology Research Associate Program, National Institute of General Medical Sciences, National Institutes of Health, Westwood Building/Room 919, Bethesda MD 20014.

PHARMACOPEIAL FORUM. **VFOAT** Pharmacopeial Forum, with USP-NF Comment Proof. V. 1- Jan./Feb. 1975-. 0363-4655. Periodical. US. English. bm. $270.00. US Pharmacopeial Convention, 12601 Twinbrook Parkway, Rockville MD 20852. **Tel** (301)881-0666. **Ind/Abst** Life Sci. Collect. **NLM** QV 738 AA1 P45. *USP Comment Proof.*

PHARMACOPSYCHIATRY. Vol. 17, No. 1 (Jan. 1984)-. Periodical. English (German, with summaries in both languages). bm. 168.00. Georg Thieme Verlag, Rudigerstrasse 14 Postfach 732, D7000 Stuttgart 1 West Germany. **Tel** (0711)8931240. **Ed** B Muller-Oerlinghausen. **Ind/Abst** Excerpta Med., Index Med., Life Sci. Collect., Pestdoc, Ringdoc, Vetdoc. **LC** RM315. **DD** 615.78. **NLM** W1. bk rev. adv acc. **Circ** 1,100. Presents latest advances in clincial psychopharmacology. It is of interest for biologically interested psychiatrists and pharmacologists as well as for neurophysiologists. *Pharmacopsychiatria, 0720-4280.*

PHARMACOTHERAPY. Vol. 1, No. 1 (July-Aug. 1981)-. 0277-0008. Periodical. US. English. bm. $225.00. Pharmacotherapy Publ Inc, 112 School Street, Carlisle MA 01741. **Tel** (617)956-5390. **Ed** Russell R Miller. **Ind/Abst** Excerpta Med., Index Med., Biol. Abstr., Chem. Abstr. **NLM** W1 PH291E. **CODEN** PHPYDQ. bk rev. adv acc. **Circ** 2,000. Review and original research articles on drugs and therapeutics.

PHARMACY & THERAPEUTICS FORUM. (PHARMACY & THERAPEUTICS FORUM : THE BULLETIN OF THE HOSPITAL PHARMACY AND DRUG INFORMATION ANALYSIS SERVICE). **VFOAT** Pharmacy and Therapeutics Forum. Began with: Vol. 26, No. 7 (Nov./Dec. 1978). 0195-542X. Periodical. US. English. bm. Drug Information Analysis Service, 926-S-School of Pharmacy, University of California-San Francisco, San Francisco CA 94143. **NLM** W1 PH293H. *Bulletin of the Hospital Pharmacy and the Drug Information Analysis Service.*

PHARMACY IN HISTORY. V. 4- 1959-. 0031-7047. Periodical. US. English. qt. American Institute of the History of Pharmacy, PO Box 789, Piscataway NJ 08854. **Tel** (608)262-5378. **Ed** Glenn Sonnedecker. **Ind/Abst** Am. Hist. Life, Hist. Abstr., Part A, Mod. Hist. Abstr., Hist. Abst., Part B, Twent. Century Abstr., Writ. Am. Hist. **NLM** W1 PH298. bk rev. adv acc. **Circ** 1,104. History of pharmacy, drugs, drug therapy—articles, notes, reviews, departments. *AIHP Notes.*

PHARMACY INTERNATIONAL. V. 1- Jan. 1980-. 0167-3157. Periodical. English. mo. 390. Elsevier Publications, 68 Hills Road, Cambridge BC2 1LA UK. **Tel** (0223)315961. **Ed** Sara Williamson. **Ind/Abst** Life Sci. Collect., Excerpta Med., Chem. Abstr. **NLM** W1 PH299. **CODEN** PHINDQ. bk rev. adv acc. **Circ** 5,000. Recent developments in the pharmaceutical sciences and in clinical pharmacy.

PHARMACY LAW DIGEST. *See* Law.

PHARMACY NEWS AND REVIEW. (PHARMACY NEWS AND REVIEW : AN OFFICIAL PUBLICATION OF THE PENNSYLVANIA PHARMACEUTICAL ASSOCIATION). **VFOAT** Pharmacy News & Review. 8750-4790. Periodical. US. English. mo. Pennsylvania Pharmaceutical Association, 508 North Third Street, Harrisburg PA 17101. **DD** 615. *PPA Newsletter.*

PHARMACY PRACTICE. V. 10- 1975-. Periodical. US. English. mo. $15.00. American Pharmaceutical Association, 2215 Constitution Avenue NW, Washington DC 20037. **Tel** (202)628-4410 Ext 22. *Academy/GP.*

PHARMACY SCHOOL ADMISSION REQUIREMENTS. **Main/Corp** American Association of Colleges of Pharmacy. Office of Student Affairs. 1st- Ed. 0149-1113. US. English. ir. American Association of Colleges of Pharmacy, 4720 Montgomery Avenue/Suite 602, Bethesda MD 20814. **Tel** (301)654-9060. **Ed** Janet R Holsopple. **LC** RS110. **DD** 615.1071173. Provides general school information and specific admission requirements for the seventy-two colleges of pharmacy in the US and Puerto Rico. Updated weekly.

THE PHARMACY STUDENT. 0279-5272. Periodical. US. English. qt. $10.00. American Pharmaceutical Association, 2215 Constitution Avenue, Washington DC 20037. **Tel** (202)628-4410.

PHARMACY TIMES. V. 35, No. 9- Sept. 1969-. 0003-0627. Periodical. US. English. mo. $26.00. Romaine Pierson Publishing Inc, 80 Shore Road, Port

Pharmacy

Washington NY 11050. **Tel** (516)883-6350. **Ed** Irving Rubin. **Ind/Abst** Hospit. Lit. Index. **LC** RS1. **DD** 615.05. **NLM** W1 PH301T. adv acc. **Circ** 80,300. (ctrl). A mass publication designed to help independent, chain drug, hospital pharmacists, and others interested or involved in pharmacy. Scope is only health-related. *American Professional Pharmacist*, 0096-0349.

PHARMACY WEST. V. 88, No. 2- Feb. 1976-. 0191-6394. Periodical. US. English. $16.00. Western Communications, 1741 Ivar Avenue/Suite 116, Los Angeles CA 90028. **Tel** (213)462-2008. **Ed** Elroy Fitzsenry. bk rev. adv acc. **Circ** 16,000. (ctrl). Covers news and other events about pharmacy in the West. *West Coast/Rocky Mountain Druggist*.

PHARMAKOPSYCHIATRIE - NEURO-PSYCHOPHARMAKOLOGIE CEASED. Vols. 1-13-. 0031-7098. Periodical. German (English). ir. **Ind/Abst** Excerpta Med. **LC** RM315. **NLM** W1 PH306H.

PHARMAKOTHERAPIE. V. 1- 1978-. 0344-7154. Monographic Series. GW. German. bm. $60.00. Dustri Verlag, Dr Karl Feistle, Bahnofstrasse 9, Postfach 49, 8024 Deisenhofen- West Germany. **Ind/Abst** Excerpta Med., Chem. Abstr. **NLM** W1 PH306T. **CODEN** PHKTDK.

PHARMALERT. Began with: Vol. 8, No. 1 (Sept. 1976). 0278-6850. Periodical. US. English. qt. $7.00. University of Maryland, 636 W Lombard Street, School of Pharmacy, Baltimore MD 21201. **Tel** (301)528-7513. **Ed** Donald E Lewis. **NLM** W1 PH306W. **Circ** 2,000. (ctrl). Publication is directed to educators and health care workers to supplement their knowledge of drug information. Articles address pharmacological, clinical and social issues on drug use.

PHARMANUAL. 1-. 0250-6068. Monographic Series. English. ir. S Karger AG, PO Box, CH-4009 Basel Switzerland. **Ind/Abst** Chem. Abstr. **NLM** W1 PH321T. **CODEN** PARMDJ.

PHARMASCOPE. Periodical. US. English. mo. Transpharma Inc, PO Box 170, Huntington Station NY 11746. Index published separately - free - automatically sent.

PHARMASOURCES. 82-. 0730-1278. US. English. an. $85.00. Flexible Software Inc, Box 47, Prarie View IL 60069.

PHARMATHERAPEUTICA. V. 1- 1976-. 0308-051X. Periodical. UK. English (papers published in any language with summaries in English). ir. Clayton-Wray Publishers Ltd, 1A High Street, Alton Hants GU34 1BA England. **Tel** (01)874-9611. **Ind/Abst** Life Sci. Collect., Excerpta Med., Pestdoc, Ringdoc, Vetdoc, Index Med., Biol. Abstr., Chem. Abstr., Sci. Cit. Index, Abr. Ed. **NLM** W1 PH307. **CODEN** PHARDW.

PHARMAZEUTISCHE INDUSTRIE. (DIE PHARMAZEUTISCHE INDUSTRIE). 1- 1933-. 0031-711X. Periodical. GW. German (summaries in English). mo. 195.00. Editio Cantor, Postfach 12 55, D-7960 Aulendorf West Germany. **Tel** 07525/431. **Ed** Rolf Halt. **Ind/Abst** Excerpta Med., Predicasts, Pestdoc, Ringdoc, Vetdoc, Int. Packag. Abstr., Energy Res. Abstr., Chem. Abstr. **NLM** W1 PH312. **CODEN** PHINAN. bk rev. adv acc. **Circ** 3,800. Publications on all questions concerning the manufacture and distribution of pharmaceutical products.

PHARMAZEUTISCHE RUNDSCHAU. V. 1- March 1959-. 0031-7128. Periodical. GW. German. mo. $56.49. W E Saarbach GMBH, Postfach 101610, D-5000 Koeln 1 West Germany. **Tel** 02 21-23 46 31. **Ind/Abst** Excerpta Med. **LC** RS1. **NLM** W1 PH315C. **CODEN** PHMRAL.

PHARMAZEUTISCHE VERFAHRENSTECHNIK HEUTE. V. 1 (July 1980)-. 0173-1890. Periodical. GW. German. qt. **Ind/Abst** Chem. Abstr. **NLM** W1. **CODEN** PVHEDO.

PHARMAZEUTISCHE ZEITUNG. VFOAT Apotheker-Zeitung. V. 118-. 0031-7136. Periodical. GW. German. wk. Govi Verlag Pharmazeut Verlag, Beethovenplatz 1-3, PO 97-0108, 6 Frankfurt 97- West Germany. **Ind/Abst** Pestdoc, Ringdoc, Vetdoc, Energy Res. Abstr., Chem. Abstr. **NLM** W1 PH317B. **CODEN** PHZIAP. *Pharmazeutische Zeitung, Vereinigt Mit Apotheker-Zeitung, 0031-7136*.

PHARMAZIE. (DIE PHARMAZIE). Began with June 1946. 0031-7144. Periodical. SZ. German. mo. $92.13. Kunst & Wissen Erich Bieber, Dufourstrasse 51, CH-8008 Zurich Switzerland. **Tel** (011)411694420. **Ind/Abst** Life Sci. Collect., Excerpta Med., Pestdoc, Ringdoc, Vetdoc, Biol. Abstr., Chem. Abstr., Nuci. Sci. Abstr., Index Med., Sci. Cit. Index, Abr. Ed. **LC** RS1. **NLM** W1 PH3255. **CODEN** PHARAT.

PHARMAZIE HEUTE. V. 1- Oct. 1971-. 0369-979X. Periodical. GW. German. bm. Deutscher Apotheker Verlag, Postfach 40, Birkenhaldstrasse 44, D7000 Stuttgart 1 West Germany. **Ind/Abst** Chem. Abstr. **NLM** W1 PH3256E. **CODEN** PHZHAM.

PHARMAZIE IN UNSERER ZEIT. Vol. 1, No. 1 (Jan. 1972)-. 0048-3664. Periodical. GW. German. bm. Papelallee 3 Postfach 1260, 6940 Weinheim West Germany. **Ind/Abst** Excerpta Med., Pestdoc, Ringdoc, Vetdoc, Index Med., Chem. Abstr. **NLM** W1 PH3256H. **CODEN** PHUZBI. Index published separately - free - automatically sent. *Mitteilungen*.

THE PHARMCHEM NEWSLETTER. V. 1- Jan. 1972-. 0146-3128. Periodical. US. English. mo. $25.00. Pharmchem Laboratories, 3925 Bohannon Drive, Menlo Park CA 94025. **Ind/Abst** Chem. Abstr. **CODEN** PHNEDO.

PHARMINDEX. *See* Indexes/Abstracts.

PHYSICIANS' DESK REFERENCE. (PHYSICIANS' DESK REFERENCE : PDR). VFOAT PDR. Began with 1974 issue. 0093-4461. US. English. an. Physicians Desk Reference, PO Box 2017, Mahopac NY 10541. **Tel** (914)628-1929. **LC** RS75. **DD** 615.1. **NLM** QV 772 P578. *Physicians' Desk Reference to Pharmaceutical Specialties and Bioliogicals*, 0093-447X.

PHYSICIANS' DESK REFERENCE FOR NONPRESCRIPTION DRUGS. VFOAT PDR for Nonprescription Drugs. 1st- Ed. US. English. an. $17.95. Medical Economics Inc, 680 Kinderkamack Road, Oradell NJ 07649. **Tel** (201)262-3030. **LC** RM671.A1. **DD** 615.105. **NLM** QV 772 P575.

PHYSICIANS' GUIDE TO WHOLESALE PRESCRIPTION DRUG PRICES. 0161-6897. US. English. Howard Spriggle Publishers, 1010 Chestnut Street, Collingdale PA 19023. **LC** HD9666.4. **DD** 338.4361510973.

PHYSIOLOGIC AND PHARMACOLOGIC BASES OF DRUG THERAPY. *See* Biology - Physiology.

PHYSIOLOGICAL PHARMACOLOGY : A COMPREHENSIVE TREATISE. *See* Biology - Physiology.

PLANTA MEDICA. 1.- Yearly. 0032-0943. Periodical. German (English and French). mo. 318,- Domestic. George Thieme Verlag Stuttgart, Postfach 732 Rudigerstrasse 14, D-7000 Stuttgart 30 West Germany. **Tel** 0711/8931-0. **Ed** E Reinhard. **Ind/Abst** Life Sci. Collect., Excerpta Med., Pestdoc, Ringdoc, Vetdoc, Index Med., Energy Res. Abstr., Biol. Abstr., Chem. Abstr., Nuci. Sci. Abstr., Bibliogr. Agric., Sci. Cit. Index, Abr. Ed. **LC** RS164. **DD** 615.3205. **NLM** W1 PL106. **CODEN** PLMEAA. adv acc. **Circ** 800. Publishes full papers, communications, letters and reviews about pharmacology, phytochemistry, biochemistry, physiology and genetics of medicinal plants.

PLANTA MEDICA. SUPPLEMENT. Periodical. English (French or German). ir. Thieme-Stratton Inc, 381 Park Avenue South, New York NY 10016. **Ind/Abst** Index Med., Chem. Abstr.

PMD. PHARMACEUTICAL MARKETERS DIRECTORY. *See* Yearbooks, Almanacs, Directories.

POLISH JOURNAL OF PHARMACOLOGY AND PHARMACY. V. 25- Jan./Feb. 1973-. 0301-0244. Periodical. PL. English. bm. ARS Polona, Krakowskie Przedmiescie 7, 00-068 Warsaw Poland. **Ind/Abst** Life Sci. Collect., Excerpta Med., Pestdoc, Ringdoc, Vetdoc, Index Med., Biol. Abstr., Chem. Abstr., Sci. Cit. Index, Abr. Ed., Curr. Abstr. Chem. Index Chem. **NLM** W1 PO23M. **CODEN** PJPPAA. *Dissertationes Pharmaceuticae et Pharmacologicae, 0012-3870*.

PR. PHARMACEUTICAL REPRESENTATIVE. VFOAT Pharmaceutical Representative. V. 8, No. 7- July 1978-. 0161-8415. Periodical. US. English. mo. $18.00. McKnight Medical Communications Inc, 550 Frontage Road, Northfield IL 60093. **Tel** (312)446-1622. **Ed** James Bowe. **Circ** 17,000. The news source for sales representatives of pharmaceutical companies. *Pharmaceutical Salesman*.

PRESCRIBERS' JOURNAL. Vol. 1, No. 1 (Mar. 1961)-. 0032-7611. Periodical. UK. English. **NLM** WI. **CODEN** PRJOBY. *Prescribers' Notes*.

PRESCRIPTION DRUG NEWS. Began in 1984?. 0882-8628. Periodical. US. English. bm. $26.00. FC&A Publishing, 103 Clover Green, Peachtree City GA 30269. **DD** 615.

PRESCRIPTION DRUGS. 8756-8950. US. English. an. Prescription Drugs, 3841 West Oakton Street, Skokie IL 60076. **LC** RM301.15. **DD** 615.1.

PRESCRIPTION PROPRIETARIES GUIDE. VFOAT P.P. Guide. 5th issue (1968-69-70)-. 0729-2333. AT. English. an. 46.50. Australian Journal of Pharmacy, 35 Walsh Street/4th Floor, West Melbourne Victoria 3002 Australia. **Tel** 329-5799. **Ed** Stuart Dickson. **NLM** QV 772 P933. adv acc. **Circ** 8,000. Describes the latest drugs on the market, their uses and side effects in alphabetical order and also the name of the manufacturers who make and supply them.

PRINCIPLES AND PRESENTATION : PHARMACEUTICALS. Main/Corp Peat, Marwick, Mitchell & Co. 0193-9343. US. English. an. $10.00. Peat Marwick Mitchell & Company, 345 Park Avenue, New York NY 10022. **LC** HF5686.D7. **DD** 657.867.

PROCEEDINGS - INTERNATIONAL CONGRESS OF NEURO-PSYCHOPHARMACOLOGY. *See* Medicine - Neurology.

PROCEEDINGS - NATIONAL SYMPOSIUM ON PROGRESS AND PROBLEMS OF BLACK PHARMACISTS IN AMERICA. Main/Conf National Symposium on Progress and Problems of Black Pharmacists in America. 1st- 1976-. 0145-6091. US. English. National Pharmaceutical Foundation, 969 Thayer Avenue/Suite No 2, Silver Spring MD 20910. **LC** RS122.5. **DD** 331.6396073.

PROCEEDINGS OF THE ANNUAL MEETING - NATIONAL ASSOCIATION OF BOARDS OF PHARMACY. Main/Corp National Association of Boards of Pharmacy. US. English. an. $15.00. National Association of Boards of Pharmacy, 1 East Wacker Drive/Suite 2210, Chicago IL 60601.

PROCEEDINGS OF THE ANNUAL MEETING OF DISTRICT NO. 4 OF THE NATIONAL ASSOCIATION OF BOARDS OF PHARMACY AND THE AMERICAN ASSOCIATION OF COLLEGES OF PHARMACY. Main/Corp National Association of Boards of Pharmacy. District 4. US. English. an.

PROCEEDINGS OF THE AUSTRALIAN PHYSIOLOGICAL AND PHARMACOLOGICAL SOCIETY. *See* Biology - Physiology.

PROCEEDINGS OF THE WESTERN PHARMACOLOGY SOCIETY. Main/Corp Western Pharmacology Society. V. 1- 1958-. 0083-8969. US. English. **Tel** (213)825-5447. **Ind/Abst** Life Sci. Collect., Excerpta Med., Int. Aerosp. Abstr., Energy Res. Abstr., Biol. Abstr., Chem. Abstr., Index Med., Nuci. Sci. Abstr. **NLM** W1 PR587HN. **CODEN** PWPSA8. **Circ** 600. (ctrl). Papers presented at the annual meeting of the Society.

PROGRESOS EN PSICOARMACOLOGIA. 0211-8351. Monographic Series. Spanish. ir. **Ind/Abst** Excerpta Med., Chem. Abstr. **NLM** W1 PR6648. **CODEN** PRPSDA.

PROGRESS IN BIOCHEMICAL PHARMACOLOGY. V. 1- 1965-. 0079-6085. Monographic Series. US. English. ir. S Karger Ag, PO Box, CH-4009 Basel Switzerland. **Tel** 061-39 08 80. **Ed** R Paoletti. **Ind/Abst** Pestdoc, Ringdoc, Vetdoc, Sci. Cit. Index, Abr. Ed., Index Med. **CODEN** PBPHAW. Thorough assessment of the most recent laboratory and clinical findings in drug research.

PROGRESS IN CLINICAL PHARMACOLOGY. VFOAT Fortschritte der Klinischen Pharmakologie. 1-. 0721-4049. Periodical. English. ir. Dustri Verlag, Dr Karl Feistle, Bahnhofstrasse 9, Postfach 49, 8024 Deisenhofen West Germany. **Ind/Abst** Pestdoc, Ringdoc, Vetdoc, Chem. Abstr. **CODEN** PCPHD8.

PROGRESS IN DRUG RESEARCH. VFOAT Fortschritte der Arzneimittelforschung, Progres des Recherches Pharmaceutiques. V. 12-

Pharmacy

1968-. 0071-786X. English (French or German). ir. Birkhauser Boston Inc, 380 Green Street, PO Box 3005, Cambridge MA 02139. **Tel** (617)876-2333. **Ed** E Jucker. **Ind/Abst** Life Sci. Collect., Index Med., Biol. Abstr., Chem. Abstr., Pestdoc, Ringdoc, Vetdoc, Sci. Cit. Index, Abr. Ed. **NLM** W1 PR668Q. **CODEN** FAZMAE. *Fortschritte der Arzneimittelforschung.*

PROGRESS IN HORMONE BIOCHEMISTRY AND PHARMACOLOGY. *See* Biology - Biochemistry.

PROGRESS IN NEURO-PSYCHOPHARMACOLOGY CEASED. V. 1-5. 0364-7722. Periodical. UK. English. bm. $45.00. Subscription Fulfillment Manager, Pergamon Press Ltd, Headington Hill Hall, Oxford OX3 0BW England. **Ind/Abst** Biol. Abstr., Chem. Abstr. **NLM** W1 PR6745. **CODEN** PRNPDP. Available on microfilm and microfiche.

PROGRESS IN PHARMACOLOGY. V. 1-. 0340-465X. Monographic Series. US. English. ir. VCH Publishers Inc, 303 NW 12th Avenue, Deerfield Beach FL 33442. **Tel** (305)428-5566. **Ind/Abst** Life Sci. Collect., Chem. Abstr. **NLM** W1 PR677M. **CODEN** PRPHDB.

PROLACTIN. 1974-. 0702-8903. Periodical. CN. English. an. Eden Press, 4626 St Catherine Street West, Montreal Quebec H3Z 1S3 Canada. **Tel** (514)931-3910. **DD** 615.363. **NLM** W1 PR7207.

PSYCHOPHARMACOLOGY. VFOAT Psychopharmacology Series. V. 1-. 0161-0139. Periodical. US. English. ir. Marcel Dekker Inc, 270 Madison Avenue, New York NY 10016. **Ed** E Usdin. **Ind/Abst** Chem. Abstr. **LC** UNC. **NLM** W1 PS7727. **CODEN** PSPHDI.

PSYCHOPHARMACOLOGY. V. 47- 1976-. 0033-3158. Periodical. WB. English (articles in French or German). mo. $681.00. Springer Verlag New York Inc, 175 5th Avenue, New York NY 10010. **Tel** (212)460-1500. **Ed** D Casey and J Gerlach. **Ind/Abst** Excerpta Med., Life Sci. Collect., Ringdoc, Pestdoc, Vetdoc, Index Med., Biol. Abstr., Chem. Abstr., Psychol. Abstr., Curr. Contents. **NLM** W1 PS7725. **CODEN** PSCHDL. Also available on microfilm. Provides a medium for the prompt publication of scientific contributions concerned with the analysis and synthesis of the effects of drugs on behavior. *Psychopharmacologia, 0033-3158.*

PSYCHOPHARMACOLOGY. (PSYCHOPHARMACOLOGY : A BIENNIAL CRITICAL SURVEY OF THE INTERNATIONAL LITERATURE). 1, Pt. 1-. 0167-9198. English. be. **Ed** D G Grahame-Smith, H Hippius, and G Winokur. **Ind/Abst** Chem. Abstr. **LC** RC483. **DD** 615.7805. **NLM** W1 PS772. **CODEN** PSYCEF.

P.T.A. HEUTE. (PTA HEUTE). VAT Pharmazeutisch-Techischer Assistent Heute. 20.- Yearly V. 0302-167X. Periodical. GW. German. mo. Deutscher Apotheker Verlag, Postf 40, Birkenwaldstrasse 44, D7000 Stuttgart 1 West Germany. **Ind/Abst** Chem. Abstr. **NLM** W1 P978H. **CODEN** PTAHAF. *Apothekerpraktikant und Pharmazeutisch-Technischer Assistent, 0303-6219.*

PUBLICATION - AMERICAN INSTITUTE OF THE HISTORY OF PHARMACY. No. 1-. 0270-0611. Monographic Series. US. English. ir. **NLM** W1 PU673.

Q.S. 1951 -Spring 1953. 0480-5895. Periodical. US. English. sm. University of Florida, College of Pharmacy, Gainesville FL 32601.

QUALITY CONTROL REPORTS. *See* Manufacturing.

QUANTITATIVE STRUCTURE-ACTIVITY RELATIONSHIPS IN PHARMACOLOGY, CHEMISTRY AND BIOLOGY. (QUANTITATIVE STRUCTURE-ACTIVITY RELATIONSHIPS IN PHARMACOLOGY, CHEMISTRY, AND BIOLOGY). Vol. 1, No. 1 (Aug. 1982)-. 0722-3676. Periodical. US. English. qt. $168.00. Verlag Chemie International, Plaza Centre/ Suite E, 1020 NW Sixth Street, Deerfield Beach FL 33441. **Ind/Abst** Chem. Abstr. **LC** RM301.42. **DD** 615.7. **NLM** W1 QU158MG. **CODEN** QSARDI.

QUARTERLY JOURNAL OF CRUDE DRUG RESEARCH CEASED. VFOAT Vierteljahrliche Zeitschrift fur Drogen-Forschung. Revue Trimestrielle des Recherches sur les Matieres Premieres. Began with V. 1-19. 0033-5525. Periodical. English (French or German). ir. **LC** RS1. **NLM** W1 QU254. *Acta Phytotherapeutica.*

QUEBEC PHARMACIE. No. 146- Feb. 1967-. 0048-6280. Periodical. CN. French. mo. Association Quebecoise des Phamaciens Proprietaires, 5115 rue St-Denis, Montreal Quebec H2J 2M1 Canada.

RADIOPHARMACY AND RADIOPHARMACOLOGY YEARBOOK. *See* Yearbooks, Almanacs, Directories.

RATIONAL DRUG THERAPY. V. 5- Jan. 1971-. 0031-7020. Periodical. US. English. mo. American Society of Pharmacology, 9650 Rockville Pike, Bethesda MD 20014. **Tel** (301)530-7060. **Ind/ Abst** Excerpta Med., Energy Res. Abstr., Biol. Abstr., Index Med. **NLM** W1 RA948. **CODEN** RDGTAP. *Pharmacology for Physicians, 0097-0115.*

RECENT ADVANCES IN CLINICAL PHARMACOLOGY. No. 1-. 0143-8735. UK. English. ir. Longman, 19 West 44th Street, New York NY 10036. **Ed** P Turner and D G Shand. **Ind/Abst** Chem. Abstr. **LC** RM300. **DD** 615.705. **NLM** W1 RE105TP. **CODEN** RACPD9.

RECENT ADVANCES IN CLINICAL THERAPEUTICS. Vol. 1-. 0730-8019. US. English. ir. Academic Press, 4805 Sand Lake Road, Orlando FL 32887. **Tel** (305)345-4100. **Ed** Jack Z Yetiv and Joseph R Bianchine. **Ind/Abst** Chem. Abstr. **NLM** W3 RE341. **CODEN** RETHDU.

REGULATORY TOXICOLOGY AND PHARMACOLOGY. *See* Medicine - Toxicology.

RELATORIO ANUAL - ASSOCIACAO BRASILEIRA DA INDUSTRIA FARMACEUTICA. **Main/Corp** Associacao Brasileira da Industria Farmaceutica. VFOAT Industria Farmaceutica Brasileira. 1977/78–. Periodical. BL. Portuguese. ir. Departamento de Comunicacoes, Av Beira Mar 262 70. Andar, 20021 Rio de Janeiro Brazil. *Relatorio da Presidencia - Associacao Brasileira da Industria Farmaceutica.*

REMINGTON'S PRACTICE OF PHARMACY. 7th-12th Ed. Monographic Series. US. English. ir. **LC** RS91.

REPERTOIRE DES ETABLISSEMENTS - ORDRE DES PHARMACIENS DU QUEBEC. (REPERTOIRE DES ETABLISSEMENTS). **Main/Corp** Ordre des Pharmaciens du Quebec. May 1982-. 0820-8549. CN. French. be. Free to Members. Ordre des Pharmaciens du Quebec Bureau 160, 1253 Av McGill College, Montreal Quebec H3B 2Y5 Canada. **DD** 615.4025714.

REPERTOIRE DES MEMBRES - ORDRE DES PHARMACIENS DU QUEBEC. **Main/Corp** Ordre des Pharmaciens du Quebec. 1978-. 0705-6796. CN. French. an. Free. L Ordre des Pharmaciens du Quebec, 1253 Avenue McGill College, Montreal Quebec H3B 2Y5 Canada. **DD** 615.1062714. (ctrl).

REPERTORIUM FARMACEUTISCHE SPECIALITES. VFOAT RX. 0165-8301. Periodical. NE. Dutch. an. Publisher de Toorts, PO Box 576, 2003 RN Haarlem Netherlands. **NLM** W1 RE207V. *Repertorium Verpakte Geneesmiddelen Onder Merknaam, 0377-4473.*

REPORT OF THE COMMITTEE ON SAFETY OF MEDICINES APPOINTED BY THE HEALTH MINISTERS OF THE UNITED KINGDOM. (REPORT). **Main/Corp** Great Britain. Committee on Safety of Medicine. 1971-. 0308-7042. UK. English. an. -/-/13. Her Majestys Stationery Office, PO Box 276, London SW8 5DT England. **LC** RA1190. **DD** 614.35. **NLM** W2 FA1 C93R.

REPORT OF THE SOUTH DAKOTA STATE PHARMACEUTICAL ASSOCIATION AND THE SOUTH DAKOTA BOARD OF PHARMACY. **Main/Corp** South Dakota Pharmaceutical Association. 0095-3164. US. English. SD Pharmaceutical Association, Pierre SD 57501. **LC** RS5. **DD** 615.1062783.

REPORT ON THE CANADIAN DRUG STORE MARKET. (A REPORT ON THE CANADIAN DRUG STORE MARKET). VFOAT Canadian Drug Store Market. Began with 1963 issue?. 0315-6311. Periodical. CN. English. an. Maclean Hunter Publications, 481 University Avenue, Toronto Ontario M5G Canada. **DD** 381.456154.

RESEARCH COMMUNICATIONS IN CHEMICAL PATHOLOGY AND PHARMACOLOGY. VFOAT Chemical Pathology and Pharmacology. V. 1- Jan. 1970-. 0034-5164. Periodical. US. English. mo. $155.00. PJD Publishers Ltd, PO Box 966 Westbury NY 11590. **Tel** (516)626-0650. **Ind/Abst** Life Sci. Collect., Excerpta Med., Pestdoc, Ringdoc, Vetdoc, Index Med., Energy Res. Abstr., Biol. Abstr., Chem. Abstr., Sci. Cit. Index, Abr. Ed. **LC** RM1. **DD** 615.105. **NLM** W1 RE216K. **CODEN** RCOCB8.

RESIDENCY DIRECTORY. *See* Yearbooks, Almanacs, Directories.

REVIEW OF MEDICAL PHARMACOLOGY. 0557-7519. US. English. ir. **NLM** W1 RE253EN, QV 4 R454.

REVIEWS IN PURE & APPLIED PHARMACOLOGICAL SCIENCES. VAT Reviews in Pure and Applied Pharmacological Sciences. Vol. 1, No. 1 (Jan./Mar. 1980)-. 0197-2839. Periodical. UK. English. qt. $95.00. John Wiley & Sons Ltd, Baffins Lane, Chichester Sussex PO19 1UD England. **Ind/Abst** Excerpta Med., Pestdoc, Ringdoc, Vetdoc, Index Med., Biol. Abstr., Chem. Abstr. **NLM** W1 RE257CGD. **CODEN** RPASDB.

REVIEWS OF PHYSIOLOGY, BIOCHEMISTRY AND PHARMACOLOGY. *See* Biology - Physiology.

REVIEWS ON DRUG METABOLISM AND DRUG INTERACTIONS. (QUARTERLY REVIEWS ON DRUG METABOLISM AND DRUG INTERACTIONS). VFOAT Drug Metabolism and Drug Interactions. Vol. 3, No. 1 & 2-. 0334-2190. Periodical. UK. English. qt. $95.00. Freund Publishing House, PO Box 35010, 61 Nachmani Street, Tel Aviv Israel. **Ind/Abst** Excerpta Med., Pestdoc, Ringdoc, Vetdoc, Index Med., Chem. Abstr. **LC** RM302. **DD** 615.7. **NLM** W1 QU526H. **CODEN** RDMIDP. *Reviews on Drug Interactions, 0048-7546.*

REVISTA BRASILEIRA DE FARMACIA. Began in 1940. 0370-372X. Periodical. Portuguese. bm. Associacao Brasileira de Farmaceuticos, rua dos Andradas 96 0 10 Andar, Rio de Janeiro Brazil. **Ind/Abst** Excerpta Med., Chem. Abstr. **NLM** W1 RE318. **CODEN** RBFAAH. *Revista da Associacao Brasileira de Farmaceuticos, 0370-3126.*

REVISTA CUBANA DE FARMACIA. V. 1- Apr. 30, 1967-. 0034-7515. Periodical. CU. Spanish (summaries in English, French). ir. $12.61. Empresa Ediciones Cubanas, Sub-Direccion Exportacion Oreilly, 407 Ciudad, Havana Cuba. **Ind/Abst** Excerpta Med., Chem. Abstr. **NLM** W1 RE359Q. **CODEN** RCUFAC.

REVISTA DA FACULDADE DE FARMACIA E ODONTOLOGIA DE RIBEIRAO PRETO. V. 8- Jan./June 1971-. 0100-0160. Periodical. articles in Portuguese or English. ir. **Ind/Abst** Chem. Abstr. **NLM** W1 RE3682. **CODEN** RFFPDP. *Boletim da Faculdade de Farmacia e Odontologia de Ribeirao Preto.*

REVISTA DE FARMACIA E BIOQUIMICA DA UNIVERSIDADE DE SAO PAULO. **Main/Corp** Universidade de Sao Paulo. Faculdade de Ciencias Farmaceuticas. 0370-4726. Periodical. Portuguese (summaries in English). ir. Faculdade de Ciencias Farmaceuticas, Caixa Postal 30786, Sao Paula Brazil. **Ind/Abst** Pestdoc, Ringdoc, Vetdoc, Biol. Abstr., Chem. Abstr., Bibliogr. Agric. **LC** RS1. **DD** 615.105. **NLM** W1 RE396F. **CODEN** RFBUBI. *Revista, 0014-6676.*

REVISTA DO INSTITUTO DE ANTIBIOTICOS. **Main/Corp** Pernambuco, Brazil (State). Universidade Federal. Instituto de Antibioticos. V. 6-. Periodical. BL. Portuguese. ir. Cedade Universetaria Engenho de Meio, Recife Periambuco Brazil. *Revista do Instituto de Antibioticos.*

REVUE D'HISTOIRE DE LA PHARMACIE. Yearly V. 18- (No. 67-110, 115-). Periodical. FR. French. qt. $21.29. Dawson-France SA, BP 40, 91 Palaiseau France. **Tel** 009-0122/Telex 60394.

REVUE PHARMACOCINETIQUE PHARMACOKINETIC REVIEW. 0821-5987. Periodical. CN. English. ir. Free. Pharmacokinetic Information Centre, Ottawa General Hospital, 501 Smyth Road, Ottawa Ontario K1H 8L6 Canada. **DD** 615.705.

RINGDOC. *See* Indexes/Abstracts.

RIVISTA DI FARMACOLOGIA E TERAPIA. V. 1- Mar. 1970-. 0302-1750. Periodical. English (articles in Italian). qt. $24.35. Stem-Mucchi, Via Tabboni 4, 4100 Modena Italy. **Ind/ Abst** Excerpta Med., Chem. Abstr. **NLM** W1 RI462. **CODEN** RVFTBB. Index published separately - free - automatically sent.

RIVISTA EUROPEA PER LE SCIENZE MEDICHE E FARMACOLOGICHE. VFOAT European Review for Medical and Pharmacological Sciences. Vol. 1, N. 1 (Dec. 1979)-.

Pharmacy

0392-291X. Periodical. Italian. qt. Ind/Abst Excerpta Med., Biol. Abstr., Chem. Abstr. NLM W1 RI661P. CODEN RESFDJ.

ROCHE HANDBOOK OF DIFFERENTIAL DIAGNOSIS. US. English. Roche Laboratories, Nutley NJ 07110. Tel (201)235-2478.

ROTE LISTE. 1935-. GW. German. an. $14.10. Editio Cantor, Postfach 12 55, D-7960 Aulendorf West Germany. Tel 07525/431. List of pharmaceutical products by the members of Bundesverband der Pharmazeutischen Industrie e.v. *Preisverzeichnis Deutscher Pharmazeutischer Spezial Praeparate.*

RUSSIAN PHARMACOLOGY AND TOXICOLOGY. V. 30- Jan./Feb. 1967-. 0036-0325. Periodical. UK. English (Russian). bm. $199.50. Euromed Publications, 33 Woodlands Road, Surbiton Surrey KT6 6PR England. Tel (01)399-3839. Ed H Cygielski. Ind/Abst Excerpta Med. NLM W1 RU828. Drug research in the USSR with special reference to the screening of chemical compounds for biological activity. Literature reviews of structure vs. chemical activity and new drugs under development.

RX ET CETERA. (RX ET CETERA : NEWSLETTER OF THE WASHINGTON STATE PHARMACEUTICAL ASSOCIATION). 0744-7736. Periodical. US. English. mo. Washington State Pharmaceutical Association, 1402 Third Avenue/Suite 517, Seattle WA 98101.

SAFE, EFFECTIVE AND THERAPEUTICALLY EQUIVALENT PRESCRIPTION DRUGS. Main/Corp New York (State). Office of Health Systems Management. VFOAT Therapeutically Equivalent Prescription Drugs. 1977-. 0273-0820. US. English. an. $2.00. Health Education Service, PO Box 7126, Albany NY 12224. *Safe, Effective, and Interchangeable Prescription Drugs.*

SAINNYAG HAGHOI JI. (SAENGYAK HAKHOE CHI). VFOAT Korean Journal of Pharmacognosy. 0253-3073. Periodical. KO. Korean (summaries in English). sa. $20.00. Hanguk Saengyak Hahkoe, 28 Yongon-Dong Chongno-ku, Seoul 110 Korea. Tel (02)877-3141. Ed Eung Bang Lee. Ind/Abst Chem. Abstr., Chem. Abstr. LC RS160. DD 615.32109519. CODEN SYHJAM. bk rev. adv acc. Circ 500. (ctrl). Original research reports on review on botanical drugs and natural products: chemistry, pharmacology, toxicology, mechanism of action, botany, taxonomy, and oriental drug preparations.

SCHRIFTENREIHE DER ARZNEIMITTELZULASSUNGS- UND AUFBEREITUNGSKOMMISSION C AM BUNDESGESUNDHEITSAMT. V. 1-. Monographic Series. German. ir. NLM W1.

SCHRIFTENREIHE DER BUNDESAPOTHEKERKAMMER ZUR WISSENSCHAFTLICHEN FORTBILDUNG. GRUNE REIHE. V. 1-. 0721-1457. Monographic Series. German. ir. Ind/Abst Chem. Abstr. NLM W1. CODEN SBWGDW.

SCHWEIZERISCHE APOTHEKER-ZEITUNG. VFOAT Journal Suisse de Pharmacie, Giornale Svizzero di Farmacia. V. 1- 1863-. 0036-7508. Periodical. SZ. Multilingual (German, French, and Italian). ir. 104.00. Schweiz Apothekerverein, Postfach 3006, CH-3000 Bern 7 Switzerland. Tel (031) 22 04 54. bk rev. adv acc. Circ 4,800. Scientific pharmaceutical. *Schweizerische Zeitschrift fur Pharmacie.*

SCIENTIA PHARMACEUTICA. VFOAT Oesterreichische Apothekerzeitung. 1- Year. 0036-8709. Periodical. AU. German. qt. 275. Oesterr Apothekerverlag GMBH, Spitalgasse 31, A-1094 Wien Austria. Tel 42-43-51. Ind/Abst Chem. Abstr. bk rev. adv acc. Circ 600. (ctrl). Research in pharmacy, pharmaceutical chemistry, pharmacognosy, pharmacology, pharmaceutical technology, pharmaceutical biology, pharmaceutical analysis, analytical chemistry and pharmacobotany.

SCRIP. 0143-7690. Periodical. UK. English. sw. $522.92. Pharma Books, c/o Scrip 82 Riverside Drive, New York NY 10024. Tel (212)580-8270. Ed Philip J Brown. Ind/Abst Pharm. News Index, Predicasts. CODEN SCRIDK. adv acc. Circ 43,000. World's leading international news journal on the ethical pharmaceutical market. Products, finance, world markets and people reported by scientific staff to keep decision makers well informed.

SELECTED METHODS OF CLINICAL CHEMISTRY. Began with V. 8 in 1977. 0271-4078. US. English. ir. American Association for Clinical Chemistry, 1725 K Street NW, Washington DC 20006. Tel (202)857-0717. LC RS403. DD 616.075605. NLM W1 SE32LD. (ctrl). *Standard Methods of Clinical Chemistry*, 0065-7115.

SENUR DAIHAGGYO NYAGHAG KOMMUNJIB. (SOUL TAEHAKKYO YAKHAK NONMUNJIP). Main/Corp Soul Taehakkyo. Yakhak Taehak. VFOAT Seoul University Journal of Pharmaceutical Sciences. Vol. 1- No. 0250-3336. Periodical. KO. English (Korean). ir. Seoul National University, San 56-1 Sinrim-dong, Kwanack-Ku, Seoul Korea. Ind/Abst Biol. Abstr., Chem. Abstr. LC RM1. CODEN STYNDJ.

SESION INAUGURAL - REAL ACADEMIA DE FARMACIA DE BARCELONA. (REAL ACADEMIA DE FARMACIA DE BARCELONA. SESION INAUGURAL DEL CURSO). Series/Titl Publicacoines de la Real Academia de Farmacia de Barcelona. VFOAT Publicaciones de la Real Academia de Farmacia. 1979-. 0515-1147. Periodical. Spanish. an. NLM W1 RE105FI. *Real Academia de Farmacia de Barcelona. Sesion Inaugural*, 0515-1147.

SIDE EFFECTS OF DRUGS ANNUAL. 1- 1977-. 0378-6080. Periodical. English. an. Excerpta Medica, 52 Vanderbilt Avenue, New York NY 10017. Ind/Abst Biol. Abstr., Chem. Abstr. LC RM302.5. DD 615.7042. NLM W1 SI255B. CODEN SEDAD8.

SOUL YAKSAHOE CHI. VFOAT Journal of the Seoul Pharmaceutical Association. Periodical. Korean. qt. Soul Tukpyolsi Yaksahoe, 549 Pangbae 2-Dong Kangnam-Ku, Seoul Korea. LC RS1.

SOUTH AFRICAN PHARMACEUTICAL JOURNAL. VFOAT Suid-Afrikaanse Tydskrif vir Apteekwese. V. 1- 1934-. 0038-2558. Periodical. SA. English (articles occasionally in Afrikaans). mo. $10.33. PSSA, Box 31360, Braamfontein 2000 South Africa. Tel (011)339-1752. Ed Carrie Smith. Ind/Abst Pestdoc, Ringdoc, Vetdoc, Chem. Abstr. NLM W1 SO908E. bk rev. adv acc. Circ 5,000. (ctrl). News and views on all sectors of pharmacy; industrial, retail, hospital and academic including drug and product news and clinical features. *African Chemist and Druggist.*

SOUTHERN PHARMACY JOURNAL. V. 71, No. 3- Jan. 1979-. 0192-5792. Periodical. US. English. mo. $24.00. Southern Pharmacy, 3030 Peachtree Road NW, Suite 310, Atlanta GA 30305. Tel (404)231-1267. Ed Max Ginsberg. NLM W1 SO957P. Circ 18,000. (ctrl). A business and professional magazine covering news and events of and about pharmacy in the Southeast and Southwest. Publishes ACPE-approved continuing education programs. *Southeastern Drug/Southern Pharmaceutical Journal*, 0193-9971.

SURVEY OF PHARMACY LAW. See Law.

SURVEY ON PRESCRIPTIONS. (A SURVEY ON PRESCRIPTIONS). Began with 1969 issue. 0316-9901. CN. English. an. 75.00. MacLean Hunter Limited, MacLean Hunter Building, 777 Bay Street, Toronto Ontario M5W 1A7 Canada. Tel (416)596-5287. DD 381.456154. Canadian prescriptions statistics: number of scripts, prices to patient, most commonly prescribed drugs, pharmacists' choice of prescription drugs. Statistics broken down by area. Includes comparable statistics dating back to 1975.

SVENSK FARMACEUTISK TIDSKRIFT. VFOAT Farmaceutisk Tidskrift. Began publication in 1897. 0039-6524. Periodical. SW. Swedish. tm. $21.29. Svensk Farmaceutisk Tidskrift, Box 1136, S-111 81 Stockholm Sweden. Ind/Abst Chem. Abstr., Excerpta Med., Pestdoc, Ringdoc, Vetdoc, Funk Scott Index Corp. Ind. NLM W1 SV253. CODEN SFTIAE.

SWISS PHARMA. 0251-1673. Periodical. SZ. German. mo. $34.64. Verlag Dr Felix Wuest AG, Seestrasse 5/Postfach, CH-8700 Kuesnacht Switzerland. Tel (01)9110055. Ind/Abst Excerpta Med. NLM W1 SW406P.

SYMPOSIA ON FRONTIERS OF PHARMACOLOGY. Vol. 1-. 0733-9321. Monographic Series. US. English. Ind/Abst Chem. Abstr., Chem. Abstr. LC UNC. DD 615.1. NLM W3 SY107. CODEN SFPHDS.

TARIF DES SPECIALITES PHARMACEUTIQUES. VFOAT Tarief der Pharmaceutische Specialiteiten. 0770-1772. Periodical. French (text in Dutch). an. Association Pharmaceutique Belge, 11 rue Archimede, B1040 Bruxelles Belgium. Tel 02 230 26 85. NLM W1 TA605. bk rev. adv acc.

TERAPIA I LEKI. 0137-9887. Periodical. Polish. ir. NLM W1 TE554. *Biuletyn Informacyjny - Centrala Farmaceutyczna Cefarm.*

TEXAS PHARMACY. V. 78- Jan. 1959-. 0362-7926. Periodical. US. English. mo. $15.00. Texas Pharmacy, PO Box 14709, Austin TX 78761. Tel (512)836-8350. Ed Luther R Parker. Ind/Abst Chem. Abstr. NLM W1 TH83. CODEN TXPDAE. adv acc. Circ 4,200. (ctrl). *Texas Druggist.*

THEORY IN PSYCHOPHARMACOLOGY. See Psychology.

THERAPEUTIC DRUG MONITORING. V. 1-. 0163-4356. Periodical. US. English. qt. $109.00. Raven Press, 1140 6th Avenue, New York NY 10036. Ind/Abst Life Sci. Collect., Excerpta Med., Pestdoc, Ringdoc, Vetdoc, Chem. Abstr., Curr. Contents, Biol. Abstr., Index Med. NLM W1 TH138. CODEN TDMODV.

TODO NATURAL DE NUEVA YORK. Yearly V. 1, No. 1, (Sept. 1984)-. 8755-1063. Periodical. US. Spanish. mo. $12.95. Editorial Mezquita, 20 West 22 Street/Room 1000, New York NY 10010. DD 615.

TOP 200. 1981-. Periodical. US. English. an. NLM QV 772 T147T.

TOPICS IN ANTIBIOTIC CHEMISTRY. Vol. 1-. 0140-0843. Periodical. UK. English. ir. Halsted Press, 605 Third Avenue, New York NY 10158. Tel (212)867-9800. Ind/Abst Chem. Abstr. LC RS431.A6. DD 615.329. NLM W1 TO539C. CODEN TACHD7.

TOPICS IN HOSPITAL PHARMACY MANAGEMENT. VFOAT THPM. Vol. 1, No. 1 (May 1981)-. 0271-1206. Periodical. US. English. qt. Aspen Systems Corporation, PO Box 6018, Gaithersburg MD 20760. Tel (301)251-5000. Ed Terry Trudeau. Ind/Abst Hospit. Lit. Index. NLM W1 TO539MSF. adv acc. Leading authorities present key topics of interest to pharmacy professionals-management, computers, finance, quality assurance. One topic covered in depth each month.

TOPICS IN MOLECULAR PHARMACOLOGY. Vol. 1-. 0167-7101. US. English. ir. Elsevier Science Publishing Company, 52 Vanderbilt Avenue, New York NY 10017. Ed Arnold S V Burgen and Gordon C K Roberts. Ind/Abst Chem. Abstr. LC RM1. DD 615.105. NLM W1 TO54C. CODEN TMPHDK.

TOXICON. V. 1- Oct. 1962-. 0041-0101. Periodical. UK. English (French or German with summaries in English). bm. Pergamon Press, 395 Sawmill River Road, Elmsford NY 10523. Tel (914)592-7700. Ind/Abst Life Sci. Collect., Excerpta Med., Energy Inf. Abstr., Environ. Abstr., Bibliogr. Agric., Biol. Abstr., Chem. Abstr., Index Med., Nuci. Sci. Abstr., Sci. Cit. Index, Abstr. Ed. LC QP631. DD 615.37305. NLM W1 TO95J. CODEN TOXIA6. (cum index).

TRAVAUX DE LA SOCIETE DE PHARMACIE DE MONTPELLIER. Began in 1942. 0037-9115. Periodical. FR. French. qt. Societe de Pharmacie de Montpellier, Faculte de Pharmacie de Montpellier Ave, Ch-Flabault, 34060 Montpellier France. Ind/Abst Excerpta Med. CODEN TSPMA6.

TRENDS IN PHARMACOLOGICAL SCIENCES. V. 1- 1979/80-. English. ir. NLM W1 TR341F. Index in last issue of volume - attached.

TRIBUNA FARMACEUTICA. Began publication with V. 1, 1932. 0371-6619. Periodical. BL. Portuguese. Universidad de Fed'l do Parana ru Cel Dulcidio 638, C Postal 888, 80000 Curitiba Parana Brazil. Ind/Abst Life Sci. Collect., Chem. Abstr. NLM W1 TR45. CODEN TFBRAU.

UIYAK CHONGBO. VFOAT Drug Information. Periodical. KO. Korean. mo. 30,000. Yagop Sinmunsa, 100-1 2-ka Chongpa-dong Yongsan-ku, Seoul Korea. LC RS1.

U.S. PHARMACEUTICAL MARKET. DRUG STORES. VFOAT U.S. Drug Stores. 0275-5181. US. English. IMS America Ltd, Ambler PA 19002. LC HD966.1. DD 381.4561510973.

U.S. PHARMACIST. V.1-. 0148-4818. Periodical. US. English. mo. $20.00. Jobson Publishing Company, 352 Park Avenue South, New York NY 10010. Tel (212)685-4848. Ed Allen Schwartz. NLM W1 UN724. adv acc. Circ 82,000. (ctrl). Reviews of drugs and dieases for pharmacists.

THE UNITED STATES PHARMACOPEIA. VFOAT US Pharmacopeia. (20th Revision- 1980)- – NF 15th Ed.-. 0195-7996. Periodical. US. English. ir. Mack Publishing Company, 20th Northampton Streets, Easton PA 18042. **Tel** (215)258-9111. **LC** RS141.2. **DD** 615.1173. **NLM** QV 738 AA1 P5. *Pharmacopeia of the United States of America.*

UNITED STATES PHARMACOPEIA DISPENSING INFORMATION. (UNITED STATES PHARMACOPEIA DISPENSING INFORMATION : USP DI). **VFOAT** USP DI. 1980-1981. 0276-5373. US. English. bm. $60.00. Mack Publ Company, 20th Northampton Streets, Easton PA 18042. **Tel** (215)258-9633. **LC** RM300. **DD** 615.58. **NLM** QV 740 AA1 U601.

UNLISTED DRUGS. V. 1- Jan. 1949-. 0042-0441. Periodical. US. English. mo. Pharmaco-Medical Documentation, PO Box 401, Chatam NJ 07928. **Tel** (201)635-9500. **DD** 615. **NLM** W1 UN975. (cum index).

UNLISTED DRUGS INDEX-GUIDE. See Indexes/Abstracts.

UPDATE - COLLEGE OF PHARMACY. DALHOUSIE UNIVERSITY. (UPDATE : A PUBLICATION OF CONTINUING PHARMACEUTICAL EDUCATION). Vol. 2, No. 1 (Sept./Oct. 1973)-. 0227-0692. Periodical. CN. English. qt. Free. College of Pharmacy, Dalhousie University, Halifax Nova Scotia B3H 3J5 Canada. **DD** 615.105. (ctrl). *Update (Nova Scotia Pharmaceutical Society. Continuing Education Committee). Update, 0227-0684.*

U.S.A.N. AND THE U.S.P. DICTIONARY OF DRUG NAMES. See Encyclopedias & General Reference Books.

USP DI. ADVICE FOR THE PATIENT. VFOAT Advice for the Patient. **VAT** United States Pharmacopeia Dispensing Information. Advice for the Patient. 1983-. 0740-6916. US. English. an. $21.95. United States Pharmacopeia Convention, 12601 Twinbrook Parkway, Rockville MD 20852. **LC** RM300. **DD** 615.1. *United States Pharmacopeia Dispensing Information, 0276-5373.*

USP DI. DRUG INFORMATION FOR THE HEALTH CARE PROVIDER. VFOAT U.S.P.D.I. **VAT** United States Pharmacopeia Dispensing Information. Drug Information for the Health Care Provider. 1983-. 0740-4174. US. English. an. $29.95. USPC, 2601 Twinbrook Parkway, Rockville MD 20852. **LC** RM300. **DD** 615.1. *United States Pharmacopeia Dispensing Information, 0276-5373.*

USP DI/UPDATE. (USP DI UPDATE). **VAT** United States Pharmacopeia Dispensing Information Update. V. 1, No. 1 (Jan./Feb. 1980)-. 0730-1324. Periodical. US. English. bm. **NLM** QV 740 AA1 U601A.

U.S.P. GUIDE TO SELECT DRUGS. (USP GUIDE TO SELECT DRUGS). **Main/Corp** United States Pharmacopeial Convention. **VAT** United States Pharmacopeial Guide to Select Drugs. 1973-. 0091-3839. US. English. an. 12601 Twinbrook Parkway, Rockville MD 20852. **LC** RS141.2. **DD** 615.1173.

DIE VEROFFENTLICHUNGEN DER INTERNATIONALEN GESELLSCHAFT FUR GESCHICHTE DER PHARMAZIE. NEUE FOLGE. **Main/Corp** International Society for the History of Pharmacy. V. 1- 1953-. Monographic Series. GW. German. ir. Wissenschaftliche Verlagsges, Postfach 40, D-700 Stuttgart 1 West Germany. *Veroffentlichungen der (Internationalen), Gesellschaft fur Geschichte der Pharmazie.*

VERZEICHNIS WISSENSCHAFTLICHER PUBLIKATIONEN. **Main/Corp** Akademie der Wissenschaften der DDR. Institut fur Wirkstofforschung. GW. German. an. Akademie der Wissenschaften der DDR, Institut fur Wirkstofforschung DDR Alfred-Kowalke Str 4, DDR 1136 Berlin-Friedrichsfelde West Germany. **LC** QP901. **DD** 615.105.

THE VIRGINIA PHARMACIST. Began with V. 1 in Sept. 1916. 0042-6717. US. English. mo. Virginia Pharmaceutical Association, 3119 West Clay Street, Richmond VA 23219. **NLM** W1 VI823H.

VOICE OF THE PHARMACIST. V. 1- Sept. 1957-. 0507-2379. Periodical. US. English. qt. $25.00. American College of Apothecaries, 874 Union Avenue, Memphis TN 38103. **Tel** (901)528-6037. **Ed** Edward H Clouse. **Circ** 1,000. (ctrl). This newsletter consists of articles of interest on timely topics for independent pharmacy practitioners.

WAKAN-YAKU KENKYUJO NEMPO. **Main/Corp** Toyama Daigaku. Wakan-Yaku Kenkyujo. VFOAT Annual Report. V. 1-. Japanese. ir. Toyama Daigaku Wakan-Yaku Kenkyujo, 3190 Gofuku (930), Toyama Japan. **Ind/Abst** Chem. Abstr. **LC** RS180.J3. **CODEN** WKNDDH.

WASHINGTON DRUG LETTER (1979). See Law.

WEEKLY PHARMACY REPORTS. VFOAT Green Sheet. 0043-1893. Periodical. US. English. wk. $25.00. F D C Reports Inc, 5550 Friendship Boulevard, Chevy Chase MD 20815. **Tel** (301)657-9830. **Ed** Herbert Carlson. **Ind/Abst** Pharm. News Index. **NLM** W1 W171. **CODEN** WPHRAR. Introduction and pricing of new pharmaceuticals, government regulatory activity (federal as well as state), coverage of national and state pharmacy association meetings.

WEHRMEDIZIN UND WEHRPHARMAZIE. Vol. 7- Jan./Feb. 1969-. GW. German. qt. $30.52. Special Publication Service, Postfach 2060 Karl Mand Str 2, 5400 Koblenz 1 West Germany. **Tel** 0261/803071. **LC** RC970. **NLM** W1 WE226A. bk rev. adv acc. (ctrl). A journal providing information on medical and health services in the bundeswehr. *Wehrmedizin.*

WELEDA KORRESPONDENZBLATTER FUR ARZTE. 0379-7031. Periodical. German. ir. **NLM** W1 WE255.

WEST AFRICAN JOURNAL OF PHARMACOLOGY AND DRUG RESEARCH. VFOAT Africaine Ouest Journal de Pharmacologie et Recherche Drogue. V. 1- Jan. 1974-. 0303-691X. Periodical. NR. English (title in French: Africaine Ouest Journal de Pharmacologie et Recherche Drogue). sa. University Lagos/Dr Bamgbose, College Medician, Department of Pharmacology, PMB 12003 Lagos Nigeria. **Ind/Abst** Chem. Abstr., Index Med. **NLM** W1 WE329K. **CODEN** WAJPAS.

WHOLESALE DRUGS MAGAZINE. See Business - Marketing.

THE WISCONSIN PHARMACIST. (THE WISCONSIN PHARMACIST : OFFICIAL PUBLICATION OF THE WISCONSIN PHARMACIST ASSOCIATION). 0043-6585. Periodical. US. English. mo. $30.00. Wisconsin Pharmaceutical Association, 202 Price Place, Madison WI 53705. **Tel** (608)238-5515. **Ed** Robert E Henry. **NLM** W1 WI8025. adv acc. **Circ** 2,000. (ctrl). Articles and features about the practice of pharmacy (especially professional and socioeconomic aspects), Wisconsin Pharmacists, and the Wisconsin Pharmaceutical Association. *Wisconsin Druggist.*

WOLGAN YAKKUK. VFOAT Journal of Pharmacy. Periodical. Korean. mo. 27,000. Wolgan Yakkuksa, 133-1 Sorin-Dong Chongno-Ku, Seoul Korea. **LC** RS1.

WORLD PHARMACEUTICALS DIRECTORY. See Yearbooks, Almanacs, Directories.

WRAP UP ON LATIN AMERICAN CHEMICALS, COSMETICS, PHARMACEUTICALS & MEDICAL EQUIPMENT. VFOAT Chemicals, Cosmetics, Pharmaceuticals & Medical Equipment. 0741-8558. Periodical. US. English. mo. $90.00 Libraries, $100.00 Others. Aurora International, PO Box 668, Norwalk CT 06856. Issued also in machine-readable form.

YAGHAG-HOI-JI. (YAKHAKHOE CHI). **Main/Corp** Taehan Yakhakhoe. VFOAT Yakhak Hoeji. 0377-9556. Periodical. KO. Korean (with table of contents and summaries in English). ir. c/o College of Pharmacy, Seoul National University, Seoul South Korea. **Ind/Abst** Chem. Abstr. **LC** RS1. **NLM** W1 YA435. **CODEN** YAHOA3.

YAKHAK YONGUJI. VFOAT Bulletin of Pharmaceutical Sciences. Periodical. English (Korean). ir. **LC** RM1.

YAKUBUTSU, SEISHIN, KODO. VFOAT Japanese Journal of Psychopharmacology. Vol. 1, No. 1 (Oct. 1981)-. 0285-5313. Japanese. ir. **Ind/Abst** Chem. Abstr., Life Sci. Collect., Excerpta Med., Index Med., Biol. Abstr. **NLM** W1 YA445N. **CODEN** YSKODB.

YAKUGAKU TOSHOKAN. See Library and Information Science.

YAKUGAKU ZASSHI. **Main/Corp** Nippon Yakugakkai. VFOAT Journal of the Pharmaceutical Society of Japan. No. 1- 1881-. 0031-6903. Periodical.

JA. Japanese (summaries in English). mo. Kyowa Book Company Inc, 1-38 Kanda Jinbo-Cho Chiyoda-Ku, Tokyo 101 Japan. **Tel** 293-0727. **Ind/Abst** Excerpta Med., Life Sci. Collect., Pestdoc, Ringdoc, Vetdoc, Index Med., Biol. Abstr., Chem. Abstr., Bibliogr. Agric., Curr. Abstr. Chem. Index Chem., Sci. Cit. Index, Abr. Ed. **NLM** W1 YA4493. **CODEN** YKKZAJ. Index in last issue of volume - attached. (cum index).

YAKUJI KOGYO SEISAN DOTAI TOKEI NEMPO. **Main/Corp** Japan. Koseisho. **VFOAT** Koseisho Yakuji Kogyo Seisan Dotai Tokei Nempo. Japanese. ir. 2000. Yakugyo Keizai Kenkyujo, c/o Tokyo Kurabu Building 2-6 Kasumigaseki, 3-chome Chiyoda-ku Tokyo 100 Japan. **LC** HD9672.J28.

YAKURI TO CHIRYO. VFOAT Basic Pharmacology & Therapeutics. Vol. 1- August 1973-. 0386-3603. Periodical. Japanese. ir. **Ind/Abst** Chem. Abstr., Excerpta Med. **NLM** W1 YA451N. **CODEN** YACHDS.

YAO HSUEH HSUEH PAO. VFOAT Acta Pharmaceutica Sinica. Began in 1953. 0513-4870. Periodical. CH. Chinese. mo. 30.00. China Publication Centre, PO Box 2820, Beijing China. **Tel** 33-5116. **Ed** Song Zhen-Yu. **Ind/Abst** Index Med., Chem. Abstr. **LC** RS1. **DD** 615.105. **CODEN** YHHPAL. adv acc. **Circ** 10,000. Original research articles on pharmaceutical sciences including medicinal chemistry, pharmaceutical analysis, chemistry of natural products, antibiotics, pharmacology, toxicology, pharmacy and pharmacognosy. *Chung-Kuo Yao Hsueh Tsa Chih.*

YAO HSUEH TSA CHIH. VFOAT The Journal of Pharmacy. Vol. 1, No. 1 (Apr.-June 1984)-. Periodical. CH. Chinese. qt. 550.00. Chung-Hua Min Kuo Yao Shih Kung Hui Chuan Kuo Lien Ho Hui, PO Box 110460, Taipei Taiwan.

YAO WU FEN HSI TSA CHIH. VFOAT Yaowu Penxi Zazhi. Vol. 1, (Jan. 1981)-. 0254-1793. Periodical. CC. Chinese. bm. 10.80. China Publication Centre, PO Box 2820, Beijing China. **Ind/Abst** Chem. Abstr. **LC** RS189. **DD** 615.105. **NLM** W1 YA701S. **CODEN** YFZADL.

THE YEAR BOOK OF CLINICAL PHARMACY. See Yearbooks, Almanacs, Directories.

ZENTRALBLATT FUER PHARMAZIE, PHARMOKOTHERAPIE UND LABORTORIUMSDIAGNOSTIK. (ZENTRALBLATT FUR PHARMAZIE, PHARMAKOTHERAPIE UND LABORATORIUMSDIAGNOSTIK). 0049-8696. Periodical. SZ. German (summaries in English and Russian). mo. $61.64. Kunst & Wissen Erich Bieber, Dufourstrasse 51, CH-8008 Zurich Switzerland. **Ind/Abst** Excerpta Med., Pestdoc, Ringdoc, Vetdoc, Biol. Abstr., Chem. Abstr. **LC** RM1. **NLM** W1 ZE784. **CODEN** ZPPLBF. *Pharmazeutische Zentralhalle fur Deutschland, Arzneimittelstandardisierung.*

ZHONGGUO YAOLI XUEBAO. (CHUNG-KUO YAO LI HSUEH PAO). VFOAT Acta Pharmacologica Sinica. V. 1, (Sept. 1980)-. 0253-9756. Periodical. CC. Chinese. qt. $9.90. China Publication Centre, PO Box 2820, Beijing China. **Ind/Abst** Index Med., Excerpta Med., Biol. Abstr., Chem. Abstr. **LC** RM1. **DD** 615.105. **NLM** W1 CH991C. **CODEN** CYLPDN.

PHILANTHROPY

ANNUAL INDEX OF FOUNDATION REPORTS. See Indexes/Abstracts.

ANNUAL REPORT OF THE DUKE ENDOWMENT. **Main/Corp** Duke Endowment. 1962/63-. US. English. an. 30 Rockefeller Plaza, New York NY 10020. **LC** HV97.D8. **DD** 001.440973. **NLM** W1 DU648P. *Financial Statement, Annual Reports of the Hospital and Orphan Sections.*

ARTS PATRONAGE SERIES. See The Arts (General).

CARNEGIE CORPORATION OF NEW YORK QUARTERLY CEASED. V. 5, No. 3-V. 14, No. 1. 0146-1613. Periodical. US. English. qt. Carnegie Corporation of New York, 437 Madison Avenue, New York NY 10022. **Tel** (212)371-3200. **Ed** Avery Russell. **Circ** 36,000. A newsletter that describes corporation-supported projects. *Quarterly*

Philately

Report - Carnegie Corporation of New York, 0146-1605.

CORPORATE 500. THE DIRECTORY OF CORPORATE PHILANTHROPY. See Yearbooks, Almanacs, Directories.

D.C. DIRECTORY OF NATIVE AMERICAN FEDERAL AND PRIVATE PROGRAMS / NATIVE AMERICAN-PHILANTHROPIC NEWS SERVICE. See Yearbooks, Almanacs, Directories.

DIRECTORIO NACIONAL DE INSTITUCIONES PRIVADAS FILANTROPICAS Y DE DESARROLLO SOCIAL. See Yearbooks, Almanacs, Directories.

DIRECTORY OF FOUNDATIONS OF THE GREATER WASHINGTON AREA. See Yearbooks, Almanacs, Directories.

ELHI FUNDING SOURCES NEWSLETTER. 0149-3450. Periodical. US. English. mo. $75.00. The Oryx Press, 3930 East Camelback Road, Phoenix AZ 85018.

THE FOUNDATION DIRECTORY. See Yearbooks, Almanacs, Directories.

THE FOUNDATION DIRECTORY. SUPPLEMENT. See Yearbooks, Almanacs, Directories.

FOUNDATION GRANTS TO INDIVIDUALS. See Yearbooks, Almanacs, Directories.

FOUNDATION NEWS. V. 1- Sept. 1960-. 0015-8976. Periodical. US. English. bm. $24.00. Foundation News, 1828 L Street NW, Washington DC 20036. Tel (202)466-6512. Ed Arlie Schardt. Ind/Abst Hospit. Lit. Index, Ref. Source. LC AS911.A2. DD 001.4405. NLM AS 1 F746. (cum index). bk rev. adv acc. Circ 15,000. Magazine for both grantmakers and grantseekers. Covers how-to's of reviewing proposals and evaluating programs; spotlights innovations in philanthropy; and much more. Includes corporate, research and international columns.

GIVING USA. VAT Giving United States of America. 1- 1956-. 0436-0257. US. English. an. $25.00. American Association of Fund Raising Council, 25 West 43rd Street, New York NY 10036. Tel (212)354-5799. Ed Fred Schnoue. LC HV89. DD 361.705873. Circ 3,200. (ctrl). A compilation of facts and trends on American philanthropy in 1983.

GRANTS MAGAZINE. V. 1- Mar. 1978-. 0160-9734. Periodical. US. English. qt. $90.00 Domestic, $101.00 Foreign. Plenum Publishing Corp, 227 West 17th Street, New York NY 10011. Tel (212)620-8000. Ed Frances Scadek and Eugene Stein. Ind/Abst Hospit. Lit. Index. LC H62.A1. DD 001.44. NLM W1 GR228. A broadly concerned, interdisciplinary publication that provides a forum for discussion of the various issues that affect both public and private philanthropy.

GRANTSMANSHIP NEWS. 1971. 0741-2487. Periodical. US. English. mo. $204.00. Grantsmanship News Inc, 81 Barrow Street, New York NY 10014. Tel (212)675-4264. Circ 1,000. Information on available grants and contracts for the educational and health-related institutions from government sources and private and public foundations.

THE GUIDE TO GIFTS AND BEQUESTS, CALIFORNIA. 1978/79-. 0163-383X. US. English. be. 440 Park Avenue South, New York NY 10016. LC AS28.C2. DD 001.44025.

INSIDE OXFAM. No. 23- Fall 1971-. 0319-0323. CN. English. Oxfam-Canada Ontario Region, 175 Carlton Street, Toronto Ontario M5A 2K3 Canada. Tel (416)961-3935. Ed Stephen Allen. DD 361.006271. (ctrl). Oxfam-Canada News, 0319-0331.

LETTER - FORD FOUNDATION. Main/Corp Ford Foundation. VFOAT Ford Foundation Letter. V. 1- Apr. 1970-. 0015-699X. Periodical. US. English. bm. Free. Ford Foundation, 320 East 43rd Street, New York NY 10017. Tel (212)573-5000. Ed Robert Tolles. Circ 35,000. An account of Ford Foundation grants and other matters of interest.

NATIONAL DATA BOOK. 5th Ed. (1981)-. 0732-8788. US. English. an. $55.00. The Foundation Center, 79 Fifth Avenue, New York NY 10003. Tel (212)620-4230. Ed Patricia Read. LC AS911.A2. DD 001.4402573. NLM AS 911.A2 F771. Brief listings for all of the more than 24,000 active grantmaking foundations in the US. Includes address, principle officer, assets and annual grant amounts. Foundation Center National Data Book, 0730-1677.

OUA/DATA'S GUIDE TO CORPORATE & FOUNDATION GIVING IN VERMONT. (OUA/DATA'S . . . GUIDE TO CORPORATE & FOUNDATION GIVING IN VERMONT). VFOAT OUADATA'S . . . Guide to Corporate & Production Giving in Vermont. 1984-1985-. US. English. be. $7.50. OUA/DATA, 81 Saltonstall Avenue, New Haven CT 06513. Tel (203)278-2477. Ed Mike Burns. Circ 500. A directory of 100 foundations and 50 corporate philanthropic policies, and priorities.

OUA/DATA'S GUIDE TO CORPORATE GIVING IN MAINE. See Yearbooks, Almanacs, Directories.

OUA/DATA'S GUIDE TO CORPORATE GIVING IN MASSACHUSETTS. (OUA/DATA'S . . . GUIDE TO CORPORATE GIVING IN MASSACHUSETTS). VFOAT Guide to Corporate Giving in Massachusetts. VAT Office of Urban Affairs/Development and Technical Assistance Research and Resource Center's Guide to Corporate Giving in Massachusetts. 1983-1984—. 0882-0449. US. English. be. $17.50. OUA/DATA, 81 Saltonstall Avenue, New Haven CT 06513. Tel (203)777-7279. Ed Mike Burns. LC HV98.M39. DD 361.7650973. Circ 500. (ctrl). A directory of Massachusetts (750) corporate philanthropic priorities, policies, and procedures.

OUA/DATA'S . . . GUIDE TO CORPORATE GIVING IN RHODE ISLAND. VFOAT Guide to Corporate Giving in Rhode Island. 1984-1985-. US. English. be. $7.50. OUA/DATA, 81 Saltonstall Avenue, New Haven CT 06513. Tel (203)278-2477. Ed Mike Burns. Circ 500. (ctrl). A directory of 300 Rhode Island philanthropy corporations policies, priorities and procedures.

PHILANTHROPIC DIGEST. 1954. 0480-2853. Periodical. US. English. mo. $35.00. Philanthropic Digest, 1100 17th Street NW/10th Floor, Washington DC 20036. Tel (202)785-4829. Ed John Rhea. Circ 800. (ctrl). Summary of philanthropic news and giving to education, health and hospitals, welfare, the arts and museums, libraries, religion and related philanthropy.

PHILANTHROPIST. (THE PHILANTHROPIST). VFOAT Philanthrope. V. 1- Fall 1972-. 0316-3849. Periodical. CN. English. ir. $21.67. Canadian Centre Philanthropy, 185 Bay Street/Suite 504, Toronto Ontario M5J 1K6 Canada.

THE PHILANTHROPY MONTHLY. VFOAT Non-Profit Report, Nonprofit Report, NP Report. 1968. Periodical. US. English. ir. $72.00. The Philanthropy Monthly, PO Box 989, New Milford CT 06776. Tel (203)354-7132. Ed Henry C Suhrke. adv acc. Circ 4,000. Issues concerning nonprofits including fund raising, postal rates, accounting, corporate and foundation giving practices, and new legislation.

PROCEEDINGS - NOTRE DAME INSTITUTE ON CHARITABLE GIVING, FOUNDATIONS, AND TRUSTS. Main/Conf Notre Dame Institute on Charitable Giving, Foundations, and Trusts. V. 1- 1976-. US. English. University of Notre Dame Law School, Notre Dame IN 46556. Ed R W Campfield. Each issue contains an index to its own contents - no vol index - loose.

REPERTOIRE DES ORGANISATIONS MEDICO-SANITAIRES ET SOCIALES PHILANTHROPIQUES PRIVEES ET D'ORIGINE RELIGIEUSE EN HAITI. See Sociology: General Works, Theory - Social Pathology, Welfare, Criminology.

STUDIES IN PHILANTHROPY (WASHINGTON, D.C.). (STUDIES IN PHILANTHROPY). 0882-5750. Monographic Series. US. English. Capital Research Center, 1612 K Street NW, Washington DC 20006.

WASHINGTON INTERNATIONAL ARTS LETTER. See Humanities.

WISE GIVING GUIDE. 0275-0031. Periodical. US. English. mo. $25.00. National Charities Information Bureau, 19 Union Square West, New York NY 10003. Tel (212)929-6300. Circ 3,000.

PHILATELY

1+1. 0316-5051. Monographic Series. CN. French (text in English). 55. le no. Editions Gilles Gheerbrant, 2130 rue Crescent, Montreal Que H3G 2B8 Canada. DD 769.904.

1869 TIMES. VAT Eighteen Hundred And Sixty Nine Times. V. 1- Nov. 1975-. 0363-6542. Periodical. US. English. qt. $15.00. 1505 Bank & Trust Tower, Corpus Christi TX 78477. LC HE6185.U5. DD 769.5697305.

AFA STEUROPA FRIMRKEKATALOG. Main/Corp Aarhus Frimrkehandel. VFOAT Steuropa Frimrkekatalog. VAT Aarhus Frimrkenhandel Steuropa Frimrkekatalog. Danish. ir. Aarhus Frimrkehandel, Bruunsgade 42 8000 C, Aarhus Denmark. LC HE6185.E85.

AFA VESTEUROPA FRIMRKEKATALOG. Main/Corp Aarhus Frimrkehandel. VFOAT Vesteuropa Frimrkekatalog. VAT Aarhus Frimrkehandel Vesteuropa Frimrkekatalog. Began with Vol. for 1974. Danish. ir. Aarhus Frimrkehandel, Bruunsgade 42 8000, Aarhus Denmark. LC HE6185.E842. AFA Europa Frimrkekatalog.

AIR MAIL MAGAZINE. No. 1- Mar. 1939-. Periodical. UK. English. mo. LC HE6187.

THE AMATEUR COLLECTOR'S STAMP CATALOGUE OF SWITZERLAND. VFOAT Stamp Catalogue of Switzerland. Began with 1951 issue. UK. English. Ed E H Spiro. LC HE6185.S9.

THE AMERICAN PHILATELIST. VFOAT American Philatelist and Year Book of the American Philatelic Association. Vol. 1, No. 1 (Jan. 10, 1887)-. 0003-0473. Periodical. US. English. mo. $24.00. American Philatelist, Box 8000, Altoona PA 16803. Tel (814)237-3803. Ed Bill Welch. Ind/Abst Art Archaeol. Tech. Abstr. LC HE6187. DD 769.560750973. bk rev. adv acc. Circ 50,000. (ctrl). Articles from humorous to scholarly on philately and the hobby of stamp collecting, and affairs of the American Philatelic Society.

AMERICAN STAMP NEWS. 0384-6679. CN. English. bm. Gray Stamp Company, Station F, Toronto Ontario Canada.

ARCADE STAMP CATALOGUE. SA. English. ir. Shop No. 5, Old Arcade, 100 Market Street, Johannesburg 2000 South Africa. LC HE6185.S622. DD 769.569680750968.

ATA HANDBOOK. VFOAT A.T.A. Handbook. 0360-5205. US. English. $4.00. American Topical Association, PO Box 630, Johnstown PA 15907. Tel (814)539-6301. LC HE6187. DD 769.564075. Circ 2,000. Listings of postage stamps by collector, topical interest. Topical Handbook.

AUSGABE - AMT FUR BRIEFMARKENGESTALTUNG. Main/Corp Liechtenstein. Amt fur Briefmarkengestaltung. Periodical. English (French and German). ir. LC HE6185.L5. DD 769.56943648.

AUSTRALASIAN STAMP CATALOGUE. AT. English. an. $8.95. Seven Seas Stamps, 62 Wingweabrra Street, Dubbo NSW 2830 Australia. Tel (068)82 3955. Ed Brian Moore. LC HE6185.A82. DD 769.56994. Circ 35,000. An illustrated and priced catalogue of the Australian commonwealth and Australian commonwealth (including Australian states issues) and Australian territories.

THE AUSTRALIAN COMMONWEALTH SPECIALISTS' CATALOGUE. Began with edition published in 1926. AT. English. ir. Seven Seas Stamps Pty Ltd, Dubbo NSW 2830 Australia. LC HE6185.A82. DD 769.569940750994.

AUSTRALIAN STAMP BULLETIN. No. 138- Jan. 1979. All. English. ir. Free. Australian Stamp Bulletin, Locked Bag 8, South Melbourne Vic 3205 Australia. Ed C Brown. LC HE6187. DD 769.56075. Circ 430,000. (ctrl). Publishes all new Australian and Australian Antarctic territory stamps and related Australian post philatelic items. Includes news of general philatelic interest. Philatelic Bulletin, Stamp Preview.

Philately

BALE CATALOGUE OF ISRAEL POSTAGE STAMPS. VFOAT Catalogue of Israel Postage Stamps. 10th Ed. (1979)-. UK. English. Michael H Bale, 41 High Street, Ilfracombe EX349DA England. LC HE6185.P14. DD 769.5695694075. *Bale Catalogue of Palestine & Israel Postage Stamp.*

THE BALTIC PHILATELIST NUMISMATIST. Periodical. CN. English. $3.00. Baltic Philatelist Club, A Greblis, PO Box 5, Roxboro H8Y 3E8 Canada. LC HE6187. DD 769.56948.

BNA TOPICS. (B N A TOPICS). V. 1- 1944-. 0045-3129. Periodical. CN. English. $15.00. British North America Philatelic Society, 25 Kings Circle, Malvern PA 19355. **Tel** (215)644-7838. **Ed** Mike Street. LC HE6187. DD 769.56074. adv acc. **Circ** 175. Articles on various aspects of the philately of British North America, including the stamp and postal history of Canada and the provinces.

BOLAFFI'S ROMAN STATES AND VATICAN CITY SPECIALIZED STAMP CATALOGUE. VFOAT Bolaffi Specialized Stamp Catalogue, Roman States and Vatican City. English. ir. John Raith, PO Box 144, Flushing NY 11365. LC HE6185.V32. DD 769.56945634.

BOLLETTINO PREFILATELICO E STORICO-POSTALE. N. 6- Dec. 1978-. Italian. ir. 10000. CCP 9/23511 Intestato Alleditrice del Corrier Maggiore, Via Dellarco 31, 35100 Padova Italy. LC HE6187. *Bollettino Prefilatelico Storico-Postale.*

DIE BRIEFMARKENAUSGABE VOM ... = L'EMISSION DE TIMBRES-POSTE DU .... VFOAT Emission de Timbres-Poste du ..., The Stamp Issue of .... English (French and German). ir. Amt fur Briefmarkengestaltung, GL-9490 Vaduz Liechtenstein. LC HE6185.L5. DD 769.56943648. *Ausgabe (Liechtenstein. Amt fur Briefmarkengestaltung).*

BULLETIN - EDMONTON STAMP CLUB. Main/Corp Edmonton Stamp Club. V. 1- Jan. 1965-. 0046-1318. Periodical. CN. English. mo. Edmonton Stamp Club, PO Box 399, Edmonton Alta T5J 2J6 Canada.

BULLETIN OF THE POLONUS PHILATELIC SOCIETY. Main/Corp Polonus Philatelic Society. VFOAT Polonus Bulletin. Began with Aug. 1942 issue. 0477-4612. Periodical. US. English. bm. Polonus Philatelic Society, PO Box 82, River Grove IL 60171. **Ed** M E Stexzynaki. LC HE6187. DD 769.569438. (cum index).

C P S NEWS LETTER. Main/Corp Canadian Philatelic Society. V. 1- June 1950-. 0384-7632. Periodical. CN. English (includes some text in French). mo. Canadian Philatelic Society, 73 Adelaide Street West, Toronto Ontario M5H 1PH Canada. DD 769.560971.

CAHIERS DE L'ACADEMIE. (LES CAHIERS DE L'ACADEMIE). Opus 1 (15 Nov. 1983)-. 0824-6602. CN. French. an. Academie Quebecoise d'Etudes Philateliques, CP 24 Succursale Beaubien, Montreal Quebec H2G 3C8 Canada. DD 769.5605. **Circ** 200. (ctrl) Researches about philately and postal history by our members. Many subjects from many countries.

CANADA & NEWFOUNDLAND POSTAL STATIONERY CATALOGUE. VAT Canada and Newfoundland Postal Stationery Catalogue. 1st- Ed. 0705-7067. Periodical. CN. English. $7.50 Per No. J F Webb, Hornby Ontario L0P 1E0 Canada. DD 769.56971.

CANADA SPECIALIZED POSTAGE STAMP CATALOGUE. Began with 1974. 0702-9268. CN. English. an. $15.00. Canada Specialized Ltd, Editorial Office, 330 Bay Street/Suite 703, Toronto Ontario M5H 2T8 Canada. LC HE6185.C22. DD 769.569710750971.

CANADIAN PHILATELIST. V. 1- March 1950-. 0045-5253. Periodical. CN. English. bm. $17.02. Royal Philatelic Society of Canada, PO Box 5320 Station F, Ottawa Ont K2C 3J1 Canada. **Tel** (613)224-4189. **Ed** Ronald Richards. bk rev. adv acc. (ctrl). Philatelic and postal history articles, worldwide with majority related to Canada. Letters to editor, book reviews, new Canada issues, advertising, new members and interests.

CANADIAN STAMP NEWS. V. 1- June 28/July 12, 1976-. 0702-3154. Periodical. CN. English. bw. $30.95. Canadian Stamp News, PO Box 11000, Bracebridge Ontario P0B 1C0 Canada. **Tel** (705)646-6691. **Ed** Diane Ujfalussy. DD 769.5605. bk rev. adv acc. **Circ** 20,000. *Coin, Stamp, Antique News, 0010-0439.*

THE CANAL ZONE PHILATELIST. VFOAT C.Z.S.G. Philatelic Notes. 0746-004X. Periodical. US. English. qt. $5.00 Membership. A R Bew Secretary, Canal Zone Study Group, 20 South Carolina Avenue South, Atlantic City NJ 08401. LC HE6185.C24. DD 769.5697287505.

CATALOGUE DES TIMBRES CANADIENS. (LE CATALOGUE DES TIMBRES CANADIENS). VFOAT The Canadian Stamp Market Guide. 80/81- Issue-. 0228-6998. CN. English (French). an. $4.95 Per No. DD 769.56029471.

CESKOSLOVENSKO. VFOAT Katalog Ceskoslovenskych Znamek. CS. Czech. ir. 40.- Single Issue. Postovni Filatelisticka Sluzba V Nakl Dopravy A Spoju, Praha 1 NA Prikope 13, Praha Czechoslovakia. LC HE6185.C952.

CHARLTON CANADA STAMP ALBUM & STORYBOOK. (THE CHARLTON CANADA STAMP ALBUM & STORYBOOK). VFOAT Canada Stamp Album & Storybook. 4th Ed. (1983)-. 0822-482X. CN. English. an. $6.00 Per Vol. Charlton International Inc, 299 Queen Street West, Toronto Ontario M5V 1Z9 Canada. DD 769.56971. *Charlton ... Canada Stamp & Storybook, 0709-4108.*

CHARLTON STAMP GUIDE. 1st- Ed. 0226-8426. CN. English. an. $1.50 Per No. DD 769.56971.

CHI YU. VFOAT Jiyou. Periodical. Chinese. mo. LC HE6187. DD 769.56075.

CHINA PHILATELY. VFOAT Chung-Kuo Jen Min Yu Cheng. No. 1 (Spring 1982)-. Periodical. US. English. bm. $26.00. China Books & Periodicals Inc, 2929 24th Street, San Francisco CA 94110. **Tel** (415)282-2994.

THE CHRONICLE OF THE U.S. CLASSIC POSTAL ISSUES. VFOAT Chronicle. VAT Chronicle of the United States Classic Postal Issues. V. 17- (No. 48-). 0009-6008. Periodical. US. English. qt. $3.00 Members, $3.50 Non-Members. US Philatelic Classics Society, 2030 Glenmont Avenue NW, Canton OH 44708. LC HE6187. DD 769.56973. *Chronicla of the U.S. Philatelic Classics Society.*

CHUNG-KUO YU KAN. VFOAT China Philatelic Magazine. Periodical. CH. Chinese. ir. $80.00 Non-Member. Chung-Kuo Chi Yu Hsieh Hui, PO Box 18, Taipei Taiwan. LC HE6204.T28. DD 769.56075.

THE COLLECTORS CLUB PHILATELIST. Main/Corp Collectors Club, New York. V. 1- Jan. 1922-. 0010-0838. Periodical. US. English. bm. $25.00. The Collectors Club, 22 East 35th Street, New York NY 10016. LC HE6187. (cum index).

DATZ PHILATELIC INDEX OF UNITED STATES POSTAGE STAMPS. *See* Indexes/Abstracts.

DAVID FIELD ALL-WORLD MINIATURE SHEET CATALOGUE. VFOAT All-World Miniature Sheet Catalogue. 1973-. 0308-549X. UK. English. 2.00. David Fields Holdings Ltd, 42 Berkeley Street, W1X 5FP London England. LC HE6230.M48. DD 769.56.

DEFINITIVES OF CANADA. (THE DEFINITIVES OF CANADA). 0707-3798. CN. English. an. A Chung, PO Box 299, McMaster University, Hamilton Ontario M5C 2N8 Canada. DD 769.56971.

DIRECTORY - CANADIAN STAMP DEALERS' ASSOCIATION. *See* Yearbooks, Almanacs, Directories.

ECHOS PHILATELIQUES. (ECHOS PHILATELIQUES : BULLETIN MENSUEL D'INFORMATION). 0707-7203. Periodical. CN. French. mo. $1.00 Per Number. Echos Philateliques, CP 398 Succursale A, Montreal Quebec H3C 2T1 Canada. DD 769.56060714281. *Philatelic Echos, 0707-7203.*

FEUILLETS PHILATELIQUES. (LES FEUILLETS PHILATELIQUES). 1-. 0226-7268. Periodical. CN. French. mo. $10.00. Les Feuillets Philateliques, C P 1212 Succursale Place d'Armes, Montreal Quebec H2Y 3K2 Canada. DD 769.5605.

FILATELIA CUBANA. Periodical. CU. Spanish. ir. Empresa Ediciones Cubanas, Sub-Direccion Exportacion Oreilly, 407 Ciudad Habana Cuba. LC HE6187. DD 769.5605.

FILATELISTA : DWUTYGODNIK POLSKIEGO ZWIAZKU FILATELISTOW. Periodical. PL. Polish. sm. ARS Polona, Krakowskie Przedmiescie 7, 00-068 Warsaw Poland.

FINANCIAL AND STATISTICAL SUPPLEMENT (AUSTRALIA). *See* Statistics.

FIRESIDE CHATS. 0015-2714. Periodical. US. English. bm. $9.00. Franklin D Roosevelt Philatelic Society, 154 Laguna Court, St Augustine Shores FL 32086-7031. **Tel** (904)797-3513. **Ed** Gustav Detjen Jr. LC HE6183.R67. DD 769.56499739170924. bk rev. adv acc. **Circ** 400. Information on Roosevelt stamps and related philatelic material, new issues, book reviews, historic data on Roosevelt administration, trading page and FD Roosevelt membership facts.

FLEETWOOD'S STANDARD FIRST DAY COVER CATALOG. 0190-7433. US. English. Fleetwood Publications, 1 Unicover Center, Cheyenne WY 82008. LC HE6184.C65. DD 769.5650294.

FOUNDATION BULLETIN. 0196-5034. Periodical. US. English. qt. Free. Philatelic Foundation, 270 Madison Avenue, New York NY 10016.

FRANCE SPECIALIZED CATALOGUE OF ARTIST PROOFS, DELUXE SHEETS, IMPERFORATES, COLOR ESSAYS, FIRST DAY COVERS, COLLECTIVE PROOFS, PRINTERS INSPECTION PROOFS, ILLUSTRATIONS. (FRANCE ... SPECIALIZED CATALOGUE OF ARTIST PROOFS, DE LUXE SHEETS, IMPERFORATES, COLOR ESSAYS, FIRST DAY COVERS, COLLECTIVE PROOFS, PRINTERS INSPECTION PROOFS, ILLUSTRATIONS). 1980-. 0197-7202. US. English. an. $14.00. Orzano Publishing Co, PO Box 394, Islip NY 11751. **Tel** (516)666-3744. **Ed** J Orzano. LC HE6185.F82. DD 769.569440750973. Covers pricing of French artist proofs, deluxe sheets, imperforates, color essays first day covers, collective proofs, printers inspection proofs including illustrations of each.

FROM THE DRAGON'S DEN. (FROM THE DRAGON'S DEN : OFFICIAL PUBLICATION OF THE RYUKYU PHILATELIC SPECIALIST SOCIETY). 0732-5517. Periodical. US. English. qt. $10.00 Domestic Membership, $15.00 Foreign Membership. Arthur L Askins, PO Box 4092, Berkeley CA 94704.

GERSHON'S SPECIALIZED CATALOGUE OF ISRAEL AND THE HOLY LAND. (GERSHON'S ... SPECIALIZED CATALOGUE OF ISRAEL AND THE HOLY LAND). VFOAT Specialized Catalogue of Isreal and the Holy Land. 0275-4967. US. English. $12.00. Gershon Litzman, 147 West 42nd Street, New York NY 10036. LC HE6185.I65. DD 769.5695694.

GIBBONS STAMP MONTHLY. Began with June 1977. Periodical. UK. English. mo. 16.80. Stanley Gibbons Publication Ltd, 5 Parkside Christchurch Road, Ringwood Hampshire BH24 3SH United Kingdom. **Tel** (042)54-2363. **Ed** John Holman. LC HE6187. DD 769.560750941. bk rev. adv acc. **Circ** 24,000. Britain's leading philatelic magazine with news specialized studies, market information. Competitions, new collectors, column and the exclusive Stanley Gibbons Catalogue Supplement. *Stamp Monthly.*

GRAND NEWS. Began with Sept. 1969 issue. 0316-7739. CN. English. mo. 30. Per No. Grand River Valley Philatelic Association, PO Box 575, Guelph Ontario N1H 6K9 Canada. DD 769.560627134.

THE HARRIS POSTAGE STAMP PRICE INDEX. Main/Corp Harris (H.E.) and Company, Boston. VFOAT Postage Stamp Price Index. 0273-0200. US. English. an. $2.95. H E Harris & Company Inc, 645 Summer Street, Boston MA 02117. LC HE6185.U6. DD 769.569730750973.

HEBERT'S CATALOGUE OF USED PLATE NUMBER SINGLES. 0098-2326. US. English. $4.00. George G Shapiro, Trans Pacific Stamp Company, PO Box 48715, Los Angeles CA 90048. LC HE6185.U6. DD 769.56973. *Catalogue of Used Plate Number Singles.*

HESSISCHE POSTGESCHICHTE. German. ir. Am Main Gesellschaft fur Deutshe, Postgeschichte Bezirksgruppe Hessen, Friedrich-Ebert-Anlage 58-72, Frankfurt West Germany. LC HE6996.H4.

Philately

THE ISRAEL PHILATELIST. 0161-0074. Periodical. US. English. bm. LC HE6187. **DD** 769.5695694. (cum index). *Israel-Palestine Philatelist.*

JACK KNIGHT AIR LOG. Vol. 1 (Nov. 1943/Jan. 1944)-. US. English. qt. LC HE6238. **DD** 383.22.

JAPANESE PHILATELY. 0146-0994. Periodical. US. English. bm. $10.00. International Society of Japanese Philately, 530 East Indian Drive, Silver Spring MD 20901. **Tel** (301)589-3686. **Ed** Robert M Spalding. LC HE6187. **DD** 769.56952. (cum index). bk rev. adv acc. **Circ** 1,500. (ctrl). Relates Japanese philately to the history, culture and customs of Japan.

JAPOS BULLETIN. VFOAT J.A.P.O.S. Bulletin. VAT Journalists, Authors and Poets on Stamps Bulletin. 0278-436X. Periodical. US. English. qt. $9.00. J A P O S Study Group, c/o Gustav Detjen Jr Secretary/Treasurer 154 Laguna Court, St Augustine Shores FL 32086-7031. **Tel** (904)797-3513. **Ed** Gustav Detjen Jr. LC HE6183.L59. **DD** 769.563. bk rev. adv acc. **Circ** 400. Data on journalists, authors and poets featured on world-wide postage stamps, new issues, book reviews, market place pages, anecdotes, and stories.

JOURNAL OF SPORTS PHILATELY. Vol. 1, No. 1 (Sept. 1962)-. 0447-953X. Periodical. US. English. bm. $6.00. C A Reiss, 15415 Lake Avenue, Lakewood OH 44107. **Tel** (216)221-1143. **Ed** John LaPorta. **DD** 769. adv acc. **Circ** 400. (ctrl). Periodical for stamp collectors with interests in sports or olympics. Includes articles on many topics, auctions, check lists, ads and membership information.

JUDAICA POST. V. 1-7, No. 6. 0447-9890. Periodical. US. English. bm. A Ben David, PO Box 1400/Station B, Downsview Ontario Canada M3H 5W3. **Tel** (301)881-2266. **DD** 769.564.

KATALOG (SWEDEN. POSTENS FRIMARKSAVDELNING). (KATALOG). English (text in French, German, and Swedish). ir. PFA Postens Frimarksavdelning, S-105 02 Stockholm Sweden.

KOREAN STAMPS. Began in 1964. Periodical. KO. English. bm. Korea Publications, Pyongyang DPRK Korea. LC HE6185.K7. **DD** 769.5695193.

LINN'S STAMP NEWS. V. 42, No. 28- (No. 2130-). Periodical. US. English. wk. $18.00. **Tel** (513)498-0801. **Ed** Michael Laurence. LC MICROFILM 02062HE, HE6187. adv acc. **Circ** 77,000. The world's largest weekly stamp newspaper, combining the best of comprehensive philatelic journalism, educational features and revealing market coverage. *Linn's Weekly Stamp News.*

LINN'S U.S. STAMP YEARBOOK. *See* Yearbooks, Almanacs, Directories.

LINN'S WORLD STAMP ALMANAC. *See* Yearbooks, Almanacs, Directories.

THE LONDON PHILATELIST. Vol. 1, No. 1 (Jan. 1892)-. Periodical. UK. English. bm. 15. Royal Philatelic Society London, 41 Devonshire Place, London W1N 1PE England. **Tel** 44 (1) 486 1044. **Ed** George E Barker. LC HE6187. bk rev. adv acc. **Circ** 1,600. Articles on the stamps and postal history of all territories world wide, plus news of the society and other philatelic bodies and activities.

MADRID FILATELICO. Periodical. Spanish. ir. Ed M Galvez Rodriguez. LC HE6187.

MEKEEL'S WEEKLY STAMP NEWS. VFOAT MeKeel's Weekly. V. 1- Jan. 7, 1981-. US. English. wk. $7.00. Severn Wylie Jewett Company, Box 1660, Portland ME 04104. **Tel** (207)773-4206. **Ed** George F Stilphen. LC HE6187. adv acc. **Circ** 5,000. News items and articles pertaining to stamp collecting.

MEMBERSHIP DIRECTORY - AMERICAN FIRST DAY COVER SOCIETY. *See* Yearbooks, Almanacs, Directories.

MEMBERSHIP DIRECTORY - AMERICAN STAMP DEALERS' ASSOCIATION. *See* Yearbooks, Almanacs, Directories.

MICHEL BENELUX-KATALOG ... BELGIEN, NIEDERLANDE, LUXEMBURG. GW. German. ir. Schwaneberger Verlag GMBH, Muthmannstrasse 4, D-8000 Munchen 45 West Germany. LC HE6185.B462. **DD** 769.569492075.

MICHEL BRIEFE-KATALOG DEUTSCHLAND. GW. German. ir. Schwaneberger Verlag GMBH, Muthmannstrasse 4, D-8000 Munchen 45 West Germany. LC HE6185.G3. **DD** 769.569430750943.

MICHEL DEUTSCHLAND-SPEZIAL-KATALOG. VFOAT Deutschland-Spezial-Katalog. GW. German. ir. Schwaneberger Verlag GMBH, Muthmannstrasse 4, D-8000 Munchen 45 West Germany. LC HE6185.G3.

MICHEL EUROPA-KATALOG. VFOAT Michel Europa, Katalog. 0301-6692. German. ir. Schwaweberger Verlag, Muthmannstrasse 4 8, 45 Munchen West Germany. LC HE6226. *Michel Briefmarkenkatalog: Europa, 0301-8857.*

MICHEL GANZACHEN-KATALOG DEUTSCHLAND. VFOAT Ganzsachen-Katalog Deutschland. GW. German. ir. Schwaneberger Verlag GMBH, Muthmannstrasse 4, D-8000 Munchen 45 West Germany. LC HE6184.S73. **DD** 769.5660750943.

MICHEL GROSSBRITANNIEN-SPEZIAL- KATALOG. GW. German. ir. Schwaneberger Verlag GMBH, Muthmannstrasse 4, D-8000 Munchen 45 West Germany. LC HE6185.G62. **DD** 769.569410750943.

MICHEL ITALIEN-KATALOG . . . MIT MALTA, SAN MARINO UND VATIKANSTAAT. GW. German. ir. Schwaneberger Verlag GMBH, Muthmannstrasse 4 D-8000 Munchen 45 West Germany. LC HE6185.I7. **DD** 769.569450750943.

MICHEL OSTERREICH-SPEZIAL-KATALOG. VFOAT Osterreich-Spezial-Katalog. GW. German. ir. Schwaneberger Verlag GMBH, Muthmannstrasse 4, D-8000 Munchen 45 West Germany. LC HE6185.A92.

MICHEL PRIVATGANZSACHEN-KATALOG BUNDESREPUBLIK DEUTSCHLAND, BERLIN, DEUTSCHE DEMOKRATISCHE REPUBLIK. VFOAT Privatganzsachen-Katalog Bundesrepublik Deutschland, Berlin, Deutsche Demokratische Republik. GW. German. ir. Schwaneberger Verlag GMBH, Muthmannstrasse 4, D-8000 Munchen 45 West Germany. LC HE6184.S73. **DD** 769.5560750943.

MICHEL SKANDINAVIEN-KATALOG. GW. German. ir. Schwaneberger Verlag GMBH, Muthmannstrasse 4, D-8000 Munchen 45 West Germany. LC HE6185.S382. **DD** 769.569480750943.

MINKUS STAMP & COIN JOURNAL. VFOAT Minkus Stamp and Coin Journal. Vol. 15, No. 3-. Periodical. US. English. qt. Minkus Stamp & Coin Journal, 116 West 32nd Street, New York NY 10001. *Minkus Stamp Journal.*

MONTHLY COLLECTOR. (THE MONTHLY COLLECTOR). V. 1- Apr. 1978-. 0707-2937. Periodical. CN. English. mo. $4.00. The Monthly Collector, 269-50 Shelley Drive, Sudbury Ontario P3A 4S6 Canada. **DD** 769.5605.

NOBLE OFFICIAL CATALOG OF BUREAU PRECANCELS. (THE NOBLE OFFICIAL CATALOG OF BUREAU PRECANCELS). VFOAT Noble Official Catalog of United States Bureau Precancels. US. English. ir. LC HE6185.U6. *Mitchell-Noble Official Catalog of Bureau Precancels.*

IL NUOVO CORRIERE FILATELICO. Vol. 1- Oct. 1975-. Periodical. English, French, German or Italian. ir. 10.000. Societe di Studi Filatelici E Storico Postali, Via Cavour 18, 50129 Firenze Italy. LC HE6187.

THE OFFICIAL BLACKBOOK PRICE GUIDE OF UNITED STATES POSTAGE STAMPS. 0195-3559. US. English. an. $1.95. House of Collectibles Inc, 773 Kirkman Road/No 120, Orlando FL 32811. LC HE6185.U6. **DD** 769.56973075.

OFFICIELE CATALOGUS : BELGIE, CONGO, RWANDA, BURUNDI, EUROPA. Main/Corp Belgische Syndicale Kamer van Postzegelhandelaren. Dutch. ir. LC HE6224. **DD** 769.56.

ONCE UPON A TIME. (ONCE UPON A TIME : NEWSLETTER OF THE ATA FOLKLORE-FAIRY TALE STUDY UNIT). Began with the issue for Aug.-Sept. 1975. 0882-9071. Periodical. US. English. bm. ATA Fairy-Tale, Folklore Study, Unit 2509/Buffalo Drive, Arlington TX 76013. LC HE6183.F35. **DD** 769.56493982.

OPINIONS - PHILATELIC FOUNDATION (NEW YORK, N.Y.). (OPINIONS). 1-. 8755-3562. Periodical. US. English. an. Philatelic Foundation, 270 Madison Avenue, New York NY 10016. **DD** 769.

PAKISTAN POSTAGE STAMPS CATALOGUE. 1975-. PK. English. ir. $2.00. Postage Stamps Catalogue, PO Box 190, Lyallpur Pakistan. LC HE6185.P122.

PHILA-PRESSE. V. 1- March 1975-. 0319-4094. Periodical. CN. French. mo. Federation des Societes Philateliques du Quebec, C P 502 HV, Quebec G1R 4R8 Canada. **DD** 769.56062714.

PHILATELIC AUCTION - CHARLTON AUCTIONS. (PHILATELIC AUCTION). Main/Corp Charlton Auctions. 0822-4919. Periodical. CN. English. ir. $2.50 Per No. Charlton Auctions, 299 Queen Street West, Toronto Ontario M5V 1Z9 Canada. **DD** 769.569710294713541. *Unreserved Public Mini Auction, 0822-7713.*

PHILATELIC AUCTION - TOREX. (PHILATELIC AUCTION). Main/Corp Torex. 0822-496X. Periodical. CN. English. ir. $2.50 Per No. Charlton Auctions, 299 Queen St West, Toronto Ontario M5V 1Z9 Canada. **DD** 769.560294713541.

PHILATELIC BULLETIN. Began with Aug. 1953 issue. Periodical. English. ir. Australia Postal Commission etc, Box 357E GPO 3001, Melbourne Australia. LC HE6187. **DD** 769.56075. (cum index).

PHILATELIC EXPRESS. V. 1- Apr. 1979-. 0709-3918. Periodical. CN. English. mo. 60. Per No., $6. Per Year, Canada and U.S.A.; $12. Per Year, other countries. JCM Publications, Philatelic Express, PO Box 4288, Regina Saskatchewan S4P 3W6 Canada. **DD** 769.56075.

PHILATELIC FOUNDATION ANALYSIS LEAFLET. Al-1- May 1979-. 0196-576X. Periodical. US. English. bm. The Philatelic Foundation, 270 Madison Avenue, New York NY 10016.

THE PHILATELIC JOURNALIST. 1971. 0048-3710. Periodical. US. English. bm. $20.00. The Philatelic Journalist, 154 Laguna Court, St Augustine Shores FL 32806. **Tel** (904)797-3513. **Ed** Gustav Detjen Jr. bk rev. adv acc. **Circ** 900. Information helpful to philatelic writers and publicists. Articles promote and publicize philately and philatelic literature. Also activities of members of the Society of Philaticians, a group of philatelic journalists.

PHILATELIC LITERATURE REVIEW. 1942. 0270-1707. Periodical. US. English. qt. American Philatelic Research Library, PO Box 8338, State College PA 16803. **Ed** Charles J Peterson. bk rev. adv acc. **Circ** 2,560.

PHILATELIC OBSERVER. (PHILATELIC OBSERVER : OFFICIAL ORGAN OF THE JUNIOR PHILATELISTS OF AMERICA). 0273-5598. Periodical. US. English. bm. Philatelic Observer, 16 Lancaster Avenue, Maplewood NJ 07040. **DD** 769.

PHILATELIC REVIEW. Periodical. UK. English. qt. 2.00 Domestic, 3.00 Overseas Sea, 4.00 Overseas Air. Candlish McCleery Ltd, 40 Whiteladies Road, Bristol BS8 2LG England. LC HE6185.G6. **DD** 769.569410750941.

PHILATELIE AU QUEBEC. VFOAT Philately in Quebec. V. 3, No 5-V. 6, 1971-1974. 0381-7547. Periodical. CN. French. mo. 15.00. Philatelie Quebec, 4545 Avenue Pierre de Coubertin, CP 1000 Succursale M, Montreal Quebec H1V 3R2 Canada. **Tel** (514)252-3035. **Ed** M Denis Cottin. **Ind/Abst** Point Repere. bk rev. adv acc. **Circ** 8,000. (ctrl). *Bulletin, 0381-7539; Sous le Signe de la Marque Bishop, 0228-1732.*

THE PHILATELIST AND PJGB. VAT Philatelist and Philatelic Journal of Great Britain. 0260-6739. Periodical. UK. English. bm. $18.38. Robson Lowe Ltd, 39 Poole Hill Auction House, Bournemouth England BH2 5PX. LC HE6187. **DD** 769.560750941. *Philatelist, Philatelic Journal of Great Britain.*

PHILATELY. 0031-739X. Periodical. UK. English. qt. British Philatelic Ltd, Rooms 107/107 1 Whitehall Place, London SW1A 2HE England.

PHILATELY FROM AUSTRALIA. V. 1- Mar. 1949-. Periodical. AT. English. qt $14.00. Royal Philatelic Society of Victoria, Box 2071S GPO, Melbourne Victoria 3001 Australia. **Ed** G Kellow. LC HE6187. **DD** 383.22. bk rev. adv acc. **Circ** 500. Specialized Australian philately.

Philately

PHIL'INDEX. *See* Indexes/Abstracts.

POSTAGE STAMP PRICES OF THE UNITED STATES, UNITED NATIONS, AND CANADA AND PROVINCES. **VFOAT** Harris Reference Catalog of Postage Stamp Prices for United States, United Nations, Canada & Provinces. 0272-5363. US. English. sa. $2.25. H E Harris and Company Inc, 645 Summer Street, Boston MA 02117. **LC** HE6226. **DD** 769.569730294.

POSTAGE STAMPS OF THE UNITED STATES. **Main/Corp** United States Postal Service. **VFOAT** United States Postage Stamps. 1970-. 0079-4244. US. English. an. US Government Printers Office, Washington DC 20402. **LC** HE6311, HE6185.U5. **DD** 383.08S, 769.56973. *Postage Stamps of the United States, 0079-4244.*

POSTAL STATIONERY. Began with July/Aug. 1948. 0554-8373. Periodical. US. English. bm. $6.00. United Postal Stationery Society, 212 Mecherle Drive, Bloomington IL 61701. **LC** HE6187. **DD** 769.56. *Postal Stationary Journal, 0278-6362.*

POSTGESCHICHTE. **VFOAT** Histoire Postale, Postal History. Periodical. SZ. German. qt. Postfeschichte Verlag, 8025 Zurich Switzerland. **LC** HE6007.

THE POSTHORN. **VFOAT** Post Horn. 0551-6897. Periodical. US. English. qt. free. Scandinavian Collectors Club, Box 302, Lawrenceville GA 30246. **Ed** Robert C Gross. **DD** 769. adv acc. **Circ** 2,000. (ctrl). Collection of Scandinavian philatelic items, philatelic history and related subjects.

PRICED CATALOGUE OF STAMPS OF FOREIGN COUNTRIES. **Main/Corp** Stanley Gibbons, Inc. **VFOAT** Stanley Gibbons Priced Catalogue of Stamps of Foreign Countries. US. English. be. Stanley Gibbons Magazines Ltd, Christchurch Road/Unit 5 Parkside, Ringwood Hampshire BH24 3SH England. **Tel** 042 54 2363. **Ed** David Aggersberg. A relatively detailed listing of the world's stamps. Fully priced in 21 volumes. Under constant editorial revision.

THE PRIVATE POST. Began with the Autumn 1975 Issue. Periodical. UK. English. an. 4.00. Cinderella Stamp Club, 44 The Ridgeway, London NW11 8QS England. **Tel** (01)455-8438. **Ed** L N Williams. **LC** HE6187. **DD** 769.56941. bk rev. **Circ** 500. Studies of private mail carriage in Britain 1660-to date.

PUBLIC STAMP AUCTION. (L.C.D. STAMP AUCTION). 0714-8941. CN. English. ir. Public Stamp Auction Catalog, c/o L C D Stamp Company, Suite 104/Mezzanine, 100 Richmond Street West, Toronto Ontario M5H 3K6 Canada. **DD** 769.560294. *Public Auction, 0714-8933.*

REFLETS DE LA PHILATELIE AU QUEBEC. V. 1- March 1976-. 0383-1132. Periodical. CN. French. ir. $1.50 Each Number. Y Legris, 5817 rue Madore, Montreal Quebec H1M 1H3 Canada. **DD** 769.56971.

ROMANIAN PHILATELIC STUDIES. 0748-2930. Periodical. US. English. qt. $10.00. Romanian Philatelic Club, 84-47 Kendrick Place, Jamaica Estates NY 11432. **LC** HE6185.R8. **DD** 769.569498.

R.S.A. POSTAGE STAMP CATALOGUE. English. ir. Arcade Stamp Shop, 97 Commissioner Street, Johannesburg South Africa. **LC** HE6185.S622. **DD** 769.56968.

SAID S.M.O.M. STAMP AND COIN CATALOGUE. **VFOAT** Said SMOM Stamp and Coin Catalogue. 1st Ed. (1982)-. English. ir. Emmanuel Said Publishers, 32 Melita Street, Valletta Malta. **LC** HE6224. **DD** 769.56.

THE SCOTT COLLECTORS CURRENT PRICE REVIEW. **VFOAT** Collectors Current Price Review. 0737-2647. Periodical. US. English. $3.00. Scott Attn: SSAPR, 3 East 57th Street, New York NY 10012. **LC** HE6226. **DD** 769.560750973.

SCOTT SPECIALIZED CATALOGUE OF UNITED STATES STAMPS. **VFOAT** Scott United States Stamp Catalogue. 51st- Edition. US. English. an. $22.50. Bloomsbury Books, 7618 North Rogers Avenue, Chicago IL 60626. **Tel** (312)761-2136. **Ed** William Cummings. Comprehensive pricing guide of US stamps which details UN stamps, plate blocks, first day cover, local stamps, and seals-issued each year in November. *Scott's Specialized Catalogue of United States Stamps.*

SCOTT STAMP CATALOGUE. (SCOTT ... STAMP CATALOGUE). **VFOAT** Stamp Catalogue. 1981-. 0271-9495. US. English. an. Harcourt Brace Jovanovich Publishers, 757 Third Avenue, New York NY 10017. *Pocket Book Edition of the Scott Stamp Catalogue, 0194-2956.*

SCOTT STAMP MONTHLY. **VFOAT** Stamp Monthly. Vol. 1, No. 1 (Nov. 1982)-. 0737-0741. Periodical. US. English. mo. $18.00 Domestic, $26.00 Foreign. Scott Publishing Company, Subscription Department, PO Box 2005, Makopac NY 10541. **LC** HE6187. **DD** 769.5607500973. *Scott's Monthly Stamp Journal, Scott Chronicle of New Issues, 0737-2809.*

SCOTT STANDARD POSTAGE STAMP CATALOGUE. **Main/Corp** Scott Publishing Co. **VFOAT** Standard Postage Stamp Catalogue. 129th Ed.- 1973-. 0161-5084. US. English. an. $90.00. Bloomsbury Books, 7618 No Rogers Ave, Chicago IL 60626. **Tel** (312)761-2136. **LC** HE6226. **DD** 380.14576956. Updated price list of stamps as well as other important information for the collector. *Scott's Standard Postage Stamp Catalogue, 0161-5084.*

SCOTTISH STAMP NEWS. Periodical. UK. English. 0.75. Alba Stamp Group, President & Honorary Secretary Stanley K Hunter, 34 Gray Street, Glasgow G37TY Scotland. **LC** HE6187. **DD** 769.56941.

SCOTT'S MONTHLY STAMP JOURNAL (1975) CEASED. (SCOTT'S MONTHLY STAMP JOURNAL). Vol. 57 (Dec. 1975)-V. 63, No. 9 (Sept. 1982) – Whole No. 637-715. Periodical. US. English. mo. Scott's Monthly Stamp Journal, PO Box 925, Farmingdale NY 11737. *Scott Monthly Journal.*

SEAPOSTER. Periodical. US. English. bm. $10.00. Maritime Postmark Society, 9482 Jolory Drive, c/o A Tattersall, Jacksonville FL 32221. **Tel** (904)771-3292. **Ed** Martin W Longseth. **LC** HE6187. adv acc. **Circ** 300. (ctrl). Articles of interest to collectors of maritime mail markings and the history and use of these marks.

SINGAPORE STAMP CATALOGUE IN FULL COLOUR. 1st ed.-. 0127-1563. English. ir. $6.50. International Stamp & Coin Agency, 2.4 & 2.5 Pertama Shopping Complex, 2nd Floor, Jalan Tuanku Abdul Rahman, Kuala Lumpur Malaysia. **Tel** (03)2926373. **Ed** Steven Tan. **LC** HE6185.S532. **DD** 769.569595707509595. **Circ** 3,000. (ctrl). Complete listing of stamps, F.D.C., postal stationery bookletes in full colors from 1948-1985.

SISSONS STAMP AUCTION. **Main/Corp** Sissions (J. N.) Limited. 0583-4465. Monographic Series. CN. English. J N Sissons Ltd, 37 King Street East, Toronto Ontario M5C 1E9 Canada. **DD** 769.56971.

THE SOUTH AFRICAN STAMP COLOUR CATALOGUE. Began with 1977. US. English. an. 11.80. Harry Edelman, 111-137 Lefferts Boulevard, 50 Ozone Park, New York NY 11420. **LC** HE6185.S622. **DD** 769.569680750968.

S.P.A. JOURNAL. **Main/Corp** Society of Philatelic Americans. **VAT** Society of Philatelic Americans Journal. V. 1- 1939-. 0036-181X. Periodical. US. English. mo. US Philatelic Classics Society, 2030 Glenmont Avenue NW, Canton OH 44708. **LC** HE6188 .B .S575. **DD** 383.2206273.

SPECIALIZED CATALOGUE OF CANADIAN STAMPS AND COVERS. **VFOAT** Specialized Catalogue of Canadian Stamps and Covers in Colour. CN. English. an. **LC** HE6185.C22. **DD** 769.56971075.

SPEZIALKATALOG UBER DIE BRIEFMARKEN DER SCHWEIZ UND VON LIECHTENSTEIN. German. ir. Zumstein & Cie, Postfach 2585, 3001 Bern 1 Farcher Switzerland. **LC** HE6185.S92. **DD** 769.56949407509494.

STAMP AUCTION NEWS. 0273-7078. Periodical. US. English. mo. Richards Publishing Company, PO Box 335, Ft Collins CO 80522.

STAMP COLLECTING. Vol. 1 (Sept. 20, 1913)-–No. 1-. 0038-9269. Periodical. UK. English. wk. 17.50. Stamp Collecting Ltd, 100 Fleet Street, Londong EC47 1DE England. **Tel** (01)724-0168. **Ed** Irwin Margolis. **LC** HE6187. bk rev. adv acc. **Circ** 25,000. Publication that presents news and features of interest to collectors of stamps, postcards and postal history. *Stamp Review, World of Stamps.*

STAMP COLLECTOR. V. 50- 1976-. 0277-3899. Newspaper. US. English. wk. $16.95. Van Dahl Publications Inc, P O Box 10, Albany OR 97321. **Tel** (503)928-5156. **Ed** Jim Magruder. bk rev. adv acc. **Circ** 23,000. *Western Stamp Collector, 0043-4213.*

STAMP DEALER FORUM. No. 1 (Oct. '84)-. 8755-3139. Periodical. US. English. bm. $12.00. Stamp Dealer Forum, PO Box 1013, Suisun CA 94585. **Tel** (707)429-5603. **Ed** Ken Lerner. **DD** 769. bk rev. adv acc. **Circ** 500. Award winning, with substance for success oriented stamp (philatelic) dealers. Information you can use. Including computer use in the collectibles trade.

THE STAMP JOURNALS INDEX. *See* Indexes/Abstracts.

STAMP NEWS (LONDON, ENGLAND). (STAMP NEWS). 0265-8216. Periodical. UK. English. sm. $20.00 US, $22.00 Canada. Stamp News Ltd, 100 Fleet Street, London EC4Y 1DE England. **LC** HE6187. **DD** 769.56075. *Philately, 0031-739X; Stamp & Postal History News; Stamp Collecting, 0038-9269; Philatelic Magazine, 0031-7357.*

STAMPS. V. 1- (No. 1-). 0038-9358. Periodical. US. English. wk. $13.20. H L Lindquist Publications, 153 Waverly Place, New York NY 10014. **Tel** (212)675-5407. **Ed** James A Morton. **LC** HE6187. **DD** 769.5605. bk rev. adv acc. **Circ** 15,000. Magazine for stamp collectors. News, current events, useful information on US and foreign stamps, market reports, postal history, and advertising to buy and sell.

STAMPS AND FOREIGN STAMPS. Oct. 1983-. Periodical. UK. English. mo. 16. Stamps and Foreign Stamps, Competition House, Farndon Road, Market Harborough Leics England. **LC** HE6187. **DD** 769.56075. *Stamps (Brentwood, Essex).*

STANDARD CANADIAN PLATE BLOCK CATALOGUE. (THE STANDARD CANADIAN PLATE BLOCK CATALOGUE). **VFOAT** Canada Plate Block Catalogue. 1st- Ed. 0700-5555. Periodical. CN. English. $2.00 Each Number. K Bileski, Station B, Winnipeg Manitoba Canada. **DD** 769.56971.

STANDARD STAMP CATALOGUE OF MALAYSIA-SINGAPORE-BRUNEI. 9th Ed. (1981)-. 0126-9690. English. an. $18.00. International Stamp & Coin Agency, G P O Box 2016, Kuala Lumpur 01-0 Malaysia. **LC** HE6185.M212. **DD** 769.569595075. *Malaysia-Singapore-Brunei Stamp Catalogue.*

STANLEY GIBBONS ELIZABETHAN SPECIALISED CATALOGUE OF MODERN BRITISH COMMONWEALTH STAMPS. **VFOAT** Stanley Gibbons Stamp Catalogue. 0264-0147. UK. English. an. Stanley Gibbons Magazines Ltd, Christchurch Road/Unit 5, Parkside Ringwood Hampshire BH2 3SH England. **Tel** 042 54 2363. **Ed** David Aggersberg. **LC** HE6185.G62. **DD** 769.569171241. A detailed priced listing of the stamps of Great Britain. Four convenient volumes, casebound. *Stanley Gibbons Elizabethan Postage Stamp Catalogue, 0071-0024.*

STANLEY GIBBONS SIMPLIFIED STAMP CATALOGUE. **Main/Corp** Gibbons (Stanley) Ltd., London. **VFOAT** Stamps of the World. Periodical. UK. English. an. Stanley Gibbons Ltd, Christchurch Road, Unit 5 Parkside, Ringwood Hampshire BH24 3SH England. **Tel** 042 54 2363. **Ed** David Aggersberg. **Circ** 25,000. A straightforward listing of the whole world's stamps in two volumes. Over 243,000 items. All fully priced, 54,000 illustrations.

STANLEY GIBBONS STAMP CATALOGUE. PART 1 : BRITISH COMMONWEALTH. **Main/Corp** Stanley Gibbons Publications Ltd. 0142-9752. UK. English. an. Stanley Gibbons Publications Ltd, 391 Strand, London WC2R OLX England. **LC** HE6226. **DD** 769.56075.

STANLEY GIBBONS STAMP CATALOGUE. PART 16, CENTRAL ASIA. 1st Ed. (1981)-. Periodical. UK. English. an. 8.50. Stanley Gibbons Publications Ltd, 391 Strand, London WC2R OLX England. **LC** HE6185.T92. **DD** 769.569580750941.

STANLEY GIBBONS STAMPS OF THE WORLD. **Main/Corp** Gibbons (Stanley) Ltd., London. **VFOAT** Stamps of the World. 36th- Ed. 0081-4210. UK. English. an. $60.00. Numismatic-Philatelic Supplies, Edelman/111-37 Lefferts Boulevard, South Ozone Park NY 11420. *Stanley Gibbons Simplified Stamps Catalogue.*

THE STATE REVENUE NEWSLETTER. 0883-6760. Periodical. US. English. bm. $4.00. Harold A Effner Jr, 425 Sylvania Avenue, Avon By The Sea

Philosophy

NJ 07717. **Tel** (201)775-7737. **Ed** David Drury. **DD** 769. adv acc. **Circ** 250. (ctrl). Available on microfilm from The State Historical Society of Wisconsin. Publishes information on the revenue stamps issued by the states and municipalities of the United States.

THE STONEHAM CATALOGUE OF BRITISH STAMPS. Began in 1978. 0142-615X. UK. English. Stoneham Publications Ltd, Stoenham Park, Eastleigh Hampshire SO5 3HT England. **LC** HE6185.G62. **DD** 769.569410750941.

STRICTLY U.S. V. 1- Oct. 1974-. 0095-5418. Periodical. US. English. bm. $3.00 US, $5.00 Canada and Mexico. Vancorp, Dunedin FL 33528. **LC** HE6187. **DD** 769.56973.

SVERIGES FRIMARKEN OCH HELSAKER. **VFOAT** S.F.F. Specialkatalog, Sverige-Katalogen, SFF Specialkatalog. 0347-1152. SW. Swedish (summaries in English and German). an. Sveriges Filatelist-Forbund, Vasavagen 76, 181 41 Lidingo Sweden.

THAI PHILATELY. Began with Jan. 1978 issue. 0198-7992. Periodical. US. English. qt. Free to Members. Society for Thai Philately, PO Box 454, Plattsburgh NY 12901. **LC** HE6185.T45. **DD** 769.569593.

TOPICAL NEW ISSUES. 0090-7286. US. English. an. $7.00. American Topical Association, PO Box 630, Johnstown PA 15907. **Tel** (814)539-6301. **Ed** Ruth Y Wetmore. **LC** HE6187. **DD** 769.56075. **Circ** 2,000. Listing of each year's worldwide postage stamps by topic pictured on them.

TOPICAL TIME. V. 1- (No. 1-). 0040-9332. Periodical. US. English. bm. $16.00. American Topical Association, PO Box 630, Johnstown PA 15907. **Tel** (814)539-6301. **Ed** Fred E Foldvary. **LC** HE6187. **DD** 769. bk rev. adv acc. **Circ** 8,000. (ctrl). Articles, checklists and columns on stamp collecting by topic.

TRIDENT (WASHINGTON, D.C.). (TRIDENT). **VFOAT** Visnik. 0882-1674. Periodical. US. English (with some in Ukrainian). $12.00. Ukrainian Philatelic and Numismatic Society, PO Box 14163, Washington DC 20044. **Tel** (703)451-2633. **Ed** Wes Capar. **DD** 769. bk rev. adv acc. **Circ** 300. (ctrl). A newsletter of the society dealing with Ukrainian philately and numismatics, conventions, membership information, articles, and society events. Also includes three auctions every year.

TRUMPETER. (THE TRUMPETER). 0148-673X. Periodical. CN. English (Croatian). qt. Trumpeter, 2596 East 8th Avenue, Vancouver British Columbia V5M 1WZ Canada.

UKRAINSKYI FILATELIST (SOIUZ UKRAINSKYKH FILATELISTIV I NUMIZMATYKIV). (UKRAINSKYI FILATELIST). **VFOAT** Ukrainian Philatelist. V. 22, Ch. 37-38-. 0198-6252. Periodical. US. English (Ukrainian). $12.00. Ukrainian Philatelic and Numismatic Society, PO Box 14163, Washington DC 20044. **Tel** (703)360-2559. **Ed** Ingert Kuzych. **LC** HE6185.U45. **DD** 769.5694771075. bk rev. adv acc. **Circ** 300. (ctrl). Society journal presenting articles and comprehensive studies of all aspects of Ukrainian philately (including Cinderella issues) and numismatics. Ukrainskyi Filatelist (Soiuz Ukrainskykh Filatelistiv).

U.S. COINS, CURRENCY & STAMPS. See Numismatics.

THE UTD PHILATELIC BULLETIN. **VFOAT** U.T.D. Philatelic Bulletin. **VAT** University of Texas at Dallas Philatelic Bulletin. Vol. 1, No. 1 (Apr. 1982)-. 0732-3670. Periodical. US. English. ir. Free. University of Texas at Dallas, Department of Special Collections, Box 643, Richardson TX 75080.

WESTERN EXPRESS. V. 1- Jan. 1951-. 0510-2332. Periodical. US. English. qt. Western Cover Society, 9877 Elmar Avenue, Oakland CA 94603. **Tel** (415)569-2817. **Ed** Everett C Erle. **LC** HE6185.U7. **DD** 383.2. (cum index). bk rev. adv acc. **Circ** 300. (ctrl). Exchange of information and ideas on collecting philatelic memorabilia of the Far West including diaries, letters, photos and express covers.

YEARBOOK AND PHILATELIC SOCIETIES' DIRECTORY. See Yearbooks, Almanacs, Directories.

YUSHU NENKAN. **VFOAT** Stamp Collectors' Annual. 1971-. JA. Japanese. ir. Kanai Stamp Co, c/o Osaka Kanai Building 4th Floor 22 Doshima Funadaikumachi Kita-Ku, Osaka Japan. **LC** HE6194.

PHILOSOPHY

20TH CENTURY LEGAL PHILOSOPHY SERIES. See Law.

ABHANDLUNGEN DER HEIDELBERGER AKADEMIE DER WISSENSCHAFTEN, PHILOSOPHISCH-HISTORISCHE KLASSE. Main/Corp Heidelberger Akademie der Wissenschaften. Philosophisch-Historische Klasse. 1913-. Periodical. GW. German. ir. Carl Winter Universitatsverlag, POB 106140 Lutherstrasse 59, D6900 Heidelberg West Germany. **Tel** 6221-49111. **LC** AS182. Monograph series on philosophy and history.

DAS ACHTZEHNTE JAHRHUNDERT. See History (General) - History of Europe.

ACTA PHILOSOPHICA FENNICA. V. 1-. 0355-1792. Monographic Series. FI. English (text also in German). ir. Akademiska Bokhandeln, Postbok 128, 00101 Helsinki 10 Finland. **Ind/Abst** Math. Rev., Philos. Index. **LC** B28.F5. **CODEN** APFEDB.

ACTA UNIVERSITATIS CAROLINAE. PHILOSOPHICA ET HISTORICA. 1958-. 0567-8293. Periodical. CS. Czech (summaries in English, French, German or Russian). ir. Artia, Ve-Smeckach 30, Praha 1 Czechoslovakia. **Ind/Abst** Am. Hist. Life, Hist. Abstr., Part A, Mod. Hist. Abstr., Hist. Abst., Part B, Twent. Century Abstr. **LC** AS141. Acta Universitatis Carolinae.

ADVANCES IN THANATOLOGY. Began with Vol. 4, No. 1. 0196-1934. Periodical. US. English. sa. Foundation Book & Periodical, 391 Atlantic Avenue, Brooklyn NY 11217. **Tel** (212)858-3026. **LC** BD444. **DD** 128.5. **NLM** W1 AD879T. Journal of Thanatology, 0047-2832.

AFRICA : THOUGHT AND PRACTICE. **VFOAT** Thought and Practice. V. 1-. Periodical. English. sa. $4.00. East African Literature Bureau, PO Box 30197, Nairobi Kenya. **LC** B5300. **DD** 199.6.

AFRIQUE ET PHILOSOPHIE. No. 1- Jan/July 1977-. Periodical. French. ir. $20.00. Departemente de Philosophie et Religions Africaines Faculte de Theologie Catholique de Kinshasa, B P 1534, Kinshasa/Limete Congo. **LC** B5300. **DD** 199.605.

AFRO AMERICAN JOURNAL OF PHILOSOPHY. (AFRO AMERICAN JOURNAL OF PHILOSOPHY : AAJP). **VFOAT** AAJP. Vol. 1, No. 1 (Summer 1982)-. 0742-3470. Periodical. US. English. ir. $20.00. Dasein Jupiter & Hammon, JAF Box 7831, New York NY 10116. **Tel** (212)926-7634. **Ed** Percy Johnston. **LC** B1. **DD** 191.08996073. bk rev. adv acc. **Circ** 3,000. (ctrl). Essays, critiques, articles in all areas of philosophy especially value theory and philosophical anthropology, and philosophy of science and technology.

AITIA. See Education (General).

AJATUS. Vol. 1 1926-. 0355-1725. FI. English (Finnish and German). be. Akakeeminen-Kirjakuppa, PO Box 128, 00101 Helsinki Finland. **Ind/Abst** Math. Rev., Philos. Index. **LC** B31. **DD** 105.

AKTUALNYE PROBLEMY ISTORII FILOSOFII NARODOV SSSR. Periodical. UR. Russian. .40 Per Issue. Izdatelstvo Moskovskogo Universiteta Moskva, K-9 Ul Gertsena, Moskva Russian SFSR. **LC** B4231.

AL-HIKMAH. V. 1- October 1976-. Periodical. Arabic. ir. Jamiat Al-Fatih Kulliyat Al-Tarbiyah, Qism Al-Falsafah Wa-Al-Ijtima, PO Box 2558, Tarabulus Libiya. **LC** B740.

ALEPH (MANIZALES, COLOMBIA). See Literature.

ALETHEIA. V. 1- June 1977-. 0149-2004. Periodical. US. English. ir. $15.00. International Academy of Philosophy Press, 403 South Britain Road, Irving TX 75060. **Tel** (214)253-2884. **Ed** Joseph Seifert. **Ind/Abst** Philos. Index. **LC** B1. **DD** 105. bk rev. adv acc. **Circ** 250. An attempt to reground the insights of classical and medieval philosophy on the basis of a new "phenomenological realism" to be sharply distinguished from transcendental phenomenology.

ALGEMEEN NEDERLANDS TIJDSCHRIFT VOOR WIJSBEGEERTE. V. 62E, No. 1 (Jan. 1970)-. 0002-5275. Periodical. NE. Dutch. qt. **Ind/Abst** Sociol. Abstr., Philos. Index. **LC** B8.D8. Algemeen Nederlands Tijdschrift Voor Wijsbegeerte en Psychologie.

ALLGEMEINE ZEITSCHRIFT FUR PHILOSOPHIE. 1976-. Periodical. GW. German. ty. Friedrich Frommann Verlag, Postfach 500460, 7000 Stuttgart West Germany. **LC** B3.

ALTERNATIVAS (SANTIAGO, CHILE). See Political Science - International Relations.

THE AMERICAN ATHEIST. 1958. 0516-9623. Periodical. US. English. mo. $40.00. American Atheist Press, PO Box 2117, Austin TX 78767. **Tel** (512)458-1244. **Ed** R Murray-O'Hair. **LC** BL2747.3. **DD** 211.805. bk rev. adv acc. **Circ** 30,000. Covers topics of interest to Atheists, ranging from the latest antics of the New Right to the latest deeds of Atheist activists.

AMERICAN JOURNAL OF THEOLOGY & PHILOSOPHY. **VAT** American Journal of Theology and Philosophy. V. 1- Jan. 1980-. 0194-3448. Periodical. US. English. ty. $9.00. Augusta College, c/o Creighton Peden, Augusta GA 30910. **Tel** (404)737-1709. **Ed** Creighton Peden and Larry Axel. **Ind/Abst** Philos. Index, Relig. Index One, Period. **LC** BR1. **DD** 230.05. adv acc. **Circ** 550. (ctrl). American theology and its dialogue with philosophy.

AMERICAN PHILOSOPHICAL QUARTERLY. V. 1- Jan. 1964-. 0003-0481. Periodical. UK. English. qt. $85.00. Philosophy Documentation Center, Bowling Green State University, Bowling Green OH 43403-0189. **Tel** (419)372-2419. **Ed** Nicholas Rescher. **Ind/Abst** Sociol. Abstr., Philos. Index, Humanit. Index, Lang. Lang. Behav. Abstr. **Circ** 1,520. The scope of the journal is the entire range of philosophical inquiry. Publishes articles of high quality regardless of the school of thought from which it derives.

ANALELE STIINTIFICE. SERIE NOUA. SECTIUNEA III A : ISTORIE-FILOZOFIE. Main/Corp Jassy. Universitatea. **VFOAT** Istorie-Filozofie. RM. Romanian. an. Ilexim Press Department, PO Box 1-136-1-137, Bucharest Romania. Analele Stiintifice. Serie Noua. Sectiunea III A : Istorie.

ANALELE UNIVERSITATII BUCURESTI : FILOSOFIE. Main/Corp Universitatea Din Bucuresti. Vol. 26- 1977-. Periodical. English (French, or Romanian). ir. 20.00. Ilexim Departamentul Export-Import Presa, PO Box 136-137 Str 13 Decembrie Nr 3, Bucuresti Romania. **LC** B8.R8. **DD** 105. Analele Universitatii Bucuresti. Filosofie, Istorie, Drept.

ANALELE UNIVERSITATII BUCURESTI : FILOSOFIE, ISTORIE, DREPT. Main/Corp Universitatea din Bucuresti. RM. Romanian (some summaries in English, French, or Russian). ir. 12.00. **LC** B28.R6.

ANALES DEL SEMINARIO DE HISTORIA DE LA FILOSOFIA. See Yearbooks, Almanacs, Directories.

ANALYSIS (NEW YORK (N.Y.). (ANALYSIS). Vol. 1, No. 1 (Nov. 1933)-. 0003-2638. US. English. qt. 11.75. Basil Blackwell & Mott Ltd, 108 Cowley Road/Journals Department, Oxford OX4 1JF England. **Tel** (0865)722146. **Ed** Jonathan Dunsby. **Ind/Abst** Sociol. Abstr., Philos. Index, Lang. Lang. Behav. Abstr. **LC** B1. **DD** 105. (cum index). bk rev. adv acc. **Circ** 600. Publishes short discussions of questions of detail in philosophy. These range over topics in philosophical logic. Philosophy of mind, moral and political philosophy.

ANCIENT PHILOSOPHY (PITTSBURGH, PA). (ANCIENT PHILOSOPHY). Vol. 1, No. 1 (Fall 1980)-. 0740-2007. Periodical. US. English. sa. $20.00. Duquesne University, c/o Ronald Polansky, Department of Philosophy, Pittsburgh PA 15282. **Tel** (412)434-6500. **Ed** Ronald Polansky. **Ind/Abst** Philos. Index. bk rev. adv acc. **Circ** 600. Devoted to the study of classical philosophy and science.

ANGELICUM. V. 2- Feb./Mar. 1925-. 0003-3081. Periodical. English (French, German, Italian or Latin). qt. 5.00. Amministr Rivista Angelicum, Largo Angelicum 1, 00184 Roma Italy. **Ed** Jordan Aumann. **Ind/Abst** MLA Int. Bibliogr. Books Artic. Mod. Lang. Lit., Old Testam. Abstr., New Testam. Abstr. **LC** BX800.A1. **DD** 230.205. Index in last issue of volume -

Philosophy

attached. (cum index). bk rev. **Circ** 800. A review of theology, philosophy, and Canon Law published by Pontifical University St Thomas in Rome Italy. *Unio Thomistica.*

ANNALES DE L'INSTITUT DE PHILOSOPHIE CEASED. 1969-1978. Periodical. BE. French. an. Editions Institut Sociologie, Avenue Paul Heger 26, B1050 Bruxelles Belgium. **Tel** 021642 32 93. **Ind/Abst** Sociol. Abstr. bk rev. **Circ** 7,200. Periodical of university level for the promotion of philosophical studies and the spreading of research in this field.

ANNALES UNIVERSITATIS SCIENTIARUM BUDAPESTINENSIS DE ROLANDO EOTVOS NOMINATAE. SECTIO PHILOSOPHICA ET SOCIOLOGICA. **Main/Corp** Eotvos Lorand Tudomanyegyetem. V. 1- 1962-. 0524-9023. Periodical. English, French, German or Russian. ir. PO Box 149, HI 389 Budapest Hungary.

ANNALI DELLA FACOLTA DI LETTERE E FILOSOFIA. **Main/Corp** Universita di Bari. Facolta di Littere e Filosofia. **Series/Titl** Pubblicazioni dell'Universita di Bari. Began in 1954. IT. Italian. be. Adriatica Bara Editrice, Libreria Dell Universita, Via Andrea da Bari 122 Italy. **Ind/Abst** Philos. Index, MLA Int. Bibliogr. Books Artic. Mod. Lang. Lit. **LC** AS222.B3.

ANNALI DELLA SCUOLA NORMALE SUPERIORE DI PISA, CLASSE DI LETTERE E FILOSOFIA. See Literature.

ANSELM STUDIES. 1-. 0735-0864. Periodical. US. English (articles in French, German, or Italian). ir. Kraus International Publ, One Water Street, White Plains NY 10601. **Tel** (914)761-9600. **Ed** M Chibnall, G Evans, D P Henry, H Kohlenberger, and Sir R Southern. An occasional journal; a collection of essays on all aspects of the life, work, thought, and influence of St. Anselm.

ANVIKSIKI. Periodical. English. ir. $3.00. Varacasi-5 India. **LC** B130.

AQUINAS. Vol. 1- 1958-. 0003-7362. Periodical. IT. English (French, German, Italian, Latin, or Spanish). ty. $24.00. Pontificia University Lateranense Piazza, Giovanni In Laterano 4, 00184 Roma Italy. **Ind/Abst** MLA Int. Bibliogr. Books Artic. Mod. Lang. Lit., Philos. Index. **LC** B765.T54. (cum index).

AQUINAS JOURNAL. Vol. 1, No. 1 (June 1984)-. Periodical. English. an. 20.00, $2.00 US. Aquinas Journal, Aquinas College, Colombo 8 Sri Lanka. **Tel** 94014/94709. **LC** AS475.A1. **DD** 052. bk rev. **Circ** 250. Interdisciplinary learned journal published by Aquinas College of Colombo Sri Lanka.

THE AQUINAS LECTURE. (AQUINAS LECTURE). 0066-5614. Monographic Series. US. English. ir. Marquette University Press, 1131 Wisconsin Avenue, Milwaukee WI 53233. **Tel** (414)224-1564. **Ed** Paul McInerny. Ideal for classroom use, library additions, or private collections. The Aquinas series has received international acceptance by scholars, universities and libraries.

ARCHIV FUR GESCHICHTE DER PHILOSOPHIE. See Genealogy and Heraldry - Archives.

ARCHIVES DE PHILOSOPHIE. See Genealogy and Heraldry - Archives.

ARCHIVES DE PHILOSOPHIE DU DROIT. See Genealogy and Heraldry - Archives.

ARCHIVES OF THE FOUNDATION OF THANATOLOGY. See Genealogy and Heraldry - Archives.

ARCHIVIO DI FILOSOFIA. See Genealogy and Heraldry - Archives.

DAS ARGUMENT; BERLINER HEFTE FUR PROBLEME DER GESELLSCHAFT. VFOAT Berliner Hefte fur Probleme der Gesellschaft. Vol. 1-. 0004-1157. Periodical. GW. German. bm. $25.81. Argument Verlag GMBH Vertrieb, Tegeler Strasse 6, D-1000 Berlin 65 West Germany. **Tel** (030)461 90 61. **Ed** Wolfgang Fritz Haug and Frigga Haug. **Ind/Abst** Sociol. Abstr., Soc. Welf. Soc. Plan./Policy Soc. Dev., Energy Res. Abstr., Sci. Cit. Index, Abr. Ed., Soc. Sci. Citation Index. (cum index). bk rev. adv acc. **Circ** 5,000. Marxist debates in the field of Marxist theory, socialist politics, feminism; book reviews in philosophy, linguistics, literary criticism, sociology, pedogogics, medicine, political science, and economics.

ASIAN PHILOSOPHICAL STUDIES. No. 1-. 0066-8443. Monographic Series. US. English. ir. St Johns University Press, Grand Central & Utopian Parkways, Jamaica NY 11439.

AUGUSTINUS. See Religion, Mythology, Rationalism - Roman Catholic Church.

AUSLEGUNG. V. 1-. 0733-4311. Periodical. US. English. sa. $10.00. Auslegung, Department of Philosophy/University of Kansas, Lawrence KS 66045. **Tel** (913)864-3976. **Ed** Peter P Cvek. **Ind/Abst** Philos. Index. **LC** B1. **DD** 105. bk rev. adv acc. **Circ** 200. A forum of expression for any and all philosophical perspectives and publishes primarily the work of students pursuing the doctorate and non-tenured Ph.D's.

AUSTRALASIAN JOURNAL OF PHILOSOPHY. Vol. 25, No. 1-2 (Aug. 1947)-. 0004-8402. Periodical. AT. English. qt. $36.00. Australasian Association of Philosophy, La Trobe University/Philosophy Department, Bundoora Vic 3083 Australia. **Ed** Brian D Ellis. **Ind/Abst** Sociol. Abstr., APAIS, Aust. Public Aff. Inf. Serv., Philos. Index, Index Book Rev. Humanit., Lang. Lang. Behav. Abstr., Am. Hist. Life, Hist. Abstr., Part A, Mod. Hist. Abstr., Hist. Abst., Part B, Twent. Century Abstr. **LC** B1. **DD** 105. bk rev. adv acc. **Circ** 1,200. The journal publishes articles, discussions, critical notices, and book reviews mainly on contemporary issues in Anglo-American and Australian philosophy. *Australasian Journal of Psychology and Philosophy.*

AUT AUT. Began with Jan. 1951 issue. 0005-0601. Periodical. IT. Italian. bm. $20.79. Nuova Italia Editrice, Via Ernesto Codignola, 50018 Scandicci FL Italy. **Ind/Abst** MLA Int. Bibliogr. Books Artic. Mod. Lang. Lit. **LC** B4.

AWAKENER. See Religion, Mythology, Rationalism.

BACK TO GODHEAD. See Religion, Mythology, Rationalism.

BASIS. Vol. 1- Oct. 1951-. 0005-6138. Periodical. IO. Indonesian. mo. $10.00 US. Yayasan Badan Penerbit Basis, ABU Bakar Ali Trompolpos 20, Yogyakarta Indonesia. **Tel** 0274-88283. **Ed** Dick Hartoko. **LC** AP95.I5. bk rev. adv acc. **Circ** 2,000. (ctrl). Culture in general, esp. philosophy, literature, anthropology and history.

BEHAVIORISM. V. 1- Fall 1972-. 0090-4155. Periodical. US. English. sa. $20.00 Domestic, $25.00 Foreign. Cambridge Center for Behavioral Studies, 11 Ware Street, Cambridge MA 02138. **Tel** (617)495-9020. **Ed** George Graham and Peter Killeen. **Ind/Abst** Excerpta Med., Philos. Index, Psychol. Abstr., Soc. Sci. Citation Index. **LC** BF199. **DD** 150.194305. **NLM** W1 BE134. **CODEN** BHVMAX. bk rev. adv acc. **Circ** 1,000. Critical commentary and discussion on behaviorism as a school of philosophy and on prospects for a science of behavior.

BEIHEFTE ZUR PHILOSOPHIA NATURALIS CEASED. 0554-0704. Monographic Series. GW. German. ir. Athenaum Verlag GMBH, Adelheidstrabe 2, 6240 Konigstein/TS West Germany. **Tel** 06174/3021. **Ed** Joseph Meurers. bk rev. adv acc. **Circ** 600. Natural philosophy and philosophical borders of the exact sciences; also history of science.

BEITRAGE ZUR GESCHICHTE DER PHILOSOPHIE UND THEOLOGIE DES MITTELALTERS. VFOAT Beitrage zur Geschichte der Philosophie des MA, Texte und Untersuchungen. Begrundet von Dr Clemens Baeumker. Vol. 1- 1891-. 0067-5024. Monographic Series. GW. German. ir. Aschendorffsche Verlagsbuchhan Dlung, Postfach 1124, 4400 Muenster West Germany. **Tel** 251/5901. **Ed** Ludwig Hodi and Wolfgang Kluxen. **Ind/Abst** MLA Int. Bibliogr. Books Artic. Mod. Lang. Lit. Contributions to the history of philosophy and theology in the middle ages; texts and research.

THE BENTHAM NEWSLETTER. No. 1- May 1978-. UK. English. an. University College, Gower Street, London WC1E 6BT England. **LC** B1574.B34. **DD** 192.

BHAVAN'S JOURNAL. V.1- 1954-. 0006-0518. Periodical. II. English. 48.-. Bharatiya Vidya Bhavan, Kulpati Km Munshi Marg, Bombay 400007 India. **Tel** 351461. **Ed** S Ramakrishnan. **LC** AP8. bk rev adv acc. **Circ** 2,500. Devoted to life, literature, and culture and fostering higher values of life and living.

BIBLIOGRAFIA FILOSOFICA MEXICANA. See Bibliographies.

BIBLIOGRAPHIE DE LA PHILOSOPHIE. See Bibliographies.

BIBLIOGRAPHIE PHILOSOPHIE. See Bibliographies.

BIBLIOGRAPHIES OF FAMOUS PHILOSOPHERS. See Bibliographies.

BIBLIOTHEQUE DES ARCHIVES DE PHILOSOPHIE. See Library and Information Science.

BIBLIOTHEQUE PHILOSOPHIQUE. **Main/Corp** Louvain. Universite Catholique. Institut Superierur de Philosophie. Monographic Series. CN. French. ir. Presses de l'Universite Laval, CP 2447/Ave de la Medecine, Ste-Foy Quebec G1K 7R4 Canada. **Tel** (418)656-5106.

BIGAKU. VFOAT Aesthetics. 1- 1950-. 0520-0962. Periodical. JA. Japanese. qt. $28.50. Japan Publishing Trading Company Ltd, PO Box 5030 Tokyo International, Tokyo 100-31 Japan. **Ind/Abst** Philos. Index, RILM Abstr.

BIJDRAGEN TIJDSCHRIFT VOOR FILOSOFIE EN THEOLOGIE. V. 4- 1953-. Periodical. NE. Dutch (English, French or German). qt. $34.13. Tillmans, Postbus 19481 Keizergracht 105, 1000 GL Amsterdam Netherlands. **Tel** 020-272621. **Ind/Abst** Rev. Hist. Eccles. (cum index). bk rev. Covers systematic theological history, dogma and theology, spirit and practice, theological biblical sciences, church history, cannon law, social sciences and others related to theological book reviews. *Bijdragen Uitgegeven voor de Philosophische en Theologische Faculteiten der Noord- en Zuid-Nederlandse Jezuieten.*

BOLETIN - ASOC. LATINO-AMERICANA DE FILOSOFOS CAT. **Main/Corp** Asociacion Latino-Americana de Filosofos Catolicos. No. 1- 1974-. Portuguese and/or Spanish. ir. Directoria Central de la Asociacion, Via Anhanguera, Km 26 Caixa Postal 11 587, Sao Paulo Brazil. **LC** B1001.

BOSTON COLLEGE STUDIES IN PHILOSOPHY. 1- 1966-. 0524-112X. US. English. mo. Boston College Studies in Philosophy, 140 Commonwealth Avenue, Boston MA 02167. **Ind/Abst** Philos. Index.

BOUNDARY 2. See Literature.

BRITISH JOURNAL FOR THE PHILOSOPHY OF SCIENCE. See Science (General).

BULLETIN DE LA SOCIETE DE PHILOSOPHIE DU QUEBEC. **Main/Corp** Societe de Philosophie du Quebec. V. 1-. 0701-1385. Periodical. CN. French. ir. Societe de Philosophie du Quebec, 2910 Boulevard Edouard Montpetit, Montreal Quebec H3T 1J7 Canada. **DD** 105.

BULLETIN DE LA SOCIETE FRANCAISE DE PHILOSOPHIE. **Main/Corp** Societe Francaise de Philosophie. V. 1- 1901-. 0037-9352. Periodical. FR. French. ir. Librairie Armand Colin, 103 BD St Michel, 75005 Paris Cedex 5 France. **Tel** 543 32 11. **Ed** X Leon. **Ind/Abst** Philos. Index. **LC** B12. **DD** 106.2.

BULLETIN DE PHILOSOPHIE MEDIEVALE. Yearly V. 6-. 0068-4023. Periodical. BE. French. an. $20.00. Siepm/College Thomas More, Chemin D Aristote 1, B1348 Louvain-La-Neuve Belgium. **Tel** (01) 43 4807. **LC** B721. **DD** 189.05. adv acc. **Circ** 800. Prospecting bibliography materials for the study of medieval Latin, Arabic, and Jewish philosophy. *Bulletin de la Societe Internationale pour l'Etude de la Philosophie Medievale.*

BULLETIN DU CERCLE GABRIEL-MARCEL. **Main/Corp** Cercle Gabriel-Marcel. V. 1- April 1979-. 0708-2312. Periodical. CN. French. ir. $1.25 Per Number. Cercle Gabriel-Marcel, CP 67, Cap-de-la-Madeleine Quebec G8T 7W1 Canada. **DD** 106.071445.

BULLETIN OF THE EVANGELICAL PHILOSOPHICAL SOCIETY. **Main/Corp** Evangelical Philosophical Society. Vol. 1, 1978-. Periodical. US. English. an. $10.00. Bulletin of the Evangelical Philosophical Society, Toccoa Falls College c/o D Clark, Toccoa Falls GA 30598. **Tel** (404)886-6831. **Ed** Steve Clinton. bk rev. **Circ** 250.

Philosophy

Discussion of philosophical issues related to religious faith from an evangelical protestant point of view.

BULLETIN OF THE HEGEL SOCIETY OF GREAT BRITAIN. (THE BULLETIN OF THE HEGEL SOCIETY OF GREAT BRITAIN). No. 1 (Spring/Summer 1980)-. 0263-5232. Periodical. UK. English. sa. 3. Editor, Dr Z A Pelczynski, Pembroke College, Oxford OX1 1DW England. **Ind/Abst** Philos. Index. **LC** B2900. **DD** 193.

BULLETIN SIGNALETIQUE. SECTION 519: PHILOSOPHIE. V. 23- 1969-. 0007-554X. Periodical. FR. French. ir. 396.00. Service des Abonnements du CDSH, 54 Bd Raspail, 75270 Paris Cedex 06 France. **Tel** 544.38.49. Bulletin Signaletique. Section 19-24: Sciences Humaines.

BULLETIN - SRI AUROBINDO INTERNATIONAL CENTRE OF EDUCATION, PONDICHERRY, INDIA. See Religion, Mythology, Rationalism.

CAHIERS DE LA REVUE DE THEOLOGIE ET DE PHILOSOPHIE. See Religion, Mythology, Rationalism - Theology.

CAHIERS PHILOSOPHIQUES AFRICAINS. VFOAT African Philosophical Journal. No. 1- Jan/1972-. Periodical. English (French). ir. $5.00. University Nationale du Zaire, BP 1825, Lubumbashi Congo Zaire. **LC** B5300.

CAHIERS SIMONE WEIL. (CAHIERS SIMONE WEIL : REVUE TRIMESTRIELLE PUBLIEE PAR L'ASSOCIATION POUR L'ETUDE DE LA PENSEE DE SIMONE WEIL). Vol. 1, No. 1 (June 1978)-. 0181-1126. Periodical. FR. French. qt. 130,00. 5 rue Monticelli, 75014 Paris France. **Tel** 45405704. Ed Andie A Devaux. **Ind/Abst** MLA Int. Bibliogr. Books Artic. Mod. Lang. Lit. **LC** B2430.W474. **DD** 194. bk rev. **Circ** 600. (ctrl).

CAHIERS SPINOZA. No. 1- Summer 1977-. 0152-593X. Periodical. FR. French. ir. Ed Replique, 19 rue Gustave Courbet, 31400 Toulouse France. **LC** B3951. **DD** 199.492.

CANADIAN PHILOSOPHICAL REVIEWS. VFOAT Revue Canadienne de Comptes Rendus en Philosophie. Vol. 1, No. 1 (Spring 1981)-. 0228-491X. Periodical. CN. English (French). ir. 64.00. Academic Printing & Publishing, PO Box 4834, Edmonton Alberta T6E 5G7 Canada. **Tel** (403)461-3419. Ed Roger A Shiner. **DD** 105. bk rev. adv acc. **Circ** 300. New books in various areas of philosophical interest reviewed quickly by scholars in the field. Ten issues yearly. Valuable aid in choosing books for personal/classroom use.

CARLETON UNIVERSITY STUDENT JOURNAL OF PHILOSOPHY. (THE CARLETON UNIVERSITY STUDENT JOURNAL OF PHILOSOPHY). Began with March 1974 issue. 0317-073X. Periodical. CN. English. ty. Free. The Carleton University Student Journal of Philosophy, Carleton University, Department of Philosophy, Colonel by Drive, Ottawa Ontario K1S 5B6 Canada. **DD** 105.

CARREFOUR. V. 1- 1 Half Yearly 1979-. 0706-1250. Periodical. CN. French. sa. Free to members, $5. Societe de Philosophie de l Outaouais, Carrefour, 90 rue Wilbrod, Ottawa Ontario K1N 6NS Canada. **DD** 105.

IL CENTAURO. N. 1 (Jan. - Apr. 1981)-. Periodical. IT. Italian. ty. 36.000. Guida Editori S R L, Via Ventaglieri 83, 80135 Napoli Italy. **LC** B4. **DD** 105.

CHARLES S. PEIRCE NEWSLETTER. No. 1- Dec. 1973-. Periodical. US. English. an. $4.00. Texas Tech University, Room 304 K, Institute of Studies in Pragmaticism, Lubbock TX 79409. Newsletter.

CHE HSUEH YEN CHIU. VFOAT Zhexue Yanjiu. Periodical. CC. Chinese. mo. $10.26. China Publication Centre, PO Box 2820, Beijing China. **LC** B8.C5.

CHEZ SOPHIE. V. 1, No. 1 (Dec. 1982)-. 0715-7096. Periodical. CN. French. ir. $1.50 Per Number. Centre Humaniste Alpha, CP 11, Levis Quebec G6V 6N6 Canada. **DD** 100.

CHINESE STUDIES IN PHILOSOPHY. 0023-8627. Periodical. US. English (Chinese). qt. $178.50. M E Sharpe Inc, 80 Business Park Drive, Armonk NY 10504. **Tel** (914)273-1800. Ed Chung-Ying Cheng. **Ind/Abst** Philos. Index. **LC** B1. **DD** 105. adv acc. **Circ** 200. The journal contains unabridged translations of articles from Chinese sources. The aim is to present the more important Chinese studies in this field. Chinese Studies in History and Philosophy.

CHUNG-KUO CHE HSUEH. V. 1, (Aug. 1979)-. Periodical. CC. Chinese. ir. 1.20. San Lien Shu Tien, Pei-Ching China Mainland. **LC** B8.C5. **DD** 181.11.

CHUNG-KUO CHE HSUEH SHIH YEN CHIU. VFOAT Research in History of Chinese Philosophy. Periodical. CH. Chinese. qt. 0.70. Chung-Kuo Kuo Chi Shu Tien, PO Box 2820, Pei-Ching China. **LC** B8.C5. **DD** 181.1109.

CIENCIA E FILOSOFIA. No. 1-. Periodical. Portuguese. ir. Faculdade de Filosofia, Letras e Ciencias Humanas, Caixa Postal 8, 105 Sao Paulo Brazil. **LC** B67.

LA CIUDAD DE DIOS. See Religion, Mythology, Rationalism.

CLASSIFICATION SOCIETY BULLETIN. (THE CLASSIFICATION SOCIETY BULLETIN). Periodical. No. 1- 1965-. 0578-4565. Periodical. UK. English. an. $10.00. Union Carbide Corporation, PO Box Y, Building 9704-1, Oak Ridge TN 37830. **Ind/Abst** Libr. Inf. Sci. Abstr. **LC** BD241. **DD** 112.

COLECCION TESIS DOCTORALES. **Main/Corp** Venezuela. Universidad Central, Caracas. Instituto de Filosofia. 0505-1827. VE. Spanish. ir. Universidad Central, Instituto Filosofia, Caracas Venezuela.

COLLABORATION. 0164-1522. Periodical. US. English. qt. $12.00. Matagiri Sri Aurobindo Center, Mt Tremper NY 12457. **Tel** (914)687-9222. Ed Jeanne Kozstange. bk rev. **Circ** 1,500. (ctrl). Devoted to the spiritual, evolutionary vision of Sri Aurobindo and the mother and containing excerpts of their writings, news and photographs from Auroville, an international community.

COLUMBIA STUDIES IN PHILOSOPHY. No. 1- 1941-. 0098-9436. Monographic Series. US. English. ir. Columbia Universtiy Press, 136 South Broadway, Irvington-on-Hudson NY 10533.

CONCERN FOR DYING. See Ethics.

CONSEQUENCE. No. 1- Jan./June 1974-. 0377-6824. Periodical. English and French. ir. 1.400. Inter-African Council for Philosophy, PO Box 1268, Cotonou Dahomey. **LC** B5300. **DD** 199.6.

CONSIDERATIONS. V. 1- June 1977-. 0709-6461. Periodical. CN. French. ty. $3.50 Students. Faculte de Philosophie Secretariat, Bureau 644/Tour des Arts, Universite Laval, Quebec Quebec G1K 7P4 Canada. **DD** 105.

CONTEMPORARY BRITISH PHILOSOPHY : PERSONAL STATEMENTS. 1st- Series. UK. English. Ed J H Muirhead. **LC** B1615. **DD** 192.

CONTEMPORARY GERMAN PHILOSOPHY. Vol. 1 (1982)-. 0740-719X. US. English. Pennsylvania State University, 215 Wagner Building, University Park PA 16802. **Tel** (814)865-1327. Ed Darrel E Christensen. **LC** B3181. **DD** 105. A yearbook which makes originally German contributions to philosophical comprehension available in English. Varied articles and book reviews in each volume.

CONTEMPORARY PHILOSOPHY. V. 7, No. 5- Late Fall 1978-. 0732-4944. Periodical. US. English. bm. $25.00. Institute of Advanced Philosophic Research, PO Box 1373, Boulder CO 80306. **Tel** (303)444-0071. Ed Alfred E Koenig. bk rev. **Circ** 900. Covers philosophy and science. Philosophic Research and Analysis.

CONTRIBUTIONS IN PHILOSOPHY. 0084-926X. Monographic Series. US. English. ir. Greenwood Press, 88 Post Road West, Box 5007, Westport CT 06881. **Tel** (203)226-3571. **LC** UNC. This series combines the far-reaching work of original thinkers with important new monographs on the history of philosophy.

CORPUS PHILOSOPHORUM DANICORUM MEDII AEVI. 0589-8080. Monographic Series. Latin. ir. C E C Gads Forlag, Vimmelskaftet 32, DK-1161 Copenhagen Denmark. **Tel** (01)150558. **Circ** 600.

CRITICA: REVISTA HISPANOAMERICANA DE FILOSOFIA. V. 1- Jan. 1967-. 0011-1503. Periodical. MX. Spanish (English and Portuguese). ir. $12.00. Instituto de Investigaciones Filosoficas, Universidad Nacional Autonoma de Mexico, Apartado 27-414, Mexico City Mexico. **Tel** 548-82-08. **Ind/Abst** Philos. Index. **LC** B1. bk rev. adv acc. (ctrl). Publishes quality essays, brief discussions and critical reviews of books regardless of the author's philosophical school or point of view.

CRITICAL TEXTS. See Literary and Political Reviews.

CRYSTAL MIRROR. See Religion, Mythology, Rationalism - Buddhism.

CUADERNOS DE FILOSOFIA. Spanish (Portuguese). ir. $5.00. Instituto Central de Filosofia Universidad de Concepcion, Casilla 2092, Concepcion Chile. **Tel** 234985. **LC** B5. **Circ** 500. (ctrl). History of philosophy, logic, philosophy of science, axiolog, ethics, deontology, gnosis, and aesthetics.

CUADERNOS DE FILOSOFIA LATINOAMERICANA. Periodical. Spanish. qt. $4.50. Cuadernos de Filosofia, Latinoamericana Universidad Santo Tomas, Carrera 9A. No. 51-23, Bogota 2 Colombia. **LC** B1001. **DD** 199.805.

CUADERNOS DE LA CATEDRA MIGUEL DE UNAMUNO. 1- 1948-. 5268-5960. SP. Spanish. be. $5.88. Secretariado de Publicaciones, Apartado 325, Salamanca Spain. **Ind/Abst** MLA Int. Bibliogr. Books Artic. Mod. Lang. Lit., Am. Hist. Life, Hist. Abstr., Hist. Abstr., Part A, Mod. Hist. Abstr., Hist. Abst., Part B, Twent. Century Abstr. **LC** B4568.U54. **DD** 868.6209.

CUADERNOS DE SEMIOTICA. No. 1- 1978-. Periodical. Spanish (summaries in English). ir. Garibaldi 2844, Montevideo Uruguay.

CUADERNOS SALMANTINOS DE FILOSOFIA. V. 1-. SP. Spanish. $20.00. Universidad Pontificia de Salamanca, Calle Compania 1, Salamanca Spain. **LC** B5. **DD** 105.

LA CULTURA. Vol. 1 Jan. 1963-. Periodical. IT. Italian. sa. $23.76. Casa Edit Felice le Monnier, Post Box 202, 50100 Firenze Italy. **Tel** 055-6813801. Ed Casa Editrice Felice Le Monnier. bk rev. adv acc. **Circ** 1,300. A journal of humanistic studies founded in 1881 by Ruggero Bonghi. It publishes important contributions in the fields of philosophy, history and literature.

THE DANDELION. V. 1- (Spr. 1977-). Periodical. US. English. qt. $4.50. Michael Coughlin, 1985 Selby Avenue, St Paul MN 55104.

DARSANA (BANGLADESH DARSHAN SAMITI). (DARSANA : BAMLADESA DARSANA SAMITIRA MUKHAPATRA). VFOAT Darshan. Periodical. Bengali. qt. **LC** B8.B4.

DARSANIKA TRAIMASIKA. Periodical. Hindi. ir. **LC** B56.

DAWN. Vol. 1/No. 1 (Summer 1981)-. 0277-4461. Periodical. US. English. qt. $8.00. Himalayan Institute, Rd 1 Box 88, Honesdale PA 18431. **Tel** (717)253-5551. Ed Kay Gendrom. bk rev. **Circ** 2,200. (ctrl). A magazine devoted to yoga, meditation, philosophy, psychology and holistic living.

DEATH AND DYING. 1950/74-. 0198-7453. US. English. ir. NLM Z 5725 D2855.

DEATH & DYING. (DEATH & DYING (BOCA RATON, FLA.)). Series/Titl Social Issues Resources Series. VFOAT Death and Dying. VAT Death and Dying (Boca Raton). V. 1, Article 1-. 0273-2483. Periodical. US. English. an. Social Issues Resources Series Inc, PO Box 2507, Boca Raton FL 33432. Ed Eleanor C Goldstein. **LC** HQ1073.5.U6. **DD** 306.905.

DEATH EDUCATION CEASED. V. 1-8, No. 4. 0145-7624. Periodical. US. English. bm. **Ind/Abst** Hospit. Lit. Index, Sociol. Abstr., Soc. Welf. Soc. Plan./Policy Soc. Dev., Excerpta Med., Cumul. Index Nurs. Allied Health Lit., Curr. Index J. Educ., Psychol. Abstr. **LC** BF789.D4. **DD** 155.93705. NLM W1 DE107. CODEN DEEDDR.

DEUKALION : PERIODIKE EKDOSE TOU KENTROU PHILOSOPHIKON EREUNON. Periodical. GR. Greek, Modern (English, French, and German). qt. $50.00. Charitos 3, Athena 139 Greece.

DEUTSCHE ZEITSCHRIFT FUR PHILOSOPHIE. Vol. 1-. 0012-1045. Periodical. German. mo. $45.61. Kunst & Wissen Erich Bieber, Dufourstrasse 51, CH-8008 Zurich Switzerland. **Tel** 01/69 44 20. **Ind/Abst** Philos. Index, Soc. Sci. Citation Index, Sociol. Abstr., Lang. Lang. Behav. Abstr. (cum index).

DIALECTICA. Began publication with V. 1, No. 1 (Feb. 15, 1947). 0012-2017. Periodical. SZ. English (articles in French or German). qt. $39.58. Editions

Dialectica, Casa Case Postal 1081, CH 2501 Bienne Switzerland. **Ind/Abst** Math. Rev., Philos. Index, Lang. Lang. Behav. Abstr., Sociol. Abstr. **LC** B1. **DD** 105. bk rev. **Circ** 700. Review of philosophy of knowledge.

DIALECTICS AND HUMANISM. Autumn 1973-. 0324-8275. Periodical. PL. English (Polish). qt. ARS Polona, Krakowskie Przedmiescie 7, 00-068 Warsaw Poland. **Ind/Abst** Philos. Index. **LC** B809.7. **DD** 190.5.

DIALOGOS. Year 1- (No. 1-). 0012-2122. Periodical. PR. Spanish (English). sa. $10.00. University of Puerto Rico, College of Humanities, Department Philosophy, Rio Piedras Puerto Rico 00931. **Tel** (804)764-000. **Ed** Roberto Torretti. **Ind/Abst** Philos. Index. bk rev. **Circ** 800. A professional journal open to all currents of philosophy and philosophical scholarship.

DIALOGUE. V. 1- Apr. 1956-. 0012-2246. Periodical. US. English. ty. $5.00. Phi Sigma Tau Marquette University, c/o Department of Philosophy, Milwaukee WI 53433. **Ed** Thomas Prendergast. **Ind/Abst** Philos. Index. **LC** B1. bk rev. adv acc. **Circ** 2,000. The official journal of Phi Sigma Tau, the national honor society in philosophy. Provides a vehicle for exchange of philosophical ideas among graduates and undergraduate students.

DIALOGUE - CANADIAN PHILOSOPHICAL ASSOCIATION. (DIALOGUE). **VFOAT** Canadian Philosophical Review, Revue Canadienne de Philosophie. V. 1- June 1962-. 0012-2173. Periodical. CN. English (French). qt. $30.95. Wilfrid Laurier University Press, 75 University Avenue West, Waterloo Ontario N2L 3C5 Canada. **Tel** (519)884-1970. **Ed** Michael McDonald. **Ind/Abst** Math. Rev., Sociol. Abstr., MLA Int. Bibliogr. Books Artic. Mod. Lang. Lit., Philos. Index, Lang. Lang. Behav. Abstr. **LC** B1. **DD** 105. bk rev. adv acc. **Circ** 1,350. A journal of the Canadian Philosophical Association, it represents most of the main areas of philosophy, such as the history of philosophy, metaphysics, logic, ethics, etc.

DIOGENE. Began publication with No. 1 (Nov. 1952). 0419-1633. Periodical. FR. French. qt. 148.00. Editions Gallimard, 49 rue de la Vanne, 92120 Montrouge France. **Tel** 656 89 00. **Ind/Abst** Philos. Index.

DIOGENES. No. 1- 1953-. 0012-303X. Periodical. IT. English. qt. $22.00. Casalini Libri, Via Benedetto da Malano 3, 50014 Fiesole Italy. **Tel** 055-599941. **Ed** Jean D'Ormesson. **Ind/Abst** MLA Int. Bibliogr. Books Artic. Mod. Lang. Lit., Philos. Index, Humanit. Index, Am. Hist. Life, Hist. Abstr., Hist. Abstr., Part A, Mod. Hist. Abstr., Hist. Abst., Part B, Twent. Century Abstr. **LC** AS4. **DD** 051. (cum index). Publication of the internation Council for Philosophy and Humanistic Studies.

DIOTIMA. 1- 1973-. English, French, or Greek. ir. $10.00. Hellenic Society for Philosophical Studies, 40 Hypsilantou Street, 140 Athenai Greece. **Ind/Abst** Philos. Index. **LC** B1. **DD** 105.

DIRECTORY FOR A NEW WORLD. *See* Yearbooks, Almanacs, Directories.

DIRECTORY OF AMERICAN PHILOSOPHERS. *See* Yearbooks, Almanacs, Directories.

A DIRECTORY OF WOMEN IN PHILOSOPHY. *See* Yearbooks, Almanacs, Directories.

DISCORSI. Periodical. Italian. sa. 18.000. Viale Gramsci, 12-80122 Napoli Italy. **LC** B4. **DD** 105.

DIVUS THOMAS; COMMENTARIUM DE PHILOSOPHIA ET THEOLOGIA. *See* Religion, Mythology, Rationalism - Theology.

DOCUMENTACION CRITICA IBEROAMERICANA DE FILOSOFIA Y CIENCIAS AFINES. Year 1-2, No. 4. 0419-5248. Periodical. SP. Spanish (with occasional articles in Portuguese). qt. $10.00. Centro de Estudios de Filosof, Apartada 145 C, Consolation 8, Seville Spain. **Ind/Abst** Am. Hist. Life, Hist. Abstr., Part A, Mod. Hist. Abstr., Hist. Abst., Part B, Twent. Century Abstr., Hist. Abstr.

DRIJARKARA. Periodical. Indonesian. ir. Seksi Majalah/Publikasi, Dewan Mahasiswa Sekolah, Tinggi Filsafat Driyarkara, Jakarta Indonesia. **LC** B8.I55.

EAST WEST JOURNAL. **VFOAT** Eastwest Journal. V. 8, No. 8- Aug. 1978-. 0191-3700. Periodical. US. English. mo. $44.00. 17 Station Street, PO Box 1200, Brookline MA 02147. **Tel** (617)232-1000. **Ed** Mark Mayell. **Ind/Abst** GeoRef, Altern. Press Index, New Period. Index, Bibliogr. Index Geol. **LC** AP2. **DD** 051. bk rev. adv acc. **Circ** 80,000. For people interested in alternative lifestyles, natural foods, crafts, exercise, organic gardening, holistic health, and occidental, oriental, religious, or philosophical thought. *Eastwest.*

EICHSTATTER STUDIEN. *See* Religion, Mythology, Rationalism - Theology.

EIDOS. V. 1- July 1978-. 0707-2287. Periodical. CN. English (text in French). sa. $10. Graduate Student Association, Department of Philosophy University of Waterloo, Waterloo Ontario N2L 3G1 Canada. **DD** 105.

ELENCHOS (BIBLIOPOLIS (FIRM)). (ELENCHOS). Vol. 1, No. 1 (1980)-. Periodical. Italian. sa. **DD** 180.5.

ENRAHONAR. 1 (First issue in 1981)-. 0211-402X. Periodical. SP. Catalan (French, Italian, and Spanish). sa. Servei de Publicacions de la Universitat Autonoma de Barcelona, Bellaterra, Barcelona Spain. **LC** B5.

EPISTEME : ANUARIO DE FILOSOFIA. *See* Yearbooks, Almanacs, Directories.

EPISTEME NS : REVISTA DEL INSTITUTE DE FILOSOFIA. 1 (Jan./Dec. 1981)-. Periodical. Spanish. ty. $15.00. Instituto de Filosofia, Apartado 47342, Caracas 1041 Venezuela. **Tel** 662-47-63. **LC** B5. **DD** 105. bk rev. adv acc. Theoretical analysis of the main problems of philosophy, contemporary discussions on logics and philosophy of language, methodology and epistemological problems of natural and social sciences, etc.

EPISTEMOLOGIA. Yearly V. 1- Jan./June 1978-. Periodical. English (Italian). sa. 28.000 Domestic, $28.00 Foreign. Tilger Genova Sas, Via Assarotti 52, 16122 Genoa Italy. **Tel** (010)891140. **Ed** Evandro Agazzi. **LC** Q174. **DD** 501. bk rev. adv acc. **Circ** 1,000. A journal for the philosophy of science which pays due attention to the analytic research on methods and contents of the sciences.

EPOPTEIA. Periodical. Greek, Modern. mo. $170.00. Imago SA, 5 Paleologou Street, Halandri 15232 Attiki Greece. **Tel** (01)6832930. **Ed** Pan Drakopoulos. bk rev. adv acc. **Circ** 2,500. (ctrl). Magazine of philosophy, culture and current affairs. Emphasis on the history of consciousness.

ERASMUS IN ENGLISH. No. 1-. 0071-1063. CN. English. an. Free. University of Toronto Press, Toronto M5S 1A6 Canada. **Ed** R M Schoeffel. **Ind/Abst** Am. Hist. Life, Hist. Abstr., Part A, Mod. Hist. Abstr., Hist. Abst., Part B, Twent. Century Abstr., MLA Int. Bibliogr. Books Artic. Mod. Lang. Lit., Hist. Abstr. **LC** B785.E65. **DD** 199.492. bk rev. **Circ** 3,500. A newsletter issued annually to provide information about progress of the collected works of Erasmus and about Erasmus studies in general.

ERKENNTNIS. V. 9- May 1975-. 0165-0106. GW. English. bm. 132. Kluwer Academic Publishers Group, PO Box 322, 3300 AH Dordrecht Netherlands. **Tel** (31)78-334911. **Ed** Wilhelm K Essler. **Ind/Abst** Sociol. Abstr., Lang. Lang. Behav. Abstr., Index Book Rev. Humanit., Philos. Index. **LC** B1. **DD** 105. bk rev. adv acc. **Circ** 750. Foundational studies and scientific methodology, covering philosophy of science and analytic philosophy, philosophy of language, logic, and mathematics, foundations of ethics, law and aesthetics. *Journal of Unified Science (Erkenntnis).*

ESCRITOS DE FILOSOFIA. Yearly V. 1, 1 (Jan./June 1978)-. 0325-4933. Periodical. AG. Spanish. sa. Academia Nacional de Ciencias, Junin 1278, CP 1114, Buenos Aires Argentina. **LC** B5. **DD** 105.

ESPIRITU. (ESPIRITU : CUADERNOS DEL INSTITUTO FILOSOFICO DE BALMESIANA). 0014-0716. Periodical. Spanish. sa. Espiritu, Duran y Bas 9, Barcelona 2 Spain. **Ind/Abst** Philos. Index.

ESTUDIOS DE CIENCIAS Y LETRAS : REVISTA DEL INSTITUTO DE FILOSOFIA, CIENCIAS Y LETRAS. No. 1-. Periodical. Spanish. ir. $10.00. AVDA 8 de Octubre, 2738 Montevideo Uruguay. **LC** AS89.A1. **DD** 068.89513.

ESTUDIOS DE FILOSOFIA Y RELIGIONES DEL ORIENTE. V. 1- 1971-. Sanskrit (Spanish). ir. Universidad de Buenos Aires, Centro de Estudios de Estudios de Filosofia Oriental, 25 de Mayo 217 20 Piso, Buenos Aires Argentina. **LC** B121.

ESTUDIOS FILOSOFICOS. 1-. Periodical. SP. Spanish. ty. $30.00. Instituto Superior d'Filosofia, Plaza San Pablo 4, 47011 Villadolid Spain. **Ed** A Martinez Casado. **Ind/Abst** Philos. Index, Lang. Lang. Behav. Abstr., Sociol. Abstr. bk rev. **Circ** 900. All topics of philosophical interest: history of ideas, contemporary problems on philosophy, theoretic aspects of scientific research.

ESTUDIOS Y DOCUMENTOS. Main/Corp Universidad de Valladolid. Facultad de Filosofia y Letras. No. 1- 1954-. 0504-9806. Monographic Series. SP. Spanish. ir. Universidad de Valladolio, Valladolid Spain.

THE ETIENNE GILSON SERIES. 1-. 0708-319X. Monographic Series. CN. English. Pontifical Institute of Mediaeval Studies, 59 Queen's Park Crescent East, Toronto Ontario Canada.

LES ETUDES BERGSONIENNES. V. 1-11. Periodical. FR. French. ir. Presses Universitaires France, 12 rue Jean de Beauvais, 75005 Paris France. **LC** B2192.B4Z7.

ETUDES DE PSYCHOLOGIE ET DE PHILOSOPHIE. 1-. Monographic Series. FR. French. ir. Librairie Philosophique J Vrin, 6 Place de la Sorbonne, 75006 Paris France. **Tel** 43 54 03 47. **Ed** Vrin. Different from one book to another, but always concerning these areas: philosophy and psychology.

ETUDES MUSULMANES. *See* Religion, Mythology, Rationalism - Islam, Bahaism, Theosophy.

ETUDES PHILOSOPHIQUES. (LES ETUDES PHILOSOPHIQUES). Began publication in 1926. 0395-7632. Periodical. FR. French. qt. 260 Domestic, $28.89 Foreign. Presses Universitaires France, 12 rue Jean-de-Beauvais, 75005 Paris France. **Tel** (1)326-2216. **Ed** Pierre Aubenque, J Brun and L Millet. **Ind/Abst** MLA Int. Bibliogr. Books Artic. Mod. Lang. Lit., Philos. Index, Index Book Rev. Humanit., Recent Publ. Artic. **LC** B2. **DD** 105. In each issue an important philosopher explains the central idea of his work. Also covered are aesthetics, teaching and practical philosophy.

EUNTES DOCETE. *See* Religion, Mythology, Rationalism - Theology.

FAITH AND PHILOSOPHY. (FAITH AND PHILOSOPHY : JOURNAL OF THE SOCIETY OF CHRISTIAN PHILOSOPHERS). Vol. 1, No. 1 (Jan. 1984)-. 0739-7046. Periodical. US. English. qt. $25.00. Faith and Philosophy, Asbury College, c/o Michael L Peterson, Department of Philosophy, Wilmore KY 40390. **Ind/Abst** Philos. Index. **DD** 200.

FAITH & REASON. *See* Religion, Mythology, Rationalism - Roman Catholic Church.

FILOSOFIA. Vol. 1, Issue 1 (Jan. 1950)-. 0015-1823. Periodical. IT. Italian. ty. 30.000 Domestic. Professor Augusto Guzzo, Piazza Statuto 26, 10144 Turin Italy. **Tel** 011 487818. **Ed** Augusto Guzzo. **Ind/Abst** Philos. Index. **LC** B4. (cum index). bk rev. Everything that has to do with philosophy and with history of philosophy.

FILOSOFIA OGGI. Yearly V. 1, N. 1(Jan.-Mar. 1978)-. Periodical. English (English, French, German, Italian, and Spanish). qt. 30.000 Domestic, 50.000 Foreign. Studio Editoriale di Cultura, Cas Postfach 997, 16100 Genova Italy. **Ed** M A Raschini and P P Ottonello. **LC** B1. **DD** 105. bk rev. **Circ** 600. International review of classical and contemporary philosophy with theoretical articles and original contributions in the principal languages.

FILOSOFISKE STUDIER. V. 1-. Periodical. Danish (or English). ir. **LC** B8.D4.

FILOSOFSKA DUMKA. Periodical. UR. Ukrainian (table of contents in Russian and English). bm. $18.00. Victor Kamkin Inc (74526), 12224 Parklawn Drive, Rockville MD 20852. **Tel** (301)881-5973. **Ind/Abst** MLA Int. Bibliogr. Books Artic. Mod. Lang. Lit.

FILOSOFSKA MISUL. V. 1- Aug. 1945-. 0015-184X. Periodical. BU. Bulgarian. mo. Hemus, 6 Boulevard Rusky, Sofia Bulgaria.

FILOSOFSKIE NAUKI. No. 1- 1971-. 0320-5452. UR. Russian. bm. $28.50. Victor Kamkin Inc (71032), 12224 Parklawn Drive, Rockville MD 20852. **Tel** (301)881-5973. **Ind/Abst** Sociol. Abstr., Lang. Lang. Behav. Abstr. **LC** B809.8.

FILOZOFIA. Began in 1966 with V. 21. 0046-385X. Periodical. Slovak (summaries in Russian and English). Kubon & Sagner, Postfach 34 01 08, Hess Strasse 39/41, D-8 Munchen 34 West Germany. **Tel** (089)52 20 27. **Ind/Abst** Sociol. Abstr., Soc. Welf. Soc. Plan./Policy Soc. Dev. Orginal works by Slovak authors about basic questions of Marxist philosophy, theoretical problems of the building of socialism, and communism, philosophical questions of natural and social sciences, as well as on the subjects of historical philosophy and scientific atheism. *Otazky Marxistickej Filozofie.*

FILOZOFICKY CASOPIS (USTAV PRO FILOZOFII A SOCIOLOGII CSAV). (FILOZOFICKY CASOPIS). '76/1-. 0015-1831. Periodical. Czech. Kubon & Sagner, Postfach 34 01 08, Hess-Strasse 39/41, D-8 Munchen 34 West Germany. **Ind/Abst** Philos. Index. Publishes papers devoted to discussing the basic problems of Marxist philosophy, such as questions concerning dialectics, ontology, gnoseology and historical materialism. *Filosoficky Casopis.*

FOURTHOUGHT NEWSLETTER. No. 1 (Apr. 1, 1981)-. 0711-3897. Periodical. CN. English. ir. $8.00. Fourthought Media, Apt 708/50 Hillsboro Avenue, Toronto Ontario M5R 1S8 Canada. **DD** 105.

FRANZISKANISCHE STUDIEN. *See* Religion, Mythology, Rationalism - Roman Catholic Church.

FREE INQUIRY (BUFFALO, N.Y.). (FREE INQUIRY). Vol. 1, No. 1 (Winter 1980/1980)-. 0272-0701. Periodical. US. English. qt. $16.50. Codesh Inc, Box 5 Central Park Station, Buffalo NY 14215. **Tel** (716)834-2921. **Ed** Paul Kortz. **Ind/Abst** Public Aff. Inf. Serv. Bull., Philos. Index. **LC** BL2700. **DD** 210. bk rev. adv acc. **Circ** 15,000. Countering religious fundamentalists, the humanist scholars who write this controversial magazine are dedicated to defending freedom and secularism in the contemporary world.

THE FREE PHILOSOPHER QUARTERLY. (THE FREE PHILOSOPHER QUARTERLY : FPQ). **VFOAT** FPQ. Vol. 1 No. 1 (Summer 1983)-. 0742-3748. Periodical. US. English. qt. $16.00 US/Canada. Free Philosopher Quarterly, PO Box 6145, Bellevue WA 98007. **LC** B1. **DD** 190.5.

FREETHINKER. V. 1- May 1881-. Periodical. UK. English. mo. $12.06. G W Foote, 702 Holloway Road, London N19 3NL England. **Tel** 01-272-1266. **Ed** William McIlroy. bk rev. **Circ** 1,500. A secular-humanist monthly dealing mainly with religion, from a critical viewpoint.

FREIBURGER ZEITSCHRIFT FUR PHILOSOPHIE UND THEOLOGIE. Vol. 1-. 0016-0725. Periodical. SZ. German (also some French). ty. 50.00. Editions Saint-Paul, Perolles 42, CH-1700 Fribourg Switzerland. **Ind/Abst** MLA Int. Bibliogr. Books Artic. Mod. Lang. Lit., Philos. Index, New Testam. Abstr., Recent Publ. Artic. **LC** BR45. bk rev. adv acc. **Circ** 600. Directed toward persons interested in philosophy, theology, economics and history, especially researchers, teachers, and students. An excellent source for libraries of universities, academies, institutes, colleges and other educational institutions. *Divus Thomas.*

FRIENDS JOURNAL. *See* Religion, Mythology, Rationalism.

GADES. *See* Education (General) - Higher Education.

GIORNALE DI METAFISICA. Yr. 1- Jan./Apr. 1979-. Periodical. Italian (French or German). ir. Tilgher - Genova S A S, Via Assarotti 52, 16122 Genova Italy. **Tel** (010)891140-870653. **Ind/Abst** Philos. Index. bk rev. adv acc. **Circ** 1,000. A journal of philosophical studies reproposing the primacy of the speculative philosophy and the research of the meaning and of the value of the man through the history and the civilisation. *Giornale di Metafisica.*

GIST. 0732-7781. Periodical. US. English. mo. $10.00. God Unlimited, University of Healing, 1101 Far Valley Road, Campo CA 92006. **Tel** (619)478-5111. **Ed** Herbert L Beierle. **Circ** 2,500. Information on University of Healing and University of Philosophy, chapters from books we publish and theses/dissertations of students, also articles on positive thinking and living.

GNOSIS. V. 1- 1973-. 0316-618X. Periodical. CN. English. an. Free. Sir George Williams University, 1455 de Maisonneuve Boulevard West, Montreal Quebec H3G 1M8 Canada. **Ind/Abst** Philos. Index. **DD** 105.

GNOZIS. **VFOAT** Gnosis. 1968-. 0017-1425. Periodical. US. English (Russian). sa. Gnosis, Box 86, 527 Riverside Drive, New York NY 10027. **Tel** (212)866-2200. **LC** B1. **DD** 001.305.

GOTHENBURG STUDIES IN PHILOSOPHY. Vol. 1 1963-. 0072-5048. SW. ir. Gothenburg University, Fack S400 10, Gothenburg Sweden.

GRADUATE FACULTY PHILOSOPHY JOURNAL. V. 1- 1971-. 0093-4240. Periodical. US. English. ir. $12.50. New School for Social Research, 65 Fifth Avenue, New York NY 10008. **Tel** (212)741-5707. **Ed** Frank X White. **Ind/Abst** Philos. Index. **LC** B1. **DD** 105. bk rev. adv acc. **Circ** 2,000. (ctrl). A journal of continental philosophy which treats political, historical, literary and scientific issues.

GRAZER PHILOSOPHISCHE STUDIEN. V. 1- 1975-. 0165-9227. NE. Multilingual (English, French, or German). sa. Humanities Press, Atlantic Highlands NJ 07716. **Ed** Rudolf Haller. **Ind/Abst** Philos. Index. Aims at developing different traditions of analytic philosophy. Journal attracts contributors from all over the world.

LE GUIDE DES RELATIONS PRESSE. 1984-. FR. French. an. 180. Edinove, 135 Avenue de Wagram, 75017 Paris France.

HAMMARSKJOLD FORUMS. Periodical. US. English. ir. Oceana Publ Inc, 75 Main Street, Dobbs Ferry NY 10522.

HEGEL-STUDIEN. V. 1- 1961-. 0073-1587. GW. German. an. $30.44. W E Saarbach GMBH, Postfach 101610, D-5000 Koeln 1 West Germany. **Tel** 02 21-23 46 31. **Ed** F Nicolin and O Poggeler. **LC** B2900.

HEGEL-STUDIEN. BEIHEFT. 1- 1964-. 0440-5927. Monographic Series. GW. English. an. W E Saarbach GMBH, Postfach 101610, D-5000 Koeln 1 West Germany. **Tel** 02 21-23 46 31.

HEIDEGGER STUDIES. Vol. 1-. 0885-4580. US. English. an. Eterna Press, PO Box 1344, Oak Brook IL 60522. **DD** 193.

HESTIA. 1960/61-. 0440-7563. Periodical. GW. German. ir. **LC** WMLC L 83/754.

HEYTHROP JOURNAL. *See* Religion, Mythology, Rationalism - Theology.

HISTORY AND PHILOSOPHY OF LOGIC. Vol. 1-. 0144-5340. UK. English (French and German). sa. $76.00. Taylor & Francis Ltd, 242 Cherry Street, Philadelphia PA 19106. **Tel** (215)238-0939. **Ed** I Grattan-Guinness. **Ind/Abst** Math. Rev. **LC** BC1. **DD** 160.5. Devoted to the study of historical developments and broader philosophical concerns of logic.

HISTORY OF PHILOSOPHY QUARTERLY. (HISTORY OF PHILOSOPHY : HPQ). **VFOAT** HPQ. Vol. 1, No. 1 (Jan. 1984)-. 0740-0675. Periodical. US. English. qt. $72.00. University of Pittsburg, c/o Prof Nicholas Rescher/Editor, Pittsburg PA 15260. **Tel** (419)372-2419. **Circ** 400. Ideally, the journal's contributions regard work in the history of philosophy and in philosophy itself as parts of a seamless whole.

HSIA-MEN TA HSUEH HSUEH PAO. CHE HSUEH SHE HUI KO HSUEH PAN. **VFOAT** Xiamendaxue Xuebao. Periodical. CC. Chinese. $6.00. China National Publishing Company, 380 Bei Su Zhou Lu, Shanghai China. **LC** H8.C47. **DD** 300.5.

HUA-CHUNG SHIH YUAN HSUEH PAO. CHE HSUEH SHE HUI KO HSUEH PAN. **VFOAT** Journal of Central China Teachers College. Philosophy and Social Sciences. Periodical. CC. Chinese. bm. 0.60. Chung-Kuo Kuo Chi Shu Tien, PO Box 2820, Pei-Ching China. **LC** AS452.W84. **DD** 059.951.

HUMAN STUDIES. V. 1- Jan. 1978-. 0163-8548. Periodical. US. English. qt. $60.00. Kluwer Academic Publishing Group, PO Box 322, 3300 AH Dordrecht Netherlands. **Tel** (201)767-8450. **Ind/Abst** MLA Int. Bibliogr. Books Artic. Mod. Lang. Lit., Sociol. Abstr., Philos. Index. **LC** B1. **DD** 105.

THE HUMANIST. V. 1- Spring 1941-. 0018-7399. Periodical. US. English. bm. $14.40. American Humanist Association, 7 Harwood Drive, Synder NY 14226. **Tel** (716)839-5080. **Ed** Lloyd Morain. **Ind/Abst** Book Rev. Index, Guide Soc. Sci. Relig. Period. Lit., Index Am. Period. Verse, Media Rev. Dig., Philos. Index, Pop. Mag. Rev., Public Aff. Inf. Serv. Bull., Soc. Welf. Soc. Plan./Policy Soc. Dev., Sociol. Abstr., Women Stud. Abstr., Humanit. Index, Read. Guide Period. Lit., Mag. Index, Lang. Lang. Behav. Abstr., Curr. Index J. Educ., Film Lit. Index. **LC** B821.A1. **DD** 144. bk rev. adv acc. **Circ** 12,000. Constructively discusses social issues and personal concerns in the light of humanistic ideas and developments in philosophy, sociology, psychology, and science. *Ethical Forum.*

HUMANIST IN CANADA. No. 18-: Fall 1967-. 0018-7402. Periodical. CN. English. qt. $7.74. Canadian Humanist Publication, Box 2007 Postal Station D, Ottawa Ontario K1P 5W3 Canada. **Tel** (613)283-7210. **Ed** D F Page. **Ind/Abst** Altern. Press Index. **DD** 144.05. bk rev. adv acc. **Circ** 1,200. Available in microform. Articles dealing with capital punishment, abortion, philosophy for children, international peace, moral values without dogma humanism and feminism. *Victoria Humanist, 0506-8657; Montreal Humanist.*

HUMANISTIC JUDAISM. *See* Religion, Mythology, Rationalism - Judaism.

HUMANISTISCHE BIBLIOTHEK. REIHE III : SKRIPTEN. V. 1- 1972-. Monographic Series. German. ir.

HUMANITAS (BRESCIA, ITALY). (HUMANITAS). Began with Jan. 1946 issue. Periodical. IT. Italian. bm. 15.44. Editrice Morcelliana Spa, Via Gabrielle Rosa 71, 25100 Brescia Italy. **Tel** 030-46451. **Ed** Stefano Minelli. **Ind/Abst** MLA Int. Bibliogr. Books Artic. Mod. Lang. Lit., Philos. Index. **LC** AP37. bk rev. **Circ** 2,000. (ctrl). Philosophy, religion, history, sociology, and literature. Problems of Catholic church today, oecumenical problems, reviews of national conferences, and sometimes monographic issues.

HUME STUDIES. V. 1- Apr. 1975-. 0319-7336. Periodical. CN. English. sa. 10. University of Western Ontario, Department of Philosophy, Talbot College, London Ontario N6A 3K7 Canada. **Tel** (519)679-2177. **Ed** John Davis. **Ind/Abst** Philos. Index, Am. Hist. Life, Hist. Abstr., Hist. Abstr., Part A, Mod. Hist. Abstr., Hist. Abst., Part B, Twent. Century Abstr. **DD** 192. bk rev. **Circ** 350. Study of David Hume.

IDEA INK. *See* Religion, Mythology, Rationalism - Roman Catholic Church.

IDEALISTIC STUDIES. V. 1- Jan. 1971-. 0046-8541. Periodical. US. English. ty. $7.00. Clark University Press, 34 Engelhard Avenue, Avenel NJ 07001. **Ind/Abst** Philos. Index. **LC** B823. **DD** 105.

THE INDEPENDENT JOURNAL OF PHILOSOPHY. **VFOAT** Revue Independante de Philosophie, Unabhangige Zeitschrift fur Philosophie. V. 1- Summer 1977-. 0378-4789. Periodical. English (German). an. $21.00. George Elliott Tucker, Cobenzlgasse 13/4, A-1190 Vienna Austria. **Ind/Abst** Philos. Index. **LC** B1. **DD** 105.

INDIAN PHILOSOPHICAL ANNUAL. II. English. ir. University of Madras, Registrar University Buildings, Chepauk Madras 600 005 India.

INDIAN PHILOSOPHICAL QUARTERLY. V. 1- Oct. 1973-. 0376-415X. Periodical. II. English. qt. $16.00. Indian Philosophical Quarterly, Department of Philosophy University of Poona, Pune 411 007 India. **Ed** S S Arlingay and Rajendra Prasad. **Ind/Abst** Philos. Index. **LC** B130. **DD** 105. bk rev. adv acc. All areas of philosophy; history of philosophy, philosophy of Indian origin. *Philosophical Quarterly.*

INDIAN PHILOSOPHY & CULTURE. **VAT** Indian Philosophy and Culture. Vol. 1, No. 1 (March 15, 1956)-. 0019-6096. Periodical. II. English. qt. Institute of Oriental Philosophy, Vrindaban UP India. **Ind/Abst** Philos. Index. **LC** B130.

INDO-IRANIAN JOURNAL. V. 1- 1957-. 0019-7246. Periodical. NE. English. qt. 70. Kluwer Academic Publishers Group, PO Box 322, 3300 AH Dordrecht Netherlands. **Tel** (31)78-334911. **Ed** J Wide Jong and M Witzel. **Ind/Abst** MLA Int. Bibliogr. Books Artic. Mod. Lang. Lit., Index Book Rev. Humanit., Sociol. Abstr., Lang. Lang. Behav. Abstr. bk rev. adv acc. **Circ** 500. Ancient and mediaeval Indian languages, literature, philosophy, and religion, ancient and mediaeval Iran, and papers on Tibet.

INFORMAL LOGIC NEWSLETTER *CEASED.* **VFOAT** Informal Logic. V. 1-5, No. 3. 0226-1448. Periodical. CN. English. ir. $11.61. University of Windsor, Department of Philosophy, Windsor Ontario N9B 3P4 Canada. **Tel** (519)253-4232. **Ed** J A Blair and D R H Johnson. **DD** 160.5. bk rev. adv acc. **Circ** 350. A journal devoted to the study of argument and other forms of reasoning used in the practice of rational life.

INQUIRY. V. 1- Spring 1958-. 0020-174X. Periodical. No. English. qt. 53.00. Universitetsforlaget, PO Box 2959-Toyen, Oslo 6 Norway. **Tel** (45)-2-27 60 60. **Ed** Alastair Hannay. **Ind/Abst** ABC Pol Sci, Am. Hist. Life, Hist. Abstr., Sociol. Abstr., Index Book Rev. Humanit., Philos. Index, Abstr. Soc. Work., Lang. Lang. Behav. Abstr., Hist. Abstr., Part A, Mod. Hist. Abstr., Hist. Abst., Part B, Twent. Century Abstr. (cum index). adv acc. **Circ** 1,000. Publishes scholarly articles, discussions, and review discussions in all areas of philosophy.

INSTITUTE SCHOLAR. V. 1-. 0196-5603. Periodical. US. English. sa. Institute for Humane Studies, 1177 University Drive, Menlo Park CA 94025.

INTEGRAL YOGA. V. 1- Dec. 1969-. 0161-1380. Periodical. US. English. bm. $12.00. Satchidananda Ashram, Route 1 Box 172, Buckingham VA 23921. **Tel** (804)969-4801. **Ed** Swami Prakashananda. bk rev. **Circ** 1,600. The ecumenical yoga teachings of Swami Satchidananda, articles about all religions, health and diet. stories, and fitness.

INTERNATIONAL CLASSIFICATION. *See* Library and Information Science.

INTERNATIONAL DIRECTORY OF PHILOSOPHY AND PHILOSOPHERS. **VFOAT** Repertoire International de la Philosophie et des Philosophes. 1st- Ed. 0074-4603. US. English. ir. $47.00. Philosophy Documentation, Bowling Green State University, Bowling Green OH 43403. **Tel** (419)372-2419. **Ed** Ramona Cormier and Richard H Lineback. **LC** B35. **DD** 102.5. Handbook of philosophy covering Europe, Central and South America, Asia, Africa, and Australia. Data on universities, societies, institutes, journals, and publishers of philosophy.

INTERNATIONAL HUMANIST. 1981, No. 1-. Periodical. English. qt. $7.90. Intl Humanist and Ethical Union, Oudkerkhof 11, 3512 GH Utrecht Netherlands. **Tel** 30-31 21 55. **Ed** Gerard Soeters. **Circ** 1,500. (ctrl). Covers humanist issues, representative of the humanist philosophy or life stance. *International Humanism.*

INTERNATIONAL JOURNAL FOR PHILOSOPHY OF RELIGION. *See* Religion, Mythology, Rationalism.

INTERNATIONAL PHILOSOPHICAL QUARTERLY *CEASED.* (IPQ, INTERNATIONAL PHILOSOPHICAL QUARTERLY). **VFOAT** International Philosophical Quarterly. V. 1-22, No. 4. 0019-0365. Periodical. US. English. qt. $10.00. International Philosophical Quarterly, Rodham University, Bronx NY 10458. **Tel** (212)579-2058. **Ed** Vincent G Potter. **Ind/Abst** Humanit. Index, Book Rev. Index, Cathol. Period. Lit. Index, Philos. Index. **LC** B1. **DD** 105. bk rev. adv acc. **Circ** 1,750. Microfilm of back issues available from Johnson Associates. To promote exchange of basic philosophical ideas, especially between traditions, for a world-wide cultivated audience.

INTERNATIONAL PHILOSOPHICAL QUARTERLY. **VFOAT** I.P.Q. Vol. 23, No. 1 (Mar. 1983)- – Issue No. 89-. 0019-0365. Periodical. US. English. qt. $20.00. International Philosophical Quarterly, Fordham University, Bronx NY 10458. **Tel** (212)579-2058. **Ed** Vincent G Potter. **Ind/Abst** Annu. Bibliogr. Engl. Lang. Lit., Philos. Index, Book Rev. Index, Ref. Source, Index Book Rev. Humanit., Humanit. Index, Cathol. Period. Lit. Index. **LC** B1. **DD** 105. bk rev. adv acc. **Circ** 1,750. Available on microfiche from KTO Microform. Aims to provide an international forum in English for interchange of basic philosophical ideas between the Americas and Europe and between east and west. *IPQ, International Philosophical Quarterly, 0019-0365.*

INTERNATIONAL SERIES IN NATURAL PHILOSOPHY. V. 86-. 0731-8871. Monographic Series. US. English. ir. Pergamon Press, c/o Cashier, 395 Sawmill River Road, Elmsford NY 10523. **Ind/Abst** Math. Rev., Comput. Control Abstr., Electr. Electron. Abstr., Sci. Abstr. Sect. A. Phys. Abstr. *International Series of Monographs in Natural Philosophy, 0074-8064.*

INTERNATIONAL SERIES OF MONOGRAPHS IN NATURAL PHILOSOPHY. V. 1-85. 0074-8064. Monographic Series. US. English. ir. Pergamon Press, 395 Sawmill River Road, Elmsford NY 10523. **Ind/Abst** Math. Rev.

INTERNATIONAL STUDIES IN PHILOSOPHY. **VFOAT** Studi Internazionali di Filosofia. 6 (Fall 1974)-. 0270-5664. Periodical. US. English (French, German and Italian). ty. $30.00. Scholars Press, PO Box 1608, Decatur GA 30031. **Tel** (404)329-6950. **Ind/Abst** Philos. Index. *Studi Internazionali di Filosofia.*

IOWA PUBLICATIONS IN PHILOSOPHY. 1963-. 0075-0395. US. English. ir. Martinus Nijhoff Publishers, PO Box 163/ Spulboulevard 50, 3300AD Dordrecht Netherlands.

IUSTITIA. V. 1- Apr. 1973-. 0092-3524. Periodical. US. English. sa. 25.000 Domestic, 40.000 Foreign. Casa Editrice Dr A Giuffre, Via Statuto 2, Periodical Department, 20121 Milano Italy. **Tel** 02/652341. **Ed** Pietro Gismondi. **Ind/Abst** Public Aff. Inf. Serv. Bull. **LC** K9. **DD** 340.115. bk rev. adv acc. **Circ** 1,300. This review is edited by the Union of Italian Catholic Jurists.

IYYUN. **VFOAT** Eydon. V. 1- Heshvan 706- 1945/ 46-. 0021-3306. Periodical. IS. Hebrew (table of contents and summaries in English, 1951). qt. $15.00. Jerusalem Philosophical Society, Hebrew University, Department of Philosophy, Jerusalem Isreal. **Tel** (2) 883747. **Ed** David Heyd. **Ind/Abst** Philos. Index. bk rev. **Circ** 700. Publishes articles, critical studies, reviews in all, fields of philosophy irrespective of author's philosophical school or method of inquiry.

JBSP. JOURNAL OF THE BRITISH SOCIETY FOR PHENOMENOLOGY. (JBSP; THE JOURNAL OF THE BRITISH SOCIETY FOR PHENOMENOLOGY). **Main/Corp** British Society for Phenomenology. **VAT** Journal of the British Society for Phenomenology. V. 1- Jan. 1970-. 0007-1773. Periodical. UK. English. ty. Haigh & Hochland Ltd, The Precinct Centre, Oxford Road, Manchester M13 9 OA England. **Tel** 061 273 4156. **Ed** Wolfe Mays. **Ind/Abst** Philos. Index, Index Book Rev. Humanit. **LC** B829.5. **DD** 142.705. bk rev. adv acc. **Circ** 450. Papers on phenomenology and existential philosophy as well as contributions from other fields of philosophy.

JOURNAL FOR THE THEORY OF SOCIAL BEHAVIOUR. V. 1- Apr. 1971-. 0021-8308. Periodical. UK. English. ty. $81.00. Basil Blackwell, Journals Department, 108 Cowley Road, Oxford OX4 1JF England. **Tel** 0865-722146. **Ed** Charles W Smith, Peter Collett and Serge Moscovici. **Ind/Abst** Sociol. Abstr., Soc. Welf. Soc. Plan./Policy Soc. Dev., Philos. Index, Psychol. Abstr., Lang. Lang. Behav. Abstr., Soc. Sci. Citation Index. **NLM** W1 JO404. adv acc. Interdisciplinary journal publishing original theoretical and methodological articles relating to social behaviour.

JOURNAL OF CHINESE PHILOSOPHY. V. 1- Dec. 1973-. 0301-8121. Periodical. US. English. qt. $92.00. University of Hawaii at Manoa, Department of Philosophy, 2530 Dole Street, Honolulu HI 96822. **Tel** (808)948-8859. **Ed** Chung-Ying Cheng. **Ind/Abst** MLA Int. Bibliogr. Books Artic. Mod. Lang. Lit., Philos. Index. **LC** B5230.A1. **DD** 181.11105. bk rev. adv acc. **Circ** 500. Devoted to the study of Chinese philosophy and Chinese thought in all phases and stages of development.

JOURNAL OF INDIAN PHILOSOPHY. 022-1791. Periodical. English. qt. 68.00. Kluwer Academic Publishers Group, PO Box 322, 3300 AH Dordrecht The Netherlands. **Tel** (31)78-334911. **Ed** Bimal K Marilal. **Ind/Abst** Philos. Index, MLA Int. Bibliogr. Books Artic. Mod. Lang. Lit. bk rev. adv acc. **Circ** 550. Analytical and comparative philosophy.

THE JOURNAL OF LIBERTARIAN STUDIES. *See* Economics - Economic Theory.

THE JOURNAL OF MIND AND BEHAVIOR. *See* Psychology.

JOURNAL OF PHENOMENOLOGICAL PSYCHOLOGY. *See* Psychology.

JOURNAL OF PHILOSOPHICAL LOGIC. V. 1- Feb. 1972-. 0022-3611. Periodical. NE. English. qt. 66. Kluwer Academic Publishers Group, PO Box 322, 3300 AH Dordrecht Netherlands. **Tel** (31)78-334911. **Ed** Richmond H Thomason. **Ind/Abst** Math. Rev., MLA Int. Bibliogr. Books Artic. Mod. Lang. Lit., Sociol. Abstr., Philos. Index, Lang. Lang. Behav. Abstr. **LC** BC51. **DD** 160.5. **CODEN** JPLGA7. adv acc. **Circ** 950. Philosophical studies utilizing formal methods or dealing with topics in logical theory.

JOURNAL OF PHILOSOPHICAL STUDIES. V. 1-6 (No. 1-21). Periodical. UK. English. bm. Japan Publishers Trading Company Inc, PO Box 5030/Tokyo International, Tokyo 100-31 Japan. **Ed** S E Hooper.

THE JOURNAL OF PHILOSOPHY. V. 18- 1921-. 0022-362X. Periodical. US. English. mo. $25.00. Columbia University, 720 Philosophy Hall, New York NY 10027. **Tel** (212)280-3188. **Ed** Leigh Cauman. **Ind/Abst** Math. Rev., MLA Int. Bibliogr. Books Artic. Mod. Lang. Lit., Annu. Bibliogr. Engl. Lang. Lit., Philos. Index, Book Rev. Index, Index Book Rev. Humanit., Humanit. Index. (cum index). bk rev. adv acc. **Circ** 4,400. Available on microfilm. Contains distinguished philosophical articles of current interest and encourages the interchange of ideas especially between philosophy and the special disciplines. *Journal of Philosophy, Psychology and Scientific Methods, 0160-9335.*

THE JOURNAL OF PRE-COLLEGE PHILOSOPHY. **VFOAT** Pre-College Philosophy. 0162-9662. Periodical. US. English. qt. $6.00. Department of Philosophy, Jersey City State College, 2039 Kennedy Boulevard, Jersey City NJ 07305.

JOURNAL OF SIKH STUDIES. *See* Religion, Mythology, Rationalism.

JOURNAL OF THE DEPARTMENT OF PHILOSOPHY. **Main/Corp** Calcutta. University. Dept. of Philosophy. V. 1- 1975-. II. English. ir. 5.00 Single Copy. University of Calcutta, Department of Philosophy, Calcutta University, Publications Sales Counter, Asutosh Building, Calcutta India. **LC** B21. **DD** 105.

JOURNAL OF THE HISTORY OF IDEAS. V. 1- Jan. 1940-. 0022-5037. Periodical. US. English. qt. $10.00. Journal of the History of Ideas, Room 748/Humanities Building/Temple University, Philadelphia PA 19122. **Tel** (215)787-8591. **Ind/Abst** Soc. Sci. Citation Index, Book Rev. Index, Am. Hist. Life, Hist. Abstr., Humanit. Index, Women Stud. Abstr., Abstr. Engl. Stud., Years Work Eng. Stud., Philos. Index, MLA Int. Bibliogr. Books Artic. Mod. Lang. Lit. **LC** B1. **DD** 105. **NLM** B 1 J86. (cum index). Available on microfilm and microfiche.

JOURNAL OF THE HISTORY OF PHILOSOPHY. 1963. 0022-5053. Periodical. US. Multilingual (English, French and German). qt. $40.00. Washington University, Melanie Miller, St Louis MO 63130. **Tel** (314)432-8089. **Ed** Rudolf A Makkreel. **Ind/Abst** Philos. Index, Am. Hist. Life, Hist. Abstr., Humanit. Index, Hist. Abstr., Part A, Mod. Hist. Abstr., Hist. Abst., Part B, Twent. Century Abstr., Index Book Rev. Humanit. **LC** B1. **DD** 105. bk rev. adv acc. **Circ** 1,500. Available on microfilm from University Microfilms. International inscope consisting of articles, notes, discussions and book reviews on the history of philosophy, history of ideas, and intellectual history.

THE JOURNAL OF THE INDIAN ACADEMY OF PHILOSOPHY. **Main/Corp** Indian Academy of Philosophy. V. 1- July 1961/ Feb. 1962-. 0019-4271. Periodical. II. English. sa. $10.00. Indian Academy of Philosophy, Belgachia Villa Block F Flat 8, Calcutta 37 India. **LC** B1.

JOURNAL OF THE INTERDENOMINATIONAL THEOLOGICAL CENTER. *See* Religion, Mythology, Rationalism - Theology.

JOURNAL OF THE PHILOSOPHICAL SOCIETY. **Main/Corp** Philosophical Society (Fourah Bay College). V. 1- 1977-. SA. English. an. University of Sierra Leone, Philosophical Society, Freetown South Africa. **LC** B1. **DD** 105.

JOURNAL OF THOUGHT. *See* Education (General).

JOURNAL OF VALUE INQUIRY. (THE JOURNAL OF VALUE INQUIRY). V. 1- Spring 1967-. 0022-5363. Periodical. English. qt. Kluwer Academic Publishing Group, Distribution Center, PO Box 322, 3300 AH Dordrecht Netherlands. **Ind/Abst** Philos. Index, Index Book Rev. Humanit. **LC** BD232.

THE JOURNAL - SOCIETY FOR THE STUDY OF BLACK PHILOSOPHY (U.S.). (THE JOURNAL). **VFOAT** Journal for the Study of Black Philosophy. Vol. 1, No. 1 (Winter-Spring 1984)-. 0741-627X. Periodical. US. English. sa. $15.00. M B P I, 215 West 98th Street/ Suite 12B, New York NY 10025. **DD** 191.

KANT-STUDIEN. Vol. 1-. 0022-8877. Periodical. German (English and French). qt. $55.00. Walter de Gruyter, 200 Saw Mill River Road, Hawthorne NY 10532. **Tel** (914)747-0110. **Ed** G Funke and R Malter. **Ind/Abst** Philos. Index, Index Book Rev. Humanit. **LC** B2750. (cum index). bk rev. adv acc. **Circ** 1,000. Publishes papers, reports, and book reviews on the nvestigation and interpretation of Kantian philosophy.

KANTOVSKII SBORNIK. Vol. 6-. UR. Russian. 1.10. Kaliningradskii Gosudarstvennyi Universitet, Ul Universitetskaia 2, 236040 Kaliningrad Obl Russian SFSR. **LC** B2798. **DD** 142.305. *Voprosy Teoreticheskogo Naslediia Immanuila Kanta.*

KENNIS EN METHODE. **VFOAT** K & M. Vol. 1- 1977-. Periodical. NE. Dutch. qt. $39.71. Uitg Boom, Postbus 58, 7940 AB Meppel Netherlands. **Ed** L Bonn. **Ind/Abst** Philos. Index. bk rev. adv acc. **Circ** 600. Published for those interested in philosophy of science and methodology.

KHUDOZHESTVENNOE TVORCHESTVO. 1982-. Periodical. UR. Russian. an. 1.90. **LC** PN53.

Philosophy

KIERKEGAARDIANA. 1- 1955-. 0075-6032. DK. Danish. ir. Rosenkilde and Bagger, 3 Kron-Prinsens-Gade, Copenhagen Denmark. LC B4377. Meddelelser - Sren Kierkegaard Selskabet.

KINESIS. V. 1- Fall 1968-. 0023-1568. Periodical. US. English. sa. $7.50. Southern Illinois University, Department of Philosophy, Carbondale IL 62901. Tel (618)536-6641. Ed Stephen A Kennett. bk rev. adv acc. Circ 200. Founded to offer a forum for graduate students in all fields to express their philosophical views in a critical yet open-minded context.

KLEINE PHILOSOPHISCHE BIBLIOGRAPHIEN. See Bibliographies.

KRITIK. English. ir. Philosophical Society, c/o Philosophy Department, University of Singapore. LC B1. DD 105.

KUNST + UNTERRICHT. (KUNST + I.E. UND UNTERRICHT). VFOAT Kunst und Unterricht. Vol. 1- Sept. 1968-. 0023-5466. Periodical. GW. German. ir. $28.81. W E Saarbach GMBH, Postfach 10610, D5000 Koeln 1 West Germany. Tel 0221/20 83-1. LC BH61.

THE KUYPER NEWSLETTER. Vol. 1, No. 1 (Jan. 1980)-. Periodical. US. English. ty. Calvin College, Department of Philosophy, Grand Rapids MI 49506.

THE LAUGHING MAN. See Religion, Mythology, Rationalism.

LAVAL THEOLOGIQUE ET PHILOSOPHIQUE. See Religion, Mythology, Rationalism - Theology.

LAW AND PHILOSOPHY. See Law.

THE LIBERTARIAN DIGEST. See Political Science.

THE LIBRARY OF LIVING PHILOSOPHERS. V. 1- 1939-. 0075-9139. Monographic Series. US. English. ir. Open Court Publishing Co, Box 599, La Salle IL 61301. Tel (800)435-6850. Ed P A Schilpp.

LIBRARY OF THEORIA. Monographic Series. English. ir. Liber International, S-205 10 Malmo Sweden. Tel 46-40-70650. Ed Liber. Ind/Abst Math. Rev.

LINGUISTICS AND PHILOSOPHY. See Linguistics.

LISTENING. See Religion, Mythology, Rationalism.

THE LITTLE LAMP. See Religion, Mythology, Rationalism - Theology.

LOCKE NEWSLETTER. (THE LOCKE NEWSLETTER). No. 1- Autumn 1970-. 0307-2606. Periodical. UK. English. ir. University of York, c/o Mr Hall, Department of Philosophy, Heslington YO1 5OD England. Ind/Abst Philos. Index. LC B1250. DD 192.

LOGOS. Periodical. IT. Italian. ir. 8000. Libreria Scientifica, 80138 Napoli, Corso Umberto I, 38-40, Napoli Italy. Ind/Abst Philos. Index. LC B4. DD 105.

LOGOS. (LOGOS : PHILOSOPHIC ISSUES IN CHRISTIAN PERSPECTIVE). Vol. 1 (1980)-. 0276-5667. Periodical. US. English. an. $7.00. University of Santa Clara, c/o James W Felt SJ, Santa Clara CA 95053. Tel (408)554-4093. Ed James W Felt and George R Lucas. Ind/Abst Philos. Index. LC BR100. DD 190.5. Circ 100. Referred philosophic essays focusing in each issue on a single topic of particular interest to those concerned with philosophy's contribution to Christian humanism.

LOGOS: REVISTA DE LA FACULTAD DE FILOSOFIA Y LITRAS. Yearly V. 1- (No. 1-). Periodical. AG. Spanish. ir. Universidad de Buenos Aires, Buenos Aires Argentina. LC AP63. DD 056.

I A M. INSTITUTE OF APPLIED METAPHYSICS. (I AM). V. 1- Winter/Spring 1976-. 0381-9558. Periodical. CN. English (includes some text in French). sa. Institu ' Applied Metaphysics, 108 St-Ignace, N(ngue Quebec J0W 1R0 Canada. DD 110.5.

MACHIKANEYAMA RONSO : BIGAKUHEN. VFOAT Machikaneyama Ronso: Aesthetics. No. 9-. Japanese or French, summaries in English, French or German. ir. Osaka Daigaku Bungakubu, 1 Machikaneyamacho 1-Chome (560), Toyonaka Japan. LC BH8.J3.

MACHIKANEYAMA RONSO : TETSUGAKUHEN. VFOAT Machikaneyama Ronso. No. 5-. JA. Japanese (some summaries in English). ir. Osaka Daigaku Bungakubu, 1-1 Machikaneyamacho, Toyonaka Osaka Japan. LC B8.J3. Machikaneyama Ronso.

MAGYAR FILOZOFIAI SZEMLE. Vol. 1-. 0025-0090. Periodical. HU. Hungarian. bm. $23.50. Akademiai Kiado, PO Box 24, 1363 Budapest Hungary. Tel 111-010. Ed F Landvai. Ind/Abst Lang. Lang. Behav. Abstr., Philos. Index. Index published separately - free - automatically sent. Circ 1,950. (ctrl). Philosophical aspects of contemporary social and natural sciences as well as "traditional" philosophical issues. Results of new investigations. Critical studies.

MAINZER PHILOSOPHISCHE FORSCHUNGEN. V. 1- 1966-. 0076-2776. Monographic Series. German. ir. Verlag Herbert Grundmann, Am Hof 32 Postfach 1268, D-5300 Bonn 1 Germany.

MAN AND WORLD. V. 1- Feb. 1968-. 0025-1534. Periodical. English (articles in French, or German with summaries in English). qt. Kluwer Academic Publ Group, PO Box 322, 3300 AH Dordrecht Netherlands. Ind/Abst Philos. Index. LC B1.

MAN, ENVIRONMENT, SPACE & TIME. VFOAT Man, Environment, Space and Time. Vol. 1, No. 1 (Fall 1979)-. 0743-720X. Periodical. US. English. sa. $16.00. Man Environment Space & Time, B4 W Sibley Hall, c/o W Island, Ithaca NY 14853. Tel (607)256-652. adv acc. (ctrl).

MANUSCRITO. V. 1- Oct. 1977-. Periodical. English (French, Portuguese, and Spanish). ir. Cidade Universitaria, Barao Geraldo, Campinas Brazil. LC B1. DD 105.

MATERIALIEN ZUR GESCHICHTE DER RAMANUJA-SCHULE. 1-. Monographic Series. German. ir. LC AS142, B133.R366.

MAUM. VFOAT Journal of the Korea Philosophical Minds. V. 1-. Periodical. KO. English (Korean). ir. 900. EWHA Women's University, Department of Philosophy, Seoul 120 South Korea. LC B8.K6.

MEDIOEVO. 1- 1975-. Periodical. IT. English (Italian). $20.55. Editrice Antenore, Via G Rusca 15, 35100 Padova Italy. LC B720. DD 189.05.

MEMOIRS OF THE AMERICAN PHILOSOPHICAL SOCIETY HELD AT PHILADELPHIA FOR PROMOTING USEFUL KNOWLEDGE. (MEMOIRS OF THE AMERICAN PHILOSOPHICAL SOCIETY, PHILADELPHIA). Main/Corp American Philosophical Society. V. 1-. 0065-9738. Monographic Series. US. English. ir. American Philosophical Society, PO Box 493, Canton MA 02021. Ind/Abst Math. Rev., MLA Int. Bibliogr. Books Artic. Mod. Lang. Lit., GeoRef, Bibliogr. Index Geol. DD 506.273.

METAPHILOSOPHY. V. 1- Jan. 1970-. 0026-1068. Periodical. UK. English. qt. 36.00. Basil Blackwell Publishers, Journals Department, 108 Cowley Road, Oxford OX4 1JF England. Tel 0865-722146. Ed Terrell Ward Bynum. Ind/Abst Sociol. Abstr., Philos. Index, Lang. Lang. Behav. Abstr. LC B1. DD 105. bk rev. adv acc. Circ 600. Publishes articles and book reviews in a wide range of philosophical topics including the foundations, scope and function of philosophy.

METHOD (LOS ANGELES, CALIF.). (METHOD). Vol. 1, No. 1 (Spring 1983)-. 0736-7392. Periodical. US. English. sa. $20.00. Department of Philosophy, Loyola Marymount University, Loyola Blvd at W 80th Street, Los Angeles CA 90045. Tel (213)642-3379. Ed Mark D Morelli. LC BD241. DD 101.8. bk rev. Circ 250. Studies in interdisciplinary methodology, philosophy, and theology in contemporary thought.

METHODOLOGY AND SCIENCE. Jan. 1968-. 0543-6095. Periodical. NE. English (French). qt $28.75. Dr P H Esser, Beelslaan 20, 2012 PK Haarlem Netherlands. Tel 023-280290. Ed Piet H Esser. Ind/Abst Philos. Index. (cum index). bk rev. adv acc. Circ 250. (ctrl). Empirical study of the foundations of science and their methodology, psycho-linguistics, mutual understanding signifies.

MIDWEST STUDIES IN PHILOSOPHY. V. 1-. 0363-6550. Monographic Series. US. English. an. University of Minnesota Press, 2037 University Avenue Southeast, Minneapolis MN 55414. Tel (612)373-3266. Ed Peter French, Theodore E Uehling Jr and Howard K Wehstein. Ind/Abst Philos. Index. LC UNC. Each volume in the series is a collection of papers focusing on a single topic in philosophy.

MIND. V. 1-16 (No. 1-64), Jan. 1876-Oct. 1891. 0026-4423. Periodical. UK. English. qt. Basil Blackwell & Mott Ltd, 108 Cowley Road, Oxford OX41JF England. Ind/Abst Math. Rev., MLA Int. Bibliogr. Books Artic. Mod. Lang. Lit., Sociol. Abstr., Index Book Rev. Humanit., Humanit. Index, Philos. Index. LC B1. DD 190.5. NLM W1 MI619H. (cum index).

MIND; A QUARTERLY REVIEW OF PSYCHOLOGY AND PHILOSOPHY. See Psychology.

MITTEILUNGEN UND FORSCHUNGSBEITRAGE DER CUSANUS-GESELLSCHAFT. Main/Corp Cusanus Gesellschaft, Vereinigung zur Forderung der Cusanusforschun. Vol. 1 1961-. 0590-451X. Periodical. GW. German. an. 77.00. Matthias Grunewald Verlag KG, Max-Hufschmidt-Str 4A, D-6500 Mainz West Germany. Tel 6131-89055. Ed Rudolf Haubst. Ind/Abst MLA Int. Bibliogr. Books Artic. Mod. Lang. Lit. LC B765.N54. Articles and research on Nicholas of Crisa (1401-64) chief philosopher of 15th century, German cardinal, humanist, and early empiricist.

THE MODERN SCHOOLMAN. 1925. 0026-8402. Periodical. US. English. qt $26.00. The Modern Schoolman, St Louis University, College of Philosophy & Letters, 3700 West Pine Boulevard, St Louis MO 63108. Tel (314)652-3700. Ed Harry R Klocker SJ. Ind/Abst Cathol. Period. Lit. Index, Philos. Index. LC B1. bk rev. adv acc. Circ 650. Articles contain material dealing with all areas of philosophy for professional students.

THE MONIST. V. 1- Oct. 1890-. 0026-9662. Periodical. US. English. qt $24.00. Sugden Printing Company, Box 600, Lasalle IL 61301. Tel (815)223-1231. Ed John Hospers and Sherwood Sugden. Ind/Abst Philos. Index, Humanit. Index, Sociol. Abstr., Lang. Lang. Behav. Abstr. LC B1. DD 105. (cum index). bk rev. adv acc. Circ 1,600. International journal of philosophical inquiry, founded 1888. Each issue is devoted to a single topic in metaphysics, epistemology, ethics, aesthetics. Eight to twelve papers per issue.

MONOGRAPH OF THE SOCIETY FOR ASIAN AND COMPARATIVE PHILOSOPHY. Main/Corp Society for Asian and Comparative Philosophy. No. 1- 1974-. Monographic Series. US. English. ir. University of Hawaii Press, 2840 Kolowalu Street, Honolulu HI 96822. Tel (808)948-8697. Ed Eliot Deutsch. A monograph series on specialized topics in Asian and comparative philosophy. The monographs are more detailed than journal articles, more specialized, and of shorter length than standard books.

MONOGRAPHIEN ZUR NATURPHILOSOPHIE CEASED. Vol. 1- 1953-. 0544-8212. Monographic Series. GW. German. ir. Anthenaum Verlag GMBH, Adelhidstrabe 2, 6240 Konigstein/TS West Germany. Tel 067 53/ 24 88.

MONOGRAPHIEN ZUR PHILOSOPHISCHEN FORSCHUNG. Vol. 1- 1947-. Monographic Series. GW. German. ir. Verlag Anton Hain/Athenaeum, Postfach 1220, 6240 Koenigstein West Germany. Tel 06174/30 21. Ed Georgi Schischkoff. bk rev. adv acc. An analysis of a wide range of philosophical themes.

MOVEMENT. 1974. Newspaper. US. English. mo. $15.00. Movement, 3500 West Adams, Los Angeles CA 90018. Tel (213)737-1134. Ed Roberts C Taylor. bk rev. adv acc. Circ 5,000. (ctrl). Individual and world transformation, interviews, health, reviews, and the spiritual community.

NAUCHNYI ATEIZM. Began in 1971. UR. Russian. mo. $9.00. Victor Kamkin Inc, 12224 Parklawn Drive, Rockville MD 20852. Tel (301)881-5973. LC BL2747.3. DD 211.8.

NEKOTORYE FILOSOFSKIE VOPROSY SOVREMENNOGO ESTESTVOZNANIJA. (NEKOTORYE FILOSOFSKIE VOPROSY SOVREMENNOGO ESTESTVOZNANIIA). No. 1- 1973-. 0301-5386. UR. Russian. 0.66 Single Issue. LC B67. NLM W1 NE196C.

NEUE HEFTE FUR PHILOSOPHIE. Issue 1- 1971-. 0085-3917. GW. English or German. ir. Vandenhoeck & Ruprecht, Postfach 3753, Theaterstr

Philosophy

13, D-3400 Goettingen West Germany. Tel 0551/65061. Ed R Bubner, K Cramer and R Wiehl. Ind/Abst Philos. Index. LC B23.

NEW HUMANIST. V. 1, No. 1, May 1972. 0306-512X. Periodical. UK. English. bm. $10.73. Pemberton Publishing Company, 88 Islington High Street, London N1 8EL England. Tel 01-226-7251. LC AP4. DD 052. Humanist (London, England).

THE NEW PHILOSOPHY. V. 1- Mar. 1898-. 0028-6443. Periodical. US. English. qt. $4.00. Swedenborg, Scientific Association, Bryn Athyn PA 19009. Ed E J Broch. LC BX8701. DD 289.405. Circ 300. Studies of the philosophy of Emanuel Swedenborg and related subjects.

THE NEW SCHOLASTICISM. V. 1- Jan. 1927-. 0028-6621. Periodical. US. English. qt. American Catholic Philosophy Association, Catholic University, 403 Administration Building, Washington DC 20064. Tel (202)635-5518. Ind/Abst Annu. Bibliogr. Engl. Lang. Lit., Philos. Index, Cathol. Period. Lit. Index. LC B1. DD 105. (cum index). Circ 2,100. (ctrl).

NEW VICO STUDIES. 1983-. 0733-9542. Periodical. US. English. an. Humanities Press Inc, Atlantic Highlands NJ 07716. Ed Giorgio Tagliacozzo. LC B3580.A1. DD 195. bk rev. Circ 700. Includes Vico's works as well as ideas that are Vichian in nature involved in Vico's thoughts.

NIETZSCHE-STUDIEN. VFOAT Nietzsche Studien. Vol. 1- 1972-. 0342-1422. WB. German (English). an. Walter de Gruyter, 200 Saw Mill River Road, Hawthorne NY 10532. Tel (914)747-0110. Ind/Abst MLA Int. Bibliogr. Books Artic. Mod. Lang. Lit. LC B3310.

NOCTES ROMANAE. V. 1-. 0078-0936. Monographic Series. SZ. German. ir. Paul Haupt Bern, 3001 Bern Falkenplatz 14, 031 23 24 25 Switzerland. Tel 031 23 24 25. Ed Georg Luck. Edition of books on Roman and Greek philosophy and philology (thesis, inaugural dissertations etc.).

NOTES ET DOCUMENTS (INSTITUT INTERNATIONAL JACQUES MARITAIN). (NOTES ET DOCUMENTS). VFOAT Notes et Documents de l'Institut International Jacques Maritain. Yearly V. 1, No. 1, (Dec. 1975)-. Periodical. IT. French. qt. $20.00. Institut International, Jaques Maritain, 16 Via Rovigo 001616 Roma Italy. LC B2430.M34. DD 194.

NOTRE DAME JOURNAL OF FORMAL LOGIC. V. 1- Jan. 1960-. 0029-4527. Periodical. US. English. qt $40.00. Notre Dame Journal of Formal Logic, Box 5, Notre Dame IN 46556. Tel 2396157. Ed M Detlefsen, K Fine, M Nadel, H Wettstein. Ind/Abst Math. Rev., Electron. Commun. Abstr. J., ISMEC Bull., Pollut. Abstr. Indexes, Saf. Sci. Abstr. J., Philos. Index, Comput. Control Abstr., Electr. Electron. Abstr., Sci. Abstr. Sect. A. Phys. Abstr., Phys. Abstr. LC BC1. CODEN NDJFAM. (cum index). adv acc. Circ 800. Publishes work in areas of philosophical and mathematical logic, philosophy of language, normal semantics for natural languages, philosophy, history and foundations of logic and mathematics.

NOUS. V. 1- Mar. 1967-. 0029-4624. Periodical. US. English. ir. $38.50. Department of Philosophy, Sycamore Hall 126/Indiana University, Bloomington IN 47401. Tel (812)335-5676. Ed Hector-Neri Castaneda. Ind/Abst Index Book Rev. Humanit., Lang. Lang. Behav. Abstr., Math. Rev., Philos. Index, Sociol. Abstr. LC B1. bk rev. adv acc. Circ 1,000. Publishes outstanding essays that extend the frontiers of philosophical research, emphasizing positive theoretical work that takes full account of current philosophical developments.

NOUVEAU DIALOGUE. No. 10- Jan. 1975-. 0317-1442. CN. French. qt. 75. Per No. Service Incroyance et Foi, 2930 rue LaCombe, Montreal Quebec H3T 1L4 Canada. DD 200.1.

NOUVELLES CARTESIENNES. VFOAT Cartesian Newsletter. 1 (Sept. 1980)-. NE. French (English). ir. Quadratures, Boite Postale 6463, NL-1005 El Amsterdam Netherlands.

NOVAIA INOSTRANNAIA LITERATURA PO OBSHCHESTVENNYM NAUKAM : FILOSOFIIA I SOTSIOLOGIIA. 1976-. UR. Multilingual (Russian). mo. 0.40. Akademiia Nauk SSR, Ul Krasikova 28/45, Moskva USSR. LC Z7127, B53. Novaia Inostrannaia Literatura Po Filosofii.

NOVAIA SOVETSKAIA LITERATURA PO OBSHCHESTVENNYM NAUKAM : FILOSOFSKIE NAUKI. 1976-. UR. Russian. mo. 0.20 Single Issue. Akademiia Nauk SSSR, Ul Krasikova 28/45, Moskva Russia. LC Z7129.R9, B4201. Novaia Sovetskaia Literatura po Filosofii.

NOVINKY LITERATURY : FILOSOFIE. Multilingual (Czech). ir. 40.00. Statni Knihovna CSR, Liliova 5, Praha Czechslovakia. LC Z7127, B53. Novinky Literatury. Spolecenske Vedy. Rada I: Filosoficke Vedy.

NUOVA CORRENTE. 1- June 1954-. 0029-6155. Periodical. IT. Italian. ir. 28.000. Tilgher Genova S A S, Via Assarotti 52, 16122 Genova Italy. Tel (010)891140. Ed M Boselli, G Franck, G Sertoli and S Verdino. Ind/Abst Abstr. Engl. Stud., MLA Int. Bibliogr. Books Artic. Mod. Lang. Lit., Sociol. Abstr., Lang. Lang. Behav. Abstr. bk rev. adv acc. Circ 1,000. Particularly careful to the modern theories of textual criticism and to the relation between literature and philosophy.

THE OBJECTIVIST FORUM. Vol. 1, No. 1 (Feb. 1980)-. 0198-7607. Periodical. US. English. bm. $20.00. The Objectivist Forum, PO Box 5311, FDR Station, New York NY 10022. Tel (212)758-7848. Ed Harry Binswanger. LC B1. DD 149. bk rev. Circ 2,600. The philosophy of any Rand and its application to the humanities, the arts and current issues.

OBSHCHESTVENNYE NAUKI V SSSR. SERIIA 3 : FILOSOFSKIE NAUKI. VFOAT Filosofskie Nauki. VAT Obshchestvennye Nauki V SSSR. Seriia Tri: Filosofskie Nauki. Began in 1973. Periodical. UR. Russian. bm. Akademiia Nauk SSR, G-19 Ul Krasikova 28/45, Moskva USSR. LC Z7128.D5, B809.8.

OCCASIONAL RESEARCH PAPERS - DEPARTMENT OF RELIGIOUS STUDIES AND PHILOSOPHY, MAKERERE UNIVERSITY. See Religion, Mythology, Rationalism.

ORIGINS RESEARCH. 0748-9919. Periodical. US. English. sa. $5.00 for 2 years. Origins Research, PO Box 203, Goleta CA 93116. Tel (805)967-8951. Ed Dennis A Wagner. DD 113. bk review. Circ 5,000. Newspaper journal that examines scientific and philosophical evidence related to creation and evolution. Often features debates and reviews of current literature.

THE OWL OF MINERVA. (THE OWL OF MINERVA : QUARTERLY JOURNAL OF THE HEGEL SOCIETY OF AMERICA). Began with: Vol. 1 (Summer 1969). 0030-7580. Periodical. US. English. sa. $16.00. Villanova University, LS Stepelevich/Department of Philosophy, Villanova PA 19085. Tel (215)645-4747. Ed Lawrence S Stepelevich. Ind/Abst Philos. Index. DD 193. bk rev. adv acc. Circ 550. Official journal of Hegel Society of America features articles, book reviews and notes on Hegel and contemporaries, Hegelianism today and idealistic philosophy in general.

OXFORD STUDIES IN ANCIENT PHILOSOPHY. Vol. 1 (1983)-. Periodical. UK. English. an. Oxford University Press, Saxon Way West/Corby, Northants NN18 9ES England. LC B1. DD 180.5.

PACIFIC PHILOSOPHICAL QUARTERLY. Vol. 61, No. 1/2 (Jan./Apr. 1980)-. 0279-0750. Periodical. US. English. qt. $30.00. University of Southern California, School of Philosophy, 3518 University Avenue, Los Angeles CA 90007. Tel (213)743-5630. Ed Raymond Neal. Ind/Abst Philos. Index, Humanit. Index, Annu. Bibliogr. Engl. Lang. Lit. LC AP2. DD 105. adv acc. Circ 1,000. Philosophy journal. Personalist, 0031-5621.

PAIDEIA. V. 1- 1972-. 0190-1176. Periodical. US. English. an. Paideia Journal Fund, Faculty-Student Association, State University College of Buffalo, 1300 Elmwood Avenue, Buffalo NY 14222. Ind/Abst MLA Int. Bibliogr. Books Artic. Mod. Lang. Lit. LC B1.

THE PAKISTAN PHILOSOPHICAL JOURNAL. V. 1- July 1957-. 0552-914X. Periodical. English (Urdu). ir. Ind/Abst Philos. Index. LC B1.

PANTHEIST VISION. (PANTHEIST VISION : THE NEWSLETTER OF THE UNIVERSAL PANTHEIST SOCIETY). 0742-5368. Periodical. US. English. ir. $8.00. Universal Pantheist Society, PO Box 265, Big Pine CA 93513. Tel (209)739-8527. Ed Harold Wood. bk rev. (ctrl). Philosophical works regarding the place of people within the universe, and the value of nature as the ultimate context for human experience.

PATRISTICA ET MEDIAEVALIA. Vol. 1-. 0325-2280. Periodical. Latin (Spanish). ir. LC B5.

PENSAMIENTO. 0031-4749. Periodical. SP. Spanish. qt. Centro Loyola, Pablo Aranda 3, Madrid 6 Spain. Tel 262 49 30. Ind/Abst Philos. Index. LC B5.

PETITE REVUE DE PHILOSOPHIE. (LA PETITE REVUE DE PHILOSOPHIE). V. 1- Fall 1979-. 0709-4469. Periodical. CN. French. sa. $10.00. Secretariat General, College Edouard-Montpetit, 945 Chemin de Chambly, Longueil Quebec J4H 3M6 Canada. Tel (514)679-2630. Ed Claude Glasson. LC B2. DD 001.205. adv acc. Circ 400. (ctrl). Digest of vulgarised analysis or reflection on any subject of life, mind or facts. No thematic.

PHAENOMENOLOGICA. 1- 1958-. 0079-1350. Monographic Series. NE. French (English and German). ir. Martinus Nijhoff Publishers, PO Box 163, Spul Boulevard 50, 3300AD Dordrecht The Netherlands.

PHANOMENOLOGISCHE FORSCHUNGEN. V. 1-. Monographic Series. GW. German (English, French). ir. Verlag Karl Alber, Hermann-Herder-Strasse 4, D-7800 Freiburg West Germany.

PHENOMENOLOGICAL INQUIRY. Vol. 9 (Oct. 1985)-. 0885-3886. Periodical. US. English. an. $10.00. The World Institute for Advanced Phenomenological Research and Learning, 348 Payson Road, Belmont MA 02178. DD 142. Phenomenology Information Bulletin, 0278-8322.

PHENOMENOLOGY AND PEDAGOGY. (PHENOMENOLOGY + PEDAGOGY). VAT Phenomenology Plus Pedagogy. Vol. 1, No. 1 (1983)-. 0820-9189. Periodical. CN. English. ty. 35.00. Publication Services, 4-116 Education North/University Of Alberta, Edmonton Alta T6G 2E1 Canada. DD 370.15. A human science journal dedicated to interpretive and critical studies of a broad range of pedagogic relations and situations.

PHENOMENOLOGY INFORMATION BULLETIN. No. 1- Oct. 1977-. 0278-8322. Periodical. US. English. an. $10.00. World Institute for Advanced Phenomenological Research and Learning, 348 Payson Road, Belmont MA 02178. Tel (617)489-3696. Ed Anna-Teresa Tymieniecka. bk rev. adv acc. Circ 1,000. This journal is a unique forum for phenomenological ideas and information from the entire world.

PHI ZERO. V. 1- Jan./Feb. 1973-. 0318-4412. CN. French. ir. $11.61. University of Montreal, Department de Philosophie, CP 6128, Montreal Que H3C 3J7 Canada. Tel (514)343-6464. Ind/Abst Point Repere. DD 105.

PHILOCRITIQUE. No. 1 (Winter 81)-. 0820-7313. Periodical. CN. French. sa. $3.00 Per No., $6.00 Per Year Individuals; $10.00 Per Year Institutions. Philocritique, c/o Module de Philosophie Universite du Quebec A, Montreal C P 8888 Succursale A, Montreal Quebec H3C 3P8 Canada. DD 105.

THE PHILOSOPHER. V. 1-25. Periodical. UK. English. an. $4.60. Philosophical Society of England, Dr P Fauch, 78 St Andrews Road, Portslade Brighton E Sussex BN4 1DE England. Tel 0273 414 204. Ed Martin Hughes. LC B1. bk rev. adv acc. Circ 600. (ctrl). Philosophy studies by professionals and amateurs. The society conducts study courses for its diplomas of associate and fellow.

THE PHILOSOPHER'S ANNUAL. V. 1- 1978-. 0162-234X. US. English. an. Rowman and Littlefield, Totowa NJ. LC B1. DD 105.

THE PHILOSOPHER'S INDEX. See Indexes/Abstracts.

PHILOSOPHIA. 1- 1971-. English, French, German, or Greek with summaries in one of the languages. ir. 20.00. Kentron Ereunes Tes Hellenikes Philosophias, 14 Anagnostopoulou Street T T 136, 106 73 Athens Greece. Tel 36 00 140. Ed Anna Kelesidou. Ind/Abst Philos. Index. LC B31. DD 105. bk rev. Circ 1,000. (ctrl). Theory, history, reviews, and news.

PHILOSOPHIA. V. 1-Jan. 1971-. 0554-0690. Periodical. IS. English. qt. 19.00. Bar-Llan University, Department of Philosophy, Rmat-Gan Israel. Tel 3-718257. Ed Asa Kasher. bk rev. adv acc. All subjects of philosophy.

Philosophy

PHILOSOPHIA ANTIQUA. V.1- 1946-. 0079-1687. Monographic Series. NE. English (text in French, Greek, Italian). ir. EJ Brill, POB 9000, 2300 PA Leiden The Netherlands.

PHILOSOPHIA NATURALIS. Vol. 1. 0031-8027. Periodical. GW. English (German). ir. 145.-. Verlag Anton Hain Athenaeum, Postfach 1220, 6240 Koenigstein West Germany. **Tel** (06753)4353. **Ed** Joseph Meurers. **Ind/Abst** Math. Rev., Philos. Index, Energy Res. Abstr. **LC** B3. **DD** 105. bk rev. adv acc. **Circ** 600.

PHILOSOPHIA PATRUM. V. 1- 1971-. Periodical. NE. Dutch. ir. EJ Brill, POB 9000, 2300 PA Leiden The Netherlands.

PHILOSOPHIA REFORMATA. (PHILOSOPHIA REFORMATA : ORGAAN VAN DE VERENIGING VOOR CALVINISTISCHE WIJSBEGEERTE). Began with issue for 1. quarterly 1936. 0031-8035. NE. Dutch (and English). sa. $21.56. Association of Calvinistic Philosophy, Box 1149, 3600 BC Maarssen Netherlands. **Tel** 03465-60945. **Ind/Abst** Philos. Index. **LC** BX9401. (cum index). bk rev. adv acc. **Circ** 700. (ctrl). Scientific articles on all sorts of subjects from a reformational-philosophical point of view.

PHILOSOPHIC EXCHANGE. V. 1- 1970-. 0193-5046. US. English. ir. $5.00 Institutions, $3.00 Individuals. Center for Philosophic Exchange, State University of New York, College of Arts and Science, Brockport NY 14420. **Ind/Abst** Philos. Index. **LC** B21. **DD** 105.

PHILOSOPHICA. V. 13- 1974-. BE. Dutch (English). sa. $12.00. Rijksuniversiteir Gent, Rozier 44, B-9000 Gent Belgium. **Tel** 091/25 75 71. **Ed** Diderik Batens. **Ind/Abst** Philos. Index. **LC** B63. bk rev. adv acc. **Circ** 350. A journal of philosophical inquiry devoted to current epistemological, axiological and social political issues. *Philosophica Gandensia.*

PHILOSOPHICA, AESTHETICA. **Main/Corp** Olomouc, Moravia. Palackejp Universita. Filosoficka Fakulta. 1- 1964-. 0474-1021. Monographic Series. Czech, English or German some articles have summaries in Russian and German. ir. **LC** B26.

PHILOSOPHICAL BOOKS. V. 1- Jan. 1960-. 0031-8051. Periodical. UK. English. qt. 27.50. Basil Blackwell Publications, 108 Cowley Road, Oxford STD England. **Tel** 0865 722146. **Ed** Anthony Ellis. **Ind/Abst** Philos. Index, Index Book Rev. Humanit. **LC** Z7127. **DD** 105. bk rev. adv acc. **Circ** 700. Publishes scholarly reviews to assist both librarians and individuals in the choice of professional works of philosophy.

PHILOSOPHICAL CURRENTS. Periodical. English. ir. BR Gruner BV, Nieuwe Herengracht 31, 1011 RM Amsterdam Netherlands. **Tel** 20-264371. **Ed** David H DeGrood. **Circ** 400. Series dedicated to bringing philosophy back into mainstream of intellectual and political life and presenting works involved with important issues of our revolutionary age.

PHILOSOPHICAL FORUM. (THE PHILOSOPHICAL FORUM). V. 1-23, 1943-65. 0031-806X. Periodical. US. English. qt. $35.00. Baruch College of C U N Y, Box 239, Lexington Avenue, New York NY 10010. **Tel** (212)505-2154. **Ed** Marx Wartofsky. **Ind/Abst** Math. Rev., Philos. Index. **LC** B1. **DD** 105. bk rev. adv acc. **Circ** 2,000. Purpose is to provide open-minded discussions which aim not so much at agreement as at lively response.

PHILOSOPHICAL INVESTIGATIONS. V. 1- Winter 1978-. 0190-0536. Periodical. US. English. qt. Basil Blackwell Publisher, 108 Cowley Road, Oxford OX4 IJF England. **Tel** (217)424-6266. **LC** B1. **DD** 149.9405.

PHILOSOPHICAL MAGAZINE. B. PHYSICS OF CONDENSED MATTER. ELECTRONIC, OPTICAL AND MAGNETIC PROPERTIES. (PHILOSOPHICAL MAGAZINE B). V. 37- Jan. 1978-. 0141-8637. Periodical. UK. English (French or German with summaries in English). mo. $320.00. Bankers Trust Co, PO Box 9137 Church Street Station, New York NY 10049. **Ind/Abst** Eng. Index Annu., Eng. Index Mon., Eng. Index Bioeng. Abstr., Eng. Index Energy Abstr., GeoRef, Comput. Control Abstr., Electr. Electron. Abstr., Sci. Abstr. Sect. A. Phys. Abstr., Met. Abstr., World Alum. Abstr., Chem. Abstr. **CODEN** PMABDJ. Index in last issue of volume - attached. *Philosophical Magazine, 0031-8086.*

PHILOSOPHICAL PAPERS. V. 1- 1972-. Periodical. English. ir. **Ind/Abst** Philos. Index.

PHILOSOPHICAL QUARTERLY. (THE PHILOSOPHICAL QUARTERLY). V. 1- Oct. 1950-. 0031-8094. Periodical. UK. English. qt. 27.50. Scottish Academic Press Ltd, 33 Montgomery Street, Edinburgh EH7 5JX Scotland. **Tel** (0865)722146. **Ed** Leslie Stevenson. **Ind/Abst** Humanit. Index, Index Book Rev. Humanit., Lang. Lang. Behav. Abstr., Math. Rev., MLA Int. Bibliogr. Books Artic. Mod. Lang. Lit., Philos. Index, Sociol. Abstr. **LC** B1. **DD** 105. bk rev. adv acc. **Circ** 1,500. Available on microfilm from University Microfilms. Aims to foster and publish significant contributions in every branch of the subject, promoting discussion of recent philosophical work.

THE PHILOSOPHICAL REVIEW. V. 1- (No. 1-). 0031-8108. Periodical. US. English. qt. $34.00 Domestic, $39.00 Foreign. Philosophical Review, Cornell University, 220 Goldwin Smith Hall, Ithaca NY 14853-3120. **Tel** (607)272-6467. **Ed** Helen Taylor-Way. **Ind/Abst** MLA Int. Bibliogr. Books Artic. Mod. Lang. Lit., Sociol. Abstr., Soc. Welf. Soc. Plan./ Policy Soc. Dev., Annu. Bibliogr. Engl. Lang. Lit., Book Rev. Index, Index Book Rev. Humanit., Humanit. Index, Lang. Lang. Behav. Abstr., Philos. Index, Soc. Sci. Citation Index, Am. Hist. Life, Hist. Abstr., Hist. Abstr., Part A, Mod. Hist. Abstr., Hist. Abst., Part B, Twent. Century Abstr. **LC** B1. (cum index). bk rev. adv acc. **Circ** 3,200. (ctrl). Topics of contemporary philosophy discussed, ranging from logic to philosophy of science, mathematics, language and history of philosophy. Book reviews and articles in every issue.

PHILOSOPHICAL STUDIES. V. 1- Jan. 1950-. 0031-8116. Periodical. English. bm. $120. Kluwer Academic Publishers, PO Box 322, 3300 AH Dordrecht Netherlands. **Tel** (31)78-334911. **Ed** John Pollock. **Ind/Abst** Annu. Bibliogr. Engl. Lang. Lit., Index Book Rev. Humanit., Lang. Lang. Behav. Abstr., Math. Rev., MLA Int. Bibliogr. Books Artic. Mod. Lang. Lit., Philos. Index, Sociol. Abstr., Cathol. Period. Lit. Index. **LC** B21. **DD** 108.2. adv acc. **Circ** 900. Philosophy in the analytic tradition. Epistemalogy, philosophical logic, the philosophy of language, and ethics.

PHILOSOPHICAL STUDIES (DUBLIN, IRELAND). (PHILOSOPHICAL STUDIES). Began in June 1951. 0554-0739. Periodical. IE. English. an. 14.50 Domestic, $22.00 Foreign. Philosophical Studies, 58 Trimleston Gardens, Booterstown County, Dublin Ireland. **Tel** 692693. **Ed** James Bastalle. **Ind/Abst** Philos. Index, Cathol. Period. Lit. Index. **LC** WMLC L 82/255. bk rev. Contemporary philosophy with references to theological, social and scientific reflection.

PHILOSOPHICAL STUDIES IN EDUCATION. **Main/Corp** Ohio Valley Philosophy of Education Society. 1976-. 0160-7561. US. English. an. $8.00. Robert Morris Col, c/o Dr R J Skovira, Narrows Run Road, Coraopolis PA 15108. **Tel** (412)262-8257. **Ed** Robert J Skovira. **Ind/Abst** Philos. Index. **LC** L107. **DD** 370.1. **Circ** 200. (ctrl). Microform. An annual proceeding of refereed essays dealing with issues and topics in philosophy of education. *Proceedings of the Annual Meeting of the Ohio Valley Philosophy of Education Society, 0092-8178.*

PHILOSOPHICAL STUDIES SERIES IN PHILOSOPHY. V. 1- 1974-. 0169-7323. Monographic Series. NE. English. ir. Kluwer Academic Publishing Group, 190 Old Derby Street, Hingham MA 02043. **Ind/Abst** Math. Rev.

PHILOSOPHICAL TOPICS. Vol. 12, No. 1 (Spring 1981)-. 0276-2080. Periodical. US. English. ty. $35.00. Philosophical Topics, 605 Dale Hall, 455 West Lindsey Street, Norman OK 73019. **Tel** (501)575-3551. **Ed** Christopher Hill. **Ind/Abst** Philos. Index. **LC** B1. **DD** 105. adv acc. **Circ** 600. Issues on designated topics: epistemology, value theory, and history of philosophy. *Southwestern Journal of Philosophy, 0038-481X.*

PHILOSOPHICAL TRANSACTIONS OF THE ROYAL SOCIETY OF LONDON. SERIES B. BIOLOGICAL SCIENCES. **Main/Corp** Royal Society (Great Britain). V. 224- 1935-. 0080-4622. Monographic Series. UK. English. ir. 264.00. The Royal Society, 6 Carlton House Terrace, London SW1Y 5AG England. **Tel** (01)839-5561. **Ind/Abst** Life Sci. Collect., Excerpta Med., GeoRef, Biol. Abstr., Chem. Abstr., Index Med., Bibliogr. Agric. **NLM** W1 PH606. **CODEN** PTRBAE. Index published separately - free - automatically sent. (cum index). **Circ** 950. Original papers at post graduate level on mathematical and physical subjects. *Philosophical Transactions of the Royal Society of London. Series B. Containing Papers of a Biological Character.*

PHILOSOPHIE (PARIS, FRANCE : 1984). (PHILOSOPHIE). No. 1 (Jan. 1984)-. 0294-1805. Periodical. French. qt. **Tel** 222.37.94.

PHILOSOPHIE (TOULOUSE, FRANCE). (PHILOSOPHIE). Began with 1972 Vol. FR. French. an. $9.05. Regisseur d'Service, Publications l'Universite d'Toulouse-Mirail, 56 rue Taur, 31000 Toulouse France. **Tel** 23 07 50. **LC** B2. **DD** 105.

PHILOSOPHIQUES. V. 1- Apr. 1974-. 0316-2923. Periodical. CN. French (summaries in English). sa. $20.00. Les Editions Bellamin, 8100 Boulevard St Laurent, Montreal PQ H2P 2LP Canada. **Tel** (514)387-2541. **Ind/Abst** Point Repere, Philos. Index. **LC** B2. **DD** 105.

PHILOSOPHISCHE ABHANDLUNGEN. Monographic Series. GW. German. ir. Vittorio Klostermann, Ptfh 900601, Frauenlobstrasse 22, 6000 Frankfurt 90 West Germany. **Tel** 0611/ 77 40 11. **Ind/Abst** Math. Rev.

PHILOSOPHISCHE RUNDSCHAU. Vol. 1-. 0031-8159. Periodical. GW. German English and French. qt. 94.-. JCB Mohr and Paul Siebeck, Postfach 2040, 7400 Tuebingen West Germany. **Tel** (07071)26064. **Ed** Rudiger Bubner and Bernhard Waldenfels. **Ind/Abst** Philos. Index. **LC** B3. **DD** 105. (cum index). bk rev. adv acc. **Circ** 1,250. Has a general outlook on trends, schools and research programs and fulfills an important function in an age where the unity of philosophy yields to ever growing specialization in isolated discipines as well as national traditions.

PHILOSOPHISCHE RUNDSCHAU. BEIHEFT. 1-. 0554-0828. Monographic Series. GW. German. qt. 94.-. JCB Mohr/Paul Siebeck, Postfach 2040, 7400 Tuebingen West Germany. **Tel** (089)2717746. **Ed** Christin Waldenfels. (cum index). bk rev. **Circ** 1,250. (ctrl). Follows the international publications in philsophy with general outlook in trends, schools and research programs.

PHILOSOPHISCHER LITERATURANZEIGER. Volume 1- 1949-. 0031-8175. Periodical. GW. German. qt. 129.-. Verlag Anton Hain/Athenaeum, Postfach 180, D-6554 Meisenheim West Germany. **Tel** (06753)4353. **Ed** R Luthe, S Nachtsheim and G Wolandt. bk rev. adv acc. **Circ** 800. Reviews of philosophical books only for philosophers, students of philosophy, university libraries, etc.

PHILOSOPHISCHES JAHRBUCH. *See* Yearbooks, Almanacs, Directories.

PHILOSOPHY. (PHILOSOPHY : THE JOURNAL OF THE BRITISH INSTITUTE OF PHILOSOPHICAL STUDIES). V. 6- (No. 22-). 0031-8191. Periodical. UK. English. qt. $120.00. Cambridge University Press, 32 East 57th Street, New York NY 10022. **Tel** (212)688-8888. **Ed** Renford Bambrough. **Ind/Abst** Index Book Rev. Humanit., Humanit. Index. bk rev. adv acc. **Circ** 2,200. Promotes the study of philosophy in all its branches: logic metaphysics, epistemology, ethics, aesthetics, social and political philosophy and the philosophies of religion, science, history, language, mind and education. *Journal of Philosophical Studies.*

PHILOSOPHY. V. 1- Jan. 1926-. 0031-8205. Periodical. UK. English. bm. $120.00. Cambridge University Press, 510 North Avenue, New Rochelle NY 10801. **Ed** Renford Barnbrough. **Ind/Abst** Sociol. Abstr., Am. Hist. Life, Hist. Abstr., Humanit. Index, Lang. Lang. Behav. Abstr., Hist. Abstr., Part A, Mod. Hist. Abstr., Hist. Abst., Part B, Twent. Century Abstr. **LC** B1. bk rev. Available on microfilm. Concerned with the study of logic, metaphysics, aesthetics, social and political philosophy and the philosophies of religion, science, history, language, mind and education.

PHILOSOPHY AND HISTORY. V. 1- 1968-. 0016-884X. Periodical. GW. English. be. 39.—. German Studies, Landhausstrasse 18, 7400 Tuebingen West Germany. **Tel** (08081)262246. **Ed** H Holnholz. **LC** Z7127. **DD** 105. (ctrl). Covers philosophy and history.

PHILOSOPHY AND LITERATURE. V. 1- Fall 1976-. 0190-0013. Periodical. US. English. sa. $26.00. Johns Hopkins University Press, 701 West

Philosophy

40th Street/Suite 275, Baltimore MD 21211. Tel (301)338-6987. Ed Denis Dutton. Ind/Abst Abstr. Engl. Stud., Index Book Rev. Humanit., MLA Int. Bibliogr. Books Artic. Mod. Lang. Lit., Philos. Index. LC PN2. DD 809. bk rev. adv acc. Circ 1,066. Uses literature to illuminate philosophy, exploring the literary aspects of philosophical writing and classical philosophical texts.

PHILOSOPHY AND MEDICINE. V. 1- 1975-. 0376-7418. Monographic Series. US. English. ir. Kluwer Boston Inc, 190 Old Derby Street, Hingham MA 02043. Ed H T Engelhardt Jr and S F Spicker. Ind/Abst Biol. Abstr. NLM W3 PH609. CODEN PHIMDN.

PHILOSOPHY AND PHENOMENOLOGICAL RESEARCH. V. 1- Sept. 1940-. 0031-8205. Periodical. US. English. qt. $17.00 Domestic, $18.50 Foreign. Philosophy & Phenomenological Research, Box 1947 Brown University, Providence RI 02912. Tel (401)863-3215. Ed Roderick M Chisholm and Ernest Sosa. Ind/Abst MLA Int. Bibliogr. Books Artic. Mod. Lang. Lit., Annu. Bibliogr. Engl. Lang. Lit., Index Book Rev. Humanit., Philos. Index, Psychol. Abstr., Sociol. Abstr., Lang. Lang. Behav. Abstr. LC B1. DD 105. CODEN PPHRAI. bk rev. adv acc. Circ 2,000. Available on microfiche from Johnson Associates., Available on microfilm from Xerox University Microfilms. Published in a wide range of areas including philosophy of mind, epistemology, ethics, metaphysics, and philosophical history of philosophy.

PHILOSOPHY & RHETORIC. VAT Philosophy and Rhetoric. V. 1- Jan. 1968-. 0031-8213. Periodical. US. English. qt. Pennsylvania State University Press, 215 Wagner Building, University Park PA 16802. Tel (814)865-1327. Ind/Abst Abstr. Engl. Stud., MLA Int. Bibliogr. Books Artic. Mod. Lang. Lit., Philos. Index, Index Book Rev. Humanit., Lang. Lang. Behav. Abstr., Sociol. Abstr., Abstr. Engl. Stud. LC B1. DD 105. UD 105.

PHILOSOPHY EAST & WEST. VAT Philosophy East and West. V. 1- Apr. 1951-. 0031-8221. Periodical. US. English. qt. $20.00. University of Hawaii Press, 2840 Kolowalu Street, Honolulu HI 96822. Tel (808)948-8697. Ed Eliot Deutsch. Ind/Abst Humanit. Index, MLA Int. Bibliogr. Books Artic. Mod. Lang. Lit., Sociol. Abstr., Philos. Index, Index Book Rev. Humanit. LC B1. DD 105. bk rev. adv acc. Circ 1,400. Journal of Asian and comparative thought, with specialized articles that relate philosophy to the arts, literature, science, and social practice of Asian civilizations.

THE PHILOSOPHY FORUM CEASED. V. 7-16. 0031-823X. Periodical. US. English. qt. $51.00. Ind/Abst Math. Rev., Philos. Index, Humanit. Index. Pacific Philosophy Forum, 0275-1194.

PHILOSOPHY IN CONTEXT. V. 1- 1972-. 0742-2733. Periodical. US. English. an. $4.00. Cleveland State University Philosophy Department, Euclid Avenue at East 24th Street, Cleveland OH 44115. Tel (216)687-3900. Ed Richard M Fox. Ind/Abst Philos. Index. LC B1. DD 105. adv acc. Circ 200. Original philosophical essays on topics of current interest for students and scholars in other disciplines as well as professional philosophers.

PHILOSOPHY RESEARCH ARCHIVES. See Genealogy and Heraldry - Archives.

PHILOSOPHY TODAY. V. 1- Mar. 1957-. 0031-8256. Periodical. US. English. qt. $15.00. Philosophy Today, Carthagena Station, Celina OH 45822. Tel (419)925-4121. Ed Robert F Lechner. Ind/Abst Cathol. Period. Lit. Index, Cathol. Period. Index, Philos. Index, Repert. Bibliogr. Philos., Humanit. Index, Philos. Index. LC B1. DD 150.5. bk rev. adv acc. Circ 1,350. Available on microfilm from University Microfilms. Trends and interest of contemporary philosophy: existentialism, phenomenology, hermeneutics, post-structuralism, philosophy of language.

DE PHILSOSPHIA. No. 1- 1980-. 0228-412X. CN. English (includes some text in French). an. Student Association, Department of Philosophy, University of Ottawa, 90 Wilbrod Street, Ottawa Ontario Canada. Ind/Abst Philos. Index. DD 105.

PHRONESIS. V. 1- Nov. 1955-. 0031-8868. Periodical. NE. English (French, German or Latin). ir. $27.85. Van Gorcum & Company, BV PO Box 43, 9400 AA Assen Netherlands. Ind/Abst Philos. Index, Index Book Rev. Humanit. LC B1. DD 180. Index in last issue of volume - attached. (cum index).

PHRONESIS, A JOURNAL FOR ANCIENT PHILOSOPHY. 0031-8868. Periodical. English. ir. Tel 05920-46846. bk rev. adv acc. Circ 1,100. (ctrl). An international journal focused on the study of philosophy from its very beginning to the sixth century after Christ.

PRAJNALOKA (NAGPUR, INDIA). (PRAJNALOKA). Periodical. Marathi. qt. 10.00. Bharatiya Dharana Samiti, Ruikar Road, Nagpur 440002 India. LC DS423.

PRESENCA FILOSOFICA. No. 1/3- 1974-. BL. Portuguese. ir. $25.00. Sociedade Brasileira de Filosofos Catolicos, Via Anhanguera, KM. 26, Caixa Postal 11.587, Sao Paulo Brazil. LC B5. DD 105.

PROBLEMY DIALEKTIKI. Vol. 1-. UR. Russian. an. LC B809.8.

PROCEEDINGS AND ADDRESSES OF THE AMERICAN PHILOSOPHICAL ASSOCIATION. Main/Corp American Philosophical Association. V. 1- 1927-. 0065-972X. Periodical. US. English. ir. University of Delaware, Newark DE 19711. Ind/Abst Philos. Index. LC B11. DD 106.073. Available on microfilm from University Microfilms. Proceedings of the Annual Meeting.

PROCEEDINGS OF THE AMERICAN CATHOLIC PHILOSOPHICAL ASSOCIATION. Main/Corp American Catholic Philosophical Association. V. 11- 1935-. 0065-7638. US. English. an. $12.00. American Catholic Philosophical Association, Catholic University of America, Washington DC 20064. Tel (202)635-5518. Ed Ralph M McInerny. Ind/Abst Philos. Index, Cathol. Period. Lit. Index. bk rev. adv acc. Circ 2,100. (ctrl). Philosophy. Proceedings of the Annual Meeting of the American Catholic Philosophical Association.

PROCEEDINGS OF THE AMERICAN PHILOSOPHICAL SOCIETY. V. 1- Jan./Mar. 1838-. 0003-049X. Periodical. US. English. qt. American Philosophical Society, PO Box 493, Canton MA 02021. Tel (617)828-8450. Ind/Abst Am. Hist. Life, Hist. Abstr., Lang. Lang. Behav. Abstr., GeoRef, Soc. Sci. Citation Index, MLA Int. Bibliogr. Books Artic. Mod. Lang. Lit., Life Sci. Collect., Sociol. Abstr., Annu. Bibliogr. Engl. Lang. Lit., Int. Aerosp. Abstr., ABC Pol Sci, Artbibliogr. Mod., Writ. Am. Hist., Biol. Abstr., Public Aff. Inf. Serv. Bull., Chem. Abstr., Eng. Index, Bibliogr. Index Geol., Soc. Sci. Citation Index, Years Work Eng. Stud. NLM W1 PR584KV. CODEN PAPCAA. (cum index). Available on microfilm.

PROCEEDINGS OF THE ARISTOTELIAN SOCIETY. Main/Conf Aristotelian Society for the Systematic Study of Philosophy. New Series, V.1- 1900/01-. 0066-7374. Periodical. UK. English. an. $18.38. Element Books Ltd, Old Brewry, Tisbury Wiltsire England. Ind/Abst Philos. Index. LC B11. DD 104. (cum index). Proceedings.

PROCEEDINGS OF THE LEEDS PHILOSOPHICAL AND LITERARY SOCIETY, LITERARY AND HISTORICAL SECTION. (PROCEEDINGS OF THE LEEDS PHILOSOPHICAL AND LITERARY SOCIETY. LITERARY AND HISTORICAL SECTION). Main/Corp Leeds Philosophical and Literary Society. V. 1-. 0024-0281. Monographic Series. UK. English. ir. Central Museum, Calverley Pt, Leeds England. Tel (0532)452894. Ed P R J Burch and I S Moxon. Ind/Abst Am. Hist. Life, Hist. Abstr., Part A, Mod. Hist. Abstr., Hist. Abstr., Part B, Twent. Century Abstr., Abstr. Engl. Stud., MLA Int. Bibliogr. Books Artic. Mod. Lang. Lit., Comput. Control Abstr., Electr. Electron. Abstr., Phys. Abstr., Years Work Eng. Stud., Hist. Abstr. LC AS122. DD 062. Circ 400. Scientific section: original work reports in any areas of science; literary and historical section: scholarly works in any area of the humanities.

PROCEEDINGS OF THE UNIVERSITY OF NEWCASTLE-UPON-TYNE PHILOSOPHICAL SOCIETY. Main/Corp Newcastle-Upon-Tyne. University. Philosophical Society. V. 1- 1964-. 0078-0251. UK. English. ir. Newcastle-Upon-Tyne University, Department of Botany, Armstrong Building, Newcastle-Upon-Tyne England. Ind/Abst Comput. Control Abstr., Electr. Electron. Abstr., Sci. Abstr. Sect. A. Phys. Abstr. CODEN PUNSAI. Proceedings of the University of Durham Philosophical Society. Series A. Science.

PROCESS STUDIES. V. 1- Spring 1971-. 0360-6503. Periodical. US. English. qt. $16.00. Center for Process Studies, 1325 North College Avenue, Claremont CA 91750. Tel (714)626-3521. Ed Lewis Ford. Ind/Abst Old Testam. Abstr., Philos. Index, Relig. Index One, Period. LC BD372. DD 230. bk rev. Circ 1,000. (ctrl). Scholarly articles and book reviews exploring the wide range of applications of process philosophy from theology to natural sciences.

PRS JOURNAL. VAT Philosophy, Religion, Science Journal, Philosophical Research Society Journal. V. 1- Aug. 1941-. 0030-8250. Periodical. US. English. qt. $9.00. Philosophical Research Society, 3910 Los Feliz Boulevard, Los Angeles CA 90027. Tel (213)663-2167. Ed Manly P Hall and Edith Waldron. LC BF1995. Circ 1,600. (ctrl). Useful knowledge in the fields of philosophy, comparative religions, and psychology. Horizon.

PRUDENTIA. Vol. 1, No. 1 (May 1969)-. Periodical. NZ. English. sa. 8.00. University of Auckland, Department of Philosophy, Private Bag, Auckland New Zealand. Ed G W R Ardley and J R Hamilton. LC DE1. DD 913.38038. bk rev. adv acc.

PUBBLICAZIONI DELL'UNIVERSITA CATTOLICA DEL SACRO CUORE. CONTRIBUTI, SERIE III. SCIENZE FILOSOFICHE. Main/Corp Universita Cattolica del Sacro Cuore. 1- 1960-. 0076-8677. Monographic Series. Italian. ir. LC B29.

PUBLICATIONS - VRIJE UNIVERSITEIT BRUSSEL. POLEMOLOGICAL CENTRE. Main/Corp Vrije Universiteit Brussel. Polemological Centre. V. 1- 1970-). Monographic Series. NE. Dutch. ir. Swets Publishing Service, PO Box 800, 2160 SZ Lissee Holland.

QUELLEN UND STUDIEN ZUR PHILOSOPHIE. V. 1- 1971-. Monographic Series. German. ir. Walter de Gruyter, 200 Sawmill River Road, Hawthorne NY 10532. Tel (914)747-0110. Ind/Abst Math. Rev. LC B23. Quellen und Studien zur Geschichte der Philosophie.

RACCOLTA DI STUDI E RICERCHE. 1-. Periodical. Italian. ir. LC B4. DD 190.5.

RADICAL PHILOSOPHY. 1- Jan. 1972-. 0300-211X. Periodical. UK. English. ty. $22.98. c/o John Fauvel, Faculty of Mathematics, Open University of Milton, Keynes MK7 6AA England. LC B1.

RASSEGNA INTERNAZIONALE DI LOGICA. (INTERNATIONAL LOGIC REVIEW). No. 1- March 1970-. 0048-6779. Periodical. IT. text in English, Italian, German or French. sa. $8.91. Rassegna Internazionale Logica, Via Belmeloro 3, Bologne Italy. Ed Franco Spisani. Ind/Abst Math. Rev., Lang. Lang. Behav. Abstr., Sociol. Abstr., Philos. Index.

RATIO. V. 1- Dec. 1957-. 0034-0006. Periodical. UK. English. sa. $59.95. Basil Blackwell, 108 Crowley Road, Oxford OX1 2EU England. Tel 0865-722146. Ed Martin Houis. Ind/Abst Math. Rev., Sociol. Abstr., Philos. Index, Lang. Lang. Behav. Abstr. LC B1. bk rev. adv acc. Deals with all branches of pure and applied philosophy. Abhandlungen der Friesschen Schule.

REALITAS. 1- 1972/73-. Spanish. ir. Sociedad de Estudios y Publicaciones, Infantas 31, Madrid Spain. LC B25. DD 105.

RECHERCHES SUR LE XVIIEME SIECLE. Series/Titl Cahiers de l'Equipe de Recherche 75. VFOAT Recherches sur le XVIIE Siecle. Began in 1976. 0180-0345. Periodical. FR. French (Italian). ir. Editions du CNRS, 15 Quai Anatole France, F-75700 Paris France. Tel (212)683-4441. LC CB401. DD 909.605. French-Italian accounts dedicated to the philosophy of the Seventeenth Century.

REPERTOIRE BIBLIOGRAPHIQUE DE LA PHILOSOPHIE. See Bibliographies.

REPORTS OF INVESTIGATIONS - INSTITUTE FOR THE STUDY OF EARTH AND MAN. Main/Corp Southern Methodist University, Dallas, Texas. Institute for the Study of Earth and Man. 1-. US. English. ir. Southern Methodist University, Department of English, c/o Theresa Enos, Dallas TX 75275.

RES BUREAUX BULLETIN. No. 1- July 15, 1974-. 0383-6150. Periodical. CN. English. ir. Free. Res Bureaux, Box 1598, Kingston Ontario K7L 5C8 Canada. DD 001.9405.

RESEARCH IN PHENOMENOLOGY. VFOAT RP. V. 1- 1971-. 0085-5553. US. English. an. $22.50. Humanities Press, Atlantic Highlands NJ 07716. Ed John Sallis. Ind/Abst Philos. Index,

Humanit. Index. **LC** B829.5. **DD** 142.7. bk rev. adv acc. Dedicated to encouraging original phenomenological research. Reviews the most important current work in phenomenology.

RESEARCH IN PHILOSOPHY & TECHNOLOGY. SUPPLEMENT. *See* Technology (General).

THE REVIEW OF METAPHYSICS. V. 1- (No. 1-). 0034-6632. Periodical. US. English. qt. Catholic University of America, School of Philosophy, Washington DC 20064. **Tel** (202)635-8778. **Ed** Jude P Dougherty. **Ind/Abst** Sociol. Abstr., Index Book Rev. Humanit., Humanit. Index, Philos. Index, Soc. Sci. Index, Book Rev. Index, Am. Hist. Life, Lang. Lang. Behav. Abstr., Hist. Abstr., Hist. Abst., Part B, Twent. Century Abstr., Hist. Abstr., Part A, Mod. Hist. Abstr. **LC** B1. **DD** 110.5. (cum index). bk rev. adv acc. **Circ** 3,000. Available on microfilm from University Microfilms. Devoted to the promotion of technically competent, definitive contributions to philosophical knowledge, regardless of the writers' affiliations.

REVISTA BRASILEIRA DE FILOSOFIA. V. 1- (Fasc. 1-). 0034-7205. Periodical. BL. Portuguese. qt. $20.00. Instituto Brasileiro Filosofia, Rua Barao de Itapetininga 88, 7 Andar, Sao Paulo Brazil. **LC** B1041. **DD** 190.5.

REVISTA DE FILOSOFIA. Vol. 1- (No. 1-). 0034-8244. SP. Spanish. qt. Consejo Super Invest Cientific, Vitruvio 8 Apartado 14 458, 28006 Madrid Spain. **Ind/Abst** Philos. Index. **LC** B5.

REVISTA DE FILOSOFIA. 1968. Periodical. MX. Spanish. ty. $15.00. Univ Iberoamer/Ctr Info Acad, Ave Cerro Torres 395/Deleg Coyoacan, 04200 Mexico DF Mexico. **Ind/Abst** Philos. Index. **LC** B5. bk rev. adv acc. **Circ** 5,000. (ctrl). International articles on subjects of philosphy, theology, religion and humanities on a Christian and Catholic vision. (Book reviews and some advertising of titles on the same subject).

REVISTA DE FILOSOFIA. Periodical. CL. Spanish. mo. $9.60. Universidad de Chile, JP Alessandri 774, Santiago Chile. **LC** B5.

REVISTA DE FILOSOFIA DE LA UNIVERSIDAD DE COSTA RICA. V. 1. No. 1 (Jan./June 1957)-. 0034-8252. Periodical. CR. Spanish. sa. $10.00. Universite de Costa Rica, c/o Editorial, Apdo 75, Guidad Universite, Rodrigo Faculta, 1000 San Jose Costa Rica. **Tel** 24-77-72. **Ed** Rafael Angel. **Ind/Abst** Am. Hist. Life, Hist. Abstr., Part A, Mod. Hist. Abstr., Hist. Abst., Part B, Twent. Century Abstr., Philos. Index. **LC** B5. bk rev. **Circ** 1,000. Philosophy and matters bordering on philosophy. Any speciality and theoretical viewpoints are welcome.

REVISTA DE FILOSOFIA LATINOAMERICANA. V. 1- Jan./June 1975-. Spanish. ir. $8.00. Ediciones Castaneda, Biblioteca Fr Mamerto Esquiu, Centario 1399, San Antonio de Padua Argentina. **LC** B1001. **DD** 199.8.

REVISTA DE FILOZOFIE *CEASED.* V. 11-V. 28, No. 6. 0034-8260. Periodical. RM. Romanian (summaries and table of contents in French and Russian). mo. **Ind/Abst** Philos. Index. *Cercetari Filozofice 0255-9498.*

REVISTA LATINOAMERICANA DE FILOSOFIA. V. 1- Mar. 1975-. 0325-0725. Periodical. Portuguese (or Spanish). ty. $20.00. Centro de Investigaciones Filosoficas, Casilla-Correo 5379, 1000 Buenos Aires Argentina. **Tel** 783-1088. **Ind/Abst** Philos. Index. **LC** B5. bk rev. adv acc. **Circ** 350. One of the few Latin American philosophical journals that is issued.

REVISTA PORTUGUESA DE FILOSOFIA. V. 1- Jan./March 1945-. 0035-0400. Periodical. PO. Portuguese. qt. $35.00. Faculdade de Filosofia, 4719 Braga Codex Portugal. **Tel** 25041. **Ind/Abst** MLA Int. Bibliogr. Books Artic. Mod. Lang. Lit., Philos. Index. **LC** B5. **DD** 105. (cum index). bk rev. adv acc. **Circ** 1,100.

REVISTA PORTUGUESA DE FILOSOFIA. SUPLEMENTO BIBLIOGRAFICO. 1- 1950-. 0556-6940. Portuguese. ir.

REVISTA VENEZOLANA DE FILOSOFIA. Year 1- Jan./June 1973-. VE. Spanish. sa. 4.00. University Simon Bolivar, Department of Philosophy, Caracas Venezuela. **Tel** 9621101-9. **Ed** Angel J Cappelletti. **Ind/Abst** Philos. Index. **LC** B5. **Circ** 1,000. Articles and notes on philosophy and history of philosophy in an open and pluralist direction.

REVOLUTIONARY WORLD *CEASED.* V. 1-50. 0303-3856. Periodical. NE. English. 110.00. B R Gruner Publishing Company, PO Box 70020, Amsterdam The Netherlands. **Ind/Abst** Philos. Index. **LC** B1. **DD** 105.

REVUE CIRPHO. **Main/Corp** International Society for Computer Research in Philosophy. **VFOAT** Cirpho Review. V. 1- Fall 1973-. 0317-3569. CN. English (French). sa. $2.50 Per No.; $4.00 Per Year, Individuals; $8.00 Per Year, Institutions. McGill University, c/o A McKinnon, Department of Philosophy, PO Box 6070, Montreal Quebec H3C 3G1 Canada. **DD** 029.9105.

REVUE DE L'ENSEIGNEMENT DE LA PHILOSOPHIE AU QUEBEC. V. 1- April 1978-. 0709-8561. Periodical. CN. French. sa. $4.00 Per No., $6.00 Per Year. A Lallier, College de Trois-Rivieres, 3500 rue de Courval, Trois-Rivieres Quebec G9A 5E6 Canada. **DD** 107.11714.

REVUE DE L'ENSEIGNEMENT PHILOSOPHIQUE. Began with Oct. 1950 issue. 0035-1393. Periodical. FR. French. bm. $25.28. Association des Professeurs de Philosophie, c/o C Broachard, 1 Clos Nollet, 91200 Athis-Mons France. **Tel** 6 938 22 27. **Ind/Abst** Am. Hist. Life, Hist. Abstr., Part A, Mod. Hist. Abstr., Hist. Abst., Part B, Twent. Century Abstr. **LC** B52. Philosophy.

REVUE DE METAPHYSIQUE ET DE MORALE (PARIS, FRANCE : 1945). (REVUE DE METAPHYSIQUE ET DE MORALE). Began in 1945. 0035-1571. Periodical. FR. French. qt. Librairie Armand Colin, 103 Boulevard St Michel, 75005 Paris Cedex 5 France. **Tel** 543 32 11. **Ind/Abst** MLA Int. Bibliogr. Books Artic. Mod. Lang. Lit., Philos. Index, Sociol. Abstr., Lang. Lang. Behav. Abstr. *Etudes de Metaphysique et de Morale.*

REVUE DE THEOLOGIE ET DE PHILOSOPHIE. New Series., V. 1-38, 1913-50. 0035-1784. Periodical. SZ. English. qt. $27.70. Revue de Theologie et de Philosophie, 3 Belles-Roches, CH-1004 Lausanne Switzerland. **Ind/Abst** Old Testam. Abstr., New Testam. Abstr., Philos. Index, Relig. Index One, Period., MLA Int. Bibliogr. Books Artic. Mod. Lang. Lit. **LC** BR3. (cum index). bk rev. **Circ** 1,000. (ctrl). Religion, church history, theology, philosophy, ministry of philosophy and science of religion. *Revue de Theolofie et Philosophie et Compte-Rendu des Principales Publications Scientifiques.*

REVUE DES SCIENCES HUMAINES. New Series, Issue 45 (Jan./ Mar. 1947)-. 0035-2195. Periodical. FR. French. qt. $26.61. Faculte Lettres Science Humaines, Universite de Lille, Lille Nord France. **Ind/Abst** MLA Int. Bibliogr. Books Artic. Mod. Lang. Lit., Index Book Rev. Humanit. **LC** B2. *Revue d'Histoire de la Philosophie et d'Historie Generale de la Civilisation.*

REVUE DES SCIENCES PHILOSOPHIQUES ET THEOLOGIQUES (PARIS : 1947). (REVUE DES SCIENCES PHILOSOPHIQUES ET THEOLOGIQUES). Began publication with V. 31 in 1947. 0035-2209. Periodical. FR. French. qt. $53.00. Librarie Philosophique, J Vrin, 6 Place de la Sorbonne, 75005 Paris France. **Tel** (1)43 54 03 47. **Ed** Vrin. **Ind/Abst** MLA Int. Bibliogr. Books Artic. Mod. Lang. Lit., Philos. Index, Old Testam. Abstr., New Testam. Abstr., Relig. Index One, Period. In addition to recension of specialized reviews, the RSPT also includes original thematic recensions in the shape of ecclesiology, philosophy or patrology bulleting. Besides, each issue contains several philosophical and purely theological articles. *Sciences Philosophiques et Theologiques.*

REVUE D'ESTHETIQUE. 1974, No. 3/4-. Monographic Series. FR. French. sa. $30.59. Editions Privat, 14 rue des Arts, 31000 Toulouse France. **Tel** (61)230926. **Ind/Abst** MLA Int. Bibliogr. Books Artic. Mod. Lang. Lit., Philos. Index.

REVUE ET CORRIGEES. Vol. 1, No. 1-. 0820-8786. Periodical. CN. French. ir. $1.25 Per Issue. Cegep de Maisonneuve, 3800 Est rue Sherbrooke, Montreal Quebec H1X 2A2 Canada. **DD** 105.

REVUE INTERNATIONALE DE PHILOSOPHIE. Vol. 1 No. 1 Oct. 15, 1938-. 0048-8143. Periodical. text in French, Dutch, English and Spanish. qt. $42.78. Editions Universas, rue Hoender 24, 9200 Wetteren Belgium. **Ind/Abst** Math. Rev., MLA Int. Bibliogr. Books Artic. Mod. Lang. Lit., Sociol. Abstr., Philos. Index, Index Book Rev. Humanit., Math. Rev., Lang. Lang. Behav. Abstr. **LC** B1.

REVUE PHILOSOPHIQUE DE LOUVAIN. V. 44- 1946-. 0035-3841. Periodical. BE. French. qt. $29.64. Editions Peeters SA, Bondgenotenlaan 153, Box 41, B-3000 Leuven Belgium. **Ind/Abst** MLA Int. Bibliogr. Books Artic. Mod. Lang. Lit., Philos. Index, Cathol. Period. Lit. Index, Sociol. Abstr. adv acc. (ctrl). *Revue Neoscolastique de Philosophie.*

REVUE ROUMAINE DES SCIENCES SOCIALES. SERIE DE PHILOSOPHIE ET LOGIQUE. V. 8-. 0035-4031. Periodical. French (English, German, or Russian). qt. $48.00. Ilexim Press Department, PO Box 1-136-1-137, Bucharest Romania. **Ind/Abst** Philos. Index, Lang. Lang. Behav. Abstr., Sociol. Abstr. **LC** B1. **DD** 105. *Revue des Sciences Sociales.*

THE RIGHT OF AESTHETIC REALISM TO BE KNOWN. 0882-3731. Periodical. US. English. wk. $16.00 Domestic, $26.00 Foreign. Aesthetic Realism Foundation, 141 Greene Street, New York NY 10012. **DD** 149.

RIVISTA CRITICA DI STORIA DELLA FILOSOFIA. Vol. 1- 1946-. 0035-581X. Periodical. IT. Italian. qt. $32.67. Nuova Italia Editrice, Via Ernesto Codignola, 50018 Scandicci FI Italy.

RIVISTA CRITICA DI STORIA DELLA FILOSOFIA *CEASED.* Vols. 5-38. 0035-581X. Periodical. IT. Multilingual (English or Italian). qt. 5,000. La Nouva Italia, Via Antonio Giacomini 8, Firenze Italy. **LC** B4. *Rivista di Storia Della Filosofia (Milano, Italy : 1946).*

RIVISTA DI ESTETICA. Began with: Vol. 1 (Jan./Apr. 1956). 0035-6212. Periodical. IT. Italian. ir. 56.000 Domestic, 70.000 Foreign. Rosenberg & Sellier, Via Andrea Doria 14, 10123 Torino Italy. **Tel** (011)532150. **Ed** Vattimo Gianni. **Ind/Abst** MLA Int. Bibliogr. Books Artic. Mod. Lang. Lit., Annu. Bibliogr. Engl. Lang. Lit. bk rev. adv acc. **Circ** 1,200. One of the most useful presences of the Italian philosophical culture and has given outstanding help to aesthetics as an interdisciplinary science.

RIVISTA DI FILOSOFIA NEO-SCOLASTICA. Vol. 1- Jan. 1909-. 0035-6247. Periodical. II. Italian. qt. $41.58. Soc Edit Vita e Pensiero, Largo Agostino Gemelli 1, 20102 Milano Italy. **Ind/Abst** MLA Int. Bibliogr. Books Artic. Mod. Lang. Lit., Philos. Index. **LC** B4. **DD** 149.

RIVISTA DI STUDI CROCIANI. Year 1- 1964-. 0035-659X. Periodical. IT. Italian. qt. $20.79. Maschio Angioino, Via Luca Giordano 7, 80127 Napoli Italy. **Ind/Abst** MLA Int. Bibliogr. Books Artic. Mod. Lang. Lit., Philos. Index. **LC** B3614.C74.

RIVISTA INTERNAZIONALE DI FILOSOFIA DEL DIRITTO. *See* Law.

ROCZNIKI FILOSOFICZNE. **VFOAT** Annales de Philosophie. V. 1- 1948-. 0035-7685. Periodical. PL. Polish (added title page in French or English). qt. ARS Polona, Krakowskie Przedmiescie 7, 00-068 Warsaw Poland. **Ind/Abst** Psychol. Abstr. **LC** B31. **CODEN** RFLZBF.

ROYAL INSTITUTE OF PHILOSOPHY LECTURE SERIES. **VFOAT** Lecture Series. Began with: 13, published in 1979?. Monographic Series. UK. English. an. Humanities Press, 171 First Avenue, Atlantic Highlands NJ 07716. **Tel** (201)872-1441. *Royal Institute of Philosophy Lectures.*

RUCH FILOSOFICKY. Began in 1920. Periodical. Czech (French, German, or Serbo-Croatian). ir. **LC** B6.

RUCH FILOZOFICZNY. V. 1- Jan. 1911-. 0035-9599. Periodical. PL. Polish. ir. ARS Polona, Krakowskie Przedmiescie 7, 00-068 Warsaw Poland.

RUSSELL. 1- Spring 1971-. 0036-0163. Periodical. CN. English. sa. $15.48. McMaster University, Library Press, 1280 Main Street West, Hamilton Ontario L8S 4L6 Canada. **Tel** (416)525-9140. **Ed** Kenneth Blackwell. **Ind/Abst** Index Book Rev. Humanit., Philos. Index. **LC** B1649 .R94. **DD** 192 B. bk rev. **Circ** 650. Articles and reviews relating to Russell's work.

SALZBURGER BEITRAGE ZUR PARACELSUSFORSCHUNG. AU. German. ir. Verband Wissen Gesellschaften, Oesterreichs/Lindengasse 37, A 1070 Wien Austria. **Tel** 93 47 56. **Ed** Sepp Domandl. **Circ** 450. Publishes articles about the period of paracelsus concerning history of medicine, science, culture and humanism.

Philosophy

SALZBURGER JAHRBUCH FUR PHILOSOPHIE. *See* Yearbooks, Almanacs, Directories.

SAMBODHI. V. 1- Apr. 1972-. Periodical. II. English (Gujarati, Hindi or Sanskrit). ir. 20.00. LD Institute of Indology, Ahmedabad-9 India. LC B130. DD 181.405.

SAPIENTIA. Vol. 1- 1946?-. 0036-4703. Periodical. AG. Spanish. qt. Direccion y Administracion, Bartolome Mitre 1869, 1039 Buenos Aires Argentina. Ind/Abst Philos. Index.

SAPIENZA. Vol. 1- 1948-. 0036-4711. Periodical. IT. Italian. qt. 16.-. Rivista International Filosofia Teolog, Vicoletto S Pietro Maiella 4, 80134 Napoli Italy. Tel (081)459003. Ind/Abst MLA Int. Bibliogr. Books Artic. Mod. Lang. Lit., Old Testam. Abstr., New Testam. Abstr., Philos. Index. (cum index). bk rev. Research and discussions of problems in philosophy and theology especially those of San Tommaso and the school of Tomista.

SCHOPENHAUER-JAHRBUCH. VAT Schopenhauer Jahrbuch. 32.- 1945/48-. 0080-6935. German. an. $18.26. Verlag Waldemar Kramer, 6 Frankfurt/Main West Germany. Ind/Abst Philos. Index. *Jahrbuch der Schopenhauer-Gesellschaft.*

SCIENCE AND NATURE. 1978. 0193-3396. Periodical. US. English. an. $15.00. Dialectics Workshop, 53 Hickory Hill Road, Tappan NY 10983. Tel (914)359-2283. Ed Lester Talkington. Ind/Abst Math. Rev., Altern. Press Index. LC Q174. DD 501. bk rev. adv acc. Circ 1,500. An independent journal addressing the philosophical problems of the natural sciences (biological, physical, mathematical), demonstrating the usefulness of the Marxist world view in the practice of science.

SCIENCE ET ESPRIT. Began in 1968. 0316-5345. Periodical. CN. English (French and Italian). ty. Editions Bellarmin, 8100 St Laurent, Montreal 351 Canada. Tel (514)387-2541. Ind/Abst MLA Int. Bibliogr. Books Artic. Mod. Lang. Lit., New Testam. Abstr., Old Testam. Abstr., Point Repere, Relig. Index One, Period. LC BR3. DD 230.05. *Sciences Ecclesiastiques.*

SCIENCE OF MIND. 1927. 0036-8458. Periodical. US. English. mo $10.35. Science of Mind, PO Box 75127, Los Angeles CA 90075. Tel (213)388-2181. Ed John S Niendorff. adv acc. Circ 100,000. (ctrl). The magazine expresses the science of mind, a philosophy of successful living. Teaches how to use spiritual understanding to experience happiness, health, prosperity and greater self-awareness.

SCIENTIFIC AESTHETICS. VFOAT Sciences de l'Art. V. 1- June 1976-. 0145-5923. Periodical. US. English. qt. $32.00. Plenum Press, 227 West 17th Street, New York NY 10011. LC BH1. DD 111.85. CODEN SCAEDP.

SEMANA NACIONAL DE FILOSOFIA NO BRASIL: ANAIS. Series/Tlt Estudos Universitarios. Serie Filosofia. 1A.-. BL. Portuguese. ir. Editora Universitaria, Campus Universitario, 58.000 Joao Pessoa Paraiba Brazil. LC B1041. DD 199.81.

SH'MA. 1- Nov. 9, 1970-. 0049-0385. Periodical. US. English. bw. $12.00. SH'MA Inc, PO Box 567, Port Washington NY 11050. Tel (516)944-9791. Ed Eugene B Borowitz. bk rev. Circ 8,500. A forum for discussion of topics of interest to the Jewish community, free of any organizational censorship or restraint.

SOCIAL THEORY AND PRACTICE. V. 1- Spring 1970-. 0037-802X. Periodical. US. English. ty. $27.00 Domestic, $31.00 Foreign. Department of Philosophy, Florida State University, Tallahassee FL 32306. Tel (904)644-1483. Ed Peter Dalton and Constance Jakubcin. Ind/Abst Soc. Sci. Index, Am. Hist. Life, Hist. Abstr., Soc. Welf. Soc. Plan./Policy Soc. Dev., ABC Pol Sci, Philos. Index, Sociol. Abstr., Abstr. Criminol. Penol., Curr. Index J. Educ., Lang. Lang. Behav. Abstr., Repert. Bibliogr. Philos., Soc. Sci. Citation Index. LC H1. DD 300.5. adv acc. Circ 620. Includes discussion of important and controversial issues in social, political, legal, economic, educational, and moral philosophy. Constructive critissism is welcome.

THE SOUTHERN JOURNAL OF PHILOSOPHY. V. 1- Spring 1963-. 0038-4283. Periodical. US. English. qt. $14.00. Memphis State University, Southern Journal of Philosophy, Memphis TN 38152. Tel (901)454-2536. Ed Nancy D Simco. Ind/Abst Philos. Index. LC B1. DD 105. bk rev adv acc. Circ 1,200. Articles from all perspectives in all areas of philosophy.

SOUTHWEST PHILOSOPHICAL STUDIES. Vol. 1 (Apr. 1976)-. 0885-9310. Periodical. US. English. an. $30.00. Southwest Texas State University, Department of Philosophy, V Luizz, San Marcos TX 78666. Ind/Abst Philos. Index. DD 105. *Proceedings, Proceedings of the . . . Annual Meeting of the Southwestern Philosophical Society,* 0882-1607.

THE SOUTHWESTERN JOURNAL OF PHILOSOPHY CEASED. V. 1-11. 0038-481X. Periodical. US. English. ty. $13.00 Institutional, $6.00 Students. Southwestern Journal of Philosophy, 605 Dale Tower Hall, 455 West Lindsey, Norman OK 73069. Ind/Abst Math. Rev., Philos. Index. LC B1. DD 105.

SOVIET STUDIES IN PHILOSOPHY. V. 1- Summer 1962-. 0038-5883. Periodical. US. English (Russian). qt. $178.50. M E Sharpe Inc, 80 Business Park Drive, Armonk NY 10504. Tel (914)273-1800. Ed John Somerville. Ind/Abst Philos. Index, Soc. Sci. Citation Index. LC B1. DD 105. adv acc. Circ 300. A source for complete and unabridged translations of current articles by Soviet philosophers, taken from Soviet journals covering the entire range of philosophy.

SOVREMENNAIA ZARUBEZHNAIA FILOSOFIIA I SOTSIOLOGIIA. UR. Multilingual (Russian). 0.28 Each Issue. Ul Krasikova D 28/45, Moskva Russian SFSR. LC Z7125, B53.

THE SPRINGER SERIES ON DEATH AND SUICIDE. (THANATOS, THE SPRINGER SERIES ON DEATH AND SUICIDE). VFOAT Springer Series on Death and Suicide. V. 1- 1979-. 0271-1192. Monographic Series. US. English. ir. Springer Publishing Company Inc, 536 Broadway, New York NY 10012. Tel (212)431-4370. Ed R Kastenbaum. LC UNC. NLM W1 SP685P.

SPRINGER TRACTS IN NATURAL PHILOSOPHY. VFOAT Ergebnisse der Angewandten Mathematik. V. 1- . 0081-3877. Monographic Series. US. English (German). ir. Springer Verlag-New York Inc, 175-5th Avenue, New York NY 10010. Tel (212)460-1584. Ind/Abst Math. Rev. LC UNC. Contains articles on theory, methods, analysis, and functions of philosophy. *Ergebnisse der Angewandten Mathematik.*

SSIAL UI SORI. VFOAT Voice of the People. Began with Apr. 1970 issue. Periodical. KO. Korean. ir. 3,000. Ssial Ui Sori Sa, 70 4-ka Wonhyo Ro, Yongsan-ku 140, Seoul South Korea. LC B8.K6.

STUDI FILOSOFICI E PEDAGOGICI. 1-. Periodical. Italian (English). ir. LC B4. DD 105.

STUDIA ANSELMIANA; PHILOSOPHICA, THEOLOGICA. IT. Multilingual (English, French, German, and Latin). ir. Herder Editrice E Liberia, Piazza Montecitorio 121, Rome Italy.

STUDIA FILOZOFICZNE. 1957, No. 1-. 0039-3142. Periodical. PL. Polish (tables of contents also in Russian and English). mo. ARS Polona, Krakowskie Przedmiescie 7, 00-068 Warsaw Poland. Ind/Abst Artbibliogr. Mod., Am. Hist. Life, Hist. Abstr., Lang. Lang. Behav. Abstr., Sociol. Abstr., Hist. Abstr., Part A, Mod. Hist. Abstr., Hist. Abst., Part B, Twent. Century Abstr. LC B6. *MYSL Filozoficzna.*

STUDIA LEIBNITIANA. 0039-3185. Periodical. GW. German (French). sa. 96.-. Franz Steiner Verlag GMBH, Postfach 347, D7000 Stuttgart 1 West Germany. Tel (0711)2582229. Ed Kurt Mileler, Heinrich Scheppers, and Wilhelm Totok. Ind/Abst Math. Rev., Philos. Index. LC B2550. CODEN STLBBI. bk rev. adv acc. Circ 450. Dedicated to Leibuit, his philosophy, and the impact of his works.

STUDIA LOGICA. V. 1- 1953-. 0039-3215. Periodical. English (Polish 1953-73). qt. D Reidel Publishing Company, PO Box 17, 3300 AA Dordrecht Holland. Tel (31)78-334911. Ind/Abst Math. Rev., Philos. Index. CODEN SLOGAP. bk rev. adv acc. Circ 400. Logical systems, their semantics, methodology, and applications.

STUDIA MEDIEWISTYCZNE. 1- 1958-. 0039-3231. PL. Polish and Latin with some summaries in French. ir. ARS Polona, Krakowskie Przedmiescie 7, 00-068 Warsaw Poland. Ind/Abst MLA Int. Bibliogr. Books Artic. Mod. Lang. Lit.

STUDIA PHILONICA. V. 1- 1972-. 0093-5808. US. English. an. $5.00. McCormick Theological Seminary, 800 West Belden Avenue, Chicago IL 60614. Ind/Abst Old Testam. Abstr., New Testam. Abstr. LC B689.Z7. DD 181.3.

STUDIA PHILOSOPHIAE CHRISTIANAE. Vol. 1-. 0585-5470. Periodical. PL. Polish (summaries in English, French, and German). sa. ARS Polona, Krakowskie Przedmiescie 7, 00-068 Warsaw Poland. Ind/Abst Philos. Index. LC BR9.P6.

STUDIA UNIVERSITATIS BABES-BOLYAI. SERIES PHILOSOPHIA. Main/Corp Cluj, Transylvania. Universitatea Babes-Bolyai. VFOAT Series Philosophia. Year 11- 1966-. 0578-5480. RM. Rumanian. an. Ilexim Press Department, PO Box 1-136-1-137, Bucharest Romania. Ind/Abst Bibliogr. Index Geol. *Studia Universitatis Babes-Bolyai. Series Philosophia et Oeconcmica.*

STUDIEN UND MATERIALIEN ZUR GESCHICHTE DER PHILOSOPHIE. KLEINE REIHE. Vol. 1- 1975-. German. ir.

STUDIEN ZUR PHILOSOPHIE UND LITERATUR DES NEUNZEHNTEN JAHRHUNDERTS. Vol. 1- 1968-. 0081-735X. Monographic Series. GW. German. ir. Vittorio Klosterman Verlag, Postfach 900601, Frauenlobstrasse 22, 6000 Frankfurt 90 West Germany. Tel (0611)774011.

STUDIEN ZUR PROBLEMGESCHICHTE DER ANTIKEN UND MITTELALTERLICHEN PHILOSOPHIE. V. 1-. Monographic Series. NE. German. ir. EJ Brill, POB 9000, 2300 PA Leiden The Netherlands.

STUDIES IN HISTORY AND PHILOSOPHY. *See* History (General).

STUDIES IN HUME AND SCOTTISH PHILOSOPHY. 1-. Monographic Series. US. English. Austin Hill Press Inc, 2955 Renault Place, San Diego CA 92122.

STUDIES IN PHILOSOPHY. 1- 1963-. 0081-8399. Monographic Series. UK. English. ir. Walter de Gruyter Inc, 200 Saw Mill River Road, Hawthone NY 10532. Tel (914)747-0110.

STUDIES IN PHILOSOPHY AND THE HISTORY OF PHILOSOPHY. V. 1-. 0585-6965. US. English. ir. Catholic University of America, Press, PO Box 4852 Hampden Station, Baltimore MD 21211. Tel (301)338-7817. Ed J K Ryan. Ind/Abst Philos. Index. LC B21. DD 108.2.

STUDIES IN SOVIET THOUGHT. (STUDIES IN SOVIET STUDIES). V. 1- 1961-. 0039-3797. Periodical. English (German or French). qt. Tel (31)78-334911. Ind/Abst Am. Hist. Life, Hist. Abstr., Part A, Mod. Hist. Abstr., ABC Pol Sci, Artbibliogr. Mod., Philos. Index, Recent Publ. Artic. LC B809.8. DD 197.2. bk rev. adv acc. Circ 600. Modern and recent Soviet thought, and pre-revolutionary developments.

STUDII DE ISTORIE A FILOZOFIEI UNIVERSALE (BUCHAREST, ROMANIA : 1974). (STUDII DE ISTORIE A FILOZOFIEI UNIVERSALE). VFOAT Studies on the History of World Philosophy. 4-. Periodical. Romanian. ir. 15. Calea Victoriei, NR 125, R 79717 Bucuresti Romania. LC B8.R8. *Filozofie Moderna Si Contemporana.*

SUPPLEMENTARY VOLUME - ARISTOTELIAN SOCIETY. (SUPPLEMENTARY VOLUME). Main/Conf Aristotelian Society (Great Britain). V. 1- 1918-. 0309-7013. UK. English. an. $43.67. Element Books Limited, Old Brewery, Tisbury Wiltshire England. Ind/Abst Philos. Index. (cum index).

SYMPOSION; PHILOSOPHISCHE SCHRIFTENREIHE. 1-. Monographic Series. GW. German. ir. Verlag Karl Alber, Hermann-Herder-Strasse 4, D-7800 Freiburg West Germany.

SYMPOSIUM OF THE CONFERENCE ON SCIENCE, PHILOSOPHY AND RELIGION. *See* Science (General).

SYNAPSE. (SYNAPSE : THE MENSA PHILOSOPHY SIG NEWSLETTER). 0823-1435. Periodical. CN. English. bm. Free to Members, $1.00 Each Number to Others. Mensa Philosophy Sig, PO Box 212, Regina Saskatchewan S4P 2ZP Canada. DD 105.

SYNTHESE. 0039-7857. Periodical. NE. Multilingual (English, Dutch, French, German). mo. 264.00. Kluwer Academic Publishers Group, PO Box

Philosophy

322, 3300 AH Dordrecht Netherlands. **Tel** (31)78-334911. Ed Jaakko Hinrikka. **Ind/Abst** Lang. Lang. Behav. Abstr., Math. Rev., MLA Int. Bibliogr. Books Artic. Mod. Lang. Lit., Sociol. Abstr., Soc. Sci. Citation Index, Philos. Index. bk rev. adv acc. **Circ** 1,100. Theory of knowledge, scientific discovery, induction, probability, causation, and role of mathematics. Statistics and logic, symbolic logic, foundations of mathematics, and sociology.

TATTVALOKAH. VFOAT Tattvaloka. Periodical. English (Sanskrit). bm. $4.00. Sri Abhinava Vidyatheertha Educational Trust Navasuja, 15 Venkatakrishna Iyer Street, Raja Annamalaipuram Madras 600028 India. LC B132.V3. DD 181.4805.

TEACHING PHILOSOPHY. V. 1- Summer 1975-. 0145-5788. Periodical. US. English. qt. $32.00. Philosophy Documentation Center, Bowling Green University, Bowling Green OH 43404. **Tel** (419)372-2419. Ed Arnold Wilson. **Ind/Abst** Philos. Index, Media Rev. Dig. LC B52. DD 107. bk rev adv acc. **Circ** 850. Publishes articles, discussions, reports, and reviews on theoretical issues in philosophy, innovative methods and courses, new texts and audiovisual materials.

TEOREMA. March 1971-. 0210-1602. Periodical. SP. Spanish. qt. Universidad de Valencia, Logica Fac Filosofia, Letr Valencia Spain. **Ind/Abst** Math. Rev., Philos. Index. LC B5.

TEORIA. I, ERMENEUTICA FILOSOFICA. VFOAT Ermeneutica Filosofica. 1981/1-. Periodical. Italian. sa. $20.00. ETS, C C P 12157566 Piazza Torricelli 4, 56100 Pisa Italy. **Tel** (050)500001. Ed Vittorio Sainati and Renzo Raggiunti. LC B4. DD 149.9405. bk rev. **Circ** 1,000. Covers logic philosophy of mathematics, philosophy of languages, history of logic hermeneutics, history of philosophy, and philosophy of religion.

TETSUGAKU. VFOAT Series of Philosophy. 1- 1953-. JA. Japanaese. be. Tokyo Daigaku Shuppankai, 3-1 Hongo 7, Bunkyo-Ku 113, Tokyo Japan. LC B8.J3.

TETSUGAKU RONSHU (RYUKYU DAIGAKU. HOBUNGAKUBU). (TETSUGAKU RONSHU). VFOAT Ryudai Pholosophical Studies. JA. English (Japanese). ir. Ryukyu Daigaku Hobungakubu, 1 Tonokuracho 3 Naha-Shi, Okinawa Japan. LC B1.

TETSUGAKU RONSO. No. 1- July, 1977-. German (Japanese). ir. Osaka Daigaku Bungkabu, c/o Tetsugaku Kenkushitsu, 1-1 Mahcikaneyamacho 1, Toynaka, Osaka 560 Japan. LC B8.J3.

TETSUGAKU SHISO RONSHU. VFOAT Studies in Philosophy. No. 7- (1981)-. JA. Japanese (with some summaries in English and French). ir. Tsukuba Daigaku Tetsugaku Shiso Gakukei, 1-1 Tennodai 1-Chome Sakura-Mura Niihari-Gun, Ibaraki-Ken 305 Japan. LC B8.J3. *Tsukuba Daigaku Tetsugaku Shiso Gakukei Ronshu.*

THANATOLOGY ABSTRACTS (ST. LOUIS PARK, MINN.). *See* Indexes/Abstracts.

THEOLOGIE UND PHILOSOPHIE. *See* Religion, Mythology, Rationalism - Theology.

THEORIA. V. 1- 1935-. 0040-5825. Periodical. SW. Swedish (Vols. 1-2 in Norwegian, and Danish). ty. Theoria Bengt Hansson, Filosofiska Institutionen, S-223 50 Lund Sweden. Ed A Petzall. **Ind/Abst** Math. Rev., Philos. Index, Sociol. Abstr., Lang. Lang. Behav. Abstr. LC B1. DD 105. CODEN THRAA5. (cum index).

THEORY AND DECISION. Vol. 1 (Oct. 1970)-. 0040-5833. Periodical. NE. English (French). qt. $132.00. Kluwer Academic Publishers Group, PO Box 322, 3300 AH Dordrecht The Netherlands. **Tel** (31)78-334911. Ed W Leinfellner. **Ind/Abst** Math. Rev., Sociol. Abstr., Soc. Welf. Soc. Plan./Policy Soc. Dev., Philos. Index, Psychol. Abstr., Lang. Lang. Behav. Abstr., Soc. Sci. Citation Index. LC H61. CODEN THDCBA. Index in last issue of volume - attached. bk rev. adv acc. **Circ** 900. Philosophy and methodology of the social sciences: application of advanced methodology of philosophy of science, logic, and mathematics, discussion of empirical models, etc.

THE THOMIST. V. 1- Apr. 1939-. 0040-6325. Periodical. US. English. qt. $15.00 Domestic, $17.00 Foreign. Thomist Press, 487 Michigan Avenue NE, Washington DC 20017. **Tel** (202)529-5300. Ed Joseph A Dinoia. **Ind/Abst** Cathol. Period. Lit. Index, New Testam. Abstr., Philos. Index. LC BX801. DD 230.05. (cum index). bk rev adv acc. **Circ** 1,150. A review of theology and philosophy in the realist Aristotelian-Thomistic tradition that seeks a rapport with contemporary thought.

THE THOREAU QUARTERLY. *See* Literature.

TOEGYE HAKPO. Began with Oct. 1973 issue. Periodical. KO. Korean. ir. 3,000. Toegyehak Yonguwon, 16 1-ka Olji-Ro, Chung-Ku, Seoul South Korea. LC B5254.Y482.

TOHGAKU. *See* History (General) - History of Asia.

TOPOI. Vol. 1, No. 1 & 2 (Dec. 1982)-. 0167-7411. Periodical. English. ir. $44.00. D Reidel Publishing Company, PO Box 17, Dordrecht Holland. **Tel** (31)78-334911. Ed E Bencivenga and E Forni. **Ind/Abst** Math. Rev., Philos. Index. LC B1. DD 105. bk rev. adv acc. **Circ** 400. Philosophical studies and the history of philosophy, the most important topics that have emerged, the growth of discussing chemistry and the tendencies that developed.

TOYO GAKUJUTSU KENKYU. VFOAT Journal of Oriental Science. Began in 1963. Periodical. JA. Japanese. ir. 300. Toyo Tetsugaku Kenkyujo, 7-20 Uehara 2-chome Shibuya-ku 151, Tokyo Japan. LC B121.

TRANSACTIONS OF THE AMERICAN PHILOSOPHICAL SOCIETY.... Began in 1771. 0065-9746. Monographic Series. US. English. ir. $65.00. American Philosophical Society, PO Box 493, Canton MA 02021. **Tel** (617)828-8450. **Ind/Abst** Math. Rev., GeoRef, Recent Publ. Artic., Bibliogr. Index, Soc. Sci. Citation Index, Bibliogr. Index Geol. LC Q11. CODEN TAPSAY. Index in last issue of volume - attached.

TRANSACTIONS OF THE CHARLES S. PEIRCE SOCIETY. Main/Corp Charles S. Peirce Society. V. 1- Spring 1965-. 0009-1774. Periodical. US. English. qt. $27.00. Hare State University of New York, Philosophy Hall/Baldy Hall, Buffalo NY 14260. **Tel** (716)636-2444. Ed Peter H Hare. **Ind/Abst** Philos. Index, Ref. Source, Index Book Rev. Humanit. DD 105. bk rev. adv acc. **Circ** 500. History of American philosophy.

TRAVAUX DE LA FACULTE DE PHILOSOPHIE ET LETTRES. Main/Corp Brussels. Universite Libre. Faculte de Philosophie et Lettres. V. 1-. Monographic Series. BE. French. ir. $69.50. Universite Libre de Bruxelles, 50 Avunue F D Roosevelt, B-1050 Bruselles Belgium.

TRAVAUX DU CENTRE DE DOCUMENTATION ET DE BIBLIOGRAPHIE PHILOSOPHIQUES DE BESANCON. *See* Bibliographies.

TSUKUBA DAIGAKU TETSUGAKU SHISO GAKUKEI RONSHU CEASED. VFOAT Studies. No. 7, Issue 1975 (1980). Japanese (English). ir. LC B8.J3.

TULANE STUDIES IN PHILOSOPHY. VFOAT Studies in Philosophy. V. 1-. 0082-6766. US. English. ir. Tulane University, Department of Philosophy, New Orleans LA 70118. **Ind/Abst** Sociol. Abstr., Philos. Index, Lang. Lang. Behav. Abstr. LC B21. DD 105.

UCHENYE ZAPISKI KAFEDR MARKSISTSKO-LENINSKOI FILOSOFII VYSSHEI PARTIINOI SHKOLY PRI TSK KPSS I MESTNYKH VYSSHIKH PARTIINYKH SHKOL. 0502-9988. UR. Russian. ir. Victor Kamkin Inc, 12224 Parklawn Drive, Rockville MD 20852. **Tel** (301)881-5973. LC B6.

UCHENYE ZAPISKI KAFEDR OBSHCHESTVENNYKH NAUK VUZOV G. LENINGRADA. FILOSOFIIA CEASED. VFOAT Filosofiia. Began with V. 2- 1960. Ceased with V. 20, 1980. 0502-9996. UR. Russian. an. *UCHENYE Zapiski Kafedr Obshchestvennykh Nauk Vuzov G. Leningrada: Istoriia KPss, Polit.-Ekonomia, Filosofiia.*

ULTIMATE REALITY AND MEANING. Vol. 1, No. 1. 0709-549X. Periodical. CN. English (French). qt. $33.27. University of Toronto Press, Journals Department, 5201 Dufferin Street, Downsview Ontario M3H 5T8 Canada. **Tel** (416)667-7781. **Ind/Abst** Sociol. Abstr., Philos. Index, Relig. Index One, Period., Guide Soc. Sci. Relig. Period. Lit. LC BD331. DD 110.5.

THE VEDANTA KESARI. V. 1 - 1914-. 0042-2983. Periodical. II. English. mo. 7.00. Sri Ramakrisha Math, 16 Ramakrisha Math Road, Madras 600004 India. **Tel** 71231. Ed Swami Tapasyananda. bk rev. adv acc. **Circ** 5,000. Ideas in the areas of philosophy, religion and culture.

VERIFICHE. Vol. 1- Sept. 1972-. 0391-4186. IT. Italian (summaries in German). qt. 4000. C.C.P. 14, 12388 Recapito, Casella Postale 269, Trento Italy. **Ind/Abst** Am. Hist. Life, Recent Publ. Artic., Hist. Abstr., Part A, Mod. Hist. Abstr., Hist. Abstr., Part B, Twent. Century Abstr. LC B4.

VESTNIK MOSKOVSKOGO UNIVERSITETA. SERIIA VII : FILOSOFIIA. Main/Corp Moskovskii Gosudarstvennyi Universitet Im. M.V. Lomonosova. 1- Jan./Feb. 1977-. Periodical. UR. Russian. bm. Victor Kamkin Inc, 12224 Parklawn Drive, Rockville MD 20852. **Tel** (301)881-5973. **Ind/Abst** Lang. Lang. Behav. Abstr., Sociol. Abstr. LC B6. *Vestnik Moskovskogo Universiteta. Seriia VIII: Filosofiia.*

VINCULO. Yearly V. 1- March 1973-. French or Portuguese. ir. Faculdade de Filosofia, rua Coronel Celestino 75, 39400 Montes Clares M G Brazil. LC AS80.F85.

THE VISVA-BHARATI JOURNAL OF PHILOSOPHY. V. 1- Aug. 1964-. 0042-7187. Periodical. II. English. sa. $2.64. Visva-Bharati Journal of Philosophy, 731235 West Bengal India.

VITA E PENSIERO. Vol. 1- 1915-. 0042-725X. Periodical. IT. Italian. mo. Society Edit Vita e Pensiero, Largo Agostino Gemelli 1, 20102 Milano Italy. **Ind/Abst** MLA Int. Bibliogr. Books Artic. Mod. Lang. Lit.

VIVARIUM. V. 1- May 1963-. 0042-7543. Periodical. English (French or German). sa. 50. E J Brill, POB 9000, 2300 PA Leiden The Netherlands. Ed L M de Ryk. **Ind/Abst** MLA Int. Bibliogr. Books Artic. Mod. Lang. Lit., Philos. Index. LC B1. DD 189.05. bk rev adv acc. Devoted in particular to the profane side of medieval philosophy and the intellectual life of the Middle Ages and Renaissance.

THE VOICE OF SANKARA. VFOAT Sankara-Bharati. Began with issue for May 1976. Periodical. II. English (Hindi and Sanskrit). qt. $10.00. Adi Sankara Advaita Research Centre, 26 College Road, Nungambakkam Madras 600006 India. LC B132.A3. DD 181.48205.

VOPROSY FILOSOFII. 1- 1947-. 0042-8744. Periodical. UR. Russian (English, French, German or Spanish). mo. $59.50. Victor Kamkin Inc (70156), 12224 Parklawn Drive, Rockville MD 20852. **Tel** (301)881-5973. **Ind/Abst** Sociol. Abstr., Am. Hist. Life, Hist. Abstr., Math. Rev., Lang. Lang. Behav. Abstr.

WAI KUO CHE HSUEH. V. 1-. Periodical. CC. Chinese. ir. 1.40. Hsin Hua Shu Tien, Pei-Ching fa Hsing so, Peking China. LC B8.C5. DD 105.

WAI KUO CHE HSUEH SHIH YEN CHIU CHI KAN. VFOAT Research on Empiricism and Rationalism in the History of Modern European Philosophy. Began with Dec. 1978 issue. CC. Chinese. ir. 0.86. Hsin Hua Shu Tien, Shang-Hai fa Hsing so, Shanghai China. LC B816. DD 109.

THE WANDERER. *See* Religion, Mythology, Rationalism - Roman Catholic Church.

WIENER HUMANISTISCHE BLATTER. No. 1- 0083-9965. AU. German. an. Hermann Boehlaus Nachfolger, Postfach 200, A-1040 Wein Austria. *Mitteilungen.*

WIENER JAHRBUCH FUR PHILOSOPHIE. *See* Yearbooks, Almanacs, Directories.

WISSENSCHAFT UND WELTBILD. 1.- Volume. 0043-6798. Periodical. AU. German. ir. Dr Arthur Werner Verlag, Sandwirtgasse 21, Vienna A-1060 Austria. **Ind/Abst** Philos. Index, Lang. Lang. Behav. Abstr., Sociol. Abstr.

WOLFENBUTTELER STUDIEN ZUR AUFKLARUNG. Vol. 1- 1974-. 0342-5940. German. ir. **Ind/Abst** MLA Int. Bibliogr. Books Artic. Mod. Lang. Lit. LC B802.

WORLD FUTURES. Vol. 17, No. 1/2 (Jan. 1981) -. 0260-4027. Periodical. US. English. ir. $130.00. Gordon & Breach, PO Box 197, London WC2E 9PX England. **Tel** SCIPUB G. Ed Ervin Laszlo. **Ind/Abst** Math. Rev., Sociol. Abstr., Soc. Welf. Soc. Plan./Policy Soc. Dev., Humanit. Index. LC B1. DD 303.4. CODEN WOFUDM. bk rev. adv acc. *Philosophy Forum, 0031-823X.*

WORLD ORDER. *See* Religion, Mythology, Rationalism.

XEROGRAMMATA: HOCHSCHULSCHRIFTEN ZUR PHILOSOPHIE. V. 1- 1967-. 0512-6614. GW. German. ir. Bouvier Verlag H Gerundmann, Postfach 1268 AM HOF 32, 5300 Bonn West Germany.

YEAR BOOK - AMERICAN PHILOSOPHICAL SOCIETY. See Yearbooks, Almanacs, Directories.

YOGA LIFE. Vol. 1, No. 1 (Winter 1982/83)-. 0824-2526. Periodical. CN. English. Free. Sivananda Ashram Yoga Camp, 8th Avenue, Val Morin Quebec J0T 2R0 Canada. Tel (819)322-3226. DD 613.70460601. bk rev. Circ 60,000. Articles on yoga science, holistic health, biology, biophysics, preventive medicine, nutrition and diet, meditation, science of the mind, world peace and general news of Sivananda Yoga Vedanta Centers International. Sivananda Yoga Life, 0227-4930.

YOGA-MIMAMSA. Began in 1958. 0044-0507. Periodical. English or Sanskrit. ir. LC B132.Y6. DD 181.4505.

YOGA RESEARCH. V. 1- 1978-. 0191-3298. US. English. an. Free to members Yoga Research Society, $5.00 Members of Swami Kuvalayananda Yoga Foundation, $7.00 Others. 251 South 12th Street, Philadelphia PA 19107. LC B132.Y6. DD 158.

ZEITSCHRIFT FUR PHILOSOPHISCHE FORSCHUNG. Volume 1-1946-. 0044-3751. Periodical. GW. German. qt. 145.-. Verlag Anton Hain Meisenheim, Postfach 180, D-6554 Meisenheim West Germany. Tel (06753)4353. Ed Hans Michael Baumgartner. Ind/Abst Philos. Index, Index Book Rev. Humanit. LC B3. DD 015. (cum index). bk rev. adv acc. Circ 1,400. Research in all branches of philosophy. Written for philosphers, students of philosophy, university libraries, institutes, etc.

ZIONIST IDEAS. See Sociology: General Works, Theory.

PHOTOGRAPHY & PHOTOGRAPHS

4-H SLIDE AND TAPE CATALOGUE. Main/Corp University of Saskatchewan. VAT Four-H Slide and Tape Catalogue. 0822-7608. Periodical. CN. English. U-Learn Office, PO Box 22 University of Saskatchewan, Saskatchewan S7N 0W0 Canada. DD 017.137.

596. VFOAT Five Ninety-Six. Vol. 1, No. 3 (June/July 1983). 0822-4331. Periodical. CN. English. bm. $15.00. Canadian Centre of Photography and Film, 596 Markham Street, Toronto Ontario M6G 2L8 Canada. DD 779.0922. Focus (Canadian Centre of Photography and Film), 0822-4323.

AAS PHOTO-BULLETIN. Main/Corp American Astronomical Society. Working Group on Photographic Materials. VFOAT Photo-Bulletin. VAT American Astronomical Society Photo-Bulletin. No. 1-. 0065-7433. Periodical. US. English. ir. $10.00. American Astronomical Society, University Florida 211 Space Science, Gainesville FL 32611. Tel (904)392-2052. Ed Alex G Smith. Ind/Abst Int. Aerosp. Abstr., Chem. Abstr., Comput. Control Abstr., Electr. Electron. Abstr., Sci. Abstr. Sect. A. Phys. Abstr. CODEN ASYBBE. bk rev. Intended to communicate practical information about the materials and techniques used in modern astronomical photography.

ABSTRACTS OF PHOTOGRAPHIC SCIENCE & ENGINEERING LITERATURE. See Indexes/Abstracts.

ACTAS DE CULTURA Y ENSAYOS FOTOGRAFICOS F/8. Periodical. Spanish. qt. Grupo Fotografico de Libre Expresion, Apartado de Correos 459, Sevilla Spain. LC TR1. DD 770.5.

ADVERTISING PHOTOGRAPHY IN CHICAGO. Vol. 1-. 0742-8006. US. English. an. $30.00. Alexander Communications Inc, 212 West Superior Suite 400, Chicago IL 60610. Tel (312)944-5115. Ed Kathleen Casper. DD 779. adv acc. Circ 10,000. (ctrl). Specifically created to promote the fact that Chicago has one of the most vigorous and innovative photographic talent pools in the country. Perfect reference of the Chicago photographic community.

AFTERIMAGE. Began publication in 1972. 0300-7472. Periodical. US. English. mo. $25.00. Visual Studies Workshop, 31 Prince Street, Rochester NY 14607. Tel (716)442-8676. Ed Nathan Lyons. Ind/Abst Film Lit. Index, Art Index, Repert. Int. Litt. Art. LC TR640. DD 770.5. bk rev. Circ 8,000. Critical reviews and news pertaining to fine art photography, video, film, visual sociology, media studies, and artist's books.

AMATEUR PHOTOGRAPHER. V. 95- (No. 2954-). Periodical. UK. English. wk. Business Press International Ltd, Perrymount Road/Haywards Heath W Sussex RH163BR England. Amateur Photographer & Cinematographer.

AMERICAN CINEMEDITOR : A PUBLICATION OF . . . AMERICAN CINEMA EDITORS, INC. Vol. 21, No. 3 (Fall 1971)-. 0044-7625. Periodical. US. English. qt. American Cinema Editors Inc, 4416-1/2 Finley Avenue, Los Angeles CA 90027. Tel P11-04-81. LC TR899. DD 778.53505. Cinemeditor, 0069-4169.

AMERICAN PHOTOGRAPHER. V. 1- June 1978-. 0161-6854. Periodical. US. English. mo. CBS Publications, 1515 Broadway, New York NY 10036, (subscription address): Neodata PO Box 2606 Boulder CO 80322). Ed Sean Callahan. Ind/Abst Mag. Index, Pop. Mag. Rev. LC TR1. DD 770.5.

AMERICAN PHOTOGRAPHY SHOWCASE. 0278-8314. Periodical. US. English. an. American Showcase, 724 Fifth Avenue Tenth Floor, New York NY 10019. Tel (212)245-0981. Ed Ira Shapiro. LC TR690.4. DD 770.2573. Circ 17,000. (ctrl). Superbly printed professional sourcebook representing the best and latest work from America's most outstanding commercial advertising photographers. American Showcase, 0742-6100.

AMERICAN SHOWCASE. VFOAT American Showcase of Photography, Graphic Design, Illustration, TV, Film, and Video. Vol. 3-V. 4. 0742-6100. US. English. an. $67.90. American Showcase, 724 5th Avenue/10th Floor, New York NY 10019. Tel (212)245-0981. LC TR690. DD 770.2573. American Showcase of Photography, Illustration and Graphic Design.

ANNUAL OF INDIAN PHOTOGRAPHY. 1978-. English. ir. 12/-. Sooriya Publishing House, 52 Thaiyappa Mudali Street, V O C Nagar, Madras 600 001 India. LC TR1. DD 770.5.

ANSCONIAN. Began publication with issue for May/June 1937. 0097-5796. Periodical. US. English. bm. LC TR1. DD 770.5.

ANUARIO DE LA FOTOGRAFIA ESPANOLA. Began in 1958. Spanish. ir. Editorial Everest, Carretera Leon-Astorga KM 4 500/Apartado 339, Leon Spain. LC TR640.

APERTURE (SAN FRANCISCO, CALIF.). (APERTURE). 0003-6420. Periodical. US. English. qt. $40.00. Aperture Inc, 20 East 23rd Street, New York NY 10010. Tel (212)505-555. Ed Christopher Hudson. Ind/Abst Art Index. LC TR1. DD 770.5. bk rev. adv acc. Circ 9,000. A division of Silver Mountain Foundation Inc. It is the only publication of its kind. A forum for fine art photography.

THE ARCHIVE. See Genealogy and Heraldry - Archives.

ART GALLERY. See The Arts (General).

ARTWEEK. See The Arts (General) - Art.

ASMP BOOK. VFOAT A.S.M.P. Book. VAT American Society of Magazine Photographers Book. 0737-2841. US. English. an. Annuals Publishing Company Inc, 10 East 23rd Street/Suite 520, New York NY 10010. LC TR12. DD 770.2573.

THE ASTROGRAPH. See Astronomy.

AURA. V. 1- Feb. 1976-. 0147-4855. Periodical. US. English. qt. $10.00. Andromeda Gallery, 493 Franklin Street, Buffalo NO 14203. LC TR640. DD 779.05.

THE BEST OF PHOTOJOURNALISM. 1977-. 0161-4762. US. English. an. $14.95. Running Press, 125 South 22nd Street, Philadelphia PA 19103. LC TR820. DD 770.0973. Photojournalism, 0363-5996.

BEST PHOTO OF THE YEAR. (THE BEST PHOTO OF THE YEAR). 1971-. 0304-9108. Indonesian. ir. DJL Merdeka Selatan 11, Djakarta Indonesia. LC TR640.

BIBLIOGRAPHY SERIES - UNIVERSITY OF ARIZONA. CENTER FOR CREATIVE PHOTOGRAPHY. See Bibliographies.

BIZARRE CLASSIX. V. 1-. 0145-8000. US. English. $6.00. PO Box C Gracie Station, New York NY 10028. LC TR676. DD 760.

BKSTS JOURNAL. See Communication - Broadcasting.

BLACK PHOTOGRAPHERS ANNUAL. (THE BLACK PHOTOGRAPHERS ANNUAL). 1973-. 0090-7197. US. English. an. Another View Inc, PO Box 1921, Brooklyn NY 11202. LC TR640. DD 779.05.

THE BLATANT IMAGE. Vol. 1 No. 1 (1981)-. 0277-8181. US. English. an. $18.00. Blatant Image, 2000 King Mountain Trail SV, Wolf Creek OR 97497. LC TR1. DD 770.88042.

BLUE BOOK, ILLUSTRATED PRICE GUIDE TO COLLECTABLE CAMERAS. (BLUE BOOK ILLUSTRATED PRICE GUIDE TO COLLECTABLE CAMERAS). VFOAT Illustrated Price Guide to Collectable Cameras. 0147-0663. US. English. an. $8.95. Photographic Memorabilia, PO Box 351, Lexington MA 02173. LC TR6.5. DD 771.31075.

BOLETIM - ASSOCIACAO BRASILEIRA DO MICROFILME. Main/Corp Asociacao Brasileira do Microfilme. BL. Portuguese. ir. Associacao Brasileira do Microfilme, Av Prestes Maia, 214-14 O-Cj 1414, Sao Paulo Brazil. LC TR835.

BRAUN PHOTONEWS. VFOAT Photonews. Ed. 34- Nov. 1978-. 0709-8081. Periodical. CN. English. ir. Braun Canada Ltd, 3269 American Drive, Mississauga Ontario L4V 1B9 Canada. DD 381.457710971. Braun Professional Photonews, 0709-8073.

BRITISH IMAGE. 1-. UK. English. sa. Arts Council of Great Britain, 105 Piccadilly, London W1V 0AU England. LC TR640. DD 779.0941.

BRITISH JOURNAL OF PHOTOGRAPHY. 0007-1196. Periodical. UK. English. wk. 38. Greenwood & Co Ltd, 28 Great James Street, London WC1N 3EZ England. Tel 01-404-4202. Ed Geoffrey Crawley. Ind/Abst Print. Abstr., Art Index, Comput. Control Abstr., Electr. Electron. Abstr., Sci. Abstr. Sect. A. Phys. Abstr., Phys. Abstr. CODEN BRJFAM. bk rev. adv acc. Circ 11,000. Photography of technology and science. Photographic Journal.

THE BRITISH JOURNAL OF PHOTOGRAPHY ANNUAL. 1964-. UK. English. an. Writers Digest, 9933 Alliance Road, Cincinnati OH 45242. Tel (513)984-0171. Ed Geoffrey Crawley. bk rev. More than 140 color and black and white photos showcasing everything from fine art to photojournalism to fashion trends, plus an exclusive section with formulas and processing methods. British Journal Photographic Annual and Photographer's Daily Companion.

BULLETIN - ASMP, THE SOCIETY OF PHOTOGRAPHERS IN COMMUNICATIONS. (BULLETIN - ASMP—THE SOCIETY OF PHOTOGRAPHERS IN COMMUNICATIONS). Main/Corp ASMP—The Society of Photographers in Communications. 0361-9168. Periodical. US. English. mo. The Society of Photographs in Communications, 60 E 42 Street, New York NY 10017. LC TR820. DD 770.6273.

BULLETIN - CALIFORNIA MUSEUM OF PHOTOGRAPHY. See Museums.

BULLETIN - SOCIETE BELGE DE PHOTOGRAMMETRIE. Main/Corp Societe Belge de Photogrammetrie. Periodical. French. ir. LC TR693.A1. CODEN SBPBBE.

BULLETIN TRIMESTRIEL DE LA SOCIETE BELGE DE PHOTOGRAMMETRIE ET DE TELEDETECTION. No. 141/142 (Mar./June 1981)-. Periodical. KO. Dutch (French, Mar./June 1981- and Dec. 1981). qt. Secretariat, Boulevard Pacheco, 2E Etage, 1000 Bruxelles Belgium. LC TR693.A1. DD 526.9805. Bulletin Trimestriel de la Societe Belge de Photogrammetrie.

BUYER'S GUIDE TO MICROGRAPHIC EQUIPMENT, PRODUCTS AND SERVICES. 0362-0131. US. English. 8728 Colesville Road, Silver Spring MD 20910. LC TR835. DD 338.4768.

Photography & Photographs

LES CAHIERS DE LA PHOTOGRAPHIE. Began in 1981. Periodical. FR. French. qt. $30.00. Association Critique Contemporaine Photographie, Lascledex Brax, F-47310 Laplume France.

CAMERA CANADA. VFOAT APA Camera Canada. No. 1- March 1969-. 0008-2090. Periodical. CN. English (includes some text in French). qt. 12.00. National Association for Photographic Art, 22 Abbeville Road, Scarborough Ontario M1H 1Y3 Canada. Tel (416)438-0252. Ed Gunter Ott. bk rev. adv acc. Circ 3,700. Feature portfolios of Canadian photographers and how-to articles, book reviews, competitions, and events. See work of best Canadian photographers both amateur and professional. We represent Canada photographers.

CAMERA (DURANGO, COLO.). (CAMERA). VFOAT Orion Camera Blue Book. 0883-489X. US. English. an. $99.50. Orion Research Corporation, 1315 Main Avenue/Suite 300 Durango CO 81301. *Camera Reference Guide, 0740-1647.*

CAMERA (LUCERNE). (CAMERA). Periodical. SZ. English. $26.00. C J Bucher, Zurichstrasse 3, CH-6002 Lucerne Switzerland. DD 770.5.

CAMERA (LUCERNE, SWITZERLAND) CEASED. (CAMERA). -60. 0008-2074. Periodical. English. ir. Zurichstrasse 3, Lucerne CH-6002 Switzerland. LC TR1. DD 770.5.

CAMERA LUCIDA. 1 (Fall 1979)-. 0740-8641. Periodical. US. in English. ty. $24.00. Camera Lucida, PO Box 176, Sun Prairie WI 53590. Ed R Muffoletto. LC TR1. DD 770.5.

CAMERART. V. 1- Spring 1958-. 0008-2082. Periodical. JA. English. ir. $30.00. Camerart, Hinode Building/5-4 2-Chome, Kyobashi Chuo Ku Tokyo Japan. Tel (03)563-4871. Ed Todoriki Kunika. Ind/Abst Artbiliogr. Mod. adv acc. Circ 14,000. Only English camera magazine in Japan.

CAMERART PHOTO TRADE DIRECTORY. See Yearbooks, Almanacs, Directories.

CAMERAWORK CEASED. VFOAT Camera Work. Ceased with No. 32, 1985. 0308-1672. Periodical. UK. English. 1.50. LC TR1. DD 770.5.

CANADA'S PHOTOGRAPHY MARKET. 1975/76-. 0318-7055. Periodical. CN. English. MacLean-Hunter, PO Box 100 Station A, Toronto Ontario M5W 1A7 Canada. DD 338.47770971.

CANADIAN PHOTO ANNUAL. V. 1- (No. 1-). 0316-4713. Periodical. CN. English. an. MacLean Hunter Ltd, 481 University Avenue, Toronto Ontario M5G 1W8 Canada. DD 770.5.

CANADIAN PHOTOGRAPHY. BUYING GUIDE. VFOAT Guide d'Achat. CN. English (includes some text in French). an. $9.28. MacLean Hunter, PO Box 100 Station A, Toronto Ontario M5W 1A7 Canada. DD 338.4768141802571.

THE CAPE ROCK. See Literature - Poetry.

CATALOG OF FINE ANTIQUE CAMERAS & PHOTOGRAPHIC IMAGES. No. 1- June 1974-. US. English. ir. Allen & Hilary Weiner, 80 Central Park West, New York NY 10023. Tel (212)787-8357.

CINE NEWS. Periodical. SI. English. ir. Singapore Cine Club, 293-A Selegie Complex, Singapore 7 Singapore. LC TR845. DD 778.5305.

CINEFEX. See Motion Picture.

CLOSE-UP (CAMBRIDGE, MASS.). (CLOSE-UP). Began in Sept. 1970. 0740-5545. Periodical. US. English. qt. Close-Up Polaroid Corp, 575 Technology Square, Cambridge MA 02139.

COLOR PHOTOGRAPHY. VFOAT Color. 0069-5998. US. English. an. $1.50. Ziff Davis Publishing Company, 1 Park Avenue, New York NY 10016. LC TR510. DD 778.605. *Color Annual.*

COMBINATIONS. Vol. 1, No. 1 (Spring 1977)-. 0145-899X. Periodical. US. English. $14.00. Mary Ann Lynch, Greenfield Center, New York NY 12833. Ed M A Lynch. LC TR640. DD 770.5.

COMMERCIAL PRICE LIST FOR STILL PHOTOGRAPHS. Main/Corp National Film Board of Canada. 0709-6771. Periodical. CN. English. National Film Board of Canada, Tunney's Pasture, Ottawa Ontario K1A 0M9 Canada.

CONSUMER GUIDE PHOTOGRAPHIC EQUIPMENT TEST REPORTS. (CONSUMER GUIDE PHOTOGRAPHIC EQUIPMENT TEST REPORTS : BEST BUYS & DISCOUNT PRICES). VFOAT Photographic Equipment Test Reports. 0091-4576. US. English. an. $1.95. Consumer Guide, 3323 West Main Street, Skokie IL 60076. LC TR196. DD 771.

CONTEMPORARY PHOTOGRAPHER. Vol. 1-. 0010-7506. Periodical. US. English. ir. Contemporary Photographer, 305 East Culpepper Street, Culpepper VA 22701. DD 770.

CONTRE-JOUR. (CONTRE-JOUR : REVUE DE LA FEDERATION QUEBECOISE DU LOISIR PHOTOGRAPHIQUE). V. 1, No. 1 (Feb./March/April 1983)-. Periodical. CN. French. Federation Quebecoise du Loisir Photographique, 1415 Est rue Jarry, Montreal Quebec H2E 2Z7 Canada. DD 77023309714. *Bulletin d'Information (Federation Quebecoise du Loisir Photographique), 0821-1191.*

CORPORATE SHOWCASE. VFOAT Corporate Show Case. 2-. 0742-9975. US. English. an. $25.00. American Showcase, 724 Fifth Avenue, New York NY 10019. Tel (212)245-0981. Ed Ira Shapiro. LC TR706. DD 770.2573. adv acc. Circ 10,000. (ctrl). The only resource book devoted to photography and illustration for corporate assignments: corporate advertising, sales brochures, annual reports, etc. *Corporate Photography Showcase, 0731-9231.*

COTECFLASH. 1973-. 0376-7590. Periodical. Spanish. ir. Co Tec, Rocafort 41 Entlo, Barcelona Spain. LC TR640. DD 779.05.

COYOTI PRINTS. See Journalism.

CREATIVE CAMERA. No. 44- Feb. 1968-. 0011-0876. Periodical. UK. English. mo. 29.25 Domestic, $54.00 Foreign. COO Press Publishing Co, 19 Doughty Street, London WC21N 2PT England. Tel (01)405-7562. Ed Susan Butler and Peter Turner. Ind/Abst Art Index. LC TR640. DD 770.5. bk rev. adv acc. Circ 6,000. News and reviews of photography as a visual art in Great Britain including coverage of major photographic exhibitions with many high quality illustrations. *Creative Camera Owner.*

CREATIVE CAMERA COLLECTION. 5- 1979-. 0306-3909. Periodical. UK. English. an. COO Press Ltd, 19 Doughty Street, London WC1N SPT England. LC TR640. DD 770.5. *Creative Camera International Year Book.*

CUADERNOS DE FOTOGRAFIA. No. 1- Mayo 1972-. Periodical. Spanish (summaries in English). ir. Saf Fotografia, c/o San Bernabe 18, Madrid Spain. LC TR640.

DARKROOM PHOTOGRAPHY. Vol. 1, No 1 (Mar./Apr. 1979)-. 0163-9250. Periodical. US. English. ir. $14.97. Darkroom Photography, One Hallidie Plaza/Suite 600, San Francisco CA 94102. Tel (415)989-4360. Ed Richard Senti. LC TR287. DD 770.28305. bk rev. adv acc. Circ 75,000. Issued also on microfilm. University Microfilms. Photography for beginners, hobbyists, educators, students, professionals, and industrial users who are interested in any aspect of creative photography, especially in the darkroom.

IL DIAFRAMMA CEASED. VFOAT Fotografia Italiana. N. 172-264. Periodical. Italian. bm. LC TR1. DD 770.5. *Popular Photography Italiana.*

DIRECTORY OF PROFESSIONAL PHOTOGRAPHY. See Yearbooks, Almanacs, Directories.

LA DOCUMENTATION PHOTOGRAPHIQUE. 0419-5361. Periodical. FR. French. bm. Documentation Francaise, 124 rue Henri Barbusse, 93308 Aubervilliers CDX France. Tel 834-9275.

DUMONT FOTO. 1- 1978-. GW. German. ir. Dumont Buchverlag, Postfach 1004 68, D 5000 Koln 1 West Germany. LC TR640. DD 770.5.

EUROPEAN PHOTOGRAPHY. 81-. Periodical. GE. English. qt $20.00. Andreas Muller Pohle, Stargarder Weg 18, D3400 Gottingen West Germany. Tel (0551)75607. Ed Andreas Muller Pohle. bk rev. adv acc. Circ 5,000. The international, bilingual (English-German) magazine for creative photography, with critical essays, portfolios, news, book and exhibition reviews.

EVERFOTO. Spanish. ir. Espana, Editorial Everest, Carretera Leon-Astorga KM. 4 500, Leon Spain. LC TR640.

EXPOSURE. 1964. 0098-8863. Periodical. US. English. qt. $25.00. Society of Photography Education, PO Box 1651, FDR Post Office, New York NY 10150. Ed Jan Z Grover. LC TR1. DD 770.5. bk rev. adv acc. Circ 1,500. (ctrl). Scholarly articles with emphasis on critical dialogue, historical perspectives, and educational issues concerning the art of photography.

FORENSIC PHOTOGRAPHY. Periodical. UK. English. qt. $2.21. Forensic Publishing Company, PO Box 18, Bagnor Regis, Sussex England.

FOTO FINDER. 0272-1252. US. English. $10.00. The Photoletter, Osceola WI 54020. LC TR12. DD 770.2573.

FOTO GALAXIS. Multilingual (English and Spanish). ir. Galaxis, Zamora 46-48, Barcelona Spain. LC TR690.

FOTO MAGAZIN. Began publication with issue for Apr. 1949. 0340-6660. Periodical. GW. German. mo. Ringier Verlag GMBH, Postfach 701529 Ortlerstrasse 8, 8000 Muenchen 70 West Germany. Tel 089/769 92-0. LC TR1. *Foto-Spiegel.*

FOTO (STOCKHOLM, SWEDEN : 1983). (FOTO). Vol. 45, No. 1 (Jan. 1983)-. 0345-3626. Periodical. SW. Swedish. mo. 19.75. Specialtidningsforlaget, Sveavagen 53, 113 59 Stockholm Sweden. Ind/Abst Artbibliogr. Mod. *Foto Och Filmteknik.*

FOTO (WARSAW, POLAND). (FOTO : MAGAZYN FOTOGRAFICZNY). Vol. 1 (1) (Jan. 1975)-. 0324-8453. Periodical. PL. Polish. mo. ARS Polona, Krakowskie Przedmiescie 7, 00-068 Warsaw Poland. Ed Z Szargut.

FOTOGESCHICHTE. V. 1, No. 1-. 0720-5260. Periodical. GW. German. ir. 100.00. Fichardstrasse 52, D-6000 Frankfurt 1 West Germany. LC TR15. DD 770.9.

FOTOGRAFIA (WARSAW, POLAND). (FOTOGRAFIA). No. 1 (July 1953)-. 0015-8801. Periodical. PL. Polish. qt. ARS Polona, Krakowskie Przedmiescie 7, 00-068 Warsaw Poland.

FOTOGRAFIE. July 1974-. 0015-8836. Periodical. SZ. German (summaries in English, French and Russian). mo. $21.87. Kunst & Wissen Erich Bieber, Dufourstrasse 51, CH-8008 Zurich Switzerland. Tel 011-41-1-69 44 20. *Gebrauchsgrafik, Fotografische Rundschau; Kleinbild; Farben-Fotografie.*

FOTOGRAFIE. VFOAT Czechoslovak Review. Began publication in 1957. Periodical. Czech. ir. LC TR1.

FOTOGRAFIE (FOTOGRAFIE-VERLAG). (FOTOGRAFIE). 0344-1202. Periodical. GW. German. ir. 55.00. Fotografie Verlag GMBH, Rote Strasse 12, D-3400 Gottingen West Germany.

FOTOGRAMETRIA, FOTOINTERPRETACION Y GEODESIA. Spanish. ir. Tacuba No 5, Corredores Entrada No 4, Salon No 39, Mexico 1 Mexico. LC TA593.

FOTOTECNICA. Periodical. Spanish. ir. Secretariado Ejecutivo Union de Periodistas de Cuba, Calle 23 No 452, Esq A I Vedado, La Habana Cuba. LC TR820.

THE FREE STOCK PHOTOGRAPHY DIRECTORY. See Yearbooks, Almanacs, Directories.

FUNCTIONAL PHOTOGRAPHY. V. 10, No. 5- Sept. 1975-. 0360-7216. Periodical. US. English. bm. $7.50. PTN Publishing Corporation, 101 Crossways Park West, Woodbury NY 11797. Tel (516)496-8000. Ed David A Silverman. Ind/Abst GeoRef, Int. Aerosp. Abstr., Comput. Control Abstr., Electr. Electron. Abstr., Sci. Abstr. Sect. A. Phys. Abstr., Phys. Abstr., Bibliogr. Index Geol. LC TR692. DD 778.305. NLM W1 FU5182. CODEN FUPHDO. bk rev. adv acc. Circ 40,000. (ctrl). Readers are scientists, doctors, research personnel who use imaging as a part of their work, to document procedures or record scientific data. *Photographic Applications in Science, Technology and Medicine, 0098-8227.*

GELATINE. No. 1, May 1981-. 0712-2500. Periodical. CN. French. ir. $5.00 for 10 Issues. Gelatine, 1671 rue St-Hubert, Montreal Quebec H2L 3Z1 Canada. DD 770.9714.

Photography & Photographs

THE GERMAN PHOTOGRAPHIC ANNUAL. 1956-. 0435-5806. US. English (German). an. Hastings House Publishing Inc, 10 East 40th Street, New York NY 10016. **Tel** (212)689-5400. Ed W Strache and O Steinert.

GOOD OLD DAYS PHOTO ALBUM. 0160-3132. Periodical. US. English. qt. $3.00. Tower Press, Box 428, Seabrook NH 03874.

GUIDE TO MICROGRAPHIC EQUIPMENT. 6th- Ed. 0360-8654. US. English. an. Association for Information & Image Management, 1100 Wayne Avenue, Silver Springs MD 20910. **Tel** (301)587-8202. **LC** TR835. **DD** 380.14568165. *Guide to Microreproduction Equipment.*

HASSELBLAD. 0345-4533. Periodical. English. qt. 100.-. Victor Hasselblad, Box 220, S40123 Goteborg 1 Sweden. **Tel** 31/171960. Ed Odd Tommelsted. **Circ** 15,000. Presenting Hasselblad photographers and their pictures.

HERE'S HOW. (THE HERE'S HOW). **Main/Corp** Eastman Kodak Company. 0092-5365. US. English. $1.25. Eastman Kodak Company, 343 State Street/Department 454, Rochester NY 14651. **LC** TR147. **DD** 770.28.

HISTORY OF PHOTOGRAPHY. V. 1- Jan. 1977-. 0308-7298. Periodical. UK. English. qt. $60.00. University of Texas Press, Box 7819, Austin TX 78712. **Tel** (512)471-4531. Ed Heinz K Henisch. **Ind/Abst** Artbibliogr. Mod., Art Index, Repert. Int. Litt. Art. **LC** TR15. **DD** 770.9. adv acc. **Circ** 550. (ctrl). Deals with art - historical, aesthetic, social, technical, and scientific aspects of the medium in historical perspective.

HODO SHASHIN. JA. Japanese. ir. 1500. Chunichi Shimbun Honsha, 6-1 Sannomaru 1, Naka-Ku Nagoya Japan. **LC** TR820.

IMAGE. V. 1- Jan. 1952-. 0536-5465. Periodical. US. English. ir. $10.00. International Museum of Photography at George Eastman House Inc, 900 East Avenue, Rochester NY 14607. **Ind/Abst** Art Index, Energy Res. Abstr., Film Lit. Index, Repert. Int. Litt. Art. **LC** TR1. **DD** 770.974789. Available on microfilm from University Microfilms International.

IMAGE NATION *CEASED.* 1-26. 0317-4808. Periodical. CN. English. $10.00. 401 (Rear), Huron Street, 181 Ontario Canada. **LC** TR640. **DD** 779.0922.

IMAGEN. Yearly V. 1- August 1973-. Spanish. ir. Direccion General de Aerofotografia, Apartado Barranco-38, Lima Peru. **LC** TR810.

IMAGES & IDEAS BY PHOTOMETHODS. VFOAT Images and Ideas By Photomethods. Vol. 1, No. 1 (July 1982)-. 0732-7870. Periodical. US. English. ir. $3.00 Per Copy US, $4.00 Per Copy Others. Ziff-Davis Publishing Company, 1 Park Avenue, New York NY 10016. **LC** TR1. **DD** 770.5.

IMC JOURNAL. (IMC JOURNAL : PUBLICATION OF THE INTERNATIONAL INFORMATION MANAGEMENT CONGRESS). VFOAT I.M.C. Journal. VAT International Micrographic Congress Journal. Began with Fall 1967 issue. 0019-0012. Periodical. US. English. qt. $30.00. Compos-O-List Systems Inc, Silver Spring MD 20817. **Ind/Abst** ABI/Inform, Comput. Control Abstr., Electr. Electron. Abstr., Sci. Abstr. Sect. A. Phys. Abstr., Libr. Inf. Sci. Abstr., Ref. Source. **LC** TR835. **DD** 001.552305. **CODEN** IMGCB7.

IMPRESSIONS MONOGRAPH. Began publication in 1974?. Monographic Series. CN. English. Impressions, PO Box 5/Station B, Toronto Ontario M5T 2T2 Canada. Ed S Sugino and J Pendergrast. **DD** 779.

IMPRESSUM II. VFOAT Impressum 2. Aug. 1, (1981/1982)-. French (German and Italian). an. Burex Medienpublikationen, Niederfeldstrasse 26, 8932 Mettmenstette Switzerland. **LC** TR12. **DD** 001.4025494.

AN INDEX TO ARTICLES ON PHOTOGRAPHY. *See* Indexes/Abstracts.

INDUSTRIAL PHOTOGRAPHY. V. 1- Fall 1952-. 0019-8595. Periodical. US. English. mo. Media Horizons Inc, 50 West 23rd Street, New York NY 10010. **Tel** (212)645-1000. **Ind/Abst** Comput. Control Abstr., Electr. Electron. Abstr., Sci. Abstr. Sect. A. Phys. Abstr., Chem. Abstr., Eng. Index Annu., Sel. Water Resour. Abstr., Appl. Sci. Technol. Index, Phys. Abstr. **CODEN** INPHA5.

INDUSTRY STANDARD. VFOAT NMA Standard. No. 1- 1971-. Monographic Series. English. ir.

INTERNATIONAL ARCHIVES OF PHOTOGRAMMETRY. *See* Genealogy and Heraldry - Archives.

INTERNATIONAL FILE OF MICROGRAPHICS EQUIPMENT & ACCESSORIES. VAT International File of Micrographics Equipment and Accessories. 0148-5121. US. English. $250.00. Microform Review Inc, 520 Riverside Avenue, Westport CT 06880. **LC** TR835. **DD** 338.47681418.

INTERNATIONAL FIRE PHOTOGRAPHERS ASSOCIATION : NEWSLETTER : IFPA. VFOAT Newsletter. Periodical. US. English. qt. $6.00. PO Box 201, Elmhurst IL 60126. **Tel** (312)530-3097. Ed Robert Trivalos. bk rev. adv acc. **Circ** 750. (ctrl). Uses of fire photography to educate public and fire service. Promotion of proper uses of fire photography as evidence. Tools and techniques for fire photographers.

INTERNATIONAL PHOTOGRAPHER. 0020-8299. Periodical. US. English. mo. International Photographer, 7715 Sunset Boulevard, Hollywood CA 90046. **Tel** (213)876-0160.

INTERNATIONAL PHOTOGRAPHY INDEX. *See* Indexes/Abstracts.

THE JOURNAL FOR EDUCATION IN PHOTOJOURNALISM. VAT Journal for Education in Photo Journalism. Vol. 1, No. 1 (Winter 1981)-. 0273-9917. Periodical. US. English. qt. The Journal for Education in Photojournlism, Box 1393, Garden Grove CA 92642. **LC** TR820. **DD** 778.9907.

JOURNAL FUR SIGNALAUFZEICH. Began in 1973. 0323-598X. Periodical. SZ. German (summaries in English and Russian). bm. $54.72. Kunst & Wissen Erich Bieber, Dufourstrasse 51, CH-8008 Zurich Switzerland. **Tel** 011-41-1-69 44 20. **Ind/Abst** Comput. Control Abstr., Electr. Electron. Abstr., Sci. Abstr. Sect. A. Phys. Abstr., Energy Res. Abstr., Chem. Abstr., Sci. Cit. Index, Abr. Ed., Phys. Abstr. **LC** TR280. **CODEN** JSZMAE.

JOURNAL OF AMERICAN PHOTOGRAPHY. Vol. 1, No. 1 (Jan. 1983)-. 0737-3295. Periodical. US. English. qt. Photographic Society, 890 Supremem Drive, Bebsenville IL 60106. **LC** TR1. **DD** 770.5.

JOURNAL OF APPLIED PHOTOGRAPHIC ENGINEERING *CEASED.* V. 1-9. 0098-7298. Periodical. US. English. bm. $60.00 Domestic, $70.00 Foreign. Society of Photographic Scientists and Engineers, 7003 Kilworth Lane, Springfield VA 22151. **Ind/Abst** Eng. Index Annu., Eng. Index Mon., Eng. Index Bioeng. Abstr., Eng. Index Energy Abstr., Int. Aerosp. Abstr., GeoRef, Chem. Abstr., Print. Abstr. **LC** TR1.S76. **DD** 778.305. **CODEN** JAPEDL. (cum index).

JOURNAL OF BIOLOGICAL PHOTOGRAPHY. Began with: Vol. 48, No. 1 (Jan. 1980). 0274-497X. Periodical. US. English. qt. Biological Photographic Association, #1 Buttonwood Court, Indian Head Park IL 60525. **Tel** (312)246-9118. **Ind/Abst** Biol. Abstr., Abstr. Photogr. Sci. Eng. Lit., Index Med. **LC** TR1. **DD** 574.028. NLM W1 JO564D. **CODEN** JBPHD3. *Journal of the Biological Photographic Association, 0006-3215.*

JOURNAL OF IMAGING SCIENCE. V. 29, No. 1 (Jan./Feb. 1985)-. 8750-9237. Periodical. US. English. bm. $70.00 Domestic, $80.00 Foreign. Society of Photographic Scientists and Engineers, 7003 Kilworth Lane, Springfield VA 22151. **DD** 770. **CODEN** PSENAC. Available in microform. *Photographic Science and Engineering, 0031-8760.*

JOURNAL OF MICROGRAPHICS *CEASED.* VFOAT Micrographics. V. 3-16, No. 6. 0022-2712. Periodical. US. English. mo. Free to Members, $55.00 Nonmembers. NMA Headquarters, 8728 Colesville Road/Suite 1101, Silver Spring MD 20910. **Ind/Abst** Eng. Index, Libr. Inf. Sci. Abstr., Ref. Source, Chem. Abstr., Libr. Lit. **LC** TR835. **DD** 686.43. **CODEN** JMGPBN. *NMA Journal.*

THE JOURNAL OF PHOTOGRAPHIC SCIENCE. 0022-3638. Periodical. UK. English. bm. 60.00 Domestic, 70.00 Foreign. Royal Photographic Society, The Octagon, Milsom Street, Bath BA1 1DN England. **Tel** 0225-62841. Ed R J Cox. **Ind/Abst** Soc. Sci. Citation Index, Electr. Electron. Abstr., Phys. Abstr., Comput. Control Abstr., Chem. Abstr. bk rev. adv acc. **Circ** 3,000. All aspects of photographic scientific and technological research and its applications.

JOURNAL OF SCIENTIFIC AND APPLIED PHOTOGRAPHY AND CINEMATOGRAPHY. Began with: V. 3, No. 4, 1958. Periodical. US. English (summaries in Russian). ir. $496.00. Gordon & Breach, PO Box 197, London WC2E 9PX England. Ed K V Chibison. **LC** TR1. **DD** 778.0822. bk rev. adv acc.

KAMERA UND SCHULE. Began with: April/June 1962. 0022-8109. Periodical. GW. German. qt. 15.80. Junger Verlag GMBH, Postfach 100962, D 6050 Offenbach West Germany. **Tel** (069)840003-37. bk rev. adv acc. **Circ** 4,000. Used in photography classes in school, gives suggestions for the teacher. The subscription is read by students, teachers, and photo amateurs.

KELLNER'S MONEYGRAM. 0162-3702. Periodical. US. English. mo. Kellner's Photo Services, 1768 Rockville Drive, Baldwin NY 11510.

THE KODAK COMPASS. 1961-. 0452-2559. Periodical. US. English. qt. Eastman Kodak Company, 343 State Street, Rochester NY 14650.

KODAK HIGHLIGHTS. Periodical. US. English. qt. Eastman Kodak Company, 343 State Street, Rochester NY 14650. **Tel** (716)724-4000.

KODAK STUDIO LIGHT. **Main/Corp** Eastman Kodak Company. VFOAT Studio Light. 0094-8926. US. English. Eastman Kodak Company, 343 State Street, Rochester NY NY 14650. **LC** TR1. **DD** 770.5. *New Kodak Studio Light.*

KODAK TECH BITS. (TECH BITS). Began in 1963?. 0452-2591. Periodical. US. English. qt. Free to Qualified Audiences. Tech Bits, Eastman Kodak Company, c/o Editor, 343 State Street, Rochester NY 14650. (ctrl).

LEICA-FOTOGRAFIE. Began publication with Aug./Sept. 1949 issue. 0024-0621. Periodical. German. ir. $24.00. PDQ Distribution Inc, PO Box 2013, River Vale NJ 07675. **Tel** (201)767-1100. Ed Edmund Bugdoll. **LC** TR1. bk rev. adv acc. **Circ** 5,000. International magazine of 35mm photography. Contains photo essays, profiles of leading photographers, how-to articles, equipment news. Excellent reproductions in color and black and white.

LEICA FOTOGRAFIE (ENGLISH EDITION). (LEICA FOTOGRAFIE). 0174-0253. Periodical. GW. English. ir. Umschau Verlag, Stuttgarter Str 18-24, D-6000 Frankfurt Main West Germany. **LC** TR1. **DD** 771.31.

LEICA MANUAL. 0093-9374. US. English. Morgan & Morgan, 400 Warburton Avenue, Hastings-on-Hudson NY 10706. **LC** TR146. **DD** 771.31. *Leica Manual.*

LENS MAGAZINE. 0363-2636. Periodical. US. English. bm. $4.95. Lens c/o Sam Fisher, 645 Stewart Avenue, Garden City NY 11530. **Tel** (516)222-2500. Ed Barry Tanenbaum. **LC** TR1. **DD** 770.5. bk rev adv acc. **Circ** 100,000. (ctrl). Edited for advanced amateur photographers. Articles deal with how-to information and techniques plus the enjoyment of picture taking. Covers still, darkroom, film, video, new products, books.

LENS' ON CAMPUS MAGAZINE. VFOAT Lens' on Campus. Vol. 1, No. 1 (Feb. 1979)-. 0190-986X. Periodical. US. English. qt. United Technical Publications, 645 Stewart Avenue, Garden City NY 11530. **LC** TR1. **DD** 770.5.

MAGAZINE OVO. (LE MAGAZINE OVO). Began with 27/28 in 1978. 0704-9161. Periodical. CN. French. qt. $6. Le Magazine Ovo, CP 1431 Succursale A, Montreal Quebec H3C 2Z9 Canada. **DD** 770.5. *Ovo Photo, 0315-9507.*

MEMBERSHIP DIRECTORY OF THE PHOTOGRAPHIC HISTORICAL SOCIETY OF N.Y. *See* Yearbooks, Almanacs, Directories.

MICROGRAPHIC EQUIPMENT DIRECTORY AND BUYING GUIDE. *See* Yearbooks, Almanacs, Directories.

MICROGRAPHICS EQUIPMENT REVIEW. Series/Titl A Microform Review Publication. V. 1- Jan./July 1976-. 0362-1005. Periodical. US. English. an. Meckler Publishing, 11 Ferry Lane West, Westport CT 06880. **Tel** (203)226-6967. **Ind/Abst** Libr. Inf. Sci. Abstr.,

Photography & Photographs

Consum. Index Prod. Eval. Inf. Source. LC TR835. DD 686.43028.

THE MICROGRAPHICS INDEX. See Indexes/Abstracts.

THE MICROGRAPHICS INDEX. SUPPLEMENT. See Indexes/Abstracts.

MICROGRAPHICS TODAY. V. 10- Aug. 1975-. 0149-9300. Periodical. US. English. mo. National Micrographics Association, 8719 Colesville Road, Silver Spring MD 20910. *Micro-News Bulletin.*

MICROINFO. Periodical. UK. English. mo. $130.26. Microinfo Ltd, PO Box 3, Alton Hants GU34 2PG England. LC TR835. DD 686.4305.

MILLIMETER. Began in 1973. 0164-9655. Periodical. US. English. mo. $45.00. Millimeter Magazine Inc, 826 Broadway, New York NY 10003. **Tel** (212)867-3636. **Ind/Abst** Film Lit. Index, Media Rev. Dig. LC TR845. DD 778.505.

MINOLTA MIRROR. US. English. an. $6.00. Minolta Corporation, 101 Williams Drive, Ramsey NJ 07446. **Tel** (201)825-4000.

MODERN PHOTOGRAPHY. 0026-8240. Periodical. US. English. mo. ABC Leisure Magazines, 825 7th Avenue, New York NY 10019, (subscription address: Communication Data Services 112 Tenth Street Des Moines IA 50309). **Ind/Abst** Art Archaeol. Tech. Abstr., Book Rev. Index, Consum. Index Prod. Eval. Inf. Source, Film Lit. Index, Pop. Mag. Rev., Read. Guide Period. Lit., Biogr. Index, Access, Mag. Index. LC TR1. DD 770.5. Available on microfilm. *Minicam Photography, 0096-5863.*

MODERN PHOTOGRAPHY ANNUAL. 1970-. 0580-8162. US. English, French or German. an. $1.50. Modern Photography One Astor Plaza, New York NY 10036. LC TR640. DD 779.05.

MODERN PHOTOGRAPHY'S GUIDE TO THE WORLD'S BEST CAMERAS. VFOAT World's Best Cameras. 0197-5986. Periodical. US. English. an. $3.95. ABC Leisure Magazine, 825 7th Avenue, New York NY 10019. **Tel** (212)826-8360. LC TR250. DD 771.3.

MOSTRA DE FOTOGRAFIA. August 1, 1979-. Portuguese. ir. LC TR640. DD 779.0922.

NASA PHOTOGRAPHY INDEX. See Indexes/Abstracts.

NENKAN NIHON NO KOKOKU SHASHIN. VFOAT Nihon No Kokoku Shashin, Advertising Photography in Japan. '82-. English (Japanese). an. 7800. Kodansha, 12-21 Otowa 2 Bunkyo-ku 112, Tokyo-To-Japan. LC TR690.4. DD 659.1323.

NEW YORK PHOTO DISTRICT NEWS. 0274-7731. Periodical. US. English. mo. $29.00. Visions Unlimited Corporation, 167 Third Avenue, New York NY 10003. **Tel** (212)677-8418. Ed Liz Forst. bk rev. adv acc. **Circ** 22,000. A trade periodical serving the professional photographer nationwide.

NEWSLETTER - INTERNATIONAL CONGRESS ON HIGH SPEED PHOTOGRAPHY AND PHOTONICS. (NEWSLETTER). VFOAT HSSP Newsletter. Vol. 1, No. 1 (Winter 1981)-. 0272-7994. Periodical. US. English. ty. Society of Photo-Optical Instrumental Engineers, PO Box 10, Bellingham WA 98227.

NEWSLETTER OF THE FRIENDS OF PHOTOGRAPHY. Main/Corp Friends of Photography. Began with V. 1 in 1978. 0163-9552. Periodical. US. English. mo. $18.00 Membership. Friends of Photography, Sunset Center PO Box 239, Carmel CA 93921.

NIKON WORLD. V. 1- 1967-. Periodical. US. English. ir. $16.00. Nikoninc, PO Box 9605, Church Street Station, New York NY 10049. **Tel** (516)222-0200. Ed Nancy Stevens. LC TR1. bk rev. **Circ** 45,000. Portfolios of Nikon photographers and new product information. Winter issue is a calendar for following year.

NMA ANNUAL REPORT. Main/Corp National Microfilm Association. VAT National Microfilm Association Annual Report. 1973/74-. US. English. an. National Microfilm Association, 8728 Colesville Road, Suite 1101, Silver Spring MD 20910. LC TR835. DD 686.4306273.

NORTHLIGHT (TEMPE, ARIZ.). (NORTHLIGHT). 0277-8076. Periodical. US. English. qt. $6.50. Friends of Photography at ASU, Art Department, Arizona State University, Tempe AZ 85281. **Tel** (602)965-6517. LC TR1. DD 770.5.

NSA PHOTO ALBUM. Main/Corp Nichiren Shoshu Academy. VAT Nichiren Shoshu Academy Photo Album. 0099-0884. US. English. World Tribune Press, 1351 Ocean Front, Santa Monica CA 90407. LC BQ8401.2.N52. DD 909.837.

OBJECTIF - A.L.P.A. (L'OBJECTIF : LE JOURNAL DE L'A.L.P.A.) VFOAT Journal de l'A.L.P.A. VAT Objectif - Association Longueuilloise des Photographes Amateurs. April 81-. 0712-6107. Periodical. CN. French. qt. Free to Members. Objectif, c/o Association Longueuilloise des Photographes Amateurs, 100 rue St-Laurent, Longueuil Quebec J4H 1M1 Canada. DD 770.23305.

OVO MAGAZINE. 27/28-. 0704-9153. Periodical. CN. English. qt. $13.93. OVO Magazine, 307 West rue Ste Catherine/Suite 300, Montreal Quebec H2X 2A3 Canada. DD 770.5. *OVO Photo.*

PENTHOUSE PHOTO WORLD. V. 1- Apr./May 1976-. 0363-003X. Periodical. US. English. bm. $12.00. Penthouse Photo World Ltd, 909 3rd Avenue, New York NY 10022. LC TR1. DD 770.5.

PERIPLO. See Natural History.

PETERSEN'S PHOTOGRAPHIC. VFOAT Photographic. Vol. 8, No. 7- Nov. 1979-. 0199-4913. Periodical. US. English. mo. $9.76. Petersen Publishing Company, 6725 Sunset Boulevard, Los Angeles CA 90028. **Tel** (213)657-5100. Ed Karen Geller-Shinn. **Ind/Abst** Abr. Read. Guide, Book Rev. Index, Consum. Index Prod. Eval. Inf. Source, Pop. Mag. Rev., Read. Guide Period. Lit., Mag. Index. adv acc. **Circ** 276,600. The creative photographer's "how-to" magazine, with the latest on equipment, lenses and darkroom techniques. *Petersen's Photographic Magazine, 0048-3583.*

THE PHILADELPHIA PHOTO REVIEW. 0363-6488. Periodical. US. English. mo. $10.00. Dry Mount Press, 3619 Baring Street, Philadelphia PA 19104. LC TR640. DD 770.5.

PHOTO BUYING GUIDE. 1968-. US. English. an. $3.95. Publications International Ltd, 3841 West Oakton Street, Skokie IL 60076. LC TR196. DD 771. *Camera and Lens Buying Guide.*

PHOTO COMMUNIQUE. V. 1- Mar./Apr. 1979-. 0708-5435. Periodical. CN. English. qt. $16.50. Holocene Foundation, PO Box 129/Station M, Toronto Ont M6S 4T2 Canada. **Tel** (416)597-0068. Ed Gail Fisher-Taylor. LC TR640. DD 770.5. bk rev. adv acc. **Circ** 11,000. With diverse articles, interviews and news items, this highly visual magazine explores the way photography touches our lives.

PHOTO CRAFT NEWS. V. 1- Sept./Oct. 1979. 0194-1348. Periodical. US. English. bm. $18.00 Domestic, $20.00 Canada. Embee Press, 82 Pine Grove Avenue, Kingston NY 12401.

PHOTO-ESSAI CEASED. Vol. 1, No. 1 (Winter 1981)-. 0710-944X. Periodical. CN. English. an. $15.00. Butterfly Books, PO Box 2234, Winnipeg Man Canada R3C 3R5. Ed W P Stewart. DD 779.05.

PHOTO-FORUM. VFOAT Photo Forum. 1979. Periodical. AT. English. ir. 34.00. Iris Publishing Company Private Ltd, PO Box 143, Mona Vale New South Wales 2103 Australia. **Tel** (02)981-5511. Ed V Jarvis. bk rev. adv acc. **Circ** 1,200. (ctrl). Sent to the top 1,200 people who make up the amateur photo market in Australia. Its editorial aims at being informative whilst interesting to photo shops, mini labs, etc. *New Zealand Photography.*

PHOTO INFORMATION ALMANAC. See Yearbooks, Almanacs, Directories.

PHOTO LAB INDEX. See Indexes/Abstracts.

PHOTO LAB MANAGEMENT. Began with V. 1 in Mar./Apr. 1979. 0164-4769. Periodical. US. English. mo. $8.00. PLM Publishing Company Inc, 1312 Lincoln Boulevard, Santa Monica CA 90406. **Tel** (213)451-1344. Ed Carolyn Ryan. DD 771. adv acc. **Circ** 11,000. (ctrl). Directed to photo lab management personnel including lab owners, managers, production and quality control supervisors, and columns directed to prime areas of process chemistries, control, equipment, etc.

PHOTO LIFE. V. 1- Oct. 1976-. 0700-3021. Periodical. CN. English. mo. $32.46. Camar Publications, 100 Steelcase Road East, Markham Ontario L3R 1E8 Canada. **Tel** (416)475-8440. Ed Norm Rosen. DD 770.5. bk rev. adv acc. **Circ** 80,000. A magazine for the avid amateur photographer, providing technical tips and ideas to increase the enjoyment of the photographic hobby.

PHOTO MARKETING. V. 1- June 1924-. 0031-8531. Periodical. US. English. mo. $12.00. Photo Marketing Association, 3000 Picture Place, Jackson MI 49201. **Tel** (517)788-8100. Ed Nancy Brent. **Ind/Abst** Funk Scott Index Corp. Ind. adv acc. **Circ** 15,000. (ctrl). Association magazine for retailers and finishers in the photographic industry.

PHOTO PIPELINE. (THE PHOTO PIPELINE : NEWS FROM THE PHOTOGRAPHERS' UNION). 0826-5712. Periodical. CN. English. ir. $15.00 Per Year Membership, $10.00 Per Year for Students. Photographers' Union, 210 Napier Street, Hamilton Ontario L8R 1S7 Canada. DD 770.5.

PHOTO PORTFOLIO ANNUAL. French (German). an. Editions Jean Spinatsch, CH-1246 Corsier/Geneve Switzerland.

PHOTO RESOURCES. Vol. 1, No. 1 (Feb. 1983)-. 0736-671X. Periodical. US. English. mo. Free. AMR Company, 156 5th Avenue, New York NY 10010.

PHOTO SELECTION. Vol. 1, No 1 (Mar/Apr. 1981)-. 0226-9708. Periodical. CN. French. bm. $10.83. Photo Selection, CP 383/2026 rue Persico, Sillery Quebec G1T 2R5 Canada. **Tel** (418)687-3550. Ed Yolande Racine. DD 770.5. adv acc. **Circ** 18,000. A photography magazine for professional and amateur photographers. The content: portfolios, photo-reports, technical and informative chronics.

PHOTO TECHNIQUE INTERNATIONAL. 1/84-. Periodical. English. qt. LC TR1. DD 770.5. *International Photo Technique.*

PHOTO TECHNIQUE (LONDON, ENGLAND). (PHOTO TECHN:QUE). Periodical. UK. English. mo. $15.33. Penblade Publishing, 93 Sirdar Road, London W11 4EQ England.

PHOTO WEEKLY. 0031-8647. Periodical. US. English. wk. $35.00. Photo Weekly, PO Box 1416, Riverton NJ 08077. Available on microfiche from Bell and Howell Microphoto Division.

PHOTOGENIES. No 1, (April 1983)-. Periodical. FR. French. ir. 10. 42 Avenue des Gobelins, 75013 Paris France.

THE PHOTOGRAPH COLLECTOR. Vol. 1 (Oct. 1980)-. 0271-0838. Periodical. US. English. mo. $90.00. Photograph Collector, 127 East 59th Street, New York NY 10022. **Tel** (212)838-8640. Ed Robert S Persky. bk rev. **Circ** 1,000. News for the collector, curator, dealer and gallery director of fine art photography. Treats collectible photography as art and investment.

THE PHOTOGRAPH COLLECTORS' RESOURCE DIRECTORY. See Yearbooks, Almanacs, Directories.

PHOTOGRAPHER. V. 3- Summer 1976-. 0701-1326. Periodical. CN. English. qt. $5.00. Photographer, PO Box 24954 Station C, Vancouver British Columbia V5T 4G3 Canada. LC TR1. DD 770.5. *B C Photographer, 0315-0755.*

THE PHOTOGRAPHER. V. 1- Jan. 1966-. Periodical. UK. English. mo. $30.65. Institute of Incorporate Photographers, 2 Amwell End, Ware Hertfordshire England. Ed C Wordsworth. LC TR1. adv acc. Articles for the professional photographer. *Record.*

PHOTOGRAPHER'S FORUM. Vol. 1, No. 2 (Feb. 1979)-. 0194-5467. Periodical. US. English. qt. $12.00. Serbin Publishers, 614 Santa Barbara Street, Santa Barbara CA 93101. **Tel** (805)963-0439. Ed Glen Serbin. bk rev. adv acc. **Circ** 28,000. Dedicated to college photography. Each issue proudly interviews publications of shortest works and either articles of interest to college photographs. *Student Forum, 0148-589X.*

PHOTOGRAPHER'S MARKET. 1978-. 0147-247X. US. English. an. Writers Market, 9933 Alliance Road, Cincinnati OH 45242. **Tel** (513)984-0717. Ed Robin Weinstein. LC TR12. DD 381.457702573. Each issue contains an index to its own contents - no vol index - loose. Freelance photographers will find the facts they need to successfully market their work. More than 2,500 listing of buyers of freelance photography. *Artists & Photographer's Market, 0146-8294.*

PHOTOGRAPHER'S MARKET NEWSLETTER. Vol. 1, No. 1-. 0278-2790. Periodical. US. English. mo. $39.00. Writers Digest, 9933 Alliance Road, Cincinnati OH 45242. **Tel**

Photography & Photographs

(513)984-0717. Ed Robin Weinstein. Circ 1,700. Information on new photography markets. What is needed, payment rates, new addresses, phone numbers, contact names plus tips for improving your sales and trends in the marketplace.

PHOTOGRAPHIC ABSTRACTS. See Indexes/Abstracts.

PHOTOGRAPHIC CANADIANA. V. 1- Mar. 1975-. 0704-0024. Periodical. CN. English. bm. Free to members, $10.00 membership. Photographic Historical Society of Canada, PO Box 115 Station S, Toronto Ontario M5M 4L6 Canada. DD 770.9.

PHOTOGRAPHIC COLLECTOR (BISHOPSGATE PRESS). See Hobbies.

THE PHOTOGRAPHIC JOURNAL. V. 1- Mar. 3, 1853-. 0031-8736. Periodical. UK. English. bm. LC TRL.

PHOTOGRAPHIC JOURNAL. (THE PHOTOGRAPHIC JOURNAL : OFFICIAL ORGAN OF THE ROYAL PHOTOGRAPHIC SOCIETY OF GREAT BRITAIN AND THE PHOTOGRAPHIC ALLIANCE). Jan. 1956-. 0031-8736. Periodical. UK. English. mo. 40.00 Domestic, 45.00 Foreign. Royal Photographic Society, The Octagon/Milson Street, Bath BA1 1DN England. Tel 0225-62841. Ed R H Mason. Ind/Abst World Surf. Coat. Abstr., Print. Abstr., Art Index. LC TR1. DD 770.5. bk rev. adv acc. Circ 10,000. Published continuously for 132 years covering all aspects of photography plus details of the activities of the royal photographic society. Photographic Journal. Section A, Pictorial & General Photography.

PHOTOGRAPHIC PROCESSING. Began publication in 1964. 0031-8744. Periodical. US. English. mo. $10.00. PTN Publishing Corporation, 101 Crossways Park West, Woodbury NY 11797. Tel (212)895-8370.

PHOTOGRAPHIC PROCESSING EQUIPMENT DIRECTORY & BUYING GUIDE. See Yearbooks, Almanacs, Directories.

PHOTOGRAPHIC TECHNIQUES IN SCIENTIFIC RESEARCH. V. 1- 1973-. 0302-4210. UK. English. ir. Academic Press, 4805 Sand Lake Road, Orlando Fl 32887. Tel (305)345-4100. Ed A A Newman. Ind/Abst Chem. Abstr., GeoRef, Bibliogr. Index Geol. LC TR692. DD 778.308. NLM W1 PH67. CODEN PTSRD2.

PHOTOGRAPHIC TECHNOLOGY U.S.S.R. (PHOTOGRAPHIC TECHNOLOGY USSR). VAT Photographic Technology Union of Soviet Socialist Republics. V. 1- 1973-. 0092-4709. Periodical. US. English. bm. $50.00. Foreign Resources Associates, PO Box 2353, Fort Collins CO 80522. LC TR692. DD 770.15.

PHOTOGRAPHIC TRADE NEWS. VFOAT PTN. 0031-8779. Periodical. US. English. sm. $6.00. PTN Publishing Corporation, 101 Crossways Park West, Woodbury NY 11797. Tel (212)895-8370.

PHOTOGRAPHIC TRADE NEWS MASTER BUYING GUIDE. (MASTER BUYING GUIDE). VFOAT New Product Review. 1977-. Periodical. English. ir.

PHOTOGRAPHICA. V. 5, No. 1- Jan. 1973-. 0090-2063. Periodical. US. English. mo. Photographic Historical Society of New York, 244 Fifth Avenue, New York NY 10001. LC TR1. DD 770.9. News.

PHOTOGRAPHICONSERVATION. VAT Photographic Conservation. V. 1- Mar. 1979-. 0192-3196. Periodical. US. English. Graphic Arts Research Center, Rochester Institute of Technology, 1 Lomb Memorial Drive, Rochester NY 14623. Ind/Abst Libr. Inf. Sci. Abstr. LC TR465. DD 770.283.

PHOTOGRAPHIE. V. 1-. Periodical. SZ. German. mo. $55.55. Verlag Photographie, Seeburgstrasse 18, CH-6006 Luzern Switzerland. LC TR1.

PHOTOGRAPHIES. No. 1 (Spring 1983)-. 0758-2544. Periodical. FR. French (summaries in English). qt. Revue Photographies, 61 rue de Richelieu, 75002 Paris France. Ind/Abst Avery Index Archit. Period.

PHOTOGRAPHS (NEW YORK, N.Y. : 1982). (PHOTOGRAPHS). 0740-4158. Periodical. US. English. bm. $65.00 12 Issues. Photographs, 450 Broome Street, New York NY 10013.

PHOTOGRAPHY ANNUAL. 1951-. 0079-1849. US. English. an. $4.95. Ziff-Davis Publishing Company, 4 Park Avenue, New York NY 10016. Tel (212)719-6243. LC TR1. DD 770.58.

PHOTOGRAPHY BUYERS GUIDE (ZIFF-DAVIS PUBLISHING COMPANY). (PHOTOGRAPHY BUYERS GUIDE). 1983-. 0737-7053. US. English. an. $3.95. Ziff-Davis Publishing Company, One Park Avenue, New York NY 10016. LC TR12. DD 771. Photography Directory & Buying Guide.

PHOTOGRAPHY DIRECTORY & BUYING GUIDE. See Yearbooks, Almanacs, Directories.

THE PHOTOGRAPHY INDEX. See Indexes/Abstracts.

PHOTOGRAPHY MARKET PLACE. 1975/76-. 0095-439X. US. English. R R Bowker Co, 1180 Avenue of the Americas, New York NY 10036. LC TR12. DD 380.1457702573.

PHOTOGRAPHY YEAR CEASED. Ceased with 1982 issue. 0090-4406. US. English. an. LC TR1. DD 770.5.

THE PHOTOLETTER. 0190-1400. Periodical. US. English. sm. $75.00. The Photoletter, Route 2 Box 93, Osceola WI 54020. Tel (715)248-3800.

PHOTOMAG. V. 1- Jan. 1980-. 0226-7411. Periodical. CN. French. mo. $2. Per No. Editions du Gemeau, Photomag, 88 rue St-Louis, Ville Lemoyne Quebec J4R 2L4 Canada. DD 770.5.

PHOTOMETHODS. V. 17, No. 9- Sept. 1974-. 0146-0153. Periodical. US. English. mo. Photomethods, PO Box 5860, Cherry Hill NJ 08034. Tel (800)328-4329. Ind/Abst Predicasts, Art Archaeol. Tech. Abstr., Funk Scott Index Corp. Ind. LC TR1. PMI, Photo Methods for Industry, 0146-0153.

THE PHOTOPLATEMAKERS BULLETIN CEASED. Began with V. 58-, June 1968-. Ceased in 1984. 0031-8841. Periodical. US. English. bm. LC TR1. DD 686.23205. Photo Engravers Bulletin.

PICTURE (SANTA FE SPRINGS, CALIF.). (PICTURE). Issue 18 (Sept. 1981)-. 0732-1511. Periodical. US. English. qt. $45.00 Domestic, $52.50 Foreign. Picture, 1329 Dinard Avenue, Santa Fe Springs CA 90670. LC TR640. DD 770.5. Picture Magazine (Los Angeles, Calif.), 0279-0432.

PIN UPS. V. 6, No. 5- May/June 1975-. 0382-9286. Periodical. CN. English. bm. $5.00. Galaxy Press, 200 Chapel Street, Kitchener Ontario N2H 2V2 Canada. DD 779.2405. Quest, 0382-926X.

PINHOLE JOURNAL. Vol. 1, No. 1, Dec. 1985-. 0885-1476. Periodical. US. English. ty. $27.50 Members, $32.50 Nonmembers. Pinhole Journal, Star Route 15, PO Box 1655, San Lorenzo NM 88057. DD 770.

PLEIN CADRE. No 1- (Scene 1, Plan 1-). 0227-115X. Periodical. CN. French. qt. $7.74. Plein Cadre, 1415 rue Jarry Est, Montreal Quebec H2Z 2Z7 Canada. Tel (514)374-4700. DD 778.5349060714. Debobinons, 0319-5899.

PODO SAJIN YONGAM. VFOAT News Photography Annual. KO. Korean. an. 10,000. Hanguk Sajin Kijadan Sinmun Goegwan, 213-Hosil 31 Taepyongno, 1-ka Chung-ku Seoul Korea.

POPULAR PHOTOGRAPHY. V. 1- May 1937-. 0032-4582. Periodical. US. English. mo. CBS Publications, 1515 Broadway, New York NY 10036, (subscription address: Neodata PO Box 2606 Boulder CO 80322). Tel (212)725-3500. Ind/Abst Read. Guide Period. Lit., Mag. Index, Consum. Index Prod. Eval. Inf. Source. LC TR1. DD 770.5. Prize Photography, Photo Arts; Camera Magazine and American Photography.

POPULAR PHOTOGRAPHY SLR TEST REPORTS. (POPULAR PHOTOGRAPHY ... SLR TEST REPORTS). VFOAT SLR Test Reports. VAT Popular Photography Single Lens Reflex Test Reports. 0276-4814. US. English. an. $2.95. Ziff-Davis Publishing Company, #1 Park Avenue, New York NY 10016. LC TR261. DD 770.2822.

POPULAR PHOTOGRAPHY'S HOW-TO GUIDE. 0195-5667. Periodical. US. English. $2.50 Each Copy. Ziff-Davis Publishing Company, Editorial Circulation and Executive Office, One Park Avenue, New York NY 10016. LC TR1. DD 770. Photography How-to Guide, 0192-2246.

POPULAR PHOTOGRAPHY'S INVITATION TO PHOTOGRAPHY. VFOAT Invitation to Photography. 0075-0301. US. English. $1.50. Ziff Davis Publishing Company, One Park Avenue, New York NY 10016. LC TR1. DD 770.28.

POPULAR PHOTOGRAPHY'S SLR PHOTOGRAPHY. VFOAT S.L.R. Photography. 0747-8798. Periodical. US. English. an. $3.95. Ziff-Davis Publishing Company, One Park Avenue, New York NY 10016. LC TR1. DD 770.2822.

PORTFOLIO. 1973-. 0319-1168. CN. English. an. Centennial College Press, 651 Warden Avenue, Scarborough Ontario M1L 3Z6 Canada. Ed N Horowitz. DD 779.

PRC NEWSLETTER. VFOAT P.R.C. Newsletter. VAT Photographic Resource Center Newsletter. 8755-3902. Periodical. US. English. mo. Photographic Resource Center, 1019 Commonwealth Avenue, Boston MA 02134. DD 770. Newsletter (Photographic Resource Center).

PRESTIGE DE LA PHOTOGRAPHIE. No. 1-. Periodical. French. ir. 410. Editiones E P A, 18 rue d'Issy, 92100 Boulogne Paris France. LC TR1. DD 770.9.

THE PRINT COLLECTOR'S NEWSLETTER. V. 1- Mar./Apr. 1970-. 0032-8537. Periodical. US. English. bm. $42.00. Print Collectors Newsletter, 16 East 82nd Street, New York NY 10028. Tel (212)628-2654. Ed Jacqueline Brody. Ind/Abst Artbibliogr. Mod., Repert. Int. Litt. Art, Lit. Mod. Art., Avery Index Archit. Period., Art Index. LC NE1. DD 769.075. bk rev. adv acc. Circ 5,000. Newsletter covering prints and photographs in scholarly articles, interviews, book reviews, news and notes. Includes reviews of recent prints published and listing of recent auction prices.

THE PRO REVIEW. Vol. 1, No. 1 (June 1985)-. 0748-9099. Periodical. US. English. mo. Free (first 6 issues, professional). Dynamic Publications Inc, 901 Bonifant Road, Silver Spring MD 20904. DD 770.

PROCEEDINGS OF THE ... ANNUAL CONFERENCE AND EXPOSITION. Main/Corp National Micrographics Association. Conference and Exposition. 24th-25th. 0161-4649. US. English. an. National Micrographics Association, 1100 Wayne Avenue, Silver Springs MD 20910. Proceedings of the ... Annual Conference and Exposition.

PROCEEDINGS OF THE INTERNATIONAL CONGRESS ON HIGH SPEED PHOTOGRAPHY AND PHOTONICS. Main/Conf International Congress on High Speed Photography and Photonics. 13th- 1978-. English. be. Society for Photo-Optical Instrumentation Engineers, PO Box 10, Bellingham WA 98227. Tel (206)676-3290. Proceedings.

PROFESSIONAL PHOTOGRAPHER (MACLAREN PUBLISHERS). (PROFESSIONAL PHOTOGRAPHER). Vol. 20, No. 3 (Mar. 1980)-. 0019-784X. Periodical. UK. English. mo. 16.00. MacLaren Publishers, PO Box 109, Davis House, 69-77 High Street, Croydon CR9 1QH England. Industrial and Commercial Photographer.

PROFESSIONAL PHOTOGRAPHER (PROFESSIONAL PHOTOGRAPHERS ASSOCIATION). (THE PROFESSIONAL PHOTOGRAPHER). Began in 1964. US. English. mo. $35.00. PPA Publications, 1090 Executive Way, Des Plaines IL 60018. Tel (312)299-8161. Ed Alfred DeBat. bk rev. adv acc. Circ 28,000. Reports photographic techniques used by portrait, commercial, and industrial photographers, and the business of still and video studio and location photography operations, including marketing, promotion, advertising, and sales techniques. National Professional Photographer.

PROFESSIONAL PHOTOGRAPHERS OF CANADA. (PROFESSIONAL PHOTOGRAPHERS OF CANADA : JOURNAL). Vol. 9, No. 5 (1979)-. 0821-3666. Periodical. CN. English. Pennex Ltd, 107 Paramount Road, Winnipeg Manitoba R2X 2W6 Canada. DD 770.2320971. National News, 0048-5462.

P.S.A. JOURNAL. (PSA JOURNAL). 0030-8277. Periodical. US. English. mo. Photographic Society of America, 2005 Walnut Street, Philadelphia PA 19103. Ind/Abst Mag. Index, Int. Aerosp. Abstr., Ref. Source. Journal of the Photographic Society of America, 0096-5812.

QUICK FOOT. 0194-9055. Periodical. US. English. mo. $2.20. Kidsport Photo, 2761 North Haven/Suite 4141, Dallas TX 75229.

Physical Therapy

THE RANGEFINDER. V. 1- June 1952-. 0033-9202. Periodical. US. English. mo. $25.00. Rangefinder Publishing Company Inc, PO Box 1703, Santa Monica CA 90406. **Tel** (213)451-8506. **Ed** Arthur Stern. bk rev. adv acc. **Circ** 49,500. Trade publication dedicated to the advancement of the field of professional photography. Editorial material covers improving products and services and to increasing sales potential. *School Photographers Digest.*

RENZU. VFOAT Lens. Japanese. ir. Yomiuri Shimbun Sha, 7-1 Otemachi 1-Chome Chiyoda-Ku (100), Tokyo Japan. LC TR820.

DER REPROGRAF. Periodical. German. ir. Fachverband Reprografic, Kaiser-Friedrich-Ring 1A, 4000 11 Dusseldorf West Germany. LC TR920. DD 686.405. *Reprograf und Lichtpauser.*

REVISTA DE LA IMAGEN Y EL SONIDO : EIKONOS. VFOAT Eikonos. Spanish. ir. 1,000. Editoral Eco, Cruz 44, Barcelona Spain. LC TR1.

RIVISTA DI STORIA E CRITICA DELLA FOTOGRAFIA. Yearly V. 1, No. 1, (Oct. 1980)-. Italian (with English summaries). ty. $24.00. LC TR1. DD 770.9.

S L R CAMERA. Periodical. UK. English. mo. $27.58. Haymarket Publishing Ltd, 38/42 Hampton Road, Teddington Middlesex TW11 OJE London England. **Tel** 01 937 7288.

SADAN. Periodical. Korean. mo. Taehan Chigop Sajinga, Hyophoe 121 Myo-Dong Chongno-ku, Seoul Korea. LC TR1.

SALONFOTO INDONESIA. chiefly Indonesian. ir. LC TR646.I52.

SAN FRANCISCO CAMERAWORK QUARTERLY. VFOAT Camerawork Quarterly. Vol. 10, No. 3 (Autumn 1983)-. Periodical. US. English. qt. *Newsletter (San Francisco Camerawork).*

SANGAKU SHASHIN NENKAN. 1974-. JA. Japanese. ir. Yama To Keikoku Sha, 1-33 Shiba Daimon 1 chome Minato-ku, Tokyo 105 Japan. LC TR787.

SCHRIFTENREIHE - INSTITUT FUR PHOTOGRAMMETRIE DER UNIVERSITAT STUTTGART. See Geography.

SCIENTIFIC PUBLICATIONS FROM EASTMAN KODAK LABORATORIES. **Maln/Corp** Eastman Kodak Company. Research Laboratories. 1965/66-. 0424-2017. US. English. an. Eastman Kodak Company, Research Laboratories, Department of Information Services, Rochester NY 14650. LC TR7. *Abridged Scientific Publication from the Kodak Research Laboratories, 0097-5761.*

SHE YING CHIA TSO HSIN SHANG. VFOAT Photos Annual. V. 2-. Chinese. ir. $16.00. She Ying Hua Pao She, Lee Yuen Subscription Agencies, 1 On Ning Lane, Sai Ying Pun, Hsiang-Kang Hong Kong. LC TR1. *She Ying Chia Tso Chi.*

SHE YING SHIH CHIEH. VFOAT Photography Publishers. V. 1-. Periodical. Chinese. ir. $20.00. 802 Shih Hung Chi Ta Hsia Yu-to-li, Huang Hou Chiem, Hong Kong China. LC TR1.

SHE YING TSUNG KAN. VFOAT Sheyingcongkan. 1-. Periodical. CC. Chinese. ir. 0.78. Hsin Hua Shu Tien, Shang-Hai Fa Hsing So, Shang-Hai China. LC TR1.

SPAFOTO. Began with Vol. for 1972. Spanish. ir. 1650. Cotec, Rocafort 39-41 Edificio Avenida, 15 Barcelona Spain. LC TR690.4.

SPOT. 1972-. Periodical. Serbo-Croatian(R). ir. $16.00. Galereje Grada Zagreba, Katerenin Trg 2, Zagreb 41000 Yugoslavia. LC TR1.

SPOT. Vol. 2, No. 3 (Fall 1984)-. Periodical. US. English. qt. Houston Center for Photography, 1441 West Alabama, Houston TX 77006. *Image (Houston Center for Photography).*

S.P.S.E. NEWS. (SPSE NEWS). 0097-5931. US. English. bm. Society of Photographic Scientists and Engineers, 7003 Kilworth Lane, Springfield VA 22151. **Tel** (703)642-9090.

STEREO WORLD. 0191-4030. Periodical. US. English. bm. $12.00 Domestic, $18.00 Foreign. National Stereoscopic Association, PO Box 14801, Columbus OH 43210. **Ind/Abst** GeoRef. LC TR780. DD 778.405.

STILL. 1- 1970-. US. English. ir. Graphic Design Office, Yale Station, Box 2004, 212 York Street, New Haven CT 06520. LC TR640. DD 779.05.

STRATEGIES (MONTCLAIR, N.J.). (STRATEGIES). 0742-3861. Periodical. US. English. bm. $18.00. Simon Gallery, 20 Church Street, Montclair NJ 07042. **Tel** (201)783-5480. **Ed** Harold Simon. bk rev. Self-promotion and marketing newsletter for fine art photographers.

TECHNICAL PHOTOGRAPHY. V. 1- Dec. 1968/Jan. 1969-. 0040-0971. Periodical. US. English. mo. $10.00. PTN Publishing Corporation, 101 Crossways Park West, Woodbury NY 11797. **Tel** (516)496-8000. **Ed** David C Silverman. **Ind/Abst** Abstr. Bull. Inst. Paper Chem. LC TR1. DD 770.5. bk rev. adv acc. **Circ** 60,000. (ctrl). We reach in-house industrial, military and government, still life, video and audio-visual professionals.

UNDERWATER PHOTOGRAPHER. (THE UNDERWATER PHOTOGRAPHER). V. 1- April 1973-. 0091-1887. Periodical. US. English. qt. $6.00 Domestic, $10.00 Foreign. Fred M Roberts, Drawer 608, Dana Point CA 92629. LC TR800. DD 778.7305.

U.S. CAMERA. 1935-. US. English. US Camera Publishing Corporation, PO Box 562, Des Moines IA 50302. LC TR1. DD 770.5.

UNTITLED (CARMEL, CALIF.). (UNTITLED). No. 1 (3rd Quarter 1972)-. 0163-7916. Monographic Series. US. English. ir. $18.00. Friends of Photography, PO Box 239, Camel CA 93921.

VUODEN LUONNONKUVAT . . . . VFOAT Nature Photographs of the Year . . . . English (Finnish). ir. LC TR721. DD 779.3.

WHITE HOUSE NEWS PHOTOGRAPHERS ANNUAL AWARDS. 0163-3430. Periodical. US. English. an. $10.00. Ultimate Consultant, 117 King Street Suite 200, Alexandria VA 22314. **Tel** (703)548-4090. LC TR820. DD 770.79. adv acc. **Circ** 4,000. Award winning works from White House News Photographers Association, annual competition. Also, editorial contributions by well known individuals.

DIE WISSENSCHAFTLICHE UND ANGEWANDTE PHOTAGRAPHIE. 0084-0998. Monographic Series. AU. German. ir. Springer Verlag, Postfach 367, Moelkerbastei 5, A-1011 Vienna Austria.

WOLFMAN REPORT ON THE PHOTOGRAPHIC INDUSTRY IN THE UNITED STATES. US. English. an. $115.00. ABC Leisure Single Copy Sales Department, 825 7th Avenue, New York NY 10019. **Tel** (212)887-8339. **Ed** Lydia Wolfman. LC TR1. DD 338.4777. adv acc. **Circ** 11,000. (ctrl). The most authoritative survey of the American photographic industry. Coverage of amateur and professional photography, photofinishing, audio-visual, specialized products and imports and exports.

WOLGAN SAJIN. VFOAT Photography. Periodical. KO. Korean. ir. 700 Each Issue. Wolgan Sajin Chulpansa, 14-11 Kwanchul-Dong, Chongno-Ku, Seoul South Korea. LC TR1.

WORLD PHOTOGRAPHY SOURCES. 1982-. 0730-496X. US. English. Directories, 436 East 88th Street, New York NY 10028. LC TR12. DD 779.025.

WORLD TRIBUNE. 0049-8165. Periodical. US. English. wk. World Tribune Press, PO Box 1427, Santa Monica CA 90406. **Tel** (213)451-8811.

WRITER'S & PHOTOGRAPHER'S GUIDE TO NEWSPAPER MARKETS. VAT Writer's and Photographer's Guide to Newspaper Markets. 0277-6162. US. English. an. $9.95. Helm Publishing, Box 10512, Costa Mesa CA 92627.

ZHURNAL NAUCHNOI I PRIKLADNOI FOTOGRAFII I KINEMATOGRAFII. ENGLISH. (SCIENTIFIC & APPLIED PHOTOGRAPHY & CINEMATOGRAPHY). VFOAT Scientific and Applied Photography and Cinematography. Vol. 28, No. 1-. 0734-1504. Periodical. US. English (summaries in Russian). qt. $375.00. Gordon & Breach, One Park Avenue, New York NY 10016. DD 621. **CODEN** SAPHES.

ZOOM. Periodical. US. English. ir. $45.00. Zoom (USA), PO Box 2000, Long Island NY 11101. LC TR640. DD 770.5.

ZURNAL NAUCHOJ I PRIKLADNOJ FOTOGRAFII I KINEMATOGRAFII. (ZHURNAL NAUCHNOI I PRIKLADNOI FOTOGRAFII I KINEMATOGRAFII). Vol. 1- 1956-. 0044-4561. Periodical. UR. Russian. bm. $31.00. Victor Kamkin Inc, 12224 Parklawn Drive, Rockville MD 20852. **Tel** (301)881-5973. **Ind/Abst** Int. Aerosp. Abstr., Chem. Abstr. **CODEN** ZNPFAG.

PHYSICAL THERAPY

ABMS DIRECTORY OF CERTIFIED PHYSICAL MEDICINE & REHABILITATION PHYSICIANS. See Yearbooks, Almanacs, Directories.

ABUH PHYSIO : THE JOURNAL OF THE PHYSIOTHERAPY DEPT. OF THE INSTITUTE OF HEALTH, AHMADU BELLO UNIVERSITY, ZARIA. Began with: No. 1 (Dec. 1979). 0331-9113. Periodical. English. qt. NLM W1.

AFAQ SIHHIYAH. VFOAT Horizon Sante. No. 1-. Periodical. Tl. Arabic (French). qt. 0.5. Al-Munazzamah, 22 Bis rue Asdrubal, Tunis Tunisia. LC RM930.A1.

AMERICAN ARCHIVES OF REHABILITATION THERAPY. See Genealogy and Heraldry - Archives.

THE AMERICAN CHIROPRACTOR. 0194-6536. Periodical. US. English. mo. $36.00. American Chiropractic Magazine, 3401 Lake Avenue, Ft Wayne IN 46805. DD 615.

AMERICAN CORRECTIVE THERAPY JOURNAL. V. 21, No. 5- Sept./Oct. 1967-. 0002-8088. Periodical. US. English. bm. $27.00 Domestic, $30.00 Foreign. American Corrective Therapy Association, San Diego State University, San Diego CA 92182. **Tel** (619)461-5059. **Ed** B Robert Carlson. **Ind/Abst** Cumul. Index Nurs. Allied Health Lit., Excerpta Med., Psychol. Abstr., Index Med., Hospit. Lit. Index. **NLM** W1 AM346. **CODEN** ACOJBC. bk rev. adv acc. **Circ** 1,100. (ctrl). Research and programs in physical activity for handicapping conditions. *Journal of the Association for Physical and Mental Rehabilitation, 0098-8448.*

THE AMERICAN JOURNAL OF OCCUPATIONAL THERAPY. VFOAT AJOT. V. 34- Jan. 1980-. 0272-9490. Periodical. US. English. mo. $45.00 Domestic, $60.00 Foreign. American Occupational Therapy Association, 1383 Piccard Drive, Rockville MD 20850. **Tel** (301)948-9626. **Ed** Elaine Viseltear. **Ind/Abst** Hospit. Lit. Index, Excerpta Med., Except. Child Educ. Resour., Index Med., Curr. Index J. Educ., Psychol. Abstr., Energy Res. Abstr., Cumul. Index Nurs. Allied Health Lit. **NLM** W1 AM497B. **CODEN** AJOTAM. bk rev. adv acc. **Circ** 43,000. Available on microfilm from University Microfilms. Articles on research, practice techniques and professional trends in occupational therapy. Special topics may include home health care, spinal cord injury and others. *AJOT. The American Journal of Occupational Therapy, 0161-326X.*

AMERICAN JOURNAL OF PHYSICAL MEDICINE. V. 31- Feb. 1952-. 0002-9491. Periodical. US. English. bm. **Tel** (301)528-4000. **Ind/Abst** Excerpta Med., Index Med., Comput. Control Abstr., Cumul. Index Nurs. Allied Health Lit., Electr. Electron. Abstr., Energy Res. Abstr., Eng. Index Annu., Eng. Index Bioeng. Abstr., Eng. Index Energy Abstr., Eng. Index Mon., Life Sci. Collect., Sci. Abstr. Sect. A. Phys. Abstr. LC RM735.A1. DD 615.851505. **NLM** W1 AM501. **CODEN** AJPBA7. adv acc. **Circ** 2,050. Rehabilitation medicine journal examines acute problems and their treatment by the latest methods and equipment. *Occupational Therapy and Rehabilitation.*

ANNALES DE KINESITHERAPIE. V. 1- Jan./Feb. 1974-. Periodical. French. bm. $64.00. Masson Publishing USA Inc, 211 East 43rd Street/Room 1306, New York NY 10017. **Tel** (212)370-1937. **NLM** W1 AN336K. *Journal de Kinestitherapie, 0021-7751; Revue de Kinesitherapie, 0035-1172.*

ARBRE DE VIE. (L'ARBRE DE VIE). V. 1, No. 1 (15 Feb. 1982)-. 0713-4436. Periodical. CN. French. mo. Free. L'Arbre de Vie, 21 rue St-Laurent, Louiseville Quebec J5V 1J5 Canada. DD 615.53405.

Physical Therapy

ARCHIVES OF PHYSICAL MEDICINE AND REHABILITATION. See Genealogy and Heraldry - Archives.

ARKANSAS HEALTH MANPOWER STATISTICS. CHIROPRACTORS. See Statistics.

ARKANSAS HEALTH MANPOWER STATISTICS: PHYSICAL THERAPISTS. See Statistics.

ATEM UND MENSCH. Vol. 18-. 0341-3403. Periodical. German. ir. NLM W1 AT212BM. Atem.

AUDIT REPORT, TEXAS BOARD OF CHIROPRACTIC EXAMINERS. Main/Corp Texas Board of Chiropractic Examiners. VFOAT Texas Board of Chiropractic Examiners. US. English. State Auditor/John H Reagan State Office Building, PO Box 12067, Austin TX 78711. LC RZ205.U52. DD 353.976400841.

AUSTRALIAN JOURNAL OF PHYSIOTHERAPY. (THE AUSTRALIAN JOURNAL OF PHYSIOTHERAPY). V. 1- Oct. 1954-. 0004-9514. Periodical. AT. English. bm. $33.20. Australian Physiotherapy Association, 25-27 Kerr Street, Fitzroy 3065 Australia. Tel (03) 417 5244. Ed Margaret Nayler. Ind/Abst Excerpta Med. NLM W1 AU615. bk rev. adv acc. Circ 5,700. Physiotherapy journal.

AUSTRALIAN OCCUPATIONAL THERAPY JOURNAL. V. 10- Jan./Mar. 1963-. 0045-0766. Periodical. AT. English. qt. $11.80. Australian Occupational, 11 Grose Street, Campersown NSW 2050 Australia. Tel 511006. Ed Margaret Kennedy. NLM W1 AU515. bk rev. adv acc. Circ 2,100. (ctrl). Official publication of Australian Association of Occupational Therapists. Professional and clinical material. Bulletin of the Australian Association of Occupational Therapists.

BAD-INTERN : DER BERUFSGENOSSENSCHAFTLICHE ARBEITSMEDIZINISCHE DIENST. VFOAT Bad Intern. 1/83-. 0724-5297. Periodical. German. ir. NLM W1.

BALNEOLOGIA BOHEMICA. 1.- Yearly Vol. 0302-8070. Periodical. German (summaries in Czech, English, French and Russian). qt. Malostranske Nam 28, Praha 1 Czechoslovakia. Ind/Abst Biol. Abstr. LC RM801. NLM W1 BA496G. CODEN BLBHAE.

BIENNIAL REPORT OF EXAMINING AND LICENSING BOARDS - MINNESOTA STATE BOARD OF CHIROPRACTIC EXAMINERS. Main/Corp Minnesota State Board of Chiropractic Examiners. US. English. be. Board of Chiropractic Examiners, 717 Delaware Street SE, Department of Health, Minneapolis MN 55414. Biennial Report of Examining and Licensing Boards.

BOLLETTINO S.I.A.M.E. 1-. Periodical. Italian. ir. NLM W1 BO646.

BULLETIN - REHABILITATION INSTITUTE OF MONTREAL CEASED. Main/Corp Rehabilitation Institute of Montreal. Began with V. 13, No. 4 (Nov. 1967). Ceased with V. 26, No. 2, Dec. 1981/Jan. 1982. Periodical. CN. English (French). bm. Rehabilitation Institute of Montreal, 6300 Darlington Avenue, Montreal Quebec H3S 2JR Canada.

CHI KUNG YU KO HSUEH. VFOAT Journal of Qigong and Science. First published in 1982. Periodical. CC. Chinese. bm. 1.80. Post Office, Kuang-Chou, Shih China. LC RM727.C54. DD 613.7105.

CLINICAL MANAGEMENT IN PHYSICAL THERAPY. VFOAT Clinical Management. Vol. 1, No. 1-. 0276-8038. Periodical. US. English. bm. $10.00. American Physical Therapy Association, 1111 North Fairfax Street, Alexandria VA 22314. Tel (703)684-2782. Ed Claire Anne Coyne. Ind/Abst Cumul. Index Nurs. Allied Health Lit. adv acc. Circ 39,000. (ctrl). Articles share hands-on advice, opinions, and new ideas about physical therapy that relate to patient care and clinical management. Based on individual experience and observations.

CONTACT QUARTERLY. See Dance.

DAIHAN JAIHWAR NUIHAG HOIJI. (TAEHAN CHAEHWAL UIHAKHOE CHI). VFOAT The Journal of Korean Academy of Rehabilitation Medicine. Began with Mar. 1977 issue. 0379-752X. Periodical. KO. Korean (summaries in English). sa. Taehan Chaehwal Uihakhoe, 1 2-ka Myong-dong Chung-ku, Seoul Korea. LC RM695. NLM W1 TA392BJ.

DANSKE FYSIOTERAPEUTER. Vol. 56- 1974-. 0105-0648. Periodical. Danish. bw. NLM W1 DA697. Tidsskrift for Fysioterapeuter, 0040-7054.

DEVELOPMENTAL DISABILITIES SPECIAL INTEREST SECTION NEWSLETTER. 0279-4098. Periodical. US. English. qt. American Occupational Therapy Association, 1383 Piccard Drive, Rockville MD 20850.

DIRECTORY OF PHYSICAL THERAPISTS AND PHYSICAL THERAPISTS ASSISTANTS LICENSED AND REGISTERED IN TENNESSEE. See Yearbooks, Almanacs, Directories.

EXPANDING HORIZONS IN THERAPEUTIC RECREATION. Main/Conf Symposium on Therapeutic Recreation. 1- 1971-. 0147-393X. US. English. sa. University of Missouri, Columbia MO 65201. LC RM736.7. DD 615.8515. NLM W3 EX92.

FIZICHESKIE I KURORTNYE FAKTORY I IKH LECHEBNOE PRIMENENIE. No. 8- 1974-. Periodical. UR. Russian. an. NLM W1 FI816EA. Fizychni I Kurortni Faktory ta Ikh Likuvalne Zastosuvannia.

FLOOR 4. VFOAT Floor Four. Vol. 1, No. 2 (Apr. 1978)-. 0821-4085. Periodical. CN. English. Free. B C Telephone Employee Fitness Program, 3777 Kingsway, Burnaby British Columbia V5H 3Z7 Canada. DD 613.706071133. (ctrl). 0821-4093.

INTERNATIONAL JOURNAL OF REHABILITATION RESEARCH. VFOAT Internationale Zeitschrift fur Rehabilitationsforschung, Revue Internationale de Recherches de Readaptation. V. 1- Jan. 1978-. 0342-5282. Periodical. GW. English (articles in German). ir. $14.00. G Schindele Verlag, Rheinstrasse 5, D7512 Rheinstetten 3 West Germany. Ind/Abst Sociol. Abstr., Soc. Welf. Soc. Plan./Policy Soc. Dev., Index Med., Biol. Abstr., DSH Abstr., Except. Child Educ. Resour., Excerpta Med., Psychol. Abstr., Rehabil. Lit., Curr. Index J. Educ. NLM W1 IN785T. CODEN IJRRDK.

INTERNATIONAL REVIEW OF CHIROPRACTIC. June, 1964-Jan. 1967. 0535-1960. Periodical. US. English. qt. $30.00. International Chiropractors Association, 1901 L Street NW/Suite 800, Washington DC 20036. Tel (202)659-6476. Ed Susan Hunter. bk rev. adv acc. Circ 10,000. Professional trade journal geared to chiropractors and chiropractic students with editorial content on practice management, public relations research and legislation.

JOURNAL OF CHRONIC DISEASES AND THERAPEUTICS RESEARCH. See Pharmacy.

JOURNAL OF CLINICAL CHIROPRACTIC. VFOAT JCC. V. 3-. 0271-4817. Periodical. US. English. $17.95. JCC Publishing Company, 259 Robby Lane, New Hyde Park NY 11040. NLM W1 JO587C. J.C.C. Journal of Clinical Chiropractic, 0097-4706.

JOURNAL OF REHABILITATION IN ASIA. (THE JOURNAL OF REHABILITATION IN ASIA). VFOAT Rehabilitation in Asia. V. 1- Nov. 1959-. 0022-4162. Periodical. II. English. ty. $25.00. Indian Society of Rehabilitation Handicapped, c/o P C Hansotia Company, Simg Road, Bombay 400032 India. Ed W G Rama Rao. Ind/Abst Excerpta Med. LC RM930.A1. NLM W1 JO867. bk rev. adv acc. Concerns rehabilitation and the handicapped.

JOURNAL OF REHABILITATION RESEARCH AND DEVELOPMENT. Vol. 21, No. 1 (May 1984)-. 0748-7711. Periodical. US. English. sa. Superintendent of Documents, US Government Printing Office, Washington DC 20402. Ind/Abst Excerpta Med., Eng. Index Annu., Eng. Index Mon., Eng. Index Bioeng. Abstr., Eng. Index Energy Abstr. LC RD130. DD 617.58. NLM W1. Journal of Rehabilitation R&D.

JOURNAL OF THE CANADIAN CHIROPRACTIC ASSOCIATION. (THE JOURNAL OF THE CANADIAN CHIROPRACTIC ASSOCIATION). VFOAT Journal de l'Association Chiropratique Canadienne. 0008-3194. Periodical. CN. English. qt. Free to Members, $25.00 Nonmember. Journal of the Canadian Chiropractic Association, 1900 Bayview Avenue, Toronto Ontario M4H 3E6 Canada. DD 615.5340971. NLM W1 J223RB. Canadian Chiropractic Journal, 0410-8795.

KINESITHERAPIE. No. 116- March 1962-. Periodical. French. ir. NLM W1 KI648. Revue des Kinesitherapeutes.

KINESITHERAPIE SCIENTIFIQUE. 0023-1576. Periodical. FR. French. mo. $62.53. Spek, 9 Et 11 rue des Petits Hotels, 75010 Paris France. Tel 246 80 07. Ind/Abst Biol. Abstr. NLM W1 KI648S. CODEN KNTSAC.

KIRO COURRIER. Vol. 1, No. 1 (Jan. 1982)-. 0713-309X. Periodical. CN. French. mo. Free. Kiro Courrier, 2415 Boulevard Pere Lelievre, Duberger Quebec G1P 2X Canada. DD 615.53405. (ctrl).

KRANKENGYMNASTIK. V. 1-. 0023-4494. Periodical. GW. German. mo. $42.61. Richard Pflaum Verlag KG, Postfach 20 19 20, D-8000 Muenchen 2 West Germany. Tel 089/1 26 07-0. Ind/Abst Excerpta Med. NLM W1 KR241.

KURORTOLOGIIA I FIZIOTERAPIIA. Vol. 10- 1977-. Monographic Series. UR. Russian. qt. Hemus, 6 Boulevard Rusy, Sofia Bulgaria. NLM W1 KU708S. Fizicheskie I Kurortnye Faktory I Ikh Lechebnoe Primenenie.

LOISIRS SANTE. VFOAT Sante Loisirs. No. 1 (Sept. 1982)-. Periodical. FR. French. ir. 38 Domestic, 80 Foreign. FFEPGV, 41-43 rue de Reuilly, F-75012 Paris France. Tel 341 86 10. Gymnastique Volontaire.

NEBRASKA HEALTH MANPOWER REPORTS : CHIROPRACTORS. See Economics - Labor.

NEW ZEALAND JOURNAL OF PHYSIOTHERAPY. V. 1- Sept. 1938-. 0303-7193. Periodical. NZ. English. ty. 35. New Zealand Society of Physiotherapists, PO Box 5198, Wellington New Zealand. Tel 735-768. Ed Rocky Louden. Ind/Abst Cumul. Index Nurs. Allied Health Lit. NLM W1 NE9732E. bk rev. adv acc. Circ 1,500. (ctrl). Professional material pertaining to physiotherapy.

NRA NEWSLETTER. VAT National Rehabilitation Association Newsletter. 0279-5507. Periodical. US. English. bm. News Letter.

THE OCCUPATIONAL THERAPY JOURNAL OF RESEARCH. Vol. 1, No. 1 (Apr. 1981)-. 0276-1599. Periodical. US. English. qt. $35.00. American Occupational Therapy Foundation, 1383 Piccard Drive, Rockville MD 20850. Tel (301)953-3699. Ind/Abst Excerpta Med., Psychol. Abstr. LC RM735.A1. DD 615.85152072. NLM W1 OC604.

OUI-DIRE - SOCIETE QUEBECOISE DES THERAPEUTES EN READAPTATION PHYSIQUE. (LE OUI-DIRE). 0710-4367. Periodical. CN. French. bm. Free to Members. Societe Quebecoise des Therapeutes en Readaptation Physique, 1150 East Boulevard Saint-Joseph, Montreal Quebec H2J 1L5 Canada. DD 615.82060714.

PHYSICAL & OCCUPATIONAL THERAPY IN GERIATRICS. See Medicine - Geriatrics.

PHYSICAL & OCCUPATIONAL THERAPY IN PEDIATRICS. See Medicine - Pediatrics.

PHYSICAL THERAPY. V. 44- Jan. 1964-. 0031-9023. Periodical. US. English. mo. $24.00. American Physical Therapy Association, 1111 North Fairfax Street, Alexandria VA 22314. Tel (703)684-2782. Ind/Abst Life Sci. Collect., Excerpta Med., Cumul. Index Nurs. Allied Health Lit., Hospit. Lit. Index, Except. Child Educ. Resour., Index Med., Curr. Contents Clin. Pract., Except. Child Educ. Abstr., Sci. Cit. Index, Abr. Ed. LC RM695. DD 615.8205. NLM W1 PH749J. CODEN PTHEA.

PHYSICAL THERAPY FORUM (MIDDLE ATLANTIC EDITION). (PHYSICAL THERAPY FORUM). 8750-2119. Periodical. US. English. wk. Free to Licensed Physical Therapists. Physical Therapy Forum Inc, 251 West DeKalb Pike/Suite A-115, King of Prussia PA 19406. DD 610.

PHYSIOQUEBEC. V. 1- Sept. 1975-. 0708-1006. Periodical. CN. English (French). ir. Free to members. Professional Corporation of Physiotherapists of Quebec, 1440 West St Catherine Street/ # 816, Montreal Quebec H3G 1R8 Canada. DD 615.805.

Physical Training

PHYSIOTHERAPY. V. 34- 1948-. Periodical. UK. English. mo. 20. Chartered Society of Physiotherapy, 14 Bedford Row, London WC1R 4ED England. **Tel** 01-242 1941. **Ed** J Whitehouse. **Ind/Abst** Index Med. Index in last issue of volume - attached. bk rev. adv acc. **Circ** 23,000. The official journal of the Chartered Society of Physiotherapy. It contains original papers by leading physiotherapists, doctors, and members of other professions. *Chartered Society of Physiotherapy.*

PROGRAMMING TRENDS IN THERAPEUTIC RECREATION. Began with Vol. 1, No. 1 (Feb. 1980). 0740-5685. Periodical. US. English. bm. $14.00. Creative Leisure Services, 2225 East McKinney, Denton TX 76201. **Tel** (817)382-0000.

PROGRESS REPORT - AMERICAN PHYSICAL THERAPY ASSOCIATION. Main/Corp American Physical Therapy Association. 0162-3907. Periodical. US. English. mo. $4.00 Nonmembers. American Physical Therapy Association, 1111 North Fairfax Street, Alexandria VA 22314.

RAPPORT ANNUEL - CORPORATION PROFESSIONNELLE DES PHYSIOTHERAPEUTES DU QUEBEC. (RAPPORT ANNUEL). **Main/Corp** Corporation Professionnelle des Physiotherapeutes du Quebec. 0227-7611. CN. French. an. Corporation Professionnelle des Physiotherapeutes du Quebec, 1440 Ouest rue Ste-Catherine/Bureau 816, Montreal Quebec H3G 1R8 Canada. **LC** RM695. **DD** 615.82060714.

REHABILITACION. V. 1- 1967-. 0048-7120. Periodical. SP. Spanish. qt. $19.63. Sociedad Espanola de Rehabilitacion, Villanueva 11, Madrid 1 Spain. **Ind/Abst** Excerpta Med. **NLM** W1 RE173LK.

REHABILITATION DIGEST. V. 1- Summer 1969-. 0048-7139. Periodical. CN. English. qt. $6.97. Canadian Rehabilitation Council for Disabled, 1 Yonge Street/Suite 2110, Toronto Ontario M5E 1E5 Canada. **Tel** (416)862-0340. **Ed** Heather Ney. **Ind/Abst** Except. Child Educ. Resour. bk rev. adv acc. **Circ** 1,755. Offers news, views and in-depth articles on physical rehabilitation for professionals and disabled people. Events, reviews, and the latest and best in technology are featured.

REHABILITATION FACILITIES PLAN, ADDENDUM FOR THE ESTABLISHMENT AND IMPROVEMENT OF WORKSHOPS, MEDICALLY ORIENTED CENTERS, COMMUNITY BASED AUDIOLOGICAL FACILITIES, WORK ACTIVITY CENTERS, WORK STUDY PROGRAMS CEASED. (REHABILITATION FACILITIES PLAN, ADDENDUM FOR THE ESTABLISHMENT AND IMPROVEMENT OF WORKSHOPS, MEDICALLY ORIENTED CENTERS, COMMUNITY BASED AUDIOLOGICAL FACILITIES, WORK ACTIVITY CENTERS, AND WORK STUDY PROGRAMS). **Main/Corp** Montana. Rehabilitative Services Division. Special Projects Bureau. 0093-2973. US. English. an. **LC** RM930.A1. **DD** 362.042509786.

REHABILITATION R&D PROGRESS REPORTS. (REHABILITATION R & D PROGRESS REPORTS). **VFOAT** Rehabilitation R and D Progress Reports. **VAT** Rehabilitation Research and Development Progress Reports. 1983-. 0882-7753. US. English. an. Free. Superintendent of Documents, US Government Printing Office, Washington DC 20402.

THE STROKING TIMES. 8756-0364. Periodical. US. English. mo. $8.00. The Stroking Times, 71 West Sproul Road, Springfield PA 19064. **Tel** (215)543-9080. **Ed** David Linton. **DD** 615. bk rev. **Circ** 500. Newsletter about massage and other hands-on healing, articles, news, reviews, and opinion plus a calendar of learning opportunities nationwide for "people who knead people.".

THEORIE UND PRAXIS DER KORPERKULTUR. Vol. 1-. 0563-4458. Periodical. SZ. German. mo. $24.84. Kunst & Wissen Erich Bieber, Dufourstrasse 51, CH-8008 Zurich Switzerland. **Tel** 011-41-1-69 44 20. **LC** GV201. **NLM** W1 TH123.

TODAY'S CHIROPRACTIC. V. 1- Jan./Feb. 1972-. 0091-2360. Periodical. US. English. bm. $18.00. Life Chiropractic College, 1269 Barclay Circle, Marietta GA 30060. **Ed** Miriam Butler. **LC** RZ201. **DD** 615.53405. **NLM** W1 TO161. bk rev. adv acc. **Circ** 24,000. (ctrl). Chiropractic, health, nutrition, exercise and celebrities.

TRANSFERT. (LE TRANSFERT). V. 3, No. 3 (Feb. 1979)-. 0713-4355. Periodical. CN. French (English). qt. $15.48. Corporation Professionnelle des Ergotherapeutes, 1500 Maisonneuve Boulevard East, Montreal Quebec H1L 2B1 Canada. **Tel** (514)527-9281. **DD** 615.8515209714. *Bulletin (Corporation Professionnelle des Ergotherapeutes du Quebec).*

THE UPPER CERVICAL MONOGRAPH. V. 1- Mar. 1973-. 0364-1953. Periodical. US. English. qt. NUCCA Monograph Editor, 221 West Second Street, Monroe MI 48161. **NLM** W1 UP65.

PHYSICAL TRAINING

ACADEMY PAPERS - AMERICAN ACADEMY OF PHYSICAL EDUCATION. MEETING. Main/Corp American Academy of Physical Education. Meeting. No. 1- 1967-. 0569-2121. US. English. an. Human Kinetics Publishers, Box 5076, Champaigne IL 61820. **Tel** (217)351-5076. **LC** UNC. **Circ** 250. Leading scholars in physical education present the latest research and state-of-the-art papers on different topics related to the theme of the annual conference.

ACTA. GYMNICA. Main/Corp Prague. Universita Karlova. 1966-. Periodical. CS. Czech (summaries in English and Russian). sa. Artia, Ve-Smechkach 30, Praha 1 Czechoslovakia. **LC** GV201. *Sbornik.*

ACTUA. No. 1- JAN. 1973-. 0381-193X. Periodical. CN. English. mo. $5. Association des Professionnels de l'Activitie Physique du Quebec, 1415 East rue Jarry, Montreal Quebec H2E 2Z7 Canada. **DD** 796.4109714.

ADAPTED PHYSICAL ACTIVITY QUARTERLY. (ADAPTED PHYSICAL ACTIVITY QUARTERLY : APAQ). **VFOAT** APAQ. V. 1, No. 1-. 0736-5829. Periodical. US. English. qt. $48.00. Human Kinetics Publishers Inc, Box 5076, Champaign IL 61820. **Tel** (217)351-5076. **Ed** Geoffrey D Broadhead. bk rev. adv acc. **Circ** 620. Multidisciplinary journal dealing with physical activity for special populations of all ages. Presents the latest theoretical and applied research regarding adaptations of equipment, facilities, methodology and/or settings.

ADVANCES IN PEDIATRIC SPORT SCIENCES. See Medicine - Pediatrics.

AEROBICS. (AEROBICS : AN OFFICIAL PUBLICATION OF THE AEROBICS CENTER). 0739-8611. Periodical. US. English. mo. $15.00 US, $20.00 Canada. Aerobics Center/Communications Division, 12200 Preston Road, Dallas TX 75230.

AEROBICS & FITNESS. (AEROBICS & FITNESS : THE JOURNAL OF THE AEROBICS & FITNESS ASSOCIATION OF AMERICA). **VFOAT** Aerobics and Fitness. Began with Mar.-Apr. 1984. 0749-8942. Periodical. US. English. bm. $18.00. Aerobics and Fitness Association of America, 15250 Ventura Boulevard, Sherman Oaks CA 91403. **Tel** (818)905-0040. **Ed** Peg Angsten. **DD** 613. bk rev. adv acc. **Circ** 20,000. (ctrl). Covers aerobic exercise and sports, health and fitness education. Contains timely, in-depth editorial and articles, new products section, personal profiles, motivational pieces, photo features, and the like. *AFAA Journal.*

AMERICAN ACADEMY OF PHYSICAL EDUCATION PAPERS. VFOAT Academy Papers. No. 17-. 0741-4633. US. English. an. $12.00. Human Kinetics Publishers Inc, Box 5076, Champaign IL 61820. **Tel** (217)351-5076. **LC** UNC. Each volume of the academy papers includes invited papers from scholars in the area of sport and physical education. *Academy Papers, 0569-2121.*

ANNUAIRE (FRANCE. MINISTERE DE LA JEUNESSE, DES SPORTS ET DES LOISIRS. DIVISION DES ETUDES ET DE LA STATISTIQUE). See Yearbooks, Almanacs, Directories.

ANNUAL REPORT - NATIONAL FITNESS COUNCIL OF VICTORIA. Main/Corp National Fitness Council of Victoria. English. ir. 570 Bourke Street, 3000 Melbourne Australia. **LC** GV204.A82. **DD** 613.7062945.

ARENA. 1. Periodical. NE. English (German). sa. EJ Brill, POB 9000, 2300 PA Leiden The Netherlands. **LC** GV201.

ASCA NEWSLETTER - AMERICAN SWIMMING COACHES ASSOCIATION. (ASCA NEWSLETTER). **VFOAT** A.S.C.A. Newsletter. 0747-6000. Periodical. US. English. bm. $30.00. ASCA, 1 Hall of Fame Drive, Fort Lauderdale FL 33316. **Tel** (305)462-6297. **Ed** John Croward. bk rev. adv acc. **Circ** 2,500. Information for swimming coaches.

ATHLETIC TRAINING. Began with Mar. 1972 issue. 0160-8320. Periodical. US. English. qt. $20.00 Domestic, $25.00 Foreign. Athletic Training, 1001 East 4th Street, Greenville NC 27834. **Tel** (919)752-1725. **Ed** Steve Yates. **Ind/Abst** Excerpta Med. **LC** RC1200. **DD** 617.1027. **NLM** W1 AT387. **CODEN** ATHTA. bk rev. adv acc. **Circ** 10,000. (ctrl). Research, current literature and general information on physical fitness, diet, medical opinion, new developments in the prevention and management of sports-related injuries. *Journal.*

AUDIBLE (TORONTO, ONT.). See Recreation, Leisure - Sports.

AUDIT REPORT, GOVERNOR'S COMMISSION ON PHYSICAL FITNESS. Main/Corp Texas. Governor's Commission On Physical Fitness. US. English. **LC** GV481. **DD** 613.709764.

AUSTRALIAN JOURNAL FOR HEALTH, PHYSICAL EDUCATION AND RECREATION : AJHPER CEASED. **VFOAT** AJHPER. Began with No. 67 (Mar. 1975). Ceased with No. 98 (Summer 1982/83). 0004-9492. Periodical. AT. English. qt. *Australian Journal of Physical Education.*

BEITRAGE ZUR LEHRE UND FORSCHUNG IM SPORT. V. 59-. GW. German. ir. Verlag Karl Hofmann, Postfach 1360, D-7060 Schorndorf West Germany. **LC** GV201. *Beitrage zur Lehre und Forschung der Liebeserziehung.*

BLACK BELT. V. 1- 1962?-. 0277-3066. Periodical. US. English. mo. $18.00 Domestic, $20.50 Foreign. Rainbow Publications, 1845 West Empire Avenue, Burbank CA 91504. *Black Belt Magazine.*

BODY BULLETIN. April. 1981-. 0275-9101. Periodical. US. English. mo. $14.00. Rodale Press Inc, 33 East Minor Street, Emmaus PA 18049. **Tel** (215)967-5171.

BODYWORK (TORONTO, ONT.). (BODYWORK). 0822-6296. Periodical. CN. English. qt. $12.00. Bodywork, 732 Spadina Avenue, Toronto Ont M5S 2J2 Canada. **DD** 615.82205.

BOLETIN DE ESTUDIOS Y DOCUMENTACION DEL SEREM CEASED. **Main/Corp** Spain. Servicio de Recuperacion y Rehabilitacion de Minusvalidos Fisicos y Psiquicos. No. 1- Feb. 1975-. 0211-0334. Spanish. ty. Servicio de Publicaciones Ministerio de Sanidad y Seguridad Social, Maria de Guzman 52, Madrid Spain. **LC** HV3000.

BOLETIN DEL CONSEJO SUPERIOR DE DEPORTES. Main/Corp Spain. Consejo Superior de Deportes. Yearly V. 35 (No. 409-). Spanish. ir. Martin Fierro, S/N Ciudad Universitaria, Madrid Spain. **LC** GV273. **DD** 613.707.

BRITISH JOURNAL OF PHYSICAL EDUCATION. Vol. 14, No. 3 (May/June 1983)-. 0144-3569. Periodical. UK. English. bm. 35.00. British Journal of Physical Education, Ling House, 162 Kings Cross Road, London WC1X 9DH England. **Tel** 01-278-9311. **Ed** A J Pethgrick. **Ind/Abst** Ref. Source. bk rev. adv acc. **Circ** 6,000. (ctrl). Latest developments and information for PE teachers. *Action.*

BULLETIN - HISPA. Main/Corp HISPA. English (French and German). ir. 50.00. Professor Dr Roland Penson, K University of Leuven Teruumereul 101, B 3030 Heverlee Belgium. **LC** GV201. **DD** 613.7.

BULLETIN - INTERNATIONAL WEIGHTLIFTING FEDERATION. Main/Corp International Weightlifting Federation. English (French). ir. Tamas Ajan, General Secretary IWF, 1442 Budapest PF 116, Hungary. **LC** GV546. **DD** 796.410601.

BULLETIN OF PHYSICAL EDUCATION. 1950. 0521-0011. Periodical. UK. English. ty. $12.26. British Association of Organisers and Lecturers in Physical Education, 6 Ladywood Mead, Leeds LS8 2LZ England. **Tel** 657160. **Ed** Terry

Williamson. adv acc. **Circ** 1,000. Articles concerning current practice and developments in physical education in schools and colleges in the UK.

CAHPER JOURNAL. **Main/Corp** Canadian Association for Health, Physical Education and Recreation. **VFOAT** Journal of the Canadian Association for Health, Physical Education and Recreation. V. 35, No. 1- Oct./Nov. 1968-. 0226-5478. Periodical. CN. English (abstracts in French). bm. $30.95. Canadian Association of Health Physical Education and Recreation, 333 River Road, Ottawa Ontario K1L 8H9 Canada. **Tel** (613)748-5622. **Ed** Elie Betito. **Ind/Abst** Can. Period. Index, Can. Educ. Index. **DD** 613.7'07. bk rev. adv acc. **Circ** 25,000. Pqriodical touching on areas such as: physical education, health, recreation, dance and fitness for the professional or library reference. *Journal of the Canadian Association for Health, Physical Education and Recreation, 0008-2899.*

CANADIAN MARATHON ANNUAL. *See* Recreation, Leisure - Sports.

CARNEGIE RESEARCH PAPERS. V. 1- Dec. 1979-. Periodical. UK. English. an. 2.50 Domestic, 4.00 Foreign. Leeds Polytechnic, Calvary Street, Leeds LSI 3HE England. **Tel** 0532 462329. **Ed** John Humphries. adv acc. **Circ** 300. *Research Papers in Physical Education.*

CHEF DE FORME - RESEAU PARTICIPACTION. (CHEF DE FORME). Vol. 1, No. 2-. 0827-3502. Periodical. CN. French. qt. Free to Members. Reseau Participaction, 80 Ouest rue Richmond, Toronto Ontario M5H 2A4 Canada. **DD** 613.70971.

CHUNG-HUA WU SHU. Periodical. CC. Chinese. qt. 0.34. Post Office Peking, Peking China.

CHUNG-KUO KUO SHU. **VFOAT** Zhong Guo Guoshu. Periodical. CH. Chinese. qt. 0.30. Chin-Chou Shih Yu Tien Chu, Liao-Ning China Mainland.

CHUNG-KUO WU SHU SHIH LIAO CHI KAN. V. 1-. Chinese. ir. **LC** GV1112.

CLUB INDUSTRY. Vol. 1, No.1(Sept./Oct. 1984)-. 0747-8283. Periodical. US. English. bm. $36.00. Sportscape Inc, 1415 Beacon Street #320, Box c 9122, Boston MA 02146. **Tel** (617)277-3823. **Ed** Todd Logan. **DD** 613. adv acc. **Circ** 20,000. (ctrl). A business magazine for health and fitness club management.

COMPLETED RESEARCH IN HEALTH, PHYSICAL EDUCATION, AND RECREATION *CEASED.* 1974-. 0516-916X. Periodical. US. English. an. $8.95. 1201 16th Street NW, Washington DC 20036. **LC** Z6121, GV1. **DD** 016.79. **NLM** ZQT 180 C737. *Completed Research in Health, Physical Education, and Recreation.*

CORPORATE FITNESS & RECREATION. **VFOAT** Corporate Fitness and Recreation. Vol. 1, No. 1 Oct./Nov. 1982. 0745-0869. Periodical. US. English. bm. $40.00. Brentwood Publishing Corporation, PO Box 49045, Los Angeles CA 90049-0045. **Tel** (213)826-8388. **LC** HD7395.P45. **DD** 613.7088331. bk rev. adv acc. **Circ** 18,099. (ctrl). For fitness directors, exercise leaders, physical education consemp services, recreation leaders and administrators involved in corporate fitness.

DIET & EXERCISE. *See* Nutrition and Dietetics.

DISCOVERY YMCA. *See* Recreation, Leisure.

DZIENNIK URZEDOWY GOWNEGO KOMITETU KULTURY FIZYCZNEJ I SPORTU. **Main/Corp** Poland. Gowny Komitet Kultury Fizycznej i Sportu. 0137-6187. PL. Polish. ir. 60.00. RSW Prasas-Ksaiazka-Ruch Centrala Kolportazu Prasy I Wydawnictw, Ul Towarowa 28, 00-958 Warszawa Poland.

EDUCACION FISICA, CHILE. Periodical. CL. Spanish. qt. **LC** GV239. **DD** 613.70983. **NLM** W1 ED68T. *Revista Chilena de Educacion Fisica.*

EDUCATORS GUIDE TO FREE HEALTH, PHYSICAL EDUCATION AND RECREATION MATERIALS. *See* Education (General) - Special Aspects of Education.

EXECUTIVE FITNESS NEWSLETTER. 0014-4525. Periodical. US. English. bw. $30.00. Rodale Press Inc, Attn L Zver 33 East Minor Street, Emmaus PA 18049. **Tel** (215)967-5171. **Ed** Porter Shimer. **Circ** 46,000. Health tips for the busy executive trying to stay in shape, with topical articles on exercise, diet and stress reducing techniques.

EXERCISE FOR MEN ONLY. **VFOAT** Exercise. Vol. 1, Issue 1 (Mar./Apr. 1985)-. 0882-4657. Periodical. US. English. bm. $19.50 Domestic, $24.00 Foreign. Chelo Enterprises Ltd, 350 5th Avenue/Suite 6204, New York NY 10118.

FEELING FINE. (FEELING FINE : A DIGEST OF INFORMATION AND IDEAS FROM THE FITNESS AND NUTRITION CLUB). Vol. 2, No. 1 (Mar. 1984)-. 0826-2594. Periodical. CN. English. ir. Free to Members. F A N Club, #2 203 Beverley Street, Toronto Ontario M5T 1Y5 Canada. **DD** 641.105. *F.A.N. Club Digest, 0827-3170.*

FEELING GOOD (TORONTO, ONT.). (FEELING GOOD). V. 1, No. 1 (Winter 1981)-. 0714-7368. Periodical. CN. English. ir. Feeling Good, Canadian Cancer Society, Suite 1001/130 Bloor Street West, Toronto Ontario M5S 2V7 Canada. **DD** 613.8505. *Tobacco Road (Canadian Cancer Society), 0227-6887; Fresh Air (Canadian Cancer Society), 0229-5067.*

FIGHTING STARS NINJA. **VFOAT** Fighting Stars. 0886-8786. Periodical. US. English. bm. Rainbow Publications Inc, PO Box 7728, Burbank CA 91510-7728. **DD** 796. *Fighting Stars, 0274-5178.*

FIGHTING WOMAN NEWS. 0146-8812. Periodical. US. English. qt. $15.00. Fighting Women News, PO Box 1459 Grand Central Station, New York NY 10163. **Tel** (212)228-0900. **Ed** Valerie Eads. bk rev. adv acc. **Circ** 5,000. Martial arts, self-defense, combative sports. History, technique, how-to, reviews, etc. Aimed at literate, adult practitioners.

FIRST AIDER. Periodical. US. English. mo. $4.00. The First Aider, PO Box 1001, Gardner KS 66030. **Tel** (913)884-7511. **Ed** Katherine B Knisely. bk rev. **Circ** 120,000. (ctrl). Dedicated to sharing information concerning the care and prevention of athletic injuries; geared to high school/college coaches, athletic trainers and students.

FIT THIRD AGE. (A FIT THIRD AGE). **VFOAT** Troisieme Age en Forme. **VAT** Troisieme Age en Forme. No. 1 (1984)-. 0827-3103. Periodical. CN. English (French). ty. Free. Secretariat for Fitness in the Third Age, 333 River Road, Vanier Ontario K1L 8H9 Canada. **DD** 613.70971. (ctrl).

FITNESS AND LIFESTYLE RESEARCH REVIEWS. Jan. 1980-. 0227-7751. Periodical. CN. English. mo. $89. Per Year, Canada. Danielson Research Consultants, 217 Maki Avenue, Sudbury Ont P3E 2P3 Canada. **DD** 613.05.

FITNESS BULLETIN. (THE FITNESS BULLETIN). Vol. 5, No. 1 (Jan. 1982)-. 0820-6163. Periodical. CN. English. mo. Free to Members. Fitness Institute, 255 Yorkland Boulevard, Willowdale Ontario M2J 1S3 Canada. **DD** 613.705. *Fitness Institute Bulletin, 0826-4341.*

FITNESS LEADER. Vol. 1, No. 1 (Sept. 1982)-. 0713-3995. Periodical. CN. English. ir. $53.20. Fitness Leader c/o Pitters Publishing, Suite 405 251 Bank Street, Ottawa Ont K2P 1X3 Canada. **DD** 613.705.

FITNESS MANAGEMENT. Vol. 1, No. 1(Mar./Apr. 1985)-. 0882-0481. Periodical. US. English. bm. $25.00. Fitness Management, PO Box 1198, Solana Beach CA 92075-0910. **DD** 613.

FITNESS REPORT. (THE FITNESS REPORT). V. 1- Feb. 1980-. 0226-7810. Periodical. CN. English. mo. $75.00. Basquill Elson Inc, 102 Adelaide Street E, Toronto Ont M5C 1K9 Canada. **Tel** (416)362-4538. **Ed** Joe Taylor. **DD** 613.70971. bk rev. adv acc. Current review of events, resources, conferences, and program ideas in fitness. Book reviews, articles of interest and new equipment.

FUKUOKA DAIGAKU TAIIKUGAKU KENKYU. **VFOAT** Fukuoka University Review of Physical Education. JA. Japanese. ir. Fukuoka Daigaku Kenkyujo, 11 Nanakuma, Nishi-Ku, Fukuoka Japan. **LC** GV201.

GET FIT. **VFOAT** Fit. 8750-8079. Periodical. US. English. mo. Get Fit, 1400 Stierlin Road, Mountain View CA 94043. **DD** 613. *Fit, 0278-9760.*

GIGIENA I SANITARIJA. (GIGIENA I SANITARIIA). Began with: 1943, No. 1. 0016-9900. Periodical. UR. Russian (tables of contents also in English). mo. $33.50. Victor Kamkin Inc (70220), 12224 Parklawn Drive, Rockville MD 20852. **Tel** (301)881-5973. **Ind/Abst** Coal Abstr., Index Med., Int. Aerosp. Abstr., Biol. Abstr., CIS Abstr., Chem. Abstr. **NLM** W1 GI133. **CODEN** GISAAA. Index in last issue of volume - attached. *Gigiena I Zdorove.*

GUIA DE ENTIDADES E INSTALACIONES DEPORTIVAS. **VFOAT** Guia Deportiva de Vizcaya. Spanish. ir. D.N.E.F. y d'Instalaciones Deportivas, Jose Ma Escuza 16, Bilbao Spain. **LC** GV204.S72.

GYMNASTIKK OG TURN. 1948-. Periodical. NO. Norwegian. ir. $10.00. Norges Gymnastikk-OG, Hauger Skolovei 1, 1346 Gjettum Norway. **Ed** Rolf Rustad.

HA-HINUKH HA-GUFANI. **VFOAT** Hachinuch Hagufani. Periodical. Hebrew. ir. 12.50. **LC** GV201.

HANGUK CHEYUK HAKHOE CHI. **VFOAT** Korean Journal of Physical Education. Periodical. English (Korean). ir. **LC** GV201.

HEALTH FACT NEWS. 1981. 0279-5639. Periodical. US. English. mo. $25.00. Health Fact News, PO Box C-100, Colts Neck NJ 07722. **Tel** (201)946-4429. **Ed** Lillian Dichter. **DD** 614. bk rev. adv acc. **Circ** 100,000. New information about health nutrition and fitness collected from over 2,000 daily, weekly, and monthly world wide publications.

HOKEN TAIIKUGAKU KENKYU KIYO. **VFOAT** Annals of Physical Education. No. 1 (1965)-. 0474-795X. Periodical. JA. Japanese. ir. Osaka Shiritsu Daigaku Kyoyobu Hoken Taiiku, Kenkyushitsu 3-138 Sugimoto 3 Sumiyoshi-Ku, Osaka-Shi 558 Japan. **LC** GV201.

HOLISTIC MASSAGE. (HOLISTIC MASSAGE : NEWSLETTER OF THE INTERNATIONAL ACADEMY OF MASSAGE SCIENCE). Vol. 1, No. 1 (June 23, 1984)-. 0748-6855. Periodical. US. English. mo. $15.00. International Academy of Massage Science, 25 Price's Lane, Rose Valley PA 19063. **Tel** (215)566-6049. **Ed** Karen Carlson. **DD** 615. bk rev. adv acc. **Circ** 200. Comprehensively covers scientific Swedish massage and Holistic health-building modalities for persons interested in professional training.

HOME GYM & FITNESS. **VFOAT** Home Gym and Fitness. Vol. 1, No. 1 (Mar. 1985)-. 0885-2146. Periodical. US. English. bm. $10.00. Home Gym & Fitness, PO Box 27968, San Diego CA 92128-9990.

THE IAHPER JOURNAL. **VFOAT** Indiana Journal of Health, Physical Education and Recreation. V. 1- 19-. Periodical. US. English. qt. $10.00. c/o Jennifer Jones, Vincennes University, Vincennes IN 47591. **Tel** (812)237-4170. **Ed** Mary Ann Dunscomb. bk rev. adv acc. **Circ** 2,000. (ctrl). Educational articles for professionals in the fields of health, physical recreation and dance.

IDEA ANNUAL DIRECTORY. *See* Yearbooks, Almanacs, Directories.

INFOAAU. **Main/Corp** Amateur Athletic Union of the United States. **VFOAT** Info A.A.U. **VAT** Info Amateur Athletic Union. 0279-9863. Periodical. US. English. bm. $8.00. Amateur Athletic Union, 3400 West 86th Street, Indianapolis IN 46268. **Tel** (317)872-2900. **Ed** Mike Bowyer. adv acc. **Circ** 8,000. The official publication of the Amateur Athletic Union. It covers stories about the Union's activities as well as articles on health and physical fitness. *AAU News, 0199-6991.*

INFORMATIONSHEFT ZUM TRAINING. Periodical. German. ir. **LC** GV201.

INSIDE KUNG-FU. 0199-8501. Periodical. US. English. mo. $18.75. Unique Publications, Subscription Department, 4201 Van Woen Place, Burbank CA 91505. **Tel** (818)845-2656.

INSIGHTS. (INSIGHTS : NRA NEWS FOR YOUNG SHOOTERS). **VFOAT** In Sights. Vol. 2, Issue 1 (Jan./Feb. 1982)-. 0747-007X. Periodical. US. English. bm. $4.00. National Rifle Association of America, 1600 Rhode Island Avenue Northwest, Washington DC 20036. **DD** 799. *NRA Junior News.*

INTERNATIONAL JOURNAL OF PHYSICAL EDUCATION. **VFOAT** Internationale Zeitschrift fur Sportpadagogik. V. 10- Spring 1973-. 0341-8685. Periodical. US. English (German). qt. $30.00. ICHPER, c/o Ms Helen Metheny, 1900 Association Drive, Reston VA 22091. **Tel** (703)476-3486. **Ind/Abst** Educ. Index, Bibliogr. Index. **LC** GV201. **DD** 613.707. *Gymnasion.*

INVENTARISATIE SPORTACCOMMODATIES. **Main/Corp** Netherlands (Kingdom, 1815-). Centraal Bureau voor de Statistiek. Dutch. ir. 14.50. Centraal Bureau voor de Statistiek, Staatsuitgeverij, S-Gravenhage Netherlands. **LC** GV433.N4.

IRON MAN. 1936. 0047-1496. Periodical. US. English. bm. $12.50. Iron Man Industries, PO Box 10, Alliance NB 69301. **Tel** (308)762-5152. adv acc. Bodybuilding, power lifting and weightlifting.

JAHRBUCH DER TURNKUNST. *See* Yearbooks, Almanacs, Directories.

Physical Training

JOE WEIDER'S MUSCLE & FITNESS.
VFOAT Joe Weider's Muscle and Fitness. 0744-5105. Periodical. US. English. mo. $29.95. l'Brute, 21100 Erwin Street, Woodland Hills CA 91367. Tel (213)603-0648. Ed Joe Weider. adv acc. Circ 350,000. A comprehensive magazine on bodybuilding and weight training by the world's best. *Joe Weider's Muscle.*

THE JOURNAL OF PHYSICAL EDUCATION CEASED. (JOURNAL OF PHYSICAL EDUCATION). Began with V. 25, Sept. 1927. Ceased with V. 78, No. 3, (Jan./Feb. 1981). 0022-3662. Periodical. US. English. bm. Ed J Brown. LC GV201. DD 613.705. NLM W1. *Physical Training.*

THE JOURNAL OF PHYSICAL EDUCATION AND PROGRAM. Vol. 78, No. 4/D (Spring 1981)-. 0735-0139. Periodical. US. English. ir. $9.00. National Physical Education, 40 West Long Street, Columbus OH 43215. Tel (614)224-2514. NLM W1 JO836LM. *Journal of Physical Education (Dayton, Ohio), 0022-3662.*

JOURNAL OF PHYSICAL EDUCATION AND RECREATION CEASED. V. 46-52, No. 4. 0097-1170. Periodical. US. English. $35.00. 201 16th Street NW, Washington DC 20036. LC GV201. DD 613.705. *Journal of Health, Physical Education, Recreation, 0022-1473.*

JOURNAL OF PHYSICAL EDUCATION, RECREATION & DANCE. VFOAT Journal of Physical Education, Recreation and Dance, JOPEPD. Vol. 52, No. 5 (May 1981)-. 0730-3084. Periodical. US. English. ir. American Alliance for Health Physical Education Recreation and Dance, 1900 Association Drive, Reston VA 22091. Tel (703)476-3493. Ind/Abst Except. Child Educ. Resour., Curr. Index J. Educ., Media Rev. Dig., Educ. Index. LC GV201. DD 613.705. NLM W1 JO836MC. *Journal of Physical Education and Recreation, 0097-1170.*

JOURNAL OF TEACHING IN PHYSICAL EDUCATION. See Education (General) - Theory, Practice of Education.

JUDO. See Recreation, Leisure - Sports.

KAHPER JOURNAL (RICHMOND, KY.). See Public Health and Safety.

KARATE KEBEC. See Recreation, Leisure - Sports.

KOKURITSU KYOGIJO YORAN. Periodical. Japanese. ir. Kokuritsu Kyogijo, 10 Kasumigaokacho Shinjuku-Ku (160), Tokyo Japan. LC GV416.T634.

KULTURA FIZYCZNA. Main/Corp Poland. Gowny Urzad Statystyczny. 1949/66-. PL. Polish. bm. ARS Polona, Krakowskie Prezedmiescie 7, 00-068 Warsaw Poland. LC HA1451, GV288.P6. NLM W1 KU685.

LEADERS' QUARTERLY - PARTICIPACTION NETWORK. (LEADERS' QUARTERLY). Vol. 1, No. 1-. 0827-3499. Periodical. CN. English. qt. Free to Members. Participaction Network, Suite 805/80 Richmond Street West, Toronto Ontario M5H 2A4 Canada. DD 613.70971.

MANITOBA PHYSICAL EDUCATION TEACHERS' ASSOCIATION; JOURNAL. V. 1- Oct. 1977-. 0706-0882. Periodical. CN. English. ty. Manitoba Physical Education Teachers' Association, 191 Harcourt Street, Winnipeg Manitoba R3J 3H2 Canada. Ind/Abst Can. Educ. Index. DD 613.707. *Newsletter, 0384-7462.*

MICHIGAN COUNCIL ON PHYSICAL FITNESS AND HEALTH ANNUAL REPORT TO THE MICHIGAN DEPARTMENT OF PUBLIC HEALTH. US. English. an. Michigan Department of Public Health, PO Box 30035, 3500 North Logan, Lansing MI 48909. LC RA447.M5. DD 353.977400841.

MINCE ET SVELTE. No. 1- Sept. 1979-. 0226-7535. Periodical. CN. French. mo. $1.50 Each Number. Quebecscope, Distributions Eclair, 8320 Place de la Lorraine, Anjou Quebec H1J Canada. DD 613.2505.

MONOGRAPH - WORLD REHABILITATION FUND. (MONOGRAPH). Began with: No. 1, published 1979. 0738-128X. Monographic Series. US. English. ir. $25.00. World Rehabilitaiton Fund Inc, 400 East 34th Street, New York NY 10016. Tel (212)679-2934. Ed Diane E Woods. LC UNC. NLM W1 MO5559. Circ 4,000. (ctrl). International rehabilitation.

MOTOR SKILLS. THEORY INTO PRACTICE CEASED. (MOTOR SKILLS : THEORY INTO PRACTICE). V. 1- Fall 1976-. 0147-0302. Periodical. US. English. sa. $8.00. Herbert H Lehman College, c/o Anne Rothstein, Department of DHPER, Bronx NY 10468. Ind/Abst Excerpta Med. LC GV223. DD 613.70973. NLM W1 MO948I.

MUSCLE MAG INTERNATIONAL. V. 1- Fall 1974-. 0317-087X. Periodical. CN. English. mo. $21.63. Health Culture Inc, Unit One 2, Melanie Drive, Bramalea Ontario L6T 4K8 Canada. Tel (416)457-1019. DD 646.75.

MUSCULAR DEVELOPMENT. VFOAT Muscular Development Magazine. 0047-8415. Periodical. US. English. mo. $9.50. Strength and Health Publishing Company, PO Box 1707, York PA 17405. Tel (717)767-6481.

NATIONAL STRENGTH & CONDITIONING ASSOCIATION JOURNAL. VFOAT National Strength and Conditioning Association Journal. V. 3, No. 3 (June/July 1981). 0744-0049. Periodical. US. English. bm. National Strength Conditioning Association, PO Box 81410, Lincoln NE 68501. Tel (402)472-3000. Ed Ken Kontor. bk rev. adv acc. Circ 10,5000. (ctrl). Research journal that bridges the gap between athletic and biomechanic research and its practical application in strengthening athletes for their optimum performance. *National Strength Coaches Assocation Journal, 0199-610X.*

NAUCHNYE TRUDY. Main/Corp Vsesoiuznyi Nauchno-Issledovatelskii Institut Fizicheskoi Kultury. V. 1- 1971-. UR. Russian. 1.31 Single Issue. Kakhovka 2, Moskva Russia. LC GV201.

NAUTILUS MAGAZINE. 0278-3118. Periodical. US. English. bm. $6.00 Domestic, $8.40 Canada. Nautilus Magazine, PO Box 160, Independence VA 24348.

NETWORK (PARTICIPACTION NETWORK). (NETWORK). Vol. 1, No. 1 (Mar. 1, 1984)-. 0825-0324. Periodical. CN. English. qt. Participaction Network, Suite 805, 80 Richmond Street, Toronto Ontario M5H 2A4 Canada. DD 613.705.

NEW BODY. Vol. 1, No. 1 (May 1982)-. 0732-4782. Periodical. US. English. bm. $10.95. New Body, PO Box 943, Farmingdale NY 11737. Tel (212)541-7100. Ed Judy Jones. DD 796. adv acc.

NEW YORK STATE JOURNAL FOR HEALTH, PHYSICAL EDUCATION AND RECREATION. V. 1-. Periodical. US. English. sa. New York Association for Health Physical Education Recreation, 91 Fiddlers Lane, Latham NY 12110. Tel (518)785-7699.

NEWSLETTER - PRESIDENT'S COUNCIL ON PHYSICAL FITNESS AND SPORTS. (NEWSLETTER). 0364-8079. Periodical. US. English. m. Presidents Council on Physical Fitness, 400 6th Street SW, Washington DC 20201. NLM W1 PR448N.

OFFICIAL AAU JUDO RULES. See Recreation, Leisure - Sports.

OFFICIAL AAU PHYSIQUE HANDBOOK. OFFICIAL RULES. (OFFICIAL AAU PHYSIQUE HANDBOOK : OFFICIAL RULES). **Main/Corp** Amateur Athletic Union of the United States. **Series/Titl** Athletic Library. VFOAT AAU Official Rules: Physique. VAT Official Amateur Athletic Union Physique Handbook. Official Rules. 1977/78-. 0148-3560. US. English. $3.00. 3400 West 86th Street, Indianapolis IN 46268. LC GV514. DD 646.75.

OFFICIAL AAU POWERLIFTING RULE BOOK. Main/Corp Amateur Athletic Union of the United States. VFOAT AAU Official Rules Powerlifting. VAT Official Amateur Athletic Union Powerlifting Rule Book. 0145-1979. US. English. $3.00. 3400 West 86th Street, Indianpolis IN 46268. LC GV546. DD 796.41.

OFFICIAL AAU TAE KWON DO RULES. See Recreation, Leisure - Sports.

P5. PERSONAL PARTICIPATION IN PURSUIT OF PHYSICAL PROFICIENCY. (P5). VFOAT P5 Development Digest. VAT PFive. Vol. 1, No. 1 (Feb. 1982)-. 0713-4207. Periodical. CN. English. mo. $17.50. P5, Development Digest, 3549 Saint Claire Avenue East, Scarborough Ontario M1K 1L6 Canada. DD 613.705.

PHYSICAL EDUCATION GOLD BOOK. VFOAT Gold Book. 1982-84-. 0733-7272. US. English. be. Human Kinetics Publishers, Box 5076, 615 West Kirby, Champaign IL 61820. LC GV223. DD 613.7071173.

PHYSICAL EDUCATION INDEX (ANNUAL). See Indexes/Abstracts.

PHYSICAL EDUCATION INDEX (QUARTERLY). See Indexes/Abstracts.

PHYSICAL EDUCATION NEWSLETTER. 1956. 0031-8973. Periodical. US. English. ir. $28.00. Physical Education Publ, PO Box 8, Old Saybrook CT 06475. Tel (203)388-4239. Ed Towell A Klappholz. bk rev. Circ 1,500. (ctrl). Provides coverage of the best teaching and coaching practices used in the nation's schools in the areas of physical education and athletics. *Physical Education and School Athletics Newsletter.*

PHYSICAL EDUCATION REVIEW. V. 1- Spring 1978-. 0140-7708. Periodical. UK. English. sa. $18.38. North Western Counties Physical Education Association, c/o T Jones, 73 Wyverne Road, Manchester M21 1ZW England. Tel (061)881-3242. Ed K Hardman. bk rev. adv acc. Circ 1,000. (ctrl). Wide range of physical education disciplines including comparative studies, evaluation, dance, curriculum, aesthetics, sociology, psychology, physiology and history.

THE PHYSICAL EDUCATOR. VFOAT The Physical Educator of Phi Epsilon Kappa. V. 1- Oct. 1940-. 0031-8981. Periodical. US. English. qt. Phi Epsilon Kappa, 9030 Log Run Drive North, Indianapolis IN 46234. Ed David O Matthews. Ind/Abst Educ. Index, Curr. Index J. Educ., Bibliogr. Index. LC GV201. DD 371.7305. NLM W1 PH69. adv acc. Circ 7,600. (ctrl). A professional journal for health, physical education, and recreation.

PHYSICAL FITNESS RESEARCH DIGEST. Ser. 1-Ser. 9, No. 4. 0094-9108. Periodical. US. English. qt. President's Council on Physical Fitness & Sports, 400 6th Street Southwest, Washington DC 20202. LC GV223. DD 613.70973. NLM W1 PH69P.

PHYSICIAN'S SPORTSLIFE. VFOAT Physician's Sports Life. Began in 1984?. 0883-4938. Periodical. US. English. bm. $19.00. Medical Publishers Enterprises, One Bridge Plaza North/Suite 270, Fort Lee NJ 07024. DD 613.

POWERLIFTING USA. See Recreation, Leisure - Sports.

PRAXIS DER PSYCHOMOTORIK. See Education (General) - Special Aspects of Education.

PRO MOTION. (PRO MOTION : JOURNAL OF THE B.C. PHYSICAL EDUCATION TEACHER'S ASSOCIATION). 0821-5677. Periodical. CN. English. ir. British Columbia Physical Education Teachers Association, c/o Allan Thomas Viscount Elementary School, 3250 Flint Avenue, Port Coquitlam British Columbia V3B 4J2 Canada. Ind/Abst Can. Educ. Index. DD 613.707. *Pro Motion Newsletter, 0316-4985.*

PRO MOTION NEWSLETTER. V. 19- Sept. 1974-. 0316-4985. Periodical. English. ir. Free to Members. British Columbia Physical Education Teachers Association, c/o John Parry, 2568 Passage Drive, Coquitlam British Columbia V3H 3G5 Canada. DD 613.7062711. *Pro Motion, 0048-5381; Newsletter, 0316-4993.*

PROFESSIONAL KARATE. See Recreation, Leisure - Sports.

PROFESSIONAL PREPARATION DIRECTORY FOR ELEMENTARY SCHOOL PHYSICAL EDUCATION. See Yearbooks, Almanacs, Directories.

RESEARCH DIRECTORY OF THE REHABILITATION RESEARCH AND TRAINING CENTERS. See Yearbooks, Almanacs, Directories.

RESEARCH QUARTERLY FOR EXERCISE AND SPORT. V. 51- Mar. 1980-. 0270-1367. Periodical. US. English. qt. American Alliance of Health Education and Recreation, 1900 Association Drive, Business Office, Reston VA 22091. Tel (703)476-3400. Ind/Abst Excerpta Med., Biol. Abstr., Educ. Index, Except. Child Educ. Resour., Curr. Index J. Educ., Psychol. Abstr. LC GV201. DD 613.705. NLM W1 RE234AK. CODEN RQESD4. *Research Quarterly, 0034-5377.*

RESEAU (RESEAU PARTICIPACTION). (RESEAU). Vol. 1, No. 1 (1 March 1984)-. 0825-0332. Periodical. CN. French. qt. Reseau Participaction, Suite 805/80 rue Richmond, Toronto Ontario M5H 2A4 Canada. DD 613.705.

REVUE DE L'EDUCATION PHYSIQUE. V. 1- 196 -. Periodical. BE. French. qt. $19.76. Federation Belge d'Education, 33 Bd de la Sauveniere 33, Liege Belgium. Tel 041/236750. bk rev. adv acc. Circ 2,000. (ctrl). Sport physiology, movement education, biomechanics, psychology of sport, sport traumatology, physical training.

REVUE QUEBECOISE DE L'ACTIVITE PHYSIQUE. (LA REVUE QUEBECOISE DE L'ACTIVITE PHYSIQUE). Vol. 1, No. 1 (Sept. 1981)-. 0713-3081. Periodical. CN. French. ty. $6.97. University du Que a Trois Riviers, CP 500, Trois Riviers Quebec G9A 5H7 Canada. Tel (819)376-5763. Ed Lue Proteau. DD 613.7105. bk rev. adv acc. Circ 1,000. Physical education research.

ROCZNIKI NAUKOWE. Main/Corp Akademia Wychowania Fizycznego W Poznaniu. No. 22- 1973-. chiefly in Polish with summaries in English and French. ir. 110.00. LC GV201. *Roczniki Naukowe (Wyzsza Szkoa Wychowania Fizycznego W Poznaniu).*

RUNNER. V. 15- Spring 1977-. 0707-3186. Periodical. CN. English. qt. $1.50. Health and Physical Education Council, Alberta Teachers' Association, 11010-142 Street, Edmonton Alberta T5N 2R1. Ind/Abst Can. Educ. Index. DD 613.707. *H P E C Runner, 0318-0433.*

RUNNER'S GAZETTE. See Recreation, Leisure - Sports.

RUNNER'S WORLD. See Recreation, Leisure - Sports.

RUNNING & FITNESS. See Recreation, Leisure - Sports.

RUNNING TIMES. See Recreation, Leisure - Sports.

RUNNING TIMES WEST. See Recreation, Leisure - Sports.

SELF. V. 1- Jan. 1979-. 0149-0699. Periodical. US. English. mo. Conde Nast Publications Inc, 350 Madison Avenue, New York NY 10017, (subscription address: Neodata PO Box 2606 Boulder CO 80322). Ind/Abst Pop. Mag. Rev. LC RA778.A1. DD 613.04244.

SIVANANDA. (SIVANANDA). Vol. 1, No. 1 (Autumn 1981)-. 0713-5017. Periodical. CN. French. ty. Free. Revue Sivananda, c/o Camp de Yoga Sivananda, 8E Avenue, Val-Morin Quebec J0T 2R0 Canada. DD 613.704605. (ctrl).

SOMATICS. V. 1- Autumn 1976-. 0147-5231. Periodical. US. English. sa. $10.00. Somatics, 1516 Grant Avenue, Suite 220, Novata CA 94947. Tel (415)897-0336. Ed Thomas Hanna PhD. NLM W1 SO887L. bk rev. adv acc. Circ 1,200. (ctrl). Research articles for professionals and laypersons in the body-mind field.

SOUTHERN BODYBUILDER. VFOAT Southern Body Builder. March 1983-. 0736-6280. Periodical. US. English. mo. $17.50. Southern Bodybuilder Inc, PO Box 6322, Macon GA 31201.

S.P.E.A. BULLETIN. VAT Saskatchewan Physical Education Association Bulletin. Vol. 1, No. 1 (Jan. 1984)-. 0828-6132. Periodical. CN. English. mo. Saskatchewan Physical Education Association c/o Saskatchewan Teachers' Federation, P O Box 1108, Saskatchewan S7K 3N3 Canada. DD 613.707. *Leisure and Movement, 0828-6124.*

SPORT ONTARIO DIRECTORY OF SPORTS, RECREATION AND PHYSICAL EDUCATION. See Yearbooks, Almanacs, Directories.

SPORTERZIEHUNG IN DER SCHULE = EDUCATION PHYSIQUE A L'ECOLE = EDUCAZIONE FISICA NELLA SCUOLA. VFOAT Education Physique a l'Ecole. No. 1-. Periodical. French (German and/or Italian). ir. LC GV201. DD 613.707. *Korpererziehung.*

STADION. See Recreation, Leisure - Sports.

STOPWATCH. (THE STOPWATCH : THE PUBLICATION OF THE PHYSICAL EDUCATION COUNCIL OF THE NEW BRUNSWICK TEACHERS' ASSOCIATION). Vol. 11, No. 2 (Feb. 1983)-. 0821-2503. Periodical. CN. English. ir. Free. K Neilson, Fredericton High School, 365 Prospect Street, Fredericton New Brunswick E3B 3B9 Canada. DD 613.707. *Physical Education News, 0710-7730.*

STRENGTH & HEALTH. (STRENGTH AND HEALTH). 0039-2308. Periodical. US. English. bm. $9.50. Strength & Health Publishing Company, PO Box 1707, York PA 17405. Tel (717)767-6481. Ed Bob Hoffman. adv acc. Features principles of general physical fitness, olympic weightlifting and training for all major sports, also features women's training and articles on nutrition and sportsmedicine.

SYMPOSIUM PAPERS. Main/Corp Aahperd Research Consortium. Monographic Series. US. English. an.

TAHPER JOURNAL. V. 1-. Periodical. US. English. ir. Texas Association for Health Recreation, Physical Education and Dance, PO Box 7578 University Station, Austin TX 78713. Tel (512)471-3493. Ed Quentin A Christian. adv acc. Circ 5,000. A professional journal with news and information concerning health/physical education recreation and dance profession, with research articles, new book announcements, and reports of TAHPERD activities. *News Bulletin.*

T'AI CHI. 0730-1049. Periodical. US. English. bm. $15.00. T'ai Chi, PO Box 26156, Los Angeles CA 90026. Tel (213)665-7773. Ed Marvin Smalheiser. bk rev. Circ 1,600. Articles, photos about T'ai Chi Ch'uan, a Chinese exercise for health, self-defense and meditation.

TAIIKUGAKU KENKYU. VFOAT Japanese Journal of Physical Education. V. 1-. Periodical. JA. Japanese (summaries in English). ir. 5000. Nihon Taiiku Gakkai, 1-1 Kannami 1-chome, Shibuya-ku 150, Tokyo Japan. LC GV295.

TAKE FORTY AT-HOME BOOKLET. (THE TAKE FORTY AT-HOME BOOKLET). 0229-7809. Periodical. CN. English. bm. Take Forty, PO Box 742, Stock Exchange Tower, 800 Place Victoria, Montreal Quebec H4Z 1J9 Canada. DD 613.705.

TAPE RECORDER (NOVA SCOTIA TEACHERS UNION. TEACHERS ASSOCIATION FOR PHYSICAL EDUCATION). (TAPE RECORDER). Vol. 12, No. 2 (Dec. 1983)-. 0823-8839. Periodical. CN. English. ir. Free to members. Tape, PO Box 1060, Armdale Nova Scotia B3L 4L7 Canada. DD 613.707. *Tape, 0317-0233.*

TAPE. TEACHERS ASSOCIATION FOR PHYSICAL EDUCATION CEASED. (TAPE). Main/Corp Nova Scotia Teachers Union. Teachers Association for Physical Education. VFOAT TAPE Newsletter. Began publication in 1972? Ceased with V. 12, No. 1, Oct. 1983. 0317-0233. Periodical. CN. English. Nova Scotia Teachers Union, 106 Dutch Village Road, Halifax Nova Scotia B3L 4G1 Canada. DD 613.707.

TELESNA KULTURA. Main/Corp Zavod SR Slovenija za Statistiko. 1973-. Slovenian. ir. 57.00. Zavod SR Slovenije Za Statistiko, Vozarski Pot 12, Ljubljana Yugoslavia. LC GV647.3.S58.

TI YU KO HSUEH. See Recreation, Leisure - Sports.

TOKAI DAIGAKU KIYO : TAIIKUGAKUBU. VFOAT Bulletin, Faculty of Physical Education, Tokai University. No. 1-. Japanese (summaries in English and German). ir. Takai Daigaku Shuppankai, 11-2 Tsunohazu 1, Shinjuku-Ku Tokyo 160 Japan. LC GV201.

TOKYO NOKO DAIGAKU HOKEN TAIIKUGAKU RON SHU. VFOAT Hoken Taiikugaku Ron Shu. No. 1-. JA. Japanese. ir. 3-5-8 Saiwaicho Fuchushi, Tokyo (183) Japan. LC GV201.

TOTAL FITNESS. VFOAT Total Fitness Magazine. Vol. 11, No. 7 (Sept./Oct. 1982)-. 0745-1482. Periodical. US. English. bm. $12.00. National Reporter Publications Inc, 15115 South 76th East Avenue, Bixby OK 74008. Tel (918)366-4441. Ed Anne Thomas. bk rev. adv acc. Circ 100,000. The latest tips on exercise, diet, health and nutrition. *Racquetball & Total Fitness.*

TRADITIONAL TAEKWON-DO. See Recreation, Leisure - Sports.

TSUKUBA DAIGAKU TAIIKU KAGAKUKEI KIYO. VFOAT Bulletin of Institute of Health and Sport Science, the University of Tsukuba. V. 1-. 0386-7129. English (Japanese). ir. Tsukuba Daigaku, 1-1 Tennodai1 1-Chome (300-31),

Physically Impaired

Ibaraki-Ken Japan. Ind/Abst Chem. Abstr. LC GV201. CODEN TKKDD3.

TUDOMANYOS KOZLEMENYEK. Main/Corp Budapest. Magyar Testnevelesi Foiskola. summaries in French, German and Russian. ir. XII Alkotas Utca 44 Sz, Budapest Hungary. LC GV201.

TURN- UND SPORTFUHRER IM DRITTEN REICH. V. 1- 1970-. Monographic Series. German. ir. LC GV331.

THE VIRGINIA JOURNAL. V. 1- Nov. 1978-. 0739-4586. Periodical. US. English. sa. $5.00. James Madison University, c/o Dr Bruce/Godwin Hall, Harrisonburg VA 22807. Tel (703)433-6540. Ind/Abst Phys. Educ. Index, Bibliogr. Index Health Educ. Period.

LA VISION DU YOGA. Periodical. HT. French. ir. L'Association Haitienne du Kripalu Centre du Yoga, 9 rue Tertulien Guilbaud, Port-Au-Prince Haiti.

WISSENSCHAFTLICHE ZEITSCHRIFT - DEUTSCHE HOCHSCHULE FUR KORPERKULTUR LEIPZIG. Vol. 1-. 0457-3919. Periodical. SZ. German. ir. Kunst & Wissen Erich Bieber, Dufourstrasse 51, CH-8008 Zurich Switzerland. NLM W1 WI983J.

YOGA JOURNAL. 0191-0965. Periodical. US. English. bm. $15.00 Domestic, $18.50 Foreign. California Yoga Teachers Association, 2054 University Avenue, Berkeley CA 94704. Tel (415)841-9200. Ed Stephan Bodian. Ind/Abst New Period. Index. bk rev. adv acc. Circ 35,000. Body/mind approaches to personal and spiritual development: hatha yoga, holistic healing, transpersonal psychology, massage, meditation, eastern spirituality, western mysticism.

PHYSICALLY IMPAIRED

A.C.A. INDUSTRY GUIDE TO HEARING AIDS. INTERNATIONAL EDITION. (A.C.A. INDUSTRY GUIDE TO HEARING AIDS). Main/Corp Acoustic Corporation of America. VFOAT Industry Guide to Hearing Aids. 1973/75-. 0095-3474. US. English. an. 145 Tremont Street, Boston MA 02111. LC RF310. DD 617.89.

ACCENT ON LIVING. V. 3, No. 2- Fall 1958-. 0001-4508. Periodical. US. English. qt. $6.00. Accent on Living, PO Box 700, Bloomington IL 61702. Tel (309)378-2961. Ed Betty Garee. NLM W1 PO2155. adv acc. Circ 18,000. Ideas on how to make living easier for people with disabilities. *Polio Living.*

ACCENT ON LIVING BUYER'S GUIDE. VFOAT Accent on Living. 1978-. 0272-2461. US. English. be. $10.00. Accent on Living, PO Box 700, Bloomington IL 61702. Tel (309)378-2961. Ed Betty Garee. LC HV3011. DD 681.761. adv acc. Circ 20,000. Directory for physically handicapped individuals. Including dealer listings, manufacturers, organizations, publications, and films. Published every other year.

ACCESS. Dec. 1979-. 0227-1435. Periodical. CN. English. qt. 2.00. Coordinating Council on Deafness of Nova Scotia, 5185 Prince Street, Halifax Nova Scotia B3J 1L6 Canada. DD 362.4209716. *Newsletter, 0227-1427.*

ACCESS. Began publication in Aug. 1978. 2556-2657. Periodical. CN. English. qt. free. Canadian Rehabilitation Council for the Disabled, Suite 2110 1 Yonge Street, Toronto Ontario M5E 1E8 Canada. Tel (416)862-0340. Ed Heather Ney. DD 362.40971. bk rev. Circ 2,300. Activities and concerns of the Canadian Rehabilitation Council for the Disabled; rehabilitation issues and news for professionals and physically disabled people.

ACCESS ABILITY. Mar. 1981-. 0711-3498. Periodical. CN. English. ir. Free. Manitoba Organizing Committee, International Year of Disabled Persons, PO Box 177, 200 Vaughan Street, Winnipeg Manitoba R3C 0V8 Canada. DD 362.4097127.

ACCESSIBILITE A L'HABITATION. See Architecture.

ACCESSIBLE HOUSING BULLETIN. See Architecture.

Physically Impaired

ACTION MAGAZINE. 0309-2658. Periodical. UK. English. qt. $6.24. National Fund for Research into Crippling Diseases, Vincent House/1 Springfield House, Horsham Sussex England. NLM W1 AC97M.

AD VERBUM. Periodical. Spanish. ir. Confederacion Argentina de Sordomudos, Av Pedro Medrano 1352 Of 12, Buenos Aires Argentina. LC HV2350. NLM W1 AD1125.

ADDRESS LIST, REGIONAL AND SUBREGIONAL LIBRARIES FOR THE BLIND AND PHYSICALLY HANDICAPPED. See Library and Information Science.

ADVANCES IN AUDIOLOGY. Vol. 1-. 0254-8747. Monographic Series. English. ir. S Karger Ag, PO Box, CH-4009 Basel Switzerland. Ed M Hoke. NLM W1. Scientific reports covering progress in the management of hearing disorders.

ADVOCATE (TORONTO, ONT.). (ADVOCATE). July 1976-. 0229-5407. Periodical. CN. English. bm. $4.65. Ontario March of Dimes, 60 Overlea Boulevard, Toronto Ontario M4H 1B6 Canada. Tel (416)425-0501. Ed Gillian Kearney. DD 362.43060713. bk rev. adv acc. Circ 7,000. A tabloid newspaper for disabled adults and those interested in issues concerning disabled people. *Ability Advocate, 0710-1899.*

ALBERTA HANDICAPPED FORUM. (THE ALBERTA HANDICAPPED FORUM). V. 3-5, No. 4. 0382-5159. Periodical. CN. English. ir. $3. Alberta Handicapped Communications Society, 6811-104 Street, Edmonton Alberta T6H 2L5 Canada. DD 362.4097123. *Handicapped Forum, 0382-5140.*

ALPHA ACTION REPORTER. VAT Action League of Physically Handicapped Adults Action Reporter. Winter 1977-. 0227-0897. Periodical. CN. English. ir. Free to Members, $2.00 Membership. Alpha, 627 Maitland Street, London Ontario N5Y 2V7 Canada. DD 362.40971326.

AMERICAN ANNALS OF THE DEAF. VFOAT A.A.D. V. 31- Oct. 1886-. 0002-726X. Periodical. US. English. bm. American Annals of the Deaf, 814 Thayer Avenue, Silver Spring MD 20910. Ind/Abst Sociol. Abstr., Soc. Welf. Soc. Plan./Policy Soc. Dev., Lang. Lang. Behav. Abstr., Excerpta Med., Index Med., Curr. Index J. Educ., Educ. Index, Except. Child Educ. Resour., Psychol. Abstr., Public Aff. Inf. Serv. Bull. LC HV2510. DD 371. NLM W1 AM149H. CODEN ANDFAL. (cum index). Available on microfilm. *American Annals of the Deaf and the Dumb.*

ANALYSIS AND INTERVENTION IN DEVELOPMENTAL DISABILITIES. See Education (General) - Special Aspects of Education.

ANNUAL REPORT . . . - ARIZONA COUNCIL FOR THE DEAF. Main/Corp Arizona Council for the Deaf. US. English. an. Arizona Council for the Hearing Impaired, 1300 West Washington Room 105, Phoenix AZ 85007. Tel (602)255-3323. Ed Stuart R Brackney. LC HV2561.A6. DD 353.979100844. Circ 400. Informs governor and legislature of findings and makes recommendations on how to meet the needs of deaf and hearing impaired in Arizona.

ANNUAL REPORT - COMMITTEE FOR PURCHASE FROM THE BLIND AND OTHER SEVERELY HANDICAPPED. (ANNUAL REPORT). Main/Corp United States. Committee for Purchase from the Blind and Other Severely Handicapped. 0198-6961. US. English. an. Committee for Purchase from the Blind and Other Severely Handicapped, 2009 14th Street North/Suite 610, Arlington VA 22201. LC HV1783. DD 353.00844.

ANNUAL REPORT - GOVERNOR'S COMMITTEE ON EMPLOYMENT OF THE HANDICAPPED (MISSISSIPPI). See Economics - Labor.

ANNUAL REPORT - INTERNATIONAL CENTER FOR THE DISABLED. (ANNUAL REPORT). Main/Corp International Center for the Disabled. 1980-. 0732-8826. US. English. an. International Center for the Disabled, 340 East 24th Street, New York NY 10010. LC RD701.N8. DD 362.4048097471. *Annual Report, 0163-0806.*

ANNUAL REPORT - IOWA. COMMISSION FOR THE BLIND. Main/Corp Iowa. Commission for the Blind. US. English. an. Full Depository, 707 Savings and Loan Building, Des Moines IA 50309.

ANNUAL REPORT - MARCH OF DIMES BIRTH DEFECTS FOUNDATION. See Sociology: General Works, Theory - Social Pathology, Welfare, Criminology.

ANNUAL REPORT - NEW JERSEY STATE COMMISSION FOR THE BLIND AND VISUALLY IMPAIRED. Main/Corp New Jersey. Commission for the Blind and Visually Impaired. 1970/71-. 0363-9746. US. English. an. New Jersey State Commission for the Blind and Visually Impaired, 1100 Raymond Boulevard, Newark NJ 07102. LC HV1796.N5. DD 353.9749008441. NLM W2 AN4 C6R. *Annual Report - New Jersey State Commission for the Blind, 0363-9738.*

ANNUAL REPORT OF THE BOARD OF VISITORS AND SUPERINTENDENT OF THE NEW YORK STATE SCHOOL FOR THE BLIND. See Sociology: General Works, Theory - Social Pathology, Welfare, Criminology.

ANNUAL REPORT OF THE IDAHO COMMISSION FOR THE BLIND. (ANNUAL REPORT). Main/Corp Idaho Commission for the Blind. 0091-5874. US. English. an. Cecil D Andrus Governor State of Idaho, Idaho Commission for the Blind, Statehouse, Boise ID 83707. LC HV1796.I2.

ANNUAL REPORT OF THE NATIONAL ADVISORY COMMITTEE ON THE HANDICAPPED. Main/Corp National Advisory Committee on the Handicapped. 1974-. 0097-7888. US. English. an. Superintendent of Documents, US Government Printing Office, Washington DC 20402. LC HV1553. DD 362.40973. NLM W1 NA226.

ANNUAL REPORT OF THE ONTARIO ADVISORY COUNCIL ON THE PHYSICALLY HANDICAPPED. Main/Corp Ontario. Advisory Council on the Physically Handicapped. VFOAT Rapport Annuel de Conseil Consultatif de l'Ontario sur les Handicapes Physiques. 1st- 1976-. 0700-3730. CN. English. an. Advisory Council on Physically Handicapped, 3rd Floor/801 Bay Street, Toronto Ontario M5S 1Z1 Canada. LC HV3024.C3. DD 354.71300844.

ANNUAL REPORT OF THE SUPERINTENDENT OF THE NORTH DAKOTA STATE SCHOOL FOR THE BLIND TO THE DIRECTOR OF INSTITUTIONS. Main/Corp North Dakota State School for the Blind. 0360-3903. US. English. an. North Dakota School for the Blind, Grand Forks ND 58202. LC HV1796.N9. DD 371.911071078416.

ANNUAL REPORT OF THE U.S. DEPARTMENT OF HEALTH, EDUCATION, AND WELFARE TO THE PRESIDENT AND THE CONGRESS ON FEDERAL ACTIVITIES RELATED TO THE ADMINISTRATION OF THE REHABILITATION ACT OF 1973 AS AMENDED. See Public Administration.

THE ANNUAL REPORT ON THE FINDINGS AND RECOMMENDATIONS ON THE DEAF AND HEARING IMPAIRED OF OKLAHOMA. See Sociology: General Works, Theory - Social Pathology, Welfare, Criminology.

ANNUAL REPORT - SASKATCHEWAN AIDS TO INDEPENDENT LIVING. Main/Corp Saskatchewan Aids to Independent Living. CN. English. an. Saskatchewan Aids to Independent Living, 3475 Albert Street, Regina Saskatchewan S4S 6X6 Canada. LC RD755. DD 354.712400844.

ANNUAL REPORT - SASKATCHEWAN HEALTH, HEARING AID PLAN. (ANNUAL REPORT - HEARING AID PLAN). Main/Corp Saskatchewan. Hearing Aid Plan. 1974/75-. 0707-963X. CN. English. an. LC 300. DD 354.712400844.

ANNUAL REPORT - STATE OF CONNECTICUT, COMMISSION ON THE DEAF AND HEARING IMPAIRED. Main/Corp Connecticut. Commission on the Deaf and Hearing Impaired. 1974/75-. US. English. an. Commission on the Deaf and Hearing Impaired, 40 Woodland Street, Hartford CT 06105.

ANNUAL REPORT - THE COMMONWEALTH OF MASSACHUSETTS, COMMISSION ON EMPLOYMENT OF THE HANDICAPPED. See Economics - Labor.

ANNUAL REPORT TO THE GOVERNOR FOR THE PERIOD NOVEMBER 1 . . . THROUGH OCTOBER 31 - BOARD OF EXAMINERS FOR SPEECH PATHOLOGY AND AUDIOLOGY (OKLAHOMA). See Public Administration.

ANNUAL REPORT TO THE PRESIDENT AND THE CONGRESS ON THE ACTIVITIES OF THE REHABILITATION ACT INTERAGENCY COORDINATING COUNCIL. See Public Administration.

ANNUAL REPORT - WASHINGTON STATE COMMISSION FOR THE BLIND. See Sociology: General Works, Theory - Social Pathology, Welfare, Criminology.

AQPEHV. ASSOCIATION QUEBECOISE DES PARENTS D'ENFANTS HANDICAPES VISUELS. (AQPEHV : ASSOCIATION QUEBECOISE DES PARENTS D'ENFANTS HANDICAPES VISUELS). Vol. 1, No. 1 (Oct. 1980)-. 0228-4758. Periodical. CN. French. ir. $5,00. A.Q.P.E.H.V., 65 Est rue Sherbrooke/Suite 201, Montreal Quebec H2X 1C4 Canada. DD 362.41060714.

ARCHTYPE. (ARCHTYPE : PROMOTING AWARENESS OF LEGAL ISSUES AFFECTING THE DISABLED). VAT Advocacy Resource Centre for the Handicapped Type. Vol. 1, No. 1 (Jan. 1981)-. 0712-1873. Periodical. CN. English. qt. $6.19. Advocacy Resource Center for the Handicapped, 40 Orchad View Boulevard/Suite 255, Toronto Ontario M4R 1B9 Canada. Tel (416)482-8255. DD 344.71032405. bk rev. adv acc. Circ 650. Published by a legal clinic for the disabled. Legal, consumer, advocacy issues relating to spectrum of disabilities. Special interest in charter of rights and disability.

ASHA. See Education (General) - Special Aspects of Education.

AUDECIBEL. 1952. 0004-7473. Periodical. US. English. qt. $10.00. National Hearing Aid Society, 20361 Middlebelt Road, Livonia MI 48152. Tel (313)478-2610. Ed Anthony DiRocco. NLM W1 AU201. bk rev. adv acc. Circ 16,000. (ctrl). Information on hearing loss, hearing instrumentation, education, training, and related articles of this field.

AUDIOLOGISCHE AKUSTIK. VFOAT Audiological Acoustics. 19- Year. 0172-8261. Periodical. GW. German (text in English). bm. 48.00. Median-Verlag, POB 10 39-64, 6900 Heidelberg 1 West Germany. Tel 6221/25731. Ind/Abst Excerpta Med., Comput. Control Abstr., Electr. Electron. Abstr., Sci. Abstr. NLM W1 AU201FM. CODEN AUKADP. bk rev. adv acc. Circ 3,800. Concerns hearing and speech impairments and hearing loss. The latest surgical and technological advancements in hearing and speech. *Zeitschrift fur Horgeate-Akustik, 0044-2860.*

AUDIOLOGY & HEARING EDUCATION CEASED. VFOAT Audiology and Hearing Education. Began with V.1 Aug./Sept. 1975. Ceased with V. 6, No. 4, (Winter issue 1980-1981). 0360-1668. Periodical. US. English. qt. NLM W1 AU201GI.

AUDITION & PAROLE. VFOAT Audition et Parole. V. 1, 1-. 0222-3856. Periodical. French. qt. $45.38. Kunst und Wissen Erich Bieber, Postfach 46/ Whilmstrasse 4, 7000 Stuttgart 1 West Germany. NLM W1 AU202F.

AUSTRALIAN JOURNAL OF HUMAN COMMUNICATION DISORDERS. V. 1- June 1973-. 0310-6853. Periodical. AT. English. sa. $17.70. Australian Association of Speech & Hearing, 212 Clarendon, Melbourne Victoria 3002 Australia. Tel 03 342 0280. Ed Carl L Parsons. NLM W1 AU6122. bk rev. adv acc. Communication disorders, language, phonology, voice, stuttering, autism, mental retardation, deafness, speech pathology. *Journal of the Australian College of Speech Therapists.*

AUSTRALIAN TEACHER OF THE DEAF. (THE AUSTRALIAN TEACHER OF THE DEAF). V. 1- 1959-. 0005-0334. Periodical. AT. English. an. Australian Association of Teachers of the Deaf, PO Box 100, Croydon Parl New South Wales 2133 Australia. Ed Lilian Yang. NLM W1 AU697L. bk

Physically Impaired

rev. adv acc. (ctrl). Professional journal of teachers and professionals interested in issues of hearing impaired, children's education, development and language.

BALLOON. 8756-4661. Periodical. US. English. mo. $12.00. Balloon, 4521 Campus Drive Suite 282 PO Box 19553, Irvine CA 92715. Ed Jeff Colburn and Hedy Colburn. A publication listing current events for the hearing impaired in the following categories: leisure activities, entertainment events, and general information.

B.C. DEAF ADVOCATE. (THE B.C. DEAF ADVOCATE). VFOAT BC Deaf Advocate. VAT British Columbia Deaf Advocate. Vol. 1, No. 1 (July 1976)-. 0228-7161. Periodical. CN. English. sa. B C Deaf Advocate, 1959 East 1st Avenue, Vancouver BC V5N 1B3 Canada. DD 362.4209711.

BILDUNG UND REHABILITATION SEHGESCHADIGTER. 0172-8695. Monographic Series. German. ir. DD 362.41. NLM W1 SC325. Schriftenreihe Bildung und Rehabilitation Sehgeschadigter, 0172-8695.

BLIND WELFARE. 1959-. 0006-4823. Periodical. II. English. ty. 10.- India, 45.- Foreign. National Association for the Blind, 51 Mahatma Jhondi Road, Bombay India 400023. Tel 204 5482. Ed M K Choudhary. bk rev. adv acc. Circ 1,000. All aspects of blindness including prevention of blindness, pre-school education, education, rehabilitation, training and employment.

BLINDNESS, VISUAL IMPAIRMENT, DEAF-BLINDNESS CEASED. V. 1-7, No. 2. 0363-7689. US. English. sa. $5.00. Nevil Interagency Referral Service, Room 400/919 Walnut Street, Philadelphia PA 19107. LC Z5346.A2. DD 011. NLM Z 5346 B347BA.

BOLETIN DE ESTUDIOS Y DOCUMENTACION DEL SEREM. See Physical Training.

BRAILLE BOOK REVIEW. See Publishing - Books and Bookmaking.

BRAILLE BOOKS. Main/Corp Library of Congress. National Library Service for the Blind and Physically Handicapped. 1980-1981-. 0277-5247. US. English. be. National Library Service for the Blind and Physically Handicapped, Library of Congress, 1291 Taylor Street NW, Washington DC 20542. LC Z5346.Z9, HV1721. DD 011.63. Press Braille, Adult, 0079-502X.

BRAILLE MONITOR. (THE BRAILLE MONITOR). VFOAT Voice of the National Federation of the Blind. 1959-. 0006-8829. Periodical. US. English. mo. $15.00. National Federation of the Blind, 1800 Johnson Street, Baltimore MD 21230. Tel (301)659-9314. NLM W1 BR107. Issued also in braille and on talking book discs.

BRAILLE SCORES CATALOG. INSTRUMENTAL. See Music.

THE BRANDING IRON OF THE BILL RICE RANCH. VFOAT Branding Iron. 0738-498X. Periodical. US. English. mo. Bill Rice Ranch, Route 2 Franklin Road, Murfreesboro TN 37130.

BRITISH DEAF NEWS. 1- Jan./Feb. 1955/56-. 0007-0602. Periodical. UK. English. ir. 4.70 Domestic, 8.00 Foreign. The British Deaf Association, 38 Vicotria Place, Carlisle CA1 1HU England. Tel (0228)48844. Ed Bernard Quinn. bk rev. adv acc. Circ 25,000. News, articles and other items of interest to the deaf community of the UK. Deaf Quarterly, Deaf News; British Deaf Times.

BRITISH JOURNAL OF AUDIOLOGY. V. 7- Feb. 1973-. 0300-5364. Periodical. UK. English. qt. $82.00. Grune & Stratton, 111 5th Avenue, New York NY 10003. Tel (212)614-3232. Ind/Abst Excerpta Med., Index Med., Lang. Lang. Behav. Abstr., Hospit. Lit. Index, Sociol. Abstr. LC QP460. DD 617.8905. NLM W1 BR507. Sound.

BRITISH JOURNAL OF DISORDERS OF COMMUNICATION. (BRITISH JOURNAL OF DISORDERS OF COMMUNICATION : THE JOURNAL OF THE COLLEGE OF SPEECH THERAPISTS, LONDON). Vol. 1, No. 1 (April 1966)-. 0007-098X. Periodical. UK. English. ty. College of Speech Therapists, c/o Harold Poster, House 6/Lechmere Road, London NW2 5 BU England. Tel (01)459 8521. Ed Ruth Lesser. Ind/Abst Lang. Lang. Behav. Abstr., Index Med., Excerpta Med., Lang. Teach., Psychol. Abstr., Soc. Sci. Citation Index, Sociol. Abstr., Years Work Eng. Stud. LC RC423.A1. NLM W1 BR526L. (cum index). bk rev. adv acc. (ctrl). Papers and articles on speech defects and associated problems plus book reviews, etc., for the specialist in communication disorders. Speech Pathology and Therapy.

BRITISH JOURNAL OF DISORDERS OF COMMUNICATION. MONOGRAPH. VFOAT Monograph. Monographic Series. UK. English. ir. College of Speech Therapists, Harold Poster House, Lechmere Road, London NW2 5BU England. NLM W1 BR526LM.

THE BRITISH JOURNAL OF VISUAL IMPAIRMENT. No. 1 (Summer 1983)-. 0264-6196. Periodical. UK. English. ty. 4.50. c/o South Regional Association for the Blind, 55 Eton Avenue, London NW3 3ET England. Tel 01 722 9703. Ed Brian Eccles and Douglas Folley. LC HV1571. DD 362.4105. bk rev. adv acc. Circ $500. Issued also in Braille and on tape. A journal for those professionally concerned with children and adults who have a visual impairment. Covers education, employment, health and welfare. Insight (Birmingham, West Midlands, England), Inter-Regional Review.

BRNEKLINIKENS VEJLEDNINGER. 0106-3308. Danish. ir. NLM W1 BO135.

BUDGET REQUEST. Main/Corp Colorado. Division for Developmental Disabilities. Periodical. US. English. an. LC HV3006.C6. DD 353.978800841.

BULLETIN - CENTRE D'INFORMATION ET DE REFERENCE DU QUEBEC CONCERNANT LES PERSONNES HANDICAPEES. (LE BULLETIN). V. 1, No. 1, (Aug. 1983)-. 0824-7439. Periodical. CN. French. bm. $5.00. Centre d'Information et de Reference du Quebec Concernant les Personnes Handicapees, 91 Est rue St-Zotique, Montreal Quebec H2S 1K7 Canada. DD 362.4060714.

BULLETIN OF THE NATIONAL BRAILLE ASSOCIATION. Main/Corp National Braille Association. 1964. 0550-5666. Periodical. US. English. qt. $15.00 Domestic, $20.00 Foreign. National Braille Association, 1290 University Avenue, Rochester NY 14607. Tel (716)473-0900. Ed Sally M Hering. LC HV1788. DD 362.410973. Circ 2,500. (ctrl). Skills columns and articles about new materials and equipment, braille code changes. Geared to individuals who produce and distribute reading material for the blind.

BULLETIN - SASKATCHEWAN COUNCIL FOR CRIPPLED CHILDREN AND ADULTS. See Sociology: General Works, Theory - Social Pathology, Welfare, Criminology.

BULLETINS ON SCIENCE & TECHNOLOGY FOR THE HANDICAPPED. VFOAT Bulletins on Science and Technology for the Handicapped. Began with V. 1, No. 1 (May 1980). 0731-5775. Periodical. US. English. qt. American Association for the Advancement of Science, 1776 Massachusetts Avenue NW, Washington DC 20036. Tel (202)467-4496. NLM W1 BU936X.

BUREAU MEMORANDUM - WISCONSIN. DIVISION FOR HANDICAPPED CHILDREN. Main/Corp Wisconsin. Division for Handicapped Children. 0162-0150. Periodical. US. English. qt. Wisconsin Department of Public Instruction, Division for Handicapped Children, 126 Langdon Street, Madison WI 53702.

CAHIERS DE READAPTATION. VFOAT Tijdschrift voor Revalidatie. V. 1- 1975-. 0377-824X. Periodical. Dutch (French). ir. NLM W1 CA1396D.

CALGARY CORD. (THE CALGARY CORD). Began publication in 1965. 0380-9129. CN. English. ir. Free. The Society for Hearing Handicapped, 410-329A-6 Avenue South West, Calgary Alberta T2P 0R6 Canada. DD 362.420627123.

CALIPER. VFOAT Caliper Registered. Began publication in 194?. 0045-4001. Periodical. CN. English. qt. $11.61. Canadian Paraplegic Association, 520 Sutherland Drive, Toronto Ontario M4G 3V9 Canada. Tel (416)422-5640. Ed Peter Bernauer. NLM W1 CA444. bk rev. adv acc. Circ 4,500. (ctrl). The official journal of the Canadian Paraplegic Association. Features include a variety of items and commentaries of interest to physically disabled persons.

CANADIAN AMPUTEE SPORTS ASSOCIATION. See Recreation, Leisure - Sports.

CASSETTE BOOKS. See Publishing - Books and Bookmaking.

CATALOG OF CAPTIONED FILMS FOR THE DEAF. See Motion Picture.

CATALOG OF TAPE RECORDED BOOKS. Main/Corp Recording for the Blind. VFOAT Catalog / Recording for the Blind. US. English. ir. $5.00. Recording for the Blind, 20 Roszel Road, Princeton NJ 08540. Tel (609)452-0606. Catalogue of recorded textbooks available free to blind and reading impaired students at elementary, high school, college and postgraduate levels.

CCB NATIONAL NEWSLETTER. VAT Canadian Council of the Blind National Newsletter. March 1983-. 0824-3042. Periodical. CN. English. ir. Free to members. Canadian Council of the Blind, Suite 610, 220 Dundas Street, London Ontario N6a 1H3 Canada. DD 362.4106071. CCB Newsletter, 0824-6173.

CCB OUTLOOK. (THE CCB OUTLOOK). Main/Corp Canadian Council of the Blind. VAT Canadian Council of the Blind Outlook. V. 1- Jan. 1948-. 0007-7984. Periodical. CN. English. qt. CCB Outlook, 96 Ridout Street South, London Ontario N6C 3X4 Canada. LC HV1571. DD 362.4106271.

CHAEHWAL YONGU. VFOAT Rehabilitation Studies. Periodical. KO. Korean. an. Samyuk Adong Chaehwarwon, 722-3 Pongchon-Dong Kwanak-Ku, Seoul Korea. LC HV3024.K6.

CHAIRMAN'S REPORT - NEW MEXICO, GOVERNOR'S COMMITTEE ON EMPLOYMENT OF THE HANDICAPPED. See Economics - Labor.

COMMUNICATION - CANADIAN CO-ORDINATING COUNCIL ON DEAFNESS. (COMMUNICATION : THE NEWSLETTER OF THE CANADIAN CO-ORDINATING COUNCIL ON DEAFNESS). VFOAT Communication. VAT Communication - Conseil Canadien de Coordination de la Deficience Auditive. 0228-5401. Periodical. CN. English (text also in French, with French text on inverted pages). ir. Free to Members, $5.00 Membership. Canadian Co-Ordinating Council on Deafness, 55 Parkdale Avenue, Ottawa Ontario K1Y 1E5 Canada. DD 362.420971.

COMMUNICATION OUTLOOK. See Communication.

COMPANION. Main/Corp Minnesota. School for the Deaf, Faribault. Periodical. US. English. mo. $2.00. School for the Deaf, Faribault MN 55021.

CONTACT. Jan. 1972-. 0319-7379. Periodical. CN. English (includes some text in French). qt. $1.55. Canadian Cerebral Palsy Association, 55 Bloor Street East/Suite 301, Toronto Ontario M4W 1A9 Canada. Tel (416)923-2932. Ed Arthur M Timms. bk rev. adv acc. Circ 1,800. (ctrl). News and views of interest to the physically disabled community. Specific information about this association's policy development, events and action.

CPA FREEWHEELER. (THE CPA FREEWHEELER : NEWSLETTER OF THE CANADIAN PARAPLEGIC ASSOCIATION, ONTARIO DIVISION). Winter 1982/83-. 0824-7226. Periodical. CN. English. Free. Canadian Paraplegic Association, Ontario Division, 520 Sutherland Drive, Toronto Ontario M4G 3V9 Canada. DD 362.43. (ctrl). Freewheeler, 0225-5618.

CRANIO-FACIAL, CLEFT PALATE BIBLIOGRAPHY. See Bibliographies.

CRD NEWS. See Political Science - Civil Rights.

CRIPPLED CHILDREN'S AMBASSADOR CEASED. V. 40, No. 3. Periodical. US. English. qt.

DBPH NEWSLETTER. See Library and Information Science.

DEAF CANADIAN. (THE DEAF CANADIAN). V. 1- Sept./Oct. 1972-. 0315-145X. CN. English. qt. $10. Deaf Canadian Readers' Association, PO Box 1016, Calgary Alberta T2P 2K4 Canada. DD 362.4205.

THE DEAF OKLAHOMAN. V. 1- 1917-. 0274-7669. Periodical. US. English. qt.

DEFEKTOLOGIIA. See Education (General) - Special Aspects of Education.

Physically Impaired

DEFI. (LE DEFI). Vol. 1, No. 1 (Sept. 1979)-. 0709-2148. Periodical. CN. French. bm. Servcom Cote-Nord, c/o CRSSS de la Cote-Nord, 896 de Puyjalon, Hauterive Quebec G5C 1N1 Canada. DD 362.40971417.

DESIGN FOR SPECIAL NEEDS. *See* Architecture.

DIKTA. *See* Library and Information Science.

DIRECT LOAN PROGRAM FOR THE ELDERLY OR HANDICAPPED. *See* Sociology: General Works, Theory - Social Pathology, Welfare, Criminology.

DIRECTIONS (WASHINGTON, D.C.). (DIRECTIONS). Vol. 1, No. 1-. 0197-0224. Periodical. US. English. qt. $10.00 Domestic, $12.00 Foreign. Directions, Box 5664, Washington DC 20016. LC HV2510. DD 371.9123.

DIRECTORY, INDIANA STATE-AIDED COMMUNITY AGENCIES FOR THE MENTALLY RETARDED AND OTHER DEVELOPMENTALLY DISABLED AND AGENCIES RECEIVING DEVELOPMENTAL DISABILITY PROJECT GRANTS. *See* Yearbooks, Almanacs, Directories.

DIRECTORY OF FEDERAL SERVICES FOR THE HANDICAPPED AND DISABLED. *See* Yearbooks, Almanacs, Directories.

DIRECTORY OF INTERPRETERS FOR THE DEAF IN TEXAS. *See* Yearbooks, Almanacs, Directories.

DIRECTORY OF ORGANIZATIONS INTERESTED IN THE HANDICAPPED. *See* Yearbooks, Almanacs, Directories.

DISABLED USA. VAT Disabled United States of America. Publication began with Aug. 1977. 0148-5407. Periodical. US. English. ir. Superintendent of Documents, US Government Printing Office, Washington DC 20402. Tel (202)783-3238. Ind/Abst Except. Child Educ. Resour., Index U.S. Gov. Period. LC HD7256.U5. DD 362.85. *Performance (United States. President's Committee on Employment of the Handicapped), 0031-5214.*

DYNAMO (MONTREAL, QUEBEC). *See* Sociology: General Works, Theory - Social Pathology, Welfare, Criminology.

EDMON-TONE. (THE EDMON-TONE). 0823-6895. Periodical. CN. English. mo. Association for the Hearing Handicapped, 11342-127 Street, Edmonton Alberta T5M 0T8 Canada. DD 362.420971233. *Edmon-Tone Monthly Newsletter, 0823-6895.*

EDUCATION OF THE VISUALLY HANDICAPPED. *See* Education (General) - Special Aspects of Education.

EDUCATION SERIES. *See* Sociology: General Works, Theory - Social Pathology, Welfare, Criminology.

EDUCATIONAL OPPORTUNITIES THROUGH FEDERAL ASSISTANCE PROGRAMS - (OHIO). *See* Education (General).

EDUCAZIONE DEI SORDOMUTI. (L'EDUCAZIONE DEI SORDOMUTI). 1872-. 0390-5993. Periodical. Italian. ir. NLM W1 ED881.

EMPLOYMENT SERVICES NEWS. *See* Economics - Labor.

EUROPEAN REGISTER OF RESEARCH ON VISUAL IMPAIRMENT. 1974-. 0098-0986. Periodical. US. English. Ed J M Gill and M J Tobin. NLM WW 22 GA1 E8.

FOR YOUNGER READERS. (FOR YOUNGER READERS : BRAILLE AND TALKING BOOKS). Began with 1964/65. 0093-2825. US. English. be. National Library Service for the Blind and Physically Handicapped, Library of Congress, Washington DC 20542. LC Z5346.A2. DD 028.5205. Also available in braille edition and in sound recording.

FOREIGN LANGUAGE BOOKS. 1984-. 0748-4615. US. English (French, German, Italian, Portuguese, and Spanish). be. Library of Congress, National Library Service for the Blind and Physically Handicapped, Washington DC 20542. Tel (202)287-5100. DD 011. Circ 2,000. (ctrl). Catalog of recorded and braille books in foreign languages produced by the library of congress for blind and physically handicapped persons. *Libros Parlantes.*

FORUM. *See* Education (General).

FUTURE REFLECTIONS. (FUTURE REFLECTIONS : THE NATIONAL FEDERATION OF THE BLIND MAGAZINE FOR PARENTS OF BLIND CHILDREN). Vol. 1, No. 5 (Oct./Nov. 1983)-. 0883-3419. Periodical. US. English. ir. $15.00. Future Reflections, 1800 Johnson Street, Baltimore MD 21230. Tel (301)659-9314. Ed Barbara A Cheadle. DD 362. bk rev. Circ 7,000. Features articles written by parents, blind adults, and educators about all aspects of blindness and raising a blind or visually impaired child. *NFB Newsletter for Parents of Blind Children.*

GALLAUDET TODAY. *See* Education (General) - Special Aspects of Education.

GLAD DIRECTORY OF RESOURCES AVAILABLE TO DEAF & HARD-OF-HEARING PERSONS IN THE SOUTHERN CALIFORNIA AREA. *See* Yearbooks, Almanacs, Directories.

GOELAND. *See* Sociology: General Works, Theory - Social Pathology, Welfare, Criminology.

THE GREEN PAGES REHAB SOURCEBOOK. *See* Sociology: General Works, Theory - Social Pathology, Welfare, Criminology.

GUIA BIBLIOGRAFICA (SERVICIO INTERNACIONAL DE INFORMACION SOBRE SUBNORMALES). *See* Bibliographies.

GUIDE TO GRADUATE EDUCATION IN SPEECH-LANGUAGE PATHOLOGY AND AUDIOLOGY. *See* Education (General) - Higher Education.

HABILITES LOISIRS. (HABILITES LOISIRS : BULLETIN D'INFORMATION DE L'ASSOCIATION QUEBECOISE DE LOISIR POUR PERSONNES HANDICAPEES). V. 1, No. 1 (Feb. 1983)-. 0821-7815. Periodical. CN. French. qt. Free. Association Quebecoise de Loisir pour Personnes Handicapees, 1415 Est rue Jarry, Montreal Quebec H2E 2Z7 Canada. DD 790.19609714.

HANDICAPPED AMERICANS REPORTS. V. 1- 1978-. 0191-6734. Periodical. US. English. bw. $127.00. Plus Publications Inc, 2626 Pennsylvania Avenue NW, Washington DC 20037. DD 362.4.

HANDICAPPED FUNDING DIRECTORY. *See* Yearbooks, Almanacs, Directories.

HEARING AID JOURNAL CEASED. V. 26, No. 3 (Jan. 1973)-V. 35, No. 11 (Dec. 1982). 0091-2166. Periodical. US. English. mo. Laux Company Inc, West Bare Hill Road, Harvard MA 01451. NLM W1 HE641E. *National Hearing Aid Journal, 0027-9439.*

HEARING REHABILITATION QUARTERLY. V. 1- Fall 1975-. 0360-9278. Periodical. US. English. qt. $4.00. New York League for the Hard of Hearing, 71 West 23rd Street, New York NY 10010. Ind/Abst Psychol. Abstr. LC HV2350. DD 362.42. NLM W1 HE6418. *Highlights, 0360-9286.*

HOME SERVICES FOR THE SEVERELY HANDICAPPED. Main/Corp Illinois. Dept. of Rehabilitation Services. Began in 1980. US. English. an. Illinois Department of Rehabilitation Services, 623 East Adams/PO Box 1587, Springfield IL 62705.

HOMEHEALTH MAGAZINE. *See* Public Health and Safety.

HORGESCHADIGTEN-PADAGOGIK. *See* Education (General) - Special Aspects of Education.

HOW FEDERAL AGENCIES HAVE SERVED THE HANDICAPPED. Main/Corp United States. President's Committee on Employment of the Handicapped. 0091-4584. US. English. Presidents Committee on Employment of the Handicapped, 1111 20th Street NW, Washington DC 20210. LC HV1553. DD 362.40973. NLM W2 A P7HA.

HOW TO GET HELP FOR KIDS. *See* Sociology: General Works, Theory - Social Pathology, Welfare, Criminology.

ILRU INSIGHTS. (ILRU INSIGHTS : A PUBLICATION OF THE ILRU PROJECT). VFOAT I.L.R.U. Insights. Vol. 1, No. 1 (Mar. 1982)-. 0732-1953. Periodical. US. English. mo. Free. ILRU Project, PO Box 20095, Houston TX 77225. Tel (713)797-0200. Ed Laurel Richards. Circ 2,000. (ctrl). Addresses issues concerning programs assisting disabled people to live more independently. Includes updates on research and training activities, publications, and federal/state trends affecting independent living.

INFORMATION BULLETIN - DISABLED LIVING RESOURCE CENTER. (INFORMATION BULLETIN). Vol. 1, No. 1 (Spring '82)-. 0823-1109. CN. English. ir. Free. Kinsmen Rehabilitation Foundation of British Columbia Disabled Living Resource Centre, 2256 West 12th Avenue, Vancouver British Columbia V6K 2N5 Canada. Tel (604)736-8841. Ed Katheleen M Ellis. DD 362.409711. Circ 20,000. Selective bibliography of publications, equipment and services pertaining to independent living for physically disabled. Issues are topic oriented, e.g. gardening, sexuality, etc.

INFORMATION MANAGEMENT. *See* Business - General Management.

INFORMATION UPDATE - HUB, INFORMATION SERVICES. (INFORMATION UPDATE). VFOAT HUB Information Update. 0713-8474. Periodical. CN. English. ir. Information Services, PO Box 4397, St Johns Newfoundland A1C 6C4 Canada. Tel (709)754-0352. DD 016.3624048.

INTER-REGIONAL REVIEW. SUPPLEMENT. No. 1-. 0263-8401. Monographic Series. UK. English. Southern and Western Regional Association for the Blind, 55 Eton Avenue, London NW3 3ET England. NLM W1 IN976.

INTERCHANGE. 0196-5743. Periodical. US. English. ty. Free. Southwestern Region Deaf and Blind Center, 721 Capitol Mall, Sacramento CA 95814.

INTERNATIONAL REHABILITATION REVIEW. Issue 1- Jan. 1962-. 0020-8477. Periodical. US. English. qt. $30.00. Rehabilitation International, 25 East 21st Street/4th Floor, New York NY 10010. Tel (212)420-1500. Ed Barbara Duncan. Ind/Abst Excerpta Med. NLM W1 IN828D. CODEN IRERB. bk rev. Circ 10,000. Reports on trends concerning disability prevention and rehabilitation of disabled from an international perspective.

INTERNATIONAL TELEPHONE DIRECTORY OF THE DEAF. *See* Yearbooks, Almanacs, Directories.

JOURNAL HANDICO. *See* Sociology: General Works, Theory - Social Pathology, Welfare, Criminology.

JOURNAL OF APPLIED REHABILITATION COUNSELING. *See* Medicine.

JOURNAL OF CHILDHOOD COMMUNICATION DISORDERS. (JOURNAL OF CHILDHOOD COMMUNICATION DISORDERS : JCCD : A PUBLICATION OF THE DIVISION FOR CHILDREN WITH COMMUNICATION DISORDERS). VFOAT JCCD. Began in 1976. 0735-3170. Periodical. US. English. sa. $16.00. Council Exceptional Children, 1920 Association Drive, Reston VA 22091. Tel (703)620-3660. Ed Hiram L McDade. Ind/Abst Except. Child Educ. Resour. LC RJ496.C67. DD 618.92855. NLM W1 JO584S. adv acc. Circ 2,400. (ctrl). The journal includes articles of a professional nature dealing with the many aspects of communication disorders. Issues are often devoted to special topics in this area.

JOURNAL OF CLINICAL DYSMORPHOLOGY. (THE JOURNAL OF CLINICAL DYSMORPHOLOGY). Vol. 1, No. 1 (Spring 1983)-. 0736-4407. Periodical. US. English. qt. $85.00 Institutions, Except Medica. Center for Birth Defects, Information Services, Box 403/71 Harrison Avenue, Boston MA 02111. NLM W1. *Syndrome Identification, 0091-1747.*

JOURNAL OF DEVELOPMENTAL DISABILITIES. (THE JOURNAL OF DEVELOPMENTAL DISABILITIES). V. 1- 1974-. 0097-8892. Periodical. US. English. qt. $10.50. JFJ Educational Services Inc, PO Box 8470, New Orleans LA 70182. LC HV3000. DD 362.405.

JOURNAL OF LEISURABILITY. *See* Recreation, Leisure.

Physically Impaired

JOURNAL OF PRACTICAL APPROACHES TO DEVELOPMENTAL HANDICAP. V. 1- Feb. 1977-. 0707-7807. Periodical. CN. English (includes editorial and abstract in French). sa. $9.28. c/o Rehabilitation Studies, Education Tower/ University of Calgary, Calgary Alberta T2N 1N4 Canada. **Tel** (403)220-5661. **Ed** R I Brown. **Ind/Abst** Can. Educ. Index. **DD** 362.4'05. **NLM** W1 JO84. bk rev. **Circ** 400. Practical research in the field of developmentally handicapped individuals.

JOURNAL OF REHABILITATION ADMINISTRATION. V. 1- Jan. 1977-. 0148-3846. Periodical. US. English. qt. $30.00. c/o DePaul University, 25 East Jackson Boulevard, Chicago IL 60604. **Tel** (312)341-8845. **Ed** John F Newman. **Ind/Abst** Psychol. Abstr. **LC** HD7255.A2. **NLM** W1 JO866RE. bk rev. adv acc. **Circ** 1,900. (ctrl). Theoretical papers, applied research studies, and practice reports designed to improve the practice of administration, management, and supervision in a wide variety of rehabilitation settings.

JOURNAL OF REHABILITATION OF THE DEAF. 1967. 0022-4170. Periodical. US. English. qt. $45.00. American Deafness and Rehabilitation Association, 814 Thayer Avenue, Silver Springs MD 20910. **Tel** (301)589-0880. **Ed** Glenn Y Lloyd. **Ind/Abst** Lang. Lang. Behav. Abstr., Soc. Sci. Citation Index, Sociol. Abstr. **NLM** W1 JO867K. **CODEN** JRHDA. bk rev. adv acc. **Circ** 1,500. Offers a forum for information, ideas and reviews current publications of interest. Deals with research findings, program descriptions and articles on deafness relating to disciplines of rehabilitation.

THE JOURNAL OF SPEECH AND HEARING DISORDERS. V. 13- Mar. 1948-. 0022-4677. Periodical. US. English. qt. $33.00 Domestic, $36.00 Foreign. American Speech and Hearing Association, 10801 Rockville Pike, Rockville MD 20852. **Ind/Abst** MLA Int. Bibliogr. Books Artic. Mod. Lang. Lit., Lang. Lang. Behav. Abstr., Excerpta Med., Index Med., Annu. Bibliogr. Engl. Lang. Lit., Biol. Abstr., Except. Child Educ. Resour., Educ. Index, Curr. Index J. Educ., Psychol. Abstr., Energy Res. Abstr., Life Sci. Collect. **DD** 612.2. **NLM** W1 JO902H. **CODEN** JSHDAX. (cum index). Journal of Speech Disorders, 0885-9426.

THE JOURNAL OF THE ASSOCIATION FOR PERSONS WITH SEVERE HANDICAPS. (THE JOURNAL OF THE ASSOCIATION FOR PERSONS WITH SEVERE HANDICAPS : OFFICIAL PUBLICATION OF THE ASSOCIATION FOR PERSONS WITH SEVERE HANDICAPS). Vol. 8, No. 4 (Winter 1983)-. 0749-1425. Periodical. US. English. qt. The Association, 7010 Roosevelt Way NE, Seattle WA 98115. **Ind/Abst** Except. Child Educ. Resour., Curr. Index J. Educ. Journal of the Association for the Severely Handicapped, 0274-9483.

THE JOURNAL OF THE BRITISH ASSOCIATION OF TEACHERS OF THE DEAF. See Education (General) - Special Aspects of Education.

JOURNAL OF THE DENTAL GUIDANCE COUNCIL ON THE HANDICAPPED. See Dentistry.

JOURNAL OF THE DIVISION FOR EARLY CHILDHOOD. See Education (General) - Special Aspects of Education.

JOURNAL OF THE NEW JERSEY SPEECH AND HEARING ASSOCIATION. **Main/Corp** New Jersey Speech and Hearing Association. 0028-5935. Periodical. US. English. an. $10.00. New Jersey Speech Language and Hearing Association, PO Box 399, Orange NJ 07051. **NLM** W1 JO942Q.

JOURNAL OF THE ONTARIO SPEECH AND HEARING ASSOCIATION. **Main/Corp** Ontario Speech and Hearing Association. Began with 1960 issue. 0078-5105. CN. English. Ontario Speech and Hearing Association, c/o Association House, Taddle Creek Road, Toronto Ontario M5S 1A8 Canada. **DD** 618.9'2'85505.

JOURNAL OF VISUAL IMPAIRMENT & BLINDNESS. **VFOAT** Visual Impairment & Blindness. **VAT** Journal of Visual Impairment and Blindness. V. 71- Jan. 1977-. 0145-482X. Periodical. US. English. $25.00. American Foundation for the Blind, 15 West 16th Street, New York NY 10011. **Tel** (212)620-2154. **Ed** Mary Ellen Hulholland. **Ind/Abst** Except. Child Educ. Resour., Soc. Work Res. Abstr., Except. Child Educ. Abstr., Lang. Lang. Behav. Abstr., Abstr. Soc. Work., Rehabil. Lit., Curr. Contents, Excerpta Med., Curr. Index J. Educ., Ref. Source, Psychol. Abstr., Educ. Index. **LC** HV1571. **DD** 362.4105. **NLM** W1 JO9704. bk rev. adv acc. Available also in Braille and Recorded Editions. The interdisciplinary journal of record for practitioners and researchers professionally concerned with blind and visually impaired persons. New Outlook for the Blind, 0028-6435; Research Bulletin - American Foundation for the Blind, 0065-8367.

JUST CAUSE. See Law.

KENKYU HOKOKU SHU - TOKYO-TO SHINSHIN SHOGAISHA FUKUSHI SENTA. See Sociology: General Works, Theory - Social Pathology, Welfare, Criminology.

KEY FEDERAL REGULATIONS AFFECTING THE HANDICAPPED. **Main/Corp** National Association of State Mental Retardation Program Directors. 1977-78-. 0163-0490. US. English. be. US Department of Health Education and Welfare, Office of the Human Development Services, Office for Handicapped Individuals, Washington DC 20402. **LC** KF3738.A15. **DD** 344.730321. **NLM** WB 33.AA1 K4. Key Federal Regulations Affecting the Handicapped, 0163-0490.

THE KURZWEIL REPORT. V. 1- Spring 1978-. 0190-1656. Periodical. US. English. Free. Kurzweil Computer Products, 264 Third Street, Cambridge MA 02142. **NLM** W1 KU723.

LARGE TYPE BOOKS IN PRINT. See Publishing - Books and Bookmaking.

THE LAW OF THE HANDICAPPED : REPORTER AND COMMENTATOR. See Law.

LIBRARIES FOR COLLEGE STUDENTS WITH HANDICAPS. See Library and Information Science.

LIBRARY RESOURCES FOR THE BLIND & PHYSICALLY HANDICAPPED. See Library and Information Science.

LIGHT. See Sociology: General Works, Theory - Social Pathology, Welfare, Criminology.

LOW VISION ABSTRACTS. See Indexes/ Abstracts.

MAINSTREAM (SAN DIEGO, CALIF.). (MAINSTREAM). 0278-8225. Periodical. US. English. mo. $12.98. Mainstream, 2973 Beech Street, San Diego CA 92102. **Tel** (619)234-3138. **Ed** Cyndi Jones. bk rev. adv acc. **Circ** 13,000. An upbeat perspective on issues affecting disabled individuals: sports, travel, civil rights, education, accessibility, personal relations, and employment.

MARITIMER. (THE MARITIMER). V. 1- Spring 1977-. 0704-0652. Periodical. CN. English (Issues for Fall 1977-Spring 1978 have text also in French). qt. Free. Atlantic Provinces Resource Centre for the Hearing Handicapped, PO Box 308, Amherst Nova Scotia B4H 3Z6 Canada. **DD** 371.9'12'09715. New Scotian, 0028-6672.

MASTER TAPE LIST OF EDUCATION TEXTS FOR THE VISUALLY AND PHYSICALLY HANDICAPPED. (MASTER TAPE LIST OF EDUCATIONAL TEXTS FOR THE VISUALLY AND PHYSICALLY HANDICAPPED . . .). **Main/Corp** Trent University. Audio Library Programme. 1977-. 0229-8066. CN. English. be. Free. Audio Library Programme, Trent University, Peterborough Ontario K9J 7B8 Canada. **DD** 018.138. (ctrl). Master Tape List, 0229-8058.

MATILDA ZIEGLER MAGAZINE FOR THE BLIND. Began publication in 1907?. 0025-5955. Periodical. US. English. mo. Free. 20 West 17th Street, New York NY 10011. **Tel** (212)242-0263. **Ed** Michael Mellor. bk rev. **Circ** 10,000. Reprints, articles, short stories, humor, in braille and recorded disc and gives news and information of special interest to blind/visually impaired.

THE MEH BULLETIN. **VAT** Music Education for the Handicapped Bulletin. Vol. 1, No. 1 (Summer 1985)-. 8756-713X. Periodical. US. English. qt. $12.00 Domestic, $14.00 Foreign. MEH Bulletin, PO Box 454, Summit NJ 07901. **DD** 780.

MEMBERSHIP-TEAM DIRECTORY - AMERICAN CLEFT PALATE ASSOCIATION. See Yearbooks, Almanacs, Directories.

MENTAL AND PHYSICAL DISABILITY LAW REPORTER. See Law.

MENTAL RETARDATION AND DEVELOPMENTAL DISABILITIES. V. 5- 1973-. 0091-6315. US. English. ir. Plenum Press, 233 Spring Street, New York NY 10013. **Tel** (212)620-8000. **Ed** J Wortis. **LC** RC570. **DD** 618.92858805. **NLM** W1 ME936JE. Mental Retardation, 0076-647X.

MICHIGAN SPEECH-LANGUAGE-HEARING ASSOCIATION JOURNAL. **VFOAT** Michigan Speech Language Hearing Association Journal. 0742-3284. Periodical. US. English. an. $35.00 Active Membership, $25.00 Associate and Affiliate Membership, $5.00 Student Membership, $15.00 Nonmembers. Michigan Speech-Language-Hearing Association, 855 Grove Street, East Lansing MI 48823. **LC** RJ496.S7. **DD** 616.855005. MSHA: Journal of the Michigan Speech and Hearing Association, 0224-8398.

MONITORING & REPORTING PROJECT. **VFOAT** Monitoring and Reporting Project. US. English. an. Texas Governor's Committee on Employment of the Handicapped, 118 East Riverside Drive, Austin TX 78704. **LC** HV1555.T4. **DD** 353.976400844.

MUSIC CIRCULAR. See Music.

THE MUSICAL MAINSTREAM. See Music.

NAIGAI TOKUSHU KYOIKU KANKYU KIKAN TO ICHIRAN. Japanese. ir. Kokuritsu Tokushu Kuioku Sogo Kenkyujo, 2360 Nobi, Yokosuka 239 Japan. **LC** L900.

NATIONAL DIRECTORY OF BLIND TEACHERS. See Yearbooks, Almanacs, Directories.

NATIONAL NEWS OF THE BLIND CEASED. **VAT** CNIB National News of the Blind, Canadian National Institute for the Blind National News of the Blind. Ceased Publication with issue for summer 1981? (V. 43, No. 1?). 0027-9781. Periodical. CN. English. sa. Free. 1929 Bayview Avenue, Toronto Ontario M4G 3E8 Canada. **DD** 362.4'1'0971. **NLM** W1 NA554.

NEBRASKA SPEECH AND HEARING JOURNAL. V. 1- Mar. 1962-. 0470-570X. Periodical. US. English. an. Nebraska Speech & Hearing, PO Box 4516, Lincoln NE 68504. **Tel** (402)330-3858. **Ed** Kathy L Coufal. bk rev. adv acc. **Circ** 400. (ctrl). Data based research articles, clinical concerns and professional affairs for speech-language pathologists and audiologists.

NEWS - LIBRARY OF CONGRESS, DIVISION FOR THE BLIND AND PHYSICALLY HANDICAPPED. **Main/Corp** United States. Library of Congress. Division for the Blind and Physically Handicapped. V. 2- Jan./ Feb. 1971-. 0160-9211. Periodical. US. English. bm. Free. Publication Service Division for the Blind and Physically Handicapped, Library of Congress, Washington DC 20542. **LC** HV1783. Newsletter.

NEWS (LIBRARY OF CONGRESS. NATIONAL LIBRARY SERVICE FOR THE BLIND AND PHYSICALLY HANDICAPPED). (NEWS). V. 9, No. 3- May/ June 1978-. Periodical. US. English. qt. Library of Congress, Washington DC 20542. **LC** HV1783. **DD** 362.4105. News (Library of Congress. Division for the Blind and Physically Handicapped), 0160-9211.

NEWSLETTER (ASSOCIATION FOR THE SEVERELY HANDICAPPED (U.S.)) CEASED. (NEWSLETTER). Began with: Vol. 5, Issue 12 (Dec. 1979). Periodical. US. English. mo. Association for the Severely Handicapped, 1600 West Armory Way, Garden View Suite, Seattle WA 98119. Newsletter.

NEWSLETTER - CANADIAN HEARING SOCIETY, THUNDER BAY AND DISTRICT. (NEWSLETTER). Vol. 1, No. 4 (Oct. 1980)-. 0710-1880. Periodical. CN. English. mo. Free. Canadian Hearing Society, Suite 204/135 Syndicate Avenue North, Thunder Bay Ontario P7C 3V3 Canada. **DD** 362.4206071312. (ctrl). Canadian Hearing Society (Newsletter), 0710-1872.

NEWSLETTER - KINSMEN FOUNDATION FOR THE HANDICAPPED. (NEWSLETTER). 1974-. 0713-0198. Periodical. CN. English. ir. Kinsmen Foundation for the Handicapped, Box 1205,

Physically Impaired

Llyodminster Saskatchewan Canada. **DD** 362.4097124.

NORDISK TIDSKRIFT FOR DOVUNDERVISNINGEN. See Education (General) - Special Aspects of Education.

NORTH CAROLINA ANNUAL PROGRAM PLAN AMENDMENT. See Education (General) - Special Aspects of Education.

NOUVELLES DU SERVICE DE MAIN-D'OEUVRE. See Economics - Labor.

NTID FOCUS. VFOAT N.T.I.D. Focus. **VAT** National Technical Institute for the Deaf Focus. 0739-9278. Periodical. US. English. qt. National Technical Institute for the Deaf, One Lomb Memorial Drive, Rochester NY 14623. **Tel** (716)475-6753. **Ed** Marcia B Dugan. **Circ** 20,000. (ctrl). Articles on deafness research, education of deaf persons, successful hearing-impaired professionals.

OHIO JOURNAL OF SPEECH AND HEARING. (THE OHIO JOURNAL OF SPEECH AND HEARING). V. 1- Feb. 1965-. 0736-5381. Periodical. US. English. sa. Business Secretary/Sue Cutting, PO Box 1932, Dayton OH 45429. **Ind/Abst** Lang. Lang. Behav. Abstr.

ON THE BEAM. (ON THE BEAM : NEWSLETTER OF THE LOWE'S SYNDROME ASSOCIATION). Vol. 2, No. 2 (Summer 1983)-. 0740-218X. Periodical. US. English. ty. $7.00. Lowe's Syndrome Association, 222 Lincoln Street, West Lafayette IN 47906. **Tel** (317)743-3634. **Ed** Kaye McSpadden. bk rev. **Circ** 200. Irelands letters form families affected by Lowe's syndrome and pictures of their children, medical and educational articles, organizational news. Lowe's Syndrome Family Newsletter.

OSHA. ONTARIO SPEECH AND HEARING ASSOCIATION. (O S H A). **Main/Corp** Ontario Speech and Hearing Association. V. 2- Jan. 1977. 0705-8713. Periodical. CN. English. bm. Free. Ontario Speech and Hearing Association, Association House, 191 College Street, Toronto Ontario M5T 1P9 Canada. **DD** 618.9285505. (ctrl). Journal of the Ontario Speech and Hearing Association.

OTAZKY DEFEKTOLOGIE. See Education (General) - Special Aspects of Education.

OUTFRONT (OTTAWA, ONT.). (OUTFRONT). Summer 1983-. 0821-6258. Periodical. CN. English. qt. Free to Members. Council of the Disabled of Ottawa-Carleton, Room 1200/ 505 Smyth Road, Ottawa Ontario K1H 8M2 Canada. **DD** 362.40971384.

OVERSEAS OUTLOOK. Began with Fall 1977. 0161-1828. Periodical. US. English. sa. National Library Service for the Blind and Physically Handicapped, Library of Congress, Washington DC 20542. **LC** HV1571. **DD** 362.4105.

PALAESTRA (MACOMB, ILL.). See Recreation, Leisure - Sports.

PARA TRACKS. Began publication 196-. 0048-296X. Periodical. CN. English. ir. Canadian Paraplegic Association, Manitoba Division, 825 Sherbrook Street, Winnipeg Manitoba R3A 1M5 Canada. **DD** 362.43097127. Journal, 0380-2027.

PARAGRAPHIC. V. 1- 1957-. 0048-2935. Periodical. CN. English. qt. Canadian Paraplegic Association/B.C. Division, 780 SW Marine Drive, Vancouver Canada.

PARAPLEGIA. V. 1- 1963-. 0031-1758. Periodical. UK. English. bm. Longman Group Ltd, Fourth Avenue, Harlow Essex CM19 5AA England. **Ind/Abst** Life Sci. Collect., Excerpta Med., Index Med. **NLM W1** PA629. Index in last issue of volume - attached.

PARAPLEGIA NEWS. V. 1- 1946-. 0031-1766. Periodical. US. English. mo. $12.00. Paralysed Veterans of America Inc, 5201 North 19th Avenue/ Suite 111, Phoenix AZ 85015. **Tel** (602)246-9426. **Ed** Cliff Crase. **NLM W1** PA631. bk rev. adv acc. **Circ** 24,000. Research, legislation, news and general interest articles to particular interest and applicability to the wheelchair user.

PARAQUAD. See Sociology: General Works, Theory - Social Pathology, Welfare, Criminology.

PATHOLINGUISTICA. See Education (General) - Special Aspects of Education.

PHYSICAL DISABILITIES SPECIAL INTEREST SECTION NEWSLETTER. 0279-411X. Periodical. US. English. qt. American Occupational Therapy Association, 1383 Piccard Drive, Rockville MD 20850. **Tel** (301)948-9626. Newsletter - Physical Disabilities Specialty Section, American Occupational Therapy Association, 0194-6366.

PREVENTION RESOURCES (SASKATOON, SASK.). See Bibliographies.

PROCEEDINGS, ANNUAL GOVERNOR'S CONFERENCE ON THE HANDICAPPED. (PROCEEDINGS . . . ANNUAL GOVERNOR'S CONFERENCE ON THE HANDICAPPED). **Main/Conf** Governor's Conference on the Handicapped. Began with 1st (1961). 0436-2438. US. English. an. Indiana State Commission for the Handicapped, 1330 West Michigan Street, Indianapolis IN 46206. **LC** HV1555.I6. **DD** 362.409772. **NLM W3** GO536.

PROCEEDINGS OF NATIONAL FORUM. **Main/Corp** Council of Organizations Serving the Deaf. VFOAT National Forum. No. 1- 1968-. 0070-1106. Monographic Series. US. English. an.

PROFESSIONAL INTERPRETING JOURNAL OF REGISTRY OF INTERPRETERS FOR THE DEAF, INC. VFOAT RID Interpreting Journal. **VAT** Registry of Interpreters for the Deaf Interpreting Journal. Vol., No. 1 (Sept. 1981)-. 0277-6480. Periodical. US. English. sa. $12.50. Registry of Interpreters for the Deaf, 814 Thayer Avenue, Silver Spring MD 20910.

PROGRAMS FOR THE HANDICAPPED. Began with issue for Aug. 14, 1967. 0565-2804. US. English. bm. Programs for the Handicapped, Clearinghouse on the Handicapped, Office of Information and Resources for the Handicapped, Switzer Building/Room 1306, Washington DC 20202. **Ind/Abst** Index U.S. Gov. Period. **LC** HV3006. **DD** 362.404560973. **NLM W1** PR637. Mental Retardation Report.

PROGRESS IN COMMUNICATION. (PROGRESS IN COMMUNICATION : VIRGINIA COUNCIL FOR THE DEAF REPORT). **Main/Corp** Virginia. Council for the Deaf. 1974/76-. 0148-5342. US. English. Virginia Council for the Deaf, 4615 West Street/Suite 210, Richmond VA 23230. **LC** HV2561.V8. **DD** 353.9755008442.

PROGRESS REPORT - ILLINOIS GOVERNOR'S COMMITTEE ON EMPLOYMENT OF THE HANDICAPPED. See Economics - Labor.

PROSTHETICS AND ORTHOTICS INTERNATIONAL. V. 1- Apr. 1977-. 0309-3646. Periodical. UK. English. ty. $50.00. National Centre for Training and Education in Prosthetics and Orthotics, 131 St James Road, Glasgow G4 0LS Scotland. **Tel** 041-552-4400. **Ed** J Hughes, N Jacobs and R Donovan. **Ind/Abst** Life Sci. Collect., Excerpta Med., Index Med., Biol. Abstr., Comput. Control Abstr., Electr. Electron. Abstr., Sci. Abstr. Sect. A. Phys. Abstr. **NLM W1** PR778. **CODEN** POIND7. bk rev. adv acc. **Circ** 1,800. Prosthetics, orthotics, amputation surgery, neuromuscular and skeletal disorders, rehabilitaton engineering; and related topics. Prosthetics International.

RALAS. **VAT** Repatriation Artificial Limb and Appliance Service. 0314-5174. Periodical. AT. English. ir. Ralas Department of Repatriation, PO Box 21, Woden Australian Capital Territory 2606 Australia. **NLM W1** R1015L.

R.A.P.H.A.T. REGROUPEMENT DES ASSOCIATIONS DE PERSONNES HANDICAPEES DE L'ABITIBI-TEMISCAMINGUE. See Sociology: General Works, Theory - Social Pathology, Welfare, Criminology.

REFLECTIONS. See Sociology: General Works, Theory - Social Pathology, Welfare, Criminology.

REHABILITATION LITERATURE. 0034-3579. US. English. bm. $21.00 Domestic, $23.00 Foreign. Rehabilitation Literature, 2023 West Ogden Avenue, Chicago IL 60612. **Tel** (312)243-8400. **Ed** Stephen J Regnier. **Ind/Abst** Index Med., Excerpta Med., Psychol. Abstr., Hospit. Lit. Index, Abstr. Soc. Work., Ment. Retard. Abstr., Except. Child Educ. Abstr., Curr. Contents Educ., Curr. Index J. Educ., Lang. Lang. Behav. Abstr., DSH Abstr. **LC** Z5704. **DD** 016.36278. bk rev. adv acc. **Circ** 3,500. (ctrl). Available on microfilm from University Microfilms. Review and abstracting journal on literature pertaining to care, welfare, education, and employment of disabled people.

REHABILITATION WORLD. V. 1- July 1975-. 0360-0726. Periodical. US. English. qt. $15.00. Rehabilitation International USA, 20 West 40th Street, New York NY 10018. **Ind/Abst** Excerpta Med., Except. Child Educ. Resour. **LC** HD7255.A2. **DD** 362.85. **NLM W1** RE1769.

REPORT - FLORIDA COUNCIL FOR THE BLIND. **Main/Corp** Florida. Council for the Blind. US. English. an. Florida Council for the Blind, Tampa FL 33679. **LC** HV1796.

REPORT - NATIONAL ADVISORY COUNCIL FOR THE HANDICAPPED (AUSTRALIA). **Main/Corp** National Advisory Council for the Handicapped (Australia). English. ir. **LC** HV1559.A85. **DD** 354.940084406.

REPORT OF THE ANNUAL MEETING OF THE PRESIDENT'S COMMITTEE ON EMPLOYMENT OF THE HANDICAPPED. See Economics - Labor.

REPORT OF THE GOVERNOR AND TO THE JOINT COMMITTEE ON HUMAN SERVICES OF THE . . . CONNECTICUT GENERAL ASSEMBLY. **Main/Corp** Connecticut. Office of Protection and Advocacy for Handicapped and Developmentally Disabled Persons. US. English. 401 Trumbull Street, Hartford CT 06103. **LC** HV1555.C8. **DD** 353.97460084406.

REPORT ON VISUAL IMPAIRMENT SERVICES TEAMS. **Main/Corp** United States. Veterans Administration. Dept. of Medicine and Surgery. 0093-741X. US. English. Veterans Administration, Department of Medicine and Surgery, Washington DC 20420. **LC** UB369. **DD** 362.8. **NLM W2** A V54R.

RESEARCH DIRECTORY OF THE REHABILITATION RESEARCH AND TRAINING CENTERS : FISCAL YEAR . . . . See Yearbooks, Almanacs, Directories.

REVIEWS OF RESEARCH AND PRACTICE OF THE INSTITUTE FOR RESEARCH INTO MENTAL AND MULTIPLE HANDICAP. See Medicine - Psychiatry, Psychopathology.

REVUE A C E D A. (LA REVUE A C E D A). **Main/Corp** Association of Canadian Educators of the Hearing Impaired. VFOAT The A C E H I Journal. 0382-7976. Periodical. CN. English (French). ir. $6. ACEHI Journal, PO Box 308, Amherst NE B4H 3Z6 Canada. **Ind/Abst** Except. Child Educ. Resour., Can. Educ. Index, Curr. Index J. Educ. **DD** 371.9120971. Canadian Teacher of the Deaf, 0045-5431.

SEE WHAT'S HAPPENING. US. English. qt. $6.00. Modern Signs Press Inc, PO Box 1181, Los Alamitos CA 90720. **Tel** (213)596-8548. Newsletter for deaf children.

THE SEEING EYE GUIDE. (SEEING EYE GUIDE). 0037-0819. Periodical. US. English. qt. The Seeing Eye Inc, Washington Valley Road, Morristown NJ 07960.

SEMINARS. SPEECH, LANGUAGE, HEARING. (SEMINARS, SPEECH, LANGUAGE, HEARING). VFOAT Seminars in Speech, Language, and Hearing. Vol. 1, No. 1 (Feb. 1980)-V. 3, No. 4 (Nov. 1982). 0196-108X. Periodical. US. English. ir. $90.00. Thieme Stratton Inc, 381 Park Avenue South, New York NY 10016. **Tel** (212)683-5088/89. **LC** RC423.A1. **DD** 616.8552005. **NLM W1** SE489V.

SENSORY WORLD. No. 30 (Mar. 1978)-. 0730-9880. Periodical. US. English. qt. $16.00 Institutions and Libraries, $14.00 Individuals, $18.00 Overseas. PO Box 270, Lusby MD 20657. **Ed** Robert M Harmon. **LC** HV1551. **DD** 362.405. Review of Sensory Disability, 0146-9185.

SERVICES FOR PHYSICALLY DISABLED PEOPLE. See Sociology: General Works, Theory - Social Pathology, Welfare, Criminology.

SEXUALITY AND DISABILITY. See Sexual Life.

SHAA. (SHAA : A JOURNAL OF THE SPEECH AND HEARING ASSOCIATION OF ALABAMA). VFOAT SHAA Journal. **VAT** Speech and Hearing Association of Alabama. Began in 1970. 0743-4189. Periodical. US. English. sa. $8.00. SHAA, PO Box 1903, University of Alabama, AL 35486.

SHHH. Periodical. US. English. bm. $10.00. Self Help for Hard of Hearing People Inc, 7800 Wisconsin Avenue, Bethesda MD 20814-3524. **Tel** (301)657-2248.

Physics

Ed Howard E Stone Sr. adv acc. **Circ** 38,000. Education is the key to combat false views on hearing loss. Reaches hearing-impaired families and health professionals. Gives information on conditions, remedies and coping.

SIGCAPH NEWSLETTER. (SIGCAPH NEWSLETTER : A QUARTERLY PUBLICATION OF THE ACM SPECIAL INTEREST GROUP ON COMPUTERS AND THE PHYSICALLY HANDICAPPED). **VFOAT** S.I.G.C.A.P.H. Newsletter. **VAT** Special Interest Group on Computers and the Physically Handicapped Newsletter. 0163-5727. Periodical. US. English. qt. Association for Computing Machinery, PO Box 9209/Church Street Station, New York NY 10249. **Ind/Abst** Comput. Control Abstr., Electr. Electron. Abstr., Sci. Abstr. Sect. A. Phys. Abstr., Phys. Abstr. **CODEN** SGNWD2. *SICCAPH Newsletter*

SIKETEK ES NAGYOTHALLOK. Periodical. US. Hungarian. mo. Akademiai Kiado, POB 24, 1363 Budapest Hungary. **LC** MICROFILM 05675RF, RF290.

THE SILENT ADVOCATE. 0037-5187. Periodical. US. English. St Rita School for the Deaf and Hard of Hearing, 1720 Glendale-Milford Road, Cincinnati OH 45215.

THE SILENT WORLD. Periodical. II. English. ir. $2.50. Indian National Society for the Deaf, 15 Dadyseth Road Chowpatty, Bombay 7 India. **LC** HV2862. **DD** 362.420954.

SNATON SEL HAAGUDAH HAYISREELIT LSIQUM. (SHENATON SHEL HA-AGUDAH HA-YISREELIT LE-SHIKUM). **Main/Corp** Israel Society for Rehabilitation of the Disabled. **VFOAT** Annual of Israel National Society for Rehabilitation of the Disabled. V. 1- 1964-. 0377-0249. English or Hebrew. ir. Israel Society for Rehabilitation of the Disabled, 10 IBN Givrol Street, Tel-Aviv Israel. **LC** HV1559.I75. **NLM** W1 IS646.

SON OF PARATRACKS. **VFOAT** Son of Para Tracks. May 1976-. 0227-339X. Periodical. CN. English. qt. Sons of Paratracks, 825 Sherbrooke Street, Winnipeg Manitoba R3A 1M5 Canada. **Tel** (204)786-4753. Ed J Lane. **DD** 362.43097127. **Circ** 900. (ctrl). Local network of information on aspects of daily living for spinal cord injured persons regarding rehab, architectural barriers, transportation, etc. *Para Tracks, 0048-296X*.

SONDERPADAGOGIK. See Education (General) - Special Aspects of Education.

SOURCES OF INFORMATION AND SERVICES FOR THE HEARING IMPAIRED IN TEXAS. See Yearbooks, Almanacs, Directories.

SOUTH AFRICAN JOURNAL OF COMMUNICATION DISORDERS. See Medicine - Neurology.

SOUTH DAKOTA GOVERNOR'S ADVISORY COMMITTEE ON EMPLOYMENT OF THE HANDICAPPED. 0147-474X. US. English. SD Committee on Employment of the Handicapped, 222 East Capital, Pierre SD 57501. **LC** HD7256.U6. **DD** 331.5909783.

SPECIAL EDUCATION ANNUAL REPORT. See Education (General) - Special Aspects of Education.

SPECIAL EDUCATION : STATE PLAN. See Education (General) - Special Aspects of Education.

SPECIAL RECREATION DIGEST. Vol. 1, No. 1 (Jan.-Mar. 1984)-. 0747-0185. Periodical. US. English. qt. $28.00. Special Recreation Digest, 362 Koser Avenue, Iowa City IA 52240. **Tel** (319)337-7578. Ed John A Nesbitt. **LC** GV183.5. **DD** 790.1960973. bk rev. adv acc. **Circ** 275. (ctrl). Recreation for people with vision, hearing, mental, physical and social problems. Current information on recreation programs, services, grants, equipment, supplies, publications, etc. provided by 500 national and US organizations.

SPECTRUM (TORONTO, ONT. : 1981). See Sociology: General Works, Theory - Social Pathology, Welfare, Criminology.

SPEECH AND LANGUAGE: ADVANCES IN BASIC RESEARCH AND PRACTICE. (SPEECH AND LANGUAGE). V. 1- 1979-. 0193-3434. Periodical. US. English. sa. Academic Press, 4805 Sand Lake Road, Orlando FL 32819. **LC** RC423.A1. **DD** 616.855005. **NLM** W1 SP33L.

SPOKESMAN. (THE SPOKESMAN). V. 5, No. 6- Aug./Sept. 1976-. 0700-5229. Periodical. CN. English. mo. $3.86. Spokesman, 11625-135 Street, Edmonton Alberta T5M 1L1 Canada. **Tel** (403)455-2192. Ed Dianne Worley. **DD** 362.4097123. adv acc. **Circ** 7,000. (ctrl). Articles pertaining to or are of interest to Alberta's disabled community. *A H C S News, 0700-5210*.

SPORTS 'N SPOKES. See Recreation, Leisure - Sports.

SPRACHE, STIMME. GEHOR. (SPRACHE-STIMME-GEHOR). Vol. 1-. 0342-0477. Periodical. German. qt. Thieme-Stratton Inc, 381 Park Avenue, New York NY 10016. **Tel** (212)683-5088. **Ind/Abst** Excerpta Med. **NLM** W1 SP675.

DER SPRACHHEILPADAGOGE. See Education (General) - Special Aspects of Education.

THE STANDARD BEARER. (STANDARD BEARER). 0038-9447. Periodical. US. English. bm. Northwestern Publishing Association, PO Box 20234, Sacramento CA 95820.

STATE OF ILLINOIS REPORT ON TITLE I, PUBLIC LAW 89-313. See Education (General) - Special Aspects of Education.

STATE OF OREGON COMPREHENSIVE DEVELOPMENTAL DISABILITIES PLAN. **Main/Corp** Oregon. State Council on Developmental Disabilities. **VFOAT** Oregon Developmental Disabilities State Plan. 0149-9505. US. English. State Council on Developmental Disabilities, PO Box 25191, Portland OR 97225. **LC** HV3006.O7. **DD** 353.979500843.

STATE SERVICES FOR THE VISUALLY HANDICAPPED : RECOMMENDATIONS. **Main/Corp** Texas. Governor's Coordinating Office for the Visually Handicapped. 1979-. US. English. be. Governor's Coordinating Office for the Visually Handicapped, Stokes Building/Suite 105, Austin TX 78701. **LC** HV1796.T5. **DD** 362.41809764. *Recommendations Regarding State Services to the Visually Handicapped*.

STATISTIEK VAN HET BUITENGEWOON ONDERWIJS. See Statistics.

A SUMMARY OF SELECTED LEGISLATION RELATED TO THE HANDICAPPED. See Law.

TALKING BOOK TOPICS. See Publishing - Books and Bookmaking.

TALKING BOOKS. See Publishing - Books and Bookmaking.

TALKING BOOKS CATALOGUE SUPPLEMENT. See Publishing - Books and Bookmaking.

THE TEACHER OF THE DEAF. See Education (General) - Special Aspects of Education.

TEACHING ENGLISH TO THE DEAF. See Education (General) - Special Aspects of Education.

THERAPEUTIC RECREATION JOURNAL. V. 2, No. 3- 3rd Quarter 1968-. 0040-5914. Periodical. US. English. qt. $30.00. National Recreation and Park Association, Park Center Drive/12th Floor, Alexandria VA 22302. **Tel** (703)820-4940. Ed Peter A Witt. **Ind/Abst** Hospit. Lit. Index. **NLM** W1 TH158T. (ctrl). The journal is devoted to the advancement of therapeutic recreation services for the ill, disabled, and other groups with special needs. *TR, Therapeutic Recreation*.

THIRD EYE. (THE THIRD EYE). 0229-0715. Periodical. CN. English. qt. Boost, 100 Richmond Street East/Suite 408, Toronto Ontario M5C 2P9 Canada. **DD** 362.4109713.

TOKUSHU KYOIKU KANKEI KIKAN DANTAI NI YORU SHUPPANBUTSU ZASSHI TO MOKUROKU. See Education (General) - Special Aspects of Education.

TOKUSHU KYOKUGAKU KENKYU. See Education (General) - Special Aspects of Education.

TOPICS IN EARLY CHILDHOOD SPECIAL EDUCATION. See Education (General) - Special Aspects of Education.

TOPICS IN LANGUAGE DISORDERS. **VFOAT** T.L.D. Vol. 1, No. 1 (Dec. 1980)-. 0271-8294. Periodical. US. English. qt. $79.50. Aspen Systems Inc, PO Box 6018, Gaithersburg MD 20877. **Tel** (301)251-5000. **Ind/Abst** Sociol. Abstr., Educ. Index. **LC** RC423.A1. **DD** 616.855005. **NLM** W1 TO539Q.

EN TOUTE JUSTICE (OTTAWA, ONT.). See Law.

TRANSLATIONS OF THE BELTONE INSTITUTE FOR HEARING RESEARCH. **Main/Corp** Beltone Institute for Hearing Research. 0005-8888. Monographic Series. US. English. ir. Beltone Institute for Hearing, Institute 4201/West Victoria Street, Chicago Il 60646. **Ind/Abst** Biol. Abstr. **NLM** W1 BE485. **CODEN** TBHRAW.

VIBRATIONS (CANADIAN HEARING SOCIETY). (VIBRATIONS). 0227-6755. Periodical. CN. English. qt. $2.00. Canadian Hearing Society, 60 Bedford Road, Toronto Ontario M5R 2K2 Canada. **DD** 362.420971.

VIEWS. (AMERICAN SIGN LANGUAGE SIGN FOR INTERPRETER VIEWS : OFFICIAL PUBLICATION OF THE REGISTRY OF INTERPRETERS FOR THE DEAF, INC). **VFOAT** Interpreter Views. 0277-7088. Periodical. US. English. bm. $10.00. R.I.D. Inc, 814 Thayer Avenue, Silver Spring MD 20910.

VOCATIONAL EVALUATION AND WORK ADJUSTMENT BULLETIN. V. 1- 1968-. 0160-8312. Periodical. US. English. qt. VEWAA Office, Stout Vocational Rehabilitation Institute, University of Wisconsin, Menomonie WI 54751. **Tel** (715)232-1309. Ed D W Corthell. **Ind/Abst** Psychol. Abstr., Rehabil. Lit. **DD** 331. **CODEN** VEWBD3. bk rev. adv acc. **Circ** 2,000. Research on vocational evaluation and work adjustment of people with disabilities. Innovations in vocational evaluation and work adjustment techniques.

VOLUNTEERS WHO PRODUCE BOOKS. 0193-113X. US. English. National Library Service for the Blind and Physically Handicapped, Library of Congress, Washington DC 20542. **LC** HV1790. **DD** 362.4102573.

WARERA NINGEN. See Sociology: General Works, Theory - Social Pathology, Welfare, Criminology.

WASHINGTON REPORT. **Main/Corp** American Foundation for the Blind. 0043-0722. Periodical. US. English. wk. $44.00. American Foundation for the Blind, 15 West 16th Street, New York NY 10011. **Tel** (800)223-4155.

WASHINGTON SOUNDS. 1966-. 0043-0757. Periodical. US. English. mo. $15.00. National Association of Hearing and Speech Agencies, 814 Thayer Avenue, Silver Springs MD 20910.

WHEELERS' CHOICE. See Recreation, Leisure - Sports.

WHEELERS' LOG. (THE WHEELERS' LOG). V. 1- Oct. 1973-. 0705-1654. Periodical. CN. English. Free to members and interested groups. Canadian Paraplegic Association Atlantic Division, Fenwick Towers, 5599 Fenwick Street, Halifax Nova Scotia B3H 1R2 Canada. **DD** 362.4309715. Published by charitable association in interest of spinal cord injured persons in Maritime region, emphasizing aspects of care, positive action, benefits and access.

WISSENSCHAFTLICHE BEITRAGE AUS FORSCHUNG, LEHRE UND PRAXIS ZUR REHABILITATION BEHINDERTER KINDER UND JUGENDLICHER. See Education (General) - Special Aspects of Education.

THE WORLD AROUND YOU. 0199-8293. Periodical. US. English. ir. $5.00. Gallaudet College, Kendall Green, Washington DC 20002. **Tel** (202)651-5855. Ed Cathryn Carroll. bk rev. **Circ** 12,000. Publication for young, deaf people; focuses on hearing impairment and hearing impaired people.

YEARBOOK OF THE ASSOCIATION FOR EDUCATION AND REHABILITATION OF THE BLIND AND VISUALLY IMPAIRED. See Yearbooks, Almanacs, Directories.

PHYSICS

AAPT ANNOUNCER. **VAT** American Association of Physics Teachers Announcer. V. 1- 1971-. 0275-5696. Periodical. US. English. qt.

Physics

American Association of Physics Teachers, 5110 Roanoke Place/Suite 101, College Park MD 20740. Tel (301)345-4200. Ind/Abst Curr. Index J. Educ.

AARSRAPPORT - DET FYSISKE INSTITUT. Main/Corp Aarhus, Denmark. Universitet. Det Fysiske Institut. 1973/74-. DK. in English. ir. Aarhus Univ, Nordre Ruggade, DK 8000 Aarhus Denmark. LC QC1. DD 530.5.

ABHANDLUNGEN DER AKADEMIE DER WISSENSCHAFTEN IN GOTTINGEN. MATHEMATISCH-PHYSIKALISCHE KLASSE. See Mathematics.

ABSTRACTS OF BULGARIAN SCIENTIFIC LITERATURE. MATHEMATICAL AND PHYSICAL SCIENCES. See Indexes/Abstracts.

ACTA CIENCIA INDICA. PHYSICS. VFOAT Physics. V. 5, No. 1 (1979)-. 0253-732X. Periodical. in English. qt. 150.00. Pragati Prakashan, PO Box 62, 250001 Meerut India. Tel 73022. Ed A N Pandey. Ind/Abst Chem. Abstr., Comput. Control Abstr., Electr. Electron. Abstr., Sci. Abstr. Sect. A. Phys. Abstr. LC QC1. DD 530.5. CODEN ACIPD2. bk rev. adv acc. Circ 1,000. Acta Ciencia Indica, 0379-5411.

ACTA FACULTATIS RERUM NATURALIUM UNIVERSITATIS COMENIANAE. PHYSICA CEASED. (PHYSICA). Main/Corp Univerzita Komenskeho v Bratislave. Prirodovedecka Fakulta. 1-22. 0524-2355. Periodical. CS. Slovak (summaries in English, German, Russian, and/or Slovak). an. Ind/Abst Chem. Abstr. LC QC1. DD 530. CODEN AFRNAP.

ACTA PHYSICA. ACADEMIAE SCIENTARIUM HUNGARICAE CEASED. (ACTA PHYSICA ACADEMIAE SCIENTARIUM HUNGARICAE). VFOAT Acta Physica Hungarica. Began in 1951. Ceased with Vol. 53, No. 3-4. 0001-6705. Periodical. HU. English (and German, with summaries in Russian). $88.00. Akademiai Kiado, POB 24, 1363 Budapest Hungary. Tel 111-010. Ed I Kovacs. Ind/Abst Math. Rev., Int. Aerosp. Abstr., Met. Abstr., World Alum. Abstr., Chem. Abstr., Electr. Electron. Abstr., Comput. Control Abstr., Sci. Abstr. Sect. A. Phys. Abstr. LC QC3. NLM W1 AC916. CODEN APAHAQ. Index published separately - free - automatically sent. adv acc. Circ 1,000. Hungarica Acta Physica, 0376-6382.

ACTA PHYSICA AUSTRIACA. (ACTA PHYSICA AUSTRIACA). Vol. 1 May 1947-. 0001-6713. Periodical. English (German). qt. Springer Verlag-New York Inc, 175 5th Avenue, New York NY 10010. Tel (212)460-1500. Ind/Abst Chem. Abstr., Nucl. Sci. Abstr., Int. Aerosp. Abstr., Math. Rev., Energy Res. Abstr., Comput. Control Abstr., Electr. Electron. Abstr., Sci. Abstr. Sect. A. Phys. Abstr., Phys. Abstr., Sci. Cit. Index, Abr. Ed. LC QC1. DD 530.5. CODEN APASAP.

ACTA PHYSICA AUSTRIACA. SUPPLEMENTUM. 1 (1964)-. 0065-1559. English. ir. Springer Verlag, 44 Hartz Way, Secaucus NJ 07094. Tel (202)348-4033. Ed P Urban. Ind/Abst Math. Rev., Chem. Abstr., Comput. Control Abstr., Electr. Electron. Abstr., Sci. Abstr. Sect. A. Phys. Abstr., Nucl. Sci. Abstr., Phys. Abstr. CODEN APAUAV. Consists of yearly supplements to the journal Acta Physica Austriaca, which contain the proceedings of the "Internationale Universitaetswochen fuer Kernphysik" at Schladming.

ACTA PHYSICA HUNGARICA. Vol. 54, No. 1-2 (1983)-. 0231-4428. Periodical. English (French, German, and Russian). ir. Ind/Abst Math. Rev., Chem. Abstr., Comput. Control Abstr., Electr. Electron. Abstr., Nucl. Sci. Abstr., Sci. Abstr. Sect. A. Phys. Abstr., Int. Aerosp. Abstr. LC QC3. DD 530.05. CODEN APHUE2. Acta Physica Academiae Scientarum Hungaricae, 0001-6705.

ACTA PHYSICA POLONICA, A. V. 37- Jan. 1970-. 0587-4246. Periodical. PL. English. mo. VCH Publishers Inc, 303 Northwest 12th Avenue, Deerfield Beach FL 33442. Ind/Abst Math. Rev., Met. Abstr., World Alum. Abstr., Chem. Abstr., Energy Res. Abstr., Comput. Control Abstr., Electr. Electron. Abstr., Sci. Abstr. Sect. A. Phys. Abstr., Sci. Cit. Index, Abr. Ed., Phys. Abstr. LC QC1. NLM W1 AC919A. CODEN ATPLB6. Acta Physica Polonica, 0001-673X.

ACTA PHYSICA SLOVACA. V. 23- 1973-. 0323-0465. Periodical. CS. English. bm. $58.00. Slovart Foreign Trade Company Ltd, Gottwaldovo Nam 6, 817 64 Bratislv Czechoslovakia. Tel 48841-49. Ind/Abst Math. Rev., Int. Aerosp. Abstr., Chem. Abstr., Energy Res. Abstr., Comput. Control Abstr., Electr. Electron. Abstr., Sci. Abstr. Sect. A. Phys. Abstr., Sci. Cit. Index, Abr. Ed. LC QC1. DD 530.05. CODEN APSVCO. Fyzikalny Casopis.

ACTA UNIVERSITATIS CAROLINAE. MATHEMATICA ET PHYSICA. See Mathematics.

ACTIVE AND PASSIVE ELECTRONIC COMPONENTS. 0882-7516. Periodical. US. English. qt. $268.00. Gordon & Breach Publishers, One Bedford Street, London WC2E 9BB England. Ed Josephine A Castellano. DD 530. bk rev. adv acc. Electrocomponent Science and Technology, 0305-3091.

ADVANCED COURSE IN ASTROPHYSICS. See Astronomy.

ADVANCES IN BIOLOGICAL AND MEDICAL PHYSICS. V. 1-. 0065-2245. US. English. ir. Academic Press, 4805 Sand Lake Road, Orlando FL 32887. Tel (305)345-4100. Ind/Abst Index Med., Energy Res. Abstr. LC QH505.A1. DD 574.0153. NLM W1 AD439. (cum index).

ADVANCES IN CHEMICAL PHYSICS. See Chemistry.

ADVANCES IN CRYOGENIC ENGINEERING CEASED. VFOAT International Advances in Cryogenic Engineering. V. 1-. 0065-2482. US. English. ir. Plenum Publishing Company, 233 Spring Street, New York NY 10013. Tel (212)620-8000. Ed K D Timmerhaus. Ind/Abst Eng. Index, Chem. Abstr. LC TP490. DD 660.29368. CODEN ACYEAC.

ADVANCES IN INFRARED AND RAMAN SPECTROSCOPY. Vol. 1-. 0309-426X. UK. English. ir. John Wiley & Sons Inc, Eastern District Center, 1 Wiley Drive, Somerset NJ 08873. Ed R J H Clark and R E Hester. Ind/Abst GeoRef, Chem. Abstr., Energy Res. Abstr., Bibliogr. Index Geol. LC QC457. DD 543.0858305. CODEN AIRSDU.

ADVANCES IN PHYSICS. V. 1- Jan. 1952-. 0001-8732. Periodical. UK. English. bm. $300.00. Taylor & Francis Ltd, 242 Cherry Street, Philadelphia PA 19106. Tel (215)238-0939. Ed D Sherrington. Ind/Abst Math. Rev., Electron. Commun. Abstr. J., ISMEC Bull., Pollut. Abstr. Indexes, Saf. Sci. Abstr. J., Eng. Index Annu., Eng. Index Mon., Eng. Index Bioeng. Abstr., Eng. Index Energy Abstr., GeoRef, Met. Abstr., World Alum. Abstr., Chem. Abstr., Int. Aerosp. Abstr., Nucl. Sci. Abstr., Comput. Control Abstr., Electr. Electron. Abstr., Sci. Abstr. Sect. A. Phys. Abstr., Appl. Mech. Rev., Phys. Abstr., Sci. Cit. Index, Abr. Ed., Eng. Index. LC QC1. DD 530.5. NLM W1 AD783. CODEN ADPHAH. Aimed to meet the need for review papers in the major branches of condensed matter physics.

ADVANCES IN RAMAN SPECTROSCOPY. 0309-2534. UK. English. ir. Heyden & Sons Ltd, 247 South 41st Street, Philadelphia PA 19104. Ind/Abst Chem. Abstr. CODEN AVRSAG.

ADVENTURES IN EXPERIMENTAL PHYSICS. 1st- Jan. 1972-. 0044-6386. Periodical. US. English. sa. $24.00. World Science Communications, PO Box 683, Princeton NJ 08540. LC QC1. DD 530.05.

AIP CONFERENCE PROCEEDINGS. VFOAT A.I.P. Conference Proceedings. No. 1-. 0094-243X. Monographic Series. US. English. ir. American Institute of Physics, 335 East 45th Street, New York NY 10017. Tel (516)349-7800. Ind/Abst Math. Rev., Coal Abstr., GeoRef, Spin, Curr. Phys. Index, Chem. Abstr., Energy Res. Abstr., Comput. Control Abstr., Electr. Electron. Abstr., Sci. Abstr. Sect. A. Phys. Abstr., Phys. Abstr., Sci. Cit. Index, Abr. Ed., Bibliogr. Index Geol. CODEN APCPCS. Quarterly Bulletin - American Association of Physicists in Medicine, 0001-0162.

ALERTA INFORMATIVA. SERIE B : FISICA APLICADA. Yearly V. 16, No. 1 (Jan. 1979)-. SP. Spanish. mo. Instituto de Informacion y Documentacion en Ciencia y Technologia, Joaquin Costa 22, Madrid 6 Spain. LC QC1. DD 530.05. Resumenes de Articulos Cientificos y Tecnicos. Serie B, Fisica Aplicada.

AMERICAN JOURNAL OF PHYSICS. V. 1- Feb. 1933-. 0002-9505. Periodical. US. English. mo. $114.00 Domestic, $125.00 Foreign. American Association of Physics Teachers, 5110 Roanoke Place/Suite 101, College Park MD 20740. Tel (301)345-4200. Ed John S Rigden. Ind/Abst Math. Rev., Abstr. Bull. Inst. Paper Chem., Int. Aerosp. Abstr., Spin, Chem. Abstr., Curr. Phys. Index, Curr. Index J. Educ., Energy Res. Abstr., Appl. Sci. Technol. Index, Gen. Sci. Index, Comput. Control Abstr., Electr. Electron. Abstr., Phys. Abstr., Sci. Abstr. Sect. A. Phys. Abstr. LC QC1. DD 530.7. NLM W1 AM505. CODEN AJPIAS. (cum index). adv acc.

ANALELE UNIVERSITATII DIN TIMISOARA. SERIA STINTE FIZICE-CHIMICE. Main/Corp Timisoara, Rumania. Universitatea. 7- 1969-. Periodical. RM. English (French, German, or Romanian). sa. Ilexim Press Department, PO Box 1-136-1-137, Bucharest Romania. Ind/Abst Math. Rev., Chem. Abstr. CODEN ATFCBV. Analele Universitatii din Timisoara. Seria Stiinte Matematice-Fizice.

ANALES DE FISICA. See Yearbooks, Almanacs, Directories.

ANCIENT TL. VAT Ancient Thermoluminescence. No. 1 (Autumn 1977)-. 0735-1348. Periodical. US. English. qt. $9.20. Durham University, Archaeology Department, TL Laboratory, Fulling Mill the Banks, Durham DH1 3EB England. Tel 385-64466. Ed I K Bailiff. adv acc. Circ 150. (ctrl). For scientists engaged in the application of thermoluminescence and ESR dating techniques in archaeology and geology. Includes short research papers and date lists.

ANNALES ACADEMIAE SCIENTIARUM FENNICAE. SERIES A6: PHYSICA. (ANNALES ACADEMIAE SCIENTIARUM FENNICAE. SERIES A. VI : PHYSICA). Main/Corp Suomalainen Tiedeakatemia. No. 81- 1961-. 0066-2003. Monographic Series. FI. English (German). ir. Akakeeminen-Kirjakuppa, PO Box 128, 00101 Helsinki Finland. Ind/Abst Math. Rev., Int. Aerosp. Abstr., GeoRef, Energy Res. Abstr., Comput. Control Abstr., Electr. Electron. Abstr., Sci. Abstr. Sect. A. Phys. Abstr. CODEN AAFPA4. Toimituksia. Annales Academiae Scientiarum Fennicae. Sarja/Series A. VI : Physica.

ANNALES DE L'I.H.P. PHYSIQUE THEORIQUE. VFOAT Annales de l'I.H.P. Theoretical Physics, Annales Institut Henri Poincare. Section A. Physique Theorique, Annales de l'I.H.P. VAT Annales de l'Institut Henri Poincare. Physique Theorique. Vol. 38, No. 1-. 0246-0211. Periodical. FR. French (text in English, or German). bm. 1087. Gauthier-Villars, Centrale des Revues, 11 rue Gossing, 92543 Montrouge Cedex France. Ed J Ginibre. Ind/Abst Math. Rev. bk rev. adv acc. Circ 700. This journal, recently reorganized, welcomes high standard manuscripts from all areas of theoretical and mathematical physics. Annales de l'Institut Henri Poincare. Section A. Physique Theorique, 0020-2339.

ANNALES DE L'INSTITUT HENRI POINCARE. SECTION A. PHYSIQUE THEORIQUE. Main/Corp Institut Henri Poincare. VFOAT Physique Theorique. New Series, V. 1- 1964-. 0020-2339. Periodical. FR. French. 1087. Centrale des Revues-Gauthier Villars, 11 rue Gossin, 92543 Montrouge Cedex France. Tel 1043 20 15 50. Ed J Ginibre. Ind/Abst Math. Rev., Int. Aerosp. Abstr., Energy Res. Abstr., Comput. Control Abstr., Electr. Electron. Abstr., Sci. Abstr. Sect. A. Phys. Abstr. LC UNC. DD 530.05. CODEN AHPAAO. bk rev. adv acc. Circ 700. This journal, recently reorganized, welcomes high standard manuscripts from all areas of theoretical and mathematical physics. Annales de l'Institut Henri Poincare.

ANNALES DE PHYSIQUE. 9th Series V. 1-20, 1914-23. 0003-4169. Periodical. French (summaries and table of contents in English). bm. $186.25. Editions de Physique, ZI de Courtaboeuf BP 112, 91944 les Ulis Cedex France. Tel 6/ 907 36 88. Ind/Abst Int. Aerosp. Abstr., Met. Abstr., World Alum. Abstr., Chem. Abstr., Nucl. Sci. Abstr., Energy Res. Abstr., Comput. Control Abstr., Electr. Electron. Abstr., Sci. Abstr. Sect. A. Phys. Abstr., Phys. Abstr., Sci. Cit. Index, Abr. Ed. LC QC1. DD 530.5. NLM W1 AN375. CODEN ANPHAJ. (cum index). Annales de Chimie et de Physique.

ANNALES FRANCAISES DES MICROTECHNIQUES ET DE CHRONOMETRIE. Vol. 36, No. 1(1 Quarterly 1982)- 52e Year, 4 Series. 0294-1228. Periodical. FR. French. qt. 47.90. Annales Francaises des Microtechniques et de Chronometrie, 41 bis Avenue de l'Observatoire, F 25044 Besancon Cedex. **Tel** 81-80-22-66. **Ind/Abst** Comput. Control Abstr., Electr. Electron. Abstr., Sci. Abstr. Sect. A. Phys. Abstr. **CODEN** AFMCE5. **Circ** 400. Physics, engineering, time, frequency, domaine, frequency standards, precision measurement, time scales, time dissemination, quartz resonators, displays, systems and circuits, industrial realizations and quality control listing. *0221-0665.*

ANNALS OF PHYSICS. V. 1- Apr. 1957-. 0003-4916. Periodical. US. English. mo. Academic Press, 4805 Sand Lake Road, Orlando FL 32819. **Tel** (305)345-4100. **Ind/Abst** Electron. Commun. Abstr. J., ISMEC Bull., Pollut. Abstr. Indexes, Saf. Sci. Abstr. J., Met. Abstr., World Alum. Abstr., Spin, Chem. Abstr., Int. Aerosp. Abstr., Math. Rev., Nuci. Sci. Abstr., Energy Res. Abstr., Comput. Control Abstr., Electr. Electron. Abstr., Sci. Abstr. Sect. A. Phys. Abstr., Phys. Abstr., Sci. Cit. Index, Abr. Ed. **LC** QC1. **DD** 530.5. **NLM** W1 AN62G. **CODEN** APNYA6. (cum index).

ANNUAL REPORT (INSTITUTE OF PHYSICAL SCIENCES (COMMONWEALTH SCIENTIFIC AND INDUSTRIAL RESEARCH ORGANIZATION)). (ANNUAL REPORT). 0158-7439. Periodical. English. an. CSIRO Institute of Physical Sciences, PO Box 225, Dickson ACT 2602 Australia. **LC** QC51.A82. **DD** 500.205.

ANNUAL REPORT - INTERNATIONAL CENTER FOR THEORETICAL PHYSICS. (ANNUAL REPORT). **Main/Corp** International Centre for Theoretical Physics. 1st-1964/65-. 0304-7091. English. ir. International Atomic Energy Agency, International Centre for Theoretical Physics, PO Box 586, I-34100 Trieste Italy. **LC** QC1.I6285. **DD** 530.

ANNUAL REPORT - NATIONAL PHYSICAL RESEARCH LABORATORY. **Main/Corp** National Physical Research Laboratory. SA. English. ir. National Physical Research Laboratory, PO Box 395, TA Navors, Pretoria South Africa. **LC** QC51.S62. **DD** 530.0720682.

ANNUAL REPORT OF THE INSTITUTE OF ATMOSPHERIC PHYSICS. 0736-7198. an. Gordon And Breach Science Publishers, 1 Park Avenue, New York NY 10010.

ANNUAL REPORT - TECHNISCH-PHYSISCHE DIENST TNO-TH. **Main/Corp** Nederlandse Centrale Organisatie Voor. 0304-8292. English. an. Technisch-Physische Dienst Tno-th, Stieltjesweg 1, Delft Netherlands. **Tel** (015)788020. **Ed** A Verbreack. **LC** QC1. **DD** 530.0720492. **Circ** 2,500. (ctrl). Report of activities.

ANNUAL REPORTS ON NMR SPECTROSCOPY. **VAT** Annual Reports on Nuclear Magnetic Resonance Spectroscopy. Began with V. 3, 1970. 0066-4103. UK. English. ir. Academic Press, 4805 Sand Lake Road, Orlando FL 32887. **Tel** (305)345-4100. **Ed** G Webb. **Ind/Abst** Chem. Abstr. **LC** QC490. **DD** 538.3. **NLM** W1 AN769GP. **CODEN** NMRPAJ. *Annual Review of NMR Spectroscopy.*

ANNUARIO DELLA ACCADEMIA DELLE SCIENZE DELL'ISTITUTO DI BOLOGNA : CLASSE DI SCIENZE FISICHE. *See* Yearbooks, Almanacs, Directories.

APPLICATIONS OF MOSSBAUER SPECTROSCOPY. V. 1-. 0141-5115. Monographic Series. US. English. ir. Academic Press Inc, 4805 Sand Lake Road, Orlando FL 32887. **Tel** (305)345-4100. **Ind/Abst** Chem. Abstr. **CODEN** AMOSD9.

APPLIED MATHEMATICS AND MECHANICS (NEW YORK, N.Y.). *See* Mathematics.

APPLIED PHYSICS. A, SOLIDS AND SURFACES. **VFOAT** Solids and Surfaces. Vol. A26, No. 1 (Sept. 1981)-. 0721-7250. Periodical. US. English. mo. $325.00. Springer-Verlag New York, Inc., Service Center Secaucus, 44 Hartz Way, Secaucus, NJ 07094. **Ed** H K V Lotsch. **Ind/Abst** Eng. Index Annu., Eng. Index Mon., Eng. Index Bioeng. Abstr., Eng. Index Energy Abstr., Int. Aerosp. Abstr., Met. Abstr., World Alum. Abstr., Chem. Abstr., Energy Res. Abstr., Comput. Control Abstr., Electr. Electron. Abstr., Sci. Abstr. Sect. A. Phys. Abstr. **LC** QC1. **DD** 530.41. **CODEN** APSFDB. adv acc. **Circ** 65. For the rapid publication of experimental and theoretical research in physics of the condensed state, including surface science and engineering. *Applied Physics, 0340-3793.*

APPLIED PHYSICS. B, PHOTOPHYSICS AND LASER CHEMISTRY. **VFOAT** Photophysics and Laser Chemistry. Vol. B26, No. 1 (Sept. 1981)-. 0271-7269. Periodical. US. English. mo. $308.00. Springer-Verlag New York Inc, Service Center Secaucus, 44 Hartz Way, Secaucus NJ 07094. **Ed** H K V Lotsch. **Ind/Abst** Eng. Index Annu., Eng. Index Mon., Eng. Index Bioeng. Abstr., Eng. Index Energy Abstr., Int. Aerosp. Abstr., Chem. Abstr., Energy Res. Abstr., Comput. Control Abstr., Electr. Electron. Abstr., Sci. Abstr. Sect. A. Phys. Abstr. **LC** QC1. **DD** 535.05. **CODEN** APPCDL. adv acc. **Circ** 70. Journal for the rapid publication of experimental and theoretical investigations of applied research in the physics of the gaseous state, including the application of laser radiation. *Applied Physics, 0340-3793.*

APPLIED PHYSICS COMMUNICATIONS. Vol.1, No. 1-. 0277-9374. Periodical. US. English. qt. $55.00. Marcel Dekker Inc, PO Box 11305 Church Street Station, New York NY 10249. **Ed** Allen M Hermann, John A Woollam. **Ind/Abst** Eng. Index Mon., Eng. Index Bioeng. Abstr., Eng. Index Energy Abstr., Energy Inf. Abstr., Environ. Abstr., Met. Abstr., World Alum. Abstr., Eng. Index Annu., Chem. Abstr., Energy Res. Abstr., Comput. Control Abstr., Electr. Electron. Abstr., Sci. Abstr. Sect. A. Phys. Abstr. **LC** TA1. **DD** 620.005. **CODEN** APCODQ. bk rev. adv acc. (ctrl). Covers fields of applied physics; solid state, polymer, and physical chemistry, materials science; metallurgy; electrochemistry; engineering and electrical engineering.

APPLIED PHYSICS LETTERS. V. 1- Sept. 1962-. 0003-6951. Periodical. US. English. sm. American Institute of Physics, 335 East 45th Street, New York NY 10017. **Tel** (516)349-7800. **Ind/Abst** Electron. Commun. Abstr. J., ISMEC Bull., Pollut. Abstr. Indexes, Saf. Sci. Abstr. J., Int. Aerosp. Abstr., GeoRef, Met. Abstr., World Alum. Abstr., Spin, Curr. Phys. Index, Chem. Abstr., Energy Res. Abstr., Comput. Control Abstr., Electr. Electron. Abstr., Sci. Abstr. Sect. A. Phys. Abstr., Sci. Cit. Index, Abr. Ed., Phys. Abstr., Bibliogr. Index Geol. **LC** QC1. **CODEN** APPLAB.

APPLIED SOLID STATE SCIENCE. V. 1-. 0066-5533. US. English. an. Academic Press, Library Services, Orlando FL 32887. **Tel** (305)345-2000. **Ed** Raymond Wolfe. **Ind/Abst** Eng. Index Annu., Eng. Index Mon., Eng. Index Bioeng. Abstr., Eng. Index Energy Abstr. **LC** TK7871.85. **DD** 530.41. **CODEN** APSOB2.

APPLIED SOLID STATE SCIENCE. SUPPLEMENT. **VAT** Appl. Solid State Sci., Suppl. 0194-2891. Monographic Series. US. English. an. Academic Press, 4805 Sand Lake Road, Orlando FL 32819. **Ind/Abst** Chem. Abstr. **CODEN** ASSNDM.

APPROACH TO PHYSICAL SCIENCES. 1970- 9th-. 0518-1623. Periodical. AT. English. an. $2.95. School of Physics/University of New South Wales, PO Box 1, Kensington NSW 2003 Australia. *Approach to Chemistry.*

ARCHIWUM TERMODYNAMIKI I SPALANIA. *See* Genealogy and Heraldry - Archives.

ASTROFIZIKA. *See* Astronomy.

THE ASTROPHYSICAL JOURNAL. SUPPLEMENT SERIES. *See* Astronomy.

ATTI DELLA ACCADEMIA PELORITANA DEI PERICOLANTI. CLASSE I DI SCIENZE FIS., MAT. E NATURALI. Periodical. Italian (some summaries in English). ir. **LC** QC1. **DD** 505.

AUSTRALASIAN PHYSICAL & ENGINEERING SCIENCES IN MEDICINE. *See* Medicine.

AUSTRALIAN JOURNAL OF PHYSICS. V. 6- Mar. 1953-. 0004-9506. Periodical. AT. English. bm. 135.00. CSIRO Editorial Publishing Section, PO Box 89, 314 Albert Street, East Melbourne Victoria 3002 Australia. **Tel** 418-7333. **Ed** Peter Robertson. **Ind/Abst** Electron. Commun. Abstr. J., ISMEC Bull., Pollut. Abstr. Indexes, Saf. Sci. Abstr. J., Eng. Index Annu., Math. Rev., Bibliogr. Index Geol., Eng. Index, Eng. Index Energy Abstr., World Text Abstr., Met. Abstr., World Alum. Abstr., Math. Rev., Chem. Abstr., Phys. Abstr., Nuci. Sci. Abstr., Int. Aerosp. Abstr., Meteorol. Geoastrophys. Abstr., Comput. Control Abstr., Electr. Electron. Abstr., Sci. Abstr. Sect. A. Phys. Abstr., Sci. Cit. Index, Abr. Ed., Comput. Rev., GeoRef. **LC** QC1. **DD** 530.05. **NLM** W1 AU614. **CODEN** AUJPAS. adv acc. **Circ** 389. Reports of original research in most branches of physics. *Australian Journal of Scientific Research. Series A: Physical Science.*

AUSTRALIAN PHYSICIST. (THE AUSTRALIAN PHYSICIST). V. 1- 1964-. 0004-9972. Periodical. AT. English. mo. 35.00. Department of Nuclear Medicine, Sir Charles Gairdner Hospital, Western Australia 6009. **Tel** (09)389-2322. **Ed** G H Thompson. **Ind/Abst** Int. Aerosp. Abstr., Chem. Abstr., Ref. Source. **CODEN** AUPHBZ. (cum index). bk rev. adv acc. **Circ** 2,400. (ctrl). Mainly Australian physics content; some overseas physics review articles. News about physicists, branch news, political topics, teaching history of physics, book reviews, meetings, and advertisements.

BEITRAGE AUS DER PLASMAPHYSIK. **VFOAT** Contributions to Plasma Pysics. Vol. 1- 1960/61-. 0005-8025. Periodical. WB. German (English with German summaries). bm. Kunst & Wissen Erich Bieber, Dufourstrasse 51, CH-8008 Zurich Switzerland. **Tel** (01)694420. **Ed** R Rompe and M Steenbeck. **Ind/Abst** Math. Rev., Chem. Abstr., Int. Aerosp. Abstr., Energy Res. Abstr., Comput. Control Abstr., Electr. Electron. Abstr., Sci. Abstr. Sect. A. Phys. Abstr., Phys. Abstr. **LC** QC718. **CODEN** BPPHAA.

BENCHMARK PAPERS IN PHYSICAL CHEMISTRY AND CHEMICAL PHYSICS. *See* Chemistry - Physical and Theoretical Chemistry.

BIBLIOGRAFIA BRASILEIRA DE FISICA. V. 1- 1961/67-. 0067-6640. BL. Portuguese. ir. Institute Braslerio de Bibliografia Documents, Avenue General Justo 171-3 Rio de Janerio Brazil. **Tel** 081073. **LC** Z7143. *Bibliografia Brasileira de Matematica e Fisica.*

BIULETYN LUBELSKIE TOWARZYSTWA NAUKOWEGO. MATEMATYKA, FIZYKA-CHEMIA. *See* Mathematics.

A BIWEEKLY CRYOGENICS CURRENT AWARENESS SERVICE *CEASED.* **VFOAT** Current Awareness List. -List No. 719 (Dec. 22, 1980-Jan. 2, 1981). 0364-0868. US. English. bw. National Bureau of Standards, Cryogenic Data Center, Boulder CO 80303. *Current Awareness Service.*

BOLLETTINO DELLA SOCIETA ITALIANA DI FISICA. PARTE B. **Main/Corp** Societa Italiana di Fisica. 1- 1973-. IT. Italian. ir. 20.00 Nonmembers. Editrice Compositori, Viale XII Giugno 1, 40124 Bologna Italy. **Tel** (051)583149. **LC** QC1. **DD** 530.08. bk rev. adv acc. **Circ** 1,000. (ctrl).

BRUEL & KJAER TECHNICAL REVIEW. **VAT** Bruel and Kjaer Technical Review. No. 1 (1954)-. 0007-2621. DK. English. qt. Free. Bruel & Kjaer Instruments, 185 Forest Street, Marlborough MA 01752. **Tel** (617)481-7000. **Ind/Abst** Eng. Index Annu., Eng. Index Mon., Eng. Index Bioeng. Abstr., Eng. Index Energy Abstr., Int. Aerosp. Abstr., Comput. Control Abstr., Electr. Electron. Abstr., Sci. Abstr. Sect. A. Phys. Abstr. **CODEN** BKTRAP. **Circ** 14,000. (ctrl). Advance techniques in acoustical, electrical, and mechanical measurement.

BULGARIAN JOURNAL OF PHYSICS. **VFOAT** Bolgarskii Fizicheskii Zhurnal. V. 1- 1974-. 0323-9217. Periodical. English (Russian, with summaries in English). bm. $84.00. Izd-vo na Bulgarskata Akademiia Na Naukite, Vtd Hemus Department Periodicals, 6 Ruski Boulevard, Sofia Bulgaria. **Ind/Abst** Math. Rev., Electron. Commun. Abstr. J., ISMEC Bull., Pollut. Abstr. Indexes, Saf. Sci. Abstr. J., Int. Aerosp. Abstr., Met. Abstr., World Alum. Abstr., Chem. Abstr., Energy Res. Abstr., Comput. Control Abstr., Electr. Electron. Abstr., Sci. Abstr. Sect. A. Phys. Abstr. **LC** QC1. **CODEN** BJPHD5. *Izvestiia na Fizicheskiia Institut S Aneb, Izvestiia.*

BULLETIN DE LA SOCIETE FRANCAISE D'EDUCATION ET DE REEDUCATION PSYCHO-MOTRICE. 1960-. Periodical. FR. French. qt. 23.95. Societe Francaise de Reeducation, Psychomotrice 20 rue JB Carco, 1700 La Rochelle France. **Tel** 16(46)443919. **NLM** W1 BU518P. bk rev. Covers special aspects of education, physics, psychiatry and psychology.

BULLETIN DE L'UNION DES PHYSICIENS. 0366-3876. Periodical. FR. French. mo. Union des Physiciens, 44 Bd Saint-Michel, 75270 Paris Cedex 06 France. **Ind/Abst** Chem. Abstr., Energy Res. Abstr. **CODEN** BTUPAJ.

Physics

BULLETIN DU GROUPEMENT D'INFORMATIONS MUTUELLES AMPERE. Main/Corp Group for the Study of Atoms and Molecules from Radio-Electric Research. VFOAT Bulletin Ampere. Began publication with July 1956 issue. 0434-6971. Periodical. SZ. French (text in English). bm. $22.05. Centre Comptable Faculte des Sciences, 32 Boulevard d'Yvoy, 1211 Geneve 4 Switzerland. DD 621.38.

BULLETIN OF THE ACADEMY OF SCIENCES OF THE U.S.S.R. PHYSICAL SERIES. (BULLETIN OF THE ACADEMY OF SCIENCES OF THE USSR. PHYSICAL SERIES). Main/Corp Akademiia Nauk SSSR. V. 18, No. 3- 1954-. 0001-432X. Periodical. US. English (Russian). mo. Allerton Press, 150 5th Avenue, New York NY 10011. Tel (212)924-3950. Ind/Abst Comput. Control Abstr., Electr. Electron. Abstr., Sci. Abstr. Sect. A. Phys. Abstr., Phys. Abstr. LC QC1. DD 530.05. CODEN BUPSAA.

BULLETIN OF THE AMERICAN PHYSICAL SOCIETY. Main/Corp American Physical Society. V. 1-30, No. 8, Feb. 14, 1925- Dec. 28, 1955-. 0003-0503. Periodical. US. English. American Institute of Physics, 335 East 45th Street, New York NY 10017. LC QC1. DD 530.05. NLM W1 BU842. CODEN BAPSA6.

BULLETIN SIGNALETIQUE. 140 : ELECTROTECHNIQUE. V. 33- 1972-. FR. French. ir. Centre National de la Recherche Scientifique, Centre de Documentation, 26 rue Boyer, Paris France 75971. LC QC501. DD 016.537. *Bulletin Signaletique. 140: Physique II-Electricite.*

BULLETIN SIGNALETIQUE. 160 : PHYSIQUE DE L'ETAT CONDENSE. French. ir. Centre de Documentation, 26 rue Boyer, Paris France 75971. LC QC176.A1. *Bulletin Signaletique. 160: Structure de la Matiere I-Physique de l'Etat Condense, Physique Atomique et Moleculaire, Spectroscopie.*

BULLETIN SIGNALETIQUE. 165 : ATOMES ET MOLECULES, FLUIDES ET PLASMAS. V. 36- 1975-. French. ir. 250.00. Editions du CNRS, 26 rue Boyer, 75971 Paris France. LC QC170. *Bulletin Signaletique. 165: Physique Atomique et Moleculaire.*

BUSSEIKEN DAYORI (TOKYO). Main/Corp Tokyo Daigaku. Bussei Kenkyujo. 0385-9843. JA. Japanese. ir. 22-1 Roppongi 7-Chome, Minato-Ku Tokyo Japan. Tel 93-478-6811. Ind/Abst Chem. Abstr. LC QC176.A1. CODEN BUDADZ. Circ 700. (ctrl). Bulletin of the Institute for Solid State Physics, University of Tokyo. Contains contributed articles, abstracts of scientific meetings, and announcements.

C R E S S SPECTROSCOPIC REPORT. Main/Corp York University (Toronto, Ont.). Centre for Research in Experimental Space Science. No. 1- Mar. 1970-. 0318-1634. Monographic Series. CN. English. York University Centre for Research in Experimental Space Science, 4700 Keele Street/Suite 701, Downsview Ontario M3J 2R5 Canada. DD 539.12.

CANADIAN JOURNAL OF PHYSICS. VFOAT Journal Canadien de Physique. V. 29- Jan. 1951-. 0008-4204. Periodical. CN. English (includes some text in French). mo. $37.14. Receiver General for Canada, National Research Council, Montreal Road, Ottawa Ontario K1A OR6 Canada. Tel (613)993-0362. Ed G Rostoker. Ind/Abst Electr. Electron. Abstr., Comput. Control Abstr., Abstr. Bull. Inst. Paper Chem., Int. Aerosp. Abstr., Met. Abstr., World Alum. Abstr., Chem. Abstr., Math. Rev., Eng. Index Annu., Meteorol. Geoastrophys. Abstr., Sel. Water Resour. Abstr., Nuci. Sci. Abstr., Biol. Abstr., Eng. Index Mon., Pet. Abstr., Phys. Abstr., Sci. Cit. Index, Abr. Ed., Eng. Index. NLM W1 CA599. CODEN CJPHAD. adv acc. Circ 1,516. Papers, notes, communications on any area of physics. *Canadian Journal of Research.*

CESKOSLOVENSKY CASOPIS PRO FYSIKU. 1- 1951-. 0009-0700. Periodical. Czech. bm. Kubon and Sagner, Postfach 34 01 08, D-8000 Munchen 34 West Germany. Tel 020-738156. *Casopis Pro Pestovani Matematiky A Fysiky.*

CESKOSLOVENSKY CASOPIS PRO FYZIKU. (CESKOSLOVENSKY CASOPIS PRO FYZIKU. SEKCE A = CZECHOSLOVAK JOURNAL OF PHYSICS. SECTION A). VFOAT Czechoslovak Journal of Physics. Vol. 4-. 0009-0700. Periodical. Czech (with English titles and summaries). bm. Kubon & Sagner, Postfach 34 01 08, Hess-Strasse 39/41, D-8 Munchen 34 West Germany. Tel (089)52 20 27. Ind/Abst Comput. Control Abstr., Electr. Electron. Abstr., GeoRef, Int. Aerosp. Abstr. CODEN CKCFAH. Contains papers, short communications, reviews, articles and reports on events in the physics communities of Czechoslovakia. *Casopis Pro Pestovani Fysiki.*

CGCR. COMPRESSED GASES AND CRYOGENICS REPORT. VFOAT Compressed Gases and Cryogenics Report. V. 1- Aug. 1980-. 0270-0492. Periodical. US. English. mo. $144.00 Domestic, $168.00 Foreign. Van Nostrand Reinhold Co, 135 West 50th Street, New York NY 10020.

CHEMICAL PHYSICS LETTERS. V. 1- 1967-. 0009-2614. Periodical. English. ir. Elsevier Science Publishers, PO Box 211, 1000 AE Amsterdam Netherlands. Tel (020)5803.911. Ind/Abst Int. Aerosp. Abstr., Comput. Control Abstr., Electr. Electron. Abstr., Sci. Abstr. Sect. A. Phys. Abstr., Math. Rev., Nuci. Sci. Abstr., Chem. Abstr., Phys. Abstr., Sci. Cit. Index, Abr. Ed. CODEN CHPLBC. (cum index).

CHEMICAL PHYSICS OF SOLIDS AND THEIR SURFACES. Series/Titl Specialist Periodical Report. V. 7-. 0142-3401. Periodical. UK. English. 158.00 Vols. 1-8. The Chemical Society, Burlington House, London W1V OBN Canada. Ind/Abst Chem. Abstr. LC QC176.8.E4. DD 530.4105. CODEN CPSSD4. *Surface and Defect Properties of Solids.*

CHEMISTRY AND PHYSICS OF CARBON. See Chemistry.

CHEMISTRY AND PHYSICS OF LIPIDS. See Chemistry.

CHIAO HSUEH YU YEN CHIU. CHUNG HSUEH WU LI. VFOAT Jiaoxueyuyanjiu. Periodical. CH. Chinese. bm. 0.30. Post Office, Hang-Chou China. LC QC47.C6. DD 530.071251.

CHINESE ASTRONOMY AND ASTROPHYSICS. See Astronomy.

CHINESE JOURNAL OF ACOUSTICS. 0736-5152. Periodical. US. English. Gordon & Breach Science Publishers, PO Box 197, London WC2E 9PX England. bk rev. adv acc.

CHINESE PHYSICS. (CHINESE PHYSICS : A PUBLICATION OF THE AMERICAN INSTITUTE OF PHYSICS). VFOAT Chung Kuo Wu Li. V. 1, No. 1 (Jan./March 1981)-. 0273-429X. Periodical. US. English. qt. American Institute of Physics, 335 East 45th Street, New York NY 10017. Ind/Abst Math. Rev., Excerpta Med., Int. Aerosp. Abstr., Comput. Control Abstr., Electr. Electron. Abstr., Sci. Abstr., Spin, Curr. Phys. Index, Energy Res. Abstr. LC QC1. DD 530.05. CODEN CHPHD2.

CINDA. VFOAT Computer Index of Neutron Data. VAT C I N D A. 1935/76-. AU. English. an. UNIPUB, PO Box 1222, Ann Arbor MI 48106. Tel (800)521-8110. LC QC721. DD 016.5397213.

CIRCUIT FERME - TECCART. (LE CIRCUIT FERME). 0822-5516. Periodical. CN. French. ir. Institut Teccart, 3155 rue Hochelaga, Montreal Quebec H1W 1G4 Canada. DD 621.38105.

CLASSICAL AND QUANTUM GRAVITY. Vol. 1, No. 1 (Jan. 1984)-. 0264-9381. Periodical. UK. English. bm. $115.00. American Institute of Physics, Department N/M, 335 East 45th Street, New York NY 10017. Ind/Abst Math. Rev., Chem. Abstr. CODEN CQGRDG. *Journal of Physics A. Mathematical and General, 0305-4470.*

CLINICAL PHYSICS AND PHYSIOLOGICAL MEASUREMENT. (CLINICAL PHYSICS AND PHYSIOLOGICAL MEASUREMENT : AN OFFICIAL JOURNAL OF THE HOSPITAL PHYSICISTS' ASSOCIATION, DEUTSCHE GESELLSCHAFT FUR MEDIZINISCHE PHYSIK AND THE EUROPEAN FEDERATION OF ORGANISATIONS FOR MEDICAL PHYSICS). Began with: V. 1, No. 1 (Feb. 1980). 0143-0815. Periodical. UK. English. qt. American Institute of Physics, 335 East 45th Street, New York NY 10017. Tel (516)349-7800. Ind/Abst Electron. Commun. Abstr. J., ISMEC Bull., Pollut. Abstr. Indexes, Saf. Sci. Abstr. J., Life Sci. Collect., Excerpta Med., Index Med., Biol. Abstr., Comput. Control Abstr., Electr. Electron. Abstr., Sci. Abstr. Sect. A. Phys. Abstr. NLM W1 CL766. CODEN CPPMD5.

COLLECTED REPRINTS - ATMOSPHERIC PHYSICS AND CHEMISTRY LABORATORY. Main/Corp Atmospheric Physics and Chemistry Laboratory. VFOAT Atmospheric Physics and Chemistry Laboratory Collected Reprints. Periodical. US. English. ir. US Department of Commerce, National Oceanic and Atmospheric Administration, Washington DC 20402.

COLLECTIVE PHENOMENA. V. 1- Aug. 1972-. 0366-6824. US. English. ir. $296.00. Gordon & Breach, PO Box 197, London WC2E 9PX England. Tel (01)836-5125. Ed H Frohlich. Ind/Abst Math. Rev., Comput. Control Abstr., Electr. Electron. Abstr., Sci. Abstr. Sect. A. Phys. Abstr., Chem. Abstr., Phys. Abstr. LC QC174.17.P7. DD 530.05. CODEN CLPNAB. bk rev. adv acc.

COLLOID AND POLYMER SCIENCE. VFOAT Kolloid-Zeitschrift & Zeitschrift fur Polymere. V. 252- Jan. 1974-. 0303-402X. Periodical. GW. English, French, or German with summaries in the other languages. mo. 900.00 Domestic, $327.00 US. Dr Dietrich Steinkopff Verlag, PO Box 11 10, D-1600 Darmstadt 11 Germany. Tel 06151/26538-39. Ed H G Kilian and A Weiss. Ind/Abst Eng. Index Annu., Eng. Index Mon., Eng. Index Bioeng. Abstr., Eng. Index Energy Abstr., Life Sci. Collect., World Text Abstr., World Surf. Coat. Abstr., Abstr. Bull. Inst. Paper Chem., GeoRef, Biol. Abstr., Art Archaeol. Tech. Abstr., Chem. Abstr., Energy Res. Abstr. LC QD549. DD 541.3451. NLM W1 CO212T. CODEN CPMSB6. bk rev. adv acc. Circ 3,000. (ctrl). Covers fields such as solid state physics, polymer chemistry, biophysics, biology, pharmacology and medicine. *Kolloid-Zeitschrift & Zeitschrift fur Polymere, 0023-2904.*

COMMENTS ON ASTROPHYSICS. See Astronomy.

COMMENTS ON CONDENSE MATTER PHYSICS. 0885-4483. Periodical. English. ir. $166.00. Gordon & Breach Inc, 1 Bedford Street, London WC2E 988 England. *Comments on Solid State Physics, 0308-1206.*

COMMENTS ON PLASMA PHYSICS AND CONTROLLED FUSION. V. 1- Jan./Feb. 1972-. 0374-2806. Periodical. US. English. bm. $168.00. Gordon & Breach, 50 West 23 Street, New York NY 10010. Tel (01)836-5125. Ed B D Fried. Ind/Abst Comput. Control Abstr., Electr. Electron. Abstr., Sci. Abstr. Sect. A. Phys. Abstr., Chem. Abstr., Nuci. Sci. Abstr., Energy Res. Abstr., Phys. Abstr. LC QC717.6. DD 530.4405. CODEN CPCFBJ. bk rev adv acc.

COMMENTS ON SOLID STATE PHYSICS CEASED. V. 1- April/May 1968-. 0308-1206. Periodical. US. English. Gordon & Breach, 1 Bedford Street, London WC2E 9HD England. Tel 01 836 5125. Ind/Abst Int. Aerosp. Abstr., Comput. Control Abstr., Electr. Electron. Abstr., Sci. Abstr. Sect. A. Phys. Abstr., Met. Abstr., World Alum. Abstr., Nuci. Sci. Abstr., Chem. Abstr., Phys. Abstr. LC QC176.A1. DD 530.4105. CODEN COSPBK.

COMMUNICATIONS FROM THE KAMERLINGH ONNES LABORATORY OF THE UNIVERSITY OF LEIDEN. No. 217 (November 1931)-. Periodical. English (occasional contributions in French or German). ir. Kamerlingh Onnes, Kamerlingh Onnes Laboratory, Nieuwsteeg 18, 2311 SB Leiden Netherlands. Tel 071-148333. Ed M Durieusc. The abstracts of the articles published in one year from the Kamerlingh Onnes Laboratory. *Communications from the Physical Laboratory at the University of Leiden.*

COMMUNICATIONS IN MATHEMATICAL PHYSICS. Vol. 1 (1965/66)-. 0010-3616. Periodical. GW. English (French and German). mo. $797.00. Springer Verlag New York Inc, 175 Fifth Avenue, New York NY 10010. Tel (212)460-1500. Ed A Jaffe. Ind/Abst Math. Rev., Int. Aerosp. Abstr., Comput. Control Abstr., Electr. Electron. Abstr., Sci. Abstr. Sect. A. Phys. Abstr., Energy Res. Abstr., Sci. Cit. Index, Abr. Ed., Phys. Abstr. LC QC20. CODEN CMPHAY. Journal devoted to physics papers with mathematical content. Covers a broad spectrum from classical to quantum physics, individual editorial sections illustrate this scope.

COMMUNICATIONS IN THEORETICAL PHYSICS. See Communication.

COMMUNICATIONS OF THE DUBLIN INSTITUTE FOR ADVANCED STUDIES. SERIES A. See Mathematics.

COMPUTER PHYSICS COMMUNICATIONS. V. 1- July 1969-. 0010-4655. Periodical. English. mo. Elsevier Science Publishers, PO Box 211, 1000 AE Amsterdam Netherlands. Tel (020)5803.911. Ind/Abst Math. Rev.,

Physics

Electron. Commun. Abstr. J., ISMEC Bull., Pollut. Abstr. Indexes, Saf. Sci. Abstr. J., Eng. Index Annu., Eng. Index Mon., Eng. Index Bioeng. Abstr., Eng. Index Energy Abstr., GeoRef, Comput. Control Abstr., Electr. Electron. Abstr., Sci. Abstr. Sect. A. Phys. Abstr., Chem. Abstr., Nucl. Sci. Abstr., Sci. Cit. Index, Abr. Ed., Comput. Rev., Phys. Abstr., Bibliogr. Index Geol., Eng. Index. LC QC52. DD 530.0285. CODEN CPHCBZ. (cum index).

CONFERENCE SERIES. INSTITUTE OF PHYSICS. (CONFERENCE SERIES). Main/Corp Institute of Physics. 0305-2346. Monographic Series. UK. English. ir. Heydon & Sons, 247 South 41st Street, Philadelphia PA 19104. Ind/Abst Eng. Index Annu., Eng. Index Mon., Eng. Index Bioeng. Abstr., Eng. Index Energy Abstr., GeoRef, Comput. Control Abstr., Electr. Electron. Abstr., Sci. Abstr. Sect. A. Phys. Abstr., Phys. Abstr., Sci. Cit. Index, Abr. Ed. CODEN IPHSAC. *Institute of Physics and the Physical Society Conference Series.*

CONTEMPORARY CONCEPTS IN PHYSICS. Vol. 1-. 0272-2488. Monographic Series. SZ. English. ir. Harwood Academic Publishers, PO Box 786 Cooper Station, New York NY 10276. Tel (212)689-0360. Ind/Abst Math. Rev. LC UNC.

CONTEMPORARY PHYSICS. V. 1- Oct. 1959-. 0010-7514. Periodical. UK. English. bm. $184.00. Taylor & Francis Limited, 242 Cherry Street, Philadelphia PA 19106. Tel (215)238-0939. Ed J S Dugdale. Ind/Abst Excerpta Med., GeoRef, Comput. Control Abstr., Electr. Electron. Abstr., Sci. Abstr. Sect. A. Phys. Abstr., Met. Abstr., World Alum. Abstr., Chem. Abstr., Nucl. Sci. Abstr., Int. Aerosp. Abstr., Gen. Sci. Index, Phys. Abstr., Bibliogr. Index Geol. NLM W1 CO769P. CODEN CTPHAF. (cum index). Provides authoritative articles on important developments in physics that can be read and understood by anyone with an interest in, and fundamental grasp of, physics.

COSMIC AND SUBATOMIC PHYSICS REPORT. 0348-9329. Monographic Series. SW. English. ir. Cosmic and Subatomic Physics, Solvegatan 14, S-223 62 Lund Sweden. Ind/Abst Chem. Abstr. CODEN CSPLDN.

CRC HANDBOOK OF CHEMISTRY AND PHYSICS. See Chemistry.

CRYOGENIC INFORMATION REPORT. See Physics - Heat.

CRYOGENICS. V. 1- Sept. 1960-. 0011-2275. Periodical. UK. English (summaries in German, French, Italian and Russian). mo. 173.00 Domestic, 185.00 Foreign. Butterworth Scientific Limited, PO Box 63, Westbury House, Bury Street, Guildford GU2 5BH England. Tel 0438 31261. Ed Marija Vukovojac. Ind/Abst Eng. Index Annu., Eng. Index Mon., Eng. Index Bioeng. Abstr., Eng. Index Energy Abstr., Energy Inf. Abstr., Environ. Abstr., Int. Aerosp. Abstr., Comput. Control Abstr., Electr. Electron. Abstr., Sci. Abstr. Sect. A. Phys. Abstr., Chem. Abstr., Met. Abstr., World Alum. Abstr., Appl. Technol. Index, Comput. Abstr., Phys. Abstr., Sci. Cit. Index, Abr. Ed., Eng. Index. LC TP480. NLM W1 CR999. CODEN CRYOAX. bk rev. adv acc. Articles on low temperature engineering and research.

CRYSTAL LATTICE DEFECTS AND AMORPHOUS MATERIALS. Vol. 9, No. 4 (Oct. 1982)-. 0732-8699. Periodical. US. English. qt. Gordon and Breach Science Publishers Ltd, 42 William H Street, London WC2 England. Ed R Smoluchowski. Ind/Abst Comput. Control Abstr., Electr. Electron. Abstr., Sci. Abstr. Sect. A. Phys. Abstr., Chem. Abstr. LC QD931. DD 530.41. CODEN CLDMDJ. bk rev. adv acc. *Crystal Lattice Defects, 0011-2305.*

CURRENT PAPERS IN PHYSICS. No. 1- Jan. 10, 1966-. 0011-3786. Periodical. UK. English. sm. Institute of Electrical and Electronics Engineers, 345 East 47th Street, New York NY 10017. Tel (201)981-0060. Ind/Abst Fluidex, Ship Abstr. CODEN CPPHAL.

CURRENT PHYSICS INDEX. See Indexes/Abstracts.

CURRENT TOPICS IN CHINESE SCIENCE. SECTION A, PHYSICS. VFOAT Physics. Vol. 1 (1982). 0732-4383. Periodical. US. English. an. Gordon and Breach Science Publishers, PO Box 786, Cooper Station, New York NY 10276. LC QC1. DD 530.05.

C.W.E.A. NEWS. (C. W. E. A. NEWS). Main/Corp Canadian Wind Engineering Association. VFOAT Canadian Wind Engineering Association Newsletter. VAT Canadian Wind Engineering Association News. No. 1- 1977-. 0226-8442. CN. English. an. Free to Members. Department of Mechanical Engineering, University of British Columbia, Vancouver BC V6T 1W5 Canada. DD 621.45.

CZECHOSLOVAK JOURNAL OF PHYSICS. V. B16-. 0011-4626. Periodical. US. English, German or Russian 1966-68. ir. $110.00. Plenum Publishing Corp, 227 West 17th Street, New York NY 10011. Tel (212)620-8000. Ind/Abst Int. Aerosp. Abstr., Comput. Control Abstr., Electr. Electron. Abstr., Sci. Abstr. Sect. A. Phys. Abstr., Math. Rev., Met. Abstr., World Alum. Abstr., Chem. Abstr. LC QC1. CODEN CZYPAO. (cum index). *Chekhoslovatskii Fizicheskii Zhurnal, Czechoslovak Journal of Physics.*

DEVELOPMENTS IN FLOW MEASUREMENT. Series/Titl Developments Series. 1-. Periodical. UK. English. Applied Science Publishers Inc, Englewood NJ 07631. LC TA357. DD 532.05305.

DEVELOPMENTS IN THE QUARK THEORY OF HADRONS. V. 1- 1964/78-. US. English. an. Hadronic Press Inc, PO Box 155, Nonantum MA 02195. Tel (617)964-1684.

DIFFERENTIAL GEOMETRICAL METHODS IN MATHEMATICAL PHYSICS. 1-. 0720-485X. Periodical. ir. Springer Verlag, 175 Fifth Avenue, New York NY 10010.

DIFFUSION AND DEFECT DATA. V. 8- 1974-. 0377-6883. English. ir. $54.00. 411 Long Beach Parkway, Bay Village 44140. Ind/Abst Energy Res. Abstr. LC QD543. DD 531.7. *Diffusion Data, 0012-267X.*

DIRECTORY OF PHYSICS & ASTRONOMY STAFF MEMBERS. See Yearbooks, Almanacs, Directories.

DIRECTORY - SPECTROSCOPY SOCIETY OF CANADA. See Yearbooks, Almanacs, Directories.

EGYPTIAN JOURNAL OF PHYSICS. VFOAT Majallah Al-Misriyah Lil-Fiziqa. 0376-8724. UA. English (summaries in Arabic). sa. $30.00. National Information & Documentation Center, A1-Tahrir St Dokki, Cairo AR Egypt. Ind/Abst Chem. Abstr. LC QC1. DD 530.05. CODEN EJPHB2. *United Arab Republic Journal of Physics.*

ELECTRON SPECTROSCOPY : THEORY, TECHNIQUES, AND APPLICATIONS. V.1- 1977-. Periodical. UK. English. ir. Academic Press, 4805 Sand Lake Road, Orlando FL 32887. Tel (305)345-4100. Ed C R Brundle and A D Baker.

ESSAYS IN PHYSICS. V. 1-. 0071-1438. UK. English. an. Academic Press, 4805 Sand Lake Road, Orlando FL 32887. Tel (305)345-4100. Ed G K T Conn and G N Fowler. Ind/Abst Chem. Abstr., Nucl. Sci. Abstr. LC QC1. DD 530.05. CODEN ESPHAU.

EUROPEAN JOURNAL OF PHYSICS. (EUROPEAN JOURNAL OF PHYSICS : A JOURNAL OF THE EUROPEAN PHYSICAL SOCIETY). Began in 1980. 0143-0807. Periodical. UK. English (some summaries in French and German). qt. American Institute of Physics, 335 East 45th Street, New York NY 10017. Tel (516)349-7800. Ind/Abst Math. Rev., Int. Aerosp. Abstr., Comput. Control Abstr., Electr. Electron. Abstr., Sci. Abstr. Sect. A. Phys. Abstr., Chem. Abstr. LC QC1. DD 530.05. CODEN EJPHD4.

EUROPHYSICS CONFERENCE ABSTRACTS. See Indexes/Abstracts.

EUROPHYSICS NEWS. 0531-7479. Periodical. English. mo. European Physical Society, PO Box 39, 1213 Petit-Lancy 2 Switzerland. Ind/Abst Comput. Control Abstr., Electr. Electron. Abstr., Sci. Abstr. Sect. A. Phys. Abstr., Chem. Abstr., Energy Res. Abstr. CODEN EUPNAS.

EXPERIMENTELLE TECHNIK DER PHYSIK. 1.- Volume. 0014-4924. Periodical. SZ. German. bm. $43.34. Kunst & Wissen Erich Bieber, Dufourstrasse 51, CH-8008 Zurich Switzerland. Tel (011)411694420. Ind/Abst Math. Rev., Comput. Control Abstr., Electr. Electron. Abstr., Sci. Abstr. Sect. A. Phys. Abstr., Chem. Abstr., Energy Res. Abstr., Phys. Abstr. CODEN EXPPAL.

EXPLOSIVES AND PYROTECHNICS. See Engineering.

FERROELECTRICS. V. 1- Mar. 1970-. 0015-0193. Periodical. US. English. bm. $280.00. Gordon and Breach, PO Box 197, London WC2E 9PX England. Tel (01)836-5125. Ed George W Taylor. Ind/Abst Eng. Index Mon., Eng. Index Bioeng. Abstr., Eng. Index Energy Abstr., Int. Aerosp. Abstr., Comput. Control Abstr., Electr. Electron. Abstr., Sci. Abstr. Sect. A. Phys. Abstr., Met. Abstr., World Alum. Abstr., Chem. Abstr., Eng. Index Annu., Eng. Index, Nucl. Sci. Abstr., Sci. Cit. Index, Abr. Ed., Phys. Abstr. LC QC595. DD 537.244. CODEN FEROA8. bk rev. adv acc.

FERROELECTRICS. (FERROELECTRICS. LETTERS SECTION). Vol. 1, No. 1 (August 1983)-. 0731-5171. Periodical. US. English. ir. $142.00. Harwood Academic Publishers, PO Box 197, London WC2E 9PX England. Tel 851 25258. Ed George W Taylor. bk rev. adv acc. *Ferroelectrics. Letters Section (Gordon and Breach : 1982), 0731-5171.*

FESTKORPERPROBLEME. VFOAT Advances in Solid State Physics. 1962-. 0430-3393. Periodical. GW. Vols. 9-10 have title in German and English, articles in either language with summaries in both. ir. Friedr Vieweg Verlag, Postfach 5829, Faulbrunnenstrasse 13, D6200 Wiesbaden 1 West Germany. Ind/Abst Eng. Index, Comput. Control Abstr., Electr. Electron. Abstr., Sci. Abstr., Chem. Abstr., Phys. Abstr., Sci. Cit. Index, Abr. Ed., Eng. Index Annu., Eng. Index Mon., Eng. Index Energy Abstr., Eng. Index Bioeng. Abstr. LC TK7871.85. DD 621.3815208. CODEN FSTKA2. *Halbleiterprobleme.*

FILOSOFIIA I FIZIKA. 1972-. Periodical. UR. Russian. 0.75. Izd-Vo Voronezhshogo Universiteta, Pr Revoliutsii 33, Oblknigotorg Kniga-Pochioi, Voronezh 394000 Russia. LC QC5.56.

FISICA. VFOAT Area de Fisica. 1-. Periodical. Spanish (summeries in English). ir. Universidad Tecnica del Estado, Avda Ecuador 3469, Santiago Chile. LC QC1.

FISICA E TECNOLOGIA. V. 1- Jan./Mar. 1978-. 0391-9757. Periodical. IT. Italian. qt. 24.00 Members, 28.00 Nonmembers. Editrice Compositori SRL, Viale XII Giugno 1, 40124 Bologna Italy. Tel (051)583149. Ind/Abst Comput. Control Abstr., Electr. Electron. Abstr., Sci. Abstr. Sect. A. Phys. Abstr., Chem. Abstr., Phys. Abstr. CODEN FITEDJ. Circ 1,000. (ctrl).

FIZIKA. 1-. 0204-6946. Periodical. BU. Bulgarian. bm. $28.00. Hemus, 6 Boulevard Rusky, Sofia Bulgaria. Ind/Abst Chem. Abstr. LC QC1. CODEN FZKADD. *Matematika I Fizika.*

FIZIKA ELEMENTARNYKH CHASTITS I ATOMNOGO IADRA. VFOAT Problems of Elementary Particle and Atomic Nucleus Physics. Vol. 1- 1970-. Periodical. UR. Russian (summaries in English). qt. $60.00. Victor Kamkin Inc (71018), 12224 Parklawn Drive, Rockville MD 20852. Tel (301)881-5973. Ind/Abst Math. Rev., Chem. Abstr.

FIZIKA I KHIMIIA OBRABOTKI MATERIALOV. (PHYSICS AND CHEMISTRY OF MATERIALS TREATMENT). 0264-729X. Periodical. UK. English (summaries in Russian). bm. $125.00. V E Riecansky, 22 Horseshoe Close/Balsham, Cambridge CB1 6EG England.

FIZIKA MNOGOCHASTICHNYKH SISTEM. No. 1-. Periodical. UR. Russian. 1.60. Naukova Dumka, 252001 Kiev-1, Ul Kirova 4 USSR. LC QC173. DD 539.605.

FIZIKA PLAZMY. V. 1- Jan./Feb. 1975-. 0367-2921. Periodical. UR. Russian. bm. $87.00. Victor Kamkin Inc (71058), 12224 Parklawn Drive, Rockville MD 20852. Tel (301)881-5973. Ind/Abst Int. Aerosp. Abstr., Comput. Control Abstr., Electr. Electron. Abstr., Sci. Abstr. Sect. A. Phys. Abstr., Chem. Abstr. LC QC7176. CODEN FIPLDK.

FIZIKA TVERDOGO TELA. VFOAT Solid State Physics. Vol. 1- 1959-. 0367-3294. Periodical. UR. Russian (table of contents also in English). mo. $165.50. Victor Kamkin Inc (71023), 12224 Parklawn Drive, Rockville MD 20852. Tel (301)881-5973. Ind/Abst Comput. Control Abstr., Met. Abstr., Electr. Electron. Abstr., World Alum. Abstr., Sci. Abstr. Sect. A. Phys. Abstr., Chem. Abstr., Sci. Cit. Index, Abr. Ed., Phys. Abstr., Appl. Mech. Rev. LC QC176.A1. CODEN FTVTAC.

FIZIKA V SHKOLE : NAUCHNO-METODICHESKII ZHURNAL MINISTERSTVO PROSVESHCHENIIA SSSR. Began in 1937. 0130-5522. Periodical. UR. Russian. bm. $12.00. Victor Kamkin Inc, 12224 Parklawn Drive, Rockville MD 20852. Tel (301)881-5973. Ind/Abst Chem. Abstr. CODEN FIZSAK. *Matematika i Fizika v Shkole.*

FIZIKAI SZEMLE. Yearly V. 1- 1951-. 0015-3257. Periodical. HU. Hungarian. mo. Akademiai Kiado, POB 24, 1363 Budapest Hungary. Ind/Abst

Comput. Control Abstr., Electr. Electron. Abstr., Sci. Abstr. Sect. A. Phys. Abstr., Chem. Abstr., Phys. Abstr. **CODEN** FISZA6.

FIZIKO-MATEMATICHESKO SPISANIE. V. 1- 1958-. 0015-3265. Periodical. BU. Bulgarian. qt. $20.00. Hemus, 6 Boulevard Rusky, Sofia Bulgaria. **Ind/Abst** Chem. Abstr., Math. Rev., Ref. Z. Fizika, Ref. Z. Math. **CODEN** FMBMAC. *Spisanie.*

FORTSCHRITTE DER PHYSIK (BERLIN : 1953). (FORTSCHRITTE DER PHYSIK). Vol. 1 (1953)-. 0015-8208. Periodical. GE. German. mo. $99.54. Kunst & Wissen Erich Bieber, Dufourstrasse 51, CH-8008 Zurich Switzerland. **Tel** (011)411694420. **Ind/Abst** Math. Rev., Int. Aerosp. Abstr., Comput. Control Abstr., Electr. Electron. Abstr., Sci. Abstr. Sect. A. Phys. Abstr., Chem. Abstr., Energy Res. Abstr., Sci. Cit. Index, Abr. Ed., Phys. Abstr. **LC** QC1. **CODEN** FPYKA6. (cum index).

FOUNDATIONS OF PHYSICS. V. 1- 1970-. 0015-9018. Periodical. US. English. mo. $425.00 Domestic, $474.00 Foreign. Plenum Press, 233 Spring Street, New York NY 10013. **Tel** (212)620-8000. **Ed** Alwyn von der Merwe. **Ind/Abst** Math. Rev., Electron. Commun. Abstr. J., ISMEC Bull., Pollut. Abstr. Indexes, Saf. Sci. Abstr. J., Int. Aerosp. Abstr., Comput. Control Abstr., Electr. Electron. Abstr., Sci. Abstr., Nuci. Sci. Abstr., Spin, Energy Res. Abstr., Sci. Cit. Index, Abr. Ed., Phys. Abstr. **LC** QC1. **DD** 530.05. **CODEN** FNDPA4. bk rev. adv acc. An international journal devoted to the conceptual bases and foundamental theories of modern physics biophysics and cosmology.

FRA FYSIKKENS VERDEN. Began 1939. 0015-9247. Periodical. Norwegian. qt. Norsk Fysisk Selskap, Trondheim Norway. **Ind/Abst** Comput. Control Abstr., Electr. Electron. Abstr., Sci. Abstr. Sect. A. Phys. Abstr., Chem. Abstr., Energy Res. Abstr. **CODEN** FYVDAX.

FRONTIERS IN PHYSICS. No. 1-. 0429-7725. US. English. ir. Benjamin/Cummings Publishing Company Inc, 2727 Sand Hill Road, Menlo Park Ca 94025. **Tel** (415)854-2744. **Ind/Abst** Math. Rev.

FUNDAMENTALS OF COSMIC PHYSICS. *See* Astronomy.

FYSIK-KEMI. Periodical. Danish. ir. 44.00. Danmarks Fysik Og Kemilrerforening, Dyrl Jurgensensgade 11 3740, Svaneke Denmark. **LC** QC30.

FYSISK TIDSSKRIFT. Vol. 1-. 0016-3392. Periodical. DK. Danish. qt. Jul Gjellerups Boghandel, Solvgade 87-89, Copenhagen 1307 Denmark. **Ind/Abst** Comput. Control Abstr., Electr. Electron. Abstr., Sci. Abstr., Chem. Abstr., Energy Res. Abstr., Phys. Abstr., Sci. Abstr. Sect. A. Phys. Abstr. **LC** QC1. **CODEN** FYTIA4. (cum index).

GENERAL PHYSICS ADVANCE ABSTRACTS. *See* Indexes/Abstracts.

GENERAL RELATIVITY AND GRAVITATION. **VFOAT** GRG Journal. V. 1- 1970-. 0001-7701. Periodical. US. English. mo. $350.00 Domestic, $391.00 Foreign. Plenum Press, 233 Spring Street, New York NY 10013. **Tel** (212)620-8000. **Ed** A Held. **Ind/Abst** Math. Rev., Electron. Commun. Abstr. J., ISMEC Bull., Pollut. Abstr. Indexes, Saf. Sci. Abstr. J., Int. Aerosp. Abstr., Comput. Control Abstr., Electr. Electron. Abstr., Sci. Abstr. Sect. A. Phys. Abstr., Curr. Contents, Ref. Z., Zentralbl. Math. Ihre Grenzgeb., Phys. Abstr., Sci. Cit. Index, Abr. Ed. **LC** QC173.6. **DD** 530.11. **CODEN** GRGVA8. bk rev. adv acc. This is a journal of studies in general relativity and related topics. Publishes research papers on general relativity and related topics.

GEOFISICA INTERNACIONAL. (GEOFISICA INTERNACIONAL : REVISTA DE LA UNION GEOFISICA MEXICANA AUSPICIADA POR EL INSTITUTO DE GEOFISICA DE LA UNIVERSIDAD NACIONAL AUTONOMA DE MEXICO). Vol. 1, No. 1 Jan. 10, 1961-. 0016-7169. Periodical. MX. Spanish (French, English, or Russian). qt. $50.00. Instituto de Geofisica de la Universidad, Nacional Autonoma de Mexico, Cuidad Universitaria, Mexico 20 DF Mexico. **Tel** 550515. **Ed** Jorge Bouton. **Ind/Abst** GeoRef, Int. Aerosp. Abstr., Chem. Abstr., Bibliogr. Index Geol. **LC** QC801. **DD** 551. **CODEN** GFINAC. bk rev. **Circ** 1,200. (ctrl). Physics of the earth's interior: seismology, vulcanology, chemistry of the earth's interior, tectonics, geomagnetism aeronomy, meteorology, physics of the earth, hydrology and geophysical exploration.

GRADUATE PROGRAMS. PHYSICS, ASTRONOMY AND RELATED FIELDS. (GRADUATE PROGRAMS IN PHYSICS, ASTRONOMY AND RELATED FIELDS). **Series/Titl** AIP Publication. 1977-78-. 0147-1821. US. English. an. American Institute of Physics, 335 East 45th Street, New York NY 10017. *Graduate Programs: Physics, Astronomy, and Related Fields X, 0147-1821.*

GRAPHS OF NEUTRON INTENSITIES. **Main/Corp** Japan. Nihon Gakujutsu Kaigi. Kokusai Chikyu Kansoku Tokubetsu Iinkai. Taiyo Chikyukan Butsurigaku Bunkakai. **Series/Titl** Cosmic-Ray Intensity. JA. English. ir. Science Council of Japan, 23 34 Roppongi 7 Chome, Tokyo Japan. **LC** QC485.8.V3. **DD** 551.5276.

GUIA DAS INSTITUICOES EM FISICA NO BRASIL. 1982-. Portuguese. an. Centro Brasileiro de Pesquisas Fisicas-CBPF, Coordenacao de Documenta Cao e Informacao Cientifica-CDI, Divisao de Informacao Cientifica, Rue Xavier Sigaud 150, 4O. Andar, Ed Cesar Lattes URCA Brazil. **LC** QC47.B6. **DD** 530.071181.

HAGALO USTED MISMO - BRACE RESEARCH INSTITUTE. (HAGALO USTED MISMO-HOJA). **VFOAT** Hagalo Usted Mismo. 0824-7773. Monographic Series. CN. Spanish. ir. Brace Research Institute, PO Box 900, Ste-Anne-de-Bellevue Quebec H9X 1C0 Canada. **DD** 621.

HANDBOOK OF CYCLICAL INDICATORS. May 1977-. 0196-9366. Periodical. US. English. ir. US Government Printing Office, Superintendent of Documents, Washington DC 20402. **Tel** (202)783-3238.

HELVETICA PHYSICA ACTA. V. 1- 1928-. 0018-0238. Periodical. US. Multilingual (French, German, or Italian). bm. $198.00. Birkhauser Boston Inc, 380 Green Street, PO Box 3005, Cambridge MA 02139. **Tel** (617)576-6638. **Ind/Abst** Electron. Commun. Abstr. J., ISMEC Bull., Pollut. Abstr. Indexes, Saf. Sci. Abstr. J., Int. Aerosp. Abstr., GeoRef, Comput. Control Abstr., Electr. Electron. Abstr., Sci. Abstr. Sect. A. Phys. Abstr., Chem. Abstr., Nuci. Sci. Abstr., Math. Rev., Energy Res. Abstr., Sci. Cit. Index, Abr. Ed., Bibliogr. Index Geol., Phys. Abstr. **LC** QC1. **CODEN** HPACAK.

HIGH ENERGY PHYSICS INDEX. *See* Indexes/Abstracts.

I.E.E.E. TRANSACTIONS ON PLASMA SCIENCE. *See* Engineering - Electricity, Electrical Engineering, Electronics.

IL NUOVO CIMENTO DELLA SOCIETA ITALIANA DI FISICA SEZIONE. C. (IL NUOVO CIMENTO DELLA SOCIETA ITALIANA DI FISICA. C). Vol. 1C Jan./Feb. 1978-. 0390-5551. Periodical. IT. English (French Italian or German). bm. $200.00. Editrice Compositori SRL, Viale XII Giugno 1, 40124 Bologna Italy. **Ind/Abst** Int. Aerosp. Abstr., Comput. Control Abstr., Electr. Electron. Abstr., Sci. Abstr. Sect. A. Phys. Abstr., Chem. Abstr., Math. Rev. **CODEN** NIFCAS.

INDIAN JOURNAL OF PURE AND APPLIED PHYSICS. 0019-5596. Periodical. II. English. mo. $60.00. Publishers and Information Directorate, Hillside Road, New Delhi 110012 India. **Tel** 584846. **Ed** D S Sastry. **Ind/Abst** Electr. Electron. Abstr., Comput. Control Abstr., Eng. Index, Phys. Abstr., Sci. Cit. Index, Abr. Ed., Math. Rev., Chem. Abstr., Bibliogr. Index Geol. adv acc. **Circ** 1,000. Condensed matter physics, chemical physics, mathematical physics, nuclear physics, atomic and molecular physics, electronics, electrical engineering, elementary particles, and fields classical areas of phenomenology.

INDIAN JOURNAL OF RADIO & SPACE PHYSICS. **VAT** Indian Journal of Radio and Space Physics. V. 1- Mar. 1972-. 0367-8393. Periodical. II. English. bm. $34.00. Publishing and Information Directorate, Hillside Road, New Delhi 110012 India. **Ind/Abst** Comput. Control Abstr., Electr. Electron. Abstr., Sci. Abstr. Sect. A. Phys. Abstr., Int. Aerosp. Abstr., Chem. Abstr., Nuci. Sci. Abstr., Sci. Cit. Index, Abr. Ed., Phys. Abstr. **LC** QC801. **DD** 523.0105. **CODEN** IJRSAK.

INDIAN JOURNAL OF THEORETICAL PHYSICS. V. 1- June 1953-. 0019-5693. Periodical. II. English. qt. $20.00. Institute of Theoretical Physics, Secretary B Kutie, 4 1 Mohan Began Lane, Calcutta 700004 India. **Tel** 55-5726. **Ind/Abst** Int. Aerosp. Abstr., Comput. Control Abstr., Electr. Electron. Abstr., Sci. Abstr. Sect. A. Phys. Abstr., Chem. Abstr., Phys. Abstr. **LC** QC1. **CODEN** IJTPAL.

INFRARED PHYSICS. V. 1- Mar. 1961-. Periodical. UK. mostly English. bm. Pergamon Press, 395 Sawmill River Road, Elmsford NY 10523. **Tel** (914)592-7700. **Ind/Abst** Eng. Index, Phys. Abstr., Chem. Abstr., Sci. Cit. Index, Abr. Ed., Comput. Control Abstr., Electr. Electron. Abstr., Int. Aerosp. Abstr.

INSTRUMENTS AND EXPERIMENTAL TECHNIQUES. Apr. 1959-. 0020-4412. Periodical. US. English (Russian). mo. $745.00 Domestic, $825.00 Foreign. Plenum Publishing Corporation, 227 West 17th Street, New York NY 10011. **Tel** (212)620-8000. **Ed** A I Shalinikov. **Ind/Abst** Electron. Commun. Abstr. J., ISMEC Bull., Eng. Index Mon., Eng. Index Bioeng. Abstr., Eng. Index Energy Abstr., Fluidex, Comput. Control Abstr., Electr. Electron. Abstr., Sci. Abstr. Sect. A. Phys. Abstr., Appl. Mech. Rev., Chem. Abstr., Eng. Index Annu., Eng. Index Mon., Curr. Contents, Nuci. Sci. Abstr. **LC** QC53. **DD** 530.78. **CODEN** INETAK. Provides articles and research on physical measurement techniques and applications of various laboratory instuments, new materials used in the instrumentation industry.

INTERFACE & MEMORY DISCONTINUED DEVICES. **Series/Titl** D.A.T.A. Book Electronic Information Series. **VFOAT** Interface and Memory Discontinued Deivces. Ed. 1 (August 1983 - July 1984)-. 8755-3937. US. English. an. D A T A Inc, 9889 Willow Creek Road/PO Box 26875, San Diego CA 92126. **DD** 621.

THE INTERNATIONAL JOURNAL OF APPLIED RADIATION AND ISOTOPES. V. 1- July 1956-. 0020-708X. Periodical. UK. English (articles and summaries in French, German or Russian). mo. Pergamon Press, 395 Sawmill River Road, Elmsford MY 10523. **Tel** (914)592-7700. **Ind/Abst** Life Sci. Collect., Pestdoc, Ringdoc, Vetdoc, Excerpta Med., Coal Abstr., Energy Inf. Abstr., Environ. Abstr., Int. Aerosp. Abstr., GeoRef, Comput. Control Abstr., Electr. Electron. Abstr., Sci. Abstr. Sect. A. Phys. Abstr., Chem. Abstr., Nuci. Sci. Abstr., Biol. Abstr., Index Med., Sel. Water Resour. Abstr., Energy Res. Abstr., Eng. Index Annu., Eng. Index Mon., Sci. Cit. Index, Abr. Ed., Phys. Abstr., Hospit. Lit. Index, Bibliogr. Index Geol., Eng. Index. **LC** QC770. **DD** 539.752. **NLM** W1 IN7655. **CODEN** IJARAY. (cum index). Microfilm available from Microforms International Marketing Corp.

INTERNATIONAL JOURNAL OF MASS SPECTROMETRY AND ION PHYSICS *CEASED.* Vol. 1, No. 1 (Apr. 1968) Vol. 53 (Sept. 20, 1983). 0020-7381. Periodical. NE. English (French and German). ir. **Ind/Abst** Excerpta Med., Int. Aerosp. Abstr., GeoRef, Chem. Abstr. **LC** QC454. **DD** 539. **CODEN** IJMIBY.

INTERNATIONAL JOURNAL OF THEORETICAL PHYSICS. V. 1- May 1968-. 0020-7748. Periodical. US. English (French or German). mo. $325.00 US, $364.00 Foreign. Plenum Publishing Corporation, 233 Spring Street, New York NY 10013. **Tel** (212)620-8000. **Ed** David Finkelstein. **Ind/Abst** Electron. Commun. Abstr. J., ISMEC Bull., Pollut. Abstr. Indexes, Saf. Sci. Abstr. J., Int. Aerosp. Abstr., Comput. Control Abstr., Electr. Electron. Abstr., Sci. Abstr. Sect. A. Phys. Abstr., Chem. Abstr., Nuci. Sci. Abstr., Math. Rev., Curr. Contents, Sci. Cit. Index, Abr. Ed., Zentralbl. Math. Ihre Grenzgeb. **LC** QC1. **DD** 530.05. **CODEN** IJTPBM. A journal of orignial research and reviews in theoretical physics and related mathematics, dedicated to the unification of physics.

INTERNATIONAL JOURNAL OF THERMOPHYSICS. Vol. 1, No. 1 (Mar. 1980)-. 0195-928X. Periodical. US. English. qt. $150.00 Domestic, $168.00 Foreign. Plenum Publishing Company, 233 Spring Street, New York NY 10013. **Tel** (212)620-8000. **Ed** Ared Cezairloyan. **Ind/Abst** Eng. Index, Comput. Control Abstr., Electr. Electron. Abstr., Phys. Abstr., Sci. Abstr. Sect. A. Phys. Abstr., Curr. Contents, Met. Abstr., Ref. Z., World Alum. Abstr., Appl. Mech. Rev., Phys. Abstr., Chem. Abstr., Eng. Index Mon., Eng. Index Annu., Eng. Index Energy Abstr., Eng. Index Bioeng. Abstr. **LC** QC192. **DD** 536.7. **CODEN** IJTHDY. adv acc. This journal is an international medium for the publication of papers in the thermophysics field with the intent to serve both the generations and the users of thermophysical properties data.

INTERNATIONAL PHYSICS SERIES. 0392-3967. IT. English. ir. Editrice Compositori, Viale XII Giugno 1, 40124 Bologna Italy. **Ind/Abst** Chem. Abstr.

INTERNATIONAL SERIES OF MONOGRAPHS ON PHYSICS (OXFORD, OXFORDSHIRE). (INTERNATIONAL SERIES OF MONOGRAPHS ON PHYSICS). Monographic Series. UK. English. ir. Oxford University Press, 16-00 Pollitt Drive, Fair Lawn NJ 07410. **Ind/Abst** Math. Rev., Comput. Control Abstr., Electr. Electron. Abstr., Sci. Abstr. Sect. A. Phys. Abstr. **CODEN** IMPHAW.

INTERSCIENCE MONOGRAPHS AND TEXTS IN PHYSICS AND ASTRONOMY. **VFOAT** Monographs and Texts in Physics and Astronomy. 0074-9931. Monographic Series. US. English. ir. John Wiley & Sons Inc, 1 Wiley Drive, Somerset NJ 08873. **Ind/Abst** Chem. Abstr. **LC** UNC. **CODEN** IMTPA8.

INTERSCIENCE TRACTS ON PHYSICS AND ASTRONOMY. 0074-9958. Monographic Series. US. English. ir. John Wiley and Sons Inc, 1 Wiley Drive, Somerset NJ 08873. **LC** UNC.

ISOTOPENPRAXIS. Vol. 1-. 0021-1915. GE. English. mo. $109.94. Kunst & Wissen Erich Bieber, Dufourstrasse 51, CH-8008 Zurich Switzerland. **Tel** (011)411694420. **Ind/Abst** Energy Inf. Abstr., Environ. Abstr., Chem. Abstr., Energy Res. Abstr., Sci. Cit. Index, Abr. Ed. **NLM** W1 IS579. **CODEN** IPRXA9.

IZVESTIIA. SERIIA FIZICHESKAIA. **Main/Corp** Akademiia Nauk SSSR. Vol. 1- 1936-. Periodical. UR. title also in French, text in Russian. mo. $139.00. Victor Kamkin Inc (70356), 12224 Parklawn Drive, Rockville MD 20852. **Tel** (301)881-5973. **Ind/Abst** Phys. Abstr., Index Med., Electr. Electron. Abstr., Comput. Control Abstr. **LC** AS262.

IZVESTIIA. SERIIA FIZIKO-MATEMATICHESKIKH NAUK. **Main/Corp** Haykakan SSH Gitowtyownneri Akademia. V. 10-18. UR. Russian (title and table of contents also in Armenian). bm. Victor Kamkin Inc, 12224 Parklawn Drive, Rockville MD 20852. **Tel** (301)881-5973. *Izvestiia. Fiziko-Matematicheskie, Estestvennye I Tekhnicheskie Nauki.*

IZVESTIJA AKADEMIJA NAUK SSSR. FIZIKA ZEMLI. (IZVESTIIA. FIZIKA ZEMLI). **VFOAT** Fizika Zemli. 1965-. 0002-3337. Periodical. UR. Russian. mo. $80.00. Victor Kamkin Inc, 12224 Parklawn Drive, Rockville MD 20852. **Tel** (301)881-5973. **Ind/Abst** Math. Rev., Int. Aerosp. Abstr., Comput. Control Abstr., Electr. Electron. Abstr., Sci. Abstr. Sect. A. Phys. Abstr., Chem. Abstr., Energy Res. Abstr., Phys. Abstr. **CODEN** IAFZAK.

IZVESTIJA VYSSIH UCEBNYH ZAVEDENIJ. FIZIKA. (IZVESTIIA VYSSHIKH UCHEBNYKH ZAVEDENII. FIZIKA). Vol. 1 (1958)-. 0021-3411. Periodical. UR. Russian. mo. Victor Kamkin Inc, 12224 Parklawn Drive, Rockville MD 20852. **Tel** (301)881-5973. **Ind/Abst** Math. Rev., Comput. Control Abstr., Electr. Electron. Abstr., Sci. Abstr. Sect. A. Phys. Abstr., Chem. Abstr. **CODEN** IVUFAC.

IZVESTIJA VYSSIH UCEBNYH ZAVEDENIJ. RADIOFIZIKA. (IZVESTIIA VYSSHIKH UCHEBNYKH ZAVEDENII. RADIOFIZIKA). **VFOAT** Radiofizika. V. 1- 1958-. 0021-3462. Periodical. UR. Russian. mo. Victor Kamkin Inc, 12224 Parklawn Drive, Rockville MD 20852. **Tel** (301)881-5973. **Ind/Abst** Math. Rev., Int. Aerosp. Abstr., Comput. Control Abstr., Electr. Electron. Abstr., Sci. Abstr. Sect. A. Phys. Abstr., Chem. Abstr. **CODEN** IVYRAY.

JAARVERSLAG - TECHNISCH PHYSISCHE DIENST TNO-TH. **Main/Corp** Nederlandse Centrale Organisatie voor. Dutch. ir. Free. Technisch Physische Dienst Tno-Th, Stieltjesweg L, Postbus 155, Delft Netherlands. **Tel** (015)78 80 20. Ed A Verbraeck. **LC** QC1. **Circ** 2,500. (ctrl). Report of activities. *Verslag.*

JAHRESBERICHT - WERNER-HEISENBERG-INSTITUT FUR PHYSIK. **Main/Corp** Werner-Heisenberg-Institut fur Physik. German. an. Werner-Heisenberg-Institut fur Physik, Fohringer Ring 6, 8000 Munchen 40 West Germany.

JAPANESE JOURNAL OF APPLIED PHYSICS *CEASED.* V. 1-20. 0021-4922. Periodical. JA. English (occasional contributions in French or German). mo. **Ind/Abst** Eng. Index Annu., Eng. Index Mon., Eng. Index Bioeng. Abstr., Eng. Index Energy Abstr., GeoRef, Chem. Abstr. **LC** TA4. **CODEN** JJAPA5.

JAPANESE JOURNAL OF APPLIED PHYSICS. PART 2, LETTERS. **VFOAT** JJAP Letters. Vol. 21, No. 1 (Jan. 1982)-. Periodical. JA. English (French or German). mo. $181.15. Japanese Journal of Applied Physics, 24-8 Shinbashi 4-Chome, Minato-Ku Tokyo 105 Japan. **Ind/Abst** Eng. Index Annu., Eng. Index Mon., Eng. Index Bioeng. Abstr., Eng. Index Energy Abstr., Int. Aerosp. Abstr., Comput. Control Abstr., Electr. Electron. Abstr., Sci. Abstr. Sect. A. Phys. Abstr., Met. Abstr., World Alum. Abstr., Chem. Abstr. **CODEN** JAPLD8. *Japanese Journal of Applied Physics, 0021-4922.*

JETP LETTERS. **VFOAT** Soviet Physics. JETP. Letters to the Editor. V. 1- Apr. 1, 1965-. 0021-3640. Periodical. US. English (Russian). sm. American Institute of Physics, 335 East 45th Street, New York NY 10017. **Tel** (516)349-7800. **Ind/Abst** Spin, Comput. Control Abstr., Electr. Electron. Abstr., Sci. Abstr. Sect. A. Phys. Abstr., Met. Abstr., Energy Res. Abstr., World Alum. Abstr., Int. Aerosp. Abstr., Chem. Abstr., Phys. Abstr., Sci. Cit. Index, Abr. Ed., Appl. Mech. Rev. **CODEN** JTPLA2. (cum index).

JOURNAL DE PHYSIQUE. V. 24- Jan. 1963-. 0302-0738. Periodical. French (Articles in English, German or Russian). mo. Les Editions de Physique, Avenue DU Hoggar BP 112, 91944 Les Ulis France. **Ind/Abst** Eng. Index Annu., Eng. Index Mon., Eng. Index Bioeng. Abstr., Eng. Index Energy Abstr., GeoRef, Comput. Control Abstr., Electr. Electron. Abstr., Sci. Abstr. Sect. A. Phys. Abstr., Met. Abstr., World Alum. Abstr., Chem. Abstr., Math. Rev., Nuci. Sci. Abstr., Int. Aerosp. Abstr., Energy Res. Abstr., Sci. Cit. Index, Abr. Ed., Bibliogr. Index Geol., Eng. Index. **NLM** W1 JO331. **CODEN** JOPQAG. *Journal de Physique et le Radium.*

JOURNAL DE PHYSIQUE.COLLOQUE. 1966-. 0449-1947. Monographic Series. FR. French. ir. 1760 Domestic, 2120 Foreign. Les Editions de Physique, Avenida du Hoggar, BP 112, 91944 les Ulis Cedex France. **Tel** 69.07.36.88. **Ind/Abst** Eng. Index Annu., Eng. Index Mon., Eng. Index Bioeng. Abstr., Eng. Index Energy Abstr., GeoRef, Comput. Control Abstr., Electr. Electron. Abstr., Sci. Abstr. Sect. A. Phys. Abstr., Nuci. Sci. Abstr., Chem. Abstr., Energy Res. Abstr. **LC** UNC. **CODEN** JPQCAK. bk rev. adv acc. **Circ** 1,200. (ctrl). Includes original articles in different fields: theoretical physics mechanics, hydrodynamics, nuclear physics, atomic and molecular physics, plasma, physics, physics of condensed matter and book reviews.

JOURNAL OF APPLIED PHYSICS. V. 1- July 1931-. 0021-8979. Periodical. US. English. mo. $23.00 Members, $85.00 Nonmembers. Subscription Fulfillment Division, 335 East 45th Street, New York NY 10017. **Ind/Abst** Chem. Abstr., Eng. Index, Eng. Index Mon., Int. Aerosp. Abstr., Sel. Water Resour. Abstr., Nuci. Sci. Abstr., Sci. Cit. Index, Abr. Ed., Pet. Abstr., Fluidex, Eng. Index Energy Abstr., World Text Abstr., Coal Abstr., Abstr. Bull. Inst. Paper Chem., Comput. Control Abstr., Electr. Electron. Abstr., Sci. Abstr. Sect. A. Phys. Abstr., Met. Abstr., World Alum. Abstr., Energy Res. Abstr., Appl. Mech. Rev., Phys. Abstr. **LC** QC1. **DD** 530.5. **CODEN** JAPIAU. Available on microform.

THE JOURNAL OF CHEMICAL PHYSICS. **VFOAT** Chemical Physics. V. 1- Jan. 1933-. 0021-9606. Periodical. US. English. sm. American Institute of Physics, 335 East 45th Street, New York NY 10017. **Tel** (516)349-7800. **Ind/Abst** Can. Environ., Abstr. Bull. Inst. Paper Chem., Comput. Control Abstr., Electr. Electron. Abstr., Sci. Abstr. Sect. A. Phys. Abstr., Chem. Abstr., Curr. Phys. Index, Spin, Int. Aerosp. Abstr., Math. Rev., Nuci. Sci. Abstr., Energy Res. Abstr., Pet. Abstr., Phys. Abstr., Sci. Cit. Index, Abr. Ed., Appl. Mech. Rev. **LC** QD1. **DD** 541.05. **NLM** W1 JO581J. **CODEN** JCPSA6. Available on microfilm.

JOURNAL OF COMPUTATIONAL PHYSICS. V. 1- Aug. 1966-. 0021-9991. Periodical. US. English. mo. Academic Press, 4805 Sand Lake Road, Orlando FL 32819. **Ind/Abst** Math. Rev., Int. Aerosp. Abstr., GeoRef, Comput. Control Abstr., Electr. Electron. Abstr., Sci. Abstr. Sect. A. Phys. Abstr., Chem. Abstr., Spin, Energy Res. Abstr. **LC** QC20. **DD** 530.15. **CODEN** JCTPAH.

JOURNAL OF FLUID MECHANICS. 0022-1120. Periodical. UK. English. mo. $735.00. Cambridge University Press, 510 North Avenue, New Rochelle NY 10801. **Tel** (212)688-8885. **Ed** G K Batchelor. **Ind/Abst** Appl. Mech. Rev., Eng. Index, Int. Aerosp. Abstr., Math. Rev., Sci. Cit. Index, Abr. Ed., Pet. Abstr., Electr. Electron. Abstr., Phys. Abstr., Comput. Control Abstr., Bibliogr. Index Geol. bk rev. Publishes research into the foundations and the applications of fluid mechanics.

JOURNAL OF GEOPHYSICAL RESEARCH. A, SPACE PHYSICS. (JOURNAL OF GEOPHYSICAL RESEARCH. SPACE PHYSICS). **VFOAT** Space Physics. V. 72, No. 21 (Nov. 1, 1967)-. 0196-6928. Periodical. US. English. mo. $30.00 Member. American Geophysical Union, 1909 K Street NW, Washington DC 20006. **Ind/Abst** GeoRef, Chem. Abstr., Spin. **CODEN** JJGPD4. Available in microfiche. *Journal of Geophysical Research, 0148-0227.*

JOURNAL OF LOW TEMPERATURE PHYSICS. V. 1- Feb. 1969-. 0022-2291. Periodical. US. English. mo. $635.00 Domestic, $711.00 Foreign. Plenum Publishing Corporation, 227 West 17th Street, New York NY 10011. **Tel** (212)620-8000. **Ed** John G Daunt and John P Harrison. **Ind/Abst** Electron. Commun. Abstr. J., ISMEC Bull., Pollut. Abstr. Indexes, Saf. Sci. Abstr. J., Eng. Index Mon., Eng. Index Bioeng. Abstr., Eng. Index Energy Abstr., Int. Aerosp. Abstr., Comput. Control Abstr., Sci. Abstr. Sect. A. Phys. Abstr., Met. Abstr., World Alum. Abstr., Spin, Electr. Electron. Abstr., Nuci. Sci. Abstr., Eng. Index Annu., Appl. Mech. Rev., Chem. Abstr., Curr. Contents, Phys. Abstr., Electr. Electron. Abstr., Energy Res. Abstr. **LC** QC278. **DD** 536.5605. **CODEN** JLTPAC. An international medium for the publication of original papers on fundamental theoretical and experimental research in ion temperature physics.

JOURNAL OF MACROMOLECULAR SCIENCE. PHYSICS. (JOURNAL OF MACROMOLECULAR SCIENCE. PART B. PHYSICS). V. B1- March 1967-. 0022-2348. Periodical. US. English. qt. $225.00. Marcel Dekker Inc, Journals Department, PO Box 11305, Church Street Station, New York NY 10249. **Tel** (212)696-9000. **Ed** Phillip H Geil. **Ind/Abst** Eng. Index Annu., Eng. Index Mon., Eng. Index Bioeng. Abstr., Eng. Index Energy Abstr., Int. Aerosp. Abstr., Comput. Control Abstr., Electr. Electron. Abstr., Sci. Abstr. Sect. A. Phys. Abstr., Chem. Abstr., Nuci. Sci. Abstr., Sci. Cit. Index, Abr. Ed., Eng. Index. **LC** QD380. **DD** 547.705. **NLM** W1 JO748C. **CODEN** JMAPBR. bk rev. adv acc. (ctrl). Devoted to the publication of significant fundamental contributions to the physics of macromolecular solids and liquids. *Journal of Macromolecular Chemistry.*

JOURNAL OF MATHEMATICAL AND PHYSICAL SCIENCES. *See* Mathematics.

JOURNAL OF MATHEMATICAL PHYSICS. V. 1- Jan./Feb. 1960-. 0022-2488. Periodical. US. English. mo. American Institute of Physics, 335 East 45th Street, New York NY 10017. **Tel** (516)349-7800. **Ind/Abst** Electron. Commun. Abstr. J., ISMEC Bull., Pollut. Abstr. Indexes, Saf. Sci. Abstr. J., Comput. Control Abstr., Electr. Electron. Abstr., Sci. Abstr. Sect. A. Phys. Abstr., Spin, Curr. Phys. Index, Biol. Abstr., Chem. Abstr., Int. Aerosp. Abstr., Math. Rev., Nuci. Sci. Abstr., Energy Res. Abstr., Appl. Mech. Rev., Phys. Abstr., Sci. Cit. Index, Abr. Ed. **LC** QC20. **CODEN** JMAPAQ. Microfilm editions of back volumes available on 16 mm and 35 mm.

JOURNAL OF MOLECULAR SPECTROSCOPY. V. 1- July 1957-. 0022-2852. Periodical. US. English. mo. Academic Press, 4805 Sand Lake Road, Orlando FL 32819. **Ind/Abst** Life Sci. Collect., Abstr. Bull. Inst. Paper Chem., Comput. Control Abstr., Electr. Electron. Abstr., Sci. Abstr. Sect. A. Phys. Abstr., Bibliogr. Agric., Biol. Abstr., Chem. Abstr., Int. Aerosp. Abstr., Nuci. Sci. Abstr. **LC** QC451. **DD** 539.105. **NLM** W1 JO774. **CODEN** JMOSA3.

JOURNAL OF PHYSICS A. MATHEMATICAL AND GENERAL. (JOURNAL OF PHYSICS A : MATHEMATICAL AND GENERAL). V. 8- Jan. 1975-. 0305-4470. Periodical. UK. English. mo. $150.00. American Institute of Physics, Department N/M, 335 East 45th Street, New York NY 10017. **Ind/Abst** Math. Rev., Int. Aerosp. Abstr., GeoRef, Comput. Control Abstr., Electr. Electron. Abstr., Sci. Abstr. Sect. A. Phys. Abstr., Eng. Index, Chem. Abstr. **LC** QC1. **DD** 530.05. **NLM** W1 JO836RB. **CODEN** JPHAC5. *Journal of Physics A. Mathematical, Nuclear and General, 0301-0015.*

THE JOURNAL OF PHYSICS AND CHEMISTRY OF SOLIDS. V. 24-. 0022-3697. Periodical. UK. English. mo. Pergamon Press, 395 Sawmill River Road, Elmsford NY 10523.

Tel (914)592-7700. **Ind/Abst** Eng. Index Annu., Eng. Index Mon., Eng. Index Bioeng. Abstr., Eng. Index Energy Abstr., GeoRef, Comput. Control Abstr., Electr. Electron. Abstr., Sci. Abstr. Sect. A. Phys. Abstr., Met. Abstr., World Alum. Abstr., Energy Res. Abstr., Chem. Abstr., Nucl. Sci. Abstr., Int. Aerosp. Abstr., Appl. Mech. Rev., Phys. Abstr., Sci. Cit. Index, Abr. Ed., Bibliogr. Index Geol., Eng. Index. **NLM** W1 JO836S. **CODEN** JPCSAW. Available on microfilm from Microforms International Marketing Corporation. *Physics and Chemistry of Solids.*

JOURNAL OF PHYSICS D. APPLIED PHYSICS. (JOURNAL OF PHYSICS D : APPLIED PHYSICS). **VFOAT** Applied Physics. V. 3- Jan. 1970-. 0022-3727. Periodical. UK. English. mo. $295.00. American Institute of Physics, 335 East 45th Street, New York NY 10017. **Tel** (516)349-7800. **Ind/Abst** Eng. Index Annu., Eng. Index Mon., Eng. Index Bioeng. Abstr., Fluidex, World Text Abstr., Coal Abstr., Abstr. Bull. Inst. Paper Chem., GeoRef, CIS Abstr., Comput. Control Abstr., Electr. Electron. Abstr., Sci. Abstr. Sect. A. Phys. Abstr., Met. Abstr., World Alum. Abstr., Int. Aerosp. Abstr., Nucl. Sci. Abstr., Chem. Abstr., Eng. Index, Appl. Sci. Technol. Index, Appl. Mech. Rev., Phys. Abstr., Sci. Cit. Index, Abr. Ed. **LC** QC1. **DD** 530.05. **NLM** W1 JO836V. **CODEN** JPAPBE. *British Journal of Applied Physics. Series 2. Journal of Physics D.*

JOURNAL OF PHYSICS F. METAL PHYSICS. (JOURNAL OF PHYSICS F : METAL PHYSICS). V. 1- Jan. 1971-. 0305-4608. Periodical. UK. English. mo. American Institute of Physics, 335 East 45th Street, New York NY 10017. **Ind/Abst** Electron. Commun. Abstr. J., ISMEC Bull., Pollut. Abstr. Indexes, Saf. Sci. Abstr. J., Comput. Control Abstr., Electr. Electron. Abstr., Sci. Abstr. Sect. A. Phys. Abstr., Met. Abstr., World Alum. Abstr., Int. Aerosp. Abstr., Nucl. Sci. Abstr., Chem. Abstr., Eng. Index Annu. **LC** QC176.A1. **DD** 546.305. **CODEN** JPFMAT. Index in last issue of volume - attached. *Metal Physics.*

JOURNAL OF PLASMA PHYSICS. V. 1- Feb. 1967-. 0022-3778. Periodical. UK. English. bm. $395.00. Cambridge University Press, 510 North Avenue, New Rochelle NY 10801. **Tel** (914)235-0300. **Ed** J P Dougherty. **Ind/Abst** Electron. Commun. Abstr. J., ISMEC Bull., Pollut. Abstr. Indexes, Saf. Sci. Abstr. J., Eng. Index Annu., Eng. Index Mon., Eng. Index Bioeng. Abstr., Eng. Index Energy Abstr., Comput. Control Abstr., Electr. Electron. Abstr., Sci. Abstr. Sect. A. Phys. Abstr., Int. Aerosp. Abstr., Chem. Abstr., Nucl. Sci. Abstr., Energy Res. Abstr., Appl. Mech. Rev., Phys. Abstr., Sci. Cit. Index, Abr. Ed. **LC** QC718. **DD** 537.1605. **CODEN** JPLPBZ. bk rev. Publishes research into the behavior and uses of ionized media. Both theoretical and experimental papers are published, including numerical investigations of theoretical problems.

JOURNAL OF QUANTITATIVE SPECTROSCOPY AND RADIATIVE TRANSFER. UK. English. mo. Pergamon Press, 395 Sawmill River Road, Elmsford NY 10532. **Tel** (914)592-7700. **Ind/Abst** Sci. Cit. Index, Abr. Ed., Phys. Abstr., Appl. Mech. Rev., Chem. Abstr., Comput. Control Abstr., Electr. Electron. Abstr., Int. Aerosp. Abstr.

JOURNAL OF STATISTICAL PHYSICS PHYSICS. *See* Statistics.

JOURNAL OF TECHNICAL PHYSICS. V. 16- 1975-. 0324-8313. Periodical. US. English (summaries in Polish and Russian). VCH Publishers Inc, 303 Northwest 12th Avenue, Deerfield Beach FL 33442. **Tel** (305)428-5566. **Ind/Abst** Math. Rev., Eng. Index Annu., Eng. Index Mon., Eng. Index Bioeng. Abstr., Eng. Index Energy Abstr., Int. Aerosp. Abstr., Comput. Control Abstr., Electr. Electron. Abstr., Sci. Abstr. Sect. A. Phys. Abstr., Chem. Abstr., Appl. Mech. Rev., Sociol. Abstr., Phys. Abstr., Lang. Lang. Behav. Abstr., Eng. Index. **LC** TA355. **DD** 620.1005. **CODEN** JTPHDR. *Proceedings of Vibration Problems.*

JOURNAL OF THE ALABAMA ACADEMY OF SCIENCE. *See* Biology.

JOURNAL OF THE EARTH AND SPACE PHYSICS. **VFOAT** Journal of Earth and Space Physics. V. 1- 1972-. 0378-1046. Periodical. IR. English (French, German, or Farsi). ir. University of Tehran-Institute Geophysics, Shahreza Avenue, Tehran Iran. **Ind/Abst** GeoRef, Bibliogr. Index Geol. **CODEN** JESPCS.

JOURNAL OF THE PHYSICAL SOCIETY OF JAPAN. **Main/Corp** Nippon Butsuri Gakkai. V. 1- July/Dec. 1946-. 0031-9015. JA. English. mo. $367.20. Japan Publications Trading Company, PO Box 5030, Tokyo International, Tokyo 100-31 Japan. **Tel** (292)3751-9. **Ind/Abst** Math. Rev., Eng. Index Annu., Eng. Index Mon., Eng. Index Bioeng. Abstr., Eng. Index Energy Abstr., Int. Aerosp. Abstr., GeoRef, Comput. Control Abstr., Electr. Electron. Abstr., Sci. Abstr. Sect. A. Phys. Abstr., Met. Abstr., World Alum. Abstr., Chem. Abstr., Appl. Mech. Rev., Eng. Index, Sci. Cit. Index, Abr. Ed. **LC** QC1. **DD** 530.5. **CODEN** JUPSAU. Index in last issue of volume - attached. (cum index). Available on microfiche. *Proceedings of the Physico-Mathematical Society of Japan.*

JOURNAL OF THERMOPHYSICS AND HEAT TRANSFER. 0887-8722. Periodical. US. English. qt. American Institute of Aeronautics and Astronautics, PO Box 11312/Church Street Station, New York NY 10249.

THE JOURNAL OF UNDERGRADUATE RESEARCH IN PHYSICS. Vol. 1, No. 1 (Apr. 1982)-. 0731-3764. Periodical. US. English. sa. $10.00. Guilford College, Department of Physics, c/o R Adelberger, Greensboro NC 27410. **Tel** (919)292-5511. **Ed** Rexford E Adelberger. **Circ** 750. Devoted to research done by undergraduate students in physics and physics related fields.

JOURNAL OF VACUUM SCIENCE & TECHNOLOGY. A. VACUUM, SURFACES, AND FILMS. (JOURNAL OF VACUUM SCIENCE & TECHNOLOGY. A, VACUUM, SURFACES, AND FILMS : AN OFFICIAL JOURNAL OF THE AMERICAN VACUUM SOCIETY). **VFOAT** Journal of Vacuum Science and Technology. 2nd Ser., V. 1, No. 1 (Jan. - Mar.)-. 0734-2101. Periodical. US. English. bm. American Institute of Physics, 355 East 45 Street, New York NY 10017. **Ind/Abst** Met. Abstr., World Alum. Abstr., Spin, Chem. Abstr., Curr. Phys. Index, Coal Abstr. **LC** TJ940. **DD** 621.5505. **CODEN** JVTAD6. Issued also on microfilm. *Journal of Vacuum Science and Technology, 0022-5355.*

JOURNAL OF VACUUM SCIENCE & TECHNOLOGY. B, MICROELECTRONICS PROCESSING AND PHENOMENA. (JOURNAL OF VACUUM SCIENCE & TECHNOLOGY. B, MICROELECTRONICS PROCESSING AND PHENOMENA : AN OFFICIAL JOURNAL OF THE AMERICAN VACUUM SOCIETY). **VFOAT** Journal of Vacuum Science and Technology. 2nd Ser., V. 1, No. 1, (Jan./March 1983)-. 0734-211X. Periodical. US. English. bm. $200.00 US, $210.00 Foreign. AIP Subscription Fulfillment Division, 500 Sunnyside Boulevard, Woodbury NY 11797. **Ind/Abst** Met. Abstr., World Alum. Abstr., Spin, Chem. Abstr., Coal Abstr., Curr. Phys. Index. **DD** 621. **CODEN** JVTBD9. Issued also on microfilm. *Journal of Vacuum Science and Technology, 0022-5355.*

JURNAL FIZIK MALAYSIA. Vol. 5, No. 1 (Mar. 1984)-. Periodical. MY. English. qt. Business Manager Jurnal Fizik Malaysia, d/a Jabatan Kizit, Universiti Malaysia, Kuala Lumpur 22-11 Malaysia. *Buletin Fizik, 0126-9674.*

KHIMICHESKAIA FIZIKA. (SOVIET JOURNAL OF CHEMICAL PHYSICS). Began with: 1982, No. 1 (Nov. 1983). 0733-2831. Periodical. US. English (Russian). ir. $722.00. Gordon & Breach, PO Box 197, London WC2E 9PX England. **Ed** N N Semenov. **LC** QD450. **DD** 539. **CODEN** SJCPDF. bk rev. adv acc.

KINAM. (KINAM : REVISTA DE FISICA). Vol. 1, No. 1-. 0185-125X. Periodical. MX. English (text in French, Spanish and Portuguese with abstracts in English and Spanish). qt. $50.00. KINAM, Apartado Postal 20-454 Mexico 20 DF Mexico. **Ind/Abst** Math. Rev., Comput. Control Abstr., Electr. Electron. Abstr., Sci. Abstr. Sect. A. Phys. Abstr., Chem. Abstr., Energy Res. Abstr. **LC** QC1. **DD** 530.05. **CODEN** KINADW.

KONFERENZTERMINE ENERGIE, PHYSIK, MATHEMATIK. *See* Energy.

KONGELIGE DANSKE VIDENSKABERNES SELSKAB. MATEMATISK-FYSISKE MEDDELELSER. *See* Mathematics.

LASER APPLICATIONS. *See* Engineering - Electricity, Electrical Engineering, Electronics.

LASER INTERACTION AND RELATED PLASMA PHENOMENA. **Main/Conf** Workshop on Laser Interaction and Related Plasma Phenomena, Rensselaer Polytechnic Institute. 1st- 1969-. 0148-0987. US. English. ir. Plenum Press, 233 Spring Street, New York NY 10013. **Tel** (212)620-8000. **Ind/Abst** Chem. Abstr. **CODEN** LIPPAR.

LASER UND OPTOELEKTRONIK. 14. Vol. No. 1 (Apr. 1982)-. 0722-9003. Periodical. English (German). qt. 66.- Domestic, 85.- Foreign. AT-Fachverlag, Postfach 50 01 80, 7000 Stuttgart 50 West Germany. **Tel** 0711/52 70 41. **Ind/Abst** Comput. Control Abstr., Electr. Electron. Abstr., Sci. Abstr. Sect. A. Phys. Abstr., Energy Res. Abstr. **LC** TA1671. **DD** 621.36605. **NLM** W1. **CODEN** LAOPD3. bk rev. adv acc. **Circ** 3,015. Active in research, applications, development and manufacturing in the field of lasers and optoelectronics in technology, communications, physics, chemistry, analysis, biology and medicine. *Laser + Elektro-Optik, 0344-5186.*

LECTURE NOTES IN PHYSICS. 1-. 0075-8450. Monographic Series. English (French and German). ir. Springer Verlag-New York Inc, 175 5th Avenue, New York NY 10010. **Tel** (212)460-1584. **Ind/Abst** Comput. Control Abstr., Electr. Electron. Abstr., Sci. Abstr. Sect. A. Phys. Abstr., Chem. Abstr., Energy Res. Abstr., Appl. Mech. Rev., Sci. Cit. Index, Abr. Ed., Math. Rev., Phys. Abstr. **CODEN** LNPHA4. Contains articles on solutions of Einsteins equations, phase transitions in equilibrium nonequilibrium systems and nuclear physics.

LETTERE AL NUOVO CIMENTO. V. 1-4, 1969-1970. 0024-1318. Periodical. IT. Italian. wk. Editrice Compositori, Viale XII Giugno 1, 40124 Bologna Italy. **Ind/Abst** Chem. Abstr., Math. Rev., Comput. Control Abstr., Electr. Electron. Abstr., Sci. Abstr. Sect. A. Phys. Abstr., Energy Res. Abstr., Met. Abstr., World Alum. Abstr. **LC** QC1. **CODEN** LNUCAE.

LETTERS IN MATHEMATICAL PHYSICS. V. 1- Dec. 1975-. 0377-9017. Periodical. English. qt. 134. Kluwer Academic Publishers Group, PO Box 322, 3300 AH Dordrecht Netherlands. **Tel** (31)78-334911. **Ed** M Flato. **Ind/Abst** Math. Rev., Electron. Commun. Abstr. J., ISMEC Bull., Pollut. Abstr. Indexes, Saf. Sci. Abstr. J., Comput. Control Abstr., Electr. Electron. Abstr., Sci. Abstr. Sect. A. Phys. Abstr., Chem. Abstr., Phys. Abstr., Sci. Cit. Index, Abr. Ed. **LC** QC19.2. **DD** 530.1505. **CODEN** LMPHDY. bk rev. adv acc. **Circ** 650. Group theory and applications to physics; quantum-field theory; mathematical models for particle, nuclear, plasma, and solid-state physics; classical, quantum, and statistical mechanics.

LITOVSKIJ FIZICESKIJ SBORNIK. (LITOVSKII FIZICHESKII SBORNIK). **VFOAT** Lietuvos Fizikos Rinkinys. 1- 1961-. 0024-2969. Periodical. UR. Russian (summaries in Lithuanian, English, French, or German). bm. $39.50. Victor Kamkin Inc (76715), 12224 Parklawn Drive, Rockville MD 20852. **Tel** (301)881-5973. **Ind/Abst** Math. Rev., Electron. Commun. Abstr. J., ISMEC Bull., Pollut. Abstr. Indexes, Saf. Sci. Abstr. J., Int. Aerosp. Abstr., Comput. Control Abstr., Electr. Electron. Abstr., Sci. Abstr. Sect. A. Phys. Abstr., Met. Abstr., World Alum. Abstr., Chem. Abstr. **LC** QC1. **CODEN** LFRMA7.

LNG/CRYOGENICS. **VFOAT** Cyrogenics. V. 1- Feb./Mar. 1973-. Periodical. US. English. bm. $20.00. Barrington Publications, 825 South Barrington Avenue, Los Angeles CA 90049. **LC** TP761.L5. **DD** 665.73.

LOW TEMPERATURE PHYSICS; PROCEEDINGS. **Main/Conf** International Conference on Low Temperature Physics. English (Vol. for 1955 in French). ir. 233 Spring Street, New York NY 10013. **LC** QC278. **DD** 536.5608.

MAGYAR FIZIKAI FOLYOIRAT. Vol. 1-. 0025-0104. Periodical. HU. Hungarian. bm. 90. Medical University, PO Box 263, 1444 Budapest Hungary. **Tel** 339-599. **Ed** G Turchanyi. **Ind/Abst** Comput. Control Abstr., Electr. Electron. Abstr., Sci. Abstr. Sect. A. Phys. Abstr., Chem. Abstr., Phys. Abstr., Appl. Mech. Rev. **LC** QC1. **CODEN** MGFFAC. bk rev. **Circ** 450. Diagnostic methods and plasma scattering equipment. Nonlinear model of the anisotropic fiberstructure of the artery wall. Irreversible thermodynamic theory of the transport processes and its application for the research of the superconductors.

MAJALLAH-I FIZIK. **VFOAT** Iranian Journal of Physics. V. 1, No. 1, (Winter 1983)-. Periodical. IR. Persian, Modern. qt. 19.00. Khiyaban-I Shahid-I Duktur-I Bihishti, Khiyaban-I Park, Shumarah-I 85 Tehran Iran. **Tel** 626031. **Ed** R Mansourit. **LC** QC1. bk rev. **Circ** 3,500. Contains original research and instructional papers, review articles, translation of articles from international journals, book reviews, new books, problems, news, and news of Iranian Physical Society.

MECHANICS OF SOLIDS. **Main/Corp** Akademiia Nauk SSSR. 0025-6544. Periodical. US. English (Russian). bm. Allerton Press Inc, 150 Fifth Avenue, New York NY 10011. **Tel** (212)924-3950. **Ind/Abst** Math. Rev., Electron. Commun. Abstr. J., ISMEC

Physics

Bull., Pollut. Abstr. Indexes, Saf. Sci. Abstr. J., Eng. Index Annu., Eng. Index Mon., Eng. Index Bioeng. Abstr., Eng. Index Energy Abstr., Int. Aerosp. Abstr., Comput. Control Abstr., Electr. Electron. Abstr., Sci. Abstr. Sect. A. Phys. Abstr. LC QC176.A1. DD 530.41. **CODEN** MESOBN. *Mechanics of Solids, 0025-6544.*

MEDICAL PHYSICS. V. 1- 1974-. 0094-2405. Periodical. US. English. bm. American Institute of Physics, 335 East 45th Street, New York NY 10017. **Tel** (516)349-7800. **Ind/Abst** Electron. Commun. Abstr. J., ISMEC Bull., Pollut. Abstr. Indexes, Saf. Sci. Abstr. J., Excerpta Med., Index Med., Life Sci. Collect., Int. Aerosp. Abstr., Biol. Abstr., Comput. Control Abstr., Electr. Electron. Abstr., Sci. Abstr. Sect. A. Phys. Abstr., Energy Res. Abstr., Spin, Chem. Abstr., Curr. Phys. Index, Phys. Abstr., Hospit. Lit. Index. LC R895.A1. DD 610153. NLM W1 ME409R. **CODEN** MPHYA6. *Quarterly Bulletin - American Association of Physicists in Medicine, 0001-0162.*

MEDICAL PHYSICS HANDBOOKS. 1-. 0143-0203. Monographic Series. UK. English. **Ind/Abst** Comput. Control Abstr., Electr. Electron. Abstr., Sci. Abstr. Sect. A. Phys. Abstr. NLM W1 ME409V.

MEDICAL PHYSICS MONOGRAPH. Began in 1978?. 0163-1802. Monographic Series. US. English. LC UNC. DD 610.153. NLM W1 ME409W. *AAPM Monograph.*

MEMOIRS OF THE FACULTY OF SCIENCE, KYOTO UNIVERSITY. SERIES OF PHYSICS, ASTROPHYSICS, GEOPHYSICS AND CHEMISTRY. **Main/Corp** Kyoto Daigaku. Rigakubu. V. 32- Sept. 1967-. 0368-9689. JA. English. ir. Kyoto University, Faculty of Science, Kyoto 606 Japan. **Ind/Abst** Int. Aerosp. Abstr., Comput. Control Abstr., Electr. Electron. Abstr., Sci. Abstr. Sect. A. Phys. Abstr., Chem. Abstr. LC Q77. DD 500.208. **CODEN** MFKPAQ. *Memoirs of the College of Science, University of Kyoto. Series A.*

METHODS OF EXPERIMENTAL PHYSICS. V. 1-. 0076-695X. Monographic Series. US. English. ir. Academic Press, 4805 Sand Lake Road, Orlando FL 32887. **Tel** (305)345-4100. Ed Robert Celotta and Judah Levine. **Ind/Abst** Comput. Control Abstr., Electr. Electron. Abstr., Sci. Abstr. Sect. A. Phys. Abstr., Chem. Abstr., Nuci. Sci. Abstr., Phys. Abstr. LC UNC. **CODEN** MEEPAN.

METODOLOGICHESKIE VOPROSY FIZIKI. 2-. Periodical. UR. Russian (summaries in Estonian, and English or German). 0.47 Each Issue. Tartu Riiklik Ulikoo, Ul Iulikooki 18 Tartu, Estonia USSR. LC AS262.T22, QC6. *Filosofskie Voprosy Fiziki.*

MOLECULAR PHYSICS. V. 1- Jan. 1958-. 0026-8976. Periodical. UK. English (articles in French or German). ir. $860.00. Taylor & Francis Ltd, 242 Cherry Street, Philadelphia PA 19106. **Tel** (215)238-0939. Ed R F Barrow. **Ind/Abst** Math. Rev., Electron. Commun. Abstr. J., ISMEC Bull., Pollut. Abstr. Indexes, Saf. Sci. Abstr. J., Int. Aerosp. Abstr., Comput. Control Abstr., Electr. Electron. Abstr., Sci. Abstr. Sect. A. Phys. Abstr., Chem. Abstr., Phys. Abstr., Sci. Cit. Index, Abr. Ed. LC QC173. DD 539.605. **CODEN** MOPHAM. Index in last issue of volume - attached. (cum index). Contains original research papers on chemical physics, including all aspects of the physics of molecules and, particularly, on the molecular structure, properties, dynamics and collisions, and on the equilibrium, transport and relaxation properties of molecular assemblies.

MOSCOW UNIVERSITY PHYSICS BULLETIN. **Main/Corp** Moscow. Universitet. V. 21-. 0027-1349. Monographic Series. US. English (Russian). bm. Allerton Press Inc, 150 Fifth Avenue, New York NY 10011. **Tel** (212)924-3950. **Ind/Abst** Math. Rev., Int. Aerosp. Abstr., Phys. Abstr., Electr. Electron. Abstr., Comput. Control Abstr., Sci. Abstr. Sect. A. Phys. Abstr. LC Q4. DD 530.05. **CODEN** MUPBAC.

NACHRICHTEN DER AKADEMIE DER WISSENSCHAFTEN IN GOTTINGEN. 2. MATHEMATISCH-PHYSIKALISCHE KLASSE. *See* Mathematics.

NATIONAL BUREAU OF STANDARDS MONOGRAPH. (NBS MONOGRAPH). VFOAT N.B.S. Monograph. 1-. 0083-1832. Monographic Series. US. English. ir. National Bureau of Standards, Room E120/Adm Voice of Z39, Washington DC 20234. **Ind/Abst** GeoRef, Chem. Abstr., Nuci. Sci. Abstr. LC QC100. DD 602.18. **CODEN** NBSMA6. *National Bureau of Standards Circular, 0096-9648.*

NATIONAL BUREAU OF STANDARDS SPECIAL PUBLICATION. (NBS SPECIAL PUBLICATION). VFOAT National Bureau of Standards Special Publication. Began with: No. 295 in 1968. 0083-1883. Monographic Series. US. English. ir. National Bureau of Standards, Room E120/ADM Voice of 239, Washington DC 20234. **Ind/Abst** Eng. Index Annu., Eng. Index Mon., Eng. Index Bioeng. Abstr., Eng. Index Energy Abstr., Coal Abstr., GeoRef, Chem. Abstr., World Surf. Coat. Abstr., Nuci. Sci. Abstr. LC QC100. DD 389. **CODEN** XNBSAV.

NATO ADVANCED SCIENCE INSTITUTES SERIES. SERIES B, PHYSICS. VFOAT NATO ASI Series. Monographic Series. US. English. Plenum Press, Atten: H Feldman, 233 Spring Street, New York NY 10013. **Tel** (212)620-8000. **Ind/Abst** Chem. Abstr. **CODEN** NABPDS. *NATO Advanced Study Institutes Series. Series B, Physics.*

NEW TRENDS IN PHYSICS TEACHING = TENDANCES NOUVELLES DE L'ENSEIGNEMENT DE LA PHYSIQUE. VFOAT Tendances Nouvelles de l'Enseignement de la Physique. V. 1- 1965/66-. 0077-8907. Periodical. English (French). ir. UNIPUB, PO Box 1222, Ann Arbor MI 48106. **Tel** (800)521-8110. LC QC30. DD 530.071.

NEWSLETTER - CENTER FOR HISTORY OF PHYSICS. **Main/Corp** Center for History of Physics (American Institute of Physics). V. 5, No. 4- Oct. 1972-. 0148-5857. US. English. ir. 335 East 45th Street, New York NY 10017. LC QC9.U5. DD 530.0973. *Newsletter - Center for History and Philosophy of Physics, 0008-9060.*

NONLINEAR VIBRATION PROBLEMS. (ZAGADNIENIA DRGAN NIELINIOWYCH). 1-. 0044-1597. Periodical. Polish (summaries in English and Russian). ir. **Ind/Abst** Int. Aerosp. Abstr., Comput. Control Abstr., Electr. Electron. Abstr., Sci. Abstr. Sect. A. Phys. Abstr. **CODEN** NLVBAO.

NOTAS DE FISICA. V. 1- 1978-. Monographic Series. English. mo. Cent Brasil de Pesquisas Fisic, Av Wenceslau Braz 71 ZC82, Rio de Janeiro GB Brazil. **Ind/Abst** Energy Res. Abstr.

NOUVELLES DE L'A.Q.T. **Main/Corp** Association Quebecoise de Teledetection. VAT Nouvelles de l'Association Quebecoise de Teledetection. Vol. 1, No. 1 (Sept. 1983)-. 0826-2799. Periodical. CN. French. sa. Free to Members. Association Quebecoise de Teledetection, C P 10047, Ste-Foy Quebec G1V 4C6 Canada. **DD** 621.3678060714.

NOVINKY LITERATURY : MATEMATIKA-FYZIKA. *See* Bibliographies.

NU SCIENCE. V. 1- Mar. 1968-. Periodical. SA. English. ir. University of Natal, Science Council, King George 5th Avenue, Durban South Africa. LC QC1. DD 505.

NUOVO CIMENTO DELLA SOCIETA ITALIANA DE FISICA, SEZIONE D. (IL NUOVO CIMENTO DELLA SOCIETA ITALIANA DI FISICA. DELETE). VFOAT Condensed Matter, Atomic, Molecular and Chemical Physics, Biophysics, D, Condensed Matter, Atomic, Molecular and Chemical Physics, Biophysics. Vol. 1, No. 1 Jan.-Feb. 1982-. 0392-6737. Periodical. English (French, German, Italian or Spanish). bm. 265.00 Members, 330.00 Nonmembers. Editrice Compositori SRL, Viale XLL Guigno 1, 40124 Bologna Italy. **Tel** (051)583149. **Ind/Abst** Math. Rev., Chem. Abstr. **CODEN** NCSDDN. **Circ** 500. (ctrl). Atomic and molecular physics.

OBZORNIK ZA MATEMATIKO IN FIZIKO. *See* Mathematics.

OXFORD PHYSICS SERIES. No. 1-. Monographic Series. UK. English. ir. Oxford University Press, 16-00 Pollitt Drive, Fair Lawn NJ 07410. **Ind/Abst** Comput. Control Abstr., Electr. Electron. Abstr., Sci. Abstr. Sect. A. Phys. Abstr. **CODEN** OXPSD7.

PAPER SUMMARIES - AMERICAN SOCIETY FOR NONDESTRUCTIVE TESTING. *See* Engineering.

PARTICLE ACCELERATORS. V. 1- March 1970-. 0031-2460. Periodical. US. English. ir. $286.00. Harwood Academic Publishers, PO Box 197, London WC2E 9PX England. Ed F T Cole. **Ind/Abst** Eng. Index Mon., Eng. Index Bioeng. Abstr., Eng. Index Energy Abstr., Comput. Control Abstr., Electr. Electron. Abstr., Sci. Abstr. Sect. A. Phys. Abstr., Eng. Index Annu., Eng. Index Annu., Chem. Abstr., Nuci. Sci. Abstr., Phys. Abstr., Eng. Index. LC QC787.P3. DD 539.7305. **CODEN** PLACBD. bk rev. adv acc.

PERSPECTIVE OF PHYSICS. (A PERSPECTIVE OF PHYSICS). V. 1- 1976-. 0260-4280. UK. English. an. One Park Avenue, New York NY 10016. LC QC1. DD 530.05.

PHASE TRANSITIONS. V. 1- Sept. 1979-. 0141-1594. Periodical. US. English. ir. $188.00. Gordon & Breach, PO Box 197, London WC2E 9PX England. Ed A M Glazer. **Ind/Abst** Eng. Index Mon., Eng. Index Bioeng. Abstr., Eng. Index Energy Abstr., Comput. Control Abstr., Electr. Electron. Abstr., Sci. Abstr. Sect. A. Phys. Abstr., Met. Abstr., World Alum. Abstr., Chem. Abstr., Eng. Index Annu., Phys. Abstr., Appl. Mech. Rev., Eng. Index. LC QC176.8.P45. DD 536.40105. **CODEN** PHTRDP. bk rev. adv acc.

PHASE TRANSITIONS AND CRITICAL PHENOMENA. Vol. 1-. Monographic Series. UK. English. ir. Academic Press, 4805 Sand Lake Road, Orlando FL 32887. **Tel** (305)345-4100. Ed C Domb and M S Green.

PHILIPS JOURNAL OF RESEARCH. V. 33-. 0165-5817. Periodical. NE. English. sm. 75.00. Philips Research Laboratories, PO Box 8000, 5600 JA Eindhoven Netherlands. **Tel** 40-742880. Ed A Van Oostrom. **Ind/Abst** Math. Rev., Electron. Commun. Abstr. J., ISMEC Bull., Pollut. Abstr. Indexes, Saf. Sci. Abstr. J., Int. Aerosp. Abstr., Comput. Control Abstr., Electr. Electron. Abstr., Sci. Abstr. Sect. A. Phys. Abstr., Met. Abstr., World Alum. Abstr., Chem. Abstr. LC Q1. DD 500.205. **CODEN** PHJRD9. **Circ** 1,700. (ctrl). Research papers describing work carried out in laboratories of Philips. *Philips Research Reports, 0031-7918.*

PHOTON. (PHOTON : PHYSICS FOR FUN). VFOAT Physics for Fun. No. 1 (Sept. 1977)-. 0715-3996. Periodical. CN. English. ir. $4.00. Photon c/o I Peterson, 2912-2 Forest Laneway, Willowdale Ont M2N Canada. DD 530.02.

PHOTOVOLTAICS TECHNIQUE. Vol. 1, No. 1 (Dec. 1982)-. 0824-3794. Periodical. CN. English. bm. $50.00. Spectral Engineering Ltd, 29 Popular Plains Crescent, Toronto Ont M4V 1E9 Canada. DD 621.381542.

PHSYICA SCRIPTA. T. (PHYSICA SCRIPTA). Vol. T1-. 0281-1847. Periodical. UK. English. ir. Royal Academy of Sciences, Publications Department, Fack S-104, 05 Stockholm Sweden. LC QC1. DD 530.05.

PHYS 13 NEWS. No. 1 (Oct. 1971)-. 0710-0140. Periodical. CN. English. ir. University of Waterloo/Faculty, Science Department, Physics Waterloo Ontario N2L 3G1 Canada. **Tel** (519)885-1211. DD 530.0712.

PHYSICA A. VFOAT Theoretical and Statistical Physics. Began with Jan. 1975 issue. 0378-4371. Periodical. NE. English (text in French or German, with abstracts in English). mo. $672.00. North Holland Publishing Company, PO Box 211, 1000 AE Amsterdam The Netherlands. **Ind/Abst** Math. Rev., Comput. Control Abstr., Electr. Electron. Abstr., Sci. Abstr. Sect. A. Phys. Abstr., Energy Res. Abstr., Chem. Abstr. LC QC1. DD 530.15. **CODEN** PHYADX. (cum index). *Physica, 0031-8914.*

PHYSICA B + C. VFOAT Physica B and C. Began with Jan. 1975 issue. 0378-4363. Periodical. NE. text in English, French, or German, with abstracts in English. mo. $768.00. North-Holland Publishing Company, PO Box 211, 1000 AE Amsterdam The Netherlands. **Ind/Abst** Math. Rev., Eng. Index Annu., Eng. Index Mon., Eng. Index Bioeng. Abstr., Eng. Index Energy Abstr., Comput. Control Abstr., Electr. Electron. Abstr., Sci. Abstr. Sect. A. Phys. Abstr., Energy Res. Abstr., Chem. Abstr. LC QC1. DD 530.05. **CODEN** PHBCDQ. *Physica, 0031-8914.*

PHYSICA. D. (PHYSICA D. NONLINEAR PHENOMENA). Began with Vol. for Apr. 1980. 0167-2789. Periodical. English. ir. Elsevier Science Publishers, PO Box 211, 1000 AE Amsterdam Netherlands. **Tel** (020)5803.911. **Ind/Abst** Math. Rev., Int. Aerosp. Abstr., Comput. Control Abstr., Electr. Electron. Abstr., Sci. Abstr. Sect. A. Phys. Abstr., Chem. Abstr. LC QC1. DD 530.05. **CODEN** PDNPDT. *Physica, 0031-8914.*

PHYSICA SCRIPTA. V. 1- 1970-. 0031-8949. Periodical. SW. English (text in French or German). mo. $350.00. Royal Swedish Academy of Science, Box 50005, S-104 05 Stockholm Sweden. **Tel** 46(0)8-15 04 30. Ed Nils Robert Nilsson. **Ind/Abst** Math. Rev., Int. Aerosp. Abstr., GeoRef, Comput. Control Abstr., Electr. Electron. Abstr., Sci. Abstr. Sect. A. Phys. Abstr., Energy Res. Abstr., Met. Abstr.,

World Alum. Abstr., Chem. Abstr., Appl. Mech. Rev., Phys. Abstr., Sci. Cit. Index, Abr. Ed., Bibliogr. Index Geol. **LC** QC1. **NLM** W1 PH683. **CODEN** PHSTBO. Index in last issue of volume - attached. **Circ** 800. General physics journal with special emphasis on cross-disciplinary fields of physics; also, topical issues included in the subscription. *Arkiv for Fysik, Physica Fennica.*

PHYSICA STATUS SOLIDI A. APPLIED RESEARCH. (PHYSICA STATUS SOLIDI. A: APPLIED RESEARCH). V. 1- Jan. 1970-. 0031-8965. Periodical. WB. English (summaries in English, French, German or Russian). mo. $720.00. VCH Publishers Inc, 303 North 12th Avenue, Deerfield Beach FL 33442. **Tel** (305)428-5566. **Ind/Abst** Energy Res. Abstr., Met. Abstr., World Alum. Abstr., Chem. Abstr., Sci. Cit. Index, Abr. Ed., Eng. Index, Phys. Abstr., Comput. Control Abstr., Electr. Electron. Abstr., Electron. Commun. Abstr. J., Pollut. Abstr. Indexes, ISMEC Bull., Eng. Index Mon., Eng. Index Annu., Eng. Index Bioeng. Abstr., Saf. Sci. Abstr. J., Int. Aerosp. Abstr., GeoRef, Eng. Index Energy Abstr., Sci. Abstr. Sect. A. Phys. Abstr. **NLM** W1 PH683F. **CODEN** PSSABA. Index published separately - free - automatically sent. (cum index). *Physica Status Solidi, 0031-8957.*

PHYSICA STATUS SOLIDI. B : BASIC RESEARCH. V. 43- Jan. 1971-. 0370-1972. Periodical. English (German, French or Russian, with summaries in English and German, French or Russian). mo. $720.00. VCH Publishers Inc, 303 North West 12th Avenue, Deerfield Beach FL 33442. **Tel** (305)428-5566. **Ind/Abst** Int. Aerosp. Abstr., Comput. Control Abstr., Electr. Electron. Abstr., Sci. Abstr. Sect. A. Phys. Abstr., Energy Res. Abstr., Met. Abstr., World Alum. Abstr., Chem. Abstr., Phys. Abstr., Eng. Index, Math. Rev., Sci. Cit. Index, Abr. Ed. **CODEN** PSSBBD. Index in last issue of volume - attached. *Physica Status Solidi, 0031-8957.*

PHYSICAL REVIEW. A. GENERAL PHYSICS. (PHYSICAL REVIEW A : GENERAL PHYSICS). V. 1- Jan. 1970-. 0556-2791. Periodical. US. English. mo. American Institute of Physics, 335 East 45th Street, New York NY 10017. **Tel** (516)349-7800. **Ind/Abst** Comput. Control Abstr., Electr. Electron. Abstr., Sci. Abstr. Sect. A. Phys. Abstr., Energy Res. Abstr., Chem. Abstr., Curr. Phys. Index, Spin, Nuci. Sci. Abstr., Int. Aerosp. Abstr., Math. Rev., Sci. Cit. Index, Abr. Ed., Phys. Abstr. **LC** QC1. **DD** 530.05. **NLM** W1 PH737A. **CODEN** PLRAAN. (cum index). *Physical Review, 0031-899X.*

PHYSICAL REVIEW ABSTRACTS. *See* Indexes/Abstracts.

PHYSICAL REVIEW AND PHYSICAL REVIEW LETTERS INDEX. *See* Indexes/Abstracts.

PHYSICAL REVIEW. B. CONDENSED MATTER. (PHYSICAL REVIEW B : CONDENSED MATTER). V. 18- July 1, 1978-. 0163-1829. Periodical. US. English. sm. American Institute of Physics, 335 East 45th Street, New York NY 10017. **Tel** (212)661-9404. **Ind/Abst** GeoRef, Comput. Control Abstr., Electr. Electron. Abstr., Sci. Abstr. Sect. A. Phys. Abstr., Abstr. Bull. Inst. Paper Chem., Energy Res. Abstr., Met. Abstr., World Alum. Abstr., Spin, Chem. Abstr., Curr. Phys. Index, Nuci. Sci. Abstr., Int. Aerosp. Abstr., Math. Rev. **LC** QC176.A1. **DD** 530.41. **CODEN** PRBMDO. *Physical Review. B. Solid State, 0556-2805.*

PHYSICAL REVIEW. D. PARTICLES AND FIELDS. (PHYSICAL REVIEW. D, PARTICLES AND FIELDS). 3rd. Ser., V. 1, No. 1 (1 Jan. 1970)-. 0556-2821. Periodical. US. English. sm. American Institute of Physics, 335 East 45th Street, New York NY 10017. **Tel** (212)661-9404. **Ind/Abst** Comput. Control Abstr., Electr. Electron. Abstr., Sci. Abstr. Sect. A. Phys. Abstr., Energy Res. Abstr., Chem. Abstr., Curr. Phys. Index, Spin, Nuci. Sci. Abstr., Int. Aerosp. Abstr., Math. Rev., Sci. Cit. Index, Abr. Ed., Phys. Abstr. **NLM** W1 PH737D. **CODEN** PRVDAQ. *Physical Review, 0031-899X.*

PHYSICAL REVIEW LETTERS. V. 1- July 1958-. 0031-9007. Periodical. US. English. wk. American Institute of Physics, 335 East 45th Street, New York NY 10017. **Tel** (212)661-9404. **Ind/Abst** GeoRef, Comput. Control Abstr., Electr. Electron. Abstr., Sci. Abstr. Sect. A. Phys. Abstr., Energy Res. Abstr., Met. Abstr., World Alum. Abstr., Chem. Abstr., Curr. Phys. Index, Spin, Nuci. Sci. Abstr., Int. Aerosp. Abstr., Math. Rev., Appl. Mech. Rev., Sci. Cit. Index, Abr. Ed., Phys. Abstr. **LC** QC1. **DD** 530.5. **NLM** W1 PH739. **CODEN** PRLTAO. (cum index). *Physical Review, 0031-899X.*

PHYSICS ABSTRACTS. *See* Indexes/Abstracts.

PHYSICS ABSTRACTS. AUTHOR INDEX. *See* Indexes/Abstracts.

PHYSICS ABSTRACTS. SUBJECT INDEX. *See* Indexes/Abstracts.

PHYSICS AND CHEMISTRY IN SPACE. V. 1- 1970-. 0079-1938. Monographic Series. GW. German. ir. Springer Verlag-New York Inc, 175 5th Avenue, New York NY 10010. **Tel** (212)460-1500. **Ed** J G Roederer and J Zahringer. **Ind/Abst** Comput. Control Abstr., Electr. Electron. Abstr., Sci. Abstr. Sect. A. Phys. Abstr., Phys. Abstr. **LC** QC801. **CODEN** PCSPDD. Numbered series.

PHYSICS AND CHEMISTRY OF LIQUIDS. V. 1- Feb. 1968-. 0031-9104. Periodical. UK. English. ir. $334.00. Harwood Academic Publishers, PO Box 197, London WC2E 9PX England. **Ed** N H March. **Ind/Abst** Eng. Index Annu., Eng. Index Mon., Eng. Index Bioeng. Abstr., Eng. Index Energy Abstr., Comput. Control Abstr., Electr. Electron. Abstr., Sci. Abstr. Sect. A. Phys. Abstr., Energy Res. Abstr., Chem. Abstr., Nuci. Sci. Abstr., Appl. Mech. Rev., Sci. Cit. Index, Abr. Ed., Phys. Abstr., Eng. Index. **LC** QD541. **DD** 530.4205. **CODEN** PCLQAC. bk rev. adv acc.

PHYSICS AND CHEMISTRY OF MATERIALS WITH LAYERED STRUCTURES. 0378-1917. NE. English. ir. D Reidel Publishing Company, 160 Old Derby Street, Hingham MA 02043. **Ind/Abst** Chem. Abstr. **LC** QD478. **DD** 530.41. **CODEN** PCMSDQ.

PHYSICS AND CONTEMPORARY NEEDS. **Main/Conf** International Summer College on Physics and Contemporary Needs. V. 1- 1976-. 0163-2051. US. English. ir. Plenum Publishing Corporation, 233 Spring Street, New York NY 10013. **Tel** (212)620-8000. **Ind/Abst** Chem. Abstr. **LC** QC1. **DD** 530. **CODEN** PCONDL.

PHYSICS BRIEFS. **VFOAT** Physikalische Berichte. V. 1- Jan. 15, 1979-. 0170-7434. Periodical. US. English. sm. American Institute of Physics, 355 East 4th Street, Subscription Fulfillment, New York NY 10017. **Ind/Abst** Energy Res. Abstr., Chem. Abstr. **LC** QC1. **DD** 016.53. **NLM** Z 7141 P578. **CODEN** PHBRD3. Each issue contains an index to its own contents - no vol index - loose. *Physikalische Berichte.*

PHYSICS BULLETIN. V. 19- Jan. 1968-. 0031-9112. Periodical. UK. English. mo. American Institute of Physics, 335 East 45th Street, New York NY 10017. **Tel** (212)661-9404. **Ind/Abst** Excerpta Med., Comput. Control Abstr., Electr. Electron. Abstr., Sci. Abstr. Sect. A. Phys. Abstr., Pap. Board Abstr., Chem. Abstr. **LC** QC1. **DD** 530.05. **CODEN** PHSBB4. *Bulletin.*

THE PHYSICS, CHEMISTRY AND MECHANICS OF SURFACES. 0734-1520. Periodical. US. English. ir. $722.00. Gordon & Breach, PO Box 197, London WC2E 9PX Enland. **Ed** E P Velikhov. bk rev. adv acc.

PHYSICS EDUCATION. V. 1- May 1966-. 0031-9120. Periodical. UK. English. ir. American Institute of Physics, 335 East 45th Street Subscription Fulfillment, New York NY 10017. **Tel** (212)661-9404. **Ind/Abst** Comput. Control Abstr., Electr. Electron. Abstr., Sci. Abstr. Sect. A. Phys. Abstr., Chem. Abstr., Curr. Index J. Educ., Ref. Source, Media Rev. Dig., Phys. Abstr. **LC** QC30. **CODEN** PHEDA7. Index published separately - free - automatically sent. Available on microfiche from the publisher.

PHYSICS IN TECHNOLOGY. 0305-4624. Periodical. UK. English. bm. American Institute of Physics, 335 East 45th Street, New York NY 10017. **Ind/Abst** Eng. Index Mon., Eng. Index Bioeng. Abstr., Eng. Index Energy Abstr., Life Sci. Collect., Excerpta Med., Coal Abstr., Ship Abstr., Energy Inf. Abstr., Environ. Abstr., Int. Aerosp. Abstr., GeoRef, Comput. Control Abstr., Electr. Electron. Abstr., Sci. Abstr. Sect. A. Phys. Abstr., Chem. Abstr., Eng. Index Annu., Eng. Index, Nuci. Sci. Abstr., Bibliogr. Agric., Bibliogr. Index Geol. **LC** QC1. **DD** 620.005. **CODEN** PHYTBK. *Review of Physics in Technology, 0034-6683.*

PHYSICS LETTERS. SECTION A. (PHYSICS LETTERS : PART A). V. 24A- Jan. 2, 1967-. 0375-9601. Periodical. NE. English (French, or German). wk. N H P C, PO Box 103, 1000 AC Amsterdam The Netherlands. **Ind/Abst** Math. Rev., Comput. Control Abstr., Electr. Electron. Abstr., Sci. Abstr. Sect. A. Phys. Abstr., Energy Res. Abstr., Met. Abstr., World Alum. Abstr., Chem. Abstr. **LC** QC1. **DD** 530.05. **CODEN** PYLAAG. Index in last issue of volume - attached. (cum index). *Physics Letters, 0031-9163.*

PHYSICS MANPOWER. EDUCATION AND EMPLOYMENT STATISTICS. (PHYSICS MANPOWER, EDUCATION AND EMPLOYMENT STUDIES). **Main/Corp** American Institute of Physics. **Series/Titl** AIP Pub. 0569-5716. US. English. ir. American Institute of Physics, Attn: S Ellis, 335 East 45th Street, Subscription Fulfillment, New York NY 10017. **Tel** (212)661-9404. **LC** QC29. **DD** 530.023. *Physics: Education, Employment, Financial Support.*

PHYSICS NEWS. 1975-. 0160-3353. US. English. an. $5.00. American Institute of Physics, 335 East 45th Street, New York NY 10017. **LC** QC1. **DD** 530.05. *0092-8437.*

THE PHYSICS OF FLUIDS. V. 1- Jan./Feb. 1958-. 0031-9171. Periodical. US. English. mo. American Institute of Physics, 335 East 45th Street, New York NY 10017. **Tel** (212)661-9404. **Ind/Abst** Chem. Abstr., Eng. Index, Nuci. Sci. Abstr., Int. Aerosp. Abstr., Index Med. **CODEN** PFLDAS.

PHYSICS OF QUANTUM ELECTRONICS. V. 1-. 0161-3731. Monographic Series. US. English. ir. Addison Wesley Publishing Company, 1 Jacob Way, Reading MA 01867. **Tel** (617)944-3700. **Ind/Abst** Eng. Index Annu., Eng. Index Mon., Eng. Index Bioeng. Abstr., Eng. Index Energy Abstr., Comput. Control Abstr., Electr. Electron. Abstr., Sci. Abstr. Sect. A. Phys. Abstr., Chem. Abstr. **CODEN** PHQEA2.

PHYSICS OF SEMICONDUCTORS. **Main/Conf** International Conference on the Physics of Semiconductors. 1978-. UK. English. be. Institute of Physics, 47 Belgrave Square, London SW1X 8QX England. **LC** QC612.S4. **DD** 537.622. *Proceedings.*

PHYSICS PAPERS. **Main/Corp** Uniwersytet Slaski w Katowicach. 1- 1973-. English. ir. 9.00 Single Issue. Universytet Slaski W Katowicach, Ul Bankowa 12, Katowice Poland. **LC** QC1. **DD** 530.

PHYSICS REPORTS. **VFOAT** Physics Letters. V. 1C- Mar. 1971-. 0370-1573. Periodical. English. wk. Elsevier Science Publishers, PO Box 211, 1000 AE Amsterdam Netherlands. **Ind/Abst** Math. Rev., Chem. Abstr., Comput. Control Abstr., Electr. Electron. Abstr., Sci. Abstr. Sect. A. Phys. Abstr., Phys. Abstr., Sci. Cit. Index, Abr. Ed. **LC** QC1. **CODEN** PRPLCM. *Case Studies in Atomic Physics.*

PHYSICS SOLARITERRESTRIS. **Series/Titl** Geodatische und Geophysikalische Veroffentlichungen. No. 1-. Periodical. English (German, or Russian with summaries in the other languages). ir. Nationalkomitee fur Geodasie und Geophysik bei der Akademie der Wissenschaften der DDR, Potsdam West Germany. **Ind/Abst** Int. Aerosp. Abstr. **LC** QC801. **DD** 551.05.

THE PHYSICS TEACHER. V. 1- Apr. 1963-. 0031-921X. Periodical. US. English. ir. $60.00 Domestic, $70.00 Foreign. American Association of Physics Teacher, 5110 Roanoke Place/Suite 101, College Park MD 20740. **Tel** (301)345-4200. **Ed** Clifford E Swartz. **Ind/Abst** Excerpta Med., Coal Abstr., Comput. Control Abstr., Electr. Electron. Abstr., Sci. Abstr. Sect. A. Phys. Abstr., Energy Res. Abstr., Educ. Index, Spin, Chem. Abstr., Curr. Phys. Index, Curr. Index J. Educ., Media Rev. Dig., Gen. Sci. Index, Phys. Abstr. **LC** QC30. **DD** 530.071. **CODEN** PHTEAH. adv acc. Available on microfilm.

PHYSICS TODAY. V. 1- May 1948-. 0031-9228. Periodical. US. English. mo. American Institute of Physics, 335 East 45th Street, New York NY 10017. **Tel** (516)349-7800. **Ind/Abst** Math. Rev., Mag. Index, Excerpta Med., Coal Abstr., Energy Inf. Abstr., Environ. Abstr., Pop. Mag. Rev., GeoRef, Comput. Control Abstr., Electr. Electron. Abstr., Spin, Sci. Abstr. Sect. A. Phys. Abstr., Art Archaeol. Tech. Abstr., Energy Res. Abstr., Ref. Source, Appl. Sci. Technol. Index, Read. Guide Period. Lit., Chem. Abstr., Curr. Phys. Index, Nuci. Sci. Abstr., Int. Aerosp. Abstr., Curr. Index J. Educ., Bibliogr. Index Geol., Gen. Sci. Index, Appl. Mech. Rev. **LC** QC1. **DD** 530.5. **NLM** W1 PH847. **CODEN** PHTOAD.

PHYSIK DATEN. **VFOAT** Physics Data. V. 1-. 0344-8401. GW. English (German). ir. Zentralstelle Atomkernenergie, Dokumentation/Leopoldshafen 2, 7514 Eggenstein West Germany. **Ind/Abst** Comput. Control Abstr., Electr. Electron. Abstr., Sci. Abstr.

Physics

Sect. A. Phys. Abstr., Energy Res. Abstr., Met. Abstr., World Alum. Abstr., Chem. Abstr. **CODEN** PHDADU.

PHYSIK IN UNSERER ZEIT. V. 1-. 0031-9252. Periodical. German. bm. VCH Publishers Inc, 303 NW 12th Avenue, Deerfield Beach FL 33442. Tel (305)428-5566. **Ind/Abst** Int. Aerosp. Abstr., Energy Res. Abstr., Chem. Abstr. LC QC1. DD 530.05. **CODEN** PHUZAH.

PHYSIK UND TECHNIK. GW. German. ir. Wissenschaftliche Verlagsge, Sellschaft MBH/ Postfach 40, D7000 Stuttgart 1 West Germany. Tel 0711/2582-0.

PHYSIKALISCHE BLATTER. 0031-9279. Periodical. German. mo. VCH Publishers Inc, 303 Northwest 12th Avenue, Deerfield Beach FL 33442. Tel (305)428-5566. **Ind/Abst** Excerpta Med., Int. Aerosp. Abstr., Comput. Control Abstr., Electr. Electron. Abstr., Sci. Abstr. Sect. A. Phys. Abstr., Energy Res. Abstr., Chem. Abstr. **CODEN** PHBLAG. Index published separately - free - automatically sent. (cum index). Neue Physikalische Blatter.

PISMA V ZHURNAL EKSPERIMENTALNOI I TEORETICHESKOI FIZIKI. VFOAT Pisma V Zhetf. V. 9 (Jan. 1969)-. 0370-274X. Periodical. UR. Russian. sm. Victor Kamkin Inc (70304), 12224 Parklawn Drive, Rockville MD 20852. Tel (301)881-5973. **Ind/Abst** Comput. Control Abstr., Electr. Electron. Abstr., Sci. Abstr. Sect. A. Phys. Abstr., Chem. Abstr., Met. Abstr., World Alum. Abstr. **CODEN** PZETAB. Zhuranl Eksperimentalnoi I Teoreticheskoi Fiziki Pisma V Redaktsiiu.

PISMA V ZHURNAL TEKHNICHESKOI FIZIKI. Began in 1975. 0320-0116. Periodical. UR. Russian. sm. $84.50. Victor Kamkin Inc (70768), 12224 Parklawn Drive, Rockville MD 20852. Tel (301)881-5973. **Ind/Abst** Phys. Abstr., Comput. Control Abstr., Electr. Electron. Abstr., Sci. Abstr. Sect. A. Phys. Abstr., Chem. Abstr. LC QC1. **CODEN** PZTFDD.

PMTF. Mai/Iun 1960-. 0044-4626. Periodical. UR. Russian. bm. Victor Kamkin Inc (70295), 12224 Parklawn Drive, Rockville MD 20852. Tel (301)881-5973. **Ind/Abst** Math. Rev., Int. Aerosp. Abstr., Comput. Control Abstr., Electr. Electron. Abstr., Sci. Abstr. Sect. A. Phys. Abstr., Energy Res. Abstr., Chem. Abstr., Met. Abstr., World Alum. Abstr., Phys. Abstr. LC QC1. DD 530.05. **CODEN** ZPMFAF.

POCKET PRICE GUIDE. VFOAT Case Pocket Price Guide. 0742-4442. US. English. $9.50. Knife Nook, Box 243, Burke VA 22015. Ed Jim Sargent and Jim Schleyer. LC TS380. DD 621.9320750973.

PORTUGALIAE PHYSICA. V. 1- 1943-. 2498-4903. Periodical. PO. French (English). ir. 250. Faculdade de Ciencias de Lisbon, Laboratorid de Fisica, Rua da Escola Politecnia 58& Lisbon 2 Portugal. **Ind/Abst** Math. Rev., Comput. Control Abstr., Electr. Electron. Abstr., Sci. Abstr. Sect. A. Phys. Abstr., Chem. Abstr. **CODEN** POPYA4.

POSTEPY FIZYKI. Vol. 1- 1949-. 0032-5430. Periodical. PL. Polish. bm. ARS Polona, Krakowskie Przedmiescie 7, 00-068 Warsaw Poland. **Ind/Abst** Comput. Control Abstr., Electr. Electron. Abstr., Sci. Abstr. Sect. A. Phys. Abstr., Chem. Abstr. LC QC1. **CODEN** PSTFAT.

POWERTECHNICS MAGAZINE. VFOAT Power Technics. Vol. 1, No. 1 (June 1985)-. 0882-7419. Periodical. US. English. mo. $75.00 US and Canda. Darnell Research Inc, 705 North Vine Street, Anaheim CA 92805. DD 621.

PRACE FIZYCZNE. Main/Corp Uniwersytet Jagiellonski. VFOAT Schedae Physicae. No. 1-. Polish (summaries in English). ir. **Ind/Abst** Math. Rev. LC QC1.

PRAMANA. Began with issue for July 1973. 0304-4289. Periodical. II. English. mo. $202.00. J C Baltzer, Wettsteinplatz 10, CH-4058 Basel Switzerland. Tel 61268925. **Ind/Abst** Math. Rev., Int. Aerosp. Abstr., GeoRef, Comput. Control Abstr., Electr. Electron. Abstr., Sci. Abstr. Sect. A. Phys. Abstr., Met. Abstr., World Alum. Abstr., Chem. Abstr., Appl. Mech. Rev., Bibliogr. Index Geol., Sci. Cit. Index, Abr. Ed., Phys. Abstr. LC QC1. DD 530. **CODEN** PRAMCI.

PROBLEMY KOSMICHESKOI FIZIKI. Vol. 1-. 0555-2796. UR. Russian (summaries in English). **Ind/Abst** Int. Aerosp. Abstr., Chem. Abstr. LC QC801. **CODEN** PRKFAB.

PROBLEMY MATEMATICESKOJ FIZIKI. (PROBLEMY MATEMATICHESKOI FIZIKI). Vol. 1-. 0555-2818. Periodical. UR. Russian. **Ind/Abst** Int. Aerosp. Abstr., Math. Rev. LC QC20.

PROCEEDINGS - INTERNATIONAL CONFERENCE ON HIGH ENERGY PHYSICS. Main/Conf International Conference on High Energy Physics. 0534-8706. US. French. ir. American Institute of Physics, 335 East 45th Street, New York NY 10017.

PROCEEDINGS - INTERNATIONAL CONFERENCE ON INSTRUMENTATION FOR HIGH-ENERGY PHYSICS. Main/Conf International Conference on Instrumentation for High-Energy Physics. English. ir. LC QC786.

PROCEEDINGS OF SUMMER INSTITUTE ON PARTICLE PHYSICS. Main/Conf Summer Institute on Particle Physics. Series/Titl SLAC Report. Began in 1973. 0146-1273. US. English. an. $12.75. US Department of Commerce, National Technical Information Service, 5285 Port Royal Road, Springfield VA 22161. **Ind/Abst** Chem. Abstr. **CODEN** PSIPD7. Also available on microfiche.

PROCEEDINGS OF THE ACADEMY OF SCIENCES OF THE USSR. APPLIED PHYSICS SECTIONS. Main/Corp Akademiia Nauk SSSR. VFOAT Applied Physics Sections. Vol. 112, Issues 1/6 Jan./Feb. 1957-. Periodical. US. English. mo. Consultants Bureau Inc, 233 Spring Street, New York NY 10013.

PROCEEDINGS OF THE ANNUAL EASTERN THEORETICAL PHYSICS CONFERENCE. Main/Conf Eastern Theoretical Physics Conference. 1962-. 0424-1940. US. English. an. LC QC1.

PROCEEDINGS OF THE INTERNATIONAL CONFERENCE ON LASERS. Main/Conf International Conference on Lasers. VFOAT Lasers. 1st- 1978-. 0190-4132. US. English. an. $95.00. STS Press, PO Box 177, McLean VA 22101. Tel (703)642-5835. Ed K M Corcoran. **Ind/Abst** Chem. Abstr. **CODEN** PICLDV. Circ 400. Contains papers on lasers, technology and applications in science, industry, medicine, and other fields.

PROCEEDINGS OF THE INTERNATIONAL CONFERENCE ON PRESSURE SURGES. Main/Conf International Conference on Pressure Surges. 1st-1972-. UK. English. ir. Learned Information Inc, 143 Old Marlton Pike, Medford NJ 08055. Tel (609)654-6266.

PROCEEDINGS OF THE ... INTERNATIONAL CONGRESS ON RHEOLOGY. Main/Corp International Congress on Rheology. Began publication with 1st in 1948?. US. English (French or German). ir. University Park Press, 300 North Charles Street, Baltimore MD 21201. Tel (800)638-7511. LC QC189.

PROCEEDINGS, TRUDY, OF THE P. N. LEBEDEV PHYSICS INSTITUTE. (PROCEEDINGS (TRUDY) OF THE P. N. LEBEDEV PHYSICS INSTITUTE). Main/Corp Akademiia Nauk SSSR. Fizicheskii Institut. VFOAT Proceedings of the P.N. Lebedev Physics Institute. 0568-5508. US. English. ir. Plenum Press, 233 Spring Street, New York NY 10013. Tel (212)620-8000. LC QC1.

PROGRESS IN MEDICAL AND ENVIRONMENTAL PHYSICS. Vol. 1-. Monographic Series. UK. English. ir. Blackie And Son Limited, Bishopbriggs, Glasgow G64 2NZ England. Tel 44 (41) 772 2311. Ed D Jackson. NLM W1 PR67088. A series of two books covering the state of the art for medical physicist in imaging techniques.

PROGRESS IN MEDICAL RADIATION PHYSICS. Vol. 1-. 0730-2339. US. English. ir. Plenum Press, 233 Spring Street, New York NY 10013. Ed Colin G Orton. **Ind/Abst** Chem. Abstr. NLM W1 PR6711D. **CODEN** PMRPDA.

PROGRESS OF PHYSICS. VFOAT Fortschritte der Physik. 0033-0671. Periodical. US. English. ir. Birkhauser Boston Inc, 380 Green Street, PO Box 3005, Cambridge MA 02139. **Ind/Abst** Math. Rev. LC QC1. DD 530.05.

PROGRESS OF THEORETICAL PHYSICS. Began with: Vol. 1 in July 1946. 0033-068X. Periodical. JA. English. mo. Kyoto University, c/o Yukawa Hall, 606 Kyoto Japan. **Ind/Abst** Math. Rev., Int. Aerosp. Abstr., GeoRef, Comput. Control Abstr., Electr. Electron. Abstr., Sci. Abstr. Sect. A. Phys. Abstr., Chem. Abstr., Sci. Cit. Index, Abr. Ed. LC QC1. DD 530.15. **CODEN** PTPKAV. Index in last issue of volume - attached. (cum index).

PURE AND APPLIED PHYSICS. 0079-8193. Monographic Series. US. English. ir. Academic Press, 4805 Sand Lake Road, Orlando FL 32819. Tel (305)345-4100. **Ind/Abst** Comput. Control Abstr., Electr. Electron. Abstr., Sci. Abstr. Sect. A. Phys. Abstr., Chem. Abstr., Phys. Abstr. LC UNC. **CODEN** PAPHAP.

QUANTUM PHYSICS AND ITS APPLICATIONS. V. 1- 1964-. 0481-1275. US. English. ir. Gordon & Breach, 50 West 23rd Street, New York NY 10010.

QUARTERLY REVIEWS OF BIOPHYSICS. V. 1- May 1968-. 0033-5835. Periodical. UK. English. qt. Cambridge University Press, PO Box 482, London England. **Ind/Abst** Life Sci. Collect., Excerpta Med., Index Med., Biol. Abstr., Chem. Abstr. LC QH505.A1. DD 574.19105. NLM W1 QU526E. **CODEN** QURBAW.

RAPPORT NATIONAL DE CONJONCTURE SCIENTIFIQUE : PHYSIQUE. Main/Corp France. Centre National de la Recherche Scientifique. Comite National de la Recherche Scientifique. FR. French. ir. 15 Quai Anatole, Paris France 75700. LC QC1. DD 530.05.

REFERATIVNYI ZHURNAL. FIZIKA. Referaty No. 1-. 0034-2343. Periodical. UR. Russian. ir. $1,024.50. Victor Kamkin Inc (56244), 12224 Parklawn Drive, Rockville MD 20852. Tel (301)881-5973. **Ind/Abst** Chem. Abstr. LC QC1. (cum index).

RELATORIO DA DIRECAO CIENTIFICA, CENTRO BRASILEIRO DE PESQUISAS FISICAS. Main/Corp Centro Brasileiro de Pesquisas Fisicas. Direcao Cientifica. Portuguese. ir. Centro Brasileiro de Pesquisas Fisicas, Direcas Cientifica, Av Wenceslau Braz 71, Rio de Janeiro Brazil. LC QC47.B62.

RELATORIO DA PRESIDENCIA. Main/Corp Centro Brasileiro de Pesquisas Fisicas. Portuguese. ir. Av Wenceslau Braz 71, Rio de Janeiro Brazil. LC QC47.B6.

RELATORIO DAS ATIVIDADES ADMINISTRATIVAS. Main/Corp Centro Brasileiro de Pesquisas Fisicas. Portuguese. ir. Av Wenceslau Braz 71, Rio de Janeiro Brazil. LC QC47.B6.

RENDICONTI DELLA SCUOLA INTERNAZIONALE DI FISICA ENRICO FERMI. Main/Corp International School of Physics Enrico Fermi. Vol. 1- Aug. 19/Sept. 12, 1953-. 0505-0189. Italian. ir. Elsevier Science Publishers, PO Box 1663, Grand Central Station, New York NY 10163.

REPORT - JOINT INSTITUTE FOR LABORATORY ASTROPHYSICS. (REPORT). VFOAT JILA Report. 0732-7935. US. English. University of Colorado, Joint Institute for Laboratory Astrophysics, Boulder CO 80309. Tel (303)492-7801. **Ind/Abst** Chem. Abstr. **CODEN** JILRAP. Bibliographies and evaluated compliations of data on electron and photon collisions with atoms and ions and low-energy heavy particle collisions.

REPORT OF RESEARCH CENTER OF ION BEAM TECHNOLOGY, HOSEI UNIVERSITY. SUPPLEMENT. VFOAT Hosei Daigaku Ion Bimu Kogaku Kenkyujo Kokoku. No. 1 (Dec. 1980)-. English. ir. **Ind/Abst** Chem. Abstr. LC QC702.7.B65. DD 537.56. **CODEN** RCISDS.

REPORT SERIES - UNIVERSITY OF LSLO, INSTITUTE OF PHYSICS. (REPORT SERIES). 0332-5571. Monographic Series. NO. English. ir. Institute of Physics, University of Oslo, Oslo 3 Norway. **Ind/Abst** Chem. Abstr. **CODEN** RUSPDP.

REPORTS ON MATHEMATICAL PHYSICS. V. 1- Aug. 1970-. 0034-4877. Periodical. PL. English. bm. $323.00. Pergamon Press, 395 Sawmill River Road, Elmsford NY 10523. **Ind/Abst** Math. Rev., Electron. Commun. Abstr. J., ISMEC Bull., Pollut. Abstr. Indexes, Saf. Sci. Abstr. J., Comput. Control Abstr., Electr. Electron. Abstr., Sci. Abstr. Sect. A. Phys. Abstr., Chem. Abstr., Phys. Abstr. LC QC19.2. DD 530.1505. **CODEN** RMHPBE.

REPORTS ON PROGRESS IN PHYSICS. V. 1- 1934-. 0034-4885. Periodical. UK. English. mo. American Institute of Physics, 335 East 45th Street, New York NY 10017. Tel (212)661-9404. **Ind/Abst** Math. Rev., GeoRef, Int. Aerosp. Abstr., Comput. Control Abstr., Electr. Electron. Abstr., Sci. Abstr. Sect. A. Phys. Abstr., Met. Abstr., World Alum. Abstr., Chem. Abstr., Appl. Mech.

Rev., Eng. Index, Bibliogr. Index Geol., Sci. Cit. Index, Abr. Ed., Phys. Abstr. **LC** QC3. **NLM** W1 PH747. **CODEN** RPPHAG. (cum index).

RESEARCH IN SURFACE FORCES. **Main/Conf** Konferentrsia Po Poverkhnostym Silam. US. English (summaries in Russian). ir. Plenum Press, c/o H Feldman, 233 Spring Street, New York NY 10013. **Tel** (212)620-8000.

REUNION - COMITE INTERNATIONAL DES POIDS ET MESURES, COMITE CONSULTATIF POUR LES ETALONS DE MESURE DES RAYONNEMENTS IONISANTS, SECTION II. **Main/Corp** Comite International des Poids et Mesures. Comite Consultatif pour les Etalons de Mesure des Rayonnements Ionisants. Section II. 1st- 1970-. 0379-5640. FR. French. ir. Bureau International des Poids et Mesures, Pavillon de Breteuil, F-92310 Sevres France. **Tel** (1) 45 34 00 51. **LC** QC795.42. **DD** 539.77. **CODEN** CIMRBM. **Circ** 350. Contains the proceedings of the meetings of the relevant committee whose attendees are representatives of national laboratories engaged in standardization and related researches. *Reunion - Comite International des Poids et Mesures, Comite Consultatif pour les Etalo.*

REUNION - COMITE INTERNATIONAL DES POIDS ET MESURES, COMITE CONSULTATIF POUR LES ETALONS DE MESURE DES RAYONNEMENTS IONISANTS, SECTION IV. **Main/Corp** Comite International des Poids et Mesures. Comite Consultatif pourtles Etalons de Mesure des Rayonnements Ionisants. Section IV. 1.- 1972-. 0379-5667. FR. French. ir. Bureau International des Poids et Mesures, Pavillon de Breteuil, F-92310 Sevres France. **Tel** (1) 45 34 00 51. **LC** QC795.42. **DD** 539.77. **CODEN** CIEEBB. **Circ** 350. Contains the proceedings of the meetings of the relevant committee whose attendees are representatives of national laboratories engaged in standardization and related researches.

REUNION - COMITE INTERNATIONAL DES POIDS ET MESURES, COMITE CONSULTATIF POUR LES ETALONS DE MESURE DES RAYONNEMENTS IONISANTS, SECTION III. **Main/Corp** Comite International des Poids et Mesures. Comite Consultatif pour les Etalons de Mesure des Rayonnements Ionisants. Section III. 1.- 1972-. 0379-5659. French. ir. Bureau International des Poids et Mesures, Pavillon de Breteuil, F-92310 Sevres France. **Tel** (1) 45 34 00 51. **LC** QC795.42. **DD** 539.77. **CODEN** CIMNBA. **Circ** 350. Contains the proceedings to the meetings of the relevant committee whose attendees are representatives of national laboratories engaged in standardization and related researches.

REUNION - COMITE INTERNATIONAL DES POIDS ET MESURES, COMITE CONSULTATIF POUR LES ETALONS DE MESURE DES RAYONNEMENTS IONISANTS, SECTION I. **Main/Corp** Comite International des Poids et Mesures. Comite Consultatif pour les Etalons de Mesure des Rayonnements Ionisants. Section I. 1.- 1970-. 0379-5632. French. ir. Bureau International des Poids et Mesures, Pavillon de Breteuil, F-92310 Sevres France. **Tel** (1) 45 34 00 51. **LC** QC795.42. **DD** 539.77. **CODEN** CIREB8. **Circ** 350. Contains the proceedings of the meetings of the relevant committee whose attendees are representatives of national laboratories engaged in standardization and related researches.

REVIEWS OF MODERN PHYSICS. V. 2- 1930-. 0034-6861. Periodical. US. English. qt. American Institute of Physics, 335 East 45th Street, New York NY 10017. **Tel** (212)661-9404. **Ind/Abst** Excerpta Med., GeoRef, Comput. Control Abstr., Electr. Electron. Abstr., Sci. Abstr. Sect. A. Phys. Abstr., Energy Res. Abstr., Spin, Chem. Abstr., Curr. Phys. Index, Int. Aerosp. Abstr., Math. Rev., Nuci. Sci. Abstr., Appl. Mech. Rev., Sci. Cit. Index, Abr. Ed., Phys. Abstr. **NLM** W1 RE257E. **CODEN** RMPHAT. *Physical Review Supplement.*

REVIEWS OF PLASMA PHYSICS. V. 1- 1965-. 0080-2050. US. English (Russian). ir. Plenum Press, 233 Spring Street, New York NY 10013. **Tel** (212)620-8000. **Ind/Abst** Comput. Control Abstr., Electr. Electron. Abstr., Sci. Abstr. Sect. A. Phys. Abstr., Phys. Abstr. **LC** QC718. **DD** 530. **CODEN** RPLPAK.

REVISTA BRASILEIRA DE FISICA. V. 1- April 1971-. 0374-4922. Periodical. BL. contributions in Portuguese, English, Spanish and French, with abstracts in Portuguese and English. ty. $70.00. Sociedade Brasileira de Fisca, Universite de Sao Paulo, CX Postal 10552, 01000 Sao Paulo SP Brazil. **Tel** 815. 55 99. **Ed** Nicin Fagury. **Ind/Abst** Coal Abstr., Int. Aerosp. Abstr., Comput. Control Abstr., Electr. Electron. Abstr., Sci. Abstr. Sect. A. Phys. Abstr., Chem. Abstr., Phys. Abstr. **CODEN** RBFSA3. adv acc. General physics.

REVISTA DE BIOLOGIA Y MEDICINA NUCLEAR. *See* Medicine.

REVISTA DE FIZICA SI CHIMIE. Periodical. RM. Romanian. mo. Ilexim Press Department, PO Box 1-136-1-137, Bucharest Romania. **LC** QC1. *Revista de Fizica Si Chimie. Seria A, Revista de Fizica Si Chimie. Seria B.*

REVISTA MEXICANA DE ASTRONOMIA Y ASTROFISICA. *See* Astronomy.

REVISTA MEXICANA DE FISICA. V. 1- Apr. 1952-. 0035-001X. Periodical. MX. Spanish. qt. $40.00. Sociedad Mexicana de Fisica AC, Apartado Postal 70-542, Ciudad Universidad, 04510 Mexico DF Mexico. **Tel** 550 59 10. **Ed** Sergio Hojman. **Ind/Abst** Math. Rev., Comput. Control Abstr., Electr. Electron. Abstr., Sci. Abstr. Sect. A. Phys. Abstr., Chem. Abstr., Phys. Abstr. **LC** QC1. **CODEN** RMXFAT. **Circ** 2,000. (ctrl). Original research papers on theoretical and experimental physics, scientific instrumentation history and philosophy of physics, teaching and educational policy, scientific policy.

REVUE DE PHYSIQUE APPLIQUEE. Vol. 1- March 1966-. 0035-1687. Periodical. FR. French. mo. les Editions de Physique, Avenue du Hoggar BP 112, 91944 les Ulis Cedex France. **Ind/Abst** GeoRef, Int. Aerosp. Abstr., Comput. Control Abstr., Electr. Electron. Abstr., Sci. Abstr. Sect. A. Phys. Abstr., Energy Res. Abstr., Met. Abstr., World Alum. Abstr., Chem. Abstr., Phys. Abstr., Bibliogr. Index Geol., Sci. Cit. Index, Abr. Ed. **LC** QC1. **NLM** W1 RE799K. **CODEN** RPHAAN.

REVUE ROUMAINE DE PHYSIQUE. V. 1- 1956-. 0035-4090. Periodical. English (French, German or Russian). ir. Rompresfilatelia, PO Box 1362137, Bucharest Romaina. **Ind/Abst** Electr. Electron. Abstr., Comput. Control Abstr., Math. Rev., Phys. Abstr., Sci. Cit. Index, Abr. Ed., Eng. Index, Chem. Abstr. **LC** QC1. **DD** 530.05.

RHEOLOGICA ACTA. Vol. 1- May 1958-. 0035-4511. Periodical. GW. English (text and summaries in French, or German). ir. $227.40. Springer Verlag-New York Inc, 175 5th Avenue, New York NY 10010. **Tel** (212)460-1500. **Ed** H Giesekus. **Ind/Abst** Math. Rev., Coal Abstr., World Surf. Coat. Abstr., Int. Aerosp. Abstr., Comput. Control Abstr., Electr. Electron. Abstr., Sci. Abstr. Sect. A. Phys. Abstr., Energy Res. Abstr., Chem. Abstr., Appl. Mech. Rev., Sci. Cit. Index, Abr. Ed., Phys. Abstr. **LC** QC189. **DD** 531.11. **CODEN** RHEAAK. Publishes theoretical and experimental contributions covering phenomenological rheology and structural rheology, electro- and magnetorheology, rheooptics, rheometry and applied rheology.

RIVISTA DEL NUOVO CIMENTO. (LA RIVISTA DEL NUOVO CIMENTO). Serie 1, V. 1, No. 1 (Jan./Mar. 1969)-V. 2 (1970). 0035-5917. Periodical. IT. Italian. mo. $165.00 Members, $210.00 Nonmembers. Editrice Compositori, Viale 12 Giugno 1, 40124 Bologna Italy. **Tel** (051)583149. **Ind/Abst** Math. Rev., Comput. Control Abstr., Electr. Electron. Abstr., Sci. Abstr. Sect. A. Phys. Abstr., Energy Res. Abstr., Chem. Abstr., Phys. Abstr., Sci. Cit. Index, Abr. Ed. **NLM** W1 RI351E. **CODEN** RNUCAC. **Circ** 1,000. (ctrl). Covers instellar grains, absorption and emission by minor atmospheric gases in the radiation balance of the earth, conformal quantum electrodynamics and nondecomposable representations, photoreactions above the giant-dipole resonance, etc. *Supplemento Al Nuovo Cimento.*

THE RUSHLIGHT. Began with Nov. 1934 issue. 0148-3501. Periodical. US. English. qt. Rushlight Club, Corresponding Secretary, 21 Claire Road, Vernon CT 06066. **LC** TP746. **DD** 621.32305.

SAE MULLI. **VFOAT** New Physics. 0374-4914. Periodical. KO. Korean (with summaries in English). ir. Hanguk Mulli Hakhoe, San 76-561 Yoksam-Dong Kangnam-ku, Seoul Korea. **Ind/Abst** Chem. Abstr., Comput. Control Abstr., Electr. Electron. Abstr., Sci. Abstr. Sect. A. Phys. Abstr. **LC** QC1. **CODEN** NWPYA4.

SCIENCE ABSTRACTS. SECTION A. PHYSICS ABSTRACTS. *See* Indexes/Abstracts.

THE SCIENCE REPORTS OF THE TOHOKU UNIVERSITY. EIGHTH SERIES. PHYSICS AND ASTRONOMY. **VFOAT** Physics and Astronomy. Vol. 1, No. 1 (June 1980)-. 0388-5607. Periodical. JA. English (title also in Japanese). ir. Professor S Yoshida, Faculty of Science, Tohoku University, Sendai Japan. **Ind/Abst** Comput. Control Abstr., Electr. Electron. Abstr., Sci. Abstr. Sect. A. Phys. Abstr., Chem. Abstr. **LC** Q77. **DD** 530.05. **CODEN** SRTAD9. *Science Reports of the Tohoku University. Series 1, Physics, Chemistry, Astronomy.*

SCIENCE RESEARCH ABSTRACTS JOURNAL. *See* Indexes/Abstracts.

SCIENCE RESEARCH ABSTRACTS JOURNAL. PART A. SUPERCONDUCTIVITY. MAGNETOHYDRODYNAMICS AND PLASMAS. THEORETICAL PHYSICS. *See* Indexes/Abstracts.

SEG ABSTRACTS. *See* Indexes/Abstracts.

SEMICONDUCTORS AND INSULATORS. V. 2, No.4- May 1977-. 0309-5991. Periodical. US. English. qt. $288.00. Gordon & Breach, PO Box 197, London WC2E 9PX England. **Ed** A C Damask. **Ind/Abst** Comput. Control Abstr., Electr. Electron. Abstr., Sci. Abstr. Sect. A. Phys. Abstr., Chem. Abstr. **LC** QC610.9. **DD** 537.622. **CODEN** SINSD4. bk rev. adv acc. *Journal of Nonmetals and Semiconductors, 0140-1653.*

SEMICONDUCTORS AND SEMIMETALS. V. 1-. 0080-8784. Monographic Series. US. English. ir. Academic Press, 4805 Sand Lake Road, Orlando FL 32887. **Tel** (305)345-4100. **Ed** R K Willardson and A C Beer. **Ind/Abst** Comput. Control Abstr., Electr. Electron. Abstr., Sci. Abstr. Sect. A. Phys. Abstr., Sci. Cit. Index, Abr. Ed., Phys. Abstr. **LC** QC610.9. **DD** 537.622.

SERIES OF MONOGRAPHS ON SELECTED TOPICS IN SOLID STATE PHYSICS. V. 1-. Monographic Series. English. ir. Elsevier Science Publishing, PO Box 1663 Grand Central Station, New York NY 10163. **Ind/Abst** Phys. Abstr., Electr. Electron. Abstr., Comput. Control Abstr.

SHU HSUEH WU LI HSUEH PAO. **VFOAT** Acta Mathematica Scientia. V. 1-. Periodical. Chinese (English). qt. 1.25. Acta Mathematica Scientia, PO Box 30, Wuhan 43007 People's Republic of China. **Ind/Abst** Math. Rev. **LC** QC19.2. **DD** 530.1505.

SIMON STEVIN; WIS- EN NATUURKUNDIG TIJDSCHRIFT. *See* Mathematics.

SOLAR PHYSICS. *See* Astronomy.

SOLID STATE ABSTRACTS JOURNAL. *See* Indexes/Abstracts.

SOLID STATE COMMUNICATIONS. V. 1- June 1963-. 0038-1098. Periodical. US. English (French, German, or Russian). ir. $1187.50. Pergamon Press, c/o Cashier, 395 Sawmill River Road, Elmsford NY 10523. **Tel** (914)592-7700. **Ind/Abst** Electron. Commun. Abstr. J., ISMEC Bull., Pollut. Abstr. Indexes, Eng. Index Mon., Eng. Index Bioeng. Abstr., Eng. Index Energy Abstr., Coal Abstr., Int. Aerosp. Abstr., GeoRef, Comput. Control Abstr., Electr. Electron. Abstr., Sci. Abstr. Sect. A. Phys. Abstr., Chem. Abstr., Eng. Index Annu., Eng. Index Mon., Nuci. Sci. Abstr., Met. Abstr., World Alum. Abstr., Phys. Abstr., Sci. Cit. Index, Abr. Ed., Bibliogr. Index Geol., Eng. Index. **LC** QC176.A1. **DD** 530.4105. **CODEN** SSCOA4. Available on microfilm from Microforms International Marketing Corp.

SOLID STATE PHYSICS. V. 1-. 0081-1947. US. English. an. Academic Press, 4805 Sand Lake Road, Orlando FL 32819. **Ed** F Seitz and D Turnbull. **Ind/Abst** GeoRef, Chem. Abstr., Nuci. Sci. Abstr. **LC** QC173. **DD** 539.2. **CODEN** SSPHAE. (cum index).

SOLID STATE PHYSICS : ADVANCES IN RESEARCH AND APPLICATIONS. SUPPLEMENT. **VFOAT** Supplement. 1-. Monographic Series. US. English. ir. Academic Press, 4805 Sand Lake Road, Orlando FL 32887. **Tel** (305)345-4100. **Ed** H Ehrenreich, Frederick Seitz and David Turnbull.

SOLID STATE PHYSICS LITERATURE GUIDES. **VFOAT** ORNL Literature Guides. **VAT** Oak Ridge National Laboratory Literature Guides. V. 1-. 0081-1963. Monographic Series. US. English. ir. Plenum Press, Attn H Feldman, 233 Spring Street, New York NY 10013. **Tel** (212)620-8000. **LC** Z7144.S58. **DD** 016.53041.

SOVIET JOURNAL OF PLASMA PHYSICS. V. 1- Jan./Feb. 1975-. 0360-0343. Periodical. US. English (Russian). bm. American Institute of Physics, 335 East 45th Street, New York NY 10017. **Tel** (212)661-9404. **Ind/Abst** Eng. Index Annu., Eng. Index Mon., Eng. Index Bioeng. Abstr., Eng. Index Energy Abstr., Int. Aerosp. Abstr., Comput. Control Abstr., Electr. Electron. Abstr., Sci. Abstr. Sect. A. Phys. Abstr., Energy Res. Abstr., Chem. Abstr., Spin, Curr. Phys. Index, Phys. Abstr. **LC** QC717.6. **DD** 530.4405. **CODEN** SJPPDC.

SOVIET PHYSICS. **VFOAT** Technical Physics. V. 1- Oct. 1956-. 0038-5662. Periodical. US. English (Russian). mo. American Institute of Physics, 335 East 45th Street, New York NY 10017. **Tel** (212)661-9404. **Ind/Abst** Eng. Index Annu., Eng. Index Mon., Eng. Index Bioeng. Abstr., Eng. Index Energy Abstr., Int. Aerosp. Abstr., Comput. Control Abstr., Electr. Electron. Abstr., Sci. Abstr. Sect. A. Phys. Abstr., Energy Res. Abstr., Spin, Curr. Phys. Index, Appl. Mech. Rev., Phys. Abstr. **LC** QC1. **DD** 530.947. **CODEN** SPTPA3.

SOVIET PHYSICS-COLLECTION. 0363-7891. Periodical. US. English. bm. Allerton Press Inc, 150 Fifth Avenue, New York NY 10011. **Tel** (212)924-3950. **Ind/Abst** Math. Rev., Comput. Control Abstr., Electr. Electron. Abstr., Sci. Abstr. Sect. A. Phys. Abstr., Chem. Abstr., Appl. Mech. Rev., Phys. Abstr. **LC** QC1. **DD** 530.05. **CODEN** SPCODK.

SOVIET PHYSICS. DOKLADY. (SOVIET PHYSICS, DOKLADY). V. 1- Aug. 1956-. 0038-5689. Periodical. US. English (Russian). mo. American Institute of Physics, 335 East 45th Street, New York NY 10017. **Tel** (212)661-9404. **Ind/Abst** Math. Rev., Electron. Commun. Abstr. J., ISMEC Bull., Pollut. Abstr. Indexes, Saf. Sci. Abstr. J., Int. Aerosp. Abstr., GeoRef, Comput. Control Abstr., Electr. Electron. Abstr., Sci. Abstr. Sect. A. Phys. Abstr., Energy Res. Abstr., Spin, Curr. Phys. Index, Appl. Mech. Rev., Bibliogr. Index Geol., Phys. Abstr. **LC** QC1. **DD** 530.5. **CODEN** SPHDA9. Available on microfilm.

SOVIET PHYSICS, JETP. **VFOAT** JETP. **VAT** Soviet Physics, Journal of Experimental and Theoretical Physics. V. 1- July 1955-. 0038-5646. Periodical. US. English (Russian). mo. American Institute of Physics, 335 East 45th Street, New York NY 10017. **Tel** (212)661-9404. **Ind/Abst** Math. Rev., Electron. Commun. Abstr. J., ISMEC Bull., Pollut. Abstr. Indexes, Saf. Sci. Abstr. J., Int. Aerosp. Abstr., Comput. Control Abstr., Electr. Electron. Abstr., Sci. Abstr. Sect. A. Phys. Abstr., Energy Res. Abstr., Spin, Curr. Phys. Index, Met. Abstr., World Alum. Abstr., Phys. Abstr., Appl. Mech. Rev. **LC** QC1. **DD** 530.5. **CODEN** SPHJAR. (cum index). Available on microfilm.

SOVIET PHYSICS JOURNAL. Jan./Feb. 1965-. 0038-5697. Periodical. US. English (Russian). mo. $645.00 Domestic, $715.00 Foreign. Consultants Bureau, 233 Spring Street, New York NY 10013. **Tel** (212)620-8000. **Ed** V N Petinlco. **Ind/Abst** Math. Rev., Electron. Commun. Abstr. J., ISMEC Bull., Pollut. Abstr. Indexes, Saf. Sci. Abstr. J., Eng. Index Mon., Eng. Index Bioeng. Abstr., Eng. Index Energy Abstr., Int. Aerosp. Abstr., Comput. Control Abstr., Electr. Electron. Abstr., Sci. Abstr. Sect. A. Phys. Abstr., Appl. Mech. Rev., Chem. Abstr., Eng. Index Annu., Eng. Index, Phys. Abstr. **LC** QC1. **CODEN** SOPJAQ. Publishes English translations of original Russian research by the Academy of Science of the USSR in physics.

SOVIET PHYSICS, LEBEDEV INSTITUTE REPORTS. (SOVIET PHYSICS — LEBEDEV INSTITUTE REPORTS). No. 1-. 0364-2321. Periodical. US. English (Russian). mo. Allerton Press, 150 5th Avenue, New York NY 10011. **Tel** (212)924-3950. **Ind/Abst** Eng. Index Annu., Eng. Index Mon., Eng. Index Bioeng. Abstr., Eng. Index Energy Abstr., Comput. Control Abstr., Electr. Electron. Abstr., Sci. Abstr. Sect. A. Phys. Abstr., Chem. Abstr., Appl. Mech. Rev., Phys. Abstr., Eng. Index. **LC** QC1. **DD** 530.05. **CODEN** SPLRD6.

SOVIET PHYSICS. SEMICONDUCTORS. (SOVIET PHYSICS : SEMICONDUCTORS). **VFOAT** Semiconductors. V. 1- July 1967-. 0038-5700. Periodical. US. English (Russian). mo. American Institute of Physics, 335 East 45th Street, New York NY 10017. **Tel** (212)661-9404. **Ind/Abst** Electron. Commun. Abstr. J., ISMEC Bull., Pollut. Abstr. Indexes, Saf. Sci. Abstr. J., Eng. Index Mon., Eng. Index Bioeng. Abstr., Eng. Index Energy Abstr., Int. Aerosp. Abstr., Comput. Control Abstr., Electr. Electron. Abstr., Sci. Abstr. Sect. A. Phys. Abstr., Energy Res. Abstr., Spin, Curr. Phys. Index, Chem. Abstr., Eng. Index Annu., Eng. Index, Nuci. Sci. Abstr., Met. Abstr., World Alum. Abstr., Phys. Abstr., Sci. Cit. Index, Abr. Ed. **LC** QC612.S4. **DD** 537.62205. **CODEN** SPSEBY.

SOVIET PHYSICS. SOLID STATE. (SOVIET PHYSICS, SOLID STATE). V. 1- Jan. 1959-. 0038-5654. Periodical. US. English (Russian). mo. American Institute of Physics, 335 East 45th Street, New York NY 10017. **Tel** (212)661-9404. **Ind/Abst** Electron. Commun. Abstr. J., ISMEC Bull., Pollut. Abstr. Indexes, Saf. Sci. Abstr. J., Eng. Index Annu., Eng. Index Mon., Eng. Index Bioeng. Abstr., Eng. Index Energy Abstr., Minproc, Int. Aerosp. Abstr., Comput. Control Abstr., Electr. Electron. Abstr., Sci. Abstr. Sect. A. Phys. Abstr., Energy Res. Abstr., Curr. Phys. Index, Spin, Met. Abstr., World Alum. Abstr., Eng. Index, Phys. Abstr. **LC** QC176. **DD** 531.705. **CODEN** SPSSA7. Available on microfilm.

SOVIET PHYSICS, USPEKHI. V. 1- Sept./Oct. 1958-. 0038-5670. Periodical. US. English (Russian). mo. American Institute of Physics, 335 East 45th Street, New York NY 10017. **Tel** (212)661-9404. **Ind/Abst** Math. Rev., Coal Abstr., Int. Aerosp. Abstr., GeoRef, Comput. Control Abstr., Electr. Electron. Abstr., Sci. Abstr. Sect. A. Phys. Abstr., Energy Res. Abstr., Spin, Curr. Phys. Index, Bibliogr. Index Geol., Phys. Abstr. **LC** QC1. **DD** 530.5. **CODEN** SOPUAP. Available on microfilm.

SOVIET SCIENTIFIC REVIEWS. SECTION A. PHYSICS REVIEWS. **VFOAT** Physics Reviews. V. 1- 1979-. Monographic Series. English (language translation of papers originally written in Russian). ir. **Ind/Abst** Chem. Abstr.

SOVIET TECHNICAL PHYSICS LETTERS. V. 1- Jan. 1975-. 0360-120X. Periodical. US. English (Russian). mo. American Institute of Physics, 335 East 45th Street, New York NY 10017. **Tel** (212)661-9404. **Ind/Abst** Int. Aerosp. Abstr., Comput. Control Abstr., Electr. Electron. Abstr., Sci. Abstr. Sect. A. Phys. Abstr., Energy Res. Abstr., Spin, Curr. Phys. Index, Phys. Abstr. **LC** QC1. **DD** 530.05. **CODEN** STPLD2.

SPECTROCHIMICA ACTA. PART B : ATOMIC SPECTROSCOPY. V. 23B- March 1967-. 0584-8547. Periodical. UK. English (French, or German, with summaries in English). mo. $617.50. Pergamon Press, 395 Sawmill River Road, Elmsford NY 10523. **Tel** (914)592-7700. **Ind/Abst** Electron. Commun. Abstr. J., ISMEC Bull., Pollut. Abstr. Indexes, Saf. Sci. Abstr. J., Excerpta Med., Biol. Abstr., GeoRef, Comput. Control Abstr., Electr. Electron. Abstr., Sci. Abstr. Sect. A. Phys. Abstr., Chem. Abstr., Met. Abstr., World Alum. Abstr., Phys. Abstr., Chem. Abstr., Bibliogr. Index Geol., Sci. Cit. Index, Abr. Ed. **LC** QD95. **DD** 539.7. **NLM** W1 SP315B. **CODEN** SAASBH. Available on microfilm from Microforms International Marketing Corp. *Spectrochemica Acta.*

SPRINGER SERIES IN COMPUTATIONAL PHYSICS. 0172-5726. Monographic Series. German. ir. Springer Verlag-New York Inc, 175 5th Avenue, New York NY 10010. **Tel** (212)460-1584. **Ind/Abst** Math. Rev. Contains topics on computational Galerkin methods, computer studies of phase transitions and critical phenomena, methods for fluid flow, optimal shape design for elliptic systems.

SPRINGER SERIES IN ELECTROPHYSICS. *See* Engineering - Electricity, Electrical Engineering, Electronics.

SPRINGER TRACTS IN MODERN PHYSICS. **VFOAT** Ergebnisse der Exakten Naturwissenschaften. Vol. 38-. 0081-3869. English (German). ir. Springer Verlag NY, 44 Hartz Way, Secaucus NJ 07094. **Tel** (201)348-4033. **Ed** G Hoehler. **Ind/Abst** Comput. Control Abstr., Electr. Electron. Abstr., Sci. Abstr. Sect. A. Phys. Abstr. **CODEN** STPHBM. (cum index). **Circ** 300. Devoted to reviews of a tutorial nature in which the literature is judiciously sifted by competent experts. Organized around a certain theme in the areas of atomic, elementary-particle, nuclear, and solid-state physics. *Ergebnisse der Exakten Naturwissenschaften, 0367-0325.*

SPS CHAPTER LIST. **Main/Corp** Society of Physics Students. **VAT** Society of Physics Students Chapter List. 0197-6761. US. English. an. $2.50. Society of Physics Students, American Institute of Physics, 335 East 45th Street, New York NY 10017.

THE STOPPING AND RANGES OF IONS IN MATTER. (V. 2- 1977-). Monographic Series. US. English.

STP NEWSLETTER. **VFOAT** S.T.P. Newsletter. **VAT** Solar Terrestrial Physics Newsletter. English. qt. $6.00. ICSTI, 51 Boulevard de Montmorency, 75016 Paris France.

STUDIA UNIVERSITATIS BABES-BOLYAI. PHYSICA. **Main/Corp** Universitatea Babes-Bolyai. Began in 1975. 0370-8578. Periodical. English (French, or Romanian). an. Ilexim Press Department, PO Box 1-136-1-137, Bucharest Romania. **Ind/Abst** Math. Rev., Int. Aerosp. Abstr., Chem. Abstr. **LC** QC1. **DD** 530.05. **CODEN** SBBPAJ. *Studia Universitatis Babes-Bolayi. Series Physica.*

STUDIES IN HIGH ENERGY PHYSICS. 0270-4730. Monographic Series. English. qt. $112.50. Harwood Academic Publishers, PO Box 786, Cooper Station, New York NY 10276. **Ind/Abst** Chem. Abstr. **CODEN** SEPHDL.

STUDIES IN MODERN THERMODYNAMICS. *See* Chemistry - Physical and Theoretical Chemistry.

STUDIES IN STATISTICAL MECHANICS. **Series/Titl** Series in Physics. Vol. 1-. 0081-8542. Monographic Series. NE. English. ir. Elsevier Science Publishers, PO Box 1663/Grand Central Station, New York NY 10163. **Ind/Abst** Comput. Control Abstr., Electr. Electron. Abstr., Sci. Abstr. Sect. A. Phys. Abstr., Chem. Abstr., Phys. Abstr., Math. Rev. **LC** QC175. **CODEN** SSTMBG.

STUDII SI CERCETARI DE FIZICA. 0039-3940. Periodical. RM. Romanian (summaries in English). mo. $75.00. Rompresfilatelia, PO Box 1362137, Bucharest Romania. **Ind/Abst** Math. Rev., Electron. Commun. Abstr. J., ISMEC Bull., Pollut. Abstr. Indexes, Saf. Sci. Abstr. J., Int. Aerosp. Abstr., Comput. Control Abstr., Electr. Electron. Abstr., Sci. Abstr. Sect. A. Phys. Abstr., Chem. Abstr., Met. Abstr., World Alum. Abstr., Phys. Abstr. **LC** QC1. **CODEN** SCEFAB. *Studii Si Cercetari de Fizica.*

SURFACE WAVE ABSTRACTS. *See* Indexes/Abstracts.

SURVEYS IN HIGH ENERGY PHYSICS. Vol. 1, No. 1 (Oct. 1979)-. 0142-2413. Periodical. SZ. English. qt. $120.00. Harwood Academic Publishers GMBH, PO Box 786, Cooper Station, New York NY 10003. **Tel** (212)242-4464. **Ed** J M Charap. **Ind/Abst** Comput. Control Abstr., Electr. Electron. Abstr., Sci. Abstr. Sect. A. Phys. Abstr., Chem. Abstr., Phys. Abstr. **LC** QC793. **DD** 539.72105. **CODEN** SHEPDB. bk rev. adv acc.

TECHNICAL REPORT - MASSACHUSETTS INSTITUTE OF TECHNOLOGY. SOLID STATE AND MOLECULAR THEORY GROUP. **Main/Corp** Massachusetts Institute of Technology. Solid State and Molecular Theory Group. No. 1-. US. English. **LC** QC173.

TECHNIQUES OF PHYSICS. 0308-5392. Monographic Series. UK. English. ir. Academic Press, 4805 Sand Lake Road, Orlando FL 32887. **Tel** (305)345-4100. **Ed** John F Cornwell. **Ind/Abst** Comput. Control Abstr., Electr. Electron. Abstr., Sci. Abstr. Sect. A. Phys. Abstr., Math. Rev. **CODEN** TEPHDW.

TECHNISCHE PHYSIK IN EINZELDARSTELLUNGEN. 0082-2590. Monographic Series. English (German). ir. Springer Verlag-New York Inc, 175 5th Avenue, New York NY 10010. **Tel** (212)460-1584.

TEORETICESKAJA I MATEMATICESKAJA FIZIKA. (TEORETICHESKAIA I MATEMATICHESKAIA FIZIKA). Vol. 1- 1969-. 0564-6162. Periodical. UR. Russian (summaries in English). mo. $90.00. Victor Kamkin Inc, 12224 Parklawn Drive, Rockville MD 20852. **Tel** (301)881-5973. **Ind/Abst** Math. Rev., Int. Aerosp. Abstr., Comput. Control Abstr., Electr. Electron. Abstr., Sci. Abstr. Sect. A. Phys. Abstr., Energy Res. Abstr., Chem. Abstr., Phys. Abstr. **LC** QC20. **CODEN** TMFZAL.

TEPLOFIZIKA VYSOKIH TEMPERATUR. (TEPLOFIZIKA VYSOKIKH TEMPERATUR). Vol. 1- 1963-. 0040-3644. Periodical. UR. Russian. bm. $69.50. Victor Kamkin Inc (70967), 12224 Parklawn Drive, Rockville MD 20852. **Tel** (301)881-5973. **Ind/Abst** Int. Aerosp. Abstr., Comput. Control Abstr., Electr. Electron. Abstr., Sci. Abstr. Sect. A. Phys. Abstr., Chem. Abstr., Met. Abstr., World Alum. Abstr., Phys. Abstr. **CODEN** TVYTAP.

TETRAHEDRON. V. 1- Apr. 1957-. 0040-4020. Periodical. UK. English (articles in French and German). ir. Pergamon Press, c/o Cashier, 395 Sawmill River Road, Elmsford NY 10523. **Tel** (914)592-7700. **Ind/Abst** Life Sci. Collect., Excerpta Med., Pestdoc, Ringdoc, Vetdoc, Bibliogr. Agric., Biol. Abstr., Chem. Abstr., Nucl. Sci. Abstr., Sci. Cit. Index, Abr. Ed., Ocean. Abstr. **LC** QD241. **DD** 547.05. **NLM** W1 TE636. **CODEN** TETRAB. (cum index).

TEXTS AND MONOGRAPHS IN PHYSICS. Began in 1976. 0172-5998. Monographic Series. US. English. ir. Springer Verlag-New York Inc, 175 5th Avenue, New York NY 10010. **Tel** (212)460-1584. **Ind/Abst** Math. Rev., Comput. Control Abstr., Electr. Electron. Abstr., Sci. Abstr. Sect. A. Phys. Abstr. Contains articles on quantum dynamics and foundations of quantum mechanics.

THIN SOLID FILMS. V. 1- July 1967-. 0040-6090. Periodical. English (French, or German, with English summaries). ir. $1,454.59. Elsevier Sequoia SA, PO Box 851, 1001 Lausanne Switzerland. **Ind/Abst** Electron. Commun. Abstr. J., ISMEC Bull., Pollut. Abstr. Indexes, Saf. Sci. Abstr. J., Eng. Index Mon., Eng. Index Bioeng. Abstr., Eng. Index Energy Abstr., Comput. Control Abstr., Electr. Electron. Abstr., Sci. Abstr. Sect. A. Phys. Abstr., Energy Res. Abstr., Chem. Abstr., Nucl. Sci. Abstr., Int. Aerosp. Abstr., Eng. Index Annu., Eng. Index, Met. Abstr., World Alum. Abstr., Phys. Abstr., Sci. Cit. Index, Abr. Ed. **LC** TK7871.15.F5. **DD** 082 0 621.38171. **CODEN** THSFAP.

TOPICS IN APPLIED PHYSICS. V. 1- 1973-. 0303-4216. Monographic Series. English. ir. **Tel** (212)460-1500. **Ind/Abst** Comput. Control Abstr., Electr. Electron. Abstr., Sci. Abstr. Sect. A. Phys. Abstr., Energy Res. Abstr., Chem. Abstr. **NLM** W1 TO539E. **CODEN** TAPHD4. Numbered series.

TOPICS IN CURRENT PHYSICS. 1-. 0342-6793. Monographic Series. English. Springer Verlag-New York Inc, 175 5th Avenue, New York NY 10010. **Tel** (212)460-1584. **Ind/Abst** Comput. Control Abstr., Electr. Electron. Abstr., Sci. Abstr. Sect. A. Phys. Abstr., Energy Res. Abstr., Chem. Abstr. **CODEN** TCPHDI. Contains articles on physics.

TRANSPORT THEORY AND STATISTICAL PHYSICS. *See* Statistics.

ULTRASONICS. V. 1- Jan./Mar. 1963. 0041-624X. Periodical. UK. English. bm. 84. Butterworth Scientific Ltd, PO Box 63, Westbury House, Bury Street, Guildford GU2 5BH England. **Tel** 0483 31261. **Ed** Marija Vukovojac. **Ind/Abst** Predicasts, Eng. Index Annu., Funk Scott Index Corp. Ind., Hospit. Lit. Index, Eng. Index Energy Abstr., Fluidex, Abstr. Bull. Inst. Paper Chem., Life Sci. Collect., Excerpta Med., Eng. Index Mon., Index Med., Int. Aerosp. Abstr., Comput. Control Abstr., Electr. Electron. Abstr., Sci. Abstr. Sect. A. Phys. Abstr., CIS Abstr., GeoRef, Chem. Abstr., Met. Abstr., World Alum. Abstr., Appl. Sci. Technol. Index, Sci. Cit. Index, Abr. Ed., Bibliogr. Index Geol., Appl. Mech. Rev., Phys. Abstr., Eng. Index. **LC** TA367. **NLM** W1 UL748. **CODEN** ULTRA3. bk rev. adv acc. Also available on microfiche. Papers from academies and industry describing primary research in ultrasonics.

USPEHI FIZICESKIH NAUK. (USPEKHI FIZICHESKIKH NAUK). Vol. 1- 1918-. 0042-1294. Periodical. UR. Russian (summaries and table of contents in English). mo. $83.00. Victor Kamkin Inc (71004), 12224 Parklawn Drive, Rockville MD 20852. **Tel** (301)881-5973. **Ind/Abst** Math. Rev., Int. Aerosp. Abstr., GeoRef, Comput. Control Abstr., Electr. Electron. Abstr., Sci. Abstr. Sect. A. Phys. Abstr., Chem. Abstr., Met. Abstr., World Alum. Abstr., Sci. Cit. Index, Abr. Ed. **LC** QC1. **CODEN** UFNAAG. (cum index).

USSR AND EASTERN EUROPE SCIENTIFIC ABSTRACTS. PHYSICS. *See* Indexes/Abstracts.

VAKUUM-TECHNIK. Vol. 1- Jan. 1952-. 0042-2266. Periodical. GW. German. ir. 195.-. Rudolf A Lang Verlag, Postfach 1228, 6270 Idstein, Auf der au 2 West Germany. **Tel** (06126)2476. **Ed** Rudolf A Lang. **Ind/Abst** Comput. Control Abstr., Electr. Electron. Abstr., Sci. Abstr., Chem. Abstr., Eng. Index, Int. Aerosp. Abstr., Nucl. Sci. Abstr., Phys. Abstr. **CODEN** VAKTAY. bk rev. adv acc. (ctrl). International technical journal for all areas of research development and application in the fields of physics and technology of the vacuum and of surfaces and thin coatings including measurement and transport technology, materials analysis and technology.

VESTNIK LENINGRADSKOGO UNIVERSITETA. FIZIKA, KHIMIIA. **Main/Corp** Leningradskii Universitet. **VFOAT** Fizika, Khimiia. 0024-0826. Periodical. UR. Russian (table of contents also in English). qt. Victor Kamkin Inc, 12224 Parklawn Drive, Rockville MD 20852. **Tel** (301)881-5973. **Ind/Abst** Math. Rev., Abstr. Bull. Inst. Paper Chem., GeoRef, Comput. Control Abstr., Electr. Electron. Abstr., Sci. Abstr. Sect. A. Phys. Abstr., Chem. Abstr., Energy Res. Abstr. **CODEN** VLUFBI. *Vestnik.*

VESTNIK MOSKOVSKOGO UNIVERSITETA. SERIIA III: FIZIKA, ASTRONOMIIA. (VESTNIK MOSKOVSKOGO UNIVERSITETA. SERIIA III, FIZIKA, ASTRONOMIIA). Began in 1960. 0579-9392. Periodical. UR. Russian. bm. Victor Kamkin Inc, 12224 Parklawn Drive, Rockville MD 20852. **Tel** (301)881-5973. **Ind/Abst** Math. Rev., GeoRef, Int. Aerosp. Abstr., Chem. Abstr., Bibliogr. Agric., Energy Res. Abstr., Met. Abstr., World Alum. Abstr., Comput. Control Abstr., Phys. Abstr., Electr. Electron. Abstr., Sci. Cit. Index, Abr. Ed. **CODEN** VMUFAO. *Vestnik Moskovskogo Universiteta. Seriia Matematiki, Mekhaniki, Astronomii, Fiziki, Khimii.*

LE VIDE, LES COUCHES MINCES. 34.- Year (No. 195-). 0223-4335. Periodical. FR. French (summaries in English). ir. 730. Societe Francaise du Vide, 19 rue du Renard, F-75004 Paris France. **Tel** (33-1)43781582. **Ind/Abst** Eng. Index Annu., Eng. Index Mon., Eng. Index Bioeng. Abstr., Eng. Index Energy Abstr., Comput. Control Abstr., Electr. Electron. Abstr., Sci. Abstr. Sect. A. Phys. Abstr., Chem. Abstr., Energy Res. Abstr., Met. Abstr., World Alum. Abstr. **LC** QC166. **DD** 533.505. **CODEN** VCMIDS. bk rev. adv acc. **Circ** 2,000. (ctrl). Articles about: thin films, vacuum metallurgy, vacuum science, surfaces, industrial vacuum, plasma, dry etching, and leak detection. *Vide.*

VISNYK KYIVSKOHO UNIVERSYTETU. SERIIA FIZYKY. **Main/Corp** Kiev. Universytet. **VFOAT** Seriia Fizyky. Began in 1967 with No. 8. UR. Ukrainian (summaries in English). Tarasivska 11, Kiev USSR. **LC** QC1. *Visnyk Kyivskoho Universytetu. Seriia Fizyky ta Khimii.*

WILEY MONOGRAPHS IN CHEMICAL PHYSICS. 0277-2477. Monographic Series. UK. English. ir. John Wiley & Sons Inc, 1 Wiley Drive, Somerset NJ 08873.

WILEY SERIES IN PLASMA PHYSICS. 0271-602X. Monographic Series. US. English. ir. John Wiley & Sons Inc, 1 Wiley Drive, Somerset NJ 08873.

WISSENSCHAFTLICHE ZEITSCHRIFT DER TECHNISCHEN HOCHSCHULE KARL-MARX-STADT. *See* Engineering.

WU LI HSUEH CHIN CHAN. **VFOAT** Progress in Physics. Periodical. Chinese (abstracts in English). qt. 1.20. Chung-Kuo Kuo Chi Shu Tien, PO Box 399, Pei-Ching China. **LC** QC1. **DD** 530.05.

WU LI HSUEH PAO. **VFOAT** Acta Physica Sinica. Vol. 9, No. 1 (Jan. 1953)-. 0372-736X. Periodical. CC. Chinese (with abstracts in English or Russian). mo. China Publication Centre, PO Box 2820, Beijing China. **Tel** (415)282-2994. **Ind/Abst** Math. Rev., Int. Aerosp. Abstr., Chem. Abstr., Spin, Met. Abstr., World Alum. Abstr., Energy Res. Abstr., Comput. Control Abstr., Electr. Electron. Abstr., Sci. Abstr. Sect. A. Phys. Abstr. **CODEN** WLHPAR. *Chinese Journal of Physics.*

WU LI TIEN TI. **VFOAT** The World of Physics. Chinese or English. ir. **LC** QC1.

ZAHLENWERTE UND FUNKTIONEN AUS NATURWISSENSCHAFTEN UND TECHNIK, NEUE SERIE. **VFOAT** Landolt - Bornstein. Monographic Series. English (German). ir. Springer Verlag-New York Inc, 175 5th Avenue, New York NY 10010. **Tel** (212)460-1584. **LC** QC61. *Zahlenwerte und Funktionen aus Physik, Chemie, Astronomie, Geophysik und Technik.*

ZAMP : ZEITSCHRIFT FUR ANGEWANDTE MATHEMATIK UND PHYSIK. *See* Mathematics.

ZBORNIK RADOVA PRIRODNO-MATEMATICKOG FAKULTETA. SERIJA ZA FIZIKU. **VFOAT** Physics Series. Began in 1981 with V. 11. 0352-0889. Periodical. English (Serbo-Croatian). ir. Prirodno-Matematicki Fakultet U Novom Sadu, Ul Dr Ilije Djuricica 4, 21000 Novi Sad Yugoslavia. **LC** QC1. *Zbornik Radova.*

ZEITSCHRIFT FUR NATURFORSCHUNG. *See* Chemistry.

ZEITSCHRIFT FUR PHYSIK. A. ATOMS AND NUCLEI. (ZEITSCHRIFT FUR PHYSIK A, ATOMS AND NUCLEI). V. 272- 1975-. 0340-2193. GW. Multilingual (English or German with summaries in English). mo. Springer Verlag New York Inc, 175 5th Avenue, New York NY 10010. **Tel** (212)460-1500. **Ed** M Campagna and H Horner. **Ind/Abst** Math. Rev., Comput. Control Abstr., Electr. Electron. Abstr., Sci. Abstr. Sect. A. Phys. Abstr., Chem. Abstr., Energy Res. Abstr., Phys. Abstr., Sci. Cit. Index, Abr. Ed. **LC** QC1. **CODEN** ZPAADB. Covers the physics of condensed matter and general physics. Publishes papers on physical properties of crystallines, disordered, and amorphous solids, and on classical and quantum liquids. *Zeitschrift fur Physik.*

ZEITSCHRIFT FUR PHYSIK B *CEASED.* **VFOAT** Condensed Matter and Quanta. V. 20-37. 0340-224X. US. English. ir. $421.00. Springer Verlag New York Inc, 175 5th Avenue, New York NY 10010. **Tel** (212)460-1500. **Ed** M Campagna and H Horner. **Ind/Abst** Math. Rev., Chem. Abstr., Sci. Cit. Index, Abr. Ed., Phys. Abstr., Comput. Control Abstr., Electr. Electron. Abstr. **LC** QC176.A1. **CODEN** ZPBBDJ. Covers the physics of condensed matter and general physics. Emphasis is put on quantum optics and statistical, especially in the area of nonequilibrium processes and cooperative phenomena. *Zeitschrift fur Physik, Physik der Kondensierten Materie.*

ZEITSCHRIFT FUR PHYSIK. C, PARTICLES AND FIELDS. *See* Physics - Nuclear Physics.

ZHURNAL TEKHNICHESKOI FIZIKI. **VFOAT** Fizicheskii Zhurnal. Vol. 1- 1931-. 0044-4642. Periodical. UR. Russian. mo. $116.00. Victor Kamkin Inc (70298), 12224 Parklawn Drive, Rockville MD 20852. **Tel** (301)881-5973. **Ind/Abst** Met. Abstr., Int. Aerosp. Abstr., World Alum. Abstr., Comput. Control Abstr., Electr. Electron. Abstr., Sci. Abstr. Sect. A. Phys. Abstr., Chem. Abstr., Sci. Cit. Index, Abr. Ed., Appl. Mech. Rev., Phys. Abstr. **LC** QC1. **CODEN** ZTEFA3. *Zhurnal Prikladnoi Fiziki, Fizika I Proizvodstvo.*

ZURNAL EKSPERIMENTALNOJ I TEORETICESKOJ FIZIKI. (ZHURNAL EKSPERIMENTALNOI I TEORETICHESKOI FIZIKI). Periodical. UR. Russian. mo. $227.00. Victor Kamkin Inc (70303), 12224 Parklawn Drive, Rockville MD 20852. **Tel** (301)881-5973. **Ind/Abst** Math. Rev., Int. Aerosp. Abstr., Comput. Control Abstr., Electr. Electron. Abstr., Sci. Abstr. Sect. A. Phys. Abstr. **CODEN** ZETFA7. *Fizicheskii Zhurnal. Seriia A, Zhurnal Eksperimentalnoii I Teoreticheskoi Fiziki.*

ANALYTIC AND EXPERIMENTAL MECHANICS

ANNUAL REVIEW OF FLUID MECHANICS. V. 1- 1969-. 0066-4189. US. English. an. $32.00 Domestic, $35.00 Foreign. Annual Reviews Inc, 4139 El Camino Way, Palo Alto Ca 94306. **Tel** (415)493-4400. **Ed** Milton Van Dyke and John V Wehausen. **Ind/Abst** Fluidex, Life Sci. Collect., Eng. Index Annu., Eng. Index Mon., Eng. Index Bioeng. Abstr., Eng. Index Energy Abstr., Sel. Water Resour. Abstr., Comput. Control Abstr., Electr. Electron. Abstr., Sci. Abstr. Sect. A. Phys. Abstr., GeoRef, Biol. Abstr., Chem. Abstr., Int. Aerosp. Abstr., Appl. Mech. Rev., Sci. Cit. Index, Abr. Ed., Bibliogr. Index Geol., Phys. Abstr., Eng. Index. **LC** QC145. **DD** 532.005. **CODEN** ARVFA3. (cum index). Comprehensive, thorough coverage of latest advances in fluid mechanics, written by acknowledged experts in the field. Extensive literature citations included.

ARCHIVE FOR RATIONAL MECHANICS AND ANALYSIS. *See* Genealogy and Heraldry - Archives.

ARCHIVES OF MECHANICS. *See* Genealogy and Heraldry - Archives.

CHISLENNYE METODY MEKHANIKI SPLOSHNOI SREDY. V. 1, No. 1-. UR. Russian. 0.50 Single Issue. Adademiia Nauk SSSR, 630090 Novosibirsk Russia. **Ind/Abst** Math. Rev., Energy Res. Abstr. **LC** QA808.2.

CISLENNYE METODY V DINAMIKE RAZREZENNYH GAZOV. (CHISLENNYE METODY V DINAMIKE RAZREZHENNYKH GAZOV). **Main/Corp** Akademiia Nauk SSSR. Laboratoriia Teorii

Protsessov Perenosa. No. 1- 1973-. 0302-6086. UR. Russian. 0.73 Single Issue. **Ind/Abst** Int. Aerosp. Abstr., Chem. Abstr. **LC** QA930. **CODEN** CMRGA7.

DEVELOPMENTS IN FRACTURE MECHANICS. **Series/Titl** Developments Series. 1-. UK. English. Applied Science Publishers, Englewood NJ 07631. **LC** TA409. **DD** 620.166.

DEVELOPMENTS IN THEORETICAL AND APPLIED MECHANICS. (DEVELOPMENTS IN THEORETICAL AND APPLIED MECHANICS. PROCEEDINGS). **Main/Conf** Southeastern Conference on Theoretical and Applied Mechanics. 0070-4598. US. English. Pergamon Press, 395 Sawmill River Road, Elmsford NY 10523. **LC** QA801. **DD** 620.1005.

EXPERIMENTAL MECHANICS. V. 1- Jan. 1961-. 0014-4851. Periodical. US. English. qt. Society for Experimental Stress Analysis, 14 Fairfield Drive, Brookfield Center CT 06805. **Ind/Abst** Eng. Index Mon., Eng. Index Bioeng. Abstr., Eng. Index Energy Abstr., Coal Abstr., Abstr. Bull. Inst. Paper Chem., Int. Aerosp. Abstr., Comput. Control Abstr., Electr. Electron. Abstr., Sci. Abstr. Sect. A. Phys. Abstr., Met. Abstr., World Alum. Abstr., Chem. Abstr., Eng. Index Annu., Eng. Index Mon., Nuci. Sci. Abstr., Appl. Sci. Technol. Index. **LC** TA401. **DD** 620.110287. **CODEN** EXMCAZ.

FIZIKA, A JOURNAL OF EXPERIMENTAL AND THEORETICAL PHYSICS. **VFOAT** Fizika. V. 1- 1969-. 0015-3206. Periodical. YU. English (German). qt. Commission for Physics, National Committee of IUPAP, Zagreb 3 Gric 3 Yugoslavia. **Ind/Abst** Comput. Control Abstr., Electr. Electron. Abstr., Sci. Abstr. Sect. A. Phys. Abstr. **CODEN** FZKAAA. Index published separately - free - automatically sent.

FIZIKA I TEKHNIKA VYSOKIKH DAVLENII. Began in 1980. UR. Russian (summaries in English). 1.40. Izdaetlstvo Naukova Dumka, 252601 Kiev, GSP Repina 3, Kiev Russia SFSR. **Ind/Abst** Chem. Abstr. **LC** QC281. **DD** 531.11. **CODEN** FTVDDZ.

FIZIKA TVERDOGO TELA (DONETSKII GOSUDARSTRENNYI UNIVERSITET). (FIZIKA TVERDOGO TELA). No. 1 (1970)-. 0202-2915. Russian. ir. **Ind/Abst** Chem. Abstr. **LC** QC176. **CODEN** FZTTAA.

FLUID DYNAMICS TRANSACTIONS. **Main/Conf** Symposium on Advanced Problems and Methods in Fluid Mechanics. V. 5- 1969-. 0137-6462. English (French, German, or Russian). ir. **Ind/Abst** Int. Aerosp. Abstr. **LC** QA911. **DD** 532.05. *Fluid Dynamics Transactions, 0137-6462.*

FLUID MECHANICS. SOVIET RESEARCH. (FLUID MECHANICS : SOVIET RESEARCH). V. 1- Jan./Feb. 1972-. 0096-0764. Periodical. US. English. bm. John Wiley & Sons Inc, 605 Third Avenue, New York NY 10158. **Tel** (800)526-5368. **Ind/Abst** Math. Rev., Electron. Commun. Abstr. J., ISMEC Bull., Pollut. Abstr. Indexes, Saf. Sci. Abstr. J., Eng. Index Mon., Eng. Index Bioeng. Abstr., Eng. Index Energy Abstr., Fluidex, Coal Abstr., GeoRef, Comput. Control Abstr., Electr. Electron. Abstr., Sci. Abstr. Sect. A. Phys. Abstr., Chem. Abstr., Eng. Index Annu., Phys. Abstr., Nuci. Sci. Abstr., Sel. Water Resour. Abstr., Spin, Int. Aerosp. Abstr., Energy Res. Abstr., Appl. Mech. Rev., Eng. Index. **LC** QC145.2. **DD** 532.005. **CODEN** FMSVAM.

HOMMES ET FONDERIE. Began in 1970-. 0018-4357. Periodical. FR. French. ir. $43.11. PYC Edition, 254 rue de Vangirard, 75740 Paris Cedex 15 France. **Tel** 532 27 19. **Ind/Abst** Chem. Abstr., Met. Abstr., World Alum. Abstr. **CODEN** HFONDM. *Revue Mensuelle d'Information.*

IFF-BULLETIN. (IFF BULLETIN). **Main/Corp** Kernforschungsanlage Julich. Institut fur Festkorperforschung. **VAT** Institut fur Festkorperforschung Bulletin. 0340-0743. German (English). ir. **Ind/Abst** Energy Res. Abstr. **LC** QC176.A1.

INTERNATIONAL JOURNAL FOR NUMERICAL METHODS IN FLUIDS. Vol. 1, No. 1 (Jan.-Mar. 1981)-. 0271-2091. Periodical. UK. English. mo. John Wiley & Sons Inc, Baffins Land Chichester, Sussex PO19 1UD England. **Ind/Abst** Math. Rev., Electron. Commun. Abstr. J., ISMEC Bull., Pollut. Abstr. Indexes, Saf. Sci. Abstr. J., Fluidex, Eng. Index Annu., Eng. Index Mon., Eng. Index Bioeng. Abstr., Eng. Index Energy Abstr., Ship Abstr., Abstr. Bull. Inst. Paper Chem., Int. Aerosp. Abstr. **LC** QA901. **DD** 532.005. **CODEN** IJNFDW.

INTERNATIONAL JOURNAL OF FRACTURE. V. 9- Mar. 1973-. 0376-9429. Periodical. English. mo. Kluwer Academic Publishing Group, PO Box 332, 3300 AH Dordrecht Netherlands. **Tel** 078-172811. **Ed** M L Williams. **Ind/Abst** Math. Rev., Electron. Commun. Abstr. J., ISMEC Bull., Pollut. Abstr. Indexes, Saf. Sci. Abstr. J., Eng. Index Annu., Eng. Index Mon., Eng. Index Bioeng. Abstr., Eng. Index Energy Abstr., Ship Abstr., Int. Aerosp. Abstr., Comput. Control Abstr., Electr. Electron. Abstr., Sci. Abstr. Sect. A. Phys. Abstr., Met. Abstr., World Alum. Abstr., Chem. Abstr., Phys. Abstr., Sci. Cit. Index, Abr. Ed., Eng. Index. **LC** TA409. **DD** 620.112605. **CODEN** IJFRAP. adv acc. **Circ** 1,100. (ctrl). Original or experimental contributions which provide better understanding of mechanisms that cause micro and macro fracture in all engineering manifestations and significance. *International Journal of Fracture Mechanics, 0020-7268.*

INTERNATIONAL JOURNAL OF NON-LINEAR MECHANICS. V. 1- Apr. 1966-. 0020-7462. Periodical. US. English. bm. Pergamon Press, 395 Sawmill River Road, Elmsford NY 10523. **Tel** (914)592-7700. **Ind/Abst** Electron. Commun. Abstr. J., ISMEC Bull., Pollut. Abstr. Indexes, Saf. Sci. Abstr. J., Eng. Index, Comput. Control Abstr., Electr. Electron. Abstr., Sci. Abstr., Int. Aerosp. Abstr., Math. Rev., Nuci. Sci. Abstr., Energy Res. Abstr., Phys. Abstr., Sci. Cit. Index, Abr. Ed., Sci. Abstr. Sect. A. Phys. Abstr., Eng. Index Annu., Eng. Index Mon., Eng. Index Energy Abstr., Eng. Index Bioeng. Abstr. **LC** QA427. **DD** 531. **CODEN** IJNMAG. Available on microform from Microforms Int. Marketing Corp.

INTERNATIONAL JOURNAL OF SOLIDS AND STRUCTURES. V. 1- Feb. 1965-. 0020-7683. Periodical. US. English (summaries in Russian). mo. Pergamon Press, 395 Sawmill River Road, Elmsford NY 10523. **Tel** (914)592-7700. **Ind/Abst** Electron. Commun. Abstr. J., ISMEC Bull., Pollut. Abstr. Indexes, Saf. Sci. Abstr. J., Eng. Index Mon., Eng. Index Bioeng. Abstr., Eng. Index Energy Abstr., GeoRef, Comput. Control Abstr., Electr. Electron. Abstr., Sci. Abstr. Sect. A. Phys. Abstr., Met. Abstr., World Alum. Abstr., Chem. Abstr., Eng. Index Annu., Eng. Index, Phys. Abstr., Int. Aerosp. Abstr., Math. Rev., Sci. Cit. Index, Abr. Ed., Appl. Mech. Rev. **LC** TA349. **CODEN** IJSOAD. Available on microfilm from Microfilms International Marketing Corp.

ISSLEDOVANIIA PO UPRUGOSTI I PLASTICHNOSTI. Vol. 1-. 0578-9583. UR. Russian. **Ind/Abst** Int. Aerosp. Abstr., Chem. Abstr. **LC** QA931. **CODEN** IDUPAI.

ITOGI NAUKI I TEKHNIKI : GIDROMEKHANIKA. **VFOAT** Itogi Nauki Tekhniki. UR. Russian. 1.56 Single Issue. Proizvodstvenno-Izdatelskii Kombinat Viniti, Liubertsy, Oktiabrskii Prospekt 403, Moskva Russian SFSR. **LC** QC138. *Itogi Nauki: Gedromekhanika.*

ITOGI NAUKI I TEKHNIKI : MEKHANIKA DEFORMIRUEMOGO TVERDOGO TELA. **VFOAT** Mekhanika Deformiruemogo Tverdogo Tela. V. 10-. Periodical. UR. Russian. 1.31. Liubertsy, Oktiabrskii Prospekt 403, Moskva Russian SFSR. **LC** QA801. *Itogi Nauki I Tekhniki: Mekhanika Tverdykh Deformiruemykh Tel.*

ITOGI NAUKI I TEKHNIKI : MEKHANIKA ZHIDKOSTI I GAZA. **VFOAT** Itogi Nauki I Tekhniki: Seriia Mekhanika Zhidkosti I Gaza. V. 10-. 0202-781X. Periodical. UR. Russian. 1.40 Single Issue. 140010 G Liubertsy, 10 Moskovskoi Obl, Oktiarskii Prosp, Maskva Russian SFSR. **Ind/Abst** Chem. Abstr. **LC** QC138. **CODEN** ITSGDS. *Itogi Nauki I Tekhniki: Gidromekhanika.*

ITOGI NAUKI I TEKHNIKI : OBSHCHAIA MEKHANIKA. **VFOAT** Obshchaia Mekhanika. V. 2-. Periodical. UR. Russian. 0.90. Liubertsy, 10 Moskovskoi Obl, Oktiabrskii Prosp 403, Moskva Russian SFSR. **LC** QA801. *Itogi Nauki: Obshchaia Mekhanika.*

IZVESTIJA AKADEMIJA NAUK SSSR, MEHANIKA ZIDKOSTI I GAZA. (IZVESTIIA. MEKHANIKA ZHIDKOSTI I GAZA). **Main/Corp** Akademiia Nauk SSSR. **VFOAT** Mekhanika Zhidkosti i Gaza. Jan./Feb. 1966-. 0568-5281. Periodical. UR. Russian. bm. $50.00. Victor Kamkin Inc, 12224 Parklawn Drive, Rockville MD 20852. **Tel** (301)881-5973. **Ind/Abst** Math. Rev., Int. Aerosp. Abstr., Comput. Control Abstr., Electr. Electron. Abstr., Sci. Abstr. Sect. A. Phys. Abstr., Chem. Abstr., Energy Res. Abstr., Appl. Mech. Rev., Phys. Abstr. **LC** QA901. **CODEN** IMZGAB. *Izvestiia. Mekhanika.*

JEMNA MECHANIKA A OPTIKA. Began publication in 1956. 0447-6441. CS. Czech. mo. Artia, Ve Smeckach 30, Praha 1 Czechoslovakia. **Ind/Abst** Int. Aerosp. Abstr., CIS Abstr., Comput. Control Abstr., Electr. Electron. Abstr., Sci. Abstr. Sect. A. Phys. Abstr., Phys. Abstr. **LC** TS500. **CODEN** JMKOA5.

JOURNAL DE MECANIQUE *CEASED.* V. 1-20. 0021-7832. Periodical. FR. French. qt. Gauthier-Villars, B P No 119, 93104 Montreuil Cedex France. **Ind/Abst** Eng. Index Annu., Eng. Index Mon., Eng. Index Bioeng. Abstr., Eng. Index Energy Abstr., GeoRef, Chem. Abstr., Eng. Index Mon., Int. Aerosp. Abstr., Math. Rev., Nuci. Sci. Abstr. **LC** QA801. **CODEN** JOMCAR.

JOURNAL DE MECANIQUE THEORIQUE ET APPLIQUEE. **VFOAT** Journal of Theoretical and Applied Mechanics. Vol. 1, No. 1-. 0750-7240. Periodical. FR. English (French with summaries in English and French). ir. 770. CDR Centrale des Revues, 11 rue Gossin, 92543 Montrouge Cedex France. **Ind/Abst** Math. Rev., Fluidex, Comput. Control Abstr., Electr. Electron. Abstr., Excerpta Med., Life Sci. Collect., Sci. Abstr. Sect. A. Phys. Abstr., Chem. Abstr., Energy Res. Abstr. **LC** QA801. **DD** 531. **CODEN** JMTADB. *Journal de Mecanique, 0021-7832; Journal de Mecanique Appliquee, 0399-0842.*

JOURNAL OF APPLIED MATHEMATICS AND MECHANICS. **VFOAT** Applied Mathematics and Mechanics. V. 22-. 0021-8928. Periodical. UK. English (Russian). bm. Pergamon Press, 395 Sawmill River Road, Elmsford NY 10532. **Tel** (914)592-7700. **Ind/Abst** Math. Rev., Eng. Index Mon., Eng. Index Bioeng. Abstr., Eng. Index Energy Abstr., Chem. Abstr., Eng. Index Annu., Eng. Index Mon., Int. Aerosp. Abstr., Math. Rev., Nuci. Sci. Abstr., Comput. Control Abstr., Electr. Electron. Abstr., Sci. Abstr. Sect. A. Phys. Abstr., Appl. Mech. Rev. **LC** QA801. **DD** 531.017. **CODEN** JAMMAR. (cum index).

JOURNAL OF ELASTICITY. V. 1- Sept. 1971-. 0374-3535. Periodical. NE. English (abstracts in English, French or German). qt. 356.00. Kluwer Academic Publishing Group, PO Box 322, 3300 AH Dordrecht Netherlands. **Tel** 078-172811. **Ed** D E Carlson. **Ind/Abst** Math. Rev., Electron. Commun. Abstr. J., ISMEC Bull., Pollut. Abstr. Indexes, Saf. Sci. Abstr. J., Eng. Index Annu., Eng. Index Mon., Eng. Index Bioeng. Abstr., Eng. Index Energy Abstr., Int. Aerosp. Abstr., Comput. Control Abstr., Electr. Electron. Abstr., Sci. Abstr. Sect. A. Phys. Abstr., ISMEC Bull., Phys. Abstr., Sci. Cit. Index, Abr. Ed., Appl. Mech. Rev., Eng. Index. **LC** QA931. **DD** 531.382305. **CODEN** JELSAY. adv acc. **Circ** 400. (ctrl). The journal's main purpose is to report original and significant discoveries in elasticity which will be published as full papers or research notes.

JOURNAL OF FLUID MECHANICS. V. 1- May 1956-. 0022-1120. Periodical. UK. English. mo. Cambridge University Press, 510 North Avenue, New Rochelle NY 10801. **Ed** G K Batchelor. **Ind/Abst** Math. Rev., Electron. Commun. Abstr. J., ISMEC Bull., Pollut. Abstr. Indexes, Saf. Sci. Abstr. J., Eng. Index Annu., Eng. Index Mon., Eng. Index Bioeng. Abstr., Eng. Index Energy Abstr., Fluidex, Life Sci. Collect., Ship Abstr., Abstr. Bull. Inst. Paper Chem., GeoRef, Comput. Control Abstr., Electr. Electron. Abstr., Sci. Abstr. Sect. A. Phys. Abstr., Chem. Abstr., Nuci. Sci. Abstr., Int. Aerosp. Abstr., Sel. Water Resour. Abstr. **LC** QA901. **DD** 532.505. **CODEN** JFLSA7. (cum index).

JOURNAL OF NON-NEWTONIAN FLUID MECHANICS. V. 1- Jan. 1976-. 0377-0257. Periodical. NE. English. bm. Elsevier Science Publishers, PO Box 211, 1000 AE Amsterdam Netherlands. **Tel** (020)5803911. **Ind/Abst** Eng. Index, Fluidex, Comput. Control Abstr., Electr. Electron. Abstr., Sci. Abstr., Phys. Abstr., Chem. Abstr., Sci. Cit. Index, Abr. Ed., Appl. Mech. Rev., Eng. Index Annu., Eng. Index Bioeng. Abstr., Eng. Index Energy Abstr., Eng. Index Mon., Sci. Abstr. Sect. A. Phys. Abstr. **LC** QA901. **DD** 532.005. **CODEN** JNFMDI.

JOURNAL OF RHEOLOGY. V. 22- Feb. 1978-. 0148-6055. Periodical. US. English. bm. John Wiley & Sons, 605 Third Avenue, New York NY 10158. **Tel** (800)526-5368. **Ind/Abst** Math. Rev., Eng. Index Annu., Eng. Index Mon., Eng. Index Bioeng. Abstr., Eng. Index Energy Abstr., Art Archaeol. Tech. Abstr., Int. Aerosp. Abstr., Comput. Control Abstr., Electr. Electron. Abstr., Sci. Abstr. Sect. A. Phys. Abstr., Spin, Chem. Abstr., Energy Res. Abstr. **LC** QC189. **DD** 531.1105. **CODEN** JORHD2. *Transactions of the Society of Rheology, 0038-0032.*

JOURNAL OF THE MECHANICS AND PHYSICS OF SOLIDS. V. 1- Oct. 1952-. 0022-5096. Periodical. UK. English. bm. Pergamon Press, 395 Sawmill River Road, Elmsford NY 10523.

Physics—Heat

Tel (914)592-7700. Ind/Abst Eng. Index Mon., Eng. Index Bioeng. Abstr., Eng. Index Energy Abstr., Comput. Control Abstr., Electr. Electron. Abstr., Sci. Abstr. Sect. A. Phys. Abstr., Met. Abstr., World Alum. Abstr., Chem. Abstr., Eng. Index Annu., Eng. Index, Int. Aerosp. Abstr., Math. Rev., Nucl. Sci. Abstr., ISMEC Bull., Phys. Abstr., Sci. Cit. Index, Abr. Ed., Appl. Mech. Rev. LC TA350. CODEN JMPSA8.

KENKYU ROMBUN SHOROKU SHU. Main/Corp Kyushu Daigaki, Fukuoka Japan. Tokyo Rikigaku Kenkyujo. VFOAT Abstracts of Papers. JA. English and Japanese. ir. Kyushu Daigaku Oyo Rikigaku Kenkyujo, 10-1 Hakozaki 6, Higashi-Ku 812 Fukuoka Japan. LC TA349.

KOTAI BUTSURI. A SHIRIZU. VFOAT Solid State Physics. A Series. Began in 1976. Periodical. JA. Japanese. mo. 104.00. Maruzen Company Ltd, PO Box 5050, 100-31 Tokyo Japan. Tel 03-409-5329. Ed Seizo Nagasaki. Ind/Abst Chem. Abstr. CODEN KBUADI. adv acc. Circ 6,000. (ctrl) Introduces experimentation and theory of solid state physics. *Kotai Butsusi.*

LI HSUEH CHIN CHAN. VFOAT Advances in Mechanics. Periodical. CC. Chinese. qt. 0.80. Hsin Hua Shu Tien, Peking China. LC QC120. DD 531.05.

LI HSUEH YU SHIH CHIEN. Periodical. CH. Chinese. bm. $10.80. China Publication Centre, PO Box 2820, Beijing China.

MECCANICA. V. 1- 1966-. 0025-6455. Periodical. IT. English. qt. $50.00. Pitagora Editrice, Via del Legatore 3, 40138 Bologna Italy. Tel 051-53-00-03. Ed PITSFORD. Ind/Abst Math. Rev., Electron. Commun. Abstr. J., ISMEC Bull., Pollut. Abstr. Indexes, Saf. Sci. Abstr. J., Fluidex, Int. Aerosp. Abstr., Comput. Control Abstr., Electr. Electron. Abstr., Sci. Abstr. Sect. A. Phys. Abstr., Chem. Abstr., Appl. Mech. Rev., Eng. Index, Phys. Abstr. LC QA801. CODEN MECCB9. Circ 1,000. Concerns applied mechanics.

MECHANICS RESEARCH COMMUNICATIONS. V. 1- 1974-. 0093-6413. Periodical. US. English. bm. Pergamon Press, 395 Sawmill River Road, Elmsford NY 10523. Ind/Abst Math. Rev., Int. Aerosp. Abstr., Comput. Control Abstr., Electr. Electron. Abstr., Sci. Abstr. Sect. A. Phys. Abstr., Appl. Mech. Rev., Sci. Cit. Index, Abr. Ed., Phys. Abstr. LC TA349. DD 620.1005. CODEN MRCOD2.

MECHANIKA TEORETYCZNA I STOSOWANA. V. 1- 1963-. 0079-3701. Periodical. PL. Polish (summaries in English and Russian). qt. ARS Polona, Krakowskie Przedmiescie 7, 00-068 Warsaw Poland. Ind/Abst Math. Rev., Eng. Index Annu., Eng. Index Mon., Eng. Index, Eng. Index Bioeng. Abstr., Eng. Index Energy Abstr., Int. Aerosp. Abstr., Comput. Control Abstr., Electr. Electron. Abstr., Sci. Abstr. Sect. A. Phys. Abstr., Phys. Abstr., Appl. Mech. Rev. LC QA801. CODEN MTYSAX.

MOSCOW UNIVERSITY MECHANICS BULLETIN. Main/Corp Moskovskii Gosudarstvennyi Universitet IM. M. V. Lomonosova. VFOAT Mechanics Bulletin. 0027-1330. Periodical. US. English (Russian). bm. Allerton Press Inc, 150 Fifth Avenue, New York NY 10011. Tel (212)924-3950. Ind/Abst Eng. Index Annu., Eng. Index Mon., Eng. Index Bioeng. Abstr., Eng. Index Energy Abstr., Int. Aerosp. Abstr., Chem. Abstr., Appl. Mech. Rev., Eng. Index. CODEN MUVMB8.

PROBLEMY TEORII GRAVITATSII I ELEMENTARNYKH CHASTITS. Began in 1966-. 0370-2189. Periodical. UR. Russian. an. 1.90. Energoizdat 113114, Shliuzova Nab 10, Moskva M 114 USSR. Ind/Abst Math. Rev., Int. Aerosp. Abstr., Phys. Abstr. LC QC178. DD 531.1405. CODEN PTGEA2.

REFERATIVNYI ZHURNAL. MEKHANIKA CEASED. VFOAT Mekhanika. 1953, 1 (Oct. 1953)-1981, 12 (Dec. 1981). 0034-2483. Periodical. UR. Russian. mo. Ind/Abst Math. Rev. LC QC1. (cum index).

RHEOLOGY ABSTRACTS. See Indexes/Abstracts.

SHINKU. VFOAT Journal of the Vacuum Society of Japan. Began in 1958. 0559-8516. Periodical. JA. Japanese. mo. $99.00. Maruzen Company Ltd, PO Box 5050, 100-31 Tokyo Japan. Ind/Abst Chem. Abstr., Comput. Control Abstr., Electr. Electron. Abstr., Sci. Abstr. Sect. A. Phys. Abstr. CODEN SHINAM. (ctrl). *Shinku Kogyo, Shinku Gujutsu.*

SM ARCHIVES. See Genealogy and Heraldry - Archives.

SOLID STATE IONICS. V. 1/2- Apr. 1980-. 0167-2738. Periodical. US. English. bm. $74.75. Elsevier/North-Holland Inc, 52 Vanderbilt Avenue, New York NY 10017. Ind/Abst Eng. Index Annu., Eng. Index Mon., Eng. Index Bioeng. Abstr., Eng. Index Energy Abstr., Comput. Control Abstr., Electr. Electron. Abstr., Sci. Abstr. Sect. A. Phys. Abstr., Chem. Abstr., Met. Abstr., World Alum. Abstr. LC QC176.A1. DD 530.41. CODEN SSIOD3.

STATISTICAL MECHANICS. See Statistics.

STRAIN. V. 1- Jan. 1965-. 0039-2103. Periodical. UK. English. qt. 30. British Society for Strain Measurement, Exchange Building Quayside, Newcastle-Upon-Tyne NE1 3BJ England. Tel 0632-617971. Ed R Royles. Ind/Abst Eng. Index Mon., Eng. Index Bioeng. Abstr., Eng. Index Energy Abstr., Life Sci. Collect., Ship Abstr., Int. Aerosp. Abstr., Comput. Control Abstr., Electr. Electron. Abstr., Sci. Abstr. Sect. A. Phys. Abstr., Appl. Mech. Rev., Eng. Index, Eng. Index Mon., Eng. Index Annu., Met. Abstr., World Alum. Abstr. CODEN STRNBG. Index in first issue of next volume - loose - separately paged. (cum index). bk rev. adv acc. Circ 1,750. Strain and stress measurement and analysis using strain gauges, transducers and other engineering measurements to assist product design evaluation and test.

THEORETICAL AND APPLIED MECHANICS. VFOAT Teoreticheskaia I Prikladnaia Mekhanika (Romanized Form). 1 (1975)-. 0350-2708. Periodical. YU. English (text in Russian, French, or German). an. Prirodno-Matematicki Fakultet Institut za Mehaniku, Postanski Pregradak 550, 11000 Beograd Yugoslavia. Ind/Abst Math. Rev.

USPEKHI MEKHANIKI. VFOAT Advances in Mechanics. V. 1-. Periodical. Russian (summaries in English). ir. Wydawnictwa Ippt Pan Swietokrzyska 21, 00-049 Warszawa Poland. Ind/Abst Math. Rev. LC QA801.

VACUUM. V. 1- Jan. 1951-. 0042-207X. Periodical. UK. English. mo. $65.00 Institution $25.00 Individual. Pergamon Press, Maxwell House, Fairview Park, Elmsford NY 10523. Ind/Abst Eng. Index Annu., Eng. Index Mon., Eng. Index Bioeng. Abstr., Eng. Index Energy Abstr., Fluidex, Int. Aerosp. Abstr., Comput. Control Abstr., Electr. Electron. Abstr., Sci. Abstr. Sect. A. Phys. Abstr., Chem. Abstr., Eng. Index Mon., Nucl. Sci. Abstr., Met. Abstr., World Alum. Abstr., Appl. Sci. Technol. Index. LC QC166. DD 533.12. NLM W1 VA244. CODEN VACUAV.

VOPROSY KVANTOVOI TEORII ATOMOV I MOLEKUL. Vol. 1-. Periodical. UR. Russian. ir. 2.25 Single Issue. Izdatelstvo Lgu Im AA Zhdanova, 199164 Leningrad Universitetskaia Nab 7/9, Lenningrad Russia. LC QC173.96.

YONGU NONMUNJIP (PUSAN TAEHAKKYO. MULSONG YONGUSO). (YONGU NONMUNJIP). Periodical. English (Korean). an. Pusan Taehakkyo Mulsong Yonguso, San 30 Tongnae-Ku, Pusan Korea. LC QC172.

ZEITSCHRIFT FUR NATURFORSCHUNG. TEIL A, PHYSIK, PHYSIKALISCHE CHEMIE, KOSMOPHYSIK. VFOAT Physik, Physikalische Chemie, Kosmophysik. Vol. 27A, Issue 1 (Jan. 1972)-. 0340-4811. Periodical. GW. German. mo. 485.-. Verlag der Zeitsch fur Naturforschung, Postfach 2645, D7400 Tuebingen West Germany. Tel (06131)573276. Ed S Grossmann, A Kelmm and H Pfirsch. Ind/Abst Excerpta Med., Int. Aerosp. Abstr., Comput. Control Abstr., Electr. Electron. Abstr., Sci. Abstr. Sect. A. Phys. Abstr., Math. Rev., Curr. Contents, Phys. Abstr., Energy Res. Abstr., Met. Abstr., World Alum. Abstr., Chem. Abstr., Sci. Cit. Index, Abr. Ed., Phys. Abstr. LC QC1. DD 505. Index in last issue of volume - attached. adv acc. Circ 1,100. Original papers, letter, general reviews. *Zeitschrift fur Naturforschung. A, Astrophysik, Physik, Physikalische Chemie,* 0044-3166.

HEAT

ADVANCES IN HEAT TRANSFER. V. 1- 1964-. 0065-2717. US. English. ir. Academic Press, 4805 Sand Lake Road, Orlando FL 32887. Tel (305)345-4100. Ed Thomas F Irvine Jr and James P Hartnett. Ind/Abst Energy Inf. Abstr., Environ. Abstr., Comput. Control Abstr., Electr. Electron. Abstr., Sci. Abstr. Sect. A. Phys. Abstr., GeoRef, Energy Res. Abstr., Bibliogr. Index Geol., Phys. Abstr. LC QC320.A1. DD 536.2082. CODEN AHTRAR.

ADVANCES IN TRANSPORT PROCESSES. Vol. 1-. 0271-2334. Periodical. US. English. ir. John Wiley & Sons Inc, 1 Wiley Drive, Somerset NJ 08873. Tel (212)850-6418. Ind/Abst Chem. Abstr. LC QC319.8. DD 531.1137. CODEN ATRPDU.

BULLETIN OF THERMODYNAMICS AND THERMOCHEMISTRY. (BULLETIN OF THERMODYNAMICA AND THERMOCHEMISTRY). No. 1-19. 0068-4139. US. English. an. *Thermochemical Bulletin, Bulletin of Unpublished Thermal Data.*

CRYOGENIC INFORMATION REPORT. No. 1- Apr. 1963-. 0011-2259. Periodical. US. English. ir. Impact, PO Box 1972, Estes Park CO 80517. Tel (303)586-5636. Ed Arthur L Anderson. bk rev. adv acc. Circ 300. New products, patents, research, etc., on what's happening in cryogenics worldwide.

FIZIKA NIZKIKH TEMPERATUR. VFOAT Low Temperature Physics. Vol. 1- Jan. 1975-. 0430-6244. Periodical. UR. Russian (summaries in English). mo. $81.00. Victor Kamkin Inc (74527), 12224 Parklawn Drive, Rockville MD 20852. Tel (301)881-5973. Ind/Abst Int. Aerosp. Abstr., Comput. Control Abstr., Electr. Electron. Abstr., Sci. Abstr. Sect. A. Phys. Abstr., Chem. Abstr., Phys. Abstr., Sci. Cit. Index, Abr. Ed. LC QC278. CODEN FNTEDK.

GONGCHENG REWULI XUEBAO. (KUNG CHENG JE WU LI HSUEH PAO). VFOAT Journal of Engineering Thermodynamics. V. 1, (Feb. 1980)-. 0253-231X. Periodical. CH. Chinese (abstracts in English). qt. Chung-Kuo Kuo Chi Shu Tien, PO Box 2820, Peking China Mainland. Ind/Abst Chem. Abstr., Fluidex. LC QC310.15. DD 621.402105. CODEN KCJPDF.

HEAT TECHNOLOGY. V. 1- Spring 1970-. 0017-9337. Periodical. US. English. ir. Selas Corporation of America, PO Box 200, Dresher PA 19025. Tel (215)646-6600. Ind/Abst Chem. Abstr. CODEN HTTCA7.

HEAT TRANSFER AND FLUID FLOW DATA BOOK. Main/Corp General Electric Company. Research and Development Center. 1943-. US. English. ir. $395.00. Genium Publishing Corporation, 1145 Catalyn Street, Schenctady NY 12303. Tel (518)377-8854.

HEAT TRANSFER. JAPANESE RESEARCH. (HEAT TRANSFER : JAPANESE RESEARCH). V. 1- Jan./March 1972-. 0096-0802. Periodical. US. English. qt. John Wiley & Sons Inc, 605 Third Avenue, New York NY 10158. Tel (212)692-6035. Ind/Abst Eng. Index Mon., Eng. Index Bioeng. Abstr., Eng. Index Energy Abstr., Fluidex, Comput. Control Abstr., Electr. Electron. Abstr., Sci. Abstr. Sect. A. Phys. Abstr., Int. Aerosp. Abstr., Nucl. Sci. Abstr., Chem. Abstr., Eng. Index Annu., Eng. Index Mon., Energy Res. Abstr., Phys. Abstr., ISMEC Bull., Appl. Mech. Rev., Eng. Index. LC QC320. DD 621.402205. CODEN HTJPAU.

HEAT TRANSFER. SOVIET RESEARCH. (HEAT TRANSFER : SOVIET RESEARCH). V. 1- Jan. 1969-. 0440-5749. Periodical. US. English. bm. John Wiley and Sons Inc, 605 3rd Avenue, New York NY 10158. Tel (800)526-5368. Ind/Abst Eng. Index Mon., Eng. Index Bioeng. Abstr., Eng. Index Energy Abstr., Fluidex, Coal Abstr., Chem. Abstr., Eng. Index Annu., Sci. Abstr. Sect. A. Phys. Abstr., Eng. Index, Nucl. Sci. Abstr., Energy Res. Abstr., ISMEC Bull., Phys. Abstr., Comput. Control Abstr., Appl. Mech. Rev., Electr. Electron. Abstr., Int. Aerosp. Abstr. LC QC320. DD 536.2005. CODEN HTSRAD.

HEAT TREATMENT OF METALS. See Metals & Metallurgy.

HEAT TREATMENT OF REFUSE FOR INCREASING ANAEROBIC BIODEGRADABILITY. Series Corp Stanford University. Dept. of Civil Engineering. Technical Report. (2d- Jan./June 1975-). Periodical. US. English. sa.

HIGH TEMPERATURE. V. 1- July/Aug. 1963-. 0018-151X. Periodical. US. English (Russian). bm. $645.00 Domestic, $715.00 Foreign. Consultants Bureau, 233 Spring Street, New York NY 10013. Tel (212)620-8000. Ed A E Sheidun. Ind/Abst Electron. Commun. Abstr. J., ISMEC Bull., Pollut. Abstr. Indexes, Saf. Sci. Abstr. J., Eng. Index Mon., Eng. Index Bioeng. Abstr., Eng. Index Energy Abstr., Fluidex, Comput. Control Abstr., Electr. Electron. Abstr., Sci. Abstr. Sect. A. Phys. Abstr., Chem. Abstr., Curr. Contents, Eng. Index Annu., Eng. Index Mon.,

Int. Aerosp. Abstr., Nuci. Sci. Abstr., Appl. Mech. Rev., Spin, Energy Res. Abstr., Phys. Abstr., Eng. Index. **LC** QC276. **DD** 536.5705. **CODEN** HITEA4.

HIGH TEMPERATURES. HIGH PRESSURES. (HIGH TEMPERATURES - HIGH PRESSURES). **VFOAT** High Pressures. V. 1- 1969-. 0018-1544. Periodical. UK. English (French or German with summaries in English). bm. 206.00. Pion Ltd, 207 Brondesbury Park, London NW2 5JN England. **Tel** (01)459-0066. **Ed** E Fitzer and J Lees. **Ind/Abst** Eng. Index Mon., Eng. Index Bioeng. Abstr., Eng. Index Energy Abstr., Coal Abstr., Int. Aerosp. Abstr., GeoRef, Comput. Control Abstr., Electr. Electron. Abstr., Sci. Abstr. Sect. A. Phys. Abstr., Met. Abstr., World Alum. Abstr., Chem. Abstr., Eng. Index Mon., Mineral. Abstr., Nuci. Sci. Abstr., Eng. Index Annu., Phys. Abstr., Bibliogr. Index Geol., Eng. Index. **LC** QC276. **CODEN** HTHPAK. bk rev. adv acc. **Circ** 500. Experimental and theoretical study of matter under extreme thermal and mechanical conditions. Applications to chemical, mechanical, engineering, materials science, metallurgy.

INTERNATIONAL COMMUNICATIONS IN HEAT AND MASS TRANSFER. Vol. 10, No. 1 (Jan.-Feb. 1983)-. 0735-1933. Periodical. US. English. bm. $150.00. Pergamon Press, 395 Sawmill River Road, Elmsford NY 10523. **Ind/Abst** Fluidex, Abstr. Bull. Inst. Paper Chem., Energy Res. Abstr., Chem. Abstr., Curr. Contents, Coal Abstr., Eng. Index. **LC** QC319.8. **DD** 536.2005. **CODEN** IHMTDL. Issued also on microfilm and microfiche. *Letters in Heat and Mass Transfer, 0094-4548.*

INTERNATIONAL JOURNAL OF HEAT AND MASS TRANSFER. **VFOAT** Heat and Mass Transfer. V. 1- June 1960-. 0017-9310. Periodical. UK. articles in various languages with summaries in English, French, German or Russian. mo. Pergamon Press, 395 Sawmill River Road, Elmsford NY 10523. **Tel** (914)592-7700. **Ind/Abst** Electron. Commun. Abstr. J., ISMEC Bull., Pollut. Abstr. Indexes, Saf. Sci. Abstr. J., Eng. Index Mon., Eng. Index Bioeng. Abstr., Eng. Index Energy Abstr., Fluidex, Excerpta Med., Coal Abstr., Energy Inf. Abstr., Environ. Abstr., Int. Aerosp. Abstr., GeoRef, Comput. Control Abstr., Electr. Electron. Abstr., Sci. Abstr. Sect. A. Phys. Abstr., Chem. Abstr., Sci. Cit. Index, Abr. Ed., Pet. Abstr., Energy Res. Abstr., Bibliogr. Index Geol., Phys. Abstr., Appl. Mech. Rev. **LC** QC320. **DD** 536.205. **CODEN** IJHMAK. Microform available from Microforms International Marketing Corp.

JOURNAL OF ENGINEERING PHYSICS. V. 8- Jan. 1965-. 0022-0841. Periodical. US. English (Russian). mo. $675.00 Domestic, $750.00 Foreign. Consultants Bureau, 233 Spring Street, New York NY 10013. **Tel** (212)620-8000. **Ed** A G Shashico. **Ind/Abst** Math. Rev., Eng. Index Mon., Eng. Index Bioeng. Abstr., Eng. Index Energy Abstr., Fluidex, Int. Aerosp. Abstr., Comput. Control Abstr., Sci. Abstr. Sect. A. Phys. Abstr., Appl. Mech. Rev., Chem. Abstr., Eng. Index Annu., Eng. Index, Phys. Abstr., Electr. Electron. Abstr., ISMEC Bull., Phys. Abstr., Appl. Mech. Rev. **LC** TA4. **CODEN** JEPHAL. Contains useful results and new data on all aspects of heat and mass transfer, including nucleate and film boiling fluidation and diffusion, gas dynamics, combustion, thermophysical properties, thermal stresses and design of heat transfer apparatus.

JOURNAL OF HEAT TRANSFER. V. 81- Feb. 1959-. 0022-1481. Periodical. US. English. qt. $25.00 Members, $50.00 Nonmembers. ASME United Engineering Center, 345 East 47th Street, New York NY 10017. **Ind/Abst** Appl. Sci. Technol. Index, Eng. Index Mon., Eng. Index Bioeng. Abstr., Eng. Index Energy Abstr., Energy Inf. Abstr., Environ. Abstr., Fluidex, Abstr. Bull. Inst. Paper Chem., Comput. Control Abstr., Electr. Electron. Abstr., Sci. Abstr. Sect. A. Phys. Abstr., Chem. Abstr., Spin, Coal Abstr., Eng. Index Annu., Energy Res. Abstr., Eng. Index Mon., Int. Aerosp. Abstr., Nuci. Sci. Abstr., Indexes Publ. Am. Soc. Mech. Eng. **LC** TA1. **DD** 621.402205. **CODEN** JHTRAO. *Transactions of the American Society of Mechanical Engineers, 0097-7788.*

JOURNAL OF NON-EQUILIBRIUM THERMODYNAMICS. **VFOAT** Non-Equilibrium Thermodynamics. V. 1-. 0340-0204. English. bm. $186.00. Walter de Gruyter Inc, 200 Saw Mill River Road, Hawthorne NY 10532. **Tel** (914)747-0110. **Ed** J U Keller. **Ind/Abst** Eng. Index Annu., Eng. Index Mon., Eng. Index, Eng. Index Bioeng. Abstr., Eng. Index Energy Abstr., Coal Abstr., Int. Aerosp. Abstr., Comput. Control Abstr., Electr. Electron. Abstr., Sci. Abstr. Sect. A. Phys. Abstr., Chem. Abstr., Energy Res. Abstr., Sci. Cit. Index, Abr. Ed., Appl. Mech. Rev. **LC** QC318.I7. **DD** 536.7. **CODEN** JNETDY. bk rev. adv acc. **Circ** 400. The journal deals with the physical foundations and the engineering applications of non-equilibrium thermodynamics.

JOURNAL OF THERMAL ANALYSIS. Vol. 1- 1969-. 0449-5497. Periodical. UK. English. bm. 298.-. John Wiley and Sons Ltd, Baffins Lane Chichester, Sussex PO19 1UD England. **Tel** (0243)784531. **Ed** E Buzagu and J Simon. bk rev. adv acc. Papers on all aspects of thermal investigations including the evaluation of experimental material and fundamental studies.

LETTERS IN HEAT AND MASS TRANSFER *CEASED.* V. 1-9, No. 6. 0094-4548. Periodical. US. English. bm. $110.00. Maxwell House, Fairview Park, Elmsford NY 10523. **Ind/Abst** Eng. Index Annu., Eng. Index Mon., Eng. Index Bioeng. Abstr., Eng. Index Energy Abstr., Coal Abstr., Int. Aerosp. Abstr., Chem. Abstr. **LC** QC319.8. **DD** 536.2005. **CODEN** LHMTBI. Available on microfilm.

NUMERICAL HEAT TRANSFER. V. 1- Jan./Mar. 1978-. 0149-5720. Periodical. US. English. bm. Hemisphere Publishing Corporation, 1025 Vermont Avenue NW, Washington DC 20005. **Tel** (212)725-1999. **Ind/Abst** Eng. Index Mon., Eng. Index Bioeng. Abstr., Eng. Index Energy Abstr., Fluidex, Int. Aerosp. Abstr., Comput. Control Abstr., Electr. Electron. Abstr., Sci. Abstr. Sect. A. Phys. Abstr., Met. Abstr., World Alum. Abstr., Eng. Index Annu. **LC** QC320. **DD** 536.20015194. **CODEN** NUHTD6.

PREVIEWS OF HEAT AND MASS TRANSFER. V. 1- Sept. 1974-. 0094-9477. Periodical. US. English. bm. $125.00. Pergamon Press, 395 Sawmill River Road, Elmsford NY 10523. **LC** QC319.8. **DD** 536.2.

PROCEEDINGS OF THE INTERNATIONAL HEAT TRANSFER CONFERENCE. **Main/Conf** International Heat Transfer Conference. **VFOAT** Proceedings - International Heat Transfer Conference. Periodical. US. English. ir. American Institute of Chemical Engineers, 345 East 47th Street, New York NY 10017. **LC** QC320, QC311.

QUARTERLY PROGRESS REPORT ON BLOWDOWN HEAT TRANSFER SEPARATE-EFFECTS PROGRAM FOR . . . . US. English. qt. Government Printing Office Sales Program, Division of Technical Information and Document Control, Washington DC 20555.

SOVIET JOURNAL OF LOW TEMPERATURE PHYSICS. V. 1- Jan. 1975-. 0360-0335. Periodical. US. English (Russian). mo. American Institute of Physics, 335 East 45th Street, New York NY 10017. **Tel** (212)661-9404. **Ind/Abst** Int. Aerosp. Abstr., Comput. Control Abstr., Electr. Electron. Abstr., Sci. Abstr. Sect. A. Phys. Abstr., Energy Res. Abstr., Chem. Abstr., Spin, Curr. Phys. Index, Phys. Abstr., Eng. Index. **LC** QC278. **DD** 536.5605. **CODEN** SJLPDQ.

TEMPERATURE DEVELOPMENTS. Periodical. US. English. qt. Omega Press, One Omega Drive, Box 4047, Stamford CT 06907. **Tel** (203)359-1660. (ctrl). Measurement and control handbooks for temperature, pressure flow, hand tools and ph. All books are in full color and all include prices and complete descriptions.

TEPLOPROVODNOST' I DIFFUZIIA. **Main/Corp** Riga. Politehniskais Instituts. Kafedra Promyshelnnoi Teploenergetiki. Began in 1969. UR. Russian. 0.54 Each Issue. Rigas Politehniskais Instituts, 10 Ul Auseklia 7, Riga Latvian SSR. **LC** QC319.8.

THERMAL CONDUCTIVITY. 14-. 0163-9005. US. English. an. $45.00. Plenum Press, 233 Spring Street, New York NY 10013. **Tel** (212)620-8000. **Ind/Abst** Chem. Abstr. **DD** 536. **CODEN** THCOD9. *Advances in Thermal Conductivity : Papers Presented at the International Conference on Thermal Conductivity.*

WARMELEHRE UND WARMEWIRTSCHAFT *CEASED.* GE. German. ir. Deutscher Buch Export-Import, Leninstrasse 16, DDR-701 Leipzig East Germany. **LC** TP363. **DD** 621.40208.

LIGHT, OPTICS, RADIATION

ABSORPTION SPECTRA IN THE INFRARED REGION. V. 1- 1974-. UK. English. sa. Butterworths, 88 Kingsway, London WC2B 6AB England. **LC** QC457. **DD** 547.3085.

ABSTRACTS - SYMPOSIUM ON MOLECULAR SPECTROSCOPY. *See* Indexes/Abstracts.

ADVANCES IN HOLOGRAPHY. V. 1- 1975-. 0361-2961. US. English. M Dekker, 270 Madison Avenue, New York NY 10016. **Ind/Abst** Chem. Abstr. **LC** QC449. **DD** 535.4. **CODEN** ADHODZ.

ADVANCES IN OPTICAL AND ELECTRON MICROSCOPY. *See* Biology - Microscopy.

ANNUAL REPORT OF THE RADIATION CENTER OF OSAKA PREFECTURE. Began in 1961. 0474-7879. Periodical. English. an. **Ind/Abst** Chem. Abstr. **LC** QC794.95. **DD** 539.205. **NLM** W1 OS1072. **CODEN** ARROAA.

APPLIED HEALTH PHYSICS ABSTRACTS AND NOTES. *See* Indexes/ Abstracts.

APPLIED OPTICS. V. 1- Jan. 1962-. 0003-6935. Periodical. US. English. sm. American Institute of Physics, 335 East 45th Street, New York NY 10017. **Tel** (516)349-7800. **Ind/Abst** Fluidex, Life Sci. Collect., Eng. Index Annu., Eng. Index Mon., GeoRef, Eng. Index Bioeng. Abstr., Eng. Index Energy Abstr., Coal Abstr., Excerpta Med., Abstr. Bull. Inst. Paper Chem., Int. Aerosp. Abstr., Art Archaeol. Tech. Abstr., Chem. Abstr., Curr. Phys. Index, Energy Res. Abstr., Appl. Sci. Technol. Index, Comput. Control Abstr., Electr. Electron. Abstr., Spin, Sci. Abstr. Sect. A. Phys. Abstr., Sci. Cit. Index, Abr. Ed., Phys. Abstr., Eng. Index, Comput. Abstr. **LC** QC350. **DD** 535.05. **NLM** W1 AP528J. **CODEN** APOPAI.

APPLIED OPTICS AND OPTICAL ENGINEERING. V. 1-. 0197-8535. US. English. Academic Press Inc, 4805 Sand Lake Road, Orlando FL 32819. **Ed** R Kingslake. **Ind/Abst** Comput. Control Abstr., Electr. Electron. Abstr., Sci. Abstr. Sect. A. Phys. Abstr., Chem. Abstr. **LC** TA1501. **DD** 621.36. **CODEN** AOOEDF.

APPLIED SPECTROSCOPY. V. 6- Nov. 1951-. 0003-7028. Periodical. US. English. ir. $60.00. Society for Applied Spectroscopy, PO Box 64008, Baltimore MD 21264. **Tel** (301)694-8122. **Ed** William G Fateley. **Ind/Abst** Eng. Index Annu., Eng. Index Mon., Sel. Water Resour. Abstr., Eng. Index Bioeng. Abstr., Eng. Index Energy Abstr., World Surf. Coat. Abstr., Coal Abstr., Excerpta Med., Energy Inf. Abstr., Environ. Abstr., Abstr. Bull. Inst. Paper Chem., GeoRef, Biol. Abstr., Met. Abstr., World Alum. Abstr., Ref. Source, Spin, Chem. Abstr., Bibliogr. Agric., Energy Res. Abstr., Comput. Control Abstr., Electr. Electron. Abstr., Sci. Abstr. Sect. A. Phys. Abstr. **LC** QD71. **DD** 544.605. **NLM** W1 AP529. **CODEN** APSPA4. (cum index). bk rev. adv acc. **Circ** 6,000. Original contributions covering the theory and practice of atomic, molecular and surface spectroscopy. Includes all forms of optical spectroscopy, x-ray, NMR and mass spectroscopy. *Bulletin - Society for Applied Spectroscopy, 0096-8706.*

APPLIED SPECTROSCOPY REVIEWS. V. 1- 1967-. 0570-4928. Periodical. US. English. qt. $165.00. Marcel Dekker Inc, Journal Department, PO Box 11305 Church Street Station, New York NY 10249. **Tel** (212)696-9000. **Ed** Edward G Brame Jr. **Ind/Abst** GeoRef, Chem. Abstr., Comput. Control Abstr., Electr. Electron. Abstr., Sci. Abstr. Sect. A. Phys. Abstr., Energy Inf. Abstr., Environ. Abstr., Sci. Cit. Index, Abr. Ed., Phys. Abstr., Bibliogr. Index Geol. **LC** QC450. **DD** 535.8405. **NLM** W1 AP529G. **CODEN** APSRBB. bk rev. adv acc. (ctrl). Provides the latest information on principles, methods, and applications of spectroscopy for the researcher.

ARCHIVES OF MASS SPECTRAL DATA. *See* Genealogy and Heraldry - Archives.

ATTI DELLA FONDAZIONE GIORGIO RONCHI. Year 31-Jan./Feb. 1976-. 0391-2051. Periodical. IT. Italian (articles in English and French). bm. $100.00. Fondazione Giorgio Ronchi, Largo Enrico Fermi, 1-50125 Firenze Italy. **Tel** (055)22.11.63. **Ind/Abst** Excerpta Med., Chem. Abstr., Psychol. Abstr., Comput. Control Abstr., Electr. Electron. Abstr., Sci. Abstr. Sect. A. Phys. Abstr. **NLM** W1 AT775Q. **CODEN** AFDGA2. bk rev. adv acc. **Circ** 900. (ctrl). Topics of pure and applied optics; history and philosophy of science. *Atti della Fondazione Giorgio Ronchi e Contributi dell'Istituto Nazionale de Ottica, 0365-236X.*

BIOLOGICAL EFFECTS OF ELECTROMAGNETIC RADIATION. *See* Physics - Magnetism.

BIOLOGICAL EFFECTS OF NONIONIZING ELECTROMAGNETIC RADIATION. *See* Physics - Magnetism.

BUNKO KENKYU. **VFOAT** Journal of the Spectroscopical Society of Japan. 1- June 1951-. 0038-7002. Periodical. JA. Japanese. ir. Tokyo International, PO Box 5030, Tokyo 10031 Japan. **Ind/Abst** Comput. Control Abstr., Electr. Electron. Abstr., Sci. Abstr. Sect. A. Phys. Abstr., Chem. Abstr. **NLM** W1 BU944G. **CODEN** BUKKAT.

CANADIAN SPECTROSCOPIC NEWS. V. 1- March 1972-. 0381-5447. Periodical. CN. English. ir. $5.00. Multiscience Publications Ltd, 1253 McGill College Suite 111, Montreal Quebec H3B 2Y5 Canada. **Tel** (514)866-8236. *Canadian Spectroscopy, 0008-5057.*

COLOR RESEARCH AND APPLICATION. V. 1- Spring 1976-. 0361-2317. Periodical. US. English. qt. John Wiley & Sons Inc, 605 Third Avenue, New York NY 10158. **Tel** (800)526-5368. **Ind/Abst** Eng. Index Mon., Eng. Index Bioeng. Abstr., Eng. Index Energy Abstr., World Surf. Coat. Abstr., Abstr. Bull. Inst. Paper Chem., Art Archaeol. Tech. Abstr., Comput. Control Abstr., Electr. Electron. Abstr., Sci. Abstr. Sect. A. Phys. Abstr., Chem. Abstr., Eng. Index Annu., Phys. Abstr., Sci. Cit. Index, Abr. Ed., Eng. Index. **LC** QC494. **DD** 535.605. **CODEN** CREADU.

COMPUTER ENHANCED SPECTROSCOPY. *See* Computers and Computer Science.

DIANAMIKA IZLUCAJUSCEGO GAZA. (DINAMIKA IZLUCHAIUSHCHEGO GAZA). **Main/Corp** Akademiia Nauk SSSR. Vychislitelnyi Tsentr. No. 1- 1974-. 0320-006X. UR. Russian. ir. 0.51 Each Issue. Computer Centre, Vavilova Str 40, Moscow 117333 USSR. **Tel** 1352489. **Ed** Yu Shmyglevsky. **Ind/Abst** Chem. Abstr. **LC** QA930. **CODEN** DIZGAU. adv acc. **Circ** 800. Radiative gas dynamics-methods sf solutions and solutions of problems.

ELECTRO-OPTICS REPORT. **VFOAT** Electro Optics Report. Vol. 1, No. 1 (Jan. 15, 1985)-. 8756-7180. Periodical. US. English. bw. $200.00. Pennwell Publishing Company, PO Box 557, Littleton MA 01460. **Tel** (617)486-9501. **Ed** Judd Holt. **DD** 621. Business, financial and marketing news and features about and/or of interest to the electr-optics and optics industries.

FIBER AND INTEGRATED OPTICS. V. 1-. 0146-8030. Periodical. US. English. ir. $86.00. Crane Russak & Company, 3 East 44th Street, New York NY 10017. **Tel** (212)867-1490. **Ed** Henri Hodara. **Ind/Abst** ISMEC Bull., Pollut. Abstr. Indexes, Saf. Sci. Abstr. J., Eng. Index Mon., Eng. Index Bioeng. Abstr., Eng. Index Energy Abstr., Int. Aerosp. Abstr., Comput. Control Abstr., Electr. Electron. Abstr., Sci. Abstr. Sect. A. Phys. Abstr., Chem. Abstr., Aquat. Sci. Fish. Abstr., Curr. Contents, Eng. Tech. Appl. Sci., Geotech. Abstr., Mar. Sci. Contents Tables, Ocean. Abstr. **LC** TA1800. **DD** 621.369205. **CODEN** FOIOD2. adv acc. **Circ** 800. Presents research on fiber optics and integrated optics research and procedures.

FIBER OPTICS DIRECTORY UPDATE SERVICE. *See* Yearbooks, Almanacs, Directories.

FIBER OPTICS NEWS. V. 5, No. 1 (Jan. 14, 1985)-. 8756-2049. Periodical. US. English. wk. $297.00 U.S., $330.00 Foreign. Phillips Publishing Company, 7315 Wisconsin Avenue/Suite 1200 North, Bethesda MD 20814. **DD** 535. *Fiber Laser/News, 0275-6099.*

FINNIGAN SPECTRA. 0161-2220. Periodical. US. English. ty. **Ind/Abst** Chem. Abstr. **CODEN** FISPDD.

GUANGXUE XUEBAO. (KUANG HSUEH HSUEH PAO). **VFOAT** Acta Optica Sinica. Began in 1981. 0253-2239. Periodical. Chinese (with abstracts in English). bm. 1.00. Chung-Kuo Kuo Chi Shu Tien, PO Box 2820, Peking China Mainland. **Ind/Abst** Chem. Abstr., Spin, Energy Res. Abstr. **LC** QC350. **DD** 621..3881305. **CODEN** GUXUDC.

HONGWAI YANJIU. (HUNG WAI YEN CHIU). **VFOAT** Chinese Journal of Infrared Research. Vol. 1, March 1982-. Periodical. Chinese (abstracts in English). qt. 0.70. Shang-Hai Shih Pao Kan Fa Hsing Chu, Shanghai China. **Ind/Abst** Chem. Abstr. **LC** TA1570. **DD** 621.36205. **CODEN** HOYADS.

HOSHASEN. 0285-3604. Periodical. JA. Japanese. ty. Oyo Butsuri Gakkai, Hoshasen Bunkakai Minato-Ku, Shibiya Koen 3 Chome 5 Ban 8 Go, Kikai Shinko Kaikan 209 Go 105 No 2 Tokyo Japan. **Ind/Abst** Chem. Abstr., Energy Res. Abstr. **CODEN** HOSHDJ.

INFORMATION COULEUR MONTREAL, QUEBEC). (INFORMATION COULEUR). Vol. 1, No. 1 (Jan. 1984)-. 0822-8493. Periodical. CN. French. ty. Centre Quebecois de la Coleur, Universite du Quebec A Montreal C P 888 Succursale A, Montreal Quebec H3C 3P8 Canada. **DD** 535.605.

INTER-SOCIETY COLOR COUNCIL NEWS. **VFOAT** News. 0731-2911. US. English. $35.00. Inter-Society Color Council, 2431 Linden Lane, Silver Springs MD 20910. **Tel** (301)589-4747. **Ed** Mary Ellen Zuyus. **LC** QC495. **DD** 535.605. bk rev. **Circ** 1,000. (ctrl). Reports and developments relating to the science of color from the standpoint of the artist, educator, scientist, colorist and designer. *Newsletter (Inter-Society Color Council).*

INTERNATIONAL JOURNAL OF INFRARED AND MILLIMETER WAVES. V. 1, No. 1- Mar. 1980-. 0195-9271. Periodical. US. English. mo. $215.00 Domestic, $243.00 Foreign. Plenum Press, 233 Spring Street, New York NY 10013. **Tel** (212)620-8000. **Ed** Kenneth S Button. **Ind/Abst** Electron. Commun. Abstr. J., ISMEC Bull., Pollut. Abstr. Indexes, Saf. Sci. Abstr. J., Eng. Index Mon., Eng. Index Bioeng. Abstr., Eng. Index Energy Abstr., Int. Aerosp. Abstr., Comput. Control Abstr., Electr. Electron. Abstr., Sci. Abstr. Sect. A. Phys. Abstr., Chem. Abstr., Eng. Index Annu., Ref. Z., Sci. Cit. Index, Abr. Ed., Phys. Abstr., Eng. Index. **LC** TA1570. **DD** 621.361205. **CODEN** IJIWDO. adv acc. This journal provides a common forum for rapid dissemination of the results of original research in millimeter sumbmillimeter and far infra red theory techniques devices systems spectroscopy and applications.

IPLE LIGHTING JOURNAL. **VFOAT** I.P.L.E. Lighting Journal. Vol. 48, No. 1 (Mar. 1983)-. 0265-0398. Periodical. UK. English. qt. 25.00. Institute of Public Lighting Engineers, 9 Lawford Road Rugby, Warwickshire CV21 2DZ England. **Tel** 0788 46492/3. **Ed** D Barnes. **Ind/Abst** Comput. Control Abstr., Electr. Electron. Abstr., Sci. Abstr. Sect. A. Phys. Abstr., Energy Res. Abstr. adv acc. **Circ** 2,000. (ctrl). Gives up-to-date information on lighting technology and equipment available, through advertising, section news, conference and exhibition news. *Public Lighting, 0033-3603.*

ISSLEDOVANIIA PO NELINEINOI OPTIKE I SPEKTROSKOPII. Vol. 1- 1973-. UR. Russian. 1.00 Single Issue. Izd-Vo Saratovskogo Universiteta, Universitetskaia 42, Saratov USSR. **LC** QC446.15.

JAARLIKSE STRALINGSVERSLAG. **Main/Corp** South Africa. Weather Bureau. **VFOAT** Annual Radiation Report. 0377-0311. SA. English. ir. 3.75. Government Printer, Private Bag, Pretoria 0001 South Africa. **LC** QC911. **DD** 551.52710968.

JAHRBUCH FUR OPTIK UND FEINMECHANIK. *See* Yearbooks, Almanacs, Directories.

JAHRESBERICHT (MAX-PLANCK-INSTITUT FUR QUANTENOPTIK). (JAHRESBERICHT). **VFOAT** MPQ Jahresbericht. 1981-. Periodical. GW. German. an. Max-Planck-Institut fur Quantenoptik, D-8046 Garching Bei Munchen West Germany. *PLF Jahresbericht.*

JAPAN ANNUAL REVIEWS IN ELECTRONICS, COMPUTERS & TELECOMMUNICATIONS. OPTICAL DEVICES AND FIBERS. **VFOAT** Optical Devices & Fibers. 1982-. Periodical. US. English. ir. Elsevier Science Publishing Company Inc, PO Box 1663, Grand Central Station, New York NY 10163.

JEMNA MECHANIKA A OPTIKA. *See* Physics - Analytic and Experimental Mechanics.

JENA REVIEW. 1st- Year. 0448-9497. Periodical. English (German). ir. $7.62. Kunst und Wissen Erich Bieber, Dufourstrasse 51, CH-8008 Zurich Switzerland. **Ind/Abst** Chem. Abstr., Eng. Index, Int. Aerosp. Abstr., Electr. Electron. Abstr., Phys. Abstr., Comput. Control Abstr., Bibliogr. Index Geol. **LC** TS510. **CODEN** JNRVAY.

JOURNAL OF CURRENT LASER ABSTRACTS. *See* Indexes/Abstracts.

JOURNAL OF LIGHTWAVE TECHNOLOGY. **VFOAT** I.E.E.E./O.S.A. Journal of Lightwave Technology. Vol. No. 1, No. 1 (Mar. 1983)-. 0733-8724. Periodical. US. English. bm. American Institute of Physics, 335 East 45th Street, Subscription Fulfillment, New York NY 10017.

JOURNAL OF LUMINESCENCE. V. 1/2- 1970-. 0022-2313. Periodical. English. bm. Elsevier Science Publishers, PO Box 211, 1000 AE Amsterdam Netherlands. **Tel** (020)5803.911. **Ind/Abst** Eng. Index Annu., Eng. Index Mon., Eng. Index Bioeng. Abstr., Eng. Index Energy Abstr., GeoRef, Comput. Control Abstr., Electr. Electron. Abstr., Sci. Abstr. Sect. A. Phys. Abstr., Nuci. Sci. Abstr., Biol. Abstr., Chem. Abstr., Eng. Index Mon., Bibliogr. Index Geol., Sci. Cit. Index, Abr. Ed., Eng. Index, Phys. Abstr. **LC** QC476.4. **DD** 535.3505. **CODEN** JLUMA8.

JOURNAL OF MOLECULAR SPECTROSCOPY. Periodical. US. English. mo. Academic Press, 4805 Sand Lake Road, Orlando FL 32819. **Tel** (305)345-4100. **Ind/Abst** Chem. Abstr., Comput. Control Abstr., Electr. Electron. Abstr., Phys. Abstr., Sci. Cit. Index, Abr. Ed., Int. Aerosp. Abstr.

JOURNAL OF OPTICAL COMMUNICATIONS. V. 1, No. 1 (Sept. 1980)-. 0173-4911. Periodical. English. qt. $114.44. Fachverlag Schiele und Schoen, Markgrafenstrasse 11, 1 Berlin 61 West Germany. **Tel** 030 251 60 29. **Ind/Abst** Int. Aerosp. Abstr., Comput. Control Abstr., Electr. Electron. Abstr., Sci. Abstr. Sect. A. Phys. Abstr., Chem. Abstr. **CODEN** JOCODG.

JOURNAL OF OPTICS. **VFOAT** J. Optics (Paris). V. 8- Jan./Feb. 1977-. 0150-536X. Periodical. US. English (French). bm. Masson Publishing USA Inc, 211 East 43rd Street/Room 1306, New York NY 10017. **Tel** (212)370-1937. **Ind/Abst** Eng. Index Annu., Eng. Index Mon., Eng. Index Bioeng. Abstr., Eng. Index Energy Abstr., Excerpta Med., Int. Aerosp. Abstr., GeoRef, Comput. Control Abstr., Electr. Electron. Abstr., Sci. Abstr. Sect. A. Phys. Abstr., Chem. Abstr., Energy Res. Abstr. **LC** QC350. **DD** 535.05. **NLM** W1 JO803RE. **CODEN** JOOPDB. *Nouvelle Revue d'Optique, 0335-7368.*

JOURNAL OF PHOTOACOUSTICS *CEASED.* Vol. 1, No. 1-Vol. 1, No. 4. 0278-2901. Periodical. US. English. qt. $51.00. Marcel Dekker Inc, 270 Madison Avenue, New York NY 10016. **Ind/Abst** Comput. Control Abstr., Electr. Electron. Abstr., Sci. Abstr. Sect. A. Phys. Abstr., Chem. Abstr. **LC** QD96.O6. **DD** 535.84. **NLM** W1 JO832B. **CODEN** JPHODE.

JOURNAL OF RADIATION RESEARCH. V. 1- June 1960-. 0449-3060. Periodical. English. qt. **Ind/Abst** Electron. Commun. Abstr. J., ISMEC Bull., Pollut. Abstr. Indexes, Saf. Sci. Abstr. J., Life Sci. Collect., Excerpta Med., Coal Abstr., Index Med., Biol. Abstr., Comput. Control Abstr., Electr. Electron. Abstr., Sci. Abstr. Sect. A. Phys. Abstr., Chem. Abstr., Bibliogr. Agric., Energy Res. Abstr. **LC** QH652.A1. **NLM** W1 JO864. **CODEN** JRARAX. (ctrl). Papers of radiation, biology, medicine and agriculture.

JOURNAL OF RAMAN SPECTROSCOPY. **VFOAT** JRS. V. 1- Apr. 1973-. 0377-0486. Periodical. UK. English. bm. John Wiley & Sons Ltd, Baffins Lane Chichester, Sussex PO19 1UD England. **Tel** (0243) 784531. **Ind/Abst** Excerpta Med., Abstr. Bull. Inst. Paper Chem., Int. Aerosp. Abstr., Comput. Control Abstr., Electr. Electron. Abstr., Sci. Abstr. Sect. A. Phys. Abstr., Chem. Abstr., Energy Res. Abstr., Sci. Cit. Index, Abr. Ed., Phys. Abstr. **LC** QC454.R36. **DD** 544.64. **CODEN** JRSPAF.

JOURNAL OF SOVIET LASER RESEARCH. Vol. 1, No. 1 (Jan-Mar 1980)-. 0270-2010. Periodical. US. English (Russian). bm. $245.00 Domestic, $275.00 Foreign. Consultants Bureau, 233 Spring Street, New York NY 10013. **Tel** (212)620-8000. **Ed** U E Basor. **Ind/Abst** Electron. Commun. Abstr. J., ISMEC Bull., Pollut. Abstr. Indexes, Saf. Sci. Abstr. J., Eng. Index Mon., Eng. Index Bioeng. Abstr., Eng. Index Energy Abstr., Int. Aerosp. Abstr., Eng. Index Annu., Energy Res. Abstr. **LC** TA1501. **DD** 621.3660947. **NLM** W1 JO901VH. **CODEN** JSLRDU.

JOURNAL OF THE OPTICAL SOCIETY OF AMERICA. **Main/Corp** Optical Society of America. V. 1- Jan. 1917-. 0039-3941. Periodical. US. English. sm. American Institute of Physics, 335 East 45th Street, New York NY 10017. **Tel** (516)349-7800. **Ind/Abst** Appl. Mech. Rev., Appl. Sci. Technol. Index, Comput. Control Abstr., Electr. Electron. Abstr., Eng. Index, Index Med., Math. Rev., Chem. Abstr., Psychol. Abstr., Sci. Cit. Index, Abr. Ed., Phys. Abstr., Int. Aerosp. Abstr. (cum index).

JOURNAL OF THE OPTICAL SOCIETY OF AMERICA (1930) *CEASED.* (JOURNAL OF THE OPTICAL SOCIETY OF AMERICA). **VFOAT** JOSA, J.O.S.A. Began with V. 20, No. 1 Jan. 1930. Ceased with V. 73, No. 12 (Dec. 1983). 0030-3941. Periodical. US. English. mo. **Ind/Abst** Life Sci. Collect., Abstr. Bull. Inst. Paper Chem., Int. Aerosp. Abstr., GeoRef, Ref. Source, Chem. Abstr., Curr. Phys. Index, Appl. Sci. Technol. Index, Energy Res. Abstr. **LC** QC350. **DD** 535.05. **NLM** W1 JO944G. **CODEN** JOSAAH. Index received separately bound from publisher. (cum index). *Journal of the Optical Society of America and Review of Scientific Instruments, 0093-4119.*

JOURNAL OF THE OPTICAL SOCIETY OF AMERICA. A, OPTICS AND IMAGE SCIENCE. **VFOAT** Optics and Image Science. Vol. 1, No. 1 (Jan. 1984)-. 0740-3232. Periodical. US. English. mo. $16.00 US Member, $225.00 US Nonmember, $34.00 Foreign Member, $252.00 Foreign Nonmember. Journal of the Optical Society of America, 1816 Jefferson Place Northwest, Washington DC 20036. **Ind/Abst** Math. Rev., Abstr. Bull. Inst. Paper Chem., Index Med., Curr. Phys. Index, Psychol. Abstr., Spin. **LC** QC350. **DD** 535.05. **NLM** W1. **CODEN** JOAOD6. *Journal of the Optical Society of America (1930), 0030-3941.*

JOURNAL OF THE OPTICAL SOCIETY OF AMERICA. PART B. OPTICAL PHYSICS. (JOURNAL OF THE OPTICAL SOCIETY OF AMERICA. PART B, OPTICAL PHYSICS). 0740-3224. Periodical. US. English. bm. Journal of the Optical Society of America, 1816 Jefferson Place Northwest, Washington DC 20036. *Journal of the Optical Society of America (1930), 0030-3941.*

KEP ES HANGTECHNIKA. Began in 1955. 0023-0480. Periodical. HU. Hungarian. bm. Akademiai Kiado, POB 24, 1363 Budapest Hungary. **Ind/Abst** Comput. Control Abstr., Electr. Electron. Abstr., Sci. Abstr. Sect. A. Phys. Abstr., Chem. Abstr., Phys. Abstr. **LC** TR845. **CODEN** KEHTAS.

KESSHO RAMAN DETA NO SHUSHU SEIRI BUNSEKI HYOKA TO NI KANSURU CHOSA KENKYU HOKOKU. **Main/Corp** Nihon Bunseki-Kagakukai. Japanese. ir. **LC** QC454.R36.

LASER AND PARTICLE BEAMS. Vol. 1, Pt. 1 (Feb. 1983)-. 0263-0346. Periodical. UK. English. qt. $140.00. Cambridge University Press, 32 East 57th Street, New York NY 10022. **Tel** (212)688-8888. **Ed** Heinrich Hora. **Ind/Abst** Chem. Abstr. **LC** QC689.5.L37. **DD** 535.58. **CODEN** LPBEDA. bk rev. adv acc. **Circ** 250. Covers the generation of high intensity laser and particle beams, their interaction with materials and the physics of systems with very high energy densities.

LASER FOCUS BUYERS' GUIDE. Began with Vol. for 1971. 0075-8027. Periodical. US. English. an. $70.00 US and Canada. Pennwell Publishing Co, PO Box 1111, Littleton MA 01460. **Tel** (617)486-9501. **Ed** Nancy Ferrell. **LC** TA1674. **DD** 621.366029473. adv acc. Comprehensive annual directory of products, services, and the companies that provide those products and services, for the laser, optic, electro-optic, and fiberoptic industries. *Laser Marketers' and Buyers' Guide.*

LASER FOCUS (LITTLETON, MASS. : TOWN). (LASER FOCUS). **VFOAT** Laser Focus/Electro-Optics. Vol. 20, No. 10 (Oct. 1984)-. 0740-2511. Periodical. US. English. mo. $45.00. Laser Focus/Electro-Optics, Circulation Department, PO Box 1111, Littleton MA 01460. **NLM** W1. *Laser Focus including Electro-Optics Magazine.*

LASER-RAMAN & INFRARED SPECTROSCOPY ABSTRACTS. *See* Indexes/Abstracts.

LASER REPORT. 0023-8600. Periodical. US. English. ir. $175.00 US and Canada, $190.00 Others. Pennwell Publishing Co, PO Box 1111, Littleton MA 01460. **Tel** (617)486-9501. **Ed** Barbara Akerley. **Ind/Abst** Predicasts, Funk Scott Index Corp. Ind. **Circ** 400. Business news and market trends in lasers. *Laser Focus Mid-Month Report.*

LASERS. Vol. 1 (1966)-. 0075-8035. US. English. ir. CRC Press Inc, 2000 Corporate Boulevard NW, Boca Raton FL 33431. **Tel** (305)994-0555. **Ind/Abst** Chem. Abstr. **CODEN** LASEBM.

LASERS IN THE LIFE SCIENCES. 0886-0467. Periodical. US. English. qt. Harwood Academic Publishers, 50 West 23rd Street, New York NY 10010.

LICHT-FORSCHUNG. (LICHT FORSCHUNG : ORGAN DER LICHTTECHNISCHEN GESELLSCHAFT E.V). 0172-3286. Periodical. German (summaries in English). sa. 80.00. Richard Pflaum Verlag KG, Postfach 20 19 20, 8000 Munchen 2 West Germany. **Ind/Abst** Eng. Index Annu., Eng. Index Mon., Eng. Index Bioeng. Abstr., Eng. Index Energy Abstr., Coal Abstr. **LC** TH7700. **DD** 621.3205. **CODEN** LIFODB.

LIGHTING DIMENSIONS. V. 1- Jan. 1977-. 0191-541X. Periodical. US. English. ir. $18.00. Lighting Dimensions Publ Inc, 1590 South Coast Highway, Suite 8, Laguana Beach CA 92651. **Tel** (714)494-9999. **Ed** Mike Williams. **LC** PN2091.E4. **DD** 792.02505. bk rev. adv acc. **Circ** 10,500. (ctrl). Trade magazine for the creative and entertainment lighting professional, including film, TV, theatrical, and architectural lighting.

LIGHTWAVE. **VFOAT** Light Wave. Jan. 1984-. 0741-5834. Periodical. US. English. sm. $44.00. The Journal of Fiber Optics, 235 Bear Hill Road, Waltham MA 02154. **Tel** (617)890-2700. **Ed** John Ryan. adv acc. **Circ** 11,000. (ctrl). Serves a concentrated audience of fiber optics market including telecommunications, data communications, lightwave systems and components, energy, process control, on all levels and job functions.

LIST OF LIGHTS AND FOG SIGNALS. **Main/Corp** United States. Defense Mapping Agency Hydrographic/Topographic Center. 0096-1280. US. English. Defense Mapping Agency, Building 56, US Naval Observatory, Washington DC 20305. **LC** VK1150. **DD** 623.894. *List of Lights and Fog Signals, 0096-1280.*

LIST OF LIGHTS AND FOG SIGNALS. BALTIC SEA WITH KATTEGAT, BELTS AND SOUND, AND GULF OF BOTHNIA. **VFOAT** Baltic Sea with Kattegar Belts and Sound, and Gulf of Bothnia. US. English. Defense Mapping Agency, Hydrographic/Topographic Center, Washington DC 20315. **LC** VK1185.B34. **DD** 623.8930916334.

LIUMINESTSENTNYE MATERIALY I OSOBO CHISTYE VESHCHESTVA. **Main/Corp** Vsesoiuznyi Nauchno-Issledovatelskii Institut liuminoforov i Osobo Chistykh Veshchestv. UR. Russian (summaries in English). 1.00 Single Issue. Pr Khimikov 1, Stavropol Russia. **LC** QC477.8.

MICROBEAM ANALYSIS. 1979-. 0278-1727. US. English. an. $25.00. San Francisco Press, PO Box 6800, San Francisco CA 94101-6800. **Tel** (415)524-1000. **Ind/Abst** Chem. Abstr. **LC** QD98.E4. **DD** 543.08586. **CODEN** MBANDD. **Circ** 800. Extended abstracts of papers presented at annual meeting of Microbeam Analysis Society; profusely illustrated, including high-quality micrographs. *Proceedings, 0146-6275.*

MOLEKULIARNAIA SPEKTROSKOPIIA. Vol. 1- 1960-. UR. Russian. Izd-Vo Leningradskogo Univ, Universitetskaya Nav 79, Lenningrad B 164 USSR. **LC** QC454.M6. **DD** 535.8405.

MONOGRAPHS ON APPLIED OPTICS. No. 1-. 0077-0973. Monographic Series. US. English. ir. Elsevier Science Publishing Company Inc, PO Box 1663, Grand Central Station, New York NY 10163. **LC** UNC. **NLM** W1 MO569S.

MOSSBAUER SPECTROSCOPY ABSTRACTS. *See* Indexes/Abstracts.

NATIONAL CONFERENCE ON RADIATION CONTROL. 1st- 1969-. 0160-2136. US. English. an. Free. BRH Technical Information Staff, 5600 Fishers Lane, Rockville MD 20857. **NLM** W3 NA454E.

NCRP NEWS. Periodical. US. English. National Council on Radiation, 7910 Woodmont Avenue/Suite 1016, Bethesda MD 20814. **Circ** 1,000. News of new NCRP publications and significant NCRP activity.

NRC TLD DIRECT RADIATION MONITORING NETWOR. **VAT** Nuclear Regulatory Commission's Thermoluminescent Dosimeter (TLD) Direct Radiation Monitoring Network. Vol. 1, Nos. 1, 2 (Jan.-June 1981)-. 0883-3311. US. English. qt. Superintendent of Documents, US Government Printing Office, Washington DC 20402.

NUCLEAR TRACKS AND RADIATION MEASUREMENTS. *See* Physics - Nuclear Physics.

NUOVO CIMENTO DELLA SOCIETA ITALIANA DI FISICA. SEZIONE B. (IL NUOVO CIMENTO DELLA SOCIETA ITALIANA DI FISICA. B). **VFOAT** Relativity, Classical and Statistical Physics. Vol. 1B (11 Jan. 1971)-. 0369-4100. Periodical. Italian (summaries in English and Russian). mo. 325.00 Members, 400.00 Nonmembers. Editrice Compositori S R L, Viale XII Giugno 1, 40124 Bologna Italy. **Tel** 051-58 31 49. **Ind/Abst** Chem. Abstr., Energy Res. Abstr., Excerpta Med., Life Sci. Collect., Math. Rev., Comput. Control Abstr., Electr. Electron. Abstr., Sci. Abstr. Sect. A. Phys. Abstr. **CODEN** NIFBAP. **Circ** 1,000. (ctrl). Mathematical methods in physics. Classical and quantum physics: mechanics and fields. Relativity and gravitation; electricity and magnetism, optics, acoustics, fluid, plasmas and electric discharges. Fundamental astronomy and astrophysics, instrumentation, techniques, and astronomical observations. *Nuovo Cimento. B.*

OPTICA ACTA. V. 1- 1954/55-. 0030-3909. Periodical. UK. English (French and German). mo. $490.00. Taylor & Francis Ltd, 242 Cherry Street, Philadelphia PA 19106. **Tel** (215)238-0939. **Ed** R Loudon. **Ind/Abst** Math. Rev., Electron. Commun. Abstr. J., ISMEC Bull., Pollut. Abstr. Indexes, Saf. Sci. Abstr. J., Excerpta Med., Int. Aerosp. Abstr., Comput. Control Abstr., Electr. Electron. Abstr., Sci. Abstr. Sect. A. Phys. Abstr., Chem. Abstr., Sci. Cit. Index, Abr. Ed., Phys. Abstr. **NLM** W1 OP795. **CODEN** OPACAT. Covers the whole field of classical and quantum optics.

OPTICA APPLICATA. V. 1- 1971-. 0078-5466. PL. Polish. qt. ARS Polona, Krakowskie Przedmiescie 7, 00-068 Warsaw Poland. **Ind/Abst** Comput. Control Abstr., Electr. Electron. Abstr., Sci. Abstr. Sect. A. Phys. Abstr., Chem. Abstr. **LC** QC350. **CODEN** OPAPBZ.

OPTICA PURA Y APLICADA. V. 1- 1968-. 0030-3917. Periodical. SP. English (French and Spanish). ty. $25.00. Instituto de Optica, Serrano 121 Daza de Valdes, Madrid 6 Spain. **Tel** 261 68 00. **Ed** A Corrous. **Ind/Abst** Int. Aerosp. Abstr., Comput. Control Abstr., Electr. Electron. Abstr., Sci. Abstr. Sect. A. Phys. Abstr., Chem. Abstr., Phys. Abstr. **LC** QC350. **DD** 535.05. **CODEN** OPAPAY. bk rev. (ctrl). Ideas in the areas of color, solar energy, spectroscopy, luminiscence, image formation, photography, vision, physical and theoretical optica, instruments.

OPTICAL AND QUANTUM ELECTRONICS. V. 7- 1975-. 0306-8919. Periodical. UK. English. bm. Associated Book Publishing, North Way Andover, Hampshire SP10 5BE England. **Tel** (0264)62141. **Ed** G Parry. **Ind/Abst** Eng. Index Annu., Eng. Index Mon., Eng. Index Bioeng. Abstr., Eng. Index Energy Abstr., Coal Abstr., Int. Aerosp. Abstr., Comput. Control Abstr., Electr. Electron. Abstr., Sci. Abstr. Sect. A. Phys. Abstr., Chem. Abstr., Eng. Index, Sci. Cit. Index, Abr. Ed., Phys. Abstr. **LC** TA1671. **DD** 621.3605. **CODEN** OQELDI. adv acc. Papers on optical physics, optical engineering and optoelectronics with the emphasis on fibres, nonlinear and coherent optics. *Opto-Electronics, 0030-4077.*

OPTICAL ENGINEERING. V. 11- Jan./Feb. 1972-. 0091-3286. Periodical. US. English. bm. Society of Photo-Optical Institute, PO Box 10, Bellingham WA 98227. **Tel** (206)676-3290. **Ed** Jack Gaskill. **Ind/Abst** Electron. Commun. Abstr. J., ISMEC Bull., Pollut. Abstr. Indexes, Saf. Sci. Abstr. J., Eng. Index Mon., Eng. Index Bioeng. Abstr., Eng. Index Energy Abstr., Excerpta Med., Coal Abstr., Comput. Control Abstr., Electr. Electron. Abstr., Sci. Abstr. Sect. A. Phys. Abstr., Chem. Abstr., Eng. Index Annu., Eng. Index, Int. Aerosp. Abstr., Appl. Sci. Technol. Index, Sci. Cit. Index, Abr. Ed., Phys. Abstr., Bibliogr. Index Geol., Appl. Mech. Rev. **LC** TR692.5. **DD** 621.3605. **CODEN** OPEGAR. bk rev. adv acc. **Circ** 8,300. Publishes referreed technical papers relating to the engineering, design, production, and application of optical and optoelectronic applied science and technology.

OPTICAL ENGINEERING REPORTS. Jan. 1984-. 0741-5931. Periodical. US. English. mo. Free Domestic, $25.00 Foreign. SPIE - The International Society for Optical Engineering, PO Box 10, Bellingham WA 98227-0010. **Tel** (206)676-3290. **Ed** Rich Donnelly. adv acc. **Circ** 55,000. Newspaper with articles, interviews, optics, and optoelectronics, mailed free to applied scientists, engineers, technicians, and others in the industry.

THE OPTICAL INDUSTRY & SYSTEMS ENCYCLOPEDIA & DICTIONARY. **VAT** The Optical Industry and Systems Encyclopedia and Dictionary. 25th- Ed. 0191-0639. US. English. $50.00 Domestic, $60.00 Foreign. The Optical Publishing Company Inc, PO Box 1146, Berkshire Common,

Pittsfield MA 01201. **Tel** (413)499-0514. **Ed** Teddi C Laurin. **LC** TA1509. **DD** 621.3605. bk rev. adv acc. **Circ** 52,000. (ctrl). The voice of photonics technology, optics, electro-optics, lasers, fiber optics and imaging. *Optical Industry & Systems Directory, 0078-5474.*

OPTICAL INFORMATION PROCESSING. **Main/Conf** US-USSR Science Cooperation Seminar on Optical Information Processing. V. 1- 1975-. 0162-7643. US. English. Plenum Press, 227 West 17th Street, New York NY 10011. **LC** TA1630. **DD** 621.381959.

OPTICAL SPECTRA *CEASED.* V. 1-15. 0030-395X. Periodical. US. English. mo. Free to qualified individuals, $27.00 Others/Domestic, $35.00 Others/Foreign. Optical Publishing Company, Berkshire Common, PO Box 1146, Pittsfield MA 01224. **Ind/Abst** Predicasts, Int. Aerosp. Abstr., GeoRef, Chem. Abstr., Eng. Index, Nucl. Sci. Abstr. **LC** TS510. **DD** 681.405. **NLM** W1 OP823N. **CODEN** OPTSA2. Available on microfilm from University Microfilms. *News and Notes of the Optical Industry.*

OPTICS AND LASER TECHNOLOGY. Began in Aug. 1970. 0030-3992. Periodical. UK. English. bm. 157.00. Butterworth Scientific Limited, PO Box 63, Westbury House, Bury Street, Guildford GU2 5BH England. **Tel** 483-31261. **Ed** Stephen Bailey. **Ind/Abst** Electron. Commun. Abstr. J., ISMEC Bull., Pollut. Abstr. Indexes, Saf. Sci. Abstr. J., Eng. Index, Fluidex, Comput. Control Abstr., Electr. Electron. Abstr., Sci. Abstr. Sect. A. Phys. Abstr., Ref. Source, Int. Aerosp. Abstr., Chem. Abstr., Nucl. Sci. Abstr., Electron. Pub. Abstr., Sci. Cit. Index, Abr. Ed., Phys. Abstr., Eng. Index Annu., Eng. Index Mon., Eng. Index Energy Abstr., Eng. Index Bioeng. Abstr. **LC** QC350. **DD** 535.05. **CODEN** OLTCAS. bk rev. adv acc. **Circ** 1,200. Also available on microfilm from the publisher. An international journal bridging the research/applications gap. Review articles, original research papers and news are published. *Optics Technology.*

OPTICS AND SPECTROSCOPY. V. 6- Jan. 1959-. 0030-400X. Periodical. US. English (Russian). mo. American Institute of Physics, 335 E 45th Street, New York NY 10017. **Tel** (516)349-7800. **Ind/Abst** Electron. Commun. Abstr. J., ISMEC Bull., Pollut. Abstr. Indexes, Saf. Sci. Abstr. J., Abstr. Bull. Inst. Paper Chem., Int. Aerosp. Abstr., Comput. Control Abstr., Electr. Electron. Abstr., Sci. Abstr. Sect. A. Phys. Abstr., Energy Res. Abstr., Chem. Abstr., Nucl. Sci. Abstr., Spin, Curr. Phys. Index, Appl. Mech. Rev., Phys. Abstr. **LC** QC350. **DD** 535.05. **NLM** W1 OP864. **CODEN** OPSUA3. (cum index).

OPTICS COMMUNICATIONS. V. 1- Apr. 1969-. 0030-4018. Periodical. NE. English (French or German). bm. Elsevier Science Publishers, PO Box 211, 1000 AE Amsterdam Netherlands. **Tel** (020)5803.911. **Ind/Abst** Electron. Commun. Abstr. J., ISMEC Bull., Pollut. Abstr. Indexes, Saf. Sci. Abstr. J., Eng. Index Mon., Eng. Index Bioeng. Abstr., Eng. Index Energy Abstr., GeoRef, Comput. Control Abstr., Electr. Electron. Abstr., Sci. Abstr. Sect. A. Phys. Abstr., Chem. Abstr., Nucl. Sci. Abstr., Int. Aerosp. Abstr., Eng. Index Mon., Eng. Index Annu., Phys. Abstr., Sci. Cit. Index, Abr. Ed., Eng. Index, Bibliogr. Index Geol. **LC** QC350. **DD** 535.05. **CODEN** OPCOB8. (cum index).

OPTICS INDEX. *See* Indexes/Abstracts.

OPTICS LETTERS. V. 1- July 1977-. 0146-9592. Periodical. US. English. mo. American Institute of Physics, 335 East 45th Street, New York NY 10017. **Tel** (516)349-7800. **Ind/Abst** Excerpta Med., Int. Aerosp. Abstr., Comput. Control Abstr., Electr. Electron. Abstr., Sci. Abstr. Sect. A. Phys. Abstr., Energy Res. Abstr., Spin, Chem. Abstr., Curr. Phys. Index. **LC** QC350. **DD** 535.05. **NLM** W1 OP864D. **CODEN** OPLEDP.

OPTICS NEWS. V. 1- Feb. 1975-. 0098-907X. US. English. mo. American Institute of Physics, 335 East 45th Street, New York NY 10017. **Tel** (516)349-7800. **Ind/Abst** Abstr. Bull. Inst. Paper Chem., Energy Res. Abstr., Spin, Curr. Phys. Index. **LC** QC350. **DD** 535.05. **NLM** W1 OP864G. **CODEN** ONEWDU.

OPTIK; ZEITSCHRIFT FUR LICHT- UND ELEKTRONENOPTEK. **VFOAT** Zeitschrift fur Licht- und Elektronenoptik. V. 25- 1967-. Periodical. GW. German (English). mo. 816.-. Wissenschaftliche Verlagsgesellschaft MBH, Postfach 40, D7000 Stuttgart 1 West Germany. **Tel** (0711)25820. bk rev. adv acc. **Circ** 600. Unpublished articles on subjects for light and electron optics.

OPTIKA I SPEKTROSKOPIJA. (OPTIKA I SPEKTROSKOPIIA; SBORNIK STATEI). 1- 1956-. 0030-4034. UR. Russian. mo. $126.50. Victor Kamkin Inc (70670), 12224 Parklawn Drive, Rockville MD 20852. **Tel** (301)881-5973. **Ind/Abst** Int. Aerosp. Abstr., Chem. Abstr., Sci. Cit. Index, Abr. Ed., Electr. Electron. Abstr., Phys. Abstr., Comput. Control Abstr., Bibliogr. Index Geol. **LC** QC476.5. **CODEN** OPSPAM. Index in last issue of volume - attached. (cum index).

OPTIKO-MEHANICESKAJA PROMYSLENNOST. (OPTIKO-MEKHANICHESKAIA PROMYSHLENNOST). Began in 1931. 0030-4042. Periodical. UR. Russian. mo. $49.50. Victor Kamkin Inc (70675), 12224 Parklawn Drive, Rockville MD 20852. **Tel** (301)881-5973. **Ind/Abst** Int. Aerosp. Abstr., Comput. Control Abstr., Electr. Electron. Abstr., Sci. Abstr. Sect. A. Phys. Abstr., Chem. Abstr. **LC** QC350. **CODEN** OPMPAQ.

PHOTONICS SPECTRA. **VFOAT** Photonics. Vol. 16, Issue 1 (Jan. 1982)-. 0731-1230. Periodical. US. English. mo. $50.00. Optical Publishing Company Inc, Box 1146, Pittsfield MA 01202. **Tel** (413)499-0514. **Ed** Diane L Kelley. **Ind/Abst** Predicasts, Comput. Control Abstr., Electr. Electron. Abstr., Sci. Abstr., GeoRef, Met. Abstr., World Alum. Abstr., Chem. Abstr., Eng. Index. **LC** TS510. **DD** 681.405. **NLM** W1 PH671H. **CODEN** PHSAD3. bk rev. adv acc. **Circ** 52,000. (ctrl). Available on microfilm from University Microfilms. International journal of optics, electro-optics, lasers, fiber optics and imaging technology. Directed to scientists, engineers, technicians and management personnel of the photonics industry. *Optical Spectra, 0030-395X.*

PROCEEDINGS OF THE . . . ANNUAL TRI-SERVICE CONFERENCE ON THE BIOLOGICAL EFFECTS OF MICROWAVE RADIATION. **Main/Conf** Tri-Service Conference on the Biological Effects of Microwave Radiation. 4th-. US. English. ir. Plenum Press Inc, 233 Spring Street, New York NY 10013. **Tel** (212)620-8000. **LC** QH652. **DD** 574.19.

PROGRESS IN OPTICS. Vol. 1-. 0079-6638. English. an. Elsevier North-Holland Inc, 52 Vanderbilt Avenue, New York NY 10017. **Ind/Abst** Eng. Index Annu., Eng. Index Mon., Eng. Index Bioeng. Abstr., Eng. Index Energy Abstr., Comput. Control Abstr., Electr. Electron. Abstr., Sci. Abstr. Sect. A. Phys. Abstr., Chem. Abstr. **LC** QC351. **DD** 535.05. **NLM** W1 PR676K. **CODEN** POPTAN.

PROTECTION CONTRE LES RAYONNEMENTS IONISANTS. French. ir. 26 rue Desaix, 75727 Paris Cedex 15 France.

RADIATION AND ENVIRONMENTAL BIOPHYSICS. *See* Biology - Biophysics.

RADIATION EFFECTS. V. 1- Jan. 1969-. 0033-7579. Periodical. US. English. mo. $278.00. Gordon & Breach, PO Box 197, London WC2E 9PX England. **Ed** Walter Gibson. **Ind/Abst** Eng. Index, Excerpta Med., Energy Inf. Abstr., Environ. Abstr., Int. Aerosp. Abstr., Comput. Control Abstr., Electr. Electron. Abstr., Sci. Abstr., Energy Res. Abstr., Met. Abstr., World Alum. Abstr., Nucl. Sci. Abstr., Biol. Abstr., Chem. Abstr., Phys. Abstr., Sci. Cit. Index, Abr. Ed., Sci. Abstr. Sect. A. Phys. Abstr., Eng. Index Annu., Eng. Index Mon., Eng. Index Bioeng. Abstr., Eng. Index Energy Abstr. **LC** QD601.A1. **DD** 541.3805. **NLM** W1 RA16. **CODEN** RAEFBL. bk rev. adv acc.

RADIATION EFFECTS LETTERS SECTION. Began in 1983. 0142-2448. Periodical. US. English. bm. **Ed** Walter Gibson. **Ind/Abst** Comput. Control Abstr., Electr. Electron. Abstr., Sci. Abstr. Sect. A. Phys. Abstr. **CODEN** RELRDK. bk rev. adv acc. *Radiation Effects Letters, 0142-2448.*

RADIATION PHYSICS AND CHEMISTRY. V. 9-. 0146-5724. Periodical. UK. English. mo. Pergamon Press, 395 Sawmill River Road, Elmsford NY 10523. **Ind/Abst** Electron. Commun. Abstr. J., ISMEC Bull., Pollut. Abstr. Indexes, Saf. Sci. Abstr. J., Life Sci. Collect., Excerpta Med., Coal Abstr., Int. Aerosp. Abstr., Comput. Control Abstr., Electr. Electron. Abstr., Sci. Abstr. Sect. A. Phys. Abstr., Chem. Abstr. **LC** QD601.A1. **DD** 541.3805. **NLM** W1 RA164. **CODEN** RPCHDM. Available on microfilm and microfiche. *International Journal for Radiation Physics and Chemistry, 0020-7055.*

RADIATION PHYSICS, BIOPHYSICS AND RADIATION BIOLOGY. **Main/Corp** Columbia University. Radiological Research Laboratory. US. English. US Department of Energy, Technical Information Center, Springfield VA 22161.

RADIATION PROTECTION DOSIMETRY. Vol. 1, No. 1-. 0144-8420. Periodical. UK. English. ir. $350.00. Nuclear Technology Publishing, Subscriptions Department, PO Box #7, Ashford Kent TN25 4NW England. **Tel** (0233)41683. **Ed** T F Johns. **Ind/Abst** Excerpta Med., Comput. Control Abstr., Electr. Electron. Abstr., Sci. Abstr. Sect. A. Phys. Abstr., Energy Res. Abstr., Chem. Abstr. **LC** R905. **DD** 363.179. **NLM** W1 RA164R. **CODEN** RPDODE. bk rev. adv acc. **Circ** 1,000. (ctrl). All aspects of personnel and environmental dosimetry and monitoring for ionising radiation.

RADIATION PROTECTION MANAGEMENT. Vol. 1, No. 1 (Oct. 1983)-. 0740-0640. Periodical. US. English. qt. $250.00 Domestic, $260.00 Canada. Techrite Company, PO Box 7928, Marietta GA 30065.

RADIOLOGICAL QUALITY OF THE ENVIRONMENT. (RADIOLOGICAL QUALITY OF THE ENVIRONMENT IN THE UNITED STATES). **Main/Corp** United States. Environmental Protection Agency. Office of Radiation Programs. May 1976-. 0363-9819. Periodical. US. English. an. US Environmental Protection Agency, Office of Radiation Programs, Washington DC 20460. **LC** TD196.R3. **DD** 614.839. **NLM** W1 RA335.

RADIOPHYSICS AND QUANTUM ELECTRONICS. **Main/Corp** Russia (1923- U.S.S.R.) Ministerstvo Vysshego i Srednego Spetsialnogo Obrazovaniia. 0033-8443. Periodical. US. English (translated from Russian). mo. Consultants Bureau, 233 Spring Street, New York NY 10013. **Tel** (212)620-8000. **Ed** V L Ginzury. **Ind/Abst** Math. Rev., Electron. Commun. Abstr. J., ISMEC Bull., Pollut. Abstr. Indexes, Saf. Sci. Abstr. J., Eng. Index Mon., Eng. Index Bioeng. Abstr., Eng. Index Energy Abstr., Comput. Control Abstr., Electr. Electron. Abstr., Sci. Abstr. Sect. A. Phys. Abstr., Appl. Mech. Rev., Chem. Abstr., Eng. Index Annu., Eng. Index, Phys. Abstr., Electr. Electron. Abstr., Nucl. Sci. Abstr. **LC** QC661. **DD** 539.205. **CODEN** RPQEAC. This journal reports on the properties and applications of electromagnetic radiation in the radio and optical bands Covers radio astronomy, plasma theory, millimeter and submillimeter waves, antenna and wave guide technology. *Soviet Radiophysics, 0097-1545.*

REAL-TIME SIGNAL PROCESSING. **VFOAT** Real Time Signal Processing. 1 (Aug. 28-29, 1978)-. 8755-3619. US. English. an. 405 Fieldston Road, Bellingham WA 98225. **LC** TK5102.5. **DD** 621.38043.

REFRACTORIES. (CURRENT INDUSTRIAL REPORTS. MQ-32C, REFRACTORIES). 0161-0406. Periodical. US. English. qt. $8.00. Data User Services Division, Customer Services Publication, Bureau of the Census, Washington DC 20233. **Tel** (301)763-4100. **Ind/Abst** Predicasts, Chem. Abstr., Am. Stat. Index. **LC** HD9600.R43. **DD** 380.145666720973. **CODEN** CIRRDF. Presents timely data on the production, inventories, and orders of approximately 5,000 products, which represents 40 percent of all US manufacturing.

REPORT ON ENVIRONMENTAL RADIATION SURVEILLANCE IN NORTH CAROLINA. (REPORT ON ENVIRONMENTAL RADIATION SURVEILLANCE IN NORTH CAROLINA FOR . . .). **VFOAT** Environmental Radiation Surveillance. 0147-2887. US. English. Department of Human Resources, Division of Facility Services, Radiation Section, PO Box 12200, Raleigh NC 27605. **LC** TD196.R3. **DD** 363.179. **NLM** W2 AN8 D52R.

REZA KAGAKU KENKYU. **VFOAT** Laser Science Progress Report of IPCR. Began in 1979. Periodical. Japanese (summaries in English). an. Rikagaku Kenkyujo, 2-Ban 1-Go Hirosawa Wako-Shi, Saitama-Ken 35 Japan. **Ind/Abst** Chem. Abstr. **CODEN** RKAKDK.

RICERCHE SPETTROSCOPICHE. Vol. 1, No. 1-. 0370-7342. Periodical. Italian. ir. **Ind/Abst** Comput. Control Abstr., Electr. Electron. Abstr., GeoRef, Sci. Abstr. Sect. A. Phys. Abstr. **CODEN** RSLAAU.

SCIENCE RESEARCH ABSTRACTS JOURNAL. PART B. LASER AND ELECTRO-OPTIC REVIEWS. QUANTUM ELECTRONICS AND UNCONVENTIONAL ENERGY SOURCES. *See* Indexes/Abstracts.

SOVIET JOURNAL OF OPTICAL TECHNOLOGY. Began in 1966. 0038-5514. Periodical. US. English (Russian). mo. American Institute of Physics, 335 East 45th Street, New York NY 10017. **Tel** (212)661-9404. **Ind/Abst** Electron.

Physics—Magnetism

Commun. Abstr. J., ISMEC Bull., Pollut. Abstr. Indexes, Saf. Sci. Abstr. J., Comput. Control Abstr., Electr. Electron. Abstr., Sci. Abstr. Sect. A. Phys. Abstr., Energy Res. Abstr., Chem. Abstr., Eng. Index, Nucl. Sci. Abstr., Int. Aerosp. Abstr., Spin, Curr. Phys. Index, Phys. Abstr. LC TS510. CODEN SJOTBH.

SPECTROSCOPIA MOLECULAR. V. 1- (No. 1-). 0038-6995. Periodical. US. Interlingua. mo. F Cleveland, Spectroscopia Laboratory, University of Kentucky, Lexington KY 40506. Ind/Abst Chem. Abstr. LC QC451. DD 535.8405. CODEN SPMOAX. Available on microfilm from University Microfilms International.

SPRINGER SERIES IN CHEMICAL PHYSICS. V. 1-. 0172-6218. Monographic Series. English. Springer Verlag-New York Inc, 175 5th Avenue, New York NY 10010. Tel (212)460-1584. Ind/Abst Comput. Control Abstr., Electr. Electron. Abstr., Sci. Abstr. Sect. A. Phys. Abstr., Chem. Abstr., Phys. Abstr., Math. Rev. CODEN SSCPDA. Contains articles on laser processing, chemistry of solid surfaces, atoms in strong light fields, and formations of organic solids.

SPRINGER SERIES IN OPTICAL SCIENCES. 0342-4111. Monographic Series. English. ir. Springer Verlag-New York Inc, 175 5th Avenue, New York NY 10010. Tel (212)460-1584. Ind/Abst Eng. Index Annu., Eng. Index Mon., Eng. Index Bioeng. Abstr., Eng. Index Energy Abstr., Comput. Control Abstr., Electr. Electron. Abstr., Sci. Abstr. Sect. A. Phys. Abstr., Energy Res. Abstr., Chem. Abstr. CODEN SSOSDB. Contains articles on optical phase conjugation, laser physics, scanning electron microscopy, and holography and deformation analysis.

STATE OF WASHINGTON ENVIRONMENTAL RADIATION PROGRAM ... ANNUAL REPORT. Main/Corp Washington (State). Environmental Radiation and Emergency Response Unit. VFOAT Report, Environmental Radiation Program. US. English. an. LC TD196.R3. DD 363.728.

STUDIES IN RADIATION EFFECTS IN SOLIDS. V. 1- 1966-. US. English. ir. Gordon & Breach Science Publishers, 50 West 23rd Street, New York NY 10010. Tel (212)206-8900. LC QC176.8.R3. DD 539.7222.

STUDIES IN RADIATION EFFECTS ON SOLIDS. V. 2- 1967-. Periodical. US. English. ir. Gordon & Breach Science Publishers, 50 West 23rd Street, New York NY 10010. LC QC475. CODEN SRESAJ. Studies in Radiation Effects: Series A, Physical and Chemical.

STUDIES IN RADIATION EFFECTS. SERIES A. PHYSICAL AND CHEMICAL. (STUDIES IN RADIATION EFFECTS : SERIES A, PHYSICAL AND CHEMICAL). V. 1. Periodical. US. English. ir. Gordon & Breach Science Publishers, 50 West 23rd Street, New York NY 10010. Tel (212)206-8900. LC QC475.

UV/EB NEWS. VAT Ultraviolet, Electron Beam News. Vol. 1, No. 1 (Jan. 1981)-. 0275-3901. Periodical. US. English. bm. $111.00. Technology Marketing Corporation, 17 Park Street, Norwalk CT 06851. Tel (203)846-2029. Ed Kathleen Delaney. adv acc. Circ 5,000. Newsletter featuring general industry news as they relate to ultraviolet, electron beam and infrared technologies.

VIDEODISC AND OPTICAL DISK UPDATE. (VIDEODISC & OPTICAL DISK UPDATE). 0742-5732. Periodical. US. English. sm. $157.00. Meckler Publishing, 11 Ferry Lane West, Westport CT 06880. Tel (203)226-6967. DD 001. adv acc. Circ 1,000. Provides current news on developing optical based information systems and C-D ROM and videodisc products and reports. Videodisc Update, 0733-0421.

VISION RESEARCH. V. 1- June 1961-. 0042-6989. Periodical. UK. English (French or German). mo. Pergamon Press, 395 Sawmill River Road, Elmsford NY 10523. Tel (914)592-7700. Ind/Abst Life Sci. Collect., Excerpta Med., Index Med., Biol. Abstr., Int. Aerosp. Abstr., Comput. Control Abstr., Electr. Electron. Abstr., Sci. Abstr. Sect. A. Phys. Abstr., Chem. Abstr., Psychol. Abstr., Sci. Cit. Index, Abr. Ed., Phys. Abstr., Hospit. Lit. Index. LC QP474. DD 591.18. NLM W1 VI84. CODEN VISRAM. Index in last issue of volume - attached.

X-RAY DIFFRACTION ABSTRACTS. See Indexes/Abstracts.

YUAN TZU KUANG PU FEN HSI. VFOAT Atomic Spectroscopy. CH. Chinese. ir. 0.36. Hsin Hua Shu Tien Pei-Ching fa Hsing So, Peking China. LC QC450. DD 53914.

ZURNAL PRIKLADNOI SPEKTROSKOPII. (ZHURNAL PRIKLADNOI SPEKTROSKOPII). VFOAT Vsesoiuznyi Zhurnal Prikladnoi Spektroskopii. Vol. 1- Sept. 1964-. 0514-7506. Periodical. US. Russian. mo. $83.00. Victor Kamkin Inc (70305), 12224 Parklawn Drive, Rockville MD 20852. Tel (301)881-5973. Ind/Abst Coal Abstr., Abstr. Bull. Inst. Paper Chem., Int. Aerosp. Abstr., Comput. Control Abstr., Electr. Electron. Abstr., Sci. Abstr. Sect. A. Phys. Abstr., Chem. Abstr., Energy Res. Abstr., Phys. Abstr. CODEN ZPSBAX. (cum index).

MAGNETISM

ADVANCES IN MAGNETIC RESONANCE. V. 1- 1965-. 0065-2873. US. English. ir. Academic Press, 4805 Sand Lake Road, Orlando FL 32887. Tel (305)345-4100. Ed J S Waugh. Ind/Abst Sci. Cit. Index, Abr. Ed. LC QC762. DD 538.3.

ADVANCES IN MAGNETIC RESONANCE. SUPPLEMENT. No. 1-. Monographic Series. US. English. ir. Academic Press, 4805 Sand Lake Road, Orlando FL 32819.

ANNUAIRE : MAGNETISME TERRESTRE. See Yearbooks, Almanacs, Directories.

ANNUAL REPORT FOR MAGNETIC OBSERVATORIES. VFOAT Rapport Annuel des Observatoires Magnetiques. 1970-. 0704-3023. CN. English (French). an. $4.20. Earth Physics Branch, 1 Observatory Cresent, Ottawa Ontario K1A 0E4 Canada. Ed E I Loomer. LC QC825.1. DD 538.7971.

BIOLOGICAL EFFECTS OF ELECTROMAGNETIC RADIATION. 0147-2372. US. English. qt. Franklin Institute/ Research Laboratory, Box 2266, Philadelphia PA 19103. LC QP82.2.E43. DD 574.191705.

BIOLOGICAL EFFECTS OF NONIONIZING ELECTROMAGNETIC RADIATION. Series/Titl NTIA Contractor Reports. Began with V. 1, Oct. 1976. Periodical. US. English. qt. National Telecommunications and Information Administration, Washington DC 20230. Each issue contains an index to its own contents - no vol index - loose. Vols. for (Oct. 1980-June 1981—) distributed to depository libraries in microfiche. Biological Effects of Electromagnetic Radiation.

BIOLOGICAL MAGNETIC RESONANCE. V. 1-. 0192-6020. Periodical. English. ir. Plenum Publishing Corporation, 233 Spring Street, New York NY 10013. Tel (212)620-8000. Ed L J Berliner and J Reuben. Ind/Abst Chem. Abstr. NLM W1 BI75R. CODEN BMGRDB. Each issue contains an index to its own contents - no vol index - loose.

BOLETIM GEOMAGNETICO PRELIMINAR. Main/Corp Instituto Nacional de Meteorologia e Geofisica. Portuguese. ir. Instituto Nacionel de Meteorologia e Geofisica, rua Saraiva de Carvalho 2, Lisboa Portugal. LC QC825.4. DD 538.78469.

CHUNG-HUA WU LI I HSUEH TSA CHIH. VFOAT Zhonghua Wuliyixue Zaxhi. Vol. 1. 0254-1424. Periodical. CC. Chinese. qt. 3.80. China Publication Centre, PO Box 2820, Beijing China. Tel 49153. Ed Bei Chi. NLM W1 CH985D. bk rev. adv acc. Circ 10,000. (ctrl). Ultrasound diagnosis: magnetism, light, computer, electronmicroscope sampling technique and some others used in medicine.

DATA CATALOGUE - WORLD DATA CENTER C2 FOR GEOMAGNETISM. Main/Corp World Data Center C2 for Geomagnetism. 1978-. English. ir. WDC-C2 for Geomegnetism, c/o Kyoto University Library, Yoshida Honmachi Kyoto 606 Japan. LC QC811. DD 538.7. Catalogue of Data.

DATA REPORT OF HYDROGRAPHIC OBSERVATIONS. SERIES OF GEOMAGNETISM. Main/Corp Japan. Kaijo Hoancho. Suirobu. VFOAT Suirobu Kansoku Hokoku : Chijikihen. No. 1- 1965-. 0303-5492. JA. English. ir. Nippon Yusen Kaisha, 3-2 Marunouchi 2-chome, Chiyoda-ku Tokyo Japan. LC QC830.J25.

ELECTROMAGNETIC METROLOGY CURRENT AWARENESS SERVICE. (ELECTROMAGNETIC METROLOGY). 0046-1709. US. English. mo. $100.00. Electromagnetic Metrology Information Center, Boulder CO 80302. LC QC535. DD 016.537.

ELECTROMAGNETICS. Vol. 1, No. 1 (Jan.-Mar. 1981). 0272-6343. Periodical. US. English. qt. $63.50. Hemisphere Publishing Corp, 79 Madison Avenue/Suite 1110, New York NY 10016. Tel (202)783-3958. Ed P L E Uslenghi. LC QC759.6. CODEN ETRMDV. bk rev. adv acc. Circ 440. Refereed papers in the broad field of electromagnetics, electromagnetic theory, high frequency techniques, extra and very low frequency, numerical techniques, scattering and disfraction.

ELECTRON SPIN RESONANCE SPECTROSCOPY ABSTRACTS. See Indexes/Abstracts.

FIZIKA MAGNITNYKH MATERIALOV. No. 1- 1973-. UR. Russian. 0.97 Single Issue. LC QC750.

GEOMAGNETIC DATA. Series/Titl Report UAG** IMS Data Publication. 0163-4402. US. English. World Data Center A for Solar-Terrestrial Physics, United States Department of Commerce, NOAA/ NGSDC, Boulder CO 80302. LC QC811. DD 538.7.

GEOMAGNETIC DATA. Main/Corp International Association of Geomagnetism and Aeronomy. Series Corp Its IAGA Bulletin. VFOAT Indices K and C. 1940/46-. English. ir. International Association of Geomagnetism and Aeronomy, 39 Ter Rue Gay Lussac, 75005 Paris France.

GEOMAGNETISM AND AERONOMY. V. 1- 1961-. 0016-7932. Periodical. US. English (Russian). bm. $365.00. American Geophysical Union, 2000 Florida Avenue NW, Washington DC 20009. Tel (202)462-6903. Ind/Abst GeoRef, Comput. Control Abstr., Electr. Electron. Abstr., Sci. Abstr. Sect. A. Phys. Abstr., Int. Aerosp. Abstr., Phys. Abstr., Bibliogr. Index Geol. LC QC811. DD 538.705. CODEN GMARAX. Available on microfilm. English translation of the Russian journal, Geomagnetism Aeronomiya. Covers aeronomy; geomagnetism; interplanetary, planetary, and solar phenomena; cosmic rays; and solar-terrestrial relationships.

GEOMAGNETIZM I AERONOMIJA. (GEOMAGNETIZM I AERONOMII). Vol. 1- 1961-. 0016-7940. Periodical. UR. Russian. bm. $60.00. Victor Kamkin Inc (70218), 12224 Parklawn Drive, Rockville MD 20852. Tel (301)881-5973. Ind/Abst Int. Aerosp. Abstr., GeoRef, Comput. Control Abstr., Electr. Electron. Abstr., Sci. Abstr. Sect. A. Phys. Abstr., Chem. Abstr., Energy Res. Abstr., Phys. Abstr., Sci. Cit. Index, Abr. Ed., Bibliogr. Index Geol. CODEN GEAEA6.

HYPERFINE INTERACTIONS. V. 1- June 1975-. 0304-3843. Periodical. SZ. English. bm. $675.00. JC Baltzer AG Scientific Publishing Company, Wettsteinplatz 10, CH-4058 Basel Switzerland. Tel 61 26 8925. Ind/Abst Comput. Control Abstr., Electr. Electron. Abstr., Sci. Abstr. Sect. A. Phys. Abstr., Chem. Abstr., Phys. Abstr., Sci. Cit. Index, Abr. Ed. LC QC762. DD 538.3. CODEN HYINDN.

ITOGI NAUKI I TEKHNIKI : GEOMAGNETIZM I VYSOKIE SLOI ATMOSFERY. VFOAT Itogi Nauki I Tekhniki. V. 1- 1972-. UR. Russian. 1.87 Single Issue. G Liubertsy-10, Moskovskoi Obl, Oktiabrskii Prospekt 403, Moskva Russian SFSR. LC QC811.

ITOGI NAUKI I TEKHNIKI. SERIIA FIZIKA PLAZMY. VFOAT Seriia Fizika Plazmy. V. 1, Ch. 1-. 0202-7933. Periodical. UR. Russian. 140010 G Liubertsy, 10 Moskovskoi Obl, Oktiabrskii Prospekt 403, Proizvodstvenno-Izdatelskii Kombinat Viniti, Moskva Russian SFSR. Ind/Abst Int. Aerosp. Abstr. LC QC717.6.

JOURNAL OF MAGNETIC RESONANCE. Periodical. US. English. ir. Academic Press, 4805 Sand Lake Road, Orlando FL 32819. Tel (305)345-4100. Ind/Abst Chem. Abstr., Sci. Cit. Index, Abr. Ed., Phys. Abstr., Electr. Electron. Abstr., Comput. Control Abstr., Int. Aerosp. Abstr.

JOURNAL OF MAGNETIC RESONANCE. V. 1- Jan. 1969-. 0022-2364. Periodical. US. English. Academic Press, 4805 Sand Lake Road, Orlando FL 32819. Ind/Abst Electron. Commun. Abstr. J., ISMEC Bull., Pollut. Abstr. Indexes, Saf. Sci. Abstr. J., Life Sci. Collect., Abstr. Bull. Inst. Paper Chem., Int. Aerosp. Abstr., Comput. Control Abstr., Electr. Electron. Abstr., Sci. Abstr. Sect. A. Phys. Abstr., Chem. Abstr., Nucl. Sci. Abstr. LC QC762. DD 538.3. CODEN JOMRA4.

JOURNAL OF MAGNETISM AND MAGNETIC MATERIALS. V. 1- Oct. 1975-. 0304-8853. Periodical. NE. English. mo. Elsevier Science Publishers, PO Box 211, 1000 AE Amsterdam

Physics—Nuclear Physics

The Netherlands. Tel (020)5803911. Ind/Abst Eng. Index Annu., Eng. Index Mon., Eng. Index Bioeng. Abstr., Eng. Index Energy Abstr., Int. Aerosp. Abstr., GeoRef., Comput. Control Abstr., Electr. Electron. Abstr., Sci. Abstr. Sect. A. Phys. Abstr., Met. Abstr., World Alum. Abstr., Chem. Abstr., Sci. Cit. Index, Abr. Ed., Phys. Abstr., Bibliogr. Index Geol. LC QC750. DD 538.05. CODEN JMMMDC.

MAGNETIC FUSION PROGRAM SUMMARY DOCUMENT. Main/Corp United States. Dept. of Energy. Office of Fusion Energy. US. English. an. US Department of Energy, Office of Energy Technology, Office of Fusion Energy, 5285 Port Royal Road, Springfield VA 22161.

MAGNETIC RESONANCE ANNUAL. 1985-. 8756-9787. US. English. an. Raven Press, 1140 Avenue of the Americas, New York NY 10036. Ed Herbert Y Kressel. LC QC762. DD 538.36205. NLM W1.

MAGNETIC RESONANCE REVIEW. V. 1- Jan. 1972-. 0097-7330. Periodical. US. English. qt. $168.50. Gordon and Breach Science Publishers, 1 Park Avenue, New York NY 10016. Ed Charles P Poole Nj. Ind/Abst Comput. Control Abstr., Electr. Electron. Abstr., Sci. Abstr. Sect. A. Phys. Abstr., Met. Abstr., World Alum. Abstr., Chem. Abstr., Nucl. Sci. Abstr. LC QC762. DD 538.3. CODEN MRSRBL. bk rev. adv acc.

MAGNETIC SEPARATION NEWS. Vol. 1, No. 1 (Dec. 1983)-. 0731-3632. Periodical. US. English. ir. $130.00. Gordon & Breach, PO Box 197, London WC2E 9PX England. Ed Martin Parker. CODEN MSNWDK. bk rev. adv acc.

MAGNETISM. 0464-4387. US. English. ir. Academic Press, 4805 Sand Lake Road, Orlando FL 32819. Tel (305)345-4100. Ind/Abst Chem. Abstr. CODEN MAGNAX.

MAGNETISM LETTERS CEASED. V. 1. 0308-6011. Periodical. UK. English. bm. $75.00. 42 William IV Street, London WC2 England. Ind/Abst Chem. Abstr. LC QC750. DD 538.05. CODEN MALEDY. *International Journal of Magnetism, 0020-7365.*

MAGNITNAJA GIDRODINAMIKA. (MAGNITNAIA GIDRODINAMIKA). 1965-. 0025-0015. Periodical. UR. Russian. qt. $35.00. Victor Kamkin Inc (70568), 12224 Parklawn Drive, Rockville MD 20852. Tel (301)881-5973. Ind/Abst Math. Rev., Electron. Commun. Abstr. J., ISMEC Bull., Pollut. Abstr. Indexes, Saf. Sci. Abstr. J., Int. Aerosp. Abstr., Comput. Control Abstr., Electr. Electron. Abstr., Sci. Abstr. Sect. A. Phys. Abstr., Chem. Abstr., Phys. Abstr. LC QC718. DD 538.605. CODEN MAGIAI.

NIHON OYO JIKI GAKKAISHI. Began in 1977-. 0285-0192. Periodical. JA. Japanese. ir. 2000 Single Issue. Nihon Oyo Jiki Gakkai, 12-5 Shibuya 1, Shibuya-ku, Tokyo-to 150 Japan. Ind/Abst Coal Abstr., Chem. Abstr. LC QC750. CODEN NOJGD3.

NUCLEAR MAGNETIC RESONANCE. Began with: Vol. 1, published in 1971. 0305-9804. UK. English. an. 87.00. Royal Society of Chemistry, Blackhorse Road, Letchworth Herts SG6 1HN England. Tel (04626)72555. Ed G A Webb. Ind/Abst GeoRef, Chem. Abstr. LC QC762. DD 538.3. CODEN NMRNBE.

NUCLEAR MAGNETIC RESONANCE SPECTROMETRY ABSTRACTS. See Indexes/Abstracts.

NUMERISCHE ERGEBNISSE UND MAGNETOGRAMME WINGST. Series/ Titl Erdmagnetisches Jahrbuch. 1973-. Periodical. German. an. LC QC830.W56. DD 538.794359. *Ergebnisse der Erdmagnetischen Beobachtungen im Observatorium Wingst im Jahre . . . .*

OBSERVATIONS MAGNETIQUES. M'BOUR, REPUBLIQUE DU SENEGAL. VFOAT M'Bour, Republique du Senegal. Began with No. 1 (1965). FR. French. ir. Services Scientifiques Centraux, 70-74 Route D'Aulnay, 93140 Bondy France. LC QC830.M425. DD 538.79663.

PARAMAGNITNYI REZONANS. 0370-0704. UR. Russian. 0.58 Single Issue. IZD-VO Kazanskogo Universiteta, Ul Lenina D 4/5, Kazan USSR. Ind/Abst Chem. Abstr. LC QC762. CODEN PMRZA3.

PROTON NMR COLLECTION. CUMULATIVE CHEMICAL CLASS INDEX. See Indexes/Abstracts.

REPORT OF THE GEOMAGNETIC AND GEOELECTRIC OBSERVATIONS. Main/Corp Chijike Kansokujo, Kakioka, Japan. VFOAT Geomagnetic and Geoelectric Observations. Began publication with issue for 1957/58. English. ir. Ind/Abst GeoRef. LC QC830.

RESULTS OF GEOMAGNETIC OBSERVATIONS, BELSK. Main/Corp Polska Akademia Nauk. Instytut Geofizyki. Series/Titl Publications of the Institute of Geophysics. English. ir. Panstwowe Wydawnictwo Naukowe, Ul Pasteura 3 02-093, Warszawa Poland. LC QC830.B46. DD 538.794383.

RISULTATI DELLE OSSERVAZIONI MAGNETICHE. English (Italian). an. LC QC830.L39. DD 538.7945711.

SEIDENKI GAKKAI KOEN RONBUNSHU : SEIDENKI GAKKAI ZENKOKU TAIKAI. VFOAT Seidenki Gakkai Zenkoku Taikai. No. 1-Issue (1977)-. JA. Japanese. an. Seidenki Gakkai c/o Sharumu, 80 4F 1-3 Hongo 4, Bunkyo-ku Tokyo 113 Japan. LC QC570.

SEIDENKI GAKKAI SHI. 0386-2550. English (Japanese). bm. 2000. Seidenki Gakkai c/o Gakkaishi Kanko Senta, 4-16 Yayoi 2, Bunkyo-ku Tokyo-to 113 Japan. LC QC570. DD 537.205.

SPEKTROSKOPIJA GAZORAZRJADNOJ PLAZMY. (SPEKTROSKOPIIA GAZORAZRIADNOI PLAZMY). Vol. 1-. 0134-9007. Periodical. UR. Russian. ir. 0.89 Each Issue. IZD-VO Leningradskogo Universiteta, 199164 Universitetskaia Nab 7/9, Leningrad USSR. Ind/Abst Chem. Abstr. LC QC718.5.S6. CODEN SGPLDD.

TI TZU KUAN TSE PAO KAO. VFOAT Report of Geomagnetic Observation. Vol. 1-2 (1978-1979)-. Periodical. Chinese (English). ir. Ti Chen Chu Pan She, Pei-Ching China. LC QC830.U78. DD 538.78516.

TI TZU KUAN TSE PAO KAO (KUANG-CHOU TI TZU TAI). (TI TZU KUAN TSE PAO KAO). VFOAT Report of Geomagnetic Observation. Periodical. CH. Chinese (English). ir. Ti Chen Chu Pan She, Peking China. LC QC830.C27. DD 538795129.

VOPROSY ELEKTRODINAMIKI I MEKHANIKI SPLOSHNYKH SRED. Periodical. UR. Russian. 0.66 Single Issue. Latviiskii Gosudarstvennyi Universitet, Riga 226098 B Rainisa, Riga Latvian SSR. LC QC630.

WISSENSCHAFTLICHE BERICHTE AUS DER HOCHMAGNETFELDANLAGE DER PHYSIKALISCHEN INSTITUTE DER TECHNISCHEN UNIVERSITAT BRAUNSCHWEIG. Main/Corp Technische Universitat Carolo-Wilhelmina. Hochmagnetfeldanlage der Physikalischen Institute. German. ir. mendelssohnstrasse 1B, D-3300 Braunschweig West Germany. LC QC754.2.M3.

NUCLEAR PHYSICS

ACTA PHYSICA POLONICA, B. V. 1- Jan./Mar. 1970-. 0587-4254. Periodical. English. mo. VCH Publishers Inc, 303 Northwest 12th Avenue, Deerfield Beach FL 33442. Ind/Abst Math. Rev., Met. Abstr., World Alum. Abstr., Chem. Abstr., Energy Res. Abstr., Comput. Control Abstr., Electr. Electron. Abstr., Sci. Abstr. Sect. A. Phys. Abstr., Sci. Cit. Index, Abr. Ed., Phys. Abstr. LC QC770. NLM W1 AC919B. CODEN APOBBB. *Acta Physica Polonica, 0001-673X.*

ACTIVITES SCIENTIFIQUES ET TECHNIQUES - COMMISSARIAT A L'ENERGIE ATOMIQUE. Main/Corp France. Commissariat a l'Energie Atomique. French. da. $384.00. New York Yomiuri Express, 41 East 42nd Street, New York NY 10017. Tel (212)661-5977. LC QC770. DD 539.705.

ADVANCES IN ATOMIC AND MOLECULAR PHYSICS. V. 1-. 0065-2199. US. English. ir. Academic Press, 4805 Sand Lake Road, Orlando FL 32887. Tel (305)345-4100. Ed D R Bates. Ind/Abst Comput. Control Abstr., Electr. Electron. Abstr., Sci. Abstr. Sect. A. Phys. Abstr., Chem. Abstr., Spin, Energy Res. Abstr., Sci. Cit. Index, Abr. Ed., Phys. Abstr. LC QC173. DD 539. CODEN AAMOA2.

ADVANCES IN NUCLEAR PHYSICS. V. 1- 1968-. 0065-2970. US. English. ir. Plenum Press, c/o H Feldman, 233 Spring Street, New York NY 10013. Tel (212)620-8000. Ed M Baranger and E Vogt. Ind/Abst Comput. Control Abstr., Electr. Electron. Abstr., Sci. Abstr. Sect. A. Phys. Abstr., Chem. Abstr., Spin, Energy Res. Abstr., Phys. Abstr., Sci. Cit. Index, Abr. Ed. LC QC173. DD 539.705. CODEN ANUPBZ.

ADVANCES IN NUCLEAR QUADRUPOLE RESONANCE. Began publication with Vol. 1 in 1974. 0065-2970. UK. English. ir. Heyden & Son Ltd, 247 South 41st Street, Philadelphia PA 19104. Ed J A S Smith. Ind/Abst Energy Res. Abstr.

ADVANCES IN NUCLEAR SCIENCE AND TECHNOLOGY. V. 1- 1962-. 0065-2989. US. English. ir. Plenum Publishing Corporation, 233 Spring Street, New York NY 10013. Tel (212)620-8000. Ed E J Henley and H Kouts. Ind/Abst Eng. Index Annu., Eng. Index Mon., Eng. Index Bioeng. Abstr., Eng. Index Energy Abstr., Energy Inf. Abstr., Environ. Abstr., Comput. Control Abstr., Electr. Electron. Abstr., Sci. Abstr. Sect. A. Phys. Abstr., Chem. Abstr., Energy Res. Abstr., Phys. Abstr. LC TK9001. DD 621.48058. NLM W1 AD685. CODEN ANUTAC.

ANNUAL REPORT - ATOMIC ENERGY CONTROL BOARD. Main/Corp Atomic Energy Control Board. 1st- 1946/47-. Periodical. CN. English (inverted special title page in French). an. Atomic Energy Control Board, 270 Albert Street, PO Box 1046, Ottawa Ontario K1P 5S9 Canada. Tel (613)996-8211.

ANNUAL REPORT - COMMISSION OF EUROPEAN COMMUNITIES. JOINT RESEARCH CENTRE. ISPRA ESTABLISHMENT, ITALY. (ANNUAL REPORT - JOINT RESEARCH CENTRE, ISPRA ESTABLISHMENT). Main/Corp Commission of the European Communities. Joint Research Centre. ISPRA Establishment. 0376-5482. English. ir. European Community Information Service, 2100 M Street Northwest/Suite 707, Washington DC 20037. LC QC789.I82. DD 539.707204521.

ANNUAL REPORT - KOENERUGI BUTSURIGAKU KENKYUJO (JAPAN). Main/Corp Koenerugi Butsurigaku Kenkyujo (Japan). VFOAT K.E.K. Annual Report. English. an. Technical Information Office, National Laboratory for High Energy Physics, Ibaraki-Ken 305 Japan. LC QC789.2.J32. DD 539.707205213.

ANNUAL REPORT - NUCLEAR SCIENCE. Main/Corp Lawrence Berkeley Laboratory. Nuclear Science. US. English. an. US Department of Energy, Lawrence Berkeley Laboratory, 5285 Port Royal Road, Springfield VA 22161.

ANNUAL REPORT - OAK RIDGE ASSOCIATED UNIVERSITIES. (ANNUAL REPORT). Main/Corp Oak Ridge Associated Universities. Began with: 21st (1967). 0078-2904. US. English. an. Oak Ridge Associated University, PO Box 117, Oak Ridge TN 37830. LC QC789.O3. DD 621.48072073. *Annual Report, 0742-4760.*

ANNUAL REPORT - STUDSVIK ENERGITEKNIK AB. Main/Corp Studsvik Energiteknik AB. English. ir. Studsvik Energiteknik AB, S-61182, Nykoping Sweden. LC QC792.8.S82. DD 338.762148094857. *Studsvik Energiteknik AB. Studsvik Energiteknik AB.*

ANNUAL RESEARCH REPORT - SOUTHERN UNIVERSITIES NUCLEAR INSTITUTE. Main/Corp Southern Universities Nuclear Institute. VFOAT Annual Research Report - Kerninstituut Van Die Suidelike Universiteite. 0304-839X. English. ir. PO Box 17 7131, Faure South Africa. LC QC789.S62. DD 539.705.

ANNUAL REVIEW OF NUCLEAR AND PARTICLE SCIENCE. V. 28- 1978-. 0163-8998. US. English. an. $34.00 Domestic, $37.00 Foreign. Annual Reviews Inc, 4139 El Camino Way, Palo Alto CA 94306. Tel (415)493-4400. Ed J D Jackson. Ind/Abst Comput. Control Abstr., Electr. Electron. Abstr., Sci. Abstr. Sect. A. Phys. Abstr., GeoRef, Biol. Abstr., Chem. Abstr., Spin, Energy Res. Abstr. LC QC770. DD 539.705. NLM W1 AN778BN. CODEN ARPSDF. Comprehensive, thorough coverage of latest advances in nuclear and particles science, written by acknowledged experts in the field.

Physics—Nuclear Physics

Extensive literature citations included. *Annual Review of Nuclear Science,* 0066-4243.

ANNUAL STATUS REPORT. NUCLEAR MEASUREMENTS. Series/Titl EUR. VFOAT Nuclear Measurements. English. an. LC QC784.5. DD 539.70287.

ANNUAL STATUS REPORT. THERMONUCLEAR FUSION TECHNOLOGY. VFOAT Thermonuclear Fusion Technology. English. an. LC TK9204. DD 621.484.

ARABIDOPSIS INFORMATION SERVICE. 0066-5657. GW. English, French, or German with summaries in English. an. $12.00. Goethe Universitet, Postfach 111, 932 Siesmayerstr 70, c/o A Kranz, D6000 Frankfurt West Germany. Tel (069)7984734. Ed Albert R Kranz. Ind/Abst Bibliogr. Agric., Biol. Abstr. LC QK495.C9. DD 583.123. CODEN ADISBG. adv acc. Circ 500. (ctrl). Arabidopsis research communication 'botanical drosophila, space plant' methods, materials, stock exchange, mutant lines, wildtype races, conservation, gene technology, and space biology.

ARSREDOGORELSE - STATENS RAD FOR ATOMFORSKNING. Main/Corp Statens Rad For Atomforskning. VFOAT Annual Report - Swedish Atomic Research Council. Danish, English, or Swedish. ir. Statens Rad for Atomforskning Redaktionstjansten, Box 23136, 10435 Stockholm Sweden. LC QC792.78.S8. *Redogorelse.*

ATOM INDONESIA. Vol. 1, No. 1-2 (July 1975)-. 0378-4576. Periodical. IO. English. sa. Free. Atom Indonesia, PO Box 85 KBY, Jakarta Selatan Indonesia. Tel Telex 46354. Ind/Abst Chem. Abstr., Energy Res. Abstr. LC QC791.9. DD 539.705. CODEN ATINDD. Circ 500.

ATOMIC DATA AND NUCLEAR DATA TABLES. V. 12- 1973-. 0092-640X. US. English. bm. Academic Press, 4805 Sand Lake Road, Orlando FL 32819. Tel (305)345-4100. Ind/Abst Int. Aerosp. Abstr., Chem. Abstr., Spin, Energy Res. Abstr., Comput. Control Abstr., Electr. Electron. Abstr., Sci. Abstr. Sect. A. Phys. Abstr., Phys. Abstr., Sci. Cit. Index, Abr. Ed. LC QC173. DD 539.70212. CODEN ADNDAT. *Atomic Data,* 0004-1082; *Nuclear Data Tables (New York),* 0090-0214.

ATOMIC PHYSICS; PROCEEDINGS. Main/Conf International Conference on Atomic Physics. 1st- 1968-. 0090-6360. US. English. ir. Plenum Press, 233 Spring Street, New York NY 10013. Tel (212)620-8000. Ind/Abst Chem. Abstr. LC QC173. DD 539.7. CODEN ATPHDU.

ATOMNAIA ENERGIIA. V. 1- 1956-. Periodical. UR. Russian. mo. $80.00. Victor Kamkin Inc (70026), 12224 Parklawn Drive, Rockville MD 20852. Tel (301)881-5973. Ind/Abst Chem. Abstr., Energy Res. Abstr., Comput. Control Abstr., Electr. Electron. Abstr., Sci. Abstr. Sect. A. Phys. Abstr., Pollut. Abstr. Indexes, Phys. Abstr. LC QC770. CODEN AENGAB.

BIBLIOGRAPHY OF ATOMIC AND MOLECULAR PROCESSES (WASHINGTON, D.C.). *See* Bibliographies.

BIRCH BARK ALLIANCE. (THE BIRCH BARK ALLIANCE). V. 1- Oct. 1978-. 0709-082X. Periodical. CN. English. qt. 8.00 for 2 years. Opirg-Peterborough, c/o Trent University, Peterborough Ontario K9J 7B8 Canada. DD 338.47621480971.

BOARD OF GOVERNORS AND PERMANENT MISSIONS OF MEMBER STATES. Main/Corp International Atomic Energy Agency. English. ir. Protocol Office/International Atomic Energy Agency, Wagramerstrasse 5 PO Box 100, A-1400 Vienna Austria. LC QC770. DD 341.76753.

BROOKHAVEN HIGHLIGHTS. Began with 1970/71. 0092-1548. US. English. an. National Technical Information Service, US Department of Commerce, 5285 Port Royal Road, Springfield VA 22161. LC QC789.U62. DD 539.7072074725. 0498-6520.

CNS BULLETIN. VAT Canadian Nuclear Society Bulletin, Bulletin. Societe Nucleaire Canadienne. Vol. 1, No. 1 (May 1980)-. 0714-7074. Periodical. CN. English (French). mo. Free. Canadian Nuclear Society, 11 Elizabeth Street, Toronto Ontario M5G 1P7 Canada. DD 621.4806071. (ctrl).

COMITE CONSULTATIF POUR LES ETALONS DE MESURE DES RAYONNEMENTS IONISANTS : RAPPORT. Main/Corp Comite International des Poids et Mesures. Comite Consultatif pour les Etalons de Mesure des Rayonnements Ionisants. VFOAT Rapport du Comite Consultatif pour les Etalons de Mesure des Rayonnements Ionisants . . . au Comite International des Poids et Mesures. FR. English (French). ir. Bureau International de Poids et Mesures Depositaire Offilib, 48 rue Gay-Lussac, F-75005 Paris France. LC QC795.42. DD 539.72.

COMMENTS ON ATOMIC AND MOLECULAR PHYSICS. V. 1- April/May 1969-. 0010-2687. Periodical. UK. English. ir. $168.00. Gordon & Breach, PO Box 197, London SC2E 9PX England. Tel (01)836-5125. Ed H H Stroke. Ind/Abst Comput. Control Abstr., Electr. Electron. Abstr., Sci. Abstr. Sect. A. Phys. Abstr., Chem. Abstr., Nucl. Sci. Abstr., Phys. Abstr. LC QC770. DD 539.05. CODEN CAMPBS. bk rev. adv acc.

COMMENTS ON NUCLEAR AND PARTICLE PHYSICS. V. 1- Jan. 1967-. 0010-2709. Periodical. US. English. ir. Gordon & Breach, 1 Bedford Street, London WC2E 9HD England. Tel 01 836 5125. Ind/Abst Comput. Control Abstr., Electr. Electron. Abstr., Sci. Abstr. Sect. A. Phys. Abstr., Chem. Abstr., Energy Res. Abstr., Phys. Abstr. CODEN CNPPAV.

CONFERENZBERICHTE. KERNFORSCHUNG, KERNTECHNIK. VFOAT Conference Papers. Nuclear Research, Nuclear Technology. V. 1- 0170-9003. GW. English (German). mo. 125.00. Fachinformationszentrum Energie Physik Mathematik GMBH, 7514 Eggenstein-Leopolds-Hafen 2, Karlsruhe West Germany. LC QC792.78.G3. DD 016.5397. *Informationen zur Kernforschung und Kerntechnik.*

COURRIER CERN. SZ. French. ir. Free. Public Information Office, 1211 Geneva, 23 Switzerland. Ed Gordon Fraser. LC QC788. DD 539.705. adv acc. Circ 18,000. (ctrl). International journal of high energy physics and related topics.

DIRECTORY - AMERICAN NUCLEAR SOCIETY. *See* Yearbooks, Almanacs, Directories.

FILM CATALOGUE . . . . Main/Corp Vic Library. English. ir. LC QC792.72.Z9. DD 016.62148. NLM WN 18. *Vic Library Film Catalogue.*

FUSION. 0148-0537. Periodical. US. English. bm. $20.00 Domestic, $25.00 Canada. Fusion, Fusion Energy Foundation, 1010-16th Street NW, Washington DC 20036. Ind/Abst Comput. Control Abstr., Electr. Electron. Abstr., Sci. Abstr. Sect. A. Phys. Abstr., Chem. Abstr., Energy Res. Abstr., Energy Inf. Abstr., Environ. Abstr. LC QC791.7. DD 539.764. CODEN FUSID8. *Newsletter - Fusion Energy Foundation,* 0364-2003.

GAIKOKU GENSHIRYOKU KIKAN KANKO SHIRYO GEPPO = MONTHLY LIST OF SELECTED ATOMIC ENERGY PUBLICATIONS. VFOAT Monthly List of Selected Atomic Energy Publications. V. 18-. English, French, German, Italian, Spanish or Russian. ir. Kokuritsu Kokai Toshokan, 10-1 Nagatacho 1 Chiyoda-ku (100), Tokyo Japan. LC Z5160, QC792. *Genshiryoku Kankei Shiryo Mokuroku.*

HADRONIC JOURNAL. V. 1- April 1978-. 0162-5519. Periodical. US. English. bm. $250.00. Hadronic Press, Nonantum MA 02195. Tel (617)864-9859. Ind/Abst Math. Rev., Comput. Control Abstr., Electr. Electron. Abstr., Sci. Abstr. Sect. A. Phys. Abstr., Chem. Abstr., Energy Res. Abstr. LC QC793.5.H322. DD 539.7216. CODEN HAJODX.

HE HUAXUE YU FANGSHE HUAXUE. (HO HUA HSUEH YU FANG SHE HUA HSUEH). VFOAT Journal of Nuclear and Radiochemistry. V. 1, (Nov. 1979)-. 0253-9950. Periodical. Chinese (abstracts in English). qt. 0.60. Chung-Kuo Kuo Chi Shu Tien, PO Box 2820, Peking China. Ind/Abst Comput. Control Abstr., Electr. Electron. Abstr., Sci. Abstr. Sect. A. Phys. Abstr., Chem. Abstr. LC QC770. DD 541.3805. CODEN HHHHDH.

HE JUBIAN YU DENGLIZITI WULI. (HO CHU PIEN YU TENG LI TZU TI WU LI). VFOAT Nuclear Fusion and Plasma Physics. Began in 1981. 0254-6086. Chinese (abstracts in English). qt. 0.60. Post Office, China. Ind/Abst Spin, Chem. Abstr., Energy Res. Abstr. LC QC790.95. DD 539.76405. CODEN HYDWDP.

HIGH ENERGY PHYSICS. Series/Titl Pure and Applied Physics, V. 25. Periodical. US. English. ir. Academic Press, 4805 Sand Lake Road, Orlando FL 32887. Tel (305)345-4100. Ed E H S Burhop. LC QC721. DD 539.72108.

INIS ATOMINDEX. *See* Indexes/Abstracts.

INTERNATIONAL ATOMIC ENERGY AGENCY PUBLICATIONS. CATALOGUE. 1972-. English (French, Russian, and Spanish). ir. Division of Publications, International Atomic Energy Agency, Kartner Ring 11, Box 590, A-1011 Vienna Austria. LC Z5160, QC776. DD 016.5397. *Publications in the Nuclear Sciences.*

JAHRESBERICHT - DYNAMITRON-TANDEM-LABORATORIUM, BOCHUM. Main/Corp Dynamitron-Tandem-Laboratorium (Bochum, Germany). GW. German. an. Dynamitron-Tandem-Laboratorium, Universitatsstr 150 Gebaude NT, 4630 Bochum 1 West Germany. LC QC789.G32. DD 539.705.

JAHRESBERICHT - HAHN-MEITNER-INSTITUT FUR KERNFORSCHUNG BERLIN GMBH. Main/Corp Hann-Meitner-Institut fur Kernforschung Berlin. German. ir. LC QC792.8.G32. DD 539.70720431554.

JAHRESBERICHT - KERNFORSCHUNGSANLAGE JULICH. Main/Corp Kernforschungsanlage Julich des Landes Nordrhein-Westfalen. 0341-8790. German. ir. 517 Julich 1 Postfach 365, Julich West Germany. Ind/Abst Chem. Abstr. LC QC792.78.G3. CODEN KJNJAT.

JAHRESBERICHT - OSTERREICHISCHES FORSCHUNGSZENTRUM SEIBERSDORF. Main/Corp Osterreichisches Forschungszentrum Seibersdorf. 1979-. German. an. Osterreichisches Forschungszentrum Seibersdorf Ges M B H, Lenaugasse 10, 1082 Wien Austria. LC QC792.78.A9. *Jahresberich.*

JOURNAL OF PHYSICS G. NUCLEAR PHYSICS. (JOURNAL OF PHYSICS G : NUCLEAR PHYSICS). V. 1- Jan. 1975-. 0305-4616. Periodical. UK. English. mo. $130.00. American Institute of Physics, Department N/M, 325 East 45 Street, New York NY 10017. Ind/Abst Electron. Commun. Abstr. J., ISMEC Bull., Pollut. Abstr. Indexes, Saf. Sci. Abstr. J., Int. Aerosp. Abstr., GeoRef, Comput. Control Abstr., Electr. Electron. Abstr., Sci. Abstr. Sect. A. Phys. Abstr., Chem. Abstr., Energy Res. Abstr. LC QC770. DD 539.705. CODEN JPHGBM. *Journal of Physics A. Mathematical, Nuclear and General,* 0301-0015.

JOURNAL OF RADIOANALYTICAL AND NUCLEAR CHEMISTRY. LETTERS. Vol. 85, No. 1 (20 Jan. 1984)-. 0236-5731. Periodical. English. ir. *Journal of Radioanalytical Chemistry, Radiochemical and Radioanalytical Letters.*

JOURNAL OF THE SOCIETY FOR RADIOLOGICAL PROTECTION. Vol. 1, No. 1 (Spring 1981)-. 0260-2814. UK. English. qt. $40.00. Atomic Energy Research Establishment, c/o J A B Gibson Harwall Dicot, Oxfordshire 0X11 0RA England. Tel (0235)24141. Ed J H Jackson. Ind/Abst Eng. Index Annu., Eng. Index Mon., Eng. Index Bioeng. Abstr., Eng. Index Energy Abstr., Excerpta Med., Biol. Abstr., Comput. Control Abstr., Electr. Electron. Abstr., Sci. Abstr. Sect. A. Phys. Abstr., Chem. Abstr., Energy Res. Abstr. NLM W1 JO954R. CODEN JSRPDK. bk rev. adv acc. Circ 800. Journal publishes technical papers, letters, book reviews, meetings and instrument information on operational health physics with related topics in education training and research.

KAKURIKEN KEDKYU HOKOKU. Main/Corp Tohoku Daigaku, Sendai, Japan. Genshikaku Rigaku Kenkyu Shisetsu. VFOAT Research Report of Laboratory of Nuclear Science, Tohoku University. Began in 1968. 0385-2105. JA. Japanese (English). ir. Tohoku Daigaku, 1 Tomizawa Kanayama, Sendai 982 Japan. Ind/Abst Chem. Abstr., Energy Res. Abstr. LC QC770. DD 539.705. CODEN TLNRBV.

KAO NENG WU LI. VFOAT Gaoneng Wuli. 0253-4266. Periodical. CC. Chinese. qt. $1.80. China Publication Centre, PO Box 2820, Beijing China. Ind/Abst Chem. Abstr. LC QC793. CODEN KNLIDD.

KAO NENG WU LI YU HO WU LI = PHYSICA ENERGIAE FORTIS ET PHYSICA NUCLEARIS. V. 1- Nov. 1977-. Periodical. CC. Chinese (abstracts in English). bm. China Publication Centre, PO Box 2820, Beijing China. Ind/Abst Math. Rev., Comput. Control Abstr., Electr. Electron. Abstr., Sci. Abstr. Sect. A. Phys. Abstr., Spin, Chem. Abstr., Energy Res. Abstr. LC QC793. CODEN KNWLD9.

Physics—Nuclear Physics

KARYOKU GENSHIRYOKU HATSUDEN. VFOAT The Thermal and Nuclear Power. 0387-1029. Periodical. JA. Japanese. mo. Karyoku Genshiryoku Hatsuden Gijutsu Kyokai, 7-ban 25-go Kita Aoyama 2-chome Minato-ku, Tokyo-to 107 Japan. Ind/Abst Coal Abstr.

KERNENERGIE. 1- Year. 0023-0642. Periodical. SZ. German. mo. $120.33. Kunst & Wissen Erich Bieber, Dufourstrasse 51, CH-8008 Zurich Switzerland. Tel 011-41-1-69 44 20. Ind/Abst Electron. Commun. Abstr. J., ISMEC Bull., Pollut. Abstr. Indexes, Saf. Sci. Abstr. J., Excerpta Med., CIS Abstr., Chem. Abstr., Energy Res. Abstr., Energy Inf. Abstr., Environ. Abstr., Sci. Cit. Index, Abr. Ed. CODEN KERNAQ.

KOENERUGIKEN GEPPO. Main/Corp Koenerugi Butsurigaku Kenkyujo. Japanese. ir. Koenerugi Butsurigaku Kenkyujo, Maeno 30-32, Ibaraki-Ken Japan. LC QC770.

LBL RESEARCH REVIEW. VAT Lawrence Berkeley Laboratory Research Review. Vol. 10, No. 1 (Spring 1985)-. 0882-1305. Periodical. US. English. qt. LBL Research Review, Lawrence Berkeley Laboratory, Building 80C/Room 108, Berkeley CA 94720. DD 505. *LBL Newsmagazine, 0146-2725.*

MAJALAH - B.A.T.A.N (MAJALAH). **Main/Corp** Indonesia. Badan Tenaga Atom Nasional. **VAT** Majalah - Badan Tenaga Atom Nasional. 0303-2876. Periodical. Indonesian (summaries in English). ir. 1000. Badan Tenaga Atom Nasional, Jl Palatehan I/26, Kebayoran Indonesia. Ind/Abst Chem. Abstr. LC QC792. CODEN MBTNA3. *Madjalah.*

METHODS IN SUBNUCLEAR PHYSICS. 0097-1065. Monographic Series. US. English. ir. Gordon & Breach, 1 Bedford Street, London WC2E 9HD England. Ind/Abst Comput. Control Abstr., Electr. Electron. Abstr., Sci. Abstr. Sect. A. Phys. Abstr., Chem. Abstr., Phys. Abstr. CODEN MSNPBV.

MONOGRAPHIE - INSTITUT INTERUNIVERSITAIRE DES SCIENCES NUCLEAIRES. Main/Corp Institut Interuniversitaire des Sciences Nucleaires. No. 1- 1957-. 0534-1299. BE. French, Dutch and English. ir. Institut Interuniversitaire des Sciences Nucleaires, Brussels Belgium. CODEN IINMA9.

MONTHLY REPORT ON THE NUCLEAR FUEL MARKET. 0742-4582. Periodical. US. English. mo. Nuexco, 3000 Sand Hill Road, Building 3, Menlo Park CA 90025. *Monthly Report on the Uranium Market.*

MOSSBAUER EFFECT REFERENCE AND DATA JOURNAL. See Chemistry.

I N I S REFERENCE SERIES. English. ir. UNIPUB, PO Box 1222, Ann Arbor MI 48106. Tel (212)916-1700. Ind/Abst Chem. Abstr.

NBS. REACTOR. SUMMARY OF ACTIVITIES. (NBS REACTOR, SUMMARY OF ACTIVITIES). Main/Corp National Measurement Laboratory (U.S.). Reactor Radiation Division. VFOAT N.B.S. Reactor, Summary of Activities. VAT National Bureau of Standards Reactor. Summary of Activities. Began with 1971/72. 0148-4192. US. English. an. Reactor Radiation Division, National Measurement Laboratory, Route 270, Gaithersburg MD 20234. LC QC100, QC786.4. DD 602.15, 530. CODEN NBTNAE. Vols. for 1981-1982- distributed to depository libraries in microfiche.

NMR. (NMR : BASIC PRINCIPLES AND PROGRESS). VFOAT NMR : Grundlagen und Fortschritte. VAT Nuclear Magnetic Resonance. V. 1-. 0170-5989. US. English. ir. Springer Verlag-New York Inc, 175-5th Avenue, New York NY 10010. Tel (212)460-1584. Ind/Abst Chem. Abstr. LC QC490. CODEN NBPPD3. Contains topics which deal with chemistry and the sciences.

NO NUCLEAR NEWS CEASED. VFOAT NNN. Vol. 1, No. 1 (Oct. 1977)-Vol. 7, No. 3 (Winter 1984). 0737-1942. Periodical. US. English. mo. P.I.D.C., 595 Massachusetts Avenue, Cambridge MA 02139.

NOTIZIARIO DELL'ENEA. VFOAT Notiziario dell'E.N.E.A. VAT Notiziario dell'Energia Nucleare e delle Energie Alternative. Vol. 28, N. 4/5 (Apr./May 1982)-. Periodical. IT. Italian. mo. Ind/Abst Chem. Abstr. LC QC770. DD 333.792405. CODEN NOTEDD. *Notiziario del CNEN, 0392-7121.*

NUCLEAR ACTIVE. 0048-1025. Periodical. English (summaries in French, German, Japanese, Russian, and Spanish). sa. Naomi Eliovson, POB 78687, Sandton 2146 Transvaal South Africa. Tel (011)788-9461. Ed Naomi Eliovson. Ind/Abst Comput. Control Abstr., Electr. Electron. Abstr., Sci. Abstr. Sect. A. Phys. Abstr., Energy Res. Abstr., Chem. Abstr. CODEN NULABZ. (ctrl). New developments in any scientific discipline which involve nuclear energy/techniques.

NUCLEAR AND PARTICLE PHYSICS ANNUAL. V. 1- 1967-. 0550-3035. US. English. Gordon & Breach, 50 West 23rd Street, New York NY 10010. Ed L Ederman and J Wenser. LC QC770. DD 539.05.

NUCLEAR DATA SHEETS. V. 6- July 1971-. 0090-3752. Periodical. US. English. mo. $33.00 Domestic, $36.00 Foreign. Academic Press, 4805 Sand Lake Road, Orlando FL 32819. Ind/Abst Comput. Control Abstr., Electr. Electron. Abstr., Sci. Abstr. Sect. A. Phys. Abstr., Energy Res. Abstr., Spin, Chem. Abstr. LC QC783. DD 539.70212. CODEN NDTSBA. *Nuclear Data Current Sheets. Section B, 0090-550X.*

NUCLEAR FUEL CYCLE. (NUCLEAR FUEL CYCLE : A CURRENT AWARENESS BULLETIN). Jan. 1982-. 0735-2506. Periodical. US. English. sm. National Technical Information Service, 5285 Port Royal Road, Springfield VA 22161. Tel (703)486-4630. (cum index).

NUCLEAR FUSION. VFOAT Fusion Nucleaire, Iadernyi Sintez, Fusion Nucleare. V. 1- Sept. 1960-. 0029-5515. Periodical. US. English. mo. $175.00. UNIPUB, PO Box 1222, Ann Arbor MI 48106. Tel (212)686-4707. Ind/Abst Electron. Commun. Abstr. J., ISMEC Bull., Pollut. Abstr. Indexes, Saf. Sci. Abstr. J., Eng. Index Annu., Eng. Index Mon., Eng. Index Bioeng. Abstr., Eng. Index Energy Abstr., Energy Inf. Abstr., Environ. Abstr., Int. Aerosp. Abstr., Comput. Control Abstr., Electr. Electron. Abstr., Sci. Abstr. Sect. A. Phys. Abstr., Energy Res. Abstr., Chem. Abstr., Phys. Abstr., Sci. Cit. Index, Abr. Ed., Int. Aerosp. Abstr., Eng. Index. LC QC791. DD 621.48405. CODEN NUFUAU. Index in last issue of volume - attached.

THE NUCLEAR INDEX. See Indexes/Abstracts.

NUCLEAR INSTRUMENTS & METHODS CEASED. VAT Nuclear Instruments and Methods. V. 4-184. 0029-554X. Periodical. English. sm. Ind/Abst Life Sci. Collect., Energy Inf. Abstr., Environ. Abstr., GeoRef, Art Archaeol. Tech. Abstr., Chem. Abstr., Nucl. Sci. Abstr., Int. Aerosp. Abstr., Eng. Index Annu. LC QC786. DD 539.7078. NLM W1 NU123. CODEN NUIMAL. (cum index). *Nuclear Instruments.*

NUCLEAR INSTRUMENTS AND METHODS IN PHYSICS RESEARCH. (NUCLEAR INSTRUMENTS & METHODS IN PHYSICS RESEARCH). Vol. 185, No. 1-3 (June 15, 1981)-V. 218, No. 1-3 (Dec. 15, 1983). 0167-5087. Periodical. English (articles occasionally in French). ir. Elsevier Science Publishers, PO Box 211, 1000 AE Amsterdam Netherlands. Tel 020)5803.911. Ind/Abst Eng. Index Annu., Eng. Index Mon., Eng. Index Bioeng. Abstr., Eng. Index Energy Abstr., Coal Abstr., Comput. Control Abstr., Electr. Electron. Abstr., Sci. Abstr. Sect. A. Phys. Abstr., Energy Res. Abstr., Chem. Abstr., Life Sci. Collect. LC QC786. DD 539.7028. NLM W1 NU123M. CODEN NIMRD9. *Nuclear Instruments & Methods, 0029-554X; European Synchrotron Radiation News.*

NUCLEAR INSTRUMENTS & METHODS IN PHYSICS RESEARCH. SECTION A, ACCELERATORS, SPECTROMETERS, DETECTORS AND ASSOCIATED EQUIPMENT. VFOAT Accelerators, Spectrometers, Detectors and Associated Equipment, Nuclear. Vol. 219, No. 1 (Jan. 1, 1984)-. 0168-9002. Periodical. NE. English. sm. Elsevier Science Publishers, PO Box 211, 1000 AE Amsterdam The Netherlands. Ind/Abst Life Sci. Collect., Eng. Index Annu., Eng. Index Mon., Eng. Index Bioeng. Abstr., Eng. Index Energy Abstr., Chem. Abstr. LC QC785.5. DD 539.7028. CODEN NIMAER. *Nuclear Instruments & Methods in Physics Research, 0167-5087.*

NUCLEAR MATERIALS MANAGEMENT. V. 1- Apr. 1972-. 0362-0034. Periodical. US. English. qt. $75.00 Domestic, $100.00 Foreign. Nuclear Materials Management Institute of Nuclear Materials Management, 60 Revere Drive/Suite 500, Northbrook IL 60062. Tel (312)480-9573. Ed John E Messervey. Ind/Abst Eng. Index, Excerpta Med., Energy Res. Abstr., Chem. Abstr., Nucl. Sci. Abstr., Eng. Index Annu., Eng. Index Mon., Eng. Index Energy Abstr., Eng. Index Bioeng. Abstr. CODEN NUMMB8. bk rev. adv acc. Circ 1,000. (ctrl). The official journal of the Institute of Nuclear Materials Management. The only international scholarly journal in the field of nuclear materials management.

NUCLEAR NEWS. V. 1- July 1959-. 0029-5574. Periodical. US. English. ir. $145.00 Domestic, $230.00 Foreign. American Nuclear Society, PO Box 4957, Chicago IL 60680. Tel (312)352-6611. Ed Jon Payne. Ind/Abst Excerpta Med., Comput. Control Abstr., Electr. Electron. Abstr., Sci. Abstr. Sect. A. Phys. Abstr., Met. Abstr., World Alum. Abstr., Ref. Source, Chem. Abstr., Nucl. Sci. Abstr., Environ. Abstr., Phys. Abstr. LC QC770. CODEN NUNWA8. bk rev. adv acc. Circ 18,000. Newsmagazine for nuclear industry. Feature articles. Monthly departments include power, operations, fuel, industry, international, waste management, isotopes and radiation.

NUCLEAR PHYSICS. A. V. A90- Jan. 1967-. 0375-9474. Periodical. English. ir. Elsevier Science Publishers, PO Box 211, 1000 AE Amsterdam Netherlands. Tel (020)5803.911. Ind/Abst Math. Rev., Energy Res. Abstr., Chem. Abstr., Comput. Control Abstr., Electr. Electron. Abstr., Sci. Abstr. Sect. A. Phys. Abstr., Phys. Abstr., Sci. Cit. Index, Abr. Ed. LC QC173. DD 539.705. CODEN NUPABL. (cum index). *Nuclear Physics.*

NUCLEAR PHYSICS. B. Began with: Vol. B1 (Jan. 1967). 0550-3213. Periodical. NE. English. wk. North-Holland Publishing Company, PO Box 211, 1000 AE Amsterdam The Netherlands. Ind/Abst Chem. Abstr., Comput. Control Abstr., Electr. Electron. Abstr., Energy Res. Abstr., Math. Rev., Sci. Abstr. Sect. A. Phys. Abstr. LC QC173. DD 539.705. CODEN NUPBBO. *Nuclear Physics.*

NUCLEAR PHYSICS. B, FIELD THEORY AND STATISTICAL SYSTEMS. VFOAT Field Theory and Statistical Systems. V. B170 Fs1 No. 1 (11 Aug. 1980)-. 0029-5582. Periodical. English. mo. Elsevier Science Publishers, PO Box 211, 1000 AE Amsterdam Netherlands. Tel (020)5803.911. Ind/Abst Comput. Control Abstr., Electr. Electron. Abstr., Sci. Abstr. Sect. A. Phys. Abstr., Chem. Abstr. CODEN NBSSDR.

NUCLEAR PLANT SAFETY. Began In 1983. 0742-4868. Periodical. US. English. bm. $9.00 Domestic, $12.00 Foreign. EQES Inc, 799 Roosevelt Road #6/104, Glen Ellyn IL 60137. Tel (312)858-6161. Ed K Agnihotri. bk rev. adv acc. Circ 10,000. (ctrl). Covers computer application, health physics, plant maintenance, radwaste management, plant services, and non destructive testing and evaluation related technical papers. Reports and departments for nuclear plants.

NUCLEAR SCIENCE ABSTRACTS. See Indexes/Abstracts.

NUCLEAR SCIENCE ABSTRACTS OF POLAND. See Indexes/Abstracts.

NUCLEAR SCIENCE AND ENGINEERING. See Engineering - Nuclear Engineering.

NUCLEAR SCIENCE APPLICATIONS. (NUCLEAR SCIENCE APPLICATIONS. SECTION A, SHORT REVIEWS, RESEARCH PAPERS, AND COMMENTS). Vol. 1, No. 1 (July 1980)-. 0191-1686. Periodical. SZ. English. ir. $300.00. Harwood Academic Publishers GMBH, PO Box 786, Cooper Station New York 10276. Tel (212)242-4464. Ed R Klapisch and A Zucker. Ind/Abst Comput. Control Abstr., Electr. Electron. Abstr., Sci. Abstr. Sect. A. Phys. Abstr., Energy Res. Abstr., Chem. Abstr. LC QC770. DD 539.7. CODEN NSAPDD. bk rev. adv acc. Available in microform.

NUCLEAR SCIENCE APPLICATIONS. (NUCLEAR SCIENCE APPLICATIONS. SECTION B). Vol. 1, No. 2 (Aug. 1981)-. Periodical. English. ir. $300.00. Harwood Academic Publishers, PO Box 197, London WC2E 9PX England. Ed R Klapisch and A Zucker. Ind/Abst Comput. Control Abstr., Electr. Electron. Abstr., Sci. Abstr. Sect. A. Phys. Abstr. LC QC770. DD 539.705. CODEN NSAPDD. bk rev. adv acc. Available in microform.

NUCLEAR SCIENCE INFORMATION OF JAPAN. Began with issue for May 1970. 0029-5620. JA. English. bm. Japan Atomic Energy Research Institute, Division of Technical Information Tokai-Mura Naka-Gun Ibaraki-Ken 319, Tokyo 11 Japan. LC Z7144.N8, Q776. DD 016.5397. NLM Z 7144.N8 N969. *Nuclear Science Abstracts of Japan.*

Physics—Nuclear Physics

NUCLEAR SCIENCE RESEARCH CONFERENCE SERIES. V. 1-. 0250-4375. US. English. ir. Harwood Academic Publishers, PO Box 786/Cooper Station, New York NY 10276. Tel (212)689-0360. Ind/Abst Comput. Control Abstr., Electr. Electron. Abstr., Sci. Abstr. Sect. A. Phys. Abstr., Chem. Abstr. CODEN NSRSD5.

NUCLEAR TRACKS AND RADIATION MEASUREMENTS. VFOAT Nuclear Tracks. Vol. 6, No. 1 (Mar. 1982)-. 0735-245X. Periodical. UK. English. bm. Pergamon Press, 395 Sawmill River Road, Elmsford NY 10523. Ind/Abst Comput. Control Abstr., Electr. Electron. Abstr., Sci. Abstr. Sect. A. Phys. Abstr., Energy Res. Abstr. LC QC787.N78. DD 539.7705. Nuclear Tracks, 0191-278X.

NUOVO CIMENTO DELLA SOCIETA ITALIANA DI FIZICA. SEZIONE A. (IL NUOVO CIMENTO DELLA SOCIETA ITALIANA DI FISICA. A). Vol. 1A, N. 1 (Jan. 1971)-. 0369-4097. Periodical. English. sm. 440.00 Members, 550.00 Nonmembers. Editrice Compositori S R L, Viale XII Giugno 1, 40124 Bologna, Italy. Tel (051-58 31 49. Ind/Abst Chem. Abstr., Energy Res. Abstr., Excerpta Med., Life Sci. Collect., Math. Rev., Comput. Control Abstr., Electr. Electron. Abstr., Sci. Abstr. Sect. A. Phys. Abstr. CODEN NIFAAM. (cum index). Circ 1,500. (ctrl). The physics of elementary particles and fields and nuclear physics. Nuovo Cimento. A.

PARTICLES AND FIELDS. Main/Corp American Physical Society. Division of Particles and Fields. Series/Titl AIP Conference Proceedings. Particles and Fields Subseries. 1971-. 0097-8248. US. English. American Institute of Physics, 335 East 45th Street, New York NY 10017. LC QC793. DD 539.721.

PHYSICAL REVIEW. C. NUCLEAR PHYSICS. (PHYSICAL REVIEW C: NUCLEAR PHYSICS). Ser. 3, V. 1- Jan. 1970-. 0556-2813. Periodical. US. English. mo. American Institute of Physics, 335 East 45th Street, New York NY 10017. Tel (212)661-9404. Ind/Abst Comput. Control Abstr., Electr. Electron. Abstr., Sci. Abstr. Sect. A. Phys. Abstr., Energy Res. Abstr., Chem. Abstr., Curr. Phys. Index, Spin, Nucl. Sci. Abstr., Int. Aerosp. Abstr., Math. Rev., Sci. Cit. Index, Abr. Ed., Phys. Abstr. LC QC770. DD 539.705. NLM W1 PH737C. CODEN PRVCAN. Physical Review, 0031-899X.

PHYSICS AND CHEMISTRY OF FISSION. Main/Conf Symposium on Physics and Chemistry of Fission. 1St- 1965-. English (French, or Russian with abstracts in English, French, Russian, and Spanish). ir. International Atomic Energy Agency, Wagramerstrasse 5, PO Box 100 A-1400 Vienna Austria. LC QC789.7. DD 539.76205.

PHYSICS IN COLLISION. Vol. 1-. 0733-8996. US. English. Plenum Press, 233 Spring Street, New York NY 10013. Ind/Abst Chem. Abstr. LC QC794.8.H5. DD 539.75405. CODEN PHCODX.

PHYSICS LETTERS. SECTION B. (PHYSICS LETTERS : PART B). V. 24B- Jan. 9, 1967-. 0370-2693. Periodical. NE. English (French or German). ir. Elsevier Science Publishers, PO Box 211, 1000 AE Amsterdam Netherlands. Tel (020)5803911. Ind/Abst Math. Rev., Comput. Control Abstr., Electr. Electron Abstr., Sci. Abstr. Sect. A. Phys. Abstr., Energy Res. Abstr., Chem. Abstr., Sci. Cit. Index, Abr. Ed., Phys. Abstr., Int. Aerosp. Abstr. LC QC1. DD 530.05. CODEN PYLBAJ. (cum index). Physics Letters, 0031-9163.

PHYSICS OF REACTOR SAFETY QUARTERLY REPORT. Periodical. US. English. qt. Government Printing Office, Sales Program Division of Technical Information and Document Control, US Nuclear Regulatory Commission, Washington DC 20555. Vols. for (Jan./Mar. 1983-) distributed to depository libraries in microfiche.

PLASMA PHYSICS CEASED. V. 9, No. 1 (Jan./Feb. 1967)- V. 25, No. 12 (Dec. 1983). 0032-1028. Periodical. UK. English (French). mo. Pergamon Press Inc, Maxwell House, Fairview Park, Elmsford NY 10523. Ind/Abst Math. Rev., Chem. Abstr., Int. Aerosp. Abstr., Nucl. Sci. Abstr., Appl. Sci. Technol. Index. LC QC770. DD 530.4405. CODEN PLPHBZ. Also available on microfilm and microfiche from the publisher. Plasma Physics, Accelerators, Thermounclear Research.

PLASMA PHYSICS AND CONTROLLED FUSION. VFOAT Plasma Physics. Vol. 26, No. 1A (Jan. 1984)-. 0741-3335. Periodical. UK. English. mo. $280.00 Multiple-Reader Institutions, $55.00 Individuals Belonging to Subscribing Institution. Pergamon Press, Maxwell House Fairview Park, Elmsford NY 10523. Ind/Abst Math. Rev., Electron. Commun. Abstr. J., ISMEC Bull., Pollut. Abstr. Indexes, Saf. Sci. Abstr. J., Comput. Control Abstr., Electr. Electron. Abstr., Sci. Abstr. Sect. A. Phys. Abstr. LC QC770. DD 530.4405. Plasma Physics, 0032-1028.

POWER REACTOR EVENTS. Vol. 1, No. 1 (Mar. 1979)-. 0741-1359. Periodical. US. English. bm. Superintendent of Documents, US Government Printing Office, Washington DC 20402. Tel (202)783-3238. LC TK1343. DD 363.179. Current Events. Power Reactors, 0145-1111.

PROBLEMY JADERNOJ FIZIKI I KOSMICESKIH LUCHEJ. (PROBLEMY IADERNOI FIZIKI I KOSMICHESKIKH LUCHEI). No. 1-. 0131-3142. UR. Russian. 0.79 Single Issue. Izdatelskoe Obedinenie Vyshcha Shkola, Universitetskaia 16, Kharkov Russia. Ind/Abst Math. Rev., Int. Aerosp. Abstr., Chem. Abstr. LC QC770. CODEN PIFLDC.

PROCEEDINGS OF THE INTERNATIONAL WORKSHOP ON GROSS PROPERTIES OF NUCLEI AND NUCLEAR EXCITATIONS. Main/Conf International Workshop on Gross Properties of Nuclei and Nuclear Excitations. Began in 1973-. 0720-8715. English. ir. Ind/Abst Chem. Abstr. LC QC793.S8. DD 539.72305. CODEN IWGEDH.

PROGRESS IN NUCLEAR MAGNETIC RESONANCE SPECTROSCOPY. V. 1- 1966-. 0079-6565. UK. English. ir. $218.50. Pergamon Press, 395 Sawmill River Road, Elmsford NY 10523. Ind/Abst Comput. Control Abstr., Electr. Electron. Abstr., Sci. Abstr. Sect. A. Phys. Abstr., Met. Abstr., World Alum. Abstr., Chem. Abstr., Phys. Abstr. LC QC762. DD 539.1. CODEN PNMRAT. Available on microfilm from Pergamon Press.

PROGRESS IN PARTICLE AND NUCLEAR PHYSICS. VFOAT Particle and Nuclear Physics. 0146-6410. Monographic Series. UK. English. sa. $361.00. Pergamon Press, 395 Sawmill River Road, Elmsford NY 10523. Ind/Abst Comput. Control Abstr., Electr. Electron. Abstr., Sci. Abstr. Sect. A. Phys. Abstr., Chem. Abstr. LC QC770. DD 539.721. CODEN PPNPDB. Progress in Nuclear Physics, 0079-659X.

PROTON NMR COLLECTION. CUMULATIVE CHEMICAL CLASS INDEX. See Indexes/Abstracts.

PUBLICATIONS CATALOGUE - ATOMIC ENERGY CONTROL BOARD. (PUBLICATIONS CATALOGUE). Main/Corp Canada. Atomic Energy Control Board. VAT Catalogue des Publications - Commission de Controle de l'Energie Atomique. 0711-9917. CN. English (includes French publications). an. Atomic Energy Control Board, 270 Albert Street, PO Box 1046, Ottawa Ontario K1P 5S9 Canada. DD 016.3337924.

RADIATION RESEARCH. V. 1- Feb. 1954-. 0033-7587. Periodical. US. English. mo. Academic Press, 4805 Sand Lake Road, Orlando FL 32819. Tel (305)345-4100. Ed T C Evans. Ind/Abst Electron. Commun. Abstr. J., Life Sci. Collect., Excerpta Med., Coal Abstr., Energy Inf. Abstr., Environ. Abstr., Comput. Control Abstr., Electr. Electron. Abstr., Sci. Abstr. Sect. A. Phys. Abstr., Energy Res. Abstr., Bibliogr. Agric., Biol. Abstr., Chem. Abstr., Index Med., Int. Aerosp. Abstr., Nucl. Sci. Abstr., Sel. Water Resour. Abstr., Sci. Cit. Index, Abr. Ed., Phys. Abstr., Pollut. Abstr. Indexes. LC QC770. DD 539.705. NLM W1 RA166. CODEN RAREAE. (cum index).

RADIOPROTECTION. V. 1-. 0033-8451. FR. French. qt. 180 Domestic, 255 Foreign. G E D I M, 19 rue du GD Moulin, 42019 St Etienne Cedex France. Ind/Abst Excerpta Med., CIS Abstr., Energy Res. Abstr., Chem. Abstr. LC RA569. NLM W1 RA363. CODEN RAPRBA.

RAPPORT ANNUEL - UNIVERSITE SCIENTIFIQUE ET MEDICALE DE GRENOBLE INSTITUT DES SCIENCES NUCLEAIRES. Main/Corp Universite Scientifique et Medicale de Grenoble Institut des Sciences Nucleaires. French (summaries in English). ir. Free. Universite Scientifique et Medicale de Grenoble Institute des Sciences Nucleaires, 53 Avenue des Martyrs, 38026 Grenoble Cedex France. Tel 76-47-66-36. LC QC789.F72. DD 539.7. bk rev. Circ 550. (ctrl). Nuclear/physics theory and experiment in low and medium energies, fundamental interactions, nuclear instrumentation.

RASCETY ATOMNYH I JADERNYH KONSTANT. (RASCHETY ATOMNYKH I IADERNYKH KONSTANT). Main/Corp Riga. Universitate. Skaitlosanas Centrs. Series/Titl Uchenye Zapiski Latviiskogo Gosudarstvennogo Universiteta Imeni Petra Stuchki. Began in 1970. 0302-8453. UR. Russian. 1.72 single issue. Redaktsionno-Izdatelskii Otdel Lgu Im Petra Stuchki, 50 Ul Veidenbauma 5, Riga Lavitain SFSR. LC QC770.

RELATORIO ANUAL MINAS GERAIS, BRAZIL. UNIVERSIDADE FEDERAL. INSTITUTO DE PESQUISAS RADIOATIVAS. Main/Corp Minas Gerais, Brazil. Universidade Federal. Instituto de Pesquisas Radioativas. Portuguese. ir. Universidad Federal de Minas Gerais, Instituto de Pesquisas Radioativas, Caixa Postal 1941, Cidade Universitaria, Belo Horizonte Brazil. LC QC770.

REPORT ON APPLICATIONS OF NUCLEAR SCIENCE IN NEW ZEALAND. English. ir. Executive Secretary, New Zealand Atomic Energy Committee, c/o Institute of Nuclear Sciences DSIR, Private Bag, Lower Hutt New Zealand. LC QC792.78.N45. DD 539.709931.

RESEARCH. ACCELERATORS CEASED. (RESEARCH ACCELERATORS). Main/Corp Lawrence Berkeley Laboratory. Ceased with V. 5, No. 2, March/April 1980. 0146-9193. Periodical. US. English. bm. University of California, Lawrence Berkeley Laboratory, Berkeley CA 94720. LC QC789.3.C23. DD 539.705.

RESEARCH LABORATORIES ANNUAL REPORT. English. an. Technical Information Department, Israel Atomic Commission, PO Box 7061, 61 070 Tel-Aviv Israel. LC QC770. DD 539.05. NLM W2 JI9 A8I. Research Laboratories Semi-Annual Report, 0333-5828.

RESEARCH TECHNIQUES IN NONDESTRUCTIVE TESTING. 1- 1970-. Periodical. UK. English. te. Academic Press, 4085 Sand Lake Road, Orlando FL 32887. Tel (305)345-4100. Ed R S Sharpe. DD 620.

REVIEW - OAK RIDGE NATIONAL LABORATORY. Main/Corp Oak Ridge National Laboratory. V. 1- Summer 1967-. 0362-0751. Periodical. US. English. qt. Oak Ridge National Library, Nuclear Data Project, Oak Ridge TN 37830. Ind/Abst Electron. Commun. Abstr. J., ISMEC Bull., Pollut. Abstr. Indexes, Saf. Sci. Abstr. J., Coal Abstr., Energy Inf. Abstr., Environ. Abstr., Chem. Abstr. LC QC789.3.T43. DD 505. CODEN ORNRAH.

REVUE ZAIROISE DES SCIENCES NUCLEAIRES. VFOAT Zairian Journal of Nuclear Sciences. Vol. 1, No. 1 (June 1980)-. 0252-1091. Periodical. English (French). ir. $20.00. Commissariat Generale a l'Energie Atomique, Boite Postale 868, Kinshasa XI Republic du Zaire. Ind/Abst Energy Res. Abstr. LC QC770. DD 539.705.

RIS REPORT. No. 1-. 0418-6443. Monographic Series. DK. English (No. 1 in Danish). ir. RIS National Laboratory, DK4000 Roskilde Denmark. Ind/Abst GeoRef, Met. Abstr., World Alum. Abstr., Chem. Abstr. LC QC770. DD 621.4805. NLM W1 RI285H. CODEN DATKAO.

SIN PHYSICS REPORT. Main/Corp Schweizerisches Institut fur Nuklearforschung. VAT Schweizerisches Institut fur Nuklearforschung Physics Report. No. 1- 1976-. English or German. ir. Institut fur Nuklearforschung, Ch-5234, Villigen Switzerland. LC QC789.4.S93.

SOUTH AFRICAN JOURNAL OF PHYSICS. VFOAT Suid-Afrikaanse Tydskrif vir Fisika. V. 1-. 0379-4377. Periodical. SA. English (Afrikaans). qt. 20.00. Bureau for Scientific Publishing, PO Box 1758, Pretoria 0001 South Africa. Tel (012)260207. Ed C A Engelbrecht. Ind/Abst Electron. Commun. Abstr. J., ISMEC Bull., Pollut. Abstr. Indexes, Saf. Sci. Abstr. J., Int. Aerosp. Abstr., Comput. Control Abstr., Electr. Electron. Abstr., Sci. Abstr. Sect. A. Phys. Abstr., Met. Abstr., World Alum. Abstr., Chem. Abstr. CODEN SAPHDR. bk rev. adv acc. Circ 750. Original research in any branch of physics.

SOVIET JOURNAL OF NUCLEAR PHYSICS. V. 1- July 1965-. 0038-5506. Periodical. US. English (Russian). mo. American Institute of Physics, 335 East 45th Street, New York NY 10017. Tel (516)618-3800. Ind/Abst Math. Rev., Comput. Control Abstr., Electr. Electron. Abstr., Sci. Abstr. Sect. A. Phys. Abstr., Energy Res. Abstr., Spin, Curr. Phys. Index, Phys. Abstr., Sci. Cit. Index, Abr.

Plastics

Ed. **LC** QC770. **CODEN** SJNCAS. (cum index). Available on microfilm.

SOVIET JOURNAL OF PARTICLES AND NUCLEI. 0090-4759. Periodical. US. English (Russian). bm. American Institute of Physics, 335 East 45th Street, New York NY 10017. **Tel** (212)661-9404. **Ind/Abst** Energy Res. Abstr., Math. Rev., Spin, Curr. Phys. Index, Electr. Electron. Abstr., Phys. Abstr., Comput. Control Abstr. **LC** QC793. **DD** 539.72105. **CODEN** SJPNA3.

SUMMARIES OF RESEARCH IN NUCLEAR PHYSICS. **Main/Corp** United States. Dept. of Energy. Division of Nuclear Physics. US. English. an. US Department of Energy, Office of Energy Research, Office of High Energy and Nuclear Physics, Division of Nuclear Physics, Springfield VA 22161.

SVA BULLETIN : OFFIZIELLES ORGAN DER SVA UND DESOAF. SZ. German. ir. Schweizerische Vereinigung fur Atomenergie, Barenplatz 2 Postfach 2613, CH-3001 Bern Switzerland. **LC** QC770. **DD** 539.705. *Bulletin (Schweizerische Vereinigung for Atomenergie).*

TRACE ELEMENTS INVESTIGATIONS REPORT. **VFOAT** TEI, T.E.I. 0499-5252. Monographic Series. US. English. ir. US Department of the Interior, Geological Survey, Reston VA 22092. **Ind/Abst** GeoRef. **LC** QC770. **CODEN** XGTRAZ.

TRANSACTIONS - THE ISRAEL NUCLEAR SOCIETY, THE ISRAEL HEALTH PHYSICS SOCIETY, RADIATION RESEARCH SOCIETY OF ISRAEL, THE ISRAEL SOCIETY OF MEDICAL PHYSICS, THE ISRAEL SOCIETY OF NUCLEAR MEDICINE. **Main/Corp** Agudah Ha-Yisreelit Le-Madae Ha-GArin. IS. English. ir. Israel Institute of Technology, Haifa, Technion City Israel. **LC** QC770. **DD** 539.705.

TURKISH JOURNAL OF NUCLEAR SCIENCES. Began in 1981. 0254-5446. Periodical. English. ty. Managing Editor, Atom Enerjisi Komisyonu Genel Sekreterligi Alacam Sokak, 11 Cankaya Ankara Turkey. **Ind/Abst** Coal Abstr., Chem. Abstr., Energy Res. Abstr. **CODEN** TJNSDM. *Technical Journal (Atom Enerjisi Komisyonu (Turkey)).*

VOPROSY TEORETICHESKOI I IADERNOI FIZIKI. Vol. 4- 1973-. UR. Russian. 1.05 Single Issue. Izd-Vo Saratovskogo Universiteta, Universitetskaia 42, Saratov Russia. **LC** QC770. *Kvantovo-Polevye Metody i Ikh Premenenie.*

WONJARYOK KISUL CHONGBO. Periodical. KO. Korean. ir. Hanguk Wonjaryok Yonguso, PO Box 7 Chongyangni, Seoul South Korea. **LC** QC770. (ctrl).

YUANZIHE WULI. (YUAN TZU HO WU LI). **VFOAT** Chinese Journal of Nuclear Physics. Vol. 1-. 0253-3790. Periodical. Chinese (abstracts in English). qt. China Publication Centre, PO Box 2820, Beijing China. **Ind/Abst** Comput. Control Abstr., Electr. Electron. Abstr., Sci. Abstr. Sect. A. Phys. Abstr., Chem. Abstr., Energy Res. Abstr. **LC** QC770. **DD** 539.705. **CODEN** YTHLDS.

ZEITSCHRIFT FUR PHYSIK. C, PARTICLES AND FIELDS. **VFOAT** Particles and Fields. Began in 1979. 0170-9739. Periodical. English. ir. $716.00. Springer Verlag-New York Inc, 175 5th Avenue, New York NY 10010. **Tel** (212)460-1500. Ed G Kramer & H Satz. **Ind/Abst** Math. Rev., Comput. Control Abstr., Electr. Electron. Abstr., Sci. Abstr. Sect. A. Phys. Abstr., Chem. Abstr., Energy Res. Abstr., Phys. Abstr. **LC** QC1. **DD** 539.721. **CODEN** ZPCFD2. Fields of interest: Experimental and theoretical particle physics; structure of elementary particles, high energy processes, strong, electromagnetic and weak interations, symmetry principles; quantum field theory; field theory on the lattice. *Zeitschrift Fur Physik.*

SOUND

ACOUSTICAL IMAGING. (ACOUSTICAL IMAGING : PROCEEDINGS). **Main/Conf** International Symposium on Acoustical Imaging. Began in 1979. 0270-5117. US. English. ir. Plenum Press, 233 Spring Street, New York NY 10013. **Ind/Abst** GeoRef, Eng. Index Mon., Eng. Index Bioeng. Abstr., Eng. Index Energy Abstr., Comput. Control Abstr., Electr. Electron. Abstr., Sci. Abstr. Sect. A. Phys. Abstr., Chem. Abstr., Eng. Index Annu. **LC** QC244.5. **DD** 621.3675. **CODEN** ACIGD9. *Acoustical Imaging, 0270-5117.*

ACOUSTICAL IMAGING AND HOLOGRAPHY. Vol. 1, No. 1 (1978)-. 0149-0427. Periodical. US. English. qt. $48.00. Crane Russak & Company Incorporated, 347 Madison Avenue, New York NY 10017. **Ind/Abst** Int. Aerosp. Abstr., GeoRef. **LC** QC244.5. **DD** 621.3675. **NLM** W1 AC735. **CODEN** AIHOD2.

ACOUSTICS ABSTRACTS. *See* Indexes/Abstracts.

ACOUSTICS LETTERS. V. 1- 1977-. 0140-1599. Periodical. UK. English. mo. 88.50. The Old Mill, Dorset Place, London E15 1DJ England. Ed J C Scott. **Ind/Abst** Int. Aerosp. Abstr., Chem. Abstr., Comput. Control Abstr., Electr. Electron. Abstr., Sci. Abstr. Sect. A. Phys. Abstr. **CODEN** ACLEDI. Short papers on all aspects of acoustics.

ACUSTICA. V. 1- 1951-. 0001-7884. Periodical. GW. English (French, and German). ir. $172.07. Hirzel S Verlag Stuttgart, Postfach 347, D7000 Stuttgart 1 West Germany. **Tel** 0711 2582 0. Ed C W Kosten. **Ind/Abst** Eng. Index Mon., Eng. Index Bioeng. Abstr., Eng. Index Energy Abstr., Life Sci. Collect., Lang. Lang. Behav. Abstr., Excerpta Med., Energy Inf. Abstr., Environ. Abstr., CIS Abstr., Eng. Index, Eng. Index Annu., Int. Aerosp. Abstr., Nuci. Sci. Abstr., Biol. Abstr., Chem. Abstr., Energy Res. Abstr., Comput. Control Abstr., Electr. Electron. Abstr., Sci. Abstr. Sect. A. Phys. Abstr., Phys. Abstr., Sci. Cit. Index, Abr. Ed., Sociol. Abstr., Math. Rev. **LC** QC221. **DD** 534.05. **CODEN** ACUSAY.

AKUSTICESKIJ ZURNAL. (AKUSTICHESKII ZHURNAL). V. 1- 1955-. 0002-3914. Periodical. UR. Russian. bm. $60.00. Victor Kamkin Inc (70010), 12224 Parklawn Drive, Rockville MD 20852. **Tel** (301)881-5973. **Ind/Abst** Math. Rev., Int. Aerosp. Abstr., Chem. Abstr., Comput. Control Abstr., Electr. Electron. Abstr., Sci. Abstr. Sect. A. Phys. Abstr., Sociol. Abstr., Phys. Abstr., Lang. Lang. Behav. Abstr. **CODEN** AKZHAE.

APPLIED ACOUSTICS. **VFOAT** Acoustique Applique, Angewandte Akustik. V. 1- Jan. 1968-. 0003-682X. Periodical. UK. English (articles in French or German). bm. 129.00 Domestic, $213.00 Foreign. Elsevier Applied Science Publications, Crown House Linton Road, Barking Essex IG11 8JU England. **Tel** 01 594 7272. Ed P Lord. **Ind/Abst** Fluidex, Eng. Index Annu., Eng. Index Mon., Eng. Index Bioeng. Abstr., Eng. Index Energy Abstr., Ship Abstr., Coal Abstr., Excerpta Med., Int. Aerosp. Abstr., CIS Abstr., Comput. Control Abstr., Electr. Electron. Abstr., Sci. Abstr. Sect. A. Phys. Abstr., Pollut. Abstr. Indexes, Eng. Index, Phys. Abstr. **LC** TA365. **DD** 620.205. **CODEN** AACOBL. Index in last issue of volume - attached. bk rev. adv acc. **Circ** 800. Concerned with the application of acoustic principles to design problems and materials used in their solution. Relevant to buildings, industrial equipment, transport, environmental health, etc.

ARCHIVES OF ACOUSTICS. *See* Genealogy and Heraldry - Archives.

BENCHMARK PAPERS IN ACOUSTICS. Monographic Series. US. English. ir. Academic Press, 4805 Sand Lake Road, Orlando FL 32819.

BUCHEREI DER HOCHFREQUENZTECHNIK. German. ir. Deutscher Buch Export & Import, Leninstrasse 16, DDR-701 Leipzig East Germany.

CANADIAN ACOUSTICS. **VFOAT** Acoustique Canadienne. Vol. 10, No. 1 (Jan. 1982)-. 0711-6659. Periodical. CN. English (French). qt. $15.00. Canadian Acoustics, c/o J Manuel, 5007-44 Charles Street West, Toronto Ontario M4Y 1R8 Canada. **Ind/Abst** Comput. Control Abstr., Electr. Electron. Abstr., Sci. Abstr. Sect. A. Phys. Abstr. **DD** 363.7405. **CODEN** CAACDX. *Acoustics and Noise Control in Canada, 0229-2238.*

ELECTROACOUSTIQUE. No. 1- July 1959-. 0422-888X. Periodical. BE. French. ir. Monte Fiore Institute, University of Leige, 33 rue St Gilles, Leige Belgium. **Ind/Abst** Comput. Control Abstr., Electr. Electron. Abstr., Sci. Abstr. Sect. A. Phys. Abstr., Sociol. Abstr., Phys. Abstr., Lang. Lang. Behav. Abstr. **CODEN** ELACBS.

HANGUK UMHYANG HAKHOE CHI. **VFOAT** The Journal of the Acoustical Society of Korea. V. 1- No. 1- (March 1982)-. Periodical. English (Korean). ir. Hanguk Umhyang Hakhoe, 134 Sinchon-dong, Sodaemun-ku, Seoul South Korea. **LC** TA365.

JOURNAL OF SOUND AND VIBRATION. Periodical. UK. English. sm. Academic Press, 4805 Sand Lake Road, Orlando FL 32819. **Tel** (305)345-4100. **Ind/Abst** Eng. Index, Sci. Cit. Index, Abr. Ed., Int. Aerosp. Abstr., Comput. Control Abstr., Phys. Abstr., ISMEC Bull., Math. Rev., Electr. Electron. Abstr., Pollut. Abstr. Indexes.

NOISE CONTROL ENGINEERING JOURNAL. *See* Engineering.

RUSSIAN ULTRASONICS. Vol. 1, No.1 (Jan./Mar. 1971)-. Periodical. UK. English. qt $130.00. Multi Science Publishing Company, 42/45 New Broad Street, London EC2M 1QY England.

SHENG HSUEH HSUEH PAO. **VFOAT** Acta Acustica. 1978, No. 1- - No. 1 (Aug? 1978)-. Periodical. CC. Chinese (summaries in English, (1982/3)). bm. 0.52. Guozi Shudian, PO Box 2820, Peking China. **Ind/Abst** Math. Rev., Energy Res. Abstr., Spin, Comput. Control Abstr., Electr. Electron. Abstr., Sci. Abstr. Sect. A. Phys. Abstr. **LC** QC221. **DD** 534.05. **CODEN** SHGHAS.

SOVIET PHYSICS. ACOUSTICS. **VFOAT** Acoustics. V. 1- Jan./June 1955-. 0038-562X. Periodical. US. English (Russian). bm. American Institute of Physics, 335 East 45th Street, New York NY 10017. **Tel** (212)661-9404. **Ind/Abst** Life Sci. Collect., Excerpta Med., Comput. Control Abstr., Electr. Electron. Abstr., Sci. Abstr. Sect. A. Phys. Abstr., Energy Res. Abstr., Chem. Abstr., Eng. Index, Nuci. Sci. Abstr., Int. Aerosp. Abstr., Math. Rev., Spin, Curr. Phys. Index, Phys. Abstr., Sci. Cit. Index, Abr. Ed., Appl. Mech. Rev., Eng. Index. **LC** QC221. **DD** 534.05. **CODEN** SOPAAX. Available on microfilm.

S.V. SOUND AND VIBRATION. (SV. SOUND AND VIBRATION). **VFOAT** Sound and Vibration. V. 1- Jan. 1967-. 0038-1810. Periodical. US. English. mo $10.00. Acoustical Publishing Company, 27101 East Ouiatt Road, Bay Village OH 44140. **Tel** (216)835-0101. Ed Jack Mowry. **Ind/Abst** Electron. Commun. Abstr. J., ISMEC Bull., Pollut. Abstr. Indexes, Saf. Sci. Abstr. J., Eng. Index Bioeng. Abstr., Excerpta Med., Lang. Lang. Behav. Abstr., Energy Inf. Abstr., Environ. Abstr., Ship Abstr., Comput. Control Abstr., Electr. Electron. Abstr., Sci. Abstr., CIS Abstr., Int. Aerosp. Abstr., Appl. Sci. Technol. Index, Phys. Abstr., Humanit. Index, Sociol. Abstr., Appl. Mech. Rev., Eng. Index Annu., Eng. Index, Eng. Index Energy Abstr. **LC** TA365. **DD** 620.205. **CODEN** SOVIAJ. adv acc. **Circ** 19,000. (ctrl) Noise and vibration control, structural analysis, dynamic measurements, dynamic testing, hearing conservation, and architectural acoustics.

UNDERWATER ACOUSTICS. Vol. 1 1961-. 0082-7444. English. ir. Plenum Press c/o H Feldman, 233 Spring Street, New York NY 10013. **Tel** (212)620-8000.

PLASTICS

ADHESIVES. 1978/79-. US. English. ir. $95.00. International Plastics Selector Inc & D A T A Inc, PO Box 26875, San Diego CA 92126. **Tel** (619)578-7600. Ed David Rady. adv acc. **Circ** 100,000. Property data for over 5,900 adhesives, sealants and primers. Includes paired substrate index, metal and plastic substrate chart, lap shear test data, and manufacturer/supplier cross index.

ADVANCES IN POLYMER TECHNOLOGY. Vol. 2, No. 1 (Winter 1982)-. 0730-6679. Periodical. US. English. qt. $100.00. Van Nostrand Reinhold, 135 West 50th Street, New York NY 10020. **Ind/Abst** Electron. Commun. Abstr. J., ISMEC Bull., Pollut. Abstr. Indexes, Saf. Sci. Abstr. J., Chem. Abstr., Eng. Index Annu., Eng. Index Mon., Eng. Index Bioeng. Abstr., Eng. Index Energy Abstr. **LC** TP1101. **DD** 668.905. **CODEN** APTYD5. *Advances in Plastics Technology, 0272-9504.*

ADVANCES IN URETHANE SCIENCE AND TECHNOLOGY. Vol. 1-. 0044-6378. US. English. ir. $38.50. Technomic Publishing Company Inc, 851 New Holland Avenue, Box 3535, Lancaster PA 17604. **Tel** (717)291-5609. Ed Kurt C Frisch and Daniel Klempner. **Ind/Abst** Chem. Abstr. **LC** TP1180.P8. **DD** 668.423905. **CODEN** AUSTCJ. Technology of urethane foams, elastomers,

Plastics

adhesives, and coatings and their constituent materials. Chemistry, synthesis, properties, and applications.

ANNUAL TECHNICAL CONFERENCE AND EXHIBITION - SOCIETY OF PLASTICS ENGINEERS. (ANNUAL TECHNICAL CONFERENCE AND EXHIBITION). **Main/Corp** Society of Plastics Engineers. 39th (May 4-7, 1981)-. 0733-4192. US. English. an. Society of Plastics Engineers, 14 Fairfield Drive, Brookfield CT 06805. **Tel** (203)775-0471. **Ind/Abst** Eng. Index Annu., Eng. Index Mon., Eng. Index Bioeng. Abstr., Eng. Index Energy Abstr. **CODEN** ACPED4.

AUSTRALIAN PLASTICS & RUBBER. **VAT** Australian Plastics and Rubber. 0365-8015. Periodical. AT. English. ir. $5.50. IPC Business Press, PO Box M204, Sydney Mail Exchange, Sydney New South Wales 2012 Australia. **Ind/Abst** Chem. Abstr. **LC** TP1101. **DD** 668.40994. **CODEN** AUPRCW. *Plastics in Australia.*

BP&R BRITISH PLASTICS AND RUBBER. (BRITISH PLASTICS AND RUBBER). **VFOAT** BP&R. Oct. 1975-. 0307-6164. Periodical. UK. English. mo $65.00. MCM Publishing Limited, Nelson House/265 Rotherhithe Street, London SE16 1EJ England. **Tel** (01)231-1481. Ed Ken Grace. **Ind/Abst** Predicasts, Excerpta Med., Int. Packag. Abstr., Funk Scott Index Corp. Ind. **LC** HD9661.G7. **DD** 338.4766840941. adv acc. **Circ** 11,500. (ctrl). Technical magazine for UK plastics and rubber processors. Detailing developments in materials processing machinery and ancillary equipment.

BRITISH COLUMBIA PLASTICS DIRECTORY. *See* Yearbooks, Almanacs, Directories.

CANADIAN PLASTICS. V. 1- Aug. 1943-. 0008-4778. Periodical. CN. English. mo. $42.50. Southam Communications Ltd, 1450 Don Mills Road, Don Mills Ontario M3B 1X2 Canada. **Tel** (416)445-6641. Ed Judith Nancekivell. **Ind/Abst** Predicasts, Can. Bus. Index, Chem. Abstr., Funk Scott Index Corp. Ind. **CODEN** CNPLAJ. adv acc. **Circ** 11,000. (ctrl). Trade magazine covering plastics markets and technology in Canada. *Progressive Plastics.*

CANADIAN PLASTICS DIRECTORY & BUYER'S GUIDE. *See* Yearbooks, Almanacs, Directories.

CANADIAN PLASTICS STATISTICAL YEAR BOOK. *See* Yearbooks, Almanacs, Directories.

CAOUTCHOUCS & PLASTIQUES. *See* Rubber.

CHEMIE, KUNSTSTOFFE AKTUELL. *See* Chemistry.

COLLOID AND POLYMER SCIENCE. *See* Physics.

CORPUS PLASTICS REPORT. Vol. 1, No. 1 (Jan. 12, 1982)-. 0711-561X. Periodical. CN. English. wk. Corpus Information Services, c/o Leighton, 1450 Don Mills Road, Don Mills Ontario M3B 2X7 Canada. **Tel** (416)445-7101. **DD** 338.4766840971.

CURRENT INDUSTRIAL REPORTS. MA-30D, SHIPMENTS OF SELECTED PLASTICS PRODUCTS. **VFOAT** Shipments of Selected Plastics Products. US. English. an. $1.00. Data User Services Division Customer Services Publication, Bureau of the Census, Washington DC 20233. **Tel** (301)763-4100. **LC** HD9661.U6. **DD** 381.45668490973. Presents timely data on the production, inventories and orders of approximately 5,000 products, which represents 40 percent of all US manufacturing.

DANSK PLAST. Periodical. DK. Danish. ir. 80.00. Tekinsk Forley, Skelbkgade 4, 1717 Copenhagen V Denmark. **LC** TP1101.

DEVELOPMENTS IN PLASTICS TECHNOLOGY. Series/Titl Developments Series. 1-. Monographic Series. UK. English. Elsevier Science Publishing Co, 52 Vanderbilt Avenue, New York NY 10017. **LC** TP1101. **DD** 668.405.

DEVELOPMENTS IN POLYMER STABILISATION. Series/Titl Developments Series. Began in 1979. 0262-155X. UK. English. ir. Elsevier Applied Science Publishers, Crown House, Linton Road, Barking Essex IG11 8JU England. **Tel** (01)594-7272. Ed Gerald Scott. **Ind/Abst** Eng. Index Annu., Eng. Index Mon., Eng. Index Bioeng. Abstr., Eng. Index Energy Abstr., Chem. Abstr. **LC** TP1122. **DD** 668.9. **CODEN** DPSTDI.

DEVELOPMENTS IN REINFORCED PLASTICS. Series/Titl Developments Series. 1-. 0260-9185. UK. English. Elsevier Science Publishing Co, 52 Vanderbilt Avenue, New York NY 10017. **Ind/Abst** Chem. Abstr. **LC** TP1177. **DD** 668.49405. **CODEN** DRPLDR.

DIFFUSION. (DIFFUSION PLASTIQUE). **VAT** Diffusion (Quebec). V. 1- Sept. 1973-. 0317-9850. CN. French. mo. Free. Centre de Recherche Industrielle du Quebec, Complexe Scientifique, CP 9038, Sainte-Foy Quebec G1V 4C7 Canada. **DD** 016.668405.

ELASTOMERS. Ed. 2 (1980)-. US. English. $35.00. International Plastics Selector de D A T A Inc, PO Box 26875, San Diego CA 92126. **Tel** (619)578-7600. Ed David Rady. adv acc. **Circ** 100,000. Specific property data on 3,400 elastomers, 1,300 gum stocks, 350 liquid systems, 350 thermoplastic elastomers, 1,400 formulations and their additives, natural rubber and test data. *Elastomeric Materials.*

EN BI TO PORIMA. (ENBI TO PORIMA). **VFOAT** Vinyl and Polymers. Vol. 12 (1972)-. 0367-021X. Periodical. JA. Japanese. mo. 12,360. Inst of Polymer Industry Inc, Central PO Box 1176, Tokyo Japan 100-91. **Tel** (03)211-7739. Ed SF Miyamoto. **Ind/Abst** Chem. Abstr. **CODEN** EBTPBO. bk rev. adv acc. **Circ** 10,000. *Enka Biniiru to Porima.*

ENGINEERING PLASTICS GUIDE. 1976-. Periodical. UK. English. 2.50, $6.50. European Plastics News, 40 Bowling Green Lane, London EC1R 0NE England.

EUROPEAN PLASTICS NEWS. V. 1- May 1974-. 0306-3534. Periodical. UK. English. mo. $119.60. Business Press International Ltd, Perrymount Road/Haywards Heath West Sussex RH163BR England. **Ind/Abst** Predicasts, Ship Abstr., CIS Abstr., Int. Packag. Abstr., Ref. Source, Chem. Abstr., Funk Scott Index Corp. Ind. **LC** TP1101. **DD** 668.405. **CODEN** EUPNBT.

EUROPLASTICS YEARBOOK. *See* Yearbooks, Almanacs, Directories.

EXTRUSION DIGEST. Vol. 1, No. 1 (June, 1981)-. 0276-0819. Periodical. US. English. mo. $97.00. Tracom Inc, PO Box 533, Whelling IL 60090. **Tel** (219)769-4352.

FACTS & FIGURES OF THE U.S. PLASTICS INDUSTRY. **VFOAT** Facts and Figures of the U.S. Plastics Industry. 1982 Ed.-. 0741-0859. Periodical. US. English. an. $55.00 Members, $110.00 Nonmembers. Society of Plastics Industry, 355 Lexington Avenue, New York NY 10017. **Tel** (212)503-0600. Ed Howard Kibbel. **LC** HD9661.U6. **DD** 338.4766840973. **Circ** 1,000. Statistical review of plastics industry including production, sales, capacities and markets, data on resins, feedstocks, machinery, finished products. *Facts & Figures of the Plastics Industry, 0740-8420.*

FIBERGLASS-REINFORCED PLASTIC PRESSURE VESSELS. **Main/Corp** American Society of Mechanical Engineers. Subcommittee on Reinforced Plastic Pressure Vessels. 19 -. US. English. ir. The American Society of Mechanical Engineers, United Engineering Center, 345 East 47th Street, New York NY 10017. **LC** TS283. **DD** 668.49.

FURASUCHIKKU GAIDO; GENTAIRYE FUKUZAIRYO HEN. PLASTICS YEARBOOK. *See* Yearbooks, Almanacs, Directories.

GUIA CATALOGO PLASTICOS ESPANOLES. Spanish. ir. Agrupacion Nacional Autonoma de Industriales de Plasticos, Sindicato Nacional de Industrias Quinicas, San Bernardo 62, Madrid Spain. **LC** HD9661.S7.

GUMMI, ASBEST, KUNSTSTOFFE. *See* Rubber.

GUMMI, FASERN, KUNSTSTOFFE. *See* Rubber.

HIGH PERFORMANCE PLASTICS. Vol. 1, No. 1 (Nov. 1983)-. 0264-7753. Periodical. UK. English. mo. $120.00. Elsevier International Bulletins, 52 Vanderbilt Avenue, New York NY 10017.

HIMICESKIE VOLOKNA. (KHIMICHESKIE VOLOKNA). 1959-. 0023-1118. Periodical. UR. Russian. bm. $33.50. Victor Kamkin Inc (71041), 12224 Parklawn Drive, Rockville MD 20852. **Tel** (301)881-5973. **Ind/Abst** World Text Abstr., Abstr. Bull. Inst. Paper Chem., Chem. Abstr., Energy Res. Abstr. **CODEN** KVLKA4.

IEEE CONFERENCE RECORD OF ANNUAL CONFERENCE OF ELECTRICAL ENGINEERING PROBLEMS IN THE RUBBER AND PLASTICS INDUSTRY. *See* Engineering - Electricity, Electrical Engineering, Electronics.

INTERNATIONAL JOURNAL OF POLYMERIC MATERIALS. *See* Chemistry.

INTERPLASTICS. (INTERPLASTICS : IP). VFOAT IP. Began in 1978?. 0392-3800. Periodical. US. Italian. bm. $59.40. Tecniche Nuove SRL, Via Moscova 46-9, 20121 Milan Italy. **Tel** 0331/ 576063. **Ind/Abst** Chem. Abstr. **CODEN** INPLDK.

JAPAN PLASTICS AGE. 0021-4582. Periodical. JA. English. bm. $70.00. Plastics Age Company Ltd, 10-6 Kajicho 1-chome Chiyoda-ku, Tokyo 101 Japan. Ed Eiichi Asayama. **Ind/Abst** Int. Packag. Abstr., Chem. Abstr., Funk Scott Index Corp. Ind. **CODEN** JPLAAN. adv acc. **Circ** 17,000. Review of plastics industries of Japan, with main interest in polymer technology, processing techniques, processing machine engineering and market developments. *Japan Plastics Age News.*

JAPAN PLASTICS INDUSTRY ANNUAL. Began with 1958 issue. 0448-8679. JA. English. an. $30.00. Plastics Age Company Ltd, 10-6 Kajicho 1-chome Chiyoda-ku, Tokyo 101 Japan. Ed Eiichi Asayama. **LC** TP1103. adv acc. **Circ** 17,000. Reviews in one volume the latest developments of the plastics industry of Japan. Directory section offers a source of material and equipment supplies.

JOURNAL OF CELLULAR PLASTICS. V. 1- Jan. 1965-. 0021-955X. Periodical. US. English. bm. $80.00. Technomic Publishing Company, New Holland Avenue/Box 3535, Lancaster PA 17604. **Tel** (717)291-5609. Ed Sidney H Metzger Jr. **Ind/Abst** Int. Aerosp. Abstr., Int. Packag. Abstr., Eng. Index, Chem. Abstr., Eng. Index Mon. **LC** TP1183.F6. **CODEN** JCUPAM. bk rev. adv acc. **Circ** 1,000. Foamed plastics technology. Developments in: chemistry and formulation, analysis and testing, experimental findings, chemical components, additives and systems, processing methods, machinery and equipment, fire retardance and other safety aspects.

JOURNAL OF ELASTOMERS AND PLASTICS. (THE JOURNAL OF ELASTOMERS AND PLASTICS). V. 6- Jan. 1974-. 0095-2443. Periodical. US. English. qt. $115.00. Technomic Publishing Company Inc, 851 New Holland Avenue, Box 3535, Lancaster PA 17604. **Tel** (717)291-5609. Ed Melvyn A Kohudic. **Ind/Abst** Eng. Index Annu., Eng. Index Mon., Eng. Index Bioeng. Abstr., Eng. Index Energy Abstr., Excerpta Med., Chem. Abstr., Eng. Index. **LC** TA455.P5. **DD** 668.405. **CODEN** JEPLAX. bk rev. **Circ** 400. Information for the scientific and engineering community concerned with the research, development and marketing of elastomers and plastics, and the area in between where the characteristics of both extremes are apparent. *Journal of Elastoplastics, 0022-071X.*

JOURNAL OF PLASTIC FILM & SHEETING. VFOAT Journal of Plastic Film and Sheeting. Vol. 1, No. 1 (Jan. 1985)-. 8756-0879. Periodical. US. English. qt. $125.00. Technomic Publishing Company, 851 New Holland Avenue/Box 3535, Lancaster PA 17601. **DD** 668.

JOURNAL OF REINFORCED PLASTICS AND COMPOSITES. VFOAT JRPC. Vol. 1, No. 1 (Jan. 1982)-. 0731-6844. Periodical. US. English. qt. $130.00. Technomic Publishing Company Inc, 851 Mew Holland Avenue/Box 3535, Lancaster PA 17604. **Tel** (717)291-5609. Ed Stephen W Tsai. **Ind/Abst** Int. Aerosp. Abstr., Met. Abstr., World Alum. Abstr., Chem. Abstr., Eng. Index. **LC** TA455.P55. **DD** 620.1923. **CODEN** JRPCDW. bk rev. **Circ** 400. Current technical information on materials, reinforced plastics and composites. Materials composition, properties and performance, design methods and criteria, characterization and analysis, and computer assistance are topics covered.

JOURNAL OF THERMAL INSULATION. *See* Heating, Plumbing, & Refrigeration.

JOURNAL OF VINYL TECHNOLOGY. VFOAT Vinyl Technology. V. 1- Mar. 1979-. 0193-7197. Periodical. US. English. qt. Society of Plastics Engineers, 14 Fairfield Drive, Brookfield CT 06805. **Tel** (203)775-0471. **Ind/Abst** Chem. Abstr. **LC** TP1180.V48. **DD** 668.423605. **CODEN** JVTEDI.

Plastics

KAUTSCHUK UND GUMMI. V. 1-. Periodical. GW. German. mo. $93.25. Dr Alfred Huethig Verlag Gmbh, Im Weiher 10 POB 10 28 69, 6900 Heidelberg West Germany. **Tel** (06221)489-0. **Ed** Ernst Prein and Sieghard Neufeldt. **Ind/Abst** Sci. Cit. Index, Abr. Ed., Funk Scott Index Corp. Ind., Eng. Index, Chem. Abstr. **LC** TS1870. bk rev. adv acc. International publication for high polymer raw materials- India-rubber, rubber, plastics, the rubber and plastics industry.

KOBUNSHI KAGAKU NO TEMBO. VFOAT Annual Reviews. Began with 1970 issue. JA. Japanese. ir. 3400. Kobunshi Gakkai, Maruzen 2-6 Nihonbashitoori Chuo-ku, Tokyo Japan. **LC** TP1101.

KOBUNSHI KAKO. VFOAT Polymer Processing. 0368-6426. Periodical. JA. Japanese. mo. 8800. Kabuki Kankokai, Chiekoin Marutamachi Kudaru, Kamigyo-ku 60, Kyoto Japan. **Ind/Abst** Chem. Abstr. **LC** TP1080. **CODEN** KOKABN.

KUNSTSTOFF-JOURNAL. VAT Kunststoff Journal. 0047-3766. Periodical. German (summaries in English, French, and Italian 1976-(Jan. 1979)). ir. Europa-Fachpresse-Verlag GMBH, 8 Munchen 40, Leopoldstrasse 175, Munchen West Germany. **Ind/Abst** Int. Packag. Abstr., Chem. Abstr. **LC** TP1101. **CODEN** KUNJD7.

KUNSTSTOFFBERATER, -RUNDSCHAU + -TECHNIK. (KUNSTSTOFFBERATER VEREINIGT MIT RUNDSCHAU + TECHNIK). 20.- Volume. Periodical. GW. German. mo. $49.38. Umschau Verlag, Stuttgrtr Str 18-24, Postfach 110262, 6000 Frankfurt 1 West Germany. **Tel** (069)260 01. **Ind/Abst** Comput. Control Abstr., Coal Abstr., Electr. Electron. Abstr., Sci. Abstr. Sect. A. Phys. Abstr., Phys. Abstr., Funk Scott Index Corp. Ind., Chem. Abstr. **LC** TP1101. *Kunststofftechnik, Kunststoff-Rundschau; KB.*

KUNSTSTOFFE. V. 1- Jan. 1911-. 0023-5563. Periodical. GW. German. mo. 175.20. Carl Hanser Verlag, Postfach 86 04 20, D-8000 Munchen 86 West Germany. **Tel** 92694-0. **Ind/Abst** Chem. Abstr., Predicasts, Eng. Index. **CODEN** KUNSAV. adv acc. **Circ** 11,600. Covers the whole field of plastics and rubber in a comprehensive, flexible manner. Information on new, expanding markets, the automotive industry, packaging, electrical/electronics are also included.

KUNSTSTOFFE IM BAU. 0343-3129. Periodical. GW. German. qt. 75.60. Carl Hanser Verlag, Postfach 860420/Kolbergerstr 22, 0-8 Muenchen 86 West Germany. **Tel** 089/9 26 94-0. **Ed** Wolfgang Lehmann and A Schwabe. **Ind/Abst** Eng. Index Annu., Eng. Index Mon., Eng. Index Bioeng. Abstr., Eng. Index Energy Abstr., Predicasts, Chem. Abstr., Energy Res. Abstr. **LC** TA668. **DD** 693.9. **CODEN** KUBADM. adv acc. **Circ** 4,800. Plastics in building and construction—roofs, windows, doors; advantages of plastics-architectural, physical, economical; its properties and possibilities compared to conventional materials. *Plasticonstruction, K.I.B.*

KUNSTSTOFFE IN OSTERREICH. German. ir. J Dressler Buch-Und Zeitschriftenuerlag, Wien IV Schwindgasse 5, Wien Austria. **LC** TP1112.

KUNSTSTOFFE-PLASTICS. Vol. 1-. 0023-5598. SZ. German. mo. $36.61. Vogt-Schild AG, Dornacherstrasse 39, 4501 Solothurn Switzerland. **Tel** 065/247 247. **Ind/Abst** Excerpta Med., Int. Packag. Abstr., Chem. Abstr., Eng. Index, Eng. Index Annu., Eng. Index Mon. **LC** TP986.A1. **CODEN** KUPLAK.

KYOKA PURASUCHIKKUSU. Began in 1955. 0452-9685. Periodical. JA. Japanese. mo. Maruzen Company Ltd, PO Box 5050, 100-31 Tokyo Japan. **Tel** 03-543-1531. **Ed** Takkaaki Toda. **Ind/Abst** Chem. Abstr. **CODEN** KYPUA7. adv acc. **Circ** 1,800. (ctrl). Publishes dessertation and research materials of reinforced plastics.

LABOUR SURVEY (SOCIETY OF THE PLASTICS INDUSTRY OF CANADA). *See* Economics - Labor.

MACROMOLECULES. V. 1- Jan./Feb. 1968-. 024-9297. Periodical. US. English. mo. $283.00. American Chemical Society, PO Box 57136, West End Station, Washington DC 20037. **Tel** (202)872-4600. **Ed** Field H Winslow. **Ind/Abst** Life Sci. Collect., World Text Abstr., Energy Inf. Abstr., Environ. Abstr., World Surf. Coat. Abstr., Abstr. Bull. Inst. Paper Chem., Int. Aerosp. Abstr., Bibliogr. Agric., Chem. Abstr., Nucl. Sci. Abstr., Index Med., Sci. Cit. Index, Abr. Ed. **LC** QD380. **DD** 547.8405. **NLM** W1 MA172V. **CODEN** MAMOBX. adv acc. **Circ** 2,608. Available on microfilm from the American Chemical Society. Reviews original research in fundamental aspects of polymer chemistry including synthesis, polymerization mechanisms and kinetics, chemical reactions, solution characteristics, bulk properties of organic, inorganic, biopolymers.

MANAGING CORROSION WITH PLASTICS. **Main/Conf** Intersociety Plastics Seminar. V. 1/2/3-. 0197-3967. US. English. ir. National Association Corrosion Engineers, PO Box 218340, Houston TX 77218. **Ind/Abst** Chem. Abstr. **CODEN** MCWPDY.

MANITOBA PLASTICS DIRECTORY. *See* Yearbooks, Almanacs, Directories.

MAQUINARIA PARA PLASTICOS. *See* Business - Marketing.

MATERIALE PLASTICE. Began in 1964. 0025-5289. Periodical. Romanian (summaries in English, French, German, and Russian). qt. Ilexim Press Departmant, PO Box 1 136 1 137, Bucharest Romania. **Ind/Abst** CIS Abstr., Chem. Abstr., Eng. Index Annu., Eng. Index Mon., Eng. Index Bioeng. Abstr., Eng. Index Energy Abstr. **CODEN** MPLAAM.

MATERIE PLASTICHE ED ELASTOMERI. Yearly V. 29-. 0025-5459. Periodical. IT. chiefly Italian. ir. $35.64. Industria, Viale Monte Grappa 3, 20124 Milano Italy. **Ind/Abst** Eng. Index Annu., Eng. Index Mon., Eng. Index Bioeng. Abstr., Eng. Index Energy Abstr., Predicasts. **LC** TP1101. **CODEN** MPELAK. *Materic Plastiche.*

MECHANICS OF COMPOSITE MATERIALS. V. 15- Jan./Feb. 1979-. 0191-5665. Periodical. US. English. bm. $545.00 Domestic, $605.00 Foreign. Consultants Bureau, 233 Spring Street, New York NY 10013. **Tel** (212)620-8000. **Ed** A K Malmeisler. **Ind/Abst** Electron. Commun. Abstr. J., ISMEC Bull., Pollut. Abstr. Indexes, Saf. Sci. Abstr. J., Fluidex, Int. Aerosp. Abstr., Comput. Control Abstr., Electr. Electron. Abstr., Sci. Abstr. Sect. A. Phys. Abstr., Appl. Mech. Rev., Chem. Abstr., Eng. Index, Phys. Abstr., Phys. Abstr., Appl. Mech. Rev. **LC** TA455.P58. **DD** 620.118. **CODEN** MCMAD7. *Polymer Mechanics, 0032-390X.*

MEMORIA - INSTITUTO NACIONAL DE RACIONALIZACION Y NORMALIZACION. COMISION TECNICA DE TRABAJO NO. 53 INDUSTRIAS DE PLASTICS. **Main/Corp** Instituto Nacional de Racionalizacion y Normalizacion. Comision Tecnica de Trabajo No. 53 Industrias de Plasticos y Caucho. Spanish. ir. Instituto Nacional de Racionalizacion Y Normalizacion, Serrano 150, Madrid Spain. **LC** TP1122.

MODERN PLASTICS. 0026-8275. Periodical. US. English. mo. $30.00. Modern Plastics McGraw Hill Publications Attn Cheryl Ross PO Box 416, Hightstown NJ 08520. **Tel** (609)426-5000. **Ind/Abst** Eng. Index Mon., Eng. Index Bioeng. Abstr., Eng. Index Energy Abstr., Predicasts, Energy Inf. Abstr., Environ. Abstr., Abstr. Bull. Inst. Paper Chem., Appl. Sci. Technol. Index, Chem. Abstr., Eng. Index Annu., Eng. Index, Nuci. Sci. Abstr., Funk Scott Index Corp. Ind., Sci. Cit. Index, Abr. Ed., Chem. Abstr., Appl. Sci. Technol. Index. **LC** TP986.A1. **CODEN** MOPLAY. Index published separately - free - automatically sent. adv acc. Available on microfilm. *Plastic Products.*

MODERN PLASTICS ENCYCLOPEDIA. 1954-. 0085-3518. US. English. Modern Plastics Reprint Department, PO Box 602, Hightstown NJ 08520. **Tel** (212)512-2000. *Modern Plastics Encyclopedia and Engineers Handbook.*

MODERN PLASTICS INTERNATIONAL. 0026-8283. Periodical. English. mo. Modern Plastics International, PO Box 1485, Riverton NJ 08077. **Ind/Abst** Predicasts, Ship Abstr., Int. Packag. Abstr.

MONOGRAPHS ON PLASTICS. V. 1-. 0362-0387. Monographic Series. US. English. ir. Marcel Dekker/Continuation Department, 270 Madison Avenue, New York NY 10016. **Tel** (212)696-9000. **Ed** Frisch. **Ind/Abst** Chem. Abstr. **LC** UNC. **CODEN** MGPLAC. This is an ongoing series. Each title has a different subject.

MPE JOURNAL. Periodical. English. ir. Editrice L'Industria, Piazzale Cadorna 5, Milano 20123 Italy. **Ind/Abst** Predicasts. **LC** HD9661.A1. **DD** 338.47668405.

L'OFFICIEL DE LA DROGUERIE, ET SON COMPLEMENT PLASTIQUES. VFOAT Plastiques. Began with Nov. 1949 issue. Periodical. French. ir. **LC** HD9653.1.

PLASTE UND KAUTSCHUK. 1.- Volume. 0048-4350. Periodical. SZ. English. mo. $60.96. Kunst & Wissen Erich Bieber, Dufourstrasse 51, CH-8008 Zurich Switzerland. **Tel** 011-41-1-69 44 20. **Ind/Abst** World Surf. Coat. Abstr., Comput. Control Abstr., Electr. Electron. Abstr., Sci. Abstr. Sect. A. Phys. Abstr., Int. Packag. Abstr., Energy Res. Abstr., Met. Abstr., World Alum. Abstr., Chem. Abstr., Sci. Cit. Index, Abr. Ed. **LC** TP986.A1. **CODEN** PLKAAM.

PLASTIC. Began in 1951. Periodical. DK. Danish. mo. $24.30. Dansk Bladforlag K/S, 20 Holbergsgade, DK-1057 Copenhagen K Denmark. **LC** TP986.A1.

PLASTICESKIE MASSY. (PLASTICHESKIE MASSY). Began in 1959. 0554-2901. Periodical. UR. Russian. mo. $64.00. Victor Kamkin Inc (70697), 12224 Parklawn Drive, Rockville MD 20852. **Tel** (301)881-5973. **Ind/Abst** Abstr. Bull. Inst. Paper Chem. **LC** TP986.A1.

PLASTICOS & I.E. E BORRACHA. Periodical. Portuguese. ir. 40.00. M & Z Prepresentatives Editora Abril, 112 Ferry Street, Newark NJ 07105. **LC** TP1101.

PLASTICOS UNIVERSALES. 0303-4011. Periodical. GW. Spanish. qt. 79.20. Carl Hanser Verlag, Postfach 860420, Kolbergerstr 22, 8 Muenchen 86 West Germany. **Tel** 089/9 26 94-0. **Ed** Wolfgang Glenz. **Ind/Abst** Chem. Abstr. **CODEN** PLUVBY. adv acc. **Circ** 4,000. Every issue presents topics on new industrial developments, processing machinery, raw materials, devices, accessories, applications of plastics and company literature. *Kunststoffe, Plasticos, 0023-558X.*

PLASTICS. **Main/Corp** International Plastics Selector, Inc. 1980-. US. English. ir. $125.00. International Plastics Selector Inc & D A T A Inc, PO Box 26875, San Diego CA 92126. **Tel** (619)578-7600. **Ed** David Rady. adv acc. **Circ** 100,000. Properties listed on 9,000 thermosets and thermoplastics. Over 900 manufacturers are represented. *Extruding and Molding Grades.*

PLASTICS ABSTRACTS. *See* Indexes/ Abstracts.

PLASTICS AND RUBBER INTERNATIONAL. V. 2- Jan./Feb. 1977-. 0309-4561. Periodical. UK. English. bm. $49.03. Plastics & Rubber International, 11 Hobart Place, Ms K Hyland, London SW1W 0HL England. **Tel** 01 245 9555. **Ed** Patricia Battams. **Ind/Abst** CIS Abstr., Electron. Commun. Abstr. J., ISMEC Bull., Pollut. Abstr. Indexes, Saf. Sci. Abstr. J., Excerpta Med., Predicasts, Comput. Control Abstr., Electr. Electron. Abstr., Sci. Abstr. Sect. A. Phys. Abstr., Chem. Abstr. **LC** TP1101. **DD** 668.905. **CODEN** PRUID5. bk rev. adv acc. **Circ** 11,000. Latest trends and developments related to plastics and rubber materials, products made from these materials and machinery and production processes for fabrication. *Plastics and Rubber, 0308-311X.*

PLASTICS AND RUBBER PROCESSING AND APPLICATIONS. Vol. 1, No. 1 (Mar. 1981)-. 0144-6045. Periodical. UK. English. qt. $171.00. Elsevier Applied Science Publications, Crown House, Linton Road, Barking Essex IG11 8JU England. **Ed** Geoffrey Reynolds. **Ind/Abst** Electron. Commun. Abstr. J., ISMEC Bull., Pollut. Abstr. Indexes, Saf. Sci. Abstr. J., Eng. Index Annu., Eng. Index Mon., Eng. Index Bioeng. Abstr., Eng. Index Energy Abstr., Fluidex, Comput. Control Abstr., Electr. Electron. Abstr., Sci. Abstr. Sect. A. Phys. Abstr., Chem. Abstr. **LC** TP1101. **DD** 668.405. **CODEN** PPAPDE. bk rev. adv acc. Published on behalf of the Plastics and Rubber Institute in London. *Plastics and Rubber: Processing, 0307-9422; Plastics and Rubber: Materials and Applications, 0307-9414.*

PLASTICS & RUBBER WEEKLY. Periodical. UK. English. ir. Macleren Publishers Limited, Box 109/MacLaren House/Scarbrook, Croydon CR9 1QH England. **Tel** (01)688 7788. **Ind/Abst** World Text Abstr., Coal Abstr., Fluidex, Int. Packag. Abstr., Predicasts, Funk Scott Index Corp. Ind.

PLASTICS BOTTLES *CEASED.* (CURRENT INDUSTRIAL REPORTS. M30E, PLASTICS BOTTLES). -Summary for 1983. 0145-4943. Periodical. US. English. an. $1.75. Data User Services Division, Customer Services Publication, Bureau of the Census, Washington DC 20233. **Tel** (301)763-4100. **Ind/Abst** Predicasts, Am. Stat. Index. **LC** HD9662.B69. **DD** 338.47668497. Presents timely data on the production, inventories, and orders of approximately 5,000 products, which represents 40 percent of all US manufacturing.

PLASTICS BRIEF. DESIGN & MATERIALS EDITION. (PLASTICS BRIEF). 0745-0133. Periodical. US. English. wk. $148.00. Market Search Inc, PO Box 2886, Toledo OH 43606. **Tel** (419)472-7656. **Ed** James R Best. The concise briefing for design engineers and materials engineers. *Plastic Product Design, 0194-8466.*

PLASTICS BRIEF. EXTRUSION & BLOW MOLDING EDITION. (PLASTICS BRIEF). 0745-0141. Periodical. US. English. wk. $148.00. Market Search Inc, Box 2886, Toledo OH 43606. **Tel** (419)472-7656. **Ed** James R Best. The concise briefing for reinforced termosetting plastics executives and their suppliers. *Extrusion and Blow Holding News Brief, 0194-8482.*

PLASTICS BRIEF. MARKETING EDITION. (PLASTICS BRIEF). 0745-0168. Periodical. US. English. wk. $148.00. Market Search Inc, PO Box 2886, Toledo OH 43606. **Tel** (419)472-7656. **Ed** James R Best. The concise briefing for executives in the thermoplastics industry. *Plastics Marketing News Brief, 0194-8474.*

PLASTICS BUSINESS. Vol. 1, No. 1 (Sept./Oct. 1980)-. 0229-0413. Periodical. CN. English. bm. $30.95. Plastics Business, 443 Mount Pleasant Road, Toronto Ontario M4S 2L8 Canada. **Tel** (416)482-6603. **DD** 338.4766840971.

PLASTICS BUSINESS NEWS. 0734-1784. Periodical. US. English. sm. $217.00. Canners Publishing Company, PO Box 716/Back Bay Annex, Boston MA 02117. **Tel** (617)536-7780.

PLASTICS COMPOUNDING. May/June 1978-. 0148-9119. Periodical. US. English. bm. $26.00. Plastics Compounding, Box 188-90/A, Denver CO 80218. **Tel** (218)723-9544. **Ind/Abst** Eng. Index Annu., Eng. Index Mon., Eng. Index Bioeng. Abstr., Eng. Index Energy Abstr., Predicasts, Chem. Abstr. **LC** TP1101. **DD** 668.4105. **CODEN** PLCODR.

PLASTICS DESIGN FORUM. V. 1- Mar./Apr. 1976-. 0362-9376. Periodical. US. English. bm. $35.00. Plastics Design Forum, 1 East First Street, Duluth MN 55802. **Tel** (218)723-9200. **Ed** Mel Friedman. **Ind/Abst** Predicasts, Funk Scott Index Corp. Ind. **LC** TP1101. **DD** 668.405. adv acc. (ctrl).

PLASTICS DIRECTORY OF CANADA. *See* Yearbooks, Almanacs, Directories.

PLASTICS ENGINEERING. V. 29, No. 8- Aug. 1973-. 0091-9578. Periodical. US. English. mo. $30.00. Society of Plastics Engineers, 14 Fairfield Drive, Brookfield CT 06805. **Tel** (203)775-0471. **Ed** A A Schoengood. **Ind/Abst** Appl. Sci. Technol. Index, Eng. Index Mon., Eng. Index Bioeng. Abstr., Eng. Index Energy Abstr., Excerpta Med., Abstr. Bull. Inst. Paper Chem., CIS Abstr., Comput. Control Abstr., Electr. Electron. Abstr., Int. Packag. Abstr., Sci. Abstr. Sect. A. Phys. Abstr., Eng. Index Annu., Energy Inf. Abstr., Environ. Abstr., Predicasts, Chem. Abstr., Eng. Index, Sci. Cit. Index, Abr. Ed., Phys. Abstr. **LC** TP1101. **DD** 668.405. **CODEN** PLEGBB. bk rev. adv acc. **Circ** 26,000. A trade publication with on-going coverage of the technical aspects of material use, equipment selection, product design and new product information. *SPE Journal, 0036-1844.*

PLASTICS IN BUILDING CONSTRUCTION. *See* Building and Construction.

PLASTICS IN CONSTRUCTION. VFOAT Matiere Plastique dans la Construction. V. 1- Fall 1973-. 0381-9620. Periodical. CN. English (French). qt. Dow Chemical of Canada Ltd, Construction Material Sales, 122 Arrow Road, Weston Ontario M9M 2M2 Canada. **DD** 691.9205.

PLASTICS INDUSTRIES. VFOAT Fabrication de Produits en Matiere Plastique. 1981-. 0319-9053. CN. English (French). an. $4.75 Domestic, $5.70 Foreign. Publication Sales and Services, Statistics Canada, Ottawa Ontario K1A 0V7 Canada. *Manufactueres of Plastics and Synthetic Resins, 0527-5571; Plastics Fabricating Industry, 0384-4196.*

PLASTICS MACHINERY & EQUIPMENT. VAT Plastics Machinery and Equipment. 0149-4899. Periodical. US. English. mo. $35.00. Plastics Machinery & Equipment, PO Box 18888-A, Denver CO 80218. **Tel** (218)723-9200. **Ind/Abst** Predicasts.

PLASTICS MANUFACTURING CAPABILITIES IN MISSISSIPPI. 0099-0450. US. English. be. Mississippi Research & Development Center, 3825 Ridgewood Road, Jackson MS 39205. **LC** TP1112. **DD** 338.476684025762.

PLASTICS TECHNOLOGY. VFOAT Plastics Technology Magazine. Vol. 1- Feb. 1955-. 0032-1257. Periodical. US. English. mo. $65.00. Bill Brothers Publishing, 633 3rd Avenue, New York NY 10017. **Tel** (212)986-4800. **Ind/Abst** Eng. Index Mon., Eng. Index Bioeng. Abstr., Eng. Index Energy Abstr., Excerpta Med., Predicasts, Int. Packag. Abstr., Chem. Abstr., Eng. Index Annu., Eng. Index Mon., Appl. Sci. Technol. Index, Funk Scott Index Corp. Ind., Eng. Index. **LC** TP1101. **DD** 668.405. **CODEN** PLTEAB.

PLASTICS TECHNOLOGY. MANUFACTURING HANDBOOK AND BUYERS' GUIDE. VFOAT Manufacturing Handbook and Buyers' Guide. 1974/75-1976/77. US. English. ir. $40.00. Bill Brothers Publishing Company, 633 Third Avenue, New York NY 10017. **Tel** (212)986-4800. *Plastics Technology's Annual Manufacturing Handbook and Buyers' Guide.*

PLASTICS WORLD. V. 1- Apr. 1943-. 0032-1273. Periodical. US. English. mo. $45.00. Cahners Publications, 270 St Paul Street, Denver CO 80206. **Tel** (617)964-3030. **Ed** Bernard Miller. **Ind/Abst** Predicasts, Chem. Abstr., Int. Packag. Abstr., Appl. Sci. Technol. Index, Bus. Period. Index, Energy Inf. Abstr., Environ. Abstr., Funk Scott Index Corp. Ind. **LC** TP1101. **DD** 668.405. **CODEN** PLAWA4. adv acc. **Circ** 60,000. (ctrl). The magazine for managers in the plastics industry. *Plastics Industry, 0096-9168.*

PLASTICS WORLD BUYERS GUIDE. US. English. an. $25.00. Cahners Publications, 270 St Paul Street, Denver CO 80206. **Tel** (303)388-4511. *Plastics World.*

PLASTICULTURE. (No.6- June 1970-). Periodical. FR. French (and English). qt. $26.61. International Committee for Plastics in Agriculture, 65 Rue De Prony, 75854 Paris Cedex France. **Tel** 763.12.59. **Ed** International Committee for Plastics in Agriculture. **Ind/Abst** Bibliogr. Agric. adv acc. New plastics materials and products for application in agriculture and horticulture; agricultural techniques based partially or wholly on the use of plastics.

PLASTIQUES MODERNES ET ELASTOMERES. (PLASTIQUES MODERNES ELASTOMERES). 0032-1303. English. ir. **Tel** 622 13 62. **Ind/Abst** Energy Res. Abstr., Eng. Index Annu., Eng. Index Bioeng. Abstr., Eng. Index Energy Abstr., Eng. Index Mon., Predicasts. **CODEN** PMELAW.

PLASTVERARBEITER. (DER PLASTVERARBEITER). Began with April 1950 issue. 0032-1338. Periodical. GW. German. mo. $87.17. Dr Alfred Huethig Verlag GMBH, Im Weiher 10 POB 10 28 69, D-69 Heidelberg 1 West Germany. **Tel** (06221)489-0. **Ed** Johannes Sediry, Fritz Vollmer and Lutz Rautenberg. **Ind/Abst** CIS Abstr., Int. Packag. Abstr., Eng. Index Mon., Eng. Index Bioeng. Abstr., Excerpta Med., Eng. Index Energy Abstr., Energy Res. Abstr., Chem. Abstr., Nuci. Sci. Abstr., Eng. Index Mon., Eng. Index Annu. **LC** TP986.A1. bk rev. adv acc. Covers processing and application of plastics, new procedures in the tool and machinery sector, further developments in the raw material sector.

PLASTY A KAUCUK. Vol. 11- Jan. 1974-. 0322-7340. Periodical. CS. Czech (summaries in English, German, and Russian). mo. Artia, PO Box 790, Praha 1 Czechoslovakia. **Ind/Abst** Chem. Abstr. **LC** TP1101. **CODEN** PLKCAS. *Plasticke Hmoty A Kaucuk.*

POLIMERIM VE-HOMARIM PLASTIYIM. VFOAT Polymers and Plastic Materials. 0370-2561. Hebrew (with summaries in English). ir. 10.00. Center for Industrial Research, POB 311, Hefah Israel. **Ind/Abst** Chem. Abstr. **LC** TP1101. **CODEN** PVPLAE.

POLYMER COMPOSITES. V. 1- Sept. 1980-. 0272-8397. Periodical. US. English. qt. $60.00. Society of Plastics Engineers, 14 Fairfield Drive, Brookfield Center CT 06805. **Tel** (203)775-0471. **Ed** Roger Porter. **Ind/Abst** Eng. Index Mon., Eng. Index Bioeng. Abstr., Eng. Index Energy Abstr., Int. Aerosp. Abstr., Comput. Control Abstr., Electr. Electron. Abstr., Sci. Abstr. Sect. A. Phys. Abstr., Chem. Abstr., Eng. Index Annu. **LC** TA418.9.C6. **DD** 668.49405. **CODEN** PCOMDI. **Circ** 1,000. Highly technical articles on research into polymer composites.

POLYMER DEGRADATION AND STABILITY. V. 1- Feb. 1979-. 0141-3910. Periodical. UK. English. mo. 272/245 UK. Elsevier Applied Science Publishers, Crown House/Linton Road, Barking Essex IG11 8JU England. **Ed** N Grassie. **Ind/Abst** Eng. Index Annu., Eng. Index Mon., Eng. Index, Eng. Index Bioeng. Abstr., Eng. Index Energy Abstr., Life Sci. Collect., World Surf. Coat. Abstr., Chem. Abstr., Sci. Cit. Index, Abr. Ed. **LC** QD380. **DD** 620.1920422. **CODEN** PDSTDW. bk rev. adv acc. Deals with degradation reactions and their control during processing, use and planned deterioration after use of polymer products.

POLYMER ENGINEERING AND SCIENCE. V. 5, No. 3- July 1965-. 0032-3888. Periodical. US. English. ir. $275.00. Society of Plastics Engineers, 14 Fairfield Drive, Brookfield CT 06805. **Tel** (203)775-0471. **Ed** Roger Porter. **Ind/Abst** Eng. Index Mon., Eng. Index Bioeng. Abstr., Eng. Index Energy Abstr., Comput. Control Abstr., Electr. Electron. Abstr., Sci. Abstr. Sect. A. Phys. Abstr., Chem. Abstr., Eng. Index Annu., Eng. Index Mon., Nuci. Sci. Abstr., Int. Aerosp. Abstr., Appl. Sci. Technol. Index, Phys. Abstr., Sci. Cit. Index, Abr. Ed., Eng. Index. **CODEN** PYESAZ. (cum index). **Circ** 1,200. Highly technical articles on research into polymer science and engineering. *SPE Transactions, 0096-8129.*

POLYMER NEWS. V. 1- Dec. 1970-. 0032-3918. Periodical. US. English. ir. Gordon & Breach, 1 Bedford Street, London WC2E 9HD England. **Ind/Abst** Predicasts, Comput. Control Abstr., Electr. Electron. Abstr., Sci. Abstr. Sect. A. Phys. Abstr., Ref. Source, Chem. Abstr., Funk Scott Index Corp. Ind., Phys. Abstr. **LC** TP1101. **DD** 668.405. **CODEN** PLYNBU.

POLYMER PHOTOCHEMISTRY. Vol. 1, No. 1 (Jan. 1981)-. 0144-2880. Periodical. UK. English. bm. 115 Domestic, 127 Foreign. Elsevier Applied Science Publications, Crown House Linton Road, Barking Essex IG11 8JU England. **Ed** N S Allen. **Ind/Abst** Eng. Index Annu., Eng. Index Mon., Eng. Index Bioeng. Abstr., Eng. Index Energy Abstr., Life Sci. Collect., Chem. Abstr. **LC** QD380. **DD** 547.705. **CODEN** POPHDO. bk rev. adv acc. Deals with all scientific and technical aspects of physical and chemical interactions of light and radiation with polymer systems.

POLYMER-PLASTICS TECHNOLOGY AND ENGINEERING. V. 2- 1973-. 0092-5012. Periodical. US. English. sa. $19.50. Marcel Decker, 95 Madison Avenue, New York NY 10016. **Ind/Abst** Chem. Abstr., Excerpta Med. **LC** TP1101. **DD** 668.405. **CODEN** PPTEC7. (cum index). *Journal of Macromolecular Science. Reviews in Polymer Technology, 0094-4173.*

POLYMER-PLASTICS TECHNOLOGY AND ENGINEERING. VFOAT Polymer-Plastics. 0360-2559. Periodical. US. English. qt. $220.00. Marcel Dekker, P O Box 11305 Church Street Station, New York NY 10249. **Tel** (212)696-9000. **Ed** Louis Naturman. **Ind/Abst** Appl. Mech. Rev., Chem. Abstr., Excerpta Med., Appl. Sci. Technol. Index, Curr. Contents, Eng. Tech. Appl. Sci. **CODEN** PPTEC7. bk rev. adv acc.

POLYMER TESTING. Vol. 1, No 1 (Jan/Mar 1980)-. 0142-9418. Periodical. UK. English. bm. 106 Domestic, 96 Foreign. Elsevier Applied Science Publishers, Crown House Linton Road, Barking Essex IG11 8JU England. **Ed** Roger Brown. **Ind/Abst** Eng. Index Annu., Eng. Index Mon., Eng. Index Bioeng. Abstr., Eng. Index Energy Abstr., Comput. Control Abstr., Electr. Electron. Abstr., Sci. Abstr. Sect. A. Phys. Abstr., Chem. Abstr. **LC** TA455.P58. **DD** 620.1920287. **CODEN** POTEDZ. bk rev. adv acc. Forum for developments in testing of polymers and polymeric materials.

POLYMERIC MATERIALS SCIENCE AND ENGINEERING. (POLYMERIC MATERIALS : SCIENCE AND ENGINEERING, PROCEEDINGS OF THE ACS DIVISION OF POLYMERIC MATERIALS, SCIENCE AND ENGINEERING). Vol. 49 (Aug. 28-Sept. 2, 1983)-. 0743-0515. US. English. sa. American Chemical Society, 1155 16th Street NW, Washington DC 20036. **Ind/Abst** Chem. Abstr., Coal Abstr. **LC** TP935. **DD** 668.905. **CODEN** PMSEDG. *Organic Coatings and Applied Polymer Science Proceedings, 0732-7528.*

POPULAR PLASTICS. 0032-4604. Periodical. II. English. mo. Colour Publications Private Ltd, 126 Dhyruwadi Drive, Naraman Road, Bombay 400025 India. **Ind/Abst** Chem. Abstr.

POPULAR PLASTICS (BOMBAY, INDIA : 1981). (POPULAR PLASTICS). Vol. 26, No. 6 (June 1981)-. 0253-7303. Periodical. English. mo. 50.00. Colour Publications, 126-A Dhuruwadi, Dr Nariman Road, Bombay 400 025 India. **Tel** 430 9610/9318/6319. **Ed** R V Raghavan. **Ind/Abst** Chem. Abstr. **CODEN** POPLD2. bk rev. adv acc. **Circ** 5,150. Technical articles, special columns and news reports pertaining to the plastics industries. *Popular Plastics & Rubber, 0253-7311.*

Political Science

PROCEEDINGS OF THE ANNUAL CONFERENCE - REINFORCED PLASTICS-COMPOSITES INSTITUTE. Main/Corp Reinforced Plastics/ Composites Institute. 0160-9750. US. English. an. Society of Plastics Industry, 355 Lexington Avenue, New York NY 10017. Ind/Abst Chem. Abstr. CODEN PCRPB6.

PROCEEDINGS OF THE CALIFORNIA CONFERENCE ON RUBBER-TOUGHENED PLASTICS. Main/Conf California Conference on Rubber-Toughened Plastics. V. 1-. 0271-9312. US. English. an. $80.00. Carlhaven Corporation, 1457 Firebird Way, Sunnyvale CA 94087. Tel (408)732-5325. Ind/Abst Eng. Index Annu., Eng. Index Mon., Eng. Index Bioeng. Abstr., Eng. Index Energy Abstr., Chem. Abstr. CODEN PCCPDZ.

PROCEEDINGS OF THE WATER-BORNE AND HIGHER-SOLIDS COATINGS SYMPOSIUM. Main/Conf Water-Borne and Higher-Solids Coatings Symposium. 0164-0402. Periodical. US. English. an. $55.00. University of Southern Mississippi, South Street/Box 10076, Department of Polymer Science, Hattiesburg MS 39406-0076. Tel (601)266-4868. Ed Gordon L Nelson, Charles E Hoyle, and Robson F Storey. Ind/ Abst Eng. Index Mon., Eng. Index Bioeng. Abstr., Eng. Index Energy Abstr., Chem. Abstr., Eng. Index Annu., Eng. Index. CODEN PWHSD5. Circ 500. (ctrl) Copies of papers presented at the Water-Borne and Higher-Solids Coatings Symposiums.

PRODUCTION AND SHIPMENTS OF BLOW-MOULDED PLASTIC BOTTLES. V. 1, No. 1 (Quarter ended March 31, 1982)-. 0713-9098. Periodical. CN. English (French). qt. DD 338.47668497. *Production and Shipments of Plastic Bottles, 0713-908X.*

PURASUCHIKKUSU EJI. VFOAT Plastics Age. Began in 1955. 0551-0503. Periodical. JA. Japanese. mo. $70.00. Plastics Age Company Ltd, 10-6 Kajicho 1-chome Chiyoda-ku, Tokyo 101 Japan. Ind/Abst Chem. Abstr. CODEN PLAOAE. (ctrl) Wide coverage, in-depth study of every significant step made forward! A leading trade journal with circulation reaching all corners of our industry.

REINFORCED PLASTICS. Began with Sept. 1956 issue. 0034-3617. Periodical. UK. English. mo. $35.00. McDonald Publishing London Ltd, 238A High Street, Uxbridge Middlesex UB8 1UA England. Tel 0895 30726. Ed D P McDonald. Ind/Abst Ship Abstr., Br. Technol. Index, Chem. Abstr., Predicasts, Funk Scott Index Corp. Ind. LC TA455.P55. DD 668.41605. bk rev. adv acc. Circ 3,000. Descriptions and illustrations of new applications of reinforced plastics in all industries and trades, editorial on techniques of moulding, technical articles.

ROHAGLAS S D P NEWSLETTER. No. 1-Aug. 1975-. 0383-7270. Periodical. CN. English. ir. Chemacryl Plastics, 73 Richmond Street West/Suite 500, Toronto Ontario M5H 2A2 Canada. DD 620.192305.

RUBBER & PLASTICS NEWS. See Rubber.

RUBBER & PLASTICS NEWS II. See Rubber.

SALARY SURVEY. See Economics - Labor.

SCHRIFTENREIHE KUNSTOFF - FORSCHUNG. 0174-4003. Monographic Series. German. ir. Universitatsbibliothek der Technischen Universitat, Berlin Abteilung Publikationen Strasse des 17 Juni 135, 1000 Berlin 12. Ind/Abst Chem. Abstr. CODEN SKFODY.

SOSEI TO KAKO : NIHON SOSEI KAKO GAKKAI SHI. VFOAT Journal of the Japan Society for Technology of Plasticity. Began in 1960. 0038-1586. Periodical. JA. Japanese. mo. Japan Publishers Trading Company Ltd, PO Box 5030, Tokyo International, Tokyo 100-31 Japan. Ind/Abst Met. Abstr., World Alum. Abstr., Chem. Abstr. CODEN SOKAB9. (cum index).

SPI CANADA PROGRAM, ACCOMPLISHMENTS. (SPI CANADA ... PROGRAM, ... ACCOMPLISHMENTS). Main/Corp Society of the Plastics Industry of Canada. VAT Society of the Plastics Industry of Canada Program, Accomplishments. 1981-. 0714-346X. CN. English. an. Society of the Plastics Industry of Canada, Suite 104/ 1262 Don Mills Road, Don Mills Ontario M3B 2W7 Canada. DD 338.766840971.

SPI DIMENSIONS. Main/Corp Society of the Plastics Industry of Canada. VAT Society of the Plastics Industry of Canada Dimensions, Dimensions (Don Mills). Issue 1 (Jan./Mar. 1983)-. 0821-6622. Periodical. CN. English. qt. Society of the Plastics Industry of Canada, Suite 104, 104/1262 Don Mills Road, Don Mills Ontario M3B 2W7 Canada. DD 338.766840971.

STRUCTURAL FOAM PLASTICS. See Yearbooks, Almanacs, Directories.

SYNTHETIC ORGANIC CHEMICALS. UNITED STATES PRODUCTION AND SALES OF PLASTICIZERS. (SYNTHETIC ORGANIC CHEMICALS). VFOAT Plasticizers. Periodical. US. English. an. US International Trade Commission, Washington DC 20436.

TRENDS IN END-USE MARKETS FOR PLASTICS. VFOAT End-Use Markets for Plastics. 0013-7154. US. English. mo. $335.00. Springborn Laboratories, 20 Water Street, Enfield CT 06082. Tel (203)749-8371. LC HD9661.A1. DD 338.456684. CODEN TEUMA. (cum index).

U.S. FOAMED PLASTICS MARKETS & DIRECTORY. See Yearbooks, Almanacs, Directories.

URETHANE ABSTRACTS. V. 1- Jan. 1972-. 0149-1342. US. English. mo. $105.00. Technomic Publishing Company Inc, 851 New Holland Avenue/ Box 3535, Lancaster PA 17604. Tel (717)291-5609. LC TP1180.P8. DD 668.423. CODEN URABB. Circ 225. Digest of current literature and patents on urethanes including technical, market, business, regulatory, and fire safety developments.

URETHANE PLASTICS AND PRODUCTS. Began with Jan. 1970 issue. 0049-5700. Periodical. US. English. mo. $85.00. Technomic Publishing Company, 851 New Holland Avenue, Box 3535, Lancaster PA 17604. Tel (717)291-5609. Ind/Abst Predicasts, Funk Scott Index Corp. Ind. LC TP1180.P8. DD 668.423. Circ 250. News and information on the urethane industry. New developments in urethane chemicals, market trends, regulatory/legal actions and technology.

VISION. V. 1- Spring 1969-. 0382-0424. Periodical. CN. Vol. 1, Nos. 1-2 have text in French and English. Association de Professeurs d'Arts Plastiques du Quebec, CP 424 Station Youville, Montreal Quebec H2P 2V6 Canada.

POLITICAL SCIENCE

25 I.E. VINTE E CINCO DE SETEMBRO. Periodical. Portuguese. ir. $15.00. Comissariado Politico das FRLM, Avenida Patrice Lamumba N 448, Maputo Portugal. LC DT463. DD 320.967903.

ABC POL SCI. See Bibliographies.

ACARI INDEX. See Indexes/Abstracts.

ACCESS REPORTS CEASED. VFOAT Access Reports/FOI Newsletter. V. 1- June 16, 1975-. 0364-7625. Periodical. US. English. bw. $189.00. The Washington Monitor Inc, 499 National Press Building, Washington DC 20045. LC JK468.S4. DD 323.4450973.

ACCESS REPORTS. (ACCESS REPORTS/ FREEDOM OF INFORMATION). VFOAT Access Reports. 0364-7625. US. English. bw. $200.00. Washington Monitor, 1301 Pennsylvania Avenue NW/ Suite 1000, Washington DC 20004. Tel (202)347-7757. Ed Deborah Drosnin. LC JK468.S4. DD 323.4450973. *Access Reports, 0364-7625.*

ACCIAIO. N. 1- Oct. 1976-. Periodical. IT. Italian. mo. CISIA, Pizaaz Velasca 8, 20122 Milano Italy. LC JN5657.R5.

ACCOMPLISHMENTS OF THE COMMITTEE ON INTERIOR AND INSULAR AFFAIRS OF THE HOUSE OF REPRESENTATIVES DURING THE . . . CONGRESS. Main/Corp United States. Congress. House. Committee on Interior and Insular Affairs. Periodical. US. English. be. US Government Printing Office, Superintendent of Documents, Washington DC 20402. LC JK1430.I53.

ACCOUNTS, TREASURER'S AND AUDITORS' REPORTS. Main/Corp Amnesty International. UK. English. an. Amnesty International Publications, 10 Southampton Street, London WC2E England. LC JC571. DD 323.490601.

ACHIEVEMENTS. See Economics - Labor.

ACIR STATE LEGISLATIVE PROGRAM. Main/Corp United States. Advisory Commission on Intergovernmental Relations. 1969-. US. English. an. 1701 Pennsylvania Avenue NW, Washington DC 20575. DD 352. *State Legislative Program of the Advisory Commission on Intergovernmental Relations, 0503-4744.*

ACTA POLITICA. Vol. 1- 1965/66-. 0001-6810. Periodical. NE. Dutch (summaries in English). qt. $40.61. Boomen Zoon, Postbus 58, Meppel Netherlands. Ed K Koch. Ind/Abst Sociol. Abstr., ABC Pol Sci, Am. Hist. Life, Hist. Abstr., Part A, Mod. Hist. Abstr., Hist. Abst., Part B, Twent. Century Abstr., Lang. Lang. Behav. Abstr., Hist. Abstr. bk rev. adv acc. Circ 800. Journal for political scientists, politicians, sociologists, and civil and federal administrators.

ACTAS Y DOCUMENTOS - ORGANIZATION OF AMERICAN STATES. GENERAL ASSEMBLY. Series Corp Organization of American States. Documentos Oficiales. 1- Peropdp Extraordinario de Sesiones. Periodical. US. Spanish. OAS, 1889 F Street Northwest, Washington DC 20006. LC F1402.

ADA WORLD. V. 1- Mar. 29, 1947-. 0001-0871. Periodical. US. English. qt $10.00. Americans for Democratic Action, 1411 K Street NW/Suite 850, Washington DC 20005. Tel (202)638-6447. Ed Stina Santiestevan. LC E740. DD 973.918, 973.92. Circ 80,000. Available on Microfilm. A quarterly newsletter covering the public policy concerns of ADA, liberal political action organization formed in 1947.

ADLIB. (ADLIB : A PUBLICATION OF THE LIBERAL PARTY OF CANADA). Vol. 1, No. 1 (Oct. 1979)-. 0229-3072. Periodical. CN. English (with French text on inverted pages, Oct. 1979-). Free. Liberal Party, 102 Bank Street, Ottawa Ontario K1P 5N4 Canada. DD 324.27106005. (ctrl). *Dialogue Newsletter, 0229-3080; Dialogue Bulletin, 0229-3064.*

ADMINISTRATIVE CODE COMMITTEE BIENNIAL REPORT TO THE . . . LEGISLATURE. Main/Corp Montana. Legislative Assembly. Administrative Code Committee. US. English. be. Montana Legislative Council, State Capitol/Room 138, Helena MT 59620. LC KFM9011.6. DD 328.78607658. *Biennial Report to the Legislature.*

ADVERTENTIEBLAD VAN DE REPUBLIEK SURINAME. Main/Corp Surinam. Dutch. ir. 25.00. Uitgeverij DAG, Gravenstraat 120, Paramaribo Surinam. LC J3.

AFRICA. No. 1- May 1971-. 0044-6475. Periodical. UK. English. mo. $76.63. Africa Journal Limited, Kirkman House 54A Tottenham Crt Rd, London W1P 0BT England. Tel 01-637-9341. Ed Raph Uwechue. Ind/Abst Soc. Sci. Index, Public Aff. Inf. Serv. Bull., Women Stud. Abstr., MLA Int. Bibliogr. Books Artic. Mod. Lang. Lit. LC HF46. DD 309.1603. bk rev. adv acc. Circ 90,270. Available on microfilm. Oldest pan-African English monthly presenting African affairs from African viewpoint unbiased objective news and views on rapidly changing political and economic scene in Africa.

AFRICA COMMENTARY. 8755-027X. Periodical. US. English. qt. $85.00. Baywood Publishing Company, 120 Marine Street, Farmingdale NY 11735. Tel (516)249-2464. Ed Daniel G Matthews. bk rev. A prominent international affairs forum, independent of any government, partisan, religious or social pressures, inviting a diversity of independent non-polemic comments.

AFRICAN AFFAIRS. V. 43- (No. 172-). 0001-9909. Periodical. UK. English. ir. Oxford University Press, 16-00 Pollitt Drive, Fair Lawn NJ 07410. Tel 0865/56767. Ind/Abst Humanit. Index, Am. Hist. Life, Hist. Abstr., Part A, Mod. Hist. Abstr., Hist. Abst., Part B, Twent. Century Abstr., Int. Labour Doc., Ref. Source, Soc. Welf. Soc. Plan./Policy Soc. Dev., Sociol. Abstr., Soc. Sci. Citation Index. LC DT1. DD 960.05. Available on Microfilm. *Journal of the Royal African Society.*

THE AFRICAN REVIEW. V. 1- Mar. 1971-. 0002-0117. TZ. English. sa. $28.00. University of Dar es Salaam, Department of Political Science, PO Box 35042, Dar es Salaam Tanzania. Tel 48252. Ed

Political Science

Ibrahim Msabaha. **Ind/Abst** Am. Hist. Life, Hist. Abstr., Part A, Mod. Hist. Abstr., Hist. Abst., Part B, Twent. Century Abstr., ABC Pol Sci, Int. Labour Doc., Public Aff. Inf. Serv. Bull., Hist. Abstr. **LC** DT31. **DD** 320.9603. bk rev. adv acc. **Circ** 1,000. (ctrl). Mainly the journal is concerned with African political science studies, development and international studies.

AGAINST THE CURRENT. Vol. 1, No. 1 (Fall 1980)-. 0739-4853. Periodical. US. English. qt. $24.00. Against the Current, 45 West 10th Street/Apartment 2G, New York NY 10011. **Tel** (212)777-1882. **Ed** Johanna Brenner, Robert Brenner, Samuel Farber, Nancy Holmstrom, Charles Post, Peter Drucker, and Michael Wunsch. **Ind/Abst** Altern. Press Index. bk rev. adv acc. **Circ** 3,000. Dialogue: among sectors of the revolutionary left: strategic analyses of working class and liberation movement struggles, east and west.

AGENDA FOR CITIZEN INVOLVEMENT (NEW YORK, N.Y.). (AGENDA FOR CITIZEN INVOLVEMENT). **VFOAT** Agenda. V. 1, No. 1-. 0745-368X. Periodical. US. English. bm. $15.00. NYPIRG, 9 Murray Street, New York NY 10007. **Tel** (212)349-6460. **Ed** Rachel Burd. bk rev. **Circ** 30,000. (ctrl). Articles on the environment, consumer affairs, political reform and particularly how these areas are addressed by New York's state and local governments.

AGYPTEN, FORSCHUNGSPOLITIK UND FORSCHUNGSPRAXIS. Series/Titl Marktinformation. GW. German. ir. 3.00. Bundesstelle fur Aussenhandelsinformation, Blaubach 13 Postfach 10 80 07, D-5000 Koln 1 West Germany.

AKTUELLE BEITRAGE DER STAATS- UND RECHTSWISSENSCHAFT. See Law.

AL-DIBLUMASI. VFOAT Diplomat. Arabic. mo. Wizarat Al-Kharijiyah, Dawlat Al-Imarat Al-Arabiyah, Abu Zaby United Arab Emirates. **LC** D839.

AL-GHAD AL-ARABI CEASED. (AL-GHAD AL-ARABI. AL-GHAD AL-ARABI). V. 1- Aug. 1978-. 0709-8898. Periodical. CN. Arabic (includes some text in English). mo. $.75 Per No. Al-Ghad Al-Arabi, 200 Gateway Boulevard, Don Mills Ontario M3C 1B5 Canada. **DD** 320.9174927.

AL-HUKM AL-SHABI AL-MAHALLI. Arabic or English. ir. 3.00. Wizarat Al-Hukumah Al-Mahalliyah, B P 597, Al-Khartum Sudan. **LC** JS7819.A1.

AL-NAHAR. AL-KITAB AL-SANAWI. 1974-. UA. Arabic. da. $300.00. Al-Ahram, Galaa Street, Cairo Egypt. **LC** D2.

AL-NAZEER. 0749-7415. Periodical. US. in English. Mujahed, c/o Mansour, PO Box 242, Clawson MI 48017. **DD** 323.

AL-SIYASAH AL-DAWLIYAH. V. 1- (No. 1-). 0583-4597. Periodical. UA. Arabic. qt. Al Ahram, Galaa Street, Cairo Egypt. **Ed** Butrus Ghali. **LC** D839.

AL-SIYASAH WA-AL-ISTRATIJIYAH. VFOAT Majallat Assiyasa Walistratigia. Journal 1, No. 3, (May 1983)-. Periodical. Arabic. qt. 1.00 Single Issue. S B 1850, Khartoum Sudan. **LC** JA26. Majallat Al-Siyasah Wa-Al-Istratijiyah.

AL-TALIAH; SIYASIYAH USBUIYAH. ATTALIAH WEEKLY. VFOAT Attaliah Weekly. Periodical. IS. Arabic. ir. 275.00, 200.00 Students. Shari Ibn Sina, PO Box 19372, Al-Quds Jerusalem. **LC** DS127.6.O3.

ALASKA DATA INVENTORY CATALOG. 1978-. US. English. an. Alaska State Library, Pouch G, Juneau AK 99811. **LC** Z1223.5, J87.A4. **DD** 015.798.

ALBANIA TODAY. V. 1- Nov./Dec. 1971-. 0044-7072. Periodical. AA. English. bm. $5.50. Drejtoria Qendrore Perhapjes, Ruga Knoferenca e Pezes, Tirana Albania. **LC** JN9689.A8. **DD** 320.9496503.

ALBERTA DEMOCRAT. (THE ALBERTA DEMOCRAT). V. 1- Mar. 1967-. 0382-4578. Periodical. CN. English. bm. $17.41. Alberta New Democratic Party, 5339 112 Avenue, Edmonton Alberta T5W 0N6 Canada. **Tel** (403)474-2415. **Ed** Rici Lake. **DD** 329.9'7123. bk rev. adv acc. **Circ** 8,000. Official organ of the Alberta New Democratic Party (NDP). News and features from an Albertan Democratic Socialist perspective. Information on NDP events and policies.

ALLAM- ES JOGTUDOMANY. See Law.

THE ALMANAC OF AMERICAN POLITICS. See Yearbooks, Almanacs, Directories.

THE ALMANAC OF VIRGINIA POLITICS. See Yearbooks, Almanacs, Directories.

ALTERNATIVE MEDIA. 1975. 0730-1766. Periodical. US. English. qt. $15.00. Alternative Press Syndicate, Box 1347 Ansonia Station, Manhattan NY 10023. **Tel** (212)974-1990. **Ed** R J Smith. **Ind/Abst** Altern. Press Index. bk rev. adv acc. **Circ** 5,000. Media issues and criticism, frequently spotlighting journalists and artists outside the mainstrea. Features and reviews with a commitment to progressive ideals.

AMERICA AND THE WORLD (PERGAMON PRESS). (AMERICA AND THE WORLD). **Series/Titl** Pergamon Policy Studies. Began in 1978. 0743-5819. US. English. an. $6.95. Pergamon Press, 395 Sawmill River Road, Elmsford NY 10523. **LC** E840. **DD** 327.73.

AMERICA VOTES. Began in 1956. 0065-678X. US. English. be. $75.00. Congressional Quarterly, 1414 22nd Street NW, Washington DC 20037. **Tel** (202)887-8584. **LC** JK1967. **DD** 324.973092, 324.73.

AMERICAN GOVERNMENT. VFOAT Annual Editions. 10th Ed., (1980-81)-. US. English. an. $8.95. Dushkin Publishing Group, Sluice Dock, Guilford CT 06437. **Tel** (203)453-4351. **Ed** Bruce Stinebrickner. **LC** JK1. **DD** 320.97305. Annually updated collection of public press articles covering current issues in American government. Includes topic guide and complete index. Annual Editions. Readings in American Government.

AMERICAN GOVERNMENT. TEXT. (AMERICAN GOVERNMENT : TEXT). 1973/74-. 0090-547X. US. English. Dushkin Publishing Group, Sluice Dock, Guilford CT 06437. **LC** JK8. **DD** 320.473.

AMERICAN JOURNAL OF POLITICAL SCIENCE. V. 17- Feb. 1973-. 0092-5853. Periodical. US. English. qt. $36.00. University of Texas Press, Box 7819 University Station, Austin TX 78712. **Tel** (512)471-4531. **Ed** Robert Erikson. **Ind/Abst** Soc. Sci. Citation Index, Sociol. Abstr., ABC Pol Sci, Am. Hist. Life, Hist. Abstr., Part A, Mod. Hist. Abstr., Hist. Abst., Part B, Twent. Century Abstr., Soc. Sci. Citation Index, Lang. Lang. Behav. Abstr., Hist. Abstr. **LC** JA1. **DD** 320.05. adv acc. **Circ** 2,800. (ctrl). Presents up-to-date academic research in American politics and methodology and publishes articles on international and comparative politics. Midwest Journal of Political Science, 0026-3397.

THE AMERICAN POLITICAL SCIENCE REVIEW. V. 1- Nov. 1906-. 0003-0554. Periodical. US. English. qt. **Tel** (202)483-2512. **Ind/Abst** Energy Inf. Abstr., Environ. Abstr., ABC Pol Sci, Index Econ. Artic. J. Collect. Vol., Recent Publ. Artic., Book Rev. Index, Ref. Source, Soc. Work Res. Abstr., Int. Index, Public Aff. Inf. Serv. Bull., Soc. Sci. Index, Humanit. Index, Soc. Sci. Index, Am. Hist. Life, Writ. Am. Hist., Hist. Abstr., Part A, Mod. Hist. Abstr. **LC** JA1. **DD** 320.05. (cum index). World's leading scholarly journal in the field of political science. Contains articles, review essays and book reviews in all fields of political science.

AMERICAN POLITICS QUARTERLY. V. 1- Jan. 1973-. 0044-7803. Periodical. US. English. qt. Sage Publications Inc, 275 South Beverly Drive, Beverly Hills CA 90212. **Tel** (213)274-8003. **Ind/Abst** Am. Hist. Life, Hist. Abstr., Part A, Mod. Hist. Abstr., Hist. Abst., Part B, Twent. Century Abstr., ABC Pol Sci, Writ. Am. Hist., Public Aff. Inf. Serv. Bull., Soc. Sci. Citation Index, Sociol. Abstr., Lang. Lang. Behav. Abstr., Hist. Abstr. **LC** JK1. **DD** 320.973092.

AMERICAN POLITICS (WASHINGTON, D.C. : 1983). (AMERICAN POLITICS). V. 1, No. 1 (Nov. 1983)-. 0741-1111. Periodical. US. English. mo. American Politics Inc, 810 18th Street/Suite 802, Washington DC 20006. **Tel** (202)347-1100.

AMERICAN POLITICS YEARBOOK. See Yearbooks, Almanacs, Directories.

AMERICAN SENTINEL (WASHINGTON, D.C.). (THE AMERICAN SENTINEL). Issue #266 (Sept. 7, 1981)-. 0278-0585. Periodical. US. English. bw. $57.00. Phillips Publishing Company, 7315 Wisonsin Avenue/Suite 1200-N, Washington DC 20814. **Tel** (301)986-0666. **LC** HN90.R3. **DD** 322.40973. Pink Sheet on the Left, 0048-4180.

THE AMERICAN STATESMEN'S YEARBOOK : FROM OFFICIAL REPORTS OF THE UNITED STATES GOVERNMENT, STATE REPORTS, CONSULAR ADVICES, AND FOREIGN DOCUMENTS. See Yearbooks, Almanacs, Directories.

AMERICA'S FUTURE. Began publication in 1959?. 0003-1593. Periodical. US. English. bw. Americas Future, 514 Main Street, New Rochelle NY 10802. **Tel** (914)234-6000. **Ed** John C Wetzel. bk rev. **Circ** 13,000. A review of news and public affairs supporting the free enterprise system and constitutional form of government.

AMPO. Began with Nov. 1969 issue. Periodical. English. qt. $24.00. Ampo, Box 5250, Tokyo International Japan. **Tel** (03)291-5901. **Ed** Reiko Inove. **Ind/Abst** Int. Labour Doc. **LC** HQ799.J3. **DD** 322.4205. adv acc. **Circ** 3,000. Asia's contemporary history is being recorded by those who are making it. Contains articles on politics, economics, culture and people's movements in Japan.

AMTLICHES BULLETIN DER BUNDESVERSAMMLUNG. Main/Corp Switzerland. Bundesversammlung. Nationalrat. **VFOAT** Bulletin Officiel de l'Assemblee Federale. French and German. ir. 50.00. Bundesversammbung, Maulbeerstrasse 10, 3000 Bern Switzerland. **LC** J415. Amtliches Stenographisches Bulletin.

ANALES - ACADEMIA NACIONAL DE CIENCIAS MORALES Y POLITICAS. See Yearbooks, Almanacs, Directories.

ANALES DE LA REAL ACADEMIA DE CIENCIAS MORALES Y POLITICAS. See Yearbooks, Almanacs, Directories.

ANALES PARLAMENTARIOS. See Yearbooks, Almanacs, Directories.

ANALISIS POLITICO. Began in 1972. 0185-0040. Periodical. MX. Spanish. mo. $50.00. Jose M Velasco 110-104, Mexico 19 DF Mexico. **LC** JL1281. **DD** 320.97205.

ANNALES DE DROIT CEASED. V. 24 I.E. 25 1-V. 40, 4. Periodical. BE. French. qt. J Goemaere, 21 rue de la Limite, B1030 Bruxelles Belgium. Annales de Droit et des Sciences Politiques.

ANNALES PARLEMENTAIRES. PARLEMENTAIRE HANDELINGEN. Main/Corp Belgium. Parlement. Senat. **VFOAT** Parlementaire Handelingen. BE. French (Dutch). $9.88. Moniteur Belge, rue de Louvain 40-42, 1000 Bruxelles Belgium. **LC** J393. Annales Parlementaires.

ANNALI DELLA FACOLTA DI SCIENZE POLITICHE. Main/Corp Pisa. Universita. Facolta di Scienze Politiche. 1- 1971-. 0302-4431. Italian. ir. 5000. **LC** JA18. **DD** 320.05.

ANNALI DELLA FACOLTA DI SCIENZE POLITICHE (TRIESTE, ITALY). (ANNALI DELLA FACOLTA DI SCIENZE POLITICHE). 1980, 1 V.-. Periodical. IT. English (French and Italian). bm. A Giuffre Editore, Via Statuto 2, 20121 Milano Italy. **LC** JA18. **DD** 320.05.

THE ANNALS OF THE AMERICAN ACADEMY OF POLITICAL AND SOCIAL SCIENCE. Main/Corp American Academy of Political And Social Science. V. 1- July 1890-. 0002-7162. Periodical. US. English. bm. Sage Publications, 275 South Beverly Drive, Beverly Hills CA 90212. **Tel** (213)274-8003. **Ind/Abst** Ind. Arts Index, Pooles Index Period. Lit., Public Aff. Inf. Serv. Bull., Read. Guide Period. Lit., Soc. Sci. Index.

ANNEE POLITIQUE ET ECONOMIQUE AFRICAINE (SOCIETE AFRICAINE D'EDITION : 1981). (L'ANNEE POLITIQUE ET ECONOMIQUE AFRICAINE). 1981-. French. an. $66.52. Societe Africaine D'Edition, BP 1877, Dakar Senegal. Annee Politique Africaine (Societe Africaine d'Edition : 1970), Economie Africaine en . . . .

ANNUAIRE PARIS & I.E. ET REGION. See Yearbooks, Almanacs, Directories.

ANNUAIRE SUISSE DE SCIENCE POLITIQUE. See Yearbooks, Almanacs, Directories.

ANNUAIRE TOURISTIQUE ET DIPLOMATIQUE DU CAMEROUN. See Yearbooks, Almanacs, Directories.

Political Science

ANNUAL DEPARTMENTAL REPORT - HONG KONG. Main/Corp HongKong. HongKong Government Office in London. English. ir. $12.00. Government Printer Hong Kong Government Office in London, Java Road, Hong Kong. LC J613. DD 354.51250082.

ANNUAL EDITIONS : READINGS IN AMERICAN GOVERNMENT. Periodical. US. English. an. Dushkin Publishing Company, Sluice Dock, Guilford CT 06437. Tel (203)453-4351.

THE ANNUAL INSIDER INDEX TO PUBLIC POLICY STUDIES. See Indexes/Abstracts.

THE ANNUAL REGISTER OF INDIAN POLITICAL PARTIES. V. 1- 1972/73-. II. English. ir. 140.00. H S, 30 Kailash Colony Market, New Delhi 110048 India. LC JQ298.A1. DD 329.954.

ANNUAL REPORT - AMERICAN COMMITTEE ON AFRICA. (ANNUAL REPORT). Main/Corp American Committee on Africa. 0743-1287. US. English. an. American Committee on Africa, 198 Broadway, New York NY 10038. LC DT1. DD 320.96006073.

ANNUAL REPORT - AMERICAN LEGISLATIVE EXCHANGE COUNCIL. (ANNUAL REPORT). Main/Corp American Legislative Exchange Council. 0737-0504. US. English. an. American Legislative Exchange Council, 418 C Street NE, Washington DC 20002. LC JK2430. DD 328.306073.

ANNUAL REPORT - AUSTRALIAN INDUSTRY DEVELOPMENT CORPORATION. Main/Corp Australian Industry Development Corporation. AT. English. ir. $0.30. Commonwealth Government Printing Office, PO Box 84, Canberra ACT 2600 Australia. LC J905. DD 328.9401 S, 338.0994.

ANNUAL REPORT - BETTER GOVERNMENT ASSOCIATION. Main/Corp Better Government Association (Ill.). 0194-3715. US. English. an. Better Government Association, 230 North Michigan Avenue, Chicago IL 60601. LC JK5745. DD 320.977305.

ANNUAL REPORT - DEPARTMENT OF JUSTICE (SOUTH AFRICA). Main/Corp South Africa. Dept. of Justice. VFOAT Jaarverslag - Departement Van Justisie. SA. Afrikaans and English. ir. 1.65. The Government Printer, Bosman Street, Private Bag X85, Pretoria 0001 South Africa. LC J705.

ANNUAL REPORT - FLORIDA COMMISSION ON HUMAN RELATIONS. Main/Corp Florida. Commission on Human Relations. 0147-5584. US. English. an. 2571 Executive Center Circle East, Tallahassee FL 32301. LC JC599.U5. DD 353.975900996.

ANNUAL REPORT FOR THE YEAR ENDING 31ST DECEMBER - UNITED NATIONAL INDEPENDENCE PARTY (ZAMBIA). Main/Corp United National Independence Party (Zambia). Office of the Member of the Central Committee (Luapula Province, Zambia). VFOAT Luapula Province Annual Report. English. an. Office of the Member of the Central Committee UNIP, PO Box 65, Manss Luapula Zambia. LC J725.3. DD 354.6894.

ANNUAL REPORT - MISSOURI ELECTIONS COMMISSION. Main/Corp Missouri. Elections Commission. 0149-2403. US. English. an. Missouri Elections Commission, 631 West Main Street, Jefferson City MO 65101. LC KFM8220.85.C2. DD 353.9778091.

ANNUAL REPORT - OFFICE OF THE SECRETARY OF STATE (TEXAS). Main/Corp Texas. Secretary of State. 0160-1520. US. English. Secretary of State, Capitol Station, Austin TX 78711. LC J87. DD 353.97641.

ANNUAL REPORT ON THE ACTIVITIES OF THE INDEPENDENT COMMISSION AGAINST CORRUPTION (HONGKONG). Main/Corp HongKong. Independent Commission Against Corruption. VFOAT Tsung Tu Te Pai Lien Cheng Chuan Yuan Kung Shu Kung Tso Nien Pao. 1974-. Chinese and English. ir. $3.50. The Secretary to the Independent Commission Against Corruption, Hutchinson House 6th Floor, Hong Kong. LC JQ675.A55. DD 354.512500995.

ANNUAL REPORT - SNOWY MOUNTAINS ENGINEERING CORPORATION. Main/Corp Snowy Mountains Engineering Corporation. AT. English. ir. $0.50. Commonwealth Government Printing Office, PO Box 84, Canberra Australian Capital Territory 2600 Australia. LC J905, TA217.S6. DD 328.9401 S, 338. 761658460994.

ANNUAL REPORT - UNIVERSITY OF SOUTH CAROLINA. BUREAU OF GOVERNMENTAL RESEARCH AND SERVICE. Main/Corp University of South Carolina. Bureau of Governmental Research and Service. US. English. an. University of South Carolina, Bureau of Governmental Research and Service, Columbia SC 29208. LC JA89.S56. DD 300.72075771.

ANNUAL REPORT - WEST TEXAS COUNCIL OF GOVERNMENTS. Main/Corp West Texas Council of Governments. US. English. an. West Texas Council of Governments, Mills Building/Suite 700, El Paso TX 79901. LC HC107.T4. DD 352.076493.

THE ANNUAL STATISTICAL REPORT OF EXPENDITURES MADE IN CONNECTION WITH ELECTIONS (MISSOURI). See Statistics.

ANNUARIO POLITICO. See Yearbooks, Almanacs, Directories.

A.P.E.P. (ENGLISH EDITION). (A.P.E.P). No. 78 (Apr. 1, 1976)-. Periodical. CN. English. ir. $4.00. National Publications Centre, PO Box 727, Adelaide Station, Toronto Ontario M5C 2J9 Canada. DD 320.946.

APPEARANCES OF SOVIET LEADERS. 0145-0700. US. English. an. Document Expediting (Docex) 20, National Technical Information Service, 5285 Port Royal Road, Springfield VA 22161. LC JN6521. DD 354.47002. Vols. for Jan.-Dec. 1981- distributed to depository libraries in microfiche.

THE APS REVIEW. Main/Corp Georgetown University, Washington, D.D. Graduate School. Academy in the Public Service. V. 1- Spring 1978-. US. English. ty. $10.00. Academy in the Public Service, Georgetown University/Graduate School, 2135 Wisconsin Avenue Northwest/Suite 403, Washington DC 20007. LC JS39. DD 320.

A.P.S.A. DEPARTMENTAL SERVICES PROGRAM. SURVEY OF DEPARTMENTS. (APSA DEPARTMENTAL SERVICES PROGRAM, SURVEY OF DEPARTMENTS). Main/Corp American Political Science Association. 0094-7954. US. English. an. $20.00. American Political Science Association, 1527 New Hampshire Avenue NW, Washington DC 20036. Tel (202)483-2512. LC JA28. DD 320.071173. adv acc. Circ 800. (ctrl). Report of extensive questionnaire sent to departments of political science. Includes salary information, enrollment trends, etc.

APSA DIRECTORY OF DEPARTMENT CHAIRPERSONS. See Yearbooks, Almanacs, Directories.

APSA DIRECTORY OF MEMBERS. See Yearbooks, Almanacs, Directories.

AR STAATKUNDE IN CHRISTEN-DEMOCRATISCH PERSPECTIEF. Periodical. Dutch. ir. 40.00. Dr A Kuyerstichting, Postbus 130, Kampen Netherlands. LC JA26. Antirevolutionaire Staatkunde.

ARAB-ASIAN AFFAIRS. VAT Arab Asian Affairs. No. 84- Jan. 1980-. 0196-3538. Periodical. UK. English. mo. $135.00 US. World Reports Limited, 108 Horseferry Road, London SW1P 2EF England. Tel 01-222-3836. Afro-Asian Affairs, 0163-819X.

ARCHIV DES OFFENTLICHEN RECHTS. See Genealogy and Heraldry - Archives.

ASIA YEARBOOK. See Yearbooks, Almanacs, Directories.

ASIAN AFFAIRS. (ASIAN AFFAIRS, AN AMERICAN REVIEW). V. 1- Sept./Oct. 1973-. 0092-7678. Periodical. US. English. qt. $45.00. Heldref Publications, 4000 Albemarle Street NW/Suite 302, Washington DC 20016. Tel (202)362-6445. Ed Barbara Kahn. Ind/Abst Am. Hist. Life, ABC Pol Sci, Public Aff. Inf. Serv. Bull., Hist. Abstr., Part A, Mod. Hist. Abstr., Recent Publ. Artic., Hist. Abst., Part B, Twent. Century Abstr., Hist. Abstr. LC DS33.4.U6. DD 327.5073. adv acc. Circ 416. Focuses on United States policy in Asia, as well as on domestic politics, economics, and international relations of the Asian countries from Japan to Afghanistan. Southeast Asian Perspectives, 0042-577X.

ASIAN OUTLOOK. Vol. 1, No. 1 (Aug. 1965)-. 0004-4628. Periodical. CH. English. mo. $10.00. Asian Outlook, PO Box 22992, Taipei Taiwan Republic of China. Tel (02)341-7027. Ed Joseph Yu-Jui Ku. Ind/Abst Public Aff. Inf. Serv. Bull. LC DS1. DD 950.05. Circ 21,000. (ctrl). Editorial, commentaries, inside mainland China report, etc., all Anti-Communist oriented. Free China and Asia.

ASPECTS DE LA FRANCE. 1.- Year. Periodical. FR. French. ir. $66.52. Aspects de la France, 10 rue Croix des Petits Champs, Paris 75001 France. Tel (1)42 96 1206. Ed Sniep. LC AP20. DD 054.1. bk rev. adv acc. Circ 30,000. Political analysis of politics, events and monarchy promotion.

ASSOCIATION PARLEMENTAIRE DU COMMONWEALTH. CONFERENCE REGIONALE CANADIENNE CEASED. (CONFERENCE REGIONALE CANADIENNE). Main/Corp Association des Parlementaires du Commonwealth. Conference Regionale Canadienne. 0708-7659. CN. French. an. Association des Parlementaires du Commonwealth, CP 950-EC Edifices du Parlement, Ottawa Ontario K1A 0A6 Canada. DD 328.306071.

ATLANTIC REPORT (NEW DEMOCRATIC PARTY). (ATLANTIC REPORT). No. 4 (Spring 1982)-. 0824-3743. Periodical. CN. English. ir. Free. New Democratic Party, House of Commons, Ottawa Ontario K1A 0A6 Canada. DD 330.971504. NDP Atlantic Report, 0824-3751.

AURORA SOCIAL. No. 1- Jan. 1965-. Periodical. Spanish. ir.

AUSSENPOLITIK (ENGLISH EDITION). (AUSSENPOLITIK). Began in 1970. 0587-3835. Periodical. GW. English. qt. 50.00. Interpress Verlag GMBH, Holsteinischer Kamp 14, D2000 Hamburg 76 West Germany. Tel 040/2290609. Ind/Abst ABC Pol Sci, Foreign Lang. Index, Recent Publ. Artic., Writ. Am. Hist., Soc. Sci. Citation Index, Am. Hist. Life, Hist. Abstr., PAIS Foreign Lang. Index. LC D839. DD 327.105. bk rev. adv acc. Circ 7,000. German foreign affairs review.

AUSSENPOLITIK KOMMUNISTISCHER LANDER UND DRITTE WELT. 1980/1-1981/2. Periodical. GW. German. mo. $31.20. Verlag Neue Gesellschaft GMBH, Godesberger Allee 143, D5300 Bonn 2 West Germany. Entwicklungspolitik Kommunistischer Lander.

THE AUSTRALIAN JOURNAL OF POLITICS AND HISTORY. V. 1- Nov. 1955-. 0004-9522. Periodical. AT. English. ty. $39.72. University of Queensland Press, PO Box 42, St Lucia Queensland 4067 Australia. Tel 3772438. Ed John A Moses. Ind/Abst Am. Hist. Life, Hist. Abstr., Part A, Mod. Hist. Abstr., Hist. Abst., Part B, Twent. Century Abstr., Sociol. Abstr., Soc. Welf. Soc. Plan./Policy Soc. Dev., ABC Pol Sci, Hist. Abstr., Writ. Am. Hist., APAIS, Aust. Public Aff. Inf. Serv., Soc. Sci. Citation Index, Lang. Lang. Behav. Abstr., Recent Publ. Artic. LC DU80. bk rev. Circ 1,000. History and political theory of Australia and overseas. Regular articles on Australian foreign policy and a political chronicle of both state and federal Australian politics.

AUSTRALIEN, FORSCHUNGSPOLITIK UND FORSCHUNGSPRAXIS. Series/Titl Marktinformation. GW. German. an. 3.00. Bundesstelle fur Aussenhandelsinformation, Blaubach 13, Postfach 10 80 07, D-5000 Koln 1 West Germany.

EIN AUSZUG AUS DEN TATIGKEITSBERICHTEN DER GRUPPEN UND ABTEILUNGEN DES AMTES DER NO LANDESREGIERUNG. Main/Corp Lower Austria (Austria). VFOAT Agenden Aktivitaten. German. an. Herrengasse 11-13, 1014 Wien Austria. LC J314. DD 354.436120005.

BALLOT BILLBOARD. V. 1-. Periodical. US. English. mo. New York State Board of Elections, Empire State Plaza Agency Building 2, Albany NY 12223.

BANGLADESH POLITICS. Vol. 1-. Periodical. English. an. $6.00 US. Centre for Social Studies, Room No 1107 Arts Building Dacca University, Dacca-2 Bangladesh. LC DS393. DD 320.95492.

THE BARON REPORT. No. 1- Sept. 14, 1976-. 0363-549X. Periodical. US. English. bw. $125.00. Baron Report, 910 Independence Avenue SE, Washington DC 20003. Tel (202)543-7007. Ed Alan J Baron. Circ 1,800. In depth analysis of the American political scene. Considered essential reading for liberals and conservatives by the Washington Post.

Political Science

BEFREIUNG. No. 1- 1973-. Periodical. GW. German. qt. Redaktion Befreiung, Martin-Lutherstrasse 78, 1 Berlin 62 West Germany. LC JA14. DD 320.05.

BEITRAGE ZUR GESCHICHTE DES PARLAMENTARISMUS UND DER POLITISCHEN PARTEIEN. No. 1-. 0522-6643. Monographic Series. GW. German. ir. Droste Verlag, Postfach 1122, D-4000 Dusseldorf Germany.

BEITRAGE ZUR POLITISCHEN WISSENSCHAFT. V. 1-. 0582-0421. Monographic Series. GW. German. ir. Duncker Und Humblot Verlag, Dietrich-Schafer-Weg 9, 1000 Berlin 41 West Germany.

BIBLIOGRAPHIES AND INDEXES IN LAW AND POLITICAL SCIENCE. See Indexes/Abstracts.

BIENNIAL REPORT - BUREAU OF GOVERNMENTAL RESEARCH AND SERVICE. Main/Corp University of Oregon. Bureau of Governmental Research and Service. US. English. be. LC JS303.O7.

BIENNIAL REPORT - STATE OF FLORIDA DEPARTMENT OF STATE. Main/Corp Florida. Department of State. 0099-1600. US. English. be. Florida Department of State, Tallahassee FL 32301. LC J87. DD 353.97593. Biennial Report - Secretary of State.

BIPAC ACTION REPORT. Main/Corp Business-Industry Political Action Committee. Political Action Division. VFOAT Action Report. 0272-1694. Periodical. US. English. qt. $1.00. Business-Industry Political Action Committee Political Education Division, 1747 Pennsylvania Avenue Northwest, Washington DC 20006.

BIPAC POLITICS. (POLITICS). VAT Business-Industry Political Action Committee Politics. V. 1- Nov./Dec. 1964-. 0032-3276. Periodical. US. English. qt. $30.00. Business Industry Political Action Committee Political Education Division, 1747 Pennsylvania Avenue Northwest, Washington DC 20006. Tel (202)833-1880. Ed Bernadette A Budde. Ind/Abst Soc. Sci. Citation Index. Circ 30,000. Political trends and developments of interest to the business community.

BIRMINGHAM WORLD : A STANDARD RACE JOURNAL. 1928?-. 0006-3754. Newspaper. US. English. wk. $12.50. Birmingham World, 312 North 17th Street, Birmingham AL 35202. Tel (205)251-6523. Ed Marcel Hopson Sr. bk rev. adv acc. Circ 37,000. Non partisan independent philosophy, non-secterian general news reporting features, and independent political persuasion.

THE BLACK PANTHER CEASED. V. 1-20, No. 9. 0523-7238. Periodical. US. English. wk. LC AP2. DD 323.20973. Available on microfilm from University Microfilms.

BOLETIN OFICIAL DE LAS CORTES GENERALES, CONGRESO DE LOS DIPUTADOS. SERIE E, OTROS TEXTOS. Main/Corp Spain. Cortes Generales. Congreso de los Diputados. VFOAT Otros Textos. Spanish. ir. LC J409. DD 328.4607205.

BOLETIN OFICIAL DE LAS CORTES GENERALES, CONGRESO DE LOS DIPUTADOS. SERIE I, INFORMACION SEMANAL. Main/Corp Spain. Cortes Generales. Congreso de los Diputados. Spanish. ir. LC J409. DD 328.4607205.

BOSTON OBSERVER. Vol. 1, No. 1 (Mar. 19, 1982)-. 0733-2556. Periodical. US. English. mo. Boston Observer, 8 Newbury Street, Boston MA 02116. Tel (617)267-4345. Ed Steven Pearlstein. bk rev. adv acc. Circ 5,000. Boston and Massachusetts politics, includes commentary and analysis, media criticism, business and the law.

BREAKTHROUGH. V.1, No. 1- Mar. 1977-. Periodical. US. English. ir. $6.00. John Brown Book Club, PO Box 14422, San Francisco CA 94114. Tel (415)681-9040.

BRIEFING. Began in 1975. Periodical. TU. English. wk. $310.00. Briefing, Ekonomik Basin Olgunlar Sokak, 2-1 Bakanlikar/Ankara Turkey. Tel 25 76 77-78. Ed Yavuz Tolun. bk rev. adv acc. Circ 2,000. (ctrl). Inside perspective on Turkish political, economic and business affairs analysis, commentary, economic facts and figures.

BRITISH COLUMBIA INSIGHT. VFOAT Insight. 0229-9100. Periodical. CN. English. Liberal Party in British Columbia, Suite 201/1894 West Broadway, Vancouver British Columbia V6J 1Y9 Canada. DD 324.27110605. Liberal News, 0709-9789.

BRITISH JOURNAL OF POLITICAL SCIENCE. V. 1- Jan. 1971-. 0007-1234. Periodical. UK. English. qt. $104.00. Cambridge University Press, 510 N Avenue, New Rochelle NY 10801. Tel (914)235-0300. Ed Ivor Crewe and Anthony King. bk rev. Covers all branches of political science, and articles from scholars in related disciplines. Emphasis being placed on political behavior, comparative politics and the politics of public policy.

BRITISH-SOVIET FRIENDSHIP. 1956-. 0007-1803. Periodical. UK. English. bm. 5.00. British-Soviet Friendship, 36 St Johns Square, London EC1V 4JH England. Tel 253 4161. Ed H Cousins. bk rev. adv acc. Circ 3,000. (ctrl). British-Soviet relations. Russia Today.

BULLETIN - ASSEMBLY OF FIRST NATIONS. (BULLETIN). Vol. 1, No. 1-. 0827-228X. Periodical. CN. English. mo. $18.00. Assembly of First Nations, 222 Queen Street/Suite 500, Ottawa Ontario K1P 5V9 Canada. DD 323.1197071.

BULLETIN - CONSEIL DES AFFAIRES FRANCO-ONTARIENNES. Main/Corp Ontario. Council for Franco-Ontarian Affairs. VFOAT Newsletter - Council for Franco-Ontarian Affairs. No. 13- Mar. 1978-. 0706-5361. Periodical. CN. English (French in parallel columns). ir. Council for Franco-Ontarian Affairs, 4th Floor/77 Bloor Street West, Toronto Ontario M7A 2R9 Canada. Bulletin, 0706-5353.

BULLETIN DE LIAISON - CEDE. PROGRAMME PECED. (BULLETIN DE LIAISON - C E D E, PROGRAMME P E C E O). Main/Corp Centre d'Etudes et de Documentation Europeennes. Programme de Politique Etrangere Comparee des Etats d'Europe Occidentale. First issue in 1975?. 0317-5472. Periodical. CN. French. Centre d'Etudes et de Documentation Europeennes, 5255 Av DeCelles, Montreal Quebec H3T 1V6 Canada. DD 327'.4.

BULLETIN FOR OSTSTATSSTUDIER I NORDEN. No. 1, 1979-. 0349-3709. Periodical. Danish (text in English, German, Norwegian, and Swedish). qt. Free to Members, 35.00 Nonmembers. Bulletin Oststatforskning, Svartbachsgatan 7, S-753 20 Uppsala Sweden.

BULLETIN - IDOC INTERNATIONAL. NEW SERIES. (IDOC BULLETIN). VFOAT IDOC Documentation Service. New Ser., Jan./Feb. 1977-. 0250-7633. Periodical. IT. English. mo. 35,000 Domestic, $18.00 Foreign. International Documentation Communication Centre, Via S Maria Dell'Anima 30, 00186 Rome Italy. Tel 06/6568332. Ind/Abst Relig. Index One, Period. bk rev. adv acc. Circ 1,500. (ctrl). Social and political development trends in the Third World and the impact of ideologies and religion. IDOC Bulletin.

BULLETIN - JOHN BIRCH SOCIETY. Main/Corp John Birch Society. 1959. 0449-0754. Periodical. US. English. mo. $12.00. John Birch Society, 395 Concord Avenue, Belmont MA 02178. Tel (617)489-0600. Ed Charles O Mann. LC E740.J6. Circ 50,000. The only official publication of the John Birch Society, the world's leading conservative, anit-communist, educational organization.

BULLETIN - LABORATOIRE D'ETUDES POLITIQUES ET ADMINISTRATIVES, UNIVERSITE LAVAL. Main/Corp Universite Laval. Laboratoire d'Etudes Politiques et Administratives. No. 1- Mar. 1975-. 0703-9816. Periodical. CN. French. Laboratoire d'Etudes Politiques et Administratives, Dep de Science Politique, Universite Laval, Quebec G1K 7P4 Canada. DD 320.05.

BULLETIN OF PEACE PROPOSALS. V. 1- 1970-. 0007-5035. Periodical. UR. English (French and German). qt. 48.00. Universitetsforlaget, PO Box 2959-Toyen, Oslo 6 Norway. Tel (45)2-27 60 60. Ed Marek Thee. Ind/Abst Am. Hist. Life, Hist. Abstr., Part A, Mod. Hist. Abstr., Hist. Abstr., Part B, Twent. Century Abstr., Energy Res. Abstr., Soc. Sci. Citation Index, Hist. Abstr. LC JX1901. adv acc. Circ 800. Main concern is with: armaments, the first priority - disarmament; the second - narrowing the gap between rich and poor; the third - implementation of human rights.

BULLETIN SUR LES POLITIQUES LIBERALES. Oct. 1980-. 0227-0234. Periodical. CN. French. ir. Free. Parti Liberal du Canada, 102 rue Bank, Ottawa Ontario K1P 5N4 Canada. DD 324.2710605. (ctrl).

BUSINESS & PUBLIC AFFAIRS (AMERICAN POLITICAL RESEARCH CORPORATION). (BUSINESS & PUBLIC AFFAIRS). VFOAT Business and Public Affairs. 0735-1496. Periodical. US. English. sm. $118.00. American Political Research Company, 4312 Montgomery Avenue, Bethesda MD 20814. Tel (301)654-4990.

CADERNOS DCP. Main/Corp Universidade Federal de Minas Gerais. Departamento de Ciencia Politica. No. 1- March 1974-. BL. Portuguese. ir. Universidade Federal, Caixa Postal 1621, Belo Horizonte 30.000 Brazil. LC JA5.

CADERNOS FUNDAP. V. 1, No. 1, (June 1981)-. Periodical. BL. Portuguese. qt. 1000.00. Fundacao do Desenvolvimento Administrativo, Rua Cristiano Viana 428, CEP 05411 Sao Paulo SP Brazil. LC JA5. DD 350.0005.

CAHIERS D'ECONOMIE POLITIQUE. No. 1- Oct. 1974-. 0339-3437. Periodical. FR. French. ir. Ed Anthropos, 96 Bd Auquste, Blanqui, 75013 Paris.

CAHIERS DES AMERIQUES LATINES. SERIE SCIENCES DE L'HOMME. See General Interest - General Interest-South America.

CAHIERS D'HISTOIRE DE L'INSTITUT MAURICE THOREZ CEASED. Institut Maurice Thorez. New Ser. 6-14 Vol. (No 1-34). 0021-5047. Periodical. FR. French. ir. Ind/Abst Foreign Lang. Index. Cahiers de l'Institut Maurice Thorez, 0020-2363.

CAHIERS DU SAMIZDAT. VFOAT Tetradi Samizdata. Periodical. BE. French. mo. 700. Cahiers du Samizdat, rue du lac 48/periodique mensl, 1050 Bruxelles Belgium. Tel (2)6485947. Ed A de Meeus. LC DK274.A2. DD 054. bk rev. adv acc. Circ 1,500. Underground press of the Soviety Union.

CAHIERS ZAIROIS DE LA RECHERCHE ET DU DEVELOPPEMENT. VFOAT Cahiers Zairois. 1971-. Periodical. French. ir. $8.00. ONRD, BP 3119, Kinshasa Zaire. LC JQ3601.A1. DD 320.9675103. Cahiers Congolais de la Recherche et du Developpement.

THE CALCUTTA JOURNAL OF POLITICAL STUDIES. Vol. 1, No. 1 (Winter 1980)-. Periodical. II. English. sa. Calcutta University, Asutosh Building, Calcutta 700073 India. LC JQ201. DD 320.95405.

CALIFORNIA COMMON CAUSE NEWSLETTER. 8755-1136. Periodical. US. English. sa. California Common Cause, 636 South Hobart Boulevard, Los Angeles CA 90005. DD 322.

THE CALIFORNIA EYE. 1979. 0279-0246. Periodical. US. English. bw. $125.00. The Political Animal, PO Box 3249, Torrance CA 90510. Tel (213)649-4400. Ed Joseph Scott. bk rev. Circ 1,000. Non-partisan newsletters on government and politics.

CALIFORNIA GOVERNMENT AND POLITICS ANNUAL. 0084-8271. US. English. an. $4.95. California Journal, 1714 Capitol Avenue, Sacramento CA 95814. Tel (916)444-2840. Ed Hoeber and Price. LC JK8701. DD 320.4794. Circ 6,000. Reprints of articles from California Journal regarding California government and politics.

CALIFORNIA JOURNAL. V. 1- Jan. 1970-. 0008-1205. Periodical. US. English. mo. $30.00 Library and Governmental Agency, $50.00 Corporation and Association. California Center for Research and Education in Government, 1617 10th Street, Sacramento CA 95814. Ind/Abst Infobank, Public Aff. Inf. Serv. Bull. LC JK8701. DD 320.9794.

CALIFORNIA VOTER. V. 1- Sept. 1949-. Periodical. US. English. bm. $1.00. League of Women Voters of California, 942 Market Street/ Suite 505, San Francisco CA 94102.

CAMPAIGN PEOPLE. V. 1, No. 1 (March 8, 1982)-. 0733-9771. Periodical. US. English. bw. $69.00. Campac Publications Inc, 306 A Street SE, Washington DC 20003. Tel (202)544-6300.

CAMPAIGN PRACTICES REPORTS. See Law.

CAMPAIGNS & ELECTIONS. VAT Campaigns and Elections. V. 1- Spring 1980-. 0197-0771. Periodical. US. English. qt. $120.00. Campaigns & Elections, 1621 Brookside Road, McLean VA 22102. Tel (704)534-7774. Ed Robert Abeshouse. Ind/Abst Public Aff. Inf. Serv. Bull. LC JK1976. DD 324.70973. bk rev. adv acc. Circ 2,500.

Political Science

Devoted to political campaign technology; concentrates on computer applications. Regular columns cover fund raising, election law, parties and campaign history.

CANADIAN ANNUAL REVIEW OF POLITICS AND PUBLIC AFFAIRS. 1971-. 0315-1433. CN. English (includes some text in French). an. University of Toronto Press, Front Campus, Toronto Ontario M5S 1A6 Canada. Tel (416)978-2229. Ed J Saywell. LC F1001. DD 320.971064. *Canadian Annual Review, 0068-8215.*

CANADIAN GOVERNMENT SERIES. 1-. 0068-8835. Monographic Series. CN. English. ir. University of Toronto Press, Front Campus, Toronto Ontario M5S 1A6 Canada. Tel (416)667-7791.

CANADIAN JOURNAL OF POLITICAL AND SOCIAL THEORY. See Sociology: General Works, Theory.

CANADIAN JOURNAL OF POLITICAL SCIENCE. VFOAT Revue Canadienne de Science Politique. V. 1- Mar. 1968-. 0008-4239. Periodical. CN. English (text in French). qt. University of Toronto Press, Journals Department, 5201 Dufferin Street, Downsview Ontario M3H 5T8 Canada. Ind/Abst Am. Hist. Life, Hist. Abstr., Part A, Mod. Hist. Abstr., ABC Pol Sci, Can. Period. Index, Foreign Lang. Index, Point Repere, Public Aff. Inf. Serv. Bull., Writ. Am. Hist., Ref. Source, Soc. Sci. Index, Soc. Welf. Soc. Plan./Policy Soc. Dev., Sociol. Abstr., Recent Publ. Artic. *Canadian Journal of Economics and Political Science, 0315-4890.*

CANADIAN NEWSLETTER FOR OPEN GOVERNMENT. (THE CANADIAN NEWSLETTER FOR OPEN GOVERNMENT). VFOAT Newsletter, Le Bulletin Canadien pour le Droit a l'Information Publique. VAT Newsletter - Access, Access. V. 1- Nov. 1976-. 0703-1378. Periodical. CN. English (includes some text in French). Free. Access, Box 855 Station B, Ottawa Ontario K1P 5P9 Canada. DD 354.71008105. (ctrl).

CANADIAN PARLIAMENTARY HANDBOOK. 1982-. 0714-8113. CN. English (French). be. Borealis Press, 9 Ashburn Drive Napean, Ottawa Ontario 6N4 K2E Canada. DD 328.7100202.

CANADIAN POLITICAL SCIENCE BULLETIN. VFOAT Bulletin de la Science Politique au Canada. V. 7, No. 1- Sept. 1977-. 0705-341X. Periodical. CN. French (text also in English). ir. Societe Canadienne de Science Politique, Carleton University, c/o J Pond, Promenade Colonel By, Ottawa Ontario K1S 5B6 Canada. DD 320.06271. *Bulletin, 0319-6461.*

CANADIAN REVIEW OF STUDIES IN NATIONALISM. BIBLIOGRAPHY. See Bibliographies.

CAPITAL TO CAPITAL. V. 7, No. 10 (June 28, 1982)-. 0749-4734. Periodical. US. English. bw. $25.00. National Conference of State Legislature, 444 North Capital Street NW/2nd Floor, Washington DC 20001. Tel (202)737-7004. DD 328. *Dateline Washington.*

CAPITALISM (LONDON, ONT.). (CAPITALISM). 1st Issue Aug. (1982)-. 0821-2643. Periodical. CN. English. bm. $0.50 Per No. Capitalism, c/o M Pettigrew, London Ontario N6A 4E3 Canada. DD 320.512.

CARIBBEAN DIALOGUE. Began with Aug./Sept. 1975 issue. 0384-1464. Periodical. CN. English. mo. $15. US and Canada. Caribbean Dialogue, PO Box 442 Station J, Toronto Ontario M4J 4Y8 Canada. DD 320.972905.

CARTA DEL ESTE. Yearly V. 1, No. 1 (Feb. 16, 1978)-. Periodical. SP. Spanish. ir. 1500. Prima-Press International, Carta del Este, Avenida General Peron 32, 24-I Madrid 20 Spain. LC DK274.A2. DD 323.40947.

CATALOGUE - JOHN F. KENNEDY SCHOOL OF GOVERNMENT. Main/Corp John F. Kennedy School of Government. US. English. John F Kennedy School of Government, Harvard University, 79 John F Kennedy Street, Cambridge MA 02138.

CATO POLICY REPORT. Vol. 6, No. 5 (May/June 1984)-. 0743-605X. Periodical. US. English. bm. Cato Institute, 224 Second Street Southeast, Washington DC 20504. DD 320. *Policy Report, 0190-325X; Cato's Letter.*

CENTRAL AMERICA UPDATE. 1979. 0823-7689. Periodical. CN. English. bm. 30.00. Latin American Working Group, Box 2207 Station P, Toronto Ontario M5S 2T2 Canada. Tel (416)533-4221. Ed Timothy P Draimin. DD 972.805205. adv acc. Circ 1,500. (ctrl). Opens a vital window on the critical political changes occuring in the Americas. Provides facts and interpretations to understand the rapidly changing situations in Central America.

CHECK LIST OF BRITISH OFFICIAL SERIAL PUBLICATIONS. 1967-. 0084-8085. UK. English. an. British Library, Reference Division Publication, Great Russell Street, London WC1B 3DG England. LC Z2009, J301. DD 015.41.

CHECKLIST OF OFFICIAL PENNSYLVANIA PUBLICATIONS. See Bibliographies.

CHECKLIST OF SASKATCHEWAN GOVERNMENT PUBLICATIONS. Main/Corp Saskatchewan. Legislative Assembly. Library. VAT Legislative Library of Saskatchewan Checklist of Saskatchewan Government Publications. 1976-. 0705-4122. CN. English. an. Saskatchewan Legislative Library, 234 Legislative Building, Regina Saskatchewan Canada. LC Z1373.5.S26, J119. DD 015.7124.

CHENG CHIH CHIAO YU. VFOAT Zheng Zhi Jiao Yu. Periodical. CH. Chinese. bm. .26. Shang-Hai Shih Pao Kan Fa Hsing Chu, Shanghai China. LC JA88.C45. DD 320.072051.

CHENG CHIH YU FA LU. VFOAT Cheng Chih Yu Fa Lu Tsung Kan. Periodical. CH. Chinese. ir. 0.55. Hsin Hua Shu Tien, Shang-Hai Fa Hsing So, Shanghai China. LC JA26. DD 320.05.

CHINA AKTUELL. Began in 1972. 0341-6631. Periodical. GW. German (English). mo. $63.15. Institute of Asian Affairs, Rothenbaumchaussee 32, D2000 Hamburg 13 West Germany. Tel 44-30-01. LC DS701. DD 951.005. Circ 1,200. News from and on China. Analyses. Chronological presentation of events in the fields of domestic and foreign politics and economic development and relations.

CHINA QUARTERLY. (THE CHINA QUARTERLY). No. 1- Jan./March 1960-. 0305-7410. Periodical. UK. English. qt. 17.50 Domestic, $35.00 Foreign. School of Oriental & African Study, Malet Street, c/o University of London, London WC1E 7HP England. Tel (01)637-2388. Ed Brian Hook. Ind/Abst Soc. Sci. Index, MLA Int. Bibliogr. Books Artic. Mod. Lang. Lit., Public Aff. Inf. Serv. Bull., Soc. Sci. Citation Index, ABC Pol Sci: bibliogr. contents, Women Stud. Abstr. LC DS701. DD 951.005. Index in last issue of volume - attached. (cum index). bk rev. adv acc. Circ 3,000. Leading journal of modern Chinese studies covering arts, politics, economics, agriculture, social structure and developments and popular arts, with continuing documentation of events.

CHINESE FOR AFFIRMATIVE ACTION NEWSLETTER. 0743-2291. Periodical. US. Chinese (English). mo. $10.00 Student or Elderly. Chinese for Affirmative Action, 121 Waverly Place, San Francisco CA 94108. LC F868.S156. DD 323.11951079461.

CHIU SHIH NIEN TAI. VFOAT 90 Nien Tai, The Nineties. V. 172, May 1984-. Periodical. Chinese. mo. $27.00. Chinese Periodical Distribution, 712-716 North Figueroa Street, Los Angeles CA 90012. *Chi Shih Nien Tai.*

CHOICES (HALIFAX, N.S.). (CHOICES). Jan. 1982-. 0711-0677. Periodical. CN. English. ir. Institute for Research on Public Policy, PO Box 3670, Postal Station Halifax South, Halifax Nova Scotia B3J 3K6 Canada. DD 320.05.

CHOIX (HALIFAX, N.E.). (CHOIX). Jan. 1982-. 0711-0685. Periodical. CN. French. ir. Institut de Recherches Politiques, CP 3670/Succursale Halifax-Sud, Halifax Nova Scotia B3J 3K6 Canada. DD 320.05.

CHUAN MIN CHENG CHIH CHI KAN. VFOAT Chuan Min Cheng Chih, Direct Democracy Quarterly. First published in May 1983. Periodical. CH. Chinese. qt. Chuan Min Cheng Chih Chi Kan, 40 Lane, 269 Li San Street, Nei-Hu Taipei Taiwan. LC JQ1521.A1. DD 951.249057.

CHUNG HSUEH CHENG CHIH KO CHIAO HSUEH. VFOAT Zhongxue Zheng Zhike Jiaoxue. Periodical. CH. Chinese. mo. 0.26. Post Office Peking, Peking China. LC JA88.C45. DD 320.071251.

CHUNG KU LO. VFOAT Political Monitor. First published in Jan. 1983. Periodical. CH. Chinese. mo. $500.00. Chung Ku Lo Tsa Chih She, PO Box 1687333, Taipei Taiwan.

CHUNGANG CHODAL. Periodical. KO. Korean. ir. Chodalchong, 48-26 Inui-dong, Chongno-ku, Seoul South Korea. LC JQ1726.Z36.

CHURCH & STATE. VAT Church and State. V. 1- May 1948-. 0009-6334. Periodical. US. English. mo $10.00. Church and State, 8120 Fenton Street, Silver Spring MD 20910. Tel (301)589-3707. Ed Joseph L Conn. LC BR516. DD 322.10973. bk rev. Circ 50,000. News and analysis about church-state relations.

CITIZEN PARTICIPATION. Began in 1979. 0198-8468. Periodical. US. English. qt. $12.00. Lincoln Filene Center for Citizenship & Public Affairs, Tufts University, Medford MA 02155. Tel (617)381-3456. Ed Ken Thomson. Ind/Abst Altern. Press Index. bk rev. Circ 5,000. (ctrl). Useful models and careful analysis of citizen roles in government decisionmaking at local, state and federal levels. For citizen group leaders, government officials, and social scientists.

THE CITIZENS LEAGUE'S GREATER CLEVELAND. VFOAT Greater Cleveland. V. 33- Jan. 1957-. 0746-9209. Periodical. US. English. bm. Citizens League of Greater Cleveland, 820 Citizens Building, 850 Euclid Avenue, Cleveland OH 44114-3394. *Greater Cleveland.*

CIVIL AFFAIRS JOURNAL AND NEWSLETTER. 0045-7035. Periodical. US. English. bm. $4.80. Civil Affairs Association, 4317 Westbrook Lane, Kensington MD 20895. *Military Government Journal and News Letter.*

CIVITAS. New Series, Year 1- June 1950-. 0009-8191. Periodical. IT. Italian (summaries in Spanish, French, English, German and Croatian). bm. 20.000 Domestic, 30.000 Foreign. Edizioni Civitas, Via Tirso 92, 00198 Roma Italy. Tel 865.651. Ind/Abst Am. Hist. Life, Hist. Abstr., Part A, Mod. Hist. Abstr., Hist. Abst., Part B, Twent. Century Abstr. LC H7. adv acc. Circ 6,000. Political and economic studies.

CLEMENTS' ENCYCLOPEDIA OF WORLD GOVERNMENTS. BIANNUAL SUPPLEMENT. See Encyclopedias & General Reference Books.

COIN, INDEXED CHECKLIST TO COLORADO STATE PUBLICATIONS. See Indexes/Abstracts.

COLORADO LEGISLATIVE ALMANAC. See Yearbooks, Almanacs, Directories.

COMBAT. V. 1- 23 Nov. 1946-. 0588-5620. Periodical. CN. French. ir. $10.06. Combat /Canada/, 185 Est rue Ontario, Montreal Quebec H2X 1H5 Canada. Tel (514)524-2896. Ed Claire da Sylva. bk rev. adv acc. Circ 3,000. Left-wing political, economic, social and cultural commentary from labor standpoint.

COMMITTEE IN SUPPORT OF SOLIDARITY REPORTS. Issue No. 1(April 1982)-. 0740-316X. Periodical. US. English. mo. $15.00. Committee in Support of Solidarity, 275 Seventh Avenue, 25th Floor, New York NY 10001. Tel (212)989-0909. Ed Eric Chenoweth. Circ 1,000. Publishes accounts from the Underground Polish Press on the solidarity movement and human rights.

COMMONSENSE. V. 1- Summer 1978-. 0163-3023. Periodical. US. English. ir. Republican National Committee, 310 First Street SE, Washington DC 20003. Tel (202)863-8500. LC JK2351. DD 329.6005.

COMMONWEALTH. V. 13- Feb. 1970-. 0010-3411. UK. English. mo. $23.00. Longman Group Ltd, Journals Department, Fourth Avenue, Harlow Essex CM19 1AA England. Tel 0279 442601. Ed Derek Ingram. Ind/Abst Access. LC DA10. DD 910.09171242. bk rev. adv acc. Journal of politics, arts, science and technology, sports in the commonwealth countries. *Commonwealth Journal.*

COMMONWEALTH PARLIAMENTARY ASSOCIATION. ANNUAL CANADIAN REGIONAL CONFERENCE. (COMMONWEALTH PARLIAMENTARY ASSOCIATION, ANNUAL CANADIAN REGIONAL CONFERENCE). 14th-20th. 0383-6630. Periodical. CN. English (includes some text in French). DD 328.306171. *Report of the Proceedings of the Canadian Area Conference, Commonwealth Parliamentary Association, 0069-715X.*

COMPARATIVE POLITICAL STUDIES. VFOAT CPS. V. 1- April 1968-. 0010-4140. Periodical. US. English. qt. Sage Publications, 275 South Beverly Drive, Beverly Hills CA 90212. Tel (213)274-8003. Ind/Abst Am. Hist. Life, Hist. Abstr., ABC Pol Sci, Public Aff. Inf. Serv. Bull., Soc. Sci. Index, Soc. Sci. Citation Index, Sociol. Abstr., Lang. Lang. Behav. Abstr., Hist. Abstr., Part A, Mod. Hist. Abstr., Hist. Abst., Part B, Twent. Century Abstr. LC JA3.

COMPARATIVE POLITICS. V. 1- Oct. 1968-. 0010-4159. Periodical. US. English. qt. $65.00. Comparative Politics, 49 Sheridan Avenue, Albany NY 12210. Tel (518)436-9686. Ind/Abst Soc. Sci. Index, Am. Hist. Life, Hist. Abstr., Public Aff. Inf. Serv. Bull., ABC Pol Sci, Int. Polit. Sci. Abstr., Writ. Am. Hist., Soc. Sci. Citation Index, Sociol. Abstr., Lang. Lang. Behav. Abstr., Hist. Abstr., Part A, Mod. Hist. Abstr., Hist. Abst., Part B, Twent. Century Abstr. LC JA3. DD 320.5. Available on microfilm from University Microfilms.

COMPARATIVE POLITICS (GUILFORD, CONN.). (COMPARATIVE POLITICS). VFOAT Annual Editions. 83/84-. 0741-7233. Periodical. US. English. an. $8.95. Dushkin Publishing Group Inc, Sluice Dock, Guilford CT 06437. Tel (203)453-4351. Ed Christian Soe. LC JF37. DD 320.305. Updated collection of current public press articles covering current issues in comparative politics. Includes topic guide and complete index.

CONCEPTS (MCGILL UNIVERSITY. POLITICAL SCIENCE STUDENTS' ASSOCIATION). (CONCEPTS). Spring 1982-. 0713-2735. CN. English (includes some text in French). an. Free. McGill Political Science Students' Association, 855 Sherbrooke Street, West McGill University, Montreal Quebec H3A 2T7 Canada. DD 327.05. (ctrl).

CONFLICT. V. 1-. 0149-5941. Periodical. US. English. qt. $60.00. Crane Russak & Company, 3 East 44th Street, New York NY 10017. Tel (212)867-1490. Ed George Tanham. Ind/Abst ABC Pol Sci, Predicasts, Am. Hist. Life, Hist. Abstr. LC JA1. DD 320.05. CODEN CONFDZ. bk rev. adv acc. Circ 500. Focuses on guerrilla warfare, terrorism, revolution, and conflicts of a nonphysical nature, such as economic, social, political and psychological.

CONGRESS AND THE NATION. US. English. Congressional Quarterly Service, 1414 22nd Street NW, Washington DC 20037. DD 320.973.

CONGRESS & THE PRESIDENCY. VFOAT Congress and the Presidency. V. 9, No. 1 (Winter, 1981-82)-. 0734-3469. Periodical. US. English. sa. $23.00. American University, Congress & the Presidency, Washington DC 20016. Tel (202)885-6250. Ind/Abst Am. Hist. Life, Hist. Abstr., Part A, Mod. Hist. Abstr., Hist. Abst., Part B, Twent. Century Abstr., ABC Pol Sci, Int. Polit. Sci. Abstr., Public Aff. Inf. Serv. Bull. LC JK1041. DD 328.73005. *Congressional Studies, 0194-4053.*

THE CONGRESSIONAL DIGEST. (CONGRESSIONAL DIGEST). 0010-5899. Periodical. US. English. ir. $42.00. Congressional Digest, Congressional Digest Building, 3231 P Street Northwest, Washington DC 20007. Tel (202)333-7332. Ind/Abst Mag. Index, Energy Inf. Abstr., Environ. Abstr., Pop. Mag. Rev., Read. Guide Period. Lit., Public Aff. Inf. Serv. Bull., Abr. Read. Guide, Soc. Sci. Index. Index in last issue of volume - attached. Available on microfilm. *Capitol Eye.*

CONGRESSIONAL INSIGHT. V. 1- Dec. 31, 1976-. 0196-0784. Periodical. US. English. wk. $248.00. Congressional Quarterly, 1414 22nd Street NW, Washington DC 20037. Tel (202)887-8500.

CONGRESSIONAL RESEARCH SERVICE REVIEW. March 1978-. 0193-8029. Periodical. US. English. mo. $21.00. Superintendent of Documents, US Government Printing Office, Washington DC 20402. Tel (202)783-3238. Ind/Abst Index U.S. Gov. Period. LC JK1. DD 320.973092. *Congressional Research Service Bulletin.*

CONGRESSIONAL YELLOW BOOK. VFOAT Washington Monitor's Congressional Yellow Book. Began in 1976. 0191-1422. US. English. qt. $103.00. The Washington Monitor, 1301 Pennsylvania Avenue NW/Suite 1000, Washington DC 20004. Tel (202)347-7757. Ed Jodi Scheiber. LC JK1083. DD 328.730761025. *Bimonthly Directory of Key Congressional Aides, 0099-1376.*

CONJONCTURE POLITIQUE AU QUEBEC. VFOAT Revue Conjoncture Politique au Quebec. VAT Conjoncture (Montreal. 1982). No. 1 (Winter 1981/82)-. 0711-6691. Periodical. CN. French. sa. 30.00. Conjoncture Politique, 4073 rue St Hubert/Suite 201, Montreal Quebec H2L 4A7 Canada. Ind/Abst Point Repere. DD 971.40405. adv acc. Circ 1,000. Political, Quebec and sociology.

CONNAISSANCE POLITIQUE. 1 (Feb. 1983)-. Periodical. FR. French. ir. 80. 11 rue Soufflot, 75240 Paris Cedex 05 France.

CONNECTICUT DIGEST OF ADMINISTRATIVE REPORTS TO THE GOVERNOR. Main/Corp Connecticut. Dept. of Administrative Services. VFOAT Digest of Connecticut Administrative Reports to the Governor. Began with Vol. 32 (1977/78) issue. 0277-5700. US. English. an. LC J87. DD 353.97460006. *Connecticut Digest of Administrative Reports to the Governor, 0277-5700.*

CONSEQUENCES. 0275-892X. Periodical. US. English. qt. $10.00. MLP Enterprises, 236 East Durham Street, Philadelphia PA 19119. Ed Marvin L Peebles. bk rev. adv acc. Addresses the relationship between contemporary events and the future. Chronicles everyday parallels to "1984" and "Brave New World".

CONSERVATIVE. (THE CONSERVATIVE). V. 1, No. 1 (Nov. 1981)-. 0712-2616. Periodical. CN. English. ty. Free. The Conservative, c/o Willowdale Progressive Conservative Association, PO Box 13/Station A, Willowdale Ontario M2N 5S6 Canada. DD 324.27104060713541. (ctrl).

CONSIGNA. VFOAT Consigna Politica. Periodical. Spanish. sm. Diagonal, 34 No 5-11, Bogota Columbia.

CONTACT - PC CANADA FUND. (CONTACT). VAT Contact - Progressive Conservative Canada Fund. 1st issue-. 0713-0635. Periodical. CN. English. qt. Free. Contact PC Canada Fund, 161 Laurier Avenue West, Ottawa Ontario K1P 5J2 Canada. DD 324.2710405. (ctrl).

CONTEMPORARY CRISES. V. 1- Jan. 1977-. 0378-1100. Periodical. NE. English. qt. $70.00. Kluwer Academic Publishers Group, Spui Boulevard 50, PO Box 989, 3300 AZ Dordrecht Netherlands. Tel (78)334247. Ed Stan Cohen. Ind/Abst Sociol. Abstr., Soc. Welf. Soc. Plan./Policy Soc. Dev., ABC Pol Sci, Soc. Sci. Citation Index, Public Aff. Inf. Serv. Bull. LC HV6001. DD 362.05. bk rev. A forum for critical scholars interested in theory and policy in those areas shated by criminology, law, sociology and political science.

CONTEMPORARY SOUTHEAST ASIA. V. 1- May 1979-. 0129-797X. Periodical. SI. English. qt. 16.00 US. Institute of Southeast Asian Studies, Heng Mui Keng Tr, Pasir Panjang, Singapore 0511 Republic of Singapore. Tel 7780955. LC DS520. DD 959.005. bk rev. adv acc. Circ 800. Journal dealing analytically with current issues and important developments in the region. Essential to decision makers, planners, political analysts, business executives, financiers, scholars and students of Southeast Asian Affairs.

CONTRIBUTIONS IN POLITICAL SCIENCE. No. 1-. 0147-1066. Monographic Series. US. English. ir. Greenwood Press Inc, 51 Riverside Avenue, Westport CT 06880. LC UNC.

CONVEGNO REGIONALE SULLA PARTECIPAZIONE POPOLARE ALLE SCELTE E ALLA GESTIONE DELLA COSA PUBBLICA. ATTI. 1.- 1972-. Italian. ir. LC JS5701.

COOPERATION AND CONFLICT. 0010-8367. Periodical. NO. English. qt. 32.-. Universitetsforlaget, PO Box 2959 Toyen, Oslo 6 Norway. Tel (45)-2-27 60 60. Ed Arild Underdal. Ind/Abst Am. Hist. Life, Hist. Abstr., Part A, Mod. Hist. Abstr., Hist. Abst., Part B, Twent. Century Abstr., ABC Pol Sci, Public Aff. Inf. Serv. Bull. bk rev. adv acc. Circ 600. Devoted to the studies of the foreign policies of the Nordic countries and to studies of international politics by Nordic scholars.

COPENHAGEN POLITICAL STUDIES ABSTRACTS. *See* Indexes/Abstracts.

COSMOPOLITAN CONTACT. 0010-955X. Periodical. US. English. ir. $5.00. Cosmopolitan Contact, PO Box 1566, Fontana CA 92335. Tel (716)829-4108. Ed Romulus Rexner. bk rev. adv acc. Circ 1,500. A polyglot magazine with worldwide circulation, established in 1961 by Planetary Legion for Peace to promote intercultural understanding and bonds of spiritual unity by means of contacts.

C.P.C. : PUBLICATIONS. Began publication with No. 1. Monographic Series. UK. English. ir. Conservative Political Centre, 32 Smith Square, London SW1P 3HH England.

THE CREATIVE INTERFACE. V. 1-. 0070-1459. Monographic Series. US. English. American University/Center for the Study of Private Enterprise, Massachusetts & Nebraska Avenues NW, Washington DC 20016. LC HD3616.U46. DD 322.30973.

CRESCENT INTERNATIONAL. VFOAT Crescent. VAT Crescent (Willowdale). Began publication in 1977. 0705-3754. Periodical. CN. English (Urdu). sm. $20.00. Crescent International, 300 Steelcase Road West Unit #8, Markham Ontario L3R 2W2 Canada. Tel (416)474-9292. Ed Z Bangash. DD 954.910505. bk rev. adv acc. Circ 15,000. (ctrl). Reporting Islamic movement. *Fortnightly Crescent, 0700-6942.*

CRITIQUE. V. 1- Spring 1973-. 0301-7605. Periodical. UK. English. sa. $3.00. 31 Cleveden Road, G12 OPH Glasgow Scotland. Ind/Abst Am. Hist. Life, Hist. Abstr., Part A, Mod. Hist. Abstr., Hist. Abst., Part B, Twent. Century Abstr. LC DK246. DD 320.947084.

CRITIQUE POLITIQUE. Began in 1978. Periodical. BE. French. qt. 700. Revue de Critique Politique, rue Faider 19 A, 1050 Bruxelles Belgium. LC JA11. DD 320.05.

CRITIQUE SOCIALISTE. 0045-9089. Periodical. FR. French. ir. $13.30. Librairie Syros, 9 rue Borromee, 75015 Paris France.

CURRENT AFFAIRS BULLETIN. V. 1- Sept. 29, 1947-. 0011-3182. Periodical. AT. English. mo. Current Affairs Bulletin, University of Sydney, Department of Adult Education, Sydney New South Wales Australia 2006. Ind/Abst APAIS, Aust. Public Aff. Inf. Serv. LC D839.

CURRENT AMERICAN GOVERNMENT. VFOAT CQ Guide to Current American Government. Fall 1970-. 0196-612X. US. English. sa. $18.50. Congressional Quarterly Inc, 1414-22nd Street NW, Washington DC 20037. Tel (202)887-8581. LC JK1. DD 320.97305. *CQ Guide to Current American Government, 0007-8956.*

THE CURRENT DIGEST OF THE SOVIET PRESS. VFOAT Digest of the Soviet Press. V. 1- Feb. 1, 1949-. 0011-3425. Periodical. US. English. wk. $115.00. Current Digest of Soviet Press, 1314 Kinnear Road, Columbus OH 43212. Tel (614)422-4234. Ed Fred Schulze. Ind/Abst Nexis, Public Aff. Inf. Serv. Bull. LC D839. DD 057. Circ 1,000. (ctrl). Available on microfilm and microfiche. A journal of translations and abstracts in English of significant articles from 100 Soviet newspapers and periodicals. Quarterly indexes included; annual indexes sold separately. *Current Abstracts of the Soviet Press, 0011-3166.*

CURRENT ISSUES. 0161-6641. US. English. an. $7.00. Educational Publications Close Up Foundation, 1235 Jefferson Davis Highway, Arlington VA 22202. Tel (703)892-5400. Ed Patricia Bandy. LC JK1. DD 309.173092. Handbook on 10 foreign and 10 domestic issues facing the nation and the world.

CURRENT SOVIET POLICIES. 19th-. 0590-3890. Periodical. US. English. ir. Current Digest of Soviet Press, 1314 Kinnear Road, Columbus OH 43212. Tel (614)422-4234. Ed Robert Ehlers. LC JN6598. DD 947.085. Proceedings of Soviet party congresses. Volumes I through VIII cover 19th through 26th congresses. Volumes sold separately; prices vary.

DANISH GALLUP ELECTORATE DATA. Series/Titl Data Material. English. ir. DDA Odense University, Campusvej 55, DK-5230 Odense M Denmark.

DDR REPORT. VAT Deutsche Demokratische Republik Report. 1- Yearly Volume. Periodical. GW. German. mo. $20.29. Verlag Neue Gesellschaft GMBH, Godesberger Allee 149, 5300 Bonn 2 West Germany. Tel 0228/883627. bk rev. adv acc. Circ 3,000. German Democratic Republic society discussing politics, economics, culture and law.

DEBATE (LIMA, PERU). (DEBATE). 1 (Sept./Oct. 1979)-. Periodical. Spanish. bm. $25.00. Gonzales Larranagea 265, Lima 18 Peru South America. Tel 467070-455946. (cum index). bk rev. adv acc. Circ 8,000. A magazine designed to be a forum for informed, authoritative discussion of Peru's main problems and possibilities with regards to economic and political development as well as a cultural heritage.

DEBATES AND PROCEEDINGS - LEGISLATIVE ASSEMBLY OF MANITOBA. Main/Corp Manitoba. Legislative Assembly. V. 1- Oct. 23, 1958-. 0542-5492. Periodical. CN. English. ir. 40.00. Queens Printer, 200 Vaughn

Political Science

Street, Winnipeg Manitoba B3C 0P8 Canada. **Tel** (204)945-3103. LC J109. **Circ** 300. (ctrl).

DEBATES OF THE NATIONAL ASSEMBLY. **Main/Corp** Transkei. National Assembly. VFOAT N. A. Hansard. 1st- Assembly. SA. English. ir. 1.00. Pretoria Duplicating Company, 10 van der Stel Buildings/Pretorius Street, Pretoria South Africa. LC J707.T3. DD 328.687. *Debates.*

DEBATES OF THE SENATE. **Main/Corp** Canada. Parliament. Senate. VFOAT Debats du Senat. 1867/68-. Periodical. CN. text in English and French, 1869-. da. 36.00 Domestic, 43.20 Foreign. Receiver General for Canada, Supply & Services, Ottawa Ontario K1A 0S9 Canada.

DEBATES. OFFICIAL REPORT - PROVINCIAL ASSEMBLY OF SIND. (DEBATES : OFFICIAL REPORT - PROVINCIAL ASSEMBLY OF SIND). **Main/Corp** Sind, Pakistan. Provincial Assembly. 0376-8120. English, Sindhi or Urdu. ir. Manager Sind Government Book Depot and Record Office, Abdullah Haroon Road, Karachi 4 Pakistan. LC J577.T3. DD 328.54918008.

DEBATS DE L'ASSEMBLEE NATIONALE. **Main/Corp** France. Parlement (1946-). Assemblee Nationale. FR. French. ir. Direction Journax Officiels, 26 rue Dessaix, 75732 Paris Cedex 15 France. LC J341. DD 328.4402.

DEBATTE VAN STAANDE KOMITEES. **Main/Corp** South Africa. Parliament. House of Assembly. VFOAT Debates of Standing Committees. SA. Afrikaans (English). ir. Govt Printer, Private Bag X85, Pretoria 0001 South Africa. LC J705. DD 328.6802. *Debates.*

DEFENSE & FOREIGN AFFAIRS HANDBOOK. VAT Defense and Foreign Affairs Handbook. 1976/77-. 0160-5836. US. English. an. $185.00. Perth Corporation, 1777 T Street NW, Washington DC 20009. **Tel** (202)223-4934. Ed Michael Dunn. LC UA10. DD 355.0330047. adv acc. A complete compendium of the world's nations political and defense structures— governmental and military organization, defense industries, and defense capalititics.

DEFIS QUEBECOIS (MONTREAL, QUEBEC). (DEFIS QUEBECOIS). Feb./March 1984-. 0828-4911. Periodical. CN. French. mo. $1.50 Per Nov. Parti Quebecois, 7370 rue St-Hubert, Montreal Quebec H2R 2N3 Canada. DD 324.2714093. *Defis (Montreal, Quebec : 1983), 0828-4903.*

DEMOCRAT. V. 1- Nov. 1961-. 0070-3346. Periodical. CN. English. Democrat, 64-8th Street, New Westminster British Columbia V3M 3P1 Canada. *CCF News for British Columbia and the Yukon.*

LE DEMOCRATE. No. 1- Nov. 1974-. Periodical. French. ir. 4.500. Parti Democratique Senegalais, 7 rue de Thiong, Dakar Senegal. LC JQ3396.A98. DD 329.9663.

DEMOCRATE. (LE DEMOCRATE). V. 1, No. 1, (Dec. 1963)-. 0228-488X. Periodical. CN. French (text in English, Dec. 1963-). bw. Free. Nouveau Parti Democratique du Quebec, 180 Est Boulevard Dorchester/Suite 220, Montreal Quebec H2X 1N4 Canada. DD 324.27140705. (ctrl).

DEMOCRATIC FOCUS. (THE DEMOCRATIC FOCUS). 0094-7903. Periodical. US. English. bm. $10.00. 4024 North Stuart, Arlington VA 22207. LC HK2311. DD 329.3005.

DEMOCRATIC FORUM. English. ir. 6.00. 9 Dharmatala Street, Calcutta-13 India. LC DS401. DD 915.4005.

DEMOCRATIC GERMAN REPORT CEASED. V. 1-24, No. 22. 0011-8206. Periodical. English. bw. Deutscher Buch Export-Import, Leninstrasse 16, DDR-701 Leipzig East Germany.

DEMOCRATIC LEFT. V. 7, No. 2- Feb. 1979-. 0164-3207. Periodical. US. English. bm. $15.00. Democratic Socialist of America, 853 Broadway/Suite 801, New York NY 10003. **Tel** (212)260-3270. Ed Michael Harrington and Barbara Ehronralih. **Ind/Abst** Altern. Press Index. bk rev. adv acc. **Circ** 9,000. Published by Democratic Socialists of America. *Newsletter of the Democratic Left.*

DEMOCRATIC LETTER. No. 1- May 25, 1973-. Periodical. US. English. 2800 Virginia Avenue, Washington DC 20037. *Straight Talk.*

DEMOCRATIC PARTY. YEAR BOOK. (DEMOCRATIC PARTY). **Main/Corp** Illinois. State Board of Elections. 0147-6769. US. English. an. State Board of Education, 1020 South Spring, Springfield IL 62704. LC JK2311. DD 329.30025773.

DEMOCRATIC REVIEW. V. 1- Nov. 1974-. 0363-1834. Periodical. US. English. bm. $10.00. Democratic Forum, 1621 Conneticut Avenue NW, Washington DC 20009. **Ind/Abst** Public Aff. Inf. Serv. Bull. LC JK2311. DD 329.3005.

DEMOCRATS TODAY. 0882-1615. Periodical. US. English. ir. Democratic National Committee, 1625 Mass. Avenue NW, Washington DC 20036. LC JK2311. DD 324.2736.

DEUTSCHER KURIER. Periodical. GW. German. ir. 1.20. Postfach 1580, 3 Hannover 1 West Germany. LC DD259.4. DD 320.943087.

DEUTSCHES HANDBUCH DER POLITIK. V. 1- 1960-. 0418-985X. Periodical. GW. German. ir. Guenter Olzog Verlag GMBH, Thierschstrasse 11, D-8000 Munich 22 West Germany.

DEUTSCHLAND ARCHIV. See Genealogy and Heraldry - Archives.

THE DEVELOPING COUNTRY COURIER. V. 1- Feb. 1978-. 0160-8037. Periodical. US. English. qt. $9.00. Developing Country Courier, PO Box 239, McLean VA 22101-0239. **Tel** (703)356-7561. Ed Allan F Matthews. bk rev. Independent newsletter of the North-South issues. Covers political, economic, and social trends in news, statistics, and publications about interdependence toward a New International Order.

DF ACTUALITES. VFOAT D.F. Actualites. 0338-4187. FR. French. mo. 30. 29-31 Quai Voltaire, 75340 Paris Cedex 07 France. LC Z2169, J341. DD 015.44. *Actualites DF.*

DIALOGUE ON LIBERTY. Began in 1971. 0276-4563. Periodical. US. English. qt. $1.00. Dialogue on Liberty, Rt 1 Box 1002 Woodland Road, Sterling VA 22170.

DIARI DE SESSIONS DEL PARLAMENT DE CATALUNYA. **Main/Corp** Catalonia (Spain). Parlament. 1A. Legislatura, No. 1-. SP. Catalan. ir. 1500. Seccio de Publicacions del Parlament de Cataluyna, Palau del Parlament Parc de la Ciutadella, Barcelona 3 Spain. LC J409.T3. DD 328.46701.

THE DIPLOMATIC SERVICE LIST. **Main/Corp** Great Britain. Diplomatic Service Administration Office. 1966-. 0419-1714. UK. English. an. H M Stationery Office, PO Box 276, London SW8 5DT England. LC JX1783. DD 354.42061, 341.7. *Foreign Office List and Diplomatic and Consular Year Book for . . ., Commonwealth Relations Office Year Book.*

THE DIPLOMAT'S ANNUAL. Ed. 1- 1950-. 0070-4962. Periodical. UK. English. an. Diplomatic Press & Publishing Company, 29 March Lane, London NW7 England.

DIRECTORY - AMERICAN POLITICAL SCIENCE ASSOCIATION. See Yearbooks, Almanacs, Directories.

DIRECTORY OF UNDERGRADUATE POLITICAL SCIENCE FACULTY. See Yearbooks, Almanacs, Directories.

DISTRICT AND PRECINCT BOUNDARIES, STATE OF HAWAII. **Main/Corp** Hawaii. Office of the Lieutenant Governor. 0361-9508. US. English. Lieutenant Governor's Office, PO Box 2359, Honolulu HI 96804. **Tel** (808)548-2544. LC KFH420.85.A6. DD 328.96907345. Election district and precinct maps, polling place boundary for state of Hawaii.

D.O., DIARIO OFICIAL, ESTADO DO RIO DE JANEIRO. PARTE II. **Main/Corp** Rio de Janeiro (Brazil : State). Portuguese. ir. 516. Caixa Postal N Po S 597, Niteroi Brazil. LC J6.B9. *Diario Oficial do Estado do Rio de Janeiro. Parte II.*

DR. MCBIRNIE'S NEWSLETTER. VAT Doctor McBirnie's Newsletter. Periodical. US. English. mo. Free. Dr W S McBirnie, Community Churches of America, Box 90, Glendale CA 91209. **Tel** (818)240-4871. Ed McBirnie & MacCollom. Conservative news broadcast.

DOCUMENTARY HISTORY OF THE FIRST FEDERAL CONGRESS OF THE UNITED STATES OF AMERICA, MARCH 4, 1789-MARCH 3, 1791. 1972-. Periodical. US. English. ir. Johns Hopkins University, Box 442, Baltimore MD 21218. Ed Linda Grant de Pauw. LC JK1059 1ST. DD 328.7301.

DOCUMENTATION POLITIQUE COURANTE. No. 1- Sept. 1979-. 0225-6487. Periodical. CN. French (English). sa. Bibliotheque de l'Assemblee Nationale du Quebec, Parliament, Quebec Quebec Canada. DD 328.71401.

DOKUMENTE ZUR DEUTSCHLANDPOLITIK. **Main/Corp** Germany (Federal Republic, 1949-). Bundesministerium fur Innerdeutsche Beziehungen. GW. German. ir. Alfred Metzner Verlag, Postfach 970148, D-6000 Frankfurt West Germany.

DOSSIER SOCIO-POLITIQUE. VFOAT Dossier Socio Politique. Periodical. French. ir. Al Asas, B P 543, Sale Maroc. *Dossier Economique (Sale, Morroco).*

DRP BULLETIN. **Main/Corp** Minju Konghwadang. VFOAT Bulletin. VAT Democtatic Republican Party Bulletin. V. 1-. 0011-5134. Periodical. KO. English. ir. Publicity Department Democratic Republican Party, Central Office/Central Post Office Box 196, Seoul Korea.

DUKE POLITICAL SCIENCE JOURNAL. Vol. 1 (Spring 1983)-. 8755-3783. Periodical. US. English. Duke Political Science Journal, 214 Perkins Library, Duke University, Durham NC 27706. LC JA1. DD 320.05.

EAST EUROPE REPORT. POLITICAL, SOCIOLOGICAL, AND MILITARY AFFAIRS. VFOAT Political, Sociological, and Military Affairs. No. 1694- July 2, 1979-. Periodical. US. English (Multilingual). ir. Executive Office of the President, Foreign Broadcast Information Service, Joint Publications Research Service, 5285 Port Royal Road, Springfield VA 22161. *Translations on Eastern Europe. Political, Sociological, and Military Affairs.*

EASTERN EUROPEAN POLITICS AND SOCIETIES. 0888-3254. Periodical. US. English. ty. $40.00. 2120 Berkeley Way, Berkeley CA 94720.

EDITORIALS ON FILE. V. 1- Jan. 1/15, 1970-. 0013-0966. US. English. sm. $260.00. Facts on File, 460 Park Avenue South, New York NY 10016. **Tel** (212)683-2244. Ed Carol C Collins. LC D839. DD 081. **Circ** 1,500. Collection of editorials and political cartoons from US and Canadian newspapers (over 125) on current topics of interest in US world affairs.

EGALITE (ASSOCIATION DES ECRIVAINS ACADIENS). (EGALITE). 1 Year, No 1 (Fall 1980)-. 0226-6873. Periodical. CN. French. ty. $11.61. Societe Academy d'Analyse Politique, CP 2815 Succ A, Moncton New Brunswick E1C 8T8 Canada. **Tel** (506)858-4145. Ed Melvin Gallant. DD 971.5004114. bk rev. adv acc. **Circ** 300. An independent journal of political studies established to promote understanding and discussion in respect to political, economic, social, and cultural aspects of Acadian society (French-Canadian).

ELECTION LAWS OF IOWA. **Main/Corp** Iowa. US. English. ir. State of Iowa, Core Depository, 707 Savings and Loan Building, Des Moines IA 50309. *Primary and General Election Laws.*

ELECTION POLITICS. Vol. 1, No. 1 (Winter 1983-1984)-. 0742-5279. Periodical. US. English. sa. $10.00. Free Congress Research and Education Foundation, Institute for Government and Politics 721 Second Street Northeast, Washington DC 20002. **Tel** (202)546-3004. Ed Stuart Rothenberg. LC JK1976. DD 324.973005. bk rev. **Circ** 300. Articles about campaigns, elections, electoral trends, voting behavior, public opinion and PACS.

END PAPERS. VFOAT Endpapers. 1 (Winter 1981-82!). 0262-7922. Periodical. UK. English. ty. Bertrand Russell Peace Foundation Ltd, Bertrand Russell House, Gamble Street, Nottingham NG7 4ET England. **Tel** (0)602 784504. Ed Ken Coates. LC JX1974.7. DD 327.174. bk rev. adv acc. **Circ** 2,000. A regular medium for longer articles about European nuclear disarmament and associated issues, published by the Bertrand Russell peace foundation, originators of end. *Spokesman.*

ENDERCOS DOS SENHORES SENADORES (BRAZIL). **Main/Corp** Brazil. Congresso. Senado. Secao de Telex e Telefonia. Periodical. BL. Portuguese. ir. Senado Federal, Diretoria-Gerl, Brasilia Brazil. LC J207. DD 328.81071025.

ENLIGHTENMENT AND DISSENT. No. 1 (1982)-. 0262-7612. Periodical. UK. English. $9.00. Martin Fitzpatrick, Department of History, University College of Wales, Aberystwyth Dyfed SY23 3DY Great Britain. LC DA485. DD 320.01. *Price-Priestley Newsletter, 0140-8437.*

Political Science

ESP. EXPERIMENTAL STUDY OF POLITICS. (EXPERIMENTAL STUDY OF POLITICS). VFOAT ESP. 0046-2926. Periodical. US. English. ty. $12.00. Department of Political Science, Florida Atlantic University, Boca Raton FL 33431. LC JA1. DD 320.05.

ESSAYS ON LIBERTY. V. 1. 0532-3061. US. English. Foundation for Economic Education, Irvington on Hudson, New York NY 10533. LC HM271. DD 320.51.

EST & OUEST. VAT Est et Ouest. Vol. 1 (No. 1-). 0014-1267. Periodical. FR. French. mo. Est et Quest, 15th Avenue and Raymond-Poincare, Paris 75116 France. Tel 704 24 02. LC D839. DD 327.0904. (cum index). Journal of international political studies.

ESTUDIOS POLITICOS (MEXICO CITY, MEXICO). (ESTUDIOS POLITICOS). V. 1, No. 1 (April/June 1975)-. 0185-1616. Periodical. MX. Spanish. qt. Facultad de Ciencias Politicas y Sociales, Universidad Nacional Autonoma de Mexico, Ciudad Universitaria, Mexico City Mexico. Ind/Abst Am. Hist. Life, Hist. Abstr., Part A, Mod. Hist. Abstr., Hist. Abst., Part B, Twent. Century Abstr. LC JA5.

EUROPAISCHE ZEITUNG. Vol. 28, No. 6 (June 1977)-. Periodical. GW. German. mo. $13.19. Europa Union Verlag, Bachstrasse 32 Postfach 1529, D-5300 Bonn 1 West Germany. Tel 0 228/ 72 900 10. bk rev. adv acc. Circ 40,000. The cardinal subject in the articles of the Europaische Zeitung is the "European Integration" in politics and economics. Europa Union.

EUROPEAN JOURNAL OF POLITICAL RESEARCH. V. 1- Apr. 1973-. 0304-4130. Periodical. NE. English. qt. $104.00. Elsevier Science Publishers, PO Box 211, 1000 AE Amsterdam Netherlands. Tel (020)5803911. Ind/Abst Sociol. Abstr., Soc. Welf. Soc. Plan./Policy Soc. Dev., ABC Pol Sci, Soc. Sci. Citation Index, Recent Publ. Artic. LC JA88.E9. DD 320.05.

EUROPEAN POLITICAL DATA NEWSLETTER. Periodical. NO. English. qt. Dis Norwegian Social Science, Hans Holmboesgt 22, N-5014 Nergen University, Norway. Tel 05 21 00 40.

EXECUTIVE'S HANDBOOK ON POLITICAL CONTRIBUTIONS. 1978-. 0738-4297. Periodical. US. English. an. $225.00 New, $195.00 Renewals. S & FA Reporting Services Inc, 1101-15th Street NW, Washington DC 20005.

EXILE (PASADENA, CALIF.). (EXILE). 0743-9849. Periodical. US. English. mo. $15.00. Exile, PO Box 4272, Pasadena CA 91106. Tel (818)798-4745. Ed Bete Mariam. LC DT387.95. DD 963.0705. Circ 500. (ctrl). This newsletter deals with the life of Ethiopian political exiles and the problem in Ethiopia today.

THE FACT FINDER. 0014-651X. Periodical. US. English. sm. $14.50. Everingham Company, 2422 East Indian School Road, Phoenix AZ 85016.

LE FEDERALISTE; REVUE DE POLITIQUE. Vol. 1-. 0014-925X. Periodical. Vols. for 1959-1961 issued in Italian with title Federalista. ir.

FEUILLE. (LA FEUILLE). V. 1- May 1974-. 0381-9574. Periodical. CN. French. Association Max Stirner du Quebec, CP 95 Succursale Place d'Armes, Montreal Quebec H2Y 3E9 Canada. DD 320.5705.

FIRST MONDAY. V. 1- Aug. 1971-. 0145-1677. Periodical. US. English. mo. $15.00. Republican National Committee, 310 First Street SE, Washington DC 20003. LC JK2351. DD 320.9730924. *Republican* (1969), 0034-5059.

FLINDERS JOURNAL OF HISTORY AND POLITICS. V. 1- July 1969-. 0726-7215. Periodical. AT. English. an. 5.00. Flinders University, School of Social Sciences, Bedford Park SA Australia. Tel (08)275-2225. Ed B Dickey. Ind/Abst Am. Hist. Life, Hist. Abstr., Part A, Mod. Hist. Abstr., Hist. Abst., Part B, Twent. Century Abstr., APAIS, Aust. Public Aff. Inf. Serv., Hist. Abstr. bk rev. Circ 400. Academic essays some by students, relecting range of scholarship in history and politics at this university. Australia, China, political theory, British public administration.

THE FLORIDA VOTER. Began publication in 1924?. 0426-6072. Periodical. US. English. bm. $1.50. League of Women Voters of Florida, 1035-S South Florida Avenue, Lakeland FL 33803. Tel (813)682-1636.

FOCUS ON POLITICAL REPRESSION IN SOUTHERN AFRICA. No. 1- Nov. 1975-. 0308-3586. Periodical. UK. English. bm. $12.00. IDAF Publications, 104 Newgate Street, London EC1A 7AP England. Tel (617)491-8343. LC DT737. DD 320.96806. News on political trials and detentions in Southern Africa. *Southern Africa Information Service.*

FOREIGN REPORT. 0532-1328. Periodical. UK. English. wk. 200.00. The Economist Publications, 40 Duke Street, London W1M 5DG England. Tel (01)493-6711. Ed Roland Dallas. Circ 5,000. A confidential newsletter based on a continuous flow of information from high level sources in business and politics. A vital background for political forecasting and business decisionmaking.

FORUM - FORUM FOR YOUNG CANADIANS. (FORUM). 84-. 0826-1458. CN. English (text in French). an. Free. Forum for Young Canadians, 800-77 Metcalfe Street, Ottawa Ontario K1P 5L6 Canada. DD 320.97106. (ctrl). *Bulletin*, 0705-1581.

THE FREE CHINA JOURNAL. VFOAT Tzu Yu Chung-Kuo Chi Shih Pao. Vol. 1, No. 1 (Jan. 1, 1984)-. Newspaper. English. wk. 200.00 Domestic, $5.00 Foreign. Kwang Hwa Publishing Company, PO Box 337, Taipei Republic of China. Tel (02)332-6753. Ed Tang Wang. Circ 25,000. To keep friends overseas informed about news, views, and developments in the Republic of China. *Free China Weekly.*

FREE THE FIVE NEWSLETTER. Issue #4 (June 3, 1983)-. 0824-3123. Periodical. CN. English. ir. Free. Free the Vancouver Five Defense Group, PO Box 48296 Bentall Station, Vancouver British Columbia V7X 1A1 Canada. DD 322.440971133. *Newsletter of the Free the Five Defense Group,* 0824-3115.

FREE ZANZIBAR VOICE. UK. English. ir. Zanzibar Organization, 68 Hudson Road, Southsea P05 1HD England. LC DT435.62. DD 320.9678104.

FREEMEN DIGEST (WASHINGTON, D.C.). (FREEMEN DIGEST). Began with Nov. 1983. 8755-4364. Periodical. US. English. mo. Free to Contributors. National Center for Constitutional Studies, Editorial Offices, PO Box 31776, Salt Lake City UT 84131. DD 320.

FREIBURGER RECHTS- UND STAATSWISSENSCHAFTLICHE ABHANDLUNGEN. Vol. 1- 1955-. 0429-6524. Monographic Series. GW. German. ir. CF Muller Juristischer Verlag, Postfach 102640, D69 Heidelberg 1 West Germany.

FRENCH POLITICS AND SOCIETY. Issue 8 (Dec. 1984)-. 0882-1267. Periodical. US. English. qt. $12.00. Center for European Studies, Harvard University 5 Bryant Street, Cambridge MA 02138. Tel (617)495-4303. Ed Stanley Hoffmann and George Ross. DD 944. bk rev. adv acc. Circ 350. (ctrl). This journal contains articles and book reviews on contemporary issues and debates in France. It is of interest to political scientists, sociologists, historians, and general France-watchers. *Newsletter (Conference Group on French Politics and Society).*

GACETA DEPARTAMENTAL. Main/Corp Magdalena, Colombia (Dept.). Spanish. ir. LC J6.C8.

THE GALLUP POLL. Began with 1935/71 Vol. 0195-962X. US. English. an. $49.50. Scholarly Resources, 104 Greenhill Avenue, Wilmington DE 19805. Ed George H Gallup. LC HN90.P8. DD 303.380720973. Index in last issue of volume - attached. Circ 1,000. Public opinion polls conducted by the Gallup Organization, published in annual editions.

GALLUP REPORT. (THE GALLUP REPORT). Began with Dec. 27, 1967 issue. 0576-5455. Periodical. CN. English. sw. $85.12. Gallup Report, 45 Charles Street East, Toronto Ontario M4Y 152 Canada. Tel (416)961-2811. Ed Clara M Hatton. Ind/Abst Can. Bus. Index, Funk Scott Index Corp. Ind. Circ 165. (ctrl).

THE GALLUP REPORT. No. 184 (Jan. 1981)-. Periodical. US. English. mo. $45.0G. Gallup Report, PO Box 628, Princeton NJ 08540.

GANDHI MARG. V. 1- Apr. 1979-. Periodical. II. English. mo. $20.00. Gandhi Peace Foundation, 221-223 Deen Dayal Upadhyaya Marg, New Delhi 110002 India. Ind/Abst Am. Hist. Life, Hist. Abstr., MLA Int. Bibliogr. Books Artic. Mod. Lang. Lit. LC DS481.G3. DD 909.82. *Gandhi Marg.*

GEOPOLITICA (INSTITUTO DE ESTUDIOS GEOPOLITICOS (BUENOS AIRES, ARGENTINA)). (GEOPOLITICA). No. 1 (Oct. 1975)-. 0325-2035. Periodical. Spanish. ir. 7.000 Per Issue. Instituto de Estudios Geopoliticos, Corrientes 1994 1 P, Buenos Aires Argentina. LC F2834. DD 327.1011.

GEOPOLITICA (INSTITUTO URUGUAYO DE ESTUDIOS GEOPOLITICOS). (GEOPOLITICA : ORGANO OFICIAL DEL INSTITUTO URUGUAYO DE ESTUDIOS GEOPOLITICOS). V. 1, No. 1, (August 1976)-. UY. Spanish. sa. $40.00 Four Issues. Revista Geopolitica, Soriano 1585 - 10 -6, Montevideo Uruguay. LC JC319. DD 327.101105.

GERMAN POLITICAL STUDIES. V. 1- 1974-. 0307-7233. UK. English. an. Sage Publications, 28 Banner Street, London EC1Y 8QE England. LC JA55. DD 320.05.

GERMAN STUDIES NEWSLETTER. 0882-7079. Periodical. US. English. ty. $12.00 Domestic, $15.00 Foreign. Center for European Studies, 5 Bryant Street, Cambridge MA 02138. Tel (617)495-4303. Ed James Cooney, Lily Gardner Feldman and Guido Goldman. DD 943. bk rev. Circ 300. (ctrl). A triannual which includes articles and book reviews on German politics and culture as well as descriptions of programs on Germany and conference reports.

GESELLSCHAFT UND POLITIK. Began in 1965. 0016-9099. Periodical. German. qt. 180.00. Ebendorferstrasse 6/14, Wien Austria. LC HN401. DD 361.6109436. *Schriftenreihe des Institutes fur Sozialpolitik und Sozialreform.*

GESETZBLATT DER DEUTSCHEN DEMOKRATISCHEN REPUBLIK. TEIL 2. Main/Corp Germany (Democratic Republic, 1949-). German. ir. Kunst & Wissen Erich Bieber, Dufourstrasse 51, CH-8008 Zurich Switzerland.

GIDS (UTRECHT, NETHERLANDS). (DE GIDS). Periodical. Dutch. mo. 98.50 Domestic, 124.50 Foreign. Meulenhoff BV, Postbus 100, 1017 DG Amsterdam Netherlands. Tel 02-710919. Ed K L Poll. adv acc.

GLOBAL OUTLOOK. V. 101 I.E. V. 1- March 22/April 5, 1980-. 0226-8205. Periodical. CN. English. bw. $300. Domestic, $150. Public Libraries and Other Non-Profit Organizations. Global Outlook, 30 The Driveway, Ottawa Ontario K2P 1C9 Canada. DD 905.

GLOBAL RISK ASSESSMENTS: ISSUES, CONCEPTS, AND APPLICATIONS. (GLOBAL RISK ASSESSMENTS, ISSUES, CONCEPTS & APPLICATIONS IN BUSINESS ENVIRONMENT RISK ASSESSMENT, COUNTRY, INVESTMENT & TRADE RISK ANALYSIS, POLITICAL RISK ASSESSMENT & MANAGEMENT). VFOAT Global Risk Assessments, Issues, Concepts and Applications. Book 1-. 0739-4640. US. English. $19.95. Global Risk Assessments, 3638 University Avenue/Suite 215, Riverside CA 92501. Tel (714)788-0672. LC HG4538. DD 658. bk rev. Circ 2,000. Edited book series on political risk analysis.

GLOBAL VILLAGE (NANAIMO, B.C.). (GLOBAL VILLAGE). 0827-2229. Periodical. CN. English. ir. $5.00. Global Village (Nanaimo), #202 259 Pine Street, Nanaimo British Columbia V9R 2B7 Canada. DD 320.91724. *Nidea Newsletter.*

GOLDEN STATE REPORT. Vol. 1, No. 1 (Fall 1985)-. 0884-9072. Periodical. US. English. mo. $35.00. Golden State Report Inc, 444 North 3rd Street, Sacramento CA 95814. DD 320.

GOVERNMENT AND OPPOSITION. Vol. 1, No. 1 (Oct. 1965)-. 0017-257X. Periodical. UK. English. qt. Government and Opposition, Houghton St Aldwych, London WC2 2AE England. Tel 01 405 5991. Ed G Laneser. Ind/Abst Sociol. Abstr., Soc. Welf. Soc. Plan./Policy Soc. Dev., ABC Pol Sci, Recent Publ. Artic., Public Aff. Inf. Serv. Bull., Soc. Sci. Citation Index, Am. Hist. Life, Hist. Abstr., Lang. Lang. Behav. Abstr., Soc. Sci. Index, Hist. Abstr., Part A, Mod. Hist. Abstr., Hist. Abst., Part B, Twent. Century Abstr. LC JA8. (cum index). bk rev. adv acc. Circ 1,500. A journal of comparative politics with worldwide coverage and an interest in modern political philosophy, political history and political sociology.

GOVERNMENT GAZETTE. Main/Corp Papua New Guinea. VFOAT Papua and New Guinea Gazette. English. wk. $80.62. Papua New Guinea Government Printing Office, PO Box 1280, Port Moresby, Papua New Guinea. LC J8. *Territory of Papua Government Gazette.*

GOVERNMENT GAZETTE. Main/Corp Saint Vincent and the Grenadines. English. wk. LC J3.B8. DD 354.7298440005. *Saint Vincent Government Gazette.*

Political Science

GOVERNMENT PUBLICATIONS DIRECTORY. See Yearbooks, Almanacs, Directories.

GOVERNOR'S BIENNIAL REPORT (MONTANA). US. English. be. $6.11. State of Montana, Office of the Governor, Helena MT 59601. LC J87. DD 353.97860006.

G.P.S.A. JOURNAL CEASED. (GPSA JOURNAL). **Main/Corp** Georgia Political Science Association. Vol. 1, No. 1 (Fall 1973)-V. 8 No. 2 (Fall 1980). 0092-9395. Periodical. US. English. sa. $8.00. Larry Taulbee Managing Editor, Department of Political Science, Emory University, Atlanta GA 30322. LC JA1. DD 320.05.

GRANMA. V. 1- Oct. 4, 1965-. Newspaper. CU. Spanish. da. $55.71. Empresa Ediciones Cubanas, Sub-Direccion Exportacion, Oreilly 407 Ciudad Habana Cuba.

GRASS ROOTS FORUM. 0017-3517. Periodical. US. English. qt. $5.00. Grass Roots Publishing Company, PO Box 472, San Gabriel CA 91778. LC UNC. Available in microform from University Microfilms.

GREEK OPINION. Vol. 1, No. 1 (Jan./Feb. 1984)-. Periodical. GR. English. mo. 130.00. Eurodim, 82 Constantinople Avenue, GR-104 35 Athens Greece. Tel (301)347-2226. Ed Panayote Elias Dimitras. adv acc. Circ 100. A survey of Greek public opinion and politics that includes analyses of comprehensive polls, political commentary and articles from scholarly journals and international conferences.

GREEK REPORT. Vol. 1 1969-. 0017-3908. Periodical. UK. English. mo. Greek Report, 20 Eccleston Street, London SW1 England. LC DF701. DD 320.9495.

GROUP RESEARCH REPORT. 0017-4742. Periodical. US. English. mo. $40.00. Group Research Inc, 419 New Jersey Avenue SE, Washington DC 20003. Tel (202)546-2090. LC E838. DD 320.50973.

LA GUARDIA CEASED. V. 1 (No. 1, 3, 5-7), August 1969-August 1970. Periodical. US. English. La Guardia, 805 South 5th Street, Milwaukee WI 53204. Tel 647-2470. Ed John Torres. bk rev. adv acc. Circ 20,000.

GUIDE TO GRADUATE STUDY IN POLITICAL SCIENCE. (A GUIDE TO GRADUATE STUDY IN POLITICAL SCIENCE). Began with Vol. for 1972. 0091-9632. US. English. an. $20.00. American Political Science Association, 1527 New Hampshire Avenue Northwest, Washington DC 20015. Tel (202)483-2512. Ed Patricia B Spellman. LC JA88.U6. DD 320.071173. adv acc. Circ 3,000. Lists over 300 graduate programs in political science in the US and Canada. Describes programs, lists faculty with fields of specialization.

GUIDE TO THE AUSTRALIAN FEDERAL PARLIAMENT. VFOAT Guide to the Federal Parliament. AT. English. ir. 95.00. Australian Press Services, Government Printing Office E160, Canberra Australian Capital Territory 2600 Australia. Tel (062)95-9475. Ed J M Hutchison. Comprehensive detail of members of parliament, heads of government departments, industrial and business organisations, parliamentary press gallery and maps of electoral boundaries.

GUIDE TO THE HOUSE OF COMMONS. VFOAT Times Guide to the House of Commons. 1970-. UK. English. ir. 7.95. Times Books Ltd, 16 Golden Square, London W1R 4BN England. Tel 01-434 3767. Ed Alan Wood. LC JN956. DD 328.420922. Circ 10,000. (ctrl). Complete guide to results of British general election including photos and biographies of all MPS. Published after each general election. House of Commons.

GUYANA JOURNAL. V. 1- April 1968-. 0046-6654. Periodical. GY. English. ir. Ministry of External Affairs, Georgetown Guyana.

HA-SHILTH-SA. Vol. 1, No. 3 (Mar. 11, 1974)-. 0715-4143. Newspaper. CN. English. mo. 8.00. Ha-Shilth-Sa, R R #3, Port Alberni British Columbia V9Y 7L7 Canada. Tel (604)724-5757. Ed Bob Soderlund. DD 971.100497. bk rev. adv acc. Circ 2,000. (ctrl). A native Indian publication concentrating on native issues on the west coast of Vancouver islands. Includes politics, culture, social events, sports and human interest. Your Paper Needs a Name, 0715-4143.

HAFTEN FOR KRITISKA STUDIER. 0345-4789. Periodical. SW. Swedish. bm. $20.62. Haften for Kritiska Studier, Box 5220, 102 45 Stockholm Sweden. Tel 08/620737. Ed Goran Fredriksson. bk rev. adv acc. Circ 2,400. An independent socialist magazine providing an alternative in Sweden to bourgeois scholarship. Special attention on the labor movement and the development of capitalism in the Nordic countries.

HAMBURG HANDBUCH. 0302-9247. German. ir. Distributor: Verlag P Hartung, Heidenkampsweg 82, 1 Hamburg West Germany. LC JN4287.

THE HAMLYN LECTURES. See Law.

HANDBOOK OF ILLINOIS GOVERNMENT. Main/Corp Illinois. Office of Secretary of State. 0095-2842. US. English. Office of Illinois Secretary of State, Room 300/Centennial Building, Springfield IL 62756. LC JK5730. DD 320.4773.

THE HANDBOOK OF POLITICAL BEHAVIOR. Vol. 1-. US. English. ir. $49.50. Plenum Publishing Corporation, 227 West 17th Street, New York NY 10011.

THE HANDBOOK OF STATE LEGISLATIVE LEADERS. 1983-1984-. 0743-0728. US. English. an. Ballinger Publishing Company, 54 Church Street, Cambridge MA 02138. LC JK2484. DD 328.36202573.

HANDBOOK OF THE NATIONS. 1st- Ed. 0194-3790. US. English. ir. $74.00. Gale Research Company, Book Tower, Detroit MI 48226. Tel (313)961-2242. Emphasizing up-to-date economic and governmental data, it also provides details on each political unit's land, people, communications, and defense forces.

HANSARD OFFICIAL REPORT OF DEBATES - LEGISLATIVE ASSEMBLY OF ONTARIO. SELECT COMMITTEE ON THE OMBUDSMAN. (HANSARD OFFICIAL REPORT OF DEBATES). Main/Corp Ontario. Legislative Assembly. Select Committee on the Ombudsman. No. OM-1, 3rd Session, 32nd Parliament (Nov. 2, 1983)-. 0824-9202. Periodical. CN. English. da. $15.00 Per Session. Sessional Subscription Service Information Services Branch, Ministry of Government Services, 5th Floor/880 Bay Street, Toronto Ontario 7M4 1N8 Canada. LC JL269.5.O4. DD 328.71307452.

HANSARD OFFICIAL REPORT OF DEBATES - LEGISLATIVE ASSEMBLY OF ONTARIO. STANDING COMMITTEE ON ADMINISTRATION OF JUSTICE. (HANSARD OFFICIAL REPORT OF DEBATES). Main/Corp Ontario. Legislative Assembly. Standing Committee on Administration of Justice. 3rd Sess., 32nd Parliament, No. 1- (May 25 1983)-. 0822-1871. CN. English. tw. $15.00 Per Session. Sessional Subscription Service, Information Service Branch, Ministry of Government Services, 5th Floor/880 Bay Street, Toronto Ontario M7A 1N8 Canada. LC J108. DD 328.71402. Legislature of Ontario Debates, 0824-7307.

THE HARRIS SURVEY. No. 1 (Jan. 1, 1981)-. 0273-1037. Periodical. US. English. ir. Louis Harris & Associates, 630 Fifth Avenue, New York NY 10111. Tel (212)975-1600. Ed Louis Harris. Circ 200. Public opinion attitudes on current events, politics and foreign affairs. ABC News-Harris Survey, 0163-4836.

HARVARD POLITICAL STUDIES. Monographic Series. US. English. ir. Harvard University Press, 79 Garden Street, Cambridge MA 02138. Tel (617)661-3761.

HASTINGS CONSTITUTIONAL LAW QUARTERLY. See Law.

HAWLIYAT SIYASIYAH. VFOAT Annales Politiques. V. 1, No. 1, (Winter 1982)-. Periodical. Arabic and English. ir. $75.00. Hasad Editions, 2 rue Christine, Paris 75006 France. LC DS63.1.

HEIDELBERGER POLITISCHE SCHRIFTEN CEASED. Vol. 1- 1970-. Monographic Series. GW. German. ir. Athenaum Verlag GMBH, Adelheidstrabe 2, 6240 Konigstein/TS West Germany.

HEMISPHERE HOTLINE. Vol. 10, No. 1 (Jan. 5, 1979)-. 0734-9181. Periodical. US. English. bw. $100.00. Virginia Prewett Association, 4545 Connecticut Avenue NW, Washington DC 20008. LC F1401. DD 320.54098. Hemisphere Hotline Report, 0092-377X.

HERODOTE. Began with Jan./Mar. 1976 issue. 0338-487X. Periodical. FR. French. qt. $35.92. Editions La Decouverte, 1 Place Paul Painleve, 75005 Paris France. Tel (1)4633 41 16. LC JC319. DD 327.101105. bk rev. (ctrl). One of the major French geographical publications which does not only concern geographers but all sorts of other disciplines and which helps to understand the complexity of geopolitical phenomena of the modern times.

HISPO. VFOAT Historie et Science Politique. Journal 1 (Jan. 1983)-. Periodical. French. sa. Hispo Case Postale 3000, Berne 16 Switzerland.

HISTORICAL REPORT OF THE SECRETARY OF STATE, ARKANSAS. Main/Corp Arkansas. Office of Secretary of State. 1958-. 0196-4720. US. English. Secretary of State, State Capitol, Little Rock AR 72114. LC J87. DD 320.976705. Report.

HISTORY OF POLITICAL THOUGHT. Vol. 1, Issue 1 (Spring 1980)-. 0143-781X. Periodical. UK. English. ty. $49.70. Imprint Academic, 32 Haldon Road, Exeter Devon EX44D2 England. Tel 0392-51329. Ed J Coleman and I P Hampsher-Monk. Ind/Abst Am. Hist. Life, Hist. Abstr., Part A, Mod. Hist. Abstr., Hist. Abst., Part B, Twent. Century Abstr., Philos. Index, Recent Publ. Artic. LC JA8. DD 320.0105. bk rev. adv acc. Circ 600. The study of political thought in its international and historical context, from ancient Greece to the Modern period.

HITOTSUBASHI JOURNAL OF LAW & POLITICS. VFOAT Hitotsubashi Journal of Law and Politics. Began with: Vol. 1 (Apr. 1960). 0073-2796. JA. English (and German). ir. $13.50. Japan Publications Trading Company Ltd, PO Box 5030, Tokyo Internatioal, Tokyo 100-31 Japan. Ind/Abst Writ. Am. Hist., Public Aff. Inf. Serv. Bull. DD 320.05. Annals of the Hitotsubashi Academy, 0439-2841.

HOUSE JOURNAL OF THE . . . LEGISLATURE OF THE STATE OF MONTANA. Main/Corp Montana. Legislature. House of Representatives. VFOAT House Journal. US. English. Montana Legislative Council, Room 138/State Capitol, Helena MT 59620. LC J87. DD 328.78601. House Journal.

HRVATSKI PUT. VFOAT Croatian Way. V. 11- (No. 122-). 0702-3855. Periodical. CN. Serbo-Croatian -R (includes some text in English). mo. 24.00. Croatian Republicans, Box 78/Station M, Toronto Ontario M6S 4T2 Canada. Tel (416)762-3045. Ed Rudi Tomic. LC F1035.C7. bk rev. Circ 3,000. Covers world affairs and Croatian national culture and political activity throughout the world. Nas Put, 0027-8092.

HSUEH HSI TSA CHIH. VFOAT Xue Xi Za Zhi. Periodical. CH. Chinese. mo. 0.20. Post Office Chung-tu Shih, Cheng-tu Shih China. LC AP95.C4. DD 320.53230951.

HUMAN EVENTS. V. 1- Feb. 2, 1944-. 0018-7194. Periodical. US. English. wk. $25.00. Human Events, 422 1st Street SE, Washington DC 20003. Tel (202)546-0856. Ed Thomas S Winter. Ind/Abst Book Rev. Index, Am. Hist. Life, Hist. Abstr. LC D410. DD 940.5305. bk rev. adv acc. Circ 47,000. National conservative weekly reports. Analyzes domestic and foreign political and economic events.

HUMANITY CALLS. June 1978-. Periodical. II. English. ir. Sudhir Singh, A-1/57 Safdarjang Enclave, New Delhi 110 016 India. LC JX1903. DD 327.1705.

IBERO-AMERIKANISCHES ARCHIV. See Genealogy and Heraldry - Archives.

ICSSR JOURNAL OF ABSTRACTS AND REVIEWS : ECONOMICS. See Indexes/Abstracts.

ICSSR JOURNAL OF ABSTRACTS AND REVIEWS: POLITICAL SCIENCE. See Indexes/Abstracts.

THE IDAHO POLITICAL HANDBOOK. 1978-. US. English. be. University of Idaho, Bureau of Public Affairs, Moscow ID 83843. Ed M Donovan. LC JK7595. DD 324.09796.

IFDA DOSSIER. 1- Jan. 1978-. Periodical. English (French). bm. $30.00. International Foundation Development Alternatives, 2 Place du Marche, CH-1260 Nyon Switzerland. Tel 41-22-618282. bk rev. Circ 15,000. Articles and informations on development alternatives concepts,

Political Science

activities and factors, from local to global space (including future of the United Nations). Is essentially a vehicle for mutually educating dialogues.

ILLINOIS ISSUES. V. 1- 1975-. 0738-9663. Periodical. US. English. mo. $30.00. Illinois Issues, Sangamon State University, Springfield IL 62708. **Tel** (217)786-6084. Ed Caroline Gheradini. **Ind/Abst** Public Aff. Inf. Serv. Bull. bk rev. adv acc. **Circ** 4,500. (ctrl). Monthly magazine providing in-depth coverage of the issues and people behind them in the Illinois Political-Governmental arena. Covers economics, education, business, environment, etc.

IMPACT P C. First issued Sept. 1973. 0317-8560. CN. French (text in English). mo. Free to Members. Impact PC, 225 East rue Roy/Bureau 22, Montreal Quebec H2W 1M5 Canada. DD 329.9714.

IN COMMON CEASED. V. 5, No. 5-V. 11, No. 1. 0196-6677. Periodical. US. English. qt. $15.00. 2030 M Street NW, Washington DC 20036. LC JK1. DD 320.97305. *Common Cause Report from Washington.*

IN POLITICS. Vol. 1, No. 1 (Summer 1981)-. 0275-8954. Periodical. US. English. ir. $1.25 Single Issue. In Politics, Connecticut College/Box 1322, New London CT 06320.

IN THESE TIMES. Vol. 1- Nov. 15-21, 1976-. 0160-5992. Periodical. US. English. ir. $59.00. Institute for Public Affairs, 1300 West Belmont, Chicago IL 60613. **Tel** (312)472-5700. Ed James Weinstein. **Ind/Abst** Altern. Press Index. LC AP2. DD 051. bk rev. adv acc. **Circ** 25,000. Committed to democratic social change with its weekly coverage of the nation, the world and the arts.

THE INDEPENDENT AMERICAN. Periodical. US. English. bm. The Independent American, PO Box 636, Littleton CO 80120. Also available on microfilm. *Free Men Speak.*

INDEPENDENT REPUBLICAN. Vol. 22, No. 1 (Aug. 1984)-. 8750-2364. Periodical. US. English. qt. $15.00. Vail-Smith Company, 3301 Adams Avenue, San Diego CA 92116. DD 322. *Republican, 0199-4549.*

INDEX - CANADA. PARLIAMENT. STANDING JOINT COMMITTEE ON REGULATIONS AND OTHER STATUTORY INSTRUMENTS. See Indexes/Abstracts.

INDIAN JOURNAL OF POLITICAL SCIENCE. V. 1- July/Sept. 1939-. 0019-5510. Periodical. II. English. qt. Osmania University, c/o Professor Bav Sharma, Hyderbad 500 007 India. **Ind/Abst** ABC Pol Sci, Chem. Abstr., Sociol. Abstr., Lang. Lang. Behav. Abstr. LC JA26. DD 320.5.

INDIAN JOURNAL OF POLITICS. V. 1- Jan./June 1967-. 0303-9951. Periodical. II. English. sa. 75.- Domestic, $25.00 Foreign. Aligarh Muslim University, Department of Political Science, Alegarn 202001 India. **Tel** 6720. Ed S A H Bilgrami. **Ind/Abst** Am. Hist. Life, Hist. Abstr., Part A, Mod. Hist. Abstr., Hist. Abstr., Part B, Twent. Century Abstr., ABC Pol Sci. LC JA26. DD 320.05. bk rev. **Circ** 300. (ctrl). A nonprofit, nonofficial, independent, academic journal dedicated to the advancement of research in all subfields of political science and their wider interdisciplinary nature.

THE INDIAN POLITICAL SCIENCE REVIEW CEASED. V. 1, Nos. 1 & 2 (Oct. 1966/March 1967)-V. 19 Nos. 1 & 2 (Jan./Dec. 1985). 0019-6126. Periodical. II. English. sa. University of Delhi, Department of Political Science and Arts, Faculty Building, Delhi 110007 India. **Tel** 591774. Ed Harnam Singh. **Ind/Abst** Am. Hist. Life, Hist. Abstr., Part A, Mod. Hist. Abstr., Hist. Abst., Part B, Twent. Century Abstr., ABC Pol Sci, Recent Publ. Artic. bk rev. adv acc. **Circ** 2,000. (ctrl). Concerns political science.

INDO ASIA. Vol. 1-. 0019-719X. Periodical. GW. German. qt. $29.22. Burg Verlag GMBH, Untere AU 41, 7123 Sachsenheim 3 West Germany. **Ind/Abst** PAIS Foreign Lang. Index, Foreign Lang. Index, Recent Publ. Artic. LC DS401.

INDOCHINA ISSUES. 1- Mar. 1979-. 0738-4548. Periodical. US. English. mo. $9.00. Center for International Policy, 120 Maryland Avenue Northeast, Washington DC 20002. **Tel** (202)546-8181. **Circ** 2,000. Impact of US foreign policies on human rights, social and economic conditions in nations of Indochina.

INFO JEUNES PC. VFOAT Info PC. VAT Info Jeunes Progressistes-Conservateurs du Canada (1983), Info JPC (1983). Vol. 1, No. 1 (Oct. 1983)-. 0826-2616. Periodical. CN. French. Free. Federation des Jeunes Progressistes-Conservateurs du Canada, Bureau 200 161 Ouest AV Laurier, Ottawa Ontario K1P 5J2 Canada. DD 324.27104. *Info P.C., 0820-6279.*

INFORMATIONEN ZUR POLITISCHEN BILDUNG. Monographic Series. GW. German. qt. $10.96. C W Leske Verlag, Postfach 300 406, Furstenbergstr 23, 5090 Leverkusen 3 West Germany. LC JA88.G3. DD 320.05. *Staatsburgerliche Information.*

INFRASTRUCTURE. Vol. 1, No. 1 (Oct. 1982)-. 0742-1990. Periodical. US. English. bw. $197.00 US. $202.20 Canada. Business Publishers, 951 Pershing Drive, Silver Spring MD 20910.

THE INITIATIVE NEWS REPORT. Vol. 1, No. 1 (July 1980)-. 0273-3196. Periodical. US. English. bw. $195.00. Capitol Publications Inc, 1300 North 17th Street, Arlington VA 22209. **Tel** (703)528-5400.

INSTITUT. (L'INSTITUT). Vol. 4, No. 1 (25 Jan. 1982)-. 0714-668X. Periodical. CN. French. $20.00. Institut de Recherches Politiques, C P 3670, Halifax-Sud Nova Scotia B3J 3K6 Canada. **Tel** (902)424-3801. Ed T Kent. DD 354.7105. bk rev. **Circ** 6,000. (ctrl). A forum for diverse views on all issues of public policy. *Institut de Recherches Politiques, 0227-7913.*

THE INTELLECTUAL ACTIVIST. 1979. 0730-2355. Periodical. US. English. ir. Intellectual Activist, 131 5th Avenue 101, New York NY 10003. **Tel** (212)982-8357. Ed Peter Schwartz. bk rev. Political and economic analysis from a pro laissez-faire capitalism viewpoint.

INTELLIGENCE DIGEST : WEEKLY REVIEW. Periodical. UK. English. wk. 55.00 Domestic, $165.00 US and Canada, $75.00 Others. Intelligence International Ltd, 17 Rodney Road Cheltenham, Glouchester GL50 1HX England. **Tel** 44 242 517774. LC D839. DD 327.05. bk rev. **Circ** 15,000. (ctrl). Provided with an unrivalled and complete source of inside trends throughout the world.

INTERCONTINENTAL PRESS COMBINED WITH INPRECOR. VFOAT Intercontinental Press/Inprecor. V. 16, No. 2- Jan. 16, 1978-. 0162-5594. Periodical. US. English. bw. $30.00. Intercontinental Press, 410 West Street, New York NY 10014. **Tel** (212)929-3486. Ed Doug Jenness. **Ind/Abst** Altern. Press Index, Public Aff. Inf. Serv. Bull. LC D839. DD 327.05. bk rev. **Circ** 3,500. Political analysis and interpretation of events of particular interest to labor, socialist, colonial independence, black and women's liberation movements internationally. *Intercontinental Press, 0020-5303; Inprecor.*

INTERFAITH ACTION FOR ECONOMIC JUSTICE. VFOAT Interfaith Action. Began with: issue for Sept. 1984. 8755-9404. Periodical. US. English. mo. $7.00. Interfaith Action for Economic Justice, 110 Maryland Avenue Northeast, Washington DC 20002. DD 322.

INTERIM REPORT OF THE ELECTORAL BOUNDARIES COMMISSION OF THE PROVINCE OF ALBERTA. Main/Corp Electoral Boundaries Commission for the Province of Alberta (Canada). VFOAT Interim Report. CN. English. LC JL333. DD 328.712307345.

INTERNATIONAL JOURNAL OF POLITICS. V. 1- Spring 1971-. 0012-8783. Periodical. US. English. qt. $178.50. M E Sharpe Inc, 80 Business Park Drive, Armonk NY 10504. **Tel** (914)273-1800. Ed Arnold C Tovell. **Ind/Abst** Am. Hist. Life, Hist. Abstr., Part A, Mod. Hist. Abstr., Hist. Abst., Part B, Twent. Century Abstr., Hist. Abstr. LC JA1.A1. DD 320. adv acc. **Circ** 300. A worldwide forum for the scholarship of the left, right, and center on current political theory and practice.

INTERNATIONAL MARXIST REVIEW : IMR. Began with: No. 1 (June 1971). Periodical. UK. English. IMR Publications, 2 rue Richard Lenoir, 93108 Montrevil France.

INTERNATIONAL POLITICAL SCIENCE ABSTRACTS. See Indexes/Abstracts.

INTERNATIONAL REPORT (IRVINE, CALIF.). (INTERNATIONAL REPORT). Vol. 1, No. 1 (Mar. 1983)-. 0740-669X. Periodical. US. English. ty. $15.00. International Report, PO Box 4882, Irvine CA 92716. **Tel** (714)856-5272. Ed Paul Ferandez and Rosalinda Gonzalez. LC D839. DD 905. **Circ** 300. (ctrl). A political and economic analysis of international events, exposing actions of undemocratic governments and presenting popular resistance and organization against those governments. *Colombia Report, 0730-1073.*

INTERNATIONALE KORRESPONDENZ. Vol. 1- Mar. 1973-. GW. German. ir. 3.00 Single Issue. Arno Nickel, Postfach 3971, 1 Berlin 30 West Germany. LC HX11.I5. DD 329.07205.

INTERPRETATION. V. 1- Summer 1970-. 0020-9635. Periodical. US. English. ty. $12.00. Queens College Press, G-101 Queens College, Flushing NY 11367. **Tel** (718)520-7099. Ed Hilail Gildin. **Ind/Abst** MLA Int. Bibliogr. Books Artic. Mod. Lang. Lit., Philos. Index. LC JA26. DD 320.05. bk rev.

INTERSEARCH. 0163-0997. Periodical. US. English. bw. $36.00. International Terrorist Research Center, PO Box 26804 El Paso TX 79926. *Counterforce, 0146-812X.*

IOWA ELECTION HANDBOOK WITH ELECTION LAWS OF IOWA. Main/Corp Iowa. 0360-7526. US. English. an. Box 1168, Cedar Rapids IA 52406. LC KFI4620.A29. DD 342.7770702632.

IOWA PEACE DIRECTORY. See Yearbooks, Almanacs, Directories.

IOWA VOTER. 0199-4212. Periodical. US. English. qt. LWV of Iowa, 111 Wilson Community Center, Des Moines IA 50317.

IPSR. INTERNATIONAL POLITICAL SCIENCE REVIEW. (RISP, REVUE INTERNATIONALE DE SCIENCE POLITIQUE). VFOAT IPSR, International Political Science Review. V. 1- Jan. 1980-. 0192-5121. Periodical. US. English (French). qt. Sage Publications Inc, 275 South Beverly Drive, Beverly Hills CA 90212. **Tel** (213)274-8003. **Ind/Abst** ABC Pol Sci. LC JA1.A1. DD 320.05.

IRAN-UNITED STATES CLAIMS TRIBUNAL REPORTS. See Law - International Law.

IRIS (TERRASSE-VAUDREUIL). (L'IRIS). Nov. 1974-. 0316-9065. Periodical. CN. French. ir. .60 Per No. Editions de l'Iris, 59 - 1ER Boulevard, Terrasse-Vaudreuil Quebec J7V 5S6 Canada. DD 320.9714.

ISRAEL HORIZONS. See Religion, Mythology, Rationalism - Judaism.

JACK ANDERSON'S WASHINGTON LETTER. VFOAT Washington Letter. Apr. 1984-. 0743-0825. Periodical. US. English. mo. Jack Anderson's Washington Letter, 1401 Sixteenth Street Northwest, Washington DC 20036. DD 320.

JAHRBUCH ASIEN-AFRIKA-LATEINAMERIKA. See Yearbooks, Almanacs, Directories.

JAHRBUCH DES OFFENTLICHEN RECHTS DER GEGENWART. See Yearbooks, Almanacs, Directories.

JAHRBUCH FUR GESCHICHTE DES FEUDALISMUS. See Yearbooks, Almanacs, Directories.

JAHRBUCH POLITIK. See Yearbooks, Almanacs, Directories.

THE JAMES SPRUNT STUDIES IN HISTORY AND POLITICAL SCIENCE. See History (General).

JANATA. VFOAT Janata Annual. V. 1- Jan. 26, 1946-. 0021-4221. Periodical. II. English. wk. $8.00. GG Pskikh Publishing, National House, 6 Tulloch Road, Bombay 1 India. LC DS401. DD 329.954.

JOURNAL - ANDHRA PRADESH, INDIA. LEGISLATURE. LEGISLATIVE COUNCIL. Main/Corp Andhra Pradesh, India Legislature. Legislative Council. II. English. ir. India Legislature/Legislative Council Hyderabad, Andra Pradesh Hyderabad India. LC J601.A4. DD 328.548101.

JOURNAL DES DEBATS CEASED. Main/Corp Quebec (Province). National Assembly. CN. French. $8.00. Ministre des Finances, Comptable de l'Assemblee Nationale, Quebec Canada. LC J107. *Debats de l'Assemblee Legislative de la Province de Quebec.*

JOURNAL DES DEBATS : COMMISSIONS PARLEMENTAIRES. Main/Corp Quebec (Province). National Assembly. CN. French. $8.00. Ministre des Finances, Comptable de l'Assemblee Nationale, Quebec Canada. LC J107.

JOURNAL DES DEBATS (QUEBEC). (JOURNAL DES DEBATS). Main/Corp Quebec (Province) Assemblee Nationale. 30. Legislature, 4

Session- (V.17-). CN. French. ir. $23.21. Service Documents Parliamenta, 1060 Conroy Rez de Chaussee CP 28, Quebec PC G1R 5E6 Canada. **Tel** (418)643-2754. The content shows the debates of the National Assembly of our representatives elected in the Province of Quebec. *Journal des Debats.*

JOURNAL DU RCM. (LE JOURNAL DU R C M). **Main/Corp** Rassemblement des Citoyens de Montreal. **VAT** Journal du Rassemblement des Citoyens de Montreal. June 1978-. 0709-6003. Periodical. CN. French (English). Rassemblement des Citoyens de Montreal, Bureau 101/1012 rue Mont-Royal, Montreal Quebec H2J 1X6 Canada. **DD** 329.9714281. *Bulletin Info - R. C. M., 0703-9786.*

JOURNAL OF AUSTRALIAN POLITICAL ECONOMY. (THE JOURNAL OF AUSTRALIAN POLITICAL ECONOMY). No. 1- Oct. 1977-. 0156-5826. Periodical. AT. English. ty. 20 Domestic, 25 Foreign. Australian Political Economy Movement, PO Box 805/Parkville 3052, Melbourne Victoria 3000 Australia. **Ind/Abst** APAIS, Aust. Public Aff. Inf. Serv., Energy Res. Abstr. bk rev. adv acc. **Circ** 1,000. Theoretical and empirical research on Australian society from a labour movement perspective.

JOURNAL OF CHURCH AND STATE. (A JOURNAL OF CHURCH AND STATE). V. 1- Nov. 1959-. 0021-969X. Periodical. US. English. ir. $15.00. Baylor University, Box 380, Waco TX 76798. **Tel** (817)755-1510. **Ed** James E Wood. **Ind/Abst** Am. Hist. Life, Hist. Abstr., Part A, Mod. Hist. Abstr., Hist. Abst., Part B, Twent. Century Abstr., Leg. Resour. Index, Hist. Abstr., Writ. Am. Hist., Book Rev. Index, Relig. Index One, Period., Christ. Period. Index, Educ. Adm. Abstr., Public Aff. Inf. Serv. Bull., Relig. Theol. Abstr., Curr. Law Index, Recent Publ. Artic. **LC** BV630.A1. **DD** 322.105. (cum index). bk rev. adv acc. **Circ** 1,400. Interfaith, international and interdisciplinary. Seeks to stimulate interest, dialogue, research, and publication in the broad area of religion and the state.

JOURNAL OF COMMON MARKET STUDIES. V. 1- 1962-. 0021-9886. Periodical. UK. English. qt. $78.95. Basil Blackwell Journals Department, 108 Cowley Road, Oxford OX4 1JF England. **Tel** 0865-722146. **Ed** Peter Robson. **Ind/Abst** Am. Hist. Life, Hist. Abstr., Part A, Mod. Hist. Abstr., Hist. Abst., Part B, Twent. Century Abstr., Manage. Contents, Int. Labour Doc., Predicasts, Index Econ. Artic. J. Collect. Vol., ABC Pol Sci, ABI/Inform, Manage. Market. Abstr., Hist. Abstr., Ref. Source, Public Aff. Inf. Serv. Bull., Bus. Period. Index, Energy Res. Abstr., Soc. Sci. Citation Index, Funk Scott Index Corp. Ind., Recent Publ. Artic. **LC** HC241. (cum index). adv acc. Devoted to the analysis of international integration and the experience of regional groupings.

JOURNAL OF COMMONWEALTH & COMPARATIVE POLITICS. (THE JOURNAL OF COMMONWEALTH & COMPARATIVE POLITICS). **VAT** Journal of Commonwealth and Comparative Politics. V. 12- Mar. 1974-. 0306-3631. Periodical. UK. English. ty. $18.00. F Cass Company, 67 Great Russell Street, London WC1B 3BT England. **Ind/Abst** Sociol. Abstr., Soc. Welf. Soc. Plan./Policy Soc. Dev., ABC Pol Sci, Ref. Source. **LC** JN248. **DD** 320.9171241. *Journal of Commonwealth Political Studies, 0021-9908.*

JOURNAL OF COMMONWEALTH AND COMPARATIVE POLITICS. Periodical. UK. English. ir. 44. Frank Cass & Company Ltd, 11 Gainsborough Road, London E11 1RS England. **Tel** 01-530-4226. **Ed** Richard Crook and James Manor. **Ind/Abst** ABC Pol Sci, Am. Hist. Life, Hist. Abstr., Soc. Sci. Citation Index. bk rev. adv acc. **Circ** 500. Presents research on the processes of politics in commonwealth countries, in the context of historical development.

JOURNAL OF CONSTITUTIONAL AND PARLIAMENTARY STUDIES. *See* Law.

JOURNAL OF EAST AND WEST STUDIES. **VFOAT** Tongso Yongu. V. 1- 1973-. Periodical. KO. English. sa. Institute of East and West Studies, Yonsei University, 134 Shinchon-dong-Seodaemoon-Gu. **LC** CB251.

JOURNAL OF GOVERNMENT AND POLITICAL STUDIES. V. 1- Sept. 1976-. Periodical. II. English. ir. 10.00 Domestic, $3.00 US. Punjabi University, Editorial Office/Department of Political Science, Patiala 147002 India. **LC** JQ201. **DD** 320.05.

JOURNAL OF HISPANIC POLITICS. Vol. 1, No. 1 (1985)-. 0888-2355. Periodical. US. English. an. c/o Center for Business and Government, 504 Belfar, JFK School of Government/Harvard University, Cambridge MA 02138. **DD** 323.

JOURNAL OF LAW AND POLITICS. *See* Law.

JOURNAL OF POLITICAL SCIENCE. V. 1- 1973-. 0098-4612. Periodical. US. English. sa. $11.00. Clemson University, Department of Political Science, Clemson SC 29631. **Tel** (803)656-3235. **Ed** Martin Slann. **Ind/Abst** Am. Hist. Life, Hist. Abstr., Part A, Mod. Hist. Abstr., Hist. Abst., Part B, Twent. Century Abstr., ABC Pol Sci, Hist. Abstr. **LC** JA1. **DD** 320.05. bk rev. adv acc. **Circ** 300. A publication that includes all the sub-discipline areas of political science and prefers brief articles that are written in readable and understandable prose. *South Carolina Journal of Political Science.*

THE JOURNAL OF POLITICS. V. 1- Feb. 1939-. 0022-3816. Periodical. US. English. qt. $30.00. Journal of Politics, University of Florida, Gainesville FL 32611. **Tel** (904)392-0262. **Ed** Michael Giles. **Ind/Abst** Am. Hist. Life, Hist. Abstr., Part A, Mod. Hist. Abstr., Hist. Abst., Part B, Twent. Century Abstr., Sociol. Abstr., Soc. Welf. Soc. Plan./Policy Soc. Dev., ABC Pol Sci, Annu. Bibliogr. Engl. Lang. Lit., Hist. Abstr., Writ. Am. Hist., Book Rev. Index, Public Aff. Inf. Serv. Bull., Soc. Sci. Index, Soc. Sci. Citation Index, Recent Publ. Artic. **LC** JA1. **DD** 320.5. bk rev. adv acc. **Circ** 3,500. Available on microfilm beginning with V. 15, 1953 from University Microfilms. Published by Southern Political Science Association, containing articles and book reviews on various sub-fields in political science.

JOURNAL OF PUBLIC POLICY. Vol. 1, Pt. 1 (Feb. 1981)-. 0143-814X. Periodical. UK. English. qt. $75.00. Cambridge University Press, 510 North Avenue, New Rochelle NY 10801. **Tel** (914)235-0300. **Ed** Richard Rose. **Ind/Abst** Sociol. Abstr., ABC Pol Sci, Public Aff. Inf. Serv. Bull. bk rev. Publishes articles that use concepts derived from the social sciences to illuminate a significant problem facing contemporary governments.

JOURNAL OF SOUTHERN AFRICAN AFFAIRS. V. 1- Oct. 1976-. 0275-5327. Periodical. US. English. qt. Kings Court Communications, PO Box 429, Brunswick OH 44212. **Ind/Abst** Am. Hist. Life, Hist. Abstr., Part A, Mod. Hist. Abstr., Hist. Abst., Part B, Twent. Century Abstr. **LC** DT727. **DD** 052.

JOURNAL OF THE POLITICAL SCIENCE SOCIETY. **Main/Corp** Singapore (City) University Political Science Society. 1970/71-. Periodical. SI. English. ir. Singapore University, Department of Political Science Society, Bukit Timak Road, Singapore. **LC** JQ745.S5. **DD** 320.05.

JOURNAL OF THE SENATE OF THE UNITED STATES OF AMERICA. **Main/Corp** United States. Congress. Senate. **VFOAT** Senate Journal. Began with 1st Congress, March 4/Sept. 1789. US. English. an. **LC** KF45. **DD** 328.7301.

JOURNAL OFFICIEL DE LA REPUBLIQUE FRANCAISE. DEBATS PARLEMENTAIRES: ASSEMBLEE NATIONALE. **Main/Corp** France. Parlement (1946-). Assemblee Nationale. FR. French. ir. 40.00. Assemblee Nationale, 26 rue Desaix, 75732 Paris Cedex 15 France. **LC** J7. **DD** 328.4402. *Debats Parlementaires.*

JOURNAL PC. **VAT** Journal Progressiste-Conservatrice. Vol. 1, No. 1 (June 1982)-. 0821-6495. Periodical. CN. French. mo. Association Progressiste-Conservatrice du Canada, 2ME Etage 161 Ouest Av Laurier, Ottawa Ontario K1P 5J2 Canada. **DD** 324.2710405. *Objectif 84, 0712-3965.*

JUDGMENTS OF THE UNITED NATIONS ADMINISTRATIVE TRIBUNAL. *See* Law - International Law.

KAIGIROKU SOSAKUIN. **Main/Corp** Kokuritsu Kokkai Toshokan, Tokyo. Chosa Oyobi Rippo Kosakyoku. **VFOAT** General Index to the Debates. No. 39- Kai Kokkai. JA. Japanese. ir. **LC** JQ1654.

KANSAI UNIVERSITY REVIEW OF LAW AND POLITICS. *See* Law.

KANSAS VOTER'S GUIDE. 1st 1952-. 0453-283X. US. English. be. $2.00. University of Kansas, Center for Public Affairs, Lawrence KS 66045. **Tel** (913)864-3701. **Ed** Wendy A Murray. **Circ** 1,200. A summary source of information on the electoral process in Kansas, including voting requirements, political party organization, election overview and candidate biographical information.

KAR. (KAR INTERNATIONAL). Fall 1980-. 0732-1074. Periodical. US. English (selected articles translated from the Persian). bm. $10.00 for 10 Issues. Kar International, PO Box 66156, Los Angeles CA 90066. **LC** DS318.8. **DD** 324.255075.

KEESING'S CONTEMPORARY ARCHIVES. *See* Genealogy and Heraldry - Archives.

KENTUCKY PRIMARY AND GENERAL ELECTION; REPORT. **Main/Corp** Kentucky. Registry of Election Finance. 1969-. 0095-6856. US. English. 310 West Liberty Street, Louisville KY 40202. **LC** JK1991. **DD** 329.025. *Kentucky General Election, Kentucky Primary Election.*

KHRONIKA TEKUSHCHIKH SOBYTII. **VFOAT** Chronicle of Current Events. Began with Apr. 1968 issue. Periodical. US. Russian. ir. Khronika Press, 505 Eighth Avenue, New York NY 10018. **LC** JC591.

KOLNER SCHRIFTEN ZUR POLITISCHEN WISSENSCHAFT. V. 1-5, 1964-65. 0075-6539. Monographic Series. GW. German. Duncker und Humbolt Verlag, Dietrich-Schaefer-Weg 9, 1000 Berlin 41 West Germany.

KOMMUNIST. 1946-. 0321-2114. Periodical. UR. Russian. mo. $13.50. Victor Kamkin Inc (76701), 12224 Parklawn Drive, Rockville MD 20852. **Tel** (301)881-5973.

KONSERVATIV HEUTE. Periodical. German. ir. 18.00. Verlag fur Konservative Publizistik, Gorresplatz 5-7 5400, Koblenz West Germany. **LC** JA14.

KOREAN SIGNAL. Oct./Dec. 1975-. KO. English. ir. $13.80. Save-The-Nation National Council, IP Box 3385, Seoul Korea. **LC** DS901. **DD** 951.9005.

KUKCHAEK YONGU. First issue (Summer, 1984)-. Periodical. KO. Korean. qt. 10.000. Minju Chonguidang Kukchaek Yonguso, 155-2 Kwanhun-Dong Chongno-Ku, Seoul Korea. **LC** DS922.

L. A. W. G. LETTER. **Main/Corp** Latin American Working Group. V. 2, No. 1/2- Mar./Apr. 1974-. 0316-3393. Periodical. CN. English. Latin American Working Group, PO Box 6300 Station A, Toronto Ontario M5W 1P7 Canada. **DD** 320.9803. *L. A. W. G. Newsletter, 0316-2850.*

LATIN AMERICAN INDEX. *See* Indexes/Abstracts.

LATIN PERSPECTIVE. Vol. 1, No. 1 (June 18, 1982)-. 0821-2570. Periodical. CN. English. ir. Free. ALAI, Suite 403/1224 St Catherine Street West, Montreal Quebec H3G 1P2 Canada. **DD** 320.98.

LATVIAN NEWS DIGEST. Periodical. US. English. bm. **Tel** (301)340-1914. bk rev. **Circ** 6,500. (ctrl). A summary of information presented in the press about Soviet-occupied Latvia, and Latvians there and in the free world.

LEADER'S REPORT. **VFOAT** Rapport du Chef. Nov. 1976-. 0702-7222. Periodical. CN. English (text in French). Free. National Headquarters, Progressive Conservative Party, 178 Queen Street, Ottawa Ontario K1P 5E1 Canada. **DD** 329.971.

LIBERAL POLICY NEWSLETTER. Oct. 1980-. 0227-0226. Periodical. CN. English. ir. Free. Liberal Party of Canada, 102 Bank Street, Ottawa Ontario K1P 5N4 Canada. **DD** 324.2710605. (ctrl).

LIBERAL UPDATE *CEASED.* (LIBERAL UPDATE : A PUBLICATION OF THE NEW BRUNSWICK LIBERAL ASSOCIATION). **Main/Corp** New Brunswick Liberal Association. **VFOAT** Actualite Liberale. Mar. 1983-. 0822-8973. Periodical. CN. English (text in French on inverted pages). ir. Free. N.B.L.A., 715 Brunswick Street, Fredericton New Brunswick E3B 1H8 Canada. **DD** 324.27150605.

LIBERTARIAN ANALYSIS. 0047-4509. Periodical. US. English. qt. $4.00. PO Box 210 Village Station, New York NY 10014. **LC** JC571. **DD** 320.505.

THE LIBERTARIAN DIGEST. Vol. 1, No. 1 (Jan. 1981)-. 0272-5959. Periodical. US. English. mo. $10.00. Libertarian Digest, 1920 Cedar Street, Berkeley CA 94709. **Tel** (415)548-3776. **Ed** Fred Foldvary. **LC** JC571. **DD** 320.512. bk rev. adv acc. **Circ** 200. Summaries of articles in libertarian publications.

LIBERTARIAN OPTION *CEASED.* Vol. 3, No. 1 (Jan./Feb. 1975)-Vol. 3, No. 6 (Jan. 1976). 0319-289X. CN. English. bm. $5.50 Domestic, $5.75 US. Libertarian Option, PO Box 603 Station F, Toronto Ontario M4Y 2L8 Canada. **DD** 323.4405. *Option, 0319-2881.*

Political Science

LIBERTARIAN VOICE. Vol. 1, No. 1 (Nov. 1981)-. 0713-021X. Periodical. CN. English. Libertarian Voice SLS, Suite 203/127 Yonge Street, Toronto Ontario M5C 2W4 Canada. DD 320.512.

LIBERTY BELL (REEDY, W. VA.). (THE LIBERTY BELL). 0145-7667. Periodical. US. English. mo. $25.00. Liberty Bell Publications, PO Box 21, Reedy WV 25270. DD 322.

LIEH SHIH YUNG SHENG. V. 1, (Nov. 1979)-. Periodical. Chinese. ir. 0.76. LC DS793.H5. DD 322.420922, B.

LIST OF CANDIDATES FOR STATE ELECTIVE OFFICES. Main/Corp Oklahoma. State Election Board. US. English. be. LC JK7195. DD 324.23.

LIST OF MEMBERS OF ROC LEGISLATIVE YUAN. VAT List of Members of Republic of China Legislative Yuan. CH. English. ir. American Embassy, Republic of China, Taipei Taiwan China. LC JQ1533. DD 328.51249073.

LISTY (BLATTER). Periodical. German. ir. 51.00. P Zottl, Postfach 114 A-2700, Wiener Neustadt Austria. LC DB215.6. DD 320.943704.

LONDON BOROUGH COUNCIL ELECTIONS. Main/Corp Greater London Council. Intelligence Unit. Series Corp Greater London Council. Publication. UK. English. Greater London Council Intelligence Unit, Bookshop The County Hall, London SE1 7PB England. LC JS3687. DD 329.023421. Metropolitan Borough Council Elections.

LUND POLITICAL STUDIES. 1- 1960-. 0460-0037. Monographic Series. SW. English or Swedish. ir. Liber International, S-205 10, S-2-5 10 Malmo Sweden.

THE MCCARVILLE REPORT. No. 1 (Oct. 3, 1980)-. 0732-0205. Periodical. US. English. wk. $95.00. The McCarville Report, 5805-B North Grand Boulevard, Oklahoma City OK 73118. Tel (405)843-3789.

MAGHREB. VFOAT Machrek. No. 1- Jan./Feb. 1964-. 0024-9890. Periodical. FR. French. qt. $17.96. Documentation Francaise, 124 rue Henri Barbusse, 93308 Aubervilliers Cedex France. Tel 834-9275. (cum index).

MAINSTREAM AMERICA. V. 1, No. 1-. 0749-2391. Periodical. US. English. mo. Urban Improvement Corporation, 2714 W Vernon Avenue, Los Angeles CA 90008. DD 324.

MAJALLAT AL-SIYASAH WA-AL-ISTIRATIJIYAH. VFOAT Majallat Assiyasa Walistratigia. Began in Oct. 1982. Periodical. Arabic. qt. 1.00 Single Issue. S B 1850 Khartoum Sudan. LC JA26.

MANITOBA GAZETTE. (THE MANITOBA GAZETTE). VFOAT Gazette de Manitoba. 0706-3350. Periodical. CN. English. wk. 25.00. Queens Printer, Minister of Fin, 200 Vaughn Street, Winnipeg Manitoba R3C 1T5 Canada. Tel (204)945-3103. LC J2. DD 354.71. Circ 1,600. (ctrl). Also available on microfilm from: Ottawa Canadian Library Association. Also available on microfilm from: Toronto: Micromedia. Public and private notices for permanent record and Manitoba regulations.

MANITOBA NEW DEMOCRAT CEASED. (THE MANITOBA NEW DEMOCRAT). Began with V. 1-3. Ceased with issue for July 1982?. 0380-0148. Periodical. CN. English. Manitoba New Democratic Party, 656 Broadway Avenue, Winnipeg Manitoba R3C 0X3 Canada.

MANUAL FOR THE GENERAL COURT. VFOAT NH Manual for the General Court, N.H. Manual for the General Court. 0196-4585. US. English. be. Office of Secretary of State, State House, Concord NH 03301. Tel (603)271-3242. LC JK2931. Circ 5,000. (ctrl). Previous year election results - state boards and commissions - miscellaneous state information.

MANUAL OF THE SENATE AND HOUSE OF DELEGATES. See Public Administration.

MARBURGER ABHANDLUNGEN ZUR POLITISCHEN WISSENSCHAFT CEASED. Vol. 1- 1964-. 0542-6480. Monographic Series. GW. German. ir. Athenaum Verlag GMBH, Adelheidstrabe 2, 6240 Konigstein/TS West Germany. Tel 067 53/ 24 88.

MARINE AFFAIRS JOURNAL. No. 1- Dec. 1973-. US. English. ir. University of Rhode Island, Mar AD Service/Narragansett Campus, Narrangansett RI 02882. Tel 792-2147. Ed Dennis Nixon. Circ 500. (ctrl). Discusses topics of marine management, national and international.

MARYLAND STATE PUBLICATIONS RECEIVED AT THE HALL OF RECORDS. (MARYLAND STATE PUBLICATIONS RECEIVED AT THE HALL OF RECORDS DURING THE MONTH OF . . .). Main/Corp Maryland. Hall of Records Commission. Mar. 1977-. 0197-243X. US. English. Department of General Services, Hall of Records, PO Box 828, Annapolis MD 214044. LC Z1223.5.M3, J87.M3. DD 015.752. Maryland State Documents Received at the Hall of Records During the Month of . . . .

THE MASSACHUSETTS POLITICAL ALMANAC. See Yearbooks, Almanacs, Directories.

MASSACHUSETTS STATE PUBLICATIONS. See Library and Information Science.

MATERIALY PO ISTORII KOMMUNISTICHESKOI PARTII TADZHIKISTANA. Main/Corp Dushanbe. Institut Istorii Partii. Began in 1963. UR. Russian. 0.63 Each Issue. Ifrom, Shevchenko 10, Dushanbe Tadzhik SSR. LC JQ1089.A55.

MEMBERSHIP DIRECTORY - AMERICAN POLITICAL SCIENCE ASSOCIATION. See Yearbooks, Almanacs, Directories.

MEMBERSHIP DIRECTORY - DIPLOMATIC AND CONSULAR OFFICERS, RETIRED. See Yearbooks, Almanacs, Directories.

MERIP REPORTS. Main/Corp Middle East Research & Information Project. VAT Middle East Research and Information Project Reports. V. 1- May 1971-. 0047-7265. Periodical. US. English. mo. $33.00. MERIP Reports, 475 Riverside Drive #518, New York NY 10115. Tel (212)870-3281. Ind/Abst Int. Labour Doc., Abstr. Iran., Altern. Press Index, Index Islam., Int. Dev. Abstr., Int. Polit. Sci. Abstr., Left Index, Middle East Abstr. Index, Middle East J., Mideast File, Public Aff. Inf. Serv. Bull., Sociol. Abstr., Recent Publ. Artic. LC DS42. DD 320.9565. bk rev. adv acc. Circ 6,000. Political, social and economic developments in contemporary Middle East; analysis of US policy in Middle East. Pakistan Forum, 0315-7725.

MESSENGER (WASAGA BEACH, ONT.). (MESSENGER). Vol. 2, No. 1 (Apr. 1977)-. 0229-7833. Periodical. CN. English. mo. $5.00. The Messenger, PO Box 345, Wasaga Beach Ontario L0L 2P0 Canada. DD 324.27130505. Social Credit Messenger, 0229-7825.

MEXICAN STUDIES. VFOAT Estudios Mexicanos. Vol. 1, No. 1 (Winter 1985)-. 0742-9797. Periodical. US. English (text or summaries in Spanish). sa. $30.00 Domestic, $32.00 Foreign. Mexican Studies, University of California Press, Berkeley CA 94720. Tel (415)642-4191. DD 972. bk rev. adv acc. Circ 400. Articles concerning socio-economic interdependence of Mexico and the US: covering labor, technology, industry resources and cultural transference.

MEZHDUNARODNYI EZHEGODNIK : POLITIKA I EKONOMIKA. 1958-. 0543-7822. UR. Russian (Vols. 1-3 have table of contents also in Chinese, English, and French). an. LC D839.

MICHIGAN JOURNAL OF POLITICAL SCIENCE. (MICHIGAN JOURNAL OF POLITICAL SCIENCE : A UNIVERSITY OF MICHIGAN STUDENT JOURNAL OF POLITICAL STUDIES). VFOAT University of Michigan Student Journal of Political Studies. Vol. 1, No. 1 (Winter 1981)-. 0733-4486. Periodical. US. English. ir. $10.00. Michigan Journal Political, University of Michigan, 6619 Haven Hall, Ann Arbor MI 48109-1045. Tel (313)763-2227. Ed Brud Rossmann. Ind/Abst Am. Hist. Life, Hist. Abstr. LC JA1. DD 320.05. bk rev. adv acc. Circ 500. The journal is a student journal of political studies.

MICHIGAN MUNICIPAL REVIEW. V. 1- Jan. 1928-. 0026-2331. Periodical. US. English. ir. $10.80. Michigan Municipal Review, PO Box 1487, Ann Arbor MI 48106. Tel (313)662-3246. Ed Joan S Hutchison. Ind/Abst Public Aff. Inf. Serv. Bull. LC JS39. DD 352.0005. bk rev. adv acc. Circ 9,200. (ctrl). Publication with information and ideas for local governments in Michigan.

MICROSTATE STUDIES. No. 1-. 0147-7935. Periodical. English. ir. $4.00 Each Issue. College of the Virgin Islands, Caribbean Research Institute, St Thomas Virgin Islands 00801. LC JC365. DD 321.08.

MIDDLE EAST CONTEMPORARY SURVEY. VFOAT MECS. Vol. 1 (1976-77)-. 0163-5476. US. English. an. Holmes & Meier Publishers, 30 Irving Place, New York NY 10003. LC DS62.8. DD 320.956046.

MIDDLE EAST MONITOR. VFOAT Monitor. Vol. 1, No. 1 (Feb. 1, 1971)-. Periodical. US. English. sm. $60.00. Middle East Monitor, 402 Godwin Avenue, Ridgewood NJ 07450. Tel (201)670-0624. Ed Amir N Ghazaii. Circ 200. Monitors and analyses politics and economic developments in Middle East.

MIDDLE EAST POLICY SURVEY. (MIDDLE EAST POLICY SURVEY : MEP SURVEY). VFOAT MEP Survey. No. 1 (Feb. 15, 1980)-. 0276-5632. Periodical. US. English. bw. $155.00. Middle East Policy Survey, 2011 Eye Street NW/Suite 305, Washington DC 20006. Tel (202)659-8311. Ed Richard Straus and Ken Wollack. LC DS63.2.U5. DD 327.56073. Circ 700. Insiders' political reporting and analysis of late breaking Middle East news not available in the general press or specialized periodicals.

THE MILITANT. V. 1- Aug. 14, 1937-. 0026-3885. Newspaper. US. English. wk. $40.00. Militant, 14 Charles Lane, New York NY 10014. Tel (212)929-3486. Ed Malik Miah. bk rev. Circ 9,000. A socialist newspaper covering the national and international workers movement and liberation struggles.

MIN CHU JEN. VFOAT Democrat. First published Jan. 16, 1983-. Periodical. CH. Chinese. sm. 50.00. Min Chu Jen Tsa Chih She, PO Box 563111, Taipei Taiwan.

MIN TSU WEN HSUEH YEN CHIU. First published in 1983. Periodical. CC. Chinese. ir. 0.60. Hsin Hua Shu Tien, Peking China.

MING PAO YUEH KAN. VFOAT Ming Pao. V. 1, Jan. 1966-. Periodical. Chinese. mo. $12.00. Chinese Material Service Center, 1716 Ocean Avenue/Suite 103, San Francisco CA 94112.

THE MINNESOTA VOTER. V.1- Jan. 10, 1921-. Periodical. US. English. qt. $2.00. League of Women Voters of Minnesota, 555 Wabasha Avenue, St Paul MN 55102. Tel (612)224-5445.

THE MINNESOTA VOTER. (THE MINNESOTA VOTER : A PUBLICATION OF THE LEAGUE OF WOMEN VOTERS OF MINNESOTA). 0740-1191. Periodical. US. English. qt. $2.00. League of Women Voters of Minnesota, 555 Wabasha, St Paul MN 55102. Tel (612)224-5445. Ed Mary Santi. Circ 3,600. (ctrl). Newsletter of the League of Women Voters of Minnesota. Articulate Voter.

MISSOURI ANNUAL CAMPAIGN FINANCE REPORT. 1978-. US. English. an. Secretary of State, State of Missouri, Jefferson City MO 65101. LC JK199L.5.M8. DD 324.7809778.

MITTEILUNG - DEUTSCHE FORSCHUNGSGEMEINSCHAFT (FOUNDED 1949). KOMMISSION FUR DRINGLICHE SOZIALPOLITISCHE PRAGEN. Main/Corp Deutsche Forschungsgemeinschaft (Founded 1949). Kommission fur Dringliche Sozialpolitische Fragen. Began with V. 1, 1964?. 0418-8454. Periodical. GW. German. ir. Franz Steiner Verlag, Friedrichstr 24 Postfach 5529, D 6200 Wiesbaden West Germany.

MODERN AGE. V. 1- Summer 1957-. 0026-7457. US. English. qt. $10.00. Intercollegiate Studies Institute, 14 South Bryn Mawr Avenue, Bryn Mawr PA 19010. Tel (215)525-7501. Ed George A Panichas. Ind/Abst Annu. Bibliogr. Engl. Lang. Lit., Abstr. Engl. Stud., Hist. Abstr., Part A, Mod. Hist. Abstr., Hist. Abst., Part B, Twent. Century Abstr., MLA Int. Bibliogr. Books Artic. Mod. Lang. Lit., Index Book Rev. Humanit., Book Rev. Index, Humanit. Index, Hist. Abstr., Soc. Sci. Index, Am. Hist. Life, Int. Polit. Sci. Abstr., Public Aff. Inf. Serv. Bull., Writ. Am. Hist., Years Work Eng. Stud., Hist. Abstr. LC AP2. DD 051. bk rev. adv acc. Circ 3,500. Available on microfilm and microfiche from University Microfilms. The principal quarterly of intellectual conservatism.

MOMENTUM. V. 1- Apr. 1972-. 0317-2112. CN. English. mo. Free. Ontario Progressive Conservative Association, 73 Richmond Street West, Toronto Ontario M5H 1Z9 Canada. DD 329.9713.

MONARCHY CANADA. V. 3- Spring 1973-. 0319-4019. Periodical. CN. English. ir. $7.74. Monarchist League of Canada, 2 Wedgewood Crescent, Ottawa Ontario KIR 4B4 Canada. Tel (416)482-4157. Ed Arthur Boosfield. bk rev. adv acc.

Political Science

Circ 8,000. Opinion and news of Canada's monarchy: political, constitutional, cultural, historical and human interest. Arts and book review. A look at Canada from the monarchist's viewpoint. *Canadian Monarchist, 0319-4000.*

MONDAY. 0093-318X. Periodical. US. English. wk. Republican National Committee, 310 First Street SE, Washington DC 20590. LC JK2351. DD 329.6005.

MONDO. Yearly V. 1- 19 -. Periodical. IT. Italian. wk. $12.36. Editoriale Corriere della Sera, Via Solferino 28, 20100 Milano Italy.

MONOGRAPHS IN POLITICAL SCIENCE. No. 1-. RH. English. ir. University of Rhodesia, PO Box MP 45, Mount Pleasant, Salisbury Rhodesia.

MORGN FRAYHAYT. VFOAT Morning Freiheit. 0747-4342. Newspaper. US. Hebrew (English). wk. $25.00. Morning Freiheit, 43 West 24th Street, New York NY 10010. Tel (313)255-7661. Ed Paul Novick. bk rev. adv acc. Circ 4,000. Progressive, independent, Yiddish language with English supplement.

MOTS. Series/Titl Travaux de Lexicometrie et de Lexicologie Politique. No. 1 (Oct. 1980)-. 0243-6450. Periodical. FR. French. sa. $22.62. Presses de la Fondation National des Sciences Politiques, 27 rue Saint Guillaume, 75341 Paris Cedex 07 France. Tel 260-3960. LC JA11. DD 320.014.

NAIMUSHO NENPO, HOKOKUSHO. Main/Corp Japan. Naimusho. VFOAT Naimusho . . . Nenpo. V. 1 issue (Ji Meiji 8-Year July 9-Year June) 1875 Year 7. JA. Japanese. ir. Sanichi Shobo, 8 Kanda Surugadai 2 Chiyoda-ku, Tokyo-to Japan. LC J674.

NAMIBIA ABSTRACTS. *See* Indexes/Abstracts.

NAQIB. Periodical. in Urdu. ir. Mustafa Kamal, Khibar Bazar, Pishavar India. LC JA26.

NARODNO ZEMEDELSKO ZNAME. (NARODNO ZEMEDELSKO ZNAME : ORGAN NA BULGARSKIIA ZEMEDELSKI NARODEN SUIUZ). VFOAT Zemedelsko Zname, People's Agrarian Banner : Organ of the Bulgarian Agrarian National Union. Began in 1982. 8755-9706. Periodical. US. Bulgarian. ir. Bulgarina Agrarian National Union, 109 Amherst Street, Highland Park NJ 08904. DD 324.

NASE TEME. V. 1- 1958-. 0547-3144. Periodical. Serbo-Croatian -R. ir. LC HQ799.Y8. DD 305.2309497.

NASHARA AL-GHADA'ID AL-ALAMIYYAH. (NASHARAH AL-GHADA'ID AL-ALAMIYYAH). VFOAT Scandalous International News. V. 1, No. 2 (1983)-. 0821-4964. Periodical. CN. Arabic. mo. 25.00. Nasharah Al-Ghadaid Al-Alamiyyah, PO Box 4190 Station E, Ottawa Ontario K1N 8V2 Canada. DD 320.0207. *Scandalous International News. English, French & Arabic, 0820-7887.*

NATIONAL CHRONICLE. 0027-898X. Periodical. US. English. ir $15.00. National Chronicle, Box NC, Hayden Lake ID 83835.

NATIONAL DEBATE. (THE NATIONAL DEBATE). V. 1- Oct./Nov. 1973-. 0302-6973. Periodical. II. English. mo. 1.50 Single Issue. Surinder Singh, 175 Jeevan Nagar, New Delhi India. LC JQ201. DD 320.95404.

NATIONAL DIRECTORY OF WOMEN ELECTED OFFICIALS. *See* Yearbooks, Almanacs, Directories.

NATIONAL JOURNAL. V. 7, No. 34- Aug. 23, 1975-. 0360-4217. Periodical. US. English. wk. $276.00. National Journal Inc, 11th Floor/1730 M Street Northwest, Washington DC 20036. Tel (202)857-1400. Ed Richard S Frank. Ind/Abst Hospit. Lit. Index, Nexis, Infobank, Public Aff. Inf. Serv. Bull., Energy Inf. Abstr., Environ. Abstr. LC JK1. DD 320.973092. bk rev. adv acc. Circ 5,000. A magazine on politics and government. It is written for policy makers and decision makers who need to know what's going on in Washington. *National Journal Reports, 0091-3685.*

NATIONAL LEGAL BIBLIOGRAPHY. SUBJECT AREA LIST. MUNICIPAL AND ADMINISTRATIVE LAW AND POLITICS. *See* Bibliographies.

NATIONAL P C PRESIDENT. (THE NATIONAL P C PRESIDENT). VFOAT President P C National. VAT National Progressive Conservative President, President Progressiste Conservateur National. Began publication in Jan. 1976. 0707-0349. Periodical. CN. English (French). Progressive Conservative Party, 178 Queen Street, Ottawa Ontario K1P 5E1 Canada. DD 329.971.

NATIONAL REVIEW. VFOAT National Review Bulletin. V. 1- Nov. 19, 1955-. 0028-0038. Periodical. US. English. ir. $34.00. National Review Inc, 150 E 35th Street, New York NY 10016. Tel (212)679-7330. Ed William F Buckley Jr. Ind/Abst Annu. Bibliogr. Engl. Lang. Lit., Pop. Mag. Rev., Art Archaeol. Tech. Abstr., Film Lit. Index, Biogr. Index, Book Rev. Index, Read. Guide Period. Lit., Infobank, Energy Inf. Abstr., Environ. Abstr., Media Rev. Dig., Abr. Read. Guide, Book Rev. Digest, Mag. Index. LC AP2. DD 051. bk rev. adv acc. Circ 100,000. (ctrl). An international publication on conservative opinion, news and articles edited for the already well-informed reader.

THE NATIONAL VOTER. Began May 15, 1951. 0028-0372. Periodical. US. English. qt. $8.00. League of Women Voters, 1730 M Street NW/10th Floor, Washington DC 20036. Tel (202)429-1965. Ed Debra Duff. LC E740. bk rev. Circ 185,000. (ctrl). In-depth coverage of selected national issues, interviews with political figures, accounts of citizen action on local issues throughout the country. An excellent current events piece.

NATO-WARSAW AND STRATEGIES. VFOAT N.A.T.O. Warsaw and Strategies. 0749-0674. Periodical. US. English. an. $300.00. Siveast Consultants, 410 South State Street, Dover DE 19901. Ed C V Ramasastry. adv acc. The journal aims to provide a forum and will examine the socio-economic, political and technological implications of NATO-Warsaw nations.

NCOBPS BIOGRAPHICAL DIRECTORY. *See* Yearbooks, Almanacs, Directories.

NEGOTIATION JOURNAL. Vol. 1, No. 1 (Jan. 1985)-. 0748-4526. Periodical. US. English. qt. $50.00 Domestic, $57.00 Foreign. Plenum Publishing Company, 233 Spring Street, New York NY 10013. Tel (212)620-8000. Ed Jeffrey Z Rubin. LC HD42. DD 302.305. CODEN NEJOEQ. This is an international journal devoted to the publication of works that advance the theory analysis and practice of negotiation and dispute statement.

NEUSEELAND, FORSCHUNGSPOLITIK UND FORSCHUNGSPRAXIS. Series/Titl Marktinformation. GW. German. ir. 3.00. Bundesstelle fur Aussenhandelsinformation, Blaubach 13, Postfach 10 80 07, D-5000 Koln 1 West Germany.

NEVADA STUDIES IN HISTORY AND POLITICAL SCIENCE. *See* History (General) - History of North, South, and Central America.

NEW AGE. V. 1- Sept. 1952-. 0047-9500. Periodical. II. English. wk. 50.00. Communist Party of India, Ajoy Bhavan Kotla Road, New Delhi 2 India. Tel 3310762. Ed Indradeep Sinha. bk rev adv acc. Circ 25,000. Interpretative journal of current events in India and abroad with particular reference to political science and economics analysed from Marxian view.

NEW AMERICA. V. 1- 1960-. 0028-419X. Periodical. US. English. bm. $20.00. Social Democrats USA, 275 7th Avenue/25th Floor, New York NY 10001. Tel (212)255-1390. Ed Lesly Chenoweth. LC UNC. adv acc. Content is political.

NEW DEMOCRAT CEASED. Began publication in 1961. 0028-4564. Periodical. CN. English (includes some text in French). mo. New Democratic Party of Ontario, 184 Main Street, Toronto Ontario M4E 2W1 Canada. Tel (416)699-6637.

NEW GUARD. V. 1- Mar. 1961-. 0028-5137. Periodical. US. English. qt. $10.00. Young Americans for Freedom, PO Box 1002, Woodland Road, Sterling VA 22170. Tel (703)450-5162. Ed Gerry O'Brien. LC AP2. DD 320.973. bk rev. adv acc. Circ 10,000. (ctrl). Available on microfilm from University Microfilms. Politics and popular culture for today's youth with a conservative perspective. Now in our 25th year.

THE NEW HAMPSHIRE POLITICAL ALMANAC. *See* Yearbooks, Almanacs, Directories.

NEW JERSEY LEGISLATIVE MANUAL. Main/Corp New Jersey. State Legislature. 1873. US. English. an. $22.00. New Jersey Legislative Manual, PO Box 2150, Trenton NJ 08608. Ed Edward J Mullin. The directory of government, politics, and public affairs in New Jersey. Published annually since 1983.

NEW JERSEY POLITICAL ALMANAC. *See* Yearbooks, Almanacs, Directories.

NEW OUTLOOK. V. 1- (No. 1-). 0028-6427. Periodical. IS. English. bm $38.00. David Furstenberg INS Inc, 295 Seventh Avenue, New York NY 10001. Ind/Abst Public Aff. Inf. Serv. Bull. LC DS41. DD 956.04005. Issued also in microform by University Microfilms.

NEW POLITICAL SCIENCE. VFOAT N.P.S. Began publication in 1972. 0739-3148. Periodical. US. English. qt $40.00. Columbia University City NY, 420 West 118th Street, New York NY 10027. Tel (212)280-3644. Ed Florinda Volpacchio. Ind/Abst Sociol. Abstr., Altern. Press Index. LC JA1. DD 320.05. bk rev. adv acc. Circ 1,000. (ctrl). Oriented towards developing alternative approaches to the social sciences within a critical framework of a left politics. *New Political Science (Caucus for a New Political Science : 1972), 0739-3148.*

NEW WORLD REVIEW. V. 1- Feb. 1932-. 0028-7067. US. English. bm. $7.50. New World Review, 162 Madison Avenue 3rd Floor, New York NY 10016. Tel (212)696-4765. Ed Marilyn Bechtel. Ind/Abst Hist. Abstr., Index Am. Period. Verse, Public Aff. Inf. Serv. Bull., Am. Hist. Life. LC DK266.A2. DD 947.084. bk rev. Circ 5,000. Microfilm. USSR and other socialist countries; US-USSR relations.

NEW YORK LEGISLATIVE RECORD AND INDEX. US. English. wk. Legislative Index Company, 100 South Swan Street, Albany NY 12210. DD 328.747. *New York Legislative Index.*

THE NEW YORK RED BOOK. 0196-4623. US. English. be. Williams Press, Patroon Station, Albany NY 12204. Tel (518)434-1141. LC JK3430. DD 320.9747. Circ 13,000. Lists facts concerning New York state, its political subdivisions and officials who administer its affairs. Bibliographies and photographs included.

THE NEW YORK STATE VOTER. Periodical. US. English. qt. $5.00. League of Women Voters of New York, 817 Broadway, New York NY 10003. Tel (212)677-5050. Ed Suzanne D LaLonde. Circ 11,000. (ctrl). Legislative lobbying. *LWV State News.*

NEW YORK UNIVERSITY JOURNAL OF INTERNATIONAL LAW & POLITICS. *See* Law.

NEW ZEALAND GAZETTE. NZ. English. wk. $70.40. Government Printing Office NZ, Private Bag, Wellington New Zealand. LC J8.

NEWMONTH. VAT New Month. 0192-1142. Periodical. US. English. mo. Newmonth, PO Box 278, Denmark WI 54208. Tel (414)863-2154.

NEWS RELEASE FROM CONGRESSMAN AL BALDUS. Periodical. US. English. Cannon House Office Building/Room 509, Washington DC 20515.

NEWS REVIEW ON WEST ASIA. Main/Corp Institute for Defence Studies and Analyses. Periodical. II. English. mo. $10.03. Institute for Defence Studies and Analyses, Sapru House, Barakhamba Road, New Delhi 110 001 India. LC DS63.1. DD 320.956. *News Review on East Asia, Australasia & West Asia.*

NEWSBANK : POLITICAL DEVELOPMENT. INDEX. *See* Indexes/Abstracts.

NEWSLETTER OF RESEARCH ON JAPANESE POLITICS. VFOAT Japan Research Newsletter. V. 1- 1970-. 0160-1164. US. English. an. $4.25. Brigham Young University, Department of Political Science, 740 SWKT, Provo UT 84602. Tel (801)378-3303. Ed Lee W Farnsworth. Circ 225. Listings of research (complete or in progress), research notes, dissertation abstracts, books in print, and list of scholars. Relates to study on any area of politics in Japan.

NEXT YEAR COUNTRY (1979). (NEXT YEAR COUNTRY). VFOAT Next Year Country Magazine. NYC Journal No. 1 (1979)-. 0824-5037. Periodical. CN. English. ir. Next Year Country, PO Box 3446, Regina Saskatchewan S4P 3J8 Canada. Ind/Abst Altern. Press Index. DD 320.531505. *Next Year Country News, 0712-5674.*

NFF UPDATE. VAT National Foundation Forum Update. 0882-6536. Periodical. US. English. bm. National Forum Foundation, 214 Massachusetts Avenue NE, Washington DC 20002. DD 320.

Political Science

NICARAGUAN PERSPECTIVES. VFOAT Nicaragua. Began with No. 1 (July 1981). Periodical. US. English. $18.00. Nicaragua Information Center, PO Box 1004, Berkeley CA 94704. **Tel** (415)549-1387. Ed Jim Eitel. **Ind/Abst** Altern. Press Index. LC F1521. **DD** 972.85005. bk rev. adv acc. **Circ** 5,500. Focuses primarily on Nicaraguan-culture, politics, history, economy, and effects of U.S. aggression.

NIGER STATE BUDGET SPEECH. **Main/Corp** Niger (Nigeria). Ministry of Information. English. ir. Ministry of Information, Malu Road Apapa, Lagos Nigeria. LC HJ86.2.N5. **DD** 354.6695.

THE NONVIOLENT ACTIVIST. (THE NONVIOLENT ACTIVIST : THE MAGAZINE OF THE WAR RESOSTERS LEAGUE). Dec. 1984-. 8755-7428. US. English. mo. $25.00. War Resisters League, 339 Lafayette Street, New York NY 10012. **Tel** (212)228-0450. Ed David Croteau. **DD** 303. bk rev. adv acc. **Circ** 20,000. Pacifist journal exploring issues of nonviolence, disarmament, feminism, international relations, and more. *WRL News*, 0042-9791.

NORTH CAROLINA MANUAL. **Main/Corp** North Carolina. Secretary of State. US. English. an. Secretary of State, Raleigh NC 27687. **Tel** (919)733-7355. Ed John L Cheney Jr. **Circ** 500. Current information on North Carolina state government by branch.

NORTH KOREA QUARTERLY. Began in 1974. 0340-014X. Periodical. GW. English. ir. $16.23. Institute of Asian Affairs, Rothenbaumchaussee 32, 2000 Hamburg 13 West Germany. **Tel** 44 30 01. Ed M Y Cho. LC DS930. **DD** 951.93. **Circ** 300. News and information topics on North Korea, chronology of events, documents, etc.

NORTHERN PERSPECTIVES. V. 1- Jan. 1973-. 0380-5522. Periodical. CN. English. bm. Free. Canadian Arctic Resources Committee, 46 Elgin Street, Street/Room 11, Ottawa Ontario K1P 5K6 Canada. **Tel** (613)236-7379. Ed Danna Leaman. **Ind/Abst** ASTIS Bibliogr., ASTIS Curr. Aware. Bull. **Circ** 12,000. Analysis of resource development, economic, social, and political issues in Canada's North and the circumpolar Arctic. Reviews and creative writings do not require regional theme.

NORTHERN POLITICS REVIEW. (NORTHERN POLITICS REVIEW : AN ANNUAL PUBLICATION OF THE NORTHERN POLITICAL STUDIES PROGRAM). VFOAT NPR. VAT NRP. Northern Politics Review. 1983-. 0823-9576. Periodical. CN. English. an. 30.00. Northern Political Studies, c/o Artic Institute of North America, University of Calgary, Calgary Alberta T2N 1N4 Canada. **Tel** (403)220-4038. Ed W Harriet Critchley and Frances Abele. **DD** 016.9719.

NOTEBOOK CFS. (NOTEBOOK CFS). **Main/Conf** Conference for Federal Studies. VFOAT Notebook C.F.S., C.F.S. Notebook, CFS Notebook. VAT Notebook Conference for Federal Studies. 0194-2840. Periodical. US. English. qt. Center for the Study of Federalism, Temple University, Gladfelter Hall, Philadelphia PA 19122. **Tel** (713)749-7261. Ed Robert Thomas. LC JC355. **DD** 321.0205. bk rev. **Circ** 1,000. (ctrl). Notices of conferences, books and research, as well as articles on American and comparative federalism and intergovernmental relations.

NOTES DE RECHERCHE - FACULTE DES SCIENCES SOCIALES. DEPARTEMENT DE SCIENCE POLITIQUE. UNIVERSITE D'OTTAWA. (NOTES DE RECHERCHE). VFOAT Working Papers. VAT Working Papers - Faculty of Social Sciences. Department of Political Science. University of Ottawa. No. 1 (Nov. 1974)-. 0713-8199. Monographic Series. CN. English (French). Department of Political Science, Faculty of Social Sciences, University of Ottawa, 75 Laurier Street East, Ottawa Ontario K1N 6N5 Canada. **DD** 320.

NOVA SCOTIA LIBERAL. (THE NOVA SCOTIA LIBERAL). V. 1- Sept./Oct. 1976-. 0703-1793. Periodical. CN. English. bm. Free. Nova Scotia Liberal Association, PO Box 723, Halifax Nova Scotia B3J 2T3 Canada. **DD** 329.971. (ctrl).

NOVOS ESTUDOS CEBRAP. VFOAT Novos Estudos. Vol. 1, No. 1 (Dec. 1981)-. 0101-3300. Periodical. BL. Portuguese. qt. $30.00. Editora Brasileira de Ciencias, Rua Morgado Mateus 615, 04015 Sao Paulo SP Brasil. **Tel** 544-4699. **Circ** 3,000. Covers politics, economy, sociology, and arts in general of Brazil and the world. *Estudos Cebrap*.

NUCLEAR TIMES (NEW YORK, N.Y.). (NUCLEAR TIMES). Vol. 1, No. 1 (Oct. 1982)-. 0734-5836. Periodical. US. English. mo. $23.00. Nuclear Times Inc, Room 512/298 Fifth Avenue, New York NY 10001. **Tel** (212)563-5940. Ed Greg Mitchell. **Ind/Abst** Altern. Press Index. LC JX1974.7. **DD** 327.17405. bk rev. adv acc. **Circ** 25,000. (ctrl). Chronicles the antinuclear weapons movement in United States reports on legislative, scholarly, and grassroots efforts, new scientific and research information reviews, calendar of nationwide events.

NUOVI STUDI POLITICI. Yearly V. 1- Jan./Feb. 1971-. IT. Italian. qt. Bulzoni Editore, Via del Liburni 14, 00185 Rome Italy. LC JN5201.

OBF, OF THE PEOPLE, BY THE PEOPLE, FOR THE PEOPLE. V. 1- Aug. 1975-. 0360-1781. Periodical. US. English. mo. $12.00. OBF Inc, PO Box 10107, Eugene OR 97401. LC JK1. **DD** 320.9730925.

OCCASIONAL PAPERS - DEPARTMENT OF POLITICAL SCIENCE. CARLETON UNIVERSITY. (OCCASIONAL PAPERS). 0229-7000. Periodical. CN. English. ir. c/o Gail Harmer, Graphic Services, 501 AB, Carleton University, Ottawa Ontario K1S 5B6 Canada. **DD** 320.05.

OCCASIONAL PAPERS - DEPARTMENT OF POLITICAL SCIENCE. UNIVERSITY OF ALBERTA. (OCCASIONAL PAPERS - DEPARTMENT OF POLITICAL SCIENCE, UNIVERSITY OF ALBERTA). **Main/Corp** University of Alberta. Dept. of Political Science. 1- 1974-. 0702-7621. Monographic Series. CN. English. Department of Political Science, University of Alberta, Edmonton Alberta T6G 2E1 Canada. **DD** 320.

OCCASIONAL PAPERS / REPRINTS SERIES IN CONTEMPORARY ASIAN STUDIES. *See* Law.

OCCIDENTE. V. 1- April 1975-. 0319-2733. Periodical. CN. Italian (English). mo. Occidente, 1756-A Ouest Av Eglinton, Toronto Ontario M6E 2H6 Canada. **DD** 320.53205.

OFFICIAL ABSTRACT OF VOTES, GENERAL ELECTION. *See* Indexes/Abstracts.

OFFICIAL ABSTRACT OF VOTES, PRIMARY ELECTION. *See* Indexes/Abstracts.

OFFICIAL CANDIDATES PAMPHLET. **Main/Corp** Washington (State). Office of the Secretary of State. 0091-0090. US. English. Washington Office of The Secretary of State, State Capital, Seattle WA 98115. LC JK2023.W3. **DD** 329.023797.

OFFICIAL ELECTION RETURNS AND REGISTRATION FIGURES FOR SOUTH DAKOTA. GENERAL ELECTION. US. English. LC JK6592. **DD** 324.9783033.

OFFICIAL JOURNAL OF THE PROCEEDINGS OF THE SENATE AND HOUSE OF REPRESENTATIVES OF THE STATE OF LOUISIANA AND THE LEGISLATIVE CALENDAR. **Main/Corp** Louisiana. Legislature. Senate. 0362-3556. US. English. 519 Fidelity Bank Building, Baton Rouge LA 10801. LC J87. **DD** 328.76301.

OFFICIAL REPORT OF DEBATES. **Main/Corp** Northern Ireland. Assembly. V. 1- July 31, 1973-. UK. English. 3.50. Her Majesty's Stationery Office, 80 Chichester Street, Belfast BT1 4JY Northern Ireland. LC J307.5. **DD** 328.41602.

OFFICIAL RETURNS BY ELECTION PRECINCT, PRIMARY ELECTION (JUNEAU, ALASKA : 1980). (OFFICIAL RETURNS BY ELECTION PRECINCT, PRIMARY ELECTION). US. English. LC JK2075.A4. **DD** 324.5409798. *State of Alaska Official Returns of Election Precincts, Primary Election*.

OHIO REPUBLICAN NEWS. 0164-6524. Periodical. US. English. mo. Ohio Republican News, 50 West Broad Street, Columbus OH 43215.

THE OKLAHOMA GAZETTE CEASED. V. 1, No. 1 (Jan. 1962)-V. 22, No. 20 (Oct. 1983). 0030-1728. Periodical. US. English. sm. $20.00. Oklahoma Department of Libraries, 200 Northeast 18th, Oklahoma City OK 73105. **Tel** (405)521-2502. LC J1.

OKLAHOMA GOVERNMENT DOCUMENTS. **Main/Corp** Oklahoma Publications Clearinghouse. V. 2, No. 8- Aug. 1978-. 0193-7685. Periodical. US. English. mo. Oklahoma Publications Clearinghouse, Allen Wright Memorial Library Building, 200 Northeast 18th Street, Oklahoma City OK 73105. **Tel** (405)521-2502. LC Z1223.5.O5, J87.O5. **DD** 015.766. **Circ** 500. (ctrl). Checklist of Oklahoma state government publications which have been received, processed, and distributed by the Oklahoma Publications Clearinghouse of the Oklahoma Department of Libraries. *Oklahoma Government Documents*, 0193-7685.

OKLAHOMA GOVERNMENT PUBLICATIONS. Vol. 5, No. 1 (Jan. 1981)-. US. English. mo. Oklahoma Publications Clearinghouse, Allen Wright Memorial Building, 200 NE 18th Street, Oklahoma City OK 73105. LC Z1223.5.O5, J87.O5. **DD** 015.766. *Oklahoma Government Documents*.

THE OKLAHOMA OBSERVER. 1969. 0030-1795. Periodical. US. English. sm. Oklahoma Observer, Box 53371, Oklahoma City OK 73152. **Tel** (405)525-5582. Ed Frosty Troy. bk rev. adv acc. **Circ** 7,500. A journal of commentary on government, politics and social problems.

ON HER MAJESTY'S SERVICE. V. 1- July 1, 1976-. 0384-5265. Periodical. CN. English. $5.00. Vancouver and Greater Vancouver Monarchist Association, 1865 Barclay Street/Suite 402, Vancouver British Columbia V6G 1K7 Canada. **DD** 321.87.

ON TARGET. Began with Aug. 1967 issue. 0380-5980. Periodical. CN. English. wk. $15.48. Canadian Intelligence Publications, Box 130, Flesherton Ontario NOC 1E0 Canada. Ed Ron Gostick. **Circ** 1,300. (ctrl). Provides facts and documentation on current issues in a brief and concise form.

ONTARIO DEMOCRAT. (THE ONTARIO DEMOCRAT). Vol. 22, No. 2 (Mar. 1984)-. 0827-2247. Periodical. CN. English. bm. $5.00. Democratic Publications, 184 Main Street, Toronto Ontario M4E 2W1 Canada. **Tel** (416)699-6637. **DD** 324.27130705. bk rev. **Circ** 25,000. (ctrl). Political and social issues. *New Democrat*, 0028-4564.

OPINION. Began in 1960. Periodical. II. English. ir. A D Gorwala, 40 C Ridge Road, Bombay India. LC DS401. **DD** 320.954.

ORBIS. V. 1- Apr. 1957-. 0030-4387. Periodical. US. English. qt. $50.00. Foreign Policy Research Institute, 3508 Market Street/Suite 350, Philadelphia PA 19104. **Tel** (215)382-0685. Ed Nils H Wessell. **Ind/Abst** Am. Hist. Life, Hist. Abstr., Part A, Mod. Hist. Abstr., Hist. Abst., Part B, Twent. Century Abstr., ABC Pol Sci, Predicasts, Public Aff. Inf. Serv. Bull., Soc. Sci. Index, Funk Scott Index Corp. Ind., Soc. Sci. Citation Index, Hist. Abstr. LC D839. **DD** 909.82. bk rev. adv acc. **Circ** 3,500. Examines political, military social, and economic dimensions of contemporary international affairs and book reviews.

ORDER OF BUSINESS AND NOTICES CEASED. **Main/Corp** Canada. Parliament. House of Commons. VFOAT Ordre des Travaux et Avis. Ceased with issue for May 9, 1974. 0384-2258. Periodical. CN. English (French). 26.00 Domestic, 31.20 Foreign. Receiver General for Canada, Supply & Services, Ottawa Ontario K1A 0S9 Canada. LC J103. **DD** 328.7105.

ORDO POLITICUS. **Main/Corp** Freiburg I.B. Arnold-Nergstraeser-Institut fur Kulturwissenschaftliche Forschung. Monographic Series. English. ir. Duncker and Humblot Verlag, Dietrich-Schaefer-Weg 9, 1000 Berlin 41 West Germany. **Tel** (030)7912026. Ed D Oberndorfer. Publishes works of the Arnold-Bergstraesser Institute of Freiburg West Germany. Studies in political science.

OREGON BARS. *See* Law.

OREGON STATE MONOGRAPHS. STUDIES IN POLITICAL SCIENCE. **Main/Corp** Oregon State College. VFOAT Studies in Political Science. No. 1- 1950-. Monographic Series. US. English. ir. Oregon State University Press, 101 Waldo Hall, Corvallis OR 97331.

OSTEUROPA. Vol. 1-. 0030-6428. Periodical. GW. German. mo. Zenit Pressevertrieb GMBH, Postfach 810640, 7000 Stuttgart 80 West Germany. **Ind/Abst** Am. Hist. Life, Hist. Abstr., Part A, Mod. Hist. Abstr., Hist. Abst., Part B, Twent. Century Abstr., MLA Int.

Bibliogr. Books Artic. Mod. Lang. Lit., Sociol. Abstr., ABC Pol Sci, Writ. Am. Hist., Bibliogr. Agric., Foreign Lang. Index, Soc. Sci. Citation Index, Lang. Lang. Behav. Abstr., Hist. Abstr., PAIS Foreign Lang. Index, Recent Publ. Artic. **LC** DR1. **DD** 947.0005. *Osteuropa.*

OTTAWA GREENS NEWSLETTER. Vol. 1, No. 1 (Fall 1983)-. 0826-1113. Periodical. CN. English. Free to Members, $5.00 Membership Green Party of Canada, $3.00 Green Party of Ontario. Ottawa Greens, PO Box 4089 Station E, Ottawa Ontario K1S 5B2 Canada. **DD** 324.27109.

OTTAWA ON THE RECORD. V. 1, No. 1 (Sept. 13, 1984)-. 0828-5713. Periodical. CN. English. wk. $275.00. Ottawa on the Record, c/o Henry & Gray Inc, 130 Slater Street/Suite 815, Ottawa Ontario K1P 5H6 Canada. **DD** 320.971.

PACIFIC AFFAIRS. V. 1- May 1928-. 0030-851X. Periodical. CN. English. qt. $30.00. University of British Columbia, 2075 Wesbrook Place, Vancouver British Columbia V6T 1W5 Canada. **Tel** (604)228-6508. **Ed** R S Milne. **Ind/Abst** Am. Hist. Life, Hist. Abstr., Part A, Mod. Hist. Abstr., Hist. Abst., Part B, Twent. Century Abstr., Int. Labour Doc., ABC Pol Sci, Hist. Abstr., Humanit. Index, Book Rev. Index, Soc. Sci. Index, Book Rev. Digest, Soc. Sci. Citation Index, Recent Publ. Artic. bk rev. adv acc. **Circ** 3,000. Scholarly international journal covering political, economic, social and diplomatic problems of Asia and the Pacific. Each issue contains research articles and comprehensive book review section. *News Bulletin.*

PAKISTAN POLITICAL SCIENCE REVIEW. V. 1- Autumn 1973-. 0377-2594. Periodical. PK. English. ir. $5.00. Asia Printers and Publishers, Karachi 32 Pakistan. **LC** JA26. **DD** 320.05.

PALESTINE-ISRAEL BULLETIN. (PALESTINE/ISRAEL BULLETIN). V. 1- Feb. 1978-. 0160-984X. Periodical. US. English. Search, PO Box 53, Waverley MA 02179.

PAPERS IN SOVIET AND EAST EUROPEAN LAW, ECONOMICS AND POLITICS. **Main/Corp** London School of Economics and Political Science. Monographic Series. UK. English. ir. Yale University Press, 92A Yale Station, New Haven CT 06520. **Tel** (203)432-4969.

PAPERS PRESENTED AND ORDER PAPERS. **Main/Corp** Cook Islands. Legislative Assembly. 13th Session, 1969-. CW. English. ir. $1.00. T Kapi, Government Printer, Rarotonga Cook Islands. **LC** J968.C6. **DD** 328.962304. *Papers and Bills Presented.*

PAPERS PRESENTED AT THE ANNUAL MEETING OF THE CANADIAN POLITICAL SCIENCE ASSOCIATION. (PAPERS PRESENTED AT THE ANNUAL MEETING). **Main/Corp** Canadian Political Science Association. **VFOAT** Contributions Presentees au Congres Annuel. 1st- 1913-. 0317-0896. Periodical. CN. English (includes some text in French). ir. $75.00. Canadian Political Science Association, 12 Henderson Avenue, University of Ottawa, Ottawa Ontario K1N 6N5 Canada. **Tel** (613)564-4026. **DD** 320.05. (ctrl). Microfiche. The annual collection of papers presented at the Learned Societies meetings of the Canadian Political Science Association. Covers a broad range of fields and subfields of discipline. Available on microfiche only.

PARLIAMENTARIAN. (THE PARLIAMENTARIAN). Vol. 47- Jan. 1966-. 0031-2282. Periodical. UK. English. qt. 16.00. Commonwealth Parliament Association Finance Department, 7 Old Palace Yard, London SW1Y 3JY England. **Tel** (01)219-4666. **Ed** Andrew Imlach. **Ind/Abst** ABC Pol Sci, Public Aff. Inf. Serv. Bull., Recent Publ. Artic. Index published separately - free - automatically sent. bk rev. adv acc. Parliamentary reports from commonwealth parliaments. *Journal of the Parliaments of the Commonwealth.*

PARLIAMENTARY DEBATES (HANSARD). HOUSE OF COMMONS OFFICIAL REPORT. **Main/Corp** Great Britain. Parliament. House of Commons. **VFOAT** House of Commons Official Report. 5th Ser., Vol. 394-5th Ser., Vol. 100. UK. English. wk. Her Majestys Stationery Office, PO Box 276, London SW8 5DT England. **Tel** 01-622 3316. **LC** J301. (cum index). *Parliamentary Debates. House of Commons Official Report.*

PARLIAMENTARY DEBATES. HOUSE OF REPRESENTATIVES. **Main/Corp** New Zealand. Parliament. 1854/55-. NZ. English. qt. $31.53. Government Printing Office, NZ Private Bag, Wellington New Zealand.

PARLIAMENTARY GOVERNMENT. **VFOAT** Gouvernement Parlementaire. V. 1- Oct. 1979-. 0709-4582. Periodical. CN. English (French, with French text on inverted pages). qt. $11.61. Parliamentary Centre, 275 rue Slarter Street, Ottawa Ontario K1P 5H9 Canada. **Tel** (613)237-0143. **Ed** Lynda Rivington. **DD** 328.71005. bk rev. **Circ** 2,000. (ctrl). Changing role of legislatures plus parliamentary and political reforms.

PARLIAMENTARY JOURNAL. Began in 1960. 0048-2994. Periodical. US. English. qt. $5.00. American Institute of Parliamentarians, 229 Army Post Road/Suite B, Des Moines IA 50315. **LC** JF515.

PARLIAMENTS, ESTATES & REPRESENTATION. **VFOAT** Parliaments, Estates and Representation, Parlements, Etats et Representation. Vol. 1, Pt. 1 (June 1981)-. 0260-6755. Periodical. UK. English (French and German). sa. $50.00. Tieto Ltd, Bank House, 8-A Hill Road, Clendon Avon BS21 7HH England. **LC** JF501. **DD** 328.305. Index in last issue of volume - attached.

PARTIINAIA ZHIZN. Began with July 1960 issue. Periodical. Russian. mo. $12.50. Victor Kamkin Inc (75359), 12224 Parklawn Drive, Rockville MD 20852. **Tel** (301)881-5973. **LC** JN6598.K4.

PARTIJNAJA ZIZN. (PARTIINAIA ZHIZN : ZHURNAL TSK VKP(B)). Began with Nov. 1946. 0132-0734. Periodical. UR. Russian. sm. $16.00. Victor Kamkin Inc (70691), 12224 Parklawn Drive, Rockville MD 20852. **Tel** (301)881-5973. *Partiinoe Stroitelstvo, Propagandist.*

PASSPORT TO LEGAL UNDERSTANDING. *See* Law.

PC DISPATCH. Vol. 1, No. 1 (May 1980)-. 0227-1745. Periodical. CN. English. mo. Free. PC Dispatch, 178 Queen Street, Ottawa Ontario K1P 5E1 Canada. **DD** 324.27104005. (ctrl). *Bulletin, 0316-814X.*

PC JOURNAL. **VAT** Progressive Conservative Journal. Vol. 1, No. 1 (June 1982)-. 0821-6487. Periodical. CN. English. mo. Progressive Conservatice Party of Canada, Suite 200/161 Laurier Avenue West, Ottawa Ontario K1P 5J2 Canada. **DD** 324.2710405.

PC YOUTH TODAY. **VAT** Progressive Conservative Youth Today. 0820-6260. Periodical. CN. English. ir. Progressive Conservative Youth Federation, Suite 200/161 Laurier Avenue West, Ottawa Ontario K1P 5J3 Canada. **DD** 324.27104. *Prospectus, 0707-7009.*

PEACE & DEMOCRACY NEWS. (PEACE & DEMOCRACY NEWS : THE BULLETIN OF THE CAMPAIGN FOR PEACE AND DEMOCRACY/EAST AND WEST). **VFOAT** Peace and Democracy News. V. 1, No. 1 (Spring 1984)-. 0749-5900. Periodical. US. English. ty. $10.00. Campaign for Peace and Democracy/East and West, 301 West 105th Street #2R, New York NY 10025. **DD** 361.

PEACE NEWS. Publication began on June 2, 1936. Periodical. UK. English. bw. 14.50 Domestic, 17.00 Foreign. Peace News Ltd, 8 Elm Avenue, Nottingham 3 England. **Tel** 0602 503587. **LC** MICROFILM 01885JX, JX1901. bk rev. adv acc. **Circ** 4,000. A belief in nonviolent revolution as means of speaking patterns of violence and oppression, constructing alternatives, using feminism, anarchism, pacifism, socialism and ecological theories and methods.

PEACE RESEARCH REVIEWS. V. 1- 1967-. 0553-4283. Periodical. CN. English. ir. 150.00. Peace Research Institute, 25 Dundana Avenue, Dundas Ontario L9H 4E5 Canada. **Tel** (416)628-2356. **Ed** Alan G Newcombe. **Ind/Abst** Am. Hist. Life, Hist. Abstr., Part A, Mod. Hist. Abstr., Hist. Abst., Part B, Twent. Century Abstr., ABC Pol Sci, Hist. Abstr. bk rev. **Circ** 500. Abstracts on publications about economics of 3rd world countries and striving for nuclear disarmament.

PEACEMAKER. (THE PEACEMAKER). V. 1- June 1949-. 0031-3602. Periodical. US. English. mo. $10.00. Peacemaker Movement, Box 627, Garberville CA 95440. **Ed** Kathy Epling and Paul Encimer. **LC** JX1901. bk rev. **Circ** 1,000. Nonviolence as guide, simple living, resisting government coercion through tax, draft, nuclear war, resistance, nonviolent economic and social revolution, consensus, community building and feminism.

PEACEWORK (CAMBRIDGE, MASS.). (PEACEWORK). **VFOAT** Peace Work. No. 6 (Jan. 1973)-. 0748-0725. Periodical. US. English. mo. $10.00. American Friends Service Committee, 2161 Massachusetts Avenue, Cambridge MA 02140. **Tel** (617)661-6130. **Ed** Pat Farren. **DD** 321. bk rev. **Circ** 2,100. A New England peace and social justice journal published by The American Friends Service Committee with grassroots organizing news, listings, original articles, listings, etc. *Final Draft/Only for Life.*

PENSAMIENTO POLITICO. V. 1- (No. 1-). 0031-4757. Periodical. MX. Spanish. ir. Mexican Academic Clearing House, Apartado Postal 7-854 Mexico 7 DF. **Ind/Abst** Foreign Lang. Index. **LC** JA5. **DD** 320.05.

IL PENSIERO POLITICO. Vol. 1- 1968-. 0031-4846. Periodical. IT. Italian. ir. $18.23. Casa Editrice Leo S Olschki, Casella Postale PO Box 66, 50100 Firenze Italy. **Ind/Abst** Am. Hist. Life, Hist. Abstr., Part A, Mod. Hist. Abstr., Hist. Abst., Part B, Twent. Century Abstr., MLA Int. Bibliogr. Books Artic. Mod. Lang. Lit., Hist. Abstr. **LC** JA18.

THE PEOPLE'S KOREA. Began with No. 1, published in 1961. 0031-5036. Newspaper. JA. English. mo. $19.20. Chosun Shinbosa Company, 5 Tsukudo Hachiman cho, Shinjuku ku, Tokyo 162 Japan. **Tel** 03-260-5881. **Ed** Di Jyo Sun. bk rev. adv acc. **Circ** 10,000. Korean affairs.

PEOPLE'S WORLD. 0031-5044. Newspaper. US. English. wk. $15.00. Pacific Publication Foundation, 1819 Tenth Street, Berkeley CA 94710. **Tel** (415)848-1373. **Ed** Carl Bloice. bk rev. adv acc. **Circ** 8,000. General left political newspaper.

PERSPECTIVA MUNDIAL. *See* Economics - Labor.

PERSPECTIVE. V. 1- Jan. 1972-. 0048-3494. Periodical. US. English. mo. Heldref Publications, 4000 Albemarle Street NW/Suite 100, Washington DC 20016. **Tel** (202)362-6445. **Ind/Abst** Book Rev. Index, Book Rev. Index Soc. Sci. Period., Am. Hist. Life, Manage. Contents. **LC** JA1. **DD** 320.05.

PERSPECTIVES ON SOUTHERN AFRICA. 1- 1971-. Monographic Series. US. English. ir. University of California Press, 1095 Essex Street, Richmond CA 94804-2112. **Tel** (415)642-4250. **Ed** William McClung. Books on politics, economics and culture in Southern Africa.

PERSUASION AT WORK. V. 1- March 1978-. 0163-5387. Periodical. US. English. mo. 418.00. The Rockford Institute, 934 North Main, Rockford IL 61103. **Tel** (815)964-5811. **Ed** Allan C Carlson. **Circ** 6,000. Investigates certain cultural and political topics and their impact on the private sector.

PERU, CRONOLOGIA POLITICA. V. 1- 1968/73-. PE. Spanish. an. Desco, AV Salaverry 1945, Lima 14 Peru. **LC** F3448.2.

THE PETTIT REPORT ON THE POLITICS OF SAN FRANCISCO. **VFOAT** Pettit Report. V. 1- July 7, 1980-. 0270-5516. Periodical. US. English. bw. $15.00. Bruce D Pettit, 186 Germania Street, San Francisco CA 94117.

PHILADELPHIA POLICY PAPERS. No. 1-. 0733-3218. Monographic Series. US. English. ir. Foreign Policy Research Institute, 3508 Market Street/Suite 350, Philadelphia PA 19104. **Circ** 3,000. Monograph series featuring authoritative studies of contemporary foreign policy issues, nuclear strategy and strategic planning. The politics of the nuclear freeze.

THE PHYLLIS SCHLAFLY REPORT. Began with: Vol. 1 in 1957?. 0556-0152. Periodical. US. English. mo. Phyllis Schlafly Report, PO Box 618, Alton IL 62002. **Tel** (618)462-5415. **Ed** Phyllis Schlafly. **Circ** 50,000. Defense, family, politics, economics, education, culture, foreign policy, equal rights amendment.

PLADOYER. *See* Law.

PLANIFICACION Y POLITICA. No. 1 (Nov. 1983)-. Periodical. VE. Spanish. ty. Ediciones Iveplan Centro Capriles-Piso, 8 Plaza Venezuela Caracas Venezuela.

PLATFORMS OF THE DEMOCRATIC PARTY AND THE REPUBLICAN PARTY. US. English. Superintendent of Documents, US Government Printing Office, Washington DC 20402. **LC** JK2255. **DD** 329. *Platforms of the Two Great Political Parties.*

PMS, PUBLIC MANAGEMENT SOURCES *CEASED.* (PUBLIC MANAGEMENT SOURCES). **VFOAT** PMS. Vol. 1, No. 1 (July 15, 1945)-. 0364-2275. US. English. mo. **LC** Z7163, JA1. **DD** 016.35. *Selected List of Additions to the Library.*

POINTS DE REPERE. **VFOAT** Points de Reperes. **VAT** Points de Reperes (Montreal). V. 1- Fall 1979-. 0226-742X. Periodical. CN. French. qt. $2.00

Per Number, $7.00 Yearly Quebec, $12.00 Others. Collectif d'Information et de Travial Anti-Imperialiste, 356 rue Ontario, Montreal Quebec H2X 1H8 Canada. DD 320.91724.

POLAND WATCH DIGEST. No. 1 (Aug. 20, 1985)-. 0884-4046. Periodical. US. English. mo. $30.00. Poland Watch Center, 1775 T Street NW, Washington DC 20009. DD 322.

POLICY AND POLITICS. Began in Sept. 1972. 0305-5736. Periodical. UK. English. qt. 39. University of Bristol, Rodney Lodge/Grange Road, Bristol BS8 3EA England. **Tel** (0272)741117. **Ed** Glen Bramley. **Ind/Abst** ABC Pol Sci, Soc. Work Res. Abstr., Soc. Sci. Citation Index, Am. Hist. Life, Hist. Abstr., Hist. Abstr., Part A, Mod. Hist. Abstr., Hist. Abst., Part B, Twent. Century Abstr. adv acc. **Circ** 700. Leading British journal in the field of public policy studies. Focussing on domestic and local policies and policy-making in a British and European context.

POLICY NOTES. 8755-9412. Periodical. US. English. wk. $12.00. Interfaith Action for Economic Justice, 110 Maryland Avenue Northeast, Washington DC 20002. DD 323.

POLICY OPTIONS. **VFOAT** Options Politiques. V. 1- March 1980-. 0226-5893. Periodical. CN. English (French). qt. $38.69. Institute for Research on Public Policy, Policy Options, PO Box 3670, Halifax South Nova Scotia B3J 3K6 Canada. **Tel** 365-1148. **Ind/Abst** Can. Bus. Index, Can. Period. Index. **LC** JL1. **DD** 320.97105. **Circ** 6,000. Intended for doctors, lawyers, and businessmen with a political career in mind.

POLICY SCIENCES. V. 1- Spring 1970-. 0032-2687. Periodical. English. qt. $72.00. Elsevier Science Publishers, PO Box 211, 1000 AE Amsterdam Netherlands. **Tel** (020)5803.911. **Ind/Abst** Sociol. Abstr., Soc. Welf. Soc. Plan./Policy Soc. Dev., Energy Inf. Abstr., Environ. Abstr., ABC Pol Sci, Soc. Sci. Citation Index, Lang. Lang. Behav. Abstr., Public Aff. Inf. Serv. Bull. **LC** H1. **DD** 300.5.

POLICY STUDIES. (POLICY STUDIES : THE JOURNAL OF THE POLICY STUDIES INSTITUTE). Vol. 1, Pt. 1 (July 1980)-. 0144-2872. Periodical. UK. English. qt. Policy Studies Institute, 1/2 Castle Lane, London SW1E 6DR England. **Ind/Abst** Int. Labour Doc., Public Aff. Inf. Serv. Bull. (cum index).

POLICY STUDIES JOURNAL. (POLICY STUDIES JOURNAL : THE JOURNAL OF THE POLICY STUDIES ORGANIZATION). Vol. 1, No. 1 (Autumn 1972)-. 0190-292X. Periodical. US. English. qt. $42.00. Policy Studies Organization, University of Illinois, 361 Lincoln Hall, Urbana IL 61801. **Tel** (217)359-8541. **Ed** David Rosenbloom and Mel Dubnick. **Ind/Abst** Hist. Abstr., Sociol. Abstr., Soc. Welf. Soc. Plan./Policy Soc. Dev., ABC Pol Sci, Energy Inf. Abstr., Soc. Sci. Citation Index, Environ. Abstr., Energy Res. Abstr., Am. Hist. Life, Curr. Contents, Soc. Behav. Sci., Hist. Abstr., Inf. Sci. Abstr., Int. Polit. Sci. Abstr., ABC Pol Sci, Policy Publ. Rev., Public Aff. Inf. Serv. Bull., Soc. Sci. Citation Index, U.S. Polit. Sci. Doc., ABC Pol Sci, Hist. Abstr., Part A, Mod. Hist. Abstr. **LC** H1. **DD** 361.6105. bk rev. adv acc. **Circ** 2,500. (ctrl). Causes and effects of alternative public policies on such subjects as the economy, the environment, civil liberties, world peace, poverty, urban problems, education and governmental reform.

POLICY STUDIES REVIEW. **VFOAT** P.S.R. Vol. 1, No. 1 (Aug. 1981)-. 0278-4416. Periodical. US. English. ir. $42.00. Policy Studies Organization, Wright University of Illinois, 361 Lincoln Hall/702 South, Urbana IL 61801. **Tel** (217)359-8541. **Ed** Dennis Palumbo. **Ind/Abst** Public Aff. Inf. Serv. Bull., ABC Pol Sci, Am. Hist. Life, Community Dev. Abstr., Curr. Contents, Soc. Behav. Sci., Dir. Publ. Proc., Educ. Adm. Abstr., Hist. Abstr., Part A, Mod. Hist. Abstr., Hum. Resour. Abstr., ICSSR Res. Abstr. Q., Soc. Sci. Index, Humanit. Index, Inf. Sci. Abstr., Int. Polit. Sci. Abstr., Sage Fam. Stud. Abstr., Sage Public Adm. Abstr., Sage Urban Stud. Abstr., Soc. Sci. Citation Index, Sociol. Abstr., U.S. Polit. Sci. Doc. **LC** H97. **DD** 361.6105. bk rev. adv acc. **Circ** 2,400. Available in microform from University Microfilms and in microfiche from KTO Microform. The nature, causes, and effects of alternative public policies including everything from agriculture to zoning, with 8 issues per year.

POLISH AFFAIRS (LONDON, ENGLAND : 1974). (POLISH AFFAIRS). No. 90 (May 1974)-. Periodical. UK. English. qt. Polish Council of National Unity, 43 Eaton Place, London SW1K 8BX England. *Polish Affairs and Problems of Central & Eastern Europe.*

POLISH POLITICAL SCIENCE. **VFOAT** Polish Political Science Yearbook. 11 (1981)-. 0208-7375. English. an. Polish Political Science Yearbook/Polish Institute of International Affairs, PO Box 1000 1A Warecka Str/Room No 71, 00-950 Warsaw Poland. **Tel** 26-30-21. **Ed** Longin Pastusiak. **LC** HM7. **DD** 301.05. bk rev. **Circ** 1,200. Covers political science in Poland, theory of politics, and international relations; chronicle of scientific life and bibliography. *Polish Round Table.*

POLISH WESTERN AFFAIRS. V. 1- 1960-. 0032-3039. Periodical. PL. English (French and German). sa. Ars Polona, Krakowskie Przedmiescie 7, 00-068 Warsaw Poland. **Ind/Abst** Am. Hist. Life, Hist. Abstr., Part A, Mod. Hist. Abstr., Hist. Abst., Part B, Twent. Century Abstr., Hist. Abstr., Lang. Lang. Behav. Abstr., Sociol. Abstr., Recent Publ. Artic. **LC** DK443. Index in last issue of volume - attached. (cum index).

POLITEIA. 0096-3135. Periodical. US. English. qt. $15.00. American Association of Political Consultants, 1000 Conneticut Avenue NW/Suite 1101, Washington DC 20036. **LC** JK1. **DD** 329.005.

POLITEIA. 1- 1972-. Periodical. VE. Spanish. ir. Universidad Central Venezuela, Dir de Biblio Info Doc Pub, Caracas Venezuela. **LC** JA5.

POLITICA. No. 1- July/Sept. 1976-. Periodical. Portuguese. ir. $50.00. Fundacao Milton Campus, Caixa Postal 04/0341 CEP 70.000, Brasilia Brazil. **LC** JA5.

POLITICA & I.E. E STRATEGIA. Yearly V. 1- Dec. 1972-. Periodical. Italian. ir. 8000. Trevi, Via Germanico 109, Roma Italy. **LC** D839.

POLITICA (ARHUS, DENMARK). (POLITICA). Began with V. 1, 1968. 0105-0710. Monographic Series. DK. Danish (English). ir. 270. Tidsskriftet Politica, c/o Institut for Statskundskab Aarhus Universitet, Universitetsparken, 8000 Arhus C Denmark. **Tel** 45-6-130111. **Ed** Niels Chr Sidenius. **LC** JA26. bk rev. adv acc. **Circ** 1,100. Analysis of politics and policies within specific areas. Each issue concentrates on one subject.

POLITICA (UNIVERSIDAD DE CHILE. INSTITUTO DE CIENCIA POLITICA). (POLITICA). Vol. 1, No. 1 (Set. 1982)-. Periodical. Spanish. ir. Calle Belgrado, No 10 Santiago De Chile. **LC** JA5. **DD** 320.05.

POLITICAL ACTION REPORT. V. 1- Apr. 1978-. 0162-3648. Periodical. US. English. mo. $25.00. Tyke Research Associates, 1628 K Street Northwest, Washington DC 20006. **LC** JK176.4. **DD** 322.40973.

POLITICAL ALERTS. 4th Quarter, 1976-. 0712-4295. Periodical. CN. English. wk. $8000.00. Political Alerts, c/o F H Deacon Hodgson Inc, 105 Adelaide Street West, Toronto Ontario M5H 1R4 Canada. **DD** 338.971005.

POLITICAL BEHAVIOR. V. 1- Spring 1979-. 0190-9320. Periodical. US. English. qt. Agathon Press Inc, 49 Sheridan Avenue, Fulfillment Department, Albany NY 12210. **Tel** (212)741-3087. **Ind/Abst** Sociol. Abstr., Soc. Welf. Soc. Plan./Policy Soc. Dev., Psychol. Abstr. **LC** JA74.5. **DD** 306.2.

POLITICAL CHANGE. Periodical. II. English. ir. 15.00. Dr S L Verma, Institute of Correspondence Studies at the University of Rajasthan, Jaipur 302004 Rajasthan India. **LC** JQ201. **DD** 320.954005.

POLITICAL COMMUNICATION AND PERSUASION. Vol. 1, No. 1 (1980)-. 0195-7473. Periodical. US. English. ir. $48.00. Crane Russak & Co Inc, 3 East 44th Street, New York NY 10017. **Tel** (212)867-1490. **Ed** Yonah Alexander. **Ind/Abst** Sociol. Abstr., ABC Pol Sci, Public Aff. Inf. Serv. Bull. **LC** JF1525.P8. **DD** 306.2. **CODEN** PCPEDX. bk rev. adv acc. **Circ** 600. Presents research on propaganda and psychological warfare and examines the roles of governmental and nongovernmental organizations as political communicators.

POLITICAL DIGEST. Vol. 1, No. 1 (June 1983)-. Periodical. English. mo. 1.00 Africa, $1.00 U.S.A., 1.00 U.K. & Europe. Spotlight Digest Ltd, PO Box 4490, Surulere Lagos. **LC** JQ3081.A1. **DD** 966.90505.

POLITICAL FINANCE LOBBY REPORTER. **VAT** Political Finance/Lobby Reporter. 0270-353X. Periodical. US. English. bw. $240.00. Political Finance & Lobby Reporter, 1023 National Press Building, Washington DC 20045.

POLITICAL GEOGRAPHY QUARTERLY. *See* Geography.

POLITICAL HANDBOOK OF THE WORLD (NEW YORK, N.Y.). (POLITICAL HANDBOOK OF THE WORLD). 1975-. 0193-175X. US. English. an. McGraw-Hill Book Company, 1221 Avenue of the Americas, New York NY 10020. **LC** JF37. **DD** 320.9047. *Political Handbook and Atlas of the World.*

POLITICAL INQUIRY. V. 1- Fall 1973-. 0092-9735. Periodical. US. English. qt. $10.00. 2250 Pierce Road, Box 58, University Center MI 48710. **LC** JA1. **DD** 320.05.

POLITICAL ISSUES SERIES. **VFOAT** Classroom Study Series. No. 1-. Monographic Series. US. English. ir. Center for Study of Armament, California State University, Los Angeles CA 90032.

POLITICAL METHODOLOGY. V. 1- Winter 1974-. 0162-2021. Periodical. US. English. qt. $42.00. Geron-X Publishers, Box 1108, Los Altos CA 94023. **Tel** (415)850-0456. **Ed** Chris Achen. **Ind/Abst** ABC Pol Sci. **LC** JA1. **DD** 320.05. bk rev. adv acc. **Circ** 600. (ctrl). Concerned with the entire range of interests and problems centering upon how political inquiry can be conducted.

POLITICAL POWER AND SOCIAL THEORY. V. 1- 1980-. 0198-8719. US. English. an. $49.50. JAI Press, PO Box 1678, Greenwich CT 06836. **Tel** (203)661-7602. **Ed** Maurice Zeitlin. **Ind/Abst** Sociol. Abstr., Soc. Welf. Soc. Plan./Policy Soc. Dev. **LC** JA1. **DD** 320.05.

POLITICAL PRACTICES REPORTS. V. 4, No. 4- Feburary 19, L980-. Periodical. US. English. bw. Plus Publications Inc, 2626 Pennsylvania Avenue NW, Washington DC 20037. **Ed** Chris Ryan. *Lobbying Reports, 0191-6742.*

POLITICAL PROFILES. (PROFILES). Vol. 1, No. 1 (Mar./Apr. 1985)-. 0882-7885. Periodical. US. English. bm. $36.00. Political Profiles Inc, 209 C Street NW, Washington DC 20002. **DD** 320.

POLITICAL PULSE. 8756-9248. Periodical. US. English. sm. $85.00. Political Pulse, 926 J Street/Suite 1218, Sacramento CA 95814. **Ed** Bud Lembke. **Circ** 500. Newsletter of California politics and government, includes news about campaigns, elected officials, issues, media and lobbyists.

POLITICAL QUARTERLY. (THE POLITICAL QUARTERLY). V. 1- Jan. 1930-. 0032-3179. Periodical. UK. English. qt. $50.00. International Thomson Publisning Ltd, Subscription Department, 23-29 Emerald Street, London WC1N 3QJ England. **Ind/Abst** Int. Labour Doc., ABC Pol Sci, Public Aff. Inf. Serv. Bull., Soc. Sci. Index, Writ. Am. Hist., Hist. Abstr., Am. Hist. Life, Soc. Sci. Citation Index, Hist. Abstr., Part A, Mod. Hist. Abstr., Hist. Abst., Part B, Twent. Century Abstr., Recent Publ. Artic. **LC** JA8.

POLITICAL SCIENCE. V. 1- Sept. 1948-. 0032-3187. Periodical. NZ. English. sa. $15.00. Information & Publishing Section, Victoria University of Wellington/Private Bag, Wellington New Zealand. **Tel** (04)721000. **Ed** R Mascarenhas and J Morrow. **Ind/Abst** Am. Hist. Life, Hist. Abstr., Soc. Sci. Citation Index. **LC** JA1. bk rev. adv acc. **Circ** 475. Broad field of political science with a focus on the Australasian and Pacific region research on any topic any field.

POLITICAL SCIENCE. **VFOAT** Publications in Political Science. V. 5-. Monographic Series. US. English. ir. Marcel Dekker, PO Box 11305, Church Street Station, New York NY 10249. **Tel** (212)889-9595. *Political Science and Public Administration.*

POLITICAL SCIENCE ABSTRACTS. ANNUAL SUPPLEMENT. *See* Indexes/Abstracts.

POLITICAL SCIENCE ANNUAL. V. 1- 1966-. 0079-3043. US. English. ir. Bobbs Merrill Company, 4300 West 62nd Street, Indianapolis IN 46268. **Ed** J A Robinson. **Ind/Abst** Am. Hist. Life, Hist. Abstr., Part A, Mod. Hist. Abstr., Hist. Abst., Part B, Twent. Century Abstr. **LC** JA51. **DD** 320.05.

POLITICAL SCIENCE, GOVERNMENT AND PUBLIC POLICY SERIES. **Main/Corp** Universal Reference System. US. English. ir.

POLITICAL SCIENCE QUARTERLY. V. 1- Mar. 1886-. 0032-3195. Periodical. US. English. qt. $35.00. Academy of Political Sciences, 2852 Broadway, New York NY 10025-7885. **Tel** (212)866-6752. **Ed** Demetrios Caraley. **Ind/Abst** Am. Hist. Life, Lang. Lang. Behav. Abstr., Hist. Abst., Part B, Twent. Century Abstr., Energy Inf. Abstr., Environ. Abstr., Index Econ. Artic. J. Collect. Vol., ABC Pol Sci, Annu. Bibliogr. Engl. Lang. Lit., Writ. Am. Hist., Book Rev. Index, Int. Index, Pooles Index Period. Lit., Public Aff. Inf. Serv. Bull., Soc. Sci. Index, Humanit. Index, Soc. Sci. Citation Index, Sociol. Abstr., Book Rev. Digest, Abstr. Soc. Work., Hist. Abst., Part B,

Twent. Century Abstr. **LC** H1. **DD** 320.05. (cum index). bk rev. adv acc. **Circ** 13,000. A nonpartisan journal devoted to the study of contemporary and historical aspects of government, politics, and public affairs.

POLITICAL SCIENCE REVIEW. V. 1- Feb. 1962-. 0554-5196. II. English. qt. $25.00. University Rajasthan, Professor VR Mehta, Managing Editor, Department Political Science, Jaipur 302004 India. **Ind/Abst** ABC Pol Sci, Am. Hist. Life, Hist. Abstr., Hist. Abstr., Part A, Mod. Hist. Abstr., Hist. Abst., Part B, Twent. Century Abstr. **LC** JA26.

POLITICAL SCIENCE REVIEWER. (THE POLITICAL SCIENCE REVIEWER). V. 1- 1971-. 0091-3715. US. English. an. $6.00. PO Box 52, Hampden Sydney VA 23943. **Ind/Abst** Book Rev. Index. **LC** JA1. **DD** 320.05.

THE POLITICAL SCIENCE UTILIZATION DIRECTORY. *See* Yearbooks, Almanacs, Directories.

POLITICAL SCIENTIST. V. 1- July/Dec. 1964-. 0032-3209. Periodical. II. English. sa. Ranchi University, Department of Political Science, Ranchi India. **LC** JA26.

POLITICAL STUDIES. V. 1- Feb. 1953-. 0032-3217. Periodical. UK. English. qt. Claredon Press, Oxford OX2 DP England. **Ind/Abst** Am. Hist. Life, Hist. Abstr., Part A, Mod. Hist. Abstr., Hist. Abst., Part B, Twent. Century Abstr., ABC Pol Sci, Sociol. Abstr., Soc. Welf. Soc. Plan./Policy Soc. Dev., Public Aff. Inf. Serv. Bull., Soc. Sci. Index, Soc. Work Res. Abstr., Recent Publ. Artic. **LC** JA1. **DD** 320.5. Index in last issue of volume - attached. (cum index).

POLITICAL STUDIES. V. 1- Feb. 1953-. 0032-3217. Periodical. UK. English. qt. $50.00. Butterworth Scientific Ltd, PO Box 63 Westbury House Bury Street, Guildford GU2 5BH England. **Tel** 0444 459188. **Ed** Jack Lively. **Ind/Abst** Am. Hist. Life, Hist. Abstr., Part A, Mod. Hist. Abstr., Hist. Abst., Part B, Twent. Century Abstr., ABC Pol Sci, Sociol. Abstr., Soc. Welf. Soc. Plan./Policy Soc. Dev., Public Aff. Inf. Serv. Bull., Soc. Sci. Index, Soc. Work Res. Abstr., Recent Publ. Artic. **LC** JA1. **DD** 320.5. Index in last issue of volume - attached. (cum index). Covers entire range of political studies, from political theory and history of political thought, through empirical politics to such fields as methodology, international relations, public administration and policy analysis.

POLITICAL THEORY. V. 1- Feb. 1973-. 0090-5917. Periodical. US. English. qt. Sage Publishers Inc, 275 South Beverly Drive, Beverly Hills CA 90212. **Tel** (213)274-8003. **Ind/Abst** Am. Hist. Life, Hist. Abstr., Part A, Mod. Hist. Abstr., Hist. Abst., Part B, Twent. Century Abstr., ABC Pol Sci, Philos. Index, Soc. Sci. Citation Index, Sociol. Abstr., Lang. Lang. Behav. Abstr., Recent Publ. Artic., Hist. Abstr. **LC** JA1.A1.

POLITICS. V. 1- May 1966-. 0032-3268. Periodical. AT. English. sa. $33.20. Australian Political Studies Association, PO Box 4, Canberra Australian Capital Territory 2600 Australia. **Tel** 62-493605. **Ed** P Weller. **Ind/Abst** ABC Pol Sci, Am. Hist. Life, Curr. Contents Behav. Soc. Educ. Sci., Int. Polit. Sci. Abstr., Soc. Sci. Citation Index, APAIS, Aust. Public Aff. Inf. Serv., Hist. Abstr., Part A, Mod. Hist. Abstr., Hist. Abstr., Hist. Abst., Part B, Twent. Century Abstr. **LC** JQ3995.A1. **DD** 320.05. Index in last issue of volume - attached. bk rev. adv acc. **Circ** 750. (ctrl). Political science, public administration, political theory, international relations, and book reviews. *A.P.S.A. News.*

POLITICS. **Main/Corp** American Federation of Labor and Congress of Industrial Organizations. Louisiana. Political Information Committee. 0194-3669. Periodical. US. English. mo. Free to members. Louisiana American Federation of Labor and Congress of Industrial Organizations (AFL-CIO), Political Information Committee, 429 Government Street, Baton Rouge LA 70821.

POLITICS & MARKETS. (POLITICS & MARKETS : A MONTHLY NEWSLETTER). **VFOAT** Political and Markets. 0749-4416. Periodical. US. English. mo. $115.00. Gallatin Institute, 1120 Connecticut Avenue/Suite 450, Washington DC 20063. **DD** 324.

POLITICS AND POLICY. (POLITICS AND POLICY : JOURNAL OF THE NORTH CAROLINA POLITICAL SCIENCE ASSOCIATION). **VFOAT** Journal of the North Carolina Political Science Association. Vol. 4 (1984)-. 0743-1082. Periodical. US. English. an. $4.00 Individuals, $8.00 Libraries. North Carolina Political Science Association, East Carolina University, Greenville NC 27834. **LC** JA1. **DD** 320.05. *Journal of the North Carolina Political Science Association, 0737-4801.*

POLITICS & SOCIETY. **VFOAT** Politics and Society. Vol. 1, No. 1 (Nov. 1970)-. 0032-3292. Periodical. US. English. qt. $22.00. Geron-X Publishers, Box 1108, Los Altos CA 94023. **Tel** (415)856-0456. **Ed** Mary Nolan. **Ind/Abst** Am. Hist. Life, Hist. Abstr., Part A, Mod. Hist. Abstr., Hist. Abst., Part B, Twent. Century Abstr., ABC Pol Sci, Altern. Press Index, Soc. Sci. Index, Soc. Sci. Citation Index, Sociol. Abstr., Lang. Lang. Behav. Abstr., Hist. Abstr. **LC** H1. **DD** 300.5. bk rev. adv acc. **Circ** 1,000. (ctrl). Original analyses of politics, including its social roots and its consequences.

POLITICS AND THE LIFE SCIENCES. (POLITICS AND THE LIFE SCIENCES : THE JOURNAL OF THE ASSOCIATION FOR POLITICS AND THE LIFE SCIENCES). V. 1, No. 1 (July 1982)-. 0730-9384. Periodical. US. English. sa. $25.00. Northern Illinois University, Association for Politics and the Life Sciences, Dekalb IL 60115. **Tel** (815)753-1901. **Ed** Thomas C Wiegele. **Ind/Abst** ABC Pol Sci. **LC** JA80. **DD** 320.01. bk rev. adv acc. **Circ** 314. Publishes articles, commentaries, and book reviews relating new biological knowledge to political behavior, public policy, and social science methodology.

POLITICS TODAY. Oct. 6, 1975-. Periodical. UK. English. mo. $30.65. Conservative & UN Central Office, 32 Smith Square, London SWIP 3HH England. **Tel** (01)222-9000. **Ed** A B Looke. **Ind/Abst** Mag. Index. **LC** JN1129.C69. **DD** 320.9410857. **Circ** 3,000. Provides detailed analysis of all the main aspects of conservative policy. *Notes On Current Politics, Old Queen Street Paper.*

POLITICS TODAY. V. 5, No. 2- Mar./Apr. 1978-. 0160-4929. Periodical. US. English. bm. $9.00 Domestic, $11.00 Foreign. Skeptic Magazine Inc, Presidio Plaza, Santa Barbara CA 93101. **Ind/Abst** Energy Inf. Abstr., Environ. Abstr. **LC** AP2. **DD** 905. *Skeptic, 0093-5050.*

POLITIK UND KULTUR. GW. German. bm. 30.-. Colloquium Verlag, Unter den Eichen 93, 1000 Berlin 45- West Germany. **Tel** 030-832 4838. **Ed** Wilhelm Wolfgang Schutz. **LC** AS181. bk rev. adv acc. (ctrl). Poltical, social and cultural developments in the two German states.

POLITIK UND WAHLER *CEASED.* Vol. 1- 1967-. 0554-534X. Monographic Series. GW. German. ir. Athenaum Verlag GMBH, Adelheidstrabe 2, 6240 Konigstein-TS West Germany. **Tel** 067 53/ 24 88.

POLITIKON. Began with June 1974 issue. Periodical. SA. Afrikaans (English). sa. $10.00. Political Science Association of South Africa, PO Box 486, Pretoria 0001 South Africa. **Ind/Abst** ABC Pol Sci. **LC** JA26.

POLITIQUE. (POLITIQUE : REVUE DE LA SOCIEETE QUEBECOISE DE SCIENCE POLITIQUE). Vol. 1, No. 1 (Jan. 1982)-. 0711-608X. Periodical. CN. French. sa. $10.00. Societe Quebecoise de Science Politique, Department de Science, Politique, Universite du Quebec A Montreal, CP 8888, Succursale A, Montreal Quebec H3C 3P8 Canada. **DD** 320.05.

POLITIQUE AFRICAINE (PARIS, FRANCE : 1981). (POLITIQUE AFRICAINE). 1, 1 (Jan. 1981)-. 0244-7827. Monographic Series. FR. French. ir. Editions Karthala, 22-24 Boulevard Arago, 75013 Paris France. **LC** UNC. **DD** 320.96.

POLITISCHE BILDUNG (STUTTGART, GERMANY). (POLITISCHE BILDUNG). 0554-5455. Periodical. GW. German. ir. $12.98. W E Saarbach GMBH, Postfach 101610, D5000 Koeln 1 West Germany. **Ind/Abst** Foreign Lang. Index.

POLITISCHE DOKUMENTATION. **VFOAT** Poldok. Volume 1- June 1965-. 0032-3438. Periodical. GW. German. ty. $135.50. K G Saur Verlag, 175 Fifth Avenue, New York NY 10010. **Tel** (212)982-1302. **Ind/Abst** PAIS Foreign Lang. Index, Foreign Lang. Index. **LC** JA14.

POLITISCHE STUDIEN. Issue 1- 1950-. 0032-3462. Periodical. GW. German. bm. $19.47. Hanns Seidel Stiftung, Lazarettstrasse 19, D 8000 Munchen 19 West Germany. **Tel** (089)293272. **Ind/Abst** Soc. Sci. Citation Index, Sociol. Abstr., Foreign Lang. Index, Am. Hist. Life, Hist. Abstr., Lang. Lang. Behav. Abstr., ABC Pol Sci. **LC** H35.

POLITISCHE VIERTELJAHRESSCHRIFT. V. 1- Oct. 1960-. 0032-3470. Periodical. GW. German. qt. 96.00. Westdeutscher Verlag GMBH, Postfach 5829, D6200 Wiesbaden 1 West Germany. **Tel** (06121)5341. **Ind/Abst** Am. Hist. Life, Hist. Abstr., Part A, Mod. Hist. Abstr., Hist. Abst., Part B, Twent. Century Abstr., PAIS Foreign Lang. Index, Foreign Lang. Index, Sociol. Abstr., Lang. Lang. Behav. Abstr., Hist. Abstr., Recent Publ. Artic. **LC** JA14. **DD** 320.05. Index in last issue of volume - attached. bk rev. adv acc. **Circ** 1,900.

POLITISCHES JAHRBUCH DER CHRISTLICH - DEMOKRATISCHEN UNION DEUTSCHLANDS. *See* Yearbooks, Almanacs, Directories.

POLITY. V. 1- Fall 1968-. 0032-3497. Periodical. US. English. qt. $15.00. University of Massachusetts, Political Science Department, Thompson Hall, Amherst MA 01002. **Tel** (413)545-1354. **Ed** Anwar H Syed. (cum index). bk rev. adv acc. **Circ** 1,200. (ctrl). A journal of political science covering all the topics in the discipline. Written by political scientists for political scientists.

POLITYKA. Began July 27, 1957. 0032-3500. Periodical. PL. Polish. wk. ARS Polona, Krakowskie Przedmiescie 7, 00-068 Warsaw Poland. **Ind/Abst** MLA Int. Bibliogr. Books Artic. Mod. Lang. Lit. **LC** AP54.

POPULAR GOVERNMENT. V. 1- Jan. 1931-. 0032-4515. US. English. qt. $8.00. Institute of Government University of North Carolina, Knapp Building 059A, Chapel Hill NY 27514. **Tel** (919)966-4119. **Ed** William A Campbell. **Ind/Abst** Public Aff. Inf. Serv. Bull. **LC** JK4101. **Circ** 6,450. (ctrl). Articles on North Carolina state and local government.

PORTER'S GUIDE TO CONGRESSIONAL ROLL CALL VOTES. SENATE. **VFOAT** Guide to Congressional Roll Call Votes. 98th Congress, 1st Session (1983)-. 0748-2329. US. English. qt. $75.00. Legislative Information Group Press, 1718 Connecticut Avenue Northwest/Suite 310, Washington DC 20009. **Tel** (301)270-8939. **Ed** Allison I Porter. bk rev. **Circ** 100. (ctrl). Reference books on congressional voting. Includes comprehensive indexes, vote descriptions, and member listings for 1983 and 1984 House and Senate sessions.

POSEV. **VFOAT** Possev. Began with Vol.1, in 1945. 0032-5201. Periodical. GW. Russian. mo. $34.09. Possev Verlag V Gorachek KG, Flurscheideweg 15, D-6230 Frankfurt West Germany. **Tel** (069)341265. bk rev. (ctrl). All about living in the Soviet Union and problems of opposition in the USSR.

PPI REPORT. **VFOAT** P.P.I. Report. 0742-8251. Periodical. US. English. sm. $115.00. Political Profiles, 209 C Street NE, Washington DC 20002. **Tel** (202)544-3833.

PRASHASNIKA. **VFOAT** Prasasanika. English. ir. HCM State Institute of Public Administration, Malviya Hagar, Jaipur 302004 India. **LC** JA26.

PRESENT TENSE. V. 1- Autumn 1973-. 0092-4091. Periodical. US. English. qt. $14.00. American Jewish Committee, 165 East 56th Street, New York NY 10022. **Tel** (212)751-4000. **Ed** Murray Polner. **Ind/Abst** Am. Hist. Life, Hist. Abstr., Part A, Mod. Hist. Abstr., Hist. Abst., Part B, Twent. Century Abstr., Pop. Mag. Rev., Mag. Index, Access. **LC** DS101. **DD** 910.03924. bk rev. adv acc. **Circ** 45,000. Covers political, economical and social life.

PRIMARY ELECTIONS. **Main/Corp** Maine. Election Division. US. English. be. **LC** JK2892.

PROBLEMY PARTIINOGO I GOSUDARSTVENNOGO STROITELSTVA. Vol. 1-. UR. Russian. an. **LC** JN6501. **DD** 320.947.

PROBLEMY VOSTOCNOJ EVROPY. (PROBLEMY VOSTOCHNOI EVROPY). **VFOAT** Problems of Eastern Europe. 1-. 0739-7119. Periodical. US. Russian. qt. $9.00 Single Issue. Chalidze Publications, 505 Eighth Avenue, New York NY 10018. **LC** DJK50. **DD** 320.947.

PROCEEDINGS OF THE ACADEMY OF POLITICAL SCIENCE. (PROCEEDINGS OF THE ACADEMY OF POLITICAL SCIENCE IN THE CITY OF NEW YORK). V. 1- Oct. 1910-. 0065-0684. Monographic Series. US. English. sa. Academy of Political Sciences, 2852 Broadway, New York NY 10025. **Tel** (212)866-6752. **Ind/Abst** Energy Inf. Abstr., Environ. Abstr., ABC Pol Sci, Soc. Sci. Index, Int.

Political Science

Index, Public Aff. Inf. Serv. Bull., Humanit. Index, Am. Hist. Life, Hist. Abstr., Soc. Work Res. Abstr., Soc. Sci. Index, Hist. Abstr., Part A, Mod. Hist. Abstr., Hist. Abst., Part B, Twent. Century Abstr. Available on microfilm.

PROCEEDINGS OF THE CONFERENCE OF THE AMERICAN COUNTRY LIFE ASSOCIATION. Main/Conf American Country Life Conference. 1st- Jan. 1919-. 0065-7999. US. English. an. American Country Life Association, 2118 South Summit Avenue, Sioux Falls SD 57105. Tel (605)336-5236. LC HT407. DD 323.35406373.

PROCESSED WORLD. See Economics.

PROGRAMMES ET ENGAGEMENTS ELECTORAUX. Main/Corp France. Parlement (1946-). Assemblee Nationale. VFOAT Barodet. 12/19 March 1978-. FR. French. ir. Impr de l'Assemblee Nationale, Parlement Secretariat General, Paris France. LC JN2957. DD 324.230944. *Recueil des Textes Authentiques des Programmes et Engagements Electoraux des Deputes Proclames Elus a la Suite des Elections Generales.*

THE PROGRESSIVE. US. English. ir. 409 East Main Street, Madison WI 53703.

PROJET. See Economics - Economic Theory.

PROTOKOLL - DEUTSCHER BUNDESTAG. Main/Corp Germany (West). Bundestag. German. ir. Verlag Dr H Hegen, Postfach 821, 53 Bonn-Bad Godesberg 1 West Germany. LC J351.

PROVINCIAL MEMBERS OF PARLIAMENT, METRO. (PROVINCIAL MEMBERS OF PARLIAMENT (METRO)). 1981 Ed. -. 0711-3943. CN. English. Community Information Centre of Metropolitan Toronto, 3rd Floor, 34 King Street East, Toronto Ontario M5C 1E5 Canada. DD 328.7130025.

PS. VAT Political Science. V. 1- Winter 1968-. 0030-8269. Periodical. US. English. qt. $100.00 Domestic, $105.00 Foreign. American Political Science Association, 1527 New Hampshire Avenue Northwest, Washington DC 20036. Tel (202)483-2512. Ind/Abst Am. Hist. Life, Hist. Abstr., Part A, Mod. Hist. Abstr., Hist. Abst., Part B, Twent. Century Abstr., Soc. Sci. Index, ABC Pol Sci, Writ. Am. Hist. LC JA28. Available on microfilm from University Microfilms. Includes articles analyzing contemporary issues of politics and policy.

PUBLIC CHOICE. V. 4- Spring 1968-. 0048-5829. English. ir. Kluwer Academic Publishing Group, PO Box 322, 3300 AH Dordrecht Netherlands. Ind/Abst ABC Pol Sci, Index Econ. Artic. J. Collect. Vol., Sociol. Abstr., Soc. Welf. Soc. Plan./Policy Soc. Dev., J. Econ. Lit., U.S. Polit. Sci. Doc., Public Aff. Inf. Serv. Bull. LC JA1. *Papers on Non-Market Decision Making.*

PUBLIC POLICY CEASED. V. 1-29. 0033-3646. US. English. qt. $22.00 Domestic, $28.00 Foreign. J Wiley & Son, Journals Department, 605 Third Avenue, New York NY 10016. Ind/Abst Index Econ. Artic. J. Collect. Vol., Public Aff. Inf. Serv. Bull., Soc. Sci. Index, Am. Hist. Life, Hist. Abstr., Part A, Mod. Hist. Abstr., Hist. Abst., Part B, Twent. Century Abstr. LC JA51. DD 380.162058. NLM W1 PU634. CODEN PBPYAF.

PUBLIC POLICY PAPER. No. 1-. Monographic Series. US. English. qt. University of Washington, Institute of Government Research, 3935 University Way NE, Seattle Washington 98105. LC JA37.

PUBLICATIONS OF NEW MEXICO STATE AGENCIES. 0091-696X. US. English. an. $1.50 per issue. Santa Fe NM 87501. LC Z1223.5.N56. DD 015.789.

PUBLICATIONS ON RUSSIA AND EASTERN EUROPE. Main/Corp Washington (State). University. Institute for Comparative and Foreign Area Studies. No. 1- 1969-. 0079-7790. Monographic Series. US. English. ir. University of Washington Press, Far Eastern and Russian Institute, Seattle WA 98104.

PUBLIUS. V. 1- 1971-. 0048-5950. Periodical. US. English. ir. $30.00. North Texas State University, Department of Political Science, Denton TX 76203-5338. Tel (817)565-2313. Ed Daniel J Elazar and John Kincaid. Ind/Abst Public Aff. Inf. Serv. Bull., Soc. Welf. Soc. Plan./Policy Soc. Dev., Sociol. Abstr., Writ. Am. Hist., Am. Hist. Life, Hist. Abstr., Soc. Sci. Citation Index, ABC Pol Sci, Lang. Lang. Behav. Abstr., Hist. Abstr., Part A, Mod. Hist. Abstr., Hist. Abst., Part B, Twent. Century Abstr. LC JK1. DD 321.02. bk rev. adv acc. Circ 1,100. Publishes articles on theory and practice of federalism and intergovernmental relations in the United States and other federal politics.

PUERTO RICO LIBRE. V. 1- Aug. 1973-. 0033-4030. Periodical. US. English. bm. $15.00. Solidarity Committee, Box 319, Cooper Station, New York NY 10003. Tel (212)741-3131.

PUNTO CRITICO. See Economics.

QUEBEC-CANADA. V. 1- Nov. 1977-. 0709-5643. Periodical. CN. English (French). mo. $3.00. Quebec-Canada, 1253 McGill College Avenue 470, Montreal Quebec H3B 2Y5 Canada. DD 329.9714.

QUEBEC NOUVEAU. V. 1- Nov. 1972-. 0700-334X. Periodical. CN. French. ir. Mouvement National des Quebecois, 1192 rue des Erables, Quebec Quebec G1R 2N4 Canada. DD 320.5405.

THE QUEBECER. Vol. 1, No. 1-. 0824-1783. CN. French. an. Free to Members, $3.00 Nonmembers. Alliance Quebec, Suite 501/1411 rue Crescent, Montreal Quebec H3G 2B3 Canada. DD 323.111120714.

QUEBECOIS DE MONTMAGNY-L'ISLET. (LE QUEBECOIS DE MONTMAGNY-L'ISLET). Vol. 1, No. 1-. 0228-9822. Periodical. CN. French. ir. Free. Mme Denise l'Bleney, RR 3, Montmagny Quebec G5V 3S1 Canada. DD 324.21473509305.

QUEBECOIS DU COMTE DE VANIER. (LE QUEBECOIS DU COMTE DE VANIER). V. 1- Spring 1977-. 0703-4784. Periodical. CN. French. qt. Free. Association du Parti Quebecois du Comite Boulay, 33 rue de Gaspe, Quebec Quebec G1L 2A4 Canada. DD 329.9714.

QUEBECOIS VAUDREUIL-SOULANGES. (LE QUEBECOIS VAUDREUIL-SOULANGES). Vol. 1, No. 1-. 0823-6321. Periodical. CN. French. Le Quebecois Vaudreuil-Soulanges, Parti Quebecois de Vaudreuil-Soulanges, 208 Lotbiniere, Vaureuil Quebec Canada. DD 324.2714093.

RADICAL. V. 1- 1969-. Periodical. AT. English. ir. 10.00. Radical, PO Box K408, c/o Australia Labor Party, Haymarket New South Wales 2000 Australia. bk rev. adv acc. Circ 20,000. (ctrl).

RADICAL AMERICA. V. 1- 1967-. 0033-7617. Periodical. US. English. ir. $70.00. Radical America, 38 Union Square, Somerville MA 02143. Tel (617)628-6585. Ed John P Demeter. Ind/Abst Am. Hist. Life, Hist. Abstr., Part A, Mod. Hist. Abstr., Hist. Abst., Part B, Twent. Century Abstr., Sociol. Abstr., Soc. Welf. Soc. Plan./Policy Soc. Dev., Altern. Press Index, LC HD4802. DD 322.20973. (cum index). bk rev. adv acc. Circ 5,000. Socialist-feminist journal on culture, politics; continuously published since 1967; analysis commentary, history on US, Europe and third world.

RADIO LIBERTY RESEARCH BULLETIN. 1955. 0148-2548. Periodical. US. English. wk. $85.00. Radio Free Europe, Radio Liberty NY Programming Center, 1775 Broadway, New York NY 10019. Tel (212)397-5300. LC DK1. DD 947.08505. Circ 1,500. (ctrl). Analyses of current Soviet internal and external developments, including political, social and economic trends, nationality affairs, and foreign relations.

RAG, REVISTA ADMINISTRATIVA DO GRANDE RIO. Periodical. Portuguese. ir. Visconde Rio Branco, 37 - 1 Andar, Rio de Janeiro Brazil. LC JL2499.R47. DD 309.1815.

RAPPORT - COMMISSION PERMANENTE DE LA REFORME DES DISTRICTS ELECTORAUX. Main/Corp Quebec (Province). Assemblee Nationale. Commission Permanente de la Reforme des Districts Electoraux. 3.-. CN. French. LC JL168.Q4. DD 328.71407345. *Rapport - Commission Permanente de la Reforme des Districts Electoraux.*

RECHTS- UND STAATSWISSENSCHAFTEN. Began in 1947. 0080-0163. Monographic Series. AU. German. ir. Springer Verlag, Postfach 367, Moelkerbastei 5, A-1011 Vienna Austria.

REFERENCE AID, CHIEFS OF STATE, AND CABINET MEMBERS OF FOREIGN GOVERNMENTS. Main/Corp United States. Central Intelligence Agency. 1972. Periodical. US. English. ir. $300.00. Documents Expediting Project Processing/Department of Exchange & Gift Division, Washington DC 20540. Tel (202)287-9527. Ed CIA. Circ 625. (ctrl). Includes economic and energy statistics, directories of foreign Governments. Maps.

REFORMED PERSPECTIVE. VAT Perspective (Winnipeg. 1982). Vol. 1, No. 1 (Jan. 1982)-. 0714-8208. Periodical. CN. English. mo. $25.00. Reformed Perspective, Box 12/Transcona Postal Station, Winnipeg Manitoba R2C 2Z5 Canada. Tel (204)222-9948. Ed W Gortemaker. DD 248.405. bk rev. adv acc. Circ 2,200. (ctrl). A social-political magazine for the family from a Biblical perspective.

REGARDS SUR ISRAEL. V. 1- Dec. 1972-. 0384-9120. CN. French. mo. Comite Canada-Israel, 1310 Av Greene, Montreal Quebec H3Z 2B2 Canada.

LE REGIONI: RIVISTA DI DOCUMENTAZIONE E GIURISPRUDENZA. VFOAT Rivista di Documentazione e Giurisprudenza. Vol. 1- Jan./Feb. 1973-. IT. Italian. bm. 130.000 Domestic, 170.000 Foreign. Societa Editrice Il Mulino Spa, Via Santo Stefano 6, 40125 Bologna Italy. Tel 051/23 34 15.

RENEWAL (WINCHESTER, VA.). (RENEWAL). Vol. 1, No. 1 (Jan. 26, 1981)-. 0279-0300. Periodical. US. English. ir. $15.00. Renewal, PO Box 3242, Winchester VA 22601. Tel (202)234-0747.

REPERTOIRE DES PUBLICATIONS OFFICIELLES, SERIES ET PERIODIQUES : ADMINISTRATION CENTRALES FRANCAISES. FR. French. ir. Documentation Francaise, 29-31 Quai Voltaire, 75340 Paris Cedex 07 France. LC Z2169, J341. DD 015.44.

REPORT - ASSOCIATION FOR REPORT ON CONFEDERATION. (REPORT; THE MAGAZINE OF PUBLIC AFFAIRS). V. 2, No. 5- Apr. 1979-. 0708-9864. Periodical. CN. English. mo. $10.00 Domestic, $13.00 Foreign. Association for Report on Confederation, PO 1681 Station H, Montreal Quebec H3G 2N6 Canada. DD 320.971. *Report on Confederation.*

REPORT - JAMMU AND KASHMIR LEGISLATIVE COUNCIL. COMMITTEE ON PRIVILEGES. (REPORT - JAMMU AND KASHMIR LEGISLATIVE COUNCIL, COMMITTEE ON PRIVILEGES). Main/Corp Jammu and Kashmir. Legislature. Legislative Council. Committee on Privileges. 0448-2433. II. English. ir. Jammu and Kashmir Legislative Council Secretariat, Committee on Privileges, Spinagar India. LC JQ620.K35. DD 328.5460747.

REPORT OF THE AUDITOR-GENERAL TO THE NATIONAL ASSEMBLY OF QUEBEC. Main/Corp Quebec (Province) Office of the Auditor-General. VFOAT le Verificateur General. 1971-. CN. English (French). an. National Assembly of Quebec, Office of the Auditor General, Quebec Canada.

REPORT OF THE CENTRAL COMMITTEE OF THE COMMUNIST PARTY OF UKRAINE TO THE CONGRESS OF THE COMMUNIST PARTY OF UKRAINE. Main/Corp Komunistychna Partiia Ukrainy. Tsentralavi Komitet. UR. English. 0.20 Each Copy. Ukraine Society, 6 Zoloti Vorota Street, Kiev Russian SFSR. LC JN6598.K77. DD 329.94771.

REPORT OF THE SENATE DELEGATION ON THE MEETING-MEXICO-UNITED STATE INTERPARLIAMENTARY GROUP. DELEGATION FROM THE UNITED STATES. (REPORT OF THE SENATE DELEGATION ON THE MEETING - MEXICO-UNITED STATES INTERPARLIAMENTARY GROUP). Main/Corp Mexico-United States Interparliamentary Group. Delegation from the United States. 1st- 1961-. 0539-6476. US. English. an. Superintendent of Documents, US Government Printing Office, Washington DC 20402. Ed M Mansfield and J Sparkman. LC E183.8.M6. DD 328.30601.

REPORT OF THE STANDING COMMISSION ON REFORM OF THE ELECTORAL DISTRICTS. Main/Corp Quebec (Province) National Assembly. Standing Commission on Reform of the Electoral Districts. VAT Report - Standing Commission on Reform of the Electoral Districts. 1st- 1972-. 0706-0890. Periodical. CN. English. Standing Commission on Reform of the Electoral Districts, National Assembly Parliament Building, Quebec Quebec G1A 1A7 Canada. DD 328.714073454.

REPORT ON FREEDOM. Periodical. US. English. mo. Liberty Amendment Committee, PO Box A, Prouo UT 84601. **Tel** (801)374-1800. *Report to America.*

REPORT ON MEETING OF APU SECRETARIES-GENERAL IN TOKYO. **Main/Corp** Asian Parliamentarians' Union. Central Secretariat. 1st- 1972-. JA. English. ir. TBR Building/Room No 807 10-2, 2-chome Nagata-cho, Chiyoda-ku Tokyo. **LC** DS35. **DD** 320.95.

RES PUBLICA. V. 1- Spring 1973-. 0092-671X. Periodical. US. English. qt. $51.00. Politologisch Instituut, Van Evenstraat 2B, B-3000 Leuven Belgium. **Tel** 016/22 83 44. **Ind/Abst** Sociol. Abstr., ABC Pol Sci, Lang. Lang. Behav. Abstr. **LC** AP2. adv acc. Concentrates on the analysis of Belgian politics (decision-making as well as policy) as well as on the general development of the political science and the contribution of Belgium in this development.

RESISTANCE (VANCOUVER, B.C.). (RESISTANCE). 0824-586X. Periodical. CN. English. ir. $15.00. Resistance c/o Friends of Durruti, P O Box 790 Station A, Vancouver British Columbia V6C 2N6 Canada. **DD** 322.405. bk rev. **Circ** 7,000. Covering militant autonomist, anti-imperialist, national liberation, feminist and anti-nuclear struggles in advanced capitalist countries, an important tool for revolutionary social change.

RESUME OF BUSINESS TRANSACTED DURING SESSION OF THE MEGHALAYA LEGISLATIVE ASSEMBLY, ASSEMBLED UNDER THE DEMOCRATIC CONSTITUTION OF INDIA. **Main/Corp** Meghalaya (India). Legislative Assembly. II. English. ir. Meghalaya Legislative Assembly Secretariat, Legislative Assembly, Shillong India. **LC** J601.M43. **DD** 328.5416.

RESURGENCE. V. 1- May/June 1966-. 0034-5970. Periodical. UK. English. bm. 30.00. Resurgence/Subscription Department, Northyvale Manor Farm/Camelfrd, Cornwall PL32 9TT England. **Tel** 02374-293. **Ed** Satish Kumar. **LC** JX1901. bk rev. adv acc. **Circ** 6,000. During the last several years the publication has been one of the poles, around which disciplined radical alternative thinking has taken shape.

REVIEW - ANDHRA PRADESH, INDIA. LEGISLATURE. LEGISLATIVE COUNCIL. **Main/Corp** Andhra Pradesh, India. Legislature. Legislative Council. II. English. ir. India Legislature/Legislative Council, Andhra Pradesh Hyderabad India. **LC** J601.A4. **DD** 328.548404.

REVISTA ARGENTINA DE POLITICA Y TEORIA. **VFOAT** Politica y Teoria. V. 1, No. 1- (April/July 1983)-. **Periodical.** Spanish. ir. C C No 3521 C Central, 1000 Buenos Aires Argentina.

REVISTA BRASILEIRA DE ESTUDOS POLITICOS. No. 1- Dec. 1956-. 0034-7191. Periodical. BL. Portuguese. sa. $20.00. Universidade de Minas Gerais Belo Horizonte, CP 1.301, Minas Gerais Brazil. **Tel** (031)224-8507. **Ind/Abst** Am. Hist. Life, Hist. Abstr., Part A, Mod. Hist. Abstr., Hist. Abst., Part B, Twent. Century Abstr., ABC Pol Sci, Foreign Lang. Index, Hist. Abstr., PAIS Foreign Lang. Index. **LC** JA5. (cum index). bk rev. adv acc. **Circ** 3,200. Political science, constitutional law, political history.

REVISTA CONTINENTE : CHILE HACIA EL MUNDO. **VFOAT** Chile Hacia el Mundo. Year 1- 19 Dec. 1974-. Periodical. Spanish. ir. $21.60. Serrano 20 2. Piso Casilla 11840, Santiago Chile. **LC** F3100.

REVISTA DE CIENCIA POLITICA. V. 10- Jan./Mar. 1967-. 0034-8023. Periodical. BL. Portuguese. ty. $11.90. Fundacao Getulio Verga, Caixa Postfach 9052, 20.000 Rio de Janeiro Brazil. **Ed** Afonso Arinos de Melo Franco. **Ind/Abst** ABC Pol Sci, Sociol. Abstr., Lang. Lang. Behav. Abstr. **LC** JA5. bk rev. **Circ** 1,500. *Revista de Direito Publico e Ciencia Politica.*

REVISTA DE CIENCIA POLITICA (SANTIAGO, CHILE). (REVISTA DE CIENCIA POLITICA). Began in 1979. Periodical. CL. Spanish. sa. Av Libertador Bernardo O Higgins, 340 of 14, Casilla 114-D, Santiago Chile. **Ind/Abst** Foreign Lang. Index. **LC** JA5. **DD** 320.05.

REVISTA DE POLITICA COMPARADA. No. 1 (Jan. 1980)-. 0211-5581. Periodical. SP. Spanish. qt. Universidad Internacional Menendez Pelayo y Departamento de Derecho Constitucional y Ciencia Politica de la Universidad de Alcala de Henares, Amador de los Rios 1 3O, Madrid-4 Spain. **Ind/Abst** Recent Publ. Artic. **LC** JA26. **DD** 320.305.

REVISTA FARABUNDO MARTI. **VFOAT** Farabundo Marti. Periodical. Spanish. ir. Editorial Farabundo Marti, Apartado 380, Curridabat Costa Rica. **LC** F1488.3. **DD** 320.97284.

REVOLUTION AFRICAINE. Began with No. 1, Feb. 1963. 0035-0621. Periodical. AE. French. wk. $42.63. Revolution Africaine, 7 rue du Stade a Hydra, Algiers Algeria. **Ind/Abst** Int. Labour Doc.

REVOLUTIONARY ZIMBABWE. Periodical. UK. English. 1.50. Zimbawe Solidarity Front, 66A Etherley Road, London N15 England. **LC** DT962.62. **DD** 968.910405.

REVUE DES SCIENCES MORALES & POLITIQUES. *See* Ethics.

REVUE D'ETUDES COMPARATIVES EST-OUEST. V. 6- March 1975-. 0338-0599. Periodical. FR. French (summaries in English). qt. 540. Centrale des Revues, 11 rue Gossin, 92543 Montrouge Cedex France. **Tel** 656 52 66. **Ed** E Zaleski. **Ind/Abst** Am. Hist. Life, Hist. Abstr., Part A, Mod. Hist. Abstr., Hist. Abst., Part B, Twent. Century Abstr., Int. Labour Doc., ABC Pol Sci, Soc. Sci. Citation Index, Hist. Abstr. **LC** HC244.A1. bk rev. Fills in the gaps of information on socialist countries. *Revue de l'Est.*

REVUE D'INTEGRATION EUROPEENNE. **VFOAT** Journal of European Integration. V. 1- Sept. 1977-. 0703-6337. Periodical. CN. English (French). sa. $13.93. Canadian Council on European Affairs, Department of Political Science, Saskatoon Saskatchewan S7N 0W0 Canada. **Tel** (306)966-5231. **Ed** H J Michelmann and P Soldatos. **Ind/Abst** Point Repere. **DD** 341.24205. bk rev. adv acc. **Circ** 400. (ctrl). Articles on European political and economic integration, and politics of the European community, theory of regional, and especially European integration.

REVUE DU DROIT PUBLIC ET DE LA SCIENCE POLITIQUE EN FRANCE ET A L'ETRANGER. *See* Law.

REVUE FRANCAISE DE SCIENCE POLITIQUE. V. 1- Jan./June 1951-. 0035-2950. Periodical. FR. French. bm. $35.92. Presses de la Fondation National des Sciences Politique, 27 rue Saint Guillaume, 75341 Paris Cedex 07 France. **Tel** 260 39 60. **Ind/Abst** Int. Labour Doc., Foreign Lang. Index, Point Repere, Soc. Sci. Citation Index, Sociol. Abstr., Am. Hist. Life, Hist. Abstr., Bibliogr. Index, Lang. Lang. Behav. Abstr., PAIS Foreign Lang. Index, Hist. Abstr., Part A, Mod. Hist. Abstr., Hist. Abst., Part B, Twent. Century Abstr., Recent Publ. Artic. **LC** JA11. Index in last issue of volume - attached. (cum index).

RIPEH, THE REVIEW OF IRANIAN POLITICAL ECONOMY & HISTORY. **VFOAT** Review of Iranian Political Economy & History. **VAT** Review of Iranian Political Economy and History. 0148-6101. Periodical. US. English. sm. $5.00. Georgetown University, PO Box 961, Washington DC 20057.

RIPON FORUM. 0035-5526. Periodical. US. English. bm. $15.00. Ripon Society, 6 Library Court SE, Washington DC 20003. **Tel** (202)546-1292. **Ed** William P McKenzie. **LC** JK2351. bk rev. adv acc. **Circ** 2,800. A Progressive Republican journal of opinion and political reporting. *Ripon Society Newsletter.*

THE RISING SUN. II. English. ir. 10.00. 3/147 Anna Salai, Madras 600006 India. **LC** DS840.84. **DD** 320.95405.

THE RISING TIDE. 1971-. 0364-7668. Periodical. US. English. mo. $10.00. Freedom Leadership Foundation, 1365 Connecticut Avenue NW, Washington DC 20036. **Tel** (202)265-9605. **LC** JC571. **DD** 323.405.

RIVISTA ITALIANA DI SCIENZA POLITICA. Vol. 1- April 1971-. 0048-8402. Periodical. IT. Italian. qt. 70.000 Domestic, 100.000 Foreign. Societa Editrice Il Mulino Spa, Via Santo Stefano 6, 40125 Bologna Italy. **Tel** 051/ 23 34 15. **Ind/Abst** Am. Hist. Life, Hist. Abstr., Part A, Mod. Hist. Abstr., Hist. Abst., Part B, Twent. Century Abstr., Sociol. Abstr., Soc. Welf. Soc. Plan./Policy Soc. Dev., ABC Pol Sci. **LC** JA18. **DD** 320.05.

ROLL CALL. V. 1- June 16, 1955-. 0035-788X. Periodical. US. English. wk. $15.00. Roll Call, 201 Mass Avenue NE, Washington DC 20002. **Tel** (202)546-3080. **Ed** Sidney L Yudain. **LC** JK1. **DD** 328.73005. bk rev. adv acc. **Circ** 7,500. Newspaper of the US Congress covering in hometown paper style, the world's most important community.

ROSENBERG'S RAG. Began in 1983. 0746-8644. Periodical. US. English. bw. $7.80. Rag Publishing Co, Pinchpenny Park PO Box 10, Litchfield CT 06759. **Tel** (203)567-8072. **Ed** Paul Mordecai Rosenberg. bk rev. adv acc. **Circ** 1,000. (ctrl). General comment from readers and editor; virtually all letters and articles published as received; no holds barred, short of libel, etc.

ROUND TABLE. (THE ROUND TABLE). V. 1-. 0035-8533. Periodical. UK. English. qt. $59.76. Round Table, Westbury House, PO Box 63, Bury Street, Gilford Surrey GU25BH England. **Tel** 0483 31261. **Ed** Peter Lyon. **Ind/Abst** Hist. Abstr., Am. Hist. Life, Soc. Sci. Index, Hist. Abstr., Part A, Mod. Hist. Abstr., Hist. Abst., Part B, Twent. Century Abstr., Energy Res. Abstr., ABC Pol Sci. **LC** AP4. **DD** 917.1241. Index published separately - free - automatically sent. (cum index). bk rev. adv acc. Commonwealth journal of international affairs.

RSA WORLD. Began in 1964. Periodical. SA. English. ir. RSA World, Box 2660, Pretoria 0001 Republic of South Africa. **Ed** Alexander Newman. **LC** DT779.9. **DD** 320.96806. **Circ** 3,500. Southern African events in context of world trends.

RULES AND DIRECTORY. *See* Yearbooks, Almanacs, Directories.

RUSLANDBULLETIN : UITGAVE VAN DE STICHTING RUSLANDBULLETIN. Vol. 1, No. 1 (Oct. 1976)-. 0166-1582. NE. Dutch. ir. 25.00. Stichting Ruslandbulletin, Finje van Salverdastraat 4, 1065 AE Amsterdam Netherlands. **LC** DK276.

SAFRICAN NEWS. 1st- Issue. 0708-1960. Periodical. CN. English. mo. $10.00 Individuals, $5.00 Institutions. Southern Africa Research Centre, Box 667/Station F, Toronto Ontario M4Y 2N6 Canada. **DD** 320.96806. *Canadian Press and the Events in Southern Africa, 0381-8659.*

SAHARA. 1963- (No. 1-). Periodical. FR. French. sm. 32.00. Agence France Presse, Boite Postale #20, 75061 Paris Cedex 02 France. **Tel** 233 44 66. **Circ** 1,000.

ST. CROIX REVIEW. (THE ST. CROIX REVIEW). **VAT** Saint Croix Review. V. 7- Feb. 1974-. 0093-2582. Periodical. US. English. bm. $20.00. Religion and Society Inc, PO Box 244, Stillwater NM 55082. **Tel** (612)439-7190. **Ed** Angus MacDonald. **LC** AS30. **DD** 081. bk rev. **Circ** 1,200. Also available on microfiche from KTO Microfilms and Xerox University Microfilms. Discussion of social issues. *Religion and Society, 0034-396X.*

SALUT LES COPAINS. 0036-3650. Periodical. FR. French. sm. Publications Filipacchi, 99 rue Amsterdam, 75008 Paris France.

THE SAMIZDAT BULLETIN. **VFOAT** Tetradi Samizdata. No. 1- May 1973-. 0361-1302. Periodical. US. English and Russian. mo. Samizdat Bulletin, PO Box 6128, San Mateo CA 94403.

SCANDINAVIAN POLITICAL STUDIES. **VFOAT** SPS. V. 1-12. 0080-6757. No. English. qt. Universitetsforlaget, PO Box 2959-Toyen, Oslo 6 Norway. **Tel** (45)-2-27 60 60. **Ed** Erik Damgaard. **Ind/Abst** Am. Hist. Life, Hist. Abstr., Part A, Mod. Hist. Abstr., Hist. Abst., Part B, Twent. Century Abstr., ABC Pol Sci, Sociol. Abstr., Lang. Lang. Behav. Abstr., Hist. Abstr. **LC** JN7001. **DD** 320.948. adv acc. **Circ** 600. Presents research articles and surveys of current events, elections, etc.

SCHRIFTEN ZUR VERFASSUNGSGESCHICHTE. Vol. 1- 1961-. 0582-0553. Monographic Series. GW. German. ir. Duncker und Humblot Verlag, Dietrich-Schaefer-WEG 9, 1000 Berlin 41 West Germany.

SCHRIFTENREIHE ZUR GESCHICHTE UND POLITISCHEN BILDUNG. V. 1- 1965-. 0080-7168. Monographic Series. GW. German. ir. A Henn Verlag, Postfach 1180, 5448 Kastellaun West Germany.

SCIENCE & GOVERNMENT REPORT INTERNATIONAL ALMANAC. *See* Yearbooks, Almanacs, Directories.

SCOTTISH JOURNAL OF POLITICAL ECONOMY. V. 1- Mar. 1954-. 0036-9292. Periodical. UK. English. ty. 30.00. Longman Group Ltd, Fourth Avenue, Harlow Essex CM19 5AA England. **Tel** (0279)442601. **Ed** R A Clarke. **Ind/Abst**

Political Science

Am. Hist. Life, Hist. Abstr., Part A, Mod. Hist. Abstr., Hist. Abst., Part B, Twent. Century Abstr., Int. Labour Doc., Index Econ. Artic. J. Collect. Vol., Public Aff. Inf. Serv. Bull., Soc. Sci. Citation Index, Hist. Abstr. LC HB1. DD 330.9411005. bk rev. adv acc. Circ 2,000. Devoted solely to the political, economic and social affairs of USSR and the communist countries of Eastern Europe.

SECHABA. V. 1- Jan. 1967-. 0037-0509. Periodical. UK. English. mo. $9.20. Sechaba, 28 Tenton Street, PO Box 38, London N1 9ER England. Tel 01 837 2012. Ind/Abst MLA Int. Bibliogr. Books Artic. Mod. Lang. Lit., Altern. Press Index. LC DT763. DD 322.440968.

SEIFU KANKOBUTSU SHIMBUN. See Bibliographies.

SEIJI HANDOBUKKU. 1973-. JA. Japanese. ir. 1360. Seiji Koho Seuta, 13-6 Akasaka 4-chome Minato-ku, Tokyo 107 Japan. Tel (03)582-2281. Ed Miyagawa Noriyashi. LC JQ1621. bk rev. adv acc. Circ 40. (ctrl). Japanese government and all members of government, elections, agendas, results of elections analysis.

SEIJI KENKYU. JA. Japanese. ir. Kyushu Daigaku Seiji Kenkyushitsu, Kyudai Seiji Kenkyukai, Kyushu Daigaku Hogakubu, Hakozaki 6-chome, Fukuoka Japan. LC JA26.

SEIJIGAKU RONSHU. VFOAT Political Science Review of Komazawa University. Began publication in 1974. Japanese. ir. c/o Komazawa Daigaku Hogakubu Kenkyushitsu, 23-1 Komazawa 1-chome, Setagaya-ku Tokyo Japan. LC JA26.

SEIRON. 1- October 1973. Periodical. JA. Japanese. ir. 1520. Sankei Shimbun Shuppankyoku, 3-15 Kanda Nishikicho Chiyoda-ku, Tokyo Japan. LC AP95.J2.

SELECTED U.S. GOVERNMENT PUBLICATIONS CEASED. Ceased with V. 11, No. 8, Aug./Sept. 1982. US. English. mo. Superintendent of Documents, US Government Printing Office, Washington DC 20402. Selected United States Government Publications.

SENATE AND HOUSE JOURNALS OF THE ... LEGISLATURE OF THE STATE OF MONTANA COMMENCING IN SPECIAL SESSION ... AND ENDING .... Main/Corp Montana. Legislature. VFOAT Senate and House Journals, Special Sessions. US. English. Montana Legislative Council, Room 138/State Capitol, Helena MT 59620. LC J87. DD 328.78601.

SENATE JOURNAL OF THE ... LEGISLATURE OF THE STATE OF MONTANA. Main/Corp Montana. Legislature. Senate. US. English. Montana Legislative Council, State Capitol/Room 138, Helena MT 59620. LC J87. DD 328.78601. Senate Journal.

SIC. V. 1- 1938-. 0049-0431. Periodical. VE. Spanish. ir. $30.00. Av Cristobal Rojas 16, Santa Monica Apartado 40225, Caracas 104 Venezuela. Tel 5635096. bk rev. adv acc. Circ 6,000. (ctrl). Political and economical analysis of Venezuela. Latinoamerica's theology of liberation.

SIND JOURNAL OF POLITICAL SCIENCE & MODERN HISTORY. VFOAT Sind Journal of Political Science and Modern History. V. 1 (1976)-. Periodical. US. English. sa. $15.00. Edinboro State University, PO Box 318, Edinboro PA 16412. Tel (814)732-2770. LC D839. DD 320.05.

SIYASAL BILGILER FAKULTESI DERGISI. Main/Corp Ankara Universitesi. Siyasal Bilgiler Fakultesi. VFOAT Review of the Faculty of Political Sciences. V. 1- 1946-. Periodical. TU. Turkish. qt. $58.00. Siyasal Bilgiler Fakultesi University of Ankara, Ankara Turkey. Siyasal Bilbiler Okulu Dergisi.

SLAVERY & ABOLITION. VFOAT Slavery and Abolition. Vol. 1, No. 1 (May 1980)-. 0144-039X. Periodical. UK. English. ty. Frank Cass & Company Ltd, 11 Gainsborough Road, London E11 1RS England. Ind/Abst Am. Hist. Life, Hist. Abstr., Part A, Mod. Hist. Abstr., Hist. Abst., Part B, Twent. Century Abstr., Sociol. Abstr., Soc. Welf. Soc. Plan./Policy Soc. Dev. LC HT851. DD 326.05.

SLOVANSKY PREHLED. Vol. 1- 1898-. 0037-6922. Periodical. GW. Czech. bm. Kubon and Sagner, Postfach 34 01 08, D8 Munchen 34 West Germany. Tel (089)52 20 27. Ind/Abst Am. Hist. Life, Hist. Abstr. Scholarly articles on the history and culture of Central, Southeast and East European nations, their mutual relations and relations with the West. Deals also with the rise and development of the world Socialist system and with the problems of the history of the Slavic peoples.

SLOVENSKA DRZAVA. Vol. 1- July 1950-. Periodical. US. Slovenian. mo. Slovenian National Federation Canada, 646 Euclid Avenue, Toronto Ontario Canada. LC Microfilm 05321 E, E184.S65. Slovenska Pravica.

SOCIEDAD Y POLITICA. Year 1- June 1972-. Periodical. Spanish. ir. $10.00. Apartado Postal 11154 Sta Beatriz, Lima Peru. LC F3401.

SOCRED NEWS. Vol. 1, No. 1 (May 1980)-. 0229-4095. Periodical. CN. English. British Columbia Social Credit Party, 3635-No 3 Road, Richmond British Columbia V6X 2B9 Canada. DD 324.27110505. Unity News, 0700-3676.

THE SOUTH AUSTRALIAN GOVERNMENT GAZETTE. Main/Corp South Australia. AT. English. wk. $66.40. South Australian Government Printer, 282 West Beach Road, Netley SA 5037 Australia. LC J8.

SOUTH-NORTH DIALOGUE IN KOREA. No. 1- July 1973-. Periodical. KO. English. ir. Public Relations Association of Korea, I P O Box 2147, Seoul Korea. LC DS901. DD 320.9519043.

SOUTHEAST ASIAN AFFAIRS. 1974-. 0377-5437. Sl. English. an. $25.00. Institute of Southeast Asian Studies, Heng Mui Keng Tr, Pasir Panjang, Singapore 0511 Republic of Singapore. Tel 7780955. Ed Triena Noeline Ong. LC DS502. DD 915.90305. Circ 1,000. Review of significant developments and trends in the region, particular emphasis on the Asian countries. Analysis made of major political, economic, social and strategic developments with southeast Asia.

SOUTHEASTERN POLITICAL REVIEW. Vol. 9, No. 1 (Spring 1981)-. 0730-2177. Periodical. US. English. sa. $12.00. West Georgia College, Department of Political Science, Carollton GA 30118. Tel (404)834-1342. Ed Donald T Wells. LC JA1. DD 320.05. bk rev. adv acc. Circ 380. Professional refereed journal of political science, publishing articles in all subfields of the discipline and utilizing a wide range of methodologies. GPSA Journal, 0092-9395.

SOUTHERN AFRICA PROJECT ANNUAL REPORT. VFOAT Annual Report. 1981-. 0749-9159. US. English. an. Lawyers Committee for Civil Rights Under Law, 1400 Eye Street NW/Suite 400, Washington DC 20005. LC Law. DD 323.490968. Annual Report of the Southern Africa Project.

SOUTHERN CHANGES. See Political Science - Civil Rights.

SOUTHERN POLITICAL REPORT. Began in 1978. 0739-3938. Periodical. US. English. bw. $115.00. Southern Political Report, 514 Constitution Avenue Northeast, Washington DC 20002. Tel (202)547-8098. Ed Hastings Wyman Jr. Circ 600. Covers the politics and politicans of twelve Southern states, Alabama, Arkansas, Florida, Georgia, Kentucky, Louisiana, Mississippi, North Carolina, South Carolina, Tennessee, Texas, and Virginia.

SOUTHERN PROVINCE ANNUAL REPORT. English. an. 0.20. Government Printer, PO Box 30136, Lusaka Zambia. LC J725.3. DD 354.6894.

SOVETY NARODNYKH DEPUTATOV. Noiabr 1977-. Periodical. UR. Russian. mo. $12.50. Victor Kamkin Inc (70870), 12224 Parklawn Drive, Rockville MD 20852. Tel (301)881-5973. LC JS6058. Sovety Deputatov Trudiashchikhsia.

SOVIET ANALYST. V. 1- Mar. 2, 1972-. 0049-1713. Periodical. UK. English. bw. $160.00. Soviet Analyst, PO Box 39, Richmond Surrey TW10 5BH England. Ed Iain Elliot. LC DK274. DD 320.947005. Fortnightly journal covering Eastern Europe and the USSR.

SOVIET LAW AND GOVERNMENT. See Law.

SOVIET WORLD OUTLOOK. V. 1- Jan. 15, 1976-. 0162-2404. Periodical. US. English. mo. Current Affairs Press, PO Box 15705, Fort Wayne IN 46885. Tel (301)951-0818. Ed Mose L Harvey, Amb Foy D Kohler and Morris Rothenberg. LC DK274. DD 320.947. Circ 2,800. (ctrl) A report of Kremlin views on issues critical to US interests.

SOZIALDEMOKRAT MAGAZIN. Periodical. German. ir. 18.00. Neuer Borwarts Verlag, Ollenhauserstrasse 1, 5300 Bonn West Germany. LC JN3971.A1.

SPARTACIST. No. 1- Feb./Mar. 1964-. 0038-6596. Periodical. US. English. bm. Spartacist Publishing Company, Box 1377 GPO, New York NY 10001. LC UNC.

SPECTRUM (WINTER HAVEN, FLA.). (SPECTRUM : A GUIDE TO THE INDEPENDENT PRESS AND INFORMATIVE ORGANIZATIONS). VFOAT Guide to the Independent Press and Informative Organizations. 15th Ed. (1984)-. US. English. $8.00. B Corbett, 762 Avenue North SE, Winter Haven FL 33880. Names the best sources covering the most vital, controversial subjects. Gives you up-to-date names and addresses to write for free information and sample copies. Censored, 0163-2280.

THE SPOTLIGHT. V. 2, No. 16- April 19, 1976-. 0191-6270. Periodical. US. English. wk. $30.00. The Spotlight, 300 Independence Avenue SE, Washington DC 20003. Tel (202)546-5611. Ed Vincent Ryan. bk rev. adv acc. Circ 150,000. Exclusive news for consumers, taxpayers and voters, covering populist politics, defense, security, fiscal responsibility and many other areas. National Spotlight.

SRBIJA. (SRBIJA : GLAS SRPSKIH BORACA). VFOAT Serbia : Voice of Serbian Fighters for Freedom. VAT Srbija (Fruitland), Serbia (Fruitland), Serbia (Winona). 0715-5921. Newspaper. CN. Serbo-Croatian -C. mo $10.00. Serbia, PO Box 70, Fruitland Ontario L0R 1L0 Canada. DD 320.9497.

STAAT UND RECHT. 0038-8858. Periodical. SZ. German. mo. $37.71. Kunst & Wissen Erich Bieber, Dufourstrasse 51, Ch-8008 Zurich Switzerland. Tel 011-41-1-69 44 20. Ind/Abst Sociol. Abstr., Lang. Lang. Behav. Abstr.

STAFF BIOGRAPHIES, HONG KONG GOVERNMENT. See Biographies.

STATE GOVERNMENT. V. 1- Jan. 1926-. 0039-0097. Periodical. US. English. qt. $20.00. Council of State Governments, PO Box 11910, Iron Works Pike, Lexington KY 40511. Tel (606)252-2291. Ed L E Purcell. Ind/Abst Public Aff. Inf. Serv. Bull., Int. Index, Soc. Sci. Index. LC JK2403. DD 353.905. Circ 5,500. Provides a forum for thoughtful discussion of state government. Highlights innovations, trends, and issues. Is of interest to public officials, community leaders, teachers, students, libraries, anyone concerned with governmental issues.

STATE LEGISLATURES. June/July 1975-. 0147-6041. Periodical. US. English. ir. $49.00. National Conference of State Legislative, 1125 17th Street/15th Floor, Denver CO 80202. Tel (303)292-6600. Ind/Abst Public Aff. Inf. Serv. Bull. LC JK2403. DD 328.73005. State Legislatures Today, 0196-1640.

STATE PUBLICATIONS INDEX. See Indexes/Abstracts.

STATE (WASHINGTON, D.C.). (STATE). No. 230 (Jan. 1981)-. 0278-1859. Periodical. US. English. mo. Superintendent of Documents, US Government Printing Office, Washington DC 20402. Ind/Abst Index U.S. Gov. Period., Public Aff. Inf. Serv. Bull. LC JX1. DD 353.00892. Newsletter (United States. Dept. of State), 0041-7629.

THE STATESMAN. V. 1- Apr. 1972-. Periodical. English. ir. Political Science Association of Nigeria c/o Okon 1 Udoh, Mellanby Hall, Ibadan Nigeria. LC JQ3081.A1. DD 320.966905.

THE STATESMAN'S YEAR-BOOK. See Yearbooks, Almanacs, Directories.

STATSVETENSKAPLIG TIDSKRIFT. Vol. 1-. 0039-0747. Periodical. SW. Swedish. qt. 100. Department of Political Science, Box 52, S-22100 Lund Sweden. Tel (046)109776. Ed Lennart Lundquist. Ind/Abst Am. Hist. Life, Hist. Abstr., ABC Pol Sci. (cum index). bk rev. adv acc. Circ 1,000. Contains main articles, reviews of recent political and scholarly developments, and book reviews, in Swedish, Norwegian, Danish and English languages. Its subscribers mainly come from the Nordic countries.

STIR. V. 1- Oct. 1, 1972-. Periodical. English. ir. 1.00 Each Issue. 1005 Akashdeep Building Barakhamba Road, New Delhi 1 India. LC DS401. DD 320.95405.

Political Science

STRIKE (TORONTO, ONT.). (STRIKE). Vol. 1, No. 11 (Aug./Sept. 1981)-. 0712-1539. Periodical. CN. English. ir. $10.00. Strike, PO Box 284 Main Station, Saint Catharines Ontario L2R 6T7 Canada. **Ind/Abst** Altern. Press Index. **DD** 322.42. *North American Anarchist*, 0227-1524.

STUDIA DIPLOMATICA. V. 27, No. 5/6-Sept./Nov. 1974-. Periodical. BE. Dutch, English, or French. bm. $59.28. Institut Royal des Relations, Avenue de la Couronne 88, B-1050 Bruxelles Belgium. **Ind/Abst** ABC Pol Sci, Foreign Lang. Index, Public Aff. Inf. Serv. Bull., Recent Publ. Artic., PAIS Foreign Lang. Index. **LC** D839. **DD** 320.904. *Chronique de Politique Etrangere.*

STUDIA NAUK POLITYCZNYCH. Periodical. PL. Polish (summaries in English and Russian). bm. ARS Polona, Krakowskie Przedmiescie 7, 00-068 Warsaw Poland. **LC** JA26.

STUDIEN ZUM POLITISCHEN SYSTEM DER BUNDESREPUBLIK DEUTSCHLAND *CEASED.* Vol. 1- 1973-. Monographic Series. GW. German. ir. Athenaum Verlag GMBH, Adelheidstrabe 2, 6240 Konigstein/TS West Germany. **Tel** 067 53/ 24 88.

STUDIES IN COMPARATIVE POLITICS. 1-8, 10. Monographic Series. US. English. ir. ABC Clio Press, 2040 APS Riviera Campus, Santa Barbara CA 93103.

STUDIES IN EAST EUROPEAN AND SOVIET RUSSIAN AGRARIAN POLICY. Vol. 1-. Monographic Series. US. English. ir. Allenheld Osmun & Company, 81 Adams Drive, Totowa NJ 07512.

STUDIES IN EUROPEAN POLITICS. 1-. Monographic Series. UK. English. Policy Studies Institute, 1/2 Castle Lane, London England.

STUDIES IN HISTORICAL AND POLITICAL SCIENCE. Main/Corp Johns Hopkins University. V. 1-. Monographic Series. US. English. sa. Johns Hopkins University Press, 701 West 40th Street/Suite 275, Baltimore MD 21211. **Tel** (301)338-6987.

STUDIES IN MARXISM (MINNEAPOLIS, MINN.). (STUDIES IN MARXISM). Vol. 1-. Monographic Series. US. English. Marxist Educational Press, c/o Department of Anthropology, University of Minnesota, 224 Church Street SE, Minneapolis MN 55455. **LC** UNC.

STUDIES IN POLITICAL ECONOMY. No. 1- Spring 1979-. 0707-8552. Periodical. CN. English. ty. $38.69 Foreign. PO Box 4729 Station E, Ottawa Ontario K1S 5H9 Canada. **Tel** (613)564-3772. Ed Wallace Clement. **Ind/Abst** Sociol. Abstr., Soc. Welf. Soc. Plan./Policy Soc. Dev., Public Aff. Inf. Serv. Bull. **DD** 330.05. bk rev. adv acc. **Circ** 750. A Canadian scholarly journal featuring original research from a socialist perspective on Canadian international and theoretical issues, with interdisciplinary approaches. It analyzes working class movements.

STUDIES IN THE STRUCTURE OF POWER. DECISION-MAKING IN CANADA. (STUDIES IN THE STRUCTURE OF POWER: DECISION MAKING IN CANADA). VFOAT Decision Making in Canada. 1964-. 0081-8690. CN. English. ir. University of Toronto Press, Front Campus, Toronto Ontario M5S 1A6 Canada.

STUDY OF THE JUCHE IDEA. Vol. 1, No. 1 (Apr. 1978)-. 0386-8494. Periodical. English. qt. **LC** DS935.55. **DD** 320.5405193.

STUTTGARTER BEITRAGE ZUR GESCHICHTE UND POLITIK. Vol. 1- 1966-. 0585-7945. Monographic Series. GW. German. ir. W E Saarbach GMBH, Postfach 101610, D5000 Koln 1 West Germany.

SUDOSTEUROPA. V. 1- 1959-. Periodical. German. ir. **Tel** (089)773007. **Circ** 1,000.

SUMMARY REPORT OF CAMPAIGN CONTRIBUTIONS AND EXPENDITURES : GENERAL ELECTION. Main/Corp Oregon. Elections Division. US. English. **LC** JK9095. **DD** 329.02509795.

SUMMARY REPORT OF CAMPAIGN CONTRIBUTIONS AND EXPENDITURES. PRIMARY ELECTION. (SUMMARY REPORT OF CAMPAIGN CONTRIBUTIONS AND EXPENDITURES, PRIMARY ELECTION). **Main/Corp** Oregon. Elections Divison. 0148-9399. US. English. **LC** JK1991.5.O7. **DD** 329.02509795.

SURVEY OF CURRENT AFFAIRS. V. 1- Jan. 1971-. 0039-6214. Periodical. UK. English. mo. $33.71. Her Majesty's Stationery Office, PO Box 276, London SW8 5DT England. **Tel** (01)622-3316. **LC** DA20. **DD** 320.942085. A unique official journal of record. It deals primarily with British affairs but there is also coverage of developments elsewhere in which Britain may have a special interest. *Survey of British and Commonwealth Affairs.*

A SURVEY OF PRESS FREEDOM IN LATIN AMERICA. Vol. 1 (1982)-. 0743-4324. US. English. an. $4.95. Council on Hemispheric Affairs, 1900 L Street Northwest/Suite 201, Washington DC 20036. **LC** PN4748.L29. **DD** 323.445.

SURVIVAL. Began with July 1970 issue. 0300-7944. Periodical. CN. English. ir. $2.00 for 4 Numbers. Survival, c/o Gordon Edwards, 1300 Raimbault, St Laurent Quebec H4L Canada. **DD** 322.4405.

SURYA INDIA. V. 1- Oct. 1976-. Periodical. II. English. ir. 335.-. Kanchanjunga 18 Bara Khamba Road, New Delhi 110001 India. **Tel** 3310202. Ed J K Jain. **LC** DS401. **DD** 954.005. bk rev. adv acc. **Circ** 40,000. (ctrl). A periodical dealing with current affairs, it provides an insight into political, economic and social development. It gives you 80 pages of steady reading matter.

TAAMULI. V. 1- July 1970-. 0049-2817. Periodical. TZ. English. sa. **Ind/Abst** Am. Hist. Life, Hist. Abstr., Part A, Mod. Hist. Abstr., Hist. Abst., Part B, Twent. Century Abstr., Recent Publ. Artic. **LC** JQ2945.A1. **DD** 320.967.

TABLE DES DEBATS DU SENAT. TABLE DES MATIERES. Main/Corp France. Parlement (1946-). Senta. Service des Archives. VFOAT Table des Debats du Senat. (Matieres). FR. French. ir. 17 Each Issue. Journaux Officiels, 26 Rue Desaix, 75727 Paris Cedex 15 France. **LC** J341. **DD** 328.4402016.

TABLES DES QUESTIONS ET DES REPONSES DES MINISTRES PUBLIEES DU . . . . VFOAT Tables des Questions Ecrites et des Questions Orales et Reponses des Ministres Publiees du . . . . FR. French. ir. 11. Journaux Officiels, 26 rue Desaix, 75727 Paris Cedex 15 France. **LC** J341. **DD** 328.4402016.

TALKING TURKEY *CEASED.* No. 1 (Feb. 1984)-. 8750-5835. Periodical. US. English. bw. $15.00. Talking Turkey Inc, 2 John Street, New York NY 10038. **Tel** (212)732-8552.

TEACHING POLITICAL SCIENCE. Vol. 1- Oct. 1973-. 0092-2013. Periodical. US. English. qt. $45.00. Heldref Publications, 4000 Albemarle Street North West/Suite 100, Washington DC 20016. **Tel** (202)362-6445. Ed Jerry Hanus and Virginia DeSimone. **Ind/Abst** Am. Hist. Life, Hist. Abstr., Part A, Mod. Hist. Abstr., Hist. Abst., Part B, Twent. Century Abstr., Educ. Index, Curr. Contents, Int. Polit. Sci. Abstr., Hum. Resour. Abstr., Sage Urban Stud. Abstr., Soc. Sci. Index, ABC Pol Sci, Curr. Index J. Educ., Soc. Sci. Citation Index, Lang. Lang. Behav. Abstr., Sociol. Abstr., Hist. Abstr. **LC** JA88.U6. **DD** 320.07. bk rev. adv acc. **Circ** 575. With a new look, and a new emphasis on the philosophical assumptions behind the Policies the journal provides the analysis and interpretation needed in today's volatile world.

TEACHING POLITICS. V. 1- 1972-. 0305-7771. Periodical. UK. English. ir. $22.00. British Politics Association, 16 Gower Street, London WC1E 6DP England. **Tel** 0322-75145. Ed Lynton Robins. **Ind/Abst** ABC Pol Sci. bk rev. adv acc. **Circ** 1,500. (ctrl). The theory and practice of political education, updating articles on British, European and United States politics.

TEACHING POLITICS. Periodical. II. English. qt. Foreign. Editor Teaching Politics, c/o Department of Political Science University of Delhi, Delhi 110007 India. **Tel** 2512266. Ed Susheela Kaushik. **LC** DS445. **DD** 320.05. bk rev. adv acc. **Circ** 500. Movement to make political science a dynamic discipline related to the concrete realities of the third world. To activate scholars to take stock of the trends in social sciences.

TELEPHONE DIRECTORY. See Yearbooks, Almanacs, Directories.

TEMPO. Nov. 1974-. Periodical. English. ir. $0.50 Each Issue. Anwer Jassan Mooraj, Golden Block Works Ltd, Golden Chambers Office I.I., Chundrigar Road, Korachi Pakistan. **LC** JA8. **DD** 954.91005.

TEMPS DE L'UNION NATIONALE. (LE TEMPS DE L'UNION NATIONALE). **Main/Corp** Union Nationale (Parti Politique). V. 1- March 1977-. 0703-5578. Periodical. CN. French. mo. Free to Members, $2.00 Others. Publications Unies, 130 Ouest Grande Allee, Quebec Quebec G1R 2G7 Canada. **DD** 329.9714.

THE TENNESSEE JOURNAL. 1974. 0194-1240. Periodical. US. English. wk. $97.00. Tennessee Journal, P O Box 2678 Arcade Station, Nashville TN 37219. **Tel** (615)242-7395. Ed Brad Forrister. **Circ** 1,200. A insiders newsletter on Tennessee government, politics and business.

TENNESSEE TOWN & CITY. VFOAT Tennessee Town and City. Began in 1950. 0040-3415. Periodical. US. English. sm. $10.00. Tennessee Municipal League, 226 Capitol Building, Nashville TN 37219. **Tel** (615)255-6416. Ed Beverly Bruninga. **LC** JS39. bk rev. adv acc. **Circ** 5,000. Municipal government affairs.

TESIS POLITICA. Spanish. ir. $5.00 Each Issue. Av Maestro Antonio Caso No 61-207, Mexico. **LC** F1235.

TEXAS JOURNAL OF POLITICAL STUDIES. V. 1- Fall 1978-. 0191-0930. Periodical. US. English. sa. $10.00. Sam Houston State University, Department of Political Science, Huntsville TX 77341. **Tel** (409)294-1462. Ed Edwin S Davis. **LC** JK4801. **DD** 320.9764. bk rev. adv acc. **Circ** 201. (ctrl). Articles, research notes and book reviews containing political studies from local to world events. Refereed, political science, public administration, sociology, history and economics represented.

TEXAS LEGISLATIVE HANDBOOK. 0193-2322. US. English. $2.75. Legislative Handbook Inc, PO Box 10512, Dallas TX 75207. **LC** JK4830. **DD** 328.76400202.

THE TEXAS OBSERVER. 1906-. Periodical. US. English. bw. $56.12. Texas Observer, 600 West 7th Street, Austin TX 78701. **Tel** (512)477-0746. Ed Geoffrey Rips. bk rev. adv acc. **Circ** 12,000. Coverage of regional political, and cultural news with a liberal slant. Some national and international reporting. *State Observer, East Texas Democrat.*

TEXAS STATE DOCUMENTS. See Bibliographies.

THESES IN CANADIAN POLITICAL SCIENCE. SUPPLEMENT. VFOAT Theses Canadiennes en Science Politique. Supplement. 1974/77-. 0228-3204. CN. French (English). **DD** 016.32. *Theses in Canadian Political Studies. Annual Supplement*, 0316-5280.

THIRD WORLD FORUM. V. 1- Aug./Sept. 1974-. 0317-0659. Periodical. CN. English. bm. Free to Prisoners, $15.00 US and Canada. Third World Forum, PO Box 685 Station C, Montreal Quebec H2L 4K4 Canada. **DD** 320.91724.

THIRD WORLD REPORTS. V. 1- March 1970-. 0049-3740. Periodical. UK. English. wk. $153.24. CSI Syndication Service, 15 Denbigh Gardens, Richmond Surrey England. **Tel** 01-940-6955. Ed Colin Legum. Two weekly reports on current affairs in Africa, Mid East and other third world countries. Written by Colin Legum, the distinguished specialist on this area.

TRANSAFRICA FORUM. Vol. 1, No. 1 (Summer 1982)-. 0730-8876. Periodical. US. English. qt. $35.00. Transaction Periodicals Consortium, Department 2000, Rutgers University, New Brunswick NJ 08903. **Tel** (201)932-2280. **LC** DT38.7. **DD** 327.6073. bk rev. adv acc. **Circ** 1,200. A journal of opinion on political, economic and cultural matters concerning Africa and the Caribbean.

TRIMESTRE POLITICO. Vol. 1- July/Sept. 1975-. Periodical. MX. Spanish. qt. $20.00. Fondo de Cultura Economica, Av Universidad 975, Mexico City Mexico. **Ind/Abst** Foreign Lang. Index. **LC** JL951.A1.

TUBINGER STUDIEN ZUR GESCHICHTE UND POLITIK. No. 1- 1955-. 0564-4267. Monographic Series. GW. German. ir. JCB Mohr-Paul Siebeck, Postfach 2040, 7400 Tuebingen West Germany.

TULANE STUDIES IN POLITICAL SCIENCE. V. 1- 1954-. 0082-6744. Monographic Series. US. English. ir. Tulane University, Department of Political Science, New Orleans LA 70118. **Tel** (504)865-5166. Ed Robert S Robins. **Circ** 1,000. Scholarly studies on political topics.

Political Science

THE UKRAINIAN QUARTERLY. V. 1- Oct. 1944-. 0041-6010. Periodical. US. English. qt. $15.00. Ukrainian Quarterly, 203 Second Avenue, New York NY 10003. Tel (212)228-6840. Ind/Abst Am. Hist. Life, Hist. Abstr., Part A, Mod. Hist. Abstr., Hist. Abst., Part B, Twent. Century Abstr., MLA Int. Bibliogr. Books Artic. Mod. Lang. Lit., Public Aff. Inf. Serv. Bull., Hist. Abstr. LC DK508.A2. DD 947.7. (cum index).

L'UNITE. Periodical. FR. French. ir. Parti Socialiste, 41 Boulevard Magenta, Paris 10E France. LC JN3007.S65. DD 320.944083.

UNITED STATES GOVERNMENT MANUAL. (THE UNITED STATES GOVERNMENT MANUAL). Main/Corp United States. Office of the Federal Register. Began with 1973/74. 0092-1904. US. English. an. $18.50. US Government Printing Office, Divison of Public Documents, Washington DC 20402. Tel (202)783-3238. LC JK421. DD 353. NLM JK 421 U57. *United States Government Organization Manual, 0083-1174.*

U.S. MILITARY AND GOVERNMENT INSTALLATION DIRECTORY SERVICE. See Yearbooks, Almanacs, Directories.

UNITED STATES POLITICAL SCIENCE DOCUMENTS. VFOAT USPSD. V. 1- 1975-. 0148-6063. US. English. sa. $300.00. NIAC, c/o Donald Gielas, 823 William Pitt Union, University of Pittsburgh, Pittsburgh PA 15260. Tel (412)624-0233. Ed Paul A McWilliams. LC Z7163, H9. DD 016.3. Contains comprehensive abstracts and indexes of articles from 150 scholarly journals. *Asian Studies Indexed Journal Reference Guide, 0149-1652.*

UNTERSUCHUNGEN UND MATERIALIEN ZUR VERFASSUNGS- UND LANDESGESCHICHTE. 1- 1973-. Monographic Series. GW. German. ir. N G Elwert Verlag, Postfach 1128-Reitgasse 7+9, D-3550 Marburg West Germany.

UPDATE USSR. Vol. 53, No. 4 (July 1985)-. 0884-6227. Periodical. US. English. mo. N W R Publications, 162 Madison Avenue/3rd Floor, New York NY 10016. Tel (212)696-4765. Ind/Abst Public Aff. Inf. Serv. Bull. DD 947. bk rev. Circ 5,000. Covers the Soviet Union and other socialist countries: economy, social programs, foreign policy, US/USSR relations, etc. *New World Review, 0028-7067.*

VALTIOLLISET VAALIT : KANSANEDESTAJAIN VAALIT. See Statistics.

VERBATIM REPORT. Main/Corp Newfoundland. General Assembly. CN. English. ty. University of Maine, 303 English/Math Building, Orono ME 04473. Tel (207)581-7307. Ind/Abst MLA Int. Bibliogr. Books Artic. Mod. Lang. Lit. LC J125. DD 328.71804.

VERMONT LEGISLATIVE DIRECTORY AND STATE MANUAL. See Yearbooks, Almanacs, Directories.

DIE VERWALTUNG. V. 1-. 0042-4498. Periodical. GW. German. qt. Duncker und Humblot Verlag, Dietrich-Schafer-Weg 9, 1 Berlin 41 West Germany. Ind/Abst ABC Pol Sci. LC JA44. DD 350'.0005.

VICTORIAN GOVERNMENT DIRECTORY. See Yearbooks, Almanacs, Directories.

VICTORIAN GOVERNMENT PUBLICATIONS RECEIVED BY THE STATE LIBRARY OF VICTORIA. 1976. AT. English. mo. 45.00. Library Council of Victoria, 304-328 Swanston Street, Melbourne Victoria 3000 Australia. LC Z4379, J931. DD 015.945. Circ 165. (ctrl). A bibliography of Victorian State Government Publications.

VIEWPOINTS. V. 1- Fall 1965-. 0042-5818. Periodical. CN. English. qt. $7.89. Canadian Labor Zionists Movement, 4770 Kent Avenue/Suite 300, Montreal Quebec H3W 1H2 Canada. LC DS101.

VIRGIN ISLANDS GOVERNMENT DOCUMENTS: A QUARTERLY CHECKLIST. Main/Corp Virgin Islands of the United States. Bureau of Libraries, Museums and Archaeological Services. V. 1- Winter 1977-. English. ir. Department of Conservation & Cultural Affairs, Bureau of Libraries, St Thomas Virgin Islands. LC Z1561.V8, J166. DD 015.729722.

VISION LETTER. (THE VISION LETTER). 0042-6962. US. English. sm. $49.00. Vision Incorporated, 13 East 75th, New York NY 10021. Tel (212)744-9126. Ed Richard Schroeder. LC F1401. DD 320.98003. bk rev. A political and economic report on Latin America.

VISNYK REPRESIJ V UKRAINI. (VISNYK REPRESII V UKRAINI). Vol. 1-. 0749-8624. Periodical. US. Ukrainian. mo. $25.00. Ukrainian Helsinki Group, PO Box 770, Cooper Station, New York NY 10003. LC JC599.S582. DD 323.

VISTAZO. Yearly V. 1- (No. 1-). Periodical. EC. Spanish. bw. $72.00 Central and South America, $78.00 US, $90.00 Europe, $100.00 Asia. Editores Nacionales, Box 1239, Buayaquil Ecuador. Tel 516-215. Ed Patricia de Burbano. LC AP63. adv acc. Circ 75,000. (ctrl). Covers general interest, politics, economics, cinema, medicine, law, science, literature, arts, theater, education, business, religion, and travel.

VOPROSY ISTORII KPSS. (VOPROSY ISTORII KPSS : ORGAN INSTITUTA MARKSIZMA-LENINIZMA PRI TSK KPSS). 1957, 1-. 0320-8907. Periodical. UR. Russian (tables of contents also in Chinese, English, and other languages). mo. $47.00. Victor Kamkin Inc (70146), 12224 Parklawn Drive, Rockville MD 20852. Tel (301)881-5973. Ind/Abst Sociol. Abstr., Am. Hist. Life, Hist. Abstr., Lang. Lang. Behav. Abstr. LC JN6598.K4.

VOPROSY SOTSIALNO-POLITICHESKOGO RAZVITIIA SOVETSKOGO OBSHCHESTVA. UR. Russian. 0.50. 43 Sovetskii Prospekt, Kemerovo 117 Russia. LC JA49.

VOTERS AND CANDIDATES PAMPHLET. Main/Corp Washington (State). Secretary of State. VFOAT State General Election. US. English. Secretary of State, Olympia WA 98504. LC JF495.W2. DD 329.023797. *Your Official State of Washington Voter's Pamphlet.*

VOTES AND PROCEEDINGS OF THE LEGISLATIVE ASSEMBLY OF MANITOBA. Main/Corp Manitoba. Legislative Assembly. VAT Votes and Proceedings - Legislative Assembly of Manitoba. 0319-3020. Periodical. CN. English. ir. 16.00. Queens Printer, 200 Vaughn Street, Winnipeg Manitoba R3C 1T5 Canada. Tel (204)945-3103. (ctrl).

WAHL ZUM ... DEUTSCHEN BUNDESTAG AM ... IN NIEDERSACHSEN. Series/Titl Statistik Niedersachsen. German. ir. LC JN4945.L6865. DD 324.94359.

WAHL ZUM NIEDERSACHSISCHEN LANDTAG DER .... Series/Titl Statistik Niedersachsen. GW. ir. Niedersachsisches Landesverwaltungsamt Statistik, Postfach 107, Hannover 1 West Germany. LC JN4945.L6865. DD 324.94359005. bk rev. Circ 500. Results of the polling act for the Parliament of Niedersachsen (lower-Saxony).

THE WASHINGTON MONTHLY. V. 1- Feb. 1969-. 0043-0633. Periodical. US. English. mo. $77.00. The Washington Monthly, 1711 Connecticut Avenue NW, Washington DC 20009. Tel (202)462-0128. Ed Charles Peters. Ind/Abst Am. Hist. Life, Hist. Abstr., Part A, Mod. Hist. Abstr., Hist. Abst., Part B, Twent. Century Abstr., Energy Inf. Abstr., Environ. Abstr., Pop. Mag. Rev., Book Rev. Index, Infobank, Public Aff. Inf. Serv. Bull., Energy Res. Abstr., Read. Guide Period. Lit., Mag. Index, Hist. Abstr. LC E838. DD 320.973092. bk rev. adv acc. Circ 35,000. Political and cultural analysis of American bureaucracies. Takes traditional liberal values without dogmatic liberal prejudices.

THE WASHINGTON PACIFIC REPORT. Vol. 1, No. 1 (Oct. 1, 1982)-. 0748-6359. Periodical. US. English. sm. $150.00. Washington Pacific Group, P O Box 14078, Washington DC 20044. DD 320.

WASHINGTON POLITICAL ANALYSIS. Vol. 1, No. 5 (Aug. 1, 1984)-. 0748-7770. Periodical. US. English. sm. $112.50. Publisher Services Inc, 80 South Early Street, Alexandria VA 22304. Tel (703)823-6966. Ed Ronald R Jensen and Robert E Berry. DD 320. (ctrl). Comprehensive analysis of American political developments based on historical perspective (actual election results, voter turnout, demographic information) predicting election outcomes with greater accuracy than polls.

WASHINGTON REPORT ON AFRICA. Vol. 1, Issue 1 (July 1, 1982)-. 0733-8104. Periodical. US. English. ir. $214.50. Welt Publishing Company, 1413 K Street NW, Washington DC 20005. Tel (202)371-0555. Ed John Matisonn. bk rev. Covers Washington DC events that have an impact on Africa. *African Business & Trade, 0732-670X; African Index, 0149-0796.*

WASHINGTON REPRESENTATIVES. V. 3- 1979-. 0192-060X. US. English. an. $47.70. Columbia Books Inc, 1350 New York Avenue NW/Suite 207, Washington DC 20005. Tel (202)737-3777. Ed Arthur C Close. LC JK1118. DD 328.73078025. Circ 3,700. Directory of 10,000 lobbyists and other special interest advocates in Washington and the organizations and causes they represent. *Directory of Washington Representatives of American Associations & Industry, 0147-216X.*

WASHINGTON STATE VOTER. 0043-0846. Periodical. US. English. qt. $1.00. League of Woman Voters, 1406 18th Avenue, Seattle WA 98122. Tel (206)329-4646.

WASHINGTON WATCH. Vol. 1, No. 1 (Aug. 1, 1981)-. 0275-1216. Periodical. US. English. mo. $195.00. Card Research Inc, One World Trade Center/Suite 7955, New York NY 10048.

WATASHITACHI NO SENKYO: SENKYO HAKUSHO UNDO NO TAIKEN KIROKU. Main/Corp Akaruku Tadashii Senkyo Nagoya-Shi Suishin Kyogikai. Vol. 4-. Japanese. ir. c/o Nagoya Shiyakusho, 1-1 Sannomaru, 3-chome, Naka-ku 460, Nagoya Japan. LC JQ1693.N315. *Watashitachi No Senkyo.*

WEEKLY ANALYSIS OF ECUADOREAN ISSUES. See Economics.

WEEKLY COMPILATION OF PRESIDENTIAL DOCUMENTS. See Bibliographies.

WEEKLY INFORMATION BULLETIN - HOUSE OF COMMONS. Main/Corp Great Britain. Parliament. House of Commons. Periodical. UK. English. wk. $78.15. Her Majestys Stationery Office, PO Box 276, London SW8 5DT England. Tel 01-211 0363. LC J301. DD 328.4107205. Provides the most comprehensive and cost-effective way for individuals and organisations to keep up with events in Parliament.

WEEKLY LIST OF MONTANA STATE PUBLICATIONS RECEIVED BY MONTANA STATE LIBRARY. Main/Corp Montana. State Library, Helena. US. English. wk. Montana State Library, 930 East Lyndale Avenue, Helena MT 59601. LC Z1223.5.M9, J87.M9. DD 015.786.

WEST EUROPEAN POLITICS. V. 1- Feb. 1978-. 0140-2382. Periodical. UK. English. qt. 55.-. Frank Cass & Company Ltd, 11 Gainsborough Road, London E11 1RS England. Tel 01 530 4226. Ed Gordon Smith and Vincent Wright. Ind/Abst Am. Hist. Life, Hist. Abstr., Part A, Mod. Hist. Abstr., Hist. Abst., Part B, Twent. Century Abstr., Sociol. Abstr., Soc. Welf. Soc. Plan./Policy Soc. Dev., ABC Pol Sci, Public Aff. Inf. Serv. Bull., Recent Publ. Artic. LC JN94.A1. DD 320.945. bk rev. adv acc. Circ 800. Analyses and discusses political and social issues relating to Western Europe.

WEST INDIAN. (THE WEST INDIAN). 0824-3328. Periodical. CN. English. mo. $5.00. West Indian People's Organization, P O Box 37 Station P, Toronto Ontario M5S 2S6 Canada. DD 322.42.

THE WESTERN POLITICAL QUARTERLY. V. 1- Mar. 1948-. 0043-4078. Periodical. US. English. qt. $25.00 US/Canada/Mexico, $29.00 all other countries. Western Political Quarterly, University of Utah, 258 Orson Spencer Hall, Salt Lake City,UT 84112. Tel (801)581-7137. Ed Dean Mann. Ind/Abst Energy Inf. Abstr., Environ. Abstr., ABC Pol Sci, Annu. Bibliogr. Engl. Lang. Lit., Book Rev. Index, Soc. Work Res. Abstr., Public Aff. Inf. Serv. Bull., Soc. Sci. Index, Soc. Sci. Citation Index, Sociol. Abstr., Hist. Abstr., Am. Hist. Life, Lang. Lang. Behav. Abstr., Hist. Abstr., Part A, Mod. Hist. Abstr., Hist. Abst., Part B, Twent. Century Abstr. LC JA1. DD 320.5. (cum index). Available on microfilm from University Microfilms.

WHITE POWER. No. 1- Sept. 1967-. 0043-4957. Periodical. US. English. ir. $3.00. National Socialist White People's Party, PO Box 5505, Arlington VA 22205. LC E743. DD 322.420973. *Rockwell Report.*

THE WIENER LIBRARY BULLETIN. See Library and Information Science.

WIN CEASED. Began with V. 1-, 1965-. Ceased with Oct. 1983. 0512-5375. Periodical. US. English. sm. Ind/Abst Altern. Press Index. LC UNC.

Political Science—Civil Rights

THE WOMAN ACTIVIST. V. 1 - Jan. 14, 1971-. 0049-7770. Periodical. US. English. mo. Woman Activist, 2310 Barbour Road, Falls Church VA 22043. Tel (703)573-8716. Ed Flora Carter. bk rev. adv acc. Circ 200. (ctrl). Political, feminist call for actions. Congressional information, summaries and current feminist activity in relation to politics.

WOMEN & POLITICS. See Women.

WOMEN'S POLITICAL REPORTER. 0735-6927. Periodical. US. English. PO Box 27519, Atlanta GA 30327.

WOMEN'S POLITICAL TIMES. V. 1- July 1976-. 0195-1688. Periodical. US. English. ir. $20.00. National Womens Political Caucus, 1275 K Street NW Suite 750, Washington DC 20005. Tel (202)898-1100. Ed Jeannine Grenier. bk rev. adv acc. Circ 30,000. (ctrl). Publication of the National Women's Political Caucus, it contains timely pertinent information on issues affecting women and includes profiles and interviews on women legislators and policy makers.

THE WORKERS' ADVOCATE SUPPLEMENT. (THE WORKERS' ADVOCATE : VOICE OF THE MARXIST-LENINST PARTY, USA). Vol. 1, No. 1 (Jan. 15, 1985)-. 0882-6366. Periodical. US. English. mo. Marxist-Leninist Publications, PO Box 11972 Ontario Street Station, Chicago IL 60611. DD 322.

WORKERS' DEMOCRACY. See Economics - Labor.

WORKERS TIME. Periodical. English. ir. Workers Time Ltd, 9 Central Avenue, Kingston 10.

WORKERS WORLD. 1- Mar. 1959-. 0043-809X. Periodical. US. English. wk. $10.00. Workers World, 46 West 21st Street, New York NY 10010. Tel (212)255-0352. Ed Deirdre Griswold. Circ 9,000. Socialist anti-racist, anti-imperialist newsweekly.

WORLD FOCUS. 1 (Jan. 1980)- – Vol. 1, No. 1-. Periodical. II. English. mo. 40.00, Domestic, $12.00. Hari Sharan Chhabra, F-15 Bhagat Singh Market, New Delhi 110001 India. LC D839. DD 320.9048.

WORLD JURIST. (THE WORLD JURIST). V. 7, No. 7/8- July/Aug. 1970-. 0043-8618. US. English. bm. World Peace Through Law Center, 400 Hill Building, Washington DC 20006. DD 340.05. Bulletin - World Peace through Law Center.

WORLD MARXIST REVIEW. V. 1- Sept. 1958-. 0043-8642. Periodical. CN. English. mo. 40.00. Progress Books, 71 Bathhurst Street, 3rd Floor, Toronto M5V 2P6 Canada. Tel (416)368-5336. Ed Y Sklyarev. Ind/Abst Soc. Sci. Index, Public Aff. Inf. Serv. Bull. bk rev. Theoretical and information journal of communist and workers parties throughout the world.

WORLD MARXIST REVIEW. V. 1- Sept. 1958-. Periodical. UK. English. mo. Central Books Ltd, 14 Leathermarket, London SE1 3ER England. Ind/Abst Am. Hist. Life, Hist. Abstr.

WORLD OF POLITICS. 0094-2316. US. English. mo. $15.00. Political Research Inc, 510 Continental Building, Dallas TX 75201. LC JK1. DD 320.973092.

WORLD POLITICS. 0198-0300. Periodical. US. English. an. $8.95. Dushkin Publishing Group, Sluice Dock, Guilford CT 06437. Tel (203)453-4351. Ed Suzanne Ogden. LC D839. DD 327.05. Collection of public press articles covering current issues in world politics. Includes topic guide and complete index.

THE WORLD THIS YEAR. 1971-. 0364-8575. US. English. an. Simon & Schuster, 1230 Avenue of the Americas, New York NY 10020. LC JF37. DD 320.9046.

WORLDVIEW. VAT World View. V. 1- Jan. 1958-. 0084-2559. Periodical. US. English. mo. $15.00. Worldview, PO Box 986, Farmingdale NY 11735. Ind/Abst Guide Soc. Sci. Relig. Period. Lit., Relig. Index One, Period., Public Aff. Inf. Serv. Bull., Index Relig. Period. Lit. LC D839. World Alliance Newsletter.

THE WREE-VIEW OF WOMEN. VFOAT WREE-View. Periodical. US. English. $5.00. Women for Racial & Economic Equality, 130 East 16th Street, New York NY 10003. Tel (212)473-6111. Ed Norma Spector. Ind/Abst Women Stud. Abstr. bk rev. adv acc. Circ 5,000. News/information regarding women and peace (effects of military budget/militarization); economic equality (jobs, affirmative action, child care, etc); battle against racism; support for Women's Bill of Rights.

YALE POLITICAL MONTHLY. 0736-6175. Periodical. US. English. mo. Yale Political Monthly, 962 Yale Station, New Haven CT 06520. LC JA1. DD 320.05.

YALE STUDIES IN POLITICAL SCIENCE. Began with: 1, published in 1954. 0084-3490. US. English. ir. Yale University Press, 92A Yale Station, New Haven CT 06520. Tel (203)436-7584. LC UNC. DD 320.

YOUNG MARCH. See Children and Youth Interests.

ZEITSCHRIFT FUR POLITIK. V. 1-35, No. 3. 0044-3360. Periodical. German. ir. Carl Heymanns Verlag KG, Gereonstrasse 18-32, 5000 Koln 1 West Germany. Tel (089)224811. Ed R Schmidt & A Grabowsky. Ind/Abst Am. Hist. Life, Hist. Abstr., Part A, Mod. Hist. Abstr., Hist. Abst., Part B, Twent. Century Abstr., ABC Pol Sci, Writ. Am. Hist., Foreign Lang. Index, Hist. Abstr., PAIS Foreign Lang. Index, Recent Publ. Artic. LC JA14. DD 320.05. bk rev. adv acc. Circ 1,000.

ZEITSCHRIFT FUR RECHTSPOLITIK. Vol. 1-. 0514-6496. Periodical. GW. German. mo. $20.29. C H Beckshe Verlagsbchhndlg Wilhelmstrasse 9, Postfach 400340, 8 Munchen 40 West Germany. Ind/Abst Energy Res. Abstr.

ZEITSCHRIFT FUR STAATSSOZIOLOGIE. Vol. 1-18, No. 4. Periodical. GW. German. qt. $1.85. Themis & Verlag, Postfach 1622, 78 Frieburg I B West Germany. Ed M T Vaerting. LC JA14.

ZESZYTY NAUKOWE UNIWERSYTETU JAGIELLONSKIEGO. PRACE Z NAUK POLITYCZNYCH. VFOAT Schedae Politicae, Prace Z Nauk Politycznych. Began with No. 1 in 1971. Periodical. PL. Polish (summaries in English and Russian). ir. LC JA49. DD 320.532.

ZPRAVA O SCHUZI SNEMOVNY LIDU. Main/Corp Czechoslovakia. Federalni Shromazdeni. VFOAT Zprava o Ustavujici Schuzi Snemovny Lidu. 1. Volebni Obdobi, 1. Schuze (29. Led. 1969)-. Czech. ir. Kancel AR Federalniho Shromazdeni, Vinohradska 1, 110 02 Praha Czechlovakia. LC J338.

ZPRAVA O SCHUZI SNEMOVNY NARODU. Main/Corp Czechoslovakia. Federalni Shromazdeni. VFOAT Zprava o Ustavujici Schuzi Snemovny Narodu. 1. Volbni Obdobi, 1. Schuze (29. Led. 1969)-. Czech. ir. Kancel AR Federalniho Shromazdeni, Vinohradska 1, 110 02 Praha Czechoslovakia. LC J338. Zprava o Schuzich Narodniho Shromazdeni Ceskoslovenske Socialisticke Republiky.

ZUR POLITIK UND ZEITGESCHICHTE. No. 1- 1960-. 0514-8294. GW. German. ir. Freie Universitaet, Otto-Suhr Institut, Altensteinstrasse 40, 1000 Berlin 33 West Germany.

CIVIL RIGHTS

ACLU NEWS. Periodical. US. English. bm. $20.00. ACLU-NC, 1663 Mission Street 4th Floor, San Francisco CA 94103.

ACTIVITIES - COLORADO CIVIL RIGHTS COMMISSION. Main/Corp Colorado. Civil Rights Commission. US. English. 1525 Sherman Street/Room 600C, Denver CO 80203. Activities Report.

ACTIVITIES REPORT - COLORADO. CIVIL RIGHTS COMMISSION. Main/Corp Colorado. Civil Rights Commission. 1954/55-. Periodical. US. English. an. Colorado Civil Rights Commission, 1525 Sherman Street/Room 600 C, Denver CO 80203.

ACTUALITE VIE. See Ethics.

ACTUELLES DES DROITS DE LA PERSONNEL. VFOAT Human Rights Today. No. 1-. 0824-3638. Periodical. CN. English (French). ir. Free. Canadian Human Rights Foundation, Suite 340/1980 Sherbrooke Street West, Montreal Quebec H3H 1E8 Canada. DD 323.40971.

ADVIESBRIEVEN EN- NOTA'S VAN DE EMANCIPATIERAAD. Main/Corp Emancipatieraad (Netherlands). Dutch. an. 4.75. Distributiecentrum Overheidspublikaties/D O P, Postbus 20014, 2500 EA Den Haag Netherlands.

AEGIS. (AEGIS : MAGAZINE ON ENGING VIOLENCE AGAINST WOMEN). Sept./Oct. 1978-. Periodical. US. English (Spanish). qt. $25.00. Feminist Alliance Against Rape, Box 21033, Washington DC 20009. Tel (202)686-9463. Ed Nancy McDonald. Ind/Abst Altern. Press Index. bk rev. adv acc. Circ 1,500. Provides information on rape, battering, child sexual assault and other forms of violence against women. Directed primarily at grassroots activists and community groups. Newsletter - Feminist Alliance Against Rape, Newsletter (National Communications Network (U.S.)).

AFFIRMATIVE ACTION PLAN - THOMAS JEFFERSON UNIVERSITY. Main/Corp Thomas Jefferson University. 1976-. English. ir.

AITSUGU SABETSU JIKEN. JA. Japanese. ir. 400. Buraku Kaiho Domei Osaka-fu Rengokai, 1247 Kuboyoshicho, Naniwa-ku Osaka Japan. LC HT725.J3.

ALBERTA HUMAN RIGHTS JOURNAL. Vol. 1, No. 1 (Summer 1982)-. 0713-4738. Periodical. CN. English. qt. Alberta Human Rights Journal, 10808 99 Avenue, Edmonton Alberta T5K 0G Canada. LC JC599.C22. DD 323.4097123.

ALTERNATIVE (PARIS, FRANCE : 1979). (L'ALTERNATIVE). No. 1 (Nov.-Dec. 1979)-. 0240-1568. Periodical. FR. French. bm. $24.61. L'Alternative, Pour les 4 rue Trousseau, 75011 Paris France. Ind/Abst Foreign Lang. Index. LC JC599.E92. DD 323.4090947.

ANNUAL REPORT - ALBERTA HUMAN RIGHTS COMMISSION. Main/Corp Alberta. Human Rights Commission. VFOAT Annual Report of the Alberta Human Rights Commission. 1973-. 0380-4518. CN. English. an. DD 354.7123008.

ANNUAL REPORT - ARIZONA CIVIL RIGHTS DIVISION, DEPARTMENT OF LAW. (ANNUAL REPORT - ARIZONA CIVIL RIGHTS DIVISION). Main/Corp Arizona. Civil Rights Division. 8th- 1972/73-. 0097-9155. US. English. an. Arizona Civil Rights Division, 1502 West Jefferson Street, Phoenix AZ 85007. LC HFA2811. DD 353.979100996. Annual Report - Arizona Civil Rights Commission.

ANNUAL REPORT - CITY OF DETROIT, HUMAN RIGHTS DEPT. Main/Corp Detroit (Mich.) Human Rights Dept. US. English. an. City of Detroit, Human Rights Department, 150 Michigan Avenue, Detroit MI 48226. LC JC599.U52. DD 352.980977434.

ANNUAL REPORT - COMMITTEE ON SCIENTIFIC FREEDOM AND RESPONSIBILITY. Main/Corp AAAS Committee On Scientific Freedom and Responsibility. 1977-. 0196-9218. US. English. an. American Association For the Advancement of Science, 1515 Massachusetts Avenue NW, Washington DC 20005. NLM W1 AM212L.

ANNUAL REPORT - DISTRICT OF COLUMBIA. OFFICE OF HUMAN RIGHTS. Main/Corp District of Columbia. Office of Human Rights. US. English. an. LC JC599.U52. DD 352.941109753.

ANNUAL REPORT FOR FISCAL YEAR - MAINE HUMAN RIGHTS COMMISSION. Main/Corp Maine Human Rights Commission. US. English. an. Maine Human Rights Commission, State House Station 51, Augusta ME 04333. LC KFM411. DD 342.741085, 347.410285.

ANNUAL REPORT - MANITOBA HUMAN RIGHTS COMMISSION. (ANNUAL REPORT - THE MANITOBA HUMAN RIGHTS COMMISSION). Main/Corp Manitoba. Human Rights Commission. 1974-. 0383-5588. CN. English. an. Manitoba Human Rights Commission, 430 Edmonton Street, Winnipeg Manitoba R3B 2M3 Canada. LC JC599.C2. DD 354.712700996.

ANNUAL REPORT OF THE COMMISSIONER FOR EQUAL OPPORTUNITY CEASED. Main/Corp Victoria. Equal Opportunity Board. 2nd (1979)-. AT. English. an. $2.40. Commissioner for Equal Opportunity, 356 Collins Street/10th Floor, Melbourne 3000 Australia. LC JC599.A8. DD 0354.94500811. Annual Report of the Equal Opportunity Board.

ANNUAL REPORT OF THE EQUAL OPPORTUNITY BOARD (VICTORIA, AUSTRALIA). Main/Corp Victoria, Australia. Equal Opportunity Board. 1st- 1977/78-. AT. English. ir. Government Printer, PO Box 203, North Melbourne

Political Science—Civil Rights

3051 Victoria Australia. LC JC599.A8. DD 354.94500104.

ANNUAL REPORT OF THE FAIRFAX COUNTY HUMAN RIGHTS COMMISSION. Main/Corp Fairfax County Human Rights Commission. US. English. an. County of Fairfax, Human Rights Commission, 9401 Lee Highway/Suite 206 Circle Towers Office Building, Fairfax VA 22030. LC JC599.U52. DD 352.941109755291.

ANNUAL REPORT OF THE INTER-AMERICAN COMMISSION ON HUMAN RIGHTS. Main/Corp Inter-American Commission on Human Rights. US. English. be.

ANNUAL REPORT OF THE MASSACHUSETTS COMMISSION AGAINST DISCRIMINATION. See Economics - Labor.

ANNUAL REPORT OF THE PRIVACY COMMISSIONER - CANADIAN HUMAN RIGHTS COMMISSION. Main/Corp Canadian Human Rights Commission. Privacy Commissioner. VFOAT Rapport Annuel du Commissaire a la Protection de la Vie Privee. CN. English (French). an. Canadian Human Rights Commission, 257 Slater Street, Ottawa Ontario K1A 1E1 Canada. LC JC596.2.C2. DD 354.710081106.

ANNUAL REPORT - OHIO CIVIL RIGHTS COMMISSION. Main/Corp Ohio. Civil Rights Commission. 1st- 1959/60-. US. English. an. Ohio Civil Rights Commission, Columbus OH 43215. Tel (614)466-6717. Ed Donna A Norris. LC JC599.U52. DD 323.409771. Circ 2,500. (ctrl).

ANNUAL REPORT - ONTARIO HUMAN RIGHTS COMMISSION. (ANNUAL REPORT OF THE ONTARIO HUMAN RIGHTS COMMISSION). Main/Corp Ontario Human Rights Commission. 0702-0538. CN. English. an. Ontario Human Rights Commission, 400 University Avenue, Toronto Ontario M5G 1R6 Canada. LC JC599.C2. DD 354.71300811.

ANNUAL REPORT - RHODE ISLAND COMMISSION FOR HUMAN RIGHTS. Main/Corp Rhode Island. Commission for Human Rights. US. English. an. Commission for Human Rights, 244 Broad Street, Providence RI 02903. LC JC599.U52. DD 353.9745093.

ANNUAL REPORT - SOUTH DAKOTA COMMISSION ON HUMAN RELATIONS. Main/Corp South Dakota. Commission on Human Relations. 0363-3322. US. English. an. South Dakota Commission on Human Relation, State Capitol Building, Pierre SD 57501. LC JC599.U52. DD 353.9783008.

ANNUAL REPORT - STATE OF NEW MEXICO, HUMAN RIGHTS COMMISSION. Main/Corp New Mexico. Human Rights Commission. US. English. Human Rights Commission of New Mexico, 303 Bataan Memorial Building, Santa Fe NM 87503. LC KFN4011. DD 353.978900996.

ANNUAL REPORTS - ILLINOIS. DEPT. OF HUMAN RIGHTS. Main/Corp Illinois. Dept. of Human Rights. 1st (July 1, 1980 through June 30, 1981)-. US. English. an. Illinois Department of Human Rights, 32 West Randolph Street, Civil Tower/Suite 8/9th Floor, Chicago IL 60601. LC JC599.U52. DD 353.977300811.

ANNUAL REVIEW - EUROPEAN COMMISSION OF HUMAN RIGHTS. Main/Corp European Commission of Human Rights. VFOAT Compte Rendu Annuel. FR. English and French. ir. European Commission of Human Rights, Council of Europe, Strasbourg France. DD 342.4085.

ANNUAL REVIEW - INTERNATIONAL LEAGUE FOR HUMAN RIGHTS. Main/Corp International League For Human Rights. US. English. an. International League for Human Rights, 777 United Nations Plaza/Suite 6F, New York NY 10017. Annual Review - International League for the Rights of Man, 0363-9347.

APRES-DEMAIN. 1957-. 0003-7176. Periodical. FR. French. mo. $35.92. Apres-Demain, 27 rue Jean-Dolent, 75014 Paris France. Ind/Abst Foreign Lang. Index, PAIS Foreign Lang. Index. adv acc. Political, economical, and social documentation review founded by the Human Rights League.

ARGENTINA OUTREACH. Began in 1976. 0194-2832. Periodical. US. English. $6.00. Argentine Information Service Center, 2700 Bancroft, Berkeley CA 94704. LC JC599.A7. DD 323.40982.

BIENNIAL REPORT - MINNESOTA. DEPT. OF HUMAN RIGHTS. Main/Corp Minnesota. Dept. of Human Rights. Began with 1975/76 vol. US. English. be. Minnesota Department of Human Rights, Bremer Tower/5th Floor/7th and Minnesota, St Paul MN 55101. LC JC599.U52. DD 353.977600811. Annual Report.

BILL OF RIGHTS IN ACTION. V. 10, No. 2- Sept. 1976-. 0160-7731. Periodical. US. English. qt. $4.00. Constitutional Rights Foundation, 6310 San Vincente Boulevard, Hollywood CA 90048. LC KF4742. DD 342.73085. Bill of Rights Newsletter.

THE BLACK LAW JOURNAL. See Law.

BULLETIN - AMNESTY INTERNATIONAL. CANADIAN SECTION. (BULLETIN). 0229-5539. Periodical. CN. English. ir. $9.28. Amnesty International Canadian Section, 294 Albert Street/Suite 204, Ottawa Ontario K1P 6E6 Canada. Tel (613)563-1891. DD 323.406071.

BULLETIN - C.A.D.HU. Main/Corp Comision Argentina por los Derechos Humanos. VAT Bulletin - Comision Argentina Por Los Derechos Humanos. FR. French. ir. Commission Argentine des Droits de L Homme, 61 rue de Meslay, 75003 Paris France. LC JC599.A7. DD 323.40982.

BULLETIN - CIVIL LIBERTIES ACTION SECURITY PROJECT. (BULLETIN). VFOAT Bulletin of the Civil Liberties Action Security Project (CLASP). Vol. 1, No. 1/2 (Aug./Sept.)-. 0824-4448. Periodical. CN. English. bm. $9.00. Civil Liberties Action Security Project (CLASP), PO Box 65369 Station F, Vancouver British Columbia V5N 5P3 Canada. DD 323.40971.

BULLETIN (DDR-KOMITEE FUR MENSCHENRECHTE). (BULLETIN). Began in 1975. Periodical. English (German). ir. Sekreteriat of the GDR, Committee for Human Rights, Thalmannplatz 8/9, Berlin 108 GDR East Germany. LC K4. DD 341.48105. Information (DDR-Komitee fur Menschenrechte).

BULLETIN - LIQUE HAITIENNE DES DROITS HUMAINS. Main/Corp Ligue Haitienne des Droits Humains. No. 1- Mar. 1978-. HT. French. ir. Ligue Haitienne des Droits Humains, 11 rue Tertullien Guilbaud, Bourdon Port-Au-Prince Haiti. LC JC599.H2. DD 323.4097294.

THE BULWARK. (THE BULWARK : A PROJECT OF CITIZENS IN DEFENSE OF CIVIL LIBERTIES). Vol. 1, No. 1 (Fall 1983)-. 0741-5788. Periodical. US. English. qt. Citizens in Defense of Civil Liberties, 343 South Dearborn Street/Suite 918, Chicago IL 60604. LC KF4742. DD 342.73085347.30285. Newsletter.

CAFE QUARTERLY. VAT Canadian Association for Free Expression Quarterly. Vol. 1, No. 1 (Winter 1981)-. 0711-2408. Periodical. CN. English. qt. $2.00. Canadian Association for Free Expression, Box 278/Station K, Toronto Ontario M4P 2G5 Canada. DD 323.4430971.

CALUMET (CHRISTIAN MOVEMENT FOR PEACE). (CALUMENT). 0229-3994. Periodical. CN. English. qt. $4. Calumet, 121 Avenue Road, Toronto Ontario M5R 2G3 Canada. DD 323.405.

CANADIAN HUMAN RIGHT REPORTER. Vol. 1, Decision 1(Jan. 1980)-. 0226-2177. CN. English (includes some text in French). mo. $174.11. Canadian Human Rights Reporter, 224 Fourth Avenue South/Suite 802, Saskatoon Saskatchewan S7K 5M5 Canada. Tel (306)664-5952. Ed Shelagh Day. DD 342.71085. Circ 800. (ctrl). Full text case reports of all human rights decisions (federal and provincial) in Canada plus expert commentary on emerging issues.

CANADIAN HUMAN RIGHTS ADVOCATE. V. 1, No. 1 (Nov./Dec. 1984)-. 0828-7252. Periodical. CN. English. ir. $25.00. Canadian Human Rights Advocate, PO Box 1703, Downsview Ontario M3J 2Z3 Canada. DD 323.40971.

CANADIAN HUMAN RIGHTS YEARBOOK. See Yearbooks, Almanacs, Directories.

CANDLE. (THE CANDLE). Winter 1984-. 0823-8650. Periodical. CN. English. sa. $12.00. Amnesty International English Speaking Branch, Suite 204/294 Albert Street, Ottawa Ontario K1P 6E6 Canada. DD 323.490601.

CARPA BULLETIN. Main/Corp Committee Against Repression in the Pacific and Asia. No. 1- 1978-. Periodical. English. ir.

CASE DIGEST - MICHIGAN. CIVIL RIGHTS COMMISSION. Main/Corp Michigan. Civil Rights Commission. 1964/75-. 0273-0642. US. English. sm. $100.00. Michigan Department of Civil Rights, Leonard Plaza/Main Floor, 309 North Washington Square, Lansing MI 48933. Tel (916)443-2017.

CASE ENFORCEMENT REPORT - DISTRICT OF COLUMBIA. OFFICE OF HUMAN RIGHTS. Main/Corp District of Columbia. Office of Human Rights. VFOAT Annual Case Enforcement Report. US. English. an. District of Columbia/Office of Human Rights, 420 Seventh Street Northwest/2nd Floor, Washington DC 20004. LC JC599.U52. DD 352.941109753.

CHARTER OF RIGHTS DECISIONS. (CHARTER OF RIGHTS DECISIONS : PROVIDING A DIGESTING SERVICE, BY SUBJECT, OF ALL DECISIONS RELATING TO CANADIAN BILL OF RIGHTS (1960) AND CANADIAN CHARTER OF RIGHTS AND FREEDOMS (1982)). VFOAT Canadian Charter of Rights & Freedoms. Vol. 1-. 0821-719X. Periodical. CN. English. bw. DD 342.7108502648.

CHE SAM IR. VFOAT The Third Day. VAT Sam Ir. 0715-5824. Periodical. CN. Korean. mo. Free. Third Day, 93 Queens Avenue, Weston Ontario M9N 2G5 Canada. DD 320.95195.

CHECKLIST OF HUMAN RIGHTS DOCUMENTS. V. 1- Jan./May 1976-. 0149-5372. US. English. mo. $75.00. Earl M Coleman Enterprises, 875 Avenue of the Americas, New York NY 10001. LC K3236. DD 016.342085. Checklist of Human Rights Documents, 0149-5372.

CHICAGO REPORTER. (THE CHICAGO REPORTER). Began in 1972. 0300-6921. Periodical. US. English. mo. Community Renewal Society, 18 South Michigan/Suite 1200, Chicago IL 60603. Tel (312)236-4830. Ed Roy Larson. LC F548.9.N3. DD 301.451960730773. Circ 4,500. The leading authority on racial issues and urban affairs in Chicago and the suburbs.

CHILE. See Economics - Labor.

CHILE ACTION BULLETIN ON POLITICAL PRISONERS AND HUMAN RIGHTS. VFOAT Chile Action Bulletin. Periodical. US. English. bm. Bay Area Nich, Box 800, Berkeley CA 94701.

A CHRONICLE OF HUMAN RIGHTS IN THE USSR CEASED. No. 1-48. US. English. bm. $20.00. 505 Eighth Avenue, New York NY 10018. DD 342.4708505, 344.7028505.

CIVIL LIBERTIES. No. 74- Sept. 1949-. 0009-790X. US. English. ir. $5.00 Membership. American Civil Liberties Union, 22 East 40th Street, New York NY 10016. LC JC599.U5. DD 323.40973. Civil Liberties Quarterly.

CIVIL LIBERTIES IN TEXAS. 0749-3061. Periodical. US. English. Texas Civil Liberties Union, 600 West 7th, Austin TX 78701. DD 323.

CIVIL LIBERTY : NEWSLETTER OF THE NATIONAL COUNCIL FOR CIVIL LIBERTIES. Main/Corp National Council for Civil Liberties (Great Britain). Vol. 1, No. 1 (Feb. 1985)-. UK. English. bm. $3.50. National Council for Civil Liberties, 21 Tabard Street, London SE1 4L4 England. Rights.

CIVIL RIGHTS. 7th Ed. (1984)-. 0824-7552. CN. English. $8.95 Per No. International Self-Counsel Press Head & Editorial Office, 306 West 25th Street, North Vancouver British Columbia V7N 2G1 Canada. DD 342.71085. Civil Rights in Canada, 0824-7560.

CIVIL RIGHTS & CIVIL LIBERTIES LITIGATION : A GUIDE TO SECTION SYMBOL 1983. US. English. ir. $80.00. Shepards McGraw Hill, PO Box 1235, Colorado Springs CO 80901. Tel (800)525-2474. (cum index). This dynamic text has been cited as an authority in many federal decisions and law reviews.

CIVIL RIGHTS DIRECTORY. See Yearbooks, Almanacs, Directories.

CIVIL RIGHTS RESEARCH REVIEW. (CIVIL RIGHTS RESEARCH REVIEW : A PUBLICATION OF THE CENTER FOR RESEARCH POLICY REVIEW). V. 9, No. 1-2 (Spring-Summer 1981)-. 0732-5738. Periodical. US. English. Center for National Policy Review, Catholic University of Law, Washington DC 22064. Ind/Abst Sociol. Abstr., Public Aff. Inf. Serv. Bull. Clearinghouse for Civil Rights Research.

CLEARINGHOUSE REPORT ON SCIENCE AND HUMAN RIGHTS. See Science (General).

Political Science—Civil Rights

COLORADO CIVIL LIBERTIES. 0413-7949. Periodical. US. English. bm. $20.00. Colorado Civil Liberties, 1711 Pennsylvania Street, Denver CO 80302.

COLUMBIA HUMAN RIGHTS LAW REVIEW. V. 4- Winter 1972-. 0090-7944. Periodical. US. English. sa. $18.00. Columbia University, School of Law, 435 West 116th Street, New York NY 10027. Tel (212)280-2171. Ed Gail McGowen. Ind/Abst Leg. Resour. Index, Index Leg. Period., Curr. Law Index, Contents Curr. Leg. Period. LC K3. DD 344.7308505. bk rev. Professional articles and student notes on human rights, international law, civil rights, and discrimination. *Columbia Survey of Human Rights Law, 0010-2008.*

CONSTITUTIONAL COMMENTARY. Vol. 1, No. 1 (Winter 1984-). Periodical. US. English. sa. Constitutional Commentary, University of Minnesota, Law School, 229 19th Avenue South, Minneapolis MN 55455.

THE CONVERSION PLANNER. V. 1- 197-. Periodical. US. English. bm. Sane, 514 C Street Northeast, Washington DC 20002.

CORNELL STUDIES IN CIVIL LIBERTY. Main/Corp Cornell University. Monographic Series. US. English. ir. Cornell University Press, 124 Roberts Place, Ithaca NY 14853.

COUNTRY REPORTS ON HUMAN RIGHTS PRACTICES. (COUNTRY REPORTS ON HUMAN RIGHTS PRACTICES. FOREIGN ASSISTANCE ACT OF 1961, AS AMENDED). Began with 1979. 0198-9669. US. English. an. Superintendent of Documents, US Government Printing Office, Washington DC 20402. LC JC571. DD 323.405. *Report on Human Rights Practices in Countries Receiving U.S. Aid.*

THE COVENANT. 0191-0353. Periodical. US. English. qt. Lawyers Committee For International Human Rights, 236 East 46th Street, New York NY 10017. LC K3236.2. DD 342.08505, 342.28505.

CRD NEWS. VFOAT C.R.D. News. VAT Committee for the Rights of the Disabled News. 0749-3177. Periodical. US. English. bm. Committee for the Rights of the Disabled, 2942 West Pico Boulevard, Los Angeles CA 90006. DD 344.

CRJ REPORTER. VFOAT C.R.J. Reporter. VAT Commission for Racial Justice Reporter. 0732-720X. Periodical. US. English. Commission for Racial Justice, 132 West 31st Street, New York NY 10001. Tel (212)683-5656. Ind/Abst Relig. Index One, Period.

CSW REPORT OF THE COMMISSION ON THE STATUS OF WOMEN. See Women.

DECISIONS AND REPORTS/COUNCIL OF EUROPE AND EUROPEAN COMMISSION FOR HUMAN RIGHTS. Main/Corp European Commission of Human Rights. VFOAT Decisions et Rapports. 1-. English (French). ir. *Collection of Decisions.*

THE DEFENDER. (THE DEFENDER : NEWSLETTER OF THE IOWA CIVIL LIBERTIES UNION). 0744-186X. Periodical. US. English. qt. Iowa Civil Liberties Union, 102 East Grand Avenue/Suite G-100, Des Moines IA 50309.

DIGEST ON GAY RIGHTS. (DIGEST ON GAY RIGHTS : I, HUMAN-CIVIL RIGHTS LEGISLATION). 0229-0812. Periodical. CN. English. qt. Gays for Equality, Box 27, University Centre, University of Manitoba, Winnipeg Manitoba R3T 2N2 Canada. DD 323.3.

DROIT ET LIBERTE. No. 1- 1942-. FR. French. ir. $14.24. Societe Droit et Liberte, 89 rue Oberkampf, 75011 Paris France. Tel 1 806 8800.

DROITS DE LA PERSONNE. BULLETIN D'INFORMATION SUR LA RECHERCHE ET L'ENSEIGNEMENT. (HUMAN RIGHTS : RESEARCH AND EDUCATION BULLETIN). VFOAT Droits de la Personne. No. 1 (Nov. 1984)-. 0826-7766. Periodical. CN. English (text in French with text on inverted pages). qt. Free. Human Rights Centre, University of Ottawa, 57 Copernicus, Ottawa Ontario K1N 6N5 Canada. DD 323.40971.

DROITS DE LA PERSONNE (MONTREAL, QUEBEC). (DROITS DE LA PERSONNE). Vol. 1 (1984)-. 0828-492X. Periodical. CN. French. Fondation Canadienne des Droits de l'Homme, Bureau 340/1980 Ouest rue Sherbrooke, Montreal Quebec H3H 1E8 Canada. DD 323.406071. *Human Rights (Montreal, Quebec), 0711-2122.*

EQUAL OPPORTUNITIES INTERNATIONAL. See Economics - Labor.

ESTIMATES. PART III, CANADIAN HUMAN RIGHTS COMMISSION. VFOAT Budget des Depenses. CN. English (French). $3.00 Domestic, $3.60 Foreign. Canadian Government Publishing Centre, Supply and Services Canada, Ottawa Ontario K1A 0S9 Canada. LC JC599.C2. DD 354.7100811.

EUROPAISCHE GRUNDRECHTE - ZEITSCHRIFT. (EUROPAISCHE GRUNDRECHTE). 0341-9800. Periodical. German. ir. $262.-. Engel Verlag, Elbinger Strasse 3, D7640 Kehl Am Rhein West Germany. Tel 07851/2463. Ed Thomas Buergenthal. Ind/Abst Energy Res. Abstr. adv acc. Circ 1,300. Provides an up-to-date systematic service reporting and commenting on international, constitutional and supreme court decisions in the human rights field from all over Europe. *Grundrechte.*

EUROPEAN CONVENTION ON HUMAN RIGHTS. Main/Corp Council of Europe. Directorate of Human Rights. English. an. Kluwer Academic Publications, PO Box 322, Orward 3300 AH Dordrecht Netherlands.

EUROPEAN HUMAN RIGHTS REPORTS. Began with issue for Jan. 1979. Periodical. UK. English. qt. $140.98. European Law Centre Limited, 4 Bloomsbury Square, London WC1A 2RL England. Tel 01-404 -4300. Ed Peter J Duffy. DD 341.48102684. adv acc. Includes all judgments of European Court of Human Rights; selected decisions of European Commission of Human Rights; summaries of other such decisions, resolutions and settlements.

FACE A LA JUSTICE. Vol. 1, No 0 i.e. V. 1, No. 1 (Oct. 1977)-. 0710-1090. Periodical. CN. French. bm. 20.00. Journal Face a la Justice, 1030 Cherrier/Suite 300, Montreal Quebec H2L 1H9 Canada. Tel (514)522-5965. Ed Jean Claude Bernheim. DD 364.971. adv acc. Circ 1,000. Publishes material concerning the penal and judicial systems.

FAIR EMPLOYMENT REPORT. See Economics - Labor.

THE FEDERAL CIVIL RIGHTS ENFORCEMENT BUDGET. Series/Titl Clearinghouse Publications. 0734-2454. US. English. US Commission on Civil Rights, Washington DC 20425. LC KF4755, JC599.U5. DD 353.0072236811.

FEDERAL CIVIL RIGHTS LITIGATION. Series/Titl Litigation Course Handbook Series. 0192-8635. US. English. an. Practising Law Institute, 810 Seventh Avenue, New York NY 10019. LC KF4749. DD 342.730850269.

FIRST PRINCIPLES. V. 1- Sept. 1975-. 0363-0447. US. English. bm. $15.00. Center for National Security Study, 122 Maryland Avenue NE, Washington DC 20002. Tel (202)544-5380. LC KF4742. DD 323.40973.

FORSCHUNGEN ZUR ANTIKEN SKLAVEREI. Vol. 1- 1967-. 0071-7665. Monographic Series. GW. German. ir. Franz Steiner Verlag GMBH, Postfach 347, D7000 Stuttgart 1 West Germany. Tel (0711) 2582229. Ed J Vogt and H Bellen. LC HT857. DD 326.08. Monographs dedicated to the history of ancient slavery.

FREEDOM APPEALS. Sept./Oct. 1979-. 0196-0695. Periodical. US. English. bm. Center for Appeals for Freedom, Freedom House, 20 West 40th Street, New York NY 10018. LC JC571. DD 323.405.

FREEDOM AT ISSUE. No. 1- Apr. 1970-. 0016-0520. Periodical. US. English. bm. $20.00. Freedom House, 48 East 21st Street, New York NY 10010. Tel (212)473-9691. Ed James Finn. Ind/Abst Hist. Abstr., Am. Hist. Life, Public Aff. Inf. Serv. Bull., Hist. Abstr., Part A, Mod. Hist. Abstr., Hist. Abst., Part B, Twent. Century Abstr. LC D839. DD 378.005. bk rev. Circ 5,000. A magazine devoted to supporting free institutions, analyzing their strengths and weaknesses, and recommending progressive, workable policies.

FREEDOM IN THE WORLD. Series/Titl Freedom House Book. 1978-. 0732-6610. US. English. an. Freedom House, Greenwood Press, 88 Post Road West, PO Box 5007, Westport CT 06881. LC JC571. DD 323.405.

FROM THE STATE CAPITALS. CIVIL RIGHTS. VFOAT Civil Rights. Jan. 1984-. 0741-353X. Periodical. US. English. wk. Wakeman/Walworth Inc, Box 1939, New Haven CT 06509. *From the State Capitals. Racial Relations and Civil Rights, 0734-0893.*

FROM THE STATE CAPITALS. RACIAL RELATIONS AND CIVIL RIGHTS. VFOAT Racial Relations and Civil Rights. Feb. 1982-. 0734-0893. Periodical. US. English. mo. $75.00. Wakeman/Walworth Inc, PO Box 1939, New Haven CT 06509. Tel (203)562-8518. *From the State Capitals. Racial Relations Developments at the State and Local Levels.*

FROM THE STATE CAPITALS. RACIAL RELATIONS DEVELOPMENTS AT THE STATE AND LOCAL LEVELS *CEASED.* VFOAT Racial Relations and Civil Rights, Racial Relations Developments at the State and Local Levels. Ceased with Jan. 1982. 0016-1896. Periodical. US. English. mo. Bethune Jones, 321 Sunset Avenue, Asbury Park NJ 07712.

FUNDAMENTAL RIGHTS AND FREEDOMS IN CANADA. Series Corp Canadian Jewish Congress. Information and Comment: Social and Economic Studies. 8th- 1956/57-. 0410-904X. Periodical. CN. English. Canadian Jewish Congress, 1590 McGregor Avenue, Montreal Quebec H3G 1C5 Canada. DD 323.40971. *0315-2790.*

GRUNDRECHTE. Vol. 1-. German. ir. 18.50 Monthly. Engel Verlag, Elbinger Straase 3, D-7640 Kehl Am Rhein West Germany. DD 341.481.

HARVARD CIVIL RIGHTS - CIVIL LIBERTIES LAW REVIEW. VAT Harvard Civil Rights Civil Liberties Review. V. 1- Spring 1966-. Periodical. US. English. sa. $15.00. Harvard Civil Rights, Publishing Center/Harvard Law School, Cambridge MA 02138. Tel (617)495-3694. Ed Robin Jacobson. Ind/Abst Curr. Index J. Educ., Leg. Resour. Index, Index Leg. Period., Public Aff. Inf. Serv. Bull. LC K8. DD 342.7308505. bk rev. Circ 1,500. A student edited journal focusing on civil rights: constitutional theory, criminal law, poverty law, and due process/equal protection.

HUMAN RIGHTS. (HUMAN RIGHTS : JOURNAL OF THE SECTION OF INDIVIDUAL RIGHTS AND RESPONSIBILITIES). Vol. 1, No. 1 (Aug. 1970)-. 0046-8185. Periodical. US. English. qt. $15.00. American Bar Association, 750 North Lake Shore Drive, Chicago IL 60611. Tel (312)988-6047. Ed Anthony Monahan. Ind/Abst Index Leg. Period., Soc. Sci. Index, Leg. Resour. Index, Curr. Law Index, Soc. Sci. Citation Index. LC K8. DD 342.7308505, 347.3028505. bk rev. adv acc. Circ 3,200. (ctrl). Read by a national and international audience of lawyers interested in the practice of human rights and civil rights. *Section of Individual Rights and Responsibilities Newsletter, 0572-3590; Edited Proceedings.*

HUMAN RIGHTS. Series/Titl Social Issues Resources Series. V. 1, Article 1-. 0273-2521. US. English. an. Social Issues Resources Series Inc, PO Box 2507, Boca Raton FL 33432. Ed Eleanor C Goldstein. LC JC571. DD 323.405.

HUMAN RIGHTS DIRECTORY WESTERN EUROPE. See Yearbooks, Almanacs, Directories.

HUMAN RIGHTS LAW JOURNAL : HRLJ. See Law - International Law.

HUMAN RIGHTS (MONTREAL, QUEBEC). (HUMAN RIGHTS). VFOAT Droits de l'Homme. VAT Droits de l'Homme (Montreal). 0711-2122. Periodical. CN. English (French). qt. $7.74. Canadian Human Rights Foundation, 1980 Sherbrooke Street West/Suite 340, Montreal Quebec H3H 1E8 Canada. Tel (514)932-7826. Ed Daniel Turp. DD 323.406071. bk rev. Circ 2,000. Activities of the Foundation. Reports of treaties, legislation and international and domestic cases involving human rights. Book reviews and bibliographies. *Newsletter (Canadian Human Rights Foundation), 0711-2114.*

HUMAN RIGHTS NEWS. Vol. 1 Nov. 1976-. CN. English. Ontario Human Rights Commission, 24 Victoria Street, Toronto Ontario Canada. LC KEQ812. DD 323.409713.

HUMAN RIGHTS ORGANIZATIONS & PERIODICALS DIRECTORY. See Yearbooks, Almanacs, Directories.

Political Science—Civil Rights

HUMAN RIGHTS QUARTERLY. Vol. 3, No. 1 (Feb. 1981)-. 0275-0392. Periodical. US. English. qt. $47.50. Johns Hopkins University Press, 701 West 40th Street/Suite 275, Baltimore MD 21211. Tel (301)338-6987. Ed Bert B Lockwood Jr. Ind/Abst Manage. Contents, Leg. Resour. Index, Am. Hist. Life, Hist. Abstr., Part A, Mod. Hist. Abstr., Hist. Abst., Part B, Twent. Century Abstr., Int. Labour Doc., Sociol. Abstr., Soc. Welf. Soc. Plan./Policy Soc. Dev., ABC Pol Sci, Public Aff. Inf. Serv. Bull. LC JC571. DD 323.405. bk rev. adv acc. Circ 811. Is an international forum for contributors to present comparative and international research on public policy within the scope of the Universal Declaration of Human Rights. *Universal Human Rights, 0163-2647.*

HUMAN RIGHTS REVIEW CEASED. (THE HUMAN RIGHTS REVIEW). V. 1-6, No. 3. 0308-0765. Periodical. UK. English. ty. $20.00 United States. Oxford Journals, Press Road, Neasden, London NW10 0DD England. Ind/Abst Sociol. Abstr., Soc. Welf. Soc. Plan./Policy Soc. Dev., Index Leg. Period. LC K8. DD 323.4094.

HUMAN RIGHTS TEACHING. Periodical. English. sa. Division of Human Rights and Peace UNESCO, 7 Place de Fontenoy 75700 Paris France. LC JC571. DD 323.405.

ICJ NEWSLETTER. Main/Corp International Commission of Jurists (1952-). No. 1 (Apr.-30 June 1979)-. Periodical. English. qt. 20.00. International Commission of Jurists, BP 120, 1224 Chene-Bougeries, Geneva Switzerland. LC K3236.2. DD 341.48105.

ICLU AND YOU. 1970-. US. English. qt. $10.00. Indiana Civil Liberties Union, PO Box 6147/445 North Pennsylvania, Indianapolis IN 46204. Tel (317)635-4059. Ed Jau Nae Hanger. bk rev. Circ 5,000. (ctrl). Publication discussing national and local civil liberties issues. *ICLU News, 0441-8549.*

INDEX. See Indexes/Abstracts.

INFORMATION BULLETIN (GUATEMALA HUMAN RIGHTS COMMISSION/USA). (INFORMATION BULLETIN). Periodical. US. English. Guatemala Human Rights Commission/USA, PO Box 91 Cardinal Station, Washington DC 20064.

IOWA CIVIL RIGHTS COMMISSION, CASE REPORTS. V. 1- 1965/77-. US. English. an. Iowa Civil Rights Commission, 8th Floor/Colony Building, 507 10th Street, Des Moines IA 50319. LC KFI4611. DD 342.7770850264, 347. 7702850264.

ISRAEL YEARBOOK ON HUMAN RIGHTS. See Yearbooks, Almanacs, Directories.

JOURNAL OF MODERN AFRICAN STUDIES. (JOURNAL OF MODERN AFRICAN STUDIES). V. 1- March 1963-. 0022-278X. Periodical. UK. English. qt. $95.00. Cambridge University Press, 510 North Avenue, New Rochelle NY 10801. Tel (914)235-0300. Ed David Kimble. Ind/Abst Soc. Sci. Citation Index, Soc. Sci. Index, Lang. Lang. Behav. Abstr., Sociol. Abstr., Guide Soc. Sci. Relig. Period. Lit., MLA Int. Bibliogr. Books Artic. Mod. Lang. Lit., ABC Pol Sci, Am. Hist. Life, Hist. Abstr., Int. Labour Doc., Soc. Welf. Soc. Plan./Policy Soc. Dev., Ref. Source, Bibliogr. Agric., Recent Publ. Artic. LC DT1. bk rev. adv acc. Circ 2,500. Survey of politics, economics and related topics on contemporary Africa. Main emphasis on people, policies, problems and progress of this dynamic and disparate continent.

LAWASIA HUMAN RIGHTS BULLETIN. VFOAT Lawasia. VAT Law Association for Asia and the Western Pacific Human Rights Bulletin. Vol. 1, No. 1 (June 1982)-. AT. English. sa. $7.38. Lawasia Human Rights Standing Committee, 170 Phillip Street, Sydney New South Wales 2000 Australia. Tel (02)2212970. Ed R M Hope. adv acc. Circ 2,000. (ctrl). Legislative, judicial and general reports on human rights matters in Asian countries.

THE LAWYERS COMMITTEE BULLETIN. (THE LAWYERS COMMITTEE BULLETIN : A PUBLICATION OF THE LAWYERS COMMITTEE FOR INTERNATIONAL HUMAN RIGHTS). Vol. 2, No. 1 (Feb. 1981)-. 0730-5532. Periodical. US. English. Lawyers Committee for International Human Rights, 236 East 46th Street, New York NY 10017. LC K3236.2. DD 341.48105. *Lawyers Committee News, 0270-5362.*

LIBERTY. Periodical. US. English. ir. Liberty Association, 6840 Eastern Avenue NW, Washington DC 20012.

MASSACHUSETTS DISCRIMINATION LAW REPORTER. See Law.

MATCHBOX CEASED. Began with V. 1- Spring/Summer 1974. Ceased with Oct. 1983. 0363-1699. Periodical. US. English. qt. $0.50 Single Issue. Amnesty International of the USA, 2112 Broadway/Room 309, New York NY 10023. Ind/Abst Altern. Press Index. LC JC571. DD 323.405.

THE NEW ENGLAND HUMAN RIGHTS DIRECTORY. See Yearbooks, Almanacs, Directories.

NEW PERSPECTIVES (WASHINGTON, D.C.). (NEW PERSPECTIVES). Vol. 16, No. 1 (Summer 1984)-. 8750-2135. Periodical. US. English. qt. Superintendent of Documents, US Government Printing Office, Washington DC 20402. LC JC599.U45. DD 323.40973. *Perspectives (Washington, D.C.), 0274-855X.*

NEWSLETTER HUMAN RIGHTS COMMISSION OF BRITISH COLUMBIA. (NEWSLETTER - HUMAN RIGHTS COMMISSION OF BRITISH COLUMBIA). Main/Corp Human Rights Commission of British Columbia. V. 1- Dec. 1979-. 0226-2770. CN. English. ir. Human Rights Commission of British Columbia, 880 Douglas Street, Victoria British Columbia V8W 2B7 Canada. DD 345.71100811.

NEWSLETTER - ILLINOIS STATE BAR ASSOCIATION. Main/Corp Illinois State Bar Association. Section on Individual Rights and Responsibilities. V. 1- Aug. 1972-. US. English. Illinois State Bar Association, Section on Individual Rights & Responsibilities, Illinois Bar Center, Springfield IL 62701. LC KF4749.A1. DD 323.40973.

NEWSLETTER - INTER-CHURCH COMMITTEE ON HUMAN RIGHTS IN LATIN AMERICA. Main/Corp Inter-Church Committee on Human Rights in Latin America. May 1977-. 0226-661X. Periodical. CN. English. ir. Free. Inter-Church Committee on Human Rights in Latin America, Suite 201/40 Saint Clair Avenue East, Toronto Ontario M4T 1M9. DD 323.4098. (ctrl).

NEWSLETTER - NOVA SCOTIA HUMAN RIGHTS COMMISSION CEASED. Main/Corp Nova Scotia. Human Rights Commission. VAT Nova Scotia Human Rights Commission Newsletter. Began publication with 1st. 0226-6954. Periodical. CN. English. qt.

NORTH AMERICAN HUMAN RIGHTS DIRECTORY. See Yearbooks, Almanacs, Directories.

NUESTRA LUCHA. 0731-2512. Periodical. US. English (Spanish). ir. $10.00. 714-1/2 South St Clair, Toledo OH 43609.

N.Y. CIVIL LIBERTIES. V. 23- Sept. 1974-. 0746-0201. Periodical. US. English. qt. New York Civil Liberties Union, 84 Fifth Avenue, New York NY 10011. *Civil Liberties in New York, 0009-7926.*

OBJECTIVE : JUSTICE. V. 1- 1969-. 0029-7593. Periodical. US. English. sa. $10.00. United Nations Publications, Sales Section/Room A-3315, New York NY 10017. Tel (212)754-8324. Ind/Abst Public Aff. Inf. Serv. Bull. LC HT1521. Reviews human rights issues such as apartheid, racial discrimination, etc.

OHIO CIVIL LIBERTIES. Began publication in 1969. 0274-5615. Periodical. US. English. qt. $10.00. American Civil Liberties of Ohio, 360 South Third Street/Suite 450, Columbus OH 43215. Tel (614)228-8951. Ed Mark B Levy. adv acc. Circ 5,500. (ctrl). News regarding activities of ACLU in Ohio to defend and advance principles of free speech, press, religion; fundamental fairness; equality under the law; and the right to privacy.

OPERATION LIBERTE. V. 1- Feb. 1978-. 0706-9294. Periodical. CN. English. 0.25 Each Number. La Ligue des Droits de l'Homme, 3836 rue Saint-Hubert, Montreal Quebec H2L 4A5 Canada. DD 323.40971.

OPTIONS (WASHINGTON, D.C.). (OPTIONS). Began in 1974. 0739-7992. Periodical. US. English. mo. REL Coalition Abortion Rights Inc, 100 Maryland Avenue NE, Washington DC 20002. Tel (202)543-7032. Ed Gaye Williams. bk rev. Circ 40,000. (ctrl). National, local and state legislative, organizational, denominational and other news on religious freedom and abortion rights.

THE ORGANIZER : NEWSLETTER OF THE NATIONAL ALLIANCE AGAINST RACIST AND POLITICAL REPRESSION. VFOAT Newsletter of the National Alliance Against Racist and Political Repression. Periodical. US. English. ir. National Alliance Against Racist and Political Repression, 27 Union Square West/Room 306, New York NY 10003.

PERSPECTIVES (WASHINGTON, D.C.). (PERSPECTIVES). V. 12, No. 1 (Spring 1980)- V. 15, No. 3 (Summer 1983). 0274-855X. Periodical. US. English. qt. US Commission on Civil Rights, 1121 Vermont Avenue/Room 700, Washington DC 20425. Tel (202)254-6600. Ind/Abst Soc. Sci. Index, Public Aff. Inf. Serv. Bull., Curr. Index J. Educ., Index U.S. Gov. Period. LC JC599.U45. DD 323.40973. *Civil Rights Digest, 0009-7969.*

POLICY GUIDE OF THE AMERICAN CIVIL LIBERTIES UNION. Main/Corp American Civil Liberties Union. 1966-. 0275-3170. US. English. ir. $20.00. American Civil Liberties Union, 132 West 43rd Street, New York NY 10036. Tel (212)944-9800. Ed Ari Korpivaara. bk rev. Circ 175,000. (ctrl). Reports on ACLU's litigation, legislative lobbying, and public education efforts in defense of free speech, equal protection, and other constitutional rights.

PRIORITIES. 0700-6543. CN. English. mo. $5.00. Priorities, 517 East Broadway, Vancouver British Columbia V5T 1X4 Canada. Tel 873-8898. Ed Janet Besterback. bk rev. A socialist feminist publication. It is the magazine fo the Women's Rights Committee of the N.D.P. in British Columbia Canada.

THE PUBLIC EYE. 0275-9322. Periodical. US. English. qt. $40.00. Citizens in Defense of Civil Liberties, #918 343 South Dearborn Street, Chicago IL 60604. Tel (202)347-2031.

PUCL BULLETIN. VFOAT P.U.C.L. Bulletin. Periodical. English. ir. People's Union for Civil Liberties, F-67 Bhagat Singh Market, New Delhi 110001. DD 323.40954.

QUARTERLY REPORT - LATIN AMERICAN WORKING GROUP. (QUARTERLY REPORT). 0827-3928. Periodical. CN. English. qt. Free. Latin American Working Group, PO Box 2207 Station P, Toronto Ontario M5S 2T2 Canada. DD 980.005.

RAPPORT ANNUEL - COMMISSION CANADIENNE DES DROITS DE LA PERSONNE. Main/Corp Canada. Commission Canadienne des Droits de la Personne. VFOAT Annual Report - Canadian Human Rights Commission. 1977/78-. 0708-5516. CN. text in English and French on inverted pages. an. Commission Canadienne des Droits de la Personne, 257 rue Slater, Ottawa Ontario K1A 1E1 Canada.

RAPPORT ANNUEL - COMMISSION DES DROITS DE LA PERSONNE DU QUEBEC. Main/Corp Commission des Droits de la Personne du Quebec. 1.- 1976-. 0703-1343. CN. French. an. Editeur Officiel du Quebec, 1283 Boul Charest Quest, Quebec Quebec G1N 2C9 Canada. LC JC599.C2. DD 354.71400811.

RAPPORT ANNUEL - COMMISSION ONTARIENNE DES DROITS DE LA PERSONNE. (RAPPORT ANNUEL). Main/Corp Ontario Human Rights Commission. Began with V. for 1980/1981. 0229-5210. CN. French. an. Free. LC JC599.C2. DD 354.71300811. *Ontario Annuel de la Commission Ontarienne des Droits de la Personne, 0229-5210.*

REPORT AND SUMMARY OF ACTIVITIES - SASKATCHEWAN HUMAN RIGHTS COMMISSION. Main/Corp Saskatchewan Human Rights Commission. 1972/75-. 0381-4408. CN. English. an. LC KES458.A72. DD 354.712400996.

REPORT - MISSOURI. COMMISSION ON HUMAN RIGHTS. Main/Corp Missouri. Commission on Human Rights. US. English. an. LC JC599.U5.

REPORT OF THE COMMISSION FOR RACIAL EQUALITY. Main/Corp Great Britain. Commission for Racial Equality. VFOAT Annual Report - Commission for Racial Equality. 1st- 1977-. UK. English. an. Her Majestys Stationery Office, PO Box 276, London SW8 5DT England. Tel (01)622-3316. LC DA125.A1. DD 301.4510941.

Political Science—International Relations

REPORT OF THE STANDING ADVISORY COMMISSION ON HUMAN RIGHTS. Main/Corp Northern Ireland. Standing Advisory Commission on Human Rights. VFOAT Annual Report - Standing Advisory Commission on Human Rights. 1st- 1974/75-. UK. English. 0.35. LC KDE420. DD 323.409416.

REPORT ON THE WORK ACCOMPLISHED DURING ITS ... SESSION. Main/Corp Inter-American Commission on Human Rights. 1st Session (Oct. 3-28, 1960)-. 0074-0772. Periodical. US. English. ir.

REPRESION. Yearly V. 2- (No. 13-). Periodical. Spanish. ir. Nuevo Mundo Jr, Camana 280 of 305, Lima Peru. LC JC599.P4. DD 323.490985. *Represion en el Peru.*

RESEARCH REPORT - NEW YORK CITY COMMISSION ON HUMAN RIGHTS. (RESEARCH REPORT - CITY COMMISSION ON HUMAN RIGHTS). Main/Corp New York (City). City Commission on Human Rights. 0545-4158. Monographic Series. US. English. New York City Commission on Human Rights, 475 Riverside Drive/Suite 448, New York NY 10027. LC JC599.U52. DD 323.4097471.

THE REVIEW - INTERNATIONAL COMMISSION OF JURISTS. See Law.

REVIEW - SASKATCHEWAN ASSOCIATION ON HUMAN RIGHTS. (REVIEW). 0713-0287. Periodical. CN. English. bm. Free to Members. Saskatchewan Association on Human Rights, 218-116 3rd Avenue South, Saskatoon Saskatchewan S7K 1L5 Canada. DD 323.4097124. *Saskatchewan Human Rights Review, 0713-0279.*

RIGHTS. V. 1- 1953-. 0035-5283. Periodical. US. English. bm. National Emergency Civil Liberties Committee, 25 East 26th Street, New York NY 10010. Ind/Abst Altern. Press Index. LC JC599.U5. DD 323.40973.

RIGHTS CEASED. V. 1- Sept. 1976-. Periodical. UK. English. bm. National Council of Civil Liberties, 21 Tabard Street, London SE1 4LA England. Tel 403 3888. Ed Nicky Harman. LC JC571. DD 323.40941. bk rev. Circ 10,000. Investigates civil liberty issues in the United Kingdom, with particular emphasis on campaigns of National Council of Civil Liberties. *Civil Liberty.*

RIGHTS AND FREEDOMS. VFOAT Droits et la Liberte. No. 14- Sept. 1974-. 0380-1225. Periodical. CN. English (includes some text in French). bm. $27.09. Canadian Rights Liberties Federation, 323 Chapes Street, Ottawa Ontario K1N 7Z2 Canada. Tel (613)235-8978. Ed Terrence Carling. LC JC599.C2. DD 323.40971. bk rev. Circ 4,000. Only magazine published in Canada devoted solely to examining all aspects of civil liberties and human rights. *National Newsletter, 0380-1217.*

THE SAMIZDAT BULLETIN. See Political Science.

SCHOOLS & CIVIL RIGHTS NEWS. VAT Schools and Civil Rights News. V. 3, No. 5- Mar. 8, 1979-. 0193-418X. Periodical. US. English. bw. $87.00. Capitol Publications, 2430 Pennsylvania Avenue NW/Suite G-12, Washington DC 20037. LC KF4151.A3. DD 344.73079805. *Title IX News, 0192-5601.*

SESQUIANNUAL REPORT - FLORIDA COMMISSION ON HUMAN RELATIONS. Main/Corp Florida. Commission on Human Relations. July 1972/Dec. 1973-. 0097-9244. US. English. ir. Florida Commission on Human Relations, 2571 Executive Center, Tallahassee FL 32301. LC JC599.U52. DD 353.975900996.

THE SIMON GREENLEAF LAW REVIEW : A PUBLICATION OF THE SIMON GREENLEAF SCHOOL OF LAW. Vol. 1 (Academic Year 1981-82)-. 0882-181X. Periodical. US. English. an. $7.00. The Simon Greenleaf School of Law, 2530 Shadow Ridge Lane, Orange CA 92667. LC K23. DD 261.5.

SITTHI SERIPHAP. V. 1- Mar. 1974-. Periodical. Thai. ir.

SMOLOSKYP (ELLICOTT CITY, MD.). (SMOLOSKYP). Vol. 1, No. 1 (Fall 1978)-. 0193-5755. Periodical. US. English. qt. $5.00. Smoloskyp, Box 561, Ellicot City MD 21043. Tel (301)465-2958. Ed Lesya Verba. bk rev. adv acc. Circ 10,000. Human rights developments in Ukraine and East Europe. Status of political prisoners, in USSR by republics. Samizdat materials. Political events are explored in feature articles and editorials.

SOUTHERN CHANGES. V. 1- Sept. 1978-. 0193-2446. Periodical. US. English. bm. $30.00. Southern Regional Council, 160 Spring Street NW/Suite 820, Atlanta GA 30303. Tel (404)522-8764. Ed Allen Tullos. Ind/Abst Am. Hist. Life, Hist. Abstr., Part A, Mod. Hist. Abstr., Hist. Abst., Part B, Twent. Century Abstr. LC JC599.U5. DD 323.40975. bk rev. adv acc. Circ 5,000. Reporting and analysis of issues affecting the South. Critical commentary, reviews and opinions across the range of regional experience in the South.

SOUTHERN VOICES. V. 1- Mar./Apr. 1974-. 0093-9293. US. English. bm. $7.00. 52 Fairlie Street NW, Atlanta GA 30303. Ind/Abst Am. Hist. Life, Hist. Abstr., Part A, Mod. Hist. Abstr., Hist. Abst., Part B, Twent. Century Abstr. LC F206. DD 917.503405. *South Today (Atlanta, GA.), New South (Atlanta, GA.).*

STATE ADVISORY COMMITTEE HANDBOOK. Main/Corp United States Commission on Civil Rights. VFOAT State Advisor Committee Hand Book. 0741-224X. US. English. United States Commission on Civil Rights, Washington DC 20425. LC JC599.U5. DD 353.00811.

THE STATE OF CIVIL RIGHTS. Main/Corp United States. Commission on Civil Rights. 1976-. 0161-9233. US. English. an. US Commission on Civil Rights, Washington DC 20402. LC KF4749. DD 323.40973.

STEUBEN NEWS. V. 1-. Periodical. US. English. bm. $3.00. National Council Steuben Society of America, 67-05 Fresh Pond Road, Ridgewood NY 11385. Tel (718)381-0900. Ed Henry Heinlein. LC NK5100. bk rev. adv acc. Circ 4,000. (ctrl). A patriotic organization comprised of American citizens of German ancestry dedicated to the task of giving force and effect to the United States Constitution and to encourage citizen participation in government.

STUDIES IN HUMAN RIGHTS. No. 1-. 0146-3586. Monographic Series. US. English. ir. Greenwood Press, 88 Post Road West Box 5007, Westport CT 06881. Tel (203)226-3571. Ed George W Shepherd. LC UNC.

SUPREME COURT LAW REVIEW. See Law.

TAI TU CEASED. VFOAT Independent Taiwan. Began with No. 1 Mar. 1972. Ceased 112, 6/28/81. 0362-9112. Periodical. US. Chinese. mo.

THUNDERBOLT, THE WHITE MAN'S VIEWPOINT. 0040-6643. Periodical. US. English. mo. The Thunderbolt Inc, PO Box 1211, Marietta GA 30060.

TRIENNIAL REPORT. Main/Corp Indiana. Civil Rights Commission. 1977-1980-. US. English. te. The Indiana Civil Rights Commission, 311 West Washington Street/Suite 319, Indianapolis IN 46204. LC KFI3411. DD 323.409772. *Annual Report, 0073-6856.*

TYDSKRIF VIR REGSWETENSKAP. See Law.

VETERANS' VOICE. No. 1435 (June 20, 1984)-. Periodical. US. English. Research & Publicity Unit Division of Veterans' Affairs Executive Department, State of New York, 194 Washington Avenue, Albany NY 12210.

THE VIOLATIONS OF HUMAN RIGHTS IN SOVIET OCCUPIED LITHUANIA. Main/Corp Lithuanian American Community. 1971-. 0360-7453. US. English. an. Lithuanian American Community, 708 Custis Road, Glenside PA 19038. DD 342.475085.

VIOLATIONS OF HUMAN RIGHTS IN SOVIET OCCUPIED LITHUANIA. (THE VIOLATIONS OF HUMAN RIGHTS IN SOVIET OCCUPIED LITHUANIA : A REPORT FOR . . .). 0360-7453. CN. English. an. Lithuanian Canadian Community, 1011 College Street, Toronto Ontario M6H 1A8 Canada. DD 323.409475.

VISNYK REPRESII V UKRAINI. (HERALD OF REPRESSION IN UKRAINE). No. 1 (Jan. 1980)-. 0749-8616. Periodical. US. English (Russian). mo. $25.00. Ukrainian Helsinki Group, PO Box 770 Cooper Station, New York NY 10003. DD 323.

WESLEYAN ANTI-SLAVERY REVIEW, CONTAINING AN APPEAL TO THE METHODIST EPISCOPAL CHURCH. Periodical. US. English. an. Taylor & Francis Inc, 242 Cherry Street, Philadelphia PA 19106. Tel (800)821-8312.

WORKER'S GUIDE TO SOCIAL LEGISLATION. (THE WORKER'S GUIDE TO SOCIAL LEGISLATION). VFOAT Worker's Social Guide. VAT Worker's Social Guide (1984). 1984-. 0826-8657. CN. English. an. Quebec Federation of Labour, 4th Floor/2100 Papineau Avenue, Montreal Quebec H2X 4J4 Canada. DD 344.71401. *Worker's Social Guide, 0826-8649.*

YEARBOOK OF THE EUROPEAN CONVENTION ON HUMAN RIGHTS, THE EUROPEAN COMMISSION AND EUROPEAN COURT OF HUMAN RIGHTS. See Yearbooks, Almanacs, Directories.

YEARBOOK ON HUMAN RIGHTS FOR . . . . See Yearbooks, Almanacs, Directories.

ZEITSCHRIFT FUR ZIVILPROZESS. See Law.

INTERNATIONAL RELATIONS

3. I.E. DRITTE WELT MAGAZIN. VFOAT Dritte Welt Magazin. No. 1/2- May/June 1975-. 0002-0362. Periodical. GW. German. qt. Progress Dritte Welt, Postfach 1528, 5300 Bonn 1 West Germany. LC D839. *Afrika Heute, III. Welt.*

AAUG MONOGRAPH SERIES. Main/Corp Association of Arab-American University Graduates. Monographic Series. US. English. ir. Association of Arab American University Graduates, 556 Trapelo Road, Belmont MA 02178. Tel (617)484-5483. Ed Patricia M Walsh. Series focuses on US-Middle East relations, Arab world, Middle East and Palestinian-Israeli conflict.

ABSTRACTS OF PAPERS PRESENTED AT THE ... WORLD CONGRESS OF THE INTERNATIONAL POLITICAL SCIENCE ASSOCIATION. See Indexes/Abstracts.

ACEL, ANUARIO DEL COMERCIO EXTERIOR LATINOAMERICANO. See Yearbooks, Almanacs, Directories.

ACTION AND REACTION. VFOAT Action. 0745-5615. Periodical. US. English. wk. $30.00. Action Comm Arab-American Relations, PO Box 416 Grand Central Station, New York NY 10017. Tel (212)682-1154. *Action.*

ACTIVITES DU CQRI. Main/Corp Centre Quebecois de Relations Internationales. No. 1- Spring 1972-. 0382-8468. Periodical. CN. French. sa. Centre Quebecois de Relations Internationales, A/S Universite Laval, Quebec G1K 7P4 Canada.

ACTIVITY OF THE POLISH INSTITUTE OF INTERNATIONAL AFFAIRS. Main/Corp Polski Instytut Spraw Miedzynarodowych, Warsaw. English. ir. Polish Institute of International Affairs, Ul Warecka 1A, POB 1000, 00-950 Warsaw Poland. LC JX38. DD 327.07114384.

ADELPHI PAPERS. Began in 1963. 0567-932X. Monographic Series. UK. English. ir. $65.00 US. Institute for Strategic Studies, 23 Tavistock Street, London WC2E 7NG England. Tel (01)379 7676. Ed Jonathan Alford. Ind/Abst Predicasts, Funk Scott Index Corp. Ind. Circ 7,500. A series of scholarly monographs dealing with issues of international security.

AEI FOREIGN POLICY AND DEFENSE REVIEW. VFOAT A.E.I. Foreign Policy and Defense Review. VAT American Enterprise Institute Foreign Policy and Defense Review. Vol. 1, No. 1-. 0163-9927. Periodical. US. English. qt. $18.00. American Enterprise Institute Public Policy Research, 1150 17th Street NW, Washington DC 20036. Tel (202)862-5931. Ind/Abst Predicasts, Public Aff. Inf. Serv. Bull., Funk Scott Index Corp. Ind., Recent Publ. Artic. LC E840. DD 327.73. *AEI Defense Review, 0149-838X.*

AFFARI ESTERI. V. 1- Jan. 1969-. 0001-964X. Periodical. IT. Italian. qt $14.26. Affari Esteri, 6 Via Giovanni Paisiello, 00198 Roma Italy. Ind/Abst Foreign Lang. Index, Hist. Abstr., Am. Hist. Life, PAIS Foreign Lang. Index, Hist. Abstr., Part A, Mod. Hist. Abstr., Hist. Abst., Part B, Twent. Century Abstr. LC D839. DD 327.0904. *Esteri.*

AFRICA INSIDER. 0748-4356. Periodical. US. English. bw. $150.00. Africa Insider, PO Box 53398 Temple Heights Station, Washington DC 20009. Tel (202)332-1622. Ed Dan Matthews. DD 327. Report on US and African-relations emphasizing vital intelligence rarely found on Congress, White House,

Political Science—International Relations

State Department, USIA, USAID, and other government agencies and private sector.

AFRICASIA (PARIS, FRANCE : 1984). (AFRICASIA : AFRICA, ARAB WORLD, ASIA, LATIN AMERICA). VFOAT Africa Asia. No. 1 (Jan. 1984)-. Periodical. English. mo. $40.00. 13 rue d'Uzes, 75002 Paris France. Tel (1) 42.96.16.66. LC D839. DD 909.09724. bk rev. adv acc. Circ 50,000. (ctrl). Devoted to the political, economic, social and cultural problems of the Third World. *Africasia.*

AFRIQUE-ASIE. Periodical. FR. French. sm. Afrique Asie, 13 rue d'Uzes, 75002 Paris France. Tel (1)42.96.16.66. LC DT1. bk rev. Circ 170,000. (ctrl). Devoted to the political, economic, social and cultural problems of the Third World.

AFRIQUE CONTEMPORAINE. No. 1 (April/May 1962)-. 0002-0478. Periodical. FR. French. qt. 120.00 Domestic, 135.00 Foreign. La Documentation Francaise, 29-31 Quai Voltaire, 75007 Paris France. Tel 834-9275. Ind/Abst Recent Publ. Artic., Foreign Lang. Index. LC DT348. (cum index).

AGECOP LIAISON. Main/Corp Agence de Cooperation Culturelle et Technique. VAT Agence de Cooperation Culturelle et Technique Liaison. 0336-2086. Periodical. French. mo. ACCT, 19 Avenue De Messine, Paris France 75008. LC DT14. DD 301.296.

AGENOR. No. 1- 1967-. Periodical. English (French). ir. $31.30. Agenor-A European Review, 22 rue de Toulouse, 1040 Bruxelles Belgium. Tel 32 (0) 2 230 4777. Ed John Lambert. (ctrl). Pamphlets reflect the critical thinking of the group on topical, political and economic issues arising in the European dimension.

AICD NEWSLETTER. Main/Corp Association for International Cooperation & Disarmament. Periodical. English. ir.

AJR INFORMATION. Main/Corp Association of Jewish Refugees in Great Britain. VAT Association of Jewish Refugees in Great Britain Information. V. 1- Jan. 1946-. Periodical. UK. English (German). mo. 15.00. 8 Fairfax Mansions, London NW3 England. Tel 01-624 9096. Ed M Stern. LC DS135.E5. bk rev. adv acc. Circ 5,000. Everything concerning the history, background and personalia of German-Jewish refugees worldwide.

AL-ANBA. Periodical. Arabic. ir. 1.00 Per Issue. Al-Hizb Al-Taqaddumi Al-Ishtiraki, PO Box 2893, Bayrut Lebanon. LC DS87.

AL-ARAB AL-DAWLIYAH. VFOAT Arab International Magazine. Periodical. SU. Arabic. ir. $2.00 Per Issue. Maktab Al-Dalil Al-Arabi, S B 7153, Juddah Saudi Arabia.

AL-ARD. VFOAT Al-Ard Magazine. Periodical. US. Arabic (English). $10.00. 5503 North East Prescott, Portland Oregon 97218.

AL-BAYADIR AL-SIYASI. VFOAT Bayader. Periodical. Arabic. mo. $150.00. Al-Bayader, PO Box 21445, 91213 Jerusalem. Tel 2-820957. Ed Jack Y Khazmo. LC DS63.1. bk rev. Circ 15,000. Specializes in reflecting the real situation in Israel and the area and publishes interviews and has many columns of general subjects.

AL-DUSTUR. VFOAT Dastour. Periodical. UK. Arabic. wk. 40.00. Ad-Dastour Ltd, 86/87 Campden Street, London W8 7EN England. LC DS36.

AL-MILAFF. VFOAT Al-Malaf. Journal 1, No. 1 (April 1984)-. Periodical. Arabic. sm. $750.00 Public Institutions, $500.00 Private Institutions. Manar Press & Publishing Agency Ltd, PO Box 4928, Nicosia Cyprus. LC DS119.7.

ALTERNATIVAS (SANTIAGO, CHILE). (ALTERNATIVAS). Vol. 1, No. 1-. Periodical. Spanish. ty. $30.00. Revista Alternativas Centro de Estudios de la Realidad Contemporanea, Academia de Humanismo Cristiano Catredal, 1063 Santiago Chile. Tel 6968379. Ed Heraldo Munoz. bk rev. adv acc. Circ 2,000. (ctrl).

AMBASSADOR. (THE AMBASSADOR). Began with Aug. 1970 issue. 0044-7439. Periodical. English. ir. $10.00. The Ambassador Journal, 148 San Juan Street, Pasay City Philippines. LC JX18. DD 327.205.

AMERICA LATINA, UNION SOVIETICA. VFOAT Union Sovietica. V. 1, No. 1 (Nov./Dec. 1983)-. Periodical. CL. Spanish. bm. $15.00. Flacso, 3213 Correo Central, Santiago Chile. Tel 56-2-2257357. Ed Augusto Varas. bk rev. Circ 5,000. Analysis of Soviet Latin American relations, government to government or party to party contacts

Soviet society and political perception on Latin America.

AMERICAN-ARAB AFFAIRS. VFOAT American Arab Affairs. No. 1 (Summer 1982)-. 0731-6763. Periodical. US. English. qt. $20.00. American Arab Affairs, 1730 M Street/Suite 411, Washington DC 20035. Tel (202)297-6767. Ed Annie Joyce. Ind/Abst ABC Pol Sci, Book Rev. Index, Public Aff. Inf. Serv. Bull., Recent Publ. Artic. LC DS63.1. DD 327.73017492705. bk rev adv acc. Circ 18,500. (ctrl). Definitive journal on US-ARAB commercial and political relations and events in the Middle East that affect US interests.

AMERICAN FOREIGN POLICY CURRENT DOCUMENTS (WASHINGTON, D.C. : 1984). (AMERICAN FOREIGN POLICY CURRENT DOCUMENTS). 1981-. 0501-9877. US. English. an. Superintendent of Documents, US Government Printing Office, Washington DC 20402. LC JX1417. DD 327.73. *American Foreign Policy Current Documents (Washington, D.C. : 1956), 0501-9877.*

AMERICAN PEACE DIRECTORY. See Yearbooks, Almanacs, Directories.

ANALISA. Indonesian. ir. Centre for Strategic and International Studies, Tanah Abang III/27, Jakarta Indonesia. LC JX18.

ANALISIS LATINOAMERICANO. VFOAT Analysis. Yearly V. 1-. 0195-9328. Periodical. US. Spanish. mo. $12.50. Associated Reporters, 130 West 42nd Street/Suite 1905, New York NY 10036.

I & P. VFOAT I and P. Periodical. English. mo. $50.00. I & P, B P 130-10, 75463 Paris Cedex 10 France. Tel (331)45262739. Ed Maxim Ghilan. LC DS119.7. DD 956.940505. bk rev. adv acc. Circ 10,000. Analysis and background of Middle East Conflict, with emphasis on Israeli-Palestinian relations, US Mideast policy. Exclusive investigative reporting. *Israel & Palestine.*

ANG KATIPUNAN. V. 1- Oct. 1-15, 1973-. Periodical. US. English. ir. $15.00. Ang Katipunan, PO Box 2759, Oakland CA 94602. Tel (415)547-6818. Ed Rene Cina Cruz. bk rev. Circ 2,000. News and news analysis on Philippines. Filipino minority experience in the U.S., domestic and international developments and featuring cultural/literary section.

ANNALES D'ETUDES INTERNATIONALES. VFOAT Annals of International Studies. V. 1- 1970-. 0066-2135. Multilingual (French and English). ir. 600. Etablissements Emile Bruylant, rue de la Regence 67, 1000 Brussels Belgium. Tel 02/512 98 45. Ind/Abst Am. Hist. Life, Hist. Abstr., Part A, Mod. Hist. Abstr., Hist. Abst., Part B, Twent. Century Abstr., Int. Labour Doc., Public Aff. Inf. Serv. Bull., Hist. Abstr.

ANNALI (ISTITUTO DI STUDI EUROPEI ALCIDE DE GASPERI). (ANNALI). Periodical. Italian. an. 12.00 Per Issue. LC JN2. DD 940.5505. *Bollettino (Istituto di Studi Europei Alcide de Gasperi).*

ANNOUNCEMENT OF PROGRAMS - JAPAN-UNITED STATES FRIENDSHIP COMMISSION. Main/Corp Japan-United States Friendship Commission. US. English (Japanese). an. Japan-United States Friendship Commission, 1875 Connecticut Avenue Northwest/Suite 709, Washington DC 20009.

ANNUAL REPORT - COUNCIL OF MARITIME PREMIERS. Main/Corp Council of Maritime Premiers. VFOAT Rapport Annuel. 1st- 1971/72-. 0380-0768. CN. English (text in French, with special title page and French text on inverted pages). an. Free. Council of Maritime Premiers, Box 2044, Halifax NS B3J 2Z1 Canada. Tel (902)424-7590. Ed Nancy MacCallum. LC HT395.C32. DD 309.2509715. Circ 2,100. Includes cooperative activities among three governments in economic development, communications, transportation, energy, education, federal-provincial relations, environment, Canada-US relations.

ANNUAL REPORT - COUNCIL ON FOREIGN RELATIONS, INC. Main/Corp Council on Foreign Relations. 0192-236X. US. English. an. Council on Foreign Relations, Harold Pratt House, 58 East Street, New York NY 10021. LC JX27.C6. DD 327.73006.

ANNUAL REVIEW - CATHOLIC INSTITUTE FOR INTERNATIONAL RELATIONS. Main/Corp Catholic Institute for International Relations. UK. English. an. 10.00 Domestic, 15.00 Foreign. CIIR, 22 Coleman Fields,

London N1 7AF United Kingdom. Tel (01)354-0883. Ed Francis McDonagh. Circ 3,200. Members receive: annual review, CIIR news, comments, church in the world, and other publications on world justice, development, and peace.

ANNUAL REVIEW - DEPARTMENT OF EXTERNAL AFFAIRS CEASED. (ANNUAL REVIEW). Main/Corp Canada. Dept. of External Affairs. VFOAT Canadian Foreign Relations, Revue Annuelle. VAT Canadian Foreign Relations. 1972-1981. 0315-9795. CN. English. an. Free. Department of External Affairs, Domestic Information Services Division, Ottawa Ontario K1A 0G2 Canada. Tel (613)996-9134. LC JX1515.A2. DD 327.71. Circ 10,000. A report on the activities of the Department of External Affairs. *Report of the Dept. of External Affairs.*

ARAB DAWN. (THE ARAB DAWN). VFOAT Al-Fajr Al-Arabiy. VAT Faja Al-Arabiu (1977). Vol. 1, No. 1 (Oct. 1977)-. 0715-4054. Periodical. CN. Arabic (text also in English). bm. $7.00. Canadian Arab Federation, PO Box 3003, Vancouver British Columbia Canada. DD 327.56940174927. *Arab Struggle, 0700-4079.*

ARAB PALESTINIAN RESISTANCE. Periodical. English. ir. Arab Palestinian Resistance, PO Box 3577, Damascus Syria. LC DS119.7. DD 327.5694017427.

ARAB PERSPECTIVES. VFOAT Mawaqqif Arabiyah. Vol. 1, No. 1 (Apr. 1980)-. 0733-5385. Periodical. US. English. mo. $10.00. Arab Perspectives, 747 Third Avenue, New York NY 10017. Ind/Abst Public Aff. Inf. Serv. Bull. LC DS36. DD 909.0492705.

ARAB REVIEW. (THE ARAB VIEW). Began in 1970. 8514-8578. English. ir. LC DS36. DD 320.9174927.

THE ARABS UNDER ISRAELI OCCUPATION. 1968-. LE. English and French. an. Institute for Palestine Studies, PO Box 11-7164, Beirut Lebanon. Tel 814174. LC DS127.6.O3. DD 956.046. Circ 3,000. Gives a day-to-day account of Israel's violations of Geneva conventions and universal declaration of rights of man in occupied Arab territories.

ARMS CONTROL TODAY. V. 4- Jan. 1974-. 0196-125X. Periodical. US. English. $40.00. Arms Control Association, 11 Dupont Circle NW, Washington, DC 20036. Tel (202)797-6450. Ed Robert Scott. Ind/Abst Predicasts, Funk Scott Index Corp. Ind. bk rev. adv acc. Circ 5,000. (ctrl). Deals with the latest developments in arms control negotiations and national security. Also provides updates on the nuclear arsenals of the superpowers. *ACA Newsletter.*

ASIAN SECURITY. 1979-. JA. English. an. $23.00. Maruzen Company Limited, PO Box 5050, 100-31 Tokyo Japan. LC DS35. DD 327.095.

ASIAN STUDIES CENTER BACKGROUNDER. VFOAT Backgrounder. No. 1 (Apr. 19, 1983)-. 0749-0062. Periodical. US. English. $2.00. The Heritage Foundation, 214 Massachusetts Avenue NE, Washington DC 20002. Tel (202)546-4400. Ed Burton Y Pines. DD 950. Periodic studies 5,000 to 20,000 words addressing issues affecting U.S.- Asian relations.

THE ATLANTIC COMMUNITY QUARTERLY. V. 1- Mar. 1963-. 0004-6760. Periodical. US. English. qt. $18.00. Heldref Publications, 4000 Albemarle Street NW, Washington DC 20016. Tel (202)362-6445. Ed Chuck Hagner. Ind/Abst Predicasts, ABC Pol Sci, Soc. Sci. Index, Public Aff. Inf. Serv. Bull., Energy Res. Abstr., Humanit. Index, Funk Scott Index Corp. Ind., Am. Hist. Life, Hist. Abstr., Part A, Mod. Hist. Abstr., Hist. Abst., Part B, Twent. Century Abstr. LC D839. adv acc. Circ 1,900. The best current thought on both sides of the Atlantic concerning the problems and prospects for more effective cooperative action among the nations of the North Atlantic area.

ATLANTIC SERIES : A COLLECTION OF STUDIES ON SUBJECTS RELATED TO THE NORTH ATLANTIC TREATY ORGANIZATION. VFOAT Serie Atlantique. Vol. 1 1963-. 0571-7868. Monographic Series. English, French or German. ir. Academic Book Services Holland, PO Box 66, Groningen The Netherlands.

AUSSENWIRTSCHAFT. VFOAT Zeitschrift fur Internationale Wirtschaftsbeziehungen. V. 1- March 1946-. 0004-8216. Periodical. German. qt. $39.09. Verlag Ruegger, Unterdorf 65, CH 7274 Grusch

Political Science—International Relations

Switzerland. Tel 081 42 22 44. Ind/Abst Public Aff. Inf. Serv. Bull., Foreign Lang. Index, PAIS Foreign Lang. Index. bk rev adv acc. (ctrl). The review is for leading personalities in economy law and politics as for scientists in economy.

AUSTRALIAN FOREIGN AFFAIRS RECORD. V. 44- Jan. 1973-. 0311-7995. Periodical. AT. English. mo. $33.94. Australia Government Publishing Service, PO Box 84, Canberra Australian Capital Territory 2600 Australia. Tel (062)954411. Ind/Abst APAIS, Aust. Public Aff. Inf. Serv., Public Aff. Inf. Serv. Bull., Energy Res. Abstr., Am. Hist. Life, Hist. Abstr., Hist. Abstr., Part A, Mod. Hist. Abstr., Hist. Abst., Part B, Twent. Century Abstr. LC JX1162. DD 327.94. *Current Notes on International Affairs.*

AUSTRALIAN OUTLOOK. (THE AUSTRALIAN OUTLOOK). V. 1- March 1947-. 0004-9913. Periodical. AT. English. ty. 23.00 Domestic, 35.00 Foreign. Australian Institute of International Affairs, Box E 181 Post Office, Canberra Australian Capital Territory 2600 Australia. Tel (062)51-5500. Ed Richard Higgott. Ind/Abst Am. Hist. Life, Hist. Abstr., Part A, Mod. Hist. Abstr., Hist. Abst., Part B, Twent. Century Abstr., Predicasts, ABC Pol Sci, Hist. Abstr., APAIS, Aust. Public Aff. Inf. Serv., Public Aff. Inf. Serv. Bull., Funk Scott Index Corp. Ind., Soc. Sci. Citation Index, Recent Publ. Artic. LC DU80. DD 327.94005. bk rev. adv acc. Circ 3,000. (ctrl). Authoritative journal on international relations articles by distinguished Australian and international scholars on foreign policy, trade, economies, diplomatic history, defense and strategic studies. *Austral-Asiatic Bulletin.*

BACKGROUND INFORMATION (COMMISSION OF THE CHURCHES ON INTERNATIONAL AFFAIRS). (BACKGROUND INFORMATION). Began publication in: 1978. English. ir. 20.-. Commission of the Churches on International Affairs of the World Council of Churches, 150 Route de Ferney, 1211 Geneva 20 Switzerland. Tel (022)916111. Ed Erich Weingartner. LC UNC. DD 261.8705. Circ 3,000. Provides for church-related institutions, information and analyses on current issues in international relations, e.g. human rights, conflict-situations, militarism, disarmament, peace, etc. *CCIA Background Information.*

BANGLADESH IN INTERNATIONAL AFFAIRS : MONTHLY BULLETIN OF THE BANGLADESH INSTITUTE OF LAW AND INTERNATIONAL AFFAIRS. Periodical. English. mo. LC DS394.7. DD 327.549205.

B.C. PEACE NEWS. (B. C. PEACE NEWS). VAT British Columbia Peace News. Sept. 1978-. 0708-0859. CN. English. British Columbia Peace Council, 712-207 West Hastings Street, Vancouver British Columbia V6B 1H7 Canada. DD 32717405. *B. C. News, 0708-0840.*

BEHIND THE HEADLINES. V. 1- Sept. 1940-. 0005-7983. CN. English. ir. $6.00. Canadian Institute of International Affairs, 15 King College Circle, Toronto Ontario M5S 2V9 Canada. Tel (416)979-1851. Ed Kim Richard Nossal. Ind/Abst Hist. Abstr., Am. Hist. Life, Hist. Abstr., Part A, Mod. Hist. Abstr., Hist. Abst., Part B, Twent. Century Abstr. LC F1034. DD 971.0082. Circ 3,000. International affairs with emphasis on economic political, social diplomatic and defence roles of Canada.

BEITRAGE ZUR KONFLIKTFORSCHUNG. Vol. 1-. 0045-169X. Periodical. GW. German. qt. $26.62. Markus Verlag GMBH, Hohenzollernring 85/87, Koeln West Germany. Ind/Abst Coal Abstr., Energy Res. Abstr., Soc. Sci. Citation Index. LC JX5.

BIBLIOGRAPHICAL SERIES - SOUTH AFRICAN INSTITUTE OF INTERNATIONAL AFFAIRS. See Bibliographies.

BIBLIOGRAPHY SERIES - NORMAN PATERSON SCHOOL OF INTERNATIONAL AFFAIRS. See Bibliographies.

BIISS JOURNAL. VFOAT B.I.I.S.S. Journal. Vol. 1, No. 1-. Periodical. English. ir. $3.00. Publications Officer, Bangladesh Institute of International and Strategic Studies, 1/46 Elephant Road, Dacca Bangladesh. LC D839. DD 327.09048.

BOLETIN DEL CENTRO DE RELACIONES INTERNACIONELES. Main/Corp Mexico (City). Universidad Nacional. Centro de Relaciones Internacionales. Periodical. Spanish. ir. LC D843.

BOLETIN DIPLOMATICO; PANORAMA MUNDIAL. VFOAT Boletin Diplomatico y Consular. Yearly V. 1- (No. 1-). Periodical. Spanish. ir.

BOZZE. V. 1, No. 1 (Jan. 1978)-. Periodical. IT. Italian. mo. 45.000. Edizioni Dedalo, Casella Postale 3628, 70100 Bari Italy. Tel (080)371555. bk rev. adv acc. Circ 6,000. Research of peace and war, arms race, love as political problem, USA-USSR, rights and liberation of peoples, Christianity, Roman Catholic Church, American bishops and deterrence in Latin America.

BRITISH JOURNAL OF INTERNATIONAL STUDIES. V. 1-6. 0305-8026. Periodical. UK. English. ty. Longman, 4th Avenue Harlow, Essex CM19 5AA England. LC JX1. DD 327.05.

BULLETIN OFFICIEL - MINISTERE DES RELATIONS EXTERIEURES. (BULLETIN OFFICIEL). 0751-0772. FR. French. ir. Journaux Officiels, 26 rue Desaix, 75727 Paris Cedex 15 France. *Bulletin Officiel (France. Ministere des Affaires Etrangeres).*

CALIFORNIA INTERNATIONAL TRADE REGISTER. 1980/81-. 0270-4862. US. English. be. $59.95. Times-Mirror Press, 1115 South Boyle Avenue, Los Angeles CA 90023. LC HF5065.C2. DD 382.0294794.

CANADA IN WORLD AFFAIRS. V. 1- 1941-. 0068-7685. CN. English. ir. Canadian Institute for International Affairs, 15 King College Circle, Toronto Ontario M5S 2V9 Canada. Tel (416)979-1851. Each volume provides a comprehensive history and analysis of Canada's activities abroad and foreign policy for the two years which the volume covers.

CANADIAN REPRESENTATIVES ABROAD AND REPRESENTATIVES OF OTHER COUNTRIES IN CANADA. Main/Corp Canada. Dept. of External Affairs. Periodical. CN. English. an. Receiver General for Canada, Supply & Services, Ottawa Ontario K1A 0S9 Canada. LC JX1729.A2. DD 327.71.

CANADIAN STRATEGIC REVIEW. (THE CANADIAN STRATEGIC REVIEW). 1982-. 0824-2216. CN. English. an. Canadian Institute of Strategic Studies, Suite 100/175 Bloor Street East, Toronto Ontario M4W 1E1 Canada. DD 355.021.

LE CANADO-AMERICAIN. V. 1-7, 1958-1972. Periodical. US. English. qt. Association Canado American, 52 Concord Street, Manchester NH 03101.

THE CARIBBEAN YEARBOOK OF INTERNATIONAL RELATIONS. See Yearbooks, Almanacs, Directories.

CARN. No. 1- Spring 1973-. Periodical. Celtic (English). ir.

CARTA DEL DESARROLLO. V. 1- June 1978-. 0250-6106. Periodical. US. Spanish. mo. General Secretariat, OAS, Washington DC 20006. LC WMLC L 83/430.

CAUSA INTERNATIONAL SEMINAR SERIES. 0882-4878. Monographic Series. US. English. mo. Causa International, 401 Fifth Avenue, New York NY 10016. DD 327.

CHATHAM HOUSE PAPERS. Began in 1979. 0143-5795. Monographic Series. UK. English. ir. 24.00. Routledge & Kegan Paul, Broadway House, Newtown Road, Henley-Thames RG9 1EN England. Tel 0491578321. LC UNC. Circ 80. These papers have become recognized as valuable and authoritative guides to some of the most important policy debates on critical issues of foreign policy.

CHINA & THE WORLD. Series/Titl Beijing Review Foreign Affairs Series. VFOAT China and the World. 1-. English. ir. Beijing Review, 24 Baiwanzhuang Road, Beijing China. LC DS779.27. DD 327.51.

CHINA INTERNATIONAL BUSINESS. See Business.

CHRISTEN DEMOCRATISCHE VERKENNINGEN : MAANDBLAD VAN HET WETENSCHAPPELIJK INSTITUUT VOOR HET CDA. 0/81-. Periodical. NE. Dutch. mo $16.17. Dr Kuyperstraat 5, 2415 Ba Den Haag Netherlands. LC JN5981. *Ar Staatkunde in Christian-Democratisch Perspectief, Christelijk Historisch Tijdschrift; Politiek Perspectief.*

UN CHRONICLE. VAT United Nations Chronicle. Vol. 12, No. 4 (Apr. 1975)-. 0379-0959. Periodical. US. English. mo. $14.00. United Nations Publications, Sales Section Room A 3315, New York NY 10017. Tel (212)754-8324. Ind/Abst Read. Guide Period. Lit., Soc. Sci. Index. LC JX1977.A1. DD 341.2305. Records and analyzes current international questions considered by the United Nations. *UN Monthly Chronicle.*

CHRONIQUE DU CONTROLE DES ARMEMENTS. (LA CHRONIQUE DU CONTROLE DES ARMEMENTS). No. 1 (Mar. 1984)-. 0825-1932. Periodical. CN. French. mo. Free to Members. Centre Canadien pour le Controle des Armements et le Desarmement, 5E Etage 275 rue Slater, Ottawa Ontario K1P 5H9 Canada. DD 327.17405.

CHRONOLOGIES OF MAJOR DEVELOPMENTS IN SELECTED AREAS OF FOREIGN AFFAIRS. CUMULATIVE EDITION. (CHRONOLOGIES OF MAJOR DEVELOPMENTS IN SELECTED AREAS OF FOREIGN AFFAIRS). 1979-. 0278-8365. US. English. an. LC D839. DD 327.09047. *Chronologies of Major Developments in Related Areas of International Relations (Cumulative Edition), 0278-8357.*

CHUNG MEI KUAN HSI PAO KAO. 1980-. CH. Chinese (English). an. Chung Yan Yen Chiu Yuan Mei-Kuo Wen Hua Yen Chiu So Nan-Kang, Taipei Taiwan China. LC E183.8.T3. DD 327.51249073.

CIRCA. CONFLITS INTERNATIONAUX, LES REGIONS ET LE CANADA. (CIRCA). Series/Titl Collection Etudes Strategiques et Militaires. VFOAT Rapport Annuel sur Les Conflits Regionaux et Intra-Regionaux. 0822-8418. CN. French (summaries in English). an. $10,00. Centre Quebecois de Relations Internationales, Pavillon de Koninck, Universite Laval, Quebec G1K 7P4 Canada. DD 327.1105.

CO-EXISTENCE (GLASGOW, STRATHCLYDE). (CO-EXISTENCE). Began in 1964. 0587-5994. Periodical. UK. English. ty. $58.00. Martinus Nijhoff Publishers, PO Box 163, Spui Boulevard 50, 3300 AD Dordrecht Netherlands. Tel 78-334248. Ed Stephen White and Rene Beermann. Ind/Abst ABC Pol Sci, Sociol. Abstr., Soc. Welf. Soc. Plan./Policy Soc. Dev., Soc. Sci. Citation Index, Am. Hist. Life, Hist. Abstr., Lang. Lang. Behav. Abstr., Hist. Abstr., Part A, Mod. Hist. Abstr., Hist. Abst., Part B, Twent. Century Abstr. LC H1. DD 300.5. bk rev. adv acc. A journal of international affairs specializing in east-west and development issues.

COLLECTION DE RELATIONS INTERNATIONALES. 1-. Monographic Series. NE. text in French and English. ir. Academic Book Services Holland, PO Box 66, Groningen the Netherlands.

COMMENTS ON CURRENT WORLD AFFAIRS. 1- (1962)-. Periodical. US. English. bw. 2372 Veteran Avenue, Los Angeles CA 90064.

COMPARATIVE STRATEGY. V. 1-. 0149-5933. Periodical. US. English. ir. $54.00. Crane Russak & Company, 3 East 44th Street, New York NY 10017. Tel (212)867-1490. Ed Richard B Foster. Ind/Abst Predicasts, Public Aff. Inf. Serv. Bull., Recent Publ. Artic. LC JX1. DD 327.05. CODEN COSTDY. bk rev. adv acc. Circ 800. Examines the political, military, and economic components of international affairs.

COMUNITA INTERNAZIONALE. (LA COMUNITA INTERNAZIONALE). Vol. 1 Jan 1946-. 0010-5066. Periodical. Italian. qt. $28.52. Cedam, Via Japelli 5, 35121 Padova Italy. Ind/Abst ABC Pol Sci, Foreign Lang. Index, Am. Hist. Life, Hist. Abstr., Hist. Abstr., Part A, Mod. Hist. Abstr., Hist. Abst., Part B, Twent. Century Abstr.

CONFLICT QUARTERLY. (CONFLICT QUARTERLY : JOURNAL OF THE CENTRE FOR CONFLICT STUDIES, UNIVERSITY OF NEW BRUNSWICK). Vol. 1, No. 1 (Summer 1980)-. 0227-1311. Periodical. CN. English. qt. University of New Brunswick, Centre for Conflict Studies, Fredericton New Brunswick E3B 5A3 Canada. Tel (506)453-4587. Ed David Charters. Ind/Abst Public Aff. Inf. Serv. Bull. DD 327.16. bk rev. adv acc. Circ 500. Low intensity conflict: terrorism, propagnada, unconventional warfare, intelligence, special operations, counterinsurgency, revolutionary and civil wars, psychological warfare.

CONFLICT STUDIES. No. 1-. 0069-8792. Monographic Series. UK. English. mo. $122.59. Institute Study of Conflict, 12/12A Golden Square, London W1R 3AF England. Tel 01-439 7381. Ed Josephine O'Connor Howe. bk rev. adv acc. Circ 1,200. Publications on all aspects of conflict.

Political Science—International Relations

CONGRESSIONAL PRESENTATION, FISCAL YEAR. (CONGRESSIONAL PRESENTATION, FISCAL YEAR . . .). Main/Corp United States. International Development Cooperation Agency. 1982-. 0276-6469. US. English. an. LC HC60. DD 338.91730172405.

CONSULAR LIST AND LIST OF INTERNATIONAL ORGANIZATIONS. Main/Corp Burma (Union). Ministry of Foreign Affairs. English. ir. 75.00. Ministry of Foreign Affairs, 529/531 Merchant Street, Ragoon Burma. LC JX1859.B8. DD 327.2025591.

CONTEMPORARY AFFAIRS. No. 1- 1939-. 0384-9333. Periodical. CN. English. ir. Canadian Institute of International Affairs, 15 Kings College Circle, Toronto Ontario M5S 2V9 Canada. Tel (416)979-1851. LC UNC. Circ 1,500. Each volume deals with some aspect of current international affairs or Canadian foreign policy.

COOPERATION; BULLETIN OF THE STUDENTS OF I.C.I. V. 1- Jan./March 1977-. 0704-1926. Periodical. CN. English (French). ir. Free. M Chibba, Editor Cooperation, Institute for International for International Co-Operation, University of Ottawa, 192 Laurier Avenue East, Ottawa Ontario K1N 6N5 Canada. DD 327.1705.

COUNCIL SPOTLIGHT BOOKNOTES. (COUNCIL SPOTLIGHT BOOKNOTES : A PUBLICATION OF THE WORLD AFFAIRS COUNCIL OF NORTHERN CALIFORNIA). VFOAT Booknotes. 0740-1183. Periodical. US. English. bm. $5.00. World Affairs Council of Northern California, World Affairs Center, 312 Sutter Street/Suite 200, San Francisco CA 94108. Tel (415)982-2541. Ed Lone C Beeson. bk rev. Circ 10,00. Recent books on world affairs and area studies annotated list and book reviews.

COVERTACTION INFORMATION BULLETIN. VFOAT Covert Action Information Bulletin. No. 1 (July 1978)-. 0275-309X. Periodical. US. English. qt $20.00. Covert Action Publications Inc, PO Box 50272, Washington DC 20004. Tel (202)737-5317. Ed Elen Ray, William Schaap and Louis Wolf. Ind/Abst Altern. Press Index. LC JK468.I6. DD 327.120973. bk rev. Circ 3,000. (ctrl). Reports on undercover actvities of US and western intelligence agencies, revealing a usually invisible level of international policymaking.

CROSSROADS. (CROSSROADS : TRENDS & ISSUES OF CONTEMPORARY SOCIETY). VAT Crossroads : Trends and Issues on Comtemporary Society. No. 1- Autumn 1978-. 0334-4649. Periodical. English. ir $40.00. Crane Russak & Company Inc, 3 East 44th Street, New York NY 10017. Tel (212)867-1490. Ed Ilya Zemtsov. Ind/Abst Sociol. Abstr., Soc. Welf. Soc. Plan./Policy Soc. Dev. LC HM1. DD 905. bk rev. adv acc. Circ 600. Focuses on the communist world, the Middle East, and international affairs.

THE CTC REPORTER. Main/Corp United Nations. Centre on Transnational Corporations. VAT Centre on Transnational Corporations Reporter. V. 1- Dec. 1976-. Periodical. US. English (summaries in French and Spanish). sa. $20.00. United Nations Publications, Sales Section Room A-3315, New York NY 10017. Tel (212)754-8324. Ind/Abst Public Aff. Inf. Serv. Bull. LC HD2755.5. DD 338.88. Reports on the activities of international transnational corporations.

CUBAN CHRONOLOGY. 0195-8135. US. English. Document Expediting Project, Exchange and Gift Division, Library of Congress, Photoduplication Service, Washington DC 20540. LC F1788. DD 327.7291.

CULTURE AND LIFE. Jan. 1957-. Periodical. UR. English (French, German, Russian and Spanish). mo. $15.20. Culture & Life, 70454. Tel (212)533-0250. LC DK1. DD 327.47.

CURRENT BIBLIOGRAPHICAL INFORMATION. See Bibliographies.

CURRENT WORLD LEADERS. VFOAT Biography & News. V. 21, No. 4- Apr. 1978-. 0192-6802. Periodical. US. English. ir. $130.00. International Academy at Santa Barbara, 2060 Alameda Padre Serra, Santa Barbara CA 93103. Tel (805)965-5010. Ed Thomas S Garrison. LC D839. DD 327.09045. Current directory of world leaders plus issues focusing on special topics or geopolitical areas; original articles, socioeconomic-political backgrounders, speeches, reports, and key biographies. Current World Leaders. Almanac, 0002-6255; Current World Leaders. Biography and News, 0002-6263; Current World Leaders. Speeches and Reports, 0092-1386.

DAILY REPORT : ASIA & PACIFIC. INDEX. See Indexes/Abstracts.

DARSTELLUNGEN ZUR AUSWARTIGEN POLITIK. 1- 1960-. 0418-3894. Periodical. GW. German. ir. W Kohlhammer Verlag, Hessbruehlstrasse 69 PF 800430, 7 Stuttgart 80 West Germany.

DEADLINE DATA ON WORLD AFFAIRS. Began with: Vol. 1, No. 1 (1955). 0011-5061. Periodical. US. English. wk. ABC-Clio Press, Box 4397 2050 APS, Santa Barbara CA 93103. Tel (805)963-4221. Ed Paul L Pearson.

DEFENSE & FOREIGN AFFAIRS' WEEKLY REPORT ON STRATEGIC AFRICAN AFFAIRS. VFOAT Weekly Report on Strategic African Affairs. VAT Defense and Foreign Affairs' Weekly Report on Strategic African Affairs. 0193-9181. Periodical. US. English. wk. $197.00 including Defense & Foreign Affairs Digest. Copely & Associates S A, 2030 M Street NW, Washington DC 20036.

DETENTE (BIRMINGHAM, WEST MIDLANDS, ENGLAND). (DETENTE). Began publication with: No. 1 (Oct. 1984). 0267-3169. Periodical. UK. English. qt. $18.00. Centre for Russian and East European Studies, University of Birmingham, PO Box 363, Birmingham B15 2TT England.

DEUTSCHE AUSSENPOLITIK. Vol. 1-. 0011-9881. Periodical. GE. German. mo. Kunst & Wissen Erich Bieber, Dufourstrasse 51, CH-8008 Zurich Switzerland. Ind/Abst Am. Hist., Life, Hist. Abstr., Part A, Mod. Hist. Abstr., Hist. Abst., Part B, Twent. Century Abstr., Energy Res. Abstr., Hist. Abstr. LC DD261.4. DD 327.

DEUTSCHE AUSSENPOLITIK. SONDERHEFTE CEASED. 0418-8152. Periodical. German. ir. Deutscher Buch Export-Import, Leninstrasse 16, DDR 701 Leipzig Germany.

DEVELOPMENT AND FOREIGN POLICY REPORT CEASED. Began with V. 1. No. 1 (May-June 1984). 8756-7466. Periodical. US. English. qt. $15.00. Association for Development Policy Research, 1309 L Street Northwest, Washington DC 20005. DD 327.

DEVELOPMENT, USE AND CONTROL OF NUCLEAR ENERGY FOR THE COMMON DEFENSE AND SECURITY AND FOR PEACEFUL PURPOSES. Main/Corp United States. Congress. Joint Committee on Atomic Energy. 1st- 1975-. 0360-4349. US. English. an. $1.30. Superintendent of Documents, US Government Printing Office, Washington DC 20402. LC JX1974.7. DD 327.174.

DIBLUMASI (JIDDAH, SAUDI ARABIA). (AL-DIBLUMASI). Periodical. SA. Arabic. ir. PO Box 7954, Juddah Saudi Arabia. LC JX18.

DIPLOMACY. Periodical. English. ir. $2.24. Diplomacy Company, CPO Box 2672, Seoul South Korea. LC D839. DD 327.05.

DIPLOMATIC AND CONSULAR LIST. Main/Corp Uganda. Ministry of Foreign Affairs. UG. English. ir. Uganda Ministry of Foreign Affairs, PO Box 33, Entebee Uganda. LC JX1873.U33. DD 327.20256761. Diplomatic Missions and Other Representatives in Uganda.

DIPLOMATIC CORPS AND CONSULAR AND OTHER REPRESENTATIVES IN CANADA CEASED. VFOAT Corps Diplomatique et Representants Consulaires et Autres au Canada. June 1969-Nov. 1982. 0486-4514. Periodical. CN. English (text in French). sa. Receiver General for Canada, Supply & Services, Ottawa Ontario K1A 0S9 Canada. LC JX1729.A2. DD 351.8920971. Diplomatic Corps, 0527-6837; Representatives of Other Countries in Canada, 0706-8433.

DIPLOMATIC CORPS AND CONSULAR, TRADE, AND OTHER FOREIGN REPRESENTATIVES IN PAKISTAN. English. ir. LC JX1859.P3. DD 351.892095491. List of the Diplomatic Corps and Consular, Trade and Other Foreign Representatives.

DIPLOMATIC CORPS. MINISTRY OF EXTERNAL AFFAIRS. (DIPLOMATIC CORPS - MINISTRY OF EXTERNAL AFFAIRS). Main/Corp Jamaica. Ministry of External Affairs. 0376-8384. English. ir. 24 East Race Course, PO Box 624, Kingston Jamaica. LC JX1753. DD 327.20257292.

DIPLOMATIC LIST. Main/Corp Burma (Union). Ministry of Foreign Affairs. 0377-6905. US. English. qt. Superintendent of Documents, US Government Printing Office, Washington DC 20402. Tel (202)783-3238. LC JX1859.B8. DD 327.2025591.

THE DIPLOMATIC WORLD BULLETIN AND DELEGATES WORLD BULLETIN. VFOAT Diplomatic World Bulletin. 1971. 0363-8200. Periodical. US. English. ir. $120.00. Diplomatic World Bulletin, 99 Wall Street, New York NY 10005. Tel (212)806-1500. LC JX1977.A1. DD 341.2305. adv acc. Circ 13,500. Delegates World Bulletin.

THE DIPLOMATIST; A REVIEW OF THE DIPLOMATIC AND CONSULAR WORLD. V. 1- Aug. 1947-. 0012-3110. Periodical. UK. English. mo. $70.00. Diplomatist Associates Ltd, Bedford Row House, 58 Theobalds Road, London WC1X 8SF England. Ed Vanessa Peet. LC JX1. adv acc. Circ 3,034. (ctrl). House journal for foreign diplomatic community in London containing coverage of diplomatic receptions, interviews with ambassadors, etc.

DIRASAT DAWLIYAH. VFOAT Etudes Internationales. No. 1. Periodical. Arabic (French). qt. $19.00. 1 rue du Venezuala, Tunis Tunisia. LC D839.

DIRECTORY OF PERSONNEL OF UNITED NATIONS ORGANIZATIONS AND THE INTERNATIONAL MONETARY FUND IN THE DEMOCRATIC REPUBLIC OF THE SUDAN. See Yearbooks, Almanacs, Directories.

DIRECTORY OF RETIRED MEMBERS - AMERICAN FOREIGN SERVICE ASSOCIATION. See Yearbooks, Almanacs, Directories.

DIRECTORY OF THE DIPLOMATIC CORPS AND INTERNATIONAL ORGANIZATIONS. See Yearbooks, Almanacs, Directories.

DISARMAMENT. V. 1- May 1978-. Periodical. US. English. ir. $6.00. United Nations, Sales Section Room A3315, New York NY 10017. Tel (212)754-8303. Ind/Abst Public Aff. Inf. Serv. Bull. LC JX1974. DD 327.17405. United Nations review on questions related to disarmament, peace and security.

DISARMAMENT NEWS & INTERNATIONAL VIEWS. VAT Disarmament News and International Views. 0363-3721. Periodical. US. English. mo. $20.00. Council on Religion and International Affairs, 170 East 64th Street, New York NY 10021. LC JX1974.7. DD 327.17405. Disarmament News & Views, 0275-794X.

DISINFORMATION. VFOAT Soviet Active Measures and Disinformation Forecast. Fall 1985-. 0885-2529. Periodical. US. English. qt. Regnery Gateway Inc, 1815 H Street NW/Suite 600, Washington DC 20006. DD 327.

DISMANTLER. (THE DISMANTLER). Vol. 1, No. 1-. 0711-3765. Periodical. CN. English. ir. $1.00 Per Number. Operation Dismantle, Box 3887, Station C, Ottawa Ontario K1Y 4M5 Canada. DD 327.17405.

DOCUMENTS LIST. See Bibliographies.

DOCUMENTS ON BRITISH FOREIGN POLICY, 1919-1939. Main/Corp Great Britain. Foreign Office. UK. English. ir. Her Majestys Stationery Office, PO Box 569, London SE1 England. Tel 01-211 3000. LC DA566.7. DD 327.42 942.08.

DOCUMENTS ON CANADIAN EXTERNAL RELATIONS. Main/Corp Canada. Department of External Affairs. VFOAT Documents on Canadian External Affairs. Vol. 1 1967-. CN. English. Receiver General for Canada Supply and Services, Ottowa Ontario K1A 0S9 Canada.

DOGAR MONTHLY GENERAL KNOWLEDGE DIGEST. VFOAT General Knowledge Digest. Periodical. English. mo. Dogar Brothers, 17 Urdu Bazar, Lahore Pakistan. LC D839. DD 909.828. Dogar's Monthly General Knowledge Digest.

DOORS TO LATIN AMERICA CEASED. V. 1-28, No. 1. 0012-5490. Periodical. US. English. qt. Ed A C Wilgus. World Affairs.

DYASON HOUSE PAPERS. V. 1- Aug. 1974-. 0311-3965. Periodical. AT. English. qt. 5.00 Domestic, 9.00 Foreign. Australian Institute of International Affairs, Victorian Branch, Dyason House,

Political Science—International Relations

124 Joliment Road, Melbourne Australia 3002. **Tel** (03)63-6199. Ed Andrew J Perry. **Ind/Abst** APAIS, Aust. Public Aff. Inf. Serv. **LC** D839. **DD** 327.05. **Circ** 1,500. *Australia's Neighbours.*

EAST ASIAN EXECUTIVE REPORTS. V. 1- Sept. 1979-. 0272-1589. Periodical. US. English. mo. $795.00. East Asian Executive Reports, 717 D Street NW/Suite 300, Washington DC 20004-2807. **Tel** (202)628-6900. Ed Stephen Sotle. **Ind/Abst** Leg. Resour. Index, Nexis. **DD** 346.507. adv acc. **Circ** 400. Publication covering the financial, legal and practical aspects of conducting business in East Asia.

EAST-WEST COMMERCIAL RELATIONS SERIES. Began publication in Aug. 1973. 0318-1316. Monographic Series. CN. English. Institute of Soviet and East European Studies, Carleton University, Ottawa Ontario K1S 5B6 Canada. **Tel** (613)564-3798. Ed C H McMillan. **LC** UNC. **DD** 382.09171301717. **Circ** 300. East-West commercial relations. Political aspects of Soviet energy resources.

EAST-WEST DIGEST. V. 1- Apr. 1965-. 0012-8627. Periodical. UK. English. bw. Foreign Affairs Publ Co, 139 Petersham Road, Richmond Surrey Twio 7AA England. **LC** D839. **DD** 327.091717.

EGYPT NEWSLETTER. VFOAT Newsletter Egypt. 0142-9310. Periodical. UK. English. bw. $350.00. International Communications Publications Ltd, Suite 1121/122 East-42nd Street, New York NY 10017.

EMBASSY. Periodical. UK. English. Novel Publishers Ltd, 132 Wardour Street, W1 London England. **LC** JX1. **DD** 327.05.

EMBASSY REPORT (AFRICA ED.). (EMBASSY REPORT). Vol. 1, No. 1 (Saturday Feb. 26-Friday Mar. 4, 1983)-. 0883-1815. Periodical. US. English. wk. Embassy Report, PO Box 6802, Falls Church VA 22043. **DD** 327.

EMBASSY REPORT (ASIA & OCEANIA EDITION). (EMBASSY REPORT). Vol. 1, No. 1 (Saturday Feb. 26-Friday Mar. 4, 1983)-. 0883-1823. Periodical. US. English. wk. Embassy Report, PO Box 6802, Falls Church VA 22046. **DD** 327.

EMBASSY REPORT (EDITION AUSTRALIA, CANADA, JAPAN, NEW ZEALAND, SCANDINAVIA & WESTERN EUROPE). (EMBASSY REPORT). Vol. 1, No. 1 (Saturday Feb. 26-Friday Mar. 4, 1983)-. 0883-1807. Periodical. US. English. wk. Embassy Report, PO Box 6802, Falls Church VA 22046. **DD** 327.

EMBASSY REPORT (EDITION EASTERN EUROPE & UNION OF SOCIET SOCIALIST REPUBLIC SIC). (EMBASSY REPORT). Vol. 1, No. 1 (Saturday Feb. 26-Friday Mar. 4, 1983)-. 0883-1785. Periodical. US. English. wk. Embassy Report, PO Box 6802, Falls Church VA 22043. **DD** 327.

EMBASSY REPORT (LATIN AMERICA & CARIBBEAN EDITION). (EMBASSY REPORT). 0882-9683. Periodical. US. English. ir. Embassy Report, PO Box 6802, Falls Church VA 22046. **DD** 327.

EMBASSY REPORT (MIDDLE EAST ED.). (EMBASSY REPORT). Vol. 1, No. 1 (Saturday Feb. 26-Friday Mar. 4, 1983)-. 0883-1793. Periodical. US. English. wk. Embassy Report, PO Box 6802, Falls Church VA 22043. **DD** 327.

EMPLOYEES OF DIPLOMATIC MISSIONS. 0501-9664. Periodical. US. English. qt. Superintendent of Documents, US Government Printing Office, Washington DC 20402. **Tel** (202)783-3238. **LC** JX1705.

ENVOY INTERNATIONAL (ASHFORD, KENT : 1981). (ENVOY INTERNATIONAL). Vol. 4, No. 1 (Mar. 1981)-. 0140-2935. Periodical. UK. English. mo. $42.50 (Air-Speeded). Envoy International, PO Box 1305, Long Island City NY 11101. **LC** AP4. **DD** 052. *Ambassador & Envoy International.*

EST & ET OUEST. VAT Est et Ouest. No. 143-145. Periodical. French. sm. **LC** D839. *B.E.I.P.I.*

ESTADOS UNIDOS, PERSPECTIVA LATINOAMERICANA. VFOAT Cuadernos Semestrales. No. 1-. Monographic Series. MX. Spanish. sa. $16.00. Cide, Apartado Postal 116-114, Mexico 01130 Mexico.

ESTUDIOS INTERNACIONALES. (ESTUDIOS INTERNACIONALES : REVISTA DEL INSTITUTO DE ESTUDIOS INTERNACIONALES DE LA UNIVERSIDAD DE CHILE). V. 1-3, No. 2. 0014-1518. Periodical. CL. Spanish. qt. $40.00. Corporacionn de Estudios Internacionales, Universidad de Chile, Casilla 14187, Sucursal 21, Santiago Chile. **Ind/Abst** Am. Hist. Life, Hist. Abstr., ABC Pol Sci, Foreign Lang. Index, Am. Hist. Life, Hist. Abstr., Part A, Mod. Hist. Abstr., Hist. Abst., Part B, Twent. Century Abstr.

ESTUDIOS INTERNACIONALES. Spanish. ir. Facultad de Ciencias Politicas y Sociales, Universidad Nacional Autonoma de Mexico, Apartado 3368, Panama 4 Panama. **LC** JX9. **DD** 327.05.

ETAT DU MONDE. See Yearbooks, Almanacs, Directories.

ETINCELLE. (L'ETINCELLE : ORGANE DU COMITE PROVISOIRE DU FRONT UNI). V. 1, No. 1 (March 22, 1975)-. 9001-2378. Periodical. CN. French. l'Etincelle, CP 185, Succursale Outremont, Montreal Quebec Canada. **DD** 327.0904.

ETUDES INTERNATIONALES. V. 1- Feb. 1970-. 0014-2123. Periodical. CN. French. qt. 40.00. Centre Quebecois Relations International, Pavillon de Koninck/Bureau 2466 University, Laval Quebec G1K 7P4 Canada. **Tel** (418)656-2462. **Ind/Abst** ABC Pol Sci, Am. Hist. Life, Foreign Lang. Index, Hist. Abstr., Int. Labour Doc., Point Repere. **LC** D849. bk rev. adv acc. **Circ** 1,500. (ctrl). A multidisciplinary journal devoted to international affairs.

ETUDES POLITIQUES. Yearly V. 5-. French. ir. 13.00. Institut Suisse de Recherche Sur les Pays de l'Est, Jubilaumsstrasse 41, CH J.A. 3000, 6 Berne Switzerland. **LC** D839. **DD** 327.05. *Bulletin d'Etudes Politiques.*

EUROPA ARCHIV. See Genealogy and Heraldry - Archives.

EUROPE. See Business - Commerce.

EUROPE AND LATIN AMERICA. 1980-. UK. English. an. 1.95. Latin America Bureau, PO Box 134, London NW1 4JY England. **LC** F1416.G7. **DD** 327.4108. *Britain and Latin America.*

EUROPE EN FORMATION. (L'EUROPE EN FORMATION). 1.- Year (No. 1-). 0014-2808. Periodical. FR. French. qt. 135. Presses d Europe, 4 Boulevard Carabacel, F-06000 Nice France. **Tel** 93 858557. bk rev. adv acc. **Circ** 2,000. Problems of European unity and international relationships, federalism and regionalism.

EUROPE INFORMATION. EXTERNAL RELATIONS. Periodical. English. ir. rue de la Loi 200, B-L049 Brussels Belgium.

EUROPE, PORTUGAL : FAITS ET IDEES. No. 6- Aug. 25, 1976-. Periodical. French. ir. 35. FPL, B P 90 C C P 24-515-00E, Paris France. **LC** D1050. **DD** 320.9469044. *Faits et Idees.*

EUROPEAN FILE. 1/79 (Jan. 1979)-. 0379-3133. Monographic Series. English. mo. Free. Commision of the European Communities, Directorate-General for Information Communication & Culture, rue de la Loi, 200-B01049 Brussels Belgium. **Ind/Abst** World Text Abstr. **LC** HC241.2. **DD** 330.94005. **Circ** 150,000. A series of short monographies about the European community, their main aspects and policies.

EVOLUTIONARY BLUES. Vol. 1, No. 1 (Summer/Fall 1981)-. 0730-0247. Periodical. US. English. qt. $12.00. Evolutionary Blues, PO Box 4448, Arcata CA 95521. **LC** JX1974.7. **DD** 327.17405.

FAR EASTERN AND RUSSIAN RESEARCH SERIES. Main/Corp University of Southern California, Los Angeles. School of International Relations. No. 1-. Monographic Series. US. English. ir. University of Southern California, School of International Relations, Los Angeles CA 90089.

F.A.S. PUBLIC INTEREST REPORT. Main/Corp Federation of American Scientists. VAT Federation of American Scientists Public Interest Report. V. 26, No. 8- Oct. 1973-. 0092-9824. Periodical. US. English. mo. $50.00. FAS Public Interest Report, 307 Massachusetts Avenue Northeast, Washington DC 20002. **Tel** (202)546-3300. Ed Jeremy J Stone. **LC** Q11. **DD** 509.73. NLM W1 F201A. bk rev. **Circ** 5,000. (ctrl). Contains timely articles on arms control, compliance, international security, US-USSR relations, energy and environment, and other topics of science and society. *F.A.S. Newsletter,* 0014-5653.

FEI CHING YUEH PAO. VFOAT Chinese Communist Affairs Monthly. Began with Apr. 1956 issue. 0014-9675. Periodical. CH. Chinese. mo. $30.00. Institute of International Relations, 64 Wan Shou Road, Mucha Taipei Taiwan Republic of China. **Tel** 9394921. **LC** DS777.55. adv acc. **Circ** 4,000. This journal is devoted to mainland China studies, and also provides a detailed monthly review of the general, personnel, transportation, communication and diplomatic activities of the Chinese Communists.

FELLOWSHIP. V. 1- Mar. 1935-. 0014-9810. Periodical. US. English. mo. $10.00. Fellowship of Reconciliation, Box 271, Nyack NY 10960. **Tel** (914)358-4601. **LC** JX1901. **DD** 172.405.

FILASTIN = FALASTINE. VFOAT Falastine. Periodical. Arabic. ir. $20.00. Al-Hayah Al-Arabiyah Al-Ulya Li-Filastin, PO Box 113/6052, Bayrut Lebanon. **LC** DS101.

FINANCIAL REPORT - CARNEGIE ENDOWMENT FOR INTERNATIONAL PEACE. Main/Corp Carnegie Endowment For International Peace. 0094-3029. US. English. an. Carnegie Endowment for International Peace, 345 East 46th Street, New York NY 10017. **LC** JX1906. **DD** 327.17206273.

FLASH OF DAMASCUS. VFOAT Adwa Dimashq. Periodical. English. ir. $5.00. POB 3320, Damascus Syria. **LC** DS92. **DD** 756.910405.

THE FLETCHER FORUM. V. 1- Fall 1976-. 0147-0981. Periodical. US. English. sa. $17.00. The Fletcher Forum, Fletcher School of Law Diplom, Tufts University, Medford MA 02155. **Tel** (617)628-7010. Ed Augusta Pipkin. **Ind/Abst** Leg. Resour. Index, ABC Pol Sci, Leg. Contents, Public Aff. Inf. Serv. Bull., Index Leg. Period. **LC** D839. **DD** 327.05. bk rev. adv acc. **Circ** 1,000. A journal of international relations. Publishes a wide range of articles, book reviews, political essays, and interviews on topics ranging from international politics and economics to law, history, and diplomacy.

A FONDO : ANALISIS DE LA ACTUALIDAD NACIONAL E INTERNACIONAL. V. 1, No. 1, (Oct. 1980)-. Periodical. AG. Spanish. mo. Av Independencia 2953 1ER Piso, Buenos Aires Argentina.

FOREIGN AFFAIRS. Began publication with Aug. 1948 issue. Periodical. UK. English. ir. Conservative Political Center, 32 Smith Square, London SW1P 3HH England. Ed U Branston. **LC** D839.

FOREIGN AFFAIRS BIBLIOGRAPHY. See Bibliographies.

FOREIGN AFFAIRS BULLETIN (BERLIN (GERMANY : EAST)). (FOREIGN AFFAIRS BULLETIN). Vol. 1, No. 1(Sept. 10, 1961)-. 0015-7139. Periodical. GW. English. ir. Ministry of Foreign Affairs DDR, Marx-Engles-Platz 2, DDR 102 Berlin East Germany.

FOREIGN AFFAIRS (COUNCIL ON FOREIGN RELATIONS). (FOREIGN AFFAIRS). V. 1- Sept. 1922-. 0015-7120. Periodical. US. English. qt. Foreign Affairs, PO Box 2615, Boulder CO 80321. **Ind/Abst** Read. Guide Period. Lit., Soc. Sci. Index, Abr. Read. Guide, ABI/Inform, Manage. Market. Abstr., Infobank, Energy Res. Abstr., Pop. Mag. Rev., Public Aff. Inf. Serv. Bull., Writ. Am. Hist., Recent Publ. Artic. **LC** D410. **DD** 327.05. CODEN FRNAA3. (cum index). Available in microform. *Journal of International Relations (Clark University, (Worcester, Mass.)).*

FOREIGN AFFAIRS RECORD. Main/Corp India (Republic). Ministry of External Affairs. V. 1- Jan. 1955-. 0536-9258. Periodical. II. English. ir. General Manager Government of India Press, Ministry of External Affairs, Minto Road, New Delhi India. **LC** DS448. **DD** 327.54.

FOREIGN AFFAIRS REPORTS. V. 1- July/Aug. 1952-. 0015-7155. Periodical. II. English. mo. $16.00. Indian Council of World Affairs, Sapru House Barakhamba Road, New Delhi 110001 India. **Tel** 38 20 51. Ed S L Poplai. **LC** D839.

FOREIGN CONSULAR OFFICES IN THE UNITED STATES. Began with Jan. 1, 1932. 0071-7320. US. English. an. US Government Printing Office, Superintendent of Documents, Washington DC 20402. **LC** JX1705. **DD** 351.892.

FOREIGN INTELLIGENCE LITERARY SCENE. VFOAT FILS. Vol. 1, No. 1 (Feb. 1982)-. 0749-9132. Periodical. US. English. bm. $25.00. University Publications of America, 44 North Market Street, Frederick MD 21701. **DD** 327.

FOREIGN POLICY. No. 1- Winter 1970/71-. 0015-7228. Periodical. US. English. qt. $25.00. Foreign Policy, 11 DuPont Circle NW, Washington DC 20036. **Tel** (202)797-6420. **Ed** Charles William Maynes. **Ind/Abst** Am. Hist. Life, Hist. Abstr., Part A, Mod. Hist. Abstr., Hist. Abst., Part B, Twent. Century Abstr., ABC Pol Sci, Hist. Abstr., Infobank, Public Aff. Inf. Serv. Bull., Read. Guide Period. Lit., Energy Res. Abstr., Soc. Sci. Index, Energy Inf. Abstr., Environ. Abstr., Predicasts, Soc. Sci. Citation Index, Mag. Index, Sociol. Abstr., Infobank, Lang. Lang. Behav. Abstr., Recent Publ. Artic., Pop. Mag. Rev. **LC** E744. **DD** 327.73. adv acc. **Circ** 25,000. Offers incisive coverage of world events and their implication for American business and diplomatic relations.

FOREIGN RELATIONS OF THE UNITED STATES. **Main/Corp** United States. Dept. of State. **Series/Titl** Department of State Publication. 1932-. US. English. an. US Government Printing Office, Superintendent of Documents, Washington DC 20402. **LC** JX233. **DD** 327.73. Each issue contains an index to its own contents - no vol index - loose.

FOREIGN SERVICE JOURNAL (WASHINGTON, D.C. : 1980). (FOREIGN SERVICE JOURNAL). Vol. 57, No. 1 (Jan. 1980)-. Periodical. US. English. mo. $15.00. American Foreign Service Association, 2101 E Street NW, Washington DC 20037. **Tel** (202)338-4045. **Ed** Stephen R Dujack. bk rev. adv acc. **Circ** 9,500. (ctrl). Available on microfilm from University Microfilm Library Services. The magazine for professionals in foreign affairs. *FSJ, Foreign Service Journal, 0015-7279.*

FORO INTERNACIONAL. V. 1, No. 1- July/Sept. 1960-. 0015-7821. Periodical. MX. Spanish. qt. $25.00. Colegio de Mexico, Camino al Ajusco 20, Mexico DF 01000 Mexico. **Tel** 568-60-33. **Ed** Bernardo Mabire. **Ind/Abst** Am. Hist. Life, Hist. Abstr., ABC Pol Sci, Foreign Lang. Index, PAIS Foreign Lang. Index. **LC** D839. (cum index). bk rev. adv acc. **Circ** 3,000. Foreign and domestic policies of Latin American countries, North-South relations, cooperation within the Third World superpowers. Foreign policy toward Latin America.

FREEDOM DIGEST. Periodical. English. qt. $10.00. Freedom Center C, PO Box 72733, Seoul Korea. **LC** D839. **DD** 320.9047. *WACL Bulletin.*

FREMTIDEN. 0016-1020. Periodical. DK. Danish. qt. $13.25. Det Udenrigspolitiske Selskab, Amaliegade 40 A, 1256 Copenhagen K Denmark. **Tel** 1-148886. **Ed** Mogens Espersen. bk rev. adv acc. **Circ** 1,000. A journal devoted to issues related to international politics and to Danish foreign policy.

FSJ, FOREIGN SERVICE JOURNAL. (FSJ. FOREIGN SERVICE JOURNAL). **VFOAT** Foreign Service Journal. V. 49, No. 6- June 1972-. 0015-7279. Periodical. US. English. mo. $15.00. AFSA, 2101 E Street Northwest, Washington DC 20037. **Tel** (202)338-4045. **Ed** Stephen R Dujack. **Ind/Abst** Hist. Abstr., Am. Hist. Life. bk rev. adv acc. **Circ** 10,000. Articles covering foreign affairs and the foreign service. *Foreign Service Journal, 0146-3543.*

GEOPOLITIQUE. (GEOPOLITIQUE : REVUE DE L'INSTITUT INTERNATIONAL DE GEOPOLITIQUE). Began with: No 1 (Jan. 1983). 0752-1693. Periodical. French. qt. $27.00. 1010 Vermont Avenue NW/Suite 1019, Washington DC 20005. **Tel** (202)638-7499. **Ed** Christine Morel-Maroger. **LC** D839. **DD** 327.05. adv acc. **Circ** 20,000. Disseminates information on East-West relations and their impact on Western security. It also publicizes the activities and studies of the Institute of Geopolitics.

GEOSUR. Year 1, No. 1 (Sept. 1979)-. Periodical. UY. Spanish. mo. 70. Geosur, Casilla de Correos 5006, Montevideo Uruguay. **Tel** 59 29 53. **LC** HC121. **DD** 330.980005. bk rev. adv acc. **Circ** 3,000. (ctrl). Journal of the South-American Association for geopolitical and international studies. Analyses of international relations of South America as a whole and to different countries.

GLOBAL AFFAIRS. 0886-6198. Periodical. US. English. qt. $20.00. International Security Council, 393 5th Avenue, New York NY 10016.

GLOBAL DIALOGUE. V. 1- Jan. 1968-. 0017-1190. Periodical. US. English. mo. Global Dialogue Publishing Inc, PO Box 385, Pelham NY 10803. **LC** JX1901. **DD** 327.05. Available on microfilm.

GLOBAL PERSPECTIVES. **VFOAT** G.P. V. 1, No. 1 (Spring 1983)-. 0741-0204. Periodical. US. English. sa. $9.00 Student Membership, $15.00 Professional Membership, $20.00 Library or Institutional Membership, $25.00 Sustaining Membership. Transnational Studies Association, PO Box 361, Orlando FL 32802. **Ind/Abst** Public Aff. Inf. Serv. Bull.

GLOBAL POLITICAL ASSESSMENT. **Main/Corp** Columbia University. Research Institute on International Change. No. 1- Oct. 1975/March 1976-. 0147-9512. Periodical. US. English. sa. $100.00. Research Institute on International Change, Columbia University, 420 West 118th Street, New York NY 10027. **Ed** W H Overholt. **LC** D839. **DD** 327.09097. Review by field's experts of significant political and economic trends from global and regional perspectives; most relevant to financial, business, and academic contexts.

GREAT DECISIONS. **Main/Corp** Foreign Policy Association. 1956-. 0072-727X. US. English. an. Foreign Policy Association Inc, 345 East 46th Street, New York NY 10017. **LC** E744. **DD** 327.05.

DE GROENE AMSTERDAMMER; ONAFHANKELIJK WEEKBLAD VOOR NEDERLAND. Began in 1977. US. Dutch. **Ed** A C J Jitta.

GUERRES ET CONFLITS D'AUJOURD'HUI. Periodical. French. ir. 280. I M P, 341 rue des Iselles, 78670 Villennes France.

HA-INTELIGENTSYAH HA-YEHUDIT BI-VERIT HA-MOATSOT *CEASED.* VFOAT Jewish Intelligentsia in the USSR, Jewish Intelligentsia in the U.S.S.R. 1-. IS. Hebrew. ir. **LC** DS135.R92.

HANGUK KWA KUKCHE CHONGCHI. **VFOAT** Korea and World Politics. V. 1-Series (1985)-. Periodical. KO. Korean. ir. 3.000. Kyongnam Taehakkyo Kuktong Munje Yonguso, 28-42 Samchong-dong Chongno-ku, Seoul Korea.

HARVARD INTERNATIONAL REVIEW. Vol. 1, No. 1 (Feb. 1979)-. 0739-1854. Periodical. US. English. ir. $12.00. Harvard International Review, PO Box 401, Cambridge MA 02138. **Tel** (617)495-9607. **Ed** David M Cutler and Thomas Burke. bk rev. adv acc. **Circ** 20,000. A journal of foreign affairs. Each issue features a symposium on a topic in international relations, as well as articles of general interest.

HARVARD POLITICAL REVIEW. 0090-1032. Periodical. US. English. qt. $10.00. Harvard Political Review, 79 JFK Street, Cambridge MA 02138. **Tel** (617)495-1377. **Ed** David Barkan. **LC** JK1. **DD** 320.05. bk rev. adv acc. **Circ** 3,000. A non-partisan journal of political thought covering both domestic and international affairs.

HARVARD STUDIES IN INTERNATIONAL AFFAIRS. No. 31-1974-. Monographic Series. US. English. ir. HUCFIA, c/o M & B Fulfillment, 27 Harrison Street, Bridgeport CT 06604. **Tel** (617)661-3761. *Occasional Papers in International Affairs.*

HEADLINE SERIES. No. 41 (Aug. 20, 1943)-. 0017-8780. Monographic Series. US. English. qt. Foreign Policy Association, 205 Lexington Avenue, c/o Mrs Gruber, New York NY 10016. **Tel** (212)481-8450. **Ind/Abst** Int. Index, Public Aff. Inf. Serv. Bull., Soc. Sci. Index, Humanit. Index. **LC** E744. **DD** 327.73. **Circ** 11,500. Current world problems and areas of critical importance, written by scholars and other experts. *Headline Books, 0884-4402.*

HETI VILAGGAZDASAG : HVG. **VFOAT** HVG. 0139-1682. Periodical. HU. Hungarian. wk. $15.00. Magyar Kereskedelmi Kamara, Budapest XIII Vag U 13, Budapest Hungary. **Tel** 409-950. **Ed** Matyas Vince. **LC** HC10. bk rev. adv acc. **Circ** 125,000. (ctrl). Covers international economics, finance and trade focusing on Hungary's international relations.

HLAS REVOLUCE. Periodical. US. Czech. wk. Artia, PO Box 790, Praha 1 Czechoslovakia. **LC** DB191.

HONDURAS UPDATE. No. 1 (Aug. 1982)-. US. English. mo. $14.00. Honduras Information Center, 1 Summer Street, Somerville MA 02143. **Tel** (617)625-7220. **Ed** Steve Lewontin. bk rev. **Circ** 1,200. (ctrl). Updated information and analysis of the impact of United States policy on Honduran economic, social and political life and in the rest of the region.

HRONIKA MEUNARODNIH DOGAAJA. 1963-. 0441-3350. Serbo-Croatian(R). ir. **LC** D410.

HSIEN TAI KUO CHI KUAN HSI. **VFOAT** Contemporary International Relations. V. 1, (Oct. 1981)-. Periodical. CH. Chinese. ir. 0.40. Hsin Hua Shu Tien Pei-Ching Fa Hsing So Peking China. **LC** D849. **DD** 327.09048.

IMPACT INTERNATIONAL (LONDON, ENGLAND). (IMPACT INTERNATIONAL). Vol. 7:1 (14/27 Jan. 1977)-. Periodical. UK. English. sm. $40.61. News and Media Ltd, 33 Strouf Green Road, London N4 3EF England. **Ed** A Irfan. **LC** BP1. **DD** 909.97671082. bk rev. adv acc. *Impact.*

INDEX : CANADA TREATY SERIES. *See* Indexes/Abstracts.

INDEX TO PROCEEDINGS OF THE ECONOMIC AND SOCIAL COUNCIL. 1st Spec. Sess., 14th Sess., 14th Sess., Resumed (24 Mar. 1952, 20 May to 1 Aug 1952, 16 and 19 Dec. 1952)-. 0082-8084. Periodical. US. English. ir. $9.50. United Nations, Sales Section/Room A 3315, New York NY 10017. **Tel** (212)754-8325. **LC** Z7161. **DD** 300, 341.759. Index published separately - Free - upon request. Proceedings of the economic and social council of the United Nations. *Disposition of Agenda Items.*

INDEX TO PROCEEDINGS OF THE GENERAL ASSEMBLY. *See* Indexes/Abstracts.

INDEX TO PROCEEDINGS OF THE SECURITY COUNCIL. *See* Indexes/Abstracts.

INDIA QUARTERLY. V. 1- Jan. 1945-. 0251-3048. Periodical. II. English. qt. $24.00. Indian Council World Affairs, Sapru House/Barakhamba Road, New Delhi 110001 India. **Tel** 38 20 51. **Ind/Abst** Am. Hist. Life, Hist. Abstr., Part A, Mod. Hist. Abstr., Hist. Abst., Part B, Twent. Century Abstr., ABC Pol Sci, Hist. Abstr., Recent Publ. Artic. **LC** D410. **DD** 052.

INDIAN AND FOREIGN REVIEW. Vol. 1, No. 1 (Oct. 15, 1963)-. 0019-4379. Periodical. II. English. sm. Ministry of Information and Broadcasting, Government of India Patiala House, New Delhi 110001 India. **Ind/Abst** MLA Int. Bibliogr. Books Artic. Mod. Lang. Lit. **LC** D839. Index published separately - free - automatically sent. *March of India.*

THE INDIAN EXPORT TRADE JOURNAL. Began publication with July 1948 issue. Periodical. English. mo. $50.00. Indian Export Trade Journal, Sayajiganj, Baroda 5 India. **Tel** 64158. **Ed** C M Pandit. **Ind/Abst** Bibliogr. Agric. bk rev. adv acc. **Circ** 7,500. (ctrl). Promotes international trade and development of exports. Puts traders in contact with each other.

THE INDIAN YEAR BOOK OF INTERNATIONAL AFFAIRS. *See* Yearbooks, Almanacs, Directories.

INFORMATIONS UNIVERSITAIRES EN RELATIONS INTERNATIONALES ET ETUDES ETRANGERES *CEASED.* 4-9. 0383-2619. Periodical. CN. French. *Informations Universitaires en Relations Internationales, 0046-9467.*

INFORME, RELACIONES MEXICO-ESTADOS UNIDOS. **VFOAT** Relaciones Mexico-Estados Unidos. Vol. 1, No. 1 (Oct. 1981)-. Periodical. MX. Spanish. ty. Programa de Estudios de las Relaciones Mexico-Estados Unidos Ceestem, Porfirio Diaz 50, San Jerinomo Mexico 20 DF. **Ind/Abst** Foreign Lang. Index. **LC** E183.8.M6. **DD** 303.4827207305.

INTER DEPENDENT. (THE INTER DEPENDENT). V. 1- April 1974-. 0094-5072. US. English. ir. $10.00. United Nations Association of USA, 300 East 42nd Street, New York NY 10017. **Tel** (212)697-3232. **LC** D839. **DD** 327.05.

INTERGOVERNMENTAL RELATIONS IN CANADA : THE YEAR IN REVIEW. 1978/79-. 0226-9341. CN. English. an. Institute of Intergovernmental Relations, Queens University, Kingston Ontario K7L 3N6 Canada. **Tel** (613)547-2619. *Federal Year in Review, 0706-1234.*

INTERNASJONAL POLITIKK (OSLO, NORWAY). (INTERNASJONAL POLITIKK). 1947-. 0020-577X. Periodical. NO. Norwegian. mo. 225.-. Norsk Utenrikspolitisk Institute, Postpoks 8159-Oslo Dep, Oslo 1 Norway. **Tel** 47-02-44 58 20. **Ed** Arne Olav Brundtland. **Ind/Abst** Am. Hist. Life, Hist. Abstr., Part A, Mod. Hist. Abstr., Hist. Abst., Part B, Twent. Century Abstr., ABC Pol Sci, Energy Res. Abstr. **LC** D839. bk rev. adv acc. **Circ** 2,500. Features articles on foreign affairs. Issues include arms control, military situation in Northern Europe, development programs for the Third World, European Economic Community and international trade and economics. *Internasjonal Politikk (Bergen, Norway).*

INTERNATIONAL AFFAIRS. V. 1- Jan. 1922-. 0020-5850. Periodical. UK. English. ir. Oxford University Press, 16-00 Pollitt Drive, Fairlawn NJ 07410. **LC** JX1.

INTERNATIONAL AFFAIRS AND DEFENSE. Vol. 14, INT 1 (Jan. 1983)-. 0737-3767. Periodical. US. English. mo. Newsbank Inc, 58 Pine Street, New Canaan CT 06840.

INTERNATIONAL AFFAIRS BULLETIN. Vol. 1, No. 1-. Periodical. SA. Afrikaans (English). ir. 16.00 Domestic, 45.00 Africa and Europe, 26.00 US. Editor International Affairs Bulletin, South African Institute of International Affairs, Jan Smuts House/PO Box 31596, Braamfontein 2017 Johannesburg South Africa. **Tel** 339-2021. **Ed** Alan Begg. **LC** DT30.5. **DD** 960.05. bk rev. **Circ** 3,500. All aspects of international affairs generally in relation to South African and Southern Africa. *Newsletter (South African Institute of International Affairs).*

INTERNATIONAL AFFAIRS (LONDON). (INTERNATIONAL AFFAIRS). Vol. 20, No. 1 (Jan. 1944)-. 0020-5850. Periodical. UK. English. qt. **Ind/Abst** Sociol. Abstr., ABC Pol Sci, Ref. Source, Public Aff. Inf. Serv. Bull., Soc. Sci. Index, Am. Hist. Life, Hist. Abstr., Part A, Mod. Hist. Abstr., Hist. Abst., Part B, Twent. Century Abstr., Recent Publ. Artic. **LC** JX1. **DD** 327.05. *International Affairs Review Supplement.*

INTERNATIONAL AFFAIRS (MOSCOW). (INTERNATIONAL AFFAIRS). Jan. 1955-. 0130-9641. Periodical. UR. English (summaries in Russian). mo. International Affairs, Mezhdunarod Naja Kniga USS, Moscow 121200 USSR. **Ind/Abst** Public Aff. Inf. Serv. Bull., ABC Pol Sci, Soc. Sci. Citation Index, Hist. Abstr., Part A, Mod. Hist. Abstr., Hist. Abst., Part B, Twent. Century Abstr. **LC** D839. **DD** 909.82. (cum index).

INTERNATIONAL BULLETIN. Periodical. Danish. ir. 60.00. International Bulletin, Postbox 2025, 1012 K Kbenhavn Denmark. **LC** D839. **DD** 327.05.

INTERNATIONAL DOCUMENTS ON PALESTINE. 1967-. LE. English (French). an. Institute for Palestine Studies, PO Box 11-7164, Beirut Lebanon. **Tel** 814174. **LC** DS119.7. **DD** 327.5694. **Circ** 3,000. Includes a selection of documentary material on the Palestine question and Arab-Israeli conflict, such as treaties, joint communiques, speeches and interviews.

INTERNATIONAL INTERACTIONS. V. 1- 1974-. 0305-0629. UK. English. mo. $85.00. International Interactions, c/o Gordon and Breach Science Publishers, One Park Avenue, New York NY 10016. **Ed** Edward E Azar. **LC** JX1. **DD** 327.072. **CODEN** INIAAH. bk rev. adv acc.

INTERNATIONAL JOURNAL. (INTERNATIONAL JOURNAL MICROFORM). Vol. 1 (Jan. 1946)-. 0020-7020. Periodical. US. English. Canadian Institute of International Affairs, 31 Wellesley Street East, Toronto Ontario M4Y 1G9 Canada. **Tel** (418)979-1851. **Ed** Robert Matthews and Charles Pentland. **Ind/Abst** Am. Hist. Life, Hist. Abstr., Part A, Mod. Hist. Abstr., Hist. Abst., Part B, Twent. Century Abstr., Int. Labour Doc., ABC Pol Sci, Can. Period. Index, Writ. Am. Hist., Sociol. Abstr., Soc. Sci. Citation Index, Lang. Lang. Behav. Abstr., Hist. Abstr., Recent Publ. Artic. **DD** 940.55. bk rev. adv acc. **Circ** 2,900. A selection of articles on post 1945 international affairs. Each issue has a theme.

THE INTERNATIONAL JOURNAL OF WORLD STUDIES. **VFOAT** World Studies. Vol. 1, No. 1 (Winter 1984)-. 0742-4698. Periodical. US. English. qt. $25.00. International Center for Democracy, 7676 New Hampshire Avenue/Suite 304, Langley Park MD 20783. **DD** 327.

INTERNATIONAL JOURNAL ON WORLD PEACE. Vol. 1, No. 1 (Autumn 1984)-. 0742-3640. Periodical. US. English. qt. $15.00 Domestic, $8.50 Central America, $12.20 Europe/ Middle East/Africa, $15.80 East Asia/Oceania. Professors World Peace Academy, GPO Box 1311, New York NY 10116. **Tel** (212)947-1756. **Ed** Panos D Bardis. **DD** 327. bk rev. adv acc. A scholarly, multi-disciplinary, and cross-cultural publication dealing with all aspects of peace from both theoretical and practical perspectives.

INTERNATIONAL ORGANISATIONS IN WORLD POLITICS YEARBOOK. *See* Yearbooks, Almanacs, Directories.

INTERNATIONAL ORGANIZATION. V. 1- Feb. 1947-. 0020-8183. Periodical. US. English. qt. $40.00. MIT Press Journals, 28 Carleton Street, Cambridge MA 02142. **Tel** (607)256-6257. **Ed** Peter J Katzenstein. **Ind/Abst** Leg. Resour. Index, Am. Hist. Life, Hist. Abstr., Part A, Mod. Hist. Abstr., Hist. Abst., Part B, Twent. Century Abstr., Int. Labour Doc., ABC Pol Sci, Int. Index, Public Aff. Inf. Serv. Bull., Soc. Sci. Index, Humanit. Index, Energy Res. Abstr., Sociol. Abstr., Soc. Sci. Citation Index, Curr. Law Index, Lang. Lang. Behav. Abstr., Hist. Abstr., Recent Publ. Artic. **LC** JX1901. **DD** 341.105. adv acc. **Circ** 2,700. International political and economic affairs, including foreign policy, history, political economy, and comparative politics.

INTERNATIONAL PEACE RESEARCH NEWSLETTER. V. 1- 1963-. 0020-8213. Periodical. US. English. qt. $12.00. International Peace Research Association, 199 West 10th Avenue/ Mershon Center, Columbus OH 43201. **Tel** (614)422-1681. **Ed** Elise Boulding. **Circ** 1,000. (ctrl). Forum for peace researchers and educators.

INTERNATIONAL POLICY REPORT. V. 1- Dec. 1975-. 0738-6508. Periodical. US. English. bm. $9.00. Center International Policy, 120 Maryland Avenue Northeast, Washington DC 20002. **Tel** (202)544-4666. **Circ** 1,500. Analysis of the impact on US foreign policies on human rights, social and economic conditions in the Third World.

INTERNATIONAL PROBLEMS. (BEAYOT BENLEUMIYOT). **VFOAT** International Relations. 1- 1963-. 0020-840X. Periodical. IS. Multilingual (Hebrew, English or French). qt. $30.00. Israel Association of Graduates, 21 Hess Street, Tel Aviv 63324 Israel. **Tel** (03)296482. **Ed** M Mushkat. **Ind/Abst** Am. Hist. Life, Foreign Lang. Index, Hist. Abstr., Part A, Mod. Hist. Abstr., Hist. Abst., Part B, Twent. Century Abstr., Public Aff. Inf. Serv. Bull., Hist. Abstr. **LC** D839. bk rev. **Circ** 750. Concerns political, social and international problems.

INTERNATIONAL RECORDS NEWS. **VFOAT** Int'l Records News. Vol. 1, No. 1 (May 1982) – (1)-. Periodical. English. mo. $25.00 US and Canada, Surface Mail, $35.00 Airmail. Fini Editions 18, Via Monte Battaglia, I-40046 Milo Italy. **Ind/Abst** Jazz Index.

INTERNATIONAL RELATIONS. (INTERNATIONAL RELATIONS : THE JOURNAL OF THE DAVID DAVIES MEMORIAL INSTITUTE OF INTERNATIONAL STUDIES). Began with Vol. 1, No. 1 (April 1954). 0047-1178. Periodical. UK. English. sa. $30.00. David Davies Memorial Institute of International Studies, 2 Chadwick Street, London SW1P 2EP England. **Tel** 222-4063. **Ed** Sheila Harden. **Ind/Abst** Am. Hist. Life, Hist. Abstr., Part A, Mod. Hist. Abstr., Hist. Abst., Part B, Twent. Century Abstr., Sociol. Abstr., Lang. Lang. Behav. Abstr. **LC** JX1. **DD** 327.05. bk rev. adv acc. **Circ** 1,000. Covers the whole range of International Relations including, politics, defence and strategic law, economics, environment and etc.

INTERNATIONAL RELATIONS. *See* Bibliographies.

INTERNATIONAL RELATIONS (BULGARSKA AKADEMIIA NA NAUKITE. INSTITUT PO MEZHDUNARODNI OTNOSHENIIA I SOTSIALISTICHESKA). (INTERNATIONAL RELATIONS : REVIEW OF THE INSTITUTE OF INTERNATIONAL RELATIONS AND SOCIALIST INTEGRATION WITH THE BULGARIAN ACADEMY OF SCIENCES). **VFOAT** Mezhdunarodni Otnosheniia. 1959. Periodical. BU. English. ir. $10.00. Hemus, 6 Boulevard Rusky, Sofia Bulgaria. **LC** D839. **DD** 327.05. Scientific theoretical magazine on the international relations, intended for scienfific workers, teachers and libraries, etc.

INTERNATIONAL REVIEW. Spring 1974-. 0306-3739. UK. English. qt. Hulton Publications Ltd, Audrey House Ely Place, Swanley Kent FC1 England. **LC** JX1. **DD** 327.05. *European Review.*

INTERNATIONAL REVIEW OF HISTORY AND POLITICAL SCIENCE. Vol. 1 (June 1964)-. 0020-8574. Periodical. II. English. qt. Review Publications, Rastogi Subash Bazar, Meerut UP 250002 India. **Ind/Abst** Am. Hist. Life, Hist. Abstr., Part A, Mod. Hist. Abstr., Hist. Abst., Part B, Twent. Century Abstr., Sociol. Abstr., Lang. Lang. Behav. Abstr., Hist. Abstr. **LC** D839.

INTERNATIONAL SECURITY. V. 1- Summer 1976-. 0162-2889. Periodical. US. English. qt. $52.00. MIT Press Journals, 28 Carleton Street, Cambridge MA 02142. **Tel** (617)495-1405. **Ed** Ashton B Carter and Steven E Miller. **Ind/Abst** Am. Hist. Life, Hist. Abstr., Part A, Mod. Hist. Abstr., Hist. Abst., Part B, Twent. Century Abstr., Predicasts, ABC Pol Sci, Soc. Sci. Citation Index, Public Aff. Inf. Serv. Bull., Energy Res. Abstr., Recent Publ. Artic., Funk Scott Index Corp. Ind., Hist. Abstr. **LC** JX1901. **DD** 327.1. adv acc. **Circ** 3,900. Analyses of critical world issues relating to defense policy in the US and abroad.

INTERNATIONAL SECURITY YEARBOOK (NEW YORK, N.Y.). *See* Yearbooks, Almanacs, Directories.

INTERNATIONAL STUDIES IN ECONOMICS. Monograph No. 1-. Monographic Series. US. English. ir. **LC** UNC.

INTERNATIONAL STUDIES IN THE NORDIC COUNTRIES NEWSLETTER. 1921. 0345-4975. Periodical. SW. English. sa. Free. Nordic Co-op Communication of International Politics, Lilla Nygatan 23, 2-111 28 Stockholm Sweden. **Tel** 08/23 40 60. **Ed** Anne-Marie Bratt. **LC** D839. **DD** 907.2048. Brief presentations of research projects, institutions, scientific seminars and conferences as well as a bibliographical section listing recent books, articles and research reports.

INTERNATIONAL STUDIES NEWSLETTER. Began with Mar. 1974 issue. 0097-8965. Periodical. US. English. mo. $20.00. International Studies Association, University of Pittsburgh, Pittsburgh PA 15260. **LC** JX1291. **DD** 327.07. *ISA Newsletter.*

INTERNATIONAL STUDIES NOTES. V. 1- Spring 1974-. 0094-7768. Periodical. US. English. ty. Bemidji State University, c/o Dr Leslie C Duly, Bemidji MN 56601. **Ed** Joan Wadlow and Leslie C Daly. **Ind/Abst** Am. Hist. Life, Hist. Abstr., Part A, Mod. Hist. Abstr., Hist. Abst., Part B, Twent. Century Abstr., ABC Pol Sci, Hist. Abstr. **LC** JX1291. **DD** 327.05. bk rev. adv acc. **Circ** 2,000. (ctrl). Challenging multi-disciplinary forum for exchange of research, curricular and program reports on international affairs.

INTERNATIONAL STUDIES QUARTERLY. V. 11- Mar. 1967-. 0020-8833. Periodical. UK. English. qt. $500.00. Butterworth Scientific Ltd, PO Box 63, Westbury House/Bury Street, Guildford GU2 5BH England. **Tel** 0483 31261. **Ed** Raymond D Duvall, P Terrence Hopmann, Brian L Job and Robert T Kudrle. **Ind/Abst** Am. Hist. Life, Predicasts, Writ. Am. Hist., ABC Pol Sci, Curr. Contents, Hist. Abstr., Part A, Mod. Hist. Abstr., Hist. Abst., Part B, Twent. Century Abstr., Hum. Resour. Abstr., Int. Polit. Sci. Abstr., Peace Res. Rev., Public Aff. Inf. Serv. Bull., Sage Urban Stud. Abstr., Soc. Sci. Citation Index, Soc. Sci. Index, U.S. Polit. Sci. Doc., Sociol. Abstr., Lang. Lang. Behav. Abstr., Funk Scott Index Corp. Ind., Pover. Hum. Resour. Abstr., Hist. Abstr. Issued also in microform by University Microfilms. The official journal of the International Studies Association, informs readers of the best work being done in international studies. *Background, 0361-5448.*

INTERNATIONAL YEARBOOK OF FOREIGN POLICY ANALYSIS. *See* Yearbooks, Almanacs, Directories.

INTERNATIONALES AFRIKA-FORUM. (INTERNATIONALES AFRIKAFORUM). 1 Volume. 0020-9430. Periodical. GW. German. qt. $41.40. Weltforum Verlags GMBH, Marienburger Strasse 22, 5000 Koln 51 West Germany. **Ind/Abst** Foreign Lang. Index, Recent Publ. Artic., PAIS Foreign Lang. Index. **LC** DT1.

INTERNATIONELLA STUDIER. **VFOAT** IS, Internationella Studier. 1968-. 0020-952X. Periodical. SW. Swedish. bm. $18.50. Bibliotekstjanst AB, Box 1706, S-221 01 Lund Sweden. **Tel** 046/14 08 80.

INTRODUCING THE WORLD. (INTRODUCING THE WORLD : NEWSPAPER). Vol. 2, No. 2 (Apr. 1981)-. 0824-4677. Periodical. CN. English. ir. Free to Members. Introducing the World, c/o Canadian Institute of International Affairs, 15 King's College Circle, Toronto Ontario M5S 2V9 Canada. **DD** 327.05. *Introducing the World—Newspaper, 0824-4677.*

IPRA STUDIES IN PEACE RESEARCH. **Main/Corp** International Peace Research Association. 1- 1966-). 0074-7289. Monographic Series. FI. English. ir. International Peace Association, Box 70, 33101 Tampere 10 Finland.

IPS PAPERS. **VFOAT** Institute for Palestine Studies Papers. No. 1-. Monographic Series. LE. English (Arabic and French). ir. Institute for Palestine Studies, PO Box 11-7164, Beirut Lebanon. **Tel** 814174. **Circ** 5,000. A series of analytical essays dealing with selected current aspects of the Palestine problem and the Arab-Israeli conflict.

Political Science—International Relations

IRAN VOICE. VFOAT Iranvoice. V. 1- 1979-. Periodical. US. English. bw. $15.00. Embassy of Islamic Republic of Iran, 3005 Massachusetts Avenue NW, Washington DC 20008. **Tel** (202)797-6561.

IRISH STUDIES IN INTERNATIONAL AFFAIRS. Vol. 1, No. 1-. 0332-1460. Periodical. IE. English. an. $7.66. Royal Irish Academy, 19 Dawson Street, Dublin 2 Ireland. **Tel** 01-764222. Ed John Bradley. LC DA964.A2. DD 327.05. **Circ** 500. A specialist journal of studies in foreign policy and international affairs.

ISAAS NEWSLETTER. Main/Corp Indian Society for Afro-Asian Studies. VFOAT I.S.A.A.S. Newsletter. No. 1 (1983)-. II. English. an. 10.00. Indian Society for Afro-Asian Studies, 75 Defence Enclave Vikas Marg, New Delhi 110092 India. **Tel** 382601. Ed Dharampal. LC DS32.9.I4. DD 950.0496. bk rev. adv acc. **Circ** 5,000. Covers the activities of general interest about African and Asian countries and cooperation between them.

ISLAH (DUBAYY, UNITED ARAB EMIRATES). (AL-ISLAH). VFOAT Al-Eslah. Periodical. Arabic. wk. 40.00. Dubayy Shari Al-Qassis, SB 4663 United Arab Emirates. **Tel** 665962. Ed Mohammed Saleh Rais. LC DS1. adv acc. **Circ** 20,000. Discusses the trends of politics and economics and tries to review the development of thought in this field with the fundamental of Islam.

ISRAEL & PALESTINE POLITICAL REPORT : I & P. VFOAT I. & P. VAT Israel and Palestine Political Report. Began publication in 1981. Periodical. FR. English. ir. $30.00. Israel and Palestine, 5 rue Cardinal Mercier, 75009 Paris France. **Tel** (1) 452 630 93. Ed Maxim Ghilan. bk rev. adv acc. **Circ** 7,000. Contemporary conflicts in the Near East. Israeli peace-camp, PLO internal politics, US involvement in that area. A conflict-resolution-oriented magazine. *Israel & Palestine monthly review.*

ISRAELI FOREIGN AFFAIRS. 0883-9832. Periodical. US. English. mo. Israeli Foreign Policy, 5825 Telegraph Avenue/#34, Oakland CA 94609. DD 956.

ISSUES BEFORE THE GENERAL ASSEMBLY OF THE UNITED NATIONS. (ISSUES BEFORE THE . . . GENERAL ASSEMBLY OF THE UNITED NATIONS). VFOAT Issues Before the United Nations. 31st (1976-1977 Ed.)-. 0193-8096. US. English. an. $11.00. United Nations Association of USA, 300 East 42nd Street, New York NY 10017. LC JX1977.A1. DD 341.2305. *Issues Before the United Nations General Assembly*, 0362-4404.

ITALIA NELLA POLITICA INTERNAZIONALE. (L'ITALIA NELLA POLITICA INTERNAZIONALE). Vol. 1- 1972/73-. 0303-4933. IT. Italian. an. Edizioni di Comunita, Via Nanzoni 12, 20121 Milan Italy. LC D839. DD 320.904.

JAARBOEK VAN HET DEPARTEMENT VAN BUITENLANDSE ZAKEN. *See* Yearbooks, Almanacs, Directories.

JAHRESBERICHT - DEUTSCHE GESELLSCHAFT FUR AUSWARTIGE POLITIK. Main/Corp Deutsche Gesellschaft fur Auswartige Politik. GW. German. ir. Gesellschaft for Auswartige Politik, Adenauerelle 133, Postfach 1425, D-5300 Bonn West Germany.

THE JERUSALEM JOURNAL OF INTERNATIONAL RELATIONS. V. 1- Fall 1975-. 0363-2865. Periodical. IS. English. qt. $25.00. The Magnes Press, The Hebrew University, Jerusalem Israel. **Ind/Abst** Am. Hist. Life, Hist. Abstr., Part A, Mod. Hist. Abstr., Hist. Abst., Part B, Twent. Century Abstr., ABC Pol Sci, Hist. Abstr. LC JX18. DD 327.05.

JERUSALEM PAPERS ON PEACE PROBLEMS. No. 1-. Monographic Series. IS. English. sa. 25.00. Leonard Davis Institute of International Relations, Hebrew University of Jerusalem, Jerusalem Israel. **Tel** (02)820014. Ed Gabriel Sheffer. bk rev. **Circ** 600. International relations in general, theory, practice, policy oriented and Middle Eastern politics in particular. Problems of war and peace. Conflict resolution and management.

JERUSALEM QUARTERLY. (THE JERUSALEM QUARTERLY). No. 1- Fall 1976-. 0334-4800. Periodical. US. English. qt. $46.00. Hochman Associates, 120 East 56th Street, New York NY 10022. **Tel** (212)371-4932. **Ind/Abst** Am. Hist. Life, Hist. Abstr., Part A, Mod. Hist. Abstr., Hist. Abstr., Part B, Twent. Century Abstr., Public Aff. Inf. Serv. Bull. LC DS101. bk rev. adv acc. Scholarly journal about affairs in the Middle East.

JERUSALEM TIMES. V. 1- Apr. 1974-. 0317-0829. CN. text in English and Arabic. mo. 4.00 English only, 8.00 English and Arabic. Jerusalem Times, PO Box 65654/Station F, Vancouver British Columbia V5N 5K7 Canada. DD 327.56940174927.

JEUNE AFRIQUE. Began in Oct. 1960. 0021-6089. Periodical. FR. French. ir. $76.10. Groupe J A, BP 250 Department Abonnements, 75827 Paris Cedex 17 France. LC AP27.

JEUNE AFRIQUE (PARIS, FRANCE : 1980). (JEUNE AFRIQUE). V. 20, No. 992 (Jan. 9, 1980)-. 0021-6089. Periodical. FR. French. wk. $73.00. Jeune Afrique, 3 rue Roquepine, 75008 Paris France. LC AP27. DD 054.1. *J.A., Jeune Afrique.*

JOERNAAL VIR EIETYDSE GESKIEDENIS EN INTERNASIONALE VERHOUDINGE. VFOAT Journal for Contemporary History and International Relations. V. 2- Mar. 1977-. Periodical. SA. Afrikaans (English). ir. 10.50. Institute for Contemporary History, University of the Orange Free State, Bloemfontein 9300, Republic of South Africa. **Tel** 70711. Ed P W Coetzer. LC D410. DD 909.82. bk rev. **Circ** 350. Articles with a historical or political nature and a tendency of international relations. *Joernaal vir die Eietydse Geskiedenis.*

JOURNAL OF ARAB AFFAIRS. Vol. 1, No. 1 (Oct. 1981)-. 0275-3588. Periodical. US. English. sa. $25.00. Middle East Research Group Inc, 2611 Fresno Street, Fresno CA 93703. **Tel** (209)226-8441. Ed Tawfic Farah. **Ind/Abst** ABC Pol Sci, Public Aff. Inf. Serv. Bull. LC DS36. DD 909.04927082. adv acc. **Circ** 1,000. Current affairs of middle East, Arab culture and political thought.

JOURNAL OF INTERNATIONAL AFFAIRS. V. 1- Spring 1947-. 0022-197X. Periodical. US. English. sa. $22.00. Columbia University, Box 4 International Affairs Building, New York NY 10027. **Tel** (212)280-4775. Ed James Ryan. **Ind/Abst** ABC Pol Sci, Ref. Source, Humanit. Index, Public Aff. Inf. Serv. Bull., Energy Inf. Abstr., Environ. Abstr., Am. Hist. Life, Hist. Abstr. LC JX1. DD 341.05. bk rev. adv acc. **Circ** 4,500. Availalbe through University Microfilms. Focuses on a single crucial issue in world affairs. Brings together scholars, journalists, public officials from around the world to examine policy choices and dilemnas. *Columbia Journal of International Affairs.*

JOURNAL OF PEACE RESEARCH. VFOAT JPR. V. 1- 1964-. 0022-3433. Periodical. NO. English (with summaries in English and Russian). qt. 41.-. Universitetsforlaget, PO Box 2959-Toyen, Oslo 6 Norway. **Tel** (45)-2-27 60 60. Ed Nils Petter Gleditsch. **Ind/Abst** Am. Hist. Life, Hist. Abstr., Part A, Mod. Hist. Abstr., Hist. Abst., Part B, Twent. Century Abstr., Sociol. Abstr., Soc. Welf. Soc. Plan./Policy Soc. Dev., ABC Pol Sci, Writ. Am. Hist., Public Aff. Inf. Serv. Bull., Soc. Sci. Index, Soc. Sci. Citation Index, Lang. Lang. Behav. Abstr., Hist. Abstr. LC AS9. DD 327.17205. adv acc. **Circ** 1,200. Articles directed towards ways and means of promoting peace will be favoured over purely empirical or theoretical articles.

JOURNAL OF THE FOREIGN POLICY RESEARCH ASSOCIATION OF THE UNIVERSITY OF REDLANDS. Main/Corp Redlands, Calif. University. Foreign Policy Research Association. VFOAT A Journal of Foreign Affairs. V. 1- Spring 1971-. Periodical. US. English. sa. LC JX1.

JOURNAL OF THE YUGOSLAV FOREIGN TRADE. 0022-5452. Periodical. YU. English. mo. $40.00. Export Press, Francuska 27, Belgrade Yugoslavia. **Tel** (011)625937. Ed Bozidar Milosavijevic. bk rev. adv acc. **Circ** 24,000. (ctrl). Dedicated to economic and political relations between Yugoslavia and different countries of the world with special interest on joint ventures and export. *Journal of Yugoslav Foreign Trade,* 0022-5452.

THE JOURNAL OF WORLD PEACE. Vol. 1, No. 1 (Spring 1984)-. 8756-8691. Periodical. US. English. sa. $13.00. Editorial Office, Social Science Division, University of Minnesota, Morris MN 56267. DD 327.

KOKUSAI KANKEI-GAKU KENKYU. VFOAT Study of the International Relations. No. 1- 1974-. Japanese or English. ir. Tsuda-Jubu Daigaku, 1491 Tsudamachi (189), Kodaira Japan. LC D410.

KOKUSAI KANKEI GAKUBU KENKYU NENPO. VFOAT Journal of the College of International Relations. No. 1- (1980)-. 0388-4279. Periodical. JA. English (Japanese, with some articles in Spanish). an. Nihon Daigaku Mishima Gakuen, Bunkyo-cho 2-chome, Mishima-shi, Shizuoka-ken 411, Tokyo Japan. LC JX18.

KOKUSAI KANKEI KENKYU (MISHIMA-SHI, JAPAN). (KOKUSAI KANKEI KENKYU). VFOAT Studies on International Relations. 0389-2603. Periodical. English (Japanese, with some articles in German). sa. Nihon Daigaku Kokusai Kankei Gakubu Kokusai Kankei, Kenkyujo Bukyo-cho 2-chome Mishima-shi, Shizuoka-ken 411 Japan. LC JX18.

KOKUSAI MONDAI SHIRYO. Periodical. JA. Japanese. ir. LC JX1954.

KOKUSAI SEIKEI JOHO. 1984, 1- Ed. JA. Japanese. mo. Gaimusho Joho Bunkakyoku Kokusai Kohoka, 2-1 Kasumigaseki 2 Chiyoda-ku, Tokyo-to 100 Japan. LC D839.

KOREA & WORLD AFFAIRS. VAT Korea and World Affairs. V. 1- Spring 1977-. Periodical. KO. English. qt. $35.60. Research Center of Peace and Unification of Korea, CPO Box 6545, Seoul 100 Korea. **Ind/Abst** Am. Hist. Life, Hist. Abstr., Part A, Mod. Hist. Abstr., Hist. Abst., Part B, Twent. Century Abstr., Public Aff. Inf. Serv. Bull. LC DS916.6. DD 951.9005.

THE KOREAN JOURNAL OF INTERNATIONAL STUDIES. Began with Summer 1970 issue. 0377-0451. Periodical. KO. English. qt. $28.00. Korean Institute of International Studies, KPO 426, Seoul South Korea. **Tel** (752)7727. Ed Chong-Ki Choi. LC JX1. DD 327.05. adv acc. **Circ** 1,500. Covers the articles of many fields, which are international politics, economics, social, strategic and security affairs, by the distinguished scholars and statesmen.

KUKCHE MUNJE. VFOAT Journal of International Studies. Periodical. KO. Korean. ir. 40.00. Kukche Munje Sa, 95 Yonji-dong, Chongno-ku, Seoul South Korea. **Tel** 763-7401/2. Ed Ho-Jik Hwang. LC D839. adv acc. **Circ** 20,000. (ctrl). Publishes articles on contemporary political, military, and international relation issues representing divergent ideas and opinions.

KULPOLITIKA. HU. Hungarian (summaries in English and Russian). ir. 48.00. Magyar Kulugyi Intezet, 1016 Budapest Berc U 23, Budapest Hungary. LC D839.

KULTUR & I.E. UND GESELLSCHAFT. Periodical. GW. German. ir. Friedrich Frommann Verlag, Postfach 500 460, 7000 Stuttgart 50 West Germany. LC DD259.4.

KULTURA I ZHIZN : EZHEMESIACHNYI ZHURNAL SOIUZA SOVETSKIKH OBSHCHESTV DRUZHBY I KULTURNOI SVIAZI S ZARUBEZHNYMI STRANAMI. Began in 1957. 0023-5199. Periodical. UR. Russian. mo. $12.00. Victor Kamkin Inc, 12224 Parklawn Drive, Rockville MD 20852. **Tel** (301)881-5973.

KUO CHI HSING SHIH NIEN CHIEN. VFOAT Survey of International Affairs. 1982-. CH. Chinese. an. 3.75. Hsin Hus Shu Tien, Shang-Hai Fa Hsing So Shang-Hai China. LC D839. DD 327.09047.

KUO CHI KUAN HSI HSUEH PAO. VFOAT Journal of International Relations. Vol. 1-. Periodical. CH. Chinese. an. LC JX91.C5.

LAMBERT'S WORLDWIDE DIRECTORY OF DEFENSE AUTHORITIES WITH INTERNATIONAL DEFENSE ORGANIZATIONS AND TREATIES. *See* Yearbooks, Almanacs, Directories.

LEGISLATIVE ACTIVITIES REPORT OF THE COMMITTEE ON FOREIGN RELATIONS, UNITED STATES SENATE. Main/Corp United States. Congress. Senate. Committee on Foreign Relations. 0146-9371. US. English. be. US Government Printers Office, Washington DC 20402. LC KF30.8. DD 327.73. Vols. for 96th Congress (Jan. 5, 1979/Dec. 16, 1980)- distributed to some depository libraries in microfiche.

LETTRE AFRICAINE. (LA LETTRE AFRICAINE). Vol. 1, No. 1 (Nov. 1982)-. 0820-0726. Periodical. CN. French. ir. $30.00. Lettre Africaine,

1080 Montee du Beaver Hall/Suite 1440, Montreal Quebec H2Z 1S8 Canada. DD 327.607105.

LISTA DIPLOMATICA Y DE LOS ORGANISMOS INTERNACIONALES. Spanish. ir. LC JX1769. DD 351.89209866. *Lista Diplomatica (Ecuador. Ministerio de Relaciones Exteriores).*

LISTA MEMBRILOR CORPULUI DIPLOMATIC DE LA BUCURESTI. (LISTA MEMBRILOR CORPULUI DIPLOMATIC). VFOAT Lista Membrilor Corpului Diplomatic de la Bucuresti. 0302-5578. Romanian. ir. LC JX1831.

LISTE DES MEMBRES DES CORPS DIPLOMATIQUE ET CONSULAIRE ET DES ORGANISATIONS INTERNATIONALES. Main/Corp Niger. Ministere des Affaires Etrangeres et de la Cooperation. French. ir. LC JX1867.N5. DD 327.20256626.

LISTE DU CORPS DIPLOMATIQUE. Main/Corp Benin. Ministere des Affaires Etrangeres et de la Cooperation. French. ir. Ministere des Affairs Entrangeres et de la Cooperation, Office National d'Edition, de Presse et d'Imprimerie, Paris France. LC JX1867.B4. DD 351.892. *Liste de MM. des Membres du Corps Diplomatique.*

LUMEA. Mar. 3, 1978-. Periodical. English. wk. $60.00. Rompresfilatelia, PO Box 1362137, Bucharest-Romania. LC DR267. DD 327.498.

MCIC NEWS. VAT Manitoba Council for International Cooperation News. 0710-457X. Periodical. CN. English. ir. Free. Manitoba Council for International Cooperation, 418 Wardlaw Avenue, Winnipeg Manitoba R3L 0L7 Canada. DD 327.1705.

MASALAH-MASALAH INTERNASIONAL MASAKINI. Indonesian. ir. Lembaga Research Kebudayaan Nasional, Jln Pejambon No 2, Jakarta Indonesia. LC D839.

MEZHDUNARODNAIA ZHIZN. 20 Mar. 1922-. 0026-1874. Periodical. UR. Russian (tables of contents also in English, French, German, and Chinese). mo. $18.00. Victor Kamkin Inc, 12224 Parklawn Drive, Rockville MD 20852. Tel (301)881-5973. LC D839.

MEZINARODNI VZTAHY. Periodical. CS. Czech. ir. Artia, VE Smeckach 30, Praha 1 Czechoslovakia.

MIDDLE EAST EXECUTIVE REPORTS. Vol. 1, No. 1 (Sept. 1978)-. 0271-0498. Periodical. US. English. mo. $145.00. Middle East Executive Reports Ltd, 717 D Street NW/Suite 300, Washington DC 20004-2807. Tel (202)628-6900. Ed Joseph Saba. Ind/Abst Nexis, Public Aff. Inf. Serv. Bull. DD 346.5607, 345.6067. adv acc. Circ 1,200. Publication covering the financial, legal and practical aspects of conducting business in the Middle East.

MIDDLE EAST FOCUS. V. 1 (May 1978)-. 0705-8594. Periodical. CN. English. bm. $15.48. Canadian Academic Foundation, 491 Lawrence Avenue West/Suite 305, Toronto M5M 1C7 Canada. Tel (416)789-3495. Ed Irving Abella. DD 327.56940174927. bk rev. Circ 4,000. (ctrl). A study and analysis of the social, political and economic issues underlying the conflict areas of the Middle East.

MIDDLE EAST REVIEW. V. 7- Fall 1974-. 0097-9791. US. English. qt. $90.00. Transaction Books & Periodicals, Rutgers University, New Brunswick NJ 08903. Tel (201)932-2280. Ed Michael Curtis. Ind/Abst Sociol. Abstr., Soc. Welf. Soc. Plan./Policy Soc. Dev., Public Aff. Inf. Serv. Bull., Soc. Sci. Citation Index. LC DS41. DD 956.005. bk rev. adv acc. Circ 10,000. Interests range from the complex problems in an Israeli-Arab settlement to the impact of petroleum resources on foreign policy of major power. *Middle East Information Series, 0026-3133.*

THE MIDEAST OBSERVER IN WASHINGTON. V. 1- Jan. 1, 1978-. 0149-743X. Periodical. US. English. sm. $100.00. Mideast Observer, PO Box 2397, Washington DC 20013. Tel (703)979-0100. Ed Allan Kellum. A newsletter about US policy toward the Middle East. The reporting focuses on statements and actions of official Washington, especially Congress.

MIDEAST PRESS REPORT. 0731-4655. Periodical. US. English. wk. $3,600.00. Claremont Research & Publishing, 160 Claremont Avenue, New York NY 10027. Tel (212)662-0707. Ed George Cavalletto. A press clipping compilation of all coverage of Middle East and North Africa from over 100 US and European sources, including the major newspapers of the US, England, France, as well as English language Middle East sources.

MILLENNIUM. 0305-8298. UK. English. ty. 27.25 Domestic, $50.00 US, 61.25 Canada. London School Of Economics, Houghton Street, London WC2A 2AE England. Tel 405 7686. Ed J Kurt Barling. Ind/Abst Hist. Abstr., Part A, Mod. Hist. Abstr., Hist. Abst., Part B, Twent. Century Abstr., Am. Hist. Life, ABC Pol Sci, Public Aff. Inf. Serv. Bull. LC JX1. DD 327.05. bk rev. adv acc. Circ 800. (ctrl). Combines extended academic articles, discussion pieces, review articles and book reviews, to provide a wide range coverage of the field of international relations.

MONOGRAPH SERIES IN WORLD AFFAIRS. Began in 1963/1964. 0077-0582. Monographic Series. US. English. ir. $24.00. Graduate School of International Studies, University of Denver, Denver CO 80208. Tel (303)871-2555. Ed Karen A Feste. Ind/Abst Soc. Sci. Citation Index. adv acc. Circ 600. Analytical studies in historical and social science frameworks dealing with comtemporary problems of international relations.

MONOGRAPH SERIES - INSTITUTE FOR PALESTINE STUDIES. Main/Corp Mu'Assasat Al-Dirasat Al-Filastiniyah. Monographic Series. LE. English. ir. Institute for Palestine Studies, PO Box 11-7164, Beirut Lebanon. Tel 814174. Circ 5,000. Series of analytical studies dealing with various aspects of the Palestine question and the Arab-Israeli conflict.

MONOGRAPH - UNIVERSITY OF MIAMI. INSTITUTE OF INTERAMERICAN STUDIES. (MONOGRAPH). No. 1984-2-. 0882-2727. Monographic Series. US. English (Spanish). ir. University of Miami North-South Center, Graduate School of International Studies, PO Box 248123, Coral Gables FL 33124. Tel (305)384-4303. Ed Alexanda H McIntire. DD 327. Represents research interests of graduate programs in international studies: interamerican relations, Soviet strategic studies, Middle East studies, international business.

MONOGRAPHS IN INTERNATIONAL AFFAIRS. Monographic Series. US. English. ir. University of Miami North-South Center, Graduate School of International Studies, PO Box 248123, Coral Gables FL 33124. Tel (305)284-4303.

MONTAGUE BURTON LECTURE ON INTERNATIONAL RELATIONS. 1- 1942-. Monographic Series. UK. English. ir.

MOT A MOT. Published since 1979. 0227-8715. Periodical. CN. French. mo. Association Quebec-France, Secretariat National, 9 Place Royale, Quebec G1K 4G2 Canada. DD 327.714044.

MUNDO NUEVO. Year 1- (No. 1-). Periodical. VE. Spanish (72-9454). qt. $24.00. Universidad Simbon Bolbivar, Apart Post #17.271-EL Conde, Caracas 101 Venezuela. bk rev. adv acc. Circ 2,000. Latin American reality and the world reality which can affect Latin American developments.

NASHRAH DAWRIYAH MUQAYYADAH HAWLA MADINAT AL-QUDS AL-ARABIYAH AL-MUHTALLAH MAKHUDHAH AN AL-JARAID AL-ARABIYAH WA-AL-AJNABIYAH. Periodical. Arabic or English. ir. PO Box 2601, Amman Jordan. LC DS109.94.

THE NATIONAL INTEREST. No. 1 (Fall 1985)-. 0884-9382. Periodical. US. English. qt. $18.00. National Affairs Inc, PO Box 3000/Department QQ, Denville NJ 07834. LC E840. DD 327.73005.

NATIONAL REPORTER (WASHINGTON, D.C.). (THE NATIONAL REPORTER). Vol. 9, No. 1 (Winter 1985)-. 0882-8563. Periodical. US. English. qt. The National Reporter, PO Box 647 Ben Franklin Station, Washington DC 20044. DD 327. *Counterspy, 0739-4322.*

NATIONAL SECURITY SERIES. 0228-9202. Periodical. CN. English. ir. Centre for International Relations, Queen's University, Kingston Ontario K7L 3N6 Canada. DD 327.401717.

NATO REVIEW. VFOAT N.A.T.O. Review. VAT North Atlantic Treaty Organization Review. Began with V. 19, No. 5/6 (May/June 1971). Periodical. US. English. bm. Free. Bureau of Public Affairs, Department of State/Room 5815A, Washington DC 20502. Ed Peter A Jenner. Ind/Abst Energy Inf. Abstr., Environ. Abstr., ABC Pol Sci, Index Free Period. LC UA646.3. DD 355.031091821. Circ 14,400. (ctrl). Subjects relating to the North Atlantic Treaty Organization, East-West Relations, and Disarmament Talks and Economic Affairs. *NATO Letter, 0027-6057.*

NATO'S FIFTEEN NATIONS. No. 1-21, Feb. 1956-Aug./Sept. 1961. 0027-6065. Periodical. GW. English. ir. $38.00. Moench Media Inc, 1350 Beverly Road/Suite 221, McLean VA 22101. Tel (703)790-5252. Ed Marvin Leibstone. adv acc. Circ 23,800. (ctrl). Reporting the development and activities of the NATO alliance. Reports on the entire spectrum of strategic decision making within the alliance.

NDP ANTI-WAR NEWSLETTER. Apr. 1983-. 0824-4456. Periodical. CN. English. qt. NDP Anti-War Committee, 184 Main Street, Toronto Ontario M4E 2W1 Canada. DD 327.17405.

NETWORK NEWS (UNITED CAMPUSES TO PREVENT NUCLEAR WAR). (NETWORK NEWS). VFOAT UCAM Network News. Vol. 2, No. 7 (May 1, 1982)-. 0882-6331. Periodical. US. English. mo. United Campuses to Prevent Nuclear War, 1346 Connecticut Avenue/Suite 706, Washington DC 20036. DD 327. Available on microfilm from the State Historical Society of Wisconsin. *Network News (Union of Concerned Scientists).*

NEUE ZURCHER ZEITUNG. *See* Economics - International Economics.

THE NEW INTERNATIONAL REVIEW. V. 1- Feb. 1977-. 0148-415X. Periodical. US. English. qt. $6.00. New International Review, 190-05 Hillside Avenue 6R, Holliswood NY 11423. Tel (212)479-3032. LC D839. DD 327.05.

NEW INTERNATIONALIST. No. 1- Mar. 1973-. 0305-9529. Periodical. UK. English. mo. $22.00. New Internationalist, 113 Atlantic Avenue, Brooklyn NY 11201. Tel (902)422-8338. Ind/Abst Energy Res. Abstr. LC D839. DD 052. adv acc. (ctrl). The people, the ideas and action in the fight for world development. *Internationalist.*

NEW TIMES. 1943-. 0029-5280. Periodical. UR. English. wk. New Times, 70622 All Editions. Ind/Abst Public Aff. Inf. Serv. Bull. LC D839. DD 940.5505. Available on microfilm from University Microfilms.

NEW ZEALAND INTERNATIONAL REVIEW. V. 1- Jan./Feb. 1976-. 0110-0262. Periodical. NZ. English. bm. 28.00. New Zealand Institute of International Affairs, PO Box 19-102, Wellington 2 New Zealand. Tel 727-430. Ed Ian McGibbon. LC D839. DD 327.05. bk rev. adv acc. Circ 1,500. (ctrl). Review of international affairs as they affect New Zealand. Independent, non-partisan outlook. The only such magazine published in New Zealand.

NEWS ON INDONESIA. 0545-8617. Periodical. US. English. bm. Indonesian Consulate, 351 California Street/Suite 700, San Francisco CA 94104. Tel (415)982-8966.

NEWS REVIEW ON CHINA, MONGOLIA AND THE KOREAS. Main/Corp Institute for Defence Studies and Analyses. 1972-. Periodical. II. English. mo. $10.03. Institute for Defence Studies and Analyses, Sapru House, Barakhamba Road, New Delhi 110001 India. Tel 324951. LC DS501. DD 355.033051. *News Review on China.*

NEWS REVIEW ON SOUTH ASIA AND INDIAN OCEAN. Feb. 1976-. Periodical. II. English. mo. $10.03. Institute for Defence Studies and Analyses, Sapru House, Barakhamba Road, New Delhi 110 001 India. *News Review on South Asia.*

NEWSLETTER - ASIAN BUREAU AUSTRALIA. Main/Corp Asian Bureau Australia. 1972. Periodical. UK. English. bm. 10.00 Domestic, 18.00 Foreign. Asian Bureau Australia, 173 Royal Parade, Parkville Victoria 3052 Australia. Tel (03)347-8595. Ed Denise Chon Allas. bk rev. adv acc. Circ 3,000. Analytical stories, features, reviews, opinions, and interviews on current development affairs in Asia and the Pacific, to promote just relations between Australia and the region.

NEWSLETTER - INTRODUCING THE WORLD *CEASED.* (INTRODUCING THE WORLD—NEWSLETTER). Issue No. 1 (Feb. 1981)-. 0824-4685. Periodical. CN. English. qt. Free to Members. c/o Canadian Institute of International Affairs, 15 King's College Circle, Toronto Ontario M5S 2V9 Canada. DD 327.06071.

Political Science—International Relations

NEWSLETTER - NORMAN PATERSON SCHOOL OF INTERNATIONAL AFFAIRS. Main/Corp Norman Paterson School of International Affairs. V. 2- Jan. 1975-. 0319-2024. CN. English. Norman Paterson School of International Affairs, Carleton University, Ottawa Ontario K1S 5B6 Canada. DD 327.071171384. *Newsletter, 0319-2016.*

NEWSLETTER - SOCIETY FOR HISTORIANS OF AMERICAN FOREIGN RELATIONS. Main/Corp Society for Historians of American Foreign Relations. VFOAT SHAFR Newsletter. V. 1- Dec. 1969-. 0740-6169. Periodical. US. English. qt. $10.00. Box 5154 Tennessee Technological University, Cookeville TN 38501. Tel (615)528-3336. Ed William J Brinker. Ind/Abst Am. Hist. Life, Hist. Abstr., Part A, Mod. Hist. Abstr., Hist. Abst., Part B, Twent. Century Abstr. LC E183.7. DD 327.73. adv acc. Circ 1,000. (ctrl). Personals, announcements, abstracts, bibliographic or historiographical essays, essays about foreign depositories, biographies, autobiographies of "elder statesmen" in the field, jokes, etc.

NIGERIAN JOURNAL OF INTERNATIONAL AFFAIRS. V. 1- 1975-. 0331-3646. NR. English. an. Nigerian Institute of International Affairs, Victoria Island, GPO Box 1727, Lagos Nigeria. Tel 015609. Ind/Abst Public Aff. Inf. Serv. Bull. LC JX18. DD 327.05. bk rev. adv acc. Circ 2,000. Covers political science, international relations and studies.

THE NON-ALIGNED WORLD CEASED. VFOAT Non Aligned World. Vol. 1, No. 1 (Jan.-Mar. 1983)-. Periodical. English. qt. $35.00. 23/90 Connaught Circus, New Delhi 110001 India. Ind/Abst Public Aff. Inf. Serv. Bull. LC JX18. DD 327.091716.

NORSK UTENRIKSPOLITISK ARBOK. See Yearbooks, Almanacs, Directories.

N.Y. JOURNAL JAPAN. VFOAT NY Journal Japan. 0742-8170. Periodical. US. Japanese (English). mo. $10.00. Japan Editorial Track, 310 East 46th Street/Suite 15H, New York NY 10017. Tel (212)557-5547. *J.O.P.*

OCCASIONAL PAPER (INSTITUTE FOR EUROPEAN DEFENCE & STRATEGIC STUDIES (LONDON, ENGLAND)). (OCCASIONAL PAPER). No. 1-. Monographic Series. UK. English.

OCCASIONAL PAPERS - NORMAN PATERSON SCHOOL OF INTERNATIONAL AFFAIRS. CARLETON UNIVERSITY. (OCCASIONAL PAPERS - NORMAN PATERSON SCHOOL OF INTERNATIONAL AFFAIRS, CARLETON UNIVERSITY). Main/Corp Norman Paterson School of International Affairs. Began publication in 1974. 0319-4876. Monographic Series. CN. English. Norman Patterson School of International Law, Ottawa Ontario K1S 5B6 Canada. DD 327. *Occasional Papers, 0319-4868.*

OFFICIAL RECORDS. Main/Corp United Nations. Security Council. 22nd Year, 1341st Meeting (24 May 1967)-. Periodical. US. English. ir. United Nations Publications, Sales Section/Room A-3315, New York NY 10017. Tel (212)754-8302. Records of the meetings of the Security Council. Contains 1) verbatim or summary records of the meetings, 2) annexes, important documents used in the meetings, and 3) supplements. *Official Records.*

OFFICIAL RECORDS - ECONOMIC AND SOCIAL COUNCIL. (OFFICIAL RECORDS). Main/Corp United Nations. Economic and Social Council. 1st Year, 1st Session -. 0082-8092. US. English. ir. United Nations Publications, Sales Section/Room A-3315, New York NY 10017. Tel (212)754-8302. LC HC59. Records of the meetings of the Economic and Social Council. Contains 1) verbatim or summary records of the meetings, 2) annexes, important documents used in the meetings, and 3) supplements.

OPTION PAIX. Vol. 1, No. 3-. 0823-9703. CN. French. ir. $1.00 Each Number. Comite Quebecois pour le Desarmement, 49 Boul Tache, Hull Quebec J8Y 3N7 Canada. DD 327.17405. *Arme A l'Oeil.*

OVERSEAS REPRESENTATIVES IN NEW ZEALAND AND NEW ZEALAND REPRESENTATIVES OVERSEAS. English. ir. New Zealand Ministry of Foreign Affairs, Private Bag, Wellington 1 New Zealand. LC JX1875. DD 327.2025931.

THE PACIFIST. V. 1- April 1961-. 0048-265X. Periodical. UK. English. mo. LC JX1901. *Journal of the Peace Pledge Union.*

PAIX D'URGENCE. (LA PAIX D'URGENCE : BULLETIN DU MRPDQ). No. 1 (Feb./March 84)-. 0826-2764. Periodical. CN. French. bm. $6.00. MRPDQ, c/o Carrefour Tiers-Monde 454 rue Caron, Quebec Quebec G1K 8K8 Canada. DD 327.17205.

PALESTINE. VFOAT Palestine Bulletin. 0377-2616. Periodical. English. bm. $20.00. Palestine Liberation Organization United Information, PO Box 145168, Beirut Lebanon. LC DS119.7. DD 327.56940174927.

PALESTINE. V. 1- Apr. 1, 1976-. 0191-7900. Periodical. US. English. Palestine Solidarity Committee, PO Box 1757, Manhattanville Station NY 10027. Tel (212)8505296. Ind/Abst Public Aff. Inf. Serv. Bull. LC WMLC L 83/976.

PALESTINE PERSPECTIVES. V. 1- May 1978-. 0163-3716. Periodical. US. English. bm. $15.00. Palestine Research and Educational Center, 818 18th Street/Suite 645, Washington DC 20006. Tel (202)466-3205. Ed Muhammad Hallaj. LC DS119.7. DD 327.56940174927. bk rev. adv acc. Circ 7,500. Deals with the Palestine question, the Arab-Israeli conflict, and the Israeli-occupied territories. Includes articles, news, and commentaries. *Free Palestine.*

PAPERS - PEACE SCIENCE SOCIETY INTERNATIONAL. (PAPERS - PEACE SCIENCE SOCIETY (INTERNATIONAL)). Main/Corp Peace Science Society (International). VFOAT Papers of the Peace Science Society (International). V. 20- 1973-. 0094-8055. US. English. an. Peace Society International, Department of Peace Science, Wharton School, University of Pennsylvania, Philadelphia PA 19174. Ind/Abst Index Econ. Artic. J. Collect. Vol., Public Aff. Inf. Serv. Bull. LC JX1930.P4. DD 327.17205.

PARTICIPATION. (PARTICIPATION : NEWSLETTER OF THE INTERNATIONAL POLITICAL SCIENCE ASSOCIATION). VFOAT Bulletin de l'Association Internationale de Science Politique. Vol. 1, No. 3-. 0709-6941. Periodical. CN. English (includes some text in French). ty. free. International Political Science Association, c/o University of Ottawa, Ottawa Ontario K1N 6N5 Canada. DD 320.0601. (ctrl). *International Participation, 0822-6431.*

PEACE AND CHANGE. Vol. 1, No. 1 (Fall 1972)-. 0149-0508. Periodical. US. English. ir. $21.00. Kent State University, Center for Peaceful Change, Kent OH 44242. Tel (216)672-3143. Ed Dennis Carey. Ind/Abst Am. Hist. Life, Hist. Abstr. LC JX1901. DD 327.17205. bk rev. adv acc. Circ 1,000. Publishes scholarly and interpretive articles related to achieving a peaceful, just and humane society, building bridges between peace research and education.

PEACE CALENDAR. (THE PEACE CALENDAR). 0824-3107. Periodical. CN. English. mo. Candis, 10 Trinity Square, Toronto Ontario M5G 1B1 Canada. DD 327.17205.

PEACE COURIER. No. 1- Sept. 1, 1970-. 0031-594X. Periodical. Fl. English. ir. World Peace Council Info Center, Box 114, 00181 Helsinki Finland. Tel 649004. bk rev.

PEACE NEWS FOR NONVIOLENT REVOLUTION. VFOAT Peace News. No. 1969 (April 26, 1974)-. 0031-3548. Periodical. UK. English. sm. Peace News Ltd, 5 Caledonian Road, London N1 England. LC JX1901. DD 327.17205. *Peace News (London, England).*

PEACE NEWSLETTER. 0735-4134. Periodical. US. English. mo. $12.00. Syracuse Peace Council, 924 Burnet Avenue, Syracuse NY 13203. Tel (315)472-5478. Ind/Abst Altern. Press Index. bk rev. adv acc. Circ 5,000. We offer alternative analysis of political issues which cover local organizing events, and discuss peace movement issues. Focuses on South Africa, Central America, and disarmament.

PEACE RESEARCH. V. 1- Nov. 1969-. 0008-4697. Periodical. CN. English. te. 30.00 Domestic, $32.00 Foreign. Brandon University, c/o Dr M V Naidu, Brandon Manitoba R7A 6A9 Canada. Tel (204)727-9720. Ed M U Naidu. Ind/Abst Am. Hist. Life, Hist. Abstr., Part A, Mod. Hist. Abstr., Hist. Abst., Part B, Twent. Century Abstr., Hist. Abstr. LC JX1904.5. DD 327.172072. bk rev. (ctrl). This journal publishes, scientific and scholarly work on world peace, focusing upon problems of violence, war, international organizations, development, and a better world order.

PEACE RESEARCH ABSTRACTS JOURNAL. See Indexes/Abstracts.

PEACE RESEARCH IN JAPAN. 1967-. JA. English. an. Japan Peace Research Group, c/o Prof Yoshikazu Sakamoto, University of Tokyo, Faculty of Law, Tokyo Japan. LC JX1903. DD 327.17205.

PEACE THROUGH STRENGTH REPORT. Periodical. US. English. mo. American Security Council Foundation, Washington Communications Center, Boston VA 22713. *Washington Report.*

PERMANENT MISSIONS TO THE UNITED NATIONS. Main/Corp United Nations. Series Corp Its Document. US. English. sa. $13.00. United Nations Publications, Sales Section Room A-3315, New York NY 10017. Tel (212)754-8324. LC JX1977. DD 341.13. Lists of all United Nations member states.

PERUVIAN-AMERICAN DIGEST. VAT Peruvian American Digest. 0276-6000. Periodical. US. English. Peruvian-American Association Inc, 50 West 34th Street, New York NY 10001.

PLOUGHSHARES MONITOR. VFOAT Ploughshares Monitor Newsreport. V. 1- Apr. 1977-. 0703-1866. Periodical. CN. English. bm. $10. Project Ploughshares, School for Peace and Conflict Studies, Conrad Grebel College, Waterloo Ontario N2L 3G6 Canada. DD 327.17405.

POLICY PAPERS IN INTERNATIONAL AFFAIRS. No. 1-. 0731-6321. Monographic Series. US. English. ir. Regents of The University of California, Institute of International Studies 215 Moses Hall, Berkeley CA 94720. Tel (215)642-4065.

POLITICA INTERNACIONAL (HAVANA CUBA). (POLITICA INTERNACIONAL: REVISTA DEL INSTITUTO DE POLITICA INTERNACIONAL). Began with: Vol. 1, No. 1 10th Quarterly 1963). 0032-3098. Periodical. CU. Spanish. ir. Instituto de Politica Intertional, Ministerio de Relaciones Exter, La Havana Cuba.

POLITICA INTERNAZIONALE (ROME, ITALY). (POLITICA INTERNAZIONALE). Periodical. English. mo. $17.82. Nuova Italia Editrice, Via Ernesto Codignola, 50018 Scandicci FI Italy.

POLITIQUE ETRANGERE. V. 1- Feb. 1936-. [032-342X. Periodical. FR. French. qt. $47.90. Institut Francais des Relation, 6 rue Ferrus, Paris 75014 France. Tel 580-9108. Ind/Abst Point Repere, Int. Labour Doc., ABC Pol Sci, Recent Publ. Artic., Foreign Lang. Index, Am. Hist. Life, Hist. Abstr., Part A, Mod. Hist. Abstr., Hist. Abst., Part B, Twent. Century Abstr., PAIS Foreign Lang. Index. LC JX3. bk rev. adv acc. Circ 3,000. Publishes in-depth articles on major current international issues as well as reference material (official texts, treaties, etc.). Also includes important bibliographical section.

POLITIQUE INTERNATIONALE. No 1- Autumn 1978-. 0221-2781. Periodical. FR. French (summaries in English). bm. $36.59. S A R L Politique Intle, 11 rue de Bois de Boulogne, 75116 Paris France. Tel (1)500.27-60. Ed Gurselves. Ind/Abst Foreign Lang. Index. LC D839. DD 327.05. bk rev. adv acc. Circ 100,000. The most influential French publication dealing with international affairs, read by decision makers throughout the world and often compared with America's foreign affairs.

POUVOIRS. 1- 1977-. 0152-0768. Monographic Series. FR. French. qt. 330 Domestic, $36.67. Presses Universitaires France, 12 rue Jean-de-Beauvais, 75005 Paris France. Tel (1)326-2216. Ed Philippe Ardant and Oliver Duhamel. This review of constitutional and political studies looks behind the scenes of contemporary political confusion and the over-abundance of news in order to highlight the actions of the political powers of our day.

PRAHA-MOSKVA. Began in 1951. Periodical. CS. Czech. bm. Artia, PO Box 790, Praha 1 Czechoslovakia. LC AP52.

PRC OFFICIAL ACTIVITIES AND MONTHLY BIBLIOGRAPHY. See Bibliographies.

PRESIDENT'S REPORT - COUNCIL ON FOREIGN AFFAIRS. (PRESIDENT'S REPORT). Main/Corp Council on Foreign Relations. 0093-4615. US. English. an. Council on Foreign Relations, Harold Pratt House, 58 E Street, New York NY 10021. LC JX27.C6. DD 327.73.

Political Science—International Relations

PROBLEMY PRAWNE HANDLU ZAGRANICZNEGO. Series/Titl Prace Naukowe Uniwersytetu Slaskiego W Katowicach. Periodical. Polish (summaries in French and Russian). ir. Uniwersytet Slaski, Ul Bankowa 14, 40-007 Katowice Poland.

PROCEEDINGS OF THE STANDING SENATE COMMITTE ON FOREIGN AFFAIRS. Main/Corp Canada. Parlement. Senat. Comite Permanent des Affaires Etrangeres. VAT Proceedings of the Senate Committee on Foreign Affairs, Deliberations du Comite Senatorial Permanent des Affaires Etrangeres (Edition Anglaise et Francais). Feb. 6, 1969-. 0576-3819. Periodical. CN. French (text in English and French Nov. 2, 1976-). DD 327.71. *Deliberations du Comite Senatorial Permanent des Affaires Etrangeres, 2 Nov. 1976, 0226-8191.*

PROCEEDINGS OF THE STANDING SENATE COMMITTEE ON FOREIGN AFFAIRS. Main/Corp Canada. Parliament. Senate. Standing Committee on Foreign Affairs. VFOAT Deliberations du Comite Senatorial Permanent des Affairs Etrangeres. VAT Proceedings of the Senate Committee on Foreign Affairs, Deliberations du Comite Senatorial Permanent des Affaires Etrangeres (Editions Anglaise et Francaise). Feb. 6, 1969-. 0576-3819. CN. English (French, Nov. 2, 1976-). Canadian Government Publishing Centre, Supply and Services Canada, Hull Quebec K1A 0S9 Canada. LC JX354. DD 327.71. *Deliberations du Comite Senatorial Permanent des Affaires Etrangeres, 0226-8191.*

PROGRAMME OF ACTION - WORLD PEACE COUNCIL. Main/Corp World Peace Council. English. an. Information Centre of the World Peace Council, Lonnrotinkatu 25 A 5 KRS, 00180 Helsinki 18 Finland. LC JX1907. DD 327.1720601.

THE PROGRESSIVE. V. 1-4. 0033-0736. Periodical. US. English. mo. $35.00. The Progressive, PO Box 2049, Marion OH 43306. Tel (608)257-4626. Ed Erwin Knoll. Ind/Abst Altern. Press Index, Book Rev. Index, Environ. Abstr., Media Rev. Dig., Read. Guide Period. Lit., Energy Inf. Abstr., Mag. Index, Pop. Mag. Rev. LC AP2. DD 051. bk rev. adv acc. Circ 50,000. Committed to the publication of articles and editorials that promote peaceful solutions to international disputes; the attainment of economic justice, and the protection of individual rights. *La Follette's Magazine.*

PROSPETTIVE NEL MONDO. Yearly V. 1- July 1976-. Periodical. Italian. ir. 15000. c/c Postale N 5/2173, Intestato a Casa Editrice le Monnier, Firenze Italy. LC D839. DD 327.05.

PRZEGLAD STOSUNKOW MIEDZYNARODOWYCH. Periodical. PL. Polish. ir. RSW "Prasa-Kriazka-Ruch", Centrala Kolporta Zu Prasy I Wydawnictw, Ul Towarowa 28, 00-958 Warszawa Poland. LC D839.

PUBLICATION. Main/Corp Hoover Institution on War, Revolution, and Peace. 1- 1932-. Monographic Series. US. English. ir. Stanford University, Hoover Institution Press, Stanford CA 94305.

PULA. V. 1-. Periodical. BS. English. ir. 4.65. Editor Pula, Department of Sociology, University College of Botswana and Swaziland, Private Bag 0022, Gaborane Botswana. Ind/Abst Recent Publ. Artic. LC DT1. DD 960.05.

PYONGHWA YON'GU. VFOAT Peace Research. Periodical. English (Korean). ir. LC DS917.25. DD 327.05.

QUEBEC INTER. V. 1, No. 1 (Jan. 1980)-. 0225-9745. Periodical. CN. French. mo. Free. Ministere des Affaires Intergouvernementales du Quebec, 1225 Place George V, Quebec Quebec G1R 4Z7 Canada. DD 327.714005.

QUESTIONS AFFECTING SOUTH AFRICA AT THE UNITED NATIONS. Main/Corp United Nations. Security Council. 0304-1794. US. English. ir. South Africa Institute of International Affairs, United Nations Security Council Jan Smuts House PO Box 31596, Johannesburg South Africa. LC JX1977.2.A44. DD 341.2368.

RDI MONOGRAPHS ON FOREIGN AID AND DEVELOPMENT. VFOAT R.D.I. Monographs on Foreign Aid and Development. VAT Rural Development Institute Monographs on Foreign Aid and Development. #1-. 0748-0644. Monographic Series. US. English. ir. Rural Development Institute, 4120 Brooklyn Avenue NE #508, Seattle WA 98105. DD 327.

REKAMAN SEJARAH. IO. Indonesian. an. Pt Gunung Argung, Kwitang 8, Jakarta Pusat Indonesia. LC DS644.4.

RELACIONES INTERNACIONALES. New Series V. 1- April/June 1973-. 0185-0814. Periodical. MX. Spanish. qt. Facultad de Ciencias Politicas, Unam Cubiculo 46/Cuidad Universitaria, Mexico 20 DF Mexico. Tel 6551344. LC JX9. bk rev. adv acc. Circ 2,000. Monographic studies on international relations, theoretical and practical subjects. Latin American politics and foreign policy of Mexico.

RELATIONS INTERNATIONALES. No. 1- May 1974-. 0335-2013. Periodical. FR. French. qt. $30.00. Sehric Relations Internationales, 17 rue de la Sorbonne, 75230 Paris Cedex 05 France. Ind/Abst Writ. Am. Hist., Recent Publ. Artic. LC D410. DD 327.05.

RELAZIONI INTERNAZIONALI. (RELAZIONI INTERNAZIONALI, SETTIMANALE DI POLITICA ESTERA). Yearly V. 1- 1935-. 0034-3846. Periodical. Italian. ir.

RELAZIONI INTERNAZIONALI. Began with issue for Jan. 1, 1935. 0034-3846. Periodical. IT. Italian. wk. Instutut Per Gli Studi di Politica, Via Clerici 5 Milan Italy. Ind/Abst Am. Hist. Life, Hist. Abstr. LC D410. DD 055.

REPERTOIRE DES ORGANISATIONS INTERNATIONALES ET DE LEUR PERSONNEL PARTICIPANT AUX PROGRAMMES DE COOPERATION TECHNIQUE DES NATIONS-UNIES AU CAMEROUN. CM. French. ir. Programme des Nations Unies Pour de Developpement Bureau du Representant Resident Cameroun, rue Joseph Clere Face au College de la Retraite, BP 836, Yaounde Cameroun.

REPORT OF A VANTAGE CONFERENCE. Main/Conf Vantage Conference. May 13-16, 1984-. 0748-0571. Monographic Series. US. English. ir. Free. The Stanley Foundation, 420 East Third Street, Muscatine IA 52761. Tel (319)254-1500. DD 327. Circ 10,000. Report from a conference discussing the evolving world situation and addressing timely, emerging issues. *Vantage Conference Report, 0145-8833.*

REPORT OF THE COMMISSION TO STUDY THE ORGANIZATION OF PEACE. Main/Corp Commission to Study the Organization of Peace. VFOAT Transitional Period. 1st- Nov. 1940-. US. English. ir. Commission to Study the Organization of Peace, 866 United Nations Plaza, New York NY 10017. LC JX1908.U6. DD 940.53144.

REPORT OF THE COMMITTEE ON FOREIGN AFFAIRS FOR THE . . . SESSION OF THE . . . NATIONAL ASSEMBLY APPOINTED ON . . . . Main/Corp Zambia. National Assembly. Committee on Foreign Affairs. 2nd Session, 4th National Assembly (1980)-. English. an. 1.50. Government Printer, POB 30136, Lusaka Zambia. Tel (01)215401. LC JX1865.Z332. DD 328.689407658. bk rev. adv acc.

REPORT OF THE STRATEGY FOR PEACE US FOREIGN POLICY CONFERENCE. (REPORT OF THE . . . STRATEGY FOR PEACE US FOREIGN POLICY CONFERENCE). Main/Conf Strategy for Peace US Foreign Policy Conference. 0748-9641. US. English. an. Free. Stanley Foundation, 420 East 3rd Street, Muscatine IA 52761. Tel (319)264-1500. Circ 20,000. Recommendations for US foreign policy as developed through conference discussions among policy shapers from the US government, academia, and the private sector. *Strategy for Peace.*

REPORT OF THE UNITED NATIONS ISSUES CONFERENCE. (REPORT OF THE . . . UNITED NATIONS ISSUES CONFERENCE). Main/Conf United Nations Issues Conference. 15th (Apr. 13-15, 1984)-. 0743-9180. US. English. an. Free. The Stanley Foundation, 420 East 3rd Street, Muscatine IA 52761. Tel (319)264-1500. DD 327. Circ 10,000. Report of an informal three-day conference where 25 UN diplomats, secretariat officials, and academic specialists discussed a current UN concern or organizational procedure. *Report of the . . . United Nations Procedures Conference, 0748-2361.*

REPORT OF THE UNITED NATIONS OF THE NEXT DECADE CONFERENCE. (REPORT OF THE . . . UNITED NATIONS OF THE NEXT DECADE CONFERENCE). Main/Conf United Nations of the Next Decade Conference. 19th (June 17-22, 1984)-. 0748-433X. US. English. an. Free. Stanley Foundation, 420 East Third Street, Muscatine IA 52761. Tel (319)264-1500. DD 354. Circ 15,000. Brings together 25 UN ambassadors, secretariat officials, foreign ministry officials, and international experts from the private sector to discuss a major UN issue and its future implications. *Report - Conference on the United Nations of the Next Decade.*

REPORT OF THE . . . WORLD CONGRESS. Main/Corp International Confederation of Free Trade Unions. English. bm. 650 Domestic, $15.00 Foreign. ICFTU, rue de la Montagen Aux Herbes Potageres 37-41, Bruxelles Belgium. Tel 217-80-85. (ctrl). Activities in worldwide international trade union movement.

REPORT ON PUBLICATIONS OF THE SCHOOL OF INTERNATIONAL AFFAIRS AND THE REGIONAL INSTITUTES. Main/Corp Columbia University. School of International Affairs. Vol. 1 1962/63. 0084-8921. Periodical. US. English. sa. $22.00. Columbia University, School of International Affairs, New York NY 10027. Tel (212)280-4775. Ed James Ryan. bk rev. adv acc. Circ 4,000. Each issue we invite distinguished experts to analyse a different topic in world affairs.

REPORT ON THE PALESTINIANS UNDER ISRAELI RULE. Periodical. English. mo. $80.00. Magelan S A R L, Boite Postale 130-10, 75463 Paris Cedex 10 France. Tel (331)45262739. Ed Maxim Ghilan. LC DS119.7. DD 956.94004927, No. Circ 4,000. Comprehensive report on Palestinians living in Israel, the West Bank, Gaza and Golan, their human rights, political life and opposition to occupation. Israeli sources.

REPORT ON WORLD AFFAIRS. Began in 1919. Periodical. UK. English. qt. 15.00. R W A, 3 Alma Square, London NW8 9QD England. LC D410. DD 327.0904.

RESEARCH PAPER - HEBREW UNIVERSITY OF JERUSALEM, SOVIET AND EAST EUROPEAN RESEARCH CENTRE. Main/Corp Jerusalem. Hebrew University. Soviet and East European Research Centre. 1976. Monographic Series. IS. English. mo. Free to Middle East or Soviet Union Subscription, $2.00 Each Copy. Hebrew University Jerusalem, Soviet & East European Research, Jerusalem Isreal. Tel (2)88-3180. Ed Edith Rogovin Frankel. Circ 600. Occasional papers on wide variety of Soviet and East Europe related themes historical, contemporary, internal, international, economic and political.

RESEARCH REPORT (INSTITUTE OF JEWISH AFFAIRS). See Religion, Mythology, Rationalism - Judaism.

RESEARCH SERIES - UNIVERSITY OF CALIFORNIA, BERKELEY. INSTITUTE OF INTERNATIONAL STUDIES. (RESEARCH SERIES). No. 3-. 0068-6093. Monographic Series. US. English. ir. Regents of the University of California, 210 Sproul Hall, Berkeley CA 94720. Tel (415)642-4065. Ed Paul M Gilchrist. Ind/Abst GeoRef. Scholarly research studies in the social sciences relating to international and comparative themes, especially political science and economics. *Research Series (University of California, Berkeley. Center for Chinese Studies).*

REVIEW OF INTERNATIONAL AFFAIRS. V. 1- June 7, 1950-. 0486-6096. Periodical. YU. English (published in Serbo-Croat, French, Spanish, German and Russian). sm. $26.00. Review of International Affairs, PO Box 413, 11001 Belgrade Yugoslavia. Ind/Abst Public Aff. Inf. Serv. Bull. LC D839. Index published separately - free - automatically sent.

REVIEW OF INTERNATIONAL STUDIES. Vol. 7, No. 1 (Jan. 1981)-. 0260-2105. Periodical. UK. English. qt. $52.00. Butterworth Scientific Limited, PO Box 63, Westbury House, Bury Street, Guildford GU2 5BH England. Tel 0444 4591888. Ind/Abst Am. Hist. Life, Hist. Abstr., Part A, Mod. Hist. Abstr., Hist. Abst., Part B, Twent. Century Abstr., ABC Pol Sci, Recent Publ. Artic. LC JX1. DD 327.05. Also available on microfiche. *British Journal of International Studies, 0305-8026.*

REVISTA ARGENTINA DE RELACIONES INTERNACIONALES. Vol. 1, No. 1 (Jan./April 1975)-. 0325-1888. Periodical. AG. Spanish. ty. $18.00. Fundacion Para la

Political Science—International Relations

Educacion, Defensa 251, 1065 Buenos Aires Argentina. LC HF1509.

REVISTA DE ESTUDIOS INTERNACIONALES. V. 1, No. 1 (Jan./March 1980)-. 0210-9794. Periodical. SP. Spanish. qt. $20.00. Centro de Estudios Constitucionales, Plaza de la Marina Espanola 9, Madrid 13 Spain. **Ind/Abst** Am. Hist. Life, Hist. Abstr., Part A, Mod. Hist. Abstr., Hist. Abst., Part B, Twent. Century Abstr., ABC Pol Sci. LC D839. DD 327.05. Revista de Politica Internacional (Centro de Estudios Constitucionales).

REVISTA ROMANA DE STUDII INTERNATIONALE. (REVUE ROUMAINE D'ETUDES INTERNATIONALES). 1-2-. 0048-8178. Periodical. French, Russian, and English. bm. $56.00. Rompresfilatelia, PO Box 1362137, Bucharest Romania. **Ind/Abst** Am. Hist. Life, Hist. Abstr., Part A, Mod. Hist. Abstr., Hist. Abst., Part B, Twent. Century Abstr. LC DR201.

REVISTA URUGUAYA DE ESTUDIOS INTERNACIONALES. Yearly V. No. 1, (July/August/September 1982)-. Periodical. Spanish (summaries in English). qt. Plaza Independencia, 830 P 8 Casilla de Correo 903, Montevideo Uruguay. LC D839. DD 909.82.

REVUE ANNUELLE CEASED. **Main/Corp** Canada. Dept. of External Affairs. VFOAT Relations Etrangeres du Canada. 1972-1977. CN. French. an. Information Canada/Receiver General Canada, Statistics Canada, Ottawa Ontario K1A 0T6 Canada. LC F1034.2. DD 327.71.

REVUE ANNUELLE - MINISTERE DES AFFAIRES EXTERIEURES. Main/Corp Canada. Dept. of External Affairs. VFOAT Annual Review. CN. French. an. Information Canada, 171 Slater Street, Ottawa Ontario K1A 0S9 Canada. LC JX1515.A2. DD 327.71.

REVUE D'ETUDES PALESTINIENNES : REVUE TRIMESTRIELLE PUBLIEE PAR L'INSTITUT DES ETUDES PALESTINIENNES. VFOAT Palestiniennes. No. 1 (Autumn 1981)-. 0252-8290. Periodical. French. qt. 160 Domestic, $20.00 US. Institute of Palestine Studies, PO Box 11-7164, Beirut Lebanon. **Tel** 814174. Ed Elias Sanbar. bk rev. adv acc. **Circ** 6,000. Deals exclusively with the Palestine question and the Arab-Israeli conflict.

REVUE D'HISTOIRE DIPLOMATIQUE. Began publication in 1887. 0035-2365. Periodical. FR. French. qt. $21.29. Editions a Pedone, 13 rue Soufflot, 75005 Paris France. LC JX3. (cum index).

RIVISTA DI STUDI POLITICI INTERNAZIONALI. Year 1- Jan./June 1934. 0035-6611. Periodical. IT. Italian. qt. $23.76. Rivista di Studi Politici, Lungarno del Tempio 40, 50121 Florence Italy. **Tel** 666-384. Ed Giuseppe Vedovato. **Ind/Abst** Int. Labour Doc., ABC Pol Sci, Hist. Abstr., Am. Hist. Life, Recent Publ. Artic., Hist. Abst., Part B, Twent. Century Abstr. Hist. Abstr., Part A, Mod. Hist. Abstr. LC JX7. (cum index). bk rev. **Circ** 1,200. (ctrl). Covers international law and relations, diplomatic history, European and world economic financial relations, East-West relations, Third World, Latin America, European economic community and regional organizations.

ROMANIA VIEWPOINTS. Periodical. RM. English. ir. Agerpres, Scinteia Square, Bucharest 1 Romania. LC D839. DD 327.05.

SAGE INTERNATIONAL YEARBOOK OF FOREIGN POLICY STUDIES. See Yearbooks, Almanacs, Directories.

SAIS REVIEW (JOHNS HOPKINS UNIVERSITY. SCHOOL OF ADVANCED INTERNATIONAL STUDIES: 1981). (SAIS REVIEW). VFOAT S.A.I.S. Review. VAT School of Advanced International Studies Review. No. 1 (Winter 1981)-. 0036-0775. Periodical. US. English. sa. $18.00. SAIS Review, Business Manager, 1740 Massachusetts Avenue NW, Washington DC 20036. **Tel** (202)332-1975. Ed J Duncan Moore. **Ind/Abst** Am. Hist. Life, Hist. Abstr., Part A, Mod. Hist. Abstr., Hist. Abst., Part B, Twent. Century Abstr., ABC Pol Sci, Writ. Am. Hist., Public Aff. Inf. Serv. Bull., Recent Publ. Artic. LC D839. DD 327.0904. bk rev. adv acc. **Circ** 2,500. Journal of international affairs featuring articles on security, international politics, trade and monetary matters, third world issues, US, foreign policy; plus book reviews. SAIS Review (Johns Hopkins University. School of Advanced International Studies : 1956), 0036-0775.

SAMID. VFOAT Samed. Periodical. Arabic. ir. 1.50. Jamiyat Maamil Abna Shuhada Filastin, PO Box 155024, Bayrut Lebanon. LC DS119.7.

SANE WORLD. V. 1- Feb. 1962-. 0036-4304. Periodical. US. English. mo. $20.00. Sane, 711 G Street SE, Washington DC 20003. **Tel** (202)546-7100. Ed Beth Baker. LC JX1974.7. DD 327.17405. **Circ** 89,000. News and analysis of nuclear weapons issues, military spending, economic conversion and disarmament. Sane/USA.

SCANDALOUS INTERNATIONAL NEWS. (SCANDALOUS INTERNATIONAL NEWS NEWS : SIN). VFOAT Nouvelles. Internationales Scandaleuses. Vol. 1, No. 2 (Jan./Feb. 1983)-. 0820-7887. Periodical. CN. English. mo. $25.00 Per Year, $13.00 for 6 Months. Scandalous International News, PO Box 4190 Station E, Ottawa Ontario K1N 8V2 Canada. DD 320.0207. Scandalous International News. English, French & Arabic, 0820-7887.

SCREAM (OTTAWA, ONT.). (SCREAM). No. 1-. 0828-6604. Periodical. CN. English. ir. $1.00 Per No., Free to Unemployed. Youth Information Network, PO Box 4136 Station E, Ottawa Ontario K1S 5B2 Canada. DD 327.17205.

SEMIANNUAL REPORT BY THE PRESIDENT TO THE COMMISSION ON SECURITY AND COOPERATION IN EUROPE. (SEMIANNUAL REPORT BY THE PRESIDENT TO THE COMMISSION ON SECURITY AND COOPERATION IN EUROPE : REPORT SUBMITTED TO THE COMMITTEE ON INTERNATIONAL RELATIONS). **Main/Corp** United States. President. 0147-9407. US. English. sa. Superintendent of Documents, US Government Printing Office, Washington DC 20402. LC JX1393.C65. DD 327.17094.

SEREN KENKYU. Began with May 1959 issue. Periodical. JA. Japanese. ir. 300. Sekai Rempo Kensetsu Domei, 15-10 Uchi Kanda 1-chome, Chiyoda-ku Tokyo Japan. LC JX1903.

SHIH CHIEH CHIH SHIH. VFOAT Shijie Zhishi. Periodical. CC. Chinese. sm. 1000000. China Publication Centre, PO Box 2820, Beijing China. **Tel** 552331. **Ind/Abst** Am. Hist. Life, Hist. Abstr., Part A, Mod. Hist. Abstr., Hist. Abst., Part B, Twent. Century Abstr. LC AP95.C4. DD 909. bk rev. adv acc. **Circ** 250,000. (ctrl). Explains China's foreign policies, comments on current world events, analyses the world situation, and provides information on individual countries and helps it's readers to understand what is happening in the world.

SHIH SHIH TZU LIAO SHOU TSE. CC. Chinese. ir. 0.50. Hsin Hua Shu Tien, Pei-Ching Fa Hsing So, Peking China. LC DS779.15. DD 951.05805.

SINO-AMERICAN RELATIONS. V. 1- Spring 1975-. Periodical. CN. English. qt. $14.00. Sino-American Relations, Chinese Culture University, Taiwan-13 Republic of China. Ed Yu-Tang Daniel Lew. LC E183.8.T3. DD 327.51249073. bk rev. adv acc. **Circ** 1,500. Includes international affairs, history, humanities, economic relations, memoirs and culture.

SOCIALISMO OGGI. Year 1, N. 1 (10 Jan. 1984)-. Periodical. IT. Italian. sm. 50.000. Via di Ripetta 66, Roma Italy. LC HX286. DD 335.00945.

THE SOVIET UNION AND THE MIDDLE EAST. Vol. 5, No. 1 (1980)-. 0334-4142. Periodical. IS. English. mo. $15.00. Soviet & East European Research Center, Fac-Social Science, Mount Scopus, Jerusalem 91905 Israel. **Tel** 2-88-3180. Ed Stefani Hoffman. LC DS63.2.S65. DD 327.47056. **Circ** 400. Survey and analysis of Soviet and East European press on the Middle East covering both internal affairs and international relations. Bulletin . . . the Soviet Union and the Arab-Israeli Conflict.

SPEARHEAD. No. 1- Aug. 1964-. Periodical. UK. English. mo. $13.10. Spearhead, 52 Westbourne Villas, Hove Sussex England. bk rev. adv acc. **Circ** 2,000. Commentaries on British and international affairs.

SPECIAL REPORT - UNITED STATES DEPARTMENT OF STATE, BUREAU OF PUBLIC AFFAIRS. (SPECIAL REPORT). 0271-1486. Monographic Series. US. English. US Department of State, Bureau of Public Affairs, Washington DC 20520. LC E840. DD 327.73005. Special Report - Department of State, Bureau of Public Affairs, Office of Public Communication, 0271-1508.

SPETTATORE INTERNAZIONALE. (LO SPETTATORE INTERNAZIONALE). Ceased in 1982. 0584-8776. Periodical. IT. English. qt. $11.88. Organizzazione Rab Srl, Casella Postale 30101, 00100 Roma 47 Italy. **Ind/Abst** Am. Hist. Life, Hist. Abstr., Part A, Mod. Hist. Abstr., Hist. Abst., Part B, Twent. Century Abstr., Hist. Abstr. LC D839.

SPRAWY MIEDZYNARODOWE. VFOAT International Affairs. Vol. 1-Oct. 1948-. 0038-853X. Periodical. PL. Polish (added title and table of contents in English and Russian. Table of contents also in French and German. Voprosy. Table of contents also in French and German). mo. ARS Polona, Krakowskie Przedmiescie 7, 00-068 Warsaw Poland. **Ind/Abst** Am. Hist. Life, Hist. Abstr. LC D839.

STATEMENTS AND SPEECHES - EXTERNAL AFFAIRS CANADA. (STATEMENTS AND SPEECHES). **Main/Corp** Canada. Dept. of External Affairs. Public Affairs Branch. 0712-0761. Monographic Series. CN. English. LC JX351. DD 327.71. Statements and Speeches - Bureau of Information, Department of External Affairs, 0712-0761.

STRATEGIC SURVEY. Began in 1966. 0459-7230. UK. English. an. $13.00. Marketing International Inc, 13 Park Avenue, Gaithersburg MD 20877. **Tel** (301)670-1766. LC U162. DD 355.43.

STRATEGY PAPERS. No. 1- 1969-. 0580-4105. Monographic Series. US. English. ir. National Strategy Information Center, 150 East 58th Street, New York NY 10155. **Tel** (212)838-2912.

STREITKRAFTEVERGLEICH NATO-WARSCHAUER PAKT. VFOAT Streitkraftevergleich Nato Warschauer Pakt. German. ir. Free. Streitkrafteamt Offentlichkeitsarbeit, Wiesendef 49, 5309 Meckenheim West Germany.

STUDIEN ZUR REGIERUNGSLEHRE UND INTERNATIONALEN POLITIK. NE. German. ir. Martinus Nijhoff Publishers, PO Box 163, Spulboulevard 50, 3300 AD Dordrecht Netherlands.

STUDIES IN INTERNATIONAL AFFAIRS. Main/Corp Washington Center of Foreign Policy Research. No. 1- 1967-. 0081-802X. Monographic Series. US. English. ir. Johns Hopkins University Press, 701 West 40th Street/Suite 275, Baltimore MD 21211. **Tel** (301)338-6987.

STUDIES ON INTERNATIONAL RELATIONS CEASED. No. 1-15. 0324-8283. English. sa. $5.00. RSW Prasa-Ksiazka-Ruch Chz. **Ind/Abst** Public Aff. Inf. Serv. Bull. LC JX18. DD 327.05.

SURVEY OF ACTIVITIES - COMMITTEE ON INTERNATIONAL RELATIONS. Main/Corp United States. Congress. House. Committee on International Relations. VFOAT Committee on International Relations Survey of Activities. 1976-. Periodical. US. English. ir. Superintendent of Documents, US Government Printing Office, Washington DC 20402. Survey of Activities - Committee on Foreign Affairs.

SURVIVING TOGETHER. Periodical. US. English. ir. Institute for Soviet-American Relations, 2738 McKinley Street NW, Washington DC 20015.

SWISS REVIEW OF WORLD AFFAIRS. V. 1- Jan. 1951-. 0039-7490. Periodical. SZ. English. mo. $28.00. Credit Suisse, 100 Wall Street, New York NY 10005. **Ind/Abst** Int. Labour Doc. LC D839. Index published separately - free - automatically sent.

TERRORISM. V. 1-. 0149-0389. Periodical. US. English. qt. $56.00. Crane Russak & Company, 3 East 44th Street, New York NY 10017. **Tel** (212)867-1490. Ed Yonah Alexander. **Ind/Abst** Am. Hist. Life, Predicasts, Hist. Abstr., Part A, Mod. Hist. Abstr., Hist. Abst., Part B, Twent. Century Abstr., Sociol. Abstr., Soc. Welf. Soc. Plan./Policy Soc. Dev. LC HV6431. DD 364.13105. CODEN TERRD4. bk rev. adv acc. **Circ** 800. Presents research on the types, causes, control, consequences, and meaning of all forms of terrorist activity.

THIRD WORLD UNITY. No. 1- Jan. 1978-. Periodical. English. ir. $25.00. M C Menon, 20/3771 Regharpura Karol Bagh, New Delhi 110005 India. LC D839.

THE TIMES YEARBOOK OF WORLD AFFAIRS. See Yearbooks, Almanacs, Directories.

TOWARD FREEDOM. 1952. 0040-9898. Periodical. US. English. bm. $10.00. Toward Freedom, 345 South Dearborn Street/Room 1213, Chicago IL

Political Science—International Relations

60604. **Tel** (312)427-3877. Ed William B Lloyd. **LC** D839. **DD** 327.05. bk rev. **Circ** 1,000. Economic, social and political progress of third world countries; also affairs of Soviet satellite nations.

TOWSON STATE JOURNAL OF INTERNATIONAL AFFAIRS. 0041-0063. Periodical. US. English. sa. $2.00. Towson State College, Box 1951, Baltimore MD 21204. **Ind/Abst** Am. Hist. Life, Hist. Abstr., Part A, Mod. Hist. Abstr., Hist. Abst., Part B, Twent. Century Abstr. **LC** JX1. **DD** 327.05. *Journal of International Affairs (Baltimore, Md.).*

TRADE OF NON-NATO EUROPE, JAPAN, WITH COMMUNIST COUNTRIES. See Business - Commerce.

TRANSLANTIC PERSPECTIVES. (TRANSATLANTIC PERSPECTIVES : A PUBLICATION OF THE GERMAN MARSHALL FUND OF THE UNITED STATES). **VFOAT** Perspectives. No. 1 (June 1979)-. 0192-477X. Periodical. US. English. sa. Free. The German Marshall Fund of the United States, Suite 900/11 Dupont Circle Northwest, Washington DC 20036. **Tel** (202)745-3950. Ed Elizabeth McPherson. bk rev. **Circ** 10,500. Articles of about 2,000 words in which grantees report on their German Marshall fund-supported work. Topics include technology, jobs, international economics, trade, environment and the media.

TRANSLATIONS ON JAPAN. No. 1- Oct. 28, 1975-. Periodical. US. English (Japanese). mo. National Technical Information Service, Joint Publications Research Service, 5285 Port Royal Road, Springfield VA 22161.

TRANSNATIONAL ASSOCIATIONS. (INTERNATIONAL TRANSNATIONAL ASSOCIATIONS). **VFOAT** Associations Transnationales Internationales. 29th- Year. 0250-4928. Periodical. BE. English (French). bm. $24.00. **LC** AS1. **DD** 050. **NLM** AS 1 N116. *International Associations, 0020-6059.*

TRAVAUX ET RECHERCHES - CENTRE DE RECHERCHES RELATIONS INTERNATIONALES DE L'UNIVERSITE DE METZ. **Main/Corp** Universite de Metz. Centre de Recherches Relations Internationales. French or German. ir. 40.00. Ile De Saulcy, Paris France 57000. **LC** D1. **DD** 327.05.

TREATIES AND OTHER INTERNATIONAL ACTS SERIES. Publication began with 1501, 1946. 0083-0186. Monographic Series. US. English. ir. Superintendent of Documents, US Government Printing Office, Washington DC 20402. **Tel** (202)783-3238. **LC** JX235.9. **DD** 341.273.

TREATY SERIES. **Main/Corp** Australia. Dept. of Foreign Affairs. No. 10- 1970-. Periodical. AT. English. an. Australian Government Printing Office, PO Box 84, Canberra Australian Capitol Territory 2600 Australia. **Tel** 062-95 4411. *Treaty Series.*

LA TRIBUNE DIPLOMATIQUE. Periodical. French. ir. BP 391, Kinshasa Congon. **LC** D839. **DD** 327.05.

UFSI REPORTS. **VAT** Universities Field Staff International Reports. No. 1- 1982-. 0743-9644. Monographic Series. US. English. ir. $30.00. Universities Field Staff International, Box 150, Hanover NH 03755. **Tel** (603)448-5741. Ed Manon Spitzer. **Ind/Abst** Int. Labour Doc. **LC** L13. **DD** 909.8205. **Circ** 1,400. Developments in international politics, economics, culture, emphasis on third world. *Reports - American Universities Field Staff, 0161-0724.*

UNESCO COURIER CEASED. (THE UNESCO COURIER). **VFOAT** Courier. **VAT** United Nations Educational, Scientific and Cultural Organization Courier. Vol. 7, No. 3 (July 1954). Ceased with 37th Year, No. 11 (Nov. 1984). 0041-5278. Periodical. FR. English. $12.00. UNESCO, Place de Fontenoy, 75700 Paris France. **Tel** (800)521-8110. **Ind/Abst** Read. Guide Period. Lit., Int. Labour Doc., Women Stud. Abstr., Curr. Contents Educ., Public Aff. Inf. Serv. Bull., Mag. Index. **LC** AS4.U8. **DD** 060. **NLM** W1 U576. Articles take the reader to every area of human endeavor, in every part of the world. Each issue contains color illustrations. *Courier (Paris, France).*

UNESCO PRIZE FOR PEACE EDUCATION. **VFOAT** Prize for Peace Education. 1981-. English. ir. UNESCO, 7 Place de Fontenoy, 75700 Paris France. **LC** JX1904.5. **DD** 327.17207.

THE UNITED NATIONS DISARMAMENT YEARBOOK. See Yearbooks, Almanacs, Directories.

UNITED NATIONS NEWS DIGEST. Periodical. US. English. wk.

U.S. CHINA RELATIONS : NOTES FROM THE NATIONAL COMMITTEE. **VFOAT** US China Relations. **VAT** United States China Relations. Vol. 1 No. 1 (Fall 1970)-. Periodical. US. English. qt. $3.00. National Committee on US & China Relations, 777 United Nations Plaza/12th Floor, New York NY 10017.

U.S. FIRMS & REPRESENTATIVES IN MALAYSIA. **VFOAT** United States Firms & Representatives in Malaysia. '80-. English. an. 30.00. Gray & Associates, Lot 2-63 1st Floor Wisma Central, Jalan Ampang, Kuala Lumpur Malaysia.

U.S. PARTICIPATION IN THE UN. **Series/Titl** International Organization and Conference Series. **VFOAT** Report on the United Nations. **VAT** United States Participation in the United Nations. 1948-. 0083-0208. US. English. an. US Department of State, Bureau of International Organization Affairs, Washington DC 20402. *United States and the United Nations, 0272-6769.*

UNITED STATES PARTICIPATION IN THE UNITED NATIONS; ANNUAL REPORT. **Main/Corp** United States. President. **Series Corp** United States. Department of State. Department of State Publication. **VFOAT** U.S. Participation in the U.N. 3rd- 1948-. 0083-0208. US. English. an. Superintendent of Documents, US Government Printing Office, Washington DC 20402. **DD** 327. *United States and the United Nations.*

US-CHINA REVIEW. **VFOAT** U.S.-China Review. **VAT** United States-China Review. Vol 4, No 3 (May-June 1980)-. 0164-3886. Periodical. US. English. bm. $14.00. US China Peoples Friendship, 2025 Eye Street NW/Suite 715, Washington DC 20006. **Tel** (202)296-4147. Ed Duncan McFarland. **Ind/Abst** Predicasts, Funk Scott Index Corp. Ind. **DD** 327. bk rev. adv acc. **Circ** 7,000. *New China, 0161-0643.*

U.S.C.-F.A.R. CONSOLIDATED PLAN FOR FOREIGN AFFAIRS RESEARCH. (USC/FAR CONSOLIDATED PLAN FOR FOREIGN AFFAIRS RESEARCH). **Main/Corp** United States. National Security Council. Subcommittee on Foreign Affairs Research. 0093-7517. US. English. National Security Council, Subcommittee on Foreign Affairs Research, Washington DC 20520. **LC** JX1293.U6. **DD** 327.072073.

USSR AND THIRD WORLD. V. 1- Dec. 7, 1970/Jan. 10, 1971-. 0041-5545. Periodical. UK. English. ir. Central Asian Research Centre, 8 Wakley Street, Islington London EC1 England. **Tel** 01 278 9441. Ed David L Morison. **LC** DK266.A2. **DD** 327.47. adv acc. Comprehensive current development of relations of the USSR and of China with all Third World countries comprehensively.

UST CUMULATIVE INDEXING SERVICE : CUMULATIVE INDEX TO UNITED STATES TREATIES AND OTHER INTERNATIONAL AGREEMENTS. See Indexes/Abstracts.

VEREINTE NATIONEN. 0042-384X. Periodical. GW. German. bm. Vereinte-Nationen, Postfach 1560, 54 Koblenz West Germany. **Tel** (02628)7667. **Ind/Abst** Foreign Lang. Index, PAIS Foreign Lang. Index.

VIETNAM FOREIGN AFFAIRS REVIEW. V. 1- Nov. 1973-. VM. English. Republic of Vietnam/Ministry of Foreign Affairs, Saigon South Vietnam. **LC** DS556. **DD** 327.597.

VIETNAM REPORT. V. 1- 1972-. Periodical. English. ir. *Vietnam Newsletter, Vietnam Economic Report.*

VIETNAM TODAY. V.1- 1977-. Periodical. AT. English. qt. 5.00 Domestic, 7.00 Foreign. Vietnam Today, PO Box 53, O'Connor Australian Capital Territory 2601 Australia. **Tel** (062)473612. Ed David Marr. bk rev. adv acc. **Circ** 1,000. (ctrl) Vietnam's international relations and internal politics and society given an Australian slant by writers from many fields.

VOW NEWSLETTER. 0229-9577. Periodical. CN. English. ir. Voice of Women, 175 Carlton Street, Toronto Ontario M5A 2K3 Canada. **DD** 327.1720601. *Voice of Women, 0382-0874.*

EN VRAC. March 1979-. 0706-1048. Periodical. CN. French. bm. Free. Association Quebecoise des Organismes de Cooperation Internationale, Bureau 200, 1115 Est Boul. Gouin, Montreal Quebec H2C 1B3 Canada. **DD** 327.17060714. (ctrl).

WASHINGTON INQUIRER. 0749-1050. Periodical. US. English. wk. $30.00. Washington Inquirer, POB 28526, Washington DC 20038. **Tel** (202)78-4294. Ed Peter LaBarbera. **DD** 320. bk rev. adv acc. **Circ** 7,000. Available on microfilm from the State Historical Society of Wisconsin. Foreign affairs and economic news and columns that are rarely found anywhere else. We print the news that the big media does not.

THE WASHINGTON QUARTERLY. V. 1, No. 4- Autumn 1978-. 0163-660X. Periodical. US. English. qt $40.00. MIT Press Journals, 28 Carleton Street, Cambridge MA 02142. **Tel** (617)253-2889. Ed Richard E Bissell. **Ind/Abst** Am. Hist. Life, Hist. Abstr., Part A, Mod. Hist. Abstr., Hist. Abst., Part B, Twent. Century Abstr., Energy Inf. Abstr., Predicasts, Environ. Abstr., ABC Pol Sci, Nexis, Recent Publ. Artic. **LC** D839. **DD** 327.09045. bk rev. adv acc. **Circ** 1,800. Foreign policy journal focusing on strategic balance between East and West. Deep and immediate coverage of the whole range of defense and international problems. *Washington Review of Strategic and International Studies, 0147-1465.*

WASHINGTON REPORT CEASED. 0003-1011. US. English. mo. $10.00. Washington Communications Center, Boston VA 22713. **LC** D839. **DD** 327.05.

THE WASHINGTON REPORT ON MIDDLE EAST AFFAIRS. Vol. 1, No. 1 (Apr. 5, 1982)-. 8755-4917. Periodical. US. English. sm. $45.00. AET, Suite 500/918 16th Street Northwest, Washington DC 20006. **DD** 327.

WASHINGTON REPORT ON THE HEMISPHERE. **VFOAT** C.O.H.A.'S Washington Report on the Hemisphere. Vol. 1, No. 4 (Nov. 11, 1980)-. 0275-5599. Periodical. US. English. bw. $115.00. Council on Hemisphere Affairs, 1612 20th Street NW, Washington DC 20009. **Tel** (202)745-7000. Ed Laurence R Birns. bk rev. **Circ** 2,000. US and Canadian political, economic, and diplomatic relationship with Latin America, emphasizing Central American crisis, legislative sections and human rights and foreign policy formulation. *COHA's Washington Report on The Hemisphere.*

THE WASHINGTON SPECTATOR AND BETWEEN THE LINES. **VFOAT** Washington Spectator. V. 2, No. 11- June 15, 1976-. 0145-160X. Periodical. US. English. $10.00. The Washington Spectator, PO Box 32280, Washington DC 20007. **Tel** (703)691-1271. Ed Trishram Coffin. **LC** E839.5. **DD** 973.905. bk rev. **Circ** 30,000. *Washington Spectator, 0162-3133; Between the Lines, 0006-0305.*

WASHINGTON SPECTATOR (SEATTLE, WASH.). (THE WASHINGTON SPECTATOR). Vol. 1, No. 1 (Jan. 1983)-. Periodical. US. English. Washington Spectator, University of Washington, c/o Student Activities Hub 207 FK-30, Seattle WA 19185. **Tel** (703)691-1271. bk rev. **Circ** 30,000. Watch-dog on Capitol Hill. World-wide reporting of political events.

THE WEEKLY REVIEW. Feb. 8, 1975-. Periodical. KE. English. wk. $160.00. Weekly Review Ltd, PO Box 42271, Nairobi Kenya Africa. **LC** HF1410. **DD** 338.91.

WEST COAST SOUTH AMERICA SERIES. V. 1-. 0363-3489. Periodical. US. English. bm. $100.00. Universities Field Staff International, 620 Union Drive, Indianapolis IN 46202. **Tel** (317)264-4122. Ed Manon Spitzer and Maseem Ahmed. **LC** F2213. **DD** 980.008 S. **Circ** 900. Forty reports covering international political, economic, social, and cultural issues and developments, emphasizing Third World and developing nations and regions.

WORKING PAPERS CEASED. **Main/Corp** Australian National University, Canberra. Department of International Relations. No. 1-11. 0067-2025. Periodical. AT. English. Australian National University, GPO Box 4, Canberra Australian Capital Territory 2601 Australia. **Tel** (062)493690. Ed J O Langtry. **Circ** 500. Includes topics such as superpower relationships arms control, regional strategic relationships, and Australian Defence Policy.

WORLD AFFAIRS. 0043-8200. Periodical. US. English. qt. $25.00. Heldref Publications, 4000 Albemarle Street NW/Suite 100, Washington DC

Political Science—Socialism, Communism, Anarchism, Utopianism

20016. **Tel** (202)362-6445. Ed Joyce Horn. **Ind/Abst** Energy Inf. Abstr., Environ. Abstr., ABC Pol Sci, Public Aff. Inf. Serv. Bull., Soc. Sci. Index, Soc. Sci. Citation Index, Am. Hist. Life, Hist. Abstr., Guide Soc. Sci. Relig. Period. Lit., Hist. Abstr., Part A, Mod. Hist. Abstr., Hist. Abst., Part B, Twent. Century Abstr. **LC** JX1901. **DD** 341.05. adv acc. **Circ** 665. The oldest journal of international affairs in the US. Illuminates issues involved in international conflict, and special issues bring together divergent views and analyses of important topics. *Advocate of Peace.*

WORLD AFFAIRS JOURNAL. Vol. 1, No. 1 (Spring 1982)-. 0731-4728. Periodical. US. English. qt. $12.00. Los Angeles World Affairs Council, 900 Wilshire Boulevard/Suite 2301, Los Angeles CA 90017. **Tel** (213)628-2333. Ed Leslie A Dorman. **Ind/Abst** Public Aff. Inf. Serv. Bull. **LC** D839. **DD** 327.0904. **Circ** 10,000. (ctrl). Compendium of addresses delivered to Los Angeles World Affairs Council by world leaders, statesmen, diplomats, scientists, journalists, and business leaders.

WORLD AFFAIRS REPORT. Main/Corp California Institute of International Studies. V. 3- Mar. 1973-. 0090-7103. Periodical. US. English. qt. $20.00. California Institute of International Studies, 766 Santa Ynez, Stanford CA 94305. **Tel** (415)322-2026. Ed Ronald Hilton. **Ind/Abst** Am. Hist. Life, Hist. Abstr., Part A, Mod. Hist. Abstr., Hist. Abst., Part B, Twent. Century Abstr., ABC Pol Sci, Hist. Abstr. **LC** D839. **DD** 327.0904. bk rev. adv acc. **Circ** 500. Country by country and subject by subject analysis of world developments, contrasting Soviet and Western, especially US accounts and interpretations. *Report - California Institute of International Studies, 0068-564X.*

WORLD ARMAMENTS AND DISARMAMENT. *See* Yearbooks, Almanacs, Directories.

WORLD EVENTS. V. 48- Jan. 1971-. 0747-0347. Periodical. US. English. ir. Chicago Council Foreign Relations, 116 South Michigan Avenue, Chicago IL 60003. *Notes on World Events.*

WORLD PEACE. Periodical. English. ir. International Society of United Modern Enterprise, 60A Campbell Street/PO Box 1944, Lagos Nigeria. **LC** JX1901. **DD** 327.17205.

WORLD PEACE NEWS. 1970. 0049-8130. Periodical. US. English. ir. $20.00. 777 United Nations Plaza/11th Floor, New York NY 10017. **Tel** (212)686-1069. Ed Thomas Liggett. bk rev. **Circ** 2,000,000. The development of world political unity- as seen at the U.N., with national governments, and among non-governmental "peace" organizations worldwide.

WORLD POLICY. No. 1 (1983)-. 0229-6942. CN. English. an. $10.00 Each Volume. World Policy, c/o Dr P Sarbadhikari, Department of Political Studies Lakehead University, Thunder Bay Ontario P7B 5E1 Canada. **DD** 327.05.

WORLD POLICY JOURNAL. Vol. 1, No. 1 (Fall 1983)-. 0740-2775. Periodical. US. English. qt. $48.00. World Policy Institute, 777 United Nations Plaza, New York NY 10017. **Tel** (212)490-0010. Ed Sherle Schwenninger. **Ind/Abst** Public Aff. Inf. Serv. Bull., Soc. Sci. Citation Index, Curr. Contents, Sociol. Abstr. **LC** D839. **DD** 327.09047. adv acc. **Circ** 8,600. Provides alternative economic and security policies for the US and the world based on world order value.

WORLD POLITICS. V. 1- Oct. 1948-. 0043-8871. Periodical. US. English. qt. $25.00. World Politics, Princeton University Press, Princeton, NJ 08540. Ed W T R Fox. **Ind/Abst** ABC Int. Labour Doc., Am. Hist. Life, Hist. Abstr., Part A, Mod. Hist. Abstr., Hist. Abst., Part B, Twent. Century Abstr., Humanit. Index, Public Aff. Inf. Serv. Bull., ABC Pol Sci, Book Rev. Index, Book Rev. Digest, Hist. Abstr., Int. Polit. Sci. Abstr., Soc. Sci. Index, Mon. Period. Index, U.S. Polit. Sci. Doc., Energy Inf. Abstr., Environ. Abstr. **LC** D839. **DD** 909.82. Available on microfilm or xerographic copies from University Microfilm. Available on microfiche from Johnson Associates.

WORLD PRESS REVIEW. V. 27, No. 3- Mar. 1980-. 8945-8895. Periodical. US. English. mo. $19.95. Stanley Foundation, 420 East Third Street, Muscatine IA 52761. **Tel** (319)264-1500. Ed Alfred Balk. **Ind/Abst** Energy Inf. Abstr., Environ. Abstr., Pop. Mag. Rev., Read. Guide Period. Lit., Infobank, Public Aff. Inf. Serv. Bull., Mag. Index. **LC** AP2. **DD** 051. adv acc. **Circ** 126,195. Unique, widely-quoted digest of the leading publications around the world. Information not readily available from other sources. *Atlas World Press Review, 0161-6528.*

WORLD TODAY. (THE WORLD TODAY). VFOAT Chatham House Review. V. 1- July 1945-. 0043-9134. Periodical. UK. English. mo. 40.00. 10 St Laurier's Square, London SW1 England. **Tel** (01)930-2233. Ed Christopher Cviic. **Ind/Abst** ABC Pol Sci, Int. Labour Doc., Public Aff. Inf. Serv. Bull., Soc. Sci. Index, Soc. Sci. Citation Index, Am. Hist. Life, Hist. Abstr., Hist. Abstr., Part A, Mod. Hist. Abstr., Hist. Abst., Part B, Twent. Century Abstr. **LC** D410. **DD** 940.5505. bk rev. adv acc. **Circ** 4,000. Journal of Royal Institute of International Affairs. Read in over 70 countries by political and business leaders, academics, and media. Also libraries and research institutions. *Bulletin of International News.*

WORLD TOPICS YEAR BOOK. *See* Yearbooks, Almanacs, Directories.

XX CENTURY AND PEACE. VAT Twentieth Century and Peace. Periodical. English. mo. Victor Kamkin Inc, 12224 Parklawn Drive, Rockville MD 20852. *Twentieth Century and World Peace.*

THE YEAR BOOK OF WORLD AFFAIRS. *See* Yearbooks, Almanacs, Directories.

YEARBOOK OF FINNISH FOREIGN POLICY. *See* Yearbooks, Almanacs, Directories.

YEARBOOK OF INTERNATIONAL ORGANIZATIONS. *See* Yearbooks, Almanacs, Directories.

YEARBOOK OF THE UNITED NATIONS. *See* Yearbooks, Almanacs, Directories.

YEARBOOK ON HUMAN RIGHTS FOR . . . . *See* Yearbooks, Almanacs, Directories.

YEARBOOK ON INDIA'S FOREIGN POLICY. *See* Yearbooks, Almanacs, Directories.

ZEITSCHRIFT NEUTRALITAT. Periodical. SZ. German. ir. 31.00. 6 Denzlerstrasse 10, CH-3000 Bern Switzerland. **LC** JX5.

SOCIALISM, COMMUNISM, ANARCHISM, UTOPIANISM

ADY FARANY. French or Malagasy. ir. 1200. CCP 16 434, Tananarive Madagascar. **LC** JQ3469.A515.

THE AFRICAN COMMUNIST. No. 1-. 0001-9976. Periodical. UK. English. qt. Inkululeko Publ, 39 Goodge Street, London W1P1FD England. **Tel** 636-7062. **Ind/Abst** Recent Publ. Artic. **LC** HX3. **DD** 335.43096. Available on microfilm from University Microfilms.

AFRICAN RED FAMILY. V. 1- Oct./Dec. 1972-. Periodical. UK. English. bm. $36.00. Hamibantu Publications, 107 Pevensey Road, E7 OAH London England. **LC** HX3. **DD** 335.43096.

AGITATION. Periodical. SZ. German. ir. 8025 Zurich Postfach 329, Zurich Switzerland. **LC** HX6.

AL-BARLAMAN. No. 1, (May 25, 1983)-. Periodical. SJ. Arabic. ir. Sudanese Socialist Union, P O Box 1850, Khartoum Sudan.

AL-ISHTIRAKI. V. 1-. Periodical. Arabic. ir. Al-Ittihad Al-Ishtiraki Al-Sudani, S B 185, Al-Khartum Sudan. **LC** HX9.A7.

AL-YASAR AL-ARABI. VFOAT Al-Yassar Al-Arabi, La Gauche Arabe. Periodical. Arabic. ir. 70.00. 102 Bd Beaumarchais, 75011 Paris France. **LC** HX434.A6.

ALBANIE SOCIALISTE. (L'ALBANIE SOCIALISTE). V. 1- Jan. 1978-. 0707-5057. Periodical. CN. French. bm. $4.00. Association d'Amitie Canada-Albanie, C P 654 Succursale R, Montreal Quebec Canada. **DD** 320.531094965.

THE AMERICAN LEGION FIRING LINE. V. 1- 1952-. Periodical. US. English. mo. National Americanism Commission, PO Box 1055, Indianapolis IN 46206. **Tel** (317)635-8411. **LC** HX81. **DD** 335.405. *Firing Line.*

ANARCHY. V. 1-10 (No. 1-118). 0003-2751. Periodical. UK. English. ir. $7.66. Anarchy Magazine, Box A, Freedom Angel Alley, London E1 England. **LC** HX821.

A.N.CH.A. AGENCIA NOTICIOSA CHILENA ANTIFASCISTA. (A.N.CH.A. : AGENCIA NOTICIOSA CHILENA ANTIFASCISTA). 0229-1347. Periodical. CN. English. mo. National Publications Centre, PO Box 727 Adelaide Station, Toronto Ont M5C 2J8 Canada. **DD** 335.430983.

A.N.CH.A. AGENCIA NOTICIOSA CHILENA ANTIFASCISTA. (A.N.CH.A. : AGENCIA NOTICIOSA CHILENA ANTIFASCISTA). 0229-1339. Periodical. CN. Spanish. mo. $0.25 Per No. National Publications Centre, PO Box 727, Adelaide Station, Toronto Ont M5C 2J8 Canada. **DD** 335.430983.

A.N.CH.A. AGENCIA NOTICIOSA CHILENA ANTIFASCISTA. (A.N.CH.A. : AGENCIA NOTICIOSA CHILENA ANTIFASCISTA). 0229-1355. Periodical. CN. French. mo. $0,25 Per No. Centre National de Publications, CP 727, Succursale Adelaide, Toronto Ont M5C 2J8 Canada. **DD** 335.430983.

ANNALI - FONDAZIONE GIANGIACOMO FELTRINELLI. Main/Corp Fondazione Giangiacomo Feltrinelli. Year 16- 1974/75-. Periodical. IT. Italian (some articles have summaries in French and English). ir. Giangiacomo Feltrinelli, Via Rommagnosi 3, 20121 Milano Italy. **Tel** 803911-874175-806732. **Ind/Abst** Am. Hist. Life, Hist. Abstr., Part A, Mod. Hist. Abstr., Hist. Abst., Part B, Twent. Century Abstr., Recent Publ. Artic. **LC** HX15. **DD** 335. **Circ** 2,000. One of the most significant scientific publications on labour movement history in Italy and abroad. Also including descriptions of Feltrinelli Foundation archives and funds. *Annali-Istituto Giangiacomo Feltrinelli, 0544-1374.*

ARBEITERKAMPF. Periodical. German. ir. 1.00 Single Issue. Verlag Arbeiterkampf, Rutschbahn 35 2 13, Hamburg West Germany. **LC** HX6.

ARCHIPELAG : A. VFOAT A. Periodical. Polish. mo. 152.10 Europe, $67.60. Andrzej Wieckowski, Wilhelmsruher Damm 139, D-1000 Berlin 26 West Germany. **Tel** 4151623. Ed Andrzej Wieckowski. bk rev. adv acc. **Circ** 10,000. (ctrl). Covers socialism, communism, anarchism, utopianism.

ARENA. No. 1- Sept. 1963-. 0004-0932. Periodical. AT. English. qt. 8.85. Arena Publishing Association, PO Box 18, Carlton North Victoria 3054 Australia. **Tel** (03)489-9244. **Ind/Abst** APAIS, Aust. Public Aff. Inf. Serv. bk rev. adv acc. **Circ** 2,000. Indendant Marxist journal of criticism and discussion which carries interpretative comment on political issues in Australasia and internationally, and on cultural and social theory and practice.

ARGUMENTOS. Yearly V. 1-(No. 1-)-. Periodical. SP. Spanish. ir. 1.2000. Proprensa, Maude 15, Madrid-3 Spain. **LC** HC381.

ARGUMENTY (MOSCOW, R.S.F.S.R.). (ARGUMENTY). Periodical. UR. Russian. 0.25. Politizdat, 125811 GSP Moskva, A-47 Miusskaia Pl 7, Moskva Russian SFSR. **LC** HX536.

AUSTRALIAN LEFT REVIEW. No. 1- June/July 1966-. 0004-9638. Periodical. AT. English. bm. $8.85. Communist Party of Australia, PO Box A247, Sydney South Post Office, Sydney New South Wales 2600 Australia. **Ind/Abst** APAIS, Aust. Public Aff. Inf. Serv. **LC** HX9. **DD** 335.4305. (cum index). *Communist Review.*

AUTOGESTION, L'ALTERNATIVE. No. 1 (Aug. 18-Dec. 24 1982)-. 0294-0698. Periodical. FR. French. wk. 150. PSU Service des Abonnements, 9 rue Borromee, 75015 Paris France. **LC** HX5. **DD** 335.005. *Tribune Socialiste (Paris, France : 1979).*

AUTOGESTION Y SOCIALISMO. No. 1-. Periodical. Spanish. ir. M Castellote, Editor, Rios Rosas, 51 Bajo B, Madrid Spain. **LC** HX9.S7. **DD** 335.005.

AUTONOMIE. German. ir. 6.00 Single Issue. c/o Trikont-Verlag, Josephburgstr 16, 8 Munchen 80 West Germany. **LC** HX6.

BANDIERA ROSSA. 0404-8172. Periodical. IT. Italian. wk. $29.70. Bandiera Rossa, Via Varchi #1, Milano Italy. **Tel** 02 3760027.

BIDRAG. V. 1- (No. 1-). Danish. ir. 19 Single Issue. Blabaervej 206, 5260 Jallese Denmark. **LC** HX9.D3.

BIG RED DIARY. UK. English. Pluto Press, Unit 10 Spencer Court, 7 Chalcot Road, London NW1 8LH England. **LC** HX3. **DD** 335.4305.

Political Science—Socialism, Communism, Anarchism, Utopianism

BLACK ROSE. Vol. 1, No. 1 (Spring 1979)-. Periodical. US. English. qt. $12.00. Black Rose Lectures and Learning, PO Box 1075, Boston MA 02103.

BULLETIN - CENTRE INTERNATIONAL DE RECHERCHES SUR L'ANARCHISME. Main/Corp Centre International de Recherches sur l'Anarchisme. 29- Spring 1975-. Periodical. SZ. French. sa. 10.00. Bibliotheque du C I R A, Case Postale 51, CH-1211 Geneve 13 Switzerland. LC HX821. DD 335.8305. *CIRA Bulletin.*

BULLETIN DER BOLSCHEWIKI-LENINISTEN. Main/Corp Osterreichische Bolschewiki-Leninisten. German. ir. Osterreichische Bolschewiki-Leninisten, Ehbrusterg 1, 2320 Schwechat Austria. LC HX6.

BULLETIN - WORKERS LEAGUE (U.S.). CENTRAL COMMITTEE. (BULLETIN : TWICE WEEKLY ORGAN OF THE CENTRAL COMMITTEE OF THE WORKERS LEAGUE). Vol. 4, No. 12 – 78 (Mar. 4, 1968)-. 0279-0165. Periodical. US. English. ir. $30.00. Labor Publications, PO Box 33023, Detroit MI 48216. Tel (313)875-4745. *Bulletin of International Socialism.*

CAHIERS DU COMMUNISME. Yearly V. 16, No. 7- July 1939-. 0008-0136. Periodical. FR. French. ir. $33.26. Cahiers du Communisme, 6 Boulevard Poissonniere 6, 75009 Paris France. Tel 246 82 69. Ind/Abst Foreign Lang. Index, Recent Publ. Artic. LC HX5. DD 335.405. *Cahiers du Bolchevisme.*

CAHIERS DU SOCIALISME. (LES CAHIERS DU SOCIALISME). 1 (Spring 1978)-. 0705-5846. Periodical. CN. French. sa. 12.00. Les Cahiers du Socialisme, CP 660 Succursale Desjardins, Montreal Quebec H5B 1B7 Canada. Ind/Abst Point Repere. DD 971.404.

CAHIERS MARXISTES. VFOAT C.M. Periodical. French. mo $20.00. Fondation Joseph Jacquemotte, Avenue de Stalingrad 20, 1000 Brussels Belgium. LC HX5. DD 335.405.

CALIFORNIA SOCIALIST. V. 1-. 0745-6697. Periodical. US. English. mo. California Socialist, 2404 West 7th Street/Room 202, Los Angeles CA 90057.

CAMPAIGNER. (THE CAMPAIGNER). V. 1- Sept./Oct. 1973-. 0045-4109. Periodical. US. English. mo. $19.00. Campaigner Publications, 304 West 58th Street, New York NY 10019. LC HX1. DD 320.53105.

CANADIAN DIMENSION. V. 1- 1963-. 0008-3402. Periodical. CN. English. bm. $15.48. Canadian Dimension, 801-44 Princess St, Winnipeg Manitoba R3B 1K2 Canada. Tel (204)957-1519. Ind/Abst Am. Hist. Life, Hist. Abstr., Part A, Mod. Hist. Abstr., Hist. Abst., Part B, Twent. Century Abstr., Mag. Index, Can. Environ., Can. Period. Index, Altern. Press Index, Hist. Abstr. bk rev. adv acc. Circ 4,000. Collectively operated, non-profit, responsible and 20- years old. It represents the voluntary works, ideas and hopes of socialists of many persuasions. Provides a forum for the left.

CHANGES SOCIALIST JOURNAL. VFOAT Socialist Journal Changes. V. 5, No. 10-11 (Nov./Dec. 1983)-. 0746-6335. Periodical. US. English. bm. $10.00 U.S., $25.00 Supporting, $25.00 Institutions, $15.00 Foreign, Surface, $30.00 Foreign, Air. Changes Socialist Journal, 17300 Woodward Avenue, Detroit MI 48203. Ind/Abst Altern. Press Index. LC HX1. DD 335.005. *Changes Socialist Monthly, 0194-8350.*

CHANGES SOCIALIST MONTHLY CEASED. VFOAT Changes. V. 1, No. 1 (Feb. 1979)-V. 5, No. 9 (Oct. 1983). 0194-8350. Periodical. US. English. bm. $25.00. Center for Changes, 17300 Woodward Avenue, Detroit MI 48203. Tel (313)869-4749. Ed David Finkel. Ind/Abst Altern. Press Index. LC HX1. DD 335.005. bk rev. Circ 1,000. (ctrl). A journal focusing on movements for social and political change. Special emphasis on labor, feminist, the economic crises, militarism, and problems of socialist theory. *Workers' Power.*

CHIEH FANG CHUN HUA PAO. VFOAT Jiefangjun Huabao. Periodical. CH. Chinese. mo. 1.00. Chung-kuo Chi Shu Tien, PO Box 2820, Pei-Ching China.

CHINESE COMMUNIST AFFAIRS. V. 1-6, No. 2. 0577-8999. Periodical. CH. English. mo. Institute of International Relations, 64 Wan Shou Road, Mucha Taipei Republic of China. Ed Tsao Po-I. LC DS777.55. Circ 2,700. Study of Mainland China. Also reviews of the general, personnel, transportation, communication and diplomatic activities of Chinese Communists.

CHING CHI HSUEH CHI KAN. See Economics - Economic Theory.

CHRISTIAN ANTI-COMMUNISM CRUSADE. 1961. 0195-9387. Periodical. US. English. sm. Free. Christian Anti-Communism, PO Box 890, 227 East 6th Street, Long Beach CA 90801. Tel (213)437-0941. Ed Fred C Schwarz. Circ 55,000. Accurate, up-to-date, documented information concerning doctrines, organizations, methods, programs, and objectives of communism, both within the US and internationally.

THE CHRISTIAN SOCIALIST. No. 15- 1963-. 0009-5648. Periodical. UK. English. qt. Christian Socialist Movement, Kingsway Hall, London WC2 England. LC HX51. DD 335.705. *CSM News.*

CHRONIQUES CEASED. No. 1-29/32. 0383-6959. Periodical. CN. French. mo. $2.00 Per No. Chroniques, CP 747 Succursale N, Montreal Quebec H2X 3N4 Canada. DD 301.1609714.

CHUNG KUNG YEN CHIU. VFOAT Studies on Chinese Communism. Vol. 3, No. 5 (May 1969)-. 0014-9667. Periodical. CH. Chinese. $33.40. Institute for Study of Chinese Communist Problems, PO Box 351, Taipei Taiwan. *Fei Ching Yen Chiu.*

CHUNG-KUO CHING NIEN (PEKING, CHINA : 1948). (CHUNG-KUO CHING NIEN). VFOAT Zhongguo Quignian. Began in 1948. Periodical. CH. Chinese. mo. $6.21. China Publication Centre, PO Box 2820, Beijing China. LC HX9.C5. DD 305.2350951. *Chung-Kuo Ching Nien.*

LA CITTA FUTURA. 1- 11 MAGG. 1977-. Periodical. Italian. ir. 17500. Federazione Giovanile Comunista Italiana, Conto Corrente N 24124000, La Citta Futura Via Delle Vite 13, 001 Roma Italy. LC HX547.

CIVIS MUNDI. Began with issue for Jan. 1971. 0030-3283. Periodical. NE. Dutch. bm. Stichting Civis Mundi, Van Stolkweg 10, Den Haag Netherlands. LC AP15. (cum index). *Oost-West.*

CLASS STRUGGLE. No. 1- Spring, 1975-. US. English. qt. $6.00. Class Struggle, PO Box 5539, Chicago IL 60680.

COMBAT. Main/Corp Communist League (Gt. Brit.). No. 1- March 1975-. UK. English. qt. Communist League, 26 Cambridge Road, Ilford Essex England.

COMBAT SOCIALISTE. V. 1, No. 1 (Oct. 11, 1980)-. 0227-6224. Periodical. CN. French. mo. $0.25 Per No. Combat Socialiste, CP 152 Succursale N, Montreal Quebec H2X 3M6 Canada. DD 335.430971.

COMMUNISM : QUESTIONS AND ANSWERS. No. 1-. Periodical. UR. English (Russian). 0.24 Single Issue. Progress Publishers, 21 Zubovsky Boulevard, Moscow USSR. LC HX15. DD 335.4308.

COMMUNISME (PARIS, FRANCE : 1982). (COMMUNISME). 1982/1-. Periodical. FR. French. sa. 156. Presses Universitaires de France, Service des Periodiques, 12 rue Jean-de-Beauvais, 75005 Paris France. LC HX5. DD 335.430944.

THE COMMUNIST. (THE COMMUNIST : THEORETICAL JOURNAL OF THE CENTRAL COMMITTEE OF THE REVOLUTIONARY COMMUNIST PARTY, USA). Vol. 1, No. 1 (Oct. 1976)-. 0193-3469. Periodical. US. English. $2.50 Per Vol. RCP Publications, PO Box 3486 Merchandise Mart, Chicago IL 60654. LC HX1. DD 335.4305.

COMMUNIST AFFAIRS (GUILDFORD, SURREY). (COMMUNIST AFFAIRS). Vol. 1, No. 1 (Jan. 1982)-. 0260-9819. Periodical. UK. English. qt. Magsub Ltd, Oakfield House/ Perrymount Road, Harwards Heath RHG 3D6 England. LC HX44. DD 335.43. *Documents in Communist Affairs.*

COMMUNIST PROGRAM : ORGAN OF THE INTERNATIONAL COMMUNIST PARTY. No. 1 (Oct. 1975)-. Periodical. English. an. $4.00. Editions Programme, 20 rue Jean-Bouton, Paris France 75012. LC HX3. DD 324.1.

COMMUNIST STATES AND DEVELOPING COUNTRIES. AID AND TRADE. (COMMUNIST STATES AND DEVELOPING COUNTRIES, AID AND TRADE). Main/Corp United States. Dept. of State. Bureau of Intelligence and Research. 0148-2998. US. English. an. Department of State, Bureau of Intelligence & Research, Washington DC 20036. LC HC60. DD 338.91172401717.

COMMUNIST VIEWPOINT. V. 1- March/ April 1969-. 0010-3756. Periodical. CN. English. qt. 15.00 Domestic, 24.00 Foreign. Progress Books, 71 Bathurst Street 3rd Floor, Toronto Ontario M5V 2P6 Canada. Tel (416)368-5336. Ed Anna Larsen. Ind/Abst Am. Hist. Life, Hist. Abstr. DD 335.430971. bk rev. Marxist, theoretical and political journal. Focus on Canada and international issues. *Horizons, 0441-2281.*

COMMUNISTE. (LE COMMUNISTE). V. 1- Jan./ Feb./March 1979-. 0709-3845. Periodical. CN. French. qt. $7.74. Nouvelles Frontieres, 185 Est rue Ontario, Montreal Quebec Canada. DD 335.4305.

COMPASS. Main/Corp Communist League (Gt. Brit.). UK. English. ir. Communist League, 26 Cambridge Road, Ilford Essex England.

CONTEMPORARY MARXISM. No. 1 (Spring 1980)-. 0193-8703. Periodical. US. English. qt. $18.00. Synthesis Publications, 2703 Folsom Street, San Francisco CA 94110. Tel (415)550-1284. Ed Marlene Dixon. Ind/Abst Soc. Welf. Soc. Plan./Policy Soc. Dev., Altern. Press Index, Sociol. Abstr., Public Aff. Inf. Serv. Bull. LC HX1. DD 320.53205. bk rev. adv acc. Circ 3,000. Relevant, divergent and often conflicting views on the most important questions facing our world today by leading scholars, authors, and activitists. *Synthesis.*

CORRESPONDANCE INTERNATIONALE (MONTREAL, QUEBEC). (CORRESPONDANCE INTERNATIONALE). No. 1 (Spring/Summer 1980)-. 0229-1185. Periodical. CN. French. qt. $3,50 Per No. Correspondance Internationale, CP 892 Succursale Tour de la Bourse, Montreal Quebec H4Z 1K2 Canada. DD 335.4305.

COSMOPOLITAN CONTACT. See Political Science.

CRITICA MARXISTA. Yearly V. 1- Jan./Feb. 1963-. 0011-152X. Periodical. IT. Italian. bm. Editori Riuniti, Via Serchio 9/11, 00198 Roma Italy. Tel 06 866 383. LC HX7. (cum index). Circ 6,000. Reflections on the leading idea of the present, political theory, economy and culture.

CRITIQUE COMMUNISTE. Periodical. FR. French. mo. $135.00. Presse Edition Communication, Rue Richard Lenoir, 93100 Montreuil France. LC HX5. DD 335.4305. bk rev. Review of political analysis on French and foreign political life.

CSP. CRITICAL SOCIAL POLICY. (CRITICAL SOCIAL POLICY : CSP). VFOAT CSP. Vol. 1, No. 1 (Summer 1981)-. Periodical. UK. English. ty. 27.00 Domestic, $47.00 Foreign. Longman Group Limited, 6th Floor/Westgate House The High, Harlow Essex CM20 1NE England. Tel (0279)442601. Ind/Abst Sociol. Abstr., Public Aff. Inf. Serv. Bull. bk rev. adv acc. Circ 1,000. Presents an analysis of social policy and welfare issues from a socialist viewpoint.

CUBA UPDATE. (CUBA UPDATE : A PUBLICATION OF THE CENTER FOR CUBAN STUDIES). VFOAT Main Report, Second Congress of the Communist Party of Cuba. Vol. 1, No. 1 (Apr. 1980)-. 0196-0830. Periodical. US. English. ir. $35.00. Center for Cuban Studies, 220 East 23rd Street, New York NY 10010. *Cuba Update, 0196-0830; Cuba in Focus, 0197-5277.*

DEWAN MASYARAKAT. See Economics - Labor.

DISSENT. V. 1- Winter 1954-. 0012-3846. Periodical. US. English. qt. $21.00. Foundation for Study of Ind Society Ideas, 521 Fifth Avenue, New York NY 10017. Tel (212)687-0890. Ed Irving Howe and Michael Walzer. Ind/Abst ABC Pol Sci, Sociol. Abstr., Soc. Welf. Soc. Plan./Policy Soc. Dev., Film Lit. Index, Book Rev. Index, Soc. Work Res. Abstr., Altern. Press Index, Soc. Sci. Index, Am. Hist. Life, Hist. Abstr., Part A, Mod. Hist. Abstr., Hist. Abst., Part B, Twent. Century Abstr., Public Aff. Inf. Serv. Bull., Lang. Lang. Behav. Abstr., Abstr. Soc. Work., Hist. Abstr. LC HX1. DD 335.05. (cum index). bk rev adv acc. Circ 10,000. A magazine of political and social concern. It stands for unyielding opposition to all forms of authoritarianism, with an emphasis on the importance of democratic values.

DYNAMIC. (DYNAMIC : PUBLICATION OF THE YOUNG COMMUNIST LEAGUE OF THE U.S.A) Vol. 1, No. 1 (August 1983)-. 0741-0263. Newspaper. US. English. mo. $2.50. Young Communist League of the

Political Science—Socialism, Communism, Anarchism, Utopianism

U.S.A., 235 West 23rd Street/Suite 500, New York NY 10011.

EAST ASIA QUARTERLY. Periodical. CH. English. qt. $8.00. Institute of International Relations, 64 Wan Shou Road, Mucha Taipei Taiwan China. **Tel** 9394921. adv acc. **Circ** 1,500. This journal is devoted to East Asian politics with emphasis on the Communist movement in the area.

ERA SOCIALISTA. Periodical. Romanian. ir. 72.00. Rompres-Filatelia Serviciul Import-Export-Presa, Calea Grivitei NR 64-66, POB 2001, Bucharest Romania. **LC** HX8. *Lupta de Clasa.*

EST & OUEST. *See* Political Science.

EURORED. VAT Euro-Red. No. 1-. Periodical. UK. English. ir. Communisty Party of Great Britain, Eurored, 49A Tabley Road, London N7 England.

FEMMES DEMOCRATIQUES. (FEMMES DEMOCRATIQUES : ORGANE DE L'UNION DES FEMMES DEMOCRATIQUES DU CANADA). 0828-6558. Periodical. CN. French. mo. $0,50 Le No. Union des Femmes Democratiques du Canada, CP 382 Succursale U, Toronto Ontario M8Z 5P7 Canada. **DD** 335.0088042.

FIFTH ESTATE. 0015-0800. Newspaper. US. English. bm. $10.00. The Fifth Estate, PO Box 02548, Detroit MI 48202. **Tel** (313)831-6800. **Ind/Abst** Altern. Press Index. bk rev. **Circ** 10,000. Anti-technology, anti-civilization, utopianism.

FILOSOFIIA I NAUCHNYI KOMMUNIZM. Began in 1974. Periodical. UR. Russian. an. 1.51. Ul Korova 24, Minsk USSR. **LC** HX8.

FILOSOFSKIE NAUKI. *See* Philosophy.

LA FORGE. VFOAT Forge. V. 1- Dec. 1975-. 0703-4539. Periodical. CN. French (French and English on inverted pages, Dec. 1975- Feb. 12, 1976). bw. 25. Per No. Ligue Communiste Marxist-Leniniste, Ducarada, CP 364 Succursale Place Barnes, Montreal Quebec H2Y 3H2 Canada. **DD** 335.430971.

FORGE. (THE FORGE). V. 1- Dec. 1975-. 0703-4520. Periodical. CN. English (text in French). bw. $7.00. Canadian Communist League Marxist-Leninist, PO Box 364 Station Place d'Armes, Montreal Quebec H2Y 3H2 Canada. **DD** 335.430971.

FORO INTERNACIONAL POR LA UNIDAD DEL MOVIMIENTO MARXISTA-LENINISTA. (FORO INTERNACIONAL : POR LA UNIDAD DEL MOVIMIENTO MARXISTA-LENINISTA). V. 1, No. 1 (April 1980)-. 0229-172X. Periodical. CN. Spanish. ir. $9.00 Canada/US, 36,00 France. May First Distribution, 1407 d'Iberville Street, Montreal Quebec H2K 3B1 Canada. **DD** 320.532205.

FRATERNITE (PARTI SOCIAL CHRETIENE D'HAITI). (FRATERNITE). Periodical. French. ir. Le Parti, 17 Fontamara PO Box 609, Port-Au-Prince Haiti. Ed G Eugene.

THE FREEDOM SOCIALIST. *See* Women.

GAUCHE SOCIALISTE. Vol. 1, No. 1 (Mar. 1984)-. 0823-9177. Periodical. CN. French. mo. 20.00. Gauche Socialiste NPI, 3575 Boulevard St-Laurent/Suite 908, Montreal Quebec H2X 2T7 Canada. **Tel** (514)845-6797. **DD** 320.53105. **Circ** 1,000. On issues and topics of international and local political actuality; on worker's, youth's and women's movements; on national liberation and anti-imperialist struggles.

GEKKAN SHAKAITO. VFOAT Shakaito. Sokan Sareta No wa 1957-Nen . . . 6-Gatsugo to Natte Iru. JA. Japanese. ir. 250. Nihon Shakaito Kikanshikyoku, 8-1 Nagatacho 1-chome Chiyoda-ku, Tokyo Japan. **LC** HX411.

HA-KIBUTS. VFOAT Kibbutz. 1- July 1973-. Hebrew (with summaries in English). ir. Ha-Rashut Le-Haskalah Ve-Heker, Shel Berit Ha-Tenuah Ha-Kibutsit, POB 303, Tel-Aviv Israel. **Ind/Abst** Sociol. Abstr., Soc. Welf. Soc. Plan./Policy Soc. Dev. **LC** HX765.P3.

HA-SHAVUA. Hebrew. ir. Leonardo de Vinci 13, PO Box 40009, Tel-Aviv Israel. **LC** HX765.P3. *Shavua Ba-Kibuts Ha-Artsi.*

HALGAN : ORGAN OF THE SOMALI REVOLUTIONARY SOCIALIST PARTY. VFOAT Struggle. Vol. 1, No. 1 (Oct. 1976)-. Periodical. SO. English. ir. $30.00. Somali Revolutionary Socialist Party, Peoples Hall PO Box 1204, Mogadishu SRD Somalia. **LC** DT407. **DD** 967.73005.

HALLESCHE STUDIEN ZUR GESCHICHTE DER SOZIALDEMOKRATIE. Periodical. GW. German. ir. Martin-Luther-Universitat Halle-Wittenberg DDR, 401 Halle, August-Bebel-Strasse 13 West Germany. **LC** HX6. **DD** 335.505.

HUNG CHI. VFOAT Hongqi. Vol. July 1958-. 0441-4381. Periodical. CC. Chinese. sm. China Publication Centre, PO Box 2820, Beijing China. (cum index).

HUNG CHI. (CHINA REPORT. RED FLAG). VFOAT Red Flag. Periodical. US. English (Chinese). mo. National Technical Information Service, Foreign Broadcast Information Service, Joint Publications Research Service, 5285 Port Royal Road, Springfield VA 22161. *Translations from Red Flag.*

A IDEIA. Periodical. PO. Portuguese. ir. $6.00. A Ideia, Apartado 3122, 1303 Lisboa Portugal. Ed Joao Freire. **LC** HX739.A3. **DD** 335.8309469. bk rev. **Circ** 1,500. (ctrl). Portuguese review of cultural and libertarian thought.

IDEOLOGIA I POLITYKA. Polish. ir. 72.00. Wiejska 12, Warszawa Poland. **LC** HX40.

INTERNATIONAAL MARXISTISCH TIJDSCHRIFT. Periodical. Dutch. ir. 40 Single Issue. nstituut voor Marxistische Vorming, Stalingraadlaan 18-20, 1000 Brussel Belgium. **LC** HX9.D8.

INTERNATIONAL CORRESPONDANCE (MONTREAL, QUEBEC). (INTERNATIONAL CORRESPONDANCE). No. 1 (Spring-Summer 1980) -. 0228-9962. Periodical. CN. English. qt. $3.50 Per Issue. International Correspondance, PO Box 892, Succursale Tour de la Bourse, Montreal Quebec H4Z 1K2 Canada. **DD** 335.4305.

INTERNATIONAL FORUM POUR L'UNITE DU MOUVEMENT MARXISTE-LENINISTE. (INTERNATIONAL FORUM : POUR L'UNITE DU MOUVEMENT MARXISTE-LENINISTE). V. 1, No. 1, (April 1980)-. 0227-633X. Periodical. CN. French. ir. $8.00 Canada. Distribution Premier Mai, 1407 rue d'Iberville, Montreal Quebec H2K 3B1 Canada. **DD** 320.532205.

INTERNATIONAL SOCIALISM. No. 1 (Spring 1960)-. Periodical. UK. English. ir. $13.02. International Socialism, c/o Bookmarics, 265 Seven Sisters Road, London N4 2DE England. **Tel** 1-802-6145. Ed Peter Binns. bk rev. **Circ** 4,000. Theoretical journal of the British socialist workers party.

DIE INTERNATIONALE. Periodical. GW. German. ir. 1.00 Single Issue. Verlag Arbeiterkampf, Rutschbahn 35, 2000 Hamburg 13 West Germany. **LC** HX6.

THE IRISH COMMUNIST. Periodical. IE. English. mo. $8.13. British Irish Communist Organ, 10 Athol Street, Belfast BT12 EGX North Ireland. **Tel** 225851. Ed British Irish Communist Organisation. bk rev. **Circ** 500. A wide-ranging commentary on all aspects of Irish politics, history and culture.

ISSUES & STUDIES. VFOAT Issues and Studies. Vol. 1, No. 1 (Oct. 1964)-. 0021-2377. Periodical. CH. English. mo. $33.50. Institute of International Relations, 64 Wan Shou Road Mucha, Taipei Republic of China. Ed David S Chou. **Ind/Abst** ABC Pol Sci, Soc. Sci. Citation Index, Am. Hist. Life, Hist. Abstr. bk rev. adv acc. **Circ** 3,000. An inter-disciplinary journal devoted to the discussion and analysis of problems relating to Chinese communism and other communist systems. *Analysis of Current Chinese Communist Problems, 0517-7065; Chinese Communist Affairs, Facts and Features, 0577-9006; Catalog of Current Research Publications on Modern China, 0576-8845.*

IZ ISTORII SOTSIALISTICHESKOGO I KOMMUNISTICHESKOGO STROITELSTVA V SSSR. Periodical. UR. Russian. 0.80 Single Issue. **LC** DK266.

JAPAN SOCIALIST REVIEW. No. 1- Nov. 1, 1961-. 0021-4655. Periodical. JA. English. mo. Japan Publs Trading Company Ltd, PO Box 5030/Tokyo International, Tokyo 100-31 Japan. **LC** HX9.

JOURNAL OF AFRICAN MARXISTS. VFOAT Journal des Marxistes Africanis. Issue 1 (Nov. 1981)-. 0263-2268. Periodical. UK. English (French with some summaries in French and Portuguese). sa. 17.00. Journal of African Marxists, 57 Caledonian Road, London N1 9DN England. **LC** HX436. **DD** 335.43096. bk rev. adv acc. Analysis of current African political economy from Marxist perspective.

KICK IT OVER. 0823-6526. Periodical. CN. English. qt. $0.75 Per No. PO Box 5811/Station A, Toronto Ontario M5W 1P2 Canada. **Ind/Abst** Altern. Press Index. **DD** 335.8305.

KOMMUNIST. V. 1- Aug. 1976-. German. ir. $5.00 Single Issue. Kommunistischer Bund Osterreichs, Halbbasse 12, 1070 Wien Austria. **LC** HX6. *Kommunist.*

KOMMUNIST AZERBAIDZHANA. Began in 1920. 0207-1355. Periodical. UR. Russian. mo. $10.00. Victor Kamkin Inc (76303), 12224 Parklawn Drive, Rockville MD 20852. **Tel** (301)881-5973. **LC** HX8. **DD** 324.2479107505.

KOMMUNIST ESTONII. (KOMMUNIST ESTONII : OBSHCHESTVENNO-POLITICHESKII ZHURNAL TSK KOMPARTII ESTONII). Began in 1953. 0321-2122. Periodical. UR. Russian. mo. $12.50. Victor Kamkin Inc (78165), 12224 Parklawn Drive, Rockville MD 20852. **Tel** (301)881-5973. *Bolshevik Estonii.*

KOMMUNIST (MOSKVA). (KOMMUNIST). 1952 G., No. 20-. 0023-3099. Periodical. UR. Russian. ir. $17.00. Victor Kamkin Inc, 12224 Parklawn Drive, Rockville MD 20852. **Tel** (301)881-5973. **Ind/Abst** Sociol. Abstr., Soc. Welf. Soc. Plan./Policy Soc. Dev. *Bolshevik (Moscow, R.S.F.S.R.).*

KOMMUNIST SOVETSKOJ LATVII. (KOMMUNIST SOVETSKOI LATVII : OBSHCHESTVENNO-POLITICHESKII ZHURNAL TSK KOMMUNISTICHESKOI PARTII LATVII). Began in 1952. 0321-2092. Periodical. UR. Russian. mo. $11.00. Victor Kamkin Inc (77173), 12224 Parklawn Drive, Rockville MD 20852. **Tel** (301)881-5973. *Bolshevik Sovetskoi Latvii.*

KOMMUNISTISCHE HEFTE. Periodical. German. ir. 25.00. Gruppe Revolutionare Marxisten, 1090 Liestkandlgasse 4, Wien Austria. **LC** HX6.

KOMUNIST UKRAINY. Began in 1946?. 0130-2434. Periodical. UR. Ukrainian. mo. $12.00. Victor Kamkin Inc, 12224 Parklawn Drive, Rockville MD 20852. **Tel** (301)881-5973. **LC** HX8. *Bilshovyk Ukrainy.*

KOMUNISTAS. Began publication in 1918. Periodical. UR. Lithuanian. mo. $13.50. Victor Kamkin Inc (76702), 12224 Parklawn Drive, Rockville MD 20852. **Tel** (301)881-5973. **LC** HX8.

KONGSANKWON KYONGJE. VFOAT Economic Survey of Socialist Countries. V. 1- No. 1- (1984, 3)-. Periodical. KO. Korean. qt. 2.000. Hanguk Sanop Kyongje Kisul Yonguwon, PO Box 205 Chongnyangni Ucheguk, Seoul 131 Korea. **LC** HC701. *Kongsankwon Kyongje Tonghyang.*

LABOUR WEEKLY. Periodical. UK. English. wk. 27.00. Labour Party, 150 Walworth Road, London SE1 1JT England. **Tel** (01)701-7288. Ed Donald Ross. **Ind/Abst** Am. Hist. Life, Hist. Abstr. **LC** JN1129.L3. **DD** 320.942085. bk rev. adv acc. **Circ** 16,000. Official Labour Party publication.

THE LEFT INDEX. 1982, No. 1 (Spring 1982)-. 0733-2998. US. English. qt. $50.00. Reference & Research Services, 511 Lincoln Street, Santa Cruz CA 95060. **Tel** (408)426-4479. Ed Joan Nordquist. **LC** Z7164.S67, HX1. **DD** 016.33543. Current author/subject index to the contents of periodical literature of the left perspective; includes book review index, documents section, annual cumulated subject index.

LEFT REVIEW. V. 1- MAR. 1977-. 0195-7333. Periodical. US. English. ty. $5.00. Kent Left History Forum, Kent State University, Department of History, Kent OH 44242. **LC** HX1. **DD** 335.005.

LEFTWARD. V. 1- 1974-. 0381-7350. Periodical. CN. English. Leftward, PO Box 429 Station E, Toronto Ontario M6H 4E3 Canada. **DD** 335.005.

IL LEVIATANO. 1- May/June 1976-. Periodical. Italian. ir. 9000. Savelli, Via Cicerone 44, Roma 00193 Italy. **LC** HX7.

LI SHIH WEI WU CHU I LUN TSUNG. V. 1, (Sept. 1982)-. Periodical. CH. Chinese. ir. 0.85. Ching Hua Ta Hsueh Chu Pan, She Fa Hsing Ko, Pei-Ching China. **LC** D16.9. **DD** 335.4119.

LIGNE DE MASSE. (LA LIGNE DE MASSE). V. 1- July 24, 1970-. 0704-1969. Periodical. CN. French. ir. National Publications Centre, PO Box 727/Adelaide Station, Toronto Ontario M5C 2J8 Canada. **DD** 335.4305.

LINE OF MARCH. (LINE OF MARCH : A MARXIST-LENINIST JOURNAL OF RECTIFICATION). Vol. 1, No. 1 (May-June 1980)-. 0739-3571. Periodical. US. English. bm. $12.00 Domestic, $15.00 Foreign. Institute for Scientific Socialism, Box 2729, Oakland CA 94602. **Ind/Abst** Altern. Press Index. **LC** HX1. **DD** 335.4305.

LUTTE OUVRIERE. V. 1- Nov. 1964-. 0701-8746. Periodical. CN. French. bw. 25. Per No. Lutte Ouvriere, CP 641 Succursale N, Montreal Quebec H2X 3M6 Canada. **DD** 335.4309714. *Liberation, 0048-0029; Combat Socialiste pour la Republique des Travailleurs du Quebec, 0821-4972.*

MA-KO-SSU CHU I LAI YUAN YEN CHIU LUN TSUNG. V. 1, (Nov. 1981)-. Periodical. CC. Chinese. ir. 1.20. Hsin Hua Shu Tien, Pei-Ching Fa Hsing SO, Peking China. **LC** HX9.C5. **DD** 335.409.

MA-KO-SSU CHU I YEN CHIU TSUNG KAN. **VFOAT** Ma-Ko-Ssu Chu I Yen Chiu, Makesizhuyiyanjiu. 1983, 1-. Periodical. CC. Chinese. ir. 0.96. Hsin Hua Shu Tien, Peking China. **LC** HX9.C5. **DD** 335.405.

MACHETE (MEXICO CITY, MEXICO : 1980). (EL MACHETE). No. 1 (May 1980)-. Periodical. MX. Spanish. mo. Medicina 56 Copilo, Mexico 21 DF. **LC** HX111. **DD** 335.430972.

MARX-ENGELS-JAHRBUCH. **VAT** Marx Engels Jahrbuch. 1- 1978-. GW. German. ir. 38.-. Dietz Verlag Berlin, Wallstr 76-79 Postfach 273, DDR 1020 Berlin West Germany. **Tel** 27030. **LC** HX6. **DD** 335.405. (ctrl). An indispensable supplement to the Marx-Engels Complete Edition (MEGA) as well as an important source of information on the origin of Marxism and the work of Marx and Engels.

MARXISM AND THE MASS MEDIA. *See* Bibliographies.

MARXISM TODAY. V. 1- Oct. 1957-. 0025-4118. Periodical. UK. English. mo. $30.65. Communist Party Great Britian, 16 St John Street, London EC1M 4AY England. **Tel** (01)608 0265. **Ed** Martin Jacques. **LC** AP4. **DD** 335.4305. bk rev. adv acc. **Circ** 13,000. Current affairs and political strategy with an emphasis on open debate and controversy also contains a major culture and lifestyle section. *Marxist Quarterly.*

MARXIST (NEW DELHI, INDIA). (THE MARXIST : THEORETICAL QUARTERLY OF THE COMMUNIST PARTY OF INDIA (MARXIST)). **VFOAT** Theoretical Quarterly of the Communist Party of India (Marxist). Vol. 1, No. 1 (July-Sept. 1983)-. Periodical. English. qt. $12.00. **LC** HX391. **DD** 335.430954.

THE MARXIST REVIEW. V. 1- July 1967-. 0542-7762. Periodical. English. ir. **LC** HX3. **DD** 335.4305.

MARXISTISCHE BLATTER. Vol. 1-. 0542-7770. Periodical. GW. German. bm. $11.50. Verlag Marxistische Blatter, Heddernheimer Landstr 78A, 6000 Frankfurt 50 West Germany. **Tel** 57 10 51. **Ind/Abst** Energy Res. Abstr., Foreign Lang. Index, PAIS Foreign Lang. Index. **LC** HX6. bk rev. adv acc. (ctrl). Marxist review on problems of society, politics, economies and scientific discussions.

MARXISTISCHE STUDIEN. 1.- 1978-. GW. German. an. 60.-. Inst Marxistische Studien und Forschungen, Hoberlinoau 15, 6000 Frankfurt 1 West Germany. **Tel** (069)724914. **LC** HX6. **DD** 335.405. bk rev. adv acc. **Circ** 3,000. (ctrl). Marxist analysis and discussions on political economy, social theory, class structure and social movements, especially the working class movement in the Federal Republic of Germany.

MASS LINE. V. 1- Oct. 1974-. English. ir. $8.00. K N Ramachandran, Cochin India 682106. **LC** HX3. **DD** 335.434.

MATERIALY . . . ZIZDU KOMUNISTYCHNOI PARTII UKRAINY. **Main/Corp** Komunistychna Partiia Ukrainy. Zizd. UR. Ukrainian. ir. **LC** JN6598.K75. **DD** 335.43094771.

META. V. 1- Sept. 1975-. 0702-8415. Periodical. CN. English. qt. $6.00 Canada and US. Meta Editorial Collective, PO Box 324 Station P, Toronto Ontario Canada. **DD** 320.947.

MIBI-FENIM. 1923. IS. Hebrew. qt. Hakibbutz Hameuchad Publ House PO Box 16040, Tel-Aviv Israel. **Tel** 972-3-724938. **Ed** Zerubavel Gilead. **LC** HX765.P32. Journal of the United Kibbutz movement. Discusses political, economic, social, and cultural issues of Israeli society, especially from the Kibbutz point of view.

THE MINDSZENTY REPORT. *See* Religion, Mythology, Rationalism - Roman Catholic Church.

MOLODOI KOMMUNIST. 10- Ig. Izd., No. 20 (Okt. 1952)-. 0026-9077. Periodical. UR. Russian. mo. $14.50. Victor Kamkin Inc (70546), 12224 Parklawn Drive, Rockville MD 20852. **Tel** (301)881-5973. *Molodoi Bolshevik.*

MONDOPERAIO. Periodical. IT. Italian. ir. 12.000. CCP N 1/32239, Intestato A Mondo Operaio, Via Dei Pontefici 3, 00188 Roma Italy. **LC** HX7. *Mondo Operaio.*

MONTHLY REVIEW. V. 1- May 1949-. 0027-0520. Periodical. US. English. mo. $36.00 Domestic, $39.00 Foreign. National Marine Fisheries Service, 155 West 23rd Street, New York NY 10011. **Ed** Paul M Seezy, Harry Magdoff. **Ind/Abst** Sociol. Abstr., Soc. Welf. Soc. Plan./Policy Soc. Dev., Soc. Sci. Index, Altern. Press Index, Public Aff. Inf. Serv. Bull., Am. Hist. Life, Hist. Abstr., Part A, Mod. Hist. Abstr., Hist. Abst., Part B, Twent. Century Abstr. **LC** HX1. **DD** 335.05. bk rev. adv acc. **Circ** 10,000. Independent socialist monthly providing analysis of world and national events from a political and economic point of view.

NATIONAL SOCIALIST (ARLINGTON, VA.). (THE NATIONAL SOCIALIST). 0740-9508. US. English. qt. National Socialist, Box 88, Arlington VA 22210. **LC** DD256.5. **DD** 320.533.

NAUCHNOE UPRAVLENIE OBSHCHESTVOM. Vol. 1-. 0548-0108. UR. Russian. an. **LC** HX542. **DD** 361.610947.

NAUCHNYE DOKLADY VYSSHEI SHKOLY. NAUCHNYI KOMMUNIZM. **Main/Corp** Russia (1923- U.S.S.R.) Ministerstvo Vysshego I Srednego Spetsialnogo Obrazovaniia. **VFOAT** Nauchnyi Kommunizm. Began in 1973. Periodical. UR. Russian. bm. $27.00. Victor Kamkin Inc (74831), 12224 Parklawn Drive, Rockville MD 20852. **Tel** (301)881-5973. **LC** HX8.

NEW INTERNATIONAL (NEW YORK, N.Y. : 1983). (NEW INTERNATIONAL). Vol. 1, No. 1 (Fall 1983)-. 0737-3724. Periodical. US. English. ir. $12.00/4 issues. 408 Printing and Publishing Inc, 14 Charles Lane, New York NY 10014. **LC** HX1. **DD** 320.53205.

NEW LEFT REVIEW. No. 1- Jan./Feb. 1960-. 0028-6060. Periodical. UK. English. bm. $50.57. New Left Review, 15 Greek Street, London W1E 6QZ England. **Ind/Abst** Recent Publ. Artic., Altern. Press Index, Public Aff. Inf. Serv. Bull., Soc. Sci. Citation Index, Hist. Abstr., Am. Hist. Life, Hist. Abstr., Part A, Mod. Hist. Abstr., Hist. Abst., Part B, Twent. Century Abstr. **LC** HX3. **DD** 335.005. (cum index). *New Reasoner, Universities & Left Review.*

THE NEW ORDER. No. 13- Apr./May 1978-. 0740-3283. Periodical. US. English. bm. $10.00. NSDAP-AO, PO Box 6414, Lincoln NE 68506. **Ed** Gerhard Lauck. Organ of the National Socialist, German foreign branch. Covers international National Socialist (NS) activism, legalization of NSDAP in Germany, creation of a NS state and world wide Aryan new order. *NS Report.*

THE NEW SOCIALIST. (THE NEW SOCIALIST : S). **VFOAT** S. 0731-034X. Periodical. US. English. sa. New Socialist, Box 18026, Denver CO 80218. **Tel** (303)333-1095.

NEW SOCIALIST (LONDON, ENGLAND). (NEW SOCIALIST). No. 1 (Sept./Oct. 1981)-. 0261-6912. Periodical. UK. English. bm. $30.00. Labour Party, 150 Walworth Road, London SE17 1JT England. **Tel** 01-703 5298. **Ed** Stuart Weir. **LC** HX3. **DD** 335.005. bk rev. adv acc. **Circ** 19,000. Discussion magazine of the British Labour Party. Popular and attractive with a mix of politics, interviews and wide coverage of cultural issues.

NEW WORLD REVIEW. *See* Political Science.

NEWS & LETTERS. **VAT** News and Letters. Began with June 1955 issue. 0028-8969. Periodical. US. English. mo. $2.50. News & Letters, 59 E van Buren Street/Suite 707, Chicago IL 60605. **Tel** (312)663-0839. **Ed** Eugene Walker. **LC** HX1. **DD** 335.005. bk rev. **Circ** 7,000. Labor, women's liberation, civil rights and peace news, with analysis of world events from Marxist-Humanist perspective.

NEWSLETTER - COMMITTEE ON SOCIALIST STUDIES. (NEWSLETTER). No. 1 (Oct. 1, 1970)-. 0712-5275. Periodical. CN. English. qt. Free to Members. Committee on Socialist Studies, University of Manitoba, Winnipeg Manitoba R3T 2M8 Canada. **DD** 335.006071.

NIHON KYOSANTO KOKUSAI MONDAI JUYO ROMBUN SHU. 9-. Japanese. ir. 960. 26-7 Sendagaya 4, Shibuya-ku, (151) Tokyo Japan. **LC** HX411. *Nihon Kyosanto Juyo Rombun Shu.*

NOUVELLES RECHERCHES QUEBECOISES. V. 1- 1st Quarterly 1978-. 0705-6982. Periodical. CN. French. qt. $10.00. Les Editions du Courant, 10746 Av Grande Allee, Montreal Quebec H3L 2M7 Canada. **DD** 320.9714.

NOVA MYSL. Began in 1947. 0322-905X. Periodical. CS. Czech (Vols. for 19(48)-53, 1960-(61) have tables of contents also in Russian). mo. Artia, PO Box 790, Praha 1 Czechoslovakia. **Ind/Abst** Am. Hist. Life, Hist. Abstr. **LC** HX8. **DD** 335.4305.

NOVINKY LITERATURY. MARXISMUS-LENINISMUS, SPOLECENSKE VEDY. **VFOAT** Marxismus-Leninismus, Spolecenske Vedy. CS. Czech. qt. 64.00. Statni Knihovna Csr Klementinum 190, 110 01 Praha 1 Czechoslovakia. **LC** Z7161 H85.

N.R.S., LA NOUVELLE REVUE SOCIALISTE. **VFOAT** Nouvelle Revue Socialiste. No.33- Sept. 1978-. Periodical. FR. French. ir. 270.00.-. La Nouvelle Revue Socialiste, 10 rue de Solferino, 75333 Cedex 07 Paris France. bk rev. adv acc. General and specific political and social problems. *Nouvelle Revue Socialiste.*

NUEVA ERA (PARTIDO COMUNISTA DE LA ARGENTINA : 1983). (NUEVA ERA). Second Series, Yearly V. 1, No. 1, (April 1983)-. Periodical. Spanish. mo. Entre Rios, 1041 Capital Federal, CP 1080, Buenos Aires Argentina. *Comentarios (Buenos Aires, Argentina).*

NUTCRACKER. (THE NUTCRACKER). V. 1- Nov. 17, 1916-. 0384-1499. Periodical. CN. English. ir. $1. Woodsworth-Irvine Socialist Fellowship, Box 1602, Edmonton Alberta T5J 2N9 Canada. **DD** 335.0097123.

OBSHCHESTVENNYE NAUKI. *See* Social Sciences (General).

OBSHCHESTVENNYE NAUKI ZA RUBEZHOM. SERIIA 1 : PROBLEMY NAUCHNOGO KOMMUNIZMA. **VAT** Obshchestvennye Nauki za Rubezhom. Seriia Odin : Problemy Nauchnogo Kommunizma. Began in 1972. UR. Russian. qt. Akademiia Nauk SSSR, Ul Krasikova D 28/45, Moskva USSR. **LC** HX8.

OCTOBER. (OCTOBER : THEORETICAL JOURNAL OF MARXISM-LENINISM AND MAO-TSETUNG THOUGHT). Vol. 1, No. 1 (Summer 1977)-. 0226-112X. Periodical. CN. English. qt. Red Flag Publications, PO Box 40/Station N, Montreal Quebec Canada. **DD** 335.4305.

OCTOBRE. (OCTOBRE : REVUE THEORIQUE DU MARXISME-LENINISME ET DE LA PENSEE MAOTSETOUNG). V. 1, No. 1 Summer 1977-. 0226-1138. Periodical. CN. French. qt. Red Flag Publications, PO Box 40/Station N, Montreal Quebec Canada. **DD** 335.4305.

OFFENSIV LINKS. 1- March 1974. Periodical. German. ir. 50.00. FOJ Bewegung fur Sozialismus, Franz-Hockedlingergasse 6, 1060 Wien Austria. **LC** HX6.

OKTOBER. V. 1-. Periodical. Danish. ir. 100. Forlaget Socialisten, Wildersgade 35 1408 K, Kbenhavn Denmark. **LC** HX9.D3.

OPEN ROAD. Issue 1- Summer 1976-. 0703-525X. Periodical. CN. English. ir. $15.48. The Open Road, Box 6135 Station 6, Vancouver British Columbia Canada. **Ed** OR Collective. **Ind/Abst** Altern. Press Index. **DD** 335.8305. bk rev. **Circ** 7,000. International news journal covering news and views of anarchists throughout the world, with an emphasis on direct action.

OSAWATOMIE. Spring 1975-. 0097-8906. Periodical. English. ir. **LC** HX1. **DD** 322.420973.

OUR GENERATION. Vol. 3, No. 4/V. 4, No. 1-. 0030-686X. CN. English. sa. $10.83. 3981 Boulevard St Laurent, Montreal Quebec H2W 1Y5 Canada. **Tel** (514)844-4076. **Ed** Dimitrios Rovssopoulos. **Ind/Abst** Can. Period. Index, Altern. Press Index. **DD** 327.17205. bk rev. **Circ** 4,800. An independent journal dealing with the theory and practice of contemporary anarchism and libertarian socialism. *Our Generation Against Nuclear War, 0383-8765.*

OUR SOCIALISM. Vol. 1, No. 1 (Mar. 1983)-. 0738-3436. Periodical. US. English. mo. $25.00. OS Publications, PO Box 42489, San Francisco CA

Political Science—Socialism, Communism, Anarchism, Utopianism

94142. LC HX1. DD 335.005. *Plain Speaking, 0275-4401.*

LA PAROLA DEL POPOLO. Periodical. US. English or Italian. bm. $6.00. La Parola del Popolo Publishers Inc, 6740 West Diversey Avenue, Chicago IL 60635. LC HX7.

PARTTORTENETI KOZLEMENYEK. Main/Corp Magyar Szocialista Munkaspart. Kozponti Bizottsag. Parttorteneti Intezet. Began in 1955?. 0464-476X. Periodical. HU. Hungarian (summaries in French and Russian). qt. Akademiai Kiado, POB 24, 1363 Budapest Hungary. Ind/Abst Am. Hist. Life, Hist. Abstr., Part A, Mod. Hist. Abstr., Hist. Abst., Part B, Twent. Century Abstr., Hist. Abstr. LC JN2191.S92. DD 335.4305. (cum index).

PARTY LIFE. 0377-2667. Periodical. II. English. bw. Peoples Publ House Pvt Ltd, Rani Jhansi Road New Delhi 110055 India. LC HX3. DD 329.954.

THE PEOPLE. V. 89, No. 34- Dec. 15, 1979-. 0199-350X. US. English. bw. $7.00. Socialist Labor Party, 914 Industrial Avenue, Palo Alto CA 94303. **Tel** (415)494-1532. LC HX1. DD 335.005. bk rev. **Circ** 10,000. Marxist newspaper offering analysis of national and world news. Advocates a socialist industrial union government based on worker ownership and control of the economy. *Weekly People, 0043-1885.*

PEOPLE'S POWER. V. 1- Oct. 1972-. 0377-2713. English. ir. J P Dixit, Unity Compound Juhu -54, Bombay India. LC HX3. DD 335.430954.

POCH. Periodical. German. ir. Progressiven Organisationen, 4001 Basel Postfach 338, Basel Switzerland. LC HX6.

POD ZNAMENEM LENINIZMA. Began in 1941. Periodical. UR. Russian. sm. $19.00. Victor Kamkin Inc, 12224 Parklawn Drive, Rockville MD 20852. **Tel** (301)881-5973. LC JN6598.K75.

POLITICAL AFFAIRS. Vol. 24, No. 1 (Jan. 1945)-. 0032-3128. Periodical. US. English. mo. $15.00. Political Affairs Publishers, 235 West 23 Street, New York NY 10011. **Tel** (212)989-4994. Ed Gus Hall. Ind/Abst Altern. Press Index, Public Aff. Inf. Serv. Bull. LC HX1. DD 335.4305. bk rev. adv acc. **Circ** 5,000. Also available on microfilm from University Microfilms. A journal of Marxist thought. *Communist.*

POLITICS & POWER. VFOAT POLITICS AND POWER. VAT Politics and Power. 1- 1980-. 0144-0918. UK. English. sa. Routledge and Kegan Paul Ltd, Broadway House Newton Road, Henley on Thames Oxon England. LC HX3. DD 335.00941.

POLITIQUE AUJOURD'HUI. Began with Jan. 1969 Issue. 0556-2902. Periodical. PR. French. bm. $29.27. Politique Aujourd Hui, 14-16 rue des Petits-Hotels, 75010 Paris France. Ind/Abst Int. Labour Doc. LC HX5. DD 335.005.

POTOMAC. Year 1- May 1975-. 0149-0893. Periodical. US. English. qt. Editor Alexander E Ronnett MD, 502 Garwood Avenue, Mount Prospect IL 60056. LC HX1. DD 335.4305.

PRACTICE (NEW YORK, N.Y.). (PRACTICE). Vol. 1, No. 1 (Spring 1983)-. 0742-9940. Periodical. US. English. ty. $14.95. New York Institute for Social Therapy and Research, 865 West End Avenue #1C, New York NY 10025. LC HX1. DD 335.4305.

PRAXIS INTERNATIONAL. VFOAT Praxis. Vol. 1, No. 1 (Apr. 1981)-. 0260-8448. Periodical. UK. English (French, or German, with summaries in other languages). qt. $95.00 US. Basil Blackwell Publisher, 108 Cowley Road, Oxford OX4 1JF England. Tel 0865-722146. Ed Mihailo Markovic. Ind/Abst Sociol. Abstr., Philos. Index, Altern. Press Index. LC B809.8. DD 335.05. adv acc. Forum for the critical analysis of social systems, their institutions and ideologies, social movements, and theories. *Praxis (Zagreb, Croatia).*

PRIMERNYE TEMATIKA I PLANY TEORETICHESKIKH SEMINAROV. Main/Corp Dom Politicheskogo Prosveshcheniia Mk I Mgk Kpss. UR. Russian. an. 0.22. Moskovskii Rabochii, Ul Kuibysheva 21, Moskva USSR. LC HX19.

PRIORITIES. See Political Science - Civil Rights.

PROBLEME DES FRIEDENS UND DES SOZIALISMUS. Vol. 1-. 0032-9258. Periodical. GE. German. mo. 15.60. H B Buchexport, Leninstrasse 16, DDR-7010 Leipzig East Germany. Tel 27030. LC HX6. DD 335.4305. bk rev. (ctrl). The periodical of the communist and workers' parties is edited by the Publishing House of Peace and Socialism in Prague in 40 languages.

PROBLEMI DEL SOCIALISMO. Began with: Yearly V. 1, No. 1 (Jan. 1958). 0552-1807. Periodical. IT. Italian. ty. $22.58. Franco Angeli Editore Riviste, Via le Monza 106, 20127 Milano Italy. Tel (02)28.27.651/2/3. LC HX7. DD 335.005.

PROBLEMS OF COMMUNISM. 1974. Periodical. UK. English. ir. $6.89. British Irish Communist Organ, 10 Athol Street, Belfast BT12 4GX North Ireland. Tel 225851. LC HX3. DD 335.4305. bk rev. Circ 1,000. Examines particular political/historical problems for the communist movement in depth. Not to be confused with its American namesake.

PROBLEMS OF COMMUNISM (WASHINGTON, D.C.). (PROBLEMS OF COMMUNISM). No. 1-. 0032-941X. Periodical. US. English. bm. US Government Printing Office, Superintendent of Documents, Washington DC 20402. Ind/Abst Am. Hist. Life, Hist. Abstr., Part A, Mod. Hist. Abstr., Hist. Abst., Part B, Twent. Century Abstr. ABC Pol Sci, Index U.S. Gov. Period., Int. Polit. Sci. Abstr., Soc. Sci. Index, Public Aff. Inf. Serv. Bull., U.S. Polit. Sci. Doc., Recent Publ. Artic. LC HX1. DD 335.4305, 335.4082. Index in last issue of volume - attached. (cum index). Available in microform.

PROBLEMS OF NATIONAL LIBERATION. V. 1- Nov. 1974-. English. ir. 3.00. R Dasgupta, 10 Bondel Road, Calcutta 700019 India. LC HX3. DD 335.4305.

PROBLEMY MIRA I SOTSIALIZMA. V. 1- Sept. 1958-. Periodical. Russian. mo. $23.50. Victor Kamkin Inc (70709), 12224 Parklawn Drive, Rockville MD 20852. Tel (301)881-5973. LC HX8.

PROBLEMY MIROVOGO REVOLIUTSIONNOGO PROTSESSA. Vol. 1-. Periodical. UR. Russian. 1.20. LC HX8. DD 335.4305.

PROLETARIAN INTERNATIONALISM. Vol. 1, No. 1 (Jan. 1979)-. 0276-3621. Periodical. US. English. bm. $11.00. Marxist Lenninst Publ, PO Box 11972/Ft Dearborn Station, Chicago IL 60611. LC HX1. DD 335.4305.

THE PROLETARIAN LINE. Periodical. English. bm. LC DS480.853. DD 335.4305.

PROLETARIAN PATH. Periodical. II. English. bm. 2.00 Single Issue. Moni Guha, 25/1, Jyotish Roy Road, 53 Calcutta India. LC HX3. DD 335.4305.

PROLETARIAN REVOLUTION (MONTREAL, QUEBEC). (PROLETARIAN REVOLUTION). 0229-0685. Periodical. CN. English. mo. $6.00. Lines of Demarcation, PO Box 892, Tour de la Bourse, Montreal Quebec H4Z 1K2 Canada. DD 335.4305.

PROLETARIAN UNITY CEASED. V. 1, Sept. 1976. Ceased with V. 6, No. 1. 0700-9925. Periodical. CN. English. $1.50 Per Number. En Lutte, 4933 rue de Grand Pre, Montreal Quebec Canada. DD 335.430971.

QUADERNI PIACENTINI. -74. 0048-6094. Periodical. IT. Italian. qt. $29.70. Franco Angeli Editore, V le Monza 106, 20127 Milano Italy. Tel (02)28.27.651/2/3/. LC HX7. DD 335.005.

QUE FAZER? No. 1- Nov. 1974-. Portuguese. ir. $480.00. Edicoes Maria da Fonte, rua da Fe 26 -20 2, Lisboa Portugal. LC HX9.P65.

QUESTIONS ACTUELLES DU SOCIALISME. 0033-6351. Periodical. YU. French. mo. Jugoslovenska Knjica, PO Box 36, Beograd Yuguslavia. Ind/Abst Int. Labour Doc. LC HX365.5.

QUOTIDIEN DU CANADA POPULAIRE. (LE QUOTIDIEN DU CANADA POPULAIRE). VAT QCP. Quotidien du Canada Populaire. First issue in 1972?. 0703-8054. Periodical. CN. French. ir. 0.10 Per No. Parti Communiste du Canada, Centre National de Publications, C P 727 Succursale Adelaide, Toronto Ontario M5C 2J8 Canada. DD 335.430971.

RADICAL HISTORY REVIEW. No. 7. 0163-6545. Periodical. US. English. ty. $30.00. Marho John Jay College, 445 West 59th Street, New York NY 10019. Tel (212)489-3698. Ind/Abst Am. Hist. Life, Hist. Abstr., Part A, Mod. Hist. Abstr., Hist. Abst., Part B, Twent. Century Abstr., Writ. Am. Hist., Altern. Press Index, Recent Publ. Artic. LC HX1. DD 909.08. bk rev. adv acc. Circ 3,000. Publishes the best Marxist and non-Marxist radical scholarship in jargon-free English. It scrutinizes conventional history and encourages controversy over current historical questions. *MARHO Newsletter.*

RCDA, RELIGION IN COMMUNIST DOMINATED AREAS. (RCDA. RELIGION IN COMMUNIST DOMINATED AREAS). V. 11, No. 1/3-. 0361-1086. Periodical. US. English (Multilingual). qt. $20.00. Research Center for Religion and Human Rights, 475 Riverside Drive/Suite 448, New York NY 10115. Tel (212)870-2481. Ed Blahoslav Hrudy and Olga S Hruby. bk rev. Circ 2,500. Documentation and analysis of policies of communist parties regarding religious organizations with particular attention to violation of religious freedom and human rights in communist countries. *Religion in Communist Dominated Areas, 0034-3978.*

RED MENACE. (THE RED MENACE). Vol. 1, No. 1 (Feb. 1976)-. 0711-2270. Periodical. CN. English. ir. $0.25 Per Number. The Red Menace, PO Box 171, Station D, Toronto Ontario M6P 3J8 Canada. DD 335.00971.

RELIGIOUS SOCIALISM. V. 1- Spring 1977-. 0278-7784. Periodical. US. English. qt. $2.00. Religious Socialism, 1 Maolis Road, Nahant MA 01908.

LE REVEIL ANARCHISTE. Began in 1900. Periodical. FR. French. qt. 20. BP 121, 25014 Besancon Cedex France. LC HX821. DD 335.8305.

REVIEW OF SOCIALIST LAW. See Law.

LA REVOLUTION PROLETARIENNE. V. 1, 1925-. Periodical. French. ir. LC HX821. Available also on Microfilm.

REVOLUTION PROLETARIENNE (MONTREAL, QUEBEC). (REVOLUTION PROLETARIENNE). Vol. 1, No. 1 May 1, 1978-. 0229-0693. Periodical. CN. French. mo. $6.00. Lignes de Demarcation, CP 892, Succursale Tour de la Bourse, Montreal Quebec H4Z 1K2 Canada. DD 335.4305.

REVOLUTIONARY AGE. V. 1- 1968-. 0556-7165. Periodical. US. English. qt. Freedom Socialist Publication, 3117 E Thomas, Seattle WA 98102. LC HX1. DD 335.4.

RIBERUTERU. VFOAT Libertaire. Edition No. 1-. Periodical. in Japanese. ir. 100. Riberuteru No Kai, 2190 Oizum Gakuencho Nerima-ku, Tokyo Japan. LC HX947.

ROAD OF THE PARTY. (THE ROAD OF THE PARTY : THEORETICAL ORGAN OF THE CENTRAL COMMITTEE OF THE COMMUNIST PARTY OF CANADA (MARXIST-LENINIST). Vol. 1, No. 1 (Mar. 1980)-. 0227-6089. Periodical. CN. English. $1.50 Per No. National Executive Committee of CPC, PO Box 666 Station C, Montreal Quebec H2L 4L5 Canada. DD 324.2710975.

RORAIMA. Periodical. in English. ir. LC HX1. DD 335.009881.

ROTFRONT. Periodical. AU. German. ir. 60.00. Gruppe Revolutionare Marxisten, Postfach 354, 1010 Wien Austria. LC HX6.

RRUGA E PARTISE. Periodical. AA. Albanian. mo. $9.25. Book Distribution Enterprise, rue Konferenca e Pezes, Tirana Albania. LC HX8. DD 335.4305.

SBORNIK PRACI. MARXISMUS-LENINISMUS. Main/Corp Universita Palackeho v Olomouci. Pedagogicka Fakulta. CS. Czech (summaries in Russian and German). qt. Artia, Po Box 790-VA-Smeckach 30, Praha 1 Czechoslovakia. LC HX15.

SCOTTISH JOURNAL OF POLITICAL ECONOMY. See Political Science.

SCOTTISH MARXIST. Periodical. UK. English. 0.25 Per Copy. Scottish Committee of the Communist Party of Great Britain, Gallacher House 69 Albert Road, Glasgow Scotland. LC HX250.S3. DD 335.430941.

SEKIRAH AL PEULOT HA-AGUDAH. Main/Corp Kibutse Ha-Shomer Ha-Tsair, Agudah Shitufit Merkazit. Hebrew. ir. LC HX765.P3.

SEZD MONGOLSKOI NARODNO-REVOLIUTSIONNOI PARTII. Main/Corp Mongolskaia. Series/Titl Dokumenty I Materialy Zarubezhnikh Kommunisticheskikh I Rabochiky Partii. UR. Russian. ir. LC JQ1519.M6.

SHORASHIM. VFOAT Roots. Periodical. Hebrew. ir. LC HX742.2.A3.

SOCIALISM AND DEMOCRACY. (SOCIALISM AND DEMOCRACY : THE BULLETIN OF THE RESEARCH GROUP ON SOCIALISM AND DEMOCRACY). 1 (Fall 1985)-. 0885-4300. Periodical.

Political Science—Socialism, Communism, Anarchism, Utopianism

US. English. sa. Research Group on Socialism and Democracy, PO Box 375, Graduate Center/33 West 42nd Street, New York NY 10036-8099. **DD** 335.

SOCIALISM IN THE WORLD. VFOAT Socialisme dans le Monde. NO. 1-. Periodical. English (French). ir. **LC** HX3. **DD** 335.4305. (cum index).

SOCIALISM : PRINCIPLES, PRACTICE, PROSPECTS : A MONTHLY DIGEST OF THE SOVIET PRESS. 1978, No. 1-. 0201-4432. Periodical. UR. English. mo. APN Pub House, SPPP Editorial Office, 7 Bolshaya Pochtovaya Street, Moscow 107082 Russia. **LC** HX3. **DD** 320.53205.

SOCIALISM, THEORY AND PRACTICE. VFOAT Soviet Monthly Digest of Theoretical and Political Press. No. 1- 1965-. 0583-7138. Periodical. UR. English. mo. $5.00. Eastern News Distributors Inc, 55 West 15th Street, New York NY 10011. **LC** HX1. **DD** 335.4305.

SOCIALISME. No. 1- Jan. 1954-. 0037-8127. Periodical. French. bm. Libresso B V, PO Box 878, 7400 AW Deventer Netherlands. **Ind/Abst** Foreign Lang. Index, PAIS Foreign Lang. Index. **LC** HX5. *Cahiers Socialistes.*

SOCIALISME EN DEMOCRATIE. VFOAT S & D. Socialisme en Democratie. Vol. 1-. Periodical. NE. Dutch. mo Kluwer B V, PO Box 23, Deventer The Netherlands. **LC** HX8. **DD** 320.531505. *Socialsitische Gids.*

SOCIALISME MONDIAL. V. 1- 1973-. 0318-1685. CN. French. $1.00 for 6 numbers. Socialisme Mondial, CP 244, Pointe-Aux-Trembles Quebec H1B 5K3 Canada. **DD** 335.005.

SOCIALISMO & DEMOCRACIA. VFOAT Socialismo e Democracia. Year 1, No. 1 (Jan./Mar. 984)- 1984)-. Periodical. BL. Portuguese. qt. Editora Alfa-Omega Ltda, 05413 rua Lisboa, 500 Sao Paulo Brazil. **LC** HX9.P65. **DD** 335.005.

SOCIALISMO Y PARTICIPACION. 1 (Oct. 1977)-. Periodical. PE. Spanish. qt. $40.00. C E D E P, 6 de Agosto 425 Jesus Maria, Lima 11 Peru. **Tel** 23-44-23. **LC** JL3401. **DD** 985.0633. bk rev adv acc. **Circ** 1,100. This journal studies and inquires about the next subjects: political, economical, social science and agricultural needs.

SOCIALIST AFFAIRS. V. 21- Jan. 1971-. 0049-0946. Periodical. UK. English. bm. 15.00 Domestic, 25.00 US. Socialist International, Steve Thomas Associates, 2240 Queen Street East, Toronto Ontario M4E 1G1 Canada. **Tel** 01-586-1101. Ed Robin V Sears. **DD** 335.005. bk rev. adv acc. **Circ** 5,000. News, information and reports on the democratic left in international politics. Topics covered range from disarmament and economic crisis to the environment and the role of women. *Socialist International Information.*

SOCIALIST ALBANIA. V. 1- Jan. 1978-. 0707-5065. Periodical. CN. English. bm. $4.00. Canada-Albania Friendship Association, PO Box 654 Station R, Montreal Quebec Canada. **DD** 320.531094965.

SOCIALIST CHALLENGE. No. 1- 1977-. Periodical. UK. English. wk. $52.10. Socialist Challenge, PO Box 50, London N1 2XP England. *Red Weekly.*

SOCIALIST CHALLENGE (MONTREAL, QUEBEC). (SOCIALIST CHALLENGE). No. 1 (Nov. 20, 1980)-. 0821-4980. Periodical. CN. English. ir. $10.00 per 11 number Domestic, $15.00 per 11 others. Socialist Challenge, P O Box 152 Terminal N, Montreal Quebec H2X 3M6 Canada. **DD** 335.430971.

SOCIALIST DIGEST; A QUARTERLY ANTHOLOGY OF SOCIALIST LITERATURE. No. 1- Mar. 1968-. 0037-8186. Periodical. English. ir. **LC** HX2. **DD** 335.4305.

SOCIALIST ECONOMIC REVIEW. 1981-. UK. English. an. Merlin Press, 3 Manchester Road, London E14 England. **LC** HX241. **DD** 335.00941.

SOCIALIST FULCRUM. V. 10, No. 3- 1977-. 0707-5472. Periodical. CN. English. ir. $4.65. Socialist Party of Canada, Box 4280 Station A, Victoria British Columbia V8X 3X8 Canada. **DD** 335.005. *Fulcrum, 0707-5464.*

SOCIALIST PERSPECTIVE. V. 1- June 1973-. Periodical. II. English. ir. 7.50. 140/20E South Sinthee Road, 1st Floor, Calcutta 700050 India. **Tel** 525351. Ed A K Mukhopadhyay. **LC** HX3. **DD** 335.00954. bk rev. adv acc. **Circ** 1,000. Covers articles on theoretical and empirical issues of contemporary social science. Marxism is a special interest. *Transition.*

SOCIALIST POLITICS. 1970-. Periodical. NZ. English. qt. $2.26. Zew Nealand Socialist Publishing Distribution, PO Box 1987, Auckland 1 New Zealand. **Tel** 734 046.

SOCIALIST POLITICS (NORTHAMPTON, MASS.). (SOCIALIST POLITICS). Vol. 1, No. 1 (Apr. 1984)-. 0882-7710. Periodical. US. English. $20.00. Socialist Politics Circulation, PO Box 704, Northampton MA 01060. **DD** 320.

THE SOCIALIST REGISTER. VFOAT Socialist Register. 1964-. 0081-0606. UK. English. an. Humanities Press, Atlantic Highlands NJ 07716. Ed R Miliband and J Saville. **Ind/Abst** Altern. Press Index. **LC** HX15. **DD** 320. A collection of essays covering issues of major significance for socialist theory and practice.

THE SOCIALIST REPUBLIC. (THE SOCIALIST REPUBLIC : PUBLICATION OF THE LEAGUE FOR SOCIALIST RECONSTRUCTION). Began with: Vol. 1, in Jan./Feb. 1973. 0090-7405. Periodical. US. English. sa. $3.00. Industrial Union Party, Box 711, Red Bank NJ 07701. **Tel** (201)758-0449. Ed W Petrovich and M Block. bk rev. **Circ** 1,200. (ctrl). Advocates a new social and economic system that places the majority working class in a democratic industrial system whose principle is: production for people's needs and not profit.

SOCIALIST REVIEW. V. 8- (No. 37-). 0161-1801. Periodical. US. English. bm. $34.00. Center Social Research & ED Education, 3202 Adeline, Berkeley CA 94703. **Tel** (415)547-3732. Ed Jeffrey Escoffier. **Ind/Abst** Sociol. Abstr., Altern. Press Index. **LC** HX1. **DD** 335.005. bk rev. adv acc. **Circ** 8,000. American politics, feminism, democratic movements, labor struggles, organizing strategies, leftist, perspectives on culture. *Socialist Revolution, 0037-8240; Marxist Perspectives, 0149-8681.*

SOCIALIST REVIEW. No. 1- April 1978-. 0141-2442. Periodical. UK. English. bm. $30.65. Socialist Review, PO Box 82, London E2 England. **LC** HX3. **DD** 335.005.

SOCIALIST STANDARD. V. 1- 1904-. 0037-8259. Periodical. UK. English. mo. 5.50. Socialist Party Great Britain, 52 Clapham High Street, London SW4 England. **Tel** (01)622-3811. **LC** HX3. **DD** 335.05. bk rev. **Circ** 4,000.

SOCIALIST THOUGHT AND PRACTICE. No. 1- June 1961-. 0583-7200. Periodical. English. mo. $30.00. Jugoslovenska Knjica, PO Box 36, Beograd Yuguslavia. **Tel** 621-992. **LC** HX365.5. **DD** 335.005. (cum index).

SOCIALIST VOICE. V.1-. 0705-8519. Periodical. CN. English. bw. $40.00. Socialist Voice, CP 280 Succursale de Lorimer, Montreal Quebec 82H 2N7 Canada. **Tel** (514)521-2791. Ed Joan Campana. **DD** 335.00971. adv acc. **Circ** 2,000. Covers international affairs of Central America, South Africa, the Caribbean and Pacific Islands; the role of Canada in international events; labor and radical movements in Canada; the nationalist movement of Quebec. *Labor Challenge, 0047-3847; Militant, 0705-8500; Young Socialist, 0044-0884.*

THE SOCIALIST WORKER. (SOCIALIST WORKER). No. 1-. Periodical. US. English. mo. $15.00. Socialist Worker, Box 18037, Cleveland OH 44118. **Ind/Abst** Altern. Press Index.

SOCIALIST WORKER REVIEW. Issue 68 (Sept. 1984)-. Periodical. UK. English. mo. 16.50. Socialist Worker Review, PO Box 82, London E2 England. *Socialist Review, 0141-2442.*

SOCIALIST WORLD PERSPECTIVES. V. 1- Aug. 1977-. Periodical. II. English. ir. $16.00. S S Chauhan, C-19 Amar Colony Lajpat Nagar-4, New Delhi 110024 India. **LC** HX3. **DD** 335.005.

SOCIALISTA (P.S.O.E. (POLITICAL PARTY) : WEEKLY). (EL SOCIALISTA). Periodical. SP. Spanish. sm. 2.000. El Socialista, Ferraz 70, 28008 Madrid Spain. **Tel** 4791111. **LC** JN8101. **DD** 335.00946. adv acc. **Circ** 180,000. (ctrl). The publication of the work's Spanish Party.

SOCIALISTISK POLITIK. No. 1- Dec. 1975-. Periodical. DK. Danish. qt. Modtryk Socialistisk Forlag, Mejlgade 21-23, DK 8000 Aarhus C Denmark.

SOSALISTA PANORAMA. VFOAT Socialist Panorama. Periodical. Hindi. ir. 10.00. Omaprakasa Mantri, B-71 Gulmohar Park, Journalists' Colony 49, Nai Dilli India. **LC** H8.

SOSIALISTINEN AIKAKAUSLEHTI. Joulukuu 1905-. Periodical. Finnish. ir. **LC** HX9.

SOSIALT FORUM/SOSIALT ARBEID. Vol. 46-. Periodical. NO. Norwegian. ir. Olaf Norlis Forlag, KR Augusts GY 7A, Oslo Norway. *Sosialt Forum, Sosialt Arbeid.*

SOVIET STUDIES. V. 1- June 1949-. 0038-5859. Periodical. UK. English. qt. $55.00. Soviet Studies, PO Box C-399, Birmingham AL 35283-0399. **Tel** (205)991-6925. Ed R A Clarke. **Ind/Abst** Am. Hist. Life, Hist. Abstr., Part A, Mod. Hist. Abstr., Hist. Abstr., Part B, Twent. Century Abstr., Energy Inf. Abstr., Environ. Abstr., ABC Pol Sci, Ref. Source, Soc. Sci. Index, Humanit. Index, Public Aff. Inf. Serv. Bull., Soc. Sci. Citation Index, Recent Publ. Artic. **LC** DK266.A2. **DD** 947.005. bk rev. adv acc. An academic devoted to the political, economic, and social affairs of the USSR and the communist countries of Eastern Europe.

SOZIALISTISCHE ARBEITSWISSENSCHAFT. Began publication in 1957. 0038-6111. Periodical. SZ. German. bm. $14.65. Kunst & Wissen Erich Bieber, Dufourstrasse 51, CH-8008 Zurich Switzerland. **Tel** (011)411694420. **Ind/Abst** Foreign Lang. Index.

SPARTACIST CANADA. VFOAT Spartacist. VAT Spartacist (Toronto). No. 1 (Oct. 1975)-. 0229-5415. Periodical. CN. English. bm. $.25 Each Number. Spartacist Canada Publishing Association, PO Box 6867 Station A, Toronto Ontario M5W 1X6 Canada. **DD** 335.430971.

SPW. VFOAT S.P.W. 0170-4613. Periodical. German. ir. 7.70 Each Issue. SPW-Verlag/Redaktion GMBH, Moltkestr 21, D-1000 Berlin 45 East Germany. **LC** HX6. **DD** 335.005.

STATE. Periodical. English. ir. 16.00. 457 Union Place 2, Colombo Sri Lanka (Ceylon). **LC** HX385.8.A75. **DD** 335.43095493.

STENOGRAFISKI PROTOKOL - KONGRES NA BULGARSKATA KOMUNISTICHESKA PARTIIA. Main/Corp Bulgarska Komunisticheska Partiia. Kongres. Bulgarian. ir. **LC** JN9609.A8.

STENOGRAFSKE BILJESKE. Main/Corp Savez Komunista Hrvatske., Kongres. Serbo-Croatian -R. ir. **LC** JN2199.C46. *Izvesteji.*

STP. SOCIALISM : THEORY AND PRACTICE. VFOAT Socialism: Theory and Practice. Periodical. UR. English. mo. Socialism: Theory and Practice. *Socialism, Theory and Practice, 0583-7138.*

STUDIES IN COMMUNISM, REVISIONISM, AND REVOLUTION. 14- 1969-. 0081-8054. Monographic Series. US. English. ir. Massachusetts Institute of Technology, 28 Carlton Street, Cambridge MA 02142. *Studies in International Communism.*

SUNGGONG NONMUNJIP. V. 1-. Periodical. KO. Korean. ir. 7,000. Tongil Sasang Yonguwon, 8-3 Chongpa-dong 2-ka Yongsan-ku, Seoul Korea. **LC** HX9.K65.

SZAKSZERVEZETI SZEMLE. Vol. 1-. Periodical. HU. Hungarian. ir. 40.00. Tancsics Konyvkiado, Dozsa Gyorgy UT 84/B, Budapest Hungary. **LC** HX9.H8.

TARSADALMI SZEMLE. Vol. 1-. 0039-971X. Periodical. HU. Hungarian. mo. **Ind/Abst** Am. Hist. Life, Hist. Abstr., Part A, Mod. Hist. Abstr., Hist. Abstr., Part B, Twent. Century Abstr. **LC** HX8.

TEORIIA I PRAKTIKA NA PROPAGANDATA I AGITASIIA. Began in 1946. Bulgarian. ir. UL Gurko 1, Sofiia Bulgaria. **LC** Z7164.S67, HX44.

THESIS ELEVEN. See Sociology: General Works, Theory.

TIJDSCHRIFT VOOR SOCIALE GESCHIEDENIS. Vol. 1-. Periodical. NE. Dutch. ty. 20.00. Nederlandse Vereniging Tot Beoefening Vau de Sociale Gerschiedenis, Herengracht 262-266, Amsterdam Netherlands. **Ind/Abst** Recent Publ. Artic. **LC** HX9.D8.

TOWARD FREEDOM. See Political Science - International Relations.

TRENDS IN COMMUNIST MEDIA.
VFOAT FBIS Trends in Communist Media. US.
English. wk. National Technical Information Service,
5285 Port Royal Road, Springfield VA 22161. *Trends in Communist Propaganda.*

TRIBUNE SOCIALISTE. Periodical. FR.
French. ir. 130. Service Abonnements 9, rue
Borromee, 75015 5826-65 Paris France. LC HX5. DD
335.005. *TS, Tribune Socialiste.*

TRIBUNE SOCIALISTE CEASED. No. 1-
March 1979-. Periodical. FR. French. mo. $26.61.
Societe Nouvelle Presse Polt, 9 rue Borromee, 75015
Paris France. Tel 566-45-37. LC HX5. DD 335.005.

UCHENYE ZAPISKI. Main/Corp
Kommunisticheskaia Partiia Sovetskogo Soiuza.
Vysshaia Partiinaia Shkola. 1974, Vol. 2-. UR.
Russian. 1.14 Each Issue. MYSL, 117071 B-71
Leninskii Prospekt 15, Moskva USSR. LC HX15.

UCHENYE ZAPISKI KAFEDR MARKSISTSKO-LENINSKOI FILOSOFII VYSSHEI PARTIINOI SHKOLY PRI TSK KPSS I MESTNYKH VYSSHIKH PARTIINYKH SHKOL. See Philosophy.

L'UNITE POUR LE SOCIALISME. VFOAT
Unite Africaine. Periodical. French. ir. LC HX464.5.
DD 335.009663. *Unite Africaine.*

UNITE PROLETARIENNE. 1st Edition in
1976. 0707-7696. Periodical. CN. French. bm. $1.50
Each Number. En Lutte, 4933 de Grand Pre, Montreal
Quebec H2T 2H9 Canada. DD 335.430971.

UNTER DEM PFLASTER LIEGT DER STRAND. V. 1-. German. ir. Karin Kramer Verlag,
1000 Berlin 44, Postfach 106, Berlin West Germany.
LC HX821. DD 335.8305.

UNTERSUCHUNGEN ZUR GEGENWARTSKUNDE SUDOSTEUROPAS. 1- 1957-. 0566-2761.
Monographic Series. GW. German. ir. 60.-. R
Oldenbourg Verlag, Postfach 801360, D-8000 Munich
80 West Germany. Tel 089/ 41 12. Circ 1,000. Actual
reports and comments on Albany, Bulgaria,
Yugoslavia, Romania, Hungary and their political,
economic, social and cultural developments.

VESTNIK (INSTITUT ZA MARKSISTICNE STUDIJE (SLOVENSKA AKADEMIJA ZNANOSTI IN UMETNOSTI)). (VESTNIK).
VFOAT Vestnik Instituta za Marksisticne Studije Sazu.
Letnik 1, St. 1- – 1980/1-. Slovenian. sa. LC HX8.

VESTNIK MOSKOVSKOGO UNIVERSITETA. SERIIA XII : TEORIIA NAUCHNOGO KOMMUNIZMA. Main/Corp Moscow.
Universitet. Jan./Feb. 1977-. Periodical. UR. Russian.
bm. Victor Kamkin Inc, 12224 Parklawn Drive,
Rockville MD 20852. Tel (301)881-5973. Ind/Abst Am.
Hist. Life, Hist. Abstr., Chem. Abstr. LC HX8. *Vestnik. Seriia XIII: Teoriia Nauchnogo Kommunisma.*

VOICE OF THE PEOPLE. (VOICE OF THE
PEOPLE : NATIONAL NEWSPAPER OF THE
PEOPLE'S FRONT AGAINST RACIST AND FASCIST
VIOLENCE). Vol. 1, No. 1 (Sept. 1982)-. 0824-2461.
Periodical. CN. English. ir. People's Front, P O Box
37 Station P, Toronto Ontario M5S 2S6 Canada. DD
335.40971.

VOICE OF THE YOUTH. (THE VOICE OF THE
YOUTH : ORGAN OF THE COMMUNIST YOUTH
UNION OF CANADA (MARXIST-LENINIST)). Vol. 1,
No. 1 (June 1979)-. 0229-4834. Periodical. CN.
English. ir. $0.25 Each Issue. National Publications
Centre, PO Box 727 Adelaide Station, Toronto
Ontario M5C 2J8 Canada. DD 320.532205.

VOIE DU PARTI. (LA VOIE DU PARTI : ORGANE
THEORIQUE DU COMITE CENTRAL DU PARTI
COMMUNISTE DU CANADA (MARXISTE-
LENINISTE)). Vol. 1, No. 1 (Mar. 1980)-. 0227-6097.
Periodical. CN. French. $1.50 Per Number. Comite
Executif National du PCC, CP 666 Succursale C,
Montreal Quebec H2L 4L5 Canada. DD 324.2710975.

VOIX DES JEUNES. (LA VOIX DES JEUNES :
ORGANE DE L'UNION DE LA JEUNESSE
COMMUNISTE DU CANADA (MARXISTE-
LENINISTE)). Vol. 1, No 1 (15 June 1979)-. 0229-4842.
Periodical. CN. French. ir. $0.25 Each Number.
Centre National de Publications, CP 727 Succursale
Adelaide, Toronto Ontario M5C 2J8 Canada. DD
320.532205.

VOIX DU PEUPLE. (LA VOIX DU PEUPLE :
JOURNAL NATIONAL DU FRONT DU PEUPLE
CONTRE LA VIOLENCE RACISTE ET FASCISTE).
Vol. 1, No 1 (Sept. 1982)-. 0824-247X. Periodical. CN.
French. ir. Front du Peuple, C P 37 Succursale P,
Toronto Ontario M5S 2S6 Canada. DD 335.40971.

VOPROSY TEORII I ZHIZN'. 1- 1967-.
Russian. ir. LC HX542.

THE WESTERN SOCIALIST. V. 1- (No. 1-).
0043-4191. Periodical. US. English. bm. $2.00. World
Socialist Party, 295 Huntington Avenue/Room 212,
Boston MA 02115. LC HX1. DD 335.05.

WIDERSPRUCH. No. 1 (March 1981)-.
Periodical. SZ. German. sa. 7.00 Each issue.
Redaktionskollektiv Widerspruch, Postfach 8026,
Zurich Switzerland. LC HX6. DD 335.005.

THE WORKER'S ADVOCATE. (THE
WORKERS' ADVOCATE : VOICE OF THE MARXIST-
LENINIST PARTY OF THE USA). 0276-363X.
Periodical. US. English. mo. $9.00. Marxist Leninist
Publications, PO Box 11972/Ontario St STN, Chicago
IL 60611. A newspaper of the Marxist- Leninist party,
USA which guides the American workers in
developing their revolutionary struggle to overthrow
the bourgeoisie and establish socialism.

WORLD STRENGTH OF THE COMMUNIST PARTY ORGANIZATIONS. 0084-2257. US. English.
an. US Department of State, 2201 C Street NW,
Washington DC 20520.

YEARBOOK ON INTERNATIONAL COMMUNIST AFFAIRS. 1966-. 0084-4101.
US. English. an. $49.95. Stanford University, Hoover
Institute/Room 116, Stanford CA 94305. Tel
(415)497-3373. LC HX1. DD 335.4305. One chapter on
each country having an active communist movement,
plus information on front organizations-describing the
year's events in the country relative to the Communist
Party size, changes, leadership, etc.

YOUNG SOCIALIST. V. 16- Oct. 1972-.
0360-0157. Periodical. US. English. mo. 14 Charles
Lane, New York NY 10014. Tel (212)989-7570. Ed
Ellen Haywood. LC HX1. DD 335.005. bk rev. adv acc.
Circ 4,500. Coverage of issues and activities from
opposition to US intervention in Central America,
protests against apartheid, to defense of legal
abortion, and union rights. *Young Socialist—The Organizer.*

YOUNG SOCIALIST-THE ORGANIZER.
VFOAT Organizer. 1970-72. 0044-0892. Periodical.
US. English. bm. $3.00. Young Socialist, 14 Charles
Lane, New York NY 10014. LC HX1. DD 335.005.
Young Socialist.

YUGOSLAV INFORMATION BULLETIN OF THE LEAGUE OF COMMUNISTS OF YUGOSLAVIA & THE SOCIALIST ALLIANCE OF WORKING PEOPLE OF YUGOSLAVIA. Periodical. YU. English. ir.
League of Communists of Yugoslavia and the
Socialist Alliance of Working People of Yugoslavia,
POB 25, Belgrade 11000 Yugoslavia. LC DR370. DD
320.949702.

Z POLA WALKI. Vol. 1- (No. 1-). 0044-149X.
Periodical. PL. Multilingual (tables of contents also in
French, German, and Russian). qt. ARS Polona,
Krakowskie Przedmiescie 7, 00-068 Warsaw Poland.
Ind/Abst Am. Hist. Life, Hist. Abstr., Part A, Mod. Hist.
Abstr., Hist. Abst., Part B, Twent. Century Abstr., Hist.
Abstr. LC HX315.7. (cum index).

ZBIERKA ZAKONOV, CESKOSLOVENSKA SOCIALISTICKA REPUBLIKA. Main/
Corp Czechoslovakia. Slovak. ir. 68.00. Federalny
Statisticky Urad, Trziste 8, Praha - Mala Strana
Czechoslovakia. *Zbierka Zakonov Republiky Ceskoslovenskej.*

ZEITDIENST; UNABHANGIGE SOZIALISTISCHE INFORMATION. Vol.
1.-23., No. 34. Periodical. SZ. German. wk. Zur
Socialistischen Information Postfach 195, CH 8025
Zurich Switzerland. (cum index).

ZIVOT STRANY. Vol. 1- Sept. 1954-. 0322-8118.
Periodical. CS. Czech. ir. Artia, Ve Smeck 30, Praha 1
Czechoslovakia. LC JN2229.A5.

ZU FRAGEN DES SOZIALISTISCHEN WELTSYSTEMS; AUSWAHLBIBLIOGRAPHIE. See
Bibliographies.

Population Studies

POPULATION STUDIES

ABHANDLUNGEN ZUR HUMANGEOGRAPHIE. 1-. Monographic
Series. AU. German. ir. Verlag Dr A Schendl MBH Co
Kg, Postfach 29/Karlsgasse 15, A-1041 Wien Austria.

ADDRESS LIST - NATIONAL CLEARINGHOUSE FOR CENSUS DATA SERVICES. (ADDRESS LIST). Jan.
1981-. 0744-1010. US. English. US Department of
Commerce, Bureau of the Census, Washington DC
20233. Tel (301)763-4100. LC HA37. DD 310.6073.
Lists, by state, all registrants in the National
Clearinghouse for Census Data Services including
name, address, and telephone number. *Summary Tape Processing Centers and State Data Centers.*

ALUMNI DIRECTORY - POPULATION COUNCIL. See Yearbooks, Almanacs,
Directories.

AMERICAN DEMOGRAPHICS. V. 1- Jan.
1979-. 0163-4089. Periodical. US. English. mo. $48.00.
American Demographics, PO Box 6543, Syracuse NY
13217. Tel (607)273-6343. Ed Cheryl Russel. Ind/Abst
Manage. Contents, Predicasts, Energy Inf. Abstr.,
Environ. Abstr., Popul. Index, ABI/Inform, Infobank,
Public Aff. Inf. Serv. Bull., Bus. Period. Index. LC
HB3505. DD 301.32973. bk rev. adv acc. Circ 13,000.
Provides information about consumer trends,
population shifts, and their future implications.

ANNALES DE DEMOGRAPHIE HISTORIQUE. Began publication with Vol. for
1964 under title: Etudes et Chronique. 0066-2062. FR.
French. an. 166.54. Europeriodiques SA, B P 104,
78191 Trappes Cedex France. Tel (1)30 62 93 86.
Ind/Abst Am. Hist. Life, Hist. Abstr.

ANNUAIRE ET RAPPORT D'ACTIVITES - DEPARTEMENT DE DEMOGRAPHIE. UNIVERSITE DE MONTREAL. See Yearbooks, Almanacs,
Directories.

ANNUAL DEMOGRAPHIC DATA FOR MIGRANT FAMILY HOUSING CENTERS. US. English. an. California
Department of Housing and Community Development,
921 Tenth Street, Sacramento CA 95814. Tel
(916)323-6165. LC HD7289.U7. DD 305.563. Migrant
farmworkers and family composition.

ANNUAL ESTIMATE OF POPULATION FOR THE STATE OF GEORGIA. Main/
Corp Georgia. State Data Center. 0361-6053. US.
English. an. 270 Washington Street SW, Atlanta GA
30334. LC HA321. DD 312.09758.

ANNUAL REPORT - COMMISSION ON POPULATION AND THE HAWAIIAN FUTURE. Main/Corp Hawaii. Commission on
Population and the Hawaiian Future. US. English. an.
Commission on Population and the Hawaiian Future,
550 Halekauwila Street/Room 206, Honolulu HI
96813. LC HB3525.H3. DD 353.99690081506.

ANNUAL REPORT - EAST-WEST POPULATION INSTITUTE. Main/Corp
East-West Population Institute. 0097-6032. US.
English. an. East-West Population Institute, 1777
East-West Road, Honolulu HI 96822. LC HB850. DD
301.32.

ANNUAL REPORT - INTERNATIONAL INSTITUTE FOR POPULATION STUDIES. Main/Corp International Institute for
Population Studies. II. English. an. International
Institute for Population Studies, Deonar Bombay 400
08 India. LC HB850.5.A75. DD 301.3207205.

ANNUAL REPORT - NATIONAL CENSUS AND STATISTICS OFFICE (PHILIPPINES). See Statistics.

ARBITRON TELEVISION POPULATION BOOK. Main/Corp Arbitron Company. VFOAT
Population Book. 0731-3721. US. English. an. Arbitron
Company, 1350 Avenue of the Americas, New York
NY 10019.

AREA AND ESTIMATED POPULATION IN EACH QUEENSLAND LOCAL AUTHORITY AREA. Main/Corp Australian
Bureau of Statistics. Queensland Office. 1972/73-.
0312-9047. AT. English. an. Australian Bureau of

Population Studies

Statistics, 320-330 Adelaide Street, Brisbane Queensland Australia. LC HB3683. DD 31209943. *Area and Estimated Population in Each Queensland Local Authority Area, 0312-9047.*

ASIAN-PACIFIC POPULATION PROGRAMME NEWS. VFOAT Asian & Pacific Population Programme News, Asian and Pacific Population Programme News. VAT Asian Pacific Population Programme News. V. 7- (No. 1-). 0125-6718. Periodical. TH. English. qt. ESCAP Population Division, United Nations Building, Rajdamnern Avenue, Bangkok 2 Thailand. LC HB850.5.A75. DD 304.6095. NLM W1 AS139C. *Asian Population Programme News.*

ASIAN POPULATION STUDIES SERIES. Series Corp United Nations. Document - United Nations. No. 1-. 0066-8451. US. English. ir. United Nations Publications, Sales Section/Room A-3315 New York NY 10017. Ind/Abst Popul. Index. LC JX1977. DD 301.3295.

BEFOLKNINGEN I KOMMUNERNE. Jan. 1, 1983-. 0108-8076. Danish. an. 48.00. Danmarks Statistik, Sejrgade 11, Kbenhaven Denmark. Tel 01 29 82 22. Circ 1,550. Populations of municipalities. *Befolkningen I de Enkelte Kommuner Pr. . . . Fordelt Efter Kn, Alder Og Gteskabelig Stilling.*

DIE BEVOLKERUNG IN NORDRHEIN-WESTFALEN. *See* Statistics.

BEVOLKERUNG UND ERWERBSTATIGKEIT. REIHE 1, GEBIET UND BEVOLKERUNG. VFOAT Gebiet und Bevolkerung. Periodical. GW. German. qt. 4.40. Verlag W Kohlhammer GMBH, Stuttgart West Germany.

BEVOLKERUNGSSTRUKTUR UND WIRTSCHAFTSKRAFT DER BUNDESLANDER. 1950/1961-. 0072-1867. GW. German. an. Kohlhammer Verlag GMBH, Hessbruhlstrasse 69 PF 800430, 7000 Stuttgart 80- West Germany. LC HA1235.

BEVOLKING EN GEZIN. Dutch. ir. 340.00. Botanic Building, 13E Verdieping, Sint Lazaruslaan, 10 Bus 2, 1030 Brussels Belgium. Ind/Abst Recent Publ. Artic. LC HB3603. *Bevolking en Gezin.*

BIBLIOGRAPHIE INTERNATIONALE DE LA DEMOGRAPHIE HISTORIQUE. *See* Bibliographies.

BILANZ DER WOHNBEVOELKERUNG IN DEN GEMEINDEN DER SCHWEIZ. *See* Statistics.

BIORESEARCH TODAY. POPULATION, FERTILITY & BIRTH CONTROL. VFOAT Population, Fertility & Birth Control. VAT Bioresearch Today. Population, Fertility and Birth Control. 0149-0915. US. English. mo. $100.00. Bioscience Information Service, 2100 Arch Street, Philadelphia PA 19103. Tel (215)587-4800. Current awareness journal covering population, fertility and birth control.

A BIRTH-ORIGIN STUDY OF TEXAS NEWBORNS DURING . . . . VFOAT Migration for Birth. US. English. an. Bureau of State Health Planning and Resource Development, Texas Department of Health, 1100 Westes 49th Street, Austin TX 78756. *Birth-Origin Survey of Texas Newborns.*

BIRTHS. Main/Corp Australian Bureau of Statistics. 1973-. AT. English. an. Australian Bureau of Statistics, PO Box 84, Canberra Australian Capital Territory 2600 Australia. LC HB1085. DD 312.194. *Births.*

BOLETIM DEMOGRAFICO. Began in 1970. 0101-0662. Periodical. BL. Portuguese. qt. LC HB3563.

BOLETIN DEMOGRAFICO - CENTRO LATINOAMERICANO DE DEMOGRAFIA. (BOLETIN DEMOGRAFICO). Main/Corp Celade (Organization). Year 1- Jan. 1968-. 0378-5386. Periodical. CL. Spanish (English). sa. $10.00. Calade, Casilla 91, Santiago Chile. Tel 228-3206. Ind/Abst Popul. Index. Circ 900. Contains population projections and estimates, birth and death rates, for the Latin American and Caribbean countries.

BOLIGTLLINGEN. 1. Jan. 1980-. 0107-8909. DK. Danish. ir. 33.61. Danmarks Statistik, Sejrgade 11, 2100 Kbenhavn Denmark. Tel 01 29 82 22. LC HD7347.A3. Circ 1,800. Population and housing census, national tables.

BULLETIN DE LIAISON (CENTRE REGIONAL D'ETUDES DE POPULATION). (BULLETIN DE LIAISON). Periodical. CX. French. qt. Centre Regional d'Etudes de Population, B P 1418, Bangui Central African Republic. LC HB3664.8.A3. DD 304.609660097541.

BUREAU OF THE CENSUS CATALOG. MONTHLY SUPPLEMENT CEASED. Main/Corp United States. Bureau of the Census. Ceased with Dec. 1980 issue. Periodical. US. English. mo. Ind/Abst Am. Stat. Index.

CAHIERS QUEBECOIS DE DEMOGRAPHIE. V. 4- March 1975-. 0380-1721. Periodical. CN. French. sa. 18.00 Domestic, 24.00 Foreign. INRS-Urbanisation, 3465 Durocher, Montreal Quebec H2X 2C6 Canada. Tel (514)842-4191. Ind/Abst Point Repere, Popul. Index, Foreign Lang. Index, PAIS Foreign Lang. Index. DD 301.3205. bk rev. adv acc. Circ 800. Topics covered: fertility, migration, mortality, historical demography, demolinguistics, health, social demography, methods and models of population analysis. *Bulletin de l'Association des Demographes du Quebec, 0380-1713.*

CANADIAN STUDIES IN POPULATION. V. 1- 1974-. 0380-1489. CN. English (includes some text in French). an. $15.48. Canadian Studies in Population, Department of Sociology, University of Alberta, Edmonton Alberta T6G 2H4 Canada. Tel (403)432-4659. Ind/Abst Popul. Index, Public Aff. Inf. Serv. Bull. DD 301.32971.

CAROLINA POPULATION CENTER PAPERS. No. 1 (March 1978)-. Periodical. US. English. Ind/Abst Popul. Index.

CASE STUDIES OF ARRANGEMENTS FOR EVALUATION AND UTILIZATION OF POPULATION CENSUS RESULTS. Main/Corp United Nations. Department of Economic and Social Affairs. Series Corp United Nations. Document. 1959-. English. ir. United Nations, Department of Economic and Social Affairs, Sales Section/Room A 3315, New York NY 10017. LC JX1977. DD 312.09624.

CAUSES OF DEATH (BRISBANE, QUEENSLAND). *See* Statistics.

CENSUS BUREAU METHODOLOGICAL RESEARCH. Main/Corp United States. Bureau of the Census. Began with 1963-1966. 0565-0828. US. English. an. Bureau of the Census, Data Users Division, Customer Services Publications, Washington DC 20233. LC Z7554.U5, HA37. DD 016.001433. NLM Z 7554.U5 C396.

CENSUS OF POPULATION AND HOUSING (1980). (1980 CENSUS OF POPULATION AND HOUSING CENSUS TRACTS). Series/Titl 1980 Census of Population and Housing PHC80-2-. US. English. ir. US Department of Commerce, Bureau of the Census, Washington DC 20122.

CENTER PAPER - YALE UNIVERSITY. ECONOMIC GROWTH CENTER. Main/Corp Yale University. Economic Growth Center. No. 1-. 0513-1529. Monographic Series. US. English. ir. Yale University, Economic Growth Center, Box 1987 Yale Station, New Haven CT 06520. Ind/Abst Popul. Index.

CERTIFIED POPULATION OF TENNESSEE INCORPORATED MUNICIPALITIES. US. English. an. Local Planning Assistance Office, 1800 James K Polk Building, Nashville TN 37219.

CHARACTERISTICS OF THE POPULATION BELOW THE POVERTY LEVEL. Series/Titl Current Population Reports. Series P-60. Began with: 1974. US. English. an. Superintendent of Documents, US Government Printing Office, Washington DC 20402. NLM W2.

CITY POPULATION ESTIMATES - GEORGIA. STATE DATA CENTER. Main/Corp Georgia. State Data Center. 0362-3904. US. English. 270 Washington Street SW, Atlanta GA 30334. LC HA321. DD 312.09758.

CONSUMER ATTITUDES AND BUYING PLANS. 0547-7204. Periodical. US. English. mo. $1950.00. Conference Board, 845 Third Avenue, New York NY 10022. Tel (212)759-0900. Ed Fabian Linden. Ind/Abst Funk Scott Index Corp. Ind. Circ 150. (ctrl). Demographic and regional breakdown of results of monthly consumer attitudes survey. Also a wealth of consumer, economic, and demographic statistics reported periodically.

COUNTRY DEMOGRAPHIC PROFILES. 1st-30, No. 1-. 0360-8514. Monographic Series. US. English. US Department of Commerce, Bureau of Census, Social & Economic Statistics Administration, Washington DC 20233. Ind/Abst Popul. Index. LC HB848. DD 312.

CURRENT POPULATION REPORTS : FARM POPULATION. SERIES P-27. Main/Corp United States. Bureau of the Census. VFOAT Farm Population. No. 1- Jan. 14, 1945-. US. English. ir. US Department of Commerce, Bureau of the Census, Washington DC 20402.

CURRENT POPULATION REPORTS. SER. P-25, POPULATION ESTIMATES AND PROJECTIONS. (CURRENT POPULATION REPORTS. SERIES P-25, POPULATION ESTIMATES AND PROJECTIONS). VFOAT Population Estimates and Projections. 0738-453X. Monographic Series. US. English. mo. $30.00. Superintendent of Documents, US Government Printing Office, Washington DC 20402. Tel (202)783-3238. Ind/Abst Popul. Index, Am. Stat. Index. LC HA195. DD 312.0973. NLM W2 A B9CUB. *Current Population Reports. Series P-25, Population Estimates.*

CURRENT POPULATION REPORTS. SERIES P-20, POPULATION CHARACTERISTICS. VFOAT Population Characteristics. Began with No. 1. 0363-6836. Monographic Series. US. English. ir. $76.00. Superintendent of Documents, US Government Printing Office, Washington DC 20402. Tel (202)783-3238. Ind/Abst Popul. Index, Am. Stat. Index. LC HA195. DD 312.9. NLM W2 A B9CU.

CURRENT POPULATION REPORTS. SERIES P-23, SPECIAL STUDIES. VFOAT Special Studies. No. 27-. 0498-8485. Periodical. US. English. Superintendent of Documents, U S GPO, Washington DC 20402. Ind/Abst Popul. Index, Am. Stat. Index. LC HA203. NLM W2 A B9CUE. *Current Population Reports. Series P-23, Technical Studies.*

CURRENT POPULATION REPORTS. SERIES P-26, LOCAL POPULATION ESTIMATES. VFOAT Local Population Estimates. No. 82-3-C (Feb. 1984)-. 0743-9431. Periodical. US. English. ir. US Government Printing Office, Superintendent of Documents, Washington DC 20402. LC HA203. DD 312.80973. NLM W2. *Current Population Reports. Series P-26, Federal-State Cooperative Program for Population Estimates, 0565-0917.*

CURRENT POPULATION REPORTS. SERIES P-28, SPECIAL CENSUSES. VFOAT Special Censuses. Began with No. 232. 0270-6660. Monographic Series. US. English. Subscriber Services, Bureau of the Census, Washington DC 20233. Ind/Abst Popul. Index, Am. Stat. Index. NLM W2 A B9CUC. *Current Population Reports. Series P-SC, Special Censuses.*

CURRENT POPULATION REPORTS. SERIES P-60, CONSUMER INCOME. *See* Economics.

DEMOGRAFIA Y ECONOMIA. V. 1- 1967-. 0011-8257. Periodical. MX. Spanish. qt. Colegio de Mexico, Camino Al Ajusco 20 Pedregal Sta Teresa, 10740 Mexico D F Mexico. Tel 5 68-60-33. Ind/Abst Am. Hist. Life, Hist. Abstr., Sociol. Abstr., Soc. Welf. Soc. Plan./Policy Soc. Dev., Popul. Index, Foreign Lang. Index, Lang. Lang. Behav. Abstr., Hist. Abstr., Part A, Mod. Hist. Abstr., Hist. Abst., Part B, Twent. Century Abstr. LC HB881. DD 301.3'2. (cum index). bk rev. adv acc. Circ 12,000. Demographic and economic topics, specialized in Latin American problems. Methodology and research advancements of those sciences.

DEMOGRAFIE; REVUE PRO VYZKUM POPULACNIHO VYVOJE. Vol. 1- 1959-. 0011-8265. Periodical. CS. Czech (tables of contents also in Russian and English). qt. 40. Artia, PO Box 790, VE-Smeckach 30, Praha 1 Czechoslovakia. Tel 8142257. Ind/Abst Popul. Index, Lang. Lang. Behav. Abstr., Sociol. Abstr. LC HB3592.C9. NLM W1 DE134U. (cum index). bk rev. Circ 1,800. (ctrl). A review dealing with contemporary and past population development. It also provides latest demographic data concerning Czechoslovakia.

Population Studies

DEMOGRAPHIC AND RELATED SOCIO-ECONOMIC DATA SHEETS FOR COUNTRIES OF THE ECONOMIC COMMISSION FOR WESTERN ASIA. Main/Corp United Nations. Economic Commission for Western Asia. English. ir. United Nations Economic Commission for Western Asia, Population Division ECWA, PO Box 4656, Beirut Lebanon. LC HA1660. DD 312.0956.

DEMOGRAPHIC BULLETIN. V. 1- Aug. 1977-. 0702-0031. Monographic Series. CN. English. mo. Ontario Government Bookstore, 880 Bay Street, Toronto Ontario M7A 1N8 Canada. LC HA747.O6. DD 304.609713.

DEMOGRAPHIC BULLETIN (WELLINGTON, N.Z.). (DEMOGRAPHIC BULLETIN). Series/Titl Department of Statistics Publication. Vol. 4, No. 1-. 0111-8102. Periodical. English. sa. $5.64. Demographic Bulletin, Department of Statistics, Private Bag, Wellington 1 New Zealand. Ind/Abst Popul. Index. LC HA3173. DD 312.09931. *Quarterly Demographic Bulletin, 0111-2643.*

DEMOGRAPHIC MONOGRAPHS. V. 1-. 0275-9594. Monographic Series. US. English. ir. Gordon & Breach, 1 Bedford Street, London WC2E England. Tel 01 836 5125.

DEMOGRAPHIC PROFILES, SOCIOECONOMIC PROFILES, AND PER CAPITA INCOMES OF THE RESIDENT POPULATIONS OF WASHINGTON STATE SCHOOL DISTRICTS. Main/Corp Washington (State). Dept. of Education. VFOAT Demographic Profiles, Washington State School Districts. US. English. State Superintendent of Public Instruction, Olympia WA 98504. LC LC132.W3. DD 371.219797.

DEMOGRAPHIC REPORT, HEW. Main/Corp United States. Dept. of Health, Education, and Welfare. Region III. VAT Demographic Report, Health, Education, and Welfare. 0148-6284. US. English. PO Box 13716, Philadelphia PA 19101. LC HB3509. DD 301.32974.

DEMOGRAPHIC STATISTICS. See Statistics.

DEMOGRAPHIC YEARBOOK. See Yearbooks, Almanacs, Directories.

DEMOGRAPHY. V. 1-. 0070-3370. Periodical. US. English (summaries in Spanish). qt. $25.00. Business Manager, Population Association of Demography of America, PO Box 14182, Benjamin Franklin Station, Washington DC 20044. Ind/Abst Soc. Sci. Index, Energy Inf. Abstr., Energy Res. Abstr., Environ. Abstr., Index Med., Index Econ. Artic. J. Collect. Vol., Int. Labour Doc., Popul. Index, Public Aff. Inf. Serv. Bull., Women Stud. Abstr., ABI/Inform. LC HB881.A1. DD 304.605. NLM W1 DE136K. (cum index).

DEMOGRAPHY INDIA. V. 1- Oct. 1972-. Periodical. II. English. sa. $35.00. Asia Books & Periodicals Co, 11 Darya Ganj, New Delhi 110002 India. Ed P B Desai. Ind/Abst Popul. Index. LC HB848. DD 301.320954.

DEMOSTA. Began in 1968. 0011-8338. Periodical. articles in English, French, Russian, and Spanish, V. (4)-5. ir. Federalni Statisticky Urad-Institut Demographie, Sokolovska 142, Praha Canal Zone. Ind/Abst Sociol. Abstr., Soc. Welf. Soc. Plan./Policy Soc. Dev., Popul. Index. LC HB848. DD 301.3205.

DOCPAL RESUMENES SOBRE POBLACION EN AMERICA LATINA. See Indexes/Abstracts.

EDMONTON AREA SERIES REPORT. No. 1-. 0703-8763. Monographic Series. CN. English. Free. Population Research Laboratory, Department of Sociology University of Alberta, Edmonton Alberta T6G 2H4 Canada. Tel (403)432-4659. DD 309.171233. Circ 100. Reports on the findings of our annual Edmonton area study. This is a survey of Edmonton residents gathering basic demographic data plus information on a special topic each year.

THE ELDERLY POPULATION: ESTIMATES BY COUNTY. (THE ELDERLY POPULATION, ESTIMATES BY COUNTY). Series/Titl DHHS Publication. Began with 1976. 0190-3896. Periodical. an. National Clearinghouse on Aging, 330 Independence Avenue Southwest, Washington DC 20201. LC HQ1064.U5. DD 312.920973.

ENQUETE SOCIO-ECONOMIQUE. See Statistics.

ENTRELINEAS. V. 1- Feb./Mar. 1971-. 0013-9017. Periodical. US. English (text in Spanish). sa.

EQUILIBRIUM. V. 1- Jan. 1973-. 0090-7871. Periodical. US. English. qt. $3.00. Zero Population Growth Inc, 1346 Connecticut Avenue NW, Washington DC 20036. Ind/Abst Energy Inf. Abstr., Environ. Abstr. LC HB848. DD 301.32973.

ESTIMATED AGE DISTRIBUTION OF POPULATION, QUEENSLAND. Main/Corp Australian Bureau of Statistics. Queensland Office. AT. English. ir. Auatralian Bureau of Statistics/Queensland Office, GPO Box 796, Sydney New South Wales 2110 Australia. LC HB1823. DD 312.9209943.

ESTIMATED INTERNAL MIGRATION BULLETIN (TRINIDAD AND TOBAGO). Main/Corp Trinidad and Tobago. Central Statistical Office. Series Corp Its Continuous Sample Survey of Population. 1- 1973-. 0303-4410. English. ir. Trinidad & Tobago Statistical Office, 1 Edward Street, Port-of-Spain Trinidad. LC HA867, HB2017. DD 317.2983 S, 312.8.

ESTIMATED RESIDENT POPULATION IN LOCAL GOVERNMENT AREAS. English. ir. Australian Bureau of Statistics, Ground Floor Annexe City Mutual Centre/10-20 Pulteney Street, Adelaide South Australia 5000 Australia. Tel (08)228 9439. LC HA3091. DD 312.099423. Population for local government areas: census count adjusted for under-enumeration. *Population in Local Government Areas.*

ESTIMATES OF POPULATION BY SEX AND AGE FOR CANADA AND THE PROVINCES. Main/Corp Statistics Canada. Demography Division. VFOAT Estimations de la Population Selon le Sexe et l'Age, Canada et Provinces. CN. English (French). an. $5.40. Publications Distribution, Statistics Canada, Ottawa Ontario K1A 0T6 Canada. LC HA741. DD 312.80971. *Estimates of Population by Sex and Age for Canada and the Provinces, 0707-3194.*

ESTUDIOS DE POBLACION. V. 1, No. 1- Jan. 1976-. Periodical. Spanish. ir. Asociacion Colombiana Para el Estudios de la Poblacion, Carrera 23 No 39-82, Bogota Colombia. LC HQ763. NLM W1 ES96S.

ETUDES DU CENTRE DE RECHERCHES ET D'ETUDES DEMOGRAPHIQUES. Main/Corp Centre de Recherche et d'Etudes Demographiques. VFOAT Sukkan, Soukan. MR. French. ir. LC HB3661.3.A3. DD 301.32964.

FACTFINDER FOR THE NATION. Main/Corp United States. Bureau of the Census. 0193-8762. US. English. Bureau of the Census, Subscriber Services, Washington DC 20233. Tel (301)763-4100. Describes, in a series of reports, the range of Census Bureau materials available on a given subject and suggests some of their uses.

FAMILY PLANNING. POPULATION REPORTER. See Birth Control.

FERTILITY OF AMERICAN WOMEN. Series/Titl Current Population Reports. Series P-20. Began with June 1975. 0272-6505. US. English. an. Superintendent of Documents, US Government Printing Office, Washington DC 20402. NLM W2 A B9CU No.301 Etc. *Fertility Expectations of American Women.*

FLORIDA ACCIDENTAL DEATH STATISTICS. See Statistics.

FLORIDA ESTIMATES OF POPULATION. (FLORIDA ESTIMATES OF POPULATION, STATE, COUNTIES, AND MUNICIPALITIES). 0145-4668. US. English. an. $14.70. Bureau of Economic & Business Research, University of Florida, Gainesville FL 32611. Tel (904)392-0171. LC HB3525.F6. DD 312.09759.

GEMEINDEUBERSICHT. See Geography.

GENUS. V. 1- June 1934-. 0016-6987. Periodical. IT. Italian. sa. $30.00. Edizioni Scienfifiche Ingles, Via Sommacampagna 11/13, 00185 Rome Italy. Tel 06/4750050. Ed Nora Federici. Ind/Abst Am. Hist. Life, Hist. Abstr., Part A, Mod. Hist. Abstr., Hist. Abst., Part B, Twent. Century Abstr., Popul. Index, Biol. Abstr. LC HB881. DD 304.605. NLM W1 GE357. CODEN GNUSA7. bk rev. Circ 3,000. Demographical analysis, as well as historical demography, bio-demography, economical demography, social demography, theory of population and demographical models.

GEOGRAFISKA ANNALER. SERIES B, HUMAN GEOGRAPHY. See Housing and Urban Development.

GEOGRAPHICAL MOBILITY. Series/Titl Current Population Reports. Series P-20. Began with Mar. 1975 - Mar. 1976. US. English. an. US Government Printing Office, Superintendent of Documents, Washington DC 20402. *Mobility of the Population of the United States.*

GRNLAND. 1953-. 0017-4556. Periodical. DK. Danish. mo. 195. Det Gronlakdske Seldkab, Le Bruunsvej 10, 2920 Charlottenlund Denmark. Tel 009451635733. Ind/Abst GeoRef, ASTIS Bibliogr., ASTIS Curr. Aware. Bull., Energy Res. Abstr., Bibliogr. Index Geol. LC G725. CODEN GRGSAX. bk rev. adv acc. Circ 2,000. Greenland and the Artic environments and populations.

GUIDE TO SOURCES OF INTERNATIONAL POPULATION ASSISTANCE. Series/Titl Population Programmes and Projects V. 1-. 1976-. US. English. te. United Nations Fund for Population Activities, 485 Lexington Avenue, New York NY 10017. LC HB848. DD 309.223.

HIGHLIGHTS (LONDON, ONT.). (HIGHLIGHTS). VFOAT PSC-CCPS Newsletter. VAT Population Studies Centre - Centre for Canadian Population Studies Highlights. Vol. 1, No. 1 (Sept. 1982)-. 0712-5828. Periodical. CN. English. sa. Free. Highlights, c/o Centre for Canadian Population Studies, University of Western Ontario, London Ontario N6A 5C2 Canada. Tel (519)679-3462. Ed Suzanne Shiel. DD 304.6071171326. Circ 300. A newsletter describing the activities ongoing in the centre for Canadian population studies.

HUWELIKE EN EGSKEIDINGS, BLANKES, KLEURLINGE EN ASIERS . . . SUID-AFRIKA. VFOAT Marriages and Divorces, Whites, Coloureds and Asians . . . South Africa. Periodical. Afrikaans (English). an. LC HB1283.4.A3.

IGU NEWSLETTER. VAT International Geographical Union Newsletter. No. 7-. 0251-0464. Periodical. CN. English (includes some text in French). ir. Free. Professor L A Kosinski, Department of Geography, University of Alberta, Edmonton Alberta T6G 2H4 Canada. DD 304.60601. *Newsletter (International Geographical Union. Commission on Population Geography), 0251-0456.*

IHSAAT AL-MARDA AL-MUALAJIN FI AL-MUSTASHFAYAT AL-URDUNIYAH. VFOAT Morbidity Statistics in Hospitals. Arabic (English). ir. LC HB1464.3.A3.

IIPS NEWSLETTER. Main/Corp International Institute for Population Studies. V. 19- Jan. 1978-. Periodical. II. English. qt. Free. International Institute for Population Studies, Deonar, Bombay 400 08 India. Tel 5511347. Ed Kamla Gupta. LC HB850.5.I4. DD 304.6072054. Circ 1,400. (ctrl). Newsletter giving details about the teaching and research activities of the International Institute for Population Sciences. *Newsletter - International Institute for Population Studies, 0047-0716.*

ILLINOIS POPULATION TRENDS FROM 1970 TO 2025. 1982 Ed.-. US. English. an. Illinois Bureau of the Budget, Division of Planning and Financial Analysis, 605 Stratton Building, Springfield IL 62706. LC HA341. DD 312.809773. *Illinois Population Projections.*

INGU POGON NONJIP. VFOAT Journal of Population and Health Studies. Periodical. Korean (English). sa. Korean Institute for Population and Health, San 42 14 Bulgwang dong, Eunpyung ku, Seoul Korea. Ind/Abst Popul. Index. LC HB3652.5.A3.

INITIATIVES IN POPULATION. (INITIATIVES IN POPULATION : QUARTERLY MAGAZINE OF THE POPULATION CENTER FOUNDATION OF THE PHILIPPINES). Vol. 1, No. 1 (Sept. 1975)-. 0115-2181. Periodical. PH. English. qt. 20.00. Population Center Foundation, PO box 2065 Makati Central Puyat Avenue, Makati Philippines. Tel 855-111. Ed Virgilio F Lacaba. LC HQ763. DD 363.9609599. NLM W1 IN4511. bk rev. adv acc. Circ 10,000. (ctrl). Seeks to bring scientific, technical and population program information to professionals, workers and managers.

INTERCHANGE. 1972. 0047-0465. Periodical. US. English. qt. Part of Library Membership $50.00. Population Reference Bureau, 2213 M Street NW, Washington DC 20037. Tel (202)785-4664. Ed Patricia

Population Studies

H Cancellier. bk rev. **Circ** 6,000. A newsletter which presents information on population-related issues; teaching activities; and new developments and materials in the field.

INTERCOM. V. 1- Jan. 1979-. 0163-7223. Periodical. US. Spanish. mo. Population Reference Bureau, 1337 Connecticut Avenue NW, Washington DC 20036.

INTERNATIONAL AND INTERPROVINCIAL MIGRATION IN CANADA. **Main/Corp** Statistics Canada. Demography Division. **VFOAT** Migrations Internationales et Interprovinciales au Canada. **CN.** English (French). an. $5.40. Publications Distribution, Statistics Canada, Ottawa Ontario K1A 0T6 Canada. **LC** HB1989. **DD** 304.820973. *International and Interprovincial Migration in Canada, 0703-6698.*

INTERNATIONAL DEMOGRAPHICS. Vol. 1, No. 1 (Apr. 1982)-. 0731-5414. Periodical. US. English. mo. $148.00. American Demographics, PO Box 6543, Syracuse NY 13217. **Tel** (607)273-6343. Ed Doris Walsh. **Ind/Abst** Predicasts. bk rev. **Circ** 500. Information on international consumer trends and markets. Country profiles examine income, labor, housing, age groups, etc.

INTERNATIONAL POPULATION CENSUS PUBLICATIONS, JAMAICA. **Series/Titl** International Population Census Publications. Latin America & The Caribbean. 18 -. Periodical. US. Spanish. ir. Department of Statistics, 9 Swallowfield Road, Kingston 5 Jamacia.

INVENTORY AND ANALYSIS OF FEDERAL POPULATION RESEARCH. Began with 1976. 0160-6247. US. English. an. National Institute of Child Health and Human Development, Office of Planning and Evaluation, 9000 Rockville Pike, Bethesda MD 20205. **LC** HB850.5.U5. **DD** 301.32072073. **NLM** WP 22 AA1 I6. *Inventory of Federal Population Research, 0092-7457; Analysis of Federal Population Research, 0092-850X.*

INVENTORY OF POPULATION PROJECTS IN DEVELOPING COUNTRIES AROUND THE WORLD. **Series/Titl** Population Programmes and Projects. 1973/74-. 0363-5155. US. English. an. Un Fund for Population Activities, 485 Lexington Avenue, New York NY 10017. **LC** HQ763. **DD** 363.96091724.

IOWA'S PEOPLE. V. 1, No. 1- Fall 1974-. Periodical. US. English. qt. Iowa Department of Social Services, Hoover Building, Des Moines IA 50319.

JEN KOU HSUEH KAN. **VFOAT** Journal of Population Studies. Periodical. CH. Chinese (English). an. Population Study Center, National Taiwan University, Taipei Taiwan. **Ind/Abst** Popul. Index. **LC** HB3656.A3. **DD** 304.60951249.

JEN KOU YEN CHIU. **VFOAT** Renkou Yanjiu. Began in 1980. Periodical. CC. Chinese. bm. 0.35. Chung-Kuo Kuo Chi Shu Tien, PO Box 2820, Pei-Ching China Mainland. **Ind/Abst** Popul. Index. **LC** HB3654.A3. **DD** 304.60951.

JINKO MONDAI KENKYUJO JIGYO HOKOKUSHO. Japanese. ir. **LC** HB850.5.J3.

JINKO MONDAI KENKYUJO YORAN. **VFOAT** Brochure of the Institute of Population Problems, Ministry of Health and Welfare. JA. Japanese and English. ir. 2-2 Kasumigaseki 1-chome, Chiyoda-ku (100) Japan. **LC** HB850.5.J3.

JINKOGAKU KENKYU. **VFOAT** Journal of Population Studies. No. 1- (March, 1978)-. 0386-8311. JA. Japanese (includes some summaries in English). an. Kokon Shoin, 2-10 Kanda Surugadai, Chiyoda-ku 100, Tokyo Japan. **Ind/Abst** Popul. Index. **LC** HB3651.

LAW AND POPULATION BOOK SERIES. See Law.

LAW AND POPULATION PROGRAMME NEWSLETTER. See Law.

LOCAL POPULATION STUDIES. No. 5 (Autumn 1970)-. 0143-2974. Periodical. UK. English. sa. $7.66. Local Population Studies, 24 St Margarets Road, Torquay Deton England. **Ind/Abst** Am. Hist. Life, Hist. Abstr., Part A, Mod. Hist. Abstr., Hist. Abstr., Part B, Twent. Century Abstr., Popul. Index, Hist. Abstr. **NLM** W1 LO1016H. *Local Population Studies Magazine and Newsletter.*

MAASAAMUUTTO MUUTON SUUNNAN MUKAAN KUNNITTAIN . . . . **VFOAT** Inrikes Omflyttning Efter Flyttningens Riktning Kommunvis . . . . Fl. Finnsih (Swedish). an. Government Printing Centre, PO Box 516, SF-00101 Helsinki 10 Finland. **LC** HB2068.3.A3. *Maassamuutto Kunnittain.*

MAJALAH DEMOGRAFI INDONESIA. V. 1- June 1974-. 0126-0251. IO. Multilingual (English or Indonesian). sa. 1000. Lembaga Demografi, Universitas Indonesia, Jln Salemba 4, Jakarta Indonesia. **Ind/Abst** Popul. Index. **LC** HA1815.

MARRIAGE, DIVORCE AND MORTALITY : A LIFE TABLE ANALYSIS FOR CANADA. **VFOAT** Marriage, Divorce et Mortalite : Analyse des Tables de Mortalite, Canada. **CN.** English (text in French in parallel columns). Foreign Countries. **LC** HB1359. **DD** 312.0971.

MEMORIA IDESPO. **Main/Corp** Universidad Nacional (Costa Rica). Instituto de Estudios Sociales en Poblacion. Spanish. ir. **LC** HB850.5.C8.

MIGRATION REPORT. **Main/Corp** Western Samoa. Dept. of Statistics. 1976-. English. ir. Department of Statistics, PO Box 1151, Apia Western Samoa. **LC** HB2153.8. **DD** 301.3299614.

MISSOURI POPULATION ESTIMATES, BY COUNTY, BY AGE, BY SEX. **Series/Titl** Missouri Center for Health Statistics Publication. **VFOAT** Missouri Population Estimates. Began with: 1971-1975. 0734-032X. US. English. an. Missouri Center for Health Statistic, PO Box 570, Jefferson City MO 65102. **NLM** W2 AM8 C4MC.

DE MOBILITEIT VAN DE NEDERLANDSE BEVOLKING IN . . . . **VFOAT** Mobility of Dutch Population in . . . . NE. Dutch. ir. 15.90. Centraal Bureau Voor de Statistiek, Prinses Beatrixlaan 428 Postbus 959, 2270 AZ Voorburg Netherlands. **LC** HB2065.

MONEY INCOME AND POVERTY STATUS OF FAMILIES AND PERSONS IN THE UNITED STATES. **Series/Titl** Current Population Reports. Series P-60. US. English. an. US Government Printing Office, Superintendent of Documents, Washington DC 20402.

MONTANA MORBIDITY REPORT. 0745-5429. US. English. mo. Free to Qualified Personnel. Department of Health and Environmental Sciences, Health Services Division, Cogswell Building, Helena MT 59620.

MONTHLY PRODUCT ANNOUNCEMENT. No. 1 (Jan. 1981)-. Periodical. US. English. mo. Free. Data User Services Division Customer Services Publication, Bureau of the Census, Washington DC 20233. **Tel** (301)763-4100. Ed Bernice L Baker. Lists all the Census Bureau's publications, microfiche, maps, data files and documentation that became available during the previous month.

MORTALITY. 1979-. 0732-6947. US. English. an. New Jersey Department of Health, John Fitch Plaza, PO Box 1540, Trenton NJ 08625. **LC** HB1355.N5. **DD** 312.209749. *New Jersey Health Statistics, 0545-2368.*

MORTALITY STATISTICS. See Statistics.

NEW ZEALAND POPULATION REVIEW. **VFOAT** Population Review. Vol. 6, No. 1 (Mar. 1980)-. 0111-199X. Periodical. NZ. English. qt. $16.90. New Zealand Demographic Society, PO Box 225, Wellington New Zealand. Ed Charles Crothers. **Ind/Abst** Popul. Index. bk rev. **Circ** 250. Research articles, methodological and topical comments and summaries of key statistics about the demography of New Zealand and the South Pacific. *New Zealand Population Newsletter.*

NEWBORN. See Statistics.

NEWS LETTER (POPULATION CENTRE BANGALORE). See Birth Control.

NORTH CAROLINA POPULATION PROJECTIONS. **Main/Corp** North Carolina. Division of State Budget and Management. Research and Planning Services. US. English. be. $3.50. Division of State Budget and Management/Librarian, 116 West Jones Street, Raleigh NC 27603. **LC** HA554. **DD** 312.809756.

NOTAS DE POBLACION. Vol. 1- Apr. 1973-. 0303-1829. Periodical. CL. Spanish (summaries in English). ir. $20.00. Celade, Casilla 91, Infante 9, Santiago Chile. **Tel** 228-3206. Ed Jorge Arevalo. **Ind/Abst** Popul. Index, Foreign Lang. Index, PAIS Foreign Lang. Index. **LC** HB3530.5.A3. **Circ** 1,000. Recent studies on population dynamics in Latin America and the Caribbeans and information on work being carried out in the field of population. *Boletin Informativo.*

THE NUMBERS NEWS. Vol. 1, No. 1 (Dec. 15, 1980)-. 0732-1597. Periodical. US. English. mo. $76.00. American Demographics, PO Box 6543, Syracuse NY 13217. **Tel** (800)828-1133.

NY MPONIN'I MADAGASIKARA. No 1- Tahona 1975-. French or Malagasy. ir. B P 4096, Tananarive Madagascar. **LC** HB3668.M3. **DD** 301.329691.

OHIO POPULATION ESTIMATES. **Main/Corp** Ohio. Dept. of Economic and Community Development. 0149-1520. US. English. an. Ohio Department of Economic and Community Development, Office of Research, Box 1001, Columbus OH 43216. **LC** HB3525.O3. **DD** 312.809771.

ONTARIO POPULATION STATISTICS. See Statistics.

OREGON'S DRIVING POPULATION CEASED. 1971-1980. 0091-5769. US. English. **LC** HE5633.O7.

P.A.A. AFFAIRS. **Main/Corp** Population Association of America. **VAT** Population Association of America Affairs. 0300-6816. Periodical. US. English. qt. $5.00. Population Association of America, PO Box 14182, Ben Franklin Station, Washington DC 20044. **Tel** (202)393-3253.

PENDUDUK CINA JAWA-MADURA : HASIL REGISTRASI PENDUDUK. **Main/Corp** Indonesia. Biro Pusat Statistik. **VFOAT** Chinese Population of Java-Madura : Results of Population Registration. 1973/75-. English and Indonesian. ir. $3.60. Jakarta Biro Pusat Statistik, J1 Dr Sutomo No 8, PO Box 3, Jakarta Indonesia. **Tel** 372808. **LC** HA1817.J3. bk rev. adv acc. (ctrl).

PENNSYLVANIA VITAL STATISTICS, ANNUAL REPORT. See Statistics.

PERSONS OF SPANISH ORIGIN IN THE UNITED STATES . . . ADVANCE REPORT. **Series/Titl** Current Population Reports. Series P-20. Began with Mar. 1973. US. English. an. Superintendent of Documents, US Government Printing Office, Washington DC 20402.

POCKETBOOK OF STATISTICS: JAMAICA. See Statistics.

POPULACNI ZPRAVY. Periodical. Czech. ir. Sedreatariat Vladni Populacni Komise Pri Federalnim Ministerstvu Prace A Socialnichveci, Palackeho Namesti 4, Praha 2 Czechoslovakia. **Ind/Abst** Popul. Index. **LC** HB848.

POPULATION. 1.- Yearly Vol. 0032-4663. Periodical. FR. French. bm. 235. Institut National d'Etudes Demographiques, 27 rue du Commandeur, 75675 Paris Cedex France. **Tel** (33)(1)43.20.13.45. **Ind/Abst** Biol. Abstr., Foreign Lang. Index, Int. Labour Doc., Popul. Index, Am. Hist. Life, Hist. Abstr., Part A, Mod. Hist. Abstr., Hist. Abstr., Part B, Twent. Century Abstr., Lang. Lang. Behav. Abstr., Women Stud. Abstr., Sociol. Abstr., Soc. Sci. Citation Index, Recent Publ. Artic. **LC** HB881. **DD** 312.05. **NLM** W1 PO592. **CODEN** POPUAQ. (cum index). bk rev. **Circ** 4,000. Populations studies and demographics.

POPULATION ANALYSIS OF THE ILLINOIS ADULT PRISON SYSTEM. See Sociology: General Works, Theory - Social Pathology, Welfare, Criminology.

POPULATION AND DEVELOPMENT REVIEW. V. 1- Sept. 1975-. 0098-7921. Periodical. US. English. qt. $24.00. The Population Council, One Dag Hammarskjold Plaza, New York NY 10021. **Tel** (212)644-1300. Ed Ethel P Churchill. **Ind/Abst** Am. Hist. Life, Hist. Abstr., Part A, Mod. Hist. Abstr., Hist. Abstr., Part B, Twent. Century Abstr., Int. Labour Doc., Sociol. Abstr., Soc. Welf. Soc. Plan./Policy Soc. Dev., Energy Inf. Abstr., Environ. Abstr., Index Econ. Artic. J. Collect. Vol., Popul. Index, ABC Pol Sci, Ref. Source, Public Aff. Inf. Serv. Bull., Soc. Sci. Citation Index, Recent Publ. Artic. **LC** HB848. **DD** 301.32072. **NLM** W1 PO597. **Circ** 5,000. Advances knowledge on the relationship between population growth and socioeconomic change. Discusses related issues of public policy.

POPULATION AND DWELLINGS, STATISTICAL DIVISIONS, SUB-DIVISIONS, AND LOCAL GOVERNMENT AREAS, WESTERN AUSTRALIA. See Statistics.

POPULATION AND ENVIRONMENT. V. 3- Spring 1980-. 0199-0039. Periodical. US. English. qt. $38.00. Human Sciences Press, 72 5th Avenue, New York NY 10011. **Ind/Abst** Biol. Abstr., Sociol. Abstr., Soc. Work Res. Abstr., Saf. Sci. Abstr. J.,

Population Studies

Marriage Fam. Rev., Curr. Index J. Educ., Popul. Index, Curr. Contents, Soc. Behav. Sci., Soc. Sci. Citation Index, Coll. Stud. Pers. Abstr., Energy Inf. Abstr., Environ. Abstr., Environ. Abstr., Environ. Index, Public Aff. Inf. Serv. Bull., Psychol. Abstr. **LC** HB848. **DD** 304.605. **NLM** W1 PO597E. **CODEN** PENVDK. *Journal of Population*, 0146-1052.

POPULATION AND MIGRATION. VFOAT New Zealand Population and Migration. 1971/72-. NZ. English. an. $0.60. Department of Statistics, Private Bag, Wellington New Zealand. **LC** HA3173. **DD** 312.09931. **NLM** W2 KN4 D64P. *Population, Migration, and Building*, 0077-9903.

POPULATION AND VITAL STATISTICS REPORT. Main/Corp United Nations. Statistical Office. V. 1- Jan. 1949-. US. English. qt. $18.00. United Nations Publications, Sales Section/Room A-3315, New York NY 10017. **Tel** (212)745-8324. **LC** JX1977. **DD** 312.05. Provides latest worldwide demographic statistics on birth and mortality.

POPULATION (BOCA RATON, FLA.). (POPULATION). Series/Titl Social Issues Resources Series. Vol. 1, Article 1-. 0273-2548. US. English. an. Social Issues Resources Series Inc, PO Box 2507, Boca Raton FL 33432. Ed E C Goldstein. **LC** HB848. **DD** 304.605. *Hydrographic Office,*, 1-.

POPULATION BULLETIN. Vol. 1- Sept. 1945-. 0032-468X. Periodical. US. English. ir. $50.00. Population Reference Bureau, 1337 Connecticut Avenue, Washington DC 20036. Ind/Abst Soc. Sci. Index, Int. Labour Doc., Biol. Abstr., Popul. Index, Public Aff. Inf. Serv. Bull., Soc. Sci. Citation Index, Curr. Contents, Soc. Behav. Sci., Energy Inf. Abstr., Environ. Abstr. **LC** HB881.A1. **DD** 312.05. **NLM** W1 PO643. **CODEN** POPBA3. *Population Bulletin*, 0032-468X.

POPULATION BULLETIN OF THE UNITED NATIONS. No. 3 (Oct. 1953)-. US. English. ir. United Nations Sales Section, Room A/3315, New York NY 10017. Ind/Abst Popul. Index. *Population Bulletin*.

POPULATION BULLETIN OF THE UNITED NATIONS ECONOMIC COMMISSION FOR WESTERN ASIA. (POPULATION BULLETIN OF ECWA). VFOAT Population Bulletin of E.C.W.A. No. 18 (June 1980)-. 0378-679X. Periodical. English. sa. Population Division, ECWA, PO Box 4656, Beirut Lebanon. Ind/Abst Popul. Index, Recent Publ. Artic. **LC** HB3633.3.A3. **DD** 304.60956. **NLM** W2. *Population Bulletin of the United Nations Economic Commission for Western Asia.*

THE POPULATION COUNCIL ANNUAL REPORT. (ANNUAL REPORT). Main/Corp Population Council (New York, N.Y.). VFOAT Population Council Annual Report. 1968-. 0361-7858. US. English. an. Population Council, One Dag Hammarskjold Plaza, New York NY 10017. Ind/Abst Biol. Abstr. **LC** HB848. **DD** 304.60607471. **NLM** W1 PO645. **CODEN** POPCA6. *Annual Report for the Year ended December 31 . . . .*

POPULATION ESTIMATE AND HOUSING INVENTORY FOR THE CITY OF LOS ANGELES AS OF OCTOBER 1 . . . (LOS ANGELES (CALIF.)). *See* Housing and Urban Development.

POPULATION ESTIMATES AND . . . PER CAPITA INCOME ESTIMATES FOR COUNTIES, INCORPORATED PLACES, AND MINOR CIVIL DIVISIONS. OHIO. 1982-. US. English. be. Superintendent of Documents, US Government Printing Office, Washington DC 20402.

POPULATION ESTIMATES AND . . . PER CAPITA INCOME ESTIMATES FOR COUNTIES, INCORPORATED PLACES, AND SELECTED MINOR CIVIL DIVISIONS. INDIANA. Series/Titl Current Population Reports. Series P-26. 1982-. US. English. be. Superintendent of Documents, US Government Printing Office, Washington DC 20402.

POPULATION ESTIMATES FOR MINOR CIVIL DIVISIONS BY COUNTY, MAINE. US. English. an. **LC** HA411. **DD** 312.809741.

POPULATION ESTIMATES FOR NEW JERSEY (TRENTON, N.J. : 1981). (POPULATION ESTIMATES FOR NEW JERSEY). US. English. an. Office of Demographic and Economic Analysis, Division of Planning and Research Center 388, Trenton NJ 08625-0388. **Tel** (609)292-0076. **LC** HA521. **DD** 312.809749. **Circ** 2,500. Population estimates for New Jersey, its counties, and its municipalities. *Provisional Population Estimates for New Jersey.*

POPULATION ESTIMATES FOR NORTH CAROLINA COUNTIES AND MUNICIPALITIES. Main/Corp North Carolina. Demographic Research Branch. 0160-5127. US. English. 116 West Jones Street, Raleigh NC 27602. **LC** HA551. **DD** 312.809756.

POPULATION ESTIMATES FOR OHIO. Main/Corp Ohio. Dept. of Development. Economic Research Division. VFOAT Population Series A. 0473-9418. US. English. sa. Economic Research Division Development Department, Box 1001, Columbus OH 43216. **LC** HB3525.O3. **DD** 312.809771.

POPULATION ET FAMILLE. 26/27-. 0523-1159. Periodical. BE. French (summaries in English). ir. 500. Centre d'Etude de la Population et de la Famille, Office International de Librairie, Avenue Marnix 30-1050, Bruxelles Belgium. Ind/Abst Sociol. Abstr., Soc. Welf. Soc. Plan./Policy Soc. Dev., Popul. Index, Foreign Lang. Index, Public Aff. Inf. Serv. Bull. **LC** HB848. **DD** 301.3205. **NLM** W1 PO648. *Bevolking en Gezin.*

POPULATION ET SOCIETES. No. 1- March 1968-. 0184-7783. Periodical. FR. French. mo. $6.66. Institut National D'Etudes Demographique, 27 rue du Commandeur, 75675 Paris Cedex 14 France. **Tel** (1)4 320 13 45. Ed INED. Ind/Abst Popul. Index. **LC** HB848. **NLM** W1 PO649. **Circ** 40,000. Contains science, French society, demography, world population, development.

POPULATION-FOOD PAPER. (POPULATION/FOOD PAPER). VFOAT Population/Food Fund Papers. No. 1-. 0148-4842. Monographic Series. US. English. Population/Food Fund, 265 McCannel Hall, Room 329, Grand Forks ND 58206. **NLM** W1 PO653.

POPULATION INDEX. *See* Indexes/Abstracts.

POPULATION MOBILITY IN HAWAII. Main/Corp Hawaii. Dept. of Health. 1971-. 0094-0348. US. English. PO Box 3378, Honolulu HI 96801. **LC** HB1985.H3. **DD** 301.32609969.

POPULATION MOVEMENT. *See* Sociology: General Works, Theory - Social Pathology, Welfare, Criminology.

POPULATION NEWSLETTER. No. 1- Apr. 1968-. 0048-4849. Periodical. US. English. sa. United Nations Publications, Sales Section/Room A3315, New York NY 10017. **LC** HB848. **NLM** W1 PO654.

POPULATION. PERSPECTIVE. (POPULATION : PERSPECTIVE). Main/Corp American Universities Field Staff. 1971-. 0091-5610. US. English. Freeman/Cooper, 1736 Stockton Street, San Francisco CA 94133. **LC** HB871. **DD** 301.32.

POPULATION PROFILE OF THE UNITED STATES. Began with: 1974. US. English. an. Superintendent of Documents, US Government Printing Office, Washington DC 20402. **NLM** W2.

POPULATION PROGRAM ASSISTANCE. US. English. an. Superintendent of Documents, US Government Printing Office, Washington DC 20402. **DD** 301.321.

POPULATION PROJECTIONS BY MINOR CIVIL DIVISIONS, SEX, AGE GROUP, AND COUNTY. US. English. Division of Data and Research Bureau of Health Planning and Development, Department of Human Services State House Station 11, Augusta ME 04333. **Tel** (207)289-3001. Ed Ellen Noor. **LC** HA415. **DD** 312.809741. **Circ** 400. Population projections for 1984-1993, by minor civil division, sex, age group and county. Estimated population for 1983 is also included.

POPULATION REPORT. SERIES C-D : STERILIZATION FEMALE AND MALE. 0091-9241. Periodical. US. English. **NLM** W1 PO671L.

POPULATION REPORT. SERIES E. LAW AND POLICY. (POPULATION REPORTS. SERIES E : LAW AND POLICY). VFOAT Law and Policy. No. 1- July 1974-. 0097-9082. Periodical. US. English. Department of Medical and Public Affairs, George Washington University Medical Center, 2001 S Street NW, Washington DC 20009. Ind/Abst Index Med. **NLM** W1 PO671ME.

POPULATION REPORT. SERIES I. PERIODIC ABSTINENCE. (POPULATION REPORTS. SERIES I : PERIODIC ABSTINENCE). VFOAT Periodic Abstinence. No. 1- June 1974-. 0097-9090. Periodical. US. English. Department of Medical and Public Affairs, George Washington University Medical Center, 2001 S Street NW, Washington DC 20009. Ind/Abst Index Med. **NLM** W1 PO671R.

POPULATION REPORTS. CUMULATIVE INDEX. *See* Indexes/Abstracts.

POPULATION REPORTS. SERIES D. STERILIZATION. (POPULATION REPORTS. SERIES D : STERILIZATION MALE). VFOAT Sterilization Male. No. 1- Dec. 1973-. 0093-4488. Periodical. US. English. ir. Department of Medical & Public Affairs, George Washington University Medical Center, 2001 S Street NW, Washington DC 20009. Ind/Abst Index Med., Energy Res. Abstr. **NLM** W1 PO671M.

POPULATION REPORTS. SERIES F. PREGNANCY TERMINATION. (POPULATION REPORTS. SERIES F : PREGNANCY TERMINATION). VFOAT Pregnancy Termination. No. 1- Apr. 1973-. 0091-9284. Periodical. US. English. Department of Medicine and Public Affairs, George Washington University Medical Center 2001 S Street Northwest, Washington DC 20009. Ind/Abst Index Med. **NLM** W1 PO671N.

POPULATION REPORTS. SERIES G. PROSTAGLANDINS. VFOAT Prostaglandins. No. 1- Apr. 1973-. 0091-9276. Periodical. US. English. ir. The George Washington University, Department of Medical and Public Affairs, 2001 South Street NW, Washington DC 20009. Ind/Abst Index Med., Chem. Abstr. **NLM** W1 PO671P. **CODEN** PRGPDO. *Research in Prostaglandins.*

POPULATION REPORTS. SERIES K. INJECTABLES AND IMPLANTS *CEASED*. (POPULATION REPORTS. SERIES K : INJECTABLES AND IMPLANTS). VFOAT Injectables and Implants. No. 1-2. 0097-9104. US. English. ir. Department of Medical and Public Affairs, George Washington University Medical Center, 2001 South Street Washington DC 20009. Ind/Abst Index Med. **NLM** W1 PO671SC. **CODEN** PRSIDT.

POPULATION REPORTS. SERIES L. ISSUES IN WORLD HEALTH. (POPULATION REPORTS. SERIES L : ISSUES IN WORLD HEALTH). VFOAT Issues in World Health. No. 1-. 0197-5838. US. English. ir. Hampton House 624 North Broadway, Baltimore MD 21205. Ind/Abst Excerpta Med., Index Med., Popul. Index. **NLM** W1 PO671SD.

POPULATION REPORTS (WASHINGTON, D.C.). (POPULATION REPORTS. SRIE M, SUJETS SPECIAUX). 8756-4432. Periodical. US. French. Population Information Program, Johns Hopkins University, Hampton House 624 North Broadway, Baltimore MD 21205. **DD** 304.

POPULATION REPRINTS. No. 1- 1972-. 0317-3100. Monographic Series. CN. English. Population Research Laboratory, Department of Sociology Tory Building University of Alberta, Edmonton Alberta T6G 2H4 Canada. **DD** 301.32.

POPULATION RESEARCH AND POLICY REVIEW. Vol. 1, No. 1 (Jan. 1982)-. 0167-5923. Periodical. English. ty. Kluwer Academic Publishing Group, Spui Boulevard 50, PO Box 989, 3300 AZ Dordrecht Netherlands. Ind/Abst Sociol. Abstr., Energy Inf. Abstr., Environ. Abstr., Popul. Index, Public Aff. Inf. Serv. Bull. **LC** HB848. **DD** 304.605.

POPULATION, RESEARCHES AND STUDIES. (POPULATION RESEARCHES AND STUDIES). 0255-898X. Periodical. English (Arabic). ir.

POPULATION REVIEW. V. 1- Jan. 1957-. 0032-471X. Periodical. US. English. $25.00. Indian Institute for Population Studies, 8976 Cliffridge Avenue, La Jolla CA 92037. **Tel** (619)455-6283. Ed S Chandraseuhar. Ind/Abst Sociol. Abstr., Popul. Index, Public Aff. Inf. Serv. Bull. **LC** HB881. **DD** 301.3205. **NLM** W1 PO672. bk rev. adv acc. **Circ** 2,500. Deals with Asia and other developing countries. Subjects include population, family planning, economics, environment and sociology.

POPULATION STUDIES. V. 1- June 1947-. 0032-4728. Periodical. UK. English. ty. $60.00. Population Investigation Committee, London School of Economics, Houghton Street, London WC2A 2AE England. Ed E Grebenik, J Hobcraft, and R Schofield. Ind/Abst Sociol. Abstr., Biol. Abstr., Energy Inf. Abstr., Environ. Abstr., Excerpta Med., Index Econ. Artic. J. Collect. Vol., Int. Labour Doc., Popul. Index,

Population Studies

Public Aff. Inf. Serv. Bull., Hist. Abstr., Ref. Source, Soc. Welf. Soc. Plan./Policy Soc. Dev., Women Stud. Abstr., Am. Hist. Life, Hist. Abstr., Part A, Mod. Hist. Abstr., Soc. Sci. Citation Index, Lang. Lang. Behav. Abstr., Hist. Abstr., Hist. Abst., Part B, Twent. Century Abstr. **LC** HB848. **DD** 304.605. **NLM** W1 PO675. **CODEN** POSTA4. bk rev. adv acc. **Circ** 3,100. Leading English language journal in population. Covers socio-economic and biomedical causes and consequences of fertility, family, marriage, mortality, migration theory, methods and models; worldwide trends.

POPULATION STUDIES. **Main/Corp** United Nations. Dept. of Economic and Social Affairs. No. 1- 1948-. 0082-805X. Monographic Series. US. English. ir. United Nations Publications, Sales Section/Room A-3315, New York NY 10017. **Tel** (212)754-8302. **Ind/Abst** Index Med., Women Stud. Abstr. Covers all aspects of population trends, problems and policies.

POPULATION STUDIES. II. English. ir. Professor & Head of Department of Demography and Population Studies, University of Kerala, Kariavattom 695581 India. **Tel** (0471)8057. Ed R Ramakumar. **LC** HB3640.K4. **DD** 301.3295483. adv acc. **Circ** 200. (ctrl). Research articles in demography slant towards methodology, technical demography, statistical models. Results of population studies from any part of the world.

POPULATION STUDIES BULLETIN. US. English. ir. $24.00. Bureau of Economics & Business Research, 221 Matherly Hall University of Florida, Gainesville FL 32611. **LC** HB3525.F6. **DD** 301.329759.

POPULATION TODAY. Vol. 12, No. 1 (Jan. 1984)-. 0749-2448. Periodical. US. English. mo. $40.00 Libraries, $200.00 Institutions or Corporations. Population Reference Bureau, 2213 M Street NW, Washington DC 20037. **DD** 304. *Intercom, 0092-444X.*

POPULATION TRENDS. **Main/Corp** Great Britain. Office of Population Censuses and Surveys. 1- Autumn 1975-. 0307-4463. Periodical. UK. English. qt. Her Majestys Stationery Office, PO Box 276, London SW8 5DT England. **Tel** (01)622 3316. **Ind/Abst** Sociol. Abstr., Soc. Welf. Soc. Plan./Policy Soc. Dev., Popul. Index, Public Aff. Inf. Serv. Bull. **LC** HB3583. **DD** 301.32941. **NLM** W1 PO676. Contains regular series of statistical tables on population change, vital statistics summaries, births, marriages, divorces, migration, deaths and abortions.

POPULI. 0251-6861. US. English. qt. $20.00. UNIPUB, PO Box 1222, Ann Arbor MI 48106. **Tel** (800)521-8110. **Ind/Abst** Energy Inf. Abstr., Environ. Abstr., Popul. Index, Public Aff. Inf. Serv. Bull. **LC** HB848. **DD** 301.3205. **NLM** W1 PO678. Provides up-to-date coverage of demographic trends and population problems throughout the world.

PRB REPORT. **Main/Corp** Population Reference Bureau. **VAT** Population Reference Bureau Report. Vol. 1, No. 1 (1975)-. 0146-7646. Periodical. US. English. ir. Population Reference Bureau, 1337 Connecticut Avenue NW, Washington DC 20036. *Population Profile, PRB Selection.*

PROBLEMY REGIONALNOGO DEMOGRAFICHESKOGO PROGNOZIROVANIIA V SISTEME NARODNOKHOZIAISTVENNOGO PLANIROVANIIA. UR. Russian. **LC** HB3607.

PROJECTIONS OF THE POPULATION OF THE UNITED STATES . . . (ADVANCE REPORT). **Series/Titl** Current Population Reports. Series P-25. 1982 to 2050-. US. English. Superintendent of Documents, US Government Printing Office, Washington DC 20402.

PROJECTIONS OF THE POPULATION OF VOTING AGE FOR STATES. **Series/Titl** Current Population Reports. Series P-25. Began with Nov. 1966-1968. US. English. be. Superintendent of Documents, US Government Printing Office, Washington DC 20402. *Estimates of the Civilian Population of Voting Age, for States.*

PUBLICACIONES. **Main/Corp** Mexico (City) Colegio de Mexico. Centro de Estudios Economicos y Demograficos. 1- 1967-. Periodical. MX. Spanish. ir. Colegio de Mexico, Camino Al Ajusco, 20 Pedergal Sta Teresa, 10740 Mexico DF Mexico. **Tel** (525)568-6033.

QUARTERLY POPULATION BULLETIN. **Main/Corp** New Zealand. Dept. of Statistics. V. 1-3, No. 2. 0110-4055. NZ. English. Department of Statistics, Private Bag, Wellington New Zealand. **Ind/Abst** Public Aff. Inf. Serv. Bull. **LC** HA3173. **DD** 312.09931.

QUARTERLY POPULATION GROWTH, ALBERTA. 3d Quarter 1977-. 0225-3003. Periodical. CN. English. Free. Economic and Demographic Models Unit, Bureau of Statistics, Alberta Treasury 21st Floor Park Square, Edmonton Alberta T5J 3B6 Canada. **DD** 304.62097123.

QUEENSLAND DEMOGRAPHY. **Main/Corp** Australian Bureau of Statistics. Queensland Office. 1973-. AT. English. ir. Australian Bureau of Statistics, 345 Ann Street, Brisbane Queensland 400 Australia. **LC** HA3088.Q45. **DD** 312.09943. *Statistics of the State of Queensland. Part A: Population and Vital.*

RAPPORT DE L'ANNEE - PROGRAMME DE RECHERCHE EN DEMOGRAPHIE HISTORIQUE. DEPARTEMENT DE DEMOGRAPHIE. UNIVERSITE DE MONTREAL. (RAPPORT DE L'ANNEE - PROGRAMME DE RECHERCHE EN DEMOGRAPHIE HISTORIQUE, DEPARTEMENT DE DEMOGRAPHIE). **Main/Corp** Universite de Montreal. Programme de Recherche en Demographie Historique. Published since 1971?. 0226-2924. CN. French. an. Dep de Demographie, Universite de Montreal, CP 6128 Montreal Succursale A, Montreal Quebec H3C 3J7 Canada. **DD** 304.60720714.

THE REGISTRAR GENERAL'S ANNUAL ESTIMATES OF THE POPULATION OF ENGLAND AND WALES AND OF LOCAL AUTHORITY AREAS. **Main/Corp** Great Britain. Office of Population Censuses and Surveys. UK. English. an. 0.22 1/2. H M Stationery Office, 49 High Holborn, WC1V 6HB London England. **LC** HA1123. **DD** 312.0942.

THE REGISTRAR GENERAL'S REVISED ESTIMATES OF THE POPULATION OF ENGLAND AND WALES, REGIONS, AND LOCAL AUTHORITY AREAS. **Main/Corp** Great Britain. Office of Population Censuses and Surveys. UK. English. Her Majestys Stationery Office, PO Box 276, London SW8 5DT England. **LC** HB3583. **DD** 312.0942.

REGISTRATION OF BIRTHS & DEATHS ACT. ANNUAL REPORT. (REGISTRATION OF BIRTHS & DEATHS ACT, ANNUAL REPORT). **VFOAT** Registration of Births and Deaths Act, Annual Report. Began in 1969. 0376-5288. II. English. an. Delhi Administration, Room No 148/Old Secretariat, New Delhi 110054 India. **LC** HB3640.D4. **DD** 312.095466.

REGISTRO CIVIL DO BRASIL : RESULTADOS PRELIMINARES. **Main/Corp** Centro Brasileiro de Estudos Demograficos. BL. Portuguese. ir. Centro Brasileiro de Estudos Demograficos, Av Beira Mar 436 12 O Andar, Rio de Janeiro Brazil. **LC** HA984.

REPORT BY THE EXECUTIVE DIRECTOR OF THE UNITED NATIONS FUND FOR POPULATION ACTIVITIES. **Main/Corp** United Nations Fund for Population Activities. **VFOAT** Report. Began with Vol. for 1974. US. English. an. United Nations Fund for Population Activities, 220 East 42nd Street, New York NY 10017. **LC** HB848. **DD** 354.1815. **NLM** W2 MU5 F9R. *Report on the United Nations Fund for Population Activities.*

REPORT CTC. US. English. Hawaii State Census, Statistical Areas Committee, State of Hawaii, PO Box 2359, Honolulu HI 96804. *Report CTC.*

REPORT OF THE POPULATION COMMISSION - UNITED NATIONS. **Main/Corp** United Nations. Economic and Social Council. Population Commission. **VFOAT** Report to the Economic and Social Council on the . . . Session of the Commission. 1st Session (Feb. 6/19, 1947)-. US. English (French). ir. United Nations, Sales Section Room A 3315, New York NY 10017. **LC** JX1977. **DD** 312.0611.

A REPORT ON FAMILY PLANNING SERVICES AND POPULATION RESEARCH. *See* Birth Control.

REPORT ON REGISTRATION OF BIRTHS AND DEATHS. 1980-. 0217-278X. English. an. **NLM** W2 JS6 R3R. *Report on the Registration of Births and Deaths and Marriages.*

REPORT ON THE ACTIVITIES OF THE IGU COMMISSION ON POPULATION GEOGRAPHY. **Main/Corp** International Geographical Union. Commission of Population Geography. CN. English. Professor Leszek A Kosinski, Department of Geography University of Alberta, Edmonton Alberta T6G 2H4 Canada. **LC** HB848. **DD** 301.320601.

REPORTS FROM POPULATION RESEARCH CENTERS AND PROGRAM PROJECTS. **Main/Corp** United States. National Institute of Child Health and Human Development. Center for Population Research. Began publication with 1st in 1973. 0095-6295. Periodical. US. English. an. Center for Population Research, 2213 M Street NW, Washington DC 20037. **LC** QP251.A1. **DD** 612.6005. *Annual Summary Progress Reports of Population Research Centers and Program Projects.*

RESEARCH IN POPULATION ECONOMICS. V. 1- 1978-. 0163-7878. US. English. ir. $49.50. JAI Press, PO Box 1678, Greenwich CT 06836. **Tel** (203)661-7602. Ed Paul Shultz Simon. **Ind/Abst** Popul. Index. **LC** HB848. **DD** 301.3205.

RESEARCHES ON POPULATION ECOLOGY. **VFOAT** Kotai-Gunseigaku No Kenkyu. V. 1- Mar. 1952-. 0304-5466. Periodical. JA. English (Vols. 1-3, 1952-56 in Japanese with summaries). sa. Kyowa Book Company, 1-33 Kanda Jimbo Cho, Chiyoda-ku Tokyo Japan. **Tel** 293-0727. **Ind/Abst** Life Sci. Collect., Energy Inf. Abstr., Environ. Abstr., Biol. Abstr., Sci. Cit. Index, Abr. Ed. **CODEN** KOGSBN.

RESENA DE ACTIVIDADES - CENEP. **Main/Corp** Centro de Estudios de Poblacion, (Buenos Aires, Argentina). AG. Spanish. ir. Casilla 4397, Correo Central, 1000 Buenos Aires Argentina. **LC** HB850.5.A7. **DD** 304.6072082.

REVIEW OF POPULATION REVIEWS. No. 7 (Jan./Mar. 1978)-. 0377-8967. Periodical. English. qt. Cicred 27, rue du Commandeur 75675, Paris Cedex 14 France. **Ind/Abst** Popul. Index. **LC** HB848. **DD** 304.605.

REVISTA BRASILEIRA DE ESTUDOS DE POPULACAO. Vol. 1, No. 1/2 (Jan./Dec. 1984)-. Periodical. Portuguese. ir.

REVISTA DOCPOP. **VFOAT** DOCPOP. V. 1, No. 1 (Dec. 1982)-. 0101-7217. Periodical. Portuguese (English). sa.

REZULTATI SAMOPOPISIVANJA I POSTANSKIH METODA U BEOGRADU . . . GODINE. **Series/Titl** Studije, Analize i Prikazi. **VFOAT** Results of Self-Enumeration and Mail Methods in Beograd. YU. Serbo-Croatian. ir. 50.00. Savezni Zavod za Statistiku, Kneza Milosa, Br 20, Beograd Yugoslavia. **LC** HA37.Y8, HA1635.B4.

RIVISTA ITALIANA DI ECONOMIA, DEMOGRAFIA E STATISTICA. *See* Statistics.

RURAL DEMOGRAPHY. V. 1- Summer 1974-. Periodical. BG. English. sa. $6.00. Institute of Statistical Research & Training, Secretary, Dacca 2 Bangladesh. **Ind/Abst** Popul. Index. **LC** HB850.5.B3. **DD** 301.3295492.

SEAPRAP RESEARCH REPORT. (SEAPRAP RESEARCH REPORT : A REPORT OF RESEARCH UNDERTAKEN WITH THE ASSISTANCE OF AN AWARD FROM THE SOUTHEAST ASIA POPULATION RESEARCH AWARDS PROGRAM (SEAPRAP), INSTITUTE OF SOUTHEAST ASIAN STUDIES). 0129-5101. Monographic Series. SI. English. ir. Institute of Southeast Asian Studies, Singapore Singapore. **Ind/Abst** Popul. Index. **NLM** W1.

SELECTED ANNOTATED BIBLIOGRAPHY OF POPULATION STUDIES IN THE NETHERLANDS. *See* Bibliographies.

THE SOURCEBOOK OF DEMOGRAPHICS AND BUYING POWER FOR EVERY ZIP CODE IN THE USA. (THE . . . SOURCEBOOK OF DEMOGRAPHICS AND BUYING POWER FOR EVERY ZIP CODE IN THE USA). **VFOAT** Source Book of Demographics and Buying Power for Every Zip Code in the USA. 1984-. 8755-4704. US. English. an. C A C I 1815 North Fort Myer Drive, Arlington VA 22209. **Tel** (800)292-2224. **LC** HA203. **DD** 304.60973021. A complete description of each residential zip code in the USA. Includes 1980, current year, and five year projections of over 75 demographic descriptors.

STATISTICAL POCKET BOOK, NEPAL. See Statistics.

STATISTICAL YEAR BOOK, THAILAND. See Yearbooks, Almanacs, Directories.

STATISTIQUES DEMOGRAPHIQUES. See Statistics.

STERFTETAFELS VOOR NEDERLAND CEASED. Main/Corp Netherlands. Centraal Bureau Voor de Statistiek. NE. Dutch (summaries in English). ir. LC HB1435. NLM W2 GN4 C3ST.

STUDI DI STATISTICA. See Statistics.

STUDIA DEMOGRAFICZNE. 1.- 1963-. 0039-3134. Periodical. PL. Polish (tables of contents and summaries in Russian and English). qt. ARS Polano, Krakowskie Przedmiescie 7, 00-068 Warsaw Poland. Ind/Abst Popul. Index. LC HB881.A1.

TABLEAUX DE L'ECONOMIE CHAMPENOISE. See Statistics.

TEACHING NOTES ON POPULATION. V. 1- Spring/Summer 1972-. 0363-3144. US. English. Foreign Area Materials Center, State Education Department, 60 East 42 Street, New York NY 10017.

TECHNICAL BULLETINS (WORLD FERTILITY SURVEY). (TECHNICAL BULLETINS). Began with: No. 1 (Oct. 1976). Monographic Series. English. ir. Ind/Abst Popul. Index. NLM W1.

U.S. DECENNIAL LIFE TABLES. SOME TRENDS AND COMPARISONS OF UNITED STATES LIFE-TABLE DATA. VFOAT Some Trends and Comparisons of United States Life-Table Data. Periodical. US. English. US Department of Health, Education and Welfare, Public Health Service, Health Service, Health Resources Administration, Washington DC 20402.

U.S. DECENNIAL LIFE TABLES. STATE LIFE TABLES. (U.S. DECENNIAL LIFE TABLES; STATE LIFE TABLES). VFOAT State Life Tables. Periodical. US. English. National Center for Health Statistics, Rockville MD 20402.

UNITED STATES LIFE TABLES. Main/Corp National Center for Health Statistics (U.S.). VFOAT U.S. Decennial Life Tables. V. 1- 1969/71-. US. English. an. National Center of Health Statistics, Scientific Technology Information Branch/Room 1-57, Hyattsville MD 20782. **Tel** (301)436-8500. LC HB1355. DD 312.20973. NLM HG 8781 U58L.

VERMONT POPULATION ESTIMATES, STATE, COUNTY, CITIES, TOWNS, VILLAGES. Main/Corp Vermont. Dept. of Health. Series/Titl Public Health Statistics Bulletin. US. English. 115 Colchester Avenue, Burlington VT 05401. LC HA674. DD 312.809743.

VITAL AND HEALTH STATISTICS. SERIES 23. DATA FROM THE NATIONAL SURVEY OF FAMILY GROWTH. See Statistics.

WARTA DEMOGRAFI. Periodical. Chiefly Indonesian. ir. Lembaga Demografi Fakultas Ekonomi Universitas, Jl Salemba Raya 4, Jakarta Pusat Indonesia. LC HB848.

WASHINGTON REGION. Main/Corp Washington Center for Metropolitan Studies. 1974-. 0099-2046. US. English. Washington Center for Metropolitan Studies, 1717 Massachusetts Avenue NW, Washington DC 20036. LC HB3527.W3. DD 312.09753.

WESTERN CANADA SERIES REPORT. No. 1- 1974-. 0317-3127. Monographic Series. CN. English. Population Research Laboratory, Department of Sociology Tory Building University of Alberta, Edmonton Alberta T6G 2H4 Canada. DD 301.329712.

WILDLIFE POPULATIONS AND RESEARCH UNIT PROJECT DESCRIPTIONS. See Conservation & Natural Resources.

WORKING PAPER - FLORIDA STATE UNIVERSITY. CENTER FOR THE STUDY OF POPULATION. (WORKING PAPER). 0740-9095. Monographic Series. US. English. ir. Director, Center for the Study of Population, Institute for Social Research, Florida State University, 659 Bellamy, Tallahassee FL 32306.

WORKING PAPERS IN DEMOGRAPHY. 1-. Monographic Series. AT. English. ir. Australian National University, Department of Demography, Research School of Social Sciences, Canberra Australian Capital Territory 2600 Australia. LC UNC. DD 304.6.

WORLD FERTILITY SURVEY. (THE WORLD FERTILITY SURVEY. REPORT). 1972/75-. 0377-6646. NE. English. ir. Free. Intl Statistical Institute, 428 Prinses Beatrixlaan, Voorburg Netherlands. **Tel** 70-694341. LC HB903.F4. DD 301.32105. **Circ** 3,000. Reports and analysis findings of world fertility surveys in 61 countries.

WORLD FERTILITY SURVEY (SERIES : SUMMARY OF FINDINGS). (WORLD FERTILITY SURVEY : SUMMARY OF FINDINGS). Monographic Series. English. ir. NLM W1.

WORLD POPULATION. Began with 1973. 0099-1139. US. English. be. Superintendent of Documents, US Government Printing Office, Washington DC 20402. LC HB848. DD 301.320212. NLM W2 A B9W.

WORLD POPULATION. ADVANCE REPORT. US. English. be. Subscribers Services Section (Publications), Bureau of The Census, Washington DC 20233.

WORLD POPULATION ESTIMATES. 0163-2361. US. English. an. Environmental Fund, 1302 18th Street Northwest, Washington DC 20036. LC HA155. DD 312.805.

WORLD STATISTICS IN BRIEF. See Statistics.

ZEITSCHRIFT FUR BEVOLKERUNGSWISSENSCHAFT. 0340-2398. Periodical. German. ir. 28.00 Each issue. Ind/Abst Popul. Index, Foreign Lang. Index. LC HB848.

ZERO POPULATION GROWTH NEWSLETTER. 1971-. Periodical. US. English. mo. $10.00. Zero Population Growth, 571 P Street, Sacramento CA 95814.

PRINTING

AAUP BOOK SHOW CATALOGUE. See Education (General) - Higher Education.

ADVANCES IN PRINTING SCIENCE AND TECHNOLOGY. V. 1-. 0065-3209. Monographic Series. UK. English. Maxwell House, Fairview Park, Elmsford NY 10523. Ind/Abst Abstr. Bull. Inst. Paper Chem., Chem. Abstr. LC UNC. CODEN AVPSA6.

ADVANCES IN PRINTING SCIENCE AND TECHNOLOGY : PROCEEDINGS OF THE . . . INTERNATIONAL CONFERENCE OF PRINTING RESEARCH INSTITUTES. Main/Conf International Conference of Printing Research Institutes. 13th (May 1975)-. UK. English. be. Pentech Press, Estover Road, Plymouth Devon PL6 7PZ England. LC Z120.5. DD 338.82616862. Proceedings of the . . . International Conference of Printing Research Institutes.

ALBION. Periodical. UK. English. ty. 12.00. 26 West Hill Hitchin, Hertfordshire England. Ed Roger Burford Mason. bk rev. adv acc. **Circ** 450. A journal about printing history and practice, publishing and literary reviews, etc.

ALE SEFER. VFOAT Alei Sefer. No. 1- June/July? 1975-. IS. Hebrew. sa. Bar Ilan University, Department Bibliography and Librarian, Ramat Gan Israel. LC Z228.H4.

AMERICAN INK MAKER (1981). (AMERICAN INK MAKER). Vol. 59, No. 6 (June 1981)-. 0002-8916. Periodical. US. English. mo. $18.00 Domestic, $32.00 Canada. American Ink Maker, 101 West 31st Street, New York NY 10001. Ind/Abst Abstr. Bull. Inst. Paper Chem., World Surf. Coat. Abstr. DD 667. American Inkmaker, 0002-8916.

AMERICAN PRINTER. Vol. 188, No. 4 (Jan. 1982)-. Periodcial. US. English. mo. $35.00. American Printer, 300 West Adam Street, Chicago IL 60606. **Tel** (312)726-2802. Ed E G Berglund. Ind/Abst Trade Ind. Index, Abstr. Bull. Inst. Paper Chem., Print. Abstr., Bus. Period. Index, Predicasts. LC Z119. DD 686.205. bk rev. adv acc. **Circ** 88,000. (ctrl). Serving managers and owners of printing and publishing companies . . . to aid them in remaining competitive and profitable. American Printer and Lithographer, 0192-9933.

AMERICAN PRINTMAKERS. 1st- Ed. 0094-7490. US. English. an. Graphics Group, 30 East Santa Clara Street, Arcadia CA 91006. LC NE508. DD 769.973.

THE AMERICAN REGISTER OF PRINTING AND GRAPHIC ARTS SERVICES. VFOAT American Register. 1981-. 0276-5519. US. English. an. $20.00. In-Register Inc, 1485 Bayshore Boulevard, San Francisco CA 94124. **Tel** (415)467-8760. LC Z244.6.U5. DD 686.202573.

ANAIS DO . . . CONGRESSO LATINO-AMERICANO DE MICROGRAFICA. Main/Conf Congresso Latino-Americano de Industria Micrografica. Began with Vol. for 1978. Portuguese (and Spanish). ir. LC Z265. DD 686.43.

T & E CENTER. VFOAT T and E Center. VAT Technical and Education Center. Vol. 9, No. 5 (July 1981)-. Periodical. US. English. Rochester Institute of Technology, Lomb Memorial Drive, Rochester NY 14623. Ind/Abst Abstr. Bull. Inst. Paper Chem., Print. Abstr. T & E Center Newsletter.

ANNUAL REPORT - ILLINOIS BUDGETARY COMMISSION. (ARTES GRAFICAS). Spanish. ir. Editorial Ter, Parana 624 40 P, Buenos Aires Argentina. LC Z244.6.L35. DD 338.4768620258.

ANTHRACITE TRI-DISTRICT NEWS. US. English. mo. International Printing Company, Vine & Green Street, Hazelton PA 18201.

ANUARIO BRASILEIRO DE TIPOS ALLTYPE. See Yearbooks, Almanacs, Directories.

THE APHA NEWSLETTER : A PUBLICATION OF THE AMERICAN PRINTING HISTORY ASSOCIATION. VAT American Printing History Association Newsletter. 69 (Jan. 1986)-. Periodical. US. English. bm. PO Box 4922, Grand Central Station, New York NY 10017. APHA Letter.

AUDIT REPORT. DIVISION OF PRINTING. (AUDIT REPORT, DIVISION OF PRINTING). Main/Corp Tennessee. Division of State Audit. 0148-3862. US. English. Tennessee Comptroller of the Treasury, Nashville TN 37202. LC JK5249.P8. DD 353.9768007232.

AUSTRALASIAN PRINTER. (THE AUSTRALASIAN PRINTER). Began in 1950. Periodical. AT. English. mo. 50.00. Calmor & Associates Pty Ltd, PO Box 1316, North Sydney 2060 Australia. **Tel** (02)9226560. Ed Paul Callahan. Ind/Abst CIS Abstr., Print. Abstr. LC Z119. bk rev. adv acc. **Circ** 8,500. (ctrl). Directed to senior management and production managers in the printing industry and allied areas such as typesetters, publishers, art studios, advertisement agencies, repro houses, etc.

THE AUSTRALIAN LITHOGRAPHER, PRINTER AND PACKAGER. 1964. Periodical. AT. English. bm. 22.00 Domestic, 29.00 Foreign. Prestige Publishing Party Limited, GPO 5158, Sydney New South Wales 2001 Australia. **Tel** (01)211-4052. Ed F Stern. bk rev. adv acc. **Circ** 7,500. Covers printing, publishing, packaging, and converting. Australian Lithographer.

BEITRAGE ZUR INKUNABELKUNDE. No. 1-7, 1907-35. 0067-5091. German or English. ir. Deutscher Buch Export-Import, Leninstrasse 16, DDR-701 Leipzig East Germany. LC Z240.

THE BEST IN POSTERS CEASED. Series/Titl The Print Casebooks. 1975-. 0360-8085. US. English. an. $13.95. R C Publications, 6400 Goldsboro Road Northwest, Washington DC 20034. LC NC1807.U5. DD 769.5.

BIENNALE INTERNAZIONALE DELLA GRAFICA. CATALOGO. Began with 1970. Italian. be. LC NE45.I8. Mostra Biennale Internazionale Della Grafica. Catalogo.

BOOK PRODUCTION (BENN PUBLICATIONS LTD.). See Publishing - Books and Bookmaking.

THE BRITISH PRINTER. Vol. 1-. 0007-1684. Periodical. UK. English. bm. $42.91. MacLean Hunter Ltd, 76 Oxford Street, London W1N 9FD England. **Tel** 01-434-2233. Ed Andrew Parker. Ind/Abst Abstr. Bull.

Printing

Inst. Paper Chem., Print. Abstr. LC Z119. bk rev. adv acc. Circ 13,934. (ctrl). Serves executive plus technical management in commercial printing companies and major inplant departments. Keeping them informed of all technological developments across all printing processes. *British Bookmaker, British Lithographer; Printers' International Specimen Exchange.*

THE BULLETIN - INTERNATIONAL TYPOGRAPHICAL UNION. Main/Corp International Typographical Union of North America. V. 1- Aug. 1, 1912-. 0020-904X. Periodical. US. English. mo. International Typographical Union, PO Box 157, Colorado Springs CO 80901. **Tel** (303)636-2341.

BULLETIN (PRINTING HISTORICAL SOCIETY). (BULLETIN). 1 (Sept. 1980)-. 0144-7505. Periodical. UK. English. ty. Printing Historical Society, St Bride Institute, Bride Lane, Fleet Street, London EC4 England. *Newsletter (Printing Historical Society).*

CANADIAN PRINT & PORTFOLIO. VFOAT Print & Portfolio. Vol. 1, No. 1 (1984)-. 0824-6904. Periodical. CN. English. qt. $10.00. Canadian Print & Portfolio, Suite 030-74/65 Front Street West, Toronto Ontario M5J 1E6 Canada. **DD** 769.05.

CANADIAN PRINTER & PUBLISHER. VFOAT Canadian Printer and Publisher. 0008-4816. Periodical. CN. English. an. MacLean Hunter, PO Box 100/Station A, Toronto Ontario M5W 1A7 Canada. **Ind/Abst** Abstr. Bull. Inst. Paper Chem., Can. Bus. Index, Print. Abstr. Also available in microform. *Printer & Publisher, 0317-1213.*

CARACTERE. Vol. 1- April/May 1949-. 0008-6126. Periodical. FR. French. mo. 268.00 Domestic, 407.00 Foreign. CEP Information Industrie, 23 rue Laugier, 75017 Paris France. **Tel** 622.13.62. **Ind/Abst** Print. Abstr. LC Z119. *Industries et Techniques Graphiques.*

CARACTERE - TPG. 1978-. 0151-1041. Periodical. French. ir. Caractere - TPG, 40 rue du Colisee, 75381 Paris Cedex 08 France.

CHING TSAO MU KO. Periodical. CH. Chinese. ir. 0.40. Hsin Hua Shu Tien, Tien-Chin Shih China. LC NE1183.3. **DD** 769.951.

CHUNG-KUO PAN HUA NIEN CHIEN. 1982-. CH. Chinese. an. 4.65. Liao-Ning Sheng Hsin Hua Shu Tien, Shen-Yang China. LC NE1183.3. **DD** 769.951.

CONTEMPORARY JAPANESE PRINTS. 1-. Periodical. US. English. ir. Kodansha International, 10 East 53rd Street, New York NY 10022. **Tel** (212)207-7050. LC NE771.4. **DD** 769.952.

COUNTERPROOF. Vol. 1, No. 1 (Fall 1978)-. 0275-7516. Periodical. US. English. qt. $1.00. The Print Club, 1614 Latimer Street, Philadelphia PA 19103. LC NE1. **DD** 760.5.

CREATIVE. See Business - Marketing.

DANSK GRAFIA. DK. Danish. ir. 160.00. Grafisk Kartel, Lytgten 16, 2400 Kbenhavn NV Denmark. LC Z119. *Typograf-Tidende.*

DE L'ESTAMPE. (DE L'ESTAMPE : BULLETIN D'INFORMATION DU CONSEIL DE LA GRAVURE DU QUEBEC). V. 1, No. 1, (April 1982)-. 0712-6700. Periodical. CN. French. ir. Free for Citizens. Conseil de la Gravure du Quebec, 420 Est rue Ontario, Montreal Quebec H2L 1M6 Canada. **DD** 760.60714.

DER DRUCKSPIEGEL. (DER DRUCKSPIEGEL : DIE ZEITSCHRIFT FUR DEUTSCHE UND INTERNATIONALE DRUCKTECHNIK). Began with: 1. Year. (May 30, 1946). 0012-6500. Periodical. GW. German. mo. **Ind/Abst** Print. Abstr.

DEVIL'S ARTISAN. (THE DEVIL'S ARTISAN). No. 1- Feb. 1980-. 0225-7874. Periodical. CN. English. ir. $3. Three Issues. The Devil's Artisan, 354 Markham Street, Toronto Ontario M6G 2K9 Canada. **DD** 686.205.

DIPPY. DIRECT INPUT PHOTOTYPESETTING NEWSLETTER. VFOAT Direct Input Phototypesetting Newsletter. 1975. 0196-4127. Periodical. US. English. ir. $40.00. Graphic Dimensions, 8 Frederick Road, Pittsford NY 14534. **Tel** (716)381-3428. Ed Michael Kleper. bk rev. Covers the desktop publishing and personal typesetting field for word processing, micro, and typesetting users worldwide.

DORSET CEASED. Series/Titl Cape Dorset Annual Graphics Collection. -1983. 0382-7747. CN. English (text in French and Inuit, -19—). an. M F Feheley Publishers, 5 Drumsnab Road, Toronto Ontario Canada. LC E99.E7. **DD** 769.97195. *Cape Dorset Prints, 0319-0463.*

DRUCK PRINT. VFOAT Druck-Print, Druck. Vol. 105-. 0012-6462. Periodical. GW. German (with summaries in English and French). mo. $54.97. P Keppler Verlag KG, Industriestrasse 2, 6056 Heusenstamm West Germany. **Ind/Abst** Print. Abstr. LC Z119. Index published separately - free - automatically sent. *Archiv fur Drucktechnik.*

DRUCKINDUSTRIE. VFOAT Druck Industrie. Jan. 7 1971-. 0046-0737. Periodical. SZ. German. sm. $36.12. Zollikofer & Company AG, Bunh und Offsetdruck, 9001 St Gallen Switzerland. **Tel** 071/ 29 22 22. **Ind/Abst** Print. Abstr.

DRUCKWELT. 1950. 0012-6519. Periodical. GW. German. sm. 115.-. Schluetersche Verlag Druckerei, Postfach 5440, D-3000 Hannover 1 West Germany. **Tel** 0511/1236-0. **Ind/Abst** Predicats, Print. Abstr. LC Z119. bk rev adv acc. (ctrl). Journal for contractors and managers of the printing industry. *Graphische Woche.*

ENGRAVERS JOURNAL. (THE ENGRAVERS JOURNAL). V. 1- July/Aug. 1975-. 0099-0043. Periodical. US. English. bm. Engravers Journal, Box 318, 26 Summit Street, Brighton MI 48116. **Tel** (313)229-5725. Ed James J Farrell. LC NE2720. **DD** 338.47739. adv acc. Education and advancement of the engraving industry.

EXPORT POLYGRAPH INTERNATIONAL. VFOAT Export Polygraph. No. 14 (1958)-. 0344-2039. Periodical. English (Spanish and French). bm. $21.11. Polygraph Verlag, Postfach 700940, Schaumainkai 85, 6000 Frankfurt 70 West Germany. **Tel** 0611-639066. **Ind/Abst** Print. Abstr.

FINE PRINT. Began with Jan. 1974 issue. 0361-3801. Periodical. US. English. qt. $52.00. Fine Print, PO Box 3394, San Francisco CA 94119. **Tel** (415)776-1530. Ed Sandra Kirshenbaum. **Ind/Abst** Art Archaeol. Tech. Abstr., Book Rev. Index. LC Z119. **DD** 686.20973. bk rev. adv acc. **Circ** 3,000. Provocative articles about contemporary fine printing, typography, graphic design, illustration, papermaking, calligraphy, bookbinding, and the history of books and printing, as well as critical reviews of fine books.

FRANKLIN OFFSET CATALOG. 0738-6427. Periodical. US. English. mo. $75.00 Foreign. Porte Publishing Company, 952 East 21st Street South, Salt Lake City UT 84106. **Tel** (801)486-5954. For the offset worker of different types of printing, binding and also a section for commercial printing plants, with 16 different sections.

GORDON'S PRINT PRICE ANNUAL. 1978-. 0160-6298. US. English. an. Martin Gordon Inc, 25 East 83rd Street, New York NY 10028. LC NE85. **DD** 769.12.

GOVERNMENT PRINTING & BINDING REGULATIONS. Main/Corp United States. Congress. Joint Committee on Printing. VAT Government Printing and Binding Regulations. No. 1- July 1, 1948-. 0161-5181. US. English. US Government Printing Office, Superintendent of Documents, Washington DC 20402. LC Z232.U6. **DD** 655.173. *Regulations of the Joint Committee on Printing Relative to Periodicals and Field Printing.*

GRAFICAS. (GRAFICA; REVISTA DE LAS TECNICAS DELL LIBRO). Began publication with July 1944 issue. 0017-2901. Periodical. SP. Spanish. mo. $16.35. Felipe de Pablo Cereceda, C/Blasco Degaray 76 F, Madrid 15 Spain. **Ind/Abst** Abstr. Bull. Inst. Paper Chem. LC Z119.

GRAPHIC ARTS MONTHLY AND THE PRINTING INDUSTRY. See The Arts (General) - Graphic Arts.

GRAPHIC MONTHLY. (THE GRAPHIC MONTHLY). Vol. 1, No. 1 (Jan. 1980)-. 0227-2806. Periodical. CN. English. bm. $19.35. The Graphic Monthly, 2065 Dundas Street East/Suite 205, Mississauga Ontario L4X 2W1 Canada. **Tel** (416)625-7070. **DD** 686.205.

GRAVURE BULLETIN. 0160-8789. Periodical. US. English. Gravure Technical Association, 60 East 42nd Street, New York NY 10017. **Ind/Abst** Print. Abstr. LC Z258. **DD** 686.2305. *Bulletin.*

GREMI : PUBLICACION DEL GREMIO DE INDUSTRIAS GRAFICAS DE BARCELONA Y SU PROVINCIA. See The Arts (General) - Graphic Arts.

GRI NEWSLETTER. Main/Corp Gravure Research Institute. No. 1- 196-. 0534-0489. Periodical. US. English. ir. Gravure Research Institute, 22 Manhasset Avenue, Port Washington NY 11050. **Ind/Abst** Print. Abstr. LC TR980.

HIGH VOLUME PRINTING. (HIGH VOLUME PRINTING : HVP). VFOAT HVP. Vol. 1, No. 1 (July-Aug 1982)-. 0737-1020. Periodical. US. English. bm. Innes Publishing Company, PO Box 368, Northbrook IL 60065. **Tel** (312)564-5940. Ed Bill Esler. **Ind/Abst** Predicats, Print. Abstr. LC Z119. **DD** 070.505. bk rev adv acc. **Circ** 25,000. (ctrl). For large book, magazines and commercial printers. *Book and Magazine Production, 0273-8724.*

IMPRINT (NEW YORK, N.Y. : 1976). (IMPRINT : JOURNAL OF THE AMERICAN HISTORICAL PRINT COLLECTORS SOCIETY). Began with issue for Apr. 1976. 0277-7061. US. English. sa. American Historical Print Collectors Society, Suite 711/25 West 43rd Street, New York NY 10036. LC NE505. **DD** 769.973.

IN-PLANT PRINTER. 1960. 0019-3232. Periodical. US. English. bm. Innes Publishing Company, PO Box 368-425/Huehl Road 11-B, Northbrook IL 60062. **Tel** (312)564-5940. Ed Kraig J Debus. **Ind/Abst** Print. Abstr. adv acc. **Circ** 30,000. (ctrl). Corporate and organizational in-house printing and composition departments serving 80,000 printing establishments in the US. *In-Plant Offset Printer.*

IN-PLANT REPRODUCTIONS. VAT In Plant Reproductions. V. 29, No. 12- Dec. 1979-. 0198-9065. Periodical. US. English. mo $65.00. North American Publishing Company, 401 North Broad Street, Philadelphia PA 19108. **Tel** (215)238-5300. **Ind/Abst** Abstr. Bull. Inst. Paper Chem., Print. Abstr. LC Z252.5.O5. **DD** 686.2305. (ctrl). *Reproductions Review & Methods, 0164-4327.*

INDEX AURELIENSIS. See Indexes/Abstracts.

INDEX TO MICROGRAPHICS EQUIPMENT EVALUATIONS. See Indexes/Abstracts.

INK & PRINT. VFOAT Ink and Print. Vol. 1, No. 1 (Summer 1982)-. 0263-497X. Periodical. UK. English. qt. Batiste Publications, Pembroke House/Campsbourne Road, London N8 7BR England. **Ind/Abst** Predicats, World Surf. Coat. Abstr., Abstr. Bull. Inst. Paper Chem., Print. Abstr. LC TP949. **DD** 667.405. *British Ink Maker, 0007-0831.*

INSATSU ZASSHI. VFOAT Japan Printer. Began 1917. Periodical. JA. Japanese. mo. 12000. Insatsu Gakkai Shuppanbu, c/o Shippo Building, 6-2 Ginza 5, Chuo-ku Tokyo-to 104 Japan. **Tel** (03)571-6025. Ed Akio Sato. LC Z119. adv acc.

INSTANT PRINTER. Vol. 1, No. 1 (Jan. 1982)-. 0744-3854. Periodical. US. English. bm. $50.00. Innes Publishing, Northbrook Business Center, PO Box 358/425 Huehl Road/Building 11-B, Northbrook IL 60062. **Tel** (312)564-5940. Ed Dan Witte. LC Z252.5.I49. **DD** 686.22544. bk rev adv acc. **Circ** 25,000. (ctrl). Trade publication serving the interest of the instant (retail) and small commercial print shop. Aimed at owners, managers, and equipment operators.

INSWAEGYE. Periodical. KO. Korean. ir. Inswaegyesa, 148-73 2-ka Ulchiro, Chung-ku, Seoul South Korea. LC Z119.

THE INTERNATIONAL STEREOTYPERS AND ELECTROTYPERS UNION JOURNAL. Began publication with Vol. 1 in 1906?. Periodical. US. English. mo. J J Kelley/Editor, 90 East 214th Street, Cleveland OH 44123.

THE I.S.C.A. QUARTERLY. See The Arts (General) - Graphic Arts.

L'ITALIA GRAFICA. Main/Corp Associazione Nazionale Industrie Grafiche Cartotecniche E Transformatrici. Year 7, N. 13- 1 May. 1952-. Periodical. IT. Italian. ir. Impricar, P ZA Della Conciliazione 1, 20123 Milano Italy. **Ind/Abst** Print. Abstr. LC Z119. **DD** 686.20945. *Italia Grafica.*

ITU REVIEW. Main/Corp International Typographical Union. 0019-0853. Periodical. US. English. mo. International Typographical Union, PO Box 157, Colorado Springs CO 80901. **DD** 686.

Printing

JAARVERSLAG - KONINKLIJK NEDERLANDS VERBOND VAN DRUKKERIJEN. Main/Corp Nederlands Verbond Van Drukkerijen. Dutch. ir. Koninklijk Nederlands Verbond Van Drukkeijen, Postbus 5454, Van Eeghenstraat 70, Amsterdam Netherlands. LC Z244.6.N4.

JAHRBUCH DER GRAPHISCHEN UNTERNEHMUNGEN OSTERREICHS. See Yearbooks, Almanacs, Directories.

THE JOURNAL OF INFORMATION AND IMAGE MANAGEMENT. (THE JOURNAL OF INFORMATION AND IMAGE MANAGEMENT : JIIM). VFOAT JIIM. Vol. 16, No. 7 (July 1983)-. 0745-9963. Periodical. US. English. mo. $55.00. The Journal of Information and Image Management, 8719 Colesville Road, Silver Spring MD 20910. Ind/Abst Hospit. Lit. Index, ABI/Inform, Comput. Control Abstr., Electr. Electron. Abstr., Sci. Abstr. Sect. A. Phys. Abstr., Libr. Inf. Sci. Abstr., Print. Abstr., Libr. Lit. LC TR835. DD 686.4305. Issued also in microform by University Microfilms International. Journal of Micrographics, 0022-2712.

JOURNAL OF THE PRINT WORLD. Began in 1978. 0737-7436. Periodical. US. English. qt. $6.00 US, $10.00 Canada. Journal of the Print World, Route 2, Meridith NH 03253.

THE KEMBLE OCCASIONAL. 1964-. 0453-4867. US. English. ir. $10.00. The Kemble Collections, California Historical Society Library, 2099 Pacific, San Francisco CA 94109. Tel (415)567-1848. Ed Glenn E Humphreys. Ind/Abst Am. Hist. Life, Hist. Abstr., Part A, Mod. Hist. Abstr., Hist. Abstr., Part B, Twent. Century Abstr. bk rev. Circ 200. (ctrl). Devoted to printing, publishing, and ancillary trades in the Western United States.

KIKAN HANGA. VFOAT La Gravure. No. 1 (Oct. 1968)-. Periodical. Japanese. qt. LC NE1. Hanga.

LATINGRAFICA. 1-. Spanish. ir. Parana 140 2 Piso, Buenos Aires Argentina. LC Z244.6.L35.

THE LITHOPRINTER. V. 1- Jan. 1958-. 0024-4929. Periodical. UK. English. mo. Haymarket Publishing Ltd, 1214 Annsdell Street, Kensingston London W85TR. Tel (01)937-7288. LC Z252.5.O5. DD 655.325.

LITHOPRINTER WEEK. V. 1- Oct. 3, 1979-. Periodical. UK. English. wk. $137.92. Haymarket Publishing Ltd, 1214 Annsdell Street, Kensingston London W85TR England. Tel 01 937 7288. LC Z252.5.O5. DD 686.2315. Litho-Printer.

LE LIVRE ET L'ESTAMPE. See Publishing - Books and Bookmaking.

MAGAZINE DESIGN & PRODUCTION. VFOAT Magazine Design and Production. Periodical. US. English. mo. $36.00 Domestic, $48.00 Canada. Globecom Publishers Ltd, 4551 West 107th Street, #210, Overland Park KS 66207. Tel (913)642-6611. Ed Michael Scheibach. bk rev. adv acc. Circ 21,000. (ctrl). Articles on magazine design and production techniques and technologies, such as paper, printing, prepress, computers, and typesetters.

MAITRE IMPRIMEUR. (LE MAITRE IMPRIMEUR). 1st Issue in 1937. 0025-0996. Periodical. CN. French. mo. 7.74. Association des Arts Graphiques du Quebec Inc, 480 Est Avenue Mont-Royal CH-22, Montreal Quebec H2J 1W4 Canada. Tel (514)842-2751. Ed Helene Lagadec. Ind/Abst Point Repere. adv acc. Circ 4,000. (ctrl). All matters related to printing and allied trades, new technological developments, trends in the industry, and who's who in the printing world.

MATRIX : A REVIEW FOR PRINTERS AND BIBLIOGRAPHIES. See Bibliographies.

MEMBERS - BRITISH PRINTING SOCIETY. Main/Corp British Printing Society. 0306-820X. UK. English. an. British Printing Society, 14 Penrose Avenue 23 West Bowring Park, Liverpool L14 6UT England. LC Z120.B84. DD 070.502542.

MICRODOC CEASED. V. 1-20, No. 3. 0026-2684. Periodical. UK. English. qt. Microfilm Association of Great Britain, 8 High Street, Guilford Surrey GU2 5AJ England. Ind/Abst Libr. Inf. Sci. Abstr. LC Z265. DD 686.4305. CODEN MICDB6. (cum index).

THE MOSSTYPER. Main/Corp Mosstype Corporation. 0148-5539. Periodical. US. English. sa. Mosstype Corporation, Waldwick NJ 07463. LC Z119. DD 686.205.

NATIONAL PRESERVATION REPORT. Vol. 1, No. 1 (Apr. 1979)-. 0190-9819. Periodical. US. English. ty. Central Services Division, Library of Congress, Washington DC 20541. Ind/Abst Libr. Inf. Sci. Abstr. LC Z265. DD 016.07. Newspaper and Gazette Report, 0361-0152.

NEW ENGLAND PRINTER & PUBLISHER. VFOAT New England Printer and Publisher. 0162-8771. Periodical. US. English. ir. $12.00. New England Printer & Publisher, PO Box 810, 12 Carlton Drive, Newburyport MA 01950. Ed Jean Hansen. adv acc. News of people, clubs, events and products pertinent to the graphic arts community in New England printers, marketing, and business management. New England Printer and Lithographer.

NEWSLETTER. GRAVURE ENVIRONMENTAL. (NEWSLETTER, GRAVURE ENVIRONMENTAL). VFOAT Environmental Newsletter of the Gravure Industry. No. 9- Aug. 1979-. 0271-1699. Periodical. US. English. Gravure Research Institute, 22 Manhasset Avenue, Port Washington NY 11050. Ind/Abst Print. Abstr. LC TD195.P7. DD 686.2. Gravure Environmental and O.S.H.A. Newsletter, 0091-5203.

NEWSLETTER - MICROFICHE FOUNDATION. Main/Corp Microfiche Foundation, Delft. VFOAT MF Newsletter. No. 1- Mar. 1963-. 0076-8480. English. ir. LC Z265. DD 686.43. NLM TR 835 M626N.

NIGERIAN BOOKS IN PRINT. See Publishing - Books and Bookmaking.

NIHON TAIPOGURAFI NENKAN. VFOAT Japan Typography Annual. 1974-. JA. Japanese. ir. 4500. Gurafikkusha, PO Box 102, 1-9-12 Kudan Kita Chiyoda-ku, Tokyo Japan. LC NK3600. Nihon Retaringu Nenkan.

NOTER-UP SERVICE FOR THE STATUTES OF SINGAPORE. Main/Corp Singapore. Began with 1980, No. 1. English. sa. Singapore National Printers, 303 Upper Serangoon Road, Singapore 1334 Singapore.

NOUVELLES DE L'ESTAMPE. Jan. 1963-. Periodical. French. ir. Ind/Abst Repert. Int. Litt. Art. LC NE1.

P V. PRINTING VIEWS. VFOAT Printing Views. 0030-8439. Periodical. US. English. mo. $14.00. Midwest Publ Company, 8328 North Lincoln Avenue, Skokie IL 60077. Tel (312)539-8540. Ed Len Berman. bk rev. adv acc. Circ 14,000,000. (ctrl). Midwest printing inudstry news involving new developments, legislative events, trade shows and meetings, personnel notes, calendar, installations.

PACIFIC PRINTERS PILOT. 0552-7511. Periodical. US. English. mo. Pacific Printers Pilot, 583 Monterey Pass Road, Monterey Park CA 91754. Tel (213)576-1538.

PACK & PRINT. See Packaging.

PAINTINDIA. ANNUAL. See Paints and Painting.

PAN HUA SHIH CHIEH : BHSJ. VFOAT B.H.S.J. 1983, 1-. Periodical. CH. Chinese. ir. 1.20. Hsin Hua Shu Tien, Pei-Ching Fa Hsing So, Peking China. LC NE1000. DD 769.05.

PAPER, FILM & FOIL CONVERTER. See Packaging.

PAPIER UND DRUCK CEASED. 1.- Yearly. 0031-1375. Periodical. GE. German. mo. 85.80 Domestic. Deutscher Buch Export, Leninstrasse 16, DDR 701 Leipzig East Germany. Tel 49500. Ind/Abst Abstr. Bull. Inst. Paper Chem., Print. Abstr. LC TS1080. DD 676.205. adv acc. Special journal for printing, printing machinery and paper-coverting; reports on printing machines, new processes, results of type and book design, art of illustration and cover. Buchgewerbe, Polygraphische Industrie.

PAPIRIPAR ES MAGYAR GRAFIKA. See Paper & Pulp Industry.

PDQ. 0194-2530. Periodical. US. English. mo. $150.00. Printing Industries of America, 1730 North Lynn Street, Arlington VA 22209. Tel (703)841-8113.

POINT OF SALE & SCREENPRINTING. VFOAT Point of Sale and Screenprinting. 0036-9586. Periodical. UK. English. mo. $33.71. Batiste Publications Ltd, Pembroke House, Campsbourne Road, Hornsey London N8 England. Tel 01-340 3291. Ed Geoffrey Ellis. Ind/Abst Print. Abstr. Circ 6,000. Point of Sale News.

POLIGRAFICHESKAIA PROMYSHLENNOST. BIBLIOGRAFICHESKAIA INFORMATSIIA : NOVOSTI TEKHNICHESKOI LITERATURY. VFOAT Novosti Tekniicheskoi Literatury. Began in 1969. UR. Multilingual (Russian). mo. 0.10 Single Issue. Kniga, K-9 Ul Nezhdanovoi 8/10, Moskva USSR. LC Z117.

POLIHRAFIIA I VYDAVNYCHA SPRAVA. Began in 1964. UR. Ukrainian. LC Z119.

POLYGRAPH. (DER POLYGRAPH). V. 1- 20. March 1948-. 0032-3845. Periodical. GW. German. sm. $50.32. Polygraph Verlag GMBH, Postfach 700940/Schaumainkai 85, 6000 Frankfurt West Germany. Tel 0611/ 639066. Ind/Abst Excerpta Med., CIS Abstr. LC Z119. Klimschs Druckerei-Anzeiger.

PORTFOLIO. Main/Corp Old Print Shop, Inc., New York. VFOAT Old Print Shop Portfolio. V. 1- Sept. 1941-. Periodical. US. English. mo. Old Print Shop, 150 Lexington Avenue at 30th Street, New York NY 10016. LC NE1. DD 760.5.

THE PREPRESS BULLETIN. See The Arts (General) - Graphic Arts.

PRINT. V. 1- June 1940-. 0032-8510. Periodical. US. English. bm. $40.00. RC Publishing Inc, 6400 Goldsboro Road, Bethesda MD 20817. Tel (301)229-9040. Ed Martin Fox. Ind/Abst Artbibliogr. Mod., Film Lit. Index, Print. Abstr., Art Index. LC Z119. DD 070.5068. bk rev. adv acc. Circ 40,000. America's graphic design magazine. Presents features on every facet of graphic design: advertising, illustration photography, typography, television film, environmental graphics.

PRINT ACTION. V. 1- Oct. 1971-). 0380-2752. Periodical. CN. English. mo. $11.61. Youngblood Publishing Company, 75 Roselawn Avenue, Toronto Ontario M4R 1E5 Canada. Tel (416)447-8536. Ed Pat Trusty. bk rev. adv acc. Circ 16,000. Complete coverage of international printing industry.

PRINT BUYER (LONDON, ENGLAND : 1982). (PRINT BUYER). Vol. 17, No. 1 (Oct. 1982)-. 0264-5424. Periodical. UK. English. bm. Benn Publications Limited, Sovereign Way, Tonbridge Kent TN9 1RW England. Tel 0732 364422. Ind/Abst Print. Abstr. Print & Promotion.

PRINT EDUCATION MAGAZINE. V. 1- Oct. 1976-. Periodical. US. English. mo. $13.00. Westana Publications, 298 Harbor Drive/PO Box Drawer G, Sausalito CA 94965. LC Z119. DD 686.205.

PRINT-EQUIP NEWS. 0048-5314. Periodical. US. English. mo. Printing, Publishing. P E N Publications Inc, 215 Allen Avenue POB 10820, Glendale CA 91209. Tel (818)954-9495. Ed Paul B Kissel. bk rev. adv acc. Circ 25,000. (ctrl). Regional graphic arts publication covering 19 western states. Circulation to management, supervisory personnel, and buyers of graphic arts equipment, supplies, and services.

PRINT QUARTERLY. VFOAT P.Q., PQ. Vol. 1, No. 1 (Mar. 1984). 0265-8305. Periodical. UK. English. qt. $39.85. Print Quarterly, 80 Carlton Hill, London MN8 OER England. Tel 01 625 6332. Ed David Landau. bk rev. adv acc. Circ 1,000. The history of printmaking from the Fifteenth Century to the present.

PRINTERS HOT LINE. 0192-6314. Periodical. US. English. wk. Hot Line Inc, PO Box 1709, Fort Dodge IA 50501.

PRINTER'S NEWS. 1975. 0191-8966. Periodical. US. English. mo. $25.00. Printers News, PO Box 2354, Lufkin TX 75901. Tel (409)639-1314. Ed Libby Stapleton. bk rev. adv acc. Circ 16,000. (ctrl). Newspaper for the graphic arts industry in Texas, Louisiana, Arkansas, and Oklahoma.

PRINTERS' NEWS. V. 1- Aug. 1943-. 0048-5330. Periodical. English. mo. $50.00. Printing Industries Federation Of New Zealand Inc, P O Box 1422, Wellington New Zealand. Tel 723-497. Ed L James Mauger. Ind/Abst Print. Abstr. LC Z119. DD 655.305. adv acc. Circ 1,100. (ctrl). Information for members of the printing industry, and suppliers of machinery and supplies.

PRINTERS YEARBOOK : THE COMPREHENSIVE GUIDE TO THE PRINTING INDUSTRY. See Yearbooks, Almanacs, Directories.

PRINTING ABSTRACTS. See Indexes/Abstracts.

Printing

PRINTING AND GRAPHIC ARTS BUYERS. (PRINTING AND GRAPHIC ARTS BUYERS : PGAB). **VFOAT** PGAB. 1984 ed.-. 0741-1979. US. English. an. $79.00. Hilary House Publishers Inc, 1033 Channel Drive, Hewlett Harbor NY 11557. **Tel** (516)295-2376. Ed Edward L Stern. **LC** Z475. **DD** 070.502573. adv acc. **Circ** 2,500. Names, addresses, and phone numbers of over 5,800 national key buyers and purchasing agents, of printing, advertising, direct mail, catalogs, sales promotion, displays, papers, ink, envelopes, composition, separations, etc.

PRINTING HISTORY. V. 1- 1979-. 0192-9275. Periodical. US. English. sa. $15.00. Columbia University, 516 Butler Library, c/o Susan Thompson, New York NY 10027. **Ind/Abst** Writ. Am. Hist., Libr. Inf. Sci. Abstr., Libr. Lit., Recent Publ. Artic. **LC** Z124.A2. **DD** 686.209.

PRINTING IMPRESSIONS. Vol. 1, No. 1 (June 1958)-. 0032-860X. Periodical. US. English. mo. North American Publishing Company, 401 North Broad Street, Philadelphia PA 19108. **Tel** (215)238-5300. **Ind/Abst** Abstr. Bull. Inst. Paper Chem., Print. Abstr. (ctrl).

PRINTING IMPRESSIONS. GRAPHIC ARTS MARKETPLACE. **VFOAT** Graphic Arts Marketplace. 1st Ed. (1982)-. 0736-4946. US. English. an. Printing Impressions, 401 North Broad Street, Philadelphia PA 19108. **LC** Z249. **DD** 681.6.

PRINTING IMPRESSIONS. WHO'S WHO IN COMMERCIAL WEB OFFSET. See Biographies.

PRINTING INDUSTRIES. V. 73, No. 2- Feb. 1974-. 0307-7195. Periodical. UK. English. mo. 30. British Printing Industries Federation, 11 Bedford Row, London WC1R 4DX England. **Tel** 01-242-6904. Ed Lynn Underwood. **Ind/Abst** Print. Abstr. **LC** Z120. **DD** 331.881168620941. bk rev. adv acc. **Circ** 4,503. (ctrl). Unique source of management information directly related to the printing industry. *Members Circular.*

PRINTING JOURNAL. 1974. 0191-8273. Periodical. US. English. mo. Free to industry. Printing Journal, PO Box 5515, Pasadena CA 91107. **Tel** (213)681-1122. Ed Noel Jeffrey. adv acc. **Circ** 20,000. Printing industry news and advertising journal for western states.

PRINTING NEWS. 1928. 0032-8626. Periodical. US. English. wk. $7.50. Printing News inc, 468 Park Avenue South, New York NY 10016. **Tel** (212)689-9690. Ed Leo H Joachim. **Ind/Abst** Abstr. Bull. Inst. Paper Chem. **LC** Z119. adv acc. **Circ** 8,300. (ctrl). Weekly newspaper of the printing industry-news in the world of graphic arts. *New York Printing News.*

PRINTING PRODUCT GUIDE. Apr. 1981-. 0710-2836. Periodical. CN. English. Free to Subscribers of Canadian Printer & Publisher, $16.50 Others in Canada. Printing Product Guide, PO Box 9100 Station A, Toronto Ontario M5W 1V5 Canada. **DD** 681.6.

PRINTING, PUBLISHING AND ALLIED INDUSTRIES. Main/Corp Canada. Statistique Canada. Division des Industries Manufacturieres et Primaires. **Series/Titl** Recensement Annuel des Manufactures. **VFOAT** Imprimerie, Edition et Activites Annexes. 1970-. 0575-9412. CN. text in English and French. an. 20.00 Domestic, 21.00 Foreign. Receiver General for Canada, Statistics Canada Publications, Ottawa Ontario K1A 0T6 Canada. **Tel** (800)268-1151. *Printing, Publishing and Allied Industries, 0575-9412.*

PRINTING TRADES BLUE BOOK. 1962/63-. 0079-5356. US. English. be. A F Lewis, 853 Broadway, New York NY 10003. **LC** Z475. **DD** 686.202574. *Printing Trades Blue Book.*

PRINTING TRADES BLUE BOOK. 0193-3949. US. English. be. $65.00. A F Lewis & Company Inc, 79 Madison Avenue, New York NY 10016. **Tel** (212)679-0770. Ed Barbara Costa. **LC** Z244.6.U5. **DD** 686.202574. adv acc. **Circ** 10,000. (ctrl). Graphic arts directory of the printing industry.

PRINTING TRADES BLUE BOOK. METROPOLITAN NEW YORK EDITION. (PRINTING TRADES BLUE BOOK). **VFOAT** Blue Book. No. 1- 1916-. 0079-5348. Periodical. US. English. an. A F Lewis, 853 Broadway, New York NY 10003. **LC** Z475.

PRINTING TRADES BLUE BOOK. SOUTHEASTERN EDITION. (PRINTING TRADES BLUE BOOK). **VFOAT** Blue Book. 0079-5364. US. English. be. $50.00. A F Lewis and Company Inc, 79 Madison Avenue, New York NY 10016. *Printing Trades Blue Book. Eastern Edition.*

PRINTING TRADES DIRECTORY. See Yearbooks, Almanacs, Directories.

PRINTING WORLD. Began publication with Vol. 154 in 1954. 0032-8715. Periodical. UK. English. wk. $90.41. Benn Publications Limited, Sovereign Way, Tonbridge Kent TN9 1RW England. **Tel** 364422. Ed Roy Coxhead. **Ind/Abst** Print. Abstr. **LC** Z119. bk rev. adv acc. **Circ** 12,200. A news weekly for the printing industry. *British and Colonial Printer and Stationer.*

PRINTS. V. 1- Winter 1978/79-. 0274-5097. Periodical. US. English. bm. $20.00 Domestic, $24.00 Canada, $40.00 Foreign. Art on Paper Incorporated, PO Box 1468, Alton IL 62002. **LC** NE1. **DD** 760.5.

PRINTWORLD DIRECTORY OF CONTEMPORARY PRINTS AND PRICES. See Yearbooks, Almanacs, Directories.

PRIVATE PRESS BOOKS. See Bibliographies.

PRODUCTION EMPLOYEES COST SURVEY. 0277-4119. US. English. $25.00. International Business Forms Industries, 1730 North Lynn Street, Arlington VA 22209. **Tel** (203)841-9191. Ed Douglas Taylor. **LC** Z243.U5. **DD** 331.2816862. Wage and benefit cost data for production employees of business forms plants. Categorized by plant location and job category.

PROFESSIONAL PRINTER. V. 17- Jan. 1973-. 0308-4205. Periodical. UK. English. bm. $27.58. Institute of Printing, 8 Lonsdale Gardens, Turnbridge Wells Kent TN1 1NU England. **Tel** 0892 38118. Ed Ian Kingsley. **Ind/Abst** Abstr. Bull. Inst. Paper Chem., Libr. Inf. Sci. Abstr., Print. Abstr. **LC** Z120. **DD** 686.205. bk rev. adv acc. **Circ** 4,000. (ctrl). Journal of the Institute of Printing for members and subscribers. Published six times per year, alternate months from January. *Printing Technology.*

A PUBLICATION WITH CATALOGUE OF ETCHING PROOFS EXHIBITED AT THE NATIONAL ACADEMY OF DESIGN, NEW YORK. Main/Corp New York Etching Club. 1882- New Ser., No. 1- 1891-. Periodical. US. English. an. **LC** NE1952.

PUBLICATIONS FILED WITH THE STATE RECORDS CENTER FOR THE YEAR . . . . US. English. State Records Center, State Rules and Publications Division/404 Montezuma, Santa Fe NM 87503. **LC** Z1223.5.N56, J87.N6. **DD** 015.789. *Publications and Rules Filed.*

QUARTERLY NEWS-LETTER - BOOK CLUB OF CALIFORNIA. See Publishing - Books and Bookmaking.

QUICK PRINTING. 1977. 0191-4588. Periodical. US. English. mo. $14.00. Coast Publishing, 3255 South US 1, Fort Pierce FL 33450. **Tel** (305)465-9450. Ed Robert Schweiger. adv acc. **Circ** 27,000. (ctrl). The information source for commercial copyshops and printshops.

REPORT OF THE PROCEEDINGS. ANNUAL MEETING AND TECHNICAL FORUM. (REPORT OF THE PROCEEDINGS : ANNUAL MEETING AND TECHNICAL FORUM). Main/Corp Flexographic Technical Association. 1st- 1959-. 0428-5670. US. English. an. Flexographic Technical Association, 50 Jericho Turnpike, Jericho NY 11753. **LC** Z252.5.F6. **DD** 686.231.

REPORT - PRINTING DEPT. Main/Corp Fiji. Printing Dept. FJ. English. ir. Government Printer, Ganilav House, Government Buildings, Suva Fiji Islands. **LC** J961, Z232.F48. **DD** 070.5099611.

REPRODUCTION. Began with: V. 1, No. 1 (Jan. 1964). 0034-4958. Periodical. UK. English. mo. $18.38. Bed Business Journals Ltd, 44 Wallington Square, Wallington Surrey SM6 8RG England. **Tel** 01-647 1001. Ed Charles Walker. **Ind/Abst** Print. Abstr. bk rev. adv acc. **Circ** 16,000. (ctrl). The only magazine in UK which deals expertly with inplant reprographics and the whole spectrum of the reproduction market. *Small Offset User, Repro: The Journal of the Institute of Reprographic Technology.*

DER REPROGRAF. See Photography & Photographs.

REPROGRAPHICS QUARTERLY. V. 7- Winter 1973/74-. 0306-2880. Periodical. UK. English (summaries in French and German). qt. National Reprographic Centre for Documentation, The Hatfield Polytechnic, Endymion Road Annex, Herts AL10 8 England. **Ind/Abst** Comput. Control Abstr., Electr. Electron. Abstr., Sci. Abstr. Sect. A. Phys. Abstr., Libr. Inf. Sci. Abstr., Consum. Index Prod. Eval. Inf. Source, Print. Abstr. **LC** Z48. **DD** 686.4305. **CODEN** RPGQAW. *NRCD Bulletin.*

SCREEN PRINTING. 0036-9594. US. English. mo. Signs of the Times Publishing Company, 407 Gilbert Avenue, Cincinnati OH 45202. **Ind/Abst** Abstr. Bull. Inst. Paper Chem., Print. Abstr. **LC** TT273. **DD** 686.231605. *Screen Printing Magazine.*

SCREEN PRINTING TECHNIQUES. 0362-160X. US. English. US. English. Signs of the Times Publishing Company, 407 Gilbert Avenue, Cincinnati OH 45202. **Tel** (513)421-2050. Ed Tamas S Frecska. **LC** TT273. **DD** 686.2316. bk rev. adv acc. **Circ** 12,000. Technical magazine for the screen printing industry, dealing with the process and products used in its application. *Screen Process Printing.*

SERIGRAFIA (MILANO, ITALY). (SERIGRAFIA). Began in 1956. Periodical. Italian. bm. 48.000. Via Kolbe 8, 20137 Milano Italy. **LC** TT273. **DD** 686.2316.

SHOWCASE (OLD PRINT GALLERY (WASHINGTON, D.C.)). (SHOWCASE). Vol. 2, No. 1 (Jan. 1975)-. 0743-7609. US. English. The Old Print Gallery Inc, 1220 31st Street NW, Washington DC 20007. **LC** NE70. **DD** 769.0294753. *Catalog (Old Print Gallery (Washington, D.C.)), 0748-1640.*

SUMMARY OF MEETING. Main/Corp Depository Library Council to the Public Printer (U.S.). Periodical. US. English. sa. Superintendent of Documents, US Government Printing Office, Washington DC 20402.

TEXTILE DYER & PRINTER : ANNUAL NUMBER. See Textiles.

TGC TYPEFACE DIRECTORY. See Yearbooks, Almanacs, Directories.

TRANCIATURA STAMPAGGIO. Began in 1964. 0041-1027. Periodical. IT. Italian. ir. Editoriale Tecnica Macchine, C So Venezia 18, 20121 Milano Italy. **Ind/Abst** Met. Abstr., World Alum. Abstr. **LC** TS200. **DD** 671.3305.

TYPE TALK. V. 1- Nov. 1979-. 0228-3131. Periodical. CN. English. Saskatchewan Government Printing Company, 2045 Broad Street/3rd Floor, Regina Saskatchewan S4P 3V7 Canada. **DD** 686.205.

TYPOGRAFISCHE MONATSBLATTER. Periodical. English (French or German). mm $47.50. Zollikofer & Company, Fuerstenlandstr 122, CH-9001 St Gallen Switzerland. **Tel** 071292222.

THE TYPOGRAPHER. 1975. 0279-0327. Periodical. US. English. bm. $10.00. Typographers Intl Association, 2262 Hall Pl NW/Suite 101, Washington DC 20007. **Tel** (202)965-3400. Ed Geoff Lindsay. bk rev. adv acc. **Circ** 10,500. (ctrl). Management-oriented publication for commercial typesetting companies. Features news and product information on the typesetting industry.

TYPOGRAPHIC. 0564-5883. Periodical. US. English. qt. $10.00. Typographers International Association, 2262 Hall Place NW, Box C, Washington DC 20007. **Tel** (202)965-3400. **LC** Z119. **DD** 686.205.

TYPOGRAPHICAL JOURNAL. 0041-4832. Periodical. US. English. mo. Internation Typographical Union, Box 2341, Colorado Springs CO 80901.

TYPOGRAPHY. (TYPOGRAPHY : THE ANNUAL OF THE TYPE DIRECTORS CLUB). 1-. 0275-6870. US. English. an. $25.00. Watson-Guptill Publications, 1515 Broadway, New York NY 10036. **LC** Z243.A2. **DD** 686.224.

U & LC. VAT Upper and Lower Case. Began in 1974. 0362-6245. Periodical. US. English. qt. International Typeface Corporation, 216 East 45th Street, New York NY 10017. **Ind/Abst** Print. Abstr. **LC** Z119. **DD** 686.205.

UNION WAGES AND HOURS. PRINTING TRADES, SELECTED CITIES. See Economics - Labor.

VERKAUFSAUSSTELLUNG. Main/Corp Verband Deutscher Antiquare. GW. German. ir. Verband Deutscher Antiquare, Zum Talblick 2, 6246 Glashutten Im Taunus West Germany. **LC** NE70. *Verkaufsausstellung des Verbandes Deutscher Antiquare, Autographen- und Graphikhandler.*

Psychology

VISIBLE LANGUAGE. V. 5- Winter 1971-. 0022-2224. Periodical. US. English. qt. Visible Language, Box 1972 CMA, Cleveland OH 44106. **Tel** (216)421-7340. Ed Merald E Wrolstad. **Ind/Abst** Math. Rev., Abstr. Engl. Stud., MLA Int. Bibliogr. Books Artic. Mod. Lang. Lit., Lang. Lang. Behav. Abstr., Comput. Control Abstr., Electr. Electron. Abstr., Sci. Abstr. Sect. A. Phys. Abstr., Print. Abstr., Electron. Pub. Abstr., Sociol. Abstr., Phys. Abstr. **LC** Z119. **DD** 001.55205. **CODEN** VSLGAO. adv acc. **Circ** 1,600. Research and ideas that help to define the unique role and properties of written language. *Journal of Typographic Research.*

VISUAL COMMUNICATIONS JOURNAL. V. 1- 1965-. 0507-1658. Periodical. US. English. mo. $7.50. International Graphic Arts Education Association Inc, 4615 Forbes Avenue, Pittsburgh PA 15213. **LC** Z122. **DD** 686.22.

WAYZGOOSE. (WAYZGOOSE ANTHOLOGY). '81-. 0715-4720. CN. English. an. 50.00. Wayzgoose, c/o Grimsby Public Art Gallery, 25 Adelaide Street, Grimsby Ontario L3M 1X2 Canada. **Tel** (416)945-3246. **DD** 686.2. **Circ** 135. (ctrl) A collection of signatures representing the scope of private press printers talents and includes a portfolio of limited edition prints.

WORLD-WIDE PRINTER. VAT Worldwide Printer. 0147-4804. Periodical. US. English (table of contents in Spanish, Arabic, French, Japanese, Italian, Russian and German). bm. **Tel** 31 2997 1324. **Ind/Abst** Print. Abstr. **LC** Z119. **DD** 686.205. adv acc. **Circ** 22,000. (ctrl). World trade magazine for the printing and graphic communications industries. Published in association with the Spanish language edition El Arte Tipografico. *Arte Tipografico.*

PSYCHOLOGY

ABASS NEWSLETTER. *See* Social Sciences (General).

ABSTRACTS OF RESEARCH IN PASTORAL CARE AND COUNSELING. *See* Indexes/Abstracts.

ACADEMIC PSYCHOLOGY BULLETIN. V. 1- May 1979-. 0193-1709. Periodical. US. English. ty. Michigan Psychological Association, University of Detroit Attn: Midlarsky, Detroit MI 48221. **Tel** (313)927-1267. Ed Elizabeth Midlarsky. **Ind/Abst** Psychol. Abstr. **LC** BF1. **DD** 150.5. **NLM** W1 AC33P. bk rev. **Circ** 1,100. Theoretical and empirical treatments in all areas of psychology.

ACTA PAEDOLOGICA. Vol. 1, No. 1 (Jan. 1984)-. 0737-5166. Periodical. US. English. qt. $25.00 Institutions. Acta Paedologica, PO Box 1344, Oak Brook IL 60521. **DD** 155. **NLM** W1.

ACTA PSIQUIATRICA Y PSICOLOGICA DE AMERICA LATINA. *See* Medicine - Psychiatry, Psychopathology.

ACTA PSYCHOLOGICA. V. 1- 1935-. 0001-6918. English (contributions in French, or German). ir. Elsevier Science Publishers, PO Box 211, 1000 AE Amsterdam Netherlands. **Tel** (020)5803.911. **Ind/Abst** Life Sci. Collect., Sociol. Abstr., Soc. Welf. Soc. Plan./Policy Soc. Dev., Index Med., Int. Aerosp. Abstr., Psychol. Abstr., Soc. Sci. Citation Index, Bibliogr. Index, Lang. Lang. Behav. Abstr. **LC** BF1. **DD** 150.5, 159.905. **NLM** W1 AC933. **CODEN** APSOAZ.

ACTA PSYCHOLOGICA TAIWANICA. VFOAT Kuo Li T'Ai-Wan Ta Hsueh Li Hsueh Yuan Hsin Li Hsueh Hsi Yen Chiu Pao Kao. No. 1- Nov. 1958-. 0065-1613. CH. English (Chinese). sa. $10.00. Chinese Psychological Association, National Taiwan University, Department of Psychology, Taipei 107 Taiwan ROC China. **Tel** (02)3510231. Ed Chao-Ming Cheng. **Ind/Abst** Psychol. Abstr., Soc. Sci. Citation Index. **LC** RC321. **DD** 616.89005. **CODEN** APSTCI. bk rev. adv acc. **Circ** 400. Publishes both empirical and theoretical articles.

ADVANCES IN ANALYSIS OF BEHAVIOUR. VFOAT Wiley Series on Advances in Analysis of Behaviour. Vol. 1-. 0271-9738. Monographic Series. UK. English. ir. John Wiley & Sons Inc, 605 3rd Avenue, New York NY 10158. Ed P Harzem and Michael D Zeiler. **LC** UNC. **DD** 150. **NLM** W1 AD432M.

ADVANCES IN APPLIED DEVELOPMENTAL PSYCHOLOGY. Vol. 1-. 0748-8572. US. English. an. Psychology, Medicine. Ablex Publishing Corp, 355 Chestnut Street, Norwood NJ 07648. **Tel** (201)767-8450. Ed Irving E Sigel. **DD** 155. Book series reporting applications of research in applied developmental psychology to educational, clinical, and pediatric settings.

ADVANCES IN APPLIED SOCIAL PSYCHOLOGY. Vol. 1-. US. English. qt. Lawrence Erlbaum Associates, 365 Broadway/Suite 102, Hillsdale NJ 07642.

ADVANCES IN BEHAVIORAL MEDICINE. Vol. 1 (1985)-. 0885-0836. Periodical. US. English. an. Jai Press, 36 Sherwood Place, Greenwich CN 06836. **LC** R726.5. **DD** 616.0019.

ADVANCES IN BEHAVIORAL PHARMACOLOGY. V. 1-. 0147-071X. US. English. ir. Academic Press, 4805 Sand Lake Road, Orlando FL 32887. **Tel** (305)345-4100. Ed Travis Thompson and Peter B Dews. **Ind/Abst** Life Sci. Collect. **LC** RC483. **DD** 615.7805. **NLM** W1 AD436G. **CODEN** ABPHD6.

ADVANCES IN BEHAVIOUR RESEARCH AND THERAPY. V. 1-. 0146-6402. Periodical. UK. English. qt. Pergamon Press, 395 Sawmill River Road, Elmsford NY 10523. **Ind/Abst** Psychol. Abstr. **LC** RC489.B4. **DD** 616.8914. **NLM** W1 AD436I. **CODEN** ABRTDI. Available on microfilm.

ADVANCES IN CHILD DEVELOPMENT AND BEHAVIOR. V. 1-. 0065-2407. US. English. ir. Academic Press, 4805 Sand Lake Road, Orlando FL 32887. **Tel** (305)345-4100. Ed Lewis P Lipsitt and Charles C Spiker. **Ind/Abst** Index Med., Biol. Abstr., Soc. Sci. Citation Index. **LC** BF721. **DD** 136.7082. **NLM** W1 AD53P. **CODEN** ADCDA8.

ADVANCES IN CLINICAL CHILD PSYCHOLOGY. V. 1-. 0149-4732. US. English. ir. Plenum Publishing Company, 233 Spring Street, New York NY 10013. **Tel** (212)620-8000. **LC** RJ503.3. **DD** 618.9289. **NLM** W1 AD54H.

ADVANCES IN CLINICAL NEUROPSYCHOLOGY. *See* Medicine - Neurology.

ADVANCES IN COGNITIVE-BEHAVIORAL RESEARCH AND THERAPY. VAT Advances in Cognitive Behavioral Research and Therapy. Vol. 1-. 0730-5389. US. English. ir. Academic Press, 4805 Sand Lake Road, Orlando FL 32887. **Tel** (305)345-4100. Ed Philip C Kendall. **LC** RC489.C63. **DD** 616.8914. **NLM** W1.

ADVANCES IN DESCRIPTIVE PSYCHOLOGY. (ADVANCES IN DESCRIPTIVE PSYCHOLOGY : OFFICIAL ANNUAL PUBLICATION OF THE SOCIETY FOR DESCRIPTIVE PSYCHOLOGY). Vol. 1 (1981)-. 0276-9913. US. English. ir. $52.50. JAI Press, PO Box 1678, Greenwich CT 06836. **Tel** (203)661-7602. Ed Keith E Davis and Thomas O Mitchell. **Ind/Abst** Psychol. Abstr. **LC** BF1. **DD** 150.19. **NLM** W1 AD546M.

ADVANCES IN DEVELOPMENTAL AND BEHAVIORAL PEDIATRICS. *See* Medicine - Pediatrics.

ADVANCES IN DEVELOPMENTAL PSYCHOLOGY. Vol. 1-. 0275-3049. US. English. Lawrence Erlbaum Associates, 365 Broadway, Hillsdale NJ 07642. Ed M E Lamb and A L Brown. **LC** BF712. **DD** 155. **NLM** W1 AD548.

ADVANCES IN EXPERIMENTAL SOCIAL PSYCHOLOGY. *See* Sociology: General Works, Theory.

ADVANCES IN FORENSIC PSYCHOLOGY AND PSYCHIATRY. *See* Medicine - Forensic Medicine, Medical Jurisprudence.

ADVANCES IN HUMAN PSYCHOPHARMACOLOGY. V. 1- 1980-. 0272-068X. US. English. ir. $57.50. JAI Press, PO Box 1678, Greenwich CT 06836. **Tel** (203)661-7602. Ed Graham D Burrows and John S Werry. **Ind/Abst** Chem. Abstr., Psychol. Abstr. **LC** RC483. **DD** 615.78. **NLM** W1 AD64P. **CODEN** AHPSDD.

ADVANCES IN INFANCY RESEARCH. *See* Medicine - Pediatrics.

ADVANCES IN INSTRUCTIONAL PSYCHOLOGY. V. 1-. 0163-5379. US. English. ir. Lawrence Erlbaum Associates, 365 Broadway, Hillsdale NJ 07642. **Tel** (201)666-4110. **LC** LB1051. **DD** 370.15. **NLM** W1 AD652.

ADVANCES IN LAW AND CHILD DEVELOPMENT. *See* Law.

ADVANCES IN MOTIVATION AND ACHIEVEMENT. (ADVANCES IN MOTIVATION AND ACHIEVEMENT : A RESEARCH ANNUAL). 1984-. 0749-7423. US. English. an. **LC** BF501. **DD** 153.8.

ADVANCES IN NEUROPSYCHOLOGY AND BEHAVIORAL NEUROLOGY. *See* Medicine - Neurology.

ADVANCES IN PERSONALITY ASSESSMENT. Vol. 1-. 0278-2367. US. English. an. Lawrence Erlbaum Associates Publishers, 365 Broadway, Hillsdale NJ 07642. **LC** BF698.4. **DD** 155.28.

ADVANCES IN PSYCHOLOGICAL ASSESSMENT CEASED. V. 1-6. 0065-325X. US. English. Jossey-Bass Publishers, 433 California Street, San Francisco CA 94104. **LC** BF698.4. **DD** 150.28. **NLM** W1 AD798.

ADVANCES IN PSYCHOSOMATIC MEDICINE. V. 5-. 0065-3268. Monographic Series. English. ir. S Karger AG, PO Box, CH-4009 Basel Switzerland. **Tel** 061-39 08 80. Ed T N Wise. **Ind/Abst** Index Med., Hospit. Lit. Index. **NLM** W1 AD81. Balanced information on the relationships between psychological and biological phenomena. *Fortschritte der Psychosomatischen Medizin.*

ADVANCES IN SUBSTANCE ABUSE. BEHAVIORAL AND BIOLOGICAL RESEARCH. *See* Drug Abuse and Alcoholism.

ADVANCES IN TEST ANXIETY RESEARCH. VFOAT Test Anxiety Research. Vol. 1-. English. ir. **LC** BF575.A6. **DD** 152.287. **NLM** W1.

ADVANCES IN THE BEHAVIORAL MEASUREMENT OF CHILDREN. Vol. 1 (1984)-. 8755-2018. US. English. an. JAI Press, 36 Sherwood Place, Greenwich CT 06836. **LC** BF721. **DD** 150.

ADVANCES IN THE PSYCHOLOGY OF HUMAN INTELLIGENCE. VOL. 1-. 0278-2359. Periodical. US. English. sa. Lawrence Erlbaum Associates, 365 Broadway, Hillsdale NJ 07642. **NLM** W1.

ADVANCES IN THE STUDY OF AGGRESSION. Vol. 1-. 0748-6103. US. English. Academic Press, 4805 Sand Lake Road, Orlando FL 32887. **Tel** (305)345-2000. **LC** BF575.A3. **DD** 302.54. Each volume of this interdisciplinary serial publication consists of contributions by major researchers in the field of agression, integrating work on humans and animals.

ADVANCES IN THE STUDY OF BEHAVIOR. V. 1-. 0065-3454. US. English. ir. Academic Press, 4805 Sand Lake Road, Orlando FL 32887. **Tel** (305)345-4100. Ed Daniel S Lehman, Robert A Hinde and Evelyn Shaw. **Ind/Abst** Life Sci. Collect., Biol. Abstr., Chem. Abstr., Sci. Cit. Index, Abr. Ed. **LC** QL750. **DD** 591.51. **NLM** W1 AD88. **CODEN** ADSBBF.

ADVANCES IN THE STUDY OF COMMUNICATION AND AFFECT. V. 1- 1974-. 0190-9703. US. English. Plenum Press, Attn H Feldman, 233 Spring Street, New York NY 10013. **Tel** (212)620-8000. **LC** UNC. **NLM** W1 AD8801.

ADVENTURES IN TOTAL DEVELOPMENT. (ADVENTURES IN TOTAL DEVELOPMENT : ATD). VFOAT ATD. 0883-5659. Periodical. US. English. bm. $30.00. Asbury Associates Inc, PO Box 141, Wilmore KY 40390. **DD** 158.

AGGRESSION AND ANTI-SOCIAL BEHAVIOR IN CHILDHOOD AND ADOLESCENCE. *See* Sociology: General Works, Theory - Social Pathology, Welfare, Criminology.

AGGRESSIVE BEHAVIOR. V. 1- 1974-. 0096-140X. Periodical. US. English. qt. Alan R Liss Inc, 41 East 11th Street, New York NY 10003. **Tel** (212)741-2515. **Ind/Abst** Life Sci. Collect., Excerpta Med., Biol. Abstr., Chem. Abstr., Psychol. Abstr., Soc. Sci. Citation Index, Sci. Cit. Index, Abr. Ed. **LC**

BF575.A3. **DD** 152.52. **NLM** W1 AG341. **CODEN** AGBEDU.

AGRESSOLOGIE. V. 1- April 1960-. 0002-1148. Periodical. FR. French (articles in English, German, and Spanish with summaries in all languages). mo. $120.00. Masson Publ USA Inc, 211 East 43rd Street/ Room 1306, New York NY 10017. **Tel** (212)370-1937. **Ind/Abst** Life Sci. Collect., Pestdoc, Ringdoc, Vetdoc, Excerpta Med., Biol. Abstr., Chem. Abstr., Nucl. Sci. Abstr., Index Med. **LC** BF575.A3. **NLM** W1 AG38. **CODEN** AGSOA6.

AL-DIRASAT AL-NAFSIYAH WA-AL-TARBAWIYAH. VFOAT Etudes Psychologiques et Pedagogiques. Periodical. Arabic. sa. 70.00 Institutions, 30.00 Others. P O Box 823, Al-Rabat Morocco.

AL-INSAN WA-AL-TATAWWUR. VFOAT Man and Evolution. Periodical. Arabic. qt. 1.20. Al-Jamiyah, 17 Shari 19 Madinat Al-Muqattam, Al-Qahirah United Arab Republic. **LC** BF8.A73.

AMERICAN IMAGO. V. 1- Nov. 1939-. 0065-860X. Periodical. US. English. qt. $28.00. Wayne State University Press, 5959 Woodward Avenue, Detroit MI 48202. **Tel** (313)577-4602. **Ed** Harry Slochower. **Ind/Abst** MLA Int. Bibliogr. Books Artic. Mod. Lang. Lit., Abstr. Engl. Stud., Mag. Index, Annu. Bibliogr. Engl. Lang. Lit., Recent Publ. Artic., Film Lit. Index, Read. Guide Period. Lit., Psychol. Abstr., Index Med., Soc. Sci. Citation Index, Years Work Eng. Stud. **NLM** W1 AM435I. **CODEN** AMIAAO. (cum index). **Circ** 1,100. (ctrl). Available on microfilm. Psychoanalytic journal for culture, literature, science and the arts.

AMERICAN JOURNAL OF COMMUNITY PSYCHOLOGY. V. 1- Jan./ Mar. 1973-. 0091-0562. Periodical. US. English. bm. $175.00 Domestic, $196.00 Foreign. Plenum Publishing Corporation, 233 Spring Street, New York NY 10013. **Tel** (212)620-8000. **Ed** John C Glidewell. **Ind/Abst** Electron. Commun. Abstr. J., ISMEC Bull., Pollut. Abstr. Indexes, Saf. Sci. Abstr. J., Sociol. Abstr., Coal Abstr., Cumul. Index Nurs. Allied Health Lit., Excerpta Med., Index Med., Women Stud. Abstr., Psychol. Abstr., Hospit. Lit. Index, Soc. Sci. Citation Index. **LC** RA790.A1. **DD** 361.0019. **NLM** W1 AM45LE. **CODEN** AJCPCK. bk rev. adv acc. This journal is devoted to research and theory concerned with interaction between individuals and communities, organizations, institutions and human groups.

AMERICAN JOURNAL OF ORTHOPSYCHIATRY. *See* Medicine - Psychiatry, Psychopathology.

THE AMERICAN JOURNAL OF PSYCHOLOGY. V. 1- Nov. 1887-. 0002-9556. Periodical. US. English. qt. $30.00 Domestic, $32.50 Foreign. University Illinois Press, East Gregory Drive, Champaign IL 61820. **Tel** (217)333-0950. **Ed** David Birch. **Ind/Abst** Sociol. Abstr., Index Med., Int. Aerosp. Abstr., CIS Abstr., Biol. Abstr., Book Rev. Index, Psychol. Abstr., Ref. Source, Soc. Sci. Index, Soc. Sci. Citation Index, Sociol. Abstr., Lang. Lang. Behav. Abstr. **LC** BF1. **DD** 150.5. **NLM** W1 AM517. **CODEN** AJPCAA. (cum index). bk rev. adv acc. **Circ** 2,900. Articles on general experimental psychology, original research and theoretical issues.

THE AMERICAN PSYCHOLOGIST. V. 1- Jan. 1946-. 0003-066X. Periodical. US. English. mo. $104.00. American Psychological Association, 1400 North Uhle Street, Arlington VA 22201. **Tel** (703)247-7802. **Ed** Susan Knapp. **Ind/Abst** MLA Int. Bibliogr. Books Artic. Mod. Lang. Lit., Life Sci. Collect., Hospit. Lit. Index, Sociol. Abstr., Soc. Welf. Soc. Plan./Policy Soc. Dev., Energy Inf. Abstr., Environ. Abstr., Women Stud. Abstr., Index Med., Int. Aerosp. Abstr., Soc. Work Res. Abstr., Psychol. Abstr., Curr. Index J. Educ., Gen. Sci. Index, Soc. Sci. Index, Lang. Lang. Behav. Abstr., Soc. Sci. Citation Index, Abstr. Soc. Work. **LC** BF1. **DD** 150.5. **NLM** W1 AM7297. **CODEN** AMPSAB. adv acc. **Circ** 70,000. Official journal of the association, publishes empirical, theoretical and practical articles.

AMHC FORUM. Began with: Vol. 26, No. 1 (Oct. 1973). Periodical. US. English. ty. AMHC Forum, 1213 Court Street, Utica NY 13502. **Tel** (315)797-6800. **Ind/ Abst** Hospit. Lit. Index. **NLM** W1. *AMHC Newsletter.*

ANALELE UNIVERSITATII BUCURESTI : PSIHOLOGIE. **Main/Corp** Universitatea Din Bucuresti. RM. Romanian (with summaries in French and Russian). ir. Universitatea din Bucuresti, B-Dul Gh Gheorghiu-Dej Nr 64, Bucuresti Romania. **LC** BF8.R7.

ANALISE PSICOLOGICA. V. 1- Oct. 1977-. Periodical. Portuguese. ir. 2.500 Domestic, $30.00 rest of Europe. Analise Psicologica, R Jardim do Tabaco, 44-1100 Lisboa Portugal. **Tel** 863184. **Ed** Frederico Pereira. **LC** RC500. bk rev. adv acc. **Circ** 1,000. Educational, clinical, social psychology, organizational psychology, general psychology, epistemology/history of psychology, developmental psychoanalysis, comparative psychology.

ANALYTISCHE PSYCHOLOGIE : OFFIZIELLES ORGAN DER DEUTSCHEN GESELLSCHAFT FUR ANALYTISCHE PSYCHOLOGIE, DER SCHWEIZERISCHEN GESELLSCHAFT FUR ANALYTISCHE PSYCHOLOGIE UND DER INTERNATIONALEN GESELLSCHAFT ARZT UND SEELSORGER. Vol. 5 , No. 1-. 0301-3006. Periodical. SZ. German (summaries in English). qt. 94.-. S Karger AG, PO Box, CH-4009 Basel Switzerland. **Tel** (061)39 08 80. **Ed** H Diekmann and CA Meier. **Ind/Abst** Life Sci. Collect., Psychol. Abstr., Curr. Contents. **LC** RC500. **DD** 616.891705. **NLM** W1 AN1919J. **CODEN** ANAPC4. adv acc. Includes works on classical topics of individualism of arch type, dream interpretation typology and mythology. Also current clinical and methodical questions, problems of addiction, etc. *Zeitschrift fur Analytische Psychologie und Ihre Grenzgebiete, 0049-8580.*

ANDA. Periodical. IO. Indonesian. ir. Mulyono & Associates, Gedung Pant Trisula Jl Menteng Raya 35 PO Box 3216, Jakarta Pusat Indonesia. **LC** BF8.I5.

ANNALES MEDICO PSYCHOLOGIQUES. 1-12, 1843-48. 0003-4487. Periodical. French. bm. $144.00. Masson Publishing USA Inc, 211 East 43rd Street/Room 1306, New York NY 10017. **Tel** (212)370-1937. **Ind/Abst** Life Sci. Collect., Pestdoc, Ringdoc, Vetdoc, Excerpta Med., Index Med., CIS Abstr., Psychol. Abstr. **NLM** W1 AN457P. **CODEN** AMPYAT.

ANNALS OF CHILD DEVELOPMENT. (ANNALS OF CHILD DEVELOPMENT : A RESEARCH ANNUAL). Vol. 1 (1984)-. 0747-7902. US. English. an. $49.50. JAI Press Inc, 36 Sherwood Place/PO Box 1678, Greenwich CT 06836. **Tel** (203)661-7602. **Ed** Grover Whitehurst. **LC** BF712. **DD** 155.405.

ANNALS OF THEORETICAL PSYCHOLOGY. Vol. 1-. 0747-5241. US. English. an. Plenum Press, 233 Spring Street, New York NY 10013. **LC** BF38. **DD** 150.5.

L'ANNEE PSYCHOLOGIQUE. Vol. 1 Yearly. 0003-5033. FR. French. ir. 450 Domestic, $50.00 Foreign. Presses Universitaires France, 12 rue Jean-de-Beauvais, 75005 Paris France. **Tel** (1)326-2216. **Ed** Paul Fraisse and George Noizet. **Ind/Abst** Sociol. Abstr., Index Med., Psychol. Abstr., Lang. Lang. Behav. Abstr., Soc. Sci. Citation Index. **LC** BF2. **DD** 150.5. **NLM** W1 AN673. (cum index). This is one of the most important sources for psychologists in the entire world. Research reports and findings, critical reviews and biographical analyses make this a comprehensive collection.

ANNUAL EDITIONS. READINGS IN HUMAN DEVELOPMENT *CEASED.* (ANNUAL EDITIONS : READINGS IN HUMAN DEVELOPMENT). VFOAT Readings in Human Development. 1973/74-1979/80. 0090-5348. US. English. an. Dushkin Books, Sluice Dock, Guilford CT 06437. **Tel** (203)453-4351. **LC** HQ768. **DD** 612.65.

ANNUAL EDITIONS : READINGS IN SOCIAL PSYCHOLOGY. VFOAT Readings in Social Psychology. 1977/78-. US. English. an. Dushkin Publishing Corporation, Sluice Dock, Guilford CT 06437. **Tel** (203)453-4351. **LC** HM251. **DD** 301.105.

THE ANNUAL OF PSYCHOANALYSIS. *See* Medicine - Psychiatry, Psychopathology.

ANNUAL REPORT - DEVELOPMENTAL BEHAVIORAL SCIENCES STUDY SECTION, NATIONAL INSTITUTES OF HEALTH. **Main/Corp** United States. National Institutes of Health. Developmental Behavioral Sciences Study Section. US. English. an. National Institutes of Health, 9000 Rockville Pike, Bethesda MD 20014.

ANNUAL REPORT - OKLAHOMA. STATE BOARD OF EXAMINERS OF PSYCHOLOGISTS. (ANNUAL REPORT FOR FY . . .). **Main/Corp** Oklahoma. State Board of Examiners of Psychologists. 0733-3609. US. English. an. State Board of Examiners of Psychologists, Room 503 Northeast Tenth and Stonewall, PO Box 53551, Oklahoma City OK 73152. **LC** BF80.8. **DD** 353.9766008243046.

ANNUAL REPORT TO THE GOVERNOR - NEW MEXICO STATE BOARD OF PSYCHOLOGIST EXAMINERS. **Main/Corp** New Mexico State Board of Psychologist Examiners. US. English. an. **LC** BF80.8. **DD** 353.9789008243.

ANNUAL REVIEW OF PSYCHOLOGY. V. 1- 1950-. 0066-4308. US. English. an. $31.00 Domestic, $34.00 Foreign. Annual Reviews Incorporated, 4139 El Camino Way, Palo Alto CA 94306. **Tel** (415)493-4400. **Ed** Mark R Rosenzweig and Lyman W Porter. **Ind/Abst** Life Sci. Collect., Energy Inf. Abstr., Environ. Abstr., Index Med., CIS Abstr., Biol. Abstr., Chem. Abstr., Psychol. Abstr., Soc. Sci. Index, Soc. Sci. Citation Index, Sci. Cit. Index, Abr. Ed., Sociol. Abstr., Hospit. Lit. Index, Lang. Lang. Behav. Abstr. **LC** BF30. **DD** 150.58. **NLM** W1 AN7796. **CODEN** ARPSAC. Comprehensive, thorough coverage of latest advances in psychology, written by acknowledged experts in the field. Extensive literature citations included.

APA MEMBERSHIP REGISTER. **Main/ Corp** American Psychological Association. **VFOAT** A.P.A. Membership Register. **VAT** American Psychological Association Membership Register. 1982-. 0737-1446. Periodical. US. English. ir. $25.00. American Psychological Association, 1400 North Uhle Street, Arlington VA 22201. **Tel** (202)955-7600. **Ed** John A Lazo. **LC** BF30. **DD** 150.2573. **NLM** BF 11 A51M. adv acc. **Circ** 5,000. Published to provide a current record of the association membership including mailing addresses, telephone numbers, and membership status.

APA MONITOR. **Main/Corp** American Psychological Association. **VAT** American Psychological Association Monitor. V. 1- Oct. 1970-. 0001-2114. US. English. mo. $25.00. American Psychological Association, 1400 North Uhle Street, Arlington VA 22201. **Tel** (703)247-7802. **Ed** Jeffrey Mervis. **LC** BF1. **DD** 150.5. **NLM** W1 A142V. adv acc. **Circ** 76,400. Reports news about psychology and psychologists, professional meetings and members. Features coverage of legislative developments, editorials, listings of employment opportunities.

APPLIED DEVELOPMENTAL PSYCHOLOGY. Vol. 1-. 0735-164X. US. English. an. Academic Press, 4805 Sand Lake Road, Orlando FL 32819. **LC** BF712. **DD** 155.

APPLIED PSYCHOLOGICAL MEASUREMENT. V. 1- Winter 1977-. 0146-6216. Periodical. US. English. qt. $50.00 Domestic, $60.00 Foreign. Applied Psychological, University of Minnesota, N658 Elliot Hall, Minneapolis MN 55455. **Tel** (612)376-7378. **Ed** David J Weiss. **Ind/ Abst** Psychol. Abstr. **LC** BF39. **DD** 150.182. **NLM** W1 AP528N. bk rev. adv acc. **Circ** 850. Research and reviews on methodologies for the measurement of psychological variables in all settings. Applications of psychological measurement to all areas of psychology and education.

ARCHITECTURAL PSYCHOLOGY NEWSLETTER. V. 1- July 1969-. Periodical. UK. English. qt. $12.26. Kingston Polytechnic, Kingston Upon Thames, Surrey KT1 2QJ England. **Tel** 01 549 6151. **Ed** Sue-Ann Lee. bk rev. **Circ** 300. Research summaries, articles, reviews, and information on courses, meetings and publications concerning the inter-relationship between people and their physical environment.

ARCHIVES DE PSYCHOLOGIE. *See* Genealogy and Heraldry - Archives.

ARCHIVES OF THE BEHAVIORAL SCIENCES. *See* Genealogy and Heraldry - Archives.

ARCHIVIO DI PSICOLOGIA, NEUROLOGIA E PSICHIATRIA. *See* Genealogy and Heraldry - Archives.

ARQUIVOS BRASILEIROS DE PSICOLOGIA. Vol. 31, N0. 1 (Jan./Mar. 1979)-. 0100-8692. Periodical. BL. Portuguese. qt. $11.90. Fundacao Getulio Vargas, Caixa Postal 9052, Rio de Janeiro GB Brazil. **Tel** 253-0227. **Ed** Athayde Ribeiro da Silva. **Ind/Abst** Psychol. Abstr., Soc. Sci. Citation Index, Lang. Lang. Behav. Abstr., Sociol. Abstr. **LC** BF5. **DD** 150.5. **NLM** W1 AR879B. bk rev. **Circ** 2,200. Publishes behaviorism, clinical, cognitive, counselling; educational, epistemology, ergonomy,

Psychology

industrial, projective and expressive techniques; psychoanalysis, social sport, arts, and culture. *Arquivos Brasileiros de Psicologia Aplicada.*

ART THERAPY. (ART THERAPY). Vol. 1, No. 1 (Oct. 1983)-. 0742-1656. Periodical. US. English. qt. Free to Members, $30.00 Domestic, $34.00 Foreign. Art Therapy, 5999 Stevenson Avenue, Alexandria VA 22304. Tel (703)437-6012. bk rev. adv acc. Circ 3,200. Scholarly papers, viewpoints, books, and media reviews and Association news regarding adjunct of art therapy to psychological well-being.

ASIS SPECIAL INTEREST GROUP IN THE BEHAVIORAL AND SOCIAL SCIENCES NEWSLETTER. Main/Corp American Society for Information Science. Special Interest Group in the Behavioral and Social Sciences. Periodical. US. English. ir. American Society for Information Science, 1010 16th Street NW/2nd Floor, Washington DC 20036.

AUDIT REPORT, BOARD OF PSYCHOLOGY (TENNESSEE). Main/Corp Tennessee. Division of State Audit. 0148-3420. US. English. Tennessee Comptroller of the Treasury, Nashville TN 37022. LC RA790.65.T35. DD 353.976800842.

AUSTRALIA AND NEW ZEALAND JOURNAL OF DEVELOPMENTAL DISABILITIES. V.8 No.1 (Mar. 1982.). 0726-3864. Periodical. AT. English. qt. 36.90. MacQuarie University, School Education Unit for Rehabilitation Studies, North Ryde New South Wales 2113 Australia. Tel 02 889530. Ed Trevor R Parmenter. Ind/Abst Excerpta Med., APAIS, Aust. Public Aff. Inf. Serv., Psychol. Abstr., Biol. Abstr., Except. Child Educ. Resour. NLM W1 AU388. CODEN ANZDDQ. bk rev. adv acc. Circ 1,500. (ctrl) Scholarly reports of the scientific study of the causes, prevention and intervention programs for persons with developmental disabilities. *Australian Journal of Developmental Disabilities, 0159-9011.*

AUSTRALIAN AUTISM REVIEW. V. 1- Sept. 1975-. 0312-8857. Periodical. AT. English. an. $4.43. National Association for Austin, PO Box 607 Chatswood, New South Wales 2067 Australia. Ed R Q Allen & K F Kennett. NLM W1 AU516. bk rev. adv acc. Circ 1,000. (ctrl). Medical and educational research into problems of autism including services to autistic persons and their families.

AUSTRALIAN JOURNAL OF PSYCHOLOGY. V. 1- June 1949-. 0004-9530. Periodical. AT. English. ty. $22.13. Australian Psychological Society, 191 Royal Parade, Parkville Victoria 3052 Australia. Tel (0)347 2720. Ind/Abst Life Sci. Collect., Sociol. Abstr., Women Stud. Abstr., Ref. Source, Biol. Abstr., Nuci. Sci. Abstr., Psychol. Abstr., APAIS, Aust. Public Aff. Inf. Serv., Soc. Sci. Citation Index, Lang. Lang. Behav. Abstr. LC BF1. DD 150.5. NLM W1 AU618. CODEN ASJPAE. (cum index).

AUSTRALIAN JOURNAL OF PSYCHOTHERAPY. Began with: Vol. 1, No. 1, in 1982. 0728-6155. Periodical. English. ir. $35.00. NLM W1.

AUSTRALIAN PSYCHOLOGIST. V.1- July 1966-. 0005-0067. Periodical. AT. English. ty. $22.13. Australian Psychological Society, 191 Royal Parade, Parkville VIC 3052 Australia. Tel (03)347-2720. Ind/Abst APAIS, Aust. Public Aff. Inf. Serv., Psychol. Abstr., Soc. Sci. Citation Index. NLM W1 AU644G. CODEN AUPCBK.

L'AVE : LE MAGAZINE FREUDIEN. No. 1 (April/May 1981)-. Periodical. French. qt.

BASIC AND APPLIED SOCIAL PSYCHOLOGY. Vol. 1, No. 1 (Mar. 1980)-. 0197-3533. Periodical. US. English. qt. Lawrence Erlbaum Associates, 365 Broadway/Suite 112, Hillsdale NJ 07642. Tel (201)666-4110. Ind/Abst Psychol. Abstr.

THE BEHAVIOR ANALYST. (BEHAVIOR ANALYST). Vol. 1, No. 1 (Spring 1978)-. 0738-6729. Periodical. US. English. sa. $20.00. Society for the Advancement of Behavior Analysis, Department of Psychology Western Michigan University, Kalamazoo MI 49008. Tel (616)383-0452. Ed Edward K Morris. Ind/Abst Soc. Sci. Citation Index, Psychol. Abstr., Behav. Abstr., Curr. Contents, Soc. Behav. Sci. LC BF199. DD 150.5. NLM W1 BE122D. bk rev. adv acc. Circ 2,500. (ctrl). Contains articles on trends, issues, policies, and developments in the field of behavior analysis.

BEHAVIOR IMPROVEMENT NEWS. (BEHAVIOR IMPROVEMENT NEWS : THE BEHAVIOR MODIFICATION NEWSLETTER). V. 1, No. 1- Sept. 1977-. 0193-6271. Periodical. US. English. mo. $36.00. Subscription Desk/Research Press Company, 2612 North Mattis Avenue, Champaign IL 61820.

BEHAVIOR MODIFICATION. V. 1- Jan. 1977-. 0145-4455. Periodical. US. English. qt. Sage Publications Inc, 275 South Beverly Drive, Beverly Hills CA 90212. Tel (213)274-8003. Ind/Abst Excerpta Med., Index Med., Psychol. Abstr., Soc. Sci. Citation Index. LC BF637.B4. DD 158. NLM W1 BE124T. Index in last issue of volume - attached.

BEHAVIOR RESEARCH METHODS AND INSTRUMENTATION *CEASED.* VFOAT Behavior Research Methods & Instrumentation. Vol. 1, No. 1 (Sept. 1968)-V. 15, No. 6 (Dec. 1983). 0005-7878. Periodical. US. English. bm. Ind/Abst Life Sci. Collect., Sociol. Abstr., Int. Aerosp. Abstr., Biol. Abstr., Comput. Control Abstr., Electr. Electron. Abstr., Sci. Abstr. Sect. A. Phys. Abstr. LC BF180. DD 150.724. NLM W1. CODEN BRMIAC.

BEHAVIOR RESEARCH METHODS, INSTRUMENTS, & COMPUTERS. (BEHAVIOR RESEARCH METHODS, INSTRUMENTS, & COMPUTERS : A JOURNAL OF THE PSYCHONOMIC SOCIETY, INC). VFOAT Behavior Research Methods, Instruments, and Computers. Vol. 16, No. 1 (Feb. 1984)-. 0743-3808. Periodical. US. English. bm. $60.00. Psychonomic Society, 2904 Guadalupe Street, Austin TX 78705. Tel (512)476-9687. Ed Joseph B Sidowski. Ind/Abst Life Sci. Collect. DD 150. NLM W1 BE126H. adv acc. Circ 1,250. Deals with methods, techniques, and instrumentation of research in experimental psychology with special focus on the use of computer technology in experimental psychology. *Behavior Research Methods and Instrumentation, 0005-7878.*

THE BEHAVIOR THERAPIST. 0278-8403. Periodical. US. English. ir. $22.00. Association For Advancement of Behavior Therapy, 15 West 36th Street, New York NY 10018. Tel (212)279-7970. Ed Jerry Martin. Ind/Abst Psychol. Abstr. NLM W1 BE128C. bk rev. adv acc. Circ 3,800. News magazine specializing in developments in behavior therapy/modification, special education, & mental health.

BEHAVIOR THERAPY. V. 1- Mar. 1970-. 0005-7894. Periodical. US. English. ir. $90.00. Association For Advancement of Behavior Therapy, 15 West 36th Street, New York NY 10018. Tel (212)279-7970. Ed David H Barlow. Ind/Abst Excerpta Med., Women Stud. Abstr., Biol. Abstr., Psychol. Abstr., Soc. Sci. Citation Index. LC RC489.B4. DD 616.89. NLM W1 BE128D. CODEN BHVTAK. bk rev. adv acc. Circ 3,200. An interdisciplinary journal which presents original research, both clinical and experimental, treatment procedures and methodological evaluation employed in the field of behavior therapy.

BEHAVIOR THERAPY WITH CHILDREN. 1- 1971-. 0360-6341. US. English. Aldine Publishing Company, 529 South Wabash Avenue, Chicago IL 60605. LC RJ505.B4. DD 618.92891.

BEHAVIOR TODAY. V. 1- 1970-. 0005-7924. Periodical. US. English. ir. $82.00. Atcom Company, 2315 Broadway, New York NY 10024. Tel (212)873-5900. Ed Suzanne Presod. Ind/Abst Lang. Lang. Behav. Abstr., Sociol. Abstr. NLM W1 BE128K. Circ 1,700. (ctrl). A newsletter for professionals in all areas of the behavioral and helping professions.

BEHAVIORAL AND BRAIN SCIENCES. (THE BEHAVIORAL AND BRAIN SCIENCES). V. 1- March 1978-. 0140-525X. Periodical. US. English. qt. $128.00. Cambridge University Press, 510 North Avenue, New Rochelle NY 10801. Tel (914)235-0300. Ed Stevan Harnad. Ind/Abst Life Sci. Collect., Excerpta Med., Biol. Abstr., Psychol. Abstr. LC QP360. DD 152.05. NLM W1 BE129K. CODEN BBSCDH. Provides an opportunity for an extraordinary form of scientific communication among researchers in all areas of psychology, neuroscience, behavioral biology and cognitive science.

BEHAVIORAL COUNSELING QUARTERLY. Vol. 1, No. 1 (Spring 1981)-V. 2, No. 3/4 (Fall/Winter 1982). 0190-1028. Periodical. US. English. qt. $53.63. Human Science Press, 3 Henrietta Street, c/o M Gleean, London WC2E 8LU England. Tel 01-240 0856. Ind/Abst Psychol. Abstr. LC BF637.C6. DD 158.3. NLM W1 BE13BL. CODEN BCQUDY.

BEHAVIORAL ENGINEERING. 0362-0298. Periodical. US. English. qt. Farrall Instruments, PO Box 1473, Grand Island NE 68801. Ind/Abst Psychol. Abstr. LC BF637.B4. DD 153.85. NLM W1 BE13E. CODEN BEENDZ.

BEHAVIORAL GROUP THERAPY. 1979-. 0191-5681. US. English. an. Research Press Company, 2612 North Mattis Avenue, Champaign IL 61820. LC RC489.B4. DD 616.8914205. NLM W1 BE13G.

BEHAVIORAL MEDICINE AND STRESS MANAGEMENT NEWS. V. 1- Mar. 1980-. 0227-8278. Periodical. CN. English. ir. Free. Western Center for Preventive and Behavioral Medicine, 208-125 East 13th Street North, Vancouver BC V7L 2L3 Canada. DD 616.0019.

BEHAVIORAL MEDICINE UPDATE. (BEHAVIORAL MEDICINE UPDATE : A PUBLICATION OF THE SOCIETY OF BEHAVIORAL MEDICINE). 0742-5554. Periodical. US. English. qt. $25.00. Society of Behavioral Medicine, PO Box 8530 University Station, Knoxville TN 37996. Ind/Abst Psychol. Abstr.

BEHAVIORAL NEUROSCIENCE. Vol. 97, No. 1 (Feb. 1983)-. 0735-7044. Periodical. US. English. bm. $106.00. American Psychological Association, 1400 North Uhle Street, Arlington VA 22201. Tel (703)247-7802. Ed Susan Knapp. Ind/Abst Life Sci. Collect., Excerpta Med., Index Med., Psychol. Abstr., Biol. Agric. Index, Soc. Sci. Index. NLM W1 BE13M. adv acc. Circ 2,600. Research in the broad field of biological bases of behavior, as well as occasional review and theoretical articles that make original and important contributions to the field. *Journal of Comparative and Physiological Psychology, 0021-9940.*

BEHAVIORAL RESEARCH AND SERVICE NEWSLETTER. V. 1- Sept. 1972-. 0381-5668. Periodical. CN. English. ty. 13.00. B K Sinha, Department of Psychology, Biological Sciences Building, University of Alberta, Edmonton Alberta T6G 2E9 Canada. DD 158.097123.

BEHAVIORAL SCIENCE. Vol. 1, No. 1 (Jan. 1956)-. 0005-7940. Periodical. US. English. qt. Behavioral Science, PO Box 64249, Baltimore MD 21264. Tel (301)528-4105. Ind/Abst MLA Int. Bibliogr. Books Artic. Mod. Lang. Lit., Phys. Abstr., Sociol. Abstr., Soc. Welf. Soc. Plan./Policy Soc. Dev., Excerpta Med., Index Med., ABC Pol Sci, Int. Aerosp. Abstr., Recent Publ. Artic., Comput. Control Abstr., Electr. Electron. Abstr., Energy Res. Abstr., Sci. Abstr. Sect. A. Phys. Abstr., Psychol. Abstr., Soc. Sci. Index, Comput. Rev., Soc. Sci. Citation Index, Am. Hist. Life, Hist. Abstr., Abstr. Anthropol., Math. Rev. LC BF1. DD 150.5. NLM W1 BE132. CODEN BEHSAS. (cum index).

BEHAVIORAL SCIENCE SERIES. No. 1- 1973-. 0091-2425. Monographic Series. US. English. ir. University of South Carolina Press, Columbia SC 29208. NLM W1 BE132S.

BEHAVIORAL SCIENCES NEWSLETTER. 1972. 0361-4646. Periodical. US. English. sm. $72.00. Roy W Walter & Associates, Whitney Road, Mahwah NJ 07430. Tel (201)891-5757. Ed John V Hickey. bk rev. (ctrl). Reports ways to increase productivity, motivate employees, and reduce absenteeism. Special areas of interest include organizational development, work effectiveness and change implementation.

BEHAVIORISM. See Philosophy.

BEHAVIORMETRIKA. Began with July 1974 issue. 0385-7417. Periodical. English. sa. $20.00. Japan Publications Trading Company, POB 5030, Tokyo Internationl Tokyo 100-31 Japan. LC BF76.5. DD 150.72.

BEHAVIOURAL ABSTRACTS. See Indexes/Abstracts.

BEHAVIOURAL PSYCHOTHERAPY. Began with: V. 6, No. 1 (Jan. 1978). 0141-3473. Periodical. UK. English. qt. $59.00. Academic Press, 4805 Sand Lake Road, Orlando FL 32819. Tel (305)345-4100. Ind/Abst Excerpta Med., Cumul. Index Nurs. Allied Health Lit., Psychol. Abstr. NLM W1 BE135H. *BABP Bulletin.*

BEITRAGE ZUR VERHALTUNGSFORSCHUNG. No. 1-. 0522- 719. Monographic Series. GW. German. ir. Duncker und Humblot Verlag, Dietrich-Schafer-Weg 9, 1000 Berlin 41 West Germany.

Psychology

BIBLIOGRAPHIC GUIDE TO PSYCHOLOGY. See Bibliographies.

BIBLIOGRAPHIE DER DEUTSCHSPRACHIGEN PSYCHOLOGISCHEN LITERATUR. See Bibliographies.

BIBLIOGRAPHIE SOZIALISATION UND SOZIALPADAGOGIK. See Bibliographies.

BIBLIOGRAPHIES AND INDEXES IN PSYCHOLOGY. See Indexes/Abstracts.

BIENNIAL REPORT OF EXAMINING AND LICENSING BOARDS - MINNESOTA. BOARD OF PSYCHOLOGY. Main/Corp Minnesota. Board of Psychology. US. English. be. Minnesota Board of Psychology, 717 Delaware Street SE/Room 343, Minneapolis MN 55414. Tel (612)642-0587. LC BF80.8. DD 353.9776008243. Circ 20. A report to Governor re-lisensure. Data Activities, time spent of board members and disciplinary actions taken by the board of psychology.

BIOFEEDBACK. Series/Titl Annual Research Reviews. V.2- 1977-. 0227-843X. CN. English. an. $10.00. Eden Press, 1538 Sherbrooke Street West 201, Montreal Quebec H3G 1L5 Canada. Ind/Abst Psychol. Abstr. DD 152.188. NLM W1 BI664D.

BIOFEEDBACK AND SELF-REGULATION. VFOAT Biofeedback and Self Regulation. V. 1- Mar. 1976-. 0363-3586. Periodical. US. English. qt. $125.00 Domestic, $140.00 Foreign. Plenum Press, 227 West 17th Street, New York NY 10011. Tel (212)620-8000. Ed Albert Fax. Ind/Abst Life Sci. Collect., Excerpta Med., Index Med., Biol. Abstr., Psychol. Abstr., Comput. Control Abstr., Electr. Electron. Abstr., Sci. Abstr. Sect. A. Phys. Abstr., Phys. Abstr. LC BF319.5.B5. DD 615.851. NLM W1 BI664R. CODEN BSELDP. bk rev. adv acc. This interdisclpinary journal is devoted to the rapid dissemination of information in this field. It deals with aspects of psychology, psychiatry, psychosomatic medicine, physical medicine, and cybernetics.

BIOGRAPHICAL DIRECTORY - AMERICAN PSYCHOLOGICAL ASSOCIATION. See Yearbooks, Almanacs, Directories.

BIOLOGICAL PSYCHOLOGY. V. 1- 1973-. 0301-0511. Periodical. NE. English. bm. Elsevier Science Publishers, PO Box 211, 1000 AE Amsterdam Netherlands. Tel (020)5803.911. Ind/Abst Life Sci. Collect., Excerpta Med., Index Med., Biol. Abstr., Chem. Abstr., Psychol. Abstr., Soc. Sci. Citation Index. NLM W1 BI754P. CODEN BLPYAX.

BIOLOGICAL PSYCHOLOGY BULLETIN. V. 1- Sept. 1971-. 0093-1004. Periodical. US. English. qt. PO Box 26901, Oklahoma City OK 73190. Ind/Abst Excerpta Med., Psychol. Abstr. NLM W1 BI754PB. CODEN BPCBAT.

BOLETIN DE PSICOLOGIA. Began in 1978. 0253-5742. CU. Spanish. ty. Hspt Psiquiatrico de la Habana Ministerio de Salud Publica, Habana Cuba. Ind/Abst Psychol. Abstr. NLM W1 BO266.

BOLLETTINO DI PSICOLOGIA APPLICATA. No. 37/39 (Feb./June 1960)-. 0006-6761. Periodical. IT. Italian. ir. Orginizzazioni Speciali, Via Franchi 5, Florence Italy. Ind/Abst Psychol. Abstr. NLM W1 BO563. Bollettino di Psicologiae Sociologia Applicata.

BRAIN AND LANGUAGE. V. 1- Jan. 1974-. 0093-934X. Periodical. US. English. bm. Academic Press, 4805 Sand Lake Road, Orlando FL 32819. Tel (305)345-4100. Ind/Abst MLA Int. Bibliogr. Books Artic. Mod. Lang. Lit., Life Sci. Collect., Lang. Lang. Behav. Abstr., Excerpta Med., Index Med., Psychol. Abstr., Sci. Cit. Index, Abr. Ed., Soc. Sci. Citation Index, Sociol. Abstr., Hospit. Lit. Index. LC RC423.A1. DD 612.7805. NLM W1 BR112L. CODEN BRLGA.

BRAIN MIND BULLETIN. See Medicine - Neurology.

BRITISH JOURNAL OF CLINICAL PSYCHOLOGY. (THE BRITISH JOURNAL OF CLINICAL PSYCHOLOGY). Vol. 20, Pt. 1 (Feb. 1981)-. 0144-6657. Periodical. UK. English. qt. $64.50. British Psychological Society, Blackhorse Road, Letchworth SG6 1HN England. Tel (04626)72555. Ind/Abst Life Sci. Collect., Sociol. Abstr., Excerpta Med., Cumul. Index Nurs. Allied Health Lit., Index Med., Biol. Abstr., Psychol. Abstr. LC BF1. DD 616.89005. NLM W1 BR519V. CODEN BJCPDW. British Journal of Social and Clinical Psychology, 0007-1293.

BRITISH JOURNAL OF COGNITIVE PSYCHOTHERAPY. Vol. 1, No. 1 (1983)-. 0264-5432. UK. English. sa. $30.00. DR. W. DRYDEN (ED. Ind/Abst Psychol. Abstr. NLM W1.

BRITISH JOURNAL OF DEVELOPMENTAL PSYCHOLOGY. (THE BRITISH JOURNAL OF DEVELOPMENTAL PSYCHOLOGY). Vol. 1, Pt. 1 (Mar. 1983)-. 0261-510X. Periodical. UK. English. qt. $64.50. The British Psychological Society, Blackhorse Road Letchworth, Herts SG6 1HN England. Ind/Abst Psychol. Abstr. LC BF712. DD 155.05.

BRITISH JOURNAL OF EDUCATIONAL PSYCHOLOGY. (THE BRITISH JOURNAL OF EDUCATIONAL PSYCHOLOGY). V. 1- Feb. 1931-. 0007-0998. Periodical. UK. English. ty. $40.00. Scottish Academic Press Ltd, 33 Montgomery Street, Edinburgh EH7 5JX Scotland. Tel (031)556 2796. Ed C W Valentine. Ind/Abst Sociol. Abstr., Index Med., Women Stud. Abstr., Lang. Teach., Educ. Index, Psychol. Abstr., Curr. Index J. Educ., Soc. Sci. Citation Index, Lang. Lang. Behav. Abstr. LC LB1051.A2. NLM W1 BR527. CODEN BJESAE. (cum index). Forum of Education.

BRITISH JOURNAL OF MATHEMATICAL & STATISTICAL PSYCHOLOGY. (THE BRITISH JOURNAL OF MATHEMATICAL & STATISTICAL PSYCHOLOGY). VFOAT British Journal of Mathematical and Statistical Psychology. Began with: Vol. 18 (May 1965). 0007-1102. Periodical. UK. English. sa. $79.50. British Psychological Society, Blackhorse Road, Letchworth SG6 1HN England. Ind/Abst Math. Rev., Index Med., Psychol. Abstr., Soc. Sci. Citation Index, Sociol. Abstr., Lang. Lang. Behav. Abstr. LC BF1. NLM W1 BR56. British Journal of Statistical Psychology.

BRITISH JOURNAL OF MEDICAL PSYCHOLOGY. VFOAT Medical Section. Began with: Vol. 3 (Jan. 1923). 0007-1129. Periodical. UK. English. qt. $90.50. British Psychological Society, Distribution Center, Blackhorse Road, Letchworth SG 6 1HN England. Tel 04626 72555. Ind/Abst Life Sci. Collect., Excerpta Med., Cumul. Index Nurs. Allied Health Lit., Chem. Abstr., Biol. Abstr., Psychol. Abstr., Nuci. Sci. Abstr., Index Med., Sci. Cit. Index, Abr. Ed., Soc. Sci. Citation Index, Hospit. Lit. Index, Lang. Lang. Behav. Abstr., Sociol. Abstr. LC RC321. NLM W1 BR581. CODEN BJMPAB. (cum index). British Journal of Psychology. Medical Section.

BRITISH JOURNAL OF MENTAL SUBNORMALITY. V. 17- (No. 32-). 0374-633X. Periodical. UK. English. sa. 14.00. S E F A Publications Ltd, The Globe, 4 Grt William Street, Stratford-Avon CV37 6RY England. Tel 0789/287764. Ed H C Gunzburg. Ind/Abst Excerpta Med., Psychol. Abstr., Soc. Sci. Citation Index. NLM W1 BR579. CODEN BJMSBL. bk rev. (ctrl). Covers all aspects of mental retardation: education, habilitation, environmental issues, sociology, training, and epidemiology. Journal of Mental Subnormality, 0022-2666.

BRITISH JOURNAL OF PROJECTIVE PSYCHOLOGY AND PERSONALITY STUDY. 0309-7757. Periodical. UK. English. sa. 26.00. British Rorschach Forum Trust, Psychology Department Park Prewett Hospital, Basingstoke Hants England. Ind/Abst Psychol. Abstr. NLM W1 BR614. CODEN BJPSD4. bk rev. adv acc. Articles about clinical work and research work related to projective psychology.

BRITISH JOURNAL OF PSYCHOLOGY. (THE BRITISH JOURNAL OF PSYCHOLOGY). V. 1, Jan. 1904-. 0007-1269. Periodical. UK. English. qt. $110.00. British Psychological Society, Blackhorse Road, Letchworth SG6 1HN England. Ind/Abst Biol. Abstr., Nuci. Sci. Abstr., Index Med., Psychol. Abstr., Soc. Sci. Index, MLA Int. Bibliogr. Books Artic. Mod. Lang. Lit., Lang. Lang. Behav. Abstr., Sociol. Abstr., Soc. Sci. Citation Index. LC BF1. CODEN BJSGAE. (cum index).

BRITISH JOURNAL OF SOCIAL AND CLINICAL PSYCHOLOGY CEASED. Vol. 1, Part 1 Feb. 1962)-V. 19, Pt. 4 (Nov. 1980). 0007-1293. Periodical. UK. English. qt. Ind/Abst Sociol. Abstr., Soc. Welf. Soc. Plan./Policy Soc. Dev., Excerpta Med., Women Stud. Abstr., Biol. Abstr., Psychol. Abstr., Index Med. LC BF1. DD 302.05. NLM W1 BR633. CODEN BJCPBU.

BRITISH JOURNAL OF SOCIAL PSYCHOLOGY. (THE BRITISH JOURNAL OF SOCIAL PSYCHOLOGY). Vol. 20, Pt. 1 (Feb. 1981)-. 0144-6665. Periodical. UK. English. qt. $64.50. British Psychological Society, Blackhorse Road, Letchworth SG6 1HN England. Tel (04626)72555. Ind/Abst Life Sci. Collect., Sociol. Abstr., Excerpta Med., Index Med., Biol. Abstr., Psychol. Abstr., Recent Publ. Artic. LC BF1. DD 302.05. NLM W1 BR635F. CODEN BJSPDA. British Journal of Social and Clinical Psychology, 0007-1293.

THE BULLETIN - CHRISTIAN ASSOCIATION FOR PSYCHOLOGICAL STUDIES CEASED. Main/Corp Christian Association for Psychological Studies. VFOAT CAPS Bulletin. Began with V. 1- Summer 1975-. Ceased in 1981. 0147-7978. US. English. qt $25.00. CAPS Bulletin, 27000 Farmington Road, Farmington Hills MI 48018. LC BV4012. DD 150.190882. Newsletter - Christian Association for Psychological Studies.

BULLETIN DE PSYCHOLOGIE. 0007-4403. Periodical. FR. French. ir. $37.92. Groupe Etudes Psychologie Universite, 17 rue de la Sorbonne, Paris 5E France. Ind/Abst Psychol. Abstr. NLM W1 BU564. Bulletin (Universite de Paris. Groupe d'Etudes de Psychologie).

BULLETIN DE PSYCHOLOGIE SCOLAIRE ET D'ORIENTATION. 1- 1952-. 0007-4411. Periodical. BE. French. qt. $15.81. Fed Centre Psycho-Medico-Socia, 222 BTE 8 Avenue de Tervueren, 1150 Bruxelles Belgium. Tel 762-28-44. Ind/Abst Psychol. Abstr.

BULLETIN - HUMAN FACTORS SOCIETY. Main/Corp Human Factors Society. V. 1- Jan. 1958-. 0438-1629. Periodical. US. English. mo. $25.00. Human Factors Society, Box 1369, Santa Monica CA 90406. Tel (213)394-9793. Ed Dieler Jahns. LC Q300. DD 607.2. bk rev. adv acc. Circ 5,000. Newsletter of interest to human factors practitioners/ergonomists. Feature articles, society announcements, book reviews, events, calendar, some new product notes.

BULLETIN - NATIONAL PSYCHOLOGICAL ASSOCIATION FOR PSYCHOANALYSIS. Main/Corp National Psychological Association for Psychoanalysis. 0077-5339. US. English. an. National Psychological Association for Psychoanalysis, 140 West 13th Street, New York NY 10011.

BULLETIN OF THE AUSTRALIAN PSYCHOLOGICAL SOCIETY. Vol. 1, Issue 1 (May 1979)-. Periodical. AT. English. ty. 20.00. Australian Psychological Society, 191 Royal Parade Parkville, Victoria 3052 Australia. Tel (03)347-2622. Ed Allan Anderson. adv acc. Circ 4,500. (ctrl). Gives news of members, etc. Some articles regarding professional matters and informs its members of matters which related to their society and what it is doing for them.

BULLETIN OF THE BRITISH PSYCHOLOGICAL SOCIETY. V. 1- Jan. 1948-. 0007-1692. UK. English. mo. $27.58. St Andrews House, 48 Princess Road East, Leicester LE1 7DR England. Tel 0533 549658. Ed M Boyle and R Bull. Ind/Abst Psychol. Abstr., Soc. Sci. Citation Index. NLM W1 BU844K. CODEN BBPSAD. bk rev. adv acc. Circ 11,000. (ctrl). General articles of topical interest to psychologists: news and diary of current events and conferences worldwide.

BULLETIN OF THE BUREAU OF EDUCATIONAL AND PSYCHOLOGICAL RESEARCH. CALCUTTA. (BULLETIN OF THE BUREAU OF EDUCATIONAL AND PSYCHOLOGICAL RESEARCH, CALCUTTA). Main/Corp Bureau of Educational and Psychological Research, Calcutta. No. 1- Jan. 1971-. 0376-6675. II. English. ir. Bureau of Educational and Psychological Research, 25/3 Ballygunge Circular Road, Calcutta 19 India. LC LB7. DD 370.5.

BULLETIN OF THE INTERNATIONAL TEST COMMISSION AND OF THE DIVISION OF PSYCHOLOGICAL ASSESSMENT OF THE IAAP. VFOAT Bulletin de la Commission Internationale des Tests et de la Division Evaluation en Psychologie de l'AIPA. No. 20 (Sept. 1984)-. Periodical. FR. English (French). sa. Editions du Centre de Psychologie Apliquee, 48 Avenue Victor-Hugo, 75783 Paris France. Ind/Abst Excerpta Med. Newsletter of the International Test Commission and of the Division Psychological Assessment of the IAAP.

BULLETIN OF THE MENNINGER CLINIC. See Medicine - Psychiatry, Psychopathology.

BULLETIN OF THE PSYCHONOMIC SOCIETY. Main/Corp Psychonomic Society. V. 1- Jan. 1973-. 0090-5054. Periodical. US. English. bm. $58.00. Psychonomic Society Inc, 2904 Guadalupe Street, Austin TX 78705. **Tel** (512)476-9687. **Ed** Debra Chambers. **Ind/Abst** MLA Int. Bibliogr. Books Artic. Mod. Lang. Lit., Life Sci. Collect., Excerpta Med., Int. Aerosp. Abstr., Biol. Abstr., Chem. Abstr., Psychol. Abstr., Soc. Sci. Citation Index, Sociol. Abstr., Lang. Lang. Behav. Abstr. **LC** BF1. **DD** 150.5. **NLM** W1 BU886V. **CODEN** BPNSBY. adv acc. **Circ** 1,350. (ctrl). A short-report journal providing prompt publication of articles covering all areas of experimental psychology. All articles authored or sponsored by members of the Psychonomic Society. *Psychonomic Science, 0033-3131.*

BULLETIN OF THE STUDY GROUP OF THE PSYCHOSOCIAL SEQUELS OF THE HOLOCAUST. No. 2-3-. Periodical. English. ir. $15.00. **NLM** W1. *Bulletin of the Holocaust Study Group.*

BULLETIN - YORK UNIVERSITY, TORONTO. INSTITUTE FOR BEHAVIOURAL RESEARCH. Main/Corp York University (Toronto, Ont.) Institute for Behavioural Research. No. 1- 196 -. Periodical. CN. English. ir. York University Institute for Behavioural Research, 4700 Keele Street, Downsview Ontario Canada.

CADERNOS DE PSICOLOGIA APLICADA. V. 1- Jan./July 1973-. Periodical. English, Portuguese or Spanish. ir. Centro de Orientacao e Selecao Psicotecnica, Rua Jacinto Gomes 540 5. Andar, Porto Alegre Brazil. **LC** BF636.A1.

CAHIERS CONFRONTATION. VFOAT Confrontation. No. 1, Spring 1979-. Periodical. FR. French. sa. $42.57. Aubier Montaigne, 13 Quai de Conti, Paris 6 France. **LC** BF173.A2. **DD** 150.19505.

CAHIERS DE PSYCHOLOGIE COGNITIVE. Vol. 1, No. 1 (April 1981)-. 0249-9185. Periodical. French (English). bm. 66.52. Cahiers de Psychologie, I B H O P, rue des Geraniums, 13014 Marseille France. **Tel** (91) 66 00 69. **Ed** Jean Pailhous. **Ind/Abst** Psychol. Abstr. Cognition, psychophysiology, neuropsychology, neurophysiology, psycholinguistics, ethology, and social psychology. All cognitive approaches of behaviors. *Cahiers de Psychologie, 0373-8965.*

CAHIERS INTERNATIONAUX DE SYMBOLISME. No. 1- 1963-. 0008-0284. Periodical. BE. French. qt. $23.71. Universite de l'Etat, 17 Place Warocque, B-7000 Mons Belgium. **Tel** 065/ 31 34 93. **Ind/Abst** MLA Int. Bibliogr. Books Artic. Mod. Lang. Lit., Sociol. Abstr., Lang. Lang. Behav. Abstr. **LC** BF458. **DD** 001.51.

CALIFORNIA STATE PSYCHOLOGIST. V. 1-13, 19 -Sept. 1972. Periodical. US. English. ir. California State Psychological Association, 2100 Sawtelle Boulevard/Suite 201, Los Angeles CA 90025.

CANADIAN JOURNAL OF BEHAVIORAL SCIENCE. (CANADIAN JOURNAL OF BEHAVIOURAL SCIENCE). VFOAT Revue Canadienne des Sciences du Comportement. V. 1- Jan. 1969-. 0008-400X. Periodical. CN. includes some text and summaries in French. qt. $60.00. Canadian Psychological Association, 558 King Edward Avenue, Ottawa Ontario K1N 7N6 Canada. **Tel** (613)238-4409. **Ed** Robert C Gardner. **Ind/Abst** Sociol. Abstr., Soc. Welf. Soc. Plan./Policy Soc. Dev., Women Stud. Abstr., Psychol. Abstr., Biol. Abstr., Can. Educ. Index, Soc. Sci. Citation Index, Lang. Lang. Behav. Abstr., Sci. Cit. Index, Abr. Ed. **NLM** W1 CA569P. **CODEN** CJBSAA. bk rev. **Circ** 2,500. (ctrl). Applied psychology including abnormal, child and developmental, community, educational, environmental, organizational development, personality psychometrics and social psychology.

CANADIAN JOURNAL OF PSYCHOLOGY. VFOAT Revue Canadienne de Psychologie. V. 1- 1947-. 0008-4255. Periodical. CN. English (includes some text in French, with abstracts in English and French). qt. Canadian Psychological Association, 558 King Edward Avenue, Ottawa Ontario K1N 7N6 Canada. **Tel** (613)238-4409. **Ind/Abst** Life Sci. Collect., Sociol. Abstr., Int. Aerosp. Abstr., Nuci. Sci. Abstr., Psychol. Abstr., Biol. Abstr., Index Med., Can. Educ. Index, Soc. Sci. Index, Soc. Sci. Citation Index, Lang. Lang. Behav. Abstr. **NLM** W1 CA603. **CODEN** CJPSAC. *Bulletin of the Canadian Psychological Association, 0382-8654.*

CANADIAN PSYCHOLOGY. VFOAT Psychologie Canadienne. V. 21- Jan. 1980-. 0708-5591. Periodical. CN. English (French). qt. 55.00 Domestic, 57.00 US, 60.00 Foreign. Canadian Psychological Association, 558 King Edward Avenue, Ottawa Ontario K1N 7N6 Canada. **Tel** (416)595-6022. **Ed** Helen Annis. **Ind/Abst** Biol. Abstr., Can. Period. Index, Can. Educ. Index, Psychol. Abstr. **LC** BF1. **DD** 150.5. **NLM** W1 CA647H. **CODEN** CPSGD2. bk rev. adv acc. **Circ** 3,500. (ctrl). A generalist professional affairs and applied journal published by the Canadian Psychological Association. *Canadian Psychological Review, 0318-2096.*

CATALOG OF SELECTED DOCUMENTS IN PSYCHOLOGY *CEASED.* V. 1-12. 0045-5938. Periodical. US. English. qt. American Psychological Association, 1200 17th Street Northwest, Washington DC 20036. **LC** BF1. **DD** 150.5. **NLM** Z 7203 C357. **CODEN** CSPPD9. (cum index).

CENTURY PSYCHOLOGY SERIES. 0271-9223. Monographic Series. US. English. ir. Irvington Publishers Inc, 551 Fifth Avenue, New York NY 10017.

CERTIFIED PSYCHOLOGISTS : STATE OF KANSAS. 1980-. US. English. an. Kansas State Board of Examiners of Psychologists, Secretary's Office, Topeka KA 66602. **LC** BF30. **DD** 150.25781. *Kansas Directory of Certified Psychologists.*

CESKOSLOVENSKA PSYCHOLOGIE. Vol. 1- 1957-. 0009-062X. Periodical. CS. Czech (table of contents also in Russian and French, summaries in English and Russian). bm. Kubon and Sagner, Postfach 34 01 08, D8 Muenchen 34 West Germany. **Tel** (089)52 20 27. **Ind/Abst** Soc. Sci. Citation Index, Sociol. Abstr., Lang. Lang. Behav. Abstr., Psychol. Abstr., CIS Abstr. **LC** BF8.C9. **NLM** W1 CE902S. **CODEN** CEPSBC. Articles cover a wide range of subjects in theoretical and applied psychology. General preference is given to basic research studies and surveys.

CHARACTER POTENTIAL. V. 1- Nov. 1962-. 0009-1669. Periodical. US. English. ir. $4.00 Domestic, $5.00 Foreign. Union College Character, Research Project, 207 State Street, Schenectady NY 12305. **Ind/Abst** Psychol. Abstr. **LC** BF818. **CODEN** CPOTAI. (cum index). Back issues and complete vols. in Micro-Edition are available from University Microfilms. *Adventures in Character Education.*

CHILD DEVELOPMENT. V. 1- Mar. 1930-. 0009-3920. Periodical. US. English. bm. $85.00. Child Development, 5801 Ellis Avenue, Chicago IL 60637. **Tel** (312)962-7600. **Ed** Willard Hartup. **Ind/Abst** MLA Int. Bibliogr. Books Artic. Mod. Lang. Lit., Sociol. Abstr., Soc. Welf. Soc. Plan./Policy Soc. Dev., Lang. Lang. Behav. Abstr., Index Med., Women Stud. Abstr., Biol. Abstr., Educ. Index, Except. Child Educ. Resour., Psychol. Abstr., Curr. Index J. Educ., Soc. Sci. Index. **LC** HQ750.A1. **DD** 136.705. **NLM** W1 CH647. **CODEN** CHDEAW. (cum index). adv acc. **Circ** 8,300. Available on microfilm from University Microfilms International. Reprinted Vols. 1-40 available from Kraus Reprints. Devoted to original contributions on topics in child development from the fetal period through adolescence.

CHILD PERSONALITY AND PSYCHOPATHOLOGY. *See* Medicine - Pediatrics.

CHILD STUDY JOURNAL. V. 1- Fall 1970-. 0009-4005. Periodical. US. English. qt. $30.00 Domestic, $35.00 Foreign. State University College of Buffalo, 1300 Elmwood Avenue, Buffalo NY 14222. **Tel** (716)878-5302. **Ed** Donald E Carter. **Ind/Abst** Sociol. Abstr., Soc. Welf. Soc. Plan./Policy Soc. Dev., Educ. Index, Psychol. Abstr., Curr. Index J. Educ. **LC** LB1101. **DD** 115.405. **NLM** W1 CH6911. **CODEN** CSJOD2. bk rev. **Circ** 500. Available on microfilm from University Microfilms International. Covers educational and psychological aspects of human development (child and adolescent). *Child Study Center Bulletin, 0193-8924.*

CHILD STUDY JOURNAL MONOGRAPHS *CEASED.* Began with Vol. for 1973. 0099-0116. Periodical. US. English. ir. $30.00. State University College, c/o D E Carter, 1300 Elmwood Avenue, Bacon Hall 312J, Buffalo NY 14222. **Tel** (716)878-5302. **Ed** Donald E Carter. **Ind/Abst** Sociol. Abstr., Lang. Lang. Behav. Abstr., Soc. Sci. Citation Index. **LC** LB1101. **DD** 155.405. bk rev. **Circ** 500. Educational and psychological aspects of human development (child and adolescent).

CHIRON (WILMETTE, ILL.). (CHIRON). 1984-. 0742-0897. Periodical. US. English. an. $14.95. Chiron Publications, 400 Linden Avenue, Wilmette IL 60091. **Tel** (815)223-2520. **Ed** Murray Stein and Nathan Schwartz-Salant. **DD** 150. adv acc. **Circ** 2,500. First professional Jungian journal in US to be specifically clinical in content. Contributors are Jungian analysts and psychoanalytically oriented therapists with Jungian interests.

CLASSICS IN PSYCHOANALYSIS. Monograph No. 1-. 0735-0341. Monographic Series. US. English. ir. International Universities Press, 315 Fifth Avenue, New York NY 10016. **NLM** W1.

CLASSICS IN PSYCHOANALYSIS MONOGRAPH SERIES. VFOAT Classics in Psychoanalysis. 0735-0341. Monographic Series. US. English. ir. International University Press, 80 Northfield Avenue, Building #424, Edison NJ 08837.

CLINICAL BEHAVIOR THERAPY REVIEW. V. 1- Spring 1979-. 0162-2269. Periodical. US. English. qt. $45.00 Libraries/ Domestic, $42.00 Other Institutions/Domestic, $50.00 Libraries/Foreign, $47.00 Other Institutions/Foreign. The Haworth Press, 149 Fifth Avenue, New York NY 10010. **Ind/Abst** Psychol. Abstr. **LC** WMLC L 83/839. **NLM** W1 CL668M.

CLINICAL BIOFEEDBACK AND HEALTH. (CLINICAL BIOFEEDBACK AND HEALTH. AN INTERNATIONAL JOURNAL). Vol. 8, No. 1 (Spring/Summer 1985)-. 0827-1038. Periodical. CN. English. sa. $36.00. Hans Huber Publishers, 14 Bruce Park Avenue, Toronto Ontario M4P 2S3 Canada. **Tel** (416)482-6339. **DD** 615.8. bk rev. adv acc. **Circ** 2,000. The journal publishes original articles dealing with the practice, research, and theory of behavioral medicine and health enhancement. *American Journal of Clinical Biofeedback, 0190-4019.*

THE CLINICAL PSYCHOLOGIST. V. 20- 1966-. 0009-9244. Periodical. US. English. qt. $6.00. University of Delaware, 26 East Main Street, Department Psychology, c/o L Cohen, Newark DE 19716. **Tel** (302)451-2738. **Ed** Lawrence H Cohen. **Ind/Abst** Psychol. Abstr. **DD** 157. adv acc. **Circ** 6,000. Newsletter for mental health professionals. *Newsletter - Division of Clinical Psychology.*

CLINICAL PSYCHOLOGY REVIEW. Vol. 1, No. 1-. 0272-7358. Periodical. US. English. bm. Pergamon Press, 395 Sawmill River Road, Elmsford NY 10523. **Tel** (914)592-7700. **Ind/Abst** Psychol. Abstr. **LC** RC467. **DD** 616.89005. **NLM** W1 CL768E.

THE CLINICAL SUPERVISOR. Vol. 1, No. 1 (Spring 1983)-. 0732-5223. Periodical. US. English. qt. $87.00. Haworth Press, 28 East 22nd Street, New York NY 10010. **Tel** (212)228-2800. **Ed** Carlton E Munson. **Ind/Abst** Electron. Commun. Abstr. J., ISMEC Bull., Pollut. Abstr. Indexes, Saf. Sci. Abstr. J., Cumul. Index Nurs. Allied Health Lit., Psychol. Abstr., Abstr. Res. Pastor. Care Couns., Bull. Signal., Rehabil. Lit. **LC** RC336. **DD** 616.8900683. **NLM** W1 CL795R. bk rev. adv acc. **Circ** 978. The first journal designed to reflect the concerns, needs, and interests of supervisors in a variety of professional settings.

CLINICIAN'S RESEARCH DIGEST. Began in 1983?. 8756-3207. Periodical. US. English. sm. $42.00. Clinical Information Services, PO Box 6272, Altadena CA 91001. **DD** 157.

COGNITION. V. 1-. 0010-0277. Periodical. English (summaries in French). ir. Elsevier Science Publishers, PO Box 211, 1000 AE Amsterdam Netherlands. **Tel** (020)5803.911. **Ind/Abst** MLA Int. Bibliogr. Books Artic. Mod. Lang. Lit., Life Sci. Collect., Sociol. Abstr., Lang. Lang. Behav. Abstr., Philos. Index, Biol. Abstr., Lang. Teach., Psychol. Abstr., Soc. Sci. Citation Index. **LC** BF311. **DD** 153.05. **NLM** W1 CO107N. **CODEN** CGTNAU.

COGNITION AND BRAIN THEORY. VFOAT Cognition & Brain Theory. Began with V. 3, 1979/80. 0193-5488. Periodical. US. English. qt. $50.00. Cognition and Brain Theory, Vassar College, Box 525, Poughkeepsie NY 12601. **NLM** W1 CO107P. *SISTM Quarterly Incorporating the Brain Theory Newsletter, 0194-0902.*

COGNITIVE DEVELOPMENT. 0885-2014. Periodical. US. English. qt. Ablex Publishing Corporation, 355 Chestnut Street, Norwood NJ 07648.

COGNITIVE NEUROPSYCHOLOGY. Vol. 1, No. 1 (Feb. 1984)-. 0264-3294. Periodical. UK. English. qt. $60.00. Lawrence Erlbaum Associates Ltd, c/o The Distribution Centre, Blackhorse Road,

Psychology

Letchworth Herts SG6 1HN United Kingdom. **NLM** W1.

COGNITIVE PSYCHOLOGY. V. 1- Jan. 1970-. 0010-0285. Periodical. US. English. qt. $54.00 Domestic, $62.00 Foreign. Academic Press, 4805 Sand Lake Road, Orlando FL 32819. **Tel** (305)345-4100. **Ind/Abst** MLA Int. Bibliogr. Books Artic. Mod. Lang. Lit., Sociol. Abstr., Lang. Lang. Behav. Abstr., Comput. Control Abstr., Electr. Electron. Abstr., Sci. Abstr., Psychol. Abstr., Soc. Sci. Index, Soc. Sci. Citation Index, Curr. Index J. Educ., Phys. Abstr. **LC** BF309. **DD** 150. **NLM** W1 CO107R. **CODEN** CGPSBQ.

COGNITIVE SCIENCE. V. 1- Jan. 1977-. 0364-0213. Periodical. US. English. qt. $69.50. Ablex Publishing Corporation, 355 Chestnut Street, Norwood NJ 07648. **Tel** (201)767-8450. **Ed** David L Waltz. **Ind/Abst** Math. Rev., MLA Int. Bibliogr. Books Artic. Mod. Lang. Lit., Sociol. Abstr., Lang. Lang. Behav. Abstr., Excerpta Med., Biol. Abstr., Psychol. Abstr. **LC** BF311. **DD** 155.405. **NLM** W1 CO107T. **CODEN** COGSD5. adv acc. **Circ** 2,000. This journal provides a timely flow of information in the field of cognitive science.

COGNITIVE STUDIES. V. 1- 1970-. 0069-4975. Periodical. US. English. an. Brunner Mazel Inc, 19 Union Square West, New York NY 10003. **Ed** J Hellmuth. **LC** BF309. **DD** 153.405.

COGNITIVE THEORY. V. 1- 1975-. 0163-2035. US. English. L Erlbaum Associates, 62 Maria Drive, Hillsdale NJ 07642. **LC** BF309. **DD** 153.405.

COGNITIVE THERAPY AND RESEARCH. V.1- March 1977-. 0147-5916. Periodical. US. English. bm. $120.00 Domestic, $135.00 Foreign. Plenum Press, 233 Spring Street, New York NY 10013. **Tel** (212)260-8000. **Ed** Steven O Hollon. **Ind/Abst** Adolesc. Ment. Health Abstr., Behav. Med. Abstr., Br. J. Guid. Couns., Clin. Behav. Therapy Rev., Curr. Contents, Ref. Z., Soc. Sci. Citation Index, Excerpta Med., Biol. Abstr., Psychol. Abstr. **LC** BF311. **DD** 616.811705. **NLM** W1 CO107W. **CODEN** CTHRD8. bk rev. adv acc. Broadly conceived interdisciplinary journal whose main function is to stimulate and communicate research and theory on the role of cognitive processes in human adaptation and adjustment.

COLLEAGUE. No. 1 1976-. Periodical. US. English. Rational Island Publishers, 719 Second Avenue North, Seattle WA 98109. **Ed** P Roby.

COMMUNICATION & COGNITION. See Communication.

COMMUNIQUE - NATIONAL ASSOCIATION OF SCHOOL PSYCHOLOGISTS. Main/Corp National Association of School Psychologists. 1973. 0164-775X. Periodical. US. English. ir. $15.00. National Association of School Psychologists, PO Box 184, Kent OH 44240. **Tel** (703)568-6454. **Ed** Tom Fagan. bk rev. adv acc. **Circ** 9,500. (ctrl) Describes practices of school psychologists who consult about behavior or learning problems, help develop remedial and prevention programs for pupils, parents, teachers and other staff.

COMPARATIVE STUDIES IN BEHAVIORAL SCIENCE. 0190-1079. Monographic Series. US. English. ir. John Wiley & Sons Inc, 1 Wiley Drive, Somerset NJ 08873.

COMPLEX HUMAN BEHAVIOR. 0271-9193. Monographic Series. US. English. ir. John Wiley & Sons, One Wiley Drive, Somerset NJ 08873.

CONSCIOUSNESS AND SELF-REGULATION. V. 1-. 0146-5457. Monographic Series. US. English. ir. Plenum Publishing Corporation, 233 Spring Street, New York NY 10013. **Tel** (212)620-8000. **Ed** G E Schwartz and D Shapiro. **NLM** W1 CO737.

CONTEMPORARY PROBLEMS OF CHILDHOOD. No. 1-. 0147-1082. Monographic Series. US. English. ir. Greenwood Press, 88 Post Road West, PO Box 5007, Westport CT 06881. **Tel** (203)226-3571. **Ed** Carol Ann Winchell. **LC** UNC. **NLM** ZWA 320 C761.

CONTEMPORARY PSYCHOLOGY. V. 1- Jan. 1956-. 0010-7549. Periodical. US. English. mo. $106.00. American Psychological Association, 1400 North Uhle Street, Arlington VA 22201. **Tel** (703)247-7802. **Ed** Susan Knapp. **Ind/Abst** Women Stud. Abstr., Book Rev. Index, Lang. Lang. Behav. Abstr., Soc. Sci. Citation Index, Sociol. Abstr. **LC** BF1. **DD** 150.5. **NLM** Z 7203 C761. adv acc. **Circ** 6,000.

Available in microform editions from Johnson Associates, University Microfilms, or Princeton Microfilms. Critical reviews of books, films, tapes, and other media representing a cross section of psychological literature.

CONTRIBUTIONS IN PSYCHOLOGY. No. 1-. 0736-2714. Monographic Series. US. English. ir. Greenwood Press, 88 Post Road West, PO Box 5007, Westport CT 06882. **NLM** W1.

CONTRIBUTIONS TO THE STUDY OF CHILDHOOD AND YOUTH. No. 1-. 0273-124X. Monographic Series. US. English. ir. Greenwood Press, 88 Post Road West, Westport CT 06881. **Tel** (203)226-3571. This series examines childhood and adolescence throughout the world within a historical as well as contemporary perspective.

CONVENTION PROCEEDINGS - NATIONAL ASSOCIATION OF SCHOOL PSYCHOLOGISTS. Main/Corp National Association of School Psychologists. 6th- 1974-. Monographic Series. US. English. an.

COUNSELING AND VALUES. See Religion, Mythology, Rationalism - Roman Catholic Church.

THE COUNSELING INTERVIEWER. 0160-6794. Periodical. US. English. qt. $15.00. Missouri School Counselor Association, PO Box 402, Jackson MO 63755. **Tel** (314)243-3611. **Ed** Paul Cameron. bk rev. adv acc. **Circ** 1,000. Provides up-to-date counseling information and materials for the school counselor. Current trends, theories and applications are discussed.

THE COUNSELING PSYCHOLOGIST. V. 1-. 0011-0000. Periodical. US. English. qt. $89.00. Sage Publications, 275 South Beverly Drive, Beverly Hills CA 90212. **Tel** (213)274-8003. **Ind/Abst** Women Stud. Abstr., Curr. Index J. Educ., Psychol. Abstr., Soc. Sci. Index, Soc. Sci. Citation Index. **LC** BF637.C6. **DD** 158. **NLM** W1 CO964. **CODEN** CPSYB.

COURRIER P.R.H. MONTREAL. VAT Courrier Personnalite et Relations Humaines-Montreal. No. 1 (Oct. 1977)-. 0821-0101. Periodical. CN. French. ir. $10.00. Sessions P R H, Bureau 1, 2130 Boul, Rosemont Quebec H2G 1T4 Canada. **DD** 158.1060714281.

CREATIVE LIVING TODAY. 8755-884X. Periodical. US. English. bm. $8.00. Creative Living Today, PO Box 808, Gatlinburg TN 37738. **DD** 158.

CREATIVITY IN ACTION. 1972. 0093-5263. Periodical. US. English. mo. $60.00. Creativity in Action, Sharon Valley Road, PO Box 603, Sharon CT 06069. **Tel** (203)364-0480. **Ed** Sidney X Shore. bk rev. Ideas, assistance for enhancement of creative thinking and action for individuals and groups. Tools for creativity, participation programs, creative puzzles, "Creativity Fitness Program" (copyrighted).

CRIMINAL JUSTICE AND BEHAVIOR. See Sociology: General Works, Theory - Social Pathology, Welfare, Criminology.

CRISIS. (CRISIS : INTERNATIONAL JOURNAL OF SUICIDE- AND CRISIS- STUDIES). VFOAT International Zeitschrift fur Selbstmord- und Krisen-Studien Revue International Sic pour l'Etude du Suicide et des Etats de Crise. Vol. 1, No. 1 (Apr. 1980)-. 0227-5910. Periodical. CN. English (includes some text in French and German). sa. 24.00 Domestic, $20.00 Foreign. C J Hogrefe Inc, 12/14 Bruce Park Avenue, Toronto Ontario M4P 2S3 Canada. **Tel** (416)482-6339. **Ed** Raymong Battegay. **Ind/Abst** Psychol. Abstr. **DD** 364.152205. **NLM** W1 CR202M. bk rev. adv acc. **Circ** 2,000. Serves as a forum for suicide studies, for the exchange and discussion of information, investigations, and results of suicide researchers from around the world. Vita.

CRITICAL PERSPECTIVES ON CONTEMPORARY PSYCHOLOGY. Vol. 1, No. 1 (Spring 1980)-. 0276-5330. Periodical. US. English. sa. $3.50 Domestic, $4.00 Foreign. Graduate Faculty of the New School for Social Research, 65-5th Avenue, New York NY 10003. **LC** BF1. **DD** 150.5.

CROSS-CULTURAL PSYCHOLOGY BULLETIN. (CROSS-CULTURAL PSYCHOLOGY BULLETIN : OFFICIAL PUBLICATION). Vol. 15, No. 1/ 2 (Feb/May 1981)-. 0710-068X. Periodical. CN. English. qt. Free to Members. Cross-Cultural Psychology Bulletin, c/o Dr J C Lasry, PO Box 6128 Station A, Montreal Quebec H3C 3J7 Canada. **DD** 155.80601. Cross-Cultural Psychology Newsletter, 0702-6056.

CUADERNOS DE PSICOLOGIA (BARCELONA, SPAIN). (CUADERNOS DE PSICOLOGIA). VFOAT Quaderns de Psicologia. Spanish (Catalan). ir. **Ind/Abst** Psychol. Abstr. **NLM** W1.

CUADERNOS SIGMUND FREUD. No. 1- May 1971-. Periodical. Spanish. ir.

CUMULATIVE AUTHOR INDEX TO PSYCHOLOGICAL ABSTRACTS. See Indexes/Abstracts.

CUMULATIVE SUBJECT INDEX TO PSYCHOLOGICAL ABSTRACTS. See Indexes/Abstracts.

CURRENT ISSUES IN CLINICAL PSYCHOLOGY. Main/Conf Merseyside Course in Clinical Psychology. Vol. 1-. 0741-9724. US. English. Plenum Press, 233 Spring Street, New York NY 10013. **Tel** (212)620-8000. **Ed** Eric Earas. **LC** RC469. **DD** 616.89005. **NLM** W3 ME56.

CURRENT ISSUES IN EUROPEAN SOCIAL PSYCHOLOGY. Series/Titl European Studies in Social Psychology. Vol. 1-. 0264-4517. UK. English. ir. Press Syndicate of the University of Cambridge, 32 East 57th Street, New York NY 10022. **LC** HM251. **DD** 302.05.

CURRENT PSYCHOLOGICAL RESEARCH. Began in 1981. 0144-3887. Periodical. UK. English. qt. $24.50. Transaction Books & Periodical, Rutgers University, New Brunswick NJ 08903. **Tel** (201)932-2280. **Ed** Antony J Chapman. **NLM** W1 CU807H. Publishes significant empirical contributions from all areas of psychology including critical review articles, book reviews and reports on new instrumentation and computer software.

CURRENT PSYCHOLOGICAL RESEARCH & REVIEWS. VFOAT Current Psychological Research and Reviews. Vol. 3, No. 1 (Spring 1984)-. 0737-8262. Periodical. US. English. qt. $36.00. Transaction Periodicals Consortium, Rutgers University, New Brunswick NJ 08903. **Ind/Abst** Curr. Contents, Soc. Sci. Citation Index, Soc. Sci. Index, Psychol. Abstr., ABC Pol Sci. **LC** BF1. **DD** 150.5. **NLM** W1. Current Psychological Research, 0144-3887; Current Psychological Reviews, 0144-3895.

CURRENT PSYCHOLOGICAL REVIEWS. Vol. 1, No. 1 (Jan.-Apr. 1981-). 0144-3895. Periodical. UK. English. ty. $90.00. Transaction Periodicals Consortium, Rutgers University, Department 2000, New Brunswick NJ 08903. **Tel** (201)832-2280. **Ed** Antony J Chapman. **NLM** W1 CU807I. bk rev. adv acc. **Circ** 700. Provides psychologists in applied fields with a means of keeping in touch with developments in diverse areas of psychology.

CURRENT TOPICS IN HUMAN INTELLIGENCE. Vol. 1-. 8755-0040. Monographic Series. US. English. an. Ablex Publishing Corp, 355 Chestnut Street, Norwood NJ 07648. **Tel** (201)767-8450. **Ed** Douglas Detterman. **DD** 153. Book series focusing on selected topics on human intelligence of current interest to researchers.

DAWN. See Philosophy.

DEATH STUDIES. Vol. 9, No. 1-. 0748-1187. Periodical. US. English. bm. $84.00. Hemisphere Publishing Corporation, 1010 Vermont Avenue NW, Washington DC 20005. **Tel** (202)783-3958. **Ed** Hannelore Wass. **Ind/Abst** Hospit. Lit. Index. **DD** 306. **NLM** W1. **CODEN** DESTEA. bk rev. adv acc. **Circ** 1,210. Referred papers covering death education, death-related counseling and terminal care, including all aspects of hospice and bereavement counseling, law and ethics related to terminally ill patients. Death Education, 0145-7624.

DEVELOPMENTAL PSYCHOBIOLOGY. See Biology.

DEVELOPMENTAL PSYCHOLOGY. Began in 1969. 0012-1649. Periodical. US. English. bm. $104.00. American Psychological Association, 1400 North Uhle, Arlington VA 22201. **Tel** (703)247-7802. **Ed** Susan Knapp. **Ind/Abst** Women Stud. Abstr., MLA Int. Bibliogr. Books Artic. Mod. Lang. Lit., Psychol. Abstr., Soc. Sci. Citation Index, Soc. Sci. Index, Sociol. Abstr., Lang. Lang. Behav. Abstr., Curr. Index J. Educ. adv acc. **Circ** 5,100. Articles that advance knowledge about human development across the life span.

DEVELOPMENTAL REVIEW. (DEVELOPMENTAL REVIEW : DR). VFOAT DR. Vol. 1, No. 1 (Mar. 1981)-. 0273-2297. Periodical. US.

Psychology

English. qt. $47.50. Academic Press, 4805 Sand Lake Road, Orlando FL 32819. **Tel** (305)345-4100. **Ind/Abst** Psychol. Abstr. LC BF721. DD 155. NLM W1 DE997UU.

THE DEVEREUX PAPERS. V. 1- Fall 1972-. Periodical. US. English. Devereux Foundation, Devon PA 19333. LC BF637.C45. DD 153.

DEVIANCE ET SOCIETE. See Sociology: General Works, Theory - Social Pathology, Welfare, Criminology.

DEVIANT BEHAVIOR. V. 1- 1979-. 0163-9625. Periodical. US. English. qt. $64.50. Hemisphere Publishing Corporation, 79 Madison Avenue, New York NY 10016. **Tel** (202)783-3958. Ed Clifton D Bryant. **Ind/Abst** Sociol. Abstr., Psychol. Abstr., Soc. Sci. Citation Index. LC HM1. DD 302.5. NLM W1 DE999H. **CODEN** DEBEDF. bk rev. adv acc. **Circ** 440. A forum for covering deviance and norm violation in society. A broad range of deviant behavior is presented and analyzed.

DIAGNOSTICA (GOTTINGEN, GERMANY). (DIAGNOSTICA). Began with Apr. 1955 issue. 0012-1924. Periodical. German. ir. **Tel** (416)482-6339. **Ind/Abst** Int. Aerosp. Abstr., Psychol. Abstr. NLM ZBF 431 D536. **CODEN** DGNSAQ. Pertains to the practical side of psychology: diagnostics and differential psychology. Special attention is paid to the development of tests and their application.

DIALOGUES, BEHAVIORAL SCIENCE RESEARCH. V. 1- , 1963-. 0419-0823. Periodical. US. English. Western Commission for Higher Education, PO Drawer P, Boulder CO 80302.

DIRECTORIO - COLEGIO DE PSICOLOGOS DE VENEZUELA. See Yearbooks, Almanacs, Directories.

DIRECTORIO DE MIEMBROS - SOCIEDAD INTERAMERICANA DE PSICOLOGIA. See Yearbooks, Almanacs, Directories.

DIRECTORY. See Yearbooks, Almanacs, Directories.

DIRECTORY - CANADIAN PSYCHOLOGICAL ASSOCIATION. See Yearbooks, Almanacs, Directories.

DIRECTORY, HANDBOOK - CALIFORNIA STATE PSYCHOLOGICAL ASSOCIATION. See Yearbooks, Almanacs, Directories.

DIRECTORY, HANDBOOK - PENNSYLVANIA PSYCHOLOGICAL ASSOCIATION. See Yearbooks, Almanacs, Directories.

DIRECTORY OF HANDWRITING ANALYSTS. See Yearbooks, Almanacs, Directories.

DIRECTORY OF MEMBERS - DISTRICT OF COLUMBIA PSYCHOLOGICAL ASSOCIATION. See Yearbooks, Almanacs, Directories.

DIRECTORY OF PSYCHOLOGISTS AND PSYCHOLOGICAL EXAMINERS LICENSED AND REGISTERED IN TENNESSEE. See Yearbooks, Almanacs, Directories.

DIRECTORY OF PSYCHOLOGISTS REGISTERED IN THE PROVINCE OF ONTARIO. See Yearbooks, Almanacs, Directories.

DIRECTORY OF THE AMERICAN PSYCHOLOGICAL ASSOCIATION. See Yearbooks, Almanacs, Directories.

DIRECTORY OF UNPUBLISHED EXPERIMENTAL MENTAL MEASURES. See Yearbooks, Almanacs, Directories.

DIRECTORY - THE NEW YORK SOCIETY OF CLINICAL PSYCHOLOGISTS, INC. See Yearbooks, Almanacs, Directories.

DISCIPLINE (NATIONAL CENTER FOR THE STUDY OF CORPORAL PUNISHMENT AND ALTERNATIVES IN THE SCHOOLS). (DISCIPLINE). Vol. 1, No. 1 (Winter 1980)-. Periodical. US. English. ir. $6.00. National Center for the Study of Corporal Punishment and Alternatives in the Schools, 833 Ritter Hall Temple University, Philadelphia PA 19122. **Tel** (215)787-6091. Ed Cynthia Strauss. bk rev. adv acc. **Circ** 200. (ctrl). The National Center for the study of corporal punishment and alternatives in the school's on-going journal highlights new research and topics of interest in the area of discipline.

DISCOURSE PROCESSES. See Linguistics.

DOBUTSU SHINRIGAKU NENPO. VFOAT Annual of Animal Psychology. V. 1- 1951-. 0003-5130. Periodical. JA. Japanese (text in English, with English summaries). sa. $12.00. Japan Publishers Trading Company Ltd, PO Box 5030/Tokyo International, Tokyo 100-31 Japan. **Ind/Abst** Life Sci. Collect., Psychol. Abstr. NLM W1 DO157.

THE DOWNSTATE SERIES OF RESEARCH IN PSYCHIATRY AND PSYCHOLOGY. V. 1-. 0162-2315. Monographic Series. US. English. ir. Plenum Press, 233 Spring Street, New York NY 10013. **Tel** (212)620-8000. NLM W1 DO945.

DRAGONFLIES. V. 1- Fall 1978-. 0190-7093. Periodical. US. English. $5.00. Editor Dragonflies, Department of Psychology, University of Dallas, Irving TX 75061. LC BF455.A1. DD 150.192.

DREAMWEAVER MAGAZINE. Vol. 1, No. 1 (Spring 1983)-. 0823-2180. Periodical. CN. English. qt. Dreamweaver Magazine, 6 Charles Street East, Toronto Ontario M4Y 1T2 Canada. DD 154.605. Dreamweaver (Toronto, Ont.), 0228-9342.

DREAMWORKS. VAT Dream Works. V. 1- Spring 1980-. 0192-2890. Periodical. US. English. qt. Human Sciences Press, 72-5th Avenue, New York NY 10011. **Tel** (212)243-6000. LC BF1074. DD 154.6305.

DUQUESNE STUDIES. PSYCHOLOGICAL SERIES. Began publication with V. 1 (1963). 0070-7716. Monographic Series. US. English. ir. Humanities Press, Atlantic Highlands NJ 07716. **Tel** (201)872-1441.

EARLY CHILD DEVELOPMENT AND CARE. (EARLY CHILD DEVELOPMENT AND CARE : ECDC). VFOAT ECDC, E.C.D.C. Began with July 1971 issue. 0300-4430. Periodical. UK. English. qt. $128.00. Gordon & Breach, PO Box 197, London WC2E 9PX England. **Tel** (01)836 5125. Ed Roy Evans. **Ind/Abst** Excerpta Med., Biol. Abstr., Educ. Index, Curr. Index J. Educ., Psychol. Abstr., Bibliogr. Index. LC HQ767.8. DD 305.2305. NLM W1 EA75. **CODEN** ECDCAD. bk rev. adv acc.

EDUCATIONAL AND PSYCHOLOGICAL RESEARCH. See Education (General).

EDUCATIONAL PSYCHOLOGIST. See Education (General) - Theory, Practice of Education.

EDUCATIONAL PSYCHOLOGY. Vol. 1, No. 1 (1981)-. 0144-3410. UK. English. qt. $126.00. Academic Press, 4805 Sand Lake Road, Orlando FI 32887. Ed Leo H T West. **Ind/Abst** Psychol. Abstr. LC LB1051. DD 370.15. NLM W1 ED875N.

EDUCATIONAL PSYCHOLOGY (GUILFORD, CONN.). See Education (General).

EKSPERIMENTALNOE ISSLEDOVANIE LICHNOSTI I TEMPERAMENTA. VFOAT Eksperimentalnye Issledovaniia Lichnosti I Temperamenta. UR. Russian. 0.50 Single Issue. LC AS262.P37, BF798.

EMOTION. Vol. 1-. Monographic Series. US. English. Ed Robert Plutchik and Henry Kellerman. NLM W1 EM668.

EMOTIONAL FIRST AID (NEW YORK, N.Y.). (EMOTIONAL FIRST AID). Vol. 1, No. 1 (Spring 1984)-. 0739-828X. Periodical. US. English. qt. $50.00. Brunner/Mazel Inc, 19 Union Square West, New York NY 10003. **Tel** (212)924-3344. Ed James L Greenstone. NLM W1. bk rev. adv acc. Offers a wide range of topics, both theoretical and practical, related to crisis intervention. Emotional First Aid, 0739-828X.

ENERGY AND CHARACTER. Volume 1- Jan. 1970-. 0013-7472. Periodical. UK. English. sa. 7.00 Domestic, $15.00. Abbotsbury Publications, Abbotsbury Weymouth, Dorset England. **Tel** (0305)441418. Ed David Boadella. bk rev. **Circ** 1,000. (ctrl). Somatic psychology, bioenergetics, remedial work, prevention of neurosis sociology of emotional I and disfunction.

ENSENANZA E INVESTIGACION EN PSICOLOGIA. Vol. 1, No. 1- June 1975-. Periodical. MX. Spanish. sa. $12.00. Enzenanza Investigation, Apdo Postal 19-174, Mexico 03910 Mexico DF. **Ind/Abst** Psychol. Abstr.

ENVIRONMENTAL PERCEPTION RESEARCH. WORKING PAPER. VAT Working Paper. Environmental Perception Research. No. 1-. 0710-0396. CN. English. $2.00 per No. Institute for Environmental Studies, University of Toronto, Toronto Ontario M5S 1A4 Canada. DD 155.9114.

ESSENCE CEASED. V. 1-5, No. 3. 0384-8833. Periodical. CN. English. qt. Dr S Fleming, Department of Psychology, Atkinson College, York University, 4700 Keele Street, Downsview Ontario Canada. **Ind/Abst** Psychol. Abstr. NLM W1 ES674W.

ESTUDIOS DE PSICOLOGIA. 1-. 0210-9395. Periodical. SP. Spanish. qt. 1.800. Estudios de Psicologia, Elog Gonzalo 19, Madrid -10 Spain. NLM W1 ES96SG.

ETHOLOGY AND SOCIOBIOLOGY. V. 1- Oct. 1979-. 0162-3095. Periodical. US. English. qt. Elsevier Science Publiahing Company, PO Box 1663/Grand Central Station, New York NY 10163. **Ind/Abst** Life Sci. Collect., Sociol. Abstr., Psychol. Abstr. LC BF1. DD 150.5. NLM W1 ET448. **CODEN** ETSOD8.

ETHOS. V. 1- Spring 1973-. 0091-2131. Periodical. US. English. qt. $30.00. Society for Psychological Anthropology, 1703 New Hampshire Avenue NW, Washington DC 20009. **Tel** (202)232-800. Ed Robert A Paui. **Ind/Abst** Sociol. Abstr., Psychol. Abstr. LC GN270. DD 155.805. **CODEN** ETHSAU. adv acc. **Circ** 1,045. (ctrl). Thought and research in psychological anthropology and cross-cultural psychology. Encompassing culture and cognition, transcultural psychiatry, ethnopsychiatry, socialization, psychoanalytic, anthropology and other psychocultural topics.

ETUDES DE PSYCHOLOGIE ET DE PHILOSOPHIE. See Philosophy.

EUROPAISCHE HOCHSCHULSCHRIFTEN. REIHE 6. PSYCHOLOGIE. (EUROPAISCHE HOCHSCHULSCHRIFTEN. REIHE 6, PSYCHOLOGIE). VFOAT Psychologie, Publications Universitaires Europeennes. Serie 6, Psychologie, European University Papers. Series 6, Psychology. Began with: V. 1, in 1968. 0531-7347. Monographic Series. German. ir. LC UNC. NLM W1 EU586D.

EUROPEAN MONOGRAPHS IN SOCIAL PSYCHOLOGY. 1- 1971-. 0071-2957. Monographic Series. UK. English. ir. Academic Press, 4805 Sand Lake Road, Orlando FL 32887. **Tel** (305)345-4100. **Ind/Abst** Psychol. Abstr. NLM W1 EU721F.

EXPRESS DE LA MONTAGNE. (MOUNTAIN EXPRESS). VFOAT Express de la Montagne. VAT Mountain Express (Montreal). Vol. 1, No. 1 (Winter '82/'83). 0821-669X. Periodical. CN. English (text in and French with French text on inverted pages). qt. $20.00. Quebec Society for Autism, 1181 Montagne Street, Montreal Quebec H3G 1Z2 Canada. **Tel** (514)861-1803. Ed Louise Linschoten. DD 618.928982. bk rev. **Circ** 1,500. (ctrl). Information on newest publications, research, government, social services, programs and conference calender. Memo, 0713-5742.

THE FLORIDA PSYCHOLOGIST. VFOAT FP. Vol. 10, No. 3 (summer issue 1960)-. 0046-4171. US. English. qt. Florida Psychological Association, 1731 Mockingbird Lane Gessner, Lakeland FL 33801. F.P.A. Newsletter.

FURTHER ASPECTS OF PIAGET'S WORK. 1-. English. ir. Routledge & K Paul, Broadway House/Newtown Road, Henley Thames RG9 1EN England. LC BF721.

THE G. STANLEY HALL LECTURE SERIES. Vol. 1-. 8756-7865. US. English. an. American Psychological Association, PO Box 2710, Hyattsville MD 20784. **Ind/Abst** Psychol. Abstr. DD 150.

GEDRAG. Began in 1973. 0377-7308. Periodical. NE. Dutch (English). bm. Gedrag, Tijdschrift Voor Erasmuslaan 16, Nijmegen Netherlands. **Ind/Abst** Psychol. Abstr., Soc. Sci. Citation Index. LC BF8.D8. NLM W1 GE103H. **CODEN** GEDRDT. Nijmeegs Tijdschrift Voor Psychologie, 0029-0475; Hypothese, 0018-8352.

GENES AND GENDER. 0271-6488. Monographic Series. US. English. an. $8.95. Gordian Press Inc, 85 Tompkins Street, Staten Island NY 10304. **Tel** (718)273-4700. **Ed** John Corta. adv acc. **Circ** 5,000. Genes and Gender Collective examines the issues of 'Genetic Determinism', as a widely accepted ideology requiring exposure as a perversion of science and an instrument of oppression of the most vulnerable sectors in the United States.

GENESIS OF BEHAVIOR. V. 1-. 0195-5594. Monographic Series. US. English. ir. Plenum Press, 233 Spring Street, New York NY 10013. **Tel** (212)620-8000. **NLM** W1 GE275.

THE GENETIC EPISTEMOLOGIST. (THE GENETIC EPISTEMOLOGIST : THE QUARTERLY JOURNAL OF THE JEAN PIAGET SOCIETY). Began with Oct. 1976 issue. 0740-9583. Periodical. US. English. qt. $20.00. Genetic Epistemologist, Jean Piaget Society, 113 Willard Hall, University of Delaware, Newark DE 19716. **Tel** (302)451-2311. **Ed** Frank B Murray. **LC** BF712. **DD** 155.41805. bk rev. adv acc. **Circ** 500. Reviews of empirical or theoretical literature on current topics of genetic epistemology or practical applications. *Newsletter - Jean Piaget Society.*

GENETIC PSYCHOLOGY MONOGRAPHS *CEASED.* V. 1- Jan. 1926. Ceased with Vol. 110, second half. 0016-6677. Periodical. US. English. qt. $42.00. Heldref Publications, 4000 Albemarle Street NW/Suite 302, Washington DC 20036. **Tel** (202)362-6445. **Ed** Doris Chalfin. **Ind/Abst** Life Sci. Collect., Lang. Lang. Behav. Abstr., Women Stud. Abstr., Biol. Abstr., Psychol. Abstr., Nuci. Sci. Abstr., Index Med., Soc. Sci. Citation Index, Sociol. Abstr. **LC** LB1101. **DD** 155. **NLM** W1 GE282. **CODEN** GPMOA3. adv acc. **Circ** 942. Founded in 1891 by G Stanley Hall, the journal is devoted to developmental and clinical psychology monographs in each issue.

GENETIC, SOCIAL, AND GENERAL PSYCHOLOGY MONOGRAPHS. Vol. 111, No. 1 (Feb. 1985)-. 8756-7547. Periodical. US. English. qt. $42.00. Heldref Publications, 4000 Albemarle Street NW, Washington DC 20016. **Tel** (202)362-6445. **Ed** Mary Morello Shafer. **Ind/Abst** Abstr. Soc. Work., Biol. Abstr., Child Dev. Abstr. Bibliogr., Curr. Aware. Biol. Sci., DSH Abstr., Except. Child Educ. Abstr., Excerpta Med., Index Med., Indian Psychol. Abstr., Psychol. Abstr., Rev. Relig. Res., Sociol. Educ. Abstr. **DD** 150. adv acc. **Circ** 875. Issued also in microform. Publishes articles of monograph length, devoted to research and theory. Monographs may deal with the biological as well as the behavioral and social aspects of psychology. *Genetic Psychology Monographs, 0016-6677.*

GENETIC STUDIES OF GENIUS. 1925-. US. English. ir. Stanford University Press, Stanford CA 94305. **LC** BF412. **DD** 136.765082.

GERMAN JOURNAL OF PSYCHOLOGY. (THE GERMAN JOURNAL OF PSYCHOLOGY). V. 1- Jan. 1977-. 0705-5870. CN. English. qt. 58.00 Domestic, $48.00 US. Hogrefe International Inc, 12-14 Bruce Park Avenue, Toronto Ontario M4P 2S3 Canada. **Tel** (416)482-6339. **Ed** R Amthauer, H Feger, K Foppa, G Lueer, E Mittenecker, K Pawlik, H Sydow and W H Tack. **Ind/Abst** Psychol. Abstr. **LC** BF1. **DD** 150.5, 150.8. **NLM** Z 7203 G373. Contains in each issue a comprehensive look at a particular field of modern German psychology in the form of a review article or report.

GESTALT THEORY. (GESTALT THEORY : OFFICIAL JOURNAL OF THE SOCIETY FOR GESTALT THEORY AND ITS APPLICATIONS (GTA)). Vol. 1, No. 1 (Oct. 1979-). 0170-057X. Periodical. GW. English (German). sa. Dr Dietrich Steinkopff Verlag, PO Box 1008/Saalbaustrasse 12, 6100 Darmstadt 11 West Germany. **Ind/Abst** Psychol. Abstr. **LC** BF203. **DD** 150.198205. **NLM** W1 GE831.

GIORNALE ITALIANO DI PSICOLOGIA (BOLOGNA (ITALY) : 1978). (GIORNALE ITALIANO DI PSICOLOGIA). Began with issue for Apr. 1978. 0390-5349. Periodical. IT. Italian. ty. 90.000 Domestic, 120.000 Foreign. Societa Editrice Il Mulino Spa, Via Santo Stefano 6, 40125 Bologna Italy. **Ind/Abst** Psychol. Abstr. **NLM** W1 GI814G. *Giornale Italiano di Psicologia.*

GIORNALE STORICO DI PSICOLOGIA DINAMICA. V. 1- (Issue 1-). 0391-2515. Periodical. IT. Italian (with summaries in English). ir. 100.00. C C Postale No 19932003, Intestato a Rivista di Psicologia Analitica, Via Gallonio 8, 00161 Roma Italy. **Tel** 4270177. **Ed** Aldo Carotenuto. **Ind/Abst** Psychol. Abstr. **LC** BF84. **Circ** 1,000.

GRADUATE STUDY IN PSYCHOLOGY *CEASED.* Began in 1968/69. Ceased with 16th Ed. 0072-5277. Periodical. US. English. an. American Psychological Association, 1200 17th Street NW, Washington DC 20036. **LC** BF77. **DD** 150.71173. **NLM** BF 77 G733.

GRADUATE STUDY IN PSYCHOLOGY AND ASSOCIATED FIELDS. 1983-. 0742-7220. Periodical. US. English. be. American Psychological Association, 1400 North Uhle Street, Arlington VA 22201. **Tel** (703)591-7225. **LC** BF77. **DD** 150.71173. **NLM** BF 77. *Graduate Study in Psychology.*

GROUP. V. 1- Spring 1977-. 0362-4021. Periodical. US. English. qt. $44.00. Brunner/Mazel Inc, 19 Union Square West, New York NY 10003. **Tel** (212)924-3344. **Ed** Dorothy Flapan, Peter Schlachet. **Ind/Abst** Excerpta Med., Abstr. Soc. Work., Psychol. Abstr. **LC** RC488.A1. **DD** 616.8915. **NLM** W1 GR799. **CODEN** GROUDE. bk rev. adv acc. **Circ** 1,000. Group psychotherapy-its conceptualizations and clinical applications to diverse populations.

GRUPPENDYNAMIK. Began publication in 1970. 0046-6514. Periodical. GW. German. qt. $30.03. W E Saarbach Gmbh, Postfach 101610, D5000 Koln 1 West Germany. **Ind/Abst** Psychol. Abstr. **CODEN** GRUPDT.

GUIDEPOST. *See* Education (General).

HAKSUL CHAPCHI MOKCHA SOKPO. KYOYUKHAK, SIMNIHAK, SAHOEHAK PYON. *See* Education (General).

THE HANDBOOK OF CERTIFICATION/LICENSURE REQUIREMENTS FOR SCHOOL PSYCHOLOGISTS. 1st- Ed. US. English. ir. National Association of School Psychologists, 10 Overland Drive, Stratford CT 06497. **Tel** (203)377-4249. **Ed** Timothy J Sewall and Douglas T Brown.

HANDBOOK OF PERCEPTION. V. 1- 1974-. Monographic Series. US. English. ir. $500.00. Academic Press, 4805 Sand Lake Road, Orlando FL 32819. **Ed** Carterette and Friedman. A multivolume treatise which serves as an authoritative reference source for all scientists and scholars interested in human perception.

HEARTWOOD. V. 1, No. 1 (Autumn 1982)-. 0825-5318. Periodical. CN. English. $8.00. Cortes Centre for Human Development, 3675 West 16th Avenue, Vancouver British Columbia V6R 3C3 Canada. **DD** 155.2505.

HISTORY OF PSYCHOANALYSIS MONOGRAPH. *See* Medicine - Psychiatry, Psychopathology.

HISTORY OF PSYCHOLOGY IN AUTOBIOGRAPHY. (A HISTORY OF PSYCHOLOGY IN AUTOBIOGRAPHY). V. 1- 1930-. 0097-6091. US. English. Prentice Hall, Route 8 West, Englewood Cliffs NJ 07632. **LC** BF105. **DD** 150.922, B. **NLM** W1 HI86.

HISTORY OF PSYCHOLOGY SERIES. 0146-0331. Monographic Series. US. English. ir. Scholars Facsimiles & Reprints, PO Box 344, Delmar NY 12054. **Tel** (518)439-5978.

HUMAN BEHAVIOR AND ENVIRONMENT. (HUMAN BEHAVIOR AND ENVIRONMENT. ADVANCES IN THEORY AND RESEARCH). V. 1- 1976-. 0148-8686. Periodical. US. English. ir. Plenum Publishing Corporation, 233 Spring Street, New York NY 10013. **Tel** (212)620-8000. **Ed** Irwin Altman and Joachim F Wohlwill. **Ind/Abst** Psychol. Abstr. **NLM** W1 HU444Q.

HUMAN DEVELOPMENT. V. 8- 1965-. 0018-716X. Periodical. English (text in French or German with summaries in all three languages). bm. 214.-. S Karger AG, PO Box, CH-4009 Basel Switzerland. **Tel** (061)39 08 80. **Ed** W Edelstrin, J A Meacham H Sinclair. **Ind/Abst** Biol. Abstr., Curr. Index J. Educ., Excerpta Med., Life Sci. Collect., MLA Int. Bibliogr. Books Artic. Mod. Lang. Lit., Psychol. Abstr., Soc. Welf. Soc. Plan./Policy Soc. Dev., Sociol. Abstr., Women Stud. Abstr., Educ. Index, Index Med., Nuci. Sci. Abstr., Curr. Index J. Educ. **NLM** W1 HU446C. **CODEN** HUDEA8. adv acc. Publishes original articles on all aspects of development throughout the human life span, from infancy through aging. Both social and cognitive development are covered. *Vita Humana, 0375-4774.*

HUMAN DEVELOPMENT. (HUMAN DEVELOPMENT . . .). **VFOAT** Annual Editions Human Development. 80/81-. 0278-4661. US. English. an. $8.95. Dushkin Publishing Group Inc, Sluice Dock, Guilford CT 06437. **Tel** (203)453-4351. **Ed** Hiram Fitzgerald and Michael Walraven. **LC** HQ768. **DD** 305.2. Updated collection of public press articles covering current issues in human development. Includes topic guide and complete index. *Annual Editions. Readings in Human Development, 0090-5348.*

HUMAN DEVELOPMENT (NEW YORK, N .Y. : 1980). (HUMAN DEVELOPMENT). Vol. 1, No. 1 (Spring 1980)-. 0197-3096. Periodical. US. English. qt. $18.00. Le Jacq Publishing Inc, 53 Park Place, New York NY 10007. **Tel** (212)766-4300. **Ed** James J Gill. **Ind/Abst** Cathol. Period. Lit. Index, Energy Inf. Abstr., Environ. Abstr., Women Stud. Abstr., Curr. Index J. Educ. **LC** BV4012. **DD** 253.5. bk rev. **Circ** 13,000.

HUMAN FACTORS. V. 1- Sept. 1958-. 0018-7208. Periodical. US. English. bm. $50.00. Human Factors Society, PO Box 1369, Santa Monica CA 90406. **Tel** (213)394-1811. **Ed** Charles O Hopkins. **Ind/Abst** CIS Abstr., Coal Abstr., Comput. Control Abstr., Electr. Electron. Abstr., Electron. Pub. Abstr., Energy Inf. Abstr., Energy Res. Abstr., Eng. Index, Soc. Sci. Citation Index, Sci. Cit. Index, Abr. Ed., Phys. Abstr., Comput. Rev., Comput. Abstr., Environ. Abstr., Excerpta Med., Index Med., Int. Aerosp. Abstr., Life Sci. Collect., Manage. Market. Abstr., Sci. Abstr. Sect. A. Phys. Abstr., Psychol. Abstr., Ship Abstr., Appl. Sci. Technol. Index, Biol. Abstr., Nuci. Sci. Abstr. **LC** T58.A2. **DD** 658.01. **NLM** W1 HU447. **CODEN** HUFAA6. (cum index). **Circ** 6,000. Available on microfilm from University Microfilms. Scholarly journal investigating the relationship between humans, their systems, products and environments, ergonomics, design, human-computer interface, industrial psychology, etc.

HUMAN STRESS. 0885-1174. Periodical. US. English. an. AMS Press Inc, 56 East 13th Street, New York NY 10003. **Tel** (212)777-4700. Behavioral, environmental and physiological original studies examining causes of human stress and techniques of stress reduction.

IACD QUARTERLY. **VAT** Illinois Association for Counseling and Development Quarterly. 8756-2189. Periodical. US. English. qt. IACD, Box 220, Charleston IL 61920. **DD** 158. *Illinois Guidance and Personnel Association Quarterly.*

IMAGE UNDERSTANDING. *See* Computers and Computer Science.

IMAGINATION, COGNITION AND PERSONALITY. **VFOAT** Journal of Imagination, Cognition, and Personality. Vol. 1, No. 1 (1981-82)-. 0276-2366. Periodical. US. English. qt. $69.00. Baywood Publishing, 120 Marine Street, PO Box D, Farmingdale NY 11735. **Tel** (516)249-2464. **Ed** Jerome L Singer & Kenneth S Pope. **Ind/Abst** Excerpta Med., Psychol. Abstr. **LC** BF311. **DD** 153.05. **NLM** W1 IM457T. bk rev. Presents the current understanding of the nature functions, and resources of the stream of consciousness, along with practice, scientifically based applications and interventions. *Journal of Altered States of Consciousness.*

IMPRINT. 0279-0408. Periodical. US. English. mo. Northern New Jersey Mensa, c/o Janet Cuccinelli Editrix, 17 Wierimus Lane, Hillsadle NJ 07642.

THE INDEX OF PSYCHOANALYTIC WRITINGS. *See* Indexes/Abstracts.

INDEX TO CURRENT ELECTROENCEPHALOGRAPHIC LITERATURE. *See* Indexes/Abstracts.

INDIAN JOURNAL OF APPLIED PSYCHOLOGY. Vol. 1, No. 1 (Jan. 1964)-. 0019-5073. Periodical. II. English. sa. $21.00. The Madras Psychology Society, Department of Psychology, University of Madras, Madras 600 005 India. **Ind/Abst** Biol. Abstr., Psychol. Abstr. **LC** BF636.A1. **DD** 158.05. **NLM** W1 IN206PH. **CODEN** IJAPBI.

INDIAN JOURNAL OF BEHAVIOUR. Periodical. II. English. qt. 100 Domestic, 50 Foreign. Indian Journal of Behaviour, 515 Tonachikoppal Extension, Mysore 570009 India. **Ed** T R Rao. **Ind/Abst** Psychol. Abstr. **LC** BF1. **DD** 150.5. bk rev. adv acc. **Circ** 500.

INDIAN JOURNAL OF CLINICAL PSYCHOLOGY. V. 1- Mar. 1974-. 0303-2582. Periodical. II. English. sa. 25.00. Impex India, 2118 Ansari Road, New Delhi 110002 India. **Tel** 278034. **Ed** A C Moudgil. **Ind/Abst** Sociol. Abstr., Soc. Welf. Soc. Plan./Policy Soc. Dev., Psychol. Abstr., Lang. Lang. Behav. Abstr. **LC** RC467. **DD** 616.89005. **NLM** W1 IN207B. bk rev. adv acc. **Circ** 700. Devoted to research in areas of clinical psychology mental health psychiatry and other allied and behavioural sciences.

INDIAN PSYCHOLOGICAL ABSTRACTS. *See* Indexes/Abstracts.

INDIAN PSYCHOLOGICAL REVIEW. V. 1- July 1964-. 0019-6215. Periodical. II. English. mo. 123.50. Tiwari Kothi Belanganj Afra, c/o Managing Editor, Afra 282094 India. **Tel** 64965. **Ed** S Jalota and M C Joshi. **Ind/Abst** Psychol. Abstr. **LC** BF1. **NLM** W1 IN27R. bk rev. adv acc. **Circ** 2,000. The first regular journal of India covering all the fields of psychology.

INDIAN PSYCHOLOGIST. Vol. 1, No. 1 (Apr. 1982)-. Periodical. English. sa. 30 Domestic, $8.00. Centre of Advanced Study in Psychology, Utkal University, Bhubaneswar-751, 004 Orissa India. **Tel** 53639. **Ed** S K Misra. **Ind/Abst** Psychol. Abstr. **LC** BF1. **DD** 150.5. adv acc. **Circ** 700. The journal publishes empirical and theoretical research articles of high standard half yearly. American Psychological Association's style is followed strictly.

THE INDIVIDUAL PSYCHOLOGIST *CEASED.* V. 1-18. 0019-7149. Periodical. US. English. sa. **LC** BF1. **DD** 150.5. **NLM** W1 IN352U. **CODEN** IPSYAH.

INDIVIDUAL PSYCHOLOGY. Vol. 38, No. 1 (Mar. 1982)-. 0277-7010. Periodical. US. English. qt. $30.00. University of Texas Press, Box 7819, Austin TX 78713. **Tel** (512)471-4531. **Ed** Guy J Manaster. **Ind/Abst** Sociol. Abstr., Psychol. Abstr. **LC** BF1. **DD** 150195405. **NLM** W1 IN352W. bk rev. adv acc. **Circ** 700. (ctrl). Current scholarly and professional research dealing with all aspects of the social, psychological, and personality theory founded by Alfred Adler. *Journal of Individual Psychology, 0022-1805; Individual Psychologists, 0019-7149.*

THE INDUSTRIAL-ORGANIZATIONAL PSYCHOLOGIST. **VFOAT** T.I.P. Began with Dec. 1972 issue. 0739-1110. Periodical. US. English. qt. $20.00. Industrial Organizational, 550 Madison Avenue, New York NY 10022. **Tel** (515)294-6402. **Ed** Paul M Muchinsky. **LC** HF5548.7. **DD** 158.705. adv acc. **Circ** 3,200. (ctrl). Provides up-to-date information on human resources issues in industrial-organizational psychology-selection, productivity, careers, graduate programs, international issues. *Industrial Psychologist.*

INFANT BEHAVIOR & DEVELOPMENT. **VAT** Infant Behavior and Development. V. 1- Jan. 1978-. 0163-6383. Periodical. US. English. qt. $72.50. Ablex Publishing Company, 355 Chestnut Street, Norwood NJ 07648. **Tel** (201)767-8450. **Ed** Carolyn Rovee-Collier. **Ind/Abst** MLA Int. Bibliogr. Books Artic. Mod. Lang. Lit., Sociol. Abstr., Soc. Welf. Soc. Plan./Policy Soc. Dev., Lang. Lang. Behav. Abstr., Excerpta Med., Biol. Abstr., Psychol. Abstr. **LC** BF719. **DD** 155.42205. **NLM** W1 IN3994. **CODEN** IBDEDP. adv acc. **Circ** 800. First journal devoted exclusively to infancy, providing original empirical and theoretical studies.

INFANT MENTAL HEALTH JOURNAL. *See* Medicine - Pediatrics.

INNOVATIONS IN CLINICAL PRACTICE. Vol. 1-. 0737-125X. US. English. Professional Resource Exchange Inc, PO Box 15560, Sarasota FL 34277-1560. **Ed** Peter A Keller and Lawrence G Ritt. **NLM** W1 IN455C.

INSIGHT & HINDSIGHT. **VFOAT** Insight and Hindsight. Vol. 1, No. 1 (Spring 1982)-. 0737-7215. Periodical. US. English. $6.00. **LC** BF1. **DD** 150.5.

INTELLIGENCE. V. 1- Jan. 1977-. 0160-2896. Periodical. US. English. qt. $65.00. Ablex Publishing Corporation, 355 Chestnut Street, Norwood NJ 07648. **Tel** (201)767-8450. **Ed** Douglas Detterman. **Ind/Abst** Curr. Index J. Educ., Psychol. Abstr., Biol. Abstr. **LC** BF431. **DD** 153.905. **NLM** W1 IN651K. **CODEN** NTLLDT. adv acc. **Circ** 700. Journal devoted to original research in all facets of intelligence studies.

INTERAMERICAN PSYCHOLOGIST. 0146-034X. Periodical. US. English and Spanish. Interamerican Society of Psychology, Department of Psychology, De Paul University, 2323 North Seminary Avenue, Chicago IL 60614.

THE INTERBEHAVIORIST. 8755-612X. Periodical. US. English. qt. $12.00. Edward K Morris/ Editor, Department of Human Development, 212 B Hawoth Hall/University of Kansas, Lawrence KS 66045. **Tel** (913)864-4840. **Ed** Edward K Morris. **DD** 150. bk rev. adv acc. **Circ** 150. A publication of news, discussion, reviews, and articles on interbehavioral psychology. A contestualistic, field-theory approach to a natural science of psychology.

INTERFACES IN PSYCHOLOGY. No. 1 (1984)-. 0743-2135. Periodical. US. English. an. Texas Technical Press, Texas Technical University, Lubbock TX 79409. **Tel** (806)742-2468. **Ed** John Harvey. **DD** 150. **Circ** 500. The series results from annual symposia organized by the Texas Tech University Department of Psychology. They are numbered serially, paged separately and priced individually.

INTERNATIONAL FLASH. No. 1- Oct. 1976-. 0146-0145. Periodical. US. English. qt. $24.00 Institution, Free to Members. International Council of Psychologists, 4014 Cody Road, Sherman Oaks CA 91403.

THE INTERNATIONAL FORUM FOR LOGOTHERAPY. **VFOAT** Logotherapy. Vol. 1, No. 1 (Winter 1978-Spring 1979)-. 0191-3379. Periodical. US. English. sa. $36.00. The International Forum for Logotherapy, 2000 D Dwight Way, Berkeley, CA 94704. **Tel** (415)845-2522. **Ed** Joseph Fabry. **Ind/Abst** Psychol. Abstr. **LC** RC489.L6. **DD** 616.8914. **CODEN** IFLODL. bk rev. adv acc. **Circ** 800. (ctrl). Philosophy and methods of Viktor Frankl's Logotherapy helping people find meaning and direction in their lives. *Uniquest, 0360-8182.*

INTERNATIONAL FORUM FOR PSYCHOANALYSIS. Vol. 1, No. 1-. 0738-8217. Periodical. US. English. qt. $45.00. Analytic Press, 365 Broadway, Hillsdale NJ 07642. **Ind/Abst** Chicago Psychoanal. Lit. Index. **NLM** W1.

INTERNATIONAL JOURNAL OF BEHAVIORAL DEVELOPMENT. (INTERNATIONAL JOURNAL OF BEHAVIORAL DEVELOPMENT : IJBD). **VFOAT** IJBD. Vol. 1, No. 1 (Jan. 1978)-. 0165-0254. Periodical. English. qt. $83.59. North-Holand Publication Company, Box 211, 1000 AE Amsterdam Netherlands. **Ind/Abst** Cumul. Index Nurs. Allied Health Lit., Biol. Abstr., Curr. Index J. Educ., Psychol. Abstr. **LC** BF712. **DD** 155.05. **NLM** W1 IN7655L. **CODEN** IJBDDY.

THE INTERNATIONAL JOURNAL OF CLINICAL NEUROPSYCHOLOGY. Vol. 6, No. 1-. 0749-8470. Periodical. US. English. qt. $105.00. Melnic Press Inc, PO Box 6216, Madison WI 53716. **Tel** (608)222-6611. **Ed** Charles J Golden. **Ind/Abst** Excerpta Med., Life Sci. Collect. **DD** 616. bk rev. adv acc. **Circ** 1,500. (ctrl). A quarterly journal devoted to the understanding, measurement and treatment of maladaptive human behavior dependent upon brain functioning. *Clinical Neuropsychology, 0197-3681.*

INTERNATIONAL JOURNAL OF PSYCHO-ANALYSIS. (THE INTERNATIONAL JOURNAL OF PSYCHO-ANALYSIS). V. 1- 1920-. 0020-7578. Periodical. UK. English. qt. 46.00 Domestic, $91.00 Foreign. Bailliere Tindall, 1 St Annes Road, Eastbourne East Sussex BN21 3UN England. **Tel** 01 580 4952. **Ed** T T S Hayley. **Ind/Abst** Excerpta Med., Biol. Abstr., Psychol. Abstr., Index Med., Soc. Sci. Citation Index. **LC** BF173.A2. **NLM** W1 IN777. **CODEN** IJPSAA. (cum index). bk rev. adv acc. **Circ** 7,000. Contributions to the theory and practice of psychoanalysis.

INTERNATIONAL JOURNAL OF PSYCHOLOGY. **VFOAT** International Union of Psychological Science, Journal International de Psychologie, Union Internationale de Psychologie Scientifique. V. 1- 1966-. 0020-7594. Periodical. NE. English (French). bm. Elsevier Science Publishers, PO Box 211, 1000 AE Amsterdam Netherlands. **Tel** (020)5803.911. **Ind/Abst** Psychol. Abstr., Bibliogr. Index, Lang. Lang. Behav. Abstr., Sociol. Abstr., Soc. Sci. Citation Index. **LC** BF1. **DD** 150.5. **NLM** W1. **CODEN** IJPSBB.

INTERNATIONAL PSYCHOLOGIST. 0047-116X. Periodical. US. English. qt. $24.00. c/o Patricia Cautley/Secretary General, 4805 Regent Street, Madison WI 53705. **Tel** q213)224-3156. **Ed** Carleton Shay. **LC** UNC. **NLM** W1 IN827Y. bk rev. adv acc. **Circ** 1,700. (ctrl). News of organization, of practice of psychology in different countries, own convention and other international meetings, crosscultural exchange, and book reviews.

INTERNATIONAL REVIEW OF MENTAL IMAGERY. **VFOAT** International Review of Mental Imagery Series. Vol. 1-. 0741-0131. US. English. $29.95. **Ed** Anees A Sheikh. **DD** 153. **NLM** W1 IN833 (P.

INTERNATIONAL REVIEW OF PSYCHO-ANALYSIS. (THE INTERNATIONAL REVIEW OF PSYCHO-ANALYSIS). V. 1- 1974-. 0306-2643. Periodical. UK. English. qt. $89.50. Bailliere Tindall, 1 St Annes Road/ Eastbourne, E Sussex BN21 3UN England. **Ind/Abst** Psychol. Abstr. **LC** BF173.A2. **DD** 616.891705. **NLM** W1 IN834H. **CODEN** IRPADF.

INTERNATIONAL SERIES IN EXPERIMENTAL PSYCHOLOGY (OXFORD, OXFORDSHIRE : 1977). (INTERNATIONAL SERIES IN EXPERIMENTAL PSYCHOLOGY). Began with: Vol. 22, Published in 1977. Monographic Series. UK. English. ir. **LC** UNC. **DD** 150.724. **NLM** W1 IN835JEA. *International Series of Monographs in Experimental Psychology (Oxford, Oxfordshire : 1977).*

INTERNATIONAL SERIES OF MONOGRAPHS IN EXPERIMENTAL PSYCHOLOGY (OXFORD, OXFORDSHIRE: 1977). (INTERNATIONAL SERIES OF MONOGRAPHS IN EXPERIMENTAL PSYCHOLOGY). V. 21. 0149-8908. Monographic Series. UK. English. ir. Pergamon Press, c/o Cashier, 395 Sawmill River Road, Elmsford NY 10523. **Ed** H J Eysenck. **NLM** W1 IN835K. *International Series in Experimental Psychology, 0364-0841.*

INTERPRETATION. Jan./Mar. 1967-. CN. French. sa. $7.00 Per No. Societe d Editions Interpretation, 772 rue Davaar, Montreal Quebec H2V 3B2 Canada. **DD** 157.205. **NLM** W1 IN97.

IPO ANNUAL PROGRESS REPORT. **Main/Corp** Institute for Perception Research. **VFOAT** Annual Progress Report. No. 1- 1966-. Periodical. NE. English. an. Insitute Plantenziektekundig Onder Bibnnehaven 12, Wageningen The Netherlands. **Ind/Abst** Psychol. Abstr. **NLM** W1 I266G.

IRCS MEDICAL SCIENCE. PSYCHIATRY AND CLINICAL PSYCHOLOGY. *See* Medicine - Psychiatry, Psychopathology.

IRISH JOURNAL OF PSYCHOLOGY. (THE IRISH JOURNAL OF PSYCHOLOGY). V. 1- May 1971-. 0303-3910. Periodical. IE. English. ir. The Irish Journal of Psychology, Woodlands Renmore, Galway Ireland. **Ind/Abst** Br. Educ. Index, Psychol. Abstr., Biol. Abstr., Psychol. Read. Guide, Curr. Contents Behav. Soc. Educ. Sci., Soc. Sci. Citation Index. **NLM** W1 IR434. **CODEN** IRJPAR.

ISPT JOURNAL OF RESEARCH. **Main/Corp** Institute for Studies in Psychological Testing. V. 1- Jan. 1977-. Periodical. English. sa. $20.00. Institute for Studies in Psychological Testing, 110 Karanpur, Dehradun 248001 India. **LC** BF176. **DD** 150.287.

ISRAEL JOURNAL OF PSYCHIATRY AND RELATED SCIENCES. *See* Medicine - Psychiatry, Psychopathology.

ISSUES IN MENTAL HEALTH NURSING. *See* Medicine - Nursing.

ISSUES IN RADICAL THERAPY (SPRINGFIELD, ILL. : 1982). (ISSUES IN RADICAL THERAPY). Vol. 10, No. 1 (Spring 1982)-. Periodical. US. English. ir. $20.00. Issues in Radical Therapy, Rural Route 1, Springfield IL 62707. **Tel** (217)523-8663. **Ed** Robert B Sipe. **Ind/Abst** Altern. Press Index. bk rev. adv acc. **Circ** 1,500. Explores the many issues in the psychotherapeutic world today, using the perspective of radical therapy. RT clarifies the relationship between one's personal psychological problems and the larger social/political arenas. *Issues in Cooperation & Power, 0199-8242; State and Mind, 0161-1089.*

JAHRESKATALOG PSYCHOLOGIE UND VERWANDTE WISSENSCHAFTEN. **VFOAT** Psychologie Jahrestatalog. Began publication in 1964?. 0075-2924. German. ir.

JAPANESE PSYCHOLOGICAL RESEARCH. V. 1- Mar. 1954-. 0021-5368. Periodical. JA. English. qt. $48.00. Japan Publishers Trading Company Ltd, PO Box 5030, Tokyo International, Tokyo 100-31 Japan. **Ind/Abst** Life Sci.

Psychology

Collect., Biol. Abstr., Psychol. Abstr., Soc. Sci. Citation Index, Sociol. Abstr., Lang. Lang. Behav. Abstr. **LC** BF76.5. **NLM** W1 JA979. **CODEN** JPREAV.

JORNAL BRASILEIRO DE PSIQUIATRIA. *See* Medicine - Psychiatry, Psychopathology.

JOURNAL - AMERICAN PSYCHOANALYTIC ASSOCIATION. **Main/Corp** American Psychoanalytic Association. V. 1- Jan. 1953-. Periodical. US. English. qt. **LC** BF173.A2. **DD** 131.3405.

JOURNAL DE PSYCHOLOGIE NORMALE ET PATHOLOGIQUE *CEASED.* Vol. 1-80. 0021-7956. Periodical. FR. French. qt. Presses Universitaires de France, 108 Boulevard Saint-Germain, Paris France. Ed P Janet and G Dumas. **Ind/Abst** MLA Int. Bibliogr. Books Artic. Mod. Lang. Lit., Excerpta Med., Psychol. Abstr. **LC** BF2. **NLM** W1 JO335. **CODEN** JPNPAA.

THE JOURNAL FOR SPECIALISTS IN GROUP WORK. V. 3, No. 2- Summer 1978-. 0193-3922. Periodical. US. English. qt. $12.00. American Association of Counseling Development, 5999 Stevenson Avenue, Alexandria VA 22304. **Tel** (703)823-9800. Ed Barbara Fuhrmann. **Ind/Abst** Sociol. Abstr., Curr. Index J. Educ., Psychol. Abstr. **LC** BF637.C6. **DD** 158. adv acc. **Circ** 264. (ctrl). Available in microfilm from University Microfilms, Inc. Articles that assist and further the best interest of children, youth and adults through services in the group medium. *Together (Washington. 1975)*, 0161-0333.

JOURNAL FUR ANGEWANDTE SOZIALFORSCHUNG *CEASED.* VFOAT Meinung. Vol. 9.-20. Periodical. AU. German. qt. 300.00. Matia-Theresien-Strasse 9, A-1090 Wien Austria. **LC** HM261. *Meinung.*

JOURNAL OF ABNORMAL CHILD PSYCHOLOGY. *See* Medicine - Pediatrics.

JOURNAL OF ABNORMAL PSYCHOLOGY. V. 70- Feb. 1965-. 0021-843X. Periodical. US. English. qt. $82.00. American Psychological Association, 1400 North Uhle Street, Arlington VA 22201. **Tel** (703)247-7802. Ed Susan Knapp. **Ind/Abst** MLA Int. Bibliogr. Books Artic. Mod. Lang. Lit., Excerpta Med., Women Stud. Abstr., Int. Aerosp. Abstr., Soc. Work Res. Abstr., Biol. Abstr., Psychol. Abstr., Index Med., Soc. Sci. Index, Lang. Lang. Behav. Abstr., Hospit. Lit. Index, Sociol. Abstr., Soc. Sci. Citation Index, Abstr. Soc. Work. **LC** RC321. **DD** 157.05. **NLM** W1 JO533P. **CODEN** JAPCAC. adv acc. **Circ** 5,800. Available on microfilm from Johnson Associates, University Microfilms, and Princeton Microfilms. Theory and research on determinants and correlates of abnormal behavior. *Journal of Abnormal and Social Psychology,* 0096-851X.

JOURNAL OF ADOLESCENT RESEARCH. 0743-5584. Periodical. US. English. qt. $50.00. H.E.L.P. Books, 1201 East Calle Elena, Tucson AZ, 5718. **Tel** (602)297-6452. bk rev. adv acc. **Circ** 1,000. (ctrl). Developmental and social characteristics of children ages 10 to 14. Articles cover all aspects of development, including health and education.

JOURNAL OF ALTERED STATES OF CONSCIOUSNESS *CEASED.* V. 1-5, No. 4. 0094-5498. Periodical. US. English. qt. $15.00. Baywood Publishing Company, 43 Central Drive, Farmingdale NY 11735. **Ind/Abst** Excerpta Med. **LC** BF311. **DD** 154. **NLM** W1 JO534Y. **CODEN** JACODK.

JOURNAL OF ANALYTICAL PSYCHOLOGY. V. 1- 1955-. 0021-8774. Periodical. UK. English. qt. $48.00. Academic Press, 4805 Sand Lake Road, Orlando FL 32819. **Tel** (305)345-4100. **Ind/Abst** Excerpta Med., Biol. Abstr., Psychol. Abstr., Index Med., Soc. Sci. Citation Index. **LC** BF173.A2. **DD** 131.3405. **NLM** W1 JO536. **CODEN** JANPA7.

JOURNAL OF APPLIED BEHAVIOR ANALYSIS. V. 1- Spring 1968-. 0021-8855. Periodical. US. English. qt. Journal of Applied Behavior, Department Human Development, University of Kansas, Lawrence KS 66044. **Tel** (913)843-0008. **Ind/Abst** Soc. Sci. Index, Index Med., Except. Child Educ. Resour., Psychol. Abstr., Curr. Index J. Educ., Energy Res. Abstr., Biol. Abstr., Bibliogr. Index, Lang. Lang. Behav. Abstr., Hospit. Lit. Index, Educ. Index, Sociol. Abstr., Soc. Sci. Citation Index. **LC** BF636.A1. **DD** 159.05. **NLM** W1 JO539N. **CODEN** JOABAW.

JOURNAL OF APPLIED DEVELOPMENTAL PSYCHOLOGY. V. 1- Winter 1980-. 0193-3973. Periodical. US. English. qt. $49.50. Ablex Publishing Corporation, 355 Chestnut Street, Norwood NJ 07648. **Tel** (201)767-8450. Ed Irving Sigel. **Ind/Abst** Psychol. Abstr. **LC** BF636.A1. **DD** 155.05. **NLM** W1 JO541E. bk rev. adv acc. **Circ** 600. Devoted to study of humans over time to bridge gap between research in developmental psychology and application of such research.

JOURNAL OF APPLIED PSYCHOLOGY. V. 1- Mar. 1917-. 0021-9010. Periodical. US. English. qt. $82.00. American Psychological Association, 1400 North Uhle Street, Arlington VA 22201. **Tel** (703)247-7802. Ed Susan Knapp. **Ind/Abst** Manage. Contents, Int. Labour Doc., Hospit. Lit. Index, Cumul. Index Nurs. Allied Health Lit., Index Med., Women Stud. Abstr., ABI/Inform, Soc. Work Res. Abstr., Educ. Index, Psychol. Abstr., Soc. Sci. Index. **LC** BF1. **DD** 158.05. **NLM** W1 JO543. **CODEN** JAPGBP. (cum index). adv acc. **Circ** 6,300. Available in microform from Johnson Associates, University Microfilms, and Princeton Microfilms. Research on applications of psychology in work settings such as industry, correctional systems, government, and educational institutions.

JOURNAL OF APPLIED SOCIAL PSYCHOLOGY. V. 1- Jan/Mar 1971-. 0021-9029. Periodical. US. English. ir. $165.00 Domestic, $185.00 Foreign. V H Winston & Sons Inc, 7961 Eastern Avenue, Silver Springs MD 20910. **Tel** (301)587-3356. Ed Andrew Baum. **Ind/Abst** Women Stud. Abstr., Psychol. Abstr., Soc. Sci. Index, Soc. Sci. Citation Index. **LC** HM251. **DD** 301.105. **NLM** W1 JO544G. **CODEN** JASPBX. bk rev. adv acc. **Circ** 1,100. Leading journal in the field of psychology devoted to application of experimental behavioral science research to problems of society.

JOURNAL OF BEHAVIORAL ASSESSMENT *CEASED.* Began with Vol. 1, Mar. 1979. Ceased with Vol. 6. 0164-0305. Periodical. US. English. qt. $39.00. Plenum Publishing Corporation, 227 West 17th Street, New York NY 10011. **Ind/Abst** Excerpta Med., Psychol. Abstr. **LC** BF698.4. **NLM** W1 JO555H. **CODEN** JBASDT.

JOURNAL OF BIO-FEEDBACK. (THE JOURNAL OF BIO-FEEDBACK). 0093-3597. US. English. $10.00. Bio-Feedback Technology Inc, 1804 East Ocean Boulevard, Long Beach CA 90802. **LC** BF319.5.B5. **DD** 615.8. **NLM** W1 JO564BJ.

JOURNAL OF BLACK PSYCHOLOGY. (THE JOURNAL OF BLACK PSYCHOLOGY). V. 1- Aug. 1974-. 0095-7984. Periodical. US. English. sa. $26.82. Association of Black Psychologists, PO Box 2929, Washington DC 20013. **Tel** (202)289-3663. Ed Curtis Banks. **Ind/Abst** Psychol. Abstr. **LC** E185.625. **DD** 155.8496. **NLM** W1 JO568T. bk rev. adv acc. **Circ** 1,000. Research studies, survey reports on psychological issues related to black and other ethnic populations.

JOURNAL OF CHILD AND ADOLESCENT PSYCHOTHERAPY. Vol. 1, No. 1 (June 1984)-. 0748-8793. Periodical. US. English. qt. $25.00. Rivendell Foundation, 210 Jackson Avenue, Suite 619/Bamy Building, Memphis TN 38105. **DD** 616.

JOURNAL OF CHILD DEVELOPMENT. V. 1- 1965?-. 0449-2293. JA. English. an. $19.50. Hikari Book Trading Company Ltd, 26 Sakamachi Nagatani Building, 201 Tokyo 160 Japan. **Ind/Abst** Psychol. Abstr. **CODEN** JCDVAN.

JOURNAL OF CHILD PSYCHOLOGY AND PSYCHIATRY AND ALLIED DISCIPLINES. VFOAT Journal of Child Psychology and Psychiatry. V. 1- Jan. 1960-. 0021-9630. Periodical. UK. English. qt. Pergamon Press, 395 Sawmill River Road, Elmsford NY 10523. **Tel** (914)592-7700. **Ind/Abst** Life Sci. Collect., Excerpta Med., Cumul. Index Nurs. Allied Health Lit., Educ. Index, Biol. Abstr., Psychol. Abstr., Nuci. Sci. Abstr., Index Med., Curr. Index J. Educ., Soc. Sci. Citation Index, Bibliogr. Index. **LC** RJ499.A1. **NLM** W1 JO584F. **CODEN** JPPDAI. Available on Microfilm from International Marketing Corporation.

THE JOURNAL OF CLASSROOM INTERACTION. *See* Education (General).

JOURNAL OF CLINICAL AND EXPERIMENTAL NEUROPSYCHOLOGY. Vol. 7, No. 1 (Feb. 1985)-. 0168-8634. Periodical. NE. English. ir. Swets Publishing Service, 347B Heereweg, 2161 Ca Lisse The Netherlands. **Ind/Abst** Behav. Med. Abstr., Child Dev. Abstr. Bibliogr., Curr. Contents, Excerpta Med., Index Med., Psychol. Abstr., Psychol. Read. Guide, Sci. Cit. Index, Abr. Ed., Soc. Sci. Citation Index. **NLM** W1. *Journal of Clinical Neuropsychology.*

JOURNAL OF CLINICAL CHILD PSYCHOLOGY. V. 1- Winter 1971/72-. 0047-228X. Periodical. US. English. qt. American Psychological Association, 1400 North Uhle Street, Arlington VA 22201. **Ind/Abst** Women Stud. Abstr., Except. Child Educ. Resour., Psychol. Abstr., Ref. Source. **LC** BF721. **DD** 362.7. **NLM** W1 JO587B. **CODEN** JCCPD3. *Clinical Child Psychology Newsletter.*

JOURNAL OF CLINICAL PSYCHOLOGY. V. 1- Jan. 1945-. 0021-9762. Periodical. US. English. bm. $60.00 Domestic, $64.00 Foreign. Clinical Psychology Publishing Company, 4 Conant Square, Brandon VT 05733. Ed F C Thorne. **Ind/Abst** Life Sci. Collect., Excerpta Med., Index Med., Cumul. Index Nurs. Allied Health Lit., Women Stud. Abstr., Biol. Abstr., Soc. Work Res. Abstr., Curr. Index J. Educ., Psychol. Abstr., Soc. Sci. Index. **LC** RC321. **DD** 616.805. **NLM** W1 JO591. **CODEN** JCPYAO.

JOURNAL OF CLINICAL PSYCHOLOGY. Periodical. US. English. bm. $80.00. Clinical Psychology Publishers, 4 Conant Square, Brandon VT 05733. **Tel** (802)247-6871. Ed Vladimir Pishkin. **Ind/Abst** Soc. Sci. Index, Index Med., Psychol. Abstr., Sci. Cit. Index, Abr. Ed., Soc. Sci. Citation Index, Sociol. Abstr., Lang. Lang. Behav. Abstr., Women Stud. Abstr., Hospit. Lit. Index, Sci. Cit. Index, Abr. Ed., Abstr. Soc. Work., Curr. Index J. Educ. adv acc. **Circ** 2,400. Current research in clinical psychology.

JOURNAL OF COMMUNITY PSYCHOLOGY. V. 1- Jan. 1973-. 0090-4392. Periodical. US. English. qt. Clinical Psychology Publishing Company, 4 Conant Square, Brandon VT 05733. **Tel** (802)247-6871. Ed J R Newbrough. **Ind/Abst** Hospit. Lit. Index, Sociol. Abstr., Women Stud. Abstr., Psychol. Abstr., Soc. Sci. Citation Index. **LC** RC467. **DD** 362.2205. **NLM** W1 JO593S. **CODEN** JCPSD9. bk rev. adv acc. **Circ** 700. Research and opinions in community psychology. *Journal of Clinical Psychology,* 0021-9762.

JOURNAL OF COMPARATIVE AND PHYSIOLOGICAL PSYCHOLOGY *CEASED.* (THE JOURNAL OF COMPARATIVE AND PHYSIOLOGICAL PSYCHOLOGY). Vol. 40, No. 1 (Feb. 1947)-V. 96, No. 6 (Dec. 1982). 0021-9940. Periodical. US. English. bm. $45.00 Domestic, $47.00 Foreign, $15.00 Members. APA, 1400 North Uhle Street, Arlington VA 22201. **Ind/Abst** Excerpta Med., Int. Aerosp. Abstr., Chem. Abstr., Biol. Abstr., Nuci. Sci. Abstr., Index Med., Bibliogr. Agric., Biol. Agric. Index, Energy Res. Abstr., Soc. Sci. Index. **LC** BF1. **DD** 152.05. **NLM** W1 JO594. **CODEN** JCPPAV. (cum index). *Journal of Comparative Psychology (Baltimore, MD.),* 0093-4127.

JOURNAL OF COMPARATIVE PSYCHOLOGY (WASHINGTON, D.C. : 1983). (JOURNAL OF COMPARATIVE PSYCHOLOGY). Vol. 97, No. 1 (Mar. 1983)-. 0735-7036. Periodical. US. English. qt. $40.00. American Psychological Association, 1400 North Uhle Street, Arlington VA 22201. **Tel** (703)247-7802. Ed Susan Knapp. **Ind/Abst** Excerpta Med., Index Med., Psychol. Abstr., Biol. Agric. Index, Soc. Sci. Index. **LC** BF1. **DD** 156.05. adv acc. **Circ** 2,000. Available in microform. Laboratory and field studies of the behavioral patterns of various species as they relate to evolution, development, ecology, control, and functional significance. *Journal of Comparative and Physiological Psychology,* 0021-9940.

JOURNAL OF CONSULTING AND CLINICAL PSYCHOLOGY. V. 32- Feb. 1968-. 0022-006X. Periodical. US. English. bm. $124.00. American Psychological Association, 1400 North Uhle Street, Arlington VA 22201. **Tel** (703)247-9800. Ed Susan Knapp. **Ind/Abst** Life Sci. Collect., Excerpta Med., Women Stud. Abstr., Soc. Work Res. Abstr., Biol. Abstr., Psychol. Abstr., Nuci. Sci. Abstr., Index Med., Curr. Index J. Educ., Soc. Sci. Index, Soc. Sci. Citation Index, Sociol. Abstr., Hospit. Lit. Index, Lang. Lang. Behav. Abstr. **LC** BF1. **DD** 616.89005. **NLM** W1 JO595R. **CODEN** JCLPBC. adv acc. **Circ** 11,000. Also available in microform. Research on techniques of diagnosis and treatment in disordered behavior as well as studies of populations of clinical interest. *Journal of Consulting Psychology,* 0095-8891.

JOURNAL OF COUNSELING AND DEVELOPMENT. (JOURNAL OF COUNSELING AND DEVELOPMENT : JCD). **VFOAT** JCD. Vol. 63, No. 1 (Sept. 1984)-. 0748-9633. Periodical. US. English. mo. $32.00 Nonmembers US, $35.00 Nonmembers, Foreign. American Association for Counseling and Development, 5999 Stevenson Avenue, Alexandria VA 22304. **Ind/Abst** Coll. Stud. Pers. Abstr., Book Rev. Index, Work Relat. Abstr., Curr. Index J. Educ., Educ. Index, Educ. Adm. Abstr., Except. Child Educ. Resour., Pers. Lit., Hum. Resour. Abstr., Soc. Sci. Citation Index, Soc. Work Res. Abstr., Work Relat. Abstr., Curr. Contents, Soc. Behav. Sci. **DD** 158. Issued also in microfilm by University Microfilms. *Personnel and Guidance Journal, 0031-5737.*

JOURNAL OF COUNSELING PSYCHOLOGY. V. 1- Feb. 1954-. 0022-0167. Periodical. US. English. qt. $72.00. American Psychological Association, 1400 North Uhle Street, Arlington VA 22201. **Tel** (703)247-7802. **Ed** Susan Knapp. **Ind/Abst** Women Stud. Abstr., Educ. Index, Soc. Work Res. Abstr., Curr. Index J. Educ., Psychol. Abstr., Soc. Sci. Index, Soc. Sci. Citation Index, Sociol. Abstr., Bibliogr. Index, Lang. Lang. Behav. Abstr., Abstr. Soc. Work. **LC** BF637.C6. **DD** 150.13. **NLM** W1 JO602. adv acc. **Circ** 6,300. Microform editions available from Johnson Associates, University Microfilms, and Princeton Microfilms. Empirical studies about counseling processes and interventions, theoretical articles about counseling, and studies dealing with evaluation of counseling applications and programs.

THE JOURNAL OF CREATIVE BEHAVIOR. V. 1- Winter 1967-. 0022-0175. Periodical. US. English. qt. $16.00. Creative Education Foundation, 437 Franklin Street, Buffalo NY 14202. **Tel** (716)878-6221. **Ed** Angelo M Biondi. **Ind/Abst** Sociol. Abstr., Soc. Welf. Soc. Plan./Policy Soc. Dev., Educ. Index, Soc. Work Res. Abstr., Except. Child Educ. Resour., Curr. Index J. Educ., Psychol. Abstr., Soc. Sci. Citation Index, Bibliogr. Index, Lang. Lang. Behav. Abstr. **LC** BF408. **DD** 153.3555. **NLM** W1 JO604. bk rev. **Circ** 2,500. Available on Microfilm from University Microfilms. For general readers, focusing on creativity in a broad range of subjects: education, psychology, business, and industry, the sciences and research.

JOURNAL OF CROSS-CULTURAL PSYCHOLOGY. V. 1- Mar. 1970-. 0022-0221. Periodical. US. English. qt. Sage Publications, 275 Beverly Drive, Beverly Hills CA 90212. **Tel** (213)274-8003. **Ind/Abst** Sociol. Abstr., Soc. Welf. Soc. Plan./Policy Soc. Dev., Women Stud. Abstr., Curr. Index J. Educ., Psychol. Abstr., Soc. Sci. Citation Index, Lang. Lang. Behav. Abstr., Abstr. Anthropol. **LC** BF728. **DD** 155.805. **NLM** W1 JO612A. **CODEN** JCPGB5.

THE JOURNAL OF EARLY ADOLESCENCE. Vol. 1, No. 1 (Spring 1981)-. 0272-4316. Periodical. US. English. qt. $45.00. Journal of Early Adolescence Help Books, 1201 East Calle Elena, Tucson AZ 85718. **Tel** (602)297-6452. **Ed** Hershel D Thornburg. **Ind/Abst** Psychol. Abstr. **LC** HQ796. **DD** 305.2350973. **NLM** W1 JO626N. bk rev. adv acc. **Circ** 1,000. (ctrl). Developmental and social characteristics of children ages 10 to 14. Articles cover all aspects of development, including health and education.

JOURNAL OF EDUCATION AND PSYCHOLOGY. Began in 1943. Periodical. II. English. qt. $10.00. Registrar/Sardar Patel University, Vallabh Vidyanagar, 38 120 Dist Kaira, Gujarat India. **Ed** B V Pald. adv acc. **Circ** 300. (ctrl).

THE JOURNAL OF EMOTIONAL EDUCATION. V. 1- Jan. 1961-. 0022-0779. Periodical. US. English. qt. Emotional Education Press, 112 East 19th Street, New York NY 10003. **LC** BF636.A1. **DD** 158.05. **NLM** W1 JO639.

JOURNAL OF ENVIRONMENTAL PSYCHOLOGY. Vol. 1, No. 1 (Mar. 1981)-. 0272-4944. Periodical. UK. English. qt. $86.00. Academic Press, 4805 Sand Lake Road, Orlando FL 32819. **Tel** (305)345-4100. **Ind/Abst** Archit. Period. Index, Psychol. Abstr. **LC** BF353. **DD** 155.905. **NLM** W1 JO644BFN.

JOURNAL OF EVOLUTIONARY PSYCHOLOGY. *See* Literature.

JOURNAL OF EXPERIMENTAL CHILD PSYCHOLOGY. V. 1- Apr. 1964-. 0022-0965. Periodical. US. English. bm. Academic Press, 4805 Sand Lake Road, Orlando FL 32819. **Tel** (305)345-4100. **Ind/Abst** Women Stud. Abstr., Soc. Work Res. Abstr., Biol. Abstr., Psychol. Abstr., Index Med., Curr. Index J. Educ., Soc. Sci. Index, Soc. Sci. Citation Index, Sociol. Abstr., Bibliogr. Index, Lang. Lang. Behav. Abstr., Abstr. Soc. Work. **LC** BF721. **DD** 155.4. **NLM** W1 JO644IF. **CODEN** JECPAE.

JOURNAL OF EXPERIMENTAL PSYCHOLOGY. GENERAL. Periodical. US. English. qt. $62.00. American Psychological Association, 1400 North Uhle Street, Arlington VA 22201. **Tel** (703)247-7802. **Ed** Susan Knapp. **Ind/Abst** Soc. Sci. Index, Psychol. Abstr., Soc. Sci. Citation Index, Sociol. Abstr., Lang. Lang. Behav. Abstr. adv acc. **Circ** 3,400. Longer, more integrative reports of interest to all experimental psychologists.

JOURNAL OF EXPERIMENTAL PSYCHOLOGY. HUMAN LEARNING AND MEMORY *CEASED.* (JOURNAL OF EXPERIMENTAL PSYCHOLOGY : HUMAN LEARNING AND MEMORY). **VFOAT** Human Learning and Memory. V. 1-V. 7, No. 6. 0096-1515. Periodical. US. English. bm. $28.00 Nonmembers, $10.00 Members. 1200 Seventeenth Street NW, Washington DC 20036. **Ind/Abst** Biol. Abstr., Chem. Abstr., Index Med., Int. Aerosp. Abstr., Nuci. Sci. Abstr., Soc. Sci. Index. **LC** LB1051. **DD** 370.15. **NLM** W1 JO644VD. **CODEN** JPHMD8. Available on microfilm from Johnson Associates, Inc., University Microfilms, and Princeton Microfilms. *Journal of Experimental Psychology, 0022-1015.*

JOURNAL OF EXPERIMENTAL PSYCHOLOGY. HUMAN PERCEPTION AND PERFORMANCE. (JOURNAL OF EXPERIMENTAL PSYCHOLOGY : HUMAN PERCEPTION AND PERFORMANCE). **VFOAT** Human Perception and Performance. V. 1- Feb. 1975-. 0096-1523. Periodical. US. English. bm. $15.00 Members, $30.00 Nonmembers. American Psychological Association, 1200 17th Street Northwest, Washington DC 20036. **Ind/Abst** Excerpta Med., Biol. Abstr., Chem. Abstr., Index Med., Int. Aerosp. Abstr., Nuci. Sci. Abstr., Psychol. Abstr., Curr. Index J. Educ., Energy Res. Abstr., Soc. Sci. Index. **LC** BF311. **DD** 152.05. **NLM** W1 JO644VF. **CODEN** JPHPDH. Available on microfilm from Johnson Associates, Inc., University Microfilms, and Princeton Microfilms. *Journal of Experimental Psychology.*

JOURNAL OF EXPERIMENTAL PSYCHOLOGY. HUMAN PERCEPTION AND PERFORMANCE. (JOURNAL OF EXPERIMENTAL PSYCHOLOGY : HUMAN PERCEPTION AND PERFORMANCE). V. 1- Feb. 1975-. 0096-1523. Periodical. US. English. $16.00 Nonmembers. American Psychological Association, 1200 17th Street Northwest, Washington DC 20036. **Ind/Abst** Excerpta Med., Biol. Abstr., Chem. Abstr., Index Med., Int. Aerosp. Abstr., Nuci. Sci. Abstr., Psychol. Abstr., Curr. Index J. Educ., Energy Res. Abstr., Soc. Sci. Index. **LC** BF311. **DD** 152.05. **NLM** W1 JO644VF. **CODEN** JPHPDH. Available on microfilm from Johnson Associates, Inc., University Microfilms, and Princeton Microfilms. *Journal of Experimental Psychology.*

JOURNAL OF EXPERIMENTAL PSYCHOLOGY. LEARNING, MEMORY, AND COGNITION. VFOAT Learning, Memory and Cognition. Vol. 8, No. 1 (Jan. 1982)-. 0278-7393. Periodical. US. English. qt. $84.00. American Psychological Association, 1400 North Uhle Street/Room 410, Arlington VA 22201. **Tel** (703)247-7802. **Ed** Susan Knapp. **Ind/Abst** Excerpta Med., Index Med., Curr. Index J. Educ., Psychol. Abstr., Energy Res. Abstr., Soc. Sci. Index. **LC** LB1051. **DD** 370.15. **NLM** W1 JO644VJ. adv acc. **Circ** 3,800. Issued also in microfilm. Experimental studies on fundamental encoding, transfer, memory, and cognitive processes in human behavior. *Journal of Experimental Psychology. Human Learning and Memory, 0096-1515.*

JOURNAL OF EXPERMENTAL PSYCHOLOGY. ANIMAL BEHAVIOR PROCESSES. (JOURNAL OF EXPERIMENTAL PSYCHOLOGY : ANIMAL BEHAVIOR PROCESSES). **VFOAT** Animal Behavior Processes. V. 1- Jan. 1975-. 0097-7403. Periodical. US. English. $16.00 Nonmembers. American Psychological Association, 1200 17th Street Northwest, Washington DC 20036. **Tel** (703)247-7802. **Ed** Susan Knapp. **Ind/Abst** Soc. Sci. Index, Excerpta Med., Life Sci. Collect., Biol. Abstr., Chem. Abstr., Index Med., Int. Aerosp. Abstr., Nuci. Sci. Abstr., Psychol. Abstr., Energy Res. Abstr. **LC** QL750. **DD** 599.05. **NLM** W1 JO644VB. **CODEN** JPAPDG. adv acc. **Circ** 2,600. Experimental studies on the basic mechanisms of perception, learning, motivation, and performance, especially in nonhuman animals. *Journal of Experimental Psychology, 0022-1015.*

THE JOURNAL OF GENERAL PSYCHOLOGY. V. 1- Jan. 1928-. 0022-1309. Periodical. US. English (beginning with V. 1, No. 3/4, each article is followed by resumes in French, German, and Russian). qt. $42.00. Heldref Publications, 4000 Albemarle Street NW/Suite 302, Washington DC 20016. **Tel** (202)362-6445. **Ed** Doris Cahlfin. **Ind/Abst** Sociol. Abstr., Women Stud. Abstr., Int. Aerosp. Abstr., Except. Child Educ. Resour., Biol. Abstr., Psychol. Abstr., Index Med., Gen. Sci. Index, Soc. Sci. Index, Soc. Sci. Citation Index, Lang. Lang. Behav. Abstr., Abstr. Soc. Work. **LC** BF1. **DD** 150.5, 159.905. **NLM** W1 JO668G. **CODEN** JGPSAY. adv acc. **Circ** 1,424. Concerned with experimental, physiological, and comparative psychology. Publishes articles about human and animal laboratory studies, and mathematical and other theoretical investigations.

THE JOURNAL OF GENETIC PSYCHOLOGY. V. 84- Mar. 1954-. 0022-1325. Periodical. US. English. qt. $42.00. Managing Editor, 4000 Albemarle Street NW, Washington DC 20016. **Tel** (202)362-6445. **Ed** Mary Morello Shafer. **Ind/Abst** Sociol. Abstr., Women Stud. Abstr., Except. Child Educ. Resour., Psychol. Abstr., Biol. Abstr., Index Med., Nuci. Sci. Abstr., Curr. Index J. Educ., Soc. Sci. Index. **NLM** W1 JO669. **CODEN** JGPYAI. adv acc. **Circ** 1,325. Devoted to research and theory in developmental and clinical psychology. Emphasizes empirical research and the exposition and criticism of theory, as well as applied and descriptive articles. *Pedagogical Seminary and Journal of Genetic Psychology, 0885-6559.*

JOURNAL OF HUMAN BEHAVIOR AND LEARNING. Vol. 1, No. 1-. Periodical. US. English. qt.

JOURNAL OF HUMANISTIC PSYCHOLOGY. (JOURNAL OF HUMANISTIC PSYCHOLOGY). V. 1- Spring 1961-. 0022-1678. Periodical. US. English. qt. Sage Publications Inc, 275 South Beverly Drive, Beverly Hills CA 90212. **Ind/Abst** Psychol. Abstr., Soc. Sci. Citation Index, Sociol. Abstr., Women Stud. Abstr., Lang. Lang. Behav. Abstr., Soc. Welf. Soc. Plan./Policy Soc. Dev., Curr. Index J. Educ. **LC** BF1. **DD** 150.192. **NLM** W1 JO673Y. (cum index). Available on microfilm from University Microfilms.

JOURNAL OF INDIAN PSYCHOLOGY. V. 1- Jan. 1978-. 0379-3885. Periodical. II. English. ir. $9.00. Andhara University Press, Waltair, Visakhapatnam 530 003, Waltair India. **Ind/Abst** Psychol. Abstr. **LC** BF1. **DD** 150.954. **NLM** W1 JO703D.

JOURNAL OF INDIVIDUAL PSYCHOLOGY *CEASED.* V. 13-37. 0022-1805. Periodical. US. English. sa. $15.00. G J Manaster, Department of Educational Psychology, University of Texas, Austin TX 78712. **Ind/Abst** Women Stud. Abstr. **LC** BF1. **DD** 150.5. **NLM** W1 JO703E. *American Journal of Individual Psychology, 0091-7788.*

JOURNAL OF INSTRUCTIONAL PSYCHOLOGY. V. 1- Winter 1974-. 0094-1956. Periodical. US. English. qt. Journal of Instructional Psychology, Box 8826/Spring Hill Station, Mobile AL 36608. **Tel** (205)460-6277. **Ed** G E Uhlig. **Ind/Abst** Educ. Index, Psychol. Abstr., Sociol. Abstr., Lang. Lang. Behav. Abstr. **LC** LB1051. **DD** 370.1505. bk rev. **Circ** 250. Contains general and professional education research.

JOURNAL OF LANGUAGE AND SOCIAL PSYCHOLOGY. Vol. 1, No. 1-. 0261-927X. UK. English. qt. $76.00. Tieto Ltd, Bank House/8A Hill Road, Clevedon Avon BS21 7HH England.

JOURNAL OF MATHEMATICAL PSYCHOLOGY. Periodical. US. English. qt. $127.00. Academic Press, 4805 Sand Lake Road, Orlando FL 32819. **Tel** (305)345-4100. **Ind/Abst** Comput. Rev., Math. Rev., Soc. Sci. Citation Index, Sociol. Abstr., Psychol. Abstr., Lang. Lang. Behav. Abstr.

JOURNAL OF MATHEMATICAL PSYCHOLOGY. V. 1- Feb. 1964-. 0022-2496. Periodical. US. English. qt. $110.00. Academic Press, 4805 Sand Lake Road, Orlando FL 32819. **Ind/Abst** Life Sci. Collect., Int. Aerosp. Abstr., Biol. Abstr.,

Psychology

Psychol. Abstr., Nuci. Sci. Abstr., Math. Rev. LC BF1. NLM W1 JO748T. CODEN JMTPAJ.

JOURNAL OF MEMORY AND LANGUAGE. Vol. 24, No. 1 (Feb. 1985)-. 0749-596X. Periodical. US. English. bm. $105.00 US and Canada. Academic Press, 111 Fifth Avenue, New York NY 10003. DD 153. *Journal of Verbal Learning and Verbal Behavior 0022-5371.*

JOURNAL OF MENTAL IMAGERY. V. 1- Spring 1977-. 0364-5541. Periodical. US. English. sa. $55.00. Brandon House, PO Box 240, Bronx NY 10471. Tel (914)423-9200. Ed Akhter Ahsen. Ind/Abst Psychol. Abstr. LC BF367. DD 153.3. NLM W1 JO76LM. bk rev. adv acc. Circ 11,000. In its ninth year as the sole, definitive source for imagery articles by leading experts.

THE JOURNAL OF MIND AND BEHAVIOR. V. 1, No. 1 (Spring 1980)-. 0271-0137. Periodical. US. English. qt $85.00. Journal of Mind and Behavior, PO Box 522/Village Station, New York NY 10014. Tel (718)783-1471. Ed Raymond Russ. Ind/Abst Curr. Contents, Philos. Index, Psychol. Abstr., Resour. Educ., Soc. Sci. Citation Index, Sociol. Abstr. LC BF1. DD 150.5. bk rev. adv acc. Circ 950. (ctrl). An interdisciplinary journal publishing in the areas of mind/body epistemology, the scientific method, psychiatry and social philosophy, and sociology of knowledge.

THE JOURNAL OF MUSIC THERAPY. See Music.

JOURNAL OF NONVERBAL BEHAVIOR. V. 4- Fall 1979-. 0191-5886. Periodical. US. English. qt. Human Sciences Press, 72 5th Avenue, New York NY 10011. Tel (212)243-6000. Ind/Abst Psychol. Abstr., Soc. Sci. Citation Index. LC BF353. DD 153.6. NLM W1 JO795J. CODEN JNVBDV. *Environmental Psychology and Nonverbal Behavior, 0361-3496.*

JOURNAL OF OCCUPATIONAL PSYCHOLOGY. V. 48- Mar. 1975-. 0305-8107. Periodical. UK. English. qt. $79.50. British Psychological Society, Blackhorse Road, Letchworth SG6 1HN England. Tel (04626)72555. Ind/Abst Manage. Contents, Trade Ind. Index, ABI/Inform, Int. Labour Doc., Sociol. Abstr., Ship Abstr., Cumul. Index Nurs. Allied Health Lit., CIS Abstr., Psychol. Abstr., Soc. Sci. Citation Index. LC HF5548.8. DD 158.705. NLM W1 JO802P. CODEN JOCPDJ. *Occupational Psychology, 0029-7976.*

JOURNAL OF ORGANIZATIONAL BEHAVIOR MANAGEMENT. V. 1- Summer 1977-. 0160-8061. Periodical. US. English. qt. $112.00. Haworth Press, 28 East 22nd Street, New York NY 10010. Tel (212)228-2800. Ed Thomas C Mawhinney. Ind/Abst Manage. Contents, ABI/Inform, Bibliogr. Agric., Psychol. Abstr. LC HD58.7. DD 658.3005. NLM W1 JO804LM. adv acc. Circ 981. The only professional journal devoted entirely to behavior management in organizations. Top researchers provide proven methods—backed by facts, to show the best practical ways to apply behavior management in the workplace.

JOURNAL OF PASTORAL PSYCHOTHERAPY. 0886-5477. Periodical. US. English. qt $32.00 Institutions, $42.00 Libraries. The Haworth Press, 75 Griswold Street, Binghamton NY 13904.

JOURNAL OF PEDIATRIC PSYCHOLOGY. See Medicine - Pediatrics.

JOURNAL OF PERSONALITY. V. 14- Sept. 1945-. 0022-3506. Periodical. US. English. qt. $36.00. Duke University Press, College Station/Box 6697, Durham NC 27708. Tel (919)684-2173. Ed C Peter Herman. Ind/Abst Sociol. Abstr., Index Med., Women Stud. Abstr., Psychol. Abstr., Soc. Sci. Index, Soc. Work Res. Abstr., Soc. Sci. Citation Index, Hospit. Lit. Index, Lang. Lang. Behav. Abstr., Abstr. Soc. Work. LC BF1. DD 137.05. NLM W1 JO828P. CODEN JOPEAE. bk rev. adv acc. Circ 2,000. Devoted to scientific investigations in the field of personality, especially experimental studies of personality and behavior dynamics, personality development, and individual differences in the cognitive, affective, and interpersonal domains. *Character and Personality, 0730-6407.*

JOURNAL OF PERSONALITY AND SOCIAL PSYCHOLOGY. V. 1- Jan. 1965-. 0022-3514. Periodical. US. English. mo. $320.00. American Psychological Association, 1400 North Uhle Street, Arlington VA 22201. Tel (703)247-7802. Ed Susan Knapp. Ind/Abst MLA Int. Bibliogr. Books Artic. Mod. Lang. Lit., Index Med., Women Stud. Abstr., Soc. Work Res. Abstr., Curr. Index J. Educ., Psychol. Abstr., Soc. Sci. Citation Index, Hospit. Lit. Index, Soc. Sci. Index, Lang. Lang. Behav. Abstr., Sociol. Abstr. LC HM251. DD 301.1. NLM W1 JO828PC. CODEN JPSPB2. adv acc. Circ 6,000. Research in three major areas: attitudes and social cognition, interpersonal relations and group processes, and personality processes and individual differences. *Journal of Abnormal and Social Psychology, 0096-851X.*

JOURNAL OF PERSONALITY ASSESSMENT. Periodical. US. English. bm. Society for Personality Assessment, 1070 East Angeleno Avenue, Burbank CA 91501. Tel (818)846-5550. Ind/Abst Index Med., Psychol. Abstr., Soc. Sci. Citation Index, Sociol. Abstr., Hospit. Lit. Index, Lang. Lang. Behav. Abstr., Women Stud. Abstr.

JOURNAL OF PHENOMENOLOGICAL PSYCHOLOGY. V. 1- Fall 1970-. 0047-2662. Periodical. US. English. sa. $28.50. Humanities Press, 171 1st Avenue, Atlantic Highlands NJ 07716. Tel (201)872-1441. Ed Amedeo Giorgi. Ind/Abst Psychol. Abstr., Soc. Sci. Citation Index. LC BF204.5. DD 150 .192. NLM W1 JO831F. CODEN JPHPAE. adv acc. Circ 800. Approaches phenomenology in broadest sense possible to encompass entire range of experience and behavior of man.

JOURNAL OF PSYCHEDELIC DRUGS CEASED. V. 1-12. 0022-393X. Periodical. US. English. qt. Ind/Abst Excerpta Med., Biol. Abstr. LC BF207. NLM W1 JO857G. CODEN JPSDAX.

THE JOURNAL OF PSYCHOHISTORY. V. 4- Summer 1976-. 0145-3378. Periodical. US. English. qt. $48.00. Atcom Inc, 2315 Broadway, New York NY 10024. Tel (212)873-5900. Ed David R Beisel. Ind/Abst Sociol. Abstr., Writ. Am. Hist., Psychol. Abstr., Child Dev. Abstr. Bibliogr., Hist. Abstr., Am. Hist. Life, Lang. Lang. Behav. Abstr., Hist. Abstr., Part A, Mod. Hist. Abstr., Hist. Abstr., Part B, Twent. Century Abstr. LC D16.16. DD 155. NLM W1 JO857H. bk rev. Circ 700. (ctrl). Available on microfilm from Xerox University Microfilms. A journal exploring all aspects of the rapidly developing discipline of psychohistory. *History of Childhood Quarterly, 0091-4266.*

JOURNAL OF PSYCHOLOGICAL RESEARCHES. Began with Jan. 1957 issue. 0022-3972. Periodical. Il. English. ir. $21.00. Department of Psychology, University of Madras, Madras 5 India. Ind/Abst Psychol. Abstr., Sociol. Abstr., Lang. Lang. Behav. Abstr. LC BF1. NLM W1 JO857T. CODEN JPSRB8.

THE JOURNAL OF PSYCHOLOGY. V. 1- 1935/36-. 0022-3980. Periodical. US. English. bm. $63.00. Heldref Publications, 4000 Albemarle Street NW/Suite 302, Washington DC 20016. Tel (202)362-6445. Ed Mary Morello. Ind/Abst Sociol. Abstr., Life Sci. Collect., Lang. Lang. Behav. Abstr., Int. Aerosp. Abstr., Biol. Abstr., Chem. Abstr., Psychol. Abstr., Index Med., Curr. Index J. Educ., Women Stud. Abstr., Cumul. Index Nurs. Allied Health Lit., Abstr. Soc. Work., Soc. Sci. Citation Index, Hospit. Lit. Index. LC BF1. DD 150.5, 159.905. NLM W1 JO858. CODEN JOPSAM. adv acc. Circ 1,633. An interdisciplinary journal that publishes research and theoretical articles in the general field of psychology, and explores the newly developing areas of behavior.

THE JOURNAL OF PSYCHOLOGY AND CHRISTIANITY. See Religion, Mythology, Rationalism - Protestantism.

JOURNAL OF PSYCHOLOGY AND JUDAISM. V. 1- Fall 1976-. 0700-9801. Periodical. CN. English. ir. 40.00. Center for the Study of Psychology and Judaism, 1747 Featerstone Drive, Ottawa Ontario K1H 6P4 Canada. Tel (613)731-9119. Ed Reuven P Bulka. DD 296. bk rev. adv acc. Circ 1,000. (ctrl). Investigates areas of similarities and differences between psychology and judaism with intent to establish better mutual understanding and interaction.

JOURNAL OF PSYCHOLOGY AND THEOLOGY. V. 1- Jan. 1973-. 0091-6471. Periodical. US. English. qt $20.00 Domestic, $24.00 Foreign. Journal of Psychology and Theology, Biola University, 13800 Biola Avenue, La Mirada CA 90639. Tel (213)944-0351. Ed William F Hunter. Ind/Abst Old Testam. Abstr., Psychol. Abstr., Relig. Index One, Period., Soc. Sci. Citation Index, Guide Soc. Sci. Relig. Period. Lit., Christ. Period. Index. LC BF1. DD 253.5019. NLM W1 JO858E. CODEN JPSTDG. bk rev. Circ 2,000. (ctrl). Recent scholarly thinking and research on the interrelationships of psychological and theological concepts and their application to a variety of professional and pastoral settings.

JOURNAL OF PSYCHOSOCIAL ONCOLOGY. Vol. 1, No. 1 (Spring 1983)-. 0734-7332. Periodical. US. English. qt. $89.00. Haworth Press Inc, 28 East 22nd Street, New York NY 10010. Tel (212)228-2800. Ed Grace H Christ. Ind/Abst Electron. Commun. Abstr. J., ISMEC Bull., Pollut. Abstr. Indexes, Saf. Sci. Abstr. J., Life Sci. Collect. LC RC261.A1. DD 362.1969940019. NLM W1 JO858VC. bk rev. adv acc. Circ 1,718. The only multidisciplinary journal published specifically responsible for the psychosocial needs of cancer patients and their families.

JOURNAL OF READING, WRITING, AND LEARNING DISABILITIES INTERNATIONAL. See Education (General) - Special Aspects of Education.

JOURNAL OF RELIGION AND THE APPLIED BEHAVIORAL SCIENCES. See Religion, Mythology, Rationalism.

JOURNAL OF REPRODUCTIVE AND INFANT PSYCHOLOGY. VFOAT JRIP. Vol. 1, Pt. 1 (May 1983)-. 0264-6838. Periodical. UK. English. sa. NLM W1.

JOURNAL OF RESEARCH IN PERSONALITY. V. 7- June 1973-. 0092-6566. Periodical. US. English. qt $40.00 Domestic, $49.00 Foreign. Academic Press, 4805 Sand Lake Road, Orlando FL 32819. Tel (305)345-4100. Ind/Abst Psychol. Abstr., Soc. Sci. Citation Index, Women Stud. Abstr., Lang. Lang. Behav. Abstr., Sociol. Abstr., Excerpta Med., Biol. Abstr., Curr. Index J. Educ. LC BF1. DD 150.5. NLM W1 JO869T. CODEN JRPRA6. *Journal of Experimental Research in Personality, 0022-1023.*

JOURNAL OF RURAL COMMUNITY PSYCHOLOGY. VFOAT Rural Community Psychology. Vol. 1, No. 1 (Spring 1980)-. 0276-2285. Periodical. US. English. sa. $30.00. California School Professional Psychology, 1350 M Street, Fresno CA 93721. Tel (209)486-8420. Ed Mary Beth Kenkel. Ind/Abst Psychol. Abstr. LC RA790.A1. DD 362.20425. NLM W1 JO871J. bk rev. adv acc. Circ 300. Human behavior in rural environments, rural mental health interventions and psychological impact of rural environment.

JOURNAL OF SCHOOL PSYCHOLOGY. See Education (General).

JOURNAL OF SOCIAL AND CLINICAL PSYCHOLOGY. Vol. 1, No. 1-. 0736-7236. Periodical. US. English. qt $65.00 Domestic, $80.00 Foreign. Guilford Press, 200 Park Avenue South, New York NY 10003. Tel (212)674-1900. Ed John H Harvey. LC RC467. DD 616.89005. adv acc. Circ 500. Designed to promote communication and scholarship at the interface of social and clinical psychology. The journal features reports of clinical and empirical research on various topics.

JOURNAL OF SOCIAL AND PERSONAL RELATIONSHIPS. See Sociology: General Works, Theory.

JOURNAL OF SOCIAL BEHAVIOR AND PERSONALITY. Vol. 1, No. 1 (Jan. 1986)-. 0886-1641. Periodical. US. English. qt. $56.00. Select Press, 5093 Paradise Drive, Tiburon CA 94920. DD 155. CODEN JSBPE9.

THE JOURNAL OF SOCIAL PSYCHOLOGY. Periodical. US. English (summaries in French and German). bm. $63.00. Heldref Publications, 4000 Albemarle Street NW/Suite 302, Washington DC 20016. Tel (202)362-6445. Ed Keith Cooke. Ind/Abst Abstr. Soc. Work., Index Med., Psychol. Abstr., Soc. Sci. Index, Soc. Sci. Citation Index, Sociol. Abstr., Women Stud. Abstr., Hospit. Lit. Index, Lang. Lang. Behav. Abstr. adv acc. Circ 2,256. Journal was founded in 1929 and is concerned with studies of persons in group settings and of culture and personality; also published are cross-cultural articles and notes.

JOURNAL OF SPORT BEHAVIOR. See Recreation, Leisure - Sports.

JOURNAL OF SPORT PSYCHOLOGY. See Recreation, Leisure - Sports.

JOURNAL OF THE AMERICAN PSYCHOANALYTIC ASSOCIATION. MONOGRAPH SERIES. Main/Corp American Psychoanalytic Association. VFOAT Monograph Series. No. 1-. Monographic Series. US.

Psychology

English. ir. International University Press International, 80 Northfield Avenue/Building #424, Edison NJ 08837.

JOURNAL OF THE ASSOCIATION FOR THE STUDY OF PERCEPTION. Main/Corp Association for the Study of Perception International. VFOAT Journal of the Association for the Study of Perception International. V. 11- Spring 1976-. 0004-5454. Periodical. US. English. sa. $9.00. Association for the Study of Perception, PO Box 744, Dekalb IL 60115. Tel (815)753-1416. Ed Weldon G Bradtmueller. Ind/Abst Psychol. Abstr. CODEN JSPRBE. bk rev. adv acc. Circ 310. Topics deal with perception in any form especially educational applications also deals with topics related to types of perceptual handicaps. *Journal of the Association for the Study of Perception, 0004-5454.*

JOURNAL OF THE EXPERIMENTAL ANALYSIS OF BEHAVIOR. 1958. 0022-5002. Periodical. US. English. bm. $54.00. Indiana University, Psychology Department, Bloomington IN 47405. Tel (812)336-5416. Ed Philip N Hineline. Ind/Abst Index Med., Psychol. Abstr., Sociol. Abstr., Soc. Sci. Citation Index, Sci. Cit. Index, Abr. Ed., Lang. Lang. Behav. Abstr., Soc. Sci. Index, Chem. Abstr., Sci. Cit. Index, Abr. Ed., Life Sci. Collect., Excerpta Med., Biol. Abstr., Chem. Abstr., Int. Aerosp. Abstr., Nuci. Sci. Abstr., Psychol. Abstr., Energy Res. Abstr. LC W1 JO921. DD 150.5. NLM W1 JO921. CODEN JEABAU. bk rev. adv acc. Circ 2,750. A bi-monthly publication for the original publication of experience relevant to the behavior of single organisms.

JOURNAL OF THE HISTORY OF THE BEHAVIORAL SCIENCES. V. 1- Jan. 1965-. 0022-5061. Periodical. US. English. qt $90.00. Clinical Psychology Publishing Company, 4 Conant Square, Brandon VT 05733. Tel (802)247-6871. Ed B Ross. Ind/Abst Life Sci. Collect., Sociol. Abstr., Soc. Welf. Soc. Plan./Policy Soc. Dev., Index Med., Writ. Am. Hist., Recent Publ. Artic., Ref. Source, Psychol. Abstr., Energy Res. Abstr., Am. Hist. Life, Hist. Abstr., Part A, Mod. Hist. Abstr., Hist. Abst., Part B, Twent. Century Abstr. LC BF1. NLM W1 JO928V. CODEN JHBSA5. bk rev. adv acc. Circ 1,000. Interdisciplinary international journal on the history of the behavioral sciences.

JOURNAL OF THE INDIAN ACADEMY OF APPLIED PSYCHOLOGY. Main/Corp Indian Academy of Applied Psychology. Began in 1964. 0019-4247. Periodical. II. English. ir. LC BF636.A1. DD 158.05.

JOURNAL OF THE OTTO RANK ASSOCIATION. Main/Corp Otto Rank Association. V. 1- Fall 1966-. 0030-6711. Periodical. US. English. sa. $10.00. Otto Rank Association, 35 West State Street, Doylestown Bucks County PA 18901. Ind/Abst Psychol. Abstr. LC BF173. CODEN ORAJAU. Available on microfilm from University Microfilms.

THE JOURNAL OF TRANSPERSONAL PSYCHOLOGY. VFOAT Transpersonal Psychology. Spring 1969-. 0022-524X. Periodical. US. English. sa. $24.00. Journal Transpersonal Psychology, PO Box 4437, Stanford CA 94305. Tel (415)327-2066. Ed Miles Vich. Ind/Abst Psychol. Abstr., Soc. Sci. Citation Index. LC BF1. DD 150.5. NLM W1 JO966L. CODEN JTPSAN. bk rev. Circ 3,200. Presents theory, research, applications in full human development and awareness, especially those aspects that integrate psychological and spiritual experiences, and lead to self-transcendence.

JOURNAL OF UNDERGRADUATE PSYCHOLOGICAL RESEARCH. V. 1- Sept. 1974-. 0096-1337. US. English. West Valley College/Editor, 14000 Fruitvale Avenue, Saratoga CA 95070. LC BF1. DD 150.5.

JOURNAL OF VERBAL LEARNING AND VERBAL BEHAVIOR CEASED. V. 1-23. 0022-5371. Periodical. US. English. bm. Academic Press, 4805 Sand Lake Road, Orlando FL 32819. Ind/Abst MLA Int. Bibliogr. Books Artic. Mod. Lang. Lit., Life Sci. Collect., Lang. Lang. Behav. Abstr., Int. Aerosp. Abstr., Lang. Teach., Curr. Index J. Educ., Psychol. Abstr., Soc. Sci. Index. LC BF435.A1. NLM W1 JO97H. CODEN JVLBAY.

JOURNAL OF VOCATIONAL BEHAVIOR. See Economics - Labor.

KENNETH COLEMAN'S REALITY THEORY NEWSLETTER. VFOAT Reality Theory Newsletter. 0739-3563. Periodical. US. English. qt. Seraphim Press, 7439 La Palma Avenue/Suite 263, Buena Park CA 90620.

KIKAN GENDAI KYOIKU SHINRI. VFOAT Gendai Kyoiku Shinri. Began in 1974. JA. Japanese. ir. 690. Meiji Tosho Shuppan, 3-11 Irifune 3 Chuo-ku (104), Tokyo Japan. LC LB1051.

KINDHEIT : ZEITSCHRIFT FUR ERFORSCHUNG DER PSYCHISCHEN ENTWICKLUNG. V. 1, No. 1 (March 1979)-. 0170-625X. Periodical. GW. German. Aula, Verlag fur Wissenschaft und Forschung, Luisenplatz 2, D-6200 Wiesbaden West Germany.

THE KINESIS REPORT. V. 2- FALL 1979-. 0193-1911. Periodical. US. English. qt. $24.00 Domestic, $28.00 Foreign. Human Sciences Press, 72 5th Avenue, New York NY 10011. LC BF637.C45. DD 153.6. *Kinesis.*

KLINISCHE PSYCHOLOGIE UND PSYCHOPATHOLOGIE. See Medicine - Psychiatry, Psychopathology.

KOLNER ZEITSCHRIFT FUR SOZIOLOGIE UND SOZIALPSYCHOLOGIE. See Sociology: General Works, Theory.

KYOIKU SHINRIGAKU KENKYU. (THE JAPANESE JOURNAL OF EDUCATIONAL PSYCHOLOGY). V. 1- May 1953-. 0021-5015. Periodical. JA. Japanese. qt. $56.00. Japan Publsihgin Trading Company Ltd, PO Box 5030, Tokyo International, Tokyo 100-31. Ind/Abst Psychol. Abstr. CODEN JJEPAP.

LACAN STUDY NOTES. 0882-8466. Periodical. US. English. qt. $20.00. New York Lacan Study Group, 5 Carmine Street, New York NY 10014. DD 150.

LE LANGAGE ET L'HOMME. See Linguistics.

LAW & PSYCHOLOGY REVIEW. See Law.

LEARNING AND MOTIVATION. V. 1- Feb. 1970-. 0023-9690. Periodical. US. English. qt. Academic Press, 4805 Sand Lake Road, Orlando FL 32819. Tel (305)345-4100. Ind/Abst Life Sci. Collect., Biol. Abstr., Psychol. Abstr., Soc. Sci. Citation Index. LC BF1. DD 156.31505. NLM W1 LE289G. CODEN LNMVAV.

LEHRBUCH DER DIFFERENTIELLEN PSYCHOLOGIE. V. 1- 1978-. Monographic Series. German. ir. Ed F Merz. NLM W1 LE488.

LENINSKAIA TEORIIA OTRAZHENIIA I PROBLEMY PSIKHOLOGII. See Biology - Physiology.

LIFE-SPAN DEVELOPMENT AND BEHAVIOR. V. 1- 1978-. 0161-9454. US. English. an. Academic Press, 4805 Sand Lake Road, Orlando FL 32819. LC BF712. DD 155.05. NLM W1 LI407E.

LITERATURE AND PSYCHOLOGY. See Literature.

LITTORAL. 1-. 0751-2090. Periodical. FR. French. qt. Editions Eres, 19 rue Gustave Courbet, F-31400 Toulouse France. NLM W1 LI879.

LIVING ANEW. Vol. 1, No. 1-. 0743-0264. Periodical. US. English. mo. $21.00 Domestic, $26.00 Foreign. Lafayette Publishing Company, 90 Park Avenue, New York NY 10016. DD 158.

MAGYAR PSZICHOLOGIAI SZEMLE. VFOAT Hungarian Psychological Review. Began in 1928. 0025-0279. Periodical. HU. Hungarian (summaries in Russian and English). bm. $28.00. Akademiai Kiado, P O Box 24, Budapest 1363 Hungary. Tel 343-743. Ed P Popper. Ind/Abst Lang. Lang. Behav. Abstr., Psychol. Abstr., Sociol. Abstr. LC BF8.H8. NLM W1 MA408. bk rev. Circ 3,000. (ctrl). General, developmental, pedagogical, social, labour, art, criminal, sports psychology, history of psychology by Hungarian and foreign authors.

MANAB MON. No. 1- 1972-. Periodical. English. ir. $3.50. Pavlov Institute, 132/1-A Bidham Sarani, Calcutta-4 India. LC BF. DD 150.5.

MANABAMANA. Periodical. Bengali. ir. 5.00. 132/AA, Bidhan Sarani Calcutta-4. LC BF8.B43.

MANAGEMENT PSYCHOLOGY. 0164-4629. Periodical. US. English. mo. $36.00. H K Simon Company Inc, 1280 Saw Mill River Road, Yonkers NY 10710. Tel (914)423-6000. Monthly report of modern managerial techniques.

MANITOBA PSYCHOLOGIST. Vol. 1, No. 1 (Nov. 1981)-. 0711-1533. Periodical. CN. English. qt. $15.00. Manitoba Psychologist, 244 Niagara Street, Winnipeg Manitoba R3N 0V2 Canada. DD 150.97127.

MANPOWER AND APPLIED PSYCHOLOGY. V. 1- 1967-. 0025-2409. Periodical. IE. English. ir. Ergon Press, 45 South Mall, Cork Ireland. DD 158.705.

THE MASTER LECTURE SERIES. Vol. 1 (1981)-. Monographic Series. US. English. an. NLM W1.

MEDIATION QUARTERLY. See Law.

MEDICAL HYPNOANALYSIS. See Hypnosis.

MEGAMOT. VFOAT Megamot. V. 1- Oct. 1949-. 0025-8679. Periodical. IS. Hebrew (summeries in English). qt. Hennrietta Szold Institute, 9 Columbia Street Kiryat Menachem, Jerusalem 96583 Israel. Ind/Abst Soc. Sci. Citation Index.

MEMBERSHIP DIRECTORY - PSYCHONOMIC SOCIETY. See Yearbooks, Almanacs, Directories.

MEMBERSHIP ROSTER - AMERICAN ACADEMY OF PSYCHOANALYSIS. (MEMBERSHIP ROSTER). Main/Corp American Academy of Psychoanalysis. 0736-4385. Periodical. US. English. be. $5.00. American Academy of Psychoanalysis, 30 East 40th Street/Suite 608, New York NY 10016. Tel (212)679-4105. NLM WM 22.1 A512M.

MEMORY & COGNITION. V. 1- Jan. 1973-. 0090-502X. Periodical. US. English. bm. $60.00. The Psychonomic Society Inc, 2904 Guadalupe Street, Austin TX 78705. Tel (512)447-9687. Ed Deborah Chambers. Ind/Abst Biol. Abstr., Psychol. Abstr., Lang. Lang. Behav. Abstr., Soc. Sci. Citation Index, Sociol. Abstr., MLA Int. Bibliogr. Books Artic. Mod. Lang. Lit., Life Sci. Collect., Excerpta Med., Energy Res. Abstr. LC BF371. DD 153.105. NLM W1 ME904. CODEN MYCGAO. adv acc. Circ 2,200. Articles covering human memory and learning, conceptual processes, psycholinguistics, problem solving, thinking, decision making, and skilled performance. *Psychonomic Science, 0033-3131.*

MENSALOHA. (MENSALOHA : MENSA HAWAII PUBLICATION). 8750-4529. Periodical. US. English. mo. $2.50 Members, $5.00 Nonmembers. Mensaloha, 45-436 Makalani Street, Kaneohe HI 96744.

MENTAL HEALTH (BOCA RATON, FLA.). See Public Health and Safety.

MENTAL HEALTH SERVICE SYSTEM REPORTS. SERIES AN, EPIDEMIOLOGY. See Medicine - Psychiatry, Psychopathology.

MENTAL HEALTH SPECIAL INTEREST SECTION NEWSLETTER. See Medicine - Psychiatry, Psychopathology.

MENTAL HEALTH, UNITED STATES. Series/Titl DHHS Publication. 1983-. US. English. an. Superintendent of Documents, US Government Printing Office, Washington DC 20402. NLM W2.

MENTALITIES. VFOAT Mentalites. Vol. 1, No. 1-. 0111-8854. Periodical. English (French). sa. $15.00. Outrigger Publishers, PO Box 13-049, Hamilton New Zealand. Tel 55-910. Ed Norman Simms. LC AP7.5. DD 052. bk rev. adv acc. Circ 300. History of mentalities is a comprehensive and multidisciplinary approach to human culture, psychology and institutions especially the long hidden aspects of personal and group experience.

MERRILL-PALMER QUARTERLY (WAYNE STATE UNIVERSITY PRESS). (MERRILL-PALMER QUARTERLY). VFOAT Merrill Palmer Quarterly. Vol. 28, No. 1 (Jan. 1982)-. 0272-930X. Periodical. US. English. qt. $40.00. Wayne State University Press, 5959 Woodward, Detroit MI 48202. Ind/Abst Sociol. Abstr., Women Stud. Abstr., Educ. Index, Curr. Index J. Educ., Psychol. Abstr. DD 155. *Merrill-Palmer Quarterly, Behavior and Development, 0272-930X.*

METAPHYSICS. (METAPHYSICS : THE CONCEPT OF MUC-SUC). VFOAT Metaphysics-Muc-Suc. Issue No. 1 (Aug. 1980)-. 0228-2089. Periodical. CN. English. $2.50 Each Number, Six Issues for $12.50. F X Maier, 293 Mary Street, Orillia Ontario L3V 3E8 Canada. DD 153.4205.

METHODS IN PHYSIOLOGICAL PSYCHOLOGY. See Biology - Physiology.

METHODS IN PSYCHOBIOLOGY. V. 1- 1971-. 0309-6718. Periodical. UK. English. ir. Academic Press, 4805 Sand Lake Road, Orlando FL 32887. Tel (305)345-4100. Ind/Abst Chem. Abstr. NLM W1 ME9616S. CODEN MPBYAA.

Psychology

MICROPSYCH NETWORK. Vol. 1, No. 1-. 0748-2051. Periodical. US. English. bm. $23.95. Micropsych Network, PO Box 15560, Sarasota FL 34277-1560. **DD** 150.

MIND; A QUARTERLY REVIEW OF PSYCHOLOGY AND PHILOSOPHY. Periodical. UK. English. qt. $32.50. Oxford University Press, Walton Street, Oxford OX2 6DP England. **Tel** 0865 56767. **Ed** S Blackburn. **Ind/Abst** Humanit. Index, Lang. Lang. Behav. Abstr., Sociol. Abstr., Philos. Index, Am. Hist. Life, Hist. Abstr., Math. Rev. bk rev. **Circ** 867. Publishing original papers and discussions with a 'state of the art' series reviewing current debates in cognitive psychology and offering reviews and critical notes on recent literature.

MINERVA PSICHIATRICA. See Medicine - Psychiatry, Psychopathology.

MINNESOTA SYMPOSIA ON CHILD PSYCHOLOGY. (MINNESOTA SYMPOSIA ON CHILD PSYCHOLOGY. PAPERS). **VFOAT** Child Psychology. V. 1-. 0076-9266. US. English. an. Lawrence Erlbaum Associates, Box 112, 365 Broadway, Hillsdale NJ 07642. **Tel** (201)666-4110. **Ind/Abst** Biol. Abstr., Soc. Sci. Citation Index. **LC** BF721. **DD** 155.4. **NLM** W3 MI607. **CODEN** MSCRBG.

MODERN PSYCHOANALYSIS. V. 1- Spring 1976-. 0361-5227. Periodical. US. English. sa. $12.00. Center for Modern Psychoanalytic, 16 W 10th St, New York NY 10011. **Tel** (212)260-7052. **Ed** Phyllis W Meadow. **Ind/Abst** Cumul. Index Nurs. Allied Health Lit., Psychol. Abstr. **LC** RC500. **DD** 616.891705. **NLM** W1 MO1684. bk rev. **Circ** 1,200. Dedicated to publishing articles extending the theory and practice of psychoanalysis to the full range of emotional disorders.

MONOGRAPH - NEW YORK PSYCHOANALYTIC INSTITUTE. ERNST KRIS STUDY GROUP. (MONOGRAPH). 1-. 0077-9008. Monographic Series. US. English. ir. International University Press, 80 Northfield Avenue, Building 424, Edison NJ 08837. **LC** BF173.A2. **DD** 150.19505. **NLM** W1 MO558N.

MONOGRAPHIES FRANCAISES DE PSYCHOLOGIE. 1- 1958-. 0077-071X. Monographic Series. FR. French. ir. Editions du CNRS, 15 Quai Anatole France, F-75700 Paris France. **Ind/Abst** Psychol. Abstr. **NLM** W1 MO562N. French monograph series on psychology and child psychology.

MONOGRAPHS IN PSYCHOBIOLOGY AND DISEASE. See Biology.

MONOGRAPHS IN PSYCHOSOCIAL EPIDEMIOLOGY. Began publication in 1980. 0735-0155. Monographic Series. US. English. ir. Rutgers University Press, PO Box 4869/Distribution Center, Baltimore MD 21211. **Tel** (301)338-7791. **Ed** Ben Z Locke and Andrew Slaby. **LC** UNC. **DD** 302. **NLM** W1 MO568Q.

MONOGRAPHS OF THE AMERICAN ASSOCIATION ON MENTAL DEFICIENCY (1982). (MONOGRAPHS OF THE AMERICAN ASSOCIATION ON MENTAL DEFICIENCY). No. 5-. US. English. ir. $25.00. American Association on Mental Deficiency, 1719 Kalorama Road NW, Washington DC 20009. **Tel** (202)387-1968. **Ed** Michael J Begab. **NLM** W1 MO569QMC. **Circ** 3,000. Research, significant program and professional issues, state-of-the-art compilations on important topics in mental retardation and related disabilities. Monograph of the American Association of Mental Deficiency.

MOTIVATION AND EMOTION. V. 1- Mar. 1977-. 0146-7239. Periodical. US. English. qt. $90.00 Domestic, $101.00 Foreign. Plenum Press, 233 Spring Street, New York NY 10013. **Tel** (212)620-8000. **Ed** Mortimer H Appley. **Ind/Abst** Life Sci. Collect., Biol. Abstr., Curr. Contents, Excerpta Med., Psychol. Abstr., Ref. Z., Bibliogr. Index, Soc. Sci. Citation Index. **LC** BF683. **DD** 153.805. **NLM** W1 MO944. **CODEN** MOEMDJ. bk rev. adv acc. Primary focus is human motivation. Publishes theoretical papers, reviews position papers and original research basic or applied focussing on human motivation.

MOTIVATIONSFORSCHUNG. V. 1-. 0173-3532. Monographic Series. German. ir. Verlag fur Psychologie Hogrefe, Dr C J Hogrefe, Ghottingen West Germany. **Ed** H Heckhausen. **NLM** W1 MO79.

MULTIDISCIPLINARY RESEARCH. 0098-8553. Periodical. US. English. sa. International Multidisciplinary Research Association, 848 W Holt Avenue, Pomona CA 91768. **Ind/Abst** Comput. Control Abstr., Electr. Electron. Abstr., Sci. Abstr. Sect. A. Phys. Abstr. **LC** BF11. **DD** 051. **CODEN** MRINCS.

MULTIVARIATE BEHAVIORAL RESEARCH. **VFOAT** MBR. V. 1- Jan. 1966-. 0027-3171. Periodical. US. qt. $36.00. Society for Multivariate Experimental Psychology, PO Box 32902 TCU Station, Forth Worth TX 76126. **Tel** (817)921-7672. **Ed** A Ralph Hakstian. **Ind/Abst** Sociol. Abstr., Int. Aerosp. Abstr., Biol. Abstr., Psychol. Abstr., Curr. Index J. Educ., Bibliogr. Index, Soc. Sci. Citation Index, Lang. Lang. Behav. Abstr. **LC** BF39. **NLM** W1 MU398N. **CODEN** MVBRAV. bk rev. **Circ** 1,000. Substantive, theoretical and methodological articles of multivariate experimental psychology.

MULTIVARIATE BEHAVIORAL RESEARCH MONOGRAPHS. **VFOAT** MBR Monograph. No. 1- 1966-. 0580-1788. Monographic Series. US. English. qt. $36.00. Business Manager Multivariate Behavioral Research, Texas Christian University, Fort Worth TX 76129. **Tel** (817)921-7672. **Ed** James Steiger. **Ind/Abst** Sociol. Abstr., Biol. Abstr., Psychol. Abstr. **LC** UNC. **NLM** W1 MU398P. **CODEN** MBRMAO. **Circ** 900. Substantive, theoretical, and methodological articles of multivariate experimental psychology of interest to psychologists, psychiatrists, sociologists, educators, personnel and business managers, and related fields.

MULTIVARIATE EXPERIMENTAL CLINICAL RESEARCH. 1974. 0147-3964. Periodical. US. English. qt. $22.00 Domestic, $25.00 Foreign. Wichita State University, Department of Psychology, c/o Dr Charles Burdsal, PO Box 34, Witchita KS 67208. **Tel** (316)689-3170. **Ed** Charles A Burdsal Jr. **Ind/Abst** Excerpta Med., Biol. Abstr., Psychol. Abstr. **LC** BF698.A1. **DD** 155.280182. **NLM** W1 MU398W. **CODEN** MCREDA. **Circ** 250. Outlet for research in areas covered by the terms personality study, clinical diagnosis and therapy, extending into their learning, social, physiological applied and developmental aspects. Journal of Multivariate Experimental Personality and Clinical Psychology, 0149-9688.

MUSIC PERCEPTION. See Music.

MUSIC PSYCHOLOGY INDEX. See Indexes/Abstracts.

MUSIC THERAPY. See Music.

MUSIC THERAPY PERSPECTIVES. See Music.

MUSIKTHERAPEUTISCHE UMSCHAU. See Music.

NAROPA INSTITUTE JOURNAL OF PSYCHOLOGY. **VFOAT** Journal of Psychology. Vol. 1, No. 1-. 0271-7557. US. English. ir. $15.00. Naropa Institute Journal of Psychology, 2130 Arapahoe Avenue, Boulder CO 80302. **Tel** (303)444-0202. **Ed** Edward M Podvoll. **LC** RC489.E93. **DD** 616.8916. **NLM** W1 NA181E. **Circ** 2,000. Includes articles by pscyhotherapists and others in the helping professions who mix their clinical work with various contemplative disciplines, especially Buddhist meditation practice.

NATIONAL REGISTER OF HEALTH SERVICE PROVIDERS IN PSYCHOLOGY. 1975-. 0099-2151. US. English. Council for the National Register of Health Service, Providers in Psychology, 1200 17th Street NW, Washington DC 20036. **LC** BF30. **DD** 616.89002573. **NLM** BF 30 N27.

NATIONAL REGISTER OF HEALTH SERVICE PROVIDERS IN PSYCHOLOGY. CUMULATIVE SUPPLEMENT. Began with Winter 1975-76. 0278-6370. US. English. sa. National Register of Health Service Providers in Psychology, 1200 17th Street NW, Washington DC 20036. **LC** BF30. **DD** 150.2573.

NATIONAL REGISTER OF HEALTH SERVICE PROVIDERS IN PSYCHOLOGY. SUPPLEMENT. Winter 1975/76-. 0730-5540. US. English. sa. **CNRHSPP**, 1200 17th Street NW/Suite 403, Washington DC 20036. **Tel** (202)833-2377. **LC** BF30. **DD** 150.2573.

NEBRASKA SYMPOSIUM ON MOTIVATION. **VFOAT** Current Theory and Research in Motivation. V. 2- 1954-. 0146-7875. US. English. an. University of Nebraska Press, 901 North 17th Street, Lincoln NE 68588-0520. **Tel** (402)472-3581. **Ind/Abst** Index Med., Psychol. Abstr., Biol. Abstr. **LC** BF683. **DD** 159.4082. **NLM** W3 NE16. **CODEN** NSMPB3. Current Theory and Research in Motivation, 0070-2099.

NEUROPSYCHOLOGIA. See Medicine - Neurology.

NEUROSCIENCE AND BIOBEHAVIORAL REVIEWS. See Medicine - Neurology.

NEW DIRECTIONS FOR CHILD DEVELOPMENT. Began with: No. 1, 1978. 0195-2269. Monographic Series. US. English. qt. $40.00. Jossey Bass, 433 California Street, San Francisco CA 94104. **Tel** (415)433-1767. **Ed** William Damon. **Ind/Abst** Biol. Abstr., Psychol. Abstr. **LC** BF721. **DD** 155.4. **NLM** W1 NE374DR. **CODEN** NDCDDI. **Circ** 550. Explores the cognitive, social, emotional, moral, and linguistic development of children from infancy through adolescence.

NEW IDEAS IN PSYCHOLOGY. Vol. 1, No. 1-. 0732-118X. Periodical. UK. English. ir. Pergamon Press, 395 Sawmill River Road, Elmsford NY 10523. **Ind/Abst** Life Sci. Collect. **LC** BF1. **DD** 150.5. Available in microfiche simultaneously with the paper edition and on microfilm at the end of the subscription year.

NEW PATTERNS OF LEARNING. 0275-9578. Monographic Series. US. English. ir. John Wiley and Sons Inc, 605 Third Avenue, New York NY 10158.

NEW PSYCHOLOGIST. V. 1- Apr. 1978-. Periodical. UK. English. mo. Psychologist Magazine Ltd, 167 Ferne Park Road, Hornsey London N8 9 England. **LC** BF636.A1. **DD** 158.05. Psychologist, Practical and Personal Psychology.

NEW ZEALAND JOURNAL OF PSYCHOLOGY. Vol. 12, No. 1 (May 1983)-. 0112-109X. Periodical. English. sa. **NLM** W1. New Zealand Psychologist, 0303-6863.

NEW ZEALAND PSYCHOLOGIST CEASED. (THE NEW ZEALAND PSYCHOLOGIST). V. 1-11. 0303-6863. Periodical. NZ. English. ir. **Ind/Abst** Psychol. Abstr. **NLM** W1. **CODEN** NZPSDA.

NEWS AND ACTION - OTTAWA NETWORK. (NEWS AND ACTION). Vol. 1, No. 1 (Nov. 1983)-. 0825-0308. Periodical. CN. English. bm. $5.00. Transformation Research Network, 302-100 Gloucester Street, Ottawa Ontario K2P 0A4 Canada. **DD** 158.05.

NEWSLETTER - MENSA CANADA SOCIETY, REGINA BRANCH. (NEWSLETTER). Vol. 2, No. 10 (Oct. 1982)-. 0823-2318. Periodical. CN. English. mo. Free to Members. Mensa Canada Society, Regina Branch, PO Box 212, Regina Saskatchewan S4P 2Z9 Canada. **DD** 153.9806071244. Societe Mensa Canada. Regina (Newsletter), 0823-230X.

NEWSLETTER OF THE CPA SECTION ON WOMEN & PSYCHOLOGY. See Women.

NEWSLETTER - TASK FORCE ON WOMEN'S ISSUES. (NEWSLETTER). 0715-4283. Periodical. CN. English. qt. Free. Newsletter c/o P Stephenson Task Force on Women's Issues, 717 West 10th Avenue, Vancouver British Columbia B5Z 1L6 Canada. **DD** 155.63305.

NODAL : REVUE DE L'ASSOCIATION FREUDIENNE. 1-. Periodical. FR. French. ir. 66 rue de l'Universite, 75007 Paris France.

NORDISK PSYKOLOGI. V. 1-. 0029-1463. Periodical. DK. Danish. qt. $20.75. Akademisk Forlag, St Kannikestraede 6-8, Copenhagen Denmark. **Tel** (01)119826. **Ed** Schultz Jorgensen. **Ind/Abst** Psychol. Abstr., Lang. Lang. Behav. Abstr., Soc. Sci. Citation Index, Sociol. Abstr. **LC** BF8.D3. **NLM** W1 NO217D. **CODEN** NOPSAW. bk rev. **Circ** 3,000.

NORDISK TIDSKRIFT FOR BETEENDETERAPI. **VFOAT** Scandinavian Journal of Behaviour Therapy. V. 4- 1975-. 0345-1402. Periodical. articles mainly in Swedish with some in English. ir. **Ind/Abst** Psychol. Abstr. **NLM** W1 NO2197. Beteendeterapi.

NOUVELLE REVUE DE PSYCHANALYSE. No. 1- Spring 1970-. 0223-565X. Monographic Series. FR. French. sa. 310.00. Editions Gallimard, 49 rue de la Vanne, 92120 Montrouge France. **Tel** 656 89 00. **Ind/Abst** Psychol. Abstr. **NLM** W1 NO834G.

Psychology

NOVINKY LITERATURY : PSYCHOLOGIE. See Bibliographies.

NOVYE ISSLEDOVANIIA V PSIKHOLOGII. Began in 1973. Periodical. UR. Russian. sa. 0.65 Single Issue. 107066 Lefortovskii Per 8, Moskva Russian SFSR. **Ind/Abst** Psychol. Abstr. **LC** BF8.R8. **NLM** W1 NO9698. *Novye Issledovaniia V Psikhologii I Vozrastnoi Fiziologii.*

NUTRITION AND BEHAVIOR. See Nutrition and Dietetics.

OBSERVATIONS FROM THE TREADMILL. 0048-1335. US. English. 357 Hidden River Road, Narberth PA 19072. **LC** BF1. **DD** 081.

ODENSE UNIVERSITY STUDIES IN PSYCHIATRY AND MEDICAL PSYCHOLOGY. See Medicine - Psychiatry, Psychopathology.

OMEGA. V. 1-. 0030-2228. Periodical. US. English. qt. $64.00. Baywood Publishing Company, 43 Central Drive, Farmingdale NY 11735. **Tel** (516)249-2464. Ed Robert J Kastenbaum. **Ind/Abst** Excerpta Med., Sociol. Abstr., Soc. Welf. Soc. Plan./Policy Soc. Dev., Cumul. Index Nurs. Allied Health Lit., Curr. Index J. Educ., Psychol. Abstr., Soc. Sci. Index, Soc. Sci. Citation Index. **LC** BF789.D4. **DD** 155.937. **NLM** W1 OM423. **CODEN** OMGABX. bk rev. The international forum on the subject of thanatology. Terminal illness, suicide, violence and disaster, bereavement and grief, concepts and attitudes are explored.

ONTARIO PSYCHOLOGIST. (THE ONTARIO PSYCHOLOGIST). V. 1-. 0030-3054. Periodical. CN. English. bm. 50.00. Ontario Psychological Association, 1407 Yonge Street/Suite 402, Toronto Ontario M4T 1Y7 Canada. **Tel** (416)961-5552. Ed Mona Abbott-Kesting. **Ind/Abst** Psychol. Abstr. **LC** RC467. **DD** 150.5. **NLM** W1 ON856. bk rev. adv acc. **Circ** 1,300. (ctrl). Articles and news items about professional psychology in Ontario directed at members of the profession. *O.P.A. Quarterly, 0318-2657.*

OPA UPDATE. (O P A UPDATE). Main/Corp Ontario Psychological Association. VFOAT Update. VAT Ontario Psychological Association Update, Update (Toronto. 1977). V. 1- Feb. 1977-. 0703-8895. Periodical. CN. English. qt. Free. Ontario Psychological Association, 245 Old Forest Hill Road, Toronto Ontario M6C 2H5 Canada. **DD** 150.62713. (ctrl).

THE ORACLE. (THE ORACLE : NEWSLETTER OF ORANGE COUNTY MENSA). 0746-8822. Periodical. US. English. mo. Free to Orange County Mensa Members, $7.00 Other Mensa Members (directory not included), $10.00 Nonmembers (directory not included). The Oracle, PO Box 18265, Irvine CA 92713.

ORGANIZATIONAL BEHAVIOR AND HUMAN DECISION PROCESSES. Vol. 35, No. 1 (Feb. 1985)-. 0749-5978. Periodical. US. English. bm. $162.00. Academic Press, 111 Fifth Avenue, New York NY 10003. **Ind/Abst** Hospit. Lit. Index. **DD** 158. **NLM** W1. *Organizational Behavior and Human Performance, 0030-5073.*

ORGANIZATIONAL BEHAVIOR AND HUMAN PERFORMANCE CEASED. V. 1-34. 0030-5073. Periodical. US. English. bm. $33.00 Domestic, $36.00 Foreign. Academic Press, 4805 Sand Lake Road, Orlando FL 32819. **Ind/Abst** Manage. Contents, Int. Labour Doc., Hospit. Lit. Index, Cumul. Index Nurs. Allied Health Lit., Int. Aerosp. Abstr., ABI/Inform, Psychol. Abstr., Bus. Period. Index. **LC** BF636.A1. **DD** 158.705. **NLM** W1 OR663G. **CODEN** OBHPA5.

ORIGINS OF BEHAVIOR. (THE ORIGINS OF BEHAVIOR). V. 1- 1974-. 0094-6206. Periodical. US. English. ir. John Wiley & Sons Inc, 1 Wiley Drive, Somerset NJ 08873. **NLM** W1 OR687.

PAKISTAN JOURNAL OF PSYCHOLOGY. V. 1- July 1967-. 0030-9869. Periodical. English. sa. University of Karachi, Department of Psychology, Karachi 32 W Pakistan. **LC** BF1. **DD** 150.5. **NLM** W1 PA356V.

PAVLOVIAN JOURNAL OF BIOLOGICAL SCIENCE. (THE PAVLOVIAN JOURNAL OF BIOLOGICAL SCIENCE). V. 9- Jan./March 1974-. 0093-2213. Periodical. US. English. qt. Lippincott/Harper, 2350 Virginia Avenue, Hagerstown MD 21740. **Ind/Abst** Excerpta Med., Life Sci. Collect., Index Med., Biol. Abstr., Energy Res. Abstr., Chem. Abstr., Psychol. Abstr., Soc. Sci. Citation Index. **LC** BF1. **DD** 150.194405. **NLM** W1 PA998H. **CODEN** PJBSAH. *Conditional Reflex, 0010-5392.*

PEABODY JOURNAL OF EDUCATION. See Education (General).

PEDAGOGICHESKIE PROBLEMY FORMIROVANIIA POZNAVATELNYKH INTERESOV UCHASHCHIKHSIA. Vol. 1-. Periodical. UR. Russian. an. 1.28. Leningradskii Gos Ped, 191186 G Leningrad, Naberezhnaia Reki Moiki, 48 Leningrad USSR SFSR. **LC** AZ711.

PEDAGOGIKA IR PSICHOLOGIJA CEASED. Series/Titl Lietuvos Tsr Aukstuju Mokyklu Moskslo Darbai. 1- 1962-. UR. Multilingual (Lithuanian or Russian). mo. $9.00. Victor Kamkin Inc (70106), 12224 Parklawn Drive, Rockville MD 20852. **Tel** (301)881-5973. **LC** LB1051. **NLM** W1 LI33.

PENSAMIENTOS. No. 1 1975-. Periodical. US. English. an. Rational Island Publishers, Box 2081 Main Office Station, Seattle WA 98111.

PERCEPTION. V. 1- 1972-. 0301-0066. Periodical. UK. English. bm. 135.00. Pion Ltd, 207 Brondesbury Park, London NW2 5JN England. **Tel** (01)459-0066. Ed R Gregory. **Ind/Abst** Excerpta Med., Index Med., Life Sci. Collect., Psychol. Abstr., Soc. Sci. Citation Index. **LC** BF311. **DD** 153.705. **NLM** W1 PE78G. **CODEN** PCTNBA. bk rev. adv acc. **Circ** 700. Experimental results and theoretical ideas in fields of animal, human and machine perception.

PERCEPTION AND PERCEPTUAL DEVELOPMENT. V. 1-. 0191-2518. Monographic Series. US. English. ir. Plenum Press, 233 Spring Street, New York NY 10013. **Tel** (212)620-8000. Ed H L Pick, and R D Walk. **NLM** W1 PE78GM.

PERCEPTION & PSYCHOPHYSICS. VAT Perception and Psychophysics. V. 1- Jan. 1966-. 0031-5117. Periodical. US. English. mo. $86.00. Psychonomic Society Inc, 2904 Guadalupe Street, Austin TX 78705. **Tel** (512)476-9687. Ed Charles W Eriksen. **Ind/Abst** MLA Int. Bibliogr. Books Artic. Mod. Lang. Lit., Life Sci. Collect., Excerpta Med., Lang. Lang. Behav. Abstr., Int. Aerosp. Abstr., Biol. Abstr., Int. Aerosp. Abstr., Psychol. Abstr., Soc. Sci. Citation Index, Sociol. Abstr., Soc. Sci. Index, Abr. Ed. **LC** BF233. **DD** 153.705. **NLM** W1 PE78H. **CODEN** PEPSBJ. adv acc. **Circ** 1,775. (ctrl). Deals with sensory processes, perception and psychophysics. Although the majority of articles report experimental investigations, also included are articles that are theoretical.

PERCEPTUAL AND MOTOR SKILLS. V. 5- Mar. 1955-. 0031-5125. Periodical. US. English. bm. $160.00. Box 9229, Missoula MT 59807. **Tel** (406)243-5091. Ed R B Ammons and Carol H Ammons. **Ind/Abst** MLA Int. Bibliogr. Books Artic. Mod. Lang. Lit., Life Sci. Collect., Excerpta Med., Sociol. Abstr., Lang. Lang. Behav. Abstr., Women Stud. Abstr., Int. Aerosp. Abstr., Energy Res. Abstr., Biol. Abstr., Nucl. Sci. Abstr., Index Med., Curr. Index J. Educ., Psychol. Abstr., Soc. Sci. Index, Soc. Sci. Citation Index. **NLM** W1 PE78K. **CODEN** PMOSAZ. bk rev. Experimental or theoretical articles dealing with perception or motor skills, especially as affected by experience; articles on general methodology; new material listing and reviews. *Perceptual and Motor Skills Research Exchange, 0885-6524.*

PERCEPTUAL COGNITIVE DEVELOPMENT. V. 1-6, No. 6. Periodical. US. English.

PERFILES EDUCATIVOS. See Education (General) - Higher Education.

PERFORMANCE MANAGEMENT MAGAZINE. See Business - General Management.

PERSONAL GROWTH AND BEHAVIOR. VFOAT Annual Editions: Personal Growth and Behavior. 0732-0779. Periodical. US. English. ir. $8.95. Dushkin Publishing Group, Sluice Dock, Guilford CT 06437. **Tel** (203)453-4351. **LC** BF698.A1. **DD** 155. Annually updated collection of public press articles covering current issues in personal growth and behavior. Includes topic guide and complete index.

PERSONALITY AND INDIVIDUAL DIFFERENCES. V. 1- 1980-. 0191-8869. Periodical. UK. English. bm. $110.00. Pergamon Press, 395 Sawmill River Road, Elmsford NY 10523. **Ind/Abst** Biol. Abstr., Psychol. Abstr., Sci. Cit. Index, Abr. Ed. **NLM** W1 PE86T. **CODEN** PEIDD9.

PERSONALITY AND SOCIAL PSYCHOLOGY BULLETIN. V. 1- Winter 1975-. 0146-1672. Periodical. US. English. qt. **Ind/Abst** Soc. Sci. Index, Soc. Sci. Citation Index, Psychol. Abstr. **LC** BF698.A1. **DD** 301.105. *Proceedings of the Division of Personality and Social Psychology.*

PERSONALITY ASSESSMENT SYSTEM FOUNDATION JOURNAL. VFOAT Journal. Vol. 1, No. 1 (Spring 1982)-. 0740-4379. Periodical. US. English. qt. $3.00 (Single Issue). Alfred Couchon, c/o Personality Assessment, System Institute, PO Box 4164, Martinsville VA 24115. **LC** BF698.4. **DD** 155.28.

PERSONALITY STUDY AND GROUP BEHAVIOUR. Vol. 1, No. 1 (Jan. 1981)-. Periodical. II. English. sa. $10.00. Editor/Department of Psychology, Guru Nanak Dev University, Amritsar 143005 India. **Ind/Abst** Psychol. Abstr. **LC** BF698.9.S63. **DD** 155.205.

PERSONNEL PSYCHOLOGY. V. 1- Spring 1948-. 0031-5826. Periodical. US. English. qt. $40.00. Personnel Psychology, 9660 Hillcroft/Suite 337, Houston TX 77096. **Tel** (614)299-0508. Ed Paul R Sackett. **Ind/Abst** Manage. Contents, Bus. Period. Index, ABI/Inform, Book Rev. Index, Ref. Source, Curr. Index J. Educ., Psychol. Abstr., Women Stud. Abstr., Soc. Sci. Citation Index. **LC** HF5549.A2. **DD** 658.305. **NLM** W1 PE8702. **CODEN** PPSYAQ. (cum index). bk rev. **Circ** 3,000. Issued also in microform by University Microfilms International. Top-rated journal in industrial/organizational psychology; read by personnel managers, teachers and students in business schools and psychology departments. Refereed journal with book reviews.

PERSPECTIVAS EN PSICOLOGIA. V. 1, No. 1 (May/August 1982)-. 0120-3878. Periodical. CK. Spanish (summaries in English). ty. $4.00. Apartado Aereo, 868 Manizales Colombia. **LC** BF5. **DD** 150.5.

PERSPECTIVES IN LAW & PSYCHOLOGY. See Law.

PERSPECTIVES IN PSYCHOTHERAPY. 0735-4037. Periodical. US. English. ir. Gordon and Breach, One Park Avenue, New York NY 10016.

PERSPEKTIEWE IN DIE BEDRYFSIELKUNDE. VFOAT Perspectives in Industrial Psychology. Periodical. SA. Afrikaans (English). ir. University of South Africa, Department of Industrial Psychology, Stellenbosch 7600 Republic of South Africa. **LC** HF5548.8. **DD** 158.705.

PHARMACOLOGY, BIOCHEMISTRY AND BEHAVIOR. See Pharmacy.

PHARMACOLOGY BIOCHEMISTRY & BEHAVIOR. SUPPLEMENT. See Pharmacy.

PHYSIOLOGICAL PSYCHOLOGY. V. 1- Mar. 1973-. 0090-5046. Periodical. US. English. qt. $40.00. The Psychonomic Society Inc, 2904 Guadalupe Street, c/o P Kittrell, Austin TX 78705. **Tel** (512)476-9687. **Ind/Abst** Life Sci. Collect., Excerpta Med., Chem. Abstr., Biol. Abstr., Psychol. Abstr., Sci. Cit. Index, Abr. Ed., Sociol. Abstr., Lang. Lang. Behav. Abstr. **LC** QP360. **DD** 152.05. **NLM** W1 PH926N. **CODEN** PLPSAX. adv acc. **Circ** 1,275. (ctrl). Encompasses allied fields of neurosciences that relate to behavior and experience. Includes review and theoretical papers from many disciplines e.g. psychology, pharmacology, anatomy and physiology. *Psychonomic Science, 0033-3131.*

PHYSIOLOGY & BEHAVIOR. See Biology - Physiology.

PILGRIMAGE. V. 1- 1972-. 0361-0802. Periodical. US. English. ty. $36.00. Human Sciences Press, 72 Fifth Avenue, New York NY 10011. **LC** BF204.5. **DD** 616.891405. **CODEN** PILGDR.

THE PLAIN RAPPER. (PLAIN RAPPER). 1970. 0032-0412. Periodical. US. English. qt. $2.00. Project Eden, 22738 Mission Boulevard, Hayward CA 94541. **Tel** (415)887-0566. Ed Linda Cherry. bk rev. adv acc. **Circ** 2,400. (ctrl). Newsletter of substance abuse, education, prevention, and counseling program for youth and families in Hayward, Castro Valley, and San Lorenzo (Alameda County), California.

POLISH PSYCHOLOGICAL BULLETIN. V. 1- 1970-. 0079-2993. Periodical. PL. English. qt. ARS Polona, Krakowskie Przedmiescie 7, 00-068 Warsaw Poland. **Ind/Abst** Psychol. Abstr., Soc. Sci. Citation Index. **LC** BF1. **CODEN** PPBUDY.

Psychology

POLITICAL PSYCHOLOGY. V. 1- Spring 1979-. 0162-895X. Periodical. US. English. qt. $105.00 Domestic, $118.00 Foreign. Plenum Press, 233 Spring Street, New York NY 10013. Tel (212)620-8000. Ed Alfred M Freedman. Ind/Abst Psychol. Abstr. LC JA74.5. DD 320.019. bk rev. adv acc. This is an interdisciplinary journal dedicated to examining the relationships between psychological and political phenomena.

POPULAR PSYCHOLOGY. 0091-5157. Periodical. US. English. bm. Popular Psychology, 14018 Ventura Boulevard, Sherman Oaks CA 91403. LC BF1. DD 150.5.

PRACE PSYCHOLOGICZNE. Main/Corp Uniwersytet Slaski W Katowicach. Series/Titl Prace Naukowe Uniwersytetu Slaskiego W Katowicach. Began in 1971. PL. Polish (summaries in English and Russian). ir. 10.00 single issue. Ul Bankowa 12, Katowice Poland. Tel 589-933. LC LB1051. (ctrl). Covers human problems, at work environments, job attitudes, adjustment to work, workers appraisal, professional careers, personnel management, and leadership, organizational behavior and innovations in organizations.

PRAXIS DER PSYCHOTHERAPIE UND PSYCHOSOMATIK. Vol. 24- 1979-. 0171-791X. Periodical. German. bm. Springer Verlag-New York Inc, 175 5th Avenue, New York NY 10010. Tel (212)460-1500. Ed M Ermann and Th Seifert. Ind/Abst Excerpta Med., Biol. Abstr., Psychol. Abstr., Curr. Contents, Soc. Sci. Citation Index. NLM W1 PR321K. CODEN PRPPDZ. bk rev. Available in microform. Covers psychotherapy, application of psychotherapeutic processes in various medical branches, psychology, original articles, lectures, book reviews, list of events, and special emphasis on problems in the practice. Praxis der Psychotherapie, 0032-7077.

THE PRIMAL INSTITUTE NEWSLETTER. Main/Corp Primal Institute. 1978. 2144-5056. Periodical. US. English. mo. $11.00 Domestic/Canada, $15.00 Others. Primal Institute Newsletter, 2215 Colby Avenue, Los Angeles CA 90064. Tel (213)478-0167. Ed Cindy Naughton and Nick Barton. bk rev. Circ 1,000. (ctrl). All information pertinent to primal therapy of latest developments in psychology. Letters from patient and staff as well as non-patients. Comments, book reviews, science watch, letters, events, etc.

PROBLEME UND ERGEBNISSE DER PSYCHOLOGIE. 1-80. 0048-5403. Periodical. GE. German. qt. Detuscher Buch Export-Import, Leninstrasse 16, DDR-701 Leipzig East Germany. LC BF23. NLM W1 PR56R.

PROBLEMY INDUSTRIALNOI PSIKHOLOGII. See Business.

PROCEEDINGS AND ABSTRACTS, AMERICAN INSTITUTE FOR DECISION SCIENCES, ANNUAL MEETING, WESTERN REGIONAL CONFERENCE. See Indexes/Abstracts.

PROCEEDINGS - BIOFEEDBACK SOCIETY OF AMERICA. MEETING. (PROCEEDINGS). Main/Conf Biofeedback Society of America. Meeting. VFOAT BSA Proceedings. 14th (Mar. 18-23, 1983)-. 0739-6252. US. English. an. $12.00 Members, $16.00 Nonmembers. BSA, 4301 Owens Street, Wheat Ridge CO 80033. Proceedings of the Biofeedback Society of America Annual Meeting, 0276-2838.

PROCEEDINGS OF THE BIOFEEDBACK RESEARCH SOCIETY ANNUAL MEETING. (PROCEEDINGS OF THE ANNUAL MEETING). Main/Corp Biofeedback Research Society. 1972. 0094-0895. US. English. an. $17.00. Biofeedback Society of America, 4301 Owens Avenue, Wheat Ridge CO 80033. Tel (303)422-8436. LC BF319.5.B5. DD 615.8. NLM W1 PR5847K. bk rev. adv acc. Contains copies of brief papers for submitted presentations at annual Biofeedback Society meeting.

PROCEEDINGS, OF THE SOCIETY FOR EXPERIMENTAL STRESS ANALYSIS. Main/Conf Society for Experimental Stress Analysis. V.1- 1943-. 0036-1313. US. English. an. $75.00. Society Experimental Mechanics, 14 Fairfield Drive, Brookfield Center CT 06805. Tel (203)775-6373. (cum index).

PROFESSIONAL PRACTICE OF PSYCHOLOGY. See Law.

PROFESSIONAL PSYCHOLOGY CEASED. V. 1-13. 0033-0175. Periodical. US. English. bm. $7.00 APA member, $18.00 US Non-Member, $19.00 Foreign Non-Member. American Psychological Association, 1200 17th Street Northwest, Washington DC 20030. Ind/Abst Psychol. Abstr. LC RC467. DD 175.9.05. CODEN PFPSAP. Microform editions available from Johnson Associates, University Microfilms, or Princeton Microfilms.

PROFESSIONAL PSYCHOLOGY, RESEARCH AND PRACTICE. Vol. 14, No. 1 (Feb. 1983)-. 0735-7028. Periodical. US. English. bm. $86.00. American Psychological Association, 1400 North Uhle Street, Arlington VA 22201. Tel (703)247-7802. Ed Susan Knapp. Ind/Abst Psychol. Abstr. LC RC467. DD 616.89005. NLM W1 PR601B. adv acc. Circ 4,100. Articles on techniques and practices used in the application of psychology, including applications of research, standards of practice, interprofessional relations, delivery of services, and training. Professional Psychology, 0033-0175.

PROGRESS IN APPLIED SOCIAL PSYCHOLOGY. See Sociology: General Works, Theory.

PROGRESS IN BEHAVIOR MODIFICATION. V. 1- 1975-. 0099-037X. US. English. an. Academic Press, 4805 Sand Lake Road, Orlando FL 32887. Tel (305)345-4100. Ed Michael Hersen, Richard Eisler and Peter M Miller. Ind/Abst Index Med., Soc. Sci. Citation Index. LC BF637.B4. DD 616.8914. NLM W1 PR666GM.

PROGRESS IN PHYCOLOGICAL RESEARCH. Vol. 1-. 0167-8574. Periodical. US. English. ir. Elsevier Science Publishing Company Ltd, 52 Vanderbilt Avenue, New York NY 10017. Ind/Abst Chem. Abstr. LC QK564. DD 589.3. CODEN PPREEX.

PROGRESS IN PSYCHOBIOLOGY AND PHYSIOLOGICAL PSYCHOLOGY. See Biology - Physiology.

PROGRESS IN SOCIAL PSYCHOLOGY. Vol. 1-. Monographic Series. US. English. ir. Lawrence Erlbaum Associates, 365 Broadway, Box 112, Hillsdale NJ 07642.

PRZEGLAD PSYCHOLOGICZNY. Began in 1952. 0048-5675. Periodical. PL. Polish (tables of contents also in English, some in Russian or French). qt. ARS Polona, Krakowskie Przedmiescie 7, 00-068 Warsaw Poland. Ind/Abst Sociol. Abstr., Psychol. Abstr. LC BF26. NLM W1 PR936K. CODEN PRZPBF.

PSI CHI NEWSLETTER. Main/Corp Psi Chi. 0033-2569. Periodical. US. English. qt. $6.25. Psi Chi National Office, 1400 North Uhle Street, Arlington VA 22201. Tel (803)522-2538. Ed Ruth Hubbard Cousins. LC LJ121. DD 378.1985415. bk rev. Circ 13,000. (ctrl).

PSICODEIA. 0377-8320. Periodical. SP. Spanish. mo. $21.43. Ediciones Inapp, Habana 66, Madrid 16 Spain. LC BF5. NLM W1 PS148.

PSICOLOGIA ITALIANA. Vol. 1, N. 1-. Periodical. Italian. bm. 30.000. Cooperativa Libraria Universitaria Editrice Bologna Soc Coop, A R I. Via Marsala 24, 40126 Bologna Italy. LC BF4. DD 150.5.

PSIKHOLOGICHESKII ZHURNAL. V. 1- Jan./Feb. 1980-. Periodical. UR. Russian (summaries in English). bm. $44.00. Victor Kamkin Inc (70742), 12224 Parklawn Drive, Rockville MD 20852. Tel (301)881-5973. Ind/Abst Psychol. Abstr. LC BF8.R8.

PSYCHE. Vol. 1-. 0033-2623. Periodical. GW. German. mo. $42.61. W E Saarbach GMBH, Postfach 1016108 D-5000 Koln 1 West Germany. Tel (0221)234631. Ind/Abst Index Med., Psychol. Abstr. LC BF173.A2. DD 150.19505. NLM W1 PS225. CODEN PSYEDK. (cum index).

PSYCHOANALYTIC PSYCHOLOGY. (PSYCHOANALYTIC PSYCHOLOGY : THE OFFICIAL JOURNAL OF THE DIVISION OF PSYCHOANALYSIS, AMERICAN PSYCHOLOGICAL ASSOCIATION, DIVISION 39). Vol. 1, No. 1 (Winter 1984)-. 0736-9735. Periodical. US. English. qt. $45.00. Lawrence Erlbaum Associates Inc, 365 Broadway, Hillsdale NJ 07642. NLM W1.

THE PSYCHOANALYTIC QUARTERLY. V. 1- Apr. 1932-. 0033-2828. Periodical. US. English. qt. $48.00 Domestic, $53.00 Foreign. Psychoanalytic Quarterly, 175 Fifth Avenue Room 210, New York NY 10010. Tel (212)982-9358. Ed Sander M Abend. Ind/Abst Excerpta Med., Sociol. Abstr., Soc. Welf. Soc. Plan./Policy Soc. Dev., Index Med., Psychol. Abstr., Soc. Work Res. Abstr., Lang. Lang. Behav. Abstr., Soc. Sci. Citation Index, Hospit. Lit. Index, Abstr. Soc. Work. LC BF173.A2. DD 131.3405. NLM W1 PS437. CODEN PSQAAX. (cum index). bk rev. Circ 4,000. Articles on psychoanalysis.

PSYCHOANALYTIC REVIEW. V. 1- Nov. 1913-. 0033-2836. Periodical. US. English. qt. $69.00. Guilford Press, 200 Park Avenue South, Robin Dewender, New York NY 10003. Tel (212)674-1900. Ed Leila Lerner. Ind/Abst Biol. Abstr., Psychol. Abstr., Index Med., Abstr. Soc. Work., Psychol. Abstr., Soc. Sci. Citation Index, Sociol. Abstr., Women Stud. Abstr., Hospit. Lit. Index, Lang. Lang. Behav. Abstr., Abstr. Anthropol., Abstr. Engl. Stud. LC BF1. DD 61689. NLM W1 PS411. CODEN PSREAG. bk rev. adv acc. Circ 2,000. Leading forum for critical discourse in psychoanalytic theory and clinical practice and their application to art, literature, history and the creative process. Psychoanalysis.

THE PSYCHOANALYTIC STUDY OF THE CHILD. V. 1- 1945-. 0079-7308. US. English. an. Yale University Press, 92A Yale Station, New Haven CT 06520. Tel (203)432-4969. Ind/Abst Excerpta Med., Educ. Index, Biol. Abstr., Psychol. Abstr., Index Med., Soc. Sci. Citation Index. LC BF721. DD 131.34058. NLM W1 PS45. CODEN PYACAZ. (cum index).

PSYCHOANALYTIC STUDY OF THE CHILD. (MONOGRAPH SERIES OF THE PSYCHOANALYTIC STUDY OF THE CHILD). No. 1- 1965-. Periodical. US. English. ir. Yale University Press, 92A Yale Station, New Haven CT 06520. Tel (203)436-7583.

PSYCHOENERGETICS. Vol. 4, No. 1 (1981)-. Periodical. US. English. ir. $184.00. Gordon & Breach, PO Box 197, London WC2E 9PX England. Ed Brian Millar. Each issue contains an index to its own contents - no vol index - loose. bk rev. adv acc. Psychoenergetic Systems.

THE PSYCHOHISTORY REVIEW. V. 5- June 1976-. 0363-891X. Periodical. US. English. qt. $40.00. Charles B Strozier, Sagamon State University, Brookens 382, Springfield IL 62708. Tel (217)786-6778. Ed Charles B Strozier. Ind/Abst Am. Hist. Life, Hist. Abst., Part B, Twent. Century Abstr., Sociol. Abstr., Soc. Welf. Soc. Plan./Policy Soc. Dev., Writ. Am. Hist., Hist. Abstr., Part A, Mod. Hist. Abstr., Psychol. Abstr., Soc. Work Res. Abstr., Recent Publ. Artic., Hist. Abstr. LC D16.16. DD 155. NLM W1 PS526. CODEN PSRVD2. bk rev. adv acc. Circ 300. Makes systematic use of concepts, principles and theories of psychology to enhance understanding of particular persons and events in the past. Newsletter - Group for the Use of Psychology in History, 0162-9999.

PSYCHOLOGIA. Began with June 1957 issue. 0033-2852. Periodical. JA. English. qt. $45.00. Psychologia Society, Kyoto University, Department of Psychology, Kyoto 606 Japan. Tel (075)751-2111. Ed Noboru Sakano. Ind/Abst Sociol. Abstr., Psychol. Abstr., Soc. Sci. Citation Index, Lang. Lang. Behav. Abstr. LC BF1. DD 150.5. NLM W1 PS528T. CODEN PYLGAY. bk rev. adv acc. Circ 1,000. Original works in very broad fields of psychology.

PSYCHOLOGIA; AN INTERNATIONAL JOURNAL OF PSYCHOLOGY IN THE ORIENT. V.1- June 1957-. Periodical. JA. English. qt. Kyoto University, Department of Educational Psychology, Kyoto 606 Japan. Ed Koji Sato.

PSYCHOLOGIA UNIVERSALIS. 0555-5582. Monographic Series. GW. German. ir. Verlag Anton Hain Meisenheim, Postfach 1220, D-6240 Koenigstein/Ts West Germany. Tel 06174/3021. Ed Gustav Adolf Lienert, Thomae, Wilhelm Witte Steingruber, Hans Thomae and Wilhelm Witte. Ind/Abst Psychol. Abstr. NLM W1 PS534. CODEN PSUNDR. bk rev. adv acc. Circ 400. Covers experimental psychology.

PSYCHOLOGICA BELGICA. V. 1- 1946/53-. 0033-2879. Periodical. Dutch (1946/53, Flemish and French, (1978-) English and French, with summaries in English). sa. $17.05. Editorial Secretariat, Tiensestraat 102, B-3000 Louvain Belgium. Tel 016/23.39.41. Ed Belgian Psychological Society. Ind/Abst Life Sci. Collect., Biol. Abstr., CIS Abstr., Psychol. Abstr., Soc. Sci. Citation Index. LC BF30. DD 150.5. NLM W1 PS541. CODEN PBELAN. bk rev. adv acc. Circ 500. (ctrl). Publishes scientific contributions to various fields in psychology.

PSYCHOLOGICAL ABSTRACTS. See Indexes/Abstracts.

PSYCHOLOGICAL BULLETIN. V. 1- Jan. 1904-. 0033-2909. Periodical. US. English. bm. $124.00. American Psychological Association, 1400 North Uhle Street, Arlington VA 22201. **Tel** (703)247-7802. **Ed** Susan Knapp. **Ind/Abst** MLA Int. Bibliogr. Books Artic. Mod. Lang. Lit., Int. Labour Doc., Life Sci. Collect., Women Stud. Abstr., Int. Aerosp. Abstr., Biol. Abstr., Psychol. Abstr., Index Med., Nuci. Sci. Abstr., Curr. Index J. Educ., Soc. Sci. Index. **LC** BF1. **DD** 150.5. **NLM** W1 PS557. **CODEN** PSBUAI. adv acc. **Circ** 8,700. Evaluative reviews of research literature and interpretations of substantive, methodological and research-design issues.

PSYCHOLOGICAL DOCUMENTS. Vol. 13, No. 1 (July 1983)-. 0737-6561. US. English. sa. $6.00 Members, $14.00 Nonmembers Domestic, $16.00 Nonmembers Foreign. APA Subscription Department, 1400 North Uhle Street, Arlington VA 22201. **Ind/Abst** Psychol. Abstr. **LC** BF1. **DD** 150.5. **NLM** Z 7203. *Catalog of Selected Documents in Psychology, 0045-5938.*

PSYCHOLOGICAL ISSUES. Monograph 1-. 0048-5748. Monographic Series. US. English. ir. International University Press International, 80 Northfield Avenue Building, #424, Edison NJ 08837. **Tel** (212)684-7900. **Ind/Abst** Index Med., Psychol. Abstr., Sociol. Abstr., Lang. Lang. Behav. Abstr. **LC** UNC. **NLM** W1 PS572. **CODEN** PSYIA.

PSYCHOLOGICAL MEDICINE. V. 1- 1970-. 0033-2917. Periodical. UK. English. bm. $195.00. Cambridge University Press, 510 North Avenue, New Rochelle NY 10801. **Ed** Michael Shepherd. **Ind/Abst** Life Sci. Collect., Excerpta Med., Index Med., Cumul. Index Nurs. Allied Health Lit., Chem. Abstr., Psychol. Abstr., Soc. Sci. Citation Index, Sci. Cit. Index, Abr. Ed., Hospit. Lit. Index. **NLM** W1 PS591. **CODEN** PSMDCO. bk rev. Publishes more than 900 pages a year of original research in clinical psychiatry and the basic sciences related to it.

PSYCHOLOGICAL MEDICINE. MONOGRAPH SUPPLEMENT. **VFOAT** Monograph Supplement. 1-. 0264-1801. Monographic Series. UK. English. sa. $199.00. Cambridge University Press, 32 East 57th Street, New York NY 10022. **Tel** (212)688-8888. **Ed** Michael Shepherd. **Ind/Abst** Index Med. **NLM** W1 PS591B. bk rev. adv acc. **Circ** 3,000. Concerned with original research in clinical psychiatry and the basic sciences related to it.

PSYCHOLOGICAL PERSPECTIVES. V. 1- Spring 1970-. 0033-2925. Periodical. US. English. sa. $6.00. Psychological Perspectives, 10349 West Pico Boulevard, Los Angeles CA 90064. **Ind/Abst** Psychol. Abstr. **LC** BF173.A2. **DD** 150.5.

PSYCHOLOGICAL READER'S GUIDE. (THE PSYCHOLOGICAL READER'S GUIDE). V. 1- Jan. 1973-. 0300-0443. SZ. English. mo. 80.00. Elsevier Sequoia SA, PO Box 851, CH-1001 1 Lausanne Switzerland. **LC** Z7203 BF1. **DD** 016.15. **NLM** Z 7203 P9763.

THE PSYCHOLOGICAL RECORD. V. 1- Mar. 1937-. 0033-2933. Periodical. US. English. qt. $32.00. Kenyon College, Gambier OH 43022. **Tel** (614)427-2244. **Ed** Charles E Rice. **Ind/Abst** Sociol. Abstr., Soc. Welf. Soc. Plan./Policy Soc. Dev., Lang. Lang. Behav. Abstr., Life Sci. Collect., Ref. Source, Biol. Abstr., Psychol. Abstr., Nuci. Sci. Abstr., Soc. Sci. Index, Sci. Cit. Index, Abr. Ed., Soc. Sci. Citation Index. **LC** BF1. **DD** 150.5, 159.905. **NLM** W1 PS632. **CODEN** PYRCAI. bk rev. **Circ** 1,450. Theoretical and experimental articles on current development in psychology.

PSYCHOLOGICAL REPORTS. V. 1- Mar. 1955-. 0033-2941. Periodical. US. English. bm. $160.00. Southern Universities Press, PO Box 9229, Missoula MT 59807. **Tel** (406)243-5091. **Ed** Robert B Ammons and Carol H Ammons. **Ind/Abst** Life Sci. Collect., Excerpta Med., Sociol. Abstr., Soc. Welf. Soc. Plan./Policy Soc. Dev., Lang. Lang. Behav. Abstr., Index Med., Cumul. Index Nurs. Allied Health Lit., Women Stud. Abstr., Int. Aerosp. Abstr., Biol. Abstr., Psychol. Abstr., Soc. Sci. Index, Soc. Sci. Citation Index, Hospit. Lit. Index. **LC** BF21. **DD** 150.82. **NLM** W1 PS635. **CODEN** PYRTAZ. bk rev. Experimental, theoretical, speculative articles. Encourages scientific originality and creativity in the field of general psychology. Special reviews and listings of new books and material received.

PSYCHOLOGICAL RESEARCH. V. 37- Sept. 1974-. 0340-0727. Periodical. English (articles also in German with summaries in English or German). qt. $79.00. Springer Verlag-New York Inc, 175 5th Avenue, New York NY 10010. **Tel** (212)460-1500. **Ed** E Scheerer. **Ind/Abst** Psychol. Abstr., Index Med., Soc. Sci. Citation Index. **LC** BF3. **DD** 150.5. **NLM** W1 PS635J. **CODEN** PSREDJ. Reflects recent emphasis on cognition functions, biological substrates of behavior, psycholinguistics, psychophysics, and integrative analyses of higher mental processes from a variety of theoretical viewpoints. *Psychologische Forschung, 0033-3026.*

PSYCHOLOGICAL RESEARCH BULLETIN. 1- 1961-. 0555-5620. Periodical. SW. English. ir. $15.00. Department of Psychology, Paradisgatan 5 P, 223 50 Lund Sweden. **Tel** 046/10700. **Ed** Gudmund Smith. **Ind/Abst** Psychol. Abstr. **CODEN** PRBUDE. Empirical psychological studies, often concerned with the analysis of personality.

PSYCHOLOGICAL REVIEW. Periodical. US. English. qt. $62.00. American Psychological Association, 1400 North Uhle Street, Arlington VA 22201. **Tel** (703)247-7802. **Ed** Susan Knapp. **Ind/Abst** Soc. Sci. Index, Lang. Lang. Behav. Abstr., Sci. Cit. Index, Abr. Ed., Index Med., Sociol. Abstr., MLA Int. Bibliogr. Books Artic. Mod. Lang. Lit., Soc. Work Res. Abstr., Psychol. Abstr., Soc. Sci. Citation Index, Abstr. Soc. Work., Curr. Index J. Educ. adv acc. **Circ** 6,500. Articles that make theoretical contributions to any area of scientific psychology.

PSYCHOLOGICAL STUDIES. V. 1- 1956-. 0033-2968. Periodical. II. English. sa. $16.00. University of Calcutta, PO, Calcutta 673635 India. **Ed** M A Faroqi. **Ind/Abst** Psychol. Abstr. **NLM** W1 PS645. bk rev. adv acc. **Circ** 1,000. Covers psychological research and empirical studies.

PSYCHOLOGIE FRANCAISE. 1- 1956-. 0033-2984. Periodical. FR. French. qt. $23.28. Librairie Armand Colin, 103 BD St Michel, 75005 Paris Cedex 5 France. **Tel** 543 32 11. **Ind/Abst** Sociol. Abstr., Biol. Abstr., Psychol. Abstr., Lang. Lang. Behav. Abstr. **LC** BF2. **NLM** W1 PS65. **CODEN** PSFRAT.

PSYCHOLOGIE FUR DIE PRAXIS : ORGAN DER GESELLSCHAFT FUR PSYCHOLOGIE DER DEUTSCHEN DEMOKRATISCHEN REPUBLIK. 1983/1-. Periodical. German (with summaries in English and Russian). ir. **LC** BF23. **DD** 150.5. **NLM** W1. *Probleme und Ergebnisse der Psychologie, 0048-5403.*

PSYCHOLOGIE III I.E. DREI. No. 1- Oct. 1973-. Periodical. German. ir. I A Caruso, Anschrift der Redaktion, Salzburg Austria. **LC** BF3.

PSYCHOLOGIE-INFORMATION. Periodical. German. ir. Gesellschaft fur Psychologie der DDR, AM Kupfergraben, Berlin West Germany. **LC** BF3. **DD** 150.5.

PSYCHOLOGIE MEDICALE. Vol. 1- 1968-. 0048-5756. Periodical. French. mo. $23.95. Service de Presse, Edition, Information, Department des Editions Medicales, 14 rue Drouot, 75009 Paris France. **Tel** 824 96 93. **Ind/Abst** Psychol. Abstr. **NLM** W1.

PSYCHOLOGIE PREVENTIVE. Vol. 1, No. 1 (1982)-. 0714-3494. Periodical. CN. French. sa. $2.75 Each Number. Psychologie Preventive, c/o Societe de Recherche Enq Orientation Humaine Bureau 212, 2120 East rue Sherbrooke, Montreal Quebec H2K 1C3 Canada. **DD** 150.5.

PSYCHOLOGIE QUEBEC. V. 5, No. 3, (April 1984)-. 0824-1724. Periodical. CN. French. bm. Free to Members. Corporation Professionnelle des Psychologues du Quebec, Suite 510/1575 Ouest Boulevard Henri-Bourassa, Montreal Quebec H3M 3A9 Canada. **DD** 150.9714. *Cahiers du Psycholoque Quebecois, 0701-8932.*

PSYCHOLOGIE UND PRAXIS. Issue 1 (Year 1956 July-Aug)-. 0033-2992. Periodical. GW. German. qt. $53.10 Domestic, $44.10 US. C J Hogrefe Inc, 12 14 Bruce Park Avenue, Toronto Ontario M4P 2S3 Canada. **Tel** (416)482-6339. **Ed** Hans Wehner. **Ind/Abst** CIS Abstr., Psychol. Abstr. **NLM** W1 PS653. **CODEN** PSYPBH. bk rev. adv acc. **Circ** 1,800. Official publication of the division Work and Industrial Psychology of the Professional Association of German psychologists.

PSYCHOLOGIES. No. 1 (May 1983)-. Periodical. US. French. mo. $30.95. Periodica Inc, CP 444, Outremont Quebec H2V 4R6 Canada. **Tel** (514)274-5468. bk rev. adv acc. A magazine for everyone who wants to understand himself and others. *Psychologie.*

PSYCHOLOGISCH GESEHEN. No. 1- 1965-. Periodical. GW. German. ir. Adolph Bonz Verlag, Krahenstrasse 9, 7013 Oeffingen West Germany.

PSYCHOLOGISCHE BEITRAGE. Volume 1-1953-. 0033-3018. Periodical. GW. German. qt. 114. Verlag Anton Hain Meisenheim, Postfach 180, D-6554 Meisenheim West Germany. **Tel** (06753)4353. **Ed** Gunther Baumler. **Ind/Abst** Psychol. Abstr., Soc. Sci. Citation Index, Lang. Lang. Behav. Abstr., Sociol. Abstr. **LC** BF3. **NLM** W1 PS723. bk rev. adv acc. **Circ** 50. A journal for all fields of psychology. publication of the German Society for Psychology.

PSYCHOLOGISCHE PRAXIS. No. 1-. 0079-7413. Monographic Series. SZ. German. ir. S Karger AG, CH-4009 Basel Switzerland. **Tel** 061-39 08 80. **Ind/Abst** Psychol. Abstr. **NLM** W1 PS739. **CODEN** PSPAAS.

PSYCHOLOGISCHE RUNDSCHAU. V. 1- Oct. 1949-. 0033-3042. Periodical. German. qt. $23.90 Canada, $19.80 US. Hogrefe International Inc, 12-14 Bruce Park Avenue, Toronto Ontario M4P 2S3 Canada. **Tel** (416)482-6339. **Ed** Wolfgang Prinz. **Ind/Abst** Psychol. Abstr., Soc. Sci. Citation Index. **LC** BF3. **DD** 150.5. **NLM** W1 PS742. bk rev. adv acc. **Circ** 4,000. Europe's largest scientific journal in the field of psychology.

PSYCHOLOGISCHES KOLLOQUIUM. 0555-5701. Monographic Series. German. ir. **LC** UNC. **NLM** W1 PS744L.

PSYCHOLOGISTS REGISTERED IN ONTARIO. *See* Yearbooks, Almanacs, Directories.

PSYCHOLOGUE QUEBECOIS. (LE PSYCHOLOGUE QUEBECOIS). V. 6- Jan./Feb. 1974-. 0318-1707. CN. French. ir. Corporation des Psychologues de la Province de Quebec, 8180 Chemin Devonshire, Montreal Quebec H4P 2K3 Canada. **DD** 1505. *Bulletin de Nouvelles, 0318-1715.*

PSYCHOLOGY. **VFOAT** Core Information Series. V. 1- Jan. 1975-. 0095-1145. Periodical. US. English. mo. $75.00. 7139 Hopkins Road, PO Box 138, Mentor OH 44060. **LC** Z7203, BF1. **DD** 016.15.

PSYCHOLOGY. **VFOAT** Annual Editions: Psychology. 10th- Ed. 0272-3794. US. English. an. $8.95. Dushkin Publishing Group, Sluice Dock, Guilford CT 06437. **Tel** (203)453-4351. **Ed** Hiram Fitzgerald and Michael Walraven. **LC** BF149. **DD** 150.5. Collection of public press articles covering current issues in psychology. Includes topic guide and complete index. *Annual Editions. Readings in Psychology, 0197-0542.*

PSYCHOLOGY AND AGING. 0882-7974. Periodical. US. English. qt. $20.00 Members, $80.00 Nonmembers. American Psychological Association, 1400 North Uhle Street, Arlington VA 22201. **Tel** (703)247-7802. adv acc. **Circ** 3,500. Contains original articles on adult development and aging. Its content will represent both research and practice on the subject of psychogerontology.

PSYCHOLOGY & SOCIAL THEORY. **VFOAT** Psychology and Social Theory. No. 1 (Spring/Summer 1981)-. 0277-2469. Periodical. US. English. sa. $45.00. Psychology and Social Theory, Box 4387/Triphammer Hall, Ithaca NY 14852. **Tel** (415)585-8788. **Ind/Abst** Sociol. Abstr., Soc. Welf. Soc. Plan./Policy Soc. Dev., Altern. Press Index, Psychol. Abstr.

PSYCHOLOGY AND SOCIOLOGY OF SPORT. 0885-7423. Periodical. US. English. an. $50.00. AMS Press Inc, 56 East 13th Street, New York NY 10003.

PSYCHOLOGY IN THE SCHOOLS. V. 1-. 0033-3085. Periodical. US. English. qt. $80.00. Clinical Psychology Publishing, 4 Conant Square, Brandon VT 05733. **Tel** (802)247-6871. **Ed** G B Fuller. **Ind/Abst** Lang. Lang. Behav. Abstr., Educ. Index, Except. Child Educ. Resour., Curr. Index J. Educ., Psychol. Abstr., Bibliogr. Index, Soc. Sci. Citation Index, Sociol. Abstr. **LC** LB1101. **DD** 370.1505. **NLM** W1 PS746S. bk rev. adv acc. **Circ** 1,800. Educational psychology research for the school psychologist, administrator, counselor, researcher and educator.

PSYCHOLOGY INFORMATION GUIDE SERIES. V. 1-. 0273-3579. Monographic Series. US. English. ir. $62.00. Gale Research Company, Book Tower, Detroit MI 48226. **NLM** Z 7201 P974. A series of six annotated bibliographies listing English-language sources in the field of psychology.

Psychology

PSYCHOLOGY NEWS. No. 1 (Oct. 1979)-No. 30 (Dec. 1982). Periodical. UK. English. mo. 14 Domestic, 23 US. Psychology News, 161 Lewisham Road, London England. Tel 318-3554. Ed David Cohen. bk rev. adv acc. Circ 2,500. Covers latest research, theory and news in an accurate but amusing way. If there is an alternative psychology magazine, this is it.

THE PSYCHOLOGY OF LEARNING AND MOTIVATION. V. 1-. 0079-7421. US. English. ir. Academic Press, 4805 Sand Lake Road, Orlando FL 32887. Tel (305)345-4100. Ed K W Spence and J T Spence. Ind/Abst Life Sci. Collect., Educ. Index, Soc. Sci. Citation Index. LC BF683. DD 153.1534. NLM W1 PS746U. CODEN PYLMA.

PSYCHOLOGY OF MOTOR BEHAVIOR AND SPORT. Main/Corp North American Society for the Psychology of Sport and Physical Activity. 0162-055X. US. English. an. Human Kinetics Publishers, Box 5076, Champaign IL 61820. LC GV706.4. DD 796.01.

PSYCHOLOGY OF MUSIC. See Music.

PSYCHOLOGY OF WOMEN QUARTERLY. See Women.

PSYCHOLOGY (SAVANNAH, GA.). (PSYCHOLOGY). Began with May 1964. 0033-3077. Periodical. US. English. qt. $12.50. Alliance College, c/o Dr Cash Kowalski, Cambridge Springs PA 16403. Tel (814)398-2040. Ed Joesph Cangemi. Ind/Abst Sociol. Abstr., Lang. Lang. Behav. Abstr., Biol. Abstr., Curr. Index J. Educ., Psychol. Abstr., Soc. Sci. Citation Index, Women Stud. Abstr. LC BF1. DD 150.5. NLM W1 PS746H. CODEN PYCHBR. bk rev. adv acc. Circ 1,500. (ctrl). Research, theory, techniques, and arts of practice in the general field of psychology. Study of human behavior.

PSYCHOLOGY SURVEY. No. 1- 1978-. UK. English. ir. Allen & Unwin Inc, 9 Winchester Terrace, Winchester MA 01890. Tel (617)729-0830. LC BF1. DD 150.5.

PSYCHOLOGY TODAY. V. 1- May 1967-. 0033-3107. Periodical. US. English. mo. $15.99. American Psychological Association, 1400 Uhle Street, Arlington VA 22201, (subscription address: Neodata Corporation 1200 17th Street NW Washington DC 20036). Tel (202)955-7800. Ed Patrice Horn. Ind/Abst Read. Guide Period. Lit., Soc. Sci. Citation Index, Mag. Index, Sociol. Abstr., Abr. Read. Guide, Guide Soc. Sci. Relig. Period. Lit., Women Stud. Abstr., Lang. Lang. Behav. Abstr., Book Rev. Digest. LC BF1. NLM W1 PS746W. CODEN PSTOAM. (cum index). bk rev. adv acc. Circ 850,000,000. Available on microfilm from University Microfilms. Unlock the secrets of the human mind. Authoritative and fully illustrated, Psychology Today informs, enlightens and entertains.

PSYCHOMETRIKA. V. 1- Mar. 1936-. 0033-3123. Periodical. US. English. qt. $60.00. Psychometric Society, Department of Psychology, College of William and Mary, Williamsburg VA 23185. Tel (703)256-7280. Ed Ivo Molenaar. Ind/Abst Math. Rev., Curr. Index J. Educ., Psychol. Abstr. LC BF1. DD 150.5, 159.905. NLM W1 PS747D. (cum index). bk rev. Articles on the development of quantitative models for methodology.

LA PSYCHOMOTRICITE. V. 1-. 0151-5845. Periodical. French. qt. Masson Publishing USA NC, 211 East 43rd Street/Room 1306, New York NY 10017. Tel (212)370-1937. NLM W1 PS748E.

PSYCHOPHARMACOLOGY. See Pharmacy.

PSYCHOPHYSIOLOGY. See Biology - Physiology.

PSYCHOSOMATIC MEDICINE : PROCEEDINGS OF THE ... INTERNATIONAL CONGRESS OF THE ACADEMY OF PSYCHOSOMATIC MEDICINE. See Medicine.

PSYCHOSOZIAL. V. 1, No. 1, (May 1978)-. 0171-3434. Periodical. German. ir. Adlers Foreign Books Inc, 162 Fifth Avenue, New York NY 10010. Tel (212)691-5151.

PSYCHOTHERAPY IN PRIVATE PRACTICE. 0731-7158. Periodical. US. English. $92.00. Haworth Press, 28 East 22nd Street, New York NY 10010. Tel (212)228-2800. Ed Robert D Weitz. bk rev. adv acc. Circ 1,641. The only professional journal devoted entirely to issues and methods in the development of private practice for psychotherapists.

PSYCHOTHERAPY RESEARCH REVIEW SERIES. 0732-7986. Monographic Series. US. English. ir. Guilford Press, 200 Park Avenue South, Robin Dewender, New York NY 10003. Tel (212)674-1900.

PSYCSCAN. APPLIED PSYCHOLOGY. VFOAT Applied Pscyhology. Vol. 1, No. 1 (Jan. 1981)-. 0271-7506. Periodical. US. English. qt. $50.00. American Psychological Association, 1400 North Uhle Street, Arlington VA 22201. Tel (703)247-7802. Ed Susan Knapp. NLM Z 7204.A6 P974. adv acc. Circ 2,500. Abstracts from subscriber selected journals in the general area of applied psychology.

PSYCSCAN. CLINICAL PSYCHOLOGY. V. 1- Jan. 1980-. 0197-1484. US. English. qt. $50.00. American Psychological Association, 1400 North Uhle Street, Arlington VA 22201. Tel (703)247-7802. Ed Susan Knapp. LC RC467. DD 616.89005. NLM ZWM 105 P976. adv acc. Circ 7,000. Abstracts from subscriber-selected journals of interest to clinical psychologists.

PSYCSCAN. DEVELOPMENTAL PSYCHOLOGY. VFOAT Developmental Psychology. Vol. 1, No. 1 (Jan. 1980)-. 0197-1492. Periodical. US. English. qt. $50.00. American Psychological Association, 1400 North Uhle Street, Arlington VA 22201. Tel (703)247-7802. Ed Lois Granick. NLM Z 7203 P978. adv acc. Circ 3,000. Abstracts from subscriber-selected journals of interest to developmental psychologists.

PSYCSCAN. LD/MR. VFOAT LD/MR. VAT Psycscan. Learning Disorders, Mental Retardation. Vol. 1, No. 1 (Mar. 1982)-. 0730-1928. Periodical. US. English. qt. $50.00. American Psychological Association, 1400 North Uhle Street/Room 410, Arlington VA 22201. Tel (703)247-7802. Ed Lois Granick. adv acc. Circ 8,000. Abstracts of articles on learning disorders, communication disorders, and mental retardation. Provides comprehensive selections on dyslexia, minimal brain dysfunction, perceptual disabilities, etc.

PSZICHOLOGIA A GYAKORLATBAN. 1-. 0079-7456. Monographic Series. Hungarian (table of contents in English and Russian). ir. LC BF636.A1. NLM W1 PS98.

PSZICHOLOGIA : AZ MTA PSZICHOLOGIAI INTEZETENEK FOLYOIRATA. 1981/1-. 0230-0508. Periodical. HU. Hungarian. qt. $24.00. Akademiai Kiado, POB 24, 1363 Budapest Hungary. Tel 173-719. Ed L Halasz. LC BF8.H8. bk rev. adv acc. Circ 1,450.

PSZICHOLOGIAI TANULMANYOK. 1-. HU. Hungarian (summaries in Russian and English). ir. Akademiai Kiado, Akotmany U 21, Budapest V Hungary.

PUBLICATIONS FOR THE ADVANCEMENT OF THEORY AND HISTORY IN PSYCHOLOGY. VFOAT PATH. 1-. Monographic Series. US. English. ir. Ablex Publishing Corporation, 355 Chestnut Street, Norwood NJ 07648. Tel (201)767-8450. Ed John Broughton. Covers history and theoretical issues in psychology.

QUADRANT. No. 1- Spring 1968-. 0033-5010. Periodical. US. English. sa. $15.00. 28 East 39th Street, New York NY 10016. Tel (212)697-6430. Ed Maurice Krasnow PhD. LC BF173.A2. NLM W1 QU158D. bk rev. adv acc. Circ 2,000. Addresses wide spectrum of Jungian thought through articles and book reviews on mythology, literature and symbolism, religion and philosophy, social and natural sciences, and clinical practice.

QUARTERLY JOURNAL OF EXPERIMENTAL PSYCHOLOGY CEASED. (THE QUARTERLY JOURNAL OF EXPERIMENTAL PSYCHOLOGY). V. 1-32. 0033-555X. Periodical. UK. English. qt. Ind/Abst Nuci. Sci. Abstr., Psychol. Abstr., Biol. Abstr., Index Med. LC QP351. DD 150.72. NLM W1 QU265. CODEN QJXPAR.

THE QUARTERLY JOURNAL OF EXPERIMENTAL PSYCHOLOGY. A, HUMAN EXPERIMENTAL PSYCHOLOGY. VFOAT Human Experimental Psychology. Vol. 33A, Pt. 1 (Feb. 1981)-. 0272-4987. Periodical. UK. English. qt. $87.00. Academic Press, 4805 Sand Lake Road, Orlando FL 32819. Ind/Abst Life Sci. Collect., Index Med., Biol. Abstr., Psychol. Abstr. LC QP351. DD 153.05. NLM W1 QU265D. CODEN QJEADQ. Quarterly Journal of Experimental Psychology, 0033-555X.

THE QUARTERLY JOURNAL OF EXPERIMENTAL PSYCHOLOGY. B, COMPARATIVE AND PHYSIOLOGICAL PSYCHOLOGY. VFOAT Comparative and Physiological Psychology. Vol. 33B, Pt. 1 (Feb. 1981)-. 0272-4995. Periodical. UK. English. qt. $44.50. Academic Press, 4805 Sand Lake Road, Orlando FL 32819. Ind/Abst Life Sci. Collect., Index Med., Biol. Abstr., Psychol. Abstr. LC QP351. DD 152.05. NLM W1 QU265E. CODEN QJEBDT. Quarterly Journal of Experimental Psychology, 0033-555X.

THE QUARTERLY NEWSLETTER OF THE LABORATORY OF COMPARATIVE HUMAN COGNITION. Main/Corp California. University, San Diego. Laboratory of Comparative Human Cognition. V. 1- Sept. 1978-. 0278-4351. Periodical. US. English. qt. Laboratory of Comparative Human Cognition, University of California San Diego, La Jolla CA 92093. Tel (619)452-6828. Ed Luis Moll, Jacquelyn Mitchell and Esteban Diaz. Ind/Abst Lang. Lang. Behav. Abstr. Circ 1,000. Quarterly Newsletter of the Institute for Comparative Human Development, 0160-3361.

RAZVITIE LICHNOSTI V USLOVIIAKH SOTSIALIZMA. Periodical. UR. Russian. 0.70 Single Issue. LC BF698.A1.

READING PSYCHOLOGY. V. 1- Fall 1979-. 0270-2711. Periodical. US. English. qt. $64.50. Hemisphere Publishing Corporation, 70 Madison Avenue/Suite 1110, New York NY 10016. Tel (202)783-3958. Ed Lance M Gentle. Ind/Abst MLA Int. Bibliogr. Books Artic. Mod. Lang. Lit., Lang. Lang. Behav. Abstr., Curr. Index J. Educ., Psychol. Abstr., Soc. Sci. Citation Index. LC BF456.R2. DD 153.6. bk rev. adv acc. Circ 440. Refereed quarterly covering broad selection of material for elementary, secondary, and adult levels research. Ideas for teachers, practitioners, book and instructional materials reviewed.

READINGS IN BEHAVIOR MODIFICATION. 1st- Ed. US. English. an. Special Learning Corporation, 42 Boston Post Road, Guilford CT 06437.

READINGS IN PERSONAL GROWTH AND ADJUSTMENT. (READINGS IN PERSONAL GROWTH AND ADJUSTMENT : ANNUAL EDITIONS). VFOAT Annual Editions, Personal Growth and Adjustment. 1980/81-. 0198-912X. US. English. an. Dushkin Publishing Group Inc, Sluice Dock, Guildford CT 06437. LC BF698.A1. DD 158.105. NLM W1 RE105CM. Annual Editions. Readings in Personality and Adjustment, 0361-3836.

READINGS IN PSYCHOLOGY CEASED. Main/Corp Scientific American Resource Library. US. English. ir. $66.00. W H Freeman & Publications, 660 Market Street, San Francisco CA 94104.

REGISTER VAN SIELKUNDLIGES EN PSIGOTEGNICI VIR DIE REPUBLIEK VAN SUID-AFRIKA. VFOAT Register of Psychologists and Psycho-Technicians for the Republic of South Africa. SA. Afrikaans (English). an. Oranje-Nassau Building, 188 Schoeman Street, Posbus 205, Pretoria 0001 South Africa. LC BF30. DD 150.2568.

REHABILITATION. VFOAT Internationale Zeitschrift fur Physikalische Medizin und Rehabilitation Mit Zentralblatt. V. 15- March 1962-. 0048-7147. Periodical. GW. German (summaries in English and French). sa. 15.-. Deutsche Gesellschaft Rehab EV, Joh-Kohlmann-Str 26, D-5357 Swisttal 2 West Germany. Tel 02226/10555. Ed KH Woeber. adv acc. Human, comprehensive care for life-style finding. Internationale Zeitschrift fur Physikalische Medizin und Rehabilita.

REHABILITATION PSYCHOLOGY. Began with Vol. 19 (Spring 1972) issue. 0090-5550. Periodical. US. English. qt. $45.00 Domestic, $52.00 Foreign. Springer Publishing Company, 536 Broadway, New York NY 10012. Tel (212)431-4370. Ed Mary A Jansen. Ind/Abst Excerpta Med., Psychol. Abstr., Soc. Sci. Citation Index. LC RM930.A1. DD 617. NLM W1 RE1749M. bk rev. adv acc. Circ 1,500. Journal addresses psychosocial and behavioral aspects of rehabilitation in a wide range of settings. Psychological Aspects of Disability, 0091-178X.

REPERTOIRE DES PSYCHOLOGUES EN PRATIQUE PRIVEE. 1979-. 0226-3106. CN. French. an. Free. Corporation Professionnelle des Psychologues du Quebec, Bureau 510, 1575

Psychology

Ouest Boulevard Henri-Bourassa, Montreal Quebec H3M 3A9 Canada. DD 150.25714.

REPORT OF THE PHONOLOGY LABORATORY. See Linguistics.

RESEARCH BULLETIN - DEPARTMENT OF PSYCHOLOGY. UNIVERSITY OF WESTERN ONTARIO. (RESEARCH BULLETIN - DEPARTMENT OF PSYCHOLOGY, UNIVERSITY OF WESTERN ONTARIO). Main/Corp University of Western Ontario. Dept. of Psychology. Began publication in 1965. 0316-4675. Monographic Series. CN. English. Department of Psychology, University of Western Ontario, London Ontario N6A 3K7 Canada. DD 150.

RESEARCH COMMUNICATIONS IN PSYCHOLOGY, PSYCHIATRY AND BEHAVIOR. V. 1- 1976-. 0362-2428. Periodical. US. English. qt. PJD Publications Ltd, PO Box 966, Westbury NY 11590. Tel (516)626-0650. Ind/Abst Life Sci. Collect., Excerpta Med., Biol. Abstr., Chem. Abstr., Psychol. Abstr., Sci. Cit. Index, Abr. Ed. LC BF1. DD 150.5. NLM W1 RE216HP. CODEN RCPBDC.

RESEARCH IN COMMUNITY AND MENTAL HEALTH. V. 1- 1979-. 0192-0812. US. English. ir. $49.50. JAI Press, PO Box 1678, Greenwich CT 06836. Tel (203)661-7602. Ed James R Greenley. Ind/Abst Sociol. Abstr., Soc. Welf. Soc. Plan./Policy Soc. Dev., Psychol. Abstr. LC RA790.A1. DD 616.89. NLM W1 RE227FI.

RESEARCH IN PSYCHOTHERAPY : PROCEEDINGS OF A CONFERENCE. Main/Conf Conference on Research in Psychotherapy. 1st-3rd. 0069-8660. US. English. ir. American Psychological Association, 1400 North Uhle, Arlington VA 22201. Tel (703)247-7703. LC RC336. DD 132.075.

RESEARCH PROJECT. Main/Corp Christchurch, N.A. University of Canterbury. Dept. of Psychology and Sociology. 0069-3774. Monographic Series. NZ. English. ir. University of Canterbury, Computer Center, Christchurch New Zealand.

RESEARCH REPORT - YORK UNIVERSITY. PSYCHOSOCIAL RESEARCH PROGRAMME. INSTITUTE FOR BEHAVIOURAL RESEARCH. (RESEARCH REPORT - YORK UNIVERSITY, INSTITUTE FOR BEHAVIOURAL RESEARCH, PSYCHO-SOCIAL RESEARCH PROGRAMME). Main/Corp York University (Toronto, Ont.). Institute for Behavioural Research Psycho-Social Research Programme. N. 1- 1967-. 0316-067X. Monographic Series. CN. English. York University, Institute for Behavioural Research, 4700 Keele Street, Downsview Ontario Canada. DD 301.1.

REVIEW OF CHILD DEVELOPMENT RESEARCH. VFOAT Child Development and Social Policy. V. 1-. 0091-3065. US. English. ir. University of Chicago Press, PO Box 37005, Chicago IL 60637. LC HQ767.8. DD 155.4. NLM W1 RE252R.

REVIEW OF EXISTENTIAL PSYCHOLOGY AND PSYCHIATRY. VFOAT Review of Existential Psychology & Psychiatry. V. 11, No. 3- Oct. 1972-. 0361-1531. Periodical. US. English. ty. $40.00. Review of Existential Psychology and Psychiatry, PO Box 23220, Seattle WA 98102. Tel (206)328-2024. Ed Keith Hoeller. Ind/Abst Philos. Index, Psychol. Abstr. NLM W1 RE253BG. CODEN REXPB4. bk rev. adv acc. Circ 800. Human Inquiries, 0363-2326.

REVIEW OF PERSONALITY AND SOCIAL PSYCHOLOGY. 1-. 0270-1987. Periodical. US. English. an. Sage Publications Inc, 275 South Beverly Drive, Beverly Hills CA 90212. LC BF698. DD 302.05. NLM W1 RE253K.

REVIEW OF PSYCHOANALYTIC BOOKS. Vol. 1, No. 1-. 0738-8241. Periodical. US. English. qt. $45.00 Domestic, $54.00 Foreign. Analytic Press, 365 Broadway, Hillsdale NJ 07642. LC BF173. DD 150.5. NLM ZWM 460 R454.

REVISTA DA UNIVERSIDADE CATOLICA DE PETROPOLIS. Main/Corp Universidade Catolica de Petropolis. Portuguese (summaries in English or French). ir. $5.00 Single Issue. Universidade Catolica de Petropolis, Caixa Postal 944, 25.600 Petropolis Brazil. LC BF5.

REVISTA DE HISTORIA DE LA PSICOLOGIA. V. 1, No 1 (Jan./March 1980)-. 0211-0040. Periodical. Spanish (summaries in English). ir. Revista de Historia de la Psicologia, Departamento de Psicologia General Facultad de Filosofia, y Ciencias de la Educacion, Avenida Blasco Ebanez 28, Valencia 10 Espana Spain. Ind/Abst Psychol. Abstr. LC BF85. DD 150.9.

REVISTA DE PSICOANALISIS. Year 1- July 1943-. 0034-8740. Periodical. AG. Spanish. bm. $80.00. Asociacion Psicoanal-Argentina, Rodriguez Pena 1674, 1021 Buenos Aires Argentina. Tel 44-3518. Ind/Abst Excerpta Med., Psychol. Abstr. LC RC321. DD 131.3405. NLM W1 RE463Y. bk rev. Covers psychoanalysis.

REVISTA DE PSICOLOGIA (FORTALEZA, BRAZIL). (REVISTA DE PSICOLOGIA). Vol. 1, No. 1 (Jan./Dec. 1983)-. Periodical. Portuguese. ir. LC BF5. DD 150.5.

REVISTA DE PSICOLOGIA GENERAL Y APLICADA. V. 1- (No. 1-). 0373-2002. Periodical. SP. Spanish. qt. $40.00. Inst Nacional de Psicologia, Juan Huarte de San Juan 1, Madrid 3 Spain. Ind/Abst Sociol. Abstr., Lang. Lang. Behav. Abstr., Psychol. Abstr. LC BF5. DD 150.5. NLM W1 RE468. CODEN RPGAAI.

REVISTA DE PSIHOLOGIE. Year 1-. 0034-8759. Periodical. RM. Romanian (summaries in French and Russian). qt. $45.00. Rompresfilatelia, Box 2001, Bucharest Romania. Ind/Abst CIS Abstr., Psychol. Abstr., Sociol. Abstr., Lang. Lang. Behav. Abstr. LC BF8.R7.

REVISTA INTERAMERICANA DE PSICOLOGIA. VFOAT Interamericana Journal of Psychology. V. 9, No. 3/4- Dec. 1975-. Periodical. CK. articles in English or Spanish. sa. Interamerican Journal of Psychology, c/o B Marin, 3924 Reston Court South, San Francisco CA 94080. Ind/Abst Psychol. Abstr. NLM W1 RE594GE. Interamerican Journal of Psychology. Revista Interamericana de Psicologia.

REVISTA LATINOAMERICANA DE PSICOLOGIA. V. 1-. 0034-978X. Periodical. CK. Spanish (includes summaries in English). ty. $25.00. Revista Latinoamericana de Psicologia, Apartado 92621, Bogota Columbia. Tel 256-75-27. Ed Ruben Aedila. Ind/Abst Women Stud. Abstr., Psychol. Abstr., Soc. Sci. Citation Index. LC BF5. DD 150.5. NLM W1 RE597N. CODEN RLPSBM. bk rev. adv acc. Circ 2,500. The journal publishes scientific papers in psychology.

REVISTA MEXICANA DE ANALISIS DE LA CONDUCTA. VFOAT Mexican Journal of Behavior Analysis. V. 1, No. 1 (Jan. 1975)-. Periodical. MX. English or Spanish. sa. $30.00. Mexican Journal of Behavior Analysis, Editorial Trillas SA, Apartado Postal 69-716, Mexico 21 DF Mexico. Tel 671-5692. Ed Javier Nieto. Ind/Abst Psychol. Abstr. bk rev. adv acc. Circ 1,000. Publishes original, systematic, basic and applied studies on behavior analysis. It includes theoretical works, methodological and technical articles in the areas of pharmacology, toxicology and psychophysiology.

REVISTA MEXICANA DE PSICOLOGIA. V. 1- (No. 1- July 1963-. 0035-0079. Periodical. Spanish. ir. LC BF5.

REVISTA URUGUAYA DE PSICOLOGIA. V. 1- (No. 1-). Periodical. UY. Spanish. sa. AS Psicoanalitica del Uruguay, Casilla de Correo 813, Montevideo Uruguay.

REVUE AFRICAINE ET MALGACHE DE PSYCHOLOGIE. Periodical. French. ir. 5,000. Union Senegalaise de Banque, Compte Banchire, 500592 Dakar Senegal. LC BF2.

REVUE BELGE DE PSYCHOLOGIE ET DE PEDAGOGIE. 1934. 0035-0826. Periodical. BE. French. qt. 600. Universite libre de Bruxelles, Av FD Roosevelt/50-CP 186, 1050 Bruxelles Belgium. Tel (02)478 00 04. Ed Gerard Goosens. Ind/Abst Lang. Lang. Behav. Abstr., Psychol. Abstr., Sociol. Abstr. LC LB1051.A2. NLM W1 RE743E. CODEN RBPPAA. bk rev. Circ 1,000. Pertains to educational psychology, and educational science.

REVUE DE MEDECINE PSYCHOSOMATIQUE ET DE PSYCHOLOGIE MEDICALE. See Medicine - Psychiatry, Psychopathology.

REVUE DE MODIFICATION DU COMPORTEMENT. V. 4- June 1974-. 0383-056X. Periodical. CN. French. qt. $38.69. Association Scientifique pour la Modification du Camportement (A S M C), 5555 15E Avenue, Rosemont Quebec H1X 2T9 Canada. Tel (514)729-9949. Ind/Abst Point Repere, Psychol. Abstr. DD 616.8914. bk rev. adv acc. Circ 400. Scientific reports, case studies, and essays related to behavior modification.

REVUE DE PSYCHOLOGIE APPLIQUEE. Vol. 1- Oct. 1950-. 0035-1709. Periodical. FR. French. qt $19.96. Centre de Psychologie Applique, 48 Avenue Victor Hugo, 75783 Paris Cedex 16 France. Tel 5018326. Ind/Abst Psychol. Abstr., Soc. Sci. Citation Index. LC BF636.A1. DD 158.05. NLM W1 RE804.

REVUE FRANCAISE DE PSYCHANALYSE : ORGANE OFFICIEL DE LA SOCIETE PSYCHANALYTIQUE DE PARIS. Began with issue for July 1927. 0035-2942. Periodical. FR. French. bm. 570.00 Domestic, $63.33 Foreign. Presses Universitaires de France Service des Periodiques, 12 rue Jean-de-Beauvais, Paris 75005 France. Tel (1)326-22-16. Ed Ilse Barande. Publishes individual research by members of the Psychoanalytical Society of Paris and by non-members, considered as a continuation of Freudian theory and practice.

REVUE INTERNATIONALE DE PSYCHOLOGIE APPLIQUEE. (INTERNATIONAL REVIEW OF APPLIED PSYCHOLOGY : THE JOURNAL OF THE INTERNATIONAL ASSOCIATION OF APPLIED PSYCHOLOGY). Vol. 29, No. 1/2 (Jan. 1980)-. Periodical. UK. English (French). qt. $79.68. Sage Publications Ltd, 28 Banner Street, London EC1Y 8QE England. Tel 01-253-1516. Ind/Abst Curr. Contents, Soc. Behav. Sci., Soc. Sci. Citation Index, Psychol. Abstr. LC BF636.A1. DD 158.05. Revue Internationale de Psychologie Appliquee, 0035-340X.

REVUE QUEBECOISE DE PSYCHOLOGIE. V. 1- Feb. 1980-. 0225-9885. Periodical. CN. French. ty. 40. University of Quebec at Montreal, Department of Psychologie, CP 8888, Montreal Quebec H3C 3P8 Canada. Tel (514)282-4851. Ed P Michaud. Ind/Abst Point Repere. DD 158.05. bk rev. General review of applied psychology for psychologists and allied professions.

REVUE ROUMAINE DES SCIENCES SOCIALES. SERIE DE PSYCHOLOGIE. V. 8-. 0035-3892. Periodical. RM. French (English). sa. Ilexim Press Department, PO Box 1-136-1-137, Bucharest Romania. Ind/Abst Psychol. Abstr., Sociol. Abstr., Lang. Lang. Behav. Abstr. LC BF1. NLM W1 RE965Z. Revue des Sciences Sociales.

REVUE ZAORPOSE DE PSYCHOLOGIE ET DE PEDAGOGIE. V. 1- July 1972-. French (includes some summaries in English). ir. $8.00. Universite Nationale du Zaire, Boite Postale 2012, Kisangani Congo Zaire. LC BF2. DD 370.1505.

RICERCHE DI PSICOLOGIA. Year 1- (No. 1-). 0391-6081. Periodical. IT. Italian. qt. $35.64. Franco Angeli Editore Riviste, Via le Monza 106, 20127 Milano Italy. Tel (02)28.27.651/2/3/. Ind/Abst Life Sci. Collect., Psychol. Abstr. LC BF76.5. NLM W1 RI106. Annali dell'Istituto di Psicologia, 0391-996X.

RIVISTA INTERNAZIONALE DI PSICOLOGIA E IPNOSI. New Series, 1- Jan./June 1972-. 0035-6743. Periodical. Italian (summaries in English, French, and Spanish). qt. 18. Instituto di Indagini Psicologiche, Corso XXII Marzo 57, Milano Italy. Tel (02)74.26.489-73.88.427. Ed Marco Marchesan. Ind/Abst Psychol. Abstr. LC BF1. NLM W1 R1729. bk rev. Circ 800. Articles and reports on the subject of congresses on hypnotherapy, hypnoanesthesia, hypnobirth control, hypnosis for sports, psychosomatic medicine, psychodiagnosis, handwriting psychology, psychotherapy, and social psychology. Rivista di Psicologia della Scrittura, 0485-2419.

RORSCHACHIANA. 1- 1945-. Periodical. SZ. German. ir. Verlag Hans Huber AG, Laenggassstrasse 76 POB, CH-3000 Bern 9 Switzerland. Tel 031 24 25 33.

RUTGERS PROFESSIONAL PSYCHOLOGY REVIEW. Vol. 1-. 0277-4240. Monographic Series. US. English. an. Transaction Books, Rutgers University, New Brunswick NJ 08903. Ed Donald R Peterson. LC UNC. DD 150.5. NLM W1 RU933G.

SAYBROOK REVIEW. Vol. 4, No. 1 (Spring 1982)-. 0740-0853. Periodical. US. English. Saybrook Institute, 1772 Vallejo Street, San Francisco CA 94123. Ind/Abst Psychol. Abstr. NLM W1 SA999M. Humanistic Psychology Institute Review, 0272-1627.

SCANDINAVIAN JOURNAL OF PSYCHOLOGY. V. 1- 1960-. 0036-5564. Periodical. SW. English. qt. 50.00. Almqvist & Wiksell, 108 Drottninggatan, PO Box 45150, S-104 30

Stockholm Sweden. **Tel** 00947-90-166401. **Ed** Claes von Hofsten. **Ind/Abst** Life Sci. Collect., Sociol. Abstr., Lang. Lang. Behav. Abstr., Psychol. Abstr., Sci. Cit. Index, Abr. Ed., Soc. Sci. Citation Index, Index Med. **LC** BF1. **DD** 150.5. **NLM** W1 SC153. **CODEN** SJPYA2. Index in last issue of volume - attached. (cum index). bk rev. adv acc. **Circ** 550. (ctrl). Scientific articles from all areas in psychology written mainly by professionals within Scandinavia.

THE SCANDINAVIAN PSYCHOANALYTIC REVIEW. V. 1- 1978-. Periodical. DK. English. sa. $26.29. Munksgaard Ltd, 35 Norre Sogade, DK-1370 Copenhagen K Denmark. **Ind/Abst** Psychol. Abstr., Soc. Sci. Citation Index. **LC** RC500. **DD** 150.19505. **NLM** W1 SC154N. Concerns psychoanalysis and psychology.

SCHEDULE-INDUCED BEHAVIOR. 1977-. Periodical. CN. English. ir. Human Science Press, 72 5th Avenue, New York NY 10011. **Ed** W P Christian, R W Schaeffer, G D King. **Ind/Abst** Psychol. Abstr. **NLM** W1 SC166.

SCHOOL PSYCHOLOGY REVIEW. V. 9- Winter 1980-. 0279-6015. Periodical. US. English. qt. $30.00. National Association of School Psychologists, PO Box 184, Kent OH 44240. **Tel** (703)568-6454. **Ed** Stephen Elliott. **Ind/Abst** Educ. Index, Except. Child Educ. Resour., Curr. Index J. Educ., Psychol. Abstr., Bibliogr. Index. **LC** LB1051. **DD** 370.15. bk rev. adv acc. **Circ** 9,500. (ctrl). Describes practices of school psychologists who consult behavior/learning problems, help develop remedial and prevention programs for pupils, parents, teachers and other staff. *School Psychology Digest, 0160-5569.*

SCHRIFTEN ZUR PSYCHOANALYSE UND PSYCHOSOMATISCHEN MEDIZIN. *See* Medicine.

SCHWEIZERISCHE ZEITSCHRIFT FUR PSYCHOLOGIE UND IHRE ANWENDUNGEN. BEIHEFT. **VFOAT** Revue Suisse de Psychologie et de Psychologie Appliquee. No. 1- 1943-. Monographic Series. SZ. German or French. qt. Verlag Hans Huber AG, Laenggassstrasse 76 POB, CH-3000 Bern 9 Switzerland. **Tel** 031 24 25 33.

SECRETS OF WINNERS. Premier Issue (1985)-. 0883-8941. Periodical. US. English. mo. $36.00. Secrets of Winners, PO Box 157, Whooping Lane, Altamonte Springs FL 32701. **DD** 158.

SEINEN SHINRI. **VFOAT** Youth Problem. Feb. 1977. Periodical. Japanese. ir. Kaneko Shobo, 3-7 Otsuka 3, Bunkyo-ku Tokyo 112 Japan. **LC** HQ799.J3.

THE SELF-HELP SOURCEBOOK. **VFOAT** Self Help Sourcebook. 8756-1425. US. English. an. New Jersey Self-Help Clearinghouse, Saint Clare's Hospital Community Mental Health Center, Pocono Road, Denville NJ 07834.

THE SERIES IN CLINICAL AND COMMUNITY PSYCHOLOGY. 0146-0846. Monographic Series. US. English. ir. Hemisphere Publishing Corporation, 1025 Vermont Avenue NW, Washington DC 20005. **LC** UNC. *Series in Clinical Psychology.*

THE SERIES IN HEALTH PSYCHOLOGY AND BEHAVIORAL MEDICINE. 8756-467X. Monographic Series. US. English. ir. Hemisphere Publishing Corporation, 79 Madison Avenue, New York NY 10016. **DD** 616.

SHINRIGAKU. **Main/Corp** Tokyo Daigaku. Kyoyo Gakubu. Shinrigaku Kenkyushitsu. **VFOAT** Series of Psychology. JA. Japanese. ir. Kyoyo Gakubu Shinrigaku, 865 Kombamachi Meguro-Ku, Tokyo Japan. **LC** BF8.J3.

SHINRIGAKU HYORON. **VFOAT** Japanese Psychological Review. 0386-1058. JA. Japanese (some summaries in English or German). ir. 750. Kyoto University, c/o Department of Psychology Faculty of Letters Sakyo-ku, Kyoto 606 Japan. **Ind/Abst** Psychol. Abstr. **LC** BF8.J3. **CODEN** SHHYDJ.

SHINRIGAKU KENKYU. **VFOAT** Japanese Journal of Psychology. Began publication with Vol. 1 in 1923 and ceased with V. 3 in 1925. 0021-5236. Periodical. JA. Japanese (English or German). bm. Kyowa Book Company Inc, 1-38 Kanda Jinbocho, Chiyoda-Ku, Tokyo 101 Japan. **Tel** 293-0727. **Ind/Abst** Life Sci. Collect., Index Med., Psychol. Abstr., Soc. Sci. Citation Index, Sociol. Abstr., Lang. Lang. Behav. Abstr. **CODEN** SHKEA5.

SLEEP BULLETIN. No. 170 (Jan. 1979)-. 0037-6809. US. English. mo. BRI Publications Office, University of California, Center for the Health Sciences, Los Angeles CA 90024. *Sleep Bulletin, Including Sleep Reviews, 0360-6007.*

SOCIAL BEHAVIOR AND PERSONALITY. *See* Sociology: General Works, Theory.

SOCIAL PSYCHOLOGY (DUSHKIN PUBLISHING GROUP). (SOCIAL PSYCHOLOGY). **VFOAT** Annual Editions. 0730-6962. US. English. an. Dushkin Publishing Group Inc, Sluice Dock, Guildord CT 06437. **LC** HM251. **DD** 302. *Annual Editions. Readings in Social Psycholoty.*

SOCIAL PSYCHOLOGY QUARTERLY. Began with Vol. 42 (Mar. 1979) issue. 0190-2725. Periodical. US. English. qt. $48.00 Domestic, $51.00 Foreign. American Sociological Association, 1722 N Street Northwest, Washington DC 20036. **Tel** (202)833-3410. **Ed** Peter Burke. **Ind/Abst** MLA Int. Bibliogr. Books Artic. Mod. Lang. Lit., Sociol. Abstr., Soc. Welf. Soc. Plan./Policy Soc. Dev., Soc. Sci. Index, Psychol. Abstr., Soc. Sci. Citation Index, Index Med., Soc. Work Res. Abstr., Soc. Sci. Index. **LC** HM1. **DD** 302.05. **NLM** W1 SO123TQ. adv acc. **Circ** 3,500. Available on microfilm from University Microfilms International. Publishes papers pertaining to the processes and products of social interaction. Includes study of relations to individuals or groups as they influence or are influenced by social forces. *Social Psychology (American Sociology Association), 0147-829X.*

SOCIOMETRY. V. 1-40. Periodical. US. English. qt. $8.00 Member, $12.00 Nonmember, $16.00 Institutions. American Sociological Association, 1722 North Street NW, Washington DC 20036.

SOMATOSENSORY RESEARCH. Vol. 1, No. 1-. 0736-7244. Periodical. US. English. qt. $75.00 Domestic, $90.00 Foreign. Guilford Press, 200 Park Avenue South, New York NY 10003. **Tel** (212)674-1900. **Ed** Lawrence Kruger. **Ind/Abst** Life Sci. Collect., Chem. Abstr., Index Med. **DD** 599.0182. **NLM** W1. **Circ** 500. Publishes original papers that investigate somatic sensation and its neural mechanisms. Includes anatomical, biochemical, pharmacological and behavioral studies of humans and other animals.

SOUTH AFRICAN JOURNAL OF PSYCHOLOGY. **VFOAT** Suid-Afrikaanse Tydskrif vir Sielkunde. V. 1- 1970-. 0081-2463. Periodical. Afrikaans (articles in English). ir. **Ind/Abst** Life Sci. Collect., Cumul. Index Nurs. Allied Health Lit., Biol. Abstr., Psychol. Abstr. **LC** BF1. **DD** 150.5. **NLM** W1 SO905NP. **CODEN** SAJPDL. *Journal of Behavioral Science, South African Psychologist.*

THE SOUTHERN PSYCHOLOGIST. Vol. 1, No. 1 (Fall 1982)-. 0885-9329. Periodical. US. English. qt. The Southern Psychologist, Louisiana State University at Shreveport, Department of Psychology, Shreveport LA 71115. **Ind/Abst** Psychol. Abstr. **DD** 150.

SOVIET PSYCHOLOGY. V. 5- Fall 1966-. 0038-5751. Periodical. US. English (Russian). qt. $178.50. M E Sharpe Inc, 80 Business Park Drive, Armonk NY 10504. **Tel** (914)273-1800. **Ed** Michel Cole. **Ind/Abst** Biol. Abstr., Curr. Contents, Public Aff. Inf. Serv. Bull., Psychol. Abstr., Lang. Lang. Behav. Abstr., Sociol. Abstr. **NLM** W1 SO996R. **CODEN** SOPSBK. adv acc. **Circ** 450. A combination of important articles on current work and historically formative research. *Soviet Psychology And Psychiatry, 0584-5610.*

SPANISH-LANGUAGE PSYCHOLOGY. **VFOAT** Spanish Language Psychology. Vol. 1, No. 1 (Mar. 1981)-. 0167-5311. Periodical. English. qt. $60.00. North-Holland Publishing Company, Journal Division, Box 211, 1000 AE Amsterdam the Netherlands. **LC** BF1. **DD** 150.5. **NLM** Z 7203 S735. **CODEN** SLPSDZ.

SPIRALE. (LA SPIRALE). Vol. 1, No 4 (Sept./Oct. 1983)-. 0822-9252. Periodical. CN. French. bm. Free. Fraternite Rosicrucienne Centre de Sherbrooke, C P 1383, Sherbrooke Quebec J1H 5L9 Canada. **DD** 135.4306071466. *Spirale (Fraternite Rosicrucienne. Groupe de Sherbrooke), 0822-9252.*

SPRING. Began publication with issue 1941. 0362-0522. US. English. an. $20.00. Spring Publications, PO Box 222069, Dallas TX 75222. **Tel** (214)871-2066. **Ed** James Hillman. **Ind/Abst** Psychol. Abstr. **LC** BF173.A2. **DD** 150.195405. **NLM** W1 SP685. **CODEN** SAATDM. bk rev. adv acc. A journal of archetypal psychology and Jungian thought covering mythology, psychotherapy, dreams, cultural psychology, and imagination in life and literature.

SPRINGER SERIES IN BEHAVIOR MODIFICATION. V. 1-. 0272-9636. Monographic Series. US. English. ir. Springer Publishing Company, 536 Broadway, New York NY 10012. **Tel** (212)431-4370. **LC** UNC. **NLM** W1 SP685M.

SPRINGER SERIES IN INFORMATION SCIENCES. Vol. 1-. 0720-678X. Monographic Series. US. English. Springer Verlag-New York Inc, 175 5th Avenue, New York NY 10010. **Tel** (212)460-1584. **Ind/Abst** Comput. Control Abstr., Electr. Electron. Abstr., Sci. Abstr. Sect. A. Phys. Abstr. Studies on associative memory, image processing and analysis, pattern recognition, and mechanical foundations.

SPRINGER SERIES ON BEHAVIOR THERAPY AND BEHAVIORAL MEDICINE. Vol. 6-. 0278-6729. Monographic Series. US. English. Springer Publishing Company, 200 Park Avenue South, New York NY 10003. **Ed** C M Franks and F J Evans. **NLM** W1 SP685NB. *Springer Series in Behavior Modification, 0272-9636.*

STORIA E CRITICA DELLA PSICOLOGIA. Vol. 1, N. 1 (June 1980)-. 0392-4955. Periodical. IT. English (Italian). sa. $20.79. Societa Editrice Il Mulina Spa, Via Santa Stefano 6, 40125 Bologna Italy. **Tel** 051/ 23 34 15. **Ind/Abst** Psychol. Abstr. **LC** BF1. **DD** 150.5. **NLM** W1. *Per Un'Analisi Storica e Critica Della Psicologia.*

STRESS AND ANXIETY. V. 1-. 0364-1112. US. English. ir. Hemisphere Publishing Corporation, 1010 Vermont Avenue NW/Suite 612, Washington DC 20005. **Tel** (212)725-1999. **Ind/Abst** Psychol. Abstr. **LC** BF575.S75. **DD** 616.8522. **UD** 155.9.

STUDENT PSYCHOLOGIST. (THE STUDENT PSYCHOLOGIST). Vol. 1, No. 1 (Winter 1979/1980)-. 0225-9508. Periodical. CN. English. qt. $4.00. PO Box 145, Chomedey Laval Quebec H7W 4K2 Canada. **DD** 150.5.

STUDIA PSYCHOLOGICA. **Series/Titl** Acta Universitatis Carolinae. Philosophica et Historica. Began in 1970. Periodical. Czech (with summaries in English and Russian). ir. Kubon & Sagner, Postfach 34 01 08, Hess-Strasse 39/41, D-8 Munchen 34 West Germany. **Tel** (089)52 20 27. **LC** AS141, BF8.C9. **DD** 909 S150.5. Journal for basic research in all psychological fields. Publication of experimental and theoretical original studies of Czechoslovak as well as foreign scientists.

STUDIA PSYCHOLOGICZNE. Vol. 1- 1956-. 0081-685X. Polish (summaries in English and Russian). sa. ARS Polona, Krakowskie Przedmiescie 7, 00-068 Warsaw Poland. **Ind/Abst** Sociol. Abstr., Psychol. Abstr., Lang. Lang. Behav. Abstr. **NLM** W1 ST886F. **CODEN** SPSLBL.

STUDIEN ZUR EXPERIMENTELLEN UND KLINISCHEN PSYCHOLOGIE. Vol. 1-. German. ir. **NLM** W1 ST912R.

STUDIEN ZUR KRITISCHEN PSYCHOLOGIE. Began with Vol. 1-2, 1977?. 0721-4502. Monographic Series. German. ir. **Ed** K H Braun and K Holzkamp. **LC** UNC. **DD** 150.5. **NLM** W1 ST913J.

STUDIES IN CROSS-CULTURAL PSYCHOLOGY. V. 1- 1977-. 0162-2684. Periodical. UK. English. ir. Academic Press, 4805 Sand Lake Road, Orlando FL 32887. **Tel** (305)345-4100. **Ed** N Warren. **NLM** W1 ST919I.

STUDIES IN VISUAL COMMUNICATION. *See* Communication.

STUDIES ON THE DEVELOPMENT OF BEHAVIOR AND THE NERVOUS SYSTEM. *See* Medicine - Neurology.

SUICIDE & LIFE-THREATENING BEHAVIOR. *See* Sociology: General Works, Theory.

SYNTHESIS. V. 1- 1974-. 0098-8634. Periodical. US. English. ty. $10.00. Synthesis Press, 830 Woodside Road, Redwood City CA 94061. **NLM** W1 SY66I.

SZONDIANA. **Series/Titl** Schweizerische Zeitschrift fur Psychologie und Ihre Anwendungen. Beiheft, No. 21. 1- 1953-. 0586-3872. Monographic Series. German. ir. **Ed** E Keller-Bussmann.

TEACHING OF PSYCHOLOGY. V. 1- Oct. 1974-. 0098-6283. Periodical. US. English. qt. $25.00. Lawrence Erlbaum Associates, 365 Broadway/Suite

102, Hilldale NJ 07642. **Ind/Abst** Educ. Index, Curr. Index J. Educ., Psychol. Abstr., Soc. Sci. Citation Index. **LC** BF77. **DD** 150.7. *Teaching of Psychology Newsletter.*

TECHNIQUES (BRANDON, VT.). *See* Education (General) - Special Aspects of Education.

TECHNOLOGIE DU COMPORTEMENT. (LA TECHNOLOGIE DU COMPORTEMENT). V. 1- Jan./ 1977-. 0705-2707. Periodical. CN. French. sa. $38.69. Editions Behaviora, 6975 Boulevard Taschereau/Suite 911, Brossard Quebec J4Z 1A7 Canada. **Tel** (514)678-8100. **Ind/Abst** Point Repere. **DD** 370.15305. bk rev. adv acc. **Circ** 500. (ctrl). Journal which publishes articles on the principles of applied behavior analysis. The aims of the journal are to promote the technical and methodological aspects of behavior analysis.

TENSION CONTROL. Main/Corp American Association for the Advancement of Tension Control. 1st- 1974-. 0272-5398. US. English. an. $8.50. American Association of Advancement Tension Control, PO Box 8005, Louisville KY 40208. **Tel** (502)588-6571. **LC** RC489.R45. **DD** 616.8522306.

TESTS IN MICROFICHE. *See* Education (General) - Special Aspects of Education.

THEORIA. *See* Philosophy.

THEORY IN PSYCHOPHARMACOLOGY. Vol. 1-. 0736-7945. UK. English. ir. Academic Press, 4805 Sand Lake Road, Orlando FL 32819. **Tel** (305)345-4100. Ed S J Cooper. **LC** RM315. **DD** 615.78. **NLM** W1 TH125.

THERAPEUTISCHE KONZEPTE DER ANALYTISCHEN PSYCHOLOGIE C.G. JUNG. 1-. 0344-8967. GW. German. ir. Adolph Bonz Verlag, Krahenstrasse 9, 7013 Oeffingen West Germany. Ed Ursula Eschenbach. **LC** UNC. **DD** 150.195405. **NLM** W1 TH519.

THERAPY NOW. Spring 1984-. 0824-5436. Periodical. CN. English. qt. $11.00. Therapy Now, PO Box 683 Station P, Toronto Ontario M5S 2Y4 Canada. **DD** 616.891405.

THESAURUS OF PSYCHOLOGICAL INDEX TERMS. *See* Encyclopedias & General Reference Books.

TIRES A PART. 0823-6291. CN. French (text in English). an. Free. Tires a Part, Cegep Bois-de-Boulogne, 10555 Avenue Bois-de-Boulogne, Montreal Quebec H4N 1L3 Canada. **DD** 150.711714. (ctrl).

THE TOASTMASTER. *See* Education (General) - Special Aspects of Education.

TODAY'S CHILD. V. 6, No. 6- June 1958-. 0040-8468. Periodical. US. English. mo. Edwards Publications, School Lane, Roosevelt NJ 08555.

TOPICS IN COGNITIVE DEVELOPMENT. Vol. 1-. Monographic Series. US. English. ir. Plenum Publishing Corporation, 233 Spring Street, New York NY 10013. **Tel** (212)620-8000. Ed Marilyn H Appel. **DD** 155.413. **NLM** W1 TO539LI.

TORONTO ASSOCIATION FOR HUMANISTIC PSYCHOLOGY. Vol. 5, Letter 2 (Jan./Feb. '82)-. 0824-2321. Periodical. CN. English. bm. Association for Humanistic Psychology, PO Box 342 Station Z, Toronto Ontario M5N 2Z4 Canada. **DD** 150.192. *News & Happenings*, 0824-2313.

TOTUS HOMO. V. 2- 1970-. 0390-9604. Periodical. IT. English (French or Italian). ty. Via Console Marcello 8, 20156 Milano Italy. **LC** BF1. **NLM** W1 TO82. Each issue contains an index to its own contents - no vol index - loose.

TOWSON STATE UNIVERSITY JOURNAL OF PSYCHOLOGY. VFOAT Journal of Psychology. Vol. 1, No. 1 (Spring 1977)-. 0161-7648. Periodical. US. English. an. **Ind/Abst** Psychol. Abstr. **LC** BF1. **DD** 150.5.

TPGA JOURNAL. Main/Corp Texas Personnel and Guidance Association. VAT Texas Personnel and Guidance Association Journal. V. 1- Sept. 1972-. 0364-3409. Periodical. US. English. sa. $4.00. N T Station Box 13901, Denton TX 76203. **Ind/Abst** Psychol. Abstr. **LC** BF637.C6. **DD** 158.

TRAVAIL HUMAIN. *See* Economics - Labor.

TUTORIAL ESSAYS IN PSYCHOLOGY. V. 1-. 0277-2639. US. English. ir. John Wiley and Sons, 1 Wiley Drive, Somerset NJ 08873. **Tel** (212)867-9800. Ed N S Sutherland. **NLM** W1 TU986.

THE TWINS LETTER. (THE TWINS LETTER : A PUBLICATION OF THE TWINS FOUNDATION). Vol. 1, No. 1, 2 (Fall/Winter 1984)-. 0743-748X. Periodical. US. English. qt. $25.00. The Twins Foundation, PO Box 9487, Providence RI 02940-9487. **Tel** (401)274-6910. **DD** 155. **Circ** 5,000. (ctrl). Highly diversified, relating to twins and higher groups of multiples; their lives, achievements, needs, statistics, medical scientific and other new research for and about twins and multiples.

UNISA PSYCHOLOGIA. Main/Corp University of South Africa. V. 1- 1974-. SA. Afrikaans (English). sa. $1.30. University of South Africa, PO Box 392, Department Publ Services, Pretoria 0001 South Africa. **Tel** (012)429-3111.

UNTERRICHTSWISSENSCHAFT. *See* Education (General).

UPCOMING. No. 1 1975-. Periodical. US. English. an. Rational Island Publishers, Box 2081 Main Office Station, Seattle WA 98111.

USSR AND EASTERN EUROPE SCIENTIFIC ABSTRACTS. BIOMEDICAL AND BEHAVIORAL SCIENCES. *See* Indexes/Abstracts.

USSR REPORT. LIFE SCIENCES. BIOMEDICAL AND BEHAVIORAL SCIENCES (PUBLIC ED.). (USSR REPORT. LIFE SCIENCES. BIOMEDICAL AND BEHAVIORAL SCIENCES). VFOAT Life Sciences. VAT Union of Soviet Socialist Republics Report. Life Sciences. Biomedical and Behavioral Sciences (Public Ed.). No. 1 (Mar. 28, 1980)-. 0740-1264. Periodical. US. English. **Ind/Abst** Life Sci. Collect. **NLM** W1 US918A. *USSR Report. Biomedical and Behavioral Sciences Public Ed.*, 0197-6400.

VESTNIK MOSKOVSKOGO UNIVERSITETA. SERIIA XIV : PSIKHOLOGIIA. Main/Corp Moscow. Universitet. 1977-. Periodical. UR. Russian (summaries in English). qt. 0.50 Single Issue. Vestnik Moskovskogo Universiteta, 103009 Ul Gertsena 5/7, Moskva Russian SFSR. **LC** BF8.R8.

VOPROSY PSIHOLOGII. (VOPROSY PSIKHOLOGII). V. 1- Jan./Feb. 1955-. 0042-8841. Periodical. UR. Russian. bm. $39.50. Victor Kamkin Inc (70131), 12224 Parklawn Drive, Rockville MD 20852. **Tel** (301)881-5973. **Ind/Abst** Int. Aerosp. Abstr., Psychol. Abstr., Soc. Sci. Citation Index, Lang. Lang. Behav. Abstr., Sociol. Abstr. **LC** BF8.R8. **NLM** W1 VO643. **CODEN** VOPSAI.

VOPROSY PSIKHOLOGII OBSHCHENIIA I POZNANIIA LIUDMI DRUG DRUGA. Periodical. UR. Russian. 1.10. Kubanskii Gosudarstvennyi Universitet, Ul Im K Libknekhta 149, 35075 GSP G Krasnodar Russia. **LC** BF637.

WAYS FOR THE DISABLED. *See* Public Health and Safety.

WESTCOAST PSYCHOLOGY CEASED. Vol. 14, No. 1 (Jan./Feb. 1984)-Vol. 14, No. 6 (Nov./Dec. 1984). 0824-0280. Periodical. CN. English. bm. Free. British Columbia Psychological Association, 2150 West Broadway Street/Suite 308, Vancouver British Columbia V6K 4L9 Canada. **DD** 150.60711. (ctrl). *Newsletter (British Columbia Psychological Association)*, 0824-0272.

WILEY SERIES IN PSYCHOLOGY AND PRODUCTIVITY AT WORK. VFOAT Psychology and Productivity at Work Series. 0738-0860. Monographic Series. UK. English. ir. John Wiley & Sons Inc, 605 Third Avenue, New York NY 10158.

WILEY SERIES ON PERSONALITY PROCESSES. 0195-4008. Monographic Series. US. English. ir. John Wiley & Sons Inc, 1 Wiley Drive, Somerset NJ 08873.

YAKUBUTSU, SEISHIN, KODO. *See* Pharmacy.

YOGA JOURNAL. *See* Physical Training.

YONEN KYOIKU KENKYU NEMPO. VFOAT Annual of Research on Early Childhood. Japanese (summaries in English). ir. 730. **LC** LB1101.

YOU. V. 1- Jan. 1976-. 0146-2318. Periodical. US. English. mo. $12.00. Interplay Associates, 515 Madison Avenue, New York NY 10022. **LC** HQ800. **DD** 158.2.

ZBORNIK. PSYCHOLOGIA. Main/Corp Bratislava. Univerzita. Pedagogicka Fakulta. VFOAT Sammelbuch der Padagogischen Fakultat der Komensky-Universitat in Trnava. German. ir. **LC** BF26.

ZEITSCHRIFT FUR ENTWICKLUNGSPSYCHOLOGIE UND PADAGOGISCHE PSYCHOLOGIE. *See* Education (General) - Theory, Practice of Education.

ZEITSCHRIFT FUR EXPERIMENTELLE UND ANGEWANDTE PSYCHOLOGIE. 0044-2712. Periodical. GW. German (summaries in English and French). qt. $79.00 Canada, $66.00 US. C J Hogrefe Inc, 12 14 Bruce Park Avenue, Toronto Ontario M4P 2S3 Canada. **Tel** (416)482-6339. Ed J Droesler. **Ind/Abst** Sociol. Abstr., Index Med., Int. Aerosp. Abstr., Psychol. Abstr., Soc. Sci. Citation Index, Lang. Lang. Behav. Abstr. **LC** BF3. **DD** 150.724. **NLM** W1 ZE347. **CODEN** ZANPAX. bk rev. adv acc. **Circ** 800. This publication covers all fields of psychology, experimental and applied psychology.

ZEITSCHRIFT FUR KLINISCHE PSYCHOLOGIE. (ZEITSCHRIFT FUR KLINISCHE PSYCHOLOGIE, FORSCHUNG UND PRAXIS). V. 1- 1972-. 0084-5345. Periodical. German. qt. 38.50 Domestic, 32.00 Foreign. C J Hogrefe Inc, 12 14 Bruce Park Avenue, Toronto Ontario M4P 2S3 Canada. **Tel** (416)482-6339. Ed U Baumann. **Ind/Abst** Excerpta Med., Psychol. Abstr., Soc. Sci. Citation Index. **NLM** W1 ZE433T. bk rev. adv acc. **Circ** 2,000. Official organ of the division clinical psychology of the (a) Professional Association of German Psychologists, (b) Society for Scientific Gespraechs-Psychotherapy and (c) German Society for Behavioral Therapy.

ZEITSCHRIFT FUR KLINISCHE PSYCHOLOGIE, PSYCHOPATHOLOGIE UND PSYCHOTHERAPIE. Vol. 31, No. 1-. 0723-6557. Periodical. GW. German. qt. **Ind/Abst** Index Med. **NLM** W1 ZE433V. *Zeitschrift fur Klinische Psychologie und Psychotherapie.*

ZEITSCHRIFT FUR KLINISCHE PSYCHOLOGIE UND PSYCHOTHERAPIE. Began in 1971. Ceased with Vol. 30, No. 4. 0300-869X. Periodical. GW. German. qt. 78.00. Verlag Karl Alber GMBH, Hermann-Herder-Strasse 40, D-7800 Freiburg West Germany. **Tel** (0761)273495. Ed W J Revers. **Ind/Abst** Excerpta Med., Sociol. Abstr., Soc. Welf. Soc. Plan./ Policy Soc. Dev., Psychol. Abstr., Index Med., Lang. Lang. Behav. Abstr., Soc. Sci. Citation Index. **LC** BF3. **NLM** W1. **CODEN** ZKPPAP. bk rev. **Circ** 400. *Jahrbuch fur Psychologie, Psychotherapie und Medizinische Anthropologie.*

ZEITSCHRIFT FUR PARAPSYCHOLOGIE UND GRENZGEBIETE DER PSYCHOLOGIE. *See* Parapsychology and the Occult Sciences.

ZEITSCHRIFT FUR PSYCHOLOGIE MIT ZEITSCHRIFT FUR ANGEWANDTE PSYCHOLOGIE. Began with: Vol. 168. German. qt. $34.83. Kunst & Wissen Erich Bieber, Dufourstrasse 51, CH-8008 Zurich Switzerland. **Tel** 011-41-1-69 44 20. **Ind/Abst** Index Med., Psychol. Abstr. *Zeitschrift fur Psychologie Mit Zeitschrift fur Angewandte Psychologie und Charkaterkunde.*

ZEITSCHRIFT FUR TIERPSYCHOLOGIE. Vol. 1-. 0044-3573. Periodical. WB. German (English, French or Italian). mo. Paul Parey Scientific Publishing, 35 West 38th Street 3West, New York NY 10018. **Tel** (212)730-0518. **Ind/Abst** MLA Int. Bibliogr. Books Artic. Mod. Lang. Lit., Biol. Abstr., Curr. Contents, Agric. Biol. Environ. Sci., Index Med., Int. Abstr. Biol. Sci., Nutr. Abstr. Rev., Psychol. Abstr., Bibliogr. Agric. **LC** BF1. **DD** 151.305. **NLM** W1 ZE625N. **CODEN** ZETIAG. (cum index).

ZEITSCHRIFT FUR TRANSPERSONALE PSYCHOLOGIE. Vol. 1, No. 1-. 0722-5547. Periodical. German (English). sa. Verlag fur Transpersonale Psychologie, Postfach 608, 7800 Freiburg I Br Germany. **NLM** W1.

PUBLIC ADMINISTRATION

THE 1,000 LARGEST GOVERNMENTS. VFOAT One Thousand Largest Governments. 1983-. 0883-413X. US. English. an. $150.00. Municipal Analysis Services Inc, P O Box

Public Administration

13453, Austin TX 78711. **Tel** (512)327-3328. Ed Greg Michels. **DD** 330. adv acc. **Circ** 5,000. Twenty-two different financial and employee analyses of the many sources and uses of monies for each of the major local taxing units in your state.

ABBREVIATED ANNUAL REPORT (DEPT. OF HEALTH AND HUMAN SERVICES). Main/Corp United States. Dept. of Health and Human Services. Office of Inspector General. US. English. an. **LC** HV85. **DD** 353.842.

ACCION INAP. Main/Corp Instituto Nacional de Administracion Publica (Mexico). **VAT** Accion Instituto Nacional de Administracion Publica. Periodical. Spanish. ir. Institut Nacional de Administracion Publica, Avenida Country Club No 208, Mexico DF Mexico.

ACCION PARLAMENTARIA. Began in 1961. Periodical. AG. Spanish. mo. $25.00. Redaccion y Administracion, Viamonte 749 Piso 10 OF, 1 Buenos Aires 1053 Argentina.

ACCOUNTS, CITY OF COPENHAGEN. *See* Business - Public Finance.

ACCOUNTS COMMISSION : REPORT OF THE COMMISSION FOR LOCAL AUTHORITY ACCOUNTS IN SCOTLAND. *See* Business - Public Finance.

ACROSS FROM CITY HALL. 0001-5059. Periodical. US. English. qt. Citizens Union, 15 Park Row, New York NY 10038. *Citizens Union News.*

ACROSS THE TABLE. *See* Economics - Labor.

ACTIVE 20-30 QUARTERLY. (ACTIVE 20-30 QUARTERLY : THE OFFICIAL PUBLICATION OF ACTIVE 20-30 INTERNATIONAL OF THE UNITED STATES & CANADA). **VFOAT** Active Twenty, Thirty. 0746-3707. Periodical. US. English. qt. $6.00. Active 20-30 International, 1915 I Street, Sacramento CA 95814.

ACTIVITES - ASSOCIATION DES EMPLOYES CIVILS. (ACTIVITES). **VFOAT** A.E.C. Activites. **VAT** Association des Employes Civils. Activities. 0226-9929. Periodical. CN. French. bm. Comite d'Information de l'A.E.C., 650 Av Laurier, Quebec Quebec G1R 2L4 Canada. **DD** 354.7140005.

ACTIVITES (CHAMBRE DE COMMERCE ET D'INDUSTRIE DE NICE ET DES ALPES-MARITIMES). (ACTIVITES). 0150-5726. French. ir. Palais Consulaire, 20 Boulevard Carabacel, 06000 Nice France.

ACTIVITES UMQ. (ACTIVITES - UMQ). **Main/Corp** Union des Municipalites de la Province de Quebec. V. 1- Oct. 1974-. 0316-6929. CN. French. Union des Municipalites du Quebec, 922 Est rue Liege, Montreal Quebec H2P 1L1 Canada. **DD** 352.00062714.

ACTIVITIES AND SUMMARY REPORT OF THE COMMITTEE ON THE DISTRICT OF COLUMBIA, HOUSE OF REPRESENTATIVES. *See* Law.

ACTIVITIES CARRIED OUT UNDER THE VETERANS' ADMINISTRATION MEDICAL SCHOOL ASSISTANCE AND HEALTH MANPOWER TRAINING ACT OF 1972. (PUBLIC LAW 92-541). (ACTIVITIES CARRIED OUT UNDER THE VETERANS' ADMINISTRATION MEDICAL SCHOOL ASSISTANCE AND HEALTH MANPOWER TRAINING ACT OF 1972 (PUBLIC LAW 92-541)). **Series/Conf** Senate Committee Print. Began with 1st (1972/77). 0199-9575. US. English. an. US Government Printing Office, Superintendent of Documents, Washington DC 20402.

ACTIVITIES OF THE HOUSE COMMITTEE ON GOVERNMENT OPERATIONS. Main/Corp United States. Congress. House. Committee on Government Operations. 0739-3288. US. English. be. Superintendent of Documents, US Government Printing Office, Washington DC 20002. **LC** JK1430.G6. **DD** 328.7307658. Vols. for 96th Congress, 1st and 2nd Sessions, 1979/1980-, distributed to some depository libraries in microfiche.

ACTS OF THE GENERAL ASSEMBLY OF THE COMMONWEALTH OF KENTUCKY. Main/Corp Kentucky. 1792-. Periodical. US. English. be. Legislative Research Commission, Capitol Building, Frankfort KY 40601. **Tel** (502)564-8100.

THE ACTS OF THE PARLIAMENT OF TASMANIA *CEASED.* **Main/Corp** Tasmania. **VFOAT** Tasmanian Statutes. Vol. 1- Session of Parliament 20 Victoriae (1856-7)-1980. English. ir.

ADMINFO *CEASED.* Feb. 28, 1975-Mar. 6, 1981. Periodical. US. English. mo. *Department Newsletter.*

ADMINISTRACION PUBLICA. VFOAT Revista de la ESAP. No. 1-. Periodical. PE. Spanish. ir. Escuela Superior de Administracion Publica, Apartado No 4963, Miraflores, Lima Peru.

ADMINISTRACION Y DESARROLLO (1981). (ADMINISTRACION Y DESARROLLO). No. 19 (Dec. 1981)-. Periodical. Spanish. an. $300.00. Asesoria de la Direccion de la Esap, Diagonal 40 No 46A-37 Can Apartado Aereo No 29745, Bogota Colombia. **LC** JA5. **DD** 350.0005. (cum index). *Revista de Administracion y Desarrollo.*

ADMINISTRATION. V. 1- 1953-. 0001-8325. Periodical. IE. English. qt. $37.54. Institute of Public Administration, 59 Lansdowne Road, Dublin 4 Ireland. Ed Frank Litton. **Ind/Abst** ABC Pol Sci, Curr. Contents, Sage Public Adm. Abstr., Sociol. Abstr., Lang. Lang. Behav. Abstr. **LC** JA26. **DD** 350.0005. Index published separately - free - automatically sent. (cum index). bk rev. adv acc. **Circ** 300. Provides a forum for the discussion of law, sociology, public administration, politics, and current affairs.

ADMINISTRATION & SOCIETY. VAT Administration and Society. V. 6- May 1974-. 0095-3997. Periodical. US. English. qt. Sage Publications, 275 South Beverly Drive, Beverly Hills CA 90212. **Tel** (213)274-8003. **Ind/Abst** Am. Hist. Life, Hist. Abstr., Part A, Mod. Hist. Abstr., Hist. Abst., Part B, Twent. Century Abstr., Manage. Contents, Writ. Am. Hist., ABC Pol Sci, Int. Polit. Sci. Abstr., Sage Public Adm. Abstr., Sage Urban Stud. Abstr., Public Aff. Inf. Serv. Bull., Soc. Sci. Citation Index, Curr. Index J. Educ., Sociol. Abstr., Hist. Abstr., Bibliogr. Index, Lang. Lang. Behav. Abstr., Pover. Hum. Resour. Abstr., Sociol. Abstr. **LC** JA3. **DD** 350.0005. *Journal of Comparative Administration.*

ADMINISTRATION ET GESTION. (ADMINISTRATION ET GESTION : SOMMAIRES DE LA DOCUMENTATION COURANTE). V. 1- Dec. 1973-. 0704-9765. Periodical. CN. French (English). ir. 25.00. Bibliotheque Administrative, 1056 Conroy R C, Quebec QC G1R 5E6 Canada. **Tel** (418)643-5150. bk rev. adv acc. **Circ** 1,000. (ctrl). Book reviews, bibliography, and list reviews.

ADMINISTRATION FEDERALE DU CANADA. (L'ADMINISTRATION FEDERALE DU CANADA). 1958-. 0576-1409. Periodical. CN. French. an. $10.00 Domestic, $12.00 Foreign. Information Canada, 171 Slater Street, Ottawa Ontario K1A 0S9 Canada. **LC** JL5. **DD** 354.7104.

ADMINISTRATION FOR DEVELOPMENT. No. 1- Jan. 1974-. 0304-6028. Periodical. English. ir. Administrative College of Papua/New Guinea, PO Box 1216, Boroko New Guinea. **LC** JA1. **DD** 350.000995.

ADMINISTRATION (INSTITUT INTERNATIONAL D'ADMINISTRATION PUBLIQUE). (ADMINISTRATION). 79-. Periodical. FR. French. an. Institut International d'Administration Publique, 2 Ave de l'Observatoire, 75006 Paris France. **LC** JN2301. **DD** 354.440005.

ADMINISTRATION OF JUSTICE MEMORANDA. *See* Law.

ADMINISTRATION PUBLIQUE - INSTITUT BELGE DES SCIENCES ADMINISTRATIVES. *See* Law.

ADMINISTRATION REPORT - KERALA, INDIA (STATE). ELECTRICAL INSPECTORATE DEPT. Main/Corp Kerala, India (State). Electrical Inspectorate Dept. 1968/69-. English. ir. **LC** HD9685.I43. **DD** 354.5483008722.

ADMINISTRATION REPORT - PORT OF SPAIN, TRINIDAD AND TOBAGO. PUBLIC HEALTH DEPT. *See* Public Health and Safety.

ADMINISTRATIVE AFFAIRS IN BANGLADESH. 1979-. English. an. 20.00 Domestic, 5.00 US. Center for Administrative Studies, Room No. 4036 Arts Faculty Building/University of Dacca, Dacca-2 Bangladesh. **LC** JQ635. **DD** 354.54920005.

ADMINISTRATIVE CHANGE. Periodical. II. English. sa. $13.00. Administrative Change, 7 JHA 5/ Jawahar Nagar, Jaipur 302004 India.

ADMINISTRATIVE CHANGE. V. 1- June 1973-. English. ir. $15.00. C-13 Bal Marg Tilak Nagar, Jaipur 302004 India. **Tel** 26 86 45. **LC** JA26. **DD** 350.0005.

ADMINISTRATIVE REPORT - UTAH. STATE ARCHIVES AND RECORDS SERVICE. Main/Corp Utah. State Archives and Records Service. US. English. an. Capital Building Room 28, Salt Lake City UT 84114. **LC** CD3540. **DD** 353.9792007146.

ADMINISTRATIVE SCIENCE REVIEW. V. 1- March 1967-. 0001-8406. Periodical. BG. English. qt. $18.10. National Institute of Public Administration, Nilket Dacca 2 Bangladesh. *The Guide.*

ADMINISTRATOR *CEASED.* (THE ADMINISTRATOR). Ceased with Feb. 1984 issue. 0065-1974. CN. English.

ADMINISTRATOR'S ANNUAL FINANCIAL REPORT - NATIONAL CREDIT UNION ADMINISTRATION. (ADMINISTRATOR'S ANNUAL FINANCIAL REPORT). **Main/Corp** United States. National Credit Union Administration. 0147-4960. US. English. an. National Credit Union Administration, 1775 G Street NW, Room 7670, Washington DC DC 20456. **LC** HG2037. **DD** 353.00825.

ADVANCE BUDGETING. A REPORT TO THE CONGRESS. (ADVANCE BUDGETING). **Main/Corp** United States. Congressional Budget Office. 0147-1945. US. English. $0.70 Single Issue. Congress of the United States, Congressional Budget Office, Washington DC 20402. **LC** HJ2051. **DD** 353.00722.

AFFIRMATION. Vol. 1, No. 1 (Sept. 1980)-. 0228-5800. Periodical. CN. English. qt. Ontario Human Rights Commission, Editorial Office, 80 Grosvenor Street, Toronto Ont M7A 1A7 Canada. **DD** 354.71300996.

AFFIRMATIVE ACTION PLAN. PART 1, POLICIES & PROCEDURES - ALASKA. DEPT. OF COMMUNITY AND REGIONAL AFFAIRS. Main/Corp Alaska. Dept. of Community and Regional Affairs. **VFOAT** Policies & Procedures. US. English. an. Alaska Department of Community & Regional Affairs, Pouch B, Juneau AK 99811. **LC** HC107.A47. **DD** 353.9798008180681.

AFFIRMATIVE ACTION PLAN. PART 2, DATA ANALYSIS - ALASKA. DEPT. OF COMMUNITY AND REGIONAL AFFAIRS. Main/Corp Alaska. Dept. of Community and Regional Affairs. **VFOAT** Data Analysis. US. English. sa. Alaska Department Of Community & Regional Affairs, Pouch B, Juneau AK 99811. **LC** HC107.A47. **DD** 353.9798008180681.

AFRICA GAZETTE. V. 1- May 10, 1977-. Periodical. UK. English. bw. Africa Gazette, Wheatsheaf House/Carmelite Street, London EC4Y OAX England. **LC** HD3860. **DD** 350.711096.

AFRICAN ADMINISTRATIVE STUDIES. No. 13- Jan. 1975-. 0007-9588. Periodical. MR. English. sa. 18.00. Cafrad, BP 310, Tangier Morocco. **Tel** 36601. **Ind/Abst** Public Aff. Inf. Serv. Bull. bk rev. adv acc. **Circ** 800. The objective is to contribute to the study of administrative problems concerned with economic and social development in Africa. *Cahiers Africains d'Administration Publique. African Administrative Studies.*

AGITATOR TADZHIKISTANA. 1975-. Periodical. UR. Russian. sm. $12.50. Victor Kamkin Inc (77503), 12224 Parklawn Drive, Rockville MD 20852. **Tel** (301)881-5973. **LC** JQ1089.A55.

AGRICULTURAL ADMINISTRATION. *See* Agriculture.

AGTE QADAMU PABULIKESHANI. Periodical. in Sindhi. ir. 10.00. Sindhu, Madad Ali Sindhi, Agtay Kadam Publication Saddar, Haidrabad Pakistan. **LC** JQ201.

AKTIVNOST MESNIH ZAJEDNICA. Main/Corp Savezni Zavod Za Statistiku (Yugoslavia). Serbo-Croatian(R). ir. 5.00. Savezni Zarod Za Statistiku, Kneza Milosa 20, Beograd Yugoslavia. **LC** HA1631, JS6942.

Public Administration

AL-AMAL FI KHIDMAT LUBNAN. No. 1- Festival Year 1977-. Periodical. Arabic or French. ir. 10.00 Per Issue. PO Box 992, Bayrut Lebanon. LC JQ1825.L473.

AL-KHIDMAH AL-MADANIYAH. VFOAT Civil Service. Periodical. Arabic. mo. LC JQ1825.S34.

AL-TANZIM WA-AL-IDARAH. V. 1- October 1975-. Periodical. Arabic. ir. 0.60. LC JA26.

THE ALABAMA MUNICIPAL JOURNAL. 1945. 0002-4309. Periodical. US. English. mo. Alabama Municipal Journal, PO Box 1270, Montgomery AL 36102. Tel (205)262-2566. Ed John F Watkins. adv acc. Circ 3,800. Articles of interest to municipal officials and dealing with administration of municipal governments. *Alabama Local Government Journal.*

ALABAMA PLANNING AND DEVELOPMENT COORDINATION DIRECTORY. See Yearbooks, Almanacs, Directories.

ALASKA LEGISLATURE, ROSTER OF MEMBERS. Main/Corp Alaska. Legislature. Legislative Affairs Agency. 1913/66. US. English. Legislative Affairs Agency, State Capitol, Juneau AK 99811. LC JK9530. DD 328.7980922.

ALBERTA GAZETTE. (THE ALBERTA GAZETTE, PART II). V. 53, No. 13- July 15, 1957-. 0002-4775. Periodical. CN. English. sm. Public Affairs Bureau, 11510 Kingsway Avenue, Edmonton Alberta Canada. Tel (403)4274953. Ed Donna James. Circ 3,800. Alberta government's vehicle for publication of various public ads, official notices and regulations.

ALBERTA HANSARD. Main/Corp Alberta. Legislative Assembly. V. 1- 1972-. 0383-3623. CN. English. ir. 15.00. Legislative Assembly of Albert, 313 Legislative Building, Edmonton Alberta TK5 2B6 Canada. Tel (403)427-2490. Ed Gary Garrison. LC J112. DD 328.712301. The official record of the debates of the legislative assembly of Alberta.

ALBERTA LIST. (THE ALBERTA LIST OF OFFICIAL PERSONNEL IN FEDERAL, PROVINCIAL AND MUNICIPAL GOVERNMENTS IN THE PROVINCE OF ALBERTA). Began with 1954 issue?. 0568-9163. CN. English. an. The Alberta List, PO Box 4486, South Edmonton Alberta T6E 4T7 Canada. DD 354.712300025.

ALBUM BINA NEGARA REPUBLIK INDONESIA. Edition 1 (1981-1982)-. IO. Indonesia. ir. Hervy Dharma Publishers, Jln Melinjo No 18, Rawamangun Ti Jakarta. LC JQ767. DD 354.598602.

ALGERIEN ELEKTRIZITATSWIRTSCHAFT. Series/Titl Marktinformation. GW. German. ir. 2.00. Bundesstelle fur Aussenhandelsinformation, Blaubach 13 Postfach 108007, D-5000 Koln 1 West Germany. LC HD9685.A5. DD 338.4736362.

AMBASCIATE ESTERE IN ITALIA. Italian. ir. LC JX1799. DD 354.4500892. *Ambasciate e Legazioni Estere In Italia.*

AMERICAN GOVERNMENT. TEXT. See Political Science.

AMERICAN MOTOR CARRIER. See Transportation.

THE AMERICAN POLITICAL REPORT. 8755-562X. Periodical. US. English. bw. $120.00. American Political Research Corp, 4312 Montgomery Avenue, Bethesda MD 20814. LC JK1. DD 320.973005.

AMERICAN REVIEW OF PUBLIC ADMINISTRATION. VFOAT A.R.P.A. Vol. 15, No. 1 (Spring 1981). 0275-0740. Periodical. US. English. qt. $25.00. Midwest Review of Public Administration, Park College, Editorial Office, Kansas City MO 64152. Tel (816)741-2000. Ed Jerry Hauptmann. Ind/Abst Manage. Contents, ABC Pol Sci, ABI/Inform, Public Aff. Inf. Serv. Bull. LC JK1. DD 350.0005. Contains articles viewing administrative problems and ideas developing in federal offices away from the Potomac in state or local centers and in many diversified public administration institutions. *Midwest Review of Public Administration.*

AM/FM CHRONICLE CEASED. 0731-4590. Periodical. US. English. mo. $98.00. Kellog Corporation, 5601 South Broadway #400, Littleton CO 80121. Tel (303)794-1818.

AMTLICHES GEMEINDEVERZEICHNIS FUR RHEINLAND-PFALZ. See Statistics.

AMTSBLATT DER STADT WIEN. Main/Corp Vienna. German. ir. Presse und Informationsdienst der Stadt Wien, Volksgartenstrasse 3, 1030 Wien Austria. LC JS31.V6.

ANALE DE ISTORIE. Vol. 15-. RM. Romanian (summaries in French, English, German, and Russian (1969-)). bm. Rompresfilatelia, PO Box 1362137, Bucharest Romania. Ind/Abst Am. Hist. Life, Hist. Abstr., Part A, Mod. Hist. Abstr., Hist. Abst., Part B, Twent. Century Abstr. LC JN9639.A57. *Analele.*

ANGGARAN BELANJA MENGURUS. SENARAI PERJAWANTAN DI-KEMENTERIAN2 DAN JABATAN2 DALAM ANGGARAN PERSEKUTUAN CEASED. (ANGGARAN BELANJA MENGURUS : SENARAI PERJAWATAN DI-KEMENTERIAN2 DAN JABATAN2 DALAM ANGGARAN PERSEKUTUAN). Main/Corp Malaysia. 0303-4674. English or Malay. ir. LC JQ716.

ANJOU. (ANJOU). 0713-6803. Periodical. CN. French. mo. Free. Hotel de Ville d'Anjou, 7701 Boulevard Louis-H Lafontaine, Anjou Quebec H1K 4B9 Canada. DD 352.071428.

ANNALI DELLA FACOLTA DI SCIENZE POLITICHE (TRIESTE, ITALY). See Political Science.

ANNALS OF PUBLIC ADMINISTRATION. 1-. 0278-4289. Monographic Series. US. English. ir. Marcel Dekker, 270 Madison Avenue, New York NY 10016. Tel (212)696-9000. Ed Rabin, Miller and Bartley. This is an ongoing series. Each title has a different subject.

AN ANNOTATED GUIDE TO STATEWIDE PLANNING DOCUMENTS AND RESEARCH MATERIALS - MISSOURI. DIVISION OF BUDGET AND PLANNING. Main/Corp Missouri. Division of Budget and Planning. US. English. an. Missouri Office of Administration, Division of Budget and Planning Capitol Building, Jefferson City MO 65101.

ANNOTATED LEGISLATION SERVICE. Monographic Series. UK. English. Butterworth & Company, 88 Kingsway, London WC2B 6AB England.

ANNUAIRE ADMINISTRATIF DU QUEBEC. See Yearbooks, Almanacs, Directories.

ANNUAIRE DE L'ADMINISTRATION LOCALE. See Yearbooks, Almanacs, Directories.

ANNUAIRE DEPARTEMENTAL PRIVE : ILE DE LA REUNION. See Yearbooks, Almanacs, Directories.

ANNUAIRE DES COLLECTIVITES LOCALES. See Yearbooks, Almanacs, Directories.

ANNUAIRE DES COMMUNAUTES EUROPEENNES. See Yearbooks, Almanacs, Directories.

ANNUAIRE DES DIPLOMES DE L'ECOLE NATIONALE D'ADMINISTRATION PUBLIQUE. See Yearbooks, Almanacs, Directories.

ANNUAIRE DES RESSOURCES COMMUNAUTAIRES DU MONTREAL METROPOLITAIN. See Yearbooks, Almanacs, Directories.

ANNUAIRE DES SOCIETES ET DES ADMINISTRATEURS. See Yearbooks, Almanacs, Directories.

ANNUAIRE DU MONDE POLITIQUE, DIPLOMATIQUE, ADMINISTRATIF ET DE LA PRESSE. See Yearbooks, Almanacs, Directories.

ANNUAIRE EUROPEEN D'ADMINISTRATION PUBLIQUE. See Yearbooks, Almanacs, Directories.

ANNUAIRE NATIONAL OFFICIEL DE LA REPUBLIQUE GABONAISE. See Yearbooks, Almanacs, Directories.

ANNUAIRE OFFICIEL D'ADMINISTRATION ET DE LEGISLATION. See Yearbooks, Almanacs, Directories.

ANNUAL ACTION PLAN - UTAH COUNCIL ON CRIMINAL JUSTICE ADMINISTRATION. See Sociology: General Works, Theory - Social Pathology, Welfare, Criminology.

ANNUAL ACTION PROGRAMS - MONTANA. BOARD OF CRIME COUNCIL. See Sociology: General Works, Theory - Social Pathology, Welfare, Criminology.

ANNUAL ACTIVITIES REPORT OF THE COMMITTEE ON THE JUDICIARY, UNITED STATES SENATE. See Law.

ANNUAL ADMINISTRATION REPORT FOR THE YEAR . . . - INDIA. TEA BOARD. Main/Corp India. Tea Board. English. an. Tea Board, 14 Biplabi Trailokya Maharaj Sarani, Calcutta-700 001 India. LC HD9198.I4. DD 354.540082333. *Annual Administration Report.*

ANNUAL ADMINISTRATION REPORT FOR THE YEAR . . . - TAMIL NADU (INDIA.). AGRICULTURE DEPT. See Agriculture.

ANNUAL ADMINISTRATION REPORT - GUJARAT, INDIA (STATE). FOREST DEPARTMENT. Main/Corp Gujarat, India (State). Forest Department. CN. English. an. Receiver General For Canada, Statistics Canada Publications, Ottawa Ontario K1A 0T6 Canada.

ANNUAL ADMINISTRATION REPORT OF THE FOOD AND DRUG ADMINISTRATION, MAHARASHTRA STATE. (ANNUAL ADMINISTRATION REPORT - FOOD AND DRUG ADMINISTRATION, MAHARASHTRA STATE). Main/Corp Maharashtra, India (State). Food and Drug Administration. 1970/71-. 0376-5563. II. English. an. 0.70. Director - Government Printing and Stationery, Food and Drug Administration, Maharashtia State Director, Bombay India. LC HD9672.I53. DD 354.547920077. NLM W2 JI4.1 M3D5A.

ANNUAL ADMINISTRATION REPORT OF WORKS DEPARTMENT - ORISSA, INDIA. PUBLIC WORKS DEPT. Main/Corp Orissa, India. Public Works Dept. 0376-5555. English. an. Public Works Department, Bhubaneswar Orissa India. LC HD4295.07. DD 354.54130086.

ANNUAL ADMINISTRATION REPORT - ORISSA, INDIA. CO-OPERATIVE DEPT. Main/Corp Orissa, India. Co-Operative Dept. English. ir. LC HD3540.O7.

ANNUAL ANALYSIS OF FEDERAL COMPETITIVE PROCUREMENTS IN MANAGEMENT CONSULTING. See Business - General Management.

ANNUAL AUTOMATION REPORT TO THE ARIZONA LEGISLATURE. Main/Corp Arizona. Dept. of Administration. Data Processing Division. US. English. an. Department of Administration, Data Processing Division, State of Arizona, The Capitol, Phoenix AZ 85007. LC JK8249.A8. DD 353.979100714.

ANNUAL CATALOGUE OF COMMONWEALTH PUBLICATIONS. See Bibliographies.

ANNUAL DATA PROCESSING PLAN AND REPORT - MISSOURI. OFFICE OF ADMINISTRATION. DIVISION OF EDP COORDINATION. Main/Corp Missouri. Office of Administration. Division of EDP Coordination. 1978-. US. English. an. Office of Administration, PO Box 809, Jefferson City MO 65102. LC JK5449.A8. DD 353.97780071.

ANNUAL FINANCIAL REPORT AND INVENTORY - TEXAS. AMUSEMENT MACHINE COMMISSION. Main/Corp Texas. Amusement Machine Commission. US. English. an. PO Box 13226 Capitol Station, Austin TX 78711. LC HD9999.V443. DD 353.976400858.

ANNUAL FINANCIAL REPORT AND REPORT OF OPERATIONS - CALIFORNIA. PUBLIC EMPLOYEES' RETIREMENT SYSTEM. Main/Corp California. Public Employees' Retirement System. US. English. an. Headquarters Office/Public Employees' Retirement System, 1416 Ninth Street 10th Floor, Sacramento CA 95814. LC JK8760.P4. DD 353.979400505.

ANNUAL FINANCIAL REPORT FOR THE CALENDAR YEAR ENDED DECEMBER 31 . . . - PUBLIC EMPLOYEES RETIREMENT SYSTEM OF OHIO. Main/Corp Public Employees Retirement System of Ohio. US. English. an. PERS, 277 East Town Street, Columbus OH 43215. LC

Public Administration

JK5560.P4. **DD** 353.977100505. *Annual Financial Report to the Retirement Board, Public Employees Retirement System of Ohio for the Calendar Year Ended December 31 . . ., 0277-6251.*

ANNUAL FINANCIAL REPORT OF THE VIRGINIA SUPPLEMENTAL RETIREMENT SYSTEM FOR THE FISCAL YEAR ENDED JUNE 30 . . . . See Business - Public Finance.

ANNUAL FINANCIAL REPORT - TEXAS. EXECUTIVE DEPT. Main/Corp Texas. Executive Dept. US. English. an. Office of the Governor, State Capitol, Austin TX 78711. *Annual Financial Report of the Executive Department, State of Texas.*

ANNUAL FINANCIAL REPORT - UTAH RETIREMENT SYSTEMS. Main/Corp Utah Retirement Systems. US. English. an. Utah Retirement Systems, 540 East 200 South, Salt Lake City UT 84102. **LC** JK8460.P4. **DD** 353.9792005.

ANNUAL FINANCIAL REPORT YEAR ENDED AUG. 31 . . . - TEXAS ADVISORY COMMISSION ON INTERGOVERNMENTAL RELATIONS. Main/Corp Texas Advisory Commission on Intergovernmental Relations. US. English. an. Texas Advisory Commission on Intergovernmental Relations, Box 13206 Capitol Station, Austin TX 78711. **LC** JK4835. **DD** 353.9764909.

ANNUAL FINANCIAL STATEMENT AND EXPLANATORY MEMORANDUM ON THE BUDGET OF THE PUNJAB GOVERNMENT. See Business - Public Finance.

ANNUAL GENERAL ADMINISTRATION REPORT - HIMACHAL PRADESH, INDIA. DEPT. OF LABOUR, EMPLOYMENT AND TRAINING. Main/Corp Himachal Pradesh, India. Dept. of Labour, Employment and Training. II. English. ir. Government of Himachal Pradesh, Department of Labor, Simla India. **LC** HD8681.H5. **DD** 354.54520083.

ANNUAL MEETING - NEWFOUNDLAND AND LABRADOR ASSOCIATION OF MUNICIPAL ADMINISTRATORS. Main/Corp Newfoundland and Labrador Association of Municipal Administrators. 1st- 1972-. 0319-0145. Periodical. CN. English. an. Memorial University of Newfoundland, Extension Service, PO Box 7098, St John's Newfoundland Canada. **DD** 352.00062718.

ANNUAL OMBUDSMAN REPORT - MISSOURI. OFFICE OF THE LIEUTENANT GOVERNOR. Main/Corp Missouri. Office of the Lieutenant Governor. 0148-3315. US. English. an. Office of the Lieutenant Governor, Box 563, Jefferson City MO 65101. **LC** JK5449.O4. **DD** 353.97780091.

ANNUAL PLAN FOR THE GOVERNOR'S SPECIAL GRANT (NEVADA). See Economics - Labor.

ANNUAL PLAN - GOVERNMENT OF KARNATAKA, PLANNING DEPARTMENT. See Economics - Economic History, Conditions.

ANNUAL PROCUREMENT AND FEDERAL ASSISTANCE REPORT - UNITED STATES. DEPT. OF ENERGY. Main/Corp United States. Dept. of Energy. 0748-6278. US. English. an. National Technical Information Service, US Department of Commerce, Springfield VA 22161.

ANNUAL PROGRESS REPORT . . . - MISSISSIPPI. GOVERNOR'S OFFICE OF INTERGOVERNMENTAL PERSONNEL. Main/Corp Mississippi. Governor's Office of Intergovernmental Personnel. US. English. an. Office of Intergovernmental Personnel, Walter Sillers Building, Jackson MS 39201. **LC** JK4655. **DD** 353.9762001.

ANNUAL PROGRESS REPORT ON PAPERWORK MANAGEMENT - CALIFORNIA. DEPT. OF GENERAL SERVICES. Main/Corp California. Dept. of General Services. US. English. an. Director of General Services, 915 Capitol Mall, 5th Floor, Sacramento CA 95814. **LC** JK8749.P36. **DD** 353.979400714.

ANNUAL REPORT. Main/Corp Appalachian Regional Commission. **VFOAT** Annual Report, Including Transition Quarter. 1975/1976-. US. English. an. Appalachian Regional Commission, 1666 Connecticut Avenue NW, Washington DC 20235. *Annual Report of the Appalachian Regional Commission, 0503-5422.*

ANNUAL REPORT - ABORIGINAL AFFAIRS PLANNING AUTHORITY. Main/Corp Western Australia. Aboriginal Affairs Planning Authority. AT. English. an. Aboriginal Affairs Planning Authority, West Perth Western Australia 6004. **Tel** (09)3227044. **LC** GN667.W5. **DD** 354.941008484. **Circ** 700. (ctrl). Report on the operations of the Western Australian Government Office of Aboriginal Affairs including the Aboriginal Lands Trust and Aboriginal Consultative System.

ANNUAL REPORT - ADMINISTRATION ON AGING. Main/Corp United States. Administration on Aging. 0098-8405. US. English. an. Administration on Aging, Room 4273 Health Education and Welfare Building North, Washington DC 20201. **LC** HV1457. **DD** 353.0084605. **NLM** W2 A A15A.

ANNUAL REPORT - ADVISORY COMMISSION ON INTERGOVERNMENTAL RELATIONS. (ANNUAL REPORT). Main/Corp United States. Advisory Commission on Intergovernmental Relations. **VFOAT** Advisory Commission on Intergovernmental Relations, the Year in Review. 0082-8610. US. English. an. Advisory Commission on Intergovernmental Relations, Washington DC 20575. **LC** JK325.

ANNUAL REPORT - ADVISORY CONCILIATION AND ARBITRATION SERVICE. Main/Corp Great Britian. Advisory Conciliation and Arbitration Service. 1st- 1975-. UK. English. an. **LC** HD5545. **DD** 354.410083.

ANNUAL REPORT - ALABAMA HISTORICAL COMMISSION. Main/Corp Alabama Historical Commission. US. English. an. Alabama Historical Commission, 725 Monroe Street, Montgomery AL 36130. **LC** F321. **DD** 353.976100859.

ANNUAL REPORT - ALBERTA PUBLIC UTILITIES BOARD. Main/Corp Public Utilities Board for the Province of Alberta. 0383-3690. CN. English. an. Alberta Public Utilities Board, 11th Floor Manulife House, 10055 106 Street, Edmonton Alberta T5J 1G2 Canada. **LC** HD9685.C3. **DD** 354.71230087.

ANNUAL REPORT - ALBERTA SOLICITOR GENERAL. Main/Corp Alberta. Dept. of the Solicitor General. 1974-. 0383-3658. CN. English. an. Department of the Solicitor General, 424 Legislative Building, Legislative Circle, Edmonton Alberta T5K 2B6 Canada. **LC** HV7315.A45. **DD** 354.7123065.

ANNUAL REPORT - ANCIENT MONUMENTS BOARD FOR ENGLAND. Main/Corp Ancient Monuments Board for England. 0306-5901. UK. English. an. London/H.M. Stationery Office, PO Box 276, London SW8 5DT England. **LC** DA110. **DD** 354.420085.

ANNUAL REPORT AND ACCOUNTS - CENTRAL ELECTRICITY BOARD (MAURITIUS). Main/Corp Central Electricity Board (Mauritius). MF. English. an. Mauritius Government Printer, Place d'Ames, Port Louis Mauritius. **LC** HD9685.M35. **DD** 354.6982008722.

ANNUAL REPORT AND ACCOUNTS - LONDON TRANSPORT EXECUTIVE. Main/Corp London Transport Executive. **VFOAT** London Transport. 1970-. 0308-1605. UK. English. an. London Transport Executive, 55 Broadway, London SW1 England. **LC** HE4719.L72. **DD** 352.91509421. *Report and Accounts.*

ANNUAL REPORT AND ACCOUNTS - TANZANIA INDUSTRIAL STUDIES AND CONSULTING ORGANISATION. Main/Corp Tanzania Industrial Studies and Consulting Organisation. English. an. Tanzania Industrial Studies and Consulting Organisation, Ips Building/5th Floor, Azikiwe Street, PO Box 2650, Dar es Salaam Tanzania. **LC** HC885.A1. **DD** 354.678008206. *Annual Report & Accounts.*

ANNUAL REPORT AND ACCOUNTS - XHOSA DEVELOPMENT CORPORATION. Main/Corp Xhosa Development Corporation. **VFOAT** Jaarverslag en Rekeninge -. 0303-4372. Afrikaans (and English). an. S A Xhosa Development Corporation, PO Box 618, East London South Africa. **LC** HG3729.S62. **DD** 354.6870082.

ANNUAL REPORT AND FINANCIAL STATEMENTS - ALASKA PERMANENT FUND CORPORATION. Main/Corp Alaska Permanent Fund Corporation. 1980-. US. English. an. Alaska Permanent Fund Corporation, c/o Alaska Department of Reveune/Treasury Division, Pouch SB, Juneau AK 99811. **LC** HG3729.U49. **DD** 353.979800726.

ANNUAL REPORT AND RECOMMENDATIONS OF THE GOVERNMENTAL ETHICS COMMISSION, STATE OF KANSAS. See Ethics.

ANNUAL REPORT AND STATEMENT OF ACCOUNTS - KENYA TEA DEVELOPMENT AUTHORITY. Main/Corp Kenya Tea Development Authority. 1980-1981-. English. an. **LC** HD9198.N3. **DD** 354.67620082333. *Annual Report and Accounts (1980).*

ANNUAL REPORT AND STATEMENT OF ACCOUNTS - RURAL ELECTRIFICATION CORPORATION. Main/Corp Rural Electrification Corporation. **VFOAT** Annual Report. II. English. an. D 5 N.D.S.E. Part II, Ring Road, New Delhi 49 India. **LC** HD9688.I5. **DD** 354.5400872208.

ANNUAL REPORT - ANTI-DUMPING TRIBUNAL CEASED. Main/Corp Canada. Anti-Dumping Tribunal. **VFOAT** Rapport Annuel - Tribunal Anti-Dumping, Rapport Annuel Tribunal Antidumping. 1969-. Periodical. CN. text in English and French, 1971- . French and English texts have separate paging with French text on inverted pages, 1972-. an. **LC** HF1767. **DD** 354.7100827.

ANNUAL REPORT, AREA DEVELOPMENT FUND - KENTUCKY. Main/Corp Kentucky. Dept. of Local Government. US. English. an. Department of Local Government, 2nd Floor/Capital Plaza Tower, Frankfort KY 40601.

ANNUAL REPORT - ARIZONA. ELECTED OFFICIALS' RETIREMENT SYSTEM. Main/Corp Arizona. Elected Officials' Retirement System. 1st (June 30, 1982)-. US. English. an. Elected Officials' Retirement System, 3033 North Central/ Room 411, Phoenix AZ 85012. **LC** JK8260.P4. **DD** 353.9791005.

ANNUAL REPORT - ARKANSAS NATURAL HERITAGE COMMISSION. Main/Corp Arkansas Natural Heritage Commission. US. English. an. Arkansas Natural Heritage Commission, Continental Building/Suite 500, Main and Markham, Little Rock AR 72201 500. **LC** QH76.5.A6. **DD** 353.9767008232.

ANNUAL REPORT - AUSTRALIA. DEPT. OF SUPPLY. Main/Corp Australia. Dept. of Supply. AT. English. ir. $0.52. Commonwealth Government Printing Office, PO Box 84, Canberra ACT 2600 Australia. **LC** J905, U265. **DD** 328.9401 S, 355.6210994.

ANNUAL REPORT - AUSTRALIA. INDUSTRIAL RESEARCH AND DEVELOPMENT GRANTS BOARD. Main/Corp Australia. Industrial Research and Development Grants Board. AT. English. ir. $0.50. Commonwealth Government Printing Office, PO Box 84, Canberra ACT 2600 Australia. **LC** J905, HD3646.A8. **DD** 328.9401 S, 338.0994.

ANNUAL REPORT - AUSTRALIAN DEVELOPMENT ASSISTANCE AGENCY. Main/Corp Australian Development Assistance Agency. 1st- 1974/75-. AT. English. ir. Australian Government Publishing Service, PO Box 84, Canberra ACT 2600 Australia. **LC** HC60. **DD** 354.940082.

ANNUAL REPORT - AUSTRALIAN DRIED FRUITS RESEARCH COMMITTEE. Main/Corp Australia. Dried Fruits Research Committee. 1st- 1971/72-. 0311-9009. AT. English. ir. $0.20. Australian Government Printer, PO Box 84, Canberra ACT 2600 Australia. **LC** J905, TP440. **DD** 354.94008233.

ANNUAL REPORT - AUSTRALIAN HONEY BOARD. (ANNUAL REPORT). Main/Corp Australia. Honey Board. 0067-1894. AT. English. ir. $0.40. Australian Honey Board, 647 George Street, Sydney New South Wales 2000 Australia. **LC** J905, HD9210.A8. **DD** 328.9401 S, 354.94008233.

Public Administration

ANNUAL REPORT - BARBADOS BOARD OF TOURISM. Main/Corp Barbados Board of Tourism. 14th- 1972/73-. English. ir. LC G155.B17. DD 354.72981008243. *Annual Report.*

ANNUAL REPORT - BETHPAGE PARK AUTHORITY. (ANNUAL REPORT). Main/Corp Bethpage Park Authority. 0094-856X. US. English. an. Bethpage Park Authority, Babylon NY 11702. LC F127.L8. DD 353.974700863.

ANNUAL REPORT - BOARD OF ACTUARIES OF THE CIVIL SERVICE RETIREMENT SYSTEM. Main/Corp United States. Office of Personnel Management. Board of Actuaries of the Civil Service Retirement System. 0273-4567. US. English. an. Superintendent of Documents, US Government Printing Office, Washington DC 20402. LC JK791. DD 353.005. *Report.*

ANNUAL REPORT - BOARD OF GOVERNORS OF THE FEDERAL RESERVE SYSTEM. Main/Corp Board of Governors of the Federal Reserve System (U.S.). US. English. an. Washington Board, 12th Street & Constitution Avenue, Washington DC 20551. *Annual Report of the Board of Governors of the Federal Reserve System.*

ANNUAL REPORT - BRITISH COLUMBIA BUILDINGS CORPORATION. Main/Corp British Columbia Buildings Corporation. 1977/78-. 0702-0511. CN. English. an. British Colombia Buildings Corporation, Habour Square 400-910 Government Street PO Box 1112, Victoria BC V8W 2T4 Canada. LC JL435. DD 354.711092.

ANNUAL REPORT - CALIFORNIA CENTER FOR RESEARCH AND EDUCATION IN GOVERNMENT. Main/Corp California Center for Research and Education in Government. US. English. an. California Center for Research and Education in Government, 1617 10th Street, Sacramento CA 95814. LC JK8701. DD 353.97940015.

ANNUAL REPORT - CALIFORNIA. DEPT. OF FAIR EMPLOYMENT AND HOUSING. OFFICE OF PUBLIC INFORMATION AND EDUCATION. Main/Corp California. Dept. of Fair Employment and Housing. Office of Public Information and Education. VFOAT Annual Report of the California Department of Fair Employment and Housing. US. English. an. LC HD4903.5.U58. DD 353.979400833.

ANNUAL REPORT - CANADA. MINISTRY OF STATE FOR SOCIAL DEVELOPMENT. Main/Corp Canada. Ministry of State for Social Development. VFOAT Rapport Annuel. 1982/83-. CN. English (French). an. Ministry of State for Social Development, Ottawa Ontario K1A 1G3 Canada. *Annual Report of the Ministry of State for Social Development, 0712-8215.*

ANNUAL REPORT - CAPE BRETON DEVELOPMENT CORPORATION. (ANNUAL REPORT). Main/Corp Cape Breton Development Corporation (Canada). VFOAT Rapport Annuel. VAT Rapport Annuel - Societe de Developpement du Cap-Breton (Edition Anglaise et Francaise). 1st (1967)-. 0228-4723. CN. English (French). an. Free. Cape Breton Development Corporation, Box 1330, Sydney Novia Scotia B1P 6K3 Canada. LC HD4010.N6. DD 354.7169008.

ANNUAL REPORT - CHICAGO PARK DISTRICT. Main/Corp Chicago Park District. VFOAT Chicago Park District : Annual Report. 1- 1934/35-. US. English. an. Chicago Park District, 425 East McFetridge, Chicago IL 60605. DD 352.7.

ANNUAL REPORT - CITY OF DETROIT, DEPARTMENT OF PUBLIC INFORMATION. Main/Corp Detroit (Mich.) Dept. of Public Information. US. English. an. City of Detroit, Departmnet of Public Information, Detroit MI 48120. LC JS842.P7. DD 352.94190977434.

ANNUAL REPORT - CITY OF NEW YORK, COMMISSION ON INTERGROUP RELATIONS. (ANNUAL REPORT - COMMISSION ON INTERGROUP RELATIONS). Main/Corp New York (City). City Commission on Human Rights. 0360-4853. US. English. an. Praeger Publishers, 383 Madison Avenue, New York NY 10017. LC KFX2068. DD 352.002996097471.

ANNUAL REPORT - CIVIL SERVICE COMMISSION CEASED. Main/Corp Ontario. Civil Service Commission. VAT Annual Report - Civil Service Commission of Ontario (1968). 1968-1979/80. 0319-7263. CN. English. an. Free. *Report of the Civil Service Commission, 0706-4861.*

ANNUAL REPORT - COAST GARIBALDI HEALTH UNIT. Main/Corp British Columbia. Coast-Garibaldi Health Unit. 1964-. 0228-0248. CN. English. an. Free. Coast Garibaldi Health Unit, 5861 Arbutus Avenue, Powell River BC Canada. DD 354.7110077.

ANNUAL REPORT - COLORADO. CITIZENS' ADVOCATE OFFICE. Main/Corp Colorado. Citizens' Advocate Office. 1980-. US. English. an. Citizens' Advocate Office, 121 State Capitol, Denver CO 80203. LC JK7849.O4. DD 353.97880091. *Report for the Citizens' Advocate Office.*

ANNUAL REPORT - COLORADO. DEPT. OF ADMINISTRATION. Main/Corp Colorado. Dept. of Administration. US. English. an. Executive Director's Office Department of Administration, 1525 Sherman, Denver CO 80206. LC JK7835. DD 353.97880405.

ANNUAL REPORT - COLORADO. DIVISION OF CENTRAL SERVICES. Main/Corp Colorado. Division of Central Services. Fiscal Year 1980-1981-. US. English. an. Division of Central Services, 1525 Sherman Street/Room 15, Denver CO 80203. LC JK7888.A1. DD 353.97880071. *Division of Central Services' Annual Report.*

ANNUAL REPORT, COMMITTEE ON CORPORATIONS. Main/Corp New York (State). Legislature. Assembly. Committee on Corporations, Authorities, and Commissions. 1981-. US. English. an. Legislative Office Building, Albany NY 12248. LC KFN5337. DD 353.97470087.

ANNUAL REPORT - COMMONWEALTH OF MASSACHUSETTS, OFFICE FOR CHILDREN. Main/Corp Massachusetts. Office for Children. 0360-0076. US. English. an. Office for Children, 120 Boylston Street, Boston MA 02116. LC HV883.M4. DD 353.974400847.

ANNUAL REPORT - COMMUNITY RELATIONS SERVICE, UNITED STATES DEPARTMENT OF JUSTICE CEASED. (ANNUAL REPORT). Main/Corp United States. Community Relations Service. Began with 1964/65. Ceased with fiscal year 1981. 0565-1727. US. English. an. United States Department of Justice, Community Relations Service, Washington DC 20530. LC E184.A1.

ANNUAL REPORT - CONGRESSIONAL AWARD FOUNDATION (U.S.). (ANNUAL REPORT). Main/Corp Congressional Award Foundation (U.S.). 0882-0341. US. English. an. Congressional Award, 701 North Fairfax Street/Suite 300, Alexandria VA 22314.

ANNUAL REPORT - CONNECTICUT STATE ETHICS COMMISSION. Main/Corp Connecticut State Ethics Commission. 1978-. US. English. an. Connecticut State Ethics Commission, 30 Trinity Street, Hartford CT 06115. LC JK3345. DD 353.9746009.

ANNUAL REPORT. CONTRACTOR PROCUREMENT SYSTEM REVIEW PROGRAM. (ANNUAL REPORT, CONTRACTOR PROCUREMENT SYSTEM REVIEW PROGRAM). Main/Corp United States. Dept. of Energy. Office of Procurement Management. VFOAT Contractor Procurement System Review Program. Fiscal Year 1978-. 0272-0647. US. English. an. US Department of Energy/Office of Procurement Management, Procurement and Contracts Management Directorate, Washington DC 20545. LC HD3858. DD 353.87.

ANNUAL REPORT - COUNCIL OF STATE GOVERNMENTS. Main/Corp Council of State Governments. US. English. an. Council of State Governments, PO Box 11910, Iron Works Pike, Lexington KY 40578. LC JK2403. DD 353.905.

ANNUAL REPORT - COURT SERVICES, GOVERNMENT OF THE NORTHWEST TERRITORIES. (ANNUAL REPORT). Main/Corp Northwest Territories. Court Services. 1978-. 0713-3308. CN. English. an. Culture and Communications, Government of the Northwest Territories, PO Box 1320, Yellowknife Northwest Territories Canada. DD 354.71920088. *0701-6484.*

ANNUAL REPORT - DEMOCRATIC NATIONAL COMMITTEE (U.S.). Main/Corp Democratic National Committee (U.S.). 0737-4895. US. English. an. Democratic National Committee, 1625 Massachusetts Avenue NW, Washington DC 20036. LC JK2311. DD 324.273605.

ANNUAL REPORT - DEPARTMENT OF COMMERCE. Main/Corp Indiana. Dept. of Commerce. 0360-0866. US. English. an. Department of Commerce, State House/Room 336, Indianapolis IN 46204. LC HC107.I6. DD 353.97720082.

ANNUAL REPORT - DEPARTMENT OF ENVIRONMENTAL CONSERVATION (NEW YORK). Main/Corp New York (State). Dept. of Environmental Conservation. VFOAT State of New York's Environment. US. English. an. Department of Environmental Conservation, Albany NY 12233. LC TD171.3.N5. DD 353.9747008232.

ANNUAL REPORT - DEPARTMENT OF EXTERNAL AFFAIRS. (ANNUAL REPORT). Main/Corp Canada. Dept. of External Affairs. VFOAT Rapport Annuel. 1982/83-. 0823-9185. CN. English (French with French text on inverted pages). an. Department of External Affairs, 125 Promenade Sussex Drive, Ottawa Ontario K1A 0G2 Canada. DD 354.7106105. *Annual Review, 0315-9795.*

ANNUAL REPORT - DEPARTMENT OF INDUSTRIAL DEVELOPMENT. (ANNUAL REPORT). Main/Corp Newfoundland. Dept. of Industrial Development. 1979-1980-. 0713-1275. CN. English. an. Government of Newfoundland and Labrador, Department of Development, St John's Newfoundland A1C 5T7 Canada. LC HC117.N4. DD 354.718008206.

ANNUAL REPORT - DEPARTMENT OF LOCAL GOVERNMENT AND COMMUNITY DEVELOPMENT (PHILIPPINES). Main/Corp Philippines (Republic). Dept. of Local Government and Community Development. English. ir. LC JS7301.A1. DD 354.5990084.

ANNUAL REPORT - DEPARTMENT OF MENTAL HEALTH AND DEVELOPMENTAL DISABILITIES (ILLINOIS). Main/Corp Illinois. Dept. of Mental Health and Developmental Disabilities. 0361-3534. US. English. an. Illinois Department of Mental Health, 401 State Office Building, Springfield IL 62706. LC RA790.65.I4. DD 353.97730084205.

ANNUAL REPORT - DEPARTMENT OF SCHOOL AND PUBLIC LANDS, STATE OF SOUTH DAKOTA. (ANNUAL REPORT - DEPT. OF SCHOOL AND PUBLIC LANDS, STATE OF SOUTH DAKOTA). Main/Corp South Dakota. Dept. of School and Public Lands. 0147-801X. US. English. an. South Dakota Department of School & Public Lands, Pierre SD 57501. LC LB2827. DD 353.9783008232.

ANNUAL REPORT - DEPARTMENT OF SOCIAL AND REHABILITATION SERVICES (KANSAS). Main/Corp Kansas. Dept. of Social and Rehabilitation Services. 1973-. US. English. an. Kansas State Library, 535 Kansas Avenue, Topeka KS 66603. LC HV86. DD 353.9781008406.

ANNUAL REPORT - DEPARTMENT OF STATE (NEW YORK (STATE)). Main/Corp New York (State). Dept. of State. US. English. an. New York (State) Department of State, Albany NY 12231. LC J87.

ANNUAL REPORT - DEPARTMENT OF SUPPLY AND SERVICES (NEW BRUNSWICK). Main/Corp New Brunswick. Dept. of Supply and Services. VFOAT Rapport Annuel - Ministere de l'Approvisionnement et des Services. 119th- 1972/73-. 0383-4948. CN. English (French). an. Department of Supply & Services, Ottawa Ontario K1A 0S9 Canada. LC JL236. DD 354.7150071.

ANNUAL REPORT - DEPARTMENT OF THE INTERIOR (SOUTH AFRICA). Main/Corp South Africa. Dept. of the Interior. VFOAT Jaarverslag - Departement Van Binnelandse Sake. 1972-. 0304-694X. Afrikaans and English. ir. 0.75. Government Printer, Department of the Interior, Private Bag X85, Pretoria South Africa. LC JQ1950.I5.

ANNUAL REPORT - DIVISION OF RACING, NEW YORK STATE. Main/Corp New York (State). Division of Racing. 0096-3194. US. English. an. 717 Fifth Avenue, New York NY 10022. LC SF335.U6. DD 353.974700858.

Public Administration

ANNUAL REPORT - EAST-CENTRAL STATE, NIGERIA. MINISTRY OF WORKS, HOUSING AND TRANSPORTATION. Main/Corp East-Central State, Nigeria. Ministry of Works, Housing and Transportation. 1970/71-. English. ir. Government Printer, Nigeria Ministry of Works, Housing and Transportation, Enugu Nigeria. LC HD4350.N473. DD 354.6694.

ANNUAL REPORT - EMPLOYEES' RETIREMENT SYSTEM OF GEORGIA. Main/Corp Georgia. Employees' Retirement System. 0435-4842. US. English. an. 254 Washington Street SW, Room 592, Atlanta GA 30334. LC JK4360.P4. DD 353.9758005.

ANNUAL REPORT - FEDERAL COMMUNICATIONS COMMISSION. (ANNUAL REPORT MICROFORM). Main/Corp United States. Federal Communications Commission. VFOAT FCC Annual Report. 1st- 1934/35-. 0083-0585. Periodical. US. English. an. Superintendent of Documents, US Government Printing Office, Washington DC 20402. Annual Report of the Federal Radio Commission to the Congress of the United States.

ANNUAL REPORT - FEDERAL POWER COMMISSION. Main/Corp United States. Federal Power Commission. VFOAT Annual Report of the Federal Power Commission. 1st- 1920/21-. US. English. an. Superintendent of Documents, US Government Printing Office, Washington DC 20402.

ANNUAL REPORT - FLORIDA ADVISORY COUNCIL ON INTERGOVERNMENTAL RELATIONS. Main/Corp Florida Advisory Council on Intergovernmental Relations. 1977/78-. US. English. an. Holland Building/Room 20, House Office Building, Tallahassee FL 32304.

ANNUAL REPORT - FLORIDA. DIVISION OF PARI-MUTUEL WAGERING. See Horses and Horsemanship.

ANNUAL REPORT FOR - FIJI. SUGAR BOARD. Main/Corp Fiji. Sugar Board. VFOAT Annual Report . . . Cane Harvesting and Crushing Season. English. an. LC J961, HD9118. F529. DD 300.99611, 354.9611008233.

ANNUAL REPORT FOR THE FISCAL YEAR - MISSOURI STATE EMPLOYEES' RETIREMENT SYSTEM. Main/Corp Missouri State Employees' Retirement System. July 1, 1981 to June 30, 1982-. US. English. an. Missouri State Employees' Retirement System, 900 Leslie Boulevard/PO Box 209, Jefferson City MO 65102. LC JK5460.P4. DD 353.9778005.

ANNUAL REPORT FOR THE YEAR ENDED - ZAMBIA. DEPT. OF CENSUS AND STATISTICS. See Statistics.

ANNUAL REPORT FOR THE YEARS - ZAMBIA. MINISTRY OF LEGAL AFFAIRS. Main/Corp Zambia. Ministry of Legal Affairs. English. an. 30. DD 354.68940088.

ANNUAL REPORT - GAMBIA PRODUCE MARKETING BOARD. Main/Corp Gambia Produce Marketing Board. 22nd- 1970/71-. English. ir. LC HD9490.G24. DD 354.6651008233. Annual Report of the Gambia Oilseeds Marketing Board, 0431-0020.

ANNUAL REPORT - GOVERNMENT OF INDIA, THE ALL INDIA HANDLOOM BOARD. Main/Corp India (Republic). All India Handloom Board. II. English. ir. All-India Handloom Board, Government of India, Bombay India. LC HD9866.I6. DD 354.54008242.

ANNUAL REPORT - GOVERNOR'S OFFICE OF JOB DEVELOPMENT AND TRAINING (MISSISSIPPI). See Economics - Labor.

ANNUAL REPORT - ILLINOIS. DATA INFORMATION SYSTEMS COMMISSION. Main/Corp Illinois. Data Information Systems Commission. 1976-1977-. US. English. an. Illinois Data Information Systems Commission, 1729 State of Illinois Building, 160 North La Salle Street, Chicago IL 60601. LC JK5749.A8. DD 353.9773040285. Report of the Data Information Systems Commission, State of Illinois.

ANNUAL REPORT - ILLINOIS. DEPT. OF REHABILITATION SERVICES. Main/Corp Illinois. Dept. of Rehabilitation Services. 1980-. US. English. an. Illinois Department of Rehabilitation Services, 623 East Adams, PO Box 1587, Springfield IL 62705. LC HD7256.U6. DD 353.977300834. Annual Report.

ANNUAL REPORT - ILLINOIS. GENERAL ASSEMBLY. LEGISLATIVE INVESTIGATING COMMITTEE. (ANNUAL REPORT . . .). Main/Corp Illinois. General Assembly. Legislative Investigating Commission. Began in 1975. 0276-9468. US. English. an. Illinois Legislative Investigating Commission, 300 West Washington Street, Chicago IL 60606. LC JK5774.8. DD 328.77307452. Report of the Illinois Legislative Investigating Commission, 0094-9795.

ANNUAL REPORT - ILLINOIS JOINT COMMITTEE, LEGISLATIVE INFORMATION SYSTEM. (ANNUAL REPORT - JOINT COMMITTEE ON LEGISLATIVE INFORMATION SYSTEM, STATE OF ILLINOIS). Main/Corp Illinois. General Assembly. Joint Committee on Legislative Information System. 0360-4136. US. English. an. Joint Committee on Legislative System, 57 Lincoln Tower Plaza, Springfield IL 62706. LC JK5774. DD 328.36.

ANNUAL REPORT INCLUDING . . . OBJECTIVES AND ACTION PLANS - EQUAL OPPORTUNITIES FOR WOMEN. See Women.

ANNUAL REPORT - INDIA. DEPT. OF PERSONNEL & ADMINISTRATIVE REFORMS. Main/Corp India. Dept. of Personnel & Administrative Reforms. English. an. LC JQ245. DD 354.54001. Report.

ANNUAL REPORT - INFORMATION COMMISSIONER. (ANNUAL REPORT, INFORMATION COMMISSIONER). Main/Corp Canada. Information Commissioner of Canada. VFOAT Rapport Annuel du Commissaire A L'Information. 1983-84-. 0826-9904. CN. English (French). an. Free. Information Commissioner of Canada, 112 Kent Street 14th Floor, Ottawa Ontario K1A 1H3 Canada. Tel (613)995-2410. Ed Sally Jackson. LC JL86.S43. DD 354.710081906. Circ 7,000. Report of the specialist ombudsman who investigates complaints under Canada's Access to Information Act. Summaries of all complaints, statistics and organization chart.

ANNUAL REPORT - IOWA MERIT EMPLOYMENT DEPARTMENT. Main/Corp Iowa. Merit Employment Dept. 0363-3314. US. English. an. Merit Employment Department, Grimes State Office Building, East 14th and Grand, Des Moines IA 50319. LC JK6355. DD 353.9777001.

ANNUAL REPORT - ISRAEL ELECTRIC CORPORATION LTD. (ANNUAL REPORT - THE ISRAEL ELECTRIC CORPORATION LTD). Main/Corp Hevrat Ha-Hashmal Le-Yisrael. Periodical. IS. English. ir. LC HD9685.P154.

ANNUAL REPORT - JUSTICE DEVELOPMENT COMMISSION (BRITISH COLUMBIA). Main/Corp British Columbia. Justice Development Commission. 1977/78-. 0706-3806. CN. English. an. Justice Development Commission, 1016 Langley Street, Victoria BC V8W Canada. LC KEB532.A72. DD 354.711088.

ANNUAL REPORT - KENTUCKY DEPARTMENT OF PERSONNEL. Main/Corp Kentucky. Dept. of Personnel. 0097-7527. US. English. an. Kentucky Department of Personnel, 1923 Capitol Plaza Trail, Frankfort KY 40601. LC JK5355. DD 353.9769001.

ANNUAL REPORT - LIEUTENANT GOVERNOR (NEW MEXICO). Main/Corp New Mexico. Office of the Lieutenant Governor. 0363-0838. US. English. an. State Capitol Building, Santa Fe NM 87501. LC JK8051. DD 353.9789031806.

ANNUAL REPORT - MADHYA PRADESH ELECTRICITY BOARD. Main/Corp Madhya Pradesh Electricity Board. 1977-78-. English. an. LC HD9685.I43. DD 354.543008722006.

ANNUAL REPORT. MANITOBA MUNICIPAL EMPLOYEE BENEFITS FUND. (THE MANITOBA MUNICIPAL EMPLOYEE BENEFITS FUND ANNUAL REPORT). Main/Corp Manitoba. Municipal Employees Benefits Board. 1st- 1977-. 0706-3792. CN. English. an. Municipal Employees Benefit Board, 200 - 400 Tache Avenue, Winnipeg Manitoba R2H 3C3 Canada. LC JS1721.M3. DD 352.0055097127.

ANNUAL REPORT - MARYLAND DEPARTMENT OF GENERAL SERVICES. Main/Corp Maryland. Dept. of General Services. US. English. an. Maryland Department of General Services, 301 West Preston Street, Baltimore MD 21201.

ANNUAL REPORT . . . - MARYLAND INDUSTRIAL DEVELOPMENT FINANCING AUTHORITY. Main/Corp Maryland Industrial Development Financing Authority. US. English. an. Maryland Industrial Development Financing Authority, 2244 World Trade Center, 401 East Pratt Street, Baltimore MD 21202. LC HG3729.U49. DD 353.97520082.

ANNUAL REPORT - MARYLAND PAROLE COMMISSION. Main/Corp Maryland Parole Commission. US. English. an. Maryland Parole Commission, The Investment Building/Suite 601, One Investment Place, Towson MD 21204. LC HV9278. DD 353.975200849306. Report.

ANNUAL REPORT - MARYLAND. STATE ETHICS COMMISSION. Main/Corp Maryland. State Ethics Commission. 1st (July 1, 1979 to Dec. 31, 1980)-. US. English. an. LC JK3845. DD 353.9752009.

ANNUAL REPORT - MASSACHUSETTS STATE ETHICS COMMISSION. Main/Corp Massachusetts State Ethics Commission. 1979-. US. English. an. Massachusetts State Ethics Commission, 1 Ashburton Place/ Room 1413, Boston MA 12108. LC KFM2806. DD 353.974400995.

ANNUAL REPORT - METROPOLITAN WASHINGTON COUNCIL OF GOVERNMENTS. Main/Corp Metropolitan Washington Council of Governments. 1967/68-. 0076-7107. US. English. an. Metropolitan Washington Council of Governments, Washington DC 20036. DD 352. Report - Metropolitan Washington Council of Governments.

ANNUAL REPORT - MICHIGAN DEPARTMENT OF CIVIL SERVICE. Main/Corp Michigan. Dept. of Civil Service. 1965-. US. English. an. Department of Civil Service, Lewis Class Building/320 South Walnut Street Box 30002, Lansing MI 48909. LC JK5855. DD 353.977400605.

ANNUAL REPORT - MIDDLE TENNESSEE ELECTRIC MEMBERSHIP CORPORATION. Main/Corp Middle Tennessee Electric Membership Corporation. Periodical. US. English. an.

ANNUAL REPORT - MINISTRY OF GOVERNMENT SERVICES (ONTARIO). Main/Corp Ontario. Ministry of Government Services. 1972/73-. 0317-6827. CN. English. an. Ferguson Block, 77 Wellesley Street, Toronto Ont M7A 1N3 Canada. LC JL272. DD 354.713067.

ANNUAL REPORT - MINISTRY OF LOCAL GOVERNMENT, RURAL DEVELOPMENT & URBAN RECONSTRUCTION (LIBERIA). (ANNUAL REPORT). Main/Corp Liberia. Ministry of Local Government, Rural Development & Urban Reconstruction. VAT Annual Report - Ministry of Local Government, Rural Development and Urban Reconstruction (Monrovia). 1971/72-. 0304-730X. English. ir. Ministry of Local Government, Rural Development & Urban Reconstruction, Monrovia Liberia West Africa. LC HN83. DD 354.6662063.

ANNUAL REPORT - MINISTRY OF PROVINCIAL SECRETARY AND GOVERNMENT SERVICES (BRITISH COLUMBIA). Main/Corp British Columbia. Ministry of Provincial Secretary and Government Services. 1978-. 0226-0883. CN. English. an. Ministry of Provincial Secretary & Government Services, Victoria British Columbia Canada. LC JL432. DD 354.7110405. Annual Report - Ministry of the Provincial Secretary and Travel Industry, 0705-937X.

ANNUAL REPORT - MINNESOTA. MISSISSIPPI HEADWATERS BOARD. Main/Corp Minnesota. Mississippi Headwaters Board. 0743-0574. US. English. an. LC QH76.5.M6. DD 353.97760082325.

Public Administration

ANNUAL REPORT - MINNESOTA MUNICIPAL COMMISSION. Main/Corp Minnesota Municipal Commission. US. English. an. 304 Capital Square Building, St Paul MN 55101. LC JS344.A52. DD 352.00609776.

ANNUAL REPORT - MINNESOTA. RESIDENTIAL UTILITY CONSUMER UNIT. Main/Corp Minnesota. Residential Utility Consumer Unit. 1978-79-. US. English. an. Residential Utility Consumer, Unit 162 Metro Square Building, St Paul MN 55101. LC HD2767.M62. DD 353.97760087.

ANNUAL REPORT - MISSISSIPPI COUNCIL ON CHILDREN. Main/Corp Mississippi. Council on Children. 1st- 1975/76-. US. English. an. LC HQ767.8. DD 353.976200847.

ANNUAL REPORT - MISSOURI HISTORICAL SOCIETY. (ANNUAL REPORT). Main/Corp Missouri Historical Society. 0743-0469. US. English. an. Missouri Historical Society, Jefferson Memorial Building/Forest Park, St Louis MO 63112. LC F461. DD 353.977800859.

ANNUAL REPORT - NATIONAL GAS CONSUMERS' COUNCIL (GREAT BRITAIN). Main/Corp National Gas Consumers' Council (Great Britain). UK. English. an. National Gas Consumers Council, 5th Floor/Estate House, 130 Jermyn Street, London SW1Y 4UJ England. LC HD9581.G7. DD 354.410082042. Report of the National Gas Consumers' Council for the Year Ended March 31 . . . .

ANNUAL REPORT - NEBRASKA, JOINT MERIT SYSTEM. Main/Corp Nebraska. Joint Merit System. 0272-099X. US. English. an. LC JK6655. DD 353.978200605.

ANNUAL REPORT - NEBRASKA PUBLIC SERVICE COMMISSION. Main/Corp Nebraska. Public Service Commission. 1972/73-. 0098-2083. US. English. an. Public Service Commission, 1342 M Street, Lincoln NE 68508. LC HE28.N2. DD 353.97820087. Annual Report - Nebraska State Railway Commission.

ANNUAL REPORT - NEBRASKA STATE RACING COMMISSION. Main/Corp Nebraska. State Racing Commission. 0466-7085. US. English. an. Nebraska State Racing Commission, PO Box 442, Nebraska City NE 68410. LC SF335.U6. DD 353.978200858.

ANNUAL REPORT - NEVADA. PUBLIC EMPLOYEES RETIREMENT BOARD. Main/Corp Nevada. Public Employees Retirement Board. US. English. an. Nevada Public Employees Retirement Board, 693 West Nye la, Carson City NV 89701. LC JK8560.P4. DD 353.9793005.

ANNUAL REPORT - NEW JERSEY STATE LOTTERY. (ANNUAL REPORT). Main/Corp New Jersey State Lottery. 0732-7811. US. English. an. LC HG6133.N3. DD 353.974900726. Annual Report, 0094-5285.

ANNUAL REPORT - NEW SOUTH WALES. DEPT. OF MAIN ROADS. See Engineering - Civil Engineering.

ANNUAL REPORT - NEW YORK (STATE). LEGISLATURE. ASSEMBLY. LOCAL GOVERNMENTS COMMITTEE. Main/Corp New York (State). Legislature. Assembly. Local Governments Committee. VFOAT Annual Report of the Assembly Standing Committee on Local Government. 1979-. US. English. an. The Assembly, State of New York Standing Committee on Local Government, Albany NY 12248. LC KFN5750. DD 347.47029. The. . . . Annual Report of the Standing Committee on Local Governments.

ANNUAL REPORT - NEW YORK (STATE). LEGISLATURE. ASSEMBLY. STANDING COMMITTEE ON TOURISM, THE ARTS, AND SPORTS DEVELOPMENT. Main/Corp New York (State). Legislature. Assembly. Standing Committee on Tourism, the Arts, and Sports Development. VFOAT Annual Report of the Assembly Standing Committee on Tourism, the Arts, and Sports Development. 1979-. US. English. an. LC KFN5645. DD 353.9747008505.

ANNUAL REPORT - NEW YORK (STATE). LEGISLATURE. SENATE. SELECT COMMITTEE ON INTERSTATE COOPERATION. Main/Corp New York (State). Legislature. Senate. Select Committee on Interstate Cooperation. 1980-81-. US. English. an. New York State Senate, Select Committee on Interstate Cooperation, The Capitol, Albany NY 12247. LC JK2439. DD 353.974791. Report to the Legislature.

ANNUAL REPORT - NEW YORK (STATE). OFFICE OF ADVOCATE FOR THE DISABLED. Main/Corp New York (State). Office of Advocate for the Disabled. US. English. an. Empire State Plaza, 19th Floor, Albany NY 12223. Tel (518)474-3655. Ed Evelyn Romero-Salas. LC HV1555.N7. DD 353.97470084406. adv acc. Circ 12,000. (ctrl). Information about the Developmental Disabilities Planning Council in New York State. Contains council initiatives, legislation, grant availability in New York, special projects, etc.

ANNUAL REPORT - NEW YORK STATE PROJECT FINANCE AGENCY. (ANNUAL REPORT - NYS PROJECT FINANCE AGENCY). Main/Corp New York State Project Finance Agency. 1975-. 0275-3162. US. English. an. New York State Project Finance Agency, 1250 Broadway, New York NY 10001. LC HD7303.N7. DD 353.97470081806.

ANNUAL REPORT - NEW YORK TEMPORARY STATE COMMISSION ON REGULATION OF LOBBYING. Main/Corp New York (State). Temporary State Commission on Regulation of Lobbying. 1st- 1978-. US. English. an. New York Temporary State Commission on Regulation of Lobbying, Alfred E Smith Building/PO Box 7011, Albany NY 12225. LC JK3474.5. DD 353.974709.

ANNUAL REPORT - NORTH DAKOTA PUBLIC EMPLOYEES RETIREMENT SYSTEM. Main/Corp North Dakota Public Employees Retirement System. US. English. an. North Dakota Public Employees Retirement System, Box 1214, Bismarck ND 58505. LC JK6460.P4. DD 353.978400505.

ANNUAL REPORT - NORTH DAKOTA STATE WHEAT COMMISSION. Main/Corp North Dakota. State Wheat Commission. 0098-5295. US. English. an. North Dakota State Wheat Commission, 1305 East Central Avenue, Bismarck ND 58501. LC HD9049.W5. DD 353.9784008233.

ANNUAL REPORT - NOVA SCOTIA POWER CORPORATION. Main/Corp Nova Scotia Power Corporation. 1972/73-. 0703-0789. Periodical. CN. English. an. Free. Nova Scotia Power Corporation, Barrington Street, Tower Scotia Square, PO Box 910, Halifax Nova Scotia B3J 2W5 Canada. LC HD9685.C4. DD 338.7613636209716. Annual Report, 0078-2459.

ANNUAL REPORT, OCCUPATIONAL AND PROFESSIONAL LICENSING BOARDS. July 1, 1979-June 30, 1980-. US. English. an. State Reorganization Commission, 228 Solomon Blatt Building/1105 Pendleton Street, Columbia SC 29201. LC HD3630.U7. DD 353.97570082404606.

ANNUAL REPORT OF DEPARTMENT OF PUBLIC WORKS. NOVA SCOTIA CEASED. (ANNUAL REPORT - DEPARTMENT OF PUBLIC WORKS). Main/Corp Nova Scotia. Dept. of Public Works. 1956-1980. 0546-7748. Periodical. CN. English. an. LC HD4610.N6. Annual Report of the Department of Highways and Public Works, Nova Scotia, 0546-7748.

ANNUAL REPORT OF FEDERAL PREVAILING RATE ADVISORY COMMITTEE. Main/Corp United States. Federal Prevailing Rate Advisory Committee. 1st- 1972/73-. 0098-2296. US. English. an. Superintendent of Documents, US Government Printing Office, Washington DC 20402. LC KF5375. DD 353.0012.

ANNUAL REPORT OF GUAM'S REPRESENTATIVE IN WASHINGTON TO THE PEOPLE OF GUAM AND THE GUAM LEGISLATURE. Main/Corp Guam. VFOAT Guam's Washington Representative. 1968-. 0533-3660. US. English. ir. Superintendent of Documents, US Government Printing Office, Washington DC 20402. DD 996.

ANNUAL REPORT OF LEGISLATIVE INVESTIGATING COMMISSION. ILLINOIS. GENERAL ASSEMBLY. Main/Corp Illinois. General Assembly. Legislative Investigating Commission. US. English. an. Illinois Legislative Investigating Commission, 300 West Washington Street, Chicago IL 60606. LC JK5774.8. DD 328.77307452. Annual Report, 0276-9468.

ANNUAL REPORT OF MUNICIPAL STATISTICS. See Statistics.

ANNUAL REPORT OF THE ALASKA PUBLIC UTILITIES COMMISSION. Main/Corp Alaska. Public Utilities Commission. Q-1970-. US. English. an. Alaska Public Utilities Commission, Anchorage AK 99503. LC HD2767.A5. DD 353.979800871.

ANNUAL REPORT OF THE CALENDAR YEAR ENDING DECEMBER 31 . . . . Main/Corp Vermont Lottery Commission. US. English. an. Vermont Lottery Commission, State Office Building, Montpelier VT 05602. LC HG6133.V5. DD 353.974300726.

ANNUAL REPORT OF THE CALIFORNIA HORSE RACING BOARD FOR THE PERIOD JULY 1 . . . TO JUNE 30 . . . . See Horses and Horsemanship.

ANNUAL REPORT OF THE CHICAGO PARK DISTRICT. Main/Corp Chicago Park District. 1979-. US. English. an. Chicago Park District, 425 East McFetridge, Chicago IL 60605.

ANNUAL REPORT OF THE COMMISSION ON ELECTION CONTRIBUTIONS AND EXPENSES ADMINISTERING THE ELECTION FINANCES REFORM ACT. (THE ANNUAL REPORT OF THE COMMISSION ON ELECTION CONTRIBUTIONS AND EXPENSES ADMINISTERING THE ELECTION FINANCES REFORM ACT (ONTARIO)). Main/Corp Ontario. Commission on Election Contributions and Expenses. 2nd- 1976-. 0704-3414. CN. English. an. Commission on Election Contributions and Expenses, 8th Floor 151 Bloor Street West, Toronto Ont M7A 1A2 Canada. LC JL278. DD 354.713091.

ANNUAL REPORT OF THE COMMISSIONER OF PUBLIC SAFETY FOR THE YEAR ENDING JUNE 30 - MASSACHUSETTS. See Public Health and Safety.

ANNUAL REPORT OF THE COMMISSIONER OF THE NORTHWEST TERRITORIES. Main/Corp Northwest Territories. Commissioner. VFOAT Rapport Annuel du Commissaire des Territoires du Nord-Oeust. 0549-9879. CN. English. an. Canada Department of Information, Ottawa Ont Canada. LC JL461.A1. DD 354.71920006, 352.

ANNUAL REPORT OF THE COMMITTEE ON PROGRAM REVIEW (CONNECTICUT). Main/Corp Connecticut. General Assembly. Program Review Committee. 1st- 1973-. 0098-132X. US. English. an. Connecticut General Assembly, State Capitol, Hartford CT 06115. LC JK3301. DD 328.7460765.

ANNUAL REPORT OF THE COMMUNITY RELATIONS SERVICE. Main/Corp United States. Community Relations Service. 1982-. US. English. an. US Department of Justice/ Community Relations Service, 5550 Friendship Boulevard, Chevy Chase MD 20815.

ANNUAL REPORT OF THE DEPARTMENT OF ADMINISTRATION MONTANA. (ANNUAL REPORT). Main/Corp Montana. Dept. of Administration. 0093-0911. US. English. an. State of Montana, Department of Administration, Directors Office Mitchell Building, Helena MT 59601. LC JK7335. DD 353.9786.

ANNUAL REPORT OF THE DEPARTMENT OF ANIMAL HUSBANDRY AND VETERINARY SERVICES IN KARNATAKA, INDO-DANISH PROJECT HESSARGHATTA AND BANGALORE DAIRY, BANGALORE. See Veterinary Medicine, Animal Culture.

ANNUAL REPORT OF THE DEPARTMENT OF BACKWARD CLASSES AND MINORITIES, GOVERNMENT OF KARNATAKA. See Economics - Economic History, Conditions.

ANNUAL REPORT OF THE DEPARTMENT OF INDUSTRIAL PARTICIPATORY DEMOCRACY (ZAMBIA). Main/Corp Zambia. Dept. of Industrial Participatory Democracy. 1976-. ZA. English. an. 15. PO Box 136, Lusaka Zambia. LC HD5660.Z35. DD 354.68940082.

Public Administration

ANNUAL REPORT OF THE DEPARTMENT OF PROVINCIAL SECRETARY (PRINCE EDWARD ISLAND). Main/Corp Prince Edward Island. Dept. of Provincial Secretary. CN. English. an. Providence of Prince Edward Island, Department of Provincial Secretary, Charlottetown Canada. LC J106. DD 354.717.

ANNUAL REPORT OF THE DEPARTMENT OF PUBLIC WORKS FOR THE PROVINCE OF PRINCE EDWARD ISLAND. Main/Corp Prince Edward Island. Dept. of Public Works. 1976/77-1980. 0708-6318. CN. English. an. Prince Edward Island, Department of Public Works, PO Box 2000, Charlottetown Prince Edward Island Canada. Tel (902)892-7431. Annual Report of the Department of Public Works and Highways for the Province of Prince Edward Island, 0708-6318.

ANNUAL REPORT OF THE DIRECTOR GENERAL - MULTINATIONAL FORCE AND OBSERVERS. Main/Corp Multinational Force and Observers. VFOAT Report of the Director General. 1983-. English. an. Office of Public Affairs, Multinational Force and Observers, C P 642, 00187 Rome Italy.

ANNUAL REPORT OF THE DIRECTOR TO THE BOARD OF GOVERNORS (GREAT BRITAIN). Main/Corp Great Britain. Commonwealth Institute. 1958-. Periodical. UK. English. an. Free. Commonwealth Institute, Press & Public Relations Office, Kensington High Street, London W8 6NQ England. Tel 01-603-4535. Circ 1,500. (ctrl). Annual report giving a summary of the year's events, activities, future aims, etc. Annual Report.

ANNUAL REPORT OF THE DISTRICT OF COLUMBIA CITY COUNCIL. (ANNUAL REPORT). Main/Corp District of Columbia. City Council. 1st- 1967/69-. 0092-8364. US. English. an. City Council, Room 509, City Hall 14th and E Streets Northwest, Washington DC 20004. LC JK2730. DD 352.008309753.

ANNUAL REPORT OF THE ELECTRICITY DIVISION FOR THE YEAR . . . (SEYCHELLES). Main/Corp Seychelles. Electricity Division. English. an. LC HD9685.S47. DD 354.696008722006. Annual Report.

ANNUAL REPORT OF THE GENERAL SERVICES AGENCY (LIBERIA). Main/Corp Liberia. General Services Agency. English. ir. General Services Agency, PO Box 9027, Monrovia Liberia. LC JQ3928. DD 354.6662007.

ANNUAL REPORT OF THE GOVERNMENT STORES DEPARTMENT (ZAMBIA). Main/Corp Zambia. Government Stores Dept. 0304-7679. English. ir. 10. LC JQ2879. DD 354.689400712.

ANNUAL REPORT OF THE INTERAGENCY ADVISORY GROUP. Main/Corp United States. Civil Service Commission. Interagency Advisory Group. 1974/75-. US. English. an. US Civil Service Commission, 1900 E Street NW, Washington DC 20415. LC JK631. DD 353.001.

ANNUAL REPORT OF THE KEEPER OF PUBLIC RECORDS ON THE WORK OF THE PUBLIC RECORD OFFICE AND THE REPORT OF THE ADVISORY COUNCIL ON PUBLIC RECORDS (GREAT BRITAIN). Main/Corp Great Britain. Public Record Office. 1st- 1959-. UK. English. an. Her Majestys Stationery Office, PO Box 276, London SW8 5DT England. LC JN329.P75. DD 354.4200714. Annual Report of the Deputy Keeper of the Public Records.

ANNUAL REPORT OF THE MANAGEMENT SERVICES SECTION FOR THE YEARS . . . (ZAMBIA). Main/Corp Zambia. Cabinet Office. Management Services Section. 1981 and 1982-. English. an. LC JQ2829.C55. DD 354.68940071.

ANNUAL REPORT OF THE MAYOR'S COUNCIL OF MANPOWER AND ECONOMIC ADVISORS (CHICAGO). Main/Corp Chicago. Mayor's Council of Manpower and Economic Advisors. Began with vol. for 1974. 0147-6092. US. English. an. Mayor's Council of Manpower and Economic Advisor, Chicago Civic Center/Room 302, Chicago IL 60602. LC HC108.C4. DD 352.9420977311.

ANNUAL REPORT OF THE MINES DEVELOPMENT DEPARTMENT (ZAMBIA). Main/Corp Zambia. Mines Development Dept. 1972-. English. ir. Mines Development Department, PO Box 136, Lusaka Zambia. LC HD9506.Z3. DD 354.6894008238.

ANNUAL REPORT OF THE MINISTRY OF THE SOLICITOR GENERAL (ONTARIO). Main/Corp Ontario. Ministry of the Solicitor General. (1972)-. 0380-5794. CN. English. an. Receiver General for Canada, Supply & Services, Ottawa Ont K1A 0S9 Canada.

ANNUAL REPORT OF THE NEBRASKA POWER REVIEW BOARD TO THE GOVERNOR OF NEBRASKA. Main/Corp Nebraska. Power Review Board. VFOAT Annual Report - The Nebraska Power Review Board. 1st- 1963/64-. 0470-5394. US. English. an. Nebraska Power Review Board, 301 Centennial Mall South/PO Box 94713, Lincoln NE 68509. LC HD9685.U6. DD 363.6209782.

ANNUAL REPORT OF THE NEW HAMPSHIRE GREYHOUND RACING COMMISSION TO THE GOVERNOR AND THE EXECUTIVE COUNCIL. Main/Corp New Hampshire. Greyhound Racing Commission. US. English. an. LC SF440. DD 353.974200858.

ANNUAL REPORT OF THE NEW HAMPSHIRE PARI-MUTUEL COMMISSION. Main/Corp New Hampshire Pari-Mutuel Commission. 1st Ed. (1982)-. US. English. an. Commission Office, 105 London Road/Building 1, Concord NH 03301. LC SF440. DD 353.97420076. Annual Report of the New Hampshire Greyhound Racing Commission to the Governor of New Hampshire and the Executive Council, Annual Report of the New Hampshire State Racing Commission.

ANNUAL REPORT OF THE NEW YORK STATE ASSEMBLY, STANDING COMMITTEE ON GOVERNMENTAL EMPLOYEES. Main/Corp New York (State). Legislature. Assembly. Committee on Governmental Employees. US. English. an. Albany Office, Room 621/LOB, Albany NY 12248. LC JK3455. DD 353.9747001. Annual Report.

ANNUAL REPORT OF THE NEW YORK STATE ASSEMBLY STANDING COMMITTEE ON GOVERNMENTAL OPERATIONS. Main/Corp New York (State). Legislature. Assembly. Standing Committee on Governmental Operations. 1982-. US. English. an. 839 Legislative Office Building, Albany NY 12248. Annual Report.

ANNUAL REPORT OF THE NEW YORK STATE OFFICE FOR THE AGING. Main/Corp New York (State). Office for the Aging. -1980. 0732-1783. US. English. an. New York State Office for the Aging, Empire State Plaza, Albany NY 12223. LC HV1468.N7. DD 353.97470084606.

ANNUAL REPORT OF THE OHIO REHABILITATION SERVICES COMMISSION. (ANNUAL REPORT). Main/Corp Ohio. Rehabilitation Services Commission. 0092-7430. US. English. an. Division for Information Ohio Rehabilitation Services Commission, 4656 Heaton Road, Columbus OH 43229. LC HD7256.U6. DD 353.97710084.

ANNUAL REPORT OF THE OILSEED CONTROL BOARD FOR THE PERIOD . . . (SOUTH AFRICA). Main/Corp South Africa Oilseeds Control Board. 1st- Feb. 1952/Feb. 1953-. English. an.

ANNUAL REPORT OF THE OMBUDSMAN TO THE LEGISLATIVE ASSEMBLY OF BRITISH COLUMBIA. Main/Corp British Columbia. Office of the Ombudsman. VFOAT Annual Report, Ombudsman, British Columbia. 1981-. 0713-2921. CN. English. an. Office of the Ombudsman, 8 Bastion Square, Victoria British Columbia V8W 1H9 Canada. Annual Report of the Ombudsman to the Legislature of British Columbia, 0226-8930.

ANNUAL REPORT OF THE PARLIAMENTARY COMMISSIONER. OMBUDSMAN (NEWFOUNDLAND). (ANNUAL REPORT OF THE PARLIAMENTARY COMMISSIONER (OMBUDSMAN)). Main/Corp Newfoundland. Office of the Parliamentary Commissioner (Ombudsman). 0708-7217. CN. English. an. LC JL205.A55. DD 328.71807452. Report of the Parliamentary Commissioner (Ombudsman) for the Period . . ., 0382-179X.

ANNUAL REPORT OF THE PERSONNEL DIVISION (OREGON). Main/Corp Oregon. Executive Dept. Personnel Division. US. English. an. Executive Department/Personnel Division, 100 Public Service Building, Salem OR 97310. LC JK9055. DD 353.9795001.

ANNUAL REPORT OF THE PIG MEAT PROMOTION ADVISORY COMMITTEE FOR THE YEAR ENDED 30 JUNE . . . . Main/Corp Australia. Pig Meat Promotion Advisory Committee. AT. English. an. $1.00. Pig Meat Promotion Advisory Committee, Department of Primary Industry, Canberra Australian Capitol Territory 2600 Australia. LC J905, HD9435.A8. DD 300.994 S, 354.940082656649.

ANNUAL REPORT OF THE PRESIDENT ON THE IMPLEMENTATION OF THE PRIVACY ACT OF 1974. VAT Annual Report of the President on the Implementation of the Privacy Act of Nineteen Hundred and Seventy-Four. 5th (calendar year 1979)-. 0276-9107. US. English. an. Superintendent of Documents, US Government Printing Office, Washington DC 20403. Ind/Abst Am. Stat. Index. LC JK766.5. DD 323.4450973.

ANNUAL REPORT OF THE PRINCE EDWARD ISLAND DEPARTMENT OF COMMUNITY AND CULTURAL AFFAIRS. (ANNUAL REPORT OF THE PRINCE EDWARD ISLAND DEPARTMENT OF COMMUNITY AND CULTURAL AFFAIRS FOR THE YEAR ENDING DECEMBER 31 . . .). Main/Corp Prince Edward Island. Dept. of Community and Cultural Affairs. 1982-. 0827-987X. CN. English. an. PO Box 2000, Charlottetown PEI Canada.

ANNUAL REPORT OF THE PRIVACY COMMISSIONER (CANADA). (ANNUAL REPORT). Main/Corp Canada. Privacy Commissioner of Canada. VFOAT Rapport Annuel du Commissaire a la Protection de la Vie Privee. 1983-84-. 0825-7361. CN. English (French). an. Privacy Commissioner of Canada, 112 Kent Street/14th Floor, Ottawa Ontario K1A 1H3 Canada. Tel (613)995-2410. LC JC596.2.C2. DD 354.710081106. Circ 7,000. Report of the specialist ombudsman who investigates complaints under Canada's Privacy Act and audits federal government personal records. Summaries of selected complaints. Statistics. Annual Report of the Privacy Commissioner, 0825-7361.

ANNUAL REPORT OF THE PUBLIC EMPLOYEE RETIREMENT SYSTEM OF IDAHO. Main/Corp Idaho. Public Employee Retirement Board. 1st (Apr. 20, 1965-July 1, 1966)-. US. English. an. Employee Retirement Board, State House, 820 Washington Street, Boise ID 83712. LC JK7560.P4. DD 353.97960018205.

ANNUAL REPORT OF THE PUBLIC SERVICE COMMISSION TO THE HONORABLE GOVERNOR OF PUERTO RICO. Main/Corp Puerto Rico. Public Service Commission. VFOAT Annual Report of the Public Service Commission to the Honorable Governor of Puerto Rico. Periodical. PR. English. ir. Public Service Commission, San Juan Puerto Rico. LC HD2768.P7. DD 354.

ANNUAL REPORT OF THE PUBLIC WORKS AND ELECTRICITY DEPARTMENT (MYSORE). Main/Corp Mysore. Public Works and Electricity Dept. 0304-7873. English. ir. LC HD4295.M9. DD 354.54870086.

ANNUAL REPORT OF THE PUBLIC WORKS DEPARTMENT (BELIZE). (ANNUAL REPORT OF THE PUBLIC WORKS DEPARTMENT). Main/Corp British Honduras. Public Works Department. VFOAT Annual Report - British Honduras, Public Works Department. Periodical. HO. English. ir. Government Printer, 1 Church Street, Belize City British Honduras. LC HD4019.

ANNUAL REPORT OF THE REGISTRAR GENERAL (NORTHERN IRELAND). Main/Corp Northern Ireland. General Registrar Office. UK. English. an. Her Majesty's Stationery Office, 80 Chichester Street, BT1 4JY Belfast Northern Ireland. LC HA1147.N6. DD 354.4160081.

Public Administration

ANNUAL REPORT OF THE SUBCOMMITTEE TO INVESTIGATE THE ADMINISTRATION OF THE INTERNAL SECURITY ACT AND OTHER INTERNAL SECURITY LAWS OF THE COMMITTEE ON THE JUDICIARY, UNITED STATES SENATE. Main/Corp United States. Congress. Senate. Committee on the Judiciary. Subcommittee to Investigate the Administration of the Internal Security Act and Other Internal Security Laws. Periodical. US. English. an. Superintendent of Documents, US Government Printing Office, Washington DC 20402.

ANNUAL REPORT OF THE SUBVERSIVE ACTIVITIES CONTROL BOARD. Main/Corp United States. Subversive Activities Control Board. 1st- 1950/51-. 0500-3970. US. English. an. Superintendent of Documents, US Government Printing Office, Washington DC 20402. DD 351.74.

ANNUAL REPORT OF THE SUPERVISOR OF CONSUMER CREDIT (ALBERTA). (ANNUAL REPORT OF THE SUPERVISOR OF CONSUMER CREDIT FOR YEAR ENDING . . .). Main/Corp Alberta. Alberta Consumer and Corporate Affairs. 0826-9459. CN. English. an. Alberta Consumer and Corporate Affairs, 402 Legislature Building, Edmonton Alberta T5K 2B6 Canada. LC HG3756.C3. DD 354.71230082504306.

ANNUAL REPORT OF THE SUPERVISOR OF POLITICAL FINANCING UNDER THE POLITICAL PROCESS FINANCING ACT (NEW BRUNSWICK). (THE ANNUAL REPORT OF THE SUPERVISOR OF POLITICAL FINANCING UNDER THE POLITICAL PROCESS FINANCING ACT). Main/Corp New Brunswick. Office of the Supervisor of Political Financing. VFOAT Rapport Annuel du Controleur du Financement Politique Sous la Loi sur le Financement de l'Activite Politique. 1st- 1978/79-. 0225-5839. Periodical. CN. English (French). an. Office of the Supervisor of Political Financing, Fredericton NB Canada. DD 354.715091.

ANNUAL REPORT OF THE U.S. DEPARTMENT OF HEALTH, EDUCATION, AND WELFARE TO THE PRESIDENT AND THE CONGRESS ON FEDERAL ACTIVITIES RELATED TO THE ADMINISTRATION OF THE REHABILITATION ACT OF 1973 AS AMENDED. US. English. an. Department of Health Education and Welfare, Office of the Secretary, Washington DC 20201.

ANNUAL REPORT OF THE UTAH LIQUOR CONTROL COMMISSION. Main/Corp Utah. Liquor Control Commission. US. English. an. Utah Liquor Control Commission, 1625 South 900 West PO Box 30408, Salt Lake City UT 84125. LC HV5079.U8. DD 35397920076105. *Report on Operations.*

ANNUAL REPORT OF THE VIRGINIA STATE CRIME COMMISSION. (ANNUAL REPORT - VIRGINIA STATE CRIME COMMISSION). Main/Corp Virginia. State Crime Commission. 0360-327X. US. English. an. Virginia State Crime Commission, 701 East Franklin Street, Richmond VA 23219. LC HV7296. DD 353.975500756.

ANNUAL REPORT OF THE WEST VIRGINIA DIVISION OF VOCATIONAL REHABILITATION FOR THE PERIOD . . . . Main/Corp West Virginia. Division of Vocational Rehabilitation. VFOAT Annual Report for Fiscal . . . . US. English. an. West Virginia Division of Vocational Rehabilitation, State Capitol Building, Charleston WV 25305. LC HD7256.U6. DD 353.975400834.

ANNUAL REPORT OF THE WEST VIRGINIA RACING COMMISSION TO THE GOVERNOR OF THE STATE OF WEST VIRGINIA. See Horses and Horsemanship.

ANNUAL REPORT - OFFICE OF AFFIRMATIVE ACTION (ARIZONA). Main/Corp Arizona. Office of Affirmative Action. 1976-. US. English. an. Office of Affirmative Action, 1700 West Washington/Room 804, Phoenix AZ 85007. LC JK8260.A33. DD 353.9791001.

ANNUAL REPORT - OFFICE OF RESEARCH AND DEVELOPMENT, REGION I. Main/Corp United States. Environmental Protection Agency. Region I. Office of Research and Development. Periodical. US. English. an. US Environmental Protection Agency/Region 1, Office of Research and Development, Boston MA 02203.

ANNUAL REPORT - OFFICE OF THE RENTALSMAN (SASKATCHEWAN). Main/Corp Saskatchewan. Office of the Rentalsman. 1975/76-. CN. English. an. Office of the Rentalsman, 1350 Osler Street, Regina Sask S4R 1W7 Canada. LC HD7305.S3. DD 354.712400865.

ANNUAL REPORT - OHIO LOTTERY COMMISSION. Main/Corp Ohio Lottery Commission. US. English. an. Ohio Lottery Commission, Frank J Lausche State Office Building, 615 West Superior Avenue, Cleveland OH 44113. LC HG6133.O3. DD 353.977100726.

ANNUAL REPORT - OIL SHALE ENVIRONMENTAL ADVISORY PANEL. (ANNUAL REPORT - UNITED STATES DEPARTMENT OF THE INTERIOR, OIL SHALE ENVIRONMENTAL ADVISORY PANEL). Main/Corp United States. Oil Shale Environmental Advisory Panel. 1st- 1975-. 0360-4543. US. English. an. Missouri Basin Region, United States Department of the Interior, Denver CO 80225. LC TN859.U5. DD 353.008232.

ANNUAL REPORT - OKLAHOMA PUBLIC EMPLOYEES RETIREMENT SYSTEM. Main/Corp Oklahoma. Public Employees Retirement System. US. English. an. Oklahoma Public Employees Retirement System, 580 Jim Thorphe Building PO Box 53007 Oklahoma City OK 73132. LC JK7160.P4. DD 353.9766005.

ANNUAL REPORT - OMAHA PUBLIC POWER DISTRICT. Main/Corp Omaha Public Power District. US. English. an. Executive Offices/Electric Building, 1623 Harney Street, Omaha NE 68102. LC HD9685.U6. DD 352.91220709782254.

ANNUAL REPORT ON AUCKLAND CITY COUNCIL, CITIZENS ADVICE BUREAU. Main/Corp Auckland, N.Z. City Council. English. ir. LC JS31.A92. DD 352.00820993122.

ANNUAL REPORT ON RELIEF FROM ADMINISTRATIVE ERROR. Main/Corp United States. Veterans Administration. 0360-9464. US. English. an. Superintendent of Documents, US Government Printing Office, Washington DC 20402. LC KF7706.3. DD 353.00848.

ANNUAL REPORT ON THE STATE GOVERNMENT INTERNSHIP PROGRAM. Main/Corp Rhode Island. Commission on State Government Internships. 0145-4749. US. English. an. Room 323/State House, Providence RI 02903. LC JK3260.I53. DD 353.97450015.

ANNUAL REPORT ON THE WORKING OF THE CARDAMOM BOARD. Main/Corp India (Republic). Cardamon Board. English. ir. Government of India Cardamon Board, Chittoor Road, Cochin India 682018. LC HD9210.I5. DD 354.54008233.

ANNUAL REPORT ON UTILITY AND CARRIER REGULATION OF THE NATIONAL ASSOCIATION OF REGULATORY UTILITY COMMISSIONERS. Main/Corp National Association of Regulatory Utility Commissioners. 1973-. US. English. an. National Association of Regulatory Utility Commissioners, PO Box 684, Washington DC 20044. LC HD2766. DD 353.008.

ANNUAL REPORT - ONTARIO HYDRO. (ONTARIO HYDRO ANNUAL REPORT). 1971-. 0382-2826. CN. English. an. Ontario Hydro Head Office, 700 University Avenue, Toronto Ontario M5G 1X6 Canada. LC HD9685.C3. DD 354.713008722. *Annual Report.*

ANNUAL REPORT - ONTARIO MINISTRY OF CITIZENSHIP AND CULTURE. (ANNUAL REPORT). Main/Corp Ontario. Ministry of Citizenship and Culture. 1982/1983-. 0823-504X. CN. English. an. $2.00 per issue. Publications Services Section, 5th Floor 880 Bay Street, Toronto Ontario M7A 1N8 Canada. LC JL277.A2. DD 354.71300817.

ANNUAL REPORT - PACIFIC NORTHWEST REGIONAL COMMISSION. Main/Corp Pacific Northwest Regional Commission. 1972/73-. 0362-9619. US. English. an. Pacific Northwest Regional Commission, PO Box C 34666, Seattle WA 98134. LC HT392.5.P3. DD 353.97950082.

ANNUAL REPORT - PANAMA CANAL COMPANY, CANAL ZONE GOVERNMENT. Main/Corp Panama Canal Company. VFOAT Annual Report - Canal Zone Government. 1st- 1952-. 0475-6126. Periodical. US. English. ir. Superintendent of Documents, US Government Printing Office, Washington DC 20402. LC J184.5. DD 353.8. *Annual Report of the Governor of the Panama Canal.*

ANNUAL REPORT - PENNSYLVANIA. STATE ETHICS COMMISSION. Main/Corp Pennsylvania. State Ethics Commission. 1979-80-. US. English. an. LC JK3674.7. DD 353.97480099.

ANNUAL REPORT - PHILADELPHIA. CIVIL SERVICE COMMISSION. Main/Corp Philadelphia. Civil Service Commission. US. English. an. LC JS1274.

ANNUAL REPORT - PHILIPPINES. LOCAL WATER UTILITIES ASMINISTRATION. Main/Corp Philippines. Local Water Utilities Administration. 0115-5962. PH. English. an. National Government Center, 7th Floor/NIA Building, Edsa Quezon City 3004 Philippines. LC HD4465.P54. DD 354.59900871006.

ANNUAL REPORT - PHILIPPINES. OFFICE OF THE TANODBAYAN. Main/Corp Philippines. Office of the Tanodbayan. 1979-. English. an. Republic of the Philippines, Office of the Tanodbayan, 1610 Jose P Laurel Street, San Miguel Metro Manila Phillipines. LC JQ1409.5.O4. DD 354.5990091.

ANNUAL REPORT - PLIMOTH PLANTATION, INC. Main/Corp Plimoth Plantation, Inc. VFOAT Plimoth Plantation Annual Report. Began with vol. for 1968. Periodical. US. English. an. Plimoth Plantation, PO Box 1620, Plymouth MA 02360. LC F74.P8. DD 352.94590974482.

ANNUAL REPORT - POWER AUTHORITY OF THE STATE OF NEW YORK. Main/Corp Power Authority of the State of New York. VFOAT Annual Report of the Power Authority of the State of New York. 1931-. 0275-0864. US. English. an. Power Authority of the State of New York, 10 Columbus Circle, New York NY 10019. LC HD1694. DD 627.1097.

ANNUAL REPORT - PROPERTY SERVICES AGENCY (GREAT BRITAIN). Main/Corp Great Britain. Property Services Agency. VFOAT P.S.A. Annual Report. UK. English. an. 2.25. Her Majesty's Stationery Office, 49 High Holborn, London WC1V 6HB England. LC JN851. DD 354.410086.

ANNUAL REPORT - PUBLIC EMPLOYEES' RETIREMENT ASSOCIATION OF NEW MEXICO. See Economics - Labor.

ANNUAL REPORT - PUBLIC EMPLOYEES' RETIREMENT SYSTEM OF MISSISSIPPI. Main/Corp Mississippi. Public Employees' Retirement System. 0361-6762. US. English. an. 1704 Sillers State Office Building, Jackson MS 39201. LC JK4660.P4. DD 353.9762005.

ANNUAL REPORT - PUBLIC SERVICE BOARD (AUSTRALIA). Main/Corp Australia. Public Service Board. AT. English. an. $2.84. Government Printing Office, 390-422 Harris Street, Ultimo NSW 2007 10 Australia. Tel (02) 221 3622. LC JQ4045. DD 354.9400605. *Report on the Public Service of the Commonwealth by the Public Service Board.*

ANNUAL REPORT - PUBLIC SERVICE BOARD (WESTERN AUSTRALIA). Main/Corp Western Australia. Public Service Board. 0312-5688. English. ir. LC JQ5545. DD 354.941006.

ANNUAL REPORT - PUBLIC SERVICE COMMISSION (NIGERIA). Main/Corp Anambra State (Nigeria). Public Service Commission. 1976/77-. English. ir. Government Printer, Public Service Commission, Enugu Nigeria. LC JQ3099.A834. DD 354.6694.

ANNUAL REPORT - PUBLIC UTILITY COMMISSION OF TEXAS. Main/Corp Texas. Public Utility Commission. US. English. an. Public Utility Commission of Texas, 7800 Shoal Creek Boulevard/Suite 4004, Austin TX 78757. LC HD2767.T4. DD 353.97640087.

ANNUAL REPORT, REGIME DES ALLOCATIONS FAMILIALES DU QUEBEC. Main/Corp Quebec (Province). Regie des Rentes. CN. English. an. Regie des Rentes du Quebec, Case Postale 5200, Quebec PQ G1K

Public Administration

Canada. LC HD4925.5.C2. DD 354.714008482. *Annual Report, Quebec Family Allowances Plan.*

ANNUAL REPORT - RENT REVIEW COMMISSION (BRITISH COLUMBIA). **Main/Corp** British Columbia. Rent Review Commission. 1975-. 0226-6423. CN. English. an. Rent Review Commission, 1190 Melville Street, PO Box 9600, Vancouver British Columbia V6B 4G3 Canada. LC HD7305.B2. DD 354.71100865044.

ANNUAL REPORT - REPUBLIC OF THE PHILIPPINES, NATIONAL ECONOMIC AND DEVELOPMENT AUTHORITY, TARIFF COMMISSION. **Main/Corp** Philippines (Republic). National Economic and Development Authority. Tariff Commission. English. ir. DD 354.599007246.

ANNUAL REPORT - RETIREMENT SYSTEMS OF ALABAMA. **Main/Corp** Retirement Systems of Alabama. 1976-. US. English. an. Retirement Systems of Alabama, 135 South Union Street, Montgomery AL 36130. LC JK4560.P4. DD 353.97610018205.

ANNUAL REPORT - RURAL PROJECTS AGENCY, OPERATIONS DIVISION (ETHIOPIA). **Main/Corp** Ethiopia. Rural Projects Agency. Operations Division. English. ir. LC HD4344.5. DD 354.630081806.

ANNUAL REPORT - RURAL RECONSTRUCTION AUTHORITY OF WESTERN AUSTRALIA. **Main/Corp** Rural Reconstruction Authority of Western Australia. 1st- 1971/72-. AT. English. ir. Rural Reconstruction Authority of Western Australia, Central Government Buildings Barrack Street, Perth Western Australia. LC HG2051.A82. DD 354.941008233.

ANNUAL REPORT - SAFETY AND OCCUPATIONAL HEALTH. SASKATCHEWAN POWER CORPORATION. (ANNUAL REPORT). **Main/Corp** Saskatchewan Power Corporation. Safety and Occupational Health. 0712-3612. CN. English. an. Saskatchewan Power Corporation, Libr-Archives Victoria and Scarth, Regina Saskatchewan Canada. DD 354.7124008720289.

ANNUAL REPORT - SASKATCHEWAN ECONOMIC DEVELOPMENT CORPORATION. (ANNUAL REPORT). **Main/Corp** Saskatchewan Economic Development Corporation. 1979-. CN. English. an. Saskatchewan Economic Development Corporation, 1106 Winnipeg Street, PO Box 5024, Regina Saskatchewan S4P 3M3 Canada. LC HC117.S3. DD 354.7124008206. *SEDCO Annual Report.*

ANNUAL REPORT - SASKATCHEWAN GOVERNMENT SERVICES. (ANNUAL REPORT). **Main/Corp** Saskatchewan. Saskatchewan Government Services. VFOAT Annual Report of Saskatchewan Government Services for Year Ending March 31 . . . . VAT Annual Report of Saskatchewan Government Services. 1977/78-. 0710-6831. CN. English. an. Saskatchewan Government Services, Regina Saskatchewan Canada. LC JL312. DD 354.71240071. *Annual Report, 0317-4565.*

ANNUAL REPORT - SASKATCHEWAN INTERGOVERNMENTAL AFFAIRS. (ANNUAL REPORT). **Main/Corp** Saskatchewan. Saskatchewan Intergovernmental Affairs. 1979/80-. 0710-8540. CN. English. an. Saskatchewan Intergovernmental Affairs, Legislative Building, Regina Saskatchewan Canada. LC JL301.A1. DD 354.7124061.

ANNUAL REPORT - SASKATCHEWAN PUBLIC UTILITIES REVIEW COMMISSION. **Main/Corp** Saskatchewan Public Utilities Review Commission. 1982-. 0822-2339. CN. English. an. Saskatchewan Public Utilities Review Commission, 122 3rd Ave N, Saskatoon Canada 2H6 S7K. LC HD4010.S3. DD 354.71240087.

ANNUAL REPORT - SASKATCHEWAN RURAL AFFAIRS. (ANNUAL REPORT). **Main/Corp** Saskatchewan. Saskatchewan Rural Affairs. 1980/81-. 0715-2167. CN. English. an. LC HD4010.S3. DD 354.712400818. *Annual Report, 0708-5370.*

ANNUAL REPORT - SAUDI BASIC INDUSTRIES CORPORATION. **Main/Corp** Saudi Basic Industries Corporation. English. an. LC HD4280. DD 354.538008206. *Annual Report for . . . .*

ANNUAL REPORT - SECRETARY OF STATE, MERIT COMMISSION (ILLINOIS). **Main/Corp** Illinois. Merit Commission. US. English. an. Secretary of State, 490 Centennial Building, Springfield IL 62756. LC JK5755. DD 353.977300606.

ANNUAL REPORT - SECURITIES COMMISSION. **Main/Corp** Alberta. Securities Commission. Began with 1973? issue. 0702-0724. CN. English. an. Alberta Securities Commission, 10th Floor 10065 Jasper Avenue, Edmonton Alta T5J 3B1 Canada. LC KEA318.A72. DD 354.712300825.

ANNUAL REPORT - SMALL BUSINESS ADMINISTRATION. (ANNUAL REPORT). **Main/Corp** United States. Small Business Administration. VFOAT SBA Annual Report. Began with 1966. 0083-3274. US. English. sa. $14.00. Superintendent of Documents, Government Printing Office, Washington DC 20402. Tel (202)783-3238. LC HC106.5. DD 353.0082. *Report to the President and Congress.*

ANNUAL REPORT - SOUTHERN CALIFORNIA ASSOCIATION OF GOVERNMENT. (ANNUAL REPORT). **Main/Corp** Southern California Association of Governments. 0094-050X. US. English. Southern California Association of Governments, 1111 West Sixth Street, Suite 400, Los Angeles CA 90017. LC JS303.C2. DD 352.000617949.

ANNUAL REPORT - STATE EMPLOYEES' RETIREMENT SYSTEM OF ILLINOIS. **Main/Corp** State Employees' Retirement System of Illinois. 1971-. US. English. an. State Employees' Retirement System, 1201 South Fifth Street, Springfield IL 62706. LC JK5760.P4. DD 353.9773005. *Annual Statement of the Board of Trustees.*

ANNUAL REPORT - STATE OF FLORIDA, DEPARTMENT OF STATE. (ANNUAL REPORT - STATE OF FLORIDA DEPARTMENT OF STATE). **Main/Corp** Florida. Dept. of State. 0099-1600. US. English. an. State of Florida, Department of State, Tallahassee FL 32304. LC J87. DD 353.97593.

ANNUAL REPORT - STATE OF IOWA, OFFICE FOR PLANNING AND PROGRAMMING. **Main/Corp** Iowa. Office for Planning and Programming. 1970/71-. US. English. an. Division of Municipal Affairs, 523 East 12th Street, Des Moines IA 50319. LC HC107.I7. DD 353.9777072.

ANNUAL REPORT - STATE OF NEW YORK, STATE BOARD OF ELECTIONS. **Main/Corp** New York (State). State Board of Election. 1974-. 0360-9375. US. English. an. State Board of Elections, 194 Washington Avenue, Albany NY 12225. LC JK3491.A1. DD 353.9747091.

ANNUAL REPORT - STATE OF OHIO, LEGISLATIVE BUDGET OFFICE OF THE LEGISLATIVE SERVICE COMMISSION, LEGISLATIVE BUDGET COMMITTEE. (ANNUAL REPORT - STATE OF OHIO, LEGISLATIVE BUDGET COMMITTEE). **Main/Corp** Ohio. Legislative Budget Committee. 1st- 1973/74-. 0099-1627. US. English. an. Legislative Budget Committee, 40 South Third Street, Columbus OH 43215. LC HJ9889. DD 353.977100722.

ANNUAL REPORT - STATE OF OKLAHOMA, OFFICE OF COMMUNITY AFFAIRS AND PLANNING. (ANNUAL REPORT - THE STATE OF OKLAHOMA, OFFICE OF COMMUNITY AFFAIRS AND PLANNING). **Main/Corp** Oklahoma. Office of Community Affairs and Planning. 0360-3547. US. English. an. Office of Community Affairs and Planning, 4901 North Lincoln Boulevard, Oklahoma City OK 73105. LC HN79.O5. DD 353.9766008.

ANNUAL REPORT - STEPHEN P. TEALE DATA CENTER (CALIF.). PLANNING AND ANALYSIS BRANCH. **Main/Corp** Stephen P. Teale Data Center (Calif.). Planning and Analysis Branch. US. English. an. LC JK8749.A8. DD 353.97940071.

ANNUAL REPORT SUBMITTED TO THE GOVERNOR OF OKLAHOMA. **Main/Corp** Oklahoma. Wheat Commission. 0099-1449. US. English. an. Oklahoma Wheat Commission, 3108 N W Expressway #102, Oklahoma City OK 73112. LC HD9049.W5. DD 353.9766008233.

ANNUAL REPORT - SUPPLEMENTAL ANNUITY COLLECTIVE TRUST OF NEW JERSEY. **Main/Corp** Supplemental Annuity Collective Trust of New Jersey. 0097-6040. US. English. an. 20 West Front Street, Trenton NJ 08625. LC JK3560.P4. DD 353.9749005.

ANNUAL REPORT - TENNESSEE PUBLIC SERVICE COMMISSION. **Main/Corp** Tennessee. Public Service Commission. US. English. an. Cordell Hull Building, Nashville TN 37219. *Report - Tennessee Public Service Commission.*

ANNUAL REPORT - TERRITORY OF GUAM. GU. English. ir. Guam Legislature, PO Box 373, Agana Guam. LC J951.

ANNUAL REPORT - TEXAS ADVISORY COMMISSION ON INTERGOVERNMENTAL RELATIONS. **Main/Corp** Texas Advisory Commission on Intergovernmental Relations. US. English. an. Texas Advisory Commission on Intergovernmental Relations, S F Austin Building 1700 North Congress/PO Box 13206, Austin TX 78711. LC JK6835. DD 353.9764909.

ANNUAL REPORT - TEXAS DEPARTMENT OF COMMUNITY AFFAIRS. **Main/Corp** Texas. Dept. of Community Affairs. 0360-4640. US. English. an. 611 South Congress Avenue, PO Box 13166, Capitol Station TX 78711. LC HN79.T43. DD 353.97640084.

ANNUAL REPORT - TEXAS MUNICIPAL RETIREMENT SYSTEM. (ANNUAL REPORT). **Main/Corp** Texas Municipal Retirement System. 0733-1525. US. English. an. Texas Municipal Retirement System, 1200 North Interstate 5, Box 2225, Austin TX 78768. LC JS451.T47. DD 352.00518209764.

ANNUAL REPORT - TEXAS. STATE PENSION REVIEW BOARD. **Main/Corp** Texas. State Pension Review Board. 1st-. US. English. an. State Pension Review Baord, PO Box 13498, Austin TX 78711. LC JK4860.P4. DD 353.976400505.

ANNUAL REPORT - TEXAS SURPLUS PROPERTY AGENCY. **Main/Corp** Texas Surplus Property Agency. Fiscal Year 1980-. US. English. an. Texas Surplus Property Agency, Administrative Office, PO Box 8120, Wainwright Station, San Antonio TX 78208. LC JK4888.A1. DD 358.9764007130450 6. *Annual Report on the Operations of the Texas Surplus Property Agency for the Fiscal Year.*

ANNUAL REPORT - THAILAND. KANFAIFA SUAN PHUMIPHAK. **Main/Corp** Thailand. Kanfaifa Suan Phumiphak. English. an. LC HD9685.T5. DD 354.593008722006.

ANNUAL REPORT : THE ANNUAL REPORT ON THE ACTIVITIES OF THE COMMISSION OF CALIFORNIA STATE GOVERNMENT ORGANIZATION AND ECONOMY. **Main/Corp** Commission on California State Government Organization and Economy. US. English. an. Commission on California State Government Organization and Economy, 11th and L Building/Suite 550, Sacramento CA 95814.

ANNUAL REPORT - THE COMMONWEALTH OF MASSACHUSETTS, SECURITY AND PRIVACY COUNCIL. **Main/Corp** Massachusetts. Security and Privacy Council. 0098-5759. US. English. an. Security Privacy Council, 904 Saltonstall Building, Boston MA 02202. LC HV7271. DD 353.97440075.

ANNUAL REPORT - THE DIVISION OF VOCATIONAL REHABILITATION. **Main/Corp** New Mexico. Division of Vocational Rehabilitation. US. English. an. Vocational Rehabilitation, 231 Washington Avenue/PO Box 1830, Santa Fe NM 87501. LC HD7256.U6. DD 353.978900845.

ANNUAL REPORT - THE URBAN TRANSIT AUTHORITY OF BRITISH COLUMBIA. *See* Transportation.

ANNUAL REPORT TO THE CONGRESS FOR FISCAL YEAR . . . . *See* Economics - Labor.

ANNUAL REPORT TO THE FLORIDA LEGISLATURE. **Main/Corp** Florida Commission on Ethics. 1974/75-. US. English. an. Florida Commission on Ethics, Room 2105 The

Public Administration

Capitol, Tallahassee FL 32301. **LC** JK4445. **DD** 353.9759009.

ANNUAL REPORT TO THE GOVERNOR FOR THE PERIOD NOVEMBER 1 . . . THROUGH OCTOBER 31 - BOARD OF EXAMINERS FOR SPEECH PATHOLOGY AND AUDIOLOGY (OKLAHOMA). **Main/Corp** Oklahoma. Board of Examiners for Speech Pathology and Audiology. US. English. an. Board of Examiners for Speech Pathology and Audiology, PO Box 53592, Oklahoma City OK 73105. **LC** RC423.A1. **DD** 353.976608243046.

ANNUAL REPORT TO THE GOVERNOR - MINNESOTA. GOVERNOR'S OFFICE OF ECONOMIC OPPORTUNITY. **Main/Corp** Minnesota. Governor's Office of Economic Opportunity. US. English. an. 404 Metro Square/7th & Robert Street, St Paul MN 55101. **LC** HC79.P63. **DD** 353.977600845.

ANNUAL REPORT TO THE GOVERNOR OF OKLAHOMA. **Main/Corp** Oklahoma Pork Commission. 0364-1171. US. English. an. Oklahoma Pork Commission, Stillwater OK 74074. **LC** HD9435.U53. **DD** 353.976600863.

ANNUAL REPORT TO THE GOVERNOR - OKLAHOMA PECAN COMMISSION. (ANNUAL REPORT TO THE GOVERNOR). **Main/Corp** Oklahoma Pecan Commission. Began with 1973. 0736-797X. US. English. an. Oklahoma Pecan Commission, PO Box 426, Luther OK 73054. **LC** HD9259.P35. **DD** 353.97660082333.

ANNUAL REPORT TO THE LEGISLATURE - MISSISSIPPI. STATE CENTRAL DATA PROCESSING AUTHORITY. **Main/Corp** Mississippi. State Central Data Processing Authority. US. English. an. 508 Robert E Lee Building, Jackson MS 39202.

ANNUAL REPORT TO THE LEGISLATURE ON THE OPEN MEETINGS LAW (NEW YORK STATE). **Main/Corp** New York (State). Committee on Public Access to Records. 4th (Jan. 29, 1980)-. US. English. an. Department of State, 162 Washington Avenue, Albany NY 12231. **LC** KFN5747.P83. *Annual Report to the Governor and the Legislature on the Open Meetings Law.*

ANNUAL REPORT TO THE OKLAHOMA TURNPIKE AUTHORITY. 0748-5077. US. English. an. Benham Group, 1200 NW 63rd Street/PO Box 20400, Oklahoma City OK 73156. **LC** HE356.O5. **DD** 388.12209766.

ANNUAL REPORT TO THE PRESIDENT AND THE CONGRESS ON THE ACTIVITIES OF THE REHABILITATION ACT INTERAGENCY COORDINATING COUNCIL. **Main/Corp** Rehabilitation Act Interagency Coordinating Council (U.S.). Began with 1979. 0738-131X. US. English. an. Superintendent of Documents, US Government Printing Office, Washington DC 20402. **NLM** W2 A R22.

ANNUAL REPORT TO THE SECRETARY OF THE INTERIOR - UNITED STATES. ADVISORY COMMITTEE ON COAL MINE SAFETY RESEARCH. (ANNUAL REPORT TO THE SECRETARY OF THE INTERIOR). **Main/Corp** United States. Advisory Committee on Coal Mine Safety Research. 1974-. 0360-1374. US. English. an. Secretary of the Interior, Advisory Commission on Coal Mine Safety Research, Washington DC 20402. **LC** TN805. **DD** 353.008232.

ANNUAL REPORT TO THE UTAH STATE LEGISLATURE. **Main/Corp** Utah. Legislative Auditor General. 1975/76-. 0146-2385. US. English. an. State Capitol Building, Salt Lake City UT 84114. **LC** HJ9907. **DD** 353.9792007232.

ANNUAL REPORT TO THE WEST VIRGINIA LEGISLATURE - JOINT COMMITTEE ON GOVERNMENT AND FINANCE. **Main/Corp** West Virginia. Legislature. Joint Committee on Government and Finance. Commission on Special Investigations. 1st, June 30, 1981-. US. English. an. West Virginia Legislature Joint Committee on Government and Finance, Commission on Special Investigations, 1301 Quarrier Street, Charleston WV 25301. **LC** JK4088.A1. **DD** 353.975400992. *Report to the Legislature.*

ANNUAL REPORT - UNITED STATES. DEPT. OF ENERGY. OFFICE OF INSPECTOR GENERAL. **Main/Corp** United States. Dept. of Energy. Office of Inspector General. 0194-0414. US. English. an. DOE Technical Information Center, PO Box 62, Oak Ridge TN 37830. **LC** HD9502.U5. **DD** 353.00823.

ANNUAL REPORT - UNITED STATES. DEPT. OF STATE. OFFICE OF THE INSPECTOR GENERAL, FOREIGN SERVICE. (ANNUAL REPORT). **Main/Corp** United States. Dept. of State. United States. Office of the Inspector General of the Dept. of State and the Foreign Service. VFOAT Annual Report of the Inspector General, Department of State and Foreign Service. No. 1 (1980)-. 0740-5774. US. English. an. Department of State, Office of the Inspector, General Foreign Service, Washington DC 20520. **LC** JX1705. **DD** 353.105. Vols. for 1982- distributed to depository libraries in microfiche.

ANNUAL REPORT - UNITED STATES. INTERAGENCY TASK FORCE ON ACID PRECIPITATION. (ANNUAL REPORT). **Main/Corp** United States. Interagency Task Force on Acid Precipitation. VFOAT Annual Report . . . to the President and Congress. 1983-. 0882-1739. US. English. an. Executive Director NAPAP, c/o EOP Publications, 726 Jackson Place NW/Room 2202, Washington DC 20503. *Annual Report to the President and the Congress of the United States.*

ANNUAL REPORT - U.S. MERIT SYSTEMS PROTECTION BOARD. (ANNUAL REPORT). **Main/Corp** United States. Merit Systems Protection Board. 1st (1979)-. 0271-9791. US. English. an. US Merit Systems Protection Board, 1120 Vermont Avenue, Washington DC 20419. **LC** JK631. **DD** 353.006. **NLM** W2 A M5A.

ANNUAL REPORT - UNITED STATES. WESTERN AREA POWER ADMINISTRATION. **Main/Corp** United States. Western Area Power Administration. US. English. an. Western Area Power Administration, PO Box 3402, Golden CO 80401. **LC** HD9685.U6. **DD** 353.00872200978.

ANNUAL REPORT - UPPER MISSISSIPPI RIVER BASIN COMMISSION. **Main/Corp** Upper Mississippi River Basin Commission. US. English. an. Upper Mississippi River Basin Commission, Federal Building Room 510 Fort Snelling, Twin Cities MN 55111. **LC** TC425.M6. **DD** 353.008232.

ANNUAL REPORT - URBAN AFFAIRS. (RAPPORT ANNUEL - AFFAIRES URBAINES). **Main/Corp** Canada. Urban Affairs Canada. CN. French. an. Information Canada, 171 Slater Street, Ottawa Ontario K1P 1S0 Canada. **LC** HT169.C3. **DD** 354.71008.

ANNUAL REPORT - UTAH. DEPT. OF NATURAL RESOURCES. (ANNUAL REPORT). **Main/Corp** Utah. Dept. of Natural Resources. 1982-83-. 0882-7583. US. English. an. Department of Natural Resources, 1636 W North Temple, Salt Lake City UT 84116. **LC** HC107.U8. **DD** 353.97920082306. *Annual Report, 0741-5532.*

ANNUAL REPORT - UTAH OFFICE OF PERSONNEL MANAGEMENT. **Main/Corp** Utah Office of Personnel Management. US. English. an. Utah Office of Personnel Management, 130 State Capitol, Salt Lake City UT 84114. **LC** JK8455. **DD** 353.979200105.

ANNUAL REPORT - VICTORIA. RAILWAY CONSTRUCTION AND PROPERTY BOARD. **Main/Corp** Victoria. Railway Construction and Property Board. English. an. Railway Construction and Property Board, 35 Spring Street, Melbourne Victoria 3000 Australia. **LC** HE3531. **DD** 354.94500875306.

ANNUAL REPORT - VIRGIN ISLANDS OF THE UNITED STATES. WATER AND POWER AUTHORITY. **Main/Corp** Virgin Islands of the United States. Water and Power Authority. US. English. an. Water and Power Authority, PO Box 1492, St Thomas Virgin Islands 00801. **LC** TK33.V57. **DD** 354.7297220087.

ANNUAL REPORT - VIRGINIA. BUREAU OF FRUIT, VEGETABLE, AND PEANUT MARKETING SERVICES. **Main/Corp** Virginia. Bureau of Fruit, Vegetable, and Peanut Marketing Services. July 1, 1980-June 30, 1981-. US. English. an. Bureau of Fruit Vegetable and Peanut Marketing Services, Main Office, Washington Building/Room 701, 1100 Bank Street, Richmond VA 23219. **LC** HD9240.9.U7. **DD** 353.9755008261506. *Annual Report.*

ANNUAL REPORT - VIRGINIA DEPARTMENT OF PERSONNEL AND TRAINING. **Main/Corp** Virginia. Dept. of Personnel and Training. 1st- 1979-. US. English. an. Office of Communications Department of Personnel and Training, 320 State Finance Building, Richmond VA 23219. **LC** JK3955. **DD** 353.975500106.

ANNUAL REPORT - VIRGINIA. OFFICE OF EMPLOYEE RELATIONS COUNSELORS. *See* Economics - Labor.

ANNUAL REPORT - WATER WORKS BOARD OF THE CITY OF BIRMINGHAM. **Main/Corp** Water Works Board of the City of Birmingham. US. English. an. The Board, 3600 1st Avenue North, Birmingham AL 35212. **LC** TD225.B62. **DD** 352.6109761781.

ANNUAL REPORT - WEST VIRGINIA GOVERNOR'S HIGHWAY SAFETY ADMINISTRATION. **Main/Corp** West Virginia. Governor's Highway Safety Administration. 0360-0246. US. English. an. 922 Quarrier Street, Charleston WV 25301. **LC** HE5614.3.W4. **DD** 353.975400878314.

ANNUAL REPORT - WEST VIRGINIA PUBLIC EMPLOYEES RETIREMENT SYSTEM. **Main/Corp** West Virginia. Public Employees Retirement Systems. 1968/69-. US. English. an. West Virginia Public Employees Retirement System, Building 6, Room 430, Charleston WV 25305. **LC** JK4060.P4. **DD** 353.9755005. *Annual Financial Report.*

ANNUAL REPORT - WESTERN AUSTRALIA. SETTLEMENT AGENTS SUPERVISORY BOARD. **Main/Corp** Western Australia. Settlement Agents Supervisory Board. 1st July 1981 to 30th June 1982-. English. an. **LC** HD1039.W47. **DD** 354.941008243.

ANNUAL REPORT WITH RECOMMENDATIONS - GEORGIA. STATE COMMISSION ON COMPENSATION. **Main/Corp** Georgia. State Commission on Compensation. VFOAT Report of State Commission on Compensation. US. English. an. State Commission on Compensation, 401 State Capitol, Atlanta GA 30334. **LC** JK4357. **DD** 353.97580012305.

ANNUAL REPORT - WYOMING DEPARTMENT OF LABOR AND STATISTICS. *See* Statistics.

ANNUAL REPORT - WYOMING. LEGISLATIVE SERVICE OFFICE. **Main/Corp** Wyoming. Legislative Service Office. Began with vol. for 1978. US. English. an. Legislative Service Office, 213 Capitol Building, Cheyenne WY 82002. **LC** JK7674. **DD** 328.7870761. *Annual Report.*

ANNUAL REPORT - ZAMBIA COUNCIL FOR THE HANDICAPPED. **Main/Corp** Zambia Council for the Handicapped. English. ir. **LC** HD7256.Z3. **DD** 354.689400844.

ANNUAL REPORT - ZAMBIA. EDUCATIONAL AND OCCUPATIONAL ASSESSMENT SERVICE. **Main/Corp** Zambia. Educational and Occupational Assessment Service. English. ir. Government Printer/Educational and Occupational Assessment Service, PO Box 2186, Lusaka Zambia. **LC** HD5841.Z3. **DD** 354.68940015.

ANNUAL REPORT - ZAMBIA ELECTRICITY SUPPLY CORPORATION. **Main/Corp** Zambia Electricity Supply Corporation. English. ir. Zambia Electricity Supply Corporation, PO Box 40, Lusaka Zambia. **LC** HD9685.Z3. **DD** 354.6894008722.

ANNUAL REPORT - ZAMBIA. MINISTRY OF HOME AFFAIRS. **Main/Corp** Zambia. Ministry of Home Affairs. 0514-5562. ZA. English. ir. Zambia Ministry of Home Affairs, Government Printer, Lusaka Zambia.

ANNUAL REPORT - ZAMBIA NATIONAL TOURIST BOARD. **Main/Corp** Zambia National Tourist Board. English. an. Zambia National Tourist Board, Century House, Cairo Road, Box 31014, Lusaka Zambia. **LC** G155.Z33. **DD** 354.689400827.

ANNUAL REVIEW - AGRICULTURE CANADA, RACE TRACK DIVISION. (ANNUAL REVIEW). **VAT** Revue Annuelle - Agriculture Canada, Division des Hippodromes.

Public Administration

1979-. 0713-3138. CN. French (English). an. Agriculture Canada, Race Track Division, Ottawa Ontario Canada. DD 354.710076. *Race Track Supervision, 0713-312X.*

ANNUAL REVIEW - CROWN AGENTS. Main/Corp Great Britain. Crown Agents' Office. 1974-. UK. English. an. Crown Agents, 4 Millbank, London England. LC JV1043. DD 354.41. *Crown Agents Report, 0308-5287.*

ANNUAL REVIEW OF OPERATIONS - COMMITTEE ON CROWN CORPORATIONS (BRITISH COLUMBIA). (ANNUAL REVIEW OF OPERATIONS). Main/Corp British Columbia. Legislative Assembly. Committee on Crown Corporations. 4th (Apr. 1, 1981-Mar. 31, 1982)-. 0715-0016. CN. English. an. Committee on Crown Corporations, 600-700 West Georgia Street, Box 10085, Vancouver British Columbia V7Y 1B6 Canada. LC HD4010.B7. DD 354.711092. *Annual Review of Activities, 0715-0024.*

ANNUAL STATISTICAL REPORT OF THE PROCEEDINGS OF THE LOCAL AUTHORITIES PENSION BOARD PURSUANT TO THE LOCAL AUTHORITIES PENSION ACT (ALBERTA). See Statistics.

ANNUAL STATISTICAL REPORT OF THE PROCEEDINGS OF THE PUBLIC SERVICE MANAGEMENT PENSION BOARD PURSUANT TO THE PUBLIC SERVICE MANAGEMENT PENSION ACT (ALBERTA). See Statistics.

ANNUAL STATISTICAL REPORT OF THE PROCEEDINGS OF THE PUBLIC SERVICE PENSION BOARD PURSUANT TO THE PUBLIC SERVICE PENSION ACT (ALBERTA). See Statistics.

ANNUAL TITLE VI PROGRAM REVIEW AND UPDATE. Main/Corp New Jersey. Dept. of Transportation. VFOAT Title VI Program Review and Update. 1978/79-. US. English. an. LC HE28.N5. DD 353.974900104.

ANUARIO ESTADISTICO - INSTITUTO NACIONAL DE JUBILACIONES Y PENSIONES DE LOS EMPLEADOS Y FUNCIONARIOS DEL PODER EJECUTIVO. See Yearbooks, Almanacs, Directories.

ANUDANOM KI MANGEM (INDIA. DEPT. OF COMPANY AFFAIRS). Main/Corp India (Republic). Dept. of Company Affairs. VFOAT Demands for Grants. II. Hindi and English. ir. Government of India Press, Patiala House, New Delhi India. LC HD2897. DD 354.540082.

AOR REPORTER. Main/Corp California. Legislature. Assembly. Office of Research. VAT Assembly Office of Research Reporter. V.1- June 1975-. 0146-0579. Periodical. US. English. qt. Assembly Office of Research Legislature, 1116 Ninth Street, Sacramento CA 95814. LC JK8701. DD 328.794076.

APPEARANCES OF LEADING CHINESE OFFICIALS. (APPEARANCES OF LEADING CHINESE OFFICIALS DURING . . .). 1979-. 0744-1630. US. English. an. Document Expediting Project, Exchange and Gift Division, Library of Congress, Washington DC 20540. LC JQ1507. DD 354.51002.

APPROPRIATIONS AND LETTERS OF INTENT FOR . . . . US. English. an. State Legislative Research Council, State Capitol, Pierre SD 57501. LC KFS3467. DD 353.9783007223605.

APPROPRIATIONS REPORT (MICHIGAN). Main/Corp Michigan. Legislature. Senate. Fiscal Agency. US. English. an. Senate Fiscal Agency, PO Box 30036, Lansing MI 48909.

APPROVAL MEMORANDUM FROM THE GOVERNOR (NEW YORK STATE). Main/Corp New York (State). Governor. US. English. ir.

THE APS REVIEW. See Political Science.

ARABIAN GOVERNMENT AND PUBLIC SERVICES DIRECTORY. See Yearbooks, Almanacs, Directories.

ARBEIT UND BERUF. GW. German. mo. 72.-. Verlag Arbeit und Beruf, Viatisstr 202, 8500 Nuernberg West Germany. Tel (0911)405642. Ed Walter Lutz. LC HD8443. bk rev. adv acc. Circ 10,000. Labor administration in general with special regard to the responsibility of the Federal Institute for Labour Administration. *Arbeit, Beruf und Arbeitslosenhilfe.*

ARCHIV FUR DIPLOMATIK, SCHRIFTGESCHICHTE, SIEGEL- UND WAPPENKUNDE. See Genealogy and Heraldry - Archives.

ARCHIV FUR KOMMUNALWISSENSCHAFTEN. See Genealogy and Heraldry - Archives.

ARCHIVES PARLEMENTAIRES DE 1787 A 1860. See Genealogy and Heraldry - Archives.

ARIZONA ADMINISTRATIVE DIGEST. VFOAT Administrative Digest. Vol. 1, Issue 1 (Aug. 3, 1981)-. US. English. mo. $25.00. Office of Secretary of State Publications Division, State Capitol West Wing Suite 706, Phoenix AZ 85007. Tel (602)255-4285. Ed Miriam J McClennen. LC KFA2436. DD 348.791025, 347.910825. Circ 500. Contains all governor's executive orders, proclamations of general applicability, all notices of proposed rule action, all emergency rule adoptions, governor's appointments to boards and commissions.

ARIZONA ASSOCIATION OF COUNTIES SALARY AND BENEFIT SURVEY. July 1973-. 0096-3399. US. English. an. $5.00. 3001 West Indian School Road/ Suite 303, Phoenix AZ 85017. LC JS451.A67. DD 352.0051209791.

ARIZONA DIRECTORY OF STATE REGULATORY AGENCIES FOR BUSINESSES AND OCCUPATIONS. See Yearbooks, Almanacs, Directories.

ARIZONA REVIEW. See Business.

ARIZONA STATE UNIVERSITY, TEMPE, PUBLIC AFFAIRS BULLETIN. VFOAT Public Affairs Bulletin. V. 1-5, No. 4. 0272-3085. Periodical. US. English. ir. Arizona State University, Bureau of Government Research, Tempe AZ 85281.

ARKANSAS STATE DIRECTORY. See Yearbooks, Almanacs, Directories.

ARSBERETNING (DENMARK) CEASED. 1970/71-. Danish. ir. LC JN7195.

ARSBOK FOR SVERIGES KOMMUNER. See Yearbooks, Almanacs, Directories.

ASBESTOS MA VILLE. (ASBESTOS MA VILLE : BULLETIN MUNICIPAL D'INFORMATION). Main/Corp Asbestos (Quebec). Vol. 1, No. 1 (May 1980)-. 0711-8031. Periodical. CN. French. qt. Asbestos Ma Ville, c/o Directeur des Loisirs, CP 88, Asbestos Quebec J1T 3M9 Canada. DD 352.071465.

THE ASIAN JOURNAL OF PUBLIC ADMINISTRATION. VFOAT Ya-Chou Kung Kung Hsing Cheng Hsueh. Vol. 5, No. 1 (June 1983)-. Periodical. English. sa. $12.00. Asian Journal of Public Administration, University of Hong Kong/ Department Political Science, Hong Kong HK. Tel (5)8592389. Ed Katheleen Cheek-Milby and Ian Scott. Ind/Abst Doc. Public Adm., Hum. Resour. Abstr., Int. Polit. Sci. Abstr., Sage Public Adm. Abstr., Sage Urban Stud. Abstr. bk rev. adv acc. Circ 7,500. Seeks to promote the study, research, and dissemination of information on public administration in the Asian region. *Hong Kong Journal of Public Administration.*

ASVASANA SAMITI (VIDHANAPARISHAD). Main/Corp Maharashtra, India (State). Legislature. Legislative Council. Committee on Government Assurances. English or Marathi. ir. 2.20. Maharashtra Vidhanamandala Sacivalaya, Legislative Council Secretariat, Napapura India. LC JQ620.M263.

ATTORNEYS' DIRECTORY OF SERVICES AND INFORMATION. See Yearbooks, Almanacs, Directories.

AU COURANT. VAT Au Courant (Commission de la Fonction Publique. Bureau Regional de la Capital Nationale). 0228-1139. Periodical. CN. English (text in French with parallel columns). Public Service Commission, 300 Laurier Avenue West, Ottawa Ontario K1A 0M7 Canada. DD 354.71001005.

AUDIT OF SAINT LAWRENCE SEAWAY DEVELOPMENT CORPORATION FINANCIAL STATEMENTS. See Business - Accounting.

AUDIT OF THE UNITED STATES CAPITOL HISTORICAL SOCIETY. (AUDIT OF THE UNITED STATES CAPITOL HISTORICAL SOCIETY FOR THE YEAR ENDED . . .). Began with 1972. 0091-5483. US. English. an. US General Accounting Office, Document Handling and Information Services Facility, PO Box 6015, Gaithersburg MD 20760. LC F191.U55. DD 353.007232.

AUDIT REPORT. COMMISSION TO CONTROL THE SUPREME COURT BUILDING AT NASHVILLE. (AUDIT REPORT, COMMISSION TO CONTROL THE SUPREME COURT BUILDING AT NASHVILLE). Main/Corp Tennessee. Division of State Audit. 0148-3870. US. English. Tennessee Comptroller of the Treasury, Nashville TN 37202. LC KFT512. DD 353.976800713.

AUDIT REPORT, DEPARTMENT OF GENERAL SERVICES, MOTOR VEHICLE MANAGEMENT DIVISION. Main/Corp Tennessee. Division of State Audit. 1973/ 75-. 0148-5202. US. English. Tennessee Comptroller of the Treasury, Nashville TN 37202. LC JK5288.M7. DD 353.97680087841. *Audit Report, Division of Motor Vehicle Management, 0148-5210.*

AUDIT REPORT. DIVISION OF PRINTING. See Printing.

AUDIT REPORT : SECRETARY OF STATE. Main/Corp Georgia. Dept. of Audits and Accounts. US. English. State of Georgia/Department of Audits, 115 State Capitol, Atlanta GA 30334. LC J87.

AUDIT REPORT. STATE OF NEVADA, CLARK COUNTY TAXICAB AUTHORITY. (AUDIT REPORT, STATE OF NEVADA, CLARK COUNTY TAXICAB AUTHORITY). Main/Corp Nevada. Legislative Auditor. 0160-5356. US. English. Legislative Building Capitol Complex, Carson City NV 89710. LC HE5633.N3. DD 353.979300878321.

AUDIT REPORT - STATE OF NEVADA. DEPARTMENT OF ADMINISTRATION. PERSONNEL DIVISION. (PERSONNEL DIVISION AUDIT REPORT). Main/Corp Nevada. Legislative Counsel Bureau. 0093-0202. US. English. an. Nevada Legislative Counsel Bureau Legislative Building, Carson City NV 89701. LC JK8555. DD 353.9793001.

AUDIT REPORT. STATE OF NEVADA, DEPARTMENT OF COMMERCE, HOUSING DIVISION. (AUDIT REPORT, STATE OF NEVADA, DEPARTMENT OF COMMERCE, HOUSING DIVISION). Main/Corp Nevada. Legislative Auditor. 0160-5380. US. English. an. Legislative Building Capitol Complex, Carson City NV 89710. LC HD7303.N4. DD 353.979300865.

AUDIT REPORT. STATE OF NEVADA, DEPARTMENT OF COMMERCE, REAL ESTATE DIVISION. (AUDIT REPORT, STATE OF NEVADA, DEPARTMENT OF COMMERCE, REAL ESTATE DIVISION). Main/Corp Nevada. Legislative Auditor. 0160-5348. US. English. Legislative Building Capitol Complex, Carson City NV 89710. LC HD266.N3. DD 353.9793008232.

AUDIT REPORT. STATE OF NEVADA, DEPARTMENT OF COMMERCE, REAL ESTATE EDUCATION RESEARCH AND RECOVERY FUND. (AUDIT REPORT, STATE OF NEVADA, DEPARTMENT OF COMMERCE, REAL ESTATE EDUCATION RESEARCH AND RECOVERY FUND). Main/Corp Nevada. Legislative Auditor. 0160-533X. US. English. an. Legislative Auditor, Legislative Building Capitol Complex, Carson City NV 89710. LC HJ9875. DD 353.9793007232.

AUDIT REPORT, STATE OF NEVADA, OFFICE OF THE GOVERNOR. Main/ Corp Nevada. Legislative Auditor. US. English. an. Legislative Building Capitol Complex, Carson City NV 89710.

AUDIT REPORT - STATE OF NEVADA. PUBLIC SERVICE COMMISSION. (PUBLIC SERVICE COMMISSION AUDIT REPORT). Main/Corp Nevada. Legislative Counsel Bureau. 0092-9239. US. English. an. Nevada Legislative

Public Administration

Counsel Bureau, Legislative Building, Carson City NV 89701. **LC** HD2767.N32. **DD** 353.9793008.

AUDIT REPORT. TEXAS BOARD OF LICENSURE FOR NURSING HOME ADMINISTRATORS. See Medicine - Medical Centers, Hospitals.

AUDITED ANNUAL REPORT. Main/Corp Texas. Public Utility Commission. **VFOAT** Annual Financial Report. US. English. an. Public Utility Commission of Texas, 7800 Shoal Creek Boulevard Suites 400-450N, Austin TX 78757. **LC** HD2767.T4. **DD** 353.97640087.

AUSTRALIAN GOVERNMENT GAZETTE. Main/Corp Australia. **AT.** English. ir. $0.05 Single Issue. Government Printer, PO Box 84, Canberra Australian Capital Territory 2600 Australia. **LC** J8. **DD** 354.940005. *Commonwealth of Australia Gazette.*

AUSTRALIAN GOVERNMENT PUBLICATIONS (1961). See Bibliographies.

AUSTRALIAN GOVERNMENT PUBLICATIONS. MONTHLY LIST. Main/Corp Australia. Commonwealth Government Printing Office. Publications Branch. **AT.** English. mo. Australian Government Publishing Service, PO Box 84, Canberra Australian Capital Territory 2600 Australia. **Tel** 062-95 4411.

AUSTRALIAN JOURNAL OF PUBLIC ADMINISTRATION. V. 35- Mar. 1976-. 0313-6647. Periodical. **AT.** English. qt. $18.45. Australian Institute of Public Administration, Box 904 GPO, Sydney NSW 2001 Australia. **Tel** 02/2411920. Ed M Paynter. **Ind/Abst** Int. Labour Doc., APAIS, Aust. Public Aff. Inf. Serv., Soc. Sci. Citation Index. **LC** JA26. **DD** 350.0005. bk rev. adv acc. **Circ** 5,000. Review of issues affecting public administration in Australia.

THE AUSTRALIAN MUNICIPAL JOURNAL. V. 1- 1921-. 0004-9808. Periodical. English. ir.

AUTOMATIC DATA PROCESSING ACTIVITIES SUMMARY IN THE UNITED STATES GOVERNMENT. (AUTOMATIC DATA PROCESSING ACTIVITIES SUMMARY IN THE UNITED STATES GOVERNMENT AS OF THE END OF FISCAL YEAR . . .). Began with 1976/77. 0163-111X. US. English. an. Automated Data and Telecommunications Service, Federal Supply Service, Arlington VA 20390. **LC** JK468.A8. **DD** 353.0071. *Summary of Federal ADP Activities.*

AUTORIDADES BRASILEIRAS. Began in 1957. **BL.** Portuguese. an. Empresa Brasileira de Noticias EBN Departamento de Comercializacao SCS, Ed Toufic Bl C No 256 40 Andar, CEP 70.3000 Brasilia DF Brazil. **LC** JL2421.A2. **DD** 354.81002.

AUTORIDADES E EXECUTIVOS. Portuguese. ir. Associacao Brasileiro de Telecomunicacoes, Rua da Quitanda 191-Grupo 704, Rio de Janeiro Brazil. **LC** JL2421.A2.

AVIS MUNICIPAL - VILLE DE CHARNY. (L'AVIS MUNICIPAL : BULLETIN D'INFORMATION DE LA VILLE DE CHARNY). **Main/Corp** Charny (Quebec). Vol. 1, No. 1 (Sept. 1982)-. 0820-6503. Periodical. **CN.** French. ir. Free to Residents. L'Avis Municipal, 333 20E rue, Charny Quebec G6W 5R6 Canada. **DD** 352.071459. *Vos Affaires, 0713-6773.*

AWWA SEMINAR PROCEEDINGS. VAT American Water Works Association Seminar Proceedings. 0271-5422. Monographic Series. US. English. an. $5.00 Members, $10.00 Non-Members. American Water Works Association, 6666 West Quincy Avenue, Denver CO 80235. **Ind/Abst** GeoRef. **LC** UNC.

BACKGROUND (ONTARIO. MINISTRY OF MUNICIPAL AFFAIRS AND HOUSING). (BACKGROUND). 81/27 (6 July 1981)-. 0709-1141. Periodical. **CN.** English. wk. Ministry of Municipal Affairs and Housing, Mr Dewar, Toronto Ontario M5G 2E5 Canada. **Tel** 585-6283. **DD** 354.7130005. **Circ** 2,300. (ctrl) Ontario government and municipal associations general information relating to above. *Background, 0709-1141.*

BARBADOS DIPLOMATIC AND CONSULAR LIST. BB. English. ir. Ministry of Foreign Affairs Barbados, 3rd Floor, Marine House, Hastings Christ Church, Bridgetown Barbados. **LC** JX1757.B35. **DD** 351.8920972981.

BASELINE DATA REPORT. Series/Titl Urban Data Service Publication. Vol. 15, No. 1 (Jan. 1983)-. 0739-6279. Periodical. US. English. ir. $240.00. International City Managers Association, 1120 G Street NW, Washington DC 20005. **Tel** (202)626-4600. Ed Mary Schellinger. **Ind/Abst** Public Aff. Inf. Serv. Bull. **Circ** 500. Data and text on local government activities and issues such as expenditures, employment, salaries, administrative arrangements and provide services. *Urban Data Service Report, 0049-5654.*

BEAU LIEU. (LE BEAU LIEU). Mar. 1981-. 0823-7662. Periodical. **CN.** French. mo. Municipalite du Village de Ste-Petronille, 3 Chemin l'Eglise, Ste-Petronille Ile d'Orleans Quebec G0A 4C0 Canada. **DD** 352.071448. *Information Municipale.*

BEGROTING VAN DIE UITGAWES WAT UIT INKOMSTEREKENING (SOUTH AFRICA). See Business - Public Finance.

BERITA PEKERJAAN UMUM. V. 6., No. 23/24-. IO. Indonesian. ir. Bagian Hubungan Masyarakat, Departemen Pekerjaan Umun, Jl Pattimura No 20, Kebayoran Baru, Jakarta Selatan, Djakarta Indonesia. **LC** HD4301.

BERNAN ASSOCIATES' CHECKLIST OF CONGRESSIONAL HEARINGS & COMMITTEE PRINTS. VFOAT Bernan Associates' Checklist of Congressional Hearings and Committee Prints. 0195-3761. Periodical. US. English. wk. $68.00. Bernan Associates, 9730 East George Palmer Highway, Lanhar MD 20706. **Tel** (301)459-7666. Ed Mary Ann Kenney. **Circ** 400. Weekly listing, with abstracts of Congressional hearings and prints made available for public distribution in recent days. Includes ordering information. *Bernan Associates' Checklist of Congressional Hearings, 0009-2096.*

BESTUURSMEMORIAAL. Main/Corp Antwerp (Belgium : Province). Periodical. **BE.** Dutch. ir. Provinciebestuur Van Antwerpen Grif/Koningin, Elisabethlei 22, 2018 Antwerpen Belgium. **LC** JS7.N3.

BGR NEWSLETTER. Main/Corp University of Rhode Island. Bureau of Government Research. **VAT** Bureau of Government Research Newsletter. Summer 1980-. 0273-7884. Periodical. US. English. qt. Bureau of Government Research, University of Rhode Island, Kingston RI 02881. **Tel** (401)792-2158. *BGR. Bureau of Government Research, University of Rhode Island, 0195-4431.*

BI-ANNUAL REPORT. Main/Corp Council on Black Minnesotans. **VFOAT** Biannual Report. US. English. be. **LC** E185.93.M55. **DD** 353.9776008l496073.

BI-ANNUAL REPORT - PUBLIC SERVICE COMMISSION. Main/Corp Indiana. Public Service Commission. US. English. be. Public Service Commission, 901 State Office Building 100 North Senate Avenue, Indianapolis IN 46204. **LC** HD2767.I6. **DD** 353.9772008706. *Annual Report.*

BI-LINGUAL MAGAZINE. See Transportation - Ships & Shipping.

BIBLIOGRAPHIC GUIDE TO CONFERENCE PUBLICATIONS. See Bibliographies.

BIBLIOGRAPHIC GUIDE TO GOVERNMENT PUBLICATIONS. FOREIGN. See Bibliographies.

BIBLIOTECA DE ADMINISTRACAO PUBLICA. Periodical. Portuguese. ir. **LC** JA40.

BIDS. BUSINESS INFORMATION DATA SERVICES. (B I D S, BUSINESS INFORMATION DATA SERVICES). **VAT** Business Information Data Services (April 25, 1978). V. 1, No. 13- April 25, 1978. 0707-1884. Periodical. **CN.** English. sw. $175. Business Information Data Services, PO Box 1090, Shediac New Brunswick E0A 3G0 Canada. **DD** 354.71500711. *Business Information Data Services, 0707-1892.*

BIENNIAL REPORT, AGENCIES OF THE STATE OF WASHINGTON. VFOAT Agencies of the State of Washington. 1981-1983-. US. English. be. Office of Financial Management, 300 Insurance Building, Olympia WA 98504. **LC** JK9201. **DD** 353.9797006. *Biennial Report, Education Agencies, 0735-2255; Biennial Report, General Government Agencies; Biennial Report, Human Resources Agencies; Biennial Report, Natural Resources and Recreation Agencies; Biennial Report Transportation Agencies.*

BIENNIAL REPORT COVERING AGENCIES OF THE GOVERNMENT OF THE STATE OF KANSAS. Main/Corp Kansas. **VFOAT** Biennial Report Covering All Agencies of the Government of the State of Kansas. 1958/60-. 0198-7437. US. English. be. Secretary of State, c/o Jack H Brier, State of Kansas/2nd Floor, Topeka KS 66612. **LC** JK6835. **DD** 353.9781. **NLM** W2 AK3 S45B.

BIENNIAL REPORT - DEPT. OF ADMINISTRATION, STATE OF WISCONSIN. Main/Corp Wisconsin. Dept. of Administration. 1967/69-. US. English. be. Department of Administration, 1 West Wilson, Madison WI 53702. **LC** JK6035. *Annual Report - Dept. of Administration.*

BIENNIAL REPORT - DEPARTMENT OF PROPERTY RECORDS AND INSURANCE. Main/Corp Virginia. Dept. of Property Records and Insurance. **VFOAT** Records of State Buildings and Insurance. 0363-9924. US. English. be. Department of Property Records and Insurance, 203 Governor Street, Richmond VA 23219. **LC** JK1669.V8. **DD** 353.975500862. *Records of State Buildings and Insurance.*

BIENNIAL REPORT - ILLINOIS COMMISSION ON ATOMIC ENERGY. (BIENNIAL REPORT SUBMITTED TO THE GOVERNOR AND THE GENERAL ASSEMBLY). **Main/Corp** Illinois Commission on Atomic Energy. 0732-8222. US. English. be. Illinois Commission on Atomic Energy, Lincoln Tower Plaza/ 524 South Second Street, Springfield IL 62706. **LC** HD9698.U53. **DD** 353.977300823.

BIENNIAL REPORT - KANSAS. LEGISLATURE. LEGISLATIVE DIVISION OF POST AUDIT. See Business - Accounting.

BIENNIAL REPORT - MINNESOTA. IRON RANGE RESOURCES AND REHABILITATION BOARD. (BIENNIAL REPORT). **Main/Corp** Minnesota. Iron Range Resources and Rehabilitation Board. 17th (1974-6)-. 0741-5354. US. English. be. **LC** HC107.M6. **DD** 353.977600823206. *Biennial Report.*

BIENNIAL REPORT - NEBRASKA ACCOUNTABILITY AND DISCLOSURE COMMISSION. Main/Corp Nebraska Accountability and Disclosure Commission. US. English. be. Nebraska Accountability and Disclosure Commission, 11th Floor State Capitol PO Box 95086, Lincoln NE 68509. **LC** JK1991.5.N2. **DD** 353.978200995. *Annual Report.*

BIENNIAL REPORT OF EMPLOYMENT BY GEOGRAPHIC AREA. See Economics - Labor.

BIENNIAL REPORT OF EXAMINING AND LICENSING BOARDS - MINNESOTA. BOARD OF EXAMINERS FOR NURSING HOME ADMINISTRATORS. Main/Corp Minnesota. Board of Examiners for Nursing Home Administrators. US. English. be. Minneapolis Board of Examiners for Nursing Home Administrators, 717 Delaware Street South East, Room 340, Minneapolis MN. **LC** RA997.5.M6. **DD** 353.9776008243.

BIENNIAL REPORT OF NEVADA STATE AGENCIES - NEVADA. GOVERNOR'S OFFICE OF PLANNING COORDINATION. Main/Corp Nevada. Governor's Office of Planning Coordination. 1978-. US. English. be. Governor's Office of Planning Coordination, Capitol Complex, Carson City NV 89710. **LC** JK8530. **DD** 353.97930405.

BIENNIAL REPORT OF THE DEPARTMENT OF SOCIAL AND REHABILITATION SERVICES OF THE STATE OF IDAHO. Main/Corp Idaho. Dept. of Social and Rehabilitation Services. 0094-8578. US. English. be. **LC** HD7256.U6. **DD** 353.97960084.

BIENNIAL REPORT OF THE DEPARTMENT OF WATER RESOURCES. See Water Resources.

BIENNIAL REPORT OF THE PROFESSIONAL AND OCCUPATIONAL LICENSING BUREAU, DEPARTMENT OF COMMERCE. Main/Corp Montana. Professional & Occupational Licensing Bureau. For the biennium ending June 30, 1982-. US. English. be. **LC** HD3630.U7. **DD** 353.978600824046.

Public Administration

BIENNIAL REPORT OF THE STATE LABORATORIES AND CONSUMER AFFAIRS DEPARTMENT. Main/Corp North Dakota. State Laboratories Dept. US. English. be. Box 937, Bismarck ND 58505. LC HD9000.9.U6. DD 353.97840077.

BIENNIAL REPORT OF WISCONSIN STATE ELECTIONS BOARD. Main/Corp Wisconsin. State Elections Board. 1977/78-. Periodical. US. English. be. State Elections Board, 121 South Pinckney Street, Madison WI 53703. LC JK1954. DD 353.9775091. *Annual Report of Wisconsin State Elections Board, 0362-9635.*

BIENNIAL REPORT - OKLAHOMA INDIAN AFFAIRS COMMISSION. Main/Corp Oklahoma. Indian Affairs Commission. 0360-7518. US. English. be. Indian Affairs Commission, 4901 Lincoln Blouvard, Oklahoma City OK 73105. LC E78.O45. DD 353.9766008484.

BIENNIAL REPORT - PUBLIC SERVICE COMMISSION. Main/Corp Public Service Commission of Wisconsin. 1932-. 0364-5096. US. English. be. LC HD2767.W6. DD 380.61.

BIENNIAL REPORT - STATE OF MINNESOTA, DEPARTMENT OF CIVIL SERVICE. Main/Corp Minnesota. Dept. of Civil Service. 0540-1887. Periodical. US. English. be. 215 Administration Building, St Paul MN 55155. LC JK6155. DD 354.7127001.

BIENNIAL REPORT - STATE OF MINNESOTA DEPARTMENT OF PUBLIC SERVICE. Main/Corp Minnesota. Dept. of Public Service. US. English. be. Minnesota Department of Public Service, 211 State Highway Building, St Paul MN 55155. LC HE28.M6. DD 380.309776. *Report for the Biennium.*

BIENNIAL REPORT - STATE OF WISCONSIN ETHICS BOARD. See Ethics.

BIENNIAL REPORT - STATE OF WISCONSIN, PERSONNEL COMMISSION. Main/Corp Wisconsin. Personnel Commission. 1977/79-. US. English. be. Wisconsin Personnel Commission, 131 West Wilson Street, Madison WI 53702. LC KFW2835.15. DD 353.977500106.

BIENNIAL REPORT TO LEGISLATURE - BUREAU OF PUBLIC LANDS (MAINE). Main/Corp Maine. Bureau of Public Lands. 1st- 1976/77-. 0148-9275. US. English. be. Department of Conservation, Augusta ME 04333.

BIENNIAL REPORT TO THE FLORIDA LEGISLATURE - OFFICE OF THE INSPECTOR GENERAL. Main/Corp Florida. Office of the Inspector General. 1979-1980-. US. English. be. LC JK4435. DD 353.97590006.

BIENNIAL REPORT TO THE GENERAL ASSEMBLY - CONNECTICUT. COMMISSION ON COMPENSATION OF ELECTED STATE OFFICIALS AND JUDGES. Main/Corp Connecticut. Commission on Compensation of Elected State Officials and Judges. US. English. be. Commission on Compensation of Elected State Officials and Judges, State Capitol, Hartford CT 06115. LC JK3357. DD 353.974600123.

BIENNIAL REPORT TO THE GOVERNOR. Main/Corp Pennsylvania. State Civil Service Commission. Periodical. US. English. be.

BIENNIAL REPORT TO THE LEGISLATURE - MINNESOTA. LEGISLATURE. LEGISLATIVE COMMISSION ON MINNESOTA RESOURCES. Main/Corp Minnesota. Legislature. Legislative Commission on Minnesota Resources. 1984-. US. English. be. Legislative Commission on Minnesota Resources, B-46 State Capitol, St Paul MN 55155. *Report to the Legislature.*

BIENNIAL REPORT - WISCONSIN. LEGISLATURE. JOINT COMMITTEE FOR REVIEW OF ADMINISTRATIVE RULES. Main/Corp Wisconsin. Legislature. Joint Committee for Review of Administrative Rules. US. English. be. David G Berger Co-Chairman / Joint Committee for Review of Administrative Rules, Room 329 South State Capitol, Madison WI 53702. LC KFW2821.5.O85. DD 328.77507456.

BIENNIAL REPORT - WISCONSIN. PERSONNEL BOARD. Main/Corp Wisconsin. Personnel Board. 1979/1981-. US. English. an. LC JK6055. DD 353.9775001.

BIENNIAL REVIEW - SUPPLY & SERVICES CANADA. Main/Corp Canada. Dept. of Supply and Services. VFOAT Revue Biennale - Approvisionnements et Services Canada. 0700-3773. CN. English (French in parallel columns). an. LC JL186. DD 354.710071.

BIENNIUM LEGISLATIVE REPORT - NORTH DAKOTA. ENERGY DEVELOPMENT IMPACT OFFICE. (BIENNIUM LEGISLATIVE REPORT). Main/Corp North Dakota. Energy Development Impact Office. VFOAT Biennial Report to the Legislature. 1981/83-. 0743-5568. US. English. be. LC HD9502.U53. DD 353.978400823. *Biennium Legislative Report.*

BLACK ELECTED OFFICIALS. 1984-. 0882-1593. US. English. an. $29.50. UNIPUB, Box 1222, Ann Arbor MI 48108. Tel (212)916-1654. LC E185.615. DD 353.0022208996073. Gives complete, current information on each of the 6,056 black Americans holding elective office today. *National Roster of Black Elected Officials, 0092-2935.*

BLAGOUSTROIAVANE I KOMUNALNO STOPANSTVO. Bulgarian. ir. LC HD4691.5.

BLUE BOOK - NATIONAL ASSOCIATION OF PARLIAMENTARIANS. Main/Corp National Association of Parliamentarians. US. English. be. National Association of Parliamentarians, 3706 Broadway Suite 300, Kansas City MO 64111. LC JF515. DD 328.306073.

BOARDS AND COMMISSIONS, STATE OF ALASKA. 0149-3205. US. English. LC JK9530. DD 353.979804025.

BOISBRIAND. (LE BOISBRIAND). May 1983-. 0822-5133. Periodical. CN. French. mo. Boisbriand, c/o Hotel de Ville, 940 Grande Allee, Broibrianc Quebec J7G 2J7 Canada. DD 352.071424. *Boisbriand Express, 0820-0734.*

BOISE. (LE BOISE). Main/Corp Bois-des-Filion (Quebec). 1 (Sept. 1980)-. 0712-8126. Periodical. CN. French. mo. Ville de Bois-des-Filion, 60-36E Avenue Sud, Bois-des-Filion Quebec J6Z 2G6 Canada. DD 352.071424.

BOLETIM DO SERVIDOR. Main/Corp Minas Gerais (Brazil). Secretaria de Estado de Administracao. Portuguese. ir. Secretaria de Estado de Administracao, Rua da Bahia 1.148 - 4 Andar, Belo Horizonte Brazil. DD 354.815001005.

BOLETIM DOS MUNICIPIOS. Main/Corp Fundacao de Assistencia Aos Municipios do Estado do Parana. Yearly V. 1- Oct./Dec. 1972. Portuguese. ir. Rua Mariano Torres No 135, Curitiba Brazil. LC JS2423.P38.

BOLETIM ESTATISTICO ANUAL - COMPANHIA DE ELETRICIDADE DE CEARA. See Statistics.

BOLETIM ESTATISTICO - COMPANHIA PAULISTA DE FORCA E LUZ. See Statistics.

BOLETIM ESTATISTICO. CONSUMO E CONSUMIDORES POR CLASSE E MUNICIPIO ESTADO DE SAO PAULO. See Statistics.

BOLETIM INFORMATIVO. Main/Corp Sao Paulo (Brazil). Secretaria Municipal da Administracao. Portuguese. qt. Secretaria Municipal da Administraco Cao Alameda Santos, 2356, 8O Andar CEP 01418 Sao Paulo Brazil. LC JS2425.S36. DD 352.08161.

BOLETIN ANUAL DEL MINISTERIO DE JUSTICIA. Main/Corp Uruguay. Ministerio de Justicia. 1 (1980)-. Spanish. an. DD 354.895065.

BOLETIN - COMISION DE INTEGRACION ELECTRICA REGIONAL. Main/Corp Comision de Integracion Electrica Regional. UY. Spanish. mo. $55.00. Comision de Integracion Electrica Regional, Bulevar Arlegas, 1040 Montevideo Uruguay. LC HD9685.S6.

BOLETIN DE INFORMACION DEL SECRETARIADO IBEROAMERICANO DE MUNICIPIOS. Periodical. SP. Spanish. qt. Secretariado de Congresos y Relaciones Internacionales, Santa Engracia #7, Madrid 10 Spain. LC JS6301. DD 352.046.

BOLETIN DE LEGISLACION DE LAS COMUNIDADES AUTONOMAS : BCA. Main/Corp Spain. Cortes Generales. VFOAT BCA. 1 (Jan./Feb. 1983)-. 0212-4750. SP. Spanish. qt. Servicio de Publicaciones Senado, Plaza de la Marina Espanola 8, Madrid 13 Spain.

BOLETIN OFICIAL. Main/Corp Tangier (Morocco : Province). Spanish. sm. LC J9.M65. DD 354.640005.

BOOK BOUNTY ACT RETURN. (BOOK BOUNTY ACT, RETURN). Main/Corp Australia. Parliament. 0312-5734. AT. English. ir. $0.25. Commonwealth Government Printing Office, PO Box 84, Canaberra Australian Capital Territory 2600 Australia. LC J905, HF2651.B6. DD 328.9401 S, 382.450705.

THE BOOK OF THE STATES. V. 1- 1935-. 0068-0125. US. English. be. $42.50. Council of State Governments, PO Box 11910 Iron Works Pike, Lexington KY 40578. Tel (606)252-2291. Ed L E Purcell. LC JK2403. DD 353.932. Circ 10,000. Comprehensive reference of indexed information on state government: taxes, education and finance.

BOOK REVIEWS IN PUBLIC ADMINISTRATION. V. 1- Jan./June 1974-. II. English. ir. $3.50. Indian Institute of Public Administration, Indraprastha Estate Ring Road, New Delhi 110002 India. LC JA1. DD 350.

BOUNDARY AND ANNEXATION SURVEY. Series/Titl Series GE-30. Began with 1972. 0272-4472. US. English. be. Superintendent of Documents, US Government Printing Office, Washington DC 20402. LC JS344.A5. DD 352.0060973.

BRADDOCK'S FEDERAL-STATE-LOCAL GOVERNMENT DIRECTORY. See Yearbooks, Almanacs, Directories.

BRIEF OUTLINE OF ACTIVITIES OF THE COMMITTEES OF THE ASSOCIATION. Main/Corp Association of County Councils. UK. English. Eaton House, 66A Eaton Square, Westminister SW1W 9BH England. LC JS3260. DD 352.0073.

BRITISH COLUMBIA GAZETTE. (THE BRITISH COLUMBIA GAZETTE MICROFORM). VFOAT British Columbia Gazette. 0007-0505. Periodical. CN. English. Micromedia Limited, 144 Front Street West, Toronto Ontario M5J 1G2 Canada. DD 354.7110005. Also available on microfilm from St. Paul MN, microfilmed for the New York Public Library by 3M Co IM Press.

BRITISH COLUMBIA LIST OF OFFICIAL PERSONNEL IN FEDERAL, PROVINCIAL AND MUNICIPAL GOVERNMENTS IN THE PROVINCE OF BRITISH COLUMBIA. (BRITISH COLUMBIA LIST OF OFFICIAL PERSONNEL IN FEDERAL, PROVINCIAL, AND MUNICIPAL GOVERNMENTS IN THE PROVINCE OF BRITISH COLUMBIA). VFOAT British Columbia List. VAT List of Official Personnel in Federal, Provincial and Municipal Government in the Province of British Columbia. 0711-7442. CN. English. an. 32.00. British Columbia List, 2525 Manitoba Street, British Columbia V5Y 3A5 Canada. DD 354.71100025.

BROSSARD. 1982-. 0822-5664. CN. French. an. Ville de Brossard, 3200 rue Lapiniere, Brossard Quebec J4Z 2L4 Canada. DD 352.071434.

BUDGET. COMMUNIQUES. Main/Corp Quebec (Province) Ministere des Finances. Direction des Communications. 1979/80-. 0226-4390. CN. French. an. Ministere des Finances, Parliament Building, Quebec Canada. DD 354.7140072253. *Budget. Discours sur le Budget, Budget. Credits.*

BUDGET. DISCOURS SUR LE BUDGET. Main/Corp Quebec (Province). Ministere des Finances. 1978/79-. 0226-4382. CN. French. an. Ministere des Finances, Parliament Building, Quebec Canada. DD 354.714007225. *Discours sur le Budget, 0319-7271.*

BUDGET DU QUEBEC. PREVISIONS DE DEPENSES. (BUDGET DU QUEBEC : PREVISIONS DE DEPENSES). 1975/76-. 0709-9894. Periodical. CN. French. 1. Editeur Officiel du Quebec, 675 Est Boul. Saint-Cyrille, Quebec Que G1R 4Y7 Canada. DD 354.7140072253.

BUDGET ESTIMATES - U.S. NUCLEAR REGULATORY COMMISSION. Main/Corp U.S. Nuclear Regulatory Commission. US. English. an. US Nuclear Regulatory Commission, Washington DC 20555. Vols.

Public Administration

for (1982-) distributed to depository libraries in microfiche.

BUDGET HIGHLIGHTS - UNITED STATES. DEPT. OF ENERGY. OFFICE OF THE CONTROLLER. (BUDGET HIGHLIGHTS - UNITED STATES. DEPT. OF ENERGY. OFFICE OF THE CONTROLLER). Main/Corp United States. Dept. of Energy. Office of the Controller. 0743-5487. US. English. an. Department of Energy, Office of the Controller, Washington DC 20585. LC HD9502.U5. DD 353.87.

THE BUDGET OF THE UNITED STATES GOVERNMENT. See Business - Public Finance.

BUDGET. PRESS RELEASES. Main/Corp Quebec (Province) Ministere des Finances. Direction des Communications. 1979/80-. 0226-4412. CN. English. an. Ministere des Finances, Parliament Building, Quebec Canada. DD 354.7140072253. Budget. Estimates, Budget. Budget Speech.

BUDGET REQUEST - U.S. CONSUMER PRODUCT SAFETY COMMISSION. Main/Corp United States. Consumer Product Safety Commission. VFOAT CPSC Budget Request. VAT Budget Request - United States Consumer Product Safety Commission. 0193-0362. Periodical. US. English. an. United States Consumer Product Safety Commission, 1111 18th Street Northwest, Washington DC 20207. LC HC110.C63. DD 353.0077.

BULLETIN - CITE DE COTE SAINT-LUC. (BULLETIN). VAT Newsletter - Cite de Cote Saint-Luc. Vol. 1, No. 1 (Feb. 1975)-. 0712-9661. CN. English (French, text in English only Feb. 1975 and Feb. 1976). ir. Cite de Cote Saint-Luc, 5490 Avenue Westminister, Cote Saint-Luc Quebec H4X 2A6 Canada. DD 352.071428.

BULLETIN - CITIZENS' GOVERNMENTAL RESEARCH BUREAU, MILWAUKEE. See Business - Public Finance.

BULLETIN (CIVIC FEDERATION (CHICAGO ILL.)). (BULLETIN). Began in Mar. 1941?. Periodical. US. English. ir. Civic Federation, 29 East Madison Street, Chicago IL 60602. LC JS701. DD 352.07731. Bulletin (Civic Federation and Bureau of Public Efficiency (Chicago, Ill.)).

BULLETIN DE CARIGNAN. (LE BULLETIN DE CARIGNAN). VFOAT Carignan. V. 1, No. 1 (4th Quarter 1983)-. 0822-8310. Periodical. CN. French (English). qt. Le Bulletin de Carignan, 670 rue St-Pierre, Chambly Quebec J3L 1L9 Canada. DD 352.071437.

BULLETIN DE CHATEAUGUAY. (LE BULLETIN DE CHATEAUGUAY). Main/Corp Chateauguay (Quebec). Vol. 1, No. 1-. 0712-6808. Periodical. CN. English (French on inverted pages). qt. Free. Bulletin de Chateauguay c/o Office of the Town Clerk, 5 Youville Boulevard, Chateauguay Quebec J6J 2P8 Canada. DD 352.071433.

BULLETIN DE VANIER CEASED. VFOAT Bulletin of Vanier. Vol. 5, No. 2 (April/May/June 1980)-V. 5, No. 4 (Oct./Nov./ Dec. 1980). 0712-9327. Periodical. CN. English (French in parallel columns). qt. Citizens Information Committee, 297 Dupuis, Vanier Ontario K1L 6H8 Canada. DD 352.071383. Municipal Information, 0382-0114.

BULLETIN DES MARCHES PUBLICS. Vol. 9, No. 1 (Jan. 21, 1982)-. 0713-133X. Periodical. CN. French. wk. Approvisionnements et Services Canada, Publishing Centre, Ottawa Ontario K1A 0S9 Canada. DD 354.7100712. Bulletin Hebdomadaire des Marches Publics, 0700-1185.

BULLETIN D'INFORMATION (QUEBEC PROVINCE). BUREAU. (BULLETIN D'INFORMATION). Vol. 1, No. 1 (Mar. 1984)-. 0822-9961. Periodical. CN. French. mo. Bureau d'Audiences Publiques l'Environnement, 12 rue Sainte Anne, Quebec Quebec G1R 3X2. DD 354.714093.

BULLETIN D'INFORMATION - UNION DES MUNICIPALITES DE LA PROVINCE DE QUEBEC. Main/Corp Union des Municipalites de la Province de Quebec. V. 1-. 0316-5140. Periodical. CN. French. Union des Municipalites de la Province de Quebec, 822 Est rue Sherbrooke, Montreal Quebec H2L 1K4 Canada. DD 352.00062714.

BULLETIN - EUROPEAN PARLIAMENT. See Law - International Law.

BULLETIN - FRANCE. PARLEMENT (1946-). ASSEMBLEE NATIONALE. Main/Corp France. Parlement (1946-). Assemblee Nationale. Periodical. French. ir. Secretariat General, Service des Informations Parlementaires, Palais-Bourbon, Paris France. LC J341. DD 328.4401.

BULLETIN (GERMANY (WEST). PRESSE- UND INFORMATIONSAMT : 1979). ENGLISH. (BULLETIN). 1 (June 6, 1979)-. Periodical. English. ir. Press and Information Office of the Federal Government, 11 Welckerstrasse, D-5300 Bonn 1 West Germany. Bulletin (Germany (West). Presse- und Informationsamt). English.

BULLETIN HEBDOMADAIRE - COMMISSION DES VALEURS MOBILIERES DU QUEBEC. Main/Corp Quebec (Province) Commission des Valeurs Mobilieres. V. 5, No. 8- Feb. 26, 1974-. 0707-8420. Periodical. CN. text in English and French, Feb. 26, 1974-Sept. 27, 1977. wk. Commission des Valeurs Mobilieres du Quebec, CP 246 Tour de la Bourse, Montreal Quebec H4Z 1G3 Canada. DD 354.714008258. Sommaire Hebdomadaire.

LE BULLETIN LEGISLATIF DALLOZ. Began publication with V. 1 in 1918. Periodical. FR. French. sm. $56.73. Dalloz, 11 rue Soufflot, 75240 Paris Cedex 05 France.

BULLETIN MENSUEL DE L'ENERGIE ELECTRIQUE. VFOAT Maandelikjs Bulletin van de Electrische Energie. Dutch and French. ir. Nubustere des Affaires Economiques, Administration de l'Energie, rue de Treves 49-51-1040, Bruxelles Belgium. LC HD9685.B4.

BULLETIN MUNICIPAL - CONSEIL MUNICIPAL DE SAINT-LOUIS-DE-TERREBONNE. (BULLETIN MUNICIPAL). V. 1, No. 1, (April 30, 1978)-. 0711-7744. Periodical. CN. French. qt. Free. Corporation Municipale de la Paroisse de St-Louis-de-Terrebonne, 4580 Croissant Dauphin, Saint-Louis-de-Terrebonne Quebec J0N 1N0 Canada. DD 352.071424. (ctrl).

BULLETIN MUNICIPAL D'INFORMATION - MUNICIPALITE DU CANTON DE CHERTSEY. (BULLETIN MUNICIPAL D'INFORMATION). No. 1- Jan. 1979-. 0226-8582. Periodical. CN. French. mo. Free. Canton de Chertsey, Secretariat Municipal, CP 120, 453 rue Dupuis, Chertsey Quebec J0K 3K0 Canada. DD 352.0714415.

BULLETIN MUNICIPAL - L'ANNONCIATION. (BULLETIN MUNICIPAL). V. 1, No. 1, Mar. 15, 1980-V. 2, No. 5 Sept. 1981. 0712-2527. Periodical. CN. French. ir. Free. Bulletin Municipal, Corporation du Village de l'Annonciation, Sud rue Principale, l'Annonciation Quebec J0T 1T0 Canada. DD 352.0714225. (ctrl).

BULLETIN MUNICIPAL - OUTREMONT. (BULLETIN MUNICIPAL). Main/Corp Outremont (Quebec). VFOAT Bulletin Municipal d'Outremont. No. 91 (April 1981)-. 0820-9278. Periodical. CN. French (English). mo. Free to Citizens. Hotel de Ville d'Outremont, 510 Avenue Davaar, Outremont Quebec H2V 2B9 Canada. DD 352.0714281. Bulletin d'Outremont, 0700-4508.

BULLETIN MUNICIPAL - VILLE DE MONTREAL-NORD. (BULLETIN MUNICIPAL). Main/Corp Montreal-Nord (Quebec). VFOAT Bulletin Municipal de Montreal-Nord. No. 2, (April 1983)-. 0822-0395. Periodical. CN. French. Free to Citizens. Hotel de Ville de Montreal-Nord, 4242 Place de l'Hotel de Ville, Montreal-Nord Quebec H1H 1S5 Canada. DD 352.0714281. Bulletin Special sur le Budget, 0823-5643.

BULLETIN (NATIONAL ASSOCIATION OF REGULATORY UTILITY COMMISSIONERS). (BULLETIN). 0027-8645. Periodical. US. English. wk. $65.00. National Association of Regulatory Utility Commissioners, 1102 Interstate Commerce Commission Building, PO Box 684, Washington DC 20004. LC HD2766.A3. DD 363.60973. Bulletin (National Association of Railroad and Utilities Commissioners).

BULLETIN - NORTH DAKOTA LEAGUE OF CITIES. Main/Corp North Dakota League of Cities. V. 37, No. 5- May 1969-. 0279-800X. Periodical. US. English. mo. $3.50. North Dakota League of Cities Bulletin, Box 2235, Bismarck ND 58501. Tel (701)223-3518. Ed Robert B Johnson. adv acc. Circ 2,800. (ctrl). For city officials, government administrators, employees and those interested in such matters.

BULLETIN OFFICIEL D'ANNONCES DES DOMAINES (FRANCE. MINISTERE DE L'ECONOMIC ET DES FINANCES : 20 JUIN 1981). (BULLETIN OFFICIEL D'ANNONCES DES DOMAINES). FR. French. sm. 50. Service Central de Publicite des Domaines, 17 rue Scribe, 75436 Paris Cedex 09 France. LC JN2751. DD 354.4400713. Bulletin Officiel d'Annonces des Domaines (France. Ministere du Budget).

BULLETIN OFFICIEL DES SERVICES DU PREMIER MINISTRE (FRANCE). Main/Corp France. Premier Ministre. 0249-6046. FR. French. ir. 96.00. 26 rue Desaix, 75727 Paris Cedex 15 France.

BULLETIN OFFICIEL DU SECRETARIAT D'ETAT AUX DEPARTEMENTS ET TERRITOIRES D'OUTRE-MER (FRANCE). See Law.

BULLETIN OFFICIEL - FRANCE. MINISTERE DE L'AMENAGEMENT DU TERRITOIRE, DE L'EQUIPEMENT, DU LOGEMENT ET DU TOURISME. Main/Corp France. Ministere de l'Amenagement du Territoire, de l'Equipement, du Logement et du Tourisme. French. ir. 85.00. Direction des Journaux Officiels, 26 rue Desaix, 75727 Paris Cedex 15 France. DD 354.440086.

BULLETIN PIERREFONDS. VFOAT Pierrefonds Newsletter. Vol. 1, No. 2 June 1978-. 0712-4015. Periodical. CN. English (French). ir. Free. L'Dussault Hotel de Ville, 11072 Gouin Boulevard West, Pierrefonds Quebec H8Y 1X5 Canada. DD 352.071428. (ctrl). Bulletin d'Informations (Pierrefonds, Quebec), 0712-4007.

BULLETIN - PUBLIC SERVICE COMMISSION OF CANADA. Main/Corp Public Service Commission of Canada. VFOAT Bulletin - Commission de la Fonction Publique du Canada. Began publication in 1967?. 0706-0564. Periodical. CN. text in English and French in parallel columns. ir.

BULLETIN ROUTIER. QUEBEC. (BULLETIN ROUTIER; QUEBEC). V. 5- April/June 1979-. 0226-1014. Periodical. CN. French. qt. Ministere des Transports, 1995 Boulevard Charest-Ouest, Edifice Branly 2E Etage, Ste-Foy Quebec H1N 2E6 Canada. DD 354.714008640971417. (ctrl). Bulletin Routier.

BULLETIN SAINT-LAURENT. VFOAT Saint-Laurent Newsletter. 0710-961X. Periodical. CN. English (French). City of Saint-Laurent, 777 Laurentien Boulevard, Saint-Laurent Quebec H4M 2M7 Canada. DD 352.071428. Ville de Saint-Laurent Bulletin, 0710-9601.

BULLETIN SIGNALETIQUE. 528. BIBLIOGRAPHIE INTERNATIONALE DE SCIENCE ADMINISTRATIVE. See Bibliographies.

BULLETIN SIGNALETIQUE D'INFORMATION ADMINISTRATIVE. No. 1 (Mar.1982)-. 0293-9614. Periodical. French. LC Z2169, J341. DD 015.44. Bibliographie Selective des Publications Officielles Francaises.

BULLETIN (UNITED STATES. OFFICE OF MANAGEMENT AND BUDGET). (BULLETIN). Periodical. US. English. Office of Management and Budget, Washington DC 20503.

BULLETIN USTREDNEHO VYBORU NARODNEHO FRONTU SLOVENSKEJ SOCIALISTICKEJ REPUBLIKY. Main/Corp Narodny Front Slovenskej Socialistickej Republiky. Ustredny Vybor. Slovak. ir. Narodneho Frontu Slovenskej Socialistickej Republiky, Sturova 5, Bratislava Czechoslovakia. LC JN2199.S44.

BULLETIN - VILLE DE MONT-LAURIER. (BULLETIN). Main/Corp Mont-Laurier (Quebec). Vol. 1, No. 1 (Oct. 1981)-. 0710-3689. Periodical. CN. French. qt. Free. Hotel de Ville, 485 rue Mercier, Mont-Laurier Quebec J9L 3N8 Canada. DD 352.0714225. (ctrl).

BUNDESANZEIGER - GERMANY (FEDERAL REPUBLIC, 1949-). 0344-7634. GW. German. $82.78. Bundesanzeiger Verlagsges MBH, Postfach 10 80 06-5, Koln 1 West Germany. Ind/Abst Coal Abstr.

DIE BUNDESREPUBLIK DEUTSCHLAND STAATSHANDBUCH. LANDESAUSGABE FREISTAAT BAYERN. VFOAT Bundesrepublik Deutschland. August 1981-. German. ir. Carl Heymanns Verlag KG, Gereonstrasse 18-32, 5000 Koln 1 West Germany. LC JN4161. DD 354.43300025. Bundesrepublik Deutschland Staatshandbuch. Teilausgabe Freistaat Bayern.

Public Administration

DIE BUNDESREPUBLIK DEUTSCHLAND STAATSHANDBUCH. LANDESAUSGABE LAND FREIE UND HANSESTADT HAMBURG. VFOAT Land Freie und Hansestadt Hamburg. August 1981-. GW. German. ir. Carl Heymanns Verlag KG, Gereonstrasse 18-32, 5000 Koln 1 West Germany. LC JN4287. DD 354.4351500025. *Bundesrepublik Deutschland Staatshandbuch. Teilausgabe Land Freie und Hansestadt Hamburg.*

DIE BUNDESREPUBLIK DEUTSCHLAND STAATSHANDBUCH. LANDESAUSGABE LAND NORDRHEIN-WESTFALEN. VFOAT Landesausgabe Lane Nordrhein-Westfalen. GW. German. ir. Carl Heymanns Verlag KG, Koln West Germany. LC JN4945.N62. DD 354.435500025. *Teilausgabe Land Nordrhein-Westfalen.*

BUREAU COUNTY, ILLINOIS, TAM SERVICE. VFOAT Bureau County TAM Service. VAT Bureau County, Illinois, Township Maps, Alphabetical Locator, Mailing List Service. 0883-4865. US. English. an. $32.00. R C Booth Enterprises, Harlan IA 51537.

THE BUREAUCRAT. V. 1- Spring 1972-. 0045-3544. Periodical. US. English. qt. $35.00. The Bureaucrat Inc, PO Box 347, Arlington VA 22210. Tel (202)287-6070. Ed Thomas W Novotny. Ind/Abst ABI/Inform, ABC Pol Sci, Curr. Contents, Hum. Resour. Abstr., Sage Public Adm. Abstr., Sage Urban Stud. Abstr., Soc. Sci. Citation Index, Urban Aff. Abstr., Bus. Period. Index, Sociol. Abstr., Manage. Contents, Lang. Lang. Behav. Abstr., Bus. Period. Index. LC JK1. DD 353.0005. bk rev. adv acc. Circ 4,000. Dedicated to fostering, developing, and otherwise encouraging the utmost in professionalism and performance by public managers at all levels.

THE BUREAUCRAT. V. 1- Jan./Mar. 1973-. Periodical. English. ir. $3.00 US, 4.00 Canada. Mr S E Okotie, Business Manager, The Bureaucrat, c/o Ministry of Finance, Accounting Division, Benin City Nigeria. LC JQ3092.Z1. DD 354.669300605.

BUSINESS & GOVERNMENT NEWS. VFOAT B & G News. VAT Business and Government News. V. 1- Jan. 1979-. 0707-1949. Periodical. CN. English. mo. DD 016.330971.

BUSINESS AND PUBLIC ADMINISTRATION STUDENT REVIEW. See Business.

BUTLLETI OFICIAL DEL PARLAMENT DE CATALUNYA. Main/Corp Catalonia (Spain). Parlement. 1A. Legislature, No. 1 (June 12, 1980)-. Catalan. ir. 1500. Seccio de Publicacions del Parlament de Catalunya Palau de Parlament, Parc de la Ciutadella, Barcelona 3 Spain. LC J409.T3. DD 328.467005.

BY-LAWS, RULES AND REGULATIONS. INTERNATIONAL MONETARY FUND. (BY-LAWS, RULES AND REGULATIONS). Main/Corp International Monetary Fund. Began in 1947. 0250-7307. US. English. International Monetary Fund, Washington DC 20431.

CADASTRO ORGANIZACIONAL. Main/Corp Parana (Brazil : State). Coordenadoria de Modernizacao Administrativa. Portuguese. ir. LC J208.P3. DD 354.8162000202. *Cadastro Organizacional do Estado do Parana.*

CADERNOS DE ADMINISTRACAO MUNICIPAL. No. 1-. BL. Portuguese. ir. Secretaria do Estado do Interior e Justica, Rua Paraiba 755, Belo Horizonte Brazil. LC JS2423.M5. DD 352.008098151.

CADERNOS MUNICIPAIS. Vol.1, June 1978-. Periodical. Portuguese. ir. Fundacao Antero de Quental, Ru Mestre de Aviz 15, Alges Brazil. LC P. DD 352.007209469.

CAHIERS DE L'ENAP. (LES CAHIERS DE L'ENAP). VAT Cahiers de l'Ecole Nationale d'Administration Publique (1981). No. 1 (June 1981)-. 0711-5024. Periodical. CN. French. Ecole Nationale d'Administration Publique, 945 Avenue Wolfe, Sainte-Foye Quebec G1V 4A2 Canada. LC JA4. DD 350.0005.

CAHIERS ZAIROIS DE LA RECHERCHE ET DU DEVELOPPEMENT. See Political Science.

CAL-OSHA REPORTER. See Industrial Health & Safety.

CALENDARS OF THE UNITED STATES HOUSE OF REPRESENTATIVES AND HISTORY OF LEGISLATION. Main/Corp United States. Congress. House. 0364-0558. US. English. ir. US Government Printing Office, Superintendent of Documents, Washington DC 20402. Tel (202)783-3238. LC J47. DD 328.73.

CALIFORNIA JOURNAL ALMANAC OF STATE GOVERNMENT AND POLITICS. See Yearbooks, Almanacs, Directories.

CALIFORNIA LEGISLATIVE DIRECTORY AND REFERENCE GUIDE. See Yearbooks, Almanacs, Directories.

CALIFORNIA MUNICIPAL BOND ADVISOR. Vol. 1, Issue 1 (Nov. 1, 1984)-. 0749-2375. Periodical. US. English. mo. $110.00. Arenas Building/Suite 3, PO Box 1962, Palm Springs CA 92262.

CALIFORNIA POLICY CHOICES. 1984-. 0742-0927. US. English. an. $14.95. Sacramento Public Affairs Center, 921 11th Street/Suite 200, Sacramento CA 95814. Tel (916)442-69119. Ed John J Kirlin and Donald R Winkler. LC JK8701. DD 353.97940005. Circ 1,500. (ctrl). Analyses of policy choices confronting California. Fiscal, welfare, toxics, health, prisons, pensions, demographics, economics and schools have been analyzed.

CALIFORNIA POLITICAL WEEK. 0195-6175. Periodical. US. English. wk. $37.50. California Political Week, PO Box 1468, Beverly Hills CA 90213. Tel (213)274-6385. Circ 1,120. News analysis of key public policy issues and analysis of current trends and developments in California.

CALIFORNIA PUBLIC EMPLOYEE RELATIONS. VFOAT CPER. No. 16- Mar. 1973-. 0194-3073. Periodical. US. English. ir. University of California, Institute of Industrial Relations, Berkeley CA 94720. Tel (415)642-0323. Ind/Abst Public Aff. Inf. Serv. Bull.

THE CAMPAIGNER SPECIAL REPORT. 0161-9039. Periodical. US. English. $1.50. Campaigner Publications, GPO Box 1920, New York NY 10001. LC JK2361. DD 329.81.

CANADA GAZETTE. PART 1. (CANADA GAZETTE MICROFORM). VFOAT Gazette du Canada. 0045-4192. Periodical. CN. English (French). Micromedia Limited, 144 Front Street West, Toronto Ontario M5J 1G2 Canada. DD 354.710005.

CANADA PENSION PLAN CONTRIBUTION AND UNEMPLOYMENT INSURANCE PREMIUM TABLES. See Insurance.

CANADIAN JEWISH CONGRESS INTERIM REPORT. See Ethnic.

CANADIAN LEGISLATURES. Began with 1980. 0715-7118. CN. English. an. 9.50. Director of Administration, Room 188/Legislative Building, Queen's Park, Toronto Ontario M7A 1A1 Canada. Tel (416)965-9494. Ed Robert J Fleming. LC JL179. DD 328.71076. Circ 1,500. Study of salaries, allowances, services for elected members of U.S. and Canadian legislatures and administrative arrangements and structures presently in place. *Comparative Study of Administrative Structures of Canadian Legislatures, 0715-7843.*

CANADIAN PARLIAMENTARY GUIDE. (THE CANADIAN PARLIAMENTARY GUIDE). VFOAT Guide Parlementaire Canadien. 1909-. 0315-6168. CN. English (French). ir. $25.53. Canadian Parliamentary Guide, PO Box 3453 Station C, Ottawa Ontario K1Y 4J6 Canada. Tel (613)225-5485. Ed Pierre G Normandin. DD 328.710025. Circ 3,800. (ctrl). Information on Canada and provincial parliaments, members with biographies and results of general elections. Also senate, governor general and embassies. *Canadian Parliamentary Guide and Work of General Reference for the Dominion of Canada, 0315-6168.*

CANADIAN PARLIAMENTARY REVIEW. V. 3, No. 4 (Winter 1980/81)-. 0229-2548. Periodical. CN. English. qt. $12.38. Canadian Region/CPA, PO Box 950/Conference Building, Ottawa Ontario K1A 0A6 Canada. Tel (613)996-6111. Ed Gary Levy. Ind/Abst Can. Period. Index, Public Aff. Inf. Serv. Bull. LC JL148. DD 328.71005. bk rev. adv acc. Intended to inform Canadian legislators about activities of their federal and provincial branches, and to promote study of parliamentary institutions in Canada. *Canadian Regional Review, 0707-0837.*

CANADIAN PUBLIC ADMINISTRATION. VFOAT Administration Publique du Canada. V. 1- March 1958-. 0008-4840. Periodical. CN. English (includes some text in French). qt. $46.43. Institute of Public Administration of Canada, 897 Bay Street, Toronto Ontario M5S 1Z7 Canada. Ed Kenneth Kernaghan. Ind/Abst Am. Hist. Life, Lang. Lang. Behav. Abstr., Hist. Abst., Part B, Twent. Century Abstr., Hist. Abstr., Part A, Mod. Hist. Abstr., Manage. Contents, Hospit. Lit. Index, ABC Pol Sci, Can. Bus. Index, Can. Period. Index, Public Aff. Inf. Serv. Bull., Public Manage. Source, Int. Polit. Sci. Abstr., Public Adm. Abstr. Index Artic., Index Can. Leg. Period. Vit., Pover. Hum. Resour. Abstr., Foreign Lang. Index, Sociol. Abstr. bk rev.

CANADIAN PUBLIC POLICY. See Economics.

CANAL-ISEP. VAT Canal-Information Scolaire et Professionnelle. No. 1 (81-12)-. 0711-7027. Periodical. CN. French. ir. Gouvernement du Quebec, 600 St Amable 4E Etage, Quebec Quebec G1R 4Z1 Canada. DD 354.7140085105.

CAPITAL BRIEFING. See Economics - Economics: Industry & Production.

CAPITAL IMPROVEMENT PROGRAM - FAIRFAX CO., VA. Main/Corp Office of Comprehensive Planning. Fairfax Co., Va. VFOAT CIP. Capital Improvement Program for Fairfax County, Virginia. 0147-7749. US. English. an. Office of Comprehensive Planning/County of Fairfax, 4100 Chain Bridge Road, Fairfax VA 22030. LC HD3890.V8. DD 352.1209755291.

CAPITAL LIST. (THE CAPITAL LIST). 1978-. 0703-9441. CN. English. an. Capital List Limited, PO Box 2770 Station D, Ottawa Ontario K1P 5W7 Canada. Tel (613)235-6700. LC F1059.5.O9. DD 354.7100922.

CAREERS IN THE UNITED STATES DEPARTMENT OF THE INTERIOR. See Occupations and Careers.

A CARTA. Periodical. Portuguese. ir. $600. Av 9 de Julho 3805, Sao Paulo Brazil. LC JL2401.

CASE STUDIES IN AFRICAN DIPLOMACY. Series/Titl Dar-Es-Salaam. University College. Institute of Public Administration. Study, 8-9. No. 1- 1969-. English. ir. Oxford University Press, Journals Department/Walton Street, Oxford OX2 6DP England. LC DT31. DD 320.96 S.

CASES IN PUBLIC POLICY AND MANAGEMENT. Series/Titl Intercollegiate Bibliography. 1978-. US. English. ir. Intercollegiate Case Clearing House, Soldiers Field, Boston MA 02163.

CATALOG OF STATE ASSISTANCE PROGRAMS (MARYLAND). Main/Corp Maryland. Dept. of State Planning. 0097-9309. US. English. an. $5.00. Department of State Planning, 301 West Preston Street, Baltimore MD 21201. Tel (301)225-4490. Ed Guy W Hager. LC HJ485. DD 336.185. Circ 300. (ctrl). Identifies and describes Maryland state financial assistance and technical service programs.

CATALOGUE DES PUBLICATIONS EN FRANCAIS DU GOUVERNEMENT DE L'ONTARIO. V. 1- 1979-. 0706-2923. CN. French. Centre des Publications, 880 rue Bay 5E Etage, Toronto Ontario M7A Canada. DD 015.713.

CATALOGUE OF CGSB STANDARDS. Main/Corp Canada. Government Specifications Board. VFOAT Catalogue des Normes de l'ONGC. VAT Catalogue of Canadian Government Specifications Board Standards. Jan. 1974-1980. 0700-043X. Periodical. CN. English (French). *Catalogue of Standards, 0703-1181.*

CATALOGUE OF GOVERNMENT PUBLICATIONS. GOVERNMENT OF TAMIL NADU. See Bibliographies.

CATALOGUE OF GOVERNMENT PUBLICATIONS - KENYA. See Bibliographies.

CATALOGUE OF PUBLICATIONS - COUNCIL OF EUROPE. See Bibliographies.

Public Administration

CAYMAN ISLANDS GOVERNMENT CIVIL LIST. English. ir. LC JL629.5.A4. DD 354.72921002.

CEA CONGRESSIONAL LEDGER. VFOAT Congressional Ledger. VAT Congressional Education Associates Congressional Ledger. 0737-3007. US. English. an. $5.00. Congressional Education Associates, 1411 K Street NW, Suite 801, Washington DC 20005. LC JK1051. DD 328.730775.

CEGEP-PRESSE. 0706-182X. Periodical. CN. French. Department of Manpower & Immigration, 222 Nepean Street, Ottawa Ontario K1A 0J5 Canada. DD 354.7100833.

CENSUS OF SELECTED SERVICE INDUSTRIES. Main/Corp United States. Bureau of the Census. 1972-. Periodical. US. English. ir. $12.00 V.1, $18.00 V. 2, Pt. 1, $19.00 V. 2, Pt. 2, $18.00 V. 2, Pt. 3. US Department of Commerce, Social and Economic Statistics Administration, Bureau of the Census, Washington DC 20402. *Census of Business.*

CHARLESBOURG. V. 7, No. 3 (March 1982)- V. 7, No. 8 (Oct. 1982). 0820-0599. Periodical. CN. French. Charlesbourg, 7575 Boulevard Henri-Bourassa, Charlesbourg Quebec G1H 3A5 Canada. DD 352.071447. *Informations Charlesbourg, 0703-9719.*

CHASSE QUEBEC. Main/Corp Quebec (Province). Ministere du Loisir, de la Chasse et de la Peche. 0226-2681. CN. French. an. Gouvernement du Quebec, 600 St Amable 4E Etage, Quebec G1R 4Z1 Canada. DD 354.71400858. *Chasse au Quebec, 0226-2681.*

CHECKLIST : PUBLICATIONS OF CONNECTICUT STATE AGENCIES. See Bibliographies.

CHENE. (LE CHENE : BULLETIN D'INFORMATION). 0228-5037. Periodical. CN. French. mo. Free. Ville de Lachenaie, 2953 Boul St-Charles, Lachenaie Quebec J6W 3T8 Canada. DD 352.0714416. (ctrl).

CHESNAIE. (LA CHESNAIE : BULLETIN OFFICIEL DE LA MUNICIPALITE DE BEAUMONT). Main/Corp Saint-Etienne-de-Beaumont (Quebec). 0822-6342. Periodical. CN. French. qt. Free to Citizens. Municipalite de Beaumont, 6 Boulevard Mercier, Beaumon Quebec G0R 1 Canada G0R 1. DD 352.0714733.

CHEZ VOUS. Main/Corp Mascouche (Quebec). Vol. 1, No. 1 (Nov. 1981)- 0715-920X. Periodical. CN. French. bm. Free for Citizens. Ville de Mascouche, 3034 rue Sainte-Marie, Mascouche Quebec J0N 1C0 Canada. DD 352.0714416.

CHIEF COUNSEL OFFICE DIRECTORY (INTERNAL REVENUE SERVICE). See Yearbooks, Almanacs, Directories.

CHIEFS OF STATE AND CABINET MEMBERS OF FOREIGN GOVERNMENTS. 0162-2951. Periodical. US. English. mo. Document Expediting (Docex), Exchange and Gift Division, Library Congress, Washington DC 20540. LC JF37. DD 351.0031305.

CHIEFS OF STATE AND CABINET MINISTERS OF THE AMERICAN REPUBLICS. Main/Corp Organization of American States. General Secretariat. 1966-. 0250-6114. US. English. ir. OAS General Secretariat Department of Publications, 1889 T Street NW, Washington DC 20006. LC F1402. DD 351.003130251812. *Chiefs of State and Cabinet Ministers of the American Republics.*

CHIH PU SHENG HUO. CHUNG-CHING. VFOAT Zhibu Shenghuo. Periodical. CC. Chinese. ir. 0.15. Post Office, Chung-Ching Shih China. LC JQ1519.A5. DD 324.251075.

CHIH PU SHENG HUO. KUANG-TUNG. VFOAT Zhibushenghuo. Periodical. CC. Chinese. mo. 0.15. Post Office, Kuang-Chou Shih China. LC JQ1519.A5. DD 324.251075.

CHIH PU SHENG HUO. SSU-CHUAN. VFOAT Zhibushenghuo. Periodical. CC. Chinese. mo. 0.15. Post Office, Cheng-Tu China. LC JQ1519.A5. DD 324.251075.

CHIHO JICHI NENKAN. Began with Vol. for 1978. JA. Japanese. an. Daiichi Hoki Shuppan, Kabushiki Kaisha 11-17, Minami Aoyama 2, Minato-Ku Tokyo-To-107 Japan. LC JS7371.A1.

CHIHO SENKYO NO TEBIKI. Main/Corp Japan. Jichisho. Senkuobu. JA. Japanese. ir. Teikoku Chiho Gyosei Gakkai, 52 Nishigokencho Shinjuku-Ku, Tokyo Japan. *Chiho Senkyo No Tebiki.*

CHINCHUL. V. 1-. Periodical. KO. Korean. ir. 6,000. Kihoek Chulpansa, 277-29 3-Ka Wonhyoro, Yongsan-Ku, Seoul Korea. LC JQ1726.Z13.

CHINESE LAW AND GOVERNMENT. See Law.

CHRONICLE OF PARLIAMENTARY ELECTIONS AND DEVELOPMENTS. Began with Vol. for 1966/67. SZ. English. an. Inter-Parliamentary Union, c/o Secretaria, Place du Petit-Saconnex, 1209 Geneva Switzerland. LC JF501. DD 328.305. *Chronique des Elections Parlementaires.*

CHUNG KUNG YUAN SHIH TZU LIAO HSUAN CHI. VFOAT Tsung Ho Lei. Periodical. CH. Chinese. qt. $12.00. Chung Kung Yen Chiu Tsa Chih She 64, Lane Chih Cheng Road, Section 1, Tai-Pei Shih-Lin Chu Taiwan. LC JQ1519.A5. DD 324.25107509.

CIA PUBLICATIONS RELEASED TO THE PUBLIC. Main/Corp United States. Central Intelligence Agency. Directorate of Intelligence. VFOAT C.I.A. Publications Released to the Public. VAT Central Intelligence Agency Publications Released to the Public. 1972-81-. 0734-9602. US. English. an. Document Expediting Project, Exchange and Gift Division, Library of Congress, Washington DC 20540. LC Z7163, JF35. DD 016.3512. *CIA Publications Released to the Public, 0734-9602.*

CIA PUBLICATIONS RELEASED TO THE PUBLIC THROUGH LIBRARY OF CONGRESS DOCEX. Main/Corp National Foreign Assessment Center (U.S.). VAT Central Intelligence Agency Publications Released to the Public Through Library of Congress Document Expediting Project. 1972/77-. US. English. an. Document Expediting Project, Exchange and Gift Division, Library of Congress, Washington DC 20540.

CIENCIAS ADMINISTRATIVAS. Year 5- (No. 14-). 0009-6784. Periodical. AG. Spanish. ir. $20.00. Facultad de Ciencias Economcas, Inst Invest Adm-Calle 53 #419, La Plata Argentina. Ind/Abst Int. Labour Doc. ECA.

CIS/INDEX TO PUBLICATIONS OF THE UNITED STATES CONGRESS. See Indexes/Abstracts.

CITADIN DE LA GARDEUR. (CITADIN). VFOAT Bulletin d'Information de la Ville de le Gardeur. V. 2, No. 8, (Aug. 21, 1978)-. 0712-2888. Periodical. CN. French. ir. Citadin Ville de le Gardeur, 1 Montee des Arsenaux, Le Gardeur Quebec J5Z 2C1 Canada. DD 352.0714416. *Citadin de le Gardeur, 0712-2888.*

CITIES & VILLAGES. VAT Cities and Villages. V. 18, No. 2-. 0009-7535. Periodical. US. English. mo. $10.00. Ohio Municipal League, 40 South Third Street/Suite 540, Columbus OH 43215. Tel (614)221-4349. Ed William H Edwards. bk rev. adv acc. Circ 10,000. Information concerning Ohio municipal government. *Ohio Cities and Villages.*

THE CITIZEN. V. 1- 1955-. 0578-3283. Periodical. US. English. mo $10.00. The Citizen, 254 East Griffith Street, PO Box 1675, Jackson MS 39205. LC E185.61. Available on microfilm from University Microfilm.

CITIZENS' GUIDE TO LOCAL GOVERNMENT (OLYMPIA, WASH.). (CITIZENS' GUIDE TO LOCAL GOVERNMENT). US. English. an. $2.00. Washington Research Council, 906 South Columbia, Olympia WA 98501. Tel (206)357-6643.

CITOYEN. (LE CITOYEN). Vol. 1, No. 1 (Jan. 12, 1976)-. 0712-4228. Periodical. CN. French. mo. La Citoyen, 194 Route 138, Cap-Sante Quebec G0A 1L0 Canada. DD 352.0714466.

CITY & TOWN. See Business - Public Finance.

CITY EMPLOYMENT. (CITY EMPLOYMENT IN . . .). Began with 1965. 0091-9209. US. English. an. US Department of Commerce, Customer Services Section Publications, Washington DC 20233. LC JS358. DD 352.0050973.

CITY HALL DIGEST. V. 1- Nov. 1976-. 0190-0005. Periodical. US. English. mo. $48.00. City Hall Digest, PO Box 309, Seabrook MD 20706. Tel (301)949-0376. Ed Raymond L Bancroft. bk rev. An informative report on what's happening in America's municipal governments, including community development, public safety, management techniques, finances, environmental programs, reviews and more.

CITY MAGAZINE (WINNIPEG, MAN. : 1983). (CITY MAGAZINE). Vol. 6, No. 1 (Spring issue)-. 0822-790X. Periodical. CN. English. $12.00. City Magazine, 71 Cordova Street, Winnipeg Manitoba R3N 0Z9 Canada. DD 307.760971. *City Magazine Annual, 0821-5650.*

CITY OF BALTIMORE ANNUAL REPORT. Main/Corp Baltimore (MD.). 1975/76-. Periodical. US. English. an. City Hall, 100 North Holliday. Street, Baltimore MD 21202. LC JS571. DD 352.07526.

CITY OF CALGARY ADMINISTRATION MANUAL. Main/Corp Calgary, (Alta.). 1959-. 0383-1922. CN. English. City of Calgary, Data Processing Services Department, PO Box 1200, Calgary Alberta T2P 2M7 Canada. DD 352.071233.

CITY PROBLEMS : THE ANNUAL PROCEEDINGS OF THE UNITED STATES CONFERENCE OF MAYORS. Main/Conf United States Conference of Mayors. US. English. an. $10.00. United States Conference of Mayor's, 1620 Eye Street NW, Washington DC 20006. Tel (202)293-7330. LC JS304. DD 352.073.

CITY RECORD (BOSTON). Main/Corp Boston (Mass.). 1898. US. English. wk. $12.00. City of Boston, Room 203, City Hall, Boston MA 02201. Tel (617)725-4607. Ed Arnold I Epstein. LC JS13. DD 352.074461. Circ 1,000. News of interest to residents, employees and vendors of the city of Boston.

THE CITY RECORD (CLEVELAND). Main/Corp Cleveland (Ohio). V. 1- Jan. 7, 1914-. 0196-8327. US. English. wk. $20.00. Cleveland City Record, Room 216, City Hall, Cleveland OH 44114. Tel (216)664-2840. LC JS13. DD 352.077132. Circ 250.

THE CITY RECORD (NEW YORK CITY). Main/Corp New York (City). V. 1- (No. 1-). US. English. da. $250.00. Director of the City Record, 2213 Municipal Building, New York NY 10007. Tel (212)566-2613. LC JS13. DD 352.0747.

CIUDAD Y TERRITORIO. Periodical. SP. Spanish. qt $25.00. Inst Estudios Admon Local, Garcia Morato 7, Madrid 10 Spain.

CIVIC CEASED. V. 24, No. 1-V. 30, No. 4. 0315-1972. Periodical. CN. English. mo. 15.00 Domestic, 18.00 US, 35.00 Foreign. MacLean-Hunter Limited, 777 Bay Street, Toronto Ontario M5W 1A7 Canada. Ind/Abst Can. Bus. Index, Can. Environ. LC JS1701. DD 352.00720971. *Civic Administration, 0009-7764.*

CIVIC AFFAIRS. Sept. 29, 1948-. 0045-7027. Periodical. CN. English. qt. Bureau of Municipal Research, 4 Richmond Street East/Suite 406, Toronto Ontario M5C 1M6 Canada. LC JS1789.A1. DD 352.009409713541. *Monthly Letter.*

CIVIC CINEMA. Main/Corp South Bend Civic Planning Association. 1949-. 0489-8850. US. English. an. South Bend Civic Planning Association, 403 Lincoln Way West, South Bend IN 46601. LC JS1459.S4.

CIVIL LIST OF GAZETTED EMPLOYEES UNDER THE GOVERNMENT OF MEGHALAYA, AS ON 1ST JANUARY . . . . Main/Corp Meghalaya (India). 1979-. English. ir. m/s Firma DLM Pvt Ltd, Publishers & Distributors, Regd Office 257-B/B, B Ganguly Street, Calcutta 12 India. LC JQ620.M45. DD 354.54164001025.

CIVIL LIST OF THE CAYMAN ISLANDS. (THE CIVIL LIST OF THE CAYMAN ISLANDS). 0376-7906. English. ir. LC JL629.5.A4. DD 354.72921002.

CIVIL SERVANT. (THE CIVIL SERVANT). V. 1- Dec. 1971-. 0331-085X. Periodical. English. mo. 2/6. Nigerian Civil Service Union, Western State Branch, PO Box 1640, Ibadan Nigeria. LC JQ3092.Z1. DD 331.88113546690005.

CIVIL SERVICE COMMISSION'S REPORT. Main/Corp Nova Scotia. Civil Service Commission. Periodical. CN. English. an. LC JL312. DD 351.1.

CIVIL SERVICE LEADER. 0163-2434. Periodical. US. English. wk. $9.00. Leader Publications, 233 Broadway, New York NY 10007.

Public Administration

CIVIL SERVICE REPORTER. Main/Corp Philippines (Republic). Civil Service Commission. Began in 1956. 0300-3620. Periodical. PH. English. ir. Civil Service Commission, Finance Building, Rizal Park Manila. LC JQ1412. DD 354.599006.

CIVIL SERVICE REVIEW CEASED. (THE CIVIL SERVICE REVIEW). VFOAT Revue du Service Civil. Began with V. 1-54, No. 4. 0009-8035. Periodical. CN. English (French). qt. Public Service Alliance of Canada, 233 Gilmour Street, Ottawa Ontario K2P 0P1 Canada.

THE CIVIL SERVICE YEAR BOOK. See Yearbooks, Almanacs, Directories.

CJ SOUTH. Vol. 1, No. 1 (Dec. 1981)-. 0824-5630. Periodical. CN. English. ir. Free. CJ South, c/o B Lowe, 1450 M Heatherington Road, Ottawa Ontario K1V 6S1 Canada. DD 352.071384. *Citizen's Journal (Ottawa, Ont.), 0824-2739.*

CLASSIFICATION AND PAY PLAN - DEPARTMENT OF ADMINISTRATION. DIVISION OF PERSONNEL. (CLASSIFICATION AND PAY PLAN). Main/Corp Florida. Dept. of Administration. Division of Personnel. 0092-0142. US. English. Florida Department of Administration, Division of Personnel, Carlton Building, Tallahassee FL 32304. LC JK4457. DD 353.975900103.

CLASSIFICATION MANAGEMENT. VFOAT NCMSJ. V. 1-5, No. 2. 0009-8434. Periodical. US. English. an. $18.00. National Classification Management Society, 6116 Roseland Drive, Rockville MD 20852. Tel (301)231-9191. Ed R J Suto. LC JK468.S4. Circ 1,200. (ctrl). Information security, classification of government information proprietary data, protection of classified information in government and industry.

CLASSIFICATION PLAN AND SALARY SCHEDULE. VFOAT State of Indiana Salary Schedule. US. English. an. State Personnel Department, 100 North Senate Avenue, Indianapolis IN 46204. LC JK5657. DD 353.977200103.

CLEMENTS' ENCYCLOPEDIA OF WORLD GOVERNMENTS. See Encyclopedias & General Reference Books.

CLERICAL OFFICERS AND TYPISTS LISTS (HONGKONG). 0376-7914. English. ir. J R Lee, Java Road, Hong Kong Hong Kong. LC JQ674. DD 354.5125002.

COAST PROVINCE ANNUAL REPORT. Main/Corp Coast Province, Kenya. Provincial Commisioner. English. ir. Provincial Commissioner, Mombosa Kenya 90424. LC J731.T3. DD 354.67623.

CODE OF FEDERAL REGULATIONS : LIST OF CFR SECTIONS AFFECTED. US. English. mo. Superintendent of Documents, US Government Printing Office, Washington DC 20402. Tel (202)783-3238.

CODE OF THE CITY OF DETROIT, MICHIGAN. Periodical. US. English.

COG NOTES - DENVER REGIONAL COUNCIL OF GOVERNMENTS. Main/Corp Denver Regional Council of Governments. VAT Council of Governments Notes. Periodical. US. English. mo. 1776 South Jackson Street, Denver CO 80210.

COLECTIA DE HOTARIRI ALE CONSILIULUI DE MINISTRI SI ALTE ACTE NORMATIVE. RM. Romanian. qt. Ilexim Press Department, PO Box 1-136-1-137, Bucharest Romania. Tel P11-03-77.

COLORADO MUNICIPALITIES. V. 1-1925-. 0010-1664. Periodical. US. English. bm. $12.00. Colorado Municipal League, 1500 Grant/Suite 200, Denver CO 80203. Tel (303)831-6411. Ed Kay Mariea. LC JS39. DD 352.0788. adv acc. Circ 4,500. (ctrl). Current interests and concerns of municipal officials, activities of Colorado municipalities and individuals involved in local government.

COLORADO PUBLIC POLICY RESEARCH. VFOAT Public Policy Research. V. 1- Summer 1978-. US. English. Bureau of Governmental Research and Services, Campus Box 330, Boulder CO 80309.

COMMITTEES AND MEMBER AGENCIES OF THE SOUTHERN LEGISLATIVE CONFERENCE, THE COUNCIL OF STATE GOVERNMENTS. (COMMITTEES AND MEMBER AGENCIES OF THE SOUTHERN LEGISLATIVE CONFERENCE). Main/Corp Council of State Governments. Southern Legislative Conference. 0146-5201. US. English. an. Southern Office, 3384 Peachtree Road NE, Room 610, Atlanta GA 30326. LC JK2683. DD 353.90006175.

COMMON CAUSE (WASHINGTON, D.C.). (COMMON CAUSE). V. 6, No. 4 (Oct. 1980)-. 0271-9592. Periodical. US. English. bm. $20.00. Common Cause, PO Box 220, Washington DC 20044. Tel (202)833-1200. Ind/Abst Public Aff. Inf. Serv. Bull. LC JK1. DD 329.97305. Political activism, and public awareness.

COMMONWEALTH. Main/Corp Great Britain. Commonwealth Office. No. 1- 1967-. UK. English. ir. Her Majesty Stationery Office, PO Box 276, London SW8 5DT England. LC JV33.G7. DD 325.342.

COMMONWEALTH CAPITAL FUND FOR ABORIGINAL ENTERPRISES. Main/Corp Australia. Office of Aboriginal Affairs. 1971/72-. AT. English. ir. $0.37. Commonwealth Government Printing Office, PO Box 84, Canberra Australian Capital Territory 2600 Australia. LC J905, HD2346.A85. DD 328.9401 S, 338.040994.

COMMONWEALTH OFFICE YEAR BOOK. See Yearbooks, Almanacs, Directories.

COMMONWEALTH RECORD. Began with July 1/11, 1976 issue. AT. English. wk. $160.85. Australian Government Publishing Service, PO Box 84, Canberra 2600 Australia. Tel (062) 95 4411.

COMMUNICATOR. (THE COMMUNICATOR). V. 1- Jan. 1978-. 0707-9133. Periodical. CN. English. bm. Newfoundland Association of Public Employees, PO Box 1085, St John's Newfoundland A1C 5M5 Canada. DD 354.71800173. *N A P E News, 0318-1723; N A P E Journal, 0381-6826.*

COMP NEWSLETTER. Main/Corp Council on Municipal Performance. VAT Council on Municipal Performance Newsletter. 0146-8901. Periodical. US. English. mo. $15.00 Membership. Council on Municipal Performance, 84 Fifth Avenue, New York NY 10011.

COMPARATIVE STATE POLITICS NEWSLETTER. Vol. 1, No. 1 (Oct. 1979)-. 0273-1347. Periodical. US. English. 8m. $10.00. Illinois Legislative Study Center, Sangamon State University, Springfield IL 62708. Tel (217)786-6574. LC JK2403. DD 320.97305. bk rev. Circ 300. Articles on legislative developments in the United States.

COMPARISON OF NET QUARTERLY BILLS OF WISCONSIN WATER UTILITIES AS OF JANUARY 1 . . . . 1980-. US. English. an. Public Service Commission, Accounts & Finance Division, Madison WI 53703. LC HD2767.W6, HD4464. W6. DD 363.609775 S, 338.433636109775.

COMPENDIUM OF COMMONWEALTH SERVICE INFORMATION. AT. English. ir. Australian Government Public Service, PO Box 84, Canberra Australian Capital Territory 2600 Australia. LC JQ4045. DD 331.76135494.

COMPENDIUM OF PUBLICLY AVAILABLE REPORTS ON PROCUREMENT AND FINANCIAL ASSISTANCE AWARDS - (DEPT OF ENERGY). See Energy.

COMPENSATION REPORT. Main/Corp United States. Office of Personnel Management. 8756-6834. US. English. United States Office of Personnel Management, 1900 East Street NW, Washington DC 20415. LC JK791. DD 353.00505. *Federal Fringe Benefit Facts, 0193-2772.*

COMPENSATION REPORT : U.S. CIVIL SERVICE RETIREMENT SYSTEM, FEDERAL EMPLOYEES HEALTH BENEFITS PROGRAM, FEDERAL EMPLOYEES GROUP LIFE INSURANCE PROGRAM. See Economics - Labor.

COMPENSATION (WASHINGTON, D.C.: 1982). (COMPENSATION). Vol. 1 (1982)-. 0732-5282. US. English. an. $90.00. International City Management Association, 1120 G Street NW, Washington DC 20005. Tel (202)626-6400. Ed Ross Hoff. LC JS361. DD 352.0051230973. Circ 800. Data on the salaries of top managers and department heads in municipalities and counties throughout the country.

COMPILATION OF GAO'S WORK ON TAX ADMINISTRATION ACTIVITIES. See Business - Accounting.

COMPOSITE REPORT - DEVELOPMENT AND SERVICES BOARD. Main/Corp Natal. Development and Services Board. VFOAT Saamgestelde Verslag - Raad op Ontwikkeling en Dienste. Afrikaans (English). ir. LC HD4722.N37. DD 352.9409684.

COMPREHENSIVE ANNUAL FINANCIAL REPORT FOR THE FISCAL YEAR ENDING DECEMBER 31, . . . - (OREGON). Main/Corp Oregon Public Employes Retirement System. VFOAT Annual Report. 1980-. US. English. an. Public Employees Retirement System, 1099 Southwest Columbia Street, Box 73, Portland OR 97201. LC JK9060.P4. DD 353.9795005. *Annual Financial Report.*

COMPREHENSIVE ANNUAL FINANCIAL REPORT OF THE MINNESOTA STATE RETIREMENT SYSTEM. Main/Corp Minnesota State Retirement System. VFOAT Comprehensive Annual Report. US. English. an. Minnesota State Retirement System, 529 Jackson Street, St Paul MN 55101. LC JK6160.P4. DD 353.97760018205.

COMPTE RENDU ANALYTIQUE - REPUBLIQUE DU ZAIRE. CONSEIL LEGISLATIF NATIONAL. (COMPTE RENDU ANALYTIQUE - REPUBLIQUE DU ZAIRE, CONSEIL LEGISLATIF NATIONAL). Main/Corp Zaire. Conseil Legislatif National. No. 36- Oct. 26, 1972-. 0376-7531. BE. French. ir. Conseil Legislatif National, Rue de Louvain 40 42, 1000 Bruxelles Belgium. LC J831. DD 328.675101. *Compte Rendu Analytique - Republique du Zaire. Assemblee Nationale, 0376-7523.*

COMPTE RENDU D'ACTIVITE - EDF, DIRECTION DE LA DISTRIBUTION. Main/Corp Electricite de France. Direction de la Distribution. FR. French. ir. EDF/Direction de la Distribution, 2 rue Louis Murat, 75784 Paris Cedex 08 France. LC HD9685.F84. DD 354.4400872.

COMPTROLLER GENERAL'S PROCUREMENT DECISIONS. Main/Corp United States. General Accounting Office. 0095-2117. Periodical. US. English. mo. $150.00. Federal Publications Inc, 1120 20th Street Northwest/Suite 500 South, Washington DC 20036. Tel (202)337-7000. LC JK1673. DD 353.00712. Index received separately bound from publisher.

COMPTROLLER'S REPORT OF COOK COUNTY. Main/Corp Cook Co., Ill. Office of the Comptroller. VFOAT Report of the Cook County Comptroller. 1912/13-. US. English. ty. Cook County Office of the Comptroller, Room 500, 118 North Clark Street, Chicago IL 60602. *Cook County Comptroller's Report.*

IL COMUNE DEMOCRATICO. Periodical. IT. Italian. mo. $17.82. Agenda della Lega Autonomie e Poteri Locali/Via C Balbo N 43 00184 Rome Italy. LC JS41. DD 352.00720945.

CONFERENCE OF PRESIDING OFFICERS AND CLERKS OF THE PARLIAMENTS OF AUSTRALIA, FIJI, NAURU, PAPUA NEW GUINEA AND WESTERN SAMOA. (CONFERENCE OF PRESIDING OFFICERS AND CLERKS OF THE PARLIAMENTS OF AUSTRALIA, FIJI, NAURU, PAPUA NEW GUINEA AND WESTERN SAMOA. PROCEEDINGS). Main/Conf Conference of Presiding Officers and Clerks of the Parliaments of Australia, Fiji, Nauru, Papua New Guinea and Western Samoa. 0311-9513. PP. English. ir. Government Printing Office, PO Box 84, Canberra 2600 Australian Capital Territory Australia. LC J905, JQ4059. DD 328.9401 S, 328.9405.

CONFERENCIAS - CATEDRA CALVO SOTELO. Main/Corp Spain. Instituto de Estudios de Administracion Local. Catedra Calvo Sotelo. 1974-. Spanish. ir. Instituto de Estudios de Administracion Local, Martinez Paje, Madrid 5 Spain. LC JS6302.

CONFERENCIER. (LE CONFERENCIER : BULLETIN D'INFORMATION DE LA CONFERENCE DES MAIRES DE LA BANLIEUE DE MONTREAL). V. 1, No 1 (Feb. 28, 1980)-. 0822-4137. Periodical. CN. French (English). mo. Free. Conference des Maires de la Banlieue de Montreal, CP 126 Succursale Place Desjardins, Montreal Quebec H5B 1B3 Canada. DD 352.071427.

EL CONGRESISTA. Periodical. Spanish. ir. Calle Guacanagarix Esq Privada Ensanche Quisqueya, Santo Domingo Dominican Republic. LC JL1133.

CONGRESS AND HEALTH. See Public Health and Safety.

CONGRESS IN PRINT. US. English. wk. $159.00. Congressional Quarterly, 1414 22nd Street NW, Washington DC 20037. Tel (202)887-8625.

CONGRESS : INTRODUCTORY REPORT. VFOAT Congres : Rapport Introducrif, Kongress : Einfuhrungsbericht. English (papers in French or German, with preliminary material and summaries in all three languages). ir. International Association for Bridge and Structural Engineering, ETH Honggerberg, CH-8093 Zurich Switzerland.

CONGRESS MARCHES AHEAD. Dec. 1, 1969/May 1970-. 0376-5776. II. English. ir. All India Congress Committee, 5 Dr Rajendra Prasad Road, New Delhi-1 India. LC JQ298.I5. DD 329.954.

CONGRESSI. Periodical. Italian. ir. LC AS1.

CONGRESSIONAL AND STATE OFFICERS. VFOAT Georgia Official Directory of United States Congressmen, State and County Officers. Jan. 15, 1982-. 0735-8512. US. English. an. Commissions Division, Room 219/State Capital, Atlanta GA 30334. LC JK4330. DD 353.975800025. *United States Congressmen and State Officers.*

CONGRESSIONAL DISTRICT ATLAS. See Geography.

CONGRESSIONAL DISTRICT ZIP CODES. Began with Vol. for 94th Congress. 0192-883X. US. English. Tyson Belzer and Associates Inc, 7735 Old Georgetown Road, Bethesda MD 20014. LC JK1341. DD 328.7307345025.

CONGRESSIONAL QUARTERLY ALMANAC. See Yearbooks, Almanacs, Directories.

CONGRESSIONAL RECORD (DAILY EDITION). See Law.

CONGRESSIONAL RECORD INDEX. See Indexes/Abstracts.

CONGRESSIONAL RECORD INDEX. HEALTH, EDUCATION AND WELFARE. See Indexes/Abstracts.

CONGRESSIONAL STAFF DIRECTORY. See Yearbooks, Almanacs, Directories.

CONGRESSIONAL STAFF DIRECTORY. ADVANCE LOCATOR FOR CAPITOL HILL. See Yearbooks, Almanacs, Directories.

CONNECTICUT GUIDE TO LEGISLATIVE SERVICES. 1981-. US. English. an. Matech Inc, 60 Washington Street/Suite 202, Hartford CT 06106. LC JK3330. DD 328.74600202. *Connecticut Legislator's Guide to Services.*

CONSENSUS. V. 1- Jan. 1974-. 0380-1314. Periodical. CN. English. qt. Standards Council of Canada, 350 Sparks Street, Ottawa Ontario K1R 7S8 Canada.

CONSOLIDATED FEDERAL FUNDS REPORT. VOLUME II, SUBCOUNTY AREAS. See Business - Banking & Finance.

CONSOLIDATED INDEX TO GOVERNMENT PUBLICATIONS - (GREAT BRITAIN). See Indexes/Abstracts.

CONSTITUTIONAL AND PARLIAMENTARY INFORMATION. Main/Corp Inter-Parliamentary Union. New Series, 1st-2nd Year, 1948-49. 0010-6623. Periodical. FR. English. qt. $3.32. Association of Secretaries General of Parliaments, Assamblee Nationale, 75355 Paris France. Ind/Abst Public Aff. Inf. Serv. Bull. LC JF8. (cum index).

CONTACT. V. 18 I.E. 17- Jan. 1976-. 0382-2079. Periodical. CN. English. mo. British Columbia, Parliament Building, Victoria British Columbia V8V 1X4 Canada. DD 354.711001005. *Public Service Contact, 0382-2060.*

CONTACT (SAINT-ANACLET-DE-LESSARD, QUEBEC). (CONTACT). V. 1, No. 1 (June 1982)-. 0820-0084. Periodical. CN. French. Municipalite de St-Anaclet-de-Lessard Bureau, Municipal 20 rue de la Gare, St-Anaclet-de-Lessard Quebec G0K 1H0 Canada. DD 352.0714771.

CONTEST AND LOTTERY NEWS. Vol. 1, No. 1-. 0710-6297. Periodical. CN. English. mo. $12.00. Excalibur Publishers, Suite 302B, 160 Eglinton Avenue East, Toronto Ontario M4P 1G3 Canada. DD 790.1340971.

CONTRACT MANAGEMENT. See Law.

COOPERATIVE SALARY SURVEY REPORT. Main/Corp Local Government Personnel Institute. 0147-0167. US. English. an. LC JK9057. DD 331.2813520795.

THE COST OF SOCIAL SECURITY. See Sociology: General Works, Theory - Social Pathology, Welfare, Criminology.

LA COTE D'IVOIRE : ANNUAIRE INTERNATIONAL. See Yearbooks, Almanacs, Directories.

COUNCIL COMMENTS. Main/Corp Citizens Research Council of Michigan. Vol. 1 1946-. US. English. ir. Citizens Research Council of Michigan, 625 Shelby Street, Detroit MI 48226-4154. Tel (313)961-5377.

COUNCILS, COMMITTEES & BOARDS. 1st- Ed. UK. English. ir. CBD Research Ltd, 154 High Street, Beckenham Kent BR3 1EA England. Tel 01-650-7745. Ed Lindsay Sellar. A handbook of advisory, consultative, executive and similar bodies in British public life.

COUNTERVAILING DUTY & ANTIDUMPING CASE REFERENCE LIST. VFOAT Countervailing Duty and Antidumping Case Reference List. Periodical. US. English. qt. Department of Treasury, US Customs Service, 1301 Constitution Avenue NW, Washington DC 20229.

COUNTY EXECUTIVE DIRECTORY. See Yearbooks, Almanacs, Directories.

COUNTY GOVERNMENT EMPLOYMENT. See Economics - Labor.

COUNTY OFFICERS. Began with 1979. US. English. an. State Board of Elections, State of Illinois, 1020 South Spring Street, PO Box 4187, Springfield IL 62708. LC JS451.I35. DD 352.0052025773. *State and County Officers, 0145-6199.*

COUNTY PROGRESS. V.1- 1924-. 0011-0353. Periodical. US. English. mo. $15.00. Associated Publ Co, PO Box 519, Brownwood TX 76802. Tel (915)643-2995. Ed Nancy Stephens. adv acc. Circ 1,700. Official publication for County Judges and Commissioners Association of Texas.

COURRIER DIPLOMATIQUE DE L'OCEAN INDIEN. No. 1- Nov. 1975/Jan. 1976-. French. ir. Societe de Presse de Madagascar, Banque Commerciale de Madagascar, Compte No. 420-1352, Tannanarive Madagascar. LC DT468.

THE COURTHOUSE JOURNAL. Mar. 1960-. Periodical. US. English. mo. Washington Association of County Officials, 105 East 8th Avenue/Suite 307, Olympia WA 98501.

CQ WEEKLY REPORT. VFOAT Congressional Quarterly. 0010-5910. Periodical. US. English. wk. Congressional Quarterly Inc, 1414-22nd Street NW, Washington DC 20037. LC JK1. DD 328.73.

CREDIT MANAGER'S REPORT. 8750-278X. Periodical. US. English. bw. $119.40. Executive Reports Corp, 113 Sylvan Avenue, Englewood Cliffs NJ 07632.

CROWN CORPORATIONS COMMITTEE MINUTES AND VERBATIM REPORT. Main/Corp Saskatchewan. Legislative Assembly. Crown Corporations Committee. CN. English. Crown Corporations Committee, Legislative Assembly, Regina Saskatchwan Canada. LC HD4010.S3. DD 354.7124092.

CRS STUDIES IN THE PUBLIC DOMAIN. VFOAT C.R.S. Studies in the Public Domain. VAT Congressional Research Service Studies in the Public Domain. Began with issue for 1978. 0277-125X. Periodical. US. English. sa. $9.25. Superintendent of Documents, US Government Printing Office, Washington DC 20402. Tel (202)783-3238. LC Z733.L735. DD 016.027573. NLM Z 1223.A2 C15.

CSG BACKGROUNDER. VFOAT Backgrounder. VAT Council of State Governments Backgrounder. US. English. mo. $160.00. Council of State Government, PO Box 11910, Iron Works Pike, Lexington KY 40578. Tel (606)252-2291. Ed L Edward Purcell. adv acc. (ctrl). Brief up-to-date special issue reports on current concerns and trends in the states.

Public Administration

CSI FEDERAL INDEX. See Indexes/Abstracts.

THE CUMULATED INDEX TO THE U.S. DEPARTMENT OF STATE PAPERS RELATING TO THE FOREIGN RELATIONS OF THE UNITED STATES. See Indexes/Abstracts.

CUMULATIVE SUPPLEMENT TO FIFTY SEVENTH (1964) ANNUAL REPORT, WITH SUMMARY INDEX OF EFFECTIVE GENERAL ORDERS. See Indexes/Abstracts.

CURRENT AMERICAN GOVERNMENT. See Political Science.

CURRENT FEDERAL EXAMINATION ANNOUNCEMENTS. Began with Sept./Oct. 1973. 0364-2704. Periodical. US. English. qt. US Office of Personnel Management, Washington DC 20415. *Current Federal Civil Service Announcements.*

CURRENT MUNICIPAL PROBLEMS. V. 1- 1959/76-. 0161-5122. Periodical. US. English. an. Callaghan and Co, 6141 North Cicero Avenue, Chicago IL 60646. LC JS39. DD 352.0080973.

CURRENT SELECTED SERVICES REPORT, MONTHLY SELECTED SERVICES RECEIPTS. Main/Corp United States. Bureau of the Census. VFOAT Monthly Selected Services Receipts. Began with BS 66-1, Nov. 1966. 0565-1018. US. English. mo. US Department of Commerce, Washington DC 20233.

CURRENT SOVIET LEADERS. VFOAT Leaders Sovietiques Contemporains. V. 1- 1974-. 0318-2037. CN. English. an. Mosaic Press, PO Box 1032, Oakville Ontario L6J 5E9 Canada. Tel (416)844-0963. LC JN6521. DD 354.4700205.

DAILY BULLETIN - INSTITUTE OF GOVERNMENT, UNIVERSITY OF NORTH CAROLINA AT CHAPEL HILL. See Law.

DAILY CHECKLIST OF CANADIAN GOVERNMENT PUBLICATIONS. VFOAT Liste Quotidienne des Publications du Gouvernement Canadien. Apr. 12, 1976-Nov. 10, 1978. 0700-2904. Periodical. CN. English (French). da. Receiver General for Canada, Supply & Services, Ottawa Ontario K1A 0S9 Canada. Tel (819)997-2560. *Daily Checklist of Government Publications, 0318-6768.*

DAILY LEGISLATIVE REPORT. 1949-. 0277-4917. Periodical. US. English. ir. $520.00. State Capitol Information Service, 527 East Capitol Avenue Room 900, Springfield IL 62701. Tel (217)523-6422. Ed Joseph L Harris. Issued every day, Illinois General Assembly meets. Includes the digests of all bill introductions, committee hearing schedules, committee and floor actions.

DAILY LIST OF GOVERNMENT PUBLICATIONS FROM HER MAJESTY'S STATIONERY OFFICE. 0263-743X. Periodical. UK. English. ir. 49.50. Her Majestys Stationery Office, PO Box 276, London SW8 5DT England. Tel 01-211 0363. Ind/Abst World Text Abstr. Comprises parliamentary, non-parliamentary and international organisation publications, statutory instruments and all Northern Ireland publications.

DALIL AL-HUKUMAH WA-AL-QITA AL-AMM FI JUMHURIYAT MISR AL-ARABIYAH. Arabic. ir. 11 Abd El-Khaliq Tharwat Street, Al-Qahirah United Arab Republic. LC JQ3831.

DATA PROCESSING ANNUAL REPORT AND LONG-RANGE PLAN FOR FISCAL YEARS . . . . Main/Corp Louisiana. Data Processing Coordinating and Advisory Council. 1982-1984-. US. English. an. $1.66. Louisiana Data Processing, Coordinating and Advisory Council Office of the Governor, 555 St Tammany Street, Baton Rouge LA 70806. LC JK4749.A8. DD 353.976630071.

DATA PROCESSING SURVEY. OREGON COUNTIES. Sept. 1980-. US. English. an. $6.00. LC JS451.O75. DD 352.0073.

DATELINE, VICTORIA. 0821-3429. Periodical. CN. English. Employers' Council of British Columbia, Suite 1130/800 West Pender, Vancouver British Columbia V6E 2E9 Canada. DD 354.7110005.

DATOS ESTADISTICOS - EMPRESA NACIONAL DE ENERGIA ELECTRICA. See Statistics.

Public Administration

DAUPHIN COUNTY REPORTS. See Law.

D.C. DIRECTORY OF NATIVE AMERICAN FEDERAL AND PRIVATE PROGRAMS. See Yearbooks, Almanacs, Directories.

D/C : NATIONAL NEWSLETTER FOR STATE ADMINISTERED DEFERRED COMPENSATION PROGRAMS. Vol. 1, No. 1 (Summer 1980)-. Periodical. US. English. qt. Illinois Department of Personnel, Deferred Compensation Office, 501 Stratton Building, Springfield IL 62506.

DEBATES AND PROCEEDINGS - NOVA SCOTIA HOUSE OF ASSEMBLY. Main/Corp Nova Scotia. House of Assembly. VAT Debates and Proceedings of the House of Assembly (Halifax) Official Report of the Debates and Proceedings of the Legislative Council (Halifax). 0707-8315. Periodical. CN. English. ir. Nova Scotia Communication, PO Box 2206, Halifax Nova Scotia Canada.

DEBATES; OFFICIAL REPORT. Main/Corp Jammu and Kashmir. Legislature. Legislative Council. II. English. ir. Jammu & Kashmir Legislature, Legislative Council, Jammu India. LC JQ620.K3.

DEBATS DE L'ASSEMBLEE LEGISLATIVE DU QUEBEC. (DEBATS DE L'ASSEMBLEE LEGISLATIVE). Main/Corp Quebec (Province). Assemblee Legislative. 1st Legislature- 1867/1868-. 0709-3616. Periodical. CN. French (English). ir. Editeur Officiel du Quebec, 1283 Ouest Boul Charest, Quebec G1N 2C9 Canada.

DEBATTE VAN DIE STAANDE KOMITEE OOR BEGROTINGSWETSONTWERP. Main/Corp South Africa. Parliament. House of Assembly. Standing Committee on Appropriation Bill. VFOAT Debates of the Standing Committee on Appropriation Bill. SA. Afrikaans (English). ir. 8.75. Govt Printer, Bosman Street Private Bag X85, Pretoria 0001 South Africa. DD 354.68007223405.

DECISIONS DE LA COMMISSION DES AFFAIRES SOCIALES. Main/Corp Quebec (Province) Commission des Affaires Sociales. Published since V. 1, 1975. 0702-9683. Periodical. CN. French. $5.00 Per Number.

DECISIONS OF THE DEPARTMENT OF THE INTERIOR. Main/Corp United States. Dept. of the Interior. Began in Jan. 1955. Periodical. US. English. mo. Superintendent of Documents, Government Printing Office, Washington DC 20402. Tel (202)783-3238.

DECISIONS OF THE PUBLIC UTILITIES COMMISSION OF THE STATE OF CALIFORNIA. Main/Corp California Public Utilities Commission. VFOAT Opinions and Orders of the Public Utilities Commission of California. Vol. 47 (Nov. 15, 1946 to Apr. 6, 1948)-. US. English. an. Public Utilities Commission of the State of California, California State Building, San Francisco CA 94102. LC HD2767.C2. DD 353.97940087. Decisions of the Railroad Commission of the State of California.

DECISIONS OF THE UNITED STATES DEPARTMENT OF THE INTERIOR. Main/Corp United States. Dept. of the Interior. Began with V. 68, 1961. 0193-5070. US. English. an. Superintendent of Documents, US Government Printing Office, Washington DC 20402. Decisions of the Department of the Interior, 0011-7331.

DELAWARE ANNUAL REPORT. US. English. an. Executive Department, Office of the Budget, Townsend Building, Dover DE 19901. LC JK3701. DD 353.97510006.

DELEGACIJE OSNOVNIH SAMOUPRAVNIH ORGANIZACIJA I ZAJEDNICA I SKUPSTINE DRUSTVENO-POLITICKIH ZAJEDNICA. See Statistics.

DEMAND SURVEY. PROFESSIONAL AND MANAGEMENT COURSES. (DEMAND SURVEY, PROFESSIONAL AND MANAGEMENT COURSES . . .). Main/Corp Public Service Commission of Canada. Staff Developmemt Branch. VFOAT Enquete sur les Besoins de Formation Professionnelle et en Gestion. 1978/79-. 0713-083X. Periodical. CN. English (text in French with French text on inverted pages). Public Service Commission, 300 Laurier Avenue West, Ottawa Ontario K1A 0M7 Canada. DD 354.71001505. Professional and Management Courses and Services, 0700-2378.

DEMANDS FOR GRANTS AND APPROPRIATIONS . . . (DEVELOPMENT). Main/Corp Bangladesh. Artha Bibhaga. English. ir. LC HJ67.8. DD 354.5492007225205.

DEMOCRACIA 76 I.E. SETENTA E SEIS. Periodical. Portuguese. ir. $12.50 Single Issue. Partido de Centro Democratico Socical, Largo do Caldas 5, Lisboa Portugal. LC JN8651.C45. DD 329.9469.

DEMOCRAZIA NAZIONALE. Yearly V. 1- April 19, 1977-. Periodical. Italian. ir. Democrazia Nazionale-Constituento di Destra, Via del Corso 75, Roma Italy. LC JN5657.C68.

DEPARTMENT OF REVENUE ANNUAL REPORT. Main/Corp Arizona. Dept. of Revenue. VFOAT Annual Report. 1975-1976-. US. English. an. Capitol Building, 1700 West Washington, Phoenix AZ 85007. DD 351.726. Annual Report of the Department of Revenue.

DEPARTMENT OF THE TREASURY NEWS. Main/Corp United States. Treasury Dept. US. English. ir. Treasury Department, 15 Pennsylvania Avenue/Room 2315, Washington DC 20220. Tel (202)566-2041. Circ 4,000. Includes all information regarding treasury bureaus, treasury securities and policy/planning statements issued by treasury officials. News - Department of the Treasury.

DESCRIPTIVE INVENTORY OF FEDERAL-PROVINCIAL PROGRAMS AND ACTIVITIES. (A DESCRIPTIVE INVENTORY OF FEDERAL-PROVINCIAL PROGRAMS AND ACTIVITIES). VFOAT Federal-Provincial Programs and Activities, a Descriptive Inventory. Began with Vol. for 1973. 0707-1639. CN. English. an. Federal-Provincial Relations Office, 59 Sparks Street, Ottawa Ontario K1A 0A3 Canada. LC JL27. DD 354.71082.

DESPACHOS PUBLICOS. Spanish. an. Carrera 12 No 15-95 of 307 Apartado A-718, Bogota Columbia. LC JL2821. DD 354.861002.

DETAILED DEMAND FOR GRANTS OF HOME DEPARTMENT. Main/Corp Jammu and Kashmir. Home Dept. 0376-8252. II. English. ir. Ranbir Government Press, Jammu and Kashmir/ Home Department, Jammu India. LC HV7809.K3. DD 354.54600722.

DETAILED DEMAND FOR GRANTS OF POWER DEVELOPMENT DEPARTMENT. Main/Corp Jammu and Kashmir. Power Development Dept. 0376-8309. II. English. ir. Ranbir Government Press, Jammu and Kashmir/Power Development Department, Jammu India. LC HD9556.I43.

DETAILED DEMAND FOR GRANTS OF WORKS DEPARTMENT. GOVENMENT OF JAMMU AND KASHMIR. (DETAILED DEMAND FOR GRANTS OF WORKS DEPARTMENT). Main/Corp Jammu and Kashmir. Public Works Dept. 0303-948X. II. English. ir. Ranbir Government Press, Jammu and Kashmir Works Department, Jammu India. LC HD4295.K3. DD 354.540086.

DETAILED ESTIMATES OF REVENUE OF THE PUNJAB GOVERNMENT FOR THE YEAR . . . . See Business - Public Finance.

DETAILED LISTING OF REAL PROPERTY OWNED BY THE UNITED STATES AND USED BY CIVIL AGENCIES THROUGHOUT THE WORLD AS OF . . . . US. English. an. General Services Administration, Washington DC 20405. LC JK1613. DD 353.00713.

DEVELOPMENT POLICY AND ADMINISTRATION REVIEW. V. 1- Jan./ June 1975-. Periodical. II. English. sa. $8.00. HCM State Institution Public Administration, Taipur 302004 India. Tel 64003. Ed M Hasan. LC JF1338.A2. DD 354.5400072. bk rev. adv acc. Circ 500. Developmental and administrative issues and policies confronting Third World countries. Review of existing policies and their execution to obtain alternative solutions.

DIARY OF THE CORPORATION OF THE CITY OF GLASGOW & C. Main/Corp Glasgow (Strathclyde). VFOAT City of Glasgow Corporation Diary. UK. English. 197 Pollokshawa Road, Glasgow Scotland. LC JS4274.A1. DD 352.041443.

DICTIONARY CATALOG OF OFFICIAL PUBLICATIONS OF THE STATE OF NEW YORK. See Bibliographies.

DIE BAUVERWALTUNG. (BAUVERWALTUNG). V. 1- 1952-. 0005-6847. Periodical. German. mo. Werner/Verlag GMBH, Postfach 6247, 3 Hannover Germany. Ind/Abst Energy Res. Abstr.

DIGEST OF ADVISORY OPINIONS. Main/Corp Hawaii. State Ethics Commission. US. English. State Ethics Commission, 250 South King Street #405, PO Box 616, Honolulu HI 96809. LC KFH406.A59. DD 353.996900995.

DIGEST OF OPINIONS OF THE ATTORNEY GENERAL OF TEXAS CEASED. Main/Corp Texas. Attorney-General's Office. 1947-1981. 0275-2646. US. English. an. $150.00. Texas Attorney Generals Office, PO Box 12548 Capitol Station, Austin TX 78711. DD 353.97645. (cum index). Annual Report of the Opinions of the Attorney General of the State of Texas, 0277-5530; Monthly Report of the Opinions of the Attorney General of the State of Texas, 0277-5549.

DIGEST OF PUBLIC GENERAL BILLS AND RESOLUTIONS. Main/Corp Library of Congress. Legislative Reference Service. 74th-91st Congress. US. English. ir. Superintendent of Documents, US Government Printing Office, Washington DC 20402. Tel (292)783-3238.

DIGESTO NOTARIAL. Main/Corp Argentine Republic. VFOAT Boletin de Legislacion. V. 1- 1968/ 69-. Spanish. ir.

DIMENSIONS MUNICIPALES. Vol. 1, No. 1 (7 Oct. 1982)-. 0820-7712. CN. French. ir. Federation Canadienne des Municipalites Bureau 1318, 112 rue Kent, Ottawa Ontario K1P 5P2 Canada. DD 352.07105.

DIPLOMATIC, CONSULAR AND OTHER REPRESENTATION IN CEYLON. Main/Corp Ceylon. Ministry of Defence and External Affairs. English. ir. LC JX1840.Z8.

DIPLOMATIC, CONSULAR, AND OTHER REPRESENTATIVES IN CANADA. VFOAT Representants Diplomatiques, Consulaires, et Autres au Canada. 0825-6683. CN. English (French with French text on inverted pages). be. $4.15 Canada, $5.00 Foreign. Canadian Government Publishing Center, Supply & Services Canada, Ottawa Ontario K1A 0S9 Canada. LC JX1729.A2. DD 351.8920971. Diplomatic Corps and Consular and Other Representatives in Canada, 0486-4514.

DIPLOMATIC CORPS AND CONSULAR AND OTHER REPRESENTATIVES IN CANADA CEASED. (CORPS DIPLOMATIQUE ET REPRESENTANTS CONSULAIRES ET AUTRES AU CANADA). June 1969-Nov. 1982. 0486-4514. Periodical. CN. text in French and English on inverted pages, June 1971-Nov. 1982. sa. DD 351.8920971. Corps Diplomatique, 0527-6837; Representants des Autres Pays au Canada, 0706-8433.

DIPLOMATIC LIST. Main/Corp India. Protocol Division. II. English. ir. 6.00 Domestic, $2.16 US. Controller of Publications, Publ Branch Old Secretariat, Civil Lines Delhi India. LC JX1839. DD 351.892.

DIPLOMATIC POST. Sept. 1982.-. 0714-6604. Periodical. CN. English. ir. $20.00. Diplomatic Post, 23-270 MacLaren Street, Ottawa Ontario K2P 0M3 Canada. DD 351.8920971.

DIPLOMATIC PRESS DIRECTORY OF THE REPUBLIC OF CYPRUS INCLUDING TRADE INDEX AND BIOGRAPHICAL SECTION. See Yearbooks, Almanacs, Directories.

DIRECTORIO DE DESPACHOS PUBLICOS. See Yearbooks, Almanacs, Directories.

DIRECTORIO DE LA ADMINISTRACION PUBLICA CENTRALIZADA Y PARAESTATAL. See Yearbooks, Almanacs, Directories.

DIRECTORIO . . . DE TIENDAS DEL SECTOR PUBLICO Y ASOCIADAS. See Yearbooks, Almanacs, Directories.

Public Administration

DIRECTORS' REPORT AND FINANCIAL STATEMENT. Main/Corp Mifal Ha-Payis. 1965/66-. English. ir. Mifal Ha-Payis, 3 Heftman Street, Tel Aviv Israel. LC HG6255.I8. DD 354.56940072.

DIRECTORY. BOROUGH & CITY OFFICIALS. See Yearbooks, Almanacs, Directories.

DIRECTORY - NATIONAL ASSOCIATION OF REGIONAL COUNCILS. See Yearbooks, Almanacs, Directories.

DIRECTORY. NORTH DAKOTA CITY OFFICIALS. See Yearbooks, Almanacs, Directories.

DIRECTORY OF CHINESE OFFICIALS. PROVINCIAL ORGANIZATIONS. See Yearbooks, Almanacs, Directories.

DIRECTORY OF CZECHOSLOVAK OFFICIALS. See Yearbooks, Almanacs, Directories.

DIRECTORY OF ELECTRIC LIGHT AND POWER COMPANIES. See Yearbooks, Almanacs, Directories.

DIRECTORY OF FEDERALLY SUPPORTED INFORMATION ANALYSIS CENTERS. See Yearbooks, Almanacs, Directories.

DIRECTORY OF FLORIDA GOVERNMENT. See Yearbooks, Almanacs, Directories.

DIRECTORY OF GOVERNMENT OFFICIALS. FEDERAL, STATE, COUNTY, CITY, TOWNSHIP AND SPECIAL DISTRICT OFFICIALS IN NORTH DAKOTA. See Yearbooks, Almanacs, Directories.

DIRECTORY OF GOVERNMENTAL OFFICES AND SERVICES IN NORTH CAROLINA. See Yearbooks, Almanacs, Directories.

DIRECTORY OF GOVERNMENTS IN METROPOLITAN TORONTO. See Yearbooks, Almanacs, Directories.

DIRECTORY OF KANSAS PUBLIC OFFICIALS. See Yearbooks, Almanacs, Directories.

DIRECTORY OF LOCAL CHIEF EXECUTIVES. See Yearbooks, Almanacs, Directories.

DIRECTORY OF LOCAL OFFICIALS. See Yearbooks, Almanacs, Directories.

DIRECTORY OF MAYORS. See Yearbooks, Almanacs, Directories.

DIRECTORY OF MEMBERS, NEW YORK STATE LEGISLATURE, AND MEMBERS OF CONGRESS. See Yearbooks, Almanacs, Directories.

DIRECTORY OF MICHIGAN MUNICIPAL OFFICIALS. See Yearbooks, Almanacs, Directories.

DIRECTORY OF MINNESOTA CITY OFFICIALS. See Yearbooks, Almanacs, Directories.

DIRECTORY OF MINNESOTA MUNICIPAL OFFICIALS. See Yearbooks, Almanacs, Directories.

DIRECTORY OF MISSISSIPPI ELECTIVE OFFICIALS. See Yearbooks, Almanacs, Directories.

DIRECTORY OF MUNICIPAL AND COUNTY OFFICIALS IN COLORADO. See Yearbooks, Almanacs, Directories.

DIRECTORY OF MUNICIPAL MANAGEMENT ASSISTANTS. See Yearbooks, Almanacs, Directories.

DIRECTORY OF MUNICIPAL OFFICIALS OF NEW MEXICO. See Yearbooks, Almanacs, Directories.

DIRECTORY OF OFFICIALS OF THE DEMOCRATIC PEOPLE'S REPUBLIC OF KOREA. See Yearbooks, Almanacs, Directories.

DIRECTORY OF OFFICIALS OF THE GERMAN DEMOCRATIC REPUBLIC. See Yearbooks, Almanacs, Directories.

DIRECTORY OF OFFICIALS OF VIETNAM. See Yearbooks, Almanacs, Directories.

DIRECTORY OF OKLAHOMA. See Yearbooks, Almanacs, Directories.

DIRECTORY OF OKLAHOMA'S CITY AND TOWN OFFICIALS. See Yearbooks, Almanacs, Directories.

DIRECTORY OF PUBLIC OFFICIALS IN THE LAKE ERIE REGION. See Yearbooks, Almanacs, Directories.

DIRECTORY OF RECOGNIZED LOCAL GOVERNMENTS. See Yearbooks, Almanacs, Directories.

DIRECTORY OF SERVICES FOR THE CITY OF TORONTO. See Yearbooks, Almanacs, Directories.

DIRECTORY OF SOVIET OFFICIALS. See Yearbooks, Almanacs, Directories.

DIRECTORY OF SOVIET OFFICIALS. NATIONAL ORGANIZATIONS. See Yearbooks, Almanacs, Directories.

DIRECTORY OF SOVIET OFFICIALS. REPUBLIC ORGANIZATIONS. See Yearbooks, Almanacs, Directories.

DIRECTORY OF STAFF ASSISTANTS TO THE GOVERNORS. See Yearbooks, Almanacs, Directories.

A DIRECTORY OF STATE AGENCIES, COUNCILS OF GOVERNMENTS, UNIVERSITIES AND COLLEGES, TECHNICAL COLLEGES, AND ASSOCIATIONS. See Yearbooks, Almanacs, Directories.

DIRECTORY OF STATE, COUNTY AND FEDERAL OFFICIALS. See Yearbooks, Almanacs, Directories.

DIRECTORY OF TENNESSEE COUNTY OFFICIALS. See Yearbooks, Almanacs, Directories.

DIRECTORY OF THE STATE AND COUNTY OFFICIALS OF NORTH CAROLINA. See Yearbooks, Almanacs, Directories.

DIRECTORY OF U.S. GOVERNMENT AUDIOVISUAL PERSONNEL. See Yearbooks, Almanacs, Directories.

DIRECTORY OF UTAH LOCAL OFFICIALS. See Yearbooks, Almanacs, Directories.

DIRECTORY : PROGRAMS IN PUBLIC AFFAIRS AND ADMINISTRATION. See Yearbooks, Almanacs, Directories.

DIRECTORY. REPUBLIC OF SENEGAL. See Yearbooks, Almanacs, Directories.

DISCOURS ET DECLARATIONS DU PRESIDENT DE LA REPUBLIQUE FRANCAISE. 0396-5988. Periodical. FR. French. mo. Documentation Francaise, 124 rue Henri Barbusse, 93308 Aubervilliers France. Tel 834-9275.

DISCOURS ET ENTRETIENS - PRESIDENCE DE LA REPUBLIQUE. Main/Corp Rwanda. Presidence. French or Kinyarwanda. ir. B P 15, Kigali Rwanda. LC J816M. DD 354.67571035.

DISTRICT COUNCIL JOURNAL. (DISTRICT COUNCIL JOURNAL : AN INDEPENDENT MONTHLY NEWS REPORT OF D.C. GOVERNMENT LEGISLATIVE ACTIVITY). V. 1, No. 1 (May 1983)-. 0748-1179. Periodical. US. English. mo. $53.00. District Council Journal, PO Box 39151, Washington DC 20016. Tel (202)364-8696. Ed Ruth Dixon. LC JK2701. DD 328.753005. Circ 400. Report on legislative activity of Council of the District of Columbia.

DISTRICT OF COLUMBIA REGISTER. Began with July 19, 1954 issue. 0419-439X. US. English. wk. $50.00. DC Treasurer, Room 114/District Building, 14th East Street NW, Washington DC 20004. Tel (202)727-5090.

DLAD NEWSLETTER. Main/Corp Wisconsin. Dept. of Local Affairs and Development. Apr. 1975-. Periodical. US. English. mo. Department of Local Affairs and Development, 123 West Washington Avenue, Madison WI 53702. DLAD, Official Newsletter.

DOCUMENTACION ADMINISTRATIVA. No. L-. 0012-4494. Periodical. SP. Spanish. qt. Gabinete Tecnico, Boletin Oficial Estado-Elox, Gonzalo 19-Madrid 10 Spain. Ind/Abst Int. Labour Doc., Foreign Lang. Index. LC JA26. (cum index).

DOCUMENTATION IN PUBLIC ADMINISTRATION. V. 1- Jan./Mar. 1973-. 0377-7081. Periodical. II. English. qt. $5.00. Indian Institute of Public Administration, Inderaprastha Estate Ring Road, New Delhi 110002 India. LC Z7164.A2. DD 016.35.

DOCUMENTATION TECHNIQUE - COMMISSION DE LA FONCTION PUBLIQUE DU QUEBEC. (DOCUMENTATION TECHNIQUE). No. 1, (April 1981)-. 0712-0451. Monographic Series. CN. French. ir. Comm de la Fonction Publique du Quebec, 300 Laurier Avenue West, Ottawa Ontario K1A 0M7 Canada. DD 351.1005.

DOD'S PARLIAMENTARY COMPANION. 33rd- Year. Periodical. UK. English. an. $61.30. Elm Cottage, Chilsham Lane, Herstmonceux/Hilsham East Sussex BN27 4QQ England. Ed J B Smith. adv acc. Circ 4,500. (ctrl). Contains photos and biographies of all 1,854 Lords and members of Parliament in the UK. It also contains details of all senior officials in government. Eight hundred pages, 250,000 facts and figures. Parliamentary Companion.

DOMESTIC AFFAIRS STUDIES. Main/Corp American Enterprise Institute for Public Policy Research. Vol. 1 Feb. 1972. US. English. Enterprise Institute for Publ Policy, 1150-17th Street NW, Washington DC 20036.

DORS OPENERS : NEWSLETTER OF THE DEPARTMENT OF REHABILITATION SERVICES, STATE OF ILLINOIS. VFOAT D.O.R.S. Openers. Vol. 1, No. 1 (July 1980)-. Periodical. US. English. bm. Department of Rehabilitation Services, PO Box 1587, Springfiled IL 62705.

DOSSIERS DOCUMENTAIRES. Main/Corp Algeria. Wizarat Al-Akhbar Wa-Al-Thaqafah. French. ir. 119 rue Didouche Mourad, Algeria. LC J763. DD 354.650008. Dossiers Documentaires.

DOT EMPLOYMENT FACTS. Main/Corp United States. Dept. of Transportation, Office of the Assistant Secretary for Administration. VAT Department of Transportation Employment Facts. Began with July/Dec. 1977. 0273-3609. US. English. an. US Department of Transportation, Office of the Secretary, Personnel Systems Division, Washington DC 20590. LC HE206.3. DD 353.86. Vols. for 1981/1982-(1982/1983) distributed to depository libraries in microfiche.

DROITS ET LIBERTES. V. 1- Oct. 1978-. 0706-0408. Periodical. CN. French. bm. Free. Service de l Accueil et des Communications, Commission des Droits de la Personne, 360 rue Saint-Jacques, Montreal Quebec H2Y 1P5 Canada. DD 354.71400811.

DUKE POLICY NEWS. Vol. 9, No. 1 (Oct. 1980)-. 8755-3899. Periodical. US. English. bm. Institute of Policy Science and Public Affairs, Duke University, 4875 Duke Station, Durham NC 27706. DD 350. Policy News.

ECHO MUNICIPAL. (L'ECHO MUNICIPAL). Vol. 1, No 2 (Jan. 1981)-. 0713-8024. Periodical. CN. French. mo. Free. Municipalite de l'Anse St-Jean, 3 rue du Couvent Anse, Saint-Jean Quebec G0V 1J0 Canada. DD 352.071416. (ctrl). Journal Municipal (Anse Saint-Jean, Quebec), 0713-8032.

ECONOMIC CENSUSES : MANUFACTURING ESTABLISHMENTS AND ELECTRICITY AND GAS ESTABLISHMENTS. See Economics - Economics: Industry & Production.

ECONOMIC GROWTH & REVITALIZATION REPORT. VFOAT Economic Growth and Revitalization Report. No. 85-1 (Jan. 15, 1985)-. Periodical. US. English. sm. Tel (301)588-6380. News and advice stressing, economic development of regions, states, and localities, neighborhood revitalization, with state/local case studies. Local Economic Growth & Neighborhood Reinvestment Report.

EKONOMIKA. See Economics - Economics: Industry & Production.

ELECTION RESULTS AND STATISTICS (OKLAHOMA). Main/Corp Oklahoma. State Election Board. US. English. be. State Election Board, State Capitol, Oklahoma City OK 73105. LC JK7192. DD 324.9766053.

Public Administration

ELECTION RESULTS DATABOOK FOR CUYAHOGA COUNTY. Main/Corp Governmental Research Institute, Cleveland. VFOAT Databook, Cuyahoga County Election Results. 1972/74-. 0362-6903. US. English. $3.00. 502 Ten-Ten Euclid Building, Cleveland OH 44115. LC JS451.O39. DD 329.0237713104.

ELECTIVE AND APPOINTIVE STATE OFFICERS, STATE OF MICHIGAN. 0363-2571. US. English. Department of Management and Budget, Records and Publications Center, Lansing MI 48913. LC JK5830. DD 353.9774002.

ELECTORAL STATISTICS (GREAT BRITAIN). See Statistics.

ELECTORAL STUDIES. Vol. 1, No. 1 (Apr. 1982)-. 0261-3794. Periodical. UK. English. ty. Butterworth Scientific Limited, PO Box 63, Westbury House/Bury Street, Guildford GU2 5BH England. Ind/Abst Am. Hist. Life, Hist. Abstr., Part A, Mod. Hist. Abstr., Hist. Abst., Part B, Twent. Century Abstr. LC JF1001. DD 342.05.

ELECTRIC UTILITY INDUSTRY REVIEW. See Economics - Economics: Industry & Production.

ELECTRICAL WORLD DIRECTORY OF ELECTRIC UTILITIES IN LATIN AMERICA, BERMUDA AND THE CARIBBEAN ISLANDS. See Yearbooks, Almanacs, Directories.

ELECTRICAL WORLD INTERNATIONAL DIRECTORY OF ELECTRICITY SUPPLIERS. See Yearbooks, Almanacs, Directories.

ELEZIONE DELLA CAMERA DEI DEPUTATI. IT. Italian. ir. 11.500. Istituto Centrale di Statistica, C/C Postale N 619007, Roma Italy. LC JN5609. DD 324.9450927.

EMDAH. Hebrew. ir. $14.00. PO Box 4088, Tel-Aviv Israel. LC JQ1825.P3.

EMPIRE STATE REPORT. V. 5, No. 6- Dec. 1979-. 0363-7190. Periodical. US. English. ir. $37.50. Empire State Report Inc, 17 Lexington Avenue, New York NY 10010. Tel (212)725-3313. Ind/Abst Public Aff. Inf. Serv. Bull. LC JK3401. DD 974.7043. Empire.

EMPIRE STATE REPORT (1982). (EMPIRE STATE REPORT). VFOAT E.S.R. Magazine. Vol. 8, No. 10 (Mar. 1982)-. 0747-0711. Periodical. US. English. mo. $85.00. Empire State Report Inc, 545 Eighth Avenue/16th Floor, New York NY 10010. Tel (212)239-9797. Ed Berb Beitel. Ind/Abst Public Aff. Inf. Serv. Bull. LC JK3401. DD 974.7043. adv acc. Circ 10,500. (ctrl). Offers objective reporting on public policy events and issues regarding state, county and local government, as well as business, labor and finance in the state of New York.

EMPIRE STATE REPORT WEEKLY. Vol. 9, No. 1 (Jan. 3-9, 1983)-. 0745-8622. Periodical. US. English. ir. $25.00, or $60.00 if combined with ESR Monthly. Empire State Report Weekly, 17 Lexington Avenue, New York NY 10010. LC JK3401. DD 974.7043. Empire State Report.

EMPLOYEE TRAINING IN THE FEDERAL SERVICE. Main/Corp United States. Civil Service Commission. Bureau of Training. 0565-1441. US. English. an. Superintendent of Documents, US Government Printing Office, Washington DC 20402. LC JK719. DD 353.0015.

EMPLOYEES RETIREMENT AND JUDICIAL RETIREMENT SYSTEMS OF TEXAS, ANNUAL REPORT. See Economics - Labor.

ENAP NOUVELLES. VAT Ecole Nationale d'Administration Publique Nouvelles, Ecole Nationale d'Administration Publique du Quebec Nouvelles. Vol. 1, No. 1 (Nov. 1980)-. 0229-592X. Periodical. CN. French. mo. Free. Secretariat General Enap, 31 rue Mont-Carmel, Quebec Quebec G1R 4A6 Canada. DD 350.000711714. (ctrl).

ENCYCLOPEDIA OF GOVERNMENTAL ADVISORY ORGANIZATIONS. See Encyclopedias & General Reference Books.

END OF YEAR REPORT - NORTHWEST FEDERAL REGIONAL COUNCIL. (END OF YEAR REPORT). Main/Corp United States. Northwest Federal Regional Council. 0147-4294. US. English. an. Northwest Federal Regional Council, 1321-2nd Avenue, Seattle WA 98101.

END OF YEAR REPORT. REGIONAL PLANS ASSESSMENT. (END OF YEAR REPORT : REGIONAL PROGRAM PLANS ASSESSMENT). Main/Corp United States. Environmental Protection Agency. Office of Planning and Management. 0147-7587. US. English. an. US Environmental Protection Agency, Room 3101/401 M Street SW, Washington DC 20460. LC TD171. DD 353.008232.

ENDERECOS DOS SENHORES DEPUTADOS E GUIA TELEFONICO DA CAMARA DOS DEPUTADOS (BRAZIL). Main/Corp Brazil. Congresso Nacional. Camara dos Deputados. Diretoria Legislativa. Portuguese. ir. Centro de Documentacao d Informacao, Palacio do Congresso Nacional, 70000 Brasilia Brazil. LC JL2463.

ENQUETE ANNUELLE D'ENTREPRISE. ENERGIE, EAU, CHAUFFAGE URBAIN, MINERAIS ET MATERIAUX DIVERS, METALLURGIE. Series/Titl Tratis Fondamentaux du Systeme Industriel Francais. VFOAT Energie, Eau, Chauffage Urbain, Minerais et Materiaux Divers, Metallurgie. French. an. 29-31 Quai Voltaire, 75340 Paris Cedex 07 France. LC HD9502.F7. DD 333.790944. Enquete Annuelle d'Entreprise : Energie.

ENTRE NOUS GENS DE BERNIERES. (ENTRE NOUS GENS DE BERNIERES : BULLETIN D'INFORMATION DE LA CORPORATION MUNICIPALE DE BERNIERES). 0712-967X. Periodical. CN. French. ir. Free. Entre Nous, c/o Corporation Municipale de Bernieres, 1250 Chemin de la Coop, Bernieres Quebec G0S 1C0 Canada. DD 352.071459. (ctrl).

ENTREFILETS. Vol. 1, No. 1 (Oct. 1980)-. 0710-6211. Periodical. CN. French. mo. Gouvernement du Quebec, 600 St Amable 4E Etage, Quebec G1R 4Z1 Canada. DD 354.71008236209714.

EQUAL EMPLOYMENT OPPORTUNITY REPORT. MINORITIES AND WOMEN IN STATE AND LOCAL GOVERNMENT. 0737-7207. US. English. an. US Equal Employment Opportunity Commission, 2401 E Street NW, Washington DC 20506. LC JK2480.M5. DD 353.93104. Minorities and Women in State and Local Government, 0161-4398.

EQUAL EMPLOYMENT OPPORTUNITY STATISTICS. See Statistics.

ESSAYS IN PUBLIC AFFAIRS. Vol. 1, No. 1 (Sept. 1980)-. 0711-2645. Periodical. CN. English. $3.00 Per No. Essays in Public Affairs, School of Community and Public Affairs, Concordia University, 1455 de Maisonneuve Boulevard, Montreal Quebec H3G 1M8 Canada. DD 971.005.

ESTABLISHMENT REGISTER. Main/Corp Botswana. English. ir. LC JQ2760.A691. DD 354.6810012.

ESTADO DE SANTA CATARINA : LIVRO DE ATORIDADES. Portuguese. ir. Palacio dos Despachos, Praca XV de Novembro, 88.000 Florianopolis Brazil. LC JL2499.S12. DD 354.8164002.

ESTATISTICA DAS INSTALACOES ELECTRICAS EM PORTUGAL. See Statistics.

ESTIMATE OF THE ADDITIONAL EXPENDITURE TO BE DEFRAYED FROM REVENUE AND LOAN ACCOUNTS. See Business - Public Finance.

ESTIMATE OF THE ADDITIONAL EXPENDITURE TO BE DEFRAYED FROM REVENUE, LOAN, BANTU EDUCATION AND SOUTH-WEST AFRICA ACCOUNTS. See Business - Public Finance.

ESTIMATES COMMITTEES A, B, C, D AND E, REPORTS TO THE SENATE ON DEPARTMENTAL ESTIMATES. Main/Corp Australia. Parliament. Senate. AT. English. ir. $1.60. Commonwealth Government Printing Office, PO Box 84, Canberra Australian Capital Territory 2600 Australia. LC J905. DD 328.9401 S, 354.9400722.

ESTIMATES - COUNCIL OF THE NORTHWEST TERRITORIES. (ESTIMATES). Main/Corp Northwest Territories. Dept. of Finance. Budgets and Fiscal Planning Division. VFOAT Northwest Territories Estimates. VAT Government of the Northwest Territories. Main Estimates. 1976/77-. 0700-2858. CN. English. an. Government of Northwest Territories, Department of Information, Yellowknife Northwest Territories Canada. DD 354.71920072225. Estimates, 0700-2858.

ESTIMATES OF EXPENDITURE. SUPPLEMENTARY INFORMATION. RECONCILIATION OF HISTORICAL DATA. (ESTIMATES OF EXPENDITURE : SUPPLEMENTARY INFORMATION). Main/Corp Alberta. Treasury Dept. 1976/77-. 0713-0872. CN. English. an. Treasury Department, Legislative Building, Edmonton Alberta T5K 2B6 Canada. LC HJ13. DD 354.712300722.

ESTIMATES OF RECURRENT EXPENDITURE OF THE GOVERNMENT OF KENYA. (ESTIMATES OF RECURRENT EXPENDITURE OF THE GOVERNMENT OF KENYA FOR THE YEAR ENDING 30TH JUNE . . .). Main/Corp Kenya. VFOAT Estimates-Recurrent Expenditure. 0453-5855. KE. English. an. Government of Kenya, PO Box 30128, Nairobi Kenya. LC HJ81.3. DD 354.67620072225305.

ESTIMATES OF THE GOVERNMENT OF NIGER STATE OF NIGERIA. See Business - Public Finance.

ESTIMATES. PART III, AUDITOR GENERAL OF CANADA. CN. English (French). $6.00 Domestic, $7.20 Foreign. Canadian Government Publishing Centre, Supply and Services Canada, Ottawa Ontario K1A 0S9 Canada. LC HJ9921. DD 354.71007232.

ESTIMATES. PART III, CANADIAN INTERGOVERNMENTAL CONFERENCE SECRETARIAT. VFOAT Budget des Depenses. CN. English (French). $3.00 Domestic, $3.60 Foreign. Canadian Government Publishing Centre, Supply and Services Canada, Ottawa Ontario K1A 0S9 Canada. LC JL27. DD 354.7108.

ESTIMATES. PART III, CONSUMER AND CORPORATE AFFAIRS EXPENDITURE PLAN (CANADA). VFOAT Budget des Depenses. CN. English (French). $6.00 Domestic, $7.20 Foreign. Canadian Government Publishing Centre, Supply and Services Canada, Ottawa Ontario K1A 0S9 Canada. LC HC120.C63. DD 354.9710082042.

ESTIMATES. PART III, ECONOMIC COUNCIL OF CANADA. VFOAT Budget des Depenses. CN. English (French). $3.00 Domestic, $3.60 Foreign. Canadian Government Publishing Centre, Supply and Services Canada, Ottawa Ontario K1A 0S9 Canada. LC HC111. DD 354.710082.

ESTIMATES. PART III, IMMIGRATION APPEAL BOARD. CN. English (French). $3.00 Domestic, $3.60 Foreign. Canadian Government Publishing Centre, Supply and Services Canada, Ottawa Ontario K1A 0S9 Canada. LC JV7242. DD 354.7100817.

ESTIMATES. PART III, NATIONAL RESEARCH COUNCIL CANADA. VFOAT Budget des Depenses. CN. English (French). $12.00 Domestic, $14.40 Foreign. Canadian Government Publishing Centre, Supply and Services Canada, Ottawa Ontario K1A 0S9 Canada. LC Q180.C2. DD 354.7100855.

ESTIMATES. PART III, OFFICE OF THE CHIEF ELECTORAL OFFICER. VFOAT Budget des Depenses. 1984-85-. CN. English (French). $6.00. Canadian Government Publishing Center, Supply and Services Canada, Ottawa Ontario K1A 0S9 Canada. Estimates. Part III, Chief Electoral Officer.

ESTIMATES. PART III, PRIVY COUNCIL OFFICE. VFOAT Budget des Depenses. CN. English (French). $6.00 Domestic, $7.20 Foreign. Canadian Government Publishing Centre, Supply and Services Canada, Ottawa Ontario K1A 0S9 Canada. LC JL1. DD 354.71072.

ESTIMATES. PART III, PUBLIC SERVICE COMMISSION OF CANADA. VFOAT Budget des Depenses. CN. English (French). $9.00 Domestic, $10.80 Foreign. Canadian Government Publishing Centre, Supply and Services Canada, Ottawa Ontario K1A 0S9 Canada. LC JL105. DD 354.71006.

Public Administration

ESTIMATES. PART III, PUBLIC SERVICE STAFF RELATIONS BOARD (CANADA). VFOAT Budget des Depenses. CN. English (French). $3.00 Domestic, $3.60 Foreign. Canadian Government Publishing Centre, Supply and Services Canada, Ottawa Ontario K1A 0S9 Canada. LC HD8005.6.C22. DD 354.710017.

ESTIMATES. PART III, SUPPLY AND SERVICES CANADA. VFOAT Budget des Depenses. CN. English (French). $12.00 Domestic, $14.40 Foreign. Canadian Government Publishing Centre, Supply and Services Canada, Ottawa Ontario K1A 0S9 Canada. LC JL196. DD 354.710071.

ESTIMATES. PART III, TAX REVIEW BOARD. CN. English (French). $3.00 Domestic,, $3.60 Foreign. Canadian Government Publishing Centre, Supply and Services Canada, Ottawa Ontario K1A 0S9 Canada. LC KE5717.A72. DD 354.00724.

ESTUDIOS DEL CENTRO DE INVESTIGACION Y ADIESTRAMIENTO POLITICO ADMINISTRATIVO. No. 1 (Nov./Dec. 1979)-. Monographic Series. Spanish. ir. Centro de Investigacion y, Adiestramiento Politico Administrativo, Apartado 4224, San Jose Costa Rica. LC UNC.

ESTUDOS LEGISLATIVOS. V. 1- Jan./June 1973-. Periodical. BL. Portuguese. sa. Centro de Documentacao e Informacao Coodenacao de Publicacoes Directoria Legislativa, Palacio do Congresso Nacional, 70.000 Brazil. LC JL2454.

EUROPAEISCHE RUNDSCHAU. Yearly V. 1-. 0304-2782. Periodical. German. ir. $12.00. Europa Verlags-Ag, A-1232 Wien Altmannsdorfer Strasse 154-156, Wien Austria. Ind/Abst Foreign Lang. Index. LC JN12.

EUROPE, OUTREMER. VFOAT Outremer. No. 517- Feb. 1973-. 0223-5862. Periodical. FR. French. ir. 220.00. Societe Nouvelle des Editions France Outremer SA, 6 rue de Bassano, 75116 Paris France. Ind/Abst Foreign Lang. Index. LC JV1801. DD 301.294406.

EUROPEAN PARLIAMENT DIGEST. V. 1- 1973-. 0095-7607. US. English. Rowman and Littlefield, 81 Adams Drive, Totowa NJ 07512. LC JN32. DD 341.242.

DE EUROPISKE FLLESSKABERS PUBLIKATIONER. See Bibliographies.

EXAMINATION OF FINANCIAL STATEMENTS OF THE PENNSYLVANIA AVENUE DEVELOPMENT CORPORATION. Main/Corp United States. General Accounting Office. 0098-6798. US. English. Comptroller General of the US, 490 l'Efant Plaza SW, Washington DC 20219. LC HT177.D6. DD 353.0081809753.

EXAMINATION OF PRESIDENTIAL AND VICE PRESIDENTIAL CERTIFIED EXPENDITURES. (EXAMINATION OF FISCAL . . . PRESIDENTIAL AND VICE PRESIDENTIAL CERTIFIED EXPENDITURES). 1979-. 0272-7013. US. English. an. US General Accounting Office, Document Handling and Information Services Facility, PO Box 6015, Gaithersburg MD 20760. LC JK779. DD 353.031.

THE EXECUTIVE BIO-PICTORIAL DIRECTORY. See Yearbooks, Almanacs, Directories.

EXECUTIVE BUDGET - NEW MEXICO. VFOAT Budget in Brief. 67th Fiscal Year (1978-1979)-. US. English. an. New Mexico Department of Finance and Administration, State Budget Division, Santa Fe NM 87503. *Executive Budget in Brief.*

EXECUTIVE BUDGET POLICY ISSUE PAPERS - WISCONSIN. 1977/79-. US. English. be. State Budget Office, 1 West Wilson, Madison WI 53702. LC JK6001. DD 309.177504. *Executive Budget Policy Papers.*

EXECUTIVE CAPITAL CONSTRUCTION BUDGET - NEBRASKA. 0090-841X. US. English. Nebraska Governor/Department of Administrative Services, State Capitol Building, Lincoln NE 68509. LC JK1651.N2. DD 353.978200712.

EXECUTIVE COMPENSATION SURVEY - EDISON ELECTRIC INSTITUTE. See Economics - Labor.

EXECUTIVE MANPOWER MANAGEMENT TECHNICAL ASSISTANCE PAPER. 0093-3678. US. English. $0.65 Single Issue. Executive Manpower Management Technical Assistance Center, Washington DC 20402. LC JK723.E9. DD 353.00153.

EXECUTIVE PERSONNEL IN THE FEDERAL SERVICE. Main/Corp United States. Bureau of Executive Personnel. 1977-. 0149-502X. US. English. an. $1.15. US Civil Service Commission, Bureau of Executive Personnel, Washington DC 20402. LC JK723.E9. DD 353.001005. *Executive Personnel in the Federal Service, 0149-502X.*

EXPANSION. Periodical. MX. Spanish. wk. $134.00. Grupo Editorial Expansion, Homero 136, Mexico 5 DF. Tel 593-61-91. Ed Charles H Oppenheim. adv acc. Circ 22,500. (ctrl). A fortnightly magazine, readership executives in responsible management positions in both business and government in Mexico.

EXPENDITURES FOR STAFF DEVELOPMENT AND TRAINING ACTIVITIES. Main/Corp National Center for Social Statistics. 0095-6813. US. English. National Center for Social Statistics, Washington DC 20201. LC HV91. DD 353.0084.

EXPENSE BUDGET - CITY OF NEW YORK. Main/Corp New York (City). 0094-9957. US. English. an. $5.50. The City Record Sales Office, Municipal Building, New York NY 10007. LC HJ9013. DD 352.12097471.

EXTERNAL RESEARCH STUDY. Main/Corp United States. Dept. of State. Office of External Research. Monographic Series. US. English. US Department of State, Bureau of Intelligence and Research, Office of External Research, Washington DC 20520.

F C M FORUM. Main/Corp Federation of Canadian Municipalities. V. 1- Nov. 1976-. 0381-1352. Periodical. CN. English. bm. $13.16. Federation of Canadian Municipalities, 1318 112 Kent, Ottawa Ontario K1P 5P2 Canada. Tel (613)237-5221. Ed Sheila Keating-House. DD 352.071005. bk rev. adv acc. Circ 2,800. All subjects of concern to local governments, legislation, innovations, finance.

F-M AUTOMATION NEWSLETTER. (F/M AUTOMATION NEWSLETTER). VFOAT FM Automation Newsletter. Began in 1984. 0742-468X. Periodical. US. English. mo. $98.00. Automation Group, 9501 West Devon Street/Suite 203, PO Box 507, Rosemont IL 60018. Tel (321)823-0555. *AM/FM Chronicle, 0731-4590.*

FACT AND FIGURES ON GOVERNMENT FINANCE. See Business - Public Finance.

FACTS ABOUT SOUTH DAKOTA. Main/Corp South Dakota. State Legislative Research Council. 0094-4262. US. English. be. South Dakota Legislative Research Council, State Capitol, Pierre SD 57501. LC JK6535. DD 353.9783.

FAIRFAX COUNTY GOVERNMENT ORGANIZATION MANUAL. 1974-. 0094-3967. US. English. an. $4.25 Single Issue. Office of Research and Statistics, 4100 Chain Bridge Road, Fairfax VA 22030. LC JS3.V8. DD 352.0755291.

FAMILY ALLOWANCES. VFOAT Allocations Familiales. Began with V. for 1977. 0226-6903. CN. English (French). an. LC HD4925.5.C2. DD 354.71008482. *Report on the Administration of the Family Allowances Act for the Fiscal Year Ended March 31 . . ., 0226-692X.*

FAZENDA DO ULTRAMAR. Periodical. Portuguese. ir. 150. Joaquim de Carvalho, Rua S Francisco Xavier 49, 3 Lisboa Portugal. LC JV4263.

FCNL WASHINGTON NEWSLETTER. Main/Corp Friends Committee on National Legislation, Washington, D.C. VFOAT Washington Newsletter. 1943. Periodical. US. English. mo. $15.00. Friends Committee on National Legislation, 245 2nd Street NE, Washington DC 20002. Tel (202)547-6000. Circ 8,000. Up-to-date news and analysis of legislative actions on issues of concern to friends. *Washington Newsletter of the Friends Committee on National Legislation.*

FDA BY-LINES CEASED. VFOAT F.D.A. By-Lines. VAT Food and Drug Administration By-Lines. Began with V. 1, July 1970. Ceased with V. 12, No. 4, Oct. 1982. 0092-5225. Periodical. US. English. qt. Food and Drug Administration, 200 C Street SW, Washington DC 20024. *Interbureau By-Lines, 0565-5455.*

FDA CLINICAL EXPERIENCE ABSTRACTS. See Indexes/Abstracts.

FDA QUARTERLY ACTIVITIES REPORT. Main/Corp United States. Food and Drug Administration. Program Information and Analysis Group. VAT Food and Drug Administration Quarterly Activities Report. 0145-126X. Periodical. US. English. qt. Health Education & Welfare, 5600 Fisher Lane, Rockville MD 20857. Tel (301)443-3160. Ind/Abst Am. Stat. Index.

FEDERAL ACQUISITION REPORT. V. 1, No. 1 (Sept. 1984)-. 8755-9285. Periodical. US. English. mo. $48.00. Management Concepts Incorporated, 8111 Old Courthouse Road, Vienna VA 22180. DD 353.

FEDERAL ADVISORY COMMITTEES. (FEDERAL ADVISORY COMMITTEES . . . ANNUAL REPORT OF THE PRESIDENT, COVERING THE CALENDAR YEAR . . .). VFOAT Annual Report on Federal Advisory Committees. Began with 1st, 1972. 0270-4277. US. English. an. Superintendent of Documents, US Government Printing Office, Washington DC 20402. LC JK468.C7. DD 353.093.

FEDERAL BENEFITS FOR VETERANS AND DEPENDENTS. 0883-3370. US. English. an. Superintendent of Documents, US Government Printing Office, Washington DC 20402.

THE FEDERAL CIVIL SERVICE, HISTORY, ORGANIZATION AND ACTIVITIES. Main/Corp United States. Office of Personnel Management. Library. US. English. Superintendent of Documents, US Government Printing Office, Washington DC 20402. *Federal Civil Service, History, Organization, and Activities.*

FEDERAL CONTRACT OPPORTUNITIES. ENERGY/ENVIRONMENT CEASED. (FEDERAL CONTRACT OPPORTUNITIES, ENERGY/ENVIRONMENT). V. 1- 1979-. 0276-2862. Periodical. US. English. wk. $175.00. Business Publishers, 951 Pershing Drive, Silver Spring MD 20910.

THE FEDERAL DIRECTORY. See Yearbooks, Almanacs, Directories.

THE FEDERAL EMPLOYEE. See Economics - Labor.

FEDERAL EMPLOYEES ALMANAC. See Yearbooks, Almanacs, Directories.

FEDERAL EXECUTIVE DIRECTORY. See Yearbooks, Almanacs, Directories.

FEDERAL FAST FINDER. 0278-4580. US. English. $10.00. Washington Researchers Publishing, 2613 P Street NW, Washington DC 20017. Tel (202)333-3533. LC JK404. DD 353.00025. More than 1,000 government offices are at your fingertips in this book. It is arranged in alphabetical order by key word to make finding federal departments, agencies, boards, and commissions simple.

FEDERAL FUNDING GUIDE. Began in 1980. 0273-4435. US. English. an. $78.95. Government Information Services, 1611 North Kent Street/Suite 508, Arlington VA 22209. LC HJ275. DD 353.00725305. *Federal Funding Guide for Local Governments, 0362-4285.*

FEDERAL FUNDS FOR RESEARCH AND DEVELOPMENT. Series/Titl Surveys of Science Resources Series. Began with V. 27, Fiscal Years 1977, 1978, and 1979. 0198-8700. US. English. an. National Science Foundation, Washington DC 20550. LC Q180.U5. DD 338.973. NLM W2 A N37FE. Vols. for 1983- distributed to depository libraries in microfiche. *Federal Funds for Research, Development, and Other Scientific Activities, 0083-2359.*

FEDERAL GOVERNMENT EMPLOYMENT. VFOAT L'Emploi dans l'Administration Federale. V. 22- Jan./Mar. 1973-. 0575-8491. Periodical. CN. English. qt. $2.80. Statistics Canada, Publications Distribution, Ottawa Ontario K1A 0T6 Canada. LC JL105. DD 331.76135471.

FEDERAL GOVERNMENT EMPLOYMENT IN METROPOLITAN AREAS. Main/Corp Canada. Statistics Canada. Federal Government Section. VFOAT Emploi dans l'Administration Publique Federale dans les Regions

Public Administration

Metropolitaines. 1970-. 0527-5148. Periodical. CN. English (French, 1972-). an. Receiver General for Canada, Statistics Canada Publications, Ottawa Ontario K1A 0T6 Canada. *Federal Government Employment in Metropolitan Areas.*

THE FEDERAL INDEX. *See* Indexes/Abstracts.

FEDERAL INFORMATION PROCESSING STANDARDS PUBLICATION. VFOAT FIPS Pub. 1968-. 0083-1816. Periodical. US. English. ir. Superintendent of Documents, US Government Printing Office, Washington DC 20402. LC JK468.A8. DD 350.00018.

FEDERAL INFORMATION SOURCES & SYSTEMS. (FEDERAL INFORMATION SOURCES AND SYSTEMS). Series/Titl Congressional Sourcebook Series. Began with 1976. 0148-8724. US. English. General Accounting Office, Washington DC 20548. LC Z7165.U5, JK585. DD 016.353. NLM Z 1223.A12 F293.

FEDERAL MOTOR VEHICLE FLEET REPORT. *See* Transportation.

FEDERAL PERSONNEL GUIDE. 1979-. 0163-7665. US. English. an. $30.00. Federal Personnel Publications, PO Box 274, Washington DC 20044. Tel (703)532-1635. Ed Lee E Sharff. LC JK671. DD 353.0060202. bk rev. Circ 75,000,000. (ctrl). The most complete reference book on pay, benefits, employment, retirement, health care, insurance, policies, and many more subjects of vital importance and interest too all federal employees.

FEDERAL PERSONNEL GUIDE WEEKLY NEWS UP-DATE. 1983. US. English. ir $21.00. Federal Personnel Publications, PO Box 274, Washington DC 20044. Tel (703)532-1635. Ed Sol Gordon. Circ 4,000. (ctrl). A newsletter providing accurate, concise information of value and interest to federal government employees. Covers the Congress, OPM, courts and other major news sources.

FEDERAL PERSONNEL MANUAL. Main/Corp United States. Civil Service Commission. US. English. ir. $1512.00. Cottonwood Systems Ltd, 1901 North Moore Suite, Arlington VA 22906. Tel (703)528-3520.

FEDERAL PERSONNEL MANUAL SYSTEM. FPM SUPPLEMENT 271-1. DEVELOPMENT OF QUALIFICATION STANDARDS. VFOAT Development of Qualification Standards. Periodical. US. English. ir. US Civil Service Commission, Washington DC 20402.

FEDERAL PERSONNEL MANUAL SYSTEM. FPM SUPPLEMENT 271-2. TESTS AND OTHER APPLICANT APPRAISAL PROCEDURES. VFOAT Tests and Other Applicant Appraisal Procedures. Periodical. US. English. ir. US Civil Service Commission, Washington DC 20402.

FEDERAL PERSONNEL MANUAL SYSTEM. FPM SUPPLEMENT 296-31. PROCESSING PERSONNEL ACTIONS. VFOAT Processing Personnel Actions. Periodical. US. English. ir. Superintendent of Documents, Attn SSO US Government Printing Office, Washington DC 20402. Tel (202)783-3238.

FEDERAL PERSONNEL MANUAL SYSTEM. FPM SUPPLEMENT 330-1. EXAMINING PRACTICES. VFOAT Examining Practices. Periodical. US. English. ir. US Civil Service Commission, Washington DC 20402.

FEDERAL PERSONNEL MANUAL SYSTEM. FPM SUPPLEMENT 512-1. JOB GRADING SYSTEM FOR TRADES AND LABOR OCCUPATIONS. VFOAT Job Grading System for Trades and Labor Occupations. Periodical. US. English. ir. Superintendent of Documents, Attn SSO US Government Printing Office, Washington DC 20402. Tel (202)783-3238.

FEDERAL PERSONNEL MANUAL SYSTEM. FPM SUPPLEMENT 711-1. LABOR-MANAGEMENT RELATIONS PROGRAMS PROVISIONS AND TECHNICAL GUIDE. VFOAT Labor-Management Relations Programs Provisions and Technical Guide. US. English. ir. US Civil Service Commission, Washington DC 20402.

FEDERAL PERSONNEL MANUAL SYSTEM. FPM SUPPLEMENT 731-1. DETERMINING SUITABILITY FOR FEDERAL EMPLOYMENT. VFOAT Determining Suitability for Federal Employment Labor. Periodical. US. English. ir. US Civil Service Commission, Washington DC 20402.

FEDERAL PERSONNEL MANUAL SYSTEM. FPM SUPPLEMENT 752-1. ADVERSE ACTIONS BY AGENCIES. VFOAT Adverse Actions by Agencies. Periodical. US. English. ir. US Civil Service Commission, Washington DC 20402.

FEDERAL PERSONNEL MANUAL SYSTEM. FPM SUPPLEMENT 990-3. NATIONAL EMERGENCY STANDBY REGULATIONS (PERSONNEL AND MANPOWER). (FEDERAL PERSONNEL MANUAL SYSTEM. FPM SUPPLEMENT 990-3. NATIONAL EMERGENCY STANDBY REGULATIONS PERSONNEL AND EMERGENCY STANDBY REGULATIONS (PERSONNEL AND MANPOWER)). VFOAT National Emergency Standby Regulations (Personnel and Manpower). Periodical. US. English. ir. US Civil Service Commission, Washington DC 20402.

FEDERAL PROCUREMENT REGULATIONS. Periodical. US. English. ir US General Services Administration, Washington DC 20402.

FEDERAL PRODUCTIVITY MEASUREMENT. 0278-0488. US. English. an. O P M Office of Productivity Programs, Measurement and Analysis Division, 1900 E Street Northwest, Washington DC 20145. LC JK404. DD 353.0014705. *Measuring Federal Productivity, 0272-460X.*

FEDERAL REAL AND PERSONAL PROPERTY INVENTORY REPORT (CIVILIAN AND MILITARY). Main/Corp United States. Congress. House. Committee on Government Operation. 1st- 1955-. 0498-9791. Periodical. US. English. ir. Superintendent of Documents, US Government Printing Office, Washington DC 20402. LC JK1661. DD 353.

FEDERAL RECREATION FEE REPORT. *See* Recreation, Leisure.

FEDERAL REGIONAL EXECUTIVE DIRECTORY. *See* Yearbooks, Almanacs, Directories.

FEDERAL REGISTER. *See* Law.

FEDERAL REGULATORY DIRECTORY. *See* Yearbooks, Almanacs, Directories.

FEDERAL SCIENCE EXPENDITURES AND PERSONNEL. Main/Corp Canada. Ministry of State, Science and Technology. 1977/78/1979/80-. 0226-3726. CN. English. Ministry of State Science and Technology, 270 Albert Street, Ottawa Ontario K1A 1A1 Canada. DD 354.7100819. *Federal Science Expenditures and Manpower, 0226-3718.*

FEDERAL STAFF DIRECTORY. *See* Yearbooks, Almanacs, Directories.

FEDERAL TAXES ADMINISTRATION REPORT. Main/Corp Pakistan. Central Board of Revenue. PK. English. ir. Government of Pakistan/Central Board of Revenue, Karachi 1 5 B Pakistan. DD 354.549100724.

FEDERAL TIMES. Began in 1965. 0014-9233. Periodical. US. English. wk. Army Times Publications Company, Springfield VA 22159. Tel (703)750-2000.

FEDERAL YELLOW BOOK. VFOAT Washington Monitor's Federal Yellow Book. Began in 1976. 0145-6202. US. English. bm. $271.00. The Washington Monitor, 1301 Pennsylvania Avenue NW/Suite 1000, Washington DC 20004. Tel (202)347-7757. Ed Betsy Cook. LC JK6. DD 353.00025. NLM JK 6 F293.

FEDERAL YELLOW BOOK (LIMITED ED.). (FEDERAL YELLOW BOOK). VFOAT Washington Monitor's Federal Yellow Book. Began with March 1983 issue. US. English. 1301 Pennsylvania Avenue NW, Washington DC 20004. NLM JK 6 F293.

THE FEDERALIST. (THE FEDERALIST : NEWSLETTER OF THE SOCIETY FOR HISTORY IN THE FEDERAL GOVERNMENT). V. 1, No. 1 (Summer 1980)-. 0736-8151. Periodical. US. English. qt. $12.00 Membership. Society for History in the Federal Government, Box 14139, Ben Franklin Sta, Washington DC 20044.

FEDERATION REVIEW. Vol. 8, No. 2 (Mar./Apr. 1985)-. 0882-5793. Periodical. US. English. bm. National Federation of State Humanities Councils, 12 South 16th Street/Suite 527, Minneapolis MN 55402. DD 351. *Federation Reports, 0276-1491.*

FELDVERSUCHSWESEN DER STAATLICHEN LANDWIRTSCHAFTSVERWALTUNG BADEN-WURTTEMBERG. ERGEBNISSE, BERICHTE. VFOAT Beitrage zur Produktionstechnischen Beratung auf dem Gebiet der Pflanzlichen Erzeugung. Periodical. German. ir.

FEMA NEWSLETTER. VFOAT F.E.M.A. Newsletter. VAT Federal Emergency Management Agency Newsletter. March/April 1984-. 0748-2779. Periodical. US. English. bm. FEMA, PO Box 8181, Washington DC 20024. LC HV555.U6. DD 350.7540973. *Newsletter (United States. Federal Emergency Management Agency).*

FEUILLET D'INFORMATION DE LA VILLE DE SAINT-LEONARD. (LE FEUILLET D'INFORMATION DE LA VILLE DE SAINT-LEONARD). Main/Corp Saint Leonard (Le-de-Montreal, Quebec). Vol. 1, No. 1 (1st Quarterly 1980)-. 0711-396X. Periodical. CN. French. qt. Free. La Ville, 8400 Boulevard Lacordaire, Saint-Leonard Quebec H1R 3B1 Canada. DD 352.071428. (ctrl)

FEUILLETON DE L'ASSEMBLEE NATIONALE DU QUEBEC *CEASED.* (FEUILLETON DE L'ASSEMBLEE NATIONALE). Main/Corp Quebec (Province). National Assembly. VFOAT Agenda Paper of the National Assembly. VAT Agenda Paper - National Assembly of Quebec, Feuilleton - Assemblee Nationale du Quebec. Feb. 25, 1969-Mar. 13, 1984. 0709-8715. Periodical. CN. text in English and French in parallel columns. National Assembly, Parliament Buildings, Quebec G1A 1A7 Canada. *Feuilleton = Agenda, 0709-8723.*

FINANCES OF EMPLOYEE-RETIREMENT SYSTEMS OF STATE AND LOCAL GOVERNMENTS. *See* Economics - Labor.

FINANCIAL DISCLOSURE REPORTS OF MEMBERS OF THE U.S. HOUSE OF REPRESENTATIVES. (FINANCIAL DISCLOSURE REPORTS OF MEMBERS OF THE U.S. HOUSE OF REPRESENTATIVES OF THE . . . CONGRESS FROM . . . SUBMITTED TO THE CLERK OF THE HOUSE PURSUANT TO 2 U.S.C. SECTION 703(A)). Main/Corp United States. Congress. House. 0272-6211. US. English. an. Superintendent of Documents, Crop Printing Office, Washington DC 20402. LC JK1308. DD 328.730766. Vols. for (1981-) distributed to some depository libraries in microfiche.

FINANCIAL DISCLOSURES BY MEMBERS OF CONGRESS. Main/Corp Congressional Quarterly, Inc. 0098-7352. US. English. Congressional Quarterly Inc, 1414 22nd Street Northwest, Washington DC 20037. LC JK1140. DD 328.73076.

FINANCIAL PROCEDURES BULLETIN. 2-. 0709-4981. Monographic Series. CN. English. $1., Per Vol. Publications Centre, 880 Bay Street/5th Floor, Toronto Ontario M7A 1N8 Canada. DD 352.109713. *Finance Bulletin, 0709-4973.*

FINANCIAL STATISTICS OF PUBLIC UTILITIES. ELECTRIC AND GAS COMPANIES. *See* Statistics.

FINANCIAL STATISTICS OF SELECTED ELECTRIC UTILITIES. *See* Statistics.

FINANCIAL STATISTICS OF TELEPHONE AND WATER COMPANIES. *See* Statistics.

FINANCIAL STATISTICS OF THE MAJOR PRIVATELY OWNED UTILITIES IN NEW YORK STATE. *See* Statistics.

FINNISH STATE COMPUTER CENTRE REPORT ON ACTIVITY. Main/Corp Finland. Valtion Tietokonekeskus. English. ir. LC JN6709.5.A8. DD 354.4710002854.

THE FISCAL LETTER. *See* Business - Public Finance.

FISHERIES DEVELOPMENT ACT, ANNUAL REPORT. *See* Fish Culture and Fisheries.

FLORIDA ADMINISTRATIVE WEEKLY. Vol. 1- Jan. 10, 1975-. 0098-874X. US. English. wk. $154.35. Florida Department State Bureau Administration Code, Room 1802 The Capitol, Tallahassee FL 32301. Tel (904)488-8427. Ed Liz Cloud. LC KFF36. DD 348.75901. Circ 2,000. Contains

Public Administration

information on proposed rule changes, a large bid section concerning public meetings, workshops, and public hearings.

FLORIDA GOVERNMENT SERIES. No. 1-1963-. 0071-5972. Monographic Series. US. English. ir. Florida State University, Institute of Governmental Research, Tallahassee FL 32303.

FLORIDA GOVERNOR . . . BIENNIAL BUDGET RECOMMENDATION. AMENDMENT. Main/Corp Florida. Office of the Governor. VFOAT Biennial Budget Recommendation. US. English. be. Office of the Governor, The Capitol, Tallahassee FL 32301. LC HJ2053.F6. DD 353.9759007225605.

FLORIDA MUNICIPAL RECORD. 1928. 0015-4164. Periodical. US. English. mo. $10.00. Florida League of Cities Inc, 201 West Park Street, PO Box 1757, Tallahassee FL 32302. Tel (904)222-9684. Ed Terri J Ganson. LC JS39. adv acc. Circ 4,500. Subjects of interest to local government officials in the state of Florida.

FLORIDA SENATE. (THE FLORIDA SENATE). Main/Corp Florida. Legislature. Senate. 0093-4089. US. English. be. Florida Senate, State Capitol Building, Publishers Office, Tallahassee FL 32304. Tel (904)487-5270. Ed Joe Brown. LC JK4476. DD 328.759071. Circ 75,000. This is a booklet about the Florida Senate, its organization, function and members.

FLORIDA'S GOVERNMENT. 1939-. US. English. ir. Florida Department of State Elections/ Room 1801, Tallahassee FL 32301. LC JK4416.

FLOW OF FUNDS SUMMARY STATISTICS. See Statistics.

FOCUS ON GOVERNMENTAL AFFAIRS. (FOCUS ON GOVERNMENTAL AFFAIRS : A PUBLICATION OF THE OFFICE FOR GOVERNMENTAL AFFAIRS, LUTHERAN COUNCIL IN THE USA). VFOAT Focus. Began with: Vol. 10 in 1976. 0740-3267. Periodical. US. English. mo. $6.00. Lutheran Council in the USA, 122 C Street NW/Suite 300, Washington DC 20001. Tel (202)783-7501. Focus on Public Affairs.

LA FONCTION PUBLIQUE DE L'ETAT EN . . . . SECRETARIAT D ETAT. 1984-. FR. French. an. 110. 29-31 Quai Voltaire, 75340 Paris France. Fonction Publique En . . . .

FOOD AND DRUG ADMINISTRATION PUBLIC ADVISORY COMMITTEES : AUTHORITY, STRUCTURE, FUNCTIONS, MEMBERS. VFOAT Public Advisory Committees. English. ir.

FOOTNOTE. 0533-1250. US. English. an. Department of Health Education and Welfare, Audit Agency, Office of the Assistant Secretary Comptroller, 330 Independence Avenue SW, Washington DC 20201.

FORMACION POLITICA PARA LA DEMOCRACIA. 1 (Sept. 6, 1980)-. Periodical. Spanish. wk. Editorial Redaccion S A, Bartolome Mitre 2 Piso, Buenos Aires Argentina. LC JL2001. DD 982.06405.

FORSCHUNGSFORDERUNGEN UND FORSCHUNGSAUFTRAGE. Main/Corp Austria. Bundesministerium fur Wissenschaft und Forschung. 1975-. German. ir. Bundesministerium for Wissenschaft und Forschung, Minoritenplatz 5, Wien Austria. Tel (0222)66 20-0. LC Q180.A85. Circ 1,000. Research funds and contracts contracted by federal ministry to institutions or experts outside the government.

FORTFUHRUNGSNACHWEIS ZUR BEREINIGTEN SAMMLUNG DER VERWALTUNGSVORSCHRIFTEN DES BAYERISCHEN STAATSMINISTERIUMS DES INNERN FUR DIE ZEIT VOM . . . . German. an. Bayer Staatsministerium des Innern, Odeonsplatz 3, Munchen 22 West Germany.

FORUM FCM. (FORUM F C M). Main/Corp Federation of Canadian Municipalities. V. 1, No. 3- Jan. 1977-. 0704-7177. Periodical. CN. English. mo. $10.00. Federation Canadienne des Municipalites, 600-220 Ouest rue Laurier, Ottawa Ontario K1P 5Z9 Canada. DD 352.071. Circulating, 0702-8237; F C M Forum, 0381-1360.

FPC NEWS. Main/Corp United States. Federal Power Commission. VAT Federal Power Commission News. V. 1- Jan. 5, 1968-. 0014-6080. Periodical. US. English. wk. US Government Printing Office, Superintendent of Documents, Washington DC 20402.

FRANCE MODERNE. Periodical. French. ir. 25.00. Federation Nationale des Republicains Independants, 195 Bd Saint-Germain (7E), Paris France. LC JN3007.F45. DD 320.944083.

FREIE ARGUMENTE. Periodical. German. ir. Freiheitliches Bildungswerk, Kolingasse 10/26, 1090 Wien Austria. LC JN2031.F73. DD 324.243603.

FROM THE STATE CAPITALS. FEDERAL ACTION AFFECTING THE STATES. VFOAT Federal Action Affecting the States. 0734-1202. Periodical. US. English. ir. $170.00. Wakeman/Walworth Inc, PO Box 1939, New Haven CT 06509. Tel (203)562-8518. Highlights developments in Washington that impact on states, from block grants and job programs to social security and welfare legislation, also environmental protection, unemployment and state. From the State Capitals. Federal Action.

FROM THE STATE CAPITALS. GENERAL TRENDS. Vol. 37, No. 43 (Jan. 16, 1984)-. 0741-3475. Periodical. US. English. wk. Wakeman/Walworth Inc, Box 1939, New Haven Ct 06509. From the State Capitals. General Bulletin, 0016-1691.

FROM THE STATE CAPITALS. PARKING REGULATIONS. VFOAT Parking Regulations. Jan. 1984-. 0741-3513. Periodical. US. English. wk. Wakeman/Walworth Inc, Box 1939, New Haven CT 06509. From the State Capitals. Off-Street Parking (New Haven, Conn.), 0734-161X.

FROM THE STATE CAPITALS. PUBLIC UTILITIES. VFOAT Public Utilities. 0016-1888. Periodical. US. English. wk. $175.00. Wakeman/Walworth Inc, PO Box 1939, New Haven CT 06509. Tel (203)562-8518.

FROM THE STATE CAPITALS. UNEMPLOYMENT COMPENSATION. See Economics - Labor.

FROM THE STATE CAPITALS. WORKER'S COMPENSATION. See Economics - Labor.

FUKUMU SHOROPPO. Main/Corp Japan. Began with 1960 issue. Japanese. ir.

FUNDING REPORT. Main/Corp New York State Council on the Arts. 1980-1981-. US. English. an. New York State Council on the Arts, 80 Centre Street, New York NY 10013. LC N6530.N7. DD 353.974700854. Three Year Funding Report.

FYLKESTINGSVALGET. See Statistics.

GARDEN STATE REPORT. VFOAT G.S.R. 8756-6605. Periodical. US. English. mo. Garden State Report, 204 Eagle Rock Avenue, Roseland NJ 07068. Tel (201)228-7088. adv acc. Circ 10,500. (ctrl). Offers objective reporting on public policy events and issues regarding state, county and local governments, as well as business, labor and finance in the state of New Jersey.

GAS UTILITIES; TRANSPORT AND DISTRIBUTION SYSTEMS. VFOAT Services du Gaz. 1959-. 0527-5318. CN. English (text in French). an. Receiver General for Canada, Statistics Canada/Publications, Ottawa Ontario K1A 0T6 Canada. LC HD9581.C3.

GASTOS INCURRIDOS Y PUESTOS AUTORIZADOS EN EL SISTEMA DE JUSTICIA CRIMINAL DE PUERTO RICO. Main/Corp Puerto Rico. Dept. of Justice. 1972/73-. Spanish. ir. LC HV7328. DD 353.972955.

GAZETTE DE QUEBEC. (LA GAZETTE DE QUEBEC : JOURNAL MUNICIPAL DE LA VILLE DE QUEBEC). V. 1, No. 1, (Dec. 1980)-. 0710-1686. Periodical. CN. French. ir. Free. La Ville de Quebec, Service des Communications, 2 rue des Jardins, Quebec Quebec G1R 4S9 Canada. DD 352.071447105.

GEMA D.P.R.D. TINGKAT I JAWA TENGAH. Main/Corp Jawa Tengah, Indonesia. Dewan Perwakilan Rakyat Daeran. VAT Gema Dewan Perwakilan Rakyat Daerah Tingkat Pertama Jawa Tengah. Periodical. Indonesian. ir. D P R D Tingkat I Jawa Tengah, Jl Letjen Soeprapto No 43, Semarang Indonesia. LC JS7191.A1.

GEMEINDESCHLUSSELVERZEICHNIS FUR BAYERN. Main/Corp Bayerisches Statistisches Landesamt. English. ir. 8 Munchen 2 Neuhauser Str 51, Muchen West Germany. LC JS5471.B4.

GENERAL ACCOUNTING OFFICE POLICY AND PROCEDURES MANUAL FOR GUIDANCE OF FEDERAL AGENCIES. Main/Corp United States. General Accounting Office. Periodical. US. English. mo. US Government Printing Office, Superintendent of Documents, Washington DC 20402. Tel (202)783-3238.

THE GENERAL ASSEMBLY OF GEORGIA. Main/Corp Georgia. Dept. of Archives and History. 0098-6534. US. English. Department of Archives and History, Atlanta GA 30334. LC JK4330. DD 328.758083.

GENERAL ELECTION, OFFICIAL VOTE FOR COUNTY OFFICERS. Main/ Corp Maine. Dept. of State. US. English. LC JS3.M3 D46A. DD 324.9741043.

GENERAL ELECTION. REPORT OF THE CHIEF ELECTORAL OFFICER. Main/Corp Canada. Chief Electoral Office. Periodical. CN. English (French). ir.

GENERAL REPORT OF THE LEGISLATIVE COUNCIL TO THE LEGISLATURE. Main/Corp Wisconsin. Legislative Council. 0362-9686. US. English. Legislative Council, North State Capitol/Room 147, Madison WI 53702. LC JK6074. DD 328.775076. Report of the Wisconsin Legislative Council.

GEOGRAPHIC INDEX TO PUBLIC ADMINISTRATION SERIES. See Indexes/Abstracts.

GEORGIA OFFICIAL AND STATISTICAL REGISTER. See Statistics.

GIKAI SHIRYO. Japanese. ir. Okinawa Kengikai Jimukyoku, 2-14 Senzaki 1, Naha Japan. LC JQ1699.O54.

GLIEDERUNG DES LANDTAGS RHEINLAND-PFALZ . . . WAHLPERIODE. Main/Corp Rheinland-Palatinate (Germany). Landtag. German. ir. Landtag Rheinland-Pfalz, Deutschhausplatz 12 Postfach 3040, 6500 Mainz West Germany.

GOBIERNOS DEPARTAMENTALES : EJECUCION PRESUPUESTAL. See Business - Public Finance.

GOVERNING BODIES OF FEDERALLY RECOGNIZED INDIAN GROUPS, EXCLUDING ALASKA. 0270-7233. US. English. Superintendent of Documents, US Government Printing Office, Washington DC 20402. LC E98.T77. DD 353.008484. Governing Bodies of Indian Groups Under Federal Supervision.

GOVERNING NORTH DAKOTA. 0271-3497. US. English. Bureau of Governmental Affairs, University of North Dakota, Grand Forks ND 58201. Ed Boyd L Wright. LC JK6401. DD 320.4784.

GOVERNMENT ACTIVITIES IN THE NORTH. (GOVERNMENT ACTIVITIES IN THE NORTH : REPORT AND PLANS). 1953-. 0575-7681. Periodical. CN. English. an. Canada Advisory Commitee on Northern Development, Department of Indian Affairs, Publishing Division, Ottawa Ontario K1A 0H4 Canada. LC HC111. DD 354. Annual Northern Expenditure Plan, 0382-2486.

GOVERNMENT AFFAIRS REPORT. 0146-8405. Periodical. US. English. ir. $20.00. National Parking Association, 1112 16th Street NW/ Suite 2000, Washington DC 20036.

GOVERNMENT ANNUAL REPORT OF THE REPUBLIC OF VENDA. Main/Corp Venda (South Africa). English. an. 5.00. Department of Information & Broadcasting, Private Bag X2309, Sibasa Venda South Africa.

THE GOVERNMENT CONTRACTOR. V. 1- Jan. 9, 1959-. 0017-2596. US. English. bw. $480.00. Federal Publishing Inc, 1120 20th Street NW, Washington DC 20036. Tel (202)337-7000. Ed Marvin I Friedman. DD 351.711. (ctrl). Analysis of developments in government contracting.

GOVERNMENT CONTRACTS CITATOR. 1958-. 0434-2593. Periodical. US. English. qt. $440.00. Federal Pubs, 1120 20th Street NW, Washington DC 20036. Tel (202)337-7000.

Public Administration

GOVERNMENT CONTRACTS DIRECTORY. See Yearbooks, Almanacs, Directories.

GOVERNMENT DATA SYSTEMS. V. 1- Nov./Dec. 1970-. 0046-6212. Periodical. US. English. bm. $25.00. Media Horizons Inc, 50 West 23rd Street, New York NY 10010. Tel (212)645-1000. Ed Stephen Adler. Ind/Abst Predicasts, Comput. Control Abstr., Electr. Electron. Abstr., Sci. Abstr. Sect. A. Phys. Abstr., Phys. Abstr., Funk Scott Index Corp. Ind., Comput. Rev. LC JK468.A8. DD 350.000285. CODEN GVDSB. bk rev. adv acc. Circ 24,000. (ctrl). The authoritative voice of ADP, communications, IRM, training and office automation managers.

GOVERNMENT DIRECTORY FOR BRITISH COLUMBIA WITH SELECTED FEDERAL CONTACTS. See Yearbooks, Almanacs, Directories.

GOVERNMENT EMPLOYEE RELATIONS REPORT. V. 1- (No. 1-). 0017-260X. Periodical. US. English. $448.00. Bureau of National Affairs, 9435 Key West Avenue, Rockville MD 20850. Tel (301)258-1033. LC HD8008.A1. DD 353.001705.

GOVERNMENT EXECUTIVE. V. 1- March 1969-. 0017-2626. Periodical. US. English. ir. $49.00. Government Executive, 1725 K Street/Suite 512, Washington DC 20006. Tel (202)785-2593. Ed John F Judge. Ind/Abst Manage. Contents. LC JK1. DD 353. CODEN GVEXAW. bk rev. adv acc. Circ 76,000. (ctrl). Government marketing, advertising and sales.

GOVERNMENT GAZETTE. See Political Science.

GOVERNMENT GAZETTE OF THE STATE OF NEW SOUTH WALES. Main/Corp New South Wales. No. 1- 1832-. AT. English. wk. $132.81. Government Printing Office, PO Box 75 Ultimo New South Wales, Pyrmont New South Wales 2009 Australia. LC J8. DD 354.9440005.

THE GOVERNMENT MANAGER. No. 1- Jan. 5, 1973-. 0148-7949. Periodical. US. English. ir. $96.00. Bureau of National Affairs Inc, 1231 25th Street NW, Washington DC 20037. Tel (301)258-1033.

GOVERNMENT OF CANADA PUBLICATIONS. QUARTERLY CATALOGUE. (GOVERNMENT OF CANADA PUBLICATIONS). VFOAT Publications du Gouvernement du Canada. V. 27- Jan./Mar. 1979-. 0709-0412. Periodical. CN. English (French). qt. 25.20. Receiver General for Canada, Supply & Services, Ottawa Ontario K1A 0S9 Canada. Tel (819)997-2560. Ind/Abst Popul. Index. DD 015.71. Canadian Government Publications.

THE GOVERNMENT OF NEW SOUTH WALES DIRECTORY OF ADMINISTRATION AND SERVICES. See Yearbooks, Almanacs, Directories.

GOVERNMENT PAPER SPECIFICATION STANDARDS. Main/Corp United States. Congress. Joint Committee on Printing. VFOAT Paper Specification Standards. 1959-. 0364-1260. US. English. ir. Superintendent of Documents, Attention SSO, Government Printing Office, Washington DC 20402. Tel (202)783-3238.

GOVERNMENT PRIME CONTRACTS MONTHLY. VFOAT GDP's Government Prime Contracts Monthly. VAT Government Data Publications Government Prime Contracts Monthly. Periodical. US. English. mo. $72.00. Government Data Publications', 1120 Connecticut Avenue NW, Washington DC 20036. Tel (718)627-0819. Ed Siepfried Lobel. Lists government contracts. Each listing is complete and contains name and address of awardee, agency, description of material, quantity, contract number and amount.

GOVERNMENT PRODUCT NEWS. V. 13, No. 3- Mar. 1974-. 0017-2642. Periodical. US. English. mo. $40.00. Penton/IPC, PO Box 95759, Cleveland OH 44101. Tel (216)696-7000. Ed Leslie Drahos. Ind/Abst Trade Ind. Index. bk rev. adv acc. Circ 85,079. (ctrl). Detailed information about products, services and systems of interest to government officials who plan, specify or buy for local, state and federal governments. Government Product News and Purchasing Digest.

GOVERNMENT PROGRAMS AND PROJECTS DIRECTORY. See Yearbooks, Almanacs, Directories.

GOVERNMENT PUBLICATIONS GUIDE. See Bibliographies.

GOVERNMENT PUBLICATIONS REVIEW (NEW YORK, N.Y. : 1982). See Bibliographies.

GOVERNMENT R & D REPORT. See Science (General).

GOVERNMENT REFERENCE BOOKS. See Bibliographies.

GOVERNMENT RELATIONS NOTE. See Medicine.

GOVERNMENT REPORTS : INDEXES OF CHAIRMEN AND SUBJECTS. See Indexes/Abstracts.

GOVERNMENT TENDER REPORT. 0738-3096. US. English. da. $325.00. ATA, 1616 P Street NW, Washington DC 20036.

GOVERNMENT TRAINING NEWS. 0161-1623. Periodical. US. English. mo. Business Publisher Inc, 951 Pershing Drive, Silver Springs MD 20910. Tel (301)587-6300. Ed Leonard Eiserer. A report on training trends and opportunities, cost and effectiveness studies, and over all personnel training, policies at the federal, state and local government levels.

GOVERNMENT YEARBOOK. See Yearbooks, Almanacs, Directories.

GOVERNMENTAL AFFAIRS NEWSLETTER. Main/Corp University of Missouri—Columbia. Governmental Affairs Program. 0148-4664. Periodical. US. English. mo. Governmental Affairs Program, 306 Watson Place, Columbia MO 65201. LC JK5401. DD 320.977804.

GOVERNMENTAL FLEET MANAGEMENT. V. 1- Sept./Oct. 1979-. 0193-4775. Periodical. US. English. bm. $14.00 Domestic, $22.50 Foreign. Fleet Technology Inc, PO Box 11130, Antioch Station, Kansas City MO 64119.

GOVERNMENTAL GUIDE. FLORIDA EDITION. VFOAT Governmental Guides. 0735-7753. US. English. an. Florida Governmental Guide, 0735-7761.

GOVERNMENTAL GUIDE. TENNESSEE EDITION. VFOAT Tennessee Governmental Guide. US. English. an. Ed C H Boone. LC JK5201.

GOVERNMENTAL NEWS. Vol. No. 1, Issue No. 1 (July 1949)-. 0738-5498. Periodical. US. English. qt. George F Breitbach and Sons, 952 North 12th Street, Milwaukee WI 53233. LC JS39. DD 352.073.

GOVERNOR'S ANNUAL WORK FORCE REPORT. Main/Corp Pennsylvania. Bureau of Personnel. Work Force Analysis Division. US. English. an. Work Force Analysis Division, Bureau of Personnel Governor's Office of Budget and Administration, Room 513 Finance Building, Harrisburg PA 17120. LC JK3655. DD 353.974800605.

GOVERNORS' BULLETIN. 1935. Periodical. US. English. wk. $25.00. National Governors Association, c/o Paula Simmons, 444 North Capitol, Washington DC 20001. Tel (202)624-5300. Ed Bernard S Chabel. Circ 3,500. (ctrl). Reports on the week's major developments in Washington D.C. and the states. Contains analytical articles and feature stories on policy initiatives undertaken by states and on emerging federal and state issues.

GOVERNOR'S COORDINATION AND SPECIAL SERVICES PLAN FOR THE PERIOD OF . . . . Main/Corp Illinois. Governor. US. English. an. Illinois Department of Commerce & Community Affairs, Division of Job Training Program, 320 West Washington, Springfield IL 62706. LC HD5715.3.I3. DD 353.977300833.

THE GOVERNOR'S LEGISLATIVE MESSAGE AND BUDGET REPORT. Main/Corp Kansas. Governor. US. English. an. Topeka Kansas Office of the Governor, Topeka KS 66603. LC J87. DD 353.97810352.

GOVERNOR'S RECOMMENDED BUDGET . . . : SUBMITTED TO THE . . . LEGISLATIVE ASSEMBLY. Main/Corp Oregon. Executive Dept. 1981-1983-. US. English. be. Office of the Governor, State Capitol, Salem OR 97310. Governor's Budget Recommendations.

GRA REPORTER. VAT Governmental Research Association Reporter. Began with: Vol. 1 (Jan./Feb. 1949). Periodical. US. English. qt. LC JS302.

THE GRANTSEEKER. VFOAT Grant Seeker. Began with: Oct. 1981. Periodical. US. English. bw. $137.00. Revenue Sharing Advisory Service, 1725 K Street NW Suite 200, Washington DC 20006. Tel (202)872-1766. Ed Kathy Dunten. Circ 729. Newsletter covering recent developments in federal government that would be of interest to state and local goverment and people looking for grants.

GREATER LONDON COUNCIL MINUTES. UK. English. Greater London Council, The County Hall, London S E 1 England. LC JS16. DD 328.42101. Meeting.

GREATER LOS ANGELES PUBLIC SERVICE GUIDE. VFOAT Public Service Guide to Los Angeles City, County, State & Federal Offices. 1972/73-. Periodical. US. English. ir. Public SCS Publications, 1523 West 8th Street, Los Angeles CA 90017. Tel (213)484-1088. Ed Barbara Rosien. bk rev. adv acc. Complete listings of government functions & services in Los Angeles, CA; Sacramento, San Francisco & partial Washington, DC.

GREENHILL JOURNAL OF ADMINISTRATION. V. 1- April/June 1974-. 0379-8658. Periodical. GH. English. qt. $16.00. Ghana Institute of Management & Public Administration, PO Box 50, Greenhill Achimota Ghana. LC JA26. DD 350.0005. Greenhill Bulletin.

GSA SUPPLY CATALOG (UNITED STATES. GENERAL SERVICES ADMINISTRATION : 1983). (GSA SUPPLY CATALOG). VFOAT G.S.A. Supply Catalog. VAT General Services Administration Supply Catalog. Jan. 1983-. US. English. ty. Superintendent of Documents, US Government Printing Office, Washington DC 20402. GSA Supply Catalog. Furniture, GSA Supply Catalog. Industrial Products; GSA Supply Catalog. Office Products; GSA Supply Catalog. Tools.

GUIA DEL TERCER MUNDO. 1976-. Spanish. ir. Technical Press, Paraguay 2028 20.-14, Buenos Aires Argentina. LC JF60.

GUIA RELACIONES INSTITUCIONALES DEL ESTADO ARGENTINO. VFOAT Guia Relaciones Institucionales del Estado. 1982-. Spanish. an. Graform SA Editora, Av Cordoba 669, 120 PA 1054 Argentina. LC JL2021. DD 354.8204025.

GUIDE MUNICIPAL - VILLE DE BLACK-LAKE. (GUIDE MUNICIPAL). Main/Corp Black-Lake (Quebec). Vol. 1, No. 1 (Jan. 1982)-. 0713-6447. CN. French. an. Guide Municipal, c/o Ville de Black-Lake, 350 rue Saint Hubert, CP 310, Black-Lake Quebec G0N 1A0 Canada. DD 352.0714575.

GUIDE PRATIQUE DE L'USAGER DES PREFECTURES. FR. French. ir. Centre de Diffusion et d'Informations, 10 Boulevard Bonne Nouvelle, Paris France. DD 352.044.

GUIDE. PUBLIC SERVICES, ORGANISATION OF PUBLIC AND PRIVATE LAW, BANKS, DIPLOMATIC CORPS, AIR COMPANIES, CONCISE GUIDE TO THESSALONIKI. English. ir. .500 Each. Horizon, Public Relations Organization, 50A Nikis Str, Athens Greece 119. LC JN5060.A1. DD 354.495002.

GUIDE TO FEDERAL CAREER LITERATURE. See Occupations and Careers.

GUIDE TO FEDERAL FUNDING FOR EDUCATION. See Education (General).

GUIDE TO FEDERAL MINORITY ENTERPRISE AND RELATED ASSISTANCE PROGRAMS. 1982-. 0739-6066. US. English. be. Minority Business Development Agency, US Department of Commerce, Washington DC 20006. LC HD2346.U5. DD 353.0082048. Guide to Federal Assistance Programs for Minority Business Development, 0277-5972.

GUIDE TO FEDERAL PROCUREMENT. 0276-9891. US. English. an. Northeast-Midwest Institute Publications Office, Box 37209, Washington DC 20013. LC JK1673. DD 353.00712024658.

GUIDE TO GOVERNMENT IN HAWAII. 1st Ed. (1961)-. 0072-8454. US. English. ir. Legislative Reference Bureau, State Capitol, Honolulu HI 96813. Tel (808)548-7853. LC JQ6121. DD 353.9. Circ 2,000. Organization, description of departments and

Public Administration

agencies of the state, county and federal governments in Hawaii. *Directory, Agencies and Officers, Territory of Hawaii.*

GUIDE TO NEBRASKA STATE AGENCIES. 0091-0716. US. English. Nebraska Publications Clearinghouse, 1420 P Street NE, Lincoln NE 68508. LC JK6630. DD 353.978204025.

GUIDE TO SERVICES; AN ANNUAL REPORT. Main/Corp Texas. Office of State-Federal Relations. 0148-7841. US. English. an. Office of State-Federal Relations, 1019 19th Street Northwest/Suite 830, Washington DC 20036. LC JK4801. DD 353.976492.

GYOSEI KANRI BENRAN. JA. Japanese. ir. 2000. Nihon Densan Kikaku Kabushiki Kaisha c/o Dai 12 Mori Bldg, 17-3 Toranomon 1 Minato-Ku, Tokyo-To Japan. LC JQ1642.

GYOSEI KANRI KENKYU. No. 1-. Periodical. Japanese. ir. Gyosei Kanri Mondai Kenkyukai, 1-1 Kasumigaseki 3-chome Chiyoda-ku, Tokyo 100 Japan. LC JQ1601.

GYOSEI KANRICHO NO ARAMASHI. Main/Corp Japan. Gyosei Kanricho. 1978-. JA. Japanese. ir. Gyosei Kanricho, c/o Chuo Godo Chosa Dai, 4-Gokan 1-1, Kasumigaseki 3, Chiyoda-Ku 100, Tokyo Japan. LC JQ1650.G9.

GYOSEI KANRICHO NO SHIORI. Main/Corp Japan. Gyosei Kanricho. JA. Japanese. ir. Gyosei Kanricho, 1-1 Kasumigaseki 3 Chiyoda-Ku, Tokyo Japan. LC JQ1650.G9.

HAENGJONG KWALLI YONBO. English. an. LC JQ1726.Z37.

HAENGJONG YON'GU. V. 1- Series. Periodical. Korean. ir. LC JA26.

HANDBOOK FOR GEORGIA LEGISLATORS. 1st- Ed. 0438-5047. US. English. University of Georgia, Institute of Government, Athens GA 30602. Tel (404)542-2736. Ed Edwin L Jackson and Mary E Stakes. LC JK4330. DD 328.7588. Handbook describing the powers and duties of the Georgia legislators, and the workings of the Georgia General Assembly.

HANDBOOK - NATIONAL ASSOCIATION OF SECRETARIES OF STATE. Main/Corp National Association of Secretaries of State. 1st-. 0547-4221. US. English. ir. National Association of Secretaries of State, State Capitol Building, Albany NY 12225. LC JK2403.

HANDBOOK OF BENDEL STATE OF NIGERIA. Main/Corp Bendel State (Nigeria). VFOAT Bendel State of Nigeria Handbook. English. ir. Ministry of Information, Social Development and Sports, Benin City Nigeria. LC JQ3099.B43. DD 354.66930005.

HANDBOOK OF ILLINOIS GOVERNMENT. See Political Science.

HANDBOOK OF STATE PROGRAMS FOR LOCAL GOVERNMENTS. Main/Corp Oregon. Intergovernmental Relations Division. 1978-. US. English. an. Executive Department Intergovernmental Relations Division, 306 State Library Building, Salem OR 97310. LC JK9035. DD 309.179504.

HANDBOOK OF THE NEVADA LEGISLATURE. Main/Corp Nevada. Legislature. US. English. be. Nevada Legislative Counsel Bureau, State Printing Office, Carson City NV 89701. LC JK8571. *Handbook of Nevada Legislature.*

THE HANDY-WHITMAN INDEX OF PUBLIC UTILITY CONSTRUCTION COSTS. BULLETIN. VFOAT Public Utility Construction Costs. No. 53- 1951-. US. English. Whitman Requardt and Associates, 1304 Saint Paul Street, Baltimore MD 21202. *Handy Index of Public Utility Construction Costs.*

HAN'GUK CHONJA KONGOP TONGGYE YON'GAM. See Yearbooks, Almanacs, Directories.

HANSARD OFFICIAL VERBATIM REPORT OF THE DEBATES. Main/Corp Malawi. Parliament. English. ir. Government Printer, Zomba Malawi. LC J728. DD 328.689702.

HARYANA SARAKARA KA BAJATA RAJASVA TATHA KHARCA KE VISTRTA AMUNANOM SAHITA JAISA SAMSADA KE SAMMUKHA PRASTUTA KIYA GAYA. See Business - Public Finance.

HEALTH FUNDS DEVELOPMENT LETTER. See Medicine.

THE HENNEPIN REPORTER CEASED. Began with V. 1, No. 1, Nov. 1965. Ceased V. 17, No. 3, Apr./May 1981. Periodical. US. English. mo.

HER MAJESTY'S CONSULS' LIST. Began publication in 1903. UK. English. bm. National Mutual House, South Park-Sevenoaks, Kent England. LC JX1784. DD 327.42.

HER MAJESTY'S MINISTERS AND SENIOR STAFF IN PUBLIC DEPARTMENTS. Main/Corp Great Britain. Civil Service Dept. UK. English. -/25. H M Stationery Office, 49 High Holborn, London WC1V 6HB England. LC JN406. DD 354.4104.

HERE IS YOUR INDIANA GOVERNMENT. Began publication in 1944. US. English. be. $4.00. Indiana Chamber of Commerce, 1 North Capitol/Suite 200, Indianapolis IN 46204. Tel (317)634-6407. Ed Carl Henn Jr. LC JK5601. DD 320.9772, 342.7723. Book contains complete description of state and local government, budgeting, taxes, courts, school corporations, Constitution of Indiana, plus miscellaneous information and statistics.

HERRI-ARDURALARITZAZKO EUSKAL ALDIZKARIA. See Law.

THE HIGHER EDUCATION PUBLIC ADMINISTRATION DIRECTORY. See Yearbooks, Almanacs, Directories.

HIGHLIGHTS. 0196-2523. Periodical. English. mo. Public Information Office, Trust Territory of the Pacific Islands, Saipan Mariana Islands 96950.

HISTORICAL SUMMARY OF CAPITAL IMPROVEMENTS AUTHORIZED BY GENERAL ASSEMBLY. Main/Corp Maryland. Dept. of State Planning. US. English. an. Department of State Planning, State Office Building, Baltimore MD 21201. LC HD3890.M3. DD 353.975200722253405.

THE HONG KONG GOVERNMENT GAZETTE. Main/Corp Hongkong. No. 1-93, Sept. 24, 1853-June 30, 1855. Periodical. HK. English. wk. 1,220 Domestic, 1,770 Foreign. Director Information Services, Beaconsfield House/Queens Road, Central Hong Kong China. adv acc. Circ 4,000. Provides authoritative information on latest government legislation, notices, tenders, appointments and various ordinances, regulations and bills of Hong Kong.

HOUSE BILL SUMMARIES. Main/Corp Virginia. General Assembly. House of Delegates. 0148-3005. US. English. Commonwealth of Virginia, 706 North 12th Street, Richmond VA 23201. LC KFV2407. DD 348.75501.

HOUSE OF COMMONS DEBATES. (HOUSE OF COMMONS DEBATES : OFFICIAL REPORT). Main/Corp Canada. Parliament. House of Commons. Oct. 9, 1951-. 0704-559X. Periodical. CN. English (French). 36.00 Domestic, 43.20 Foreign. Receiver General for Canada, Supply and Services, Ottawa Ontario K1A 0S9 Canada.

HOUSE OF COMMONS DEBATES = DEBATS DE LA CHAMBRE DES COMMUNES. Main/Corp Canada. Parliament. House of Commins. 1867/68-. Periodical. CN. English (French). Canadian Parlement Chambre of Communes, 180 Wellington Street/Room 435, CRS Ottawa Ontario K1AA 0A6 Canada. Tel (613)992-1254.

HOW OTTAWA SPENDS. 1983-. 0822-6482. CN. English. an. $10.95 Paperback, $17.95 Cloth. How Ottawa Spends, c/o J Lorimer and Company, 35 Britain Street, Toronto Ontario M5A 1R7 Canada. DD 354.7100722. *How Ottawa Spends your Tax Dollars, 0711-4990.*

HOW TO BECOME A CITIZEN OF THE UNITED STATES. US. English. LC JK1829.

HSIN SHIH. Began with July 1980 issue. 0250-8869. Periodical. CH. Chinese. ir. $.095. Chung-Kuo Kuo Chi Shu Tien PO Box 2820, Peking China. LC HD9502.A1. DD 333.705.

HSING CHENG YUAN SO SHU KO CHI KUAN . . . YEN CHIU FA CHAN CHENG KUO NIEN PAO. Chinese. an. LC JQ1530. DD 354.51249078.

ICAP, ADMINISTRACION, DESARROLLO, INTEGRACION - INSTITUTO CENTROAMERICANO DE ADMINISTRACION PUBLICA. Main/Corp Instituto Centroamericano de Administracion Publica. VAT Instituto Centroamericano de Administracion Publica, Administracion, Desarrollo, Integracion. V. 1- Sept./Oct. 1970-. 0044-6262. Periodical. Spanish. qt. LC JA34.

ICMA NEWSLETTER. Main/Corp International City Management Association. VAT International City Management Association Newsletter. V. 50, No. 13- July 1969-. 0047-0651. Periodical. US. English. bw. $60.00. International City Management Association, 1120 G Street Northwest, Washington DC 20005. Tel (202)626-4600. Ed Beth Payne. Circ 7,500. Contains legal issues, association news, board information, conference information, member highlights, position vacancies, appointments, applications, and calendar of events. *City Managers' Newsletter.*

IDAHO LEGISLATIVE FISCAL REPORT TO THE JOINT SENATE FINANCE-HOUSE APPROPRIATIONS COMMITTEE : A PUBLICATION OF THE LEGISLATIVE BUDGET OFFICE. Main/Corp Idaho. Legislature. Legislative Budget Office. US. English. an. Legislative Budget Office, Statehouse/Room 334, Boise ID 83720. LC HJ11. DD 353.9796007223605. *Legislative Fiscal Report to the Joint Senate Finance-House Appropriations Committee, 0362-1987.*

IDENTICAL BIDDING IN PUBLIC PROCUREMENT. (IDENTICAL BIDDING IN PUBLIC PROCUREMENT : REPORT OF THE ATTORNEY GENERAL UNDER EXECUTIVE ORDER 10936). Began with 1961/62. 0501-9575. US. English. an. Superintendent of Documents, US Government Printing Office, Washington DC 20402. LC HD3860. DD 353.00711.

IJA REVIEW. Vol. 1, No. 1 (Spring 1982)-. Periodical. US. English. Institute of Judicial Administration, 1 Washington Square Village, New York NY 10012. LC KF8700.A1. DD 016.34773005, 016.347307005.

ILKE. Vol. 1- Jan. 1974-. Periodical. Turkish. ir. 200.00. Y Z Bahadnl, P K 1222 Ankara Cad, Babiali Han Kat, Istanbul Turkey. LC JQ1801.A1.

ILLINOIS COUNTY AND TOWNSHIP OFFICIAL. VFOAT Illinois County & Township Official. 0019-1949. Periodical. US. English. mo. Illinois County Township Office, PO Box 455, Astoria IL 61501.

ILLINOIS GOVERNMENT RESEARCH. Began with vol. for Jan. 1975. 0195-7783. US. English. ir. University of Illinois, 1201 West Nevada Street, IGPA, Urbana IL 61801. Tel (217)333-3340. LC JK5701. DD 320.9773. *Illinois Government, 0073-4837.*

ILLINOIS LEGISLATIVE DIRECTORY. See Yearbooks, Almanacs, Directories.

ILLINOIS MUNICIPAL DIRECTORY. See Yearbooks, Almanacs, Directories.

ILLINOIS MUNICIPAL PROBLEMS. Main/Corp Illinois. Cities and Villages Municipal Problems Commission. 1st- 1959-. 0442-0713. US. English. be. Cities and Villages Municipal Problems Commission, Springfield IL 62706. LC JS3.I29. DD 352.0773.

ILLINOIS MUNICIPAL REVIEW (SPRINGFIELD, ILL.). (ILLINOIS MUNICIPAL REVIEW). 0019-2139. Periodical. US. English. mo. $5.00. Illinois Municipal League, PO Box 3387, Springfield IL 62708. LC JS39. DD 352.007209773. *Illinois Municipal Review, to Improve the Quality and Decrease the Cost of Municipal Service.*

THE ILLINOIS PUBLIC EMPLOYEE RELATIONS REPORT. Vol. 1, No. 1 (Mar. 1984)-. Periodical. US. English. qt. University of Illinois at Urbana-Champaign, 504 East Armory, Champaign IL 61820.

ILLINOIS STATE OFFICERS. US. English. State Board of Elections, State of Illinois, PO Box 4187, Springfield IL 62708. LC JS3.I29. DD 353.9773002. *State and County Officers, 0145-6199.*

IMPACT JOURNAL. VFOAT Impact. 1972. 0162-1300. Periodical. US. English. bm. Al Louis Ripskis, Box 23126, Washington DC 20024. Tel (202)755-0738. Ed Al Louis Ripskis. bk rev. Exposure of waste mismanagement and debate of serious policy issues in federal government, particularly HUD.

IN PROCESS. (IN PROCESS : AN UP-DATE FROM THE PUBLIC PARTICIPATION GROUP, PROGRAM AND POLICY BRANCH, PLANNING DEPARTMENT). VFOAT En Marche. VAT En Marche (Ottawa. Edition Anglaise et Francaise). Jan. 3, 1979-. 0711-2971. Periodical. CN. English. Free. Public Participation Group, Planning Department, Regional

Public Administration

Municipality of Ottawa-Carleton, 8th Floor/222 Queen Street, Ottawa Ontario K1P 5Z3 Canada. **DD** 352.960971383. (ctrl). *En Marche (Ottawa-Carleton (Ont.). Planning Dept. Public Participation Group).*

INCORPORATED MUNICIPALITIES, MUNICIPAL OFFICIALS AND STATE STREET AID ALLOCATIONS. 0098-6933. US. English. an. Department of Transportation and Highway Safety, PO Box 25202, Raleigh NC 27611. **LC** JS451.N85. **DD** 352.00809756. *Incorporated Municipalities, Municipal Officials and State Street Aid Allocations.*

INDEKS PEMILU. See Indexes/Abstracts.

INDEPENDENT SECTOR. (INDEPENDENT SECTOR : IS). **VFOAT** IS. 0743-1236. US. English. an. Independent Sector, 1828 L Street Northwest, Washington DC 20036. **LC** HV97.I57. **DD** 351.763060753.

INDEX DIGEST OF PUBLISHED DECISIONS OF THE COMPTROLLER GENERAL OF THE UNITED STATES (WASHINGTON, D.C. : 1971-1976). See Indexes/Abstracts.

INDEX, FEDERAL EMPLOYEE APPEALS DECISIONS. See Indexes/Abstracts.

INDEX, JOURNALS OF THE SENATE AND HOUSE OF THE STATE OF MISSOURI. See Indexes/Abstracts.

INDEX KOMMUNALWISSENSCHAFTLICHER LITERATUR : BUCHER. See Indexes/Abstracts.

INDEX OF ONTARIO GOVERNMENT STATISTICS FOR MUNICIPALITIES. See Indexes/Abstracts.

INDEX TO FEDERAL PROGRAMS AND SERVICES. See Indexes/Abstracts.

INDEX TO GOVERNMENT ORDERS (GREAT BRITAIN). See Indexes/Abstracts.

INDEX TO PUBLIC ADMINISTRATION SERIES—BIBLIOGRAPHY. See Indexes/Abstracts.

THE INDIAN JOURNAL OF PUBLIC ADMINISTRATION. V. 1- Jan./Mar. 1955-. 0019-5561. Periodical. II. English. qt. $15.00. DIR- Indian Institute of Public Administration, Indraprastha Estate Ring Road, New Delhi 110002 India. **Ind/Abst** Int. Labour Doc., ABC Pol Sci, Recent Publ. Artic., Sociol. Abstr., Lang. Lang. Behav. Abstr. **LC** JQ201. Index published separately - free - automatically sent.

INDIANA GENERAL ASSEMBLY LEGISLATIVE DIRECTORY. See Yearbooks, Almanacs, Directories.

INDIANA PUBLIC MANAGEMENT. V. 1- Spring 1975-. 0099-1023. Periodical. US. English. qt. 400 East Seventh Street, 47401. **LC** JK5601. **DD** 353.97720005.

INDONESHIA NO GUN-SEI SHIDOSHA ICHIRAN. JA. Japanese. ir. Tonan Ajia Chosakai, c/o Kotsu Kosha Building, 602 6-4 Marunouchi, 1-chome Chiyoda-ku, Tokyo Japan. **LC** JQ767.

L'INDUSTRIE ELECTRONIQUE FRANCAISE. Main/Corp Federation Nationale des Industries Electroniques. FR. French. ir. 15 rue de Presles, Paris France 75740. **LC** HD9696.A3. **DD** 338.47621381.

INFO-BEAUPORT. Vol. 1, No. 4 (Feb. 1983)-. 0821-0152. Periodical. CN. French. mo. Ville de Beauport Services des Communications, 577 Av Royale, Beauport Quebec G1E 1Y5 Canada. **Tel** (418)667-8554. **DD** 352.071447. **Circ** 22,000. Municipal administration. *Information (Beauport, Quebec), 0821-0144.*

INFO-BOURG. (INFO-BOURG : LE JOURNAL DE LA VILLE DE CHARLESBOURG). Main/Corp Charlesbourg (Quebec). **VFOAT** Journal de la Ville de Charlesbourg. V. 7, No. 9, Dec. 1982)-. 0715-7592. Periodical. CN. French. ir. Free to Residents. Info-Bourg, c/o Bureau d'Information Ville de Charlesbourg, 7575 Boulevard Henri-Bourassa, Charlesbourg Quebec G1H 9Z9 Canada. **DD** 352.071447. *Charlesbourg, 0820-0599.*

INFO LONGUEUIL. V. 1- July 1975-. 0383-1272. Periodical. CN. French (comprend un Resume en Anglais). ir. Le Bureau d'Information de la Ville de Longueuil, 100 Ouest rue Saint-Charles, Longueuil Quebec J4H 1E6 Canada. **DD** 352.071437.

INFO - NORTH YORK. (INFO). Main/Corp North York (Ont.). 0821-2368. CN. English. an. Info, Public Information Office/City of North York, 5100 Yonge Street, Willowdale Ontario M2N 5V7 Canada. **DD** 352.0713541.

INFO-POINTELIERE. **VFOAT** Journal Patme. Vol. 4, No. 1 (June 1980)-. 0712-3949. Periodical. CN. French. ir. Free. Info-Pointeliere, Service des Relations Publiques, Ville de Pointe-aux-Trembles, 11953 East rue Notre-Dame, Pointe-aux-Trembles Quebec H1B 2Y6 Canada. **DD** 352.071428. *Cite (Pointe-aux-Trembles, Quebec), 0712-3930.*

INFO-SAINT-BRUNO. (INFO-SAINT-BRUNO : BULLETIN MUNICIPAL DE LA VILLE DE SAINT-BRUNO-DE-MONTARVILLE). V. 1, No. 1, (Dec. 1980)-. 0714-3885. Periodical. CN. English (French). ir. Free. Information Office, City of Saint-Bruno-de-Montarville, 1585 Montarville Street, Saint-Bruno-de-Montarville Quebec J3V 3T8 Canada. **DD** 352.071437. (ctrl).

INFORMATION CIRCULAR - ALBERTA TREASURY, CORPORATE TAX ADMINISTRATION. (INFORMATION CIRCULAR/EDMONTON). Jan. 81-. 0711-5431. Periodical. CN. English. ir. Free. **DD** 354.7123007244.

INFORMATION COLLECTION BUDGET OF THE UNITED STATES GOVERNMENT. Main/Corp United States. Office of Management and Budget. Began with 1981/82 vol. 0743-4928. US. English. an. National Technical Information Service, c/o Documents Sales, 5285 Port Royal Road, Springfield VA 22161. **LC** JK468.P34. **DD** 353.00714.

INFORMATION LISTING - REGIONAL CLERK'S DEPARTMENT. (INFORMATION LISTING). Main/Corp Sudbury (Ont. : Regional Municipality). Clerk's Dept. 1979-. 0826-0613. CN. English. an. Free. Regional Municipality of Sudbury/Clerk's Department, PO Box 370, Sudbury Ontario P3E 4P2 Canada. **DD** 354.71300025. (ctrl).

INFORMATION MONT-ROLLAND. Main/Corp Mont-Rolland (Quebec). Mar. 1979-. 0710-586X. Periodical. CN. French. mo. Information Mont-Rolland, c/o La Corporation Municipale de Mont-Rolland, 245 Morin, Mont-Rolland Quebec J0R 1G0 Canada. **DD** 352.071424.

INFORMATION PRACTICES IN WYOMING STATE GOVERNMENT. Main/Corp Wyoming. Office of Information Practices. 0364-9334. US. English. an. **LC** JC599.U52. **DD** 353.978700714.

INFORMATION SAINT-CONSTANT. 0714-508X. Periodical. CN. French. ir. Free. Information Saint-Constant, Hotel de Ville Saint-Constant, 147 rue Saint-Pierre, Saint-Constant Quebec J0L 1X0 Canada. **DD** 352.071434. *Bulletin d'Information (Saint-Constant (Quebec)).*

INFORMATION SYSTEMS TECHNOLOGY IN STATE GOVERNMENTS. See Computers and Computer Science.

INFORMATION U. C. C. Q. Main/Corp Union des Conseils de Comte du Quebec. V. 1-4, No. 1. 0701-0621. Periodical. CN. French. bm. Free. Union des Conseils de Comte du Quebec, Bureau 204/2835 Chemin Gomin, Ste-Foy Quebec G1V 2K1 Canada. **DD** 352.00062714. (ctrl).

INFORMATION U.M.R.C. Main/Corp Union des Municipalites Regionales de Comte et des Municipalites Locales du Quebec. **VAT** Information Union des Municipalites Regionales de Comte et des Municipalites Locales du Quebec, Inc. Vol. 8, No. 1 (Jan. 1983)-. 0821-1094. Periodical. CN. French. bm. Free to Members. Suite 430/2795 Boulevard Laurier, Ste-Foy Quebec G1V 4M7 Canada. **DD** 352.0714. *Information U.C.C.Q. (Union des Conseils de Comte et des Municipalites Locales du Quebec), 0701-0621.*

INFORMATIONS D'ILE DE FRANCE. See Building and Construction.

L'INFORMATIQUE DANS LES ADMINISTRATIONS ET LES ENTREPRISES PUBLIQUES EN FRANCE AU . . . . FR. French. an. Documentation Francaise, 29-31 Quai Voltaire, 75340 Paris Cedex 07 France. **LC** HD4161. **DD** 354.440002854. *Informatique dans les Administrations Francaises, Informatique dans les Entreprises Publiques.*

L'INFORMATIQUE DANS LES ADMINISTRATIONS FRANCAISES. 1975-. French. ir. 15.00. Documentation Francaise, 29-31 Quai Voltaire, Paris France 75340. **LC** JN2738.E4. **DD** 354.440002854. *Informatique dans les Administrations Francaises et Son Evolution au Cours des Trois Prochaines Annees.*

L'INFORMATIQUE DANS LES ENTREPRISES PUBLIQUES. French. ir. Documentation Francaise, 29-31 Quai Voltaire, Paris France 75340. **LC** HD4161. **DD** 354.44008202854. *Informatique dans les Entreprises Pulbiques et Son Evolution au Cours des Trois Prochaines Annees.*

INFORME ANUAL . . . A LOS HONORABLES REPRESENTANTES DE CORREGIMIENTOS. Main/Corp Instituto de Recursos Hidraulicos y Electrificacion. Spanish. an. Apartado 5285, Panama.

INFORME ANUAL - ESTADO LIBRE ASOCIADO DE PUERTO RICO, COMISION DE SERVICIO PUBLICO. (INFORME ANUAL - COMISION DE SERVICIO PUBLICO). Main/Corp Puerto Rico. Public Service Commission. **VFOAT** Informe Anual - Comision de Servucui Publico del Estado Libre Asociado de Pureto Rico. 0478-8583. Periodical. PR. Spanish. ir. Public Service Commission, San Juan Puerto Rico. **LC** HD2768.P7. **DD** 354.

INFORME FINANCIERO Y ESTADISTICO, INSTITUTO NACIONAL DE ELECTRIFICACION, Y ESTADISTICAS DEL SECTOR ELECTRICO NACIONAL. See Statistics.

INFOSTAT. No. 1- Jan. 1980-. 0707-9419. Periodical. CN. French. qt. Free. Societe d Habitation du Quebec, 1054 rue Conroy Edifice G, Bloc 2M 4E Etage, Quebec Quebec G1R 5E7 Canada. **DD** 354.71400865042.

INITIATIVE AND REFERENDUM REPORT. 0734-4090. Periodical. US. English. mo. $25.00. Free Congress Research and Education Foundation, 721 2nd Street NE, Washington DC 20002. **Tel** (202)546-3004. **Ed** Patrick McGrugan. (ctrl).

INSIDE INTERIOR. No. 1- July 1974-. 0364-6688. Periodical. US. English. bm. Inside Interior, Room 7219/Department of the Interior, Washington DC 20240. *Inside Interior, 0364-6688.*

INSTITUT. (THE INSTITUTE). Vol. 4, No. 1 (Jan. 25, 1981)-. 0714-6698. Periodical. CN. English. mo. Institute for Research on Public Policy, PO Box 3670, Halifax South Nova Scotia B3J 3K6 Canada. **DD** 354.7105. *Institute for Research on Public Policy, 0227-7905.*

INTER. (L'INTER). Published since June 1978. 0225-9281. Periodical. CN. French. bm. Ministere du Travail et de la Main-d'Oeuvre, 425 rue Saint Amable, Quebec G1R 4Z1 Canada. **DD** 354.714068305.

INTER URBA. Vol. 1, No. 1 (28 Nov. 1980)-. 0710-7307. Periodical. CN. French. ir. Union des Municipalites du Quebec, Bureau 301/315 East Boulevard Dorchester, Montreal Quebec H2X 3P3 Canada. **DD** 352.0714.

INTERACTION (INTERGOVERNMENTAL COMMITTEE ON URBAN AND REGIONAL RESEARCH). (INTERACTION). No. 1- Jan. 1976-. 0226-2878. Periodical. CN. French (English). bm. Comite Intergouvernemental de Recherches Urbaines et Regionales, 36 rue Wellesley Ouest, Toronto Ontario M4Y 1G1 Canada.

INTERAGENCY TRAINING CATALOG OF COURSES. Main/Corp United States. Office of Personnel Management. 1979-81-. 0360-5019. US. English. be. $2.50. Office of Personnel Management, PO Box 7230, Washington DC 20044. **Tel** (202)254-6940. **Ed** Ernestine Blakcuore. **LC** JK639, JK718. **DD** 658.0715. (ctrl). A listing of in-service training courses available from the US office of personnel management. *Interagency Training Catalog of Courses, 0360-5019.*

INTERAGENCY TRAINING PROGRAMS. **VFOAT** Interagency Training Programs Bulletin. Spring 1959-. 0501-8188. Periodical. US. English. an. US Civil Service Commission, 1900 East Street NW, Washington DC 20415. **LC** JK718. **DD** 371.42.

INTERGOVERNMENTAL AFFAIRS FELLOWSHIP PROGRAM. (INTERGOVERNMENTAL AFFAIRS FELLOWSHIP PROGRAM, REPORT). Main/Corp United States. Civil

Public Administration

Service Commission. Bureau of Training. 0097-7780. US. English. US Civil Service Commission, Bureau of Training, 1900 E Street NW, Washington DC 20415. LC JK723.E9. DD 353.0015.

INTERGOVERNMENTAL PERSPECTIVE. Vol. 1, No. 1 (Fall 1975)-. 0362-8507. Periodical. US. English. qt. US Advisory Commission on Intergovernmental Relations, Washington DC 20575. Ind/Abst Index U.S. Gov. Period. LC JK325. DD 353.0005.

INTERIM REPORT - B.C. HYDRO. (INTERIM REPORT - B. C. HYDRO). Main/Corp B.C. Hydro. Began with Sept. 1976? issue. 0226-3351. Periodical. CN. English. qt. British Columbia Hydro and Power Authority, 970 Burrard Street, Vancouver British Columbia V6Z 1Y3 Canada. DD 354.7110087.

THE INTERIOR BUDGET IN BRIEF. Main/Corp United States. Dept. of the Interior. 0743-2844. US. English. an. US Department of the Interior, Washington DC 20240. LC JK864. DD 353.3. *Budget Highlights.*

INTERNATIONAL CONGRESS CALENDAR. Series Corp Union of International Associations. Publication. 1960/61-. 0538-6349. English. qt. $130.00. K G Saur Publications, 175 5th Avenue, New York NY 10010. LC AS8. DD 060.58. Complete information on over 7,000 international events scheduled for next 12-15 Months. Each issue is completely recumulated and is organized in 3 sections- geographical, chronological subject index.

INTERNATIONAL JOURNAL OF GOVERNMENT AUDITING. VFOAT Journal International des Institutions Superieures de Controle, Revista Interancional de Entidades Fiscalizadoras Superiores. V. 1- Sept. 1971-. 0047-0724. Periodical. CN. English (text in French and Spanish). qt. $5.00. International Journal of Government Auditing, PO Box 50009, Washington DC 20004. Tel (202)275-5682. Ed Elaine L Orr. Ind/Abst Manage. Contents, Account. Index. Suppl., ABI/Inform, Can. Bus. Index. LC HJ9701. DD 350.7232. CODEN IJGADG. Also available in microfilm format. International government auditing.

INTERNATIONAL JOURNAL OF PUBLIC ADMINISTRATION. 0190-0692. Periodical. US. English. qt. $125.00. Marcel Dekker Inc, Journals Department, PO Box 11305, New York NY 10249. Tel (212)696-9000. Ed Jack Rabin. Ind/Abst Manage. Contents, ABI/Inform, Soc. Work Res. Abstr., Curr. Contents, Soc. Behav. Sci., Int. Polit. Sci. Abstr., Sage Public Adm. Abstr., Soc. Sci. Citation Index, Autom. Subj. Citation Alert. LC JA1.A1. DD 350.0005. CODEN IJPADR. bk rev. adv acc. (ctrl). Lively, perceptive and up-to-the-minute single graphs, tables, and charts for academicians and practitioners involved in all areas of public administration.

INTERNATIONAL OMBUDSMAN INSTITUTE DIRECTORY OF OMBUDSMEN AND OTHER COMPLAINT-HANDLERS. See Yearbooks, Almanacs, Directories.

INTERNATIONAL REVIEW OF ADMINISTRATIVE SCIENCES. Began in 1957. 0020-8523. Periodical. BE. English (French, and Spanish with summaries in English). qt. $48.00. International Institute of Administrative Sciences, 25 rue de la Charite, 1040 Brussels Belgium. Ind/Abst Manage. Contents, ABC Pol Sci, Foreign Lang. Index, Public Aff. Inf. Serv. Bull. bk rev. adv acc. Articles on comparative public administration. A special section for schools and institutes and a bibliography on recent outstanding publications. Distributed all over the world. *Revue Internationale des Sciences Administratives, Progress in Public Administration.*

INTERNATIONAL TREASURY SERVICES. 0883-4601. US. English. an. Greenwich Research Associates, Office Park Eight, Greenwich CT 06830.

INTERSTATE COMPACT ON JUVENILES : ROSTER OF OFFICIAL ADMINISTRATORS AND DIRECTIONS FOR CORRESPONDENCE. Main/Corp Council of State Governments. 0589-9737. US. English. an. Council of State Governments, 36 West 44th Street, New York NY 10036.

INTERSTATE COMPACTS AND AGENCIES. Series/Titl RM. 1979-. 0198-9146. US. English. $5.00. Council of State Governments, Iron Works Pike, Lexington KY 40578. LC JS308, JK2441. DD 353.9 S, 353.9291. *Interstate Compacts, Directory of Interstate Agencies, 0589-9702.*

INTERSTATE MOVEMENT OF JUVENILES; ANNUAL REPORT. Main/Corp Council of State Governments. 0574-2846. US. English. an. Council of State Governments, 1500 Broadway, New York NY 10036.

INVENTORY OF AUTOMATIC DATA PROCESSING EQUIPMENT IN THE FEDERAL GOVERNMENT. See Office Equipment & Services.

THE IOWA MUNICIPAL SALARY SURVEY FOR . . . . See Economics - Labor.

IOWA MUNICIPALITIES. V. 15- Mar. 1960-. 0021-0595. Periodical. US. English. mo. League of Iowa Municipalities, Suite 100/900 Des Moines Street, Des Moines IA 50316. Tel (515)265-9961. LC JS303.155. *League of Iowa Municipalities Monthly Magazine.*

IOWA REVIEW QUARTERLY. 0741-2924. Periodical. US. English. qt. State of Iowa, Office for Planning and Programming, 523 East 12th Sttreet, Des Moines IA 50319. LC JK6301. DD 353.9777072.

THE IPA INTERGOVERNMENTAL ASSIGNMENT PROGRAM, REPORT. (THE IPA INTERGOVERNMENTAL ASSIGNMENT PROGRAM : REPORT). Main/Corp United States. Civil Service Commission. Bureau of Intergovernmental Personnel Programs. VAT Intergovernmental Personnel Act Intergovernmental Assignment Program: Report. 0360-6260. US. English. LC JK765. DD 353.0014.

IPS LOCAL GOVERNMENT NEWSLETTER. Main/Corp University of Connecticut. Institute of Public Service. VAT Institute of Public Service Local Government Newsletter. 0045-8139. Periodical. US. English. mo. Institute of Public Service, University of Connecticut, Storrs CT 06268.

IR VE-EZOR. VFOAT City and Region. Vol. 1- October 1972-. Periodical. IS. Hebrew (summaries in English). qt. Misrael Ha-Penim, Box 7103, Tel Aviv Israel. LC JS7499.I8.

IRELAND : A PARLIAMENTARY DIRECTORY. See Yearbooks, Almanacs, Directories.

IRS PRACTICE AND PROCEDURES. VAT Internal Revenue Service Practice and Procedures. 0194-8210. Periodical. US. English. mo. $70.00. Mark A Stephens Ltd, 10018 Colesville Road, Silver Springs MD 20901. Tel (301)593-0443. Ed Lavaughn T Davis.

THE ISRAEL ANNUAL OF PUBLIC ADMINISTRATION AND PUBLIC POLICY. 15- 1976-. IS. Englsih. ir. $12.00. Israel Institute of Public Administration, PO Box 7458, Jerusalem Israel. LC JQ1825.P3. DD 320.95694. *Public Administration in Israel and Abroad.*

ISSUES IN ILLINOIS POLICY. V. 1- 1974-. 0360-411X. US. English. Illinois Legislative Studies Center, Sangamon State University, Springfield IL 62708. LC JK5701. DD 309.1773.

ISTIQLAL. Periodical. Urdu. ir. 30.00. Abu Sayyid Anvar, Weekly Istiqlal, Lahaur Pakistan. LC JQ201.

IULA NEWSLETTER : MONTHLY REVIEW OF THE INTERNATIONAL UNION OF LOCAL AUTHORITIES. VFOAT I.U.L.A. Newsletter. VAT International Union of Local Authorities Newsletter. Began with: Vol. 1, published in 1967. 0019-087X. Periodical. NE. English. mo. International Union of Local Authority, 45 Wassenaarseweg, 2596 CG The Hague Netherlands. Tel 070/244032. LC JS42. DD 352.000601. *Local Government Throughout the World.*

IZBORI NA DELEGACII I DELEGATI ZA SOBORITE NA SOBRANIJATA. See Statistics.

IZVESTIIA VYSSHIKH UCHEBNYKH ZAVEDENII. PRAVOVEDENIE. July 1957-. 0579-3017. Periodical. UR. Russian. bm. $35.00. Victor Kamkin Inc, 12224 Parklawn Drive, Rockville MD 20852. Tel (301)881-5973.

J4B-INFO. July 11 1979-. 0713-0147. Periodical. CN. French. ir. Free to Citizens of Boucherville. Ville de Boucherville, 500 Riviere-Aux-Pins, Boucherville Quebec J4B 2Z7 Canada. DD 352.071437.

JAARVERSLAG (NETHERLANDS. RIJKSINKOOPBUREAU). (JAARVERSLAG). NE. Dutch. an. Rijksinkoopbureau, Rechterland 1, Postbus 10200, 8000 GE Zwolle The Netherlands.

JAARVERSLAG VAN DE PERMANENTE COMMISSIE VOOR OVERHEIDSDOCUMENTATIE. Main/Corp Netherlands (Kingdom, 1815-). Permanente Commissie voor Overheidsdocumentatie. Dutch. ir. Permanente Commissie voor Overheidsdocumentatie, Binnenhof 19, S-Gravenhage Netherlands. LC JN5853.

JAHRBUCH DER SOZIALDEMOKRATISCHEN PARTEI DEUTSCHLANDS. See Yearbooks, Almanacs, Directories.

JERNAL PENTADBIR. July 1978-. Periodical. English (Malay). ir. LC JA26. DD 320.05.

JICHI NO UGOKI. JA. Japanese. ir. Jichisho Bunsho Kohoka, 1-2 Kasumigaseki 2 Chome Chiyoda-Ku, Tokyo Japan. LC JS7371.A1.

JIM. JOURNAL INFORMATION MUNICIPALE. (JIM : JOURNAL INFORMATION MUNICIPALE). VAT Journal Information Municipale. 0821-0810. Periodical. CN. French. mo. Gratuit Pour les Citoyens. Ville de Donnacona, 138 Avenue Pleau, Donnacona Quebec G0A 1T0 Canada. DD 352.0714466.

JOHANNAIS. (LE JOHANNAIS : BULLETIN D'INFORMATION DE LA VILLE DE SAINT-JEAN). Main/Corp Saint-Jean (Saint-Jean, Quebec). V. 1, No. 1, (April 1976)-. 0710-5835. Periodical. CN. French. qt. Free. Service de l'Information de la Ville, CP 1025 Saint-Jean-sur-Richelieu Quebec J3B 7B2 Canada. DD 352.071438.

JOINT RULES, RULES OF THE SENATE AND RULES OF THE HOUSE OF THE STATE LEGISLATURE OF WASHINGTON. Main/Corp Washington (State) Legislature. VFOAT Legislative Manual. 0145-1916. US. English. State of Washington Legislature, Olympia WA 98504. LC JK9271. DD 328.79705.

JOINT SITTING OF THE SENATE AND THE HOUSE OF ASSEMBLY. Main/Corp South Africa. Parliament. SA. English. ir. House of Assembly, Government Printer, Bouquet Street or Bosman Street, Cape Town Pretoria South Africa. LC J705. DD 328.6801. *Joint Sitting on Both Houses of Parliament.*

JOLISO EXPRESS. Vol. 1, No. 1 (Nov. 1981)-. 0714-4199. Periodical. CN. French. ir. Joliso Express Hotel de Ville, 204 rue Principale, Saint-Basile-le-Grand Quebec J0L 1S0 Canada. DD 352.071437.

JOLISO (SAINT-BASILE-LE-GRAND). (JOLISO). V. 1, No. 1, (Dec. 1980)-. 0711-4397. Periodical. CN. French. ir. Free. Joliso Bureau du Greffier Hotel de Ville, 204 rue Principale, St-Basile-Le-Grand Quebec J0L 1S0 Canada. DD 352.071437. (ctrl).

JONCTION (ASTON-JONCTION, QUEBEC). (JONCTION). 0821-218X. Periodical. CN. French. ir. Free to Residents. Jonction, C P 94, Aston-Jonction Quebec G0Z 1A0 Canada. DD 352.071455.

JOURNAL (AMERICAN WATER WORKS ASSOCIATION). See Water Resources.

JOURNAL DE ST-DOMINIQUE. 0822-6938. Newspaper. CN. French. mo. Journal de St-Dominique, St-Damase, Quebec J0H 1S0 Canada. DD 352.0714525. *Information Regionale, St-Damase, St-Pie, St-Cesaire, 0822-692X.*

JOURNAL OF ADMINISTRATION OVERSEAS CEASED. V. 1- Jan. 1962-1980. 0021-8472. Periodical. UK. English. qt. LC JS40. *Journal of African Administration.*

THE JOURNAL OF DEVELOPMENT AND ADMINISTRATIVE STUDIES. See Economics - Economics: Industry & Production.

THE JOURNAL OF H.M. CUSTOMS AND EXCISE. Main/Corp Customs and Excise Federation. Began publication in 1910. Periodical. UK. English. sm. LC HD8013.G7. DD 351.1.

JOURNAL OF LOCAL ADMINISTRATION OVERSEAS. V. 1-4. Periodical. English. ir.

JOURNAL OF POLICY ANALYSIS AND MANAGEMENT. VFOAT Journal of the Association for Public Policy Analysis and Management. Vol. 1 (Fall 1981)-. 0276-8739. Periodical. US. English. qt. John Wiley & Sons Inc, 605 Third Avenue, New York NY 10158. Tel

Public Administration

(615)692-6035. *Policy Analysis*, 0098-2067; *Public Policy*, 0033-3646.

JOURNAL OF RURAL DEVELOPMENT AND ADMINISTRATION. Began with Vol. 4. 0047-2751. Periodical. qnglish. ir. Pakistan Academy of Rural Development, Peshawar Pakistan. *Academy Quarterly*.

JOURNAL OF STATE POLITICS AND ADMINISTRATION. V. 1- Jan./June 1978-. Periodical. English. ir. Dr A P Padhi, C/18 Jyoti Vihar Burla, 768017 Sambalpur Orissa India. **LC** JQ298.8. **DD** 320.954.

JOURNAL OF THE HOUSE. Main/Corp Iowa. General Assembly House of Representatives. 1st Session (1846/47)-. US. English. an. General Assembly House of Representatives, Core Depository/707 Savings and Loan Building, Des Moines IA 50309.

JOURNAL OF THE SOCIETY FOR STUDY OF STATE GOVERNMENTS. Main/Corp Society for Study of State Governments. V. 1- Jan./June 1968-. Periodical. Il. English. ir. Kopparti Place Karaunoi, Varanasi 5 India. **LC** JS7001. **DD** 354.540005.

JOURNAL OF URBAN AFFAIRS. See Social Sciences (General).

JOURNAL OF VOLUNTARY ACTION RESEARCH. See Sociology: General Works, Theory.

JOURNALS OF THE SENATE. Main/Corp Australia. Parliament. Senate. 1967, No. 1 (21, Feb. 1967)- 26th Parliament-. AT. English. ir. $14.16. Australian Government Printing Office, PO Box 84, Canberra Australian Capital Territory 2600 Australia. **Tel** 062-95 4411. *Records of the Proceedings and the Printed Papers*.

THE JUSTICE SYSTEM JOURNAL. See Law Enforcement.

K W I C INDEX TO THE GOVERNMENT OF ONTARIO. See Indexes/Abstracts.

KAIGAI SEIKATSU NO TEBIKI. JA. Japanese. ir. Nihon Denshin Denwa Kosha Kaigui Renrakushitsu, 1-1-6 Uchisaiwaicho Chiyoda-ku, Tokyo Japan. **LC** JV8721.Z8.

KAKUSHOCHO KOHO YOTEI JIKO. JA. Japanese. ir. 6-1 Nagatacho 1 Chiyoda-Ku, Tokyo Japan. **LC** JQ1649.P85.

KAMLOOPS FOREST REGION NEWSLETTER. Main/Corp British Columbia. Ministry of Forests. Vol. 1, No. 1 (Sept. 1980)-. 0228-4944. Periodical. CN. English. ir. Province of British Columbia, 1450 Government Information Service, Victoria British Columbia V8W 3E7 Canada. **DD** 354.71100823380971141.

KANKAI. V. 1-. Periodical. JA. Japanese. ir. 380. Gyosei Mondai Kenkyujo, 1-36 Yoyogi Shibuya-ku (15l), Tokyo Japan. **LC** JQ1642.

KANSANEDUSTAJAIN VAALIT. Main/Corp Finland. Tilastokeskus. **Series/Titl** Suomen Virallinen Tilasto. **VFOAT** Riksdagsmannavalen, Parliamentary Elections. English (Finnish and Swedish). ir. Tilastokeskus, Valtion Painatuskeskus, Annankatu 44 00100 10, Helsinki Finland. **LC** HA1448, JN6719.

KANSAS DIRECTORY. SUPPLEMENT. See Yearbooks, Almanacs, Directories.

KANSAS GOVERNMENT. Series Corp League of Kansas Municipalities. Publication. 1st- Ed. US. English. League of Kansas Muncipalities, 112 West 7th Street, Topeka KS 66603. **LC** JK6801. **DD** 353.9781.

KANSAS GOVERNMENT JOURNAL. 1914. 0022-8613. Periodical. US. English. mo. $18.00. League of Kansas Municipalities, 112 West 7th Street, Topeka KS 66603. **Tel** (913)/354-9565. **Ed** E A Mosher. bk rev. adv acc. **Circ** 7,300. (ctrl). Local, state and federal government issues affecting local governments.

KANSAS LEGISLATIVE REPORT. V. 1- June 1, 1979-. 0277-397X. Periodical. US. English. sm. $56.00. Government Research Service, 701 Jackson/Room 304, Topeka KS 66603. **Tel** (913)232-7720. **Ed** L Hellebust.

KAO-HSIUNG SHIH CHENG FU ... SHIH CHENG CHI HUA. CH. Chinese. an. Kao-Hsiung Shih Cheng Fu, Kao-Hsiung Taiwan. **LC** JS7366.9.K35.

KAPITALISTATE. No. 3- Spring 1975-. Periodical. US. English. ir. Kapitalistate, PO Box 5138, Berkeley CA 94705. **Ind/Abst** Sociol. Abstr., Altern. Press Index. *Working Papers on the Kapitalistate*.

KEIKAKU GYOSEI. See Housing and Urban Development.

KENTUCKY ADMINISTRATIVE REGULATIONS SERVICE. Main/Corp Kentucky. Legislative Research Commission. **VFOAT** Kentucky Administrative Regulations. 1975-. US. English. ir. Kentucky State Treasurer, Administrative Relations Service, State Capitol/Room 300, Frankfort KY 40601. **Tel** (502)564-3136. **Ed** Susan C Harding. **Circ** 600. (ctrl). Kentucky regulations in effect as of July 1984.

KENTUCKY CITY (LEXINGTON, KY. : 1968). (THE KENTUCKY CITY). Vol. 1, No. 1 (June 1968)-. 0453-5677. Periodical. US. English. mo. $9.00. Kentucky Municipal League, PO Box 22736, Lexington KY 40522. **Tel** (606)257-3285. **Ed** Emily Adams. **LC** JS39. **DD** 352.0769. bk rev. adv acc. **Circ** 4,050. Information on city government in Kentucky and articles of general interest on municipal government procedures and administration. *Kentucky City Bulletin*, 0734-4996.

KENTUCKY DIRECTORY OF BLACK ELECTED OFFICIALS. See Yearbooks, Almanacs, Directories.

KENTUCKY LOCAL OFFICIALS. US. English. ir. Department of Highways, Public Affairs Officer/State Office Building, Frankfort KY 40601. **LC** JS451.K45.

KEY OFFICIALS HANDBOOK. Main/Corp United States. Embassy (Sudan) Economic Section. English. ir. U S Embassy(Sudan), Economic Section, Khartoum Sudan. **LC** JQ3981.S82. **DD** 354.624002.

KGST MITTEILUNGEN. Main/Corp Kommunale Gemeinschaftsstelle fur Verwaltungsvereinfachung. **VAT** Kommunale Gemeinschaftsstelle fur Verwaltungsvereinfachung Mitteilungen. Jan. 10, 1971-. Periodical. German. sm. KGST Lindenallee, 13017 Postface 51 0720, 5000 Koln 51 West Germany. *Mitteilungen der Kommunalen Gemeinschaftsstelle fur Verwaltungsvereinfachung (KGST)*.

KIKAN GYOSEI KANRI KENKYU. **VFOAT** Gyosei Kanri Kenkyu. Periodical. JA. Japanese. ir. 4800. Gyosei Kanri Kenkyu Senta, c/o Dai 12 Mori Building 17-3, Toranomon 1, Minato-Ku 105, Tokyo Japan. **LC** JA26.

KIKAN JICHITAIGAKU KENKYU. **VFOAT** Jichitaigaku Kenkyu. Began with 1979-No. May issue. Periodical. JA. Japanese. ir. 300 Single Issue. Kanagawa-Ken Kosaikai Koeki Jigyoka, 75 Yamashitacho, Naka-Ku, Yokohama-Shi Japan. **LC** JS7371.A1.

KIKAN JINJI GYOSEI. **VFOAT** Jinji Gyosei. No. 1-. Periodical. JA. Japanese. ir. 800. Gakuyo Shobo, 7-5 Fujimi 1, Chiyoda-Ku Tokyo Japan. **LC** JQ1601.

KIKAN KOKKAI GIIN. **VFOAT** Kokkai Giin. Edition- (No. 1-4)-. Periodical. JA. Japanese. ir. 10.000. Ariyama Toredo Sabisu, 13-8 Esakacho 1-Chome, Suita 564 Japan. **LC** Z7165.J3, JQ1626.1945.

KNIZKA PARTIJNOGO AKTIVISTA. (KNIZHKA PARTIINOGO AKTIVISTA). 0302-8445. UR. Russian. 0.31. Izd-Vo Polit Lit-ry, A-47 Miussakaia Pl 7, Moskva Poland. **LC** JN6598.K7. *Zapisnaia Knizhka Partinogo Aktivista*.

KNOW YOUR CONGRESS. 1943. 0197-5730. US. English. an. $7.50. Capital Publishers Inc, PO Box 6235, Washington DC 20015. **Tel** (202)362-3769. **Ed** Diosdado M Yap. **Circ** 5,000. *Pictorial Directory of Congress*.

KOMMUNAL HANDBOG. **VFOAT** KH. DK. Danish. an. 240.00. Mostrups Forlag, Hestemllestrde 6, 1464 Kbenhavn Denmark. **LC** JS6152.

KOMMUNALWIRTSCHAFT. Began in 1912. 0450-7169. Periodical. GW. German. mo. $34.50. Kommunal Verlag, Rosseggerstr 5A, Dusseldorf West Germany. **Ind/Abst** Excerpta Med., Chem. Abstr., Energy Res. Abstr. **LC** HD4659. **CODEN** KMLWAB.

KOMMUNEVALGET. See Statistics.

KOMUNALNI FONDOVI U GRADSKIM NASELJIMA. See Statistics.

KONSULTATSII I OTVETY NA VOPROSY. V POMOSHCH RABOTNIKAM SOVETOV I DEPUTATAM. Vol. 1-. UR. Russian. Izd-Vo Izvestiia, Pushkinskaia Pl 5, Moskva Russia. **LC** JS6058.

KOSI WOLBO. Periodical. KO. Korean. mo. 22.000. Taemyong Kosi Yonguhoe, 6 Chongjin-Dong Chongno-Ku, Seoul Korea. **LC** JQ1726.Z13.

HAI KUAN TUNG CHI. See Statistics.

KUKHOE UIWON CHONGNAM. Korean. ir. 35.000. Tongsong Misul Chulpansha Konguk Samho, B/D 366-Ho 64-4 Kyongun-Dong Chongno-Ku, Seoul Korea. **LC** JQ1727.

KUKKA KOSI. Periodical. KO. Korean. mo. 22.000. Popchisa, 30-21 Mukchong-Dong Chung-Ku, Seoul Korea. **LC** JQ1726.Z13.

KUNNALLISTEN VIRANHALTIJOIDEN JA KUUKAUSIPALKKAISTEN TYONTEKIJOIDEN JA TOIMIHENKILOIDEN PALKAT. Main/Corp Finland. Tilastokeskus. Fl. Finnish. an. Valtion Painatuskeskus, Markkinointosasto Pl 516, 00101 Helsinki 10 Finland. **LC** JS6124.A35.

KWIC INDEX TO THE GOVERNMENT OF ONTARIO. See Indexes/Abstracts.

KWIC INDEX TO YOUR ONTARIO GOVERNMENT SERVICES. See Indexes/Abstracts.

LA REVUE ADMINISTRATIVE. (LA REVUE ADMINISTRATIVE, REVUE BIMESTRIELLE DE L'ADMINISTRATION MODERNE). Vol. 1- Jan./Feb. 1948-. 0035-0672. Periodical. FR. French. bm. 540. Revue Administrative, 2 rue de Viarmes, Paris 1er France. **Tel** 42362390. **Ind/Abst** Index Foreign Leg. Per. Collect. Essays, Foreign Lang. Index. **LC** JA11. **DD** 351.05. Index in last issue of volume - attached. bk rev. adv acc. **Circ** 35,000. Covers administrative law, public administration, and general management for all countries.

LABOR ARBITRATION IN GOVERNMENT. See Economics - Labor.

LABOR-MANAGEMENT RELATIONS IN STATE AND LOCAL GOVERNMENTS. See Economics - Labor.

LABOR MANAGEMENT RELATIONS ISSUES IN STATE AND LOCAL GOVERNMENTS. See Economics - Labor.

LABOR STUDIES JOURNAL. See Economics - Labor.

LACHINE 300. (LACHINE 300 : A MUNICIPAL NEWSLETTER SERVING THE CITIZENS OF THE CITY OF LACHINE). **VAT** Lachine Three Hundred, Lachine Trois Cent. No. 1-. 0710-5657. Periodical. CN. English (French on inverted pages). qt. City of Lachine, City Hall, 1800 St-Joseph Boulevard, Lachine Quebec Canada. **DD** 352.071428.

LAMBERT'S WORLDWIDE GOVERNMENT DIRECTORY WITH INTER-GOVERNMENTAL ORGANIZATIONS. See Yearbooks, Almanacs, Directories.

LANDESHAUSHALT. Series/Titl Salzburg Dokumentationen. German. ir. **LC** HJ44.S35. **DD** 354.4363007225205.

LAPORAN - WALIKOTA JAKARTA PUSAT. Main/Corp Jakarta Pusat, Indonesia. Walikota. IO. Indonesian. ir. Jakarta Pusat, Jln Pegangasaan Barat No 4, Jakarta Indonesia. **LC** JS33.J3.

LAPORAN - WALIKOTA JAKARTA TIMUR. Main/Corp Jakarta Timur (Indonesia). Wali Kota. IO. Indonesian. ir. Jakarta Timur, Jln Raya Jatinegara Timur No 55, Jakarta Indonesia. **LC** JS7206.D5. *Laporan Bulanan Walikota Jakarta Timur*.

LAPURAN TAHUNAN - SURUHANJAYA PERKHIDMATAN AWAM NEGERI SABAH. Main/Corp Sabah. Suruhanjaya Perkhidmatan Awam Negeri. 1972-. Malay. ir. *Annual Report of the Sabah State Public Service Commission*, 0304-7938.

Public Administration

LAPURAN TAHUNAN SURUHANJAYA PERKHIDMATAN AWAM NEGERI SABAH. Main/Corp Sabah. Public Service Commission. Malay. ir. Bangunam HongKong Dan Shanghai Bank, Peti Surat POS 998, Jesselton Malaysia. LC HD2768.M35.

LARU STUDIES. VFOAT Studies Laru. VAT Latin American Research Unit Studies. Vol. 1- Oct. 1976-. 0704-1217. Monographic Series. CN. English. ty. Latin American Research Unit, PO Box 673, Adelaide Street Post Office, Toronto Ontario Canada. LC JL966. DD 980'.005.

LBA HANDBOOK. Main/Corp London Boroughs Association. Began with 1970 issue. UK. English. be. London Boroughs Association, Westminster City Hall, Victoria Street, London SW1E 6QW England. LC JS3551. DD 352.00809421.

LEAFLETS, FOLDERS, ETC. - DEPT. OF HUMAN RESOURCES. Main/Corp British Columbia. Dept. of Human Resources. Monographic Series. CN. English. Free. Queen's Printer, Department of Human Resources, Victoria British Columbia Canada.

LEGISLATING FOR THE NATION'S CAPITAL. Main/Corp United States. Congress. Senate. Committee on the District of Columbia. 0161-7060. Periodical. US. English. ir. LC KFD1215. DD 348.753026.

LEGISLATION AFFECTING SOUTH DAKOTA MUNICIPALITIES. Main/Corp South Dakota Municipal League. 0093-2280. US. English. an. University of South Dakota, Center for Continuing Education, Vermillion SD 57069. LC KFS3431.A29. DD 342.78309.

LEGISLATIVE BUDGET BOOK : A PUBLICATION OF THE LEGISLATIVE BUDGET OFFICE. Main/Corp Idaho. Legislature. Legislative Budget Office. VFOAT Idaho Legislative Budget Book. Fiscal Year 1984-. US. English. an. Idaho Legislative Budget Office, Room 334/Statehouse, Boise ID 83720. LC HJ11. DD 353.97960072205.

LEGISLATIVE BUDGET ESTIMATES. See Business - Public Finance.

LEGISLATIVE CALENDAR. Main/Corp United States. Congress. House. Committee on Energy and Commerce. 97th Congress, No. 1 (Apr. 10, 1981)-. Periodical. US. English. Committee on Energy and Commerce, Rayburn House Office Building/Room 2125, Washington DC 20515. Ind/Abst CIS/Index Publ. U.S. Congr. LC KF22. DD 328.7307652. Legislative Calendar.

LEGISLATIVE CALENDAR. Main/Corp United States. Congress. Senate. Select Committee on Intelligence. Periodical. US. English. Select Committee on Intelligence, US Senate, US Government Printing Office, Washington DC 20510.

LEGISLATIVE CALENDAR, CUMULATIVE RECORD - UNITED STATES SENATE. SELECT COMMITTEE ON INTELLIGENCE. (LEGISLATIVE CALENDAR, CUMULATIVE RECORD). Main/Corp United States. Congress. Senate. Select Committee on Intelligence. 94th Congress, 2nd Session- Jan. 19, 1976-. 0148-0510. US. English. ir. Superintendent of Documents, US Government Printing Office, Washington DC 20402. LC KF21. DD 328.730765.

LEGISLATIVE CALENDAR - UNITED STATE HOUSE OF REPRESENTATIVES. COMMITTEE ON VETERANS' AFFAIRS. (LEGISLATIVE CALENDAR). Main/Corp United States. Congress. House. Committee on Veterans' Affairs. 0364-4200. US. English. Ind/Abst CIS/Index Publ. U.S. Congr. LC JK1430.V4. DD 355.115.

LEGISLATIVE CALENDAR - UNITED STATES HOUSE OF REPRESENTATIVES, COMMITTEE ON BANKING, FINANCE, AND URBAN AFFAIRS. (LEGISLATIVE CALENDAR). Main/Corp United States. Congress. House. Committee on Banking, Finance, and Urban Affairs. 0190-5473. US. English. Ind/Abst CIS/Index Publ. U.S. Congr. LC JK1430.B3. DD 328.730765. Legislative Calendar, 0364-9652.

LEGISLATIVE CALENDAR - UNITED STATES HOUSE OF REPRESENTATIVES, COMMITTEE ON RULES. (LEGISLATIVE CALENDAR). Main/Corp United States. Congress. House. Committee on Rules. 0190-5805. US. English. an. US Government Printing Office, Superintendent of Documents, Washington DC 20402. Ind/Abst CIS Abstr. LC KF22. DD 328.730765.

LEGISLATIVE CALENDAR - UNITED STATES HOUSE OF REPRESENTATIVES. COMMITTEE ON THE BUDGET. (LEGISLATIVE CALENDAR). Main/Corp United States. Congress. House. Committee on the Budget. 0147-3638. US. English. US Government Printing Office, Superintendent of Documents, Washington DC 20402. Ind/Abst CIS/Index Publ. U.S. Congr. LC KF22. DD 328.73075.

LEGISLATIVE CALENDAR - UNITED STATES SENATE. COMMITTEE ON AGRICULTURE, NUTRITION, AND FORESTRY. (LEGISLATIVE CALENDAR). Main/Corp United States. Congress. Senate. Committee on Agriculture, Nutrition, and Forestry. Began with 95th Congress, 1st Session, Jan. 4, 1977. 0147-4103. US. English. US Government Printing Office, Superintendent of Documents, Washington DC 20402. Ind/Abst CIS/Index Publ. U.S. Congr. LC JK1240.A46. DD 328.730765. Legislative Calendar, 0364-4170.

LEGISLATIVE CALENDAR - UNITED STATES SENATE. COMMITTEE ON GOVERNMENTAL AFFAIRS. (LEGISLATIVE CALENDAR). Main/Corp United States. Congress. Senate. Committee on Governmental Affairs. Began with 95th Congress, 1st Session, Jan. 4, 1977. 0147-6572. US. English. US Government Printing Office, Superintendent of Documents, Washington DC 20402. Ind/Abst CIS/Index Publ. U.S. Congr. LC JK1240.E8. DD 328.730765. Legislative Calendar, 0364-4251.

LEGISLATIVE MANUAL - GENERAL ASSEMBLY OF SOUTH CAROLINA. Main/Corp South Carolina. General Assembly. 0362-272X. US. English. an. $4.00. Clerk of the House, PO Box 11867, Columbia SC 29211. Tel (803)758-8343. Ed Lois T Shealy. LC JK4271. Circ 15,000. Pictures and biographies of members of the General Assembly, judicial system, state officers and Congress, county, state offices and US offices.

A LEGISLATOR'S GUIDE. VFOAT Legislative Guide. US. English. an. Office of Legislature, Room 333/State House, Augusta ME 04333. LC JK2830. DD 328.74100202.

LGC LOCAL GOVERNMENT CHRONICLE. VFOAT Local Government Chronicle. No. 5314- Jan. 1969-. Periodical. UK. English. wk. $65.00. IPC Magazine Ltd, Oakfield Hse Hse/Perrymount Rd, Haywards Heath W Sussex RH163BR England. Also available on microfilm. LOCAL GOVERNMENT CHRONICLE.

LIAISON. V. 1- Nov. 1975-. 0701-0532. Periodical. CN. French. Union des Municipalites du Quebec, 922 East rue Liege, Montreal Quebec H2P 1L1 Canada. DD 352.00062714.

EL LIBRO DE PUERTO RICO. 1983-. PR. Spanish. ir. Ediciones Nuevas de Puerto Rico, Apartado 2648, San Juan Puerto Rico 00903. Ed A Quinones Calderon. LC JL1041. DD 320.972950202.

LICENSEE CONTRACTOR AND VENDOR INSPECTION STATUS REPORT. US. English. qt. Superintendent of Documents, US Government Printing Office, Washington DC 20402. Tel (202)783-3238.

LIST AND ANALYSIS OF STATE PAPERS, FOREIGN SERIES : ELIZABETH I. Main/Corp Great Britain. Public Record Office. UK. English. ir. Her Majestys Stationery Office, PO Box 569, London SE1 England. Tel (01)211-5656.

LIST OF CLASSES OF UNITED STATES GOVERNMENT PUBLICATIONS AVAILABLE FOR SELECTION BY DEPOSITORY LIBRARIES. Began with 1960. 0882-4045. Periodical. US. English. qt. Superintendent of Documents, US Government Printing Office, Washington DC 20402. DD 011. List of Classes of United States Government Publications Distributed to Depository Libraries.

LIST OF MEMBERS OF THE DIPLOMATIC CORPS. English. ir. LC JX1853. DD 351.8920955.

LIST OF MEMBERS OF THE HOUSE OF COMMONS OF CANADA. (LIST OF MEMBERS OF THE HOUSE OF COMMONS OF CANADA WITH THEIR RESPECTIVE CONSTITUENCIES AND ADDRESSES). Main/Corp Canada. Parliament. House of Commons. VFOAT Liste des Deputes a la Chambre des Communes du Canada Avec Indication de la Circonscription Electorale et de l'Adresse du Depute. Nov. 12, 1953-. 0316-1641. Periodical. CN. text in English and French. Information Canada, 171 Slater Street, Ottawa Ontario K1A 0S9 Canada. DD 328.71073. List of Members of the House of Commons with Their Constituencies and Post Office Addresses.

LIST OF WORKING DOCUMENTS. Main/Corp European Parliament. 0531-4348. US. English. ir. $48.00. European Comm Info Service, Suite 707/2100 M Street NW, Washington DC 20037. LC JN32. DD 341.242.

LISTE DE MESSIEURS LES MEMBRES DU CORPS DIPLOMATIQUE ET CONSULAIRE. See Law - International Law.

LISTE DER DIPLOMATISCHEN MISSIONEN UND ANDEREN VERTRETUNGEN IN BONN. Main/Corp Germany (West). Auswartiges Amt. GW. German. ir. Stollfuss-Verlag, Dechenstrasse 7-11, 53 Bonn West Germany. LC JX1795. DD 354.4300892. Liste des Diplomatischen Korps in Bonn.

LISTE DES MEMBRES DU CORPS CONSULAIRE. Main/Corp Switzerland. Departement des Auswartigen. French. ir. LC JX1823. DD 351.89209494.

LISTE DES PERIODIQUES - ENAP. CENTRE DE DOCUMENTATION. (LISTE DES PERIODIQUES). Main/Corp Ecole Nationale d'Administration Publique (Quebec) Centre de Documentation. VAT Liste des Periodiques - Ecole Nationale d'Administration Publique. Centre de Documentation. 0711-5849. CN. French. an. Free. Centre de Documentation Ecole Nationale d'Administration Publique, 945 Avenue Qolfe, Ste-Foy Quebec G1V 3J9 Canada. DD 018.134. (ctrl).

LISTE DIPLOMATIQUE - REPUBLIQUE TOGOLAISE, MINISTERE DES AFFAIRES ETRANGERES ET DE LA COOPERATION. Main/Corp Togo. Ministere des Affaires Etrangeres et de la Cooperation. French. an. Ministere des Affaires Etrangeres et de la Cooperation, Service de Comptabilite, Lome Togo. LC JX1867.T6. DD 351.892096681.

LISTE MENSUELLE DES PUBLICATIONS DU GOUVERNEMENT DU QUEBEC. V. 1, No. 2, (April 1981)-. 0229-1894. Periodical. CN. French. mo. $15.48. Ministere des Communications, CP 1005, Quebec Canada G1K 7B5. Liste des Publications du Gouvernement du Quebec.

LIVING CITY. Began with Winter 1967 Issue. Periodical. AT. English. sa. Free. Melbourne & Met Board Works, 625 Little Collins Street, Melbourne Australia. Tel 615-4163. Ed Michael Petit. LC HT169.A82. DD 711.409945. Circ 50,000. (ctrl). Periodic report of developments in water resource management, parks and waterways developments and other public resource areas under the jurisdiction of the Melbourne and Metropolitan Board of Works.

LOBBYING IN THE FLORIDA HOUSE OF REPRESENTATIVES. Main/Corp Florida. Legislature. House of Representatives. Office of the Clerk. 0148-4354. Periodical. US. English. Florida House of Representatives, Tallahassee FL 32304. LC JK4474.5. DD 328.7590738025.

LOCAL AUTHORITY ELECTION STATISTICS. See Statistics.

LOCAL AUTHORITY STATISTICS. See Statistics.

LOCAL COUNCIL REVIEW. 0308-3594. Periodical. UK. English. qt. 2.65. National Association of Local Councils, 18 Stone Park Drive, Forest Row East, Sussex RH18 5DG England. Tel 034 282 3042. Ed Valerie A Shepard. LC JS3001. DD 352.041. bk rev. adv acc. Circ 24,773. Matters of interest of parish, town and community councils in England and Wales. Parish Councils Review, 0031-2061.

LOCAL GOVERNMENT. Periodical. English. ir. 25.00. 14 Japan Mansion Preedy Street, Karachi Pakistan. LC JS7091.A1. DD 352.05491.

LOCAL GOVERNMENT EMPLOYMENT. See Economics - Labor.

LOCAL GOVERNMENT IN SOUTHERN AFRICA. VFOAT Plaaslike Regering in Suidelike Africa. Periodical. Afrikaans (English). mo. 12.00. Melton Publications Pty Ltd, 137 Greenway, PO Box

Public Administration

84248, Greenside 2034 South Africa. **Ind/Abst** Excerpta Med. **LC** JS7531.A1. **DD** 352.068. *Municipal Administration and Engineering.*

LOCAL GOVERNMENT NEWSLETTER (NASHVILLE, TENN.). (LOCAL GOVERNMENT NEWSLETTER : A COMPTROLLER OF THE TREASURY PUBLICATION FOR LOCAL GOVERNMENT AND THE PUBLIC). Vol. 1, No. 1 (Mar. 1981)-. Periodical. US. English. bm. Division of Local Government, James K Polk State Office Building, 505 Deadrick Street, Nashville TN 37219. *Tennessee Assesors' Newsletter, Newsletter (Tennessee. Office of Local Government).*

LOCAL GOVERNMENT QUARTERLY. V. 1- Mar. 1972-. Periodical. II. English. ir. $4.50. 217 B Dhanmandi Residential Area, Road No 15, Dacca 5 India. **LC** JS7100.A1. **DD** 352.05492.

THE LOCAL GOVERNMENT REPORTS OF AUSTRALIA. V. 1- 1956-. 0076-0242. AT. English. ir. Methuen Law Book Co Ltd, 35 Mitchell Street c/o Bennett Nth, Sydney New South Wales 2060 Australia. Ed A M Cohen, J Bales, K H Gifford and R J Banton. **DD** 352.094.

LOCAL GOVERNMENT REVIEW. Periodical. UK. English. wk. $81.21. Barry Rose Law Periodicals Ltd, E Row Little London, Chichester West Sussex London PO19 1PGEngland. **LC** K12. **DD** 352.042. *Justice of the Peace and Local Government Review.*

LOCAL GOVERNMENT REVIEW IN JAPAN. No. 7- 1979-. English. an. **Ind/Abst** Public Aff. Inf. Serv. Bull. **LC** JS7371.A1. **DD** 320.80952. *Local Government Review.*

LOCAL GOVERNMENT STUDIES. Oct. 1971-. 0300-3930. Periodical. UK. English. ty. 60.00. Charles Knight & Company Limited, 209 High Street, Croydon Surrey CR0 1QR England. **Tel** 01686-9141. Ed Kieron Walsh. **Ind/Abst** Soc. Sci. Citation Index. bk rev. adv acc. **Circ** 800. A management journal for those involved in the process of decision making and in the delivery of local services by local authorities, with an emphasis on policy and management control.

LOCAL PLANNING NEWS. Vol. 1, No. 1 (Jan./Feb. 1969)-. Periodical. US. English. mo. Tennessee State Planning Office, 600 Capitol Hill Building, Nashville TN 37219. **Tel** (615)741-2211.

LOK SABHA. PARLIAMENTARY COMMITTEES. SUMMARY OF WORK. (PARLIAMENTARY COMMITTEE : SUMMARY OF WORK). **Main/Corp** India. Parliament. House of the People. 0445-6793. II. English. ir. Lok Sabha Secretariat, India Parliament House of the People, New Delhi India. **LC** JQ257.C6. **DD** 328.540765.

LONDON METROBULLETIN. No. 1 (Mar. 1983)-. 0824-4596. Periodical. CN. English. mo. Free. London Metrobulletin, c/o M Emery, PO Box 2214 Station A, London Ontario N6A 4E3 Canada. **DD** 051. (ctrl). *Downtown London Metrobulletin, 0824-4588.*

LOOSELEAF REGULATIONS SYSTEM. SERVICE 5. PROCEDURE AND ADMINISTRATION. **Main/Corp** United States. Internal Revenue Service. **VFOAT** Procedure and Administration. Periodical. US. English. ir. Procedure and Administration, US Treasury Department, Internal Revenue Service, Washington DC 20402.

LORETTAIN. (LE LORETTAIN : JOURNAL MUNICIPAL DE LA VILLE DE L'ANCIENNE-LORETTE). **Main/Corp** Ancienne-Lorette (Quebec). Vol. 1, No 1 (Sept. 1, 1981)-. 0822-7888. Periodical. CN. French. mo. Ville de l'Ancienne-Lorette, 1575 rue Turmel, Ancienne-Lorette Quebec G2E 3J5 Canada. **Tel** (418)872-9811. **DD** 352.071447. **Circ** 4,500. (ctrl). General information.

LORRAIN. (LE LORRAIN). 0715-8599. Periodical. CN. English (French on inverted pages). mo. Free to Residents. Ville de Lorraine, 100 Grande-Cote, Lorraine Quebec J6Z 1L9 Canada. **DD** 352.071424.

LOS ANGELES COUNTY ALMANAC; A GUIDE TO GOVERNMENT. See Yearbooks, Almanacs, Directories.

LOTO-LIAISON. V. 1- Sept. 1979-. 0706-196X. Periodical. CN. French. mo. Bulletin d'Information de Loto-Quebec, 2000 rue Berri, Montreal Quebec H2L 4N5 Canada. **DD** 354.71400726.

LOTTERY PLAYER'S MAGAZINE. Vol. 1, No. 1 (Aug. 1981)-. 0277-5565. Periodical. US. English. mo. $18.00. Lottery Players, PO Box 5013, Cherry Hill NJ 08034. **Tel** (609)783-0910. Ed Samuel W Valenza Jr. adv acc. **Circ** 220,000. (ctrl) Winning numbers, news and features relating to state and foreign lotteries including Western and Eastern recreational gaming information.

LOUISIANA MUNICIPAL REVIEW. V. 1- May/June 1938-. 0164-3622. Periodical. US. English. bm. **LC** JS39. **DD** 352.0763. (cum index).

LUSAKA PROVINCE ANNUAL REPORT FOR THE YEAR . . . . **Main/Corp** Zambia. Office of the Prime Minister. 1980-. English. an. 1.50. Government Printer, PO Box 30136, Lusaka Zambia. **Tel** (01)215401. **LC** J725.3. **DD** 354.6894. bk rev. adv acc. *Lusaka Province Annual Report.*

MAALAISKUNTIEN JA KUNTAINLIITTOJEN TUNTIPALKKAISTEN TYONTEKIJOIDEN PALKAT. **Main/Corp** Finland. Tilastokeskus. **VFOAT** Landskommunernas Och Kommunalforbundens Timavlonade Arbetstagares Loner. Finnish and Swedish. ir. Tilastokeskus, Annankatu 44, 00100 10 Helsinki Finland. **LC** JS6124.

MACHINE MANUAL OF INSTRUCTIONS FOR JUDGES OF ELECTION. PRIMARY ELECTION. **Main/Corp** Illinois. State Board of Elections. 0272-8389. US. English. State Board of Elections, 1020 S Spring Street, Springfield IL 62704. **LC** JK2023.I3. **DD** 324.609773.

MAFIA 67. **VFOAT** Journal Mafia 67. **VAT** Mafia Soixante-Sept. Vol. 1, No. 1 (Nov. 1981)-. 0711-5504. Periodical. CN. French. ir. Free. Mafia 67, Escadron 67, CP 1716, 50 rue Couture, Sherbrooke Quebec J1H 4B4 Canada. **DD** 358.412232.

MAINE TOWNSMAN. 1937. 0025-0791. Periodical. US. English. mo. $9.00. Maine Municipal Association, Local Government Center Community Drive, Augusta ME 04330. **Tel** (207)623-8428. Ed Michael L Starn. adv acc. **Circ** 4,100. Information about municipal governments in the state of Maine. *New England Townsman.*

MAJOR MATTERS BEFORE THE FEDERAL COMMUNICATIONS COMMISSION. See Communication.

MAKTABAT AL-IDARAH. **VFOAT** I.P.A. Library Bulletin. V. 1- March 1970-. Periodical. Arabic (or English). ir. PO Box 205, Al-Rujad Saudi Arabia. **LC** JA26.

MANAGEMENT IMPROVEMENT AND COST REDUCTION GOALS. **Main/Corp** United States. General Services Administration. US. English. Superintendent of Documents, US Government Printing Office, Washington DC 20402. **LC** JK1672. **DD** 353.0071.

MANAGEMENT IN GOVERNMENT. V. 1- April/June 1969-. 0047-570X. Periodical. II. English. qt. 14.00. Management in Government, Personnel and Administration Reform, Sardar Patel Bhawan Parliament, New Delhi 110001 India. **Tel** 312325. Ed S Regunathan. **Ind/Abst** Public Aff. Inf. Serv. Bull. **LC** JA26. **DD** 354.540005. bk rev. (ctrl). To disseminate, among practising managers and administrators, modern trends and techniques in management and public administraiton.

MANAGEMENT IN GOVERNMENT (LONDON, ENGLAND). (MANAGEMENT IN GOVERNMENT). V. 37, No. 1 (Feb. 1982)-. 0263-4678. Periodical. UK. English. qt. 7.72. Her Majesty's Stationery Office, PO Box 276, London SE1 9NH England. **Ind/Abst** Manage. Contents, Comput. Control Abstr., Electr. Electron. Abstr., Sci. Abstr. Sect. A. Phys. Abstr., Public Aff. Inf. Serv. Bull., World Text Abstr. **LC** JA8. **DD** 350.0005. **CODEN** MAGOD5. *Management Services in Government, 0307-8558.*

MANAGEMENT INFORMATION SERVICE REPORT CEASED. **VFOAT** MIS Reports, Management Information Service, Automating the Office. Vol. 1, No. 1 (Jan. 1969)-Vol. 15, No. 12 (Dec. 1983). 0730-0239. Periodical. US. English. mo. International City Management Association, 1140 Connecticut Avenue NW, Washington DC 20036. **Ind/Abst** Public Aff. Inf. Serv. Bull. **LC** JS39. **DD** 352.073.

MANAGEMENT REPORT - GENERAL SERVICES ADMINISTRATION. (MANAGEMENT REPORT). **Main/Corp** United States. General Services Administration. 0091-6242. US. English. an. US General Services Administration, Washington DC 20405. **LC** JK1672. **DD** 353.0071.

MANAGEMENT SELECTION AND DEVELOPMENT, ANNUAL STATUS REPORT. **Main/Corp** Oregon. Governor's Steering Committee for Management Selection and Development. 1972-. US. English. an. 240 Cottage Street SE, Salem OR 97310. **LC** JK9060.5.E9. **DD** 353.9795034.

MANAGEMENT SERVICES IN GOVERNMENT CEASED. V. 28-36. 0307-8558. Periodical. UK. English. qt. 1/-/-. **Ind/Abst** World Text Abstr., Ship Abstr., CIS Abstr., Public Aff. Inf. Serv. Bull. **LC** JA8. **DD** 350.0005. **CODEN** MNSGBS. *O & M Bulletin.*

MANAGING THE NATION'S PUBLIC LANDS : A PROGRAM REPORT PREPARED PURSUANT TO REQUIREMENTS OF THE FEDERAL LAND POLICY AND MANAGEMENT ACT OF 1976. See Business - General Management.

MANPOWER PLANNING DATA. See Business - Personnel Management.

MANUAL OF THE GENERAL ASSEMBLY OF THE STATE OF GEORGIA. **Main/Corp** Georgia. Secretary of State. **VFOAT** Legislative Manual. 0098-8103. US. English. an. Secretary of State, State Capitol/Room 214, Atlanta GA 30334. **LC** JK4330. **DD** 328.75805. *Handbook of the General Assembly of the State of Georgia, 0361-459X.*

MANUAL OF THE SENATE AND HOUSE OF DELEGATES. **Main/Corp** Virginia. General Assembly. 0363-1184. US. English. be. Free. House of Delegates, State Capitol, Richmond VA 23219. **Tel** (804)786-7210. Ed George A Williams. **LC** JK3930. **DD** 328.75505. **Circ** 5,000. Legislative information on senate and house members, rules, committee assignments, biographies, districts, etc.

MANUAL - STATE OF RHODE ISLAND AND PROVIDENCE PLANTATIONS. (MANUAL - THE STATE OF RHODE ISLAND AND PROVIDENCE PLANTATIONS). **Main/Corp** Rhode Island. Dept. of State. **VFOAT** State of Rhode Island Manual, Rhode Island Manual. 1975/76-. 0197-4238. US. English. be. Rhode Island Department of State, 219 State House, Providence RI 02903. **LC** JK3230. **DD** 320.4745. *Manual, with Rules and Orders, for the Use of the General Assembly of the State of Rhode Island, 0190-5309.*

MARAD. See Transportation - Ships & Shipping.

MARCHES PUBLICS. Periodical. FR. French. ir. Documentation Francaise, 124 rue Henri Barbusse, 93308 Aubervilliers Cedex France. **Tel** 834-9275. **LC** JN2758.

MARYLAND MANUAL. **VFOAT** Manual, State of Maryland. 0094-4491. Periodical. US. English. be. Hall of Records, PO Box 828, Annapolis MD 21404. **Tel** (301)269-3914. **LC** JK3831. **NLM** JK 3831 M393. Concerns Maryland government and history.

MASSACHUSETTS MUNICIPAL DIRECTORY. See Yearbooks, Almanacs, Directories.

MASSACHUSETTS MUNICIPAL GUIDE. **Main/Corp** Massachusetts Selectmen's Association. 1st- Ed. US. English. Organization Services Corporation, Executive Offices, 1616 Soldiers Field Road, Brighton MA 02135. **LC** JS451.M43. **DD** 352.008025744.

MAST. MANITOBA ASSOCIATION OF SCHOOL TRUSTEES. (M A S T). **Main/Corp** Manitoba Association of School Trustees. **VAT** Manitoba Association of School Trustees. V. 3, No. 2- Sept. 1976-. 0381-9531. Periodical. CN. English. ir. $4.00. Manitoba Association of School Trustees, 191 Provencher Boulevard, Winnipeg Manitoba R2H OG4 Canada. **Tel** (204)233-1595. Ed Judith C Neumann. **Ind/Abst** Can. Educ. Index. **DD** 370.97127. bk rev. adv acc. **Circ** 2,100. (ctrl). Articles pertaining to education.

THE MAYOR. V. 38, No. 20- Oct. 15, 1971-. Periodical. US. English. sm. $12.00. US Conference of Mayors, 1620 Eye Street Northwest, Washington DC 20006. **Tel** (202)293-7330. Index in last issue of volume - attached. *United States Municipal News.*

Public Administration

MEMBERSHIP DIRECTORY - AMERICAN SOCIETY FOR PUBLIC ADMINISTRATION, NATIONAL CAPITAL AREA CHAPTER. See Yearbooks, Almanacs, Directories.

MESNE ZAJEDNICE. Main/Corp Savezni Zavod za Statistiku (Yugoslavia). **Series Corp** Its Statisticki Bilten. Serbo-Croatian(R). ir. 5.00. Savezni Zavod za Statistiku, Knexa Milosa 20, Beograd Yugoslavia. LC HA1631, JS6942.

METRIC CONVERSION. (METRIC CONVERSION : BULLETIN). **VFOAT** Conversion au Systeme Metrique : Bulletin. No. 10 (Dec. 1975)-. 0713-7990. Periodical. CN. French (English in parallel columns). ir. Free. Transports Canada, Public Affairs Branch, Ottawa Ontario K1A 0N5 Canada. **DD** 354.7100821. (ctrl). *Conversion au Systeme Metrique, 0713-7990.*

METRO MONITOR : A PUBLICATION OF THE METROPOLITAN COUNCIL. **VFOAT** Monitor. Vol. 1, No. 1 (May 1979)-. Periodical. US. English. ir. Metropolitan Council, 300 Metro Square, 7th & Roberts Streets, St Paul MN 55101. **Tel** (612)291-6464. *Metropolitan Council's Monthly Review for Community Leaders, Perspectives (Saint Paul, Minn.).*

METROPOLITAN WASHINGTON REGIONAL DIRECTORY. See Yearbooks, Almanacs, Directories.

MICHIGAN COUNTIES. Periodical. US. English. mo. $10.00. Michigan Association of Counties, 319 West Lenawee, Lansing MI 48933. *Michigan Counties Today.*

MICHIGAN ENVIRONMENTAL REPORT. (MICHIGAN ENVIRONMENTAL REPORT : THE OFFICIAL PUBLICATION OF THE MICHIGAN ENVIRONMENTAL COUNCIL). 0747-735X. Periodical. US. English. bw. $55.00. Michigan Environmental Council, 115 Allegan/Suite 325, Lansing MI 48933. **Tel** (517)487-9539. Ed Howard L Meyerson. **Circ** 500. A publication reporting on environmental policy developments, agency activities, and major state decisions relating to environmental protection in Michigan.

MICHIGAN GOVERNMENTAL STUDIES. No. 1-. Monographic Series. US. English. ir. University of Michigan Press, 839 Greene Street, Ann Arbor MI 48106.

MICHIGAN MANUAL. 1959/60-. 0091-1933. US. English. be. State of Michigan, PO Box 30026, Deptartment of Management and Budget, Lansing MI 48909. **Tel** (517)322-1897. **LC** JK5830. **DD** 353.97740202. **Circ** 7,500. (ctrl). A book of facts and statistics on the State of Michigan. *Michigan Official Directory and Legislative Manual.*

MICHIGAN STATE EMPLOYEES' RETIREMENT SYSTEM. See Statistics.

MIDWEST REVIEW OF PUBLIC ADMINISTRATION CEASED. V. 1-14. 0026-346X. Periodical. US. English. qt. **LC** JK1.

MIM. MENSUEL D'INFORMATION MUNICIPALE. (MIM : MENSUEL D'INFORMATION MUNICIPALE). 0229-7507. Periodical. CN. French. mo. Free. Municipalite de Saint-Augustin-de-Desmaures, 200 Boul Fossambault, Saint-Augustin-de-Desmaures Quebec G0A 3E0 Canada. **DD** 352.0714466. (ctrl). *Trait d'Union (Saint-Augustin-de-Desmaures, Quebec).*

MINI-SCRIBE. Vol. 1, No 1 (Jan. 1980)-. 0228-7064. Periodical. CN. French. Corporation des Secretaires Municipaux du Quebec, Bureau 801/250 Ouest Grande Allee, Quebec Quebec G1R 2H4 Canada. **DD** 352.0714.

MINISTRY OF WORKS AND DEVELOPMENT STATEMENT. Main/Corp New Zealand. Ministry of Works and Development. 1973/74-. 0110-2729. NZ. English. an. $0.35. Govt Printer, Attn A R Shearer Private Bag, Wellington New Zealand. **LC** HD44155. **DD** 354.9310086. *Ministry of Works Statement.*

MINNESOTA ADMINISTRATIVE RULES AND REGULATIONS. Main/Corp Minnesota. Department of Administration. US. English. ir. National Insurance Law Service, 20675 Bahama Street, Chatsworth CA 91311. **Tel** (213)998-8830.

MINNESOTA CITIES. V. 61, No. 10- Sept. 1976-. 0148-8546. Periodical. US. English. mo. $15.00. League of Minnesota Cities, 183 University Avenue East, St Paul MN 55101. **Tel** (612)227-5600. Ed Jean Mehle. **Ind/Abst** Public Aff. Inf. Serv. Bull. **LC** JS39. **DD** 352.00809776. bk rev. adv acc. **Circ** 9,500. Publication on issues of concern and interest to city officials. *Minnesota Municipalities.*

MINNESOTA ELECTED OFFICIALS . . . . 1977-. US. Englsih. be. 180 State Office Building, St Paul MN 55155. *Minnesota State, Congressional, Legislative, Judicial, and County Officers.*

MINNESOTA ELECTION RESULTS : PRIMARY AND GENERAL ELECTIONS. US. English. Minnesota Election Division, Office of the Secretary of State, 180 State Office Building, St Paul MN 55155. **LC** JK6192. **DD** 329.02377605. *Minnesota General Election Results, 0095-6872.*

MINNESOTA GOVERNMENT REPORT, THE TWICE-WEEKLY NEWSLETTER ON STATE GOVERNMENT. V. 1- July 3, 1978-. Periodical. US. English. sw. $185.00. Minnesota Government Report, PO Box 441, Attn Jean Dawson, Willernie MN 55090. **Tel** (612)429-0423. Ed Jean L Dawson. **Circ** 200. (ctrl). A newsletter covering the activities of Minnesota state government, with appellate court opinions. *Capitol Reporter.*

MINNESOTA GUIDEBOOK TO STATE AGENCY SERVICES. **VFOAT** State Agency Services. 1st- Ed. US. English. be. $12.50. Minnesota State Documents Center, 117 University Avenue, St Paul MN 55155. **Tel** (612)297-3000. Ed Robin Panlener. **LC** JK6130. **DD** 353.9776000202. **Circ** 10,000. Comprehensive directory and resource to Minnesota state government operations within the executive, legislative, and judicial branches. Includes historical tourist, recreation, arts, and attractions, parks and campground data.

MINNESOTA JOURNAL. Began with issue for Nov. 15, 1983?. 0741-9449. Periodical. US. English. sm. $40.00. Minnesota Journal, 84 South 6th Street, Minneapolis MN 55402. **Tel** (612)338-0791. **Circ** 3,200. (ctrl). Analysis and reporting on state, metropolitan, local, and regional government, including public finance, transportation, education, and social services. *CL News, 0045-6969.*

MINNESOTA LEGISLATIVE MANUAL. (THE MINNESOTA LEGISLATIVE MANUAL). 1967/68-. US. English. be. Secretary of State of Minnesota, 180 State Office Building, St Paul MN 55155. **LC** JK6131. **DD** 328.77605. *Legislative Manual (Minnesota. Secretary of State).*

MINUTES : LEGISLATIVE ASSEMBLY OFFICIAL REPORT. Main/Corp Cayman Islands. Legislative Assembly. English. ir. Legislative Assembly Cayman Islands, Georgetown West Indies. **LC** J137.5. **DD** 328.7292104.

MINUTES OF PROCEEDINGS AND EVIDENCE OF THE SPECIAL COMMITTEE ON THE FEDERAL-PROVINCIAL FISCAL ARRANGEMENTS. LES PR. Main/Corp Canada. Parlement. Chambre des Communes. Comite Special sur les Accords Fiscaux Entre le Gouvernement Federal et les Provinces. **VFOAT** Proces-Verbaux et Temoignages du Comite Special sur les Accords Fiscaux Entre le Gouvernement Federal et les Provinces. Les Provinces. **VAT** Accords Fiscaux Entre le Gouvernement Federal et les Provinces, Federal-Provincial Fiscal Arrangements. Issue No. 1 (Mar. 23, 1981)-. 0710-9733. Periodical. CN. French (English in parallel columns). Queens Printer for Canada, Receiver General for Canada, Ottawa Ontario K1A 0S9 Canada. **DD** 354.71007252.

MINUTES OF PROCEEDINGS AND EVIDENCE OF THE SPECIAL JOINT COMMITTEE OF THE SENATE AND OF THE HOUSE OF COMMONS ON SENATE REFORM. Main/Corp Canada. Parliament. Special Joint Committee on Senate Reform. **VFOAT** Report of the Special Joint Committee of the Senate and the House of Commons on House Reform, Proces-Verbaux et Temoignages du Comite Mixte Special du Senat et de la Chambre des Communes sur la Reforme du Senat. Issue No 1 (Apr. 28/May 31, 1983)-. 0825-0251. CN. English (French). Canadian Government Publishing Centre, Supply & Services Ottawa Ontario K1A 0S9 Canada.

MINUTES OF PROCEEDINGS AND EVIDENCE OF THE SUB-COMMITTEE B OF THE SPECIAL COMMITTEE ON EMPLOYMENT OPPORTUNITIES FOR THE '80S. Main/Corp Canada. Parliament. House of Commons. Special Committee on Employment Opportunities for the '80s. Sub-Committee B. **VFOAT** Proces-Verbaux et Temoignages du Sous-Comite B du Comite Special sur les Perspectives d'Emploi pour les Annees 80. 1st Session of the 32nd Parliament, 1980, Issue No. 1 (Sept. 22, 1987). CN. English (French). Canadian Government Publishing Centre, Supply & Services Canada, Hull Quebec K1A 0S9 Canada.

MINUTES OF PROCEEDINGS AND EVIDENCE OF THE SUB-COMMITTEE ON DREE PROGRAMMES (QUEBEC) OF THE STANDING COMMITTEE ON REGIONAL DEVELOPMENT. ECONOMIQUE REGIONALE. Main/Corp Canada. Parlement. Chambre des Communes. Sous-Comite des Programmes du Meer (Quebec). **VFOAT** Proces-Verbaux et Temoignages du Sous-Comite des Programmes du Meer (Quebec) du Comite Permanent de l'Expansion Economique Regionale. Economique Regionale. **VAT** Dree Programmes (Quebec), Programmes du Meer (Quebec). Issue No. 1 (June 18, 1981)-. 0713-651X. Periodical. CN. French (English). Queens Printer for Canada, Receiver General of Canada, Ottawa Ontario K1A 0S9 Canada. **DD** 354.710082044.

MINUTES OF PROCEEDINGS - COUNCIL OF EUROPE, PARLIAMENTARY ASSEMBLY. Main/Corp Council of Europe. Parliamentary Assembly. FR. English. ir. Council of Europe Parliamentary Assembly, Ave l' Europe, 67 Strasbourg France. **LC** JN22. **DD** 341.242.

MINUTES OF THE PROCEEDINGS OF THE SELECT COMMITTEE ON PROCEDURE. Main/Corp Great Britain. Parliament. House of Commons. Select Committee on Procedure. **Series/Titl** Great Britain. Parliament House of Commons. Reports and Papers. UK. English. 40. Her Majesty's Stationery Office, PO Box 276, London SW8 5DT England. **LC** JN683. **DD** 328.4105. *Minutes of Evidence Taken Before the Select Committee on the Procedure in the Public Business.*

MIRABEL, A VOL D'OISEAU. (MIRABEL—A VOL D'OISEAU). Vol. 1, No. 1 (Nov. 1977)-. 0229-3285. Periodical. CN. French. ir. Free. Ville de Mirabel, Hotel de Ville, 14111 rue St-Jean Ste-Monique, Mirabel Quebec J0N 1R0 Canada. **DD** 352.071425.

MIS REPORT. Vol. 16, No. 1 (Jan. 1984)-. Periodical. US. English. mo. International City Management Association, 1120 G Street NW, Washington DC 20005. **LC PAR.** *Management Information Service Report, 0730-0239.*

MISSISSIPPI MUNICIPALITIES. V. 1- 1955-. 0026-6337. Periodical. US. English. mo. $7.00. Mississippi Municipal Association, 230 Barefield Complex, Jackson MS 39202. **Tel** (601)353-5854. Ed Pat Dunne. **LC** JS303.M7. bk rev. adv acc. **Circ** 4,000. (ctrl). Of primary interest to municipal elected and appointed officials.

MISSISSIPPI OFFICIAL AND STATISTICAL REGISTER. See Statistics.

MISSOES DIPLOMATICAS, CONSULARES E REPRESENTACOES ORGANIZACOES INTERNACIONAIS. Portuguese. ir. **LC** JX1873.M6. **DD** 351.89209679. *Missoes Diplomaticas e Representacoes de Organizacoes Internacionais.*

MISSOURI MUNICIPAL REVIEW. Began in 1936. 0026-6647. Periodical. US. English. mo. $12.00. Missouri Municipal League, 1913 William Street, Jefferson City MO 65101. Ed Diane Peck. **LC** JS39. **DD** 352.0778. adv acc. **Circ** 5,050. (ctrl). Contains articles and department coverage of full spectrum municipal administration and operation in Missouri and activities in individual cities.

MISSOURI STATE EXECUTIVE BRANCH DIRECTORY. See Yearbooks, Almanacs, Directories.

MN SMALL BUSINESS PROCUREMENT PROGRAM FOR SOCIALLY OR ECONOMICALLY DISADVANTAGED VENDORS F.Y. . . . ANNUAL REPORT. Main/Corp Minnesota. Dept. of Administration. Division of Procurement. **VFOAT** M.N. Small Business Procurement Program for Socially or Economically Disadvantaged Vendors F.Y. . . . Annual Report. **VAT** Minnesota Small Business Procurement Program for Socially or Economically Disadvantaged Vendors F.Y.

Public Administration

... Annual Report. 1982-. US. English. an. LC JK6188.A1. **DD** 353.97760071205. *Annual Report to the Legislature on the Small Business Procurement Act.*

MONITA NENPO. JA. Japanese. an. Naikaku Sori Daijin Kanbo Kohoshitsu Kochogakari, 6-1 Nagata-Cho 1 Chiyoda-Ku, Tokyo-To 100 Japan. **LC** JQ1601.

MONOGRAPH - MAXWELL GRADUATE SCHOOL OF CITIZENSHIP AND PUBLIC AFFAIRS. METROPOLITAN STUDIES PROGRAM. (MONOGRAPH). 0738-3207. Monographic Series. US. English. Maxwell School, Metropolitan Studies Program, 409 Maxwell Hall, Syracuse NY 13210. **Tel** (315)423-3114. Ed Allison Evans Henry. (ctrl). Metropolitan Studies Program conducts research on a wide range of public policy issues: domestic, urban and regional studies, international studies, and health and income security.

MONTHLY CATALOG OF UNITED STATES GOVERNMENT PUBLICATIONS. No. 672 (Jan. 1951)-. 0362-6830. Periodical. US. English. mo. US Government Printing Office, Superintendent of Documents, Washington DC 20402. **Tel** (202)783-3238. **Ind/Abst** Mintec, Min. Technol. Abstr., Minproc. **DD** 015. **NLM** Z 1223 U58M. (cum index). Vols. for Jan. 1984- also available in microfiche. *United States Government Publications Monthly Catalog, 0041-767X.*

MONTHLY CATALOG OF UNITED STATES GOVERNMENT PUBLICATIONS. UNITED STATES CONGRESSIONAL SERIAL SET SUPPLEMENT. VFOAT United States Congressional Serial Set Supplement. 97th Congress (1981-1982)-. 8756-095X. US. English. ir. Superintendent of Documents, US Government Printing Office, Washington DC 20402. Vols. for 97th Congress, 1981-1982- distributed to some depository libraries in microfiche. *Numerical Lists and Schedule of Volumes of the Documents and Reports of the ... Congress, ... Session.*

MONTHLY RELEASE. Periodical. US. English. mo. Superintendent of Documents, US Government Printing Office, Washington DC 20402. **Ind/Abst** Am. Stat. Index. **LC** JK639, JK671. **DD** 3531.006 S, 353.001.

MONTREALITES. V. 1, No. 1, (Dec. 1981)-. 0821-4573. Periodical. CN. French. ir. Free. Cidem-Communications Bureau 224, 155 Est rue Notre-Dame, Montreal Quebec H2Y 1B5 Canada. **DD** 352.0714281. (ctrl).

MOODY'S PUBLIC UTILITY MANUAL. VFOAT Public Utility Manual. 1983-. Periodical. US. English. an. Moody's Investors Service, 99 Church Street, New York NY 10007. *Moody's Manual of Investments: American and Foreign. Public Utility Securities.*

MPWH BULLETIN : OFFICIAL QUARTERLY PUBLICATION OF THE MINISTRY OF PUBLIC WORKS AND HIGHWAYS. Vol. 21, No. 1 (June 1982)-. Periodical. English. qt. MPWH Building Bonifacio Drive, Port Area, Manila Philippines. **LC** HD4306. **DD** 354.59908606. *MPW Bulletin.*

MR-1. Main/Corp California. University. University at Los Angeles. Institute of Government and Public Affairs. Periodical. US. English. ir.

MRI INFORMATIVO. Main/Corp Venezuela. Ministerio de Relaciones Interiores. Yearly V. 1- (No. 1-). VE. Spanish. ir. Ministerio de Relaciones Interiores, Caracas Venezuela. **LC** J257. **DD** 354.87305.

MULTI-UNIT AGREEMENTS IN THE FEDERAL GOVERNMENT. Periodical. US. English. an. US Civil Service Commission, Office of Labor-Management Relations, Washington DC 20415.

MUNCA DE PARTID. Periodical. RM. Romanian. mo. Ilexim Press Department, PO Box 1-136-1-137, Bucharest Romania. **LC** JN9639.A57.

MUNICIPAL CORPORATIONS. US. English. $175.00. Michie Bobbs Merrill, c/o Jim Shroyer, PO Box 717, Pelham AL 35124.

MUNICIPAL DIMENSIONS. Vol. 1, No. 1 (Oct. 7, 1982)-. 0820-7704. CN. English. ir. Federation of Canadian Municipalities, Suite 1318/112 Kent Street, Ottawa Ontario K1P 5P2 Canada. **DD** 352.07105.

MUNICIPAL DIRECTORY. *See* Yearbooks, Almanacs, Directories.

MUNICIPAL DIRECTORY. *See* Yearbooks, Almanacs, Directories.

MUNICIPAL DIRECTORY. *See* Yearbooks, Almanacs, Directories.

MUNICIPAL EXECUTIVE DIRECTORY. *See* Yearbooks, Almanacs, Directories.

MUNICIPAL HANDBOOK. THE CITY OF CALGARY. (MUNICIPAL HANDBOOK : THE CITY OF CALGARY). Main/Corp Calgary (Alta.). 1976-. 0384-840X. CN. English. an. Public Information Department, City of Calgary, PO Box 2100, Calgary Alberta T2P 2M5 Canada. **DD** 352.071233. *Municipal Manual, 0381-582X.*

MUNICIPAL INFORMATION CEASED. Main/Corp Vanier, (Ont.). Municipal Information Committee. VFOAT Information Municipale. V. 1-5, No. 1. 0382-0114. Periodical. CN. English (French). ir. Citizen's Information Committee, 297 Dupuis, Vanier Ontario K1L 7H8 Canada. **DD** 352.071383.

MUNICIPAL INSTRUCTORS' SECTION NEWS. 0739-4918. Periodical. US. English. qt. ISFSI, 20 Main Street, Ashland MA 01721.

MUNICIPAL JOURNAL. V. 78, No. 25-. 0027-3430. Periodical. UK. English. wk. Municipal Journal, 3 Clements Inn, London WC2 England. *Municipal and Public Services Journal.*

MUNICIPAL MANAGEMENT. V. 1- Summer 1978-. 0164-7296. Periodical. US. English. qt. $22.50. University of Hartford, Department of Public Administration, West Hartford CT 06117. **Tel** (203)243-4609. Ed Shalom Saar. **LC** JS39. **DD** 352.00805. Oriented articles about public management at the local government level.

MUNICIPAL MANAGEMENT DIRECTORY. *See* Yearbooks, Almanacs, Directories.

MUNICIPAL NEWS. 0027-352X. Periodical. US. English. mo. $50.00. Municipal League Seattle King, 414 Central Building, Seattle WA 98104. **Tel** (206)622-8333. Ed Stephen C Forman. **Circ** 2,000. (ctrl). Information on local public policy and emerging issues analysis with possible solutions. Opportunities for the community to get involved through forums and committee meetings.

MUNICIPAL ORDINANCE REVIEW. VFOAT NIMLO Municipal Ordinance Review. V. 6-1953-. 0027-3538. Periodical. US. English. mo. National Institute of Municipal Law Officers, 1000 Connecticut Avenue NW/Suite 800, Washington DC 20036. Index in last issue of volume - attached. *Municipal Legislative Bulletin.*

MUNICIPAL POLICY STATEMENT - LEAGUE OF ARIZONA CITIES & TOWNS. (MUNICIPAL POLICY STATEMENT). Main/Corp League of Arizona Cities and Towns. 0090-6875. US. English. an. 1820 West Washington Street, Phoenix AZ 85007. **LC** JS303.A6. **DD** 352.0791.

MUNICIPAL PROGRESS. 0146-8758. Periodical. US. English. mo. $48.00. Educational Service Bureau, 1835 K Street Northwest, Washington DC 20006. **LC** JS39. **DD** 352.0080973.

THE MUNICIPAL REPORTER. 0028-6257. Periodical. US. English. mo. $20.00. New Mexico Municipal League, PO Box 846, Santa Fe MN 87501. **Tel** (505)982-5573.

MUNICIPAL REVIEW & AMA NEWS. VFOAT Municipal Review and A.M.A. News. Vol. 51/52, No. 610 (Jan. 1981)-. 0027-3562. Periodical. UK. English. mo. 4.50 Domestic and Foreign, 3.00 Bulk Subscriptions (5 or more). Association of Metropolitan Authorities, 36 Old Queen Street, London SW1H 9JE England. **LC** JS3001. **DD** 352.007240941. *Municipal Review, 0027-3562.*

MUNICIPAL SALARY SURVEY. Main/Corp New Jersey. Dept. of Community Affairs. Municipal Information Service. 0363-1729. US. English. an. NJ Department of Community Affairs, Local Government Service, 363 West State Street, Trenton NJ 08625. **LC** JS451.N57. **DD** 353.974900123.

MUNICIPAL SALARY SURVEY. BENCH-MARK JOBS. *See* Economics - Labor.

MUNICIPAL SOUTH. V. 1- Jan. 1954-. 0027-3570. Periodical. US. English. bm. Free to Qualified Individuals, $6.00 Others Domestic, $7.00 Others Foreign. Municipal South Magazine Company, Route 2 Box 799, PO Box 1053, Lincolnton NC 28092. **LC** JS39. **DD** 352.075.

THE MUNICIPAL YEAR BOOK. *See* Yearbooks, Almanacs, Directories.

THE MUNICIPAL YEAR BOOK AND PUBLIC SERVICES DIRECTORY. *See* Yearbooks, Almanacs, Directories.

THE MUNICIPAL YEAR BOOK DIRECTORIES. *See* Yearbooks, Almanacs, Directories.

MUNICIPAL YEAR BOOK, KERALA. *See* Yearbooks, Almanacs, Directories.

MUNICIPAL/COUNTY EXECUTIVE DIRECTORY. *See* Yearbooks, Almanacs, Directories.

MUNICIPALITY (1916). (THE MUNICIPALITY). Vol. 16, No. 1 (Jan. 1916)-. 0027-3597. Periodical. US. English. mo. League of Wisconsin Municipalities, 122 West Washington Avenue, Madison WI 53703. **Tel** (608)267-2380. **Ind/Abst** Public Aff. Inf. Serv. Bull. **DD** 352. *Wisconsin Municipality (1914).*

MUNICIPALITY OF SHUNIAH. V. 1- Mar. 1975-. 0319-4167. Periodical. CN. English. Free to Citizens and Property Holders of Shuniah. Municipal Offices, 420 Leslie Avenue, Thunder Bay Ontario P7A 1X8 Canada. **DD** 352.071312.

NATAT'S NATIONAL COMMUNITY REPORTER. 0735-9691. Periodical. US. English. mo. $18.00. National Association of Towns and Townships, 1522 K Street Northwest/Suite 730, Washington DC 20005. **Tel** (202)737-5200. Ed Bruce Rosenthal. bk rev. adv acc. **Circ** 14,000. National news journal devoted to the interests of small-town and rural government. *National Community Reporter.*

NATIONAL CIVIC REVIEW. V. 1- Jan. 1912-. 0027-9013. Periodical. US. English. ir. $25.00. National Municipal League, 55 West 44th Street, New York NY 10036. **Tel** (212)535-5700. **Ind/Abst** Int. Index, Public Aff. Inf. Serv. Bull., Humanit. Index, Sociol. Abstr., Book Rev. Index, ABC Pol Sci, Am. Hist. Life, Hist. Abstr., Lang. Lang. Behav. Abstr., Soc. Sci. Index. **LC** JS39. **DD** 352.007205. *Equity, Short Ballot Bulletin; Proportional Representation Review.*

NATIONAL DIRECTORY OF STATE & LOCAL GOVERNMENT TRAINERS. *See* Yearbooks, Almanacs, Directories.

NATIONAL INDEPENDENT STUDY CENTER FISCAL YEAR ... COURSE CATALOG. VFOAT Course Catalog. US. English. an. National Independent Study Center, US Civil Service Commission/Building 20, Denver Federal Center, Denver CO 80225.

NATIONAL ISSUES-OUTLOOK. (NATIONAL ISSUES OUTLOOK). 0092-9778. Periodical. US. English. mo. Government Research Corporation, 1730 M Street Northwest, Washington DC 20036. **LC** JK1. **DD** 309.173092. *Issues-Outlook, 0147-9520.*

NATIONAL MUNICIPAL POLICY. Main/Corp National League of Cities. 1965-. US. English. an. $10.00. National League of Cities, 1301 Pennsylvania Avenue NW, Washington DC 20004. **Tel** (202)626-3000. **Circ** 2,000. Policy document outlining priorities of the nation's cities and actions. The federal government should take to address urban problems. *National Municipal Policy.*

NATIONAL NEWS REPORT. 0049-044X. Periodical. US. English. ir. $15.00. National News Report Member Service, Sierra Club 530 Bush Street, San Francisco CA 94108. **Tel** (415)981-8634. Ed Anthony Antico. **Circ** 5,000. (ctrl). Keeps readers informed about developments in environmental politics on national issues before Congress, administrative agencies, and the courts.

THE NATIONAL NOTARY. Periodical. US. English. bm. $18.00. National Notary Association, 23012 Ventura Boulevard, Woodland Hills CA 91364. **Tel** (818)347-2035. Ed Charles Faerber. adv acc. **Circ** 45,000. (ctrl). Contans instructional "how to" articles for notaries public, reports on pertinent current events and features regular departments, including "notary adviser".

NATIONAL PARLIAMENTARIAN. Began in 1938?. 8755-7592. Periodical. US. English. qt. $8.00. National Association of Parliamentarians, 3706 Broadway/Suite 300, Kansas City MO 64111. **DD** 060.

NATIONAL ROSTER OF BLACK ELECTED OFFICIALS CEASED. -1982. 0092-2935. US. English. an. $6.00. 1426 H Street NW/Suite 926, Washington DC 20005. **LC** E185.615. **DD** 353.002.

NATIONAL SECURITY AFFAIRS MONOGRAPH SERIES. VFOAT National Security Affairs Monograph. 76-1-. 0270-7241. Monographic Series. US. English. Superintendent of Documents, US Government Printing Office, Washington DC 20402.

NATIONALRAT UND BUNDESRAT AMTLICHES VERZEICHNIS DER MITGLIEDER, AUSSCHUSSE UND KLUBS. Main/Corp Austria. Nationalrat. German. ir. Nationalrat, Osterreichische Staatsdruckerei, Wien Austria. **LC** JN2023.A2.

NEBRASKA MUNICIPAL REVIEW. 0028-1905. Periodical. US. English. mo. $10.00. League of Nebraska Municipalities, 1335 L Street, Lincoln NE 68508. **Tel** (402)476-2829. Ed David L Chambers. adv acc. **Circ** 3,100. (ctrl). Issues of interest to local governments.

NENKAN NIPPON. VFOAT Nippon. 1983-. Japanese. an. 25000. Rokaru Nihonsha c/o Homei Building, 3-19 Akasaka 1 Minato-Ku, Tokyo-To 107 Japan. **LC** JQ1621.

NEUER WEG. Began in 1946. Periodical. SZ. German. sm. Kunst & Wissen Erich Bieber, Dufourstrasse 51, CH-8008 Zurich Switzerland. **Tel** 011-41-1-69 44 20. **LC** JN3971.5.A98.

NEVADA GAMING ABSTRACT. SUPPLEMENT. See Indexes/Abstracts.

NEVADA GOVERNMENT TODAY. V. 1- Oct. 1973-. 0360-9731. Periodical. US. English. qt. $6.00. Nevada League of Cities, Box 2307, Carson City NV 89701. **Tel** (702)882-2121. Ed G P Etcheverry. **LC** JS451.N35. **DD** 352.0793. adv acc. **Circ** 400. (ctrl). Local government topics.

NEVADA PUBLIC AFFAIRS REVIEW. 1978/79-. 0196-7355. Periodical. US. English. ir. $9.00. University of Nevada, Reno Nevada Public Affairs, Reno NV 89557. **Tel** (702)784-6718. Ed Richard Siegel. **LC** JK8501. **DD** 320.979305. **Circ** 2,500. (ctrl). Publishes basic and applied research related to public affairs in Nevada and promotes public education on public affairs issues. *Nevada Public Affairs Report, 0364-3921*.

THE NEW ENGLAND JOURNAL OF PUBLIC POLICY. 0749-016X. Periodical. US. English. ir. McCormick Institute of Public Affairs, Healey Library Harbor Campus, University of Massachusetts, Boston MA 02125.

NEW GOVERNMENTAL ADVISORY ORGANIZATIONS. Began with No. 1 (1976). 0730-269X. US. English. ir. Gale Research Company, Book Tower, Detroit MI 48226. **Tel** (800)521-0707. **LC** JK468.C7. **DD** 353.093025.

NEW HAMPSHIRE PUBLIC UTILITIES COMMISSION REPORTS. Vol. 58, 59-60 (1973, 1974-1975)-. US. English. New Hampshire Public Utilities Commission, 8 Old Suncock Road, Concord NH 03301. *Reports and Orders -State of New Hampshire Public Utilities Commission*.

NEW HAMPSHIRE TOWN AND CITY. V. 1- May, 1957-. 0545-171X. Periodical. US. English. mo. $8.00. New Hampshire Municipal Association, PO Box 617 North Main Street, Concord NH 03301. **Tel** (603)224-7447. Ed Karen Gomes Moore. adv acc. **Circ** 2,400. Municipal government issues and concerns.

NEW JERSEY ADMINISTRATIVE REPORTS. Vol. 1-. US. English. qt. $195.00. Administrative Publishing and Filing, Quakerbridge Plaza Building 9, Trenton NJ 08625. **Tel** (609)292-6060. **LC** KFN2240. **DD** 342.7490602642, 347. 4902602642. Index in last issue of volume - loose - separately paged.

NEW JERSEY MAYORS. US. English. Department of Community Affairs, 363 W State Street CN800, Trenton NJ 08625. **LC** JS451.N55. **DD** 352.008025749.

NEW JERSEY MUNICIPALITIES. V. 1-4, 1917-20. 0028-5846. Periodical. US. English. mo. $9.00. State League of Municipalities, 407 West State Street, Trenton NJ 08618. **LC** JS39.

NEW JERSEY REGISTER. (NEW JERSEY REGISTER). V. 1- Sept. 25, 1969-. 0300-6069. Periodical. US. English. sm. $75.00. Division of Administrative Procedure, Department of State, 10 North Stockton Street, Trenton NJ 08608. **Tel** (609)292-6060.

NEW JERSEY REPORTER. V. 9, No. 3- Sept. 1979-. 0195-3192. Periodical. US. English. ir. $25.00. Center Analysis Public Issues, 16 Vandeventer Avenue, Princeton NJ 08542. **Tel** (609)924-9750. Ed Rick Sinding. **LC** JK3501. **DD** 361.6109749. **Circ** 3,000. A magazine specializing in in-depth coverage of New Jersey's public policy and political events and issues. *New Jersey Magazine, 0164-6958*.

NEW YORK LEGISLATIVE SERVICE. 1943-. Periodical. US. English. wk. New York Legislative Service, 299 Broadway, New York NY 10007.

THE NEW YORK STATE DIRECTORY. See Yearbooks, Almanacs, Directories.

NEW YORK STATE LEGISLATIVE ANNUAL. 1946-. 0197-3983. US. English. an. $95.00. New York Legislative Service Inc, 299 Broadway, New York NY 10007. **LC** JK3401. **DD** 328.747.

NEW YORK STATE MUNICIPAL BULLETIN. US. English. New York State Conference of Mayors and Municipal Training Institute, 6 Elk Street, Albany NY 12207. **LC** JS39. **DD** 352.0747.

THE NEW YORK STATE REGISTER. VFOAT State Register. V. 1- Apr. 11, 1979-. 0197-2472. Periodical. US. English. wk. $80.00. Department of State, Division of Information Service, 162 Washington Avenue, Albany NY 12231. **Tel** (518)473-7210. Ed Maureen L Bigness. **LC** KFN5036. **DD** 348.74701. **Circ** 18,000. Information on rule making activities on New York state agencies. *New York State Bulletin*.

NEW ZEALAND LOCAL GOVERNMENT. Periodical. NZ. English. mo. 40.00. Trade Publications Ltd, PO Box 37549, Auckland New Zealand. **Tel** (09)795-500. Ed Chris Black. **LC** JS8331. **DD** 352.0931. bk rev. adv acc. **Circ** 2,500. (ctrl). New Zealand's only magazine serving all areas of local (i.e. municipal) government, aimed mainly at senior staff. *Local Body Review*.

NEWS - ADMINISTRATIVE CONFERENCE OF THE UNITED STATES. Main/Corp United States. Administrative Conference. 0197-2316. Periodical. US. English. Administrative Conference of the United States, 2120 L Street NW, Suite 500, Washington DC 20037.

NEWS BULLETIN. Main/Corp Japan. Sorifu. Tokeikyoku. JA. English. ir. Bureau of Statistics/Office of the Prime Minister, 95 Wakamatsucho, Shinjujy-ku, 162 Tokyo Japan. **LC** HA37. **DD** 354.520081.

NEWS DIGEST - INTERNATIONAL INSTITUTE OF MUNICIPAL CLERKS. Main/Corp International Institute of Municipal Clerks. 0145-2290. Periodical. US. English. mo. $15.00. The International Institute of Municipal Clerks, 160 North Altadena Drive, Pasadena CA 91107. **LC** JS42. **DD** 352.00805. *IIMC Newsletter*.

NEWS SPOT. VFOAT IMFRA News Spot. V. 1- Mar. 1980-. 0271-7980. Periodical. US. English. mo. **LC** JK723.M54. **DD** 353.00104.

NEWSLETTER - FEDERAL PROFESSIONAL ASSOCIATION. (NEWSLETTER). Main/Corp Federal Professional Association (U.S.). VFOAT FPA Newsletter. VAT Federal Professional Association Newsletter. 0735-1070. Periodical. US. English. bm. Federal Professional Association, 1302-18th Street NW, Washington DC 20036. **Tel** (202)223-6274.

NEWSLETTER - INTERNATIONAL OMBUDSMAN INSTITUTE. (NEWSLETTER). V. 1, No. 1 (Jan. 1979)-. 0229-2181. Periodical. CN. English. ir. $15.00. International Ombudsman, Institute Law Centre, University of Alberta, Edmonton Alberta T6G 2H5 Canada. **DD** 350.91.

NEWSLETTER - LEAGUE OF OREGON CITIES. (NEWSLETTER). June 1980-. 0731-1435. Periodical. US. English. mo. $15.00. League of Oregon Cities, 1201 Court Street Northeast PO Box 928, Salem OR 93708. Each issue contains an index to its own contents - no vol index - loose. *Information Update for Oregon Cities*.

NEWSLETTER - NOVA SCOTIA GOVERNMENT EMPLOYEES ASSOCIATION. Main/Corp Nova Scotia Government Employees Association. V. 9, No. 8- Oct. 1971-. 0380-1810. Periodical. CN. English. mo. 5435 Spring Garden Road, Halifax Nova Scotia Canada. *Newsletter, 0380-1829*.

NEWSLETTER (UNITED STATES. FEDERAL EMERGENCY MANAGEMENT AGENCY). (NEWSLETTER). VFOAT Federal Emergency Management Agency Newsletter. Jan./Feb. 1984. Periodical. US. English. bm. Federal Emergency Management Agency, 1735-1st Street NW, Washington DC 20472. **Tel** (202)287-0300.

NIGERIA NEWSLETTER. See Business.

THE NIGERIAN JOURNAL OF PUBLIC AFFAIRS. V. 1- Oct. 1970-. Periodical. NR. English. sa. Ahmadu Bello Univ, Institute of Admn, Zaria Nigeria. **LC** JQ3081.A1. **DD** 354.6690005.

NINMEN KANKEI HOREISHU. Main/Corp Japan. JA. Japanese. ir. Okurasho Insatsukyoku, 2-4 Toranomon 2, Minato-ku 105, Tokyo-to-Japan.

NORDISK ADMINISTRATIVT TIDSSKRIFT. V. 1-. 0029-1285. Periodical. DK. Danish. qt. $29.71. Nordisk Administrativt Tidsskrift V, Forlaget Rhodos Strandgade 36, D-1401 Copenhagen K Denmark. Ed Marius Ibsen. **Ind/Abst** Energy Res. Abstr., Am. Hist. Life, Hist. Abstr., Hist. Abstr., Part A, Mod. Hist. Abstr., Hist. Abst., Part B, Twent. Century Abstr. (cum index). bk rev. **Circ** 2,000. For public servants and officials in Scandinavia about the public administration in Denmark, Finland, Iceland, Norway and Sweden.

NORTH CAROLINA ADMINISTRATIVE CODE. LIST OF RULES AFFECTED. Vol. 1, No. 1 (Feb. 2, 1981)-. Periodical. US. English. mo. State of North Carolina Department of Justice, PO Box 629, Raleigh NC 27602-0629. Available in microform.

NORTHWEST TERRITORIES GAZETTE HANDBOOK. 1979-. 0225-5901. Periodical. CN. English. ir. Free with subscription to Northwest Territories Gazette. Culture and Communications, Government of the Northwest Territories, PO Box 1320, Yellowknife Northwest Territories X1A 2L9 Canada. **DD** 354.71920005.

NORTHWEST TERRITORIES GAZETTE. PART 1. (NORTHWEST TERRITORIES GAZETTE; PART I). V. 1- 12 Oct. 1979-. 0225-5898. Periodical. CN. English. mo. Culture and Communications, Government of the Northwest Territories, PO Box 1320, Yellowknife Northwest Territories X1A 2L9 Canada. **DD** 354.71920005.

NORTHWEST TERRITORIES GAZETTE. PART 2. (NORTHWEST TERRITORIES GAZETTE; PART II). V. 1- Oct. 26, 1979-. 0713-2123. Periodical. CN. English. bm. Culture and Communications, Government of the Northwest Territories, PO Box 1320, Yellowknife Northwest Territories X1A 2L9 Canada. **DD** 354.71920005.

NOTES - MUNICIPAL REFERENCE AND RESEARCH CENTER. Main/Corp Municipal Reference and Research Center. V. 1-45, No. 5, Oct.28, 1914-May 1971. 0027-3554. Periodical. US. English. mo. $5.00. Municipal Reference and Research Center/Room 2230 Municipal Building, New York NY 10007.

NOTES - NEW YORK (N.Y.) DEPT. OF RECORDS AND INFORMATION SERVICES. (NOTES). Vol. 1, No. 1 (Fall 1982)-. 0731-2385. Periodical. US. English. qt. $10.00. New York City Department of Records & Information Services, 31 Chambers Street/Room 305, New York NY 10007. **Tel** (212)566-0598. Ed Joan M Nichols. **Circ** 5,000. Newsletter of agency activities in library, archives, and records management. Announcements of exhibitions. *Notes (Municipal Reference and Research Center (New York, N.Y.)), 0027-3554*.

NOTICE PAPER. Main/Corp Australia. Parliament. House of Representatives. Periodical. English. ir. Australian Government Public Service, PO Box 84, Canberra Australian Capital Territory 2600 Australia. **Tel** 062-95 4411.

NOTICES TO AIRMEN. VFOAT Class Two Notams. Began with April 6, 1978. Periodical. US. English. bw. Superintendent of Documents, US

Public Administration

Government Printing Office, Washington DC 20402. **Tel** (202)783-3238. *Airman's Information Manual. Pt. 3A, Notices to Airmen.*

NOTIZIARIO GIURIDICO REGIONALE. See Law.

NRRI QUARTERLY BULLETIN. (NRRI QUARTERLY BULLETIN : ARTICLES AND ABSTRACTS FOR STATE REGULATORY AGENCY COMMISSIONERS AND STAFF). 8756-632X. Periodical. US. English. qt. $120.00. NRRI, 2130 Neil Avenue, Columbus OH 43210. **Tel** (614)422-9407. **Ed** Vivian Witkind Davis. **DD** 351. **Circ** 1,200. (ctrl). Articles and abstracts on state actions and issues in regulation of electric, gas, telecommunications and water utilities.

NUCLEAR REGULATORY COMMISSION ISSUANCES. Main/Corp U.S. Nuclear Regulatory Commission. Division of Technical Information and Document Control. Vol. 13, No. 2 (Feb. 1981)-. US. English. mo. $107.00. US Government Printing Office, Superintendent of Documents, Washington DC 20402. **Tel** (202)783-3238. *Nuclear Regulatory Commission Issuances (Monthly), 0147-2909.*

NUCLEAR REGULATORY COMMISSION ISSUANCES : OPINIONS AND DECISIONS OF THE NUCLEAR REGULATORY COMMISSION WITH SELECTED ORDERS. Main/Corp U.S. Nuclear Regulatory Commission. Division of Technical Information and Document Control. Vol. 9 (Jan.-June 1979)-. US. English. sa. NRC/GPO Sales Program, Division of Technical Information and Document Control, US Nuclear Regulatory Commission, Washington DC 20555. *Nuclear Regulatory Commission Issuances (Semiannual).*

OCCASIONAL PAPER - INTERNATIONAL OMBUDSMAN INSTITUTE. (OCCASIONAL PAPER . . .). No. 1 (July 1979)-. 0711-6349. Periodical. CN. English. International Ombudsman Institute, Faculty of Law, University of Alberta, Edmonton Alberta T6G 2H5 Canada. **LC** UNC. **DD** 351.91.

OCCASIONAL PAPER - MAXWELL GRADUATE SCHOOL OF CITIZENSHIP AND PUBLIC AFFAIRS. METROPOLITAN STUDIES PROGRAM. See Economics.

OCTAGON; A QUARTERLY JOURNAL FOR DISCERNING COLLECTORS. Periodical. UK. English. qt.

ODTU : GELISME DERGISI = METU : STUDIES IN DEVELOPMENT. See Economics.

OFF. MAN., STATE MO. (OFFICIAL MANUAL, STATE OF MISSOURI). **VFOAT** Official Manual, Missouri. 0196-4739. US. English. be. Missouri Office of the Secretary of State, Jefferson City MO 65101. **LC** JK5430. **DD** 353.977800025. *Official Manual of the State of Missouri, 0196-4739.*

OFFICE AND QUARTERS LIST : RIVERS STATE. Main/Corp Rivers State, Nigeria. Printing and Stationery Division. **VFOAT** Rivers State Office and Quarters List. English. ir. Printing and Stationery Division 1, Rail Crescent Off Industry Road, Port Harcourt Nigeria. **LC** JQ3099.R58. **DD** 354.6694.

OFFICE DIRECTORY - DEPT. OF ESTABLISHMENT & TRAINING. See Yearbooks, Almanacs, Directories.

OFFICE DIRECTORY : LAGOS AREA. See Yearbooks, Almanacs, Directories.

OFFICERS AND COMMITTEE DIRECTORY INCLUDING POLICY STATEMENTS AND OFFICIAL DOCUMENTS. See Yearbooks, Almanacs, Directories.

OFFICIAL CANDIDATES PAMPHLET. See Political Science.

OFFICIAL COMPILATION OF ADMINISTRATIVE RULES AND REGULATIONS. Main/Corp Arizona. Secretary of State. **VFOAT** Arizona Official Compilation, Administrative Rules and Regulations. 1975-. US. English. **Tel** (602)255-4285. **Circ** 500. Contains all rules and regulations (of all regulatory agencies) adopted, amended, or repealed.

OFFICIAL CONGRESSIONAL DIRECTORY. See Yearbooks, Almanacs, Directories.

OFFICIAL DIRECTORY OF THE LEGISLATURE, STATE OF IOWA. See Yearbooks, Almanacs, Directories.

OFFICIAL ELECTION RETURNS BY COUNTIES FOR THE STATE OF SOUTH DAKOTA. GENERAL ELECTION. Main/Corp South Dakota. Secretary of State. US. English. .19 Each Copy. **LC** JK6592. **DD** 324.9783033.

OFFICIAL JOURNAL OF THE EUROPEAN COMMUNITIES : DEBATES OF THE EUROPEAN PARLIAMENT. 0378-5041. US. English. mo. European Communities Information Service, Suite 707/2100 M Street NW, Washington DC 20037. **LC** JN32. **DD** 341.242.

OFFICIAL RECORD OF PROCEEDINGS. Main/Corp Hong Kong. Urban Council. English. ir. Government Printer, Jarval Road, Hong Kong. **LC** HT147.H85. **DD** 352.9418095125.

OFFICIAL REPORT OF DEBATES. Main/Corp Council of Europe. Parliamentary Assembly. 26th Session, 2nd Pt. Vol. 2, Sittings 7/15 (Sept. 24-30, 1974)-. FR. English. ir. Manhattan Publishing Company, 80 Brook Street, Croton-on-Hudson NY 10520. **LC** JN22. **DD** 341.242. *Official Report of Debate.*

OFFICIAL REPORTS OF THE PARLIAMENTARY DEBATES (HANSARD). Main/Corp South Australia. Parliament. 33D Parliament, 3rd Session- 1952-. AT. English. ir. 145. South Australia Government Printer, 282 Richmond Road, Netley South Australia 5037 Australia. **Tel** 2973999. **LC** J921. **DD** 329.942302. Record of Parliamentary debates of both Houses of the South Australian Parliament (Hansard). *Official Reports of the Parliamentary Debates.*

OFFICIAL RETURNS OF THE PRIMARY AND GENERAL ELECTIONS. US. English. Office of the Secretary of State, Capitol Building/Room 157, Charleston WV 25305. **LC** JK4092. **DD** 324.9754043. *Official Returns of the General Election, Official Returns of the Primary Election.*

OFFICIAL ROSTER, FEDERAL, STATE, COUNTY OFFICERS AND DEPARTMENTAL INFORMATION. Main/Corp Ohio. Secrerary of State. **VFOAT** Federal, State, and County Roster. Began in 1911. 0741-9988. US. English. be. Secretary of State, 30 East Broad Street/14th Floor, Columbus OH 43215. **LC** JS451.O37. **DD** 352.005209771. *Federal, State, and County Officers (1909), 0741-7845.*

OFFICIAL SOUTH AFRICAN MUNICIPAL YEARBOOK. See Yearbooks, Almanacs, Directories.

OFFICIAL SUMMARY OF SECURITY TRANSACTIONS AND HOLDINGS. 0364-2267. Periodical. US. English. mo. US Government Office, Washington DC 20402. **Tel** (202)783-3238. **Ind/Abst** Am. Stat. Index.

OFPP PAMPHLET. Main/Corp United States. Office of Federal Procurement Policy. **VAT** Office of Federal Procurement Policy Pamphlet. No. 1-. Monographic Series. US. English. ir. Superintendent of Documents, US Government Printing Office, Washington DC 20402.

THE OGC ADVISOR. See Business - Accounting.

OHIO DOCUMENTS. See Indexes/Abstracts.

OKLAHOMA GOVERNMENT DOCUMENTS. See Political Science.

OKLAHOMA UTILITIES DIRECTORY. See Yearbooks, Almanacs, Directories.

OLIPHANT WASHINGTON SERVICE. 0733-0200. Periodical. US. English. ir. Oliphant Washington Service, 1819 H Street NW/Suite 330, Washington DC 20006. **Tel** (202)296-0924. **Ed** John Oliphant. bk rev. **Circ** 200. Factual personalized information service meeting needs of energy industries for actions in all branches of Federal Government affecting them so informed decisions can be made.

OMBUDSMAN AND OTHER COMPLAINT-HANDLING SYSTEMS SURVEY. Began publication with issue 1971/72. 0711-0383. CN. English. an. $5.00 Each Number. International Ombudsman Institute Law Centre, University of Alberta, Edmonton Alberta T6G 2H5 Canada. **Ed** Bernard Frank. **DD** 350.91. *Ombudsman Survey.*

ONTARIO COUNCIL BULLETIN. Main/Corp St. John Ambulance. Ontario Council. Jan. 1968-. 0380-8831. Periodical. CN. English. St John Ambulance Association, 46 Wellesley Street East, Toronto Ontario Canada. *Ontario Provincial Bulletin, 0380-884X.*

ONTARIO GOVERNMENT PUBLICATIONS ANNUAL CATALOGUE. (ONTARIO GOVERNMENT PUBLICATIONS ANNUAL CATALOGUE . . .). 1979-. 0227-2628. CN. English (includes French publications). an. $4.65. Treasurer of Ontario, Ministry of Government Services, 880 Bay Street/5th Floor, Toronto Ontario M7A 1N8 Canada. **LC** Z1373.5.O7, J108. **DD** 015.713. *Ontario Government Publications, 0317-4115.*

ONTARIO GOVERNMENT PUBLICATIONS MONTHLY CHECKLIST. VFOAT Publications du Gouvernement de l'Ontario Liste Mensuelle. V. 1- May 1971-. 0316-1617. Periodical. CN. English. mo. $4.00. Treasurer of Ontario, Ministry of Government Service, 880 Bay Street, 5th Floor, Toronto Ontario M7A 1N8 Canada. **DD** 015.713.

ONTARIO HYDRO STATISTICAL YEARBOOK. See Yearbooks, Almanacs, Directories.

OPERATING BUDGET - TEXAS. STATE PURCHASING AND GENERAL SERVICES COMMISSION. (OPERATING BUDGET). **Main/Corp** Texas. State Purchasing and General Services Commission. 0732-0493. US. English. an. Texas State Purchasing and General Services Commission, Austin TX 78701. **LC** JK4888.A1. **DD** 353.97640072236712.

OPERATING REVENUE AND EXPENSE STATISTICS CLASS A AND B PRIVATE GAS UTILITIES IN WISCONSIN. See Statistics.

OPERATING SUMMARY - UNITED STATES. GENERAL SERVICES ADMINISTRATION. (OPERATING SUMMARY). **Main/Corp** United States. General Services Administration. 0743-3905. US. English. an. US General Services Administration, 18th and F Streets, Washington DC 20405. **LC** JK1672. **DD** 353.007105.

ORCAMENTO EMPRESAS. Main/Corp Minas Geraid (Brazil). Superintendencia de Orcamento. Portuguese. ir. **LC** HD4095.M55. **DD** 354.8151092.

ORDER PAPER AND NOTICES. Main/Corp Canada. Parliament. House of Commons. **VFOAT** Feuilleton et Avis. Oct. 1, 1974-. 0317-8420. Periodical. CN. English (text with French in parallel columns). qt. Queen's Printer, Parliament Buildings, Ottawa Ontario Canada. **LC** J103. **DD** 328.7105. *Order of Business and Notices = Ordre des Travaux et Avis, 0384-2258.*

ORDER PAPER AND NOTICES. Main/Corp Quebec (Province). Assemblee Nationale. March 13, 1984-. Periodical. CN. English. $15.48. Les Publications du Quebec, Ministere des Comm, CP 1005, Quebec Quebec G1K 7B5 Canada. **Tel** (418)643-5150. *Feuilleton de l'Assemblee Nationale du Quebec.*

ORDER PAPER AND NOTICES - LEGISLATIVE ASSEMBLY OF THE PROVINCE OF ONTARIO. (ORDER PAPER AND NOTICES - THE LEGISLATIVE ASSEMBLY OF THE PROVINCE OF ONTARIO). **Main/Corp** Ontario. Legislative Assembly. Began with No. 1, Mar. 29, 1977 issue. 0826-6980. Periodical. CN. English. da. 26.00 Domestic, 31.20 Foreign. Receiver General for Canada, Supply & Services, Ottawa Ontario K1A 0S9 Canada. *Order Paper.*

ORDERS OF THE DAY, MINUTES OF PROCEEDINGS. Main/Corp Council of Europe. Parliamentary Assembly. **VFOAT** Ordres du Jour, Proces-Verbaux. 26th Session, 2nd Pt.- Sept. 1974-. US. English and French. ir. Manhattan Publishing Co, 80 Brook Street, Croton-on-Hudson

Public Administration

NY 10520. **LC** JN22. **DD** 341.242. *Orders of the Day, Minutes of Proceedings.*

ORDINANCES OF THE YUKON TERRITORY PASSED BY THE YUKON COUNCIL. (ORDINANCES OF THE YUKON TERRITORY). **Main/Corp** Yukon Territory. 1903-1980. 0513-3998. **CN.** English. ir. Government of Yukon, Box 2703, Whitehourse Yukon Y1A 2C6 Canada. **Tel** (403)667-5169.

THE OREGON BLUE BOOK. *See* Yearbooks, Almanacs, Directories.

ORGANIZATION OF FEDERAL EXECUTIVE DEPARTMENTS AND AGENCIES. **Main/Corp** United States. Congress. Senate. Committee on Government Operations. July 1, 1952-. Periodical. US. English. ir. US Government Printing Office, Superintendent of Documents, Washington DC 20402. **LC** JK646.3. *Organization of Federal Executive Department and Agencies.*

ORGANIZATION OF THE GOVERNMENT OF ALBERTA. 0226-286X. **CN.** English. an. Alberta Treasury Administrative Services, 423 Terrace Building 9515-107 Street, Edmonton Alberta T5K 2C3 Canada. **LC** JL331. **DD** 354.72104.

ORGANIZATION OF THE GOVERNMENT OF KOREA. English. ir. **LC** JQ1726. **DD** 354.519504.

ORGANIZATION OF VIRGINIA STATE GOVERNMENT. US. English. **LC** JK3901. **DD** 353.9755073.

ORGANIZATIONAL MEETING OF THE COMMITTEE ON ARMED SERVICES, HOUSE OF REPRESENTATIVES. **Main/Corp** United States. Congress. House. Committee on Armed Services. 0732-0108. US. English. be. Superintendent of Documents, US Government Printing Office, Washington DC 20402. **LC** JK1430.A75. **DD** 328.7307658.

ORGANIZING NOTES. Began in March 1977-. 0278-4440. Periodical. US. English. ir. Campaign for Political Rights, 201 Mass Avenue NE Room 316, Washington DC 20002. **Tel** (202)547-4705. **LC** JK468.I6. **DD** 327.120973.

OTTAWA. DIRECTORY OF MUNICIPAL SERVICES. *See* Yearbooks, Almanacs, Directories.

OTTAWA LETTER. V. 13- Jan. 4, 1977-. 0702-8210. Periodical. CN. English. 80.00. CCH Canadian Ltd, 6 Garamond Court, Don Mills Ontario M3C 1Z5 Canada. **DD** 320.971064. Provides news and comments on what's going on in Parliament, government departments. *View from Ottawa, 0049-6383.*

OUTLINE OF ACTIVITIES - FOOD AND CIVIL SUPPLIES DEPARTMENT, GOVERNMENT OF MAHARASHTRA. **Main/Corp** Maharashtra (India). Food and Civil Supplies Dept. English. an. **LC** HD9016.I43. **DD** 354.5479200826.

OUTLINE OF ACTIVITIES - GOVERNMENT OF MAHARASHTRA. **Main/Corp** Maharashtra (India). II. English. ir. Government of Maharashtra, Government Central Press, Taredio Bombay 34 WB India. **LC** JQ620.M262. **DD** 309.250954792.

OVERZICHT SPECIFIEKE UITKERINGEN DIE VOOR GEMEENTEN EN PROVINCIES VAN BELANG ZIJU. NE. Dutch. an. Beheerscommissie Gegevensbestand Specifieke, Uitkeringen Kamer L613 Postbus 2001, S'Gravenhage Netherlands.

PA. TOWNSHIP NEWS. 1948. 0162-5160. Periodical. US. English. mo. $15.00. Pennsylvania Township News, 3001 Gettysburg Road, Camp Hill PA 17011. **Tel** (717)763-0930. **Ed** Diane Altemose. adv acc. **Circ** 12,000. Concerns local government, and municipal management. *Pennsylvania Township News.*

PAKISTAN JOURNAL OF LOCAL GOVERNMENT. V. 1- June 1974-. Periodical. PK. English. sa. $2.00 Per Issue. Pakistan Group for the Study of Local Government, 252 Sarwar Shaheed Road, Karachi Pakistan. **LC** JS7091.A1. **DD** 352.05491.

PAKISTAN JOURNAL OF PUBLIC ADMINISTRATION. V. 12- June 1973-. 0303-9404. Periodical. English. sa. $5.00. National Institute of Public Administration, Nilket, Dacca 2 Bangladesh. **LC** JQ541.A1. **DD** 354.54910005. *NIPA Journal, 0027-6715.*

PALCHON CHONGCHAEK YON'GU. **VFOAT** Korean Development Policy Studies. Periodical. Korean. ir. **LC** JQ1721.A1.

PAMPHLET - CIVIL SERVICE COMMISSION. **Main/Corp** United States. Civil Service Commission. **VFOAT** United States Civil Service Commission Pamphlet. No. 1- 1961-. Monographic Series. US. English. ir. Superintendent of Documents, US Government Printing Office, Washington DC 20402. **LC** JK639.

PANCAYATA DARPANA. NP. Nepali. ir. Talima Samagri Utpadana Kendra, Jawalakhel, Lalitapura Nepal. **LC** JQ1825.N45.

PAPER KURSUS PENGAWASAN DEPARTEMEN DALAM NEGERI. **Main/Corp** Indonesia. Departemen Dalam Negeri. Indonesian. ir. **LC** JF1338.A2.

PAPERS IN PUBLIC ADMINISTRATION. No. 15-. 0078-9151. Monographic Series. US. English. ir. Arizona State University, Institute of Public Administration, Tempe AZ 85281. **LC** JK8201. **DD** 320.08. *Public Affairs Series (Arizona State University. Bureau of Government Research).*

PAPERWORK AND RED TAPE; NEW PERSPECTIVES, NEW DIRECTIONS. **Main/Corp** United States. Office of Management and Budget. June 1978-. 0196-5786. US. English. sa. US Government Printing Office, Superintendent of Documents, Washington DC 20402. **LC** JK468.P34. **DD** 353.0071406.

PAR. PUBLIC ADMINISTRATION REVIEW. (PUBLIC ADMINISTRATION REVIEW). **VFOAT** PAR. V. 1- Autumn 1940-. 0033-3352. Periodical. US. English. bm. $40.00. American Society for Public Administration, 1120 G Street NW/Suite 500, Washington DC 20005. **Tel** (202)393-7878. **Ed** L D White. **Ind/Abst** ABC Pol Sci, Int. Labour Doc., Hospit. Lit. Index, ABI/Inform, Int. Aerosp. Abstr., Public Aff. Inf. Serv. Bull., Soc. Sci. Index, Book Rev. Index, Soc. Sci. Citation Index, Abstr. Soc. Work., Manage. Contents, Curr. Law Index, Leg. Resour. Index, Am. Hist. Life, Hist. Abstr., Hist. Abstr., Part A, Mod. Hist. Abstr., Hist. Abst., Part B, Twent. Century Abstr. **LC** JK1. **DD** 350.0005. **NLM** W1 PU101K. Index in last issue of volume - attached. (cum index). Available on microfilm from University Microfilms.

PARLEMENT EN KIEZER : JAARBOEK. *See* Yearbooks, Almanacs, Directories.

PARLIAMENTARY AFFAIRS. V. 1- Winter 1947-. 0031-2290. Periodical. UK. English. qt. Oxford University Press, Journals Department Walton Street, Oxford OX2 6DP England. **Tel** 0865/ 56767. **Ind/Abst** Am. Hist. Life, Hist. Abstr., Part A, Mod. Hist. Abstr., Hist. Abst., Part B, Twent. Century Abstr., ABC Pol Sci, Sociol. Abstr., Soc. Welf. Soc. Plan./Policy Soc. Dev., Public Aff. Inf. Serv. Bull., Soc. Sci. Index, Soc. Sci. Citation Index, Lang. Lang. Behav. Abstr., Hist. Abstr. **LC** JN101. **DD** 328.42.

PARLIAMENTARY ALERT. Vol. 1, No. 1-. 0821-5154. Periodical. CN. English. wk. $100.00. Henry & Gray Inc, 130 Slater Street/Suite 815, Ottawa Ontario K1P 5H6 Canada. **DD** 328.71005.

PARLIAMENTARY DEBATES. **Main/Corp** Zimbabwe. Parliament. House of Assembly. Began with May 1980 issue. English. ir. $0.03 Single Issue. House of Assembly, POB 8062 Causeway, Salisbury Zimbabwe. **LC** J725.5. **DD** 328.689102. *Parliamentary Debates.*

THE PARLIAMENTARY DEBATES (HANSARD), HOUSE OF LORDS OFFICIAL REPORT. **Main/Corp** Great Britain. Parliament. House of Lords. **VFOAT** Parliamentary Debates (Hansard). 5th Ser., Vol. 130 (1943/44)-. Periodical. UK. English. wk. Her Majestys Stationery Office, PO Box 276, London SW8 5DT England. **Tel** (01)622 3316. (cum index). *Parliamentary Debates, House of Lords Official Report.*

PARLIAMENTARY DEBATES (HANSARD), THE SENATE. **Main/Corp** Fiji. Parliament. Senate. FJ. English. ir. $0.75. Parliament of Fiji, Bureau of Statistics, Box 2221, Suva Fiji Island. **LC** J961. **DD** 328.961102.

PARLIAMENTARY DEBATES, HOUSE OF REPRESENTATIVES, WEEKLY HANSARD. **Main/Corp** Australia. Parliament. House of Representatives. 20th Parliament, 1st Session 7th Period- (V. 1-). 0519-6124. Periodical. AT. English. wk. $7.38. Australian Government Printing Office, PO Box 84, Canberra Australian Capital Territory 2600 Australia. **Tel** 062-95 4411. **LC** J905. Index published separately - free - automatically sent. *Parliamentary Debates. Senate and House of Representatives.*

PARLIAMENTARY DEBATES, SENATE, WEEKLY HANSARD. **Main/Corp** Australia. Parliament. Senate. 20th Parliament, 1st Sess., 7th Period- Sept. 8, 1953-. 0519-6140. Periodical. AT. English. wk. $7.38. Australian Government Printing Office, PO Box 84, Canberra Australian Capitol Territory 2600 Australia. **Tel** 062-95 4411. **LC** J905. **DD** 328.9402. Index published separately - free - automatically sent. *Parliamentary Debates Senate and House of Representatives.*

PARLIAMENTARY HISTORY. *See* Yearbooks, Almanacs, Directories.

PASSPORT OFFICE WORKLOADS AND ACCOMPLISHMENTS. **Main/Corp** United States. Passport Office. 0362-8469. US. English. an. US Passport Office, 1425 K Street NW Room 338, Washington DC 20524. **LC** KF4794.5. **DD** 353.0089.

PAY STRUCTURE OF THE FEDERAL CIVIL SERVICE. **Main/Corp** United States. Office of Personnel Management. Agency Compliance and Evaluation. US. English. an. Superintendent of Documents, US Government Printing Office, Washington DC 20402. **LC** JK639, JK774. **DD** 353.001 S, 331.281353. *Pay Structure of the Federal Civil Service, 0161-2964.*

PEER ANNUAL REPORT AND CUMULATIVE SUMMARIES OF REPORTS ISSUED THROUGH . . . . US. English. an. Peer Committee, PO Box 1204, Jackson MS 39205. **LC** JK4674. **DD** 328.7620745605.

PENNSYLVANIA COMPREHENSIVE STATE PLAN FOR MENTAL HEALTH SERVICES. **Main/Corp** Pennsylvania. Office of Mental Health. 1977-. US. English. **NLM** W2 AP4 O31P. *Pennsylvania State Plan for Mental Health Services.*

PENNSYLVANIA INTERGOVERNMENTAL QUARTERLY. Vol. 1, No. 1 (Fall 1982)-. 0739-3105. Periodical. US. English. qt. Pennsylvania Intergovernmental Council, PO Box 1288, Harrisburg PA 17108. **LC** JK3601. **DD** 353.9748905.

PENNSYLVANIA STATE EMPLOYES' RETIREMENT SYSTEM. 0146-5260. US. English. Pennsylvania State Employees Retirement System, 204 Labor & Industry Building, Harrisburg PA 17120. **LC** JK3660.P. **DD** 331.25209748.

PENNSYLVANIAN. V. 1- June 1962-. 0031-4714. Periodical. US. English. mo. $15.00. Local Pennsylvanian, 2941 North Front Street, Harrisburg PA 17110. **Tel** (717)236-6591. **Ed** Susan B Shultz. **LC** JS39. **DD** 352.0009748. adv acc. **Circ** 6,500. (ctrl). Educational and informative needs of local government officials, particularly pertaining to the practical application of new administrative and program development and legislative findings. *Assessors' Newsletter, Authority; Borough Bulletin; Hub; Pennsylvania League of Cities; Township Commissioner.*

PENYATA TAHUNAN - SURUHANJAYA PERKHIDMATAN AWAM NEGERI PERAK. **Main/Corp** Perak. Suruhanjaya Perkhikmatan Awam. Malay. ir. Suruhanjaya Perkhidmatan Awam Negeri Perak, 17 Jalan Douglas, Ipoh Malaysia. **LC** HD2768.M35.

PENYATA - UMNO. **Main/Corp** United Malays National Organisation. Malay. ir. United Malays National Organisation, JL T UB Rahman Bangunan Umno, Kuala Lumpur Malaysia. **LC** JQ719.A8.

PEOPLE'S REPUBLIC OF CHINA BIOGRAPHICAL APPEARANCES. **Main/Corp** Harvard University. East Asian Research Center. 0145-7586. US. English. mo. East Asian Research Center, Harvard University, Cambridge MA 02138. **LC** JQ1507. **DD** 354.51002.

PEOPLES SECTOR. *See* Business.

PERFIL. **VFOAT** Perfil da Administracao do Estado de Sao Paulo. April 1972-. BL. Portuguese. ir. $25.00. Sociedade Editorial Viscao, Rua 7 de Abril 345 30 Andar, Sao Paulo Brazil. **LC** JL2499.S199.

Public Administration

PERFIL DE EMPRESAS BENEFICIARIAS. VFOAT Perfil de Empresas. 8 de Outubro, 1980-. Portuguese. ir. O Fundo, Finam Av Presidente Vargas/800 4 Andar, Belem Para Brazil 66000. *Perfis de Empresas Beneficiarias.*

PERFORMANCE BUDGET - WEST BENGAL STATE ELECTRICITY BOARD. Main/Corp West Bengal State Electricity Board. II. English. an. West Bengal State Electricity Board, 48/1 Diamond Harbour Road, Calcutta-700 027 India. LC HD9685.I44. DD 354.541400722253.

PERFORMANCE REPORT - MINISTRY OF PUBLIC ADMINISTRATION AND HOME AFFAIRS. Main/Corp Sri Lanka. Rajya Paripalana Ha Svadesa Katayutu Amatyamsaya. English. ir. Ministry of Public Administration and Home Affairs, Independence Square, Colombo 7 Ceylon. LC JQ656. DD 354.54930005.

PERFORMANCE REPORT TO THE LEGISLATURE- LEGISLATIVE BUDGET BOARD. (PERFORMANCE REPORT TO THE LEGISLATURE). Main/Corp Texas. Legislative Budget Board. 1st- 1975-. 0360-9405. US. English. Box 12666 Capital Station, Austin TX 78711. LC JK4835. DD 353.9764.

PERIODICITE. (PERIODICITE : BULLETIN DE LIAISON DE LA CITE DE DRUMMONDVILLE). Vol. 1, No. 1-. 0712-3019. Periodical. CN. French. ir. Periodicite Hotel de Ville, 413 rue Lindsay, Drummndville Quebec J2B 1G8 Canada. DD 352.9714563.

PERS INFORMATION BULLETIN. Main/Corp Public Employment Relations Services. V. 1- Feb./Mar. 1978-. Periodical. US. English. Public Employment Relations Services, 1215 Western Avenue, Albany NY 12203.

PERSONAL IM OFFENTLICHEN DIENST. GW. an. 6.30. Niedersachsisches Landesverwaltungsamt Statistik, Postfach 107, 3000 Hannover 1 West Germany. LC JN4945.L684. DD 354.4359001. bk rev. Circ 500.

PERSONNEL. Main/Corp Canadian Public Personnel Management Association. Ottawa-Hull Chapter. July 1978-. 0715-5514. Periodical. CN. English (with French in parallel columns, July 1978-Feb. 1981). ir. Free to Members. Personnel, c/o CPPMA, PO Box 2179 Station D, Ottawa Ontario K1P 5W4 Canada. DD 354.71001006071384. *Personnel, 0715-5514.*

PERSONNEL DIRECTORY - NEW BRUNSWICK DEPARTMENT OF AGRICULTURE AND RURAL DEVELOPMENT. See Yearbooks, Almanacs, Directories.

PERSPECTIVE. July 1974-. 0316-5388. Periodical. CN. English. mo. Alberta Union of Provincial Employees, 10975-124th Street, Edmonton Alberta T5M 0J2 Canada. DD 354.712300173. *News, 0316-5396.*

PERSPECTIVES. 0743-0388. US. English. an. Close Up Foundation, 1055 Thomas Jefferson Street North West, Washington DC 20007. LC JK1. DD 320.973.

PERSPECTIVES ET REALITES. Periodical. French. ir. 20.00. 41 rue de la Bienfaisance, 75008 Paris France. LC JN2594.2.A3. DD 320.444083.

PETIT RAPPORTEUR DE STONEHAM, TEWKSBURY ET ST-ADOLPHE. (LE PETIT RAPPORTEUR DE STONEHAM, TEWKESBURY ET ST-ADOLPHE). 0710-085X. Periodical. CN. French. bm. Free. Corp Municipale des Cantons Unis de Stoneham et Teskesbury, 545 1st Avenue, Stoneham Quebec G0A 4P0 Canada. DD 352.071447.

PHILIPPINE JOURNAL OF PUBLIC ADMINISTRATION. V. 1- Jan. 1957-. 0031-7675. Periodical. PH. English. ir. $25.00. Philippine Journal of Public Administration, PO Box 474, Manila Philippine. Tel 59-95-55. Ed Jose P Tabbada. Ind/Abst Am. Hist. Life, Hist. Abstr., Part A, Mod. Hist. Abstr., Hist. Abst., Part B, Twent. Century Abstr., Sociol. Abstr., ABC Pol Sci, Public Aff. Inf. Serv. Bull. LC JA26. DD 350.0005. bk rev. Circ 1,000. Publishes articles which contribute to the advancement of public administration in general, with particular emphasis on the Philippines, Asia and the Third World.

PLAN D'ACTION, REGION 07. (PLAN D'ACTION. PREMIERE PARTIE : REGION 07). Main/Corp Quebec (Province). Ministere de l'Education. Direction Generale des Reseaux. Direction Regionale de l'Outaouais. 0229-7981. CN. French. an. Gouvernement du Quebec, 600 St Amable 4E Etage, Quebec G1R 4Z1 Canada. DD 354.714008510971422.

PLAN FOR ILLINOIS DEPARTMENT OF REHABILITATION SERVICES. Main/Corp Illinois. Dept. of Rehabilitation Services. Series/Titl Illinois Human Services Plan. VFOAT Data Report. US. English. an. 623 East Adam, PO Box 1587, Springfield IL 62705. DD 353.977300834.

PLAN TRIENNIAL DE DEVELOPPEMENT - ECOLE NATIONALE D'ADMINISTRATION PUBLIQUE. (PLAN TRIENNAL DE DEVELOPPEMENT). Main/Corp Ecole Nationale d'Administration Publique (Quebec). 0229-5946. CN. French. te. Free. Secretariat General/Ecole Nationale d'Administration Publique, 945 Avenue Wolfe, Ste-Foy Quebec G1V 3J9 Canada. DD 350.000711714.

PLANNING AND ADMINISTRATION. V. 1- Winter 1974-. Periodical. NE. English. sa. 90.-. International Union of Local Authority, 45 Wassenaarseweg, 2596 CG The Hague Netherlands. Tel (070)24.40.32. Ed Eileen M Harloff. Ind/Abst Energy Inf. Abstr., Environ. Abstr., ABC Pol Sci, Soc. Sci. Citation Index. LC JS42. DD 350.0005. bk rev. adv acc. Circ 1,100. Articles relating to the structure, planning, housing, management and functions of human settlements, and the interrelationship between governments at local and other levels, and citizen participation in local and regional government decision-making and implementation. *Studies in Comparative Local Government.*

PLANNING & PUBLIC POLICY. VAT Planning and Public Policy. V. 1- Winter 1974/75-. Periodical. US. English. qt. $1.00. University Illinois at Urbana Champagne, 909 W Nevade Bureau Urban Regional Planning, Urbana IL 61801. Tel (217)333-3020. Ed Albert Guttenberg. Circ 5,000. (ctrl). Urban and regional planning and policy issues.

PLATEAU STATE OF NIGERIA GAZETTE. Main/Corp Plateau, Nigeria. NR. English. ir. $12.00. *Gazette.*

POCKET DIRECTORY OF THE CALIFORNIA LEGISLATURE. See Yearbooks, Almanacs, Directories.

POINT OF VIEW. Began publication in 1968?. 0032-2318. Periodical. US. English. bw. $25.00. Point of View, PO Box 99530, Cleveland OH 44199. Tel (216)851-3654. Ed Roldo Bartimole. Circ 1,200. Examines local government, business, and news media and how they inter-relate to make public decisions.

POLICY AND POLITICS. See Political Science.

POLICY AND PROCEDURES MANUAL FOR GUIDANCE OF FEDERAL AGENCIES. TITLE 4. CLAIMS. Main/Corp United States. General Accounting Office. VFOAT GAO Manual for Guidance of Federal Agencies. Periodical. US. English. ir. General Accounting Office, Washington DC 20402.

POLICY FOCUS. (POLICY FOCUS : NEWSLETTER FOR THE RESEARCH UNIT FOR PUBLIC POLICY STUDIES). Vol. 1, No. 1 (June 1984)-. 0824-0450. Periodical. CN. English. sa. Free. Research Unit for Public Policy Studies, University of Calgary, Room SS/706-2500 University Drive North-West, Calgary Alberta T2N 1N4 Canada. DD 350.000971. (ctrl).

POLICY POSITIONS. Main/Corp National Governors' Association. 0160-7456. US. English. an. $2.00. National Governors Association, Center for Policy Research, 444 North Capitol Street, Washington DC 20001. LC JK2403. DD 353.9. *Policy Positions of the National Governors' Conference, 0361-7262.*

POLICY POSITIONS. SUPPLEMENT. Main/Corp National Governors' Association. 0160-7456. US. English. an. $2.00. National Governors' Association, 444 North Capitol Street, Washington DC 20001. LC JK2403.

POLICY POSITIONS. WINTER MEETING SUPPLEMENT. Main/Corp National Governors' Association. 0160-7456. US. English. $2.00. National Governors' Association, 444 North Capitol Street, Washington DC 20001. LC JK2403. DD 353.9.

POLICY RESEARCH PROJECT REPORT. Main/Corp Lyndon B. Johnson School of Public Affairs. No. 1-. 0196-0369. US. English. ir. Lyndon Johnson School of Public Affairs, University of Texas, Austin TX 79112.

POLICY STUDIES JOURNAL. See Political Science.

POLICY STUDIES REVIEW. See Political Science.

THE POLITICAL COMPANION CEASED. -No. 33. 0032-3152. Periodical. UK. English. qt. LC JN672. DD 382.420025.

POLITICS, ADMINISTRATION, AND CHANGE : BI-ANNUAL JOURNAL OF THE CENTER FOR ADMINISTRATIVE STUDIES, DACCA, BANGLADESH. Periodical. English. sa. 40.00 Domestic, $8.00 US. Center for Administrative Studies, Room No 4036/Arts Faculty Building, University of Dacca, Dacca-2 Bangladesh. LC JA26. DD 320.05. *Public Administration.*

POLITIEK MEMO. NE. DUTCH. an. Libresso BV, Postbus 23, 7400 GA Deventer Netherlands. LC JN5703.

POLITINFORMATOR I AGITATOR. Began in 1932. Periodical. UR. Russian. sm. 0.06. Izd-Vo TSK KP Belorussii, Leninskii Prospekt 77, 220041 Minsk Belorussian SSR. LC JN6598.K86.

POPULAR GOVERNMENT. See Political Science.

PORTER'S GUIDE TO CONGRESSIONAL ROLL CALL VOTES. HOUSE. VFOAT Guide to Congressional Roll Call Votes. 98th Congress, 1st Session (1983)-. 0748-2310. US. English. qt. $250.00. Legislative Information Group Press, 1710 Connecticut Avenue Northwest, Washington DC 20009.

PORTFOLIO. Spring 1977-. 0707-2481. Periodical. CN. English. sa. Free. Hamilton Harbour Commissioners, 605 James Street North, Hamilton Ontario L8L 1K1 Canada. *Port of Hamilton Dimension, 0381-0453.*

PORTFOLIO OF STATE ISSUES. Periodical. US. English. Cortlandt Group Inc, 175 Main Street, Ossining NY 10562. LC RZA 0508.

POSITION-CLASSIFICATION STANDARDS FOR WHITE COLLAR POSITIONS UNDER THE GENERAL SCHEDULE. Periodical. US. English. ir. Civil Service Commission, Bureau of Policies and Standards, Washington DC 20402.

POWER PROGRAM SUMMARY. Main/Corp Tennessee Valley Authority. Fiscal year ended Sept. 30, 1980-. 0730-4889. US. English. an. Tennessee Valley Authority, 400 Commerce Avenue, Knoxville TN 37902. LC HD9685.U6. DD 363.62. *Operations. Municipal and Cooperative Distributors of TVA Power, 0362-3432; Power Annual Report, 0146-2687; OEDC Annual Report.*

PRAYERS OFFERED AT DAILY SESSIONS OF THE ASSEMBLY. Main/Corp California. Legislature. Assembly. VFOAT Assembly Prayers. 0149-3167. Periodical. US. English.

PRECEDENCE OF CANADIAN DIGNITARIES AND OFFICIALS CEASED. Main/Corp Canada. Secretary of State. VFOAT Preseance. Ceased with issue for Dec. 1981. 0713-1534. Periodical. CN. English (French, each with special title page and separate paging. French on inverted pages).

PRELIMINARY DETERMINATION OF EPICENTERS (WEEKLY). (PRELIMINARY DETERMINATION OF EPICENTERS). Periodical. US. English. mo. Superintendent of Documents, Government Printing Office, Washington DC 20402. Tel (202)783-3238.

PRESIDENTIAL ADDRESS - THE ENGLISH ASSOCIATION. (PRESIDENTIAL ADDRESS). Main/Corp English Association (Great Britain). 1936-. UK. English. an. English Association, 1 Priory Gardens, London W4 1TT England.

PRESIDENTIAL STUDIES QUARTERLY. V. 4, No. 2- Spring 1974-. 0360-4918. Periodical. US. English. qt. $15.00. Center for Study of Presidency, 208 East 75th Street, New

York NY 10021. **Tel** (212)249-1200. Ed R Gordon Hoxie. **Ind/Abst** Am. Hist. Life, Hist. Abstr., Part A, Mod. Hist. Abstr., Hist. Abst., Part B, Twent. Century Abstr., ABC Pol Sci, Writ. Am. Hist., Public Aff. Inf. Serv. Bull., Recent Publ. Artic., Hist. Abstr. **LC** JK501. **DD** 353.0313. bk rev. adv acc. **Circ** 12,500. (ctrl). Presidency, Congress and major public policy issues including foreign and national security affairs and domestic policies also decision making and constitutional concerns. *Center House Bulletin.*

PREVIEW OF THE INSTITUTO NACIONAL DE HIDROCARBUROS ANNUAL REPORT FOR . . . . **Main/Corp** Instituto Nacional de Hidrocarburos (Spain). SP. English. an. Instituto Nacional de Hidrocarburos, Paseo de la Castellana 89, Madrid 16 Spain.

PRIMARY AND GENERAL ELECTION RETURNS. **Main/Corp** Louisiana. Dept. of State. Nov. 1, 1975 and Dec. 13, 1975-. US. English. ir. **LC** JK4792. **DD** 324.9763. *Primary Election Returns, General Election Returns.*

PRIME CONTRACT AWARDS BY STATE. US. English. sa. Washington Headquarters Services, Directorate for Information Operations and Reports, Room 3E843/The Pentagon, Washington DC 20301. Vols. for (FY 1981-) distributed to depository libraries in microfiche.

PRIME SOURCE MINI REFERENCE DIRECTORY. MOST WANTED NAMES AND ADDRESSES OF: FOREIGN CONSULATE IN U.S.A. *See* Yearbooks, Almanacs, Directories.

PRIVATE ACTS OF THE STATE OF TENNESSEE PASSED BY THE GENERAL ASSEMBLY. **Main/Corp** Tennessee. 57th- 1911-. 0196-4224. US. English. be. General Assembly, Nashville TN 37203. **DD** 348.768023. (cum index). *Acts of the State of Tennessee.*

PRO FORUM. V. 1- Fall 1979-. 0709-9673. Periodical. CN. French. qt. Free. Institut Professionnel de la Fonction Publique du Canada, 786 Avenue Bronson, Ottawa Ontario K1S 4G4 Canada. **DD** 354.71001005. (ctrl). *Journal de l'Institut Professionnel, 0318-2746.*

PRO FORUM. V. 1- Fall 1979-. 0709-9665. Periodical. CN. English. qt. Professional Institute of the Public Service of Canada, 786 Bronson Avenue, Ottawa Ontario K1S 4G4 Canada. **DD** 354.71001005. *Journal of the Professional Institute, 0318-2746.*

PROBLEM-SOLVING INFORMATION FOR STATE & LOCAL GOVERNMENTS. (PROBLEM SOLVING INFORMATION FOR STATE & LOCAL GOVERNMENTS). **VAT** Problem Solving Information for State and Local Governments. 0364-6459. US. English. wk. National Technical Information Service, 5285 Port Royal Road, Springfield VA 22161.

PROBLEMY RAD NARODOWYCH. 1-. 0079-5801. Periodical. Polish (summaries in Russian, English or French). ir. **LC** JS6132.A15. (cum index).

PROCEEDINGS . . . ANNUAL CONVENTION AND REGULATORY SYMPOSIUM, NATIONAL ASSOCIATION OF REGULATORY UTILITY COMMISSIONERS. **Main/Corp** National Association of Regulatory Utility Commissioners., Convention and Regulatory Symposium. **VFOAT** NARUC Annual Convention. Began with: 86th (1974). US. English. an. $30.00. National Association of Regulatory Utility Commissioners, 684, Washington DC 20044. **Tel** (202)628-7324. Ed Paul Rodgers. NARUC Committee reports, speeches and panel discussions from the 95th annual convention proceedings. *Proceedings, Regulatory Symposium, . . . Annual Convention.*

PROCEEDINGS - COUNTY JUDGES' AND COMMISSIONERS' CONFERENCE. **Main/Corp** County Judges' and Commissioners' Conference. 0590-0123. Periodical. US. English. an. County Judges and Commissioners Conference, Texas A & M University/Tax Accesor, College Station TX 77843.

PROCEEDINGS - GOVERNOR'S CONFERENCE ON STATE, COUNTY, AND MUNICIPAL RELATIONS. **Main/Conf** Governor's Conference on State County, and Municipal Relations. 10th- 1958-. English. ir. *Proceedings.*

PROCEEDINGS OF THE ANNUAL CONFERENCE FOR MUNICIPAL CLERKS. **Main/Corp** Conference for Municipal Clerks, Rutgers University. 1st-. 0573-2913. US. English. an. **LC** JS304. **DD** 352.073.

PROCEEDINGS OF THE . . . ANNUAL CONFERENCES. **Main/Corp** United States. Office of Government Ethics. Conference. 1st and 2nd (1980-81)-. US. English. an. Office of Government Ethics, Office of Personnel Management, 1900 East Street NW/Room 436H, Washington DC 20415. **LC** JK468.E7. **DD** 353.0099.

THE PROCEEDINGS OF THE ANNUAL FINANCIAL MANAGEMENT CONFERENCE. (THE PROCEEDINGS OF THE . . . ANNUAL FINANCIAL MANAGEMENT CONFERENCE). **Main/Conf** Financial Management Conference. Began with 3rd (1974) issue. 0740-3453. US. English. an. **LC** JK404. **DD** 353.04. *Proceedings.*

PROCEEDINGS OF THE ANNUAL IOWA STATE UNIVERSITY REGULATORY CONFERENCE ON PUBLIC UTILITY VALUATION AND THE RATE MAKING PROCESS. **Main/Conf** Iowa State University Regulatory Conference on Public Utility Valuation and the Rate Making Process. **VFOAT** Regulatory Conference on Public Utility Valuation and the Rate Making Process. 0162-5128. US. English. an. Iowa State University, Ames IA 50010. **LC** HD2766. **DD** 363.60973.

PROCEEDINGS OF THE NATIONAL GOVERNORS' ASSOCIATION ANNUAL MEETING. **Main/Corp** National Governors' Association. 69th- 1977-. 0191-3441. US. English. an. National Governors' Association, Hall of the States, 444 North Capitol Street, Washington DC 20001. **LC** JK2403. **DD** 353.9. *Proceedings of the Annual Meeting.*

PROCEEDINGS OF THE SPECIAL COMMITTEE OF THE SENATE ON THE CANADIAN SECURITY INTELLIGENCE SERVICE. **Main/Corp** Canada. Parliament. Senate. Speical Committee on the Canadian Security Intelligence Service. **VFOAT** Deliberations du Comite Senatorial Special du Service Canadien du Renseignement de Securite. 32nd Parliament, 1st Session, Issue No. 1-. CN. English (French). Canadian Government Publishing Centre, Supply and Services Canada, Ottawa Ontario K1A 0S9 Canada. **LC** JL86.I58. **DD** 327.120971.

PROCEEDINGS OF THE STANDING SENATE COMMITTEE ON NATIONAL FINANCE. *See* Statistics.

PROCES-VERBAUX DE L'ASSEMBLEE NATIONALE DU QUEBEC CEASED. **Main/Corp** Quebec (Province). National Assembly. **VFOAT** Votes and Proceedings of the National Assembly of Quebec. Feb. 25, 1969-Dec. 21, 1983. 0703-5004. Periodical. CN. English (French in parallel columns). ir. **LC** J107. **DD** 328.714. *Proces-Verbaux de l'Assemblee Legislative = Votes and Proceedings of the Legislative Assembly, 0703-5039.*

PROCUREMENT AND SUPPLY : THE INTERAGENCY TRAINING PROGRAM. **Main/Corp** GSA Training Center (U.S.). US. English. US General Services Administration, PO Box 15608, Arlington VA 22215.

PROFESSIONAL EMPLOYEES IN STATE GOVERNMENT. (PROFESSIONAL EMPLOYEES IN STATE GOVERNMENT : PEG). **VFOAT** PEG. 0744-6721. Periodical. US. English. mo. Professional Employees in State Government, 2276 East Reservoir, Springfield IL 62702.

PROGRAM ANALYSIS OF OFFICE SPACE FOR STATE AGENCIES. **Main/Corp** New Jersey. Legislature. Office of Fiscal Affairs. Division of Program Analysis. 0092-8453. US. English. Office of Fiscal Affairs, State House Annex, Trenton NJ 08625. **LC** JK1651.N5. **DD** 353.974900862.

THE PROGRAM AND RESOURCE DIGEST. **Main/Corp** United States. Dept. of Justice. 1978/79-. 0197-8187. US. English. an. US Department of Justice, Washington DC 20530. **LC** KF5107. **DD** 353.5.

LE PROGRAMME, L'ACTION POLITIQUE, LES STATUTS ET REGLEMENTS. **Main/Corp** Parti Quebecois. 1969-. CN. French. 5675 Christophe Colomb, Montreal Quebec Canada. **LC** JL259.A56. **DD** 329.9714.

PROGRESS. V. 1- Jan. 1950-. 0555-3806. Periodical. CN. English. qt. British Columbia Hydro and Power Authority, Public and Customer Relations Division, 970 Burrard Street, Vancouver British Columbia V6Z 1Y3 Canada.

Public Administration

A PROGRESS REPORT TO THE PRESIDENT. (A PROGRESS REPORT TO THE PRESIDENT : EFFORTS TO PREVENT FRAUD, WASTE, AND MISMANAGEMENT). **VFOAT** Efforts to Prevent Fraud, Waste, and Mismanagement. 0883-6450. US. English. sa.

PROPERTY HIGHLIGHTS. **Main/Corp** Wisconsin. Federal Property Program. Highlights No. 78-1- July 1978-. Periodical. US. English. mo. Federal Property Program, 201 South Dickinson, Box 1585, Madison WI 53701. *Property Bulletin.*

PROVINCIAL FINANCIAL ASSISTANCE AND SERVICES FOR LOCAL GOVERNMENT. 0711-7736. CN. English. Saskatchewan Urban Affairs, 2151 Scarth Street, Regina Saskatchewan S4P 3V7 Canada. **LC** HJ795.S2. **DD** 354.712400725305.

PROVINCIAL GOVERNMENT EMPLOYMENT CEASED. **Main/Corp** Statistics Canada. Provincial Government Section. **VFOAT** L'Emploi dans les Administrations Publiques Provinciales. **VAT** Emploi dans les Gouvernements Provinciaux. V. 13, No. 2-V. 26. No, 1 1971-. 0527-608X. Periodical. CN. English (French). qt. Receiver General for Canada, Statistics Canada Publications, Ottawa Ontario K1A 0T6 Canada. *Provincial Government Employment, 0527-608X.*

PROVINCIAL GOVERNMENT ENTERPRISE FINANCE. (PROVINCIAL GOVERNMENT ENTERPRISE FINANCE, INCOME AND EXPENDITURE, ASSETS, LIABILITIES AND NET WORTH). **VFOAT** Finance des Entreprises Publiques Provinciales, Revenus et Depensus i.e. Depenses. Actif, Passif et Valeur Nette. 1969-. 0575-9463. CN. English (French). an. $1.05. Statistics Canada, Publications Distribution, Ottawa Ontario K1A 0T6 Canada. **LC** HD4001. **DD** 354.71092. *Provincial Government Enterprise Finance, Assets, Liabilities and Net Worth, Current Revenue and Expenditure.*

PUBLIC ADMINISTRATION. V. 4- 1926-. 0033-3298. Periodical. UK. English. qt. $82.65 US. Basil Blackwell Publisher, 108 Cowley Road, Oxford OX4 1JF England. **Tel** 0865-722146. Ed O M Lee and Christopher Pouitt. (cum index). bk rev. adv acc. Official journal of Royal Institute of Public Administration essential reading for anyone with an interest in the public sector. *Journal of Public Administration.*

PUBLIC ADMINISTRATION ABSTRACTS AND INDEX OF ARTICLES. *See* Indexes/Abstracts.

PUBLIC ADMINISTRATION AND DEVELOPMENT. (PUBLIC ADMINISTRATION AND DEVELOPMENT : A JOURNAL OF THE ROYAL INSTITUTE OF PUBLIC ADMINISTRATION). Vol. 1, No. 1 (Jan.-Mar. 1981)-. 0271-2075. Periodical. UK. English. qt. John Wiley & Son, Baffins Lane Chichester, Sussex PO19 1UD England. **Ind/Abst** Manage. Contents, Int. Labour Doc., ABC Pol Sci, Curr. Contents, Soc. Sci. Citation Index, Public Aff. Inf. Serv. Bull. **LC** JF60. **DD** 350.0078091724. **CODEN** PADEDR. *Journal of Administration Overseas, 0021-8472.*

PUBLIC ADMINISTRATION AND PUBLIC POLICY. Monographic Series. US. English. ir. Marcel Dekker, 270 Madison Avenue, New York NY 10016. **Tel** (212)696-9000. Ed Henry Frederickson Rabin. This is an ongoing series. Each title has a different subject.

PUBLIC ADMINISTRATION BULLETIN (LONDON, ENGLAND). (PUBLIC ADMINISTRATION BULLETIN). No. 13 (Dec. 1972)-. 0144-2171. Periodical. UK. English. ty. $25.29. Joint University Council, Social Publication, Hamilton House Mabledon Place Ripa, London WC1H9BD England. **Tel** 01 388 0211. Ed D Pitt. **Circ** 300. Articles on public administration, covering both central and local government. *PAC Bulletin.*

PUBLIC ADMINISTRATION (LONDON, ENGLAND). (PUBLIC ADMINISTRATION). Vol. 4, No. 1 (Jan. 1926)-. 0033-3298. Periodical. UK. English. qt. Public Administration. Basil Blackwell Journals Department, 108 Cowley Road, Oxford OX4 1JF England. **Tel** 0865 722146. Ed J M Lee and Christopher Pollitt. **Ind/Abst** ABC Pol Sci, Public Aff. Inf. Serv. Bull., Soc. Sci. Index, Ref. Source, Am. Hist. Life, Hist. Abstr., Part A, Mod. Hist. Abstr., Hist. Abst., Part B, Twent. Century Abstr. (cum index). bk rev. adv acc. **Circ** 4,400. Essential reading for anyone with an interest in the public sector. Includes insights into the policy making process and the actual workings of the public sector. *Journal of Public Administration (London, England).*

Public Administration

PUBLIC ADMINISTRATION QUARTERLY. VFOAT P.A.Q. V. 7, No. 1 (Spring 1983)-. 0734-9149. Periodical. US. English. qt. $24.00. Public Administration, PO Box 632, Randallstown MD 21133. Tel (301)655-2137. Ind/Abst Manage. Contents, ABI/Inform. LC JA1. DD 350.0005. bk rev. Circ 500. (ctrl). Available in microform from University Microfilms International. *Southern Review of Public Administration, 0147-8168.*

PUBLIC ADMINISTRATION TIMES. V. 1- Jan. 1978-. 0149-8797. Periodical. US. English. sm. $25.00. American Society of Public Administration, 1120 G Street NW/Suite 500, Washington DC 20005. Tel (202)393-7878. *ASPA News & Views, 0360-4233.*

PUBLIC ADMINISTRATION (UNIVERSITY OF DACCA. (PUBLIC ADMINISTRATION). Periodical. English. qt. LC JA26. DD 320.05.

PUBLIC ADMINISTRATION UPDATE. VFOAT PAU. V. 1- Aug. 1977-. 0148-4168. Periodical. US. English. qt. $5.00. Public Administration Update, PO Box 4434, Montgomery AL 36101. Tel (205)269-2849.

THE PUBLIC ADMINISTRATOR AND THE COURTS. Vol. 1, No. 1 (July 1981)-. 0735-4703. Periodical. US. English. qt. $79.50. Research Publications Inc, 92 Fairway Drive, PO Box 9267, Asheville NC 28815. Tel (704)298-8291. Ed John C Pine. LC KF5401.A75. DD 342.73062648, 347.302602648. (ctrl). Briefs of selected significant higher court decisions affecting the field of public administration.

PUBLIC AFFAIRS. V. 1- May 15, 1960-. 0555-5914. Periodical. US. English. qt. Free. University of South Dakota, Governmental Research Bureau, Vermillion SD 57069. Tel (605)677-5702. Ed Russell Smith. Ind/Abst Public Aff. Inf. Serv. Bull. LC JK6501. DD 320.09783. Circ 2,000. Articles on public policy issues pertaining to rural areas and South Dakota.

PUBLIC AFFAIRS ADMINISTRATION. May 15, 1974-. 0700-3455. Periodical. CN. English (includes some text in French). Institute of Public Affairs, Dalhousie University, Halifax Nova Scotia B3H 4H8 Canada. DD 354.710005.

PUBLIC AFFAIRS BULLETIN. No. 1- Oct. 1978-. Periodical. US. English. ir. $10.00. University of South Carolina, Publishing Program, Bureau of Government Research & Service, Columbia SC 29208. Tel (803)777-8156. Ed Charlie B Tyer. Circ 2,500. Reports on political, social, and economic issues affecting state and local governments. *Unviersity of South Carolina Governmental Review.*

PUBLIC AFFAIRS REVIEW. (PUBLIC AFFAIRS REVIEW : JOURNAL OF THE PUBLIC AFFAIRS COUNCIL). Began with vol. for 1980. 0276-0843. Periodical. US. English. an. Public Affairs Council, 1220 16th Street NW, Washington DC 20036. LC JK467. DD 322.30973.

PUBLIC AND LOCAL ACTS OF THE LEGISLATURE OF THE STATE OF MICHIGAN. See Law.

PUBLIC AUTHORITIES DIRECTORY. See Yearbooks, Almanacs, Directories.

PUBLIC BODIES. 1982-. UK. English. LC JN409. DD 354.410405.

PUBLIC CLEANSING SERVICE IN TOKYO. Main/Corp Tokyo. Seisokyoku. English. ir. LC HD4485.J3. DD 363.6.

PUBLIC EMPLOYEE. See Economics - Labor.

THE PUBLIC EMPLOYEE. See Economics - Labor.

PUBLIC EMPLOYEE PRESS. See Economics - Labor.

PUBLIC EMPLOYEE RELATIONS COUNSELLOR. See Economics - Labor.

PUBLIC EMPLOYEE RELATIONS LIBRARY. See Economics - Labor.

PUBLIC EMPLOYEES' AND TEACHERS' RETIREMENT SYSTEMS, ANNUAL FINANCIAL REPORT. See Economics - Labor.

PUBLIC EMPLOYEES CONFERENCE PROCEEDINGS. See Economics - Labor.

PUBLIC EXECUTIVE PROJECT BULLETIN. VFOAT Management Seminars for Public Executives Bulletin. 0730-1863. US. English. an. Public Executive Project, Graduate School for Public Affairs, State University of New York at Albany, Mohawk Tower/Room 1304, Albany NY 12222. *Public Executive Project Program, 0730-1855.*

PUBLIC INFORMATION CIRCULAR. Monographic Series. US. English. ir. The Survey, Box 3008/University Station, Laramie WY 82071.

PUBLIC LANDS DIGEST. VFOAT Public Land Digest. US. English. an. BLM Montana State Office, Office of Public Affairs, PO Box 30157, Billings MT 59107.

PUBLIC LAWS OF THE STATE OF RHODE ISLAND AND PROVIDENCE PLANTATIONS PASSED AT THE GENERAL ASSEMBLY. See Law.

PUBLIC MANAGEMENT. (PM, PUBLIC MANAGEMENT). V. 50, No. 7- July 1968-. Periodical. US. English. mo. $24.00. International City Management Association, 1120 G Street Northwest, Washington DC 20005. Tel (202)626-4600. Ed Beth Payne. Ind/Abst Manage. Contents, Mag. Index, Public Aff. Inf. Serv. Bull., Soc. Sci. Index. bk rev. adv acc. Circ 14,100. Available on microfilm from University Microfilms. Contains solicited and unsolicited feature articles, book reviews, profiles of public administrators, innovations, letters to the editor, legal news, international subjects and viewpoints. *Public Management, 0033-3611.*

PUBLIC MANAGEMENT RESEARCH DIRECTORY. See Yearbooks, Almanacs, Directories.

PUBLIC MONEY. See Business - Public Finance.

PUBLIC PAPERS OF THE PRESIDENTS OF THE UNITED STATES. Main/Corp United States. President. 0079-7626. US. English. an. Superintendent of Documents, US Government Printing Office, Washington DC 20402. LC J80. DD 353.035. (cum index).

PUBLIC POWER. V. 1- Dec. 10, 1942-. 0033-3654. Periodical. US. English. bm. $35.00. American Public Power Association, 2301 M Street NW, Washington DC 20037. Tel (202)775-8300. Ed Vic Reinemer. Ind/Abst Coal Abstr., Energy Inf. Abstr., Environ. Abstr., Energy Res. Abstr., Ref. Source. LC HD9685.U4. DD 338.4736362. bk rev. adv acc. Circ 18,000. (ctrl). Articles and pictures about local publicly owned electric systems, including annual directory and annual report on public power innovation.

PUBLIC POWER WEEKLY NEWSLETTER. 0195-7325. Periodical. US. English. wk. $250.00. American Public Power Association, 2301 M Street NW, Washington DC 20037. Tel (202)775-8300. Ed Jeanne Wickline LaBella. LC HD9685.U4. DD 363.62. Circ 7,100. (ctrl). Current events affecting local publicly owned electric utilities. *Weekly Newsletter - American Public Power Association, 0196-2957.*

PUBLIC PRODUCTIVITY REVIEW. V. 1- Sept. 1975-. 0361-6681. Periodical. US. English. qt. $20.00. Public Productivity Review, 445 West 59th Street, New York NY 10019. Tel (212)489-5031. Ed Elaine Niederhoffer and Marc Holzer. Ind/Abst Manage. Contents, Cumul. Index Nurs. Allied Health Lit., ABI/Inform. LC JF1411. DD 331.118. bk rev. adv acc. Circ 1,700. (ctrl). Articles and views on present trends in government and academic productivity. Also concerns the quality of work life and its improvement.

PUBLIC SECTOR. (THE PUBLIC SECTOR). V. 1- Oct. 10, 1977-. 0700-2092. Periodical. CN. English. wk. $95.00. Corpus, 151 Bloor Street West, Toronto Ontario M5S 1S4 Canada. DD 338.971.

PUBLIC SERVICE COMMISSIONER ANNUAL REPORT (ALBERTA). Main/Corp Alberta. Office of the Public Service Commissioner. 1967-. 0701-5461. Periodical. CN. English. an. Free. Alberta Personnel Administration Office, Room 1101/Jarvis Building, 9925-107 Street, Edmonton Alberta T5K 2H9 Canada. LC HD2768.C38. DD 354.71230086. *Annual Report of the Public Service Commissioner, 0701-5461.*

PUBLIC SERVICE LIST. Main/Corp Western Australia. Public Service Board. English. ir. LC JQ5521. DD 354.941002.

PUBLIC TECHNOLOGY NEWS. 1979. 0194-1623. Periodical. US. English. mo. $35.00. Public Technology Inc, 1301 Pennsylvania Avenue NW, Washington DC 20004. Tel (202)626-2400. Ed Tod Newcombe. bk rev. Circ 3,000. Illustrated articles on cost-effective technologies for local governments and how they are being implemented. Also reports on new research and technological trends.

PUBLIC UTILITIES ACT 1951. Main/Corp Barbados. Public Utilities Board. BB. English. ir. Barbados Public Utlities Board, Barbados Statistical Service, National Insurance Building, Bridgetown Barbados. LC HD2768.B37. DD 354.729810087.

PUBLIC UTILITIES AND TRANSPORTATION NEWSLETTER. Main/Corp Illinois State Bar Association. Section on Public Utilities and Transportation. 0147-359X. US. English. LC KFI1485.A15. DD 343.7730905.

PUBLIC UTILITIES FORTNIGHTLY. (PUBLIC UTILITIES FORTNIGHTLY MICROFORM). Vol. 3, No. 2 (Jan. 24, 1929)-. 0033-3808. Periodical. US. English. Ind/Abst Coal Abstr., Energy Inf. Abstr., Environ. Abstr., Account. Index. Suppl., ABI/Inform, Energy Res. Abstr., Public Aff. Inf. Serv. Bull., Bus. Period. Index. LC Microfilm (O). *Public Utilities Reports Fortnightly.*

PUBLIC UTILITIES LAW ANTHOLOGY. See Law.

PUBLIC UTILITIES, OTHER THAN AUTO TRANSPORTATION, SERVING NORTH DAKOTA. Main/Corp North Dakota. Public Service Commission. Accounting Dept. 0361-7696. US. English. LC HD2767.N9. DD 363.6025784.

PUBLIC UTILITY PROPERTY : ASSESSED VALUE OF PUBLIC UTILITY REAL AND PERSONAL PROPERTY, BY COUNTY AND CLASS OF UTILITY. Main/Corp Ohio. Dept. of Taxation. US. English. Department of Taxation, Research and Statistics Section, PO Box 530, Columbus OH 43216. LC HD2767.O3. DD 333.332.

PUBLIC UTILITY REGULATORY POLICIES ACT OF 1978. ANNUAL REPORT TO CONGRESS. (PUBLIC UTILITY REGULATORY POLICIES ACT OF 1978, ANNUAL REPORT TO CONGRESS). VAT Public Utility Regulatory Policies Act of Nineteen Seventy Eight. Annual Report to Congress. 1979-. 0272-1260. US. English. an. National Technical Information Service, US Department of Commerce, 5285 Port Royal Road, Springfield VA 22161. LC HD2766.A3. DD 353.0087005.

PUBLIC WORKS. See Engineering.

PUBLIC WORKS MANUAL. See Engineering.

PUBLIC WORKS NEWS. 0146-5473. Periodical. US. English. ir. $90.00. Reynolds Publ Company, PO Box 578, Glen Echo MD 20768.

PUBLIC WORKS PROGRESS. Main/Corp Chicago (Ill.). Dept. of Public Works. 0148-5814. Periodical. US. English. qt. Department of Public Works, Room 406/City Hall, Chicago IL 60602. LC HD4606.C5. DD 363.50977311.

PUBLICATION (ILLINOIS. GENERAL ASSEMBLY. LEGISLATIVE COUNCIL). (PUBLICATION). Began with: No. 5, published in Nov. 1938. Monographic Series. US. English. State of Illinois, Illinois Legislative Council, Springfield IL 62706. LC JK5774. DD 328.773. *Research Report.*

PUBLICATIONS - ALBERTA MUNICIPAL AFFAIRS. See Biographies.

PUBLICATIONS OF THE NATIONAL INSTITUTE OF JUSTICE. SUPPLEMENT. Main/Corp National Institute of Justice (U.S.). 1980-. US. English. an. National Institute of Justice, Washington DC 20531. *Publications of the National Institute of Law Enforcement and Criminal Justice. Supplement, 0198-1455.*

PUBLICUS (BASEL, SWITZERLAND). (PUBLICUS). French (German). an. Verlag Schwabe & Company AG, Steinentorstrasse 13 Postfach, CH-4010 Basel Switzerland. *Schweizer Jahrbuch des Offentlichen Lebens.*

Public Administration

THE P.U.R. ANALYSIS OF INVESTOR-OWNED ELECTRIC AND GAS UTILITIES. (THE P.U.R. . . . ANALYSIS OF INVESTOR-OWNED ELECTRIC AND GAS UTILITIES). VFOAT PUR . . . Analysis of Investor-Owned Electric and Gas Utilities. VAT Public Utilities Reports Analysis of Investor-Owned Electric and Gas Utilities. 1982-. 0733-4915. US. English. an. $175.00. Public Utilities Reports Inc, Suite 2100/Rosslyn Center Building, 1700 North Moore Street, Arlington VA 22209. LC HD9685.U4. DD 338.76136362.

QUADERNI BIANCHI. Yearly V. 1, No. 1, (Jan./Feb. 1979)-. Periodical. IT. Italian. bm. $23.76. Citta e Societa, Piazza S Ambrogio 21, 20123 Milano Italy. LC JN5201. DD 945.0927.

QUALIFICATION STANDARDS FOR WHITE COLLAR POSITIONS UNDER THE GENERAL SCHEDULE. Periodical. US. English. ir. US Civil Service Commission, Washington DC 20402.

QUARTERLY BULLETIN. Main/Corp United States. Bureau of Alcohol, Tobacco, and Firearms. 1983, V. 1-. Periodical. US. English. qt. US Government Printing Office, Superintendent of Documents, Washington DC 20402. *Alcohol, Tobacco and Firearms Quarterly Bulletin.*

QUARTERLY DIGEST OF UNPUBLISHED DECISIONS OF THE COMPTROLLER GENERAL OF THE UNITED STATES. CONTRACTS. (QUARTERLY DIGEST OF UNPUBLISHED DECISIONS OF THE COMPTROLLER GENERAL OF THE UNITED STATES : CONTRACTS). Main/Corp United States. General Accounting Office. Office of the General Counsel. V. 1- Sept./Dec. 1957-. 0499-499X. Periodical. US. English. qt. United States General Accounting Office, Washington DC 20548.

QUARTERLY FINANCIAL REPORT FOR MANUFACTURING, MINING, AND TRADE CORPORATIONS. 4th Quarter 1982-. Periodical. US. English. qt. Superintendent of Documents, US Government Printing Office, Washington DC 20402. Tel (202)783-3238. *Quarterly Financial Report for Manufacturing, Mining, and Trade Corporations, 0098-681X.*

QUARTERLY JOURNAL OF THE LOCAL SELF GOVERNMENT INSTITUTE (BOMBAY). Main/Corp Local Self-Government Institute (Bombay State). V. 1- July 1930-. 0024-5623. Periodical. II. English. qt. $8.00 Foreign 30. Domestic. All India Institution of Local Self-G, 11 Horniman Circle, Fort Bombay India. Tel 572473. Ed H D Kopardekar. Ind/Abst Sociol. Abstr., Lang. Lang. Behav. Abstr. LC JS7001. bk rev. Circ 1,000. Local government administration and urban development.

QUARTERLY PROGRESS REPORT OF GOVERNMENT DEPARTMENTS AND STATUTORY AUTHORITIES. VFOAT Quarterly Progress Report. No. 28 (Mar. 1982) I.E. Mar. 1983-. AT. English. qt. Policy and Research Branch, Department of the Premier and Cabinet, 1 Treasury Place, Melbourne 3002 Australia. *Quarterly Progress Report.*

QUAT. (LE QUAT : BULLETIN DU CENTRE SOCIAL DES FONCTIONNAIRES MUNICIPAUX DE MONTREAL). Main/Corp Centre Social des Fonctionnaires Municipaux de Montreal. Vol. 2, No. 1-. 0712-6158. Periodical. CN. French. bm. Free to Members. Le Quat, c/o Centre Social des Fonctionnaires Municipaux de Montreal, 429 Est rue de la Gauchetiere, Montreal Quebec H2L 2M7 Canada. DD 352.0714281. *Detente, 0712-614X.*

QUESTIONS ET REPONSES. Main/Corp Belgium. Parlement. Chambre des Representants. VFOAT Vragen en Antwoorden. Periodical. BE. Flemish and French. ir. $9.88. Moniteur Belge, rue de Louvain 40-42, 1000 Bruxelles Belgium. LC J393. DD 328.49301.

RAADGEVENDE INTERPARLEMENTAIRE BENELUXRAAD : VERSLAG. VFOAT Conseil Interparlementaire Consultatif de Benelux : Report. Periodical. BE. Dutch (French). ir. Vast Sekretariaat Van de Interparlementaire Beneluxraad, Paleis der Natie, Brussels Belgium.

RANGE IMPROVEMENT PROGRAMS. Main/Corp Alberta. Public Lands Division. 1980/81-. 0715-0164. CN. English. an. Alberta Energy and Natural Resources, 11th Floor/South Petroleum Plaza, Edmonton Alberta T5K 2C9 Canada. DD 354.71230082326.

RAPPORT ANNUEL - BELGIUM. CONSEIL SUPERIEUR DES CLASSES MOYENNES. Main/Corp Belgium. Conseil Superieur des Classes Moyennes. BE. French. an. Conseil Superieur des Classes Moyennes Secretariat, rue de la Charite 24, 1040 Bruxelles Belgium. *Rapport Annuel du Secretaire General.*

RAPPORT ANNUEL - COMMISSION MUNICIPALE DU QUEBEC. (RAPPORT ANNUEL). Main/Corp Commission Municipale du Quebec. Began in 1979. 0229-8139. CN. French. an. LC KEQ820.A72. DD 352.0714.

LE RAPPORT ANNUEL DE LA DATAR. Main/Corp France. Delegation a l'Amenagement du Territoire et a l'Action Regionale. FR. French. an. 1 Avenue Charles Floquet, 75007 Paris France.

RAPPORT ANNUEL DES ACTIVITES DU BUREAU REGIONAL DE PLACEMENT DE L'OUTAOUAIS, REGION 07. Main/Corp Quebec (Province). Ministere de l'Education. Bureau Regional de Placement de l'Outaouais. VFOAT Rapport d'Activities. VAT Rapport d'Activites - Bureau Regional de Placement de l'Outaouais. 1980/1981-. 0228-6769. CN. French. an. Gouvernement du Quebec, 600 St Amable 4E Etage, Quebec G1R 4Z1 Canada. DD 354.714008510971422.

RAPPORT ANNUEL DU CONSEIL DE L'INFORMATION SUR L'ENERGIE ELECTRONUCLEAIRE. Main/Corp France. Conseil de l'Information sur l'Energie Electronucleaire. VFOAT Iformation sur l'Energie Electronucleaire. FR. French. ir. Documentation Francaise, 29-31 Quai Voltaire, 75340 Paris Cedex 07 France. LC HD9698.F7. DD 354.44008722.

RAPPORT ANNUEL - FEDERATION PROFESSIONNELLE DES PRODUCTEURS ET DISTRIBUTEURS D'ELECTRICITE DE BELGIQUE. Main/Corp Federation Professionnelle des Producteurs et Distributeurs d'Electricite de Belgique. French. ir. 31 rue Belliars, 1040 Bruxelles Belgium. LC HD9685.B4. DD 363.6209493. *Rapport du Conseil d'Administration a l'Assemblee Generale sur la Situation de l'Industrie de l'Electricite et sur l'Activite.*

RAPPORT ANNUEL INFORMATIQUE - MINISTERE DE L'EDUCATION, SERVICE DE L'INFORMATIQUE. (RAPPORT ANNUEL INFORMATIQUE). Main/Corp Quebec (Province). Ministere de l'Education. Service de l'Informatique. 0711-687X. CN. French. an. Gouvernement du Quebec, 600 St Amable 4E Etage, Quebec G1R 4Z1 Canada. DD 354.714068510285.

RAPPORT ANNUEL - INSTITUT NATIONAL DE PRODUCTIVITE. (RAPPORT ANNUEL). Main/Corp Quebec (Province). Institut National de Productivite. 1978/1979-. 0229-8538. CN. French. an. 51 rue d'Auteuil, Quebec Quebec G1R 4C2 Canada. DD 354.7140082.

RAPPORT ANNUEL - MINISTERE DE LA JUSTICE (QUEBEC. 1980). (RAPPORT ANNUEL). Main/Corp Quebec (Province). Ministere de la Justice. Began with 1979/80 Vol. 0715-9889. CN. French. an. LC KEQ787.A72. DD 354.7140088. *Rapport d'Activites, 0710-6653.*

RAPPORT ANNUEL - MINISTERE DE L'AGRICULTURE, DES PECHERIES ET DE L'ALIMENTATION. (RAPPORT ANNUEL). Main/Corp Quebec (Province). Ministere de l'Agriculture, des Pecheries et de l'Alimentation. 1979-1980-. 0715-6219. CN. French. an. LC HD1790.Q4. DD 354.71406823306. *Rapport Annuel, 0383-4484.*

RAPPORT ANNUEL - OFFICE DU RECRUTEMENT ET DE LA SELECTION DU PERSONNEL DE LA FONCTION PUBLIQUE. (RAPPORT ANNUEL). Main/Corp Quebec (Province). Office du Recrutement et de la Selection du Personnel de la Fonction Publique. 1979-1980-. 0227-2253. CN. French. an. Editeur Officiel du Quebec, 1283 Boul Charest Quest, Quebec PQ G1N 2C9 Canada. LC JL252.Z13. DD 354.710013.

RAPPORT ANNUEL - REGIE DE L'ELECTRICITE ET DU GAZ. (RAPPORT ANNUEL). Main/Corp Quebec (Province). Electricity and Gas Board. VAT Annual Report - Electricity and Gas Board (Quebec. 1975). 1975/76-. 0711-7132. CN. English (text in French only). an. Gouvernement du Quebec, 600 St Amable 4E Etage, Quebec G1R 4Z1 Canada. DD 354.71400872. *Annual Report.*

RAPPORT ANNUEL - REGIE DES PERMIS D'ALCOOL DU QUEBEC. (RAPPORT ANNUEL). Main/Corp Regie des Permis d'Alcool du Quebec. 1980/1981-. 0710-376X. CN. French. an. LC HV5087.C2. DD 354.7140076106. *Rapport Annuel - Commission de Controle des Permis d'Alcool du Quebec, 0714-0428.*

RAPPORT ANNUEL - SERVICE DE RECHERCHE EN DEFENSE DES CULTURES. (RAPPORT ANNUEL). Main/Corp Quebec (Province). Service de Recherche en Defense des Cultures. 1980-. 0713-4711. Periodical. CN. French. Free. Gouvernement du Quebec, 600 St Amable 4E Etage, Quebec G1R 4Z1 Canada. DD 354.7140082333042. (ctrl). *Repertoire des Travaux de Recherche en Defense des Cultures.*

RAPPORT AU PRESIDENT DE LA REPUBLIQUE ET AU PARLEMENT. Main/Corp France. Commission Nationale de l'Informatique et des Libertes. VFOAT Rapport d'Activite. Began with 1978-1980 Volume. FR. French. ir. La Documentation Francaise, 29-31 Quai Voltaire, 75340 Paris Cedex 07 France. LC JC599.F8. DD 354.4400811.

RAPPORT D'ACTIVITE - CAISSE NATIONALE DE L'INDUSTRIE (FRANCE). Main/Corp Caisse Nationale de l'Industrie (France). 1982-. 0755-2211. French. ir. LC HD4161. DD 354.4409206.

RAPPORT D'ACTIVITES CONCERNANT LES ELECTIONS DANS CERTAINES MUNICIPALITES. Main/Corp Quebec (Province). Directeur General des Elections du Quebec. 2nd (1981)-. 0229-9585. CN. French. an. LC JS1721.Q4. DD 324.971404. *Rapport Annuel.*

RAPPORT D'ACTIVITES - OFFICE DE LA CONSTRUCTION DU QUEBEC. Main/Corp Quebec (Province) Office de la Construction. 1978-. 0226-3084. CN. French. an. Office de la Construction du Quebec, 3530 rue Jean-Talon Ouest, Montreal Quebec H3R 2G3 Canada. LC HD9715.C33. DD 354.714008242. *Rapport Annuel, 0707-3399.*

RAPPORT D'ACTIVITIES - SERVICE DE L'HABITATION ET DE L'URBANISME. VILLE DE MONTREAL. (RAPPORT D'ACTIVITES - VILLE DE MONTREAL, SERVICE DE L'HABITATION ET DE L'URBANISME). Main/Corp Montreal, Quebec. Service de l'Habitation et de l'Urbanisme. 1974-. 0317-7742. Periodical. CN. French. Service de l'Habitation et de l'Urbanisme, 330 Est rue St-Paul, Montreal Quebec H2Y 1H2 Canada. DD 352.960971481. *Rapport des Activites, 0317-7734.*

RAPPORT DE LA DIRECTION DES EXPLOSIFS. Main/Corp Canada. Direction des Explosifs. 1968/1975-. 0710-7196. Periodical. CN. French. Energie Mines et Resources, 580 Booth Street, Ottawa Ontario K1A 0E4 Canada. DD 354.710075. *Rapport de la Division des Explosifs, 0710-7188.*

RAPPORT DU MEDIATEUR AU PRESIDENT DE LA REPUBLIQUE ET AU PARLEMENT. Main/Corp France. Mediateur. VFOAT Rapport du Mediateur. FR. French. an. President de la Republique et au Parlemen, 26 rue Desaix, 75727 Paris Cedex 15 France. *Rapport Annuel du Mediateur.*

RAPPORT GENERAL. Main/Corp France. Comite Central d'Enquete sur le Cout et le Rendement des Services Publics. FR. French. ir. 29-31 Quai Voltaire, 75340 Paris Cedex 07 France. LC JN2717. DD 354.4400147.

RAPPORT GENERAL D'ACTIVITE. Main/Corp France. Ministete de l'Agriculture. Direction de la Qualite. Yearly V. 1977-. FR. French. an. 40. Direction de la Qualite Sous-Direction des Affaires Communes, 44 Bd de Grenelle, 75732 Paris Cedex 15 France. LC HD9000.9.F7. DD 354.44007782.

RASHTRIYA PANCAYATA NIYAMAVALI. Main/Corp Nepal. National Panchayat. Nepali. ir. Rashtriya Pancayata Sacivalaya, Singha Durbar, Kathamadaum India. LC JQ1825.N45.

RECENT PUBLICATIONS ON GOVERNMENTAL PROBLEMS. VFOAT RPGP. 1932. 0034-1185. Periodical. US. English. mo. $25.00. Charles Merriam Center Library, 1313 East

Public Administration

60th Street, Chicago IL 60637. **Tel** (312)947-2165. Ed Charlotte Ullman. **Ind/Abst** Energy Res. Abstr., Public Aff. Inf. Serv. Bull. **LC** Z7164.A2. **DD** 016.32. bk rev. **Circ** 600. Lists pieces about the environment, architecture, finance, taxation, economics, personnel, public works, planning, utilities, public safety, public administration and the law. *Recent Publications on Legislative problems.*

RECOMMENDATIONS AND REPORTS. **Main/Corp** Administrative Conference of the United States. Periodical. US. English. an.

RECOMMENDATIONS AND REPORTS - ADMINISTRATIVE CONFERENCE OF THE UNITED STATES. (RECOMMENDATIONS AND REPORTS). **Main/Corp** Administrative Conference of the United States. 1978-. 0882-9217. US. English. an. Office of the Chairman, Administrative Conference of the United States, Washington DC 20037. *Recommendations and Reports of the Administrative Conference of the United States, 0882-9217.*

RECOMMENDED SALARIES AND BENEFITS FOR CAREER SERVICE EMPLOYEES. **Main/Corp** Florida. Dept. of Administration. Division of Personnel. 0146-9916. US. English. Department of Administration, Division of Personnel, 660 Apalachee Parkway, Tallahassee FL 32304. **LC** JK4457. **DD** 331.2813539759.

RECUEIL DES ACTES ADMINISTRATIFS. *See* Law.

RECUEIL DES ACTES ADMINISTRATIFS DE LA PREFECTURE DE PARIS ET DE LA PREFECTURE DE POLICE. **Main/Corp** Paris (France). Prefecture. FR. French. ir. 70. M le Regisseur de la Caisse Interieure, Hotel de Ville, 75196 Paris RP France. **LC** JS7.F7. **DD** 352.044361. *Recueil des Actes Administratifs de la Prefecture de la Seine et de la Prefecture de Police.*

RECURRENT ESTIMATES. **Main/Corp** Nigeria. Interim Common Services Agency. English. ir. -/10/6. Government Printer, Private Mail Bag 2020, Kaduna Nigeria. **LC** HD4350.N47. **DD** 354.6690084.

RECURRENT ESTIMATES OF THE COMMONWEALTH OF DOMINICA. **Main/Corp** Dominica. VFOAT Estimates. 1981/82-. English. ir. **LC** HJ28.5.D65. **DD** 354.729841007222505. *Estimates of the Commonwealth of Dominica.*

REFERATEBLATT ZUR RAUMENTWICKLUNG. 1975-. 0341-2512. Periodical. German. ir. Carl Heymanns Verlag KG, Gereonstrasse 18-32, 5000 Koln 1 West Germany. **Ind/Abst** Foreign Lang. Index. *Referateblatt zur Raumordnung.*

REGARDS SUR L'ACTUALITE. No. 1- May 1974-. 0337-7091. Periodical. FR. French. ir. Documentation Francaise, 124 rue Henri Barbusse, 93308 Aubervilliers Cedex France. **Tel** 834-9275. **LC** JN2301. **DD** 309.144. (cum index).

REGARDS SUR MA VILLE. (REGARDS SUR MA VILLE : BULLETIN D'INFORMATION DE LA VILLE DE SAINT-JEROME). V. 1, No 2 (Summer 81)-. 0822-9147. Periodical. CN. French. ty. Free. Ville de Saint-Jerome, 280 rue Labelle, Saint-Jerome Quebec J7Z 5L1 Canada. **DD** 352.071424. (ctrl). *Bulletin Municipal de la Ville de Saint-Jerome, 0226-1359.*

REGION (WASHINGTON D.C.). See Housing and Urban Development.

REGIONAL DIRECTORY - CAPITAL AREA PLANNING COUNCIL. *See* Yearbooks, Almanacs, Directories.

REGIONAL NEWSLETTER - CONSUMERS' ASSOCIATION OF CANADA. BRITISH COLUMBIA BRANCH. (REGIONAL NEWSLETTER). **Main/Corp** Consumers' Association of Canada. British Columbia Branch. 1976-. 0703-5446. Periodical. CN. English. bm. Free. Greater Vancouver Regional District, 4330 Kingsway, Burnaby British Columbia V5H 4G8 Canada. **Tel** (604)432-6200. Ed D J Elsie. **DD** 640.7309711. **Circ** 15,000. (ctrl). Activities of the regional government in greater Vancouver. . . parks, sewers, water, labour relations, pollution control, planning etc. *B. C. Regional Newsletter, 0703-5454.*

REGIONAL NOTES. **Main/Corp** Mississippi River Regional Planning Commission. Vol. 1, No. 1-. Periodical. US. English. bm. Mississippi River Regional Planning Commission, 315 South Front Street, La Crosse WI 54061.

REGIONAL PLAN NEWS. No. 1- Feb. 17, 1941-. 0034-3374. Periodical. US. English. ir. $25.00. Regional Planning Association, 1040 Avenue of the Americas, New York NY 10018. **Tel** (212)398-1140. Ed William B Shore. bk rev. **Circ** 4,000. Research and analysis of economic development, transportation, open space, social conditions, and land use decisions that affect the New York metropolitan region.

REGIONAL REFLECTIONS. 0715-5050. Periodical. CN. English. qt. Free. Clerks Office Region of Peel, 10 Peel Centre Drive, Brampton Ontario L6T 4B9 Canada. **Tel** 791-9400. Ed Deb Phillips-Jamieson. **DD** 917.13535005. Magazine-format publication providing an overview of the regional municipality of Peel, emphasizing the government's activities and services.

REGISTER AND MANUAL - STATE OF CONNECTICUT. **Main/Corp** Connecticut. Secretary of the State. 0270-6245. US. English. an. State of Connecticut/Secretary of State Public Division, 30 Trinity Street, Hartford CT 06115. **Tel** (203)566-2508. **LC** JK3331. **DD** 353.974600205. *Connecticut State Register and Manual.*

REGISTER OF ACTIVE COMMITTEES. US. English. an. **LC** JQ5301. **DD** 354.945040202.

REGISTRANTS, LOBBYISTS. VFOAT Registrants/Lobbyists. US. English. ir. State Ethics Commission, 301 West Preston Street/Room 1515, Baltimore MD 21201. **LC** JK3874.5. **DD** 328.38025752.

REGISTRY OF VEHICLES SINGAPORE ANNUAL REPORT. **Main/Corp** Singapore. Registry of Vehicles. **Series/Titl** CMD. English. an. **LC** HE5693.6.S5. **DD** 354.59570087834. *Annual Report.*

IL REGNO. VFOAT Regno, Documento. Periodical. IT. Italian. sm. Centro Dehoniano, Via Nosadella 6, 40123 Bologna Italy.

REGULAR MEETING - BOARD OF MISSISSIPPI LEVEE COMMISSIONERS. **Main/Corp** Mississippi. Board of Mississippi Levee Commissioners. 0544-4462. Periodical. US. English. sa. Board of Mississippi Levee Commissioners, Greenville MS 38701. **LC** TC425.M63. **DD** 353.97620086.

REGULATED ELECTRIC STUDY. (A REGULATED ELECTRIC STUDY). **Main/Corp** Missouri Public Service Commission. 1962/71-. 0093-0741. US. English. an. $5.50. Missouri Public Service Commission, Jefferson Building, Jefferson City MO 65101. **LC** HD9685.U6. **DD** 363.6209778.

REGULATORY WATCHDOG SERVICE. ALERT BULLETIN. VFOAT Alert Bulletin. 0275-0902. US. English. wk. $592.00. Washington Business Information Inc, 1117 North 19th Street/Suite 200, Arlington VA 22209. **Tel** (703)247-3421. Ed Judy Haberek. Bulletin describing pertinent materials from CPSC, FDA, Congress and other agencies. *Product Safety Watchdog Service. Alert Bulletin, 0146-4639.*

RELACAO DE AUTORIDADES - ASSESSORIA DE RELACOES PUBLICAS. **Main/Corp** Goias, Brazil (State). Assessoria de Relacoes Publicas. Portuguese. ir. Assessoria de Relacoes Publicas da Secretaria do Governo, Centro Administrativo 9O. Andar, Goiania Brazil. **LC** JL2499.G55.

RELATORIO ANUAL - CONSELHO DE DESENVOLVIMENTO INDUSTRIAL (BRAZIL). SECRETARIA EXECUTI. **Main/Corp** Conselho de Desenvolvimento Industrial (Brazil). Secretaria Executiva. VFOAT Relatorio Anual C.D.I. Portuguese. an. Conselho de Desenvolvimento Industrial, Secretaria Executiva, Setor de Autarquias Sul Quadra 5, Lote 5, Bloco H, Brasilia DF Brazil. **LC** HC186. **DD** 354.81008206.

RELATORIO ANUAL - FUNDACAO PREFEITO FARIA LIMA. **Main/Corp** Fundacao Prefeito Faria Lima. Portuguese. an. **LC** JS2423.S5. **DD** 352.08161.

RELATORIO ANUAL - SERVICO SOCIAL DO COMERCIO. ADMINISTRACAO NACIONAL. **Main/Corp** Servico Social do Comercio. Administracao Nacional. Portuguese. an. **LC** HV193. **DD** 354.81008406.

RELATORIO ANUAL SEST. **Main/Corp** Brazil. Secretaria de Controle de Empresas Estatais. Portuguese. an. **LC** HJ9769.B6. **DD** 354.81092.

RELATORIO - BRAZIL. SERVICO NACIONAL DE APRENDIZAGEM COMMERCIAL. ADMINISTRACAO REGIONAL DE MATO GROSSO. **Main/Corp** Brazil. Servico Nacional de Aprendizagem Comercial. Administracao Regional de Mato Grosso. Portuguese. an. **LC** HF1135.B7. **DD** 354.817200851. *Relatorio Anual.*

RELATORIO DA DIRETORIA EXECUTIVA. **Main/Corp** Companhia Docas do Rio de Janeiro. Portuguese. ir. **LC** HE556.R5. **DD** 354.81008771098153. *Relatorio da Diretoria.*

RELATORIO DA PRESIDENCIA REFERENTE AOS TRABALHOS DA . . . . Portuguese. ir. **LC** JL2461. **DD** 328.8104.

RELATORIO DAS ATIVIDADES. **Main/Corp** Companhia de Eletricidade de Brasilia. 1971-. Portuguese. ir. SCRS-W3-Quadra, 508 Bloco A, Brazil. **LC** HD9685.B83.

RELATORIO DE ATIVIDADES - PARA (BRAZIL : STATE). DEPARTAMENTO DE ESTRADAS DE RODAGEM. DIRETORIA DE PLANEJAMENTO. *See* Transportation - Roads and Traffic.

RELATORIO DE ATIVIDADES - SECRETARIA DE ADMINISTRACAO DO ESTADO DO ESPIRITO SANTO. **Main/Corp** Espirito Santo (Brazil : State). Secretaria de Administracao. Portuguese. ir. Secretaria de Administracao, Av Jeronimo Monteiro 103, Vitoria Brazil. **LC** J208.E8.

RELATORIO DE ATIVIDADES - SECRETARIA DE ESTADO DE ADMINISTRACAO. **Main/Corp** Para Brazil (State). Secretaria de Estado de Administracao. BL. Portuguese. ir. Rua Manoel Barata No 50 - 10O. Andar Sala 1006 66.000, Belem Brazil. **LC** JL2499.P33.

RENCONTRE. V. 1- Sept. 1979-. 0709-9495. Periodical. CN. English. qt. Free. Sagmai, 875 Grande-Allee Estate, Quebec Quebec G1R 4Y8 Canada. **Tel** (418)643-3166. **DD** 354.7140081497. bk rev. **Circ** 34,500. Information on the Government du Quebec and on organizations which may be of particular interest.

REPERTOIRE ADMINISTRATIF DU QUEBEC CEASED. 1975-1980. 0318-2665. CN. French. an. Free. **LC** JL241.A1. **DD** 354.71400025. *Annuaire Administratif du Quebec, 0318-2673.*

REPERTOIRE DE L'ADMINISTRATION QUEBECOISE. **Main/Corp** Quebec (Province). Ministere des Communications. 1983-. 0715-7258. CN. French. an. **DD** 354.71400025. *Repertoire Administratif du Quebec, 0318-2665.*

REPERTOIRE DES MUNICIPALITES ET DES COMMISSIONS SCOLAIRES. 1973-. CN. French. $3.00. Section Repertoire et Recensements Hotel du Gouvernement, l'Editeur Officiel du Quebec, Quebec Canada. **LC** JS4.Q4. **DD** 352.007209714.

REPERTOIRE DES PUBLICATIONS OFFICIELLES, SERIES ET PERIODIQUES. ADMINISTRATIONS LOCALES DE L'ETAT. *See* Bibliographies.

REPERTOIRE DES PUBLICATIONS OFFICIELLES, SERIES ET PERIODIQUES. ETABLISSEMENTS PUBLICS. *See* Bibliographies.

REPERTOIRE DES SYSTEMES INFORMATIQUES AU GOUVERNEMENT DU QUEBEC. *See* Computers and Computer Science.

REPERTOIRE MENSUEL DU MINISTERE DE L'INTERIEUR. **Main/Corp** France. Ministere de l'Interieur. 0240-4729. FR. French. mo. 75. S A des Publications Periodiques de l'Impr Paul Dupont, 38 rue Croix-des-Petits-Champs, Paris 1ER France. *Bulletin Officiel du Ministere de l'Interieur.*

REPERTOIRE PERMANENT DE L'ADMINISTRATION FRANCAISE. Feb. 15, 1945-. FR. French. an. Documentation Francaise, 124 rue Henri Barbusse, 93308 Aubervilliers Cedex France. **Tel** 834-9275. **LC** JN2304.

REPORT - ADMINISTRATIVE CONFERENCE OF THE UNITED STATES. **Main/Corp** United States. Administrative Conference. 1969-. 0566-621X. US. English. an. Superintendent of Documents, US

Public Administration

Government Printing Office, Washington DC 20402. **LC** KF5407. **DD** 353.

REPORT - ADMINISTRATIVE CONFERENCE OF THE UNITED STATES. Main/Corp Administrative Conference of the United States. Began with 1970/71. US. English. an. Administrative Conference of the United States, 2120 L Street Northwest, Washington DC 20037. *Annual Report.*

REPORT - ADVISORY COMMISSION ON INTERNATIONAL EDUCATIONAL AND CULTURAL AFFAIRS. Main/Corp United States. Advisory Commission on International Educational and Cultural Affairs. VAT Report - United States Advisory Commission on International Educational and Cultural Affairs. 1st- April 1963-. 0501-4158. US. English. an. US Advisory Commission on International Education and Cultural Affairs, Washington DC 20402.

REPORT - AGRICULTURAL FINANCE CORPORATION OF RHODESIA. Main/Corp Agricultural Finance Corporation of Rhodesia. **Series Corp** Rhodesia, Southern Parliament CMD. R.R. 1971-. English. ir. $0.50. Government Printer/Publication Office, PO Box 8062 Causeway, Salisbury Rhodesia. **LC** JQ2921.A2., HG2051. R5. **DD** 328.6891008 S, 354.6891092.

REPORT AND ACCOUNTS - CONSORZIO DI CREDITO PER LE OPERE PUBBLICHE. Main/Corp Consorzio di Credito per le Opere Pubbliche. English. an. Consorzio di Credito per le Opere Pubbliche, Via Quintino Selle 2, Rome Italy. **LC** HD4186. **DD** 354.4500725306.

REPORT AND PROCEEDINGS OF THE COMMITTEE - TAMIL NADU. LEGISLATURE. Main/Corp Tamil Nadu. Legislature. Legislative Assembly. Committee of Privileges. English or Tamil. ir. Legislative Assembly Department, Fort St George, Madras India. **DD** 328.54820747. *Report and Proceedings.*

REPORT AND STATEMENT OF ACCOUNT - MAURITIUS SUGAR SYNDICATE. Main/Corp Mauritius Sugar Syndicate. English. ir. The Mauritius Sugar Syndicate, Plantation House, Place d'Armes, Port Louis Mauritius. **LC** HD9118.M45. **DD** 354.69820082333.

REPORT AND STATEMENT OF ACCOUNTS TOGETHER WITH THE REPORT OF THE COMPTROLLER AND AUDITOR-GENERAL. Main/Corp Health and Safety Agency for Northern Ireland. 1st (1 Feb. 1979 to 31 Mar. 1979)-. IE. English. ir. 1.25. Her Majesty's Stationery Office, Government Bookshops, 80 Chichester Street, Belfast BT1 4JY Northern Ireland. **LC** T55.A1. **DD** 354.416007706.

REPORT - AUSTRALIAN CAPITAL TERRITORY ELECTRICITY AUTHORITY. Main/Corp Australian Capital Territory Electricity Authority. AT. English. ir. $0.32. Commonwealth Government Printing Office, PO Box 84, Canberra Australian Capital Territory 2600 Australia. **LC** J905, HD9685.A83. **DD** 328.9401 S, 354.947008722.

REPORT BY THE U. S. GENERAL ACCOUNTING OFFICE. *See* Business - Accounting.

REPORT - CANBERRA COLLEGE OF ADVANCED EDUCATION. COUNCIL. Main/Corp Canberra College of Advanced Education. Council. AT. English. ir. $0.62. Commonwealth Government Printing Office, PO Box 84, Canberra Australian Capital Territory 2600 Australia. **LC** J905. **DD** 328.9401 S, 378.947.

REPORT - COMMITTEE ON GOVERNMENT ASSURANCES. *See* Insurance.

REPORT - COMMITTEE ON GOVERNMENT ASSURANCES. Main/Corp Meghalaya (India). Legislative Assembly. Committee on Government Assurances. 1st- 1977-. English. ir. **LC** JQ620.M45. **DD** 328.541640765.

REPORT - COMMONWEALTH EDISON COMPANY. US. English. an. **LC** HD9685.U7.

REPORT - DEPARTMENT OF PERSONNEL AND ADMINISTRATIVE REFORMS (ADMINISTRATIVE REFORMS). Main/Corp India (Republic). Dept. of Personnel and Administrative Reforms (Administrative Reforms). 1972/73-. MY. English. ir.

Government of India, PO Box 1023, Kuala Lumpar 1002 Malaysia. **LC** JQ231. **DD** 354.54001.

REPORT - DEPARTMENT OF THE ENVIRONMENT AND CONSERVATION. Main/Corp Australia. Dept. of the Environment and Conservation. 1972/74-. AT. English. ir. $2.25. Canberra Department of Environment and Conservation, PO Box 1875, Canberra City Australian Capital Territory 2001 Australia. **LC** J905, HC610.E5. **DD** 328.940 S, 354.94008232.

REPORT - FLORIDA. LEGISLATURE. JOINT INTERIM COMMITTEE ON MENTAL HEALTH. Main/Corp Florida. Legislature. Joint Interim Committee on Mental Health. V. 1- 1957-. 0428-6383. US. English. ir. Florida Legislature, Joint Interim Committee on Mental Health, Tallahassee FL 32304.

REPORT - FLORIDA. STATE PERSONNEL BOARD. Main/Corp Florida. State Personnel Board. 1956/58-. Periodical. US. English. ir.

REPORT FOR THE FINANCIAL YEAR ENDING 30 SEPTEMBER .... Main/Corp South Africa. Wheat Board. VFOAT Annual Report for the . . . Season. SA. English. an. 2,00. Wheat Board, PO Box 908, Pretoria South Africa. **LC** HD9049.W3. **DD** 354.6800826131106. *Annual Report.*

REPORT FROM THE WHITE HOUSE CONFERENCE ON FAMILIES. Publication began with Aug. 1979. US. English. ir. White House Conference on Families, 330 Independence Avenue Southwest, Washington DC 20201.

REPORT - GOVERNMENT OF INDIA, MINISTRY OF HOME AFFAIRS. Main/Corp India (Republic). Ministry of Home Affairs. 1950/51-. 0442-5316. II. English. ir. Government of India, Ministry of Home Affairs, New Delhi India. **LC** J500. **DD** 354.54.

REPORT - GOVERNMENT OF INDIA, MINISTRY OF INDUSTRY AND CIVIL SUPPLIES. Main/Corp India (Republic). Ministry of Industry and Civil Supplies. 1974/75-. II. English. ir. Government of India, Ministry of Industry and Civil Supplies, Civil Lines Delhi 110054 India. **LC** HC431. **DD** 354.540082.

REPORT (HAWAII. LEGISLATURE. LEGISLATIVE REFERENCE BUREAU). (REPORT - STATE OF HAWAII, LEGISLATIVE REFERENCE BUREAU). US. English. Legislative Reference Bureau, State Capital, Honolulu HI 96813. **Tel** (808)548-6237. **LC** KFH20. **DD** 027.65. *Report.*

REPORT - IDAHO. PUBLIC UTILITIES COMMISSION. Main/Corp Idaho Public Utilities Commission. US. English. an. Idaho Public Utilities Commission, Boise ID 83707. **LC** KFI285. **DD** 343.7960902646.

REPORT - INDIA. DEPT. OF SUPPLY. Main/Corp India. Dept. of Supply. English. an. **LC** JQ279. **DD** 354.5400712. *Annual Report.*

REPORT (IOWA. OFFICE OF THE STATE COMPTROLLER). (REPORT). US. English. Office of The State Comptroller, State Capitol, Des Moines IA 50319. **LC** HJ2053.I8. **DD** 353.9777007232.

REPORT - JAMMU AND KASHMIR. LEGISLATIVE ASSEMBLY. COMMITTEE ON PUBLIC UNDERTAKINGS. Main/Corp Jammu and Kashmir Legislature. Legislative Assembly. Committee on Public Undertakings. II. English. ir. Jammu & Kashmir, Legislative Assembly Committee on Public Undertakings, Jammu India. **LC** HD4295.K3. **DD** 354.54600825.

REPORT - JAMMU AND KASHMIR LEGISLATIVE COUNCIL, COMMITTEE ON PETITIONS. Main/Corp Jammu and Kashmir. Legislature. Legislative Council. Committee on Petitions. 1st- 1973-. English or Urdu. ir. **LC** JQ620.K35.

REPORT - JOINT COMMITTEE ON OFFICES OF PROFIT. Main/Corp India (Republic). Parliament. Joint Committee on Offices of Profit. 0537-0280. English. ir. **LC** JQ229.C56.

REPORT - KARNATAKA LEGISLATIVE ASSEMBLY, COMMITTEE OF PRIVILEGES. Main/Corp Karnataka, India. Legislature. Legislative Assembly. Committee of Privileges. English. ir. Karnataka Legislative Assembly, Vidhana Soudha, Bangalore India. **LC** JQ620.M75, JQ620.K296. **DD** 328.54870747. *Report.*

REPORT - LOUISIANA DEPT. OF VETERANS' AFFAIRS. Main/Corp Louisiana. Dept. of Veterans' Affairs. US. English. an. State of Louisiana, Department of Veterans Affairs, Baton Rouge LA 70804. **LC** UB358.L8. **DD** 355.115.

REPORT - NEW YORK (STATE). DIVISION OF THE LOTTERY. Main/Corp New York (State). Division of the Lottery. US. English. an. Division of the Lottery, Swan Street Building, Empire State Plaza, Albany NY 12223. **LC** HG6133.N7. **DD** 353.974700726. *Empire Stakes, New York State Lottery Annual Report,* 0272-0043.

REPORT OF ATTORNEY GENERAL TO THE GOVERNOR AND THE LEGISLATURE. *See* Law.

REPORT OF EXAMINATION, PUBLIC EMPLOYEES' PENSION FUNDS - ILLINOIS. DEPT. OF INSURANCE. Main/Corp Illinois. Dept. of Insurance. US. English. be. Illinois Department of Insurance, Springfield IL 62727. **LC** JK5760.P4. **DD** 353.9773005. *Report of Examination, Public Employees' Pension Funds.*

REPORT OF GIFTS, GRANTS/CONTRACTS AND DONATION RECEIVED. Main/Corp Texas. Dept. of Mental Health and Mental Retardation. Grants Management Section. US. English. an. Texas Department of Mental Health, Box 12668 Capitol Station, Austin TX 78711.

REPORT OF MEDICAL ASSISTANCE & COUNTY INDIGENT STATISTICS. *See* Statistics.

REPORT OF PROCEEDINGS OF THE COMMONWEALTH PARLIAMENTARY CONFERENCE. Began publication with 1st in 1948?. 0573-0856. UK. English. an. Headquarters Secretary, Commonwealth Parliamenty Association, 7 Old Palace Yard, Finance Department, London SW1P 3JY England. **LC** JN248. **DD** 942.

REPORT OF SOUTH DAKOTA'S PROFESSIONAL AND OCCUPATIONAL LICENSING BOARDS AND COMMISSIONS. Main/Corp South Dakota. Dept. of Commerce and Consumer Affairs. US. English. an. Department of Commerce and Consumer Affairs, State Capitol, Pierre SD 57501. **LC** HD3630.U7. **DD** 353.97830082404606.

REPORT OF THE ACTIVITIES OF THE INSTITUTE. Main/Corp Institute of Development Management. 1972/73-. English. ir. Institute of Development Management, PO Box 604 Morogoro, Mzumbe Tanzania. **LC** JF1338.I457. **DD** 309.23071167825.

REPORT OF THE ADVISORY BOARD FOR THE RESEARCH COUNCILS. Main/Corp Great Britain. Advisory Board for the Research Councils. 1st- 1973-. UK. English. 0.20. H M Stationery Office, PO Box 276, London SW8 5DT England. **LC** Q180.G7. **DD** 354.410081.

REPORT OF THE ADVISORY COMMITTEE ON CONFEDERATION. Main/Corp Ontario. Advisory Committee on Confederation. VFOAT Rapport du Comite Consultatif de la Confederation. 1st- 1978-. 0704-9641. CN. English (French). Advisory Committee on Confederation Frost Building, North Queen's Park, Toronto Ontario M7A 1Z1 Canada. **LC** JL1. **DD** 354.713093.

REPORT OF THE ANDHRA PRADESH VIGILANCE COMMISSION. Main/Corp Andhra Pradesh Vigilance Commission. English. an. **LC** JQ620.A78. **DD** 354.5484009.

REPORT OF THE AUDITOR-GENERAL FOR . . . ON THE ACCOUNTS OF PARASTATAL BODIES - ZAMBIA. AUDITOR-GENERAL. Main/Corp Zambia. Auditor-General. VFOAT Report of the Auditor-General for . . . on the Accounts of Parastatal Bodies, Presented to the National Assembly. 1979-. English. an. **LC** HJ9929.Z35. **DD** 354.6894007232.

REPORT OF THE AUDITOR-GENERAL ON THE ACCOUNTS OF THE DECIDUOUS FRUIT BOARD AND THE SOUTH AFRICAN PLANT IMPROVEMENT ORGANISATION. Main/Corp South Africa. Controller and Auditor-General. VFOAT Verslag van die Ouditeur-Generaal

Public Administration

vor die Rekeningen van die Sagtevrugteraad en die Suid-Afrikaanse Plant- Verbeteringsorganisasie. SA. Afrikaans (English). ir. 2.05. Government Printer, Private Bag X85, Pretoria 0001 South Africa. LC HD9257.S7. DD 354.68008233.

REPORT OF THE AUDITOR GENERAL TO THE LEGISLATIVE ASSEMBLY - NEW BRUNSWICK. Main/Corp New Brunswick. Office of the Auditor-General. VFOAT Rapport du Verificateur General a l'Assemblee Legislative. 0382-1420. CN. English (French). an. WA Peterson, Queens Printer, Office of the Auditor-General Legislative Building, Fredericton New Brunswisk Canada. LC HJ9921.Z9. DD 354.715007232.

REPORT OF THE AUDITOR-GENERAL UPON THE DEPARTMENT OF ABORIGINAL AFFAIRS. Main/Corp Australia. Auditor-General's Office. AT. English. ir. Australian Government Publishing Service, PO Box 84, Canberra Australian Capital Territory 2600 Australia. LC GN665. DD 354.94008484.

REPORT OF THE BENDEL STATE CIVIL SERVICE COMMISSION. Main/Corp Bendel State Civil Service Commission. English. an. 50.00. Civil Service Commission, PMB 1066, Benin City Bendel State of Nigeria. LC JQ3099.B434. DD 354.6693006.

REPORT OF THE BENDEL STATE PUBLIC SERVICE COMMISSION. Main/Corp Bendel (Nigeria). Public Service Commission. English. ir. 50. Public Service Commission, P M B 1066, Benin City Bendel State of Nigeria. LC JQ3099.B434. DD 354.6693006.

REPORT OF THE CHIEF ELECTORAL OFFICER ON THE GENERAL ENUMERATION. (REPORT OF THE CHIEF ELECTORAL OFFICER ON THE . . . GENERAL ENUMERATION). Main/Corp Alberta. Chief Electoral Officer. Began with 1978. 0708-3998. CN. English. an. free. Alberta Legislative Assembly Office of the Chief Electoral Officer, West Chambers Building Main Floor/12220 Stony Plain Road, Edmonton Alberta T5N 3Y4 Canada. Tel (403)427-7191. LC JL338. DD 324.97123. Circ 1,500. (ctrl). Door-to-door visit to obtain the names and addresses of qualified electors to establish lists of electors.

REPORT OF THE CIVIL SERVICE PAY RESEARCH UNIT BOARD AND THE CIVIL SERVICE PAY RESEARCH UNIT. Main/Corp Great Britain. Civil Service National Whitley Council. Civil Service Pay Research Unit Board. UK. English. an. Her Majesty's Stationery Office, PO Box 276, London SW8 5DT England. LC JN443. DD 354.410012.

REPORT OF THE CO-ORDINATOR-GENERAL OF PUBLIC WORKS, QUEENSLAND. Main/Corp Queensland. Department of the Co-Ordinator General of Public Works. VFOAT Report - Co-Ordinator-General of Public Works. 0480-970X. Periodical. AT. English. ir. Government Printer, Box 680 GPO 102/George Street, Brisbane Queensland 4001 Australia. DD 354.

REPORT OF THE COMMITTEE ON GOVERNMENT ASSURANCES FOR THE . . . SESSION OF THE . . . NATIONAL ASSEMBLY, APPOINTED ON . . . . Main/Corp Zambia. National Assembly. Committee on Government Assurances. 2nd Session, 4th National Assembly (1980)-. English. an. 0.80. Government Printer, POB 30136, Lusaka Zambia. LC JQ2854. DD 328.689407456.

REPORT OF THE CONTROLLER AND AUDITOR-GENERAL ON THE ACCOUNTS OF THE ADMINISTRATION OF COLOURED AFFAIRS. Main/Corp South Africa. Control and Audit Office. VFOAT Verslag van die Kontroleur on Ouditeur-Generaal oor die Rekeninge van die Administrasie van Kleurlingsake. 1st- 1969/70-. SA. Afrikaans and English. ir. 1.55. Government Printer, Private Bag X85, Pretoria 0001 South Africa. LC DT763. DD 354.6800723205.

REPORT OF THE CONTROLLER AND AUDITOR-GENERAL ON THE ACCOUNTS OF THE CANNING FRUIT BOARD AND THE BALANCE SHEET. Main/Corp South Africa. Controller and Auditor-General. VFOAT Verslag van die Kontroleur en Ouditeur-Generaal oor die Rekeninge van die Raad vir Inmaakvrugte en die Balansstaat. Afrikaans (English). ir. 1.44. The Government Printer, Private Bag X85, Pretoria South Africa. LC HD9257.S7. DD 354.68008242.

REPORT OF THE CONTROLLER AND AUDITOR-GENERAL ON THE ACCOUNTS OF THE COTTON BOARD. Main/Corp South Africa. Controller and Auditor-General. VFOAT Verslag Van Die Kontroleur en Ouditeur-Generaal Oor Die Rekeninge Van Die Katoenraad. 1974/75-. English (Afrikaans and). ir. 1.15. Government Printer, Private Bag X85, Pretoria 0001 South Africa. LC HD9887.S7. DD 354.68008233.

REPORT OF THE CONTROLLER AND AUDITOR-GENERAL ON THE ACCOUNTS OF THE DAIRY BOARD AND THE BALANCE SHEET. Main/Corp South Africa. Controller and Auditor-General. VFOAT Verslag van die Kontroleur en Ouditeur-Generaal oor die Rekeninge van die Suiwelraad en die Balansstaat. Afrikaans (English). ir. 2.55. Private Bag X85, 0001 Pretoria South Africa. LC HD9275.S5. DD 354.68008233.

REPORT OF THE CONTROLLER AND AUDITOR-GENERAL ON THE ACCOUNTS OF THE DRIED FRUIT BOARD. Main/Corp South Africa. Controller and Auditor-General. VFOAT Verslag van die Kontroleur en Ouditeur-Generaal oor die Rekeninge van die Droevrugteraad. Afrikaans (English). ir. 2.30. The Government Printer, Private Bag X85, Pretoria 0001 South Africa. LC HD9257.S7. DD 354.68008233. *Verslag Oor die Rekenings Van die Droevrugteraad en Balansstaat.*

REPORT OF THE CONTROLLER AND AUDITOR-GENERAL ON THE ACCOUNTS OF THE MEAT TRADE CONTROL BOARD OF SOUTH-WEST AFRICA. Main/Corp South Africa. Controller and Auditor-General. VFOAT Verslag van die Kontroleur en Ouditeur-Generaal oor die Rekeninge van die Vleishandelbeheerraad van Suidwes-Afrika. SA. Afrikaans (English). ir. 0.75. Pretoria Government Printer, Private Bag X85, Pretoria 0001 South Africa. LC HD9427.S6. DD 354.68008233.

REPORT OF THE CONTROLLER OF WORKS - RHODESIA, SOUTHERN. Main/Corp Rhodesia, Southern. Dept. of Works. English. ir. Government Printer, PO Box 8081 Causeway, Salisbury Rhodesia. LC HD4350.R45. DD 354.68910086.

REPORT OF THE DIRECTOR OF DEFENCE SERVICE HOMES OF OPERATIONS IN RELATION TO INSURANCE. Main/Corp Australia. Director of Defence Service Homes. AT. English. ir. Australian Government Publishing Service, PO Box 84, Canberra Australian Capital Territory 2600 Australia. LC HG8732. DD 354.9400825.

REPORT OF THE DIVISION OF PUBLIC UTILITY CONTROL (CONNECTICUT). Main/Corp Connecticut. Division of Public Utility Control. 1978/79-. US. English. an. Division of Public Utility Control, Department of Business Regulation, 165 Capitol Avenue, State Office Building, Hartford CT 06115. LC HD2767.C8. DD 363.609746.

REPORT OF THE FISCAL COMMITTEES ON THE EXECUTIVE BUDGET. Main/Corp New York (State). Legislature. Senate. Committee on Finance. US. English. an. LC KFN5010.7. DD 353.974700722205.

REPORT OF THE GEORGIA DEPARTMENT OF TRANSPORTATION TO THE GOVERNOR AND GENERAL ASSEMBLY OF THE STATE OF GEORGIA. Main/Corp Georgia. Dept. of Transportation. VFOAT Quadrennial Report of the Georgia Department of Transportation. 33d/34th- 1969/73-. US. English. ir. No 2 Capitol Square, Atlanta GA 30334. LC TE24.G4. DD 353.975800875.

REPORT OF THE HEALTH SERVICE COMMISSIONER. 1st- 1973/74-. UK. English. an. -/7. Her Majesty's Stationery Office, PO Box 276, London 5W8 5DT England. LC KD3210. DD 354.4100841. NLM W2 FA1 P32R.

REPORT OF THE JOHNSONVILLE LICENSING TRUST FOR THE YEAR ENDED 31 MARCH . . . . Main/Corp Johnsonville Licensing Trust (N.Z.). English. an. $0.75. LC HD9368.N47. DD 352.9426.

REPORT OF THE JOINT LEGISLATIVE COMMITTEE ON METROPOLITAN AREAS STUDY. TO THE LEGISLATURE OF THE STATE OF NEW YORK. Main/Corp New York (State). Legislature. Joint Legislative Committee on Metropolitan and Regional Areas Study. Periodical. US. English. an.

REPORT OF THE JUDICIAL COUNCIL OF THE STATE OF NEW HAMPSHIRE. See Law.

THE . . . REPORT OF THE LONDON HOUSING STAFF COMMISSION. Main/Corp London Housing Staff Commission. 1st (1979-1980)-. UK. English. an. Her Majesty's Stationery Office, Government Bookshop, 49 High Holborn, London WC1V 6HB England. LC HD7288.78.G72. DD 352.7509421.

REPORT OF THE MISSISSIPPI RIVER PARKWAY COMMISSION OF MINNESOTA. Main/Corp Mississippi River Parkway Commission of Minnesota. US. English. be. 130 State Office Building, St Paul MN 55101. Tel (612)224-9903. Ed John F Edman. LC HE356.M6. DD 353.977600864206. Annual report of 1983-1984.

REPORT OF THE NEW MEXICO VETERANS' SERVICE COMMISSION. Main/Corp New Mexico. Veterans' Service Commission. 0094-7326. US. English. be. Villagra Building/408 Galisteo Street, Santa Fe New Mexico. LC UB358.N6. DD 353.978900848.

REPORT OF THE NEW YORK STATE ADMINISTRATIVE REGULATIONS REVIEW COMMISSION. Main/Corp New York (State). Legislature. Administrative Regulations Review Commission. VFOAT Report. 1983-. US. English. an. Administrative Regulations Review Commission of Capitol, Albany NY 12247. *Annual Report of the New York State Administrative Regulations Review Commission.*

REPORT OF THE OFFICE OF THE PUBLIC COUNSEL, STATE OF MISSOURI. Main/Corp Missouri. Office of the Public Counsel. Sept. 1974/Dec. 1976-. US. English. Office of the Public Counsel, PO Box 1216, Jefferson City MO 65102.

REPORT OF THE OMBUDSMAN. Main/Corp Hawaii. Office of the Ombudsman. No. 1- 1969/70-. 0073-1137. US. English. an. Kanaina Building, Iolani Palace Grounds, Honolulu HI 96813. LC JK9349.O4. DD 353.99690091.

REPORT OF THE OMBUDSMAN. Main/Corp Alberta. Office of the Ombudsman. 1974-. 0319-8197. CN. English. an. Office of the Ombudsman, 729 Centennial Building, 10015 103rd Avenue, Edmonton Alberta Canada. LC JL329.5.O4. DD 354.71230091.

REPORT OF THE OMBUDSMAN. Main/Corp Alaska. Office of Ombudsman. 1st- 1975-. 0363-5376. US. English. an. LC JK9549.O4. DD 353.97980091.

REPORT OF THE PARLIAMENTARY OMBUDSMAN, SUMMARY AND ANNOTATIONS. Main/Corp Finland. Eduskunta. Oikeusasiamies. 0355-9211. English. ir. LC JN6709.5.O4. DD 328.489707452.

REPORT OF THE PLANNING DIVISION, STATE DEPARTMENT OF FINANCE. Main/Corp Arizona. State Dept. of Finance. Planning Division. 0098-1338. US. English. an. State Department of Finance, 1700 West Washington, Phoenix AZ 85007. LC JK1651.A7. DD 353.979100862.

REPORT OF THE PUBLIC SERVICE COMMISSION. Main/Corp Mauritius. Public Service Commission. English. ir. 10.00 Single Issue. Mauritus Goverment Printer, Port Louis Mauritius. LC JQ3172. DD 354.6982001.

REPORT OF THE PUBLIC SERVICE COMMISSION. Main/Corp Oyo, Nigeria (State). Public Service Commission. Periodical. NR. English. ir. 50. Oyo State of Nigeria, Public Service Commission, Ibadan Nigeria. LC JQ3099.O924. DD 354.6692.

REPORT OF THE SECRETARY FOR PUBLIC WORKS. Main/Corp South Africa. Dept. of Public Works. VFOAT Verslag van die Sekretaris van Openbare Werke. 1952/57-. Afrikaans

Public Administration

and English (1952/57-1960/61,) English only. ir. 3.05. Department of Public Works, Private Bag X85, Bosman Street, Pretoria South Africa. LC TA119.S8. DD 354.680086. *Annual Report.*

REPORT OF THE SECRETARY OF THE COMMONWEALTH TO THE GOVERNOR AND GENERAL ASSEMBLY OF VIRGINIA. Main/Corp Virginia. Secretary of the Commonwealth. 0145-1928. Periodical. US. English. an. $15.50. Secretary Commonwealth of Virginia, PO Box IB, Richmond VA 23201. Tel (804)786-2441. *Biennal Report of the Secretary of the Commonwealth to the Governor and General Assembly of Virginia.*

REPORT OF THE SELECT STANDING COMMITTEE ON PUBLIC ACCOUNTS AND PRINTING, TOGETHER WITH MINUTES AND VERBATIM REPORT OF PROCEEDINGS. Main/Corp Saskatchewan. Legislative Assembly. Select Standing Committee on Public Accounts and Printing. VFOAT Report and Minutes. V. 1- 1968-. Periodical. CN. English. Legislative Assembly Office, Legislative Building, Regina Saskatchewan Canada.

REPORT OF THE SENATE COMMITTEE ON COMMERCE, SCIENCE, AND TRANSPORTATION TO THE SENATE COMMITTEE ON THE BUDGET. Main/Corp United States. Congress. Senate. Committee on Commerce, Science, and Transportation. 0196-7096. US. English. an. Superintendent of Documents, US Government Printing Office, Washington DC 20402. LC HJ2052. DD 353.0072255. Vols. for (1984-) distributed to some depository libraries in microfiche. *Report to the Budget Committee from the Committee on Commerce of the United States Senate, 0363-7603.*

REPORT OF THE STATE AUDITOR OF MINNESOTA ON THE REVENUES, EXPENDITURES, AND DEBT OF THE CITIES AND VILLAGES IN MINNESOTA. Main/Corp Minnesota. State Auditor. 1972/73-1973/74. 0095-3199. US. English. an. LC HJ9777.M55. DD 352.109776.

REPORT OF THE STATE CO-ORDINATION COUNCIL. Main/Corp State Co-Ordination Council (Victoria). English. ir. LC JQ5301. DD 354.94504.

REPORT OF THE STATE EMPLOYEES RETIREMENT BENEFITS BOARD FOR THE YEAR ENDED 30 JUNE .... Main/Corp Victoria. State Employees Retirement Benefits Board. English. an. $1.00. State Employees Retirement Benefits Board, 35 Spring Street, Melbourne 3000 Australia. LC JQ5349.S2. DD 354.945005.

REPORT OF THE UNITED STATES ATTORNEY FOR THE DISTRICT OF CONNECTICUT TO ... THE ATTORNEY GENERAL. Main/Corp United States Attorney for the District of Connecticut. US. English. US Attorney for the District of Connecticut, New Haven CT 06510. LC KF8700. DD 353.97460088.

REPORT OF THE WATERFRONT INDUSTRY COMMISSION FOR THE YEAR ENDED 30 SEPTEMBER .... Main/Corp New Zealand. Waterfront Industry Commission. 1977-. English. an. LC HD8039.L82. DD 354.9310087716406. *Annual Report and Statement of Accounts.*

REPORT - OHIO DEPARTMENT OF ADMINISTRATIVE SERVICES. Main/Corp Ohio. Dept. of Administrative Services. 1974-. US. English. Department of Administrative Services, Columbus OH 43215. LC JK5535. DD 353.977104.

REPORT - OMBUDSMAN. ONTARIO. (REPORT - THE OMBUDSMAN/ONTARIO). Main/Corp Ontario. Office of the Ombudsman. 2nd- July 1976/Mar. 1977-. 0704-5204. CN. English (includes some text in French). sa. LC JL269.5.O4. DD 354.7130091. *Annual Report, 0704-5212.*

A REPORT ON ACTIVITIES OF THE COUNTY GOVERNMENT DURING THE FISCAL YEAR. Main/Corp Montgomery Co., Md. Office of Information. VFOAT Annual Report on Activities of the Government of Montgomery County. US. English. an. Montgomery County Government, Office of Information, County Office Building, Rockville MD 20850. LC JS451.M39. DD 352.075284. *Annual Report - Montgomery County, Md.*

REPORT ON AGENCIES, BOARDS, AND COMMISSIONS. Main/Corp Ontario. Legislative Assembly. Standing Committee on Procedural Affairs. CN. English. an. LC JL261.A1. DD 354.7130405. *Report on Agencies, Boards and Commissions, 0711-8724.*

REPORT ON AUDIT - STATE OF MONTANA. DEPARTMENT OF INTERGOVERNMENTAL RELATIONS. ECONOMIC OPPORTUNITY DIVISION. *See* Economics - Economic History, Conditions.

REPORT ON FEDERAL REVENUE SHARING TRUST FUND TOGETHER WITH THE ANTIRECESSION FISCAL ASSISTANCE PROGRAM. VFOAT Auditors' Report, Federal Revenue Sharing Trust Fund Together with the Antirecession Fiscal Assistance Program. Began with 1977. US. English. Auditors of Public Accounts, State Capitol, Hartford CT 06115. LC HJ11. DD 353.9746007232. *Report on Federal Revenue Sharing Trust Fund, Fiscal Year Ended June 30.*

REPORT ON FRINGE BENEFITS AND RELATED PRACTICES AFFECTING GENERAL EMPLOYEES OF CITIES. Main/Corp New York (State). Public Employment Relations Board. 0361-0314. US. English. Public Employment Relations Board, 50 Wolf Road, Albany NY 12205. LC JS3.N7. DD 352.0051234097471.

REPORT ON MANDATES AND MEASURES AFFECTING LOCAL GOVERNMENT FISCAL CAPACITY. US. English. an. Florida Advisory Council on Intergovernmental Relations, Suite 400/Lewis State Bank Building, Tallahassee FL 32304. LC KFF488. DD 353.9759007253.

REPORT ON OFFICE OF THE LIEUTENANT GOVERNOR. Main/Corp Connecticut. Auditors of Public Accounts. US. English. an. State of Connecticut, Auditors of Public Accounts, State Capitol, Hartford CT 66612. LC JK3353.L5. DD 353.97460318.

REPORT ON OPERATION OF THE STATE MOTOR VEHICLE POOL. (REPORT ON OPERATION OF THE STATE MOTOR VEHICLE POOL, DEPARTMENT OF HIGHWAYS). Main/Corp Montana. Office of the Legislative Auditor. 0093-6162. US. English. Office of the Legislative Auditor, State Capitol, Helena MT 59601. LC JK7388.M7. DD 353.97860087832.

REPORT ON STATE COMPTROLLER-RETIREMENT DIVISION. CONNECTICUT MUNICIPAL EMPLOYEES' RETIREMENT AND SOCIAL SECURITY SYSTEMS, FISCAL YEAR ENDED JUNE 30 .... VFOAT Connecticut Municipal Employees' Retirement and Social Security Systems, Fiscal Year Ended June 30 .... 1981-. US. English. an. State of Connecticut, Auditor of Public Accounts, State Capitol, Hartford CT 06106. LC JS451.C87. DD 352.005509746. *Report on State Comptroller-Retirement Division. Connecticut Municipal Employees' Retirement Fund, Fiscal Year Ended June 30 ....*

REPORT ON STATE ELECTIONS COMMISSION. Main/Corp Connecticut. Auditors of Public Accounts. Periodical. US. English. State of Connecticut, Auditors of Public Accounts, Hartford CT 06115. LC JK1954. DD 353.9746008.

REPORT ON STATE PENSION COMMISSIONS. 0278-8837. US. English. an. Director Pension Commission Clearinghouse, Edward H Friend and Company, 1800 K Street NW/Suite 500, Washington DC 20006. LC JK2474. DD 353.935.

REPORT ON THE ACCOUNTS OF THE DECIDUOUS FRUIT BOARD AND THE BALANCE SHEET. Main/Corp South Africa. Controller and Auditor-General. VFOAT Verslag oor die Rekeninge van die Sagtevrugteraad en die Balansstaat. 1946/47-. SA. English (Afrikaans). ir. 1.75. Government Printer, Private Bag X85, Pretoria 0001 South Africa. LC HD9257.S7. DD 354.68008233. *Verslag ten Opsigte van die Rekeninge van die Sagtevrugteraad en die Droevrugteraad met die Staat Rekening.*

REPORT ON THE ACTIVITIES IN THE CONGRESS OF THE SELECT COMMITTEE ON AGING, U.S. HOUSE OF REPRESENTATIVES. (REPORT ON THE ACTIVITIES IN THE ... CONGRESS OF THE SELECT COMMITTEE ON AGING, U.S. HOUSE OF REPRESENTATIVES). Main/Corp United States. Congress. House. Select Committee on Aging. 0731-3519. US. English. Superintendent of Documents, Government Printing Office, Washington DC 20402. LC JK1430.A52. DD 328.7307658. NLM W2 A C814A.

REPORT ON THE CIVIL SERVICE. Main/Corp Hongkong. Civil Service Branch. English. ir. $9.00 Each Copy. Civil Service Branch, Java Road, Hong Kong Hong Kong. LC JQ676. DD 354.5125006.

REPORT ON THE FISCAL ... PAY INCREASE UNDER THE FEDERAL STATUTORY PAY SYSTEMS : ANNUAL REPORT OF THE ADVISORY COMMITTEE ON FEDERAL PAY. Main/Corp United States Advisory Committee on Federal Pay. US. English. an. Advisory Committee on Federal Pay, 1730 K Street Northwest, Washington DC 20006.

REPORT ON THE WORKING OF THE PUBLIC SERVICE COMMISSION OF KENYA. Main/Corp Kenya. Public Service Commission. Began in 1963. English. ir. 1/50. Kenya Public Service Commission, PO Box 30095, Nairobi Kenya. LC JQ2947.A65. DD 354.6762006.

REPORT - PENNSYLVANIA GENERAL ASSEMBLY. SPECIAL JOINT COMMITTEE TO REVIEW RETIREMENT COST-OF-LIVING SUPPLEMENTS AND FUNDING SOURCES. Main/Corp Pennsylvania. General Assembly. Special Joint Committee to Review Retirement Cost-of-Living Supplements and Funding Sources. 1981-82-. US. English. be. Joint State Government Commission, Room 108/Finance Building, Harrisburg PA 17120. LC JK3660.P4. DD 353.974800505.

REPORT - PIPELINE AUTHORITY. Main/Corp Pipeline Authority. 1973/74-. English. ir. $0.40. Pipeline Authority, Tasman House, Hobart Place, Canberra Australian Capital Territory Australia. LC J905, HD9580.A8. DD 328.9401 S, 354.94008232.

REPORT - PUBLIC SERVICE ADVISORY COUNCIL. Main/Corp Ireland (EIRE). Public Service Advisory Council. 1st- 1973/74-. English. ir. LC JN1445.

REPORT. PUNJAB, INDIA (STATE). LEGISLATURE. LEGISLATIVE COUNCIL. COMMITTEE ON PUBLIC UNDERTAKINGS. Main/Corp Punjab, India (State). Legislature. Legislative Council. Committee on Public Undertakings. 1st- 1967-. Periodical. English. ir. LC HD4295.P8.

REPORT - SARAWAK ELECTRICITY SUPPLY CORPORATION. Main/Corp Sarawak Electricity Supply Corporation. English. ir. LC HD9685.S36.

REPORT - SOUTH AFRICA. DRY BEAN BOARD. Main/Corp South Africa. Dry Bean Board. VFOAT Verslag. SA. English and Afrikaans. ir. Arcadia Telegrams Boneraad, 45 Hamilton Street/PO Box 678, Pretoria South Africa. LC HD9235.B42. DD 354.68008233.

REPORT - STAFF SELECTION COMMISSION. Main/Corp India. Staff Selection Commission. II. English. ir. Lok Nayak Bhavan, Kha Market New Delhi 110003 India. LC JQ247. DD 354.540013.

REPORT - TAMIL NADU LEGISLATIVE ASSEMBLY COMMITTEE ON PUBLIC UNDERTAKINGS. Main/Corp Tamil Nadu. Legislature. Legislative Assembly. Committee on Public Undertakings. 1st- 1973/74-. II. English. ir. Legislative Assembly Department, Fort St George, -9, Madras India. LC HD4295.T35. DD 354.54820086.

REPORT - TASK FORCE HYDRO. Main/Corp Ontario. Task Force Hydro. No. 1- 1972-. Monographic Series. CN. English. Ontario Government Bookstore, 880 Bay Street, Toronto M7A 1N8 Ontario Canada.

REPORT TO CONGRESS. ANNUAL REPORT ON IMPLEMENTATION OF THE FEDERAL EQUAL OPPORTUNITY RECRUITMENT PROGRAM. (REPORT TO CONGRESS, ANNUAL REPORT ON IMPLEMENTATION OF THE FEDERAL EQUAL OPPORTUNITY RECRUITMENT PROGRAM). Main/Corp United States. Office of Personnel Management. Office of Affirmative Employment Programs. VFOAT Civil Service Reform Act of 1978.

Public Administration

Began in 1980. 0277-5255. US. English. an. US Office of Personnel Management, Office of Affirmative Employment Programs, Washington DC 20415. LC JK766.4. DD 353.00104.

A REPORT TO CONGRESS FROM THE OFFICE OF SPECIAL COUNSEL. Main/Corp United States. Merit Systems Protection Board. Office of the Special Counsel. US. English. an. Office of the Special Counsel, US Merit Systems Protection Board, 1120 Vermont Avenue NW, Washington DC 20419. LC KF5337. DD 353.006. *Annual Report, 0278-5714.*

REPORT TO PARLIAMENT. OLYMPIC (1976) ACT. OLYMPIC COINS. (RAPPORT AU PARLEMENT). Main/Corp Canada. Ministere des Finances. VFOAT Report to Parliament, Olympic (1976) Act, Olympic Coins. March 1974-. 0225-5944. CN. text in French with English on inverted pages. sa. Department of Finances, Information Services, 160 Elgin Street, 26th Floor, Ottawa Ontario K1A 0G5 Canada. DD 354.7100822.

REPORT TO THE COMMITTEE ON THE BUDGET CONTAINING THE VIEWS AND ESTIMATES OF THE COMMITTEE ON PUBLIC WORKS AND TRANSPORTATION ON THE BUDGET. Main/Corp United States. Congress. House. Committee on Public Works and Transportation. 0148-9003. US. English. LC HJ2052. DD 353.00722.

REPORT TO THE CONGRESS - OFFICE OF FEDERAL PROCUREMENT POLICY. (REPORT TO THE CONGRESS). Main/Corp United States. Office of Federal Procurement Policy. Began with 1975. 0362-8310. US. English. Office of Federal Procurement Policy, Washington DC 20503. LC JK1673. DD 353.00712.

REPORT TO THE EXECUTIVE COUNCIL OF THE GOVERNMENT OF ONTARIO. Main/Corp Ontario. Committee on Government Productivity. CN. English. Ontario Government Bookstore, Queen's Printer, 880 Bay Street, Toronto Ontario M7B 1N8 Canada. LC JL270. DD 352.0713.

REPORT TO THE GENERAL ASSEMBLY OF THE STATE OF ILLINOIS. Main/Corp Illinois. Spanish Speaking Peoples Study Commission. 0094-2146. US. English. an. Spanish Speaking Peoples Study Commission, State of Illinois, Springfield IL 62756. LC F550.S75. DD 353.9773008484.

REPORT TO THE GOVERNOR AND THE LEGISLATURE ON THE ANNUAL CENSUS OF STATE EMPLOYEES CEASED. Main/Corp California State Personnel Board. -1982. 0362-3726. US. English. an. California State Personnel Board, 801 Capitol Mall, Sacramento CA 95814. LC JK8755. DD 353.9794001. *Report to the Governor and the Legislature, Annual Ethnic Census of California State Employees.*

REPORT TO THE GOVERNOR - NEW MEXICO. REGULATION AND LICENSING DEPARTMENT. Main/Corp New Mexico. Regulation and Licensing Dept. 1983-. US. English. an. State of New Mexico, Regulation and Licensing Department, Bataan Memorial Building, Santa Fe NM 87503.

REPORT TO THE GOVERNOR OF IOWA AND THE . . . GENERAL ASSEMBLY BY THE IOWA CITIZENS' AIDE/OMBUDSMAN. Main/Corp Iowa. Office of Citizens' Aide/Ombudsman. US. English. an. Iowa Citizens' Aide/Ombudsman, 515 East 12th Street, Des Moines IA 50319. LC JK6349.O4. DD 353.97770091. *Report to the Governor of Iowa and the General Assembly by the Iowa Citizens' Aide, 0361-6789.*

REPORT TO THE GOVERNORS. VFOAT CSPA State Scanning Network. 1985, No. 1-. 0882-679X. Periodical. US. English. bm. Council of State Planning Agencies, 400 North Capitol Street NW/Suite 291, Washington DC 20001. DD 353.

REPORT TO THE HEADS OF GOVERNMENT BY THE COMMONWEALTH SECRETARY-GENERAL. Main/Corp Commonwealth Secretariat. VFOAT Report of the Commonwealth Secretary-General. UK. English. Marlborough House, 36 Gordon Square, London WC1H 0PE England. LC JN248. DD 320.9171241.

REPORT TO THE HONOURABLE . . . MINISTER OF COMMUNITY SERVICES & CORRECTIONS FROM THE SOCIAL SERVICES ADVISORY COMMITTEE. Main/Corp Manitoba. Social Services Advisory Committee. VFOAT Report. 1979, 1980, 1981-. CN. English. te. Social Services Advisory Committee, 202-323 Portage Avenue, Winnipeg Manitoba R3B 2C1 Canada. LC HV109.M4. DD 354.7127008405. *Report to the Honourable . . . Minister of Health & Community Services from the Social Services Advisory Committee, 0704-4585.*

REPORT TO THE JOINT STANDING COMMITTEE ON PUBLIC UTILITIES, MAINE LEGISLATURE. Main/Corp Maine. Public Utilities Commission. US. English. an. Public Utilities Commission, 242 State Street, State House Station 18, Augusta ME 04333. LC HD2767.M2. DD 363.609741.

REPORT TO THE LEGISLATURE CEASED. Main/Corp New York (State). Legislature Senate. Select Committee on Interstate Cooperation. 1974-. US. English. LC JK2439. DD 353.9291. *Report to the Legislature.*

REPORT TO THE SENATE COMMITTEE ON THE BUDGET PURSUANT TO SECTION 301(C) OF THE CONGRESSIONAL BUDGET AND IMPOUNDMENT COUNCIL ACT OF 1974, FROM THE SENATE COMMITTEE ON ENVIRONMENT AND PUBLIC WORKS. Main/Corp United States. Congress. Senate. Committee on Environment and Public Works. 0731-3578. US. English. an. Superintendent of Documents, US Government Printing Office, Washington DC 20402. LC JK1240.P8. DD 353.00823. Vols. for (1981-) distributed to some depository libraries in microfiche. *Report to the Senate Committee on the Budget Pursuant to Section 301(C) of the Congressional Budget and Impoundment Control Act of 1974 from the Senate Committee.*

REPORT - VICTORIA. STATE SUPERANNUATION BOARD. Main/Corp Victoria. State Superannuation Board. English. an. LC JQ5349.S8.

REPORTER. Main/Corp Canada. Supply and Services Canada. VFOAT Reporter. VAT Reporter (Approvisionnements et Services Canada). Vol. 1, No. 1 (Apr. 1976)-. 0710-815X. Periodical. CN. English (French). ir. Supply & Services Canada, 88 Metcalfe Street, Ottawa Ontario Canada. DD 354.710671205. *Intendant.*

REPORTER - AMERICAN PUBLIC WORKS ASSOCIATION. (THE APWA REPORTER). Main/Corp American Public Works Association. V. 29- Jan. 1962-. 0092-4873. Periodical. US. English. mo. $5.00. American Public Works Association, 1313 East 60th Street, Chicago IL 60637. LC TA23. DD 363.50973.

REPORTS ON THE WORKING OF GOVERNMENT DEPARTMENTS FOR THE YEAR . . . . Main/Corp Malta. Information Division. English. an. LC JN1586. DD 354.45850405. *Report on the Working of Government Departments.*

REPORTS: OPINIONS, ORDERS, RULES, AND REGULATIONS - NEW YORK (STATE). PUBLIC SERVICE COMMISSION. Main/Corp New York (State). Public Service Commission. VFOAT PSC Reports. US. English. Public Service Commission, Empire Street, Plaza Agency Building 3, Albany NY 12223. LC KFN5455. DD 343.7470902646.

REPORT/TECHNICAL STUDY : REPORTED LOBBYING EXPENDITURES. Main/Corp Washington (State). Public Disclosure Commission. US. English. Public Disclosure Commission, 403 Evergreen Plaza, Mail Stop FJ-42, Olympia WA 98504. LC JK9274.5. DD 322.4309797.

REPRESENTABLE COMPENSATION PLAN. Main/Corp Oregon. Executive Dept. Personnel Division Operations and Development Unit. US. English. Operations and Development Unit, Personnel Division, Executive Department, 155 Cottage Street NE, Salem OR 97310. LC JK9057. DD 353.979500123. *Compensation Plan.*

REPUBLICAN ALMANAC. See Yearbooks, Almanacs, Directories.

REPUBLICANS ABROAD. 0738-193X. Periodical. US. English. qt. Republicans Abroad, c/o Republican National Committee 310 1st Street Southeast, Washington DC 20003. LC JK2351. DD 324.273405.

REQUIREMENTS FOR RECURRING REPORTS TO THE CONGRESS. (REQUIREMENTS FOR RECURRING REPORTS TO THE CONGRESS : A DIRECTORY). Series/Titl Congressional Sourcebook Series. Began with 1977. 0277-4496. US. English. be. LC Z7165.U5, JK585. DD 016.353. NLM Z 1223.A12 R311. *Recurring Reports to the Congress, 0148-8716.*

RES PUBLICA. See Political Science.

THE RESEARCH COUNCIL'S HANDBOOK. 1st- Ed. 0363-3543. US. English. ir. Washington Research Council, 906 South Columbia/Suite 350, Olympia WA 98501. Tel (206)357-6643. LC JK9230. DD 353.9797000202.

RESEARCH MEMORANDA - THE CITIZENS CONFERENCE ON STATE LEGISLATURES. Main/Corp Citizens Conference on State Legislatures. 1- Jan. 1967-. 0578-3364. US. English. ir. Center Legislative Research, 7503 Marin Drive/Suite 2A, Englewood CO 80110.

RESEARCH MEMORANDUM - MUNICIPAL RESEARCH AND SERVICES CENTER OF WASHINGTON. (RESEARCH MEMORANDUM). Main/Corp Municipal Research and Services Center of Washington. 0092-5500. US. English. $2.00. Municipal Research and Service Center of Washington, 4719 Brooklyn Avenue NE, Seattle WA 98105. LC JS451.W25. DD 352.00809797.

RESEARCH MONITOR. V. 1- Jan. 1978-. Periodical. US. English. wk. $495.00. National Information Service, 1754 Church Street Northwest, Washington DC 20036. Tel (202)234-5149. Ed Dale Hudelson. Circ 100. A news and reference service including a directory of all federal programs supporting extramural research and development and a weekly newsletter on policy and budget developments of federal research programs.

RESEARCH NOTE - COMMUNITY COUNCIL OF GREATER NEW YORK. Main/Corp Community Council of Greater New York. Research and Program Planning Information Dept. Periodical. US. English. Community Council of Greater New York, 225 Park Avenue South, New York NY 10003.

RESEARCH STUDIES - GREAT BRITAIN. LOCAL GOVERNMENT COMMISSION FOR ENGLAND. Main/Corp Great Britain. Local Government Commission for England. No. 1- 1968-. UK. English. ir. Her Majesty's Stationery Office, PO Box 276, London SW8 5DT England. LC JS3111. DD 352.000942.

RESOLUTION - PARLIAMENTARY ASSEMBLY OF THE COUNCIL OF EUROPE. Main/Corp Council of Europe. Parliamentary Assembly. FR. English and French. ir. Council of Europe, Avenue de l'Europe, 67 Strasbourg France. LC JN22. DD 341.242. *Resolution.*

RETAIL PRICES AND INDEXES OF FUELS AND UTILITIES. July 1971-. 0160-9882. US. English. bm. US Department of Labor, Bureau of Statistics, Washington DC 20212. *Retail Prices and Indexes of Fuels and Electricity.*

RETIREMENT LIFE. V. 1- 1922-. 0034-6179. Periodical. US. English. mo. LC JK791.

A REVIEW OF IMPORTANT ACTIVITIES AND STUDIES. Main/Corp India. Planning Commission. 0537-0329. II. English. ir. Government of India, Planning Commission, New Delhi India. LC HC435. DD 354.54008.

REVIEW OF PARLIAMENT AND PARLIAMENTARY DIGEST. Began with Oct. 20, 1972 issue. Periodical. UK. English. wk. Parliamentary Digest Ltd, 171 Queen Victoria Street, EC4 London England. LC JN101. DD 328.4203.

REVIEW OF THE UNITED STATES SYNTHETIC FUELS CORPORATIONS FINANCIAL STATEMENTS. (REVIEW OF THE UNITED STATES SYNTHETIC FUELS CORPORATION'S FINANCIAL STATEMENTS FOR THE YEAR ENDED SEPTEMBER 30 . . .). 0738-842X.

US. English. an. US G A O Document Handling and Information Services Facility, PO Box 6015, Gaithersburg MD 20760. **LC** HD9502.5.S964. **DD** 353.092.

REVISTA BRASILEIRA DOS MUNICIPIOS. Yearly V. 1- (No. 1/2-). Periodical. Portuguese. ir. **LC** JS2401.A1R48.

REVISTA CENTROAMERICANA DE ADMINISTRACION PUBLICA. No. 1, (July/Dec. 1981)-. Periodical. Spanish. sa. **LC** JL1401.A1. **DD** 354.7280005.

REVISTA DA PROCURADORIA FISCAL. **Main/Corp** Pernambuco, Brazil (State). Procuradoria Fiscal do Estado. V. 1- July/Dec. 1978-. Periodical. Portuguese. ir. Procuradoria Fiscal do Estado, Secretaria da Fazenda de Pernambuco, rua do Imperador Pedro II S/N, 4. Andar 50.000 Recife Pe Brazil. **DD** 354.813400724.

REVISTA DE ADMINISTRACAO MUNICIPAL. Periodical. Portuguese. ir. $8.00. Largo Ibam, 1 50. Andar Botafogo ZC 02, 20000 Rio de Janeiro Brazil. **LC** JS41.

REVISTA DE ADMINISTRACAO PARA O DESENVOLVIMENTO. Periodical. Portuguese. ir. INAD, Caixa Postal 1817, Recife Brazil. **LC** JA5. **DD** 350.0005.

REVISTA DE ADMINISTRACAO PUBLICA. V. 1- 1967-. 0034-7612. Periodical. BL. Portuguese. qt. $11.90. Fundacao Getulio Verga, Caxia Postal 9052, 188 ZC02 Rio de Janeiro Brazil. Ed Ana Maria G Marquesini. **LC** JA5. bk rev. **Circ** 1,700.

REVISTA FACULTAD DE ADMINISTRACION PUBLICA Y COMERCIO. **Main/Corp** Panama (City). Universidad. Facultad de Administracion Publica y Comercio. Periodical. Spanish. ir. **LC** JF1338.P33.

REVISTA LATINOAMERICANA DE ADMINISTRACION PUBLICA. Spanish. ir. Instituto Nacional de Administracion Publica, Barranca del Muerto 210 P B, Mexico Mexico. **LC** JA5.

REVISTA MEXICANA DE POLITICA EXTERIOR : PUBLICACION TRIMESTRAL DEL INSTITUTO MATIAS ROMERO DE ESTUDIOS DIPLOMATICOS. (Oct./Dec. 1983)-. Periodical. MX. Spanish. qt. Av Peralvillo 124 Col Morelos, Delegacion Cuauhtemo, C P 06200 Mexico DF Mexico.

REVISTA SINDICAL. No. 1-. Periodical. Spanish. ir. Congreso Permanente de Unidad Sindical de los Trabajodores de America Latina, Apartado Postal 32-269, Mexico 1 DF Mexico.

REVISTA UNIVERSIDAD EAFIT. VFOAT Revista Universidad E.A.F.I.T., Temas Administrativos y de Ingenieria, Rivista Universidad Eafit—Temas Administrativos y de Ingenieria. 49 (Jan.-Mar. 1983)-. 0120-033X. Periodical. CK. Spanish. qt. $12.00. Escuela Administracion y Finance, Zas Techn Centro Invest, Medellin Columbia. **Tel** 2660 500. **LC** HD28. **DD** 350.0009861. bk rev. adv acc. **Circ** 2,000. The articles published are three contributions of the teachers, documents of seminars sponsored by the University and results of some researches in the field of technology. *Temas Administrativos*.

REVISTA VENEZOLANA DE DESARROLLO ADMINISTRATIVO. No. 1 (Jan. 1982)-. Periodical. Spanish. ty. $15.00. Ediciones Funacademus, Revista Venezolana de Desarrollo Administrativo, Av Andres Bello Edificio Vam, Torre Oeste Mezzanina Caracas.

REVUE FRANCAISE D'ADMINISTRATION PUBLIQUE. No. 1- Jan./Mar. 1977-. Periodical. FR. French. qt. 260.00 Domestic, 320.00 Foreign. La Documentation Francaise, 29-31 Quai Voltaire, 75007 Paris France. **Tel** 834-9275. *Bulletin de l'Institut International d'Administration Publique, 0020-2355.*

REVUE GABONAISE D'POLITIQUES, ECONOMIQUES, ET JURIDIQUES. French. ir. 500.00. Compagnie Generale de Diffusion de la Culture Immeuble Branly, BP 14, 201 Libreville Gabon. **Ind/Abst** Foreign Lang. Index. **LC** JQ3407.A1. **DD** 320.96721.

REVUE INTERNATIONALE DES SCIENCES ADMINISTRATIVES. VFOAT International Review of Administrative Sciences. -22. Year, No. 4 (1956)-. Periodical. BE. French (English or Spanish). qt. International Instutut Administrative Sciences, 25 rue de la Charite, 1040 Brussels Belgium. **Ind/Abst** Int. Labour Doc. bk rev. adv acc. Articles on comparative public administration. A special section for schools and institutes and a bibliography on recent outstanding publications. Distributed all over the world.

REVUE MUNICIPALE. (LA REVUE MUNICIPALE). VFOAT Revue Municipale du Canada. V. 1- June 1923-. 0035-3728. Periodical. CN. French (text also in English). mo. $15.48. Revue Municipale, 6841 rue St Hubert/Suite 201, Montreal Quebec H2S 2M7 Canada. **Tel** (514)273-7261. Ed Jacqueline Lebrun. **Ind/Abst** Environ., Point Repere. bk rev. adv acc. **Circ** 9,245. (ctrl). Municipal and public works. *Cites et Villes, 0009-7500.*

REVUE PARLEMENTAIRE CANADIENNE. V. 3, No. 4 (Winter 1980/1981)-. 0229-2556. Periodical. CN. French. ir. Free. La Revue, CP 950, Edifice de la Confederation, Ottawa Ontario K1A 0A6 Canada. **DD** 328.71005. *Revue de la Region Canadienne, 0707-0845.*

RIVISTA AMMINISTRATIVA DELLA REPUBBLICA ITALIANA. Year 1- 1850-. Periodical. Italian. ir.

RIVISTA TRIMESTRALE DI DIRITTO PUBBLICO. *See Law.*

RIVISTA TRIMESTRALE DI SCIENZA DELLA AMMINISTRAZIONE. V. 19- Jan.-Mar. 1972-. Periodical. IT. Italian. qt. $29.70. Franco Angeli Editore Riviste, Vie Monza 106, Milano Italy. **Tel** (02)28.27.651/2/3/. *Scienza e la Tecnica della Organizzazione Nella Pubblica Amministrazione.*

ROADSIDE VEHICLE INSPECTION REPORT. 1980/1981-. US. English. US Department of Transportation, Federal Highway Administration, 400 Seventh Street SW, Washington DC 20590. Volumes for 1982 distributed to depository libraries in microfiche. *Roadside Vehicle Inspections.*

ROSEMERE-NOUVELLES. (ROSEMERE NEWS). Vol. 1, No. 1 Mar. 1979-. 0712-2993. Periodical. CN. English (French on inverted pages). mo. Free. Rosemere News, Town of Rosemere, 100 Charbonneau, Rosemere Quebec J7A 3W1 Canada. **DD** 352.071424. (ctrl).

ROSTER AND LIST OF COMMITTEES OF THE GENERAL ASSEMBLY OF MARYLAND. **Main/Corp** Maryland. General Assembly. US. English. Maryland General Assembly, Printing Division, Annapolis MD 21404. **LC** JK3830. **DD** 328.752073025.

ROSTER : CALIFORNIA STATE, COUNTY, CITY AND TOWNSHIP OFFICIALS, STATE OFFICIALS OF THE UNITED STATES. VFOAT California State, County, City and Township Officials of the United States. 1973/74-. US. English. Office of Procurement Documents Section, PO Box 20191, Sacramento CA 95820. **LC** JK8730. **DD** 353.9794002. *Roster: Federal, State, County, City, and Township Officials.*

ROSTER OF BLACK ELECTED OFFICIALS IN THE SOUTH. 0093-9951. US. English. ir. Voter Education Project Inc, 52 Fairlie Street NW, Atlanta GA 30303. **Tel** (404)522-7495. **LC** JK1929.A2. **DD** 353.975002.

ROSTER OF LEGISLATIVE STANDING COMMITTEES AND CHAIRMEN. VFOAT Legislative Standing Committees and Chairmen. 1973-. 0098-5007. US. English. $2.50. Council of State Governments, PO Box 11910 Iron Works Pike, Lexington KY 40505. **LC** JK2495. **DD** 328.730765.

ROSTER. STATE, DISTRICT, COUNTY OFFICERS. VFOAT State, District, County Officers. US. English. be. **LC** JK5430. **DD** 350.2025778. *Roster of State, District and County Officers of the State of Missouri.*

ROYAL GAZETTE. **Main/Corp** Nova Scotia. Periodical. CN. English. wk. $61.80. Office of the Royal Gazette Department of Government Services/Finance & Administration, 13th Floor Maritime Centre, PO Box 54, Halifax Nova Scotia B3J 2L4 Canada. **Tel** (902)424-8575. Ed Susan MacIsaac. **LC** J2. **Circ** 500. (ctrl). Also available on microfilm from: Toronto, Micromedia., Also available on microfilm from: New York, Public Library. Official government record of cabinet proclamations, orders-in-council, regulations and non-government legal notices.

Public Administration

ROYAL GAZETTE. NEW BRUNSWICK. (THE ROYAL GAZETTE MICROFORM). **Main/Corp** New Brunswick. VFOAT Gazette Royale. 0703-8623. Periodical. CN. English (French, June 30, 1977-). sa. Micromedia Limited, 144 Front Street West, Toronto Ontario M5J 1G2 Canada. **DD** 354.7150005.

ROYAL THAI GOVERNMENT GAZETTE. **Main/Corp** Thailand. No. 1- Dec. 1946-. TH. English. ir. $165.00. Nibondh & Company Ltd, PO Box 402, Bangkok Thailand. **DD** 349.59302.

RULES OF THE ASSEMBLY. **Main/Corp** New York (State). Legislature. Assembly. 0275-0821. US. English. an. New York Legislature, State Legislative Office Building, Albany NY 12224. **LC** JK3478. **DD** 328.74705.

RURAL ELECTRIC NEWS LETTER. (RURAL ELECTRIC NEWSLETTER). VFOAT RE. 0747-4784. Periodical. US. English. wk. $14.00. National Rural Electric Co-Op Association, 1800 Massachusetts Avenue Northwest, Washington DC 20036. **Tel** (202)857-9500. Ed J C Brown. bk rev. adv acc. **Circ** 23,000. Edited for managers and employees of rural electric utilities. Technical information news and opinions that strengthen skills and provide a background of regulatory, legislative and utility developments.

RURAL UTILITIES NEWSLETTER. V. 1- Feb. 1980-. 0226-658X. Periodical. CN. English. qt. Alberta Utilities, 12323 Stoney Plaine Road/7th Floor, Edmonton Alberta T5N 3Y9 Canada. **DD** 354.71230087.

THE SACRAMENTO NEWSLETTER. *See Law.*

SAGE PUBLIC ADMINISTRATION ABSTRACTS. *See Indexes/Abstracts.*

SAGE YEARBOOKS IN POLITICS AND PUBLIC POLICY. *See Yearbooks, Almanacs, Directories.*

SAINT-HUBERT, NOTRE VILLE. (NOTRE VILLE). **Main/Corp** Saint-Hubert (Quebec). VFOAT Saint-Hubert Notre Ville. Vol. 1, No. 1 (June 1981)-. 0712-7308. Periodical. CN. French. qt. Free. Service d'Information, Ville Saint-Hubert, 5900 Boulevard Cousineau, Saint-Hubert Quebec J3Y 7K8 Canada. **DD** 352.071437. *Ingo Loisir (Saint-Hubert, Quebec : 1980), 0712-7286; Entre-Nous, 0712-7294.*

SAIPA. VFOAT Tydskrif vir Publieke Administrasie. V. 1- (No. 1-). 0036-0767. Periodical. SA. Afrikaans (English). qt. $8.26. South African Institute of Public Administration, 113 Northvaal Building Box 2752, Pretoria South Africa. **Tel** (012)263184. Ed J J N Cloete. **Ind/Abst** ABC Pol Sci. **LC** JA26.

SAJJANAGADA. Periodical. Marathi. ir. 10.00. Srisamartha Seva Mandala, Srisamartha Sadan, 179 Somwar Peth, Satara City India. **LC** BL1245.S26.

SALARY ORDINANCE OF THE COUNTY OF LOS ANGELES. **Main/Corp** Los Angeles Co., Calif. Periodical. US. English. an. 222 North Grand Avenue, Los Angeles CA 90012.

SALARY PLAN, STATE OF NORTH CAROLINA. **Main/Corp** North Carolina. Office of State Personnel. 0099-0477. US. English. an. North Carolina Office of State Personnel, 116 West Jones Street, Raleigh NC 27609. **LC** JK4157. **DD** 353.97560012.

SANGAT. Periodical. Urdu. ir. 25.00. Manzur Ahmad Baloc, Gajyan Baloch General Manager Sangat, Koitah Pakistan. **LC** JQ201.

SANGIIN GIIN SENKYO NO KIROKU. **Main/Corp** Tokyo, Japan. Senkyo Kanri Iinkai. JA. Japanese. ir. Senkyo Kanri Iinkai, 2-13 Yurakucho, Chiyoda-ku, Tokyo Japan. **LC** JQ1693.T58.

SANPHAKON SAN. V. 1- 1954-. 0058-4973. Periodical. Thai. ir.

SASKATCHEWAN GAZETTE. (THE SASKATCHEWAN GAZETTE MICROFORM). 0036-4894. Periodical. CN. English. Micromedia Limited, 144 Front Street West, Toronto Ontario M5J 1G2 Canada. **DD** 354.71240005.

SASKATCHEWAN MUNICIPAL DIRECTORY. *See Yearbooks, Almanacs, Directories.*

SASKATCHEWAN POWER CORPORATION. CN. English. Sturdy-Stone Centre, 122 3rd Avenue North, Saskatoon Saskatchewan S7K 2H6 Canada. **LC** HD9685.C4. **DD** 363.62097124.

Public Administration

SASTAV ORGANA SKUPSTINA OPSTINA. Main/Corp Bosnia and Hercegovina. Republicki Zavod Za Statistiku. Serbo-Croatian(R). ir. LC JS6949.B6.

SCA, STATE & COUNTY ADMINISTRATOR. VFOAT State & County Administrator. VAT State County Administrator, State and County Administrator. V. 1- Jan./Feb. 1976-. 0363-9401. Periodical. US. English. bm. $10.00. Security World Publishing Company, 2639 South La Cienega Boulevard, Los Angeles CA 90034. LC JK2403. DD 353.905.

SCAG : A RECORD OF ACCOMPLISHMENT. Main/Corp Southern California Association of Governments. US. English. an. 1111 West Sixth Street/Suite 400, Los Angeles CA 90017. LC JS303.C2. DD 352.0094097949.

SCHMOLLERS JAHRBUCH FUR GESETZGEBUNG, VERWALTUNG UND VOLKSWIRTSCHAFT IM DEUTSCHEN REICH. See Yearbooks, Almanacs, Directories.

SCHRIFTEN. Main/Corp Deutsche Wahlergesellschaft. Vol. 1- 1947-. Periodical. English. ir. LC JN3971.A95.

SCHRIFTENREIHE DES DEUTSCHEN STADTE- UND GEMEINDEBUNDES. Main/Corp Deutscher Stadte-und Gemeindebund. V. 18-. Monographic Series. GW. German. ir. Verlag Otto Schwartz & Co, Annastrasse 7, D-3400 Gottingen West Germany. *Schriftenreihe, 0418-9590.*

SCIENCE & PUBLIC POLICY. VAT Science and Public Policy. V. 1- Jan. 1974-. 0302-3427. Periodical. UK. English. bm. Beechtree Publishing, 10 Watford Close, Guilford Surrey GUI 2EP England. Tel (0483)67497. Ed Maurice Goldsmith. Ind/Abst Excerpta Med., Sociol. Abstr., Soc. Welf. Soc. Plan./Policy Soc. Dev., Coal Abstr., GeoRef, Energy Inf. Abstr., Environ. Abstr. LC Q179.9. DD 301.243. NLM W1 SC683K. Index in first issue of next volume - loose - separately paged. bk rev. adv acc. Interactions of science, technology, policy, economic development, sociology, business, Third World, hi-tech, R&D, tech assessment, hi-technology, research and development, technology assessment, and impact. Articles, books, news, teaching, diary, etc. *Science Policy.*

SCRIBE. (LE SCRIBE). V. 1- March 1975-. 0383-7262. Periodical. CN. French. bm. Corporation des Secretaires Municipaux du Quebec Inc, CP 307, Val-David Quebec J0T 2N0 Canada. DD 352.00062714.

SEC NO-ACTION LETTERS INDEX AND SUMMARIES. See Indexes/Abstracts.

SECRETARY-GENERAL'S REPORT. Main/Corp Malaysian Chinese Association. General Assembly. VFOAT Report, Ma Hua Kung Hui Tai Piao Ta Hui Chang Nien Hui I. MY. English (Chinese). ir. Malaysian-Chinese Association, General Assembly, Kuala Lumpur Malaysia. LC JQ719.A8. DD 329.9595.

SECRETARY'S ANNUAL REPORT TO CONGRESS. Main/Corp United States. Dept. of Energy. Began with 2nd, 1980. 0199-9648. US. English. an. Superintendent of Documents, US Government Printing Office, Washington DC 20402. LC HD9502.U5. DD 353.8706. *Annual Report to Congress, 0196-4356.*

SECTOR ELECTRICO. Periodical. MX. Spanish. mo. Departamento de Informacion Comision Federal de Electricidad, Rio Atoyac No 97, Col Cuauhtemoc, Mexico 5 DF Mexico. LC HD9685.M63. DD 363.62.

SECULAR DEMOCRACY. 0582-3730. Periodical. English. ir. LC JQ201.

SEIFU KANKOBUTSU TO SOGO MOKUROKU. JA. Japanese. an. 350. Zenkoku Kampo Hambai Kyodo Kumiai, 2-4 Toranomon 2 Minato-ku, Tokyo 105 Japan. LC Z3305, JQ1601.

SEIFU KOHO YOTEI JIKO. JA. Japanese. ir. Naikau Sori Daijinkambo Kohoshitsu, 6-1 Nagatacho 1-chome, Chiyoda-ku 100 Tokyo Japan. LC JS1649.P85.

SEISAKU SHIRYO. Main/Corp Nihon Shakaito (Founded 1945). Fukkan No. 1-. JA. Japanese. ir. 800. Nihon Shakaito Seisaku Shingikai, c/o Shugiin Daiichi Kaikan Nagatocho Chiyoda-ku, Tokyo Japan. LC JQ1698.S5.

SELECTED STATE DEPARTMENT PUBLICATIONS. Main/Corp United States. Dept. of State. Bureau of Public Affairs. Began with June 1980. US. English. qt. United States Department of State, Bureau of Public Affairs, Washington DC 20052. *Recent Releases.*

SELECTED STATE OFFICIALS AND THE LEGISLATURES *CEASED.* Began in 1975. Ceased in 1975. 0191-944X. US. English. be. Council of State Governments, PO Box 11910, Iron Works Pike, Lexington KY 40578. Tel (606)252-2291. LC JK2403. DD 353.932. *State Elective Officials and the Legislatures, 0191-9431.*

THE SELF DETERMINATION QUARTERLY JOURNAL. V. 1- Mar. 1977-. 0148-2653. Periodical. US. English. qt. Self Determination, 2435 Forest Avenue, San Jose CA 95128. Tel (408)984-8134. LC JK8701. DD 3220.979405.

SEMI-ANNUAL REPORT OF THE INSPECTOR GENERAL, U.S. SMALL BUSINESS ADMINISTRATION. (SEMI-ANNUAL REPORT OF THE INSPECTOR GENERAL, U.S. SMALL BUSINESS ADMINISTRATION : PURSUANT TO PUBLIC LAW 95-452). Main/Corp United States. Small Business Administration. Office of Inspector General. Began with Apr. 1979/Sept. 1979. 0742-3802. US. English. sa. Office of Inspector General, United States Small Business Administration, 1441 L Street NW, Washington DC 20416. LC HD2346.U5. DD 353.998204806.

SEMIANNUAL REPORT TO THE CONGRESS. Main/Corp United States. General Services Administration. Office of Inspector General. US. English. sa. General Services Administration, Office of Inspector General, Washington DC 20405. LC JK1672. DD 353.007105.

SEMIANNUAL REPORT - UNITED STATES. DEPT. OF THE INTERIOR. OFFICE OF INSPECTOR GENERAL. (SEMIANNUAL REPORT). Main/Corp United States. Dept. of the Interior. Office of Inspector General. Oct. 1, 1979-Mar. 31, 1980-. 0736-7864. US. English. sa. US Department of the Interior, Office of Inspector General, Washington DC 20240. Vols. for (1983-) distributed to depository libraries in microfiche. *Semiannual Report on Operation of the Office of Inspector General.*

THE SEMSCOPE. 0361-1310. Periodical. US. English. ir. Free. Southeast Michigan Council of Governments, 1249 Washington Boulevard, Book Building/8th Floor, Detroit MI 48226. Tel (313)961-4266. Ed Natalynne Stringer & Carol Wiles. Circ 11,800. (ctrl). Southeast Michigan Council of Governments in a short and long-range planning organization for housing, economic development, population, transportation, environment, public safety in southeast Michigan.

SENATE INQUIRIES AND INVESTIGATIONS. Main/Corp United States. Congress. Senate. Committee on Rules and Administration. US. English. an. US Government Printers Office, Washington DC 20402. LC JK1239. DD 328.730741.

SENATE ISSUES YEARBOOK. See Yearbooks, Almanacs, Directories.

SENATE ROLL CALL. Vol. 1, No. 1 (Sept. 1979)-. 0730-9910. US. English. sa. $15.00 Per Copy; Free to contributors of $25.00 or more annually. The Conservative Caucus Research Analysis and Education Foundation, 422 Maple Avenue East, Vienna VA 22180. LC JK1161. DD 328.730775.

SENATORS AND MEMBERS. Main/Corp Australia. Parliament. 0706-3598. AT. English. ir. Australian Bureau of Statistics, PO Box 84, Canberra Australian Capital Territory 2061 Australia. LC JQ4051. DD 328.94073025.

SENKYO NO AYUMI. JA. Japanese. ir. Yokohama-shi Senkyo Kanri Iinkai Jimukyoku, 1 Minato-cho 1 Naka-ku, Yokohama-shi 231 Japan. LC JQ1693.Y64.

SEPARATIONS, STATE SERVICE. Main/Corp New Jersey. Dept. of Civil Service. 1960/61-. US. English. an. Department of Civil Service, Trenton NJ 08625. LC JK3558. DD 353.97490018.

SERI P.M.S.T. (SERI PMST). Main/Corp Indonesia. Direktorat Pembangunan Masyarakat Suku-Suku Terasing. VAT Seri Pembangunan Masyarakat Suku-Suku Terasing. 0302-8879.
Indonesian. ir. Department Social, JL IR H Juanda, Jakarta Indonesia. LC HN710.Z9.

SERIE RAPPORTS ET DOCUMENTS. SERIES REPORTS AND DOCUMENTS. Main/Corp Inter-Parliamentary Union. VFOAT Series Reports and Documents. Monographic Series. SZ. French (English). ir. Inter-Parliamentary Union, Place du Petit Saconnex, 1211 Geneva 28 Switzerland. LC JF8. DD 320.3.

SERVING YOU IN BOTH OFFICIAL LANGUAGES. VFOAT A Votre Service dans les Deux Langues Officielles. Began in 1982. English (French). ir. LC JL71. DD 354.7100025.

THE SESSION MONTHLY. Vol. 1, No. 1-. Periodical. US. English. mo. House Information Office, State Capitol/Room 9, St Paul MN 55155.

SESSION REPORT - GEORGIA. GENERAL ASSEMBLY. HOUSE OF REPRESENTATIVES. STATE PLANNING AND COMMUNITY AFFAIRS COMMITTEE. Main/Corp Georgia. General Assembly. House of Representatives. State Planning and Community Affairs Committee. US. English. an. State Planning and Community Affairs Committee, 142-C State Capitol, Atlanta GA 30334.

THE SHIELD. 0037-3672. Periodical. US. English. wk. $17.25. The Shield, 155 Broad Avenue, PO Box 505, Fairview NJ 07022. Tel (201)941-4400. Ed Leo Steiner. Ind/Abst Predicasts. LC JK3501. DD 353.9749006. adv acc. (ctrl). Newspaper devoted to municipal, county, and state civil service employees.

SHINKEN KAWARABAN (SHUSATSUBAN). (SHINKEN KAWARABAN). 1 (75-Winter/76-Summer)-. Periodical. JA. Japanese. an. 1000 Single Issue. Asahi Shinbun Rodo Kumiai Honbu Shinbun Kenkyu Iinkai Asahi Shinbun Nai, 3-2 Tsukiji 5 Chuo-Ku, Tokyo-To 104 Japan. LC JC599.J3.

THE SHIRE & MUNICIPAL RECORD. V. 1- 1908/09-. Periodical. AT. English. mo. Methuen Law Book Company Ltd, 35 Mitchell Street, NTH Sydney NSW 2060 Australia.

SHOKUIN JIMU HANDOBUKKU. 1974-. Japanese. ir. Kitakyushu-shi Kikakukyoku, Jimi Kanribu Gyosri, 1-Ban 1-Go Kokuraku Jonai, Kitakyushu Japan. LC JS7374.A1.

SHOTOKUZEIHO SOCHIHO SANRIN SHOTOKU JOTO SHOTOKU KIHON TSUTATSU. Main/Corp Japan. Kokuzeicho. VFOAT Shotokuzeiho Sochiho Kihon Tsutatsu. Japanese. ir. 22.00. Nozei Kyokai Rengokai, 14-1 Minami Ogicho Kita-ku 530, Osaka Japan.

SHUCHO. JA. Japanese. ir. Zenkoku Chosonkai, 1-11-35 Nagata-cho Chiyoda-ku, Tokyo Japan. LC JS7371.A1.

SIARAN UMUM - DEPARTEMEN PENERANGAN R.I. Main/Corp Indonesia. Departemen Penerangan. IO. Indonesian. ir. Direktorat Publikasi, Jl Merdeka Barat 7, Jakarta Indonesia. LC JQ761.A1.

SIGNIFICANT ARREARAGES DUE THE UNITED STATES GOVERNMENT AND UNPAID 90 DAYS OR MORE BY OFFICIAL FOREIGN OBLIGORS. Periodical. US. English. qt. US Treasury Department, Office of the Assistant Secretary for International Affairs, Washington DC 20220.

SILLERY VOUS INFORME. 0713-682X. Periodical. CN. French. ir. Free. Sillery Vous Informe, Ville de Sillery, 1445 Avenue Maguire, Sillery Quebec G1T 1Z2 Canada. DD 352.071447.

SINGAPORE GOVERNMENT DIRECTORY. See Yearbooks, Almanacs, Directories.

THE SITTINGS - EUROPEAN PARLIAMENT. Main/Corp European Parliament. Jan. 1, 1975-. LU. English. ir. European Parliament, PO Box 1601, Luxembourg LU. LC JN32. DD 341.242.

SOCIAL AUDIT. V. 1- Summer 1973-. Periodical. UK. English. qt. 5.00. Research Publications Services Ltd, Victoria Hall, East Greenwich, SE10 0RF London England. LC JC507. DD 659.2.

SOCIAL POLICY & ADMINISTRATION. VAT Social Policy and Administration. V. 13- Spring 1979-. 0144-5596. Periodical. UK. English. ir. Basil Blackwell Ltd, 108 Cowley Road, Oxford OX4 IJF

England. Ind/Abst Sociol. Abstr., Soc. Welf. Soc. Plan./Policy Soc. Dev., Soc. Sci. Citation Index. LC H1. DD 361.005. NLM W1 SO122T. *Social and Economic Administration.*

SOMMAIRES DE LA DOCUMENTATION COURANTE. ADMINISTRATION MUNICIPALE. Vol. 1, No. 1 (Feb. 1982)-. 0711-7892. Periodical. CN. French. ir. Gouvernement du Quebec, 600 St Amable 4E Etage, Quebec G1R 4Z1 Canada. DD 016.352. *Sommaires de la Documentation Courante. Administration Locale et Regionale, 0225-3674.*

SOUTH DAKOTA JOURNAL OF COUNTY GOVERNMENT. V. 1- Aug. 1954-. 0300-6174. Periodical. US. English. bm. $6.00. South Dakota Association of Colorado Commissioners, 214 East Capitol, Pierre SD 57501. Tel (605)224-4554. Ed Mary Jorgenson. LC T12. adv acc. Circ 1,000. (ctrl). Technical assistance to county government.

SOUTH DAKOTA MUNICIPALITIES. 0300-6182. Periodical. US. English. mo. $20.00. South Dakota Municipalities, 214 East Capitol, Pierre SD 57501. Tel (605)224-8654. *Bulletin - League of South Dakota Municipalities.*

SOUTH DAKOTA STATE CEMENT PLANT OPERATING FUND ANNUAL FINANCIAL REPORT FOR THE PERIOD JANUARY 1, THROUGH DECEMBER 31. VFOAT South Dakota State Cement Plant Operating Fund for the Period January 1, through December 31. US. English. an. State of South Dakota, Department of Legislative Audit, State Capitol, Pierre SD 57501. LC HD9622.U54. DD 353.9783008242.

SOUTH DAKOTA STATE CEMENT PLANT RETIREMENT FUND ANNUAL FINANCIAL REPORT FOR THE PERIOD JANUARY 1, THROUGH DECEMBER 31. VFOAT South Dakota State Cement Plant Retirement Fund for the Period January 1, through December 31. US. English. an. State of South Dakota, Department of Legislative Audit, State Capitol, Pierre SD 57501. LC HD7116.C382. DD 353.978300835.

SOUTHERN CITY. V. 1- 1949-. 0361-7130. Periodical. US. English. bm. $6.00. North Carolina League of Muncipalities, Margot Christensen, PO Box 3069, Raleigh NC 27602. Tel (919)834-1311. Ed Margot F Christensen. adv acc. Circ 5,400. Issues and topics concerning municipal Government in North Carolina.

SOUTHERN REVIEW OF PUBLIC ADMINISTRATION CEASED. V. 1-6. 0147-8168. Periodical. US. English. qt. $10.00. Southern Review of Public Administration, Auburn University at Montgomery, Montgomery AL 36117. LC JA1. DD 350.0005.

SPBR REVIEW. Main/Corp Ohio. State Personnel Board of Review. Periodical. US. English. SPBR Review, 30 East Broad Street 28th Floor, Columbus OH 43215. LC KFO435. DD 353.977100105.

SPECIAL ANALYSES, BUDGET OF THE UNITED STATES GOVERNMENT. See Business - Public Finance.

SPECIAL REPORT - AMERICAN PUBLIC WORKS ASSOCIATION. Main/Corp American Public Works Association. VFOAT APWA Special Report. No. 22-. 0065-9932. Monographic Series. US. English. ir. American Public Works Association, 1313 East 60th Street, Chicago IL 60637. Tel (312)667-2200. Ed Kenneth Bauder. Ind/Abst Eng. Index Mon., Eng. Index Bioeng. Abstr., Eng. Index Energy Abstr., GeoRef, Eng. Index Annu. LC UNC. CODEN SRAADG. Research reports of the American Public Works Association. *Public Works Engineers' Special Report.*

SPECIAL REPORT - BOSTON MUNICIPAL RESEARCH BUREAU. Main/Corp Boston Municipal Research Bureau. No. 1-44, Mar. 1963-May 1972. 0520-6561. US. English. ir. Boston Municipal Research Bureau, 294 Washington Street, Boston MA 02108.

STAATS-ZEITUNG; STAATSANZEIGER FUR RHEINLANDJ-PFALZ. Main/Corp Rhineland-Palatinate. Vol. 1- May 1950-. Periodical. German. wk. $39.40. German News Company Inc, 220 East 86th Street, New York NY 10028. Tel (212)288-5500.

DER STADTETAG. N.F. Year. 1- July/Aug. 1948-. 0038-9048. Periodical. GW. German. mo. W E Sarrbach GMBH, PO Box 101610, D-5000 Koeln 1 West Germany. Ind/Abst Excerpta Med., Coal Abstr., Energy Res. Abstr., Foreign Lang. Index, PAIS Foreign Lang. Index. LC JS41. *Gemeindetag.*

STAFF LIST, HONG KONG GOVERNMENT. Main/Corp Hongkong. Government Secretariat. VFOAT Hsiang-Kang Cheng fu Chih Yuan Ming Tse. 66th- Issue. HK. English. ir. 286.- Domestic, $38.10. J R Lee Government Printer, Beaconsfield House Queens Road, Ctr Victoria Hong Kong. LC JQ674. DD 354.5125002. Circ 400. Includes the names of all officers in ranks, their salaries and the master pay scale. *Staff List, Hong Kong Government.*

STAFF LIST - MID-WESTERN STATE, NIGERIA. MINISTRY OF ESTABLISHMENTS. Main/Corp Mid-Western State, Nigeria. Ministry of Establishments. NR. English. ir. Nigeria Ministry of Establishments, Benin City Nigeria. LC JQ3099.M54. DD 331.2813546693.

STAFF LIST - SOUTH-EASTERN STATE OF NIGERIA. Main/Corp South-Eastern State, Nigeria. English. ir. 75/-. Cabinet Office, Government Printer, Calabar Nigeria. LC JQ3099.S6. DD 354.6694002.

THE STANDARD-BEARER. V. 1-. 0049-206X. Periodical. US. English. ty. National Accreditation Council, 79 Madison Avenue, New York NY 10016.

STANDARDIZED REGULATIONS : GOVERNMENT CIVILIANS, FOREIGN AREAS. Main/Corp United States. Dept. of State. Periodical. US. English. mo. Superintendent of Documents, US Government Printers Office, Washington DC 20402.

STANDARDS DEVELOPMENT. (STANDARDS DEVELOPMENT : STATUS SUMMARY REPORT : DATA FOR DECISIONS, MANAGEMENT BY OBJECTIVES). Vol. 1, No. 1 (Jan. 31, 1981)-. 0737-8416. Periodical. US. English. qt. Superintendent of Documents, US Government Printing Office, Washington DC 20402. Tel (202)783-3238.

STATE ACTIONS. Main/Corp United States. Advisory Commission on Intergovernmental Relations. 0096-9915. US. English. Superintendent of Documents, Government Printing Office, Washington DC 20402. LC JK2403. DD 353.929. *State Action on Local Problems.*

STATE ADMINISTRATIVE OFFICIALS CLASSIFIED BY FUNCTION. VFOAT State Administrative Officials. 1981-82-. 0191-9423. US. English. be. $12.00. Iron Works Pike, Lexington KY 40578. LC JK2403. DD 353.932. *State Administrative Officials Classified by Functions, 0191-9423.*

STATE & LOCAL GOVERNMENT REVIEW. VAT State and Local Government Review. V. 8- Jan. 1976-. 0160-323X. Periodical. US. English. ty. $25.00. University of Georgia, Institute of Government, Terrell Hall, Athens GA 30602. Tel (404)542-2736. Ed Joseph W Whorton. Ind/Abst Public Aff. Inf. Serv. Bull., ABC Pol Sci. LC JK2403. DD 353.9. Circ 800. A journal of current research and viewpoints in state and local government. *Georgia Government Review.*

STATE COASTAL ZONE MANAGEMENT ACTIVITIES. Main/Corp United States. Office of Coastal Zone Management. 0147-0566. US. English. an. US Department of Commerce, Office of Coastal Zone Management, Washington DC 20230. LC HT392. DD 353.008232.

STATE CONSTITUTIONAL CONVENTION STUDIES. Main/Corp National Municipal League. 0081-4474. Monographic Series. US. English. ir. National Municipal League, 55 West 44th Street, New York NY 10036.

STATE DIRECTORY OF KENTUCKY. See Yearbooks, Almanacs, Directories.

STATE DIRECTORY OF PUBLIC OFFICIALS IN GEORGIA. See Yearbooks, Almanacs, Directories.

STATE ELECTIVE OFFICIALS AND THE LEGISLATURES (LEXINGTON, KY. : 1977). (STATE ELECTIVE OFFICIALS AND THE LEGISLATURES). 1977-. 0191-9466. US. English. be. $10.00. Iron Works Pike, Lexington KY 40578. LC JK2403. DD 353.932. *Selected State Officials and the Legislatures, 0191-944X.*

STATE ENTERPRISE CEASED. Vol. 1, No. 1 (Jan.-Mar. 1982)-. Periodical. II. English. qt. $30.00. Central News Agency Private Ltd, 23/90 Connaught Circus, PO Box 375, New Delhi 11 00 01 India. LC HD4291. DD 354.5409205.

STATE ETHICS COMMISSION ENFORCEMENT ACTIONS, ADVISORY OPINIONS. See Ethics.

STATE EXECUTIVE DIRECTORY. See Yearbooks, Almanacs, Directories.

STATE GOVERNMENT NEWS. V. 1- July 1958-. 0039-0119. Periodical. US. English. qt. $25.00. Council of State Government, PO Box 11910, Iron Works Pike, Lexington KY 40505. Tel (606)252-2291. Ed Elaine S Knapp. Ind/Abst Energy Abstr., Environ. Abstr., Public Aff. Inf. Serv. Bull., Soc. Sci. Citation Index, Hospit. Lit. Index, Am. Hist. Life, Soc. Sci. Index, Hist. Abstr., Manage. Contents, ABC Pol Sci. LC JK2403. adv acc. Circ 13,000. (ctrl). News from all branches of state government for all 50 states. Covers new state laws, trends, court decisions, administrative actions and federal state relations. *Legislative Session Sheet, 0193-3833.*

STATE GOVERNMENT RESEARCH CHECKLIST. Began in Feb. 1979. 0190-6623. US. English. bm. Council of State Governments, PO Box 11910, Iron Works Pike, Lexington KY 40578. Tel (606)252-2291. *Legislative Research Checklist, 0024-0486.*

STATE INDICATORS REPORT. Main/Corp Mississippi. Legislature. Peer Committee. US. English. Legislative Audit Committee, PO Box 1204, Jackson MS 39205. LC JK4635. DD 353.976204.

STATE INFORMATION BOOK. 1975-. US. English. ir. $72.95. Infax Corporation, 450 Maple Avenue East, Vienna VA 22180. Tel (703)281-0685. Ed Geraldine U Jones and Leonard P Hirsch. Circ 4,000. Provides name, address and phone number for leaders, administration, legislature, judiciary, and regional authorities and agencies, with statistical and historical data. Divided into state chapters for easy reference. *State Information and Federal Region Book.*

STATE LEGISLATION IMPACTING MUNICIPALITIES. See Law.

STATE LEGISLATIVE LEADERSHIP, COMMITTEES, AND STAFF. 1979-. 0195-6639. US. English. an. $13.00. Council of State Governments, Iron Works Pike, Lexington KY 40578. LC JK2495. DD 353.9 S, 328.730025. *Principal Legislative Staff Offices.*

STATE LIBRARIAN. See Library and Information Science.

STATE OF DELAWARE DEFERRED COMPENSATION COUNCIL'S ANNUAL REPORT FOR THE FISCAL YEAR ENDED JUNE 30 . . . . Main/Corp Delaware. Deferred Compensation Council. VFOAT Annual Report. US. English. an. LC JK3757. DD 353.97510012305.

STATE OF LOUISIANA, ACTS OF THE LEGISLATURE. Main/Corp Louisiana. VFOAT Acts, State of Louisiana. 1955-. US. English. ir. Acts of Legislature, Box 44125, Baton Rouge LA 70804. *Laws, etc. Acts of the Legislature, State of Louisiana.*

STATE OF MONTANA OFFICE OF THE SUPERINTENDENT OF PUBLIC INSTRUCTION AND BOARD OF PUBLIC EDUCATION : REPORT ON AUDIT. Main/Corp Montana. Office of the Legislative Auditor. 0146-4914. US. English. an. LC LB2826.M9. DD 379.15209786.

THE STATE OF MUNICIPAL SERVICES. VFOAT State of Municipal Services in New York City. 0743-7447. US. English. an. 110 East 42nd Street, New York NY 10017. LC HD4606.N5. DD 352.7097471.

STATE OF NEVADA, DEPARTMENT OF CONSERVATION AND NATURAL RESOURCES, DIVISION OF STATE PARKS AUDIT REPORT. Main/Corp Nevada. Legislative Auditor. US. English. Legislative Building, Capitol Complex, Carson City NV 89710. LC SB482.N3. DD 353.9793007232. *Audit Report - State of Nevada. Department of Conservation and Natural Resources. Division of State Parks, 0093-6596.*

STATE OF NEW MEXICO OFFICIAL RETURNS . . . GENERAL AND PRIMARY RETURNS. Main/Corp New Mexico. Secretary of State. US. English. be. State of New Mexico Office of the Secretary of State,

Public Administration

Executive Legislative Building, Santa Fe NM 87503. LC JK8092. DD 324.9789053.

STATE OF THE UNION ADDRESS. **Main/Corp** United States. President. US. English. ir. US Congress, Washington DC 20036.

STATE PLAN FOR DEVELOPMENTAL DISABILITIES. **Main/Corp** Pennsylvania Developmental Disabilities Planning Council. 0743-5916. US. English. Pennsylvania Developmental Disabilities Planning Council, Room 569/Forum Building, Commonwealth Avenue, Harrisburg PA 17120. **LC** HV3006.P4. **DD** 353.974800844. *Pennsylvania State Plan, Developmental Disabilities Services and Facilities Construction Act of 1970, 0193-1423.*

STATE REGISTER. V. 1, No. 1- , July 13, 1976- . Monographic Series. US. English. wk. $130.00. State Register Public Document, 117 University Avenue, St Paul MN 55155. **Tel** (612)297-3000. Index in last issue of volume - loose - separately paged. (cum index).

STATE REGULATORY PERMITS INVENTORY. 1980-. US. English. an. The Governor's Development Office, John W McCormack Building, One Ashburton Place, Room 2101, Boston MA 02108. **LC** JK3130. **DD** 353.9744091025.

STATE ROSTER, LIST OF STATE OFFICERS. **VFOAT** List of State Officers. 1981-. US. English. an. Code Depository, 707 Savings and Loan Building, Des Moines IA 50309. **LC** JK6330. **DD** 353.9777002.

STATE SALARY SURVEY. **Main/Corp** United States. Office of Personnel Management. Intergovernmental Personnel Programs. 1979-. Periodical. US. English. an. *State Salary Survey.*

STATE SERIES. **Main/Corp** Vermont. University. Government Research Center. No. 1 1959-. 0506-7588. US. English. ir. University of Vermont, Government Research Center, Burlington VT 05401.

STATE SERVICE. Periodical. UK. English. mo. Institute of Professional Civil Service, 3-7 Northumberland Street, London WC-2 Great Britain. *State Technology.*

STATEHOUSE OBSERVER. (THE STATEHOUSE OBSERVER). 0091-1402. Periodical. US. English. mo. Nebraska Department of Personnel, Room 1319, State Capitol Building, Lincoln NE 68509. **LC** JK6655. **DD** 331.7613539782.

STATEMENT OF POSTS AND SCALES OF PAY. **Main/Corp** Maharashtra (India). English. an. 5.00. **LC** JQ620.M264. **DD** 331.28135454792.

THE STATES AND DISTRESSED COMMUNITIES : A REPORT. **VFOAT** Distressed Communities. 1980-. US. English. an. US Advisory Commission on Intergovernmental Relations, Washington DC 20575.

STATISTICAL ABSTRACT - NEW YORK STATE DEPARTMENT OF STATE. See Indexes/Abstracts.

STATISTICAL REPORT ON GAMBLING. See Statistics.

STATISTICAL SERVICES OF THE UNITED STATES GOVERNMENT. See Statistics.

STATISTICAL TRAINING PROGRAMS BY THE U.S. BUREAU OF THE CENSUS. See Statistics.

STATISTICS OF ELECTRIC COMPANIES. See Statistics.

STATISTICS OF ELECTRIC, GAS, STEAM HEAT, TELEPHONE, TELEGRAPH AND WATER COMPANIES. See Statistics.

STATISTICS OF GAS COMPANIES. See Statistics.

STATISTIEK DER VERKIEZINGEN. GEMEENTERADEN. **Main/Corp** Netherlands (Kingdom, 1815-). Centraal Bureau voor de Statistiek. Dutch. ir. **LC** JS5948.

STATISTIEK VAN DE ELEKTRICITEITS—VOORZIENING IN NEDERLAND. See Statistics.

STATISTIEKE VAN ADMINISTRASIERADE. See Statistics.

STATUS OF AFFIRMATIVE ACTION IN CONNECTICUT STATE GOVERNMENT. **Main/Corp** Connecticut. Commission on Human Rights and Opportunities. 1978-. US. English. an. Commission on Human Rights and Opportunities, 90 Washington Street, Hartford CT 06115. **LC** JK3360.A33. **DD** 353.974600104. *Affirmative Action.*

STATUS OF MAJOR ACQUISITIONS AS OF . . . . See Business - Purchasing.

STATUS REPORT - COUNTY RESTRUCTURING STUDIES PROGRAM. (COUNTY RESTRUCTURING STUDIES PROGRAM : STATUS REPORT). **Main/Corp** Ontario. Ministry of Treasury, Economics and Intergovernmental Affairs. Local Government Organization Branch. 1-. 0382-1293. CN. English. Local Government Organization Branch Ministry of Treasury Economics and Intergovernmental Affairs, Forest Building North Queen's Park, Toronto Ontario Canada. **LC** JS4.O7. **DD** 352.007309713.

STATUTES OF THE PROVINCE OF ONTARIO. **Main/Corp** Ontario. **VAT** Statutes of Ontario. 1868-. 0709-227X. CN. English. ir. Treasurer of Ontario, Ministry Government Service, 880 Bay Street, 5th Floor, Toronto Ontario M7A 1N8 Canada. **Tel** (416)965-2054.

STATUTORY INSTRUMENTS. **Main/Corp** Great Britain. 1952-. UK. English. an. $107.28. Her Majestys Stationery Office, PO Box 276, London SW8 5DT England. **Tel** (01)211-0363. *Statutory Instruments Other Than Those of a Local, Personal or Temporary Character.*

STATUTORY REPORT - CHIEF ELECTORAL OFFICER OF CANADA. (STATUTORY REPORT - THE CHIEF ELECTORAL OFFICER). **Main/Corp** Canada. Office of the Chief Electoral Officer. **VFOAT** Rapport Statutaire du Directeur General des Elections du Canada. 1979-. 0225-9486. Periodical. CN. English (French). ir. Free. Information Canada, 131 Slater Street, Ottawa Ontario K1A 0S9 Canada. **DD** 354.71091. *Report of the Chief Electoral Officer, 0700-1568.*

STATUTORY SALARIES. MISSOURI STATE OFFICIALS. (STATUTORY SALARIES, MISSOURI STATE OFFICIALS). **Main/Corp** Missouri. General Assembly. Committee on State Fiscal Affairs. 0092-4687. US. English. General Assembly, State Capitol, Room 132, Jefferson City MO 65101. **LC** JK5457.

STC . . . PERFORMANCE REVIEW. **Main/Corp** State Trading Corporation of India, Ltd. **VFOAT** S.T.C. . . . Performance Review. English. an. State Trading Corporation of India Ltd, Chandralok 36 Janpath, New Delhi 110001 India. **LC** HD4293. **DD** 354.5400826.

STUDY - GEORGIA. UNIVERSITY. BUREAU OF PUBLIC ADMINISTRATION. **Main/Corp** Georgia. University. Bureau of Public Administration. Vol. 1-10, 1952-57. 0433-5643. US. English. ir. University of Georgia, Bureau of Public Administration, Athens GA 30602. **LC** JA37.

SUMMARIES OF CONCLUSIONS AND RECOMMENDATIONS ON THE OPERATIONS OF CIVIL DEPARTMENTS AND AGENCIES. (SUMMARIES OF CONCLUSIONS AND RECOMMENDATIONS ON THE OPERATIONS OF CIVIL DEPARTMENTS AND AGENCIES : REPORT TO THE HOUSE AND SENATE COMMITTEES ON APPROPRIATIONS BY THE COMPTROLLER GENERAL OF THE UNITED STATES). **Main/Corp** United States. General Accounting Office. 0193-2926. US. English. an. US General Accounting Office, Information Handling and Support Facility, PO Box 6015, Gaithersburg MD 20877. **LC** JK671. **DD** 353.0405.

SUMMARY, ANNUAL MEETING - NATIONAL ASSOCIATION OF STATE BUDGET OFFICERS. (SUMMARY : ANNUAL MEETING - NATIONAL ASSOCIATION OF STATE BUDGET OFFICERS). **Main/Corp** National Association of State Budget Officers. 0360-3377. US. English. an. National Association of State Budget, PO Box 11910 Iron Works Pike, Lexington KY 40505. **LC** HJ2053.A1. **DD** 353.9372. *Resume of Annual Meeting.*

SUMMARY OF IPA PROJECTS IN RECRUITING, EXAMINING AND SELECTION. **Main/Corp** United States. Civil Service Commission. Bureau of Intergovernmental Personnel Programs. **VFOAT** IPA Projects in Recruiting, Examining and Selection. **VAT** Summary of Intergovernmental Personnel Act Projects in Recruiting, Examining and Selection. 1972. US. English. US Civil Service Commission, Bureau of Intergovernmental Personnel Programs, Personnel Management Information Service, 1900 E Street NW, Washington DC 20415.

SUMMARY OF PROCEEDINGS. ANNUAL MEETING OF THE SOUTHERN GOVERNORS' ASSOCIATION. (SUMMARY OF PROCEEDINGS : ANNUAL MEETING OF THE SOUTHERN GOVERNORS' ASSOCIATION). **Main/Corp** Southern Governors' Association (U.S.). Meeting. 0278-4815. US. English. an. Southern Governors' Association, Suite 610/3384 Peachtree Road NE, Atlanta GA 30326. **LC** JK2403. **DD** 353.975031306. *Summary of Proceedings.*

SUMMARY OF PROCEEDINGS, ANNUAL MEETING. SOUTHERN LEGISLATIVE CONFERENCE OF THE COUNCIL OF STATE GOVERNMENTS. (SUMMARY OF PROCEEDINGS . . . ANNUAL MEETING : SOUTHERN LEGISLATIVE CONFERENCE OF THE COUNCIL OF STATE GOVERNMENTS). **Main/Conf** Council of State Governments. Southern Legislative Conference. 0194-0368. Periodical. US. English. $4.00. Council of State Governments, 3384 Peachtree Road/Room 610, Atlanta GA 30326. **LC** HC107.A13. **DD** 338.975. *Record of Proceedings . . . Annual Meeting, Southern Legislative Conference of the Council of State Governments, 0743-0949.*

SUMMARY OF . . . REDUCTIONS IN LOCAL GOVERNMENT FISCAL ASSISTANCE. 1983-84-. Periodical. US. English. an. Assembly Publications Office, Box 90 State Capitol, Sacramento CA 95814. *Reductions in Local Government Fiscal Relief.*

SUMMARY OF SELECTED IPA PRODUCTS. **Main/Corp** United States. Civil Service Commission., Bureau of Intergovernmental Personnel Programs. **VFOAT** Selected IPA Products. **VAT** Summary of Selected Intergovernmental Personnel Act Products, Selected Intergovernmental Personnel Act Products. US. English. US Civil Service Commission, Bureau of Intergovernmental Personnel Programs, 1900 E Street NW, Washington DC 20415.

SUMMARY PROCEEDINGS OF THE ANNUAL CONFERENCE - FEDERATION OF CANADIAN MUNICIPALITIES. (SUMMARY PROCEEDINGS OF THE . . . ANNUAL CONFERENCE). **Main/Corp** Federation of Canadian Municipalities. Conference. **VAT** Summary Proceedings of the Annual Conference of the Federation of Canadian Municipalities. 43rd (June 8/ 11, 1980)-. 0710-5134. CN. English. an. Federation of Canadian Municipalities, 1318-112 Kent Street, Ottawa Ontario K1P 5P2 Canada. **DD** 352.071. *Proceedings of the Annual Conference, 0708-9511.*

SUMULA DE PARECERES. **Main/Corp** Brazil. Congresso. Senado. Subsecretaria de Comissoes. Portuguese. ir. **LC** JL2461.

SUPLEMENTO ESPECIAL AL BOLETIN OFICIAL CONTENIENDO LOS TEXTOS DEL SERVICIO DE LA PROTECCION DE LA PROPIEDAD INDUSTRIAL. **Main/Corp** Tangier (Morocco : Province). Service de la Protection de la Propriete Industrielle. **VFOAT** Boletin Oficial de la Propiedad Industrial. No. 15- April/June 1948-. Spanish. ir. **LC** J9.M65. **DD** 354.642. *Boletin Oficial Especial del Servicio de la Proteccion de la Propieded Industrial.*

SUPPLEMENT TO ORGANIZATION OF FEDERAL EXECUTIVE DEPARTMENTS AND AGENCIES. (SUPPLEMENT TO . . . ORGANIZATION OF FEDERAL EXECUTIVE DEPARTMENTS AND AGENCIES). Began with 1977. 0730-983X. US. English. an. **LC** JK646. **DD** 353.0405. Vols. for (1982-) distributed to some depository libraries in microfiche.

SURV-HULL. (SURV-HULL : PUBLICATION MENSUELLE DU SERVICE DE L'INFORMATION ET DES RELATIONS PUBLIQUES). Vol. 1, No. 3 (March 1982)-. 0823-6704. Periodical. CN. French. mo. Free. Ville de Hull Maison du Citoyen, C P 1970 Succursale B, Hull Quebec J8X 3Y9 Canada. **DD** 352.0714221.

A SURVEY OF FINANCIAL REPORTING AND ACCOUNTING DEVELOPMENTS IN THE PUBLIC UTILITY INDUSTRY. See Business - Accounting.

Public Administration

SURVEY OF GRANT-MAKING FOUNDATIONS WITH ASSETS OF OVER $1,000,000 OR GRANTS OF OVER $200,000. VAT Survey of Grant Making Foundations with Assets of Over One Million Dollars or Grants of Over Two Hundred Thousand Dollars. 0190-5163. US. English. Public Service Materials Center, 355 Lexington Avenue, New York NY 10017.

SURVEY OF INCOME OF CIVIL SERVICE ANNUITANTS. Main/Corp United States. Civil Service Commission. 0093-7150. US. English. Superintendent of Documents, US Government Printing Office, Washington DC 20402. LC JK791. DD 353.005.

THE SURVEY OF LOCAL RETIREMENT SYSTEMS : REPORT TO THE LEGISLATURE. See Economics - Labor.

SYSTEMISIERUNGSPLAN DER KRAFT-, LUFT- UND WASSERFAHRZEUGE DES BUNDES FUR DAS JAHR . . . . Main/Corp Austria. Bundesministerium fur Finanzen. Series/Titl Anlage Zum Bundesvorlanschlag fur das Jahr . . . . German. an. LC JN1941. DD 354.436007134.

TABLAS DE RETRIBUCIONES PARA FUNCIONARIOS DE ADMINISTRACION LOCAL. Spanish. ir. LC JS6314.A35. DD 352.0051230946.

THE TABLE. Main/Corp Society of Clerks-at-the-Table in Commonwealth Parliaments. V. 1- 1932-. UK. English. an. Society of Clerks Commonwealth, c/o J M Davies, House of Parliament, London SWI England. LC JN102. DD 328.1. Journal of the Society of Clerks-at-the-Table in Empire Parliaments.

TABLE DES DEBATS DU SENAT. TABLE NOMINATIVE. Main/Corp France. Parlement (1946-). Senta. Service des Archives. VFOAT Table des Debats du Senta. (Nominative). FR. French. ir. 17 Each Issue. Journaux Officiels, 26 rue Desaix, 75727 Paris Cedex 15 France. LC J341. DD 328.4402016.

TABLE OF GOVERNMENT ORDERS, COVERING THE GENERAL INSTRUMENTS. Main/Corp Great Britain. 1671-1966-. UK. English. an. H M Stationery Office, 49 High Holborn, London WC1V 6HB England.

TANG SHIH YEN CHIU TZU LIAO. Periodical. CH. Chinese. ir. 1.76. Ssu-Chuan Sheng Hsin Hua Shu Tien Cheng-Tu China. LC JQ1519.A5. DD 324.25107509.

TANG TI CHIAO YU. VFOAT Nung Tsun Pan, Dangde Jiaoyu. Periodical. English. mo. Ha-Ho-Hao-Te Shih Yu Chu. LC JQ1519.A5. DD 324.25107505.

TC MEMORANDUM DECISIONS. Main/Corp United States. Tax Court. Vol. 12 (1943)-. US. English. ir. Prentice Hall Inc, Route 9, Englewood Cliffs NJ 07632. Tel (201)592-2724. BTA-TC Memorandum Decisions.

TECHNICAL BULLETIN - INSTITUTE OF MUNICIPAL ASSESSORS OF ONTARIO. Main/Corp Institute of Municipal Assessors of Ontario. No. 1- 1965-. 0020-2991. Periodical. CN. English. Institute of Municipal Assessors of Ontario, 9 Clintwood Gate, Don Mills Ontario M3A 1M3 Canada. DD 352.131.

TECHNICAL REPORT - BUREAU OF GOVERNMENTAL RESEARCH, UNIVERSITY OF NEVADA. Main/Corp University of Nevada, Reno. Bureau of Governmental Research. No. 1- 1965-. 0548-3646. Periodical. US. English. ir. University of Nevada, Bureau of Governmental Research, Box 8037 University Station, Reno NV 89507. LC JK8501. DD 353.9.

T.E.L. THE ELECTRIC LETTER. (TEL, THE ELECTRIC LETTER). VFOAT Electric Letter. 1972. 0093-5379. Periodical. US. English. bw. $65.00. Electric Letter, Route 2 Box 238, Mt Vernon IL 62824. Tel (618)242-6549. Ed John Turrel. bk rev. adv acc. Circ 999. Electric utility marketing and communication.

TENNESSEE BLUE BOOK. 0364-5746. US. English. be. LC JK5230. DD 353.9768.

TENNOSEI KENKYU. Vol. 1-. Periodical. JA. Japanese. ir. JCS Shuppan, c/o Nitto Building, 42 Kanda JimboCho 1-chome, Chiyoda-ku Tokyo Japan. LC JQ1601.

TERRITORY OF NORFOLK ISLAND. Main/Corp Australia. Dept. of Territories. AT. English. ir. Commonwealth Government Printing Office, PO Box 84, Canberra ACT 2600 Australia. LC J905, HC607.N56. DD 309.1948.

TEXAS GOVERNMENT NEWSLETTER. 1973-. 0164-9221. Periodical. US. English. ir. $24.70. Texas Government Newsletter, PO Box 13274, Austin TX 78711. Tel (512)474-2110. Ed Thomas L Whatley. Circ 2,000. Objective review of Texas government and politics. Weekly analysis of single topic of general interest, plus summary of current events in Texas.

TEXAS PUBLIC UTILITY NEWS. (TEXAS PUBLIC UTILITY NEWS : A PUBLICATION OF RESEARCH & PLANNING CONSULTANTS, INC). 0744-7981. Periodical. US. English. bw. $300.00. Texas Public Utility News, 500 Southwest Tower, Austin TX 78701. Tel (512)472-7765. Ed Bonnie Sonnek. Circ 65. Covers public utility issues including gas, electric and water rates, civil and state court action and final orders by RRC and PUC. Patton Utility News, 0164-3355.

TEXAS REGISTER. Main/Corp Texas. Secretary of State. 0362-4781. Periodical. US. English. sw. $80.00. Secretary of State, PO Box 13824 Capitol Station, Austin TX 78711. Tel (512)475-7886. Ed Dave Harrell. LC KFT1236. DD 348.764025. Circ 4,500. Publishes regulations, open meetings, governor appointments. Attorney General opinions, and other general information submitted by state agencies.

TEXAS STATE DIRECTORY. See Yearbooks, Almanacs, Directories.

TEXAS TOWN & CITY. VFOAT Texas Town and City. V. 46- Jan. 1959-. 0040-473X. Periodical. US. English. mo. Texas Municipal League, 1020 Southwest Tower, Austin TX 78701. LC JS39. DD 352.0764. Texas Municipalities.

TEXTS ADOPTED BY THE ASSEMBLY. Main/Corp Council of Europe. Parliamentary Assembly. VFOAT Textes Adoptes par l'Assemblee. 26th Session, 2nd Pt.- Sept. 1974-. FR. Multilingual (English and French). ir. Manhattan Publishing Company, 80 Brook Street, Croton-on-Hudson NY 10520. LC JN22. DD 341.242. Texts Adopted.

TITLE LIST OF DOCUMENTS MADE PUBLICLY AVAILABLE. Vol. 1, No. 1 (Jan. 1979)-. US. English. mo. Superintendent of Documents, US Government Printing Office, Washington DC 20402. Tel (202)783-3238. U.S. Nuclear Regulatory Commission Publications.

TITLE XX COMPREHENSIVE ANNUAL SERVICES PROGRAM FOR THE STATE OF LOUISIANA. VFOAT Title Twenty Comprehensive Annual Services Program for the State of Louisiana. US. English. an. $2.50. Department of Health and Human Resources, Office of Human Development, PO Box 44367, Baton Rouge LA 70804. Tel (504)342-2297. LC HV98.L7. DD 361.609763. Circ 325. This is the state's plan and application for social services Block Grant Funds. Comprehensive Annual Services Program Plan for Social Services under Title XX.

TITLES AND CONTENTS TO THE PARLIAMENTARY PAPERS (HOUSE OF COMMONS AND COMMAND). See Bibliographies.

TOKYO MUNICIPAL NEWS. V. 1- Mar. 1951-. 0040-893X. Periodical. JA. English. qt. Free. Tokyo Metropolitan Government, 5-1 Marunochi 3-Chome, Chiyoda-Ku Tokyo Japan. Tel (03)212-6033. Ind/Abst Public Aff. Inf. Serv. Bull. LC DS896. (ctrl). To introduce the administration of the Tokyo Metropolitan Government in the wide-ranging aspects of the people's life.

TOKYO TOGIKAI GIIN SENKYO NO KIROKU. Main/Corp Tokyo. Senkyo Kanri Iinkai. JA. Japanese. ir. Senkyo Kanri Iinkai, 13 Yurakucho 2-Chome Chiyoda-Ku, Tokyo Japan. LC JS7385.T63.

TOPICS (WASHINGTON, D.C.). (TOPICS). 0145-1375. Periodical. US. English. qt. Office of Public and Congressional Affairs, Overseas Private Investment Corporation, 1129 20th Street NW, Washington DC 20527. Ind/Abst Index U.S. Gov. Period.

TOSEI. Main/Corp Tokyo. 1973-. JA. Japanese. ir. Tokyo-To Kohoshitsu 5-1, Marunouch 3, Chiyoda-Ku, Tokyo Japan. LC JS7385.T6. Tokyo Tosei Gaiyo.

TOWARD CLOSER TIES. VFOAT University of Maryland Public Service Directory. 1981-. 0882-9012. US. English. be. $4.00. Office of Public Service, Institute for Governmental Service, Suite 2101/Woods Hall, The University of Maryland, College Park MD 20742.

TOWN & COUNTRY PLANNING. (TOWN & COUNTRY PLANNING : THE JOURNAL OF THE TOWN & COUNTRY PLANNING ASSOCIATION). Vol. 38, No. 7 (July/Aug. 1970)-. 0040-9960. Periodical. UK. English. $76.63. Town & Country Planning, 17 Carlton House Terrace, London SW1Y 5AS England. Tel 01 930 8903. Ed David Boyle. Ind/Abst Archit. Period. Index, Art Index, Ref. Source, Life Sci. Collect. bk rev. adv acc. Circ 4,000. The magazine of the Town and Country Planning Association concerned with planning and the environment worldwide. Town and Country Planning, 0040-9960.

TOWN AND DISTRICT COUNCILS ESTIMATES OF REVENUE AND EXPENDITURE. See Business - Public Finance.

TRAIT D'UNION. V. 1- Aug. 1977-. 0225-2627. Periodical. CN. French. Commission de la Fonction Publique du Canada, Direction Generale de la Formation Linguistique, Ottawa Ontario K1A 0M7 Canada. DD 354.71001505.

TRAIT D'UNION. (LE TRAIT D'UNION : BULLETIN MUNICIPAL DE ROUYN). Main/Corp Rouyn (Quebec). Vol. 1, No. 1 (Oct. 82)-. 0820-7720. Periodical. CN. French. Free. Ville de Rouyn, C P 220, Quebec J9X 5C3 Canada. Tel (819)762-1741. DD 352.0714212. Circ 7,500. (ctrl). Municipal information: bylaw, municipal finance, investment (public and private), urbanism.

TRAKTANDUM. V. 1, No. 1 (Dec. 1,1981)-. German. ir. 160.00. Verlag Steiner und Gruninger, AG Haus Zum Adler, 8226 Schleitheim Germany. LC JS6401. DD 352.0494.

TRANSITIONS (CINCINNATI, OHIO). See Transportation.

TRANSLATION - BUREAU OF RECLAMATION. Main/Corp United States. Bureau of Reclamation. Monographic Series. English. ir.

TRAVAUX. See Sanitation, Environmental Technology.

TRIENNIAL ASSESSMENT OF THE TENNESSEE VALLEY AUTHORITY. Main/Corp United States. General Accounting Office. Fiscal years 1977-1979-. 0272-2623. US. English. te. US General Accounting Office, Document Handling and Information Services Facility, PO Box 6015, Gaithersburg MD 20760. LC HN79.A135. DD 353.0082309768. Vols. for 1977/1979- distributed to depository libraries in microfiche. Examination of Financial Statements, Tennessee Valley Authority, 0565-5803.

TRL ANALYZES DEVELOPMENTS IN TEXAS STATE AND LOCAL GOVERNMENT. Main/Corp Texas Research League. VAT Texas Research League Analyzes Developments in Texas State and Local Government. Periodical. US. English. ir. PO Box 12456, Austin TX 78711.

TURKISH PUBLIC ADMINISTRATION ANNUAL. No. 1- 1974-. 0251-2955. TU. English. ir. 1 No.1u Cadde Yucetepe, Ankara Turkey. Ind/Abst Int. Labour Doc. LC JQ1801.A1. DD 354.5610005.

TYPICAL ELECTRIC BILLS. 1978-. US. English. an. US Government Printinf Office, Superintendent of Documents, Washington DC 20402. Typical Electric Bills.

UGYVITEL ES INFORMACIO AZ ALLAMIGAZGATASBAN. 0302-9778. Periodical. Hungarian. ir. Lapkiado Vallalat, 1906 Budapest PF 223 VII Lenin Korut 9-11, Budapest Hungary. Ind/Abst Comput. Control Abstr., Electr. Electron. Abstr., Sci. Abstr. Sect. A. Phys. Abstr. LC JF1525.A8. CODEN UIALD8.

UNDZER SHTIME. VFOAT Our Voice. Periodical. IS. Yiddish. mo. AKI, POB 12133, Tel-Aviv 61121 Israel. LC JQ1825.P3.

THE UNITED KINGDOM, THE COMMONWEALTH OF NATIONS, A DIRECTORY OF GOVERNMENTS. See Yearbooks, Almanacs, Directories.

UNITED NATIONS PUBLICATIONS. Main/Corp United Nations. Department of Public Information. US. English. United Nations Publications, Sales Section/Room A-3315, New York NY 10017.

UNITED STATES CODE CONGRESSIONAL AND ADMINISTRATIVE NEWS. VFOAT U.S. Code Congressional & Administrative News. 1951-. Periodical. US. English. sm. West Publishing

Public Administration

Company, 50 West Kellogg Boulevard PO Box 3526, St Paul MN 55165. *United States Code Congressional Service.*

THE U.S. CONGRESS HANDBOOK. VFOAT Congress Handbook. VAT United States Congress Handbook. 1st- 1974-. 0196-7614. US. English. an. $6.95. Congress Handbook, PO Box 566, McLean VA 22101. Tel (703)356-3572. Ed Barbara Pullen. LC JK1012. DD 328.730025. adv acc. Circ 100,000. Features how congress is organized and operates with members pictures, biographies, addresses, telephone numbers, committee assignments key staff aides listed alphabetically and by state and much more.

U.S. CONGRESSMAN JACK BRINKLEY REPORTS FROM WASHINGTON. VFOAT Jack Brinkley Reports from Washington. 0735-6021. Periodical. US. English. 2470 Rayburn House Office Building, Washington DC 20515.

U.S. DEPARTMENT OF ENERGY BUDGET TO CONGRESS : BUDGET HIGHLIGHTS. Main/Corp United States. Dept. of Energy. VFOAT Budget Highlights. VAT United States Department of Energy Budget to Congress: Budget Highlights. 0193-1040. US. English. an. US Department of Energy, Washington DC 20402. LC HD9502.U5. DD 353.87.

UNITED STATES DIRECTORY OF FEDERAL REGIONAL STRUCTURE. *See* Yearbooks, Almanacs, Directories.

UNITED STATES GOVERNMENT ANNUAL REPORT. VFOAT Annual Report of the United States Government for the Fiscal Year Ended September 30 . . . . 1984-. US. English. an. Financial Management Service, Financial Reporting Division, Budget Reports Branch, Treasury Annex No. 1, Attn GAO Building/Room 1415, Washington DC 20226. *Treasury Combined Statement of Receipts, Expenditures, and Balances of the United States Government for the Fiscal Year Ended . . .*, 0191-2062.

UNITED STATES GOVERNMENT DIRECTORY. *See* Yearbooks, Almanacs, Directories.

UNITED STATES GOVERNMENT GRANTS UNDER THE FULBRIGHT-HAYS ACT. UNIVERSITY LECTURING, ADVANCED RESEARCH. (UNITED STATES GOVERNMENT GRANTS UNDER THE FULBRIGHT-HAYS ACT : UNIVERSITY LECTURING, ADVANCED RESEARCH). Main/Corp Conference Board of the Associated Research Councils. Committee on International Exchange of Persons. 0362-6792. US. English. Committee on International Exchange of Persons, 2101 Constitution Avenue NW, Washington DC 20418.

U.S. GOVERNMENT OFFICES IN CALIFORNIA : A DIRECTORY. *See* Yearbooks, Almanacs, Directories.

UNITED STATES NUCLEAR REGULATORY COMMISSION STAFF PRACTICE AND PROCEDURE DIGEST. Main/Corp U.S. Nuclear Regulatory Commission. Office of the Executive Legal Director. Began with Dec. 1977. Periodical. US. English. qt. $40.00. National Technical Information Service, 5285 Port Royal Road, Springfield VA 22161. Tel (703)487-4650.

UNIVERSITY STUDIES IN PUBLIC ADMINISTRATION. II. English. ir. University of Rajasthan, Department of Public Administration, Jaipur 4 India. LC JF1338.U54. DD 350.000711544.

UNPUBLISHED HOUSE OF COMMONS SESSIONAL PAPERS. Main/Corp Canada. Parliament. House of Commons. VFOAT Unpublished Sessional Papers. 12th Parliament, 6th Session (12 Jan. 1916/18 May 1916)-. CN. English (French). Micromedia Limited, 144 Front Street West, Toronto Ontario M5J 1G2 Canada. DD 328.7107205. *Poincare. Section A. Physique Theorique, 0030-2339.*

UPDATE. 76-1- Oct. 29, 1976-. 0276-8909. Periodical. US. English. wk. US Department of the Interior, Office of Public Affairs/Room 7224, Washington DC 20240.

UPDATE - PROVINCE OF BRITISH COLUMBIA. MINISTRY OF FORESTS. (UPDATE). Main/Corp British Columbia. Ministry of Forests. 0713-7141. Periodical. CN. English. ir. Province of British Columbia, 1450 Government Street, Information Service, Victoria British Columbia V8W 3E7 Canada. DD 354.7110682338.

URBA. V. 1- Dec. 1979-. 0709-9444. Periodical. CN. French. bm. Free. Union des Municipalites du Quebec, 992 Est rue de Liege, Montreal Quebec H2P 1L1. DD 352.0714. (ctrl).

URBAN AFFAIRS ABSTRACTS. *See* Indexes/Abstracts.

URBAN DATA SERVICE REPORT. V. 1- Jan. 1969-. 0049-5654. Monographic Series. US. English. mo. $100.00. International City Management Association, 1140 Connecticut Avenue Northwest, Washington DC 20036.

URBAN FOCUS CEASED. V. 1-12, No. 5. 0315-0143. Periodical. CN. English. qt.

URBAN GEORGIA. 0042-0875. Periodical. US. English. ir. $10.00. Georgia Municipal Association, 34 Peachtree Street NW/Suite 2300, Atlanta GA 30303. Tel (404)488-0472. LC JS39. DD 352.00809758. *Georgia Municipal Journal.*

URBAN INNOVATION ABROAD. V.1- Nov. 1977-. 0163-6499. Periodical. US. English. mo. $116.00. Council for International Urban Liaison, 444 North Capitol Street/Suite 349, Washington DC 20001. Tel (202)638-1445. Ed George G Wynne. bk rev. Circ 5,000. News service promoting the international exchange of practical solutions to common problems at the state, county and city levels of government.

URBAN OUTLOOK. Vol. 4, No. 10 (May 4, 1982)-. 0732-8265. Periodical. US. English. sm. $117.00. Alexander Research & Communications Inc, 1133 Broadway/Suite 1407, New York NY 10010. Tel (212)206-7979. Ed Laurence A Alexander. bk rev. News, ideas and trends affecting urban areas emphasizing practical solutions in the actionable future. *Urban Planning Reports, Urban Futures Idea Exchange, 0147-7137.*

UTAH INFORMATION PRACTICES ACT, AS PASSED BY THE 1975 UTAH LEGISLATURE. REPORT TO THE GOVERNOR AND THE LEGISLATURE OF THE STATE OF UTAH BY LIEUTENANT GOVERNOR-SECRETARY OF STATE. (UTAH INFORMATION PRACTICES ACT, AS PASSED BY THE 1975 UTAH LEGISLATURE : REPORT TO THE GOVERNOR AND THE LEGISLATURE OF THE STATE OF UTAH BY LIEUTENANT GOVERNOR/SECRETARY OF STATE). Main/Corp Utah. Secretary of State. 1st- 1975-. 0363-9703. US. English. an. LC JK8449.R. DD 353.97920081.

UTILITY INVESTMENT STATISTICS, UTILITY APPROPRIATIONS. *See* Statistics.

VACHER'S PARLIAMENTARY COMPANION. VFOAT Parliamentary Companion. Began in 1832. UK. English. qt. Leeder House, Erskine Road, London NW3 3AJ England. LC JN500.

VALTIOLLISET VAALIT : TASAVALLAN PRESIDENTIN VALITSIJAMIESTEN VAALIT = STATLIGA VAL : VAL AV ELEKTORER FOR VALET AV REPUBLIKENS PRESIDENT. *See* Statistics.

VALTION TILASTOJULKAISUT. STATENS STATISTISKA PUBLIKATIONER. GOVERNMENT STATISTICS. *See* Statistics.

VALTION VIRALLISJULKAISUT. PUBLICATIONS IN FINLAND. Main/Corp Finland. Eduskunta. Kirjasto. VFOAT Statens Officiella Publikationer, Government Publications in Finland. Fl. Finnish (English and Swedish). an. $6.41. Akakeeminen-Kirjakuppa, PO Box 128, 00101 Helsinki Finland.

VALTION VIRKAMIESTEN PALKAT MARRASKUUSSA. Main/Corp Finland. Tilastokeskus. Finnish. ir. 3.00. Tilastokeskus, Annankatu 44 00100 10, Helsinki Finland. LC JN6712.Z2.

VALUE OF PUBLIC UTILITY REAL AND PERSONAL PROPERTY, BY COUNTY. (VALUE OF PUBLIC UTILITY REAL AND PERSONAL PROPERTY BY COUNTY). Main/Corp Ohio. Dept. of Taxation. 0147-6971. US. English. an. Department of Taxation, Research and Statistics Section, PO Box 530, Columbus OH 43216. LC HD2765. DD 333.336.

VARSHIKA VITTIYA VIVARANA. Main/Corp Rajasthan State Electricity Board. VFOAT Annual Financial Statement : Budget Estimates. English (Hindi). ir. LC HD9685.I43. DD 354.544008722.

VEHICLE REGISTRATION AND MOTOR FUEL TAXES. AMOUNTS DISTRIBUTED TO LOCAL GOVERNMENTS, BY COUNTY. (VEHICLE REGISTRATION AND MOTOR FUEL TAXES, AMOUNTS DISTRIBUTED TO LOCAL GOVERNMENTS, BY COUNTY). Main/Corp Ohio. Dept. of Taxation. 8669-0303. US. English. PO Box 530, Columbus OH 43216.

VERBATIM REPORT, . . . CANADIAN REGIONAL CONFERENCE - COMMONWEALTH PARLIAMENTARY ASSOCIATION. (VERBATIM REPORT, . . . CANADIAN REGIONAL CONFERENCE). Main/Corp Commonwealth Parliamentary Association. Canadian Regional Conference. VFOAT Proces-Verbal, . . . Conference Regionale Canadienne. 21st (Aug. 2/7, 1981)-. 0826-1970. CN. English (includes some text in French). an. Commonwealth Parliamentary Association, Canadian Region, PO Box 950, House of Parliament, Ottawa Ontario K1A 0A6 Canada. DD 828.30971. *Commonwealth Parliamentary Association, Annual Canadian Regional Conference, 0383-6630.*

VERSLAG VAN DIE KOMITEE OOR DIE REGLEMENT VAN ORDE. Main/Corp South Africa. Parliament. House of Assembly. Committee on Standing Rules and Orders. VFOAT Report of the Committee on Standing Rules and Orders. SA. Afrikaans (English). ir. 0.60. House of Assembly, The Government Printer, Private Bag X85 Pretoria 0001 South Africa. LC JQ1964.

VERSLAG VAN DIE OUDITEUR-GENERAAL OOR DIE REKENINGS VAN DIE ADMINISTRASIERAAD, SENTRAAL-TRANSVAALGEBIED. Main/Corp South Africa. Control and Audit Office. VFOAT Report of the Auditor-General on the Accounts of the Central Transvaal Area Administration Board. SA. Afrikaans (English). ir. 2.70. Controller and Auditor-General, Government Printer, Private Bag X85, Pretoria 0001 South Africa. LC JS7624.A13.

VERSLAG VAN DIE OUDITEUR-GENERAAL OOR DIE REKENINGS VAN DIE OLIESADEBEHEERRAAD. Main/Corp South Africa. Control and Audit Office. VFOAT Report of the Auditor-General on the Accounts of the Oilseeds Control Board. SA. Afrikaans (English). ir. 2.95. Government Printer, Bosman St Private Bag X85, Pretoria 0001 South Africa. LC HD9490.S6. DD 354.68007232.

VERSLAG VAN DIE OUDITEUR-GENERAAL OOR DIE REKENINGS VAN DIE SYBOKHAARRAAD. Main/Corp South Africa. Controller and Auditor-General. VFOAT Report of the Auditor-General on the Accounts of the Mohair Board. 1975/76-. SA. Afrikaans (English). ir. Government Printer, Bosman Street, Private Bag X85, Pretoria 0001 South Africa. LC HD9907.S6. DD 354.68007232. *Report of the Controller and Auditor-General on the Accounts of the Mohair Board.*

VERZEICHNIS DES DIPLOMATISCHEN KORPS UND ANDERER VERTRETUNGEN IN OSTERREICH. German. ir. LC JX1791. DD 351.89209436.

VICTORIA GOVERNMENT GAZETTE. AT. English. wk. 107.00. Victorian Government Printing Office, 66-112 Macaulay Road, North Melbourne 3051 Victoria Australia. Tel (03)3200100. LC J8. Circ 1,700. (ctrl).

VIDESA MANTRALAYA KI ANUDANOM KI MANGEM. Main/Corp India (Republic). Ministry of External Affairs. VFOAT Demands for Grants of Ministry of External Affairs. English and Hindi. ir. Ministry of External Affairs, Minto Road, New Delhi India. LC JQ250.I48. *Demands for Grants.*

VIE MUNICIPALE. 0713-6846. Periodical. CN. French. ir. Free. Vie Municipale, Ville de Becancour, Hotel de Ville, 1295 Nicolas Perrot, Becancour

Public Administration

Quebec G0X 1B0 Canada. **DD** 352.071455. (ctrl). *Becancour.*

VIE MUNICIPALE A JONQUIERE. (LA VIE MUNICIPALE A JONQUIERE). **Main/Corp** Jonquiere (Quebec). Mar. 1978-. 0712-3248. **CN.** French. an. Free. Service d'Information de Ville de Jonquiere, CP 2000, Jonquiere Quebec G7X 7W7 Canada. **DD** 352.071416.

VIEW FROM SPRINGFIELD. 0277-4844. Periodical. US. English. wk. $60.00. Commerce Clearing House Inc, 4025 West Peterson Avenue, Chicago IL 60646. **Tel** (217)523-6422. Ed Joseph L Harris. Features news about hearings, investigations, appointments, Governor's actions, Supreme Court and Attorney General opinions and political developments in Illinois.

VIRGINIA MUNICIPAL REVIEW CEASED. Began in Jan. 1924. Ceased with V. 59, No. 8, (Aug. 1981). 0042-6660. Periodical. US. English. mo. **LC** JS39. **DD** 352.0755.

VIRGINIA REVIEW. Vol. 59, No. 9 (Sept./Oct. 1981)-. 0732-9156. Periodical. US. English. bm. $7.00. County Publications, 1601 Pinebark Road, Chester VA 23831. **Tel** (847)748-4467. Ed Wanda N Norton. **LC** JS39. **DD** 352.0755. adv acc. **Circ** 2,000. (ctrl). *Virginia Municipal Review, 0042-6660.*

VIRGINIA STATE GOVERNMENT REPORT. US. English. be. Department of Planning and Budget, Room 443/Ninth Street, Office Building, Richmond VA 23219. **LC** JK3930. **DD** 353.9755000202.

VIRGINIA TOWN & CITY. **VAT** Virginia Town and City. V. 1- Jan. 1966-. 0042-6784. Periodical. US. English. mo. $8.00. Virginia Municipal League, PO Box 12203, Richmond VA 23241. **Tel** (804)649-8471. Ed Christine A Everson. **LC** JS39. adv acc. **Circ** 4,500. (ctrl). Articles addressing local government issues, management, and activities of the Virginia Municipal League.

VOIX DE L'A.M.S.A. (LA VOIX DE L'A.M.S.A). **VAT** Voix de l'Alliance Municipale de Sainte-Adele. V. 1, No. 1 (Jan. 1978)-. 0704-7770. Periodical. CN. French. bm. Free. Alliance Municipale de Ste-Adele, CP 1166, Ste-Adele Quebec J0R 1L0 Canada. **DD** 352.071424.

VOLITVE. **Main/Corp** Zavod sr Slovenije za Statistiko. 1974-. YU. Slovenian. ir. Zavod sr Slovenije za Statistiko, Vozarski Pot 12, Ljubljana Yugoslavia. **LC** JN9679.S6. *Volitve v Predstavniska Telesa.*

VOPROSY ISTORII KPSS. NEKOTORYE VOPROSY ORGANIZATORSKOI I IDEOLOGICHESKOI DEIATELNOSTI KPSS, NA MATERIALAKH BELORUSSKOI SSR. UR. Russian. UI Kirova 24, Minsk Russia. **LC** JN6598.K86.

VOS AFFAIRES MUNICIPALES. 0713-6714. Periodical. CN. French. ir. Free. Vos Affaires Municipales, Hotel de Ville, CP 489, Thetford-Mines Quebec G6G 5T3 Canada. **DD** 352.0714575. (ctrl).

VOTES AND PROCEEDINGS. (VOTES AND PROCEEDINGS - HOUSE OF COMMONS). **Main/Corp** Canada. Parliament. House of Commons. **VFOAT** Proces-Verbaux - Chambre des Communes. 0384-224X. Periodical. CN. English (text also in French, Oct. 12, 1976-). da. 32.00 Domestic, 38.40 Foreign. Receiver General of Canada, Supply & Services, Ottawa Ontario K1A 0S9 Canada. *Proces-Verbaux de la Chambre des Communes du Canada, 0384-2223.*

VOTES AND PROCEEDINGS OF THE HOUSE OF REPRESENTATIVES. **Main/Corp** Australia. Parliament. House of Representatives. 1967-68- — 26th Parliament-. AT. English. ir. $14.02. Australian Government Printing Office, PO Box 84, Canberra Australian Capital Territory 2600 Australia. **Tel** 062-95 4411. *Records of the Proceedings and Printed Paper.*

V.R.A. BULLETIN BOARD. (VRA BULLETIN BOARD). **Main/Corp** United States. Dept. of Health, Education, and Welfare. Vocational Rehabilitation Administration. 0090-4465. US. English. mo. US Department of Health Education & Welfare, Vocational Rehabilitation Administration, 330 Independence Avenue, Washington DC 20201. **LC** HD7256U5. **DD** 362.85. *OVR Bulletin Board.*

W-MEMO. 0163-8300. Periodical. US. English. ir. $50.00. American Public Welfare Association, 1125 15th Street Northwest/Suite 300, Washington DC 20005. **Tel** (202)293-7550. Ed David Racine. **Circ** 800. Up-to-minute detailed information and analysis of agency action affecting human service programs.

WAS UND WIE. No. 1- 1973-. German. ir. 0.30 Single Issue. AM Marx-Engels-Platz 102, Berlin East Germany. **LC** JN3971.5.A98.

WASHINGTON ACTION REPORTER. 0195-5233. Periodical. US. English. mo. Vets of Foreign Wars, 200 Maryland Avenue NE, Washington DC 20002.

WASHINGTON INFORMATION WORKBOOK. 1978-. 0192-8848. US. English. ir. Washington Researchers, 2612 P Street NW, Washington DC 20007. **Tel** (202)333-3499. **LC** JK404. **DD** 353.00025. **NLM** JK 404 W319.

WASHINGTON LETTER (JOINT MARITIME CONGRESS). (WASHINGTON LETTER). **VFOAT** Joint Maritime Congress Washington Letter. Began publication with Vol. 1 in 1979. Periodical. US. English. wk. Joint Maritime Congress Washington Letter, 444 North Capitol Street Suite 801, Washington DC 20001.

WASHINGTON MUNICIPAL SALARIES AND FRINGE BENEFITS. See Economics - Labor.

WASHINGTON REPORT - INTERSTATE CONFERENCE ON WATER PROBLEMS. (WASHINGTON REPORT). 0737-3503. Periodical. US. English. ICWP, 1919 Pennsylvania Avenue NW/Suite 300, Washington DC 20005.

WASHINGTON SOCIAL LEGISLATION BULLETIN. **VFOAT** Social Legislation Bulletin. V. 24, Issue 33- May 1976-. 0149-2578. Periodical. US. English. sm. Social Legislation Information Service, 1346 Connecticut Avenue NW, Washington DC 20036. **NLM** W1 WA639. *Washington Bulletin.*

WASHINGTON STATE. V. 1- Oct. 1973-. 0092-380X. US. English. Office of Program Planning & Fiscal Management/Information Services Division, House Office Building, Olympia WA 98504. **Ind/Abst** Public Aff. Inf. Serv. Bull. **LC** JK9230. **DD** 353.9797.

WASHINGTON STATE REGISTER. 78-01-—. 0164-6389. US. English. sm. $140.00. Washington State Register/Code Revisers Office/Legislative Building, Olympia WA 98504. **Tel** (206)753-6804. Full text of proposed, emergency and permanent rules of state agencies, and other state government information. Cumulative tables and index. *Washington Administrative Code Bulletin.*

WASHINGTON STATE YEARBOOK. See Yearbooks, Almanacs, Directories.

WATER JOURNAL. See Water Resources.

WAYS & MEANS. **VAT** Ways and Means. 0193-4716. Periodical. US. English. bm. $20.00. Ways & Means Conference on Alternative State and Local Public Policies, 1901 Q Street Northwest, Washington DC 20009.

WEEK-IN-REVIEW. (THE WEEK-IN-REVIEW). **VFOAT** Information. 0226-160X. Periodical. CN. English. wk. Free. New Brunswick Information Service, PO Box 6000, Mrs Janet Amirault, Fredericton New Brunswick E3B 5H1 Canada. **DD** 354.7150005.

WEEKLY CHECKLIST OF CANADIAN GOVERNMENT PUBLICATIONS. Nov. 17, 1978-. 0706-4659. Periodical. CN. English (French). wk. 62.40. Receiver General for Canada, Supply & Services, Ottawa Ontario K1A 0S9 Canada. *Daily Checklist of Canadian Government Publications, 0700-2904.*

WEEKLY FEDERAL EMPLOYEES' NEWS DIGEST. **VFOAT** Federal Employees' News Digest. V. 1- Aug. 10, 1951-. 0430-1692. Periodical. US. English. ir. $32.00. Federal Employees News Digest, PO Box 7528/510 North Washington Street/Suite 200, Falls Church VA 22046. **Tel** (703)533-3031. Ed Joseph Young. **LC** HD8008.A1. **Circ** 36,000. Weekly reporting of legislation and news from departments and agencies which have a bearing on benefits and working conditions of government employees.

WEST VIRGINIA BLUE BOOK. V. 1- 1916-. 0364-7323. US. English. an. West Virginia Blue Book, c/o Clerk of Senate, State Capital Charleston WV 25305. **Tel** (304)357-7800. Ed Todd C Willis. **LC** JK4031. **DD** 353.9754. **Circ** 20,000. (ctrl). General information and statistics on federal state and local government in West Virginia.

WEST VIRGINIA CIVIL SERVICE SYSTEM; ANNUAL REPORT. 1st- 1961/62-. US. English. an. **LC** JK4055.

WEST VIRGINIA MEMBERSHIP IN INTERSTATE COMPACTS. **Main/Corp** West Virginia. Legislative Services. US. English. an. Legislative Services, E-132 State Capitol, Charleston WV 25405. **LC** KFW1610.I6. **DD** 353.929109754.

WESTCHESTER PLANNING. V. 1- Summer 1973-. 0363-356X. Periodical. US. English. qt. Westchester County Department of Planning, 910 County Office Building, White Plains NY 10601.

WESTERN CITY (LEAGUE OF CALIFORNIA CITIES : 1976). (WESTERN CITY). Vol. 52, No. 9 (Sept. 1976)-. 0279-5337. Periodical. US. English. mo. $15.00. League of California Cities, 1400 K Street, Sacramento CA 95814. **Tel** (916)444-8960. Ed Victoria Clark. **Ind/Abst** Am. Hist. Life, Hist. Abstr., Part A, Mod. Hist. Abstr., Hist. Abst., Part B, Twent. Century Abstr., Hist. Abstr. **LC** TD1. **DD** 363.0978. adv acc. **Circ** 9,300. (ctrl). A magazine to keep California city leaders up to date on theoretical and practical developments in city administration. *Western City Magazine, 0043-356X.*

THE WESTERN PLANNER. Vol. 1, No. 1 (Jan.-Feb. 1980). 0279-0602. Periodical. US. English. mo. $30.00. Western Planner, 201 Isle Hall/EWLL, Cheney WA 99004. **Tel** (509)359-2288. Ed Stan Steadman. bk rev. adv acc. **Circ** 1,400. (ctrl). A journal of information and ideas for community planners, their boards and constituents, and the elected officials they serve.

THE WHITE HOUSE FELLOWSHIPS. **Main/Corp** President's Commission on White House Fellowships (U.S.). Began with 1975/76. 0149-2837. US. English. an. US President's Commission on White House Fellowships, Washington DC 20415. *White House Fellows.*

WHITE LIST OF CUSTOMS OFFICERS IN CANADA. (THE WHITE LIST OF CUSTOMS OFFICERS IN CANADA). 1976-. 0703-5926. CN. English. an. Canadian Importers Association Inc, Suite 602/2180 Yonge Street, Toronto Ontario M4S 2B9 Canada. **DD** 354.71007246002571.

WHO'S WHAT IN FLORIDA GOVERNMENT. US. English. an. Florida Chamber of Commerce, PO Box 11309, Tallahassee FL 32302.

WHO'S WHO IN FEDERAL GOVERNMENT PRIME CONTRACTORS. See Biographies.

WISCONSIN ADMINISTRATIVE CODE. **Main/Corp** Wisconsin. US. English. ir. $340.00. Document Sales & Distribution, 202 South Thornton Avenue, Department Administration, Madison WI 53702. **Tel** (608)266-6938.

THE WISCONSIN BLUE BOOK. **VFOAT** State of Wisconsin Blue Book. 1862-. US. English. Wisconsin Department of Administrative Document Sales, 202 South Thornton Avenue, Madison WI 53702. **Tel** (608)266-3358. **LC** JK6031.

WISCONSIN COUNTIES. V. 1- July 1938-. 0749-6818. Periodical. US. English. mo. $12.00. Wisconsin Counties Association, 802 West Broadway Suite 308, Madison WI 53713-1897. **Tel** (608)266-6480. Ed Mark M Rogacki. adv acc. **Circ** 3,500. (ctrl). Mainly serves county elected officials. Topics covered include: insurance, roads, job training, economic development, law enforcement, legislative action and laws affecting counties.

WISCONSIN MUNICIPALITIES OVER 2,500 EMPLOYEE WAGE AND BENEFIT SURVEY . . . INCLUDING SELECTED TOWNS. See Economics - Labor.

WYOMING OFFICIAL DIRECTORY. 1976-. 0146-700X. US. English. an. $3.50. Secretary of State of Wyoming, State Capital Building, Cheyenne WY 82002. **Tel** (307)777-7378. **LC** JK7630. **DD** 353.9787002. **Circ** 6,000. Listing of all Wyoming state and county officials, including all state boards and commissions and their members.

YEAR BOOK - ASSOCIATION OF COUNTY COUNCILS. See Yearbooks, Almanacs, Directories.

YEN KAO YUEH KAN. Periodical. CH. Chinese. mo. $300.00. Yu Ying She, 63 Chung-Ching South Road., Sec 1, Tai-Pei Shih Taiwan. **LC** JQ1521.A1. **DD** 354.512490005.

Public Health and Safety

YOJANA. V. 1- 1957-. 0044-0515. Periodical. II. English. bw. $29.47. Ministry of Information Broadcasting, Government of India, Patiala House, New Delhi 110 001 India. LC DS401.

ZEITSCHRIFT FUR AUSLANDISCHES OFFENTLICHES RECHT UND VOLKERRECHT. See Law - International Law.

ZEITSCHRIFT FUR PARLAMENTSFRAGEN. Vol. 1-. 0340-1758. Periodical. GW. German. qt. $22.24. Westdeutscher Verlag GMBH, Postfach 5829, D6200 Wiesbaden 1 West Germany. Ind/Abst Energy Res. Abstr. LC JN3971.A7.

ZENJINREN NINYO BUKAI KENKYU KEKKA HOKOKUSHO. Main/Corp Zenkoku Jinji Iinkai Rengokai. Ninyo Bukai. VAT Zenkoku Jinji Iinkai Rengokai Ninyo Bukai Kenkyu Hokokusho. Japanese. ir. LC JQ1649.A6.

ZENKOKU CHIHO KOKYO DANTAI KODO. Japanese. ir. LC JS7373.A6.

ZONES PETROLIFERES ET GAZIFERES AU LARGE DES COTES. 0228-4995. Periodical. CN. French. sa. Ministere de l'Energie des Mines et des Ressources, 580 Booth Street, Ottawa Ontario K1A 0E4 Canada. DD 354.710082388046. Permis d'Exploration du Petrole et du Gaz au Large des Cotes, 0228-4987.

ZPRAVA O SPOLECNE SCHUZI SNEMOVNY LIDU A SNEMOVNY NARODU. Main/Corp Czechoslovakia. Federalni Shromazdeni. 1. Volebni Obdobi, 6. Schuze (20. A 21. Pros. 1970)-. Czech. ir. Kancel AR Federalniho Shromazdeni, Vinohradska 1, 110 02 Praha Czechoslovakia. LC J338. Tesnopisecka Zprava o Spolecne Schuzi Snemovny Lidu a Snemovny Narodu.

PUBLIC HEALTH AND SAFETY

ABSTRACTS & REVIEWS IN ALCOHOL & DRIVING. See Indexes/Abstracts.

ABSTRACTS OF CONTRIBUTED PAPERS - MEDICAL CARE SECTION. See Indexes/Abstracts.

ABSTRACTS OF RESEARCH PAPERS. See Indexes/Abstracts.

ABSTRACTS ON HYGIENE. See Indexes/Abstracts.

ABSTRACTS ON HYGIENE AND COMMUNICABLE DISEASES. See Indexes/Abstracts.

ACCELERATION AND PASSING ABILITY. See Transportation.

ACCIDENT ANALYSIS AND PREVENTION. V. 1- July 1969-. 0001-4575. Periodical. UK. English. bm. Pergamon Press, 395 Sawmill River Road, Elmsford NY 10523. Tel (914)592-7700. Ind/Abst Electron. Commun. Abstr. J., ISMEC Bull., Pollut. Abstr. Indexes, Saf. Sci. Abstr. J., Eng. Index Annu., Eng. Index Mon., Eng. Index Bioeng. Abstr., Eng. Index Energy Abstr., Excerpta Med., CIS Abstr., Ref. Source, Biol. Abstr., Psychol. Abstr., Soc. Sci. Citation Index, Eng. Index. LC HV675.A1. DD 614.805. NLM W1 AC69K. CODEN AAPVB5. Available on microfilm and microfiche from Microforms International Marketing Corporation.

ACCIDENT AND HEALTH BUSINESS. VFOAT Summary of Accident and Health Insurance Business in North Carolina. US. English. an. North Carolina Department of Insurance, Raleigh NC 27611. LC HG9338.N8. DD 368.38009756.

ACCIDENT FACTS. Began in 1921?. 0148-6039. US. English. an. $2.80. National Safety Council, 425 North Michigan Avenue, Chicago IL 60611. LC HA217. DD 312.40973.

ACCIDENT FACTS. Main/Corp Illinois. Dept. of Transportation. US. English. an. Illinois Department of Transportation, 2300 South Dirkson Parkway, Springfield IL 62764. LC HE5614.3.I4. DD 312.4409773.

ACCIDENT FATALITIES. CANADA. (ACCIDENT FATALITIES, CANADA). 1969-. 0316-7283. Periodical. CN. English. an. Canada Safety Council, 30 The Driveway, Ottawa Ontario K2P 1C9 Canada. DD 312.27. Accident Facts, Canada, 0547-891X.

ACCIDENTAL DEATHS IN CONNECTICUT. Main/Corp Connecticut. Safety Commission. 0098-0560. US. English. Connecticut Safety Commission, 79 Elm Street, Hartford CT 06115. LC HB1323.A2. DD 312.2709746.

ACCIDENTAL POISONING IN WISCONSIN. Main/Corp Wisconsin. Division of Health. 0094-5927. US. English. Division of Health, Box 309, Madison WI 53701. LC RA11965.W6. DD 312.4.

ACCIDENT/INCIDENT BULLETIN. VAT ACCIDENT INCIDENT BULLETIN. Began with No. 144, 1975. 0163-4674. US. English. an. Federal Railroad Administration/Office of Safety, 400 Seventh Street SW, Washington DC 20590. LC HE1780. DD 312.440973. Accident Bulletin, 0092-1645.

ACCIDENTS DE LA CIRCULATION SUR LA VOIE PUBLIQUE. Main/Corp Institut National de Statistique (Belgium). French. ir. LC HE5614.5.B4. DD 312.4409493.

ACCIDENTS IN NORTH AMERICAN MOUNTAINEERING. See Recreation, Leisure - Outdoor Life.

ACCIDENTS OF MOTOR CARRIERS OF PASSENGERS. Began with 1973/74. 0147-6904. US. English. an. U S Department of Transportation, Federal Highway Administration, 400 7th Street SW, Washington DC 20590. LC HE5614.2. DD 388.314. NLM W2 A B8702A. Vols. for 1976, 1980/1981- distributed to depository libraries in microfiche. Accidents of Class I Motor Carriers of Passengers.

ACCIDENTS OF MOTOR CARRIERS OF PROPERTY. Began with 1973. US. English. an. Federal Highway Administration, Bureau of Motor Carrier Safety, 400 7th Street SW, Washington DC 20590. LC HE5614.2. DD 388.314. Vols. for 1979- distributed to depository libraries in microfiche. Accidents of Large Motor Carriers of Property, 0565-0089.

ACTA HOSPITALIA. 0044-6009. Periodical. Dutch (text also in English or French with summaries in English and French). qt. 1,200 Domestic, 1,500 Foreign. Acta Hospitalia, Vital de Kosterstraat 102, 3000 Leuven Belgium. Tel (016)22.07.64. Ed J E Blanpain. Ind/Abst Hospit. Lit. Index, Excerpta Med. NLM W1 AC811. bk rev. adv acc. (ctrl). Covers health care management and health care financing.

ACTUALITES PREVENTION. Vol. 1, No. 1 (Autumn 1979)-. 0711-169X. Periodical. CN. French. qt. Free. Actualite Prevention Health Marketing Systems, CP 490 Succursale A, Scarborough Ontario M1K 2N0 Canada. DD 614.05. (ctrl).

ADMINISTRATION IN MENTAL HEALTH. Series/Titl DHEW Publication. Winter 1972-. 0090-1180. Periodical. US. English. qt. Human Sciences Press, 72 5th Avenue, New York NY 10011. Ind/Abst Sociol. Abstr., Soc. Welf. Soc. Plan./Policy Soc. Dev., Excerpta Med., Soc. Work Res. Abstr., Hospit. Lit. Index, Soc. Work Res. Abstr., Psychol. Abstr., Curr. Index J. Educ., Index Med., Soc. Sci. Citation Index, Abstr. Soc. Work. LC RA790.A1. DD 350.84205. NLM W1 AD339. CODEN ADMHA2.

ADMINISTRATION OF THE TOXIC SUBSTANCES CONTROL ACT, ANNUAL REPORT. 1st- 1977-. US. English. an.

ADMINISTRATION REPORT - PORT OF SPAIN, TRINIDAD AND TOBAGO. PUBLIC HEALTH DEPT. Main/Corp Port of Spain, Trinidad and Tobago. Public Health Dept. English. ir. Public Health Department, Government Printing Office, Port of Spain Trinidad & Tobago. LC RA194.T7. DD 362.10972983.

ADVANCE DATA. See Statistics.

ADVANCES. (ADVANCES : JOURNAL OF THE INSTITUTE FOR THE ADVANCEMENT OF HEALTH). Vol. 1, No. 1 (Winter 1984)-. 0741-9783. Periodical. US. English. qt. $75.00. Institute for the Advancement of Health, 16 East 53rd Street, New York NY 10022. Tel (212)832-8282. Ed Harris Dienstfrey. bk rev. adv acc. Circ 3,000. Reports on developments in the scientific study of mind-body interactions and health; it is written for professionals and the interested public.

ADVANCES IN HEALTH ECONOMICS AND HEALTH SERVICES RESEARCH. Vol. 2 (1981)-. 0731-2199. US. English. ir. $52.50. JAI Press, PO Box 1678, Greenwich CT 06836. Tel (203)661-7602. Ed Richard M Scheffler and Louis F Rossiter. Ind/Abst Hospit. Lit. Index. LC RA410.A1. DD 338.473621. NLM W1 AD621T. Research in Health Economics, 0197-0690.

AECQ SAFETY. (AECQ SAFETY : ASSOCIATION OF BUILDING CONTRACTORS OF QUEBEC OFFICIAL NEWSLETTER). VAT Association des Entrepreneurs en Construction du Quebec. Safety, A.E.C.Q.-Safety. Vol. 1, No. 1 (Nov. 13, 1980)-. 0228-6750. Periodical. CN. English. Free to Members. Association of Building Contractors of Quebec Head Office, Suite 100/7777 Louis-H Lafontaine Boulevard, Anjou Quebec H1K 4E4 Canada. DD 363.11969009714.

AEROSPACE SAFETY. See Aeronautics, Astronautics.

AFFIRMATIVE ACTION PLAN - MAINE. DEPT. OF MENTAL HEALTH AND CORRECTIONS. (AFFIRMATIVE ACTION PLAN). Main/Corp Maine. Dept. of Mental Health and Corrections. 0731-3446. US. English. an. LC RA790.65.M3. DD 353.97410084.

AFFIRMATIVE ACTION PLAN - OKLAHOMA HEALTH PLANNING COMMISSION. Main/Corp Oklahoma Health Planning Commission. US. English. an. Oklahoma Health Planning Commission, 1000 NE 10th Street, Oklahoma City OK 73105. LC RA134. DD 353.976600770683.

AFFIRMATIVE ACTION PROGAM - ILLINOIS DEPT. OF MENTAL HEALTH AND DEVELOPMENTAL DISABILITIES. Main/Corp Illinois Dept. of Mental Health and Developmental Disabilities. US. English. an. Department of Mental Health & Developmental Disabilities, 160 North Lasalle Street Room 1500, Chicago IL 60601. LC RA790.65.I4. DD 353.9773001.

AFRO TECHNICAL PAPERS. No. 1- 1970-. Monographic Series. CG. English. ir. World Health Organization, P O Box 5284 Church Street Station, New York NY 10249. Tel (518)436-9686. NLM W1 ALL545.

AL-SIHHAH WA-AL-HAYAH. Periodical. Arabic. ir. 0.21 Single Issue. LC RA773.

ALABAMA MEDICUS. No. 1 (May/June 1980)-. 0883-1572. Periodical. US. English. bm. University of Alabama at Birmingham, Lister Hill Library of the Health Sciences University Station, Birmingham AL 35294. DD 614.

ALABAMA'S HEALTH. 0145-6857. Periodical. US. English. mo. Alabama Department of Public Health Bureau of Primary Prevention, Room 206/State Office Building, Montgomery AL 36130. Tel (205)261-5095. Ed Arrol Sheehan. Circ 1,500. (ctrl). Official publication of the Alabama Department of Public Health. Articles include descriptions of department activities, accomplishments and a calendar of events.

ALBANY BULLETIN ON HEALTH AND WELFARE LEGISLATION OF THE STATE COMMUNITIES AID ASSOCIATION : BULLETIN. Main/Corp State Communities Aid Association. US. English. wk. State Communities Aid Association, 105 East 22nd Street, New York NY 10010. Tel (212)677-0250. Albany Bulletin On Health and Welfare Legislation. Family and Child Welfare.

ALCOHOL HEALTH AND RESEARCH WORLD. See Drug Abuse and Alcoholism.

ALERTE. V. 1- March 1977-. 0704-6340. Periodical. CN. French. qt. 6.50. Service National des Sauveteurs, 1415 East rue Jarry, Montreal Quebec H2E 2Z7 Canada. Tel 252-3100. Ed Normand Laberge. DD 797.2109714. bk rev. adv acc. Circ 8,000. (ctrl). Lifesaving and lifeguarding, safety in and around pools and beaches, equipment and teaching/lifesaving, first aid and medical emergencies.

ALLIED HEALTH TRENDS. 0275-7699. Periodical. US. English. ir. $40.00. American Society of Allied Health Professions, 1101 Connecticut Avenue Suite 700, Washington DC 20036. Tel (202)293-3422.

Public Health and Safety

ALTERNATIVE DESIGNS. Began with: Vol. 1, No. 1 (June 1983). 0747-9263. Periodical. US. English. mo. $90.00. Pracon Inc, 10390 Democracy Lane, Fairfax VA 22030. **NLM** W1. *Blueprint For Healthcare Program Development.*

AMERICAN HEALTH. VFOAT A.H. V. 1, No. 1 (Mar./Apr. 1982)-. 0730-7004. Periodical. US. English. ir. $40.00. American Health Partners, 80 5th Avenue, New York NY 10011, (subscription address: Communication Data Services PO Box 4966 Des Moines IA 50340). **Tel** (800)247-5470.

AMERICAN JOURNAL OF EPIDEMIOLOGY. V. 81- 1965-. 0002-9262. Periodical. US. English. mo. $84.00 Domestic, $89.00 Foreign. American Journal Epidemiology, 615 North Wolfe Street, Department A, Baltimore MD 21205. **Tel** (301)955-3441. **Ed** George W Comstock. **Ind/Abst** Electron. Commun. Abstr. J., ISMEC Bull., Pollut. Abstr. Indexes, Saf. Sci. Abstr. J., Life Sci. Collect., Coal Abstr., Excerpta Med., Index Med., CIS Abstr., Biol. Abstr., Energy Res. Abstr., Sci. Cit. Index, Abr. Ed., Hospit. Lit. Index. **NLM** W1 AM451D. **CODEN** AJEPAS. (cum index). adv acc. **Circ** 5,000. (ctrl). Publishes original field and laboratory studies on the occurrence and distribution of endemic and epidemic diseases including infectious and non-infectious acute and chronic diseases and statistical methodology. *American Journal of Hygiene, 0096-5294.*

AMERICAN JOURNAL OF INFECTION CONTROL. V. 8- Feb. 1980-. 0196-6553. Periodical. US. English. bm. $60.00. C V Mosby Company c/o R E Kinnes, 11830 Westline Industrial Drive, St Louis MO 63146. **Tel** (314)872-8370. **Ed** Mary Castle. **Ind/Abst** Life Sci. Collect., Hospit. Lit. Index, Excerpta Med., Index Med., Cumul. Index Nurs. Allied Health Lit. **LC** RA969. **DD** 614.4405. **NLM** W1 AM468N. bk rev. adv acc. **Circ** 7,920. Serves infection control practitioners concerned with the control of infections associated with hospitals and other health care facilities. *APIC Journal, 0161-6005.*

AMERICAN JOURNAL OF PUBLIC HEALTH. VFOAT JPH. V. 61- 1971-. 0090-0036. Periodical. US. English. mo. $60.00. American Public Health Association, 1015 15th Street Northwest, Washington DC 20005. **Tel** (202)780-5600. **Ed** Alfred Yankauer. **Ind/Abst** Soc. Work Res. Abstr., Appl. Sci. Technol. Index, Public Aff. Inf. Serv. Bull., Biol. Abstr., Chem. Abstr., Cumul. Index Nurs. Allied Health Lit., Environ. Period. Bibliogr., Excerpta Med., Hospit. Lit. Index, Index Med., Nuci. Sci. Abstr., Public Health Rev., Saf. Sci. Abstr. J., Curr. Index J. Educ., Energy Res. Abstr., Gen. Sci. Index, Soc. Sci. Index, Bibliogr. Agric., Med. Socioecon. Res. Source, Abstr. Anthropol., Book Rev. Index, Sci. Cit. Index, Abr. Ed. **NLM** W1 AM521C. **CODEN** AJHEAA. (cum index). adv acc. **Circ** 35,000. Available on microfilm from University Microfilms International. Peer reviewed journal publishes latest original studies and research in 45 public health disciplines. *American Journal of Public Health and the Nation's Health, 0002-9572.*

AMERICAN JOURNAL OF RURAL HEALTH. (AMERICAN JOURNAL OF RURAL HEALTH). VFOAT Rural Health. 0278-9388. Periodical. US. English. qt. $20.00. American Rural Health Association, Suite 731/1717 11th Avenue South, Birmingham AL 35205. *Rural Health Communications.*

THE AMERICAN MEDICAL ASSOCIATION'S COST EFFECTIVENESS PLAN. VFOAT A.M.A. Cost Effectiveness Plan. 0743-4073. US. English. an. Order Department OP-149, American Medical Association, PO Box 10946, Chicago IL 60610. **LC** RA410.A1. **DD** 362.1042.

AMERICA'S HEALTH. Periodical. US. English. mo. Pfizer Inc, 235 East 42nd Street, New York NY 10017. **Tel** (212)421-4000.

ANAIS DA CONFERENCIA NACIONAL DE SAUDE. Main/Conf Conferencia Nacional de Saude (Brazil). BL. Portuguese. be. Ctr Documentacao Ministerio de Saude, Bloco G Terreo, 70058 Brasilia DF Brazil. **LC** RA463.

ANALYSIS OF RESEARCH PUBLICATIONS SUPPORTED BY NIH AND NHLBI. Main/Corp National Institutes of Health (U.S.). VFOAT Analysis of Research Publications Supported by NIH. 1970-1976-. US. English. National Institutes of Health, Office of Program Planning and Evaluation/Program Evaluation Branch, 9000 Rockville Pike, Bethesda MD 20205.

ANALYSIS OF RESEARCH PUBLICATIONS SUPPORTED BY NIH AND NIAID. Main/Corp National Institutes of Health (U.S.). VFOAT Analysis of Research Publications Supported by NIH. 1970-1976-. US. English. National Institutes of Health, Office of Program Planning and Evaluation/Program Evaluation Branch, 9000 Rockville Pike, Bethesda MD 20205.

ANNALES DE L'UNIVERSITE DE MADAGASCAR. BIOLOGIE-CLINIQUE-SANTE PUBLIQUE. *See* Biology.

ANNALI DELL'ISTITUTO SUPERIORE DI SANITA. V. 1- 1965-. 0021-2571. Periodical. IT. text mainly in Italian with some articles in English or German. qt. $23.47. Instituto Poligrafico d Stato, Piazza Verdi 10, 00100 Rome Italy. **Ind/Abst** Sel. Water Resour. Abstr., Excerpta Med., Index Med., Biol. Abstr., Chem. Abstr., Bibliogr. Agric., Electr. Electron. Abstr., Comput. Control Abstr., Phys. Abstr. **NLM** W1 AN486G. **CODEN** AISSAW. *Rendiconti - Istituto Superiore di Sanita, 0370-5811.*

ANNUAIRE - ASSOCIATION GENERALE DES HYIGENISTES ET TECHNICIENS MUNICIPAUX (FRANCE). *See* Yearbooks, Almanacs, Directories.

ANNUAL ACTIVITIES SUMMARY - DIVISION OF MEDICAL SERVICES, TENNESSEE VALLEY AUTHORITY. *See* Medicine.

ANNUAL CONFERENCE PROCEEDINGS - B.C. HEALTH ASSOCIATION. (ANNUAL CONFERENCE PROCEEDINGS - B.C. HEALTH ASSOCIATION). VAT Annual Conference Proceedings - British Columbia Health Association. 60th- 1977-. 0702-0163. Periodical. CN. English. an. **NLM** W1 AN748M. *Proceedings of the Annual Meeting - British Columbia Health Association, 0702-0155.*

ANNUAL EDITIONS. READINGS IN HEALTH. (ANNUAL EDITIONS : READINGS IN HEALTH). VFOAT Readings in Health. 0360-9766. US. English. an. Dushkin Books, Sluice Dock, Guilford CT 06437. **Tel** (203)453-4351. **LC** RA773. **DD** 613.05.

ANNUAL FINANCIAL REPORT - TEXAS. DEPT. OF HEALTH. Main/Corp Texas. Dept. of Health. US. English. an. Texas Department of Health, PO Box 12067, Austin TX 78711. **LC** RA157. **DD** 353.976400841. *Audit Report.*

ANNUAL FISCAL REPORT - WISCONSIN. DEPT. OF HEALTH AND SOCIAL SERVICES. DIVISION OF MANAGEMENT SERVICES. Main/Corp Wisconsin. Dept. of Health and Social Services. Division of Management Services. US. English. an. State Department of Health & Social Services, 1 West Wilson Street, Box 309, Madison WI 53701. **LC** HV86. **DD** 353.9775007231. *Annual Fiscal Report, 0098-0412.*

AN ANNUAL IMPLEMENTATION PLAN FOR NORTHERN INDIANA. Main/Corp Northern Indiana Health Systems Agency. Periodical. US. English. an. Northern Indiana Health Systems Agency, 900 East Colfax Avenue, South Bend IN 46617.

ANNUAL IMPLEMENTATION PLAN - HAWAII. STATE HEALTH PLANNING AND DEVELOPMENT AGENCY. Main/Corp Hawaii. State Health Planning and Development Agency. US. English. an. Hawaii State Health Planning and Development Agency, 600 Kapioleni Boulevard/Suite 205, Honolulu HI 96813. **LC** RA49. **DD** 362.109969.

ANNUAL IMPLEMENTATION PLAN - HEALTH PLANNING COUNCIL (MADISON, WIS.). Main/Corp Health Planning Council (Madison, Wis.). US. English. an. Health Planning Council Inc, 310 Price Place/Suite 206, Madison WI 53705.

ANNUAL IMPLEMENTATION PLAN. HSA BOARD ADOPTED. Main/Corp Health Systems Agency of Southwestern Pennsylvania. 1984-. US. English. an.

ANNUAL IMPLEMENTATION PLAN - MONTANA HEALTH SYSTEMS AGENCY. Main/Corp Montana Health Systems Agency. 1978-. US. English. an. Montana Health Systems Agency, 324 Fuller Avenue, Helena MT 59601. **LC** RA395.A4. **DD** 362.109786.

ANNUAL IMPLEMENTATION PLAN - VERMONT. HEALTH POLICY CORPORATION. Main/Corp Vermont. Health Policy Corporation. 0273-2203. US. English. an. 103 South Main Street, Waterbury VT 05676. **LC** RA395.A4. **DD** 362.109743.

ANNUAL PERFORMANCE REPORT - WYOMING. MENTAL HEALTH AND MENTAL RETARDATION SERVICES. Main/Corp Wyoming. Mental Health and Mental Retardation Services. 0098-5627. US. English. an. Mental Health and Mental Retardation Services, State Office Building West, Cheyenne WY 82002. **LC** RA790.65.W8. **DD** 362.209787.

ANNUAL POPULATION, MENTAL INSTITUTIONS. Series/Titl Statistical Bulletin MH. VFOAT Annual Population Report, Mental Institutions. US. English. an. **LC** RC445.W54. **DD** 362.21.

ANNUAL PROGRESS REPORT - AFRICAN MEDICAL AND RESEARCH FOUNDATION. HEALTH BEHAVIOUR AND EDUCATION DEPT. Main/Corp African Medical and Research Foundation. Health Behaviour and Education Dept. English. an. Health Behaviour and Education Department, African Medical and Research Foundation, Box 3012, Nairobi Kenya. **LC** RA440.3.A4. **DD** 362.1042096.

ANNUAL PROGRESS REPORT - SOUTHWEST OKLAHOMA MIGRANT HEALTH PROJECT. Main/Corp Southwest Oklahoma Migrant Health Project. VFOAT Annual Report. US. English. an. Oklahoma State Department of Health, Northeast 10th Street & Stonewall, Oklahoma City OK 73152. **LC** RA448.5.M5. **DD** 362.10425.

ANNUAL PROGRESS REPORT - U.S. ARMY MEDICAL RESEARCH INSTITUTE OF INFECTIOUS DISEASES. (ANNUAL PROGRESS REPORT). 0361-6800. US. English. an. United States Army Medical Research, Institute of Infectious Diseases, Fort Detrick, Frederick MD 21701. **LC** RC110. **DD** 616.9072075288. **NLM** W1 AN758S.

ANNUAL REPORT - ALABAMA. DEPT. OF MENTAL HEALTH. Main/Corp Alabama. Dept. of Mental Health. US. English. an. State of Alabama, Department of Mental Health, 135 South Union Street, Montgomery AL 36130. **LC** RA790.65.A2. **DD** 353.976100842.

ANNUAL REPORT - ALABAMA. DEPT. OF PUBLIC HEALTH. Main/Corp Alabama. Dept. of Public Health. US. English. an. Alabama Department of Public Health, State Office Building, Montgomery AL 36130. **LC** RA446.5.A3. **DD** 353.9761007705.

ANNUAL REPORT - ALBERTA HEALTH AND SOCIAL SERVICES DISCIPLINES COMMITTEE. Main/Corp Alberta Health and Social Services Disciplines Committee. 1st- 1976/77-. 0707-1434. CN. English. an. Free. Alberta Health and Social Services Disciplines Committee, 424 Legislative Building, Edmonton Alberta T5K 2B6 Canada. **Tel** (403)427-6904. **LC** RA410.9.C2. **DD** 354.712300841. **Circ** 700. Contains information on history, mandates, membership, major activities of committee, manpower planning, surveys of personnel, associations, training programs, manpower indicators, and liason activities of committee.

ANNUAL REPORT - ALBERTA HEALTH CARE INSURANCE PLAN. *See* Insurance.

ANNUAL REPORT - ARKANSAS. DIVISION OF COMMUNICABLE DISEASE CONTROL. Main/Corp Arkansas. Division of Communicable Disease Control. US. English. an. **LC** RA24. **DD** 614.42767.

ANNUAL REPORT - BOARD OF SCIENTIFIC COUNSELORS, NINDS, NATIONAL INSTITUTES OF HEALTH. *See* Medicine - Neurology.

ANNUAL REPORT - BOPHUTHATSWANA (SOUTH AFRICA) DEPT. OF HEALTH AND SOCIAL WELFARE. Main/Corp Bophuthatswana (South Africa) Dept. of Health and Social Welfare. English. an. **LC** RA352.S75. **DD** 354.6829400841.

ANNUAL REPORT - BUREAU OF HEALTH FACILITIES. Main/Corp United States. Bureau of Health Facilities. 1978/79-. US. English. an. United States Deparment of Health and

Public Health and Safety

Human Services, Health Resources Administration Bureau of Health Facilities, Hyattsville MD 20782. LC RA981.A2. DD 353.00841. *Annual Report - Bureau of Health Facilities Financing, Compliance, and Conversion.*

ANNUAL REPORT - CENTRAL DISTRICT HEALTH DEPARTMENT. (ANNUAL REPORT). Main/Corp Idaho. Central District Health Dept. 1971/72-. 0094-0410. US. English. LC RA51. DD 353.9796007705.

ANNUAL REPORT - CITY OF CHICAGO/HSA. Main/Corp City of Chicago/HSA. VAT Annual Report - City of Chicago, Health Systems Agency. 1977/78-. 0271-339X. US. English. an. City of Chicago Health Systems Agency, 180 North Lasalle Street/Suite 700, Chicago IL 60601. LC RA55.C56. DD 352.94410977311.

ANNUAL REPORT - COMMONWEALTH OF MASSACHUSETTS, RATE SETTING COMMISSION. Main/Corp Massachusetts. Rate Setting Commission. 1974/75-. 0362-7101. US. English. an. 1 Ashburton Place, Boston MA 02108. LC RA410.54.M4. DD 338.43362109744.

ANNUAL REPORT - DELAWARE. COMMISSION ON THE TRANSPORTATION OF HAZARDOUS MATERIALS. Main/Corp Delaware. Commission on the Transportation of Hazardous Materials. US. English. an. Department of Public Safety, PO Box 818, Dover DE 19901. LC T55.3.H3. DD 353.9751008750289.

ANNUAL REPORT - DEPARTMENT OF HEALTH AND SOCIAL SECURITY. Main/Corp Great Britain. Dept. of Health and Social Security. 1968-. UK. English. an. Her Majestys Stationery Office, PO Box 276, London SW8 5DT England. Tel 01-622 3316. *Annual Report of the Ministry of Health, Report of the Ministry of Social Security.*

ANNUAL REPORT - DEPARTMENT OF HEALTH AND SOCIAL SERVICES. *See* Sociology: General Works, Theory - Social Pathology, Welfare, Criminology.

ANNUAL REPORT - DEPARTMENT OF PUBLIC HEALTH (PAPUA). (ANNUAL REPORT). Main/Corp Papua-New Guinea (Ter.) Dept. of Public Health. VFOAT Annual Report - Dept. of Public Health. Papua-New Guinea. 0377-9203. Periodical. English. ir. NLM W2 LP2 D4A.

ANNUAL REPORT - DEPARTMENT OF PUBLIC SAFETY (ALABAMA). Main/Corp Alabama. Dept. of Public Safety. 0146-8499. US. English. an. State of Alabama, Department of Public Safety, Montgomery AL 36104. LC HV7571.A2. DD 353.97610075.

ANNUAL REPORT - DEPARTMENT OF SAFETY (TENNESSEE). Main/Corp Tennessee. Dept. of Safety. 0095-1994. US. English. an. Andrew Jackson State Office Building, Nashville TN 37219. LC HE5614.3.T2. DD 353.976800783.

ANNUAL REPORT - DIVISION OF HEALTH, DEPARTMENT OF HEALTH AND REHABILITATIVE SERVICES, STATE OF FLORIDA. (ANNUAL REPORT - DIVISION OF HEALTH (FLORIDA)). Main/Corp Florida. Division of Health. 1969-. 0148-1894. US. English. an. Division of Health, 1217 Pearl Street, PO Box 210, Jacksonville FL 32202. LC RA44. DD 614.09759. NLM W2 AF4 D64A. *Annual Report - State Board of Health, State of Florida, 0275-1534.*

ANNUAL REPORT - DIVISION OF MENTAL HYGIENE AND MENTAL RETARDATION (NEVADA). Main/Corp Nevada. Division of Mental Hygiene and Mental Retardation. US. English. an. Nevada Division of Mental Hygiene and Mental Retardation, Suite 108/4600 Kietzke Lane, Reno NV 89502.

ANNUAL REPORT - ENERGY ACTION STAFF. (ANNUAL REPORT - ENERGY ACTION STAFF, U.S. HEALTH RESOURCES ADMINISTRATION). Main/Corp United States. Health Resources Administration. Energy Action Staff. 1975/76-. 0147-491X. US. English. an. Maryland Department of Health Education & Welfare, 5600 Fishers Lane, Rockville MD 20852. LC RA981.A2. DD 333.7.

ANNUAL REPORT - EPIDEMIOLOGY & DISEASE CONTROL STUDY SECTION, NATIONAL INSTITUTES OF HEALTH. Main/Corp United States. National Institutes of Health. Epidemiology and Disease Control Study Section. VAT Annual Report - Epidemiology and Disease Control Study Section, National Institutes of Health. US. English. an. National Institutes of Health, 9000 Rockville Pike, Bethesda MD 20014.

ANNUAL REPORT - FLORIDA. DEPT. OF HEALTH AND REHABILITATIVE SERVICES. Main/Corp Florida. Dept. of Health and Rehabilitative Services. US. English. an. Florida Department of Health and Rehabilitative Services, 1323 Winewood Boulevard, Tallahassee FL 32301. LC RA447.F6. DD 353.97590077.

ANNUAL REPORT FOR PERIOD - NATAL (SOUTH AFRICA). DEVELOPMENT AND SERVICES BOARD. Main/Corp Natal (South Africa). Development and Services Board. VFOAT Jaarverslag vir die Tydperk .... Afrikaans (English). an. LC RA352.S75. DD 362.109684.

ANNUAL REPORT FOR THE YEAR ENDING MARCH 31 - SASKATCHEWAN HEALTH. Main/Corp Saskatchewan. Saskatchewan Health. VFOAT Annual Report. CN. English. an. Saskatchewan Health, T C Douglas Building, 3475 Albert Street, Regina Saskatchewan S4S 6X6 Canada. LC RA185.S3. DD 362.1097124.

ANNUAL REPORT - GEORGIA. DEPT. OF PUBLIC SAFETY. Main/Corp Georgia. Dept. of Public Safety. 1959-. US. English. an. Georgia Department of Public Safety, PO Box 1456, Atlanta GA 30371. *Report.*

ANNUAL REPORT - GEORGIA. DEPT. OF PUBLIC SAFETY. Main/Corp Georgia. Dept. of Public Safety. 1957-. Periodical. US. English. an. LC HV7571.G4.

ANNUAL REPORT - GOVERNMENT OF THE VIRGIN ISLANDS OF THE UNITED STATES, DEPARTMENT OF PUBLIC SAFETY. Main/Corp Virgin Islands of the United States. Dept. of Public Safety. 0505-6373. VI. English. ir. Government of the Virgin Islands of the US/Department of Public Safety, Charlotte Amalie, St Thomas VI 00801. LC HV7683.

ANNUAL REPORT - GREENE VALLEY DEVELOPMENTAL CENTER. Main/Corp Greene Valley Developmental Center. VFOAT GVDC Annual Report. 0149-7251. US. English. an. PO Box 3087, Greeneville TN 37743. LC HV3006.T352. DD 362.3.

ANNUAL REPORT - HAWAII STATE HEALTH PLANNING AND DEVELOPMENT AGENCY AND HAWAII STATEWIDE HEALTH COORDINATING COUNCIL. Main/Corp Hawaii. State Health Planning and Development Agency. 1977/78-. US. English. an. LC RA49. DD 353.996900841.

ANNUAL REPORT - HEALTH SURVEILLANCE REGISTRY (BRITISH COLUMBIA). (ANNUAL REPORT). Main/Corp British Columbia. Health Surveillance Registry. 1975-. 0226-496X. CN. English. an. Health Surveillance Registry for the Ministry of Health, PO Box 34020 Station D, Vancouver British Columbia V6J 4M3 Canada. NLM W2 DC2.1 B8H4A. *Annual Report - Registry for Handicapped Children and Adults, 0486-3070.*

ANNUAL REPORT, HIGHWAY SAFETY IMPROVEMENT PROGRAMS IN VIRGINIA. VFOAT Annual Report, Highway Safety Improvement Programs. US. English. an. Virginia Department of Highways and Transportation, 1401 East Broad Street, Richmond VA 23219. LC HE5614.3.V8. DD 363.125609755.

ANNUAL REPORT - INTERIM AMBULANCE AUTHORITY (TASMANIA). Main/Corp Tasmania. Interim Ambulance Authority. English. ir. LC RA996.A82. DD 354.94600841. *Report.*

ANNUAL REPORT - JOINT COMMITTEE ON PUBLIC HEALTH AND SAFETY OF THE CONNECTICUT GENERAL ASSEMBLY (CONNECTICUT). *See* Law.

ANNUAL REPORT - JOINT LEGISLATIVE COMMITTEE ON THE PROBLEMS OF PUBLIC HEALTH, MEDICARE, MEDICAID AND COMPULSORY HEALTH AND HOSPITAL INSURANCE (NEW YORK (STATE)). *See* Law.

ANNUAL REPORT - KANSAS. LONG TERM CARE OMBUDSMAN. Main/Corp Kansas. Long Term Care Ombudsman. Federal Fiscal Year 1982-. US. English. an. Kansas Department of Aging, 610 West 10th Street, Topeka KS 66612. LC RA644.7.K2. DD 353.978100841.

ANNUAL REPORT - LIPID METABOLISM ADVISORY COMMITTEE, NATIONAL INSTITUTES OF HEALTH. Main/Corp National Heart, Lung, and Blood Institute. Lipid Metabolism Advisory Committee. 1975/76-. US. English. an. National Heart Lung and Blood Institute, National Institutes of Health, 9000 Rockville Pike, Bethesda MD 20014. *Annual Report - Lipid Metabolism Advisory Committee, National Institutes of Health.*

ANNUAL REPORT - MARYLAND HIGH BLOOD PRESSURE COMMISSION. (ANNUAL REPORT FOR THE FISCAL YEAR - MARYLAND HIGH BLOOD PRESSURE COMMISSION). Main/Corp Maryland High Blood Pressure Commission. 8755-707X. US. English. an. Maryland High Blood Pressure Commission, 201 West Preston Street, Baltimore MD 21201.

ANNUAL REPORT - MICHIGAN. DEPT. OF MENTAL HEALTH. OFFICE OF RECIPIENT RIGHTS. Main/Corp Michigan. Dept. of Mental Health. Office of Recipient Rights. US. English. an. LC RA790.65.M5. DD 362.209774.

ANNUAL REPORT - MINISTRY OF HEALTH (BRITISH COLUMBIA). Main/Corp British Columbia. Ministry of Health. VFOAT Ministry of Health Annual Report. VAT Ministry of Health Annual Report (Victoria). 1977-. 0706-4810. CN. English. an. LC RA185.B7. DD 354.7110077. NLM W2 DC2.1 B8D4A. *Annual Report, 0701-5372.*

ANNUAL REPORT - MINISTRY OF HEALTH (ONTARIO). Main/Corp Ontario. Ministry of Health. 47th- 1971-. 0702-6684. CN. English. an. Ministry of Health, Hepburn Block Queen's Park, Toronto Ontario M7A 1R3 Canada. LC RA185. DD 354.71300841. NLM W2 DC2.1 O5P9A.

ANNUAL REPORT - MINNESOTA OFFICE OF HEALTH FACILITY COMPLAINTS. Main/Corp Minnesota Office of Health Facility Complaints. US. English. an. Minnesota Office of Health Facility Complaints, 717 Delaware Street SE, Minneapolis MN 55440. LC RA981.M6. DD 353.977600841.

ANNUAL REPORT - MISSISSIPPI HEALTH CARE COMMISSION. Main/Corp Mississippi Health Care Commission. July 1, 1979-June 30, 1980-. US. English. an. $3.00. Mississippi Health Care Commission, 2688 Insurance Center Drive, Jackson MS 39216. Tel (601)981-6880. LC RA395.A4. DD 353.97620084105. *Annual Report.*

ANNUAL REPORT - MISSISSIPPI STATE BOARD OF HEALTH. Main/Corp Mississippi. State Board of Health. 93D- 1969/70-. 0197-940X. US. English. an. NLM W2 AM7 S7B. *Biennial Report Being the Annual Reports of the State Board of Health of the State of Mississippi, 0197-8276.*

ANNUAL REPORT - MISSISSIPPI. STATE DEPT. OF HEALTH. Main/Corp Mississippi. State Dept. of Health. US. English. an. Office of Public Relations, Mississippi State, Department of Health, PO Box 1700, Jackson MS 39205.

ANNUAL REPORT - MONTANA HEALTH SYSTEMS AGENCY. Main/Corp Montana Health Systems Agency. US. English. an. Montana Health Systems Agency, 324 Fuller Avenue, Helena MT 58601. LC RA101. DD 353.97860084.

ANNUAL REPORT - NATIONAL ADVISORY RESEARCH RESOURCES COUNCIL. Main/Corp National Institutes of Health. National Advisory Research Resources Council. US. English. an. 9000 Rockville Pike, Bethesda MD 20014.

ANNUAL REPORT - NATIONAL BLOOD RESOURCE PROGRAM ADVISORY COMMITTEE, NATIONAL INSTITUTES OF HEALTH. Main/Corp National Heart and Lung Institute. National Blood Resource Program Advisory Committee. US. English. an. National Heart and Lung Institute, National Institutes of Health, 9000 Rockville Pike, Bethesda MD 20014.

Public Health and Safety

ANNUAL REPORT - NATIONAL COUNCIL ON HEALTH PLANNING AND DEVELOPMENT. Main/Corp United States. National Council On Health Planning and Development. 0197-5005. US. English. an. US Department of Health Education and Welfare/Public Health Service Health Resources, Administration Center Building/3700 East-West Highway, Hyattsville MD 20782. LC RA395.A3. DD 353.00841.

ANNUAL REPORT - NATIONAL DRINKING WATER ADVISORY COUNCIL. Main/Corp United States. National Drinking Water Advisory Council. 1975-. 0148-3323. US. English. an. National Drinking Water Advisory Council, 2626 Pennsylvania Avenue NW, Washington DC 20037. LC RA592.A1. DD 353.00871.

ANNUAL REPORT - NATIONAL INSTITUTE OF ENVIRONMENTAL HEALTH SCIENCES. (ANNUAL REPORT). 0160-2187. US. English. an. National Institute of Environmental Health Sciences, Research Triangle Park NC 27711. LC RA566.26. NLM W1 NA486CG.

ANNUAL REPORT - NATIONAL INSTITUTE OF HYGIENE. 1978-. 0208-595X. Periodical. English. ir. NLM W 20.5 A614. *Annual Report - State Institute of Hygiene, 0208-5887.*

ANNUAL REPORT - NEBRASKA. DEPT. OF HEALTH. Main/Corp Nebraska. Dept. of Health. 0090-3795. US. English. an. Nebraska Department of Health, 1007 State Capital, Lincoln NE 68509. LC RA447.N2. DD 353.97820077.

ANNUAL REPORT - NEW MEXICO TRAFFIC SAFETY COMMISSION. *See* Transportation - Roads and Traffic.

ANNUAL REPORT - NEW YORK (STATE). OFFICE OF MENTAL HEALTH. (ANNUAL REPORT - NEW YORK STATE OFFICE OF MENTAL HEALTH). Main/Corp New York (State). Office of Mental Health. 1978-. 0273-5199. US. English. an. Office of Public Affairs, New York State Office of Mental Health, 44 Holland Avenue, Albany NY 12229. LC RA790.65.N7. DD 353.974700842. NLM W2 AN6 O27A.

ANNUAL REPORT - NORTHERN INDIANA HEALTH SYSTEMS AGENCY. Main/Corp Northern Indiana Health Systems Agency. US. English. 900 East Colfax Avenue, South Bend IN 46617.

ANNUAL REPORT - NORTHERN IRELAND. EASTERN HEALTH AND SOCIAL SERVICES BOARD. Main/Corp Northern Ireland. Eastern Health and Social Services Board. 0144-7084. English. an. 2.00. Eastern Health and Social Services Board, 65 University Street, Belfast BT7 1HN Northern Ireland. LC RA246. DD 354.4160084094165.

ANNUAL REPORT OF BUREAU OF HEALTH PLANNING. (HEALTH PLANNING UNDER WAY : ANNUAL REPORT). Main/Corp United States. Bureau of Health Planning. Fiscal 1978. Periodical. US. English. an.

ANNUAL REPORT OF INTRAMURAL ACTIVITIES - NATIONAL INSTITUTE OF ALLERGY AND INFECTIOUS DISEASES (U.S.). (ANNUAL REPORT OF INTRAMURAL ACTIVITIES). Main/Corp National Institute of Allergy and Infectious Diseases (U.S.). 0882-2239. US. English. an. LC RC109. DD 616.9072073.

ANNUAL REPORT OF THE ACTIVITIES OF THE ALABAMA DEPT. OF PUBLIC HEALTH. Main/Corp Alabama. Dept. of Public Health. US. English. an. Department of Public Health, 206 State Office Building, Montgomery AL 36130. Tel (205)261-5095. LC RA15. DD 353.9761007705. Circ 1,000. (ctrl). Describes the activities of the various bureaus of the Alabama Department of Public Health, including statistics and graphs of services rendered. *Activities Report - Alabama Dept. of Public Health.*

ANNUAL REPORT OF THE ALASKA DIVISION OF PUBLIC HEALTH. Main/Corp Alaska. Division of Public Health. 0095-3407. US. English. an. State of Alaska, Division of Public Health, Juneau AK 99801. LC RA18. DD 353.97980084105.

ANNUAL REPORT OF THE ALBERTA HEALTH OCCUPATIONS BOARD FOR THE PERIOD OF JANUARY 1 ... TO DECEMBER 31 .... Main/Corp Alberta Health Occupations Board. 1982 ... 1982-. CN. English. an. Alberta Health Occupations Board, 8th Floor 7th Street Plaza South/10030-107 Street, Edmonton Alberta T5J 3E4 Canada. LC RA185.A5. DD 354.712300841.

ANNUAL REPORT OF THE ARIZONA DEPARTMENT OF HEALTH SERVICES. Main/Corp Arizona. Dept. of Health Services. 1974-. 0362-1421. US. English. an. Department of Health Services, 1740 West Adams Street, Phoenix AZ 85007. LC RA21. DD 353.979100841. NLM W2 AA7 S6A. *Annual Report - Arizona State Department of Health, 0190-0633.*

ANNUAL REPORT OF THE COMMISSIONER OF PUBLIC SAFETY FOR THE YEAR ENDING JUNE 30 - MASSACHUSETTS. Main/Corp Massachusetts. Dept. of Public Safety. VFOAT Annual Report. US. English. an. Massachusetts Department of Public Safety, 1010 Commonwealth Avenue, Boston MA 02215. LC JS3.M38. DD 353.9744076. *Report.*

ANNUAL REPORT OF THE DIRECTOR - PAN AMERICAN SANITARY BUREAU. Main/Corp Pan American Sanitary Bureau. 1902-. 0085-462X. Periodical. US. English. an. NLM W2 MP2 P9A.

THE ANNUAL REPORT OF THE INDIANA DEPARTMENT OF MENTAL HEALTH. Main/Corp Indiana. Dept. of Mental Health. 0098-4205. US. English. an. 1315 West 10th Street, Indianapolis IN 46202. LC RA790.65.I5. DD 353.97720084205.

ANNUAL REPORT OF THE MEDICAL OFFICER OF HEALTH (LUSAKA, ZAMBIA). Main/Corp Lusaka, Zambia. Health and Welfare Dept. 0304-7725. English. ir. Health and Welfare Department, PO Box 789, Lusaka Zambia. LC RA352.Z25. DD 362.1096894.

ANNUAL REPORT OF THE MENTAL HEALTH DIVISION OF THE DEPARTMENT OF HEALTH OF THE PROVINCE OF ONTARIO. Main/Corp Ontario. Mental Health Division. CN. English. an. Ontario Mental Health Foundation, 365 Bloor Street East, Toronto Ontario M4W 3L4 Canada. LC RC448. DD 362.209713. *Annual Report of the Hospitals Division, Department of Health Upon the Ontario Mental Hospitals and Mental Health Services of the Province of Ontario.*

ANNUAL REPORT OF THE STATE ADVISORY COUNCIL ON MENTAL HEALTH AND RETARDATION (MASSACHUSETTS). Main/Corp Massachusetts. State Advisory Council on Mental Health and Retardation. US. English. an. Department of Mental Health, 190 Portland Street, Boston MA 02114. LC RA790.65.M35. DD 362.209744.

ANNUAL REPORT OF THE STATE DEPARTMENT OF HEALTH OF NEW YORK. Main/Corp New York (State). Dept. of Health. 22nd- 1901-. US. English. an. New York State Department of Health, Room 1456/Tower Building, Empire State Plaza, Albany NY 12237. *Annual Report of the State Board of Health, 0275-3367.*

ANNUAL REPORT - OHIO. DEPT. OF MENTAL HEALTH. Main/Corp Ohio. Dept. of Mental Health. Fiscal Year 1981-. US. English. an. Department of Mental Health, Bureau of Statistics, 30 East Broad Street/Suite 1205, Columbus OH 43215. LC RA790.65.O3. DD 353.97710084206.

ANNUAL REPORT - OKLAHOMA. DEPT. OF MENTAL HEALTH. Main/Corp Oklahoma. Dept. of Mental Health. 1982-. US. English. an. Department of Mental Health, 4545 North Lincoln, Oklahoma OK 73105. LC RA790.65.O5. DD 353.976600842. *Annual Report of Mental Health Care in Oklahoma.*

ANNUAL REPORT - OKLAHOMA DEPARTMENT OF PUBLIC SAFETY. Main/Corp Oklahoma. Department of Public Safety. US. English. an. Oklahoma Department of Public Safety, PO Box 11415, Oklahoma City OK 73136. LC HE5614.3.O5. DD 614.86209766.

ANNUAL REPORT ON HIGHWAY SAFETY IMPROVEMENT PROGRAMS. *See* Transportation - Roads and Traffic.

ANNUAL REPORT ON MONITORING AND IMPLEMENTATION OF THE INDIANA PLAN FOR HEALTH. 1983-. US. English. an. Indiana State Board of Health, 1330 West Michigan Street, PO Box 1964, Indianapolis IN 46206-1964. Tel (317)633-8507. LC RA395.A4. DD 353.977200841. Circ 150. Report issued by the Indiana State Board of Health.

ANNUAL REPORT ON THE HEW/USDA RURAL HEALTH FACILITIES AGREEMENT. Main/Corp United States. Farmers Home Administration. 1978/79-. US. English. an. LC RA771.5. DD 362.10425. NLM W2 A F124A.

ANNUAL REPORT ON THE OPERATIONS OF THE 911 EMERGENCY NUMBER SYSTEMS BOARD IN WISCONSIN. Main/Corp Wisconsin. Emergency Number Systems Board. US. English. an. State of Wisconsin, Emergency Number Systems Board, 101 South Webster Street/8th Floor, Madison WI 53702. LC TK6024.W6. DD 363.108.

ANNUAL REPORT ON THE PUBLIC INFORMATION AND EDUCATION COUNTERMEASURE OF ALCOHOL SAFETY ACTION PROJECTS. *See* Transportation - Roads and Traffic.

ANNUAL REPORT - PARKLAWN COMPUTER CENTER. Main/Corp Parklawn Computer Center. 1976-. 0147-9016. US. English. an. Maryland Department of Health Education & Welfare, 5600 Fishers Lane, Rockville MD 20852. LC RA409.5. DD 353.00841.

ANNUAL REPORT - PRINCE EDWARD ISLAND. DEPT. OF HEALTH AND SOCIAL SERVICES. Main/Corp Prince Edward Island. Dept. of Health and Social Services. 1st (1980/1981)-. 0820-9979. CN. English. an. LC RA185.P8. DD 354.717068406. *Annual Report, 0701-5291; Annual Report of the Department of Health, 0317-4530.*

ANNUAL REPORT - PUBLIC SAFETY PERSONNEL RETIREMENT SYSTEM OF THE STATE OF ARIZONA. Main/Corp Arizona. Public Safety Personnel Retirement System. US. English. an. 3033 North Central/Room 411, Phoenix AZ 85012. LC HV7571.A6. DD 353.9791005.

ANNUAL REPORT - RHODE ISLAND. DEPT. OF HEALTH. (ANNUAL REPORT . . .). Main/Corp Rhode Island. Dept. of Health. 1978-1979-. 0731-244X. US. English. an. NLM W2 AR4 D3A. *Department of Health, State of Rhode Island, 0731-7042.*

ANNUAL REPORT, SAFETY. *See* Transportation - Roads and Traffic.

ANNUAL REPORT - SASKATCHEWAN HEALTH. COMMUNITY SERVICES, SWIFT CURRENT REGION. (ANNUAL REPORT - SASKATCHEWAN. SWIFT CURRENT HEALTH REGION). Main/Corp Saskatchewan. Swift Current Health Region. 0709-4930. CN. English. an. Swift Current Health Region, No 1 E I Wood Building, 350 Cheadle Street West, Swift Current Saskatchewan Canada. LC RA185.S3. DD 362.10971243.

ANNUAL REPORT - SASKATCHEWAN HEALTH RESEARCH BOARD. (ANNUAL REPORT). Main/Corp Saskatchewan Health Research Board. 1st (1980)-. 0715-9714. CN. English. an. Saskatchewan Health Research Board, 2302 Arlington Avenue, Saskatoon Saskatchewan S7J 3L3 Canada. LC R854.C3. DD 354.712400841042.

ANNUAL REPORT - SCHISTOSOMIASIS CONTROL COUNCIL (PHILIPPINES). Main/Corp Schistosomiasis Control Council (Philippines). VFOAT S.C.C. Annual Report. English. an. LC RA644.S3. DD 614.553.

ANNUAL REPORT - SOUTH AFRICA. DEPT. OF HEALTH & WELFARE. Main/Corp South Africa. Dept. of Health & Welfare. VFOAT Jaarverslag. Afrikaans (English). an. LC RA352.S75. DD 354.68007706. *Annual Report.*

ANNUAL REPORT, SOUTH DAKOTA GOVERNOR'S TRAFFIC SAFETY PROGRAM. *See* Transportation - Roads and Traffic.

ANNUAL REPORT - STATE HEALTH PLANNING AND DEVELOPMENT AGENCY, OFFICE OF THE GOVERNOR, STATE OF MISSISSIPPI. (ANNUAL REPORT - STATE OF MISSISSIPPI, STATE HEALTH PLANNING AND DEVELOPMENT AGENCY). Main/Corp Mississippi. State Health Planning and Development Agency. 1976/77-. 0162-8682. US. English. an. Watkins

Public Health and Safety

Building, Suite 100, 510 George Street, Jackson MS 39201. **LC** RA395.A4. **DD** 353.97620084105.

ANNUAL REPORT - STATE OF NEW JERSEY, DEPARTMENT OF LAW & PUBLIC SAFETY. *See* Law.

ANNUAL REPORT - TENNESSEE. DEPARTMENT OF PUBLIC HEALTH. **Main/Corp** Tennessee. Department of Public Health. 1937/38-. US. English. an. Department of Public Health, Health Education Service, Nashville TN 37219. **LC** RA154. **DD** 614.09768. *Biennial Report.*

ANNUAL REPORT - TEXAS COORDINATING COMMISSION FOR STATE HEALTH AND WELFARE SERVICES. **Main/Corp** Texas Coordinating Commission For State Health and Welfare Services. 1st- 1976-. 0161-2166. US. English. an. Executive Office Building, 411 West 13th Street, Austin TX 78701. **LC** RA395.A4. **DD** 353.976400841.

ANNUAL REPORT, THE INDIAN HEALTH CARE IMPROVEMENT ACT, P.L. 94-437. (ANNUAL REPORT : THE INDIAN HEALTH CARE IMPROVEMENT ACT, P.L. 94-437). **VFOAT** Indian Health Care Improvement Act, P.L. 94-437, Annual Report. 0748-9021. US. English. an. US Department of Health and Human Services/Public Service Health Resources and Services Administration/Indian Health Service, Parklawn Building/ 5600 Fishers Lane, Rockville MD 20857. **LC** RA448.5.I5. **DD** 362.108997. Vols. for 1981- distributed to depository libraries in microfiche.

ANNUAL REPORT TO CONGRESS - NATIONAL TRANSPORTATION SAFETY BOARD. *See* Transportation.

ANNUAL REPORT TO THE CONGRESS BY THE SECRETARY OF HEALTH, EDUCATION, AND WELFARE ON THE PROFESSIONAL STANDARDS REVIEW ORGANIZATIONS PROGRAM. **Main/Corp** United States. Health Standards and Quality Bureau. **VFOAT** Professional Standards Review Organizations Program. 1st- 1976/77-. 0192-7493. US. English. an. Department of Health Education and Welfare, Health Care Financing Administration 330 C Street Southwest, Washington DC 20201. **LC** RA399.A3. **DD** 353.00841. **NLM** W2.

ANNUAL REPORT TO THE GOVERNOR AND LEGISLATURE OF THE STATE OF CALIFORNIA. **Main/Corp** California Health Facilities Commission. US. English. an. California Health Facilities Commission, 555 Capitol Mall Room 525, Sacramento CA 95814. **LC** RA981.C3. **DD** 362.1109794.

ANNUAL REPORT TO THE GOVERNOR AND THE LEGISLATURE ON PILOT PROGRAMS - CALIFORNIA. DEPT. OF HEALTH. **Main/Corp** California. Dept. of Health. 0146-745X. US. English. an. California Department of Health Commission, 717 K Street, Sacramento CA 95814. **LC** RA27. **DD** 362.109794.

ANNUAL REPORT : TUBERCULOSIS CONTROL IN THE PROVINCE OF NEW BRUNSWICK. **Main/Corp** New Brunswick. Division of Tuberculosis Control. CN. English. an. New Brunswick Tuberculosis and Respiratory Disease Association, PO Box 1345, Fredericton New Brunswick Canada. **LC** RA644.T7. **DD** 614.54209715.

ANNUAL REPORT - UNITED STATES. INDIAN HEALTH SERVICE. NAVAJO AREA. OFFICE OF ENVIRONMENTAL HEALTH AND ENGINEERING. (ANNUAL REPORT). **Main/Corp** United States. Indian Health Service. Navajo Area. Office of Environmental Health and Engineering. **VFOAT** Navajo Area E.H.E. 0734-5690. US. English. an. United States Public Health Service, Indian Health Service Navajo Area, Office of Environmental Health and Engineering, Window Rock AZ 86515. **LC** RA448.5.I5. **DD** 353.0084108997.

ANNUAL REPORT . . . - UNITED STATES. OFFICE OF HEALTH RESOURCES OPPORTUNITY. 0147-7579. Periodical. US. English.

ANNUAL REPORT - VERMONT HEALTH POLICY CORPORATION. **Main/Corp** Vermont Health Policy Corporation. Began with 1977/78. US. English. an. Vermont Health Policy Corporation, PO Box 1051, Montpelier VT 05602. **LC** RA395.A4. **DD** 353.974300841.

ANNUAL REPORTS TO LEGISLATURE, STATE HOSPITAL ADVISORY BOARDS (CALIFORNIA). **Main/Corp** California. Dept. of Health. US. English. an. **LC** RA790.65.C2. **DD** 362.2109794.

ANNUAL REVIEW AND PROGRESS PLAN - CONNECTICUT. DEPT. OF MENTAL HEALTH. **Main/Corp** Connecticut. Dept. of Mental Health. US. English. an. **LC** RA790.65.C8. **DD** 353.974600842.

ANNUAL REVIEW AND PROGRESS REPORT - MASSACHUSETTS. DEPT. OF MENTAL HEALTH. **Main/Corp** Massachusetts. Dept. of Mental Health. 1977-. US. English. an. Massachusetts Department of Mental Health, 190 Portland Street, Boston MA 02114. **LC** RA790.65.M35. **DD** 353.974400842.

ANNUAL REVIEW AND PROGRESS REPORT - NEBRASKA. DEPT. OF PUBLIC INSTITUTIONS. MEDICAL SERVICES DIVISION. **Main/Corp** Nebraska. Dept. of Public Institutions. Medical Services Division. **VFOAT** Annual Review & Progress Report on the Nebraska State Comprehensive Mental Health Plan. US. English. an. **LC** RA790.65.N2. **DD** 362.209782.

ANNUAL REVIEW OF PUBLIC HEALTH. v. 1- 1980-. 0163-7525. US. English. an. $31.00 Domestic, $34.00 Foreign. Annual Reviews Inc, 4139 El Camino Way, Palo Alto CA 94306. **Tel** (415)493-4400. Ed Lester Breslow. **Ind/Abst** Life Sci. Collect., Hospit. Lit. Index, Cumul. Index Nurs. Allied Health Lit., Index Med., Chem. Abstr. **LC** RA421. **DD** 362.105. **NLM** W1 AN7796K. **CODEN** AREHDT. Comprehensive, thorough coverage of latest advances in public health, written by acknowledged experts in the field. Extensive literature citations included.

ANNUAL STATISTICAL REPORT FOR INDIANA MENTAL HEALTH CLINICS. *See* Statistics.

ANNUAL STATISTICAL REPORT. MENTAL HEALTH SERVICES. MENTAL RETARDATION SERVICES. VETERANS' HOMES SERVICE (NEBRASKA). *See* Statistics.

ANNUAL STATISTICS - MANITOBA HEALTH SERVICES COMMISSION. *See* Statistics.

ANNUAL SUMMARY - IOWA. STATE DEPT. OF HEALTH. DIVISION OF DISEASE PREVENTION. (ANNUAL SUMMARY). **Main/Corp** Iowa. State Dept. of Health. Division of Disease Prevention. 0730-6814. US. English. an. Lucas State Office Building, Des Moines IA 50319. **LC** RA643.6.I8. **DD** 312.3909777.

ANNUAL SUMMARY OF THE UTILIZATION OF INPATIENT AND DAY CARE FACILITIES, ISRAEL. English. an. **LC** RA990.I7. **DD** 362.11095694.

ANNUAL WORK PLAN . . . FOR THE OFFICE OF HEALTH PROTECTION, COLORADO DEPARTMENT OF HEALTH. **Main/Corp** Colorado. Office of Health Protection. US. English. an. **LC** RA31. **DD** 353.97880077.

ANNUAL WORK PROGRAM - WASHINGTON TRAFFIC SAFETY COMMISSION. **Main/Corp** Washington (State). Traffic Safety Commission. 0095-3385. US. English. an. PO Box 1399, Olympia WA 98504. **LC** HE5614.3.W2. **DD** 614.86209797.

APPENDIX TO THE DIABETES MELLITUS COORDINATING COMMITTEE . . . ANNUAL REPORT TO THE DIRECTOR, NATIONAL INSTITUTES OF HEALTH. 6th (Fiscal Year 1979)-. US. English. an. Diabetes Mellitus Coordinating Committee, National Institutes of Health, Bethesda MD 20205.

ARCHIVIO SICILIANO DI MEDICINA E CHIRURGIA. 2, ACTA MEDITERRANEA DI PATOLOGIA INFETTIVA E TROPICALE. *See* Genealogy and Heraldry - Archives.

ARIZONA PUBLIC SAFETY SURVEY. US. English. an. Classification and Compensation Division, City of Phoenix Personnel Department, 10 North Third Avenue, Phoenix AZ 85003. **LC** HV8145.A7. **DD** 331.281363209791.

ARIZONA VITAL HEALTH STATISTICS. *See* Statistics.

ASEPTIC MENINGITIS SURVEILLANCE. (ASEPTIC MENINGITIS SURVEILLANCE, ANNUAL SUMMARY). **VFOAT** Aseptic Meningitis Surveillance. 1976-. 0195-556X. US. English. an. United States Department of Health and Human Services, Public Health Service Centers for Disease Control, Atlanta GA 30333. **NLM** W2 A C2N. *Neurotropic Viral Diseases Surveillance. Aseptic Meningitis, Annual Summary.*

ASIAN JOURNAL OF INFECTIOUS DISEASES. V. 1- June/Sept. 1977-. 0129-4024. Periodical. SI. English. qt. $18.00. Medical Book Center, Crawford PO Box 666, Singapore 7 Republic of Singapore. **Ind/Abst** Life Sci. Collect., Excerpta Med., Chem. Abstr. **NLM** W1 AS139K. **CODEN** AJIDDF.

ASPECTS TECHNIQUES DE LA SECURITE ROUTIERE. *See* Transportation - Roads and Traffic.

AU NATUREL. (AU NATUREL : BULLETIN DE LA FEDERATION QUEBECOISE DE NATURISME). Vol. 1, No. 1 (Summer 1982)-. 0715-4690. Periodical. CN. French. qt. $1.25 Per No. Au Naturel, c/o Federation Quebecoise de Naturisme, Porte 3-37, 1415 Est rue Jarry, Montreal Quebec H2E 2Z7 Canada. **DD** 613.19405. *Information Naturistes Quebecoises,* 0715-4682.

THE AUSTRALIAN HEALTH CARE SYSTEM. **Series/Titl** Australian Studies in Health Service Administration. 1979-. English. an. **NLM** W1.

AVIATION SAFETY. *See* Aeronautics, Astronautics.

AWARE (DARBY, PA.). (AWARE). 0742-471X. Periodical. US. English. bm. $5.00 Donation. Mercy Catholic Medical Center, Lansdowne Avenue & Baily Road, Darby PA 19023. **DD** 613.

N B C NEWS NFC. *See* Building and Construction.

BACKFLOW PREVENTION. *See* Water Resources.

BALANCED PERSPECTIVE ON THE HEALTH OF KANSAS. (BALANCED PERSPECTIVE ON : THE HEALTH OF KANSANS). **Main/Corp** Kansas. Dept. of Health and Environment. **VFOAT** Health of Kansans. 1976/77-. 0161-2212. US. English. an. Kansas State Department of Health and Environment, Topeka KS 66620. **LC** RA67. **DD** 362.109781.

BASIC BIBLIOGRAPHIES FOR EDUCATORS IN HEALTH. *See* Bibliographies.

BASIC DOCUMENTS. **Main/Corp** World Health Organization. 1st- Ed. 0512-3003. SZ. English. ir. 27 Av Appia CH 1211, Geneva 27 Switzerland. **LC** RA8. **DD** 614.0611.

BEITRAGE ZUR HYGIENE UND EPIDEMIOLOGIE *CEASED.* Vol. 1- 1943-. 0067-5083. Periodical. GE. German. ir. Detuscher Buch Export-Import, Leninstrasse 16, DDR-701 Leipzig East Germany. **Ind/Abst** Excerpta Med., Index Med. **NLM** W1 BE341.

BEST'S EXECUTIVE DATA SERVICE. LIFE-HEALTH INDUSTRY MARKETING RESULTS. FIVE YEAR EXPERIENCE BY STATE LIFE LINES. *See* Business - Marketing.

BEST'S SAFETY DIRECTORY. *See* Yearbooks, Almanacs, Directories.

BESTWAYS. *See* Nutrition and Dietetics.

BETTER HEALTH (BIRMINGHAM, ALA.). (BETTER HEALTH). Vol. 1, No. 1 (July 1984)-. 8750-1228. Periodical. US. English. mo. $15.00. Better Health, University of Alabama in Birmingham, University Station, Birmingham AL 35294.

BIBLIOGRAPHY OF PUBLICATIONS RESULTING FROM NCHSR EXTRAMURAL RESEARCH. *See* Bibliographies.

BIBLIOGRAPHY ON HEALTH INDEXES. *See* Indexes/Abstracts.

Public Health and Safety

BIENIAL REPORT OF THE STATE DEPARTMENT OF HEALTH OF NORTH DAKOTA. (BIENIAL REPORT OF THE STATE DEPARTMENT OF HEALTH OF NORTH DAKOTA FOR THE BIENNIAL PERIOD ENDED . . .). **Main/Corp** North Dakota. State Dept. of Health. 18th (June 30, 1924)-25th (June 30, 1938). 0731-888X. US. English. be. **NLM** W2 AN9 S7B. *Biennial Report of the State Board of Health to the Governor of North Dakota for the Years, 0731-1397.*

BIENNIAL REPORT - MINNESOTA DEPARTMENT OF HEALTH. Main/Corp Minnesota. Dept. of Health. US. English. be. Minnesota Department of Health, 717 SE Delaware Street, Minneapolis MN 55440. **LC** RA91. **DD** 362.109776. **NLM** W2 AM6 D4B.

BIENNIAL REPORT OF EXAMINING AND LICENSING BOARDS - MINNESOTA. ADVISORY COMMITTEE OF EXAMINERS IN MORTUARY SCIENCE. Main/Corp Minnesota. Advisory Committee of Examiners in Mortuary Science. US. English. be. 717 Delaware Street SE, Minneapolis MN 55440. **LC** RA623.A3. **DD** 353.977600772.

BIENNIAL REPORT OF THE N.H. ADVISORY COMMISSION ON HEALTH AND WELFARE. (BIENNIAL REPORT OF THE N. H. ADVISORY COMMISSION ON HEALTH AND WELFARE). **Main/Corp** New Hampshire. Advisory Commission on Health and Welfare. **VAT** Biennial Report of the New Hampshire Advisory Commission on Health and Welfare. 1st- 1973/75-. 0362-6202. US. English. be. New Hampshire Advisory Commission on Health and Welfare, 8 Loudon Road, Concord NH 03301. **LC** RA111. **DD** 353.9742008405. **NLM** W2 AN3 A2A. *Annual Report of the Advisory Commission on Health and Welfare, 0545-1418.*

BIENNIAL REPORT OF THE REGIONAL DIRECTOR TO THE . . . SESSION OF THE REGIONAL COMMITTEE. VFOAT Biennial Report of the Who Regional Director for the Eastern Mediterranean. 1 July 1977-30 June 1979-. English. be. **LC** RA541.N36. **DD** 362.10956.

BIENNIAL REPORT - TEXAS DEPARTMENT OF HEALTH. Main/Corp Texas. Dept. of Health. 1977/79-. US. English. be. Texas Department of Health, 1100 West 49th Street, Austin TX 78756. **LC** RA157. **DD** 353.97640084106. *Biennial Report - Texas Department of Health Resources, 0163-1667.*

BIENNIAL REPORT - VIRGINIA. DEPT. OF HEALTH REGULATORY BOARDS. Main/Corp Virginia. Dept. of Health Regulatory Boards. 1978-1980-. US. English. be. Department of Health Regulatory Boards, Virginia Commission of Health Regulatory Boards, Seaboard Building/Suite 453, 3600 West Broad Street, Richmond VA 23230. **LC** RA396.A4. **DD** 353.975500841.

BIOGRAPHICAL DIRECTORY OF THE AMERICAN PUBLIC HEALTH ASSOCIATION. *See* Yearbooks, Almanacs, Directories.

BOATING SAFETY TRAINING MANUAL. Series/Titl Comdtinst. 0190-5481. US. English. an. G-BEL-3 U S Cosst Guard, Washington DC 20593. **LC** KF2558.P5. **DD** 623.888.

BODY-MIND NETWORKS. VFOAT Body Mind Networks. Began in 1984. 8756-8551. Periodical. US. English. $20.00. Networks Main Office, 4139 Chestnut Street, Philadelphia PA 19104. **LC** RA773. **DD** 613.05. *Networks (Philadelphia, Pa.), 8756-8543.*

BRAKES. Main/Corp United States. National Highway Traffic Safety Administration. **Series/Titl** Consumer Aid Series. 0095-1854. US. English. Superintendent of Documents, Government Printing Office, Washington DC 20402. **LC** TL242. **DD** 629.208 S, 629.246. *Brakes, 0095-1854.*

BRIEFS OF ACCIDENTS INVOLVING AERIAL APPLICATION OPERATIONS, U. S. GENERAL AVIATION. *See* Aeronautics, Astronautics.

BRIEFS OF ACCIDENTS INVOLVING AMATEUR-HOME BUILT AIRCRAFT, U.S. GENERAL AVIATION. *See* Aeronautics, Astronautics.

BRIEFS OF AIRCRAFT ACCIDENTS INVOLVING TURBINE POWERED AIRCRAFT. U.S. GENERAL AVIATION. *See* Aeronautics, Astronautics.

BRIEFS OF FATAL ACCIDENTS INVOLVING WEATHER AS A CAUSE-FACTOR, U.S. GENERAL AVIATION. *See* Aeronautics, Astronautics.

BRUCELLOSIS SURVEILLANCE. (BRUCELLOSIS SURVEILLANCE ANNUAL SUMMARY). **Series/Titl** DHEW Publication. **VFOAT** Brucellosis Surveillance. Began with 1971. 0090-1156. US. English. an. Center for Disease Control, Atlanta GA 30333. **LC** RA644.B7. **DD** 312.395700973. **NLM** W2 A C7CT. *Zoonosis Surveillance. Brucellosis, 0091-0341.*

BULLETIN A.S.P.Q. VAT Bulletin Association pour la Sante Publique du Quebec. Vol. 6, No. 5 (Feb. 1984)-. 0826-9203. Periodical. CN. French. ir. Association pour la Sante Publique du Quebec, 2E Etage 284 Carre St-Louis, Montreal Quebec H2X 1A4 Canada. **DD** 614.060714. *Bulletin (Association pour la Sante Publique du Quebec : 1980), 0228-426X.*

BULLETIN - CROIX-ROUGE LIBANAISE. (BULLETIN). **Main/Corp** Croix-Rouge Libanaise. 0253-9349. Periodical. French. mo. **NLM** W1 RE156UQT.

BULLETIN DU MINISTERE DE LA SANTE PUBLIQUE ET DE LA FAMILLE. Main/Corp Belgium. Ministere de la Sante Publique et de la Famille. 0304-9450. Periodical. BE. French. ir. 200. CCP 26, Bruxelles 392 Belgium. **LC** RA254. **DD** 614.09493. **NLM** W2 GB4 M6B. *Bulletin de la Sante Publique.*

BULLETIN - HEALTH SCIENCES ASSOCIATION OF ALBERTA. *See* Economics - Labor.

BULLETIN - HOLMES SAFETY ASSOCIATION. *See* Engineering - Mining Engineering.

BULLETIN - NATIONAL INSTITUTES OF HEALTH (U.S.). Main/Corp National Institutes of Health (U.S.). US. English. **LC** RA421.

BULLETIN OF THE HIGH INSTITUTE OF PUBLIC HEALTH. (THE BULLETIN OF THE HIGH INSTITUTE OF PUBLIC HEALTH). Began in 1971. 0379-7988. Periodical. English. ir. **NLM** W1 BU848.

BULLETIN OF THE PAN AMERICAN HEALTH ORGANIZATION. Main/Corp Pan American Sanitary Bureau. **VFOAT** PAHO Bulletin. V. 7, No. 3-. 0301-5750. Periodical. US. English. qt. $32.00. Pan American Health Organization, 525 23rd Street NW, Washington DC 20037. **Tel** (202)861-3200. **Ed** Manuel A Bobenrieth. **Ind/Abst** CIS Abstr., Hospit. Lit. Index, Excerpta Med., Energy Inf. Abstr., Environ. Abstr., Index Med., Ref. Source, Bibliogr. Agric. **LC** RA10. **DD** 362.109181. **NLM** W1 BU884D. bk rev. **Circ** 11,000. (ctrl). Medical research, preventative and social medicine, health systems, administration, health, manpower, common diseases, veterinary, public health, environmental health, maternal and child health, food and nutrition, health technology and chronical diseases. *Boletin de la Oficina Sanetaria Panamericana. English Edition, 0085-4638.*

BULLETIN OF THE SOCIETY OF VECTOR ECOLOGISTS. Main/Corp Society of Vector Ecologists. V. 1- 1974-. 0146-6429. US. English. sa. $20.00. Society of Vector Ecologists, PO Box 87, Santa Ana CA 92702. **Tel** (714)971-2421. **Ed** James P Well. **Ind/Abst** Chem. Abstr. **LC** RA639. **DD** 614.4305. **NLM** W1 BU889X. **CODEN** BSVEDL. adv acc. **Circ** 300. Publication of manuscripts on the subjects of biology, ecology and management of arthropods of public health significance.

BULLETIN - ONTARIO DIVISION. CANADIAN RED CROSS SOCIETY. (BULLETIN). Feb./Mar. 1976-. 0715-366X. Periodical. CN. English. ir. Canadian Red Cross Society, Ontario Division, 460 Jarvis Street, Toronto Ontario M3Y 2H5 Canada. **DD** 363.1005. *News Bulletin, 0045-5288.*

BUNDESGESUNDHEITSBLATT. 31. Jan. 1958-. 0007-5914. Periodical. German. bw. 105.00. Carl Heymanns Verlag KG, Gereonstrasse 18-32, 5000 Koln 1 West Germany. **Tel** (0221)134022. **Ed** Gunther Beitzke and Dieter Briggemauu. **Ind/Abst** Excerpta Med., CIS Abstr., Int. Packagu. Abstr., Energy Res. Abstr. **NLM** W2 GG4 B7B. Index published separately - free - automatically sent. bk rev. adv acc. **Circ** 2,500. (ctrl). Statements and treatises on juvenile law and juvenile aid in court justice-adolescents and family.

BUSINESS AND HEALTH. *See* Business.

BUSINESS, HEALTH AND EDUCATIONAL DISCIPLINES. *See* Business.

BYOIN NEMPO - KOKURITSU KYOTO BYOIN. Main/Corp Kokuritsu Kyoto Byoin. Japanese. ir. Kokuritsu Kyoto Byoin, Fushimi-ku (612), Kyoto Japan. **LC** RA990.J6. **NLM** WX 2 JJ3 K2K2B.

C A H P E R NEWS CEASED. **Main/Corp** Canadian Association for Health, Physical Education and Recreation. V. 2, No. 2-V. 8, No.6. 0318-1960. CN. English. ir. Canadian Association for Health Physical Education and Recreation, 333 River Road, Vanier City Ontario K1L 8B9 Canada. **DD** 613.706071. *C A H P E R Across Canada, 0318-1979.*

CAHIERS DE SANTE COMMUNAUTAIRE. (LES CAHIERS DE SANTE COMMUNAUTAIRE). No. 1, (June 1978)-. 0228-4308. CN. French. an. $6.50 Per No. Les Cahiers de Sante Communautaire, c/o l'Association pour la Sante Publique du Quebec, Universite de Montreal, Ste-Foy Quebec G1K 7P4 Canada. **DD** 614.09714.

CALIFORNIA STATE HEALTH PLAN. Main/Corp California. Office of Statewide Health Planning and Development. 1980/85-. 0272-9164. US. English. **NLM** W2 AC2 O4C. *California State Plan for Health.*

CALIFORNIA STATE PLAN FOR COMMUNITY MENTAL HEALTH CENTERS. Main/Corp California. Dept. of Mental Health. Grants Section. 1978/79-. 0191-9806. US. English. an. State of California, Department of Mental Health, Sacramento CA 95814. **LC** RA790.65.C2. **DD** 354.979400842. **NLM** W2 AC2 B943C. *California State Plan for Community Mental Health Centers, 0191-9806.*

CAMPUS SAFETY NEWSLETTER. *See* Education (General) - Higher Education.

CAMPUS SAFETY REPORT NEWSLETTER. *See* Education (General) - Higher Education.

CANADA'S MENTAL HEALTH. Began publication in 1953. 0008-2791. Periodical. CN. English. qt. $4.26. Receiver General for Canada, Supply and Services, Ottawa Ontario K1A 0S9 Canada. **Ind/Abst** Hospit. Lit. Index, Cumul. Index Nurs. Allied Health Lit., Can. Period. Index, Can. Educ. Index, Psychol. Abstr., Public Aff. Inf. Serv. Bull., Abstr. Soc. Work. **NLM** W1 CA492. **CODEN** CAMHA3.

CANADIAN JOURNAL OF PUBLIC HEALTH. VFOAT Revue Canadienne de Sante Publique. V. 34- Jan. 1943-. 0008-4263. Periodical. CN. English (French). bm. 29.50 Domestic, 35.00 Foreign. Canadian Public Health Association, 1335 Carling Avenue/Suite 210, Ottawa Ontario K1Z 8N8 Canada. **Tel** (613)725-3769. **Ed** J M Last. **Ind/Abst** Hospit. Lit. Index, Excerpta Med., Energy Inf. Abstr., Environ. Abstr., Cumul. Index Nurs. Allied Health Lit., ASTIS Bibliogr., ASTIS Curr. Aware. Bull., Nuci. Sci. Abstr., Biol. Abstr., Chem. Abstr., Index Med., Bibliogr. Agric., Soc. Sci. Citation Index. **NLM** W1 CA605. **CODEN** CJPEA4. bk rev. adv acc. **Circ** 4,000. (ctrl). Original articles only which are of interest to public health officers, nurses, doctors and public health researchers. *Canadian Public Health Journal, 0319-2652.*

CANADIAN SECURITY. V. 1- Sept./Oct. 1979-. 0709-3403. Periodical. CN. English. bm. 20.00. Security Publishing Limited, PO Box 430 Station O, Toronto Ontario M4A 2P1 Canada. **Tel** (416)755-4343. **Ed** Jack Percival. **DD** 658.47. bk rev. adv acc. **Circ** 15,000. (ctrl). Dedicated to the protection of persons and property including mobile communications, fire and emergency services, health and safety and all aspects of security. *Resources Protection, 0315-3231.*

CAPITAL PLAN (OHIO). Main/Corp Ohio. Dept. of Mental Health and Mental Retardation. 1976/81-. 0149-1393. Periodical. US. English. be. Ohio Department of Mental Health and Mental Retardation, Office of the Director, 2929 Kenny Road AM A204, Columbus OH 43221. **LC** RA790.65.O3. **DD** 362.209771.

CATALOG OF PUBLICATIONS OF THE NATIONAL CENTER FOR HEALTH STATISTICS. *See* Statistics.

Public Health and Safety

CATALOG OF PUBLICATIONS - UNITED STATES. HEALTH RESOURCES ADMINISTRATION. See Bibliographies.

CATALOG OF UNIVERSITY PRESENTATIONS. Main/Corp National Center for Health Statistics (U.S.). 0748-5093. US. English. an. National Center for Health Statistics, 3700 East-West Highway, Hyattsville MD 20782. LC RA407.3. DD 016.36210973021.

CATALOGO DE POS-GRADUACAO EM SAUDE COLETIVA DO BRASIL. 1983-. Portuguese. ir. LC RA440.7.B6. DD 614.071181.

CATALOGUE OF STATE MATERIALS - MEDICAID/MEDICARE MANAGEMENT INSTITUTE. Main/Corp Medicaid/Medicare Management Institute. 0271-857X. US. English. Medicaid/Medicare Management Institute Clearinghouse, 389 East Highrise, 6401 Security Building, Baltimore MD 21235. LC Z6673.6.U6, RA395.A3. DD 016.3621.

CAUSES OF DEATH. BULLETIN. AUSTRALIAN BUREAU OF STATISTICS. See Statistics.

CESKOSLOVENSKE ZDRAVOTNICTVI. Vol. 1- 1953-. 0009-0689. Periodical. CS. Czech (Russian). mo. Artia, Ve Smeckach 30, PO Box 790, Praha 1 Czechoslovakia. Ind/Abst Coal Abstr., Index Med., CIS Abstr. NLM W1 CE9155. Index in first issue of next volume - attached.

CHA GUIDEBOOK. See Religion, Mythology, Rationalism - Roman Catholic Church.

CHAC INFO. See Religion, Mythology, Rationalism - Roman Catholic Church.

CHAN. CONSUMER HEALTH ACTION NETWORK. See Consumer Interests.

CHEMECOLOGY. See Conservation & Natural Resources.

CHIBA-KEN EISEI KENKYUJO KENKYU HOKOKU. VFOAT Bulletin of the Public Health Laboratory of Chiba Prefecture. 0386-6742. Japanese. an. Chiba-Ken Eisei Kenkyujo, 666-2 Nitona-cho, Chiba-shi 280 Japan. Ind/Abst Chem. Abstr. LC RA532.C45. CODEN CEKHDO.

CHILD PROTECTION REPORT. 0147-1260. Periodical. US. English. bw. $135.00. Child Protection Report, 1346 Connecticut Avenue NW, Washington DC 20036. Tel (202)785-4055. Ed William E Howard. NLM W1 CH668I. bk rev. Circ 1,000. (ctrl) An independent news service for professionals working with children and youth.

CHOSA GEPPO - KOKURITSU EISEI SHIKENJO. Main/Corp Kokuritsu Eisei Shikenjo. JA. Japanese. ir. c/o Kokuritsu Eisei Shikenjo Fosoku Toshokan, 1-18 Kamiyoga 1-chome Setagaya-ku, Tokyo Japan. LC RA421.

CHRA RECORDER. (C H R A RECORDER). Main/Corp Canadian Health Record Association. VAT Canadian Health Record Association Recorder, Recorder (Oshawa). Dec. 1976-. 0227-3748. Periodical. CN. English (includes some text in French). Free to Members. Canadian Health Record Association, Suite 2/187 King Street East, Oshawa Ontario L1H 1C3 Canada. DD 651.5042610971. CAMRL Recorder, 0316-0637.

THE CHRONICLE. VFOAT Omaha District Dental Society Journal. 1938?-. 0030-2201. Periodical. US. English. ir. $10.00. Chronicle, 119 North 51st Street, Omaha NE 68132. Tel (402)554-1333. Ed D O de Shazer. Ind/Abst Index Dent. Lit. NLM W1 CH962K. bk rev. adv acc. Circ 2,000. Dental and good health nutrition interest, cooking, recipes, and book reviews. Chronicle of the Omaha District Dental Society.

CHUNG-KUO HUAN CHING KO HSUEH. See Sanitation, Environmental Technology.

CICH NEWSLETTER. (C I C H NEWSLETTER). Main/Corp Canadian Institute of Child Health. VFOAT Bulletin de l'I C S I. VAT Canadian Institute of Child Health Newsletter, Bulletin de l'ICSI, Bulletin de l'Institut Canadien de la Sante Infantile. V. 1- Nov. 1978-. 0225-5502. Periodical. CN. English (French). qt. Canadian Institute of Child Health, 410 Laurier Avenue West/Suite 803, Ottawa Ontario K1R 7T3 Canada. Tel (613)238-8425. DD 613.0432.

CLINICAL ELECTIVES FOR MEDICAL AND DENTAL STUDENTS AT THE NATIONAL INSTITUTES OF HEALTH. Main/Corp National Institutes of Health (U.S.). US. English. an. US Department of Health & Human Services, Public Health Service, National Institutes of Health, Bethesda MD 20205. Clinical Electives for Medical Students at the National Institutes of Health.

CLOTHED WITH THE SUN. (CLOTHED WITH THE SUN : THE QUARTERLY JOURNAL OF CLOTHES-OPTIONAL LIVING). Began in June 1981?. 0883-4326. Periodical. US. English. qt. $15.00. The Naturists Inc, PO Box 132, Oshkosh WI 54902. DD 613.

C.O.A. BULLETIN. Main/Corp Commissioned Officers Association of the United States Public Health Service. VAT Commissioned Officers Association Bulletin. 0526-6742. Periodical. US. English. mo. $5.00. COA Bulletin, 1750 Pennsylvania Avenue NW, Washington DC 20006. NLM W1 C541.

COCUK SAGLIGI VE HASTALIKLARI DERGISI. 0010-0161. Periodical. TU. Turkish. qt. Burhan Say, Hacettepe University Cocuk Sagligi, Ankara Turkey. Ind/Abst Biol. Abstr. NLM W1 CO103H. CODEN CSHDAO.

CODE OF FEDERAL REGULATIONS. 42, PUBLIC HEALTH. Main/Corp United States. Dept. of Health and Human Services. VFOAT Public Health. US. English. an. Superintendent of Documents, US Government Printing Office, Washington DC 20402. NLM KF 70.A3 C669. Vols. for (1984-) distributed to depository libraries in microfiche. Code of Federal Regulations. 42, Public Health.

COLORADO'S HEALTH. Vol. 1 1967-. 0588-506X. Periodical. US. English. bm. Colorado State Department of Public Health, 4210 East 11th Avenue, Denver CO 80220. Colorado Health News.

COMMUNICABLE DISEASE NEWSLETTER. Periodical. US. English. bw. New York State Department of Health, Empire State Plaza, Tower Building, Albany NY 12237. Tel (518)474-3224.

COMMUNICABLE DISEASE STATISTICS. See Statistics.

COMMUNICABLE DISEASE SUMMARY. 0744-7035. Periodical. US. English. bm. Oregon Health Division, PO Box 231, Portland OR 97207.

COMMUNIQUE NATIONAL - ASSOCIATION CANADIENNE POUR LA SANTE MENTALE. Main/Corp Canadian Mental Health Association. VFOAT National Newsletter - Canadian Mental Health Association. V. 1, No. 2- Autumn 1976-. 0705-811X. Periodical. CN. English (French text on alternate pages). Canadian Mental Health Association, 2160 Younge Street, Toronto Ontario M4S 2Z3 Canada. DD 362.206271. National Volunteer Newsletter, 0702-0309.

COMMUNITY HEALTH BULLETIN. No. 1- July/Sept. 1975-. 0312-6579. Periodical. English. ir. Australian Government Publication Service, Editor, PO Box 100, Woden Australian Capital Territory 2606 Australia. NLM W1 CO4288H.

COMMUNITY HEALTH IN SA : OFFICIAL JOURNAL OF THE INSTITUTE OF PUBLIC HEALTH. VFOAT Volksgesondheid in SA : Offisiele Blad van die Instituut vir Openbare Gesondheid. VAT Community Health in South Africa. June 1979-. Periodical. English (articles in Afrikaanse). ir. NLM W1 CO429C. Volksgesondheid.

COMMUNITY HEALTH INSTITUTE CLEARINGHOUSE NEWS. (THE COMMUNITY HEALTH INSTITUTE CLEARINGHOUSE NEWS). 0191-3972. Periodical. US. English. NLM W1 CO429CI. Newsletter Supplement - National Association of Community Health Centers, Inc, 0191-3980.

COMMUNITY HEALTH SERVICES BULLETIN CEASED. Nov. 1973-March 1981. 0708-3874. Periodical. CN. English. qt. Free. Local Health Services Bulletin.

COMMUNITY HEALTH STUDIES. V. 1- Oct. 1977-. 0314-9021. Periodical. AT. English. ty. 40.00. University of Adelaide, Department of Community Medicine, Adelaide 5000 South Australia. Tel 223 0230. Ed John D Potter. Ind/Abst Excerpta Med., Index Med., APAIS, Aust. Public Aff. Inf. Serv., Soc. Sci. Citation Index. NLM W1 CO429G. bk rev. Circ 1,200. Journal of the Australian and New Zealand Society for Epidemiology and Research in Community Health, covering a wide range of human natural and social sciences as well as epidemiology research.

COMPARATIVE IMMUNOLOGY, MICROBIOLOGY AND INFECTIOUS DISEASES. V. 1- 1978-. 0147-9571. Periodical. UK. English. qt. Pergamon Press, 395 Sawmill River Road, Elmsford NY 10523. Ind/Abst Life Sci. Collect., Excerpta Med., Index Med., Biol. Abstr., Bibliogr. Agric. NLM W1 CO435K. CODEN CIMIDV.

COMPREHENSIVE ENVIRONMENT, HEALTH, AND SAFETY PROGRAM REPORT. See Sanitation, Environmental Technology.

COMPREHENSIVE HEALTH PLAN FOR NEW JERSEY. Main/Corp New Jersey. Comprehensive Health Planning Agency. 1973/74-. 0094-1336. Periodical. US. English. an. John Fitch Plaza, PO Box 1540, Trenton NJ 08625. LC RA395.A4. DD 362.109749.

CONCEPTS FOR TRAFFIC SAFETY. See Transportation - Roads and Traffic.

CONCERN. (CONCERN : A PAPER FOR PEOPLE WHO CARE ABOUT PEOPLE). Vol. 1, No. 1-. 0229-2661. Periodical. CN. English. qt. Food for the Hungry/Canada, 210-6th Street, New Westminster British Columbia V3L 3 Canada. DD 363.857505.

CONGRES ANNUEL - CONSEIL CANADIEN DA LA SECURITE. Main/Corp Conseil Canadien de la Securite. 0700-6659. Periodical. CN. French. an. 6.50. Conseil Canadien de la Securite, 1765 Boulevard Saint Laurent, Ottawa Ontario K1G 3V4 Canada. Tel (416)445-7101. Ed Frances Sgro. DD 614.805. Circ 200,000. For safety education in the home, traffic and recreational environments. Canada Safety Council Conference.

CONGRESS AND HEALTH. Series/Titl Government Relations Handbook Series, No. 1, Rev., etc. 1st- Ed. 0195-9840. Periodical. US. English. ir. National Health Council Inc, 622 Third Avenue, New York NY 10017-6765. Tel (212)972-2700. NLM W1 CO595. One-step, 88-page resource document on the 99th Congress and its involvement in the health field. Describes legislative process and lists all key individuals involved.

CONSOLIDATED ANNUAL REPORT ON STATE AND TERRITORIAL PUBLIC HEALTH LABORATORIES. VFOAT Consolidated Annual Report. 0743-5908. US. English. an. US Department of Health and Human Services, Public Health Service Centers for Disease Control, Laboratory Improvement Program Office, Atlanta GA 30333. LC RA428. DD 614.072073. NLM W1 AS753M.

CONSOLIDATED PLAN. APPENDICES - MISSOURI. DEPT. OF MENTAL HEALTH. (CONSOLIDATED PLAN. APPENDICES). Main/Corp Missouri. Dept. of Mental Health. 0732-2658. US. English. te. Missouri Department of Mental Health, 2002 Missouri Boulevard, Jefferson City MO 65101. LC RA790.65.M8. DD 353.977800842.

CONSOLIDATED PLAN - MISSOURI. DEPT. OF MENTAL HEALTH. (CONSOLIDATED PLAN). Main/Corp Missouri. Dept. of Mental Health. 0732-264X. US. English. te. Missouri Department of Mental Health, 2002 Missouri Boulevard, Jefferson City MO 65101. LC RA790.65.M8. DD 353.977800842.

CONSUMER HEALTH PERSPECTIVES. V. 5- 1978-. 0191-3921. Periodical. US. English. bm. $25.00. Consumer Commission on Accreditation of Health Services, 377 Park Avenue South, New York NY 10016. Ind/Abst Hospit. Lit. Index. NLM W1 CO755H. Health Perspectives, 0097-0069; Quarterly - Consumer Commission on the Accreditation of Health Services, 0361-9907.

CONSUMER PRODUCT HAZARD INDEX. See Indexes/Abstracts.

CONSUMING PASSIONS. 0741-7748. Periodical. US. English. bm. Consuming Passions, PO Box 77, Norwood NJ 07648. Tel (201)768-0201. Ed Barbara May. DD 613. bk rev. Circ 5,000. (ctrl). A newsletter devoted to the conflicting relationship between people and food.

Public Health and Safety

CONTEMPORARY HEALTH JOURNAL. VFOAT CHJ. Vol. 1, No. 1 (March 1983)-. 0882-4479. Periodical. US. English. mo. Contemporary Health Journal, PO Box 443, Racine WI 53401-0443. **DD** 614.

CONTINUING EDUCATION FOR THE HEALTH PROFESSIONS, STATISTICAL REPORT. See Statistics.

CONTRIBUTIONS TO EPIDEMIOLOGY AND BIOSTATISTICS. V. 1-. 0377-3574. Monographic Series. SZ. English. ir. S Karger AG, PO Box, CH-4009 Basel Switzerland. **Tel** 061-39 08 80. Ed S A Klingberg. **Ind/Abst** Chem. Abstr., Index Med. **NLM** W1 CO778RC. **CODEN** CEPBDV. Problems of public health studied through the integrated use of epidemiologic and biostatistical methods.

CONTROL OF COMMUNICABLE DISEASES IN MAN. (CONTROL OF COMMUNICABLE DISEASES IN MAN : AN OFFICIAL PUBLICATION OF THE AMERICAN PUBLIC HEALTH ASSOCIATION). 8755-4046. US. English. ir. American Public Health Association, 1015 Fifteenth Street NW, Washington DC 20005. **DD** 614.

CPHA HEALTH DIGEST. (C P H A HEALTH DIGEST). **Main/Corp** Canadian Public Health Association. **VAT** Canadian Public Health Association Health Digest. V. 1- Feb. 1977-. 8403-5624. Periodical. CN. English. bm. Canadian Public Health Association, 1335 Carling Avenue/Suite 210, Ottawa Ontario K1Z 8N8 Canada. **Tel** (613)725-3769. **DD** 614.0971. *C P H A Newsletter, 0703-5594.*

CPR POPULATION RESEARCH. **Main/Corp** United States. National Institute of Child Health and Human Development. Center for Population Research. **VAT** Center for Population Research Population Research. 0190-7190. Monographic Series. US. English. National Institute of Child Health and Human Development, Center for Population Research, Bethesda MD 20014. **NLM** W1 C548.

CSSR ZDRAVOTNICTVI. VFOAT Zdravotnictvi CSSR. 0514-2431. Periodical. Czech. ir. **NLM** W2 GC8 M6Z. *Zdravotnictvi CSSR.*

CUMULATED ANNOTATIONS - CLEARINGHOUSE ON HEALTH INDEXES. See Bibliographies.

CURRENT AWARENESS IN HEALTH EDUCATION. Began with Oct. 1978. 0196-2426. Periodical. US. English. mo. Superintendent of Documents, US Government Printing Office, Washington DC 20402. **LC** Z5814.H43, RA440.5. **NLM** ZWA 18 C976.

CURRENT CHARGES FOR SELECTED HOSPITAL SERVICES . . . . See Medicine - Medical Centers, Hospitals.

CURRENT CLINICAL TOPICS IN INFECTIOUS DISEASES. 1-. 0195-3842. US. English. an. McGraw-Hill Book Company, 1221 Avenue of the Americas, New York NY 10020. **Tel** (212)997-3355. **LC** RC111. **DD** 616.905. **NLM** W1 CU786T.

CURRENT ESTIMATES FROM THE NATIONAL HEALTH INTERVIEW SURVEY, UNITED STATES. Series/Titl DHHS Publication. 1981-. US. English. an. Superintendent of Documents, US Government Printing Office, Washington DC 20402. *Current Estimates from the Health Interview Survey, United States, 0502-2673.*

CURRENT HEALTH 1. VAT CURRENT HEALTH ONE. 0199-820X. Periodical. US. English. mo. $4.95. Curriculum Innovations Inc, 3500 Western Avenue, Highwood IL 60035. **Tel** (312)432-2700. **Ind/Abst** Child. Mag. Guide.

CURRENT HEALTH 2. VFOAT Current Health Two. 0163-156X. Periodical. US. English. mo. $4.95. Curriculum Innovations Inc, 3500 Western Avenue, Highwood IL 60035. **Tel** (312)432-2700. **Ind/Abst** Pop. Mag. Rev., Read. Guide Period. Lit.

CURRENT TOPICS IN INFECTION. No. 1-. Monographic Series. US. English. ir. Elsevier Science Publ Co Inc, PO Box 1663 Grand Central Station, New York NY 10163. **NLM** W1 CU82IM (P.

CURRENT TOPICS IN VECTOR RESEARCH. Vol. 1-. 0737-8491. US. English. $35.95. Praeger Publishers, 521 Fifth Avenue, New York NY 10175. **Tel** (215)574-4973. Ed Kerry F Harris. **LC** RA639. **DD** 614.43. **NLM** W1. **Circ** 500. Topics in vector research whose purpose is to establish continuous communication among researchers of all types of vector-related problems.

CURRENTS. 0146-874X. Periodical. US. English. qt. Horizon House Institute, 1019 Stafford House, 5555 Wissahicken Avenue, Philadelphia PA 19144. **LC** RA790.6. **DD** 362.20973. **NLM** W1 CU826B.

DANGEROUS GOODS REGULATIONS. **Main/Corp** International Air Transport Association. **VFOAT** IATA Dangerous Goods Regulations. **VAT** IATA Dangerous Goods Regulations, International Air Transport Association Dangerous Goods Regulations. Began publication with Jan. 1983 issue. 0256-3223. CN. English. an. $35.00. International Air Transport Association, 2000 Peel Street, Montreal Quebec H3A 2R4 Canada. **DD** 363.177. *Restricted Articles Regulations.*

DATEN DES GESUNDHEITSWESENS. **Main/Corp** Germany (West). Bundesministerium fur Jugend, Familie und Gesundheit. 1977-. German. ir. Bundesminister fur Jugend Familie und Gesundheit, 5300 Bonn-Bad Godesberg, Bonn West Germany. **LC** RA407.5.G4.

DEFENDER. (THE DEFENDER). 1- Oct. 1968-. 0379-5071. Periodical. KE. English (with some Swahili). qt. 2.00. African Medical Research & Education Foundation, PO Box 30125, Nairobi Kenya. Ed Elly Oduol. **NLM** W1 DE114. **Circ** 15,000. Ideas in the area of family health, sex education, chronic illness, first aid, personal hygiene, and environmental health.

DEFICIENCE MENTALE CEASED. VFOAT Mental Retardation. V. 13, No. 2-V. 30 No. 4. Periodical. CN. English (text in only, Apr. 1963-Summer 1967). qt. Canadian Association for the Mentally Retarded, Kinsmen National Institute on Mental Retardation Building, York University, 4700 Keele Street, Downsview Ontario M3J 1P3 Canada. **Ind/Abst** Can. Educ. Index. **NLM** W1 DE117K.

DEVELOPMENTS IN ENVIRONMENTAL CONTROL AND PUBLIC HEALTH. Series/Titl Developments Series. 1-. 0260-0862. UK. English. ir. Elsevier Applied Science Publ, Crown House Linton Road, Barking Essex IG11 8JU England. **Tel** 01 594 7272. Ed A Porteous. **Ind/Abst** GeoRef, Chem. Abstr. **NLM** W1 DE997VWF. **CODEN** DCPHDC.

DIAL CODES. **Main/Corp** North Carolina. Office of Emergency Medical Services. US. English. an. North Carolina Office of Emergency Medical Services, PO Box 12200, Raleigh NC 27605. **LC** RA645.6.N8. **DD** 363.348025756.

DIFESA SOCIALE. V. 1- Jan. 1922-. 0012-2653. Periodical. Italian. qt. **Ind/Abst** Biol. Abstr., CIS Abstr. **NLM** W1 DI518. **CODEN** DISOAJ. (cum index).

THE DIGEST. **Main/Corp** Texas. Dept. of Public Safety. Division of Disaster Emergency Services. Periodical. US. English. bm. Public Safety Department State of Texas, 5805 North Lamar Boulevard, Disaster Emergency Service, Austin TX 78773. **Tel** (512)452-0331.

A DIRECTORY OF FULL-TIME COUNTY AND URBAN HEALTH DEPARTMENTS. See Yearbooks, Almanacs, Directories.

DIRECTORY OF MENTAL HEALTH AND ALCOHOLISM PROGRAMS IN MARYLAND. See Yearbooks, Almanacs, Directories.

DIRECTORY OF STATE, TERRITORIAL, AND REGIONAL HEALTH AUTHORITIES. See Yearbooks, Almanacs, Directories.

DISCUSSION PAPER (LEONARD DAVIS INSTITUTE OF HEALTH ECONOMICS). (DISCUSSION PAPER). VFOAT Discussion Paper Series. No. 44-. Monographic Series. US. English. **NLM** W1 DI745F. *Discussion Paper (National Health Care Management Center (U.S.)).*

DISCUSSION PAPER - WASHINGTON (STATE). UNIVERSITY. CENTER FOR HEALTH SERVICES RESEARCH. **Main/Corp** Washington (State). University. Center for Health Services Research. Series/Titl Health Policy Research Series. Monographic Series. US. English. ir. Center for Health Services, Research Department of Health Services, School of Public Health and Community Medicine, University of Washington, Seattle WA 98195.

DISEASE CONTROL NEWSLETTER. Periodical. US. English. mo. Division of Personal Health, Minnesota Department of Health, Minneapolis MN 55101. **Tel** (612)296-5201.

DRAFT HEALTH SYSTEMS PLAN FOR SOUTH CAROLINA HEALTH SERVICE AREA III. **Main/Corp** Pee Dee Regional Health Systems Agency, Inc. VFOAT Health Systems Plan. No. 2-. US. English. an. PO Box 5959, Florence SC 29502.

THE DRINKING AND DRUG PRACTICES SURVEYOR. See Drug Abuse and Alcoholism.

ECOLOGICAL ILLNESS LAW REPORT. See Law.

ECOLOGY OF DISEASE. Vol. 1, No. 1-. 0278-4300. Periodical. UK. English. qt. $75.00. Pergamon Press, Maxwell House Fairview Park, Elmsford NY 10523. **Ind/Abst** Life Sci. Collect., Excerpta Med., Index Med., Biol. Abstr. **LC** RA565.A1. **DD** 614.42. **NLM** W1 EC916M. **CODEN** EYDIDI.

EDUCACION MEDICA Y SALUD. V. 1-. 0013-1091. US. Spanish. qt. $32.00. Pan American Health Organization, 525 23rd Street NW, Washington DC 20037. **Tel** (203)642-1214. **Ind/Abst** Index Med. **NLM** W1 ED69. bk rev. **Circ** 6,000. (ctrl). Published to support manpower development activities in the countries of the Region and to disseminate modern techniques for the teaching-learning process in the health sciences in general.

EDUCATION SANITAIRE. VFOAT Health Education Sanitaire. **VAT** Health Education (Ottawa. French Edition), Health Education Sanitaire (French Edition). 0700-1991. Periodical. CN. French. qt. **Tel** (613)990-7853. **Ind/Abst** Can. Educ. Index. bk rev. **Circ** 3,000. Information for Canadian health promotion professionals on new policies, programs, resources and events.

EFFECTIVE HEALTH CARE. Vol. 1, No. 1 (June 1983)-Vol. 2, No. 6. 0167-871X. Periodical. English (summaries in French and German). bm. Elsevier Science Publishers, PO Box 211, 1000 AE Amsterdam Netherlands. **Tel** (020)5803.911. **Ind/Abst** Hospit. Lit. Index. **NLM** W1. **CODEN** EHCAD6.

EGESZSEGNEVELES. VFOAT Educatio Sanitaria. Periodical. HU. Hungarian. bm. Akademiai Kiado, POB 24, 1363 Budapest Hungary. **LC** RA440.3.H9. *Egeszsegugyi Felvilagositas.*

EIS DIRECTORY. See Yearbooks, Almanacs, Directories.

EISEI GYOSEI GYOMU HOKOKU. **Main/Corp** Japan. Koseisho. Daijin Kambo. Tokei Johobu. 1973-. Japanese. ir. **LC** RA531. **NLM** W2 JJ3 K8EI. *Eisei Gyosei Gyomu Hokoku.*

EISEI SHIKENJO HOKOKU. **Main/Corp** Kokuritsu Eisei Shikenjo. VFOAT Bulletin of National Institute of Hygienic Sciences. No. 67-. 0077-4715. JA. Japanese (summaries in English). an. Kokuritsu Eisei Shikenjo, 18-1 Kamiyoga 1-chome Setagaya-ku, Tokyo 158 Japan. **Ind/Abst** Life Sci. Collect., Excerpta Med., Index Med., Int. Packag. Abstr., Chem. Abstr., Bibliogr. Agric. **LC** RA421. **NLM** W1 EI573. **CODEN** ESKHA5. *Eisei Shikenjo Iho.*

EMERGENCY. V. 10, No. 2- Feb. 1978-. 0162-5942. Periodical. US. English. mo. $17.59. Emergency, PO Box 159, Carlsbad CA 92008. **Tel** (619)438-2511. Ed Kim Pallas. **Ind/Abst** Cumul. Index Nurs. Allied Health Lit. **LC** RA995.A1. **DD** 616.02505. **NLM** W1 EM661Q. bk rev. adv acc. **Circ** 37,000. To meet the needs and interests of various providers of emergency health care. *Emergency Product News, 0098-2180.*

EMS MESSENGER. VFOAT E.M.S. Messenger. **VAT** Emergency Medical Services Messenger. Began with V. 1, Sept. 1978. 0164-8971. Periodical. US. English. bm. Free. Texas Department of Health, EMS Division, 1100 West 49th Street, Austin TX 78756.

THE EMT JOURNAL CEASED. **VAT** Emergency Medical Technicians Journal. Began with V. 1, Mar. 1977. Ceased with Dec. 1981 issue. 0147-5851. Periodical. US. English. bm. $35.75 Domestic, $40.75 Foreign. C V Mosby Co, 11830 Westline Industrial Drive, St Louis MO 63141. **Ind/Abst** Cumul. Index Nurs. Allied Health Lit. **LC** RA645.5. **DD** 362.1. **NLM** W1 E37.

L'ENFANT EN MILIEU TROPICAL. Began with: No. 1, published in 1961. Periodical. FR. French. bm. 20. Centre Internationale de l'Enfance, Chateau de Longchamp, Bois de Boulogne, 75106 Paris France. **Tel** 506-79-92. Ed Anne-Marie Masse-Raimbault. **NLM** W1 EN575. bk rev. **Circ** 10,000. (ctrl). Journal furnishes practical information that can be directly applied to health, and Information agents for development. Each issue deals with a specific topic.

Public Health and Safety

ENVIRONMENT, SAFETY, HEALTH AT DOE FACILITIES. See Sanitation, Environmental Technology.

ENVIRONMENTAL ACCIDENT STATISTICS. See Statistics.

ENVIRONMENTAL HEALTH REVIEW. See Sanitation, Environmental Technology.

ENVIRONMENTAL MANAGEMENT FOR THE PUBLIC HEALTH INSPECTOR. 1970-. 0316-0661. Periodical. CN. English. an. Institution of Public Affairs, Dalhousie University, Halifax Nova Scotia B3H 4H8 Canada. **DD** 614.05. *Environmental Hygiene for the Public Health Inspector, 0071-092X.*

ENVIRONMENTAL RADIATION SURVEILLANCE IN WASHINGTON STATE. See Sanitation, Environmental Technology.

ENVIRONMENTAL TECHNOLOGY & ECONOMICS. See Sanitation, Environmental Technology.

EPI NEWSLETTER. VAT Expanded Program on Immunization Newsletter. V. 1- May 1979-. 0251-4710. Periodical. US. English. bm. Free. Expanded Program on Immunization Paho, 525-23rd Street NW, Washington DC 20037. **Tel** (202)861-3247. Ed Ciro de Quadros. **NLM** W1 E42. bk rev. adv acc. **Circ** 4,000. (ctrl). Articles on epidemiology of diseases (polio, tuberculosis, tetanus, diphtheria, measles, whooping cough) in countries of Americas. Includes vaccination coverage, data and morbidity.

EPIDEMIOLOGIC NOTES & COMMUNICABLE DISEASE MORBIDITY REPORT (NORTH CAROLINA). Main/Corp North Carolina. Division of Health Services. Epidemiology Section. 0095-313X. Periodical. US. English. mo. Free. PO Box 2091, Raleigh NC 27602. **Tel** (919)733-3421. Ed Hazel King. **LC** RA124. **DD** 614.42756. **NLM** W2 AN8 B3R. **Circ** 850. (ctrl). Notes on epidemiology programs of North Carolina State Division of Health Services; monthly communicable disease morbidity statistics.

EPIDEMIOLOGIC REVIEWS. V. 1- 1979-. 0193-936X. US. English. an. $84.00 Domestic, $89.00 Foreign. American Journal of Epidemiology, 624 North Broadway/Room 225, Baltimore MD 21205. **Tel** (301)955-3441. Ed George W Comstock. **Ind/Abst** Life Sci. Collect., Excerpta Med., Index Med., Biol. Abstr. **LC** RA648.5. **DD** 614.405. **NLM** W1 EP449. **CODEN** EPIRD7. adv acc. **Circ** 4,800. (ctrl). Original and laboratory studies on occurence of disease with articles on infectious and non-infectious diseases and statistical methodology.

EPIDEMIOLOGICAL BULLETIN. V. 1-. Periodical. US. English. bm. Free. Pan Amer Health Organization, 525-23rd Street NW c/o Dr Tigre-Hce, Washington DC 20037. **Tel** (202)861-4356. Ed Renate Plant. **LC** RA650. **DD** 614.42705. **NLM** W1 EP449P. bk rev. **Circ** 10,000. (ctrl). Periodical publication of short accounts of and comments on epidemiological activities of priority public concern and information regarding technical aspects involved in health prevention in the Region of the Americas. *Weekly Epidemiological Report.*

EPIDEMIOLOGICAL COMMENTS. SA. Afrikaans (English). mo. Department of Health, Welfare & Pensions, Health Services Building c/o Struben & Andries Streets, Pretoria South Africa. **LC** RA650.8.S6. **DD** 614.4268.

ESTABLISHMENTS AND PRODUCTS LICENSED UNDER SECTION 351 OF THE PUBLIC HEALTH SERVICE ACT. Main/Corp United States. Food and Drug Administration. Bureau of Biologics. Series/Titl DHHS Publication. ?1971-. Periodical. US. English. 8800 Rockville Pike, Bethesda MD 20205.

ESTIMATES. PART III, HEALTH AND WELFARE CANADA. CN. English (French). $12.00 Domestic, $14.40 Foreign. Canadian Government Publishing Centre, Supply and Services Canada, Ottawa Ontario K1A 0S9 Canada. **LC** RA184. **DD** 354.7100841.

THE ETA SIGMA GAMMAN. Periodical. US. English. ir. $10.00. ETA Sigma Gamma, Ball State University, Muncie IN 47306. **Tel** (317)285-5961. Ed Denis H Amschier. bk rev. **Circ** 2,500. Publishes articles dealing with a broad range of health-related topics of interest to students, school health educators, public health professionals, and those in related areas.

EXCERPTA MEDICA. SECTION 17. PUBLIC HEALTH, SOCIAL MEDICINE AND HYGIENE. See Indexes/Abstracts.

EXECUTIVE HEALTH CEASED. Began in Feb. 1963. 0423-8966. Periodical. US. English. mo. $30.00. Executive Health Report, PO Box 589/Rancho, Sante Fe CA 92067. **Tel** (619)756-2600. **NLM** W1 EX201. A newsletter on different areas of health.

EXPLORING MENTAL HEALTH PARAMETERS. Vol. 1-. US. English. **LC** RA790.65.G4. **DD** 362.209758231.

FACTS AT YOUR FINGERTIPS. Series/Titl DHHS Publication. Began with 3rd Ed., Fall 1978. 0196-6294. US. English. US Department of Health & Human Services, Public Health Service, Office of Health Research Statistics & Technology, National Center for Health Statistics, 3700 East-West Highway, Hyattsville MD 20782. **NLM** ZWA 900 AA F14. *Facts at Your Fingertips, Almost, 0196-6278.*

FAMILLE AVERTIE. V. 1- Fall 1974-. 0315-954X. Periodical. CN. French. qt. $4.65. Canada Safety Council, 1765 St Laurent Boulevard, Ottawa Ontario K1G 3V4 Canada. **Tel** (514)482-9110. **DD** 614.805.

FAMILY & COMMUNITY HEALTH. VAT Family and Community Health. V. 1- Apr. 1978-. 0160-6379. Periodical. US. English. qt. $64.00. Aspen Systems Corporation, 1600 Research Boulevard, Rockville MD 20850. **Tel** (301)251-5000. **Ind/Abst** Hospit. Lit. Index, Cumul. Index Nurs. Allied Health Lit., Bibliogr. Agric., Psychol. Abstr. **LC** RA421. **DD** 362.1. **NLM** W1 FA432BK.

FAMILY SAFETY CEASED. Began with V. 21, No. 3- 1961. Ceased with V. 42, No. 3, Fall 1983. 0014-7397. Periodical. US. English. qt. $2.50. National Safety Council, 444 North Michigan Avenue, Chicago IL 60611. **DD** 613. **NLM** W1 FA454K. *Home Safety Review.*

FAMILY SAFETY AND HEALTH (CANADIAN EDITION). (FAMILY SAFETY AND HEALTH). Vol. 42, No. 4 (Winter 1983-84). 0749-3118. Periodical. US. English. qt. National Safety Council, 444 North Michigan Avenue, Chicago IL 60611. **DD** 613. *Family Safety (Canadian Edition), 0749-3231.*

FAMILY SAFETY AND HEALTH (UNITED STATES EDITION). (FAMILY SAFETY AND HEALTH). V. 42, No. 4 (Winter 1983-84)-. 0749-310X. Periodical. US. English. qt. National Safety Council, 444 North Michigan Avenue, Chicago IL 60611. **DD** 613. **NLM** W1 FA454K. *Family Safety, 0014-7397.*

FATAL ACCIDENT FACTS. Main/Corp Tennessee. Dept of Safety. Planning and Research Section. 0363-3373. US. English. Department of Safety, Andrew Jackson State Office Building, Nashville TN 37219. **LC** HE5614.3.T2. **DD** 312.274.

FDA CONSUMER. VAT Food and Drug Administration Consumer. Vol. 6, No. 6 (July/Aug. 1972)-. 0362-1332. Periodical. US. English. Superintendent of Documents, US Government Printing Office, Washington DC 20402. **Tel** (202)783-3238. **Ind/Abst** Mag. Index, Hospit. Lit. Index, Energy Inf. Abstr., Environ. Abstr., Pop. Mag. Rev., Index U.S. Gov. Period., Consum. Index Prod. Eval. Inf. Source, Public Aff. Inf. Serv. Bull., Bibliogr. Agric., Read. Guide Period. Lit. **LC** HD9000.9.U5. **DD** 640.73. **NLM** W1 F203E. **CODEN** FDACB. *FDA Papers, 0014-5750.*

FEDERAL MOTOR VEHICLE SAFETY STANDARDS AND REGULATIONS. See Transportation.

FILM AND PAMPHLET CATALOG. Main/Corp Kansas. Health and Environmental Education Services. VFOAT Film Library. 13th- Ed. US. English. Kansas Department of Health & Environment, Health and Environmental Services, Topeka KS 66620. **LC** RA440.5. **DD** 016.613. *Films and Pamphlets Catalog.*

FINANCIAL REPORT - DEPARTMENT OF HEALTH & SOCIAL SERVICES, DIVISION OF HEALTH. (FINANCIAL REPORT - DIVISION OF HEALTH). Main/Corp Wisconsin. Division of Health. 0362-7187. US. English. an. Wisconsin Department of Health & Social Services, Division of Health, PO Box 309, Madison WI 53701. **LC** RA177. **DD** 353.97750077.

FINANCIAL REPORT, OHIO'S LOCAL HEALTH DEPARTMENT. US. English. an. Ohio Department of Health, 246 N High Street PO Box 118, Columbus OH 43216. **LC** RA410.54.O3. **DD** 353.97710072236841. *Financial Report of Ohio Local Health Departments.*

FIRE AND POLICE PERSONNEL REPORTER. (FIRE AND POLICE PERSONNEL REPORTER : A MONTHLY PUBLICATION OF THE PUBLIC SAFETY PERSONNEL RESEARCH INSTITUTE). 0164-6397. Periodical. US. English. mo. $39.00. Public Safety Research Institute, PO Box 2105, San Francisco CA 94080. **Tel** (415)877-0735. **LC** HV8138. **DD** 350.740973. *Fire Department Personnel Reporter.*

FLIGHT SAFETY. See Aeronautics, Astronautics.

FLORIDA SUMMARY OF ACCIDENT DATA. See Transportation - Roads and Traffic.

FLORIDA'S HEALTH. V. 68- Jan. 1976-. 0362-0654. Periodical. US. English. mo. Health Program Office, PO Box 210, Jacksonville FL 32201. **LC** RA44. **DD** 613.05. **NLM** W1 FL925. *Florida Health Notes, 0015-4105.*

THE FLOWER ESSENCE JOURNAL. 0732-8389. Periodical. US. English. an. Flower Essence Society, PO Box 459, Nevada City CA 95959. *Flower Essence Quarterly, 0273-7868.*

FOCAL POINTS. VFOAT Health Education Focal Points. Began with Aug. 1975. 0278-1808. Periodical. US. English. bm. Superintendent of Documents, US Government Printing Office, Washington DC 20402. **NLM** W1 FO1001P.

FOCUS ON HEALTH. (FOCUS ON HEALTH : ISSUES AND EVENTS OF . . . FROM THE NEW YORK TIMES INFORMATION BANK). Series/Titl News in Print. Began in 1978. 0271-3152. US. English. an. Arno Press Inc A New York Times Company, 3 Park Avenue, New York NY 10016. **LC** R101.F63A. **DD** 610.5. **NLM** ZWA 100 F625.

FOGARTY INTERNATIONAL CENTER SERIES ON PREVENTIVE MEDICINE. Series/Titl DHEW Publication. VFOAT Preventive Medicine. V. 1-. 0161-553X. Monographic Series. US. English. ir. **NLM** W3 FO492.

FOOD AND NUTRITION BULLETIN. See Nutrition and Dietetics.

FOOD IRRADIATION INFORMATION. See Food & Drink.

FOODBORNE DISEASE SURVEILLANCE. ANNUAL SUMMARY. (FOODBORNE DISEASE SURVEILLANCE, ANNUAL SUMMARY). VFOAT Foodborne Disease Surveillance. Began with 1978. 0270-4072. US. English. an. US Department of Health and Human Services, Public Health Service, Centers for Disease Control, Atlanta GA 30333. **LC** RC143. **DD** 615.9540973. **NLM** W2 A C2FA. Vols. for 1978 Rev.-(1981) distributed to depository libraries in microfiche. *Foodborne & Waterborne Disease Surveillance, 0737-1241.*

FOREIGN TRAVEL IMMUNIZATION GUIDE. 5th Ed.-. 0193-0338. US. English. an. Medical Economics Company, Oradell NJ 07649. **LC** RA638. **DD** 614.470202. **NLM** W1 FO562.

FORESIGNT (TORONTO, ONT.). (FORESIGHT). Vol. 1, No. 1 (Spring 1981)-. 0710-0663. Periodical. CN. English. qt. Free to Members. The Association, Foresight, 175 College Street, Toronto Ontario M5T 1P8 Canada. **DD** 629.28307071.

FORSCHUNGSPROGRAMM - BUNDESANSTALT FUR STRASSENWESEN, BEREICH UNFALLFORSCHUNG. See Transportation - Roads and Traffic.

FORWARD PLAN FOR HEALTH. 1976/80-1977/81. 0363-5031. Periodical. US. English. an. **NLM** W2 A P9F.

FORWARD PLAN FOR THE HEALTH SERVICES ADMINISTRATION. Main/Corp United States. Health Services Administration. VFOAT Forward Plan. 1976/80-. 0196-4909. US. English. an. Department of Health Education and Welfare, Public Health Service, Health Services Administration, 5600 Fishers Lane, Rockville MD 20857. **NLM** W2 A H6F.

FRIENDS. (FRIENDS : THE VOICE OF RED CROSS IN NOVA SCOTIA). Vol. 1, No. 1 (Sept. 1981)-. 0821-638X. Periodical. CN. English. qt. Free. Nova Scotia Red Cross, PO Box 366, Halifax Nova Scotia B3J 2P8 Canada. **DD** 361.763409716. (ctrl). *A.I.D. News, Blood Programme Roundup, 0712-6484; Link*

Public Health and Safety

Up (Halifax, N.S.), 0229-9763; Red Cross Goes to School, 0229-9828; Sand and Surf, 0315-677X.

FROM THE STATE CAPITALS. MOTOR VEHICLE REGULATION. See Transportation - Automobiles.

FROM THE STATE CAPITALS. PUBLIC SAFETY. VFOAT Public Safety. Sept. 1984-. 0749-2782. Periodical. US. English. mo. $125.00. Wakeman/Walworth Inc, PO Box 1939, New Haven CT 06509. From the State Capitals. Disaster and Emergency Planning, 0734-0869; From the State Capitals. Fire Administration, 0734-1059; From the State Capitals. Police Administration, 0734-1148.

FUKUOKA-SHI EISEI SHIKENJOHO. See Sanitation, Environmental Technology.

GEOCHEMISTRY AND THE ENVIRONMENT. See Sanitation, Environmental Technology.

GEOGRAPHIA MEDICA. 1- 1969/70-. 0300-807X. Periodical. HU. English (French or German). ir. Akademiai Kiado, POB 24, 1363 Budapest Hungary. Ind/Abst Excerpta Med., Index Med., Biol. Abstr. LC RA791. NLM W1 GE359S. CODEN GMDCB4. Geographia Medica Hungarica, 0435-3730.

DAS GESUNDHEITSWESEN DER BUNDESREPUBLIK DEUTSCHLAND. VFOAT Public Health in the Federal Republic of Germany. V. 1- 1963-. text in German, English and French. ir.

DAS GESUNDHEITSWESEN IN NORDRHEIN-WESTFALEN. See Statistics.

GESUNDHEITSWESEN. REIHE 2, MELDEPFLICHTIGE KRANKHEITEN. VFOAT Meldepflichtige Krankheiten. 1981-. GW. German. an. 7.70. Verlag W Kohlhammer GMBH, Philipp-Reis-Strasse 3, Postfach 42 11 20, 6500 Mainz 42 West Germany. NLM W2. Gesundheitswesen. Reihe 2.1, Geschlechtskrankheiten, 0173-3834; 0172-8946.

GESUNDHEITSWESEN. REIHE 2.3, SONSTIGE MELDEPFLICHTIGE KRANKHEITEN. (GESUNDHEITSWESEN. REIHE 2.3 : SONSTIGE MELDEPFLICHTIGE KRANKHEITEN). VFOAT Sonstige Meldepflichtige Krankheiten. 0173-3869. Periodical. German. qt. NLM W2 GG4 S772GC. Bevolkerung und Kultur. Reihe 7: Gesundheitswesen. 1: Meldepflichtige Krankheiten.

GIFU-KEN SEISHIN EISEI SENTA SHOHO. No. 1- 1971-. JA. Japanese. ir. c/o Gifu-ken Gifu Sofo Chosha, Gifu-shi Japan. LC RA790.7.J3.

GIGIENA NASELENNYKH MEST. Vol. 12- 1973-. 0301-2468. UR. Ukrainian. an. NLM W1 GI134HB. Hihiena Naselenykh Mists', 0301-2468.

GIORNALE DI MALATTIE INFETTIVE E PARASSITARIE. V. 1- Jan./Feb. 1949-. 0017-0321. Periodical. IT. Italian. mo. 65.00. Giornale di Malattie Infettive, Via A Appiani 5, 20121 Milano Italy. Tel (02)6555 472. Ed Francesco Colonnells. Ind/Abst Life Sci. Collect., Excerpta Med. NLM W1 GI615. bk rev. adv acc. Circ 1,250. (ctrl) Writings dealing with clinical biological and experimental studies concerning infectious and parasitical diseases. Proceedings of conferences held by the Society of Infectious Diseases.

GOOD HEALTH GUIDE. V. 1- Jan. 1949-. Periodical. US. English. qt. LC RA421. DD 616.05.

GRANT APPLICATION FOR CONTINUATION OF FULL DESIGNATION. Main/Corp Montana Health Systems Agency. US. English. Montana Health Systems Agency Inc, 324 Fuller Avenue, Helena MT 59601. LC RA395.A4. DD 353.978600841.

GRANTS FOR TRAINING, CONSTRUCTION, MEDICAL LIBRARIES (BETHESDA, MD. : 1983). (GRANTS FOR TRAINING, CONSTRUCTION, MEDICAL LIBRARIES). Fiscal year 1983 funds-. 8756-551X. US. English. an. US Department of Health & Human Services, Public Health Service, National Institutes of Health, Building WB/Room 449, Bethesda MD 20205. DD 338. Grants for Training, Construction, Cancer Control, Medical Libraries, 0194-3987.

THE GREEN SHEET - UNITED STATES. DEPT. OF HEALTH AND HUMAN SERVICES. (THE GREEN SHEET : NEWS ABOUT THE U.S. DEPARTMENT OF HEALTH AND HUMAN SERVICES). 0732-9385. Periodical. US. English. da. United States Department of Health and Services, Office of Public Affairs, 638E Hubert H Humphrey Building, Washington DC 20201.

THE GROUP HEALTH JOURNAL. Began winter 1980. 0196-6332. Periodical. US. English. sa. $25.00. Group Health Association of America, 624 9th Street NW/ Suite 700, Washington DC 20001. Tel (202)737-4311. Ed Peggy Pond. Ind/Abst Hospit. Lit. Index. LC RA413. DD 362.10425. NLM W1 GR858R. bk rev.

GROUP HEALTH NEWS. V. 18- 1977-. 0164-0542. Periodical. US. English. mo $50.00. Group Health Association of America, 624 Ninth Street NW/Suite 700, Washington DC 20001. Tel (202)737-4311. Ed J Cohen. NLM W1 GR8581H. Circ 4,500. Group Health & Welfare News, 0017-470X.

GROUP HEALTH PULSE. VFOAT Pulse. 8750-5231. Periodical. US. English. mo. $1.00 Included in Membership. Group Health Pulse, 2829 University Avenue SE, Minneapolis MN 55414. DD 362. Pulse (Minneapolis, Minn.), 0745-578X.

GUIDE TO AUDIOVISUAL RESOURCES FOR THE HEALTH CARE FIELD. VFOAT Audiovisual Resources for the Health Care Field. 1981-. 0278-3444. US. English. an. American Hospital Publishing, 211 East Chicago Avenue, Chicago IL 60611. LC R835. DD 610.78. NLM WA 18 G945.

GUIDE TO NIH PROGRAMS AND AWARDS. Main/Corp National Institute of Health (U.S.). VAT Guide to National Institutes of Health Programs and Awards. Mar. 1976-. 0363-0218. Periodical. US. English. ir. LC RA11. DD 610.72073. NLM WA 20.5 G948. Guide to Grant and Award Programs of the National Institutes of Health.

NA HAKHOE CHI. VFOAT Korean Leprosy Bulletin. Periodical. KO. English (Korean). ir. Taehan Na Hakhoe, 1 2-ka Myong-dong, Chung-ku, Seoul South Korea. LC RC154.A1.

HALSOUPPLYSNING. Main/Corp Sweden. Socialstyrelsen. Namnden for Halsoupplysning. SW. Swedish. ir. Socialstyrelsens Namnd for Halsoupplysning, 106 30 Stockholm Sweden. LC RA440.3.S8.

HANGUK YOK HAKHOE CHI. VFOAT Korean Journal of Epidemiology. Periodical. KO. Korean (summaries in English). ir. Hanguk Yok Hakhoe, 28 Yongon-dong, Chongno-ku 110, Seoul South Korea. LC RA648.5.

HANSENIASE : RESUMOS E NOTICIAS. See Indexes/Abstracts.

HARVARD PUBLIC HEALTH ALUMNI BULLETIN. V. 1- May 1944-. 0017-8152. Periodical. US. English. sa. Ind/Abst Biol. Abstr., Nuci. Sci. Abstr. NLM W1 HA639. CODEN HPHBAI.

HARYANA HEALTH JOURNAL. Vol. 1, No. 1 (Jan. 1970)-. 0017-8241. Periodical. English. qt. LC RA312.H37. DD 362.10954558. NLM W1 HA71E.

HASIL-HASIL RAPAT KERDJA KESEHATAN NASIONAL. Main/Conf Rapat Kerdja Kesehatan Nasional. 0216-9053. Indonesian. ir. NLM W1 HA716.

HAZARDOUS AND TOXIC SUBSTANCES. See Medicine - Toxicology.

HAZARDOUS MATERIALS TRANSPORTATION. See Transportation.

HEALTH CEASED. Ceased with Autumn 1981 issue. 0017-8837. Periodical. CN. English. Health League of Canada, 76 Avenue Road, Toronto Ontario M5R 2H1 Canada. Ind/Abst CIS Abstr., Can. Period. Index. NLM W1 HE179.

HEALTH. 1970-. Periodical. US. English. mo. NLM Microfiche 40. (cum index).

HEALTH. Main/Corp Rhode Island. Department of Health. Periodical. US. English. an. LC RA144.

HEALTH. (HEALTH : JOURNAL OF THE COMMONWEALTH DEPARTMENT OF HEALTH). 0046-7006. Periodical. English. qt. Ind/Abst Energy Res. Abstr. NLM W1 HE165.

HEALTH AFFAIRS. Vol. 1, No. 1 (Winter 1981)-. Periodical. US. English. qt. $32.00. Project Hope, Millwood VA 22646. Tel (703)837-2100. Ed John R Fglehart. bk rev. Circ 4,500. A multidisclpinary journal dedicated to the serious explanation of major domestic health policy issues, with special emphasis on issues involving both the public and private sectors.

HEALTH ALERT (PASADENA, CALIF.). (HEALTH ALERT). V. 1, No. 1 (Sept. 1984)-. 8755-4763. Periodical. US. English. mo. $78.00. Health Alert Publications, 180 South Lake Avenue/ Suite 235, Pasadena CA 91101. DD 613.

HEALTH AND ENVIRONMENT DEPARTMENT RESOURCE DIRECTORY. See Yearbooks, Almanacs, Directories.

HEALTH AND HEALTH INSURANCE : THE PUBLIC'S VIEW. See Insurance.

HEALTH & MEDICAL HORIZONS. VFOAT Health and Medical Horizons. 0734-5003. US. English. an. MacMillan Publishing Company, 866 Third Avenue, New York NY 10022. Tel (212)702-4264. Ed Robert Famighetti. LC RA773. DD 610.5. Latest advances in all branches of medicine and in health preservation explained in nontechnical language for general public.

HEALTH & MEDICINE. (HEALTH&MEDICINE : JOURNAL OF THE HEALTH AND MEDICINE POLICY RESEARCH GROUP). Began with: Vol. 1, No. 1 (Winter 1982). 0741-2339. Periodical. US. English. qt. $35.00. Ind/Abst Hospit. Lit. Index, Public Aff. Inf. Serv. Bull. NLM W1 HE414F.

HEALTH AND PERSONAL SOCIAL SERVICES STATISTICS FOR ENGLAND WITH SUMMARY TABLES FOR GREAT BRITAIN. See Statistics.

HEALTH AND POPULATION. PERSPECTIVES AND ISSUES. (HEALTH AND POPULATION. PERSPECTIVE AND ISSUES : JOURNAL OF NATIONAL INSTITUTE OF HEALTH AND FAMILY WELFARE). VFOAT Health and Population. V. 1, No. 1 (Jan./Mar. 1978)-. 0253-6803. Periodical. English. qt. Tel 665482. Ind/Abst Excerpta Med., Popul. Index. LC RA529. DD 362.10954. NLM W1 HE263D. bk rev. Circ 800. Deals with health problems and issues. NIHAE Bulletin, 0378-6196; Journal of Population Research, 0377-0478.

HEALTH AND SOCIAL SERVICE JOURNAL. V. 83- Jan. 6, 1973-. 0300-8347. Periodical. UK. English. wk. $103.00. MacMillan Journals, Frandon Road, Market Harborough, Leicester LE16 9NR England. Tel (0256)29242. Ind/Abst Hospit. Lit. Index, Excerpta Med., Cumul. Index Nurs. Allied Health Lit. LC HV1. DD 362.941. NLM W1 HE265E. British Hospital Journal and Social Service Review, 0007-0793; Community Medicine, 0300-5917.

HEALTH CARE DEMONSTRATION SERIES. Monographic Series. US. English. ir. University of Iowa, Graduate Program in Hospital and Health Administration, Iowa City IA 52242.

HEALTH CARE EDUCATION. V. 6, No. 2- Apr. 1977-. 0160-7006. Periodical. US. English. bm. $18.00. Health Care Education, 60 East 42nd Street, New York NY 10017. Ind/Abst Cumul. Index Nurs. Allied Health Lit. NLM W1 HE299E. In-Service Training and Education, 0090-2225.

HEALTH CARE EXPENDITURES IN KANSAS. 1966-1976-. 0883-3699. US. English. an. Kansas Department of Health and Environment, Office of Health Planning, Topeka KS 66620.

HEALTH CARE FINANCING. GRANTS FOR RESEARCH AND DEMONSTRATIONS. (GRANTS FOR RESEARCH AND DEMONSTRATIONS). Series/Titl Health Care Financing. 0271-1389. US. English. an. ORDS Publications, Oak Meadows Building Room 1A9 6230 Security Boulevard, Baltimore MD 21235. LC RA410.53. DD 353.00841045. NLM W2 A H24HA.

HEALTH CARE FINANCING REVIEW. Vol. 1, issue 1 (Summer 1979)-. 0195-8631. Periodical. US. English. qt. $18.00. HCFA ORDS Publications, 6325 Security Boulevard/1A9 Oak Mds, Baltimore MD 21207. Tel (301)597-2420. Ed Gerri Michael. Ind/Abst Predicasts, Soc. Work Res. Abstr., Abstr. Health Care Manage. Stud., Am. Stat. Index, Excerpta Med., Index U.S. Gov. Period., MEDOC, Hospit. Lit. Index, Public Aff. Inf. Serv. Bull., Funk Scott Index Corp. Ind. LC RA410.53. DD 338.4336210973. NLM W1 HE299KF. bk rev. Circ 4,000. Health care financing issues and innovative delivery systems as related to the Medicare and Medicaid programs.

HEALTH CARE FINANCING TRENDS. Vol. 1, No. 1 (Fall 1979)-. 0882-8946. Periodical. US. English. qt. ORD Publications, Room 1-E-9 Oak Meadows Building 6340 Security Boulevard, Baltimore MD 21207. Ind/Abst Excerpta Med. NLM W2.

HEALTH CARE IN CANADA. V. 20, No. 10- Oct. 1978-. Periodical. CN. English. mo. $24.00 US. Southam Business Publications, 1450 Don Mills Road, Don Mills Ontario M3B 2X7 Canada.

Public Health and Safety

HEALTH CARE SYSTEMS. V. 14, No. 5- Sept./Oct. 1975-. 0149-2888. Periodical. US. English. bm. American Hospital Association, 840 North Lake Shore Drive, Chicago IL 60611. **NLM** W1 HE303. *Management Systems.*

HEALTH CAREER OPPORTUNITY GRANTS FOR THE DISADVANTAGED. See Occupations and Careers.

THE HEALTH CONSEQUENCES OF SMOKING. (THE HEALTH CONSEQUENCES OF SMOKING : A REPORT OF THE SURGEON GENERAL). **Main/Corp** United States. Office on Smoking and Health. **VFOAT** Changing Cigarette, Cancer, Chronic Obstructive Lung Disease. 0098-311X. US. English. an. Office on Smoking and Health, 5600 Fishers Lane/Room 1-58, Rockville MD 20857. **Tel** (301)443-1575. **LC** RA1242.T6. **DD** 615.952379. **NLM** W1 HE313G. *Health Consequences of Smoking, 0098-311X.*

HEALTH DATA ANNUAL. V. 1- 1974-. 0097-7306. US. English. an. Massachusetts Department of Public Health, 150 Tremont Street 5th Floor, Boston MA 02111. **Tel** (617)727-2977. **Ed** Maureen Dipietro. **LC** RA407.4.M45. **DD** 362.109744. **Circ** 1,500. (ctrl). A report on health facility utilization in Massachusetts.

HEALTH DATA INVENTORY. 0735-0848. US. English. an. US Department of H H S, Health Data Advisory Committee, 200 Independence Avenue SW, Washington DC 20201. **LC** RA445. **DD** 362.1072073. Vols. for 1982- distributed to depository libraries in microfiche.

HEALTH DATA SUMMARIES FOR CALIFORNIA COUNTIES. 1980-. 8755-240X. US. English. an. **LC** RA407.4.C2. **DD** 362.109794.

HEALTH DEVELOPMENT IN AFRICA. 1-. Monographic Series. English. ir.

HEALTH DEVICES ALERTS. ABSTRACTS. See Indexes/Abstracts.

HEALTH EDUCATION JOURNAL. (THE HEALTH EDUCATION JOURNAL). Began publication in 1943. 0017-8969. Periodical. UK. English. qt. $4.60. Health Education Council Ltd, 78 New Oxford Street, London WC1A 1AH England. **Tel** 631 0930. **Ed** Michael Jacob. **Ind/Abst** Hospit. Lit. Index, Excerpta Med., Ref. Source. **LC** RA421. **DD** 613.05. **NLM** W1 HE322. bk rev. adv acc. **Circ** 4,500. A lively look at the full spectrum of health education and health promotion in Britain and overseas, through research papers, opinion pieces, letters and reviews.

HEALTH EDUCATION (OTTAWA, ONT.). (HEALTH EDUCATION). **VAT** Education Sanitaire (Edition Anglaise), Health Education Sanitaire (English Edition). 1962. 0017-8950. Periodical. CN. English. qt. Free to Canadians. Health & Welfare Canada, Ottawa K1A 1B4 Ontario Canada. **Tel** (613)990-7853. **Ed** Kay Rawlings. **Ind/Abst** Can. Educ. Index, Media Rev. Dig. **LC** RA440.3.C2. **DD** 613.07071. **NLM** W1 HE321F. bk rev. **Circ** 7,500. Information for Canadian health promotion professionals on new policies, programs, resources and events.

HEALTH EDUCATION QUARTERLY. V. 7- Spring 1980-. 0195-8402. Periodical. US. English. qt. John Wiley & Sons, 605 Third Avenue, New York NY 10158. **Tel** (800)526-5368. **Ind/Abst** Hospit. Lit. Index, Sociol. Abstr., Soc. Welf. Soc. Plan./Policy Soc. Dev., Excerpta Med., Index Med., Psychol. Abstr., Energy Res. Abstr., Soc. Sci. Citation Index. **LC** RA440.A1. **DD** 613.071. **NLM** W1 HE325H. **CODEN** HEQUDC. *Health Education Monographs, 0073-1455.*

HEALTH EDUCATION REPORT. V. 1- Nov./Dec. 1973-. 0193-7138. Periodical. US. English. bm. $9.00. Daniel Sullivan, PO Box 728, Ojai CA 93023.

HEALTH EDUCATION REPORTS. **VFOAT** HE Reports. V. 1- Feb. 9, 1979-. 0193-5232. Periodical. US. English. bw. Health Education Reports, 2626 Pennsylvania Avenue NW, Washington DC 20037. **NLM** W1 HE325M.

HEALTH (FAMILY MEDIA, INC.). (HEALTH). V. 13, No. 7 (July/Aug. 1981)-. 0279-3547. Periodical. US. English. mo. $15.00 Domestic, $18.00 Canada, $19.00 all Other Countries. Family Health Inc, 149 Fifth Avenue, New York NY 10010. **Ind/Abst** Abr. Read. Guide, Gen. Sci. Index, Read. Guide Period. Lit., Cumul. Index Nurs. Allied Health Lit., Pop. Mag. Rev. **LC** RA773. **DD** 613.05. **NLM** W1 HE181B. *Family Health, 0014-7249.*

HEALTH FREEDOM NEWS : THE JOURNAL OF THE NATIONAL HEALTH FEDERATION. Vol. 1, No. 1 (June 1982)-. Periodical. US. English. mo. National Health Foundation, PO Box 1307, Monrovia CA 91016. **Tel** (213)357-2181. **NLM** W1. *National Health Federation's Public Scrutiny.*

HEALTH GRANTS & CONTRACTS WEEKLY. **VAT** Health Grants and Contracts Weekly. 0194-2352. Periodical. US. English. ir. $179.00. Capitol Publishing, 1300 North 17th Street, Arlington VA 22209. **Tel** (703)528-5400.

HEALTH GROUPS IN WASHINGTON, A DIRECTORY. (HEALTH GROUPS IN WASHINGTON : A DIRECTORY). **Series/Titl** Government Relations Handbook Series. Began with 3rd Ed., 1977. 0278-5323. US. English. ir. National Health Council Inc, 622 Third Avenue, New York NY 10017. **Tel** (212)869-8100. **NLM** W 22 AD6 H434. Directory of national health organizations in the Greater Washington, DC area. *Private Health Organizations' Government Relations Directory.*

HEALTH HAPPENINGS CEASED. Ceased publication July 1980. Periodical. US. English. mo.

HEALTH IN NEW ZEALAND. English. ir. New Zealand Department of Health, PO Box 5013, Wellington New Zealand. **LC** RA555. **DD** 614.09931.

HEALTH IN SCOTLAND. 1980-. UK. English. an. 3.60. Her Majesty's Stationery Office, Government Bookshops, 13A Castle Street, Edinburgh EH2 3AR Scotland. **LC** RA243. **DD** 362.109411. *Health Services in Scotland, 0302-3397.*

HEALTH IN THE UNITED STATES. **Main/Corp** National Center for Health Statistics (U.S.). 0148-7450. US. English. 5600 Fishers Lane, Rockville MD 20852. **LC** RA407.3. **DD** 362.10973.

HEALTH IN WISCONSIN. V. 22-. 0146-2768. Periodical. US. English. ir. Department of Health & Social Science, 1 West Wilson Street, Box 309, Madison WI 53701. **LC** RA177. **DD** 362.109775. **NLM** W1 HE35K. *Wisconsin's Health, 0043-6747.*

HEALTH INFORMATION BULLETIN. KE. English. ir. Health Information System, PO Box 20781, Nairobi Kenya. **LC** RA407.5.K45. **DD** 614.426762021.

HEALTH INFORMATION FOR INTERNATIONAL TRAVEL. See Travel.

HEALTH INFORMATION RESOURCES IN THE DEPARTMENT OF HEALTH AND HUMAN SERVICES. **Main/Corp** United States. Dept. of Health and Human Services. **Series/Titl** DHHS (PHS) Publication. 1980-. US. English. an. **NLM** W 22 AA1 U53H.

HEALTH INSURANCE UNDERWRITER. See Insurance.

HEALTH ISSUES ON CAPITOL HILL. V. 1- Jan. 1976-. 0145-336X. US. English. mo. $19.00 Domestic, $20.90 Foreign. Health Issues on Capitol Hill, PO Box 2936, Washington DC 20013. **NLM** W1 HE373.

THE HEALTH LETTER. V. 1, No. 1-. 0739-4217. Periodical. US. English. sm. $22.00. Communications Inc, PO Box 326, San Antonio TX 78292. **Ed** Lawrence E Lamb. **Ind/Abst** Mag. Index. **DD** 614. **Circ** 11,000.

HEALTH LITERATURE REVIEW. (HEALTH LITERATURE REVIEW : HLR). **VFOAT** HLR. V. 1, No. 1-. 0740-7262. Periodical. US. English. bm. $32.00. True to Form Press, PO Box 8029, St Paul MN 55113. **NLM** ZWB 100.

HEALTH MANPOWER PILOT PROJECTS PROGRAM. ANNUAL REPORT TO THE LEGISLATURE AND THE HEALING ARTS LICENSING BOARDS. (HEALTH MANPOWER PILOT PROJECTS PROGRAM). **Main/Corp** California. Office of Statewide Health Planning and Development. 0192-6101. US. English. an. Health & Welfare Agency, Office of Statewide Health Planning & Development, Sacramento CA 95814. **LC** RA396.A4. **DD** 362.109794. *Experimental Health Manpower Pilot Projects, 0190-4825.*

HEALTH MANPOWER RESOURCES. **Main/Corp** New Zealand. Dept. of Health. Management Services and Research Unit. UK. English. **LC** RA410.9.N42. **DD** 331.11.

HEALTH (NEW YORK, N.Y.). (HEALTH). V. 13, No. 7 (July/Aug. 1981)-. 0014-7249. Periodical. US. English. mo. Palm Coast Data Ltd, PO Box 6007, Palm Coast FL 32037. **Tel** (904)445-4662.

HEALTH (NEW ZEALAND). (HEALTH). Periodical. English. qt. Department of Health, PO Box 5013, Wellington New Zealand. **NLM** W1 HE181.

THE HEALTH OF KANSANS CHART BOOK. Began with Vol. for 1978. 0276-606X. US. English. an. Free. Research and Analysis Section Department of Health and Environment, Bureau of Registration and Health Statistics, Topeka KS 66620. **LC** RA407.4 .K3. **DD** 362.109781.

HEALTH ORGANIZATIONS OF THE UNITED STATES, CANADA AND INTERNATIONALLY. **VFOAT** Health Organizations. 1st-4th Ed. 0440-5609. US. English. ir. $85.00. Gale Research Company, Book Tower, Detroit MI 48226. **Ed** P Wasserman and M Kaszubski. **LC** R711. **DD** 610.62. Contains complete details for more than 1,600 voluntary associations, professional societies and other groups concerned with health, medical, hospital, pharmaceutical, and related fields.

HEALTH ORGANIZATIONS OF THE UNITED STATES, CANADA AND THE WORLD. 0277-8653. US. English. ir. Gale Research, Book Tower, Detroit MI 48226. **DD** 610.6073. Contains complete details for more than 1,600 voluntary associations, professional societies, and other groups concerned with health, medical, hospital, pharmaceutical, and related fields. *Health Organizations of the United States, Canada, and Internationally, 0440-5609.*

HEALTH PATHWAYS. 0164-7598. Periodical. US. English. mo. Health Pathways, Office of Statewide Health Planning and Development Program Office, 455 Capitol Mall/Suite 120, Sacramento CA 95814.

HEALTH PLANNING & HEALTH SERVICES RESEARCH. **VAT** Health Planning and Health Services Research. Began with Oct. 9, 1979. 0199-9974. US. English. wk. NTIS, 5285 Port Royal Road, Springfield VA 22161. **NLM** ZWA 540 AA1 H4. *Health Planning, 0017-9086.*

HEALTH PLANNING INFORMATION SERIES. 1-. 0149-2659. Monographic Series. US. English. ir. Superintendent of Documents, US Government Printing Office, Washington DC 20402. **LC** UNC. **NLM** W2 A B8693H.

HEALTH POLICY. Vol. 1-. 0733-9143. Monographic Series. US. English. ir. Marcel Dekker Inc, 270 Madison Avenue, New York NY 10016. **Tel** (212)696-9000. **Ed** Roemer. **LC** UNC. **NLM** W1 HE473S. This is an ongoing series. Each title has a different subject.

HEALTH POLICY QUARTERLY. V. 1, No. 1 (Spring 1981)-. 0163-5107. Periodical. US. English. qt. Human Sciences Press, 72 5th Avenue, New York NY 10011. **LC** RA1. **DD** 362.105. **NLM** W1 HE475. **CODEN** HPEUDT.

HEALTH POLICY WEEK. (HEALTH POLICY WEEK : HPW). **VFOAT** HPW. 0732-7439. Periodical. US. English. wk. $235.00. Health Policy Week, 4853 Cordell Avenue/ #1022, Bethesda MD 20814. **Tel** (301)656-0450. **Ed** Frank S Joseph. *Morris Report on Federal Health Policy, 0277-3902.*

HEALTH PROMOTION NEWSLETTER. V. 1, No. 1-. 0882-0252. Periodical. US. English. mo. $18.00. Health Promotion Publications, 2952 Mesquite Drive, Riverside CA 92503. **DD** 614.

HEALTH RESEARCH GRANTS AND AWARDS. **Main/Corp** Ontario. Ministry of Health. 1983/84-. 0714-6760. CN. English. an. **LC** RA440.3.C22. **DD** 610.720713. *Health Personnel and Research Grant Programs, 0709-3535.*

HEALTH RESOURCES ADMINISTRATION FORWARD PLAN. **VFOAT** Forward Plan. 1978/82-. 0163-0830. Periodical. US. English. an. **NLM** W2 A P9F.

HEALTH RESOURCES STATISTICS. See Statistics.

HEALTH SCIENCES AUDIOVISUALS. (HEALTH SCIENCES AUDIOVISUALS MICROFORM). **Main/Corp** National Library of Medicine (U.S.). Fall 1983-. 0278-7318. US. English. **NLM** W 18 N28015H (P.

HEALTH SERVICES ADMINISTRATION EDUCATION. 1979-. 0160-4961. US. English. be. $40.00. Association of University Programs in Health Administration, 1911

Public Health and Safety

North Fort Myer Drive/Suite 503, Arlington VA 22209. **Tel** (703)524-5500. Ed Gary L Fiherman. **LC** RA440.7.U6. **DD** 362.1068. **NLM** W 22.1 H434. bk rev. **Circ** 1,500. An international journal of management development for health services, including topics of interest to educators and practitioners involved in the education of health managers.

HEALTH SERVICES IN CZECHOSLOVAKIA. English. ir. Institute For Health Information and Statistics, Praha 10 Vinohrady, T R W Piecka 98 Czechoslovakia. **LC** RA407.5.C95. **DD** 362.109437.

HEALTH SERVICES INFORMATION. V. 1- Mar. 11, 1974-. 0094-6036. Periodical. US. English. ir. $275.00. Healthcare Publishers, 1341 G Street NW, Washington DC 20005. **Tel** (202)347-5500. **NLM** W1 HE575I.

HEALTH SERVICES: JOURNAL OF THE CONFEDERATION OF HEALTH SERVICE EMPLOYEES. See Economics - Labor.

HEALTH SERVICES RESEARCH. V. 1- Summer 1966-. 0017-9124. Periodical. US. English. bm. $38.00. Health Administration Press, University of Michigan, School of Public Health, Ann Arbor MI 48109. **Tel** (313)764-1380. **Ind/Abst** Manage. Contents, Hospit. Lit. Index, Excerpta Med., Cumul. Index Nurs. Allied Health Lit., Index Med., ABI/Inform, Energy Res. Abstr., Soc. Sci. Citation Index. **LC** RA960. **DD** 362.105. **NLM** W1 HE576E. **CODEN** HESRA.

HEALTH SERVICES RESEARCH NOTES. Feb. 1981-. 0749-6354. Periodical. US. English. qt. University of Washington, Department of Health Services, Seattle WA 98105. **Tel** (206)543-3866. **DD** 362. *Centernotes, 0749-9612.*

HEALTH STATISTICS IN THE NORDIC COUNTRIES. See Statistics.

HEALTH STATISTICS PLAN. See Statistics.

HEALTH SYSTEMS AGENCIES, STATE HEALTH PLANNING AND DEVELOPMENT AGENCIES, AND STATEWIDE HEALTH COORDINATING COUNCILS. VFOAT Directory, Health Systems Agencies, State Health Planning and Development Agencies, Statewide Health Coordinating Councils. Feb. 1, 1979-. US. English. ir. Bureau of Health Planning Information Office, Room 6-22/Center Building, 3700 East-West Highway, Hyattsville MD 20782. **NLM** WA 22. *Directory, Health Systems Agencies, State Health Planning and Development Agencies, Statewide Health Coordinating Councils, 0273-3943.*

HEALTH SYSTEMS PLAN: PURSUANT TO THE NATIONAL HEALTH PLANNING AND RESOURCES DEVELOPMENT ACT OF 1974 (PUBLIC LAW 93-641). See Law.

HEALTH SYSTEMS UPDATE. V. 1- Aug. 1978-. 0164-6621. Periodical. US. English. mo. Health Systems Management, Rockerfeller Empire Street/Plaza, Albany NY 12237. **Tel** (518)474-7354.

HEALTH TRENDS. 0017-9132. Periodical. UK. English. qt. 4.00. Department of Health & Social Science, Alexander Fleming House/Elephant and Castle, London SE1 6BY England. **Tel** 407-5522. Ed Dr J L Hunt. **Ind/Abst** Hospit. Lit. Index, Biol. Abstr. **LC** RA485. **DD** 362.10941. **NLM** W1 HE5996. **CODEN** HETBAT. **Circ** 65,000. (ctrl). A review for the medical profession on subjects relevant to the management of the British national service including statistics and epidemiological studies. *Monthly Bulletin of the Ministry of Health & The Public Health Laboratory Service.*

HEALTH, UNITED STATES. Series/Titl DHHS Publication. VFOAT Health, United States... with Prevention Profile. Began with 1st report, 1975. 0361-4468. US. English. an. Maryland Department of Health Education and Welfare, 5600 Fishers Lane, Rockville MD 20852-0402. **LC** RA407.3. **DD** 362.10973. **NLM** W2 A N1479H.

HEALTHCARE MARKET RESEARCH, REPORTS, STUDIES, & SURVEYS. VFOAT Health Care Market Research, Reports, Studies, & Surveys. 8755-9153. US. English. an. Find/Svp, 500 5th Avenue, New York NY 10109.

HEALTHLINES (ANN ARBOR, MICH.). (HEALTHLINES). VFOAT Health Lines. 8756-453X. Periodical. US. English. mo. $15.00. University of Michigan Fitness Research Center, 401 Washtenaw, Ann Arbor MI 48109. **Tel** (313)763-2462. Ed Marilyn P Edington. **DD** 613. bk rev. **Circ** 3,400. (ctrl). A newsletter that focuses on self-responsibility and preventive health behavior as vital components of a healthy lifestyle.

HEALTHMARKETING. VFOAT Health Marketing. Vol. 1, Issue No. 1 (Nov.-Dec. 1982)-. 0745-4538. Periodical. US. English. bm. $24.00. Healthmark, 4641 North Lee Highway, Cleveland TN 37311. **Ind/Abst** Hospit. Lit. Index. **NLM** W1. *Hospital Management Communications, 0274-5429.*

HEALTH/PAC BULLETIN. VFOAT Health PAC Bulletin. VAT Health/Policy Advisory Center Bulletin. June 1968-. 0017-9051. Periodical. US. English. bm. $35.00. Health Policy Advisory Center, 17 Murray Street, New York NY 10007. **Tel** (212)267-8890. Ed Jon Steinberg. **Ind/Abst** Altern. Press Index, Hospit. Lit. Index. **NLM** W1 HE468. bk rev. adv acc. **Circ** 2,000. (ctrl). The bulletin analyzes health policy for its effect on all Americans — toward the goal of affordable, appropriate, quality health care for everyone.

HEALTHSHARING. V. 1- Nov. 1979-. 0226-1510. Periodical. CN. English (includes some text in French). qt. $11.61. Women Healthsharing, 101 Niagara Street/Room 200A, Toronto Ontario M5V 1C3 Canada. **Tel** (416)862-1791. Ed Connie Clement, Elizabeth Amer. **Ind/Abst** Altern. Press Index. **DD** 613.0424405. bk rev. adv acc. **Circ** 3,000. (ctrl). Focus on critical analysis of health issues from feminist perspective with information on personal and social concerns. And features: news, reviews, resources. *Women's Health Quarterly.*

HEALTHSPAN. See Law.

HEALTHSPAN. VFOAT Health Span. Vol. 2, No. 1 (Jan. 1985)-. 8755-2205. Periodical. US. English. mo. Law & Business Inc, 855 Halley Road, Clifton NJ 07013. *Healthscan.*

HEALTHWISE. VFOAT Health Wise. 0740-1086. Periodical. US. English. mo. $19.70. Healthwise, PO Box 1786, Indianapolis IN 46206.

HEALTHWISE EXECUTIVE. VFOAT Health Wise Executive. 0740-1094. Periodical. US. English. mo. $39.70. Alexander Grant, MD and Associates, PO Box 1786, Indianapolis IN 46206.

HEALTHY PEOPLE. Vol. 1, No. 1-. 0884-2094. Periodical. US. English. mo. Health Management Communications, Harwood Building/Room 319, Scarsdale NY 10583. **DD** 614.

HELPER (AMERICAN SOCIAL HEALTH ASSOCIATION). (THE HELPER: A PROGRAM SERVICE OF THE AMERICAN SOCIAL HEALTH ASSOCIATION). Vol. 1, No. 1 (July 1979)-. Periodical. US. English. qt. $55.00. Herpes Resource Center, PO Box 100, Palo Alto CA 94302. **Tel** (415)321-5134. Ed John Graves. bk rev. (ctrl). To inform the public about all aspects of herpes simplex virus disease using current, factual information.

HIGHWAY & VEHICLE SAFETY REPORT. See Transportation - Roads and Traffic.

HIGHWAY SAFETY LITERATURE. HUMAN FACTORS BIBLIOGRAPHY. See Bibliographies.

HIGHWAY SAFETY LITERATURE (NATIONAL RESEARCH COUNCIL (U.S.). TRANSPORTATION RESEARCH BOARD). See Transportation - Roads and Traffic.

HIGHWAY SAFETY PLAN. See Transportation - Roads and Traffic.

HIGHWAY SAFETY PLAN. See Transportation - Roads and Traffic.

HIGHWAY SAFETY PLAN. See Transportation - Roads and Traffic.

HIGHWAY SAFETY PLAN. See Transportation - Roads and Traffic.

HIGHWAY SAFETY PLAN FOR MISSOURI. See Transportation - Roads and Traffic.

HIGHWAY SAFETY PROGRAM, ANNUAL REPORT OF ACTIVITIES. See Transportation - Roads and Traffic.

HIGINA. Vol. 1, No. 1 (Nov. 1979)-. 0126-3331. Periodical. Indonesian. mo. **NLM** W1 HI406B.

HIMA DIRECTORY. See Yearbooks, Almanacs, Directories.

HMO EXECUTIVE SALARY SURVEY. See Economics - Labor.

HMO, OFFICE OF HEALTH MAINTENANCE ORGANIZATIONS, ANNUAL REPORT TO THE CONGRESS. Main/Corp United States. Office of Health Maintenance Organizations. 1977/78-. 0195-816X. US. English. an. US Department of Health Education and Welfare, Office of Health Maintenance Organizations, 12420 Parklawn Drive, Rockville MD 20857. **LC** RA413.5.U5. **DD** 353.0084105. **NLM** W2 A O22H. *HMO, Health Maintenance Organizations, Annual Report to the Congress, 0163-6243.*

HMTC UPDATE. VFOAT Update. VAT Hazardous Materials Technical Center Update. 0882-1976. Periodical. US. English. bm. HMTC, PO Box 8168, Rockville MD 20856-8168. **DD** 363.

HOKENJO UNEI HOKOKU. Main/Corp Japan. Koseisho. Tokei Johobu. 1973-. Japanese. ir. **LC** RA531. *Hokenjo Unei Hokoku.*

HOKKAIDORITSU SEISHIN EISEI SENTA NEMPO. JA. Japanese. an. Hokkaidoritsu Seishin Eisei Senta, Kita 6-ben 34-go, Hondori 16-chome, Shiroishi-ku 003, Sapporo-shi Japan. **LC** RA790.7.J3.

HOME CARE SERVICES IN NEW YORK STATE. 0277-7401. US. English. an. Bureau of Home and Health Care Services, Office of Health Systems, Management Room 1970/Empire State Plaza/Tower Building, Albany NY 12237.

HOME HEALTH CARE SERVICES QUARTERLY. V. 1- Spring 1979-. 0162-1424. Periodical. US. English. qt. $112.00. Haworth Press, 28 East 22nd Street, New York NY 10010. **Tel** (212) 228-2800. Ed Laura Reif, RN and Brahna Trager, ACSW LCSW. **Ind/Abst** Hospit. Lit. Index, Sociol. Abstr., Soc. Welf. Soc. Plan./Policy Soc. Dev. **LC** RA645.3. **DD** 362.1405. **NLM** W1 HO502R. bk rev. adv acc. **Circ** 1,039. This journal will cover major areas of interest and concern to policy makers, planners, and providers of home health care and related services.

HOMEHEALTH MAGAZINE. VFOAT Homehealth. Vol. 1, No. 1 (Jan./Feb. 1985). 0883-0835. Periodical. US. English. bm. $10.00. Healthmark Associates, PO Box 1996, Columbia MD 21044. **Tel** (301)730-8439. Ed Mary T Cronin. **DD** 362. adv acc. **Circ** 20,000. A publication for consumers of health care products and services. Articles focus on the concerns of persons with minor or severe health problems.

HOPE NEWS. V. 1- May 1963-. Periodical. US. English. qt. **NLM** W1 HO587P.

HOSPITAL SECURITY AND SAFETY MANAGEMENT. See Medicine - Medical Centers, Hospitals.

HOW TO: EVALUATE HEALTH PROGRAMS. VFOAT How to. V. 1- Aug. 1978-. 0191-3727. Periodical. US. English. mo. $37.00. Capitol Publications, Suite G-12/2430 Pennsylvania Avenue NW, Washington DC 20037. **NLM** W1 HO96A.

HSV REPORTS. VFOAT H.S.V. Reports. VAT Herpes Simplex Virus Reports. Vol. 1, No. 1 (Fall 1984)-. 0749-7628. Periodical. US. English. qt. $20.00. Vital Interests Inc, PO Box 33342, Washington DC 20033. **DD** 616.

HYGIE. 1982/1-. 0751-7149. Periodical. FR. English (French and Spanish). qt. $22.00. International Union of Health Education, 9 rue Newton, 75116 Paris France. **Tel** (1) 47 20 97 93. Ed F J Tomiche. **Ind/Abst** Index Med., Excerpta Med. **NLM** W1 HY353. bk rev. adv acc. **Circ** 3,500. (ctrl). Publishes field and research activities, interviews or reports. Each issue includes a round up on a particular health education theme. Gives international news in brief on meetings, and events.

IAEA SAFETY SERIES. (SAFETY SERIES). Began with No. 1 (1958). 0074-1892. Monographic Series. US. English. an. UNIPUB, PO Box 1222, Ann Arbor MI 48106. **Tel** (800)521-8110. **Ind/Abst** GeoRef, Bibliogr. Index Geol., Pollut. Abstr. Indexes. **LC** HD7269.A6. **DD** 363.179 #2. **NLM** W1 SA125M. **CODEN** SSAEAW.

IDAHO DEPARTMENT OF HEALTH & WELFARE ANNUAL REPORT. VAT Idaho Department of Health and Welfare Annual Report. 0272-5916. US. English. **NLM** W2 AI2 D28I.

IGIENE E SANITA PUBBLICA. 0019-1639. Periodical. IT. Italian. ir. 80.000. Gaetano del Vecchio, Via Stamira 7 I, 00162 Rome Italy. **Tel** 06/42.70.948. Ed Gaetano del Vecchio. **Ind/Abst** Chem. Abstr., Biol.

Public Health and Safety

Abstr. **NLM** W1 IG445. **CODEN** ISPRA2. bk rev. adv acc. **Circ** 2,000. Original articles, unedited and experimental, that concern hygiene and public health. Original, unedited contributions on microbiology, parasitology, immunology, statistics, and infectious diseases.

IGIENE MODERNA. Vol. 1- Jan. 1908-. 0019-1655. Periodical. IT. Italian. bm. $20.00. Igiene Moderna/Antonio Sanna, Via Zandonai No 11, 00194 Roma Italy. **Ind/Abst** Electron. Commun. Abstr. J., ISMEC Bull., Pollut. Abstr. Indexes, Saf. Sci. Abstr. J., Life Sci. Collect., Sel. Water Resour. Abstr., CIS Abstr., Biol. Abstr., Chem. Abstr., Nuci. Sci. Abstr. **NLM** W1 IG585. **CODEN** IGMPAX.

ILLINOIS HEALTH SCIENCES LIBRARIES SERIAL HOLDINGS LIST. See Library and Information Science.

ILLINOIS JOURNAL OF HEALTH, PHYSICAL EDUCATION AND RECREATION. Began with issue for Fall 1967. 0019-2074. Periodical. US. English. sa. Western Illinois University, Brophy Hall, Ethel Docherty Ed, Macomb IL 61455. **Tel** (309)438-2331.

IMMUNIZATION ABSTRACTS AND BIBLIOGRAPHY. See Indexes/Abstracts.

IMPACT. See Law.

INDEX OF STATISTICS PUBLISHED BY THE DEPARTMENT OF HEALTH. See Indexes/Abstracts.

INDEX TO HEALTH AND SAFETY EDUCATION (MULTIMEDIA). See Indexes/Abstracts.

THE INDIAN HEALTH PROGRAM OF THE U.S. PUBLIC HEALTH SERVICE. Main/Corp United States. Health Services and Mental Health Administration. US. English. Superintendent of Documents, US Government Printing Office, Washington DC 20402. **LC** RA448.5.I5. **DD** 362.

INDIAN JOURNAL OF DERMATOLOGY, VENEREOLOGY, AND LEPROLOGY. See Medicine - Dermatology.

INDIAN JOURNAL OF ENVIRONMENTAL HEALTH. See Sanitation, Environmental Technology.

INDIAN JOURNAL OF LEPROSY. Vol. 56, No. 1 (Jan.-Mar. 1984). 0254-9395. Periodical. English. qt. $15.00. Hind Kusht Nivaran Sangh, 1 Red Cross Road, New Delhi 110001 India. **Tel** 606608. Ed Dv Dharmemdra. **Ind/Abst** Index Med., Excerpta Med. **NLM** W1. bk rev. adv acc. **Circ** 1,500. Publishes research articles, abstracts from current literature, reviews, reports on leprosy and allied subjects of medicine. Leprosy in India.

INDIAN JOURNAL OF PUBLIC HEALTH. Began publication with January issue 1957. 0019-557X. Periodical. II. English. qt. $10.00. Indian Public Health Association, 110 Chittaranjan Avenue, Calcutta India. **Ind/Abst** Biol. Abstr., Chem. Abstr., Index Med., Hospit. Lit. Index. **NLM** W1 IN229. **CODEN** IPBHAH.

THE INDIANA STATE BOARD OF HEALTH BULLETIN. VFOAT Bulletin. 0019-6754. Periodical. US. English. qt. Free. Indiana State Board of Health, 1330 West Michigan Street, Indianapolis IN 46206. **Tel** (317)633-0109. Ed Woodrow A Myers. **LC** RA61. **DD** 353.97720077. **NLM** W2 AI6 S6M. **Circ** 15,000. Magazine on wide range of public health related subjects. Monthly Bulletin (Indiana State Board of Health).

INDICE BOLIVIANO DE CIENCIAS DE LA SALUD. See Indexes/Abstracts.

INDORAIR. Vol. 3 I.E. V. 2, No. 3 (Fall 1976)-. 0712-2063. Periodical. CN. English. qt. Non-Smokers' Rights Association, 455 Spandina Avenue/Suite 201, Toronto Ontario M5S 2G8 Canada. **Tel** (416)595-1538. **DD** 363.19509713. Non-Smokers' Rights Association Newsletter, 0712-2071.

INF MEMO. Periodical. US. English. National High Blood Pressure Education Program, National Heart Lung and Blood Institute, US Department of Health and Human Services, Public Health Service, National Institutes of Health, Bethesda MD 20014.

INFECTION CONTROL. 0195-9417. Periodical. US. English. mo. $65.00. Slack Inc, 6900 Grove Road, Thorofare NJ 08086. **Ind/Abst** Excerpta Med., Index Med., Cumul. Index Nurs. Allied Health Lit., Biol. Abstr. **LC** RA969. **DD** 614.44. **CODEN** IICODV. IC, Infection Control, 0195-9417.

INFECTIOUS DISEASE REVIEWS. V. 1- 1971?-. 0090-6549. US. English. 295 Main Street, Mt Kisco NY 10549. **Ind/Abst** Chem. Abstr. **LC** RC110. **DD** 616.905. **NLM** W3 IN103Q. **CODEN** IFDRAL.

INFECTIOUS DISEASES. V. 1- Jan. 1971-. 0090-8886. Periodical. US. English. mo. Medical Information Systems, 3845 North Meridian Street, Indianapolis IN 46208. **Tel** (317)923-1575. **NLM** W1 IN406K.

INFECTIOUS DISEASES AND ANTIMICROBIAL AGENTS. 1-. 0734-4627. Monographic Series. US. English. ir. Marcel Dekker Inc, 270 Madison Avenue, New York NY 10016. **Tel** (212)696-9000. Ed H Neu. **Ind/Abst** Chem. Abstr. **DD** 616.905. **NLM** W1 IN406L. **CODEN** IDAADC. This is an ongoing series. Each title has a different subject.

INFECTIOUS DISEASES CAPSULE & COMMENT. VFOAT Infectious Diseases Capsule and Comment. Vol. 1, No. 1 (Feb. 1982)-. 0741-7462. Periodical. US. English. mo. Free. HP Publishing Company, 575 Lexington Avenue, New York NY 10022.

INFECTIOUS DISEASES NEWSLETTER. (INFECTIOUS DISEASES NEWSLETTER : IDN). **VFOAT** IDN. Vol. 1, No. 1 (Oct. 1981)-. 0278-2316. Periodical. US. English. mo. $112.00. Elsevier Science Publishing Company, Inc, PO Box 1663 Grand Central Station, New York NY 10163. **Tel** (212)370-5520. Ed Paul D Hoeprich. **NLM** W1 IN406T. **Circ** 960. Offers concise reports of the current state of knowledge and practice in infectious diseases.

INFECTOLOGIKA. V. 4, No. 1 (Jan./Feb. 1983)-. Periodical. Spanish. bm. **NLM** W1. Immunologika.

INFOAAU. See Physical Training.

INFORMACAO PARA A SAUDE : BOLETIM MENSAL DE NOTIFICACAO CORRENTE EDITADO PELO CENTRO DE DOCUMENTACAO DO MINISTERIO DA SAUDE. 0101-5486. Periodical. Portuguese. mo. **LC** RA421.

INFORMATION FROM HEATH/ CLOSER LOOK RESOURCE CENTER. VFOAT Information from Heath/Closer Look. Vol. 1, No. 1 (Jan. 1981)-. Periodical. US. English. qt. Heath/Closer Look Resource Center, Box 1492, Washington DC 20013.

INFORMATION GUIDE - ARIZONA DEPARTMENT OF HEALTH SERVICES. Main/Corp Arizona. Bureau of Vital Records and Information Services. Research and Statistical Analysis. 1979-. US. English. Bureau of Vital Records and Information Services, Arizona Department of Health Services, 1740 West Adams Street, Phoenix AZ 85007. **LC** RA21. **DD** 353.979100841042. Information Guide - Arizona Department of Health Services, 0161-6722.

INFORMATSIONEN BIULETIN - SONS, UPRAVLENIE NARODNO ZDRAVE I SOTSIALNI GRIZHI. No. 1- 1979-. Bulgarian. ir. **NLM** W1 IN438U.

INFORME AL HONORABLE CONGRESO DE LA REPUBLICA DE COLOMBIA. Main/Corp Colombia. Ministerio de Salud Publica. Began in 1968. Spanish. ir. **LC** RA214. **DD** 362.109861. **NLM** W2 DC7 M608I. Informe Al H. Congreso de la Republica.

INFORME ANUAL DE ACTIVIDADES - SERVICIO ESPECIAL DE SALUD PUBLICA. (INFORME ANUAL DE ACTIVIDADES). **Main/Corp** Peru. Servicio Especial de Salud Publica. Began in 1960. 0253-8326. Spanish. an. **NLM** W2 DP6 S5I.

INFORME ANUAL - SERVICIO NACIONAL DE ERRADICACION DE LA MALARIA. 0253-5610. Spanish. an. **NLM** W2 DC8 S6I.

INGEGNERIA AMBIENTALE INQUINAMENTO E DEPURAZIONE. 0302-7775. Periodical. IT. Italian. mo. $47.52. Inst di Ingegneria Sanitario, Piazza Leonarda de Vinvi 32, 20133 Milano Italy. **Ind/Abst** Chem. Abstr. **CODEN** IGEABH.

INNOVATIVE PROGRAMS IN MENTAL HEALTH. ABSTRACTS BOOK. See Indexes/Abstracts.

INSIGHT. (INSIGHT : OFFICIAL PUBLICATION OF THE SINGAPORE ASSOCIATION FOR MENTAL HEALTH). '78-. 0129-6078. English. an. **NLM** W1 IN458J.

INSTRUCTIONAL MANUAL. DATA PREPARATION. VITAL STATISTICS. See Statistics.

INTERCHANGE. V. 1- Fall 1978-. 0195-9549. Periodical. US. English. National Health Care Management Center, The University of Pennsylvania, 3641 Locust Walk CE, Philadelphia PA 19104. **NLM** W1 IN669M.

INTERNATIONAL CONGRESS OF THE INTERNATIONAL COUNCIL ON HEALTH, PHYSICAL EDUCATION, AND RECREATION. Main/Corp International Council on Health, Physical Education, and Recreation. 1st- 1958-. 0074-4417. Periodical. US. English. be. International Council on Health Physical Education and Recreation, 1900 Association Drive, Reston VA 22091. **LC** GV205. **DD** 371.7.

INTERNATIONAL DIGEST OF HEALTH LEGISLATION. V. 1- 1948-. Periodical. US. English. ir. $60.00. World Health Organization, PO Box 5284, Church Street Station, New York NY 10249. **Tel** (202)861-3200. **LC** Microfiche K3569.2.

INTERNATIONAL HEALTH PLANNING SERIES. Began with: 1, 1979. 0731-6615. US. English. ir. **NLM** W1 IN764F.

INTERNATIONAL JOURNAL OF AVIATION SAFETY. See Aeronautics, Astronautics.

INTERNATIONAL JOURNAL OF EPIDEMIOLOGY. V. 1- Spring 1972-. 0300-5771. Periodical. UK. English. qt. 48 Domestic, $85.99 US, 55 Others. Oxford University Press, Walton Street, Oxford OX2 6DP England. **Tel** (0865)56767. Ed C Duv Florey. **Ind/Abst** Life Sci. Collect., Excerpta Med., Index Med., Biol. Abstr., CIS Abstr., Hospit. Lit. Index, Sci. Cit. Index, Abr. Ed. **LC** RA651. **DD** 614.405. **NLM** W1 IN766I. **CODEN** IJEPBF. bk rev. adv acc. **Circ** 2,500. Research, teaching and application of epidemiology.

INTERNATIONAL JOURNAL OF HEALTH EDUCATION. See Education (General).

INTERNATIONAL JOURNAL OF HEALTH EDUCATION (1982). See Education (General) - Special Aspects of Education.

THE INTERNATIONAL JOURNAL OF HEALTH PLANNING & MANAGEMENT. VFOAT Health Planning and Management. 0749-6753. Periodical. UK. English. qt. John Wiley & Sons, Baffin Lane, Chichester Sussex United Kingdom.

INTERNATIONAL JOURNAL OF HEALTH SERVICES. V. 1- Feb. 1971-. 0020-7314. Periodical. US. English. qt. Baywood Publishing Company, PO Box D, Farmingdale NY 11735. **Tel** (516)249-2464. Ed Vicente Manarro. **Ind/ Abst** Sociol. Abstr., Soc. Welf. Soc. Plan./Policy Soc. Dev., Abstr. Hospit. Manage. Stud., Excerpta Med., Hospit. Lit. Index, Index Med., Med. Care Rev., Med. Socioecon. Res. Source, Energy Res. Abstr. **LC** RA421. **DD** 362.105. **NLM** W1 IN768. **CODEN** IJHSC. A multidisciplinary publication devoted to health and social policy, political economy, sociology, history and philosophy, ethics and law.

INTERNATIONAL JOURNAL OF LEPROSY AND OTHER MYCOBACTERIAL DISEASES. V. 34- Jan./Mar. 1966-. 0148-916X. Periodical. US. English (French or Spanish). qt. $80.00. International Journal of Leprosy, 1262 Broad Street, Bloomfield NJ 07003. **Tel** (201)338-9197. **Ind/Abst** Excerpta Med., Life Sci. Collect., Chem. Abstr. **NLM** W1. International Journal of Leprosy, 0020-7349.

INTERNATIONAL JOURNAL OF MENTAL HEALTH. V. 1- Spring/Summer 1972-. 0020-7411. Periodical. US. English. qt. $148.05. M E Sharpe Inc, 80 Business Drive, Armonk NY 10504. **Tel** (914)273-1800. Ed Martin Gittelman. **Ind/ Abst** Excerpta Med., Public Aff. Inf. Serv. Bull., Psychol. Abstr., Soc. Sci. Citation Index. **LC** RA790.A1. **DD** 614.5805. **NLM** W1 IN769W. **CODEN** IJMHBV. adv acc. **Circ** 300. This journal bridges the gaps in knowledge globally, conceptually speaking, as well as geographically for mental health scientists.

INTERNATIONAL PERSPECTIVES IN PUBLIC HEALTH. **VFOAT** IPPH. Vol. 1, issue 1 (Spring 1984)-. 8755-5328. Periodical. US. English. qt. $20.00. Ministry of Concern for Public Health, 5495 Main Street/Suite 147, Buffalo NY 14221. **Tel** (416)533-7351. **Ed** R Bertell. **DD** 614. bk rev. adv acc. **Circ** 350. Environmental health, including health problems related to military production and weapon testing and ways of preventing further problems.

INTERNATIONAL QUARTERLY OF COMMUNITY HEALTH EDUCATION. *See* Education (General) - Special Aspects of Education.

INTERNATIONAL RESEARCH AND DEMONSTRATION PROJECTS. AN ANNOTATED LISTING. **VFOAT** Social and Rehabilitation International Research and Demonstration Projects. Periodical. US. English. an. Department of Health Education and Welfare, Social and Rehabilitative Services, Washington DC 20201.

INTRAMURALE GEZONDHEIDSZORG. **VFOAT** Intramural Health Care. 1981-. NE. Dutch (summaries in English). an. Centraal Bureau Voor de Statistik, Prinses Beatrixlaan 428, Postbus 959, 2270 AZ Voorburg Netherlands. **LC** RA407.5.N37. *Intramurale Gezondhiedszorg in Nederland.*

IOWA ACCIDENT FACTS. US. English. an. Iowa Department of Transportation, Office of Safety Programs/Lucas Building, Des Moines IA 50319. **LC** HE5614.3.I8. **DD** 363.12509777.

THE IPM PRACTITIONER. *See* Agriculture.

ISHIKAWA-KEN EISEI KOGAI KENKYUJO NEMPO. JA. Japanese. an. Ishikawa-Ken Eisei Kogai Kenkyujo, 251 Minma 2-chome, Kanazawa-shi 921 Japan. **LC** RA566.5.J3.

ISSUE PAPER - UNIVERSITY OF PENNSYLVANIA, NATIONAL HEALTH CARE MANAGEMENT CENTER. (ISSUE PAPER - NATIONAL HEALTH CARE MANAGEMENT CENTER). No. 1- Feb. 1979-. 0195-5551. Monographic Series. US. English. ir. **NLM** W1 IS6672.

ITOGI NAUKI I TEKHNIKI : MEDITSINSKAIA GEOGRAFIIA. **VFOAT** Itogi Nauki I Tekhniki: Seriia Meditsinskaia Geografiia. UR. Russian. 2.81. Liubertsy Oktiabrskii Prospekt 403, Moskva USSR. **LC** RA791. *Itogi Nauki: Meditsinskaia Geografiia.*

IWATE-KEN EISEI KENKYUJO NENPO. **VFOAT** Annual Report of the Iwate Prefectural Institute of Public Health. Began in 1952. Japanese. an. Iwate-Ken Eisei Kenkyujo, 15-Ban 25 Go Uchimaru, Morioka-shi 020 Japan. **Ind/Abst** Chem. Abstr. **LC** RA532.I9. **CODEN** IKENDI.

JIGYO YORAN - KOKURITSU KOSHU EISEIIN. **Main/Corp** Kokuritsu Koshu Eiseiin, Tokyo. 1978-. JA. Japanese. ir. Kokuritsu Koshu Eiseiin, 6-1 Shirokanedai 4, Minato-ku 108, Tokyo Japan. **LC** RA532.T64.

JOURNAL - ADDICTION RESEARCH FOUNDATION. (THE JOURNAL - ADDICTION RESEARCH FOUNDATION). **Main/Corp** Addiction Research Foundation of Ontario. V. 1- June 1972-. 0044-6203. Periodical. CN. English. mo. $12.38 Domestic, 24.00 Foreign. Addiction Research Foundation, 33 Russell Street, Toronto Ontario M5S 2S1 Canada. **Tel** (416)595-6053. **Ed** Anne MacLennan. **NLM** W1 JO222P. bk rev. adv acc. **Circ** 24,000. News publication for professionals in addictions and related health, enforcement, research, and education fields.

JOURNAL - AMERICAN HEALTH CARE ASSOCIATION. **Main/Corp** American Health Care Association. V. 1- July 1975-. 0360-4969. US. English. bm. $36.00. American Health Care Association, 1200 15th Street Northwest, Washington DC 20005. **Tel** (202)833-2050. **Ed** Sheran Hartwell. **Ind/Abst** Hospit. Lit. Index, Cumul. Index Nurs. Allied Health Lit. **LC** RA973.5. **DD** 362.104250973. **NLM** W1 JO222UH. bk rev. adv acc. **Circ** 20,000. The magazine for long term care professionals and features expert opinion and reports on current management and patient care techniques and services.

JOURNAL DE L'A.I.H.P.Q. (LE JOURNAL DE L'A. I. H. P. Q). **Main/Corp** Association des Insepcteurs en Hygiene Publique du Quebec. **VAT** Journal de l'Association des Inspecteurs en Hygiene Publique du Quebec. V. 17- May 1976-. 0705-0003. Periodical. CN. French. Association des Inspecteurs en Hygiene Publique du Quebec, CP 39 Succursale N, Montreal Quebec H2X 3M2 Canada. **DD** 614.09714. *Journal de l'A.I.S.P.Q., 0315-4300.*

JOURNAL OF ALLIED HEALTH. Began publication in 1972. 0090-7421. Periodical. US. English. qt. $24.00. 300 North Zeeb Road, Ann Arbor MI 48106. **Tel** (202)857-1150. **Ed** John Burke. **Ind/Abst** Hospit. Lit. Index, Index Med., Cumul. Index Nurs. Allied Health Lit., Curr. Index J. Educ. **LC** R690. **DD** 610.695305. **NLM** W1 JO534V. adv acc. (ctrl).

JOURNAL OF COMMUNICABLE DISEASES. (THE JOURNAL OF COMMUNICABLE DISEASES). Began in 1969. 0019-5138. Periodical. II. English. qt. $15.00. Indian Society for Malaria and Communicable Diseases, 22 Alipur Road, Delhi 6 India. **Ind/Abst** Excerpta Med., Index Med., Biol. Abstr. **NLM** W1 JO593E. **CODEN** JCDSBF. *Bulletin of the Indian Society for Malaria & Other Communicable Diseases, 0537-2526.*

JOURNAL OF COMMUNITY HEALTH. V. 1- Fall 1975-. 0094-5145. Periodical. US. English. qt. Human Sciences Press, 72 5th Avenue, New York NY 10011. **Tel** (212)243-6000. **Ind/Abst** Electron. Commun. Abstr. J., ISMEC Bull., Pollut. Abstr. Indexes, Saf. Sci. Abstr. J., Hospit. Lit. Index, Life Sci. Collect., Sociol. Abstr., Soc. Welf. Soc. Plan./Policy Soc. Dev., Excerpta Med., Index Med., Cumul. Index Nurs. Allied Health Lit., Energy Res. Abstr., Gen. Sci. Index. **LC** RA421. **DD** 362.1205. **NLM** W1 JO593Q. **CODEN** JCMHB.

JOURNAL OF ENVIRONMENTAL HEALTH. Began in 1938. 0022-0892. Periodical. US. English. bm. $15.00. National Environmental Health Association, 1200 Lincoln #704, Denver CO 80203. **Ind/Abst** Biol. Abstr., Chem. Abstr., Sel. Water Resour. Abstr., Bibliogr. Agric., Hospit. Lit. Index, Environ. Period. Bibliogr. **LC** RA565.A1. **DD** 614.705. **CODEN** JEVHAH. Available on microfilm from University Microfilms.

JOURNAL OF EPIDEMIOLOGY AND COMMUNITY HEALTH. V. 33, No. 2- June 1979-. 0143-005X. Periodical. UK. English. qt. $72.03. British Medical Journal, Tavistock Square, London WC1H 9JR England. **Ind/Abst** Hospit. Lit. Index, Life Sci. Collect., Excerpta Med., Index Med., Biol. Abstr., Psychol. Abstr., Sci. Cit. Index, Abr. Ed., Abstr. Soc. Work. **NLM** W1 JO644BQ. **CODEN** JECHDR. *Epidemiology and Community Health, 0142-467X.*

JOURNAL OF FOOD QUALITY. **VFOAT** FNP Journal of Food Quality. V. 1- Apr. 1977-. 0146-9428. Periodical. US. English. qt. Food and Nutrition Press, 155 Post Road East/PO Box 71, Westport CT 06881. **Tel** (203)227-6596. **Ed** M P de Figueiredo. **Ind/Abst** Excerpta Med., Chem. Abstr., Bibliogr. Agric. **LC** TP372.5. **DD** 664.07. **NLM** W1 JO65W. **CODEN** JFQUD7. bk rev. adv acc. Publishes all aspects of food quality assurance and regulations including environmental factors.

JOURNAL OF FOOD SAFETY. **VFOAT** FNP Journal of Food Safety. V. 1- Aug. 1977-. 0149-6085. Periodical. US. English. qt. $75.00. Food and Nutrition Press, 155 Post Road East/PO Box 71, Westport CT 06881. **Tel** (203)227-6596. **Ed** M Solberg and J Rosen. **Ind/Abst** Life Sci. Collect., Chem. Abstr., Bibliogr. Agric. **LC** TX501. **DD** 614.3105. **NLM** W1 JO65Y. **CODEN** JFSADP. bk rev. adv acc. Emphasizes chemical and microbiological coverage of food safety. Chemical includes toxicology, metabolism, and environmental conversion of materials entering the food supply.

THE JOURNAL OF HEALTH ADMINISTRATION EDUCATION. Vol. 1, No. 1 (Winter 1983)-. 0735-6722. Periodical. US. English. qt. $40.00. AUPHA, 1911 North Fort Myer Drive, Arlington VA 22209. **Ind/Abst** Hospit. Lit. Index. **LC** RA440.6. **DD** 362.1068. bk rev. **Circ** 1,500. Chronicles advances in univeristy-based and management development for health administrators. Also includes health services research and policy discussion.

JOURNAL OF HEALTH AND HUMAN RESOURCES ADMINISTRATION. *See* Sociology: General Works, Theory.

JOURNAL OF HEALTH AND SOCIAL BEHAVIOR. *See* Sociology: General Works, Theory.

JOURNAL OF HEALTH CARE MARKETING. *See* Business - Marketing.

THE JOURNAL OF HOLISTIC HEALTH. V. 1- 1975/76-. 0161-5491. Periodical. US. English. an. $10.00. Mandala Holistic Health, PO Box 1233, Del Mar CA 92014. **LC** RA773. **DD** 613.05. **NLM** W1 JO671E.

JOURNAL OF HYGIENE, EPIDEMIOLOGY, MICROBIOLOGY, AND IMMUNOLOGY. 1- 1957-. 0022-1732. Periodical. CS. English (articles in French or German). qt. $92.00. Karger Libri AG, Petersgraben 31, CH-4009 Basel 11 Switzerland. **Tel** 061/390880. **Ind/Abst** Index Med., CIS Abstr., Index Dent. Lit., Chem. Abstr., Bibliogr. Agric., Sci. Cit. Index, Abr. Ed., Hospit. Lit. Index, Saf. Sci. Abstr. J., Life Sci. Collect., Excerpta Med., Coal Abstr., Electron. Commun. Abstr. J., ISMEC Bull., Pollut. Abstr. Indexes. **LC** RA421. **NLM** W1 JO674L. **CODEN** JHEMA2.

THE JOURNAL OF LATIN COMMUNITY HEALTH. Vol. 1, No. 1 (Fall, 1982)-. 0740-2279. Periodical. US. English. sa. $12.00. Journal of Latin Community Health Inc, Box 273/107 Avenue Louis Pasteur, Boston MA 02115. **LC** RA448.5.H57. **DD** 362.108968073.

JOURNAL OF MARKETING FOR MENTAL HEALTH. 0883-7589. Periodical. US. English. qt. $52.00 Institutions, $60.00 Libraries. Haworth Press, 75 Griswold Street, Binghamton NY 13904.

JOURNAL OF MEDICAL ENTOMOLOGY. V. 1- Apr. 1964-. 0022-2585. Periodical. US. English. bm. $30.00. Bishop Museum Press, PO Box 19000-A, Honolulu HI 96819. **Tel** (808)847-3511. **Ind/Abst** Life Sci. Collect., Excerpta Med., Pestdoc, Ringdoc, Vetdoc, Bibliogr. Agric., Biol. Abstr., Chem. Abstr., Index Med., Nuci. Sci. Abstr., Sel. Water Resour. Abstr., Energy Res. Abstr., Sci. Cit. Index, Abr. Ed. **LC** RA639.5. **NLM** W1 JO75E. **CODEN** JMENA6.

THE JOURNAL OF PRIMARY PREVENTION. 0278-095X. Periodical. US. English. qt. $45.00. Human Sciences Press, 72 5th Avenue, New York NY 10011. **Ind/Abst** Sociol. Abstr., Soc. Welf. Soc. Plan./Policy Soc. Dev., Excerpta Med., Psychol. Abstr. **LC** RA790.A1. **DD** 362.205. **NLM** W1 JO841H. **CODEN** JPPRDT. *Journal of Prevention, 0163-514X.*

JOURNAL OF PUBLIC HEALTH POLICY. V. 1- Mar. 1980-. 0197-5897. Periodical. US. English. qt. $60.00. Journal of Public Health, 208 Meadowood Drive, South Burlington VT 05401. **Tel** (802)658-0136. **Ed** Milton Terris. **Ind/Abst** Hospit. Lit. Index, Sociol. Abstr., Soc. Welf. Soc. Plan./Policy Soc. Dev., Excerpta Med., Energy Inf. Abstr., Environ. Abstr., Index Med., Cumul. Index Nurs. Allied Health Lit., Biol. Abstr., Public Aff. Inf. Serv. Bull. **LC** RA421. **DD** 614.05. **NLM** W1 JO859UH. **CODEN** JPPODK. bk rev. adv acc. **Circ** 1,600. All aspects of public health policy, including prevention, medical care, and the physical and social environment.

JOURNAL OF SCHOOL HEALTH. (THE JOURNAL OF SCHOOL HEALTH). **VFOAT** JOSH. The Journal of School Health. V. 7- Jan. 1937-. 0022-4391. Periodical. US. English. ASHA, PO Box 708, Kent OH 44240. **Tel** (216)678-1601. **Ed** R Morgan Pigg Jr. **Ind/Abst** Index Med., Cumul. Index Nurs. Allied Health Lit., Women Stud. Abstr., Int. Nurs. Index, Psychol. Abstr., Index Med., Biol. Abstr., Educ. Index, Bibliogr. Agric., Curr. Index J. Educ., Media Rev. Dig., Energy Res. Abstr. **LC** LB3401. **DD** 371.705. **NLM** W1 JO873S. **CODEN** JSHEA2. (cum index). bk rev. adv acc. Articles on current trends, research and developments on the physical and mental health of school-age children. *School Physicians' Bulletin.*

JOURNAL OF THE ASSOCIATION OF PUBLIC ANALYSTS. *See* Nutrition and Dietetics.

JOURNAL OF THE EGYPTIAN PUBLIC HEALTH ASSOCIATION. (THE JOURNAL OF THE EGYPTIAN PUBLIC HEALTH ASSOCIATION). 1926?-. 0013-2446. Periodical. UA. added title in Arabic on back cover. $16.00. Shousha Building/ Block A 31, Sharia 26, Cairo Egypt. **Ind/Abst** Excerpta Med., Biol. Abstr., Chem. Abstr., Nuci. Sci. Abstr., Index Med. **NLM** W1 JO92F. **CODEN** JEGPAY.

JOURNAL OF THE ROYAL SOCIETY OF HEALTH. **VFOAT** J.R.S.H., JRSH. Vol. 103, No. 1 (Feb. 1983)-. 0264-0325. Periodical. UK. English. bm. Royal Society of Health, 13 Grosvenor Place, London SW1X 7EN England. **Tel** 01 235 9961. **Ind/Abst** Excerpta Med., Energy Inf. Abstr., Environ.

Public Health and Safety

Abstr., Index Med., Biol. Abstr., Chem. Abstr., Nutr. Abstr. Rev. NLM W1 JO951G. *Royal Society of Health Journal.*

KAHPER JOURNAL (RICHMOND, KY.). (KAHPER JOURNAL). VFOAT K.A.H.P.E.R. Journal. VAT Kentucky Association for Health, Physical Education and Recreation Journal. Vol. 1, No. 1 (Oct. 1964)-. 0022-7269. Periodical. US. English. sa. $10.00. Kentucky Association of Health Physical Education and Recreation, c/o Don Calitri, 128 East Kentucky University, Richmond KY 40475-0933. Tel (606)622-1898. Ed Paul Motley and Hal Holmes. bk rev. adv acc. Circ 500. (ctrl). Official publication of the Kentucky Association for Health, Physical Education, Recreation and Dance. Professional journal with articles dealing with health, physical education and recreation.

KANAGAWA-KEN EISEI KENKYUJO KENKYU HKOKU. VFOAT Bulletin of the Kamagawa Prefectural Public Health Laboratories. Began with Oct. 1971 issue. 0303-0350. Periodical. JA. Japanese (some summaries in English). an. Kanagawa-Ken Eisei Kenkyujo, 52-2 Nakaocho Asahi-ku, Yokohama-shi 241 Japan. Ind/Abst Chem. Abstr. LC RA532.K36. NLM W1 KA429M. CODEN KEKHB8.

KANSENSHOGAKU ZASSHI. VFOAT The Journal of the Japanese Association for Infectious Diseases. Began in 1970. 0387-5911. Periodical. JA. Japanese. mo. Japan Publications Trading Company Inc, PO Box 5030, Tokyo International, Tokyo 100-31 Japan. Ind/Abst Index Med., Chem. Abstr. CODEN KSSZAT. *Nihon Densenbyo Gakkai Zasshi.*

KENENKEN DAYORI. No. 1 (Aug. 1979)-. Periodical. JA. Japanese. ir. 2000. Aki Shobo, 9 Kanda Jinbocho 2 Chiyoda-ku, Tokyo-to 101 Japan. LC HV5770.J3.

KESEHATAN MASYARAKAT. VFOAT Journal of Public Health. 0126-0979. Periodical. English or Indonesian. ir. Bagian Penerbitan Dan Perpustakaan Birov Department, Jl Prapatan No 10, Jakarta Indonesia. LC RA317. NLM W1 KE758C. *Kesehatan Masjarakat.*

KIRO SANTE. V. 1- Nov. 1974-. 0317-0519. Periodical. CN. French. bm $5.42. Kirosante, 33 Ste Agathe, Monts Quebec J8C 2J6 Canada. Tel (819)326-1666. Ed Gaston Arguin. DD 615.53405. bk rev. adv acc. Circ 8,500. Various informations dealing with the many aspects of global health and the different methods leading to the achievement and the maintenance of that state of well-being.

KOKURITSU EISEI SHIKENJO YORAN = NATIONAL INSTITUTE OF HYGIENIC SCIENCES. JA. Japanese. ir. Kokuritsu Eisei Shikenjo, 18-1 Kami Yoga 1-chome, Setagaya-ku 158, Tokyo Japan. LC RA428.3.K64.

KOKURITSU KOSHU EISEIIN NEMPO. Began with the report for 1948. JA. Japanese. ir. Kokuritsu Koshu Eiseiin, 39 Shiba Shirokane Kaimachi L-chome Minato-ku, Tokyo 108 Japan. LC RA440.6.

KOKURITSU YOBO EISEI KENKYUJO NEMPO. VFOAT Nempo. Began with the report for 1947. Japanese. ir. Kokuritsu Yobo Eisei Kenkyujo, 10-35 Kami Osaki 2-chome Shinaga-ku, Tokyo 141 Japan. LC RA421. NLM W1 KO308.

KONGANG SAENGHWAL. VFOAT Health Life. V. 1- (Dec. 1982)-. Periodical. KO. Korean. mo. 27.500. Chusik Hoesa Kongang Saenghwal, 170-33 Kaebong-dong Kuro-ku, Seoul 150-04 Korea. LC RA773.

KONGANG SIDAE. V. 1- (1983. 12)-. Periodical. KO. Korean. mo. 3.000. Kongang Sidaesa, 51-3 Nonhyon-dong Kangnam-ku, Seoul Korea. LC RA773.

KOSHU EISEI NI KANSURU KENKYU HOKOKU. Periodical. JA. Japanese. ir. Tokyo-to Eiseikyoku, 5-1 Marunouchi 3 Chiyoda-ku, Tokyo 100 Japan. LC RA421. NLM W1 KO623L.

KOSHU EISEIIN KENKYU HOKOKU = BULLETIN OF THE INSTITUTE OF PUBLIC HEALTH. Main/Corp Kokuritsu Koshu Eiseiin, Tokyo. V. 1-. Periodical. Japanese (English). ir. Kokuritsu Koshu Eiseiin, 6-ban 1-go Shirokanedai 4-chome, Minato-ku, Tokyo Japan. LC RA421.

KOSTEN EN FINANCIERING VAN DE GEZONDHEIDSZORG. VFOAT Cost and Financing of Health Care. 0075-6954. NE. Dutch (summaries in English). an. 14.40. Centraal Bureau Voor de Statistiek, Prinses Beatrixlaan 428, Postbus 959, 2270 AZ Voorburg Netherlands. *Kosten en Financiering van de Gezondheidszorg in Nederland.*

KOTSU ANZEN KOGAI KENKYUJO NEMPO. *See* Transportation - Roads and Traffic.

KRANKENHAUSHYGIENE + INFEKTIONSVERHUTUNG. (KRANKENHAUS-HYGIENE + INFEKTIONSVERHUTUNG). VFOAT Krankenhaus-Hygiene und Infektionsverhutung. Began with: 1 (Feb. 1979). 0720-3373. Periodical. German. bm. Fischer & Pflaum Verlag, Lazarettstrasse 4, 8000 Munchen 4 West Germany. Ind/Abst Excerpta Med. NLM W1 KR257M.

KUMAMOTO-KEN EISEI KOGAI KENKYUJO HO. 1971/72-. JA. Japanese. ir. Kumamoto-Ken Eisei Kogai Kenkyujo, 4-33 Minami-Sendanbatamachi, Kumamoto 860 Japan. LC RA565.A1.

KUMPULAN PIDATO MENTERI KESEHATAN RI. VFOAT Kumpulan Pidato Menteri Kesehatan R.I. English (Indonesian). an. Departemen Kesahatan Republik Indonesia, J1 Prapatan No 10, Jakarta Indonesia. LC RA317.

KYOTO-SHI EISEI KENKYUJO NEMPO. JA. Japanese. an. Kyoto-Shi Eisei Kenkyujo, 1-2 Mibu Higashi Takadacho, Nakagyo-ku, Kyoto-shi Japan. LC RA532.K96. NLM W2 JJ3.2 K9E3N.

LAPORAN TENTANG KESEHATAN RAKJAT DI PROPINSI DJAWA TENGAH. Main/Corp Djawa Tengah (Indonesia). Djawatan Kesehatan Rakjat. Indonesian. ir. LC RA318.D54. *Laporan Dari Djawatan Kesehatan Rakjat Propinsi Djawa Tengah.*

LAURISTON S. TAYLOR LECTURES IN RADIATION PROTECTION AND MEASUREMENTS. VFOAT Lauriston S. Taylor Lecture Series in Radiation Protection and Measurements. Began with: Lecture No. 1 (Mar. 17, 1977). 0277-9196. Monographic Series. US. English. an. National Council of Radiation Protection Publications, 7910 Woodmont Avenue/Suite 1016, Bethesda MD 20814. Tel (301)657-2652. NLM W1 LA826.

LEGISLATIVE STATUS REPORT - NATIONAL ASSOCIATION OF COMMUNITY HEALTH CENTERS. *See* Law.

LEPROSY IN INDIA CEASED. Began with July 1929 issue. Ceased with Oct. 1983 issue. 0024-1024. Periodical. I. English. qt. $7.00. Hind Kusht Nivaran Sangh, 1 Red Cross Road, New Delhi 110001 India. Tel 666008. Ind/Abst Excerpta Med., Hospit. Lit. Index. LC RC154.7.I6. DD 616.998. NLM W1.

LEPROSY RELIEF CANADA INC. (THE LEPROSY RELIEF (CANADA) INC). 0382-7682. Periodical. CN. English. ir. Leprosy Relief Canada, PO Box 1672 Station B, Montreal Quebec H3B 3L3 Canada. DD 362.19699805. *Help for the Leper, 0382-7674.*

LEPTOSPIROSIS SURVEILLANCE, ANNUAL SUMMARY (1977?). (LEPTOSPIROSIS SURVEILLANCE, ANNUAL SUMMARY). VFOAT Letosprirosis Surveillance. US. English. ir. Center for Disease Control, Atlanta GA 30333. *Leptospirosis, Annual Summary, 0091-0295.*

LIFE AND HEALTH; THE HEALTH MAGAZINE. 0024-3035. Periodical. US. English. mo. $9.00. Review & Herald Publishing Association, 6856 Eastern Avenue NW, Washington DC 20012. Ed W H Maxson, MC Wilcox, and G H Heald. LC RA773. NLM W1 LI38W.

THE LIFE BOAT. No. 1 (Jan. 1858)-. Periodical. US. English. $3.86. Royal National Lifeboat Institute, West Quay Road Poole, Dorset BH15 1H2 England. Tel 0202 671133. Ed Edward Wake-Walker. bk rev. adv acc. Circ 125,000. Articles about the work of the Royal National Lifeboat Institution. Includes accounts of rescues by lifeboats. Fund raising stories and covers all aspects of lifeboating.

LIFE STYLES HEALTH SERIES. No. 1-. 0277-545X. Monographic Series. US. English. ir. Institute Research of Social Science, Manning Hall 026A University of North Carolina, Chapel Hill NC 27514. NLM W1 LI407H.

LIFEGUARD. V. 1- Dec. 1975-. 0381-1565. Periodical. CN. English. Project Life, 17 Dundas Street East, Mississauga Ontario L5A 1W1 Canada. DD 615.852.

LIFELINE (SORRENTO, B.C.). (LIFELINE). 0712-2462. Periodical. CN. English. bm. $13.00. Editor Lifeline, PO Box 206, Sorrento British Columbia V2E 2W0 Canada. DD 363.35.

LIFELINES SASKATCHEWAN. Main/Corp Royal Life Saving Society Canada. Saskatchewan Branch. Vol. 6, No. 12 (June 1981)-. 0711-4257. Periodical. CN. English. qt. Royal Life Saving Society Canada, Saskatchewan Branch, 2205 Victoria Avenue, Regina Saskatchewan S4P 0S4 Canada. DD 363.14. *Lifelines, 0706-7933.*

LIFESAVER. (LIFESAVER : THE U.S. COAST GUARD SAFETY AND OCCUPATIONAL HEALTH REVIEW). Vol. I, No. 1 (Winter 1980)-. 0270-4102. Periodical. US. English. qt. Commandant G-CSP, US Coast Guard Headquarters, Washington DC 20593. LC VG53. DD 363.12372.

LINK LINE. *See* Education (General).

LIVING CEASED. VFOAT Visa-Vie. Vol. 1-V. 3, No. 2. 0317-4522. Periodical. CN. English (text in French). qt. $0.25 Per Issue. Health and Welfare Canada Headquarters, Brook Claxton Building, Ottawa Ontario K1A 0K9 Canada. LC RA184. DD 614.0971.

LIVING SAFETY FOR THE CANADIAN FAMILY. VFOAT Living Safety. Spring 1983-. 0714-5896. Periodical. CN. English. qt. Free. Canadian Safety Council, 1765 St Laurent Boulevard, Ottawa Ontario K1G 3V4 Canada. DD 363.1005. (ctrl).

LOCAL HEALTH DEPARTMENTS IN OREGON. 1976-. 0146-1516. US. English. ir. NLM W2 AO7 L8Y. *Tabulation of Local Health Services, Annual Summary, 0362-4080.*

LOUISIANA STATE PLAN FOR COMPREHENSIVE MENTAL HEALTH SERVICES. Main/Corp Louisiana. Office of Mental Health. 0162-8461. US. English. an. Office of Mental Health, 655 North 5th Street/Room 303, Baton Rouge LA 70804. LC RA790.65.L8. DD 362.209763.

MAINE MENTAL HEALTH PLAN. Main/Corp Maine. Dept. of Mental Health and Corrections. 0147-2585. US. English. Department of Mental Health and Corrections, State Office Buiding, Augusta ME 04333. LC RA790.65.M3. DD 362.209741.

MALARIA SURVEILLANCE, ANNUAL SUMMARY. VFOAT Malaria Surveillance. US. English. an. US Department of Health and Human Services, Public Health Service Centers for Disease Control, Atlanta GA 30333. LC RC156.A1. DD 614.5320973. NLM W2 A C7CM. Vols. for 1982-distributed to depository libraries in microfiche.

MATERIALY KRAEVOI EPIDEMIOLOGII I GIGIENY. Periodical. UR. Russian. NLM W1 MA9425F.

MEASLES SURVEILLANCE REPORT. VFOAT Measles Surveillance. Began with No. 1, Aug. 1966. 0198-6899. US. English. ir. US Department of Health and Human Services, Public Health Service, Centers for Disease Control, Atlanta GA 30333. LC RA644.M5. DD 614.5230973. NLM W2 A C2G.

MEDIA PROFILES. THE HEALTH SCIENCES EDITION. VFOAT Health Sciences Edition. Vol. 10, Issue 1-. 0740-1892. Periodical. US. English. bm. $87.50. Olympic Media Information, 70 Hudson Street, Hoboken NJ 07030. Tel (201)963-1600. Ed Walt Carroll. LC RA440.55. DD 016.61. NLM WA 18 M489. bk rev. Critical reviews of film video and other audiovisual media for the education and health sciences professionals and patient education. *Hospital/Health Care Training Media Profiles, 0095-0580.*

MEDICAL AND HEALTH ANNUAL. *See* Medicine.

MEDICAL CARE. ANNUAL REPORT. (ANNUAL REPORT. MEDICAL CARE). VFOAT Medical Care. Began with: 1975/76?. 0710-8613. CN. English (text also in French). NLM W2 DC2 H3A. *Annual Report of the Minister of National Health and Welfare Respecting Operations of the Medical Care Act, 0710-8605.*

MEDICARE— USE OF HOME HEALTH SERVICES (HEALTH CARE FINANCING PROGRAM STATISTICS). (MEDICARE— USE OF HOME HEALTH SERVICES). Series/Titl Health Care Financing Program Statistics. US. English. an. Free to libraries. ORD Publications, Oak Meadows Building, Room 1A9, 6325 Security Boulevard, Baltimore MD 21207. Tel (301)594-9346. Ed Linda Cantale. Circ

Public Health and Safety

2,000. (ctrl). Presents data on the use of home health agency services by medicare beneficiaries in 1980.

MEDIGUIDE TO INFECTIOUS DISEASES. Vol. 1, Issue 1-. 0737-6030. Periodical. US. English. qt. Dellacorte Publications Inc, 767 Lexington Avenue, New York NY 10021. **NLM** W1 ME787FL.

MEDITSINSKAIA GAZETA. V. 25, No. 90- (No. 2148-). 0025-8318. Periodical. UR. Russian. sw. $20.00. Victor Kamkin Inc (50075), 12224 Parklawn Drive, Rockville MD 20852. **Tel** (301)881-5973. **NLM** W1 ME7951. **CODEN** MEGZAT. *Meditsinskii Rabotnik.*

MEMORIA - DONIMICAN REPUBLIC. SECRETARIA DE ESTADO DE SALUD PUBLICA Y ASISTENCIA SOCIAL. Main/Corp Dominican Republic. Secretaria de Estado de Salud Publica y Asistencia Social. Spanish. an. **LC** RA456.D6. **DD** 362.1097293.

MEMORIA - HONDURAS, MINISTERIO DE SALUD PUBLICA Y ASISTENCIA SOCIAL. Main/Corp Honduras. Ministerio de Salud Public y Asistencia Social. Spanish. ir. **LC** RA191.H6.

MENTAL HEALTH AND DEVELOPMENTAL DISABILITIES CODE, WITH ANNOTATIONS OF REQUIRED FORMS. See Law.

MENTAL HEALTH ANNUAL REPORT. FY 1980-. US. English. an. Division of Mental Health and Developmental Disabilities, Department of Health and Social Services, Pouch H-04, Juneau AK 99811. **LC** RA790.65.A4. **DD** 362.209798. *Analysis of Patient and Program Characteristics, Community Mental Health Client and Services Summary.*

MENTAL HEALTH (BOCA RATON, FLA.). (MENTAL HEALTH). Series/Titl Social Issues Resources Series. V. 1, Article 1-. 0272-9962. US. English. an. Social Issues Resources Series Inc, PO Box 2507, Boca Raton FL 33432. Ed E C Goldstein. **LC** RA790.A1. **DD** 362.2.

MENTAL HEALTH IN AUSTRALIA. V. 1- Aug. 1973-. 0310-5776. Periodical. AT. English. sa. 7.00. Australia National Association of Mental Health, Suite 23-20/Commerical Road, Melbourne Victoria 3004 Australia. **Tel** (03)266-1938. Ed G C Collins. **Ind/Abst** APAIS, Aust. Public Aff. Inf. Serv., Psychol. Abstr. **NLM** W1 ME9258. bk rev. **Circ** 1,000. (ctrl). Articles and reviews in promotion of mental health and prevention of mental illness. *Mental Health in Australia, 0025-9667.*

MENTAL HEALTH NEWS BULLETIN. VAT Guelph/Wellington Mental Health News Bulletin. Began publication with Spring 1979 issue. 0827-2700. Periodical. CN. English. qt. Free to Members. Canadian Mental Health Association Guelph-Wellington Branch, 15 Yarmouth Street PO Box 932, Guelph Ontario N1H 6M6 Canada. **DD** 362.20971343.

MENTAL HEALTH PLAN. Main/Corp Maine. Dept. of Mental Health and Mental Retardation. VFOAT Maine Mental Health Plan. 1982-83-. 0743-9113. US. English. an. Maine Department of Mental Health and Mental Retardation, 411 State Office Building/ Station 40, Augusta ME 04333. **LC** RA790.65.M3. **DD** 362.2042509741.

MENTAL HEALTH PLAN AND ... ANNUAL REPORT. US. English. an. State of Pennsylvania, Department of Public Welfare, Harrisburg PA 17120. **LC** RA790.65.P4. **DD** 353.97480084206.

MENTAL HEALTH RESOURCES IN THE GREATER WASHINGTON AREA. 0092-5403. US. English. an. N I M H Public Inquiries, 5600 Fishers Lane, Rockville MD 20852. **LC** RA790.65.W18. **DD** 362.2042509753. **NLM** WM 22 AD6 M5.

MENTAL HEALTH SERVICE SYSTEM REPORTS. SERIES EN. MENTAL HEALTH ECONOMICS. (MENTAL HEALTH SERVICE SYSTEM REPORTS. SERIES EN, MENTAL HEALTH ECONOMICS). Series/Titl DHHS Publication. VFOAT Mental Health Economics. No. 1-. 0733-9852. US. English. **NLM** W1 ME928EU.

MENTAL HEALTH STATISTICS. See Statistics.

MENTAL HEALTH STATISTICS. See Statistics.

MENTAL HEALTH SYSTEM DESCRIPTION AND BUDGET REQUESTS FOR THE STATE OF OKLAHOMA. Series/Titl Combined Drug, Alcohol & Mental Health Plan. US. English. an. Oklahoma Department of Mental Health, PO Box 53277, Capitol Station, Oklahoma City OK 73152. **LC** RA790.65.O5. **DD** 353.97660084206.

MENTAL RETARDATION. VFOAT MR. V. 1- Feb. 1963-. 0047-6765. Periodical. US. English. bm. $30.00. American Association on Mental Deficiency, 1719 Kalorama Road NW, Washington DC 20009. **Tel** (202)387-1968. Ed Louis Rowitz. **Ind/Abst** Excerpta Med., Index Med., Energy Res. Abstr., Educ. Index, Except. Child Educ. Resour., Soc. Work Res. Abstr., Curr. Index J. Educ., Psychol. Abstr., Soc. Sci. Citation Index, Sociol. Abstr., Educ. Index, Lang. Lang. Behav. Abstr., Abstr. Soc. Work. **LC** RC569.7. **DD** 362.3. **NLM** W1 ME936J. **CODEN** MRTDAH. bk rev. adv acc. **Circ** 12,000. Journal for persons working in mental retardation - administrators, educators, therapists, advocates. Material relevant to improving life opportunities of people who are mentally retarded.

MENTAL RETARDATION AND LEARNING DISABILITY BULLETIN. (THE MENTAL RETARDATION AND LEARNING DISABILITY BULLETIN). Vol. 11, No. 1 (1983)-. 0822-4277. Periodical. CN. English. sa. $11.61. University of Alberta, Faculty of Education, 4-116 Education North, Edmonton Alberta H6G 2G5 Canada. **Tel** (403)432-4204. Ed J P Das and Lyle Barton. **Ind/Abst** Psychol. Abstr., Can. Educ. Index. **DD** 362.305. bk rev. adv acc. **Circ** 500. Emphasizes articles with direct application to the education/ treatment of mentally retarded, learning disabled, and handicapped persons. *Mental Retardation Bulletin (Centre for the Study of Mental Retardation), 0707-9761.*

MENTAL RETARDATION AND THE LAW. See Law.

MERGE. See Transportation - Roads and Traffic.

METHODOLOGY REPORTS. See Statistics.

MH, MARYLAND'S HEALTH. V. 1- Jan./Feb. 1971-. Periodical. US. English. qt. Public Information Services, Maryland State Department of Health and Mental Hygiene, 301 West Preston Street, Baltimore MD 21201. **LC** RA81. **DD** 362.109752. **NLM** W2 AM3 S72M. *Maryland's Health.*

MICHIGAN HEALTH & SAFETY DIGEST. VFOAT Michigan Health and Safety Digest. 0746-0368. Periodical. US. English. mo. $60.00. Pathfinder Associates, 208 California Avenue North, Muskegon MI 49445.

MICHIGAN HEALTH STATISTICS. See Statistics.

THE MICHIGAN HOLISTIC HEALTH DIRECTORY. See Yearbooks, Almanacs, Directories.

MICHIGAN SCHOOL BUS ACCIDENTS. See Transportation.

MICROBIAL DISEASES. 1980 Ed.-. Periodical. US. English. ir. Ed Carl W May. **NLM** W1 MI262U.

MIGRANT HEALTH PROJECTS; SUMMARY OF PROJECT DATA. Main/Corp United States. Health Services Administration. Bureau of Community Health Services. Division of Monitoring and Analysis. 1975-. 0145-1340. Periodical. US. English. qt. **LC** RA448.5.M5. **DD** 362.85. **NLM** W2 A H64M.

THE MILBANK MEMORIAL FUND QUARTERLY. HEALTH AND SOCIETY. (MILBANK MEMORIAL FUND QUARTERLY. HEALTH AND SOCIETY). VFOAT Health and Society. V. 51- Winter 1973-. 0160-1997. Periodical. US. English. qt. $55.00. Massachusetts Institute of Technology, 28 Carlton Street, Cambridge MA 02142. **Ind/Abst** Bus. Period. Index, Manage. Contents, Energy Res. Abstr., Hospit. Lit. Index, Index Med., Int. Labour Doc., Life Sci. Collect., Soc. Welf. Soc. Plan./Policy Soc. Dev., Soc. Work Res. Abstr., Sociol. Abstr., Soc. Sci. Citation Index, Lang. Lang. Behav. Abstr. **NLM** W1 MI483D. *Milbank Memorial Fund Quarterly, 0026-3745.*

MINNESOTA ALCOHOL PROGRAMS FOR HIGHWAY SAFETY. Main/Corp Minnesota. Highway Safety and Research Station. 1972-. 0093-2558. US. English. 210 State Highway Building, St Paul MN 55155. **LC** HE5620.D7. **DD** 614.862.

MINNESOTA HEALTH STATISTICS. See Statistics.

MISSOURI ANNUAL HIGHWAY SAFETY WORK PROGRAM. See Transportation - Roads and Traffic.

MISSOURI C.H.P. IN RETROSPECT. Main/Corp Missouri. Governor's Advisory Council on Comprehensive Health Planning. 0094-0429. Periodical. US. English. Office of Comprehensive Health Planning, 303 Missouri Boulevard, Jefferson City MO 65101. **LC** RA395.A4. **DD** 362.109778.

MISSOURI HEALTH PROGRAMS PERFORMANCE REPORTS. Main/Corp Missouri. Division of Health. 0275-8156. US. English. an. PO Box 570, Broadway State Office Building, Jefferson City MI 65102. **LC** RA97. **DD** 353.977800841.

MISSOURI HEALTH REPORT. Main/Corp Missouri. Division of Health. 1973/75-. 0149-1857. US. English. be. Division of Health, PO Box 570, Jefferson City MO 65101. **LC** RA97. **DD** 362.109778. **NLM** W2 AM8 D41A. *Biennial Report - Missouri Division of Health, 0164-2766.*

MISSOURI STATE HEALTH PLAN. Main/Corp Missouri. Statewide Health Coordinating Council. VFOAT State Health Plan. 1978-. US. English. Missouri State Health Planning and Development Agency, Broadway State Office Building, Jefferson City MO 65101. **LC** RA395.A4. **DD** 362.109778.

MISSOURI STATE PLAN FOR HIGH BLOOD PRESSURE CONTROL. Fiscal Year 1980-. 0742-1354. US. English. an. **LC** RA645.H9. **DD** 362.19616132. *Missouri State Plan for Hypertension Control, 0742-1362.*

MISSOURI VITAL STATISTICS. See Statistics.

MMWR : MORBIDITY AND MORTALITY WEEKLY REPORT. ANNUAL SUMMARY. VFOAT M.M.W.R. 1979-. US. English. an. Center for Disease Control, Public Health Service, US Department of Health and Human Services, Atlanta GA 30333. *MMWR Annual Summary.*

MMWR. SURVEILLANCE SUMMARIES. MORBIDITY AND MORTALITY WEEKLY REPORT. SURVEILLANCE SUMMARIES. VFOAT Morbidity and Mortality Weekly Report Surveillance Summaries. Vol. 32, No. 1st (Feb. 1983)-. Periodical. US. English. qt. $69.00 Domestic, $86.25 Foreign. Centers for Disease Control, Atlanta GA 30333. **Tel** (404)321-2100. Ed Michael B Gregg. **Ind/Abst** Index Med. **LC** RA407.3. **DD** 614.427305. **NLM** W2 A C7CMA. **Circ** 43,000. Provides analysis and statistics on the occurrence of disease and death due to all causes in the United States.

MONOGRAPH SERIES - POLICY AND PLANNING DIVISION, COMMONWEALTH DEPARTMENT OF HEALTH. (MONOGRAPH SERIES). No. 1 (Apr. 1978)-. 0157-5503. Monographic Series. English. ir. **NLM** W1 MO559Q.

MONOGRAPH SERIES - WORLD HEALTH ORGANIZATION. (MONOGRAPH SERIES). Main/Corp World Health Organization. No. 1-. 0512-3038. Monographic Series. US. English (French). ir. World Health Organization, 49 Sheridan Avenue, Albany NY 12210. **Ind/Abst** Excerpta Med., Biol. Abstr., Index Med. **NLM** W1 WO879. **CODEN** WHOMAP.

MONOGRAPHS IN EPIDEMIOLOGY AND BIOSTATISTICS. Vol. 1-. 0740-0845. Monographic Series. US. English. ir. Oxford University Press, 16 00 Pollitt Drive, Fairlawn NJ 07410. Ed Abraham M Lilienfeld.

MONTANA STATE HEALTH PLAN. Main/Corp Statewide Health Coordinating Council (Mont.). 1979/80-. US. English. an. Department of Health & Environmental Science, Bureau of Health Planning & Resource Development, Helena MT 59601. **LC** RA395.A4. **DD** 362.109786.

MONTANA VITAL STATISTICS. See Statistics.

MONTHLY SUMMARY OF VITAL STATISTICS. See Statistics.

Public Health and Safety

MORBIDITY AND MORTALITY WEEKLY REPORT. (MORBIDITY AND MORTALITY WEEKLY REPORT : MMWR). VFOAT MMWR, M.M.W.R. Began with V. 25, No. 10, (March 19, 1976)-. 0149-2195. Periodical. US. English. wk. $69.00. US Government Printing Office, Superintendent of Documents, Washington DC 20402. **Tel** (404)321-2100. Ed Michael B Gregg. **Ind/Abst** Index Med., Am. Stat. Index. LC RA407.3. DD 614,4273. NLM W2 A N25M. **Circ** 43,000. Provides analysis and statistics on the occurrence of disease and death due to all causes in the United States. *Morbidity and Mortality (Washington, D.C. : 1952), 0091-0031.*

THE MORRIS REPORT ON FEDERAL HEALTH POLICY. VFOAT Health Systems Report. Vol. 10, No. 40 (Oct. 23, 1981)-. 0277-3902. Periodical. US. English. wk. $140.00. Morris Inc, 1346 Connecticut Avenue, Washington DC 20036. **NLM** W1 MO916B. *Health Systems Report, 0194-0899.*

MOSQUITO BORNE DISEASES BULLETIN. VFOAT MBD. Vol. 1, No. 1 (July/Sept. 1984)-. 0857-0817. Periodical. English. qt. **NLM** W1.

MOTOR ACCIDENTS IN NEW ZEALAND. See Transportation.

MOTOR CRASH ESTIMATING GUIDE. See Transportation - Automobiles.

MOTOR VEHICLE TRAFFIC ACCIDENTS. See Transportation - Roads and Traffic.

MOTORIK. Vol. 1-. 0170-5792. Periodical. GW. German. mo. 42.-. Verlag Karl Hofmann, Postfach 1360, D-7060 Schorndorf West Germany. **Tel** (07181)7811. bk rev. adv acc. **Circ** 3,500.

MOUNT CARMEL CLINIC TALKS ABOUT YOUR HEALTH. VFOAT Your Health. Began with May 1974 issue. 0317-0748. CN. English. mo. Free. Mount Carmel Clinic, 120 Selkirk Avenue East, Winnipeg Manitoba R2W 2L2 Canada. DD 362.120971274.

MUTUAL AID. (MUTUAL AID : THE EMS MANAGEMENT NEWSLETTER). 0734-9998. Periodical. US. English. bm. $9.00. EMS Management Institute, PO Box 102, Sterling VA 22170. **Tel** (703)450-6097. Ed Joseph V Saitta. bk rev. adv acc. **Circ** 1,000. (ctrl). A review of current public safety issues with emphasis on pre-hospital emergency medical services management.

MVP-BERICHTE. (MVP BERICHTE). VAT Max-Von-Pettenkofer Berichte. Began in 1978-. 0173-0452. Monographic Series. German. ir. **Ind/Abst** Chem. Abstr. LC UNC. NLM W1 MV993. CODEN MVBEDT.

NAGOYA-SHI EISEI KENKYUJO HO. VFOAT Annual Report of Nagoya City Health Research Institute. Began in 1951. JA. Japanese. an. Nagoya-shi Eisei Kenkyujo, 1-11 Ogiyamacho Mizuho-ku, Nagoya Japan. **Ind/Abst** Chem. Abstr. CODEN NEKSD8.

NARRATIVE ANNUAL REPORT - HAWAII. DEPT. OF HEALTH. (NARRATIVE ANNUAL REPORT). **Main/Corp** Hawaii. Dept. of Health. 0732-2925. US. English. an. LC RA49. DD 353.99690077. *Hawaii State Health Department Narrative Annual Report, 0196-819X.*

NATIONAL ANNUAL MEDICAID STATISTICS. See Statistics.

THE NATIONAL COMMITTEE ON VITAL AND HEALTH STATISTICS. See Statistics.

NATIONAL DIRECTORY OF HEALTH PROFESSIONS ADVISORS. See Yearbooks, Almanacs, Directories.

NATIONAL DIRECTORY OF SAFETY CONSULTANTS. See Yearbooks, Almanacs, Directories.

NATIONAL HEALTH DIRECTORY. See Yearbooks, Almanacs, Directories.

NATIONAL HEALTH FEDERATION BULLETIN CEASED. Began in Apr. 1955. Ceased with V. 26, No. 9 Oct. 1980. 0027-9420. Periodical. US. English. LC RA421. DD 614.05. NLM W1 NA471.

NATIONAL HEALTH SERVICE ACTS, 1946 TO 1968. ACCOUNTS. (NATIONAL HEALTH SERVICE ACTS, 1946 TO 1968, ACCOUNTS, SUMMARISED ACCOUNTS OF REGIONAL HOSPITAL BOARDS, BOARDS OF GOVERNORS OF TEACHING HOSPITALS, HOSPITAL MANAGEMENT COMMITTEES, AND EXECUTIVE COUNCILS (INCLUDING JOINT PRICING COMMITTEES) AND THE ACCOUNT OF THE DENTAL). **Main/Corp** Great Britain. Exchequer and Audit Dept. 0302-3559. UK. English. an. 0.34. Her Majesty's Stationery Office, PO Box 276, London SW8 5DT England. LC RA241. DD 354.4100841.

NATIONAL HMO CENSUS. Series/Titl DHHS Publication. VFOAT National H.M.O. Census. VAT National Health Maintenance Organizations Census. June 30, 1981-. 0737-2965. US. English. an. DHHS Public Health Service, Office of Health Maintenance Organizations, Division of Program Promotion, Rockville MD 20857. LC RA413.5.U5. DD 362.10425. *National HMO Census of Prepaid Plans.*

NATIONAL INSTITUTES OF HEALTH RESEARCH PLAN. VFOAT NIH Research Plan. Began in 1980-1982. 0278-6834. US. English. an. NLM W2 A N2058N.

NATIONAL MONTHLY MEDICAID STATISTICS. See Statistics.

NATIONAL NOSOCOMIAL INFECTIONS STUDY REPORT. (NATIONAL NOSOCOMIAL INFECTIONS STUDY REPORT, ANNUAL SUMMARY). Began with 1974. 0147-443X. US. English. an. US Department of Health and Human Services, Public Health Service Centers for Disease Control, Atlanta GA 30333. LC RA969. DD 614.44. NLM W2 A N229Q. *National Nosocomial Infections Study, 0146-7417.*

NATIONAL POISON PREVENTION WEEK, ANNUAL REPORT. 1st- 1962-. US. English. an. Consumer Product Safety Commission, PO Box 1543, Washington DC 20013.

NATIONAL SAFETY AND HEALTH NEWS. VFOAT National Safety News. Vol. 131, No. 5 (May 1985). 8756-5366. Periodical. US. English. mo. $20.50 Members, $25.75 Nonmembers. National Safety Council, 444 North Michigan Avenue, Chicago IL 60611. DD 614. *National Safety News, 0028-0100.*

NATIONAL TRAFFIC SAFETY NEWSLETTER CEASED. -Nov. 1980. 0364-846X. Periodical. US. English. ir. US Department of Transportation, National Highway Traffic Safety Administration, Washington DC 20590.

NATIONAL TRANSPORTATION SAFETY BOARD DECISIONS. See Transportation.

THE NATION'S HEALTH. V. 1- Jan. 1971-. 0028-0496. Periodical. US. English. mo. $8.00. American Public Health Association, 1015 15th Street, Washington DC 20005. **Tel** (202)789-5600. Ed Kathryn Foxhall. bk rev. adv acc. Health policy, APHA business, environmental health, nutrition, occupational health, safety congress, federal agencies, and health statistics. *American Journal of Public Health and the Nation's Health, 0002-9572.*

NATURAL DISASTER SCIENCE. Vol. 1, No. 1 (Nov. 1, 1979)-. 0388-4090. Periodical. JA. English. sa. 40.00. Maruzen Co Ltd, PO Box 5050, 100-31 Tokyo Japan. **Ind/Abst** Eng. Index Annu., Eng. Index Mon., Eng. Index Bioeng. Abstr., Eng. Index Energy Abstr., GeoRef. CODEN NDISDP. (ctrl). A unified forum for scientific works on natural hazards and prevention or mitigation of natural disasters.

NATURAL HEALTH BULLETIN. 0047-9152. Periodical. US. English. mo. $31.25. Princeton Educational Publishers, CN 5245, Princeton NJ 08540. **Tel** (609)924-9329.

NCHSR PROGRAM SOLICITATION : GRANTS FOR HEALTH SERVICES RESEARCH DISSERTATIONS. Main/Corp National Center for Health Services Research. Series/Titl DHHS Publication. VFOAT N.C.H.S.R. Program Solicitation. VAT National Center for Health Services Research Program Solicitation. US. English. an. US Department of Health and Human Services, Public Health Service, Office of Health Research Statistics and Technology, National Center for Health Services Research, 3700 East-West Highway, Hyattsville MD 20782. Vol. for 1983 distributed to depository libraries in microfiche.

NCRP REPORT. VAT National Council on Radiation Protection and Measurements Report. No. 32-. 0083-209X. US. English. ir. National Council on Radiation Protection and Measurements Report, 7910 Woodmont Avenue/Suite 1016, Bethesda MD 20814. **Tel** (301)657-2652. **Ind/Abst** GeoRef, Biol. Abstr., Bibliogr. Index Geol. LC UNC. CODEN NCRDBG. *NCRP Report, 0083-209X.*

NEBRASKA HEALTH MANPOWER REPORTS : PHYSICIAN'S ASSISTANTS. Main/Corp Nebraska. Division of Health Data and Statistical Research. US. English. an. 301 Centennial Mall South, PO Box 95007, Lincoln NE 68509.

NEBRASKA STATE COMPREHENSIVE MENTAL HEALTH PLAN. Main/Corp Nebraska. Dept. of Health. US. English. LC RA790.65.N2.

NEIGHBORHOOD HEALTH CENTERS. SUMMARY OF PROJECT DATA. REPORT. (NEIGHBORHOOD HEALTH CENTERS : SUMMARY OF PROJECT DATA. REPORT). **Main/Corp** United States. Health Services Administration. Bureau of Community Health Service. Division of Monitoring and Analysis. No. 9- 4th Quarter 1974-. 0161-4533. Periodical. US. English. qt. US Health Services Administration, Rockville MD 20852. LC RA445. DD 362.1. *Comprehensive Health Service Projects. Summary of Project Data. CHSP Report, 0161-4525.*

NEISS DATA HIGHLIGHTS : NATIONAL ELECTRONIC INJURY SURVEILLANCE SYSTEM. VAT National Electronic Injury Surveillance System Data Highlights. -V. 6, No. 3 (July-Sept. 1982). Periodical. US. English. an. Free. US Consumer Product Safety Commission, WTB Rm #625, Washington DC 20207. **Tel** (301)492-6424. **Ind/Abst** Am. Stat. Index. **Circ** 3,000. (ctrl). Publication provides national estimates of products juridiction of CPSC treated in hospital emergency departments. *Neiss News, 0364-6475.*

NEPEGESZSEGUGY. VFOAT Vengerskoe Zdravookhranenie. Began in 1920. 0369-3805. Periodical. Hungarian (summaries in English, French, German, and Russian). ir. NLM W1 NE204.

NETWORK NEWS - NATIONAL WOMEN'S HEALTH NETWORK (U.S.). (NETWORK NEWS : THE NEWSLETTER OF THE NATIONAL WOMEN'S HEALTH NETWORK). Vol. 7, No. 4 (July/Aug. 1982)-. 8755-867X. Periodical. US. English. bm. $50.00. National Women's Health Network, 224 Seventh Street SE, Washington DC 20003. DD 362. *National Women's Health Network News, 0277-0385.*

NEVADA HEALTH. Periodical. US. English. Nevada State, Division of Health, Capitol Complex, Carson City NV 89710.

NEW DIRECTIONS FOR MENTAL HEALTH SERVICES. No. 1- 1979-. 0193-9416. Monographic Series. US. English. qt. $40.00. Jossey-Bass Inc, 433 California Street, San Francisco CA 94104. **Tel** (415)433-1767. Ed H Richard Lamb. **Ind/Abst** Index Med., Psychol. Abstr. LC UNC. NLM W1 NE374E. **Circ** 500. Describes new mental health treatment techniques, approaches and offers guidance on providing effective services in light of recent social and legal developments.

NEW HAMPSHIRE'S FATAL TRAFFIC ACCIDENT FACTS. See Transportation - Roads and Traffic.

NEW MEXICO EPIDEMIOLOGY REPORT. Dec. 15, 1983-. 8750-4642. Periodical. US. English. mo. PO Box 968-Crown Building, Santa Fe NM 87504-0968. DD 614. *New Mexico Communicable Disease Summary, 0279-1919.*

NEW MEXICO SELECTED HEALTH STATISTICS. See Statistics.

NEW YORK STATE DEPARTMENT OF HEALTH MONOGRAPH. No. 10- 1975-. 0190-1648. Monographic Series. US. English. ir. NLM W2 AN6 D3NF.

NEW ZEALAND HEALTH REVIEW. (NEW ZEALAND HEALTH REVIEW : JOURNAL OF THE COLLEGE OF COMMUNITY MEDICINE, THE NZ INSTITUTE OF HEATH ADMINISTRATORS AND THE NZ NURSES ASSOCIATION). 0111-6304. Periodical. English. ir. $10.00. The Editor, PO Box 10-245, The Terrace, Wellington New Zealand. NLM W1 NE9729.

NEWS & FEATURES FROM NIH. VFOAT News and Features from N.I.H. Periodical. US. English. mo. NIH News Branch, Building 31 Room 2B-10, Bethesda MD 20205. **Ind/Abst** Index U.S. Gov. Period.

Public Health and Safety

NEWS - CANADIAN HEALTH EDUCATION SOCIETY. (NEWS). Autumn 1982-. 0822-4129. Periodical. CN. English. qt. Free to Members. Canadian Health Education Society, PO Box 2305, Ottawa Ontario K1P 5K0 Canada. **DD** 613.07071.

NEWS LETTER - WOMEN'S HEALTH CLINIC. See Women.

NEWS OF THE COOPERATIVE HEALTH STATISTICS SYSTEM. See Statistics.

NEWSLETTER FOR RESEARCH IN MENTAL HEALTH AND BEHAVIORAL SCIENCES. V. 15, No. 1- Feb. 1973-. 0092-394X. Periodical. US. English. Vetrans Administration Hospital, Perry Point MD 21902. **LC** RA790.A1. **DD** 616.89. **NLM** W1 NE998I. **CODEN** NRMSD7. *Newsletter for Research in Psychology.*

NEWSLETTER - MINISTRY OF HEALTH. Main/Corp British Columbia. Ministry of Health. Nov. 1- Nov. 1978-. 0226-2789. CN. English. Ministry of Health, Health Promotion Programs Information Services, 1515 Blanshard Street, Victoria British Columbia Canada. **DD** 354.7110677.

NEWSLETTER - NATIONAL BOARD OF OCCUPATIONAL SAFETY AND HEALTH. No. 1- 1976-. 0348-7598. Periodical. English. ir. **NLM** W1 NE998L.

NEWSLETTER - OCCUPATIONAL HYGIENE ASSOCIATION OF ONTARIO. (NEWSLETTER). No. 8 (Aug. 1982)-. 0823-4558. Periodical. CN. English. ir. Free. Newsletter Occupational Hygiene Association of Ontario, c/o C Dumschat, 254 Maris Street, Sarnia Ontario N7T 4T3 Canada. **DD** 613.62060713. *Newsletter (American Industrial Hygiene Association. Ontario Section), 0828-5829.*

NEWSLETTER - ONTARIO ASSOCIATION OF LEGAL CLINICS. (NEWSLETTER). **VFOAT** Ontario Association of Legal Clinics Newsletter. Vol. 1, No. 1 (Jan. 1984)-. 0827-2379. Periodical. CN. English. bm. Free to Members, $10.00 Others. Ontario Association of Legal Clinics, Suite 226, 69 Sherbourne Avenue, Toronto Ontario M5A 3X9 Canada. **DD** 347.71301706.

NHSC HEALTH CARE PRACTITIONERS. Main/Corp National Health Service Corps (U.S.). **VAT** National Health Service Corps Health Care Practitioners. US. English. Department of Health, Education and Welfare, Public Health Service, Health Services Administration, Bureau of Community Health Services, National Health Services Corps, 5600 Fishers Lane, Rockville MD 20857. **NLM** W 22.AA1 N101.

NIHON EISEIGAKU ZASSHI. **VFOAT** Japanese Journal of Hygiene. V. 1- Aug. 1946-. 0021-5082. Periodical. JA. Japanese. bm. $44.50. Japan Publishing Trading Co Ltd, PO Box 5030 Tokyo International, Tokyo 100-31 Japan. **Ind/Abst** Excerpta Med., Index Med., Biol. Abstr., CIS Abstr., Chem. Abstr. **NLM** W1 NI889M. **CODEN** NEZAAQ.

NORTH CAROLINA FIVE YEAR PLAN FOR COMPREHENSIVE MENTAL HEALTH SERVICES : ANNUAL REPORT AND UPDATE. Main/Corp North Carolina. Division of Mental Health and Mental Retardation Services. US. English. an. **LC** RA790.65.N8. **DD** 362.209756.

NORTH CAROLINA LOCAL HEALTH DEPARTMENTS, BUDGETARY, ECONOMIC AND OTHER PERTINENT DATA. (NORTH CAROLINA LOCAL HEALTH DEPARTMENTS : BUDGETARY, ECONOMIC, AND OTHER PERTINENT DATA). Main/Corp North Carolina. Division of Health Services. Office of Local Administration. 0098-5783. US. English. PO Box 2091, Raleigh NC 27602. **LC** RA124. **DD** 353.975600841.

NORTH DAKOTA HIGHWAY SAFETY IMPROVEMENT PROGRAM, ANNUAL REPORT. See Transportation - Roads and Traffic.

NSRY BHDST YRN. (IRANIAN JOURNAL OF PUBLIC HEALTH). **VFOAT** Nashriyan-i Bihdasht-i Iran. 0304-4556. Periodical. IR. English (each issue has separately paged sections in English and Persian, with some articles and summaries also in French). qt. $25.00. Iranian Public Health Association, Ghodes Avenue Number 43, PO Box 1310, Tehera Iran. **Ind/Abst** Excerpta Med., Chem. Abstr. **NLM** W1 IR329. **CODEN** IJPHCD.

NUCLEAR TIMES (NEW YORK, N.Y.). See Political Science.

NUDISTES DU QUEBEC. V. 1- April 1976-. 0702-8504. Periodical. CN. French. bw. 50. Per No. Entreprises Jemapro, CP 135 Succursale, Ste-Therese de Blainville Quebec J7E 4J1 Canada. **DD** 613.19405.

NURSING SCAN. WOMEN'S HEALTH. **VFOAT** Women's Health. Vol. 1, No. 1-. 0883-4369. Periodical. US. English. qt. $15.00. Nursing Scan: Women's Health, University of Illinois at Chicago, College of Nursing, 845 St Damen, Chicago IL 60612. **Tel** (312)996-0153. Ed B J McElmurry, D Webster, A Dan, D Biordi, D Boyer, and S Swider. **DD** 610. Current awareness document (periodicals) in women's health.

NY-PENN NEWS. **VAT** NY Penn News, New York Penn News. Periodical. US. English. mo. $10.00. NY Penn Health Systems Agency, 306 Press Building/9 Chennago Street, Binghamton NY 13902. **Tel** (607)722-3445.

OAMR ACTION ALERT. **VFOAT** Action Alert. **VAT** Ontario Association for the Mentally Retarded Action Alert. 0229-1126. Periodical. CN. English. ir. Free. Ontario Association for the Mentally Retarded, 1376 Bayview Avenue, Toronto Ontario M4G 3A3 Canada. **DD** 362.3809713. (ctrl).

OBJECTIF PREVENTION. V. 1- Nov. 1977-. 0705-0577. Periodical. CN. French. bm. $4.65. Assn Sante Securite du Travail, 294 Carre Saint Louis 5 Etage, Montreal Quebec H2X 1A4 Canada. **Tel** (514)524-6871. **DD** 614.79305. *Vie, 0380-9234.*

OCCUPATIONAL THERAPY IN HEALTH CARE. Vol. 1, No. 1 (Spring 1984)-. 0738-0577. Periodical. US. English. qt. $42.00. Haworth Press Inc, 28 East 22nd Street, New York NY 10010. **Tel** (212)228-2800. Ed Florence S Cromwell. **NLM** W1. adv acc. **Circ** 515. The professional journal designed to provide timely information on significant clinical questions to the growing number of occupational therapy practitioners.

OCCUPATIONAL THERAPY IN MENTAL HEALTH. V. 1- Spring 1980-. 0164-212X. Periodical. US. English. qt. $102.00. Haworth Press, 28 East 22nd Street, New York NY 10010. **Tel** (212)228-2800. Ed Diane Gibson. **Ind/Abst** Excerpta Med., Cumul. Index Nurs. Allied Health Lit., Biol. Abstr., Psychol. Abstr. **LC** RC487. **DD** 616.89165205. **NLM** W1 OC601N. **CODEN** OTMHDX. bk rev. adv acc. **Circ** 1,295. The journal presents timely material specifically for occupational therapists in mental health clinics, hospitals, schools, human service agencies and transitional living programs.

OFFICE OF HEALTH MAINTENANCE ORGANIZATIONS . . . ANNUAL REPORT TO CONGRESS. Main/Corp United States. Office of Health Maintenance Organizations. 5th (Fiscal Year 1979)-. US. English. an. US Department of Health and Human Services, Health Resources and Services Administration, Bureau of HMOS and Resources Development, Office of Health Maintenance Organizations, Rockville MD 20857. *HMO, Office of Health Maintenance Organizations . . . Annual Report of the Congress, 0195-816X.*

OHIO COMPREHENSIVE MENTAL HEALTH SERVICES STATE PLAN. Main/Corp Ohio. Division of Mental Health. Office of Planning. **VFOAT** Ohio Comprehensive Mental Health Services State Plan P. L. 94-63. 0161-0678. US. English. an. 30 East Broad Street, Columbus OH 43215. **LC** RA790.65.O3. **DD** 362.209771. **NLM** W2 AO3 D460.

OKLAHOMA HEALTH STATISTICS. See Statistics.

OKLAHOMA TRIENNIAL STATE HEALTH PLAN. 0740-7343. US. English. te. **LC** RA395.A4. **DD** 362.109766. *Oklahoma State Health Plan, 0740-7351.*

ON THE STATE OF THE PUBLIC HEALTH. Main/Corp Great Britain. Dept. of Health and Social Security. 1968-. 0072-6087. UK. English. an. Her Majesty's Stationery Office, PO Box 276, London SW8 5DT England. **LC** RA241. **DD** 614.0942. *On the State of the Public Health.*

OPINION AND ORDER. Main/Corp United States. National Transportation Safety Board. US. English. ir. National Transportation Safety Board, 800 Independence Avenue SW, Washington DC 20594.

ORDNUNGSPOLITIK IM GESUNDHEITSWESEN. V. 1-. Monographic Series. German. ir. Ed Philipp Herder-Dorneich and Alexander Schuller. **NLM** W1.

OREGON PUBLIC HEALTH STATISTICS REPORT. See Statistics.

ORIENTATION M. French. ir. 300. Editions Mutalistes, Rue de la Loi 121, 1040 CCP 790.00, Bruxelles Belgium. **Tel** (02)230-7890. **LC** HD7186. **DD** 368.4009493. **Circ** 3,025. (ctrl). Actual problems concerning health insurance and health policy; organisation and facilities concerning health, health economics, medical law, and social security. *Orientation Mutualiste.*

OUT HEALTH. **VFOAT** Out Magazine's Quarterly Guide to Health in Gay Life. Vol. 1, No. 1 (Winter 1981)-. 0278-5811. Periodical. US. English. qt. $10.00. Out Health, 1522 14th Street Northwest, Washington DC 20005.

AN OVERVIEW. Main/Corp Washington (State). Dept. of Social and Health Services. Periodical. US. English. mo. Office of Public Affairs, Department of Social & Health Services, OB-44Q, Olympia WA 98504. **Tel** (206)753-2745. *Overview of Social and Health Services.*

A P C O PUBLIC SAFETY COMMUNICATIONS. Periodical. US. English. mo. $30.00. Association of Public Communications, PO Box 669 105 1/2 Canal Street, New Smyrna Beach FL 32070. **Tel** (904)427-3461. Ed Bob Buttgen. adv acc. **Circ** 6,000. (ctrl). Articles detailing the latest news of public safety communications for law enforcement, fire, 9-1-1 centers, forestry and conservation. Two-way radios, microwave, data transmission.

PAI BOLETIN INFORMATIVO. **VAT** Programa Ampliado de Inmunizacion Boletin Informativo. 0251-4729. Periodical. US. Spanish. bm. Free. Programa Ampliado de Inmunizacion OPS, 525 23rd Street NW, Washington DC 20037. **Tel** (202)861-3248. Ed Ciro de Quadros. bk rev. **Circ** 8,000. (ctrl).

PAKISTAN JOURNAL OF HEALTH. Vol. 1- Apr. 1951-. 0030-9834. Periodical. English. ir. **LC** RA541.P27.

PAN AMERICAN HEALTH. V. 7, No. 2- 1975-. 0377-5119. Periodical. US. English. qt. Pan American Health Organization, 525 23rd Street Northwest, Washington DC 20037. **Ind/Abst** Excerpta Med. **LC** RA421. **DD** 362.1097. **NLM** W1 PA4012. **CODEN** PAHED. *Gazette.*

PARAMETERS IN HEALTH CARE. V. 1- Spring 1976-. 0163-1594. Periodical. US. English. qt. **NLM** W1 PA626E.

PARENTHESE (HULL, QUEBEC). (PARENTHESE). 0228-6688. Periodical. CN. French. mo. Free. Productions Claude Savoie, 327 Boulevard St-Joseph 8065, Quebec J8Y 3Z1 Canada. **DD** 362.2109714221.

PATIENT EDUCATION NEWSLETTER. Vol. 4, No. 6 (Dec. 1981). 0278-8209. Periodical. US. English. bm. $20.00. UAB School of Public Health, 720 20th Street, Birmingham AL 35294. **Tel** (205)934-7178. Ed Edward E Bartlett. **Ind/Abst** Hospit. Lit. Index. adv acc. **Circ** 2,300. (ctrl). Newsletter for health professionals on patient education developments. *Physician's Patient Education Newsletter.*

PERFORMANCE BUDGET - MINISTRY OF HEALTH AND FAMILY PLANNING, GOVERNMENT OF INDIA. Main/Corp India (Republic)., Ministry of Health and Family Planning. II. English. ir. **LC** RA311. **DD** 354.5406841.

PERFORMANCE BUDGET OF HEALTH AND FAMILY WELFARE DEPARTMENT. Main/Corp Gujarat (India). Health and Family Welfare Dept. II. English. ir. 2.95. The Government Press, Vadodara India. **LC** RA312.G8. **DD** 354.547500841.

PERSPECTIVES. (PERSPECTIVES - CENTER FOR HEALTH ADMINISTRATION STUDIES, UNIVERSITY OF CHICAGO). A9- 1971-. 0094-4483. Periodical. US. English. ir. University of Chicago, Center for Health Administration Studies, Chicago IL 60637. **Tel** (312)962-7104. **NLM** W1 PE8705K. *Health Administration Perspectives, 0577-702X.*

PESTICIDE-PCB IN FOODS PROGRAM. See Food & Drink.

PESTICIDRESTER I DANSKE LEVNEDSMIDLER. **VFOAT** Pesticide Residues in Danish Food. 1978-79-. 0108-2086. Danish (text in English). ir. 20.00. Miljministriet,

Public Health and Safety

Statens Levnedsmiddelinstitut Mrkhj Bygade 19, DK-2860 Sborg Denmark. **LC** TX571.P4. **DD** 363.192. *Rapport Over Pesticidrester I Danske Levnedsmidler.*

PHI : PLANNING FOR HEALTH ISSUES. VFOAT Planning for Health Issues. Vol. 1, No. 1 (Spring 1980)-. Periodical. US. English. qt. $10.00. Planning for Health Issues, 19 Garfield Place/Suite 700, Cincinnati OH 45202. **Tel** (513)621-2434.

PHS GRANTS POLICY MEMORANDUM. Main/Corp United States. Public Health Service. VFOAT Public Health Service Supplementation to the DHEW Grants Administration Manual. No. 1- Jan. 22, 1974-. Periodical. US. English. Department of Health Education and Welfare, Public Health Service, 5600 Fishers Lane, Rockville MD 20852.

PHYSICAL CONDITION REPORT OF COMMERCIAL DRIVERS INVOLVED IN ACCIDENTS. See Transportation.

POCKET BOOK OF HEALTH STATISTICS. See Statistics.

POLIOMYELITIS SURVEILLANCE (CENTERS FOR DISEASE CONTROL (U.S.)). (POLIOMYELITIS SURVEILLANCE). VFOAT Poliomyelitis Surveillance Summary. Summary 1977-1978-. 0734-6611. US. English. an. U S Department of Health and Human Services, Public Health Service, Center for Disease Control, Atlanta GA 30333. **LC** RA644.P9. **DD** 614.549. **NLM** W2 A C7CNA. *Neurotropic Diseases Surveillance. Poliomyelitis.*

POLLUTING INCIDENTS IN AND AROUND U.S. WATERS. See Sanitation, Environmental Technology.

POST ROCK. V. 9- (No. 32-). 0149-3744. Periodical. US. English. qt. Free. Kansas Bureau of Health and Environmental Education, Building 740, Forbes Air Force Base, Topeka KS 66620. **LC** RA447.K2. **DD** 614.09781. *Community Health.*

POSTEPY HIGIENY I MEDYCYNY DOSWIADCZALNEJ. Vol. 1-. 0032-5449. Periodical. PL. Polish. bm. ARS Polona, Krakowskie Przedmieccie 7, 00-068 Warsaw Poland. **Ind/Abst** Life Sci. Collect., Biol. Abstr., Chem. Abstr., Index Med. **NLM** W1 PO941. **CODEN** PHMDAD. *Postepy Wiedzy Medycznej, 0477-7891.*

PRAEGER MONOGRAPHS IN INFECTIOUS DISEASE. VFOAT MID. Vol. 1-. Monographic Series. US. English. **Ed** David Schlossberg. **NLM** W1.

PRAVENTION. V. 1-. 0170-2602. Periodical. GW. German. qt. W Kohlhammer Verlag GMBH, Hessbruehlstr 69, Postfach 800430, 7000 Stuttgart 80-West Germany. **NLM** W1 PR204.

PRAVENTIVMEDIZIN. VFOAT Revue de Medecine Preventive. V. 14-18. 0301-0988. Periodical. English (text in German, French, or with some summaries in the same languages). ir. 49.-. Verlag Vogt & Schild AG, Dornacherstrasse 39, CH4500 Soloturn 1 West Germany. **Tel** 065-247 247. **Ind/Abst** CIS Abstr. **NLM** W1 PR205. bk rev. adv acc. **Circ** 2,200. A high standard periodical covering public health, environmental hygienics. *Zeitschrift Fur Praventivmedizin.*

PRAXIS. Feb. 1980-. Periodical. BL. Portuguese. ir. Centro de Estudos Margarida Terapia Ocupacional, Rua Corcovado 74 Jardim Botanico, Rio de Janeiro Brazil. **LC** RA790.A1. *Abertura.*

PRELIMINARY NATIONAL MEDICAID STATISTICS. See Statistics.

PRELIMINARY NATIONAL MONTHLY MEDICAID STATISTICS. See Statistics.

PREVENT BLINDNESS NEWS. V. 1-. Periodical. US. English. ty. National Society to Prevent Blindness, 79 Madison Avenue, New York NY 10016. *Prevention of Blindness News, 0032-8014; Wise Owl News, 0043-6755.*

PREVENTION. V. 1- June 1950-. 0032-8006. Periodical. US. English. mo. Rodale Press, 33 East Minor Street, Emmaus PA 18049. **Tel** (215)967-5171. **Ind/Abst** Pop. Mag. Rev., Chem. Abstr., Bibliogr. Agric., Read. Guide Period. Lit., Abr. Read. Guide, Mag. Index, Mag. Index. **LC** RA421. **DD** 613.05. **NLM** W1 PR496. **CODEN** PRVEAT.

PREVENTION AU CANADA. (LA PREVENTION AU CANADA). March 1969-. 0317-5987. Periodical. CN. French. Conseil Canadien de la Securite, 30 The Driveway, Ottawa Ontario K2P 1C9 Canada. **DD** 614.805. *Nouvelles de Securite Routiere, 0319-3373.*

PREVENTION IN HUMAN SERVICES. Vol. 1, No. 1/2 (Fall/Winter 1981)-. 0270-3114. Periodical. US. English. qt. $112.00. Haworth Press, 28 East 22nd Street, New York NY 10010. **Tel** (212)228-2800. **Ed** Robert Hess. **Ind/Abst** Excerpta Med., Hospit. Lit. Index, Sociol. Abstr., Biol. Abstr., Soc. Work Res. Abstr., Psychol. Abstr. **LC** RA421. **DD** 362.1. **NLM** W1 PR497. **CODEN** PHSEDF. adv acc. **Circ** 780. A journal devoted entirely to the application of the philosophy of prevention in mental health and other human services. *Community Mental Health Review, 0363-1605.*

PREVENTION PREVIEW. Vol. 1, No. 1 (Fall 1979)-. 0711-1681. Periodical. CN. English. qt. Free. Prevention Preview, Health Marketing Systems, PO Box 490, Station A, Scarborough Ontario M1K 2N0 Canada. **DD** 614.05. (ctrl).

PREVENTION (WASHINGTON, D.C.). (PREVENTION). '80-. 0730-7888. US. English. an. Department of Health and Human Services, Public Health Service, Office of Disease Prevention and Health Promotion, 200 Independence Avenue SW, Washington DC 20201. **LC** RA445. **DD** 614.440973. **NLM** W2 A P97P.

PREVOYANCE. Vol. 1, No. 1 Spring 1981-. 0710-0671. Periodical. CN. French. qt. Free to Members. Prevoyance, 175 rue College, Toronto Ontario M5T 1P8 Canada. **DD** 629.28307071.

PRIDE INSTITUTE JOURNAL OF LONG TERM HOME HEALTH CARE. VFOAT Journal of Long Term Home Health Care. Vol. 1, No. 1 (Summer 1982)-. 0743-5088. Periodical. US. English. qt. $24.00. Pride Institute Journal, St Vincent's Hospital, 153 West 11th Street, New York NY 10011. **Ind/Abst** Hospit. Lit. Index. **NLM** W1 PR516H.

PRIMARY CARE FOCUS. Began with: Vol. 1, No. 1 (Mar. 1981). 0732-1260. Periodical. US. English. bm. $50.00. National Association of Community Health Centers, 1625 I Street NW/Suite 403, Washington DC 20006. **NLM** W1 PR522AD.

PRIORITY HEALTH PROBLEMS OF MICHIGAN. Main/Corp Michigan. Dept. of Public Health. US. English. an. Michigan Department of Public Health, 3500 North Logan Street, Box 30035, Lansing MI 48909. **LC** RA87. **DD** 362.109774.

PROBLEMI NA ZDRAVEOPAZVANETO. V. 8, No. 1-. 0205-0315. Periodical. Bulgarian. qt. **NLM** W1 PR572JM. *Klinichni Nabliudeniia.*

PROCEEDINGS . . . ANNUAL GROUP HEALTH INSTITUTE. Main/Corp Group Health Institute. US. English. an. $16.95. Group Health Association of America, 624 Ninth Street NW/Suite 700, Washington DC 20001. **Tel** (202)737-4311.

PROCEEDINGS OF THE ANNUAL MEETING OF THE CANADIAN PUBLIC HEALTH ASSOCIATION. Main/Corp Canadian Public Health Association. VFOAT Travaux de l'Assemblee Generale de l'Association Canadienne d'Hygiene Publique. 65th-1974-. 0319-2644. CN. English and French. Canadian Public Health Association, 55 Parkdale Avenue, Ottawa Ontario K1Y 1E5 Canada. **DD** 614.05.

PROCEEDINGS OF THE ANNUAL SEMINAR OF THE CALIFORNIA COMMUNITY HEALTH INSTITUTE. Main/Conf California Community Health Seminar. 1st-1974-. 0162-0657. US. English. an. **NLM** W3 C11.

PROCEEDINGS OF THE HEALTH POLICY FORUM. Main/Conf Health Policy Forum. No. 1-. 0195-976X. Monographic Series. US. English. United Hospital Fund of New York, 3 East 54th Street, New York NY 10022. **NLM** W3 HE375.

PROCEEDINGS OF THE NATIONAL HEALTH LAWYERS ASSOCIATION'S ANNUAL PROGRAM ON LONG TERM CARE AND THE LAW. See Law.

PROCEEDINGS OF THE U.S. PUBLIC HEALTH SERVICE COOPERATIVE STUDIES, RENAL DISEASE AND HYPERTENSION. Main/Corp United States. Health Services Administration. Division of Hospitals and Clinics. VFOAT Renal Disease and Hypertension. V. 11- 1974-. US. English. an. Federal Center Building #3, Prince George Center, 6525 Belcrest Road West, Hyattsville MD 20782. *Proceedings of the Public Health Service Cooperative Studies, Renal Disease and Hypertension.*

PRODUCT SAFETY & LIABILITY REPORTER. 0092-7732. Periodical. US. English. wk. $516.00. Bureau of National Affairs Inc, 1231 25th Street NW, Washington DC 20037. **Tel** (202)452-4417. **Ed** William A Beltz and Stanley J Gilbert. **LC** KF3945.A73. **DD** 344.73042. bk rev. **Circ** 1,206. Weekly notification and reference service covering federal regulatory activities in consumer product safety, including motor vehicles. Reference file has text of pertinent law and regulations.

PRODUCT SAFETY & THE LAW. See Law.

PRODUCT SAFETY UP TO DATE. Main/Corp National Safety Council. 0091-8954. US. English. National Safety Council, 425 North Michigan Avenue, Chicago IL 60611. **LC** TS175. **DD** 658.56.

PROFESSIONAL STANDARDS REVIEW ORGANIZATION : PROGRAM EVALUATION. Main/Corp United States. Health Care Financing Administration. Office of Research, Demonstrations, and Statistics. Series/Titl Health Care Financing Research Report. 1977-. US. English. an. Department of Health, Education, and Welfare, Health Care Financing Administration, 330 C Street SW, Washington DC 20201.

PROGRAM BUDGET STATEMENT. Main/Corp Michigan. Dept. of Public Health. 0192-9747. US. English. an. Michigan Department of Public Health, 3500 North Logan, Lansing MI 48914. **LC** RA87. **DD** 353.977400841.

PROGRAM EVALUATION IN THE HEALTH FIELDS. Series/Titl Social Problems Series. V. 1- 1969-. 0731-8073. Monographic Series. US. English. Human Sciences Press, 72 Fifth Avenue, New York NY 10011. **Ed** H C Schulberg, A Sheldon, and F Baker. **NLM** W1 PR632H.

PROGRAM POLICY GUIDELINES - MICHIGAN. DEPT. OF MENTAL HEALTH. Main/Corp Michigan. Dept. of Mental Health. US. English. **LC** RA790.65.M5. **DD** 362.20425. *Annual Program Policy Guidelines.*

PROGRAM, STRALINGSBESKYTTELSE. VFOAT Stralingsbeskyttelse, Programme, Strahlenschutz, Programme, Radiation Protection. US. English (French and German). ir. $46.00. European Community Information Service, 2100 M Street NW/Suite 707, Washington DC 20037. **LC** RA569. **DD** 363.179.

PROGRESS REPORT - HEALTH AND SAFETY RESEARCH DIVISION. (HEALTH AND SAFETY RESEARCH DIVISION PROGRESS REPORT FOR THE PERIOD . . .). Series/Titl ORNL. VFOAT Progress Report. Began with: 1977/78. 0731-7050. US. English. an. National Technical Information Service, Oak Ridge National Laboratory, 5285 Port Royal Road, Springfield VA 22161. **NLM** W1 HE264J.

PROMOTING HEALTH. V. 1- Jan./Feb. 1980-. 0272-9709. Periodical. US. English. bm. $74.00. American Hospital Association, 840 North Lake Shore Drive, Chicago IL 60611. **Tel** (312)280-6076. **Ed** Sharyn Sweeney Bills. **Ind/Abst** Hospit. Lit. Index, Cumul. Index Nurs. Allied Health Lit. **NLM** W1 PR721M. bk rev. **Circ** 2,500. Focuses on issues relevant to management of hospital-based health promotion programs, emphasizing practical "how-to" information.

PROPOSED PROGRAM AND BUDGET ESTIMATES. Main/Corp Pan American Health Organization. Series/Titl Official Document of the Pan American Health Organization; Corporate Law and Practice Course Handbook Series. Periodical. US. English. an. **NLM** W2 MP2 P92PE. *Proposed Program and Budget Estimates.*

PROSPECTIVE ET SANTE. Began with No. 1. 0152-2108. Periodical. FR. French. qt. $15.96. P S P, 9 rue Alfred de Vigny, 75008 Paris France. **Tel** 01/763 41 33. **NLM** W1 PR767. Interdisciplinary journal for the science of life and health.

PROTECTION OFFICER NEWSLETTER. (THE PROTECTION OFFICER NEWSLETTER). Vol. 1, No. 1 (May 1984)-. 0823-9630. Periodical. CN. English. Protection Officer Publications, PO Box 6004 Station A, Calgary Alberta T2H 1L3 Canada. **Tel** (403)932-6979. **Ed** Ronald R Minion. **DD** 363.289. bk rev. adv acc. **Circ** 600. (ctrl).

Public Health and Safety

Covering protection of the home, family, neighborhood, business, executive. Protection of personnel assets and information. Providing ongoing information for private, government and corporate security personnel that deals with security training and administration.

PSITTACOSIS SURVEILLANCE. (PSITTACOSIS SURVEILLANCE, ANNUAL SUMMARY). **VFOAT** Psittacosis Surveillance. 1975-1977-. 0195-573X. US. English. ir. Center for Disease Control, Atlanta GA 30333. **LC** RA644.P95. **DD** 614.5660973. **NLM** W2 A C7CZA. *Zoonosis Surveillance. Psittacosis, Annual Summary, 0271-7816.*

PUBLIC ADVISORY COMMITTEES, AUTHORITY, STRUCTURE, FUNCTIONS, MEMBERS. Main/Corp United States. Food and Drug Administration. 0147-4251. US. English. Food and Drug Administration, 5600 Fishers Lane, Rockville MD 20852. **LC** RA401.A3. **DD** 353.00841.

PUBLIC AFFAIRS PAMPHLET. No. 1-. 0197-8152. Monographic Series. US. English. ir. $10.00. Public Affairs Committee Inc, 381 Park Avenue South, New York NY 10016. **Tel** (212)683-4331. Ed Adele Broude. **LC** UNC. **Circ** 11,500. Concise pamphlets focusing on health and mental health family life, drug abuse, and social and economic issues.

PUBLIC HEALTH. 0033-3506. Periodical. UK. English. bm. $102.50. H Holt MacMillan Press, Houndmills, Basingstoke Hants RG21 2XS United Kingdom. **Tel** (305)345-4100. **Ind/Abst** Excerpta Med., CIS Abstr., Biol. Abstr., Chem. Abstr., Life Sci. Collect., Index Med., Sel. Water Resour. Abstr., Energy Inf. Abstr., Environ. Abstr., Soc. Sci. Citation Index, Sci. Cit. Index, Abr. Ed., Hospit. Lit. Index. **NLM** W1 PU309. **CODEN** PUHEAE.

PUBLIC HEALTH ENGINEER (LAHORE, PAKISTAN). (PUBLIC HEALTH ENGINEER : JOURNAL OF PAKISTAN SOCIETY OF PUBLIC HEALTH ENGINEERS). Periodical. English. ir. **NLM** W1 PU457L.

THE PUBLIC HEALTH LABORATORY. 0033-3522. Periodical. US. English. bm. Public Health Laboratory, Box 438, Boiling Springs NC 28017. **Ind/Abst** Excerpta Med. **NLM** W1 PU47. **CODEN** PHLAA.

PUBLIC HEALTH PAPERS. No. 1-. 0555-6015. Monographic Series. English. ir. World Health Organization, CH 1211, Geneve 27 Switzerland. **Ind/Abst** Life Sci. Collect., Excerpta Med., Index Med., Biol. Abstr. **NLM** W1 PU542. **CODEN** WHOPAY.

PUBLIC HEALTH REPORTS (UNITED STATES. PUBLIC HEALTH SERVICE : 1982). (PUBLIC HEALTH REPORTS). Vol. 97, No.4 (July/Aug. 1982)-. Periodical. US. English. bm. Superintendent of Documents, US Government Printing Office, Washington DC 20402. **Tel** (202)783-3238. **Ind/Abst** Pestdoc, Am. Stat. Index, Index U.S. Gov. Period., Ringdoc, Vetdoc, Cumul. Index Nurs. Allied Health Lit. **LC** RA11. **DD** 614.0973. *Public Health Reports (United States. Health Resources Administration), 0090-2818.*

PUBLIC HEALTH REPORTS (WASHINGTON, D.C. : 1974). (PUBLIC HEALTH REPORTS). Vol. 89, No. 4 (July/Aug. 1974)-. 0033-3549. Periodical. US. English. bm. US Government Printing Office, Superintendent of Documents, Washington DC 20402. **Ind/Abst** Am. Stat. Index, Bibliogr. Agric., Energy Res. Abstr., Index Med., Popul. Index, Predicasts, Public Aff. Inf. Serv. Bull., Soc. Work Res. Abstr., Index U.S. Gov. Period., Soc. Sci. Index. **LC** RA11. **DD** 614.0973. **NLM** W1 PU545. *Health Services Reports (United States. Health Services Administration), 0090-2918.*

PUBLIC HEALTH REVIEWS. Began publication with Vol. 1 (1972). 0301-0422. Periodical. IS. English. qt. 89.00. Technosdar Ltd/International Scientific Publishers, 5 Levontin Street/POB 31684, 61 316 Tel Aviv Israel. **Tel** (03)622418. Ed Suigmund Geller. **Ind/Abst** Excerpta Med., Energy Inf. Abstr., Environ. Abstr., Cumul. Index Nurs. Allied Health Lit., Biol. Abstr., Curr. Contents, Soc. Behav. Sci., Hospit. Lit. Index, Soc. Sci. Citation Index, Index Med. **NLM** W1 PU547. **CODEN** PBHRAM. bk rev. adv acc. **Circ** 1,000. The only journal devoted to authoritative, evaluative reviews of current studies in the broad field of public health. For both specialist and nonspecialist.

PUBLIC HEALTH STATISTICS. See Statistics.

PUBLIC HEALTH STATISTICS (MADISON, WIS. : 1977). See Statistics.

PUBLIC SAFETY MANAGEMENT. 0748-9927. Periodical. US. English. wk. $130.00. Ministerium Communications, 19 Joslin Street, Providence RI 02909. **Tel** (401)751-8509. Ed Thomas J Lopatosky. Newsletter covering ideas, news, and other material targeted to county and municipal officials responsible for fire protection, law enforcement, and emergency medical services.

PUBLIC SCRUTINY (NATIONAL HEALTH FEDERATION). (PUBLIC SCRUTINY). Vol. 26, No. 10 (Nov. 1980)-. Periodical. US. English. mo. $0.60 Single Issue. Public Scrutiny, PO Box 688, Monrovia CA 91016. *Bulletin (National Health Federation), 0027-9420.*

PUBLIC SECTOR: HEALTH CARE RISK MANAGEMENT. (PUBLIC SECTOR HEALTH CARE RISK MANAGEMENT). **VFOAT** Health Care Risk Management. June 1980-. 0270-8973. Periodical. US. English. mo. $140.00. Cox Publications, PO Box 958, El Cerrito CA 94530. **Tel** (415)527-2552. **NLM** W1 PU638F.

PUBLICACION CIENTIFICA - ORGANIZACION PANAMERICANA DE LA SALUD. 0553-0016. Monographic Series. US. Spanish. ir. **NLM** W1 PU656KA. *Publicacion Cientifica - Oficina Sanitaria Panamericana, 0254-2668.*

PUBLICATIONS OF THE NATIONAL INSTITUTE OF MENTAL HEALTH. Periodical. US. English. qt. National Clearinghouse for Mental Health Information, Public Inquiries Section, 5600 Fishers Lane, Rockville MD 20857.

PUBLICATIONS OF THE UNIVERSITY OF KUOPIO. COMMUNITY HEALTH. SERIES ORIGINAL REPORTS. VFOAT Community Health. 0357-3346. Monographic Series. English. ir. **NLM** W1 PU736U.

PUBLICATIONS OF THE UNIVERSITY OF KUOPIO. COMMUNITY HEALTH. SERIES STATISTICS AND REVIEWS. See Statistics.

PUBLICATIONS OF THE WORLD HEALTH ORGANIZATION : A BIBLIOGRAPHY. See Bibliographies.

QUARTERLY VITAL STATISTICS REVIEW. See Statistics.

R & S REPORT. See Statistics.

RADIATION CONTROL FOR HEALTH AND SAFETY. Main/Corp United States. Dept. of Health, Education, and Welfare. 0094-8608. US. English. Superintendent of Documents, US Government Printing Office, Washington DC 20402. **LC** RA569. **DD** 614.83905.

RAILROAD ACCIDENT REPORT. BRIEF FORMAT. See Transportation - Railroads.

RAPPORT ANNUEL DU CURATEUR PUBLIC. Main/Corp Quebec (Province). Curatelle Publique. 1977-. 0824-8567. CN. French. an. Editeur Officiel du Quebec, 1283 Boul Charest Quest, Quebec Province of Quebec G1N 2C9 Canada. **LC** RA790.7.C2. **DD** 354.7140042. *Rapport Annuel - Curatelle Publique du Quebec, 0824-8559.*

RAPPORT ANNUEL - MINISTERE DE LA SANTE PUBLIQUE. Main/Corp Rwanda. Ministere de la Sante Publique. French. ir. **LC** RA352.R95. **DD** 354.675710077.

RAPPORT ANNUEL - MINISTERE DE LA SANTE PUBLIQUE ET DE LA FAMILLE. Main/Corp Belgium. Ministere de la Sante Publique et de la Famille. French. ir. **LC** RA254. **DD** 354.4930084105.

RAPPORT ANNUEL - REUNION. DIRECTION DEPARTEMENTALE DES AFFAIRES SANITAIRES ET SOCIALES. Main/Corp Reunion. Direction Departementale des Affaires Sanitaires et Sociales. French. an. D.D.A.S.S. Route du Campus Universitaire, le Chaudron 97490, Ste-Clotilde Reunion. **LC** RA363.R4. **DD** 354.69810084.

RAPPORT D'ACTIVITE - INSTITUT D'HYGIENE ET D'EPIDEMIOLOGIE. Main/Corp Institut d'Hygiene et d'Epidemiologie. French. ir. Institut d Hygiene et d Epidemiologie, 14 rue Juliette Wytsman, Bruxelles Belgium. **LC** RA428.3.I57. **DD** 610.720493.

RATIONAL LIVING CEASED. Vol. 1 (Feb. 1966)-V.18, No. 1 (Spring 1983). 0034-0049. Periodical. US. English. sa. **Ind/Abst** Sociol. Abstr., Soc. Welf. Soc. Plan./Policy Soc. Dev. **LC** RA790.A1. **DD** 614.5805. **NLM** W1 RA948L. **CODEN** RTLVBX.

RECENT ADVANCES IN COMMUNITY MEDICINE. No. 0144-1256. UK. English. ir. Churchill Livingstone Inc, 1560 Broadway, New York NY 10036. **Tel** (212)819-5400. Ed A E Bennett. **NLM** W1 RE105UE.

RECENT ADVANCES IN INFECTION. No. 1-. 0144-1078. UK. English. ir. Lonman Inc, 95 Church Street, White Plains NY 10601. Ed D Reeves and A Geddes. **Ind/Abst** Chem. Abstr. **LC** RC111. **DD** 616.9. **NLM** W1 RE105UMG. **CODEN** RAIFD9.

RECENT ADVANCES IN SEXUALLY TRANSMITTED DISEASES. No. 1-. 0143-6805. Periodical. UK. English. ir. Churchill Livingstone Inc, 1560 Broadway, New York NY 10036. **Tel** (212)819-5400. Ed R S Morton and J R W Harris. **NLM** W1 RE105YI.

RECURSOS HUMANOS. Main/Corp Santa Catarina, Brazil. Secretaria da Saude. 1974-. Portuguese. ir. **LC** RA410.9.B7.

REHABILITATION. See Psychology.

RELATORIO - DIRECCAO PROVINCIAL DOS SERVICOS DE SAUDE E ASSISTENCIA. Main/Corp Mozambique. Direccao dos Servicos de Saude e Assistencia. Seccao de Estatistica. 1964-. 0254-0282. Portuguese. an. **NLM** W2 HM7 D45R. *Relatorio Anual da Direccao dos Servicos de Saude e Higiene, 0254-0266; Estatistica dos Servicos de Saude.*

RELEVE EPIDEMIOLOGIQUE HEBDOMADAIRE. VFOAT Weekly Epidemiological Record. 0049-8114. Periodical. English (French). wk. $60.00. World Health Organization, PO Box 5284, Church Street Station, New York NY 10249. **Tel** (202)861-3200. Contains notifications made under the International Health Regulations and information concerning their application. Also contains epidemiological notes on communicable diseases of international importance.

REPERTOIRE DES ETABLISSEMENTS DE SANTE ET DE SERVICES SOCIAUX. 1974-. 0318-6067. CN. French. an. Ministere des Affaires Sociales, 1075 Chemin Saint-Foy, Quebec Ontario G1S 2M1 Canada. **LC** RA983.A4. **DD** 362.1025714.

REPORT - DIVISION OF HEALTH SERVICES RESEARCH AND DEVELOPMENT. UNIVERSITY OF BRITISH COLUMBIA. (REPORT - DIVISION OF HEALTH SERVICES RESEARCH AND DEVELOPMENT, UNIVERSITY OF BRITISH COLUMBIA). **Main/Corp** University of British Columbia. Division of Health Services Research and Development. Began publication in 197-. 0225-901X. Periodical. CN. English. ir. Office of the Coordinator, Division of Health Science Research and Development Health Center, University of British Columbia, Vancouver British Columbia V6T 1W5 Canada. **DD** 610.6909711.

REPORT - FLORIDA. LEGISLATURE. JOINT INTERIM COMMITTEE ON MENTAL HEALTH. See Public Administration.

REPORT - GOVERNMENT CHEMICAL LABORATORY. Main/Corp Government Chemical Laboratory (Queensland). **VFOAT** Annual Report - Queensland Government Chemical Laboratory. 0481-3308. Periodical. AT. English. ir. Queensland Government Printer, Government Printing Office, Box 680, Brisbane Queensland Australia. **DD** 614.

REPORT - GOVERNMENT OF INDIA, MINISTRY OF HEALTH AND FAMILY WELFARE, DEPARTMENT OF HEALTH & DEPARTMENT OF FAMILY WELFARE. Main/Corp India (Republic) Dept. of Health. 1976/77-. Periodical. English. ir. **NLM** W2 JI4 D37R.

REPORT - GREAT BRITAIN. COMMITTEE ON SAFETY OF DRUGS. Main/Corp Great Britain. Committee on Safety of Drugs. 1964-. 0436-3779. UK. English. ir.

REPORT - KENTUCKY. DEPT OF HEALTH. Main/Corp Kentucky. Dept. of Health. US. English. ir. State of Kentucky, Department of Health, Frankfort KY 10601. **LC** RA71. **DD** 614.061769.

Public Health and Safety

REPORT - NATIONAL HEALTH COUNCIL. Main/Corp Ireland (Eire). National Health Council. English. ir. 25. Stationery Office, G P O Arcade 1, Dublin Ireland. **LC** RA273. **DD** 362.109417.

REPORT - NEW ZEALAND. DEPT. OF HEALTH. Main/Corp New Zealand. Dept. of Health. English. ir. **LC** RA372.N6. **DD** 614.09931.

REPORT - NORTH DAKOTA STATE DEPARTMENT OF HEALTH. Main/Corp North Dakota. State Dept. of Health. **VFOAT** Health in North Dakota. 0094-1816. US. English. **LC** RA127. **DD** 362.109784. **NLM** W2 AN9 S7B.

A REPORT OF HEALTH, PHYSICAL EDUCATION, AND RECREATION RESEARCH PROJECTS COMPLETED OR IN PROGRESS IN THE STATE OF INDIANA. (A REPORT OF HEALTH, PHYSICAL EDUCATION, AND RECREATION RESEARCH PROJECTS COMPLETED OR IN PROGRESS IN THE STATE OF INDIANA IN . . .). 0275-7494. US. English. an. State Board of Health, Public Health Statistics, 1330 West Michigan Street, Indianapolis IN 46206. **LC** RA440.A1. **DD** 613.0720772.

REPORT OF MEDICAL ASSISTANCE & COUNTY INDIGENT STATISTICS. See Statistics.

REPORT OF THE ADMINISTRATOR - ALCOHOL, DRUG ABUSE, AND MENTAL HEALTH ADMINISTRATION. See Drug Abuse and Alcoholism.

REPORT OF THE ADMINISTRATOR - UNITED STATES. HEALTH SERVICES ADMINISTRATION. (REPORT OF THE ADMINISTRATOR - UNITED STATES. HEALTH SERVICES ADMINISTRATION). **Main/Corp** United States. Health Services Administration. **Series/Titl** DHHS Publication. 0276-8321. US. English. an. US Department of Health and Human Services, Public Health Services Administration, 5600 Fishers Lane, Rockville MD 20857. **LC** RA412.5.U6. **DD** 353.0084106. **NLM** W2 A H635R.

REPORT OF THE COMMISSIONER OF PUBLIC HEALTH - WESTERN AUSTRALIA. Main/Corp Western Australia. Public Health Dept. **VFOAT** Report, Commissioner of Public Health,. 1947-. Periodical. English. ir. **NLM** W2 KA8 D43R. Report of the Public Health Department.

REPORT OF THE COMMITTEE ON SAFETY OF MEDICINES APPOINTED BY THE HEALTH MINISTERS OF THE UNITED KINGDOM. See Pharmacy.

REPORT OF THE DIRECTOR, NATIONAL HEART, LUNG, AND BLOOD INSTITUTE. Began with 7th, 1980. US. English. an. National Institute of Health, 9000 Rockville Pike, Bethesda MD 20014. Report of the Director of the National Heart, Lung, and Blood Institute, 0193-7340.

REPORT OF THE DIRECTOR OF MENTAL HEALTH SERVICES. (WESTERN AUSTRALIA). Main/Corp Western Australia. Mental Health Services. **VFOAT** Annual Report of the Director of Mental Health Services. English. ir. **LC** RA790.7.A8. **DD** 354.94100842. **NLM** W2 KA8.1 W5M5R.

REPORT OF THE GENERAL CONFERENCE - ROYAL NEW ZEALAND SOCIETY FOR THE HEALTH OF WOMEN AND CHILDREN (INC.). (REPORT OF THE GENERAL CONFERENCE - ROYAL NEW ZEALAND SOCIETY FOR THE HEALTH OF WOMEN AND CHILDREN). **Main/Corp** Royal New Zealand Society for the Health of Women and Children. **VFOAT** Report of the General Conference - Plunket Society. 0110-991X. NZ. English. be. **NLM** W1 RO712C. Report of the General Conference - Society for the Health of Women and Children.

REPORT OF THE HEALTH SERVICE COMMISSIONER. See Public Administration.

REPORT OF THE NATIONAL HEALTH AND MEDICAL RESEARCH COUNCIL. Main/Corp National Health and Medical Research Council (Australia). AT. English. ir. **LC** RA371. **DD** 614.0994. **NLM** W2 KA8 N2R.

REPORT OF THE NATIONAL HEART, LUNG, AND BLOOD ADVISORY COUNCIL. Main/Corp National Heart, Lung, and Blood Advisory Council. **VFOAT** 30 Years of Progress for the People in Heart, Lung, and Blood Disease. Began with 4th, 1976. 0161-1917. US. English. an. US Department of Health and Human Services, Public Health Service, National Institutes of Health, American Heart Lung and Blood Advisory Council, Bethesda MD 20205. **LC** RA645.H4. **DD** 362.1961. **NLM** W2 A N162R. Report of the National Heart and Lung Advisory Council, 0193-2225.

REPORT OF THE SASKATCHEWAN SAFETY COUNCIL PUBLIC OPINION POLL. (A REPORT OF THE SASKATCHEWAN SAFETY COUNCIL PUBLIC OPINION POLL). **Main/Corp** Saskatchewan Safety Council. **VFOAT** Traffic Safety Public Opinion Poll. **VAT** Traffic Safety Public Opinion Poll (1976). 1976-. 0707-1973. CN. English. an. Saskatchewan Safety Council, 348 Victoria Avenue, Regina Saskatchewan S4N 0P6 Canada. **DD** 301.1543614862097124. Report of the Traffic Safety Public Opinion Poll, 0707-7645.

REPORT OF VITAL STATISTICS FOR OHIO. See Statistics.

REPORT ON HEALTH CONDITIONS IN THE NORTHWEST TERRITORIES. CN. English. Regional Health Services Advisor Medical Services Health And Welfare Canada, Bag 7777, Yellowknife Northwest Territories Canada. **LC** RA450.N57. **DD** 362.109719021.

REPORT ON THE WORLD HEALTH SITUATION. VFOAT World Health Situation. 6th- 1973-77-. English. ir. Report on the World Health Situation.

REPORT . . . REVIEWS OF PROPOSED INSTITUTIONAL HEALTH SERVICES AND CAPITAL EXPENDITURE PROJECTS UNDER CERTIFICATE OF NEED AND SECTION 1122. Main/Corp Oklahoma Health Planning Commission. US. English. an. Oklahoma Health Planning Commission, 100 NE 10th Street/ Room 1106, PO Box 53551, Oklahoma City OK 73152. Report - Reviews of Proposed Institutional Health Services and Capital Expenditure Projects in Oklahoma.

REPORT SERIES ON MENTAL HEALTH STATISTICS. SERIES B. ANALYTICAL AND SPECIAL STUDY REPORTS. See Statistics.

REPORT TO THE GOVERNOR - MARYLAND. HEALTH SERVICES COST REVIEW COMMISSION. Main/Corp Maryland. Health Services Cost Review Commission. **VFOAT** Annual Report to the Governor. US. English. an. Health Services Cost Review Commission, 201 West Preston Street, Baltimore MD 21201.

REPORT TO THE GOVERNOR - NEW YORK STATE FACILITIES DEVELOPMENT CORPORATION. Main/Corp New York State Facilities Development Corporation. 1974-. 0145-7306. US. English. an. New York State Facilities Development Corporation, 44 Holland Avenue, Albany NY 12208. **LC** RA790.65.N7. **DD** 362.209747. Report to the Governor - New York State Health and Mental Hygiene Facilties Improvement Corporation, 0094-2545.

REPORT TO THE PEOPLE. See Transportation - Roads and Traffic.

REPORT - WHO EXPERT COMMITTEE ON FILARIASIS. Main/Corp World Health Organization. Expert Committee on Filariasis. **Series Corp** World Health Organization. Technical Report Series. English. ir. World Health Organization, Distribution and Sales Service, 1211 Geneva Switzerland. **LC** RA8, RA644.F5. **DD** 610.8 S, 614.5552.

REPORTABLE DISEASE BULLETIN. US. English. **LC** RA643.6.N9. **DD** 312.3909784.

REPORTED MORBIDITY AND MORTALITY IN TEXAS. ANNUAL SUMMARY. (REPORTED MORBIDITY AND MORTALITY IN TEXAS, ANNUAL SUMMARY). V. 1- 1978-. 0273-5202. US. English. an. **LC** RA643.6.T4. **DD** 312.3909764.

THE REPORTER - NEW JERSEY ASSOCIATION FOR HEALTH, PHYSICAL EDUCATION AND RECREATION. (NEW JERSEY ASSOCIATION FOR HEALTH, PHYSICAL EDUCATION AND RECREATION REPORTER). **Main/Corp** New Jersey Association for Health, Physical Education and Recreation. 0034-477X. Periodical. US. English. qt. NJ Association for Health Physical Education & Recreation, Pitman Richwood Road, c/o B Jenkins, Pitman NJ 08071.

RESEARCH BULLETIN OF THE HIMALAYAN INTERNATIONAL INSTITUTE/ELEANOR N. DANA LABORATORY. 0276-4148. Periodical. US. English. qt. Free to Members, $10.00 Others Domestic, $15.00 Other Foreign. Himalayan International Institute of Yoga Science and Philosophy, RD1 Box 88, Honesdale PA 18431. **LC** RA781.7. **DD** 613.7046.

RESEARCH FINDINGS - CENTRAL HEALTH EDUCATION BUREAU, DIRECTORATE GENERAL OF HEALTH SERVICES. (RESEARCH FINDINGS). Began with: Vol. 1, No. 1 (Apr. 1968). 0254-9581. Periodical. English. qt. Free. **NLM** W1 RE225C.

RESEARCH GRANTS. VFOAT N.I.H. Research Grants. Began with fiscal year 1968. US. English. an. US Department of Health and Human Services, Public Health Service, National Institutes of Health Building WB/Room 449, Bethesda MD 20205. **NLM** WA 22 AA1 R46.

RESEARCH REPORT SERIES - HEALTH SERVICES RESEARCH CENTER, KAISER FOUNDATION HOSPITALS. (RESEARCH REPORT SERIES - HEALTH SERVICES RESEACH CENTER). Report No. 1- 1976-. 0147-023X. Monographic Series. US. English. ir. Ed P Turner. **NLM** W1 RE234HC.

RESEARCH SERIES - BLUE CROSS OF WESTERN PENNSYLVANIA. 1- Oct. 1965-. 0196-0474. Monographic Series. US. English. bm. Blue Cross-Western Pennsylvania, One Smithfield Street, Research Department, Pittsburgh PA 15222. **Tel** (412)255-7837. **NLM** W1 RE234WC.

RESOLUTIONS AND DECISIONS, ANNEXES, SUMMARY RECORDS. See Law - International Law.

RESOURCE DIRECTORY, HEALTH INFORMATION SHARING PROJECT. See Yearbooks, Almanacs, Directories.

RESOURCES FOR HEALTH R & D REPORT. VAT Resources for Health Research and Development Report. No. 21-. 0360-7933. US. English. US Department of Health Education and Welfare, Public Health Service, Washington DC 20204. **LC** R854.U5. **DD** 610.72073. **NLM** W2 A N213R. Resources for Biomedical Research, 0163-3481.

RESPONSE. (RESPONSE : OFFICIAL JOURNAL OF THE NATIONAL ASSOCIATION FOR SEARCH AND RESCUE). Vol. 1, No. 1 (Winter 1982)-. 0732-2933. Periodical. US. English. bm. $14.95. Jems Publishing Company, PO Box 1026, Solana Beach CA 92075. **Tel** (619)481-1185. Ed Rick Minerd. **LC** TL553.8. **DD** 363.34805. bk rev. adv acc. **Circ** 10,000. Magazine of search and rescue management published by Jems publishing for the National Association for Search and Rescue. Discusses rescue techniques, equipment, disaster management, missions, etc.

REVIEW OF ALLIED HEALTH EDUCATION. 1- 1974-. 0095-7224. US. English. $7.50. University Press of Kentucky, Editorial and Sales Office, Lexington KY 45506. **LC** R847.A1. **DD** 610.71073. **NLM** W1 RE252L.

REVIEWS OF CLINICAL INFECTIOUS DISEASES. 1982-. 0731-9266. US. English. an. Academic Press, 4805 Sand Lake Road, Orlando FL 32819. **DD** 616.

REVIEWS OF INFECTIOUS DISEASES. V. 1- Jan./Feb. 1979-. 0162-0886. Periodical. US. English. bm. $135.00. University of Chicago Press, PO Box 37009, Chicago IL 60637. **Ind/Abst** Life Sci. Collect., Pestdoc, Ringdoc, Vetdoc, Index Med., Biol. Abstr., Chem. Abstr. **LC** RC110. **DD** 616.905. **NLM** W1 RE257DG. **CODEN** RINDDG.

REVISTA CENTROAMERICANA DE CIENCIAS DE LA SALUD. Yearly V. 1- (No. 1-) 1975-. 0379-7090. Periodical. CR. Spanish. ty. Universitaria Centroamericana CSUCA-Confederacion, Apartado 37, Cuidad Univ R Facio, San Jose Costa Rica. **Tel** 25-27-44. bk rev. **Circ** 500. Deals with public health in Central America, process of health and disease, theoretical and methodological principles, laws of biological and social sciences.

Public Health and Safety

REVISTA CUBANA DE ADMINISTRACION DE SALUD. VFOAT R.C.A.S. V. 1- Jan./June 1975-. 0252-1903. Periodical. CU. Spanish (tables of contents in English). qt. $21.01. Empresa Ediciones Cubanas, Sub-Direccion Exportacion Oreilly, 407 Ciudad, Havana Cuba. **Ind/Abst** Popul. Index. **LC** RA456.C7. **NLM** W1 RE359BR.

REVISTA CUBANA DE HIGIENE Y EPIDEMIOLOGIA. Year 13- Jan./August 1975-. 0253-1151. Periodical. CU. Spanish. ir. Empresa Ediciones Cubanas, Oreilly 407, Ciudad Havana Cuba. **Ind/Abst** Excerpta Med., Biol. Abstr., Chem. Abstr. **NLM** W1 RE3596. **CODEN** RCHEDF. Boletin Higiene y Epidemiologia, 0006-629X.

REVISTA DA FUNDACAO S.E.S.P. (REVISTA DA FUNDACAO SESP). **Main/Corp** Fundacao Servicos de Saude Publica. VAT Revista da Fundacao Servicos de Saude Publica. V. 17, No. 2-. 0304-2138. Periodical. BL. Portuguese (summaries in English). ir. Fundacao Servicos de Saude, Publica Avenue, Rio Branco 251 120 Andar, Rio de Janeiro Brazil. **Ind/Abst** Chem. Abstr. **LC** RA463. **NLM** W1 RE37V. **CODEN** RFSEAK. Revista do Servico Especial de Saude Publica, 0100-0101.

REVISTA DO INSTITUTO ADOLFO LUTZ. **Main/Corp** Sao Paulo, Brazil (City). Instituto Adolfo Lutz. V. 1- July 1941-. 0370-5374. BL. Portuguese (summaries in English). an. Instituto Adolfo Lutz, Sao Paulo Brazil. **Ind/Abst** Life Sci. Collect., Excerpta Med., Chem. Abstr., Bibliogr. Agric. **LC** R25. **DD** 610.5. **NLM** W1 RE521. **CODEN** RIALA6.

REVISTA LATINOAMERICANA DE SALUD. 1-. Periodical. Spanish. ir. $20.00. Editorial Nueva Imagen, Apartado Postal 600, Mexico 1 D F Mexico. **LC** RA450.5. **DD** 362.1098.

REVUE DE DROIT SANITAIRE ET SOCIAL. No. 61, (Jan./March 1980)- . Yearly V. 16-. 0245-9469. Periodical. FR. French. qt. $50.82. Dalloz, 11 rue Soufflot, 75240 Paris Cedex 05 France. **NLM** W1 RE778EE. Revue Trimestrielle de Droit Sanitaire et Social.

REVUE D'EPIDEMIOLOGIE ET DE SANTE PUBLIQUE. V. 24- Jan./Feb. 1976-. 0398-7620. Periodical. US. English (French, with summaries and tables of contents in both languages). bm. Masson Publishers USA Inc, 211 East 43rd Street/Room 1306, New York NY 10017. **Tel** (212)370-1937. **Ind/Abst** CIS Abstr., Life Sci. Collect., Excerpta Med., Index Med., Biol. Abstr., Energy Res. Abstr. **NLM** W1 RE798R. **CODEN** RESPDF. Revue d'Epidemiologie, Medecine Sociale et Sante Publique, 0035-2438.

REVUE D'HYGIENE ET DE MEDECINE SCOLAIRE ET UNIVERSITAIRE. VFOAT Revue Francaise d'Hygiene et Medecine Scolaire et Universitaire. V. 26- 1973-. Periodical. FR. French. qt. Doin Editeurs, 8 Place de 1 Odeon, 75 Paris 6EME France. **Tel** 325.34.02. Revue d'Hygiene et Medecine Scolaires et Universitaires.

RHODE ISLAND COMMUNITY HEALTH PROFILES. No. 1- 1976-. 0163-349X. Periodical. US. English. **NLM** W1 RH453.

RISK ABSTRACTS. See Indexes/Abstracts.

ROAD TRAFFIC SAFETY RESEARCH COUNCIL REPORT. See Transportation - Roads and Traffic.

ROBOT. See Transportation - Roads and Traffic.

ROSTER OF MEMBERS & AUTHORITY STRUCTURE FUNCTIONS. (HRA, HSA, CDC & ADAMHA PUBLIC ADVISORY COMMITTEES : AUTHORITY, STRUCTURE, FUNCTIONS, ROSTER). VAT Roster of Members and Authority Structure Functions, Health Resources Administration, Health Services Administration, Center for Disease Control, Alcohol, Drug Abuse, and Mental Health Administration Public Advisory Committees. 0095-6163. US. English. Health Resources Administration, Office of the Administrator, DMS Committee Management Branch, 5600 Fishers Lane, Rockville MD 20852. **LC** RA11. **DD** 353.00841. **NLM** WA 22 AA1 H103.

RUBELLA SURVEILLANCE. US. English. U S Department of Health and Human Services, Public Health Service Centers for Disease Control, Atlanta GA 30333.

RUMAH TANGGA DAN KESEHATAN. 0485-6015. Periodical. Indonesian. ir.

RUNDSCHAU FUR FLEISCHBESCHAUER, TRICHINENSCHAUER UND GEFLUGELFLEISCHKONTROLLEURE . Vol. 26, No. 4, Apr. 1974-. 0340-1219. Periodical. German. mo. M & H Schaper Verlag, Ptch 810669, Grazer Strasse, D3000 Hannover 81 West Germany. **Tel** 05 11/83 00 18. **NLM** W1 RU684. Rundschau fur Fleischbeschauer und Trichenenschauer, 0340-126X.

THE RYAN ADVISORY FOR HEALTH SERVICES GOVERNING BOARDS. V. 5, No. 4- Apr. 1977-. 0161-7680. Periodical. US. English. mo. $12.00. **NLM** W1 RY33. Ryan Advisory for Hospital Governing Boards, 0196-9242.

SAFETY EFFECTIVENESS EVALUATION : REPORT NO. NTSB-SEE. **Main/Corp** United States. National Transportation Safety Board. VFOAT Report No. NTSB-SEE. Periodical. US. English. National Transportation Safety Board, 800 Independence Avenue SW, Washington DC 20594.

SAFETY IMPROVEMENT WORK PROGRAM. See Transportation - Roads and Traffic.

SAFETY I.S.H.C. See Transportation - Roads and Traffic.

SAFETY JOURNAL. 0036-2506. US. English. bm. Safety Journal, PO Box 4189 Station B, Anderson SC 29621. **Tel** (803)226-5327. **Ind/Abst** Electron. Commun. Abstr. J., ISMEC Bull., Pollut. Abstr. Indexes, Saf. Sci. Abstr. J.

SAFETY RECOMMENDATIONS. **Main/Corp** United States. National Transportation Safety Board. US. English. mo. National Technical Information Service, 5285 Port Royal Road, Springfield VA 22161. **Tel** (703)487-4630.

SAFETY RELATED RECALL CAMPAIGNS FOR MOTOR VEHICLES AND MOTOR VEHICLE EQUIPMENT, INCLUDING TIRES. DETAILED REPORTS. See Transportation - Automobiles.

SAFETY ROAD CHECKS, MOTOR CARRIERS OF PROPERTY. **Main/Corp** United States. Bureau of Motor Carrier Safety. 0098-0250. US. English. Bureau of Motor Carrier Safety, Washington DC 20590. **LC** TL230.A1. **DD** 388.344. Selected Safety Road Checks, Motor Carriers of Property.

SAFETY SADISTICS. **Main/Corp** Arizona. Office of Highway Safety. VFOAT Arizona Safety Sadistics. 0147-3743. Periodical. US. English. qt. Office of Highway Safety, Arizona Department of Transportation, 1655 W Jackson, Phoenix AZ 85007. **LC** HE5614.3.A6. **DD** 614.86209791. Arizona Safety Sad-istics, 0044-8869.

SAFETY UPDATE. V. 1- Apr. 1979-. 0704-4739. Periodical. CN. English. qt. Free. Ontario Safety League, 409 King Street West, Toronto Ontario M5V 1K1 Canada. **DD** 363.109713. (ctrl). News, 0700-9844.

SAGE ANNUAL REVIEWS OF COMMUNITY MENTAL HEALTH. See Medicine - Psychiatry, Psychopathology.

SAGE STUDIES IN COMMUNITY MENTAL HEALTH. VFOAT Sage Series in Community Mental Health. 1-. 0730-3807. Monographic Series. US. English. ir. Sage Publications, PO Box 5024, Beverly Hills CA 90210. Ed R H Price. **NLM** W1 SA126M.

SAITAMA-KEN EISEI KENKYUJO HO. REPORT OF THE SAITAMA INSTITUTE OF PUBLIC HEALTH. JA. Japanese. ir. Saitama-ken Eisei Kenkyujo, 639-1 Kami Okubo Higashi, Urawa 338 Japan. **LC** RA421.

SALUBRITAS. V. 1- Jan. 1977-. 0191-5789. Periodical. US. English. qt. $10.00. American Public Health Association, 1015 15th Street Northwest, Washington DC 20005. **Tel** (202)789-5688. **NLM** W1 SA352. bk rev. **Circ** 2,500. Information exchange on primary health care in developing countries including articles on "How to . . .", family planning, health eduction, immunizations, conferences, training publications, etc.

SALUD PANAMERICANA. 0250-5975. Periodical. US. Spanish. qt. 525 23rd Street NW, Washington DC 20037. **LC** RA421. **DD** 614.098. Gaceta.

LA SANTE DE L'HOMME. Periodical. FR. French. ir. $9.84. Comite Francais Ed pour la San, 9 rue Newton, 75116 Paris France. **LC** RA421.

SANTE PUBLIQUE. (LA SANTE PUBLIQUE). Year 1- 1958-. 0048-9107. Periodical. RM. French (English or German). qt. Ilexim Press Department, PO Box 1-136-1-137, Bucharest Romania. **Ind/Abst** Excerpta Med., Index Med., CIS Abstr., Hospit. Lit. Index. **NLM** W1 SA832.

SASKATCHEWAN PROVINCIAL HIGHWAYS ACCIDENT STATISTICS. See Statistics.

SAUDE. **Main/Corp** Bahia (Brazil : State). Secretaria da Saude Publica. Portuguese. ni. **LC** RA464.B33. **DD** 614.098142.

SCANDINAVIAN JOURNAL OF INFECTIOUS DISEASES. V. 1-. 0036-5548. SW. English. qt. $60.00. Almqvist & Wiksell, 108 Drottninggatan, PO Box 45150, S-104 30 Stockholm Sweden. **Tel** Telex 85413160. **Ind/Abst** Life Sci. Collect., Excerpta Med., Pestdoc, Ringdoc, Vetdoc, Index Med., Biol. Abstr., Chem. Abstr., Sci. Cit. Index, Abr. Ed., Hospit. Lit. Index. **NLM** W1 SC15K. **CODEN** SJIDB7.

SCHOOL HEALTH DIGEST. V. 1-. Periodical. US. English. State University of New York, Division of Drug and Health Services, Albany NY 12234.

SCHRIFTENREIHE DER AKADEMIE FUR OFFENTLICHES GESUNDHEITSWESEN IN DUSSELDORF. (SCHRIFTENREIHE DER AKADEMIE FUR OEFFENTLICHES GESUNDHEITSWESEN IN DUSSELDORF). V. 1-. 0172-2131. Monographic Series. English (German). ir. **NLM** W1 SC326F.

SCHS STUDIES. No. 8 (Aug. 1980)-. US. English. Free. PO Box 2091, Raleigh NC 27602. **Tel** (919)733-4728. Ed Charles J Rothwell. **LC** RA407.4.N8. **DD** 362.109756. **Circ** 500. Studies on health topics of current interest are presented in newsletter form. PHSB Studies.

SCOTTISH HEALTH SERVICES. **Main/Corp** Scotland. Scottish Home and Health Dept. UK. English. Her Majesty's Stationery Office, 13 A Castle Street, Edinburgh EH2 3AR Scotland. **LC** RA243. **DD** 362.109411.

SCOTTISH HEALTH STATISTICS. See Statistics.

SEAMIC HEALTH STATISTICS. See Statistics.

SEAMIC INFORMATION RETRIEVAL ON CURRENT LITERATURE. SERIES A: TYPHOID AND PARA-TYPHOID FEVERS, AND SALMONELLA FOOD POISONING. Series/Titl SEAMIC-IR. VFOAT Typhoid and Para-Typhoid Fevers, and Salmonella Food Poisoning. No. 3- Mar. 1979-. Periodical. English. ir. **NLM** ZWC 260 S106. SEAMIC Information Retrieval on Current Literature. Series A: Typhoid Fever & Salmonellosis.

SEAMIC INFORMATION RETRIEVAL ON CURRENT LITERATURE. SERIES F, HEALTH STATUS INDICATORS. (SEAMIC INFORMATION RETRIEVAL ON CURRENT LITERATURE. SERIES F : HEALTH STATUS INDICATORS). Series/Titl SEAMIC-IR. VFOAT Health Status Indicators. No. 1- Jan. 1980-. 0254-2870. English. ir. **NLM** ZWA 900.1 S104.

SEAMIC INFORMATION RETRIEVAL ON CURRENT LITERATURE. SERIES L. VENEREAL DISEASE. Series/Titl SEAMIC-IR. VFOAT Venereal Disease. No. 1 (Dec. 1981)-. 0254-8720. Monographic Series. English. ir. **NLM** ZWC 140 S438.

SEARCH AND RESCUE MAGAZINE. 1975. 0092-5136. Periodical. US. English. qt. Search & Rescue Magazine, 4195 Polaris Avenue, Lompac CA 93436. **Tel** (805)733-3986. Ed Kimberly Plummer. **LC** TL553.8. **DD** 614.8. (ctrl). Our publication describes the happenings in the search and rescue world.

SECOND OPINION (SAN FRANCISCO, CALIF.). (SECOND OPINION). VFOAT 2nd Opinion. 0748-9528. Periodical. US. English. mo. $50.00. CMRW, 2845 24th Street, San Francisco CA 94110. **Tel** (415)826)4401. **DD** 362. bk rev. **Circ** 1,500. (ctrl). Gives our members the latest news on health care issues that affect women and children: sexually

Public Health and Safety

transmitted diseases, PMS, toxic shock syndrome, osteoporosis, hazards from cleaning, endometriosis, and perinatal health.

SEISHIN EISEI SHIRYO. VFOAT Annual Report on Mental Health. No. 1-. 0454-2010. Japanese. ir. Kokuritsu Seishin Eisei Kenkyujo, 7-3 Konodai 1 (272), Ichikawa Japan. Ind/Abst Psychol. Abstr. LC RA790.A1. CODEN SESHAX.

SELECTION SANTE ACHP. Main/Corp Association Canadienne d'Hygiene Publique. VFOAT Selection Sante. VAT Selection Sante. Association Canadienne d'Hygiene Publique. V. 1- Feb. 1977-. 0705-1204. Periodical. CN. French. bm. Association Canadienne d'Hygiene Publique, 1335 Avenue Carling/Suite 210, Ottawa Ontario K1Z 8N8 Canada. Tel (613)725-3769. DD 614.06271. *Bulletin d'Information, 0705-1190.*

SEXUALLY TRANSMITTED DISEASE (STD) STATISTICAL LETTER. See Statistics.

SEXUALLY TRANSMITTED DISEASES. V. 4- Jan./Mar. 1977-. 0148-5717. Periodical. US. English. qt. $57.00. J B Lippincott Company, East Washington Square, Philadelphia PA 19105. Tel (215)238-4273. Ed William M McCormack. Ind/Abst Life Sci. Collect., Excerpta Med., Index Med., Biol. Abstr. LC RC201.A1. DD 616.951005. NLM W1 SE99U. CODEN STRDDM. adv acc. Circ 2,073. Published in order to disseminate information on all human sexually transmitted diseases. *Journal of the American Venereal Disease Association, 0095-148X.*

SEXUALLY TRANSMITTED DISEASES. ABSTRACTS & BIBLIOGRAPHY. See Indexes/Abstracts.

SEXUALLY TRANSMITTED DISEASES IN CANADA. VFOAT Sexually Transmitted Diseases Canada. 1976-. 0711-8929. CN. English. an. Department of National Health and Welfare, Bureau of Epidemiology, Ottawa Ontario K1A 0K9 Canada. DD 312.395100971. *Sexually Transmitted Disease in Canada, 0711-8910.*

SHENG HUO YU CHIEN KANG. VFOAT Life and Health. First published in Aug. 1976-. Periodical. HK. Chinese. ir. $2.00 Single Issue. Ta Kuang Chu Pan She, 64 Marble Road, Hsiang-Kang Hong Kong. LC RA773.

SHOKUHIN EISEI KANKEI JIGYO HOKOKU. Main/Corp Tokyo. Eiseikyoku. Kankyo Eiseibu. Japanese. ir. Kankyo Eiseibu, 5-1 Marunouch, Chiyoda-ku 100 Tokyo Japan. LC RA601.

SHOKUHIN EISEI KENKYU. VFOAT Food Sanitation Research. 0559-8974. Periodical. JA. Japanese. mo. 6000. Nihon Shokuhin Eisei Kyokai, 6-1 Jingumae 2 Shibuya-ku, Tokyo 150 Japan. Ind/Abst Chem. Abstr. LC RA601. NLM W1 SH514. CODEN SHEKAR.

SHOKUHIN EISEIGAKU ZASSHI. VFOAT Journal of the Food Hygienic Society of Japan. 0015-6426. Periodical. Japanese (articles in English). bm. Japan Publishing Trade Company Ltd, PO Box 5030, Tokyo International Tokyo 100-31 Japan. Ind/Abst Life Sci. Collect., Excerpta Med., Biol. Abstr., Bibliogr. Agric., Chem. Abstr. LC RA601. NLM W1 SH514K. CODEN SKEZAP.

SIGNAL. VFOAT Signal. V. 1- Nov. 1974-. 0037-4911. Periodical. CN. English (French on inverted pages). Quebec Safety League, 5576 Upper Lachine Road, Montreal Quebec H4A 2A7 Canada. DD 614.805. *Le Signal.*

SINGAPORE COMMUNITY HEALTH BULLETIN. (THE SINGAPORE COMMUNITY HEALTH BULLETIN). No. 19- July 1978-. 0129-7457. English. ir. Ind/Abst Excerpta Med. NLM W1 SI519J. *Singapore Public Health Bulletin, 0304-4378.*

SMART'S HEALTH & SAFETY NEWSLETTER. VFOAT Smart's Health and Safety Newsletter. 1 (Dec. 1982)-. 0736-8356. Periodical. US. English. $35.00. Darrell Hepprer, 154 Sunnyside Drive, San Leandro CA 94577.

SMOKE SIGNALS. 0583-659X. Periodical. US. English. mo. $4.95. Narcotics Education Inc, 6830 Laurel Street NW, Washington DC 20012.

SMOKING AND HEALTH BULLETIN. Began with Feb./Mar. 1970. 0081-0363. US. English. mo. Technical Information Center, Office on Smoking and Health, Park Building Room 116/5600 Fishers Lane, Rockville MD 20857. Ind/Abst Am. Stat. Index. LC RA1242.T6. DD 615.952379. NLM ZQV 137 S666. *Smoking and Health Bibliographical Bulletin.*

SMOKING AND HEALTH REPORTER. Vol. 1, No. 1 (Oct. 1983)-. 0738-4920. Periodical. US. English. qt. $5.00 General, Free to Non-Profit Libraries. Smoking and Health Reporter, Indiana University, HPER Building/Room 116, Bloomington IN 47405. Ind/Abst Bibliogr. Index Health Educ. Period.

SOCIALNYTT. 1968-. 0037-7619. Periodical. SW. Swedish. mo. $15.97. Socialnytt, Liber Foerlag, 16289 Stockholm Sweden. NLM W1 SO139K. *Sociala Meddelanden.*

SOCIETA E SALUTE. 0391-5913. Monographic Series. IT. Italian. ir. IL Pensiero Scientifico Edit, Via Panama 48, 00198 Rome Italy. Ed G Berlinguer and A Seppilli. LC UNC. NLM W1 SO3315.

SOCIOECONOMIC ISSUES OF HEALTH. 1979-. 0198-7399. US. English. an. American Medical Association, PO Box 821, Monroe WI 53566. LC RA410.53. DD 338.4336210973. NLM W1 SO878MH. *Reference Data on Socioeconomic Issues of Health, 0092-8836.*

SOCIOLOGY OF HEALTH & ILLNESS. See Sociology: General Works, Theory.

SOKOTO STATE HEALTH STATISTICS. VFOAT Health Statistics. 1980-. 0189-8035. English. an. LC RA407.5.N44. DD 362.1096695.

SONDERHEFT. Main/Corp Landesarbeitsgemeinschaft zur Bekampfund der Geschlechtskrankheiten und fur Geschlechtserziehung Nordrhein-Westfalen. Monographic Series. German. ir. Koln-Sulz, Zulpicher Strasse 337, Koln West Germany. LC RA644.V4.

SONGSIM CHUNGANG YUJI CHAEDAN YONBO. VFOAT Annual Report. English (Korean). an. Songsim Chungang Yuji Chaedan, 94-195 Yongdungpo-dong Yongdungpo-ku, Seoul Korea. LC RA990.K64.

SOURCES OF MORBIDITY DATA FROM THE CLEARINGHOUSE ON CURRENT MORBIDITY STATISTICS PROGRAMS. See Statistics.

THE SOUTHEAST ASIAN JOURNAL OF TROPICAL MEDICINE AND PUBLIC HEALTH. V. 1- March 1970-. 0038-3619. Periodical. TH. English. qt. $20.00. Seameo-Tropmed Publications, 420/6 Rajvithi Rd-Tropmed Proj, Bangkok 10400 Thailand. Tel 2457193. Ed Tranakchit Harinasuta. Ind/Abst Life Sci. Collect., Excerpta Med., Index Med., Biol. Abstr., Chem. Abstr., Bibliogr. Agric., Hospit. Lit. Index. NLM W1 SO924P. CODEN SJTMAK. bk rev. adv acc. Circ 1,000. Tropical diseases, parasitology, entomology, nutritional disorders, public health, infectious diseases, immunology, clinical trials, case reports, SEAMEO symposia proceedings, technical meetings, etc.

SOVETSKOE ZDRAVOOKHRANENIE. Began in 1943. 0038-5239. Periodical. UR. Russian (summaries in English, 1959-). mo. $33.50. Victor Kamkin Inc (70867), 12224 Parklawn Drive, Rockville MD 20852. Tel (301)881-5973. Ind/Abst Index Med., Int. Aerosp. Abstr., CIS Abstr. NLM W1 SO993. *Za Sotsialisticheskoe Zdravookhranenie.*

SOZIAL- UND PRAVENTIVMEDIZIN. VFOAT Medecine Sociale et Preventive. V. 19- Jan./Feb. 1974-. 0303-8408. Periodical. articles in English, French, or German with summaries in all three languages. bm. 70.00. Vogt Schid AG, Dorcacherstrasse 39, 4501 Solothurn Switzerland. Tel 061 73 38 38. Ind/Abst Life Sci. Collect., Excerpta Med., Index Med., CIS Abstr., Chem. Abstr. NLM W1 SO999B. CODEN SZPMAA. bk rev. adv acc. Circ 1,000. Scientific, medical journal dedicated to preventive medical services, health statistics, community medicine, including occupational health and medicine and environmental health. *Praventivmedizin, 0301-0988.*

SPECIAL GRANTS PROJECTS. ABSTRACTS OF FINAL REPORTS. See Indexes/Abstracts.

SPM. SALUD PUBLICA DE MEXICO. VFOAT Salud Publica de Mexico. V. 18, No. 3- May/June. 1976-. 0036-3634. Periodical. MX. Spanish. bm. $30.00. Av Fco de P Miranda, Apartado Postal 37-500, 06696 Mexico DF Mexico. Tel 593-08-33. Ind/Abst Excerpta Med., Index Med. NLM W1 SA368. Circ 5,000. (ctrl). Public health in Mexico, endocrinology, etc. *Salud Publica de Mexico.*

STANDARD METHODS FOR THE EXAMINATION OF DAIRY PRODUCTS. Main/Corp American Public Health Association. 12th- ed. 8755-3554. US. English. ir. American Public Health Association, 1015 15th Street NW, Washington DC 20005. DD 637.

STANDARDS AND CRITERIA, MENTAL HEALTH PROGRAMS IN OKLAHOMA, ALCOHOL, DRUG, AND COMMUNITY MENTAL HEALTH. VFOAT Mental Health Programs in Oklahoma. 0732-6459. US. English. Oklahoma Department of Mental Health, PO Box 53277, Capitol Station, Oklahoma OK 73152. LC RA790.65.O5. DD 353.976600842.

THE STAR. V. 1- Sept. 1941-. 0049-2116. Periodical. US. English. bm. $2.00. Star, Box 325, Carville LA 70721. Ind/Abst Excerpta Med. NLM WX2 A5L6M3S.

STATE HEALTH PLAN. (STATE HEALTH PLAN . . .). Main/Corp Arkansas State Health Planning and Development Agency. 1979-. 0735-0880. US. English. an. Arkansas State Health Planning & Development Agency, 4815 West Markham, Little Rock AR 72201. LC RA24. DD 353.976700841.

STATE HEALTH PLAN FOR IOWA. VFOAT Iowa S.H.P. 0276-5268. US. English. Iowa State Department of Health, Lucas State Office Building, Des Moines IA 50319. LC RA395.A4. DD 362.109777. NLM W2 AI8 D6S.

STATE LEGISLATION ON SMOKING AND HEALTH. Began with 1975. 0146-017X. US. English. an. Centers for Disease Control, Center for Health Promotion and Education, Atlanta GA 30333.

STATE MEDICAL FACILITIES PLAN. Main/Corp North Carolina. Dept. of Human Resources. Division of Facility Services. 1979-1980-. 0741-0573. US. English. an. Division of Facility Services, 1330 St Mary's Street, Raleigh NC 27605. LC RA981.N82. DD 362.1109756. *North Carolina State Medical Facilities Plan.*

STATE OF COLORADO ANNUAL HIGHWAY SAFETY WORK PROGRAM. See Transportation - Roads and Traffic.

STATE PLAN PROGRESS REPORT FOR FISCAL YEAR . . . . Main/Corp South Carolina. State Dept. of Mental Health. 1979-80-. US. English. an. South Carolina State Department of Mental Health 2414, Bull Street, PO Box 485, Columbia SC 29202. LC RA790.65.S6. DD 362.209757.

STATE PLAN (SOUTH CAROLINA. STATE DEPT OF MENTAL HEALTH). Main/Corp South Carolina. State Dept. of Mental Health. US. English. an. South Carolina State Department of Mental Health, 2414 Bull Street, PO Box 485, Columbia SC 29202. LC RA790.65.S6. DD 362.209757.

STATE PLAN (UTAH. DIVISION OF MENTAL HEALTH). Main/Corp Utah. Division of Mental Health. VFOAT Utah State Plan. US. English. an. LC RA790.65.U8. DD 362.209792. *State Plan for Community Mental Health Services.*

STATISTICAL AND ACCOUNTING REPORT. See Statistics.

STATISTICAL INFORMATION RELEVANT TO THE HEALTH SERVICES. See Statistics.

STATISTICAL NEWS FROM THE HEALTH DATA CENTER. See Statistics.

STATISTICAL NOTES FOR HEALTH PLANNERS. See Statistics.

STREET PHARMACOLOGIST. See Drug Abuse and Alcoholism.

STUDY - ROYAL COMMISSION ON MATTERS OF HEALTH AND SAFETY ARISING FROM THE USE OF ASBESTOS IN ONTARIO. (STUDY). VFOAT Study Series. VAT Study Series - Royal Commission on Matters of Health and Safety Arising from the Use of Asbestos in Ontario. No. 1-. 0714-0169. Periodical. CN. English. DD 363.177509713.

SUMMARY AND ANALYSIS. RAILROAD OPERATIONAL ACCIDENTS. See Transportation - Railroads.

Public Health and Safety

SUMMARY OF ACCIDENT DATA. See Transportation - Roads and Traffic.

SUMMARY OF GRANTS AND CONTRACTS. (SUMMARY OF GRANTS AND CONTRACTS ACTIVE ON . . .). Main/Corp National Center for Health Services Research. Series/Titl NCHSR Research Management Series. Began with June 30, 1974. 0094-7741. US. English. an. US Department of Health and Human Services, Public Health Service, National Center for Health Services Research, 1-46 Park Building, 5600 Fishers Lane, Rockville MD 20857. LC RA440.6. DD 362.1072073. Vols. for 1977-1978, 1980-1983 distributed to depository libraries in microfiche. *Summary of Grants and Contracts Administered by the National Center for Health Services Research and Development, 0094-7741.*

SUMMARY OF HEALTH AND PERSONAL SOCIAL SERVICES ACCOUNTS. Main/Corp Northern Ireland. Dept. of Health and Social Services. UK. English. LC RA247.N6. DD 354.41600841. *Summary of Health Services Accounts.*

SUMMARY OF OFFICE OF HEALTH MAINTENANCE ORGANIZATIONS ANNUAL REPORT TO THE CONGRESS. Main/Corp United States. Office of Health Maintenance Organizations. 4th- 1977/78-. 0198-9324. US. English. an. US Department of Health Education and Welfare, Public Health Service, Washington DC 20857. LC RA413.5.U5. DD 353.00841.

SUMMARY OF RECEIPTS, DISBURSEMENTS, AND BALANCES. Main/Corp Florida. Division of Health. US. English. ir. PO Box 210, Jacksonville FL 32201. LC RA44.

SUMMARY OF SAFETY MANAGEMENT AUDITS. 0748-2949. US. English. an. Federal Highway Administration, 400 7th Street SW, Washington DC 20590. LC HE5623.A216. DD 363.1259.

SUMMARY STATEMENTS OF NIEHS-SUPPORTED RESEARCH PROJECTS. VFOAT Summary Statements of N.I.E.H.S.-Supported Research Projects. US. English. an. National Institute of Environmental Health Sciences, Research Triangle Park NC 27711. NLM WA 22 AA1 S956.

SUNDHEDSTILSTANDEN I GRNLAND. VFOAT The State of Health in Greenland. Danish. an. LC RA407.5.G75. DD 362.109982.

SUNDHEDSTILSTANDEN I KBENHAVN; STADSLGENS ARSBERETNING. Main/Corp Copenhagen. Stadslgeembedet. VFOAT State of Health in Copenhagen. Danish, with some English. ir. LC RA258.C6. *Arsberetning Angaende Sundhedstilstanden I Kbenhavn.*

SUPERVISOR'S SAFETY CLINIC. 0194-8717. Periodical. US. English. sm. $27.00. Bureau of Business Practice, 24 C Rope Ferry Road, Waterford CT 06386. Tel (203)442-4365.

SURVIVE (BOULDER, COLO.). (SURVIVE). Vol. 1, Issue No. 1 (Fall/1981)-. 0277-5271. Periodical. US. English. qt. $12.00 Six Issues. Survive Publications Inc, 5735 Arapahoe Avenue, Boulder CO 80303. Ind/Abst Pop. Mag. Rev. LC GF86. DD 613.69.

TABULATION OF DATA FROM NATIONAL ELECTRONIC INJURY SURVEILLANCE SYSTEM, NEISS. (TABULATION OF DATA FROM NATIONAL ELECTRONIC INJURY SURVEILLANCE SYSTEM). Main/Corp National Injury Information Clearinghouse. 0360-9952. US. English. an. US Consumer Product Safety Commission, 5401 West Bard Avenue, Washington DC 20207. LC RD93.8. DD 312.4.

TAKING CARE. 1978. US. English. mo. $15.00. Center for Consumer Health Education, 11490 Commerce Park Drive/Suite 140, Reston VA 22091. Tel (703)860-9090. Ed Judith Roman Eichner. Circ 125,000.

TALLYBOARD. See Forestry.

TECHNICAL JOURNAL - ONTARIO BRANCH. RLSSC. (TECHNICAL JOURNAL). 0227-6577. Periodical. CN. English. ir. $3.00. Royal Life Saving Society Canada, Ontario Branch, 8 York Street, Toronto Ontario M5J 1R2 Canada. DD 363.14.

TECHNICAL REPORT - NATIONAL INSTITUTE OF HEALTH AND FAMILY WELFARE, NEW DELHI. Main/Corp National Institute of Health and Family Welfare (India). 1-. 0253-6757. Monographic Series. II. English. ir. LC UNC. NLM W1 TE148E.

TERVEYDENHUOLLON LAITOKSET JA VIRANOMAISET. VFOAT Halsovardens Inrattningar och Myndigheter. 0357-8607. Fl. Finnish (Swedish). ir. Government Printing Centre, Marketing Department, PO Box 516, SF-00101 Helsinki 10 Finland. *Terveydenhuollon Organisaatio, 0357-1343.*

TERVEYDENHUOLTO. HALSOVARD. HEALTH SERVICES. Main/Corp Finland. Laakintohallitus. Series/Titl Suomen Virallinen Tilasto. VFOAT Halsovard. 1971/77-. 0303-2442. Fl. Finnish (Swedish, with summaries in English). an. Valtion Painatuskeskus, Annankatu 44, 00100 Helsinki 10 Finland. LC HA1448, RA299.F5. DD 362.109471. NLM W2 GF5 L2Y. *Yleinen Terveyden- Ja Sairaanhoito.*

TETANUS SURVEILLANCE; REPORT. Main/Corp Center for Disease Control. No. 4-. 0094-6605. US. English. Chief Special Pathogens Sections, Bacterial Diseases Division, Bureau of Epidemiology, Atlanta GA 30333. LC RA644.T4. DD 614.51280973. NLM W2 A N151K. *Tetanus Surveillance, 0094-6605.*

TEXAS COMPENDIUM OF HEALTH RELATED DATA. Main/Corp Texas. Bureau of State Health Planning & Resource Development. 1979-. US. English. an. Texas Department of Health, 1100 West 49th Street, Austin TX 78756. LC RA7.6.T4. DD 362.109764.

TEXAS PREVENTABLE DISEASE NEWS. VFOAT Preventable Disease News. June 26, 1982-. 8750-9474. Periodical. US. English. wk. Texas Department of Health, 1100 West 49th Street, Austin TX 78756-3180. *Texas Morbidity This Week.*

TIRES. Main/Corp United States. National Highway Traffic Safety Administration. Series/Titl Consumer Aid Series. 1972-. 0095-2001. US. English. Superintendent of Documents, Government Printing Office, Washington DC 20402. LC TL242. DD 629.208 S, 629.248. *Tires, 0095-2001.*

TODAY IN HEALTH PLANNING. V. 1- Jan. 22, 1979-. 0164-498X. US. English. bw. $70.00. American Health Planning Association, 1110 Vermont Avenue NW Street, Washington DC 20005. Tel (202)861-1200.

TODAY'S HEALTH (TORONTO, ONT.). (TODAY'S HEALTH). Vol. 1, No. 1 (Feb./Mar. 1983)-. 0821-6819. Periodical. CN. English. ir. $9.00. Today's Health, 296 Richmond Street West, Toronto Ontario M5V 1X2 Canada. DD 613.05.

TOPICS IN ENVIRONMENTAL HEALTH. V. 1-. 0166-2082. Monographic Series. NE. English. ir. Elsevier Science Publication, PO Box 1663 Grand Central Station, New York NY 10163. Ind/Abst Life Sci. Collect., Chem. Abstr., Bibliogr. Agric. NLM W1 TO539LM. CODEN TEHEDH.

TORO KYOTONG. See Transportation - Roads and Traffic.

TOT TALK. 0824-507X. Periodical. CN. English. ir. Alberta Safety Council, 10526 Jasper Avenue, Edmonton Alberta T5J 1Z7 Canada. DD 363.13088054.

TOTAL HEALTH. V. 2- Mar./Apr. 1980-. 0274-6743. Periodical. US. English. bm. $9.00. Total Health, 6001 Tapanga Canyon, Woodland Hills CA 91367. Tel (818)887-6484. Ed Robert L Smith. bk rev. adv acc. Circ 70,000. Dedicated to preventive health care; covers nutrition, exercise, fitness, mental health; practical tips on care of body, mind and spirit. *Trio.*

TRAFFIC ACCIDENT FACTS. See Transportation - Roads and Traffic.

TRAFFIC SAFETY ANNUAL REPORT. See Transportation - Roads and Traffic.

TRANSACTIONS OF SHASE JAPAN. See Technology (General).

TRANSMISSION/DISTRIBUTION HEALTH & SAFETY REPORT. See Engineering - Electricity, Electrical Engineering, Electronics.

TRICHINOSIS SURVEILLANCE, ANNUAL SUMMARY. Series/Titl DHHS Publication. VFOAT Trichinosis Surveillance. Began with 1966. US. English. an. US Department of Health and Human Services, Public Health Service, Centers for Disease Control, Atlanta GA 30333. LC RC186.T185. DD 614.5620973.

TRUDY NAUCHNO-PRAKTICHESKOI KONFERENTSII DERMATO-VENEROLOGOV IRKUTSKOI OBLASTI. Series/Titl Nauchnye Trudy - Irkutskii Gosudarstvennyi Meditsinskii Institut. Periodical. UR. Russian. NLM W1 NA995.

UNITED STATES IMMUNIZATION SURVEY. Series/Titl DHEW Publication. 0095-2168. US. English. an. Center for Prevention Services, Division of Immunization, Data Management Branch, Atlanta GA 30333. LC RA638. DD 614.470973. NLM W2 A N1495U.

UNITED STATES UNDERWATER FATALITY STATISTICS. See Statistics.

URBAN HEALTH. Began with V. 1, Apr. 1972. 0191-8257. Periodical. US. English. $21.00. Urban Publishing Company, 1814 Washington Road, Atlanta GA 30344. Tel (404)762-7668. Ed Harold Hamilton. Ind/Abst Hospit. Lit. Index. LC RA395.A3. DD 610. NLM W1 UR157K. bk rev. adv acc. Circ 42,000. (ctrl). Interesting articles of practical value to the health professions and students. Articles on health care delivery, medical problems, and health care programs.

UTAH STATE PLAN FOR HEALTH SERVICES. Main/Corp Utah. State Division of Health. US. English. Division of Health, 44 Medical Drive, Salt Lake City UT 84113. LC RA161. DD 362.109792.

VAGTRAFIKOLYCKOR MED PERSONSKADA. See Transportation - Roads and Traffic.

VARDFACKET. V. 1- 1977-. 0347-0911. Periodical. SW. Swedish. ir. Svenska Halso Och Sjukvardens Tjanstemannaforbund, Box 3260, 103 65 Stockholm Sweden. Tel (08)22 58 40. Ind/Abst Int. Nurs. Index. NLM W1 VA125. *Tidskrift for Sveriges Sjukskoterskor, 0037-6027.*

VD NEWS. VAT Veneral Disease News. V. 1- 1976-. US. English. qt. American Social Health Association, 260 Sheridan Avenue, Palto Alto CA 94306. *Social Health News.*

VDT NEWS. See Computers and Computer Science.

VEGETARIAN VOICE. 1974. 0271-1591. Periodical. US. English. qt. $12.00. North American Vegetarian Society, PO Box 72, Dolgeville NY 13329. Tel (518)568-7970. Ed Jennie Collura. bk rev. adv acc. Circ 3,000. Information about vegetarianism, animal rights, health, recipes, and related topics.

VERMONT STATE PLAN FOR THE PROVISION OF COMPREHENSIVE MENTAL HEALTH SERVICES : ANNUAL REVIEW AND PROGRESS REPORT. Main/Corp Vermont. Department of Mental Health. US. English. an. LC RA790.65.V5. DD 362.209743.

VERSLAG - NEDERLANDS INSTITUUT VOOR PRAEVENTIEVE GEZONDHEIDSZORG. Main/Corp Nederlands Instituut voor Praeventieve Gezondheidszorg. 1978-. NE. Dutch (English). ir. Nederlands Instituut voor Praeventieve Gezondheidszorg, Wassernaarseweg 56, 2333 Al-PO Box 124, 2300 AC Leiden Netherlands. LC RA440.85. DD 613. *Verslag.*

VERSLAG VAN DE DELEGATIE VAN HET KONINKRIJK DER NEDERLANDEN NAAR DE WERELDGEZONDHEIDSVERGADERING. Main/Corp Netherlands. Delegatie naar de Wereldgezondheidsvergadering. Dutch or English. ir. Staatsuitgeverij, S-Gravenhage Netherlands. LC RA8.

VERSLAGEN, ADVIEZEN, RAPPORTEN - MINISTERIE VAN VOLKSGEZONDHEID EN MILIEUHYGIENE. 1974-. 0166-3976. Monographic Series. NE. Dutch. ir. Staatsuitgeverij, Christoffel Plantijnstraat 1, 2515 TZ'S-Gravenhage Netherlands. NLM W2 GN4 G4V. *Volksgezondheid, 0300-1032.*

VIBRANT LIFE. Vol. 1, No. 1 (Jan./Feb. 1985)-. 0749-3509. Periodical. US. English. bm. $12.00 Domestic, $14.00 Foreign. Review and Herald Publishing Association, 55 West Oak Road,

Public Health and Safety

Hagerstown MD 21740. **DD** 613. *Your Life and Health*, 0279-2680.

THE VIDEOLOG : PROGRAMS FOR THE HEALTH SCIENCES. 1979-. 0195-7295. US. English. $35.00. Esselte Video Inc, Order Center Department 100, PO Box 978, Edison NJ 08817. **LC** R835. **DD** 016.61. **NLM** WA 18 V652. *Health Sciences Video Directory*, 0363-0781.

VITAL AND HEALTH STATISTICS. SER. 14. DATA ON NATIONAL HEALTH RESOURCES. See Statistics.

VITAL AND HEALTH STATISTICS. SERIES 3, ANALYTICAL STUDIES. See Statistics.

VITAL AND HEALTH STATISTICS. SERIES 4, DOCUMENTS AND COMMITTEE REPORTS. See Statistics.

VITAL AND HEALTH STATISTICS. SERIES 13 : DATA FROM THE NATIONAL HEALTH SURVEY. DATA ON HEALTH RESOURCES UTILIZATION. See Statistics.

VITAL STATISTICS ANNUAL REVIEW. See Statistics.

VITAL STATISTICS. PART 2D, NCHS PROCEDURES FOR MORTALITY MEDICAL DATA SYSTEM FILE PREPARATION AND MAINTENANCE. See Statistics.

VITASANA. (VITA SANA). **VFOAT** Vitasana Magazine. Yearly V. 1, No. 1, (Jan./Feb. 1984)-. 0826-2756. Periodical. CN. Italian. mo. $2.00 Each Number. Vita Sana, Suite 405/1017 Wilson Avenue, Downsview Ontario M3K 1Z1 Canada. **DD** 613.05.

THE VOICE OF THE PEDESTRIAN. **VFOAT** La Voix du Pieton, Die Stimme des Fussgangers. Periodical. Dutch (English, French, or German). sa. 20.00. General Secretary, 61/III Passage, The Hague Netherlands. **LC** HE5601. **DD** 388.41.

VOLUME OF PAPERS - ANNUAL CONFERENCE AUSTRALIAN INSTITUTE OF HEALTH SURVEYORS SOUTH AUSTRALIAN DIVISION. (ANNUAL CONFERENCE). **VFOAT** SA Health Surveyors Conference. 1st- Oct. 1974-. 0312-1267. Periodical. English. ir. **NLM** W1 AN748W.

VOPROSY INFEKTSIONNOI PATOLOGII I IMMUNOLOGII. Vyp. 3- 1963-. 0372-5952. Periodical. UR. Russian. **NLM** W1 VO628J. *Voprosy Infektsionnoi Patologii i Immunologii*.

WABOLU-BERICHTE. (WABOLU BERICHTE). 0172-7702. Monographic Series. German. ir. **Ind/Abst** Chem. Abstr. **NLM** W1. **CODEN** WBLBD6.

WARTA KESEHATAN. (WARTA DINAS KESEHATAN). **Main/Corp** Jakarta Raya (Indonesia). Dinas Kesehatan. No. 5- August 1972-. 0377-6549. Periodical. Indonesian. ir. Dinas Kesehatan, Jl Kesehatan No 100, Jakarta Indonesia. **LC** RA318.J34. **NLM** W1 WA287. *Warta Kesehatan*, 0377-6549.

WASHINGTON ACTIONS ON HEALTH (WASHINGTON, D.C. : 1981). (WASHINGTON ACTIONS ON HEALTH). Vol. 7, No. 1 (Jan. 5, 1981)-. 0194-5416. Periodical. US. English. ir. Capitol Publications, 1300 North 17th Street, Arlington VA 22209. **Tel** (703)528-5400. **NLM** W1 WA57J. *Washington ACtions on Health & Health Care Week*, 0194-5416.

WASHINGTON HEALTH RECORD. 0164-1514. Periodical. US. English. wk. $157.00. McGraw Hill Publishers, 1120 Vermont Avenue NW/ Suite 1200, Washington DC 20005. **Tel** (202)463-1700. Ed Susan Namovicz. **NLM** W1 WA603. **Circ** 300. Calendar of regulations, legislation, publications, meetings, developments and happenings in the health field.

WASHINGTON REPORT ON HEALTH LEGISLATION & REGULATION. See Law.

WASHINGTON REPORT ON MEDICINE & HEALTH. See Medicine.

WAYS FOR THE DISABLED. 0882-9659. Periodical. US. English. bm. $36.00. First Publications, PO Box 5072, Evanston IL 60204. **Tel** (312)869-7210. Ed Mark Russell and Tom Terez. bk rev. adv acc. **Circ** 30,000. For everyone who wants to bring a better life to people with mental disabilities. Approximately 7 million people are retarded, and some 10 million people are mentally ill in the United States.

THE WELLNESS JOURNAL. 0739-4411. Periodical. US. English. mo. $18.50 Domestic, $21.00 Canada. Earl Hipp, PO Box 19095, Minneapolis MN 55419. *Minnesota Wellness Journal*.

THE WELLNESS NEWSLETTER. 0740-8498. Periodical. US. English. bm. $24.00. The Wellness Newsletter, 9300 Oak Street Northeast, St Petersburg FL 33702. **Tel** (813)578-2352. Ed Carolyn Chambers Clark. bk rev. adv acc. Health promotion/ disease prevention focus. Topics includes: stress, nutrition, fitness, self-care, relationships, environment, current research, wellness, events and free resources.

WELLNESS PERSPECTIVES. Vol. 1, No. 1 (Winter 1984)-. 0748-1764. Periodical. US. English. qt. $12.00. Wellness Perspectives, 120 C Leverton Hall, University of Nebraska, Lincoln NE 68583-0837. **Tel** (402)472-1665. Ed Leor H Rottmann. **DD** 613. bk rev. **Circ** 1,200. Health promotion, wellness, health enhancement, improvement of lifestyle, self-care, family and individual well-being.

WELLSPRING. (WELLSPRING : QUARTERLY MAGAZINE OF THE SELF-CARE NETWORK). Vol. 1, No. 1 (Summer 1983)-. 0822-1049. Periodical. CN. English. qt $10.00 Domestic, $12.00 Foreign. Network Centre For Self-Care, 435 Simcoe Street, Victoria British Columbia V8V 4T4 Canada. **DD** 613.

WEST COAST LIFELINER. **Main/Corp** Royal Life Saving Society Canada. B.C. & Yukon Branch. 0225-4255. Periodical. CN. English. Free. Royal Life Saving Society, Canada B C & Yukon Branch, 100-1200 Hornby Street, Vancouver British Columbia V6Z 2E2 Canada. **DD** 363.14. (ctrl).

WHEELERS' LOG. See Physically Impaired.

WHITE CLOUD JOURNAL OF AMERICAN INDIAN MENTAL HEALTH. **VFOAT** Journal of American Indian Mental Health. Vol. 2, No. 4-. Periodical. US. English. sa. $15.00. National Center American Indian Mental Health, University South Dakota, Room 360/Julian Hall, Vermillion SD 57069. **Tel** (605)677-5298. **Ind/ Abst** Sociol. Abstr., Psychol. Abstr., Soc. Work Res. Abstr. *White Cloud Journal of American Indian/ Alaska Native Mental Health*, 0190-2482.

WHO FOOD ADDITIVES SERIES. See Food & Drink.

WHO OFFSET PUBLICATION. **VAT** World Health Organization Offset Publication. No. 1- 1973-. 0303-7878. Periodical. SZ. English. World Health Organization, 20 Ave Appia, CH-1211 Geneva Switzerland. **Ind/Abst** Excerpta Med., Index Med., Biol. Abstr. **NLM** W1 W15E. **CODEN** WHOPBZ.

WISCONSIN ANNUAL HIGHWAY SAFETY WORK PROGRAM. See Transportation - Roads and Traffic.

WISCONSIN MENTAL HYGIENE REVIEW. V. 1- Jan. 1966-. 0043-6550. Periodical. US. English. qt. Wisconsin Division of Mental Hygiene, 1 West Wilson Street, Madison WI 53702. **LC** RA790.65.W6.

WN TRENDS, HEALTH CARE AND MANAGEMENT. **VFOAT** W.N. Trends, Health Care and Management. Vol. 1, No. 1 (Jan. 1984)-. 0742-1052. Periodical. US. English. mo. $240.00. Wenz-Neely Company, 1009 South 4th Street, Louisville, KY 40203. **LC** RA410.A1. **DD** 362.1068.

WORKING PAPER (INTERNATIONAL CENTRE FOR DIARRHOEAL DISEASE RESEARCH, BANGLADESH). (WORKING PAPER). Began in 1979. Monographic Series. English. ir. **Ind/Abst** Popul. Index. **NLM** W1 WO848D. *Working Paper (Cholera Research Laboratory)*.

WORKING PAPER SERIES - HEALTH SERVICES MANAGEMENT UNIT. DEPARTMENT OF SOCIAL ADMINISTRATION. UNIVERSITY OF MANCHESTER. (WORKING PAPER SERIES). Began with: No. 1, Published in 1978. 0141-2647. Monographic Series. UK. English. ir. **NLM** W1 WO848M.

WORLD HEALTH. (WORLD HEALTH : THE MAGAZINE OF THE WORLD HEALTH ORGANIZATION). Began in 1957. 0043-8502. Periodical. US. English. ir. World Health Organization, 49 Sheridan Avenue, Albany NY 12210. **Tel** (518)436-9686. **Ind/Abst** Energy Inf. Abstr., Environ. Abstr., Cumul. Index Nurs. Allied Health Lit., Int. Aerosp. Abstr., Public Aff. Inf. Serv. Bull., Read. Guide Period. Lit., Mag. Index, Pollut. Abstr. Indexes. **NLM** W2 MW6 W9W. (cum index). Written for the lay reader with a general interest in public health, and reflects not only WHO activities around the world but also the broad themes of health and development. *Who Newsletter*.

WORLD HEALTH FORUM. V. 1-. 0251-2432. Periodical. English. ir. World Health Organization, Distribution & Sales Service, 1211 Geneva 27 Switzerland. **Ind/Abst** Life Sci. Collect., Excerpta Med., Energy Inf. Abstr., Environ. Abstr., Biol. Abstr., Public Aff. Inf. Serv. Bull. **LC** RA441. **DD** 362.105. **NLM** W1 WO873. **CODEN** WHFODN. Provides a medium for the presentation and discussion of new concepts in public health and new approaches to health problems.

WORLD HEALTH ORGANIZATION TECHNICAL REPORT SERIES. (TECHNICAL REPORT SERIES). No. 1-. 0512-3054. Monographic Series. US. English (French). bw. $33.00. World Health Organization, PO Box 5284, Church Street Station, New York NY 10249. **Tel** (202)861-3200. **Ind/Abst** Life Sci. Collect., Excerpta Med., Index Med., Biol. Abstr. **LC** RA8. **NLM** W2 MW6 W9T. **CODEN** WHOTAC.

WORLD HEALTH STATISTICS ANNUAL. See Statistics.

WORLD HEALTH STATISTICS QUARTERLY. See Statistics.

WORLD OF ASP. **Main/Corp** American Self-Protection Association. V. 1- Nov./Dec. 1975-. 0380-4712. Periodical. CN. English. bm. Stewart Fraser, PO Box 302, Kingston NC B0P 1RO Canada.

WORLD SMOKING & HEALTH. See Tobacco.

WORLDWIDE REPORT. EPIDEMIOLOGY. **VFOAT** Epidemiology. No. 146 (5 July 1979)-. 0740-0918. Periodical. US. English (Multilingual). National Technical Information Service, 5285 Port Royal Road, Springfield VA 22161. **NLM** ZWA 100 E64. Available on microfilm. *World Epidemiology Review*.

YAMAGUCHI-KEN EISEI KENKYUJO NEMPO. Japanese. an. **LC** RA532.Y35.

YEAR BOOK OF INFECTIOUS DISEASES. See Yearbooks, Almanacs, Directories.

YEAR BOOK - ROYAL SOCIETY OF TROPICAL MEDICINE AND HYGIENE. See Yearbooks, Almanacs, Directories.

YELLOW-FEVER VACCINATING CENTRES FOR INTERNATIONAL TRAVEL. **Main/Corp** World Health Organization. **VFOAT** Centres de Vaccination Contre la Fievre Jaune pour les Voyages Internationaux. 0510-8675. English (French). ir. **LC** RA644.Y4. **DD** 614.541. **NLM** WC 22 MW6 W9C.

YORAN - KOKURITSU KOSHU EISEIIN. **Main/Corp** Kokuritsu Koshu Eiseiin, Tokyo. Japanese. ir. 6-1 Shirokanedai 4, Minato-ku Tokyo 108 Japan. **LC** RA532.T64.

ZDRAVOOHRANENIE KIRGIZII. (ZDRAVOOKHRANENIE KIRGIZII). 0132-8867. Periodical. UR. Russian. bm. $33.50. Victor Kamkin Inc (77393), 12224 Parklawn Drive, Rockville MD 20852. **Tel** (301)881-5973. **Ind/Abst** Int. Aerosp. Abstr., Chem. Abstr., Index Med. **LC** RA421. **NLM** W1 ZD853K. **CODEN** ZDKIDZ.

ZDRAVOOKHRANENIE ROSSIJSKOJ FEDERACII. (ZDRAVOOKHRANENIE ROSSIISKOJ FEDERATSII). Vol. 1- 1957-. 0044-197X. Periodical. UR. Russian. mo. $32.50. Victor Kamkin Inc (73164), 12224 Parklawn Drive, Rockville MD 20852. **Tel** (301)881-5973. **Ind/Abst** Int. Aerosp. Abstr., Index Med. **NLM** W1 ZD854.

ZDRAVOTNICKE NOVINY. Periodical. US. Czech. wk. Artia, Ve Smeckach 30, PO Box 790, Praha 1 Czechoslovakia.

ZDRAVSTVENA ZASTITA. Vol. 1- 1972-. 0350-3208. Periodical. Serbo-Croatian -R. ir. **NLM** W1 ZD8634.

ZDROWIE PUBLICZNE. Began publication with Aug. 1885 issue. Periodical. PL. Polish (tables of contents also in Russian and English). mo. ARS Polona, Krakowskie Przedmiescie 7, 00-068 Warsaw Poland. LC RA421.

ZEITSCHRIFT FUR DIE GESAMTE HYGIENE UND IHRE GRENZGEBIETE. Vol. 1-. 0049-8610. Periodical. GE. German (summaries in English and Russian). mo. Kunst & Wissen Erich Bieber, Dufourstrasse 51, CH-8008 Zurich Switzerland. Tel 011-41-1-69 44 20. Ind/Abst Life Sci. Collect., Excerpta Med., Coal Abstr., Index Med., CIS Abstr., Chem. Abstr. LC RA421. NLM W1 ZE265. CODEN ZHYGAM.

ZEITSCHRIFT FUR HEILPADAGOGIK. See Education (General) - Special Aspects of Education.

ZEITSCHRIFT FUR VERKEHRSSICHERHET. See Transportation - Roads and Traffic.

ZENTRALBLATT FUR BAKTERIOLOGIE, MIKROBIOLOGIE UND HYGIENE. 1. ABT. ORIGINALE B, HYGIENE. VFOAT Hygiene. VAT Zentralblatt fur Bakteriologie, Mikrobiologie and Hygiene. Erste Abteilung Originale B, Hygiene. Began with issue for June 1980. 0174-3015. Periodical. GW. English (and German). bm. Gustav Fischer Verlag, Postfach 720143, D-7000 Stuttgart 70 West Germany. Ind/Abst Excerpta Med., Chem. Abstr., Index Med., Life Sci. Collect., Pestdoc, Ringdoc, Sel. Water Resour. Abstr., Vetdoc, Curr. Contents. LC QR46 .Z453. DD 616.0105. CODEN ZAOMDC. Zentralblatt fur Bakteriologie. 1 Abt. Originale B, Hygiene, Krakenhaushygiene, Betriebshygiene, Praventive Medizin, 0172-5602.

ZENTRALBLATT FUR BAKTERIOLOGIE, MIKROBIOLOGIE UND HYGIENE. 1. ABT. : REFERATE, MEDIZINISCHE MIKROBIOLOGIE, PARASITOLOGIE, HYGIENE, PRAVENTIVE MEDIZIN. HYGIENE, PREVENTIVE MEDICINE. See Indexes/Abstracts.

ZHONGHUA FANGSHE YIXUE YU FANGHU ZAZHI. See Medicine - Radiology.

ZOO-SANITARY SITUATION IN MEMBER COUNTRIES IN . . . . See Veterinary Medicine, Animal Culture.

ZYCIE I ZDROWIE. No. 1- 6, Jan. 1974-. Periodical. Polish. ir. Czasopism RSW Prasa-Ksiazka-Ruch, Wronia 23 00840 Konto PKO NR, 1-6-100024 Warszawa Poland. LC RA421.

PUBLISHING

AADE EDITORS' JOURNAL. VFOAT AADE Journal. VAT American Association of Dental Editors Editors' Journal. V. 1- 1974-. 0160-6999. Periodical. US. English. ty. American Association of Dental Editors, 30 East 42nd Street/Suite 1606, New York NY 10017. Ind/Abst Index Dent. Lit. NLM W1 A102BJ. Bulletin - American Association of Dental Editors, 0569-2555; Transactions - American Association of Dental Editors.

ABA BOOK BUYER'S HANDBOOK. VAT American Booksellers Association Book Buyer's Handbook. 0277-3104. US. English. an. American Booksellers Association, 122 East 42nd Street, New York NY 10168. LC Z475. DD 070.502573. Book Buyer's Handbook.

ACP NOTEBOOK. (A C P NOTEBOOK). Main/Corp Association of Canadian Publishers. VAT Association of Canadian Publishers Notebook. No. 10- March 1978-. 0705-6621. Periodical. CN. English. mo. Free. 70 The Esplanade/3rd Floor, Toronto Ontario M5E 1R2 Canada. DD 070.50971. Notebook, 0705-6613.

AFRICAN BOOK PUBLISHING RECORD. (THE AFRICAN BOOK PUBLISHING RECORD). V. 1- Jan. 1975-. 0306-0322. Periodical. UK. English. qt. Hans Zell Publishers, PO Box 56, Oxford OX1 3EL England. Ed Hans M Zell. Ind/Abst MLA Int. Bibliogr. Books Artic. Mod. Lang. Lit. LC Z465.7. DD 070.573096. Bibliography of African published titles. Features news, reports, interviews, articles, book and magazine reviews. A buying and acquisitions tool.

AL-NASHIR AL-ARABI. VFOAT Arab Publisher. Periodical. Arabic. qt. 50. P O Box 4607, Tarabulus Libya. LC Z464.A65.

ALBION. See Printing.

AMERICAN BOOK PUBLISHING RECORD. VFOAT BPR. V. 1- Feb. 1960-. 0002-7707. Periodical. US. English. mo. $65.00. RR Bowker Company, 1180 Avenue of the Americas, New York NY 10036, (subscription address: Bowker Subscription Service, PO Box 1429 Riverton NJ 08077). Tel (800)521-8110. Ind/Abst Abstr. Bull. Inst. Paper Chem. LC Z1219. DD 015. NLM Z 1219 A512.

AMERICAN BOOK PUBLISHING RECORD CEASED. (AMERICAN BOOK PUBLISHING RECORD. BPR CUMULATIVE). VFOAT BPR Cumulative, B.P.R. Cumulative. 1960-1964-. 0002-7707. US. English. an. R R Bowker Company, PO Box 1807, Ann Arbor MI 48106. Tel (800)521-0600. LC Z1201. DD 015.73.

AMERICAN BOOK PUBLISHING RECORD. BPR CUMULATIVE. VFOAT BPR Cumulative. 1973-. 0002-7707. Periodical. US. English. an. R R Bowker, 205 East 42nd Street, New York NY 10017. DD 015.73. Each issue contains an index to its own contents - no vol index - loose.

ANNUAIRE - SOCIETE DE DEVELOPPEMENT DU LIVRE ET DU PERIODIQUE. See Yearbooks, Almanacs, Directories.

ANNUAL REPORT - ASSOCIATION OF AMERICAN PUBLISHERS. (ANNUAL REPORT). Main/Corp Association of American Publishers. 0276-5349. US. English. an. Association of American Publishers Inc, 1 Park Avenue, New York NY 10016. LC Z477. DD 070.50973.

ASNE : PROCEEDINGS OF THE . . . CONVENTION OF THE AMERICAN SOCIETY OF NEWSPAPER EDITORS. Main/Corp American Society of Newspaper Editors. Convention. VFOAT A.S.N.E., Convention of the American Society of Newspaper Editors. 1982-. US. English. an. $25.00. American Society of Newspaper Editors, PO Box 17004, Washington DC 20041. Tel (703)620-6087. Ed Elise Burroughs. Circ 1,200. Proceedings of the annual convention. Problems of Journalism (1948).

THE ASSOCIATION OF AMERICAN UNIVERSITY PRESSES DIRECTORY. See Yearbooks, Almanacs, Directories.

AUSTRALIAN BOOKSELLER & PUBLISHER. Began with V. 51, 1971 issue. Periodical. AT. English. ir. $5.90. D W Thorpe Pty Ltd, PO Box 146 20-24 Stokes Street, Port Melbourne 3207 Australia. Tel (03) 645 1511. Ed Michael Webster. LC Z533.7. DD 070.50994. bk rev. adv acc. Circ 8,000. (ctrl). Australian and New Zealand equivalent to "Publisher's Weekly" and the British "Bookseller". Ideas: Book Trade Journal.

THE AUSTRALIAN LITHOGRAPHER, PRINTER AND PACKAGER. See Printing.

AUTHOR-PUBLISHER NEWS & VIEWS. (AUTHOR/PUBLISHER NEWS & VIEWS). No. 1- Aug. 1975-. 0381-727X. CN. English. an. McGraw-Hill Ryerson Ltd, 330 Progress Avenue, Scarborough Ontario M1P 2Z5 Canada. DD 070.50971.

AUTHOR'S NEWS. No. 1 (Mar. 1981)-. 0713-0171. Periodical. CN. English. mo. $9.00. Author's News, 4340 Coldfall Road, Richmond British Columbia V7C 1P8 Canada. DD 808.0205.

BEGINNING (IOWA CITY, IOWA). (BEGINNING). Vol. 1, No. 1 & 2 (Spring/Summer 1983)-. 0739-6694. Periodical. US. English. qt. $10.00. Community Writers Association, Department, P-1 PO Box 2191, Iowa City IA 52244.

THE BEST IN COVERS & POSTERS. Series/Titl Print Casebooks. VFOAT Best in Covers and Posters. Began with: 2nd Ed. (1977). US. English. be. R C Publications, 6400 Goldsboro Road Northwest, Washington DC 20034. Best in Covers, Best in Posters.

BIBLIOGRAPHIE DER UBERSETZUNGEN DEUTSCHSPRACHIGER WERKE. See Bibliographies.

BNA ONLINE. VFOAT B.N.A. Online. VAT Bureau of National Affairs Online. Vol. 1, No. 1 (Apr. 1984)-. 0747-5438. Periodical. US. English. bm. Free. BNA Online, 1231 25th Street NW, Washington DC 20037.

BOEKBLAD. Volume 147, No. 40 (Oct. 3, 1980)-. 0167-4765. Periodical. NE. Dutch. WYT Uitgevers, Postbus 268, 3000 AG Rotterdam Netherlands. LC Z2435. Nieuwsblad voor den Boekhandel.

BOOK & PERIODICAL DEVELOPMENT COUNCIL NEWSLETTER CEASED. No. 1-No. 6. 0701-0931. Periodical. CN. English. Book & Periodical Development Council, 86 Bloor Street West/Suite 215, Toronto Ontario M5S 1M5 Canada. DD 070.50971.

BOOK NEWS FOR BOOKSELLERS AND LIBRARIANS. No. 1- Oct. 1975-. 0381-7261. Periodical. CN. English. qt. McGraw-Hill Ryerson Ltd, 330 Progress Avenue, Scarborough Ontario M1P 2Z5 Canada. DD 070.50971.

BOOK PUBLISHERS DIRECTORY. See Yearbooks, Almanacs, Directories.

THE BOOK PUBLISHING ANNUAL. 1984 Ed.-. 0000-0787. US. English. an. R R Bowker Company, 205 East 42nd Street, New York NY 10017. LC Z477. Publishers Weekly Yearbook, 0000-0469.

BOOKS IRELAND. No. 1- Mar. 1976-. 0376-6039. IE. English. ir. $14.00. Books Ireland, 683 Osceola Avenue, St Paul MN 55105. Tel (612)647-5678. Ed Bernard Share. Ind/Abst Libr. Inf. Sci. Abstr. LC Z331.7. DD 658.80907057309415. bk rev. adv acc. Circ 5,000. Ireland's leading magazine of book reviews and news about publishing in Ireland. Available in US from Irish Books and Media.

BORSENBLATT FUR DEN DEUTSCHEN BUCHHANDEL. Year 1- 1834-. Periodical. SZ. German. ir. $50.56. Kunst & Wissen Erich Bieber, Dufourstrasse 51, CH-8008 Zurich Switzerland. Tel 01/69 44 20.

BUCH DER ZEIT. Began publication in 1959. 0007-2761. Periodical. German (English). mo. Free. Buchexport, Leninstrasse 16, DDR-7010 Leipzig East Germany. Tel 71370. DD 015. bk rev. adv acc. Circ 12,000. (ctrl). An illustrated selection of the most important publications, editors' articles regarding the publishing programme and the authors. Deutscher Buch-Kurier.

BUCH UND BUCHHANDEL IN ZAHLEN. Vol. 1-. 0068-3051. GW. German. an. Buchhandler Vereinigung GMBH, Grosser Hirschgraben 17-21, 6 Frankfurt 1 - West Germany. LC Z313.

A C P NEWSLETTER. Main/Corp Association of Canadian Publishers. V. 4, No. 3- Apr. 1976-. 0700-3579. Periodical. CN. English. Association of Canadian Publishers, 56 the Esplanade/Suite 401, Toronto Ontario M5E 1A8 Canada. DD 070.50971. I P A Newsletter, 0316-3792.

CABELL'S DIRECTORY OF PUBLISHING OPPORTUNITIES IN EDUCATION. See Yearbooks, Almanacs, Directories.

CALIFORNIA PUBLISHER. 0008-1434. Periodical. US. English. mo. $15.00. California Newspaper Publishing Association, 1127 11th Street/Suite 1040, Sacramento CA 95814. Tel (916)443-5991. LC PN4700. DD 071.94.

CANADIAN BOOK PUBLISHERS' COUNCIL COMMUNIQUE. V. 3- Jan. 1976-. 0384-6873. CN. English. mo. Free. Canadian Book Publishers' Council, 45 Charles Street East/Suite 701, Toronto Ontario M4Y 1S2 Canada. DD 070.57306271. Newsletter, 0319-5104.

CANADIAN COMMUNITY PUBLISHER. (THE CANADIAN COMMUNITY PUBLISHER). Jan./Feb. 1972-. 0045-4583. Periodical. CN. English. wk. $10.00. Canadian Community Newspaper Association, 88 University Avenue/Suite 705, Toronto Ontario M5J 1T6 Canada. Tel (416)598-4277. Ed Kay Dills. bk rev. adv acc. Circ 2,000. (ctrl). Canadian Weekly Publisher, 0008-5316.

CANADIAN ISBN AGENCY. See Yearbooks, Almanacs, Directories.

CANADIAN REPORT. (THE CANADIAN REPORT). No. 1- June 1, 1978-. 0705-5137. Periodical. CN. English. $50. E C Witmer, The Canadian Report, 1607-145 Marlee Avenue, Toronto Ontario M6B 3H3 Canada. DD 070.50971.

Publishing

CASSELL AND PUBLISHERS ASSOCIATION DIRECTORY OF PUBLISHING IN GREAT BRITAIN, THE COMMONWEALTH, IRELAND, SOUTH AFRICA & PAKISTAN. See Yearbooks, Almanacs, Directories.

CATALOG AGE. Vol. 1, No 1 (March 1984)-. 0740-3119. Periodical. US. English. qt. Free to qualified subscribers, $16.00 Others. Catalog Age, PO Box 4006, New Canaan CT 06840-4006.

THE CATALOG MARKETER. 1981. 0730-9937. Periodical. US. English. bw. $159.00. Maxwell Sroge Publishing Inc, 731 North Cascade, Colorado Springs CO 80903. Tel (303)633-5556. Ed Cecile Wood. (ctrl) How to produce a catalog. Expert and proven methods of catalog production: art, copy, printing, lists, law, photography, creative, fulfillment.

CATALOGUE DE L'EDITEUR OFFICIEL DU QUEBEC. Main/Corp Quebec Official Publisher. 1974-. 0316-1560. Periodical. CN. English (French). an. Quebec Official Publisher, 675 Saint-Cyrille Boulevard, Quebec Quebec G1R Canada. DD 015.714. *Publications - Bureau de l'Editeur Officiel du Quebec, 0316-1579.*

CHU PAN SHIH LIAO. VFOAT Chuban Shiliao. 1-. Periodical. CH. Chinese. ir. 0.60. Hsin Hua Shu Tien, Shang-hai Fa Hsing So, Shang-hai China. LC Z462.7. DD 079.51.

COLLANA DI STUDI SULLA PUBBLICITA. 1- 1957-. 0413-4028. Periodical. IT. Italian. ir. Via Giovanni Pascoli 55, 20133 Milano Italy.

CONTEMPORARY AUTHORS BIBLIOGRAPHICAL SERIES. See Bibliographies.

COSMEP EAST NEWSLETTER. Main/Corp Committee of Small Magazine/Press Editors & Publishers. East Region. 0148-6152. Periodical. US. English. qt. Free to Members, $10.00 Others. Cosmep-East, PO Box 237, Youngstown OH 44501.

COSMEP NEWSLETTER (SAN FRANCISCO, CALIF. : 1981). (COSMEP NEWSLETTER). V. 12, No. 6 (March 1981)-. Periodical. US. English. mo. $85.00. Committee Small Editors & Publishers, PO Box 703, San Francisco CA 94101. Tel (415)922-9490. Ed Richard Morris. bk rev. Circ 1,200. Newsletter for small book and periodical publishers; published by COSMEP, the national trade association for small publishers. *Independent Publisher.*

CPH COMMENTATOR. Main/Corp Concordia Publishing House. 0007-8905. Periodical. US. English. qt. Concordia Publ House, 3558 South Jefferson Avenue, St Louis MO 63118.

CURIOSPRESS INTERNATIONAL. No. 1- 1974-. 0398-8074. FR. French, English, German, Spanish, and Italian. ir. Pierre Birukoff, c/o Infos A1 International, BP 127, 75563 Cedex France. LC Z282. DD 011.

DIRECTORIO DE EDITORES Y DISTRIBUIDORES LATINOAMERICANOS. See Yearbooks, Almanacs, Directories.

DIRECTORY - ASSOCIATION OF AMERICAN UNIVERSITY PRESSES. See Yearbooks, Almanacs, Directories.

DIRECTORY - ASSOCIATION OF CANADIAN PUBLISHERS. See Yearbooks, Almanacs, Directories.

DIRECTORY OF MEMBERS - FEDERATION OF INDIAN PUBLISHERS. See Yearbooks, Almanacs, Directories.

DIRECTORY OF MEMBERS - SINGAPORE BOOK PUBLISHERS ASSOCIATION. See Yearbooks, Almanacs, Directories.

DIRECTORY OF PUBLISHING OPPORTUNITIES IN JOURNALS AND PERIODICALS. See Yearbooks, Almanacs, Directories.

LES EDITEURS ET DIFFUSEURS DE LANGUE FRANCAISE. VFOAT Repertoire International des Editeurs et Diffuseurs de Langue Francaise. Began with 1979 Vol. 0245-1875. FR. French. an. Cercle de la Librairie, 35 rue Gregoire-de-Tours, 75006 Paris France. LC Z282. DD 015.44. *Repertoire International des Editeurs et Diffuseurs de Langue Francaise.*

EDITING HISTORY. Vol. 1, No. 1 (June 1984) -. 0883-3532. Periodical. US. English. sa. $25.00. R V Schnucker, Northeast Missouri State University, LB115 Kirksville MO 63501. Tel (816)785-4665. Ed R V Schnucker. DD 905. bk rev. adv acc. Circ 200. A newsletter for history editors, covering all aspects of publishing.

EL EDITOR. Periodical. US. English (a bilingual publication). wk. $35.00. Amigo Publications, 1191-16th Street, Lubbock TX 79401. Tel (806)763-3841.

L'EDITORE. Yearly V. 1- Jan. 1978-. Periodical. IT. Italian. mo. $23.76. Ed Fabbri, V Mecenate 91, 20138 Milano Italy. LC Z344. DD 070.50945.

THE EDITORIAL EYE. Began in 1978. 0193-7383. Periodical. US. English. ir. $46.20 Domestic, $51.45 Canada, $57.75 Foreign. Editorial Experts Inc, 85 South Bragg Street/Suite 400, Alexandria VA 22312. Tel (703)642-3040. Ed Bruce Boston. bk rev. Circ 2,000. Newsletter for publications professionals. Focuses on editorial standards and practices, covers writing, editing, proofreading, grammar style and usage. *Freelancer's Newsletter, 0016-0636.*

ELECTRONIC PUBLISHER. No. 1 (Aug. 6, 1981)-. 0277-9846. Periodical. US. English. sm. $395.00. Paul Kagan Associates Inc, 126 Clock Tower Place, Carmel CA 93923. Tel (408)624-1536. Ed Larry Garbrandt. Newsletter on publishing via television. Latest developments in videotex and newspaper-cable joint ventures.

ELECTRONIC PUBLISHING AND BOOKSELLING. (ELECTRONIC PUBLISHING AND BOOKSELLING : EPB). VFOAT EPB. Vol. 1, No. 1 (June 1983)-. 0737-5336. Periodical. US. English. bm. $75.00. Oryx Press, 2214 North Central at Encanto/Suite 103, Phoenix AZ 85004. Tel (602)254-6156. Ed Meyers. Ind/Abst Electron. Pub. Abstr. DD 070. bk rev. adv acc. Circ 500. (ctrl). Covers computer systems serving publishers and booksellers in activities from editing and composition to information dissemination; designed for informaton professionals interested in current technology.

ELECTRONIC PUBLISHING REVIEW. Vol. 1, No. 1 (Mar. 1981)-. 0260-6658. Periodical. UK. English. qt. $120.00. Learned Information Ltd, 143 Old Marlton Pike, Medford NJ 08055. Tel (609)654-6266. Ind/Abst Electron. Commun. Abstr. J., ISMEC Bull., Pollut. Abstr. Indexes, Saf. Sci. Abstr. J., Fluidex, Predicasts, Comput. Control Abstr., Electr. Electron. Abstr., Sci. Abstr. Sect. A. Phys. Abstr., Libr. Inf. Sci. Abstr., Print. Abstr., Electron. Pub. Abstr. LC Z286.E43. DD 070.502854. CODEN EPURDX.

EPHEMERA NEWS. 0734-3337. Periodical. US. English. qt. Ephemera Society of America Membership Lois Meredith, PO Box 943, Hillsboro NH 03244.

EXHIBITS DIRECTORY - ASSOCIATION OF AMERICAN PUBLISHERS. See Yearbooks, Almanacs, Directories.

FLORIDA NEWS MEDIA DIRECTORY. See Yearbooks, Almanacs, Directories.

THE FOLIO 400. VFOAT Folio Four Hundred. 0742-0625. US. English. an. $25.00. Folio Publishing Corporation, 125 Elm Street, PO Box 697, New Canaan CO 06840. LC Z286.P4. DD 070.50973.

FOR IMMEDIATE RELEASE. Began with June 1976 issue. 0701-0664. Periodical. CN. English. ir. Free. Canadian Book Information Centre, 70 The Esplanade, Toronto Ontario M5E 1R2 Canada. DD 070.50971. (ctrl).

GIORNALE DELLA LIBRERIA. 0017-0216. Periodical. IT. Italian. mo. Editrice Bibliografica, Viale Vittorio Veneto 24, 20124 Milano Italy. Tel (02)6597950. Ed Carlo Enrico Rivolta. LC Z2345. adv acc. Circ 5,000. Organ of Italian Publisher Association. Covers book publishing and marketing. Three sections: publishers, booksellers, librarians. Lists the books of the month - about 1,000. *Giornale Della Libreria, Della Tipografia, e Della Arti e Industrie Affini.*

GUIA DAS EDITORAS BRASILEIRAS. 1978-. BL. Portuguese. ir. Sindicato Nacional dos Editores de Livros, Av Rio Branco 37-150 Andar, 20.000 Rio de Janeiro Brazil. LC Z521.5. DD 070.502581.

GUIDE TO PUBLISHERS AND RELATED INDUSTRIES IN JAPAN. JA. English. ir. Free. Publishers Association for Cultural Exchange, No 2-1 Saragaku-cho 1 chome Chiyoda-ku, 101 Tokyo Japan. Tel (03)291-5685. Ed Hiroyasu Ochiai. LC Z463.5. DD 070.502552. adv acc. Circ 4,000.

HSIN SHU YUEH KAN. First published in Oct. 1983. Periodical. CH. Chinese. mo. $15.00. Yu Chen Shu Pao She 6, 230 Lane Yen Ping S Road, Tai-Pei Shih Taiwan. LC Z464.T357. DD 079.51249.

HUMBER MAGAZINE WORLD. Spring 1980-. 0711-3269. Periodical. CN. English. qt. Free to Canadian Editors Publishers and Freelance Writers, Others $2.00 Per Issue. Humber College of Applied Arts and Technology, 205 Humber College Boulevard, Rexdale Ontario M9W 5L7 Canada. DD 070.57205.

IDEAS FOR EDITORS. 1- 1978-. US. English. an. Decathlon Books, 1500 Carter Avenue/PO Box 591, Ashland NY 41101. Ed David E Carter.

ILLINOIS SMALL PRESS DIRECTORY. See Yearbooks, Almanacs, Directories.

THE INDIAN PUBLISHER AND BOOKSELLER. VFOAT Pustaka-Vyavasayi Patrika. V. 1- Nov. 1950-. 0019-6223. Periodical. II. English. mo. Indian Publisher and Bookseller, Popular Book Depot, Bombay 7 India. LC Z457.

THE INDIANA PUBLISHER. 0019-6711. Periodical. US. English. mo. $5.00. Hoosier State Press Association Inc, 1542 Consolidate Building/116 North Penn, Indianapolis IN 46204. Tel (317)637-3966.

INFORMATION EXPRESS. Began in 1983. Periodical. US. English. mo. National Standards Association Inc, 5161 River Road, Bethesda MD 20816. Tel (301)951-1310.

INTERNATIONAL DIRECTORY OF SCHOLARLY PUBLISHERS. See Yearbooks, Almanacs, Directories.

INTERNATIONAL PUBLISHING NEWSLETTER. Vol. 1, No. 1 (Oct. 1983)-. 0740-7513. Periodical. US. English. mo. $60.00. Publisher Services Inc, 80 South Early Street, Alexandria VA 22304. Tel (703)823-6966.

INTERNATIONALES VERLAGSADRESSBUCH. See Yearbooks, Almanacs, Directories.

ISRAEL BOOK TRADE DIRECTORY. See Yearbooks, Almanacs, Directories.

IZDATELSKOE DELO. Began in 1973. Periodical. UR. Russian (Multilingual). mo. 0.06 Single Issue. Kniga, K-9 Ul Nezhdanovoi 8/10, Moskva USSR. LC Z279. *Izdatelskoe Delo, Knigovedenie, Knizhnaia Torgovlia l Gosudarstvennaia Bibliografiia.*

JERSEY PUBLISHER. 0021-5961. Periodical. US. English. mo. $12.00. New Jersey Press, Association of Rutgers University, College Avenue at Somerset, New Brunswick NJ 09901.

THE KEMBLE OCCASIONAL. See Printing.

KNIZNY MAGAZIN. Czech. ir. 24.00. Zdruzeni Slvenskych Vdavatelstiev a Podnikov, Knizneho Obchodu Vo Vydavatelstve Obzor, Ul Cs Armady 29 A, Bratislava Czechoslavakia. LC Z301.7.

LEGAL BRIEFS FOR EDITORS, PUBLISHERS, AND WRITERS. V. 1- June 1977-. 0149-1695. Periodical. US. English. $48.00. McGraw Hill Book Co, Suite 2600/1221 Avenue of the Americas, New York NY 10020. LC KF2750.A15. DD 343.730998.

MAGAZINE AGE. V. 1- Jan. 1980-. 0194-2506. Periodical. US. English. mo. $36.00. Magazine Age, PO Box 4006, 125 Elm Street, New Canaan CT 06840. Tel (203)972-0761.

MAGAZINE & BOOKSELLER. VFOAT Magazine and Bookseller. V. 37, No. 2 (Feb. 1982)-. 0744-3102. Periodical. US. English. mo. North American Publishing Company, 401 North Broad Street, Philadelphia PA 19108. Tel (215)238-5300. *Marketing Bestsellers, 0164-9876; Profitways.*

MAGAZINE DESIGN & PRODUCTION. See Printing.

MAGAZINE PEOPLE. '84-. 8756-3827. US. English. an. $50.00. Min Publishing Company, 18 East 53rd Street, New York NY 10022. Tel (212)751-2670. Ed William E Barlow. LC Z479. DD 070.502573. A who's who of magazine publishing.

Publishing

MASSON TODAY. Main/Corp Masson Publishing USA. V. 1-. 0272-5541. Periodical. US. English. qt. Masson Publishing USA Inc, 14 East 60 Street, New York NY 10022.

MEDIA MANAGEMENT MONOGRAPH. No. 1- Sept. 1978-. 0192-7663. Monographic Series. US. English. ir. $147.00. Jim Mann and Associates, 9 Mt Vernon Drive, Gales Ferry CT 06335. Tel (203)464-2511. Ed Jim Mann. Circ 310. Each issue treats one aspect of periodical publishing and consists of an interview with an expert, an in-depth analysis of the subject and a check list for practical application.

MEDIA SCANDINAVIA. 16.- Udg. 0076-5821. DK. Danish (English). ir. 415.00. Danske Reklamebueauers Brancheforening, Gl Strand 44, 1202 Kbenhavn Denmark. Tel (01)134444. Ed Borge O Madsen. LC Z6941. adv acc. Circ 2,100. Covering all Scandinavian countries. Information on newspapers, magazines, tradepapers, etc. Data on readerships rates circulations and production details. *Media.*

MEMBRES DE LA C A P A C CEASED. Main/Corp Composers, Authors and Publishers Association of Canada. VFOAT C A P A C Membership List. 1975-1982. 0319-4035. CN. text in French and English. an. Composers Authors and Publishers Association of Canada, 1240 Bay Street, Toronto Ontario M5R 2C2 Canada. DD 780.6271. *C A P A C Members, 0317-8145.*

MEMORANDUM - AMERICAN NEWSPAPER PUBLISHERS ASSOCIATION. Main/Corp American Newspaper Publishers Association. Began with Mar. 1976 issue. 0270-9864. Periodical. US. English. $100.00. American Newspaper Publishers Association, PO Box 17407, Dulles International Airport, Washington DC 20041. Tel (703)648-1109. Ed James E Donahue. LC Z675.N37. DD 026.0713. bk rev. adv acc. Circ 10,000. (ctrl). Journal of the American Newspapers Association, content includes press freedom, government affairs, circulation, advertising, labor and personnel, telecommunications, newsprint, promotion, education, news editorial, production technologies, and readerships. *Library Bulletin, 0402-0170.*

MEXICO EDITOR. Annual 1979-. MX. Spanish. ir. LC Z497. DD 070.50972.

MICROFORM MARKET PLACE. VFOAT MMP, Microform Market Place. 1974/75-. 0362-0999. US. English. be. $34.95. Meckler Publishing, 11 Ferry Lane West, Westport CT 06880. Tel (203)226-6967. LC Z286.M5. DD 070.57. NLM Z 286.M5 M619. adv acc. Circ 1,000. Directory to worldwide micropublishers.

MICROFORM REVIEW. V. 1- Jan. 1972-. 0002-6530. Periodical. US. English. qt. $67.50. Meckler Publishing, 11 Ferry Lane West, Westport CT 06880. Tel (203)226-6967. Ed Thomas A Bourke. Ind/Abst Comput. Control Abstr., Electr. Electron. Abstr., Sci. Abstr. Sect. A. Phys. Abstr., Libr. Lit., Inf. Sci. Abstr., Libr. Inf. Sci. Abstr., Curr. Index J. Educ., Phys. Abstr. LC Z265. DD 025.179. CODEN MFRVA. (cum index). bk rev. adv acc. Available on microfiche. Reviews micropublications for libraries.

MICROLOG NEWSLETTER. June 1979-. 0708-790X. Periodical. CN. English. mo. Free with Subscription to Microlog Index. Micromedia Ltd, 144 Front Street West, Toronto Ontario M5J 1G2 Canada. DD 070.50971.

MISSOURI PRESS NEWS. Began publication in 1938. 0026-6671. Periodical. US. English. mo. $7.50. Missouri Press Association, 802 Locust, Columbia MO 65201. Tel (314)449-4167. Ed Doug Crews. adv acc. Circ 1,100. (ctrl). Official publication of Missouri Press Association for newspaper publishers, editors, printers, advertising and circulation managers and allied graphic arts trade.

MONTHLY REPORT - ASSOCIATION OF AMERICAN PUBLISHERS. (MONTHLY REPORT : A NEWSBULLETIN FOR MEMBERS OF THE ASSOCIATION OF AMERICAN PUBLISHERS). Vol. 1, No. 1 (Sept. 1984)-. 0748-8173. Periodical. US. English. mo. AAP, 2005 Massachusetts Avenue Northwest, Washington DC 20036. DD 070. *AAP Capital Letter, 0162-3303; Trade Voices; AAP International News and Notes; Paperback Publishing Division Information Bulletin; AAP School Division Newsletter; Higher Education Division Information Bulletin.*

NASZE PROBLEMY. Periodical. Polish. ir. 40.00 Single Issue. Warszawskii Wydawn Prasowe RSW Prasa-Ksiazka-Ruch, Ul Wiejska 12, Warszawa Poland. LC PN4705.

NEW BOOK NEWS FROM QUEBEC. V. 1- Oct. 1978-. 0709-0641. Periodical. CN. English. mo. Free. Societe de Promotion du Livre Inc, Suite 40 445 Saint-Francois-Xavier Street, Montreal Quebec H2Y 2T1 Canada. DD 028.105.

NEW ENGLAND PRINTER & PUBLISHER. *See* Printing.

NEW PAGES. Began in 1980. 0271-8197. Periodical. US. English. ir. New Pages Press, 4426 South Balsay Road, Grand Blanc MI 48439. Tel (313)742-9583. Ind/Abst Altern. Press Index.

NEW POLISH PUBLICATIONS. VFOAT Nouvelles Publications Polonaises. 0028-6486. Periodical. PL. English. mo. ARS Polona, Krakowskie Przedmiescie 7, 40-068 Warsaw Poland. Tel 26 76 22. LC Z2521. DD 015.438.

NEWS PREVIEWS. 0095-2680. Periodical. US. English. mo. Springer Verlag-New York Inc, 175-5th Avenue, New York NY 10010. Tel (212)460-1500. Announcement of new titles available from Springer-Verlag.

NEWSLETTER - CANADIAN TELEBOOK AGENCY. (NEWSLETTER). 4 (Spring 1983)-. 0825-7752. Periodical. CN. English. qt. Free to Members. Canadian Telebook Agency, Suite 209/31 Wellesley Street, Toronto Ontario M4Y 1G7 Canada. DD 070.502854. *Information Newsletter (Canadian Telebook Agency), 0823-1893.*

NEWSLETTER OF THE ASSOCIATION FOR DOCUMENTARY EDITING. Main/Corp Association for Documentary Editing. V. 2- Feb. 1980-. 0196-7134. Periodical. US. English. qt. $15.00. Association for Documentary Editing Ratification Project, University of Wisconsin History Department, 455 North Park Street, Madison WI 53706. Tel (608)263-1865. Ed Sharon R Ritenour. bk rev. adv acc. Circ 400. (ctrl). Deals with issues related to editing and publishing documents. *ADE Newsletter.*

NEWSPAPER TECHNIQUES (DARMSTADT, GERMANY). (NEWSPAPER TECHNIQUES : THE MONTHLY PUBLICATION OF THE INCA-FIEJ RESEARCH ASSOCIATION). VFOAT IFRA Newspaper Techniques. Periodical. English. ir. $30.44. International Research Association Newspaper, Technology/Washingtonplatz 1, 61 Darmstadt West Germany. Tel (0049)6151-76057. Ed George B Smith. Ind/Abst Print. Abstr. LC Z119. DD 070.57205. bk rev. adv acc. Circ 4,220. Technical magazine dealing with the latest developments in the newspaper industry and the news media on an international basis.

NEWSREAL. VFOAT News Real. 0730-224X. Periodical. US. English. mo. $8.00. Newsreal, PO Box 40323, Tucson AZ 85717. Tel (301)951-1310. Available on microfilm from Bell & Howell. *Tucson's Mountain Newsreal.*

NIGOG +. (LE NIGOG +). VAT Nigog Plus. Feb. 1983. 0820-8255. Periodical. CN. French. bm. Free. Association des Editeurs de Periodiques Culturels Quebecois, C P 786 Succursale Place d'Armes, Montreal Quebec H2Y 3J2 Canada. DD 070.572060714. (ctrl).

NIHON SHUPPANJIN SOKAN. 1976-. JA. Japanese. ir. 5000. Bunka Tsushinsha, 1-12 Yushima 4-chome Bunkyo-ku, Tokyo 113 Japan. LC Z463.5.

NOTICIAS DO LIVRO. No. 1- Nov. 1978-. Periodical. PO. Portuguese. $22.00. Noticias do Livro, Liberdade 266, 1200 Lisboa Portugal. LC Z1035.A1.

OREGON PUBLISHER. 0745-6379. Periodical. US. English. mo. Oregon Newspaper Publishers Association, 2130 5th Street SW/Suite 2, Portland OR 97201.

OSTERREICHS PRESSE, WERBUNG, GRAPHIK HANDBUCH CEASED. Vol. 15-. 0030-0004. AU. German. ir. Verlag Osterreichs Presse, Schreyvogelgasse 3, A-1010 Wien Austria. LC Z6956.A9, PN5164. DD 079.94025. NLM Z 6956.A9 O29. *Handbuch Osterreichs Presse, Werbung, Graphik, 0030-0004.*

OUTPUT MODE. 1- July 1979-. 0193-7391. Periodical. US. English. mo. $24.00. Padre Productions, Box 1275, San Luis Obispo CA 93406. Tel (805)543-5404.

P-H EXECUTIVE ACTION REPORT. Main/Corp Prentice-Hall, Inc. VFOAT Executive Action Report. VAT Prentice Hall Executive Action Report. June 5, 1976-. 0164-9825. Periodical. US. English. wk. $141.00. Prentice-Hall Inc, Sylvan Avenue, Englewood Cliffs NJ 07632. *Prentice Hall Executive Report.*

PAGES. *See* Publishing - Books and Bookmaking.

PAN AFRICAN BOOK WORLD. Vol. 1, No. 1 (Aug. 1981)-. Periodical. English. ir. Fourth Dimension Publishers, 179 Zik Avenue Enugu, Anambra State Nigeria. LC Z465. DD 070.5096.

PEMBIMBING PEMBACA. Periodical. Indonesian. ir. Balai Pustaka, Jl Dr Wahidin 1, Jakarta Indonesia. LC Z460.7. *Pembimbing Pembatja.*

PERSONAL PUBLISHING. Vol. 1, No. 1 (Oct. 1985)-. 0884-951X. Periodical. US. English. mo. $30.00. Renegade Co, 549 Hawthorn, Bartlett IL 60103. DD 070. *Professional Publishing, 0736-7457.*

PNPA PRESS. VAT Pennsylvania Newspaper Publisher's Association Press. 1929. 0030-8196. Periodical. US. English. mo. $17.75. PA Newspaper Publication Association, 2717 North Front Street, Harrisburg PA 17110. Tel (717)234-4067. Ed Rick White and Marcia Janiczek. bk rev. adv acc. Circ 900. Edited for the newspaper and publishing industry of Pennsylvania. Comment on journalism, advertising circulation, marketing, personnel etc. *PNPA Press Bulletin.*

POLICY PUBLISHERS AND ASSOCIATIONS DIRECTORY. *See* Yearbooks, Almanacs, Directories.

PRESSTIME. VAT Press Time. V. 1- Oct. 1979-. 0194-3243. Periodical. US. English. mo. $100.00. American Newspaper Publishers Association, Box L7407, Dulles International Airport, Washington DC 20041. Tel (703)620-9500. Ind/Abst Abstr. Bull. Inst. Paper Chem., Print. Abstr., Electron. Pub. Abstr. LC PN4700. DD 070.05.

PRINTING, PUBLISHING AND ALLIED INDUSTRIES. *See* Printing.

PROCEEDINGS OF THE ANNUAL MEETING OF THE SOCIETY FOR SCHOLARLY PUBLISHING. (PROCEEDINGS OF THE . . . ANNUAL MEETING OF THE SOCIETY FOR SCHOLARLY PUBLISHING). Main/Corp Society for Scholarly Publishing (U.S.). Meeting. 2nd (June 2-4, 1980)-. 0734-8509. US. English. an. Society for Scholarly Publishing, 2000 Florida Avenue Northwest, Washington DC 20009. Tel (202)328-3555. Circ 500. Collection of papers presented at annual meeting. Topics include the creation, publishing, and dissemination of scholarly works. *SSP Proceedings, 0196-6146.*

PRODUCTION JOURNAL. 1958. 0032-9878. Periodical. UK. English. bm. 3.00. The Newspaper Society, Whitefriars House, 6 Carmelite Street, London EC4Y 0BL England. Tel (01)583-3311. Ed Basil Loven. Ind/Abst Abstr. Bull. Inst. Paper Chem., Print. Abstr. adv acc. Circ 3,000. All matters connected with newspaper publishing.

PROFESSIONAL PUBLISHING. Vol. 1, No. 1 (Mar./Apr. 1983)-. 0736-7457. Periodical. US. English. mo $15.00. Renegade Company, 4318 North Paulina Street, Chicago IL 60613. Ind/Abst Electron. Commun. Abstr. J., ISMEC Bull., Pollut. Abstr. Indexes, Saf. Sci. Abstr. J. LC Z284. DD 070.502854.

PROOF. V. 1- 1971-. 0079-6980. US. English. an. J Faust & Company Publishers, Box 5615, Columbia SC 29205. Ind/Abst MLA Int. Bibliogr. Books Artic. Mod. Lang. Lit. LC Z1219. DD 010.5.

PUBLICATION DESIGN. 12-. US. English. Society of Publication Designers, 25 West 43rd Street/Suite 711, New York NY 10036.

PUBLISHERS' CATALOGS ANNUAL. US. English. an. Meckler Publishing, 520 Riverside Avenue, Westport CT 06880.

PUBLISHERS DIRECTORY. *See* Yearbooks, Almanacs, Directories.

PUBLISHERS, DISTRIBUTORS, & WHOLESALERS OF THE UNITED STATES. VFOAT Publishers, Distributors, and Wholesalers of the United States. 3rd Ed.-. 0000-0671. US. English. an. R R Bowker Company, 1180 Avenue of the Americas, New York NY 10036. LC Z475. DD 070.502573. NLM Z 475 P976. *Publishers and Distributors of the United States, 0000-0620.*

Publishing—Books and Bookmaking

PUBLISHERS IN THE UNITED KINGDOM AND THEIR ADDRESSES. 1965-. 0079-7839. Periodical. UK. English. ir. $4.98. J Whitaker & Sons Ltd, 12 Dyott Street, London WC1A 1DF England. **Tel** 01-836 8911. **LC** Z327. **DD** 655.402542. adv acc. Listing of over 2,000 of the most active publishers, telex and telephone numbers, ISBN, publisher prefix and type of book published. *Publishers and Their Addresses.*

PUBLISHERS' INTERNATIONAL DIRECTORY WITH ISBN INDEX. *See* Yearbooks, Almanacs, Directories.

PUBLISHER'S MONTHLY. Began publication in 1959. Periodical. II. English (Hindi). mo. $8.80. Shyam Lal Gupta, Cen Elec Pr, Ravindra Mansion Ram Nager, New Delhi 110055 India. **LC** Z284.

THE PUBLISHERS' TRADE LIST ANNUAL. 1874-. 0079-7855. US. English. an. R R Bowker Company, PO Box 1385, Ann Arbor MI 48106. Ed F Leypoldt. **LC** Z1215. **DD** 015.73. *Uniform Trade List Annual.*

PUBLISHERS WEEKLY. V. 3- Jan. 1873-. 0000-0019. Periodical. US. English. wk. $59.00. RR Bowker Company, 1180 Avenue of the Americas, New York NY 10036, (subscription address: Bowker Subscription Service PO Box 1428 Riverton NJ 08077). **Ind/Abst** Libr. Lit., Bus. Period. Index, Read. Guide Period. Lit., Pop. Mag. Rev., Libr. Inf. Sci. Abstr., Book Rev. Index, Ref. Source. **LC** Z1219. Available on microfilm from University Microfilms. *Publishers' and Stationers' Weekly Trade Circular.*

THE PUBLISHING & BOOKSELLING DIRECTORY. *See* Yearbooks, Almanacs, Directories.

PUBLISHING EDUCATION NEWSLETTER. V. 1- Jan. 1979-. 0190-048X. Periodical. US. English. qt. Association of American Publishers Inc, 1 Park Avenue, New York NY 10016. **Tel** (212)689-8920.

PUBLISHING HISTORY. 1-. 0309-2445. Periodical. UK. English. sa. $60.00. Chadwick-Healey Inc, 1021 Prince Street, Alexandria VA 22314. **Tel** (703)683-4890. Ed Michael Turner. **Ind/Abst** Am. Hist. Life, Hist. Abstr., Part A, Mod. Hist. Abstr., Hist. Abst., Part B, Twent. Century Abstr. **LC** Z280. **DD** 658.8090705730941. bk rev. adv acc. **Circ** 800. A scholarly journal devoted to the social, economic and literary history of book, newspaper and magazine publishing.

PUBLISHING POLICY FILE. VFOAT ACP Publishing Policy File. VAT Association of Canadian Publishers Publishing Policy File. Vol. 1, No. 1 (Oct. 1980)-. 0228-720X. Periodical. CN. English. mo. Association of Canadian Publishers, 3rd Floor/70 The Esplanade, Toronto Ontario M5E 1R2 Canada. **DD** 070.50971.

PUBLISHING TRADE. Vol. 1, No. 1 (Jan./Feb. 1982)-. 0730-6741. Periodical. US. English. bm. $20.00. Publishing Trade, 464 Central Avenue, Northfield IL 60093. **Tel** (312)441-7488. Ed Rosanne M Ullman. **Ind/Abst** Electron. Commun. Abstr. J., ISMEC Bull., Pollut. Abstr. Indexes, Saf. Sci. Abstr. J., ABI/Inform. **LC** Z286.P4. bk rev. adv acc. **Circ** 6,800. (ctrl). Magazine for non-consumer magazines.

QUALIS. *See* Yearbooks, Almanacs, Directories.

REPERTOIRE DE LA LECTURE FRANCOPHONE. (LE REPERTOIRE DE LA LECTURE FRANCOPHONE). Vol. 1, No. 1 (Nov. 1983)-. 0823-969X. Periodical. CN. French. S O P Services de Presse Inc, 9756 Boul St-Laurent, Montreal Quebec H3L 2N3 Canada. **DD** 015.710241.

REPERTOIRE DES EDITEURS ET DE LEURS DISTRIBUTEURS. Nov. 1983-. 0826-5631. Periodical. CN. French. st. Repertoire des Editeurs et de Leurs Distributeurs, 1151 rue Alexandre-Deseve, Montreal Quebec H2L 2T7 Canada. **DD** 070.5025714. *Repertoire des Editeurs et de Leurs Distributeurs a l'Usage Exclusif des Libraires, 0228-0264.*

REPERTOIRES LIVRES HEBDO. VFOAT Un an de Nouveautes. 2 1980-. Periodical. US. English. qt. (cum index).

SCHOLARLY PUBLISHING. V. 1- Oct. 1969-. 0036-634X. Periodical. CN. English. qt. $30.18. University of Toronto Press, 5201 Dufferin Street, Downsview Ontario M3H 5T8 Canada. **Tel** (416)667-7781. **Ind/Abst** Am. Hist. Life, Hist. Abstr., Part A, Mod. Hist. Abstr., Hist. Abst., Part B, Twent. Century Abstr., Abstr. Engl. Stud., MLA Int. Bibliogr. Books Artic. Mod. Lang. Lit., Libr. Inf. Sci. Abstrs., Ref. Source, Libr. Lit., Soc. Sci. Citation Index, Hist. Abstr. **LC** Z286.S37. **DD** 655.4. (cum index). Microform available from Micromedia Limited, Toronto Canada.

SELF-PUBLISHING WRITER. (THE SELF-PUBLISHING WRITER). V. 1- Oct. 1972-. 0091-6226. Periodical. US. English. qt. $7.50. S S Morril, 547 Howard Street, San Francisco CA 94105. **LC** Z285.5. **DD** 051.

SESAME (MEDFORD, OR.). (SESAME). Vol. 1, No. 1 (Apr. 1985)-. 0883-1467. Periodical. US. English. mo. $26.00. Windyridge Press, PO Box 327, Medford OR 97501. **Tel** (503)772-5399. Ed Gene Olsen. **DD** 808. bk rev. **Circ** 100. Instruction and marketing advice for professional writers. Most phases of writing and publishing covered.

THE SEYBOLD REPORT ON PUBLISHING SYSTEMS. Vol. 11, No. 9 (Jan. 18, 1982)-. 0736-7260. Periodical. US. English. sm. $240.00 Domestic, $252.00 Canada, $284.00 Foreign. Seybold Publications, POB 644, Media PA 19063. **Tel** (215)565-2480. Ed Jonathan Seybold. **Ind/Abst** Electron. Pub. Abstr., Print. Abstr. (ctrl). Covers, typesetting equipment, page make-up facilities, and related electronic pre-press systems for the printing and publishing market. *Seybold Report, 0364-5517.*

SHUPPAN JANARU & SHUPPANKAI JOHO. Vol. 1, Oct. 1979-. JA. Japanese. ir. 5700. Riso Shuppansha, 10-3 Kanda Jimbocho 3-chome Chiyoda-ku 101, Tokyo Japan. **LC** Z463.7.

SHUPPAN KAIHATSU KENKYU. Vol. 1-. JA. Japanese. ir. 3000. Shuppan Kaihatsusha, 22 Kanda Jimbocho Chiyoda-ku (101), Tokyo 101 Japan. **LC** Z284.

SIGNATURE. 1- Apr. 1979-. 0708-515X. Periodical. CN. English. ty. Free. Association of Book Publishers of British Columbia, 1622 West 7th Avenue, Vancouver British Columbia V6J 1S5 Canada. **DD** 338.47070509711. (ctrl).

SRI LANKA JATIKA GRANTHA NAMAVALIYA. *See* Bibliographies.

SUARA PENERBIT INDONESIA. IO. Indonesian. ir. **LC** Z460.7.

TENKANKI NI ARU SHUPPANGYOKAI. V. 4-. JA. Japanese. ir. 40000. Marunouchi Risachi Senta, c/o Nihon Building 6-2 Otemachi, 2-chome Chiyoda-ku (100), Tokyo Japan. **LC** Z463.5. *Shuppansha Chosaroku.*

TEXAS PUBLISHERS & PUBLICATIONS DIRECTORY. *See* Yearbooks, Almanacs, Directories.

VIKING COLLEGE CATALOG. Main/Corp Viking Press, Inc., New York. 0362-997X. US. English. Viking Press, 625 Madison Avenue, New York NY 10022. **LC** Z473.V5. **DD** 017.8097471.

VIREO. No. 1 (Spring 1981)-. 0823-6127. Periodical. CN. French. qt. Free. Centre Vireo, 2215 rue Marie-Victoria, Sillery Quebec G1T 1J6 Canada. **DD** 015.714.

WHO DISTRIBUTES WHAT AND WHERE. VAT Who Distributes What & Where. 2nd- 1982-. 0000-0426. Periodical. US. English. ir. $63.50. R R Bowker Company, 1180 Avenue of the Americas, New York NY 10036. **LC** Z282. **DD** 070.5025. **NLM** Z 282 W628 1980.

THE WRITER'S MARKET. 1922-. 0084-2729. US. English. an. $19.95. Writers Digest, 9933 Alliance Road, Cincinnati OH 45242. **Tel** (513)984-0717. Ed Paula Deimling. **LC** PN161. **DD** 808.0250977178. **Circ** 130,000. A directory listing 4,000 publishers of all types of writing, with complete contact details. Also includes articles on the business of writing and interviews with writers and editors.

BOOKS AND BOOKMAKING

A-D : AN INTIMATE JOURNAL FOR ART DIRECTORS, PRODUCTION MANAGERS, AND THEIR ASSOCIATES. V.1- Sept. 1934-. Periodical. English. bm. **LC** Z119.

AB BOOKMAN'S YEARBOOK. *See* Yearbooks, Almanacs, Directories.

ADRESSBUCH DES DEUTSCHSPRACHIGEN BUCHHANDEL. *See* Yearbooks, Almanacs, Directories.

THE ADVENT. Periodical. II. English. qt. Hindustan Book Agency of India, 17 UB Jawahar Nagar, Delhi 7 India.

AFRICAN BOOK TRADE DIRECTORY. *See* Yearbooks, Almanacs, Directories.

THE AFRICAN BOOK WORLD & PRESS : DIRECTORY. *See* Yearbooks, Almanacs, Directories.

AFRICAN BOOKS IN PRINT. VFOAT Livres Africains Disponibles. 1975-. 0306-9516. UK. English. be. International Scholarly Book Services, PO Box 4347, Portland OR 97207. **LC** Z3501. **DD** 015.6.

AIGA BOOK SHOW. Main/Corp American Institute of Graphic Arts. VAT American Institute of Graphic Arts Book Show. 1976-. 0160-0427. US. English. American Institute of Graphic Arts, 1059 Third Avenue, New York NY 10021. **LC** Z208. **DD** 070.5730973. *Fifty Books of the Year, 0145-1723.*

ALAM AL-KUTUB. VFOAT World of Books. Journal 1- May 1980-. Periodical. Arabic. ir. 100. Dar Thaqif, PO Box 1590, Al-Riyad Al-Mamlakah Al-Arabiyah Al-Saudiyah, Al-Taif Saudi Arabia.

AMERICAN BOOK COLLECTOR. *See* Hobbies.

AMERICAN BOOK PRICES CURRENT. V. 1- 1894/95-. 0091-9357. US. English. an. $93.05. Bancroft Parkman Inc, P O Box 236, Washington CT 06793. **Tel** (212)737-2715. **LC** Z1000. **DD** 018.3. **NLM** Z 1000 A512. (cum index).

AMERICAN BOOK TRADE DIRECTORY. *See* Yearbooks, Almanacs, Directories.

AMERICAN BOOKSELLER. 0148-5903. Periodical. US. English. mo. $68.00. American Booksellers Association, 122 East 42nd Street, New York NY 10017. **Tel** (212)867-9060. **LC** Z477. **DD** 658.8090705730973.

AMPHORA. 1- 1967-. 0003-200X. Periodical. CN. English. qt. $35.00. Alcuin Society, PO Box 3216, Vancouver British Columbia V6B 3X8 Canada. **Tel** (604)688-2341. Ed Ron McAmmond. **LC** Z990. **DD** 020.75. bk rev. adv acc. **Circ** 300. (ctrl). Items of interest to members who are fond of fine books and with various crafts which produce fine books. *Notes from the Alcuin Society, 0568-935X.*

AMTMANN CIRCLE BULLETIN. VFOAT Bulletin du Cercle Amtmann. Vol. 1, No. 1 (Mar. 1983)-. 0820-8972. Periodical. CN. English (includes some text in French). ty. 25. Amtmann Circle, PO Box 3336 Station D, Ottawa Ontario K1P 6H8 Canada. Ed Peter E Greig. **DD** 002.075. bk review. **Circ** 150. Antiquarian book trade and book collecting in Canada.

ANCIEN DU CANADA FRANCAIS. (LES CAHIERS DU LIVRE ANCIEN DU CANADA FRANCAIS). Vol. 1, No. 1 (Jan. 1984)-. 0822-4315. Periodical. CN. French. qt. $36.00 Domestic, $38.00 Foreign Cahiers du Livre. Institut Canadien-Francais de Bibliophilie, C P 8493, Ste-Foy Quebec G1V 4N5 Canada. **DD** 002.07509714.

ANNOTATED CATALOGUE OF BOOKS PUBLISHED IN JAPAN. No. 2- 1975/76-. JA. English. ir. Publishers Association for Cultural Exchange, 2-1 sarugaku-cho 1 chome, chiyoda-ku 101, Tokyo Japan. **LC** Z3301. **DD** 015.52. *Annotated Catalogue of 270 Books Published in Japan.*

ANNUAL DIRECTORY OF BOOKSELLERS IN THE BRITISH ISLES SPECIALISING IN ANTIQUARIAN AND OUT-OF-PRINT BOOKS. *See* Yearbooks, Almanacs, Directories.

ANNUAL PAPERBOUND BOOK GUIDE FOR HIGH SCHOOLS. 1963-. 0570-2577. US. English. R R Bowker Company, 205 East 42nd Street, New York NY 10017. **LC** Z1033.P3. **DD** 028.52.

ANNUAL REPORT OF THE AMERICAN RARE, ANTIQUARIAN AND OUT-OF-PRINT BOOK TRADE CEASED. VFOAT American Rare, Antiquarian and Out-of-Print Book Trade. 1978/79. US. English. ir. $9.95. BCAR Publishing, PO Box 50 Cooper Station, New York NY 10003. **LC** Z479. **DD** 070.50973.

Publishing—Books and Bookmaking

ANNUAL REVIEW OF ENGLISH BOOKS ON ASIA. 1974-. 0098-7379. US. English. an. Brigham Young University Press, Attn Alreia Walker, 358 JRCB, Provo UT 84602. LC Z3001, DS5. DD 016.95.

ANTIQUARIAN TRADE LIST ANNUAL. (ANTIQUARIAN TRADE LIST ANNUAL : (ALTA)). VFOAT Atla. (1980)-. 0197-0364. US. English. ir. Pergamon Press, 395 Sawmill River Road, Elmsford NY 10523. DD 017.8.

ANTIQUARIAT. Periodical. German. ir. 56.00. Dr L Rossipaul Verlagsgesellschaft, 7621 Stammheim Finkenweg 6, Stammheim W Germany. LC Z286.A55.

ANZEIGER DES OSTERREICHISCHEN BUCHHANDELS. German. sa. Hauptverband des Osterreichischen Buchhandels, Grunangergasse 4 1010 1, Wien Austria. Tel 52-15-35. LC Z2105. bk rev. adv acc. News from international and Austrian booktrade and advertising. *Anzeiger des Osterreichischen Buch-, Kunst- und Musikalienhandels.*

ARCHIV FUR GESCHICHTE DES BUCHWESENS. See Genealogy and Heraldry - Archives.

L'ARGUS DU LIVRE ANCIEN & MODERNE. VFOAT Argus du Livre Ancien et Moderne. No. 16 (July 1982). 0242-5823. FR. French. qt. $61.87. Promodis, 18 rue Dauphine, 75006 Paris France. Tel (1)634-77-68. Ed Promodis. bk rev. adv acc. Recording book auctions especially in France and giving regular information about book-exhibitions, book dealers, catalogues or bibliographies. *Argus Mensuel du Livre Ancien & Moderne.*

L'ARGUS DU LIVRE DE COLLECTION & DE L'ANTOGRAPHIE. VFOAT Argus du Livre de Collection et de l'Autographie. No. 29 (Oct. 1985)-. Periodical. French. qt. Promodis, 18 rue Dauphine, 75006 Paris France. *Argus du Livre Ancien & Moderne, 0242-5823.*

ARHEOGRAFSKI PRILOZI. 1-. Periodical. YU. Serbo-Croatian -C. ir. Narodna Biblioteka Srbije, Arheografsko Odeljenje, Skerliceva 1, 11 000 Beograd Yugoslavia. LC Z115.5.S45.

ART ET METIERS DU LIVRE. Vol. 83, No. 45- Nov. 1973-. Periodical. FR. French. ir. 250. Art et Metiers du Livre, 31 Place Saint Ferdinand, 75017 Paris France. Tel 4574 67 43. Ed R Baschet. adv acc. Circ 2,400. Handicraft bookbinding and all subjects concerned with art books. *Reliure-Brochure-Dorure.*

ASIAN BOOK DEVELOPMENT NEWSLETTER. V. 10- July 1978-. Periodical. English. ir. Asian Cultural Centre, No 6 Fukuromachi Shinjuku-ku, Tokyo 162 Japan. LC Z448.7. DD 070.573095. *Newsletter - Tokyo Book Development Centre.*

ASIAN BOOKS NEWS LETTER. V. 1-. Periodical. English. $48.00. K K Roy Private LTD, PO Box 10210/55 Gariahat Road, Calcutta 700019 India. Tel 91 33-474872. Ed K K Roy. Circ 1,500. Bibliographic listings of material published in all Asian countries.

AUSTRALIAN BOOK REVIEW. No. 1- June 1978-. 0155-2864. Periodical. AT. English. mo. Australian Book Review, PO Box 89, Parkville 3052 Australia.

AUSTRALIAN BOOK SCENE. AT. English. ir. D W Thorpe Pty Ltd, 384 Spencer Street, West Melbourne Victoria 3003 Australia. LC Z533.7. DD 070.50994.

AUSTRALIAN BOOKS. 1933-. 0067-1738. Periodical. AT. English. an. 6.50. National Library of Australia, Canberra Australia Capital Territory 2600 Australia. Tel (062)621646. LC Z4011. DD 016.994. A current reference and reading list of works dealing with Australia or of Australian authorship which are authoritative of outstanding quality.

AUSTRALIAN BOOKS IN PRINT. AT. English. an. D W Thorpe Pty Ltd, PO Box 146, 20-24 Stokes Street, Port Melbourne 3207 Australia. Tel 03 645 1511. LC Z4011. DD 015.94. NLM Z 4011 A935. *Bookbuyers Reference Book, 0524-0603.*

BA, BESPRECHUNGEN/ANNOTATIONEN. VFOAT Besprechungen/Annotationen. Periodical. German. ir. Einkaufszentrale fur Offentliche Bibliotheken GMBH, 7410 Reutlingen, Postfach 96, Bismarckstrasse 3, Reutlingen West Germany. LC Z1035.A1.

BAI. Main/Corp National Book Centre of Pakistan. 1-1965-. Periodical. Bengali. ir. LC Z459.7.

THE BEAN HOME NEWSLETTER. Vol. 1, No. 1 (Nov. 1, 1984)-. 0882-4428. Periodical. US. English. qt. $10.00 for 2 years. Friends of Freddy, 15-C Laurel Hill Road, Greenbelt MD 20770. Tel (301)474-1982. Ed Lee Secrest. DD 002. adv acc. Circ 100. Dedicated to the preservation and perpetuation of the writings of Walter R. Brooks and his alter ego, Freddy the Pig. Emphasizes literary criticism, biographical data on Brooks, and how to locate these books (now mostly out of print).

LES BEAUX LIVRES DE L'ANNEE. 1973-. FR. French. ir. Comite des Expositions du Livre et des Arts Graphiques Francais, Office de Promotion de l'Edition Francaise, Cercle de la Librairie, 117 Bd Saint-Germain, 75279 Cedex 06 Paris France. LC Z1033.F5. DD 011. *Cinquante Beaux Livres de l'Annee.*

BEITRAGE ZUR GESCHICHTE DES BUCHWESENS. Vol., 1-. 0067-5040. German. Deutsher Buchexport-Import, Leninstrasse 16, DDN-701 Leipzig East Germany. Tel 49500. LC Z285. History of editing, booktrade, binding, and printing.

BEST BOOKS BY CONSENSUS. 1983-84-. 8755-9633. US. English. an. $5.00. Information Digest, PO Box 165, Morton Grove IL 60053. Tel (312)965-1456. Ed Chung I Park. LC Z1035. DD 017. Annotated list of current books chosen by consensus of reviews, prizes, and recommendations. *Best Sellers & Best Choices, 0275-0945.*

BEST BOOKS FOR YOUNG ADULTS. Main/Corp American Library Association. Young Adult Services Division. 0882-0708. Periodical. US. English. an. .25. American Library Association, 50 East Huron Street, Chicago IL 60611. DD 028.

BEST BUYS IN PRINT. 1- Spring 1978-. 0161-7001. Periodical. US. English. qt. $25.00. Pierian Press, PO Box 1808, Ann Arbor MI 48106. LC Z1036. DD 017.4.

BIBLIOFILIA. (LA BIBLIOFILIA). Vol. 1-. 0006-0941. Periodical. IT. Italian. ty. $21.98. Casa Editrice, Leo S Olschki, Casella Postale, PO Box 66, 50100 Firenze Italy. Ind/Abst MLA Int. Bibliogr. Books Artic. Mod. Lang. Lit. LC Z1007. (cum index).

BIBLIOGRAPHIE DER BUCH- UND BIBLIOTHEKSGESCHICHTE : BBB. See Bibliographies.

BIBLIOGRAPHY OF SELECTED INDIAN BOOKS. See Bibliographies.

BIBLIONEWS AND AUSTRALIAN NOTES AND QUERIES. 2 Ser. V. 1- Jan. 1966-. 0045-1940. Periodical. AT. English. an. 10.00. Book Collectors Society of Australia, 234A Raglan Street, Mosman New South Wales 2088 Australia. Tel (02)960-3804. Ed John Fletcher. Ind/Abst Annu. Bibliogr. Engl. Lang. Lit. bk rev adv acc. Circ 400. (ctrl). Quarterly journal posted to members of the Book Collectors' Society of Australia. Articles, reviews and notes and queries. *Biblionews.*

BINDEREPORT. VFOAT Allgemeiner Anzeiger fur Buchbindereien. 12. May 1977-. 0342-3573. Periodical. GW. German. mo. 110.-. Schlueterstsche Verlag Druckerei, Postfach 5440, D-3000 Hannover 1 West Germany. Tel 0511-12360. Ind/Abst Print. Abstr. bk rev. adv acc. (ctrl). Manufacturing process of books, printing process in trade-industry and publishing industry. *Allgemeiner Anzeiger fur Buchbindereien.*

BINDERIJEN. Series/Titl Produktiestatistieken Industrie. VFOAT Binderies. NE. Dutch (summaries in English). an. 12.10. Centraal Bureau voor de Statistiek, Prinses Beatrixlaan 428 Postbus 959, 2270 AZ Voorburg Netherlands. LC Z270.N43. DD 686.309492.

BOK OG SAMFUNN A-UTGAVE CEASED. Vol. 98, No. 12-101. Vol. Periodical. NO. Norwegian. mo. Norwegian Booksellers Association, Ovre Voligate 15-0158 Oslo 1 Norway. Tel 41 07 59. *Bok og Samfunn.*

BOK OG SAMFUNN (OSLO, NORWAY : 1981) CEASED. (BOK OG SAMFUNN). Vol. 102, No. 1 (12 Jan. 1981)-102. Vol., No. 36 (10 Dec. 1981). Periodical. NO. Norwegian. Norwegian Booksellers Association, Ovre Voligate 15, Oslo Norway. bk rev. adv acc. Circ 2,500. *Bok Og Samfunn A-Utgave, Bok Og Samfunn B-Utgave.*

BOKVANNEN. Vol. 1- Sept. 1946-. 0006-5846. Periodical. SW. Swedish. qt. 13.70. Bokvannen, Kommendorsg 33, S-114 58 Stockholm Sweden. Tel 08-60 53 64. Ed Jan Jerring. Ind/Abst MLA Int. Bibliogr. Books Artic. Mod. Lang. Lit. LC Z1007. (cum index). bk rev. adv acc. Circ 1,500. (ctrl). Magazine for those interested in literature, books, fine bindings, book collections, the history of books and literature.

BOLETIN BIBLIOGRAFICO CERLAL CEASED. Main/Corp Centro Regional Para el Fomento del Libro en America Latina. VAT Boletin Bibliografico Centro Regional Para el Fomento del Libro en America Latina. Vol. 1- July 1974-. CK. Spanish. qt. $25.00. Centro Regional Fomento Libro, Amer Lat Caribe Cer/Calle 70 No. 9-52, Bogota Colombia. LC Z1601, F1408. NLM Z 1601.U5A B688.

BOOK AUCTION RECORDS. Began in 1903. Periodical. UK. English. an. LC Z1000. DD 017.3. NLM Z 1000 B723. *Sale Records.*

THE BOOK COLLECTOR. V. 1- Spring 1952-. 0006-7237. Periodical. UK. English. qt. $24.00. The Collector Ltd, 3 Bloomsbury Place, London WCIA 2QA England. Ind/Abst Abstr. Engl. Stud., MLA Int. Bibliogr. Books Artic. Mod. Lang. Lit., Annu. Bibliogr. Engl. Lang. Lit., Libr. Lit., Book Rev. Index, Ref. Source, Index Book Rev. Humanit., Recent Publ. Artic. LC Z990. DD 020.75. (cum index). *Book Handbook.*

BOOK INDUSTRY TRENDS. 1977-. 0160-970X. US. English. an. $150.00. R R Bowker Company, PO Box 1807, Ann Arbor MI 48106. Tel (203)655-2473. LC Z477. DD 658.8090705730973.

BOOK MARKETS IN THE AMERICAS, ASIA, AFRICA & AUSTRALASIA. 1979/1980-. UK. English. Euromonitor Publications, 41 Russell Square, London WC1B 5DL England. LC Z284. DD 07050212.

BOOK MARKETS IN WESTERN EUROPE. 1st Ed. UK. English. an. 95. Euromonitor Publications Ltd, 87-88 Turnmill Street, London EC1M 5QU England. Tel 01 251 8024. LC Z291. DD 070.5094.

THE BOOK-MART. VAT Book Mart. 0161-5556. Periodical. US. English. mo. Book Mart - Mae McKinley, PO Box 72, Lake Wales FL 33853.

BOOK PRODUCTION (BENN PUBLICATIONS LTD.). (BOOK PRODUCTION). Periodical. UK. English. sa. Printing World, 25 New Street Square, London EC4A 3JA England. LC Z119. DD 070.505.

BOOK PROMOTION NEWS. No. 1- Aug. 1973-. English. ir. United Nations Educational, Place de Fontenoy, Paris France 75700. Ind/Abst Print. Abstr. LC Z1003. DD 028.

THE BOOK REVIEW. V. 1- Jan. 1976-. II. English. qt. 10.00. Perspective Publications, F-24 Bhagat Singh Market, New Delhi 110001 India. LC Z1035.A1. DD 028.10954.

BOOK REVIEW DIGEST. Began with: Vol. 1 in Jan. 1906. 0006-7326. Periodical. US. English. mo. H W Wilson Company, 950 University Avenue, Bronx NY 10452. Tel (212)588-8400. Ed Martha Mooney. LC Z1219. NLM Z 1219 B723. The only international bibliography of hardcover and paperback English language books. *Cumulative Book Review Digest.*

BOOK REVIEW INDEX. See Indexes/Abstracts.

BOOK TALK. V. 1- 1972-. 0145-627X. US. English. ir. $5.00. New Mexico Book League, 8632 Horacio Place NE, Albuquerque NM 87111. Tel (505)299-8940. Ed Carol A Myers. bk rev. adv acc. Circ 500. (ctrl). Articles, book reviews and book listings of interest to libraries, booksellers and collectors interested in southwestern United States.

BOOK TRADE IN CANADA. (THE BOOK TRADE IN CANADA). VFOAT Industrie du Livre au Canada. Began with Vol. for 1976. 0700-5296. Periodical. an. $21.28. Ampersand Publishing Services, Rural Route #1, Caledon Ontario 10N 1C0 Canada. Tel (519)927-3321. Ed Eunice Thorne and Ed Matheson. LC Z485. DD 070.502571. Directory of Canadian publishers, services to the industry and booksellers. *Book Publishers in Canada, 0317-6975.*

BOOK WORLD. VFOAT Chicago Tribune Book World. V. 1- Sept. 10, 1967-. 0006-7369. Periodical. US. English. wk. $10.00. Washington Post Newspaper, 1150 15th Street NW, Washington DC 20071. Ind/

Abst Book Rev. Index. (cum index). *Books Today, Book Week, 0524-059X.*

BOOK WORLD. 1978-. English. ir. 20.00. Bookworld Publications, Kitab Mahal Chaura Rasta, Jaipur 302003 India. **LC** Z284. **DD** 658.809070573.

BOOKDEALERS IN NORTH AMERICA. 7th- Ed. UK. English. ir. $25.00. Sheppard Press Ltd, PO Box 42 Russell Chambers, London WC2E 8AX England. **Tel** (01)240 0406. **Ed** T Rendall Davies. adv acc. **Circ** 4,000. Directory of dealers in secondhand and antiquarian books in Canada and USA, - tenth edition. *Book Dealers in North America.*

BOOKLETTER/SOUTHEAST. **VFOAT** Bookletter Southeast. V. 1, No. 1 (Nov./Dec. 1977)-. Periodical. US. English. qt. $12.00. Route 2 Box 440, Greenwood SC 29646.

BOOKNOTES (PORTLAND, ORE.). (BOOKNOTES). **VFOAT** Book Notes. July 1984-. 0747-847X. Periodical. US. English. mo. $35.00. Interpub, PO Box 42265, Portland OR 97242.

BOOKS AND ART IN THE USSR. 0201-8500. Periodical. UR. English. qt. **LC** Z2491. **DD** 015.47.

BOOKS AND BOOKMEN. V. 1- Oct. 1955-. 0006-744X. Periodical. UK. English. mo. $30.48. Brevet Publishing Ltd, 43 B Gloucester Road, Croydon CR0 2DH England. **Ed** Sally Emerson. **Ind/Abst** Book Rev. Index, Abstr. Engl. Stud. **LC** Z2005. *John O'London's Books of the Month, Argosy; Book Guide; Books-in-Print; Technical Books-in-Print; Books-in-Britain.*

BOOKS & RELIGION. *See* Religion, Mythology, Rationalism.

BOOKS AT BROWN. V. 1- June 1938-. 0147-0787. Periodical. US. English. an. $10.00. Friends of the Library of Brown University, PO Box A, Providence RI 02912. **Tel** (401)863-2146. **Ind/Abst** MLA Int. Bibliogr. Books Artic. Mod. Lang. Lit. **LC** Z733.P958. **DD** 027.7745. **Circ** 400. (ctrl). Prints articles and bibliographic essays from research based on the collections of Brown University Library. Also considers profiles of book collectors, articles on book collecting, fine printing, and graphic arts.

BOOKS FROM FINLAND. V. 1- 1967-. 0006-7490. Periodical. FI. English. sa. 125.00. Akakeeminen-Kirjakuppa, PO Box 128, 00101 Helsinki Finland. **Tel** (90)651 122. **Ind/Abst** MLA Int. Bibliogr. Books Artic. Mod. Lang. Lit. **LC** Z2520. **DD** 015.471.

BOOKS FROM ISRAEL. **Main/Corp** Israel Export Institute. Book and Printing Center. 0578-932X. IS. English. an. Free. Israel Book & Printing Center, 29 Hamered Street PO Box 29732, 68125 Tel Aviv Israel. **Tel** (03)630-830. bk rev. adv acc. **Circ** 2,500. (ctrl). A review of books published in Israel in the current year. Short annotations with relevant information about books. Covers all subject areas. *Catalogue of Selected Books from Israel for the International Book Trade.*

BOOKS IN ARABIC. (BOOKS IN ARABIC : RECENT ACQUISITIONS). **Main/Corp** Metropolitan Toronto Library Board. **VFOAT** Lughah Al-Arabiyyah. Vol. 1, No. 1 (Aug. 1980)-. 0713-4460. Periodical. CN. English. ir. Free. Metropolitan Toronto Library Board, 789 Yonge Street, Toronto Ontario M4W 2G8 Canada. **DD** 017.12927. (ctrl). *Arabic, 0713-4452.*

BOOKS IN ARABIC; ADDITIONS. **Main/Corp** Metropolitan Toronto Central Library. Languages Centre. Began publication in 1969?. 0705-7172. Periodical. CN. English. qt. Languages Centre of the Metropolitan Toronto Central Library, 214 College Street, Toronto Ontario M5T 1R3 Canada. **DD** 016.8927.

BOOKS IN ARMENIAN. **Main/Corp** Metropolitan Toronto Library Board. Languages Co-Ordinator. 0705-8209. Periodical. CN. English. qt. Metropolitan Toronto Library Board, Languages Co-ordinator, 229 College Street West, Toronto Ontario M5R 1R3 Canada. **DD** 016.891992. *Books in Armenian.*

BOOKS IN BENGALI. (BOOKS IN BENGALI : RECENT ACQUISITIONS). **Main/Corp** Metropolitan Toronto Library Board. Vol. 1, No. 1 (Aug. 1980)-. 0713-5335. Periodical. CN. English. ir. Free. Metropolitan Toronto Library Board, 789 Yonge Street, Toronto Ontario M4W 2G8 Canada. **DD** 017.129144. (ctrl). *Bengali, 0713-5327.*

BOOKS IN CANADA. V. 1- July 1971-. 0045-2564. Periodical. CN. English. ir. 13.95 Domestic, 16.95 Foreign. Canadian Review of Books, 366 Adelaide Street East/Suite 432, Toronto Ontario M5A 3X9 Canada. **Tel** (416)363-5426. **Ed** Michael Smith. **Ind/Abst** Can. Period. Index, Book Rev. Index, Book Rev. Index, Ref. Source. **LC** Z1369. **DD** 028.10971. bk rev. adv acc. **Circ** 30,000. Literary book review magazine for consumers. In addition to reviews, contains articles about, and profiles and interviews of, Canadian authors.

BOOKS IN CHINESE. (BOOKS IN CHINESE : RECENT ACQUISITIONS). **Main/Corp** Metropolitan Toronto Library Board. Vol. 1, No. 1 (Aug. 1980)-. 0713-4495. Periodical. CN. English (in Chinese). ir. Free. Metropolitan Toronto Library Board, 789 Yonge Street, Toronto Ontario M4W 2G8 Canada. **DD** 017.12951. (ctrl). *Chinese, 0713-4487.*

BOOKS IN CROATIAN. (BOOKS IN CROATIAN-SERBIAN : RECENT ACQUISITIONS). **Main/Corp** Metropolitan Toronto Library Board. **Series/Titl** Multilanguage Collections in the Public Libraries of Metropolitan Toronto. Vol. 1, No. 1 (Aug. 1980)-. 0713-4568. Periodical. CN. English. ir. Free. Metropolitan Toronto Library Board, 789 Yonge Street, Toronto Ontario M4W 2G8 Canada. **DD** 017.129182. (ctrl). *Croatian Serbian, 0713-455X.*

BOOKS IN CZECH. **Main/Corp** Metropolitan Toronto Library Board. Languages Co-Ordinator. July/Sept. 1973-. 0705-2308. Periodical. CN. English. qt. Languages Co-Ordinator of the Metropolitan Toronto Library Board, 229 College Street, Toronto Ontario M5T 1R4 Canada. **DD** 016.89186. *Books in Czech.*

BOOKS IN DANISH. **Main/Corp** Metropolitan Toronto Library Board. Languages Co-Ordinator. 0705-2332. Periodical. CN. English. qt. Languages Co-Ordinator of the Metropolitan Toronto Library Board, 229 College Street, Toronto Ontario M5T 1R4 Canada. **DD** 016.83981. *Books in Danish.*

BOOKS IN DUTCH. (BOOKS IN DUTCH : RECENT ACQUISITIONS). **Main/Corp** Metropolitan Toronto Library Board. **VFOAT** Nederlands. Vol. 1, No. 1 (Aug. 1980)-. 0713-4533. Periodical. CN. English. ir. Free. Metropolitan Toronto Library Board, Regional Multi-Language Department, 789 Yonge Street, Toronto Ontario M4W 2G8 Canada. **Tel** (416)928-5326. **Ed** Jaswinder Gundara. **DD** 018.123931. **Circ** 307. (ctrl). A list of multi-language acquisitions in the public library system of Metropolitan Toronto. *Dutch, 0713-4525.*

BOOKS IN ESTONIAN. (BOOKS IN ESTONIAN : RECENT ACQUISITIONS). **Main/Corp** Metropolitan Toronto Library Board. **VFOAT** ESTI Keel. Vol. 1, No. 1 (Aug. 1980)-. 0714-2129. Periodical. CN. English. ir. Free. Metropolitan Toronto Library Board, 789 Yonge Street, Toronto Ontario M4W 2G8 Canada. **DD** 017.1294545. (ctrl). *Estonian, 0714-2110.*

BOOKS IN FINNISH. (BOOKS IN FINNISH : RECENT ACQUISITIONS). **Main/Corp** Metropolitan Toronto Library Board. **VFOAT** Suomenkieii. Vol. 1, No. 1 (Aug. 1980)-. 0714-2382. Periodical. CN. English. ir. Free. Metropolitan Toronto Library Board, Regional Multi-Language Department, 789 Yonge Street, Toronto Ontario M4W 2G8 Canada. **Tel** (416)928-5326. **Ed** Jaswinder Gundara. **DD** 018.1294541. **Circ** 307. (ctrl). A list of multi-language acquisitions in the public library systems of Metropolitan Toronto. *Finnish, 0714-2374.*

BOOKS IN FRENCH *CEASED.* (BOOKS IN FRENCH : RECENT ACQUISITIONS). **Main/Corp** Metropolitan Toronto Library Board. Languages Co-Ordinator. **Series/Titl** Multilanguage Collections in the Public Libraries of Metropolitan Toronto. V. 1, No. 1 (Aug. 1980)-V. 3, No. 4 (Jan. 1983). 0714-2404. Periodical. CN. English. ir. Free. Metropolitan Toronto Library Board, 789 Yonge Street, Toronto Ontario M4W 2G8 Canada. **DD** 018.1241. (ctrl). *French, 0714-2390.*

BOOKS IN FRISIAN. **Main/Corp** Metropolitan Toronto Library Board. Languages Co-Ordinator. Began publication in 1973. 0705-2286. Periodical. CN. English. qt. Languages Co-Ordinator of the Metropolitan Toronto Public Library Board, 229 College Street, Toronto Ontario M5T 1R4 Canada. **DD** 016.8392.

BOOKS IN FRISIAN. (BOOKS IN FRISIAN : RECENT ACQUISITIONS). **Main/Corp** Metropolitan Toronto Library Board. Vol. 1, No. 1 (Aug. 1980)-. 0714-2420. Periodical. CN. English. ir. Free. Metropolitan Toronto Library Board, 789 Yonge Street, Toronto Ontario M4W 2G8 Canada. **DD** 01812392. (ctrl). *Frisian, 0714-2412.*

BOOKS IN GERMAN. (BOOKS IN GERMAN : RECENT ACQUISITIONS). **Main/Corp** Metropolitan Toronto Library Board. **VFOAT** Deutsch. Vol. 1, No. 1 (Aug. 1980)-. 0714-2455. Periodical. CN. English. ir. Free. Metropolitan Toronto Library Board, 789 Yonge Street, Toronto Ontario M4W 2G8 Canada. **DD** 018.1231. (ctrl). *German, 0714-2447.*

BOOKS IN GREEK. (BOOKS IN GREEK : RECENT ACQUISITIONS). **Main/Corp** Metropolitan Toronto Library Board. **VFOAT** Ellinika. Vol. 1, No. 1 (Aug. 1980)-. 0714-2471. Periodical. CN. English. Free. Metropolitan Toronto Library Board, 789 Yonge Street, Toronto Ontario M4W 2G8 Canada. **DD** 018.1289. (ctrl). *Greek, 0714-2463.*

BOOKS IN GUJARATI. (BOOKS IN GUJARATI : RECENT ACQUISITIONS). **Main/Corp** Metropolitan Toronto Library Board. **Series/Titl** Multilanguage Collections in the Public Libraries of Metropolitan Toronto. **VFOAT** Gajarati. Vol. 1, No. 1 (Aug. 1980)-. 0714-2501. Periodical. CN. English. ir. Free. Metropolitan Toronto Library Board, 789 Yonge Street, Toronto Ontario M4W 2G8 Canada. **DD** 017.1291471. (ctrl). *Gujarati, 0714-2498.*

BOOKS IN HINDI. (BOOKS IN HINDI : RECENT ACQUISITIONS). **Main/Corp** Metropolitan Toronto Library Board. Vol 1, No. 1 (Aug. 1980)-. 0714-2528. Periodical. CN. English. ir. Free. Metropolitan Toronto Library Board, 789 Yonge Street, Toronto Ontario M4W 2G8 Canada. **DD** 017.1291431. (ctrl). *Hindi, 0714-251X.*

BOOKS IN HUNGARIAN. (BOOKS IN HUNGARIAN : RECENT ACQUISITIONS). **Main/Corp** Metropolitan Toronto Library Board. **VFOAT** Magyar. Vol. 1, No. 1 (Aug. 1980)-. 0714-2544. CN. English. ir. Free. Metropolitan Toronto Library Board, Regional Multi-Language Department, 789 Yonge Street, Toronto Ontario M4W 2G8 Canada. **Tel** (416)928-5326. **Ed** Jaswinder Gundara. **DD** 018.1294511. **Circ** 307. (ctrl). A list of multi-language acquisitions in the public library systems of Metropolitan Toronto. *Hungarian, 0714-2536.*

BOOKS IN ITALIAN. (BOOKS IN ITALIAN : RECENT ACQUISITIONS). **Main/Corp** Metropolitan Toronto Library Board. **VFOAT** Italianio. Vol. 1, No. 1 (Aug. 1980)-. 0714-2609. CN. English. ir. Free. Metropolitan Toronto Library Board, 789 Yonge Street, Toronto Ontario M4W 2G8 Canada. **DD** 018.1251. (ctrl). *Italian, 0714-2595.*

BOOKS IN JAPANESE. **Main/Corp** Metropolitan Toronto Library Board. Languages Co-Ordinator. 0705-6486. Periodical. CN. English. qt. Languages Co-Ordinator of the Metropolitan Toronto Library Board, 229 College Street, Toronto Ontario M5T 1R4 Canada. **DD** 016.8956. *Books in Japanese.*

BOOKS IN LATVIAN. **Main/Corp** Metropolitan Toronto Library Board. Languages Co-Ordinator. 0705-8381. Periodical. CN. English. qt. Languages Co-Ordinator of the Metropolitan Toronto Library Board, 229 College Street, Toronto Ontario M5T 1R4 Canada. **DD** 016.89193. *Books in Latvian.*

BOOKS IN LITHUANIAN. **Main/Corp** Metropolitan Toronto Library Board. Languages Co-Ordinator. 0705-8225. Periodical. CN. English. qt. Languages Co-Ordinator of the Metropolitan Toronto Library Board, 229 College Street, Toronto Ontario M5T 1R4 Canada. **DD** 016.89192. *Books in Lithuanian.*

BOOKS IN MARATHI. **Main/Corp** Metropolitan Toronto Library Board. Languages Co-Ordinator. 0317-2406. Periodical. CN. English. qt. Metropolitan Toronto Library Board Languages Co-Ordinator, 229 College Street, Toronto Ontario M5T 1R4 Canada. **DD** 016.89146. *Books in Marathi.*

BOOKS IN PANJABI. (BOOKS IN PANJABI : RECENT ACQUISITIONS). **Main/Corp** Metropolitan Toronto Library Board. **Series/Titl** Multilanguage Collections in the Public Libraries of Metropolitan Toronto. Vol. 1, No. 1 (Aug. 1980)-. 0714-282X. Periodical. CN. English. ir. Free. Metropolitan Toronto Library Board, 789 Yonge Street, Toronto Ontario M4W 2G8 Canada. **DD** 017.129142. (ctrl). *Panjabi, 0714-2811.*

BOOKS IN PERSIAN. (BOOKS IN PERSIAN : RECENT ACQUISITIONS). **Main/Corp** Metropolitan Toronto Library Board. **Series/Titl** Mutlilanguage Collections in the Public Libraries of Metropolitan Toronto. **VFOAT** Farsi. Vol. 1, No. 1 (Aug. 1980)-. 0227-2741. Periodical. CN. English. qt. Free. Metropolitan Toronto Library Board, Regional Multi-Language Department, 789 Yonge Street, Toronto Ontario M4W 2G8 Canada. **Tel** (416)928-5326. **Ed**

Jaswinder Gundara. DD 017.129155. Circ 307. (ctrl). A list of multi-language acquisitions in the Metropolitan Toronto Library systems. *Persian, 0714-2757.*

BOOKS IN POLISH. (BOOKS IN POLISH : RECENT ACQUISITIONS). **Main/Corp** Metropolitan Toronto Library Board. **Series/Titl** Multilanguage Collections in the Public Libraries of Metropolitan Toronto. **VFOAT** Jezyk Polski. Vol. 1, No. 1 (Aug. 1980)-. 0714-2773. Periodical. CN. English. ir. Free. Metropolitan Toronto Library Board, Regional Multi-Language Department, 789 Yonge Street, Toronto Ontario M4W 2G8 Canada. **Tel** (412)928-5326. **Ed** Jaswinder Gundara. **DD** 018.1291851. **Circ** 307. (ctrl). A list of multi-language acquisitions in the public library systems of Metropolitan Toronto. *Polish, 0714-2765.*

BOOKS IN POLISH OR RELATING TO POLAND. V. 1- 1950-. Periodical. UK. English. qt. Polish Library, 238-246 King Street, London W6 ORF England.

BOOKS IN PORTUGUESE. (BOOKS IN PORTUGUESE : RECENT ACQUISITIONS). **Main/Corp** Metropolitan Toronto Library Board. **Series/Titl** Multilanguage Collections in the Public Libraries of Metropolitan Toronto. **VFOAT** Portuguese. Vol. 1, No. 1 (1980)-. 0714-279X. Periodical. CN. English. ir. Free. Metropolitan Toronto Library Board, 789 Yonge Street, Toronto Ontario M4W 2G8 Canada. **DD** 018.1269. (ctrl). *Portuguese, 0714-2781.*

BOOKS IN PORTUGUESE; ADDITIONS. **Main/Corp** Metropolitan Toronto Central Library. Languages Centre. Began with Oct./Dec. 1969 issue. 0705-6745. Periodical. CN. English. qt. Languages Centre of the Metropolitan Toronto Central Library, 214 College Street, Toronto Ontario M5T 1R3 Canada. **DD** 016.869. *Books in Portuguese.*

BOOKS IN PRINT MICROFORM. 1948-. US. English. an. $199.95. R R Bowker Company, PO Box 1807, Ann Arbor MI 48106. **Tel** (212)916-1600. Provides bibliography data on virtually all US books in print and forthcoming.

BOOKS IN PRINT SOUTH AFRICA. **VFOAT** Suid-Afrikaanse Boeke Tans in Druk. Began with Vol. for 1979. Afrikaans (English). ir. 42.90. Cedarwood Text, PO Box 51254, Randburg 2125 South Africa. **LC** Z3603. **DD** 015.68.

BOOKS IN PRINT SUPPLEMENT. 1972/73-. 0000-0310. US. English. an. R R Bowker, PO Box 1807, Ann Arbor MI 48106. **Tel** (212)916-1600. **LC** Z1215. **DD** 015.73. **NLM** Z 1215 B724A. A supplement to books in print, a comprehensive bibliographic reference listing every US book in print.

BOOKS IN RUSSIAN; ADDITIONS. **Main/Corp** Metropolitan Toronto Central Library. Languages Centre. Began with Oct./Dec. 1969 issue. 0705-6737. Periodical. CN. English. qt. Languages Centre of the Metropolitan Toronto Central Library, 214 College Street, Toronto Ontario M5T 1R3 Canada. **DD** 016.8917. *Books in Russian.*

BOOKS IN SCOTLAND. No. 1 (Spring-Summer 1978)-. 0143-1285. Periodical. UK. English. ir. $8.89. Ramsay Head Press, 36 North Castle Street, Edinburgh Scotland. **Tel** 031-225 5666. **Ed** Norman Wilson. bk rev. adv acc. **Circ** 3,000. A review of books in general, new books by Scottish writers and books about Scotland. Also, articles on contemporary writing and authors who's who.

BOOKS IN SERIES. 3rd Ed.-. US. English. an. $360.50. R R Bowker, PO Box 1807, Ann Arbor MI 48106. **NLM** Z 1033.S5 B724. *Books in Series in the United States, 0000-0515.*

BOOKS IN SPANISH. (BOOKS IN SPANISH : RECENT ACQUISITIONS). **Main/Corp** Metropolitan Toronto Library Board. **Series/Titl** Multilanguage Collections in the Public Libraries of Metropolitan Toronto. Vol. 1, No. 1 (Aug. 1980)-. 0713-5998. Periodical. CN. English. ir. Free. Metropolitan Toronto Library Board, 789 Yonge Street, Toronto Ontario M4W 2G8 Canada. **DD** 018.1261. (ctrl). *Spanish, 0713-598X.*

BOOKS IN SWEDISH. **Main/Corp** Metropolitan Toronto Library Board. Languages Co-Ordinator. 0705-8489. Periodical. CN. English. qt. Languages Co-Ordinator of the Metropolitan Toronto Library Board, 229 College Street, Toronto Ontario M5T 1R4 Canada. **DD** 016.8397. *Books in Swedish.*

BOOKS IN TAGALOG. (BOOKS IN TAGALOG : RECENT ACQUISITIONS). **Main/Corp** Metropolitan Toronto Library Board. **Series/Titl** Multilanguage Collections in the Public Libraries of Metropolitan Toronto. 0824-5592. Periodical. CN. English. ir. Free. Metropolitan Toronto Library Board, 789 Yonge Street, Toronto Ontario M4W 2G8 Canada. **DD** 017.1299211. (ctrl). *Tagalog, 0714-2994.*

BOOKS IN UKRAINIAN. (BOOKS IN UKRAINIAN : RECENT ACQUISITIONS). **Main/Corp** Metropolitan Toronto Library Board. Vol. 1, No. 1 (Aug. 1980)-. 0714-2927. Periodical. CN. English. ir. Free. Metropolitan Toronto Library Board, 789 Yonge Street, Toronto Ontario M4W 2G8 Canada. **DD** 017.1291791. (ctrl). *Ukrainian, 0714-2919.*

BOOKS IN URDU. (BOOKS IN URDU : RECENT ACQUISITIONS). **Main/Corp** Metropolitan Toronto Library Board. Vol. 1, No. 1 (Aug. 1980)-. 0714-296X. Periodical. CN. English. ir. Free. Metropolitan Toronto Library Board, 789 Yonge Street, Toronto Ontario M4W 2G8 Canada. **DD** 017.1291439. (ctrl). *Urdu, 0714-2951.*

BOOKS IN VIETNAMESE. (BOOKS IN VIETNAMESE : RECENT ACQUISITIONS). **Main/Corp** Metropolitan Toronto Library Board. **Series/Titl** Multilanguage Collections in the Public Libraries of Metropolitan Toronto. Vol. 1, No. 1 (Aug. 1980)-. 0227-2776. Periodical. CN. English. ir. Free. Metropolitan Toronto Library Board, 789 Yonge Street, Toronto Ontario M4W 2G8 Canada. **DD** 018.1295922. (ctrl). *Languages Co-Ordinator. Vietnamese, 0714-2854.*

BOOKS IN YIDDISH. **Main/Corp** Metropolitan Toronto Library Board. Vol. 1, No. 1 (Aug. 1980)-. 0705-8268. Periodical. CN. English. ir. Free. Metropolitan Toronto Library Board, 789 Yonge Street, Toronto Ontario M4W 2G8 Canada. **DD** 017.1237. (ctrl). *Books in Yiddish, 0705-8268.*

BOOKS INDIA. II. English. ir. National Book Trust, A-5 Green Park, New Delhi 110016 India. **LC** Z3203. **DD** 015.54.

BOOKS NOW. *See* Literature.

BOOKS ON DEMAND: AUTHOR GUIDE. INTERNATIONAL ED. (BOOKS ON DEMAND; AUTHOR GUIDE). 1983-. 0736-9034. US. English. University Microfilms International, 300 N Zeeb Road, Ann Arbor MI 48106.

BOOKS OUT-OF-PRINT. **VFOAT** Books Out of Print. 1980-1983-. 0000-0736. US. English. an. R R Bowker Company, 205 East 42nd Street, New York NY 10017. **LC** Z1000.5. **DD** 015. **NLM** Z 1000.5.

BOOKSELLER (1927). (THE BOOKSELLER). No. 1139 (Sept. 16, 1927)-No. 1167 (Mar. 30, 1928) – New Weekly Series. Periodical. UK. English. wk. 53.00. J Whitaker & Sons Ltd, 12 Dyott Street, London WC1A 1DF England. **Tel** (01)836-8911. **Ed** Louis Baum. bk rev. adv acc. **Circ** 20,000. Book trade newspaper containing news views and reviews including a listing of all books published in the UK in that week. *Bookseller and the Stationery Trades' Journal.*

BOOKSELLERS CHOICE. 1977-. 0705-3169. CN. English. an. Free. Canadian Booksellers Association, Suite 400/56 The Esplanade, Toronto Ontario M5E 1A7 Canada. **DD** 015.71. *Canadian Basic Books, 0317-6037.*

BOOKSTORE JOURNAL REVIEWS. V. 1- Fall 1973-. 0092-6264. Periodical. US. English. ty. 2031 W Cheyenne Road, Colorado Springs CO 80906. **LC** Z286.R4. **DD** 028.1.

BORSENBLATT FUR DEN DEUTSCHEN BUCHHANDEL. FRANKFURTER AUSGABE. SONDERNUMMER. Vol. 1-. Periodical. GW. German. ir. Buchhandler Vereinigung GMBH, Grosser Hischgraben 17-21, D-60 Frankfurt 1 West Germany.

BP REPORT ON THE BUSINESS OF BOOK PUBLISHING. **VFOAT** BP Report. 0145-9457. Periodical. US. English. wk. $275.00. Knowledge Industry Publications Inc, 701 Westchester Avenue, White Plains NY 10604. **Tel** (914)328-9157. **Ed** Morilynn Mcgeehon. Newsletter on business of book publishing. Covers financial, personnel, product and general news about book publishing.

BRAILLE BOOK REVIEW. Began publication in 1932. 0006-873X. Periodical. US. English. bm. Publication Services, National Library Service for the Blind and Physically Handicapped, Library of Congress, Washington DC 20542. **LC** Z5346.Z9. **DD** 011.63. Also available in a braille edition.

BRAILLE BOOKS. *See* Physically Impaired.

BRITISH BOOKS IN PRINT. 1965-. 0068-1350. UK. English. an. R R Bowker Company, 205 East 42nd Street, New York NY 10017. **Tel** (800)521-0600. **LC** Z2001. **DD** 015.41. **NLM** Z 2001 R332. *Reference Catalogue of Current Literature.*

BRITISH BULLETIN OF PUBLICATIONS ON LATIN AMERICA, THE CARIBBEAN, PORTUGAL AND SPAIN. No. 59 (Oct. 1978)-. Periodical. UK. English. sa. 10.00. Bailey Brothers & Swinfen Ltd, Warner House, Folkestone Kent CT19 6PH England. **Tel** 01 235 2303. **Ed** Noel Treacy. bk rev. **Circ** 1,000. (ctrl). Informs readers of recently published books in English on the countries included in the title. *British Bulletin of Publications on Latin America, The West Indies, Portugal and Spain.*

BRITISH PAPERBACKS IN PRINT. 1982-. 0262-9763. UK. English. an. $47.50. J Whitaker & Sons Ltd, 12 Dyott Street, London WC1A 1DF England. **Tel** 01-836 8911. **LC** Z1033.P3. **DD** 019.40941. Listing of more than 65,000 titles in print and in paperback, published or distributed in the United Kingdom. A list of series and their publishers. *Paperbacks in Print (J. Whitaker & Sons).*

BUCH + I.E. UND LESER. German. ir. Hauptabteilung Information und Offentlichkertsarbeit, 6 1 Postfach 3914, Frankfurt AM Main W Germany. **LC** Z319.

BUCHERSCHIFF; DIE DEUTSCHE BUCHERZEITUNG. 1- May 1951-. 0007-3059. Periodical. GW. German. ir. Altkonig-Verlag Dr G Dietrich, Gartenstrasse 13, Postfach 460, 6370 Oberursel West Germany.

BULGARIAN ACADEMIC BOOKS. Began in 1969. 0324-0509. English. an. Bulgarian Academy of Sciences, 36th Street, Sofia Bulgaria. **LC** Z5055.B9. **DD** 015.4977.

BULLETIN D'INFORMATION - FOIRE INTERNATIONALE DU LIVRE DE MONTREAL. **Main/Corp** Montreal International Book Fair. **VFOAT** Newsletter - Montreal International Book Fair. No. 1- Dec. 1, 1975-. 0700-5083. Periodical. CN. English (French). Montreal International Book Fair, 436 Sherbrooke Street East, Montreal Quebec H2L 1J6 Canada. **DD** 338.4707050740114281.

BULLETIN OF INFORMATION - REGIONAL CENTRE FOR BOOK PROMOTION IN AFRICA. **Main/Corp** Regional Centre for Book Promotion in Africa. **VFOAT** Bulletin d'Information - Centre Regional de Promotion du Livre en Afrique. V. 1- Jan./Mar. 1978-. English (French). ir. The Director, Regional Centre for Book Promotion in Africa, PO Box 1646, Yaounde Cameroon. **LC** Z465.7. **DD** 658.809070573096.

BULLETIN OF THE CENTER FOR CHILDREN'S BOOKS. **Main/Corp** University of Chicago. Center for Children's Books. V. 12- Sept. 1958-. 0008-9036. Periodical. US. English. mo. University of Chicago Press, PO Box 37005, Chicago IL 60637. **Tel** (312)753-3347. **Ind/Abst** Book Rev. Index. **LC** Z1037.A1. *Bulletin of the Children's Book Center.*

BUTT. V. 1-. 0146-7182. Periodical. US. English. qt. $5.00. Len Andersen, 156 Pleasant Street, Arlington MA 02174.

BUY BOOKS WHERE, SELL BOOKS WHERE. (BUY BOOKS WHERE - SELL BOOKS WHERE). Began with 1978 Vol. 0732-6599. US. English. ir. $21.50. Ruth E Robinson Books, Route 7 Box 162A, Morgantown WV 26505. **Tel** (304)594-3140. **Ed** Ruth E Robinson and Daryush Farudi. **LC** Z475. **DD** 070.502573. bk rev. adv acc. A directory of out-of-print booksellers and their author/subject specialties by author/subject and geographic location of bookseller.

CAHIERS DE BIBLIOLOGIE. 1-. 0228-6556. Periodical. CN. French. ir. $4.00 Per Number. Librairie Jean Gagnon, 498 rue d'Aiguillon/CP 653 HV, Quebec Quebec G1R 4S2 Canada. **DD** 010.

CANADA BOOK AUCTIONS. Sale No. 121- Oct. 25, 1979-. 0225-0543. Periodical. CN. English. ir. **DD** 018'.3. *Montreal Book Auctions.*

CANADA BOOK AUCTIONS RECORDS. Vol. 6 (1979/1980)-. 0711-7299. CN. English. be. $27.09. Canada Book Auctions, 35 Front Street East, Toronto Ontario M5E 1B3 Canada. **Tel**

Publishing—Books and Bookmaking

(416)368-4326. **DD** 018.3. *Montreal Book Auction Records, 0226-0107.*

CANADIAN BOOKS IN PRINT CEASED. VFOAT Catalogue des Livres Canadiens en Librairie. 1967-1974. 0702-0201. Periodical. CN. French (English). an. University of Toronto Press, Front Campus, Toronto Ontario M5S 1A6 Canada. **DD** 015.71. **NLM** Z 1365 C211.

CANADIAN BOOKS IN PRINT. AUTHOR AND TITLE INDEX. See Indexes/Abstracts.

CANADIAN BOOKSELLER. (THE CANADIAN BOOKSELLER). Jan. 1979-. 0225-2392. Periodical. CN. English. ir. 20.00. Canadian Booksellers Association, 49 Laing Street, Toronto Ontario M4L 2N4 Canada. Tel (416)469-5976. Ed Gillian O'Reilly. **DD** 658.809070570971. Circ 1,300. Journal of the Canadian retail book trade. Net 30, 0225-6622.

CARNETS DU GOBELET. (LES CARNETS DU GOBELET : BULLETIN DES GENS DU LIVRE). No. 1 (3 Nov. 1980)-. 0820-0475. Periodical. CN. French. mo. $5.00. Carnets du Gobelet, c/o H Tranquille, App 5, 1480 rue Crevier, Saint Laurent Quebec H4L 2X3 Canada. **DD** 028.8.

CASSETTE BOOKS. Main/Corp Library of Congress. National Library Service for the Blind and Physically Handicapped. Began with 1977/78. 0363-9029. US. English. an. Library of Congress, National Library Service for the Blind and Physically Handicapped, Washington DC 20542. **LC** Z5347, HV1721. *Cassette Books, 0363-9029.*

CATALOG OF PRINTED BOOKS. SUPPLEMENT. See Bibliographies.

CATALOGUE - LAURENCE WITTEN RARE BOOKS. Main/Corp Laurence Witten Rare Books. 8756-7083. US. English. sa. $15.00 Domestic, $25.00 Foreign. Laurence Witten Rare Books, 181 Old Post Road, PO Box 490, Southport CT 06490. **DD** 018. *Catalogue.*

CATALOGUE OF RARE BOOKS. Main/Corp Meisei Daigaku. Toshokan. No. 1- 1974-. Japanese. ir. Library of Meisei University, 377 Hodokubo (191), Hino Japan. **LC** Z1029.

CCBC : COOPERATIVE CHILDREN'S BOOK CENTER CIRCULAR. Main/Corp Cooperative Children's Book Center, Madison, Wis. VFOAT Cooperative Children's Book Center Circular. V. 1, No. 1-. Periodical. US. English. ir. Cooperative Children's Book Center, 4290 Helen C White Hall, 600 Park Street, Madison WI 53706.

CERLAL, NOTICIAS SOBRE EL LIBRO. VFOAT Noticias Sobre el Libro. No. 30 (July 1981)-. 0120-0887. Periodical. CK. Spanish. qt. Cerlal, Apartado Aereo 17438, Bogota Colombia. **Ind/Abst** Libr. Inf. Sci. Abstr. **LC** Z490. **DD** 070.5098. *Noticias Sobre el Libro y Bibliografia.*

CHILDREN'S BOOKS IN PRINT (LONDON, ENGLAND). (CHILDREN'S BOOKS IN PRINT). VFOAT Whitaker Children's Books in Print. Began in 1969. 0577-781X. UK. English. an. 31. J Whitaker & Sons, 12 Dyott Street, London WC1 1DF England. Ed Edward Heron. **LC** Z1037. **DD** 028.52. adv acc. Listing of over 24,000 children's books in print with alphabetical and classified sections of titles published or distributed in UK plus directory of publishers and distributors.

CHOICE. VFOAT Books for College Libraries. V. 1- March 1964-. 0009-4978. Periodical. US. English. mo. $100.00 Domestic, $110.00 Foreign. Choice, 100 Riverview Center, Middletown CT 06457. Tel (203)347-6933. Ed Patricia Sabosik. **Ind/Abst** Book Rev. Index, Libr. Lit., Ref. Source. **LC** Z1035. bk rev. adv acc. Circ 5,000. Books and nonprint selection journal published by the Association of College and Research Libraries, a division of the American Library Association.

CHONGHAP TOSO MONGNOK. VFOAT Catalogue of KPC Books. KO. Korean. ir. Hanguk Chulpan Hyoptong Chohap, 91 2-ka Sinmun-no, Chongno-ku, Seoul Korea. **LC** Z316.

CHRISTIAN BOOKSELLER & LIBRARIAN CEASED. VFOAT Christian Bookseller and Librarian. Vol. 28, No. 10 (Oct. 1982)-V. 29, No. 11 (Nov. 1983). 0736-0649. Periodical. US. English. ir. $18.00. 396 East Street Charles Road, Wheaton IL 60188. Tel (312)653-4200. Ed Karen Tornberg. **LC** BV2369. **DD** 070.57. bk rev. adv acc. Circ 9,700. (ctrl). Readership is primarily Christian booksellers, publishers, etc. Contains current book and reviews as well as articles on store management, trends in the industry, etc. *Christian Bookseller, 0009-5273.*

CHRISTIAN BOOKSELLER (WHEATON, ILL. : 1983). (CHRISTIAN BOOKSELLER). Vol. 29, No. 12 (Dec. 1983)-. 0749-2510. Periodical. US. English. mo. $18.00. Christian Life Missions, 396 E Street, Charles Road, Wheaton IL 60187. Tel (312)653-4200. Ed Karen Tornberg. **LC** BV2369. **DD** 381.45002. bk rev. adv acc. Circ 10,000. (ctrl). We are a Christian publication going to religious bookstores, publishers, etc. We carry articles on management, industry information, and book reviews. *Christian Bookseller & Librarian, 0736-0649.*

CHULPAN MUNHWA. VFOAT Korean Books Journal, Korean Publishers Association Journal. 0009-6245. Periodical. KO. Korean. mo. 300 Single Issue. Taehan Chulpan Munhwa Hyophoe, 105-2 Saryon-dong, Chongno-ku Seoul 110 Korea. **LC** Z464.K67.

CLE DIRECTORY OF THE IRISH BOOK TRADE. See Yearbooks, Almanacs, Directories.

COMIC BOOKS, PAPERBACKS, MAGAZINES. Series/Titl The Official Collector's Price Report. VFOAT Comics, Paperbacks, and Magazines. 1st Ed.-. 0747-5225. US. English. an. $3.50. The House of Collectibles Inc, Orlando Central Park, 1900 Premier Row, Orlando FL 32809. **LC** Z1000.5. **DD** 017.8.

CORANTO. V. 1-. 0010-8669. Periodical. US. English. ir. University of Southern California Library, Gifts and Exchange Department, Los Angeles CA 90089-0182. Tel (213)743-6055. Ed Steven Hanson. **Ind/Abst** MLA Int. Bibliogr. Books Artic. Mod. Lang. Lit., Abstr. Engl. Stud. **LC** AP2. **DD** 051. Circ 750. Concerns itself with books and people of interest in the realm of book collecting and writing, especially those with some special interest in USC.

CUMULATIVE BOOK INDEX. See Indexes/Abstracts.

UN AN DE NOUVEAUTES. 1981-. 0294-1090. FR. French. an. Editions Professionnelles du Livre, 18 rue Dauphine, F-75006 Paris France. *An de Nouveautes (Edition Avec Prix Cession de Base), 0223-5218; An de Nouveautes (Edition Destinee a l'Etranger), 0223-5226.*

DEUTSCHE BUCHER. Began publication 1974. Periodical. German. ir. Editions Rodopi, Keizersgracht 302-304, Amsterdam Netherlands. *Duitse Boek, 0046-080X.*

DIRECTORY OF AMERICAN BOOK SPECIALISTS. See Yearbooks, Almanacs, Directories.

A DIRECTORY OF DEALERS IN SECONDHAND AND ANTIQUARIAN BOOKS IN THE BRITISH ISLES. See Yearbooks, Almanacs, Directories.

DK NEWSLETTER. See Bibliographies.

DOCUMENTATION ON BOOKS. Began in 1972. Periodical. English. bm. European Foundation for Management Development, Place Stephanie 20, B - 1050 Brussels Belgium.

DOCUMENTI SULLE ARTI DEL LIBRO. 1-. 0070-6906. IT. Italian. ir. Edizoni Polifilo, Via Borgonuovo 2, 20121 Milano Italy. **LC** Z4.

DRITA. Began with 1961 issues. Periodical. Albanian. wk. $7.72. Book Distribution Enterprise, rue Konferenca E Pezes, Tirana Albania. **LC** UNC.

EARLY ENGLISH BOOKS, 1475, 1640, SELECTED FROM POLLARD AND REDGRAVE'S SHORT-TITLE CATALOGUE. VFOAT Early English Books, 1475-1640. 1-. US. English. University Microfilms International, 300 North Zeeb Road, Ann Arbor MI 48106. **LC** Z2002. **DD** 015.42. *English Books, 1475-1640. Consolidated Cross Index by STC Number.*

ECONOMIC SURVEY. Main/Corp Booksellers Association of Great Britain and Ireland. Charter Group. UK. English. an. 154 Buckingham Palace Road, London SW1W 9TZ England. **LC** Z329. **DD** 658.8090705730941.

ELLENIKA BIBLIA (TORONTO, ONT.). (ELLENIKA BIBLIA). 1st Ed. (1981)-. 0710-5223. CN. English (text in Greek). be. Ellenika Biblia. **DD** 011.289.

ERWACHSENENBILDUNG IN OSTERREICH. See Education (General).

THE EUROMONITOR BOOK READERSHIP SURVEY. VFOAT Book Readership Survey. UK. English. an. Euromonitor Publications, PO Box 26/18 Doughty Street, London WC1N 2AN England. *Book Readership Survey.*

FACSIMILES IN COLLOTYPE OF IRISH MANUSCRIPTS. Main/Corp Ireland (Eire). Irish Manuscripts Commission. 1931-. IE. English. ir. Government Publ Sales Office, Government Printing Office, Arcade Dublin Ireland, Dublin Ireland. **LC** Z115IR. **DD** 091.

FICHERO BIBLIOGRAFICO HISPANOAMERICANO. See Bibliographies.

THE FOLIO. V. 1- Sept./Oct. 1947-. 0015-5772. Periodical. UK. English. ir. Folio, 33 Bedford Place, London, WC1B SJX England. **LC** Z990. **DD** 655.405.

FORTHCOMING BOOKS. VFOAT FB, Forthcoming Books. V. 1- Jan. 1966-. 0015-8119. US. English. bm. RR Bowker Company, 1180 Avenue of the Americas, New York NY 10036. (subscription address: Bowker Subscription Service PO Box 1429, Riverton NJ 08077). Tel (800)257-7894. **LC** Z1219. **DD** 015.73. *Interim Index to Forthcoming Books.*

GENEALOGICAL & LOCAL HISTORY BOOKS IN PRINT. 0146-616X. Monographic Series. US. English. ir. $5.95. Genealogical and Local History, 6818 Lois Drive, Springfield VA 22150. Tel (703)922-7550. Ed Netti Schreiner-Yantis. **LC** Z5313.U5. Each issue contains an index to its own contents - no vol index - loose. adv acc. Circ 15,000. A bibliography of over 30,000 books and microforms valuable to those tracing their ancestry; with full ordering information for each. *Genealogical Books in Print, 0147-426X.*

THE GET READY SHEET. See Library and Information Science.

GODT BOGARBEJDE (FORENING FOR BOGHAANDVRK (DENMARK) : 1972). (GODT BOGARBEJDE). Danish. an. **LC** Z121. *Arets Bedste Bogtryk.*

GUIA A LAS RESENAS DE LIBROS DE Y SOBRE HISPANOAMERICA. VFOAT Guide to Reviews of Books from and About Hispanic America. 1972-. US. Spanish (English). an. Index each issue contains an index to its own contents - no vol index - loose.

GUIA DAS LIVRARIAS E PONTOS DE VENDA DE LIVROS NO BRASIL. 1-. Ed. Portuguese. ir. Sindicato Nacional dos Editores de Libros, Av Rio Branco 37 - 150 Andar S/1503/6 1510/12, Rio de Janeiro Brazil. **LC** Z521.5.

GUIA DE COMPRAS DEL LIBRERO. Spanish. ir. Pueyrredon 1753, Buenos Aires Argentina. **LC** Z519.5.

GUILD OF BOOK WORKERS JOURNAL. VFOAT Journal of the Guild of Book Workers. V. 1- Fall 1962-. 0434-9245. Periodical. US. English. sa. $30.00. Guild of Book Workers, 521 Fifth Avenue, New York NY 10175. Tel (212)757-6454. Ed Virginia Wiseneski-Klett. **Ind/Abst** Art Archaeol. Tech. Abstr. **LC** Z1008. **DD** 686.305. (cum index). bk rev. adv acc. Circ 900. History of book arts related subjects, and modern practices, reviews of exhibitions.

GUNZO. Began in 1946. Periodical. JA. Japanese. mo. $72.00. Kinokuniya Bookstores America, 1581 Webster Street, San Francisco CA 94115. Tel (415)567-7625. bk rev. adv acc. Novels.

HANGUK KYOGWASO MONGNOK. Korean. ir. **LC** Z5817, L B3048.K6.

HEAD AND HAND : NEWSLETTER OF THE CSE BOOKCLUB CEASED. VFOAT Head & Hand. No. 1-. UK. English. ty. 4.00. Head and Hand, c/o John Goodman, CSE, 25 Horsell Road, London N5 1XL England.

HEIDELBERGER TASCHENBUCHER. 0073-1684. Monographic Series. German. ir. Springer Verlag-New York Inc, 175 5th Avenue, New York NY 10010. Tel (212)460-1584. **Ind/Abst** Math. Rev., Biol. Abstr. CODEN HDTSAB.

HINDI PRACARAKA PATRIKA. V. 1- Jan. 1973-. Periodical. Hindi. ir. 6.00. Hindi Pracaraka Samsthana, PO Box 106 Pisachmochan, 221001 Varanasi India. **LC** Z457.

Publishing—Books and Bookmaking

HODEGOS GRAPHIKON TECHNON.
Greek and Modern. ir. Mikras Asias 1, 610 Athenai Germany. **LC** Z249.

HON (YUSHODO SHOTEN). (HON : A BOOK-BIN FOR SCHOLARS). VAT Hon, A Book Bin for Scholars. Vol. 1, No. 1 (Jan. 1970)-. 0046-7839. Periodical. JA. English. an. Export Division Yushodo, 29 Sanei-cho, Tokyo 160 Japan.

HUNGARIAN BOOK REVIEW. V. 14- Jan./Mar. 1972-. 0324-3451. Periodical. HU. English. qt. Akademiai Kiado, POB 24, 1363 Budapest Hungary. **LC** Z2143. **DD** 015.439. *Books from Hungary.*

IMPRIMATUR; EIN JAHRBUCH FUR BUCHERFREUNDE. *See* Yearbooks, Almanacs, Directories.

INDEX TO SCIENTIFIC BOOK CONTENTS. *See* Indexes/Abstracts.

INDIAN BOOK REPORTER CEASED. Began publication in 1964. II. English. ir. Prabhu Book Service, Gurgaon Haryana India. **LC** Z3201. **DD** 015.54.

INDIAN BOOK REVIEW. Jan. 1981-. English. mo. Kalaikathir Coimbatore-37. **LC** Z1035.A1. **DD** 028.1.

INDIAN BOOKS. V. 1- Jan. 1968-. 0019-445X. Periodical. II. English. mo $40.00. Mukherji Book House, 1 Gopi Mohan Dutta Lane, Calcutta 700 003 India. **LC** Z3201.

INDIAN BOOKS IN PRINT. 1st- Ed. 0300-8363. English. Bowker Publishers Company, Erasmus High Street Epping, Essex CM 1 6 4BU England. **Tel** (212)685-9351. **LC** Z3201. **DD** 015.54. NLM Z 3201 I405.

THE INDIAN PUBLISHER AND BOOKSELLER. *See* Publishing.

INTERNATIONAL BIBLIOGRAPHY OF THE BOOK TRADE AND LIBRARIANSHIP. *See* Bibliographies.

INTERNATIONAL BOOK COLLECTORS ALMANAC/NEWSLETTER. *See* Yearbooks, Almanacs, Directories.

INTERNATIONAL BOOK TRADE DIRECTORY. *See* Yearbooks, Almanacs, Directories.

THE INTERNATIONAL BOOKBINDER. 0020-6180. Periodical. US. English. mo. International Bookbinder, Room 506/AFLCIO Building, Washington DC 20401.

INTERNATIONAL BOOKS IN PRINT. Began in 1979. 0170-9348. English. ir. $3.50. K G Saur Inc, 175 5th Avenue, New York NY 10010. **Tel** (212)982-1302. Ed Archie Rugn. **LC** Z2005. **DD** 018.4. NLM Z 2005 I61. Listing of English-language titles published out of US and UK. Includes over 140,000 title entries and 140,000 cross references from over 5,000 publishers. Also two part-author title lists and subject guide.

INTERNATIONAL DIRECTORY OF BOOKSELLERS. *See* Yearbooks, Almanacs, Directories.

INTERNATIONAL PRINT BUYER'S DIRECTORY. *See* Yearbooks, Almanacs, Directories.

IRISH BOOKLORE. Vol. 1, No. 1 (Jan. 1971)-. 0044-8346. Periodical. UK. English. sa. Queens University of Belfast, Department of Library and Information Services, Belfast BT7 1NN North Ireland.

ISRAEL BOOK NEWS : IBN. VFOAT I.B.N. No. 1 (Winter 1983)-. 0333-953X. English. qt. **LC** Z449.7. **DD** 070.5095694.

ISRAEL BOOK TRADE DIRECTORY. *See* Yearbooks, Almanacs, Directories.

ISRAEL BOOK WORLD CEASED. No. 1-38. 0021-1974. Periodical. English. **LC** Z449. **DD** 070.5095694.

JAPAN ENGLISH PUBLICATIONS IN PRINT. 1st Ed. (1985-87)-. 0910-7908. English. ir. Japan Publications Guide Service, CPO Box 971, Tokyo 100-91 Japan. Lists all books, monographs and substantial booklets, to list all annuals, magazines and other periodicals that are published wholly or partly in English in Japan. *Japan English Magazine Directory, Japan English Books in Print.*

JOURNAL OF RARE OLD BOOKS. (THE JOURNAL OF RARE OLD BOOKS). No. 1 (1984)-. 0826-1067. Periodical. CN. English (includes some text in French). $5.50 Per Volume. Journal of Rare Old Books, PO Box 9542, Sainte-Foy Quebec G1V 4B8 Canada. **DD** 002.075.

KNIZHNAIA TORGOVLIA. BIBLIOGRAFICHESKAIA INFORMATSIIA. Vol. 1- 1973-. UR. Miltilingual (Russian). bm. 0.05 Single Issue. Kniga, K-9 UI Nezhdanovoi 8/10, Moskva USSR. **LC** Z279. *Izdatelskoe Delo, Knigovedenie, Knizhnaia Torgovlia I Gosudarstvennaia Bibliografiia.*

KNIZHNAIA TORGOVLIA. OPYT, PROBLEMY, ISSLEDOVANIIA. 0320-1244. Periodical. UR. Russian. **LC** Z165.

KNIZHNAIA TORGOVLIA. REFERATIVNAIA INFORMATSIIA. Vol. 1- 1973-. UR. Russian. bm. 0.15 Single Issue. Kniga, K-9 UI Nezhdanovoi 8/10, Moskva USSR. **LC** Z278.

LARGE PRINT BOOKS - GEORGIAN BAY REGIONAL LIBRARY SYSTEM. (LARGE PRINT BOOKS). **Main/Corp** Georgian Bay Regional Library System. 0229-4370. CN. English. ir. Free. Georgian Bay Regional Library System, 30 Morrow Road, Barrie Ontario L4N 3V8 Canada. **DD** 018.163. (ctrl).

LARGE TYPE BOOKS IN PRINT. 1970-. 0163-3198. US. English. ir. $62.00. Bowker Company, 205 East Forty-Second Street, New York NY 10017. **LC** Z5348, HV1731. **DD** 011.

LATIN AMERICA IN BOOKS. V. 1- Dec. 1977-. 0738-7113. Periodical. US. English. sa. $10.00 US and Canada, $11.00 Foreign. Latin America in Books, University of New Orleans, POB 1387, New Orleans LA 70148. **Tel** (540)286-6294. Ed Charles M Nissly. bk rev. **Circ** 250. Annotated bibliography of recently published books in English on Latin America and the Caribbean (includes US Southwest). All categories except children's literature.

LAW BOOKS IN PRINT. *See* Law.

LAW BOOKS PUBLISHED. *See* Law.

LESELAND. Periodical. GE. German. an. Borsenverein der Deutschen Buchhandler, Gerichtsweg 26, Postfach 16, 7010 Leipzig East Germany. **LC** Z321.7. **DD** 380.145070509431.

LIBRARIUM. Vol. 1-. 0024-2152. Periodical. SZ. English (French and German). ty. Schweizerische Bibliophile, Gesellschaft Zahringerplatz 6, 8001 Zurich Switzerland. **Ind/Abst** MLA Int. Bibliogr. Books Artic. Mod. Lang. Lit. **LC** Z990. *Stultifera Navis.*

LIBRERIA. Spanish. ir. 20 Single Issue. Mallorca 274 1 Planta, Barcelona Spain. **LC** Z416.

LIBRES HEBDO (EDITION DESTINEE A L'ETRANGER). (LIVRES HEBDO). No 1- 4 Sept. 1979-. 0223-4815. Periodical. FR. French. sm. $179.60. Diffusion Cercle d la Librarie, 30 rue Daulphin, 75006 Paris France. **Ind/Abst** Math. Rev. **LC** Z2165. **DD** 015.44. *Bibliographie de la France, Biblio, 0335-5675; Bulletin du Livre, 0007-456X.*

EL LIBRO ESPANOL. V. 1- (No. 1-). 0024-273X. SP. Spanish. mo. Institut Nacional, Libro Espanol Santiago Rusinol, 8 Madrid 3 Spain. **Ind/Abst** Am. Hist. Life, Hist. Abstr. **LC** Z2685. **DD** 015.46. NLM Z 2685 L693. *Bibliografia Hispanica, Libros del Mes; Novedades Editoriales.*

LIBROS. Periodical. Spanish. ir. Camara Columbiana de la Industria Editorial, Calle 15 Num 9-30, Oficina 206 Apartado Aereo 8998, Bogota Columbia. **LC** Z523.7.

LIBROS AL DIA. Yearly V. 1- (No. 1-). Periodical. Spanish. ir. 35.00. Edificio la Linea, Oficina 153 A Avenida Liberatador, Caracas Venezuela. **LC** F2308.

LIBROS DE LA SOCIEDAD ESPANOLA DE CRITICA DE LIBROS. VFOAT Libros. Periodical. Spanish. mo. *Libros (Madrid, Spain).*

LIBROS EN ESPANOL ... TITULOS. VFOAT Publicaciones Editadas en Espanol. Spanish. ir. **LC** Z2685. **DD** 056.1. *Publicaciones Editadas en Espanol.*

THE LICENSING BOOK. VFOAT Licensing. Vol. 1, No. 1 (Oct. 1983)-. 0741-0107. Periodical. US. English. mo. The Licensing Book, 145 East 49th Street, New York NY 10017.

LINK. No. 1- Spring 1973-. Periodical. UK. English. qt. $2.60. Central Books Ltd, 14 The Leathermarket, London SE1 3ER England.

LIST OF PRINTED BOOKS ADDED TO THE LIBRARY . . . . *See* Bibliographies.

LISTE DES LIVRES DISPONIBLES DE LANGUE FRANCAISE DES AUTEURS ET DES EDITEURS CANADIENS. (LA LISTE DES LIVRES DISPONIBLES DE LANGUE FRANCAISE DES AUTEURS ET DES EDITEURS CANADIENS). VFOAT Canadian Authors & Publishers French Books in Print. Sept./Oct. 1981-. 0708-4889. Periodical. CN. French. ir. $120.00. Agence Internationale d'Abonnements Periodica Inc, CP 220, Ville Mont-Royal Quebec H3P 3C4 Canada. **DD** 015.7140241. Also available in microform.

LIVRE D'ICI (MENSUEL). (LIVRE D'ICI). Vol. 8, No 1 (Nov. 1982)-. 0714-9948. Periodical. CN. French. mo. $1,00 le No. Societe de Promotion du Livre, Bureaus 48-49/445 rue St-Francois Xavier, Montreal Quebec H2Y 2T1 Canada. **DD** 028.109714.

LE LIVRE ET L'ESTAMPE. Dec. 1954-. 0024-533X. Periodical. BE. French. si. 1100. Societe Royale Bibliophiles des Iconophiles Belgium, 4 et Boulevard de l'Empereur, 1000 Brussels Belgium. **Tel** (02)5195311. Ed Eugene Rouir. **LC** Z990. (cum index). bk rev. adv acc. **Circ** 300. History of books (old and contemporary) and prints.

LES LIVRES DE L'ANNEE. 1922/25-1930/33. Monographic Series. French. ir. **LC** Z2165.B58.

LES LIVRES DISPONIBLES. VFOAT French Books in Print. 1977-. French. $515.00. Cercle de la Libraries, PO Box 1445, Mrs Goldberg, Long Island City NY 11101. **Tel** (212)937-4606. **LC** Z2161. **DD** 015.44. NLM Z 2161 L788. *Repertoire des Livres de Langue Francaise Disponibles, 0080-1003; Catalogue de l'Edition Francaise.*

LIVROS EM PORTUGUES. 1st Ed. (1981)-. 0710-5231. CN. English (Portuguese). be. Livros Em Portugues. **DD** 011.269.

MANHATTAN BOOK HOUND. Apr. 1980-. 0198-9960. Periodical. US. English. mo. $15.00. Butler Communications, PO Box 5347, New York NY 10150.

MARATHI PRAKASANA VARSHIKA ANI PRAKASANA DAYARI. VFOAT Prakasana-Dayari. II. Marathi. an. 18.00. Aniruddha Sahitya, 1493 K Sadashiv, Pune 411030 India. **Tel** 441004. Ed Gajanan Kshirsagar. adv acc. **Circ** 3,500. Covers list of books printed during the year, lists of publishers, booksellers, periodicals, colleges, artists, etc.

MARGINALIEN; ZEITSCHRIFT FUR BUCHKUNST UND BIBLIOPHILE. No. 1- Jan. 1957-. 0025-2948. Periodical. German. ir. **Ind/Abst** MLA Int. Bibliogr. Books Artic. Mod. Lang. Lit. (cum index).

MEDBOOKS. Periodical. SZ. English. sa. Karger Libri AG, CH-3009 Basel Switzerland.

MEDIAEVAL ACADEMY BOOKS. No. 89-. Monographic Series. US. English. ir. Mediaeval Academy of America, 1430 Mass Avenue, Cambridge MA 02138. Medieval civilization. *Publication.*

MEDICAL AND HEALTH CARE BOOKS AND SERIALS IN PRINT. 1985-. 0000-085X. US. English. an. R R Bowker Company, 205 East 42nd Street, New York NY 10017. **LC** Z6658. **DD** 016.61. *Medical Books and Serials in Print, 0000-0574.*

MEMBERSHIP LIST - CANADIAN BOOKBINDERS AND BOOK ARTISTS GUILD. (MEMBERSHIP LIST). **Main/Corp** Canadian Bookbinders and Book Artists Guild. 1983-. 0824-1864. CN. English. an. Canadian Bookbinders and Book Artists Guild, 26 Morningside Avenue, Toronto Ontario M6S 1C3 Canada. **DD** 686.3006071.

MERKBLATTER - KOMMISSION FUR EINBANDFRAGEN VEREINS DEUTSHER BIBLIOTHEKARE. **Main/Corp** Verein Deutscher Bibliothekare. Kommission fur Einbandfragen. German. ir. Kommission fur Eingandfragen, Fehrbelliner Platz 3, 1000 Berlin 3 West Germany. **LC** Z267. *Einband Buchpflege.*

MILWAUKEE READER. **Main/Corp** Milwaukee. Public Library. 1942. 0026-4377. Periodical. US. English. wk. $3.00. Milwaukee Public Library, 814 West Wisconsin Avenue, Milwaukee WI

Publishing—Books and Bookmaking

53233. Tel (414)278-3031. Ed Lorelei Starck. bk rev. Circ 4,500. (ctrl). Newsletter on books, events, and community affairs.

MINIATURE BOOK NEWS. No.1-32. 0026-5128. Periodical. US. English. $9.00. Miniature Book News, 16 Dromara Road, St Louis MO 63124. LC Z1033.M6.

NEDERLANDSE BOEKEN. 1st Ed. (1981)-. 0710-5207. CN. English (text in Dutch). be. Nederlandse Boeken. DD 011.23931.

NEW & FORTHCOMING CANADIAN BOOKS. July/Dec. 1976-. 0703-8690. Periodical. CN. English. sa. $7.74. Quill and Quire Magazine, 56 The Esplanade/Suite 213, Toronto Ontario M5E 1A7 Canada. Tel (416)364-3333. DD 015.71.

NEW BOOK ANNOUNCEMENTS. ANNUAL BOOK CATALOG. Main/Corp AMACOM. US. English. an. AMACOM, 135 W 50th Street, New York NY 10020. *AMACOM Resources for Professional Management.*

THE NEW BOOKBINDER : JOURNAL OF DESIGNER BOOKBINDERS. Vol. 1 (1981)-. Periodical. UK. English. an. $22.98. Designer Bookbinders, 6 Queen Square, London WC1N 3AR England. Ind/Abst Art Archaeol. Tech. Abstr., Libr. Inf. Sci. Abstr. bk rev. adv acc. Circ 700. (ctrl). Modern designer bookbindings exhibitions, binding techniques and design. Review of books. Profiles of contemporary bookbinders. *Designer Bookbinders Review.*

NEW BOSTON REVIEW CEASED. Vol. 1, No. 1 (June 1975)-V. 6, No. 6 (Dec. 1981). 0361-168X. Periodical. US. English. bm. $4.50. New Boston Review, 77 Sacramento Street, Somerville MA 02143. Ind/Abst Book Rev. Index.

THE NEW REVIEW OF BOOKS AND RELIGION. *See* Religion, Mythology, Rationalism.

NEW ZEALAND BOOKS IN PRINT. English. an. $18.45. D W Thorpe Pty Ltd, PO Box 146/20-24 Stokes Street, Port Melbourne 3207 Australia. Tel (03)645-1511. adv acc. Circ 1,100. Lists all New Zealand books in print by title, author, subject classification with full details, as well as other New Zealand book trade information. *List of New Zealand Books in Print.*

NEWS-LETTER OF THE AMERICAN ANTIQUARIAN SOCIETY. Main/Corp American Antiquarian Society. No. 1- Jan. 1968-. 0569-2229. Periodical. US. English. sa. American Antiquarian Society, 185 Salisbury Street, Worcester MA 01609. Tel (617)755-5221. Ed M VC Callahan. LC E172. DD 973.06273. Circ 1,649. (ctrl). Presents news and information about the activities of the society's members and staff, as well as news of collections and acquisitions of the society.

NEWSLETTER - CANADIAN BOOKBINDERS AND BOOK ARTISTS GUILD. (NEWSLETTER). Vol. 1, No. 1-. 0822-9538. Periodical. CN. English. ir. Free to Members, Membership $15.00 per year. Canadian Bookbinders and Book Artists Guild, 26 Morningside Avenue, Toronto Ontario M6S 1C3 Canada. DD 686.3006071.

NEWSLETTER - GUILD OF BOOKWORKERS. Main/Corp Guild of Book Workers. VFOAT Guild of Book Workers Newsletter. VAT Newsletter - Guild of Bookworkers. 0730-3203. Periodical. US. English. Guild of Book Workers, 663 Fifth Avenue, New York NY 10022.

NIGERIAN BOOKS IN PRINT. 1967-. NR. English (Multilingual). ir. Nigerian Book Suppliers Ltd, PO Box 3870, Lafos Nigeria. LC Z965, Z3597. DD 027.5669 S, 015.669.

NIHONGO-NO-TOSHO. 1st. Ed. (1981)-. 0710-5304. CN. English (text in Japanese and with Japanese text romanized on opposite pages). be. Nihongo-No-Tosho. DD 011.2956.

NISSHOREN ZENKOKU SHOTEN MEIBO. Main/Corp Nihon Shoten Kumiai Rengokai. VFOAT Zenkoku Shoten Meibo. 1973-. JA. Japanese. ir. Nihon Shoten Kumiai Rengokai, 2 kanda Surguadai 1-chome Chiyoda-ku, Tokyo Japan. LC Z463.5.

NOS LIVRES. Vol. 8, No. 1 (Jan. 1977)-. 0384-7446. Periodical. CN. French. ir. 14.00 Domestic, 20.00 Foreign. Office des Communications, 4005 de Bellechasse, Montreal Quebec H1X 1J6 Canada. Tel (514)729-6391. DD 028.105. Journal of evaluation of books in French published in Canada. More than 500 book reviews included. *Livre Canadien, 0381-7776.*

NOUVELLES DU LIVRE ANCIEN. 0335-752X. French. qt. Service du Livre Ancien Bibliotheque Nationale, 58 rue de Richelieu, 75084 Paris Cedex 02 France. LC Z4. DD 002.05.

THE OFFICIAL PRICE GUIDE TO OLD BOOKS & AUTOGRAPHS. VFOAT Old Books & Autographs. 0747-5047. US. English. an. House of Collectibles Inc, Orlando Central Park, 1900 Premier Row, Orlando FL 32809. LC Z1000.5. DD 017.8.

PAGES. 1-. US. English. $34.00. Gale Research Company, Book Tower, Detroit MI 48226. Ed Matthew J Bruccoli and C E Frazer Clark. A magazine in book form on the world of books and publishing.

PAPERBACKS BY MAIL. Main/Corp Chinook Regional Library. 0822-5818. CN. English. an. Chinook Regional Library, 1240 Chaplin Street Northwest, Swift Current Saskatchewan S9H 0G8 Canada. DD 017.532.

PAPERBOUND BOOKS IN PRINT. Mar. 1971-. 0031-1235. US. English. sa. $173.00. RR Bowker, PO Box 1807, Ann Arbor MI 48106. Tel (212)916-1600. LC Z1033.P3. DD 011. Reference providing bibliographic data on all U.S. paperbound books in print.

PERMANENCE-DURABILITY OF THE BOOK. (PERMANENCE/DURABILITY OF THE BOOK). VFOAT Publication. No. 1-. 0553-6774. Monographic Series. US. English. W J Barrow Research Laboratory, Virginia Historical Society Building, Box 7311, Richmond VA 23221. LC Z701. DD 025.84.

POLSKIE KSIAZKI (TORONTO, ONT.). (POLSKIE KSIAZKI). 1st Ed. (1981)-. 0710-5290. CN. English (text in Polish). be. Polskie Ksiazki. DD 011.291851.

POLYGRAPH ADRESSBUCH DER DRUCKINDUSTRIE. German. ir. LC Z291. *Polygraph Adressbuch der Graphischen Industrie.*

PROCEEDINGS OF THE ANNUAL CONFERENCE. *See* Library and Information Science.

PRZEGLED KSIEGARSKI I WYDAWNICZY. Periodical. PL. Polish. mo. ARS Polona, Krakowskie Przedmiescie 7, 00-068 Warsaw Poland. LC Z365. *Praca Ksiegarska.*

PUBLICATION - AUGUSTAN REPRINT SOCIETY. (PUBLICATIONS). 1946. Monographic Series. US. English. ir. University of California, Augustan Reprint Society, 2520 Cimarron Street, Los Angeles CA 90018. Tel (213)731-8529. Ed David S Rodes. Ind/Abst Annu. Bibliogr. Engl. Lang. Lit., MLA Int. Bibliogr. Books Artic. Mod. Lang. Lit. Circ 700. (ctrl). The Augustan Reprint Society publishes rare and significant restorations and Eighteenth-Century works in photographic facsimile, accompanied by scholarly introductions.

QUAERENDO. V. 1- Jan. 1971-. 0014-9527. Periodical. English (French or German). qt. 84.-. E J Brill, PO Box 9000, 2300 PA Leiden The Netherlands. Tel (071)312-624. Ed A R A Crouset van Uchelen. Ind/Abst Recent Publ. Artic. bk rev. adv acc. Contains articles, notes and news in the field of the science of manuscripts and books.

QUARTERLY - NATIONAL BOOK CENTRE BANGLADESH. Main/Corp National Book Centre Bangladesh. V. 1- Winter 1974-. Periodical. English. ir. National Book Centre, 67-A Purana Paltan, Dacca India. LC Z1003.5.B36. DD 028.9095492.

QUARTERLY NEWS-LETTER - BOOK CLUB OF CALIFORNIA. Main/Corp Book Club of California. V. 1- May 1933-. 0006-7202. Periodical. US. English. qt. $40.00. Book Club of California, 312 Sutter Street/Room 510, San Francisco CA 94108. Tel (415)781-7532. Ed D Steven Corey. Ind/Abst Funk Scott Index Corp. Ind., MLA Int. Bibliogr. Books Artic. Mod. Lang. Lit. LC Z1008. DD 028. (cum index). bk rev adv acc. Circ 1,045. (ctrl).

QUEBEC BOOKS. VFOAT QB. Vol. 1, No 1 (Fall 1983)-. 0739-070X. Periodical. US. English (French). sa. $6.00 Domestic, $7.00 Foreign. Information Center on Canada, PO Box 627, Burlington VT 05402.

QUILL AND QUIRE. (QUILL & QUIRE). Began in 1935. 0033-6491. Periodical. CN. English. ir. $30.95. Quill & Quire, 56 The Esplanade/Suite 213, Toronto Ontario M5E 1A7 Canada. Tel (416)364-3333. Ind/Abst Book Rev. Index, Bibliogr. Agric., Can. Bus. Index, Can. Period. Index, Libr. Inf. Sci. Abstr. LC Z487. DD 655.505.

QUILL & QUIRE. GENERAL INDEX. *See* Indexes/Abstracts.

RARE BOOKS : TRENDS, COLLECTIONS, SOURCES. 1983-84-. Periodical. US. English. an. $44.94. R R Bowker Company, PO Box 1807, Ann Arbor MI 48106. Ed Alice D Schreyer. NLM Z 1029.

RBMS NEWSLETTER. VFOAT R.B.M.S. Newsletter. VAT Rare Books and Manuscripts Section Newsletter. No. 1 (Apr. 1984)-. 0743-1481. Periodical. US. English. sa. Free to Members of ALA. American Library Association, Association of College and Research Libraries, c/o Executive Director, 50 East Huron Street, Chicago IL 60611.

RECENT BOOKS IN MEXICO. V. 1- Nov. 1954-. 0486-1205. Periodical. MX. English (Spanish). bm. $6.00. CTRO Mexicano Excrit, LG Inclan 2709, VLA Cortes/Deleg B Juarez 03530 Mexico 13 DF Mexico. Tel 579 78 10. LC Z1411. Circ 1,000. Bibliographical reviews of books written originally in spanish and printed in Mexico.

REPERTOIRE. LIVRES ET PERIODIQUES DES PROFESSEURS. (REPERTOIRE : LIVRES ET PERIODIQUES DES PROFESSEURS). 1983-. 0715-8130. CN. French. an. Universite du Quebec A Montreal, C P 8888 Succursale A, Montreal Quebec H3C 3P8 Canada. DD 013.37909714281. *Repertoire des Productions, 0822-4722.*

REVIEW OF BOOKS AND RELIGION (FORWARD MOVEMENT PUBLICATIONS). *See* Religion, Mythology, Rationalism.

REVISTA DE CLUBE DO LIVRO. Main/Corp Clube do Livro, Sao Paulo, Brazil. No. 1- July/August 1977-. Periodical. Portuguese. ir. LC Z521.7.

REVISTA DO LIVRO. No. 1- March/April 1973-. Periodical. Portuguese. ir. Circulo do Livro, Caixa Postal 7413, CEP 01310 Sao Paulo Brazil. LC Z1035.A1. DD 028.1.

REVUE D'HISTOIRE DES TEXTES. V. 1- 1971-. 0373-6075. FR. English or French. an. $29.27. Editions du CNRS, 15 Quia Anatole, 75700 Paris France. LC Z4.

ROMANIAN BOOKS. Periodical. RM. English. ir. Cartimex Inc, 126 Calea Victoriei, Box 134-35, Bucharest Romania. LC Z2921. DD 015.498. *Rumanian Books.*

ROMANIAN BOOKS IN FOREIGN LANGUAGES. English. ir. Centrala Cartii, 7 Biserica Amzei Street, Bucuresti Romania. LC Z2921. DD 015.498.

RUSSKIE KNIGI (TORONTO, ONT.). (RUSSKIE KNIGI). 1st Ed. (1981)-. 0710-5282. CN. English (Russian). be. Russkie Knigi. DD 011.29171.

SACH VIET. 1st Ed. (1981)-. 0710-5258. CN. English (Vietnamese). be. Metropolitan Toronto Library Board, Toronto Ontario Canada. DD 011.295922.

SALON DU LIVRE DE MONTREAL. (PROGRAMME DES ACTIVITES). Main/Corp Salon du Livre de Montreal. VAT Salon du Livre, Montreal. 21/26 Nov. 1979-. 0822-5443. CN. French. an. Free. Salon du Livre de Montreal, 1151 rue Alexandre-de-Seve, Montreal Quebec H2L 2T7 Canada. DD 002.0740114281. (ctrl).

SARVODAYA. Began with July(?) 1952. 0036-4835. Periodical. English. ir. Hindustan Book Agency, 17 UB Jawahar Nagar, Delhi 7 India. *Khadi World.*

SCHOLARLY BOOKS IN AUSTRALIA. AT. English. ir. Association of Australian University Presses, University of Queensland, Box 42 Post Office, St Lucia Queensland 4067, Victoria Australia. LC Z1033.U64. DD 016.0705940994.

SCHOLARS FACSIMILES & REPRINTS. (SCHOLARS' FACSIMILES & REPRINTS). VAT Scholars Facsimiles and Reprints. 0161-7729. Monographic Series. US. English. Scholars Facsimiles and Reprints Inc, PO Box 344, Delmar NY 12054. Tel (518)439-5978. Ed Norman

Real Estate

Mangouni. **Ind/Abst** MLA Int. Bibliogr. Books Artic. Mod. Lang. Lit. **LC** UNC. Facsimile reprints of rare books of scholarly interest, primarily in English and American literature, history, philosophy, and religion.

DIE SCHONSTEN BUCHER DER BUNDESREPUBLIK DEUTSCHLAND. See Bibliographies.

SCRIPTORIUM. V. 1- 1946/47-. 0036-9772. Periodical. BE. English (French, German, or Italian). sa. $83.70. Drukkerij Cultura, Hoenderstraat 22, 9200 Wetteren Belgium. Ed F Lyna and C Gaspar. **Ind/Abst** MLA Int. Bibliogr. Books Artic. Mod. Lang. Lit., New Testam. Abstr. **LC** Z108. **DD** 417.05. **NLM** Z 108 S434.

SHOSHIGAKU. V. 1, 1933-Jan. 1942. Japanese. ir. (cum index).

SINGAPORE BOOK WORLD. **VFOAT** Dunia Buku Singapura. Began with issue for Apr. 1970. 0080-9659. SI. English (text in Chinese, and Malay). an. $2.47. Chopmen Publishers, 865 Mountbatten Road 05 28/29, Singapore 1543 Rep Singapore. **Ind/Abst** Libr. Inf. Sci. Abstr. **LC** Z464.S55. **DD** 338.470705095957. (cum index).

SINGAPORE BOOKS IN PRINT. 1977/78-. 0129-4431. English. ir. National Book Development Council of Singapore, c/o Shanghai Book Store Pte Ltd, 81 Victoria Street, Singapore 7 Singapore. **LC** Z3248.S5. **DD** 015.5952.

SMALL PRESS RECORD OF BOOKS IN PRINT. **VFOAT** Small Press Record of Books. 5th- Ed. 0148-9720. US. English. an. Dustbooks, PO Box 1056, Paradise CA 95969. Ed L Fulton. **LC** Z1033.L73. **DD** 070.593. *Small Press Record of Books, 0361-364X.*

SOUTH DAKOTA AUTHORS' CATALOG. 1981-. 0742-8936. US. English. an. $5.00. 909 East 34th Street, Sioux Falls SD 57105. **Tel** (605)361-6942. Ed Janet Leih. bk rev. adv acc. **Circ** 500. Catalog of current books by South Dakota writers.

SRPSKO-HRVATSKE KNJIGE. 1st Ed. (1981)-. 0710-5274. CN. English (Serbo-Croatian). be. Metropolitan Toronto Library Board, 214 College Street, Toronto Ontario M5T 1R3 Canada. **DD** 011.29182.

SUBJECT GUIDE TO BOOKS IN PRINT. 1957-. 0000-0159. US. English. an. R R Bowker Company, PO Box 1807, Ann Arbor MI 48106. **Tel** (800)521-8110. **LC** Z1215. **DD** 015.73. **NLM** Z 1215 S941.

SUBJECT GUIDE TO CANADIAN BOOKS IN PRINT. 1973-. 0315-1999. Periodical. CN. English. an. 50.00. University of Toronto Press, 5201 Dufferin Street, Downsview Ontario M3H Canada. **Tel** (416)667-7791. Ed Marian Butler. **DD** 015.71. **Circ** 1,200. A complete reference and buying guide to Canadian Books currently in print, by subject.

SUBJECT GUIDE TO CHILDREN'S BOOKS IN PRINT. 1970. 0000-0167. Monographic Series. US. English. an. R R Bowker Company, PO Box 1807, Ann Arbor MI 48106. **LC** Z1037.A1. **DD** 028.52. *Children's Books for Schools and Libraries.*

SUBJECT GUIDE TO FORTHCOMING BOOKS. V. 1- Jan. 1967-. 0000-0264. Periodical. US. English. bm. $65.00. RR Bowker Company, 1180 Avenue of the Americas, New York NY 10036, (subscription address: Bowker Subscription Service PO Box 1429 Riverton NJ 08077). **Tel** (800)257-7894.

SUGGESTED LIST OF MEDICAL BOOKS & JOURNALS. Sept. 1982-. 0821-1582. CN. English. be. Ontario Medical Association, 240 St George Street, Toronto Ontario M5R 2P4 Canada. **DD** 016.61. *Suggested List of Basic Books & Journals, 0821-1558.*

SUOMENKIELISIA KIRJOJA. 1st Ed. (1981)-. 0710-5215. CN. English (Finnish). be. Suomenkielisia Kirjoja. **DD** 011.294541.

SUPPLEMENT ONE, HEALTH SCIENCES BOOKS & JOURNALS. Sept. 1982-. 0821-1590. CN. English. be. Ontario Medical Association, 240 St George Street, Toronto Ontario M5R 2P4 Canada. **DD** 016.61. *Supplement One, Medical Books & Journals, 0821-1566; Supplement Two, Health Sciences Books & Journals, 0821-1574.*

SWANN GALLERIES, INC. (CATALOGUE - SWANN GALLERIES, INC). **Main/Corp** Swann Galleries, Inc. 1940. 0193-5526. Periodical. US. English. ir. $100.00. Swann Galleries Inc, 104 East 25th Street, New York NY 10010. **Tel** (212)254-4710. **Circ** 1,000. (ctrl). Book auction catalogues, including prints, maps, autographs and manuscripts, and photographica.

SWEDISH BOOK REVIEW. SUPPLEMENT. 0265-8119. UK. English. an. Valerie Gustaveson, 260 East San Jose Avenue, Claremont CA 91711.

SWEDISH BOOKS. Ceased publication in 1982?. 0348-4211. Periodical. SW. English. qt $12.50. Swedish Books, PO Box 2387, S-40316 Gotenborg Sweden.

TALKING BOOK TOPICS. 0039-9183. Periodical. US. English. bm. Publication Services, National Library Service for the Blind and Physically Handicapped, Library of Congress, Washington DC 20542. **LC** HV1708.

TALKING BOOKS. **Main/Corp** South Central Regional Library System (Ont.). 1975-. 0707-5391. CN. English. an. South Central Regional Library System, 200 Dundurn Street South, Hamilton Ontario L8P 4K7 Canada. **DD** 018.1.

TALKING BOOKS. 1st- Ed. 0225-5723. Periodical. CN. English. be. Free. Southwestern Regional Library System, 660 Ouellette Avenue Suite 216, Windsor Ontario N9A 1L1 Canada. **DD** 018.138. (ctrl).

TALKING BOOKS AVAILABLE IN THE PUBLIC LIBRARIES OF METROPOLITAN TORONTO. 1st- Ed. 0700-3277. Periodical. CN. English. Metropolitan Toronto Library Board, 214 College Street, Toronto Ontario M5T 1R3 Canada. **DD** 011. *0380-2973.*

TALKING BOOKS CATALOGUE. **Main/Corp** Northwestern Regional Library System (Ont.). 1981-. 0711-7434. Periodical. CN. English. ir. Talking Books Catalogue, Northwestern Regional Library System, 910 Victoria Avenue, Thunder Bay Ontario P7C 1B4 Canada. **DD** 018.138. *Talking Books for the Handicapped, 0703-8887.*

TALKING BOOKS CATALOGUE SUPPLEMENT. **Main/Corp** Northwestern Regional Library System (Ont.). 0229-4028. CN. English. ir. Northwestern Regional Library System, 910 Victoria Avenue, Thunder Bay F Ontario P7C 1B4 Canada. **DD** 018.138.

TALKING BOOKS IN THE PUBLIC LIBRARIES OF METROPOLITAN TORONTO, PACKING LIST. June 1977-. 0710-3573. Periodical. CN. English. Metropolitan Toronto Library Board, 214 College Street, Toronto Ontario M5T 1R3 Canada. **DD** 018.138.

TASCHENBUCH-KATALOG. **VFOAT** Taschenbuch Katalog. GW. German. ir. Koch, Neff & Oetinger & Company und Koehler & Volckmar, Koch, Neff, & Oetinger & Company, Stuttgart, Koln West Germany.

TEXAS BOOKS IN REVIEW. Began with V. 1, 1977 issue. 0739-3202. US. English. an. $2.00. Texas Books in Review, Box T-159 Tarleton Station, Stephenville TX 76402. **LC** F381. **DD** 976.4.

TEXTBOOK NEWS. See Education (General).

TODOS LOS LIBROS. Periodical. Spanish. ir. 1,000. Sedmay Ediciones, Lopez de Hoyos 36, Madrid Spain. **LC** Z1035.A1. **DD** 028.1.

TRENDS UPDATE. Vol. 1, No. 1 (May 1982)-. 0731-5589. Periodical. US. English. mo. $240.00. Book Industry Study Group, 160 5th Avenue, New York NY 10010. **Tel** (212)929-1393. Ed John Dessaver. Enhances and expands upon the statistics provided in the Trends annual, explains the forecasting techniques used in preparing the data and highlites areas of importance.

UKRAINSKI KNYZHKY. 1st Ed. (1981)-. 0710-5266. CN. English (Ukrainian). be. Ukrainski Knyzhky. **DD** 011.291791.

UNIVERSITY PUBLISHING. 1984. 0191-4146. Periodical. US. English. qt. University of California Press, 2120 Berkeley Way, Berkeley CA 94720. **Tel** (415)642-4247. Ed William McClung, Leonard Michaels, and Christine Taylor. **LC** Z1033.U64. **DD** 070.594. bk rev. adv acc. **Circ** 1,500. Independent, international, quarterly review of University Press books.

VERZEICHNIS LIEFERBARER BUCHER. ERGANZUNGSBAND. See Bibliographies.

VERZEICHNIS LIEFERBARER BUCHER. SCHLAGWORT-VERZEICHNIS. See Bibliographies.

THE WASHINGTON POST BOOK WORLD. **VFOAT** Book World. Began with Vol. 1 Sept. 10, 1967. Periodical. US. English. wk. $13.00 Domestic, $15.60 Foreign. Washington Post, Mail Subscription Department, 1150 15th Street NW, Washington DC 20071. **Tel** 334-7881. Ed Brigitte Weeks. bk rev. adv acc. *Book Week, Books Today.*

WHAT'S NEW IN BOOKS. V. 47- Jan. 1965-. 0043-4566. Periodical. US. English. an. $40.00. Chicago Public Library, North Michigan and East Washington, Chicago IL 60602. **Ind/Abst** MLA Int. Bibliogr. Books Artic. Mod. Lang. Lit. *Book Bulletin.*

WHITAKER'S BOOKS OF THE MONTH & BOOKS TO COME. **VFOAT** Books of the Month & Books to Come. **VAT** Whitaker's Books of the Month and Books to Come. Jan. 1970-. 0043-4868. Periodical. UK. English. mo. 34.00. J Whitaker & Sons Ltd, 12 Dyott Street, London WC1A 1DF England. **Tel** (01)836-8911. **LC** Z2005. **DD** 015.42. Complete listing of new English language books added to Whitaker's database plus, forthcoming books for the next two months under author title and keyword.

WOLFENBUTTELER NOTIZEN ZUR BUCHGESCHICHTE. Vol. 1- May 1976-. 0341-2253. Periodical. German. ir. 40.00. DR E Hauswedell and Company, 3400 Wolfenbuttel, Postfach 227, Hamburg West Germany. **LC** Z119. (cum index).

WOLGAN TOKSO. **VFOAT** Tokso. Periodical. KO. Korean. ir. 5,000. Wolgan Tokso, 73 Soron-dong, Chongno-ku, Seoul South Korea. **LC** Z1003.5.K8.

THE WORTHWHILE PRICE GUIDE. See Bibliographies.

REAL ESTATE

ABA SECTION OF TAXATION ANNUAL ADVANCED STUDY SESSIONS. SELECTED PROBLEMS AND TECHNIQUES IN ESTATE PLANNING. See Law.

ACCREDITED RESIDENT MANAGER NEWS. See Business - General Management.

ACTUALITE IMMOBILIERE. V. 1- Oct. 1976-. 0701-0516. Periodical. CN. French. qt. 22.00. Laboratoire Rech Sciencos Immo, C P 8888 Succursale A, Montreal Quebec H3C 3P8 Canada. **Tel** (514)282-7936. Ed Jacques Saint-Pierre. **Ind/Abst** Point Repere. **DD** 333.3309714. adv acc. **Circ** 4,000. Studies in real estate applied to Montreal, Quebec, and Canada.

ADVANCED REAL ESTATE LAW COURSE. 1st- 1979-. 0198-9448. US. English. an. State Bar of Texas, PO Box 12487/Capitol Station, Austin TX 78711. **LC** KFT1326. **DD** 346.7640437.

AGRICULTURAL REAL ESTATE VALUES IN ALBERTA. **Main/Corp** Alberta. Alberta Agriculture. Resource Economics Branch. 1976-. 0701-7502. CN. English. an. **LC** HD319.A4. **DD** 333.335097123. *Rural Real Estate Values in Alberta, 0383-3585.*

AIM. APPRAISAL INSTITUTE MAGAZINE. (A I M, APPRAISAL INSTITUTE MAGAZINE). **Main/Corp** Appraisal Institute of Canada. V. 20-28, Book 1. 0383-6649. Periodical. CN. English (includes some text in French). qt. A I M, 309-93 Lombard Avenue, Winnipeg Manitoba R3B 3B1 Canada. **Tel** (204)942-0751. **Ind/Abst** ABI/Inform, Can. Bus. Index. *Appraisal Institute Magazine, 0044-846X.*

AIREA NEWSLETTER. **VFOAT** Newsletter. **VAT** American Institute of Real Estate Appraisers Newsletter. 0748-9072. Periodical. US. English. Free. AIREA, 430 North Michigan Avenue, Chicago IL 60611-4088. **Tel** (312)329-8520. Ed Mark L Roth. **DD** 333. **Circ** 1,000. Articles on the uses of computers in the real estate appraisal office, product

Real Estate

announcements, and user group notices, user tips, computer systems for trade and sale.

ALI-ABA COURSE OF STUDY. ABA SECTION OF TAXATION, ANNUAL OF TAXATION, ANNUAL ADVANCED STUDY SESSIONS, ADVANCED TAX PLANNING FOR REAL ESTATE TRANSACTIONS: MATERIALS. (ADVANCED TAX PLANNING FOR REAL ESTATE TRANSACTIONS : ALI-ABA COURSE OF STUDY, MATERIALS). VFOAT ALI-ABA Course of Study, Materials. 0277-3252. US. English. an. ALI-ABA, 4025 Chestnut Street, Philadelphia PA 19104. LC KF6540.Z9. DD 343.730546, 347.303546.

ALI-ABA COURSE OF STUDY. FOREIGN INVESTMENT IN U.S. REAL ESTATE. MATERIALS. (ALI-ABA COURSE OF STUDY. FOREIGN INVESTMENT IN U.S. REAL ESTATE : MATERIALS). VAT American Law Institute-American Bar Association Course of Study. Foreign Investment in United States Real Estate. Materials. 0270-9708. US. English. an. American Law Institute-American Bar Association, Committee on Continuing Professional Education, 4025 Chestnut Street, Philadelphia PA 19104. LC KF573. DD 346.73043.

ALI-ABA COURSE OF STUDY : MODERN REAL ESTATE TRANSACTIONS : MATERIALS. See Law.

ALI-ABA COURSE OF STUDY. REAL ESTATE CONDOMINIUMS AND PUDS : MATERIALS. See Law.

ALL ABOUT HOMES. Apr. 15, 1977-. 0703-9743. Periodical. CN. English. wk. 25 Per Issue. All About Homes, 1261 Don Mills Road, Don Mills Ontario M3B 2W7 Canada. DD 333.33709713541.

ALLMAN FASTIGHETSTAXERING. Main/Corp Sweden. Statistiska Centralbyran. Series/Titl Sveriges Officiella Statistik. VFOAT General Assessment of Real Estate. Swedish (English). ir. LC HJ4373.

ALMANAK PERUMAHAN DAN KOMPONEN BAHAN BANGUNAN. See Yearbooks, Almanacs, Directories.

ANNUAL ASSESSMENT AND SALES INFORMATION - SOUTH DAKOTA. PROPERTY TAX DIVISION. Main/Corp South Dakota. Property Tax Division. 0364-0248. US. English. an. LC HJ4267. DD 336.222.

ANNUAL OF INDUSTRIAL PROPERTY LAW. See Law.

ANNUAL REPORT - BRITISH COLUMBIA PLACE LTD. Main/Corp British Columbia Place Ltd. CN. English. an. LC HD319.B8. DD 338.761333380971.

ANNUAL REPORT - IOWA REAL ESTATE COMMISSION. Main/Corp Iowa. Real Estate Commission. US. English. an. Free. Real Estate Commission, 1223 East Court Avenue, Des Moines IA 50319. LC HD266.I8. DD 353.9777008243.

ANNUAL REPORT - NEW MEXICO. REAL ESTATE COMMISSION. (ANNUAL REPORT). Main/Corp New Mexico. Real Estate Commission. 0092-413X. US. English. an. Real Estate Commission, Room 1031, 505 Marquette NW, Albuquerque NM 87101. LC HD266.N6. DD 353.9789008243.

ANNUAL REPORT OF THE REAL ESTATE AND BUSINESS AGENTS SUPERVISORY BOARD FOR THE PERIOD 1ST JULY . . . TO 30TH JUNE . . . (WESTERN AUSTRALIA). Main/Corp Western Australia. Real Estate and Business Agents Supervisory Board. English. an. LC HD1039.W47. DD 354.941008243.

ANNUAL REPORT - SUPERINTENDENT OF INSURANCE AND REAL ESTATE (ALBERTA). See Insurance.

ANNUAL REPORT - TEXAS REAL ESTATE COMMISSION. Main/Corp Texas Real Estate Commission. US. English. an. Texas Real Estate Commission, PO Box 12188 Capitol Station, Austin TX 78711. LC HD266.T4. DD 353.9764008243.

APARTMENT & CONDOMINIUM NEWS. VFOAT Apartment and condominium News. 8756-1387. Periodical. US. English. mo. $20.00. Relocation Consultants Inc, 579 West North Avenue Suite 302, Elmhurst IL 60126. DD 333.

APARTMENT MANAGEMENT NEWSLETTER. VFOAT Apartment Newsletter. 1925. 0744-9143. Periodical. US. English. mo. $64.00. Apartment Management Publishing Company Inc, 155 East 56th Street, New York NY 10022. Tel (212)935-4804. Ed Harold Mann. adv acc. Practical information and news for better cost-saving apartment management to maximize cash flow, renting and marketing, finance, tenant relations, maintenance, legal.

THE APPRAISAL JOURNAL. V. 7, No. 2- 1939-. 0003-7087. Periodical. US. English. qt. $60.00. American Institute of Real Estate Appraisal, 430 North Michigan, Chicago IL 60611. Tel (312)329-8559. Ed Charles W Olson. Ind/Abst Manage. Contents, Account. Index. Suppl., ABI/Inform, Ref. Source, Public Aff. Inf. Serv. Bull., Bibliogr. Agric., Bus. Period. Index. LC HD251. DD 333.33205. CODEN APPJA5. (cum index). bk rev. Circ 16,000. Available on microfilm from University Microfilms. Professional articles on real estate appraisal or closely related subjects. Journal of the American Institute of Real Estate Appraisers.

APPRAISAL REVIEW JOURNAL. V. 1- Winter 1978-. 0195-4407. Periodical. US. English. ty. $64.00. National Association of Review Appraisers, 8715 Via de Commercio, Scottsdale AZ 85258. Tel (602)998-3000. Ed Robert G Johnson. LC HD1387. DD 333.33205. bk rev. adv acc. Circ 30,000. Consist of articles concerning all areas of review appraisal and mortgage underwriting.

THE APPRAISER. V. 1- Jan. 1944-. 0003-7095. Periodical. US. English. ir. $10.00. American Institute of Real Estate Appraisers, 430 North Michigan, Chicago IL 60611. Tel (312)329-8520. Ed James E Garner. LC HD251. adv acc. Circ 12,200. News and opinion on real estate finance, construction, investment, and long-term trends, directed toward professional real estate appraisers and consultants.

THE APPRAISERS' INFORMATION EXCHANGE. 8755-4348. Periodical. US. English. bm. International Society of Appraisers, PO Box 726, Hoffman Estates IL 60195. Tel (312)882-0706. Ed Maurice E Fry. DD 332. bk rev. adv acc. Circ 2,500. (ctrl). Newsletter about appraisers, appraising of appraisals pertaining to personal property of all types for all reasons.

AREA DEVELOPMENT. V. 1- June 1965-. 0004-0908. Periodical. US. English. mo. $40.00 Domestic, $60.00 Foreign. Halcyon Business Publications, 525 Northern Boulevard, Great Neck NY 11021. Tel (516)829-8990. Ed Tom Bergeron. Ind/Abst Energy Inf. Abstr., Environ. Abstr. LC HD58. DD 658.2105. adv acc. Circ 32,000. (ctrl). Available on Microfilm from University Microfilms International. Serves the field of facility planning, site selection, plant expansion for manufacturers and service companies.

ARIZONA REAL ESTATE PRESS. VFOAT Real Estate Press. V. 3, Issue 18- Oct. 12, 1978-. 0199-0314. Periodical. US. English. sm. Arizona Real Estate Press, 828 East Washington, Phoenix AZ 85004. Tel (602)256-6666. Arizona Business, Financial Real Estate Press, 0270-8566.

ARIZONA REALTOR DIGEST. Vol. 1, No.1 (Mar./Apr. 1979)-. 0199-9206. Periodical. US. English. bm. $6.00 US and Canada. Arizona Association of Realtors, 4414 North 19th Avenue/Suite R, Phoenix AZ 85015. LC HD266.A7. DD 333.3309791.

THE ARNOLD ENCYCLOPEDIA OF REAL ESTATE. YEARBOOK. See Yearbooks, Almanacs, Directories.

ASSESSMENT DIGEST. V. 1- Jan./Feb.1979-. 0731-0277. Periodical. US. English. bm. $25.00. International Association Assessing Officer, PO Box 94573, Chicago IL 60690-4573. Tel (312)947-2053. bk rev. adv acc. Circ 8,500. (ctrl). Magazine of news on issues in valuation and property taxation as well as association announcements, etc. International Assessor.

ASSESSOR'S DATA EXCHANGE. Vol. 1, No. 1 (July 1, 1981)-. 0741-501X. Periodical. US. English. qt. $90.00 General, $70.00 IAAO Members, Discounts available for subscribers who submit sales data for publication. Assessor's Data Exchange, International Association of Assessing Officers, 1313 East 60th Street, Chicago IL 60637.

AT HOME IN CANADA'S CAPITAL. VAT At Home (Ottawa). V. 1- Sept. 1979-. 0225-9761. Periodical. CN. English. mo. $8.00. At Home in Canada's Capital, Suite 2/430 Maclaren Street, Ottawa K2P 0M8 Canada. DD 643.120971384. (ctrl).

AUDIT REPORT, DEPARTMENT OF INSURANCE, TENNESSEE REAL ESTATE COMMISSION. See Insurance.

BAHAMAS DATELINE. See Business - Investments.

BESSOCHI NENKAN. 1974-. JA. Japanese. ir. 18000. Housing Enterprise, 32-6 Hongo 5 chome Bunkyo-ku, Tokyo 113 Japan. LC HD911.A1.

BLACK'S OFFICE SPACE GUIDE TO THE BALTIMORE/WASHINGTON MARKET. VFOAT Black's Guide. Oct. 1981-. 0733-2009. US. English. an. $49.95. Black's Guide, 332 Broad Street, PO Box 2090, Red Bank NJ 07701. Tel (301)942-3600. Ed James F Black Jr. LC HD268.W3. DD 333.338. adv acc. Circ 10,000. (ctrl). A commercial real estate publishing company that publishes an office space leasing directory which lists available office space in their various stages of development: Proposed, under construction for the Baltimore/Washington area. Black's Guide. Baltimore/Washington Office Space Market, 0199-8145.

BOMA INTERNATIONAL SKYLINES. VFOAT Skylines. VAT Building Owners and Managers Association International Skylines. Vol. 6, No. 6 (June 1981)-. 0279-2044. Periodical. US. English. mo. $95.00. Builder Owner Management Association, 1250 Eye Street NW/Suite 200, Washington DC 20005. Tel (202)289-7000. Ed Kathryn N Hamilton. adv acc. Circ 6,000. Covers all aspects of building management operating tips, energy saving ideas, marketing trends, financing tips and legislative news. Building Owner and Manager.

BUSINESS OPPORTUNITIES JOURNAL. See Business - Investments.

THE CAIN AND SCOTT APARTMENT LETTER. 0882-4177. Periodical. US. English. sa. $10.00. Cain and Scott Inc, 220 West Mercer, Seattle WA 98119-3954. Tel (206)285-7100. Ed Mike W Scott. Publication dealing with financing, sales, rent control, marketing, vacancies, and construction in the Seattle area.

CALIFORNIA REAL ESTATE (CALIFORNIA ASSOCIATION OF REALTORS). (CALIFORNIA REAL ESTATE). V. 56- Dec. 1975-. 0008-1450. Periodical. US. English. mo. $12.00. California Association of Realtors, 525 South Virgil Avenue, Los Angeles CA 90020. Tel (213)739-8320. Ed Pat McLean. Circ 100,000. (ctrl). Practical information that serves to improve real estate agents business approach, professionalism, and basic day-to-day procedures in the form of generic, how-to articles. California Real Estate Magazine, 0732-2194.

CALIFORNIA REAL PROPERTY LAW REPORTER. See Law.

CAMP RESORT LAW REPORT. See Law.

CANADIAN PROFESSIONAL REAL ESTATE DIRECTORY FOR THE PROVINCE OF BRITISH COLUMBIA. See Yearbooks, Almanacs, Directories.

CANADIAN REAL ESTATE. VFOAT l'Immobilier Canadien. V. 1-2, No. 8. 0225-7912. Periodical. CN. English (includes some text in French). mo. Free to Members. Canadian Real Estate Association, 99 Duncan Mill Road, Don Mills Ontario M3B 1Z2 Canada. DD 333.330971. C R E A Reporter, 0315-3843.

CANADIAN REAL ESTATE (1983). (CANADIAN REAL ESTATE). VFOAT L'Immobilier Canadien. VAT Immobilier Canadien (1983). 0823-8197. Periodical. CN. English (text also in French). qt. Free to Members. CREA, 99 Duncan Mill Road, Don Mills Ontario M3B 1Z2 Canada. DD 333.330971.

CANADIAN REAL ESTATE ANNUAL CEASED. (THE CANADIAN REAL ESTATE ANNUAL). 1964-73. 0068-9564. Periodical. CN. English. an. $6.97. MacLean Hunter/Circulation/ Accounting Department, PO Box 100 Station A, Toronto Ontario M5W 1A7 Canada. LC HD311.A1. DD 338.476900971.

CANADIAN REALTY NEWS. V. 1- May 1974-. 0381-7687. Periodical. CN. French. ir. Tankoos Yarmon Ltd, 8 Est rue King, Toronto Ontario M5C 1B5 Canada. DD 333.00971.

CHICAGOLAND'S REAL ESTATE ADVERTISER CEASED. VFOAT Real Estate Advertiser. Ceased in 1983. 0009-3769. Periodical. US. English. wk. $32.00. Real Estate Advertiser, 415 North State Street, Chicago IL 60610. Tel (312)922-9278.

Real Estate

CIT REAL ESTATE REPORT. VFOAT C.I.T. Real Estate Report. Vol. 1, No. 1 (May 1984)-. 0743-5630. Periodical. US. English. mo. Free to clients. HBJ Newsletter Bureau, 757 Third Avenue, New York NY 10017.

COASTAL BEND APARTMENT & RENTAL GUIDE. VFOAT Coastal Bend Apartment and Rental Guide. Feb. '84-. 0748-2019. Periodical. US. English. mo. Free. Coastal Bend Apartment & Rental Guide, PO Box 72925, Corpus Christi TX 78472.

COMMERCIAL INVESTMENT JOURNAL. See Business - Investments.

THE COMMERCIAL REAL ESTATE BROKERS DIRECTORY. See Yearbooks, Almanacs, Directories.

COMMERCIAL REAL ESTATE LEASES. Series/Titl Real Estate Law and Practice Course Handbook Series. 0192-3897. US. English. an. Practising Law Institute, 810 Seventh Avenue, New York NY 10019. Ed M R Friedman. LC KF593.C6. DD 346.7304346.

THE COMMERCIAL RECORD. 1882. 0010-3098. Periodical. US. English. wk. Commercial Record, 750 Old Main Street, Rocky Hill CT 06067. Tel (203)563-3796. Ed Nena Groskind. adv acc. Circ 4,000. (ctrl) Information from real estate deeds; sales price, seller, buyer, mortgage, address, liens, attachments, bankruptcies, new corps, and building permits.

CONDO SALES REPORT. Began in 1983?. 8750-1236. US. English. mo. $225.00. Yale Robbins Inc, 31 East 28th Street, New York NY 10016.

CONDOMINIUM. (THE CONDOMINIUM). V. 1-6, No. 11. 0383-8021. Periodical. CN. English. ir. PO Box 286 Station R, Toronto Ontario M4G 3Z9 Canada. Tel (416)429-4600. Ed Cindy Woods. DD 301.5409713541. adv acc. Circ 2,000. Condominium management, from owners' and manager's viewpoint. Issues: reserve funds, condominium insurance, taxes, special assessments, budgets, lifestyle, legislation, etc.

CONTACT. V. 1- Jan. 1977-. 0703-119X. Periodical. CN. English. mo. Real Estate Institute of Canada, 99 Duncan Mill Road, Don Mills Ontario M3B 1Z2 Canada. DD 333.3306271. Journal, 0703-6914.

COUNTRY PROPERTY BUYERS' GUIDE. Began publication in Aug. 1974. 0703-1955. Periodical. CN. English. mo. $5.40. Datalist Ltd, 1262 Don Mills Road, Don Mills Ontario M3B 2W7 Canada. DD 333.3309713.

CREA REPORTER CEASED. (C R E A REPORTER). Main/Corp Canadian Real Estate Association. V. 1-10, No. 2. 0315-3843. Periodical. CN. English (includes some text in French). mo. Canadian Real Estate Association, 99 Duncan Mill Road, Don Mills Ontario M3B 1Z2 Canada. DD 333.33'0971. Canadian Realtor, 0008-4905; Newsletter.

CREATIVE REAL ESTATE MAGAZINE. VFOAT Creative Real Estate. 0194-7222. Periodical. US. English. mo. $40.00. Creative Real Estate, Drawer L, Rancho Santa Fe CA 92067. Tel (619)756-1441. Ed A D Kessler. bk rev. adv acc. Circ 40,000. National reference journal for creative real estate investors and professionals with how-to formulas by recognized experts, includes directory of exchange groups and an educational calendar. Real Estate News Observer.

CREATIVE TAX PLANNING FOR REAL ESTATE TRANSACTIONS. (CREATIVE TAX PLANNING FOR REAL ESTATE TRANSACTIONS : ALI-ABA COURSE OF STUDY, MATERIALS). VFOAT ALI-ABA Course of Study, Materials. 0732-751X. US. English. an. ALI-ABA Committee on Continuing Professional Education, 4025 Chestnut Street, Philadelphia PA 19104. LC KF6540.Z9. DD 343.730546, 347.303546.

DENVER LIVING. VFOAT Living. Ceased in 1983. 0192-9100. Periodical. US. English. bm. $12.00. Baker Publications, 5757 Alpha Road/Suite 409, Dallas TX 75240. Tel (303)695-8440. Ed Patt Dodd. adv acc. Circ 85,000. (ctrl). Housing guide for newcomers and local residents looking for homes in the Metro Denver area.

THE DIGEST OF STATE LAND SALES REGULATIONS. (DIGEST OF STATE LAND SALES REGULATIONS). VFOAT State Digest. 0739-6368. Periodical. US. English. qt. Land Development Institute Ltd, 1401 16th Street NW, Washington DC 20036. Tel (202)232-2144. Circ 400. (ctrl). State-by-state summary of laws and administrative policy affecting real estate, land development, campgrounds, timesharing, advertising, and related laws.

DIRECTORY - CANADIAN REAL ESTATE ASSOCIATION. See Yearbooks, Almanacs, Directories.

DIRECTORY - INTERNATIONAL REAL ESTATE FEDERATION. See Yearbooks, Almanacs, Directories.

DIRECTORY, LICENSED REAL ESTATE BROKERS AND SALES ASSOCIATES. See Yearbooks, Almanacs, Directories.

DIRECTORY, LICENSED REAL ESTATE BROKERS AND SALESMEN - (SOUTH CAROLINA). See Yearbooks, Almanacs, Directories.

DIRECTORY OF LICENSED REAL ESTATE APPRAISERS. See Yearbooks, Almanacs, Directories.

DIRECTORY OF LICENSED REAL ESTATE BROKERS AND SALESMEN, STATE OF NEBRASKA. See Yearbooks, Almanacs, Directories.

DIRECTORY OF LICENSED REAL ESTATE BROKERS AND SALESPERSONS. See Yearbooks, Almanacs, Directories.

DIRECTORY OF LICENSED REAL ESTATE BROKERS AND SALESPERSONS. See Yearbooks, Almanacs, Directories.

DIRECTORY OF MEMBERS - AMERICAN INSTITUTE OF REAL ESTATE APPRAISERS. See Yearbooks, Almanacs, Directories.

DIRECTORY OF MEMBERS - NATIONAL ASSOCIATION OF REAL ESTATE INVESTMENT TRUSTS. See Yearbooks, Almanacs, Directories.

DIRECTORY OF REAL ESTATE AND BUSINESS CHANCE BROKERS AND SALESMEN. See Yearbooks, Almanacs, Directories.

THE DIRECTORY OF REAL ESTATE INVESTORS. See Yearbooks, Almanacs, Directories.

DIRECTORY, PROFESSIONAL REAL ESTATE MANAGEMENT WHO'S WHO. See Yearbooks, Almanacs, Directories.

DIRECTORY - SOCIETY OF INDUSTRIAL REALTORS. See Yearbooks, Almanacs, Directories.

DIRECTORY - SOUTH DAKOTA REAL ESTATE BOARD. See Yearbooks, Almanacs, Directories.

DISCLOSURE. VFOAT Neighborhoods First Disclosure. 0196-8203. Periodical. US. English. mo. National Training and Information Center, 1123 West Washington Boulevard, Chicago IL 60607.

DISTRICT OF COLUMBIA REAL ESTATE REPORTER. VFOAT Real Estate Reporter. 0738-6931. Periodical. US. English. mo. $75.00. Real Estate Reporter Ltd, 1401 16th Street NW, Washington DC 20036. Tel (202)232-2144. Circ 250. (ctrl). Reports on the latest in land use, historic preservation, zoning, licensing and permits, rental housing, administrative and court decision.

EDUCATION QUARTERLY CEASED. Spring 1977-Winter 1985. 0703-1173. CN. English. qt. Real Estate Institute of Canada, 99 Duncan Mill Road, Don Mills Ontario Canada. DD 333.330971. Journal, 0703-6914.

EJENDOMSSALG. VFOAT Sales of Real Property. 0917-0172. DK. Danish (English). ir. 16.39. Danmarks Statistik, Sejrgade 11, 2100 Kbenhavn Denmark. Tel (01)298222. LC HD731.A1. Circ 1,150. Total sales of real property, agricultural holdings, residential, commercial and industrial properties, etc.; building sites and announcements of forced sales of real property.

EMERGING TRENDS IN REAL ESTATE. US. English. an. LC HD251. DD 333.330973.

ERC DIRECTORY. See Yearbooks, Almanacs, Directories.

EURO AFRICA'S REVIEW OF THE NAIROBI PROPERTY MARKET. Main/Corp Euro Africa International Ltd. VFOAT Euro Africa Property Review. 1979/80-. Periodical. English. an. Euro Africa International Ltd, POB 40889, Nairobi Kenya. LC HD983.Z9. DD 333.330967625.

EXISTING HOME SALES. Main/Corp National Association of Realtors. Dept. of Economics and Research. 1976-. 0161-5882. US. English. an. $24.00 Member, $36.00 Non-Members. National Association of Realtors, Headquarters Office, 430 North Michigan Avenue, Chicago IL 60611. LC HD255. DD 333.338. Existing Home Sales Series, Annual Report.

EXPENSE ANALYSIS, CONDOMINIUMS, COOPERATIVES, & PLANNED UNIT DEVELOPMENTS. 1978-. 0191-2208. US. English. an. $59.00. Institute of Real Estate Management, 430 North Michigan Avenue, Chicago IL 60611. Tel (312)661-1930. Ed Kenneth Anderson. LC HD7287.67.U5. DD 658.15933. Circ 5,500. Survey of homeowners association operating costs, including administration, maintenance, contract services, amenities and replacement research. Income-Expense Analysis. Apartments, Condominiums & Cooperatives, 0161-5262.

FARM REAL ESTATE MARKET DEVELOPMENTS. Main/Corp United States. Dept. of Agriculture. Economics, Statistics, and Cooperatives Service. Cd 85- Aug. 1980-. US. English. an. Department of Agriculture, Economics Statistics and Cooperatives Service, Washington DC 20250. Farm Real Estate Market Developments.

FEDERAL INCOME TAXATION OF REAL ESTATE. SUPPLEMENTS. US. English. ir. $72.00. Warren Gorham and Lamont Inc, 210 South Street, Boston MA 02111. Tel (800)225-2363.

FIABCI INTERNATIONAL DIRECTORY. See Yearbooks, Almanacs, Directories.

FIABCI REPORTER. Main/Corp International Real Estate Federation. Periodical. FR. English (French, German and Spanish). ir. FIABCI Paris, 68 rue Des Archives, Paris (3E) France. LC HD251. DD 333.3305. FIABCI.

FINANCIAL FREEDOM REPORT. See Business - Investments.

FIRST TUESDAY. 1979. 0272-8230. Periodical. US. English. mo. $59.50. First Tuesday, PO Box 20068, Riverside CA 92506. Tel (714)686-8005. Ed Simon Sykes. LC HD251. DD 33.330973. Circ 5,000. A journal for the Real Estate Industry.

FLORIDA REAL ESTATE & DEVELOPOMENT UPDATE. VFOAT Florida Real Estate and Development Update. Vol. 1, No. 1-. 0887-3208. Periodical. US. English. sm. $100.00. Data Directions Inc, PO Box 912, Port Washington DC 11050. DD 332.

THE FLORIDA REAL ESTATE BROKER & THE LAW. VFOAT Florida Real Estate Broker and the Law. 0735-9071. Periodical. US. English. $24.00. CE Hartle Associates, PO Box 23091, Jacksonville FL 32223. LC KFF126.A59. DD 333.3309759.

FLORIDA REAL ESTATE COMMISSION HANDBOOK. VFOAT F.R.E.C. Handbook. US. English. $4.50. Florida Division of Real Estate, PO Box 1900, Orlando FL 32802. LC KFF282.R4. DD 346.7590437, 347.5906437. Board of Real Estate Handbook, 0734-8363.

FLORIDA REAL ESTATE COMMISSION NEWS & REPORT. 0744-6152. Periodical. US. English. qt. $00.55. Florida Real Estate Commission, 400 West Robinson Street, Orlando FL 32801. Florida Board of Real Estate News & Report, 0199-4565.

FLORIDA'S MOBILE HOME GUIDE. VFOAT Florida Mobile Home Guide. 0192-1363. US. English. an. $4.75. Mobile Home News, PO Box 1219, Altamonte Springs FL 32701. Tel (305)830-7300. Ed Joe Hoeddinghaus. LC TX1107.2.F6. DD 647.94759. bk rev. adv acc. Circ 25,000. Mobile/manufactured home living in Florida - industry, product and lifestyle information. Mobile Home Guide.

FUDOSAN KANKEI HOREI SHU. Main/Corp Japan. JA. Japanese. ir. 2600. Jutaku Shimpo Sha, c/o Tokyo Toranomon Building 10 Shiba Toranomon Minato-ku, Tokyo 105 Japan.

FUDOSAN SHINROPPO. Main/Corp Japan. Japanese. ir. 2600. Shukan Jutaku Shimbun Sha, 9-4 Shinjuku 1, Shinjuku-ku 160 Tokyo Japan.

Real Estate

GENERAL SERIES - CENTER FOR REAL ESTATE AND URBAN ECONOMIC STUDIES, SCHOOL OF BUSINESS ADMINISTRATION, UNIVERSITY OF CONNECTICUT. (GENERAL SERIES - CENTER FOR REAL ESTATE AND URBAN ECONOMIC STUDIES). Main/Corp University of Connecticut. Center for Real Estate and Urban Economic Studies. No. 1-. 0069-9047. Monographic Series. US. English. ir. Center for Real Estate and Urban Economic Studies, U-41Re Attn: Publications School of Business Administration, University of Connecticut, Storrs CT 06268. LC HD251. DD 333.33.

THE GOLD BOOK OF MULTI-HOUSING. VFOAT Who's Who in the Multifamily Housing Industry. Began in 1979. 0195-847X. US. English. CMR Associates Inc, 2129-1 Baldwin Avenue, Crofton MD 21114. LC HD1390. DD 338.769083102573.

GOLD POST. Vol. 1, Issue 1-. 0229-0723. Periodical. CN. English. mo. Free. Gold Post, Suite 204/1992 Yonge Street, Toronto Ontario Canada. DD 333.330971.

HAWAII INVESTOR. VFOAT Hawaii Inve$tor. 0745-7073. Periodical. US. English. mo. $15.00 Domestic, $26.00 Foreign. Hawaii Invester, 1 North King Street/Suite 202, Honolulu HI 96817. *Hawaii Real Estate Investor, 0273-5806.*

HGS INTERNATIONAL'S REAS LETTER. VFOAT H.G.S. International's R.E.A.S. Letter. VAT Henry G Sobeck International's Real Estate Agent's Survival Letter. Vol. 1, No. 1 (May 1983)-. 0733-1304. Periodical. US. English. mo. $147.00. Sobeck International, 516 Jackson Avenue, Westwood NJ 07675.

HOMEOWNER'S ADVISOR. Vol. 1, No. 1 (June 1983)-. 0738-6109. Periodical. US. English. mo. Circulation Department, Homeowners Advisor, 10076 Boca Entrada Boulevard, Boca Raton FL 33433.

HOUSE PRICE TRENDS AND RESIDENTIAL CONSTRUCTION COSTS IN THE TORONTO REAL ESTATE BOARD MARKET AREA AND IN CANADA. 1978- Ed. 0705-9515. CN. English. an. $2.00 Per No. Toronto Real Estate Board, Research Department, 1883 Yonge Street, Toronto Ontario M4S 1Y7 Canada. DD 338.4369080971354I. *House Price Trends and Residential Construction Costs in Metropolitan Toronto and Canada, 0319-7522.*

INCOME/EXPENSE ANALYSIS. APARTMENTS. (INCOME/EXPENSE ANALYSIS : APARTMENTS). VAT Income Expense Analysis: Apartments. 1978-. 0194-1941. US. English. an. $75.00. Institute of Real Estate Management, 430 North Michigan Avenue, Chicago IL 60611. Tel (312)661-1930. Ed Kenneth Anderson. LC HD7287.6.U5. DD 333.338. Circ 10,000. Statistical summaries of the financial operations of apartment buildings in the US and Canada - by metropolitan area and building type. *Income-Expense Analysis. Apartments, Condominiums & Cooperatives, 0161-5262.*

INCOME/EXPENSE ANALYSIS. OFFICE BUILDINGS, DOWNTOWN AND SUBURBAN. 1982 Ed.-. US. English. an. Institute of Real Estate Management, c/o Sharon Shelton, 430 North Michigan Avenue, Chicago IL 60611. Tel (312)661-1930. *Income/Expense Analysis. Suburban Office Buildings, 0146-9360.*

INDICATOR. (THE INDICATOR). Main/Corp Vancouver Island Real Estate Board. 1976-. 0381-0917. CN. English. an. 15.00. Vancouver Island Real Estate Board, PO Box 592, Nanaimo British Columbia V9R Canada. Tel (604)390-4212. Ed D Gardner. DD 333.330971134. Circ 1,500. (ctrl). A statistical review of market activities in real estate, also a review of demographics and commercial development.

INTERNATIONAL DIRECTORY OF MEMBERS. See Yearbooks, Almanacs, Directories.

INTERNATIONAL PROPERTY INVESTMENT JOURNAL. Vol. 1, No. 1 (Aug. 1982 issue)-. 0731-4639. Periodical. UK. English. ir. $146.00. Harwood Academic Publishers, PO Box 197, London WC2E 9PX England. Ed Alan J Placa. Ind/Abst Leg. Resour. Index. LC K9. DD 346.043, 342.643. CODEN IPRIDZ. bk rev. adv acc. Issued also in microform.

INTERNATIONAL REAL ESTATE JOURNAL. Vol. 1, 1-. 8755-6138. Periodical. US. English. ty. $64.00. International Institute, International Office, 8715 Via de Commercio, Scottsdale AZ 85258. Ed E K Twichell. DD 333. bk rev. adv acc. Circ 30,000. Journal specializes on international real estate concerning investment, development, finance and real estate on a general basis.

JOURNAL OF PROPERTY MANAGEMENT. V. 1- June 1934-. 0022-3905. Periodical. US. English. bm. $12.50. Institute of Real Estate Management, 430 North Michigan Avenue, Chicago IL 60611. LC TX955.

JOURNAL OF REAL ESTATE EDUCATION. (JOURNAL OF REAL ESTATE EDUCATION : PUBLICATION OF THE NATIONAL ASSOCIATION OF REALTORS). Vol. 1, No. 1 (Fall 1982)-. 0732-1821. Periodical. US. English. qt. Free. National Association of Realtors, 777 14th Street NW, c/o C Cuttings, Washington DC 20005. Ed Cynthia Cutting. bk rev. adv acc. Circ 10,200. (ctrl). Serious forum for scholarly articles, training articles, profiles of educators, philosophies of education, and general information on real estate education nationally.

JOURNAL OF REAL ESTATE TAXATION. See Business - Public Finance.

JUST COMPENSATION; A MONTHLY REPORT ON CONDEMNATION CASES. See Law.

KANSAS REALTOR. (KANSAS REALTOR : OFFICIAL PUBLICATION OF THE KANSAS ASSOCIATION OF REALTORS). 0279-9960. Periodical. US. English. mo. *Jayhawk Realtor.*

LANDLORD-TENANT RELATIONS REPORT. See Housing and Urban Development.

LAPORAN PASARAN HARTA. VFOAT Property Market Report. 1978-. English (Malay). ir. LC HD890.6.Z63. DD 333.33209595.

LAURENTIAN REAL ESTATE HIGHLIGHTS. Vol. 1, No. 1 (May 1983)-. 0822-1030. Periodical. CN. English. qt. Entreprises de l'Arpent Perdu, R R 2, Ste Agathe des Monts Quebec J8C 2Z8 Canada. Tel (819)326-4963. Ed Sheila Eskenazi. DD 333.330971424. adv acc. Circ 750. (ctrl). Real estate market and upper Laurentians for selected clients and potential clients.

LIVING (SOUTH FLORIDA EDITION). (LIVING). VFOAT South Florida Living. Vol. 3, No. 3 (June/July 1983)-. 0741-3440. Periodical. US. English. bm. Baker Publications Inc, 5757 Alpha Road/Suite 400, Dallas TX 75234. LC HD266.F6. DD 333.3309759. *South Florida Living, 0279-8506.*

LOWER BUCKS COUNTY REAL ESTATE DIRECTORY. See Yearbooks, Almanacs, Directories.

LUSK'S ANNE ARUNDEL COUNTY REAL ESTATE DIRECTORY, PROPERTY TRANSFERS. See Yearbooks, Almanacs, Directories.

LUSK'S BALTIMORE COUNTY REAL ESTATE DIRECTORY, PROPERTY TRANSFERS. See Yearbooks, Almanacs, Directories.

LUSK'S CARROLL COUNTY REAL ESTATE DIRECTORY. See Yearbooks, Almanacs, Directories.

LUSK'S DISTRICT OF COLUMBIA REAL ESTATE DIRECTORY SERVICE. See Yearbooks, Almanacs, Directories.

LUSK'S EAST SUFFOLK COUNTY REAL ESTATE DIRECTORY. See Yearbooks, Almanacs, Directories.

LUSK'S FAIRFAX COUNTY, VIRGINIA REAL ESTATE DIRECTORY SERVICE. See Yearbooks, Almanacs, Directories.

LUSK'S MONTGOMERY COUNTY, MARYLAND, ASSESSMENT DIRECTORY. See Yearbooks, Almanacs, Directories.

LUSK'S NORTHERN VIRGINIA REAL ESTATE GUIDE. VFOAT Northern Virginia Real Estate Guide. 0745-8878. US. English. wk. $230.00. Rufus S Lusk & Son Inc, 1824 Jefferson Place NW, Washington DC 20036.

LUSK'S PRINCE WILLIAM COUNTY REAL ESTATE DIRECTORY SERVICE. See Yearbooks, Almanacs, Directories.

THE MARION STAR. VFOAT Marion Star and Southern Real Estate Advertiser. Began in 1846. Newspaper. US. English. wk. PO Box 880, Marion SC 29571. Ed W J McKerall.

MEMBERSHIP PROFILE. 0735-3235. US. English. an. National Association of Realtors, 430 North Michigan Avenue, Chicago IL 60611. LC HD251. DD 331.761333330973.

MEMBERSHIP/COMMITTEE DIRECTORY - BUILDING OWNERS AND MANAGERS ASSOCIATION INTERNATIONAL. See Yearbooks, Almanacs, Directories.

MINNEAPOLIS REALTOR. 0745-3906. Periodical. US. English. sm. Minneapolis Realtor, 6101 Wayzata Boulevard, Minneapolis MN 55416.

MINNESOTA REAL ESTATE DIRECTORY. See Yearbooks, Almanacs, Directories.

MINNESOTA REAL ESTATE LAW JOURNAL. See Law.

MOBILITY. See Business.

MONEY & REAL ESTATE. VFOAT Money and Real Estate. 8756-9124. Periodical. US. English. mo. $120.00 Charter, $180.00 Regular. Executive Enterprise Publishing Company, 33 West 60th Street, New York NY 10023.

MORGUARD REPORT. 0712-9769. Periodical. CN. English. qt. Free. Morguard Group Ltd, 6 Crescent Road, Toronto Ontario M4W 3K9 Canada. DD 332.63240971.

THE MORTGAGE AND REAL ESTATE EXECUTIVES REPORT. (MORTGAGE AND REAL ESTATE EXECUTIVES REPORT). 0047-813X. Periodical. US. English. sm. $125.00. Warren Gorham & Lamont Inc, 210 South Street, Boston MA 02111. Tel (800)225-2363.

MOVING TO & AROUND WINNIPEG & MANITOBA. See Travel.

MOVING TO OTTAWA/HULL. VAT Emmanager a Ottawa/Hull (1978). 1978-. 0226-7837. CN. English (French). an. Moving to Publications, PO Box 272 Station C, Winnipeg Manitoba R3M 3S7 Canada. DD 917.1384. *Emmenager a Ottawa/Hull, 0226-7837.*

MUNICIPAL BONDS. See Law.

NATIONAL ASSOCIATION OF REALTORS STATEMENT OF POLICY. VFOAT Statement of Policy and Position on Current Issues. 0740-9419. US. English. National Association of Realtors, 430 North Michigan Avenue, Chicago IL 60611. LC HD1361. DD 333.330973.

NATIONAL MARKET LETTER CEASED. Began with V. 1, May 1946-. Ceased with Sept. 1981. Periodical. US. English. mo. $20.00. 73 West Monroe, Chicago IL 60603. LC HD251. DD 333.33.

NATIONAL REAL ESTATE INVESTOR. See Business - Investments.

NATIONAL REAL ESTATE INVESTOR. DIRECTORY ISSUE. See Yearbooks, Almanacs, Directories.

NATIONAL ROSTER OF REALTORS. 0090-1741. US. English. an. $25.00. National Roster of Realtors, PO Box 1888, Cedar Rapids IA 52406. Tel (310)364-6032. Ed Evelyn Oldridge. LC HD253. DD 333.33. adv acc. Circ 11,000. The official directory of the entire membership of the National Association of Realtors. It also contains information on the association and its institutes, councils, national and state officers.

NATIONAL THRIFT NEWS. See Business - Banking & Finance.

NEBRASKA REAL ESTATE LAW JOURNAL. See Law.

NEW ENGLAND REAL ESTATE JOURNAL. 1963. 0028-4890. Periodical. US. English. wk. $52.00. New England Real Estate, Box 55, Accord MA 02018. Tel (617)749-6947. Ed Ben Summers. bk rev. adv acc. Circ 25,000. (ctrl).

Real Estate

NEW HOMES AND APARTMENTS GUIDE, GREATER TORONTO AREA. 0710-2283. Periodical. CN. English. qt. Free. Toronto Home Builders' Association, 5218 Yonge Street, Willowdale Ontario M2N 5P6 Canada. **DD** 333.3309713541. *Houses for Sale.*

NEW HOMES MAGAZINE. 0192-4893. Periodical. US. English. bm. $6.00. New Homes Magazine, 3151 Air Way Avenue/Building J1, Costa Mesa CA 92626. **Tel** (714)751-5813. **Ed** Kele Bock. adv acc. (ctrl). For over 17 years, our magazine has been finding buyers for builders throughout California. We feature some of the finest new home developments in excellent locations.

NEW JERSEY REALTOR. 0028-5919. Periodical. US. English. mo. $10.00. New Jersey Association of Real Estate, 295 Pierson Avenue Box 2098, Edison NJ 08818. **Tel** (201)494-5616. **Ed** Marianne Astalos. bk rev. adv acc. **Circ** 28,000. (ctrl). Trends of the New Jersey Association of Realtors; including legal questions and guidelines, real estate issues and member inquiries.

NEWSLETTER ESTATES. *See* Business - Investments.

N.Y. HABITAT. VFOAT NY Habitat. Vol. 1, No. 1 (May 1982)-. 0745-0893. Periodical. US. English. ir. $25.00. New York Habitat, 928 Broadway, New York NY 10010. **Tel** (212)505-2030. **Ed** Carol J Ott. bk rev. adv acc. **Circ** 10,000. (ctrl). A business magazine for co-op and condo Boards of Directors, owners and would-be owners. Covering all aspects of ownership-management, value sales, group leadership. *Loft Living.*

OKLAHOMA REALTOR. 0745-5046. Periodical. US. English. bm. Oklahoma Realtor, 9807 North Broadway, Oklahoma City OK 73114.

ONTARIO HOME BUYERS GUIDE. MISSISSAUGA EDITION CEASED. (ONTARIO HOMES BUYERS GUIDE). Feb. 1975-. 0316-1463. CN. English. mo. Stelijes Publications Ltd, 45 Charles Street East, Toronto Ontario M4Y 1S2 Canada. **DD** 333.3370971353.

ONTARIO HOMES BUYERS GUIDE. V. 5, No. 1- Jan. 22, 1975-. 0316-1471. CN. English. 0.50 Each Number. Ontario Homes Magazines, 45 Charles Street East, Toronto Ontario M4Y 1S2 Canada. **DD** 333.33709713541. *Ontario Homes Magazines, 0317-5197.*

OPERATIONS MANUAL OF THE NATIONAL ASSOCIATION OF REALTORS. Main/Corp National Association of Realtors. 0147-1929. US. English. $4.00. 430 North Michigan Avenue, Chicago IL 60611. LC HD251. **DD** 333.33.

PHOTO ROSTER. Main/Corp Society of Industrial Realtors. 0190-5449. US. English. be. Society of Industrial Realtors, 925 15th Street NW, Washington DC 20005. LC HD251. **DD** 333.3302573.

PINELLAS REVIEW. 1953-. Periodical. US. English. wk. $25.00. Pinellas Review, PO Box 14446, St Petersburg FL 33733. **Tel** (813)546-4635. **Ed** Theodore Serrill. bk rev. adv acc. **Circ** 3,100. (ctrl). Financial, banking, real estate legal newspaper. All deeds, mortgages, judgements, new business, law matters, and politics.

THE PRACTICAL REAL ESTATE LAWYER. *See* Law.

PRESERVATION LAW REPORTER. *See* Law.

PREVIEWS GUIDE TO THE WORLD'S FINE REAL ESTATE. Main/Corp Previews Incorporated. VFOAT Previews' International Real Estate Guide. US. English. an. $19.95. Previews Inc, Greenwich Office Park, Greenwich CT 06830. **Tel** (800)782-2222. **Ed** Helene Nichols. LC HD1361. **DD** 333.3305. adv acc. **Circ** 20,000. Guide showing the world's finest real estate for sale around the world.

PRIVATE REAL ESTATE LIMITED PARTNERSHIPS. Series/Titl Real Estate Law and Practice Course Handbook Series. 1977-. 0271-0897. Periodical. US. English. an. Practising Law Institute, 810 Seventh Avenue, New York NY 10019. LC KF1079. **DD** 346730437.

PROFESSIONAL REAL ESTATE REPORTS. Vol. 1, No. 1 (Sept. 1984)-. 0749-8012. Periodical. US. English. bm. $235.00. Tribune Media Services, 1909 Cinnaminson Avenue, Cinnaminson NJ 08077. **DD** 333.

PROFILE OF REAL ESTATE FIRMS. 0742-5074. US. English. an. $10.00. National Association of Realtors, Economics and Research Division 777 14th Street Northwest, Washington DC 20005. LC HD278. **DD** 338.761333330973.

PROPERTIES. 0033-1287. Periodical. US. English. mo. Properties Magazine, 4900 Euclid Avenue, Cleveland OH 44103.

PROPERTY MARKET REPORT . . . . Began with Vol. for 1979. English. an. $16.00. LC HD890.6.Z63. **DD** 333.33209595. *Laporan Pasaran Harta.*

QUESTOR REAL ESTATE SYNDICATION YEARBOOK. *See* Yearbooks, Almanacs, Directories.

THE RAM DIGEST. *See* Housing and Urban Development.

RATING APPEALS. *See* Law.

REAL ESTATE ANALYSIS AND PLANNING SERVICE. 0882-9144. US. English. Data Resources Inc, 24 Hartwell Avenue, Lexington MA 02173. LC HD251. **DD** 333.330973.

THE REAL ESTATE ANALYST. Main/Corp Wenzlick (Roy) and Company. Periodical. US. English. Roy Wenzlick Research, 595 Olive Street, St Louis MO 63101. LC HD251. **DD** 333.33.

REAL ESTATE AND CONSTRUCTION REPORT. Main/Corp Real Estate Research Council of Southern California. 1977-. 0147-9946. Periodical. US. English. qt. Real Estate Research Council of Southern California, Sherman Oaks CA 91423. LC HD266.C22. **DD** 333.3309794. *Residential Research Report, 0147-9636.*

REAL ESTATE AND PUBLIC UTILITY PROPERTY TAXES. (REAL ESTATE AND PUBLIC UTILITY PROPERTY TAXES. GROSS TAXES LEVIED, TAXES CHARGED, AND VALUE OF PROPERTY, BY CLASS OF PROPERTY AND CITY, CALENDAR YEAR . . .). Series/Titl Table PD. 1976-. 0732-0701. US. English. an. Ohio Department of Taxation, Research and Statistics Section, PO Box 530, Columbus OH 43216. LC HJ4255. **DD** 336.2209771. *Property Taxes, Real Estate and Public Utility.*

REAL ESTATE & THE LAW. VAT Real Estate and the Law. V. 1- Sept. 1979-. 0270-7683. Periodical. US. English. mo. $29.00. Philip Clarke Baten Reports, PO Box 2171, Washington DC 20013. LC KF2042.R4. **DD** 346.7304305.

THE REAL ESTATE APPRAISER AND ANALYST. V. 44, No. 5- Sept./Oct. 1978-. 0271-258X. Periodical. US. English. ir. $7.50. Society of Real Estate Appraisers, 645 North Michigan Avenue, Chicago IL 60611. **Tel** (312)346-7422. **Ed** Gerri Rothbauer. LC HD1387.A1. **DD** 333.33205. bk rev. **Circ** 17,000. Articles on valvation of specific property types, discussion of the appraisal process and refinement of individual techniques, land planning and its effects on value. *Real Estate Appraiser, 0034-0677.*

REAL ESTATE ASSESSMENT, SALES RATIO STUDY. *See* Business - Public Finance.

REAL ESTATE ASSESSMENT/SALES RATIO STUDY. Began in 1979. US. English. an. $1.50. Kansas Department of Revenue. LC HJ4217. **DD** 336.22209781. *Kansas Assessment Sales Ratio Study.*

THE REAL ESTATE BOARD REPORT. Vol. 1, No. 1 (Apr. 1981)-. 0276-4792. Periodical. US. English. mo $72.00. Newsletter Management Corporation, 10076 Boca Entrada Boulevard, Boca Raton FL 33433. **Tel** (305)483-2600.

REAL ESTATE BULLETIN. (REAL ESTATE BULLETIN : OFFICIAL PUBLICATION OF THE CALIFORNIA DIVISION OF REAL ESTATE). 0734-7839. Periodical. US. English. qt. Real Estate Bulletin, 1719 24th Street, Sacramento CA 95816.

REAL ESTATE CLOSINGS. Main/Corp New York (City). Practising Law Institute. Series/Titl Real Estate Law and Practice Course Handbook Series. 4th- 1973-. 0148-2718. Periodical. US. English. Practising Law Institute, 810 Seventh Street, New York NY 10019. LC KF665. **DD** 346.730437. *Real Estate Closing Workshop, 0148-2645.*

REAL ESTATE: DEBTORS' AND CREDITOR'S RIGHTS. (REAL ESTATE, DEBTORS' AND CREDITORS' RIGHTS : ALI-ABA COURSE OF STUDY, MATERIALS). VFOAT Ali-Aba Course of Study, Materials. 0734-9653. Periodical. US. English. an. ALI-ABA Committee on Continuing Professional Education, 4025 Chestnut Street, Philadelphia PA 19104. LC KF1501.Z9. **DD** 346.73077, 347.30677.

REAL ESTATE DEVELOPMENT ANNUAL. (THE REAL ESTATE DEVELOPMENT ANNUAL). 1974-. 0319-1087. CN. English. an. $57.96. MacLean Hunter, PO Box 100 Station A, Toronto Ontario M5W 1A7 Canada. **DD** 338.476900971. *The Canadian Real Estate Annual, 0068-9564.*

THE REAL ESTATE DIGEST. 0882-8733. Periodical. US. English. mo. $48.00. The Real Estate Digest, PO Box 26555, Birmingham AL 35226. **Tel** (205)967-4232. **Ed** Richard E Dewberry. **DD** 332. adv acc. **Circ** 10,000. How-to-do-it guide for real estate investing, creative financing techniques, and up-to-date strategies. Plus guest authors famous in the real estate field.

REAL ESTATE DIRECTORY OF MANHATTAN. *See* Yearbooks, Almanacs, Directories.

REAL ESTATE EDUCATION AND RESEARCH SPECIAL ACCOUNT. US. English. an. Department of Commerce, Two Nationwide Plaza, Columbus OH 43215. LC HD1381.5.U5. **DD** 353.977100826533333.

REAL ESTATE FINANCE. Vol. 1, No. 1 (Spring 1984)-. 0748-318X. Periodical. US. English. qt. $58.00. Federal Research Press, 65 Franklin Street, Boston MA 02110. **DD** 332.

REAL ESTATE FINANCE LAW JOURNAL. *See* Law.

REAL ESTATE FINANCE TODAY. Vol. 1, No. 1 (Feb. 1984)-. 0742-0021. Periodical. US. English. sm. $48.00. Mortgage Bankers Association of America, 1125 15th Street NW, Washington DC 20005. **DD** 333.

REAL ESTATE FINANCING REPORT. *See* Business - Public Finance.

REAL ESTATE FORUM. VFOAT Forum. Began in 1946?. 0034-0707. Periodical. US. English. ir. $60.00. Real Estate Forum, 12 West 37th Street/3rd Floor, New York NY 10018. **Tel** (212)563-6460.

REAL ESTATE INSIDER. 0034-0715. Periodical. US. English. ir. $88.00. Atcom Inc, 2315 Broadway, New York NY 10024. **Tel** (212)873-5900. **Ed** Robert Reis. **Circ** 2,100. (ctrl). A newsletter for owners and managers and brokers of real estate firms.

REAL ESTATE INTELLIGENCE REPORT. V. 1- Nov. 1978-. 0194-6900. Periodical. US. English. mo. $95.00. Phillips Publishing Inc, 7315 Wisconsin Avenue/Suite 1200-N, Washington DC 20014. **Tel** (301)986-0666.

REAL ESTATE INVESTING LETTER. *See* Business - Investments.

REAL ESTATE ISSUES. V. 1- Fall 1976-. 0146-0595. US. English. sa. $18.00. American Society of Real Estate Counselors, 430 North Michigan Avenue, Chicago IL 60611. **Tel** (312)329-8431. **Ed** Linda Magad. Ind/Abst ABI/Inform. LC HD251. **DD** 333.33. bk rev. adv acc. **Circ** 1,500. The journal contains articles that focus on theoretical and empirical approaches to timely problems and topics in the field of real estate.

REAL ESTATE LAW AND PRACTICE COURSE HANDBOOK SERIES. *See* Law.

REAL ESTATE LAW BRIEF CASE. 0034-0758. Periodical. US. English. mo. $10.00. Legal Research Institute, PO Box 26, San Antonio TX 78291.

REAL ESTATE LAW JOURNAL. *See* Law.

REAL ESTATE LAW REPORT. *See* Law.

REAL ESTATE LETTER. (THE REAL ESTATE LETTER). Vol. 1, No. 1 (Oct. 15, 1979)-. 0228-8737. Periodical. CN. English. mo. $75.00. Real Estate Letter, 716 Gordon Baker Road, Willowdale Ontario M2H 3M8 Canada. **DD** 333.330971.

REAL ESTATE LICENSE LAW AND RULES AND REGULATIONS. *See* Law.

REAL ESTATE MAGAZINE (CHICAGO, ILL.). (REAL ESTATE MAGAZINE). VFOAT Real Estate. Vol. 70, No. 31 (Friday, Aug. 5, 1983)-. 0746-164X. Periodical. US. English. bw. Free to Qualified Personnel, $32.00 Others. Law Bulletin

Real Estate

Publishing Company, 415 North State Street, Chicago IL 60610. *Chicagoland's Real Estate Advertiser, 0009-3769.*

REAL ESTATE MANUAL. Main/Corp Iowa Real Estate Commission. US. English. Iowa Real Estate Commission, Executive Hills, 1223 East Court Avenue, Des Moines IA 50319. LC HD266.I8. DD 333.33068.

THE REAL ESTATE MARKET IN NEW ZEALAND. Main/Corp New Zealand. Valuation Dept. 1975-. NZ. English. ir. 10.00. Valuation Department, PO Box 12-343, Wellington New Zealand. Tel 738-555. LC HD1387, HD11205. DD 333.3309931 S, 333.33509931. Circ 350. Shows provisional national real estate sales statistics in New Zealand. *Rural Real Estate Market in New Zealand.*

REAL ESTATE NEWS. METRO EDITION. (REAL ESTATE NEWS). V. 1- Oct. 5, 1979-. 0225-2783. Periodical. CN. English. wk. Free. Toronto Real Estate Board, 1883 Yonge Street, Toronto Ontario M4S 1Y7 Canada. DD 333.3309713541. *Toronto Real Estate, 0225-2775.*

REAL ESTATE NEWSLETTER (TORONTO, ONT.). (REAL ESTATE NEWSLETTER). Nov. 1982-. 0821-6541. Periodical. CN. English. qt. Free. Real Estate Newsletter, Levanthol & Howarth, 120 Adelaide Street West, Toronto Ontario M5H 1T6 Canada. Ind/Abst ABI/Inform. DD 333.330971.

REAL ESTATE NEWSLINE. Vol. 1, No. 1 (Nov. 1984)-. 0749-8640. Periodical. US. English. mo. Free. Kenneth Leventhal & Company, 2049 Century Park East/Suite 1700, Los Angeles CA 90067. Tel (213)277-0880. Ed James Carberry. DD 332. Circ 10,000. (ctrl). Real estate news and analysis.

REAL ESTATE PERIODICALS INDEX. *See* Indexes/Abstracts.

REAL ESTATE QUARTERLY. Vol. 1, No. 1 (Summer 1982)-. 0742-2644. Periodical. US. English. qt. $32.00 Members, $48.00 Nonmembers. National Association of Realtors, Economics and Research Division, 777 14th Street NW, Washington DC 20005. Tel (202)383-1059. LC HD1361. DD 333.3305. adv acc. Circ 3,000. Market trends and analysis of residential, commercial, industrial, farm and land real estate.

REAL ESTATE RECORD AND BUILDER'S GUIDE. VFOAT Record and Guide. V. 148- July 5, 1941-. 0034-0774. Periodical. US. English. wk. $325.00. Real Estate Data Inc, 475 Fifth Avenue/Suite 1901, New York NY 10017. Tel (212)532-2705. Ed Venice Kelly. adv acc. Circ 1,200. Lists real estate information on properties that have sold in Manhattan. Includes owner's name, address and phone number as well as financial data. *Real Estate Record.*

REAL ESTATE REPORT. 0079-9890. US. English. ir. University of Connecticut, School of Business Administration, Storrs CT 06268. LC HD251.

REAL ESTATE REPORT (REAL ESTATE RESEARCH CORPORATION). (REAL ESTATE REPORT). Periodical. US. English. qt. Real Estate Research Corporation, 72 West Adams, Chicago IL 60603.

REAL ESTATE REVIEW (BOSTON, MASS.). (REAL ESTATE REVIEW). Vol. 1, No. 1 (Spring 1971)-. 0034-0790. Periodical. US. English. qt. $56.70. Warren Gorham & Lamont Inc, 210 South Street, Boston MA 02111. Tel (800)225-2363. Ind/Abst Manage. Contents, Account. Index. Suppl., ABI/Inform, Public Aff. Inf. Serv. Bull., Bus. Period. Index, Energy Inf. Abstr., Environ. Abstr., Soc. Sci. Citation Index. LC HD251. DD 333.330973.

REAL ESTATE SALES/CLOSINGS LAW BULLETIN. VFOAT Real Estate Sales Closings Law Bulletin. Began with issue for Oct. 1984?. 8755-8262. US. English. mo. $36.50. Entre Deux Mers Ltd, 7 South River Lane East, Duxbury MA 02332. DD 346.

THE REAL ESTATE SECURITIES JOURNAL. *See* Business - Investments.

REAL ESTATE SECURITIES LETTER. (REAL ESTATE SECURITIES LETTER : AN INFORMATION SERVICE OF QUESTOR ASSOCIATES). 0275-1127. Periodical. US. English. mo. $150.00. Questor Associates, 115 Sansome Street, San Francisco CA 94104. *Real Estate Syndication Reporter Newsletter, 0197-1107.*

REAL ESTATE SYNDICATIONS. Series/Titl Real Estate Law and Practice Course Handbook Series. US. English. an. Practising Law Institute, 810 Seventh Avenue, New York NY 10019. LC KF1079.Z9. DD 346.73043, 347.30643.

REAL ESTATE SYNDICATIONS REPORTER. Vol. 1, No. 1 (Mar. 1984)-. 0748-3171. Periodical. US. English. mo. $128.00. Federal Research Press, 65 Franklin Street, Boston MA 02110. *Real Estate Tax Shelter Review, 0737-5263.*

THE REAL ESTATE TAX DIGEST. 8756-3835. Periodical. US. English. mo. Matthew Bender & Company, PO Box 2329, San Francisco CA 94126. LC KF6535.A15. DD 343.7305405, 347.3035405.

REAL ESTATE TAX IDEAS. Began in Apr. 1972. 0162-7538. Periodical. US. English. mo. $75.60. Warren Gorham & Lamont Inc, 210 South Street, Boston MA 02111. Tel (800)225-2363 Outside Massachusetts.

REAL ESTATE TODAY. V.1- 1968-. 0034-0804. Periodical. US. English. an. $10.00 Institute Members, Libraries, Educational Institutions, Faculty and Students, $18.00 Others. National Association of Realtors, 430 North Michigan Avenue, Chicago IL 60611. Tel (312)329-8277. Ed Karen L Nelson. Ind/Abst Trade Ind. Index, Mag. Index, Ref. Source. LC HD251. DD 333.3305. bk rev. adv acc. Circ 700,000. (ctrl). An educational magazine for real estate salespeople and brokers covering all aspects of residential, commercial-investment, brokerage management, real estate, mortgage finance, and business industry trends.

REAL ESTATE TRENDS IN METROPOLITAN VANCOUVER. 5th- Ed. 0085-5405. Periodical. CN. English. ir. Real Estate Board of Greater Vancouver, 1101 West Broadway, Vancouver British Columbia V6H 1G2 Canada. DD 333.30971133. *Real Estate and Business Trends in Metropolitan Vancouver and British Columbia, 0318-6083.*

REAL ESTATE VALUATION GUIDE. Vol. 13, Issue 142-. 0743-9377. US. English. mo. $15.00 Each Copy. E H Boeckh Company, 615 East Michigan Street, PO Box 664, Milwaukee WI 53201. LC HD1387. DD 333.33205. *Real Estate Evaluation Guide, 0743-9415.*

REAL ESTATE VENTURE ANALYSIS. 0092-3672. US. English. Practising Law Institute, 810 7th Avenue, New York NY 10019. LC HD1375. DD 333.33.

REAL PROPERTY SECTION NEWS. *See* Law.

REALTOR. Jan. 1977-. 0704-6707. Periodical. CN. English. mo. Free. Toronto Real Estate Board, 1888 Yonge Street, Toronto Ontario M4S 1Y7 Canada. Tel (416)481-6151. Ed Leslie A Ironstone. DD 333.33062713541. bk rev. adv acc. Circ 82,000. Real estate (residential and ICI) related to homebuying, selling, market conditions, community interest, home improvement, government concerning ownership, interest rates, etc. *Listings Magazine, 0317-9605.*

REALTOR NEWS. 0279-6309. Periodical. US. English. wk. $12.00. National Association of Realtors, 430 North Michigan Avenue, Chicago IL 60611-4087. Tel (312)329-8449. Ed Bill Adkinson. adv acc. Circ 604,220. (ctrl). Provides timely, up-to-date news and information concerning all aspects of the real estate industry.

REALTY. 0481-9004. Periodical. US. English. bw. $12.00. Leader-Observer Inc, 80-34 Jamaica Avenue, Woodhaven NY 11421. Tel (212)296-2233. Ed Lester A Sobel. bk rev. adv acc. Important news of real estate, finance, regulation, management, sales, leases, mortgages, trends, personnel.

REALTY AND BUILDING. VFOAT Realty & Building. Vol. 115, No. 19 (May 11, 1946)-. 0034-1045. Periodical. US. English. wk. $14.00. Realty and Building Inc, 12 East Grand Avenue, Chicago IL 60611. Tel (312)944-1204. Ed George R Stearns. LC HG1. DD 333.330977311. adv acc. Circ 9,000. News articles of property sales and construction and organizational activities mostly local. We have a national section. Regular features, names of buyers and sellers of real estate, building permits, wrecking permits, and weekly construction reports. *Economics (Chicago, Ill.).*

REALTY BLUEBOOK. 0090-399X. US. English. an. Professional Pub Corporation, PO Box 4187, San Rafael CA 94903. LC HD253. DD 333.33.

REGARDIE'S. Vol. 1, No. 3 (Jan./Feb. 1981)-. 0279-5965. Periodical. US. English. bm. $30.00. Regardie's Magazine, 1010 Wisconsin Avenue NW, Washington DC 20007. LC HC108.W3. DD 330.9753005. *Regardie's Business & Real Estate Washington, 0274-984X.*

REIT FACT BOOK. Main/Corp National Association of Real Estate Investment Trusts. VAT Real Estate Investment Trusts Fact Book. 1974-. 0095-1374. US. English. an. $40.00. National Association of Real Estate Investment Trusts, 1101 Seventeenth Street NW, Washington DC 20036. Tel (202)785-8717. Ed Michael E Dunbar. LC HG5095. DD 332.6324. Circ 3,000. Annual summary of status of the real estate investment trust industry.

REIT HANDBOOK OF MEMBER TRUSTS. *See* Business - Investments.

THE RELOCATION REPORT. 0275-7613. Periodical. US. English. sm. $65.00. The Kinsale Corporation, 117 Gutzon Borglum Road, Stamford CT 06903. Tel (203)322-4666. Ed Liam Murphy. bk rev. Circ 2,000. Newsletter concerning the employee relocation industry.

RE/MAX INTER. Vol. 1, No. 1 (Oct. 1982)-. 0712-5976. Periodical. CN. French. Re/Max Quebec, 1200 Ouest Boulevard St Martin, Laval Quebec H7S 2E4 Canada. DD 333.33060714.

RESEARCH IN REAL ESTATE. (RESEARCH IN REAL ESTATE : A RESEARCH ANNUAL). Vol. 1 (1982)-. 0731-7999. US. English. an. $49.50. JAI Press Inc, PO Box 1678, Greenwich CT 06836. Tel (203)661-7602. Ed C F Sirmans. LC HD251. DD 333.330973.

RESSI REVIEW. (THE RESSI REVIEW). Main/Corp Real Estate Securities and Syndication Institute. VFOAT Real Estate Securities and Syndication Institute Review. 0199-3534. Periodical. US. English. mo. $25.00. Real Estate Securities, 430 North Michigan Avenue, Chicago IL 60611. Tel (312)670-6760. Ed Lisa B Johnson. bk rev. Circ 4,000. (ctrl). Provides RESSI's membership with timely reporting on current regulatory and legislative issues affecting the real estate securities industry as well as institute affairs.

RIGHT OF WAY. Began with Feb. 1954 issue. 0035-5275. Periodical. US. English. bm. $16.00. International Right Way Association, 9920 la Cienega Boulevard/Suite 515, Inglewood CA 90301. Tel (213)649-5323. Ed Mike Powell. Ind/Abst Energy Inf. Abstr., Environ. Abstr. DD 333. bk rev. adv acc. Circ 9,000. (ctrl). Land acquisition for public use, engineering, appraisal, acquisition, real property law, and property management. *News.*

ROBERT G. ALLEN'S REAL ESTATE ADVISOR. 8756-7784. Periodical. US. English. mo. $126.00. The Allen Group, 145 Center Street, PO Box 8000, Provo UT 84603. DD 332. *Nothing Down Advisor.*

RON JANOFF'S GUIDE TO COMMERCIAL REAL ESTATE. VFOAT Guide to Commercial Real Estate. 1st- 1977-. 0194-3723. US. English. $50.00. Ronald C Janoff, 2300 North Campbell Avenue, Tucson AZ 85719. LC HD7287.6.U5. DD 333.337.

ROSTER OF LICENSED REAL ESTATE BROKERS AND SALESMEN BY COMPANY. 0098-0315. US. English. Delaware Real Estate Comm/Dept of Administrative Services, Division of Business and Occupational Regulations, State House Annex, Dover DE 19901. LC HD266.D3. DD 658.8933333. *Roster of Real Estate Brokers and Salesmen.*

ROSTER OF REAL ESTATE LICENSEES (IOWA). Main/Corp Iowa Real Estate Commission. VFOAT Roster of Licensed Real Estate Brokers and Salespersons. Began with 1977 issue. an. Iowa Real Estate Commission, Suite 205/1223 East Court Avenue, Des Moines IA 50319. LC HD266.I8. DD 333.33025777. *Roster of Licensed Real Estate Brokers and Sales Persons.*

ROSTER - REAL ESTATE INSTITUTE OF CANADA. Main/Corp Real Estate Institute of Canada. VFOAT Liste - Institut Canadien de l'Immeuble. Began publication 1971?. 0319-0226. Periodical. CN. text in English and French. Real Estate Institute of Canada, 99 Duncan Mill Road, Don

Mills Ontario M3B 1Z2 Canada. DD 333.3306271. *C I R Membership Roster.*

ROYAL TRUST FOCUS ON REAL ESTATE. (THE ROYAL TRUST FOCUS ON REAL ESTATE). VFOAT Current Perspectives of Canadian Real Estate. VAT Current Perspectives of Canadian Real Estate. 0227-6844. Periodical. CN. English. sa. Free. Royal Trust Marketing, c/o D Bloore, PO Box 7500, Station A, Toronto Ontario M5W 1P9 Canada. DD 333.330971.

ROYAL TRUST SURVEY OF CANADIAN HOUSE PRICES. Feb. 1, 1978-. 0706-8506. Periodical. CN. English. ty. Free. Royal Trust Corporation, PO Box 7500 Station A, Toronto Ontario M5W 1P9 Canada. DD 338.436908640971. (ctrl). *Survey of House Prices, 0706-8484.*

RUMAH-RUMAH YANG DITAWARKAN KEPADA ANDA DI JAKARTA. Vol. 1 (Period Oct. 1982 to March 1983-). Indonesian. sa. 1500. PT Pondok Press, PO Box 132, Mampang KBY, Jakarta Selatan Indonesia. LC HD900.J34.

RUNZHEIMER REPORTS ON RELOCATION. VFOAT Reports on Relocation. Vol. 1, No. 1 (Mar. 1982)-. 0731-9150. Periodical. US. English. mo. $197.00. Runzheimer International, 555 Skokie Boulevard/Suite 245, Northbrook IL 60062. Tel (312)291-9011. Ed Kenneth Groh. Covers all aspects of corporate employee transfer programs.

RURAL REAL ESTATE MARKET IN NEW ZEALAND (WELLINGTON, N.Z. : 1981). (RURAL REAL ESTATE MARKET IN NEW ZEALAND). 0549-0111. English. mo. 20.00. Valuation Department, PO Box 5098, Wellington North New Zealand. Tel 738-555. LC HD1120. DD 333.335. Circ 350. Bulletins showing real estate sales and price indexes by districts in New Zealand with some historical series.

THE SALT LAKE REAL ESTATE NEWS. VFOAT Real Estate News. Vol. 1, No. 1 (Aug. 1982)-. 0745-0036. Periodical. US. English. mo. $18.00. The Salt Lake Real Estate News, PO Box 11778, Pioneer Station, Salt Lake City UT 84147-0778.

SERVICE CORPORATION DIRECTORY. See Yearbooks, Almanacs, Directories.

SHOPPING CENTER WORLD. V. 1- Feb. 1972-. 0049-0393. Periodical. US. English. mo. $39.00. Communication Channels Inc, 6255 Barfield Road, Atlanta GA 30328. Tel (404)256-9800.

SKATTER OG AFGIFTER. See Business - Public Finance.

SOCIETY OF INDUSTRIAL REALTORS INDUSTRIAL REAL ESTATE MARKET SURVEY. VFOAT Industrial Real Estate Market Survey. Began with issue for Spring 1980. 0730-0131. US. English. sa. $50.00. Society Industrial Realtors, 777 14th Street NW, Washington DC 20005. Tel (202)383-1147. LC HD1393.5. DD 333.3360973. Circ 700. Current prices for industrial and office space by states and specific areas.

SOFTWHERE. REAL ESTATE. VFOAT Software. Jan. 1984-. 8755-6065. US. English. $21.90. Moore Data Management Services, Division of Moore Business Forms Inc, 1660 South Highway 100, Minneapolis MN 55416. LC HD1380. DD 333.330285425.

SOUND ADVICE. (SOUND ADVICE : THE ENGLISH & CARDIFF REAL ESTATE & INVESTMENT ADVISORY LETTER). 0733-4605. Periodical. US. English. qt. $78.00. Wes English's Sound Advice, 2120 Omega Road, San Ramon CA 94583. Tel (415)838-8100. Ed John Wesley English. bk rev. Circ 1,000. Advisory letter containing original and in-depth research in all sectors of real estate. Clearly-written articles on tax matters and laws affecting investors. *English & Cardiff Real Estate Advisory Letter.*

SOUTH FLORIDA LIVING CEASED. VFOAT Living. Vol. 1, No. 1 (Mar.-Apr. 1981)-V. 3, No. 2 (Apr.-May 1983). 0279-8506. Periodical. US. English. bm. $12.00. 700 West Hillboro Boulevard Building 3/Suite 102, Deerfield Beach FL 33441. Tel (305)428-5602. Ed Marcy N Jay. adv acc. Circ 120,000. New home buyers guide for South Florida includes map guides, financial information and other editorial for new home buyer market.

SOUTHEAST REAL ESTATE NEWS. 0192-1630. Periodical. US. English. $23.00. Communication Channels Inc, 6255 Barfield Road, Atlanta GA 30328. Tel (404)256-9800.

SOUTHWEST REAL ESTATE NEWS. V. 1- 197 -. 0192-9194. Periodical. US. English. ir. $23.00. Communication Channels Inc, 6255 Barfield Road, Atlanta GA 30328. Tel (404)256-9800. *Texas Real Estate News.*

SREA BRIEFS. Main/Corp Society of Real Estate Appraisers. VAT Society of Real Estate Appraisers Briefs. V. 15, No. 21- Oct. 15, 1980-. 0273-8236. Periodical. US. English. bw. *Appraisal Briefs, 0194-8555.*

SUMMARY OF REAL ESTATE ASSESSMENT/SALES RATIO STUDY. US. English. an. Free. State of Iowa Department of Revenue, Hoover State Office Building, Des Moines IA 50319. LC HD266.I8. DD 333.33209777.

SUN BELT BUILDINGS JOURNAL. 0745-354X. Periodical. US. English. mo. Real Estate Press Inc, 824 East Washington, Phoenix AZ 85012.

A SURVEY OF ACCOUNTING AND REPORTING PRACTICES OF REAL ESTATE DEVELOPERS. Main/Corp Price, Waterhouse and Company. VFOAT Real Estate Developers. US. English. an. Price Waterhouse and Company, 1251 Avenue of the Americas, New York NY 10020.

SURVEY OF BUILDING, CONSTRUCTION, AND REAL ESTATE SECTORS. See Building and Construction.

TAX MANAGEMENT REAL ESTATE JOURNAL. See Law.

TIERRA GRANDE. 0164-5781. Periodical. US. English. qt. Texas A & M University, Texas Real Estate/Research Ctr, College Station TX 77843. Tel (409)845-0369. Ed David S Jones. Circ 65,000. Report on latest real estate research results, emphasizing on Texas. Audience primarily licensed real estate brokers.

TIMESHARING LAW REPORTER BRIEFS. Began in Oct. 1981-. 0738-6923. Periodical. US. English. mo. $62.00. Land Development Institute Ltd, 1401 16th Street NW, Washington DC 20036. Tel (202)232-2144. Ed Stuart Marshall Bloch and William B Ingersoll. LC KF598.A15. DD 346.730432, 347.306432. Circ 250. (ctrl). News on federal, state, and local laws regarding timesharing and related court and administrative decisions. *Resort Timesharing Law Reporter (Washington, D.C. : 1981), 0749-3681.*

TRUST ROYAL ETUDE SUR LE PRIX DES MAISONS AU CANADA. Main/Corp Compagnie Trust Royal. Feb. 1, 1978-. 0706-8514. Periodical. CN. French. ty. Free. Trust Royal, C P 7500 Succursale A, Toronto Ontario M5W 1P9 Canada. DD 338.436640971. *Etude sur les Prix des Maisons, 0706-8492.*

U.S. REAL ESTATE REGISTER. VFOAT US Real Estate Register. Vol. 1 (1984/1985)-. 8755-1608. US. English. an. Barry Inc, PO Box 262, Woburn MA 01801. LC HD1394. DD 332.632402573. *Industrial/Commercial Real Estate Managers' Directory, 0737-1950.*

URBAN REAL ESTATE MARKET IN NEW ZEALAND. Main/Corp New Zealand. Valuation Dept. NZ. English. mo. 20.00. Valuation Department, PO Box 5098, Wellington New Zealand. Tel 7380555. LC HD1387 HD1120.5. DD 333.33 S 333.33709931. Circ 350. Bulletins showing real estate sales and price indexes by districts in New Zealand with some historical series.

VALUATION. Periodical. US. English. be. $8.00. American Society of Appraisers, PO Box 17265 Dulles Airport, Washington DC 20041. Tel (703)620-3838. Ed Shirley Belz. Ind/Abst Manage. Contents, Account. Index. Suppl. Circ 5,500. (ctrl). Articles concerned with the appraisal of real estate, fine arts, business valuation, antiques, machinery/equipment public utilities, aircraft and other properties. *Technical Valuation.*

THE VALUER. V. 1-1930-. 3782-241X. Periodical. AT. English. qt. 20.00. Australian Institute of Valuers/General Registrar, 3/5 McKay Gardens, Turner Canberra CT 2601 Australia. Tel (062)472155. Ed H O Thomas. Ind/Abst APAIS, Aust. Public Aff. Inf. Serv. bk rev. Circ 5,500. (ctrl). Technical articles of current valuation topics contributed by experts together with relevent synopsis of most recent cases that effect values.

THE WISCONSIN REALTOR. Vol. 1, No. 1 (June 1981)-. 0279-2583. Periodical. US. English. mo. $5.00 Members (included in dues), $10.00 Nonmembers. Wisconsin Realtors Association, 4801 Hayes Road, Madison WI 53704.

YANKEE HOMES. 8756-0259. Periodical. US. English. mo. $12.00. Yankee Publishing, Depot Square, Peterborough NH 03458. Tel (603)563-8111. Ed Georgia Orcutt. bk rev. adv acc. Circ 15,000. Features New England real estate for sale, from seaside to mountaintop, in styles from Federal to contemporary, including homes, inns, farms, and cabins.

YUKON REAL ESTATE SURVEY. Mar. 1978-. 0711-9321. Periodical. CN. English. qt. Government of Yukon, Box 2703, Whitehorse Yukon Y1A 2C6 Canada. DD 333.3322097191.

ZENKOKU SHIGAICHI KAKAKU SHISU. Main/Corp Nihon Fudosan Kenkyujo. VFOAT Zenkoku Mokuzo Kenchikuhi Shisu. JA. Japanese. sa. Nihon Fudosan Kenkyuju, c/o Kangin Fujiya Building 3-2 Toronomon 1-chome Minto-ku, Tokyo Japan. LC HD918.

RECREATION, LEISURE

ALBERTA PROVINCIAL PARKS USER STATISTICS. See Statistics.

ANNUAIRE - ASSOCIATION DES. See Yearbooks, Almanacs, Directories.

ANNUAL NATIONAL CONFERENCE ON RECREATION PLANNING AND DEVELOPMENT. (ANNUAL NATIONAL CONFERENCE ON RECREATION PLANNING AND DEVELOPMENT : PROCEEDINGS OF THE SPECIALTY CONFERENCE). Main/Conf National Conference On Recreation Planning and Development. 1st- 1979-. 0197-9426. US. English. an. $36.00. American Society of Civil Engineers, 345 East 47th Street, New York NY 10017. LC GV53. DD 790.0973.

ANNUAL REPORT - MISSISSIPPI PARK COMMISSION. Main/Corp Mississippi. Park Commission. US. English. an. 717 Robert E Lee Building, Jackson MS 39201. LC SB482.M7. DD 353.97620086305. *Annual Report.*

ANNUAL REPORT OF THE PARKS AND BEACHES COMMISSION (BARBADOS). See Conservation & Natural Resources.

ANNUAL REPORT - OKLAHOMA TOURISM AND RECREATION DEPARTMENT. See Travel.

ANNUAL REPORT - RECREATION, PARKS AND WILDLIFE FOUNDATION. (ANNUAL REPORT). Main/Corp Alberta. Recreation, Parks and Wildlife Foundation. 0711-2815. CN. English. an. Recreation/Parks and Wildlife Foundation, PO Box 4732, Edmonton Alberta T6E 5G6 Canada. LC GV56.A4. DD 354.7123008635.

ANNUAL REPORT - RECREATIONAL AND CULTURAL FACILITIES CAPITAL GRANTS (SASKATCHEWAN). Main/Corp Saskatchewan. Recreational and Cultural Facilities Capital Grants Program. 1977/78-. 0708-3831. CN. English. an. Minister of Culture & Youth, Legislative Building, Regina Saskatchewan S4S 0B3 Canada. LC GV433.C32. DD 338.47790097124.

ANNUAL REPORT - STATE PARK AND RECREATION COMMISSION (NEW MEXICO). Main/Corp New Mexico. State Park and Recreation Commission. US. English. an. State Capitol Building, Santa Fe NM 87503. LC GV191.42.N6. DD 333.7809789.

APPALACHIA BULLETIN ISSUE. N.S., V. 40, No. 8- Aug./Sept. 1974-. Periodical. US. English. ir. $15.50. Appalachia Mountain Club, 5 Joy Street, Boston MA 02108. Tel (617)523-0636. Ed Diane Welebit. bk rev. adv acc. Circ 35,000. (ctrl). Ten issues a year devoted to nature, outdoor sports, conservation and travel. Published by the nation's oldest conservation and outdoor recreation organization. *Appalachia Bulletin.*

ARQTICLE. (L'ARQTICLE). VAT Association des Recreologues du Quebec Article. Vol. 1, No. 1-. 0821-4190. Periodical. CN. French. qt. Free to

Recreation, Leisure

Members, $6.00 Others. Association des Recreologues du Quebec, c/o Bureau des Projets Speciaux, Universite du Quebec A Trois-Rivieres, C P 500, Trois-Rivieres Quebec G9A 5H7 Canada. **DD** 790.060714.

ASPEN VACATION GUIDE. 0147-0043. Periodical. US. English. sa. Advertising and Editorial Office, Box 10456, Aspen CO 81611.

ATLANTA SINGLES MAGAZINE & DATE BOOK. VFOAT Atlanta Singles Magazine and Date-Book. Nov./Dec. 1977-. 8750-8435. Periodical. US. English. bm. $9.00. Atlanta Singles Magazine & Datebook, PO Box 80158, Atlanta GA 30302.

AUSTRALIAN PARKS AND RECREATION. Feb. 1976-. 0311-8223. Periodical. AT. English. qt. 30.00. Royal Australian Institute, Parks and Recreation, PO Box 102, Dickson Australian Capital Territory 2602 Australia. **Tel** (062)414-371. Ed Graham Yapp and Dianne Coward Coward. **Ind/Abst** Bibliogr. Agric. bk rev. adv acc. **Circ** 1,200. (ctrl). Professional journal dealing with all aspects of parks and recreation, sporting facilities, recreation planning, horticulture/arboreta and leisure pursuits. *Australian Parks.*

BALLOON. See Physically Impaired.

BALLOON LIFE. Vol. 1, No. 1 (Feb. 1986)-. 0887-6061. Periodical. US. English. mo. 3381 Pony Express Drive, Sacramento CA 95834-1422. **DD** 797.

BAND & FESTIVAL GUIDE. See Music.

BIENNIAL REPORT OF THE NORTH CAROLINA RECREATION COMMISSION. Main/Corp North Carolina. Recreation Commission. Periodical. US. English. ir. North Carolina Recreation Commission, Raleigh NC 27603. **LC** GV54.N8.

BIENNIAL REPORT OF THE VERMONT RECREATION BOARD. Main/Corp Vermont. Recreation Board. VFOAT Recreation in Vermont. 0503-9967. Periodical. US. English. be. Vermont Recreation Board, Montpelier VT 05602. **LC** GV54.V5. **DD** 790.

BIENNIAL REPORT - VIRGINIA COMMISSION OF OUTDOOR RECREATION. Main/Corp Virginia. Commission of Outdoor Recreation. 1st- 1966/68-. 0507-0503. Periodical. US. English. be. Virginia Commission of Outdoor Recreation, 101 North 14th Street/Monroe Building, Richmond VA 23219-3679. **LC** GV191.42.V8. **DD** 301.57.

THE BULLETIN - AMERICAN SUNBATHING ASSOCIATION. (THE BULLETIN). 0279-8158. Periodical. US. English. mo. $15.00. American Sunbathing Association, 1703 North Main Street, Kissimmee FL 32743-3396. **Tel** (305)933-2064. Ed Bill Belleville. adv acc. **Circ** 30,000. (ctrl). Newspaper of nudist news and club events.

BULLETIN - CENTRE OF LEISURE STUDIES. ACADIA UNIVERSITY CEASED. (BULLETIN - CENTRE OF LEISURE STUDIES, ACADIA UNIVERSITY). Main/Corp Acadia University. Centre of Leisure Studies. No. 1, 1976. Ceased with V. 9, No. 2, 1984?. 0383-8005. Periodical. CN. English. bm. Free. Centre of Leisure Studies, Acadia University, Wolfville Nova Scotia B0P 1X0 Canada. **DD** 790.05. (ctrl).

CALIFORNIA PARKS & RECREATION. VFOAT California Parks and Recreation Magazine. VAT California Parks and Recreation. 1954. 0733-5326. Periodical. US. English. qt. $20.00. California Park Recreation Society, 1400 K Street/Suite 302, Sacramento CA 95814. **Tel** (916)441-0254. Ed Norma Minas. bk rev. adv acc. **Circ** 4,000. (ctrl). Magazine and professional journal of primary interest to park and recreation professionals. *California Park and Recreation Magazine.*

CALIFORNIA RECREATION ACTION PROGRAM REPORT. Main/Corp California. Dept. of Parks and Recreation. 1981-82-. US. English. an. State of California/Resources Agency, Department of Parks and Recreation, PO Box 2390, Sacramento CA 95811. **LC** GV54.C2. **DD** 333.78309794.

CAMPING AND TRAILERING GUIDE. VFOAT Camping Guide. 0361-5812. Periodical. US. English. mo. $6.45. Rajo Publications, PO Box 1014, Grass Valley CA 95945. **LC** GV191.68. **DD** 796.540973.

CANADIAN POOL & PATIO CEASED. VFOAT Pool & Patio. V. 1-7, No. 4. 0317-2791. CN. English. qt. $6. Southam Business Publications Limited, 1450 Don Mills Road, Don Mills Ontario M3B 2X7 Canada. **DD** 643.55.

CANADIAN POOL & PATIO CONSUMERS HANDBOOK. Vol. 8, No. 1 (Spring 1981)-. 0711-6470. CN. English. an. $2.00 Per Issue. Canadian Pool and Patio Consumers Handbook, c/o Southam Business Publishers, 1450 Don Mills Road, Don Mills Ontario M3B 2X7 Canada. **DD** 643.55. *Canadian Pool & Patio, 0317-2791.*

CANSPA COMMUNICATOR. VAT Canadian Swimming Pool Association Communicator. Vol. 3, No. 3 (June 1982)-. 0823-0145. Periodical. CN. English. ir. Free to Members. Canadian Swimming Pool Association, Suite 503/6303 Airport Road, Mississauga Ontario L4V 1R8 Canada. **DD** 690.57406071. (ctrl). *National Newsletter (Canadian Swimming Pool Association), 0229-2866.*

CARAVAN CAMPING DIRECTORY. See Yearbooks, Almanacs, Directories.

CARNIVAL & CIRCUS BOOKING GUIDE. 1972-. 0090-2985. US. English. an. $1.00. 2160 Patterson Street, Cincinnati OH 45214. **LC** GV1851.A3. **DD** 658.917910680973.

CARTE-CALENDRIER DES FETES POPULAIRES DU QUEBEC. 0821-4158. CN. French. an. $50.00. Societe des Festivale Populaires du Quebec, 1415 Est rue Jarry, Montreal Quebec H2E 2Z7 Canada. **Tel** (514)252-3037. **DD** 394.25025714. bk rev. adv acc. **Circ** 75,00. Directory of festivals in Quebec. *Fetes Populaires au Quebec, 0229-2963.*

CATALOGUE OF CURRENT ONTARIO UNIVERSITY RECREATION AND LEISURE RESEARCH. 1973-. 0316-9278. Periodical. CN. English. Ontario Research Council on Leisure, c/o Department of Graphic Services, University of Waterloo, Waterloo Ontario N2L 3G1 Canada. **DD** 301.570720713.

CATALYST. April 1977-. 0705-3991. Periodical. CN. English. bm. Free. Recreation Society of British Columbia, 1200 Hornby Street, Vancouver British Columbia V6Z 1W2 Canada. **DD** 790.062711. (ctrl). *Newsletter.*

CHURCH RECREATION MAGAZINE. V. 1- Oct./Dec. 1970-. 0162-4652. Periodical. US. English. qt. $7.75. Materials Service Department, 127 Ninth Avenue North, Nashville TN 37234. **Tel** (615)251-2289. Ed Joe Williamson. **DD** BV1620. **DD** 259. bk rev. Reaching people for Christ through recreation. Exciting reading for church leaders and for families and individuals. Includes step-by-step how-to articles. *Church Recreation, 0529-7028.*

CONNECTICUT WALK BOOK. See Recreation, Leisure - Outdoor Life.

CORPORATE FITNESS & RECREATION. See Physical Training.

COUNTRY VACATIONS IN ALBERTA. 0229-5229. Periodical. CN. English. Alberta Department of Agriculture, 9718-197th Street, Edmonton Alberta Canada. **DD** 796.56097123. *Alberta Country Vacations, 0229-5199.*

COUNTY AND MUNICIPAL RECREATION AND PARK SERVICES STUDY. Main/Corp Maryland. Office of Recreation and Leisure Services. Fiscal Year 1982-. US. English. an. Director, Office of Recreation and Leisure Services, Maryland Department of Natural Resources, Tawes State Office Building, Annapolis MD 21401. **LC** GV54.M3. **DD** 353.975200858. *County and Municipal Recreation and Park Services Study.*

COUNTY RECREATION & PARK SERVICES STUDY. Main/Corp North Carolina. Recreation Division. VAT County Recreation and Park Services Study. 0360-4667. US. English. 436 North Harrington Street, Raleigh NC 27603. **LC** GV54.N8. **DD** 338.473015709756.

COUP D'OEIL SUR LE SAGUENAY-LAC-ST-JEAN ENR. V. 1- July./Aug./Sept. 1978-. 0709-2679. Periodical. CN. French. qt. Les Promotions Gm Enr, 623 rue Louis-Hemon, Chicoutimi Quebec G7H 3W2 Canada. **DD** 790.0971416.

COURIER (WASHINGTON, D.C.). (COURIER : THE NATIONAL PARK SERVICE NEWSLETTER). VFOAT National Park Service Newsletter. Began with 1977. Periodical. US. English. mo. National Park Service, Room 5103/1100 L Street Northwest, Washington DC 20240. *Newsletter (United States. National Park Service).*

DISCOVERY YMCA. Vol. 1, No. 1 (Oct. 1982)-. Periodical. US. English. bm. $9.00. YMCA of the USA, 101 North Wacker Drive, Chicago IL 60606. **Tel** (312)269-0520. Ed Anthony Ripley. adv acc. **Circ** 75,000. (ctrl). Articles for volunteer board members and professional staff of YMCA's on buildings, fitness, and sports, social services, family, youth, international, new ideas, and current national issues.

DISNEY NEWS. V. 1- Winter 1965/66-. 0095-7178. Periodical. US. English. qt. $8.00. Disney News, PO Box 3310, Anaheim CA 92803. **Tel** (714)999-4168. Ed Margery Lee. **LC** GV1853.D5. **DD** 791.06879496. Behind the scenes disney information.

DOCTOR'S REVIEW. Vol. 1, No. 1 (Jan./Feb 1983)-. 0821-5758. Periodical. CN. English. mo. $5.00 Per Number. Doctor's Review, 4342 Sherbrooke Street West, Westmount Quebec H3Z 1E3 Canada. **DD** 790.05.

DOCUMENTATION TOURISTIQUE. See Travel.

DURHAM SPECTRUM RECREAT. (DURHAM SPECTRUM AND RECREATION). 0821-5847. Newspaper. CN. English. mo. $0.15 Per Number. Durham Spectrum and Recreation, 1730 McPherson Court, Pickering Ontario L1W 3E6 Canada. **DD** 790.0971356.

EASTERN CAMPGROUNDS & TRAILER PARKS. VAT Eastern Campgrounds and Trailer Parks. 1974-. 0194-0198. US. English. an. Rand McNally & Company Campground Publications, PO Box 728, Skokie IL 60076. **Tel** (312)673-9100. Ed Mary Niles. **LC** GV191.4. **DD** 647.9473. bk rev. adv acc. **Circ** 260,000. About 10,000 public and private campground listings in chart form, park name, address, phone, directions, number of sites, fees, etc. The directory preferred by Americas campers.

EASTERN CAMPING & TRAILERING AREAS IN EASTERN UNITED STATES AND CANADA. US. English. an. American Automobile Association, 8111 Gatehouse Road, Falls Church VA 22047. **LC** GV191.35. **DD** 647.947. *Eastern Campground Directory: Areas in the Eastern United States and Canada.*

ECONOMIC RESEARCH REPORT. See Economics.

ETUDES ET MEMOIRES. See Travel.

EYE. (THE EYE). Vol. 2 (June 14, 1984)-. 0828-6310. Periodical. CN. English. mo. Free. Eye, c/o Rye Eye Publishing, 80 Victoria Street, Toronto Ontario M58 1W7 Canada. **DD** 790.09713541. *Eye Newspaper, 0828-6302.*

FACILITIES DIRECTORY. See Yearbooks, Almanacs, Directories.

FEDERAL RECREATION FEE REPORT. (FEDERAL RECREATION FEE REPORT : INCLUDING FEDERAL AND STATE AND PRIVATE SECTOR RECREATION VISITATION AND FEE DATA : A REPORT TO CONGRESS). Main/Corp United States. National Park Service. 1981-. 0736-8364. US. English. an. **LC** GV191.4. **DD** 333.780973. *Federal Recreation Fee Program, 0192-5369.*

FRIDAY (TORONTO, ONT.). (FRIDAY). Vol. 1, No. 12 (Aug. 21, 1980)-. 0229-2319. Periodical. CN. English. Free. Friday Magazine, 130 Merton Street/Suite 306, Toronto Ontario M4S 1A4 Canada. **DD** 790.09713541. *Friday In and About Toronto, 0229-2300.*

FROM THE STATE CAPITALS. (FROM THE STATE CAPITALS. PARKS AND RECREATION TRENDS). VFOAT Parks and Recreation Trends. 0734-113X. Periodical. US. English. mo. $75.00. Wakeman/Walworth Inc, PO Box 1939, New Haven CT 06509. **Tel** (203)562-8518. Keeps you current on what states and municipalities are doing in conservation, land management and development, financial assistance, special taxes and fees, as well as parks and recreation personnel. *From the State Capitals. Parks and Recreation.*

GO (EDMONTON). (GO). Began publication in 1965. 0046-6042. CN. English. Free. Go Publishing Ltd, PO Box 2675 Postal Station A, Edmonton Alberta T5J 2G4 Canada. **DD** 790.0971233.

Recreation, Leisure

GRIST (WASHINGTON, D.C.). (GRIST). VFOAT Park Practice Grist. Began with V. 15, No. 5, Sept./Oct. 1971. 0533-2933. Periodical. US. English. bm. $20.00. National Recreation & Parks Board, 3101 Park Center Drive/12th Floor, Alexandria VA 22302. Tel (703)820-4940. Ind/Abst Park Pract. Prog. LC SB482.A4. DD 333.780973.

THE GUIDE TO SUMMER CAMPS AND SUMMER SCHOOLS. 0072-8705. US. English. be. $18.94. Porter Sargent Publisher, 11 Beacon Street, Boston MA 02108. Tel (617)523-1670. LC GV193. Information on location and enrollment, director's winter address, fees, length of camping period, and other pertinent facts. *Sargent Guide to Summer Camps and Summer Schools.*

THE HAMPTONS : THE MAGAZINE OF THE WORLD'S MOST SOPHISTICATED RESORT. Periodical. US. English. The Hamptons, PO Drawer AR, Bridgehampton NY 11932.

HAPPENINGS IN KAMLOOPS. VFOAT Happenings. V. 1- March 1979-. 0225-7009. Periodical. CN. English. mo. Free. Suncastle Holdings, Happenings in Kamloops, PO Box 869 Station Main, Kamloops British Columbia V2C 5M8 Canada. DD 790.097114.

HIGHLIGHTS - CONGRESS FOR RECREATION & PARKS. (HIGHLIGHTS). Main/Conf Congress for Recreation and Parks. 1970-. 0092-0975. US. English. LC GV53. DD 301.57.

HOME ENTERTAINMENT GUIDE. Vol. 13, No. 5 (May 1983)-. 0827-2484. Periodical. CN. English. mo. $1.95 Per No. Home Entertainment Guide, 1659 Bayview Avenue, Toronto Ontario M4G 3C1 Canada. DD 790.05. *FM Guide, 0316-2400.*

HONEYMOON HIDEAWAYS. See Travel.

IDAHO STATE PARKS AND RECREATION. Main/Corp Idaho. Dept. of Parks and Recreation. 0149-662X. US. English. an. State House, 2263 Warm Springs Avenue, Boise ID 83720. LC GV191.42.I2. DD 353.979600863.

IDEAS. No. 1-4-. Periodical. US. English. Youth Specialities, 1224 Greenfield Drive, El Cajun CA 92021. Index received separately bound from publisher. (cum index).

ILAM : JOURNAL OF THE INSTITUTE OF LEISURE & AMENITY MANAGEMENT. VFOAT I.L.A.M. Vol. 1, No. 1 (Jan. 1983)-. 0031-2223. Periodical. UK. English. 30 Foreign. Journal of Park Administration Ltd, Berry House/41 High Street, Cambridge CB4 5NB England. Tel 0954-30940. Ed Peter Coulson. LC GV75. DD 333.7830941. bk rev. adv acc. Contains essential reading for all involved in the management of leisure facilities and departments within the public or private sectors. *Parks and Recreation.*

ILLINOIS PARKS & RECREATION. VAT Illinois Parks and Recreation. V. 26, No. 5- Sept./Oct. 1970-. 0019-2155. Periodical. US. English. bm. $10.00. Illinois Association of Park Districts, 217 East Monroe Street/Suite 101, Springfield IL 62701. Tel (217)523-4554. Ed Barbara Valiukenas. adv acc. Circ 4,000. Reflects current trends, problems, solutions, programs and services affecting parks, recreation and the leisure field. *Illinois Parks, Illinois Park and Recreation Quarterly.*

INFO SAINTE-CATHERINE. V. 1, No. 1 (Aug./Sept. 1984)-. 0824-1473. Periodical. CN. French. ir. Free. Conseil Municipal Sainte Catherine, 5585 Boulevard Marie-Vitorin Sainte-Catherine, Portneuf Quebec J0L 1E0 Canada. DD 352.071434. (ctrl).

INFORMO-LOISIR. (L'INFORMO-LOISIR). Vol. 5, No. 2 (Mar. 1983)-. 0823-4620. Periodical. CN. French. Conseil Regional des Loisirs Aritibi-Temiscaminque, 768 3E Av, Valdor Quebec J9P 1S9 Canada. DD 790.0971413. *P'tites Vites, 0823-4612.*

INTERNATIONALES SAUNA-ARCHIV : ORGAN DER VEREINIGUNGEN, INTERNATIONAL SAUNA SOCIETY, HELSINKI, DEUTSCHER SAUNA-BUND E.V., BIELEFELD, SCHWEIZERISCHER SAUNA-VERBAND, ZURICH. VFOAT Internationales Sauna Archiv. V. 1, 1 (March 1984)-. Periodical. Fl. German. qt. NLM W1. *Sauna Nachrichten Mit Sauna-Archiv.*

JOURNAL OF LEISURABILITY. Vol. 7, No. 3 (July 1980)-. 0711-222X. Periodical. CN. English. an. $11.61. Leisurability Publications, 36 Bessemer Court/Unit 3, Concord Ontario L4K 2T1 Canada. Tel (416)669-5373. Ed Peggy Hutchison. DD 362.405. NLM W1 J0745E. Concerned with leisure, disability, and human services. *Leisurability, 0317-2317.*

JOURNAL OF LEISURE RESEARCH. Periodical. US. English. qt. $30.00. National Recreation and Park Association, 3101 Park Center Drive/12th Floor, Alexandria VA 22302. Tel (703)820-4940. Ind/Abst Soc. Sci. Citation Index, Soc. Sci. Index, Psychol. Abstr., Avery Index Archit. Period., Curr. Index J. Educ.

JOURNAL OF LEISURE RESEARCH. V. 1- Winter 1969-. 0022-2216. Periodical. US. English. qt. National Recreation and Park Association, 3101 Park Center Drive/12th Floor, Alexandria VA 22302. Ind/Abst Sociol. Abstr., Energy Inf. Abstr., Environ. Abstr., Curr. Index J. Educ., Psychol. Abstr., Soc. Sci. Index. LC GV1. DD 790.05. CODEN JLERA.

JOURNAL OF PARK AND RECREATION ADMINISTRATION. (JOURNAL OF PARK AND RECREATION ADMINISTRATION : A PUBLICATION OF THE AMERICAN ACADEMY FOR PARK AND RECREATION ADMINISTRATION). Vol. 1, No. 1 (Jan. 1983)-. 0735-1968. Periodical. US. English. qt. $35.00. Indiana University, Room 133/Health Physical Education Recreation Building, Bloomington IN 47405. Tel (812)335-4711. Ed Daniel R Sharpless. LC GV181.5. DD 790.069. bk rev. Circ 1,000. (ctrl). The journal provides a forum for the analysis of management and organization of the delivery of park, recreation, and leisure services.

LAND, WATER, RECREATION. REPORT. (LAND, WATER, RECREATION; REPORT). VFOAT Report - N. H., State Planning Project. No. 1- 19 -. 0548-4863. Monographic Series. US. English. ir. New Hampshire State Planning Project, Concord NH 03301. LC GV54.N4. DD 711.

LEAFLETS, FOLDERS, ETC. - DEPT. OF RECREATION AND CONSERVATION. Main/Corp British Columbia. Dept. of Recreation and Conservation. Monographic Series. CN. English. Free. Queens Printer, Victoria British Columbia Canada.

LEISURABILITY CEASED. VFOAT Journal of Leisurability. V. 1-7, No. 2. 0317-2317. CN. English. qt. $11.00. Journal of Leisurability, PO Box 281 Station A, Ottawa Ontario K1N 8V2 Canada. DD 790.19605. NLM W1 LE671.

LEISURE AND RECREATION STATISTICS ESTIMATES. See Statistics.

LEISURE BUSINESS. 0739-0890. Periodical. US. English. sm. $195.00. Leisure Information Service, 804 D Street NE, Washington DC 20002.

LEISURE FORUM. V. 4- Jan./Feb. 1977-. 0704-643X. Periodical. CN. English. ir. Free to Members, 0.50 Others. Leisure Forum, 2799 Roblin Boulevard, Winnipeg Manitoba R3R 0B8 Canada. DD 7900627127. *Newsletter, 0704-6448.*

LEISURE INDUSTRY DIGEST. Vol. 1, No. 1 (June 1, 1981)-. 0276-0916. Periodical. US. English. sm. $95.00. Leisure Industry Digest, PO Box 27488, Washington DC 20038. Tel (202)965-7295. Ed Marj Jensen. bk rev. adv acc. Circ 300. (ctrl). Trade reports on various leisure industries: theme parks, concerts, recordings, movies, Broadway, travel, tourism, economic and financial briefs, trends and demographics, publishing and media.

LEISURE INFORMATION NEWSLETTER CEASED. (LEISURE INFORMATION NEWSLETTER : LIN). VFOAT LIN. Ended with Vol. 10, No. 1, Summer 1983. 0740-9206. Periodical. US. English. qt. Department of Recreation Leisure Physical Education and Sports, 635 East Building, Washington Square, New York University, New York NY 10003. Tel (212)598-3455.

LEISURE INFORMATION QUARTERLY. Vol. 10, No. 1 (Summer 1983)-. Periodical. US. English. qt. Department of Recreation and Leisure, New York University, New York NY 10003. Tel (212)598-3455. bk rev. Circ 400. Refereed journal of topical issues related to society and leisure, social sciences, handicapped, counseling and education. Also, trends in service need and delivery. *Leisure Information Newsletter.*

LEISURE LINES. VFOAT Leisurelines. 0733-5377. Periodical. US. English. ir. $15.00. California Park Recreation Society, 1400 K Street/Suite 302, Sacramento CA 95814. Tel (916)441-0254. Ed Norma Minas. bk rev. Circ 4,100. In-house newsletter for park and recreation professionals.

LEISURE OPPORTUNITIES IN RICHMOND. No. 1-. 0711-5792. CN. English. an. $0.75 Per No. Leisure Opportunities in Richmond, Corporation of the Township of Richmond Municipal Offices, 6911 No 3 Road, Richmond British Columbia V6Y 2C1 Canada. DD 790.0971133. *0227-0889.*

LEISURE, RECREATION, AND TOURISM ABSTRACTS. See Indexes/Abstracts.

LEISURE SCIENCES. V. 1- 1977-. 0149-0400. Periodical. US. English. qt. $48.00. Crane Russak & Company, 3 East 44th Street, New York NY 10017. Tel (212)867-1490. Ed Donald R Field and Robert B Ditton. Ind/Abst Psychol. Abstr. CODEN LESCDC. bk rev. adv acc. Circ 600. Available on microfilm from University Microfilms International. Presents scientific inquiries into the study of leisure, recreation, travel and their impact on the physical and social environment.

LEISURE STUDIES. See Social Sciences (General).

LEISUREWAYS. VFOAT Leisure Ways. Vol 1 (Feb. 1982)-. 4562-5747. Periodical. CN. English. ir. $2.50. Leisureways, 2 Carlton Street, Toronto Ontario M5B 1K4 Canada. DD 790.05. *Canadian Motorist, 0008-4530.*

LOISIR ET SOCIETE. VFOAT Society and Leisure. V. 1- April 1978-. 0705-3436. Periodical. CN. English (French). sa. 35.00. Universite du Quebec, CP 500, Trois Rivieres Quebec G9A 5H7 Canada. Tel (819)376-5355. Ed Gilles Pronovost and Max d'Amours. Ind/Abst Sociol. Abstr., Soc. Welf. Soc. Plan./Policy Soc. Dev., Point Repere. LC GV14.45. DD 301.5705. bk rev. Circ 1,000. Multidisciplinary journal on leisure studies, thematic issues twice a year. Publishes in authors' language: French or English. Summaries in 4 languages. *Society and Leisure, 0037-9670.*

LOISIR. INFORMATION CEASED. (LOISIR INFORMATION). VFOAT Leisure Newsletter. V. 4, No. 2, 1976. Ceased with V. 9, No. 3. 0701-1342. Periodical. CN. English (French). ty. $8.00. Universite du Quebec a Trois-Rivieres, PO Box 500, Trois-Rivieres Quebec G9A 5H7 Canada. Tel 30-5318882. Ed T J Kamphorst. DD 790.05. bk rev. adv acc. Circ 400. (ctrl). Sociology of leisure, leisure research, leisure research policy. *Leisure Newsletter, 0701-1334.*

LOISIR LONGUEUIL. Summer- 81. 0711-3293. Periodical. CN. French. Bureau d'Information, Direction du Loisir, CP 5000 Longueuil Quebec J4K 4Y7 Canada. DD 790.0971437.

LOISIR MUNICIPAL. (LE LOISIR MUNICIPAL : BULLETIN D'INFORMATION DU SERVICE DE DEVELOPPEMENT COMMUNAUTAIRE DU CLEQ). 0227-4418. Periodical. CN. French. bw. C.L.E.Q., 100 Ouest rue de l'Eveche, Rimouski Quebec G5L 4H7 Canada. DD 790.097147.

LOISIR-QUEBEC. 1971-. 0384-7705. Periodical. CN. French. Confederation des Loisirs du Quebec, 1135 Chemin Saint-Louis, Quebec Quebec G1S 1E7 Canada. DD 790.09714.

LONG ISLAND RECREATION & VISITORS GUIDE. VFOAT Long Island Recreation and Visitors Guide. Began with V. for 1975. 0882-1895. US. English. an. LI/Business, 303 Sunnyside Boulevard, Plainview NY 11803. *Long Island U.S.A.*

LONG ISLAND'S NIGHTLIFE MAGAZINE. VFOAT Long Island's Nightlife. 0744-7590. Periodical. US. English. mo. $36.00. Long Island's Nightlife, 1770 Deer Park Avenue, Deer Park NY 11729. Tel (516)242-7722. Ed Bill Ervilino. bk rev. adv acc. Circ 22,500. New York - exciting places to visit.

LOST TREASURE. See Romance and Adventure.

MANAGING THE LEISURE FACILITY. See Business - General Management.

MEMBERSHIP ROSTER - CANADIAN PARKS/RECREATION ASSOCIATION. Main/Corp Canadian Parks/Recreation Association. VFOAT Listes des Membres - Association Canadienne des Loisirs/Parcs. 1973-. 0316-9847. CN. English and French. English title only, 1973-1974. an. Canadian Parks/Recreation Association, 333 River Road, Vanier City Ottawa Ontario K1L 8B9 Canada. DD 790.06271.

METROPARKS EMERALD NECKLACE. See Recreation, Leisure - Outdoor Life.

Recreation, Leisure

MILIEU DE VIE. V. 1- June 1977-. 0708-9627. Periodical. CN. French. qt. $3.86. Federation Quebecoise des Centres Communautaires, 804 Cote Abraham Road, Quebec Quebec G1R 1A3 Canada. Tel (418)647-4536. DD 790.062714.

MINUTES OF THE FLORIDA OUTDOOR RECREATIONAL DEVELOPMENT COUNCIL. FLORIDA OUTDOOR RECREATIONAL PLANNING COMMITTEE. (MINUTES OF THE FLORIDA OUTDOOR RECREATIONAL DEVELOPMENT COUNCIL, FLORIDA OUTDOOR RECREATIONAL PLANNING COMMITTEE). Main/Corp Florida Outdoor Recreational Development Council. 1963/64-. 0428-6472. Periodical. US. English. ir. Florida Outdoor Recreational Planning Committee, Tallahassee FL 32304. LC GV54.F6. DD 790.

MONDE DES LOISIRS. (LE MONDE DES LOISIRS). -1981. 0702-858X. CN. French. an. $4.65. Regroupement Organismes Nationaux de Loisir du Quebec, 1415 rue Sarry Est, Montreal Quebec H2E Z27 Canada. DD 790.025714.

MONTREAL CALENDAR MAGAZINE. 1st- Year. 0315-0534. Periodical. CN. English. mo. 30.00. Mondo Media, 1844 William Street, Montreal Quebec H3J 1R7 Canada. Tel (514)937-5771. Ed Kevin McKeown. adv acc. Circ 50,000. (ctrl) Lifestyle magazine focussing on Montreal comprehensive events, plus restaurant listings.

MONTREAL CE MOIS-CI. V. 1- Oct. 11/Nov. 14, 1974-. 0316-8530. Periodical. CN. French. mo. 30. Mondo-Media, 1844 William Street, Montreal H3J 1R5 Canada. Tel (514)937-5771. Ed Andre Ducharme. DD 790.09714281. adv acc. Circ 90,000. (ctrl). Lifestyle magazine focussing on Montreal. Comprehensive events plus restaurant listings.

MOTOR HOMES, CAMPERS, VAN CONVERSIONS, SURFER VANS. See Transportation.

MUNICIPAL RECREATION & PARK SERVICES STUDY. Main/Corp North Carolina. Recreation Division. VAT Municipal Recreation and Park Services Study. 0360-6716. US. English. 436 North Harrington Street, Raleigh NC 27602. LC GV54.N8. DD 353.97560085.

NATIONAL CONFERENCE TASK FORCE ON RECREATION USE AND RESOURCE MANAGEMENT. Main/Corp Edison Electric Institute. Task Force on Recreation Use and Resource Management. National Conference. 3rd (1980)-. US. English. Edison Electric Institute, 1111 19th Street NW, Washington DC 20036. National Conference on Recreation and Resource Management.

NATIONAL PARK GUIDE. Began in 1971. 0734-7960. US. English. an. Rand McNally & Company, 8225 North Central Park, Skokie IL 60076. Tel (312)673-9100. Ed Michael Frome. bk rev. adv acc. Circ 35,000. The guide to your trip to our nation's national parks. Covers all national parks, plus about 300 other areas in the national park service. Rand McNally National Park Guide.

NATIONAL PARK SERVICE POPULAR STUDY SERIES. HISTORY. Main/Corp United States. National Park Service. No. 1- 1941-. Periodical. US. English. ir. US Department of the Interior, National Park Service, Washington DC 20240. LC E160. DD 917.3.

NATIONAL PARK SERVICE SOURCE BOOK SERIES. Main/Corp United States. National Park Service. No. 1- 1941-. 0083-2316. Monographic Series. US. English. ir. Superintendent of Documents, US Government Printing Office, Washington DC 20402. LC E160.

NATIONAL RECREATIONAL, SPORTING AND HOBBY ORGANIZATIONS OF THE UNITED STATES. (NATIONAL RECREATIONAL, SPORTING, AND HOBBY ORGANIZATIONS OF THE UNITED STATES). VFOAT National Recreational, Sporting & Hobby Organizations. 1st Annual Ed. (1981)-. 0276-5276. US. English. an. $31.80. Columbia Books Inc, 1350 New York Avenue NW/Suite 207, Washington DC 20005. Tel (212)737-3777. Ed Regina Germain. LC GV53. DD 790.02573. Circ 1,000. Directory of 1,250 national organizations serving vocational and recreational interests of Americans.

NEW ENGLAND ENTERTAINMENT DIGEST MICROFORM. VFOAT N.E.E.D., NEED. Vol. 1, No. 1 (Aug. 6, 1979)-. Newspaper. US. English. sm. $10.00. Paul Reale, PO Box 735, Marshfield MA 02050. Tel (617)837-0538.

NEWFOUNDLAND AND LABRADOR CAMPGROUND GUIDE. (NEWFOUNDLAND AND LABRADOR : CAMPGROUND GUIDE). VFOAT Newfoundland and Labrador : Accommodation Guide. 0713-7745. CN. English. an. Province of Newfoundland and Labrador, 95 Bonaventure Avenue, St Johns Newfoundland A1C 5T7 Canada. DD 647.94718.

NEWSLETTER - NEWFOUNDLAND & LABRADOR PARKS RECREATION ASSOCIATION. (NEWSLETTER). Main/Corp Newfoundland and Labrador Parks Recreation Association. Sept. 1981-. 0712-1032. Periodical. CN. English. Newsletter NLPRA, Building 25, Torbay Airport, c/o Confederation Building, St John's Newfoundland A1C 5T7 Canada. DD 790.069. Newsletter, 0707-5405.

NORTH CAROLINA RECREATIONAL AND PARK REVIEW. 0164-4254. Periodical. US. English. ir. $12.00. North Carolina Recreation and Park Society, 436 North Harrington Street, Raleigh NC 27603. Tel (919)832-5868.

NOW (TORONTO, ONT. : 1981). (NOW). Vol. 1, No. 1 (Sept. 10, 1981. 0712-1326. Periodical. CN. English. wk. $27.09. Now, 150 Danforth Avenue, Toronto Ontario M4K 1N1 Canada. Tel (416)461-0871. Ed Michael Hollett. DD 790.09713541. bk rev. adv acc. Circ 70,000. (ctrl). Young adult, news and entertainment weekly with an emphasis on the downtown scene.

OFFICIAL BULLETIN - RECREATION ASSOCIATION OF NOVA SCOTIA. (OFFICIAL BULLETIN). No. 1-. 0711-7760. Periodical. CN. English. Free to Members. Recreation Association of Nova Scotia, PO Box 3010, South Halifax Nova Scotia B3J 3G6 Canada. DD 790.09716. Official Bulletin of— R.A.N.S., 0711-7752.

ON S'PARLE. No. 1- June 10 1972-. 0382-8220. Periodical. CN. French. Communication Inter-Media, Sherbrooke Local 120, 180 Acadie, Sherbrooke Quebec J1H 2T3 Canada. DD 791.4506271466.

ORC REPORT. (THE ORC REPORT). Series Corp Life. No. 1 (Oct. 1983)-. 0826-3019. Periodical. CN. English. ir. Free. Outdoor Recreation Council of British Columbia, 1200 Hornby Street, Vancouver British Columbia V6Z 2E2 Canada. DD 796.509711. (ctrl).

OUTDOOR RECREATION ACTION. Main/Corp United States. Bureau of Outdoor Recreation. No. 1- Aug. 1966-. 0030-7130. Periodical. US. English. qt. $4.15 Domestic, $5.20 Foreign. Superintendent of Documents, US Government Printing Office, Washington DC 20402. Ind/Abst Public Aff. Inf. Serv. Bull. LC GV53. DD 790.01.

OUTDOOR RECREATION IN GEORGIA. V. 1- 1977-. 0148-401X. US. English. an. $4.95. Terminus Media Inc, 1819 Peachtree Road, Atlanta GA 30309. LC GV191.42.G4. DD 647.94758.

OUTDOOR RECREATION IN ILLINOIS . . . ACTION PROGRAM. 1980-1981-. US. English. an. LC GV191.42.I3. DD 790.09773. Outdoor Recreation in Illinois, Action Plan.

PASSE-TEMPS. V. 1- Sept. 1977-. 0703-5497. Periodical. CN. French. mo. $9. Domestic, $10. Others. Bert-Hold, Passe-Temps, Service des Abonnements, CP 1050 Succursale Anjou, Montreal Quebec H1K 4H2 Canada. DD 790.05.

PENNSYLVANIA DIRECTORY OF RECREATION, PARK, AND CONSERVATION AGENCIES. See Yearbooks, Almanacs, Directories.

PENNSYLVANIA RECREATION & PARKS. VFOAT Pennsylvania Recreation and Parks. 0742-793X. Periodical. US. English. qt. $6.00. PRPS, 723 South Atherton Street, State College PA 16801. Tel (814)234-4272. Ed Robert D Griffith. adv acc. Circ 1,300. (ctrl). Information on a range of topics related to recreation, parks, and conservation focused toward the interests of professional society members.

PENNSYLVANIA RECREATION & PARKS YEARBOOK & DIRECTORY. See Yearbooks, Almanacs, Directories.

POOL INDUSTRY CANADA. V. 22, No. 1- Jan./Feb. 1979-. 0708-1847. Periodical. CN. English. $6.50. DD 647.9674. Pools, Parks & Rinks, 0384-5206.

POOL SCOPE. 0199-6207. Periodical. US. English. National Spa & Pool Institute, 2000 K Street NW, Washington DC 20006. Tel (202)331-8844.

PROGRAMME SOUVENIR. FESTIVAL DU VOYAGEUR, ST. BONIFACE, MANITOBA. (PROGRAMME SOUVENIR). Main/Corp Festival du Voyageur (St-Boniface, Man.). VFOAT Souvenir Program. Feb. 16/23, 1975-. 0229-2572. CN. English (French). an. Festival du Voyageur, PO Box 10, 219 Provencher Boulevard, Saint Boniface Manitoba R2H 2B5 Canada. DD 791.6240971274. Official Program, 0229-2564.

PROGRESS REPORT - OREGON STATE PARKS AND RECREATION DIVISION. See Conservation & Natural Resources.

PUBLICATION - STATE OF CALIFORNIA RECREATION COMMISSION. Main/Corp California. Recreation Commission. VFOAT Recreation in California. No. 1- 1948-. Monographic Series. US. English. ir. State of California, Recreation Commission, Sacramento CA 95814. DD 790.61794.

RAPPORT ANNUEL - CONSEIL QUEBECOIS DE LA JEUNESSE, DES LOISIRS, DES SPORTS ET DU PLEIN AIR. Main/Corp Quebec (Province). Conseil Quebecois de la Jeunesse, des Loisirs, des Sports et du Plein Air. 1973/74-. Periodical. CN. French. an. EOQ, Montreal Quebec Canada.

RECREACTION. #1 (80)-. 0710-6025. Periodical. CN. English (includes some text in French). ir. Canadian Parks/Recreation Association, 333 River Road, Vanier City Ontario K1L 8B9 Canada. DD 790.06071.

RECREATIE. 0486-1825. Periodical. NE. Dutch. ir. Stichting Recreatie, Postbus 80547, 2508 GM Den Haag Netherlands.

RECREATION AND CULTURAL FACILITIES INDEX. See Indexes/Abstracts.

RECREATION AND PARK EDUCATION CURRICULUM CATALOG. 0148-2882. US. English. ir. National Recreation and Park Association, 3101 Park Center Drive/12th Floor, Alexandria VA 22302. Tel (703)820-4940. LC GV181.35. DD 375.7900973.

RECREATION AND PARK YEARBOOK. See Yearbooks, Almanacs, Directories.

RECREATION CANADA. No. 27/5- Sept. 1969-. 0031-2231. Periodical. CN. English (French). ir. $23.21. Canadian Parks and Recreation Association, 333 River Road, Vanier City Ontario K1L 8H9 Canada. Tel (613)748-5651. Ed Denny Neider. Ind/Abst Can. Environ. adv acc. Circ 3,500. (ctrl). Timely, pertinent articles and expert opinion essential to the education and professional development of anyone involved or interested in the provision of parks, recreation and leisure services. P & R, 0380-2558.

RECREATION MANAGEMENT CEASED. Began with Jan. 1958 issue. Ceased with V. 24, No. 9, Nov. 1981. 0034-1770. Periodical. US. English. mo.

THE RECREATION MANAGEMENT YEARBOOK. See Yearbooks, Almanacs, Directories.

RECREATION PRACTITIONERS BULLETIN. Feb. 1983-. 0824-7323. Periodical. CN. English. qt. Free to Members. N/LP/RA Torbay Recreation Centre, c/o Confederation Building, St John's Newfoundland A1C 5T7 Canada. DD 790.06909718.

RECREATION REPORTER. Mar./Apr. 1971-. 0380-2647. Periodical. CN. English. bm. $13.93. British Columbia Recreation Association, 1200 Hornby Street, Vancouver British Columbia V6Z 2E2 Canada. Tel (604)687-3333. Ed William D Webster. bk rev. adv acc. Circ 1,500. (ctrl). Magazine contains information regarding trends developments and management in the field of recreation and parks.

RECREATION RESEARCH REVIEW. V. 5, No. 2, (Nov. 1976)-. 0702-9284. Periodical. CN. English. qt. $15.00. Ontario Research Council on Leisure, 36 Bessemer Court/Unit 3, Concord Ontario L4K 2T1 Canada. Tel (519)885-1211. Ed Ronald Johnson. DD 790.05. bk rev. adv acc. Circ 2,000. Research articles aimed at both the academic and practitioner in the area of recreation and leisure. All aspects of recreation are considered from outdoor to municipal, sport to administration. Recreation Review, 0318-7713.

Recreation, Leisure

RECREATION, SPORTS & LEISURE. Vol. 1, No. 1 (Sept. 1981)-. 0277-707X. Periodical. US. English. ir. $50.00. Lakewood Publications, 50 South Ninth Street, Minneapolis MN 55402. **Tel** (612)333-0471. Ed Bill Anderson. bk rev. adv acc. **Circ** 51,000. (ctrl). New ideas for managers of leisure fitness and recreation facilities.

RECREATION, SPORTS & LEISURE RESOURCE. VFOAT Recreation, Sports, and Leisure Resource. 84-. 0883-279X. US. English. an. $24.00. Lakewood Publications, 50 South 9th Street, Minneapolis MN 55402. **Tel** (612)333-0471. **Ed** Bill Anderson. bk rev. adv acc. **Circ** 51,000. (ctrl). New product tabloid magazine serving the informational needs of managers of recreation, sports and leisure facilities.

RECREATION STATISTICS. See Statistics.

REKURIESHON KENKYU. VFOAT Journal of Leisure and Recreation Studies. V. 1, No. 1, (Nov. 1971)-. JA. Japanese (abstracts in English). an. Nihon Rekurieshon Gakkai c/o Kishimoto Kinen Taiikukan, 1-1 Jinnan 1 Shibuya-ku, Tokyo-to 150 Japan.

REPERTOIRE DES ORGANISMES DU LOISIR DU QUEBEC. (REPERTOIRE DES ORGANISMES DE LOISIRS DU QUEBEC). 1982/1983-. 0714-9840. CN. French. an. **DD** 790.025714. Monde des Loisirs, 0702-858X.

REVIEW OF SPORT & LEISURE. See Recreation, Leisure - Sports.

REVIEW OF THE NEW ZEALAND COUNCIL FOR RECREATION AND SPORT. Main/Corp New Zealand. State Services Commission. English. an. State Services Commission, Private Bag, Wellington New Zealand. LC GV149. **DD** 796.060931.

REVUE DU C.L.E.Q. (LA REVUE DU C.L.E.Q). VAT Revue du Conseil des Loisirs de l'Est du Quebec, Revue du Cleq. 0228-6440. Periodical. CN. French. qt. Free. C L E Q, 100 Ouest rue de l'Eveche, Rimouski Quebec G5L 4H7 Canada. **DD** 790.0971477. (ctrl).

ROCKY MOUNTAIN VISITOR. 0821-5146. Periodical. CN. English. mo. 3.00. Rocky Mountain Visitor, 125 9 Avenue SE/Suite 250, Calgary Alberta Canada T2G OP6. **Tel** (403)266-5085. **Ed** Jack Newton. **DD** 917.11. adv acc. **Circ** 300,000. (ctrl). Comprehensive and current information on major events, activities, attractions, shops, restaurants, and accommodation in Banff, Canmore, Lake Louise and Jasper (resorts in the Canadian Rockies).

ROLLER SKATING BUSINESS. 0191-7617. Periodical. US. English. bm. Roller Skating Rink Operators Association, 7700 A Street, Lincoln NE 68501. **Tel** (402)489-8811. **Ed** Nance Kirk. LC GV859.4. **DD** 796.210682. adv acc. **Circ** 1,600. (ctrl). Management, marketing, maintenance, and news features for skating center operators. Available only to members of the Roller Skating Rink Operators Association.

RURAL RECREATION AND TOURISM ABSTRACTS. See Indexes/Abstracts.

RV WORLD. V. 1- June 1973-. Periodical. US. English. bm. $7.50. Hi-Torque Publications, Box 317, Encino CA 91316. LC SK600. **DD** 796.5405.

S I R L S. STANDARD FILE NO. 42. ADOLESCENCE, SPORT AND LEISURE. See Recreation, Leisure - Sports.

SAGAMIE. V. 1, No. 1 (Summer 1980)-. 0229-7698. Periodical. CN. French. qt. Free. Sagamie, 85 Jean-Allard, Jonquiere Quebec G7X 3E8 Canada. **DD** 790.0971416.

SCORP DIGEST. VAT Statewide Comprehensive Outdoor Recreation Planning Digest. Vol. 1, No. 1 (July 1980)-. US. English. Heritage Conservation and Recreation Service, US Department of the Interior Information Exchange, Washington DC 20243.

SEA PEN. See Zoology-Vertebrate and Invertebrate.

SEEKER (SARNIA). (SEEKER). V. 1- May 15, 1975-. 0318-9279. CN. English. wk. $5.00. Seeker Publishing Company, PO Box 82, Sarnia Ontario N7T 7H8 Canada. **DD** 790.0971327. Pleasure Seeker, 0318-9287.

SIRLS. STANDARD FILE NO. 38. HISTORY OF SPORT & LEISURE. RENAISSANCE TO MODERN. See Bibliographies.

SOCIAL ACTIVITIES FOR ADULTS. VFOAT Social Activities for Adults in Metropolitan Toronto. 0712-3205. Periodical. CN. English. be. $3.00 Each Volume. Community Information Centre of Metropolitan Toronto, 3rd Floor/34 King Street East, Toronto Ontario M5C 1E5 Canada. **DD** 367.025713541.

SPECIAL RECREATION DIGEST. See Physically Impaired.

LO SPETTACOLO IN ITALIA. Began with issue for 1936. Italian. an. LC GV85. **DD** 790.945.

A STEWARDSHIP REPORT. Main/Corp California. Dept. of Parks and Recreation. 1973/74-. 0362-6563. US. English. Department of Parks and Recreation, PO Box 2390, Sacramento CA 95811. LC SB482.C2. **DD** 333.7809794. California State Park System, A Stewardship Report.

SUMMER IN CANADA. See Economics - Labor.

SWIMMING POOL AGE & SPA MERCHANDISER. VFOAT Swimming Pool Age and Spa Merchandiser. VAT Swimming Pool Age and Swimming Pool Age Merchandiser. Vol. 55, No. 12 (June 15, 1981)-. 0279-134X. Periodical. US. English. sm. $19.00. Communication Channels Inc, 6255 Barfield Road, Atlanta GA 30328. **Tel** (404)256-9800. LC GV837.A1. **DD** 338.4769089. Swimming Pool Weekly and Swimming Pool Age, 0039-7393.

TEMPS FORT. (TEMPS FORT : BULLETIN D'INFORMATION DU CRL RIVE SUD). No. 1 (March 1977)-. 0229-4052. Periodical. CN. French. mo. Free. Temps Fort, 780 rue St-Jean, Longueuil Quebec J4H 2Y7 Canada. **DD** 790.097143. (ctrl). Bulletin d'Information (Conseil Regional des Loisirs de la Rive Sud), 0229-4036.

THERAPEUTIC RECREATION JOURNAL. See Physically Impaired.

TORONTO TONIGHT. Began with V. 1, No. 1 (Dec. 1983). 0827-4207. Periodical. CN. English. sm. Free. Toronto Tonight, 531 Lawrence Avenue West, Toronto Ontario M6A 1A3 Canada. **DD** 790.09713541.

TOUR DE SUTTON. (LE TOUR DE SUTTON). Vol. 1, No. 1 (Sept. 1983)-. 0826-5224. Periodical. CN. English (French). qt. Free. Bureau du Tourisme et des Congres de Sutton, PO Box 810, Sutton Quebec J0E 2K0 Canada. **DD** 790.0971464.

TOURIST ATTRACTIONS & PARKS. VAT Tourist Attractions and Parks. 0194-4894. Periodical. US. English. bm. Tourist Attractions & Parks, 401 North Broad Street, Philadelphia PA 19108. **Tel** (215)925-9744. bk rev. adv acc. **Circ** 20,000. (ctrl). Trade publication for the amusement, fair, carnival, arena, arcade, and traveling show industry.

TOUT A LOISIR. 0822-5524. Periodical. CN. French. mo. Conseil Regional des Loisirs Saguenay-Lac-Saint-Jean, 414 rue Collard, Alma Quebec G8B 1N2 Canada. **DD** 790.0971416.

TRENDS (PARK PRACTICE PROGRAM (U.S.)). (TRENDS). Vol. 6 I.E. V. 7, No. 2 (Apr. 1970)-. Periodical. US. English. qt. National Recreation and Park Association, 3101 Park Center Drive, Alexandria VA 22302. Ind/Abst Park Pract. Prog., Park Pract. Index, Index U.S. Gov. Period. Trends in Parks & Recreation.

UITVOERINGSORGANEN BUURT- EN KLUBHUISWERK. Main/Corp Netherlands. Centraal Bureau voor de Statistiek. VFOAT Community Works Units. 1976-. Dutch. ir. 10.75. Centraal Bureau voor de Statistiek, Staatsuitgeverij, S-Gravenhage Netherlands. LC HN46.N4.

VARIA BELADIRI. 923-. Periodical. US. Indonesian. mo. 350. Pt Badan Penerbit & Percetakan Vaira, Jl Abdulrachman Saleh No 40, Jakarta Pusat Indonesia. LC GV111. Varia.

VAYAGEUR. (LE VOYAGEUR). Vol. 1, No. 1 (Jan. 82)-. 0713-3073. Periodical. CN. French. Le Voyageur, Conseil Regional des Loisirs de l'Outaouais, 111 rue Carillon, Hull Quebec J8X 2P8 Canada. **DD** 790.097142. Ouaisir, 0711-6489.

VIE ET CAMPING. Vol. 1, No. 1 (1976). 0710-2054. Periodical. CN. French. ir. $3.09. CRV Publishing Company Ltd, 414 Park Avenue, Montreal Quebec H2X 2H5 Canada. **Tel** (514)282-0191. **Ed** J G Langlois. **DD** 796.5409714. bk rev. adv acc. **Circ** 100,000.

VISIONS IN LEISURE AND BUSINESS. V. 1, (1) (Spring 1982)-. 0277-5204. Periodical. US. English. qt. $40.00 Domestic, $75.00 Foreign. Appalachina Association, 615 Pasteur Avenue, Bowling Green OH 43402. **Tel** (419)352-9111. **Ed** David L Groves. (ctrl). An international Journal of personal services, programming and administration.

VISITATION AND OUTDOOR RECREATION STATISTICAL REPORT. See Statistics.

THE WATER SKIER. See Recreation, Leisure - Sports.

W.D. FARMER'S VACATION & RETIREMENT HOMES FOR PLEASANT LIVING. See Travel.

WHEELERS RV RESORT & CAMPGROUND GUIDE. VFOAT RV Resort & Campground Guide. VAT WHEELERS RECREATIONAL VEHICLE RESORT AND CAMPGROUND GUIDE. 1979-. 0194-0384. US. English (Vols. for 1979- have introduction in French and Spanish). an. $9.95. Print Media Services Ltd, 1301 Jarvis Avenue, Elk Grove Village IL 60007. **Tel** (312)981-0100. **Ed** Gloria Telander. adv acc. **Circ** 180,000. Guide to campgrounds and RV resorts in North America and a toll-free reservation directory for its US advertisers. Plus travel articles and information. Wheelers Recreational Vehicle Resort and Campground Guide. North American Edition, 0362-9759.

THE WHITE BOOK OF SKI AREAS. U.S. AND CANADA. (THE WHITE BOOK OF SKI AREAS : U.S. AND CANADA). VAT White Book of Ski Areas. United States and Canada. 3rd- Ed. 0163-9684. US. English. an. $7.95. PO Box 3635, Georgetown Station, Washington DC 20007. **Tel** (202)342-0886. **Ed** Robert G Enzel. LC GV854.4. **DD** 796.9302573. **Circ** 20,000. Directory of all ski areas in the US and Canada and the various services provided by the areas. Rates and photos are included in the white book. White Book of U.S. Ski Areas, 0145-6075.

WINTER RECREATION DIRECTORY. See Yearbooks, Almanacs, Directories.

WLRA BULLETIN CEASED. Main/Corp World Leisure and Recreation Association. VFOAT W.L.R.A. Bulletin. V. 16, No. 3-V. 22. Periodical. English. ir. IRA Bulletin (International Recreation Association).

WLRA JOURNAL. VFOAT W.L.R.A. Journal. Vol. 23, No. 1 (Jan./Feb. 1981)-. Periodical. US. English. bm. World Leisure and Recreation Association, 345 East 46th Street, New York NY 10017. WLRA Bulletin.

WOODALL'S FLORIDA & SOUTHERN STATES RETIREMENT AND RESORT COMMUNITIES. VFOAT Florida & Southern States Retirement and Resort Communities. VAT Woodall's Florida and Southern States Retirement and Resort Communities. 0163-4313. US. English. an. $5.95. Woodall's Publishing Company, 500 Hyacinth Place, Highland Park IL 60035. LC HQ1063. **DD** 301.435.

WOODALL'S RETIREMENT AND RESORT COMMUNITIES. EASTERN EDITION. (WOODALL'S RETIREMENT AND RESORT COMMUNITIES). VFOAT Woodall's Eastern Edition Retirement & Communities Directory. 0145-577X. US. English. $2.95. Woodall Publishing Company, 500 Hyacinth Place, Highland Park IL 60035. LC HQ1063. **DD** 301.435.

WOODALL'S RETIREMENT AND RESORT COMMUNITIES. NATIONAL EDITION. (WOODALL'S RETIREMENT AND RESORT COMMUNITIES). VFOAT Woodall's National Edition Retirement & Resort Communities Directory. 0146-4892. US. English. $5.95. Woodall Publishing Company, 500 Hyacinth Place, Highland Park IL 60035. LC HQ1063. **DD** 301.54.

WORCESTER MAGAZINE. 1976. 0191-4960. Periodical. US. English. wk. $15.00. Worcester Magazine, PO Box 1000, Worcester MA 10614. **Tel** (617)799-0511. **Ed** Dan Kaplan. adv acc. **Circ** 50,000. (ctrl). Local art and entertainment guide, alternative newsweekly.

YOUR GUIDE TO THE LEISURE LIFE OF SOUTHWESTERN ONTARIO. VFOAT Leisure Life. VAT Leisure Life (Goderich). Spring & Summer 1980-. 0712-2225. Periodical. CN. English. ir. $0.25 Per Number. Leisure Life, c/o Signal-Star Publishing, PO Box 220, Goderich Ontario N7A 4B6 Canada. **DD** 790.097132.

Recreation, Leisure—Games & Amusements

GAMES & AMUSEMENTS

ACTIVITY PROGRAMMERS SOURCEBOOK. See Education (General).

ALMANAC. SPORTS AND GAMES. See Yearbooks, Almanacs, Directories.

THE AMAZING SPIDER-MAN. VFOAT Spider-Man. VAT Amazing Spider Man. Began with No. 1, Mar. 1963. 0274-5232. Periodical. US. English. mo. $7.80. Marvel Comics, 387 Park Avenue South, New York NY 10016. Tel (212)576-9259. Ed Jim Shooter. adv acc. Circ 350,000. Comic book adventures of Spider-Man.

AMERICAN FIREWORKS NEWS. VFOAT A.F.N. 8755-3163. US. English. mo. $13.50. American Fireworks News, S R Box 30, Dingmans Ferry PA 18328. Tel (717)828-8417. Ed J M Drewes. DD 662. bk rev. adv acc. World's only newsletter devoted exclusively to fireworks.

THE AMERICAN GO JOURNAL. Began in 1949. 0148-0243. Periodical. US. English (Japanese). qt. $15.00. American GO Association, PO Box 397 Old Chelsea Station, New York NY 10011. Ed Roy J Laird. LC GV1459. DD 794.05. bk rev. adv acc. Circ 900. How-to articles, game commentary, news, book reviews, and other material concerning GO, the world's oldest and most fascinating game.

AMUSEMENT BUSINESS. V. 73- Jan. 9, 1961-. 0003-2344. Periodical. US. English. wk. $88.00. Amusement Business, PO Box 24970, Nashville, TN 37202. Tel (609)786-1669. Ind/Abst Trade Ind. Index. LC GV1851.A3. DD 338.76179006805. Available on microfilm from University Microfilms. *Funspot, Billboard, 0006-2510.*

AMUSEMENT JEUNESSE. First issue in May 1978?. 0709-2415. Periodical. CN. French. ty. $1. Canada, $1.25 Others. Les Editions Publiitee, CP 71 Succursale R, Montreal Quebec H2S 3K8 Canada. DD 793.7305.

AMUSEMENT PARK JOURNAL. 0271-7999. Periodical. US. English. qt. $30.00. Amusement Park Journal, PO Box 157, Natrona Heights PA 15065. Tel (412)226-1178. LC GV1851.A3. DD 791.06805.

AMUSEMENT RIDES & GAMES BUYERS' GUIDE. VAT Amusement Rides and Games Buyers' Guide. 0149-8010. US. English. an. $10.00. Amusement Business, PO Box 24970, Nashville TN 37202. Tel (615)748-8120. LC GV1851.A3. DD 380.1456887.

ANECDOTA SCOWAH. US. English.

ANNUAIRE DE LA BANDE DESSINEE DANS LA COMMUNAUTE FRANCAISE DE BELGIQUE. See Yearbooks, Almanacs, Directories.

ANNUAL HANDBOOK - BADMINTON ASSOCIATION OF ENGLAND. Main/Corp Badminton Association of England. UK. English. an. 40. 81A High Street, Bromley BR1 1JY Kent England. LC GV1007. DD 796.3450942.

ANNUAL REPORT - ALBERTA GAMES. (ANNUAL REPORT). Main/Corp Alberta Games Council. 1st (1978/79)-. 0228-3042. CN. English. an. Alberta Games, Alberta Place, 3rd Floor, 1520-4 Street South West, Calgary Alberta T2R 1H5 Canada. LC GV722.5.A43. DD 354.712300858.

ANNUAL REPORT OF THE PALISADES INTERSTATE PARK IN NEW JERSEY. Main/Corp Palisades Interstate Park Commission. 1st-. US. English. an. Palisades Interstate Park Commission, Administrative Building, Bear Mountain NY 10911. DD 710.

ANNUAL U.S. OPEN CHESS CHAMPIONSHIP. English. ir. LC GV1313. DD 794.1 S, 794.157.

APOCALYPSE. V. 1, No.1- Spr. 1975-. Periodical. US. English. mo. Apocalypse, 62 Jane Street c/o Harry Lorayne, New York NY 10014. Tel (212)989-5694. Ed Harry Lorayne. adv acc. Magical effects contributed by magicians.

APPRENTICE. (THE APPRENTICE). No. 1- May 1978-. 0706-7399. Periodical. CN. English. qt. $5.50 (6 Issues) Canada and US. D Berman, 24 Seguin Street, Ottawa K1J 6P3 Canada. DD 796.1.

ARCHIE. Series/Titl Archie Series. 0735-6455. Periodical. US. English. bm. Archie Comic Publications, 325 Fayette Avenue, Mamaroneck NY 10543. Tel (914)381-5155. *Archie Comics.*

ARCHIE'S GIRLS BETTY AND VERONICA. Series/Titl Archie Series. VFOAT Betty & Veronica, Veronica. Began with No. 1 (1950). 0735-6463. Periodical. US. English. bm. Archie Comics, 325 Fayette Avenue, Mamaroneck NY 10543. Tel (914)381-5155.

ARN SABA'S NEIL THE HORSE, COMICS AND STORIES. VFOAT Neil the Horse, Comics and Stories. Vol. 1, No. 1 (Feb. 1983)-. 0715-8572. Periodical. CN. English. bm. $1.60 Per No. Neil The Horse Comics And Stories, P O Box 1674 Station C, Kitchener Ontario N2G 4R2 Canada. DD 741.5971.

THE AVENGERS. VFOAT Mighty Avengers. 0274-5240. Periodical. US. English. mo. $7.80. Marvel Comics, 387 Park Avenue South, New York NY 10016. Tel (212)576-9259. Ed Jim Shooter. adv acc. Circ 210,000. The adventures of one of the world's foremost teams of superhuman crimefighters banded together to battle menaces too big for anyone else to handle.

BADMINTON REVIEW. See Recreation, Leisure - Sports.

BALOUNE. No. 1- Feb. 1977-. 0707-9672. Periodical. CN. French. mo. $1. Per No. Editions Baloune Enrg, #161 East Ontario, Montreal Quebec H2X 1H Canada. DD 741.59714.

BATTLE STATIONS. Aug. 1983-. 0822-9651. Periodical. CN. English. mo. $9.00. Battle Stations, 1001-1239 12th Avenue SW, Calgary Alberta T3C 3R8 Canada. DD 794.205.

BEST OF THE RIP OFF PRESS. (THE BEST OF THE RIP OFF PRESS). Main/Corp Rip Off Press. V. 1- 1973-. 0092-5314. US. English. PO Box 14158, San Francisco CA 94114. LC PN6726. DD 741.5923.

BETTY AND ME. Series/Titl Archie Series. Archie Comics Group. VFOAT Betty & Me. Began with No. 1 (Aug. 1965). 0006-0267. Periodical. US. English. bm. Betty & Me c/o Archie Enterprises Inc, 325 Fayette Avenue, Mamaroneck NY 10543.

BILLIARDS DIGEST. V. 1- Sept./Oct. 1978-. 0164-761X. Periodical. US. English. bm. $17.00. Billiards Digest, 875 North Michigan Avenue/Suite 3734, Chicago IL 60611. Tel (312)266-7179.

BLACK POWDER TIMES. 0745-1385. Periodical. US. English. mo. Black Powder Times, Box 842, Mt Vernon WA 98273. Tel (206)336-2969.

BLUE RIBBON CROSSPATCHES. VFOAT Crosspatches. 0194-3103. Periodical. US. English. bm. Official Publications Inc, 201 East 57th 3rd Avenue, New York NY 10022. Tel (212)355-5001.

BLUE RIBBON FILL-IT-INS. VFOAT Fill-It-Ins. 0194-3111. Periodical. US. English. bm. Official Publications Inc, 201 East 57th 3rd Avenue, New York NY 10022. Tel (212)355-5001.

BLUE RIBBON WORD-FINDS. VFOAT Word-Finds. VAT Blue Ribbon Word Finds. 0194-312X. Periodical. US. English. mo. Official Publications Inc, 201 East 57th 3rd Avenue, New York NY 10022. Tel (212)355-5001.

BRAVE AND BOLD. US. English. mo. DC Comics, PO Box 1308F Department R6, Fort Lee NJ 07024.

BREATHING. V. 1- Sept./Oct. 1978-. 0707-7319. Periodical. CN. English. bm. Breathing Enterprises, PO Box 55 Station Z, Toronto Ontario M5N 2Z3 Canada. DD C817.5408.

BRIDGE. 0045-2823. Periodical. US. English. qt. $5.00 Domestic, $5.00 Foreign. Bridge, PO Box 477 Canal Street Station, New York NY 10013. *Bridge Magazine.*

THE BRIDGE. Periodical. UK. English. mo. 14.95. Bridge Publications Limited, 30 Fleet Street, London EC4Y 1AH England. Tel 353 9095. Ed Alan Hiron. bk rev. adv acc. Circ 7,000. For over 50 years the leading journal on bridge. Sells to over 85 countries. News, stories, letters, theory, bookshop, all regularly featured.

THE BRIDGE WORLD. Began publication 1929. 0006-9876. Periodical. US. English. mo. Bridge World, 39 West 94th Street, New York NY 10025. Tel (212)866-5860.

BRISEBOIS ET COMPAGNIE. No 1- Jan. 1977-. 0383-8498. Periodical. CN. French. 50. Distributions Eclaire, 8320 Place de Lorraine, Anjou Quebec H1J 1E6 Canada. DD 741.59714.

THE BRITISH CHESS MAGAZINE. V.1- 1881-. Periodical. UK. English. mo. 15.60 Domestic, $24.60 Foreign. British Chess Magazine, 9 Market Street Saint Leonards on Sea, Sussex TN38 0DQ Great Britian. Tel 0424-424009. Ed B Cafferty. LC GV1313. bk rev. adv acc. Circ 4,000. Chess news, games, and puzzles from the whole world.

BROKEN CUE NEWS. (THE BROKEN CUE NEWS). Began with Jan. 1974 issue. 0317-1917. Periodical. CN. English. bm. $3. Editor Broken Cue News, 16 Kenora Street, Ottawa Ontario K1Y 3K8 Canada. DD 794.7205.

BULLETIN - SOCIETE DES JEUX DU QUEBEC. (LE BULLETIN - SOCIETE DES JEUX DU QUEBEC). Main/Corp Societe des Jeux du Quebec. V. 1- June 1976-. 0381-0003. Periodical. CN. French. bm. Free to Clients of the Society. Societe des Jeux de Quebec Inc, 1415 Est rue Jarry, Montreal Quebec H2E 2Z7 Canada. DD 796.062714.

BUYERS' GUIDE FOR THE MASS ENTERTAINMENT INDUSTRY. 0362-6180. US. English. an. $15.00. Amusement Business Magazines, PO Box 24970, Nashville TN 37202. Tel (615)748-8120. LC GV1851.A3. DD 381.45790068.

CANADIAN BRIDGE DIGEST. V. 7, No. 3- Sept. 1977-. 0707-9524. Periodical. CN. English. Free to Members. Canadian Bridge Federation, 2692 Bendale Place, North Vancouver British Columbia V7H 1G9 Canada. DD 795.41506271. *Bridge Digest, 0317-9281.*

CANADIAN CHESS CHAT. V.4, No.6- 1950-. Periodical. CN. English. mo. 24.00. Canadian Chess Chat, Box 304 Station B, Hamilton Ontario Canada. Tel 549-2342. Ed Frank J Szarka. Circ 5,000. International chess, and chess problems. *Maritime Chess Chat.*

CANADIAN HERO COMICS. 1st issue-. 0821-5960. Periodical. CN. English. $7.95. Canadian Hero Comics, PO Box 190 Clarkson Station, Mississauga Ontario L5J 3Y1 Canada. Tel (416)844-4669. Ed Robert Edward Livesey. DD 971.00992. Circ 3,000. Illustrated stories of real-life Canadian heroes and heroines designed for schools and libraries.

CAPTAIN CANUCK. No. 1- July 1975-. 0383-0462. Periodical. CN. English. $3. Comely Comix, 1854 Portage Avenue, Winnipeg Manitoba R3J 0G9 Canada. DD 741.5971.

CAPTAIN GEORGE'S YELLOW JOURNAL. V. 1- April 4, 1975-. 0317-6134. CN. English. Vast Whizzbang Organization, 594 Markham Street, Toronto Ontario M6G 2L8 Canada. DD 741.5.

CASCADE COMIX MONTHLY. No. 1- March 1978-. Periodical. US. English. mo. Everyman Studios, 432 South Cascade, Colorado Springs CO 80903.

CASINO DIGEST. Vol. 101 (Nov. 1984)-. 8755-6103. Periodical. US. English. mo. $36.00 Domestic, $46.00 Foreign. Casino Digest, Suite 804/L-123, 323 Frankling Building South, Chicago IL 60606. DD 795.

CEREBUS. VAT Cerebus the Aardvark (1979). No. 11 (Aug. 1979)-. 0712-7774. Periodical. CN. English. ir. $1.50 Per No. Cerebus, PO Box 1674/Station C, Kitchener Ontario N2G 4R2 Canada. DD 741.5971. *Cerebus the Aardvark, 0229-0103.*

CHESS. V. 1- (No.1-). 0009-3319. Periodical. UK. English. r. $35.00. Chess Ltd, Sutton, Coldfield B73 6AZ England. Tel 021-354-2536. Ed B H Wood. bk rev. adv acc. Circ 8,000. Chess world-wide. Presented in a challenging and witty style. *Canadian Chessner, Social Chess Quarterly.*

THE CHESS CORRESPONDENT. 0009-3327. Periodical. US. English. mo. $7.50. Correspondence Chess League of America, PO Box 3363, Decatur IL 62525. Ed Jerry Honn. LC GV1313. DD 794.105. bk rev. adv acc. Circ 1,500. Chess games, articles and columns by America's leading correspondence players.

CHESS DIGEST MAGAZINE. VFOAT Chess Digest. V. 1- Jan. 1968-. 0009-3335. Periodical. US. English. ir. $13.50. Chess Digest Magazine, PO Box 210225, Dallas TX 75211. LC GV1313. DD 794.105.

Recreation, Leisure—Games & Amusements

CHESS HORIZONS. 0147-2569. Periodical. US. English. bm. $7.00. Massachusetts Chess Association, c/o George Mirijanian, 46 Beacon, Fitchburg MA 01420. **Tel** (617)345-5011. **Ed** Frank Niro. bk rev. adv acc. **Circ** 2,000. New England and international chess news and feature articles by top US and foreign players. Tournament reports and annotated games.

CHESS LIFE. VFOAT Chess Life & Review. V. 35- Jan. 1980-. 0197-260X. Periodical. US. English. mo. $25.00. US Chess Federation, 186 Route 9 West, New Windsor NY 12550. **Tel** (914)562-8350. **Ed** Larry Parr. **LC** GV1313. **DD** 794.105. bk rev. adv acc. **Circ** 55,000. Membership publication of US Chess Federation. World and national chess news; instruction and analysis of the game of chess. *Chess Life & Review*, 0009-3351.

CHESS LIFE & REVIEW. (CHESS LIFE AND REVIEW). V. 1- 1946-. 0009-3351. Periodical. US. English. mo. $15.00. United States Chess Federation, 186 Rt 9W, New Windsor NY 12550.

CHILD LIFE. *See* Children and Youth Interests.

CHILDRENS' MYSTERY WORD. V. 1- Dec. 1977-. 0705-3819. Periodical. CN. English. ir. $1. Per No. Mystery Word Publications, 5 Highburn Crescent, Blackburn Hamlet Ontario K1B 3H7 Canada. **DD** 793.7305.

CIRCLE-A-WORD PUZZLES. VAT Circle a Word Puzzles. 0194-3146. Periodical. US. English. ir. $9.00. Editorial Services Inc, PO Box 687, Old Lyme CT 06371.

CLASSIC CROSSWORD PUZZLES. 0199-5588. Periodical. US. English. mo. $14.50. Penny Press Inc, 185 East Avenue, Norwalk CT 06855. **Tel** (203)866-6688.

THE COMIC BOOK PRICE GUIDE. 1st- Ed. 0730-2916. US. English. an. $10.95. Overstreet Publications Inc, 780 Hunt Cliff Drive NW, Cleveland TN 37311. **Tel** (615)472-4135. **LC** Z1000. **DD** 016.7415973. adv acc. **Circ** 70,000. Lists all American comic books from 1900 to present with average market valves, lists major artists, characters, origin issues, etc etc. The number one guide for comics.

COMIC RESEARCH LIBRARY NEWSLETTER. *See* Library and Information Science.

THE COMICS BUYER'S GUIDE. No. 482 (Feb. 11, 1983)-. 0745-4570. Periodical. US. English. wk. $10.00. Krause Publications Inc, 700 East State Street, Iola WI 54990. *Buyer's Guide for Comic Fandom*.

COMICS FEATURE. V. 1- Mar. 1980-. 0199-7459. Periodical. US. English. bm.

COMPOSITE ANNUAL REPORT - PALISADES INTERSTATE PARK COMMISSION. (COMPOSITE ANNUAL REPORT; NEW YORK-NEW JERSEY). **Main/Corp** Palisades Interstate Park Commission (New York and New Jersey). 1959-. 0479-270X. US. English. an. Palisades Interstate Park Commission, Administrative Building, Bear Mountain NY 10911. **DD** 710.

COMPUTER GAMES. V. 2, No. 3 (Dec./Jan. 1984)-. 0748-4461. Periodical. US. English. bm. $15.00. Carnegie Publications Corp, 888 Seventh Avenue, New York NY 10106. **LC** GV1469.3. **DD** 794.8205. *Video Games Player*, 0748-4453.

COMPUTER GAMING WORLD. 1981. 0744-6667. Periodical. US. English. bm. $13.50. Computer Gaming World, PO Box 4566, Anaheim CA 92803. **Tel** (714)535-4435. **Ed** Russell Sipe. bk rev. adv acc. **Circ** 25,000. (ctrl). The authoritative source for reviews of computer games. Focus is on games of strategy and adventure.

CONAN THE BARBARIAN. V. 1- (No. 1-). 0273-0782. US. English. mo. $7.80. Marvel Comics, 387 Park Avenue South, New York NY 10016. **Tel** (212)576-9259. **Ed** Jim Shooter. adv acc. **Circ** 165,000. The steel-thewed Cimmerian swashbuckles through sorcerors, mad kings, pirates and giant spiders on his quest for the Topaz Throne of Aquilonia.

CONAN THE KING. 20 (Jan. 1984)-. 0746-8237. Periodical. US. English. bm. $12.00 Domestic, $14.00 Canada. Marvel Comics Group, 387 Park Avenue South, New York NY 10016. *King Conan*, 0279-0076.

CONTEMPORARY GAMES. US. English. ir. Gale Research Co, Book Tower, Detroit MI 48226. **Ed** J Belch. A single volume directory of some 900 games, plus a separate bibliographical volume citing 2,372 books and articles.

CONTEST HOTLINE. 0195-9735. Periodical. US. English. ir. Contest Hotline, PO Box 1255, Chico CA 95927. **Tel** (714)970-0790.

THE CONTRACT BRIDGE BULLETIN. 0010-7840. Periodical. US. English. mo. American Contract Bridge League, PO Box 161192, Accounting Department, Memphis TN 38186. **Tel** (901)332-5586.

COOPERATIVE GAMES NEWSLETTER. VFOAT Jeux Cooperatifs Newsletter. **VAT** Bulletin Jeux Cooperatifs, Jeux Cooperatifs. Bulletin, Bulletin de Jeux Cooperatifs. Vol. 1, No. 1 (May 1979)-. 0229-9852. Periodical. CN. English (issued as a single folded sheet with French text on verso of May 1979-). qt. $2.00. Cooperative Games Newsletter, c/o S Olsen, 12 Bedale Drive, Ottawa Ontario K2H 5M1 Canada. **DD** 613.71019.

CORRESPONDENCE CHESS. V. 1- 1954-. Periodical. UK. English. qt. $7.00. British Corrsspondence Chess Association, Whitestones Maddox Lane, Leatherhead Surrey XT23 3BS England. **Ed** G E Finch. bk rev. adv acc. **Circ** 800. Correspondence chess games and related material. *B.C.C.A. Magazine*.

CROSSWORD TREAT. 0194-3154. Periodical. US. English. bm. Official Publications Inc, 201 East 57th-3rd Avenue, New York NY 10022. **Tel** (212)355-5001.

CROSSWORD VARIETIES. 0194-3162. Periodical. US. English. bm. Official Publications Inc, 201 East 57th-3rd Avenue, New York NY 10022. **Tel** (212)355-5001.

CROSSWORDS GALORE. Began in 1984. 0743-7005. Periodical. US. English. bm. $6.98. American Astrology, 475 Park Avenue South, New York NY 10016. **DD** 793.

CRYPTOGRAPHY MAGAZINE. *See* Hobbies.

DAREDEVIL. 0279-8271. Periodical. US. English. mo. $7.80. Marvel Comics, 387 Park Avenue South, New York NY 10016. **Tel** (212)576-9259. **Ed** Jim Shooter. adv acc. Daredevil is blind. His sight has been replaced with an internal rader sense, his other senses have been heightened to an extreme degree, and this helps in his war against organized crime.

DAVID LORD'S WORLD OF CRICKET. VFOAT World of Cricket. V. 1- 1973-. 0311-0435. Periodical. AT. English. mo. David Lord Publ Pty Ltd, Suite 5 & 6/340 Victoria Avenue, Chatswood New South Wales 2067 Australia. **LC** GV911. **DD** 796.35805.

DAZZLER. Vol. 1, No. 1 (Mar. 1981)-. 0279-2354. Periodical. US. English. mo. $7.20. Marvel Comics, 387 Park Avenue South, New York NY 10016. **Tel** (212)576-9259. **Ed** Jim Shooter. adv acc. **Circ** 93,000.

DELL CHAMPION VARIETY PUZZLES. VFOAT Champion Variety Puzzles. 0747-5888. Periodical. US. English. bm. $6.25 US, $7.75 Canada. Dell Champion Variety Puzzles Subscription Service, Box 4800, Marion OH 43305.

DELL CROSSWORD PUZZLES. VFOAT Crossword Puzzles. 0274-6301. Periodical. US. English. mo. $12.50. Dell Publishing Company, 1 Dag Hammarskjold Plaza, 245 East 47th Street, New York NY 10017, (subscription address: Fulfillment Corporation of America 381 West Center Marion OH 43302). **Tel** (212)605-3000.

DELL OFFICIAL CROSSWORD PUZZLES. VFOAT Official Crossword Puzzles. 0274-6239. US. English. mo. Dell Publishing Co Inc, PO Box 4800, Marion OH 43305. **Tel** (212)605-3000.

DELL PENCIL PUZZLES & WORD GAMES. VFOAT Pencil Puzzles & Word Games. **VAT** Dell Pencil Puzzles and Word Games. 0274-6220. Periodical. US. English. bm. Dell Publishing Co Inc, PO Box 4800, Marion OH 43305. **Tel** (212)605-3000.

DELL POCKET CROSSWORD PUZZLES. VFOAT Pocket Crossword Puzzles. 0274-6425. US. English. bm. $9.97. Dell Publishing Co Inc, PO Box 4800, Marion OH 43305. **Tel** (212)605-3000.

DELL WORD SEARCH PUZZLES. VFOAT Word Search Puzzles. 0274-6190. Periodical. US. English. mo. $9.97. Dell Publishing Co Inc, PO Box 4800, Marion OH 43305. **Tel** (212)605-3000.

DEUTSCHE SCHACHZEITUNG. V. 27, No. 1, (Jan. 1872)-. 0012-0669. Periodical. German. mo. Walter de Gruyter Inc, 200 Saw Mill River Road, Hawthorne NY 10532. **Tel** (914)747-0110. **LC** GV1313. *Schachzeitung, Deutsche Schachrundshau*.

DRAGON. 0279-6848. Periodical. US. English. mo. Dragon Publishing, PO Box 72089, Chicago IL 60690. **Tel** (414)248-3625. **Ed** Kim Mohan. bk rev. adv acc. **Circ** 115,000. Articles on role-playing games, especially the Advanced Dungeons and Dragons game. Some fiction, and reviews of games and books.

ECHEC +. VAT Echec Plus. #34 (March/April 1984)-. 0825-0049. Periodical. CN. French. bm. $25.00. Federation Quebecoise des Echecs, CP 640 Succursale C, Montreal Quebec H2L 4L5 Canada. **Tel** (514)844-5104. **DD** 794.105. bk rev. adv acc. **Circ** 3,000. (ctrl). International and national tournament news, games, analysis, problems, contests, authorities articles, chronicles on middle and end games also on chess computers, reports, and activities calender. *Petit Rocque*, 0227-8340.

ELECTRONIC GAMES SOFTWARE ENCYCLOPEDIA. (ELECTRONIC GAMES . . . SOFTWARE ENCYCLOPEDIA). VFOAT E.G. Software Encyclopedia. No. 1 (1983)– – Vol. 1, No. 1 (1983)–. 0736-8488. Periodical. US. English. an. $3.95 Single Issue. Reese Publishing Co, 460 West 34th Street, New York NY 10001. **LC** GV1469.2. **DD** 794.8205.

EPIC ILLUSTRATED. 0279-246X. Periodical. US. English. bm. Marvel Comics Group, 387 Park Avenue South, New York NY 10016. **Tel** (212)576-9259.

FANTASTIC FOUR. 0274-5291. Periodical. US. English. mo. $7.80. Marvel Comics, 387 Park Avenue South, New York NY 10016. **Tel** (212)576-9259. **Ed** Jim Shooter. adv acc. **Circ** 237,000. Super-heroic team defending the world against various perils. Team's made up of four members: mister fantastic, invisible woman, human torch, and she-hulk or the thing.

FEATURED FILL-IT-INS. VAT Featured Fill It Ins. 0194-3170. Periodical. US. English. mo. Official Publication Company, 201 East 57th 3rd Avenue, New York NY 10022. **Tel** (212)355-5001.

FLAMING CARROT COMICS. VFOAT Flaming Carrot. Vol. 1, No. 1 (May 1984)-. 0826-256X. Periodical. CN. English. bm. $2.00 Per No. Flaming Carrot Comics, PO Box 1674 Station C, Kitchener Ontario N2G 4RC Canada. **DD** 741.5971.

FU-CHUN-CHIANG HUA PAO : FCJ. VFOAT Fuchunjianghuabao. Periodical. Chinese. ir. 0.32. Chung-Kuo Kuo Chi Shu Tien, PO Box 2820, Pei-Ching China. **LC** PN6700. **DD** 741.5951.

FUNPARKS DIRECTORY. *See* Yearbooks, Almanacs, Directories.

GAMBLERS WORLD. V. 1- Dec. 1973/Jan. 1974-. 0092-069X. Periodical. US. English. $15.00 (11 issues). 527 Madison Avenue, New York NY 10022. **LC** GV1301. **DD** 795.01.

GAMBLING TIMES. V. 1- Feb. 1977-. 0149-0214. Periodical. US. English. mo. Gambling Times, 1018 North Cole, Hollywood CA 90038. **Tel** (213)466-5261. **LC** GV1301. **DD** 795.0105.

GAMES. 0199-9788. Periodical. US. English. mo. $15.97. Playboy Enterprise Inc, 919 North Michigan Avenue, Chicago IL 60611, (subscription address: Communication Data Services PO Box 4966 Des Moines IA 50340). **LC** GV1199. **DD** 794.05.

GAMES MERCHANDISING. *See* Business - Marketing.

GAMING BUSINESS. VFOAT Gaming Business Magazine. 0736-0916. Periodical. US. English. mo. $180.00. BMT Publications, 254 West 31st Street, New York NY 10001. **Tel** (212)594-4120. **Ed** Paul Dworin. **LC** HV6715. **DD** 363.420973. adv acc. GWB deals with the major issues, news and developments affecting the various segments of the legalized gambling and wagering industry. *Gaming Business Magazine*, 0196-2213.

GENERAL STAFF JOURNAL. (THE GENERAL STAFF JOURNAL). Aug. 1982-. 0828-4733. Periodical. CN. English. ir. General Staff Journal, c/o M L Tohver #1414/141 Davisville Avenue, Toronto Ontario M4S 1G7 Canada. **DD** 793.9.

GENII. 0016-6855. Periodical. US. English. mo. $20.00. The Conjurors Magazine, PO Box 36068, Los Angeles CA 90084. **Tel** (213)851-5333. **Ed** William Larsen Jr. bk rev. adv acc. **Circ** 10,000. A specialty

Recreation, Leisure—Games & Amusements

publication describing the arts/performance of magic. *Conjurors' Magazine.*

G.I. JOE. VFOAT GI Joe. 0746-7397. Periodical. US. English. mo. Marvel Comics Group, 387 Park Avenue South, New York NY 10016.

GLOBE GIANT PUZZLEBOOK. 0278-5544. US. English. qt. Globe Communications Corporation, 2455 East Sunrise Boulevard, Fort Lauderdale FL 33304. DD 793.7305.

GO WORLD. No. 1 (May-June 1977)-. JA. English. qt. $20.00. Ishi Press Inc, CPO Box 2126, Tokyo Japan. Tel 0467-83-4369. Ed John Power. LC GV1459. DD 794.2. bk rev. adv acc. (ctrl). Quarterly magazine on the Japanese game of GO news, tournament games and instructional articles.

GOREN BRIDGE LETTER. Vol. 1, No. 1 (May 1984)-. 8756-3908. Periodical. US. English. mo $27.95. Goren Bridge Letter, 1909 Cinnaminson Avenue, Cinnaminson NJ 08077. DD 795.

GRAN TORNEO INTERNACIONAL DE AJEDREZ DE MADRID. Main/Corp Madrid (Spain). Ayuntamiento. Began in 1943. SP. Spanish. ir. LC GV1455. DD 794.157.

GRATIS (SCARBOROUGH, ONT.). (GRATIS). 1st Issue (Mar. 1979)-. 0225-381X. Periodical. CN. English. qt. $1.25. Gratis Publications, 36 Ivy Green Crescent, Scarborough Ontario M1G 2X Canada. DD 741.505.

GROUPUSCULE. Published since Dec. 1977?. 0226-6237. Periodical. CN. French. bm. $1. Per. No. Groupuscule, 965 Sud Avenue Concorde, St-Hyacinthe Quebec J2T 3L4 Canada. DD 741.59714.

GUIDE TO AMUSEMENT RIDES. 0145-8159. US. English. Amusement Business, PO Box 2150, Radnor PA 19089. LC HD9999.A68. DD 338.4768.

THE GUIDE TO SIMULATIONS/ GAMES FOR EDUCATION AND TRAINING. See Education (General).

THE HULK. No. 1- Oct. 1978-. 0195-3060. Periodical. US. English. bm. $9.50. Marvel Comics, 387 Park Avenue South, New York NY 10016. Tel (212)576-9259. Ed Jim Shooter. adv acc. Circ 130,000.

HUMOR GRAPHIC. Began in 1960. Italian. an. 10.000. Via A Della Pergola North 11, 20159 Milano Italy. LC NC1528.H85. DD 741.5945.

IDEAS. No. 1-. Periodical. US. English. ir. Ed Mike Yaconelli. Each issue contains an index to its own contents - no vol index - loose. (cum index).

THE INCREDIBLE HULK. Vol. 1, No. 101- Apr. 1968-. 0274-5275. Periodical. US. English. mo. $7.80. Marvel Comics, 387 Park Avenue South, New York NY 10016. Tel (212)576-9259. Ed Jim Shooter. adv acc. Circ 130,000. A mild-mannered scientist becomes a huge, raging monster when angered. *Tales to astonish (1959).*

INFORMA' JEUX. V. 1- Nov. 1977-. 0705-3835. Periodical. CN. French. Federation Quebecoise des Jeux Recreatifs, 1415 East rue Jarry, Montreal Quebec H2E 2Z7 Canada. DD 794.05. *Bulletin, 0383-8048.*

THE INTERNATIONAL PLAYERS CHESS NEWS. (THE INTERNATIONAL PLAYERS CHESS NEWS : OFFICIAL PUBLICATION OF THE COMMITTEE ON PUBLICATIONS OF F.I.D). VFOAT Players Chess News. Began in 1983?. 0742-700X. Periodical. US. English. wk. $68.00 US, $72.72 Canada and Mexico. Players Chess Association, Circulation Department, PO Box 5721, Pasadena CA 91107. DD 794. *Players Chess News, 0744-4222.*

JACKPOT. VAT Jackpot Magazine (Toronto). V. 1- June/July 1977-. 0703-1785. Periodical. CN. English. ir. $5.00. Jackpot Magazine, 41 Roehampton Avenue, Toronto Ontario M4P 1P9 Canada. DD 795.0971.

JACQUES. Dec. 1979-. 0227-4450. Periodical. CN. English. ir. $1.25 Per No. Jacques, PO Box 8008, Ottawa Ontario K1G 3H6 Canada. DD 741.59713.

JAQUE MATE. Began with issue for Mar./Apr. 1964. 0021-3683. Periodical. CU. Spanish. mo. $5.65. 'Empresa Ediciones Cubanas, Sub-Direccion Exportacion, Oreilly 407 Ciudad Habana Cuba.

JEU DES 8 ERREURS. (JEU DE 8 ERREURS). Vol. 1, No. 1- 0822-4013. Periodical. CN. French. ty. Jeu des 8 Erreurs, 8023 East rue Jarry, Montreal Quebec H1J 1H6 Canada. DD 793.73.

THE JOURNAL OF MAGIC HISTORY. V. 1- Mar. 1979-. 0192-9917. Periodical. US. English. ty. $11.00. The Journal of Magic History, PO Box 7149, Toledo OH 43615. Ind/Abst Am. Hist. Life, Hist. Abstr., Part A, Mod. Hist. Abstr., Hist. Abst., Part B, Twent. Century Abstr., Writ. Am. Hist. LC GV1541. DD 793.805.

THE JOURNAL OF THE TRAVELLERS' AID SOCIETY. No. 1-. 0193-3124. Periodical. US. English. qt. $9.00 US and Canada, $18.00 Foreign. Journal, PO Box 1646, Bloomington IL 61701. LC GV1469.T75. DD 794.2.

THE JOY OF CROSSWORDS. No. 1 (Feb. 1984)-. 8750-2291. Periodical. US. English. bm. $17.25 Domestic, $21.25 Foreign. Penny Press Inc, Box 3211, Stamford CT 06905.

JUNIOR BOWLER. V. 1- Nov. 1964-. 0273-9100. Periodical. US. English. mo. American Junior Bowling Congress, 1572 East Capitol Drive, Milwaukee WI 53211. LC GB901. DD 794.605. *Prep Pin Patter.*

KEBEK KOMIK. V. 1- June 1976-. 0700-9054. Periodical. CN. French. ir. 50 Per No. Editions La Feuille de Chou, CP 1845, Succursale Place d Armes, Montreal Quebec H2Y 3L9 Canada. DD 741.59714.

KIDO. Periodical. Japanese. ir. 480. Nihon Kiin, 7-2 Goban, Chiyoda-ku Tokyo 102 Japan. LC GV1459.

KILLSHOT. 0711-7094. Periodical. CN. English. qt. Free to Members. Killshot, c/o Group Sport Office, 160 Vanderhoof Avenue, Toronto Ontario M4G 4B8 Canada. DD 796.3109713.

KING CONAN. Began with No. 1 (March 1980). 0279-0076. Periodical. US. English. mo $12.00. Marvel Comics, 387 Park Avenue South, New York NY 10016. Tel (212)576-9259. Ed Jim Shooter. adv acc. Sword and sorcery adventure in pre-cataclysmic hyperborea featuring the greatest barbarian hero of all time.

LAUGH COMICS DIGEST MAGAZINE. Series/Titl Archie Digest Library. VFOAT Laugh. 8750-0612. Periodical. US. English. bm $6.00 Domestic, $7.50 Canada. Close-Up Inc, 325 Fayette Avenue, Mamovoneck NY 10543.

THE LINKING RING. V. 1- 1923-. 0024-4023. Periodical. US. English. mo. LC GV1541. (cum index).

THE LOG. 0024-5801. Periodical. US. English. mo. $10.00. United States Naval Academy, Annapolis MD 21412. adv acc. Circ 5,500. Humor magazine for midshipmen. Includes humor, satire and entertainment. Most valuable advertising for career, starting assistance firms, e.g. banks, insurances, car dealers and credit cards.

LOISIRS JEUNESSE. No 1- Feb. 15, 1974-. 0381-7113. Periodical. CN. French. ir. $16.25. Loisirs Jeunesse, 5609 rue des Pensees, Montreal H1G 1W1 Canada. Tel (514)321-7264. DD 790.192.

THE LONE STAR HUMOR DIGEST. 8756-7369. Periodical. US. English. ty. $16.00. Lone Star Publications, PO Box 29000/Suite 103, San Antonio TX 78229. Tel (512)433-6076. bk rev adv acc. A humor 'book-by-subscription' for the comedy connoisseur and general reader. Each issue contains jokes, cartoons, essays, reviews, letters and stories. *Lone Star (Houston, Tex. : 1983), 0735-1623.*

LPV; LISTOS PARA VENCER. 1- 1961-. Periodical. CU. Spanish. wk. Empresa Ediciones Cubanas, Sub-Direccion Exportacion, Oreilly 407 Ciudad Habana Cuba.

MAD. Began Nov. 1958. 0024-9319. Periodical. US. English. ir. $10.75. EC Publ Inc, 485 Madison Avenue, New York NY 10022. Tel (212)752-7685. Ed John Ficirra and Nick Meglin. Circ 1,000,000. Funny stuff. *New Mad.*

THE MAGIC DIRECTORY. See Yearbooks, Almanacs, Directories.

MAGIC MAGAZINE. (THE MAGIC MAGAZINE). 0097-5176. Periodical. US. English. mo. $10.00. Magic Industries, 20 East 46th Street, New York NY 10017. LC GV1541. DD 793.8.

MAGYAR SAKKELET. Began in 1951. Periodical. HU. Hungarian. mo. Akademiai Kiado, POB 24, 1363 Budapest Hungary. LC GV1313.

MARVEL AGE. Began in 1983. 8750-4367. Periodical. US. English. mo. Marvel Comics Group, 387 Park Avenue South, New York NY 10016.

MARVEL FANFARE. 0746-7664. Periodical. US. English. bm. $15.00. Marvel Comics Group, 387 Park Avenue South, New York NY 10016.

MARVEL TEAM-UP. VAT Marvel Team Up. V. 1- Mar. 1972-. 0274-5313. Periodical. US. English. mo. $7.80. Marvel Comics, 387 Park Avenue South, New York NY 10016. Tel (212)576-9259. Ed Jim Shooter. adv acc. Circ 250,000. Mystery-suspense adventures set in exotic locales at home and abroad starring everyone's favorite web-slinger.

MASS ENTERTAINMENT BUYERS GUIDE. VFOAT Buyers Guide for the Mass Entertainment Industry. 0748-1675. US. English. $15.00 Each Copy. Amusement Business, 14 Music Circle East, Nashville TN 37203. LC GV1851.A3. DD 338.76179106802573. *Buyers' Guide for the Mass Entertainment Industry, 0362-6180.*

MATOU. (MATOU : LA REVUE DE LA LIGUE D'ECHECS DE L'OUTAOUAIS INC). No 1 (May 1980)-. 0711-2246. Periodical. CN. French. ir. $5.00 Per Issue. c/o G Jobin, 135 rue Lorrain, Buckingham Quebec J8L 1R3 Canada. DD 794.105.

MICHAEL T. GILBERT'S STRANGE BREW. VFOAT Strange Brew. Dec. 1982-. 0820-8840. Periodical. CN. English. qt. Michael T Gilbert's Strange Brew, P O Box 1674 Station C, Kitchener Ontario N2G 4R2 Canada. DD 741.5971.

MINI-JEUX. (LES MINI-JEUX). No. 1- 0711-3307. Periodical. CN. French. ty. $2.50 Per No. Les Mini-Jeux, CP 71 Succursale R, Montreal Quebec H2S 3K8 Canada. DD 793.7305.

MINI RECREATION. (MINI RECREACTION). No. 1-. 0714-489X. Periodical. CN. French. ir. $2.50 Per No. Messageries Dynamiques, 775 Boulevard Lebeau, St-Laurent Quebec H4N 1S5 Canada. DD 793.73.

MOT A TROUVER MYSTERIEUX. VAT Mot Mysterieux Eclair. Vol. 1, No. 2-. 0228-569X. Periodical. CN. French. bm. $6.00. Mot a Trouver Mysterieux Bert-Hold Inc, CP 1050 Succursale Anjou, Montreal Quebec H1K 4H2 Canada. DD 793.7305. *Mot Mystere, 0228-5681.*

MOT MYSTERE. VAT Mot Mystere Eclair. Vol. 1, No 1. 0228-5681. Periodical. CN. French. DD 793.7305.

MOTS A TROUVER POPULAIRES. Vol. 1, No 1-. -. 0228-6475. Periodical. CN. French. qt. $4.00. Distribution Eclair, 8320 Place de Lorraine, Montreal Quebec H1J 1E6 Canada. DD 793.7305.

MOTS A TROUVER RG. No. 1-. 0823-7123. Periodical. CN. French. qt. 10.00 Domestic, 11.00 Foreign. Mots A Trouver RG, 8050 Est Boul Metropolitain, Montreal Quebec H1K 1A1 Canada. Tel (514)353-7660. DD 793.7305. adv acc. Circ 12,000. Crossword book.

MOTS CACHES J'AIME. (LES MOTS CACHES J'AIME). 1-. 0826-4740. Periodical. CN. French. qt. 10.00 Domestic, 11.00 Foreign. Les Mots Caches J'Aime, 8050 Boul Metropolitain Est, Montreal Quebec H1K 1A1 Canada. Tel (514)353-7660. DD 793.73. adv acc. Circ 12,000.

MOTS CACHES SUPERMAGAZINE. Vol. 1, No 1-. 0822-4145. Periodical. CN. French. bm. 13.00. Mots Caches Supermagazine, 8050 Pretropolitan Boulevard East, Montreal Quebec H8K 1A1 Canada. Tel (514)353-7660. DD 793.73. adv acc. Circ 10,000. Crosswords book.

MOTS CROISES ECLAIR. V. 1- Jan. 1977-. 0384-8191. Periodical. CN. French. mo. $1.50 Each Number. Distributions Eclair, 8320 Place de Lorraine, Montreal Quebec H1J 1E4 Canada. DD 793.7305.

MOTS CROISES FRANCAIS ANGLAIS. V. 1, No. 1, (Fall '83)-. 0822-8728. Periodical. CN. English (French). qt. $1.50 Each Number. Mots Croises Francais Anglais c/o Roland Dolce, 580 71st Street East, Charlesbourge Quebec G1H 1M1 Canada. DD 793.73205.

MOTS CROISES POUR TOUT L'MONDE. VFOAT Mots Croises Pour Tout le Monde. Vol. 1, No 1-. 0712-5631. Periodical. CN. French. mo. Mot Croises Pour Tout l'Monde, 9393 Avenue Edison, Montreal Quebec H1J 1T4 Canada. DD 793.73205.

MOTS CROISES T V HEBDO. VFOAT T V Hebdo. No 1 1974-. 0319-7115. Periodical. CN. French. $1.25 Each Number. Les Publications Eclair Ltee, 9393 Av Edison, Montreal Quebec H1J 1T5 Canada. DD 793.73205.

MOTS ENTRE-CROISES POPULAIRES. Vol. 1, No 1-. -. 0228-6483. Periodical. CN. French. qt. $1.00 Each Number. Distributions Eclair, 8320 Place de Lorraine, Montreal Quebec H1J 1E6 Canada. DD 793.7305.

Recreation, Leisure—Games & Amusements

THE NATIONAL OBSERVER BOOK OF CROSSWORDS. 0192-6837. Periodical. US. English. mo. $11.88. CBS Publications, 1515 Broadway, New York NY 10036, (subscription address: Neodata PO Box 2606 Boulder CO 80322). Tel (212)685-5589.

NEW COMIC WORLD. (THE NEW COMIC WORLD). No. 1- 1976-. 0382-7313. Periodical. CN. English. ir. Vast Whizzbang Organization, 594 Markham Street, Toronto Ontario M6G 2L8 Canada. DD 741.5971.

NEW YORK HERALD TRIBUNE CROSSWORD PUZZLES. VFOAT Crossword Puzzles. 0164-1425. US. English. bm. $4.95. I H T Corporation, 850 Third Avenue, New York NY 10022. Tel (212)715-2628. Ed Michelle Arnot. bk rev. adv acc. Circ 100,000. Puzzles and related pastimes, including features on celebrities who enjoy puzzles, reviews of games and books about them.

NEW YORK HERALD TRIBUNE CROSSWORD PUZZLES. POCKET SIZE. VFOAT Crossword Puzzles. Pocket Size. 0195-2641. Periodical. US. English. bm. $4.00. I H T Corporation, 850 Third Avenue, New York NY 10022.

THE NEW YORK TIMES CROSSWORD PUZZLES. VFOAT Crossword Puzzles. V. 1- 1976-. 0364-3700. US. English. Quadrangle/New York Times Book Co, 10 East 53rd Street, New York NY 10022. LC GV1507.C7. DD 793.732.

NO FIXED ADDRESS (LONDON, ONT.). (NO FIXED ADDRESS). Vol. 1 (Aug. 30, 1982)-. 0821-5731. Periodical. CN. English. ir. $6.50 for 10 Issues. No Fixed Address, 704 Brant Street, London Ontario N5Y 3NI Canada. DD 793.705.

NORTHWEST CHESS. VFOAT Northwest Chess Magazine. No. 1- Nov. 1947-. 0146-6941. Periodical. US. English. $12.00. Northwest Chess, PO Box 5370, Lynnwood WA 98046.

OFFICIAL'S FUN PUZZLES. 8755-9293. Periodical. US. English. bm. Official Publications, 201 East 57th Street, New York NY 10022. *Children's Fun Puzzles, 0194-3138.*

ONTARIO CHESS NEWS. Issue 1 (May 1981)-. 0712-2195. Periodical. CN. English. ty. Free to OCA Members, $1.00 Each Number. Ontario Chess News, c/o Erik Malmsten, #1715 620 James Street, Toronto Ontario M4Y 2R8 Canada. DD 794.105.

ORBEN'S COMEDY FILLERS. VFOAT Comedy Fillers. 0048-2099. Periodical. US. English. mo. Comedy Center, PO Box 1992, Wilmington DE 19899. Ed R Orben.

ORBEN'S CURRENT COMEDY. VFOAT Current Comedy. 0048-2102. Periodical. US. English. sm. Comedy Center, Division Reports Inc, 700 Orange Street, Wilmington DE 19801. Tel (302)656-2209. Ed R Orben.

PADUK. Periodical. KO. Korean. mo. 24,000. Hanguk Kiwon, 13-4 Kwanchol-Dong Chongno-Ku, Seoul Korea. LC GV1459.

EN PASSANT. No. 62 (9/10 1983)-. 0822-5672. Periodical. CN. English (includes some text in French). ir. $12.00. En Passant, 289 Olmstead Street/ Suite 2, Vanier Ontario K1L 7G9 Canada. DD 794.106071. *Chess Canada, 0225-7351.*

PENNY PRESS. (THE PENNY PRESS). June 15, 1976-. 0700-9127. Periodical. CN. English (includes some text in French, Sept. 19, 1976-June 5, 1977). The Penny Press, PO Box 4346/Station E, Ottawa Ontario K1S 5B3 Canada. DD 917.1384005.

PEP (MAMARONECK, N.Y.). (PEP). Series/Titl Archie Series. Archie Comics Group. 0031-5060. Periodical. US. English. bm. $3.60 Domestic, $4.50 Canada. Pep, c/o Archie Enterprises Inc, 325 Fayette Avenue, Mamaroneck NY 10543.

PETER PARKER, THE SPECTACULAR SPIDER-MAN. 0273-6632. Periodical. US. English. mo. $7.80. Marvel Comics, 387 Park Avenue South, New York NY 10016. Tel (212)576-9259.

PETIT INTELLECTUEL. (LE PETIT INTELLECTUEL). V. 1- Oct. 1979-. 0709-3497. Periodical. CN. French. bw. 0.75. Editions le Compagnon, CP 143 Succursale A, Hull Quebec J8Y 6M8 Canada. DD 793.7305.

PLASTIZINE. No. 1 (May 1982)-. 0715-5719. Periodical. CN. English. ir. Free. Plastizine c/o Vancouver Comic Book Club, P O Box 48873 Bentall Station, Vancouver British Columbia V7X 1A8 Canada. DD 741.5971134.

PLAY METER. 0162-1343. Periodical. US. English. sm. $50.00. Play Meter, PO Box 24170, New Orleans LA 70184. Tel (504)488-7003. Ed David Pierson. LC HD9993.E453. DD 338.4768824. adv acc. Circ 6,000. Trade magazine for the coin-op amusement game industries. Contains features, interviews, technical information and new products.

POPULAR BRIDGE. V. 1- July/Aug. 1967-. 0032-4450. Periodical. US. English. bm. Miller Magazines Inc, 2660 E Main Street, Ventura CA 93003. Tel (805)643-3664. LC GV1281.

POPULAR CROSSWORDS. 0194-6749. Periodical. US. English. mo. $11.88. CBS Publications, 1515 Broadway, New York NY 10036, (subscription address: Neodata PO Box 2606 Boulder CO 80322). Tel (800)243-8005.

POPULAR WORD GAMES. VFOAT Word Games. 0194-6757. Periodical. US. English. mo. $12.88. CBS Publications, 1515 Broadway, New York NY 10036, (subscription address: Neodata PO Box 2606 Boulder CO 80322).

POST SCRIPTS. 0162-3060. Periodical. US. English. mo. $12.00. Curtis Publishing Company, Bonnie Kanter, 1000 Waterway Boulevard, Indianapolis IN 46202. Tel (317)633-2061. Ed James Thom. Circ 1,500. Wit, wisdom, and amusing anecdotes from cover to cover.

PRISME. VFOAT Revue Prisme. No. 1- March 1976-. 0383-1833. Periodical. CN. French. ir. $1.00 Each Number. Editions Phase, CP 454 Succursale Place d'Armes, Montreal Quebec H2Y 3H3 Canada. DD 741.59714.

PUBLIC GAMING NEWSLETTER. 0196-2558. Periodical. US. English. sm. Public Gaming Research Institute, PO Box 17241, Rockville MD 20850.

QUEBEC AU BOUT DES DOIGTS. V. 1- May 1975-. 0381-6443. Periodical. CN. Multilingual (text in English and French). mo. Publicites Cascades Inc, 1155 Ste-Foy Road, Quebec Quebec G1S 2M8 Canada. DD 790.09714471.

RADIO MODELLER. 0144-0713. Periodical. UK. English. mo. 14.50. Model & Allied Publications, PO Box 35 Bridge Street, Hemel Hempstead England. Tel (0442) 21221. Ed Alec Gee. bk rev. adv acc. All aspects of radio controlled model aircraft e.g. building, flying. Also vintage aircraft, gliders, waterplanes and scale aircraft.

REVUE CEASED. VFOAT Ottawa Arts & Entertainment Revue. June 12, 1977-Nov. 24/30 1977. 0826-0656. Periodical. CN. English (includes some text in French). sw. $38.69. The Penny Press Ltd, PO Box 4346 Station E, Ottawa Ontario K1S 5B3 Canada. Tel (613)563-0151. DD 790.0971384005. *Penny Press, 0700-9127.*

REVUE JEUNESSE. No. 1-. 0711-3455. Periodical. CN. French. ty. $2.50 Per Number. Revue Jeunesse, c/o Les Editions Publi, CP 123 Succursale R, Montreal Quebec H2S 3K6 Canada. DD 793.7305.

REVUE QUEBECOISE DE BRIDGE. (LA REVUE QUEBECOISE DE BRIDGE). Vol. 1, No. 1 (Oct. 1984)-. 0828-5012. Periodical. CN. French. qt. $1.00 Per No. Federation Quebecoise de Bridge, 1415 East rue Jarry, Montreal Quebec H2E 2Z7 Canada. DD 795.41505.

RING-A-WORD PUZZLES. VAT Ring a Word Puzzles. 0194-3189. Periodical. US. English. mo $9.00. Editorial Services Inc, PO Box 687, Old Lyme CT 06371.

RINGETTE REVIEW. (RINGETTE REVIEW : RINGETTE CANADA'S NATIONAL NEWSLETTER). VFOAT Revue Ringuette. Vol. 1, No. 1 (Apr. 1979)-. 0821-5782. Periodical. CN. English (some text in French, 1983-). ir. Free. Ringette Canada, PO Box 2162, Stettler Alberta T0C 2L0 Canada. DD 796.96. (ctrl).

ROBERT CAMPBELL'S SOUP TO NUTS. VFOAT Soup to Nuts. No. 1-. 0227-5953. Periodical. CN. English. mo. $1.00 for 4 Mo. Soup to Nuts, c/o R Campbell, 63 Lanyard Road, Weston Ontario M9M 1Y8 Canada. DD 793.905. *Cheader's Digest, 0703-8186.*

SAHOVSKI GLASNIK. Periodical. YU. Slovak. mo. Sahovska Nakzada, Preradoviceva 18, Zagreb Yugoslavia. Tel 041-273-692. Ed Drazen Marovic. LC GV1313. bk rev. adv acc. Circ 5,500. (ctrl). Chess-review bringing great number of important commented games of international tournaments theoretical news, results and scores, photos, etc.

SCHAAK JAARBOEK. *See* Yearbooks, Almanacs, Directories.

SCRABEQ. (SCRABEQ : LA REVUE DES SCRABBLEURS DU QUEBEC). 1 (Sept./Oct. 81)-. 0710-1724. Periodical. CN. French. bm. $2.00 Per Issue. SCRABEQ, CP 133 Succursale E, Montreal Quebec H2T 3H5 Canada. DD 793.73.

SHAKHMATNYI BIULLETIN. Began publication in 1955. 0037-3230. Periodical. UR. Russian. mo. $27.00. Victor Kamkin Inc (71085), 12224 Parklawn Drive, Rockville MD 20852. Tel (301)881-5973. LC GV1313.

SHAKHMATY V SSSR. 1931-. 0132-0947. Periodical. UR. Russian. mo. $22.50. Victor Kamkin Inc, 12224 Parklawn Drive, Rockville MD 20852. Tel (301)881-5973. LC GV1313. *Shakhmatnyi Listok.*

SHOU HUO. VFOAT Shouhuo. V. 1, (July 1957)- V. 20, (July 1960). Periodical. CC. Chinese. bm. China Publication Centre, PO Box 2820, Beijing China.

SIMGAMES. *See* Education (General) - Special Aspects of Education.

SIMON AND SCHUSTER CROSSWORD PUZZLE BOOK. VAT Simon and Schuster Cross Word Puzzle Book. 0196-7231. US. English. $3.95. Simon & Schuster Building, Rockefeller Center, 1230 Avenue of the Americas, New York NY 10020. LC GV1507.C7. DD 793.7305.

SNAFU (LOW, QUEBEC). (SNAFU). 0715-5522. Periodical. CN. English. ir. $8.00, 10 No. SNAFU, RR #1, Low Quebec J0X 2C0 Canada. DD 794.2.

SOAP OPERA WORD-FIND HIDDEN WORD PUZZLES. VAT Soap Opera Word Find Hidden Word Puzzles. 0194-3197. Periodical. US. English. bm. Official Publications Inc, 201 East 57th Street 3rd Avenue, New York NY 10022. Tel (212)355-5001.

THE SPACE GAMER. 1975. 0194-9977. Periodical. US. English. bm. $23.00. Space Gamer, PO Box 18957, Austin TX 78760. Tel (512)447-7866. Ed Warren Spector. bk rev. adv acc. Circ 5,600. News, reviews, scenarios, designer notes, articles, fiction, humor and other items of interest to adventure gamers (players of science fiction and fantasy games).

SPECHECS. (SPECHECS : BULLETIN DU CLUB LE SPECIALISTE DES ECHECS). No. 1 (Dec. 1979)-. 0227-0846. Periodical. CN. French. ir. $2.00 Each Number. Spechecs, 1111 Est Boul. de Maisonneuve, Montreal Quebec H2L 1Z6 Canada. DD 794.1060714281.

STANFORD WONG'S BLACKJACK NEWSLETTER. VFOAT Blackjack Newsletter. 0197-5595. Periodical. US. English. mo. $75.00. Pi Yee Press, 7910 Ivanhoe #34, La Jolla CA 92037.

STAR WARS. No. 1-. 0274-5356. Periodical. US. English. mo. $7.80. Marvel Comics, 387 Park Avenue South, New York NY 10016. Tel (212)576-9259. Ed Jim Shooter. adv acc. Circ 130,000. Luke Skywalker, Han Solo, Princess Leia and the rest of the heroes made famous by George Lucas' ''Star Wars'' trilogy continue their adventures throughout the universe.

STARLOG PRESENTS COMICS SCENE. VFOAT Comics Scene. 0732-5622. Periodical. US. English. bm. $11.98 US/Canada, $16.00 Others. Comics Scence, 75 Park Avenue South, New York NY 10016. LC WMLC L 83/292.

STARSLAYER. Began in 1983?. 0746-6552. Periodical. US. English. mo. $11.00 Domestic, $13.75 Canada. First Comics Inc, 1014 Davis Street, Evanston IL 60201.

SUPER MAZE CRAZE PUZZLE PICTURES. VFOAT Super Maze Craze. 0732-5657. Periodical. US. English. $7.50. Canam Media Inc, 151 Hempstead Turnpike, West Hempstead NY 11552.

SUPERB CROSSWORD PUZZLES. VFOAT Crossword Puzzles. 0194-3219. Periodical. US. English. bm. Official Publication Company, 201 East 57th 3rd Avenue, New York NY 10022. Tel (212)355-5001.

SUPERB FILL-IT-INS. VFOAT Fill-It-Ins. VAT Superb Fill It Ins. 0194-3227. Periodical. US. English. mo. Official Publications Inc, 201 East 57th 3rd Avenue, New York NY 10022. Tel (212)355-5001.

SUPERB WORD-FIND PUZZLES. VFOAT Word-Find Puzzles. VAT Superb Word Find Puzzles. 0194-3235. Periodical. US. English. mo. $9.60. Official Publications, 201 East 57th 3rd Avenue, New York NY 10022. Tel (212)355-5001.

Recreation, Leisure—Outdoor Life

SUPERB WORD-TWISTS. VAT Superb Word Twists. 0199-218X. Periodical. US. English. bm. Official Publications Inc, 201 East 57th 3rd Avenue, New York NY 10022. Tel (212)355-5001.

SYSTEMS & METHODS. VAT Systems and Methods. V. 1-. 0161-2530. Periodical. US. English. bm. $10.00. GBC Press, 630 South 11th Street, PO Box 4115, Las Vegas NV 89127. LC GV1302. DD 795.01.

TEEN WORD-FINDS. VAT Teen Word Finds. 0194-326X. Periodical. US. English. bm. $6.00. Office Publications Inc, PO Box 1231, Stamford CT 06904.

THOSE ANNOYING POST BROS. VFOAT Post Bros. No. 1 (Jan. 1985)-. 0827-4703. Periodical. CN. English. bm. $2.25 Each Number. Vortex Comics, 9th Floor/96 Spadina Avenue, Toronto Ontario M5V 2J6 Canada. DD 741.5971.

TOURNAMENT CHESS. Vol. 1 1982-. 0276-7090. Periodical. UK. English. qt. 54.00. Tui Enterprises, 35 Ceres Road, Plumstead London SE 18 1HR England. Tel 316-1484. Ed Nigel Davies. LC GV1455. DD 794.157. adv acc. Circ 1,000. Provides quick and accurate coverage of the strongest modern grandmaster tournaments, plus a major openings survey. Completely indexed. Ideal for aspiring or established internationals.

TOYS & GAMES. See Gifts, Toys.

TRANSFORMERS (NEW YORK, N.Y.). (THE TRANSFORMERS). VFOAT Trans Formers. Began with: 1 (Sept. 1984). 0887-5960. Periodical. US. English. mo. Marvel Comics Group, 387 Park Avenue South, New York NY 10016.

TRUE MARKET PRICE GUIDE TO COMIC BOOK RETAIL VALUES. 1973/74-. 0317-6657. CN. English. an. 'True Market" Price Guide to Comic Book Retail Values, 5165 Metropolitan Boulevard East, Montreal Quebec H1R 1Z7 Canada. DD 381.4574159029.

TVB. (T V B). Began with Jan. 1977 issue (No. 4). 0703-8178. Periodical. CN. English. ir. $1.00. Games by Mail, 48 Elsfield Road, Toronto Ontario M8Y 3R5 Canada. DD 793. Vulgar Bloatman, 0705-7024.

THE UNCANNY X-MEN. VFOAT X-Men. VAT Uncanny X Men. No. 114- Oct. 1978-. 0274-5372. Periodical. US. English. mo. $7.80. Marvel Comics, 387 Park Ave South, New York NY 10016. Tel (212)576-9259. Ed Jim Shooter. adv acc. Circ 430,000. A group of young mutant outcasts from all over the world band together at Professor Xavier's school for gifted youngsters and use their varied superpowers to protect humanity from itself. X-Men.

VARIETY WORD-FIND PUZZLES. VAT Variety Word Find Puzzles. 0194-3286. Periodical. US. English. mo. Official Publications Inc, 201 East 57th 3rd Avenue, New York NY 10022. Tel (212)355-5001.

VENDING TIMES. V. 1- 1961-. 0042-3327. Periodical. US. English. mo. $25.00. Vending Times Inc, 545 8th Avenue, New York NY 10018. Tel (212)714-0101. Ed Arthur E Yohalem. Ind/Abst Trade Ind. Index, Predicasts, Funk Scott Index Corp. Ind. bk rev. adv acc. Circ 15,000. (ctrl). Covers vending, coin-operated music and amusement machines, and coffee service fields. Vend, V/T Music & Games.

VIDEOMANIA. VFOAT Video. Vol. 1, No. 1-. 0711-7914. Periodical. CN. English. mo. $23.21. Videomania Publ Company, 920 Alness Street/Suite 110, Downsview Ontario M3J 2H7 Canada. Ed Salah Bachir. DD 778.59905. bk rev. adv acc. Circ 38,000. Video and home entertainment monthly with focus on films and video hardware. Background and interviews with film personalities and test reports of new equipment.

VORTEX (TORONTO, ONT.). (VORTEX). Vol. 1 No. 1 (Nov. 1982)-. 0823-7034. Periodical. CN. English. bm. $1.95 Each Number. Vortex Magazine, 93A Bloor Street West, Toronto Ontario M5S 1Y2 Canada. DD 741.5971.

VOTRE BOTTIN DE CROSSE. See Recreation, Leisure - Sports.

THE WARGAMER. 8750-3433. Periodical. US. English. mo. $72.00. 3W Inc, PO Box F, Cambria CA 93428. Tel (805)927-5439. Ed Keith Poulter. bk rev. adv acc. Circ 8,500. The leading publisher of games, reviews, and articles for historical board game players. Each issue contains a new and complete game.

WARP. Began in 1983?. 0746-6544. Periodical. US. English. mo. $11.00 Domestic, $13.75 Canada. First Comics Inc, 1014 Davis Street, Evanston IL 60201.

THE WHITE TOPS. 1929. 0043-499X. Periodical. US. English. bm. $15.00. Circus Fans Association of America, PO Box 69, Camp Hill PA 17011. Tel (717)761-4819. Ed James G Saunders. bk rev. adv acc. Circ 2,600. (ctrl). Past and present history of the circus. News items regarding the local Tent and Top activities of the members and legislation as it relates to circus animals. Chatter from Around the White Tops.

WINNING. Jan. 1977-. 0700-4990. Periodical. CN. English. bm. $8.00. Winning, Box 263 La Salle Station, Niagara Falls NY 14304. DD 795.01. Gambling Quarterly, 0316-6163.

WINNING. 0744-2467. Periodical. US. English. mo. $12.00. National Reporter Publishers Inc, 15115 South 76th Avenue, Bixby OK 74008. Tel (918)366-4441. Ed Andre Hinds. bk rev. adv acc. Circ 250,000. Tips on winning contests, sweepstakes, and lotteries, including monthly listings of current sweepstakes and lotteries.

WORD WAYS. See Linguistics.

WORLD'S FINEST COMICS. VFOAT World's Finest. 0745-1326. Periodical. US. English. mo. DC Comics Inc, PO Box 1308F Department R6, Fort Lee NJ 07024.

YUKON KOMIX. Vol. 1, No. 1-. 0229-0383. Periodical. CN. English. J Lodder, PO Box 87, Dawson Yukon Y0B 1G0 Canada. DD 741.5971.

ZANY WORD SEARCH & FIND PUZZLES. VFOAT Zany Word Search and Find Puzzles. 0732-5649. Periodical. US. English. ir. Can-Am Media Inc, 313 West 53rd Street, New York NY 10019.

OUTDOOR LIFE

ACCIDENTS IN NORTH AMERICAN MOUNTAINEERING. Began in 1968. 0065-082X. US. English. an. $4.00. American Alpine Club, 113 East 90th Street, New York NY 10028. LC GV199.8. DD 363.14. Accidents in American Mountaineering.

THE ADIRONDAC. VFOAT Ad-I-Ron-Dac. V. 1- 1937-. 0001-8236. Periodical. US. English. mo. $15.00. Adirondack Mountain Club Inc, 172 Ridge Street, Glens Falls NY 12801. Tel (513)793-7737. Ed Neal Burdick. bk rev. adv acc. Circ 8,500. Promotes preservation, conservation and education in the 6 million acre Adirondack state park. Focus on history, hiking, backpacking, skiing, snowshoeing, ecology and current issues.

ADVENTURE GUIDE. VFOAT Saskatchewan Adventure Guide. 0826-9513. CN. English. Free. Saskatchewan Tourism And Renewable Resources, 3211 Albert Street, Regina Saskatchewan S4S 5W6 Canada. LC GV191.46.S2. DD 647.947124.

ALABAMA GAME & FISH. VAT Alabama Game and Fish. 0279-6783. Periodical. US. English. mo. $11.95. Game & Fish Publications, P O Box 741, Marietta GA 30061. Tel (404)953-9222.

ALASKA. V. 35, No. 10- Oct. 1969-. 0002-4562. Periodical. US. English. mo. $21.00. Alaska Northwest Publishing Company, 130 2nd Avenue South, Edmonds WA 98020. Tel (206)774-4111. Ed Tom Gresham. Ind/Abst Pop. Mag. Rev., GeoRef, Mag. Index, Access. LC SK1. DD 799.09798. adv acc. Circ 160,000. Captures the vitality and excitement of Alaskan life... news, stories and superb color photography! Special hunting and travel issues each year. Alaska Sportsman.

ALASKA FISHING GUIDE. 0361-3984. US. English. $3.95. Alaska Northwest Pub Co, Box 4-EEE, Anchorage AK 99509. LC SH467. DD 799.109798.

ALASKA HUNTING GUIDE. 0095-5760. US. English. an. $3.95. Alaska Northwest Publishing Company, Box 4-EEE, Anchorage AK 99506. LC SK49. DD 799.209798.

ALASKA OUTDOORS. 1978. 0274-8282. Periodical. US. English. bm. $12.95. Swensens Publishing Company, PO Box 6324, Anchorage AK 99502. Tel (907)276-2672. Ed Christopher M Batin. bk rev. adv acc. Circ 300,000. If it's in the outdoors and in Alaska, it's in Alaska Outdoors.

ALGOMA OUTDOORS. 1977-. 0707-3151. CN. English. an. Free. Algoma Kinniwabi Travel Association, 553 Queen Street East Sault Ste, Marie Ontario P6A 2A3 Canada. DD 917.13132044. (ctrl).

ALMANACH CHASSE ET PECHE. See Yearbooks, Almanacs, Directories.

ALMANACH DE KUYPER DE CHASSE ET PECHE. See Yearbooks, Almanacs, Directories.

ALPES (QUARTERLY). (LES ALPES : REVUE DU CLUB ALPIN SUISSE). VFOAT Alpi, Le Alpi : Rivista del Club Alpino Svizzero. Began in 1957. Periodical. SZ. French (German, Italian, and Romansh). qt. 40.00. Hallerstrasse 79, Postfach 2728, CH 3001 Berne Switzerland. LC DQ820. DD 914.947005.

ALPINE JOURNAL. (THE ALPINE JOURNAL). V. 1- March 1863-. 0065-6569. UK. English. an. 16.00. West Col Productions, Goring Reading, Berks RG8 9AA England. Ind/Abst GeoRef, Bibliogr. Index Geol. LC DQ821. DD 949.47005. (cum index). bk rev. adv acc. Circ 3,500. Is unique in mountain literature. Published as a record of mountain adventure and scientific observation and follows peaks, passes and glaciers.

ALTITUDES MONT TREMBLANT (1981). (ALTITUDES MONT TREMBLANT). VFOAT Altitudes. VAT Altitudes (Mont Tremblant). Vol. 2, No. 4 (July 1981)-. 0711-5857. Periodical. CN. English (French in parallel columns). ir. $10.00. Altitudes Mont Tremblant, Publications Altitude Mont Tremblant, PO Box 284, Mont-Tremblant Quebec J0T 1Z0 Canada. DD 971.424005. Mont-Tremblant Altitudes, 0227-4477.

THE A.M.C. MAINE MOUNTAIN GUIDE. Main/Corp Appalachian Mountain Club. VFOAT Maine Mountain Guide. VAT Appalachian Mountain Club Maine Mountain Guide. 1st- Ed. 0514-9738. Periodical. US. English. ir. Appalachian Mountain Club, 5 Joy Street, Boston MA 02108. LC F17.3. DD 917.410443. A.M.C. Katahdin Guide.

THE AMERICAN ALPINE JOURNAL. V. 1- 1929-. 0065-6925. Periodical. US. English. an. Ind/Abst Int. Aerosp. Abstr., GeoRef.

AMERICAN FIELD. 1874. 0002-8452. Periodical. US. English. wk. $22.00. American Field, 222 West Adams Street, Chicago IL 60606. Tel (312)372-1383. Ed William F Brown Sr. LC Ski. bk rev. adv acc. Circ 13,000. Sporting dog and hunting magazine, field trials and bird dog competition. Chicago Field.

AMERICAN HIKER. (AMERICAN HIKER : THE OFFICIAL PUBLICATION OF THE AMERICAN HIKING SOCIETY AND INTERNATIONAL BACKPACKERS ASSOCIATION). Vol. 1, No. 1 (Mar., 1981)-. 0279-9472. Periodical. US. English. bm. $6.00. The American Hiking Society, 1701 18th Street NW, Washington DC 20009. Tel (202)234-4609. American Hiking Society News, 0164-5722.

AMERICAN HUNTER. (THE AMERICAN HUNTER). V. 1- Oct. 1973-. 0092-1068. Periodical. US. English. mo. $40.00. National Rifle Association of America, 1600 Rhode Island Avenue NW, Washington DC 20036. Tel (800)368-5714. LC SK1. DD 799.205.

AMERICAN RIFLEMAN. See Recreation, Leisure - Sports.

THE AMERICAN SHOTGUNNER. See Recreation, Leisure - Sports.

AMERICANA (BRAUNSCHWEIG, GERMANY). (AMERICANA : ZEITSCHRIFT FUR INDIANISTIK-CORRAL BRAUNSCHWEIG). Began in 1981?. Periodical. GW. German. qt. $13.80. Americana, Schuetzenstrasse 15/M Grieger, D33 Braunschweig West Germany. Tel 531-43146.

ANDERSON'S CAMPGROUND DIRECTORY. See Yearbooks, Almanacs, Directories.

ANGLER & HUNTER IN ONTARIO. (THE ANGLER & HUNTER IN ONTARIO). V. 1, No. 2- V. 3, No. 10. 0700-5032. Periodical. CN. English. mo. $22.44. Ontario Outdoor Publishing Ltd, Box 1541, Peterborough Ontario K9J 7H7 Canada. Tel (705)748-3891. Ed Jack Davis. DD 799.09713. bk rev. adv acc. Circ 54,000. Informative and entertaining fiction pertaining to fishing, hunting, wildlife and environmental concerns, plus official news of the Ontario Federation of Anglers and Hunters (OFAH). Angler & Hunter, 0700-5024.

Recreation, Leisure—Outdoor Life

L'ANNEE MONTAGNE. 1981-82-. FR. French. an. Editions Acla, 7 rue de Lille, Paris France 75007. LC GV199.8. DD 796.522.

ANNUAL FINANCIAL REPORT - SOUTH DAKOTA DEPARTMENT OF WILDLIFE, PARKS AND FORESTRY. Main/Corp South Dakota. Dept. of Wildlife, Parks and Forestry. US. English. an. Department of Wildlife Parks and Forestry, Sigurd Anderson Building, Pierre SD 57501. LC SK447. DD 353.9783007231. *Annual Financial Report - South Dakota Department of Game, Fish and Parks, 0146-8987.*

ANNUAL PROGRESS REPORT (DENVER WILDLIFE RESEARCH CENTER). (ANNUAL PROGRESS REPORT). VFOAT Annual Report. US. English. an. LC SB993. DD 639.905.

ANNUAL REPORT OF SURVEY-INVENTORY ACTIVITIES. Main/Corp Alaska. Division of Game. 0362-6962. US. English. an. Alaska Department of Fish and Game, PO Box 32000, Juneau AK 99802. LC SK367. DD 353.979800823305.

ANNUAL SPRING BROWSE UTILIZATION SURVEY. SOUTH DAKOTA. (ANNUAL SPRING BROWSE UTILIZATION SURVEY : SOUTH DAKOTA). Periodical. US. English. an.

APPALACHIA (APPALACHIAN MOUNTAIN CLUB : 1876). (APPALACHIA). V. 1- (No. 1-). 0003-6587. Periodical. US. English. sa. Applachian Mountain Club, 5 Joy Street, Boston MA 02108. Ind/Abst GeoRef, Bibliogr. Agric. LC G505. (cum index).

APPALACHIAN TRAILWAY NEWS. See Conservation & Natural Resources.

THE APPALACHIAN VOICE. See Conservation & Natural Resources.

AUSTRALIAN GEM & TREASURE HUNTER. VAT Australian Gem and Treasure Hunter. No. 43-. 0159-6322. Periodical. AT. English. mo. $16.23. Gemcraft, 291-295 Wattletree Road, East Malvern Victoria 3145 Australia. Tel 03-5091181. Ed Gladys Rangott. Ind/Abst GeoRef. bk rev. adv acc. Circ 12,000. Family outdoor activities of prospecting, mining, detecting, gold prospecting, treasure hunting, gemstones and minerals, camping, etc. *Australian Gems & Crafts Magazine.*

BACKPACKER (ZIFF-DAVIS PUBLISHING COMPANY : 1980). (BACKPACKER). V. 8, No. 5 (Oct./Nov. 1980)-. 0277-867X. Periodical. US. English. bm. Backpacker, Ziff-Davis Publishing Co, 1 Park Avenue, New York NY 10016. Ind/Abst Mag. Index, Pop. Mag. Rev., Consum. Index Prod. Eval. Inf. Source. *Backpacker including Wilderness Camping, 0199-3097.*

BACKPACKING JOURNAL. V. 1- Spring/Summer 1975-. 0098-3594. Periodical. US. English. qt. $5.95 US, $6.95 Foreign. Backpacking Journal, Box 1885 GPO, New York NY 10001. LC GV199.6. DD 796.5.

BADGER SPORTSMAN. 1943. 0005-3775. Periodical. US. English. mo. $6.00. Vereauteren Publishing, 19 East Main Street, Chilton WI 53014. Tel (414)849-4651. Ed Mark Ibach. bk rev. adv acc. Circ 18,600. A fishing, hunting and camping guide to Wisconsin and the midwest.

B.C. NATURALIST. See Conservation & Natural Resources.

BC OUTDOORS. (B C OUTDOORS). V. 23, No. 4- July/Aug. 1967-. 0045-3013. Periodical. CN. English. mo. $21.01. Special Interest Publications, 202-1132 Hamilton Street, Vancouver British Columbia V6B 2S2 Canada. Tel (604)687-1581. Ed Henry L Frew. Ind/Abst Can. Environ., Can. Period. Index. bk rev. adv acc. Circ 35,000. Outdoor recreation in BC - fishing, camping, hunting, hiking, cross-country skiing, backroad travel, wildlife, conservation, outdoor equipment, and book reviews. *British Columbia Digest, 0382-5639.*

BERGWELT. Jan. 1974-. 0340-1294. German. ir. 36.00. Berverlag R Rother, 8 Munchen 19 Landshuter Allee 49, Munchen W Germany. LC DQ820. *Winter, Bergkamerad, 0005-8939.*

BOWBENDER MAGAZINE. VFOAT Bowbender. Vol. 1 (Aug. 1984)-. 0827-2638. Periodical. CN. English. qt $2.00. Bowbender Magazine, PO Box 912, Carstairs Alberta T0M 0N0 Canada. Tel (403)337-3023. Ed Kathleen Windsor. DD 799.32097123. bk rev. adv acc. Circ 10,000. Intended to provide information and enjoyment for the archery enthusiast. Regardless of the type of bow, shafting, shooting style or pursuit, if your launching of arrows employs healthy and responsible attitudes, then we salute you.

BOWHUNTING GUIDE. VAT Bow Hunting Guide. 1979/80-. 0197-0488. US. English. Aqua-Field Publications, 728 Beaver Dam Road, Point Pleasant NJ 08742. LC SK36. DD 799.20285.

THE BRITISH ARCHER. V. 1- June/July 1949-. Periodical. UK. English. bm. $16.00 US. BA Publishing Company Ltd, 74 South Street, Reading RG1 4RA England. Tel (0734) 55444. Ed John Histead. bk rev. adv acc. Circ 3,000. A magazine for target and field archers.

BRITISH COLUMBIA SPORTSMAN. VAT B.C. Sportsman. Vol. 10, No. 1 (Mar. 1980)-. 0228-815X. Periodical. CN. English. qt. DD 799.09711. *BCWF Newsletter, 0228-8141.*

BRUCE TRAIL NEWS. (THE BRUCE TRAIL NEWS). Began publication in 196-. 0383-9249. Periodical. CN. English. ty. $3.86. Bruce Trail Association, PO Box 857, Hamilton Ontario L8N 3N9 Canada. Tel (416)529-6821. DD 796.5105.

BUCK FOR WILDLIFE. ANNUAL REPORT. (BUCK FOR WILDLIFE : ANNUAL REPORT). Main/Corp Alberta. Fish and Wildlife Division. 0712-3604. CN. English. an. Alberta Recreation Parks and Wildlife/Fish and Wildlife Division, Sun Building, 10363 - 108 Street, Edmonton T5J 1L7 Canada. LC SK471.A3.

BUL' D'AIR. (BUL' D'AIR : BULLETIN D'INFORMATION DE PLEIN AIR DU CONSEIL DES LOISIRS DE L'EST DU QUEBEC). 0228-4545. Periodical. CN. French. bw. Free. C.L.E.Q., 100 Ouest rue de l'Eveche, Rimouski Quebec G5L 4H7 Canada. DD 790.097147.

BULLETIN A L'USAGE DES TRAPPEURS. See Recreation, Leisure - Sports.

BULLETIN - UNION INTERNATIONALE DES ASSOCIATIONS D'ALPINISME. Main/Corp International Union of Alpine Associations. Periodical. English, French or German. ir. 20.00. International Union of Alpine Associations, 29 rue des Delices, Geneva 1211 Switzerland. LC DQ820. DD 914.94700621.

CACHE CREEK CHECK. Series/Titi Wildlife Management Harvest Statistics. 1970-. 0317-4425. Periodical. CN. English. an. DD 799.29711.

CALEDON COMMENT. (CALEDON COMMENT : THE MAGAZINE OF THE CALEDON HILLS BRUCE TRAIL CLUB). 0821-235X. Periodical. CN. English. qt. Free to Members. Caledon Hills Bruce Trail Club, PO Box 302, Waterloo Ontario N2Y 4A4 Canada. DD 796.51060713535.

CALIFORNIA EXPLORER. See Travel.

CAMP DIRECTORY. See Yearbooks, Almanacs, Directories.

CAMPBOOK. EASTERN CANADA. VFOAT Eastern Canada Campbook. Began with 1980. US. English. an. 8111 Gatehouse Road, Falls Church VA 22047. LC GV191.46.M4. DD 647.9471. *Eastern Canada Camping.*

CAMPBOOK. MIDEASTERN. VFOAT Camp Book. Mideastern. Began with issue for 1980. 0734-2705. US. English. an. American Automobile Association, 8111 Gatehouse Road, Falls Church VA 22047. LC GV191.42.A84. DD 647.9474. *Mideastern Camping, 0147-7285.*

CAMPBOOK. NORTH CENTRAL. VFOAT Camp Book. 0732-2585. US. English. an. American Automobile Association, 8111 Gatehouse Road, Falls Church VA 22047. LC GV198.65.N67. DD 647.9477. *North Central Camping, 0147-8613.*

CAMPBOOK. NORTHEASTERN. VFOAT Camp Book. 0732-7315. US. English. an. American Automobile Association, 8111 Gatehouse Road, Falls Church VA 22047. LC GV191.42.N74. DD 917.4. *Northeastern Camping, 0196-6456.*

CAMPBOOK. NORTHWESTERN. VFOAT Camp Book. 0732-2577. US. English. an. American Automobile Association, 8111 Gatehouse Road, Falls Church CA 22047. LC GV191.35. DD 647.9779. *Northwestern Camping, 0095-4411.*

CAMPBOOK. SOUTH CENTRAL. Began with 1980 Ed. 0731-535X. US. English. an. American Automobile Association, 8111 Gatehouse Road, Falls Church VA 22047. LC GV198.65.S68. DD 647.94767. *South Central Camping.*

CAMPBOOK. SOUTHEASTERN. VFOAT Camp Book. Began with 1980 Ed. 0731-5112. US. English. an. American Automobile Association, 8111 Gatehouse Road, Falls Church VA 22047. LC GV191.42.S83. DD 647.9475. *Southeastern Camping, 0162-9166.*

CAMPBOOK. SOUTHWESTERN. VFOAT Camp Book. Began with 1980 Ed. 0731-8103. US. English. an. American Automobile Association, 8111 Gatehouse Road, Falls Church VA 22047. LC GV191.42.A165. DD 6479479. *Southwestern Camping, 0094-2855.*

CAMPBOOK. WESTERN CANADA AND ALASKA. VFOAT Camp Book. Began in 1980. 0732-5347. US. English. an. American Automobile Association, 8111 Gatehouse Road, Falls Church VA 22047. LC GV198.67.C2. DD 647.9471. *Western Canada. Alaska Camping.*

CAMPER'S GUIDE TO AREA CAMPGROUNDS. 0094-0054. US. English. be. $3.95. M B Pearsall, Box 305, Hillsdale IL 61257. LC GV191.42.M53. DD 917.7043.

CAMPGROUND & TRAILER PARK DIRECTORY. UNITED STATES, CANADA, MEXICO. See Yearbooks, Almanacs, Directories.

CAMPING CANADA. V. 1- 1972-. 0384-9856. Periodical. CN. English. an. 11.00. CRV Publishing, 3414 Park Avenue, Montreal Quebec H2X 245 Canada. Tel (514)282-0191. Ed Reg Fife. DD 917.104644. adv acc. Circ 56,000. (ctrl).

CAMPING, CARAVANING FRANCE. VFOAT Camping, Caravaning. French (introductory material in English, German, and Dutch). ir. Pneu Michelin, 46 Avenue de Breteuil, 75341 Paris Cedex 07 France. LC GV191.48.F8. DD 914.404837. *Camping, Caravanning en France.*

CAMPING CLUES. 0822-6474. Periodical. CN. English. ir. Town Talk Publications, 89 Oriole Parkway, Toronto Ontario M5P 2G7 Canada. DD 796.542. *Town Talk About Toronto Presents Camping Clues, 0822-6466.*

CAMPING DIRECTORY - ONTARIO PRIVATE CAMPGROUND ASSOCIATION. See Yearbooks, Almanacs, Directories.

CAMPING FHUHRER BAND II : DEUTSCHLAND, MITTEL- UND NORD-EUROPA. VFOAT Campingfuhrer Band II: Deutschland, Mittel- und Nordeuropa. VAT Camping Fuhrer Bank Zwei: Deutschland, Mittel- und Nord-Europa. German. ir. Postfach 70 00 86, 8 Munich 70 West Germany. LC GV191.48.E8.

CAMPING-FUHRER. BAND 1 : SUDEUROPA. German. an. Free. ADAC Verlag, 8 Munchen 70, Postfach 70 00 86, Munchen West Germany. Tel (089)76762315. Ed Horst Nitschke. LC GV198.67.E855. adv acc. Circ 251,000. (ctrl). Guide to European camping-sites, based on accurate inspection and research. Insertions: multicoloured map; special brochure with listings of campingsites ordered into fields of interest.

CAMPING HOTLINE. 8755-9773. Periodical. US. English. mo. Free to Members, $15.00 Others. HAP Enterprises Inc, 500 Hyacinth Place, Highland Park IL 60035. LC GV191.4. DD 796.540973. *Woodall's Camping Hotline, 0277-0075.*

CAMPING IN THE NATIONAL PARK SYSTEM. Began with 1965. US. English. an. Superintendent of Documents, US Government Printing Office, Washington DC 20402. *Camping Facilities in Areas Administered by the National Park Service.*

CAMPING JOURNAL. 0527-446X. Periodical. US. English. mo.

CAMPING MAGAZINE. (THE CAMPING MAGAZINE). V. 1- Jan. 1930-. 0740-4131. Periodical. US. English. ir. American Camping Association, 5000 State Road 67 North, Martinsville IN 46151. Tel (317)342-8456. Ed Glenn Job. Ind/Abst Read. Guide Period. Lit., Mag. Index. LC SK601.A1. adv acc. Circ 8,000. Issued in microform by University Microfilms International. Ideas in area of organized camping for camping professionals. *Camping (Cambridge, Mass.).*

CAMPING MAPS, CANADA. 0575-7584. CN. English. LC G1116.E6.

Recreation, Leisure—Outdoor Life

CAMPING QUATRO RODAS. 1980-. Portuguese. ir. Editora Abril Ltda, Caixa Postal 5095, Sao Paulo SP 7 CEP 01390 Brazil. **LC** GV191.48.B6. **DD** 647.9481.

CAMPNEWS. (CAMPNEWS : OFFICIAL PUBLICATION OF THE PATRIOTIC ORDER SONS OF AMERICA). **VFOAT** Camp News. 0746-1259. Periodical. US. English. bm. Patriotic Order Sons of America, 115 Rochelle Avenue, Philadelphia PA 19128.

CANADIAN ALPINE JOURNAL. (THE CANADIAN ALPINE JOURNAL). **VFOAT** Journal Alpin Canadien. V. 1- 1907-. 0068-8207. Periodical. CN. English. an. 14.00. Alpine Club of Canada, PO Box 1026, Banff Alberta T0L0C0 Canada. **Tel** (403)762-4481. Ed Moira Irvine. **Ind/Abst** GeoRef, Bibliogr. Index Geol. **DD** 796.5220971. **CODEN** CNAJA6. bk rev. (ctrl). Canadian mountaineering journal and expeditions.

CANADIAN CAMPER. (THE CANADIAN CAMPER). V. 3, Issue 4- July 1970-. 0316-280X. Periodical. CN. English. bm. $2.32. Canadian Family Camping Federation, Box 397, Rexdale Ontario Canada. *C.F.C.F. News for the Canadian Camper, 0045-4729.*

CANADIAN CAMPING. Began with Feb. 1949 issue. 0008-3119. Periodical. CN. English (includes some text in French). qt. $4.65. Canadian Camping Association, 1806 Avenue Road/Suite 2, Toronto Ontario M5M 3Z1 Canada. **Tel** (416)781-4717. Ed Jay Haddad. bk rev. adv acc. **Circ** 2,000. (ctrl). Organized children's camps in Canada- fitness at camp, standards, camping advisor, letters to the editor, environment, etc.

CASCADES EAST. V. 1- May 1976-. 0194-8954. Periodical. US. English. qt. $8.00. Sun Publishing Co, PO Box 5784 716 Northeast 4th Street, Bend OR 97708. **Tel** (503)382-0127. Ed Geoff Hill. bk rev. adv acc. For all ages as long as they are interested in outdoor recreation in Central Oregon: fishing, hunting, sight-seeing, hiking, bicycling, mountain climbing, backpacking, rockhouding, skiing, snowmobiling, etc.

CHURCH CAMPING (TORONTO, ONT.). (CHURCH CAMPING). 0713-3650. Periodical. CN. English. ir. Free. United Church of Canada, Division of Mission in Canada, 85 St Clair Avenue East, Toronto Ontario M4T 1M8 Canada. **DD** 796.5422.

CINEMA SOCIETA. N. 1- June 1966-. 0009-7152. Periodical. IT. Italian. qt. Cinema Societa, Via Monte Cervialto 102, 00139 Rome Italy.

CINEMANTICS. No. 1- Jan. 1970-. Periodical. UK. English. qt. 117 Hartfield Road, London SW19 England.

C.O.E.Q. JOURNAL. *See* Education (General).

COLEMAN GUIDE TO CAMPING & THE GREAT OUTDOORS. **VFOAT** Coleman Guide to Camping and the Great Outdoors. 0734-7251. Periodical. US. English. $2.50 Domestic, $2.95 Foreign. Aqua-Field Publications Inc, PO Box 721, 728 Beaver Dam Road, Point Pleasant NJ 08742. **LC** GV191.68. **DD** 796.5405. *Coleman Outdoor Annual, 0195-3958.*

COLORADO OUTDOORS. V. 1- Jan./Feb. 1952-. 0010-1699. Periodical. US. English. bm. Division of Wildlife, 6060 Broadway, Denver CO 80216. **Tel** (303)297-1192. Ed Charles Hjelte. **Ind/Abst** Energy Inf. Abstr., Environ. Abstr. **Circ** 60,000. Articles on conservation of animals, fish, soil forests and camping, hunting, fishing and related outdoor activities in Colorado. *Colorado Conservation, Colorado Conservation Comments.*

COLORADO WILDLIFE RESEARCH REVIEW. 1977-1979-. 0276-8992. US. English. $1.50. Research Center Library, Division of Wildlife, 317 West Prospect, Fort Collins CO 80526. **LC** SK375. **DD** 596.0978805. *Colorado Game Research Review.*

CONNECTICUT WALK BOOK. Series Corp Connecticut Forest and Park Association. Publication. 1st- Ed. 0092-5764. US. English. $3.50. Connecticut Forest and Park Association, 1010 Main Street, East Hartford CT 06108-8537. **Tel** (203)289-3637. Ed John E Hibbard. **LC** SD1, F92.3. **DD** 333.7809746, 917.46044. Scenery, wildlife, and outdoor recreation in Connecticut.

CORD SPORTSFACTS HUNTING. (CORD SPORTSFACTS : HUNTING). **VFOAT** Hunting. 0092-8216. US. English. an. $2.25. Cord Communications Corp, 25 West 43rd Street, New York NY 10036. **Tel** (212)695-5525. **LC** SK1. **DD** 799.205.

COURANT. (LE COURANT : BULLETIN DE LA FEDERATION QUEBECOISE DU CANOT-CAMPING). June/July 1982-. 0712-4570. Periodical. CN. French. bm. 14.00. Federation Quebecoise du Canot-Camping, 4545 Pierre de Coubertin, C P 1000 Succ M, Montreal Quebec H1V 3R2 Canada. **Tel** (514)252-3001. **DD** 797.122060714. adv acc. **Circ** 2,000. (ctrl). Recreational canoeing and canoe camping activities in Quebec province. *Contre-Courant (Federation Quebecoise du Canot-Camping), 0229-8813.*

DAISY SHOOTING ANNUAL. 0362-7160. US. English. an. $1.75. Aqua-Field Publications Inc, 342 Madison Avenue, New York NY 10017. **LC** GV1151. **DD** 799.05.

DEER AND DEER HUNTING. *See* Recreation, Leisure - Sports.

DEER HUNTING. *See* Recreation, Leisure - Sports.

DEER SPORTSMAN. *See* Recreation, Leisure - Sports.

DUCKS UNLIMITED. *See* Conservation & Natural Resources.

EASTERN CANADA CAMPING. Main/Corp American Automobile Association. 0363-2091. US. English. an. American Automobile Association, 8111 Gatehouse Road, Falls Church VA 22042. **LC** GV191.46.M4. **DD** 917.1.

EXPEDITION (LONGUEUIL, QUEBEC). (EXPEDITION). **VFOAT** Magazine Expedition. April/May 1982-. 0714-4008. Periodical. CN. French. bm. $10.00. Magazine Expedition, #6 140 Place du College, Longueuil Quebec J4J 1G2 Canada. **DD** 796.505.

EXPLORE (CALGARY, ALTA.). (EXPLORE). No. 4 (Jan. 1982)-. 0714-816X. Periodical. CN. English. bm. $14.95. Explore, PO Box 2197, Calgary Alberta T2T 5M9 Canada. **Tel** (403)678-2713. Ed Al Gordon. **DD** 917.12304305. bk rev. adv acc. **Circ** 35,000. Editorial is aimed at "self-propelled" outdoor enthusiasts (e.p. skiers, hikers, canoeists, bicyclists) travel destinations and equipment for these sports are covered. *Explore Alberta Magazine, 0706-8174; Whiskey Jack Magazine, 0226-7462.*

FELD WALD WASSER. SCHWEIZERISCHE JAGDZEITUNG. V. 24, No. 1- Jan. 1973-. Periodical. SZ. German. mo. 64.-. Meier & Cie Ag Schaffhausen, Offset Buchdruck, 8200 Schaffhausen Switzerland. **Tel** 053/881 11. Ed Jakob W Reiff. **Ind/Abst** Bibliogr. Agric. bk rev. adv acc. **Circ** 8,000. Hunting, dogs, fishing, book reviews, nature, news from the advertiser, hunting club news, and reports on hunting.

FIELD & STREAM. (FIELD AND STREAM). V. 2, No. 8- Jan. 1898-. 0015-0673. Periodical. US. English. mo. CBS Publications, 1515 Broadway, New York NY 10036, (subscription address: Neodata PO Box 2606 Boulder CO 80322). **Tel** (800)525-0643. **Ind/Abst** Pop. Mag. Rev., Biogr. Index, Read. Guide Period. Lit., Consum. Index Prod. Eval. Inf. Source, Mag. Index. **LC** Ski. **DD** 799. *Western Field and Stream, Forest and Stream.*

FIELD & STREAM DEER HUNTING ANNUAL. **VAT** Field and Stream Deer Hunting Annual. 0163-5042. US. English. an. $1.50. CBS Publications, 1 Fawcett Place, Greenwich CT 06830. **LC** SK301. **DD** 799.277357.

FIELD & STREAM (FAR WEST ED.). (FIELD & STREAM). **VFOAT** Field and Stream. 8755-8572. Periodical. US. English. mo. $13.94 U.S., $18.94 Foreign. CBS Magazines, 3807 Wilshire Boulevard/Suite 1204, Los Angeles CA 90010. **DD** 799. *Field & Stream, 0015-0673; Living Outdoors.*

FIELD & STREAM GUIDE TO CAMPING ON WHEELS. **VFOAT** Guide to Camping on Wheels. 1973-. US. English. an. $1.25. CBS Publications, 383 Madison Avenue, New York NY 10017. **LC** TL298. **DD** 338.47629226. *Field & Stream Camping on Wheels.*

FIELD & STREAM HUNTING ANNUAL. *See* Recreation, Leisure - Sports.

FIELD & STREAM (MIDWEST ED.). (FIELD & STREAM). **VFOAT** Field and Stream. 8755-8599. Periodical. US. English. mo. $13.94 U.S., $18.94 Foreign. CBS Magazines, 3807 Wilshire Boulevard/Suite 1204, Los Angeles CA 90010. **DD** 799. *Field & Stream, 0015-0673; Living Outdoors.*

FIELD & STREAM (NORTHEAST ED.). (FIELD & STREAM). **VFOAT** Field and Stream. 8755-8580. Periodical. US. English. mo. $13.94 U.S., $18.94 Foreign. CBS Magazines, 3807 Wilshire Boulevard/Suite 1204, Los Angeles CA 90010. **LC** SK1. **DD** 799.05. *Field & Stream, 0015-0673; Living Outdoors.*

FIELD & STREAM (SOUTH ED.). (FIELD & STREAM). **VFOAT** Field and Stream. 8755-8602. Periodical. US. English. mo. $13.94 U.S., $18.94 Foreign. CBS Magazines, 3807 Wilshire Boulevard/Suite 1204, Los Angeles CA 90010. **DD** 799. *Field & Stream, 0015-0673; Living Outdoors.*

FIELD & STREAM (WEST ED.). (FIELD & STREAM). **VFOAT** Field and Stream. 8755-8610. Periodical. US. English. mo. $13.94 U.S., $18.94 Foreign. CBS Magazines, 3807 Wilshire Boulevard/Suite 1204, Los Angeles CA 90010. **DD** 799. *Field & Stream, 0015-0673; Living Outdoors.*

FIELD (LONDON, ENGLAND : 1983). (THE FIELD). **VFOAT** Field, The Farm, The Garden. UK. English. wk. $88.00 US and Canada. The Harmsworth Press Ltd, Watling Street, Bletchley Buckinghamshire England. **LC** GV1. **DD** 799.0941.

FINS AND FEATHERS (MISSOURI EDITION). (FINS AND FEATHERS). **VFOAT** Missouri Fins and Feathers. Began in 1978?. 0741-4048. Periodical. US. English. mo. $12.95 Domestic, $15.95 Canada. PO Box 3986, Glenstone Station, Springfield MO 65804.

FINS AND FEATHERS (NEW MEXICO EDITION). (FINS AND FEATHERS). **VFOAT** New Mexico Fins and Feathers. V. 1, No. 1 (May 1984)-. 0748-7924. Periodical. US. English. mo. $12.95 U.S., $15.95 Canada. Fins and Feathers Publishing Company, PO Box 27160, Albuquerque NM 87125.

FINS AND FEATHERS (RHODE ISLAND EDITION). (FINS AND FEATHERS). **VFOAT** Rhode Island Fins and Feathers. Began in 1982. 0741-384X. Periodical. US. English. mo. $12.95 U.S., $15.95 Canada. Fins and Feathers Publishing Company, PO Box 9347, Providence RI 02940.

FISH AND GAME CODE (CALIFORNIA). Main/Corp California. 19 -. Periodical. US. English. be. California Fish & Game Commission, PO Box 1015, North Highlands CA 95660. **Tel** (916)445-4711.

FISH AND WILDLIFE REFERENCE SERVICE NEWSLETTER. No. 28- Sept. 1974-. 0160-4740. Periodical. US. English. qt. Fish and Wildlife Reference Service, 2100 West Mississippi Avenue, Denver CO 80223. **Tel** (303)573-5152. *Newsletter, Library Reference Service, Federal Aid in Fish and Wildlife Restoration, 0190-4353.*

FISHING & HUNTING JOURNAL. **VFOAT** Fishing and Hunting Journal. 0886-3008. Periodical. US. English. mo. $29.95. Fishing & Hunting Journal, 2141 Schuetz Road, St Lousi MO 63146.

FROM THE STATE CAPITALS. FISH AND GAME REGULATION. *See* Fish Culture and Fisheries.

FULL CRY. 1939. 0016-2620. Periodical. US. English. mo. $11.00. Wright Publications Inc, PO Box 10, Boody IL 62514. **Tel** (217)865-2332. Ed Seth R Gault. bk rev. adv acc. **Circ** 37,000. Edited for trail and treehound enthusiasts; racoon, lion and bear hunters. Club news, breed association and state news, stories, articles and training material for the entire family.

FUR DIE SICHERHEIT IM BERGLAND; JAHRBUCH. *See* Yearbooks, Almanacs, Directories.

FUR-FISH-GAME. **VAT** Fur Fish Game. 1905. 0016-2922. Periodical. US. English. mo. $9.00. A R Harding Publishing Company, 2878 East Main Street, Columbus OH 43209. **Tel** (614)231-9585. Ed Jim Maccracken. adv acc. **Circ** 180,000. (ctrl). Contains fishing, camping, dogs, guns and ammunition, hunting in US, trapping fur bearing animals, sale of pelts and prices, outdoor questions and answers, conservation.

GARDEN IDEAS & OUTDOOR LIVING. *See* Horticulture and Plant Culture.

Recreation, Leisure—Outdoor Life

GENERAL INFORMATION BROCHURE. Main/Corp British Columbia Mountaineering Club. CN. English. an. British Columbia Mountaineering Club, PO Box 2674, Vancouver British Columbia V6B 3W8 Canada. DD 796.522060711.

GEORGIA SPORTSMAN. V. 1- 1976-. 0199-6517. Periodical. US. English. mo. $27.95. Game and Fish Publications, PO Box 741, Marietta GA 30061. Tel (404)953-9222.

GLEN ECHO PARK. Periodical. US. English. qt. Glen Echo Park, National Park Service, MacArthur Boulevard, Glen Echo MD 20768.

GRAY'S SPORTING JOURNAL. V. 1- Winter 1976-. 0273-6691. Periodical. US. English. qt. $24.95. Grays Sporting Journal, PO Box 2549/205 Willow Street, Hamilton MA 01982. Tel (617)486-4486. Ed Edward E Gray. LC GV191.2. DD 796.505. bk rev. adv acc. Circ 30,000. (ctrl). Each issue is written for the advanced angler and shooter. We strive to bring you the best in outdoor photography and literature.

GREAT LAKES CAMPBOOK. VFOAT Great Lakes Camp Book. 1982 Ed.-. 0734-8517. US. English. an. $3.00. American Automobile Association, 8111 Gatehouse Road, Falls Church VA 22047. LC GV198.65.G7. DD 647.9477. Great Lakes Camping, 0363-5171.

GREAT LAKES CAMPING CEASED. 0363-5171. US. English. an. 8111 Gatehouse Road, Falls Church VA 22042. LC GV198.65.G7. DD 641.9477.

GREAT OUTDOORS. 0432-5737. UK. English. mo. Holmes McDugall Ltd, Ravenseft House, 302-304 St Vincent Street, Glasgow G2 5NL Scotland.

GREENSCAPE. See Horticulture and Plant Culture.

GUIDE CHASSE ET PECHE. VFOAT Chasse et Peche. Vol. 1-. 0713-603X. CN. French. an. $4.00 Per Volume. Distributions Eclair, 8320 Place de Lorraine, Anjou 437 Quebec Canada. DD 799.09714.

GUIDEBOOK - WEST TEXAS GEOLOGICAL SOCIETY. (GUIDEBOOK FALL FIELD TRIP). Main/Corp West Texas Geological Society. VFOAT Fall Field Trip. 0510-1387. US. English. an. West Texas Geological Society, PO Box 1595, Midland TX 79701. Tel (915)683-1573. CODEN GFTSDH.

GUN DIGEST HUNTING ANNUAL. See Recreation, Leisure - Sports.

GUN DOG. See Recreation, Leisure - Sports.

GUN WORLD HUNTING GUIDE. See Recreation, Leisure - Sports.

GUTMANN PUMA/EXPLORER KNIFE ANNUAL. VFOAT Puma/Explorer Knife. VAT Gutman Puma Explorer Knife Annual. 0731-1885. Periodical. US. English. an. $2.50. Aqua-Field Publications Inc, PO Box 721, Point Pleasant NJ 08742. LC TS380. DD 621.93205. Gutmann Knife Annual, 0271-762X.

HIKING. V. 1- Spring 1974-. 0094-0291. Periodical. US. English. $2.00. Woodall Publishing Company, 500 Hyancith Place, Highland Park IL 60038. LC GV199. DD 796.505.

THE HIMALAYAN JOURNAL. V. 1- Apr. 1929-. Periodical. English. ir. 130.-. Oxford University Press, Post Box 31, Bombay 1 BR India. Tel 262461. Ed Harish B Kapadia. LC DS485.H6. DD 915.42. bk rev. adv acc. (ctrl). Mountaineering and allied activities in the Himalayan and related mountain ranges.

HOOSIER OUTDOORS. 0018-4780. Periodical. US. English. bm. Hossier Publications Inc, PO Box 552, Chesterton IN 46304. Tel (219)926-2592. Ed Thomas J Glancy. LC SK75. DD 917.72044. bk rev. adv acc. Circ 35,000. Magazine covers outdoor sports and is geared towards Indiana residents. Also contains articles on the conservation of natural resources.

HU WAI SHENG HUO. VFOAT Outdoor Life. Began with July 5, 1976 issue. Periodical. CH. Chinese. mo. $39.00. Hu Wai Sheng Huo Tsa Chi She 12 Yen Ping S Road, Taipei Taiwan. LC GV191.2. DD 796.505.

HUNTER CASUALTY REPORT. Main/Corp Arkansas Game and Fish Commission. US. English. an. Arkansas Game and Fish Commission, #2 Natural Resources Drive, Little Rock AR 72205. LC SK53. DD 363.14.

IDAHO WILDLIFE. Vol. 1, No. 1 (Jan./Feb. 1978)-. 8755-2469. Periodical. US. English. bm. $10.00. Idaho Fish & Game Department, PO Box 25, Boise ID 83707. LC SK387. DD 639.905. Idaho Wildlife Review, 0019-1248.

INDIAN MOUNTAINEER. May 1978-. Periodical. II. English. ir. 10-. Indian Mountaineering Foundation, 18-Q Block Behind South Block Central Sect, New Delhi 110055 India. LC GV199.44.I532. DD 796.5220954.

INFORM-AUX-CAMPS. (INFORM-AUX-CAMPS : BULLETIN D'INFORMATION DE L'ASSOCIATION DES CAMPS DU QUEBEC). 0710-6351. Periodical. CN. French. Free. Association des Camps du Quebec, 1415 East rue Jarry, Montreal Quebec H2E 2Z7 Canada. DD 796.542060714. (ctrl).

INTERNATIONAL DIVER INDEX. WORLD INDIVEX EDITION. See Indexes/Abstracts.

INTERNATIONAL SKI TRAILS. See Recreation, Leisure - Sports.

INTERNATIONAL WILDLIFE. 0020-9112. Periodical. US. English. ir. National Wildlife Federation, 1412 16th Street NW, Washington DC 20036.

IROQUOIAN. (THE IROQUOIAN). Main/Corp Iroquoia Bruce Trail Club. 9412-6336. Periodical. CN. English. qt. Iroquoia Bruce Trail Club, PO Box 183, Hamilton Ontario L8N 3A2 Canada. DD 796.5106071352.

ITHACAGUN HUNTING & SHOOTING ANNUAL. See Recreation, Leisure - Sports.

JACHT EN NATUURBEHEER. Periodical. Dutch. tr. Koninklijke Sint-Hubertusclub van Belgie, 1000 Brussel Jan Jacobsplein 1, Brussel Belgium. LC SK205.

JOURNAL OF THE NORTH AMERICAN FALCONERS' ASSOCIATION. (THE JOURNAL OF THE NORTH AMERICAN FALCONERS' ASSOCIATION). Main/Corp North American Falconers' Association. Began with Vol. for 1962. 0097-6253. US. English. an. North American Falconers' Association, Route 3 Box 301, Durango CO 81301. LC SK321. DD 799.2320973.

KANSAS WILDLIFE. Vol. 38, No. 1 (Jan./Feb. 1981). 0279-9030. Periodical. US. English. bm. $15.00. Information Education Division Kansas Fish & Game Commission, Box 54A Rural Route 2, Pratt KS 67124. Tel (316)672-5911. Ed Wayne Van Zwoll. LC SK397. DD 639.909781. bk rev. Circ 34,000. Descriptions of Kansas wild creatures and places, outdoor activities, and resource management. How-to articles on hunting, fishing, and photography. Kansas Fish & Game, 0022-8591.

KENTUCKY HAPPY HUNTING GROUND. V. 1- Dec. 1945-. 0023-0235. Periodical. US. English. bm. Department of Fish & Wildlife, A Mitchell Building/#1, Game Farm Road, Frankfort KY 40601. Tel (502)564-4336. Ed John Wilson. LC SK1. DD 799. bk rev. Circ 30,000. (ctrl). Official publication of Kentucky Department of Fish and Wildlife Resources; devoted to wildlife conservation, outdoor sports, wise and ethical use of natural resources.

KEY-WORD-INDEX OF WILDLIFE RESEARCH. See Indexes/Abstracts.

LONE STAR SIERRAN. See Conservation & Natural Resources.

LOUISIANA GAME & FISH. VFOAT Louisiana Game and Fish. Began in 1981?. 0744-3692. Periodical. US. English. mo. $11.95. Game and Fish Publications, PO Box 741, Marietta GA 30061. Tel (404)953-9222.

LOUISIANA OUT-OF-DOORS. (LOUISIANA OUT-OF-DOORS : OFFICIAL PUBLICATION OF THE LOUISIANA WILDLIFE FEDERATION). VFOAT Louisiana Out of Doors. 0738-8098. Periodical. US. English. mo. $5.00. Louisiana Out of Doors, PO Box 16089, Louisiana State University, Baton Rouge LA 70893. Tel (504)355-1871. Ed Randy P Lanctot. bk rev. adv acc. Circ 2,500. (ctrl). 16-Page tabloid newspaper containing articles on conservation topics, things of interest to hunters, anglers, boaters, hikers, etc. and environmental issues.

MAINE FISH AND WILDLIFE. See Fish Culture and Fisheries.

MANITOBA CAMPING DIRECTORY. See Yearbooks, Almanacs, Directories.

MANUAL OF SKI MOUNTAINEERING. 1st- Ed. US. English. Ed D R Brower. LC GV854. DD 796.93.

MASSACHUSETTS WILDLIFE. See Conservation & Natural Resources.

METROPARKS EMERALD NECKLACE. V. 24, No. 6- May 1975-. Periodical. US. English. mo. Cleveland Metroparks System, 4101 Fulton Parkway, Cleveland OH 44144. Tel (216)351-6300. Ed Debra L Haskell. Circ 50,000. Articles on resources of the park system, both natural and recreational. Monthly listing of scheduled activities and programs. Emerald Necklace.

MICHIGAN OUT-OF-DOORS. VAT Michigan Out of Doors. Began publication in 1950. 0026-2382. Periodical. US. English. mo. Michigan United Conservation Clubs, PO Box 30235, Lansing MI 48909. Tel (517)371-1041. Ed Ken Lowe. Ind/Abst Pop. Mag. Rev. bk rev. adv acc. Circ 105,000.

MICHIGAN SPORTSMAN (OSHKOSH WIS.). (MICHIGAN SPORTSMAN). 0539-8908. Periodical. US. English. ir. $9.95. Great Lakes Sportsman Group, PO Box 2266, Oshkosh WI 54903. Tel (414)231-9338. Ed Steve Smith. adv acc. Circ 32,000. Fishing, hunting and other outdoor participation activities in Michigan.

MINNESOTA OUT-OF-DOORS. 0026-5608. Periodical. US. English. mo. $10.00. Minnesota Conservation, 1034 Cleveland Avenue South, St Paul MN 55116. Tel (612)690-3077.

MINNESOTA SPORTSMAN. V. 1- July/Aug. 1977-. 0274-8622. Periodical. US. English. ir. $9.95. Great Lakes Sportsman Group, 801 Oregon Street, Oshkosh WI 54903. Tel (414)231-8160. Ed Chuck Petrie. adv acc. Circ 35,000. Fishing, hunting and other outdoor participation activities in Minnesota.

MISSISSIPPI GAME & FISH. VFOAT Mississippi Game and Fish. 0744-4192. Periodical. US. English. mo $11.95. Game and Fish Publications, PO Box 741, Marietta GA 30061. Tel (404)953-9222.

MISSISSIPPI OUTDOORS. V. 42, No. 6- Nov./Dec. 1979-. 0199-3240. Periodical. US. English. bm. Mississippi Department of Wildlife, PO Box 451, Jackson MS 39205. LC SH11.M7. DD 799.09762. Mississippi Game and Fish, 0026-6256.

MITTEILUNGEN (OSTERREICHISCHER ALPENVEREIN (1950-)). (MITTEILUNGEN). Periodical. German. bm. LC JQ821. DD 796.52205. Mitteilungen (Osterreichischer Alpenverein (1950-). Akademische Sektion).

LA MONTAGNE ET ALPINISME. No. 1- Oct. 1955-. 0047-7923. Periodical. FR. French. ir. 100. La Montagnee Alpinisme, 9 rue la Boetie, Paris 8E France. Tel 47 42 38 46. bk rev. adv acc. Circ 60,000. National magazine of the Association "Club Alpin Francais" dealing with mountain climbing, trekking, and so on. Montagne.

MONTANA OUTDOORS. See Conservation & Natural Resources.

MOTORCAMPING HANDBOOK. US. English. $1.50. Popular Science Publishing Corporation, 355 Lexington Avenue, New York NY 10017. LC SK600. DD 796.5405.

THE MOUNTAINEER. V. 1- Mar. 1907-. 0027-2620. Periodical. US. English. mo. $7.00. Mountaineer, 300 3rd Avenue West, Seattle WA 98119. Tel (206)284 6310. Ind/Abst Bibliogr. Index Geol.

MOUSQUETON. (LE MOUSQUETON). 0712-3817. Periodical. CN. French. mo. $6.00. Le Mousqueton, Federation Quebecoise de la Montagne, 1415 East rue Jarry, Montreal Quebec H2E 2Z7 Canada. DD 796.52205.

MS OUTDOORS. VFOAT Mississippi Outdoors. Vol. 44, No. 5 (Sept.-Oct. 1981)-. 0732-6602. Periodical. US. English. bm. Mississippi Department of Wildlife Conservation, POB 451, Jackson MS 39205. LC SH11.M7. DD 799.09762. Mississippi Outdoors, 0199-3240.

MUSHROOM (MOSCOW, IDAHO). See Biology - Botany.

MUSKIE : THE OFFICIAL PUBLICATION OF MUSKIES, INC. Periodical. US. English. mo. Muskies Inc International Office, 1708 University Avenue, St Paul MN 55104. LC SH691.M8. DD 799.1753. Newsletter (Muskies, Inc.).

Recreation, Leisure—Outdoor Life

MUZZLELOADER. 1974. 0274-5720. Periodical. US. English. bm. $10.00. Rebel Publishing Company Inc, Route 5 Box 347-M, Texarkana TX 75501. Tel (214)832-4726. Ed William Scurlock. bk rev. adv acc. Circ 14,000. (ctrl). The publication for black powder shooters.

N.A.D.A. RECREATION VEHICLE APPRAISAL GUIDE. See Transportation - Automobiles.

NATIONAL OUTDOOR OUTFITTERS NEWS. See Business.

NATIONAL SURVEY OF FISHING, HUNTING, AND WILDLIFE-ASSOCIATED RECREATION. 1980-. 0736-6450. US. English. ir. Superintendent of Documents, US Government Printing Office, Washington DC 20402. LC SK41. DD 333.954130973.

NATIONAL SURVEY OF FISHING, HUNTING, AND WILDLIFE-ASSOCIATED RECREATION. ALASKA. US. English. ir. US Fish and Wildlife Service, Washington DC 20240.

NATIONAL SURVEY OF FISHING, HUNTING, AND WILDLIFE-ASSOCIATED RECREATION. ARKANSAS. 0742-7174. US. English. ir. US Fish and Wildlife Service, Washington DC 20240. LC SK53. DD 333.95409767.

NATIONAL SURVEY OF FISHING, HUNTING, AND WILDLIFE-ASSOCIATED RECREATION. CONNECTICUT. 0742-7166. US. English. ir. US Fish and Wildlife Service, Washington DC 20240. LC SK59. DD 333.95409746.

NATIONAL SURVEY OF FISHING, HUNTING, AND WILDLIFE-ASSOCIATED RECREATION. IDAHO. US. English. ir. US Fish and Wildlife Service, Washington DC 20240.

NATIONAL SURVEY OF FISHING, HUNTING, AND WILDLIFE-ASSOCIATED RECREATION. ILLINOIS. 0742-7158. US. English. ir. US Fish and Wildlife Service, Washington DC 20240. LC SK71. DD 333.95409773.

NATIONAL SURVEY OF FISHING, HUNTING, AND WILDLIFE-ASSOCIATED RECREATION. LOUISIANA. 0742-714X. US. English. ir. US Fish and Wildlife Service, Washington DC 20240. LC SK83. DD 333.95409763.

NATIONAL SURVEY OF FISHING, HUNTING, AND WILDLIFE-ASSOCIATED RECREATION. MICHIGAN. US. English. ir. US Fish and Wildlife Service, Washington DC 20240. Vols. for (1980-) distributed to depository libraries in microfiche.

NATIONAL SURVEY OF FISHING, HUNTING, AND WILDLIFE-ASSOCIATED RECREATION. NEW YORK. 0742-7190. US. English. ir. US Fish and Wildlife Service, Washington DC 20240. LC SK111. DD 333.95409747.

NATIONAL SURVEY OF FISHING, HUNTING, AND WILDLIFE-ASSOCIATED RECREATION. OHIO. 0742-7182. US. English. ir. US Fish and Wildlife Service, Washington DC 20240. LC SK115. DD 333.95409771.

NEBRASKALAND. VFOAT Nebraska Land. V. 42, No. 5 (June 1964)-. 0028-1964. Periodical. US. English. mo. $9.50. Nebraska Game and Parks Commission, 2200 North 33rd Street, Box 30370, Lincoln ME 68503. Tel (402)464-0641. Ed Lowell A Johnson. bk rev. adv acc. Circ 65,000. Conservation and outdoor recreation-hunting and fishing plus historical stories about Nebraska. Outdoor Nebraskaland, 0091-6404.

NEW HAMPSHIRE NATURAL RESOURCES. See Conservation & Natural Resources.

NEW JERSEY OUTDOORS. See Conservation & Natural Resources.

NEW MEXICO WILDLIFE. 1960. 0028-6338. Periodical. US. English. bm. $5.50. Department of Fish and Game, State Capitol, Sante Fe NM 87503. Tel (505)827-7911. Ed Jeffery L Pederson. Ind/Abst Biol. Abstr. LC SK427. DD 333.95909789. CODEN NMWIAN. Circ 8,500. Wildlife, conservation, game and fish features.

NEW WILDERNESS LETTER. V. 1- Jan. 1977-. 0197-4874. Periodical. US. English. sa. New Wilderness, 325 Spring Street/Room 208, New York NY 10013. Tel (212)807-7944.

NEW YORK FISH AND GAME JOURNAL. See Conservation & Natural Resources.

NEW ZEALAND WILDLIFE. 1962. 0028-8802. Periodical. NZ. English. qt. Miss P A Hewitt, PO Box 6514, Wellington New Zealand. Tel 847-499. Ed Smelby Grant. bk rev. adv acc. Circ 10,000. Hunting, shooting, wildlife, game management and outdoor recreation articles, stories and information. New Zealand's largest circulation: hunting and shooting magazine.

NEWFOUNDLAND OUTDOORS. VFOAT Newfoundland Outdoors Magazine. V. 1- June 1976-. 0383-8943. Periodical. CN. English. mo. Newfoundland Outdoors Magazine, PO Box 219Y Holyrood CB, Newfoundland A0A 2R0 Canada. DD 796.509718.

NEWSLETTER - BLUE MOUNTAINS BRUCE TRAIL CLUB. Main/Corp Blue Mountains Bruce Trail Club. VAT News Letter - Blue Mountains Bruce Trail Club, Bulletin - Blue Mountains Bruce Trail Club. Spring 1979-. 0225-7335. Periodical. CN. English. ir. Blue Mountains Bruce Trail Club, PO Box 306, Barrie Ontario L4M 4T5 Canada. DD 796.5106071317. BMBTC Newsletter, 0708-0867.

NEWSLETTER - COLORADO RIVER ASSOCIATION. Main/Corp Colorado River Association. 0588-5035. Periodical. US. English. mo. 417 South Hill Street, Los Angeles CA 90013.

NIAGARA BRUCE TRAIL CLUB. 0706-7429. Periodical. CN. English. ir. Niagara Bruce Trail Club, PO Box 1, St Catherines Ontario L2R 6R4 Canada. DD 796.5105.

NORTH DAKOTA OUTDOORS. V. 1- July 1938-. 0029-2761. Periodical. US. English. ir. $7.00. Ed Bry, North Dakota Game & Fish Department, Bismarck ND 58505. Tel (701)221-6315. Ed Ed Bry. Ind/Abst Energy Inf. Abstr., Environ. Abstr. LC SK351. DD 799.05. bk rev. Circ 27,000. (ctrl). A state Game and Fish Department publication. North Dakota Outdoors, 0029-2761.

NORTH EAST OUT DOORS. VFOAT Northeast Outdoors. 1966. 0199-8463. Periodical. US. English. mo. $12.00. Northeast Outdoors, PO Box 2180-70 Edwin Avenue, Waterbury CT 06722-2180. Tel (203)755-0158. Ed Howard Fielding. bk rev. adv acc. Circ 14,000. (ctrl). Camping and recreational vehicle travel in northeastern United States.

THE NORTH WOODS CALL. 1953. 0029-2958. Periodical. US. English. ir. Northwoods Call, Route 1 Box 193, Charlevoix MI 49720. Tel (616)547-9797. Ed Glenn Sheppard. bk rev. adv acc. Circ 12,000. (ctrl). Regional conservation and outdoor recreation journal.

NORTHWESTERN CAMPING & TRAILERING. VFOAT Camping & Trailering. US. English. an. American Automobile Association, 1712 G Street Northwest, Washington DC 20006. LC GV191.4. DD 917.8043.

N.R.A. HUNTING ANNUAL. (NRA HUNTING ANNUAL). Main/Corp National Rifle Association of America. VFOAT North American Hunting Directory. 0090-5690. US. English. an. $1.75. National Rifle Association of America, 1600 Rhode Island Avenue Northwest, Washington DC 20036. LC SK12. DD 799.2097.

OCCASIONAL PAPER - CANADA WILDLIFE SERVICE. (OCCASIONAL PAPER - CANADIAN WILDLIFE SERVICE). VFOAT Occasional Paper Series. No. 1-. 0576-6370. Monographic Series. CN. English (issued also in French. Some no. issued also with French. Includes abstracts in French). Free. Information Canada, Ottawa Ontario Canada. Ind/Abst ASTIS Bibliogr., ASTIS Curr. Aware. Bull., Sel. Water Resour. Abstr., Biol. Abstr. LC UNC. CODEN CWOPAL.

OFF BELAY CEASED. No. 1- 1972-. 0146-339X. Periodical. US. English. bm. $7.50. Off Belay, 15630 SE 124th Street, Renton WA 98055. LC GV199.8.

OHIO FISH AND WILDLIFE REPORT. No. 1-. 0085-4468. Monographic Series. US. English. ir. Free. Ohio Division of Wildlife, c/o Ken Laub, 1500 Dublin Road, Columbus OH 43215-9912. Tel (614)265-7036. Ed Kenneth W Laub. Ind/Abst Life Sci. Collect., Biol. Abstr., Wildl. Rev. CODEN OFWRBD. Circ 1,000. (ctrl). Reports of fish and wildlife research and management. Ohio Game Monographs, 0078-4036; Ohio Fish Monographs, 0078-4028.

ONTARIO OUT OF DOORS. V. 9, Issue 11- Dec. 1977-. 0707-3178. Periodical. CN. English. mo. Ontario Out of Doors, 3 Church Street/Suite 202, Toronto Ontario M3E 1M2 Canada. Tel (416)368-3011. Ed Burt Myers. DD 799.09713. adv acc. Circ 62,000. Fishing and hunting in Ontario. Ontario Fisherman & Hunter Out of Doors, 0319-6941.

ONTARIO OUTDOOR GUIDE & CALENDAR. VFOAT Ontario Outdoor Guide. No. 1 (Spring '84)-. 0827-2352. Periodical. CN. English. ir. Ontario Outdoor Guide, 296 Glen Road, Toronto Ontario M4W 2X3 Canada. DD 799.09713.

ONTARIO OUTDOORSMAN. 0823-6453. Periodical. CN. English. ir. $10.00. Ontario Outdoorsman, PO Box 7054, Ancaster Ontario L9G 3L1 Canada. DD 799.09713.

OREGON WILDLIFE COMMISSION FINANCIAL STATEMENT. 0362-8264. US. English. Oregon Wildlife Commission, PO Box 3503, Portland OR 97208. LC SK439. DD 353.9795008232.

OUTDOOR ALBERTA. Summer 1984-. 0827-2964. Periodical. CN. English. ir. $5.00. Outdoor Alberta, 12514-124 Street, Edmonton Alberta T5L 0N5 Canada. DD 799.097123.

OUTDOOR AMERICA. V. 36, No. 7- July 1971-. 0021-3314. Periodical. US. English. bm. $20.00. Izaak Walton League of America, 1701 North Fort Meyer Drive/Suite 1100, Arlington VA 22209. Tel (703)528-1818. Ed Carol Dana. Ind/Abst Energy Inf. Abstr., Environ. Abstr. LC SK1. DD 799.0973. adv acc. Circ 50,000. Articles on national natural resources, conservation issues and outdoor recreation, pursuits such as fishing, hunting, and camping. Izaak Walton Magazine.

OUTDOOR ATLANTIC. V. 1- Oct./Nov. 1979-. 0228-0604. Periodical. CN. English. ir. 5.00. Fundy Group Publications, PO Box 128, Yarmouth Nova Scotia B5A 4BA Canada. DD 639.09715.

OUTDOOR CALIFORNIA. V. 1- July 1930-. 0030-7025. Periodical. US. English. bm. $4.00. California Department of Fish and Game, PO Box 1015 Publication Section, North Highlands CA 95660. Ind/Abst Energy Inf. Abstr., Environ. Abstr. LC SH11.

OUTDOOR CANADA. V. 1- Dec. 1972-. 0315-0542. Periodical. CN. English. ir. 14.00. Outdoor Canada Magazine Ltd, 953A Eglinton Avenue E, Toronto Ontario M4G 4B5 Canada. Tel (416)443-888. Ed Sheila Kaighin. Ind/Abst Can. Environ., Can. Period. Index. adv acc. Circ 143,000. Adult and family magazine covering outdoor recreation in Canada, including fishing camping, boating, hiking, wildlife, photography, and conservation.

THE OUTDOOR COMMUNICATOR : THE OFFICIAL JOURNAL OF THE NEW YORK STATE OUTDOOR EDUCATION ASSOCIATION. Began in 1980. Periodical. US. English. sa. Communicator.

OUTDOOR CREST. Began publication in 1975?. 0700-9909. Periodical. CN. English. ir. The Outdoor Crest, 61 Edgehill Road, Islington Ontario M9A 4N1 Canada. DD 799.062713541. Outdoor Crest Newsletter, 0700-9895.

OUTDOOR GUIDE. No. 1- 1970-. 0048-2420. Periodical. US. English. mo. Outdoor Guide, 2718 Montana Avenue, Billings MT 59101.

OUTDOOR HIGHLIGHTS. V. 3, No. 4-. 0279-8700. Periodical. US. English. sm. $5.97. Illinois Department of Conservation, 603 State Office Building, Springfield IL 62706. Tel (217)782-7454. Ed Gary C Thomas. Circ 39,000. Outdoor recreation and historic sites. News - Illinois Dept. of Conservation.

OUTDOOR INDIANA. V. 1-20, No. 2, Feb. 1934-Feb. 1953. 0030-7068. Periodical. US. English. mo. $7.50. State of Indiana, Room 612, State Office Building, Indianapolis IN 46204. Tel (317)232-4004. Ed James B Parham. Circ 34,000. Reporting on Indiana's natural resources: state parks, fish and wildlife, Flora and Fauna, state history.

OUTDOOR LIFE. V. 1- 1897-. 0030-7076. Periodical. US. English. mo. $13.94 US, $17.94 Foreign. Times Mirror, 380 Madison Avenue, New York NY 10017, (subscription address: Neodata PO Box 2606 Boulder CO 80322). Tel (303)447-9330

Recreation, Leisure—Outdoor Life

Neodata. Ind/Abst Read. Guide Period. Lit., Pop. Mag. Rev., Consum. Index Prod. Eval. Inf. Source, Abr. Read. Guide.

OUTDOOR LIFE DEER HUNTER'S YEARBOOK. See Yearbooks, Almanacs, Directories.

OUTDOOR NEWS. 0279-9065. Periodical. US. English. mo. $15.00. 4545 Lincoln Boulevard, Suite 171, Oklahoma City OK 73105. Tel (405)524-7009. Ed Mike McCormick. bk rev. adv acc. Circ 11,000. Articles on conservation issues, hunting and fishing in Oklahoma.

OUTDOOR NEWS (TORONTO). (THE OUTDOOR NEWS). V. 1, No. 10- Sept. 1974-. 0316-8468. Periodical. CN. English. mo. $3.50 for 12 issues, Canada; $4.00 for 12 issues, US. The Outdoor News, 302 Bridgeland Avenue Rear, Toronto Ontario M6A 1Z4 Canada. DD 796.505. Ontario Camping News, 0316-8476.

OUTDOOR OKLAHOMA. V. 21, No. 8- Sept. 1965-. 0030-7106. Periodical. US. English. bm. $8.00. Department of Wildlife Conservation, 1801 North Lincoln, Oklahoma City OK 73105. Tel (405)521-3855. Ed Dean G Graham. Ind/Abst Energy Inf. Abstr., Environ. Abstr. Circ 22,000. (ctrl). Hunting, fishing and conservation information. Oklahoma Wildlife, 0199-9524.

THE OUTDOOR PATH. Periodical. US. English.

OUTDOOR REPORTS. Vol. 1, No. 1 (Winter 1977)-. 0709-3470. Periodical. CN. English. qt. $2.00. Outdoor Recreation Council of British Columbia, 100-1200 Hornby Street, Vancouver British Columbia V6Z 2E2 Canada. DD 796.09711.

OUTDOOR RETAILER. See Business - Marketing.

OUTDOOR SPORTSMAN. 0272-9342. US. English. $2.25 Single Issue US, $2.75 Single Issue Canada. Aqua-Field Publications Inc, 728 Beaver Dam Road, Point Pleasant NJ 08742. LC SK1. DD 799.05.

OUTDOORS IN GEORGIA. V. 1- July 1972-. 0147-720X. Periodical. US. English. mo. $5.00. Georgia Department of Natural Resources, 270 Washington Street/Room 714, Atlanta GA 30334. LC SK67. DD 799.09758. Georgia Game & Fish, 0016-8270.

OUTDOORS WEST. Periodical. US. English. sa. $5.00. Federation of Western Outdoor Clubs, 512 Boylston East/ #106, Seattle WA 98102. Tel (206)322-3041. Ed Hazel Wolf. bk rev. Circ 1,000. Conservation issues in eight Western states. Western Outdoors Annual, 0091-7524.

OUTSIDE (CHICAGO, ILL.). (OUTSIDE). Began with Feb./March 1980 issue. 0278-1433. Periodical. US. English. mo. $18.00. Mariah Publications Corporation, 3401 W Division Street, Chicago IL 60651, (subscription address: Neodata PO Box 2606 Boulder CO 80322). Tel (312)951-0990. Ed Lawrence J Burke. Ind/Abst Pop. Mag. Rev., Access. LC GV191.2. DD 796.50973. adv acc. Circ 220,000. The complete magazine of the great outdoors. Outside emphasizes participatory outdoor activities such as backpacking, canoeing, diving, kayaking, skiing and much more. Mariah Outside, 0194-4371.

OUTWARD BOUND. 1985-. 0749-4459. Periodical. US. English. an. $3.95. Telepictures Publications Inc, 300 Madison Avenue/8th Floor, New York NY 10017. DD 910.

PARENTS' GUIDE TO ACCREDITED CAMPS (1982). (PARENTS' GUIDE TO ACCREDITED CAMPS). 1982-. US. English. an. A C A Headquarters, Bradford Woods, Martinsville IN 46151. Parents' Guide to Accredited Camps: Northeast; Parents' Guide to Accredited Camps: West; Parents' Guide to Accredited Camps: South; Parents' Guide to Accredited Camps: Midwest.

PARQUES Y JARDINES. See Conservation & Natural Resources.

PATHFINDER. (THE PATHFINDER). Winter 1980-. 0227-2881. Periodical. CN. English. qt. Free to Members. Pathfinder Great Divide Trail Association, PO Box 5322 Station A, Calgary Alberta T2H 1X6 Canada. DD 917.11005. Great Divide Trail Association Newsletter, 0227-2873.

PENNSYLVANIA GAME NEWS. V. 1- Apr. 1930-. 0031-451X. Periodical. US. English. mo. $16.50. Pennsylvania Game Commission, PO Box 1567, Harrisburg PA 17120. LC SK351.

THE PENNSYLVANIA SPORTSMAN. 0274-6336. Periodical. US. English. mo. Northwoods Publications Inc, 1718 North Second Street, Harrisburg PA 17102. Pennsylvania's Outdoor People, 0199-9494.

PETERSEN'S HUNTING ANNUAL. VFOAT Hunting Annual. 1975-. 0095-5124. US. English. an. $6.95. Petersens Publishing Company, 6725 Sunset Boulevard, Los Angeles CA 90028. Tel (213)657-5100. LC SK1. DD 799.205.

PLEIN AIR MAURICIE. Feb. 1978-. 0705-9221. Periodical. CN. French. mo. Free. Plein Air Mauricie, 564 Boulevard des Prairies, Cap-De-La-Madeleine Quebec G8T 1K9 Canada. DD 799.1209714465. (ctrl).

POLOVNICKE STUDIE. V. 1- 1973-. Monographic Series. Slovak (summaries in English, German and Russian). ir.

POTOMAC APPALACHIAN. V. 1- May 1972-. 0098-8154. US. English. mo. $6.00. Potomac Appalachian Trail Club, 1718 N Street NW, Washington DC 20036. Tel (202)638-5307. Potomac Appalachian Trail Club Bulletin, Forecast.

POTOMAC APPALACHIAN. Magazine No. 1- Spring 1973-. 0092-2226. US. English. ir. $6.00. Potomac-Appalachian Trail Club, 1718 N Street Northwest, Washington DC 20036. Tel (202)638-5307. LC F217.B6. DD 917.55. bk rev. Circ 2,700. Review of recent events and descriptions of upcoming activities.

PROCEEDINGS OF THE NATIONAL CONFERENCE ON OUTDOOR RECREATION RESEARCH. Main/Conf National Conference on Outdoor Recreation Research, Ann Arbor. 1963-. Periodical. US. English. ir.

PSE OUTDOOR ADVENTURES BOWHUNTING ANNUAL. VFOAT PSE Bowhunting. 0198-9154. US. English. an. $1.95. Aqua-Field Publications Inc, 728 Beaver Dam Road, Point Pleasant NJ 08742. LC SK36. DD 799.20285.

PUBLICATION - BUREAU OF OUTDOOR RECREATION. Main/Corp United States. Bureau of Outdoor Recreation. No. 1- 1964-. 0501-7386. Monographic Series. US. English. Superintendent of Documents, US Government Printing Office, Washington DC 20402. LC GV182.2. DD 796.

QUEBEC NATURE. V. 1- Dec. 1976-. 0381-1123. Periodical. CN. French. mo $1.25 Each Number. Quebec Nature, CP 1066 Succursale B, 111 rue Carillon, Hull Quebec J8X 2P8 Canada. DD 796.509714.

QUEENSLAND ACCOMMODATION AND CARAVANNING DIRECTORY. See Yearbooks, Almanacs, Directories.

RAND MCNALLY CAMPGROUND & TRAILER PARK GUIDE. EASTERN. (RAND MCNALLY CAMPGROUND & TRAILER PARK GUIDE, EASTERN). VFOAT Rand McNally Campground and Trailer Park Guide. 0733-8309. US. English. an. Rand McNally & Co, Campground Publications, PO Box 728, Skokie IL 60076. LC GV191.35. DD 647.9473. Rand McNally Eastern Campgrounds & Trailer Parks, 0194-4177.

RAND MCNALLY CAMPGROUND & TRAILER PARK GUIDE. WESTERN. VFOAT Rand McNally Campground and Trailer Park Guide. 0732-6068. Periodical. US. English. Rand McNally & Company, Campground Publications, PO Box 728, Skokie IL 60076. LC GV191.35. DD 647.947809.

RAND MCNALLY WESTERN CAMPGROUNDS & TRAILER PARKS. VFOAT Western Campgrounds & Trailer Parks. 1970-. Periodical. US. English. ir. Rand McNally & Company, 23 East Madison, Chicago IL 60602. LC SK601. DD 917.9043.

RAPPEL. (LE RAPPEL : JOURNAL DU CLUB DE CANOT-CAMPING LES PAGAYEURS INC). 0710-5789. Periodical. CN. French. ir. Free to Members. Les Pagayeurs, CP 579 Succursale Desjardins, Montreal Quebec H5B 1B7 Canada. DD 797.122060714.

RECORDS OF EXOTICS. See Recreation, Leisure - Sports.

RECREATION AND OUTDOOR LIFE DIRECTORY. See Yearbooks, Almanacs, Directories.

REPORT - AUDUBON SOCIETY OF RHODE ISLAND. See Zoology-Vertebrate and Invertebrate.

REPORT - KENYA NATIONAL PARKS' TRUSTEES. See Conservation & Natural Resources.

REPORT - NATIONAL PARKS AUTHORITY PF W.A. See Conservation & Natural Resources.

REPORT OF THE NATIONAL HIKING WAY BOARD. Main/Corp National Hiking Way Board (South Africa). VFOAT Verslag van die Nasionale Voetslaanpadraad. SA. Afrikaans (English). ir. 2.15. The National Hiking Way Board, Obtainable From: Government Printer, Bosman Street, Private Bag X85, Pretoria South Africa. LC GV199.44.S6.

RESEAU PLEIN-AIR. VFOAT Bulletin de la Societe Quebecoise du Plein-Air. April 81-. 0711-2572. Periodical. CN. French. ir. Free to Members, $5.00 Others. Societe Quebecoise du Plein-Air, 1415 Est rue Jarry, Montreal Quebec H2E 2Z7 Canada. DD 796.509714. P.A. (Societe Quebecoise du Plein-Air), 0711-2281.

RESOURCE PUBLICATION - U.S. FISH AND WILDLIFE SERVICE. See Conservation & Natural Resources.

RIDEAU TRAIL NEWSLETTER. (THE RIDEAU TRAIL NEWSLETTER). Began with summer 1971 issue. 0709-7085. Periodical. CN. English. qt. Free to Members. Rideau Trail Association, Box 15 Kingston Ontario K7L 4V6 Canada. DD 796.510627137.

THE ROCKY MOUNTAIN MAGAZINE WINTER GUIDE. (THE ROCKY MOUNTAIN MAGAZINE ... WINTER GUIDE). VFOAT Winter Guide. Winter 1981/82-. 0278-0194. US. English. an. $2.95. Rocky Mountain Magazine, 1741 High Street, Denver CO 80218.

ROYAL RED BALL OUTDOOR SPORTSMAN. 0197-1883. Periodical. US. English. an. $1.95 a copy. Aqua-Field Publications Inc, 728 Beaver Dam Road, Point Pleasant NJ 08742. LC SK1. DD 799.05.

SAFARI (TUCSON, ARIZ.). See Recreation, Leisure - Sports.

SAMMANFATTNING AV ARTIKLARNA. See Recreation, Leisure - Sports.

SAN. VFOAT Mountain. Periodical. KO. Korean. ir. 5,000. Sanak Munhwasa, 64-8 1-Ka Taepyong-no Chung-ku, Seoul Korea. LC GV199.8.

THE SCI RECORD BOOK OF TROPHY ANIMALS. VFOAT S.C.I. Record Book of Trophy Animals. Began in 1978?. 0195-7538. US. English. be. Safari Club International, 5151 East Broadway/Suite 1680, Tucson AZ 85711. LC SK277. DD 799.26.

SCOUT-JEUNESSE. No. 1- Feb. 1976-. 0383-0853. Periodical. CN. French. ir. $5.00. les Amis du Signe de Piste, 16 Place DuFort, Repentigny Quebec J6A 3H7 Canada. DD 769.505. (ctrl).

SENTIER CHASSE-PECHE. VFOAT Chasse-Peche. Vol. 11, No. 4 (Feb. 1982)-. 0711-7957. Periodical. CN. French. mo. 26.00. Groupe Polygone Editeur Inc, 11450 Albert Hudon, Montreal Quebec H1Z 1B1 Canada. Tel (514)327-4464. Ed Jeannot Ruel. Ind/Abst Point Repere. DD 799.09714. bk rev. adv acc. Circ 75,000. (ctrl). The only French magazine for anglers, hunters, trappers, outdoormen. Rank first-base male readers. Among 49 largest Canadian magazines for editorial interest. Quebec Chasse et Peche, 0315-260X; Sentier, 0228-3107.

SICHERHEIT IM BERGLAND. Periodical. AU. German. an. Kuratorium, Prinz-Eugen-Strasse 12, 1040 Wien Austria. LC GV200.18. DD 363.14.

SIERRA. See Conservation & Natural Resources.

THE SKEETER. See Recreation, Leisure - Sports.

SKI CANADA JOURNAL. See Recreation, Leisure - Sports.

SKI RACING REDBOOK. See Recreation, Leisure - Sports.

SKIER'S HOLIDAY GUIDE. See Recreation, Leisure - Sports.

SLOVENSKE DIVADLO. Vol. 2- 1954-. Periodical. Czech. qt. Kubon and Sagner, Postfach 34 01 08, D8 Muenchen 34 West Germany. Tel 0811 52

Recreation, Leisure—Outdoor Life

20 27. Ind/Abst MLA Int. Bibliogr. Books Artic. Mod. Lang. Lit. *Divadelnofedny Sbornik.*

SNOTRACK CEASED. 0049-0822. Periodical. US. English. bm. $5.00 Domestic, $6.00 Foreign. Market Communications Inc, 225 East Michigan, Milwaukee WI 53202.

SNOW GOER TRADE. 0279-3873. Periodical. US. English. qt. Webb Publishing Company, 1999 Shepard Road, St Paul MN 55116. Tel (612)690-7200.

SOUTHERN OUTDOORS. 0199-3372. Periodical. US. English. ir. Southern Outdoors, PO Box 1790, Montgomery AL 36117. Tel (205)277-3940. Ed Larry Teaque. Ind/Abst Pop. Mag. Rev. LC SK1. adv acc. Circ 252,000. (ctrl). Edited and written for southern sportsman, featuring articles on fishing, hunting, camping and boating in the south.

SOUTHWESTERN CAMPING & TRAILERING. VFOAT Camping & Trailering. VAT Southwestern Camping and Trailering. 0093-1977. US. English. an. American Automobile Association, 1712 G Street Northwest, Washington DC 20006. LC SK601.4.S68. DD 917.8043.

SPORTS AFIELD DEER. VFOAT Deer. 0160-1830. Periodical. US. English. an. $1.50. The Hearst Corporation, 250 West 55th Street, New York NY 10019. Tel (212)262-8830. Ed Tom Paugh. LC SK301. DD 799.277357. adv acc. Circ 300,000. How-to stories about deer hunting.

THE SPORTS AFIELD OUTDOOR ALMANAC. See Yearbooks, Almanacs, Directories.

SPORTSMAN. (FIELD & STREAM SPORTSMAN). 0091-0651. US. English. $1.25. CBS Publications, 383 Madison Avenue, New York NY 10017. LC SK1. DD 799.

SPORTSMANS BOOK OF U.S. RECORDS. See Recreation, Leisure - Sports.

SPORTSMEN. (THE SPORTSMEN). 1981-. 0711-0065. CN. English. an. Free. CRV Publications Canada Ltd, Suite 221, 3414 Park Avenue, Montreal Quebec H2X 2H5 Canada. DD 796.50971.

STUDY OF PARKS AND RECREATION DEPARTMENTS IN VIRGINIA. 8th Ed. (1980-1981)-. US. English. an. Virginia Commission of Outdoor Recreation, Recreation Services Section, James Monroe Building, 101 North 14th Street, Richmond VA 23219. LC GV191.42.V8. DD 338.4779009755. *Study of Local Parks and Recreation Departments in Virginia.*

SUMMARY OF FEDERAL HUNTING REGULATIONS. ATLANTIC FLYWAY. (SUMMARY OF FEDERAL HUNTING REGULATIONS, ATLANTIC FLYWAY). VFOAT Atlantic Flyway. US. English. an. Department of the Interior, Fish & Wildlife Service, Washington DC 20240.

SUMMARY OF FEDERAL HUNTING REGULATIONS. CENTRAL FLYWAY. (SUMMARY OF FEDERAL HUNTING REGULATIONS, CENTRAL FLYWAY). VFOAT Central Flyway. US. English. an. Department of the Interior, Fish & Wildlife Service, Washington DC 20240.

SUMMARY OF FEDERAL HUNTING REGULATIONS. MISSISSIPPI FLYWAY. (SUMMARY OF FEDERAL HUNTING REGULATIONS, MISSISSIPPI FLYWAY). VFOAT Mississippi Flyway. US. English. an. Department of the Interior, Fish & Wildlife Service, Washington DC 20240.

SUMMARY OF FEDERAL HUNTING REGULATIONS. PACIFIC FLYWAY. (SUMMARY OF FEDERAL HUNTING REGULATIONS, PACIFIC FLYWAY). VFOAT Pacific Flyway. US. English. an. Department of the Interior, Fish & Wildlife Service, Washington DC 20240.

SUMMARY OF THE HUNTING REGULATIONS. Main/Corp Ontario. Ministry of Natural Resources. 1978-. 0226-482X. Periodical. CN. English. an. Ministry of Natural Resources, Information Services, Toronto Ontario Canada. DD 346.713046954. *Hunting, 0226-188X.*

SUMMIT. 1955. 0039-5056. Periodical. US. English. bm. $12.00. Summit Magazine, PO Box 1889, Big Bear Lake CA 92315. Ed J M Crenshaw and H V J Kilness. LC G505. bk rev. adv acc. Circ 6,000. Up-to-date information on all phases of mountaineering expeditions, rockclimbing, ski mountaineering, medical notes, climbing and backpacking. *Summit Magazine.*

SVENSK JAKT. 0039-6583. Periodical. SW. Swedish. mo. Fack, S-10041 Stockholm Sweden.

TECHNICAL ASSISTANCE BULLETIN. No. 1-. 0190-2792. Monographic Series. US. English. US Bureau of Outdoor Recreation, Lake Central Region, 3853 Research Park Drive, Ann Arbor MI 48104. LC GV191.42.M52. DD 301.570977.

TECHNICAL CIRCULAR - NEW HAMPSHIRE FISH AND GAME DEPARTMENT. Main/Corp New Hampshire. Fish and Game Department. No. 1- 1937-. 0077-8389. Monographic Series. US. English. ir. State of New Hampshire, Department of Fish and Game, Concord NH 03301. DD 799.

TETON. 0049-3481. Periodical. US. English. an. $3.00. Teton Magazine, Box 1903-10 West Broadway, Jackson WY 83001. Tel (307)733-9220. Ed Gene Downer. bk rev. adv acc. Circ 15,000. Concerns nature, wildlife, individual outdoor activities, and pioneer history.

TEXAS FISH & GAME. VFOAT Texas Fish and Game. 0887-4174. Periodical. US. English. mo. $14.95. Highland Publishing, PO Box 1000, Marble Falls TX 78654. Ed Marvin Spivey.

TEXAS HUNTER'S DIRECTORY. See Yearbooks, Almanacs, Directories.

TEXAS RIVERS AND RAPIDS. 1972-. 0163-4771. US. English. $5.95. B M Nolen, PO Box 60, Pipe Creek TX 78063. LC GV776.T4. DD 917.64.

THUNDER BAY CAMPING GUIDE. 1972-. 0380-6197. CN. English. Guide Publishing, PO Box 3074 Station P, Thunder Bay Ontario P7B 5E8 Canada. DD 917.1312044.

THUNDER COUNTRY OUTDOORS. V. 2, No. 1- Oct. 1974-. 0318-8477. Periodical. CN. English. mo. Thunder Country Promotions, Box 1242 Station F, 1184 Roland Avenue, Thunder Bay Ontario P7C 4X9 Canada. DD 796.930971312. *Thunder Country Skier, 0318-8469.*

TOURISTIC ANALYSIS REVIEW. See Travel.

TRACK. English. ir. 15.00 Each Issue. International Professional Hunters Association, Eastern Hemisphere Office Hilton Hotel PO Box 40528, Nairobi Kenya. LC SK1. DD 799.205.

TRAIL AND TIMBERLINE. No. 1- Apr. 1918-. 0041-0756. Periodical. US. English. $6.00. Colorado Mountain Club, 2530 West Alameda Avenue, Denver CO 80219. Tel (303)922-8976. Ed Will Mahoney. LC F782.R6. bk rev. adv acc. Circ 6,700. (ctrl). Our members share their interests, concerns, and experiences in the mountains of Colorado and of the world. *Trail and Timberline.*

TRAIL CAMPING. V. 1- Jan. 1973-. 0090-2241. Periodical. US. English. mo $9.00. Cramax Publications Inc, PO Box 310, Canoga Park CA 91305. LC SK600. DD 796.505.

TRAILER LIFE'S RV CAMPGROUND & SERVICES DIRECTORY. See Yearbooks, Almanacs, Directories.

TRAILS-A-WAY. OHIO EDITION. (TRAILS-A-WAY). 0194-5394. Periodical. US. English. ir. $5.00. Taw Publishing Company, 9731 Riverside Drive, Greenville MI 48838.

TRAPPING SEASONS AND REGULATIONS. Main/Corp Washington (State). Dept. of Game. US. English. Washington Game Department, 600 North Capitol Way, Olympia WA 98504.

UNSERE JAGD. Periodical. SZ. German. mo. Kunst & Wissen Erich Biebert, Dufourstrasse 51, CH-8008 Zurich Switzerland. LC SK201.

URBAN WILDLIFE MANGER'S NOTEBOOK. 0882-584X. US. English. qt. National Institute for Urban Wildlife, 10921 Trotting Ridge Way, Columbia MD 21044.

URBAN WILDLIFE NEWS. 0882-5858. Periodical. US. English. qt. $15.00 Donation from Members. National Institute for Urban Wildlife, 10921 Trotting Ridge Way, Columbia MD 21044.

USA OUTDOORS. 0883-6841. Periodical. US. English. bm. $15.00. USA Outdoors, PO Box 796908, Dallas TX 75379-6908. DD 796. *Military Outdoors, 0194-6846.*

UTAH BIG GAME RANGE TREND STUDIES. See Recreation, Leisure - Sports.

UTAH BLACK BEAR HARVEST. Main/Corp Utah. Division of Wildlife Resources. 0147-2380. US. English. Utah Department of Natural Resources, 1596 West North Temple, Salt Lake City UT 84116. LC SK453, SK295. DD 333.95 S, 799.2774446.

UTAH COUGAR HARVEST. See Recreation, Leisure - Sports.

VANCOUVER ISLAND'S OUTDOOR JOURNAL. VFOAT Outdoor Journal. V. 1- Mar. 14, 1974-. 0315-1212. Periodical. CN. English. mo. $21.00. Ohio Publications, Box 8, Hubbard OH 44425. Tel (216)534-4256.

THE VIRGINIA OUTDOORS PLAN. EXECUTIVE SUMMARY. Main/Corp Virginia. Commission of Outdoor Recreation. VFOAT Executive Summary, the Virginia Outdoors Plan. US. English. Commission of Outdoor Recreation, 101 North 8th Street, Richmond VA 23219. LC GV191.42.V8. DD 790.09755.

VOICE OF THE TRAPPER. 1959. 0194-6927. Periodical. US. English. qt $12.00. National Trappers Association, PO Box 3667, Bloomington IL 61702. Tel (309)829-2422. Ed Tom Krauss. adv acc. Circ 17,000. (ctrl). To educate and promote trapping.

WESTERN & EASTERN TREASURES. 1963. Periodical. US. English. mo. $13.75. Peoples Publishing Company, 901 West Victoria Street B-2, Compton CA 90220. Tel (213)537-0896. Ed Rosemary Anderson. adv acc. Circ 100,000. 'The favorite family outdoor sports magazine," treasure hunting, gold prospecting, detecting equipment, guide to lost mines, product tests and coinshooting.

WESTERN BACKCOUNTRY MAGAZINE. VFOAT Western Backcountry. 0194-4398. Periodical. US. English. mo. Western Backcountry, PO Box Q, Quincy CA 95971. Tel (916)283-0667. *Wild Country, 0164-601X.*

WESTERN CANADA, ALASKA CAMPING. (WESTERN CANADA : ALASKA CAMPING). VFOAT Alaska Camping. 0146-6585. US. English. an. American Automobile Association, 8111 Gatehouse Road, Falls Church VA 22042. LC GV198.67.C2. DD 647.9471.

WESTERN CANADA OUTDOORS. V. 1- 1977-. 0703-8399. Periodical. CN. English. bm. $6.00. The McIntosh Publication Company Ltd, PO Box 430, North Battleford Saskatchewan S9A 2Y5 Canada. Tel (306)445-7477. Ed Stan Nowakowski. DD 639.909712. bk rev. adv acc. Circ 42,000. (ctrl). Policy statements on wildlife, habitat, fish and development of water quality. Trying to improve the quality for outdoor recreation. *0049-7592 0045-9836.*

WESTERN OUTDOOR NEWS. 0049-7479. Periodical. US. English. ir. Western Outdoors Publications, PO Box 2027, Newport Beach CA 92663.

WESTERN OUTDOORS. Began in 1953. 0043-4000. Periodical. US. English. mo. $14.95. Western Outdoors Publications, PO Box 2027, Newport Beach CA 92663. Tel (714)546-4370. Ed Burt Twilegar. Ind/Abst Pop. Mag. Rev. LC SK1. DD 799.05. bk rev. adv acc. Circ 150,114. Editorial coverage on where-to-go in the West for recreational activities, with emphasis on new places for fishing, hunting, camping and pleasure boating.

WHEELER'S TRAILER RESORT AND CAMPGROUND GUIDE. SUN BELT EDITION. (WHEELERS TRAILER RESORT AND CAMPGROUND GUIDE). 0090-600X. US. English. an. $2.95. Aventour Marketing Ltd, 1550 Northwest Highway, Park Ridge IL 60068. LC SK601.3. DD 796.540257.

WILD UND HUND. Began publication with: 11. Vol. (1885). Periodical. German. bw. $61.50. Paul Parey Scientific Publishing, 35 West 38th Street 3 West, New York NY 10018. Tel (212)730-0518. Ed H Reetz. bk rev. adv acc. Circ 75,000. Popular magazine for hunters and wildlife lovers.

WILDERNESS. See Conservation & Natural Resources.

WILDERNESS ARTS AND RECREATION. V. 2, No. 3-. 0705-3150. Periodical. CN. English. bm. 1.00 Each Number. Big Bear Wilderness Services, Box 2640, Edson Alberta T0E 0P0 Canada. DD 796.5097123. *Alberta Wilderness Arts and Recreation, 0381-6303.*

Recreation, Leisure—Sports

WILDERNESS SUMMER OUTINGS. Main/Corp National and Provincial Parks Association of Canada. 1977-. 0704-6464. CN. English. an. National and Provincial Parks Association of Canada, Suite 308/47 Colborne Street, Toronto Ontario M5E 1E3 Canada. DD 796.5. *Summer Outings, 0384-5850.*

WILDERNESS TOURS NEWS. VFOAT Bulletin Wilderness Tours. VAT Bulletin Wilderness Tours (English and French Ed.). 1979-. 0821-6118. CN. English (only, 1979). an. Free. Wilderness Tours News, PO Box 89, Beachburg Ontario K0J 1C0 Canada. DD 797.1220971. (ctrl)

WILDERNESS TRAILS 'N' TALES. Vol. 2, Issue 1 (Apr. 1983)-. Periodical. CN. English. mo. 12.00. Wilderness Trails 'N' Tales, P O Box 4321 Station A, Fredericton N B E3B 5G4 Canada. DD 799.0715.

WISCONSIN DEER AND BEAR HARVEST SUMMARY. Main/Corp Wisconsin. Dept. of Natural Resources. 1968-. US. English. an. Wisonsin Deer and Bear Harvest Summary, PO Box 7921, Madison WI 53707. DD 799.277357.

WISCONSIN OUTDOORS AND CONSERVATION NEWS. Main/Corp Wisconsin. Dept. of Natural Resources. Feb. 19-20, 1977-. Periodical. US. English. wk. Wisconsin Outdoors and Conservation News, PO Box 7021, Madison WI 53707. *Wisconsin Outdoors.*

WISCONSIN SPORTSMAN. 0361-9451. Periodical. US. English. ir. $9.95. Great Lakes Sportsman Group, PO Box 2266, Oshkosh WI 54903. Tel (414)233-1327. Ed Thomas Petrie. LC SK143. DD 977.5005. adv acc. Circ 70,000. Fishing, hunting and other outdoor participation activities in Wisconsin.

WOLGAN NAKKSI. VFOAT Nakksi. 1st Vol. ('84/5)-. Periodical. KO. Korean. mo. 36,000. Choson Ilbosa 61, 1-ka Taepyong-no Chung-ku, Seoul Korea. LC SH667.K8.

WONDERFUL WEST VIRGINIA. See Conservation & Natural Resources.

WOODALL'S BETTER CAMPING. VFOAT Better Camping. 0091-2018. Periodical. US. English. mo. $6.00. Woodall Publishing Co, 500 Hyacinth Place, Highland Park IL 60035. LC SK600. DD 796.5405.

WOODALL'S CAMPGROUND DIRECTORY. EASTERN EDITION. See Yearbooks, Almanacs, Directories.

WOODALL'S CAMPGROUND DIRECTORY. NORTH AMERICAN EDITION. See Yearbooks, Almanacs, Directories.

WOODALL'S CAMPGROUND DIRECTORY. WESTERN EDITION. See Yearbooks, Almanacs, Directories.

WOODALL'S FLORIDA CAMPGROUND DIRECTORY. See Yearbooks, Almanacs, Directories.

WOODALL'S MISSOURI/ARKANSAS CAMPGROUND DIRECTORY. See Yearbooks, Almanacs, Directories.

WOODALL'S THE TENTING DIRECTORY. See Yearbooks, Almanacs, Directories.

WOODALL'S THE TENTING DIRECTORY. See Yearbooks, Almanacs, Directories.

WOODALL'S THE TENTING DIRECTORY. See Yearbooks, Almanacs, Directories.

WOODALL'S TRAILERING PARKS AND CAMPGROUNDS DIRECTORY. See Yearbooks, Almanacs, Directories.

WOODALL'S TRAILERING PARKS & CAMPGROUNDS. WESTERN EDITION. (WOODALL'S TRAILERING PARKS & CAMPGROUNDS). VFOAT Trailering Parks & Campgrounds. 0095-9243. US. English. an. $2.95. Woodall Publishing Company, 3500 Western Avenue, Highland Park IL 60035. LC GV191.35. DD 917.8043.

WOODS N WATERS MAGAZINE. See Recreation, Leisure - Sports.

WORLDWIDE HUNTING ANNUAL. See Recreation, Leisure - Sports.

SPORTS

3WHEELING. VAT Three Wheeling, 3 Wheeling. V. 1- Spring 1980-. 0196-5549. Periodical. US. English. mo. $28.00. Wright Publishing Company Inc, Box 2260, Costa Mesa CA 92626. Tel (714)979-2560. Ed Bruce Simurda. bk rev. adv acc. Circ 65,241. Edited for all terrain vehicle and 4-wheel owners, off-road enthusiasts. Features include new models, technical articles, how-to-do-it's, and competition coverages.

4 FOR 20. VFOAT Four for Twenty. June 1980-. 0229-3684. Periodical. CN. English. bm. Ontario Association of Archers, 160 Vanderhoof Avenue, Toronto Ontario M4G 4B8 Canada. DD 799.32060713. *Ontario Association of Archers : Newsletter, 0229-3676.*

4 X 4. REGLEMENTS GENERAUX, FONDS DE POINTS. (4 X 4 : REGLEMENTS GENERAUX, FONDS DE POINTS). Main/Corp Federation Auto-Quebec. VAT Quatre Par Quatre. Reglements Generaux, Fonds de Points. 0822-5281. CN. French. an. $1,00 le vol. Federation Auto-Quebec, 1415 Est rue Jarry, Montreal Quebec H2E 2Z7 Canada. DD 796.7209714.

1001 CUSTOM AND ROD IDEAS. See Transportation - Automobiles.

AAU JUNIOR OLYMPIC HANDBOOK. Main/Corp Amateur Athletic Union of the United States. VFOAT AAU Official Handbook, Junior Olympics. VAT Amateur Athletic Union Junior Olympic Handbook. 0361-4654. US. English. an. $0.75. Amateur Athletic Union, 3400 West 86th Street, Indianapolis IN 46268. LC GV723.A45. DD 796.48.

ABILITY MAGAZINE. 8756-8934. Periodical. US. English. qt. $7.00. Majestic Press, PO Box 5311, Mission Hills CA 91345. DD 796. *0738-9280.*

ACC BASKETBALL. VAT Atlantic Coast Conference Basketball. V. 1- 1978/79-. 0193-7960. US. English. an. $2.50. Capitol Sports Network Publications, Capitol Broadcasting Company, 2619 Boulevard, Raleigh NC 28230. LC GV885.72.A85. DD 796.323630975.

ACC BASKETBALL HANDBOOK. VFOAT A.C.C. Basketball Handbook. VAT Atlantic Coast Conference Basketball Handbook. 0733-0448. Periodical. US. English. an. UMI Publications, PO Box 30036, North Tryon Street, Charlotte NC 282300. Tel (704)374-0420.

ACE. 0733-043X. Periodical. US. English. bm. $17.50 Domestic, $20.00 Canada. Burlesque Publishing Inc, 300 West 43rd Street, New York NY 10036.

ACTA - BRATISLAVA. UNIVERZITA. FAKULTA TELESNEJ VYCHOVY A SPORTU. Main/Corp Bratislava. Univerzita. Fakulta Telesnej Vychovy a Sportu. Periodical. English. ir. Slovenske Pedagogicke Nakl Univerzita, Fakulta Telesnej Vychovy a Sportu, Bratislava Czechoslovakia.

ACTIF. (L'ACTIF : BULLETIN HEBDOMADAIRE DU SERVICE DES SPORTS). 0228-4057. Periodical. CN. French. wk. Free. Universite de Montreal, Service des Sports, CP 6128 Succursale A, Montreal Quebec H3C 3J7 Canada. DD 796.060714281. (ctrl).

ACTION NOW (SAN JUAN CAPISTRANO, CALIF.). (ACTION NOW). Vol. 7, No. 9 (Apr. 1981)-. 0279-8689. Periodical. US. English. mo. PO Box 1028, Dana Point CA 92629. LC GV561. DD 796.05. *Skateboarder's Action Now, 0274-7170.*

ACUC PLUNGE. (THE ACUC PLUNGE). VAT Association of Canadian Underwater Councils Plunge. Vol. 1 (Oct. 1981)-. 0713-8261. Periodical. CN. English. ACUC Plunge, 333 River Road, Vanier Ontario K1L 8B9 Canada. DD 797.230971. *I, 0700-3706.*

ADDVANTAGE. 0149-4082. Periodical. US. English. bm. $18.00. Two Commerce Park Square Suite 100/23200 Chargrin Boulevard, Cleveland OH 44122. Tel (216)464-8546. Ed Bernice Adams. LC GV991, A26. DD 796.3420973. bk rev. adv acc. Circ 5,000. (ctrl). Tennis magazine for teaching professionals.

A.H.M.H. INC. ASSOCIATION DU HOCKEY MINEUR DE HULL INC. (A.H.M.H. INC. : ASSOCIATION DU HOCKEY MINEUR DE HULL INC). VAT Association Du Hockey Mineur de Hull Inc. Vol. 1, No 1 (Dec. 1983)-. 0826-2314. Periodical. CN. French. ir. Association du Hockey Mineur de Hull, C P 1970 Succursale B, Hull Quebec J8K 3X5 Canada. DD 796.9626.

AIAW HANDBOOK. Main/Corp Association for Intercollegiate Athletics for Women. VAT Association for Intercollegiate Athletics for Women Handbook. 1976/77-. 0362-6636. US. English. an. 1201 16th Street NW, Washington DC 20036. LC GV439. DD 796.0194. *AIAW Handbook-Directory.*

AIAW HANDBOOK-DIRECTORY. See Yearbooks, Almanacs, Directories.

A.I.A.W. HANDBOOK OF POLICIES AND OPERATING PROCEDURES. (AIAW HANDBOOK OF POLICIES AND OPERATING PROCEDURES). Main/Corp Association for Intercollegiate Athletics for Women. 0090-9106. US. English. Association for Intercollegiate Athletics for Women, 1201 16th Street Northwest, Washington DC 20036. LC GV439. DD 796.0194.

AIR GUN. V. 1- Nov. 1978-. 0164-2863. Periodical. US. English. qt. $10.00 Domestic, $13.00 Foreign. Air Gun Magazine Inc, Quaker Point Professional Center, 1100 Quaker Road, Macedon NY 14502. LC TS537.5. DD 799.3.

AL-RIYADAH WA-AL-SHABAB. VFOAT Alriada wa Ashabab. Periodical. Arabic. ir. $200.00. Muassasat Al-Bayan, Lil-Sihafah Wa-Al-Tibaah, Wa-Al-Nashr Dubayy S B 2710, Dubayy Trucial States United Arab Emirates. Tel 444400. Ed Hasher Maktoum. LC GV561.R57. bk rev. adv acc. Circ 40,000. (ctrl). Concerned with Arabic and international sports and youths. Includes interviews with stars in different olympic games. Publishes weekly arabic sport activities plus outstanding international ones.

AL-SAQR. VFOAT Alsaqer. Periodical. Arabic. ir. Al-Quwat Al-Musallahah Al-Qatariyah Al-Dawahah, PO Box 4925, Al-Dawhah Qatar. LC GV561.

A.L.B.A. BOWLS. Main/Corp American Lawn Bowls Association. VAT American Lawn Bowls Association Bowls. V. 3- (13th - Issue) 0001-1754. Periodical. US. English. qt. $3.00. American Lawn Bowls, 445 Surfview Drive, Pacific Palisades CA 90272. LC GV909. DD 796.31. *A.L.B.A. Bowls, 0001-1754.*

ALBERTA DIVER. Began publication Jan.? 1980 (V. 20, No. 1?). 0227-1923. Periodical. CN. English. mo. Free to Members. Alberta Scuba Divers Council, PO Box 205, Edmonton Alberta T5J 2J1 Canada. DD 797.230607123. *Splash, 0227-1915.*

ALL-PRO HOCKEY. 83/84-. 0824-4464. CN. English. an. $2.95 Per Vol. All-Pro Hockey, 123 Newkirk Road, Richmond Hill Ontario L4C 3G5 Canada. DD 796.96206.

THE ALL-SPORTS RECORD BOOK. US. English. LC GV741.

ALMANAC. SPORTS AND GAMES. See Yearbooks, Almanacs, Directories.

ALMANACH CHASSE ET PECHE. See Yearbooks, Almanacs, Directories.

LES ALOUETTES. Main/Corp Montreal Alouette Football Club. VFOAT Alouettes. 1973-. 0318-9759. CN. English (French). an. Montreal Alouette Football Club, Autostade Cite du Havre, Montreal Quebec Canada. DD 796.335060714281. *Montreal Alouettes.*

ALPINE SKIING COMPETITION GUIDE. EASTERN/CENTRAL EDITION. (ALPINE SKIING COMPETITION GUIDE). 1983-. 0733-9356. US. English. an. United States Ski Association, Competition Division Alpine, PO Box 100, Park City UT 84060. *Alpine Skiing Competition Guide, 0733-6659; Alpine Skiing Competition Guide, 0733-6667.*

ALPINE SKIING COMPETITION GUIDE. ROCKY MOUNTAIN EDITION. (ALPINE SKIING COMPETITION GUIDE). 1982-. 0278-2960. US. English. an. $6.75. United States Ski Association, Competition Division Alpine, PO Box 100, Park City UT 84060. LC WMLC L 83/26.

ALPINE SKIING COMPETITION GUIDE. WESTERN/ROCKY EDITION. (ALPINE SKIING COMPETITION GUIDE). 1983-. 0733-9348. US. English. an. United States Ski Association, US Alpine Office, 1750 East Baldre Street, Colorado Springs CO 80909. Tel (303)578-4600. adv acc. Circ 13,000. (ctrl). A comprehensive guide to alpine ski racing in the United States. *Alpine Skiing Competition Guide,*

Recreation, Leisure—Sports

0733-6675; Alpine Skiing Competition Guide, 0278-2960.

AMATEUR BASEBALL NEWS. 0002-6816. Periodical. US. English. bm. $5.00. American Amateur Baseball Congress, P O Box 5332, Akron OH 44313. **Tel** (216)836-5424.

THE AMATEUR BOXER. 1978. 0160-7332. Periodical. US. English. $15.00. Diversified Periodicals, Box 249, Cobalt CT 06414. **Tel** (203)342-4730. Ed Bob Taylor. **DD** 796. bk rev. adv acc. **Circ** 1,500. Everything related to amateur boxing.

AMATEUR SPORT NEWS (BRITISH COLUMBIA EDITION). (AMATEUR SPORT NEWS). 0824-4014. Periodical. CN. English. sa. Free. Amateur Sport News, 701-10240-124 Street, Edmonton Alberta T5N 3W6 Canada. **DD** 796.09711.

AMATEUR SPORT NEWS (CENTRAL ALBERTA EDITION). (AMATEUR SPORT NEWS). 0824-4065. Periodical. CN. English. sa. Free. Amateur Sport News, 701-10240-124 Street, Edmonton Alberta T5N 3W6 Canada. **DD** 796.0971233.

AMATEUR SPORT NEWS (EDMONTON EDITION). (AMATEUR SPORT NEWS). 0824-4057. Periodical. CN. English. sa. Free. Amateur Sport News, 701-10240-124 Street, Edmonton Alberta T5N 3W6 Canada. **DD** 796.0971233.

AMATEUR SPORT NEWS (NORTHERN ALBERTA EDITION). (AMATEUR SPORT NEWS). 0824-4049. Periodical. CN. English. sa. Free. Amateur Sport News, 701-10240-124 Street, Edmonton Alberta T5N 3W6 Canada. **DD** 796.097123.

AMATEUR SPORT NEWS (NORTHERN BRITISH COLUMBIA EDITION). (AMATEUR SPORT NEWS). 0824-4006. Periodical. CN. English. sa. Free. Amateur Sport News, 701-10240-124 Street, Edmonton Alberta T5N 3W6 Canada. **DD** 796.09711.

AMATEUR SPORT NEWS (NORTHERN SASKATCHEWAN EDITION). (AMATEUR SPORT NEWS). 0824-4030. Periodical. CN. English. sa. Free. Amateur Sport News, 701-10240-124 Street, Edmonton Alberta T5N 3W6 Canada. **DD** 796.097124.

AMATEUR SPORT NEWS (SOUTHERN ALBERTA EDITION). (AMATEUR SPORT NEWS). 0822-8280. Periodical. CN. English. sa. Free. Amateur Sport News, 701-10240 124 Street, Edmonton Alberta T5N 2W8 Canada. **DD** 796.097123.

AMATEUR SPORT NEWS (SOUTHERN BRITISH COLUMBIA EDITION). (AMATEUR SPORT NEWS). 0824-3999. Periodical. CN. English. sa. Free. Amateur Sport News, 701-10240-124 Street, Edmonton Alberta T5N 3W6 Canada. **DD** 796.09711.

AMATEUR SPORT NEWS (SOUTHERN SASKATCHEWAN EDITION). (AMATEUR SPORT NEWS). 0824-4022. Periodical. CN. English. sa. Free. Amateur Sport News, 701-10240-124 Street, Edmonton Alberta T5N 3W6 Canada. **DD** 796.097124.

AMATEUR SPORT REPORT. 0710-9504. Periodical. CN. English. ir. $6.00. E & M Amateur Sport Report Ltd, Suite 102/221-14th Street South West, Calgary Alberta T2T 3T2 Canada. **DD** 796.0971233.

AMATEUR WRESTLING NEWS. 0569-1796. Periodical. US. English. ir. $20.00. Amateur Wrestling News, PO Box 60387, Oklahoma City OK 73146. **Tel** (405)236-2808. Ed Ron Good. bk rev. adv acc. **Circ** 10,000. Covers all phases of amateur wrestling (Olympic to high school to college). *Wrestling News and Reports.*

AMERICAN COONER. 0002-807X. Periodical. US. English. mo. $11.00. American Cooner, PO Box 211, Sesser IL 62884. **Tel** (618)625-2711. Ed George O Slankard. adv acc. **Circ** 30,000. Coon hound events, supplies and articles. *Mountain Music.*

AMERICAN COWBOY. VFOAT American Cowboy Magazine. 0738-9795. Periodical. US. English. bm. $10.00 Domestic, $14.00 Foreign. Hoof & Horn Publishers, PO Box 311, Walsenburg CO 81089. **LC** GV1834.5. **DD** 791.8. *American Cowboy Magazine, 0199-4220.*

AMERICAN FENCING. V. 1- Nov. 1949-. 0002-8436. Periodical. US. English. bm. $9.00. United States Fencing Association, 1750 East Boulder Street, Colorado Springs CO 80909. **Tel** (303)578-4511. Ed Mary Huddleson. **LC** U860. **DD** 796.8605. bk rev. adv acc. **Circ** 8,000. (ctrl). Promotion of the sport of fencing and activities of USFA membership. *A.F.L.A. Secretary's Newsletter, Riposte.*

AMERICAN FIELD. *See* Recreation, Leisure - Outdoor Life.

AMERICAN GUN TIMES. 0743-4286. Periodical. US. English. mo. $10.00. Second Amendment Foundation, James Madison Building, 12500 NE 19th Place, Bellevue WA 98005.

THE AMERICAN HANDGUNNER. V. 1- Sept./Oct. 1976-. 0145-4250. Periodical. US. English. bm. $34.75. Publishers Development Corp, 591 Camino De La Reina Ste 200, San Diego CA 92108. **Tel** (619)297-5350. Ed Jerry Rakusan. **LC** TS537. **DD** 799.20283305. bk rev. adv acc. **Circ** 150,000. Publication devoted exclusively to the sport of handgunning.

AMERICAN HIGH SCHOOL ATHLETE. US. English. qt. Athletic Publishing Group Inc, PO Box 248, Andover MA 01810. **LC** GV697.A1. **DD** 796.0922, B.

AMERICAN HOCKEY & ARENA. VAT American Hockey and Arena. 1980. Periodical. US. English. ir. American Hockey & Arena Magazine, 2997 Broadmoor Valley Road, Colorado Springs CO 80906. **Tel** (303)576-4990. Ed Jeff Mordhorst. **LC** GV848.4.U6. **DD** 796.9620973. adv acc. **Circ** 30,000. Promotes the continuing healthy growth of the sport and the successful construction and operation of ice facilities. *United States Hockey & Arena Biz, 0162-654X.*

AMERICAN HOCKEY MAGAZINE. 8756-3789. Periodical. US. English. bm. $12.00. 2997 Broadmoor Valley Road, Colorado Springs CO 80906. **Tel** (303)576-4990. Ed Mike Schroeder. **LC** GV848.4.U6. **DD** 796.9620973. adv acc. **Circ** 30,000. (ctrl). Edited for those involved in the game of ice hockey on all levels. Covers hockey news across the U.S. with an emphasis on the amateur level. *American Hockey & Arena.*

AMERICAN JOURNAL OF SPORTS MEDICINE. *See* Medicine.

THE AMERICAN MARKSMAN. 0199-6770. Periodical. US. English. mo. $6.00. National Rifle Association of America, 1600 Rhode Island Avenue NW, Washington DC 20036. **Tel** (800)368-5714.

THE AMERICAN RACING MANUAL. 1906-. Periodical. US. English. an. $50.00. Daily Racing Form Inc, 10 Lake Drive, Hightstown NJ 08520. **Tel** (609)448-9100. **LC** SF325. *American Sporting Manual.*

THE AMERICAN RACING PIGEON NEWS. *See* Veterinary Medicine, Animal Culture.

AMERICAN RIFLEMAN. 0003-083X. Periodical. US. English. mo. National Rifle Association of America, 1600 Rhode Island Avenue NW, Washington DC 20036. **Tel** (800)368-5714. **Ind/Abst** Mag. Index, Pop. Mag. Rev., Art Archaeol. Tech. Abstr., Consum. Index Prod. Eval. Inf. Source. **LC** SK1. **DD** 799.205. *Arms and the Man, 0271-6917.*

THE AMERICAN SHOTGUNNER. 0162-153X. Periodical. US. English. mo. $50.00. The American Shotgunner, PO Box 3351, Reno NV 89505. **Tel** (702)826-3825. Ed Robert Thruston and Kerry Watkins. **LC** WMLC L 83/19. bk rev. adv acc. **Circ** 134,000. The connoisseur's hunting, fishing, outdoor recreation and travel magazine. Columns on shooting sports, exotic hunting and fishing trips, wildlife art and gun investments.

AMERICAN SWIMMING COACHES ASSOCIATION WORLD CLINIC YEARBOOK. *See* Yearbooks, Almanacs, Directories.

AMERICAN WHITEWATER. VFOAT Whitewater. 0300-7626. Periodical. US. English. bm. American Whitewater Affiliation, 146 North Broadway, Palatine IL 60067.

ANNALS OF SPORTS MEDICINE. *See* Medicine.

L'ANNEE DU RUGBY. French. ir. **LC** GV944.85. **DD** 796.333630944.

L'ANNEE DU TENNIS. Began with Vol. for 1979. French. an. **LC** GV991. **DD** 796.34205.

L'ANNEE PLANCHE A VOILE. 1980-81-. French. an. **LC** GV811.63.W56. **DD** 797.17205.

ANNUAIRE DU SPORT UNIVERSITAIRE QUEBECOIS ET CALENDRIERS DES ACTIVITES. *See* Yearbooks, Almanacs, Directories.

ANNUAIRE ET REGLES DE JEU - ASSOCIATION CANADIENNE DE VOLLEY-BALL. *See* Yearbooks, Almanacs, Directories.

ANNUAIRE (FRANCE. MINISTERE DE LA JEUNESSE, DES SPORTS ET DES LOISIRS. DIVISION DES ETUDES ET DE LA STATISTIQUE). *See* Yearbooks, Almanacs, Directories.

ANNUAL - ASSOCIATION OF TRACK AND FIELD STATISTICIANS. *See* Statistics.

ANNUAL - KAJAKS TRACK AND FIELD CLUB. Main/Corp Kajaks Track and Field Club. 1979-. 0229-0618. CN. English. an. Free. Kajaks Track and Field Club, 11540 Seabrook, Richmond British Columbia V7A 3H3 Canada. **DD** 796.420971133. (ctrl). *Annual, 0708-2150.*

ANNUAL OF THE ONTARIO CURLING ASSOCIATION CEASED. Main/Corp Ontario Curling Association. Began publication with 1893? issue. 0317-7769. CN. English. an. Free to Members. Ontario Curling Association, 85 Elginton Avenue East, Toronto Ontario M4P 1H5 Canada. **LC** GV845. **DD** 796.96.

ANNUAL REPORT - DIVISION OF RACING, NEW YORK STATE. *See* Public Administration.

ANNUAL REPORT - LOS ANGELES OLYMPIC ORGANIZING COMMITTEE. (ANNUAL REPORT). Main/Corp Los Angeles Olympic Organizing Committee. 1979-. US. English. an. Los Angeles Olympic Organizing Committee, 10100 Santa Monica Boulevard/6th Floor, Los Angeles CA 90067.

ANNUAL REPORT - NEBRASKA STATE RACING COMMISSION. *See* Public Administration.

ANNUAL REPORT OF THE EXECUTIVE COMMITTEE OF UNITED STATES GOLF ASSOCIATION. (ANNUAL REPORT OF THE EXECUTIVE COMMITTEE). Main/Corp United States Golf Association. Executive Committee. 0146-8448. US. English. an. US Golf Association, Golf House, Far Hills NJ 07931. **LC** GV969.U5. **DD** 338.477963520973.

ANNUAL REPORT OF THE FEDERAL COMMUNICATIONS COMMISSION ON THE EFFECT OF PUBLIC LAW 93-107, THE SPORTS ANTIBLACKOUT LAW, ON THE BROADCASTING OF SOLD-OUT HOME GAMES OF PROFESSIONAL FOOTBALL, BASEBALL, BASKETBALL AND HOCKEY. *See* Communication - Broadcasting.

ANNUAL REPORT OF THE NEW HAMPSHIRE GREYHOUND RACING COMMISSION TO THE GOVERNOR AND THE EXECUTIVE COUNCIL. *See* Public Administration.

ANNUAL REPORT - TOTALISATOR AGENCY BOARD. Main/Corp Totalisator Agency Board. English. ir. Free. 304 Lambton Quay, Wellington New Zealand. Tel 748-999. Ed R H Pope. **LC** SF331. **DD** 354.93100762. **Circ** 500. (ctrl). Sets out financial statement annually of totalisator agency board dealing with off-track betting on horses and dogs.

ANNUAL REPORTS OF THE NATIONAL COLLEGIATE ATHLETIC ASSOCIATION. Main/Corp National Collegiate Athletic Association. 1965/66-. 0077-3794. Periodical. US. English. an. $8.00. National Collegiate Athletic Association, PO Box 1906, Shawnee Mission KS 66222. **Tel** (913)384-3220. **LC** GV563. **DD** 796.06273. Reports of various NCAA committees, minutes of Council, Presidents Commission and Executive Committee meetings, complete financial report.

ANNUAL YEAR BOOK - UNITED STATES TROTTING ASSOCIATION, INC. *See* Yearbooks, Almanacs, Directories.

EL ANO AUTOMOVIL. Spanish. ir. 1,600. Edisport S L, Isaac Peral 12, Madrid-15 Spain. **LC** GV1029. **DD** 796.72.

Recreation, Leisure—Sports

ANUDANOM KI MANGEM, KHELA VIBHAGA (INDIA. DEPT. OF SPORTS). Main/Corp India. Dept. of Sports. VFOAT Demands for Grants of Department of Sports. English (Hindi). an. LC GV653. DD 796.0954.

AQUA-FIELD SPORTSMAN. See Manufacturing.

AQUALINE. 0714-4563. Periodical. CN. English. ir. $6.00. Aqualine, c/o R Clark, Parks and Recreation Services, Civic Centre, Etobicoke Ontario M9C 2Y2 Canada. DD 797.05.

THE ARCHER. V. 1- Autumn 1951-. 0003-8237. Periodical. US. English. qt. Camas Press, PO Box 41, Camas Valley OR 97416. Tel (503)445-2327. LC AP2. DD 811.008.

ARCHER AU QUEBEC, FEUILLET D'INFORMATION . . . . (L'ARCHER AU QUEBEC : FEUILLET D'INFORMATION DE LA FEDERATION DE TIR A L'ARC DU QUEBEC). Main/Corp Federation de Tir a l'Arc du Quebec. VFOAT Archer au Quebec (Feuillet d'Information). No. 1-. 0227-0757. Periodical. CN. French. bm. Free to Members. La Federation, 1415 Est rue Jarry, Montreal Quebec H2E 2Z7 Canada. DD 799.32060714. (ctrl).

ARCHERY WORLD. VFOAT TAM, The Archer's Magazine. V. 15, No.11- Dec. 1966-. 0003-827X. Periodical. US. English. bm. Archery World/Winter Sports Publishing, 715 Florida Avenue South, Minneapolis MN 55426. Ind/Abst Mag. Index, Consum. Index Prod. Eval. Inf. Source. DD 799. *TAM and Archery World.*

ARGO NEWS. V. 1- Feb. 1977-. 0704-0822. Periodical. CN. English. ir. 50 Per No. Argonaut Inc, Argo News Unit 52, 655 Dixon Road, Rexdale Ontario M9W 1J4 Canada. DD 796.33506.

ARKANSAS SPORTSMAN. 0744-4184. Periodical. US. English. mo. $11.95. Game and Fish Publications, PO Box 741, Marietta GA 30061. Tel (404)953-9222.

ATHLETIC ADMINISTRATION. (ATHLETIC ADMINISTRATION). Began publication in 1966. 0044-9873. Periodical. US. English. bm. $15.00. National Association of Collegiate Directors of Athletics, PO Box 16428, Cleveland OH 44116. Tel (216)331-5773. Ed Michael J Cleary and Timothy W Gleason. bk rev. adv acc. Circ 3,800. (ctrl). Covers intercollegiate athletic administration.

ATHLETIC BUSINESS. See Business.

ATHLETICS. UK. English. an. MacDonald and Jane's Publishers, Paulton House, 8 Shepherdess Walk, London N1 7LW England. LC GV1060.5. DD 796.42.

ATHLETICS (TORONTO, ONT.). (ATHLETICS). VFOAT Athletics Magazine. No. 27 (Mar./Apr. 1981)-. 0229-4966. Periodical. CN. English. ir. $44.88. Athletics, 1220 Sheppard Avenue East, Willowdale Ontario M2K 2X1 Canada. Tel (416)495-4053. Ed Greg Lockhart. DD 796.4209713. bk rev. adv acc. Circ 18,000. (ctrl). The only magazine in Canada that covers all results: interviews, rankings, training programs and the science of training. *Ontario Athletics, 0229-0014.*

ATHLETISME CEASED. -No. 2. 0381-6214. Periodical. CN. French. ir. $9.28. Federation Athletisme Quebec, 1415 Tarry Street, Montreal Quebec H2E 2Z7 Canada. Tel (514)374-4700.

ATHLETISME ET COURSE SUR ROUTE. (ATHLETISME ET COURSE SUR ROUTE : REVUE OFFICIELLE DE LA FEDERATION D'ATHLETISME DU QUEBEC). 0822-9953. CN. French. mo. 12.00. Federation d'Athletisme du Quebec, 1415 Est rue Jarry, Montreal Quebec H2E 2Z7 Canada. DD 796.4209714. *Athletisme, 0381-6214.*

ATHLON'S PRO FOOTBALL. VFOAT Pro Football. Vol. 1 (1982)-. 0734-2888. Periodical. US. English. an. $5.95. Athlon Publications, 3814 Cleghorn Avenue, Nashville TN 37215. Tel (615)297-7581. LC GV937. DD 796.332640973.

AUDIBLE (TORONTO, ONT.). (AUDIBLE). 1970. 0710-2038. Periodical. CN. English. qt. 8.00. Ontario Amateur Football Association, 1220 Sheppard Avenue East, Willowdale Ontario M2K 2X1 Canada. Tel (416)495-4290. Ed Steve Valeriote. DD 796.33509713. adv acc. Circ 2,000. (ctrl). Football related articles on techniques, systems, safety, training, and officiating with emphasis on the amateur coach and volunteer.

AUSTRALIAN JOURNAL OF SPORTS MEDICINE AND EXERCISE SCIENCES : THE OFFICIAL JOURNAL OF THE AUSTRALIAN SPORTS MEDICINE FEDERATION. See Medicine.

AUTO MODIFIEE. (L'AUTO MODIFIEE). Vol. 1, No 1-. 0822-1006. Periodical. CN. French. mo. L'Auto Modifiee, CP 848, Rawdon Quebec J0K 1S0 Canada. Tel (514)834-5359. Ed Luc Richard. DD 629.22809714. adv acc. Circ 8,000. Motorsport racing of all kind. Track and club listing (Canada-USA) information, flashback, schedules-past major event reports, and what happen/what's new-full of photos.

AUTO RACING DIGEST. V. 1- July 1973-. 0090-8029. Periodical. US. English. bm. $7.95. Auto Racing Digest, PO Box 3300, Comm Data Services, Harlan IA 51537. Tel (312)491-6440. Ed Michael Herbert. LC GV1029. DD 796.720973. bk rev. adv acc. Circ 75,000. Covers all forms of auto racing.

AUTO RACING USA. VAT Auto Racing United States of America. V. 1- Oct. 1978-. 0164-369X. Periodical. US. English. mo. $8.95 Domestic, $9.95 Canada. Auto Racing USA, PO Box 72/916 Franklin Avenue, Franklin Lakes NJ 07417.

AUTO RACING/USA. (AUTO RACING, USA). VFOAT Autoracing/USA. 1983-. 8756-9353. US. English. an. $39.95. Motorbooks International, Osceola WI 54020. LC GV1033. DD 796.720973.

AUTO SPORT. Vol. 8, Issue 3 (May 1982)-. 0714-7104. Periodical. CN. English. mo. $10.95. Wheelspin News, 3045 Universal Drive, Mississauga Ontario L4X 2E2 Canada. DD 796.72. *Auto Sport Canada, 0317-3798.*

AUTO SPORT CANADA CEASED. VFOAT Autosport Canada. V. 1-8, Issue 2. 0317-3798. CN. English. mo. $6. Autosport Canada c/o Wheelspin News Inc, 3057 Universal Drive, Mississauga Ont L4X 2E2 Canada. DD 796.720971.

B. C. TRACK MONTHLY CEASED. VFOAT British Columbia Track Monthly. Began publication in Fall 1966. 0382-5086. Periodical. CN. English. mo. $5. N Jordan, 773 No 4 Road, Richmond British Columbia V6Y 2T4 Canada. DD 796.4209711.

BABE RUTH BASEBALL'S ATHLETES OF THE YEAR. 0097-8124. US. English. an. 200 South Hull Street, Montgomery AL 36104. LC GV865.A1. DD 396.35762, B.

BADGER SPORTSMAN. See Recreation, Leisure - Outdoor Life.

BADMINTON. Main/Corp Saskatchewan High Schools Athletic Association. 0704-4933. CN. English. an. Free. Saskatchewan High Schools Athletic Association, 2220 College Avenue, Regina Saskatchewan S4P 3V7 Canada. DD 796.345097124.

BADMINTON CANADA. Vol. 1, No. 1 (Sept. 1981)-. 0711-124X. Periodical. CN. English (includes some text in French). qt. 6.00 Domestic, 8.00 Foreign. Canadian Badminton Association, 333 River Road, Ottawa Ontario K1L 8B9 Canada. Tel (613)748-5605. Ed David Kilfoyle. DD 796.3450971. bk rev. adv acc. Circ 3,000. (ctrl). News and views on badminton and players in Canada as well as information from around the world. *Badminton Review, 0382-554X.*

BADMINTON CHALLENGE. (THE BADMINTON CHALLENGE : BRITISH COLUMBIA BADMINTON ASSOCIATION NEWSPAPER). 0710-0051. Periodical. CN. English. qt. Free. British Columbia Badminton Association, 6326 Collingwood Street, Vancouver British Columbia V6N 1T6 Canada. DD 796.34509711.

THE BADMINTON MAGAZINE. Began in 1983. 0747-9069. Periodical. US. English. qt. $5.00 Domestic, $10.00 Foreign. Badminton Magazine, PO Box 3796, Manhattan Beach CA 90266. Tel (213)546-3652. Ed Cassandra Salapatas-Metz. DD 796. adv acc. Circ 1,200. (ctrl). Badminton scene in the USA.

BADMINTON NEW-NOUVEAU BRUNSWICK. (BADMINTON NEW-NOUVEAU BRUNSWICK : NEWSLETTER). Sept. 1979-. 0229-3862. Periodical. CN. English (includes some text in French). ir. Free. Badminton New-Nouveau Brunswick, 5 Neck Road, Rothesay New Brunswick E0G 2W0 Canada. DD 796.34509715. (ctrl). *Badminton New Brunswick, 0229-3854.*

BADMINTON REVIEW. V. 1-16, No. 4. 0382-554X. Periodical. CN. English. qt. 6.00 Domestic, 8.00 Foreign. Canadian Badminton Association, 333 River Road-11th Floor, Ottawa Ontario K1L 8H9 Canada. Tel (613)748-5605. Ed David Kilfoyle. DD 796.34'5'0971. bk rev. adv acc. Circ 3,000. (ctrl). Information on all aspects of badminton from coaching, recreation, elite players, and reports on major and domestic championships. News from the government's "Sport Canada", and other articles of interest.

BADMINTON REVIEW (ST. ALBERT, ALTA.). (BADMINTON REVIEW). 0822-6784. Periodical. CN. English. Alberta Badminton Association, 13 Mission Avenue, St Albert Alverta T8N 1H6 Canada. DD 796.345097123. *Alberta Badminton Review, 0714-3893.*

BADMINTON RULE BOOK. Main/Corp Alberta Badminton Association. 0826-5208. CN. English. an. Alberta Badminton Association, 13 Mission Avenue, St Albert Alberta T8N 1H6 Canada. DD 796.3450607123.

BADMINTON U S A. V. 27, No. 1- Nov. 1967-. Periodical. US. English. bm. $5.00. United States Badminton Association, PO Box 456, Waterford MI 48095. Tel (313)627-4884. Ed Don Rittman. adv acc. Circ 1,500. (ctrl). Tournament results, tournament listing, national and local stories, advertising, and action pictures.

BADMINTONIEN. (LE BADMINTONIEN). Published since May 1979. 0228-0698. Periodical. CN. French. bm. Free to Members. Federation de Badminton du Quebec, 1415 Est rue Jarry, Montreal Quebec H2E 2Z7 Canada. DD 796.34505.

'BAMA. V. 1- June 1979-. 0195-0975. Periodical. US. English. ir. $30.00. College Sports Publ Inc, PO Box 6104, University AL 35486. Tel (205)345-5074. Ed Kirk McNair. adv acc. Circ 15,000. Official full-color magazine of the University of Alabama athletics, emphasizing football and men's basketball but including all men and women's sports.

BASEBALL AMERICA. 0745-5372. Periodical. US. English. sa. $22.50. American Sports Publishing Inc, PO Box 2089, Durham NC 27702. *All-America Baseball News, 0228-6033.*

BASEBALL AMERICA'S BASEBALL DIRECTORY. See Yearbooks, Almanacs, Directories.

BASEBALL BULLETIN. 0199-0128. Periodical. US. English. qt. $10.00. Donald Publications Inc, PO Box 413, Troy MI 48099. Tel (313)879-1676. Ed Larry Donald. bk rev. adv acc. Circ 20,000. Tabloid newspaper, nostalgia and in-depth columns by nationally known writers.

BASEBALL CANADA. Vol. 1, No. 1 (July 1977)-. 0227-6518. Periodical. CN. English (includes some text in French). ir. Free. Baseball Canada, 333 River Road, Vanier Ontario K1L 8B9 Canada. DD 796.3570971. (ctrl).

BASEBALL CARDS. See Hobbies.

BASEBALL CASE BOOK. 0270-4218. US. English. National Federation of State High School Association, Federation Place Box 98, Kansas City MO 60120. LC GV877. DD 796.35702022.

BASEBALL DIGEST. V. 1- Aug. 1942-. 0005-609X. Periodical. US. English. mo. $13.95. Communications Data Services, PO Box 3300, Harlan IA 51537. Tel (312)491-6440. Ed Jack Kuenster. LC GV862. DD 796.35705. bk rev. adv acc. Circ 300,000. Baseball's only monthly magazine.

BASEBALL HOBBY NEWS. See Hobbies.

BASEBALL (MONTREAL, QUEBEC). (BASEBALL). 0821-4123. Periodical. CN. English (French). ir. $2.25 Per No. Montreal Baseball Club, PO Box 500/Station M, Montreal Quebec H1V 3P2 Canada. Tel (514)253-3434. Ed Rene Guimond. DD 796.3576409714281. adv acc. Circ 350,000. Baseball editorial content with photography. Articles on players, teams, players' families, Hall of Fame stars and special interest stories. Goal of articles is to get the fans to know the team and its players.

BASEBALL (OTTAWA, ONT.). (BASEBALL). 82-. 0713-8415. CN. French. an. $4.95 Per No. Baseball c/o Edicompo Bureau 104, 1207 rue Saint-Andre, Montreal Quebec H2L 3S8 Canada. DD 796.35706.

BASEBALL RESEARCH JOURNAL. 1972-. 0734-6891. US. English. an. Society for American Baseball Research, PO Box 323, Cooperstown NY 13326. Ind/Abst Am. Hist. Life, Hist.

Recreation, Leisure—Sports

Abstr., Part A, Mod. Hist. Abstr., Hist. Abst., Part B, Twent. Century Abstr. LC GV862. DD 796.35705.

BASEBALL RULE BOOK. NATIONAL FEDERATION EDITION. (BASEBALL RULE BOOK). 0270-1537. US. English. an. National Federation of State High School Associations, 11724 Plaza Circle/PO Box 20626, Kansas City MO 64195. Tel (816)464-5400. Ed Bradley A Rumble. LC GV877. DD 796.35702022. adv acc. Circ 55,000. The offical rules of high school baseball. *Baseball Rules*.

BASEBALL TRIVIA NEWSLETTER. VFOAT Baseball Trivia. Began with issue for Jan. 1984?. 0743-4723. Periodical. US. English. mo. $18.00 Introductory, $24.00 Regular. Baseball Trivia Newsletter, 217 Crystal Avenue, Staten Island NY 10302.

BASEBALLS FORGOTTEN HEROES. Vol. 1 (July 1984)-. US. English. Stevens Enterprises, 95 Allen Street Box 187, Netcong NJ 07857. Tel (201)347-3067. Ed Frank Stevens. LC GV865.A1. DD 796.3570922, B. adv acc. Pictures and biographies of baseball players who are not in the Baseball Hall of Fame.

BASELINE. (THE BASELINE). Vol. 1, No. 1 (Feb. 1980)-. 0229-3471. Periodical. CN. English. qt. Free to Members, $5.00 Membership. B.C.A.B.A., 1299 Hornby Street, Vancouver British Columbia V6Z 2E2 Canada. DD 796.323060711.

BASKETBALL. Main/Corp Saskatchewan High Schools Athletic Association. 0704-4941. CN. English. an. Free. Saskatchewan High Schools Athletic Association, 2220 College Avenue, Regina Saskatchewan S4P 3V7 Canada. DD 796.32362097124.

BASKETBALL BULLETIN. (THE BASKETBALL BULLETIN). 0094-9175. US. English. ir. $50.00. Sports Publishing, 6000 Camp Bowie Boulevard/Suite 197, Fort Worth TX 76116. Tel (817)737-0925. LC GV882. DD 796.323630973.

BASKETBALL CASE BOOK. 0525-4663. US. English. $1.15. National Federation of State High School Association, 400 Leslie Street, PO Box 89, Elgin IL 60120. LC GV885.45. DD 796.32362.

THE BASKETBALL CLINIC. 0146-5007. Periodical. US. English. mo. $31.25. Princeton Educational Publ, Box CN 5245, Princeton NJ 08540. Tel (609)924-5534.

BASKETBALL DIGEST. V. 1- Nov. 1973-. 0098-5988. Periodical. US. English. mo. $9.95. Basketball Digest, PO Box 3300, Comm Data Services, Harlan IA 51537. Tel (312)491-6440. Ed Michael Herbert. LC GV885.5. DD 796.32305. bk rev. adv acc. Circ 130,000. Covers all National Basketball Association basketball.

BASKETBALL FORECAST. 0160-5747. US. English. $1.25 Single Issue. Lexington Library, PO Box 1741 Grand Central Station, New York NY 10017. LC GV885.6. DD 796.3230973.

BASKETBALL OFFICIALS MANUAL. 0270-4226. US. English. an. National Federation of State High Schools, 11724 Plaza Circle Box 20626, Kansas City MO 64195. Tel (816)464-5400. LC GV885.2. DD 796.32302022.

BASKETBALL RULES SIMPLIFIED AND ILLUSTRATED FOR OFFICIALS, COACHES, PLAYERS, SPECTATORS. (BASKETBALL RULES SIMPLIFIED AND ILLUSTRATED . . . FOR OFFICIALS, COACHES, PLAYERS, SPECTATORS). Main/Corp National Federation of State High School Associations. VFOAT Official High School Basketball Rules Simplified and Illustrated. 0737-5212. US. English. an. $2.25. National Federation of State High School Associations, 11724 Plaza Circle Box 20626, Kansas City MO 64195. LC GV885.45. DD 796.32302022.

BASKETBALL STARS. 1970-. US. English. an. Pyramid Books, 757 Third Avenue, New York NY 10017. LC GV884.A1. DD 796.3230922, B. *Basketball Stars*.

BASKETBALL TIMES. 0744-2866. Periodical. US. English. mo. $18.00. Basketball Times, PO Box 960, Rochester MI 48063. Tel (313)879-1676. *College and Pro Basketball Times, 0164-3096*.

BASKETBALL WEEKLY. 0005-6170. Periodical. US. English. ir. $20.00. Basketball Weekly, 17820 East Warren, Detroit MI 48224. Tel (313)881-9555.

B.C. ALL-TIME TOP TEN PERFORMANCES AND TOP THIRTY. (B.C. ALL-TIME TOP TEN PERFORMANCES AND TOP THIRTY FOR . . .). Main/Corp British Columbia Track & Field Association. 1980-. 0821-7637. CN. English. an. British Columbia Track & Field Association, 1200 Hornby Street, Vancouver British Columbia V6Z 2E2 Canada. DD 796.4209711. *Junior Development, Top Fifty, 0225-7742*.

B.C. ARCHER. (THE B. C. ARCHER). VAT British Columbia Archer. 0226-7691. Periodical. CN. English. mo. $15. Membership. British Columbia Archery Association, J Wiebe, 1905-37th Avenue, Vernon British Columbia V1T 2W9 Canada. DD 799.32060711.

BC ATHLETICS RECORD. VAT British Columbia Athletics Record. Mar./Apr. 1983-. 0822-9759. Periodical. CN. English. bm. Free. B C Athletic, Track & Field Association, 1200 Hornby Street, Vancouver British Columbia V6Z 2E2 Canada. DD 796.4209711. Yes. *BC Track Record, 0711-0006*.

B.C. RUNNER. (B. C. RUNNER). No. 1-11. 0707-3240. Periodical. CN. English. qt. Free to Members, $4.00 to Others. Seawall Running Society, PO Box 4981, Vancouver British Columbia V6B 4A6 Canada. DD 796.42609711.

B.C. SPORTS ANNUAL. (B. C. SPORTS ANNUAL). 1974-. 0315-999X. Periodical. CN. English. an. Optimist Club of Vancouver, 164-11th Avenue East, Vancouver British Columbia V5T 2C2 Canada. DD 796.09711. *Sports Annual, 0316-0092*.

BECOIS-VOLANT. 0820-9863. Periodical. CN. French. ir. 15.00. Association de Vol Libre du Quebec, C P 332, Saint-Laurent Quebec H4L 4V6 Canada. Ed Jean Letourneau. DD 797.55. adv acc. Circ 300. Hang-gliding activity in Quebec Province training club meets, competitions and safety records.

BEHIND THE WHISTLE. 0275-3626. Periodical. US. English. bm. $8.50. Behind the Whistle, PO Box 67E36, Los Angeles CA 90067. LC GV943.9.R43. DD 796.334305.

BEIHEFT ZU LEISTUNGSSPORT. See Medicine.

BERICHTE UND ASPEKTE. Main/Corp Bundesinstitut fur Sportwissenschaft. German. ir. 5023 Lovenich (Bez Koln), Hertzstrasse1, Lovenich W Germany. LC GV563.B84.

THE BERMUDIAN. 1930. Periodical. BM. English. mo. $20.00. Bermudian Publishing Co, Bermudiana Arcade Queen Street, Hamilton Bermuda. Tel 809 29 50695. Ed Dinah Darby. bk rev. adv acc. Circ 10,000. (ctrl). Personalities, sports, and social news.

BEST OF GOAL. (THE BEST OF GOAL). 1973/74-. 0097-9767. US. English. $2.95. Spartan Publishing Company, Box 2001, New Canaan CT 06840. LC GV846. DD 796.96205.

BEYOND SIGHT. VFOAT Actualite. 0712-2446. Periodical. CN. English. Beyond Sight CBSA, c/o National Sport and Recreation Centre, 333 River Road, Vanier City Ontario K1L 8B9 Canada. DD 796.019605.

BIENNIAL REPORT - OREGON. DEPT. OF FISH AND WILDLIFE. Main/Corp Oregon. Dept. of Fish and Wildlife. 0276-0657. US. English. be. Department of Fish & Wildlife/ Office of the Director, 506 SW Mill Street/PO Box 3503, Portland OR 07208. LC SK439. DD 639.909795. *Biennial Report, 0098-387X*.

THE BIG EIGHT. 0361-588X. US. English. an. $3.50. College Sports, PO Box 1765, Norman OK 73070. Tel (405)364-1050. LC GV958.5.B53. DD 796.332630973.

BIG TEN FOOTBALL ALMANAC. See Yearbooks, Almanacs, Directories.

THE BILL JAMES BASEBALL ABSTRACT. See Indexes/Abstracts.

BLITZ. V. 1- Oct. 1977-. 0705-1484. Periodical. CN. English (text also in French). qt. Free. Montreal Alouette Football Club, PO Box 100 Station M, Montreal Quebec H1V 3L6 Canada. DD 796.335060714281. (ctrl).

THE BLUE BOOK OF COLLEGE ATHLETICS. 1931/32-. US. English. an. $12.00. Rohrich Corporation, 903 East Tallmadge Avenue, Akron OH 44310. Tel (216)633-1711. Ed A W Tinker. LC GV741. DD 371.74. bk rev adv acc. Circ 5,000. (ctrl). Includes names, addresses, telephone numbers, high ranking officials, coaches, athletic activities and records of colleges.

BLUE BOOK OF JUNIOR COLLEGE ATHLETICS. 1959-. 0520-2973. Periodical. US. English. an. $11.00. Rohrich Corporation, 903 East Tallmadge Avenue, Akron OH 44310. Tel (216)633-1711. Ed A W Tinker. LC GV583. DD 796. bk rev. adv acc. Circ 2,000. (ctrl). College data listing name, address, telephone number, high ranking officials, coaches, athletic activities and records.

BLUE JAYS YEARBOOK. See Yearbooks, Almanacs, Directories.

BOB LURTSEMA'S VIKING REPORT CEASED. VFOAT Viking Report. V. 4, No. 24- July 1978-. 0194-9942. Periodical. US. English. ir. $16.95. Viking Report, 7644 Lyndale Avenue South, Minneapolis MN 55423. Tel (612)861-7437. *Karl Kassulke's Viking Report*.

BOLETIM INFORMATIVO - CONSELHO NACIONAL DE DESPORTOS. Main/Corp Brazil. Conselho Nacional de Desportos. Portuguese. ir. Rua da Imprensa 16-11 Andar, Rio de Janeiro Brazil. LC GV597.B73A.

BOOK OF RECORDS, NATIONALS - SOFTBALL CANADA. (BOOK OF RECORDS, NATIONALS). Main/Corp Canadian Amateur Softball Association. Sept. 1980-. 0821-0098. CN. English (text also in French). an. Canadian Amateur Softball Association/National Sport And Recreation Centre, 333 River Road, Vanier Ontario K1L 8B9 Canada. DD 796.3578. *Book of Records, 0821-008X*.

BOSTON BRUINS OFFICIAL YEARBOOK. See Yearbooks, Almanacs, Directories.

BOSTON CELTICS. 0361-6894. US. English. an. $2.50. Shamrock Pub Co, PO Box 9100, Boston MA 02114. LC GV885.52.B67. DD 796.323640974461.

BOSTON RUNNING NEWS. 8750-8621. Periodical. US. English. bm. $9.00. Boston Running News, PO Box 252, Boston MA 02113. DD 796.

BOTTIN DES MEMBRES - ASSOCIATION DES PECHEURS SPORTIFS DE SAUMONS DU QUEBEC INC. (BOTTIN DES MEMBRES). Main/Corp Association des Pecheurs Sportifs de Salmons du Quebec. May 1982-. 0821-011X. CN. French. an. Association des Pecheurs Sportifs de Saumons du Quebec, Bureau 225, 1990 Ouest Boul Charest, Ste-Foy Quebec G1N 4K8 Canada. DD 799.1755025714.

BOW & ARROW. (BOW AND ARROW). Vol. 1- May/June 1963-. 0006-8403. Periodical. US. English. bm. $10.00. Gallant Publishing Company Inc, Box HH 34249 Capistrano, Capistrano Beach CA 92624. Tel (714)493-2101. Ed Jack Lewis. LC GV1183. adv acc. Circ 111,000. Concentrates on bowhunting, special bow reports and new products. Special departments are devoted to the technical aspects of equipment.

BOWBENDER MAGAZINE. See Recreation, Leisure - Outdoor Life.

BOWHUNTING GUIDE. See Recreation, Leisure - Outdoor Life.

BOWLERS JOURNAL. V. 65, No. 9- Sept. 1978-. 0164-9183. Periodical. US. English. mo. $39.00. National Bowlers Journal Inc, 875 North Michigan/ Suite 3734, Chicago IL 60611. Tel (312)266-7171. *National Bowlers Journal & Billiard Review*.

BOWLING. V. 37- Aug. 1970-. 0162-0274. Periodical. US. English. mo. American Bowling Congress, 5301 South 76th Street, Greendale WI 53129. Tel (414)421-6400. *Bowling Magazine*.

BOWLING DIGEST. Vol. 1, No. 1 (Mar./Apr. 1983)-. 8750-3603. Periodical. US. English. bm. $12.00. Bowling Digest, PO Box 10732, Des Moines IA 50340. LC WMLC L 83/129. bk rev. adv acc. Circ 110,000. Covers professional and amateur bowling.

BOWLING-FENCING GUIDE. Began with Vol. for 1973/75. 0099-0051. US. English. be. American Alliance for Health Physical Education and Recreation, National Association for Girls and Women in Sport, 1201 16th Street NW, Washington DC 20036. LC GV709. DD 796.31. *Bowling-Fencing-Golf Guide*.

BOX Y LUCHA. Periodical. Spanish. bw. $15.60. Prensa Y Libros SA, PO Box 2145, San Ysidro CA 92073.

Recreation, Leisure—Sports

BOXING TODAY. 0274-7979. Periodical. US. English. mo. Boxing Today, 155 West 29th Street, New York NY 10001. **Tel** (203)735-3381.

BRIDGEPORT JAI-ALAI OFFICIAL SOUVENIR YEARBOOK. *See* Yearbooks, Almanacs, Directories.

THE BRITISH ARCHER. *See* Recreation, Leisure - Outdoor Life.

BRITISH COLUMBIA SPORT SALMON FISHING NEWS. *See* Fish Culture and Fisheries.

BRITISH COLUMBIA SPORTS HALL OF FAME AND MUSEUM. VFOAT Sports Hall of Fame and Museum. 1977-. 0228-3263. CN. English. an. British Columbia Sports Hall of Fame and Museum, Exhibition Park, Vancouver British Columbia V5K 4A9 Canada. **DD** 796.074011133. *British Columbia Sports Hall of Fame, 0318-3645.*

BRITISH JOURNAL OF SPORTS MEDICINE. *See* Medicine.

BROWNS NEWS/ILLUSTRATED. VAT Browns News Illustrated. 0278-9973. Periodical. US. English. ir. Browns News/Illustrated, 2 Berea Commons/Suite 200, Berea OH 44017. **Tel** (216)826-4640. Ed Ray Yannucci. adv acc. **Circ** 20,000. Covers Cleveland Browns football and the NFL.

BUCKEYE SPORTS BULLETIN. 0883-6833. Periodical. US. English. ir. Buckeye Sports Bulletin, PO Box 12453, Columbus OH 43212.

BUDO. VFOAT Budo. Periodical. Japanese. ir. 2-3 Kitanomaru Koen, Chiyoda-ku 102 Japan. LC GV1112.

BULLETIN 78. (COMMONWEALTH GAMES). Main/Conf Commonwealth Games, 11th, Edmonton, Alta., 1978. V. 1- Dec. 1976-. 0382-4713. Periodical. CN. English. mo. Free. The XI Commonwealth Games Foundation, PO Box 1978, Edmonton Alberta T5J 5J5 Canada. **DD** 796.409171241.

BULLETIN A L'USAGE DES TRAPPEURS. No. 2-. 0709-2172. Monographic Series. CN. French. Direction de la Peche Sportive et de la Chasse, Ministere des Ressources Naturelles, CP 6000, Fredericton New Brunswick E3B 5H1 Canada.

BULLETIN DE NOUVELLES - FEDERATION QUEBECOISE DES SPORTS AERIENS. SECTEUR PARACHUTISME. (BULLETIN DE NOUVELLES). Main/Corp Federation Quebecoise des Sports Aeriens. Secteur Parachutisme. Vol. 3, No. 1 (March 31 1983)-. 0826-1326. Periodical. CN. French. ir. Federation Quebecoise des Sports Aeriens, 1415 Est rue Jarry, Montreal Quebec H2E 2Z7 Canada. **DD** 797.5609714. *Bulletin de Nouvelles, 0822-5249.*

BULLETIN DE NOUVELLES - FEDERATION QUEBECOISE DES SPORTS AERIENS. SECTEUR VOL LIBRE. (BULLETIN DE NOUVELLES). Main/Corp Federation Quebecoise des Sports Aeriens. Secteur Vol Libre. Vol. 3, No 1 (19 April 1983)-. 0822-854X. Periodical. CN. French. ir. Federation Quebecoise des Sports Aeriens, 1415 Est rue Jarry, Montreal Quebec H2E 2Z7 Canada. **Tel** (514)252-3055. **DD** 797.55. *Bulletin de Nouvelles, 0822-532X.*

BULLETIN DE NOUVELLES - FEDERATION QUEBECOISE DES SPORTS AERIENS, VOL A VOILE, VOL A MOTEUR, CONSTRUCTION AMATEUR. (BULLETIN DE NOUVELLES). Main/Corp Federation Quebecoise des Sports Aeriens. Vol A Voile, Vol A Moteur, Construction Amateur, Aerostation. 0822-5311. Periodical. CN. French. ir. Free to members, $7.00 Others. Federation Quebecoise des Sports Aeriens, 1415 Est rue Jarry, Montreal Quebec H2E 2Z7 Canada. **DD** 797.5309714.

BULLETIN - ESCRIME QUEBEC. (BULLETIN). Main/Corp Escrime Quebec. VAT Escrime Quebec (1982). Vol. 1, No 1 (Jan. 82)-. 0820-8131. Periodical. CN. French. Federation d'Escrime du Quebec, 1415 Est rue Jarry, Montreal Quebec H2E 2Z7 Canada. **DD** 796.8609714. *Revue, 0709-9509.*

BULLETIN - FEDERATION INTERNATIONALE DE GYMNASTIQUE. Main/Corp Federation Internationale de Gymnastique. VFOAT Bulletin d'Information de la Fig. 0428-1659. Periodical. US. French (English). qt. $25.00. US Gymnastics Federation, 200 South Capital Avenue #10, Indianapolis IN 46225. **Tel** (317)261-9704. LC UNC.

BULLETIN - FEDERATION OF CANADIAN ARCHERS INC. (BULLETIN). Main/Corp Federation of Canadian Archers. Mar. 1984-. 0823-9371. Periodical. CN. English (French, with French text on inverted pages). qt. Free to members. Federation of Canadian Archers, 333 River Road, Vanier Ontario K1L 8H9 Canada. **DD** 799.320971.

BULLETIN H B2 SO. (LE BULLETIN H B2 SO). Vol. 1, No. 1 (Mar./April 1983)-. 0823-5465. Periodical. CN. French. bm. Free to Members. Club Hachedeuzo, CP 636, Aylmer Quebec J9H 3R8 Canada. **DD** 797.2305.

LE BULLETIN HALTE. Vol. 4, No. 2 (Mar. 1984)-. 0828-4970. Periodical. CN. French. qt. Free. Association Canadienne des Entraineurs, 333 Chemin River, Vanier Ontario K1L 8H9 Canada. **DD** 796.07706071. (ctrl). *Halte (Ottawa, Ont.), 0711-091X.*

BULLETIN - HISPA. *See* Physical Training.

BULLETIN - ICSS. (BULLETIN - I C S S). Main/Corp International Committee for Sociology of Sport. 0700-8090. Periodical. CN. English. sa. Free. ICSS Secretariat, Math & Computer Building, Faculty of HKLS University of Waterloo, Waterloo Ontario N2L 3G1 Canada. **DD** 796. (ctrl).

BULLETIN - SASKATCHEWAN HIGH SCHOOLS ATHLETIC ASSOCIATION. (BULLETIN). 0229-2149. Periodical. CN. English. mo. Saskatchewan High Schools Athletic Association, 2220 College Avenue, Regina Saskatchewan S4P 3V7 Canada. **DD** 796.097124.

BULLETIN SKI NAUTIQUE. (BULLETIN SKI NAUTIQUE : BULLETIN OFFICIEL DE LA FEDERATION QUEBECOISE DE SKI NAUTIQUE). VFOAT Ski Nautique. VAT Ski Nautique (Montreal). Vol. 1, No 1 (May 1983)-. 0824-0906. Periodical. CN. French. bm. 10.00. Federation Quebecoise de Ski Nautique, 4545 Pierre de Coubertin, CP 1000 Succursale M, Montreal H1V 3R2 Canada. **Tel** (514)252-3092. Ed Pierre Laforest. **DD** 797.3505. adv acc. **Circ** 1,000. (ctrl). Instruction calendar of activities, equipment, physical conditioning, safety, and interviews.

BUSINESS DIRECTORY - NATIONAL FOOTBALL LEAGUE RETIRED PLAYERS ASSOCIATION (U.S.). *See* Yearbooks, Almanacs, Directories.

BYLAWS, RULES, AND SPECIFICATIONS - WOMEN'S INTERNATIONAL BOWLING CONGRESS. Main/Corp Women's International Bowling Congress. 0191-1902. US. English. Women's International Bowling Congress, 5301 South 76th Street, Greendale WI 53129. LC GV901.W6. **DD** 794.6.

BYU SPORTSLETTER. VFOAT B.Y.U. Sports Letter. VAT Brigham Young University Sportsletter. Began in 1984. 8750-4251. Periodical. US. English. ir. Cougar Publications Inc, 555 South State Street, Orem UT 84058.

C. A. S. C. SOLO EVENTS REGULATIONS CEASED. Main/Corp Canadian Automobile Sport Clubs. VFOAT F. C. S. A. Reglementation des Evenements Solo. VAT Canadian Automobile Sport Clubs Solo Events Regulations, Federation Canadienne du Sport Automobile Reglementation des Evenements Solo. Began with 1975-1981/82. 0382-0092. CN. English (English only 1975, 1981/82; text in English with French version at the end, 1976, 1979/80). be. Canadian Automobile Sport Clubs, PO Box 97, Willowdale Ontario M2N 5S7 Canada. **DD** 796.72. *Race & Solo Regulations, 0381-9892.*

C. C. A. RODEO NEWS. (C C A RODEO NEWS). Main/Corp Canadian Cowboys Association. 0382-4055. Periodical. CN. English. sm. $7.74. CCA Rodeo News, Box 276, North Battleford Saskatchewan S9A 2Y3 Canada. **Tel** (306)445-3233. **DD** 791.8. *C A C A Rodeo News, 0382-4268.*

CAA MAGAZINE. (CAA MAGAZINE : OFFICIAL PUBLICATION OF THE CHICAGO ATHLETIC ASSOCIATION). VAT Chicago Athletic Association Magazine. 0279-6945. Periodical. US. English. an. Chicago Athletic Association, 12 South Michigan Avenue, Chicago IL 60603. *Cherry Circle, 0009-3238.*

CALIFORNIA BOWLING NEWS. 0008-0918. Periodical. US. English. wk. $12.00. California Bowling News, 2606 West Burbank Boulevard, Burbank CA 91505. **Tel** (213)849-4664.

CANADA GUNSPORT. Began with V. 1, No. 5, Feb. 1976 issue. 0383-1191. Periodical. CN. English. Canada Gunsport, PO Box 201, Willowdale Ontario M2N 5C8 Canada. **DD** 683.400971. *Journal of Military, Police and Sporting Arms, 0383-1205.*

CANADA RUGBY NEWS. VFOAT Rugby Canada. V. 1, No. 1 (Oct./Nov. 1981)-. 0712-3280. Periodical. CN. English. ir. Canada Rugby News, Sports Marketing Consultants, 1260-1176 West Georgia Street, Vancouver British Columbia V6E 4A2 Canada. **DD** 796.3330971. *Scrum Down, 0706-7542.*

CANADA SKI. V. 1- Nov. 1968-. 0045-4222. Periodical. CN. English. qt. $2.00. Canada Ski, PO Box 180, Pointe Claire Quebec H9R 4N9 Canada. LC GV854.8.

CANADA SKI DIRECTORY. *See* Yearbooks, Almanacs, Directories.

CANADA'S SPORT MAGAZINE. VFOAT Sport. VAT Sport (Concord). Vol. 1, No. 1 (Sept. 1982)-. 0715-2043. Periodical. CN. English (includes some text in French). bm. $18.00 Domestic, $22.00 US, $38.00 Foreign. Canada's Sport Magazine, Unit 8/7777 Keele Street, Concord Ontario L4K 1B1 Canada. **DD** 381.4568870971.

CANADIAN AMPUTEE SPORTS ASSOCIATION. (CANADIAN AMPUTEE SPORTS ASSOCIATION : NEWSLETTER). VFOAT Association Canadienne des Sports pour Ampute : Journal. Vol. 1, Issue 1-. 0823-6674. Periodical. CN. English. qt. Free. Canadian Amputee Sports Association, 428 Lake Bonavista Drive SE, Calgary Alberta T2J 0M1 Canada. **DD** 796.0196. (ctrl).

CANADIAN AND PROVINCIAL GOLF RECORDS. 1972-. 0316-8131. Periodical. CN. English. an. Royal Canadian Golf Association, 696 Yonge Street, Toronto Ontario M4Y 2A7 Canada. **DD** 796.35270971. *National Tournament Records, 0316-8212.*

CANADIAN AQUATICS. Vol. 1, No. 1 (July 1982)-. 0712-5135. Periodical. CN. English. ir. Free to Aquatic Clubs and Organizations, $18.00 Canada, $21.00 Foreign. Subscription Department, Canadian Aquatics Publications, Suite 210/255 Yorkland Boulevard, Willowdale Onratio M2J 1S3 Canada. **DD** 797.20971.

CANADIAN ARCHER. (THE CANADIAN ARCHER). Mar. 1974-. 0319-2571. Periodical. CN. English (includes some text in French). bm. $11.61. Federation Canadian Archers, 333 River Road, Vanier Ontario K1L 8H9 Canada. **Tel** (613)748-5604. Ed Stan Siatkowski. adv acc. **Circ** 1,000. (ctrl). Information to archers on FCA programs, general archery information, rules, coaching, and general archery business. 0014-9454.

CANADIAN COLLEGES SPORT SCENE. VFOAT College Sport Scene. Issue No. 1-. 0228-4014. Periodical. CN. English (includes some text in French). qt. Free. Canadian Colleges Athletic Association, 333 River Road, Vanier Ontario K1L 8B9 Canada. **DD** 796.071171.

CANADIAN CRICKETER. (THE CANADIAN CRICKETER). Vol. 1, No 1 (Mar. 1972)-. 0228-9504. Periodical. CN. English. qt. $3.86. Canadian Cricket Association, PO Box 1364, Brockville Ontario K6V 5V6 Canada. **DD** 796.3580971.

CANADIAN DIVING JOURNAL. Jan. 1983-. 0715-9633. Periodical. CN. English. ir. 7.50. Canadian Diving Journal, PO Box 285 Station V, Toronto Ontario M6R 3G5 Canada. **Tel** (416)922-9948. Ed Gain Wong. **DD** 797.23. bk rev. adv acc. **Circ** 10,000. An intelligent review of holiday resorts and new equipment designed for scuba divers. Publication is strongly pro-conservation and also introduces latest developments in diving education.

CANADIAN EQUINE SPORTS. Oct. 1974-. 0319-2997. Periodical. CN. text in English and French. mo. $9. Canadien Equine Sports, 1117 St Catherine Street West, Montreal Quebec H3B 1H9 Canada. **DD** 798.205. *Equine Sports, 0319-2989.*

CANADIAN FIELD HOCKEY NEWS. Began with March 1964 issue. 0045-4788. CN. English. ty. $3.86. Canadian Field Hockey News, 333 River Road, Vanier Ontario K1L 8H9 Canada. **DD** 796.35506271.

CANADIAN HORSESHOE PITCHERS YEAR BOOK. *See* Yearbooks, Almanacs, Directories.

CANADIAN INTERPRETATIONS OF THE INTERNATIONAL AMATEUR WRESTLING RULES. VFOAT Canadian Amateur Wrestling Rules and Guide. Began with 1972 issue. 0382-4640. CN. English. an. $3. Per No.

Recreation, Leisure—Sports

Canadian Amateur Wrestling Association, 333 River Road 11th Floor, Vanier Ontario K1L 8B9 Canada. **DD** 796.8120971.

CANADIAN JOURNAL OF APPLIED SPORT SCIENCES. **VFOAT** Journal Canadien des Sciences Appliquees au Sport. Vol. 1, No. 1 (Jan. 1976)-. 0700-3978. CN. English (includes some text in French). qt. 65.00. Canadian Association of Sports Science, 333 River Road, Ottawa Ontario K1L 8H9 Canada. **Tel** (613)748-5671. Ed David Cunningham. **Ind/Abst** Chem. Abstr., Psychol. Abstr. **DD** 796.05. **NLM** W1 CA569H. **CODEN** CJASD8. bk rev. **Circ** 350. (ctrl). Contains original papers, reviews, lectures, communications, abstracts of outstanding papers, book reviews, letters to the editor, and invited papers.

CANADIAN JOURNAL OF HISTORY OF SPORT. **VFOAT** Revue Canadienne de l'Histoire des Sports. Vol. 12, No. 1 (May 1981)-. 0712-9815. Periodical. CN. English. sa. 8.00. Faculty of Human Kinetics, c/o Dr Metcalfe, University of Windsor, Windsor Ontario N9B 3P4 Canada. **Tel** (519)253-4232. Ed Alan Metcalfe. **Ind/Abst** Am. Hist. Life, Hist. Abstr., Part A, Mod. Hist. Abstr., Hist. Abst., Part B, Twent. Century Abstr. **DD** 796.09. bk rev. **Circ** 500. Sport history, in particular North American. Some articles are on international topics. *Canadian Journal of History of Sport and Physical Education, 0008-4115.*

CANADIAN JOURNAL OF HISTORY OF SPORT AND PHYSICAL EDUCATION CEASED. V. 1-11, No. 2. 0008-4115. Periodical. CN. English (includes some text in French). sa. Canadian Association for Health Physical Education and Recreation c/o Dr A Metcalfe, Faculty of Human Kinetics/ University of Windsor, Windsor Ontario N9B 3P4 Canada.

CANADIAN MARATHON ANNUAL. 1979-. 0709-0269. CN. English. an. E Thomas, Canadian Marathon Annual, 22 Findlay Avenue, Ottawa Ontario K1S 2T9 Canada. **DD** 796.4260971.

CANADIAN OLDTIMERS' HOCKEY NEWS CEASED. **VFOAT** Actualites des Veterans Canadiens du Hockey. V. 1-7, No. 3. 0381-5013. Periodical. CN. English. ir. $4. Canadian Oldtimers' Hockey News, PO Box 951, Peterborough Ontario K9J 7A5 Canada. **DD** 796.9620971.

CANADIAN RODEO NEWS. See Yearbooks, Almanacs, Directories.

CANADIAN RODEO NEWS CEASED. Began with V. 1, Mar. 17, 1964. Ceased with V. for 1984. 0008-4964. Periodical. CN. English. sm. Canadian Rodeo News, 315A-36 Avenue South East, Calgary Alberta T2G 1W1 Canada.

CANADIAN RULE BOOK FOR AMATEUR FOOTBALL. 0229-2580. CN. English. $1.00. Canadian Rule Book for Amateur Football, 333 River Road, Vanier Ontario K1L 8B9 Canada. **DD** 796.33502022.

CANADIAN RUNNER. Oct./Nov. 1979-. 0226-5257. Periodical. CN. English. ir. Canadian Runner, 6 Brentcliffe Road, Toronto Ontario M4G 3Y2 Canada. **Tel** (416)425-6699. **DD** 796.4260971. *Ontario Runner, 0226-5249.*

CANADIAN SPORTS ALMANAC AND DIRECTORY. See Yearbooks, Almanacs, Directories.

CANADIAN SPORTS AWARDS, ATHLETE OF THE MONTH. 1980-. 0823-874X. CN. English. an. Free. Sports Federation of Canada, 333 River Road, Vanier Ontario K1L 8B9 Canada. **DD** 796.0922.

CANADIAN SPORTSMAN. (THE CANADIAN SPORTSMAN). Began publication in 1870?. 0008-5073. Periodical. CN. English. ir. Canadian Sportsman, 25 Towline Road/Tillonsburg, Ottawa Ontario N4G 4H6 Canada. **Tel** (519)842-4824.

CANADIAN VOLLEYBALL ANNUAL AND RULE BOOK. 1963-. 0576-6346. Periodical. CN. English. an. Canadian Volleyball Association, 333 River Road, Vanier City Ontario K1L 8H9 Canada. **DD** 796.325.

CANADIAN WEIGHTLIFTING JOURNAL. **VFOAT** Journal Canadien d'Halterophilie. No. 1- 1977-. 0705-1727. Periodical. CN. English (includes some text in French). Free to Members. Canadian Weightlifting Federation, 333 River Road, Vanier Ontario K1L Canada. **DD** 796.41. *Official Newsletter, 0705-1719.*

CANADIAN WESTERN RIDER. (THE CANADIAN WESTERN RIDER). **VAT** Western Rider (1983). Vol. 13, No. 1 (March 1983)-. 0823-4582. Periodical. CN. English. mo. $15.00. Canadian Western Rider, PO Box 7065, Ancaster Ontario L9G 3L3 Canada. **DD** 798.205. *Canadian Rider, 0702-9071.*

CANADIAN WRESTLER. V. 2- Feb. 1977-. 0705-176X. Periodical. CN. English. qt. $12.38. Canadian Amateur Wrestling, 333 River Road, Vanier City Ontario K1L 8H9 Canada. **Tel** (613)748-5686. **DD** 796.8120971. bk rev. adv acc. **Circ** 6,000. (ctrl). Free style and G R wrestling articles, results and interviews devoted to amateur wrestling in Canada. *Wrestler, 0382-4063.*

CANADIAN YOUTH SOCCER BULLETIN. V. 1-. 0225-6169. Periodical. CN. English. ir. $4. Canadian Youth Soccer Association, 333 River Road, Ottawa Ontario K1L 8B9 Canada. **DD** 796.3340971.

CANPARA (1976)-. (CANPARA). **VFOAT** Parachutiste Canadien. Vol. 10, No. 4 (Aug. 1976)-. 0227-5880. Periodical. CN. English (includes some text in French). bm. $15.48. Canadian Sport Parachuting Association, 333 River Road, Vanier City Ontario K16 8B9 Canada. **Tel** (613)748-5650. Ed Bill Knott. **DD** 797.560971. bk rev. adv acc. **Circ** 11,000. (ctrl). Sport parachuting and other aviation sports. *Canadian Parachutist, 0319-3896.*

CAPTAIN'S MATE. 0094-5889. Periodical. US. English. mo. $9.00. 833 Dover Drive/Suite 3, Newport Beach CA 92660. **LC** GV771. **DD** 797.105.

CAROLINA RUNNER. 0883-1629. Periodical. US. English. mo. $10.00. Carolina Runner, PO Box 144, Concord NC 28026. **Tel** (704)788-4702. Ed Julia Morrison. bk rev. adv acc. **Circ** 3,000. Results of foot races held each month in North and South Carolina; also, calendar of upcoming races; readers' forum and first-person articles also used.

CATALOGUE OF SPORTS BOOKS, FILMS & VIDEO TAPES. **VFOAT** Catalogue du Sports Livres, Films et Bandes Magnetoscopique. 1980/81-. 0228-7277. CN. English (some text in French). an. Coaching Association of Canada, 333 River Road, Ottawa Ontario K1L 8B9 Canada. **DD** 016.7960971.

CATCH. Began with Jan. 1975 issue. 0703-5535. Periodical. CN. English. qt. $9.28. Catch/Canada, CARA Headquarters, 333 River Road, Ottawa Ontario K1L 8B Canada. **Tel** (613)746-5758. **DD** 797.1230971. bk rev. adv acc.

CATCHLINE. See Business.

CAVES AND CAVING. See Earth Sciences.

CAVING INTERNATIONAL. **VFOAT** Caving International Magazine. No. 1-. 0706-8166. Periodical. CN. English. qt. 3.00. Caving International, PO Box 4328, Edmonton Alberta T64 4T3 Canada. **Ind/Abst** GeoRef. **DD** 796.52505.

THE CENTER FOR SPORTS SPONSORSHIP'S SPONSOR QUEST. **VFOAT** Sponsor Quest. Began in 1984. 0747-6817. Periodical. US. English. mo. $30.00. Center for Sports Sponsorship, 34 Washington Road, Princeton Junction NJ 08550.

CENTRE THIRD. (CENTRE THIRD : THE ONTARIO AMATEUR NETBALL ASSOCIATION'S NEWSLETTER). 0712-1334. Periodical. CN. English. ir. Free. Centre Third, Ontario Amateur Netball Association, 160 Vanderhoof Avenue, Toronto Ontario M4G 4B8 Canada. **DD** 796.32. (ctrl).

CHAMPION (VANIER, ONT.). (CHAMPION). Vol. 1, No. 1 (Dec. 1977)-. 0229-3455. Periodical. CN. English (French). ir. Athlete Information Bureau of the National Sport and Recreation Center, 333 Chemin River Road, Vanier Ontario K1L 8H9 Canada. **DD** 7960971.

CHAMPIONS DU SPORT AMATEUR. (LES CHAMPIONS DU SPORT AMATEUR). **VFOAT** Champions. **VAT** Champions (Montreal-Nord). V. 1, No 1 (Summer 83)-. 0822-5621. CN. French. mo. $1.75 Per No. Les Champions du Sport Amateur, 4845 Charleroi, Montreal-Nord Quebec H1H 1V5 Canada. **DD** 796.0971427.

CHAMPIONSHIP WRESTLING YEARBOOK. See Yearbooks, Almanacs, Directories.

CHEYUGIN. First issue Sept. 1984. Periodical. KO. Korean. mo. 2,800. Supochu Nyushu Sa, 25-27 Sangdo-dong Tongjak-ku, Seoul Korea. **LC** GV561.

CHEYUK CHONGSO. **Main/Corp** Taehan Cheyukhoe. 1973-. Korean. ir. Taeham Cheyukhoe, 19 Mugyodong, Seoul Korea. **LC** GV663.K6.

CHICAGO ATHLETIC ASSOCIATION ANNUAL. **VFOAT** Annual. 0882-7346. US. English. an. **LC** GV584.5.C4. **DD** 796.06077311.

CHICAGO BOWLER. 0009-3513. Periodical. US. English. wk. Chicago Bowler, 746 West Webster Street, Chicago IL 60614.

CHINA SPORTS. **VFOAT** Chung-Kuo Ti Yu. Began in 1980. Periodical. US. English. mo. $33.00. China Books and Periodicals, 2929 24th Street, San Francisco CA 94110. **LC** GV651. **DD** 796.0951. *China's Sports, 0577-8948.*

CHINA'S SPORTS CEASED. V. 1- 1957-. 0577-8948. Periodical. English. ir.

CHUNG-HUA MIN KUO TI YU HSIEH CHIN HUI CHI KAN. **VFOAT** Republic of China Amateur Athletic Federation Quarterly. Began with Sept. 1973 issue. Periodical. Chinese. ir. **LC** GV663.T3.

CHUNG-KUO WU SHU SHIH LIAO CHI KAN. See Physical Training.

CHUO KEIBA NENKAN. See Horses and Horsemanship.

CIRCUIT ROUTIER. REGLEMENTS. (CIRCUIT ROUTIER : REGLEMENTS). **Main/Corp** Federation Auto Quebec. **VFOAT** Road Racing : Rules. 0822-5273. CN. English (French version at the end). an. $1.00 Per Vol. Federation Auto-Quebec, 1415 Jarry St West, Montreal Quebec H2E 2Z7 Canada. **DD** 796.7209714.

C'KI PASSE-PARTOUT. Vol. 1, No. 1 (June 1981)-. 0229-8236. Periodical. CN. French. qt. $20.00. C'Ki Passe-Partout, App 204, 6300-391eme Avenue, Montreal Quebec H1T 2W7 Canada. **DD** 796.0196.

CLASS. CANADIAN LADIES ASSOCIATION OF SHOOTING SPORTS. (CLASS). Vol. 1, No. 1 (Spring 1980)-. 0713-052X. Periodical. CN. English. wk. Free to Members. M Spinney Class, 1514-1050 Markham Road, Scarborough Ontario M1H 2Y7 Canada. **DD** 799.310971.

CLIMBING (ASPEN, COLO.). (CLIMBING). Began with No. 1, 1970. 0045-7159. Periodical. US. English. bm. $15.00. Climbing, Box E Joye Cole, Aspen CO 81612. **Tel** (303)925-3414. Ed Michael Kennedy. **LC** GV199.4. **DD** 796.52230973. bk rev. adv acc. **Circ** 9,000. Technical rock, snow, ice climbing and alpine mountaineering throughout North America and the world. Protusely illustrated in 4 color, news, reviews, equipment and commentary.

CLINICAL UPDATE, SPORTS MEDICINE. See Medicine.

CLINICS IN SPORTS MEDICINE. See Medicine.

CLUB DES AMIS DE GILLES VILLENEUVE INC. (LE CLUB DES AMIS DE GILLES VILLENEUVE INC. : BULLETIN). **Main/Corp** Club des Amis de Gilles Villeneuve. V. 1, No 1, (April 1979)-. 0228-4839. Periodical. CN. French. bm. Free. Club des Amis de Gilles Villeneuve, CP 1365, Place d'Armes, Montreal Quebec H2Y 3K5 Canada. **DD** 796.7205. (ctrl).

CLUB LIVING. 0160-6166. Periodical. US. English. ir. Club Living Inc, 250 Station Plaza, Hartsdale NY 10530.

CLUBS, HOBBIES AND SPORTS IN HAMILTON-WENTWORTH. See Hobbies.

THE COACHING CLINIC. 0009-9880. Periodical. US. English. $24.00. Prentice-Hall, Englewood Cliffs NJ 07632. **LC** GV711.

COACHING. MEN'S ATHLETICS. (COACHING : MEN'S ATHLETICS). V. 1- Jan./Feb. 1977-. 0146-1265. Periodical. US. English. bm. $10.00. PO Box 867, 50 South Main Street, Wallingford CT 06492. **LC** GV711. **DD** 796.077.

COACHING REVIEW. V. 1- Jan. 1978-. 0705-5617. Periodical. CN. English. bm. 16.00. Coaching Association of Canada, 333 River Road, Ottawa Ontario K1L 8H9 Canada. **Tel** (613)748-5624. Ed Steve Newman. **DD** 796.07705. bk rev. adv acc. **Circ** 12,000. Publishes material on coaching related topics. It is an educational and informational vehicle supplementing programs such as the National Coaching Certification Program. *Bulletin, 0319-0102; Communique, 0318-9562; 0710-1678.*

Recreation, Leisure—Sports

COACHING SCIENCE UPDATE. 1979/1980 Ed.-. 0226-8965. CN. English. an. Free to members, $2.50 Per Vol. for non-members. Coaching Science Update, 333 River Road, Ottawa Ontario K1L 8B9 Canada. **DD** 796.07705.

COACHING. WOMEN'S ATHLETICS CEASED. (COACHING : WOMEN'S ATHLETICS). V. 3-7. 0160-2624. Periodical. US. English. $19.95 Professional, $21.95 Nonprofessional. Coaching: Women's Athletics, 1353 Boston Post Road, Madison CT 06443. **LC** GV709.14. **DD** 796.077. *Coach. Women's Athletics*, 0145-9570.

COAST TO COAST SPORT. Sept. 15, 1976-. 0821-2066. Periodical. CN. English. ir. Sports Federation of Canada, 333 River Road, Vanier Ontario K1L 8B9 Canada. **DD** 796.06071.

COLLEGE AND JUNIOR TENNIS. 0279-1153. Periodical. US. English. mo. $15.00. Junior Tennis, 100 Harbor Road, Port Washington NY 11050. **Tel** (516)883-6601. Ed Liza DeLuca. bk rev. adv acc. Circ 5,000. (ctrl). The only publication in the world that's specifically aimed at the college and junior tennis players. We cover all match results, biographies and any other related info-worldwide. *College & Jr. Tennis*, 0164-5668.

COLLEGE FOOTBALL MODERN RECORD BOOK. Main/Corp National Collegiate Sports Services. 0092-881X. US. English. $2.00. 420 Lexington Avenue, New York NY 10170. **LC** GV956.8. **DD** 796.332630973.

COLLEGIATE BASEBALL. 1957. 0530-9751. Periodical. US. English. ir. $11.00. Lou Pavlovich, PO Box 50566, Tuscon AZ 85703. **Tel** (602)623-7495. Ed Louis Pavlovich. bk rev. adv acc. Circ 8,500. We cover technical and factual information on amateur baseball, conduct polls on leaders among schools and compile statistics. *Collegiate Baseball Digest*.

COLLEGIATE SPORTS REPORT. (COLLEGIATE SPORTS REPORT : AN OFFICIAL PUBLICATION OF THE INTERNATIONAL UNIVERSITY PRESS). Vol. 1, No. 1 (Sept. 1973)-. 0748-9668. Periodical. US. English. mo. $36.00. The International University Press, 1301 South Noland Road, Independence MO 64055.

COLORADO BIG GAME HARVEST. Main/Corp Colorado. Wildlife Services Section. 0148-0332. US. English. $3.00. Colorado Division of Wildlife, 6060 Broadway, Denver CO 80216. **LC** SK57. **DD** 799.2609788. *Colorado Big Game Harvest*, 0148-0332.

COLORADO SKI AND WINTER RECREATION STATISTICS. See Statistics.

COLT AMERICAN HANDGUNNING ANNUAL. VFOAT Colt Handgunning. 1976-. 0364-071X. US. English. an. $1.75 Single Issue. Aqua-Field Publications Inc, 342 Madison Avenue, New York NY 10017. **LC** TS537. **DD** 799.2023305.

COMMUNICATION - INTERNATIONAL SKATING UNION. Main/Corp International Skating Union. English, French and German. $5.33. International Skating Union, Postfach 7270, Davos-Platz Switzerland. **Tel** 083 37577. **LC** GV849. **DD** 769.910601. bk rev. Circ 1,550. Has Included 54 new melodies and titles that have been carefully chosen and tested in the presence of international trainers and dance couples with a view to character, rhythm and sound.

COMMUNIQUE - SYNCHRO SWIM CANADA. Main/Corp Canadian Amateur Synchronized Swimming Association. No. 1- Jan. 1979-. 0226-8701. Periodical. CN. English. ir. Free. Synchro Swim Canada, 333 River Road, Ottawa Ontario K1L 8B9 Canada. **DD** 797.2106071.

THE COMPLETE HANDBOOK OF COLLEGE FOOTBALL. 1st- Ed. 1977-. 0149-0168. Periodical. US. English. $2.25 Single Issue. The New American Library, PO Box 999, Bergenfield NJ 07621. **LC** GV951. **DD** 796.332630973.

THE COMPLETE HANDBOOK OF PRO BASKETBALL. US. English. New American Library Inc, 1301 Avenue of the Americas, New York NY 10019. **LC** GV885.55. **DD** 796.323640973.

THE COMPLETE HANDBOOK OF PRO FOOTBALL. 1975- Ed. 0361-2988. US. English. $1.95. New American Library, 1301 Avenue of the Americas, New York NY 10019. **LC** GV955. **DD** 796.332640973.

THE COMPLETE HANDBOOK OF SOCCER. 1976-. 0363-6046. US. English. an. $1.95. New American Library, PO Box 999, Bergensfield NJ 07621. **LC** GV944.U5. **DD** 796.3340973.

THE COMPLETE HANDBOOK OF THE OLYMPIC GAMES. 0749-9248. US. English. ir. $4.50. New American Library, 1633 Broadway, New York NY 10019. **LC** GV721.5. **DD** 796.4805.

THE COMPLETE HANDBOOK OF THE OLYMPIC WINTER GAMES. US. English. ir. $3.50. New American Library, 1633 Broadway, New York NY 10019. **LC** GV841.5. **DD** 796.9805.

THE COMPREHENSIVE DIRECTORY OF SPORTS ADDRESSES. See Yearbooks, Almanacs, Directories.

CONGRESS . . . PROCEEDINGS - FEDERATION DES SPORTS DU CANADA. (CONGRESS. . . : PROCEEDINGS). Main/Corp Federation des Sports du Canada. Congres. VFOAT Congres : Compte Rendus. 0229-5156. CN. French. an. Federation des Sports du Canada, 333 Chemin River, Vanier Ontario K1L 8B9 Canada. **DD** 796.06071.

CONNAISSANCE DE LA CHASSE. Periodical. FR. French. ir. 114.00. Editions Lariviere, 103 rue la Fayette, 75010 Paris France. **LC** SK1. **DD** 799.205.

CONSTITUTION. BY-LAWS. HISTORY - CANADIAN AMATEUR HOCKEY ASSOCIATION. (CONSTITUTION, BY-LAWS, HISTORY - CANADIAN AMATEUR HOCKEY ASSOCIATION). Main/Corp Canadian Amateur Hockey Association. VFOAT C. A. H. A. Hockey Handbook. Began publication with 1972 issue. 0317-9540. Periodical. CN. English. an. Canadian Amateur Hockey Association, 333 River Road, Ottawa Ontario K1L 8B9 Canada. **DD** 796.96206. *Constitution, By-Laws, Regulations, History*, 0317-9559.

CONSTITUTION. STATUTS. HISTORIQUE - ASSOCIATION CANADIENNE DE HOCKEY AMATEUR. (CONSTITUTION, STATUTS, HISTORIQUE - ASSOCIATION CANADIENNE DE HOCKEY AMATEUR). Main/Corp Association Canadienne de Hockey Amateur. 1976-. 0700-9364. Periodical. CN. French. an. Association Canadienne de Hockey Amateur, 333 rue River, Vanier Ontario K1L 8B9 Canada. **DD** 796.96206.

CONTEMPORARY BIOGRAPHY, ATHLETES. See Biographies.

CONVERSE BASKETBALL YEARBOOK. See Yearbooks, Almanacs, Directories.

CORD SPORTFACTS GUNS GUIDE. VFOAT Guns Guide. 0590-6776. US. English. $1.25. Cord Communications Corp, 145 East 52nd Street, New York NY 10020. **LC** TS532. **DD** 623.44075.

CORD SPORTFACTS HOCKEY GUIDE. 0591-0374. US. English. $0.75. Cord Communications Corporation, 25 West 43 Street, New York NY 10036. **LC** GV846. **DD** 796.96205.

CORD SPORTFACTS HUNTING. See Recreation, Leisure - Outdoor Life.

CORD SPORTFACTS PRO FOOTBALL GUIDE. VFOAT Pro Football Guide. 0197-7105. US. English. $1.50 Single Issue. Cord Communcations Corp, 25 West 43rd Street, New York NY 10036. **LC** GV955.5.N35. **DD** 796.332640973.

COUP D'OEIL SUR L'HALTEROPHILIE. 0227-6909. Periodical. CN. French. bm. $8,00. Federation d'Halterophilie du Quebec, 1415 rue Jarry Est, Montreal Quebec H2E 2Z7 Canada. **DD** 796.4109714.

COURSES ET ELEVAGE. Periodical. FR. French. bm. $39.91. Union Natl Interprofessionnell Cheval, 51 rue Dumont d'Urville, 75116 Paris France. **Tel** (1)500 03 I0. bk rev. adv acc. Circ 8,500. Racing and breeding of bloodhorses for flat, jump and trot.

CROSS COUNTRY. Main/Corp Saskatchewan High Schools Athletic Association. 0704-495X. CN. English. an. Free. Saskatchewan High Schools Athletic Association, 2220 College Avenue, Regina Saskatchewan S4P 3V7 Canada. **DD** 796.426.

CROSS-COUNTRY RULES AND REGULATIONS. Main/Corp Canadian Ski Association. 0227-6828. CN. English. an. Canadian Ski Association, Tower A, 333 River Road, Vanier Ontario K1L Canada. **DD** 796.93.

CROSS COUNTRY SKI MAGAZINE. VFOAT Cross Country. V. 7- Sept./Oct. 1980-. 0270-9643. Periodical. US. English. ty. $2.50 Single Issue. Times Mirror Magazines Inc, 380 Madison Avenue, New York NY 10017. **LC** GV854.9.C7. **DD** 796.93. *Ski Magazine's Guide to Cross Country Skiing*, 0097-7373.

CROSS COUNTRY SKIER. Vol. 1, No. 1 (Oct. 1981)-. 0278-9213. Periodical. US. English. ir. $11.97. Rodale Press Inc, 33 East Minor Street, Emmaus PA 18049. **Tel** (215)967-5171. Ed James C McCullagh. adv acc. Circ 45,000. America's leading nordic magazine for skiers of all levels. The latest on products and equipment, and information on training technique, touring and cross country vacations. 0164-6974.

THE CROSSFACE. 1972. 0273-9135. Periodical. US. English. ir. $8.00. Crossface/Wisconsins, 4715 Holm Road, Oregon WI 53575. **Tel** (608)262-4399. Ed Russell & Nancy Hellickson. adv acc. Circ 2,500. All styles and levels of wrestling are covered with emphasis on Wisconsin.

CURLING. Main/Corp Saskatchewan High Schools Athletic Association. 0704-4968. CN. English. an. Free. Saskatchewan High Schools Athletic Association, 2220 College Avenue, Regina Saskatchewan S4P 3V7 Canada. **DD** 796.96.

CURRENT THERAPY IN SPORTS MEDICINE. Series/Titl Current Therapy Series. 1985-1986-. CN. English. be. C V Mosby Company, 11830 Westline Industrial Drive, St Louis MO 63141. Ed R Peter Welsh and Roy J Shephard. **LC** RC1200. **DD** 617.102705. **NLM** W1.

CYNEGETICUS. V. 1- Jan. 1977-. 0160-2543. Periodical. US. English. qt. $8.00. Cynegeticus, Box 315, Helena MT 59624. **Tel** (406)227-8766. Ed Douglas C Stange. bk rev. A bibliographical resource and scholarly vehicle devoted to an interdisciplinary approach to the discussion and exploration of hunting.

DAC NEWS. Main/Corp Detroit Athletic Club. 0011-4707. Periodical. US. English. mo. Detroit Athletic Club, 241 Madison Avenue, Detroit MI 48226.

DALLAS COWBOYS OFFICIAL WEEKLY. VFOAT Dallas Cowboys Weekly. 1975. 0745-0370. Periodical. US. English. ir. $15.95. Dallas Cowboy Weekly, 6116 North Central Expressway, Dallas TX 75206. **Tel** (214)369-8000. Ed Steve Perkins. adv acc. Circ 83,075. (ctrl) Complete coverage of all cowboy's games, individual player stories, past and present, and a section on the Dallas Cowboy cheerleaders. *Official Dallas Cowboys Weekly*.

DAVE CAMPBELL'S ARKANSAS FOOTBALL. VFOAT Arkansas Football. 0147-1295. Periodical. US. English. ir. $15.00. Sports Communications, PO Box 95, Waco TX 76703. **Tel** (817)752-4351.

DAVE CAMPBELL'S TEXAS FOOTBALL. VFOAT Texas Football. 1960. 0147-1287. Periodical. US. English. ir. $17.50. Sports Communication Inc, PO Box 95, Waco TX 76703. **Tel** (817)752-4351. Ed Dave Campbell. adv acc. Circ 100,000. Coverage of football in the SWC.

DEER AND DEER HUNTING. 0164-7318. Periodical. US. English. bm. $18.00. The Stump Sitters, PO Box 1117, Appleton WI 54912. **Tel** (414)734-0009.

DEER HUNTING. VFOAT Petersen's Complete Guide to Deer Hunting. Began with 1977 Vol. 0270-0069. Periodical. US. English. an. $2.50 US, $3.25 Canada. Petersen Publishing Co, 6725 Sunset Boulevard, Los Angeles CA 90028. **LC** SK301. **DD** 799.277357.

DEER SPORTSMAN. 0362-1952. Periodical. US. English. bm. $6.00. PO Box 142, Marlinton WV 24954. **LC** SK301. **DD** 799.277357.

THE DELLBOOK OF SUPERWINNERS. VFOAT Superwinners. 0732-457X. US. English. an. Dell Publishing Company, 1 Dag Hammerskjold Plaza, New York NY 10017. **LC** GV1201.6. **DD** 001.440973.

DELPHIN. Began with I, 1954. Periodical. GW. German. mo. Crossohaus Wegner & Co, PO Box 10 25 40, D-2000 Hamburg 1 West Germany. **Tel** 02 21-23 46 31.

EL DEPORTE. Periodical. CU. Spanish (summaries in English and French). mo. $0.30 Single Issue. Empresa de Medios de, Propaganda Deportiva Inder, Apartado Postal No 5104, LA Habana Cuba. **LC** GV592.C9. **DD** 796.097291.

Recreation, Leisure—Sports

DERBY. See Horses and Horsemanship.

DESK-REFERENCE DIRECTORY. See Yearbooks, Almanacs, Directories.

DESPORT. (LE DESPORT). V. 1, No. 1-No. 33-. 0383-6452. Periodical. CN. French. qt. Editions Desport, 1207 rue Saint-Andre, Montreal Quebec H2L 3S8 Canada. DD 175.05.

DESPORTO. (DESPORTO : REVISTA LUSO-CANADIANA DE DESPORTO : PORTUGUESE CANADIAN SPORTS MAGAZINE). Vol. 1, No. 1 (July 1977)-. 0229-7906. Periodical. CN. Portuguese. wk. $0.50 Per No. Portuguese Business Promotions, 629 Dufferin Street, Toronto Ontario M6K 2B2 Canada. DD 796.08969071.

DESTINATION PLEIN AIR. 0822-1448. Periodical. CN. French. ir. Free. Federation Quebecoise de la Marche, 1415 Est rue Jarry, Montreal Quebec H2E 2Z7 Canada. DD 796.5109714. (ctrl).

DEUTSCHE ZEITSCHRIFT FUR SPORTMEDIZIN. See Medicine.

DIRECTORY - CANADIAN INTERUNIVERSITY ATHLETIC UNION. See Yearbooks, Almanacs, Directories.

DIRECTORY OF ADDRESSES - FEDERATION INTERNATIONALE DE FOOTBALL ASSOCIATION. See Yearbooks, Almanacs, Directories.

A DIRECTORY OF NEW ENGLAND SKI TOURING CENTERS. See Yearbooks, Almanacs, Directories.

DIRECTORY OF SCOTTISH SPORTS. See Yearbooks, Almanacs, Directories.

DIRECTORY OF UNIVERSITY ATHLETICS. See Yearbooks, Almanacs, Directories.

DIRECTORY - ONTARIO AMATEUR FOOTBALL ASSOCIATION. See Yearbooks, Almanacs, Directories.

DIRECTORY - SPORTS FEDERATION OF CANADA. See Yearbooks, Almanacs, Directories.

DIRECTORY - VIRGINIA HIGH SCHOOL LEAGUE. See Yearbooks, Almanacs, Directories.

DIRT WHEELS MAGAZINE. 0745-0192. Periodical. US. English. mo. $14.98. Hi-Torque Publications, PO Box 9502, Mission Hills CA 91345. Tel (818)365-6831. Ed Tom Webb. adv acc. Circ 120,000. Directed to three and four ATV enthusiasts, with race coverage, technical articles, testing and riding tips.

DISC SPORTS. VFOAT International Disc Sports Magazine. Oct. 1983-. 0747-9956. Periodical. US. English. bm. $7.00. Disc Wares Unlimited, PO Box 333, Amherst MA 01004.

DIVE CANADA. V. 1- Apr. 174-. 0315-114X. Periodical. CN. English. mo. Canadian Underwater Council, 559 Jarvis Street, Toronto Ontario M4Y 2J1 Canada. O.U.C. Diving News, 0315-1573.

DIVE-CANADA CEASED. (DIVE CANADA). V. 1-6, No. 1. 0317-6762. CN. English. Canadian Amateur Diving Association, 333 River Road, Ottawa Ontario K1L 8B9 Canada. DD 797.240971.

DIVER. Periodical. UK. English. mo. 16 Domestic, $35.00 Foreign. 40 Grays Inn Road, WC1X8LR London England. Tel (01)405-0224. Ed Bernard Eaton. LC GV840.S78. DD 797.23. bk rev. adv acc. Circ 36,000. Diving and underwater exploration and discovery. Triton.

THE DIVER. V. 1- Nov./Dec. 1980-. 0273-8589. Periodical. US. English. bm. $15.00. The Diver/Connecticut, PO Box 249, Cobalt CT 06414. Tel (203)342-4730. Ed Bob Taylor. bk rev. adv acc. Circ 2,000. Everything to do with platform and springboard diving.

DIVER DOWN. Fall 1975-. 0700-3994. Periodical. CN. English. qt. Free. New Brunswick Underwater Council, PO Box 382, Chatham New Brunswick E1N 3A Canada. DD 797.23062715. (ctrl).

DIVER MAGAZINE. V. 4, No. 6- Aug. 1978-. 0706-5132. Periodical. CN. English. mo. $60.00. Diver Magazine Canada, 1807 Maritime Mews/Suite 210, Granville IS Vancouver V6H 3W7 Canada. Tel (504)273-4333. Ed Neil McDaniel. DD 797.2305. bk rev. adv acc. Circ 20,000. (ctrl). Sport diving in North America and abroad with emphasis on destinations, photography, marinelife equipment, education and safety and shipwreck adventures highlighting histories of wrecks. Diver and Underwater Adventure, 0704-5220.

DIVER'S ALMANAC. See Yearbooks, Almanacs, Directories.

DODGERS. (DODGER BLUE : THE OFFICIAL NEWSPAPER OF THE LOS ANGELES DODGERS). 0744-8058. Periodical. US. English. ir. $12.50. Dodger Blue, Dodger Staduim, Los Angeles CA 90012. Tel (213)224-1500.

DRAFT GUIDE CEASED. VFOAT Sporting News Draft Guide. 1983 Ed.-. 0737-0911. US. English. an. $12.95. Sporting News, 1212 North Lindbergh Boulevard, PO Box 56, St Louis MO 63166. LC WMLC L 83/137.

DRAFT REVIEW AND PREVIEW CEASED. (DRAFT REVIEW AND . . . PREVIEW). VFOAT Sporting News . . . Draft Review and . . . Preview. 1983, 1984-. 0740-2074. US. English. an. Sporting News Publishing Co, PO Box 56, St Louis MO 63166. LC GV937. DD 796.3320922, B.

DRAG RACING WORLD. VFOAT Drag World. Began in 1984. 0747-4148. Periodical. US. English. bw. $25.00. Drag Racing World, 12425 US Highway 19S, Clearwater FL 33546. DD 796. Dragworld, 0747-0487.

DRAG RULES. Main/Corp National Hot Rod Association. 0277-4771. US. English. $3.00. National Hot Rod Association, 10639 Riverside Drive, North Hollywood CA 91602. LC GV1029.3. DD 796.72.

DUNE BUGGIES AND HOT VWS. See Transportation - Automobiles.

DUNHILL GOLF YEARBOOK. See Yearbooks, Almanacs, Directories.

DZIENNIK URZEDOWY GOWNEGO KOMITETU KULTURY FIZYCZNEJ I SPORTU. See Physical Training.

THE EAGLE. 0162-5144. Periodical. US. English. bm. $8.00 Domestic, $12.00 Foreign. USFHA National Office, 4415 Buffalo Road, North Chili NY 14514. LC GV1017.H7. DD 796.355.05.

EASTERN BASKETBALL. 1976. 0195-0223. Periodical. US. English. ir. $33.00. Eastern Basketball, Number 7 May Court, West Hempstead NY 11552. Tel (516)483-9495. Ed Rita Napolitano. bk rev. adv acc. Circ 30,000. (ctrl). College and high school basketball (including recruiting) from Maine to Georgia.

EASTERN ZONE NEWSLETTER - ONTARIO ASSOCIATION OF ARCHERS. Main/Corp Ontario Association of Archers. Eastern Zone. V. 1- Oct. 1979-. 0228-2348. Periodical. CN. English. ir. Ontario Association of Archers Eastern Zone, R Sunstrum, RR 1, Carlsbad Springs Ontario K0A 1K0 Canada. DD 799.32060713.

ECHEC +. See Recreation, Leisure - Games & Amusements.

ELITE SPORTIVE QUEBECOISE. (L'ELITE SPORTIVE QUEBECOISE). 1980-. 0229-7450. CN. French. an. $6.95 Per No. Societe des Sports du Quebec, 1415 Est rue Jarry, Montreal Quebec H2E 2Z7 Canada. DD 796.060714.

ENTRAINEUR. (L'ENTRAINEUR). VFOAT Revue de l'Entraineur. VAT Revue de l'Entraineur (1984). Jan./Mar. 1984-. 0828-4954. Periodical. CN. French. qt. $16.00. Entraineur, c/o Societe des Sports du Quebec, 1415 Est rue Jarry, Montreal Quebec H2E 2Z7 Canada. DD 796.07705. Revue de l'Entraineur, 0705-5625.

ENTREFILET. Published since Sept.?1978. 0228-071X. Periodical. CN. French. qt. Free to Members. Federation de Badminton du Quebec, 1415 Est rue Jarry, Montreal Quebec H2E 2Z7 Canada. DD 796.34505.

ENVOI. (L'ENVOI : REVUE OFFICIELLE DE LA FEDERATION DE HOCKEY SUR GAZON DU QUEBEC). Vol. 1, No. 1 (June 1983)-. 0823-1834. Periodical. CN. French. qt. Free. Federation de Hockey Sur Gazon du Quebec, 1415 Est rue Jarry, Montreal Quebec H2E 2Z7 Canada. DD 796.35505. (ctrl).

EPSCC NEWSLETTER. VFOAT E.P.S.C.C. Newsletter. VAT Eastern Pennsylvania Sports Collectors Club Newsletter. 0737-3449. Periodical. US. English. qt. $3.50 or Free to Members. Eastern Pennsylvania Sports Collectors Inc, PO Box 37, Maple Glen PA 19002.

ESCRIME. Periodical. FR. French. ir. 190. 45 rue de Liege, 75008 Paris France. LC GV1143. DD 796.86. Escrime Francaise.

ESQUIVE. (L'ESQUIVE). Vol. 1, No. 1 (10 June 1981)-. 0823-793X. Periodical. CN. French. ir. Federation Quebecoise de Boxe Amateur, 1415 Est rue Jarry, Montreal Quebec H2E 2Z7 Canada. DD 796.8309714. (ctrl).

EUROPAPOKAL. GW. German. ir. Copress-Verlag, 8 Munchen 40 Schellingstrasse 39, Munchen West Germany. LC GV943.52. DD 796.33464094.

THE EUROPEAN FOOTBALL BOOK. No. 1- 1968/69-. UK. English. an. 1.00. S Paul, 178-202 Great Portland Street, London W1 England. LC GV942. DD 796.334094.

EVALUATION OF ERRORS IN FIGURES. 1st- Ed. Periodical. US. English. US Figure Skating Association, 20 First Street, Colorado Springs CO 80906. LC GV849.A1. DD 796.91.

EXERCISE AND SPORT SCIENCES REVIEWS. See Medicine.

EXPRESS EQUESTRE. VFOAT Magazine Equestre. Vol. 1, No. 1-. 0822-7330. Periodical. CN. French. ir. $18,00. Express Equestre, C P 416 Succursale Bourassa, Montreal Quebec H2C 3G7 Canada. DD 798.209714.

EXTRA INNING. (THE EXTRA INNING). Vol. 5, No. 4 (May/June, 1983)-. 0823-0684. Periodical. CN. English. bm. Free to Members. Softball Canada, 333 River Road, Vanier Ontario K1L 8H9 Canada. DD 796.3578. Coaches Technical Bulletin (Softball Canada), 0226-918X.

F. C. B. A. REGLEMENTS OFFICIELS DU BASEBALL. Main/Corp Federation Canadienne de Baseball Amateur. 1975-. 0318-4722. Periodical. CN. French. an. Free to Members. Federation Canadienne de Baseball Amateur, 333 Chemin River, Vanier Ontario K1L 8B9 Canada. DD 796.35702022. C. F. A. B. Baseball Rules, 0318-4714.

FACT BOOK - TORONTO MAPLE LEAFS. (FACT BOOK). Main/Corp Toronto Maple Leafs (Hockey Team). VFOAT Official Fact Book of the Toronto Maple Leafs. 1980/1981-. 0229-1819. CN. English. an. Free. Maple Leaf Gardens Ltd, 60 Carleton Street, Toronto Ontario M5B 1L1 Canada. DD 796.9626. (ctrl). New Era Maple Leafs . . . Fact Book, 0229-0049.

FACTS & FIGURES - CANADIAN AMATEUR SOFTBALL ASSOCIATION. Main/Corp Canadian Amateur Softball Association. VFOAT Faits & Gestes - Association Canadienne de Softball Amateur. Began publication in 19752. 0226-577X. CN. English (French). an. Free. Canadian Amateur Softball Association, National Sport and Recreation Centre, 355 River Road, Vanier Ontario K1L 8C1 Canada. DD 796.3578. (ctrl).

FACTS AND FIGURES REPORT. VFOAT Annual Facts and Figures Report on U.S. Tennis Club Operations. 0278-1239. US. English. an. Laventhol & Horwath, 1845 Walnut Street, Philadelphia PA 19103. LC GV1000. DD 796.342068.

FELD WALD WASSER. SCHWEIZERISCHE JAGDZEITUNG. See Recreation, Leisure - Outdoor Life.

FENCING CANADA. VFOAT Escrime Canada. VAT Escrime Canada (1981). Vol. 1, No. 3 (Sept. 1981)-. 0711-5970. Periodical. CN. English (French). qt. $7.00. Fencing Canada, Canadian Fencing Association, 333 River Road, Vanier Ontario K1L 8B9 Canada. DD 796.860971. Escrime Canada, 0711-5962.

F.I.B.A. RULES CASEBOOK. Main/Corp International Amateur Basketball Federation. VFOAT FIBA Basketball Rules Casebook. VAT Federation Internationale de Basketball Amateur Rules Casebook. 0712-5585. CN. English. ir. 5.00. F I B A Rules Casebook, c/o Basketball Canada, 333 River Road, Vanier Ontario K1L 8B9 Canada. Tel (613)748-5607. Ed Allen G Rae. DD 796.32302022. adv acc. Circ 10,000. Play situations giving rule interpretations for Federation Internationale de Basketball Amateur Rules Casebook.

FIELD & STREAM DEER HUNTING ANNUAL. See Recreation, Leisure - Outdoor Life.

Recreation, Leisure—Sports

FIELD & STREAM HUNTING ANNUAL. VFOAT Hunting Annual. VAT Field and Stream Hunting Annual. 0361-3011. US. English. an. $1.25. CBS Publications, 600 Third Avenue, New York NY 10016. LC SK1. DD 799.205.

FIELD HOCKEY RULES. NATIONAL FEDERATION ED. (FIELD HOCKEY RULES). Main/Corp National Federation of State High School Associations. VFOAT Field Hockey Rule Book. 0275-5394. US. English. 11724 Plaza Circle, Box 20626, Kansas City MO 64195. Tel (816)464-5400. Ed Susan True. LC GV1017.H7. DD 796.355. adv acc. Circ 1,300. Rules governing high school competition in field hockey.

FIFA NEWS. Main/Corp Football Association International Federation. VAT Federation Internationale De Football Association News. Periodical. English. mo. $34.64. Federation Internationale de Football Association, PO Box 85, 8030 Zurich 30 Switzerland. Tel 01 55 5400. Ed FIFA. LC GV942. DD 796.3340621. Circ 4,500. (ctrl) Official results of football games international and official communications within the International Football Association.

FIGHT BEAT. VFOAT Fight. 8756-2340. Periodical. US. English. bm. $27.50 U.S., $30.00 Foreign. Fight Beat, 155 Avenue of the Americas, New York NY 10013. DD 796.

THE FIGHT DIRECTOR. Periodical. UK. English. qt. The Society of British Fight Directors, 54 Belsize Park, London NW3 England.

FIGHTING STARS. Began in 1973. 0274-5178. Periodical. US. English. bm. $7.50. Rainbow Publications Inc, 1845 West Empire Avenue, Burbank CA 91504.

FINAL REPORT. Main/Corp Intergovernmental Committee for Physical Education and Sport. English. ir. UNESCO, 7 Place de Fontenoy, 75700 Paris France. LC GV563. DD 613.705. General Report.

FIRST AIDER. See Physical Training.

FISHING & HUNTING JOURNAL. See Recreation, Leisure - Outdoor Life.

FISHING & HUNTING NEWS. 0015-301X. Periodical. US. English. wk. $29.95. Fishing & Hunting News, c/o Kim Elliott, PO Box C19000, Seattle WA 98109. Tel (206)624-3845.

FITNESS REPORT. See Physical Training.

FIZKULTURA I SPORT : FIS. VFOAT FIS. Osnovan 15 Maia 1922 Goda. Periodical. UR. Russian. mo. $16.50. Victor Kamkin Inc (71026), 12224 Parklawn Drive, Rockville MD 20852. Tel (301)881-5973.

FLORIDA GOLF DIRECTORY. See Yearbooks, Almanacs, Directories.

FLORIDA SPORTSMAN. 1- 1969-. 0015-3885. US. English. mo. $22.95. Wickstrom Publishers Inc, 5901 SW 74th Street/Suite 310, Miami FL 33143. Tel (305)661-4222. Ed Vic Dunaway. adv acc. Circ 76,000. Fishing, boating and other outdoors enjoyment in the sunshine state.

FLYPAPER. (THE FLYPAPER). V. 1-. 0317-2481. CN. English. qt. Free to Members. Alberta Hang Glider Association, PO Box 4063 Station C, Calgary Alberta T2T 5M9 Canada. DD 797.550627123.

FOCUS. (FOCUS : AN INTERNAL COMMUNICATION OF THE C.F.P.S.A.A.). 0229-7639. Periodical. CN. English (text in French with French text on inverted pages). ir. Free. C.F.P.S.A.A., 333 River Road, Vanier Ontario K1L 8B9 Canada. DD 371.89.

FOOTBALL. Main/Corp Saskatchewan High Schools Athletic Association. 0225-9524. CN. English. an. Free. Saskatchewan High Schools Athletic Association, 2220 College Avenue, Regina Saskatchewan S4P 3V7 Canada. DD 796.335.

FOOTBALL ACTION. VFOAT Football Action, Complete College & Pro Betting Annual. 0197-1891. US. English. an. $2.75. Sports Eye Inc, Great Neck NY 11025. LC GV937. DD 796.33205.

FOOTBALL CASE BOOK. 0163-6200. US. English. an. National Federation of State High School Associations, Federation Place, Box 98, Elgin IL 60120. LC GV955. DD 796.33202022.

FOOTBALL DIGEST. V. 1- Sept. 1971-. 0015-6760. Periodical. US. English. ir. $12.95. Football Digest, PO Box 3300, Harlan IA 51537. Tel (312)491-6440. Ed Michael Herbert. bk rev. adv acc. Circ 200,000. Covers NFL football.

FOOTBALL HANDBOOK. Main/Corp National Federation of State High School Associations. US. English. be. National Federation of State High School Associations, Federation Place, Box 98, Kansas City MO 60120. LC GV937. DD 796.33205.

FOOTBALL JOURNAL. VFOAT CAFA Journal. V. 1- Aug./Sept. 1974-. 0317-2163. CN. English. bm. $3.00. Canadian Amateur Football Association, 333 River Road, Vanier Ontario K1L 8B9 Canada. DD 796.33505.

FOOTBALL NEWS. 0161-9020. Periodical. US. English. ir. $19.95. Football News, 17820 East Warren, Detroit MI 48224. Tel (313)881-9554. Ed Matt Marson. adv acc. Circ 120,000. (ctrl). Complete coverage of college and pro football; weekly ratings of top teams, college and pro; outstanding predictions of all major games.

FOOTBALL OFFICIALS MANUAL. 0163-6219. US. English. an. National Federation of State High School Associations, Federation Place, Box 98, Elgin IL 60120. LC GV954.35. DD 796.3320202.

FOOTBALL RECORDS. VFOAT NCAA Football Records. Began with Vol. for 1979. 0738-1611. US. English. an. National Collegiate Athletic Association, Publishing Department, PO Box 1906, Shawnee Mission KS 66222. LC GV956.8. DD 796.332630973. Official National Collegiate Athletic Association Football Records, 0145-2630.

FOOTBALL REGISTER. Began in 1966. 0071-7258. US. English. an. $11.15. The Sporting News, PO Box 56, St Louis MO 63166. Tel (314)997-7111. Individual statistics, career highlights and personal facts on over 1,500 active players in the NFL. Updated annually.

FOOTBALL RULE BOOK. Main/Corp National Federation of State High School Associations. US. English. an. National Federation of State High School Associations, 11724 Plaza Circle, PO Box 20626, Kansas City MO 64195.

FOOTBALL STATISTICIANS' MANUAL. See Statistics.

FOOTNOTES (RESTON, VA.). (FOOTNOTES). VFOAT Foot Notes. 8755-9048. Periodical. US. English. qt. Steve Clapp, 11155 Saffold Way, Reston VA 22090. Tel (703)437-8586. Ed Steve Clapp. DD 796. bk rev. adv acc. Circ 115,000. A journal for members of the Road Runners Club of America, which promotes long distance running as a sport and as healthy exercise.

FRANCE FOOTBALL. Began in 1945. Periodical. FR. French. $90.47. C I P P, 25 Avenue Michelet, 93400 Saint-Ouen Cedex France. LC GV944.F8. DD 796.3340944.

FREE FLIGHT (OTTAWA ONT.). (FREE FLIGHT). VFOAT Vol Libre. 0827-2557. Periodical. CN. English (includes some text in French). bm. $18.00 Domestic, $24.00 Foreign. Soaring Association of Canada National Office, 485 Bank Street/2nd Floor, Ottawa Ontario K2P 1Z2 Canada. Tel (613)232-1243. Ed T Burton. DD 797.5505. bk rev. adv acc. Circ 1,500. For the enjoyment of soaring enthusiasts.

FREE THROW. V. 4, No. 4 (Dec. 1977)-. 0705-3894. Periodical. CN. English (includes some text in French). qt. $4.00. Canadian Water Polo Association, National Sport and Recreation Centre, 333 River Road, Ottawa Ontario K1L 8B9 Canada. DD 797.25. Water Polo in Canada, 0317-0543.

FRIENDLY FAIRWAYS OF MICHIGAN. 0193-0443. US. English. an. $5.70. Friendly Fairways of America, PO Box 237-A, Royal Oak MI 48068. LC GV962. DD 796.352068025774.

GAMEDAY. (GAMEDAY : AN OFFICIAL PRO PUBLICATION OF THE NFL). VFOAT Game Day. 8755-1470. Periodical. US. English. mo. National Football League Properties Inc, 410 Park Avenue, New York NY 10022. LC GV937. DD 796.332640973.

GATOR BAIT. 0744-0995. Periodical. US. English. ir. $25.00. Gator Bait, PO Box 14022, Gainesville FL 32604. Tel (904)372-1215. Ed David Stirt. adv acc. Circ 22,000. (ctrl). A sports tabloid covering all aspects of University of Florida athletic competition with a heavy emphasis on football and recruiting. Published 38 times a year.

GAZETTE SPORTIVE. (LA GAZETTE SPORTIVE). Vol. 1, No. 1-. 0229-9364. Periodical. CN. French. mo. $1.00 Per Number. Editions de la Competition, 116 Chemin Dufferin, Hampstead Quebec H3X 2Y1 Canada. DD 796.09714.

GEKKAN KENDO NIHON. VFOAT Kendo Nippon Monthly. Periodical. JA. Japanese. ir. 6200. Suki Janaru, 4-14 Kudan Minami 2-chome, Chiyoda-ku 102, Tokyo Japan. LC GV1142.

GENEESKUNDE EN SPORT. V. 1- 1968-. NE. Dutch. bm. 18.45. Uitgeversmij de Tijdstroom, 7240 BA 14, Lochem Netherlands. Tel 05730-3651. Ind/Abst Biol. Abstr. CODEN GESPBS. bk rev adv acc. Circ 4,000. Sports medicine and sport sciences, including psychology, motor skills, mental and physical training.

GENERAL COMPETITION RULES. Main/Corp Sports Car Club of America. 0196-7630. US. English. $2.50. Sports Car Club of America Inc, PO Box 22476, Denver CO 80222. LC GV1030. DD 796.720973.

GEORGIA SPORTSMAN. See Recreation, Leisure - Outdoor Life.

THE GIANTS NEWSWEEKLY. Vol. 1, No. 1 (Apr. 1, 1981)-. 0279-0238. Periodical. US. English. ir. $19.95. Giants Newsweekly, PO Box 816/43 Front Street/Suite 10, Red Bank NJ 07701. Tel (201)747-1085. Ed Randy Lange. bk rev. adv acc. Circ 48,000. Complete coverage of New York Giants football.

THE GIRLS' AND WOMEN'S TAEKWONDO NEWSLETTER. 0882-5920. Periodical. US. English. Free. The Girls' and Women's Taekwondo Newsletter, 14125 Berryville Road, Germantown MD 20874. DD 796.

GIRLS BASKETBALL RULES BOOK. NATIONAL FEDERATION EDITION. (GIRLS BASKETBALL RULES BOOK). Main/Corp National Federation of State High School Associations. 0361-5839. US. English. $0.85. National Federation of State High School Associations, 400 Leslie Street, Chicago IL 61020. LC GV886. DD 796.3238.

GIRLS GYMNASTICS JUDGING MANUAL. NATIONAL FEDERATION EDITION. (GIRLS GYMNASTICS JUDGING MANUAL). Main/Corp National Federation of State High School Associations. 0197-162X. US. English. National Federation of State High School Associations, Federation Place, PO Box 98, Elgin IL 60120. LC GV464. DD 796.41.

GO FOR SPORTS. V. 1- Fall 1977-. 0704-0385. Periodical. CN. English. Monday Publications, Box 1390, Victoria British Columbia V8W 3C4 Canada. DD 796.0971134.

GO GATORS. V. 1- June 1979-. 0194-9594. Periodical. US. English. mo. Go Gators, Inside Florida Sports, PO Box 14083, Gainesville FL 32604.

GOAL. (GOAL : THE NATIONAL HOCKEY LEAGUE MAGAZINE). 0273-5601. Periodical. US. English. ir. $19.95. Goal Magazine, PO Box Goal, Lowell MA 01852. Tel (617)452-4480.

GOALGETTER. V. 1- Feb. 28, 1979-. 0708-5427. Periodical. CN. English. bw. $12. DD 796.33409711.

GOLF & CLUB YEARBOOK. See Yearbooks, Almanacs, Directories.

GOLF ANNUAL. 0095-4071. US. English. an. Diamondhead Corporation, Mountainside NJ 07092. LC GV961. DD 796.35205.

GOLF BUSINESS. 0148-3706. Periodical. US. English. mo. Free to Qualified Management Personnel at Golf Facilities, $18.00 Others. Golf Business, 9800 Detroit Avenue, Cleveland OH 44102. LC GV961. DD 796.35205. Golfdom, 0017-1905.

GOLF CANADA. April 1967-. 0017-1751. Periodical. CN. English (includes some text in French). mo. Golf Canada, 491 Vitre Street West, Montreal Quebec H2Z 1G6 Canada.

GOLF COURSE MANAGEMENT. V. 47- Jan. 1979-. 0192-3048. Periodical. US. English. mo. $30.00. Golf Course Superintendent Association of America, 1617 St Andrews Drive, Lawrence KS 66044. Tel (913)841-2240. Ed Clay Loyd. LC GV975. DD 796.352068. bk rev. adv acc. Circ 18,000. Golf course management. Golf Superintendent, 0017-1840.

Recreation, Leisure—Sports

GOLF DIGEST. V. 1- Spring 1950-. 0017-176X. Periodical. US. English. mo. Golf Digest Inc, 495 Westport Avenue, Norwalk CT 06856, (subscription address: Communication Data Services PO Box 4966 Des Moines IA 50340). Tel (800)247-5470. Ind/Abst Consum. Index Prod. Eval. Inf. Source, Pop. Mag. Rev., Consum. Index Prod. Eval. Inf. Source. *Arrowhead Gold Digest.*

THE GOLF DIGEST ALMANAC. See Yearbooks, Almanacs, Directories.

GOLF DIRECTORY. See Yearbooks, Almanacs, Directories.

GOLF GUIDE. 0099-1783. Periodical. US. English. mo. $9.00. Werner Book Corp, 631 Wilshire Boulevard, Santa Monica CA 90401. LC GV961. DD 796.35205. *Golfguide and Golf & Club.*

GOLF ILLUSTRATED. V. 1- Summer 1973-. 0160-6808. Periodical. US. English. wk. 47.50. 47 Dartford Road, Sevenoaks Kent TN13 3TE England. Tel (0732)451861. Ed W Robertson. LC GV961. DD 796.35205. adv acc. Circ 30,000. Golf worldwide immediacy of tournament reporting being fortnightly publication good features including fashion articles.

GOLF ILLUSTRATED (NEW YORK, N.Y.). (GOLF ILLUSTRATED). Vol. 1, No. 1 (Winter 1985)-. Periodical. US. English. bm. $11.94 Domestic, $15.94 Foreign. Golf Illustrated Magazine, PO Box 6057, Palm Coast FL 32037. *Golf Illustrated, 0160-6808.*

GOLF INDUSTRY. V. 1- Oct. 1975-. 0160-6824. US. English. bm. $12.00. Industry Publishers Inc, 1545 NE 123rd Street, North Miami FL 33161. Tel (305)893-8771. LC HD9993.G65. DD 338.47688763520973.

GOLF JOURNAL. (GOLF JOURNAL : THE OFFICIAL PUBLICATION OF THE UNITED STATES GOLF ASSOCIATION). 0017-1794. Periodical. US. English. ir. $8.00. US Golf Association, Golf House, Far Hills NJ 07931. Tel (201)234-2300. Ed Robert T Sommers. Circ 140,000. (ctrl). Focuses its attention on the history, humor, latest developments, agronomy, equipment, rules, and technical issues of golf.

GOLF MAGAZINE. VFOAT Golf. Began in 1959. 0017-1808. Periodical. US. English. mo. $54.00. Kinokuniya Book Stores, 1581 Webster Street, San Francisco CA 94115. Tel 0865-51-1166. Ind/Abst Mag. Index, Pop. Mag. Rev., Access. LC GV961. DD 796.35205. bk rev. adv acc.

THE GOLF REPORTER. 0745-7502. Periodical. US. English. wk. $19.00. The Golf Reporter, PO Box 18810, Charlotte NC 28218. *Carolinas Golf Reporter, 0199-3461.*

THE GOLF TRAVELER. 0191-717X. Periodical. US. English. bm. $5.00. Golf Card International Inc, Bill Roland Associate Editor, 1137 East 2100 South, Salt Lake City UT 84106. Tel (801)486-9391. Ed Allen Cornwall. bk rev. adv acc. Circ 45,000. For the 60,000 members of "The Golf Card", the Golf Traveler serves as an excellent directory of affiliated golf courses including editorial support.

GOLF WORLD. Vol. 1 1947-. 0017-1891. Periodical. US. English. ir. $22.00. Golf World c/o Dorothy Strazza, 2100 Powers Ferry Road NW, Atlanta GA 30339. Tel (404)955-5656. Ed Richard Taylor. LC GV961. DD 796.35205. adv acc. Circ 100,000. News magazine of golf, with in-depth analysis of all PGA and LPGA action as well as collegiate, senior and amateur coverage. Comprehensive travel features and regular instructional series.

GOLF WORLD. Vol. 1- 1962-. 0017-1883. Periodical. UK. English. mo. 15.00. Golf World Ltd, 9 Saint Davids Road/Cliffton, Campville Tamworth England. Ed Peter Haslam. DD 796.352. bk rev. adv acc. Circ 80,000. Britain and Europe's largest selling golf magazine. The policy is to bring the best instruction and worldwide coverage of the golf scene.

THE GOLFER'S HANDBOOK. Began publication in 1898. UK. English. an. Munro Barr Publication Ltd, 1 Park Circus, Glasgow G3 6AS Scotland. LC GV961. DD 796.352058.

GOLFGUIDE ANNUAL. 0360-0858. US. English. an. $1.50. Werner Book Corp, 631 Wilshire Boulevard, Santa Monica CA 90401. LC GV961. DD 796.35205. *Golf & Club Annual.*

GOLFINFORMACION. VFOAT Golf Information. Spanish. ir. Ediciones Informativas y Deportivas, Avda Del Generalisimo 60, Madrid Spain. LC GV985.S7. DD 796.3520946.

GOLFING IN QUEBEC. No. 1-. 0708-5060. CN. English. an. Free. Gouvernement du Quebec, 600 St Amable 4E Etage, Quebec G1R 4Z1 Canada. DD 796.352025714. *Golf Quebec, 0707-1299.*

GOLFSHOP OPERATIONS. See Business - Marketing.

GONG FU. (KUNG FU). VFOAT Kung Fu Magazine. 0376-6535. Periodical. Chinese. ir. $2.00 Single Issue. LC GV1112.

GRAND PRIX DU CANADA. See Transportation - Automobiles.

GRAND PRIX LABATT DU CANADA. REGLEMENTS. See Transportation - Automobiles.

GRAND SLAM. Began with Nov. 1972 issue. 0701-0745. Periodical. CN. English (includes some text in French). bm. $2. Canadian Amateur Softball Association, 333 River Road, Ottawa Ontario K1L 8B9 Canada. DD 796.3578.

GRAY'S SPORTING JOURNAL. See Recreation, Leisure - Outdoor Life.

GREEN. (THE GREEN : THE OFFICIAL VOICE OF CANADIAN LAWN BOWLING COUNCIL). Issue No. 1 (Apr. 1972)-. 0823-6380. Periodical. CN. English. ir. $6.00. Canadian Lawn Bowling Council c/o Mrs Beverly Redston, 82 Kenwood Road, Beaconsfield Quebec H9W 5K4 Canada. Tel (613)748-5643. DD 796.31. adv acc. Circ 5,000. (ctrl). Information and news on the sport of lawn bowls in Canada.

GREENMASTER. (THE GREENMASTER). V. 2, No. 3- Feb. 1966-. 0380-3333. Periodical. CN. English (includes some text in French). mo. Canadian Golf Superintendents Association, 698 Weston Road, Toronto Ontario M6N 3R3 Canada. *News Bulletin, 0380-3341.*

GRIT AND STEEL. 1899. 0017-4297. Periodical. US. English. mo. $14.00. Grit and Steel, Box 280, Gaffney SC 29342. Tel (803)489-2324. Ed Mary M Hodge. adv acc. Circ 6,000. Published in the interest of those devoted to game fowl.

GUIDE CHASSE ET PECHE. See Recreation, Leisure - Outdoor Life.

GUIDE DU COUREUR - MASKI-COURONS. (GUIDE DU COUREUR). Main/Corp Maski-Courons. VAT Maski-Courons. Guide du Coureur. 1980-. 0821-0195. CN. French. an. Maski Courons, CP 68, Saint Gabriel de Brandon Quebec J0K 2N0 Canada. DD 796.42606071443.

GUIDE DU GOLF. (LE GUIDE DU GOLF . . .). 84-. 0823-8731. CN. French. an. Editions Quebecor, 225 Est rue Roy, Montreal Quebec H2W 2N6 Canada. DD 796.3526405.

GUINNESS SPORTS RECORD BOOK. 1972-. Periodical. US. English. ir. Sterling Publishing Co Ltd, 2 Park Avenue, New York NY 10016. Tel (212)532-7160. Ed David Boehm. LC GV741. DD 796.0212. Complete sports records from around the world. The biggest, fastest and best of sports.

GUN DIGEST HUNTING ANNUAL. 1st Ed. (1984)-. 0739-4403. Periodical. US. English. an. $9.95. DBI Books Inc, 1 Northfield Plaza, Northfield IL 60093. LC WMLC L 83/283.

GUN DOG. V. 1, No. 1 (Sept./Oct. 1981)-. 0279-5086. Periodical. US. English. bm. $15.97. Gun Dog, PO Box 68, Adel IA 50003. Tel (515)993-4006. Ed Bob Wilbanks. bk rev. adv acc. Circ 68,000. (ctrl). Magazine devoted exclusively for the upland bird and waterfowl hunter.

GUN WORLD. V. 1- 1960-. 0017-5641. Periodical. US. English. mo. $17.00. Gallant Publishing Company, Box HH 34249, Camino Capistrano, Capistrano Beach CA 92624. Tel (714)493-2101. Ed Jack Lewis. adv acc. Circ 136,000. Edited for shooters, hunters and target shooters. Features deal with firearms, tests of new shooting equipment with evaluations. Contents are aimed at firearms enthusiast.

GUN WORLD ANNUAL. VFOAT GWA. 0362-2495. US. English. an. $1.50. Gallant Publishing Co, Box HH 34249 Camino Capistrano, Capistrano Beach CA 92624. LC TS532. DD 683.4005.

GUN WORLD HUNTING GUIDE. Began with issue for 1973. 0362-4749. US. English. an. $1.50. Gallant Publishing Co, 34249 Camino Capistrano, Capistrano Beach CA 92624. LC SK1. DD 799.21305.

GUNS & AMMO ACTION SERIES. VFOAT Guns and Ammo Action Series. No. 1-. Monographic Series. US. English. bm. $2.95 Each Domestic, $3.50 Foreign. Petersen Publishing Co, 6725 Sunset Boulevard, Los Angeles CA 90028.

GUNS REVIEW. Periodical. UK. English. mo. 12.50 Domestic, 14.50 Foreign. Tee & Whiten Distributors Ltd, Standard House Bonhill Street, London EC2A 4DA England. Tel 01-628-4741. LC TS532. DD 683.4005.

GUTMANN PUMA/EXPLORER KNIFE ANNUAL. See Recreation, Leisure - Outdoor Life.

GYMNASTICS WORLD. Began with Jan. 1975. 0098-8677. Periodical. US. English. bm. Gymnastics World, PO Box 110, Santa Monica CA 90406. LC GV461. DD 796.4105.

N H L PRO HOCKEY. 8th- Ed. 0319-5627. CN. English. an. Simon & Schuster of Canada, Markham Ontario Canada. DD 796.96206. *Pro Hockey, 0316-5728.*

HANDBALL CANADA. V. 1- Jan. 1980-. 0226-1529. Periodical. CN. English. qt. Free to Members, $5. Others. Canadian Team Handball Federation, 333 River Road, Vanier Ontario K1L 8B9 Canada. DD 796.310971. *Bulletin.*

HANDBALL MAGAZINE. V. 1- Nov. 1976-. 0700-4664. Periodical. CN. French. ir. Federation Quebecoise de Handball Olympique, 1415 East rue Jarry, Montreal Quebec H2E 1A7 Canada. DD 796.31.

HANDBOOK AND DIRECTORY - CANADIAN FIELD HOCKEY ASSOCIATION. See Yearbooks, Almanacs, Directories.

HANDBOOK AND DIRECTORY - CANADIAN WOMEN'S FIELD HOCKEY ASSOCIATION. See Yearbooks, Almanacs, Directories.

HANDBOOK - CANADIAN BADMINTON ASSOCIATION. (HANDBOOK). Main/Corp Canadian Badminton Association. VAT Handbook - Canadian Badminton Coaches Association, Handbook - Canadian Badminton Umpires Association. 0229-5806. CN. English. an. $1.25 Per No. Canadian Badminton Association, 333 River Road, Ottawa Ontario K1L 8B9 Canada. DD 796.3450971.

THE HANDBOOK FOR OFFSHORE RACING. See Boats and Boating.

HANDBOOK - NEW YORK STATE PUBLIC HIGH SCHOOL ATHLETIC ASSOCIATION. Main/Corp New York State Public High School Athletic Association. US. English. New York State Public High School Athletic Association Inc, Executive Park South, Albany NY 12203.

HANDBOOK OF POLICIES AND PROCEDURES - CANADIAN WOMEN'S INTERCOLLEGIATE ATHLETIC UNION. Main/Corp Canadian Women's Intercollegiate Athletic Union. VFOAT CWIAU Handbook. VAT Canadian Women's Intercollegiate Athletic Union Handbook, Handbook. USICF, Handbook. Union Sportive Interuniversitaire Canadienne Feminine. 1974/75-. 0704-755X. CN. English. an. Canadian Women's Intercollegiate Athletic Union, 333 River Road, Vanier Ontario K1L 8B9 Canada. DD 796.06271.

HANDLOADER. VFOAT Handloader Magazine. 0017-7393. Periodical. US. English. bm. $16.00. Wolfe Publishing Co, Box 3030, Prescott AZ 86301. Tel (602)445-2810. Ed Dave Wolfe. bk rev. adv acc. Circ 35,000. (ctrl). Technical journal of ammunition reloading.

HANDLOADER'S DIGEST. 1st Ed. (1962)-. 0073-0211. US. English. ir. $12.95. DBI Books Inc, 4092 Commercial Avenue, Northbrook IL 60062. Tel (312)272-6310. Ed John T Amber. LC TS538. DD 683.40605.

LE HAUT COMITE DE LA JEUNESSE, DES SPORTS ET DES LOISIRS EN . . . . Main/Corp France. Haut Comite de la Jeunesse, des Sports et des Loisirs. French. ir. Le Comite, 82 rue de Lille, Paris VIIE France. LC GV79. DD 790.06.

HIKING. See Recreation, Leisure - Outdoor Life.

Recreation, Leisure—Sports

HISTORY AND RECORDS OF THE NCAA MEN'S AND WOMEN'S CHAMPIONSHIPS. Main/Corp National Collegiate Athletic Association. VFOAT National Collegiate Championships. 1981/82-. US. English. an. *History and Records of National Collegiate Championships and National College Division Championships.*

HOCKEY. V. 1- Nov. 1975-. 0361-5847. Periodical. US. English. bm. $6.00. Golf Digest Inc, 297 Westport Avenue, Norwalk CT 06856. LC GV846. DD 796.96205.

HOCKEY. V. 1- Dec. 1977-. 0704-7983. Periodical. CN. French. ir. $10.00. Publications Belseg, Hockey Inc, Bureau 2202/1115 Ouest rue Sherbrooke, Montreal Quebec H3A 1H3 Canada. DD 796.96205.

HOCKEY AMATEUR. Main/Corp Canadian Amateur Hockey Association. 0826-5313. CN. English. an. Free. Hockey Amateur, 8928 Boulevard St-Michel, Montreal Quebec H1Z 3G4 Canada. DD 796.96202022.

HOCKEY DIGEST. V. 1- Nov. 1972-. 0046-7693. Periodical. US. English. mo. $9.95. Hockey Digest, PO Box 3300, Communication Data Services, Harlan IA 51537. Tel (312)491-6440. Ed Michael Herbert. LC GV846. DD 796.96205. bk rev. adv acc. Circ 135,000. Covers the National Hockey League.

HOCKEY FIELD. Vol. 43, No. 1 (17th Sept., 1955)-. 0018-3008. Periodical. UK. English. mo. $14.00 Surface Mail, $24.00 Air Mail. Miss G Hooper, 369 Atlantic Avenue, Cohasset MA 02025. Ed J Whitehead. *Women's Hockey Field.*

HOCKEY GUIDE. VFOAT Sporting News Hockey Guide. 1981-82 Ed.-. 0278-4955. US. English. an. $7.50. Hockey Guide, 1212 North Lindbergh Boulevard, PO Box 56, St Louis MO 63166. LC GV846. DD 796.96205. *Pro and Amateur Hockey Guide, 0090-0818.*

HOCKEY HAWK OF MANITOBA. Sept. 1982-. 0821-5804. Periodical. CN. English. ir. $16.50. Hockey Hawk of Manitoba, PO Box 70, East Selkirk Manitoba R0E 0M0 Canada. DD 796.962097127.

HOCKEY ILLUSTRATED. Periodical. US. English. ir. Complete Sports, 333 Johnson Avenue, Brooklyn NY 11206.

HOCKEY NEWS. (THE HOCKEY NEWS). Began with Oct. 1, 1947 issue. 0018-3016. Periodical. CN. English. ir. 22.45. Hockey News, 85 Scarsdale Road, Toronto Ontario M3B 2R2 Canada. Tel (416)445-5702. Ed Robert McKenzie. adv acc. Circ 84,000. Statistics, features and opinions on all levels of the game.

HOCKEY ONTARIO MAGAZINE. VFOAT Hockey Ontario. Vol. 3, No. 6 (Sept./Oct. 1982)-. 0821-4700. Periodical. CN. English. ir. $4.50. Hockey Ontario Development Committee, 1220 Sheppard Avenue East, Willowdale Ontario M2K 2X1 Canada. DD 796.96205. *Hockey Scope.*

HOCKEY PROFESSIONNEL. 0712-8428. CN. French. an. $6.95 Per Volume. Hockey Professionnel, c/o Presses Metropolitaines, 175 le Mortagne, Boucherville Quebec J4B 6G4 Canada. DD 796.96206. *Hockey L N H, 0704-7894.*

HOCKEY REGISTER. 0090-2292. US. English. an. $11.15. The Sporting News, Box 44, St Louis MO 63166. Tel (314)997-7111. LC GV848.5.A1. DD 796.9620922, B. History and records of all active NHL forwards and defensemen and special section on goal tenders. Also, a listing of major award winners.

HOCKEY STARS. (HOCKEY STARS OF . . .). 0073-2869. US. English. $0.95. Pyramid Communications Inc, 919 Third Avenue, New York NY 10022. LC GV848.5.A1. DD 796.9620922 ¢B!.

HOCKEY'S HERITAGE. 1969-. 0317-9257. Periodical. CN. English. be. Hockey Hall of Fame, Canadian National Exhibition GRNDS, Toronto Ontario M6K 3C3 Canada. Tel (416)595-1345. DD 796.9620922. *Hockey Hall of Fame Book, 0317-9265.*

HOKKEJ. (KHOKKEI: KALENDAR-SPRAVOCHNIK). 0302-7260. UR. Russian. 0.11. Fizkultura 1 Sport, K-6 Kaliaevskaia Ul 27, Moskvo Russia. LC GV848.4.R8K48.

HOOF BEATS. V. 1- 1933-. 0018-4683. Periodical. US. English. mo. $18.00. US Trotting Association, 750 Michigan Avenue, Columbus OH 43215. Tel (614)224-2291. Ed Dean A Hoffman. bk rev. adv acc. Circ 27,000. (ctrl). News and feature stories about raising and racing harness horses. Extensive color photography. Historical prices accepted.

HOOP/NBA TODAY. (HOOP). Vol. 11, Issue 1 (Nov. 1984)-. 0749-5285. Periodical. US. English. bm. $15.95 US, $19.95 Canada. Hoop Magazine, Subscription Department, PO Box Hoop, Lowell MA 01852. DD 796. *NBA Today, 0279-1935.*

HOOSIER SCENE. V. 12, No. 5- Sept. 27, 1976-. Periodical. US. English. Indiana University Varsity, Club Assembly Hall, Bloomington IN 47401. *Indiana Football News.*

HORS-PISTE. Vol. 1, No. 1 (Mar, 1973)-. 0823-0919. Periodical. CN. English. ir. $20.00 Per Year. Sentiers-Quebec, 1415 East rue Jarry, Montreal Quebec H2E 2Z7 Canada. DD 796.5109714. *Information Sentiers, 0228-9865.*

HORSE RACING MAGAZINE. See Horses and Horsemanship.

THE HORSESHOE PITCHER'S NEWS DIGEST. Periodical. US. English. mo. National Horseshoe Pitcher Association of America, 9439 Camp Creek Road, c/o D Roberts, Lucasville OH 45648. Tel (614)289-4101.

HOT ROD. See Transportation - Automobiles.

HUNTER'S HORN. 0018-7860. Periodical. US. English. mo. $10.00. Hunters Horn, PO Box 707, Sesser IL 62884. Tel (618)625-2711. Ed George O Slankard. adv acc. Circ 10,000. Fox hunting events and supplies plus fox hunting stories.

HUNTING GUIDE. 0073-4101. US. English. an. $1.35. Davis Publications Inc, 229 Park Avenue South, New York NY 10003. LC SK1. DD 799.205.

HUNTING HOTSPOTS. Series/Titl A Sports Afield Special. VFOAT Sports Afield Hunting Hotspots. 0730-5052. US. English. an. $1.95. Sports Afield, 250 West 55th Street, New York NY 10019. LC SK41. DD 799.297305.

HUNTING (NEW YORK, N.Y.). (HUNTING). VFOAT Sports Afield Hunting Annual. 0276-8895. Periodical. US. English. an. Sports Afield, 250 West 55th Street, New York NY 10019. Tel (212)262-3205. Ed Mike Schwanz. LC SK7. DD 799.205. adv acc. Circ 300,000. How-to articles about big-game hunting and birdshooting. *Sports Afield Hunting Annual.*

HUSKY FEVER. Vol. 1, No. 1-. 0715-495X. Periodical. CN. mo. $10.50. Husky Fever, PO Box 2212, Yellowknife Northwest Territories X0E 1H0 Canada. DD 798.8.

I.A.A.F. DIRECTORY. See Yearbooks, Almanacs, Directories.

ICE WORM. (THE ICE WORM : THE OFFICIAL PUBLICATION OF THE EASTERN ONTARIO SECTION, C.F.S.A.). 0710-1430. Periodical. CN. English. ir. $2.00. Eastern Ontario Section, C.F.S.A., 160 Vanderhoof Avenue, Toronto Ontario M4G 4B8 Canada. DD 796.9109713.

IDAHO WILDLIFE. See Recreation, Leisure - Outdoor Life.

ILLUSTRATED DIGEST OF BASEBALL. 0091-3901. US. English. $1.50. Stadia Sports Publications, 180 Madison Avenue, New York NY 10016. LC GV877. DD 796.357640973.

ILLUSTRATED DIGEST OF PRO FOOTBALL. 0092-654X. US. English. $1.50. Stadia Sports Publishing, 180 Madison Avenue, New York NY 10016. LC GV955. DD 796.332640973.

INDEX (TULSA, OKLA.). See Indexes/Abstracts.

INDIANA RACQUET SPORTS. 0743-992X. Periodical. US. English. mo. Indiana Racquet Sports, 630 North College Avenue, Indianapolis IN 46204.

THE INDIANAPOLIS 500 YEARBOOK. See Yearbooks, Almanacs, Directories.

INDY CAR RACING. Began in 1983?. 0747-0894. Periodical. US. English. mo. $20.00. Indy Car Racing, PO Box 500, Concord NC 28025. DD 796.

INFO BASKET. No. 1 (Oct. 1970)-V. 6, No 3 (Feb. 1976). 0710-1414. Periodical. CN. French (text in English). ir. Federation de Basket-Ball du Quebec, 1415 Jarry East, Montreal Quebec H2E 2Z7 Canada. DD 796.323060714.

INFO-VOLLEY. No. 1 (1st Oct. 1980)-. 0823-6305. Periodical. CN. French. mo. Association Regionale de Volleyball de Quebec, Bureau 225/1990 Ouest Boulevard Charest, Sainte-Foy Quebec G1N 4K8 Canada. DD 796.32506071447. *Bulletin de Nouvelles (Association Regionale de Volleyball de Quebec), 0710-734X.*

INFORMO LOISIR. V. 1- Dec. 1973-. 0380-3090. Periodical. CN. French. bm. Free to Members. Conseil Regional des Loisirs de Quebec, Bureau 300/917 rue Mgr Grandin, Ste-Foy Quebec G1V 3X8 Canada. DD 790.0971447. *Servo Loisir, 0380-3082.*

INSIDE BOXING. No. 1 (Nov. 1983)-. 0742-5171. Periodical. US. English. Starlog Press, 475 Park Avenue South, New York NY 10016.

INSIDE EDGE. (INSIDE EDGE : THE OFFICIAL PUBLICATION OF THE WESTERN ONTARIO SECTION, C.F.S.A.). 0711-1126. Periodical. CN. English. ir. $3.50. Canadian Figure Skating Association, Western Ontario Section, Box 1074, Hagersville Ontario N0A 1H0 Canada. DD 796.9109713.

INSIDE KUNG-FU. See Physical Training.

INSIDE RUNNING. Began in July 1977?. 0194-6552. Periodical. US. English. mo. $8.00 U S, $16.00 Foreign. Inside Running, PO Box 36082, Houston TX 77236.

INSIDE SPORTS. V. 1- Oct. 1979-. 0195-3478. Periodical. US. English. mo. $18.00. Inside Sports Inc, PO Box 10794, Des Moines IA 50340. Tel (312)491-6440. Ed Michael Herbert. LC GV561. DD 796.05. bk rev. adv acc. Circ 400,000. Indepth look at sports today, colorful, exciting up close and personal.

INSIDE THE AUBURN TIGERS. Vol. 1, No. 1 (Aug. 1981)-. 0279-2273. Periodical. US. English. mo. $30.00. College Sports Publishing Inc, PO Box 6104, University AL 35486. Tel (205)345-5074. Ed Mark Murphy. Circ 12,000. Official full-color magazine of Auburn University athletics emphasizing football and men's basketball. Also includes all men's and women's sports.

INSIDE WATER. (INSIDE WATER : OFFICIAL MAGAZINE OF THE ONTARIO WATER POLO ASSOCIATION). Vol. 1 (Spring 1983)-. 0822-9929. Periodical. CN. English. ir. Free. Ontario Water Polo Association, 1220 Sheppard Avenue, Willowdale Ontario M2K 2X1 Canada. DD 797.25. (ctrl). *Polo Post, 0228-7420.*

INSIDE WOMEN'S TENNIS. (INSIDE WOMEN'S TENNIS : OFFICIAL PUBLICATION OF THE WOMEN'S TENNIS ASSOCIATION). 0738-7040. Periodical. US. English. bw. $25.00. Womens Tennis Association, 1604 Union Street, San Francisco CA 94123.

INSIDERS BASEBALL FACT-BOOK. VFOAT Insiders Baseball Fact Book. 0731-8162. US. English. an. $8.00 Single Issue. Research Analysis Publications, PO Box 49213, Los Angeles CA 90049. LC GV877. DD 796.3570973.

INSIDERS BASEBALL FACT-BOOK EXTRA. VFOAT Insiders Baseball Fact Book Extra. 1st Ed. (1982)-. 0731-8146. US. English. an. $7.00. Research Analysis Publications, PO Box 49213, Los Angeles CA 90049. LC GV877. DD 796.3570973.

INSPORTS. V. 1- Sept. 1975-. Periodical. US. English. qt. Creative Educational Society, 123 South Broad, Mankato MN 56001. Ind/Abst Child. Mag. Guide.

INTERNATIONAL DIVER INDEX. WORLD INDIVEX EDITION. See Indexes/Abstracts.

THE INTERNATIONAL GOLF DIRECTORY. See Yearbooks, Almanacs, Directories.

INTERNATIONAL GYMNAST (SANTA MONICA, CALIF. : 1981). (INTERNATIONAL GYMNAST). VFOAT International Gymnast Magazine. Vol. 23, No. 10 (Oct. 1981)-. 0735-7567. Periodical. US. English. mo. $36.00. Sundby Sports Publications, PO Box 110, Santa Monica CA 90406. Tel (213)451-8768. *International Gymnast Magazine, 0276-1041.*

INTERNATIONAL JOURNAL OF SPORT BIOMECHANICS. (INTERNATIONAL JOURNAL OF SPORT BIOMECHANICS : IJSB). VFOAT IJSB. Vol. 1, No. 1 (Feb. 1985)-. 0740-2082. Periodical. US. English. qt. $48.00 Domestic, $52.00 Foreign. Human Kinetics Publishers Inc, Box 5076, Champaign IL 61820. Tel (217)351-5076. Ed Richard C Nelson. DD 612. bk rev. adv acc. Circ 450. Publication devoted to sport biomechanics. Contains articles (theoretical and applied) relating to the study of the forces affecting human movement in sport and exercise.

Recreation, Leisure—Sports

INTERNATIONAL JOURNAL OF SPORT PSYCHOLOGY. (INTERNATIONAL JOURNAL OF SPORT PSYCHOLOGY : OFFICIAL JOURNAL OF THE INTERNATIONAL SOCIETY OF SPORTS PSYCHOLOGY). Began publication with V. 1, 1970. 0047-0767. Periodical. IT. Italian (articles mainly in English with some in French). qt. $48.00. Edizioni Luigi Pozzi, Via Panama 68, 00198 Roma Italy. Ind/Abst Psychol. Abstr., Soc. Sci. Citation Index. LC GV706.4. DD 796.05. NLM W1 IN791D. CODEN ISPYAN.

INTERNATIONAL JOURNAL OF SPORTS MEDICINE. See Medicine.

INTERNATIONAL REVIEW FOR THE SOCIOLOGY OF SPORT. Vol. 19, No. 1-. 0074-7769. Periodical. English. qt. LC GV706. DD 306.483. International Review of Sport Sociology.

INTERNATIONAL REVIEW OF SPORT SOCIOLOGY. V. 1- 1966-. 0074-7769. Periodical. PL. English (summaries in Russian, German and French). qt. 98.00. R Oldenbourg Verlag, Postfach 801360, 8000 Munchen 80 West Germany. Ind/Abst Sociol. Abstr., Soc. Welf. Soc. Plan./Policy Soc. Dev. LC GV706. DD 301.57.

INTERNATIONAL SKI TRAILS. 0092-1769. US. English. an. $3.95. Subscription Department, 3700 Wilshire Boulevard/Suite 538, Los Angeles CA 90010. LC GV854.A1. DD 796.93.

INTERNATIONAL SPORT SCIENCES. See Medicine.

INTERNATIONAL TENNIS WEEKLY. 0199-0853. Periodical. US. English. wk. $24.00. International Tennis Weekly, 319 Country Club Road, Garland TX 35040. Tel (214)494-5991.

THE INTERSCHOLASTIC LEAGUER. See Education (General).

INVITATION (CHICOUTIMI, QUEBEC). (INVITATION). No. 1 (July 1981)-. 0710-1295. Periodical. CN. English (text in French). mo. Free. Invitation, PO Box 1983, Chicoutimi Quebec G7H 6M6 Canada. DD 796.980971. (ctrl).

ISLANDWIDE RUNNER. VFOAT Islandwide Running Magazine. 0740-6266. Periodical. US. English. mo. $20.00. Islandwide Runner, 16 Concourse, Amityville NY 11701. Tel (516)842-7034. Ed Ralph Epifanio. bk rev. adv acc. Circ 1,500. Regional running magazine (Long Island and Metropolitan New York) covering calendar and results of track and field and road racing, also human interest stories.

ITALIAN JOURNAL OF SPORTS TRAUMATOLOGY. See Medicine.

ITHACAGUN HUNTING & SHOOTING ANNUAL. VFOAT Ithacagun Annual. V. 1- 1976-. 0361-4999. US. English. an. $1.75. Aqua-Field Publications Inc, 342 Madison Avenue, New York NY 10017. LC SK1. DD 799.05.

IT'S SPORTS. 0274-886X. Periodical. US. English. mo. $15.00. Fox and Fink, c/o J Brooks, PO Box 8077, Tampa FL 33674. Tel (813)932-4441.

J U C O REVIEW. Main/Corp National Junior College Athletic Association. 0047-2956. Periodical. US. English. ir. $10.00. National Junior Collegiate Athletic Association, 1831 Austin Bluffs Parkway/Suite 200, Colorado Springs CO 80907. Ed George E Killian. bk rev. adv acc. Circ 3,650. (ctrl). Lists all tournament results for those sports that member Junior Colleges of the NJCAA participate as well as other pertinent junior college information.

JACKPOT & RODEO NEWS. VFOAT Jackpot and Rodeo News. 8750-8680. Periodical. US. English. mo. $12.00. Jackpot and Rodeo News, 1706 Service Road, Ceres CA 95307.

J.D.P. NEWSLETTER. VAT Junior Development Program Newsletter. 0828-6337. Periodical. CN. English. ir. Free to Members. Ontario Association of Archers, 1229 Sheppard Avenue East, Willowdale Ontario M2K 2X1 Canada. DD 799.3209713. Newsletter (Ontario Association of Archers Junior Development Program), 0828-6329.

JIM RENNIE'S SPORTS LETTER. VFOAT Sports Letter. 1977. 0712-2632. Periodical. CN. English. wk. 165.00. Jim Rennie's Publications, PO Box 1000, Collingwood Ontario L9Y 4L4 Canada. Tel (705)445-7161. Ed Jim Rennie. DD 338.47688760971. bk rev. adv acc. Circ 1,200. (ctrl). Business newsletter reporting each week on developments in the Canadian sporting goods and ski trades.

JOHN HORAN'S SPORTS INK. VFOAT Sports Ink. 0882-7877. Periodical. US. English. ir. $190.00. John Horan's Sports Ink, PO Box 1263, Morrisville PA 19067. Tel (215)493-2720. Ed John Horan. DD 658. Circ 750. Business news and analysis of sports industry.

JOURNAL - CANADIAN OLDTIMERS' HOCKEY ASSOCIATION. (JOURNAL). VFOAT Canadian Oldtimers' Hockey Association Journal. VAT Coha Journal. Vol. 1, No. 1 (Oct. 1981)-. 0826-5887. Periodical. CN. English (includes some text in French). ir. Free to Members. COHA, 333 River Road, Ottawa Ontario K1R 8H9 Canada. DD 796.9626.

JOURNAL OF BASEBALL HISTORY. 0884-9501. Periodical. US. English. qt. $45.00. Meckler Publishing Company, 11 Ferry Lane West, Westport CT 06880.

JOURNAL OF GAMBLING BEHAVIOR. Vol. 1, No. 1 (Spring/Summer 1985)-. 0742-0714. Periodical. US. English. sa. Human Sciences Press, 72 Fifth Avenue, New York NY 10011. DD 795.

THE JOURNAL OF ORTHOPAEDIC AND SPORTS PHYSICAL THERAPY. See Medicine - Orthopedics.

JOURNAL OF SPORT AND SOCIAL ISSUES. See Sociology: General Works, Theory.

JOURNAL OF SPORT BEHAVIOR. Began in 1978. 0162-7341. Periodical. US. English (summaries also in French). qt. $15.00. United State Sports Academy, University of South Alabama, Mobile AL 36688. Tel (205)460-7131. Ed William F Gilley. Ind/Abst Psychol. Abstr. LC GV561. DD 796.05. adv acc. Circ 450. (ctrl). Publishes original, empirical investigations and theoretical papers dealing with studies of social behavior in the areas of games and sport.

JOURNAL OF SPORT HISTORY. V. 1- Spring 1974-. 0094-1700. Periodical. US. English. ty. $20.00. North American Society for Sport History, Ronald A Smith, Penn State University/276 Recreation Building, University Park PA 16802. Ind/Abst Am. Hist. Life, Hist. Abstr., Part A, Mod. Hist. Abstr., Hist. Abst., Part B, Twent. Century Abstr., Writ. Am. Hist., Recent Publ. Artic. LC GV571. DD 796.09.

JOURNAL OF SPORT PSYCHOLOGY. VFOAT Sport Psychology. V. 1- 1979-. 0163-433X. Periodical. US. English. qt. $53.00. Human Kinetics Publishing, Box 5076, Champaign IL 61820. Tel (217)351-5076. Ed Diane Gill. Ind/Abst Biol. Abstr., Educ. Index, Psychol. Abstr. LC GV706.4. DD 796.01. NLM W1 JO903H. CODEN JSPPDA. bk rev. adv acc. Circ 1,325. Contains both theoretical and applied articles investigating the interactions between psychological variables and sport performance.

JOURNAL OF SPORTS MEDICINE AND PHYSICAL FITNESS. V. 1-. 0022-4707. Periodical. US. English (summaries in French and Spanish). qt. $60.00. Lippincott-Harper, East Washington Square, Philadelphia PA 19105. Tel (215)238-4295. Ind/Abst Chem. Abstr., Index Med., Hospit. Lit. Index. NLM W1 JO903. CODEN JMPFA3. Articles cover medical aspects of sport and physical training for improving and maintaining health, and psychological, physiological and pathological effects of muscular activity.

JOURNAL OF SPORTS SCIENCES. Vol. 1, No. 1 (Spring 1983)-. 0264-0414. Periodical. UK. English. ty. $90.50. Associated Book Publishers, North Way, Andover Hampshire SP10 5BE England. Tel (0264)62141. Ed T Reilly. LC GV561. DD 796.05. NLM W1. bk rev. adv acc. Multidisciplinary journal covering anatomy, anthropology, behavioural sciences, biomechanics, physiology and psychology.

THE JOURNAL OF SWIMMING RESEARCH. Vol. 1, No. 1 (Fall 1984)-. 0747-5993. Periodical. US. English. qt. $35.00. Asca 1, Hall of Fame Drive, Fort Lauderdale FL 33316. DD 797.

THE JOURNAL OF THE AMERICAN SPORTING BOOK COLLECTOR. See Hobbies.

JOURNAL OF THE CANADIAN ATHLETIC THERAPISTS ASSOCIATION. See Medicine.

JOURNAL OF THE NORTH AMERICAN FALCONERS' ASSOCIATION. See Recreation, Leisure - Outdoor Life.

JOURNAL OF THE PHILOSOPHY OF SPORT. V. 1- 1974-. 0094-8705. US. English. an. $15.00. Human Kinetics Publishers, Box 5076, Champaign IL 61820. Tel (217)351-5076. Ed Klaus V Meier. Ind/Abst Philos. Index. LC GV706. DD 796.01. bk rev. Circ 300. Contains articles and discussions, synthesis statements, and critical reviews dealing with the philosophy of sport.

JUDO. V. 1- Oct. 1956-. 0022-5819. Periodical. UK. English. bm. $19.01. Judo Ltd, Candem House, 717 Manchester Old Road, Rhodes Mditn, Manchester M24 4JF England. Tel 061 653 1499. Ed Frank Smith. LC GV475.J9. bk rev. adv acc. Circ 5,000. (ctrl). Judo. Reports which include British international competitions, profiles, technical articles, training schedules, and reviews.

JUDO CANADA. (JUDO CANADA : OFFICIAL NEWSLETTER OF THE CANADIAN KODOKAN BLACK BELT ASSOCIATION). VFOAT Bulletin Officiel de l'Association Canadienne des Ceintures Noires du Kodokan. Vol. 1, No. 1 (Jan. 1983)-. 0821-2481. Periodical. CN. English (French). ir. $10.00. Canadian Kodokan Black Belt Association, 333 River Road, Vanier Ontario K1L 8H9 Canada. DD 796.815205. Information Bulletin (Canadian Kodokan Black Belt Association), 0822-6490.

JUDO ONTARIO'S NEWSLETTER (JAN./FEB. 1984). (JUDO ONTARIO'S NEWSLETTER). VFOAT Ontario Judoka. VAT Judo Ontario Newsletter (Jan./Feb. 1984). Vol. 9, No. 1 (Jan./Feb. 1984)-. 0823-812X. Periodical. CN. English. bm. Free. Judo Ontario, 1220 Sheppard Avenue East, Willowdale Ontario M2K 2X1 Canada. DD 796.8152097913. (ctrl). Ontario Judoka, 0826-0567.

JUNIOR BOWLER. See Recreation, Leisure - Games & Amusements.

JUNIOR DEVELOPMENT. TOP FIFTY. (JUNIOR DEVELOPMENT, TOP FIFTY). 1978-. 0225-7742. CN. English. an. $1. Per No. J Swan, British Columbia Track and Field Association, 2447 Sugarping Street, Abbotsford British Columbia V2T 3M7 Canada. DD 796.4209711. Statistics Annual, Junior Development, 0225-7734.

JUNIOR HOCKEY ACTION. Vol. 1, No. 1 (Sept. 1982)-. 0826-4279. Periodical. CN. English. $22.00 for 20 Issues, Canada. Junior Hockey Action, PO Box 3311, Langley British Columbia V3A 4R6 Canada. DD 796.9626.

THE KANSAS WRESTLER. 0744-4486. Periodical. US. English. mo. $10.00. The Kansas Wrestler, Box 956/218 North Culp Street, Russell KS 67665-095.

KARATE AND ORIENTAL ARTS. 1966. Periodical. UK. English. bm. $12.00. Paul H Crompton Ltd, 638 Fulham Road, London SW6 England. Ed Paul Crompton. LC GV476. DD 796.815305. bk rev. adv acc. Circ 15,500. Topics include martial arts of the East and West, health and strength, survival systems, and modern self defence systems, Zen Buddhism, etc. Karate Magazine & Oriental Arts.

KARATE ILLUSTRATED. Began in 1974. 0022-9016. Periodical. US. English. mo. Rainbow Publications Inc, 1813 Victory Place/Box 7728, Burbank CA 91510. Tel (818)849-2181. LC GV1114.3. DD 796.815305.

KARATE KEBEC. V. 1- Oct. 1975-. 0383-6517. Periodical. CN. French. $12.00. Karate Kebec, C P 10 Succursale Beaubien, Montreal Quebec H2G 3C8 Canada. DD 796.815305.

KART-TECH. Vol. 1, No. 1 (Apr. 1981)-. 0279-8816. Periodical. US. English. mo. $23.95. Kart-Tech Magazine, 31 H Street/Suite 2, Bakersfield CA 93304. Tel (919)428-4068. World Karting, 0194-7605.

KARTER NEWS. Main/Corp International Kart Federation. 0096-3216. Periodical. US. English. mo. $15.00. International Kart Federation, 4650 Arrow Highway/Suite B4, Montclair CA 91763. Tel (714)625-5497. LC GV1029.5. DD 796.76. adv acc. Circ 5,000. Karting events, photos of karts at karting events, race reports, tech and rule update, minutes of board meetings and other karting related info.

KAYHAN-I VARZISHI. Periodical. IR. Persian, Modern. ir. 50.00 Single Issue. Khiyaban-I Firdawsi Kuchah-I Atabak, Tehran Iran. LC GV657.

KENTUCKY SPORTS WORLD. V. 1- 1977-. 0192-6411. Periodical. US. English. mo.

KEY. (THE KEY). Vol. 1, No. 1 (Winter 1981)-. 0824-524X. Periodical. CN. English. qt. $6.00. Ontario Amateur Basketball Association, 160 Vanderhoof

Recreation, Leisure—Sports

Avenue, Toronto Ontario M4G 4B8 Canada. **DD** 796.32305.

KICK. (KICK : THE OFFICIAL MAGAZINE OF THE NORTH AMERICAN SOCCER LEAGUE). 0277-6111. US. English. mo. $11.97. Kick Magazine Inc, 420 Madison Avenue, New York NY 10017. **Tel** (212)575-0066. **LC** GV944.U5. **DD** 796.334097.

KICK INDOOR. (KICK INDOOR : THE OFFICIAL INDOOR PROGRAM OF THE NORTH AMERICAN SOCCER LEAGUE). Vol. 1, No. 1-. 0277-691X. Periodical. US. English. NASL Marketing Inc, 1133 Avenue of the Americas, New York NY 10036. **LC** GV943.9.I6. **DD** 796.33405.

KICK (NEW YORK, N.Y. : 1983). (KICK). Began in 1983. 0882-8180. Periodical. US. English. bm. $18.00 Domestic, $28.00 Foreign. Kick, 575 Lexington Avenue/Suite 2700, New York NY 10022. **DD** 796.

KICKER SPORTMAGAZIN. Periodical. German. sw. German News Company Inc, 220 East 86th Street, New York NY 10028. **Tel** (212)288-5500. **LC** GV611.

KIRON. (LE KIRON). 0709-8456. Periodical. CN. French. bm. Free. Le Kiron, CP 183, St-Sauveur Quebec G1K 6W3 Canada. **DD** 796.426060714. (ctrl) *Bulletin des Centaures.*

KOI USA. VFOAT KOI U.S.A. VAT Koi United States of America. 0748-7320. Periodical. US. English. bm. $8.00 US, $10.50 Canada. Associated Koi Clubs of America, PO Box 1, Midway City CA 92655. **DD** 639.

KUNG FU MI AO. VFOAT Secrets of Kung Fu. First published Sept. 1974-. Periodical. Chinese. ir. $28.50. Lung Publisher Inc, PO Box 20606, Causeway Bay Post Office, Hsiang-Kang Hong Kong. **LC** GV1112.

LACROSSE. 0194-7893. Periodical. US. English. ir. $5.50. Miss Gertrude Hooper, 369 Atlantic Avenue, Cohasset MA 02025.

LADY GOLFER. (THE LADY GOLFER). 0092-8909. Periodical. US. English. ir. $7.00. Seidal Publications, Box 1118, Scottsdale AZ 85252. **LC** GV966. **DD** 796.352024042.

LAWS OF THE GAME AND UNIVERSAL GUIDE FOR REFEREES. *See* Law.

LEISTUNGSSPORT. *See* Medicine.

LET'S CHEER. VAT Let Us Cheer. 1964. 0733-9674. Periodical. US. English. ir. $12.00. Miss Drillteam USA Pageant, 1212 Ynez Avenue, Redondo Beach CA 90277. **Tel** (213)540-3364. Ed Kay Crawford. adv acc. (ctrl). A national pep arts magazine for drill teams, flags, baton, songleaders, pom-pom and dance lines. Excellent for instructors and students. Edited by the worlds greatest authorities.

LIEN - ASSOCIATION DES PROFESSEURS DE JUDO DU QUEBEC. (LE LIEN). No. 1 (June 80)-. 0822-7306. Periodical. CN. French. mo. Association des Professeurs de Judo du Quebec, 279 Est rue St-Joseph, Quebec Quebec G1K 6Y2 Canada. **DD** 796.815209714.

LIGNE DIRECTE SUR LE MONTREAL INTERNATIONAL. V. 1- Oct. 1974-. 0319-0986. Periodical. CN. French. Free to Members, $5. others. Club Montreal International, C P 1976 Succursale C, Montreal Quebec H2L 2H0 Canada. **DD** 796.48.

LIVRE DE REGLEMENTS ADMINISTRATIFS - FEDERATION QUEBECOISE DE HOCKEY SUR GLACE. (LIVRE DE REGLEMENTS ADMINISTRATIFS). **Main/Corp** Federation Quebecoise de Hockey Sur Glace. Seasons 1982/1983 - 1983/1984-. 0821-4603. CN. French. an. Federation Quebecoise de Hockey Sur Glace, 1415 Est rue Jarry, Montreal Quebec H2E 2Z7 Canada. **DD** 796.96202022. *Livre de Reglements, 0710-4758.*

LE LIVRE D'OR DE LA MOTO. *See* Motorcycles.

LE LIVRE D'OR DU GOLF. FR. French. ir. Solar, 8 rue Garanciere, 75006 Paris France. **LC** GV961. **DD** 796.3527.

LIVRE OFFICIEL DES RECORDS - LIGUE CANADIENNE DE FOOTBALL. **Main/Corp** Ligue Canadienne de Football. First issue in 1978?. 0225-7203. CN. French. an. Ligue Canadienne de Football, Bureau 1800 11 Ouest rue King, Toronto Ontario M5H 1A3 Canada. **DD** 796.3356.

LIVRET DES REGLEMENTS DE LA FEDERATION CANADIENNE DES ARCHERS. **Main/Corp** Federation Canadienne des Archers. First issue in 1975?. 0706-3180. CN. French. ir. $1. le Vol. Federation Canadienne des Archers, 333 Chemin River, Vanier Ontario K1L 8B9 Canada. **DD** 799.320971.

LOISIRS-PRESSE. No. 1 (Jan. 15, 1982)-. 0713-553X. Periodical. CN. French. bw. Free. Loisirs-Presse, 1414 East rue Jarry, Montreal Quebec H2E 2Z7 Canada. **DD** 790.09714.

LOUISIANA GAME & FISH. *See* Recreation, Leisure - Outdoor Life.

LUCARNE. (LA LUCARNE). Vol. 1, No 1-. 0826-1202. Periodical. CN. French (text in English). ir. $8.00. Federation Quebecoise de Soccer Football, 1415 Est rue Jarry, Montreal Quebec H2E 2Z7 Canada. **DD** 796.334077.

MAGAZINE CONTRE-JOUR. VFOAT Contre-Jour. Vol. 1, No 1-. 0821-1329. Periodical. CN. French. 3,50 Domestic. Contre-Jour, C P 477 Succursale Limoilou, Quebec Quebec G1L 4W3 Canada. **DD** 796.7205.

MAGAZINE DES ARTS MARTIAUX DU QUEBEC. (LE MAGAZINE DES ARTS MARTIAUX DU QUEBEC). Vol. 1, No. 1 (May/June 1982)-. 0713-4290. Periodical. CN. French. mo. $12.00. Le Magazine des Arts Martiaux du Quebec, 4337 rue Papineau, Montreal Quebec H2H 1T3 Canada. **DD** 796.81505.

MAGAZINE EXPOS. (LE MAGAZINE EXPOS . . .). VFOAT Expos. Vol. 1 (80)-. 0712-4155. CN. French. an. $2.75 Per Number. Magazine Expos, Bureau 1100/1001 Boulevard de Maisonneuve East, Montreal Quebec H2L 4P9 Canada. **DD** 796.3576409714281.

MAINE SNOWMOBILER. 0195-2870. Periodical. US. English. mo. $2.80. Maine Snowmobiler, Box 77, Augusta ME 04330.

THE MAINE SPORTSMAN. 0199-0365. Periodical. US. English. mo. $9.50. Maine Sportsman, PO Box 507, Yarmouth ME 04096. **Tel** (207)846-9501. Ed Harry P Vanderweide. bk rev. adv acc. **Circ** 22,000. Seasonal activities: hunting, fishing, canoeing, archery, dogs, by the columnists. Some activities also covered regionally by other columnists.

MAN UNDERWATER. 1967. 0383-7777. Periodical. CN. English. mo $9.28. Manitoba Underwater Council, PO Box 711, Winnipeg Manitoba R3C 2K3 Canada. Ed Joan Eggett. **DD** 797.230627127. adv acc. **Circ** 300. (ctrl). Scuba diving publication containing information on safety, education, activities and information of interest to the Manitoba Diver. *Newsletter, 0383-7742.*

MANCHETE ESPORTIVA. Periodical. BL. Portuguese. ir. 20 Single Issue. Bloch, rua do Resenda 100, Rio de Janeiro Brazil. **LC** GV561. **DD** 796.05.

MANITOBA CURLING REVIEW. 0823-8448. Periodical. CN. English. mo. $8.00. Manitoba Curling Review, PO Box 182, Rosenfeld Manitoba R0G 1X0 Canada. **DD** 796.96.

MANITOBA HIGH SCHOOLS ATHLETIC DIRECTORY. *See* Yearbooks, Almanacs, Directories.

MANITOBA LET'S WRESTLE CEASED. (MANITOBA LET'S WRESTLE). VFOAT 'Let's Wrestle''. Began publication in 1972. 0704-6413. Periodical. CN. English. ir. Free to members. Manitoba Amateur Wrestling Association, 1301 Ellice Avenue, Winnipeg Manitoba R3G 0G1 Canada. **DD** 796.812097127.

MANUAL OF SKI MOUNTAINEERING. *See* Recreation, Leisure - Outdoor Life.

MANUAL OF THE NATIONAL COLLEGIATE ATHLETIC ASSOCIATION. **Main/Corp** National Collegiate Athletic Association. VFOAT NCAA Manual. 0077-3816. US. English. an. NCAA Publishing Department, PO Box 1906, Shawnee Mission KS 66201. **LC** GV563. **DD** 796.06073.

MANUEL - ASSOCIATION CANADIENNE DE BADMINTON. (MANUEL). **Main/Corp** Association Canadienne de Badminton. 0227-5996. CN. French. an. $1.25 Per No. Association Canadienne de Badminton, 333 River Road, Ottawa Ontario K1L 8B9 Canada. **DD** 796.34506071.

MANUEL DES REGLEMENTS OFFICIELS - ASSOCIATION CANADIENNE DE NAGE SYNCHRONISEE AMATEUR, INC. (MANUEL DES REGLEMENTS OFFICIELS). **Main/Corp** Association Canadienne de Nage Synchronisee Amateur. 0706-991X. Periodical. CN. French. Association Canadienne de Nage Synchronisee Amateur, 333 Chemin River, Ottawa Ontario K1L 8H9 Canada. **DD** 797.21.

MANUEL D'INTERPRETATION DU REGLEMENT OFFICIEL DE BASKET-BALL DE LA F.I.B.A. **Main/Corp** Federation Internationale de Basketball Amateur. VFOAT Reglement F.I.B.A.-Manuel d'Interpretation. VAT Reglement Federation Internationale de Basketball Amateur, Manuel d'Interpretation. 0823-177X. CN. French. ir. Association Canadienne de Basket-Ball Amateur, 333 Chemin River, Vanier Ontario K1L 8B9 Canada. **Tel** (613)748-5607. Ed C Stothart. **DD** 796.32302022. bk rev. adv acc. **Circ** 10,000. (ctrl). Articles on basketball competitions of national teams, college and universities. Also includes technical articles for coaches.

MARATHON HANDBOOK. 0360-9928. US. English. an. $1.95. World Publications, Box 366, Mountainview CA 94040. **LC** GV1065. **DD** 796.426.

MARATHON PLUS CEASED. Vol. 1, No 1 (Aug./Sept. 1984). Ceased with Vol. 2, No. 1 (Dec./Jan. 84/85)?. 0828-5853. Periodical. CN. French. mo. $20.00. Marathon Plus, 1028 Marie-Victorin, Laval Quebec H7E 3C1 Canada. **DD** 796.05. *Marathon (Montreal, Quebec), 0823-0870.*

MARITIME DIVING NEWS. V. 1-2, No. 3. 0225-0780. Periodical. CN. English. bm. $9.00 Domestic, $12.00 US, $25.00 Other Countries. Maritime Diving News Ltd, PO Box 2340 Dartmouth East, Dartmouth Nova Scotia B2W 3Y4 Canada. **DD** 797.2309715.

MASTERS. 1978-. 0191-8117. US. English. an. Augusta National Golf Club, Augusta GA 30901. **LC** GV970. **DD** 796.3526.

MEDALIST FLASHBACK NOTEBOOK. Began with 1976 volume. 0743-6580. US. English. an. Medalist Sports Education, 10206 North Port Washington Road, Mequon WI 53092. **LC** GV885.3. **DD** 796.323077.

MEDECINE DU SPORT. *See* Medicine.

MEDICINA DELLO SPORT. *See* Medicine.

MEDICINE AND SCIENCE IN SPORTS AND EXERCISE. V. 12- Spring 1980-. 0195-9131. Periodical. US. English. bm. $60.00. Williams & Wilkin Company, 428 East Preston Street, Baltimore MD 21202. **Tel** (301)528-4000. Ed Elsworth R Buskirk. **Ind/Abst** Electron. Commun. Abstr. J., ISMEC Bull., Pollut. Abstr. Indexes, Life Sci. Collect., Excerpta Med., Cumul. Index Nurs. Allied Health Lit., Biol. Abstr., Energy Res. Abstr., Chem. Abstr., Curr. Contents, Index Med., Nuci. Sci. Abstr., Sci. Cit. Index, Abr. Ed., Women Stud. Abstr., Psychol. Abstr., Abstr. Anthropol., Comput. Rev. **LC** RC1200. **DD** 617.102705. **NLM** W1 ME649NB. **CODEN** MSPEDA. adv acc. **Circ** 12,500. Original investigations of sports medicine topics for exercise physiologists, physiatrists, physical therapists and athletic trainers. *Medicine and Science In Sports, 0025-7990.*

MEDICINE AND SPORT SCIENCE. Vol. 17-. 0254-5020. Monographic Series. English. ir. **Tel** (061)39 08 80. Ed E Jokl and M Hebbelinck. **NLM** W1. These works invite study by anyone interested in the development of sports medicine as an active scientific discipline. *Medicine and Sport, 0076-6070.*

MEDIZIN UND SPORT. *See* Medicine.

MEMBERSHIP DIRECTORY - AMERICAN COLLEGE OF SPORTS MEDICINE. *See* Yearbooks, Almanacs, Directories.

MEMBERSHIP DIRECTORY OF THE GOLF COURSE SUPERINTENDENTS ASSOCIATION OF AMERICA. *See* Yearbooks, Almanacs, Directories.

MEMBERSHIP ROSTER - VANCOUVER LAWN TENNIS AND BADMINTON CLUB. (MEMBERSHIP ROSTER). **Main/Corp** Vancouver Lawn Tennis and Badminton Club. 0712-657X. CN. English. an. Free to Members. Vancouver Lawn Tennis and Badminton Club, 1630 West 15th Avenue, Vancouver British Columbia V6J 2K7 Canada. **DD** 796.3402571133.

Recreation, Leisure—Sports

METRO SPORTS. VFOAT Metrosports. Periodical. US. English. mo. 529 South 7th Street, Minneapolis MN 55415.

THE MIAA NEWSLETTER. Main/Corp Massachusetts Interscholastic Athletic Association. VAT Massachusetts Interscholastic Athletic Association Newsletter. 0273-6683. Periodical. US. English. mo. MIAA, 75 Central Street/PO Box 269, Ashland MA 01721.

THE MICHIGAN RUNNER. 0279-1773. Periodical. US. English. mo. Great Lakes Sports Publications Inc, PO Box 707, Ypsilanti MI 48197. **Tel** (313)227-4200.

MICHIGAN SPORTSMAN (OSHKOSH WIS.). See Recreation, Leisure - Outdoor Life.

MID AMERICAN AUTO RACING NEWS. 0199-2465. Periodical. US. English. ir.

MIDWEST RACING NEWS. VFOAT MRN. 0047-732X. Periodical. US. English. ir. $13.00. Midwest Racing News Inc, 6646 West Fairview Avenue, Milwaukee WI 53213. **Tel** (414)778-4700. **Ed** Phil Hall and James K Engel. bk rev. adv acc. **Circ** 9,000. Results, stories, features and upcoming events of general interest to the auto racing enthusiast.

MINI-FRANC JEU. First issue in 1978?. 0225-4018. Periodical. CN. French. mo. Free. Federation du Sport Scolaire du Quebec, 1415 East rue Jarry, Montreal Quebec H2E 2Z7 Canada. **DD** 796.09714. (ctrl). Franc Jeu, 0700-3374.

MINNESOTA SPORTSMAN. See Recreation, Leisure - Outdoor Life.

MINTO PHOENIX CEASED. Main/Corp Minto Skating Club. VFOAT Phoenix. Ceased with V. 28, No. 50 (April/May 1980)?. 0380-0636. Periodical. CN. English. ir. Minto Skating Club, PO Box 918 Station B, Ottawa Ontario K1P 5P9 Canada.

MINUTES OF THE ANNUAL MEETING OF THE S.H.S.A.A. Main/Corp Saskatchewan High Schools Athletic Association. Meeting. VFOAT Annual Meeting Proceedings. VAT Mintues of the Annual Meeting of the Saskatchewan High Schools Athletic Association, Annual Minutes - Saskatchewan High Schools Athletic Association, Annual Meeting Proceedings - Saskatchewan High Schools Athletic Association. 0225-0357. CN. English. an. Saskatchewan High Schools Athletic Association, 2220 College Avenue, Regina Saskatchewan S4P 3V7 Canada. **DD** 796.0607124.

MISSISSIPPI GAME & FISH. See Recreation, Leisure - Outdoor Life.

MISSISSIPPI OUTDOORS. See Recreation, Leisure - Outdoor Life.

LE MONDE DU RUGBY. Series/Titl Stock Sports. 1973/74-. French. ir. 25. Stock, 14 rue de l'Ancienne-Comedie, Paris 6E France. **LC** GV945.5. **DD** 796.33305.

MOTOR RACING YEAR. (THE MOTOR RACING YEAR). 1971-. 0090-2144. US. English. an. W W Norton & Company Inc, 500 Fifth Avenue, New York NY 10110. **LC** GV1029. **DD** 796.7205.

MOTOR SPORT YEARBOOK. See Yearbooks, Almanacs, Directories.

MOTOR TREND. See Transportation - Automobiles.

MOTORCAMPING HANDBOOK. See Recreation, Leisure - Outdoor Life.

MOTORCYCLE DRAG RACING NEWSPAPER. See Motorcycles.

THE MOTORCYCLIST'S POST. See Transportation.

MOUNTAIN GAZETTE. Began in Sept. 1972. 0160-726X. Periodical. US. English. mo. $8.00. Mountain Gazette, 745 Walnut Street, Boulder CO 80302. Skier's Gazette.

MULTIHULLS. VFOAT Multihulls Magazine. 1975. 0749-4122. Periodical. US. English. bm. Chiodi Advertising & Publishing Inc, 421 Hancock Street, North Quincy MA 02171. **Tel** (617)328-8181. **Ed** Charles Chiodi. **DD** 797. bk rev. adv acc. **Circ** 30,000. (ctrl). Complete coverage of all size multihulls, design, racing, boat tests, cruising info and safety information. The only true source for multihull sailors.

MUSCLE UP. 0279-2990. Periodical. US. English. bm. $10.00. Charlton Publications Inc, Charlton Building, Derby CT 06418. **Tel** (203)735-3381. **DD** 796.

MUZZLE BLASTS. Periodical. US. English. mo. $19.75. National Muzzle Loading Rifle Association, PO Box 67, Friendship IN 47021. **Tel** (812)667-5131. **Ed** Maxine Moss. bk rev. adv acc. **Circ** 27,000. (ctrl). History and educational material on muzzle loading firearms.

MUZZLELOADER. See Recreation, Leisure - Outdoor Life.

THE MUZZLELOADING ARTILLERYMAN. See Antiques.

NAGWS GUIDE, BASKETBALL. (NAGWS GUIDE : BASKETBALL). Main/Corp National Association for Girls & Women in Sport. VFOAT NAGWS Basketball Guide. VAT National Association for Girls and Women in Sport Guide: Basketball. 1975/76-. 0362-3254. US. English. National Association for Girls and Women in Sports, 1201 Street Northwest, Washington DC 20036. **LC** GV885.A1. **DD** 796.3238. Basketball Guide, with Official Rules and Standards.

NAGWS GUIDE : BASKETBALL CASE BOOK. Main/Corp National Association for Girls & Women in Sport. VFOAT Basketball Casebook. VAT National Association for Girls and Women in Sport Guide: Basketball Case Book. 1978/79-. 0193-5445. US. English. an. AAHPER Publications Sales, 1201 16th Street Northwest, Washington DC 20036. **LC** GV886. **DD** 796.323802022.

NAGWS GUIDE. BASKETBALL, VOLLEYBALL. (NAGWS GUIDE : BASKETBALL, VOLLEYBALL). Main/Corp National Association for Girls & Women in Sport. VFOAT NAGWS Basketball, Volleyball Guide: Tips and Techniques. VAT National Association for Girls and Women in Sport Guide. Basketball, Volleyball. 1977/79-. 0161-3650. US. English. be. National Association for Girls and Women in Sports, 1201 16th Avenue Northwest, Washington DC 20036. **LC** GV885.3. **DD** 796.323077.

NAGWS GUIDE. FIELD HOCKEY. Main/Corp National Association for Girls & Women in Sport. VFOAT Field Hockey. VAT National Association for Girls and Women in Sport Guide: Field Hockey. 1978/80-. 0749-4491. US. English. be. **LC** GV1017.H7. **DD** 796.355. NAGWS Guide: Field Hockey, Lacrosse, 0145-9554.

NAGWS GUIDE. FLAG FOOTBALL, SPEEDBALL, SPEED-A-WAY. Main/Corp National Association for Girls & Women in Sport. Series/Titl Sports Library for Girls and Women. VFOAT N.A.G.W.S. Guide. June 1980-June 1982-. Periodical. US. English. be. American Alliance for Health Physical Education Recreation and Dance, 1900 Association Drive, Reston VA 22091. Flag Football, Speedball, 0190-9363.

NAGWS GUIDE. GYMNASTICS. (NAGWS GUIDE : GYMNASTICS). Main/Corp National Association for Girls & Women in Sport. VFOAT NAGWS Gymnastics Guide. VAT National Association for Girls and Women in Sport Guide: Gymnastics. 1975/77-. 0363-9282. US. English. National Association for Girls and Women in Sports, 1201 Sixteenth Avenue Northwest, Washington DC 20036. **LC** GV464. **DD** 796.41. Gymnastics Guide.

NAGWS GUIDE. LACROSSE. (NAGWS GUIDE : LACROSSE. Main/Corp National Association for Girls & Women in Sport. VFOAT Lacrosse Guide. VAT National Association for Girls and Women in Sport Guide: Lacrosse. 1979/81-. 0749-4483. US. English. be. $2.50. A A H P E R, 1201 16th Street Northwest, Washington DC 20036. **LC** GV989.15. **DD** 796.347. NAGWS Guide: Field Hockey, Lacrosse, 0145-9554.

NAGWS GUIDE. SOCCER. (NAGWS GUIDE : SOCCER). Main/Corp National Association for Girls & Women in Sport. VFOAT NAGWS Soccer Guide. VAT National Association for Girls and Women in Sport Guide. Soccer. 1978/79-. 0163-4747. US. English. an. $2.00. American Alliance for Health Physical Education and Recreation, 1201 Sixteenth Street Northwest, Washington DC 20036. **LC** GV943.4. **DD** 796.33402022. NAGWS Guide. Soccer, Speedball, Flag Football, 0145-6601.

NAGWS GUIDE. SOFTBALL. (NAGWS GUIDE : SOFTBALL). Main/Corp National Association for Girls & Women in Sport. VFOAT NAGWS Softball Guide. VAT National Association for Girls and Women in Sport Guide: Softball. 1976/78-. 0363-2504. US. English. National Association for Girls and Women in Sports, 1201 Sixteenth Avenue Northwest, Washington DC 20036. **LC** GV881. **DD** 796.3578. Softball Guide.

NAGWS GUIDE, SYNCHRONIZED SWIMMING. (NAGWS GUIDE : SYNCHRONIZED SWIMMING). Main/Corp National Association for Girls & Women in Sport. VFOAT NAGWS Synchronized Swimming Guide. VAT National Association for Girls and Women in Sport Guide, Synchronized Swimming. 1978/79-. 0163-4267. US. English. an. American Alliance for Health Physical Education and Recreation, 1201 Sixteenth Street Northwest, Washington DC 20036. **LC** GV837. **DD** 797.2105. NAGWS Guide, Aquatics, 0361-719X.

NAGWS GUIDE. TEAM HANDBALL, RACQUETBALL, ORIENTERING CEASED. (NAGWS GUIDE : TEAM HANDBALL, RACQUETBALL, ORIENTEERING). Main/Corp National Association for Girls & Women in Sport. 1976/78-1979/81. 0145-9767. US. English. 1201 16th Street Northwest, Washington DC 20036. **LC** GV1017.T4. **DD** 796.31.

NAGWS GUIDE. TENNIS. (NAGWS GUIDE : TENNIS). Main/Corp National Association for Girls & Women in Sport. VFOAT NAGWS Tennis Guide. VAT National Association for Girls and Women in Sport Guide. Tennis. 1980/82-. 0272-863X. US. English. be. **LC** GV991. **DD** 796.3422. NAGWS Guide. Tennis, Badminton, Squash.

NAGWS GUIDE. TRACK AND FIELD. (NAGWS GUIDE : TRACK AND FIELD). Main/Corp National Association for Girls & Women in Sport. VFOAT NAGWS Track and Field Guide. VAT National Association for Girls and Women in Sport Guide. Track and Field. 1976/78-. 0362-9481. US. English. National Association for Girls and Women in Sports, 1201 Sixteenth Avenue Northwest, Washington DC 20036. **LC** GV1060.8. **DD** 796.42. Track and Field Guide, with Official Rules and Standards.

NAGWS GUIDE. VOLLEYBALL. (NAGWS GUIDE : VOLLEYBALL). Main/Corp National Association for Girls & Women in Sport. VAT National Association for Girls and Women in Sport Guide: Volleyball. 1975/77-. 0145-1987. US. English. an. National Association for Girls and Women in Sports, 1201 16th Street Northwest, Washington DC 20036. **LC** GV1017.V6. **DD** 796.325. Volleyball Guide.

NAGWS RULES : BASKETBALL CEASED. Main/Corp National Association for Girls & Women in Sport. VFOAT Basketball. Began with 1975/76 issue. Ceased with 1981/1982 issue. US. English. an. Official Basketball Rules for Girls and Women.

NAGWS RULES. SKIING. (NAGWS RULES : SKIING). Main/Corp National Association for Girls & Women in Sport. VFOAT NAGWS Skiing Rules. VAT National Association for Girls and Women in Sport Rules: Skiing. 0148-1150. US. English. American Alliance for Health Physical Education and Recreation, 1201 16th Street Northwest, Washington DC 20036. **LC** GV854.87. **DD** 796.93.

NAGWS/ABO BASKETBALL CASEBOOK. (NAGWS/ABO BASKETBALL CASEBOOK : FOR THE UNITED STATES GIRLS' AND WOMEN'S BASKETBALL RULES). Main/Corp National Association for Girls & Women in Sport. Affiliated Boards of Officials. Series/Titl Sports Library for Girls and Women. VFOAT NAGWS ABO Basketball Casebook. 1982/84-. Periodical. US. English. National Association for Girls and Women in Sports, 1201 16th Street Northwest, Washington DC 20036. NAGWS Guide: Basketball Case Book.

NAIA NEWS. Main/Corp National Association of Intercollegiate Athletics. VFOAT NAIA News and Coach. VAT National Association of Intercollegiate Athletics News. V. 1- 1950-. 0740-5995. Periodical. US. English. bm. $12.00. National Association of Intercollegiate Athletics, 1221 Baltimore Street, Kansas City MO 64105.

NASCAR NEWSLETTER. Main/Corp National Association for Stock Car Auto Racing. VAT National Association for Stock Car Auto Racing Newsletter. 0027-5999. Periodical. US. English. sm. $25.00. National Association for Stock Car Auto Racing Inc, PO Box K, Daytona Beach FL 32015. **Tel** (904)253-0611. **Ed** Chip Williams. adv acc. **Circ** 20,000. (ctrl). For stock car auto racers who are members of NASCAR.

NATIONAL 5-PIN BOWLERS NEWS. VFOAT Bowlers News. VAT National Five-Pin Bowlers News, Bowlers' News (1978). V. 3, No. 2- Jan. 1978-. 0705-7423. Periodical. CN. English. mo. National 5-Pin Bowlers News, 2487 Kaladar Avenue/Suite 215,

Recreation, Leisure—Sports

Ottawa Ontario K1V 9A9 Canada. DD 796.3582205. *Canadian 5-Pin Bowlers News, 0381-1530.*

NATIONAL AERONAUTICS. See Aeronautics, Astronautics.

THE NATIONAL BILLIARD NEWS. VFOAT Billiard News. 0747-3265. Periodical. US. English. mo. $15.00. National Billiard News, PO Box 487, Birmingham MI 48012.

NATIONAL COLLEGIATE CHAMPIONSHIPS. VFOAT History and Records of the NCAA Men's and Women's Championships. 1977/78-. 0190-4329. US. English. an. $8.00. National Collegiate Athletic Association, PO Box 1906, Shawnee Mission KS 66222. Tel (913)384-3220. LC GV741. DD 796.06273. Detailed summary of the championships of the previous year for both men and women, plus history and records of championships conducted since 1883. *National Collegiate Championships Records Book, 0148-9798.*

NATIONAL COLLEGIATE FENCING CHAMPIONSHIPS HANDBOOK. VFOAT National Collegiate Championships Handbook: Fencing. Periodical. US. English. an. The National Collegiate Athletic Association, US Highway 50 and Nall Avenue/PO Box 1906, Shawnee Mission KS 66222.

NATIONAL COLLEGIATE SKIING CHAMPIONSHIPS HANDBOOK. VFOAT National Collegiate Championship Handbook: Skiing. Periodical. US. English. an. The National Collegiate Athletic Association, US Highway 50 and Nall Avenue/PO Box 1906, Shawnee Mission KS 66222.

NATIONAL DIRECTORY OF COLLEGE ATHLETICS (WOMEN'S ED.). See Yearbooks, Almanacs, Directories.

THE NATIONAL DIRECTORY OF HIGH SCHOOL COACHES. See Yearbooks, Almanacs, Directories.

NATIONAL DIRECTORY OF WOMEN'S ATHLETICS. See Yearbooks, Almanacs, Directories.

NATIONAL DRAGSTER. 1960. 0466-2199. Periodical. US. English. ir. $28.00. National Dragster, 10639 Riverside Drive, North Hollywood CA 91602. Tel (213)980-3724. Ed George Phillips. adv acc. Circ 40,000.

NATIONAL FEDERATION HANDBOOK. Main/Corp National Federation of State High School Associations. VFOAT National Federation of State High School Associations Handbook. 0737-5204. US. English. National Federation of State High School Associations, 11724 Plaza Circle, Box 20626, Kansas City MO 64195. LC GV710. DD 371.89. *Official Handbook, 0146-8626.*

NATIONAL GYMNASTICS JUDGES ASSOCIATION MEN'S RULES INTERPRETATIONS. VFOAT United States National Gymnastics Judges Association Men's Rules Interpretations. 0272-1597. US. English. National Gymnastics Judges Association, 10409 Genesta Avenue, Granada Hills CA 91344. LC GV463.3. DD 796.41.

NATIONAL HIGH SCHOOL SPORTS RECORD BOOK. Main/Corp National Federation of State High School Associations. 1978/79-. 0192-978X. Periodical. US. English. $1.95. National Federation of State High School Associations, Federation Place Box 98, Elgin IL 60120. LC GV346. DD 796.

NATIONAL HOCKEY LEAGUE GUIDE. 1964/65-. 0316-8174. Periodical. CN. English. an. National Hockey League, 922 Sun Life Building, Montreal Quebec H3B 2W Canada. DD 796.962. *Press and Radio Guide, 0466-2997.*

THE NATIONAL PASTIME. VFOAT T.N.P. Vol. 1, No. 1 (Fall 1982)-. 0734-6905. Periodical. US. English. an. Free to Members, $5.00 Others. Society for American Baseball Research, PO Box 323, Cooperstown NY 13326. LC GV863.A1. DD 796.3570973.

NATIONAL RACQUETBALL. 0161-7966. Periodical. US. English. mo. $18.00. National Racquetball, 1800 Pickwick Avenue, Glenview IL 60025. Tel (312)724-7856. LC GV1017.R3. DD 796.3430973.

NATIONAL SKI AREA NEWS. V. 1- Spring 1973-. 0098-5945. Periodical. US. English. qt. $9.00. 61 South Main Street, West Hartford CT 06107. LC GV854.4. DD 796.930973.

NATIONAL SPEED SPORT NEWS. 1934. 0028-0208. Periodical. US. English. ir. National Speed Sport News, Box 608, Ridgewood NJ 07451. Tel (201)445-3117. Ed Chris Economaki. bk rev. adv acc. Circ 72,000.

NATIONAL STRENGTH & CONDITIONING ASSOCIATION JOURNAL. See Physical Training.

NATIONAL SURVEY OF FISHING, HUNTING, AND WILDLIFE-ASSOCIATED RECREATION. See Recreation, Leisure - Outdoor Life.

NATIONAL SURVEY OF FISHING, HUNTING, AND WILDLIFE-ASSOCIATED RECREATION. ALASKA. See Recreation, Leisure - Outdoor Life.

NATIONAL SURVEY OF FISHING, HUNTING, AND WILDLIFE-ASSOCIATED RECREATION. ARKANSAS. See Recreation, Leisure - Outdoor Life.

NATIONAL SURVEY OF FISHING, HUNTING, AND WILDLIFE-ASSOCIATED RECREATION. CONNECTICUT. See Recreation, Leisure - Outdoor Life.

NATIONAL SURVEY OF FISHING, HUNTING, AND WILDLIFE-ASSOCIATED RECREATION. IDAHO. See Recreation, Leisure - Outdoor Life.

NATIONAL SURVEY OF FISHING, HUNTING, AND WILDLIFE-ASSOCIATED RECREATION. ILLINOIS. See Recreation, Leisure - Outdoor Life.

NATIONAL SURVEY OF FISHING, HUNTING, AND WILDLIFE-ASSOCIATED RECREATION. LOUISIANA. See Recreation, Leisure - Outdoor Life.

NATIONAL SURVEY OF FISHING, HUNTING, AND WILDLIFE-ASSOCIATED RECREATION. MICHIGAN. See Recreation, Leisure - Outdoor Life.

NATIONAL SURVEY OF FISHING, HUNTING, AND WILDLIFE-ASSOCIATED RECREATION. NEW YORK. See Recreation, Leisure - Outdoor Life.

NATIONAL SURVEY OF FISHING, HUNTING, AND WILDLIFE-ASSOCIATED RECREATION. OHIO. See Recreation, Leisure - Outdoor Life.

NATIONWIDE DIRECTORY SPORTING GOODS BUYERS. See Yearbooks, Almanacs, Directories.

NAUTICA (SALEM, MASS.). (NAUTICA). Began in 1984. 8755-3112. Periodical. US. English. bm. $14.00 (8 Issues). Nautica Pickering Wharf, Salem MA 01970. DD 797.

NBA REGISTER. VFOAT Sporting News Official N.B.A. Register. VAT National Basketball Association Register. 1982-83 Ed.-. 0739-3067. US. English. an. $9.95. The Sporting News, 1212 North Lindbergh Boulevard, PO Box 56, St Louis MO 63166. Tel (314)997-7111. LC GV885.515.N37. DD 796.3230922, B. Circ 12,000. Full collegiate and professional records for every active player. Includes photos of each player. *Official National Basketball Association Register, 0271-8170.*

NCAA BASEBALL RULES. Main/Corp National Collegiate Athletic Association. VFOAT N.C.A.A. Baseball Rules. VAT National Collegiate Athletic Association Baseball Rules. 1983-. 0736-5209. US. English. an. $3.00. NCAA Publishing Department, PO Box 1906, Shawnee Mission KS 66201. Tel (913)384-3220. LC GV877. DD 796.3570973. Baseball rules. *NCAA Baseball.*

NCAA BASKETBALL. VAT National Collegiate Athletic Association Basketball. Began with issue for 1980. 0276-1017. Periodical. US. English. $5.00. National Collegiate Athletic Association, PO Box 1906, Shawnee Mission KS 66222. Tel (913)384-3220. LC GV885.45. DD 796.323630973. Contain individual and team records, statistical leaders, all-America teams, game-by-game results from last year and schedules for the upcoming season. *Official National Collegiate Athletic Association Basketball Guide, Basketball Records, 0733-8376.*

NCAA DIRECTORY. See Yearbooks, Almanacs, Directories.

NCAA FOOTBALL. Main/Corp National Collegiate Athletic Association. 1982-. 0735-5475. US. English. an. $5.00. National Collegiate Athletic Association, PO Box 1906, Shawnee Mission KS 66222. Tel (913)384-3220. *Football Records.*

NCAA FOOTBALL RULES AND INTERPRETATIONS. Main/Corp National Collegiate Athletic Association. VFOAT N.C.A.A. Football Rules and Interpretations. VAT National Collegiate Athletic Association Football Rules and Interpretations. Began in 1979. 0736-5160. US. English. an. $3.00. National Collegiate Athletic Association, PO Box 1906, Shawnee Mission KS 66222. Tel (913)384-3220. LC GV956.8. DD 796.3326302022. Football rules and interpretations. *Official National Collegiate Athletic Association Football Rules & Interpretations which Supplements the NCAA Official Football Rules, 0094-5226.*

NCAA ILLUSTRATED MEN'S BASKETBALL RULES. Main/Corp National Collegiate Athletic Association. VFOAT Illustrated Men's Basketball Rules. 1983-. 0736-5179. US. English. an. $3.00. NCAA Publishing Department, PO Box 1906, Shawnee Mission KS 66201. Tel (913)384-3220. LC GV885.45. DD 796.32302022. Men's illustrated basketball rules. *NCAA Illustrated Basketball Rules, 0272-5754.*

NCAA LACROSSE. Main/Corp National Collegiate Athletic Association. VFOAT N.C.A.A. Lacrosse. US. English. an. National Collegiate Athletic Association, PO Box 1906, Shawnee Mission KS 66201. *Official National Collegiate Athletic Association Lacrosse Guide.*

NCAA MANUAL. Main/Corp National Collegiate Athletic Association. US. English. an. National Collegiate Athletic, PO Box 1906, Shawnee Mission KS 66222. Current NCAA Legislation and by-laws. Interpretations of executive regulations and procedures. Also includes recommended policies.

NCAA MEN'S AND WOMEN'S CROSS COUNTRY AND TRACK AND FIELD RULES. Main/Corp National Collegiate Athletic Association. VFOAT N.C.A.A. Men's and Women's Cross Country and Track and Field Rules. VAT National Collegiate Athletic Association Men's and Women's Cross Country and Track and Field Rules. 1984-. 0882-3170. US. English. an. $3.00. National Collegiate Athletic Association, PO Box 1906, Shawnee Mission KS 66222. Tel (913)384-3220. Men's and women's cross country and track and field rules. *NCAA Men's and Women's Track and Field Rules, 0736-7783.*

NCAA MEN'S AND WOMEN'S SKIING RULES. Main/Corp National Collegiate Athletic Association. VFOAT N.C.A.A. Men's and Women's Skiing Rules. 1984-. 0741-9279. US. English. an. $4.00. NCAA, PO Box 1906, Shawnee Mission KS 66201. Tel (913)384-3220. LC GV854.A1. DD 796.93. Men's and women's skiing rules. *NCAA Men's Skiing Rules, 0736-5136.*

NCAA MEN'S AND WOMEN'S SWIMMING AND DIVING RULES. VFOAT Men's and Women's Swimming and Diving Rules. 0736-5128. Periodical. US. English. an. $3.00. National Collegiate Athletic Association, PO Box 1906, Shawnee Mission KS 66222. Tel (913)384-3220. LC WMLC L 83/119. Men's and women's swimming and diving rules.

NCAA MEN'S BASKETBALL RULES AND INTERPRETATIONS. Main/Corp National Collegiate Athletic Association. VFOAT Men's Basketball Rules and Interpretations. VAT National Collegiate Athletic Association Basketball Rules and Interpretations. 1983-. 0736-5187. US. English. an. National Collegiate Athletic Association, PO Box 1906, Shawnee Mission KS 66222. Tel (913)384-3220. LC WMLC L 83/183. *NCAA Basketball Rules and Interpretations.*

NCAA MEN'S ICE HOCKEY RULES AND INTERPRETATIONS. Main/Corp National Collegiate Athletic Association. VFOAT N.C.A.A. Men's Ice Hockey Rules and Interpretations. 1983-. 0735-9195. US. English. an. $3.00. NCAA Publishing Department, PO Box 1906, Shawnne Mission KS 66201. Tel (913)384-3220. LC GV847. DD 796.9620711. Men's ice hockey rules and interpretations. *NCAA Ice Hockey, 0734-5011.*

NCAA MEN'S LACROSSE RULES. Main/Corp National Collegiate Athletic Association. VFOAT N.C.A.A. Men's Lacrosse Rules. 1984-.

Recreation, Leisure—Sports

0742-4361. US. English. an. NCAA Publishing Department, PO Box 1906, Shawnee Mission KS 66201. **LC** GV989. **DD** 796.347. *NCAA Lacrosse Rules, 0736-7775.*

NCAA MEN'S SOCCER RULES. Main/Corp National Collegiate Athletic Association. **VFOAT** N.C.A.A. Men's Soccer Rules. **VAT** National Collegiate Athletic Association Men's Soccer Rules. 0735-0368. US. English. an. National Collegiate Athletic Association, PO Box 1906, Shawnee Mission KS 66222. **Tel** (913)384-3220. **LC** GV943.4. **DD** 796.33402022. Men's soccer rules.

NCAA MEN'S WATER POLO RULES. Main/Corp National Collegiate Athletic Association. **VFOAT** N.C.A.A. Men's Water Polo Rules. 1982-. 0734-0508. US. English. an. $3.00. National Collegiate Athletic Association, PO Box 1906, Shawnee Mission KS 66222. **Tel** (913)384-3220. **LC** GV839. **DD** 797.25. Men's water polo rules. *NCAA Water Polo Rules, 0271-860X.*

THE NCAA NEWS. (NCAA NEWS). **Main/Corp** National Collegiate Athletic Association. **VAT** National Collegiate Athletic Association News. 0027-6170. Periodical. US. English. $20.00. National Collegiate Athletic Association, PO Box 1906, Shawnee Mission KS 66222. **Tel** (913)384-3220. Ed Thomas A Wilson. adv acc. Thoroughly covers the business of college athletics, week after week - 46 times a year.

NCAA RIFLE RULES. VFOAT Rifle Rules. **VAT** National Collegiate Athletic Association Rifle Rules. 0736-5144. US. English. an. $4.00. NCAA Publishing Department, PO Box 1906, Shawnee Mission KS 66201. **Tel** (913)384-3220. **LC** WMLC L 83/136. Men's and women's rifle rules.

NCAA SOCCER; ANNUAL GUIDE. Main/Corp National Collegiate Athletic Association. **VAT** National Collegiate Association Soccer. 39th- 1979-. 0195-7457. US. English. an. NCAA, PO Box 1906, Shawnee Mission KS 66222. **LC** GV943.A1. **DD** 796.3340973. *Official National Collegiate Athletic Association Soccer Guide.*

NCAA SWIMMING; ANNUAL GUIDE. Main/Corp National Collegiate Athletic Association. **VAT** National Collegiate Athletic Association Swimming. 56th- 1980-. 0272-8095. US. English. an. **LC** GV837.A1. **DD** 797.21. *Official National Collegiate Athletic Association Swimming Guide.*

NCAA WOMEN'S BASKETBALL RULES. VFOAT NCAA Basketball. **VAT** National Collegiate Athletic Association Women's Basketball Rules. 1986-. 0882-6293. US. English. an. National Collegiate Athletic Association, Nall Avenue at 63rd Street, Mission KS 66201. **DD** 796.

NCAA WRESTLING RULES. Main/Corp National Collegiate Athletic Association. **VFOAT** N.C.A.A. Wrestling Rules. 1983-. 0736-511X. US. English. an. $3.00. NCAA Publishing Department, PO Box 1906, Shawnee Mission KS 66201. **Tel** (913)384-3220. **LC** GV1195. **DD** 796.812. Wrestling rules. *NCAA Wrestling, 0738-1603.*

NEPTUNUS. Periodical. Portuguese. ir. **LC** GV776.33.A2.

NEW ERA TORONTO MAPLE LEAFS . . . FACT BOOK. (THE NEW ERA TORONTO MAPLE LEAFS . . . FACT BOOK). **Main/Corp** Toronto Maple Leafs (Hockey Team). **VFOAT** Official Fact Book of the Toronto Maple Leafs. 1979/1980-. 0229-0049. CN. English. an. Free. Maple Leaf Gardens Ltd, 60 Carleton Street, Toronto Ontario M5B 1L1 Canada. **DD** 796.9626. (ctrl). *Toronto Maple Leafs Fact Book, 0229-0030.*

THE NEW GUN WEEK. See Hobbies.

THE NEW ZEALAND JOURNAL OF SPORTS MEDICINE. See Medicine.

NEW ZEALAND WILDLIFE. See Recreation, Leisure - Outdoor Life.

NEWSLETTER - CANADIAN ACADEMY OF PODIATRIC SPORTS MEDICINE. See Medicine.

NEWSLETTER - CANADIAN ACADEMY OF SPORT MEDICINE. See Medicine.

NEWSLETTER - CANADIAN ASSOCIATION OF SPORTS SCIENCES. Main/Corp Canadian Association of Sports Sciences. Began publication in 1968? 0708-9171. Periodical. CN. English (Includes some text in French). ir. Canadian Association of Sports Sciences, c/o Non Resident Sports, Sports Federation, Ottawa K1L 8B9 Canada. **DD** 796.06271.

NEWSLETTER - CANADIAN ATHLETIC THERAPISTS ASSOCIATION. See Medicine.

NEWSLETTER - CANADIAN MODERN PENTATHLON ASSOCIATION. (NEWSLETTER). **VFOAT** Bulletin. **VAT** Bulletin - Association Canadienne du Pentathlon Moderne. 0823-7948. Periodical. CN. English (includes some text in French). bm. Canadian Modern Pentathlon Association, 1893 Stonehenge Crescent, Gloucester Ontario K1B 4N7 Canada. **DD** 796.

NEWSLETTER - CANADIAN PHYSIOTHERAPY ASSOCIATION. SPORTS PHYSIOTHERAPY DIVISION. See Medicine.

NEWSLETTER - CANADIAN PODIATRIC SPORTS MEDICINE ACADEMY. See Medicine.

NEWSLETTER - FEDERATION OF MOUNTAIN CLUBS OF BRITISH COLUMBIA. Main/Corp Federation of Mountain Clubs of British Columbia. V. 1- Sept./Nov. 1974-. 0316-909X. Periodical. CN. English. Federation of Mountain Clubs of British Columbia, PO Box 2674, Vancouver British Columbia V6B 3X1 Canada. **DD** 796.522062711.

NEWSLETTER - FIGURE SKATING COACHES OF CANADA. (NEWSLETTER). **Main/Corp** Figure Skating Coaches of Canada. **VFOAT** Figure Skating Coaches of Canada Newsletter. 0826-2969. Periodical. CN. English. ir. Free to Members. FSCC, PO Box 93, Agincourt Ontario M1S 3B4 Canada. **DD** 796.9107071. *Circle, 0227-2091.*

NEWSLETTER - HANG GLIDING ASSOCIATION OF CANADA. (NEWSLETTER). **VFOAT** Bulletin. No. 1 (July 1980)-. 0229-1746. Periodical. CN. English (includes some text in French). Hang Gliding Association of Canada, PO Box 4063 Station C, Calagary Alberta T2T 5M9 Canada. **DD** 797.55.

NEWSLETTER - MANITOBA UNDERWATER COUNCIL. Main/Corp Manitoba Underwater Council. Sept. 1964-. 0383-7742. Periodical. CN. English. mo. Manitoba Underwater Council, PO Box 711, Winnipeg Manitoba R3C 2K3 Canada. **DD** 797.230627127.

NEWSLETTER-NORTH AMERICAN SOCIETY FOR SPORT HISTORY. Main/Corp North American Society for Sport History. V. 1- 1973?-. US. English.

NEWSLETTER - PRESIDENT'S COUNCIL ON PHYSICAL FITNESS AND SPORTS. See Physical Training.

NFA JOURNAL. (N F A JOURNAL). **Main/Corp** National Firearms Association (Canada). **VAT** National Firearms Association Journal. V. 1- Aug. 1978-. 0706-5086. Periodical. CN. English. mo. Free to Members. National Firearms Association, PO Box 4610 Station E, Ottawa Ontario K1S 5H8 Canada. **DD** 683.40075.

NFL FOOTBALL FORECAST. VFOAT Football Forecast. **VAT** National Football League Football Forecast. 0364-8273. US. English. $1.25. Lexington Library Inc, PO Box 1741 Grand Central Station, New York NY 10017. **LC** GV955.5.N35. **DD** 796.332640973.

NHL OFFICIAL GUIDE. Main/Corp National Hockey League. **VFOAT** N.H.L. Official Guide. 1982-1983-. Periodical. CN. English. an. $16.45. National Hockey League, 1155 Metcalf/Suite 960, Montreal Quebec H3B 2W2 Canada. **Tel** (416)531-6535. Ed Gary Meagher. **LC** GV847.5. **DD** 796.96202022. **Circ** 65,000. The only complete and official guide to the game of hockey. Complete records and statistics covering almost 100 years of play. Authorized by the National Hockey League. *National Hockey League Guide.*

NIMROD. V. 1, No. 4 - Apr. 1969-. Periodical. Hungarian. mo. Akademiai Kiado, POB 24, 1363 Budapest Hungary. **Ind/Abst** Index Am. Period. Verse.

NORDIC. 0163-5905. US. English. an. $5.00. Nordic Skiing Inc, PO Box 106, West Brattleboro VT 05301. **LC** GV855.5.E67. **DD** 688.7693.

NORDIC SKIING COMPETITION GUIDE. VFOAT Skiing Competition Guide. 1981-. 0277-7452. US. English. an. $6.00. Human Kinetics Publishers Inc, Box 5076, Champaign IL 61820. **LC** GV855.4. **DD** 796.93.

NORM EVANS' SEAHAWK REPORT. VFOAT Seahawk Report. 0197-8349. Periodical. US. English. ir. $15.75. Norm Evans' Seahawk Report, 123 Lake Street/Suite 103, Kirkland WA 98033.

NORMANDIE. French. ir. Pneu Michelin Firm, 46 Avenue de Bretevil, 75341 Paris France. **LC** GV1025.F7.

NORTH AMERICAN HUNTER. V. 1- Winter 1979-. 0194-4320. Periodical. US. English. bm. $48.00. North American Hunter Club, PO Box 35557, Minneapolis MN 55435. **Tel** (612)941-7654. Ed Mark LaBarbera. bk rev. adv acc. **Circ** 100,000. The technical, how-to, and pleasurable aspects of hunting. Distribution is to members of the North American Hunting Club. These hunters take their sport seriously.

NORTHERN LIGHTS (CANADIAN FIGURE SKATING ASSOCIATION. NORTHERN ONTARIO SECTION). (NORTHERN LIGHTS). 0711-1134. Periodical. CN. English. ir. $2.00. Canadian Figure Skating Association, 160 Vanderhood Avenue, Toronto Ontario M4C 4B8 Canada. **DD** 796.9109713.

NORTHWEST PLAYER. Began with: Vol. 1, No. 1 (Dec. 1979). 0737-5530. Periodical. US. English. mo. $4.00. Northwest Sports Foundation, 946 North 83rd, Seattle WA 98103. **Tel** (206)524-0741.

NORTHWEST RUNNER. (NORTHWEST RUNNER : A CLUB NORTHWEST PUBLICATION). Vol. 13, No. 3 (Apr. 1985)-. 0883-7945. Periodical. US. English. mo. $12.00. Club Northwest, 1231 NE 94th Street, Seattle WA 98115. *Nor'Wester (Seattle, Wash.), 8750-6076.*

NORTHWESTERN SPORTSMAN. 0164-3134. Periodical. US. English. mo. Northwestern Publishing Co Inc, PO Box 1208, Big Timber MT 59011. **Tel** (406)932-3646.

NOUVEAUTES EN SCIENCE DE L'ENTRAINEMENT. Ed. 1979/1980-. 0226-997X. CN. French. an. $2,50 le No. Association Canadienne des Entraineurs, 333 Chemin River, Ottawa Ontario K1L 8B9 Canada. **DD** 796.07705.

N.R.A. HUNTING ANNUAL. See Recreation, Leisure - Outdoor Life.

NSGA BUYING GUIDE. Main/Corp National Sporting Goods Association. 1974/75-. Periodical. US. English. an. $20.00. National Sporting Goods Association, 1699 Wall Street, Mt Prospect IL 60056. **Tel** (312)439-4000. Ed K Lindgren.

N.S.U.C. UNDERWATER NEWS. VAT Nova Scotia Underwater Council News. Issue 3 (1979)-. 0711-3986. Periodical. CN. English. ir. Free to Members. Nova Scotia Underwater Council, PO Box 34, Armdale Nova Scotia Canada. **DD** 797.23060716. *NSUC Newsletter, 0711-3994.*

OBA NEWS. VAT Ontario Broomball Association News, Federation of Broomball Associations of Ontario News. 0822-7691. Periodical. CN. English. ir. Free to Members. Federation of Broomball, Association of Ontario, 160 Vanderhoof Avenue, Toronto Ontario M4G 4B8 Canada. **DD** 796.96.

OCEANS. No. 1- Jan. 1970-. Periodical. FR. French (summaries in English, German, Italian and Spanish). ir. 178. Oceans, 122 Chemin de Sormiou, 13009 Marseille France. **Tel** (91)731740. Ed Yves Baix. **Ind/Abst** Gen. Sci. Index, Biol. Agric. Index. **LC** GV840.S78. adv acc. **Circ** 30,000. (ctrl). Diving.

OCTOPUS. (L'OCTOPUS). 0712-6883. Periodical. CN. French. ir. Free to Members, $5.00 Others. Octo-Bulles Ltee, 949 Boulevard d'Ecarie, St Laurent Quebec H4C 3M3 Canada. **DD** 797.23060714.

OFFICIAL A.A.U. BASKETBALL HANDBOOK. Main/Corp Amateur Athletic Union of the United States. 0090-4414. US. English. $5.00. 3400 West 86th Street, Indianapolis IN 46268. **LC** GV882. **DD** 796.32305.

OFFICIAL AAU DIVING RULES. Main/Corp Amateur Athletic Union of the United States. **VFOAT** Diving Rules. US. English. an. Amateur Athletic Union of US, 3400 West 86th Street, Indianapolis IN 46268. **Tel** (317)297-2900. **LC** GV837. **DD** 797.200202.

Recreation, Leisure—Sports

OFFICIAL A.A.U. GYMNASTICS HANDBOOK. (OFFICIAL AAU GYMNASTICS HANDBOOK). Main/Corp Amateur Athletic Union of the United States. VFOAT AAU Official Handbook. 0091-3391. US. English. 3400 West 86th Street, Indianapolis IN 46268. LC GV461. DD 796.4.

OFFICIAL AAU JUDO RULES. Main/Corp Amateur Athletic Union of the United States. VFOAT AAU Official Rules, Judo. US. English. ir. Amateur Athletic Union, 3400 West 86th Street, Indianapolis IN 46268. LC GV475. DD 796.8152.

OFFICIAL AAU KARATE RULES. Main/Corp Amateur Athletic Union of the United States. VFOAT AAU Official Rules: Karate. VAT Official Amateur Athletic Union Karate Rules. 1977/78-. 0148-737X. US. English. $3.00. 3400 West 86th Street, Indianapolis IN 46268. LC GV1114.3. DD 796.8153.

OFFICIAL AAU POWERLIFTING RULE BOOK. See Physical Training.

OFFICIAL AAU SYNCHRONIZED SWIMMING HANDBOOK. Main/Corp Amateur Athletic Union of the United States. VFOAT Synchronized Swimming Rules. US. English. an. Official Synchronized Swimming, 1750 East Boulder Street, Colorado Springs CO 80909. LC GV837. DD 797.210202.

OFFICIAL AAU TAE KWON DO RULES. Main/Corp Amateur Athletic Union of the United States. VFOAT Taekwondo. VAT Official Amateur Athletic Union Tae Kwon Do Rules. 1977/80-. 0198-7941. US. English. Amateur Athletic Union of the United States, 3400 West 86th Street, Indianapolis IN 46268. LC GV1114.3. DD 796.8153.

OFFICIAL AAU TRACK AND FIELD HANDBOOK. Main/Corp Amateur Athletic Union of the United States. VFOAT AAU Official Handbook, Track & Field. VAT Official Amateur Athletic Union Track and Field Handbook. 0361-347X. US. English. an. TAC/USA Book, PO Box 120, Indianapolis IN 46206. Tel (317)297-2900. LC GV1060.67. DD 796.40202.

OFFICIAL AAU TRAMPOLINE AND TUMBLING HANDBOOK. Main/Corp Amateur Athletic Union of the United States. VFOAT AUU Official Handbook:. VAT Official Amateur Athletic Union of the United States Trampoline and Tumbling Handbook. 0361-2899. US. English. an. $5.00. Amateur Athletic Union, 3400 West 86th Street, Indianapolis IN 46268. LC GV555. DD 796.47.

OFFICIAL AAU WATER POLO RULES. Main/Corp Amateur Athletic Union of the United States. VFOAT AAU Official Rules, Water Polo. Periodical. US. English. an. Amateur Athletic Union of US, 3400 West 86th Street, Indianapolis IN 46268. Tel (317)297-2900.

OFFICIAL AAU WRESTLING HANDBOOK. Main/Corp Amateur Athletic Union of the United States. US. English. an. $3.00. 3400 West 86th Street, Indianapolis IN 46268. LC GV1195. DD 796.8120202.

OFFICIAL BASEBALL DOPE BOOK CEASED. 0162-5411. US. English. an. $8.95. Sporting News, Box 44, St Louis MO 63166. Tel (314)997-7111. LC GV877. DD 796.3570973. Stadium diagrams, team rosters, win-loss records, All-Star game records, etc. Baseball Dope Book.

OFFICIAL BASEBALL GUIDE. 0078-3838. US. English. an. $9.95. The Sporting News, Box 44, St Louis MO 63166. Tel (314)997-7111. Review of baseball's previous season: day-by-day scores, team highlights, club directroies and upcoming schedule. Baseball Guide and Record Book, 0272-295X.

OFFICIAL BASEBALL RECORD BOOK (SAINT LOUIS, MO. : 1982) CEASED. (OFFICIAL BASEBALL RECORD BOOK). VFOAT Baseball Record Book. 1982 Ed.-. 0162-5438. US. English. an. $7.95. The Sporting News, 1212 North Lindbergh Boulevard, PO Box 56, St Louis MO 63166. DD 796. Sporting News . . . Official Baseball Record Book, 0882-8237.

OFFICIAL BASEBALL REGISTER. Began in 1973. 0162-542X. US. English. an. $9.95. The Sporting News, PO Box 14 St Louis MO 63166. Tel (314)997-7111. Statistical information on the major league players and active managers. Baseball Register.

OFFICIAL BASEBALL RULES. 0078-3846. US. English. an. $2.50. The Sporting News, PO Box 56, St Louis MO 63166. Tel (314)997-7111. Official baseball playing rules, updated/revised annually.

OFFICIAL BASKETBALL RULES FOR MEN AND WOMEN. Main/Corp International Amateur Basketball Federation. VFOAT Official Basketball Rules. English. ir. 5.00. Official Basketball Rules c/o Canadian Amateur Basketball Association, 10th Floor 333 River Road, Vanier Ontario K1L 8B9 Canada. Tel (613)748-5607. DD 796.32302022. Circ 20,000. Rules of basketball (international).

OFFICIAL C. F. A. B. BASEBALL RULES. Main/Corp Canadian Federation of Amateur Baseball. 1975-. 0318-4714. Periodical. CN. English. an. Free to Members. Canadian Federation of Amateur Baseball, 33 River Road, Vanier Ontario K1L 8B9 Canada. DD 796.35702022. C. F. A. B. Official Baseball Rules, 0318-4706.

OFFICIAL FIELD HOCKEY RULES FOR SCHOOL GIRLS. Main/Corp United States Field Hockey Association. 0362-3270. US. English. US Field Hockey Association, 25 Front Street, Marblehead MA 01945. LC GV1017.H7. DD 796.355.

OFFICIAL GUIDE & RECORD BOOK - NATIONAL HOCKEY LEAGUE. (OFFICIAL GUIDE & RECORD BOOK). Main/Corp National Hockey League. 1984/85-. 0828-6647. CN. English. an. $13.95 Per Vol. National Hockey League, Suite 960/1155 Metcalfe Street, Montreal Quebec K3B 2W2 Canada. DD 796.96206. Official Guide, 0826-5038; Official Record Book, 0826-0214.

OFFICIAL HANDBOOK. Main/Corp International Amateur Athletic Federation. VFOAT IAAF Handbook. UK. English. an. LC GV1060.5. DD 796.420202.

OFFICIAL HANDBOOK OF THE A.A.U. CODE. (OFFICIAL HANDBOOK OF THE AAU CODE). Main/Corp Amateur Athletic Union of the United States. VFOAT AAU Code. 0091-3045. US. English. $10.00. 3400 West 86th Street, Indianapolis IN 46268. Tel (317)872-2900. LC GV563. DD 796.0973. Code of the Amateur Athletic Union and listing of all personnel and functions within the Union.

OFFICIAL HIGH SCHOOL BASEBALL RULES. Main/Corp National Federation of State High School Associations. 0736-7821. US. English. National Federation of State High School Associations, 11724 Plaza Circle/Box 20626, Kansas City MO 64195. LC GV877. DD 796.35702022.

OFFICIAL HIGH SCHOOL BOYS GYMNASTICS RULES. Main/Corp National Federation of State High School Associations. VFOAT Boys Gymnastics Rules. 1982/83-. 0740-9532. US. English. an. National Federation of State High School Associations, 11724 Plaza Circle, Box 20626, Kansas City MO 64195. Tel (816)464-5400. Ed Susan True. LC GV461. DD 796.41. adv acc. Circ 400. Rules governing high school competition in boys gymnastics. Boys Gymnastics Rule Book, 0277-8386.

OFFICIAL HIGH SCHOOL FOOTBALL RULES. Main/Corp National Federation of State High School Associations. VFOAT Official Football Rules. 1983-. 0747-9808. US. English. an. National Federation of State High School Associations, 11724 Plaza Circle, Box 20626, Kansas City MO 64195. LC GV956.8. DD 796.33202022.

OFFICIAL HIGH SCHOOL GIRLS GYMNASTICS RULES AND MANUAL. Main/Corp National Federation of State High School Associations. VFOAT Girls Gymnastics Rules and Manual. 1982/83-. 0739-9804. US. English. an. $3.00. National Federation of State High School Associations, PO Box 20626, Kansas City MO 64195. LC GV464. DD 796.41088042. Girls Gymnastics Rule Book and Manual, 0731-8537.

OFFICIAL HIGH SCHOOL ICE HOCKEY RULES. Main/Corp National Federation of State High School Associations. 1982-83-. 0735-651X. US. English. an. National Federation of State High School Association, 11724 Plaza Circle, Box 20626, Kansas City MO 64195. LC GV847.5. DD 796.96202022. Ice Hockey Rule Book, 0732-8117.

OFFICIAL HIGH SCHOOL WRESTLING RULES. Main/Corp National Federation of State High School Associations. VFOAT Wrestling Rules. 1982/83-. 0735-8946. US. English. an. National Federation of State High School Associations, 11724 Plaza Circle, Box 20626, Kansas City MO 64195. LC GV1195. DD 796.8120712. Wrestling Rule Book, 0361-641X.

OFFICIAL NATIONAL BASKETBALL ASSOCIATION REGISTER. VFOAT Official NBA Register. 1980-81-. 0271-8170. US. English. an. $9.95. The Sporting News, PO Box 44, St Louis MO 63166. Tel (314)997-7111. LC GV885.515.N37. DD 796.3230922. B. Complete review of previous basketball season, week-by-week, containing club rosters, directories and college draft choices.

OFFICIAL NATIONAL COLLEGIATE ATHLETIC ASSOCIATION BASEBALL GUIDE. (THE OFFICIAL NATIONAL COLLEGIATE ATHLETIC ASSOCIATION BASEBALL GUIDE). VFOAT Official Collegiate Baseball Guide. Periodical. US. English. an. LC GV877.

THE OFFICIAL NATIONAL COLLEGIATE ATHLETIC ASSOCIATION BASKETBALL RULES & INTERPRETATIONS. Main/Corp National Collegiate Athletic Association. VFOAT NCAA Official Basketball Rules & Interpretations. VAT The Official National Collegiate Athletic Association Basketball Rules and Interpretations. 0163-2817. US. English. an. $1.00. National Collegiate Athletic Association, PO Box 1906, Shawnee Mission KS 66222. LC GV885.45. DD 796.32302022.

THE OFFICIAL NATIONAL COLLEGIATE ATHLETIC ASSOCIATION BASKETBALL STATISTICIANS' MANUAL. See Statistics.

OFFICIAL NATIONAL FEDERATION BASKETBALL RULE BOOK. Main/Corp National Federation of State High School Associations. VFOAT Basketball Rule Book. 0270-8280. US. English. 11724 Plaza Circle, PO Box 20626, Kansas City MO 64195. LC GV885.45. DD 796.32302022.

OFFICIAL NATIONAL FOOTBALL LEAGUE GUIDE. (OFFICIAL GUIDE). Main/Corp National Football League Guide. 1972-. 0091-0821. US. English. an. New American Library, 1301 Avenue of the Americas, New York NY 10019. LC GV955.5.N35. DD 796.332640973.

OFFICIAL NATIONAL FOOTBALL LEAGUE RECORD & FACT BOOK. (OFFICIAL . . . NATIONAL FOOTBALL LEAGUE RECORD & FACT BOOK). Main/Corp National Football League. VFOAT Official . . . National Football League Record and Fact Book. 1984-. 0883-4199. US. English. an. Workman Publishing Company, 1 West 39th Street, New York NY 10018. Official Record Manual, National Football League . . . Media Information Book, 0743-7080.

OFFICIAL NBA GUIDE. VFOAT Official National Basketball Association Guide. 1981-82-. 0078-3862. US. English. an. Sporting News, 1212 No Lindbergh Boulevard, Box 56, St Louis MO 63166. LC GV885. DD 796.3230973. National Basketball Association Official Guide.

OFFICIAL NFL AND COLLEGE SCHEDULES AND RECORDS CEASED. VFOAT Schedules and Records. VAT Official National Football League and College Schedule and Records. 0747-8623. US. English. an. $1.95. Sporting News Publishing Company, PO Box 56, St Louis MO 63166.

OFFICIAL PGA TOUR MEDIA GUIDE. Main/Corp Professional Golfers' Association of America. VAT Official Professional Golfers' Association Tour Media Guide. 0193-9653. US. English. an. Professsional Golfers Association of America, Palm Beach Gardens Box 12458, Lake Park FL 33403. LC GV969.P75. DD 796.3520973.

OFFICIAL PLAYING RULES FOR THE CANADIAN FOOTBALL LEAGUE. (THE OFFICIAL PLAYING RULES FOR THE CANADIAN FOOTBALL LEAGUE). Main/Corp Canadian Football League. VFOAT Official Playing Rules for Canadian Football. 1974-. 0316-151X. Periodical. CN. English. an. Free. Canadian Football League, 11 King Street West/Suite 908, Toronto Ontario M5H 1A3 Canada. DD 796.33502022. Official Playing Rules for the Canadian Football League and the Canadian Amateur Football Association, 0316-1501.

THE OFFICIAL PRICE GUIDE TO SPORTS COLLECTIBLES. VFOAT Sports Collectibles. 1st Ed. (1984)-. 0748-1160. US. English. an. $2.95. House of Collectibles Inc, Orlando Central Park, 1900 Premier Row, Orlando FL 32809. LC GV568.5. DD 796.0973.

OFFICIAL READ-EASY BASKETBALL RULES . . . . Main/Corp National Collegiate Athletic Association. US. English. an. $1.50. National Collegiate Athletic Association Publishing

Recreation, Leisure—Sports

Department, PO Box 1906, Shawnee Mission KS 66222. Tel (913)384-3220. Popularized versions of the official rules for each sport, easily read and understood.

OFFICIAL READ-EASY FOOTBALL RULES. (OFFICIAL READ-EASY FOOTBALL RULES . . .). Main/Corp National Collegiate Athletic Association. 0277-559X. US. English. an. $1.50. National Collegiate Athletic Association, PO Box 1906, Shawnee Mission KS 66222. Tel (913)384-3220. LC GV956.8. DD 796.33202022. Popularized versions of the official rules for each sport, easily read and understood.

OFFICIAL READ-EASY MEN'S BASKETBALL RULES. VFOAT Basketball Rules. VAT Official Read Easy Men's Basketball Rules. 0736-5195. US. English. an. $1.50. NCAA Publishing Department, POB 1906, Shawnee Mission KS 66201. Tel (913)384-3220. LC GV885.45. DD 796.32302022. Popularized versions of the official rules for each sport, easily read and understood.

OFFICIAL RECORD AND INFORMATION MANUAL - CANADIAN FOOTBALL LEAGUE. Main/Corp Canadian Football League. VFOAT Official Record Manual. 1975-. 0708-6784. CN. English. an. Canadian Football League, Suite 1800/11 King Street West, Toronto Ontario M5H 1A3 Canada. DD 796.3356. *C F L Official Yearbook, 0318-9775.*

OFFICIAL REGULATIONS AND PLAYING RULES. LITTLE LEAGUE, SENIOR LEAGUE, BIG LEAGUE SOFTBALL. Main/Corp Little League Baseball, Inc. US. English. an. Little League Baseball Inc, PO Box 3485, Williamsport PA 17701. LC GV881.2. DD 796.3578.

OFFICIAL RULE BOOK - CANADIAN AMATEUR SYNCHRONIZED SWIMMING ASSOCIATION, INC. (OFFICIAL RULE BOOK). Main/Corp Canadian Amateur Synchronized Swimming Association. 0706-9901. Periodical. CN. English. Canadian Amateur Synchronized Swimming Association, 333 River Road, Ottawa Ontario K1L 8H9 Canada. DD 797.21.

OFFICIAL RULE BOOK OF THE CANADIAN WATER SKI ASSOCIATION. (THE OFFICIAL RULE BOOK OF THE CANADIAN WATER SKI ASSOCIATION). Main/Corp Canadian Water Ski Association. 0714-4814. CN. English. an. CWSA Official Rule Book, 333 River Road, Vanier Ontario K1L 8B9 Canada. DD 797.17305.

OFFICIAL RULE BOOK OF THE NATIONAL HOCKEY LEAGUE. Main/Corp National Hockey League. VFOAT Rule Book. 0316-831X. Periodical. CN. English. an. National Hockey League, Information and Statistics Bureau, 920 Sun Life Building, Montreal Quebec H3B 2W2 Canada. LC GV847.5. DD 796.962.

OFFICIAL RULES FOR COMPETITIVE SWIMMING. Main/Corp Amateur Athletic Union of the United States. VFOAT AAU Official Rules. 0091-3413. US. English. an. $6.00. United States Swimming Rules & Regulations, 1750 East Boulder Street, Colorado Springs CO 80909. Tel (305)578-4578. Ed William A Lippman Jr and Carol Zaleski. LC GV837. DD 797.21. adv acc. Circ 22,000. Complete rules and regulations for competitive swimming in the United States. Also includes current records.

OFFICIAL RULES FOR PROFESSIONAL FOOTBALL. Main/Corp National Football League. 0196-7827. US. English. 410 Park Avenue, New York NY 10022. LC GV955. DD 796.332640973.

OFFICIAL RULES FOR WATER POLO. Main/Corp Amateur Athletic Union of the United States. VFOAT AAU Official Rules, Water Polo. 0093-5786. US. English. an. 3400 West 86th Street, Indianapolis IN 46268. LC GV839. DD 797.25.

OFFICIAL RULES - ONTARIO RINGETTE ASSOCIATION CEASED. Main/Corp Ontario Ringette Association. 1973/74-1979/80. 0316-7615. Periodical. CN. English. Ontario Ringette Association, c/o Ms M Brown, Excutive Director, 559 Jarvis Street, Toronto Ontario M4Y 2J1 Canada. DD 796.96.

OFFICIAL RULES - RINGETTE CANADA. (OFFICIAL RULES). Main/Corp Ringette Canada. 1980/1981-. 0711-0537. CN. English. c/o W Clark, Ontario Ringette Association, 160 Vanderhoof Avenue, Toronto Ontario M4G 4B8 Canada. DD 796.96. *Official Rules, 0316-7615.*

THE OFFICIAL UNITED STATES TENNIS ASSOCIATION YEARBOOK AND TENNIS GUIDE WITH THE OFFICIAL RULES. See Yearbooks, Almanacs, Directories.

OFFICIAL USFL GUIDE AND REGISTER. VFOAT Official U.S.F.L. Guide and Register. VAT Official United States Football League Guide and Register. 1984 Ed.-. 0742-4299. US. English. an. $9.95. Sporting News Publishing Company, PO Box 56, St Louis MO 63166. LC GV955.5.U8. DD 796.332640973.

THE . . . OFFICIAL VOLLEY BALL GUIDE AND RULES. 1950. US. English. an. US Volleyball Association, PO Box 77065, San Francisco CA 94107. *Official United States Volley Ball Association Volley Ball Guide . . ., with the Official Rules.*

OFFICIAL WORLD SERIES RECORDS. US. English. an. The Sporting News, PO Box 56, St Louis MO 63166. Tel (314)997-711. LC GV877. The history of the World Series games with records, recaps, box scores and player rosters. In-depth look at last year's championship games.

THE OHIO RUNNER. 0279-9634. Periodical. US. English. ir. $10.00. Ohio Runner, PO Box 20215, Columbus OH 43220. Tel (614)889-9066.

OLDTIMERS' SPORTS NEWS. Oct. 1981-. 0711-5539. Periodical. CN. English. mo. $8.51. Tatham Publications Inc, Box 951, Peterborough Ontario K9J 7A5 Canada. Tel (705)743-2679. DD 796.0192. Covers and promotes Oldtimers' sports with an emphasis on Oldtimers' hockey. *Canadian Oldtimers' Sports News, 0711-1002.*

OLIMPIISKAIA PANORAMA : ORGAN OLIMPIISKOGO KOMITETA SSSR. No. 1 (Autumn/Winter 1981)-. Periodical. UR. Russian. qt. Fizkultura I Sport, Moskva 119270, Luzhneskaia Nab 8, Moskva Russian SFSR. LC GV721.4.S65. DD 796.480947.

OLYMPIAN. (THE OLYMPIAN). V. 1- July/Aug. 1974-. 0094-9787. Periodical. US. English. $19.88. US Olympic Committee, 1750 East Boulder Street, Colorado Springs CO 80909. Tel (303)632-5551. Ed Bob Condron. LC GV721.5. DD 796.4805. adv acc. Circ 60,000. (ctrl). The official publication of the United States Olympic Committee, devoted to amateur sports and the Olympic movement in the United States.

OLYMPIAN. 0030-2163. Periodical. US. English. mo. $10.00. Olympic Club, 524 Post Street, San Francisco CA 94102. LC GV563. DD 796.05.

OLYMPIANS CEASED. (THE OLYMPIANS). 1974-1976. 0382-795X. CN. English. an. Publinova, 491 Vitre Street West, Montreal Quebec H2Z 1G6 Canada. DD 796.4809.

OLYMPIC REVIEW. Began with Oct. 1967 issue. 0377-192X. Periodical. SZ. English. bm. 45.00. Comite International Olympique, Chateau de Vidy 1007, Lausanne Switzerland. LC GV721.5. DD 796.4805.

OLYMPIENS CEASED. (LES OLYMPIENS). 1974-1976. 0382-7968. CN. French. an. Publinova, 491 Ouest rue de Vitre, Montreal Quebec H2Z 1G6 Canada. DD 796.4809.

OLYMPRESSE 1976. (OLYMPRESS 1976). V. 2, No. 3- May 1974-. 0316-6384. Periodical. CN. French and English each with separate paging. mo. Organizing Committee of the 1976 Olympic Games, PO Box 1976, Montreal Quebec H3C 3A6 Canada. DD 796.48. *Olympress 1976, Olympresse 1976.*

ON COURT. July 1983-. 0824-6629. Periodical. CN. English. Free. DD 796.340971. (ctrl).

ON THE RUN. VFOAT En Courant. 0229-088X. Periodical. CN. English. mo. Free to Members. National Capital Runners' Association, 22 Findlay Avenue, Ottawa Ontario K1S 2T9 Canada. DD 796.4260971383.

ONTARIO AMATEUR WRESTLING ASSOCIATION RESULTS BOOK. (RESULTS BOOK). Main/Corp Ontario Amateur Wrestling Association. 1981/1982-. 0822-6806. CN. English. an. 5.00. Ontario Amateur Wrestling Association, 1220 Sheppard Avenue East, Willowdale Ontario M2K 2X1 Canada. Tel (416)495-4165. Ed Ingrid Leslie. DD 796.81209713. adv acc. Circ 3,000. Results of Canadian amateur wrestlers in international, national, provincial and local competitions. *Results Book, 0820-6082.*

ONTARIO BADMINTON. No. 1- Sept. 1978-. 0709-8308. Periodical. CN. English. bm. $2.32. Ontario Badminton Association, 160 Vanderhoof Avenue, Toronto Ontario M4G 4B8 Canada. Tel (416)429-7701. DD 796.34509713. *First Seed, 0705-3134.*

ONTARIO FEDERATED SNOWMOBILER. Vol. 1, No. 1 (Oct. 1981)-. 0821-0039. Periodical. CN. English. ir. Ontario Federated Snowmobiler, 426 London Street, Peterborough Ontario K9H 3A3 Canada. DD 796.9409713.

ONTARIO FENCER. (ONTARIO FENCER : MAGAZINE). 0228-9075. Periodical. CN. English. qt. Free to Members. Ontario Fencing Association, 559 Jarvis Street, Toronto Ontario M4Y 2J1 Canada. DD 796.8609713.

ONTARIO FISH AND WILDLIFE REVIEW CEASED. V. 1-20, No. 1. 0030-2929. Periodical. CN. English. qt. Free. Ministry of Natural Resources, Division of Fish and Wildlife, Parliament Buildings, Toronto Ontario M7A 1W3 Canada. Ind/Abst Can. Environ., Biol. Abstr. LC SK152.O5. CODEN OFWRAC.

ONTARIO GOLF NEWS. VFOAT Golf News. VAT Golf News (Thornhill). Vol. 1, No. 1 (May 1981)-. 0710-2801. Periodical. CN. English. ir. $6.00. Ontario Golf News, PO Box 5400, Thornhill Ontario L3T 4S5 Canada. DD 796.35209713.

ONTARIO OUT OF DOORS. See Recreation, Leisure - Outdoor Life.

ONTARIO SPORTSCENE. V. 1- Nov. 1979-. 0225-5782. Periodical. CN. English. bm. Free. Ontario Sports Administrative Centre Inc, 160 Vanderhoof Avenue, Toronto Ontario M4G 4B8 Canada. DD 796.09713. (ctrl).

ONTARIO WATER SKIER. (THE ONTARIO WATER SKIER). V. 1- Feb. 1974-. 0226-5702. Periodical. CN. English. ir. Ontario Sports Administrative Centre, 160 Vanderhoof Avenue, Toronto Ontario M4G 4B8 Canada. DD 797.17305.

ONTARIO WRESTLER. VFOAT Newsletter. V. 1- Sept. 1979-. 0226-1561. Periodical. CN. English. ir. Free to Members. Ontario Olympic Wrestling Federation, 160 Vanderhoof Avenue, Toronto Ontario M4G 4B8 Canada. DD 796.81209713.

ORIENTEERING CANADA. 0227-6658. Periodical. CN. English. qt. $5.00, Free to Members. Canadian Orienteering Federation, 333 River Road, Vanier Ontario K1L 8B9 Canada. DD 796.42.

ORIENTEERING NORTH AMERICA. 0886-1080. Periodical. US. English. mo. $15.00 Domestic, $21.00 Canada. SM & L Berman Publishing Company, 23 Fayette Street, Cambridge MA 02139. DD 796.

OUTDOOR LIFE DEER HUNTER'S YEARBOOK. See Yearbooks, Almanacs, Directories.

OUTDOOR SPORTSMAN. See Recreation, Leisure - Outdoor Life.

OUTDOORS IN GEORGIA. See Recreation, Leisure - Outdoor Life.

PACER (WINNIPEG, MAN.). (PACER). 0229-3463. Periodical. CN. English. bm. Free. Pacer, c/o Manitoba High Schools, Athletic Association, 1301 Ellie Avenue, Winnipeg Manitoba R3G 0G1 Canada. DD 796.097127. (ctrl).

PACIFIC MOTORSPORT. V. 1- July 1975-. 0319-2113. Periodical. CN. English. mo. $5. North 60 Publications Ltd, PO Box 77, Chemainus British Columbia V0R 1K0 Canada. DD 796.7290795.

PADDLES UP. Vol. 1, No. 1 (March 1983)-. 0823-1095. Periodical. CN. English (includes some text in French). bm. Free to Members. Canadian Canoe Association, 333 River Road, Vanier Ontario K1L 8B9 Canada. DD 797.14. *Newsletter (Canadian Canoe Association), 0821-3739.*

PAKISTAN BOOK OF CRICKET. 1976-. PK. English. an. 10.00. Q Ahmed, 3rd Floor Spencers Building, II Chundrigar Road GPO Box 3721, Karachi Pakistan. LC GV928.P3. DD 796.35809549.

PALAESTRA (MACOMB, ILL.). (PALAESTRA). Vol. 1, No. 1 (Fall 1984)-. 8756-5811. Periodical. US. English. qt. $24.00. Palaestra, PO Box 508, Macomb IL 61455. Tel (309)833-1902. Ed David P Beaver. DD 796. bk rev. adv acc. Circ 4,000. (ctrl).

Recreation, Leisure—Sports

Offers well balanced feature content dealing with all aspects of sport and physical education for the disabled. Focus is on special competitive events, training techniques, biomechanics, teaching methods. Published in cooperations with the USOC's Committee on Sport for the Disabled.

PARACHUTIST. V. 1- Sept. 1957-. 0031-1588. Periodical. US. English. mo. $21.50. United States Parachute Association, 1440 Duke Street, Alexandria VA 22314. Tel (703)836-3495. LC GV770.

PARAVENTURE. V. 1, No. 1, (Fall 1982)-. 0821-6517. Periodical. CN. French. qt. Free to Members. Federation Quebecoise des Sports Aeriens, 1415 Est rue Jarray, Montreal Quebec H2E 2Z7 Canada. DD 797.5609714.

PARAVOICE. (PARAVOICE : THE NEWSLETTER FOR PARACHUTISTS). 0228-9938. Periodical. CN. English. bm. $5.00. Sport Parachuting Clubs of Ontario, 160 Vanderhoof Avenue, Toronto Ontario M4G 4B8 Canada. DD 797.5609713.

PARENTS NEWSLETTER. V. 1- Oct. 1979-. 0709-9339. Periodical. CN. English. mo. Ontario Hockey Council, Apt 610/50 Michener Road, Chatham Ontario N7L Canada. DD 796.9626.

PASSE-SPORTS. Vol. 3, No. 1 (Nov. 1980)-. 0820-070X. Periodical. CN. French. qt. Free. Passe-Sports, c/o Commission Scolaire Regionale, Honore-Mercier, 69 Boulevard St Joseph, Saint-Jean-Sur-Richelieu Quebec J3B 1V8 Canada. DD 796.0971451. (ctrl). *Mini-Franc Jeu Regional, 0226-7675.*

PECHEUR ET CHASSEUR QUEBECOIS. V. 1, No. 5- Sept. 1976-. 0703-9107. Periodical. CN. French. ir. $1. Per No. Pecheur et Chasseur Quebecois, 3580 rue Masson, Montreal Quebec H1X 1S2 Canada. DD 799.09714. *Pecheur Quebecois, 0384-1073.*

PENNSYLVANIA HIGH SCHOOL ATHLETIC YEARBOOK. See Yearbooks, Almanacs, Directories.

THE PENNSYLVANIA SPORTSMAN. See Recreation, Leisure - Outdoor Life.

PETERSEN'S ANNUAL PRO FOOTBALL. (PETERSEN'S ... ANNUAL PRO FOOTBALL). VFOAT Petersen's Pro Football ... Annual. 0731-0161. US. English. an. Petersen Publishing Company, 6725 Sunset Boulevard, Los Angeles CA 90028. LC GV955.5.N35. DD 796.332640973.

PETERSEN'S CIRCLE TRACK. See Transportation - Automobiles.

PETERSEN'S COLLEGE FOOTBALL. (PETERSEN'S ... COLLEGE FOOTBALL). VFOAT College Football. 1980-. 0276-2129. US. English. an. $2.50 Domestic, $3.25 Canada. Petersen Publishing Company, 6725 Sunset Boulevard, Los Angeles CA 90028. LC GV937. DD 796.3326305.

PETERSEN'S HUNTING. VFOAT Hunting. V. 1- Nov. 1973-. 0146-4671. Periodical. US. English. mo. $15.94. Petersens Publishing Company, 6725 Sunset Boulevard, Los Angeles CA 90028. Tel (213)657-5100. Ed Craig Boddington. LC SK1. DD 799.205. adv acc. Circ 286,400. Insight, updates, and advice on big game, small game, waterfowl, and exotics- especially for the hunting enthusiast.

PETERSEN'S HUNTING ANNUAL. See Recreation, Leisure - Outdoor Life.

PETERSEN'S PRO BASEBALL. 0148-3153. Periodical. US. English. an. $1.95 (Single Issue). Petersens Publishing Company, 6725 Sunset Boulevard, Los Angeles CA 90028. LC GV875.A1. DD 796.357640973.

PETERSEN'S PRO BASKETBALL. VFOAT Petersen's Pro Basketball Annual. 0192-2238. US. English. an. $1.95 Per Copy. Petersen Publishing Company, 6725 Sunset Boulevard, Los Angeles CA 90028. LC GV885.7. DD 796.323640973.

PETERSEN'S PRO HOCKEY. 1979/80-. 0271-2636. US. English. an. $2.50 Domestic, $3.25 Canada. Petersen Publishing Company, 6725 Sunset Boulevard, Los Angeles CA 90028. LC GV846. DD 796.9627.

PGA MAGAZINE. (PGA MAGAZINE : THE OFFICIAL PUBLICATION OF THE PROFESSIONAL GOLFERS' ASSOCIATION OF AMERICA). VFOAT P.G.A. Magazine. VAT Professional Golfers Association Magazine. Began with Oct. 1977 issue. 0161-1259. Periodical. US. English. mo. $12.00. Professional Golfers Association of America, Palm Beach Gardens/Box 12458, Lake Park FL 33403. Tel (305)626-3600. Ed Bill Burbaum. LC GV961. DD 796.35205. bk rev. adv acc. Circ 41,200. Official publication of the PGA of America for professional golfers, collegiate and other serious golfers with news roundups and feature stories covering major golfing events, personalities and history of golf. *Professional Golfer.*

PHYSICAL FITNESS/SPORTS MEDICINE. See Medicine.

PHYSICIAN AND SPORTSMEDICINE. See Medicine.

PING PANG SHIH CHIEH. VFOAT Pingpang Shijie. Periodical. CH. Chinese. qt. $2.00. Jen Min Ti Yu Chu Pan She, Peking China. Tel 757161. Ed Cen Yuefang and Ma Guanghong. LC GV1004.9. DD 796.34605. bk rev. adv acc. Circ 20,000. Studies of basic theories and techniques in table tennis, reports on major tournaments domestic and international, stories of star players, experience in training, etc.

PLACAR. No. 1 (20 Mar. 1970)-. Periodical. Portuguese. ir. Editora Abril Ltd, Caixa Postal 2372, Sao Paulo Brazil.

PLAYING RULES. Main/Corp Women's International Bowling Congress. 0361-3976. US. English. Women's International Bowling Congress, 5301 South 76th Street, Greendale WI 53129. LC GV905. DD 794.6.

PLEIN AIR MAURICIE. See Recreation, Leisure - Outdoor Life.

PLONGEE. (LA PLONGEE). V. 5, No 2-March/April 1978-. 0228-3530. Periodical. CN. French. bm. $13.93. Fec Quebecoise Activites Sub, 4545 Pierre de Coubertin, CP 1000 Succursale M, Montreal Quebec H1V 3R2 Canada. Tel (514)252-3009. Ed F A Hamel. DD 797.2305. bk rev. adv acc. Circ 5,000. Scuba diving magazine with editorial, equipment, photography, technics, news, story, instruction, and leading article. *Plongee Sous-Marine, 0704-7096.*

THE POCKET BOOK OF PRO FOOTBALL. 0148-8007. US. English. $1.95 Single Issue. 1230 Avenue of the Americas, New York NY 10020. Ed H M Furlow. LC GV955. DD 796.332640973.

POCKET PRO GOLF MAGAZINE. VFOAT Pocket Pro Golf Magazine & Course Guide. 1982 Ed.-. 0821-2023. CN. English. an. Free to Golfers. Longhurst Golf Enterprises, Suite 202/2 St Clair Avenue East, Toronto Ontario M4T 2T5 Canada. DD 796.35230971. *Pro Pocket Guide Golf Magazine, 0711-4079.*

POINT AFTER. (THE POINT AFTER : OFFICIAL NEWSLETTER OF THE O.A.F.A). Vol. 1, No. 1-. 0229-7736. Periodical. CN. English. O A F A, 160 Vanderhoof Avenue, Toronto Ontario M4G 4B8 Canada. DD 796.3350609713.

POINT DE MIRE. V. 1- Nov. 1978-. 0707-8021. Periodical. CN. French. qt. DD 799.31062714. *Pistolier, 0704-7215.*

POINT SPREAD PLAYBOOK. VAT Point Spread Play Book. 1979-. 0273-3420. US. English. an. Point Spread Playbook, 1314 Watling Road, Arlington Hiights IL 60004. LC GV955. DD 796.332640973.

POLO (GAITHERSBURG, MD.). (POLO). V. 2, No. 6- Oct./Nov. 1976-. 0146-4574. Periodical. US. English. ir. $24.00. Polo Publishers, 656 Quince Orchard Road, Gaithersburg MD 20760. Tel (301)979-3900. Ed Ami Shinitzky. LC GV1010. DD 796.35305. adv acc. Circ 5,000. Anything and everything to do with the sport of polo. *Polonews, 0146-4612.*

POLOISTE. (LE POLOISTE). Mar. 1979-. 0226-5443. Periodical. CN. French. qt. Federation de Water Polo du Quebec, 1415 East rue Jarry, Montreal Quebec H2E 2Z7 Canada. DD 797.25. *Bulletin, 0226-5435.*

POLOVNICKE STUDIE. See Recreation, Leisure - Outdoor Life.

THE POOP SHEET. 0195-0037. Periodical. US. English. ir. $29.00. Sports Letter Inc, PO Box 147, Chapel Hill NC 27514. Tel (919)967-7789.

POPULAR ROTORCRAFT FLYING. See Aeronautics, Astronautics.

POPULAR SPORTS FACE-OFF. Jan. 1973-. 0092-5969. Periodical. US. English. sa. $0.75 Per Copy. Popular Library, 355 Lexington Avenue, New York NY 10017. LC GV846. DD 796.9620973. *Face-Off.*

POPULAR SPORTS. SOCCER ILLUSTRATED. VFOAT Soccer Illustrated. 1979-. 0195-9476. US. English. an. CBS Publications-Popular Magazine Group, 1515 Broadway, New York NY 10036. LC GV942. DD 796.33405. *Popular Sports. Soccer, 0195-9441.*

POSEIDON. No. 1- 1964-. Periodical. SZ. German. mo. Kunst & Wissen Erich Bieber, Dufourstrasse 51, CH-8008 Zurich Switzerland. Tel 011-41-1-69 44 20. LC GV840.S78.

POST FOOTBALL GUIDE. UK. English. T Bailey Forman Ltd, Forman Street, PO Box 99, Nottingham NG1 4AB England. LC GV944.G7. DD 796.3340942.

POUR LA SUITE DES JEUX. (POUR LA SUITE DES JEUX : BULLETIN D'INFORMATION DE LA FONDATION DES JEUX DU QUEBEC). V. 1, No. 1, (April 1983)-. 0824-4170. Periodical. CN. English (French). ir. Free. Fondation des Jeux du Quebec, 1415 Jarry West, Montreal Quebec H2E 2Z7 Canada. DD 796.4060714. (ctrl).

POWDER. 0145-4471. Periodical. US. English. mo. $10.00. Powder Magazine, PO Box 1028, Dana Point CA 92629. LC GV854.A1. DD 796.9305.

POWERBOAT. 0032-6089. Periodical. US. English. mo. $15.00. Powerboat, PO Box 3842, Van Nuys CA 91407. LC GV835.9. DD 797.14. *Power Boat.*

POWERLIFTING USA. VAT Powerlifting United States of America. 1977. 0199-8536. Periodical. US. English. mo. $21.00. Powerlifting USA, PO Box 467, Camirillo CA 93010. Tel (805)482-2378. Ed Mike Lambert. bk rev. adv acc. Circ 10,300. Coverage of the sport of powerlifting, contest results, training techniques, and athelete profiles.

THE PREDICAMENT. 0199-0705. Periodical. US. English. ir. $10.00. Predicament, PO Box 545, Emmetsburg IA 50536. Tel (712)852-3011. Ed Ron Seaman. adv acc. Circ 2,500. Wrestling newspaper covering high schoool wrestling with some college and JR wrestling.

PREP ALL-AMERICA BASKETBALL YEARBOOK. See Yearbooks, Almanacs, Directories.

PREP ALL-AMERICA FOOTBALL YEARBOOK. See Yearbooks, Almanacs, Directories.

PREP TRACK & FIELD ATHLETES OF THE YEAR. VAT Prep Track and Field Athletes of the Year. 0361-1051. US. English. an. 200 South Hull Street, Montgomery AL 36104. LC GV697.A1. DD 796.420922, B.

PRESTO. Began in 1974?. 0318-9325. CN. text in French and English. wk. Organizing Committee of the 1976 Olympic Games, PO Box 1976, Montreal Quebec H3C 3A6 Canada. DD 796.48.

PRO. US. English. National Property Football League Properties Inc, Creative Services, 10880 Wilshire Boulevard/Suite 906, Los Angeles CA 90024. LC GV956.W3. DD 796.332640973. *Redskin.*

PRO AND AMATEUR HOCKEY GUIDE. 0090-0818. US. English. an. $3.00. 212 North Lindbergh Boulevard, St Louis MO 63166. LC GV846. DD 796.96205.

PRO BASKETBALL. 0360-2125. US. English. $1.50. Pocket Books, 630 5th Avenue, New York NY 10020. LC GV882. DD 796.323640973.

PRO FOOTBALL GUIDE. VFOAT Sporting News Pro Football Guide. 1983 ed-. 0732-1902. US. English. an. $9.95. Sporting News, 1212 North Lindbergh Boulevard, PO Box 56, St Louis MO 63166. Tel (314)997-7111. LC GV937. DD 796.332640973. Circ 15,000. Complete review of previous season-every game and every team. Includes club rosters, college draft picks, individual records. *Sporting News Pro Football Guide, 0732-1902.*

PRO FOOTBALL WEEKLY. 0032-9053. Periodical. US. English. ir. Football World Inc, 666 Dundee Road/Suite 1101, Northbrook IL 60062.

PROCEEDINGS OF THE ANNUAL CONFERENCE SOUTHEASTERN ASSOCIATION OF FISH AND WILDLIFE AGENCIES. (PROCEEDINGS OF THE ... ANNUAL CONFERENCE SOUTHEASTERN ASSOCIATION OF FISH AND WILDLIFE AGENCIES). Main/Corp Southeastern Association of Fish and Wildlife Agencies. 30th (Oct. 24-27, 1976)-. 0276-7929. US. English. ir. c/o Joe L Herring, PO Box 15570, Baton Rouge LA 70895. Tel (504)342-5881. Ind/Abst Life Sci. Collect. LC SK1. DD 333.9560975. *Proceedings.*

PROCEEDINGS OF THE ANNUAL CONVENTION OF THE NATIONAL COLLEGIATE ATHLETIC ASSOCIATION. (PROCEEDINGS OF THE ANNUAL CONVENTION). Main/Corp National Collegiate Athletic Association. VFOAT Convention

Recreation, Leisure—Sports

Proceedings. 61st- 1967-. 0077-3808. US. English. an. $12.00. National Collegiate Athletic Association, PO Box 1906, Shawnee Mission KS 66222. **Tel** (913)384-3220. Transcripts of all general sessions at the NCAA Convention, summaries of round tables and a roster of delegates and visitors. *Yearbook.*

PROCEEDINGS OF THE SPECIAL CONVENTION OF THE NATIONAL COLLEGIATE ATHLETIC ASSOCIATION. (PROCEEDINGS OF THE SPECIAL CONVENTION). **Main/Corp** National Collegiate Athletic Association. 1st- Aug. 1973-. 0094-4459. US. English. ir. $4.00. National Collegiate Athletic Association, PO Box 1906, Shawnee Mission KS 66222. **Tel** (913)384-3220. **LC** GV563. **DD** 796.06273. The proceedings of the special conventions.

PROCEEDINGS - SPORT B.C., ANNUAL GENERAL MEETING. (PROCEEDINGS - SPORT B. C., ANNUAL GENERAL MEETING). **Main/Corp** Sport B.C. General Meeting. 1978-. 0709-7069. CN. English. an. Sport B C, 1200 Hornby Street, Vancouver British Columbia V6Z 2E2 Canada. **DD** 796.060711. *Proceedings, 0709-7050.*

PROFESSIONAL KARATE. V. 1- Summer 1973-. 0098-0706. US. English. ir. $4.50. Universal Publications of America, 1880 Century Park East/Suite 325, Oklahoma City CA 90067. **LC** GV476. **DD** 796.815305.

THE PROFESSIONAL SKATER. (THE PROFESSIONAL SKATER : A NEWSLETTER OF THE PROFESSIONAL SKATERS GUILD OF AMERICA). **VFOAT** PS Magazine. **VAT** Professional Skaters Magazine. 8750-9369. Periodical. US. English. bm. $12.00. Professional Skaters Guild of America, PO Box 5904, Rochester MN 55903. **Tel** (507)281-5122. Ed Carole Shulman. **DD** 796. bk rev. adv acc. **Circ** 1,200. (ctrl). A newsletter of the Professional Skaters Guild of America. The publication brings technical advice, rule changes, trends, and articles of human interest. *Newsletter (Professional Skaters Guild of America), 0273-5571.*

PROFILE. 1974-. 0095-151X. US. English. an. $1.95. Dell Publishing Company, 10880 Wilshire Boulevard, Los Angeles CA 90024. **LC** GV955.5.N35. **DD** 796.332640973.

PROGRAMME DES ACTIVITES CULTURELLES ET SPORTIVES. (CULTURAL AND SPORTS ACTIVITIES PROGRAM). **Main/Corp** Saint-Laurent (Ile-de-Montreal, Quebec). Fall/Winter/Spring 1983/84-. 0828-5705. Periodical. CN. English (text in French with text on inverted pages). sa. Free. Centre des Loisirs de Saint-Laurent, Sports and Cultural Department, 1870 Decelles Street, Saint Laurent Quebec H4M 1A8 Canada. **DD** 790.0971428. *Programme des Activites Bulturelles et Sportives, 0828-5705.*

PROLOG. 0095-3946. US. English. an. Dell Publishing Company, 10880 Wilshire Boulevard, Los Angeles CA 90024. **LC** GV955.5.N35. **DD** 796.332640973. *Prolog.*

PROPELLER. 0194-6218. Periodical. US. English. mo. $10.00. American Power Boat Association, 17640 East Nine Mile Road Box 377, East Detroit MI 48021. **Tel** (313)375-1907. Ed Hilary R Spittle. adv acc. **Circ** 6,000. Update on American Power Boat Association racing news and technical information. Annual photo issue in November.

PRORODEO SPORTS NEWS. V. 26, No. 11- Apr. 19, 1978-. 0161-5815. Periodical. US. English. bw. $15.00. Professional Rodeo Cowboy Association, 101 Pro Rodeo Drive, Colorado Springs CO 80919. **Tel** (303)593-8840. Ed Karin Morrison. bk rev. adv acc. **Circ** 26,000. Official voice of Pro Rodeo. Inside information on the world's top rodeo cowboys, calendar of upcoming pro contests in US and Canada and information on equipment, etc. *Rodeo Sports News.*

PROSPECTUS - CONCORDES. (PROSPECTUS). **Main/Corp** Concordes (Equipe de Football). 1983-. 0822-5141. CN. French (text in English). an. Free to the Media. Prospectus, c/o Concordes de Montreal, CP 100 Succursale M, Montreal Quebec H1V 3L6 Canada. **DD** 796.3356. (ctrl).

PSE OUTDOOR ADVENTURES BOWHUNTING ANNUAL. *See* Recreation, Leisure - Outdoor Life.

PSYCHOLOGY OF MOTOR BEHAVIOR AND SPORT. *See* Psychology.

QUEBEC SOCCER. **VFOAT** Quebec Soccer Magazine. **VAT** Quebec Soccer Magazine. 0228-6351. Periodical. CN. French (text in English). ir. $10.00. Les Promotions Socbec Inc, 3270 Est rue Belanger, Montreal Quebec H2X 1A1 Canada. **DD** 796.33409714.

QUEST. V. 1- 1963-. 0033-6297. Periodical. US. English. sa. $20.00. Human Kinetics Publishers Inc, Box 5076, Champaign IL 61820. **Tel** (217)351-5076. Ed Wilma Harrington. **Ind/Abst** Coal Abstr., Curr. Index J. Educ., Women Stud. Abstr., Educ. Index, Soc. Sci. Index. **LC** GV201. **DD** 613.705. bk rev. **Circ** 1,400. Contains theoretical and applied articles synthesizing recent research development in the sport sciences and other subdisciplines of human movement.

RACECAR. V. 6, No. 5- May 1979-. 0194-6862. Periodical. US. English. mo. Formula Enterprises, PO Box 305, Dover NJ 07801. **LC** GV1029. **DD** 796.7205. *Formula.*

RACEFORM UP-TO-DATE FORM BOOK. *See* Horses and Horsemanship.

RACER. (THE RACER). V. 1- Nov. 1965-. 0380-7762. Periodical. CN. English (includes some text in French). ir. $1.93. Canadian Amateur Speed Skating, 33 River Road, Vanier Ontario K1L 8B9 Canada.

RACER. (THE RACER). Vol. 1, No. 1- 0826-7111. Periodical. CN. English. sa. $2.95 Each Number. Racer Northwest Publication Ltd, #304/1931 Nelson Street, Vancouver British Columbia V6G 1N3 Canada. **DD** 796.426.

THE RACING PIGEON. V. 1- (No. -). 0033-7390. Periodical. UK. English. wk. $47.50. Racing Pigeon Publishing Company Inc, 19 Doughty Street, London WC1N 2PT England. **Tel** 01 2420565. Ed Cae Osman. bk rev. adv acc. **Circ** 33,000. Care of, keeping, training, and showing racing pigeons.

RACING PIGEON BULLETIN. V. 1- 1946-. 0146-8383. Periodical. US. English. sa. $21.00. Racing Pigeon Bulletin, 34 East Franklin Street, Bellebrook OH 45305. **Tel** (513)848-4972. *Western Racing Pigeon Bulletin, 0195-3249.*

RACING PIGEON PICTORIAL. V. 1- (No. 1-). 0033-7404. Periodical. UK. English. mo. 14.00. Racing Pigeon Publishing Company Ltd, 19 Doughty Street, London WC1N 2PT England. **Tel** 01 242 0565. Ed Cae Osman. bk rev. adv acc. **Circ** 12,000. Care of, keeping, training and showing racing pigeons.

RACQUET (NEW YORK, N.Y. : 1985). (RACQUET). Spring 1985-. 0883-8429. Periodical. US. English. qt. $10.00 Domestic, $13.00 Canada. PO Box 3000, Denville NJ 07834. **DD** 796. *Racquet Quarterly, 0273-9194.*

RACQUET QUARTERLY. 0273-9194. Periodical. US. English. qt. $10.00. Heather & Pine International, 36 East 73rd Street, New York NY 10021. **Tel** (212)988-1065.

RACQUETBALL CEASED. V. 1, No. 1-V. 11, No. 4. 0163-2043. Periodical. US. English. mo. $12.00. International Racquetball Association, 5545 Murray Road, Memphis TN 38117. **LC** GV1017.R3. **DD** 796.34.

RACQUETBALL CANADA (MONTREAL, QUEBEC). (RACQUETBALL CANADA). Winter 1981-. 0229-7396. Periodical. CN. English. qt. $5.00. Harvid Publications Ltd, Suite 430/5180 Queen Mary Road, Montreal Quebec H3W 3E7 Canada. **DD** 796.34. *Racquetball Canada Bulletin, 0226-0069.*

RACQUETS CANADA. V. 1- June 1971-. 0315-3851. Periodical. CN. English. mo. $11.61. Racquets-Canada, 22A Cumberland Street/Suite 203, Toronto Ontario M4W 1JA Canada. **Tel** (416)961-6641.

RALLEY. REGLEMENTS. (RALLYE : REGLEMENTS). **Main/Corp** Federation Auto-Quebec. 0822-529X. CN. French. an. $1.00 Each Number. Federation Auto-Quebec, 1415 Est rue Jarry, Montreal Quebec H2E 2Z7 Canada. **DD** 796.7209714.

RALLY ONTARIO. COMPETITION NEWS. (COMPETITION NEWS). Vol. 1, No. 1 (June 1980)-. 0229-9550. Periodical. CN. English. mo. $3.00. Competition News, c/o B Zambusi, 120 Adelaide Street, Kitchener Ontario N2M 2B6 Canada. **DD** 796.7209713.

RALLY REGULATIONS. **Main/Corp** Canadian Automobile Sport Clubs. 1974/75-. 0381-9493. CN. English. Canadian Automobile Sport Clubs, PO Box 97, Willowdale Ontario M2N 5S7 Canada. **DD** 796.720971.

RALLYE. V. 1- Oct. 1975-. 0363-7697. Periodical. US. English. mo. $10.00. Spectrum IV Corporation, 2880 LBJ Freeway/Suite 243, Dallas TX 75234. **LC** GV1029.2. **DD** 796.72.

RECORDS OF EXOTICS. V. 1- 1976-. 0364-7153. US. English. T B Temple, Box 181, Mountain Home TX 78058. **LC** SK277. **DD** 799.260973.

RECORDS OF SELECTED PLAYERS. **Main/Corp** United States Tennis Association. 0363-8766. US. English. US Tennis Association, 51 East 42nd Street, New York NY 10017. **LC** GV991. **DD** 796.3420212.

REFEREE. V. 1-. 0733-1436. Periodical. US. English. mo. $21.95. Mano Enterprises Inc, PO Box 161, Franksville WI 53126. **Tel** (414)632-8855. Ed Barry Mano. bk rev. adv acc. Rule interpretations and viewpoints, miscellaneous sports, health and feature stories.

REGLEMENT OFFICIEL DE JEU POUR LA LIGUE CANADIENNE DE FOOTBALL. **Main/Corp** Ligue Canadienne de Football. **VFOAT** Reglement Officiel de Jeu du Football Canadien. 1974-. 0316-1536. Periodical. CN. French. an. Free. Ligue Canadienne de Football, 11 Ouest rue King/Bureau 908, Toronto Ontario M5H 1A3 Canada. **DD** 796.33502022. *Reglement Officiel du Jeu pour la Ligue Canadienne de Football et l'Association Canadienne de Football Amateur, 0316-1528.*

REGLEMENTS OFFICIELS - ASSOCIATION CANADIENNE D'ATHLETISME. (REGLEMENTS OFFICIELS). **Main/Corp** Association Canadienne d'Athletisme. **VFOAT** Statuts et Reglements. **VAT** Statuts et Reglements - Association Canadienne d'Athletisme. 0710-4391. CN. French. te. Reglements Officeils Association Canadienne d'Athletisme, 355 Chemin River, Vanier Ontario K1L 8C1 Canada. **DD** 796.4206071. *Manuel Oficiel, Statuts et Reglements, 0381-9701.*

REGLEMENTS OFFICIELS - ASSOCIATION DE SKI NAUTIQUE DE CANADA. (REGLEMENTS OFFICIELS). **Main/Corp** Association de Ski Nautique du Canada. 0714-4806. CN. French. an. A S N C Reglements Officiels, 333 Chemin River, Vanier Canada K1L 8B9 Canada. **DD** 797.17305.

REGLEMENTS OFFICIELS - RINGUETTE CANADA. (REGLEMENTS OFFICIELS). **Main/Corp** Ringuette Canada. 1980/1981-. 0711-0545. CN. French. c/o W Clark, Association Ontarienne de Ringuette, 160 Av Vanderhoof, Toronto Ontario M4G 4B8 Canada. **DD** 796.96.

REGLES DE JEU POUR FOOTBALL AMATEUR CANADIEN. **Main/Corp** Union Sportive Interuniversitaire Canadienne. 1982-. 0820-6651. CN. French. an. $1.50 Per Issue. Regles de Jeu pour Football Amateur Canadien, 11E Etage 333 Chemin River, Vanier Ontario K1L 8B9 Canada. **DD** 796.33502022.

REGULATIONS. SZ. English. be. International Skating Union, Promenade 73 Postfach, CH-7270 Davos Platz Switzerland.

RELATORIO - CONFEDERACAO BRASILEIRA DE FUTEBOL. **Main/Corp** Confederacao Brasileira de Futebol. 1979-. Portuguese. ir. **LC** GV943.55.C66. **DD** 796.3340981. *Relatorio.*

RELATORIO - CONSELHO NACIONAL DE DESPORTOS. **Main/Corp** Brazil. Conselho Nacional de Desportos. Portuguese. ir. **LC** GV597.

RENDEZ-VOUS 76 MONTREAL. 1- Aug. 1973-. 0318-2843. CN. English (French in parallel columns). Free. Organizing Committee of the 1976 Olympic Games, PO Box 1976, Montreal Quebec H3C 3A6 Canada. **DD** 796.48. (ctrl).

RENDEZVOUS & LONGRIFLES. **VAT** Rendezvous and Longrifles. 0828-4725. Periodical. CN. English. $10.00 Domestic, $12.00 US, $15.00 Other Countries. Rendezvous & Longrifles, 1465 Paddington Court, Burlington Ontario L7M 1W7 Canada. **DD** 683.4205.

Recreation, Leisure—Sports

REPERTOIRE D'ADRESSES - CONSEIL SUPERIEUR DU SPORT EN AFRIQUE. See Yearbooks, Almanacs, Directories.

REPORT - INTERNATIONAL CONGRESS ON PHYSICAL EDUCATION AND SPORTS FOR GIRLS AND WOMEN. Main/Conf International Congress on Physical Education and Sports for Girls and Women. VFOAT Heranwachsende Jugend Heute. Monographic Series. UR. English (text in German, and French). ir. LC GV205.

REPORT - NATIONAL ATHLETIC DIRECTORS' CONFERENCE, LOUISVILLE, KY. Main/Conf National Athletic Directors Conference, Louisville, KY. 1st-1959-. 0547-4442. Periodical. English. ir. LC GV205. DD 796.06373.

REPORT OF THE DEPARTMENT OF YOUTH, SPORT AND RECREATION. Main/Corp Victoria. Dept. of Youth, Sport and Recreation. AT. English. ir. $0.20. Department of Youth Sport and Recreation, 23rd Floor 570 Bourke Street, 3000 Melbourne Australia. LC GV153. DD 301.5709945.

REPORT OF THE NCAA FOOTBALL TELEVISION COMMITTEE TO THE ANNUAL CONVENTION OF THE NATIONAL COLLEGIATE ATHLETIC ASSOCIATION. (REPORT OF THE . . . NCAA FOOTBALL TELEVISION COMMITTEE TO THE . . . ANNUAL CONVENTION OF THE NATIONAL COLLEGIATE ATHLETIC ASSOCIATION). Main/Corp NCAA Football Television Committee. VFOAT Report of the NCAA Football Television Committee. 1981-. 0736-5101. US. English. an. $6.00. National Collegiate Athletic Association, Nall Avenue at 63rd Street, PO Box 1906, Shawnee Mission KS 66201. Tel (913)384-3220. LC GV351. DD 070.449796332630973. Television committee report to the annual convention. *Report of the NCAA Television Committee to the . . . Annual Convention.*

REPORT OF THE . . . RACING SEASON - MAINE STATE HARNESS RACING COMMISSION. Main/Corp Maine State Harness Racing Commission. US. English. an. LC SF335.U6. DD 338.477984609741. *Annual Report of the Harness Racing Commission to the Governor of Maine.*

REPORT OF THE . . . SUMMER SESSION OF THE INTERNATIONAL OLYMPIC ACADEMY. Main/Corp International Olympic Academy. Summer Session. Began with: 1st published in 1961. 0538-8910. GR. English (French). an. $5.00. Hellenic Olympic Committee, 4 Kapsali Street, Athens 138 Greece. LC GV3.

REPORT OF THE VIRGINIA ATHLETIC COMMISSION TO THE GOVERNOR OF VIRGINIA. Main/Corp Virginia. Athletic Commission. 0145-8191. US. English. Virginia Athletic Commission, 805 East Broad Street, Richmond VA 23219. LC GV584.V8. DD 796.4061755.

REPORT - OFFICE OF ATHLETIC COMMISSIONER. (REPORT). Main/Corp Nebraska. Office of Athletic Commissioner. 0091-942X. US. English. an. Office of the Athletic Commissioner, Lincoln NE 68508. LC GV1116.U5. DD 353.978200858.

REPRESENTING PROFESSIONAL ATHLETES AND TEAMS. See Law.

RESEARCH QUARTERLY FOR EXERCISE AND SPORT. See Physical Training.

RESEARCH REPORTS - NAGWS. (NAGWS RESEARCH REPORTS). Main/Corp National Association for Girls & Women in Sport. VAT National Association for Girls and Women in Sport Research Reports, Research Reports - National Association for Girls and Women in Sport. 0148-8910. US. English. 1201 Sixteen Street Northwest, Washington DC 20036. LC GV709. DD 796.05.

REVIEW OF SPORT & LEISURE CEASED. VAT Review of Sport and Leisure. Began with V. 1, Fall 1976. Ceased with V. 6, No. 2, Winter 1981?. 0148-2912. Periodical. US. English (French). Ed Benjamin Lowe. LC GV561. DD 796.05.

REVIEW OF THE NEW ZEALAND COUNCIL FOR RECREATION AND SPORT. See Recreation, Leisure.

REVUE DE L'ENTRAINEUR. (LA REVUE DE L'ENTRAINEUR). V. 1- Jan. 1978-. 0705-5625. Periodical. CN. French. qt. 16.00. Coaching Association of Canada, 333 River Road, Ottawa Ontario K1L 8H9 Canada. Tel (514)374-0925. Ed Francois Huot. DD 796.07705. bk rev. adv acc. Circ 2,000. Publishes material on coaching related topics. It is an educational and informational vehicle supplementing programs such as the National Coaching Certification Program. *Bulletin, 0319-0102; Communique, 0318-9562.*

REVUE QUEBECOISE DE L'ACTIVITE PHYSIQUE. See Physical Training.

RIFLE. VFOAT Rifle Magazine. 0162-3583. Periodical. US. English. bm. $16.00. Dave Wolfe Publishing Company, PO Box 3030, Prescott AZ 86301. Tel (602)445-7810. Ed Dave Wolfe. bk rev. adv acc. Circ 25,000. (ctrl). Technical journal of the shooting sports.

RIFLES. VFOAT Shooting Times Rifles. US. English. $3.95. PJS Publications, New Plaza, PO Box 1790, Peoria IL 61656. LC WMLC L 83/285.

RING (NEW YORK, N.Y.). (THE RING). V. 1- Feb. 15, 1922-. 0035-5410. Periodical. US. English. mo. Ring Inc, 130 West 37th Street, New York NY 10018. Tel (212)736-7464. Ed N S Fleischer. LC GV1115.

ROAD & MOTOR SPORT. Began publication in 1965. 0702-7885. Periodical. CN. English. mo. .25 Per No. Road & Motor Sport Magazine, PO Box 264, Burnaby British Columbia Canada. DD 796.7209711.

ROAD & TRACK. VAT Road and Track. V. 1- June 1947-. 0035-7189. Periodical. US. English. mo. CBS Publications, 1515 Broadway, New York NY 10036, (subscription address: Neodata PO Box 2606 Boulder CO 80322). Tel (800)243-8005. Ind/Abst Mag. Index, Pop. Mag. Rev., Consum. Index Prod. Eval. Inf. Source, Read. Guide Period. Lit. LC TL1. DD 796.7205.

ROD ACTION. 0194-7133. Periodical. US. English. mo. $17.50. Challenge Publications, 7950 Deering Avenue, Canoga Park CA 91304. Tel (213)887-0550 Mon-Thurs.

RODEO NEWS. 0149-6425. Periodical. US. English. mo. Rodeo News, PO Box 587, Pauls Valley OK 73075. Tel (405)238-3310.

RODEO SPORTS NEWS. Began in 1953. US. English. LC Microfilm 05498 GV, GV1834.

RODEO TIMES. Vol. 1, No. 1 (Sept. 1980)-. US. English. mo. $12.00. National High School Rodeo Association, Sheraton Plaza, Billings MT 59101. Tel (406)252-7325.

ROTHMANS FOOTBALL YEARBOOK. See Yearbooks, Almanacs, Directories.

THE ROYAL BANGKOK SPORTS CLUB RUGBY MAGAZINE. English. ir.

ROYAL RED BALL OUTDOOR SPORTSMAN. See Recreation, Leisure - Outdoor Life.

RUGBY. 1975. 0162-1297. Periodical. US. English. ir. $19.00. The Rugby Press Ltd, 2414 Broadway, New York NY 10024. Tel (212)787-1160. Ed Ed Hagerty. bk rev. adv acc. Circ 11,000. In-depth coverage of US and international rugby players plus up to date on changes and developments in the game.

RUGBY WORLD. V. 1- Oct. 1960-. 0035-9777. Periodical. UK. English. mo. Business Press International Ltd, Perrymound Road, Hayward Heath West Sussex RH1 63BR England.

RULE BOOK - MIDWEST 4 WHEEL DRIVE ASSOCIATION. (RULE BOOK). Main/Corp Midwest 4 Wheel Drive Association. VFOAT Off-Road Racing Rules and Regulations. VAT Rule Book - Midwest Four Wheel Drive Association. 1981-. 0278-615X. US. English. $2.00. LC GV1029.3. DD 796.72.

RULES AND BY-LAWS - CANADIAN TRACK AND FIELD ASSOCIATION. (RULES AND BY-LAWS). Main/Corp Canadian Track and Field Association. 0710-4383. CN. English. te. Rules and By-Laws, Canadian Track and Field Association, 355 River Road, Vanier Ontario K1L 8C1 Canada. DD 796.4206071. *Official C T F A Rules and Bylaws, 0381-9698.*

RULES AND STANDING ORDERS OF THE INTERNATIONAL TENNIS FEDERATION. Main/Corp International Tennis Federation. UK. English. 1.50. International Tennis Federation, Barons Court, West Kensington London W14 9EG England. LC GV991. DD 796.34202022.

RULES BOOK OF THE FEDERATION OF CANADIAN ARCHERS. Main/Corp Federation of Canadian Archers. 1978-. 0226-773X. CN. English. ir. $1.00 Per Vol. Federation of Canadian Archers, 333 River Road, Vanier Ontario K1L 8B9 Canada. DD 799.320971. *Rules Booklet of the Federation of Canadian Archers, 0318-4250.*

RULES FOR INBOARD, INBOARD ENDURANCE, UNLIMITED RACING. See Boats and Boating.

RULES FOR OUTBOARD PERFORMANCE CRAFT AND DRAG RACING. See Boats and Boating.

RULES FOR STOCK OUTBOARD, PRO OUTBOARD, MODIFIED OUTBOARD. See Boats and Boating.

THE RULES OF GOLF AS APPROVED BY THE UNITED STATES GOLF ASSOCIATION AND THE ROYAL AND ANCIENT GOLF CLUB OF ST. ANDREWS, SCOTLAND. US. English. an. United States Golf Association, Golf House, Far Hills NJ 07931. LC WMLC L 83/960.

RULES OF TENNIS. Main/Corp International Tennis Federation. UK. English. 0.40. International Tennis Federation, Barons Court, West Kensington London W1R 9EG England. LC GV1001. DD 796.34202022.

RULES OF THOROUGHBRED RACING. See Horses and Horsemanship.

THE RUNNER. V. 1- Oct. 1978-. 0149-7316. Periodical. US. English. mo. $18.00 Domestic, $20.00 Canada. The Runner, PO Box 2730, Boulder CO 80322. Ind/Abst Bibliogr. Agric., Pop. Mag. Rev. LC GV1061. DD 796.426.

THE RUNNER YEARBOOK. See Yearbooks, Almanacs, Directories.

THE RUNNER'S ALMANAC USA-CANADA. See Yearbooks, Almanacs, Directories.

RUNNER'S GAZETTE. 1976. 0199-6983. Periodical. US. English. mo. $10.00. Runners Gazette, RD1 Box 223, Lewisburg PA 17837. Tel (717)524-9713. Ed Freddi Carlip. bk rev. adv acc. Circ 6,000. Race coverage of running and triathlons, sportsmedicine features, training techniques, book reviews, and calendar listing of upcoming events.

RUNNER'S WORLD. 0035-9939. Periodical. US. English. ir. $19.95. Rodale Press, 33 E Minor Street/Vern Walther, Emmaus PA 18049. Tel (215)967-5171. Ed Chuck McCullagh. Ind/Abst Mag. Index, Pop. Mag. Rev. LC GV1061. DD 796.426. adv acc. Circ 300,000. A running magazine containing profiles on running personalities, coverage of major races, medical and training advice, diet and nutritional information. *Distance Running News.*

RUNNING & FITNESS. VFOAT Running and Fitness. Vol. 13, No. 5. (Sept./Oct. 1981) – 13th-Years – No. 79-. 0279-2214. Periodical. US. English. bm. $20.00 Domestic, Membership; $30.00 Foreign, Membership. AR & FA, 2420 K Street Northwest, Washington DC 20037. *Jogger, 0164-694X.*

RUNNING IN CONNECTICUT. 1982 Ed.-. 0278-9477. Periodical. US. English. an. $7.95. Waterford Publishing Company, 221 Waterford Parkway North, Waterford CT 06385.

RUNNING TIMES. No. 1- Jan. 1977-. 0147-2968. Periodical. US. English. mo. $17.50. Running Times, 12808 Occoquan Road, Woodbridge VA 22192. Tel (703)491-2044. Ed Ed Ayres. LC GV1061. DD 796.426. bk rev. adv acc. Circ 41,000. News and information on training, injury prevention, and forthcoming road races for recreational and competitive runners. Includes America's most complete calendar of running events.

RUNNING TIMES WEST. VFOAT Running Times. 0271-5465. Periodical. US. English. mo. $12.00. Running Times, 12808 Occoquan Road, Woodbridge VA 22192. LC GV1061. DD 796.426.

RUNNING TIMES YEARBOOK. See Yearbooks, Almanacs, Directories.

Recreation, Leisure—Sports

S I R L S. STANDARD FILE NO. 42. ADOLESCENCE, SPORT AND LEISURE. VFOAT Adolescence, Sport and Leisure. 0380-7622. CN. English. an. 20.00. SIRLS, University of Waterloo, Waterloo Ontario N2L 3G1 Canada. DD 016.30157.

SACRAMENTO SPORTS. VFOAT Sports Magazine. 0746-1585. Periodical. US. English. mo. $8.95. Anpac Publishing Inc, 2414 16th Street, Sacramento CA 59818. *Sacramento Sports News & Calendar Magazine, 0745-1156.*

SAFARI (TUCSON, ARIZ.). (SAFARI). VFOAT Safari Magazine. 0199-5316. Periodical. US. English. bm. $20.00. Safari Club International, 5151 East Broadway, Tucson AZ 84711. Tel (602)745-9109. Ed Bill Quimby. LC SK1. DD 799.2605. bk rev. adv acc. Circ 13,500. (ctrl). Articles reflect sports hunting on a worldwide basis, both from the recreational standpoint, as well as conservation.

SAIL BOARDER. VFOAT Sailboarder. Vol. 1, No. 1 (Dec. 1981)-. 0744-1886. Periodical. US. English. bm. $20.00. Surfer Publishing Inc, PO Box 1028, Dana Point CA 92629. Tel (714)496-5922.

SAMMANFATTNING AV ARTIKLARNA. (SUOMEN RIISTA). 1-. 0491-5585. Fl. Finnish (summaries in English). ir. Academic Bookstore, Box 128, SF-00101 Helsinki 10 Finland. Ind/Abst Life Sci. Collect. LC SK1.

SAN DIEGO SPORTS DIGEST. 0193-7332. Periodical. US. English. mo. San Diego Sports Digest, 3681 Fifth Avenue, San Diego CA 92103. Tel (714)295-1120.

SASKATCHEWAN PLAYER. VFOAT Player. 0824-5878. Periodical. CN. English. mo. $1.50 Single Copies, $12.00 Domestic, $15.00 Foreign. Brigdens Publications, 1150 Eighth Avenue, Regina Saskatchewan S4R 1C9 Canada. DD 796.097124.

SASKATCHEWAN SKI JOURNAL. Began publication in Dec. 1974?. 0228-2143. Periodical. CN. English. ir. $4.00. 413 Hilliard Street East, Saskatoon Saskatchewan S7K 0E7 Canada. Tel (306)653-2765. Ed Dennis Adkin. DD 796.93097124. adv acc. Circ 13,000. (ctrl). Skiing information and advertising of particular interest to Saskatchewan skiers.

SCANDINAVIAN JOURNAL OF SPORTS SCIENCES. V. 1- Aug. 1979-. 0357-5632. Periodical. Fl. English. ir. Finnish Society for Research, Annankatu 4 B/SF-00120, Helsinki 12 Finland. Tel 0-90-640306. Ed Paavo V Komi. Ind/Abst Excerpta Med., Social. Abstr. NLM W1 SC154BM. bk rev. adv acc. Circ 500. (ctrl). Original research in the field of sport and physical education. The scope is interdisciplinary, covering biological as well as social sciences. Special theme issues are also published.

SCHIESSPORTSCHULE DIALOGUES. 1-. 0160-1253. Periodical. US. English. $6.00. Reliable Productions Inc, PO Box 865, Mesa AZ 85201. LC GV1151. DD 799.205.

SCHOLASTIC COACH. VFOAT Coach. Began publication with Sept. 1931 issue. 0036-6382. Periodical. US. English. mo. $17.95. Scholastic Magazines, PO Box 2042, Marbpac NY 10541. Tel (201)505-3418. Ed Herman L Masin. Ind/Abst Educ. Index, Biogr. Index. LC GV561. bk rev. adv acc. Circ 37,000. Microform. Professional journal for high school, college, and recreational athletic directors and coaches. Features technical articles, editorials, and other helpful materials for target audience.

SCHWEIZERISCHE ZEITSCHRIFT FUR SPORTMEDIZIN. VFOAT Revue Suisse de Medecine Sportive, Revista Svizzera di Medicina Sportiva. Began in 1953. 0036-7885. Periodical. SZ. English (contains articles in German, and French). qt. $13.85. Verlag Paul Haupt Bern, Falkenplatz 14, CH-3001 Bern Switzerland. Tel 031-23-24-25. Ed Paul Haupt Bern. Ind/Abst Excerpta Med., Index Med. LC RC1200. NLM W1 SC612. bk rev. adv acc. Deals with sports-medicine.

THE SCI RECORD BOOK OF TROPHY ANIMALS. See Recreation, Leisure - Outdoor Life.

SCIENCE DU SPORT. 0822-6792. Periodical. CN. French. mo. Association Canadienne des Entraineurs, 333 Chemin River, Ottawa Ontario K1L 8B9 Canada. DD 613.7105.

SCORE. (SCORE : CANADA'S GOLF MAGAZINE). No. 1 (Apr./May 1981)-. 0711-3226. Periodical. CN. English. $13.93. Control Media Communication, 43 Madison Avenue, Toronto Ontario M5R 2S2 Canada. Tel (416)961-5141. DD 796.3520971.

THE SCOUTING REPORT. (THE SCOUTING REPORT : AN IN-DEPTH ANALYSIS OF THE STRENGTHS AND WEAKNESSES OF EVERY ACTIVE MAJOR LEAGUE BASEBALL PLAYER). 1st Ed. (1983)-. 0743-1309. US. English. an. Harper & Row Publishers, 10 East 53rd Street, New York NY 10022. LC GV877. DD 796.3570922.

SCOUT'S NOTEBOOK. 0883-4466. US. English. $12.95. Pro Football Weekly Inc, 2501 West Peterson Avenue, Chicago IL 60659.

SCWDC. VAT Ski Club of Washington, D.C. 0883-6817. Periodical. US. English. mo. Ski Club of Washington DC (SCWDC), 5309 Lee Highway, Arlington VA 22207.

SEA (LOS ANGELES, CALIF.). (SEA). VFOAT Sea Magazine. 0746-8601. Periodical. US. English. mo. $15.95 Domestic, $21.94 Foreign. Sea Magazine, PO Box 2522, Los Angeles CA 90078. Ind/Abst Pop. Mag. Rev. LC GV811.8. DD 797.105. *Sea & Pacific Skipper, 0274-905X.*

SEC SPORTS JOURNAL. VAT Southeastern Conference Sports Journal. 0279-8646. Periodical. US. English. ir. South Sports, PO Box 59238, Birmingham AL 35259. Tel (205)871-8398. *Sports Page, 0194-1984.*

SELECTION DE PRESSE - CLUB MULTI-SPORTS INTERNATIONAL DE MONTREAL. (SELECTION DE PRESSE). VFOAT Selection de Presse (Quotidiens et Hebdomadaires). May 1979/June 1980-. 0226-8728. CN. French. an. Club Multi-Sports International de Montreal, C P 1976 Succursale St Michel, Montreal Quebec H2A 2M3 Canada. DD 796.09714.

SEMANARIO DEPORTIVO LPV. VAT Semanario Deportivo Listos Para Vencer. Spanish. ir. $0.15 Single Issue. Inder, Apartado 5104, La Habana Cuba. LC GV592.C9.

SENTIER CHASSE-PECHE. See Recreation, Leisure - Outdoor Life.

SERVO LOISIR. V. 1- Jan. 1972-. 0380-3082. Periodical. CN. French. bm. Free to members of the Council. Conseil Regional des Loisirs de Quebec, Bureau 300 917 rue Mgr Grandin, Ste-Foy Quebec G1V 3X8 Canada. DD 790.0971447.

SFI BULLETIN. VFOAT Sport Fishing Institute Bulletin. Began with No. 101 (April 1960). 0085-6592. Periodical. US. English. mo. $10.00. Sport Fishing Institute, 1010 Massachusetts Avenue NW/Suite 100, Washington DC 20001. Tel (202)898-0770. Ed Gilbert Radonski. bk rev. Circ 15,000. Articles. *Bulletin - Sport Fishing Institute, 0097-0492.*

THE SHOOTER'S BIBLE. No. 44- 1953- Ed. 0080-9365. US. English. an. $15.95. Stoeger Publishing Company, 55 Ruta Court, South Hackensack NJ 07606. Ed John Olson. LC TS535. DD 683. *Stoeger's Catalog and Handbook.*

SHOOTING SPORTSMAN. V. 1- April 1978-. 0164-7881. Periodical. US. English. mo. $3.50 Members, $6.75 Nonmembers and Out-of-State. Shooting Sportsman, PO Box 1376, Eugene OR 97440.

SHOOTING TIMES. Began with Mar. 1960 issue. 0038-8084. Periodical. US. English. mo. PJS Publications Inc, PO Box 1790, News Plaza, Peoria IL 61656, (subscription address: Communication Data Services 110 Tenth Street Des Moines IA 50309). Tel (309)682-6626. Ind/Abst Consum. Index Prod. Eval. Inf. Source. LC GV1151.

SHOOTING TIMES MAGNUM BUYER'S GUIDE. VFOAT Magnum Buyer's Guide. 0883-5942. US. English. $3.95 Single Issue. PJS Publications, News Plaza, PO Box 1790, Peoria IL 61656.

SHOTGUN SPORTS. Vol. 4, No. 1 (Feb. 1982)-. 0744-3773. Periodical. US. English. mo. Shotgun Sports, 2500 A Valley Road, Reno NV 89512. *Shootin' Trap, 0194-665X.*

S.H.S.A.A. DIRECTORY OF SCHOOLS. See Yearbooks, Almanacs, Directories.

SHUTTLE. (THE SHUTTLE : NEWSLETTER OF THE SASKATCHEWAN BADMINTON ASSOCIATION). Feb. 1982-. 0712-5801. Periodical. CN. English. ir. Free to Members. Saskatchewan Badminton Association, 2205 Victoria Avenue, Regina Saskatchewan S4P 0S4 Canada. DD 796.345097124. *Newsletter, 0227-6704.*

SICHERHEIT IM BERGLAND. See Recreation, Leisure - Outdoor Life.

SIGNPOST FOR NORTHWEST HIKERS. 1966. 0583-2594. Periodical. US. English. mo. $20.00. Signpost, 16812 36th Avenue West, Lynwood WA 98036. Tel (206)743-3947. Ed Ann Marshall. bk rev. adv acc. Circ 4,000. (ctrl). The oldest general circulation periodical in the hiking/backpacking/ski touring field, serving the Northwest outdoors community with updates, reports, trail information and tips.

SIRLS. STANDARD FILE NO. 36. NATIONAL & CULTURAL PERSPECTIVES IN SPORT & LEISURE. (S I R L S. STANDARD FILE NO. 36. NATIONAL & CULTURAL PERSPECTIVES IN SPORT & LEISURE). VFOAT National & Cultural Perspectives in Sport & Leisure. 0708-7284. Periodical. CN. English. SIRLS, University of Waterloo, Faculty of Human Kinetics, Waterloo Ontario N2L 3G1 Canada. DD 016.30157. *S I R L S. Standard File No. 36. Leisure and Sport in a Cross-National and Cross-Cultural Perspective, 0380-7568.*

SIRLS. STANDARD FILE NO. 39. HISTORY OF SPORT & LEISURE. ANCIENT & MEDIEVAL. (S I R L S. STANDARD FILE NO. 39. HISTORY OF SPORT & LEISURE, ANCIENT & MEDIEVAL). 0708-7268. Periodical. CN. English. SIRLS, University of Waterloo, Faculty of Human Kinetics, Waterloo Ontario N2L 3G1 Canada. DD 016.30157. *SIRLS. Standard File No. 39. Socio-History of Sport and Leisure in Ancient and Medieval Times, 0380-7592.*

SKATE. 1937. 0037-6124. Periodical. US. English. qt. $8.00. Roller Skating Rink Open Association, Box 81846, Lincoln NE 68501. Tel (402)489-8811. Ed Nance Kirk. bk rev. adv acc. Circ 10,000. A-color magazine featuring competitive roller skating news for US amateur atheletes.

SKEET SHOOTING REVIEW. Began in 1947. 0037-6140. Periodical. US. English. mo. National Skeet Shooting Association, PO Box 28188, San Antonio TX 78228. LC GV1181. DD 799.31305.

THE SKEETER. 0745-8517. Periodical. US. English. bm. The Skeeter, PO Box 11789, Fresno CA 93775-1789. DD 799.

SKI AREA MANAGEMENT. See Business - General Management.

SKI CANADA JOURNAL. V. 1-4, No. 6. 0316-2648. Periodical. CN. English. ir. 12.00. MacLean Hunter-Circulation & Accounting Department, PO Box 100 Station A, Toronto Ontario M5W 1A7 Canada. Tel (416)596-5038. Ed Clive Hobson. adv acc. Circ 56,000. (ctrl). Canada's leading ski magazine for both downhill and cross country skiers. Covers racing, travel, skiing personalities and our own on-slope testing.

SKI CANADA NAUTIQUE CEASED. V. 1-21, No. 3. 0315-3665. Periodical. CN. English (includes some text in French). qt. 333 River Road, Place Vanier K1L 8B9 Canada.

SKI INDUSTRY BULLETIN. VFOAT Bulletin de l'Industrie du Ski. 0229-1940. Periodical. CN. English (text in French, Jan. 1973-Dec. 1982). ir. Free. National Ski Industries Association, 306A Youville Square, Montreal Quebec H2Y 2B6 Canada. DD 338.47796930971. (ctrl).

THE SKI INDUSTRY LETTER. 0197-3479. Periodical. US. English. bw. $96.00. Sport Letters Inc, 180 Cook Street, Denver CO 80206.

SKI NAUTIQUE NEWS. Feb. 1982-. 0714-8267. Periodical. CN. English (French). ty. Free. Ski Nautique News c/o CWSA, 333 River Road, Vanier Ontario K1L 8B9 Canada. DD 797.1730971. (ctrl). *Ski Canada Nautique, 0315-3665.*

SKI PRO. VFOAT Ski Pro. No. 1- Nov. 1976-. 0703-914X. Periodical. CN. English (French text on inverted pages). bm. Free. Ski Pro, Suite 350/3300 Cavendish Boulevard, Montreal Quebec H4B 2M8 Canada. DD 796.930971. (ctrl).

SKI QUEBEC. Premiere Edition in 1974?. 0703-2056. Periodical. CN. French. ir. $5.00. Publisysteme Inc 660, rue Deslauriers, Saint-Laurent Quebec H4N Canada. DD 796.9305.

Recreation, Leisure—Sports

SKI RACING. 1968. 0037-6213. Periodical. US. English. ir. $30.00. Ski Racing, 2 Bentley Avenue, Poultney VT 05764. Tel (802)287-9090. Ed Don A Metivier. bk rev. adv acc. Circ 30,000. (ctrl). Ski competition-travel coverage world wide.

SKI RACING REDBOOK. 0091-1461. US. English. an. $1.00. Paper House Inc, 1801 York Street, Denver CO 80206. LC GV854.9.R3. DD 796.93.

SKI REVY. 1978-. Periodical. Norwegian. ir. LC GV854.A1.

SKI RUN. 0195-5640. Periodical. US. English. bm. Free. Ski Run, 115 Mission Street, San Francisco CA 94112.

SKI TRAILS (VANCOUVER, B.C. : CA. 1978). (SKI TRAILS). 0710-0523. Periodical. CN. English. mo. $.50 Each Number. Raipub Enterprises, 726 Richards, Vancouver British Columbia V6B 3L2 Canada. DD 796.9309711. *Ski Trails West, 0381-8675.*

SKI X-C. VFOAT Ski XC. VAT Ski Cross-Country. 1978-79-. 0161-1054. US. English. sa. Ziff-Davis Publishing Company, One Park Avenue, New York NY 10016. LC GV855. DD 796.93.

SKIERS ADVOCATE. 0195-1300. Periodical. US. English. qt. $6.00. American Ski Association, 155 South Madison Street, Denver CO 80209. Tel (303)399-9924.

SKIERS DIRECTORY. See Yearbooks, Almanacs, Directories.

SKIER'S HOLIDAY GUIDE. UK. English. 1.20. Ski Specialists, 4 Douro Place, London W8 5PH England. LC GV854.8.E9. DD 796.930254.

SKIEUR NAUTIQUE. (LE SKIEUR NAUTIQUE : PUBLICATION OFFICIELLE DE LA FEDERATION QUEBECOISE DE SKI NAUTIQUE). 0229-0596. Periodical. CN. French. qt. Free to Members, $10.00 Others. Federation Quebecoise de Ski Nautique, 1415 Est Jarry, Montreal Quebec H2E 2Z7 Canada. DD 797.17309714.

SKIING. Began with V. 11, No. 1, Oct. 1958. 0037-6264. Periodical. US. English. mo. $10.00. CBS Publications, 1515 Broadway, New York NY 10036, (subscription address: Neodata PO Box 2606 Boulder CO 80322). Tel (212)719-6000. Ind/Abst Pop. Mag. Rev., Consum. Index Prod. Eval. Inf. Source, Read. Guide Period. Lit., Mag. Index. LC GV854.A1. DD 796.9305.

SKIING TRADE NEWS. V. 1- Sept. 1964-. US. English. an. $8.00. CBS Publications, 1515 Broadway, New York NY 10036. LC GV854.A1. DD 796.9305. *Wintersports.*

SKIN DIVER. VFOAT Skin Diver Magazine. V. 1- Dec. 1951-. 0037-6345. Periodical. US. English. mo. $15.94. Petersen Publishing Company, 6725 Sunset Boulevard, Los Angeles CA 90028. Tel (213)657-5100. Ed Bill Gleason. Ind/Abst Mag. Index, Pop. Mag. Rev., Consum. Index Prod. Eval. Inf. Source. LC SH458. adv acc. Circ 209,600. Worldwide coverage of underwater recreation, including scuba techniques, underwater photography, new products and more.

SKYDIVING. V. 1- 1979-. 0192-7361. Periodical. US. English. mo. $20.00. c/o Michael F Truffer, PO Box 1520, Deland FL 32721. Tel (904)736-9779. Ed Michael Truffer. bk rev. adv acc. Circ 7,200. (ctrl). A news magazine that covers the techniques, equipment, places, events and people of parachuting.

SLOWBALL CANADA. (SLOW PITCH RULES). Main/Corp Softball Canada. VFOAT Reglements de Balle Lente. VAT Softball Canada Slow Pitch Rules. 1980-. 0229-1452. CN. English (French). Softball Canada, 355 River Road, Vanier Ontario K1L 8C1 Canada. DD 796.3578.

SNIPES JOURNAL. VFOAT S.N.I.P.E.S. Journal. VAT Society for the National Institutes of Physical Education and Sports Journal. Began With: Vol. 1, in Jan. 1978. 0253-6706. Periodical. II. English. qt. $15.00. Netaji Subhas National Institute of Sports, Moti Bagh Patiala 147 001 India. Tel 74070. Ed R L Anand. NLM W1 S49. bk rev. adv acc. Circ 3,000. Researched articles by well-known sports scientists and coaches are published in the journal each quarter. The journal is well-received in India and abroad.

SNOMAN. 0712-256X. Periodical. CN. English. mo. Free. Snoman Inc, Box 1577, Winnipeg Manitoba R3C 2Z4 Canada. DD 796.94097127.

SNOWMOBILE. V. 1- Aug./Sept. 1980-. 0274-8363. Periodical. US. English. qt. $7.00. Winter Sports Publishing, 11812 Wayzata Boulevard, Suite 100, Minnetonka MN 55343. Tel (612)545-2662. *Snotrack, 0049-0822; Midwest Snowmobiler, 0195-1203.*

SNOWMOBILE ANNUAL. 1974/75-. 0700-3315. CN. English. an. Leisure Publications, 105 1255 Yonge Street, Toronto Ontario M4T 1W6 Canada. DD 796.9. *Snowmobile, 0700-3307.*

SNOWMOBILE SPORTS. V. 1- Sept. 1977 -. 0704-7339. Periodical. CN. English. sa. Leisure Publications, 1255 Yonge Street/Suite 105, Toronto Ontario M4T 1W6 Canada. Tel (416)922-7197. Ed Rob Johnson. DD 796.9. adv acc. Circ 62,290. (ctrl). Listing of all new snowmobiles and ATV's sold in Canada. Includes current prices, specs, photos, articles and tips for the snowmoblier.

SOCCER. Main/Corp Saskatchewan High Schools Athletic Association. 0704-4976. CN. English. an. Free. Saskatchewan High Schools Athletic Association, 2220 College Avenue, Regina Saskatchewan S4P 3V7 Canada. DD 796.334097124.

SOCCER AMERICA. V. 1- 1971-. 0163-4070. Periodical. US. English. wk. $32.00. Soccer America Weekly, PO Box 23704, Oakland CA 94623. Tel (415)549-1414. Ed Lynn Berling-Manvel. adv acc. Circ 12,000. For the soccer enthusiast covering the NISL, outdoor pros, college, amateur and international games. Stories, features, stats, playing and coaching tips and much more. *Soccer West.*

SOCCER CANADA. VAT Soccer (Toronto). V. 1- Apr. 1980-. 0227-1834. Periodical. CN. English. ir. $7.00 US, Canada, $8.50 others. Soccer Canada, 49 Saint Nicholas Street, Toronto Ontario M4Y 1W6 Canada. DD 796.3340971. *Canadian Soccer News, 0319-4469.*

SOCCER DIGEST. 0149-2365. Periodical. US. English. bm. $7.95. Soccer Digest, PO Box 3300, Comm Data Services, Harlan IA 51537. Tel (312)491-6440. Ed Michael Herbert. LC GV942. DD 796.33405. bk rev. adv acc. Circ 60,000. Covers indoor and world cup soccer.

SOCCER ILLUSTRATED (TORONTO, ONT.). (SOCCER ILLUSTRATED). Vol. 1, No. 9 (Nov. 1980)-. 0710-2577. Periodical. CN. English. mo. $30.18. Soccer Illustrated, 69 Belgrave Avenue, Toronto Ontario M5M 3S9 Canada. DD 796.3340971. *Soccer in Canada, 0710-2585.*

SOCCER JOURNAL. 0560-3617. Periodical. US. English. bm. $25.00. National Soccer Coaches Association of America, c/o Editor Tim Schum West Gym SUNY Binghamton, Binghamton NY 103901. Tel (607)777-2133. Ed Tim Schum. bk rev. adv acc. Circ 4,000. (ctrl). Information about and for soccer coaches. Contains technical pieces on soccer coaching plus information also on activities of the NSCAA.

SOCCER MATCH. 0744-964X. Periodical. US. English. sm. $9.50. Soccer Match, 302 South Brand Boulevard/Suite 1, Glendale CA 91204. Tel (213)240-0461.

SOCCER MONTHLY CEASED. Began in 1974? Ceased in 1983. 0194-7591. Periodical. US. English. mo.

SOCCER (OTTAWA, ONT.). (SOCCER). 82-. 0713-8423. CN. French. an. $4.95 Each Number. Soccer c/o Edicompo, Bureau 104, 1207 rue Saint-Andre, Montreal Quebec H2L 3S8 Canada. DD 796.33406.

SOCCER RULE BOOK. Main/Corp National Federation of State High School Associations. Began with 1979/80 vol. 0731-9541. US. English. an. National Federation of State High School Associations, 11724 Plaza Circle, PO Box 20626, Kansas City MO 64195. LC GV943.4. DD 796.33402022. *Soccer Rules, 0163-4763.*

SOCCER TEXAS. Vol. 1, No. 1 (Mar. 1985)-. 0882-9632. Periodical. US. English. mo. $3.00. Texas Sports Marketing, 13650 Rolling Hill, Dallas TX 75240.

SOCCER WORLD. VFOAT Soccer World Magazine. Began in 1974. 0098-8707. Periodical. US. English. mo. $7.50. Runner's World Magazine Company, 1400 Stierlin Road, Mountain View CA 94042. LC GV942. DD 796.33405.

SOCIOLOGY OF SPORT JOURNAL. Vol. 1, No. 1 (1984)-. 0741-1235. Periodical. US. English. qt. $48.00 Domestic, $52.00 Foreign. Human Kinetics Publishers Inc, Box 5076, Champaign IL 61820. Tel (217)351-5076. Ed Jay J Coakley. DD 306. bk rev. adv acc. Circ 495. Journal focusing on the understanding of human behavior within the context of sport and physical activity.

SOFTBALL GUIDE. 1939-. US. English. ir. American Association for Health Physical Education and Recreation, Division for Girls and Women's Sports, 1201 Sixteenth Street NW, Washington DC 20036. *Softball, Track and Field Guide.*

SOFTBALL RULE BOOK. Main/Corp National Federation of State High School Associations. VFOAT Softball Rule Book for 12-Inch Fast Pitch and 12-Inch Slow Pitch. 0732-2844. US. English. an. $2.50. National Federation of State High School Associations, 11724 Plaza Circle, Box 20626, Kansas City MO 64195. Tel (816)464-5400. Ed Bradley A Rumble. LC GV881. DD 796.3578. adv acc. Circ 55,000. The official rules for high school softball. *Softball Rules, 0146-8286.*

SOFTBALL RULES. Main/Corp Softball Canada. VFOAT Official Softball Rules, Reglements de Softball. 1979-. 0228-9644. CN. English (French). an. Softball Canada, 355 River Road, Vanier Ontario K1L 8C1 Canada. DD 796.3578.

SOLO EVENT REGULATIONS. Main/Corp Canadian Automobile Sport Clubs. VFOAT CASC Solo Event Regulations. VAT CASC Solo Event Regulations (1984), Canadian Automobile Sport Clubs Solo Event Regulations (1984). 1984-. 0828-6108. CN. English. an. $3.00 Each Volume. Canadian Automobile Sport Clubs National Office, Suite 213/5385 Yonge Street, Willowdale Ontario M2N 5R7 Canada. DD 796.720971. *C.A.S.C. Solo Events Regulations, 0382-0092.*

SOLO. REGLEMENTS. (SOLO : REGLEMENTS). Main/Corp Federation Auto-Quebec. 0822-5303. CN. French. an. $1,00 Each Volume. Federation Auto-Quebec, 1415 Est rue Jarry, Montreal Quebec H2E 2Z7 Canada. DD 796.7209714.

SOUTH CAROLINA TENNIS MAGAZINE. Vol. 1, No. 1 (Apr. 1982)-. 0744-6195. Periodical. US. English. qt. $5.00. Professional Publishing Company, 3020 Devine Street, Columbia SC 29205.

SOUTHERN CALIFORNIA TENNIS TALK & RACQUETBALLREPORT. VFOAT Tennis Talk & Racquetball Report. VAT Southern California Tennis Talk and Racquetball Report. 0199-7467. Periodical. US. English. mo. $6.00. Charles Roberts Publications Inc, 4707A la Villa Marina, Marina del Rey CA 90291. Tel (213)821-6268.

SOUTHERN GOLF. 0146-8251. Periodical. US. English. bm. $9.00. Southern Golf, PO Drawer 77, Elm Grove WI 53122. Tel (813)796-3877. LC GV975. DD 338.477963520975. *Southern Golf Course Operations for the Bermudagrass Belt, 0145-4196; Southern Landscape & Turf, 8755-2256.*

SOUTHERN MOTORACING. See Motorcycles.

SOUTHERN OUTDOORS. See Recreation, Leisure - Outdoor Life.

SOUTHERN RUNNER. 0744-3439. Periodical. US. English. bm. Greater New Orleans Runners Association Inc, PO 6524, Metairie LA 70009.

SOVIET SPORTS REVIEW. Began in Mar. 1979. 0275-598X. Periodical. US. English (Russian). qt. $49.00. Soviet Sports Review, PO Box 2878, Escondido CA 92025. Tel (619)480-0558. Ed Michael Yessis. LC GV201. DD 613.707. Circ 1,000. Sports training articles translated directly from the Russians specializing in weightlifting, sports medicine, track and field athletes, coaches and medical personnel. *Yessis Review of Soviet Physical Education and Sports, 0513-5389.*

SPEEDWAY SCENE. 0747-5403. Periodical. US. English. wk. $25.00. Speedway Scene, Box 300, North Easton MA 02356-0300. Tel (617)238-7797. Ed Val LeSievr. adv acc. The most comprehensive north east also Winston Cup racing world of outlaws, ASA and other top racing organizations covered fifty two weeks.

SPIN. (SPIN : OFFICIAL MAGAZINE OF THE U.S. TABLE TENNIS ASSOCIATION). VFOAT Spin Magazine. Vol. 1, No. 1 (July-Aug. 1983)-. 0746-1801. Periodical. US. English. mo. $12.00. USTTA Olympic House, 1750 East Boulder Street, Colorado Springs CO 80909. Tel (303)632-5551. adv acc. Circ 6,000. (ctrl). Competitive table tennis, national and international level, player profiles, coaching articles, tournament results. *Table Tennis Topics (1978), 0273-8538.*

Recreation, Leisure—Sports

SPITBALL. See Literature.

SPORT. German. ir. LC GV607.

SPORT. Vol.1 (Sept. 1946)-. 0038-7436. Periodical. US. English. mo. $12.00. Charter Data Services, 119 West 40th Street Floor #2, New York NY 10018. **Tel** (212)869-4700. Ed David Bauer. adv acc. **Circ** 932,000. Provides the best in sports journalism. Features range from monthly interviews to in-depth stories to picks, predictions, and previews. Teaches our readers to watch sports with an educated eye.

SPORT AEROBATICS. 0161-5351. Periodical. US. English. mo. $25.00. Experimental Aircraft Association Inc, Wittman Airfield, Oshkosh WI 54903. Tel (414)426-4800. LC TL711.S8. DD 797.5405.

SPORT ALBERTA NEWS. V. 1- June 7, 1974-. 0700-9046. Periodical. CN. English. bw. $6.00. Sport Alberta News, PO Box 3950 Station B, Calgary Alberta T2M 4M5 Canada. DD 796.097123.

THE SPORT AMERICANA BASEBALL CARD PRICE GUIDE. See Hobbies.

THE SPORT AMERICANA BASEBALL MEMORABILIA AND AUTOGRAPH PRICE GUIDE. VFOAT Baseball Memorabilia and Autograph Price Guide. No. 1-. 0738-1212. US. English. $8.95. Den's Collectors Den, PO Box 606, Laurel MD 20707. LC GV875.2. DD 769.497963570973.

THE SPORT AMERICANA FOOTBALL, HOCKEY, BASKETBALL, AND BOXING CARD PRICE GUIDE. VFOAT Football, Hockey, Basketball, and Boxing Card Price Guide. No. 2-. 0732-1775. US. English. an. $8.95. Den's Collectors Den, PO Box 606, Laurel MD 20810. LC GV959. DD 769.49796. *Sport Americana Football & Basketball Card Price Guide, 0270-224X.*

SPORT AND FITNESS INDEX. See Indexes/Abstracts.

SPORT AND RECREATION INDEX. See Indexes/Abstracts.

SPORT AUTO. Began in 1969. Periodical. German. mo. 54.60. Vereinigte Motor Verlag GMBH & Company, KG Postfach 1042, D7000 Stuttgart 1 West Germany. LC GV1029. DD 796.7205.

SPORT AVIATION. See Aeronautics, Astronautics.

SPORT EN CAPSULES. (LE SPORT EN CAPSULES : BULLETIN D'INFORMATION SPORTIVE DU CONSEIL DES LOISIRS DE L'EST DU QUEBEC). 0227-4396. Periodical. CN. French. bw. Free. C.L.E.Q., 100 Ouest rue de l'Eveche, Rimouski Quebec G5L 4H7 Canada. DD 796.097147. (ctrl)

SPORT FLYER. 4th year, No. 10 (Jan. 1985)-. 8750-8117. Periodical. US. English. mo. $9.00. Sport Flyer, PO Box 98786, Tacoma WA 98499. **Tel** (206)588-1743. Ed Bruce Williams. bk rev. adv acc. **Circ** 25,000. (ctrl). For enthusiasts of sport-recreational flying, including ballooning, ultralights, homebuilt, kites, etc. News articles report on new products, safety tips, competitions and people. *Ultralight Flyer, 0279-0181.*

SPORT HEALTH : OFFICIAL GAZETTE OF AUSTRALIAN SPORTS MEDICINE FEDERATION. See Medicine.

SPORT IN THE USSR. VAT Sport in the Union of Soviet Socialist Republics. Began in 1963. 0038-7908. Periodical. UR. English. mo. Sport in the USSR 70903. LC GV561.

SPORT LONDON. Vol. 1, No. 1 (Tue. Aug. 1, 1978)-. 0229-2475. Periodical. CN. English. wk. $12.00. Sport London, 370 Queen's Avenue, London Ontario N6B 1Y6 Canada. DD 796.0971326.

SPORT MEDICINE DIRECTORY. See Yearbooks, Almanacs, Directories.

SPORT ONTARIO DIRECTORY OF SPORTS, RECREATION AND PHYSICAL EDUCATION. See Yearbooks, Almanacs, Directories.

SPORT ONTARIO NEWS. V. 1- June 1972-. 0707-1906. Periodical. CN. English. bm. Free. Sport Ontario, 559 Jarvis Street, Toronto Ontario M4Y 2J1 Canada. DD 796.09713.

SPORT PARACHUTIST. Periodical. UK. English. bm. $6.89. British Parachute Association, Kimberley House, 47 Vaughn Way, Leicester LEF 4SG England. LC GV770.

SPORT PRESTIGE. 1st Year, No. 1 (1 Nov. 1979)-. 0227-7417. Periodical. CN. French. wk. Free. Journal Sport Prestige, 251 St-Georges, St-Jerome Quebec J7Z 5A1 Canada. DD 796.0971424.

SPORT QUEBEC. Oct. 1970-. 0700-8791. Periodical. CN. French. ir. Service des Communications de la Confederation des Sports du Quebec, 1415 East rue Jarry, Montreal Quebec H2E 2Z7 Canada. DD 796.09714005.

SPORT SCENE. Vol. 1, No. 1 (Dec. 1979)-. 0270-1812. Periodical. US. English. qt. $24.00. Sport Scene, 4985 Oak Garde Drive, Kernersville NC 27284. **Tel** (919)784-4926. Ed Jack Hutslar. bk rev acc. **Circ** 15,000. (ctrl). For parents, youth, coaches and others interested in sports and recreation in education. Focus is on kids, their programs and how adults can work with them in a positive, safe manner.

SPORT SOCIOLOGY BULLETIN. V. 1- Spring 1972-. 0163-187X. Periodical. US. English. sa. Governors State University, Park Forest South IL 60466. LC GV706.5. DD 301.57.

SPORT STYLE. See Clothing and Fashion.

SPORTHIRADO. VFOAT Sport News. Began publication in Dec. 1954. 0702-5033. Periodical. CN. Hungarian. mo. $27.09. Sporthirado Green Meadows, 110 Unity Road/Apt 210, Toronto Ontario M4J 4A9 Canada. **Tel** (416)461-2623. Ed Gary Super. adv acc. **Circ** 3,200. (ctrl). *Sportes Tarsadalmi Hirado, 0702-5041.*

SPORTING CLASSICS. Vol. 1, No. 1-. 0279-0998. Periodical. US. English. bm. $17.95. Sporting Classics, PO Box 1017, Camden SC 29020. **Tel** (803)425-1003. Ed John Culler. bk rev. adv acc. **Circ** 80,000,000. Rapidly becoming America's highest quality hunting and fishing magazine.

SPORTING GOODS AND TOY INDUSTRY. Main/Corp Canada. Dominion Bureau of Statistics. Industry Division. **Series/Titl** Annual Census of Manufactures. 1961-1964. 0575-979X. Periodical. CN. English. an. 20.00 Domestic, 21.00 Foreign. Receiver General for Canada, Statistics Canada Publications, Ottawa Ontario K1A 0T6 Canada. *Sporting Goods and Toy Industry, 0575-979X.*

SPORTING GOODS BUYERS. See Business - Purchasing.

SPORTING GOODS CANADA CEASED. V. 1-9, No. 6. 0381-8977. Periodical. CN. English. bm.

SPORTING GOODS CANADA. DIRECTORY ISSUE. See Yearbooks, Almanacs, Directories.

THE SPORTING GOODS MARKET. (THE SPORTING GOODS MARKET IN . . .). 0193-8401. US. English. an. $95.00. National Sporting Goods Association, 1699 Wall Street, Mt Prospect IL 60056. **Tel** (312)439-4000. LC HD9992.U5. DD 381.4568870973.

SPORTING GOODS REGISTER. (THE SPORTING GOODS REGISTER.) 0363-1478. US. English. an. Sporting Goods Dealer, PO Box 56, St Louis MO 63166. LC HD9992 .U5. DD 380.1456887602573.

SPORTING GOODS TRADE CEASED. V. 1-10, No. 1. 0381-9280. Periodical. CN. English.

SPORTING LIFE (WESTMOUNT, QUEBEC). (SPORTING LIFE). Vol. 1, No. 1 (Feb./Mar. 1984)-. 0826-5992. Periodical. CN. English. bm. $2.50 Each Number. Sporting Life, 4827-A St Catherine Street West, Westmount Quebec H3Z 1S9 Canada. DD 796.0971.

THE SPORTING NEWS. 0038-805X. Periodical. US. English. wk. $138.85. Sporting News, 1212 North Lindbergh Boulevard, St Louis MO 63166, (subscription address: Fulfillment Corporation of America 205 West Center Street Marion OH 43302). **Tel** (314)997-7111. Ind/Abst Access, Mag. Index.

THE SPORTING NEWS BASEBALL YEARBOOK. See Yearbooks, Almanacs, Directories.

THE SPORTING NEWS COLLEGE AND PRO BASKETBALL YEARBOOK. See Yearbooks, Almanacs, Directories.

THE SPORTING NEWS COLLEGE FOOTBALL YEARBOOK. See Yearbooks, Almanacs, Directories.

SPORTING NEWS' NATIONAL FOOTBALL GUIDE CEASED. (THE SPORTING NEWS' NATIONAL FOOTBALL GUIDE). VFOAT National Football Guide. 0081-3788. US. English. an. $3.00. 1212 North Lindbergh Boulevard, St Louis MO 63166. LC GV955. DD 796.332640973.

THE SPORTING NEWS OFFICIAL BASEBALL RECORD BOOK CEASED. VFOAT Official Baseball Record Book. 0162-5438. US. English. an. $8.95. The Sporting News, Box 44, St Louis MO 63166. **Tel** (314)997-7111. League records, team records, career records, historic firsts in baseball.

THE SPORTING NEWS PRO FOOTBALL YEARBOOK. See Yearbooks, Almanacs, Directories.

THE SPORTING NEWS SUPER BOWL BOOK. (SUPER BOWL BOOK). VFOAT Sporting News Super Bowl Book. 1981-. 0275-4487. US. English. an. $9.95. Sporting News Publishing Company, 1212 North Lindbergh Boulevard, St Louis MO 63166. **Tel** (314)997-7111. Ed Bob McCoy. LC GV956.2.S8. DD 796.3327. **Circ** 10,000. Recap of past Super Bowl Games records, rosters of players. Covers football championship games since 1933.

SPORTING SCENE (SCARBOROUGH, ONT.). (SPORTING SCENE). Vol. 21, (July 1982)-. 0824-9849. Periodical. CN. English. mo. Free. Sporting Scene c/o Martens Graphic Promotions, 70 Romulus Drive, Scarborough Ontario M1K 4C2 Canada. DD 796.09713541. *Scarborough Sporting Scene, 0824-9830.*

SPORTMANIA. V. 1- 7 April 1979-. 0225-4476. Periodical. CN. French. bm. le Magazine Sportmania, Case Postale 8, St Lambert PQ J4P 3N4 Canada. **Tel** (514)672-6710. DD 796.05.

SPORTMEDINFO. (SPORTMEDINFO DU CONSEIL CANADIEN DE LA MEDECINE SPORTIVE). VFOAT Sportmedinfo from the Sport Medicine Council of Canada. Vol. 1, No. 1-. 0824-4219. Periodical. CN. English (French in parallel columns). qt. $5.00. Sport Medicine Council of Canada, 333 River Road, Ottawa Ontario K1L 8B9 Canada. DD 617.1027.

SPORTS AFIELD. V. 103, No. 3- Mar. 1940-. 0038-8149. Periodical. US. English. mo. Hearst Corporation, 224 W 57th Street, New York NY 10019, (subscription address: Communication Data Services 110 Tenth Street Des Moines IA 50309). **Tel** (800)247-5470. Ind/Abst Pop. Mag. Rev., Mag. Index, Consum. Index Prod. Eval. Inf. Source, Access. *Sports Afield and Trails of the Northwoods.*

SPORTS AFIELD DEER. See Recreation, Leisure - Outdoor Life.

THE SPORTS AFIELD OUTDOOR ALMANAC. See Yearbooks, Almanacs, Directories.

SPORTS & ATHLETES. VFOAT Sports and Athletes. Vol. 5, No. 1 (Feb. 1982)-. 0730-1162. Periodical. US. English. mo. $13.50 Domestic, $18.00 Foreign. Active Markets, PO Box 97000, Bellevue WA 98009. Ind/Abst Child. Mag. Guide. LC GV561. DD 796.05. *Young Athlete, 0160-5844.*

SPORTS AND THE COURTS. See Law.

SPORTS (BOCA RATON, FLA.). (SPORTS). Series/Titl Social Issues Resources Series. Vol. 1, Article 1-. 0273-2572. US. English. an. Social Issues Resources Series Inc, PO Box 2507, Boca Raton FL 33432. Ed Eleanor C Goldstein. LC GV583. DD 796.0973.

SPORTS CLUB MAGAZINE. V. 2, No 6,- Jan./Feb. 1979-. 0225-1876. Periodical. CN. French. ir. $1.50 Each Number. Publisyteme Inc, 531 rue Deslauriers, Ville St-Laurent Quebec H4N 1W2 Canada. DD 796.05. *0703-1904.*

SPORTS COLLECTORS DIGEST. See Hobbies.

THE SPORTS COLLECTORS DIRECTORY. See Yearbooks, Almanacs, Directories.

SPORTS DIRECTORY. See Yearbooks, Almanacs, Directories.

SPORTS DOCUMENTATION MONTHLY BULLETIN. Began publication in 1971. UK. English. mo. $28.35. University of Birmingham, PO Box 363, Birmingham B15 2TT England. **Tel** (021)274 1301. **Circ** 350. (ctrl). Sport, biomechanics, psychology, physiology, sociology,

Recreation, Leisure—Sports

recreation, physical education, sports medicine, sports injuries.

SPORTS HIGH. Vol. 1, No. 1 (Sept. 1982)-. 0733-8740. Periodical. US. English. mo. $20.00 Domestic, $27.00 Foreign. Oxley International Corporation, PO Box 2836, Farmington Hills MI 48018.

SPORTS ILLUSTRATED. V. 1- Aug. 16, 1954-. 0038-822X. Periodical. US. English. Time Inc, 301 East Ohio Street Chicago IL 60611. **Tel** (312)329-6800. **Ind/Abst** Book Rev. Index, Mag. Index, Infobank, Read. Guide Period. Lit., Abr. Read. Guide, Pop. Mag. Rev., Biogr. Index. LC GV561. DD 796.05.

SPORTS IN ROMANIA : MAGAZINE OF THE ROMANIAN OLYMPIC COMMITTEE. Began in 1957. Periodical. English. ir. Romanian Olympic Committee, 16 Vasile Conta Street, Bucharest LA 70139. LC GV645. DD 796.09498.

SPORTS IN THE GDR. VAT Sports in the German Democratic Republic. 0584-9209. Periodical. English. ir. Kunst & Wissen Erich Bieber, Dufourstrasse 51, CH-8008 Zurich Switzerland. LC GV612.6.

SPORTS JOURNAL. (THE SPORTS JOURNAL). V. 2, No. 7- July 1977-. 0707-3933. Periodical. CN. English. mo. $8.00. National Sports Journal Ltd, 206-110A Meridian Road Northeast, Calgary Alberta T2A 2N6 Canada. DD 796.0971. *National Sports Journal, 0701-1253.*

SPORTS LAW REPORTER. See Law.

SPORTS LINE. VAT SPORTSLINE. 0199-1019. Periodical. US. English. qt. $2.00. Sportsline, 117 Freer Gymnasium, University of Illinois, Urbana IL 61801.

SPORTS LITERATURE INDEX. See Indexes/Abstracts.

SPORTS-LOISIRS. Vol. 1, No 1 (Summer 1984)-. 0826-5305. Periodical. CN. French. ir. Free. Sports-Loisirs, c/o Publ Antisquebec 8928 rue St-Michel, Montreal Quebec H1Z 3G4 Canada. DD 796.09714.

SPORTS MEDIA NEWS. Began in 1979. 0747-6825. Periodical. US. English. mo. $85.00. Mars Corporation, 34 Washington Road, Princeton Junction NJ 08550.

SPORTS MEDICINE. See Medicine.

SPORTS MEDICINE (AUKLAND, (N.Z.). See Medicine.

SPORTS MERCHANDISER. 0049-1985. Periodical. US. English. mo. WRC Smith Publishing Company Inc, 1760 Peachtree Road NW, Atlanta GA 30309. **Tel** (404)874-4462. Ed Gene Marnell. bk rev. adv acc. **Circ** 27,500. (ctrl). Serves dealers and distributors of sporting goods and equipment.

SPORTS 'N SPOKES. V. 1- May/June 1975-. 0161-6706. Periodical. US. English (Sports). bm. $16.00. PVA Publications, 5201 North 19th Avenue, Suite 111, Phoenix AZ 85015. **Tel** (602)246-9426. Ed Nancy Crase. LC GV709.3. DD 796.060880810973. bk rev. adv acc. **Circ** 8,000. A magazine covering wheelchair sports and recreation for spinal cord injured, amputees, polio, and some congenital disabilities such as spina bifida.

SPORTS NEWS. 0194-8016. Periodical. US. English. wk. $7.50. Aneco Publications Inc, PO Box 1656, Grand Rapids MI 49501. **Tel** (616)453-3351. Ed L J Ney. adv acc. **Circ** 7,700. (ctrl). Featuring recognition of achievement in participation of sports at participants own level of competition. *Michigan Bowling & Golfing News, 0164-9051.*

SPORTS PEOPLE. Vol. 2, No. 3 (Mar. 1982)-. 0712-5607. Periodical. CN. English. mo. $18.00 Domestic, $24.00 US. Sports People, 411 Richmond Street East/Suite 102, Toronto Ontario M5A 3S5 Canada. DD 796.05. *Sports Update (Toronto, Ont.), 0712-5593.*

THE SPORTS PERIODICALS INDEX. See Indexes/Abstracts.

SPORTS QUARTERLY PRESENTS INSIDE HOCKEY. VFOAT Inside Hockey. 0732-0043. Periodical. US. English. an. $2.25 Each Issue. Lopez Publications Inc, 23 West 26th Street, New York NY 10010.

SPORTS RETAILER. Vol. 34, No. 1 (Jan. 1981)-. 0279-6678. Periodical. US. English. mo. $30.00. National Sporting Goods Association, 1699 Wall Street, Mt Prospect IL 60056. **Tel** (312)439-4000. Ed Cal T Morken. LC GV743. DD 338.476887. adv acc. **Circ** 18,000. Management topics for top executives of retail sporting goods stores. *Selling Sporting Goods, 0037-1610.*

SPORTS. SCIENCE PERIODICAL ON RESEARCH AND TECHNOLOGY IN SPORT. (SPORTS : SCIENCE PERIODICAL ON RESEARCH AND TECHNOLOGY IN SPORT). VFOAT Science Periodical on Research and Technology in Sport. 0820-6457. Periodical. CN. English. mo. 24.00 Domestic, 30.00 Foreign. Coaching Association of Canada, 333 River Road, Ottawa Ontario K1L 8B9 Canada. **Tel** (613)748-5624. Ed Paul Patterson. DD 613.7105. **Circ** 2,000. (ctrl). Has the mandate of presenting current sport science information of interest to people involved in sport related field. Topics include psychology, strength, sport medicine, testing special topics.

SPORTS TRADE CANADA. Vol. 10, No. 2 (Apr. 1982)-. 0714-6175. Periodical. CN. English. ir. $15.00. Sports Trade Canada c/o G P Page Publications, 380 Wellington Street West, Toronto Ontario M5V 1E5 Canada. **Ind/Abst** Can. Bus. Index. DD 338.47688760971. *Sporting Goods Trade, 0381-9280; Sporting Goods Canada, 0381-8977.*

SPORTSCAPE. V. 1- Winter 1981-. 0272-7579. Periodical. US. English. qt. Free. Sportscape, Box CY366, 400 Commonwealth Avenue, Boston MA 02215.

SPORTSEARCH. (SPORT SEARCH). VFOAT Sport Search. Vol. 1, No. 1 (Sept. 1985)-. 0882-553X. Periodical. US. English. mo. $60.00 Domestic, $70.00 Foreign. Human Kinetics Publishers Inc, Box 5076, Champaigne IL 61820. **Tel** (217)351-5076. DD 796. adv acc. Contains the table of contents pages of 248 sports journals from around the world. Each issue also contains 125 abstracts of selected articles.

SPORTSFORUM (PORT WASHINGTON, N.Y.). (SPORTSFORUM). VFOAT Sports Forum. 8750-541X. Periodical. US. English. ir. Sportsforum, 18 Industrial Park Drive, Port Washington NY 11050. *Kyle Rote's Sportsforum, 0745-4732.*

SPORTSMAN. See Recreation, Leisure - Outdoor Life.

SPORTSMANS BOOK OF U.S. RECORDS. VAT Sportsmans Book of United States Records. 1980-. 0270-3513. US. English. an. New York Hunting and Fishing Guide, 45 Gibbs Street, Rochester NY 14604. LC SH455. DD 799.0212.

SPORTSMEDICINE DIGEST. See Medicine.

SPORTSTATTEN IN NORDRHEIN-WESTFALEN. Series/Titl Beitrage zur Statistik des Landes Nordrhein-Westfalen. GW. German. ir. 18.00. Landesamt fur Datenverarbeitung und Statistik Nordrhein-Westfalen, Postfach 1105, 4000 Dusseldorf 1 West Germany. LC HA1320.N6, GV433. G43N67. DD 690.58043094356.

SPORTSTYLE. VFOAT Sport Style. Vol. 1, No. 1 (Apr. 1983)-. 0733-8708. Periodical. US. English. mo. $23.94. Fairchild Publications, 7 East 12th Street, New York NY 10003. LC WMLC L 83/124.

THE SPORTSWOMAN. V. 1- Spring 1973-. 0099-0388. Periodical. US. English. bm. $4.50. Jensen-Fane Pub, PO Box 2611, Culver City CA 90230. LC GV709. DD 796.0194.

SPORTUNTERRICHT. Vol. 22-. Periodical. GW. German (some summaries in English and French). mo. 61.80. Verlag Karl Hofmann, Postfach 1360, D-7060 Schorndorf West Germany. **Tel** 07181/7811. LC GV201. bk rev. adv acc. *Leibeserziehung.*

SPORTVEZETO. Periodical. HU. Hungarian. mo. $16.00. Akademiai Kiado, POB 24, 1363 Budapest Hungary. LC GV648.H8.

SPORTWISSENSCHAFT. Began 1971. Periodical. GW. English or German, with summaries in both languages and French. qt. 16.-. Verlag Karl Hofmann, Postfach 1360, D-7060 Schorndorf West Germany. **Tel** 07181/7811. LC GV201. bk rev.

SPORTWISSENSCHAFT UND SPORTPRAXIS. 1970. Monographic Series. GW. German. ir. Verlag Ingrid Czwalina, Ressenbuttler Redder 75, D-2070 Ahrensburg West Germany. **Tel** (04102)59190. Ed Clemens Czwalina. LC GV565. Books on sport science and practice. *Schriftenreihe fur Sportwissenschaft und Sportpraxis.*

SPOTLIGHT ON YOUTH SPORTS. (SPOTLIGHT ON YOUTH SPORTS : A PUBLICATION OF THE INSTITUTE FOR THE STUDY OF YOUTH SPORTS). VFOAT Spotlight. 0740-0802. Periodical. US. English. qt. $3.00. Michigan State University, Youth Sports Institute, East Lansing MI 48824. **Tel** (517)353-6689. Ed Deborah Feltz. bk rev. **Circ** 6,000. (ctrl). Educational materials for volunteer youth sports coaches. Designed to enchance the sports experience of children through the education of adults who teach them skills and attitudes.

SQUASH LIFE. Vol. 5, No. 3 (Sept./Oct. 1981)-. 0821-025X. Periodical. CN. English. bm. Free. Squash Ontario, 160 Vanderhoof Avenue, Toronto Ontario M4G 4B8 Canada. DD 796.34309713. (ctrl). *Let Point, 0821-0241.*

SQUASH NEWS. V. 1- Apr. 1978-. 0164-7148. Periodical. US. English. ir. $8.00. Squash News, Arcadia Road Box 52, Hope Valley RI 02832. **Tel** (401)539-2381. Ed Hazel White Jones. bk rev. adv acc. **Circ** 16,000. A publication on the game of squash. Features tournament results from professional to novice level, instruction and features. US and international game covered in-depth.

SQUASH REVIEW. (SQUASH REVIEW : NATIONAL CAPITAL SQUASH RACQUETS ASSOCIATION NEWSLETTER). Vol. 1, No. 1 (Nov. 12, 1976)-. 0229-2351. Periodical. CN. English. ir. Free. Squash Review, Box 8943, Ottawa Ontario K1G 3J2 Canada. DD 796.3430971383.

STADION. 1-. 0172-4029. Periodical. GW. German. ir. 69.50. H Richarz, Postbox M65, St Augustin 1 Federal Republic of Germany. **Tel** (0221)4982384. Ed W Decker and M Laemmer. **Ind/Abst** Am. Hist. Life, Hist. Abstr., Part A, Mod. Hist. Abstr., Hist. Abst., Part B, Twent. Century Abstr. LC GV561. adv acc. **Circ** 400. (ctrl). History of sport, physical education and adjacent areas from the earliest times until today, including all cultures and people. *Arena.*

STATE LAWS GOVERNING BOXING AND WRESTLING IN CALIFORNIA WITH RULES AND REGULATIONS. See Law.

STATISTICS ANNUAL - B.C. TRACK & FIELD ASSOCIATION. See Statistics.

STAZIONI SCIISTICHE IN ITALIA. 1983-. Italian. an. LC GV854.A2. DD 796.9302545.

STOCK CAR CLASSIFICATION GUIDE. See Transportation - Automobiles.

STOCK CAR RACING. VFOAT Stock Car Racing Magazine. 0734-7340. Periodical. US. English. mo. $20.00. Lopez Publications Inc, 602 Montgomery Street, Alexandria VA 22314. **Tel** (703)836-5881. Ed Dick Berggren. LC GV1029.9.S74. DD 796.720973. bk rev. adv acc. **Circ** 81,000. America's oval track racer's "Bible". It reaches, every month, virtually every participant in closed wheel oval track racing.

STREET AND SMITH'S OFFICIAL YEARBOOK. BASEBALL. See Yearbooks, Almanacs, Directories.

STREET AND SMITH'S OFFICIAL YEARBOOK. COLLEGE FOOTBALL. See Yearbooks, Almanacs, Directories.

STREET AND SMITH'S OFFICIAL YEARBOOK. PRO FOOTBALL. See Yearbooks, Almanacs, Directories.

STREET MACHINES & BRACKET RACING. See Transportation - Automobiles.

STREET RODDER. 0277-5735. Periodical. US. English. mo. $12.00. McMullen Publications, 2145 West Lapalma, Anaheim CA 92801. **Tel** (714)635-9040.

STROKE SAVER. Vol. 1, issue 1-. 0824-4138. CN. English. an. Scorecard & Course Layout of The Woodlands Golf & Country Club, Brampton Ontario Canada. DD 796.352068713535.

SUMMARY OF FEDERAL HUNTING REGULATIONS. CENTRAL FLYWAY. See Recreation, Leisure - Outdoor Life.

SUMMARY OF FEDERAL HUNTING REGULATIONS. MISSISSIPPI FLYWAY. See Recreation, Leisure - Outdoor Life.

Recreation, Leisure—Sports

SUMMARY OF FEDERAL HUNTING REGULATIONS. PACIFIC FLYWAY. See Recreation, Leisure - Outdoor Life.

SUMMARY OF THE HUNTING REGULATIONS. See Recreation, Leisure - Outdoor Life.

SUMP CEASED. (THE SUMP). Began publication in 1955? Ceased between July/Aug./Sept. 1984 and April 1985. 0318-5443. Periodical. CN. English. Edmonton Light Car Club, PO Box 5712, Station L, Edmonton Alberta T6C 4G2 Canada. DD 796.72.

SUPER BOWL CEASED. 1-. 0747-6450. Periodical. US. English. an. $8.95. Creative Education, 123 South Broad Street, Mankato MN 56001. Tel (507)388-6273. A book on each Super Bowl and the organization. A set of 20.

SUPER BOWL FACT BOOK. VFOAT Sporting News Super Bowl Fact Book. 1982 Ed.-. 0733-1630. US. English. an. Sporting News, 1212 North Lindbergh Boulevard, Box 56, St Louis MO 63166. LC GV956.2. DD 796.3327.

SUPER STOCK & DRAG ILLUSTRATED. VFOAT Super Stock. VAT Super Stock and Drag Illustrated. 0039-5692. Periodical. US. English. mo. $13.00. Lopez Publications, 602 Montgomery Street, Alexandria VA 22314. Tel (703)836-5881. Ed Steve Collison. bk rev. adv acc. Circ 56,000. Dedicated to the drag racing enthusiast, with articles and color photos on latest events and in-depth technical features.

SUPER STOCK & DRAG ILLUSTRATED'S PULLING POWER. VFOAT Pulling Power. 0744-4362. Periodical. US. English. bm. $14.95. Lopez Automotive Group, 602 Montgomery Street, Alexandria VA 22314. Tel (703)836-5881. Ed Woody Hatten. bk rev. adv acc. Circ 55,000. Captured America's love for truck and tractor pulling enthusiasts with the best in-depth coverage available, at its colorful best.

SUPOCHU REJO. VFOAT Sports, Leisure. 1st Vol. (1984/4)-. Periodical. KO. Korean. mo. Hanguk Ilbosa, 14 Chu. ak-dong Chongno-ku, Seoul Korea. LC AP95.K6.

SUPOCHU SAJIN YONGAM. 1983-. KO. Korean. an. 30,000. Hanguk Ilbosa, 14 Chunghak-dong Chongno-ku, Seoul Korea. LC GV663.K6.

THE SURF REPORT. V. 1- July 1980-. 0270-2630. Periodical. US. English. mo. $30.00. Surfer Publications, PO Box 1028, Dana Point CA 92629. Tel (714)496-5922. Ed Rus Calisch. Circ 1,000. Summary and forecast of worldwide surf conditions.

SURFBOARD. 1980-. 0276-6582. US. English (French or Spanish). Transmedia, 9811 Edgelake Drive, La Mesa CA 92041. LC GV840.S8. DD 797.17205. Surfboard Builder's Yearbook.

SURFER. VFOAT Surfer Monthly. Began in 1960. 0039-6036. Periodical. US. English. mo. $18.00. Surfer Publications, PO Box 1028, Dana Point CA 92629. (subscription address: Communication Data Services PO Box 7300 Bergenfield NJ 07621). Tel (714)496-5922. LC GV840.S8. DD 797.17205.

SURFING. 1964. 0194-9314. Periodical. US. English. mo. $35.00. Surfing Magazine, PO Box 27889, San Diego CA 92128. Tel (714)4927873. Ed David Gilouiett. bk rev. adv acc. Circ 85,000. (ctrl).

SVENSK JAKTKALENDER. Began with vol. for 1972/73. Swedish. ir. Forlagahuset Norden, Box 305 201 23 1, Malmo Switzerland. LC SK210.

SWIM. V. 1- Feb. 1974-. 0319-0560. Periodical. CN. English. mo. $30.95. Swim Canada, 402 King Street East, Toronto Ontario M5A 1L3 Canada. DD 797.210971.

SWIM (ARLINGTON VA.). (SWIM). VFOAT Swim Magazine. Vol. 1, No. 1 (Oct./Nov. 1984)-. 8755-2027. Periodical. US. English. bm. $12.00. Swim Magazine, 523 South 26th Road, Arlington VA 22202. DD 797.

SWIM SWIM. 0195-6760. Periodical. US. English. qt. Swim Swim, PO Box 5901, Santa Monica CA 90405. Tel (213)558-3321.

SWIMMING AND DIVING RULES. Main/Corp National Federation of State High School Associations. VFOAT Swimming and Diving Rules and Case Book. 0163-2884. US. English. an. $1.75. National Federation of State High School Associations, Federation Place, PO Box 98, Elgin IL 60120. LC GV837. DD 797.2.

SWIMMING AND DIVING WATER POLO RULE BOOKS. NATIONAL FEDERATION EDITION. (SWIMMING AND DIVING WATER POLO RULE BOOKS). Main/Corp National Federation of State High School Associations. 0275-5068. US. English. National Federation of State High School Associations, PO Box 20626, Kansas City MO 64195. Tel (816)464-5400. Ed Susan True. LC GV837. DD 797.205. adv acc. Circ 2,950. Rules covering competition in high school swimming, diving, and water polo.

SWIMMING TECHNIQUE. V. 1- Apr. 1964-. 0039-7415. Periodical. US. English. qt. $10.00. Swimming World, Box 45497, Los Angeles CA 90045. Tel (213)674-2120. Ed Mark Muckenfuss. LC UNC. bk rev. adv acc. Circ 8,000. Features instructional, "how to" material on swimming for both participants and those engaged in aquatic sports.

SWIMMING TIMES. 1923. Periodical. UK. English. mo. $13.02. Sport Shelf, PO Box 634, New Rochelle NY 10802. Tel 0509-230431. Ed Richard H Brown. adv acc. Circ 15,236. Official journal of the Amateur Swimming Association and the Institute of Swimming Teachers and Coaches.

SYNCHRO CANADA. V. 5- 1975-. 0317-0578. CN. English. qt. $7.74. Canada Amateur Sychronized Swimming Association, 333 River Road, Ottawa Ontario K1L 8H9 Canada. Tel (613)748-5674. Ed Karen Vansacker. DD 797.21. bk rev. adv acc. Circ 600. An insight into Canadian synchronized swimming, at home and abroad. Covering areas of coaching, officiating, competitions, recreation, sport science, and administration. Synchronized Canada, 0316-4802.

SYNCHRONIZED CANADA CEASED. Began publication in 1970. Ceased with V. 4, No. 4. 0316-4802. Periodical. CN. English. qt. 15.00. Canadian Amateur Synchronized Swimming Association, 18 Harlowe Crescent, Ottawa Ontario K2H 5P1 Canada. Tel (613)748-5674. Ed Laurence Clark. DD 797.21. bk rev. adv acc. Circ 1,000. (ctrl). Publication (includes yearbook) on Canadian synchronized swimming; the athletes, coaches, judges and volunteers; what makes Canada number one in the world. Directed to the International Synchronized Community.

TABA. (TABA : ALBERTA BOWHUNTERS AND ARCHERS ASSOCIATION). 0821-5669. Periodical. CN. English. bm. Free. PO Box 1772, Pincher Creek Alberta T0K 1W0 Canada. DD 799.320607123. (ctrl). Alberta Bowhunter and Archer, 0044-7080.

TABLE TENNIS TECHNICAL. VFOAT Technique Tennis de Table. 0828-4539. Periodical. CN. English (some issues include some text in French). ir. Free. Canadian Table Tennis Association, 333 River Road, Vanier Ontario K1L 8B9 Canada. DD 796.34606071. (ctrl).

TAC/USA OFFICIAL RULES FOR ATHLETICS. VFOAT T.A.C. U.S.A. Official Rules for Athletics. VAT The Athletics Congress of the USA Official Rules for Athletics. US. English. The Athletics Congress of the USA, 155 West Washington Street/Suite 220, Indianapolis IN 46204.

TAUCHEN. Periodical. German. ir. 51.60. Jahr-Verlag, 2000 Hamburg 70, Schlosstrasse 6, Hamburg West Germany. LC GV840.S78. DD 797.23. Delphin, Taucher.

TEAM HANDBALL UPDATE. Winter Ed. (80/81)-. 0712-2314. Periodical. CN. English. ty. Team Handball Update O T H G, 160 Vanderhoof Avenue, Toronto Ontario M4G 4B8 Canada. DD 796.31. Team Handball News, 0229-5660.

TECHNICAL MANUAL - CANADIAN SOCCER ASSOCIATION. Main/Corp Canadian Soccer Association. V. 1- Nov. 1977-. 0705-7504. Periodical. CN. English. qt. $5.00 Domestic, $6.00 US and Caribbean, $7.00 Others. Canadian Soccer Association, 333 River Road, Ottawa Ontario K1L 8B9 Canada. DD 796.334077. Coach, 0701-001X.

TECHNIQUE. (TECHNIQUE : THE OFFICIAL TECHNICAL PUBLICATION OF THE UNITED STATES GYMNASTICS FEDERATION). 0748-5999. Periodical. US. English. qt. $12.00. USGF, 101 West Washington Street/Suite 1144E, Indianapolis IN 46204. LC GV461. DD 796.410973. USGF Technical Journal.

TEMPS LIBRE. (TEMPS LIBRE : BULLETIN DE LA SOCIETE QUEBECOISE D'HISTOIRE DU LOISIR). Vol. 4, No. 1 (May 1980)-. 0228-6629. Periodical. CN. French. Free to Members, $10.00 Others. Temps Libre, 36 Chemin du Vieux Fort, Lauzon Quebec G6V 2C5 Canada. DD 796.09714. Grhap, 0705-1573.

TENNESSEE SPORTSMAN. V. 1- Aug. 1980-. 0161-3871. Periodical. US. English. mo. $11.95. Game & Fish Publications, PO Box 741, Marietta GA 30061. Tel (404)953-9222. Tennessee Sportsman, 0161-3871.

TENNIS. V. 1- May 1965-. 0040-3423. Periodical. US. English. mo. Tennis Magazine, 495 Westport Avenue, Norwalk CT 06856. (subscription address: Communication Data Services PO Box 4966 Des Moines IA 50340). Tel (203)847-5811. Ind/Abst Consum. Index Prod. Eval. Inf. Source, Pop. Mag. Rev. LC GV991. DD 796.34205.

TENNIS BUYERS GUIDE. (TENNIS ... BUYERS GUIDE). Summer 1982-. 0733-9763. Periodical. US. English. sa. $17.00. Tennis Buyers Guide, 495 Westport Avenue, Norwalk CT 06856. Tel (203)847-5811. Ed Nick Romano. LC GV1002.5. DD 688.76342. bk rev. adv acc. Circ 14,000. (ctrl). Reaches retailers at various outlets that sell tennis products. It covers the latest product developments and the best techniques to sell them. Tennis ... Directory, 0276-3559.

TENNIS BUYER'S GUIDE (NORWALK, CONN.). (TENNIS BUYER'S GUIDE). Began in Apr. 1984. 0749-6478. Periodical. US. English. sa. Free to Qualified Personnel, $17.00 Others. Golf/Digest Tennis Inc, 495 Westport Avenue, Norwalk CT 06856. DD 688.

TENNIS INDUSTRY. V. 1- Sept. 1972-. 0191-5851. Periodical. US. English. mo. $22.00. Tennis Industry, 1545 NE 123rd Street, North Miami FL 33161. Tel (305)893-8771.

TENNIS LIFE. 0279-9979. Periodical. US. English. bm. Tennis Life Magazine, 700 Horton Drive, Silver Spring MD 20902. Tel (301)593-3222.

TENNIS WEEK. 0194-9098. Periodical. US. English. ir. $100.00. Tennis Week, 6 East 39th Street/8th Floor, New York NY 10016. Tel (212)741-2323.

TENNIS WORLD. V. 1- Apr. 1969-. 0040-3474. Periodical. UK. English. ir. $26.05. Dennis Fairey Publishing Ltd, Chiltern House, 184 High Street, Berkhamsted Herts HP43AP England. Tel 04427 74947. Ed Henry Wancke. bk rev. adv acc. Circ 15,500. British and international tennis magazine containing previews, results, instruction, competitions; richly illustrated with full color and black and white photographs.

TESTNEVELES- ES SPORTEGESZSEGUGYI SZMELE. See Medicine.

TEXAS COACH. 1958. 0040-4241. Periodical. US. English. mo. $10.00. Texas High School Coaches Association, PO Box 14627, 5300 North IH 35, Austin TX 78761. Tel (512)454-6709. Ed Eddie Joseph. bk rev. adv acc. Circ 11,000. (ctrl). Articles of interest to coaches of sports; football, basketball, baseball, track, and soccer. Articles also include sports for females.

TEXAS GOLF. 0199-3062. Periodical. US. English. mo. $20.00. Texas Golf, 4316 Main Street, Dallas TX 75226.

TEXAS HUNTER'S DIRECTORY. See Yearbooks, Almanacs, Directories.

THUMPER (ST. ALBERT, ALTA.). (THUMPER). Jan. 1981-. 0821-7114. Periodical. CN. English. ir. Alberta Volleyball Association, 13 Mission Avenue, St Albert Alberta T8N 1H6 Canada. DD 796.3250607123. Newsletter (Alberta Volleyball Association), 0821-7122.

THUNDER COUNTRY OUTDOORS. See Recreation, Leisure - Outdoor Life.

TI TSAO. VFOAT Ticao Mulu. Periodical. CC. Chinese. qt. 0.28. Chung-kuo Kuo Chi Shu Tien, PO Box 2820, Pei-ching China. LC GV461. DD 796.4105.

TI YU KO HSUEH. VFOAT Sports Science. Periodical. CC. Chinese. qt. 0.65. Chung-kuo Kuo Chi Shu Tien, PO Box 2820, Pei-ching China. LC GV561. DD 796.05.

TI YU SHIH LIAO. Periodical. CH. Chinese. ir. 0.35. Hsin Hua Shu Tien, Pei-Ching fa Hsing So, Peking China. LC GV651. DD 796.0951.

TIEN CHING. VFOAT Tian Jing. Periodical. CC. Chinese. bm. 0.28. Chung-kuo Kuo Chi Shu Tien, PO Box 2820, Pei-ching China. LC GV1060.5. DD 796.4205.

Recreation, Leisure—Sports

TIGER-CAT FACT BOOK. Main/Corp Hamilton Tiger-Cat Football Club. VFOAT Fact Book. 0710-1643. CN. English. an. $2.00 Each Number. Hamilton Tiger-Cat Football Club, PO Box 170, Hamilton Ontario L8N 3A Canada. DD 796.33560922.

THE TIGER RAG. V. 1- Sept. 1, 1978-. 0744-7604. Periodical. US. English. wk. $32.00. Bayou Bengal Publishing Company, PO Box 16540-A LSU Station, Baton Rouge LA 70893. Tel (504)343-8724. Ed Steve Myers. adv acc. Circ 12,000. Sports publication covering Louisiana State University and the southeastern conference.

TIME OUT (OTTAWA, ONT.). (TIME OUT). VFOAT CAC Newletter. No. 1 (Mar. 1981)-. 0710-1678. Periodical. CN. English. ir. Free to Members. Coaching Association of Canada, Tower B, 333 River Road, Ottawa Ontario K1L 8B9 Canada. DD 796.07706071.

THE TOLEDO SPORTSMAN. VFOAT Sportsman. 8750-6726. Periodical. US. English. mo. $7.25. Grissom Publications, PO Box 288, Carthage TX 75633. Tel (214)693-7678. Ed Loyd C Grissom. bk rev. adv acc. Circ 10,000. Fishing and hunting magazine-newspaper.

TONGGYE YONBO. See Horses and Horsemanship.

TORONTO ARGONAUTS FACT BOOK. (FACT BOOK). Main/Corp Toronto Argonaut Football Club. VFOAT Toronto Argonauts Fact Book and Media Guide. 0227-6526. CN. English. an. Free. Toronto Argonaut Football Club Exhibition Stadium, Exhibition Place, Toronto Ontario M6K 3C3 Canada. DD 796.3356. (ctrl).

TOUCHDOWN. V. 1- Nov. 1972-. 0090-4228. Periodical. US. English. ir. Touchdown Publishing Inc, 3 Embarcadero Center/Suite 980, San Francisco CA 94111. Tel (415)398-1919. LC GV955.5.N35. DD 796.332640973.

THE TOUR BOOK. (THE TOUR BOOK - TOURNAMENT PLAYERS DIVISION, PROFESSIONAL GOLFERS' ASSOCIATION OF AMERICA). Main/Corp Professional Golfers' Association of America. Tournament Players Division. 146-1796. US. English. an. 5101 River Road, Washington DC 20016. LC GV964.A1. DD 796.3520922.

TRACK. See Recreation, Leisure - Outdoor Life.

TRACK AND FIELD. Main/Corp Saskatchewan High Schools Athletic Association. 0704-4984. CN. English. an. Free. Saskatchewan High Schools Athletic Association, 2220 College Avenue, Regina Saskatchewan S4P 3V7 Canada. DD 796.42097124.

TRACK AND FIELD JOURNAL. VFOAT T F J. No. 1- Jan./Feb. 1980-. 0226-2630. Periodical. CN. English (includes some text in French). qt. $19.35. Canadian Track Field Association, 333 River Road, Ottawa Ontario K1L 8H9 Canada. Tel (613)748-5678. Ed Tom MacWilliam. DD 796.420971. bk rev. adv acc. Circ 800. (ctrl). Technical information about track and field athletics. Each issue features a different main theme, e.g., the jumps, the throws, the sprints, etc.

TRACK & FIELD NEWS. VAT Track and Field News. Began with Feb. 1948 issue. 0041-0284. Periodical. US. English. mo. $22.00. Track & Field News, PO Box 296, Los Altos CA 94023. Tel (415)948-8188. Ed Garry Hill. bk rev. adv acc. Circ 35,000. (ctrl). America's only magazine exclusively devoted to coverage of the entire sport of track and field for US and worldwide.

TRACK & FIELD QUARTERLY REVIEW (KALAMAZOO, MICH.). (TRACK & FIELD QUARTERLY REVIEW). VFOAT Track and Field Quarterly Review. Began in 1968. 0041-0292. Periodical. US. English. qt. $15.00. Track & Field Association of USA, 1705 Evanston St, Kalamazoo MI 49008. Tel (616)349-1008. Ed George Dales. bk rev. adv acc. Circ 2,000. Issued also on microfilm by Xerox University Microfilms. Technical educational journal for track and field coaches and athletes. *Quarterly Review (United States Track Coaches Association).*

TRACK AND FIELD RULE BOOK. Main/Corp National Federation of State High School Associations. 1982-. US. English. an. $2.50. National Federation of State High School Associations, 11724 Plaza Circle, Box 20626, Kansas City MO 64195. Tel (816)464-5400. Ed Thomas E Frederick. LC GV1060.67. DD 796.42. adv acc. Circ 65,000. The national high school rules for track and field competition. Also includes the national records for girls and boys competition. *National Federation Track and Field Rule Book, 0270-4129.*

TRACK NEWSLETTER. 0041-0306. Periodical. US. English. ir. $35.00. Track & Field News, c/o W Harding PO Box 296, Los Altos CA 94023. Tel (415)948-8188. Ed Garry Hill. Circ 500. (ctrl). Devoted to the US/worldwide track and field, and an in-depth statistics of all track and field results.

TRACK TECHNIQUE. 0041-0314. US. English. qt. $8.00. Track & Field News, c/o W Harding, Box 296, Los Altos CA 94203. Tel (415)948-8188. Ed Vera Gambetta. bk rev. adv acc. Circ 5,000. (ctrl). Contains the most current articles dealing with the training and technical aspects of track and field.

TRACK TECHNIQUE. (TRACK TECHNIQUE : THE OFFICIAL TECHNICAL PUBLICATION OF THE ATHLETICS CONGRESS/USA). 84 (Spring 1983)-. 0742-3918. Periodical. US. English. qt. $6.50 Domestic, $7.50 Foreign. Track & Field News Inc, PO Box 296, Los Altos CA 94022. LC GV561. DD 796.4205. *Track Technique Annual, 0731-5864.*

THE TRADITIONAL ARCHERY DIGEST. VFOAT Traditional Archery. No. 11 (Mar.-Apr. 1982)-. 0745-5666. Periodical. US. English. bm. $12.00 Domestic, $15.00 Canada. Olde Reliable Publications, Box 61, Paradise Route, Portal AZ 85632. *Longbow Shooter's Digest, 0195-1866.*

TRADITIONAL TAEKWON-DO. VFOAT Taekwondo. 0745-2365. Periodical. US. English. qt. $10.00. Traditional Taekwondo, 6202 South Sheridan, Tulsa OK 74136. Tel (918)494-9691. Ed D W Kang. bk rev. adv acc. Circ 70,000. Martial arts magazine for all ages around the world. We accept articles from our readers and cover every aspect of the martial arts world.

TRAP & FIELD. VAT Trap and Field. 0041-1760. Periodical. US. English. mo. $15.00. Trap & Field Magazine, 1000 Waterway Boulevard, Indianapolis IN 46202. Tel (317)633-2080. Ed Bonnie Nash. bk rev. adv acc. Circ 14,500. Official publication of the Amateur Trapshooting Association, governing body of the clay target sport in North America, the largest association in the world regulating clay target firing.

TRENTE POUR CENT. V. 1- (No. 1-). 0319-1478. Periodical. CN. text also in English, June 1975-. ir. Free. Mission Quebec, 76 1415 Est rue Jarry, Montreal Quebec H2E 1A7 Canada. DD 796.48.

TROPHY BIG GAME INVESTIGATIONS AND HUNTING SEASON RECOMMENDATIONS. Main/Corp Nevada. Division of Game. 1980-. 0883-2951. US. English. an. State of Nevada, Department of Wildlife, 1100 Valley Road, PO Box 10678, Reno NV 89520-0022. *Big Game Investigations and Hunting Season Recommendations, 0160-1547.*

TSU CHIU SHIH CHIEH. Periodical. CH. Chinese. bm. 0.28. Post Office, Peking China. LC GV942.

TURF AND SPORT DIGEST. 0041-4158. Periodical. US. English. bm. $8.00. Turf & Sport International Ltd, 511-513 Oakland Avenue, Baltimore MD 21212. Tel (301)323-0300. Ed Allen Mitzel. bk rev. adv acc. Circ 30,000. (ctrl). A favorite of thoroughbred racing fans. Features articles on everything that's happening in the exciting world of thoroughbred racing. Handicapping hints, racing statistics, jockey, horses, and trainer profiles.

U.I.T. JOURNAL. (U.I.T. JOURNAL). VFOAT UIT Journal. 1'81-. Periodical. English. bm. International Shooting Union, Bavariaring 21, D-8000 Munchen 2 Deutschland West Germany. LC GV1151. DD 799.305. *International Shooting Sport.*

ULTRALIGHT FLYER CEASED. No. 1 (Apr. 1981)-. 0279-0181. Periodical. US. English. mo. Ultralight Flyer, PO Box 98786, Tacoma WA 98499. Tel (206)588-1743. DD 797.

UNDERCURRENT. 0192-0871. Periodical. US. English. ir. $28.00. Atcom Inc, 2315 Broadway, New York NY 10024. Tel (212)873-5900. Ed Bed Davidson. Circ 13,600. (ctrl). A newsletter for the sport diver, featuring resort and equipment reviews safety tips and ways to have more fun under water.

UNITED STATES SWIMMING RULES AND REGULATIONS. (UNITED STATES SWIMMING RULES AND REGULATIONS : OFFICIAL PUBLICATION OF UNITED STATES SWIMMING). VFOAT Rules and Regulations. 0742-7808. US. English. United States Swimming Inc, 1750 East Boulder Street, Colorado Springs CO 80909. LC WMLC L 83/117.

UNITED STATES TENNIS CLUB REGISTRY. 1st- ed. 0364-8214. US. English. Tennis Club Registry, PO Box 4231, Irvine CA 92716. LC GV991. DD 796.3420973.

U.S. TENNIS TOURNAMENT DIRECTORY. SUPPLEMENT. See Yearbooks, Almanacs, Directories.

US SWIMMING NEWS. VAT United States Swimming News. 0883-0347. Periodical. US. English. mo. $19.95. US Swimming News, 1750 East Boulder Street, Colorado Springs CO 80909. Tel (303)578-4578. Ed Jeff Dimond. DD 797. Circ 2,000. (ctrl). Newsletter of U.S. swimming, the national governing body for competitive swimming carries items for the record about swimming.

USA GYMNASTICS. VFOAT U.S.A. Gymnastics. Vol. 13, No. 1 (Jan./Feb. 1984)-. 0748-6006. Periodical. US. English. bm. $12.00 Domestic, $14.00 Canada. USGF, Suite 1144E/101 West Washington Street, Indianapolis IN 46204. DD 796. *USGF Gymnastics.*

USDF CALENDAR OF COMPETITIONS. See Horses and Horsemanship.

USGA GREEN SECTION RECORD. Main/Corp United States Golf Association. Green Section. VAT United States Golf Association Green Section Record. Began with May 1963 issue. 0041-5502. Periodical. US. English. bm. $9.00. US Golf Association, Golf House, Far Hills NJ 07931. Ind/Abst Bibliogr. Agric. LC GV975. DD 711.558. *USGA Journal and Turf Management.*

U.S.H.L. YEARBOOK. See Yearbooks, Almanacs, Directories.

USSA SKI NEWS. VFOAT U.S.S.A. Ski News. VAT United States Ski Association Ski News. Began in 1983. 0747-1327. Periodical. US. English. qt. USSA 1750 East Boulder Street, Colorado Springs CO 80909. Tel (303)578-4600. Ed Jolene S Aubel. DD 796. adv acc. Circ 15,000. (ctrl). Current news, results and activities of the U.S. Ski Association.

USTA COLLEGE TENNIS GUIDE. VFOAT U.S.T.A. College Tennis Guide. VAT United States Tennis Association College Tennis Guide. Began publication with Vol. for 1979. US. English. be. $3.50. US Tennis Association, 729 Alexander Road, Princeton NJ 08540. Tel (609)452-2580. Ed Anne B Humes. Circ 6,000. For the college-bound tennis player, a comprehensive index to intercollegiate tennis teams and scholarships for both men and women. Nearly 1,500 colleges and universities listed alphabetically by state.

UTAH BIG GAME RANGE TREND STUDIES. 1981-. 0741-9708. US. English. an. Utah Department of Natural Resources and Energy, Division of Wildlife Resources, 1596 West North Temple, Salt Lake City UT 84116. LC SK453. DD 639.9797357. *Big Game Range Inventory.*

UTAH COUGAR HARVEST. Main/Corp Utah. Division of Wildlife Resources. VFOAT Utah Cougar Harvest Book. US. English. an. Utah Department of Natural Resources and Energy, Division of Wildlife Resources, 1596 West North Temple, Salt Lake City UT 84116. LC SK453. DD 799.2774428.

VARIA. Vol. 1- No. 1-. 0506-4155. Periodical. Indonesian. wk. Djakarta Indonesia. LC GV1111. DD 796.815.

VELI MAG. (VELIG MAG). VFOAT Velimag. V, 1, No 1 (Feb. 1984)-. 0822-8221. Periodical. CN. English. ir. $6.00. Veli Mag, Bureau 108 780 Chemin du Bord du Lac, Dorval Quebec H9S 2C4 Canada. DD 797.3309714.

VISIER. Periodical. SZ. German. mo. Kunst & Wissen Erich Bieber, Dufourstrasse 51, CH-8008 Zurich Switzerland. LC GV1151.

VOICE OF THE TRAPPER. See Recreation, Leisure - Outdoor Life.

VOILE LIBRE (MONTREAL, QUEBEC). (VOILE LIBRE). Vol. 1, No. 1 (1982)-. 0826-4511. Periodical. CN. French. qt. $9.00. Voile Libre, C P 306 Succursale Bourassa, Montreal Quebec H2C 3G1 Canada. DD 797.17205.

VOLLEYBALL. Main/Corp Saskatchewan High Schools Athletic Association. 0704-4992. CN. English. an. Free. Saskatchewan High Schools Athletic Association, 2220 College Avenue, Regina Saskatchewan S4P 3V7 Canada. DD 796.325097124.

VOLLEYBALL CASE BOOK AND OFFICIALS MANUAL. Main/Corp National Federation Volleyball Rules Committee. VFOAT Official High School Volleyball Case Book and Officials Manual. 0749-1832. US. English. National

Recreation, Leisure—Sports

Federation of State High School Associations, 11724 Plaza Circle, Box 20626, Kansas City MO 64195. LC GV1015.39. DD 796.3250202.

VOLLEYBALL MAGAZINE. Charter Issue (Winter 1976)-. 0274-6662. Periodical. US. English. qt. $12.00 Domestic, $17.00 Foreign. Volleyball Magazine, PO Box 28816, San Diego CA 92128. LC GV1015. DD 796.32505.

VOLLEYBALL RULE BOOK. Main/Corp National Federation of State High School Associations. VFOAT Volleyball Rules. 1979-80-. 0882-1372. US. English. an. National Federation of State High School Association, 11724 Plaza Circle, Box 20626, Kansas City MO 64195. Tel (816)464-5400. Ed Susan True. LC GV1017.V6. DD 796.325. adv acc. Circ 11,000. Rules covering high school competition in volleyball. *Volleyball Rules, 0363-2156.*

VOLLEYBALL TECHNICAL JOURNAL. VFOAT National Volleyball Coaches Association Technical Journal. V. 1- Jan. 1974-. 0315-0887. Periodical. CN. includes some text in French. ir. $14.40 US. Canadian Volleyball Association, 333 River Road, Vanier City Ontario K1L 3H9 Canada. Tel (613)748-5681. Ed Lorne Saurila. bk rev. adv acc. Articles on coaching at all levels. Features Canadian and international authors.

VOTRE BOTTIN DE CROSSE. Main/Corp Federation de Crosse du Quebec. 0712-757X. CN. French. an. Free. Votre Bottin de Crosse, c/o Federation de Crosse du Quebec, 1415 East rue Jarry, Montreal Quebec H2E 2Z7 Canada. DD 796.347060714.

WASHINGTON STATE SPORT CATCH REPORT. Main/Corp Washington (State). Dept. of Fisheries. 0148-4389. US. English. an. LC SH11. DD 639.2755. *Washington Salmon Sport Catch Report from Punch Card Returns.*

THE WATER SKIER. Began in 1951. 0049-7002. Periodical. US. English. ir. $10.00. American Water Ski Association, PO Box 191, Winter Haven FL 33882. Tel (813)324-4341. Ed Duke Cullimore. Ind/Abst Mag. Index. LC GV840.S5. DD 797.1730973. adv acc. Circ 18,000. Information about the sport of water skiing, both recreational and organized competition. Includes instruction, equipment, personalities, events.

DE WATERKAMPIOEN. Vol. 1 (7 Jan. 1927)- – No. 1-. Periodical. Dutch. ir. LC GV771. DD 797.05.

WATERSKI. VFOAT Water Ski. Vol. 7, No. 1 (Apr. 1985)-. 0883-7813. Periodical. US. English. bm. Waterski Magazine, PO Box 136, Mount Morris IL 61054. DD 797. *World Waterskiing Magazine, 0194-6633; Spray's Water Ski, 8750-5509.*

WEEKEND. Year 1- June 1973-. Periodical. Italian. ir. $56.00. Bolaffi and Mondadori, Via Rivalta 34 10141, Torino Italy. LC GV1.

WESTERN BOWLER. 0746-7060. Periodical. US. English. mo. Western Bowler, 941 Bench Boulevard, Billings MT 59105.

WESTERN SPORTSMAN. V. 11- Spring 1979-. 0709-1532. Periodical. CN. English. bm. $10.95 Domestic, $14.45 Foreign. Western Sportsman, PO Box 737, Regina Saskatchewan S4P 3A8 Canada. Tel (306)352-8384. Ed Rick Bates. DD 799.297123. adv acc. Circ 28,000. Covers fishing and hunting in Alberta and Saskatchewan. *Fish and Game Sportsman, 0015-2897.*

WHAT'S ON - NATIONAL SPORT AND RECREATION CENTRE. (WHAT'S ON). VFOAT Actualites. 0821-7289. Periodical. CN. English (French). mo. 40.00 Domestic, 50.00 US. National Sport and Recreation Centre, 333 River Road, Vanier Ontario K1L 8H9 Canada. Tel (613)748-5644. Ed Ken Smith. DD 796.097. adv acc. Circ 1,200. (ctrl). A listing of amateur sports events in Canada, and directory of Canadian sport associations with contacts, telephone numbers. Also listed are meetings and future events. *Calendar of Events (National Sport and Recreation Centre).*

WHEELERS' CHOICE. V. 1- Jan. 1979-. 0225-9982. Periodical. CN. English. ir. $3.86. Canadian Wheelchair Sports Association, 333 River Road, Ottawa Ontario K1L 8H9 Canada. Tel (613)741-2463. Ed Dean Mellway. DD 796.0196. bk rev. adv acc. Circ 2,500. (ctrl). Wheelchair sports in Canada.

WHISTLE. (THE WHISTLE). 0227-0862. Periodical. CN. English. bm. Free. British Columbia Youth Soccer Association, 1200 Hornby Street, Vancouver British Columbia V6Z 1W2 Canada. DD 796.33409711. (ctrl).

WHO'S WHO DIRECTORY OF SPORTS, RECREATION AND PHYSICAL EDUCATION. *See* Yearbooks, Almanacs, Directories.

WIDE WORLD OF CANOEING. VFOAT Canoeing. 0273-0111. Periodical. US. English. $1.95 Domestic, $2.50 Foreign. Aqua-Field Publications Inc, 728 Beaver Dam Road, Pt Pleasant NJ 08741. LC GV781. DD 797.12205.

WINDRIDER. VFOAT Windrider Magazine. VAT WIND RIDER. Vol. 1, Issue 1 (Fall 1981)-. 0279-4659. Periodical. US. English. bm. $27.97. Windrider, PO Box 183, Mt Morris IL 61054. Tel (305)628-4802. Ed Nancy K Crowell. adv acc. Circ 35,000. Features how-to instructional tips, detailed board/equipment reviews, descripture travel articles and stunning full-color photography.

WINDSPORT. VFOAT Windsport Canada. VAT Windsport Canada (1983). Vol. 2, Issue No. 2 (April 1983)-. 0826-5003. Periodical. CN. English. ir. $9.50. Windsport, 2nd Floor/550 Bronte Road, Oakville Ontario L6J 4Z3 Canada. DD 797.1720971. *Windsport Canada, 0714-8852.*

WINDSPORT CANADA. Vol. 1, Issue 1 (Jan/Feb 1982)-V. 2 Issue No. 1 (Feb. 1983). 0714-8852. Periodical. CN. English. mo. $10.83. Windsport Magazine, 550 Bronte Road, Oakville Ontario L6J 4Z3 Canada. Tel (416)827-5462. Ed Steve Jarrett. DD 797.1720971. bk rev. adv acc. Circ 15,000. Devoted to the sport of Windsurfing. Featuring colour action photography and information articles appealing to those involved or wishing to become involved in this exciting sport.

WINDSURF. (WIND SURF). Vol. 11, No. 4 (Nov. 81)-. 0279-9359. US. English. mo. Windsurf Magazine, PO Box 561, Dana Point CA 92629. Tel (714)661-4888. Ed Drew Kampion. LC GV811.63.W56. DD 797.17205. adv acc. Circ 40,000. The leading boardsailing magazine in the US. This editorial features on competition, high-performance surfsailing, interviews, travel, and tips. *Windsurf, 0279-9359.*

THE WINGED HEAD. Established 1910. 0043-5864. Periodical. US. English. mo.

WISCONSIN SILENT SPORTS. 0882-9640. Periodical. US. English. mo. $10.00. Wisconsin Silent Sports, PO Box 152, Waupaca WI 54981. DD 796.

WISSENSCHAFTLICHE ZEITSCHRIFT - DEUTSCHE HOCHSCHULE FUR KORPERKULTUR LEIPZIG. *See* Physical Training.

WOLGAN SSIRUM. VFOAT Ssirum. Periodical. KO. Korean. mo. 10,000. Taehan Ssirum Hyophoe, 19 Mugyo-dong Chung-ku, Seoul 100 Korea. LC GV1198.81.K6.

WOMEN'S COACHING CLINIC. Vol. 1, No. 1 (Sept. 1977)-. 0146-1133. Periodical. US. English. $31.25. Prentis-Hall Inc, Slyvan Avenue, Englewood Cliffs NJ 07632. Tel (609)924-9329. Ed Annette R van Deusen. LC GV709.14. DD 796.0194. bk rev. Circ 2,500. Each issue conveys the best thinking, the newest strategies devised by some of the most successful coaches of women's sports today.

WOMEN'S COURT. VFOAT Women's Court. 8756-8365. Periodical. US. English. mo. $13.95 Domestic, $19.50 Canada. Thomas Sports Enterprises, 4343 Lincoln Centre, Matteson IL 60443. DD 796.

WOMEN'S TRACK & FIELD WORLD (1982). (WOMEN'S TRACK & FIELD WORLD). VFOAT Women's Track and Field World. Vol. 15, No. 1 (Mar. 1982)-. 0739-0858. Periodical. US. English. mo. S F Vincent Reel, PO Box 850, Cedar Glen CA 92321. Tel (714)621-5168. Ed Vince Reel. bk rev. adv acc. Circ 20,000. Club, scholastic, collegiate and world coverage. Results, statistics, features, technique, many photos, women/girls only. *Women's Track World, 0193-8312.*

WOODS N WATERS MAGAZINE. VFOAT Woods "N" Waters. VAT Woods and Waters Magazine. 0279-0807. Periodical. US. English. mo. $10.00. Woods "N" Waters Magazine, PO Box 983, Fond du Lac WI 54935. Tel (414)921-1890. Ed Barbara Laken. adv acc. Circ 50,000. (ctrl). An outdoor fishing and hunting magazine written by sportsmen who love the outdoors, not technical writers who study fish and game.

WORLD ALMANAC GUIDE TO PRO HOCKEY. *See* Yearbooks, Almanacs, Directories.

WORLD CLINIC YEARBOOK. *See* Yearbooks, Almanacs, Directories.

WORLD SOCCER. Began in 1960. Periodical. UK. English. mo. $29.73. Websters Publications Ltd, Onslow House, 60-66 Saffron Hill, London EC 1N 8AY England. Tel (01)831-6871. LC GV942. DD 796.33405.

WORLD SOCCER NEWS. Vol. 1, No. 1 (Oct. 7, 1981)-. 0711-3919. Periodical. CN. English. wk. $1.00 Each Issue. World Soccer News, Suite 205/4250 Weston Road, Weston Ontario M9L 1W9 Canada. DD 796.33405.

WORLD TENNIS. V. 1- June 1953-. 0043-910X. Periodical. US. English. mo. $15.94. Palm Coast Data, PO Box 6007, Palm Coast FL 32037. Tel (303)442-4282. Ind/Abst Pop. Mag. Rev., Read. Guide Period. Lit., Consum. Index Prod. Eval. Inf. Source, Mag. Index. LC GV991. DD 796.34. *American Lawn Tennis, Racquet.*

WORLD-WIDE GOLF DIRECTORY. *See* Yearbooks, Almanacs, Directories.

WORLDWIDE HUNTING ANNUAL. (WORLDWIDE HUNTING ANNUAL : OFFICIAL PUBLICATION OF SAFARI CLUB INTERNATIONAL). VFOAT Safari Worldwide Hunting Annual. 1981-. 0276-4865. Periodical. US. English. an. $5.50. Safari Magazine, 5151 East Broadway, Tucson AZ 85711. LC SK1. DD 799.2605.

WRESTLING. Main/Corp Saskatchewan High Schools Athletic Association. 0706-6538. CN. English. an. Free. Saskatchewan High Schools Athletic Association, 2220 College Avenue, Regina Saskatchewan S4P 3V7 Canada. DD 796.8123097124.

WRESTLING MASTERS. Began in 1983. 8755-3767. Periodical. US. English. bm. $20.95. Sports Masters Publishing Company, PO Box 824, Brookline MA 02146. DD 796.

WRESTLING RULE BOOK CEASED. Main/Corp National Federation of State High School Associations. 0361-641X. US. English. 400 Leslie Street, PO Box 98, Elgin IL 60120. LC GV1195. DD 796.8120712.

WRESTLING USA. VFOAT Wrestling U.S.A. VAT Wrestling United States of America. V. 15, No. 6- Feb. 1, 1980-. 0199-6258. Periodical. US. English. ir. $20.00. Wrestling USA, PO Box 128 MSU, Bozeman MT 59717. Tel (406)586-4457. Ed Lanny Bryant. adv acc. Circ 10,000. (ctrl). A national magazine dedicated to amateur wrestling from the elementary school student to the olympian. A publication for the coach, athlete and wrestling fan. *Scholastic Wrestling News.*

WRESTLING'S MAIN EVENT. (WRESTLINGS MAIN EVENT). VFOAT Main Event. V. 1, No. 1 (June 1982)-. 0278-9612. Periodical. US. English. bm. $16.00. Pumpkin Press Inc, Empire State Building, Suite 6204, New York NY 10118.

WWF MAGAZINE. (WWF MAGAZINE : OFFICIAL PUBLICATION OF THE WORLD WRESTLING FEDERATION). VFOAT Official World Wrestling Federation Magazine. VAT World Wrestling Federation Magazine. 8756-7792. Periodical. US. English. bm. $14.47 Domestic, $19.47 Foreign. WWF Magazine, PO Box 1538, Greenwich CT 06836. DD 796. *Official World Wrestling Federation's Magazine, 0747-4016.*

THE YEAR BOOK OF SPORTS MEDICINE. *See* Yearbooks, Almanacs, Directories.

YEARBOOK - CANADIAN LADIES' GOLF ASSOCIATION. *See* Yearbooks, Almanacs, Directories.

YEARBOOK - CANADIAN RACING PIGEON UNION. (YEAR BOOK - CANADIAN RACING PIGEON UNION). Main/Corp Canadian Racing Pigeon Union. 0316-2559. Periodical. CN. English. an. Free to members. Canadian Racing Pigeon Union, R R 4, London Ontario N6A 4B8 Canada. DD 798.8.

YEARBOOK - ENSIGN CLASS ASSOCIATION. *See* Yearbooks, Almanacs, Directories.

YEARBOOK - UNITED STATES POLO ASSOCIATION. *See* Yearbooks, Almanacs, Directories.

YOUNG ATHLETE CEASED. V. 1-4. 0160-5844. Periodical. US. English. bm. Young Athlete Inc, 1601 114th Avenue SE, Bellevue WA 98004. LC GV561. DD 796.05.

THE YOUNG BREED: THE WORLD OF YOUTH RODEO. VFOAT World of Youth Rodeo. 1978-. US. English. an. $24.95. Triple M Publishing Company, Box 778, Lewisville TX 75067. LC GV1834.4. DD 791.80973.

Religion, Mythology, Rationalism

THE YOUNG WRESTLER. V. 1- Sept./Oct. 1974-. 0160-5771. US. English. qt. $3.00. PO Box 60387, Oklahoma City OK 73106. **LC** GV1198.12. **DD** 796.8120973.

RELIGION, MYTHOLOGY, RATIONALISM

4E JOUR. VAT Quatrieme Jour. 0820-8778. Periodical. CN. French. ir. $3,00. Mouvement Cursillo d'Ottawa, 256 Avenue King Edward, Ottawa Ontario K1N 7M1 Canada. **DD** 269.6.

AACC BULLETIN CEASED. **Main/Corp** All Africa Conference of Churches. **VAT** All Africa Conference of Churches Bulletin. V. 1-12, No. 1. Periodical. English. ir. $9.00. All African Conference of Churches, PO Box 14205, Nairobi Kenya.

AACC NEWSLETTER. Main/Corp All Africa Conference of Churches. Information Dept. KE. English. ir. All-Africa Conference on Churches, PO Box 14206, Nairobi Kenya Africa. **LC** BR1359. **DD** 276.

AAR STUDIES IN RELIGION. Main/Corp American Academy of Religion. **VFOAT** Studies in Religion. **VAT** American Academy of Religion Studies in Religion. 0145-2789. Monographic Series. US. English. ir. Scholars Press, Customer Services, PO Box 4869, Hampden Station, Baltimore MD 21211. **Tel** (301)338-6946. Ed James Wiggins. **LC** UNC. Monographs representing historical, methodological, critical, and constructive aspects of scholarship in the field of religion.

ABBEY LETTER. No. 81- June 1969-. Periodical. US. English. qt. St Gregory's Abbey, 56500 Abbey Road, Three Rivers MI 49093. *Benedicite.*

ABSTRACTS - AMERICAN ACADEMY OF RELIGION. *See* Indexes/Abstracts.

ABSTRACTS (AMERICAN ACADEMY OF RELIGION AND SOCIETY OF BIBLICAL LITERATURE). *See* Indexes/Abstracts.

ABSTRACTS OF RESEARCH IN PASTORAL CARE AND COUNSELING. *See* Indexes/Abstracts.

ACCENT ON WORSHIP. (ACCENT ON WORSHIP : A PUBLICATION OF THE LITURGICAL CONFERENCE). Vol. 1, No. 1-. 0276-2358. Periodical. US. English. qt. Free to Members, $7.50 Others. The Liturgical Conference, The Merkle Building, 806 Rhode Island Avenue NE, Washington DC 20018. **Tel** (202)529-7400. Ed Rachel Reeder. bk rev. **Circ** 4,500. (ctrl). A benefit of membership in The Liturgical Conference. It provides 2-3 articles of interest to pastoral liturgists on music, art, preaching, etc., as well as book reviews. *Accent on Liturgy, 0272-7951.*

ACCENT ON YOUTH. Periodical. English. mo. Methodist Publishing House, PO Box 801, Nashville TN 37202. **Tel** (215)749-6431.

ACT. 0001-5083. Periodical. US. English. mo. $3.00. Christian Family Movement, PO Box 272, Ames IA 50010. **Tel** (515)232-7432. Ed Laverne Sober. bk rev. **Circ** 2,800. Newsletter of Christian family movement. Ideas and resources of interest to families and family life ministers.

ACTES DU CONGRES DE LA SOCIETE CANADIENNE POUR L'ETUDE DE LA RELIGION. (LES ACTES DU CONGRES DE LA SOCIETE CANADIENNE POUR L'ETUDE DE LA RELIGION). **Main/Corp** Canadian Society for the Study of Religion. Congress. **VFOAT** Annual Proceedings of the Canadian Society for the Study of Religion. Began publication in 1968. 0317-4972. CN. English (French). M Schumaker, Queen's Theological College, Kingston Ontario K7L 3N6 Canada. **LC** BL21. **DD** 200.5.

ACTION. Mar. 1970-. 0315-6036. Periodical. CN. English. Overseas Missions Department of the Pentecostal Assemblies of Canada, 10 Overlea Boulevard, Toronto M4H 1A5 Canada.

ACTION. No. 1- July 1, 1966. Periodical. UK. English. mo. World Association for Christian Communication, 122 Kings Road, London SW3 4TR England. **Tel** 589-1484. Ed Ann Shakespeare. bk rev. **Circ** 2,200. (ctrl). Communication and church trends. *National European.*

ACTION (CENTRAL ILLINOIS CONFERENCE EDITION). (ACTION). V. 1- 1962-. 0363-731X. Newspaper. US. English. bm. $0.40. Illinois Area Commission on United Methodist Communication, 501 East Capitol Avenue, Springfield IL 62701.

ACTUALITE DIOCESAINE. (ACTUALITE DIOCESAINE : JOURNAL DE L'EGLISE DE SAINT-JEAN-LONGUEUIL). Vol. 14, No 9 (25 Fall 1983)-. 0823-552X. Periodical. CN. French. 6w. 5.00. Diocese de Saint-Jean-Longueuil, Service de l'Information, 740 Ste-Foy, Longueuil Quebec J4K 4X8 Canada. **Tel** (514)679-1100. **DD** 282.71437. bk rev. adv acc. **Circ** 7,100. News from Christian communities of the diocese plus editorial content stating the policies and position of the church on a variety of subjects. *Au Rythme de Notre Eglise, 0383-0152.*

ADRIS NEWSLETTER. VAT Association for the Development of Religious Information Systems Newsletter. V. 1, No. 1 (Summer 1971)-. 0300-7022. US. English. qt. $5.00. Rev Richard F Smith SJ/ Editor, Fordham University, Department of Theology, New York NY 10458.

ADULT LEADERSHIP. 0162-4172. Periodical. US. English. mo. $6.00. Materials Services Department, 127 Ninth Avenue North, Nashville TN 37234.

ADVANCE. V. 1- Oct. 1965-. 0001-8589. Periodical. US. English. mo. $9.00. Gospel Publishing House, 1445 Booneville Avenue, Springfield MO 65802.

AEIC JOURNAL. VFOAT Journal of the Association of Evangelical Institutional Chaplains. **VAT** Association of Evangelical Institutional Chaplains Journal. No. 1 (July 1976)-. Periodical. US. English. sa. AEIC, 2912 Chamberlayne Avenue, Richmond VA 23222.

AFER. VFOAT AFER, African Ecclesial Review. V. 7- Jan. 1965-. 0250-4650. Periodical. English. ir. Pastoral Institute of Eastern Africa GABA, PO Box 908, El Doret Kenya Africa. **Tel** 2634 Eldoret. Ed Felician N Rwehikiza. **Ind/Abst** New Testam. Abstr., Cathol. Period. Lit. Index, Relig. Index One, Period., Recent Publ. Artic. **LC** BX1675.A1. **DD** 276. bk rev. **Circ** 2,500. (ctrl). To make Christ's message relevant for Africa today: to this end it offers and invites discussion, reflection, information, and documentation. *African Ecclesiastical Review.*

AFKAR INQUIRY. VFOAT Afkar/Inquiry. Vol. 1, No. 4 (Sept. 1984)-. Periodical. UK. English. mo. Tropvale Ltd, 55 Banner Street, London EC1Y 8PX England. *Afkar.*

AFRICAN ECCLESIASTICAL REVIEW CEASED. V. 1-6. 0001-1134. Periodical. KE. English. bm. $16.00. Gaba Publications, P O Box 908, Eldoret Kenya East Africa. **Tel** 2634 Eldoret. Ed Felician N Rwehikiza. **Ind/Abst** New Testam. Abstr., Cathol. Period. Lit. Index, Relig. Index One, Period. bk rev. **Circ** 2,500. (ctrl). To make Christ's message relevant for Africa today: to this end it offers and invites discussion, reflection, information and documentation.

L'AGE D'OR. 1 (Winter 1983)-. Periodical. French. qt. 100. B P 47, 45390 Puiseaux France. **LC** BL624. **DD** 291.05.

THE AGE OF ATHEISM. English. ir. The Atheist Society of India, Thompson Street, Visakhapatnam 53001 India. **LC** BL2747.3. **DD** 211.805.

ALASKAN CHURCHMAN CEASED. Vol. -75. Periodical. US. English. qt. *Churchman.*

ALERT. Vol. 13, No. 2 (Aug. 1983)-. Periodical. US. English. qt.

ALL ABOUT ISSUES. VFOAT A.L.L. About Issues. **VAT** All About Issues for God, for Life, for the Family, for the Nation, American Life Lobby About Issues. 0733-1231. Periodical. US. English. mo. American Life Lobby, PO Box 490, Stafford VA 22554.

ALL THE WORLD. A QUARTERLY REVIEW OF THE WORLD-WIDE WORK OF THE SALVATION ARMY. *See* Sociology: General Works, Theory - Social Pathology, Welfare, Criminology.

THE ALLIANCE TEACHER. 0270-966X. Periodical. US. English. qt. $3.00. Alliance Teacher/ Christian Publications, 3825 Harzdale Drive, Camp Hill PA 17011.

THE ALLIANCE WORLD. 0270-9678. Periodical. US. English. qt. Christian Publications Inc, 25 South 10th Street, PO Box 3403, Harrisburgh PA 17105.

AMBASSADOR REPORT. 0882-2123. Periodical. US. English. qt. $20.00. Ambassador Report, PO Box 60068, Pasadena CA 91106. **Tel** (818)798-6112. Ed John Trechak. **DD** 289. bk rev. **Circ** 2,500. Exposes on Armstrongism, Ambassador College and cults in general.

THE A.M.E. CHURCH REVIEW. V. 1- July 1884-. 0360-3725. Periodical. US. English. qt. $6.50. W D Johnson/Editorial Office, 468 Lincolin Drive NW, Atlanta GA 30318. Ed B T Tanner and L J Coppin.

AMERICA. V. 1- (No. 1-). 0002-7049. Periodical. US. English. wk. $25.00. America Press, 106 West 56th Street, New York NY 10019. **Tel** (212)581-4640. Ed George W Hunt. **Ind/Abst** Pop. Mag. Rev., Cathol. Period. Lit. Index, Biogr. Index, Film Lit. Index, Read. Guide Period. Lit., Book Rev. Index, Book Rev. Digest, Media Rev. Dig., Old Testam. Abstr. **LC** BX801. **DD** 282. bk rev. adv acc. **Circ** 35,000. (ctrl). Available on microfilm from University Microfilms. Journal of opinion published by Jesuits on national and international topics. *Messenger.*

AMERICAN ACADEMY OF RELIGION ACADEMY SERIES. VFOAT AAR Academy Series. Began with No. 37, published in 1981. 0277-1071. Monographic Series. US. English. ir. Scholars Press, PO Box 2268, Chico CA 95927. *Dissertation Series - American Academy of Religion, 0145-272X.*

AMERICAN ACADEMY OF RELIGION AIDS FOR THE STUDY OF RELIGION. VFOAT Aids for the Study of Religion. 0145-3246. Monographic Series. US. English. ir. Scholars Press, PO Box 1608, Decatur GA 30029. **Tel** (404)329-6950. Ed Gene Tucker. **LC** UNC. Research and reference sources for the study of religion.

AMERICAN ACADEMY OF RELIGION TEXTS AND TRANSLATION SERIES. VFOAT Texts and Translation Series. No. 1-. 0147-8931. Monographic Series. US. English. be. Scholars Press, PO Box 1608, Decatur GA 30029. **Tel** (404)329-6950. Ed Gene Tucker. Texts, translations, and critical analyses of ancient manuscripts related to early Western history and culture.

THE AMERICAN BENEDICTINE REVIEW. V. 1- Spring 1950-. 0002-7650. Periodical. US. English. qt. $10.00. American Benedictine Review, Assumption Abbey, Richardson ND 58652. **Tel** (701)974-3315. Ed Terrence Kurdong. **Ind/Abst** Am. Hist. Life, Hist. Abstr., Part A, Mod. Hist. Abstr., Hist. Abst., Part B, Twent. Century Abstr., MLA Int. Bibliogr. Books Artic. Mod. Lang. Lit., New Testam. Abstr., Energy Res. Abstr., Writ. Am. Hist., Cathol. Period. Lit. Index, Years Work Eng. Stud., Hist. Abstr. **LC** BX3001. **DD** 271.105. **Circ** 1,000. (ctrl). Available on microfilm from University Microfilms. A scholarly publication which covers a broad spectrum of topics while at the same time addressing Benedictines in today's world.

THE AMERICAN RABBI. 0164-3916. Periodical. US. English. bm. $26.00. Pastoral Services, 7507 Melba Avenue, Canoga Park CA 91304. **Tel** (818)340-6486. Ed Harry Essrig. **LC** BM730.A1. **DD** 296.42. bk rev. **Circ** 825. (ctrl). Homiletical journal containing sermons, biblical interpretations and book reviews of special appeal to Rabbis of all branches of Judaism. *PASTORAL SERVICES.*

THE AMERICAN RATIONALIST. V. 1- May 1956-. 0003-0708. Periodical. US. English. bm. **LC** BL2700. **DD** 149.7.

AMHC FORUM. *See* Psychology.

AMIGO. V. 1- Sept./Oct. 1973-. 0318-5729. Periodical. CN. French. ir. $2.32. Service Mondi-Ami, 11011 rue Drouart, Montreal Quebec H3M 2S4 Canada. **Tel** (514)337-3846. Ed Therese Roy. bk rev. adv acc. Includes christian values, missionary projects, cross- words, crafts, biblical reflection and prayers, school year events, history.

ANALECTA ANSELMIANA. UNTERSUCHUNG UBER PERSON U. WERK ANSELMUS VON CANTERBURY. GW. Multilingual (English, French, German and Italian). ir. Minerva GMBH, Morgensternstrasse 37, D6000 Frankfurt West Germany.

ANALECTA BOLLANDIANA. V. 1- 1882-. 0003-2468. Periodical. BE. text in Latin and French. qt. $55.00. Societe des Bollandistes, 24 Boulevard Saint-Michel, B-1040 Bruxelles Belgium. **Ind/Abst** MLA Int. Bibliogr. Books Artic. Mod. Lang. Lit. (cum

Religion, Mythology, Rationalism

index). bk rev. Critical history about lives of saints, ancient and Middle Ages.

ANALECTA CARTUSIANA. 1- 1970-. Monographic Series. AU. English or German. ir. 65. Institut Fur Englishe Sprache, Univ Salzburg, A-5020 Salzburg Austria. Tel 06217 7084. Ed James Hogg. Ind/Abst MLA Int. Bibliogr. Books Artic. Mod. Lang. Lit. Circ 200. History and spirituality of the Carthusian Order.

ANALECTA SACRA TARRACONENSIA. V. 1- 1925-. 0304-4300. Periodical. SP. Spanish. ir. 2.000. Libreria Balmes, Calle Duran y Bas 11, Barcelona 2 Spain. Tel 317.94.43. Ind/Abst Am. Hist. Life, Hist. Abstr., Part A, Mod. Hist. Abstr., Hist. Abst., Part B, Twent. Century Abstr., MLA Int. Bibliogr. Books Artic. Mod. Lang. Lit., Hist. Abstr. LC BX806.C3. DD 205. (cum index). Circ 1,000.

ANANDA SANDESA. Hindi. ir. 10.00. Sri Anandapura Trasta, Karyalaya Ananda Sandesa, Dist Guna, MP, Sri Anandapura India. LC BL1100.

ANCHOR. (ANCHOR : NEWSLETTER OF THE AMERICAN MINISTERIAL ASSOCIATION). Vol. 1, Issue 1 (Mar. 1982)-. 0732-4340. Periodical. US. English. qt. $10.00 Non-Members, Free to Members. American Ministerial Association, 25920 Narbonne Avenue No 16, Lomita CA 90717.

ANCIENT CHRISTIAN WRITERS. No. 1- 1946-. 0066-1597. Monographic Series. US. English. ir. Paulist Press, 400 Sette Drive, Paramus NJ 07652.

ANCLA (EL PASO, TEX.). (ANCLA). 0279-7216. Periodical. US. Spanish. qt. $5.50. Sunday School Board of SBC, 127 Ninth Avenue North, Nashville TN 37234.

ANDOVER NEWTON QUARTERLY. CEASED. V. 1-20. 0003-2972. Periodical. US. English. qt. Andover Newton Theological School, 210 Herrick Road, Newton Centre MA 02159. Ind/Abst Relig. Index One, Period., Relig. Theol. Abstr., Elenchus Bibligr. Bibicus, Int. Zeitschriftenschan Bibelwissenschaft Grenzgeb., New Testam. Abstr., Book Rev. Mon. Andover Newton Bulletin.

ANGELICUM. See Philosophy.

ANNALS OF SAINT ANNE DE BEAUPRE. (THE ANNALS OF SAINT ANNE DE BEAUPRE). V. 88, No. 1- Jan. 1974-. 0318-434X. CN. English. mo. 6.50. The Annals of Sainte Anne de Beaupre, PO Box 1000, St Anne de Beaupre Quebec G0A 3C0 Canada. Tel (418)827-4538. Ed Rock Achard. DD 248.05. Circ 55,000. We specifically speak of Saint Anne and other Church's concerns. Various events at our shrine also family education, comments from our readers, etc. The Annals of Good Saint Anne de Beaupre, 0318-4331.

ANNALS - SOCIETY FOR THE PROPAGATION OF THE FAITH. (ANNALS). VFOAT Annals of the Propagation of the Faith. VAT Annals of the Propagation of the Faith (Scarboro. 1972). 0822-8647. Periodical. CN. English. ir. Papal Mission-Aid Societies, 2661 Kingston Road, Scarborough Ontario M1M 1M3 Canada. DD 266.205. Annals of the Propagation of the Faith, 0702-3596.

ANNUAL DIRECTORY, HOUSES OF PRAYER. See Yearbooks, Almanacs, Directories.

ANNUAL REPORT - MINDOLO ECUMENICAL FOUNDATION. Main/Corp Mindolo Ecumenical Foundation. RH. English. sa. $1.80. Mindolo Ecumenical Foundation, PO Box 1192, Kitwe Zambia Northern Rhodesia. LC BR1446.6. DD 262.001.

ANNUAL REPORT - SINGAPORE. MUSLIM RELIGIOUS AFFAIRS DIVISION. Main/Corp Singapore. Muslim Religious Affairs Division. Sl. English. an. Majlis Ugama Islam Singapura, Muslim Religious Affairs Division, Singapore 6 Singapore. LC BP10. DD 354.595700857.

ANNUAL REPORT - UNITED CHURCH BOARD FOR WORLD MINISTRIES. Main/Corp United Church Board for World Ministries. 151st- 1961-. 0145-0824. US. English. an. United Church Board for World Ministries, 475 Riverside Drive, New York NY 10027. LC BV2360. DD 262.001. Annual Report - American Board of Commissioners for Foreign Missions, 0362-7632; Treasurer's Report; Directory and Calendar of Prayer.

ANTONIANUM. Vol. 1- 1926-. 0003-6064. Periodical. IT. English (German, Italian, Latin, and Spanish). qt. $35.00. Editore Antonianum, Via Merulana 124, 00185 Rome Italy. Ind/Abst MLA Int. Bibliogr. Books Artic. Mod. Lang. Lit., Old Testam. Abstr., New Testam. Abstr., Am. Hist. Life, Hist. Abstr., Hist. Abstr., Part A, Mod. Hist. Abstr., Hist. Abst., Part B, Twent. Century Abstr. (cum index). bk rev. Circ 1,000. (ctrl). Antonianum service in faith and in Christian science.

APPELES A LA LIBERTE (LEGARDEUR, QUEBEC). (APPELES A LA LIBERTE). Jan. 84-. 0828-4695. Periodical. CN. French. qt. Free. Appeles A La Liberte, C P 81, Legardeur Quebec J5Z 2N4 Canada. DD 269.205.

APUNTES (DALLAS, TEX.). (APUNTES). Vol. 1, No. 1 (Spring 1981)-. 0279-9804. Periodical. US. Spanish (English). qt. $5.00. Apuntes, Perkins School of Theology, c/o Roy D Barton, Dallas TX 75275. Tel (214)692-2265. Ed Justo L Gonzalez. Ind/Abst Relig. Index One, Period. bk rev. Theology from an hispanic perspective; theological issues relevant to Hispanics.

ARBEITEN ZUR GESCHICHTE DES ANTIKEN JUDENTUMS UND DES URCHRISTENTUMS. German. ir. EJ Brill, POB 9000, 2300 PA Leiden The Netherlands.

ARBEITEN ZUR KIRCHENGESCHICHTE HAMBURGS. V. 1- 0518-2107. Monographic Series. GW. German. ir. Friedrich Wittig Verlag, Papenhuder Strasse 2, 2000 Hamburg 76 West Germany.

ARBEITEN ZUR KIRCHLICHEN ZEITGESCHICHTE. REIHE B : DARSTELLUNGEN. Vol. 1-. Monographic Series. GW. German. ir. Vandenhoeck & Ruprecht, Postfach 3753, Theaterstr 13, D 3400 Goettingen West Germany. Tel 0551/65061. Ed Georg Kretschmer and Klans Scholder. adv acc.

ARCHETYPAL IMAGES IN GREEK RELIGION. V. 1- 1959-. 0570-6378. Monographic Series. UK. English. ir. Princeton University Press, Box A 3175 Princeton Pike, Lawrenceville NJ 08648. Tel (609)896-2111.

ARCHIV FUR RELIGIONSPSYCHOLOGIE. See Genealogy and Heraldry - Archives.

ARCHIVES DE SCIENCES SOCIALES DES RELIGIONS. See Genealogy and Heraldry - Archives.

THE ARMENIAN CHURCH. (ARMENIAN CHURCH). V.1- 1958-. 0004-2315. Periodical. US. English. mo. Diocese of Armenian Church of America, 630 Second Avenue, New York NY 10016.

ARTE CRISTIANA. See The Arts (General).

ASCENT. V. 1- Sept. 1969-. 0315-8179. Periodical. CN. English. ty. $6.19. Yasodhara Ashram Society, Box 9, Kootenay Bay British Columbia V0B 1X0 Canada. Tel (604)227-9224. Ed Ian MacKenzie. DD 181.4805. bk rev. Circ 1,500. (ctrl). Published twice a year, and carries a major article by Swami Radha. Book reviews and contributions from friends and associates.

THE ASIAN AMERICAN JOURNEY. VFOAT TAJ. 0741-0336. Periodical. US. English. bm. $4.00 (General Issues), $5.00 (General and Religious Issues). Agape Fellowship, 332 South Virgil Avenue, Los Angeles CA 90020.

ATAMA-SAIMSA. VFOAT Atam-Science. Periodical. Punjabi. ir. 12.00. Raghabira Singha Bira, 82-A Ashutosh Mukherji Road, Calcutta 25 India. LC BL2017.

ATEISMO E DIALOGO. VFOAT Atheism and Dialogue, Atheisme et Dialogue, Ateismo y Dialogo. Began with V. 1 in 1966-. Periodical. Italian (French, Spanish, and English). ir. $9.00 Europe, $11.00 Others. Secretariato per I Non Credenti, Palazzo San Calisto, 00120 Citta del Vaticano.

ATEIZMUS. Periodical. CS. Slovak. bm. $24.00. Slovart Foreign Trade Company Limited, Gottwaldovo Nam 6, 817 64 Bratislava Czechoslovakia. Tel 48841-49. LC BL2700.

ATHEIST. (THE ATHEIST). 0304-1409. Periodical. English. ir. $2.00. LC BL2747.3. DD 211.805.

AU RYTHME DE NOTRE EGLISE CEASED. V. 1-14, No. 8. 0383-0152. Periodical. CN. text also in English. bm. G Roy 740, Boul Ste-foy, CP 40, Longueuil Quebec J4K 4X8 Canada.

AUFTRAG (BASEL, SWITZERLAND : 1967). (AUFTRAG). V. 1, No 1 (Feb./March 1967)-. 0004-7880. Periodical. SZ. German. bm. 12.-. Auftrag Administration, Missionsstr 21, 4003 Basel 3 Switzerland. Tel (061)253725. Ed Eduard Abel. Circ 47,000. Publication for church and mission. Dienst und Zeugnis, Auftrag (Basel, Switzerland : 1956); Pionier; Ostasien; Bruder Uberall.

AUGUSTINIAN STUDIES. V. 1- 1970-. 0094-5323. US. English. ir. Augustinian Institute, University of Villanova, c/o R de Sincone, Villanova PA 19085. Ind/Abst Philos. Index, Cathol. Period. Lit. Index. LC BR65.A9. DD 270.20924.

AUGUSTINIANA. See History (General).

AUJOURD'HUI CREDO. V. 21, No. 8-9 Aug./Sept. 1974-. 0383-2554. Periodical. CN. French. mo. $11.61. Aujourd'Hui Credo, 3480 Boul Decarie, Montreal Quebec H4A 3J5 Canada. Tel (514)486-9213. Credo, 0383-2546.

AUSTIN SEMINARY BULLETIN (FACULTY EDITION). (AUSTIN SEMINARY BULLETIN). 0883-7988. Periodical. US. English. mo. Austin Seminary Bulletin, 100 East 27th Street, Austin TX 78705. Ind/Abst Relig. Index One, Period. DD 285.

AUSTRALIAN FRIEND (SYDNEY, N.S.W.). (THE AUSTRALIAN FRIEND : THE ORGAN OF THE SOCIETY OF FRIENDS (QUAKERS). Periodical. English. ir. Religious Society of Friends, Friends House, 631 Orrong Road, Toorak, Victoria 3142 Australia. Friend of Australia and New Zealand.

AUTRE PAROLE. (L'AUTRE PAROLE). No. 1 (Sept. 1976)-. 0228-4146. Periodical. CN. French. ty. $2.00. Monique Dumais, Departement des Sciences Religieuses, Universite du Quebec, 300 Av des Ursulines, Rimouski Quebec G5L 3A1 Canada. DD 261.834409714.

AWAKE. 1919. 0005-237X. Periodical. US. English. sm. Watchtow Biblical & Tract Society, 117 Adams Street, Brooklyn NY 11201. Tel (914)744-2041. Ed W L Barry. Circ 8,900,000. Articles focus on God's purpose to make earth a paradise, while dealing with nature, science, health, lands, peoples, religion, and world affairs. Consolation.

AWAKENER. 0005-2388. Periodical. US. English. ir. $4.00 2 year subscription. Universal Spiritual League in America, 938 18th Street, Hermosa Beach CA 90254. Tel (213)379-2656. Ed Filis Frederick. Ind/Abst New Period. Index. bk rev. Circ 1,000. Journal devoted to the philosophy and teachings of Avatar Meher Baba, the spiritual master well-known East and West, featuring biographical material, articles, poetry, art and reviews.

BACK TO GODHEAD. 0005-3643. Periodical. US. English. mo. $10.00. Back to Godhead, PO Box 18928, Philadelphia PA 19119. Tel (215)822-0787. Ed Satsvarupa des Goswami. Circ 240,000. The magazine of the Hare Krsna movement, philosophy of Bhakti Yoga, vegetarianism, karma, reincarnation and activities of Iskcon founded 1944 AC Bhaktivedanta Swami Prabhupada.

BACKGROUND INFORMATION (COMMISSION OF THE CHURCHES ON INTERNATIONAL AFFAIRS). See Political Science - International Relations.

BARATAINKNAK A MAGYAR JEZSUITAK. 0228-9873. CN. English (text also in Hungarian). an. Free. Hungarian Jesuit Fathers, 282 Spadina Avenue, Toronto Ontario M5T 2E5 Canada. DD 255.53005. (ctrl).

BEACON. V. 5- Mar. 1970-. 0382-6384. Periodical. CN. English. bm. $6.19. Basilian Press, 286 Lisgar Street, Toronto Ontario M6J 3G9 Canada. Tel (416)656-3772. Ed Roman Kravec. bk rev. adv acc. Circ 1,500. Digest of Ukrainian press, news of Ukrainian and Roman Catholic Church, articles of spiritual value and preservation of Ukrainian cultural heritage. Life Beacon.

BEADS OF TRUTH. Periodical. US. English. sa. $10.00. 3 HO Foundation, 1620 Preuss Road, Los Angeles CA 90035. Tel (213)273-9422.

BEMA. (BEMA : THE OFFICIAL PUBLICATION OF THE DIOCESE OF THE ARMENIAN CHURCH OF AMERICA). Vol. 1, No. 1 (Apr. 1980)-. 0199-8765. Periodical. US. English. sa. $3.00. Armenian Church of America, 630 Second Avenue, New York NY 10016. Armenian Church, 0004-2315; Hayastanyaitz Yegeghetzy, 0017-8667.

Religion, Mythology, Rationalism

BENEDICTINES. 21,1 (Fall 1966)-. 0005-8726. Periodical. US. English. sa. $8.00. Mount St Scholastica, Atchison KS 66002. Tel (816)561-6479. Ed Mary Alice Guilfoil. bk rev. Circ 1,000. (ctrl). Available in microfilm from Xerox University Microfilms. A monastic journal exploring contemporary values, interpretations, contributions, monastic life, current society and church. *Benedictine Review,* 0148-947X.

BENSHEIMER HEFTE. Issue 1- 19 -. 0522-9014. Monographic Series. GW. German. ir. Vandenhoeck & Ruprecht, Postfach 3753, Theaterstr 13, D 3400 Goettingen West Germany. Tel 0551/65061. Ed Er Bund. adv acc.

BENTARA ILMUPENGETAHUAN KRISTEN. VFOAT The Herald of Christian Science. 0409-0810. Periodical. US. Indonesian (parallel text in English). qt. $2.00. Christian Science Publishing Society, 1 Norway Street, Boston MA 02115.

BHARATIYA VIDYA. V. 1- Nov. 1939-. 0378-1984. II. English. mo. 60. Bharatiya Vidya Bhavan, Chowpatty Road, Bombay 7 India. Tel 351461. Ed J H Dave and S A Upadhyaya. Ind/Abst MLA Int. Bibliogr. Books Artic. Mod. Lang. Lit. LC DS401. DD 954.005. bk rev. Circ 500. Studies in indology, Indian culture, literature, philosophy, religion, art, Sanskrit, etc.

BIBLE JOURNEYS FOR CHRISTIANS. Began in 1984. 0747-3893. Periodical. US. English. qt. $40.00. ALT Publishing Company, PO Box 400, Green Bay WI 54305.

BIBLE LANDS. V. 1- 1903-. 0006-0763. Periodical. UK. English. ir. Jerusalem & Middle East Church AS, 24 The Borough, Farnham Surrey GU9 7NJ England.

BIBLE LIVES OF FAITH SERIES. STUDENT BOOK. V. 1- Fall 1979-. 0190-1710. Periodical. US. English. qt. $4.25. Graded Press, 201 Eighth Avenue South, Nashville TN 37206. Ind/Abst United Methodist Period. Index.

THE BIBLE STANDARD AND HERALD OF CHRIST'S KINGDOM. VFOAT Bible Standard. 0006-081X. Periodical. US. English. mo. Free. Laymen's Home Missionary Movement, Chester Springs PA 19425. Tel (215)827-7665. Ed August Gohlke. Circ 7,500. Interdenominational mission dealing especially with the end of the Christian era and ushering in the coming kingdom of Christ and the church.

BIBLEBHASHYAM CEASED. VFOAT Bible Bhashyam. Began with V. 1, No. 1 (Mar. 1975). Ceased V. 6, No. 4 (Dec. 1980). English. qt. $3.00. St Thomas Apostolic Seminary, Vadavathoor, Kerala 686010 India. Ind/Abst New Testam. Abstr., Old Testam. Abstr. LC BS410. DD 220.05.

BIBLIOGRAFIA IDG. B, DIRITTO CANONICO ED ECCLESIASTICO. *See* Bibliographies.

BIBLIOGRAPHIE ZUR SYMBOLIK, IKONOGRAPHIE UND MYTHOLOGIE. *See* Bibliographies.

BIBLIOGRAPHIES AND INDEXES IN RELIGIOUS STUDIES. *See* Bibliographies.

BIBLIOTHECA THEOLOGIAE PRACTICAE. 1- 1957-. Monographic Series. Latin. ir. Liber International, S-205 10, 2-205 10 Malmo Sweden.

B.M.A.A. DIRECTORY AND HANDBOOK. *See* Yearbooks, Almanacs, Directories.

BOLETIN DE LA PROVINCIA DE SAN JOSE DE LA ORDEN DE AGUSTINOS RECOLETOS. Main/Corp Recollets (Augustinian). Provincia de San Jose. Spanish. ir. Colegio San Augustin, c/Alberite 104-122, Logrono Spain. LC BX2944.S25.

BONNES NOUVELLES - TEMOIGNAGE JEUNESSE GRANBY. Main/Corp Temognage Jeunesse Granby. V. 2, No. 2- Dec./Jan. 1979-. 0709-0722. Periodical. CN. French. mo. Free. Temoignage Jeunesse Granby, C P 725, Granby Quebec J2G 8W8 Canada. DD 269.205. *Bonnes Nouvelles de Temoignage Jeunesse,* 0709-0714.

BOOK REVIEWS OF THE MONTH. *See* Indexes/Abstracts.

BOOKS & RELIGION. VFOAT Books and Religion. Vol. 13, No 1 (Jan./Feb. 1985). 0732-7218. Periodical. US. English. mo. $16.00. Divinity School, Duke University, Durham NC 27705. Ed Christopher Walters-Burgee. Ind/Abst Relig. Index One, Period. bk rev. adv acc. Circ 15,000. A review offering panoramic coverage of religious books and all other aspects of the interplay of religion and culture. *Review of Books and Religion (Forward Movement Publications).*

BOOKSTORE JOURNAL. V. 1- June 1968-. 0006-7563. Periodical. US. English. mo. $25.00. Christian Booksellers Association, 2620 Venetucci Boulevard, PO Box 200, Colorado Springs CO 80901. Tel (303)576-7880. Ed Dave Somers. LC Z479. DD 381.45070573. bk rev. adv acc. Circ 9,000. (ctrl). Bookstore journal contains management, marketing, and new product information for christian booksellers.

BRAHMANA-GAURAVA. 0304-9272. Hindi. ir. 3.00. Moti Katra -3, Agara India. LC BL1100.

BRAHMAVADIN. (THE BRAHMAVADIN). Vol. 1, No. 1 (Jan. 1966)-. 0006-8721. Periodical. English. ir. Ind/Abst Philos. Index. LC BL1. DD 105. (cum index). *Brahmavadin (Madras, India).*

BRETHREN MISSIONARY HERALD. 1940. 0161-5238. Periodical. US. English. mo. Brethren Missionary Herald, Box 544, Winona Lake IN 46590. Tel (219)267-7158. Ed Charles W Turner. adv acc. Circ 8,000. (ctrl). Denominational interest for national fellowship of Brethren Churches.

BRITISH COLUMBIA CHURCH DIRECTORY. *See* Yearbooks, Almanacs, Directories.

BRITISH JOURNAL OF RELIGIOUS EDUCATION. V. 1- Autumn 1978-. 0141-6200. Periodical. UK. English. ty. 12.50. Christian Education Movement, 2 Chester House Pages Lane, London N10 1PR England. Tel (021)472-1301. Ed J M Hull. bk rev. adv acc. Circ 4,500. Professioanl academic journal for religious education in county schools including curriculum, theory and practice. *Learning for Living.*

THE BRITISH WEEKLY AND CHRISTIAN WORLD. VFOAT British Weekly & Christian World. Vol. 145, No. 3909 (Dec. 14, 1961)-No. 4880 (Oct. 24, 1980). 0007-1951. Periodical. UK. English. wk. $32.18. Christian Weekly Newspapers, 146 Queen Victoria Street, London EC4V 4EH England. Tel 01 248 2124. Ed Anne Tyler. adv acc. *British Weekly, Christian World (London, England).*

BULETINUL CULTULUI PENTICOSTAL : ORGANUL CULTULUI PENTICOSTAL-BISERICA LUI DUMNEZEU APOSTOLICA DIN REPUBLICA SOCIALISTA ROMANIA. 0526-3867. Periodical. RM. Romanian. bm. Ilexim Press Department, PO Box 1-136-1-137, Bucharest-Romania.

BULLETIN - ANGLICAN CHURCH WOMEN. DIOCESE OF OTTAWA. (BULLETIN - ANGLICAN CHURCH WOMEN, DIOCESE OF OTTAWA). Main/Corp Anglican Church of Canada. Anglican Church Women. Diocese of Ottawa. V. 1-10, No. 12. 0382-4985. Periodical. English. mo. *News Bulletin,* 0382-4993.

BULLETIN - CANADIAN RELIGIOUS CONFERENCE. Main/Corp Canadian Religious Conference. V. 1- Jan. 1955-. 0316-8743. Periodical. CN. English (French). CRC Bulletin, 324 Laurier Avenue East, Ottawa K1N 6P6 Canada. DD 255.006271.

BULLETIN - CONFERENCE RELIGIEUSE CANADIENNE. Main/Corp Conference Religieuse Canadienne. VFOAT Bulletin CRC. V. 1- Jan. 1955-. 0316-8751. Periodical. CN. French (issued in July 2, 1968-June 1969 V.8, No 6- Vol. 9, No. 5 in English and French). Bulletin CRC, 324 Est Avenue Laurier, Ottawa K1N 6P6 Canada. DD 255.006271.

BULLETIN - COUNCIL ON THE STUDY OF RELIGION. Main/Corp Council on the Study of Religion. VFOAT Bulletin of the Council on the Study of Religion. V. 1- June 1970-. 0002-7170. Periodical. CN. English. ir. $18.00. Council on the Study of Religion, Wilfrid Laurier University, Waterloo Ontario N2L 3C5 Canada. Tel (519)884-7300. Ed L Biallas. Ind/Abst Old Testam. Abstr., Relig. Index One, Period. LC BL1. DD 200.5. adv acc. Circ 14,400. Available on microfilm from University Microfilms. Publishes articles in the field of religious studies and news of the constituent societies of the Council on the study of religion. *Bulletin of the American Academy of Religion,* 0569-2148.

BULLETIN D'ARABE CHRETIEN CEASED. V. 1-5. Periodical. French. ir. Postliggen Heverlee 1, 3030 Heverlee Belgium.

BULLETIN DE L'A.I.M. Main/Corp AIDE a l'Implantation Monastique. VFOAT A.I.M. Bulletin. 1969. 0007-4314. Periodical. US. English. sa. $8.00. US National Center for AIDE Inter-Monasteres, 8300 Morganford Road, St Louis MO 93123. Tel (314)638-6427. Ed Dom Paul Gordan. bk rev. Circ 750. Invaluable historical witness and documentation of monastic life in the Mission World and the beginning efforts of dialogue between Christian and Non-Christian monks and nuns.

BULLETIN DE NOUVELLES - SOCIETE CANADIENNE DE DROIT CANONIQUE. Main/Corp Canadian Canon Law Society. VFOAT Newsletter - Canadian Canon Law Society. V. 1- Mar. 1974-. 0703-1963. Periodical. CN. English (French). ty. Free to members. Canadian Canon Law Society, 223 Main Street, Ottawa Ontario K1S 1C4 Canada. DD 262.905.

BULLETIN DE THEOLOGIE ANCIENNE ET MEDIEVALE. V. 1- Jan. 1929-. 0007-442X. Periodical. BE. French. an. $22.00. Dept Recher Theologie Ancienne et Medievale, Mechelse Straat 202, B-3000 Leuven Belgium. LC Z7753.

BULLETIN - NANZAN INSTITUTE FOR RELIGION AND CULTURE. Main/Corp Nanzan Institute for Religion and Culture. 0386-720X. Periodical. JA. English. ir. Nanzan University, 18 Yamazato-cho Showa-ku, Nagoya Japan.

THE BULLETIN OF CHRISTIAN INSTITUTES OF ISLAMIC STUDIES. V. 1- Jan./June 1978-. Periodical. II. English. qt. $12.00. Asia Books and Periodicals Company, 11 Darya Ganj, New Delhi 110002 India. Ed David T Lindell. Ind/Abst Relig. Index One, Period. bk rev. Circ 500. Concerns comparative religion, Islamic studies, and Christian-Muslim relations. *Basheer.*

BULLETIN OF DR. WILLIAM'S LIBRARY. Main/Corp Dr. Williams's Library. UK. English. an. 2.00. Dr Williams Trust, 14 Gordon Square, London WC1H 0AG England. Tel (01)387-3727. LC Z921.L87. Circ 2,000. Recent accessions. *Bulletin and Classified List of Accessions to the Library.*

THE BULLETIN OF THE CENTER FOR THE STUDY OF SOUTHERN CULTURE AND RELIGION. *See* Sociology: General Works, Theory - Manners and Customs.

BULLETIN OF THE EVANGELICAL PHILOSOPHICAL SOCIETY. *See* Philosophy.

THE BULLETIN OF THE SCOTTISH INSTITUTE OF MISSIONARY STUDIES. Main/Corp Scottish Institute of Missionary Studies. No. 1- June 1967-. Periodical. UK. English. ir. $4.10. Scott Institute of Missionary Studies, University of Aberdeen, Religious Studies, Aberdeen AB9 2UB Scotland.

BULLETIN - REGROUPEMENT INTERUNIVERSITAIRE POUR L'ETUDE DE LA RELIGION. Main/Corp Interuniversity Centre for the Study of Religion. VFOAT Newsletter - Interuniversity Centre for the Study of Religion. V. 1- Nov. 1979-. 0226-6067. Periodical. CN. English (French). ir. Free. Interuniversity Centre for the Study of Religion, PO Box 8888, Montreal Quebec H3C 3P8 Canada. DD 200.711714.

BULLETIN SIGNALETIQUE 527. HISTOIRE ET SCIENCES DES RELIGIONS. TABLES ANNUELLES. VFOAT Histoire et Sciences des Religions. Vol. 33 (1979)-. 0180-9296. FR. French. qt. 66. Centre Documentation Science Humaines, 54 Blvd Raspail, 75260 Paris Cedex 06 France. Tel 1.45.44.38.49. bk rev. adv acc. Circ 1,000. Covering religious sciences, ancient religion of Israel, Judaism, Christianity, Bible exegesis, theology, and history of religion. *Bulletin Signaletique 527: Sciences Religieuses. Tables Annuelles,* 0007-5620.

Religion, Mythology, Rationalism

BULLETIN - SRI AUROBINDO INTERNATIONAL CENTRE OF EDUCATION, PONDICHERRY, INDIA. Main/Corp SRI Aurobindo International Centre of Education, Pondicherry, India. Periodical. II. English (French). qt. $7.00. SRI Aurobindo Ashram, International Centre of Education, Pondicherry S 605002 India. Ed Harikant C Patel. adv acc. Circ 2,200. Main subjects contains Yoga philosophy and psychology, teachings of Sri Aurobindo and the Mother, activities of the Education Centre.

BURGENSE. 1- 1960-. 0521-8195. Periodical. Spanish. sa. Facultad de Teologia del Norte de Espana, Martinez de Compo 7, 09003 Burgos Spain. Ind/Abst Old Testam. Abstr., New Testam. Abstr. LC BR7.

BUZZ. Began with Nov. 2, 1976 issue. 0701-2837. Periodical. CN. English. mo. 9.95. Buzz Christian Ministries, 37 Elm Road New Malden, Surrey KT3 3HB England. Tel (01)942-9761. Ed Steve Goddard. DD 027.47131. bk rev. adv acc. Circ 23,616. News and current affairs regarding: significance for contemporary Christian arts, media reviews, features, etc. Newsletter, 0701-2829.

BYU STUDIES. VFOAT Brigham Young University Studies. Vol. 20, No. 1 (Fall 1979)-. 0278-1980. Periodical. US. English. qt. $8.00. Brigham Young University Press, 205 University Press Boulevard, Provo UT 84602. Tel (801)378-6691. Ed Edward Geary. Ind/Abst Am. Hist. Life, Hist. Abstr., Abstr. Engl. Stud., MLA Int. Bibliogr. Books Artic. Mod. Lang. Lit., Annu. Bibliogr. Engl. Lang. Lit., Relig. Index One, Period., Writ. Am. Hist. bk rev. A journal dedicated to the correlation of revealed and discovered truth and that the spiritual and intellectual are complementary. Avenues of knowledge point of view. High scholarly standards. Brigham Young University Studies, 0277-7363.

C. S. P. WORLD NEWS. VFOAT Congregation of St.-Paul World News. V. 2, No. 4- Apr. 1965-. 0702-7958. Periodical. CN. English. mo. CSP World News, Box 2608 Station D, Ottawa Ontario K1P 5W7 Canada. Ed G F C Hamel. DD 051. Voice of Port Royal.

CAHIERS DE L'APF. Main/Corp Association des Pasteurs de France. No. 1- May 1974-. Periodical. French. ir. 10.00. Association des Pasteurs de France, 47 rue de Clichy, Paris France 75011. Confiance.

CAHIERS DE SPIRITUALITE IGNATIENNE. V. 1- Jan./Mar. 1977-. 0705-8942. Periodical. CN. French. qt. 20.00. Centre de Spiritualite Ignatie, 2370 rue Nicolas Pinel, Ste-Foy Quebec G1V 4L6 Canada. Tel (418)653-6353. DD 248.05. Circ 800. Spirituality of Ignatius de Loyala in his spiritual exercises.

CAHIERS DES RELIGIONS AFRICAINES. V. 1- Jan./July 1967-. 0008-0047. Periodical. CG. French. sa. Presses Universitaires du Zaire, PO Box 712, Kinshasa Limete Zaire. Ind/Abst Recent Publ. Artic. LC BL2400. DD 229.605.

LES CAHIERS RATIONALISTES. Began in 1930. Periodical. FR. French. mo. 240. Union Rationaliste, 16 rue de l'Ecole Polytechnique, Paris 5E France. Tel 46330350. LC AP20. bk rev. Circ 2,500. Essays on religion, philosophy, science, and against parapsychology or other false sciences.

CALEDONIA TIMES. V. 9- Jan. 1968-. 0701-0729. Periodical. CN. English. ir. Anglican Discese of Caledonia, 208 West 4th Avenue, Prince Rupert British Columbia V8J 1P3 Canada. DD 283.71132. Caledonia Diocesan Times, 0383-6509.

CALGARY EVANGELICAL DIRECTORY. See Yearbooks, Almanacs, Directories.

CAMPUS LIFE. Began publication in 1944. 0008-2538. Periodical. US. English. mo. $14.95. CTI, 465 Gundersen Drive, Carol Stream IL 60188. Tel (312)260-6200. Ed Scott Bolinder. Ind/Abst Christ. Period. Index. adv acc. Circ 165,000. (ctrl). Also available on microfilm from Xerox University Microfilms. Exciting graphics, zany humor, fiction and inspiring true life stories written for teenagers.

CANADA MISSION DIRECTORY. See Yearbooks, Almanacs, Directories.

CANADIAN CHALLENGE (ABBOTSFORD, B.C.). (CANADIAN CHALLENGE). Vol. 1, No. 1 (Spring 1984)-. 0828-6930. Periodical. CN. English. qt. Campus Crusade for Christ of Canada, PO Box 368, Abbotsford British Columbia V2S 4N9 Canada. DD 267.61. Canadian Report (Abbotsford, B.C.), 0821-6339.

CANADIAN CHURCHMAN. V. 16- 1890-. 0008-3216. Periodical. CN. English. mo $3.09. Canadian Churchman, 600 Jarvis Street, Toronto Ont M4Y 2J6 Canada. Tel (416)924-9192. Ed Jerrold F. Hames. bk rev. adv acc. Circ 273,000. Published for Anglicans across Canada. Contains reports of current news events and human interest features from across the country and overseas, recognizing the wide diversity and interest of its readers. Dominion Churchman.

CANADIAN CHURCHMAN AND CROSSTALK. VFOAT Crosstalk. Began with Feb. 1978 issue. 0706-8069. Periodical. CN. English. Anglican Church of Canada Diocese of Ottawa, 71 Bronson Avenue, Ottawa Ontario K1R 6O6 Canada. DD 283.71384. Canadian Churchman and the Ottawa Diocesan News, 0706-8050.

CANADIAN DISCIPLE. 0008-3410. Periodical. CN. English. qt. $3.86. Canadian Disciple, PO Box 81, Milton Nova Scotia B0T 1P0 Canada. Tel (902)354-48766. Ed Fred W Gordon. Circ 800. This is the official publication of the Christian Church (disciples of Christ) in Canada. Editor chooses subjects of religious and social action plus church news.

CANADIAN QUAKER HISTORY NEWSLETTER. No. 1- Nov. 1972-. 0319-3934. Periodical. CN. English. sa. $7.74. Canadian Friends Historical Association, 60 Lowther Avenue, Toronto Ontario M5R 1R7 Canada. Tel (415)839-4328. Ed Kathleen Hertzberg and Jane Zavitz. bk rev. Circ 200. (ctrl). Publishes historic research into the history and settlement of Quakers in Canada and allied topics. Includes genealogy of Quaker ancestors, also communication and information for members.

CANADIAN UNITARIAN. (THE CANADIAN UNITARIAN). V. 1- Summer 1957-. 0527-9860. Periodical. CN. English. Canadian Unitarian Council, 175 St Clair Avenue West, Toronto Ontario M4V 1P7 Canada.

CANON LAW ABSTRACTS. See Indexes/Abstracts.

CARIBBEAN JOURNAL OF RELIGIOUS STUDIES. V. 1- Sept. 1975-. 0253-066X. Periodical. French, Spanish, or Dutch. sa. 10.00. United Theological College West Indies, PO Box 136, Golding Avenue, Kingston 7 Jamaica West Indies. Tel (809)92-79868. Ed Ashley Smith. Ind/Abst Relig. Index One, Period. LC BR1. DD 200.5. bk rev. Circ 2,100. (ctrl). Research on religious issues done especially by Caribbean scholars and persons involved in pastoral work in the region or in other third world situations.

CARMELUS. V. 1-. 0008-6673. Periodical. IT. English (French, German, Italian, and Spanish). sa. 30.00 Domestic, $25.00 Foreign. Institutum Carmelitanum, Via Sforza Pallavicini 10, 00193 Rome Italy. Tel (06)6543-513. Ed Joachim Smet. LC BX3201. DD 255.73005. bk rev. adv acc. Circ 600. Theological, philosophical, bibliographical and historical studies, especially as these relate to the Carmelite Order. Analecta Ordinis Carmelitaram.

CELEBRATE. 1970-. Periodical. US. English. bm. $5.53. Dove Communications, 60-64 Railway Road, Box 316, Blackburn Victoria 3130 Australia. Tel 03 877 1333. Ed Shirley McDonald. Junior secondary level religious education magazine: comments, stories, reflections, activities, liturgy-oriented and doctrine-based.

CENTRAL THEMES. (CENTRAL THEMES : A QUARTERLY BULLETIN OF CENTRAL PENTECOSTAL COLLEGE). Main/Corp Central Pentecostal College. 0821-4107. Periodical. CN. English. qt. Central Pentecostal College, 1303 Jackson Avenue, Saskatoon Saskatchewan S7H Canada. Tel 374-6655. Ed J Harry Faught. DD 207.71242. adv acc. Circ 1,500. Alumni news and current events of Central Pentecostal Colleges. News and needs expressed to friends of the college.

CHAINON CEASED. (LE CHAINON : BULLETIN DES FRANCISCAINS SECULIERS DE LA REGIONALE DE SHERBROOKE). 0712-4783. Periodical. CN. French (English). ir. $5,00. Franciscains Seculiers de la Regionale de Sherbrooke, CP 516, Sherbrooke Quebec J1H 5K2 Canada. DD 271.3071466.

CHINA AND OURSELVES. (CHINA AND OURSELVES : NEWSLETTER OF THE CANADA CHINA PROGRAMME). 1976. 0828-1602. Periodical. CN. English. qt. $3.86. Canadian China Program, 40 St Clari Avenue East, Toronto Ontario M4T 1M9 Canada. Tel (416)927-4152. Circ 700. (ctrl). Concerns church in China.

CHINA AND THE CHURCH TODAY. 1 : 1 (Jan. 1979)-. Periodical. English. bm. $12.00. Christian National Evangelical Commission, PO Box 15025, San Jose CA 95115. Tel (408)298-0965.

CHINA NOTES. V. 1- Sept. 1962-. 0009-4412. Periodical. US. English. qt. $10.00. China Notes, Room 616/475 Riverside Drive, New York NY 10027. Tel (212)870-2371. Ed Franklin J Woo. LC UNC. adv acc. Circ 1,000. Current developments and relationships of Chinese christian churches inside and outside of the Chinese society, religion and culture. China Bulletin of the Far Eastern Office, 0529-3146.

CHING FENG. V. 8- Winter 1964-. 0009-4668. Periodical. HK. English. qt. $14.00 US. Tao Fong Shan Ecumenical Center, Tao Fung Shan N T Shatin, Hong Kong. Tel 0-6050839. Ed Petter K H Lee. Ind/Abst Relig. Index One, Period. bk rev. adv acc. Circ 1,000. This serial is devoted to the contextualization of Christian thought in China and also in the Asian setting and deals with the encounter of christianity and encounters with Chinese religions and culture. Quarterly Notes on Christianity and Chinese Religion.

CHRISTIAN CYNOSURE CEASED. Began in 1868. Ceased Autumn 1983 issue. 0009-5311. Periodical. US. English. qt. Ed W I Phillips.

THE CHRISTIAN ENDEAVOR WORLD. V. 1- 1897-. 0009-5338. Periodical. US. English. qt. $1.30. Christian Endeavor World, 1221 East Broad Street, Box 1110, Columbus OH 43216. Tel (614)258-9545. Ed F E Clark, A R Well and Others. LC BV1420. Report and promote activities of christian endeavor groups in the United States and throughout the world. Golden Rule (1886).

CHRISTIAN FAMILY. 0279-5310. Periodical. US. English. mo. $13.95. Christian Family, PO Box 791293, Dallas TX 75379. DD 248.

CHRISTIAN LEADERSHIP LETTER. 0194-1615. Periodical. US. English. mo. Marc Publications, 919 West Hunting Drive, Monrovia CA 91016. DD 254.

CHRISTIAN MISSION. 8750-7765. Periodical. US. English. bm. Christian Aid Mission, Route 10 Box 1, Charlottesville VA 22901. DD 266.

CHRISTIAN PEACE CONFERENCE. 1- Nov. 1962-. 0009-5567. Periodical. English. bm. 2.00. Artia, PO Box 790, VE-Smeckach 30, Praha 1 Czechoslovakia. Tel 24 33 38. Ed Jiri Svoboda. bk rev. Circ 4,000. Peace and development issues from Christian view.

CHRISTIAN SCIENCE BIBLE LESSONS. 0146-7166. Periodical. US. English. mo. $2.50. Christian Science Publishing Society, 1 Norway Street, Boston MA 02115. Also available in phonodisc.

CHRISTIAN SCIENCE MONITOR (EASTERN EDITION) CEASED. (THE CHRISTIAN SCIENCE MONITOR). Vol. 52, No. 280 (Oct 24, 1960)-V. 75, No. 217 (Sept. 30, 1983). Newspaper. US. English. Ind/Abst Art Archaeol. Tech. Abstr. LC Newspaper. Also issued on microfilm by Graphic Microfilm of New England, University Microfilms and Micro Photo Div., Bell & Howell. Christian Science Monitor (Atlantic Edition).

CHRISTIAN SCIENCE MONITOR (MIDWESTERN EDITION) CEASED. (THE CHRISTIAN SCIENCE MONITOR). Newspaper. US. English. da.

CHRISTIAN STATESMAN. V. 1- 1867-. 0009-5664. Periodical. US. English. bm. $3.00. National Reform Association, 442 7th Avenue/Patterson Heights, Beaver Falls PA 15010. Tel (412)846-0159. Ed D Howard Elliott. LC HN51. DD 261.805. bk rev. adv acc. Circ 2,000. (ctrl). The application of reformational, biblical Christianity to society, culture, and political science.

CHRISTIAN WRITER'S SERVICE GUIDE. VFOAT Service Guide. 1983-. 0736-7600. Periodical. US. English. an. Christian Horizons Unlimited, PO Box 5650, Lakeland FL 33803.

CHRISTIANITY & CIVILIZATION. VFOAT Christianity and Civilization. No. 1 (Spring 1982)-. 0278-8187. Periodical. US. English. ir. Christianity and Civilization, 708 Hamvassy Road, Tyler TX 75711. Tel (214)592-0620.

Religion, Mythology, Rationalism

CHRISTIANITY & LITERATURE. See Literature.

CHRYSOSTOM : QUARTERLY BULLETIN OF THE SOCIETY OF ST JOHN CHRYSOSTOM. No. 1 (Spring 1960)-No. 32 (Winter 1967-68). 0529-5025. Periodical. UK. English. sa. $3.07. Society of St John Chrysostom, Marian House, Holden Avenue, London N12 8HY England.

CHURCH ADMINISTRATION. V. 1- Oct. 1959-. 0412-4553. Periodical. US. English. mo. $17.00. Materials Services Department, 127 Ninth Avenue North, Nashville TN 37234. Tel (615)251-2000.

CHURCH ALERT. Periodical. English. ir. $5.00. Sodepax, Ecumenical Centre, PO Box 66, 150 Route de Ferney, 1211 Geneva 20 Switzerland.

CHURCH & HOME LEAFLETS. AGES 4 - 6. VFOAT Ages 4-6 Church & Home Leaflets. Vol. 1, No. 1 (Fall 1982)-. 0276-3435. Periodical. US. English. qt. Graded Press, PO Box 801, Nashville TN 37202. *Kindergartner, 0023-1517.*

CHURCH & HOME LEAFLETS. ELEMENTARY A. VFOAT Church and Home Leaflets. Vol. 1, No. 1 (Sept. 5, 1982)-. 0278-3533. Periodical. US. English. qt. $6.25. Graded Press, PO Box 801, Nashville TN 37202. *Step by Step, 0160-4023.*

CHURCH & STATE. See Political Science.

CHURCH & SYNAGOGUE LIBRARIES. See Library and Information Science.

CHURCH GROWTH RESOURCE NEWS. Periodical. US. English. ir. Institute of American Church Growth, 150 South Los Robles/Suite 600, Pasadena CA 91101.

THE CHURCH HERALD. V. 1- Jan. 7, 1944-. 0009-6393. Periodical. US. English. sm. $10.25. Church Herald, 1324 Lake Drive Southeast, Grand Rapids MI 49506. Tel (616)458-5156. *Intelligence-Leader.*

CHURCH MANAGEMENT. See Business - General Management.

CHURCH MUSIC QUARTERLY. See Music.

CHURCH (NEW YORK, N.Y.). (CHURCH). Vol. 1, No. 1 (Spring 1985)-. 0883-5667. Periodical. US. English. qt. $30.00. National Pastoral Life Center, 299 Elizabeth Street, New York NY 10012. Tel (212)431-7825. Ed Margaret O'Brien Steinfels. DD 253. bk rev. Circ 4,500. Designed to provide information, insight, and interpretation for pastoral ministers. It combines serious longer essays on theology, scripture, history, spirituality, and scoiology with shorter, concrete articles on parish matters.

CHURCH OBSERVER. Jan. 1948-. 0009-6482. Periodical. UK. English. qt. The Church Union, Faith House, 7 Tufton Street, Westminister SWIP 3QN England. Available on microfilm from University Microfilms. *Church Union Gazette, Platform.*

THE CHURCH OF ENGLAND YEAR BOOK. See Yearbooks, Almanacs, Directories.

CHURCH OF GOD MISSIONS. 0009-6504. Periodical. US. English. mo. $5.00. Missions Education, PO Box 2337, Anderson IN 46018. Tel (317)649-7597. Ed Dondeena Caldwell. bk rev. Circ 8,500. (ctrl). Missions education materials include stories and reports from missionaries and national workers in sixty-five countries. Also considered are social issues, such as peace, hunger, and poverty.

CHURCH PROGRAMS FOR MIDDLERS & JUNIORS. VAT Church Programs for Middlers and Juniors. Vol. 1, No. 1 (Fall 1981)-. 0273-5059. Periodical. US. English. qt. $2.75 Single Issue. Gospel Publishing House, 1445 Boonville Avenue, Springfield MO 65802.

CHURCH PROGRAMS FOR PRIMARIES. Vol. 7, No. 1 (Fall 1981)-. 0273-5113. Periodical. US. English. qt. $2.75 Single Issue. Gospel Publishing House, 1445 Boonville Avenue, Springfield MO 65802. *Children's Church, 0190-4221.*

CHURCH RECREATION MAGAZINE. See Recreation, Leisure.

CHURCH RESOURCE DIRECTORY. See Yearbooks, Almanacs, Directories.

THE CHURCH SECRETARY'S SWAP SHOP. VFOAT Swap Shop. 0738-6885. Periodical. US. English. mo. $10.00. E Jane Mall, 326 Cantebury, Corpus Christi TX 78412.

THE CHURCH WOMAN. VFOAT CW. 0009-6598. Periodical. US. English. bm. $6.00. The Church Woman, 475 Riverside Drive/Room 812, New York NY 10015. LC BV4415. DD 259.

CHURCH WORLD. 1930-. 0009-6601. Periodical. US. English. wk. $13.00. Church World, PO Box 698, Brunswick ME 04011. Tel (207)729-8753. Ed Henry Gosselin. bk rev. adv acc. Circ 10,000.

EL CIERVO. Began with No. 1 in 1952. 0045-6896. Periodical. SP. Spanish. mo. $21.59. El Ciervo, Calvet 56, 08080 Barcelona Spain. Tel 200 51 45. bk rev. adv acc. Circ 5,000. The presence of free Christians in the cultural Laic world.

CINTAMANI. Periodical. English, Hindi or Sanskrit. ir. 4.00. 28/16 V G Kher Road, 40006 Bombai India. LC BL1100.

LA CIUDAD DE DIOS. Began with V. 152 in 1936. Periodical. SP. Spanish. ty. 25.00. Padres Agustinos, Monasterio de el Escorial, Madrid Spain. Tel 8905011. Ind/Abst MLA Int. Bibliogr. Books Artic. Mod. Lang. Lit., New Testam. Abstr., Public Aff. Inf. Serv. Bull., Am. Hist. Life, Hist. Abstr., Hist. Abstr., Part A, Mod. Hist. Abstr., Hist. Abst., Part B, Twent. Century Abstr. (cum index). bk rev. Circ 700. (ctrl). Ideas in the areas of philosophy and religion. *Ciudad de Dios, Religion y Cultura.*

CIVILTA CATTOLICA. (LA CIVILTA CATTOLICA). V. 1- April 1850- V. 1- April 1850-. 0009-8167. Periodical. IT. Italian. sm. $100.00. la Civilta Cattolica, Via di Porta Pinciana 1, 00187 Roma Italy. Tel 06/6798351. Ind/Abst Cathol. Period. Lit. Index, New Testam. Abstr., Am. Hist. Life, Hist. Abstr., Hist. Abstr., Part A, Mod. Hist. Abstr., Hist. Abst., Part B, Twent. Century Abstr. LC AP37. (cum index). bk rev. adv acc. Circ 18,000. Contains 140 articles, notes, comments and reviews of the press; 70 political and cultural commentaries of current interest.

CLERGY JOURNAL. V. 45, No. 9- June 1969-. Periodical. US. English. mo. $10.00. 4119 Terrace Lane, Hopkins MN 55343. Available on microfilm from University Microfilms, Ann Arbor. *Church Management.*

CLOCHER CEASED. (LE CLOCHER). No. 1, (Year 1982)-. 0714-8984. Periodical. CN. French. ir. Free. Le Clocher, CP 520 Nicolet, Quebec J0G 1E0 Canada. DD 271.00971455.

COLECCION TEMAS. Main/Corp Centro Arquidiocesano de Pastoral, Lima. 1- 1970-. Periodical. CK. Spanish. ir. Apt Aereo 4817, Bogota Colombia.

COLLABORATION. See Philosophy.

COMMAND. See Military Science.

COMMUNAUTE CHRETIENNE. V. 1- Jan./Feb. 1962-. 0010-3454. Periodical. CN. French. bm. 18.50. 2715 Chemin de la Cote, Sainte Catherine, Montreal H3T 1B6 Canada. Tel 514 739 9797. Ind/Abst Point Repere. bk rev. Pastoral theology.

COMMUNIO VIATORUM. Began in 1958. 0010-3713. Periodical. CS. English (French, German and Latin). qt. $17.50. Artia, PO Box 790 Ve-Smeckach 30, Praha 1 Czechoslovakia. Ind/Abst New Testam. Abstr., Relig. Index One, Period. LC BR1A1.

COMMUNION. Periodical. YE. qt. Communion Administration, 71250 Taize Communaute, Taize France. *Verbum Caro.*

THE CONGREGATIONALIST. V. 1-6, Feb. 1958-Dec. 1964. 0010-5856. Periodical. US. English. bm. $7.00. National Association Christian Churches, PO Box 1620, Oak Creek WI 53154. Tel (414)764-1620. Ed Mary Woolsey. LC BX7101. DD 285.805. bk rev. adv acc. Circ 5,000. (ctrl). Denominational publication of literary items and current event coverage. *Free Churches.*

CONSCIENCE ET LIBERTE. No. 1-3, 1948-50. Periodical. French. ir. 13. Association Internationale pour la Defense del la Liberte Religieuse, Schlosshaldenstrasse 17, 3006 Berne Switzerland.

CONSECRATED LIFE. V. 1-. Periodical. US. English (Multilingual). $10.00. Institute on Religious Life, 4200 North Austin Avenue, Chicago IL 60634. Tel (312)545-1946. Ed James Downey. Ind/Abst Cathol. Period. Lit. Index. bk rev. Circ 2,300. Official journal of the Vatican Congregation for Religious and Secular Institutes. Carries documents, decrees and guidelines of the congregation, studies and reports.

CONTACT (1953-). 0573-7796. Periodical. US. English. mo. $9.00. Contact, PO Box 1088, Nashville TN 37202. Tel (615)361-1010. Ed Jack Williams. bk rev. Circ 7,500. (ctrl). To provide news of interest and related articles for the Free Will Baptist denomination.

CONTEMPORARY RELIGIOUS MOVEMENTS. 0190-0986. Monographic Series. US. English. ir. John Wiley & Sons Inc, 1 Wiley Drive, Somerset NJ 08873.

CONTES EVANGELIQUES. See Children and Youth Interests.

CONTEXT; A COMMENTARY ON THE INTERACTION OF RELIGION AND CULTURE. V. 1- Oct. 15, 1969-. 0361-8854. Periodical. US. English. $24.95. Claretian Publishing, 221 West Madison Street, Chicago IL 60606. Tel (312)236-7782. Ed Martin E Marty. Circ 6,380. Martin E. Marty's commentary on the interaction of religion and culture.

CONTRIBUTIONS TO THE STUDY OF RELIGION. No. 1-. 0196-7053. Monographic Series. US. English. ir. Greenwood Press, 88 Post Road West, Westport CT 06881. Tel (203)226-3571. Ed Henry W Bowden.

COPTOLOGIA. (COPTOLOGIA : STUDIA COPTICA ORTHODOXA : A RESEARCH PUBLICATION IN COPTIC ORTHODOX STUDIES). VFOAT Gyptologia : Epchisbo Enremenkimi Enorthodoxos. Vol. 1 (1981)-. 0229-1134. CN. English. an. $5.00 Per No. St Peter's Printing & Publishing Co, Unit #4 2395 Cawthra Road, Mississauga Ontario L5A 2W8 Canada. DD 281.7.

CORBAN. V. 1- Nov. 1973-. 0382-487X. Periodical. CN. English. Corban, PO Box 965, Barrie Ontario L4M 5E1 Canada. DD 205.

CORNERSTONE (SAN ANTONIO, TEX.). (THE CORNERSTONE). Began with June 1985?. 0883-6108. Periodical. US. English. mo. $24.00. Cornerstone Publishing Co, PO Box 37226, San Antonio TX 78218. DD 277.

CORPUS CHRISTIANORUM. CLAVIS PATRUM GRAECORUM. VFOAT Clavis Patrum Graecorum. V. 1- 19 -. Periodical. BE. Latin. ir. Brepol IGP, Baron du Fourstraat 8, 2300 Turnhot Belgium. Tel 014/41.54.63. The series contains the works of Christian Latin literature of the 1st to the 12th Century and of the Greek Post-Niceme fathers.

CORPUS CHRISTIANORUM : CONTINUATIO MEDIAEVALIS. V. 1-. 0589-7963. Monographic Series. Latin. ir. Brepols, Baron Frans Fourstraat, B-2300 Turnhout Belgium. Tel (014) 41 54 63. Ed Abbey Steenbrugge. Patriotic texts of the 8th to the 19th century.

CORPUS CHRISTIANORUM : SERIES GRAECA. Monographic Series. Greek (texts in Latin and commentary in French). ir. Brepols, Rue Baron Frans du Four 8, B-2300 Turnhout Belgium. Tel 014/415463. Greek Patrology with prinicipally Post-Nicene fathers.

CORPUS SCRIPTORUM CHRISTIANORUM ORIENTALIUM. Monographic Series. BE. Latin. ir. 960.00. Editions Peeters, Bondgenotenlaan 153 PB 41, B 3000 Leuven Belgium. adv acc. (ctrl).

COUNCIL COMMUNICATOR. Main/Corp Canadian Council of Churches. V. 1- Mar. 1970-. 0045-4605. Periodical. CN. English. qt. $1.00. Canadian Council of Churches, Ruth Tillman, 40 St Clair Avenue East, Toronto Ontario M4T JM9 Canada.

CRADLE ROLL PROGRAM HELPS. 0163-8688. US. English. qt. $9.92 Domestic, $10.92 Foreign. Review & Herald Publishing Association, 6856 Eastern Avenue Northwest, Washington DC 20012. Tel (301)791-7000. Sabbath school aids for the leader of the Cradle Roll Department.

CREATION RESEARCH SOCIETY QUARTERLY. (QUARTERLY). 0092-9166. Periodical. US. English. qt. $17.00. Creation Research Society, 5093 Williamsport Drive, Norcross GA 30092. Tel (404)449-4758. Ed Emmett L Williams. LC BS651. DD 213.05. bk rev. Circ 2,000. Articles from a scientific viewpoint, that support the creation model of science.

Religion, Mythology, Rationalism

CREATION SCIENCE DIALOGUE. Winter 1980-. 0229-253X. Periodical. CN. English. qt. $2.00. Creation Science Association, Box 9075 Station E, Edmonton Alberta T5P 4K1 Canada. **DD** 213. *Creation Dialogue, 0702-7176.*

CREDO. Periodical. NO. Norwegian. ir. $13.06. Credo Forlag AS, Holbergs Plass 4, Olso 1 Norway. **Tel** 02/208935. **Ed** Anfin Skaaheim and Arne H Fjeldstad. bk rev. adv acc. **Circ** 6,500. A student magazine with theological, scientifical and other actual items for Christians. Including, family-problems and problems between faith and study.

CREER. No. 1- April/May 1975-. Periodical. AG. Spanish. mo. Editorial el Pais Saicf ei Defensa 570, Buenos Aires Argentina.

CRISTIANISMO Y SOCIEDAD. Vol. 1- (No. 1-). 0011-1457. Periodical. AG. Spanish. qt. Editorial Tierra Nueva, San Jose 28 60P, 1076 Buenos Aires Argentina. **Ind/Abst** Relig. Index One, Period. *Iglesia y Sociedad en America Latina.*

CROCKFORD'S CLERICAL DIRECTORY. *See* Yearbooks, Almanacs, Directories.

LA CROIX. **VFOAT** Croix du Dahomey. Periodical. French. ir. 1000. BP 105, Cotonou Dahoney. **LC** BX1682.D34.

CRUCIBLE (MERCEDES, TEX.). (THE CRUCIBLE). 8756-1247. Periodical. US. English. qt. $10.00. De Young Press, Box 7252, Spencer IA 51301-7252. **DD** 211.

CULTURAL INFORMATION SERVICE. 0097-952X. Periodical. US. English. ir. $25.00. Cultural Information Service, PO Box 786 Madison Square Station, New York NY 10159. **Tel** (212)691-5240. **Ed** Frederic A Brussat. **LC** BR115.C8. **DD** 261.83. bk rev. Reviews and previews of literature, television, videos, films, popular music. TV and film viewers' guides, posters and bookmarks.

CURRENT CHRISTIAN ABSTRACTS. *See* Indexes/Abstracts.

CURRENT LC SUBJECT HEADINGS IN THE FIELD OF RELIGION. **VFOAT** Library of Congress Subject Headings in the Field of Religion. **VAT** Current Library of Congress Subject Headings in the Field of Religion. Vol. 1, No. 1 (Sept. 1983)-. Periodical. US. English. qt. $6.00. Eastern Baptist Theological Sem Lancaster, City Line c/o T Gilbert, Philadelphia PA 19151. **Tel** (215)896-5000.

DAILY PRAYER REMINDER. **VAT** International Intercessors Daily Prayer Reminder. 0227-096X. Periodical. CN. English. mo. Free to Members. International Intercessors, Box 2500, Streetsville Ontario L5M 2H2 Canada. **DD** 248.32.

DAILY WORD. 0011-5525. Periodical. US. English. mo. Unity School of Christianity, Unity Village MO 64065. **Tel** (816)524-3550. **Ed** Martha Smock. Also available in large-type edition. Daily thoughts and meditations for good living. *Unity Daily Word.*

DAUGHTERS OF SARAH. Vol. 1, No. 1 (Nov. 1974)-. 0739-1749. Periodical. US. English. bm. $28.00. Daughters of Sarah, 2716 West Cortland, Chicago IL 60647. **Tel** (312)252-3344. **Ed** Lareta Halteman Finger. bk rev. adv acc. **Circ** 3,500. A Christian feminist forum. Articles on theology, Bible, social justice issues, women's history, personal issues, spirituality, marriage, children, health, and the church.

DAVANTAGE. V. 1- April 1967-. 0703-6485. Periodical. CN. French. mo. $5. Societe St-Vincent de Paul, Secretariat, Conseil Central de Quebec, 777 des Glacis, Quebec Quebec G13 3R1 Canada. **DD** 267.242714471.

DAYANANDA SANDESA. Periodical. Hindi. ir. 6.00. Arsha Sahitya Pracara Trasta, 2-F Kamla Nagar 7, Dilli India. **LC** BL1250.

THE DEACON. (DEACON). 0045-9771. Periodical. US. English. qt. $8.50. Materials Services Department, 127-9th Avenue North, Nashville TN 37234. **Tel** (615)251-2000.

DECISION (CANADIAN EDITION). (DECISION). 0820-9057. Periodical. CN. English. mo. $5.00. Billy Graham Evangelistic Association of Canada, Room 402/171 Donald Street, Winnipeg Manitoba R3C 2R3 Canada. **Tel** (612)338-0500. **Ed** Roger C Palms. **DD** 269.205. **Circ** 2,000,000. To present the good news of salvation in Jesus Christ and to encourage teach and strengthen Christians.

DECISION. EDICION EN ESPANOL. (DECISION). V. 1- Nov. 1960-. 0744-8252. Periodical. US. Spanish (International editions available: British, Australian, French, German, English, Japanese, Chinese). mo. Decision Magazine, 1300 Harmony Place, Minneapolis MN 55403. **Tel** (612)338-0500. **Ed** Roger C Palms. **Ind/Abst** Christ. Period. Index. **LC** BV3750. **DD** 269.205. (cum index). Braille edition available. A message by Billy Graham. Personal testimonies, inspirational poems, reports from around the world, articles on the spiritual life and a Bible study.

DECISION (MINNEAPOLIS, MINN.). (DECISION). V. 1- Nov. 1960-. 0011-7307. Periodical. US. English (International editions available: British, Australian, French, German, Spanish, Japanese, Chinese). mo. $5.00. Billy Graham Evangelistic Association, 1300 Harmony Place, Minneapolis MN 55403. **Tel** (612)338-0500. **Ed** Roger C Palms. **Ind/Abst** Christ. Period. Index. **LC** BV3750. **DD** 269.205. (cum index). Braille edition available. A message by Billy Graham, personal testimonies, inspirational poems, reports from around the world, articles on the spiritual life, and a Bible study.

DEFENDER OF THE FAITH *CEASED.* V. 4, No. 4- Apr. 1974. Ceased with V. 14, No. 1/2 (Jan./Feb. 1983)?. 0316-2966. Periodical. CN. English. mo. $2.00. Defender of the Faith, c/o United Pentecostal Church, 1730-46th Avenue South West, Calgary Alberta T2T 2R5 Canada. *Canadian Plains Messenger, 0316-2885.*

DHARMA MARGA. April/June 1982-. Periodical. II. Hindi. qt. 12.00. Ramayana Vidyapeeth, 15 Institutional Area/Lodi Road, New Delhi 1100 India. **LC** BL1100.

DIRECTORY - ASSOCIATED CHURCH PRESS. *See* Yearbooks, Almanacs, Directories.

DIRECTORY - CANADIAN RELIGIOUS CONFERENCE. *See* Yearbooks, Almanacs, Directories.

DIRECTORY OF CAMPUS MINISTRY. *See* Yearbooks, Almanacs, Directories.

DISCERNER. 1947-. 0416-0274. Periodical. US. English. mo. Religion Analysis Service Inc, 2708 East Lake Street, Minneapolis MN 55406. **Tel** (612)722-4463. **Ed** John Dahlin. bk rev. **Circ** 4,000. Information concerning cults and non-Christian religions.

DISCIPLESHIP JOURNAL. Vol. 1, No. 1 (Jan./Feb. 1981)-. 0273-5865. Periodical. US. English. bm. $12.00. The Navigators, PO Box 1113, Dover NJ 07801. **Tel** (303)598-1212. **LC** BV4485. **DD** 248.4.

DISCIPLIANA (INDIANAPOLIS, IND.). (DISCIPLIANA). Vol. 20, No. 1 (Mar. 1960)-. 0732-9881. Periodical. US. English. qt. $10.00. Disciples of Christ Historical Society, 1101-19th Avenue South, Nashville TN 37212. **Tel** (615)327-1444. **Ed** James M Seale. **LC** BX7301. **DD** 286.605. bk rev. **Circ** 5,400. (ctrl). The holdings of this society relate to the religious movement which began in 19th Century American and is known as the Campbell-Stone movement and embraces three distinct church bodies. *Harbinger and Discipliana.*

DISSERTATION SERIES - AMERICAN ACADEMY OF RELIGION *CEASED.* **Main/Corp** American Academy of Religion. **VFOAT** American Academy of Religion Dissertation Series. Began with No. 1-36. 0145-272X. Monographic Series. US. English.

DISSERTATIONES AD HISTORIAM RELIGIONUM PERTINENTES. V. 1-. 0419-4233. Monographic Series. NE. English. ir. E J Brill, PO Box 9000, 2300 PA Leiden The Netherlands.

DONUM DEI. 1- 1959-. 0318-0123. Periodical. CN. English. Canadian Religious Conference, 324 Laurier Street East, Ottawa Ontario K1N 6P6 Canada.

DOSSIERS VIE OUVRIERE. **VFOAT** Vie Ouvriere. No. 81-130. 0384-1146. CN. French. Dossiers Vie Ouvriere, 1201 rue Visitation, Montreal Quebec H2L 3B5 Canada. **DD** 248.88. *Pretres et Laics, 0555-0920.*

DRAUDZES VESTIS. Began publication in Jan. 1953. 0701-0214. Periodical. CN. Latvian. mo. 20.-. E Lange, 364 Pleasant Park Road, Ottawa Ontario K1H 5M8 Canada. **Tel** (613)733-3906. **Ed** Edgars Lange. **DD** 284.171384. bk rev. adv acc. **Circ** 180. Church news and Latvian community life in Canada, the USA and other countries.

THE DRUM CALL. Began with Jan. 1922. Periodical. English. ir. United Presbyterian Church in Africa, Box 32, Ebolowa Cameroun West Africa.

DUC ME HANG CUU GIUP. Periodical. VM. Vietnamese. mo. 360. Ao Hien Toan, 38 Ky Dong, Saigon South Vietnam. **LC** BX806.V5.

THE DUKE DIVINITY SCHOOL REVIEW. **Main/Corp** Duke University, Durham, N.C. Divinity School. V. 29- Winter 1964-. 0012-7078. Periodical. US. English. ty. Divinity School of Duke University, Durham NC 27706. **Ind/Abst** New Testam. Abstr., Relig. Index One, Period. *Duke Divinity School Bulletin, 0190-4523.*

EARLITEEN. **VFOAT** Early Teen. 0737-6405. Periodical. US. English. qt. $7.16 Domestic, $8.12 Foreign. Review and Herald Publishing Association, 55 West Oak Ridge Drive, Hagerstown MD 21740. **Tel** (301)791-7000. Sabbath school material for the earliteen department. *Earliteen Bible Study Guide, 0163-8807.*

EARLITEEN-JUNIOR PROGRAM HELPS. 0163-8769. Periodical. US. English. qt. $9.92 Domestic, $10.92 Foreign. Review & Herald Publishing Association, 6856 Eastern Avenue Northwest, Washington DC 20012. **Tel** (301)791-7000. Sabbath school aids for the leaders of the earliteen.

EAST ASIA MILLIONS. **VFOAT** Millions. V. 69, No. 5- May 1961-. 0012-8406. Periodical. US. English. ir. $4.00. Overseas Missionary Fellowship, 404 South Church Street, Robesonia PA 19551. **Tel** (215)693-5881. **Ed** Fay Goddard. bk rev. **Circ** 20,000. Reports of evangelism and church planting in southeast Asia, including material for prayer. *Millions (Philadelphia, Pa.), 0740-400X.*

ECOS CRISTOFOROS. 0882-3707. Periodical. US. Spanish. bm. Free. The Christophers, 12 East 48th Street, New York NY 10017. **DD** 271.

THE ECUMENICAL REVIEW. V. 1- Autumn 1948-. 0013-0796. Periodical. SZ. English. qt. 15.-. World Council of Churches, 150 Route de Ferney, 1221 Geneva 20 Switzerland. **Tel** 91.61.11. **Ed** Emilio Castro. **Ind/Abst** Old Testam. Abstr., New Testam. Abstr., Book Rev. Index, Relig. Index One, Period., Humanit. Index. **LC** BX1. **DD** 280. Index published separately - free - automatically sent. bk rev. adv acc. (ctrl). Available on microfilm from University Microfilms International. A theological forum for the discussion of ecumenical concerns such as church unity, mission, human community, peace and justice. *Christendom.*

THE ECUMENIST. V. 1- Oct. 1962-. 0013-080X. Periodical. US. English. Paulist Press, 543 Island Road, Ramsey NJ 07446. **Tel** (212)265-4028. **Ind/Abst** Old Testam. Abstr., New Testam. Abstr., Cathol. Period. Lit. Index. **LC** BX1. **DD** 262.001.

EDUCATION NOTES *CEASED.* Began with No. 1, 1974. Ceased with No. 15, 1979. 0382-7232. Periodical. CN. English. ir. Canadian Catholic Organization for Development and Peace, Suite 305/67 Bond Street, Toronto Ontario M5B 1X5 Canada. **DD** 261.805.

EN EGLISE. V. 1- Jan. 1974-. 0317-851X. Periodical. CN. French. ir. $3.86. Off Comm Soc/Ser D Iocesain, 679 rue Chabanel, Chicoutimi Quebec G7H 3S5 Canada. **Tel** (418)543-9975.

EGLISE CANADIENNE. (L'EGLISE CANADIENNE). V. 1- Jan. 1968-. 0013-2322. Periodical. CN. French. sm. $19.35. L'Eglise Canadienne, 1073 Boulevard Saint Cyrille Ouest, Quebec Quebec G1S 4R5 Canada. **Tel** (418)681-8109. **Ed** Jacques Barnard. bk rev. adv acc. **Circ** 7,000. Documents, studies and information about the life of Roman Catholic Church in Canada.

THE ELDER CHURCHMAN. V. 1- June 1969-. 0360-6120. Periodical. US. English. ty. Rev Max A Kapp, Box 1392, Vineyard Haven MA 02568.

EMMANUEL. V. 1- Jan. 1895-. 0013-6719. Periodical. US. English. mo. $18.00. 184 East 76th Street, New York NY 10021. **Tel** (212)861-1076. **Ed** Eugene A LaVerdiere. bk rev. adv acc. **Circ** 6,000. Our purpose is to meet the spiritual needs of those engaged in church ministry. The focus of our spirituality is Eucharistic.

EPHEMERIDES LITURGICAE. V. 1- Jan. 1887-. 0013-9505. Periodical. IT. English (German, Italian, and Latin). bm. $17.82. Ephemerides Liturgicae, Via Pompeo Magno 21, 00192 Rome Italy. **Ind/Abst** New Testam. Abstr.

Religion, Mythology, Rationalism

EPOCHE. V. 4, No. 2- Fall 1976-. 0149-3043. Periodical. US. English. $5.00. The History of Religions at UCLA, Department of History, Los Angeles CA 90024. **LC** BL41. **DD** 291.05. *History of Religions Newsletter, 0360-6147.*

EPS, ECUMENICAL PRESS SERVICE. 29th Year, No. 46- 14 Dec. 1962-. Periodical. SZ. English. wk. $29.50. World Council of Churches, 150 Route de Ferney, 1211 Geneve 20 Switzerland. Ed Tom Dorris. *Ecumenical Press Service.*

ESA. ENGAGE/SOCIAL ACTION. VFOAT Engage/Social Action. VAT Engage Social Action. V. 3- Jan. 1975-. 0164-5528. Periodical. US. English. mo. $27.00. Board of Church & Society, 100 Maryland Avenue Northeast, Washington DC 20002. **Tel** (202)488-5632. Ed Lee Ranck. **Ind/Abst** Relig. Index One, Period. bk rev. adv acc. **Circ** 5,500. Available on microfilm from University Microfilms. In-depth analysis of current social issues from a Christian perspective. *Engage-Social Action, 0090-3485.*

ETUDES PRELIMINAIRES AUX RELIGIONS ORIENTALES DANS L'EMPIRE ROMAIN. V. 1- 1961-. 0531-1950. Monographic Series. NE. French. ir. EJ Brill, PO Box 9000, 2300 PA Leiden the Netherlands.

ETUDES THEOLOGIQUES ET RELIGIEUSES. Vol. 1- Mar. 1926-. 0014-2239. Periodical. FR. French. qt. 20. Etudes Theologiques et Religieuses, 13 rue Louis Perrier, 34000 Montpellier France. **Tel** 67.92.61.28. **Ind/Abst** Old Testam. Abstr., New Testam. Abstr., Relig. Index One, Period. Index published separately. (cum index). bk rev. adv acc. **Circ** 2,500. Studies on religion, history, theology and philosophy of religion.

EUHEMER: PRZEGLAD RELIGIOZNAWCZY. Began publication in 1957. 0014-2298. Periodical. Polish (tables of contents also in French and English). ir. **LC** BL9.P6.

EUROPAISCHE SAGEN. V. 1- 1961-. 0531-2450. Monographic Series. German. ir. Ed Will-Erich Peuckert. European myths.

EVANGEL. 0162-1890. Periodical. US. English. wk. $4.50. Light & Life Press, Winoma Lake IN 46590. **Tel** (219)267-7161.

THE EVANGELICAL BEACON. 1931. 0014-3332. Periodical. US. English. Evangelical Beacon, 1515 East 66th Street, Minneapolis MN 55423. **Tel** (612)866-3343. Ed George M Keck. **LC** BX7548.A1. **DD** 289.9. bk rev. adv acc. **Circ** 40,200. *Evangelical Beacon and Evangelist.*

EVANGELIKUS ELET. 0133-1302. Periodical. HU. Hungarian. wk. Akademiai Kiado, POB 24, 1363 Budapest Hungary.

EVANGELIZING TODAY'S CHILD. Vol. 1, No. 1 (May/June 1974)-. Periodical. US. English. bm. $12.00. Child Evangelism Fellowship, Box 348, Warrenton MO 63383. **Tel** (615)775-3300. Ed Elsie Lippy. **Ind/Abst** Christ. Period. Index. bk rev. adv acc. **Circ** 27,000. *Child Evangelism.*

EXCHANGE. No. 1 (Apr. 1972)-. 0166-2740. Periodical. NE. English (Dutch and French). ty. $8.62. Department of Missiology lime, Rapenburg 61, NL 2311 GJ Leiden Netherlands. **Tel** (071)14 42 48. Ed L Lagerwerf. bk rev. adv acc. **Circ** 700. (ctrl). Surveys on developments in Third World theology, churches and Christianity.

EXPRESSION (WINNIPEG, MAN.). (EXPRESSION). 0824-474X. Periodical. CN. German. ir. Free. Mennonite Brethren Communications, PO Box 2 Station F, Winnipeg Manitoba R2L 2A5 Canada. **DD** 289.70607127. (ctrl).

EXPRESSION (WINNIPEG, MAN.). (EXPRESSION). Vol. 1, No. 1 (June 1983)-. 0824-4731. Periodical. CN. English. bm. Free. Mennonite Brethren Communications, PO Box 2 Station F, Winnipeg Manitoba R2L 2A5 Canada. **DD** 289.70607127. (ctrl).

FACE TO FACE; AN INTERRELIGIOUS BULLETIN. V. 1- Fall 1975-. 0361-6061. Periodical. US. English. qt. $2.50. Anti-Defamation League of Bnai Brith, 315 Lexington Avenue South, New York NY 10016.

FAITH TODAY. V. 1- Feb. 1978-. 0706-7003. Periodical. CN. English. mo. Dominican Publications, St Saviors Dominick Street, Dublin 1 Ireland. **DD** 269.20971.

FAMILY MINISTRIES. (FAMILY MINISTRIES : ASSEMBLIES OF GOD NEWSLETTER). VFOAT Family Ministries Newsletter. 0277-4518. Periodical. US. English. qt. Gospel Publishing House, 1445 Boonville, Springfield MO 65802.

FATIMA CRUSADER. (THE FATIMA CRUSADER). Issue No. 1 (Summer 1978)-. 0713-0163. Periodical. CN. English. qt. Free. National Committee for the National Pilgrim Virgin of Canada, PO Box 3394, Ottawa Ontario K1Y 4J6 Canada. **DD** 232.917.

FELLOWSHIP OF BELIEVERS BULLETIN. (BULLETIN - FELLOWSHIP OF BELIEVERS). V. 3, No. 4- July/Aug. 1971-. 0316-7909. Periodical. CN. English. bm. Fellowship of Believers, PO Box 537, Gladstone Manitoba R0J 0T0 Canada. **DD** 269.205. *Anointed Life, 0316-7895.*

FELLOWSHIP YEARBOOK. See Yearbooks, Almanacs, Directories.

FESTIVAL QUARTERLY. Began with: V. 1, No. 1 (Spring 1974). 8750-3530. Periodical. US. English. qt. $8.50. Festival Quarterly, 3513 Old Philadelphia Pike, Intercourse PA 17534. **Tel** (717)768-7171. **DD** 289.

FLASH POINT. VAT Flashpoint. 0190-5864. Periodical. US. English. mo. Free. General Conference, Sabbath School Department, 6840 Eastern Avenue NW, Washington DC 20012.

FOCUS ON SOCIAL JUSTICE. 1- Nov. 1974-. 0383-6983. Periodical. CN. English. ir. Canadian Religious Conference, 3377 Bayview Avenue, Willowdale Ontario M2M 3S4 Canada. **DD** 261.805.

FOI ET LE TEMPS. Yearly V. 1- Jan./Feb. 1968. 0430-8522. Periodical. French. bm. $13.00. La Foi et Temps, 28 rue des Jesuites, 7500 Tournai Belgium. *Revue Ecclesiastique de Liege, Revue Diocesaine de Namur.*

FOLKLORE & MYTHOLOGY. See Folklore.

FOLKLORE AND MYTHOLOGY STUDIES. See Folklore.

FRANCISCAN ESSAYS. UK. English. ir. Aberdeen University Press, Farmers Hall, Aberdeen AB9 2XT Scotland. **LC** BX3601. **DD** 271.306242, 271.304.

FRANCOIS AUJOURD'HUI. No. 1 (Sept. 1982)-. 0821-3488. Periodical. CN. French. bm. $5.00. Fraternite Provinciale de l'Ordre Franciscain Seculier, 836 rue d'Aiguillon, Quebec Quebec G1R 1M9 Canada. **DD** 271.3.

FREE CHURCH CHRONICLE. Began Jan. 1899. 0016-0326. Periodical. UK. English. qt. Free Church Federal Council, 27 Tavistock Square, London WC1H 9HH England.

FREE INQUIRY (BUFFALO, N.Y.). See Philosophy.

FREETHOUGHT TODAY. VFOAT Free Thought Today. Began in Jan. 1984. 0882-8512. Periodical. US. English. $15.00. Freedom from Religion Foundation, PO Box 750, Madison WI 53701. **Tel** (608)256-5800. Ed Annie Laurie Gaylor. **DD** 211. adv acc. **Circ** 2,500. The only freethought newspaper in the US. Hard-hitting critique of religion, Bible, advancement of freethought, state/church separation. For atheists, agnostics, humanists, and freethinkers.

FREIBURGER RUNDBRIEF. Vol. 6- (No. 21/24-). 0344-1385. Periodical. GW. German. an. $8.68. Luckner Gertrud Dr, Postfach 420, D-7800 Freiburg West Germany. **Ind/Abst** Old Testam. Abstr. *Rundbrief zur Forderung der Freundschaft Zwischen dem Alten und dem Neuen Gottesvolk in Geiste der Beiden Testamente.*

FRIENDS JOURNAL. V. 1- July 2, 1955-. 0016-1322. Periodical. US. English. ir. $15.00. Friends Journal, 1501 Cherry Street, Philadelphia PA 19102. **Tel** (215)241-7277. Ed Vinton Deming. **LC** BX7601. **DD** 289.605. bk rev. adv acc. **Circ** 9,500. Available on microfilm from University Microfilms International. Covers the spectrum of Quaker interests through meditative pieces and action stories, history and current issue analysis, poetry and art, book reviews, reports, reader's forum, etc. *Friend, Friends Intelligencer 0362-8965.*

THE FRIENDS' QUARTERLY. V. 1- 1947-. 0016-1357. Periodical. UK. English. qt. 4.72 Domestic, $10.00 US and Canada. Headley Brothers Ltd, The Invicta Press, Ashford Kent England. *Friends' Quarterly Examiner, 0144-9168.*

GALA REVIEW. VAT Gay Atheists League of America Review. Vol. 1, No. 1-. 0277-3236. Periodical. US. English. mo. $10.00. GALA, PO Box 14142, San Francisco CA 94114. **LC** BL2747.3. **DD** 261.83576.

GATHERING. Advent/Christmas 1983-. 0823-1869. Periodical. CN. English. ty. Working Unit on Worship and Liturgy, United Church of Canada, 85 St Clair Avenue East, Toronto Ontario M1T 1M8 Canada. **DD** 264.0792005. *Getting it all Together (United Church of Canada. Committee on Liturgy), 0713-3669.*

GAY CHRISTIAN WITNESS. See Sexual Life.

GEIST UND LEBEN. Yearly Vol. 20. 0016-5921. Periodical. GW. German. bm. $19.81. Echter-Verlag, Postfach 5560, Julius Promenade 64, D8700 Wuerzburg 7 West Germany. **Tel** 0931/3091-153. **Ind/Abst** New Testam. Abstr. **LC** BV5015. (cum index). bk rev. adv acc. **Circ** 4,000. Articles of spirituality (asceticism, mysticism). *Zeitschrift fur Aszese und Mystik.*

GEM (FINDLAY, OHIO). (THE GEM). 0745-3019. Periodical. US. English. mo. Churches of God Publications, PO Box 926, Findlay OH 45840.

GENERATION. (THE GENERATION). V. 1- March 1975-. 0384-1081. Periodical. CN. English. mo. Free. El Shaddai Crusaders Association, 416 Main Street 508A, Winnipeg Manitoba R3B 1A9 Canada. **DD** 243.05.

GLOBAL CHURCH GROWTH. 1964. 0731-1125. Periodical. US. English. bm. $6.00. O C Ministries Inc, 25 Corning Avenue, Milpitas CA 95035. **Tel** (408)263-1101. Ed James Montgomery. bk rev. adv acc. **Circ** 3,000. Our content is based on the belief that the main thrust of scripture is evangelization of the world thus the prime task of church and mission. *Global Church Growth Bulletin, 0273-7183.*

GOOD-NEWS-LETTER. (GOOD-NEWS-LETTER : DIALOGUE ON EVANGELISM IN THE UNITED CHURCH OF CANADA). Vol. 1, No. 1 (Jan. 1980)-. 0713-3677. Periodical. CN. English. ir. Free. United Church of Canada, Division of Mission in Canada, 85 St Clair Avenue East, Toronto Ontario M4T 1M8 Canada. **Tel** (416)925-5931. Ed Gordon Bruce Turner. **DD** 269.0971. bk rev. **Circ** 6,000. (ctrl). Commentary, critique, and resources in the field of evangelization; continuing education events in evangelism highlighted for North America and program directions of National Working Unit highlighted.

GOSPEL CHOIR. See Music.

THE GOSPEL EVANGEL. 0744-2203. Periodical. US. English. mo. Gospel Evangel, 117 River Vista Drive, Goshen IN 46526. **Tel** (219)293-4923.

THE GOSPEL HERALD. 0273-7167. Periodical. US. English. mo. The Gospel Herald, PO Box 507, Jellico TN 37762.

GOSPEL TIDINGS. 0017-2375. Periodical. US. English. mo. $6.00. Gospel Tidings, 1700 Great Oaks Drive, Round Rock TX 78681.

GOSPEL WITNESS. (THE GOSPEL WITNESS). 1922. Periodical. CN. English. bw. 10.00. Gospel Witness, 130 Gerrard Street East, Toronto Ontario M5A 3T4 Canada. **Tel** (416)925 3261. Ed W P Bauman. bk rev. **Circ** 3,000. (ctrl). Contains information on: sermons, articles, current religious interest, missionary news, sunday school lesson outlines, and book reviews. *Gospel Witness and Protestant Advocate, 0702-570X.*

GRASSROOTS. V. 1- Fall 1977-. 0740-5308. Periodical. US. English. qt. $6.00. Resource Center Small Churches, PO Box 752, Luling TX 78648. **Tel** (512)875-5155. Ed Robert B Greene. bk rev. **Circ** 1,400. Contains articles for and about life in small or rural churches and communities.

THE GREEK ORTHODOX THEOLOGICAL REVIEW. V. 1- Aug. 1954-. 0017-3894. Periodical. US. English. qt. $14.00 Domestic, $16.00 Foreign. Holy Cross Greek Orthodox School, 50 Goddard Avenue, Brookline MA 02146. **Tel** (617)731-3500. Ed Michael Vaporis. **Ind/Abst** Old Testam. Abstr., New Testam. Abstr., Hist. Abstr., Relig. Index One, Period., Relig. Theol. Abstr., Am. Hist. Life, Hist. Abstr., Hist. Abstr., Part A, Mod. Hist. Abstr., Hist. Abst., Part B, Twent. Century Abstr., Index Relig. Period. Lit., Recent Publ. Artic. **LC** BX200. **DD** 230.19. (cum index). bk rev. adv acc. **Circ**

Religion, Mythology, Rationalism

1,000. (ctrl). The review contains theological abstracts from reviewed texts spaning the globe of beliefs with a strong Orhodox Christian axis as it's theology.

DIE GRIECHISCHEN CHRISTLICHEN SCHRIFTSTELLER DER ERSTEN JAHRHUNDERTE MICROFORM. V. 1-. Periodical. GE. German (Greek or Latin). ir. Deutscher Buch Export-Import, Leninstrasse 16, DDR-701 Leipzig East Germany.

GROWTH REPORT. Vol. 1, No. 1 (1983)-. Periodical. US. English. The Institute for American Church Growth, 709 East Colorado/Suite 150, Pasadena CA 91101. Church Growth, America.

GUARDIAN OF TRUTH. Vol. 25, No. 1 (Jan. 1, 1981)-. 0273-5504. Periodical. US. English. wk. $35.00. Guardian of Truth Foundation, PO Box 9670, Bowling Green KY 42101. Tel (513)426-1736. Gospel Guardian, 0161-9888 Truth Magazine.

GUIDE TO RELIGIOUS PERIODICALS CEASED. V. 1- Sept. 1964/Feb. 1965-. US. English. sa. LC Z7753.

HALTE JEUNESSE ET FOI. (HALTE JEUNESSE ET FOI : BULLETIN D'INFORMATION DU CENTRE JEUNESSE ET FOI). VFOAT Bulletin d'Information du Centre Jeunesse et Foi. Sept. 1982-. 0823-261X. Periodical. CN. French. ir. Free. Centre Jeunesse et Foi, CP 2532, Quebec Quebec G1K 7R3 Canada. DD 259.50971447. Societe Amour des Jeunes et Centre Jeunesse et Foi : Bulletin, 0820-6139.

HANDBOOK, ANNUAL CONFERENCE - ASSOCIATED CHURCHES OF CHRIST IN NEW ZEALAND. (HANDBOOK : ANNUAL CONFERENCE). Main/Corp Associated Churches of Christ in New Zealand. 0304-1603. English. an. $0.85. Associated Churches of Christ in New Zealand, Department of Administration, PO Box 30516, Lower Hut New Zealand. LC BR1480. DD 286.6931.

THE HEALING HAND. V. 23-32, No. 1, May 1966-Summer/Autumn 1975. Periodical. UK. English. ty. 3. Edinburgh Medical Missionary Society, 12 Mayfield Terrace, Edinburgh EH9 1SA Scotland. Tel 031 667 2518. Ed J R Barclay. Circ 2,000. (ctrl). Christian medical work including reports from the society hospital in Nazareth, Israel. Quarterly Paper.

THE HELPING HAND. V. 9- Winter Quarter 1977/78. 0745-029X. US. English. qt. $4.50. American Sabbath Tract Society, 3120 Kennedy Road P O Box 1678, Janesville WI 53547. Tel (608)752-5055. Ed Linda Harris. Circ 2,300. (ctrl). Helping Hand in Bible-School Work.

THE HERALD OF CHRISTIAN SCIENCE. 0146-7174. Periodical. US. English. qt. $1.00. Christian Science Publishing Society, 1 Norway Street, Boston MA 02115.

HERALD OF HIS COMING. 1941. Periodical. US. English. mo. Herald of His Coming, Box 3457 Terminal Annex, Los Angeles CA 90051. Tel (213)790-2128. Ed Lois J Stucky. Circ 170,000. Helps for Christian Living Prayer Revival.

HIGHLIGHT QUEBEC. Vol. 4, No. 1 (Feb. 1984)-. 0825-4850. Periodical. CN. English. ir. $6.00. Highlight Quebec, PO Box 403, Lachine Province of Quebec H8S 4C2 Canada. Tel (514)878-3035. Ed Ed Hoyer. DD 289.9. bk rev. adv acc. Circ 1,600. Information about Christian activities in Quebec, and to encourage an interest in foreign missions. Highlight (Lachine, Quebec), 0823-8146.

HIMPUNAN PERATURAN PERUNDANG-UNDANGAN PRODUK DEPARTEMEN AGAMA R. I. See Law.

HINDU REGENERATION. Periodical. II. English. ir. 6.00. Hyderabad 500029 India. LC BL1100. DD 294.505.

HINDU VISVA. Periodical. Hindi. ir. 12.00. Vishva Hindu Parishad 6/10 Arya Samaj Road, Karol Bagh New Delhi 110005. LC BL1100.

HINDUISM. Jan. 1965?-. 0018-1927. Periodical. UK. English. qt. Bharat Sevashram Sangha, 17 Stanlake Villas, London W12 England.

HINDUTVA. Periodical. II. English. ir. $3.00. A-14 Green Park, New Delhi -16 India. LC BL1100. DD 294.505.

HIS DOMINION (CANADIAN CHURCH GROWTH CENTRE). (HIS DOMINION). Vol. 4, No. 1 (1977)-. 0229-7175. Periodical. CN. English. qt. $5.42. Canadian Theological Seminary, 4400 Fourth Avenue, Regina Saskatchewan S4T 0H8 Canada. Tel (306)545-1515. Ed Franklin Pyles. DD 262.001. bk rev. Circ 2,700. (ctrl). A journal of special interest to ministerial personnel covering topics of worldwide content pertaining to the thought and practice of Christianity. Church Growth Canada, 0315-8152.

HISPANIA SACRA. V. 1- (No. 1-). 0018-215X. Periodical. SP. Spanish. sa. Consejo Superior de Investigaciones Cientificas, Vitruvio 8, Apartado 14 458, 28006 Madrid Spain. Ind/Abst Am. Hist. Life, Hist. Abstr., Part A, Mod. Hist. Abstr., Hist. Abst., Part B, Twent. Century Abstr., Hist. Abstr. LC BR1020.

HISTOIRE RELIGIEUSE DU CANADA. 0440-8934. Monographic Series. CN. French. ir. Editions Fides, 235 East Boulevard Dorchester, Montreal H2X1N9 Canada.

HISTORIA RELIGIONUM. 0439-2132. Monographic Series. Multilingual (English and German). ir.

HISTORY OF RELIGIONS. V. 1- Summer 1961-. 0018-2710. Periodical. US. English. qt. University of Chicago Press, PO Box 37005, Chicago IL 60637. Tel (312)753-3347. Ind/Abst Am. Hist. Life, Hist. Abstr., Part A, Mod. Hist. Abstr., Hist. Abst., Part B, Twent. Century Abstr., Old Testam. Abstr., New Testam. Abstr., Humanit. Index, Relig. Index One, Period., Guide Soc. Sci. Relig. Period. Lit., Hist. Abstr. LC BL1. DD 220.9.

HLAS PRAVOSLAVI : ORGAN PRAVOSLAVNE CIRKVE V CESKOSLOVENSKU. Periodical. CS. Czech. ir. Artia, PO Box 790, Praha 1 Czechoslovakia.

EL HOGAR CRISTIANO. 0018-3229. Periodical. US. Spanish. qt. $6.00. The Sunday School Board of SBC, 127 Ninth Avenue North, Nashville TN 37234.

HOME LEAGUER. (THE HOME LEAGUER). Vol. 30, No. 11 (May 1983)-. 0822-5079. Periodical. CN. English. mo. $4.00 Per Year. Salvation Army Home League Department, 20 Albert Street, Toronto Ontario M5G 1A6 Canada. DD 267.15. Canadian Home Leaguer, 0008-3771.

HOME LIFE. V. 1- Jan. 1947-. 0018-4071. Periodical. US. English. mo. $9.25. Materials Services Department, 127 Ninth Avenue North, Nashville TN 37234. Tel (615)251-2271. Ed Reuben Herring. bk rev. Circ 750,000. Popular reading monthly on Christian marriage and Christian family life distributed mainly through Southern Baptist churches.

HOME MISSIONS IMPACT. Periodical. US. English. qt. Estenision and Evangelism, Home Missions Impact, Box 2000, Marion IN 46952.

HOMILETIC. V. 1- 1976-. 0738-0534. Periodical. US. English. an. $9.00 Domestic, $10.00 Foreign. Lutheran Theological Seminary, Gettysburg PA 17325. Tel (717)334-6286. Ed Richard L Thulin. bk rev. adv acc. Circ 1,000. A review of publications in religious communication.

HOMILY SERVICE. Began in 1968. 0732-1872. Periodical. US. English. mo. $36.00. Liturgical Conference, 810 Rhode Island Avenue NE, Washington DC 20018. Tel (202)529-7400. Ed Rachel Reeder. Circ 4,200. (ctrl). The publication offers aids to preachers of the various Christian churches: scriptural exegesis, "ideas and illustrations," homily models, etc.

HRVATSKI KATOLICKI GLASNIK. VFOAT Croatian Catholic Messenger. 0018-6910. Periodical. US. Serbo-Croatian(R). mo. $20.00. Croatian Franciscan Fathers, 4851 Drexel Boulevard, Chicago IL 60615. Ed Diomzije Lasic. Circ 2,000. Religion and mythology.

HUNGARIAN CHURCH PRESS. VFOAT Ungarischer Kirchlicher Pressedienst. V. 1- Mar. 26, 1949-. 0438-1920. Periodical. HU. English. sm. Akademiai Kiado, POB 24, 1363 Budapest Hungary.

HYONDAE CHONGGYO. VFOAT The Modern Religion Monthly. Periodical. KO. Korean. ir. 24.000. Hyondae Chonggyosa, 310-68 4-ka Ulchiro Chung-ku, Seoul 100 Korea. LC BL2230.

IDEAS. See Recreation, Leisure.

I.E. VAT Id Est. V. 1- 1964-. 0422-4108. Periodical. US. English. bm. The Ecumenical Institute, 344 West Congress Parkway, Chicago IL 60624.

IFMA NEWS BULLETIN. VFOAT I.F.M.A. News Bulletin. VAT Interdenomination Foreign Mission Association News Bulletin. -June 1953. Periodical. US. English. qt. Interdenomination Foreign Mission Association News, PO Box 395, Wheaton IL 60187. Claiming the World for Christ.

IMMANUEL. No. 1- Summer 1972. 0302-8127. Periodical. IS. English (descriptions, summaries and translations of recent Hebrew publications). sa. $12.00. Adl of Bnai Brith, 823 United Nation Plaza, New York NY 10017. Tel (212)490-2525. Ind/Abst New Testam. Abstr., Old Testam. Abstr., Relig. Index One, Period. bk rev. Religious thought and research in Israel.

IN UNITY. Began in 1953. 0442-3844. Periodical. AT. English. qt. Free to Australian Libraries. Australian Council of Churches, PO Box C199/ Clarence Street, Sydney 2000 Australia. Tel (02)29.2215. Ed Joan Dugdale. bk rev. Circ 6,500. (ctrl). Covers work of Australian and world councils of churches, ecumenical and inter-faith dialogue within Australia and world-wide, theology, aid, development, and education.

INDEX TO RELIGIOUS PERIODICALS LITERATURE. See Indexes/Abstracts.

INDIAN CHURCH HISTORY REVIEW. V. 1- June 1967-. 0019-4530. Periodical. II. English. sa. $8.00. Church History Association of India, Wilson College, Mackichan Hall, Bombay 7 India. Ind/Abst Relig. Index One, Period. LC BR1150. DD 275.4. bk rev. Ideas and essays on the origin, growth and present features of the church in India. Bulletin of the Church History Association of India.

INDIAN RECORD. See Sociology: General Works, Theory.

INFORMATION SERVICE - THE SECRETARIAT FOR PROMOTING CHRISTIAN UNITY. Main/Corp Catholic Church Secretariatus Ad Christianorum Unitatem Fovendam. No. 1- 1967-. Periodical. English. qt. $12.00. Secretariat-Christian Unity, 00120 Vatican City Italy.

INNOVATIONS (ELGIN, ILL.). (INNOVATIONS). Vol. 1, No. 1 (Summer 1984)-. 0743-1074. US. English. qt. $15.00. David C Cook Publishing Company, 850 North Grove Avenue, Elgin IL 60120. DD 207.

THE INQUIRER. No. 4789- April 14, 1934-. 0020-1723. Periodical. UK. English. bw. 8.50 Domestic, $20.00. Inquirer Publishing Company Inc, 1-6 Essex Street, London WC2R 3HY England. Tel (01)240-2384. Ed Frank Walker. bk rev adv acc. Circ 2,500. Religious journal. Inquirer and Christian Life.

INSIDE OUT. 0148-3714. US. English. Hanuman Foundation, 276 Riverside Drive, New York NY 10025. LC BL624. DD 248.86.

INSPIRATION. V. 1- Jan. 1978-. 0149-5917. Periodical. US. English. qt. $1.95 Single Copy. Petersen Publishing Company, 6725 Sunset Boulevard, Los Angeles CA 90029. LC BV4501.2. DD 248.405.

INTERDEPENDENCE. 1969-. 0362-4668. Periodical. US. English. ir. c/o Unitarian Church of Evanston, 1130 Ridge Avenue, Evanston IL 60201.

INTERNATIONAL BIBLIOGRAPHY OF THE HISTORY OF RELIGIONS. See Bibliographies.

INTERNATIONAL JOURNAL FOR PHILOSOPHY OF RELIGION. V. 1- Spring 1970-. 0020-7047. Periodical. English. bm. Kluwer Academic Publishing Group, PO Box 322, 3300 AH Dordrecht Netherlands. Ind/Abst Humanit. Index, Philos. Index, Relig. Index One, Period. LC BL51. DD 200.1.

INTERNATIONAL LAZARITE. V. 1- Jan/Mar. 1975-. Periodical. CN. English. qt. $25.00. Saint Lazarus Trust, Captain Donald R Puller, 32 Blue Spruce Circle, Weston CT 06880. LC CR5037. DD 255.8.

THE INTERNATIONAL LESSON ANNUAL. 1956-. 0074-6770. Monographic Series. US. English. an. $5.95. Abingdon Press, 201 8th Avenue South, PO Box 801, Nashville TN 37202. Tel (800)251-3320. Ed Horace R Weaver. LC BV1560. DD 268.61. Index in last issue of volume - attached. An interdenominational resource for teachers of Sunday school and church school. Contains step-by-step lesson plans for every Sunday from September 1985 to August 1986.

INTERNATIONAL REVIEW OF MISSION. V. 58, No. 230- Apr. 1969-. 0020-8582. Periodical. SZ. English. qt. $15.00. World Council of Churches Publications Department, 150 Route de Ferney, 1211 Geneva 20 Switzerland. **Tel** (022)916111. **Ed** Eugene I Hockwell. **Ind/Abst** Recent Publ. Artic., Relig. Index One, Period., Am. Hist. Life, Hist. Abstr., Christ. Period. Index, Hist. Abstr., Part A, Mod. Hist. Abstr., Hist. Abst., Part B, Twent. Century Abstr. Index published separately - free - automatically sent. bk rev. adv acc. **Circ** 4,500. International review of mission scholarly articles, book reviews and a bibliography in the area of mission and evangelism. Often centering on a specific ecumenical mission theme. *International Review of Missions.*

INVESTORS' BULLETIN (MILTON, ONT.). (INVESTORS' BULLETIN). **VAT** Investors' Bulletin (Cambridge), Investors' Bulletin (Willowdale), Investors Bulletin of the Ken Campbell Evangelistic Association. Jan. 1973-. 0712-9904. Periodical. CN. English. ir. Campbell-Reese Evangelistic Team, PO Box 100, Milton Ontario L9T 2Y3 Canada. **DD** 269.206071.

INWARD LIGHT. No. 1- Fall 1937-. Periodical. US. English. an. $7.00 US, Canada and Mexico. Inward Light, 749 Polo Road, Bryn Mawr PA 19010. **Tel** (401)322-1732. **Ed** Charles Perry and Eleanor Perry. bk rev. **Circ** 1,000. An organ of expression and intercommunication relating inner life to problems of our time.

IRON MOUNTAIN. Summer 1984-. 8756-3142. Periodical. US. English. sa. $9.00. Artemisia Press, PO Box 6423, Colorado Spring CO 80934. **DD** 291.

ISKCON REPORT. **VFOAT** I.S.K.C.O.N. Report. 0748-2272. Periodical. US. English. mo. Iskcon Report, 3764 Watseka Avenue, Los Angeles CA 90034. **DD** 294.

THE ISKCON WORLD REVIEW. **VFOAT** I.S.K.C.O.N. World Review. 0748-2280. Periodical. US. English. mo. $8.00 Domestic, $16.00 Foreign. The Iskcon World Review, 3764 Watseka Avenue, Los Angeles CA 90034. **Tel** (213)204-3646. **Ed** Uddhava Dasa. **DD** 294. adv acc. **Circ** 20,000. The newspaper of the Hare Krishna Movement, containing news on its worldwide network of temples, cultural centers, vegetarian restaurants, and farming communities.

ISKRA. No. 28- Mar. 4-Vol. 1945-. 0021-1761. Periodical. CN. text in English and Russian. bw. Soyuz Dukhovn Hbshchin Khrista, Box 760/Grand Forks, British Columbia Canada. **Tel** 4423757. *Sten-Gazeta Soiuza Dukhovnikh Obshchin Khrista.*

ISLAMOCHRISTIANA. ISLAMIYAT MASIHIYAT. **VFOAT** Islamiyat Masimiyat. 1 (1975)-. Periodical. Arabic (English and French). an. Pontificio Istituto/di Studi Arabi e d'islamistica, Piazza di S Appollinare 49, 00186 Rome Italy. **Tel** (6)656 11 31. **LC** BP172. **DD** 261.27. bk rev. Christian-Muslim dialogue in history and today comparative theologies and mystics bibliography about these topics. Points of convergence and co-operation between believers.

JAAR THEMATIC STUDIES. **VFOAT** J.A.A.R. Thematic Studies. **VAT** Journal of the American Academy of Religion Thematic Studies. Vol. 47, No. 2 (June 1979)-. 0735-6919. Monographic Series. US. English. ir. Scholars Press, PO Box 4869/ Hampden Station, Baltimore MD 21211. **Tel** (916)891-4541. **Ind/Abst** Relig. Index One, Period. *Journal of the American Academy of Religion. Supplement, 0146-9215.*

JAGANI. 1 (1975?)-. Periodical. English (Hindi). an. 10.-. Sri Prananath Mission, D-193 Defence Colony, New Delhi 110024 India. **Tel** 633930. **Ed** Ranjit Saha and Vimla Mehta. **Circ** 1,000. Based on philosophy of Saint Prannath this magazine is trying to bring awareness in the world that God is one and religion also is one.

JAHRBUCH FUR ANTIKE UND CHRISTENTUM. *See* Yearbooks, Almanacs, Directories.

JAPAN CHRISTIAN ACTIVITY NEWS. **VFOAT** JCAN. Began in 1952. 0021-4353. Periodical. JA. English. mo. $16.51. National Christian Council of Japan, Room 24 2 13 18, Nishi Waseda Shinji-ku, Tokyo 160 Japan. **Tel** (03)203-0372. **Ed** Aiko Y Carter. bk rev. **Circ** 400. A newsletter of the National Christian Council in Japan, with news of ecumenical activities in Japan.

THE JAPAN CHRISTIAN QUARTERLY. V. 1- Jan. 1926-. 0021-4361. Periodical. JA. English. qt. Kyowa Book Company, 1-38 Kanda Jinbo-cho, Chiyoda-ku Tokyo 101 Japan. **Tel** 293-0727. **Ind/Abst** MLA Int. Bibliogr. Books Artic. Mod. Lang. Lit., Relig. Index One, Period. **LC** BV3440. **DD** 275.2. (cum index). *Japan Evangelist.*

JAPAN HARVEST. 0021-440X. Periodical. JA. English. qt. 15.00. Japan Evangelical Missionary Association, c/o Oscc Building, 1 Kanda Surugadai, 2 Ch Chiyoda-ku Tokyo 101 Japan. **Tel** 03-295-1949. **Ed** Siegfried A Buss. bk rev. adv acc. The magazine for today's Japan missionary with special news of what's happening across Japan and around the world. Survey, testimony and information exchange.

JAPANESE JOURNAL OF RELIGIOUS STUDIES. Began with Mar. 1974 issue. 0304-1042. Periodical. JA. English. qt. $15.00. Japanese Association for Religious Studies, University of Tokyo, Tokyo Japan. **Tel** (03)812-2111. **Ed** Horiyoshi Tamaru. **Ind/Abst** Relig. Index One, Period. **LC** BL2202. **DD** 200.5. bk rev. adv acc. **Circ** 1,500. (ctrl). Studies in Japanese religious traditions. *Contemporary Religions in Japan.*

JAPANESE RELIGIONS. Began in 1959. 0448-8954. Periodical. JA. English (Japanese). ir. 9.00. NCC Center, Study Japanese Religions, Kyoto DIOC, Japan Episcopal Church, Karasuma, Shimotachiuri Kyoto 602 Japan. **Ed** Yuki Hideo. **Ind/Abst** Relig. Index One, Period., Relig. Theol. Abstr. **LC** BL2202. **DD** 291.0952. Index in last issue of volume - attached. bk rev. Studies of Japanese religions and the encounter between Christianity and Eastern religions. *Quarterly Notes (Shoshukyo Kenkyu Senta (Japan)).*

JEEVADHARA; A JOURNAL OF CHRISTIAN INTERPRETATION. V. 1- (No. 1-). Periodical. II. English. bm. 8.00. Theology Center, Kottayam 686 017, Kerala India. **Tel** 7430. **Ed** Joseph Constantine Manalel. **Ind/Abst** Old Testam. Abstr., New Testam. Abstr. bk rev. adv acc. **Circ** 1,000. (ctrl). Whole theology divided into six areas: anthropology, scriptures, doctinal theology, ecclesiology, ecumenisum and practical theology each of which is dealt with in an issue.

JOSEMARIA ESCRIVA DE BALAGUER. (JOSEMARIA ESCRIVA DE BALAGUER : FONDATEUR DE L'OPUS DEI : BULLETIN D'INFORMATION). No. 1, (Dec. 1976)-. 0703-2757. Periodical. CN. French. sa. Free. Vice-Postulation de l'Opus dei au Canada, 5643 rue Plantagenet, Montreal Quebec H3T 1S3 Canada. **DD** 271.095.

JOSEMARIA ESCRIVA DE BALAGUERI; BULLETIN. No. 1- Jan. 1977-. 0703-9093. Periodical. CN. English. sa. Free. Vice-Postulation of Opus Dei in Canada, 5643 Plantagenet Street, Montreal Quebec H3T 1S3 Canada. **DD** 255.094.

THE JOSEPHITE HARVEST. 0021-7603. Periodical. US. English. qt. $2.00. St Joseph's Society, 1130 North Calvert Street, Baltimore MD 21202. *Colored Harvest.*

JOURNAL - CHRISTIAN MEDICAL SOCIETY. *See* Medicine.

JOURNAL ECK. V. 1, No. 1, (Jan./Feb./March 1983)-. 0821-1515. Periodical. CN. French. qt. $10.00. Eckankar Centre de Quebec, 833 Avenue Marguerite-Bourgeois, Quebec G1S 3W7 Canada. **DD** 299.93.

JOURNAL FOR ANTHROPOSOPHY. Began with Spring 1965 issue. 0021-8235. Periodical. US. English. sa. $10.00. Journal of Anthroposophy, c/o Christy Barnes, Hillsdale Road, New York NY 12529. **Tel** (518)325-7182. **Ed** Christy Barnes and Arthur Zajone. **LC** BP595.A1. **DD** 212.53. bk rev. adv acc. **Circ** 1,800. New, practical impulses in science, art, education and medicine arising from the insights of the spiritual science by Rudolf Steiner.

JOURNAL FOR THE SCIENTIFIC STUDY OF RELIGION. V. 1- Oct. 1961-. 0021-8294. Periodical. US. English. qt. $35.00. Executive Office, Society for the Scientific Study of Religion, Box U68A, University of Connecticut, Storrs CT 06268. **Tel** (203)486-4424. **Ed** Don Copps. **Ind/Abst** Humanit. Index, Sociol. Abstr., Hist. Abst., Part B, Twent. Century Abstr., Am. Hist. Life, Hist. Abstr., Part A, Mod. Hist. Abstr., MLA Int. Bibliogr. Books Artic. Mod. Lang. Lit., Soc. Welf. Soc. Plan./Policy Soc. Dev., Old Testam. Abstr., Psychol. Abstr., Ref. Source, Relig. Index One, Period. **LC** BL1. **CODEN** JSSRBT. bk rev. adv acc. **Circ** 3,000. (ctrl). Theoretical, methodological and empirical studies and reviews of current books on religious institutions and experiences.

JOURNAL OF CHINESE RELIGIONS. No. 10 (Fall 1982)-. 0737-769X. Periodical. US. English. an. $10.00. Secretary-Treasurer, Department of Asian Studies, University of British Columbia, Vancouver British Columbia U6T 1W5 Canada. **LC** BL1802. **DD** 299.5105. *Bulletin (Society for the Study of Chinese Religions (U.S.)), 0271-3446.*

THE JOURNAL OF CHRISTIAN HEALING. Began in 1979. 0738-2944. Periodical. US. English. sa. $12.00 Domestic, $14.00 Foreign. Journal of Christian Healing, 103 Dudley Avenue, Narberth PA 19072. **Tel** (215)667-0460. **Ed** Douglas W Schoeninger. **LC** BT732. **DD** 150.190882. bk rev. adv acc. **Circ** 1,450. Interdisciplinary journal advancing the knowledge and practice of healing through Jesus Christ by the power of the Holy Spirit of all dimensions of the person-physical, emotional, relational and spiritual.

JOURNAL OF COMPARATIVE SOCIOLOGY AND RELIGION. *See* Sociology: General Works, Theory.

JOURNAL OF DHARMA. V. 1- July 1975-. 0253-7222. Periodical. II. English. qt. $12.00. Journal of Dharma, c/o Joan Stein 804 Grove Lane, Santa Barbara CA 93105. **Tel** (805)687-8791. **Ind/Abst** Philos. Index, Relig. Index One, Period. **LC** BL1. **DD** 291.05. bk rev. (ctrl). Religious studies.

JOURNAL OF ECCLESIASTICAL HISTORY. (THE JOURNAL OF ECCLESIASTICAL HISTORY). V. 1- April 1950-. 0022-0469. Periodical. UK. English. qt. Cambridge University Press, 510 North Avenue, New Rochelle NY 10801. **Tel** (914)235-0300. **Ed** C W Dugmore. **Ind/Abst** Am. Hist. Life, Hist. Abstr., Part A, Mod. Hist. Abstr., Hist. Abst., Part B, Twent. Century Abstr., New Testam. Abstr., Years Work Eng. Stud., Ref. Source, Humanit. Index, Relig. Index One, Period., Guide Soc. Sci. Relig. Period. Lit., Hist. Abstr., Years Work Eng. Stud., Recent Publ. Artic. **LC** BR140. **DD** 270.05. Index published separately - free - automatically sent.

JOURNAL OF ECUMENICAL STUDIES. V. 1- Winter 1964-. 0022-0558. Periodical. US. English. qt. $17.50 Domestic, $19.50 Foreign. Journal of Ecumenical Studies, Temple University, (022-38), Philadelphia PA 19122. **Tel** (215)787-7714. **Ed** Leonard Swidler. **Ind/Abst** Am. Hist. Life, Hist. Abstr., Part A, Mod. Hist. Abstr., Hist. Abst., Part B, Twent. Century Abstr., Old Testam. Abstr., New Testam. Abstr., Writ. Am. Hist., Ref. Source, Hist. Abstr., Cathol. Period. Lit. Index, Relig. Theol. Abstr., Elenchus Bibliogr. Bibicus, Humanit. Index, Relig. Index One, Period. **LC** BX1. **DD** 262.001. Index in last issue of Volume - attached. bk rev. adv acc. **Circ** 2,200. Articles, reviews and abstracts related to interreligious, interideological dialogue, worldwide, in English, but covering all major languages.

JOURNAL OF FEMINIST STUDIES IN RELIGION. Vol. 1, No. 1 (Spring 1985)-. 8755-4178. Periodical. US. English. sa. $25.00. Scholars Press, PO Box 1608, Decatur GA 30029. **Tel** (404)329-6950. **Ed** J Plaskow and E S Fiorenza. **Ind/Abst** Guide Soc. Sci. Relig. Period. Lit., Relig. Index One, Period., Relig. Theol. Abstr. **DD** 200. adv acc. Feminist research in religion. Encourages discussion and dialogue among men and women of differing feminist perspectives on studies in religion.

THE JOURNAL OF LAW AND RELIGION. *See* Law.

JOURNAL OF MENNONITE STUDIES. Vol. 1 (1983)-. 0824-5053. CN. English. an. $8.00. Journal of Mennonite Studies, University of Winnipeg, Winnipeg Manitoba R3B 2E9 Canada. **DD** 289.771.

THE JOURNAL OF RELIGION. V. 1- Jan. 1921-. 0022-4189. Periodical. US. English. qt. University of Chicago Press, PO Box 37005, Chicago IL 60637. **Tel** (312)753-3347. **Ind/Abst** Old Testam. Abstr., Annu. Bibliogr. Engl. Lang. Lit., New Testam. Abstr., Soc. Sci. Index, Book Rev. Digest, Book Rev. Index, Humanit. Index, Relig. Index One, Period., Guide Soc. Sci. Relig. Period. Lit., Am. Hist. Life, Hist. Abstr., Recent Publ. Artic., Hist. Abstr., Part A, Mod. Hist. Abstr., Hist. Abst., Part B, Twent. Century Abstr. **LC** BR1. Available on microfilm to regular subscribers only from University Microfilms. Microfiche editions available from Johnson Associates. *Biblical World, 0190-3578 American Journal of Theology.*

JOURNAL OF RELIGION AND HEALTH. **VFOAT** Religion & Health. V. 1- Oct. 1961-. 0022-4197. Periodical. US. English. qt. $30.00. Human Sciences Press, 72 Fifth Avenue, New York NY 10011. **Ind/Abst** Relig. Theol. Abstr., Psychol. Abstr., Relig. Index One, Period. **LC** RC321. **DD** 616.89005. **NLM** W1 JO868. **CODEN** JRHEAT. (cum index).

Religion, Mythology, Rationalism

JOURNAL OF RELIGION AND THE APPLIED BEHAVIORAL SCIENCES. (JOURNAL OF RELIGION AND THE APPLIED BEHAVIORAL SCIENCES : A PUBLICATION OF ASSOCIATION FOR CREATIVE CHANGE WITHIN RELIGIOUS AND OTHER SOCIAL SYSTEMS). Vol. 1, No. 2 (Fall 1979)-. 0275-1402. Periodical. US. English. ty. Free to Members, $10.00 Nonmembers. Association for Creative Change, PO Box 2212, Syracuse NY 13220. LC BL1. DD 291.65019. *Journal of Religion & the Applied Behavioral Sciences.*

JOURNAL OF RELIGION IN AFRICA. VFOAT Religion en Afrique. V. 1-. 0022-4200. Periodical. NE. English (French). ty. $24.00. E J Brill, PO Box 9000, 2300 PA Leiden The Netherlands. Tel (071)312624. Ind/Abst Am. Hist. Life, Hist. Abstr., Part A, Mod. Hist. Abstr., Hist. Abst., Part B, Twent. Century Abstr., Hist. Abstr., Relig. Index One, Period., Recent Publ. Artic. LC BL2400. bk rev. adv acc. Circ 500. (ctrl). Devoted to the study of the forms and history of religion within the African continent. Bibliographical material and instrumental studiorum are a specially prominent feature. *African Religious Research, 0044-6602.*

THE JOURNAL OF RELIGIOUS HISTORY. 1960. 0022-4227. Periodical. AT. English. sa. $33.40. Macquarie University, School of History/Philosophy and Politics, North Ryde New South Wales Australia 2113. Tel (02) 889203. Ed Bruce E Mansfield. Ind/Abst Am. Hist. Life, Hist. Abstr., Relig. Index One, Period. bk rev. adv acc. Circ 600. Articles and reviews on all fields of religious history (ancient, medieval, modern), and on bearing of religion on general history.

JOURNAL OF RELIGIOUS STUDIES. V. 1- Sept. 1969-. 0047-2735. Periodical. II. English. sa. $13.00. Punjabi University Registrar, Production and Sales Officer, Patiala 147002 India. Tel 73262. Ed Wazir Singh. LC BL1. DD 200.5. bk rev. Circ 1,000. (ctrl). Devoted to the study and understanding of the religiousness of mankind on historical, comparative and philosophical lines.

JOURNAL OF RELIGIOUS STUDIES. V. 6, No. 2/V. 7, No. 1- Fall 1978/Spring 1979-. 0193-3604. Periodical. US. English. sa. $6.00. Cleveland State University, Department of Religious Studies, Cleveland OH 44115. Tel (216)687-2170. Ind/Abst New Testam. Abstr., Relig. Index One, Period. *Ohio Journal of Religious Studies, 0094-5668.*

THE JOURNAL OF RELIGIOUS THOUGHT. V. 1- Autumn 1943-. 0022-4235. Periodical. US. English. sa. $26.00. Howard University Divinity School, 1240 Randolph Street NE, Washington DC 20017. Tel (202)636-7766. Ed Cain H Felder. Ind/Abst Am. Hist. Life, Hist. Abstr., Part A, Mod. Hist. Abstr., Hist. Abst., Part B, Twent. Century Abstr., New Testam. Abstr., Relig. Index One, Period. LC BR1. DD 205. bk rev. adv acc. Circ 800. (ctrl). Available on microfilm from University Microfilms, Ann Arbor. Focuses on issues in religion and ministry relating to Afro-American, Caribbean and African people through feature articles, pastor's corner segment and book reviews/notes.

JOURNAL OF SIKH STUDIES. Began with issue for Feb. 1974. 0379-8194. Periodical. II. English. sa. $30.00. Guru Nanak Development University, Department of Publications, Amritsar India. Tel 33911. Ed Madanjit Kaur. Ind/Abst Recent Publ. Artic. LC BL2017. DD 294.6. bk rev. adv acc. Circ 750. The journal contains original articles by eminent writers on subjects concerning Sikh history, religion and philosophy.

JOURNAL OF THE AMERICAN ACADEMY OF RELIGION. Main/Corp American Academy of Religion. V. 35- 1967-. 0002-7189. Periodical. US. English. qt. Scholars Press, PO Box 1608, Decatur GA 30031. Tel (404)329-6950. Ind/Abst Am. Hist. Life, Hist. Abstr., MLA Int. Bibliogr. Books Artic. Mod. Lang. Lit., Relig. Index One, Period., Humanit. Index, Old Testam. Abstr., New Testam. Abstr., Ref. Source, Hist. Abstr., Part A, Mod. Hist. Abstr., Hist. Abst., Part B, Twent. Century Abstr., Years Work Eng. Stud. LC BV1460. (cum index). Available on microfilm from University Microfilms. *Journal of Bible and Religion, 0885-2758.*

JOURNAL OF THE AMERICAN SCIENTIFIC AFFILIATION. Main/Corp American Scientific Affiliation. V. 1- Jan. 1949-. 0003-0988. Periodical. US. English. qt. $30.00. American Scientific Affiliation, PO Box J, Ipswich MA 01938. Tel (617)356-5656. Ed Wilbur Bullock. Ind/Abst Christ. Period. Index, Guide Soc. Sci. Relig. Period. Lit. LC BL240.2. DD 261.5. (cum index). bk rev. adv acc. Circ 4,000. Available on microfilm from University Microfilm. Papers of academic caliber which address issues pertaining both to science and the christian faith. Both the 'hard' sciences and the 'soft' sciences are represented.

JOURNAL OF THE ASSOCIATION FOR THE UNDERSTANDING OF MAN. Main/Corp Association for the Understanding of Man. V. 1- Sept. 1971-. 0146-8820. Periodical. US. English. qt $25.00 Includes Membership. Association for the Understanding of Man, PO Box 5310, Austin TX 78763. LC BL624. DD 291.405.

JOURNAL OF THE CANADIAN CHURCH HISTORICAL SOCIETY. Main/Corp Canadian Church Historical Society. V. 1- Sept. 1950-. 0008-3208. Periodical. CN. English. qt. $4.00. Canadian Historical Society, 537 Main Street, Glenn Williams Ontario L76 3T1 Canada. Ind/Abst Am. Hist. Life, Hist. Abstr., Part A, Mod. Hist. Abstr., Canadiana, Can. Hist. Rev., Hist. Abstr., Relig. Index One, Period. LC BR570. DD 283.71.

THE JOURNAL OF THE CHRISTIAN BRETHREN RESEARCH FELLOWSHIP CEASED. VFOAT CBRF Journal. Ceased with No. 30. 0306-7467. Periodical. UK. English. ir.

JOURNAL OF THE CHRISTIAN MEDICAL ASSOCIATION OF INDIA. See Medicine.

JOURNAL OF WOMEN'S MINISTRIES. No. 1 (Winter 1984)-. Periodical. US. English. qt.

JUBILEE INTERNATIONAL. (JUBILEE INTERNATIONAL : PRISON FELLOWSHIP INTERNATIONAL NEWSLETTER). VFOAT Jubliee. Spring 1981. 0736-9662. Periodical. US. English (French and Spanish). qt. Free. Prison Fellowship International, PO Box 40562, Washington DC 20016.

JUNGE KIRCHE. Vol. 1-. 0022-6319. Periodical. GW. German. mo. 48. Vertrieb Junge Kirche, Mathildenstrasse 86, D-2800 Bremen West Germany. Tel 0421-71648. Ed G Casalis, H Kloppenburg and D Soelle. LC BX8001. bk rev. adv acc. Circ 6,200. Topics include theology, ecumenism, Third World, environment, peace movements and nonviolence. *Akid.*

JUNIOR. (JUNIOR : SABBATH SCHOOL LESSON QUARTERLY OF SEVENTH- DAY ADVENTISTS). VFOAT Junior Sabbath School Lessons. V. 51, No. 1 (Jan.-Mar. 1985)-. 0748-6928. Periodical. US. English. qt. $7.16 Domestic, $8.12 Foreign. Review and Herald Publishing Association, 55 West Oak Ridge Drive, Hagerstown MD 21740. Tel (301)791-7000. Sabbath school material for the Junior department. *Junior Bible Explorer, 0163-8777.*

KATALLAGETE. Began publication in 1965. 0022-9288. Periodical. US. English. ir. Committee of Southern Churchmen, Box 2307/College Station, Berea KY 40404. Ind/Abst Relig. Index One, Period. LC BR535.

KERK & WERELD. VFOAT Kerk en Wereld. Periodical. NE. Dutch. Kon Van Gorcum & Comp, B V P B 43, Assen Netherlands.

KESTON NEWS SERVICE. Began in 1975. 0278-3169. Periodical. US. English. sm. $50.00. Society for Study of Religion Under Communism, Keston College USA/Box 1310, Framingham MA 01701. Tel (617)235-4799. Ed Alyona Kojevnikov. Ind/Abst Relig. Index One, Period. A biweekly news bulletin of events concerning the religious communities in the Soviet Union and Eastern Europe.

KHRYSTYIANS' KYI VISNYK. VFOAT Christian Herald. 0383-2740. Periodical. CN. Ukrainian. bm. Khrystiansky Wisnyk-Christian, 787 Toronto Street, Winnipeg Manitoba R3E 1Z7 Canada. Tel (204)783-3201.

KIDO (SEOUL, KOREA). (KIDO). VFOAT The Prayer. Periodical. KO. Korean. mo. 7.000. Wolgan Kidosa, 37-1 1-ka Wonhyoro Yongsan-ku, Seoul 140 Korea.

KIKAN GENDAI SHUKYO. RELIGIONS IN JAPAN. VFOAT Gendai Shukyo. JA. Japanese. ir. 4800. Enu Esu Shuppankai, 11 Nishikubo Sakuragawacho, Shipa-ku Tokyo Japan. LC BL2202.

KIRCHE IN NOT. 1- 1953-. Periodical. German. ir. Ostpriesterhilfe E V und Haus der Begegnung E V, Haus der Begegnung, 624 Konigstein/Ts, Konigstein Im Taunus West Germany. LC BR738.6.

KIRCHE UND KONFESSION. V. 1- 1962-. 0453-929X. Monographic Series. GW. German. ir. Vandenhoeck & Ruprecht, Postfach 3753, Theaterstr 13, D 3400 Goettingen West Germany. Tel (0551)65061. adv acc.

KIRCHE UND RECHT. Monographic Series. GW. German. ir. Verlag Herder Freiburg, Hermann-Herder, Strasse 4, D-7800 Freiburg - West Germany. Ed W Plochl.

KIRISUTOKYO KAGAKU SAKIGAKE. VFOAT Herald of Christian Science. 0145-8019. Periodical. US. parallel text in English. qt. $2.00. Christian Science Publishers Society, 1 Norway Street, Boston MA 02115.

KIRKE OG KULTUR. VFOAT For Kirke OG Kultur. Vol. 26-. Periodical. NO. Norwegian. ir. 175.00. Forlagsentralens Tidsskrift, Postboks 6005 Etterstad, Oslo 6 Norway. Tel 02-200710. Ind/Abst MLA Int. Bibliogr. Books Artic. Mod. Lang. Lit. LC AP45. bk rev. adv acc. Circ 3,000. (ctrl). Church and culture. *For Kirke OG Kultur.*

KOKUGAKUIN DAIGAKU NIHON BUNKA KENKYUJO HO. Began with Feb. 1964 issue. Japanese. ir. Kokugakuin Daigaku Tokyo, Higashi 4-chome Shibuya-ku 150 Tokyo Japan. Tel (03)409-0111. LC DS820.8. bk rev.

KOREAN CHURCH DIRECTORY OVERSEAS. See Yearbooks, Almanacs, Directories.

KOSMOS + OEKUMENE. VFOAT Kosmos en Oekumene. 6E Volume Number 1-. Periodical. NE. Dutch. mo. 51.50. St Willibrord Vereniging, St Janssingel 21, S-Hertogenbosch Netherlands. Tel (073)136471. bk rev. Circ 1,500. Covers issues about the ecumenical movement. *Kosmos + Oecumene.*

KRESTANSKA REVUE. 0023-4613. Periodical. CS. Czech. ir. Artia, PO Box 790, Praha 1 Czechoslovakia.

KRISTEN VIDENSKABS HEROLD. VFOAT The Herald of Christian Science. 0145-7551. Periodical. US. Danish (parallel text in English). qt. $2.00. Christian Science Publishing Society, 1 Norway Street, Boston MA 02115. *Christian Science Herold.*

KRISTEN VITENSKAPS HEROLD. VFOAT The Herald of Christian Science. 0145-7535. Periodical. US. Norwegian (parallel text in English). qt. $2.00. Christian Science Publishing Society, 1 Norway Street, Boston MA 02115. *Christian Science Herold.*

KUNDALINI QUARTERLY. Summer 1976-. 0364-3727. Periodical. US. English. qt. $15.00. KRI, 8191 Monte Vista, Claremont CA 91711. LC BL1215.K8. DD 294.543.

KYOHOE WA YOKSA. VFOAT Church and History. V. 1- (Sept. 1975)-. Periodical. KO. Korean. ir. Hanguk Kyohoesa Yonguso, 367-27 Hapchong-dong Mapo-ku, Seoul Korea.

KYRKOHISTORISK - ARSSKRIFT. (KYRKOHISTORISK ARSSKRIFT). Series/Titl Skrifter Utgivna Av Svenska Kyrkohistoriska Foreningen. VFOAT H. Lundstrom Kyrkohistorisk Arsskrift, Lundstrom Kyrkohistorisk Tidskrift, Linderholm. Kyrkohisttidskrift. Vol. 1. 0085-2619. SW. Swedish. an. Almqvist & Wiksell, 108 Drottninggatan, PO Box 45150, S-104 30 Stockholm Sweden. Tel Telex 85413160. Ed Herman Lundstrom. Ind/Abst Recent Publ. Artic., Am. Hist. Life, Hist. Abstr., Hist. Abstr., Part A, Mod. Hist. Abstr., Hist. Abst., Part B, Twent. Century Abstr. LC BR140. (cum index).

LADOC. VAT Latin America Documentation. No. 1- June 1970-. 0360-3350. Periodical. US. English. bm. $16.00. Apartado 5594, Lima 100 Peru. Tel 475210. Ed Richard Renshaw. LC BX1425.A1. DD 282.8. Circ 1,200. Documents from the Latin American churches.

LATERANUM. V. 1- 1919-. Periodical. IT. Italian. sa. Pontificia Univ Lateranense, Piazza Giovanni in Laterano 4, 00184 Roma Italy. Ind/Abst Old Testam. Abstr.

THE LAUGHING MAN. V. 1-. 0363-1664. Periodical. US. English. qt. $17.95. The Laughing Man, PO Box 3680, Clearlake Highlands CA 95422. Tel (415)492-0922. Ed Richard Schorske. LC BL1. DD 200.5. bk rev. Circ 6,000. The alternative to scientific materialism and religious provincialism. *Dawn Horse, Vision Mound, 0164-4971.*

LE-ELA. VFOAT L'Eylah. Periodical. UK. English. an. $3.07. Office of the Chief Rabbi, Adler House, Tavistock Square, London WC1H 9HN England. Tel

Religion, Mythology, Rationalism

01 203 6427. Ed J Sacks. LC BM1. DD 296.05. bk rev. adv acc. **Circ** 4,000. (ctrl) Discussion of contemporary orthodox Jewish issues.

LEBENDIGE SEELSORGE. Periodical. GW. German. bm. 42.-. Lebendige Seelsorge Verlag, Juliuspromenade 64, Postfach 5560, D-8700 Wurzburg 1 West Germany. **Tel** 0931/3091-153. Ed Echter. bk rev. adv acc. **Circ** 6,300. Articles on ministerial work and pastoral duties.

A L'ECOUTE (NICOLET, QUEBEC). (A L'ECOUTE). 0823-1451. Periodical. CN. French. mo. $7.50. Office Diocesain d'Education, C P 250, Nicolet Quebec J0G 1E0 Canada. DD 268.8271405.

LETTERS AND NOTICES. Began with V. 1 in June 1862. Periodical. UK. English. ir. $20.00. Jesuit Information Office, 114 Mount Street, London W1Y 6AH England. **Tel** (01)49-7596. Ed Hugh Kay. bk rev. **Circ** 2,300. A review of Christian thought and world affairs i.e. China in Deng's last years, God in the nuclear age, arms control: a new perspective and detente by way of Germany.

LIBER ANNUUS. See Yearbooks, Almanacs, Directories.

LINGUISTICA BIBLICA. 1- Nov. 1970-. 0342-0884. Periodical. PL. German. sa. $15.01. Linguistica Biblica Bonn, Postfach 130154, 5300 Bonn 1 West Germany. **Ind/Abst** MLA Int. Bibliogr. Books Artic. Mod. Lang. Lit., Lang. Lang. Behav. Abstr., Old Testam. Abstr., New Testam. Abstr., Sociol. Abstr. LC BL65.L2. DD 201.4.

LISTE DES RELIGIEUX, DES RESIDENCES ET DES OEUVRES - CONGREGATION DE SAINTE-CROIX, SOCIETE DES PERES, LA PROVINCE CANADIENNE. (LISTE DES RELIGIEUX, DES RESIDENCES ET DES OEUVRES). **Main/Corp** Peres de Sainte-Croix. Province Canadienne. 1980/81-. 0820-0629. CN. French. an. Province Canadienne des Peres de Sainte-Croix, 4961 rue Coronet, Montreal Quebec H3V 1C9 Canada. DD 271.79. Liste des Religieux et Catalogue des Maisons, 0228-751X.

LISTENING. V. 1- Winter 1966-. 0024-4414. Periodical. US. English. ir. $9.50. Listening, 7200 West Division Street, River Forest IL 60305. **Tel** (312)771-3030. Ed Victor S Lamonte. **Ind/Abst** Old Testam. Abstr., Cathol. Period. Lit. Index, Philos. Index. LC AP2. adv acc. **Circ** 1,000. Interested in ideas, persons, in dialogue and in explorations, it is interested in anything that is cogent. A journal of religion and culture.

LITERATURE AND BELIEF. See Literature.

LITURGICAL CONFERENCE. Monographic Series. US. English. mo. Liturgical Newsletter, Box 3554, Albuquerque NM 87110. **Tel** (505)883-0469.

LITURGICAL REVIEW CEASED. V. 2-11. Periodical. UK. English. sa. 2.50. Scottish Academic Press, 33 Montgomery Street, Edinburgh EH7 5JX England. Liturgical Studies.

LITURGY (WASHINGTON, D.C. : 1980). (LITURGY). 0458-063X. Periodical. US. English. qt. $25.00. Liturgy, 810 Rhode Island Avenue Northeast, Washington DC 20018. **Tel** (202)529-7400. Ed Rachel Reeder. **Ind/Abst** Cathol. Period. Lit. Index. LC BV169. DD 264.005. **Circ** 4,500. (ctrl). Addresses the subject of worship that is ecumenical, imaginative and free; sacramental celebrations; liturgical ministries. Explores themes in relation to worship, music, and the arts, social justice and the Bible in the assembly. Liturgy (Washington, D.C. : 1956), 0458-063X.

THE LIVING CHURCH. VFOAT Living Church and the Layman's Magazine. V. 104- Jan. 7, 1942-. 0024-5240. Periodical. US. English. wk. The Living Church, 407 East Michigan, Milwaukee WI 53202. **Tel** (414)276-5420. Ed H Boone Porter. bk rev. adv acc. **Circ** 10,300. Publishes current news of Episcopal church. Containing articles, book reviews, special reports, letters from readers and clergy changes. Living Church and the Layman's Magazine, 0161-8482.

LIVING CITY. 0193-5968. Periodical. US. English. mo. $15.00. Living City/NY, PO Box 126, Jamaica NY 11415. **Tel** (718)896-0334. Ed Sharry Silvi. LC BX809.F6. DD 270.82. bk rev. **Circ** 5,500. Articles focusing on the spirituality of the Focolare movement, a spirituality of unity; articles on ecumenism and current events regarding the Catholic Church and the Christian world in general.

LIVING MESSAGE. 0380-4267. Periodical. CN. English. mo. $3.86. Anglican Church of Canada, Box 820, Petrolia Ontario Canada N0N 1R0. **Tel** (519)882-2497.

LIVING ORTHODOXY. 1979. 0279-8433. Periodical. US. English. bm. $12.00. St John of Kronstadt Press, Agape Community, Liberty TN 37095. **Tel** (615)536-5239. Ed Gregory Williams. bk rev. **Circ** 500. Traditional Orthodox Christian material in English: Saints' lives, short articles of spiritual guidance; explanations of Orthodox liturgical practice; reviews of books of interest to strugglers in the Faith; occasional news of the publishing community.

LIVING WITH CHRIST. V. 1- Apr./May 1977-. 0703-6752. Periodical. CN. English. ir. $4.00 Canada and US, $6.75 other. Novalis, PO Box 498 Station A, Ottawa Ontario K1N 8Y5 Canada. DD 264.023. Living with Christ, 0383-2481.

LIVING WITH CHRIST. V. 42, No. 4- Apr./May 1977-. 0703-6760. Periodical. CN. English. ir. $7.74. Novalis, Box 9700 Terminal, Ottawa Ontario K1G 4B4 Canada. DD 264.023. Living with Christ, 0383-2481.

THE LOGOS. V. 1- Jan. 1968-. 0746-1534. Periodical. US. English. bm. $10.00. Logos Ministry for Orthodox Renewal, 2707 South Calhoun Street, Fort Wayne IN 46807. **Tel** (219)456-6603. Ed Eusebius Stephonon. **Ind/Abst** Philos. Index. bk rev adv acc. **Circ** 5,000. (ctrl). Messages on the subject of christian life, christian renewal and charismatic revival.

LOGOS JOURNAL. 0194-3820. Periodical. US. English. bm. $6.69 Domestic, $8.69 Foreign. Logos International Fellowship Inc, 201 Church Street, Plainfield NJ 07060. LC BR1644. DD 269. Herald of Faith-Harvest Time Magazine.

THE LOOKOUT. Periodical. US. English. wk. $15.00. Standard Publishing Company, 8100 Hamilton Avenue, Cincinnati 31 Ohio. **Tel** (513)931-4050. Ed Mark A Taylor. LC BX7312.A1. DD 268.43305. **Circ** 145,000. Helps guild Sunday schools, individual Christian commitment, and Christian family life. Deals with contemporary issues in light of Biblical teaching.

LUTHERISCHE MONATSHEFTE. Vol. 1. 0024-7618. Periodical. German. mo. 49,50. Lutherisches Verlagshaus GMBH, 3000 Hannover 1 Knochenhauer, Strasse 38-40, D-30 Hannover 1 West Germany. **Tel** 0511/1241-733. Ed Vereinigte Evangel.-Luth Kirche Deutschlands. LC BX8001. DD 261.05. bk rev. adv acc. **Circ** 6,400. Information and opinion on church and religion-culture and politics. Evangelisch-Lutherische Kirchenzeitung, Informationsblatt fur Die Gemeinden in Den Niederdeutschen Lutherischen Landeskirchen; Lutherische Nachrichten.

LUTHERJAHRBUCH. VFOAT Luther-Jahrbuch. Vol. 1- 1919-. GW. German. ir. Vandenhoeck and Ruprecht, Postfach 3753 Theaterstr 13, D-3400 Goettingen West Germany. **Tel** 0551/65061. Ed Helmar Junghans. **Ind/Abst** MLA Int. Bibliogr. Books Artic. Mod. Lang. Lit. bk rev. adv acc. **Circ** 390.

MACAE ESPIRITA. Periodical. BL. Portuguese. ir. Uniao Espirita Macaense Departamento Social, Caixa Postal 74, Macae RJ Brazil.

MAGYAR EGYHAZ. VFOAT Magyar Church. Began in 1922. 0360-5760. Periodical. US. English (Hungarian). bm. $5.00. Classic Printing Corporation, 9527 Madison Avenue, Cleveland OH 44102.

THE MAHA BODHI. Began publication in 1924. 0025-0406. Periodical. II. English. mo. $4.00. Maha Bodhi, 4A Bankim Chatterjee Street, Calcutta 73 India. **Tel** 34-1091. Ed Wipulasara Mahathera. bk rev. adv acc. **Circ** 2,000. One of the oldest and one of the most widely read journals in the world. International, devoted to Buddhism, Buddhist literature, art, culture and Buddhist news, and book reviews. Maha Bodhi and the United Buddhist World.

MAILBOX CLUB MESSENGER. (THE MAILBOX CLUB MESSENGER). No. 1-. 0227-0056. Periodical. CN. English. Free. Western Tract Mission, 401-33rd Street West, Saskatoon Saskatchewan S7L 0V5 Canada. DD 248.405.

MAILBOX CLUB UPDATE. 1st quarter, 1978-. 0227-0080. Periodical. CN. English. qt. Free. Western Tract Mission, 401-33rd Street West, Saskatoon Saskatchewan S7L 0V5 Canada. DD 248.24606071242.

MANA SAMANI. (MANASAMANI). 0377-9505. Hindi. mo. 5.00. Ramvan Satna, Madhya Pradesh, Ramavana India. LC BL1100.

MANANAM. 0276-0444. Periodical. US. English. qt. $15.00. Mananam, 6601 February Drive, Cincinnati OH 45239. **Tel** (513)385-7880. Ed Vilasini Balakrishnan. LC B130. DD 294.505. adv acc. **Circ** 800. (ctrl). A quarterly journal dedicated to the exposition of Vedantic thought, with an emphasis on the unity of all religions.

MANASABHARATI : SRI RAMACARITAMANASA CATUSSATABDI SAMAROHA SAMITI, MADHYAPRADESA, BHOPALA KI MASIKA MUKHAPATRIKA. See Literature.

MANDEMENTS, LETTRES PASTORALES ET CIRCULAIRES DES EVEQUES DE QUEBEC. V. 1-4, 1887-1888. 0383-2724. CN. French. Archeveche de Quebec la Chancellerie, CP 459, Quebec Quebec H3H 1G4 Canada.

MARANA THA. V. 1- May 1976-. 0700-9674. Periodical. CN. French. mo. Service Central du Renouveau Charismatique Catholique, 1202 rue de Bleury, Montreal Quebec H3B 3J3 Canada. DD 269.

MARANATHA. (LE SEIGNEUR VIENT). V. 1- Feb. 1972-. 0318-9147. Periodical. CN. French. qt. 15. Per No. Le Seigneur Vient Maranatha, CP 603, St-Hyacinthe Quebec J2S 7C2 Canada. DD 248.205.

MARIANUM: EPHEMERIDES MARIOLOGIAE. Vol. 1- 1939-. Periodical. IT. Latin (text in French, Italian, English, and Spanish). qt. 35.00. Admin Rivista Marianum, Viale Trenta Aprile 6, 00153 Roma Italy. **Ind/Abst** New Testam. Abstr., MLA Int. Bibliogr. Books Artic. Mod. Lang. Lit. Index in last issue of volume - attached. (cum index).

MARK-UP. Began in 1970?. Periodical. US. English. mo. Washington Office, National Council of Churches, 110 Maryland Avenue NE, Washington DC 20002.

THE MARTURION. 0047-6064. Periodical. US. English. mo. People of the Living God, 2101 Prytania Street, New Orleans LA 70130. Witness.

MASTER SERMON SERIES. (MSS, MASTER SERMON SERIES). VFOAT Master Sermon Series. V. 1- 1970-. 0362-0808. Periodical. US. English. mo. $25.00. Cathedral Publishers, PO Box 244, Royal Oak MI 48068. **Tel** (313)546-4510. Ed Carl Howie. **Circ** 2,000. Sermons and prayers to aid the minister in preparing weekly sermons.

MATURE YEARS. V. 1- Sept./Nov. 1968-. 0025-6021. Periodical. US. English. qt. $8.50. United Methodist Publishing House, PO Box 801, Nashville TN 37202. LC BV4580.A1. DD 248.85. Mature Years.

MEASURING MORMONISM. V. 1- Apr. 1974-. 0094-5633. US. English. an. Association for the Study of Religion, 3646 East 3580 South, Salt Lake City UT 84109. LC BX8601. DD 289.33.

MEDIA: LIBRARY SERVICES JOURNAL. See Library and Information Science.

MEDIUM. See Education (General).

MELANGES DE SCIENCE RELIGIEUSE. Vol. 1. 0025-8911. Periodical. FR. French. qt. $12.51. Institut Catholique, 60 Boulevard Vauban, 59046 Little Cedex France. **Tel** (50)30 88 27. **Ind/Abst** MLA Int. Bibliogr. Books Artic. Mod. Lang. Lit., Old Testam. Abstr., New Testam. Abstr., Relig. Index One, Period. LC BR3. DD 230.05. bk rev adv acc. **Circ** 500. Theology, philosophy, religious history, institutions and law history, anthropology, sociology, pedagogies, literature and art history.

MENNONITE BRETHREN HERALD. V. 1- Jan. 19, 1962-. 0025-9349. Periodical. CN. English. sm. $37.92. Mennonite Brethren Herald, 3- 169 Riverton Avenue, Winnipeg R2L 2E5 Canada. **Tel** (204)669-6575. Ed Herb Kopp. bk rev. adv acc. **Circ** 12,500. A denominational church magazine published to keep the church informed on trends, news, literature, and missions.

MENNONITE HISTORIAN. V. 1- Sept. 1975-. 0700-8066. Periodical. CN. English. qt. $3.09. Mennonite Heritage Centre, 600 Shartesbury Boulevard, Winnipeg Manitoba R3P 0M4 Canada. **Tel** (204)888-6781. Ed History/Archives Committee of the Mennonite Heritage Centre. DD 289.771. bk rev. adv acc. **Circ** 2,000. (ctrl). An 8 page quarterly publication of historical articles and reports written in popular style pertinent to Mennonites of Canadian-Russian background.

Religion, Mythology, Rationalism

THE MENNONITE QUARTERLY REVIEW. V. 1-Jan. 1927-. 0025-9373. Periodical. US. English. qt. Mennonite Quarterly Review, Goshen College, Goshen IN 46526. Tel (219)533-3161. Ed John S Oyer. Ind/Abst Hist. Abstr., Part A, Mod. Hist. Abstr., Hist. Abst., Part B, Twent. Century Abstr., Recent Publ. Artic., Writ. Am. Hist., Ref. Source, Hist. Abstr., Am. Hist. Life, Relig. Index One, Period. LC BX8101. DD 289.705. (cum index). bk rev. Circ 1,000. Information concerning Anabaptist-Mennonite history, thought, life, and current affairs. *Goshen College Record. Review Supplement.*

MENNONITE REPORTER. V. 2, No. 1- Jan. 10, 1972-. 0380-0121. Periodical. CN. English. bw. $12.38. Mennonite Publishing Service Inc, 3-312 Marsland Drive, Waterloo Ontario N2L 3Z1 Canada. Tel (519)884-3810. Ed Ron Rempel. bk rev. adv acc. Circ 9,700. (ctrl). News and comment about and for Mennonites in Canada; commentary on wider church and world issues from Anabaptist-Mennonite perspective. *Canadian Mennonite Reporter, 0380-013X.*

MENNONITE WEEKLY REVIEW. Vol. 1, No. 1 (Sept. 18, 1923)-. Newspaper. US. English. wk. $14.50. Herald Publ Company, Box 568, 129 West Sixth, Newton KS 67114. Tel (316)283-3670. Ed Robert M Schrag. bk rev. adv acc. Circ 14,000. News and comment regarding churches, agencies, institutions of Mennonite denomination in USA and abroad.

EL MENSAJERO DEL CORAZON DE JESUS. Periodical. MX. Spanish. mo. Apartado 2181, Mexico 1 DF Mexico.

MESSAGE (NASHVILLE, TENN.). (MESSAGE). Vol. 44, No. 3 (May-June 1978)-. 0026-0231. Periodical. US. English. bm. $11.95. Review and Herald Publishing Association, 6856 Eastern Avenue NW, Washington DC 20012. Tel (301)791-7000. Ed Delbert W Baker. LC BX1601. DD 286.73. bk rev. Circ 75,000. (ctrl). A Christian magazine of contemporary issues primary focus is a black minority readership. It appeals to an interdenominational audience with readers mainly in the US and also abroad. *Message Magazine, 0162-6019.*

MESSAGE OF THE CROSS. Periodical. US. English. bm. Bethany Fellowship, 6820 Auto Club Road, Minneapolis MN 55438. Tel (617)944-2121.

MESSENGER. (THE MESSENGER). V. 1- Jan. 11, 1963-. 0701-3299. Periodical. CN. English. bw. Evangelical Mennonite Conference, Box 1268, Steinbach Manitoba Canada.

MESSENGER. (THE MESSENGER). V. 186, No. 7/8- July/Aug. 1966-. 0381-5293. Periodical. CN. English. mo. The Messenger, Box 2642 Station B, Kitchener Ontario N2H 6N2 Canada. DD 289.405. *New Church Messenger, 0028-4424.*

MICHIGAN CHRISTIAN ADVOCATE. Began in 1875. 0026-2072. Periodical. US. English. wk. $8.00. Michigan Christian Advocate, 316 Springbrook Avenue, Adrian MI 49221. Tel (517)265-2075. Ed Edward L Duncan. bk rev. adv acc. Circ 21,000. (ctrl). Weekly news for Michigan United Methodist Church.

MINISTERIAL FORMATION. 1 (1978)-. Periodical. English. qt. World Council of Churches, 475 Riverside Drive/Room 770, New York NY 10115. Ind/Abst Relig. Index One, Period.

MINZOKU SHUKYO KENKYU. V. 1, No. 1, (Shukigo Fall 1980)-. Periodical. JA. Japanese. qt. 2800. Minzoku Shukyo Kenkyujo, c/o Imperiaru Ochanomizu 810, 11-2 Kanda Ogawamachi, Chiyoda-ku 101, Tokyo Japan. LC BL9.J3.

MISERE. (LA MISERE). No. 1- Dec. 1970-. 0318-9953. Periodical. CN. French. ty. 15. Per No. La Misere, CP 1238, Trois-Rivieres Quebec G9A 5K8 Canada. DD 248.05.

MISSION FRONTIERS : THE BULLETIN OF THE UNITED STATES CENTER FOR WORLD MISSION. Vol. 1:1 (Jan. 1979)-. Periodical. US. English. mo. $3.00 Domestic, $4.00 Foreign. US Center for World Mission, 1605 East Elizabeth Street, Pasadena CA 91104. Tel (818)797-1111. Ed Ralph B Winter. bk rev. Circ 52,000. (ctrl). We focus on the activities of the US Center for World Missions with a basic purpose of reaching the unreached people groups with the gospel.

MISSIONARY NEWS SERVICE. 1954. 0026-6051. Periodical. US. English. sm. $18.00. Evangelical Missions Information Service, Box 794, Wheaton IL 60189. Tel (312)653-2158. Ed James Reapsome. Circ 1,600. Reports of missionary activity around the world.

MISSIONSWISSENSCHAFTLICHE FORSCHUNGEN. Vol. 1- 1962-. 0076-9428. Monographic Series. GW. German. ir. Guetersloher Verlagshaus, Postfach 1343/Koenigstrasse 23-25, 4830 Guetersloh West Germany. Tel 5241-8620. Published by the West German Society of Mission Studies on christian missionaries in the past and in the world today.

MISSOURI NEWS. 0746-827X. Periodical. US. English. qt. Church of God Publishing House, 922 Montgomery Avenue, Cleveland TN 37311.

MODERN RATIONALIST. (THE MODERN RATIONALIST). 0304-1727. Periodical. English. ir. K Veeramani, 2 Rundalls Road 7, Madras India. LC BL2700. DD 149.705.

MON FRERE ET MOI. 1- June 1968-. 0316-0785. Periodical. CN. French. qt. Centre de L'Association Missionaire de Marie Imaculee, C P 721, Winnipeg Manitoba R3C 2K3 Canada.

MONATSHEFTE FUR EVANGELISCHE KIRCHENGESCHICHTE DES RHEINLANDES. 1.- Yearly Volume. Periodical. GW. German. ar. 30.-. Dr Rudolf Habelt GMBH, Am Buchenhang 1, 5300 Bonn 1 West Germany. Ed H Faulenbach, D Meyer, and W Schmidt. LC BX8022.R5. *Monatshefte fur Rheinische Kirchengeschichte.*

MONOGRAPH SERIES - SOCIETY FOR THE SCIENTIFIC STUDY OF RELIGION. Main/Corp Society for the Scientific Study of Religion. No. 1-. Monographic Series. US. English. ir. Society Scientific Study of Religion, University Connecticut, Box U 68 A, Storrs CT 06268. Tel (203)486-4424.

THE MONTH AT UNESCO. Periodical. English. qt. International Catholic Center for UNESCO, 9 rue Cler, 75007 Paris France. Tel (1) 470517599. LC AS4.U83. bk rev. Circ 5,000. Information for the Christian world about UNESCO activities and publications.

MONUMENTA ORDINIS FRATRUM PRAEDICATORUM HISTORICA. V. 1-. Monographic Series. IT. Latin. ir. Instituto Storico Domenicano, Convento S Sabina Avenita Roma, Rome Italy. History of the Dominican Order.

MOODY MONTHLY. V. 38, No. 7- Mar 1938-. 0027-0806. Periodical. US. English. mo. Moody Monthly, 2101 West Howard Street, Chicago IL 60645. Tel (312)274-2535. Ind/Abst Ref. Source, Christ. Period. Index, Guide Soc. Sci. Relig. Period. Lit. *Moody Bible Institute Monthly.*

MUSLIMS OF THE SOVIET EAST. English. ir. Editorial Office, 30 Navoi-Str, 700 129 Tashkent USSR. LC BP65.S58. DD 297.09584.

MUSU ZINIOS. 1- Saus. 2, 1972-. Periodical. US. Lithuanian. bw. $8.00. Tevai Jezuitai Cikugoje, 2345 West 56th Street, Chicago IL 60636. Tel (312)737-8400. Ed Anthony Saulaitis. LC BX806.L5. bk rev. adv acc. Circ 1,400. (ctrl). Information about activities of Lithuanian ethnic groups in the Lithuanian Cultural Center and of Lithuanian Jesuit Fathers.

MYSTICS QUARTERLY (IOWA CITY, IOWA). (MYSTICS QUARTERLY). Vol. 10, No. 1 (Mar. 1984)-. 0742-5503. Periodical. US. English. qt. $10.00. University of Iowa, Publications Order Department GSB, Iowa City IA 52242. Tel (319)353-8609. Ed Valerie Lagorio and Ritamary Bradley. Ind/Abst MLA Int. Bibliogr. Books Artic. Mod. Lang. Lit. LC BV5077.G7. DD 248.2205. adv acc. Circ 472. (ctrl). The international journal devoted to the study of the medieval English and continental mystics. *14th Century English Mystics Newsletter, 0737-5840.*

MYTHOLOGIE FRANCAISE. VFOAT Bulletin de la Societe de Mythologie Francaise. No. 103 (Oct./Dec. 1976)-. Periodical. FR. French. qt. 130.00. Societe de Mythologie Francaise, 175 Rue de Pontoise, 6000 Beauvais France. *Bulletin de la Societe de Mythologie Francaise.*

MYTHPRINT. VAT Myth Print. 1970. 0146-9347. Periodical. US. English. mo. $7.00. Mythopoeic Society, 1008 North Monterey Street, Alhambra CA 91801. Tel (313)284-0848. Ed David S Bratman. Ind/Abst Abstr. Engl. Stud. bk rev. adv acc. Circ 300. (ctrl). Newsletter of the Mythopoeic Society. Contains reviews and notices of current events in the field of fantasy, literature with a special emphasis on Tolkien, Lewis and Williams.

NASE ZAJEDNISTVO. VFOAT Our Croatian Community. No. 1 (1981)-. 0824-3522. Periodical. CN. Serbo-Croatian -R. qt. 1.00. Nase Zajednistvo, PO Box 664, Streetsville Ontario L5M 2C2 Canada. DD 282.08991823071.

NATIONAL BULLETIN ON LITURGY. No. 5- Sept. 1965-. 0084-8425. Periodical. CN. English. bm. 8.00 Domestic, 10.00 Foreign. Publishing Service Canadian Conference Catholic Bishops, 90 Parent Street, Ottawa Ontario K1N 7B1 Canada. Tel (613)236-9461. Ed Patrick Byrne. Canada's own liturgical journal treating all aspects of liturgical questions; written for those who are involved in liturgy. *Bulletin of the National Commission on Liturgy, 0700-7442.*

NATIONAL CHRISTIAN COUNCIL REVIEW. V. 71, No. 5- May 1951-. Periodical. English. mo. Wesley Press c/o Mr Samuel, PO Box 37 Church Road, Mysore City 570001 India. *National Christian Council Review.*

THE NATIONAL CHRISTIAN REPORTER. VFOAT Reporter. 0279-8913. Periodical. US. English. wk. PO Box 222198, Dallas TX 75222.

NATIONAL SPIRITUALIST (INDIANAPOLIS, IND.). (THE NATIONAL SPIRITUALIST). Began with: Vol. 56, No. 598 (Aug./Sept. 1974). 0882-1275. Periodical. US. English. mo. $7.00 Domestic, $8.00 Foreign. Summit Publications by Stow, 668 East 62nd Street, Indianapolis IN 46220. LC BF1001. DD 299.93. *Summit of Spiritual Understanding.*

NAUKA I RELIGIIA. Sept. 1959-. 0130-7045. Periodical. UR. Russian. mo. $15.50. Victor Kamkin Inc (70602), 12224 Parklawn Drive, Rockville MD 20852. Tel (301)881-5973. Ind/Abst Int. Aerosp. Abstr. LC BL2700.

NCCC CHRONICLES. Main/Corp National Council of the Churches of Christ in the United States of America. VAT National Council of the Churches of Christ Chronicles. V. 1- Summer 1975-. 0098-8162. Periodical. US. English. ty. $1.00. National Council of Churches of Christ, 475 Riverside Drive, New York NY 10027. Tel (212)870-2228. Ed Sarah Vilankulu. Circ 20,000. Overview of activities of the National Council of the Church of Christ and its program.

NEDERLANDS ARCHIEF VOOR KERKGESCHIEDENIS. Vol. 1-7 1884-99. 0028-2030. Periodical. NE. Dutch. ir. E J Brill, P O Box 9000, 2300 PA Leiden The Netherlands. Ed J G R Acquoy and H C Rogge. Ind/Abst Am. Hist. Life, Hist. Abstr. LC BR900. Primarily devoted to church and dogmatic history and is open to any contributions in these fields as well as in other specialised related fields.

NEEDLE'S EYE (TORONTO, ONT.). (NEEDLE'S EYE). 0710-7315. Periodical. CN. English. sa. Free. Needle's Eye, 600 Jarvis Street, Toronto Ontario M4Y 2J6 Canada. DD 261.80971. (ctrl).

NETWORK. VFOAT USPG Network. New ser., No. 7- Autumn 1977-. 0028-3037. Periodical. UK. English. qt. 2.00. United Society for the Propogation of Gospel, 15 Tufton Street, London SW1 England. Tel (01)222 4222. Ed Anthony Richmond. bk rev. Circ 16,000. (ctrl). Christian mission in a variety of political situations worldwide. *USGP Network.*

NEUE ZEITSCHRIFT FUR MISSIONSWISSENSCHAFT. NOUVELLE REVUE DE SCIENCE MISSIONAIRE. VFOAT Nouvelle Revue de Science Missionaire. 1.-. 0028-3495. Periodical. SZ. English (French, German, and Italian). qt. 30.00. Neue Zeitschrift fur Missionswissenschaft, CH6405 Immensee Switzerland. Tel 041/81 51 81. Ed J Specker. Ind/Abst Recent Publ. Artic. LC BV2130. bk rev. adv acc. Circ 800. International review which covers all branches of missionology. *Missionswissenschaft und Religionswissenschaft.*

NEW DAY. (THE NEW DAY). 0028-453X. Periodical. US. English. bw. $7.50. New Day Publishing Company, 1600 West Oxford Street, Philadelphia PA 19121. Tel 03-9940. Ed Eugene Amman. LC BX7350.A1. DD 289.9. adv acc. Available on microfilm from the New York City Library,

Religion, Mythology, Rationalism

Microfilm Department and Kraus-Thomson Organization. Publish works - works of Father and Mother Divine, and general news items included.

THE NEW ERA. 0164-5285. Periodical. US. English. mo. $7.00. Church of Jesus Christ Latter Day Saints, 50 East North Temple, Salt Lake City UT 84150. **Tel** (801)531-2951. **Ed** Brian K Kelly. **Circ** 185,000. Articles by, about, and for young (12-18) Latterday Saints and their leaders. Must have LDS point of view.

NEW ERA. (NEW ERA : A NEWSLETTER OF THE NEW ECUMENICAL RESEARCH ASSOCIATION). Vol. 1, No. 1 (March/April 1981)-. 0277-3082. Periodical. US. English. bm. International Religious Foundation Inc, 10 Dock Road, Barrytown NY 12507.

NEW FOUNDATION PAPERS. No. 1 (July 1980)-. 0748-6804. Periodical. US. English. qt. $6.00. George Fox Fund Inc, PO Box 267, Kutztown PA 19530. **Tel** (215)682-7332. **Ed** J H McCandless. bk rev. **Circ** 400. Promoting the everlasting gospel preached by George Fox and early Quakers.

NEW HORIZONS. V. 1- Mar. 1956-. 0363-6976. Periodical. US. English. qt. Missouri School of Religion, Ninth and Lowry, Columbia MO 65201.

NEW MENORAH. (NEW MENORAH : THE B'NAI OR JOURNAL OF JEWISH RENEWAL). 2nd Ser., No. 1-. 0883-0215. Periodical. US. English. mo. $24.00 Domestic, $30.00 Foreign. B'Nai or Journal of Jewish Renewal, 6723 Emlen Street, Philadelphia PA 19119. **Tel** (215)849-5385. **Ed** Arthur Wasnow and Shana Margolin. **DD** 296. adv acc. **Circ** 3,000. Theory and practice of Movement for Jewish Renewal: new liturgies, feminist, Torah-rooted politics, etc. Menorah (Philadelphia, PA.).

NEW RELIGIONS NEWSLETTER. V. 1- Apr. 1977-. 0704-5883. Periodical. CN. English. mo. $10.00. Herbert Richardson, PO Box 164, Toronto Ontario M5S 1J4 Canada.

THE NEW REVIEW OF BOOKS AND RELIGION. V. 1-4. 0146-0609. Periodical. US. English. mo. $10.00. Seabury Book Service, 815 2nd Avenue, New York NY 10017. **Ind/Abst** Relig. Index One, Period. **LC** BL1. **DD** 200.5. Review of Books and Religion, 0048-7465; New Book Review.

NEW WINE. Began with V. 1 in 1969. 0194-438X. Periodical. US. English. mo. $15.00. New Wine, PO Box Z, Mobile AL 36616. **Tel** (205)460-9010. **Ed** Bruce Longstreth. **Circ** 52,000. Practical and inspirational teaching for Christian growth. Features today's most popular Christian leaders with articles on the family, prayer, praise and worship, spiritual warfare and more.

NEW WYCLIF SOCIETY NEWSLETTER. (THE NEW WYCLIF SOCIETY NEWSLETTER). No. 1 (Fall 1979)-. 0227-5422. Periodical. CN. English. sa. $3.00 Domestic, $2.50 US. New Wyclif Society, Department of English, University of Ottawa, Ottawa Ontario K1N 6N5 Canada. **DD** 270.50924.

NEWS NOTES - NATIONAL FEDERATION OF PRIESTS' COUNCILS. (NFPC NEWS NOTES). VFOAT News Notes. Sept. 1979-. 0738-3886. Periodical. US. English. mo. $10.00. National Federation of Priests' Council, 1307 South Wabash Avenue, Chicago IL 60605. **Tel** (312)427-0115.

NEWSLETTER - BILL PRANKARD EVANGELISTIC ASSOCIATION. (NEWSLETTER). May 1983-. 0823-9606. Periodical. CN. English. ir. Free. Bill Prankard Evangelistic Association, PO Box 5555 Station F, Ottawa Ontario K2C 3M1 Canada. **DD** 269.206071.

NEWSLETTER - CANADIAN INSTITUTE OF RELIGION AND GERONTOLOGY. Main/Corp Canadian Institute of Religion and Gerontology. V. 1- Jan. 1974-. 0315-2219. Periodical. CN. English. Canadian Institute of Religion and Gerontology, 296 Lawrence Avenue East, Toronto Ontario M4N 1T7 Canada.

NEWSLETTER FROM C.A.R.E.E.'S CHRISTIAN-MARXIST ENCOUNTER TASK GROUP. VFOAT Newsletter from Caree's Christian-Marxist Encounter Task Group. VAT Newsletter from Christians Associated for Relationships with Eastern Europe's Christian Marxist Encounter Task Group. 0732-9253. Periodical. US. English. ty. $3.00. Dr Nicholas Piediscalzi, Department of Religion, Wright State University, Dayton OH 45435.

NEWSLETTER - MASSACHUSETTS BAY DISTRICT, UNITARIAN UNIVERSALIST CHURCHES. Main/Corp Unitarian Universalist Association. Massachusetts Bay District. VFOAT Mass Bay District Newsletter. V. 1- Jan. 15, 1976-. 0364-667X. Periodical. US. English. Massachusetts Bay District, Unitarian Universalist Churches, 110 Arlington Street, Boston MA 02116.

NEWSLETTER OF THE AFRO-AMERICAN RELIGIOUS HISTORY GROUP OF THE AMERICAN ACADEMY OF RELIGION. Main/Corp American Academy of Religion. AFRO-American Religious History Group. V. 1- Fall 1976-. US. English. sa. $3.00. College of the Holy Cross, Editor Office of Special Study, Worchester MA 01610. **Tel** (617)793-2011. **Ed** Randall K Burkett.

NEWSLETTER - PRAIRIE RELIGIOUS LIBRARY ASSOCIATION. (NEWSLETTER). Vol. 1, No. 1 (Mar. 1980)-. 0225-5758. Periodical. CN. English. Free to Members, Membership $15.00. PRLA Newsletter, c/o Campion College Library, University of Regina, Regina Saskatchewan S4S 0A2 Canada. **DD** 027.67060712.

NEWSLETTER - RELIGIOUS STUDIES AND MORAL EDUCATION COUNCIL. ALBERTA TEACHERS' ASSOCIATION. (NEWSLETTER - RELIGIOUS STUDIES AND MORAL EDUCATION COUNCIL, ALBERTA TEACHERS' ASSOCIATION). Main/Corp Alberta Teachers' Association. Religious Studies and Moral Education Council. V. 1- Fall 1974-. 0701-1237. Periodical. CN. English. 15.00. Alberta Teachers' Association, 11010 - 142 Street, Edmonton Alberta T5N Canada. **Tel** 453-2411. **Ed** De McMorrow. **DD** 207. bk rev. **Circ** 300. (ctrl). Reports on council happenings and explores issues of current concern to religion studies.

NEWSLETTER-REVIEW - R.M. BUCKE MEMORIAL SOCIETY FOR THE STUDY OF RELIGIOUS EXPERIENCE. (NEWSLETTER-REVIEW - THE R. M. BUCKE MEMORIAL SOCIETY FOR THE STUDY OF RELIGIOUS EXPERIENCE). Main/Corp Bucke (R. M.) Memorial Society. V. 1- 1966-. 0079-9343. Periodical. CN. English. sa. $2.50. R M Bucke Memorial Society, c/o The Secretary, 4453 Maisonneuve Boulevard West 215, Montreal Canada.

NEWSLETTER - WOMEN'S CAUCUS-RELIGIOUS STUDIES. Main/Corp Women's Caucus-Religious Studies (Organization). V. 1- Fall 1972-. 0362-4676. Periodical. US. English. qt. $5.00. Ann M Vater/Loyola University of the South, Box 58, New Orleans LA 70118.

NEWSLETTER - WOMEN'S INTER-CHURCH COUNCIL OF CANADA. (NEWSLETTER). Main/Corp Women's Inter-Church Council of Canada. 0822-2061. Periodical. CN. English. ir. Free. WICC, 77 Charles Street West, Toronto Ontario M5S 1K5 Canada. **DD** 261.834405. Hi There, 0826-3078.

NICM ASSOCIATES NEWSLETTER. VFOAT Associates Newsletter. VAT National Institute for Campus Ministries Associates Newsletter. Vol. 1, No. 1 (Aug. 1977)-. Periodical. US. English. sa. National Institute for Campus Ministries, Annabel Taylor Hall, Cornell University, Ithaca NY 14853. National Newsletter (National Institute for Campus Ministries).

THE NICM JOURNAL FOR JEWS AND CHRISTIANS IN HIGHER EDUCATION. See Education (General) - Higher Education.

THE NIGERIAN CHRISTIAN. Vol. 1- 1967-. 0029-005X. Periodical. NR. English. mo. 12.00. Daystar Press, PO Box 1261, Literature Department, Ibadan Nigeria. **Ed** Rachel Alao. **LC** BR1463.N5. bk rev. adv acc. **Circ** 1,500. Contains Christian views on contemporary issues, news and reports from Christian churches in Nigeria and overseas, especially from member churches of the Christian Council of Nigeria.

NIRMALYA : SRI JAGANNATHA MISANA MUKHAPATRA. Vol. 1, No. 1 (Aug. 1982)-. Periodical. II. Oriya. qt. 3.00. Sri Jagannath Mission, Kacheri Road, Puri 752001 India. **LC** BL1225.J3.

NORSK TIDSSKRIFT FOR MISJON. V. 2-. 0029-2206. Periodical. NO. Norwegian. qt. $27.00. Universitetsforlaget, PO Box 2959-Toyen, Oslo 6 Norway. **Tel** 02-276 0 60. Contains mission and missionary questions. Norsk Misjonstidsskrift.

THE NORTH AMERICAN MORAVIAN. V. 1- Sept. 1970-. 0027-1012. Periodical. US. English. ir. $5.50 Domestic, $6.50 Canada and Foreign. The North American Moravian, PO Box 1245, Bethlehem PA 18016. **Tel** (215)867-0594. **Ed** Bernard E Michel. bk rev. adv acc. **Circ** 26,100. A church journal publishing articles of general church interest, and going to each home of members in the US and Canada as privilege of membership. Moravian, 0196-531X; Wachovian Moravian, 0196-0296.

NORTH CAROLINA CHRISTIAN ADVOCATE. 1855. 0029-2435. Periodical. US. English. wk. $10.00. North Carolina Christian Advocate, Box 508, Greensboro NC 27402. **Ed** C A Simonton Jr. adv acc. **Circ** 19,862. United Methodist church publication; with particular emphasis on North Carolina; also national and worldwide religion news.

THE NORTH INDIA CHURCHMAN. V. 1- Feb. 1971-. Periodical. US. English. mo. $4.00. North India Churchman, c/o Ann E Strickler, 1420 Santo Domingo, Duarte CA 91010. **Tel** (213)357-4247. United Church Review.

NOTRE PAIN QUOTIDIEN (SAINT-JEROME, QUEBEC). (NOTRE PAIN QUOTIDIEN). Sept./Oct. 1981-. 0712-9114. Periodical. CN. French. mo. $6.97. Novalis, CP 700, Hull Quebec J8Z 1X2 Canada. **Tel** (613)560-2727. **DD** 242.205.

NOUVEL ESSOR MARCELLE MALLET. See Biographies.

NOUVELLES ET DOCUMENTS - PROVINCE CANADIENNE DES PERES DE SAINTE-CROIX. (NOUVELLES ET DOCUMENTS - LA PROVINCE CANADIENNE DES PERES DE SAINTE-CROIX). Main/Corp Peres de Sainte-Croix. Province Canadienne. No 1- Oct. 1977-. 0707-7211. Periodical. CN. French. ir. Archives Provinciale des Peres de Sainte-Croix, 4994 Cote-des-Neiges, Montreal Quebec H3V 1A4 Canada. **DD** 271.79.

NOVA ET VETERA. 1- 1926-. 0029-5027. Periodical. SZ. French. qt. 45.-. Editions Universitaires, Perolles 42, 1700 Fribourg Suisse. **Tel** 037-24 68 12. **Ed** Editions Universitaires. **Ind/Abst** New Testam. Abstr. **LC** AP24. bk rev. adv acc. **Circ** 650. The journal presents an instrument of research and a reflection to the light of the gospel.

NOVAIA SOVETSKAIA INOSTRANNAIA LITERATURA PO OBSHCHESTVENNYM NAUKAM : PROBLEMY ATEIZMA I RELIGII. See Bibliographies.

NOVI SKRYZHALI. Periodical. CN. Ukrainian. qt. PO Box 11 Station F, Winnipeg Manitoba Canada R2L 2A5. **LC** BL980.C2.

NOVUM TESTAMENTUM. SUPPLEMENTS. 1- 1958-. 0050-2802. Monographic Series. NE. English. ir. 100.-. E J Brill, P O Box 9000, 2300 PA Leiden The Netherlands. **Tel** (071)312624. **Ed** D K Barrett and A F J Klyn. bk rev. adv acc. **Circ** 1,350. Covers the whole area of textual and literary criticism, the language, critical interpretation, theology, and historical and literary background of the Novum Testamentum and early Christian literature.

NUMEN (INTERNATIONAL ASSOCIATION FOR THE HISTORY OF RELIGIONS). (NUMEN). VFOAT International Review for the History of Religions. Vol. 1 (Jan. 1954)-. 0029-5973. Periodical. NE. English (French, German, and Italian). sa. $28.00. E J Brill, PO Box 9000, 2300 PA Leiden The Netherlands. **Tel** (071)312624. **Ind/Abst** MLA Int. Bibliogr. Books Artic. Mod. Lang. Lit., New Testam. Abstr., Relig. Index One, Period. **LC** BL1. bk rev. adv acc. **Circ** 850. (ctrl). Ensures a regular interchange of the results of investigations carried out in the field of history of religions.

OBSERVATEUR ORTHODOXE. (L'OBSERVATEUR ORTHODOXE). No. 1 (June 1983)-. 0824-653X. Periodical. CN. French. qt. L'Eglise Orthodoxe Russe Hors Frontieres, 8011 Av Champagneur, Montreal Quebec H3N 2K4 Canada. **DD** 281.905.

OCCASIONAL BULLETIN OF MISSIONARY RESEARCH CEASED. V. 1-4. 0364-2178. Periodical. US. English. qt. $6.00. 6315 Ocean Avenue, PO Box 2057, Ventnor NJ 08406. **Ind/Abst** Christ. Period. Index, Guide Soc. Sci.

Religion, Mythology, Rationalism

Relig. Period. Lit., Relig. Theol. Abstr., Relig. Index One, Period. LC BV2350. DD 266.02305. *Occasional Bulletin from the Missionary Research Library, 0026-606X.*

OCCASIONAL PAPERS ON RELIGION IN EASTERN EUROPE. VFOAT O.P.R.E.E. Vol. 1, No. 1-. 0731-5465. Monographic Series. US. English. ir. $35.00. Caree NCC/Dr Paul Mojzes Rosemont College, Rosemont PA 19010. Tel (215)527-02000. Ed Paul Mojzes. LC BR738.6. DD 274.708205. bk rev. Circ 600. Church-state relations and religious developments in socialist Eastern Europe (includes USSR). Includes both regional and country by country academic studies.

OCCASIONAL PAPERS - UNITED METHODIST BOARD OF HIGHER EDUCATION AND MINISTRY. See Education (General) - Higher Education.

OCCASIONAL RESEARCH PAPERS - DEPARTMENT OF RELIGIOUS STUDIES AND PHILOSOPHY, MAKERERE UNIVERSITY. Main/Corp Makerere University. Dept. of Religious Studies and Philosophy. V. 8- Dec. 1972-. SA. English. ir. 40.-. Makerere University, Department of Religious Studies & Philosophy, PO Box 16022, Kampala Uganda Africa. LC BL2400. DD 200.96. *Occasional Papers in African Traditional Religion and Philosophy.*

OECUMENISME (EDITION FRANCAISE). (OECUMENISME). VFOAT Ecumenism. No 1- Feb. 1966-. 0383-4301. Periodical. CN. French. qt. Centre d'Oecumenisme, 2065 Ouest rue Sherbrooke, Montreal Quebec H3H 1G6 Canada. *Oecumenisme en Marche, 0383-428X.*

OEKUMENISCHE STUDIEN. 1- 1957-. 0473-7997. Monographic Series. NE. German and English. ir. EJ Brill, PO Box 9000, 2300 PA Leiden The Netherlands.

OKUMENISCHE FORSCHUNGEN : 2, SOTERIOLOGISCHE ABTEILUNG. V. 1-7. Monographic Series. GW. German. ir. Verlag Herder Freiburg, Hermann-Herder Strasse 4, D-7800 Freiburg West Germany.

ON GUARD; PENTECOSTAL SERVICEMEN'S MAGAZINE. 0738-758X. Periodical. US. English. bm. $5.00. On Guard/TN/, 900 Walker Street, PO Box 3330, Cleveland TN 37311. Tel (615)478-1131. Ed Robert D Crick. adv acc. Circ 13,000. Christian pentecostal servicemens magazine.

ONE WORLD. No. 1- Nov. 1974-. 0303-125X. Periodical. SZ. English. mo. $11.00. Box 66, 1211 Geneva 20 Switzerland. Ind/Abst Relig. Index One, Period. LC BR1. DD 262.001. *This Month, Justice and Service.*

ONTARIO CHURCHMAN. (THE ONTARIO CHURCHMAN). 0030-2848. Periodical. CN. English. mo. $4.00. Ontario Churchman, 90 Johnson Street, Kingston Ontario Canada. Tel (613)544-4774. Ed Gordon Hendra. bk rev. adv acc. Circ 8,500. (ctrl) Practical theology, upcoming events, news, and a Anglican Church of Canada newspaper.

ONTARIO NEW BULLETIN - WCTU. (ONTARIO NEWS BULLETIN). VFOAT Ontario WCTU News Bulletin. VAT Ontario News Bulletin - Woman's Christian Temperance Union. 0229-4540. Periodical. CN. English. ir. Free. Ontario Woman's Christian Temperance Union News Bulletin, c/o J L Armstrong, RR 2, Spencerville Ontario K0E 1X0 Canada. DD 178.060713. (ctrl).

OPEN DOORS (ORANGE, CALIF.). (OPEN DOORS). VFOAT Open Doors with Brother Andrew. 8756-5234. Periodical. US. English. bm. Free. Open Doors News Service, PO Box 2020, Orange CA 92669. Tel (714)751-4080. Ed Dan Wooding. DD 272. Circ 700. We are and international news service covering news of persecuted Christians around the world.

OPEN WINDOWS. 0162-4296. Periodical. US. English. qt. $3.75. Materials Service Department, 127 9th Avenue North, Nashville TN 37203. Tel (615)251-2000. LC BV4800. DD 242.05.

ORATORY. (THE ORATORY). 0384-1871. Periodical. CN. English. bm. 5. Oratoire St Joseph Mont Royal, 3800 Chemin Reine-Marie, Montreal Quebec H3V 1H6 Canada. Tel (514)733-8211. Ed Theresa Baron. Circ 10,000. Official reviews of the Saint Joseph oratory into Canada.

ORBIS BIBLICUS ET ORIENTALIS. 1- 1973-. Monographic Series. GW. German. ir. Vandenhoeck & Ruprecht, Postfach 3753, Theaterstr 13, D 3400 Goettingen West Germany. Tel 0551/65061. Ed Othmar Keel and Bernard Tremel. adv acc.

ORDRE HOSPITALIER. (L'ORDRE HOSPITALIER : BULLETIN D'INFORMATION). Vol. 1, No. 1 (March 78)-. 0226-9996. Periodical. CN. French. ty. Free. Comite Central, Ordre Hospitalier de St-Jean de Dieu, 555 Ouest Boul Gouin, Montreal Quebec H3L 1K5 Canada. DD 271.49.

ORIENT. V. 1- May/June 1953-. 0472-0490. Periodical. CN. French. bm. 2.00. Orient, 2600 rue Desjardins, Montreal Quebec H1V 2H7 Canada. Tel (514)731-6231. Ed Julien Alain. Circ 14,500. Awakens and examines the reflection of the man and woman of today on the presence of Christians in the world.

ORIENTE-OCCIDENTE. VFOAT Oriente Occidente. Yearly V. 1, No. 1, (Jan./June 1980)-. 0325-8823. Periodical. Spanish. sa. LC BL7. DD 105.

ORITA. V. 1- June 1967-. 0030-5596. Periodical. NR. English. sa. 16.00. Department of Religious Studies, University of Ibadan, Ibadan Nigeria West Africa. Ed M Oduyoye. Ind/Abst Recent Publ. Artic. LC BL80.2. (cum index). bk rev. adv acc. Circ 500. Promotes the study and understanding of "the phenomenon and the social implications of religion in general and religion in Africa in particular.".

ORTHODOX OBSERVER. VFOAT Orthodoxos Parateretes. V. 37- (No. 619-). 0731-2547. Periodical. US. English (Greek). sm. $12.00 Domestic, $15.00 Canada, $20.00 Foreign. Greek Orthodox Archdio N & S AM, 8 East 79th Street, New York NY 10021. Tel (212)628-2590. bk rev. adv acc. Circ 125,000. We publish the activities of our more than 500 communities. *Orthodox Observer, 0731-2547.*

OUR FAMILY. Began with Jan. 1949 issue. 0030-6843. Periodical. CN. English. mo. $14.70. Our Family, PO Box 249, Battleford Saskatchewan S0M 0E0 Canada. Tel (306)937-2663. Ed Albert Lalonde. adv acc. Circ 16,650. (ctrl). Articles that challenge, inform, and inspire our readers and that help them apply the gospel to everyday life situations.

OUR KINGDOM MINISTRY FOR CANADA. (OUR KINGDOM MINISTRY. FOR CANADA). Vol. 25, No. 1 (Jan. 1982)-. 0823-2547. Periodical. CN. English. mo. Watch Tower Bible and Tract Society, Canadian Branch, PO Box 4100, Georgetown Ontario L7G 4Y4 Canada. DD 289.9205. *Our Kingdom Service, 0382-4837.*

OUR KINGDOM MINISTRY FOR GUYANA. (OUR KINGDOM MINISTRY. FOR GUYANA). Vol. 25, No. 1 (Jan. 1982)-. 0823-2563. Periodical. CN. English. mo. Watch Tower Bible and Tract Society/Canadian Branch, PO Box 4100, Georgetown Ontario L7G 4Y4 Canada. DD 289.9205.

OUR LADY OF THE CAPE CEASED. VFOAT Annals of Our Lady of the Cape. Began with Jan.? 1945 issue. 0700-6527. CN. English. qt. Oblate Fathers of Mary Immaculate, Capde la Madelaine, Quebec G8T 3V4 Canada. *Annals of Our Lady of the Cape, 0700-6519.*

OUR LADY'S DIGEST. 0030-6886. Periodical. US. English. qt. $4.00. Our Ladys Digest, Box 777, Twin Lakes WI 53181. Tel (414)877-3886. Ed Stanley Matuszewski. LC BT595. DD 232.931. bk rev. Circ 50,000. A national Catholic quarterly on Mary, Mother of Christ, from Catholic books and magazines besides articles by and eminent staff of associate and contributing editors.

OUR SUNDAY VISITOR. 0030-6967. Periodical. US. English. wk. Our Sunday Visitor, PO Box 920, Huntington IN 46750. Tel (800)348-2440. Ind/Abst Cathol. Period. Lit. Index.

OXBRIDGE DIRECTORY OF RELIGIOUS PERIODICALS. See Yearbooks, Almanacs, Directories.

PALESTRA DEL CLERO. Began in 1921. Periodical. IT. Italian. sm. Messaggerie Italiane SPA, Via Calabria 23-20090, Milano Italy. Ind/Abst New Testam. Abstr.

PAN Z WAMI. 0274-9009. US. Polish. bm. $4.50 Domestic, $6.00 Canada. Polish-American Liturgical Center, PO Box 5042, Orchard Lake MI 48033.

PAPERS OF THE CANADIAN SOCIETY OF CHURCH HISTORY. Main/Corp Canadian Society of Church History. 1975-. 0226-3564. CN. English. an. $7.74. Canadian Society of Church History, Dr CF Johnston, St Andrews College, 1121 College, Saskatoon Saskatchewan S7N 0W3 Canada. Tel (709)737-8621. DD 277.1. *Papers, 0226-3564.*

PAPYROLOGISCHE TEXTE UND ABHANDLUNGEN. Vol. 1- 1968-. Monographic Series. GW. German. ir. Dr Rudolf Habelt GMBH, Am Buchengang 1, 5300 Bonn 1 West Germany. Ed D Hagedorn, R Kassel, L Koenen and R Merkelbach.

PAPYRUS BODMER. V. 1-. Monographic Series. SZ. French (Greek, Coptic). ir. Fondation Marine Bodmer, 19-21 Route du Guignard 1223 Cologny, Geneve Switzerland. Tel 022/36.23.70. Grecian and Coptic texts (Papyri) of the early Christianity. Also Meander's comedies (3).

PARABOLA. V. 1- Winter 1976-. 0362-1596. Periodical. US. English. qt. $18.00. University New South Wales, c/o Mr James, School of Mathematics, PO Box 1, Kensington New South Wales 2033 Australia. Tel (212)924-0004. Ed Lorraine Kisley. Ind/Abst Abstr. Engl. Stud., MLA Int. Bibliogr. Books Artic. Mod. Lang. Lit., Book Rev. Index, Relig. Index One, Period. LC BL1. DD 291.1305. bk rev. adv acc. Circ 17,000. Explores the universal themes found in myth, legend, ritual and religion of the world's traditions, relating them to our modern search for meaning.

PARACLETE (SPRINGFIELD, MO.). (PARACLETE). Began in 1967. 0190-4639. Periodical. US. English. qt. $4.50. Gospel Publishing House 1445, Boonville Avenue, Springfield MO 65802. Tel (417)862-2781. Ed H W Steinberg. bk rev. Circ 6,500. Journal concerning the person and work of the Holy Spirit.

PARISH COMMUNICATION. Vol. 1, No. 1 (Mar. 1981)-. 0279-7828. Periodical. US. English. mo. $19.50. Growth Associates, PO Box 215, Weston VT 05161-0215. Tel (802)824-3440. Ed Patty R Coleman. bk rev. Circ 1,000. Weekly aids for church bulletins, art, essays, quotes and information on communication for church leaders.

PARISH MINISTRY. 0276-0479. Periodical. US. English. bm. Paulist Press, 545 Island Road, Ramsey NJ 07446. *Parish, 0190-664X.*

THE PARISH PAPER. 1971. Periodical. US. English. mo. $5.00. Yokefellow Institute, 530 North Brainard Street, Naperville IL 60540. Tel (312)355-0817. Ed Lyle E Lehaller.

PAROPAKARI. II. Hindi. ir. 10.00. Surendra Prakassa Sarma, Srikarana Sarada Mantri Paropakarini Sabha, Ajamera India. LC BL1100.

PARTNERSHIP. (PARTNERSHIP : THE MAGAZINE FOR WIVES IN MINISTRY). V. 1, No. 1 (Jan./Feb. 1984)-. 0747-9190. Periodical. US. English. bm. $17.70 Domestic, $21.75 Foreign. Partnership Subscription Services, PO Box 1966, Marion OH 43305. DD 253.

PASTORALE SCOLAIRE. (LA PASTORALE SCOLAIRE). V. 15, No. 2- Nov./Dec. 1979-. 0227-1095. Periodical. CN. French. ir. Conference de la Pastorale Scolaire, 1073 Ouest Boulevard Saint-Cyrille, Quebec Quebec G1S 4R5 Canada. DD 259.23060714. *Bulietin de Liaison, 0227-1087.*

PATHWAY TO GOD. Periodical. II. English. ir. 10.00. Academy of Comparative Philosophy & Religion, Belgaum India. LC BL1. DD 291.05.

THE PATRISTIC AND BYZANTINE REVIEW. VFOAT PBR. Vol. 1, No. 1-. 0737-738X. Periodical. US. English. ty. $35.00. The Patristic and Byzantine Revies, Rural Route 1 Box 353-A/Minuet Lane, Kingston NY 12401. Ind/Abst Relig. Index One, Period. DD 270.

PATRISTISCHE TEXTE UND STUDIEN. 1- 1964-. 0553-4003. Monographic Series. US. German. ir. Walter de Gruyter Inc, 200 Saw Mill River Road, Hawthorne NY 10532. Tel (914)747-0110.

PELOUBET'S SELECT NOTES ON THE INTERNATIONAL BIBLE LESSONS FOR CHRISTIAN LIVING. UNIFORM SERIES. VFOAT Uniform Series. 1875. US. English. an. $7.95. Baker Book House, PO Box 6287, Grand Rapids MI 49506. Tel (800)253-7283. Ed Ralph Earle. A complete Sunday School teacher's aid for all denominations using the International Sunday School Lessons. *Select Notes on the International Sunday School Lessons. Improved Uniform Series.*

THE PENTECOSTAL MINISTER. Vol. 1, No. 1 (Spring 1981)-. 0279-7038. Periodical. US. English. qt. $12.00. Pathway Press, 1080 Montgomery Avenue, Cleveland TN 37311. Tel (615)472-3361.

PENTECOSTAL TESTIMONY. (THE PENTECOSTAL TESTIMONY). 1928. 0031-4927. CN. English. mo. $9.28. The Pentecostal Testimony, 10

Religion, Mythology, Rationalism

Overlea Boulevard, Toronto Ontario M4H 1A5 Canada. **Tel** (416)425-1010. **Ed** Robert J Skinner. **Ind/Abst** Guide Soc. Sci. Relig. Period. Lit. bk rev. adv acc. **Circ** 26,000. Denominational, inspirational articles, news of our fellowship locally and worldwide, some theological articles, letters to the editor, book reviews, some missions and social concerns articles.

PERIODICA DE RE MORALI, CANONICA, LITURGICA. V. 16- April/June 1927-. 0031-529X. Periodical. IT. Latin. qt. $40.00. Pontificio Instituto Biblico, Piazza Della Pilotts 35, 00187 Rome Italy. bk rev. *Periodica de re Canonica et Morali Utilia Praesertim Religiosis et Missionariis.*

PERKINS JOURNAL. Vol. 26, No. 1 (Fall, 1972)-. 0730-2142. Periodical. US. English. qt. Perkins School of Theology, Southern Methodist University, Dallas TX 75275. **Ind/Abst** Old Testam. Abstr., New Testam. Abstr., Relig. Index One, Period. **LC** BR1. **DD** 23007605. *Perkins School of Theology Journal.*

PERSONAL CHRISTIANITY. 0745-1288. Periodical. US. English. mo. Personal Christianity, 14952 East Pacific Avenue, Baldwin Park CA 91706.

PERSONALSTAND DER WELT- UND ORDENSGEISTLICHKEIT DER ERZDIOZESE WIEN. **Main/Corp** Vienna (Archdiocese). Erzbischofliches Ordinariat. AU. German. ir. Erzbischofliches Ordinariat, 1010 Wien Wollzeile 2, Wien Austria. **LC** BX1521.V5.

PERSPECTIVES IN RELIGIOUS STUDIES. V. 1- Spring 1974-. 0093-531X. Periodical. US. English. sa. $12.00 Domestic, $17.00 Foreign. Mercer University, c/o Watson Mills, Macon GA 31207. **Tel** (912)744-2880. **Ed** Watson E Mills. **Ind/Abst** Old Testam. Abstr., New Testam. Abstr., Relig. Index One, Period. bk rev. adv acc. **Circ** 650. Promotes communication and cooperation providing opportunities for consideration of literature, movements, and ideas developing in the field of religion. Also, provides aid to the sharing of curricular concepts, teaching methods, and new approaches to study.

PHILADELPHIA YEARLY MEETING NEWS. VFOAT Yearly Meeting News. Vol. 1, No. 1 (March 1, 1963)-. 0429-7326. Periodical. US. English. bm. Religious Society of Friends, 1515 Cherry Street, Philadelphia PA 19102. Also available on microfilm from Free Library of Philadelphia. *Messenger.*

PHILIPPINIANA SACRA. V. 1- Jan./Apr. 1966-. 0554-0577. Periodical. PH. English (Spanish, Latin). ty. 4500 Domestic, $18.00 US. University of Santo Tomas, Publications Department, Manila Philippines. **Tel** 731-05-58. **Ed** Lucio Gutierrez. **LC** BR1. bk rev. adv acc. **Circ** 600. (ctrl). Devoted to serious studies in theology, philosophy and history with special emphasis on Philipino and Asian issues.

PHILOSOPHY OF RELIGION AND THEOLOGY. PROCEEDINGS. (PHILOSOPHY OF RELIGION AND THEOLOGY : PROCEEDINGS). **Main/Corp** American Academy of Religion. Philosophy of Religion and Theology Section. 0149-4376. US. English. University of Waterloo, Waterloo Ontario N2L 3C5 Canada. **LC** BL51. **DD** 200.1.

PIONEER. V. 1- Jan. 1951-. 0480-5321. Periodical. CN. English (Dutch). mo. Reformed Churches in Canada, 201 Paradise Road North, Hamilton Ontario L8S 3T3 Canada. **Tel** (416)527-0998.

THE PLAIN TRUTH. Began with Feb. 1934 issue. 0032-0420. Periodical. US. English. Voluntary contributions. The Plain Truth, 300 West Green, Pasadena CA 91123. **Ed** H W Armstrong. **DD** 205.

EN PLEIN MONDE. VFOAT Cette Nouvelle Ecole du Quebec: le Peuple N'en Veut Pas, Pourquoi?. First issue in 1967?. 0319-4078. Periodical. CN. French. qt. $3. En Plein Monde, c/o Des Auxiliaries Franciscaines 1215 Boul Masson, Les Saules Quebec G1P 1J4 Canada. **DD** 205.

POINT (GOROKA, PAPUA NEW GUINEA). (POINT). Began in 1972. Periodical. English. sa. 13.00. Melanesian Institute Books, PO Box 571, Goroka E H P, Papua New Guinea. **Tel** 721777. **Ed** Paul Roche. **Circ** 750. Focuses on a relevant and topical theme each time, specifically on Melanesia: religious movements, cultures, religions, christian ministry, ethics and development, history, folklore, etc.

POLSKA BILBIOGRAFIA NAUK KOSCIELNYCH. See Bibliographies.

PORTALS OF PRAYER. 0032-4884. Periodical. US. English. mo. $3.00. Concordia Publishing Company, 3558 South Jefferson Street, St Louis MO 63118. **Tel** (314)664-7000.

POSTAL CHRISTIAN WITNESS CEASED. No. 1-67. 0700-7787. CN. English. qt. Christian Transportation, 512 Yonge Street, Toronto Ontario M4Y 1X9 Canada.

POUR LA VERITE : JOURNAL DE L'UNION DES EGLISES EVANGELIQUES LIBRES DE FRANCE. Periodical. FR. French. mo. $5.00. Magnificat Assoc/Domaine de Marie Coredentrice, Clemery Paris 54610 Nomeny France.

PRABUDDHA BHARATA; OR AWAKENED INDIA. VFOAT Awakened India. V. 1- July 1896-. 0032-6178. Periodical. II. English. mo. $10.00. Prabuddha Bharata, 5 Dehi Entally Road, Calcutta 700 014 India. **Ed** Swami Vivedananda. **LC** BL1100. **DD** 294.05.

PRAVOSLAVNAIA RUS'. VFOAT Orthodox Russia. 0032-7018. Periodical. US. Russian. sm. $24.00. Holy Trinity Monastery, PO Box 36, Jordanville NY 13361.

THE PREACHER'S PERIODICAL. 0744-8562. Periodical. US. English. mo. $25.00. Preachers Periodical, 109 Indian Trail, Searcy AR 72143.

THE PRESENT TRUTH AND HERALD OF CHRIST'S EPIPHANY. 0032-7700. Periodical. US. English. bm. $2.00. Laymens Home Missionary Movement, Chester Springs PA 19425. **Tel** (215)827-7665.

THE PRESENT TRUTH OF THE APOKALYPSIS. 0745-192X. US. English. bm. Laodicean Home Missionary Movement, 18386 Otsego Drive, Fort Myers FL 33908.

PRIESTHOOD AND BROTHERHOOD. See Yearbooks, Almanacs, Directories.

PRIONS EN EGLISE. V. 29, No 5A- 1 Jan. 1965-. 0383-8277. CN. French. wk. Novalis, C P 498 Succursale A, Ottawa Ontario K1N 8Y5 Canada. *Prie Avec l'Eglise*, 0383-8269.

PRITEL LIDU : CASOPIS SLEZSKE CIRKVE EVANGELICKE A.V. EWANGELICKIEGO A.W. VFOAT Przyjaciel Ludu : Pismo Slaskiego Kosciola Ewangelickiego A.W. Periodical. CS. Czech (Polish). ir. $19.80. Artia, PO Box 790, Praha 1 Czechoslovakia. **Tel** 566 56. bk rev. adv acc. **Circ** 2,250. (ctrl). Theological articles, information of the church life.

PROCEEDINGS OF THE ANNUAL CONVENTION - CHRISTIAN ASSOCIATION FOR PSYCHOLOGICAL STUDIES. (PROCEEDINGS OF THE ANNUAL CONVENTION). **Main/Corp** Christian Association for Psychological Studies. 0092-072X. US. English. an. $3.00. 6850 Division Avenue South, Grand Rapids MI 49508. **LC** BL53.A1. **DD** 201.1. **CODEN** PACSDU.

PROCEEDINGS OF THE TRIENNIAL ASSEMBLY OF THE CANADIAN COUNCIL OF CHURCHES. (THE PROCEEDINGS OF THE . . . TRIENNIAL ASSEMBLY (. . . MEETING) OF THE CANADIAN COUNCIL OF CHURCHES). **Main/Corp** Canadian Council of Churches., Assembly. 4th Triennial Assembly (1979) – 20th meeting (1979)-. 0227-4337. Periodical. CN. English. te. Canadian Council of Churches, 40 St Clair Avenue East, Toronto Ontario M4T 1M9 Canada. **DD** 277.1. *Record of Proceedings*, 0701-4309.

PROGRESSIVE WORLD. Began with issue for Mar. 1947. Periodical. US. English. mo. **LC** BL2700.

PROVIDENCE DES PAUVRES. MERE GAMELIN. (LA PROVIDENCE DES PAUVRES, MERE GAMELIN). V. 1- Feb. 1978-. 0705-0917. Periodical. CN. French. sa. Free. Centre Emilie-Gemelin, 5655 rue de Salaberry, Montreal Quebec H4J 2J5 Canada. **DD** 255.979.

PROVIDENCE OF THE POOR. MOTHER EMILIE GAMELIN. (PROVIDENCE OF THE POOR, MOTHER EMILIE GAMELIN). V. 1- Feb. 1978-. 0705-0925. Periodical. CN. English. sa. Free. Emilie Gemelin Centre, 5655 de Salaberry Street, Montreal Quebec H4J 2J5 Canada. **DD** 255.979.

PRS JOURNAL. See Philosophy.

PULPIT HELPS. Began publication in 1975. 0193-3914. Periodical. US. English. mo. $58.00. Pulpit Helps, 6815 Shallowford Road, Chattanooga TN 37421. **Tel** (800)251-7206. **Ed** Spiros Zodhiates. bk rev. adv acc. **Circ** 225,000. (ctrl). Ministerial helps for ministers. Family helps, education, and administration.

PULPIT RESOURCE. 0195-1548. Periodical. US. English. qt. $24.00. Pulpit Resource Inc, 121 Maono Place, Honolulu HI 96821. **Tel** (808)373-4410. **Ed** Glendon E Harris. **DD** 251. **Circ** 9,000. Homiletical aid designed to provide sermon approaches and illustrative material.

PULSE (WHEATON, ILL. : 1984). (PULSE). Began with V. 19 in Jan. 1984. 0747-8631. Periodical. US. English. sm. $25.00. Evangelical Missions Information Service, 25 W560 Geneva Road, Box 794, Wheaton IL 60189. **Tel** (312)653-2158. **Ed** James Reapsome. **DD** 266. **Circ** 3,000. Reports of world news in the context of world missions. *Europe Pulse*, 0739-0521; *Latin American Pulse*, 0739-0513; *Asia Pulse*, 0739-0548; *Africa Pulse*, 0739-0556; *Chinese World Pulse*, 0739-053X; *Muslim World Pulse*, 0739-0505.

Q.T.C. TODAY. (Q.T.C. TODAY : NEWS OF THE QUEEN'S THEOLOGICAL COLLEGE). VAT Queen's Theological College Today. No. 1-. 0828-5780. Periodical. CN. English. ir. Free. Queen's Theological College, Kingston Ontario K7L 3N6 Canada. **DD** 207.71372. (ctrl).

QUAKER LIFE. Sept. 1- 1960-. 0033-5061. Periodical. US. English. mo. $12.00. Friends of United Press, 101 Quaker Hill Drive, Richmond IN 47374. **Tel** (317)962-7573. **Ed** Jack Kirk. **LC** BX7601. **DD** 289.605. bk rev. adv acc. **Circ** 8,700. Denominational magazine for Friends United Meeting (Society of Friends/Quaker) with inspirational articles and news for a largely Quaker readership. *American Friend*, 0364-5878 *Quaker Action*.

DER QUAKER : MONATSHEFTE DER DEUTSCHEN FREUNDE. Began in 1932. Periodical. German. ir. Relig Ges Freunde/Gertrud Benz, Rhonbergstr 6, 816 Miesbach Pars West Germany. *Monatshefte der Deutschen Freunde.*

QUAKER MONTHLY. V. 43, No. 4- Apr. 1964-. 0033-507X. Periodical. UK. English. mo. Quaker Home Service, Friends House, Euston Road, London NW1 2BJ England. **Tel** 01-387 3601. **Ed** Meg Chignell. bk rev. **Circ** 3,500. Articles, reviews, photos and poetry by members of the Religious Society of Friends on all aspects of Quaker life and service. *Wayfarer*, 0144-915X.

THE QUARTERLY JOURNAL OF THE MYTHIC SOCIETY (BANGALORE). **Main/Corp** Mythic Society, Bangalore, India. V. 1- Oct. 1909-. Periodical. II. English. an. $10.00. Hindustan Book Agency, 17 UB Jawahar Nagar, Delhi 7 India. **LC** DS401.

A QUIET REVOLUTION : MINISTRY OF VOICE OF CALVARY MINISTRIES. Periodical. US. English. Voice of Calvary Ministries, PO Box 10562, Jackson MS 39209. **Tel** (601)353-1635.

R M MARIANNHILL. (RM MARIANNHILL). VFOAT Mariannhill. VAT Revue Missionnaire Mariannhill (1981), Mariannhill (Sherbrooke. 1981). Vol. 33, No. 1 1981-. 0712-1695. Periodical. CN. French. $3.00. Revue Mariannhill, Mont-Sainte-Anne, Sherbrooke Quebec J1H 5G9 Canada. **DD** 266.205. *Revue Missionnaire Mariannhill*, 0705-1514.

RADICAL RELIGION CEASED. V. 1-5. 0360-8212. Periodical. US. English. qt. $13.00. Community for Religious Research and Education, PO Box 9164, Berkeley CA 94709.

RADIUS (STUTTGART, GERMANY). (RADIUS). Began publication with Dec. 1955 issue. 0033-8532. Periodical. German. qt. Radius Verlag, Kniebisstrasse 29, D7000 Stuttgart 1 West Germany. **Tel** 711-28391. bk rev. adv acc. **Circ** 9,000. Monographic issues on literature and religion.

THE RAINBOW HERALD. Vol. 1, No. 1 (Oct.-Dec. 1983)-. 0748-7312. Periodical. US. English. qt. $7.00. Rainbow's End Company, PO Box 173, Baden PA 15005.

RAISON. (LA RAISON : BULLETIN RATIONALISTE DE LIBRE CRITIQUE). V. 1, No. 1 (March/April 1979)-. 0228-7870. Periodical. CN. French. bm. Free. La Raison, CP 628, Succursale Desjardins, Montreal Quebec H5B 1B7 Canada. **DD** 211.405.

RECHERCHES DE SCIENCE RELIGIEUSE. Vol. 1- 0034-1258. Periodical. FR. French. qt. 230.00 Foreign. Recherches de Science, 15 Rue Monsieur, Paris 7E France. **Tel** 473 474 77. **Ed** J Moingt. adv acc. Covers religious

Religion, Mythology, Rationalism

sciences, theology, philosophy of religion, and world religions.

RECORDS. Main/Corp Scottish Church History Society. V. 1- 1923-24—. UK. English. an. (cum index).

REFLECTION. V. 63- 1965/66-. 0362-0611. Periodical. US. English. ty. Yale Divinity School, 409 Prospect Street, New Haven CT 06510. Tel (203)436-2498. Ed Harry B Adams. bk rev. Circ 7,000. Articles of interest to clergy and other religious professionals. Deals with a broad range of topics. *Yale Divinity News, 0364-8613.*

REGULAE BENEDICTI STUDIA. V. 1 (1972)-. GW. French (German, Italian, and English). ir. Verlag Gerstenberg, Rathausstrasse 18, Postfach 390, D-3200 Hildesheim West Germany.

RELIGII MIRA. 1982-. Periodical. UR. Russian. an. 1.60. GlaV Red Vostochnoi, Lit-Ry Izd-Va Nauka Moskva K-31, UL Zhdanova 12/1 USSR.

RELIGION. V. 1- Spring 1971-. 0048-721X. Periodical. UK. English. qt. $85.00. Academic Press, 4805 Sand Lake Road, Orlando FL 32819. Tel (305)345-4100. Ind/Abst Old Testam. Abstr., New Testam. Abstr., Relig. Index One, Period. LC BL1. DD 200.5.

RELIGION AND LIFE LETTERS. 0730-2363. Periodical. US. English. bw. $20.00 Domestic, $25.00 Foreign. Spiritual Studies Center, PO Box 1104, Rockville MD 20850.

RELIGION & LITERATURE. VFOAT Religion and Literature. Vol. 16 (Winter 1984)-. 0029-4500. Periodical. US. English. ty. $10.00. University of Notre Dame, Department of English, Notre Dame IN 46556. Tel (219)239-5725. Ed Thomas Werge and James Dougherty. Ind/Abst Abstr. Engl. Stud., Am. Humanit. Index, Cathol. Period. Lit. Index, Eight. Century Curr. Bibliogr., Lit. Crit. Regist., Relig. Theol. Abstr., MLA Int. Bibliogr. Books Artic. Mod. Lang. Lit. bk rev adv acc. Circ 500. (ctrl). A forum for an on-going discussion of the relations between the religious impulses and the literary forms of any era, place or language. *Notre Dame English Journal, 0029-4500.*

RELIGION AND REASON. 1- 1971-. 0080-0848. Monographic Series. English and French. ir. Walter de Gruyter Inc, 200 Sawmill River Road, Hawthorne NY 10532.

RELIGION AND SOCIETY. Began publication in 1954. 0034-3951. Periodical. English. ir. $15.00. Religion and Society, PO Box 4600, 17 Miller Road, 560 046 Bangalore India. Tel 575981. Ed Saral K Chatterji. Ind/Abst Guide Indian Period. Lit. LC BL1. bk rev. Circ 1,100. Christian journal of research and study of social and religious issues especially from perspective of oppressed sections of society to promote social justice.

RELIGION AND THE ARTS. 1-. 0145-2738. Monographic Series. US. English. ir. Scholars Press, PO Box 1608, Decatur GA 30031. Tel (404)329-6950.

RELIGION (BOCA RATON, FLA.). (RELIGION). Series/Titl Social Issues Resources Series. V. 1, Article 1-. 0273-2556. US. English. Social Issues Resources Series Inc, PO Box 2507, Boca Raton FL 33432. Ed Eleanor C Goldstein. LC BL1. DD 291.05.

RELIGION IN COMMUNIST LANDS. 0307-5974. Periodical. UK. English. qt. 16.00 Domestic, 18.00 North Africa and Middle East, 19.00 US, 20.00 Australia. Centre for the Study of Religion and Communism, 34 Lubbock Road, BR7 5JJ Chiolehurst England. Tel (0689)50116. Ed Jane Ellis. Ind/Abst Relig. Index One, Period. LC BR738.6. DD 261.72091717. bk rev. adv acc. Circ 2,000. (ctrl). Academic articles and background information on the situation of all religious groups in countries with communist governments (emphasis on Soviet bloc).

RELIGION IN LIFE CEASED. V. 1-49. 0034-3986. Periodical. US. English. qt. Abingdon Press, PO Box 801, Nashville TN 37202. Ed John Baillie, L H Bugbee, and C K Gilbert. Ind/Abst Old Testam. Abstr., Humanit. Index. LC BR1. DD 205. Vols. 1-24 available on microfilm from ATLA Board of Microtext, New Haven, CT.

RELIGION IN SOUTHERN AFRICA. Vol. 1, No. 1 (Jan. 1980)-. Periodical. SA. English. sa. 6,00. Religion in Southern Africa, University of Durban-Westville, Department of Science and Literature, Private Bag X54001, Durban 4000 South Africa. Ind/Abst Recent Publ. Artic., Relig. Index One, Period. LC BL2463. DD 200.5.

RELIGION IN THE PEOPLE'S REPUBLIC OF CHINA. Began with Nov. 1979 issue. Periodical. UK. Chinese (English). ty. China Study Project, 6 Ashley Gardens, Rusthall Tunbridge Wells Kent TN4 8TY England. LC BL1790. DD 291.0951.

RELIGION INDEX ONE. PERIODICALS. See Indexes/Abstracts.

RELIGION INDEX TWO. MULTI-AUTHOR WORKS. See Indexes/Abstracts.

RELIGION OCH KULTUR CEASED. Began with Vol. 1, 1930. Ceased with Vol. 51. 0034-4001. Periodical. SW. Swedish. ir. 25. 752 21 Uppsala, Uppsala Sweden. LC BR6.

RELIGION TEACHER'S JOURNAL. 1966. 0034-401X. Periodical. US. English. ir. $14.00. Twenty Third Publications, Box 180, Mystic CT 06388. Tel (203)536-2611. Ed Gwen Costello. Ind/Abst Cathol. Period. Lit. Index, Media Rev. Dig. bk rev. adv acc. Circ 40,000. (ctrl). Practical and motivational articles for religion teachers.

DIE RELIGIONEN DER MENSCHHEIT. V. 1- 1961-. 0486-3585. Monographic Series. GW. German. ir. Kohlhammer Verlag, ABT Veroef Fentl Stat Bundesamt, Postfach 421120, D65 Mainz 42 West Germany. Tel 06131/59094/95.

RELIGIONI E CIVILTA. New Series, V. 1-. Monographic Series. IT. Italian. ir. Ed Dedalo, Cas Postale 362, Bari 70100 Italy. LC BL5. *Studi e Materiali di Storia Delle Religioni.*

RELIGIONSGESCHICHTLICHE VERSUCHE UND VORARBEITEN. V. 1- 1903-. Monographic Series. GW. German. ir. Walter de Gruyter, Genthiner Str 13, D-1 Berlin 30 West Germany. Tel 030/26005-0.

RELIGIONSVIDENSKABELIGT TIDSSKRIFT. Vol. 1 (Oct. 1982)-. 0108-1993. Periodical. Danish. ir. 60. Religionsvidenskabeligt Tidsskrift Institut For Kristendomskundskab Hovedbygningen, NDR Ringgade 1, 8000 Aarhus C Denmark. Tel (06)136711. Ed Armin W Geertz. bk rev. adv acc. Circ 350. (ctrl). History of religions, science of religions, theology, philosophy of religion, sociology of religion, psychology of religion, anthropology, structuralism and semiotics.

RELIGIOUS AND THEOLOGICAL ABSTRACTS. See Indexes/Abstracts.

RELIGIOUS BOOK REVIEW. Began in 1973. 0279-9588. Periodical. US. English. qt. $15.00. Michael Glazier Inc, 1210 King Street, Wilmington DE 19801. LC Z286.R4. DD 200. *Religious Book Guide, 0008-7939.*

RELIGIOUS BOOKS AND SERIALS IN PRINT. See Bibliographies.

RELIGIOUS FREEDOM REPORTER. See Law.

THE RELIGIOUS HERALD. Vol. 1, No.1 (Jan. 11, 1828)-. 0738-7318. Periodical. US. English. wk. The Religious Herald, PO Box 8377, Richmond VA 23226-0377. *Evangelical Inquirer.*

RELIGIOUS LIFE. 0279-0459. Periodical. US. English. mo. $5.00. Institute on Religious Life, 4200 North Austin Avenue, Chicago IL 60634. Tel (312)545-1946. Ed James Downey. bk rev. Circ 3,700. Newsletter of news, talks of the Holy Father, book reviews, commentaries and reflections by noted writers on the church's teaching and on spiritual life.

RELIGIOUS PERIODICALS INDEX. See Indexes/Abstracts.

RELIGIOUS PERSPECTIVES. 1-. 0486-3658. Monographic Series. US. English. ir. Lippincott/Harper, 2350 Virginia Avenue, Hagerstown MD 21740. Tel (800)242-7737.

RELIGIOUS READING. 1- 1975-. 0147-8109. US. English. an. McGrath Publishing Company, PO Box 9001, Wilmington NC 28402. LC Z7751. DD 016.2.

RELIGIOUS STUDIES. V. 1- Oct. 1965-. 0034-4125. Periodical. UK. English. qt. $105.00. Cambridge University Press, 510 N Avenue, New Rochelle NY 10801. Tel (914)235-0300. Ed Stewart Sutherland. Ind/Abst New Testam. Abstr., Philos. Index, Book Rev. Index, Ref. Source, Humanit. Index, Relig. Index One, Period. LC BL1. DD 200.5. bk rev. Articles reflect the sharpening and intensification of the study of religion in recent years using the results of research in many fields including philosophy, psychology, history of religions and sociology.

RELIGIOUS STUDIES REVIEW. Began with Sept. 1975 issue. 0319-485X. Periodical. US. English. qt $30.00 Domestic, $38.00 Foreign. Mercer University, Council on the Study of Religion, Macon GA 31207. Tel (912)744-2880. Ed Watson E Mills. Ind/Abst Old Testam. Abstr., New Testam. Abstr., Book Rev. Index, Relig. Index One, Period. LC BL1. DD 200.5. bk rev. adv acc. Circ 2,672. Review of publications in the field of religion and related disciplines.

RELIGIOUS TRADITIONS. V. 1- Apr. 1978-. 0156-1650. Periodical. AT. English. sa. $11.07. University of Sydney, c/o Arvind Sharma/Religious Studies, Sydney New South Wales 2006 Australia. Ind/Abst Relig. Index One, Period. *Journal of Studies in Mysticism.*

REPORT - CHRISTIAN INSTITUTE FOR THE STUDY OF RELIGION AND SOCIETY. Main/Corp Christian Institute for the Study of Religion and Society, Bangalore, India. 1958-. 0578-0039. US. English. mo. $29.64. Rockford Institute, 934 North Main Street, Rockford IL 61103. Tel (815)964-5811. LC BR1150. DD 261.10625487.

REPORT FROM THE CAPITAL. 0364-6661. Periodical. US. English. mo. $5.00. Report from the Capital, 200 Maryland Avenue Northeast, Washington DC 20002. Tel (202)544-4226. Ed Victor Tupitza. Index in first issue of next volume - loose - separately paged. bk rev. Circ 5,000. Religious liberty and separation of church and state: in-depth coverage of court and legislative events in this field, especially at federal level.

REPORT OF FAITH. Feb. 1982-. 0714-7120. Periodical. CN. English. ir. Bill Prankard Evangelistic Association, Box 5555 Station F, Ottawa Ontario K2C 3M1 Canada. DD 2691.20971. *Bill & Gwen Prankard's Report (1981), 0714-7112.*

REPORT - SINGAPORE HINDUS RELIGIOUS AND CULTURAL SEMINAR. Main/Conf Singapore Hindus Religious and Cultural Seminar. 1969/71-. English or Tamil. ir. LC BL1157.S55. DD 294.505.

REPORTS TO THE GENERAL ASSEMBLY OF THE UNITED FREE CHURCH OF SCOTLAND. Main/Corp United Free Church of Scotland. UK. English. an. United Free Church of Scotland, 11 Newton Place, Glasgow C3 Scotland. Tel (041)332-3435. LC BX9089. DD 262.052411. Circ 250. (ctrl). Religion report of work of assembly committees throughout the preceding year financial state of the denomination.

RES NEWS EXCHANGE. (R.E.S. NEWS EXCHANGE). Main/Corp Reformed Ecumenical Synod. VAT Reformed Ecumenical Synod News Exchange. V. 1- 1964-. 0033-6904. Periodical. US. English. mo $5.00 Domestic, $6.00 Canada, $7.00 Foreign. Reformed Ecumenical Synod, 1677 Gentian Drive SE, Grand Rapids MI 49508. Tel (616)455-1126. Ed Paul G Schrotenboer. bk rev. Circ 1,150. (ctrl). A digest of religious news articles obtained from sources throughout the world with one page devoted to a book review.

RESEARCH IN MINISTRY. 1981-. US. English. an. $40.00. Religion Index-Alta, 5600 South Woodlawn, Chicago IL 60637. Tel (312)947-9417. Ed Thomas J Davis. Circ 100. (ctrl). Indexes doctor of ministry projects and thesis from ATS accredited seminaries and divinity schools. Author abstracts are included.

RESEAU. 1- Sept. 1975-. 0704-0539. Periodical. CN. French. ir. Resau, 5353 Av Notre-Dame de Grace, Montreal Quebec H4A 7L2 Canada. DD 271.2071.

RESTORATION MAGAZINE. VAT Restoration (Regina). Vol. 1, No. 1 (Winter 82)-. 0711-8171. Periodical. CN. English. qt. Restoration Magazine, c/o Maranatha Christian Centre, 1077 Angus Street, Regina Saskatchewan S4T 1Y4 Canada. Tel (306)569-1936. Ed Dean Smith. DD 205. Circ 10,000. (ctrl). This is a Bible-based magazine which is intended to strengthen the local church and to promote the doctrine of the restoration of the church.

RESURRECTION BULLETIN. (THE RESURRECTION BULLETIN). 0714-7686. Periodical. CN. English. ty. Resurrection Bulletin, c/o Provincial Office, Resurrection College, Waterloo Ontario N2L 3G7 Canada. DD 255.79.

RETURN TO THE SOURCE. Vol. 1, No. 1 (Mar. 1982)-. 0743-1244. Periodical. US. English. Return to the Source, 3249 West Roosevelt Road, Chicago IL 60624. **Tel** (312)762-3024. **Ed** Shemuel B Israel. bk rev. adv acc. **Circ** 1,500. Analytic essays presenting historic and esoteric material which serves to provide a link between man, both ancient and modern, and his source.

REVIEW OF BOOKS AND RELIGION (FORWARD MOVEMENT PUBLICATIONS). (THE REVIEW OF BOOKS AND RELIGION). Vol. 10, No. 1 (Mid-Sept. 1981)-. 0732-5800. Periodical. US. English. bm. Duke University, Divinity School, c/o C Walters-Bugbee, Durham NC 27706. **Tel** (919)684-3569. **Ind/Abst** Relig. Index One, Period. **LC** BL1. **DD** 200.5. *New Review of Books and Religion, 0146-0609.*

REVIEW OF RELIGIONS. Began publication in 1902. 0034-6721. Periodical. English. mo. Ahmadiyya Movement Islam Inc, 2141 Leroy Place NW, Washington DC 20008. **LC** BP1. Available on microfilm from University Microfilms.

REVIEW OF RELIGIOUS RESEARCH. V. 1- Summer 1959-. 0034-673X. Periodical. US. English. qt. $30.00. Religious Research Association Inc, Box U-68-A, University of Connecticut, Storrs CT 06268. **Tel** (203)486-4424. **Ed** Ed Lehman. **Ind/Abst** Index Relig. Period., Relig. Index One, Period., Soc. Sci. Citation Index, Curr. Contents Behav. Soc. Educ. Sci., Sociol. Abstr., Soc. Welf. Soc. Plan./Policy Soc. Dev., Writ. Am. Hist., Relig. Theol. Abstr., Theol. Literaturzeitung, Lang. Lang. Behav. Abstr., Guide Soc. Sci. Relig. Period. Lit. **LC** BL1. **NLM** W1 RE254N. (cum index). bk rev. adv acc. **Circ** 1,200. (ctrl). Available on microfilm from University Microfilms. Methods, research, findings, and uses of studies on religious behavior. Articles, book reviews, and reports of research projects: academic.

REVISTA JAVERIANA (1977). (REVISTA JAVERIANA). V. 87, No. 434 (May. 1977)-. Periodical. CK. Spanish. ir. $45.00 US. Carrera 23, Number 39 69, Apartado Aerei 24773, Bogata Columbia. **Tel** 2699209. **Ind/Abst** Am. Hist. Life, Hist. Abstr. bk rev. adv acc. **Circ** 5,000. (ctrl). Publishes information concerning current Colombian problems. A Catholic journal but admits collaboration of different ideologies. *Javeriana.*

REVUE DE L'HISTOIRE DES RELIGIONS. **Series/Titl** Annales du Musee Guimet. Annual Vol. 1-. 0035-1423. Periodical. FR. French. qt. $36.25. Presses Universitaires France, 12 rue Jean-de-Beauvais, 75005 Paris France. **Tel** (1)326-22-16. **Ed** Charles Amiel. **Ind/Abst** Am. Hist. Life, Hist. Abstr., Part A, Mod. Hist. Abstr., Hist. Abst., Part B, Twent. Century Abstr., New Testam. Abstr., Relig. Index One, Period., Hist. Abstr. **LC** BL3. **DD** 200.9. Considers general history of religion and details of specific religions, ancient or modern, highly civilized or primitive.

REVUE D'HISTOIRE DE LA SPIRITUALITE. V. 48- 1972-. 0755-2068. Periodical. FR. French. qt. 52. 15 rue Monsieur, 75 Paris France. **Ind/Abst** MLA Int. Bibliogr. Books Artic. Mod. Lang. Lit. **LC** BV5015. *Revue d'Ascetique et de Mystique.*

REVUE D'HISTOIRE ECCLESIASTIQUE. Vol. 1- 1900-. 0035-2381. Periodical. BE. French. qt. 2.500. Bibliotheque de l'Universite Coll-erasme, PLC Blaise Pascal, B-1348 Louvain Belgium. **Ed** Roger Aubert. **Ind/Abst** Am. Hist. Life, Hist. Abstr., Part A, Mod. Hist. Abstr., Hist. Abst., Part B, Twent. Century Abstr., MLA Int. Bibliogr. Books Artic. Mod. Lang. Lit., New Testam. Abstr., Relig. Index One, Period., Hist. Abstr., Recent Publ. Artic. **LC** BX940. **DD** 282. (cum index). bk rev. adv acc. **Circ** 2,000. History of the church from the beginnings to our days, with systematical bibliography.

RIC SUPPLEMENT. **VAT** Repertoire Bibliographique des Institutions Chretiennes Supplement. FR. English. Cerdic Publications-Palais, Universite, 9 Place de l'Universite, 67084 Strasbourg Cedex France. **Tel** (88)355940. **Ed** Jean Schlick and Marie Zimmermann. bk rev. adv acc. **Circ** 600. International bibliographical repertory about religion and Christian churches, their organization action legislation thinking ecumenism relations with society and governments.

RICERCHE DI STORIA SOCIALE E RELIGIOSA. Vol 1- Jan./June 1972-. Periodical. Italian. ir. 9500. Edizioni di Stori e Letteratura, Via Lancellotti 18, Roma 00186 Italy. **LC** BL60.

RIVISTA DI STORIA DELLA CHIESA IN ITALIA. Vol. 1- Jan./April 1947-. 0035-6557. Periodical. IT. Italian. sa. $35.64. Herder Editrice e Liberia, Piazza Montecitorio 121, Rome Italy. **Ind/Abst** Am. Hist. Life, Hist. Abstr., Part A, Mod. Hist. Abstr., Hist. Abst., Part B, Twent. Century Abstr., Hist. Abstr. **LC** BR870.

RIVISTA DI STORIA E LETTERATURA RELIGIOSA. Vol. 1- 1965-. 0035-6573. Periodical. IT. Italian. ir. $26.73. Casa Editrice Leo S Olschki, PO Box 66, 50100 Firenze Italy. **Ind/Abst** MLA Int. Bibliogr. Books Artic. Mod. Lang. Lit., New Testam. Abstr.

RIVISTA DI VITA SPIRITUALE. Yearly V. 1- March 1957-. 0035-6638. Periodical. IT. Italian. bm. $14.26. Edizioni O C D, Via Gregorio V11 133, 00165 Rome Italy. *Vita Carmelitana.*

ROND DE TAFEL. Vol. 23 (1968)-. 0035-8169. Periodical. NE. Dutch. bm. 22 Netherlands and Belgium, 30 Foreign. Abdij van Berne, Abdijstraat 53, NL 5473 AC Heeswijk-Dinther Netherland. **Tel** 04139-1394. **Ed** N van Beijnen. bk rev. **Circ** 6. (ctrl). Articles about liturgy and information about liturgical subjects and events. *Offer.*

ROYAUME. (LE ROYAUME). No. 1 (May 1982)-. 0713-3413. Periodical. CN. French (comprend du texte en Anglais). ir. $5.00. Royaume, CP 520, Limoilou Quebec G1L 4W3 Canada. **DD** 232.9105. *Etoile, 0706-6856.*

SA. SOCIOLOGICAL ANALYSIS. **VFOAT** Sociological Analysis. V. 34- 1973-. 0038-0210. Periodical. US. English. qt. Sociological Analysis, University of Connecticut, c/o L d'Antonio, Box U-68A, Storrs CT 06268. **Tel** (203)486-4424. **Ed** Barbara Hargrove. **Ind/Abst** Curr. Contents Behav. Soc. Educ. Sci., Relig. Index One, Period., Lang. Lang. Behav. Abstr., Am. Hist. Life, Women Stud. Abstr., Ref. Source, Soc. Sci. Citation Index, Sociol. Abstr., Soc. Welf. Soc. Plan./Policy Soc. Dev., Hist. Abstr., Part A, Mod. Hist. Abstr., Hist. Abst., Part B, Twent. Century Abstr., Hist. Abstr. bk rev. adv acc. **Circ** 1,200. (ctrl). Available on microfiche from Johnson Associates. Sociology of religion: theoretical and empirical issues, comparative, historical, behavioral studies. *Sociological Analysis, 0161-0422.*

SACRIS ERUDIRI. 1- 1948-. 0771-7776. BE. Dutch (English, French and German with summaries in Latin). an. Kluwer Academic Publishing Group, PO Box 322, 3300 AH Dordrecht Netherlands. **Ind/Abst** MLA Int. Bibliogr. Books Artic. Mod. Lang. Lit., Old Testam. Abstr. **LC** BX800.A1. (cum index).

SAI SUDDHA. Periodical. English, Tamil or Telugu. ir. All India Sai Samaj, Madras-4, Madras India. **LC** BL1100. **DD** 294.505.

SAINTE ANNE DE BEAUPRE. V. 96, No 1- Jan. 1968-. 0318-4366. Periodical. CN. French. mo. 3.00. Les Annales, Basilique Sainte-Anne, Quebec Quebec G0A 1C0 Canada. **DD** 248.05. *Les Annales de la Bonne Sainte Anne de Beaupre, 0318-4358.*

SALT. **VFOAT** Journal of the Religious Studies and Moral Education Council. No. 1- Spring 1979-. 0709-616X. Periodical. CN. English. ir. Alberta Teachers Association, 11010-142 St Barnett House, Edmonton Alberta T5N 2R1 Canada. **Tel** (403)453-2411. **Ind/Abst** Can. Educ. Index. **DD** 200.7. bk rev. (ctrl).

UNA SANCTA; ZEITSCHRIFT FUR OKUMENISCHE BEGEGNUNG. Yearly V. 1-. Periodical. GW. German. qt. $11.36. Kyrios Verlag, Postfach 1740, D 8050 Freising West Germany. **Ind/Abst** New Testam. Abstr. adv acc.

SANKAYA PATRIKA. V. 1-. Periodical. English (Hindi, Pali, Prakrit, and Sanskrit). an. 32.00. Sales Department, Sampurnanand Sanskrit, Vishvavidyalaya, 221002 Varanasi India. **LC** BL2003.

SANTA SANDESA. 1973-. Hindi. ir. 10.00. Sant Kabir Chauk, 358 Nana Peth, Poona 411002 India. **LC** BL1145.

SASURA. Periodical. JA. Japanese. ir. 3000. 14-11 Chuo 5 Nakano-ku (164), Tokyo Japan. **LC** BL2216.

SAT SANDESH (MONTREAL, QUEBEC). (SAT SANDESH). Vol. 1, No. 1 (Mar. 1978)-. 0714-8003. Periodical. CN. French. qt. $7.00. Sat Sandesh, c/o Claire d'Allaire App 1014, 3555 rue Berri, Montreal Quebec H2L 4G4 Canada. **DD** 294.64405.

SCHRIFTEN ZUR ANTIKEN MYTHOLOGIE. 1- 1972-. Monographic Series. GW. German. ir. Verlag Phillipp Von Zabern, POB 4065, D-6500 Mainz West Germany. **Tel** 06131/23 22 14. Covers mythology.

SCHRIFTENREIHE DES VEREINS FUR RHEINISCHE KIRCHENGESCHICHTE. **Main/Corp** Verein fur Rheinische Kirchengeschichte. Began publication 1953. Monographic Series. GW. German. ir. Dr Rudolf Habelt GMBH, Am Buchenhang 1, 5300 Bonn 1 West Germany.

SCIENCE OF MIND. *See* Philosophy.

SCOPE. **VFOAT** Envergure. V. 1- 194 -. 0381-8187. Periodical. CN. English (includes some text in French). sa. Canadian Council of Christians and Jews, c/o J Kotick, 229 Yonge Street/Room 506, Toronto Ontario M5E 1B3 Canada.

SCOTTISH JOURNAL OF RELIGIOUS STUDIES. (THE SCOTTISH JOURNAL OF RELIGIOUS STUDIES). Vol. 1, No. 1 (Spring 1980)-. 0143-8301. Periodical. UK. English. sa. $20.00. University of Stirling, Department of Religious Studies, FK9 4LA Scotland. **Tel** 0786 73171. **Ed** Glyn Richards. **Ind/Abst** Relig. Index One, Period. **LC** BL1. **DD** 200.5. bk rev. adv acc. **Circ** 200. Promotes a critical investigation of all aspects of the study of religion.

SCP JOURNAL. **VAT** Spiritual Counterfeits Project Journal. Vol. 1, No. 1 (Apr. 1977)-. US. English. an. Spiritual Counterfeits Project, Po Box 4308, Berkeley CA 94704. **Ind/Abst** Christ. Period. Index. *Journal of the Spiritual Counterfeits Project.*

SCRIPTURE IN CHURCH. No. 1 (Spring 1971)-. 0332-1150. Periodical. English. qt. $20.00. Dominican Publications, St Saviors, Dublin 1 Ireland. **Ind/Abst** Old Testam. Abstr.

THE SEABURY JOURNAL. Vol. 1, No. 1/2 (Apr./May 1983)-. 0747-864X. Periodical. US. English. mo. The Seabury Journal, PO Box 1106 S M S, Fairfield CT 06430. **Ed** Ross B Baxter. **DD** 283.

SEMINARY NEWS. (SEMINARY NEWS : NEWS ABOUT THE GRADUATE SEMINAR OF PHILLIPS UNIVERSITY). **Main/Corp** Phillips University (Enid, Okla.). Graduate Seminary. 0745-5518. Periodical. US. English. qt. Phillips University, University Station, Enid OK 73702. *Phillips Seminary News.*

SEMIOTIQUE ET BIBLE : BULLETIN D'ETUDES ET D'ECHANGES. **VFOAT** Semiotique & Bible. No. 1 (Dec. 1975)-. Periodical. FR. French. qt. Centre pour l'Analyse, 25 rue du Plat, 6G 288 Lyon Cedex France. **Ind/Abst** New Testam. Abstr.

SENTINEL OF THE BLESSED SACRAMENT. Periodical. US. English. mo. Sentinel of the Blessed, 194 East 76th Street, New York NY 10021.

SERVICE TO REFUGEES; PROJECT LIST. **Main/Conf** All Africa Conference of Churches. Refugee Dept. English. ir. All Africa Conference on Churches, PO Box 20301, Nairobi Kenya. **LC** BV4470. **DD** 259.

SHARING THE VICTORY. *See* Religion, Mythology, Rationalism - Bible.

SHEVILIN. Year 1- (Galion 1-). Periodical. IS. Hebrew. ir. National Religious Party, 166 IBN Gabirol Street, Tel Aviv Israel.

SHIH CHIEH TSUNG CHIAO TZU LIAO. **VFOAT** Shijie Zongjiao Ziliao. No. 1 (Mar. 1980)-. Periodical. CC. Chinese. qt. $2.61. China Publication Centre, PO Box 2820, Beijing China.

SHIH CHIEH TSUNG CHIAO YEN CHIU. **VFOAT** Shijie Zongjiao Yanjiu. No. 1- Aug. 1979-. Periodical. CC. Chinese. qt. $7.38. China Publication Centre, PO Box 2820, Beijing China.

SHINTO KOTEN KENKYU : KAIHO. **VFOAT** Kaiho. 1 (Oct. 1979)-. Periodical. JA. Japanese. ir. Shinto Taikei Hansankai, c/o Nashonaru Building, 1-2 Shiba Koen 1, Minato-Ku Tokyo-To 105 Japan. **LC** BL2216.

SHINTO SHUKYO. **VFOAT** Journal of Shinto Studies. Japanese. ir. c/o Kokugakuin Daigaku, 10-28 Higashi 4-Chome, Shiuya-Ku Tokyo Japan. **LC** BL2216.

SHREE GURUDEV-VANI. English. ir. 5.00. Shree Gurudev Ashram, PO Vajreshwari Dist Thana, Ganeshpuri India. **LC** BL25.

SHUKYO KENKYU. **VFOAT** Journal of Religious Studies. Began with June 1939 issue. Periodical. Japanese. ir.

SHUKYOGAKU NEMPO. **VFOAT** Annual of Science of Religion. English. ir. **LC** BL9.J3.

SIDDHA VANI. English. ir. 3.00. Siddha Yoga Dham, M-11 Green Park Extension, New Delhi India. **LC** BL1100. **DD** 294.505.

SIDIC (ENGLISH ED.). (SIDIC). Began publication with V. 1 in 1968?. Periodical. IT. English. ty. Sidic, Via del Plebiscito 112, 00186 Rome Italy. **Tel** (396)679-53087. **Ed** Le Deaut, Gilles, and Sedawie. **Ind/Abst** Cathol. Period. Lit. Index, Old Testam. Abstr. bk rev. Contains articles by Jews and Christians on themes of interest to both. Includes documentation on dialogue, news, bibliography, and book reviews.

SIGNAL. First issue in 1970?. 0316-361X. Periodical. CN. French. ir. Service de Coordination de la Rencontre, C P 1096, Quebec Quebec G1K 7B5 Canada. **DD** 269.205.

SII VOUS INFORME. (LE SII VOUS INFORME). VAT Service d'Information Intercommunautaire vous Informe. V. 1, No 1 (Feb. 1972)-. 0821-1442. Periodical. CN. French. bm. Service d'Information Intercommunautaire, Bureau 120/1800 Ouest Boulevard Dorchester, Montreal Quebec H3H 2H2 Canada. **DD** 271.009714281.

THE SIKH COURIER. Began with Oct. 1960 issue. Periodical. UK. English. qt. 0.25 Each Issue. Sikh Cultural Society of Great Britain, 88 Mollison Way Edgeware Middlesex, London HA8 5QW England. **LC** BL2017. **DD** 294.605.

SIKH DHARMA BROTHERHOOD. 0364-8206. Periodical. US. English. qt. $6.00. Sikh Dharma Brotherhood, 1704 Q Street Northwest, Washington DC 20009. **LC** BL2017. **DD** 294.605.

SIKH RELIGIOUS STUDIES INFORMATION. No. 1- July 1979-. 0193-1466. Periodical. US. English. bm. IASWR, Melville Memorial Library, Stony Brook NY 11794. **Tel** (516)246-8362. **Ed** Christoper Chapple. **Circ** 65. Cumulative bibliographic information for study of Sikhism.

SINGLE ADULT MINISTRY INFORMATION : S. A. M. I. VFOAT S.A.M.I. Vol. 13, No. 5 (Mar. 1986)-. 0887-1167. Periodical. US. English. mo. $15.00 US, $18.00 Canada. Institute of Singles Dynamics, PO Box 11394, Kansas City MO 64112. **DD** 259. *Single I, 0737-2078.*

SOJOURNERS. Began with Jan. 1976. 0364-2097. Periodical. US. English. $12.00. Peoples Christian Coalition, 1309 L Street NW, Washington DC 20005. **Tel** (202)737-2780. **Ind/Abst** Relig. Index One, Period. **LC** BR115.W6. **DD** 261.805. *Post American, 0361-2422.*

SOLIA. (SOLIA, THE HERALD). 1935. 0038-1039. Periodical. US. English (Romanian). mo. $10.00 Domestic, $14.00 Canada and $16.00 Foreign. Romanian Orthodox Episcopate, 11341 Woodward Avenue, Detroit MI 48202. **Tel** (517)522-4800. **Ed** Nathaniel Popp. bk rev. **Circ** 4,700. (ctrl). It is the official newspaper of the Romanian Orthodox Episcopate of America. It contains religious news and deals with the issues of faith.

O SOLO. 0584-0821. Periodical. US. Portuguese. qt. Solo, PO Box 1231, Sisters OR 97759. **Ed** Jerry Jones. bk rev. adv acc. **Circ** 26,000. The Christian magazine for single adults.

SOPHIA. V. 1- Apr. 1962-. 0038-1527. Periodical. AT. English. ty. 7-50. Sophia-Deakin University, School of Humanities, Victoria 3217 Australia. **Ed** M J Charlesqorth. **Ind/Abst** Philos. Index, APAIS, Aust. Public Aff. Inf. Serv. **LC** BL1. **DD** 200.1. **Circ** 750. A journal for discussion in philosophical theology.

SOURCE (TORONTO, ONT.). (SOURCE). Sept./Oct. 1981-. 0229-4931. Periodical. CN. English. bm. $5.00. Source, 10 Overlea Boulevard, Toronto Ontario M4H 1A5 Canada. **DD** 268.899. *Cell Pak, 0707-1868.*

SOURCES FOR THE STUDY OF RELIGION IN MALAWI. No. 1-. Monographic Series. MW. English. ir. Department of Religious Studies, Chancellor College, University of Malawi, Box 280, Zomba Malawi. **LC** UNC.

SOUTH AFRICAN OUTLOOK. V. 52- 1922-. 0038-2523. Periodical. SA. English. mo. Outlook Publications Pty Ltd, PO Box 245, 7700 Rondebosch South Africa. **Tel** (021)4781389. **Ed** Francis Wilson. bk rev. **Circ** 1,300. *Christian Express.*

SOUTH CAROLINA NEWS. V. 1- 1945-. 0747-1130. Periodical. US. English. bm. Church of God Publishing House, 922 Montgomery Avenue, Cleveland TN 37311.

SOUTH DAKOTA CHURCHMAN. 1919. Periodical. US. English. ir. $3.00. South Dakota Episcopal Church, PO Box 517, Sioux Falls SD 57101. **Tel** (605)823-4346. **Ed** Mary B Hobbs. bk rev. **Circ** 4,500. (ctrl). Newsletter and bulletin board for Episcopal Diocese of South Dakota.

SOVIET CHRISTIAN PRISONER LIST. 1981-. 0278-1018. US. English. an. Society for the Study of Religion Under Communism, PO Box 2310, Orange CA 92669. **LC** BR1608.S65. **DD** 272.9.

SPIRIT. (SPIRIT). No. 1, Ed. 1, (Sept./Oct. 1985)-. 0885-0291. Periodical. US. English. bm. Spirit Ministries Inc, PO Box 1231, Sisters OR 97759. **Tel** (503)549-0443. bk rev. adv acc. **Circ** 40,000. Helps guide today's new generation of adults toward a more Biblical lifestyle and philosophical perspective. Provides a framework for making decisions and wise choices in an increasingly complicated, changing and challenging world. *Solo, 0164-4734.*

SPIRIT (DENVER, COLO.) *CEASED.* (SPIRIT). Vol. 70, No. 4 (Apr. 1985)-. 8750-9784. Periodical. US. English. mo. $7.50 Domestic, $9.50 Foreign. Spirit, 1819 East 14th Avenue, Denver CO 80218. **Tel** (303)322-7730. **Ed** D Wells. Spirtual daily study. *Aspire, 0004-4962.*

SPIRITUAL COMMUNITY GUIDE. 1- 1972-. 0160-0354. US. English. Spiritual Community Publications, Box 1080, San Rafael CA 94902. **LC** BP602. **DD** 200.257.

SPIRITUAL INDIA. V. 1- Jan. 1973-. Periodical. II. English. ir. $4.00. Shanti Villa, 1615 Madarsa Road, Kashmere Gate, Delhi India 110006. **LC** BL2001.2. **DD** 200.954.

SPIRITUAL LIFE. Began publication in 1955. 0038-7630. Periodical. US. English. qt. $9.00 Domestic, $10.50 Foreign. Spiritual Life, 2131 Lincoln Road NE, Washington DC 20002. **Tel** (202)832-6622. **Ed** Christopher Latimer. **Ind/Abst** Cathol. Period. Lit. Index. **LC** BX2350.A1. **DD** 248.05. bk rev. **Circ** 18,000. A Catholic quarterly of contemporary spirituality.

SRI AUROBINDO CENTENARY ANNUAL. 1972-. English. ir. 3.00. SRI Aurobindo Centenary Committee, 47 Galle Face Court Galle Road, Colombo -3 Ceylon. **LC** BL1270.G4. **DD** 181.45.

SRI CANKARA KRUPA. SRISANKARAKRPA. VFOAT Srisankarakrpa. Periodical. Tamil (Sanskrit or English). ir. **LC** BL1245.S5.

SRI NRUSIMHA PRIYA. SRI NRISIMHA PRIYA. VFOAT Sri Nrisimha Priya. Periodical. Tamil. ir. **LC** BL1245.V3.

SRI SABARIMALA SASTA SOVANIR. Malayalam. ir. West Coast Publicity Service, M G Road Cochin 11, Ernakulum India. **LC** BL1100.

THE STANDARD BEARER; A REFORMED SEMI-MONTHLY MAGAZINE. V. 1- 1924-. 0362-4692. Periodical. US. English. sm. $10.50. Standard Bearer, PO Box 6064, Business Office, Grand Rapids MI 49506. **Tel** (616)243-2953. **Ed** H C Hoeksema. bk rev. **Circ** 1,700. Religious and church news. Includes book reviews (religious).

STATISTICS FROM RELIGIOUS ORGANIZATIONS. *See* Statistics.

STIMMENT DER ZEIT (FREIBURG). (STIMMEN DER ZEIT). Vol. 88-. 0039-1492. Periodical. GW. German. mo. Verlag Herder Freiburg, Hermann-Herder Strasse 4, D-7800 Freiburg West Germany. **Ind/Abst** Annu. Bibliogr. Engl. Lang. Lit., New Testam. Abstr., Artbibliogr. Mod., Energy Res. Abstr., Cathol. Period. Lit. Index, MLA Int. Bibliogr. Books Artic. Mod. Lang. Lit. (cum index). *Stimmen aus Maria-Laach.*

STUDI E MATERIALI DI STORIA DELLE RELIGIONI (L'AQUILA, ITALY : 1983). (STUDI E MATERIALI DI STORIA DELLE RELIGIONI). VFOAT SMSR. Vol. 7, No. 1-. Periodical. English. sm. *Studi Storico-Religiosi.*

STUDI STORICO-RELIGIOSI. VFOAT SSR. Vol. 1, Issue. 1-. Periodical. English (German, and Italian). sa. Inst di Studi Storico-Regigios Facolta di Lettere, Univ Degli, Studi Roma Italy. *Studi e Materiali di Storia Delle Religioni.*

STUDI SUL PENSIERO FILOSOFICO E RELIGIOSO DEI SECOLI XIX E XX *CEASED.* 1- 1966-. Monographic Series. IT. Italian. Marzorati Editore, Via Piero Martinetti 6, Milano 20147 Italy. **Tel** 405050.

STUDIA LITURGICA. V. 1- Mar. 1962-. 0039-3207. Periodical. English (Latin). ir. $17.50. Studia Liturgica, PO Box 25088, 3001 HB Rotterdam Netherlands. **Tel** 10-768249. **Ed** Wiebe Vos and Geoffrey Wainwright. **Ind/Abst** New Testam. Abstr., Relig. Index One, Period. bk rev. An international ecumenical review for liturgical research and renewal.

STUDIA MONASTICA. V. 1- 1959-. 0039-3258. Periodical. SP. Multilingual (Latin, Catalan, English, French, Spanish, etc). sa. 45.00. Studia Monastica, Abadia de Montserrat, Barcelona 13 Spain. **Tel** 8350251. **Ed** Josep Massot Muntaner. **Ind/Abst** Am. Hist. Life, Hist. Abstr., Part A, Mod. Hist. Abstr., Hist. Abst., Part B, Twent. Century Abstr., MLA Int. Bibliogr. Books Artic. Mod. Lang. Lit., Hist. Abstr. **LC** BX2400. bk rev. **Circ** 800. Articles, chronicles and book reviews on themes of monatic history and spirituality of all times, in all countries.

STUDIA MORALIA. *See* Ethics.

STUDIA MYSTICA. V. 1- Spring 1978-. 0161-7222. Periodical. US. English. qt. $18.00. California State University, 6000 J Street, Sacramento CA 95819. **Tel** (916)454-6444. **Ed** Mary E Giles. **Ind/Abst** MLA Int. Bibliogr. Books Artic. Mod. Lang. Lit., Relig. Index One, Period. **LC** BL625. **DD** 291.42. bk rev. adv acc. **Circ** 400. (ctrl). Studies and expresses relationship of mystical and aesthetic in all art forms.

STUDIA POST-BIBLICA. 1- 1959-. 0585-5500. Monographic Series. NE. English, French or German. ir. E J Brill, PO Box 9000, 2300 PA Leiden the Netherlands.

STUDIA THEOLOGICA LUNDENSIA. Monographic Series. SW. Multilingual. ir. Liber International, S-205 10, Malmo Sweden. **Tel** 46-40-70650.

STUDIA Z HISTORII KAZNODZIEJSTWA I HOMILETYKI. Vol. 1- 1975-. Polish (summaries in French). ir. DZIA, Administracyjno-Gospodarczy ATK, Ul Dewajtis, 01-653 Warsaw Poland. **LC** BV4205.

STUDIE. **Main/Corp** Krestanska Akademia. Began in 1958. 0450-9250. Periodical. Czech. ir. $5.00. (Academia Cristiana Administrace Studii), Via Concordial, Rome Italy 00183. **LC** BX806.C9.

STUDIEN ZUR UMWELT DES NEUEN TESTAMENTS. Vol. 1- 1962-). 0585-6272. Monographic Series. GW. German. ir. Vandenhoeck & Ruprecht, Postfach 3753 Theatrestr 13, D 3400 Goettingen West Germany. **Tel** 0551/65061. **Ed** C H Burchard, G Jeremias, H W Vuhn and H Stegenann. bk rev. adv acc. **Circ** 700.

STUDIES IN COMPARATIVE RELIGION. V. 1- Winter 1967-. 0039-3622. Periodical. UK. English. qt. $19.50. Perennial Books Ltd, Pates Manor, Hatton Road, Bedfont Middlesex England. **Ed** J Peter Hobson, Olive Clive-Ross and Ralph Smith. **Ind/Abst** Relig. Index One, Period., Humanit. Index. **LC** BL1. bk rev. adv acc. Studies in comparative religion, metaphysics, cosmology and traditional symbolism. *Tomorrow.*

STUDIES IN ICONOGRAPHY. V. 1- 1975-. 0148-1029. US. English. an. $27.00. Arizona State University, School of Art, Anthony Gully, Tempe AZ 85287. **Tel** (602)965-6747. **Ed** Anthony Gully. **Ind/Abst** MLA Int. Bibliogr. Books Artic. Mod. Lang. Lit., Avery Index Archit. Period., Years Work Eng. Stud., Repert. Int. Litt. Art. **LC** NX1. **DD** 700. bk rev. **Circ** 350. (ctrl). The journal is interdisciplinary in nature. Articles focus on problems of iconography in critical studies of art and literature. All periods are covered.

STUDIES IN MEDIEVAL AND REFORMATION THOUGHT. V. 1- 1966-. 0585-6914. Monographic Series. English. ir. E J Brill, PO Box 9000, 2300 PA Leiden The Netherlands.

STUDIES IN RELIGION. VFOAT SR, Sciences Religieuses. V. 1- June 1971-. 0008-4298. Periodical. CN. English (also in French). qt. 30.00. Wilfred Laurier University Press, 75 University Avenue West, Waterloo Ontario N2L 3C6 Canada. **Tel** (514)282-4477. **Ed** Roland D Chagnon. **Ind/Abst** New Testam. Abstr., MLA Int. Bibliogr. Books Artic. Mod. Lang. Lit., Old Testam. Abstr., Relig. Index One, Period. **LC** BL1. **DD** 200.5. bk rev. adv acc. **Circ** 1,300. Publishes articles and reviews in the various disciplines concerned with the scientific study of religion. *Canadian Journal of Theology, 0576-5579.*

STUDIES IN RELIGION AND SOCIETY SERIES. Monographic Series. US. English. ir. Center for Scientific Study Religion, 5757 University Avenue, Chicago IL 60637.

STUDIES IN SIKHISM AND COMPARATIVE RELIGION. Vol. 1, No. 1 (Oct. 1982)-. Periodical. English. sa. 30.00 Domestic, $7.50. Guru Nanak Foundation, Near Qutab Hotel,

Religion, Mythology, Rationalism

New Delhi 110067 India. Tel 654353/652151. Ed Mohinder Singh. LC BL2017. DD 294.605. bk rev. **Circ** 750. Religion history and philosophy with major focus on comparative study of religion and Sikhism.

STUDIES IN THE HISTORY OF RELIGIONS, SUPPLEMENTS TO NUMEN. 1- 1954-. 0585-7260. Monographic Series. NE. English or German. ir. E J Brill, POB 9000, 2300 PA Leiden The Netherlands.

SUARA. Main/Corp Malaysia Inter-Religious Organisation. V. 1- 1970-. Periodical. English. ir. $3.00 Each Issue. Belangor Editorial Board M I R O, 16 Road 49E, Petaling Jaya Malaysia. LC BL1. DD 291.05.

SUMMARY OF PROCEEDINGS. ANNUAL CONFERENCE - AMERICAN THEOLOGICAL LIBRARY ASSOCIATION. See Library and Information Science.

SUNDAY SCHOOL LEADERSHIP. V. 1- Oct. 1980-. 0274-8568. Periodical. US. English. mo. $10.50. Materials Services Department, 127 9th Avenue North, Nashville TN 37234. Tel (615)251-2000. *Outreach, 0162-4318.*

SUNDAY SERMONS. 0745-3558. Periodical. US. English. bm. $61.90. Voicings Publications, PO Box 4049, Silver Spring MD 20904.

SUNDAY; THE MAGAZINE FOR THE LORD'S DAY. V. 55, No. 4- 4th Qtr. 1969-. 0039-5161. Periodical. US. English. qt. Lords Day Alliance of US, 2930 Flower Road South/Suite 107, Atlanta GA 30341. *Lord's Day Leader.*

SUNRISE. V. 1- Oct. 1951-. 0562-6048. Periodical. US. English. bm. $7.50. Theosophical University Press, PO Bin C, Pasadena CA 91109. Tel (818)798-3378. Ed Grace F Knoche. LC BP500. DD 212.05. bk rev. (ctrl). A journal with articles on philosophic, religious and scientific themes in light of ancient and modern theosophy. Includes interviews, letters, and book reviews. *Theosophical Forum.*

SUNSTONE. 0363-1370. Periodical. US. English. bm. $23.00. Sunstone Foundation, 59 West 1st Street, Salt Lake City UT 84101-1507. Tel (801)355-5926. LC AP2. DD 051. A forum featuring a variety of perspectives on complex issues in Mormonism. Includes theological, historical, and other interpretive essays; fiction, news, and book reviews.

SUPPLEMENT MENSUEL AUX CAHIERS RATIONALISTES. 0153-0380. Periodical. FR. French. mo. Union Rationaliste, 16 rue de L Ecole-Polytechique, 75005 Paris 5E France. LC AP20. DD 054.1. *Courrier Rationaliste.*

SURVIVE (VANCOUVER, B.C.). (SURVIVE). 0229-1975. Periodical. CN. English. mo. Free. Church of Scientology of British Columbia, 4857 Main Street, Vancouver British Columbia V5V 3R Canada. DD 299.936. (ctrl).

SVENSK EXEGETISK ARSBOK. See Yearbooks, Almanacs, Directories.

SVENSK MISSIONSTIDSKRIFT. Began publication in 1913. 0346-217X. Periodical. SW. Swedish. qt. 7.98. Swedish Institute of Mission Research, Swedish Missionary/Gotgatan 3, S-752 22 Uppsala Sweden. Tel (018)13-75225. Ed Jonas Jonsson. Ind/Abst Relig. Index One, Period. LC BV2355.S9. bk rev. adv acc. Religion, society and churches in the Third World Missionary research and reports.

SYMBOLON. Vol. 1- 1960-. 0082-0660. GW. German. ir. E J Brill, Antwerpener Strasse 6-12, D-5000 Koeln West Germany. LC BL600.

SYMPOSIUM OF THE CONFERENCE ON SCIENCE, PHILOSOPHY AND RELIGION. See Science (General).

THE TABLET (LONDON). (THE TABLET). V. 1- No. 1-. 0039-8837. UK. English. wk. $42.91. Tablet Publishing Company, 48 Great Peter Street, London SW1P 2HB England. Ed John Wilkins. Ind/Abst Cathol. Period. Lit. Index. LC AP4. DD 052. bk rev. adv acc. **Circ** 55,000. Each week it seeks to instruct and entertain on religion, politics, society, ethics and the arts, considered in the light of Christian principles and beliefs.

THE TAGASTAN. 0749-6451. Periodical. US. English. sa. The Tagastan, PO Box 338, Villanova PA 19085. DD 255.

TARGET (TORONTO, ONT.). (TARGET). VFOAT Piao Kan. 0712-2942. Periodical. CN. Chinese (English). bm. Ambassadors for Christ in Canada, 41 Cecil Street, Toronto Ontario M5T 1N2 Canada. DD 269.205.

TEACHING PICTURES FOR BIBLE SEARCHERS. 0040-0645. US. English. qt. $11.00. Sunday School Board of the Southern Baptist Convention, 127 North Avenue North, Nashville TN 37234.

THE TEILHARD REVIEW CEASED. Vol. 1, No. 1 (Summer 1966)-V. 16, No. 3. 0040-2184. Periodical. UK. English. ty. The Teilhard Centre Future Man, 23 Kensington Square, London W8 5HN England. Ed Michael LeMorvan. Ind/Abst Cathol. Period. Lit. Index. (cum index). bk rev. adv acc. **Circ** 1,000. Microform. An international journal of integrative studies concerned with the future of a humanity increasingly responsible for its own evolution.

TEMENOS. V. 1- 1965-. 0497-1817. Periodical. English. ir. Finnish Society for the Study of Comparative Religion, Helsinki Finland. Ind/Abst MLA Int. Bibliogr. Books Artic. Mod. Lang. Lit. LC BL1.A1. DD 291.05.

TENRI JOURNAL OF RELIGION. No. 1 (Mar. 1955)-. 0495-1492. JA. English. an. Tenri University Press, Tenri Nara Japan. LC BL1. DD 200.5.

TENRIKYO NENKAN. 1974-. JA. Japanese. ir. Tenrikyo Doyusha, Tenri 632 Japan. LC BL2222.T4.

TENRIKYO TOKEI NENKAN. VFOAT Statistical Year Book of Tenrikyo. No. 1- Issue. JA. Japanese, 1931- Japanese (an Japanese (1952-72). ir. Tenrikyo Kyokai Hombu, Mishima-cho Tenri-shi Nara-ken, Tenri Japan. LC BL2222.T4.

TER HERKENNING. Vol. 1-. Periodical. NE. Dutch. bm. Boekencentrum B V, Scheveningseweg 72, Box 84176, The Hague Netherlands. *Christus en Israel, Kerk en Israel.*

TESTAMENT. Vol. 1 No. 1 (Apr. 1984)-. 0743-572X. Periodical. US. English. qt. Church of God, PO Box 46041, Denver CO 80201.

TEXAS CHURCH WOMAN. 0746-9756. Periodical. US. English. bm. $2.00. Texas Church Woman, Rt 3 Box 176, Hereford TX 79045.

TEXTUS PATRISTICI ET LITURGICI. No. 1- 1964-. 0082-3775. Monographic Series. GW. German. ir. Verlag Friedrich Pustet, Postfach 339, 8400 Regensburg 11 West Germany.

THEORIA TO THEORY CEASED. V. 1-V. 14, No. 4. 0049-3686. Periodical. UK. English. qt. Ind/Abst Philos. Index. LC BL51.

THIS WORLD. No. 1 (Winter/Spring 1982)-. 0734-0117. Periodical. US. English. qt. $16.00. Institute for Educational Affairs, 310 Madison Avenue/Suite 1629, New York NY 10017. Ind/Abst Relig. Index One, Period. LC BL65.P7. DD 261.05.

TICKER TAPE. (TICKER TAPE). No. 1-. 0710-5061. Periodical. CN. English. qt. $6.00. Ticker Tape, 600 Jarvis Street, Toronto Ontario M4Y 2S6 Canada. DD 261.8505.

TIERRA NUEVA. Yearly V. 1- (No. 1-). Periodical. Spanish. ir. $9.00. Cedial, Calle 17 No 4-68 Apartamento 401 Apartado Aereo 20134, Botoga Colombia. LC BR600.

TODAY'S PARISH. 1968. 0040-8549. Periodical. US. English. ir. Twenty Third Publications, Box 180, Mystic CT 06388. Tel (203)536-2611. Ed Carol Clark. Ind/Abst Cathol. Period. Lit. Index. bk rev. adv acc. Proven ways to develop and renew vibrant faith communities. For professional and volunteer parish leaders and concerned parishioners.

TOHO SHUKYO. VFOAT Journal of Eastern Religions. Periodical. Japanese (with summaries in English). ir. c/o Otemon Gakuin Daigaku, 230 Al (567), Ibaraki Japan. LC BL1899.

TRACES. TEACHERS OF RELIGION AND CHRISTIAN ETHICS IN SASKATCHEWAN. See Ethics.

TRIMENIAIO PERIODIKO TES CHRISTIANIKES EPISTEMES. BIBLIKA MATHEMATA. VFOAT Christian Science Quarterly. Bible Lessons. 0145-9503. Periodical. US. English. qt. $3.25. Christian Science Publishing Society, 1 Norway Street, Boston MA 02115.

TRINITE. LIBERTE. (TRINITE, LIBERTE). No longer published after Dec. 1977?. 0318-0573. CN. French. te. Les Peres Trinitaires, 3449 Ave Ontario, Montreal Quebec H3G 2C8 Canada. DD 255.79.

TRINITY UNIVERSITY MONOGRAPH SERIES IN RELIGION. VFOAT Monograph Series in Religion. V. 1-. 0742-2393. Monographic Series. US. English. ir. Trinity University Press, 715 Stadium Drive, San Antonio TX 78284.

TRO OCH LIV. Began in 1942. 0346-2803. Periodical. SW. Swedish. bm. $9.00. Tro Och Liv, Hemrin/Kottlavagen 116, 181 41 Lidingo Sweden. Tel (08)765-7733.

TRUTH CONSCIOUSNESS JOURNAL. Vol. 1, No. 1 (Summer 1977)-. 0191-5207. Periodical. US. English. qt. $7.00. Truth Consciousness Inc, Gold Hill Salina Star Route, Boulder CO 80302. Tel (303)447-1637. Ed Rolf Norgaand and Bob Conrow. LC BP605.T78. DD 299.93. **Circ** 400. Devoted to the realization of the true self within; a vehicle for Swami Amar Jyoti's message of spiritual awakening; professes a universal outlook of religion.

THE TRUTH SEEKER. (TRUTH SEEKER). V. 1- Sept. 1873-. 0041-3712. Periodical. US. English. mo. $9.00. Truth Seeker, Box 2832, San Diego CA 92112. Tel (714)574-7600. LC BL2700.

TSUNG CHIAO SHIH CHIEH. VFOAT Religious World. Began with Oct. 1979 issue. Periodical. CH. Chinese. qt. Tsung Chiao Shih Chieh Tsa Chih She 31 Chi-nan Road, 2nd Section, Taipei Taiwan. LC BL9.C4. DD 200.5.

TULASI PRAJNA. Jan./Mar. 1975-. Periodical. Hindi. ir. Jain Vishwa Bharati, Ladnun Rajasthan, Ladanum India. LC BL1300.

UNDERSTANDING THE SUNDAY READINGS. July/Aug./Sept. 1980-. 0278-6095. US. English. mo. McGrath Publishing Company, 6231 Leesburg Pike/Suite 404, Falls Church VA 22044.

UNITED CHURCH OBSERVER. (THE UNITED CHURCH OBSERVER). V. 1- March 1, 1939-. 0041-7238. Periodical. CN. English. mo. United Church Observer, Room 410, 85 St Claire Avenue East, Toronto Ontario Canada. Tel (416)960-8500. Ed Hugh McCullum. LC BX9881.A1. DD 280. bk rev. adv acc. **Circ** 270,000. (ctrl). Also available on microfilm from University Microfilms International, Ann Arbor, MI. Local and world news on religion and religious happenings. *New Outlook, United Church Record and Missionary Review; Christian Advance.*

UNITED SYNAGOGUE REVIEW. VFOAT Review. 0041-8153. Periodical. US. English. qt. United Synagogue of America, 155 5th Avenue, New York NY 10010. Tel (212)533-7800.

UNITY. (UNITY, A WAY OF LIFE). 0162-3567. Periodical. US. English. mo. Unity School of Christianity, Unity Village MO 64065. Tel (816)524-3550. Ed Pam Yearsley. Self-improvement and motivational material.

UNIVERS. 48Ieme- Yearly V. 0381-9876. Periodical. CN. French. $3.86. Univers, 2269 Chemin Street, St Louis Quebec G1T IRF Canada. DD 266.205. *Propagation de la Foi.*

UNPUBLISHED WRITINGS ON WORLD RELIGIONS. No. 1- Oct. 1977-. 0149-0230. US. English. sa. $4.00. Institute for Advanced Studies of World Religions, 5001 Melville Memorial Library, State University of New York at Stony Brook, Stony Brook NY 11794.

UNSEARCHABLE RICHES. Began with V. 1, Jan. 1910. 0042-0476. Periodical. US. English. bm.

UPDATE (ARHUS, DENMARK). (UPDATE : A QUARTERLY JOURNAL ON NEW RELIGIOUS MOVEMENTS). Vol. 6, No. 1 (Mar. 1982)-. Periodical. DK. English. qt. $15.00. Dialog Center, Katrinebjergvej 46, DK-8200 Aarhus N Denmark. Tel (06)10 54 11. Ed Neil T Duddy. LC BL1.A1. DD 291.05. bk rev. adv acc. **Circ** 1,000. Beliefs and activities of new religious critiqued from theological, sociological and psychological perspectives. Dialogue in print, between leaders and adherents of those groups and scholars researching them. *New Religious Movements Update.*

VECTOR. 0361-8331. Periodical. US. English. Vermont Ecumerical Council and Bible Society, Box 593/30 Elmwood Avenue, Burlington VT 05401.

VEDIC LIGHT. Periodical. English. ir. Maharshi Dayananda Bhawan, Ramila Ground, Delhi India. LC BL1100. DD 294.505.

VEROFFENTLICHUNGEN. Main/Corp Institut fur Europaische Geschichte (Mainz, Germany). Vol. 1 1953-. 0537-7919. Monographic Series. GW. German. ir. Franz Steiner Verlag GMBH, Postfach 347, D7000 Stuttgart 1 West Germany. Tel

Religion, Mythology, Rationalism

(0711) 2582229. Ed K O V Aretin and P Manns. Monographs dedicated to European and church history as well as to problems of theology.

VETUS TESTAMENTUM. Vol. 1-. 0042-4935. Periodical. NE. English (Vols. for 19- in French or German). qt. 114.00. E J Brill, P O Box 9000, 2300 PA Leiden The Netherlands. Tel (071)312-624. Ed G A Emerton, W L Halladay. Ind/Abst Old Testam. Abstr., New Testam. Abstr., Relig. Index One, Period., Recent Publ. Artic. LC BS410. bk rev. adv acc. Circ 2,650.

VETUS TESTAMENTUM. SUPPLEMENTS. 0083-5889. Monographic Series. English, French or German. ir. E J Brill, P O Box 9000, 2300 PA Leiden The Netherlands. Tel (071)312-624. Ed T A Emerton and W L Halladay. Covers the whole range of O.T. study, including history, literature, religion and theology, text, versions, language, etc.

VIE SERVITE. VFOAT Servite Life. V. 1- Fall 1958-. 0709-8812. Periodical. CN. French (text in English 1958-1964?, 1969-1970). qt. Free. Ordre des Servites de Marie, Maison Provinciale, 5705 East Boulevard Gouin, Montreal Nord Quebec H1G 5X1 Canada. DD 271.79.

LA VIE SPIRITUELLE. Yearly V. 1- (No. 1-). 0042-5613. Periodical. FR. French. ir. Editions du Cerf, 29 Boulevard la Tour Maubourg, 75340 Paris Cedex 07 France. Ind/Abst Old Testam. Abstr. (cum index).

LA VIE SPIRITUELLE. SUPPLEMENT. VFOAT Supplement de la Vie Spirituelle. V. 1-22 (No. 1-91). Periodical. FR. French. ir. $49.49. Editions du Cerf, 29 Boulevard La Tour Maubourg, 75340 Paris Cedex 07 France. Ind/Abst Cathol. Period. Lit. Index. (cum index).

VIEWPOINT. V. 1- Fall 1957-. Periodical. UK. English. ty. International School of Christian Fellow, 47 Marylebone Lane, London W1M 6AX England.

VIGILIAE CHRISTIANAE. See Literature.

VIGNERON. (LE VIGNERON). March 1979-. 0225-1183. Periodical. CN. French. ir. $4.50. Le Vigneron, CP 403, Lachine Quebec H8S 4C2 Canada. Tel (514)878-3035. Ed Ed Hoyer. DD 253.709714. bk rev. adv acc. Circ 1,000. Information about Christian activities in Quebec, and to encourage an interest in foreign missions. Vision, 0225-1175.

VIRA. VFOAT Faith. Vol. 1- (No. 1-). Periodical. US. English (Ukrainian). qt. United Ukrainian Orthodox Sisterhoods, PO Box 300, South Bound Brook NJ 08880. LC BX738.U4.

VISIBLE RELIGION. Vol. 1-. English. an. LC BL1. DD 291.305.

VITA EVANGELICA. No. 1- 1966-. 0507-1690. Monographic Series. CN. English. ir. Canadian Religious Conference, 324 Laurier Avenue East, Ottawa K1N 6P6 Ontario Canada.

VITAL CHRISTIANITY. V. 1- 1881-. 0042-7381. Periodical. US. English. ir. Vital Christianity, PO Box 2499, Anderson IN 46011. Tel (317)644-7721. Ed Harold L Phillips. Ind/Abst Guide Soc. Sci. Relig. Period. Lit. Available in microform.

VOCE EVANGELICA. VFOAT Evangel Voice. V. 13- Jan/March 1974-. 0708-2479. Periodical. CN. Italian (includes some text in English). bm. Free. Voce Evangelica, Box 222 Station V, Toronto Ontario M6R 3A5 Canada. DD 289.9. (ctrl) Communicato Missionario, 0708-2460.

VOCET. VFOAT Qu'il Appelle. V. 1- Winter 1980-. 0228-2186. Periodical. CN. French. qt. Free. Vocet, Pavillon l'Assomption, Cap-Rouge Quebec G0A 1K0 Canada. DD 271.49.

VOICE OF FREEDOM. 1952-. 0042-8116. US. English. mo. $8.00 Domestic, $8.50 Foreign. Voice of Freedom, Box 24836, Dallas TX 75224.

VOX REFORMATA. No. 1- Dec. 1962-. 0728-0912. Periodical. AT. English. sa. 5.50. The Bursar Reformed Theological College, 55 Maud Street, Geelong Victoria 3220 Australia. Tel (052)214652. Ed R O Zorn. Ind/Abst New Testam. Abstr. (cum index). bk rev. Circ 200. (ctrl). A theological journal, usually containing two essays or articles by either members of faculty, visiting lecturers, or ministers of reformed church, together with many book reviews.

WARTA HINDU DHARMA. Indonesian. ir. 60. Jln Nangka-7A, Denpasar Indonesia. LC BL1100.

THE WAY. V. 1- Jan. 1961-. 0043-1575. Periodical. UK. English. qt. $12.00. The Way, 39 Fitzjohns Avenue, London NW3 5JT England. Ind/Abst New Testam. Abstr., Cathol. Period. Lit. Index. LC BX2350.A1.

WAY OF ST. FRANCIS. VFOAT Way. VAT Way of Saint Francis (1980). 0273-8295. Periodical. US. English. bm. $5.00. Way of St Francis, 107 Golden Gate Avenue, San Francisco CA 94102. Way.

WERELD EN ZENDING. Vol. 1-. 0165-988X. Periodical. NE. Dutch. qt $14.50. Wereld en Zending, Donsvlinder 46, 2317 KG Leiden Netherlands. Ed G Verstraelen-Gelbuin. Ind/Abst Am. Hist. Life, Hist. Abstr. bk rev. adv acc. Circ 2,000. Ecumenical journal for missionary information and reflection. Missiewerk, Heerbaan.

WESLEYAN WORLD. Vol. 50, No. 1 (Sept. 1968)-. 0739-0440. Periodical. US. English. mo. General Department of World Missions Weslyan Church, PO Box 2000, Marion IN 46952. Tel (317)674-3301. Ed Wayne W Wright. bk rev. Circ 16,500. To inform North American readers of the Wesleyan Church's overseas missionary program and to promote that program. Wesleyan Missionary, World Missions Bulletin.

WESTERN RECORDER. 0043-4132. Periodical. US. English. wk. $6.50. Kentucky Baptist Convention, 10701 Shelbyville Road, Middletown KY 40203. Tel (502)245-4101. Ed Jack Sanford. adv acc. Circ 65,000. (ctrl). Contains news of Southern Baptist around the world. We carry local, state and convention news to 2,200 churches in Kentucky alone.

WHEREVER IN THE WORLD, FOR JESUS' SAKE. VFOAT Wherever. Began publication with: Vol. 1, No. 1 (Spring 1976). Periodical. US. English. ir. Evangelical Alliance Mission, PO Box 969, Wheaton IL 60187. Tel (312)653-5300.

WHITE FATHERS AFRICANADA. VAT Africanada. V. 1- March 1978-. 0707-395X. Periodical. CN. English. bm. $1.00. White Fathers, 47 Colonsay Road, Thornhill Ontario L3T 3E9 Canada. DD 266.2.

WHOLE EARTH NEWSLETTER. VFOAT New Missionary Herald Whole Earth Newsletter. V. 1- 1970-. 0361-1930. Periodical. US. English. qt. United Church Board for World Ministries, 475 Riverside Drive, New York NY 10027. Missionary Herald Newsletter, 0544-4357.

WITH ONE VOICE CEASED. Main/Corp Multimedia Zambia. 1- 1971-. English. ir. LC BV652.95. DD 254.3096894.

THE WITTENBURG DOOR. VFOAT Puerta de Wittenburg. Began in 1971. 0199-8285. Periodical. US. English. bm. $12.00. Youth Specialties, 1224 Greenfield Drive, El Cajon CA 92021. Tel (619)440-2333. Ed Mike Yaconelli. Ind/Abst Christ. Period. Index. Circ 20,000. Dedicated to church reform and renewal. Contains editorials, features and interviews in humorous satire.

WOMEN'S CONCERNS. Issue 25 (Mar. 1984)-. 0827-2263. Periodical. CN. English. qt. Free. Women's Concerns Division of Mission in Canada, 85 St Clair Avenue East, Toronto Ontario M4T 1M8 Canada. Tel (416)925-5931. Ed Deborah Marshall. DD 261.8344. bk rev. Circ 5,000. A resource of the United Church of Canada. It keeps women aware of issues which affect their lives and how they impact Christian growth and wholeness. Women's Concerns Newsletter, 0713-3693.

WORLD ENCOUNTER. V. 1- 1963-. 0043-8413. Periodical. US. English. qt. $6.00. Division of World Mission and Ecumenism, Lutheran Church in America, 2900 Queen Lane, Philadelphia PA 19129. Tel (215)438-6360. Ed James E Solheim. LC BX8048.2. bk rev. adv acc. Circ 5,500. As the mission magazine of the Lutheran Church in America and the American Lutheran Church, we deal with current international issues; religious, political and sociological. Foreign Missionary, 0362-5109.

WORLD IMPACT (NIAGARA FALLS, ONT.). (WORLD IMPACT). May/June 1978-. 0710-2275. Periodical. CN. English. qt. World Impact, c/o P Younggren, PO Box 823, Niagara Falls Ontario L2E 6V6 Canada. DD 269.20971. Jesus Revival.

WORLD ORDER. V. 1- Fall 1966-. 0043-8804. Periodical. US. English. qt. $26.00. World Order, 536 Sheridan Road, Wilmette IL 60091. Tel (312)869-9039. Ed Betty Fisher. Circ 4,000. Intended to stimulate, inspire, and serve thinking people in their search to find relationships between contemporary life and contemporary religious teachings and philosophy. World Order, 0043-8804.

WORLD PARISH. V. 1- Oct. 1962-. 0043-8839. Periodical. US. English. bm. World Methodist Council, Lake Junaluska NC 28745. LC BX8201. DD 287.05.

WORSHIP. V. 26- Dec. 1951-. 0043-941X. Periodical. US. English. bm. $17.00 Domestic, $18.00 Foreign. Liturgical Press, Saint Johns Abbey, Collegeville MN 56321. Tel (612)363-2213. Ed Aelred Tegels. Ind/Abst Old Testam. Abstr., New Testam. Abstr., Cathol. Period. Lit. Index, Relig. Index One, Period. LC BV175. bk rev. adv acc. Circ 7,000. A scholarly, ecumenical review exploring the structure of Christian worship and the problems of liturgical renewal. Orate Fratres, 0196-6898.

WORSHIP AND PREACHING. V. 1- 19(70)-. 0032-7407. Periodical. UK. English. bm. 1.25. Methodist Publishing House, Wellington Road, Wimbledon SW19 8EU England. Preacher's Quarterly, 0478-0264.

WORSHIP IN INDIA SERIES. No. 1-. Monographic Series. II. English. ir. 15.00. Books Today, 24-B5 Original Road, Karol Bagh New Delhi 110005 India. Tel 4721928. Ed B C Sinha. Circ 1,000. The work is a socio-religious study and studies human nature in India since the pre-Vedic period.

YEAR BOOK AND CLERICAL DIRECTORY. See Yearbooks, Almanacs, Directories.

YEAR BOOK AND PROCEEDINGS OF THE GENERAL ASSEMBLY - PRESBYTERIAN CHURCH OF NEW ZEALAND. See Yearbooks, Almanacs, Directories.

YEAR BOOK OF THE (COLLEGIATE). See Yearbooks, Almanacs, Directories.

YEAR BOOK - UNITED REFORMED CHURCH. See Yearbooks, Almanacs, Directories.

YEAR BOOK . . . (. . . YEAR OF ISSUE). See Yearbooks, Almanacs, Directories.

YEARBOOK. See Yearbooks, Almanacs, Directories.

YEARBOOK & DIRECTORY OF THE CHRISTIAN CHURCH (DISCIPLES OF CHRIST). See Yearbooks, Almanacs, Directories.

YEARBOOK AND MINUTES OF THE ANNUAL CONFERENCE - EVANGELICAL FREE CHURCH OF AMERICA. See Yearbooks, Almanacs, Directories.

YEARBOOK - INTER-MENNONITE CONFERENCE, ONTARIO. See Yearbooks, Almanacs, Directories.

THE YEARBOOK - NATIONAL ASSOCIATION OF CONGREGATIONAL CHRISTIAN CHURCHES. See Yearbooks, Almanacs, Directories.

YEARBOOK OF AMERICAN AND CANADIAN CHURCHES. See Yearbooks, Almanacs, Directories.

YEARBOOK OF JEHOVAH'S WITNESSES. See Yearbooks, Almanacs, Directories.

YEARBOOK - UNITED MENNONITE CHURCHES IN ONTARIO. MENNONITE CONFERENCE OF ONTARIO. WESTERN ONTARIO MENNONITE CONFERENCE CEASED. (YEARBOOK - UNITED MENNONITE CHURCHES IN ONTARIO, MENNONITE CONFERENCE OF ONTARIO, WESTERN ONTARIO MENNONITE CONFERENCE). Main/Corp Conference of the United Mennonite Churches of Ontario. Began with 1974 issue, Ceased with 1980 issue. 0319-0218. Periodical. CN. English. an. Mennonite Conference of Ontario, 87 Falesy Avenue, Kitchener Ontario N2A Canada. DD 289.7713.

YFC TODAY. See Children and Youth Interests.

YOUR CHURCH. V. 1- April/June 1955-. 0049-8394. Periodical. US. English. bm. $8.00. Religious Publishing Co, 198 Allendale Road, King of Prussia PA 19406. Tel (215)265-9400. Ed Phyllis Mather Rice. Ind/Abst Int. Index Multi Media Inf. LC BV652.A1. DD 254. bk rev. adv acc. Circ 188,000.

Religion, Mythology, Rationalism—Bible

(ctrl). To provide pastors with information about all aspects of their work including building and equipment, counseling, administration, personal finances and to present a variety of thought provoking articles. *Protestant Church Buildings and Equipment*, 0555-490X.

YOUTH FOR CHRIST KINGSTON. (YOUTH FOR CHRIST KINGSTON : NEWS). VFOAT KYFC News. VAT K.Y.F.C. News, Kingston Youth for Christ News. 0822-8345. Periodical. CN. English. bm. Free. Youth for Christ/Kingston, PO Box 2077, Kingston Ontario K7L 5J8 Canada. DD 267.610971372. (ctrl).

YOUTHLETTER. VFOAT Youth Letter. Vol. 6, No. 15 (Dec. 1975)-. Periodical. US. English. mo. $15.95. Subscriber Services, PO Box 611, Holmes PA 19043. Tel (215)546-3696. Ed James W Reapsome. bk rev. Circ 6,500. News, trends, reviews, and opinion to help church youth workers keep in touch with youth culture. *Youth Today (Philadelphia, PA)*.

YUKRANDA. Periodical. II. Hindi. ir. 12.00. Directorate of Employment and Training, 790 Wright Town, Madhya Pradesh India. LC BL1100.

Z BIBLIA NA CO DZIEN. Periodical. Polish. ir. 5.00. Zwiastun Wydawnictow Kosciola Ewang-Ausgab W Prl, Ul Miodowa 21, 00-246 Warszawa Poland 21. LC BV4509.P6.

ZEITSCHRIFT FUR DIE NEUTESTAMENTLICHE WISSENSCHAFT UND DIE KUNDE DER ALTEREN KIRCHE. Vol. 1-. 0044-2615. Periodical. German. ir. Walter de Gruyter and Company, 200 Saw Mill River Road, Hawthorne NY 10532. Tel (914)747-0110. Ind/Abst New Testam. Abstr., Relig. Index One, Period. LC BS410. (cum index).

ZEITSCHRIFT FUR MISSION. Periodical. GW. German. qt $9.74. Christliches Verlagshaus GMBH, Postfach 310349 Motorstr 36, D7000 Stuttgart 31 West Germany. Tel 0711/83000-51. bk rev. adv acc. Circ 1,300. (ctrl). Scientific, theological articles about Christian mission in the whole world, many writers of the Third World. Third World problems. *Evangelisches Missions-Magazin*, *Evangelische Missions-Zetischrift*.

ZEITSCHRIFT FUR RELIGIONS- UND GEISTESGESCHICHTE. Vol. 1-. 0044-3441. Periodical. German. qt. 96.00. E J Brill, Antwerpener Street 6-12, D-5000 Koeln 1 West Germany. Tel (221)516488. Ed Kurt Toepner. Ind/Abst Am. Hist. Life, Hist. Abstr., Part A, Mod. Hist. Abstr., Hist. Abst., Part B, Twent. Century Abstr., New Testam. Abstr., Philos. Index, Relig. Index One, Period., Hist. Abstr. LC BL4. bk rev. adv acc. Circ 550. Articles on comparative religion and the corpus of scientific knowledge and history of ideas.

ZEITSCHRIFT FUR SCHWEIZERISCHE KIRCHENGESCHICHTE. VFOAT Revue d'Histoire Ecclesiastique Suisse. Yearly Vol. 1-. 0044-3484. Periodical. SZ. German (French). sa. $17.32. Paulus Verlag, Perolles 42, 1700 Freiburg Switzerland. Tel 037 24 68 12. LC BR1030. bk rev. Circ 400. Articles on church history by emminent authors and book reviews.

ZNAK. V. 1- June 1946-. 0044-488X. Periodical. PL. Polish. mo. ARS Polona, Krakowskie Przedmiescie 7, 00-068 Warsaw Poland. LC AP54.

ZYGON. V. 1- Mar. 1966-. 0044-5614. Periodical. US. English. qt. Tel (305)656-2134. Ind/Abst Am. Hist. Life, Hist. Abstr., Part A, Mod. Hist. Abstr., Humanit. Index, Book Rev. Index, New Testam. Abstr., Old Testam. Abstr., Philos. Index, Psychol. Abstr., Relig. Index One, Period., Relig. Period. Lit. LC BL240.2. DD 215. Index in last issue of volume - attached. bk rev. adv acc. Circ 2,000.

ZYGON NEWSLETTER. V. 1- Oct. 1979-. 0882-7109. Periodical. US. English. qt. Zygon Newsletter, Rollins College, Winter Park FL 32789. Ind/Abst Relig. Index One, Period. DD 215.

BIBLE

ABHANDLUNGEN ZUR THEOLOGIE DES ALTEN UND NEUEN TESTAMENTS. Vol. 1-. Monographic Series. SZ. German. ir. Schweizer Buchzentrum, Postfach, CH-4501 Olten Switzerland. Tel 062/47 61 61.

ABR-NAHRAIN. VAT Abr -Nahrain. V. 1- 1959/60-. 0065-0382. NE. English. an. E J Brill, PO Box 9000, 2300 PA Leiden The Netherlands. Ind/Abst MLA Int. Bibliogr. Books Artic. Mod. Lang. Lit., Old Testam. Abstr. Aims to appeal to all university specialists in the fields of Arabic, Syriac and Hebrew, Semitic palaeography and linguistics, and archaeological and literary studies on biblical material.

ABSTRACTS (AMERICAN ACADEMY OF RELIGION AND SOCIETY OF BIBLICAL LITERATURE). See Indexes/Abstracts.

ADULT BIBLE STUDIES. 0149-8347. Periodical. US. English. qt. $7.00. Methodist Publ House, 201 8th Avenue South, Nashville TN 37203. Tel (615)749-8421. Ed Victor J Jacobs. Ind/Abst United Methodist Period. Index. bk review. Circ 700,000. A systematic study of the bible for adults designed to relate the authority, history, and relationship of its message to life.

ALTER ORIENT UND ALTES TESTAMENT. V. 1- 1969-. Monographic Series. GW. English or German. ir. Neukirchener Verlag, Postfach 216, D-4133 Neukirchen West Germany.

AMERICAN BIBLE SOCIETY RECORD. V. 115, No. 6- July/Aug. 1970-. 0006-0801. Periodical. US. English. mo. Free. American Bible Society, 1865 Broadway, New York NY 10023. Tel (212)581-7400. Ed Cliford P MacDonald. LC BV2370. DD 205. Circ 350,000. (ctrl). Stories and articles concerning the work and mission of the American Bible Society. *Bible Society Record*.

THE ANCHOR BIBLE. 1964-. Periodical. US. English. ir. Doubleday Company Inc, 501 Franklin Avenue, Garden City NY 11530.

ANNUAL OF THE JAPANESE BIBLICAL INSTITUTE. Main/Corp Nihon Seishogaku Kenkyujo. V. 1- 1975-. Periodical. JA. English (text in French and German). an. Japanese Biblical Institute, 3-10-20 Osawa Mitaka-shi, Tokyo Japan. Ind/Abst Old Testam. Abstr., New Testam. Abstr.

ANNUAL REPORT OF THE AMERICAN BIBLE SOCIETY. Main/Corp American Bible Society. 1st-. 0740-6401. US. English. an. American Bible Society, 1865 Broadway, New York NY 10029. LC BV2370. DD 266.06273.

AUSTRALIAN BIBLICAL REVIEW. V. 1- Mar./June 1951-. 0045-0308. Periodical. AT. English. an. Queens College, University of Melbourne, Parkville Victoria 3052 Australia. Ind/Abst Old Testam. Abstr., New Testam. Abstr., Relig. Index One, Period. LC BS410. DD 220.05.

THE AUSTRALIAN JOURNAL OF BIBLICAL ARCHAEOLOGY. V. 1- 1968-. 0084-747X. AT. English. an. University of Sydney, Sydney New South Wales 2006 Australia. LC BS620.A1. DD 220.9305.

BEITRAGE ZUR GESCHICHTE DER BIBLISCHEN HERMENEUTIK. 1- 1959-. 0522-6481. Monographic Series. GW. German. ir. JCB Mohr/Paul Siebeck, Postfach 2040, 7400 Tuebingen West Germany.

BIBBIA E ORIENTE. Yearly V. 1- Jan./Feb. 1959-. 0006-0585. Periodical. IT. Italian. qt. $40.00. Centro Studi Arti Grafiche, Sardini Editrice, 25040 Bornato BS Italy. Tel 030-725123. Ed Fausto Sardini. Ind/Abst Old Testam. Abstr., New Testam. Abstr., Relig. Theol. Abstr., Recent Publ. Artic. LC BS410.

BIBEL UND GEMEINDE. Began with Yearly V. 44, No. 3, 1954. 0006-0615. Periodical. GW. German. qt $15.00. Verlag Bibel und Gemeinde, Wiesenstr 27, D7517 Waldbronn 2 West Germany. Tel 07243/67231. Ed Bibelbund. bk rev. Circ 3,500. Encourages understanding of the Bible and the value of its authority publicizing scientific and general literature concerning inerrancy and absolute trustworthiness of scritpures etc.

BIBEL UND KIRCHE. VFOAT Jahrbuch. 1.- Yearly V. 0006-0623. Periodical. GW. German. qt. Verlag Kath Bibelwork GMBH, Silberburgstrabe 121A, D7000 Stuttgart 1 West Germany. Tel 0711 626001. Ind/Abst Old Testam. Abstr., New Testam. Abstr. bk rev. adv acc. *Katholisches Bibelwerk*.

BIBEL UND LITURGIE. Began with Vol. 1 in 1926. 0006-064X. Periodical. AU. German. qt. 272.-. Osterreichisches Katholisches Bibelwerk Stiftsplatz 8, A-3400 Klosterneuburg Austria. Tel (02243)2938. Ind/

Abst Old Testam. Abstr., New Testam. Abstr. bk rev Circ 1,200. (ctrl). Journal for Bible research, pastoral Bible studies, liturgical studies and practice.

BIBLE ADVENTURES. 0162-9220. US. English. qt $4.00. David C Cook Publishing Co, 850 North Grove Avenue, Elgin IL 60120.

BIBLE AND SPADE. Vol. 1, No. 1 (Winter 1972)-. 0162-9301. Periodical. US. English. qt. $8.00 US, $10.50 Foreign. Word of Truth Productions, Box 288, Ballston Spa NY 12020. LC BS620.A1. DD 220.93.

BIBLE BHASHYAM. Vol. 7, No. 1 (Mar. 1981)-. Periodical. II. English. qt $8.00. Bible Bhashyam, PO Box I Vadavathoor Kottayam, 686 010, Kerala India. Ed Mathew Vellanickal. Ind/Abst New Testam. Abstr., Old Testam. Abstr. bk rev. adv acc. Circ 1,850. Personalities, and themes in the Bible, with special emphasis on the relevance of the theme in Indian context. *Biblebhashyam*.

BIBLE BOOK STUDY FOR YOUTH TEACHERS. V. 1- Oct./Dec. 1978-. 0162-4830. Periodical. US. English. qt. $5.50. Sunday School Board of the Southern Baptist Convention, 127 Ninth Avenue North, Nashville TN 37234.

THE BIBLE COLLECTOR CEASED. 1st- 20th year (No. 1-80). 0006-0690. Periodical. US. English. qt. $5.00. International Society of Bible Collectors, PO Box 2485, El Cajon CA 92021. LC BS410. DD 220.

BIBLE DISCOVERERS. 0162-4695. Periodical. US. English. qt. $2.25. Sunday School Board of the Southern Baptist Convention, 127 Ninth Avenue North, Nashville TN 37234.

BIBLE DISCOVERERS TEACHER. 0162-4687. Periodical. US. English. qt. $4.50. Sunday School Board of the Southern Baptist Convention, 127 Ninth Avenue North, Nashville TN 37234.

BIBLE DISTRIBUTOR. ENGLISH. (THE BIBLE DISTRIBUTOR). 0256-9361. Periodical. US. English. ty. $9.00. United Bible Societies, 1865 Broadway, New York NY 10023.

BIBLE EXPOSITOR AND ILLUMINATOR. Periodical. US. English. qt. Union Gospel Press, Box 6059, Cleveland OH 44101. Tel (216)749-2100. Ed T T Musselman Jr.

BIBLE-IN-LIFE STORIES. 0162-9573. Periodical. US. English. qt. $3.50. David C Cook Publishing Co, 850 North Grove Avenue, Elgin IL 60120.

THE BIBLE NEWSLETTER. Vol. 1, No. 1 (Feb. 1981)-. 0279-8069. Periodical. US. English. mo. $15.95. Eternity Subscriber Services, PO Box 611, Holmes PA 19043. Tel (215)546-3696.

BIBLE REVIEW (WASHINGTON, D.C.). (BIBLE REVIEW). V. 1, No. 1 (Feb. 1985)-. 8755-6316. Periodical. US. English. qt. $15.00 US, $17.00 Foreign. Biblical Archaeology Society, PO Box 601, Holmes PA 19043. DD 220.

BIBLE SCIENCE NEWSLETTER. 0164-5587. Periodical. US. English. mo. $17.00. Bible Science Association, 2911 East 42nd Street, Minneapolis MN 55406. Tel (612)724-1883. Ed Paul A Bartz. bk rev. Circ 12,000. (ctrl). Practical articles, news, features and book reviews for the Christian dealing with all areas of Bible and science relationships.

BIBLE SEARCHERS : TEACHER. 0006-0798. Periodical. US. English. qt. $4.50. Sunday School Board of the Southern Baptist Convention, 127 Ninth Avenue North, Nashville TN 37234.

THE BIBLE TODAY. No. 1- Oct. 1962-. 0006-0836. Periodical. US. English. bm. $23.00. The Liturgical Press, St Johns Abbey, Collegeville MN 56321. Tel (612)363-2213. Ed Dianne Berfant. Ind/Abst Old Testam. Abstr., New Testam. Abstr., Cathol. Period. Lit. Index. bk rev. adv acc. Circ 12,000. Promoting, understanding and appreciating scripture for life and ministry, written especially for the non-specialist reader.

THE BIBLE TRANSLATOR. VFOAT Technical Papers for the Bible Translator. V. 1- 1950-. 0006-0844. Periodical. II. English. qt. $12.00. Bible Translator, Invicta Press, Ashford Kent England. Ind/Abst Relig. Index One, Period., Christ. Period. Index, New Testam. Abstr., Old Testam. Abstr. LC BS410. DD 220.05. (cum index).

BIBLIA REVUO. No. 1-8, 1964-66. 0006-0879. Periodical. IT. Esperanto. qt. Esperanto Language Service Company, 452 Apdine/Apartment 501,

Chicago IL 60657. **Ind/Abst** Old Testam. Abstr., New Testam. Abstr.

BIBLIA Y FE. 1 (Jan./April 1975)-. 0210-5209. Periodical. SP. Spanish. ty. $11.00. Biblia Y Fe, Fermin Caballero 53, Madrid 3 Spain. **Ind/Abst** Old Testam. Abstr.

BIBLICA. V. 1-. 0006-0887. Periodical. IT. English (articles in French, German, Italian, or Spanish). qt. $35.00. Pontificio Istituto Biblico, Piazzo Della Pilotta 35, 00187 Rome Italy. **Tel** 06 678 1567. **Ind/Abst** New Testam. Abstr., Old Testam. Abstr., Relig. Index One, Period., Index Relig. Period. Lit. **LC** BS410. **DD** 220.05. (cum index). bk rev.

THE BIBLICAL ARCHAEOLOGY REVIEW. *See* Archaeology.

BIBLICAL BULLETIN. 0749-9280. Periodical. US. English. bm. Free. Biblical Seminary, 200 North Main Street, Hatfield PA 19440. **DD** 207.

BIBLICAL RESEARCH. V. 1- 1956-. 0067-6535. Periodical. US. English. an. $4.20. Chicago Society of Biblical Research, 5555 South Woodlawn Avenue, Chicago IL 60637. **Tel** (312)241-7800. **Ed** Robert G Boling. **Ind/Abst** Old Testam. Abstr., New Testam. Abstr., Relig. Index One, Period. **LC** BS410. **DD** 220.05. **Circ** 500. (ctrl). Papers of the Chicago Society of Biblical Research, contributed by members of the society. History, literature and interpretation of documents: Old Testament, Intertestamental, and New Testament.

BIBLICAL RESEARCH MONTHLY. 1937. 0746-4525. Periodical. US. English. bm. $15.00. Biblical Research Society, 4005 Verdugo Road, Los Angeles CA 90065. **Tel** (213)257-8162. **Ed** Ronald L Cooper.

BIBLICAL SCHOLARSHIP IN NORTH AMERICA. 0277-0474. Monographic Series. US. English. Scholars Press, 101 Salem Street, Chico CA 95926.

BIBLICAL THEOLOGY BULLETIN. V. 1- Feb. 1971-. 0146-1079. Periodical. US. English. qt. $16.00. St Johns University, Department of Theology, Father White, Jamaica NY 11439. **Tel** (718)990-6161. **Ed** Leland J White and David M Bossman. **Ind/Abst** Old Testam. Abstr., New Testam. Abstr., Book Rev. Index, Relig. Index One, Period. **LC** BS410. **DD** 220.05. bk rev. adv acc. **Circ** 1,500. Articles and reviews by senior and new scholars edited for non-specialized readers interested in multi- disciplinary approaches to Bible and theology. 40% non-US subscribers. *Verbum Domini.*

BIBLICAL VIEWPOINT. V. 1- Apr. 1967-. 0006-0925. Periodical. US. English. sa. $3.50. Bob Jones University, Greenville SC 29614. **Tel** (803)242-5100. **Ed** Stewart Custer. **Ind/Abst** Christ. Period. Index. bk rev. **Circ** 2,000. A journal for the reverent exposition of the Bible, maintaining the view of a Bible-believing Christian.

BIBLICUM. Periodical. SW. Swedish. qt. 60. Biblicum-Tidskrift for Biblisk Kallparksgatan 10A, 32 Uppsala Sweden. **Tel** 018-10 69 25. **Ed** Seth Erlandsson. bk rev. Theological journal and a monograph series in Scandianvian and foreign languages; also book reviews.

BIBLISCH-THEOLOGISCHE STUDIEN. 1-. Monographic Series. GW. German. ir. Neukirchener Verlag Erzieh, Postfach 216, D4133 Neukirchen West Germany. *Biblische Studien.*

BIBLISCHE BEITRAGE. SZ. German. ir. Verlag Schweizerisches Katholishces Bibelwerk, Rue de l'Hopital 1, CH-1700 Fribourg Switzerland. **LC** BS413.

BIBLISCHE NOTIZEN. Issue 1- 1976-. Periodical. GW. German. ty. $11.97. Biblische Notezin, An der Universitat 2, D-8600 Bamberg West Germany. **Ed** Manfred Gorg. **Ind/Abst** Old Testam. Abstr., Relig. Index One, Period.

BIBLISCHE UNTERSUCHUNGEN. V. 1-. 0523-5154. Monographic Series. GW. German. ir. Verlag Friedrich Pustet, Gutengergstr 8/PF 11 04 41, 84 Regensburg 11 West Germany.

BIBLISCHE ZEITSCHRIFT. No. 1- Volume. Periodical. GW. German. sa. $23.46. Ferdinand Schoeningh Verlag, Postfach 2540 Juehenplatz-Rathaus, D-4790 Paderborn West Germany. **Tel** (05251)21322. **Ind/Abst** Relig. Index One, Period.

BULLETIN OF THE CANADIAN SOCIETY OF BIBLICAL STUDIES. **Main/Corp** Canadian Society of Biblical Studies. **VFOAT** Bulletin de la Societe Canadienne des Etudes Bibliques. Began publication 1935. 0068-970X. CN. English and French, 1970-. an. $11.61. St Thomas More College, 1437 College Drive, Saskatoon Saskatchewan S7N 0W6 Canada. **Tel** (306)343-4561. **DD** 220.07.

BULLETIN - UNITED BIBLE SOCIETIES. **Main/Corp** United Bible Societies. Began in 1950. 0041-719X. US. English. ir. $3.00. United Bible Societies, 1865 Broadway, New York NY 10023. **Tel** (212)581-7400. **LC** BV2370. **Circ** 200. Information on the work of the United Bible Societies throughout the world.

BURIED HISTORY. *See* Archaeology.

CAHIERS D'ARCHEOLOGIE BIBLIQUE. V. 1-17. 0575-0474. Monographic Series. FR. French. ir. J Gabalda et Cie Editeurs, 90 rue Bonaparte, 75006 Paris France.

CARIBBEAN CHALLENGE. Began in 1957. 0008-6436. Periodical. JM. English. mo. $6.00. Christian Literature Crusade Inc, Box 186/55 Church Street, Kingston Jamaica. **Tel** 922-7878. adv acc. **Circ** 22,500.

CHILDREN'S BIBLE STUDIES. ELEMENTARY B. STUDENT BOOK. **VFOAT** Elementary B. Student. Vol. 1, No. 1 (Fall 1982)-. 0278-3746. Periodical. US. English. qt. $5.50. Graded Press, PO Box 801, Nashville TN 37202. *Middle Elementary Student, 0149-774X.*

CHILDREN'S BIBLE STUDY. AGES 3-4, TEACHER. (CHILDREN'S BIBLE STUDY. AGES 3-4. TEACHER). **VFOAT** Ages 3-4. Teacher. Vol. 1, No. 1 (Fall 1982)-. 0276-346X. Periodical. US. English. qt. Graded Press, 201 8th Avenue South, Nashville TN 37202. *Nursery 3-4 Guidebook, 0160-399X.*

CHILDREN'S BIBLE STUDY. AGES 4-6, TEACHER. (CHILDREN'S BIBLE STUDY. AGES 4-6. TEACHER). **VFOAT** Ages 4-6 Teacher. Vol. 1, No. 1 (Fall 1982)-. 0276-3451. Periodical. US. English. qt. Graded Press, PO Box 801, Nashville TN 37202. *Step by Step, 0160-4023.*

CHRISTIAN SCIENCE QUARTERLY. BIBLE LESSONS. V. 1- Jan./March 1890-. 0145-7365. Periodical. US. English. qt. $3.25. Christian Science Publishing Society, 1 Norway Street, Boston MA 02115. **LC** BX6901. **DD** 289.505. Also available in braille and phonodisc editions with the title: Christian Science Bible Lessons.

CHRISTIAN STANDARD. V. 1- April 7, 1866-. 0009-5656. Periodical. US. English. wk. $13.00. Christian Standard, 8121 Hamilton Avenue, Cincinnati OH 45231. **Tel** (513)931-4050. **Ed** Sam E Stone. **Ind/Abst** Guide Soc. Sci. Relig. Period. Lit. bk rev. **Circ** 75,000. Weekly journal of essays, news, and inspirational material. Devoted to the restoration of New Testament Christianity.

CLAIRON. (LE CLAIRON). 0710-099X. Periodical. CN. French. ir. Publications GBU, Bureau 601, 455 Ouest rue St-Antoine, Montreal Quebec H2Z 1J1 Canada. **DD** 220.060714.

COME AND SEE. V. 1- Aug. 1974-. 0316-3040. Periodical. CN. English. bm. Free. Nathanael Literature Distributors, 64 Hills Road, Ajax Ontario L1S 2W4 Canada. **DD** 220.605.

COMPREHENSIVE BIBLE STUDY. 0162-962X. Periodical. US. English. qt. $4.25. David C Cook Publishing Co, 850 North Grove Avenue, Elgin IL 60120.

CULTURA BIBLICA. V. 1- (No. 1-). Periodical. SP. Spanish. ty. Cultura Biblica, Julian Gayarre 1, Madrid Spain 7.

THE DAWN : A HERALD OF CHRIST'S PRESSENCE. Periodical. US. English. mo. Dawn Bible Students Association, 199 Railroad Avenue, East Rutherford NJ 07073.

DICTIONNAIRE DE LA BIBLE. SUPPLEMENT. **VFOAT** Supplement au Dictionnaire de la Bible. V. 1-. FR. French. ir. Letouzey et Ane, 87 BD Raspail, 75006 Paris France.

DISCOVER THE BIBLE. 1964. 0018-912X. Periodical. CN. English. wk. $13.35. Bible Center, 2065 Sherbrooke Street West, Montreal Quebec H3H 1G6 Canada. **Tel** (514)933-7311. **Ed** Walter Bedard. (ctrl).

DOSSIERS POUR L'ANIMATION BIBLIQUE. Monographic Series. FR. French. ir. Editions du Centurion, 17 rue de Babylone, 75007 Paris France.

ESTUDIOS BIBLICOS. Began publication with Nov. 29 issue. 0014-1437. Periodical. SP. Spanish. qt. Consejo Super Invest Cientific, Vitruvio 8, Apartado 14 458, 28006 Madrid Spain. **Ind/Abst** Old Testam. Abstr., New Testam. Abstr., Relig. Index One, Period. **LC** BS410. **DD** 220.02.

ETOILE DU MATIN. (L'ETOILE DU MATIN). No. 1 Sept. 1980-. 0712-2667. Periodical. CN. French. ir. Free. Etoile du Matin, CP 564, Gatineau Quebec J8P 7A2 Canada. **DD** 220.05.

EXEGETICAL RESOURCE. 0744-0448. Periodical. US. English. qt. $10.80. Pulpit Resource Inc, 121 Maono Place, Honolulu HI 96821. **Tel** (808)373-4410. **Ed** Glendon E Harris. **DD** 251. **Circ** 2,000. (ctrl). Interpretive help on Bible developed from variant readings and ancient texts. *Pulpit Resource. Supplement, 0274-6344.*

EXPLORING THE BIBLE. AGES 8-12. PACKET. **VAT** Exploring the Bible. Ages Eight to Twelve. Packet. 0149-8584. US. English. an. $5.95. Graded Press, United Methodist Publishing House, 201-8th Avenue South, Nashville TN 37202.

THE EXPOSITORY TIMES. V. 1- Oct. 1889-. 0014-5246. Periodical. UK. English. mo. 15.24. T & T Clark Ltd, 59 George Street, Edinburgh EH2 2LQ Scotland. **Tel** 031-225-4703. **Ed** Cyril Rodd. **Ind/Abst** New Testam. Abstr., Old Testam. Abstr., Relig. Index One, Period. **LC** BS410. (cum index). bk rev. adv acc. **Circ** 7,000. Continues to be one of the most popular periodicals for ministers and laymen world-wide who wish to keep informed of recent biblical and theological studies.

FACET BOOKS. BIBLICAL SERIES. No. 1- 1963-. 0071-3597. US. English. ir. Fortress Press, 2900 Queen Lane, Philadelphia PA 19129.

FEUILLET BIBLIQUE. (LE FEUILLET BIBLIQUE). No. 849- 3 Sept., 1978-. 0225-2112. Periodical. CN. French. ir. $22.44. Archdiocese of Montreal, 2065 rue Sherbrooke West, Montreal Province of Quebec H3H 1G6 Canada. **Tel** (514)931-7311. **Ed** Paul A Martin. **DD** 220.05. **Circ** 12,500. A lucid presentation of each Sunday's three Biblical readings. *Parole Dimanche, 0225-2120.*

FORSCHUNGEN ZUR RELIGION UND LITERATUR DES ALTEN UND NEUEN TESTAMENTS. Vol. 1 Issue. Monographic Series. GW. German. ir. Vandenhoeck & Ruprecht, Postfach 3753 Theaterstr 13, D-3400 Goettingen West Germany. **Tel** (0551)65061. adv acc.

THE GIDEON. Began with V. 3, No. 3, 1903. Periodical. US. English. mo. $3.50. Gideons International, 2900 Lebanon Road, Nashville TN 37214. *Gideon Quarterly.*

GOD'S REVIVALIST AND BIBLE ADVOCATE. (GOD'S REVIVALIST AND BIBLE ADVOCATE : PUBLICATION OF GOD'S BIBLE SCHOOL). **VFOAT** God's Revivalist. 1888. 0745-0788. Periodical. US. English. sm. $4.50. Gods Revivalist and Bible Advocate, 1810 Young Street, Cincinnati OH 45210. **Tel** (513)721-7944. **Ed** Hubert Hotchkiss. bk rev. **Circ** 21,000. (ctrl). Articles pertaining to Christian growth, revival in the church, and the interests and happenings of God's Bible School.

GOD'S WORD TODAY. V. 1- Oct. 1979-. 0199-3429. Periodical. US. English. mo. $10.00. God's Word Today, PO Box 7705, Ann Arbor MI 48107. **Tel** (313)761-8505. **Ed** George Martin. bk rev. **Circ** 90,000. A guide to Bible reading for Catholics.

GRACE SEMINARY SPIRE. **Main/Corp** Grace Theological Seminary, Winona Lake, Indiana. 1974. Periodical. US. English. qt. Grace Theological Seminary, 200 Seminary Drive, Winona Lake IN 46590. **Tel** (219)267-8191. **Ed** Gerald H Twombly. **Circ** 6,000. Brief articles on themes relating to biblical interpretation, ethical issues, answers to alumni questions and alumni news items.

GUIDE TO BIBLES IN PRINT. *See* Bibliographies.

HA-ALON HA-ONATI - NEOT QEDUMIM. (HA-ALON HA-ONATI - NEOT KEDUMIM). **Main/Corp** Neot Kedumim Ltd. No. 1/2, 1966-. Hebrew. ir. Neot Kedwmin Ltd, PO Box 299, Kiryat Ono Israel. **LC** BS660.

HANDBUCH ZUM NEUEN TESTAMENT. Monographic Series. GW. German. ir. JCB Mohr/Paul Siebeck, Postfach 2040, 7400 Tuebingen West Germany.

HARVARD SEMITIC SERIES. 0073-0645. Monographic Series. US. English. ir. Scholars Press, PO Box 1608, Decatur GA 30029. **Tel** (404)329-6950. **Ed** Frank M Cross Jr. Biblical criticism and research.

HENOCH. V. 1, Issue 1 (Mar. 1979)-. Periodical. IT. Italian. ty. $18.00. Marietti Editori, Via Adam 15, 1-15033 Casale Monferrato, Torino Italy. **Ind/Abst** Old Testam. Abstr., New Testam. Abstr. **LC** BS410.

Religion, Mythology, Rationalism—Bible

HERMENEIA; A CRITICAL AND HISTORICAL COMMENTARY ON THE BIBLE. US. English. ir. Fortress Press, 2900 Queen Lane, Philadelphia PA 19129. Tel (215)848-6800.

HOKHMAH. VFOAT Hokhma. No. 1-. Periodical. SZ. French. ty. 13.50. Hokhma, Case Postale 48, 1315 La Sarraz Switzerland. Tel (021)87 70 17. Ed Michel Kocher. Ind/Abst New Testam. Abstr. LC BR3. DD 230.05. Circ 1,300. Articles written by professors, pastors and students, try to approach the Bible unbiased and to relate it to the church and the world of today.

HORIZONS IN BIBLICAL THEOLOGY. V. 1- 1979-. 0195-9085. Periodical. US. English. sa. $15.00. Pittsburg Theological Seminary, 616 North Highland Avenue, Pittsburgh PA 15206. Tel (412)362-5610. Ed Ulrich Mauser. Ind/Abst Old Testam. Abstr., New Testam. Abstr., Relig. Index One, Period. LC BS543.A1. DD 230. bk rev. adv acc. Circ 800. Dialogue between old and new testament theologies and scholarly work aimed at the achievement of canonical interpretation of scripture.

IN OTHER WORDS. Vol. 1- Feb. 1975-. 0279-3172. Periodical. US. English. ir. Wycliffe Bible Translators, 19891 Beach Boulevard, Huntington Beach CA 92647. *Translation.*

INTERNATIONALE ZEITSCHRIFTENSCHAU FUR BIBELWISSENSCHAFT UND GRENZGEBIETE. VFOAT International Review of Biblical Studies, Revue Internationale des Etudes Bibliques. 1951/52-. 0074-9745. GW. Multilingual (German, English, and French). an. $64.12. FB1 Warburgerstr 100, D-4790 Paderborn West Germany. LC Z7770. Annual volume with CA 3,000 abstracts and reviews of all materials relevant to biblical studies. There are sections on religion in general, middle eastern archaeology, and theology.

JOURNAL FOR THE STUDY OF THE NEW TESTAMENT. VFOAT J.S.N.T. Issue 1 (Oct. 1978)-. 0142-064X. Periodical. UK. English. ty. $44.00. JSOT Press, University of Sheffield, Department of Biblical Studies, Sheffield S10 2TN England. Tel 0742 78555. Ed D Hill. Ind/Abst New Testam. Abstr., Relig. Index One, Period. LC BS410. DD 225.05. bk rev. adv acc. Circ 850. Critical scholarship in new testament studies.

JOURNAL FOR THE STUDY OF THE OLD TESTAMENT. Issue 1- Dec. 1976-. 0309-0892. Periodical. UK. English. ty. $44.00. JSOT Press/University of Sheffield, Department of Biblical Studies, Sheffield S10 2TN England. Tel 0742-78555. Ed D J A Clines and P R Davies. Ind/Abst Old Testam. Abstr., New Testam. Abstr., Relig. Index One, Period. LC BS410. DD 221.05. bk rev. adv acc. Circ 1,200. Critical scholarship in old testament studies.

JOURNAL OF BIBLICAL LITERATURE. V. 9- 1890-. 0021-9231. Periodical. US. English. qt. Scholars Press, PO Box 1608, Decatur GA 30031. Tel (404)329-6950. Ind/Abst Old Testam. Abstr., New Testam. Abstr., Book Rev. Index, Ref. Source, Humanit. Index, Relig. Index One, Period., Recent Publ. Artic. LC BS410. DD 220.05. (cum index). *Journal of the Society of Biblical Literature and Exegisis.*

THE JOURNAL OF PASTORAL PRACTICE. V. 1-. 0196-9072. Periodical. US. English. ir. $16.00. Christian Counseling and Education Foundation, 1790 East Willow Grove Avenue, Laverock PA 19118. Tel (215)884-7676. Ed Jay E Adams. bk rev. Circ 625. (ctrl). Biblical insights and methods dealing with the counseling of troubled people, for pastors and lay people alike.

JOY. VFOAT Canadian Home Bible League Newsletter. Jan./Feb. 1979-. 0228-8109. Periodical. CN. English. bm. Free. Joy, PO Box 524/Station A, Weston Ontario M9N 3N3 Canada. DD 220.7.

KEYNOTES. July/Sept. 1971-. 0315-2006. CN. English. qt. $8.00. Scripture Union, PO Box 452, Upper Darby PA 19082. Tel (215)352-5400. Ed C L Swanson. Ind/Abst Music Index. Circ 2,500. Commentary for young teens relating bible teaching to life situations via reflection and prayer.

KRISTEN VIDENSKABS KVARTALSHEFTE. BIBELSTUDIER. VFOAT Christian Science Quarterly. Bible Lessons. 0145-739X. Periodical. US. Danish (parallel text in English). qt. $3.25. Christian Science Publishing Society, 1 Norway Street, Boston MA 02115.

KRISTEN VITENSKAPS KVARTALSHEFTE. BIBELSTUDIER. VFOAT Christian Science Quarterly. Bible Lessons. 0145-7381. Periodical. US. English. qt. $3.25. Christian Science Publishing Society, 1 Norway Street, Boston MA 02115.

LA FOI ET LA VIE. (FOI ET VIE). Began in 1898. 0015-5357. Periodical. FR. French. ir. 160. Foi et Vie, 139 Boulevard Montparnasse, Paris 75006 France. Tel (1)42.22.15.99. Ed Jacques Ellul. Ind/Abst New Testam. Abstr., Relig. Index One, Period. bk rev. (ctrl). Covers Jewish studies, spiritual life, commemoration of the revocation of the Edit de Nantes, Bible studies on Paul, etc.

LECCIONES BIBLICAS. 0731-275X. US. Spanish. qt. $2.00. The Sunday School Board of SBC, 127 Ninth Avenue North, Nashville TN 37234.

LIVING WORD. (THE LIVING WORD). 0229-5261. Periodical. CN. English. ir. Free. Living Word Bible Institute, PO Box 969, Swan River Manitoba R0L 1Z0 Canada. DD 269.2.

LIVRETE TRIMESTRAL DA CIENCIA CRISTA. LICOES BIBLICAS. VFOAT Christian Science Quarterly. Bible Lessons. 0145-7454. Periodical. US. English. qt. $3.25. Christian Science Publishing Society, 1 Norway Street, Boston MA 02115.

MEGIDDO MESSAGE; DEVOTED TO THE CAUSE OF CHRIST. 1914. 0194-7826. Periodical. US. English. mo. $2.00. Megiddo Church, 481 Thurston Road, Rochester NY 14619. Tel (716)436-4050. Ed K E Flowerday. bk rev. Circ 8,000. (ctrl). Encouraging Bible teaching/ application, promoting inspirational and moral principles. Not affiliated with any other group. Upholds faith in God, Christ and the Bible.

MEMBER'S HANDBOOK. Main/Corp Society of Biblical Literature. US. English. ir. Scholars Press, PO Box 2268, Chico CA 95927. LC BS411. DD 220.0601.

MENDY AND THE GOLEM. Vol. 1, No. 1 (Elul 5741 1981). 0278-4432. Periodical. US. English. bm. $5.00. Mendy Enterprises, 450 7th Avenue, New York NY 10001. Tel (212)410-1155. Ed Yankel Pinson. adv acc. Circ 30,000. (ctrl). 32 pages of fun and excitement in a comic format making stories of the Bible fun, and relating them to people of all ages.

MISSIONARY MESSENGER. 0227-4949. Periodical. CN. English. ir. Free. J Bailey, 774 Elgin Street, Newmarket Ontario L3Y 3B8 Canada. DD 220.605. (ctrl).

LE MONDE DE LA BIBLE. 1- Nov./Dec. 1977-. 0154-9049. Periodical. FR. French. ir. $28.20. Bayard Presse, 3 rue Bayard, 75393 Paris Cedex 08 France. Tel 562 51 51. Ind/Abst Old Testam. Abstr. *Bible et Terre Sainte.*

MONOGRAPH SERIES - SOCIETY FOR OLD TESTAMENT STUDY. Main/Corp Society for Old Testament Study. Vol. 1 1971-. Monographic Series. UK. English. ir. Cambridge University Press, Edinburgh Building Shaftesbury Road, Cambridge CB2 2RM England.

NEUTESTAMENTLICHE ABHANDLUNGEN. Vol. 1- 1908. Monographic Series. GW. German. ir. Aschendorffsche Verlagsbuchhan Dlung, Postfach 1124, 4400 Muenster West Germany. Tel 251/6901. Ed Joachim Gnilka. Monograph volumes of commentaries to the New Testament.

NEW DIRECTION (TORONTO, ONT.). (NEW DIRECTION). Oct. 1979-. 0712-8096. Periodical. CN. English. bm. $5.00. New Direction, c/o 100 Huntley Street, Toronto Ontario M4Y 2L1 Canada. DD 220.05.

NEW DISCIPLES. MEDIA KIT. Series/Titl Youth Bible Studies. VAT New Disciples. Media Kit. Fall 1982-. 0739-3598. Periodical. US. English. qt. $5.95. Graded Press, 201 8th Avenue South, PO Box 801, Nashville TN 37202.

NEW TESTAMENT ABSTRACTS. See Indexes/Abstracts.

NEW TESTAMENT STUDIES. V. 1- Sept. 1954-. 0028-6885. Periodical. UK. English (French and German). qt. $69.00. Cambridge University Press, 510 North Avenue, New Rochelle NY 10801. Ed G N Stanton. Ind/Abst New Testam. Abstr., Recent Publ. Artic., Humanit. Index, Relig. Index One, Period. LC BS410. DD 225.05. Covers all aspects of the text and theology of the new testament. *Bulletin of the Studiorum Novi Testamenti Societas.*

NEW TESTAMENT TOOLS AND STUDIES. 0077-8842. Monographic Series. NE. English. ir. E J Brill, POB 9000, 2300 PA Leiden The Netherlands.

NOTES ON SCRIPTURE IN USE. VFOAT N.O.S. Began in 1981. 0737-2876. Periodical. US. English. qt. $6.00 Domestic, $7.00 Foreign. Dallas Center Bookstore Summer Institute of Linguistics Inc, 7500 West Camp Wisdom Road, Dallas TX 75236. Tel (214)298-3331. Ed Thomas Crowell. bk rev. adv acc. Occasional journal devoted to discussion of issues relating to promotion of scriptures in vernacular languages among native speakers of these languages.

NOTES ON TRANSLATION. 0734-0788. Periodical. US. English. qt. $1.00. Summer Institute of Linguistic, 7500 West Camp Wisdom Road, Dallas TX 75236. Tel (214)298-3331. Ind/Abst MLA Int. Bibliogr. Books Artic. Mod. Lang. Lit. LC BS449. DD 220.4. (cum index). Issued also on microfiche. A publication of the Wycliffe Bible Translators, with theoretical and practical articles on Bible translation and related topics.

NOUVELLES BIBLIQUES. Yearly V. 1, No. 1- Sept. 1976-. 0225-0489. Periodical. CN. French. qt. Free. Societe Biblique Candienne, Bureau 200/1450 Av Union, Montreal Quebec H3A 2B8 Canada. DD 220.06071.

NOVUM TESTAMENTUM. V. 1- Jan. 1956-. 0048-1009. Periodical. NE. English (French and German). qt. E J Brill, PO Box 9000, 2300 PA Leiden The Netherlands. Ind/Abst New Testam. Abstr., Relig. Index One, Period. LC BS410. DD 225.05. (cum index).

OLD TESTAMENT ABSTRACTS. See Indexes/Abstracts.

OLD TESTAMENT ESSAYS. Vol. 1 (1983)-. English (German). an. 6.00. Editor, Old Testament Essays, Department of Old Testament UNISA, PO Box 392, 0001 Pretoria Republic of South Africa. Tel 27 12 440-1940/1365. Ed J J Burden. Ind/Abst Old Testam. Abstr. Circ 500. Scholarly reports on research into the old testament.

ORIGINS. V. 1- 1974-. 0093-7495. Periodical. US. English. sa. $4.00. Geoscience Research Institute, Loma Linda University, Loma Linda CA 92350. Tel (714)824-4548. Ed Ariel A Roth. Ind/Abst GeoRef, Bibliogr. Index Geol. LC BS651. DD 213.05. CODEN ORIGD. bk rev. Circ 2,000. Publishes articles dealing with the broad question of origins, especially interpretations of science and the Bible.

OUDTESTAMENTLICHE STUDIEN. 0169-7226. Periodical. NE. Dutch (English, French, and German). ir. E J Brill, POB 9000, 2300 PA Leiden The Netherlands. Tel 071-312624. Ed A S Van Der Woude. Ind/Abst Old Testam. Abstr. Old testament studies, mainly by Dutch scholars. Both, monographs and collective volumes.

PAIN DE VIE. V. 1, No. 1 (July 1978)-. 0228-7072. Periodical. CN. French. mo. Free. Pain de Vie, CP 723, St-Hyacinthe Quebec J2S 7P5 Canada. DD 220.05.

PARABOLE. V. 1- Oct. 1978-. 0709-0056. Periodical. CN. French. bm. Parabole, 212 Boulevard St Joseph Quest, Montreal Quebec H2T 2P8 Canada. Tel (514)274-4381. DD 220.05. *Bulletin Biblique, 0709-0048.*

PARTAGE (MONTREAL, QUEBEC). (PARTAGE). 2 (April/May/June 1984)-. 0824-1821. Periodical. CN. French. qt. 7.00. Ligue pour la Lecture de la Bible, 1701 rue Belleville, Ville Lemoyne Province of Quebec J4P 3M2 Canada. Tel (514)465-0445. DD 220.605. Circ 6,000. Bible readings adapted to life every day. *Pain du Jour, 0704-187X.*

PRIMARY ONE. Vol. 19, No. 1 (Sept., Oct., Nov. 1981)-. 0273-5148. Periodical. US. English. qt. Gospel Publishing House, 1445 Boonville Avenue, Springfield MO 65802. *Bible Stories One, 0190-4256.*

PROCEEDINGS OF THE IRISH BIBLICAL ASSOCIATION. Main/Corp Irish Biblical Association. No. 1 (1976)-. 0332-4427. IE. English. an. 7.00. Trinity College, Irish Biblical Association, c/o Dublin Ireland. Tel (01)772941. Ed A D H Mayes. Ind/Abst Old Testam. Abstr., New Testam. Abstr. LC UNC. DD 220.05. Circ 200. Biblical, theological and ancient historical essays. Studies.

PSEUDEPIGRAPHA VETERIS TESTAMENTI GRAECE. Monographic Series. English. ir. E J Brill, POB 9000, 2300 PA Leiden The Netherlands.

THE REFORMATION REVIEW. V. 1- Oct. 1953-. 0034-303X. Periodical. US. English. ir. $10.00. International Council of Christian Churches, 756 Haddon Avenue, Collingswood NJ 08108. Tel

Religion, Mythology, Rationalism—Buddhism

(609)858-0700. Ed Dr. J.C. Maris and Dr. William LeRoy. bk rev. **Circ** 300. Scholarly presentation of some of the finest fundamental Biblical messages and exegesis of our day taken mainly from essays ICCC affiliated publications and conferences.

RESEARCHER. (THE RESEARCHER). V. 1- Spring 1971-. 0225-3798. Periodical. CN. English. qt. $2.00. Bible Lovers Fellowship, PO Box 232, Sudbury Ontario P3E 4N5 Canada. Ed J R Boyd. **DD** 220.1505.

REVISTA BIBLICA. Yr. 1- (No. 1-). 0034-7078. Periodical. AG. Spanish. ir. $16.00. Revista Biblica, Casilla Postal 33, 1425 Buenos Aires Argentina. Ed Eduardo Birezychudek. **Ind/Abst** Relig. Index One, Period., New Testam. Abstr. bk rev. **Circ** 500. Biblical exegesis, theology and hermeneutical studies in an ecumenical fashion by Catholic and Protestant scholars.

REVUE BIBLIQUE. VFOAT Vivre et Penser. V. 24-. 0035-0907. Periodical. FR. French. qt. 730. J Gabalda, CIE Editeurs, rue Bonaparte 90, 75006 Paris France. **Tel** 43-26-53-55. **Ind/Abst** New Testam. Abstr., Old Testam. Abstr., Relig. Index One, Period. **LC** BS410. **DD** 220.05. bk rev. *Revue Biblique Internationale.*

RICERCHE BIBLICHE E RELIGIOSE. Yearly V. 1- 1966-. 0035-502X. Periodical. IT. Italian. qt. $12.00. Facolta Biblica, Via del Bollo 5, 20123 Milano Italy. **Ind/Abst** New Testam. Abstr.

RIVISTA BIBLICA. Year 1- 1953-. Periodical. AG. some articles in English or French. qt. $16.00. Revista Biblica, Casilla Postal 33, 1425 Buenos Aires Argentina. Ed Eduardo Bierzychudek. bk rev. **Circ** 500. Biblical exegesis, theology, and hermeneutic studies in an ecumenical fashion by Catholic and Protestant scholars.

RIVISTA BIBLICA. Vol. 5- Jan./Mar. 1957-. 0035-5798. Periodical. IT. Italian (English and French). ir. 25,000.00 Domestic, 35,000.00 Foreign. Centro Dehoniano, Via Nosadella 6, 40123 Bologna Italy. **Tel** (51)330301. Ed Alfio Filippi. **Ind/Abst** New Testam. Abstr. Index in last issue of volume - attached. Publication of the Italian Bible Association. Promotes understanding of the Holy Scriptures; scientific research and disclosure of the Word of God; contains articles, bibliographical notes, and notices. *Rivista Biblica Italiana.*

SCHOOLS AND SCHOLARS. Series/Titl Studies in American Biblical Scholarship. 0147-9318. Monographic Series. US. English. Scholars Press, University of Montana, Missoula MT 59801. **LC** UNC.

SCRIPTURA. No. 1 (July 1980)-. Periodical. Afrikaans (English). qt. $4.63. Scriptura, Department of Biblical Studies, University of Stellenbosch, 7600 Stellenbosch South America. **Tel** 02231/ 71140.

SCRIPTURE BULLETIN. V. 1- Jan./Mar. 1969-. 0036-9780. Periodical. UK. English. sa. $10.00. Catholic Bible Association of Great Britain, 1 Malcolm Road, Frank O'Reilly, London SW19 AS England. Ed M Prior. **Ind/Abst** Old Testam. Abstr., Cathol. Period. Lit. Index. **LC** BS410. **DD** 220.05. bk rev. adv acc. **Circ** 550. Biblical comment, criticism and reviews. *Scripture.*

SCRIPTURE COMES ALIVE. 0747-0207. Periodical. US. English. qt. $40.00. Oil Publishing Company, PO Box 400, Green Bay WI 54305. *Fr. McBride Homily Service, 0274-550X.*

SEISHOGAKU RONSHU. Began in 1962. JA. Japanese. an. 2000. Yamamoto Shoten, 23 Ichigaya Honmura-cho Shinjuku-ku, Tokyo Japan. **LC** BS410.

SEMEIA. 1- 1974-. 0095-571X. Periodical. US. English. qt. $35.00. Scholars Press, PO Box 1608, Decatur GA 30031. **Tel** (404)329-6950. **Ind/Abst** Old Testam. Abstr., New Testam. Abstr., Relig. Index One, Period. **LC** BS410. **DD** 220.605.

SEMENCE. (LA SEMENCE). 0228-670X. Periodical. CN. French. qt. Free. La Semence, 230 rue Lupien, Cap-de-la-Madeleine Quebec G8T 6W4 Canada. **DD** 220.05.

SHARE THE WORD. V. 1- Lent 1980-. 0199-5049. Periodical. US. English. bm. Free. Share the Word, 3031 4th Street NE, Washington DC 20017. **Tel** (202)832-5022. Ed Ann Cormier. **Circ** 200,000. (ctrl). Home bible study guide that follows the Sunday Liturgical readings.

SHARING THE VICTORY. (SHARING THE VICTORY : PUBLICATION OF THE FELLOWSHIP OF CHRISTIAN ATHLETES). Vol. 1, No. 1 (Sept./Oct. 1982)-. 0745-1245. Periodical. US. English. bm. $9.00. Fellowship of Christian Athletes, 8701 Leeds Road, Kansas City MO 64129. **Tel** (816)921-0909. Ed Skip Stogsdill. bk rev. **Circ** 50,000. Presents to athletes and coaches, and all whom they influence, the challenge and adventure of receiving Jesus Christ as Savior and Lord. *Christian Athlete, 0744-0227 Widening Circle.*

SHENATON LE-MIKRA ULE-HEKER HA-MIZRAH HA-KADUM. 1- 736- 1975-. Hebrew (summaries in English). ir. Hotsaat Tanakh Yistael, Rehov Hasharon 12 Tel-Aviv, Yerushalayim Israel. **LC** BS410.

SHORE LINES. Vol. 1, No. 1 (Nov./Dec.) 1982-. 0745-4430. Periodical. US. English. qt. Gulf Shore Bible Institute, PO Box 2522, Fort Myers FL 33902.

SOCIETY OF BIBLICAL LITERATURE DISSERTATION SERIES. (DISSERTATION SERIES (SOCIETY OF BIBLICAL LITERATURE)). VFOAT SBL Dissertation Series. No. 1-. 0145-2770. Monographic Series. US. English. ir. Scholars Press, PO Box 1608, Decatur GA 30029. **Tel** (404)329-6950. Ed C Talbert and J Roberts. Dissertations of scholars of the old or new testaments of the Bible.

SOCIETY OF BIBLICAL LITERATURE MONOGRAPH SERIES. 15-. 0145-269X. Monographic Series. US. English. ir. Scholars Press, PO Box 1608, Decatur GA 30029. **Tel** (404)329-6950. Ed Adela Yarbro Collins. **LC** UNC. A series of scholarly texts in which the Bible is examined from diverse perspectives: historical, philosophical, text-critical, etc. *Journal of Biblical Literature. Monograph Series.*

SOCIETY OF BIBLICAL LITERATURE SEMINAR PAPERS. 1973-. 0145-2711. US. English. an. Scholars Press, PO Box 1608, Decatur GA 30029. **Tel** (404)329-6950. Ed Kent Richards. **Ind/Abst** Relig. Index One, Period. **LC** BS410. **DD** 220.6. A yearly publication of the papers presented at the annual AAR/SBL meeting. *Book of Seminar Papers, 0160-631X.*

STUDIA POHL; SERIES MAIOR. 1- 1969-. Monographic Series. English. ir. Biblical Institute Presss, Piazza Della Pilotta 35, 00187 Rome Italy.

STUDIEN ZUM NEUEN TESTAMENT. Vol. 1- 1969-. Monographic Series. GW. German. ir. Guetersloher Verlagshaus, Postfach 2368 Koenigstrasse 23, 4830 Guetersloh 1 West Germany. **Tel** 05241/8620. Ed Gunter Klein, Willi Marxsen and Wolfgang Schrage. Monograph series on studies of the New Testament.

STUDIES IN AMERICAN BIBLICAL SCHOLARSHIP. 0147-930X. Monographic Series. US. English. ir. Scholars Press, University of Montana, Missoula MT 59801. **LC** UNC.

STUDIES IN THE BIBLE AND EARLY CHRISTIANITY. Vol. 1-. Monographic Series. US. English. Mellen Press, PO Box 450, Lewiston NY 14092.

STUTTGARTER BIBELSTUDIEN. 1-. 0585-7961. Monographic Series. GW. German. ir. Verlag Katholisches Bibelwerk Silberburgstr 121A, D7000 Stuttgart 1 West Germany.

SYMPOSIUM ON CREATION. 1- 1968-. 0090-1954. US. English. Baker Book House, Box 6287, Grand Rapids MI 49506. **LC** BS651. **DD** 220.85.

TEXTUS; ANNUAL OF THE HEBREW UNIVERSITY BIBLE PROJECT. V. 1- 1960-. 0082-3767. Periodical. IL. English (Hebrew). ir. The Magnes Press, The Hebrew University, Jerusalem Israel. **Ind/Abst** MLA Int. Bibliogr. Books Artic. Mod. Lang. Lit. **LC** BS410. (cum index).

THAILAND BIBLE LITERATURE. 0744-7248. Periodical. US. English. bm. Salem Church of Christ, Route 5 Box 235, Florence AL 35630.

VETERA CHRISTIANORUM. Year 1-. 0506-8126. Periodical. IT. Italian (Latin). sa. 54.000. Instituto de Letteratura Cristiana Antica, S Giacomo F, Bari 70122 Italy. **Tel** (080)23.56.27. **Ind/Abst** MLA Int. Bibliogr. Books Artic. Mod. Lang. Lit., New Testam. Abstr. bk rev. adv acc. (ctrl).

VIERTELJAHRSHEFT DER CHRISTLICHEN WISSENSCHAFT. BIBELLEKTIONEN. VFOAT Christian Science Quarterly. Bible Lessons. 0145-7411. Periodical. US. English. qt. $3.25. Christian Science Publishing Society, 1 Norway Street, Boston MA 02115.

THE WAY MAGAZINE. 1953. 0277-0431. Periodical. US. English. bm. $12.00. American Christian Press, Box 328, New Knoxville OH 45871. **Tel** (419)753-2523. Ed Frank F Herron. **Circ** 13,000. (ctrl). Features Biblical research and the application of Biblical principles in such areas as health, prosperity and family matters.

WORD IN ACTION. 1972-. Periodical. UK. English. ir. British and Foreign Bible Society, 146 Queen Victoria Street, London EC4V 4BX England. *Bible in the World.*

YOUNG AMBASSADOR. 1946. 0044-071X. Periodical. US. English. ir. $10.00. Back to the Bible Broadcast, Box 82808, Lincoln NE 68501. **Tel** (402)435-2171. Ed David W Lambert. **Circ** 82,000. Bible-centered, nondenominational for young teens.

ZEITSCHRIFT FUR DIE ALTTESTAMENTLICHE WISSENSCHAFT. See Religion, Mythology, Rationalism - Theology.

ZEITSCHRIFT FUR DIE ALTTESTAMENTLICHE WISSENSCHAFT. BEIHEFTE. Monographic Series. German. ir. $65.00. Walter de Gruyter Company, 200 Sawmill River Road, Hawthorne NY 10532. **Tel** (914)747-0110. Ed O Kaiser. bk rev. adv acc. **Circ** 1,400. The journal publishes papers in different languages concerning the interpretation of biblical scholars of the Old Testament.

BUDDHISM

THE AMERICAN BUDDHIST NEWSLETTER. 0747-900X. Periodical. US. English. mo. American Buddhist Movement, 301 West 45th Street, New York NY 10036. **DD** 294.

ANNALS OF THE NYINGMA LINEAGE IN AMERICA. V. 1- 1969/75-. 0147-4839. US. English. an. Dharma Publishing, 2425 Hillstone Avenue, Berkeley CA 94704. **LC** BQ7662.2. **DD** 294.3923.

BUDDHIST-CHRISTIAN STUDIES. VAT Buddhist Christian Studies. Vol. 1 (1981)-. 0882-0945. Periodical. US. English. an. $8.00. University of Hawaii Press, 2840 Kolowalu Street, Honolulu HI 98622. **Tel** (808)948-8299. Ed David W Chappell. **DD** 261. bk rev. adv acc. **Circ** 350. (ctrl). Buddhism and Christianity and their interrelationship based on historical materials and contemporary experience, offering articles, book review, and news items.

BUDDHIST RESEARCH INFORMATION. VFOAT BRI. No. 1 (Apr. 1979)-. 0192-396X. Periodical. US. English (Chinese). sa. IASWR, Melville Memorial Library, Stony Brook NY 11794. **Tel** (516)246-8365. Ed J Gatyso. **Circ** 350. (ctrl). Lists inquiries on Buddhist studies and reports on Buddhist research planned, in progress, or completed. Intended to supplement other bibliographies which primarily concern published scholarship.

BUDDHIST STUDIES. 1974-. II. English, Hindi and Sanskrit. ir. 10.00. Department of Buddhist Studies, University of Delhi, Delhi-7, New Delhi India. **LC** BQ2. **DD** 294.305.

BUDDHIST TEXT INFORMATION. No. 1- Nov. 1974-. 0360-6112. Periodical. US. English. qt. $7.00. Inst for Adv Study World Religion, Melville Memorial Library, SUNY Stony Brook NY 11794. **Tel** (516)246-8365. Ed Richard A Gard. **LC** Z7860, BQ1020. **DD** 016.2943. (cum index). **Circ** 350. (ctrl). Cumulative bibliographic information for the study of Buddhist texts. In addition, describes texts and their published editions, translations, and studies. Special attention given to projects planned in progress.

BUDDHISTS FOR PEACE. Vol. 1, No. 1-. Periodical. English. qt. $8.00. ABCP Headquarters, Gangdanthekchenling Monastery, Ulan Bator Mongolia. **LC** BQ20.A74. **DD** 294.33787305.

BUKKYO SHIGAKU KENKYU. VFOAT Journal of the History of Buddhism. V. 1, No. 2, June, 1974-. Japanese. ir. Bukkyo Shigakukai, c/o Bukkyo Daigaku, 96 Murasa Kino Kita Hananobo Kita-ku, Kyoto Japan. **LC** BQ6. *Bukkyo Shigaku.*

BUKKYO SHISO SHI. VFOAT Journal of the History of Buddhist Thoughts. 1- 1979-. Periodical. Japanese. ir. 1800. Heirakuji Shoten, Sanjo Noboru, Higashi Doin, Nakakyo-ku, Kyoto Japan. **LC** BQ4066.

Religion, Mythology, Rationalism—Buddhism

BUKKYOSHI KENKYU (RYUKOKU DAIGAKU. BUKKYOSHI KENKYUKAI). (BUKKYOSHI KENKYU). VFOAT Journal of Studies in History of Buddhism. JA. Japanese. ir. Nagata Bunshodo Nishinotoin Nishi Iru Hanayacho, Shimogyo-ku, Kyoto-shi 600 Japan. LC BQ256.

CHAN NHU. VFOAT Hoi Phat-Giao Viet-Nam Gia-Na-Dai. 0822-0581. Periodical. CN. Vietnamese. mo. Channhu, PO Box 1536, Ottawa Ontario K1G 0M1 Canada. DD 294.305.

CHIMO. V. 1- Jan. 1975-. 0704-4909. Periodical. CN. English. mo. $20. Chimo Publications, 79 Victoria Street, Toronto Ontario M5C 2B1 Canada. DD 294.54305.

CRYSTAL MIRROR. V. 1- 1971-. 0097-7209. US. English. an. $12.95. Dharma Publishing, 2425 Hillside Avenue, Berkeley CA 94704. Tel (415)548-5407. LC BQ7662. DD 294.392305. Overview of Buddhist history with teachings on mind, consciousness, philosophy, practice and transmission.

DAIBYAKURENGE. Began in 1949. Periodical. Japanese. ir. Daibyakurenge Kankokai, 18 Shinanomachi, Shinjuku-ku 160, Tokyo Japan. LC BQ8400.

DIALOGUE (COLOMBO, SRI LANKA). (DIALOGUE). No. 1 (Sept. 1963)-No. 27 (Nov. 1973). 0012-2181. Periodical. CE. English. ty. $6.00. Ecumenical Institute of Study & Dialogue, 490-5 Havalock Road, Colombo 6 Sri Lanka. Tel 586998. Ed Aloysius Pieris. (cum index). bk rev. Circ 2,000. Buddhist Christian dialoge with particular attention to Sri Lanka.

DIALOGUE. NEW SERIES. V. 1, No. 1- Jan./Apr. 1974-. Periodical. CE. English. ir. $6.00. Ecumenical Institute for Study and Dialogue, 490/5 Havelock Road, Colombo 6 Sri Lanka (Ceylon). Tel 586998. Ed Aloysius Peiris. bk rev. Circ 2,000. Buddhist Christian dialogue in the context of contemporary Sri Lanka. *Dialogue, 0012-2181.*

DOHO DAIGAKU RONSO. VFOAT Journal of Buddhism and Cultural Science. Japanese. ir. c/o Doho Daigaku, 1 Inabajicho 7 Nakamura-Ku, Nagoya Japan. LC AS552.D54.

THE EASTERN BUDDHIST. Vol. 1, No. 1 (May 1921)-. 0012-8708. Periodical. US. English. sa. Scholars Press, PO Box 1608, Decatur GA 30031. Tel (404)329-6950. Ind/Abst MLA Int. Bibliogr. Books Artic. Mod. Lang. Lit., Relig. Index One, Period. DD 294.3205. (cum index).

FAN YIN. Began in 1976?. Periodical. Chinese. ir. LC BQ3. DD 294.305.

GEKKAN MIKKYO KOZA. VFOAT Mikkyo Koza. JA. Japanese. ir. 1200. Hirakawa Shuppan, 15-17 Hirakawacho 2-chome, Chiyda-ku 102, Tokyo Japan. LC BQ8900.

HOKKE BUNKA KENKYU. VFOAT Journal of Institute for the Comprehensive Study of Lotus Sutra. 1975 Edition-. Japanese or English. ir. Rissho Daigaku Hokekyo Bunka Kenkyujo, 2-16 Osaki 4-chome Shinagawa-ku, Tokyo 14 Japan. LC BQ2057.

HUA FAN FO HSUEH NIEN KAN. VFOAT Journal of Sino-Indian Buddhist Studies. First published in 1982-. Periodical. CH. Chinese (some summaries and articles in English). an. $10.00. Hua Fan Fo Hsueh Yen Chiu So 22 Lane 110 Yang Te Road Sec 2 Shih Lin Taipei Taiwan. LC BQ3. DD 294.305.

JOURNAL OF BUDDHIST PHILOSOPHY. Vol. 1 (1983)-. 0741-2193. Periodical. US. English. an. $30.00. Buddhist Philosophy, PO Box 2717, Bloomington IN 47402-2717.

THE JOURNAL OF SHASTA ABBEY. (THE JOURNAL OF SHASTA ABBEY : PUBLICATION OF THE ORDER OF BUDDHIST CONTEMPLATIVES). 0732-8508. Periodical. US. English. bm. $15.00. Journal of Shasta Abbey, Shasta Abbey, PO Box 199, Mt Shasta CA 96067. Tel (916)926-4208. Ed L B H Kinzan Learman. Circ 600. Articles on the practice of Buddhism in daily life. *Journal of the Zen Mission Society.*

THE JOURNAL OF THE INTERNATIONAL ASSOCIATION OF BUDDHIST STUDIES. Main/Corp International Association of Buddhist Studies. VFOAT J.I.A.B.S. V. 1- 1978-. 0193-600X. Periodical. US. English. sa. $50.00. University of Wisconsin, 1242 Van Hise Hall, Madison WI 53706. Tel (608)262-5881. Ed A K Narain. LC BQ2. DD 294.305. bk rev. adv acc. Circ 600. (ctrl). Contains scholarly articles that deal with all possible aspects of Buddhist studies.

KIKANSHI. Main/Corp Bankoku Bukkyoto Remmei. Series/Titl Seito Kokugo Waso Bunko. VFOAT Organ for the Universal Buddhist League and the Genuine Japanese Language Movement, The Japanese and English. English (Japanese). ir. LC BQ6.

KOMAZAWA DAIGAKU BUKKYO GAKUBU RON SHU. VFOAT Journal of Buddhist Studies. Began with 1971, March issue. JA. Japanese. ir. Komazawa Daigaku Bukkyo Gakubu Kenkyoshitsu, 23-1 Komazawa 1-chome Setagaya-ku, Tokyo Japan. LC BQ6.

KUMGANG. VFOAT Wolgan Kumgang. V. 1- (1985/1)-. Periodical. KO. Korean. mo. 20.000. Wolgan Kumgangsa, 174-13 Tonggyo-dong Mapo-ku, Seoul Korea. LC BQ8.K6.

MELANGES CHINOIS ET BOUDDHIQUES. Began in 1932. Monographic Series. BE. French. ir. 2000 Domestic, $35.00 US. Inst Belge des Hautes Etudes, Chinoises 10 PAPC Cinqatenaire, 1040 Bruxelles Belgique. Tel 02-733 96 10. Ed Institut Belge des Hautes Etudes Chinoises. LC BL1405. DD 294.304. Circ 1,000. Irregular serial published every two years on Chinese classical studies and Buddhism.

THE MIDDLE WAY. V. - May/June 1943-. 0026-3214. Periodical. UK. English. qt. 6. Middle Way/Journal of Buddhist, 58 Eccleston, London SW1 England. Tel 01 834 5858. Ed John Snelling. bk rev. adv acc. Circ 2,500. All aspects of Buddhist theory, practice, history, art and mythology, also news and book reviews. Traditions Represented.

NARITASAN BUKKYO KENKYUJO KIYO. VFOAT Journal of Naritasan Institute for Buddhist Studies. JA. Japanese. ir. c/o Naritasan Shinshoji, Narital 286 Narita Japan. LC BQ6.

NIHON BUKKYO SHIGAKU. 0385-5805. JA. Japanese. ir. Sankibo Busshorin, 28-4 Hongo 5, Bunkyo-Ku Tokyo Japan. LC BQ670.

NIPPON BUKKYO GAKKAI NEMPO. VFOAT Journal of the Nippon Buddhist Research Association. JA. Japanese. ir. Nippon Bukkyo Gakkai Seibu Jimusho, c/o Otani Daigaku, Koyama Kamifusacho, Kita-Ku, Kyoto Japan. LC BQ6.

NSA QUARTERLY. Main/Corp Nichiren Shoshu Academy. VAT Nichiren Shoshu Academy Quarterly. Periodical. US. English or Japanese. qt. World Tribune Press, 1351 Ocean Front, Santa Monica CA 90401. LC BQ8400. DD 294.392.

PALI PARAGU BWE YA PUGGO MYA I HTEIRUPPATTI MYA. Main/Corp Pali Takkatho Baho Ahpwe. Periodical. Burmese. ir. Pali Takkatho Baho Ahpwe, PO Box 1003, Yankonmyo Burma. LC BQ424.

POMNYUN. Periodical. KO. Korean. ir. 2,000. Pomnyun Sa, 74 Kwanhun-dong, Chongno-ku, Seoul South Korea. LC BQ8.K6.

PULGYO MUNHWA. VFOAT Buddhist Civilization. V. 1- Feb. 1974-. Periodical. Korean. ir. 400 Single Issue. 382 Sonhwa-dong, Taejon Korea. LC DS901.

PULGYO (SEOUL, KOREA). (PULGYO). VFOAT Buddhism. Periodical. Korean. mo. 7,000. Pulgyosa, 1 Pongwon-dong Sodaemun-ku, Seoul Korea. LC BQ8.K6.

RELIGIONS OF ASIA SERIES. No. 1-. Monographic Series. English. ir. Asian Humanities Press, 2512 Ninth Street, Berkeley CA 94710. Tel (415)486-8065. Ed Lewis Lancaster. Monographs which deal with the religions of Asia, especially Buddhism.

SACRED BOOKS OF THE BUDDHISTS. V. 1- 1895-. Monographic Series. UK. English. ir. LC BQ1138.

SEIKYO HODO SHASHINSHU. VFOAT Best Press Photos: The Seikyo. 1973-. JA. Japanese. ir. 850. Seikyo Shimbun Sha, 18 Shinanomachi Shinjuku-ku (160), Tokyo Japan. LC BQ8400.

SHIH FANG YUEH KAN. VFOAT Shih Fang, Universal Monthly. V. 1, (Oct. 1982)-. Periodical. CH. Chinese. mo. 150.00. Shih Fang Tsa Chih She, PO Box 91-389, Taipei Taiwan. LC BQ620. DD 294.30951.

SHINSHUGAKU. VFOAT Journal of Studies in Shin Buddism. Periodical. Japanese. sa. Ryukoku Daigaku Shinshu Gakkai, Shichijo Omiya Shimo-Gyo-ku, Kyoto 600 Japan. LC BQ8700.

SHITENNOJI KOKUSAI BUKKYO DAIGAKU BUNGAKUBU KIYO. VFOAT Review of International Buddhist University, Faculty of Letters. Japanese. ir. Shitennoji Kokusai Bukkyo, Daigaku 1308 Hanyuno, Habikino-shi Osaka-fu Japan. LC AS552.H52.

THE SOKA GAKKAI NEWS. No. 1- Feb. 25, 1975-. Periodical. JA. English. ir. International Bureau Soka Gakkai, 32 Shinano-Machi Shinjuka 160, Tokyo Japan. LC BQ8400. DD 294.365.

SOKA GAKKAI NYUSU. VFOAT The Sokagakkai News. Periodical. JA. Japanese. ir. Soka Gakkai Kohoshitsu, 32 Shinano-Machi, Shinjuku-ku Tokyo-to 160 Japan. LC BQ8400.

SON SASANG. Periodical. KO. Korean. bm. 2,000. Son Sasangsa, 42-1 5-ka Chongno Chongno-ku, Seoul 110 Korea. LC BQ9250.

SPRING WIND (TORONTO, ONT.). (SPRING WIND). Began publication in 1980?. 0825-799X. Periodical. CN. English. qt. $4.50 Each Number. Spring Wind, c/o Zen Lotus Society 46 Gwynne Avenue, Toronto Ontario M6K 2C3 Canada. DD 294.392705.

STUDIES IN EAST ASIAN BUDDHISM. No. 1-. Monographic Series. US. English. University of Hawaii Press, Honolulu HA 96822. Tel (808)948-8255. Scholarly research on buddhist history and philosophy.

STUPA. 1-. Periodical. DK. Danish. ir. 14.50 Each Issue. Helene Ree, Jellingegade 4, 2100 Kbenhavn Denmark. LC BQ7549.

TAISHO DAIGAKU KENKYU KIYO. VFOAT Taisho Daigaku Kenkyukiyo. Began in 1954. Periodical. JA. English (Japanese). ir. Taisho Daigaku Shuppanbu 20-1, Nishi Sugamo 3-chome, Toshima-ku Tokyo. LC BQ6. *TAisho Daigaku Gakuho.*

TAISHO DAIGAKU SOGO BUKKYO KENKYUJO NEMPO. VFOAT Annual of the Institute for Comprehensive Studies of Buddhism, Taisho University. Edition-. JA. English (Japanese). an. Taisho Daigaku Sogo Bukkyo Kenkyujo, 20-1 Nishi Sugamo 3-chome, Toshima-ku, Tokyo Japan. LC BQ6.

TOHOKAI. No. 1- (Dec. 1973-1978)-. Periodical. JA. Japanese. ir. 600. Toyo Bunka Suishinkai, c/o Juraku Building 108 Toganicho Kita-ku, Osaka 530 Japan. LC BQ6.

UOC TUE. VFOAT Torch of Wisdom. So Ramat- April 5, 1976-. Periodical. US. English (Vietnamese). $0.85 Each Issue. 5333 16th Street NW, Washington DC 20011. LC BQ120. DD 294.3.

VAJRA BODHI SEA. VFOAT Hai Ti Pu Kang Chin. V. 1- Apr. 1970-. 0507-6986. Periodical. US. English. mo. $30.00. Buddhist Text Translation Association, 1731 15th Street, San Francisco CA 94103. Tel (415)626-4204. Ed Bhikshuni Heng Chr. LC BQ2. bk rev. Circ 3,500. English translations of major Buddhist scriptures, biographical sketches of ancient masters, Sanskrit language lesson, and contemporary articles by practitioners. Bi-lingual: English-Chinese.

THE VAJRADHATU SUN. 0882-0813. Periodical. US. English. bm. $15.00 Domestic, $18.00 Foreign. The Vajradhatu Sun, 1345 Spruce Street, Boulder CO 80302. LC BQ2. DD 294.305.

THE WHEEL. 1958. 0049-7541. Periodical. CE. English. qt. $8.00. The Buddhist Publications Society, PO Box 61, Kandy Sri Lanka. Tel (08)03679. Ed Von Bhikkhu Bodhi. LC BL1400. Circ 45,000. Publications relating to Buddhism, its philosophy, and its practice, including translations of selected Pali texts, with notes, as found in the oldest and most reliable Buddhist tradition, the Theravada Pali Canon.

WORLD BUDDHISM. (VESAK ANNUAL). 0084-1447. English. ir. 153-3 Dutugemunu Street, Nugegoda Sri Lanka. LC BL1400. DD 294.305. Index in first issue of next volume - loose - unpaged.

WORLD BUDDHISM. V. 1- Aug. 1952-. 0043-8286. Periodical. English. qt. Paramadhamma Buddhist Institut, No 41 Lumbini Avenue, Ratmalana, Sri Lanka Ceylon. LC BL1400.

Religion, Mythology, Rationalism—Eastern Christian Churches

YOUNG BUDDHIST. (THE YOUNG BUDDHIST). 0377-8088. SI. English or Chinese. ir. 83 Silat Road, 3 Singapore Rep Singapore. LC BQ3. DD 294.305.

YOUNG EAST. V. 1-15 (No. 1-60). 0513-5974. Periodical. JA. English. qt. $10.00. Tohokai Inc, Kinsen Building, 2-17 Nishitemma 6-Chome Kita-U, Osaka 530 Japan. Tel (03)365-5131. Ed Bando Slojun. LC BL1400. bk rev. adv acc. Circ 1,200. (ctrl). A journal on Buddhism and Japanese culture. First published in 1925. *Young East.*

ZCLA JOURNAL. Main/Corp Zen Center of Los Angeles. VAT Zen Centre of Los Angeles Journal. 0360-991X. Periodical. US. English. ty. $6.00. Zen Center for Los Angeles, 927 South Normandie Avenue, Los Angeles CA 90006. LC BQ9250. DD 294.3927.

EASTERN CHRISTIAN CHURCHES

ANNIVERSARY - SAINTS CONSTANTINE AND ELENA ROMANIAN ORTHODOX CHURCH. Main/Corp Saints Constantine and Elena Romanian Orthodox Church, Edmonton, Alta. 24th- 1972-. 0380-030X. CN. English (includes some text in Romanian). an. Saints Constantine and Elena Romanian Orthodox Church, 9005-132nd Street, Edmonton Alberta T5E 4X7 Canada. DD 281.971233. *Anniversary, 0380-0318.*

BAJAVAJA USKALOS'. *See* Ethnic.

BISERICA ORTODOXA ROMANA. VFOAT Eglise Orthodoxe Roumaine. Periodical. RM. Romanian. bm. Ilexim Press Department, PO Box 1-136-1-137, Bucharest Romania. LC BX690.

COPTIC CHURCH REVIEW. V. 1- Spring 1980-. 0273-3269. Periodical. US. English. qt. $7.00. Society Coptic Church Studies, PO Box 714, East Brunswick NJ 08816. Tel (717)273-9817. Ed Rodolph Yanney. Ind/Abst Relig. Index One, Period. LC BX130. DD 281.7. bk rev. Circ 500. Biblical studies with emphasis on spiritual exegesis, liturgical life of Church, lives and writings of the Church Fathers, ascetic and mystic spirituality.

EKKLESIA KAI THEOLOGIA : EKKLESIASTIKE KAI THEOLOGIKE EPETERIS TES HIERAS ARCHIEPISKOPES THYATEIRON KAI MEGALES VRETANNIAS. VFOAT Church and Theology. V. 1 (1980)-. UK. Greek, Ancient (text in English, and French). an. 5 Graven Hill, London W.2 England. LC BX200.

EKKLESIASTIKOS PHAROS. V. 1-. Periodical. ET. Greek, Modern. qt. $20.00. Archbishop Methodos Fouyas, PO Box 571, Addis Ababa Ethiopia. (cum index).

HO EPHEMERIOS. Periodical. Greek, Modern. sm. LC BX618.

EPISKEPSIS (FRENCH ED.). (EPISKEPSIS). Began in 1970. Periodical. French. bm. $14.84. Ctr Orthodoxe Patriarcat Oecum, 37 Chemin de Chambesy, 1292 Chambesy-Geneva Switzerland.

EZEGODNIK PRAVOSLAVNOJ CERKVI V AMERIKE. (EZHEGODNIK PRAVOSLAVNOI TSERKVI V AMERIKE). Main/Corp Avtokefalnaia Amerikanskaia Pravoslavnaia Tserkov. No. 1.- 1975-. 0146-8189. US. Russian. an. Orthodox Church in America, PO Box 675, Syosset NY 11791. LC BX496.A5.

GLASUL BISERICII. Periodical. RM. Romanian. bm. Ilexim Press, PO Box 1-136-1-137, Bucharest Romania. LC BX690.

IRENIKON. V. 1- 1926-. 0021-0978. Periodical. BE. French. ir. $26.00. Monastere Benedictin, B-5395 Chevetogne Belgium. Ind/Abst Relig. Index One, Period., MLA Int. Bibliogr. Books Artic. Mod. Lang. Lit. (cum index). bk rev. Circ 7,250. Ecumenism, theology and history of Eastern and Western churches. Ecumenical church news.

THE JOURNAL OF THE MOSCOW PATRIARCHATE. Main/Corp Russkaia Pravoslavnaia Tserkov. Moskovskaia Patriarkhiia. 1971-. Periodical. UR. English. mo. $1.00. Box No 624, G-435 Moscow USSR. Ind/Abst Relig. Index One, Period. LC BX460. DD 281.947.

KANON : YEARBOOK OF THE SOCIETY OF THE LAW OF THE ORIENTAL CHURCHES. *See* Yearbooks, Almanacs, Directories.

KIRCHE IM OSTEN. (KIRCHE IM OSTEN : STUDIEN ZUR OSTEUROPAISCHEN KIRCHENGESCHICHTE UND KIRCHENKUNDE). Vol. 1 (1958)-. 0453-9273. GW. German. an. Vandenhoeck & Ruprecht, Postfach 3753/Theaterstr 13, D-3400 Goettingen West Germany. Tel 0551/65061. Ind/Abst Relig. Index One, Period. adv acc.

LOOKING EAST. Periodical. PO. English. ir. Byzantine Center, Fatima Portugal. LC BX106.3. DD 281.9.

MAJALLAT AL-NUR AL-URTHUDHUKSIYAH. VFOAT Nur Al-Urthudhuksiyah. Periodical. Arabic. ir. 30.00. Shafiq Haydar Mina Tarabulus Hayy Mar Ilyas, Box 11-2966, Beirut Lebanon. LC BX200.

MAJALLAT AL-SALAM. VFOAT Salam. Began in 1978. 0882-9756. Periodical. US. Arabic (English). mo. PO Box 3309, Detroit MI 48203. LC BX130.

MESSAGER. Periodical. French. ir. 16. 3 rue Toepffer, 1206 Geneve Suisse France. LC BX460. DD 281.94.

NADEZHDA. Vol. 1-. Periodical. GW. Russian. ty. $29.22. Possev Verlag V Gorachek KG, Flurscheideweg 15, D-6230 Frankfurt West Germany. Tel (069)341265. bk rev. (ctrl). Religious poetry and Russian national bibliographie and biographie.

NADEZHDA (FRANKFURT AM MAIN, GERMANY). (NADEZHDA). Vol. 1-. Periodical. ir. LC BX578. DD 242.

ONE CHURCH. VFOAT Edinaia Tserkov. V. 1- 1947-. 0030-2503. Periodical. US. English. bm. $6.00. One Church Circulation Department, 158 Stiles Street, Elizabeth NJ 07208. Tel (201)352-1192. Ed F Kovulchuk. bk rev. Circ 1,600. Available on microfilm from University Microfilms. Official publication of the Patriarchal Parishes of the Russian Orthodox Church in the USA, also includes Orthodox interest to all concerned with Church life in the Soviet Union.

ONE IN CHRIST. V. 1-. 0030-252X. Periodical. UK. English. ir $25.00. One in Christ, Turvey Abbey Turvey, Bedfordshire MK43 8DE England. Tel Turvey 432. Ed Paschal Anne Hardiment. Ind/Abst Old Testam. Abstr., Cathol. Period. Lit. Index, New Testam. Abstr., Relig. Index One, Period. LC BX1781. DD 282.05. bk rev. Circ 1,000. Available in microfilm. Christian unity and documentation economical initiatives. Theology, history and spirituality relating to ecumenism. *Eastern Churches Quarterly, Ecumenical Notes.*

ORIENTALIA CHRISTIANA ANALECTA. No. 101- 1935-. Monographic Series. IT. English, French, German (Italian). ir. Pontificio Istituto Orientale, Piazza 5 Maria Maggiore 7, 00185 Rome Italy. Tel 731-2254. bk rev. Circ 500. *Orientalia Christiana.*

ORIENTALIA CHRISTIANA PERIODICA. V. 1- 1935-. 0030-5375. Periodical. IT. Latin (English, French, German, Italian and Spanish). sa. Pontificio Istituto Orientale, Piazza S Maria Maggiore 7, 00185 Rome Italy. Tel (06)7312254. Ind/Abst New Testam. Abstr., Relig. Index One, Period. LC BX100. DD 281.05. (cum index).

THE ORTHODOX CHURCH. 1965. 0048-2269. Periodical. US. English. mo. $21.00. Orthodox Church in America, 14-24 154th Street, Whitestone NY 11357. Ed John Meyendorff. LC BX496.A1. DD 281.973. Circ 30,000. (ctrl).

ORTHODOX EDUCATOR. Fall 1981-. Periodical. US. English. ty. Orthodox Educator, 88 Jean Avenue c/o Arlene Kallaur, Hempstead NY 11550. Tel (516)922-0550.

ORTHODOX LIFE. V. 1- Jan./Feb. 1950-. 0030-5820. Periodical. US. English (Russian). bm. $8.00. Holy Trinity Monastery, PO Box 36, Jordanville NY 13361. LC BX460. DD 281.93.

THE ORTHODOX WORD. V. 1- 1965-. 0030-5839. Periodical. US. English. bm. $10.00. Beegum Gorge Road, Platina CA 96076. Ed Father Herman. bk rev. adv acc. Circ 2,800. Available on microfilm from University Microfilms. An illustrated church magazine of Patristic thought and tradition. Regularly features lives of Saints, ascetic writings of Church Fathers ancient and new, contemporary issues, etc.

ORTHODOXY CANADA. 0710-1635. Periodical. CN. English. mo. $7.00. Synaxis Press, PO Box 404, Chilliwack British Columbia V2P 6J7 Canada. DD 281.93. *Tlingit Herald.*

ORTODOXIA. Began in 1949?. Periodical. Romanian. ir. Institutul Biblic si de Misiune Ortodoxa, Intrarea Patriarhiei Nr 9 Secrotul 5, Bucuresti Romania. LC BX690.

OSTKIRCHLICHE STUDIEN. 1.- Volume. 0030-6487. Periodical. GW. German. ty. 33.77. Augustinus-Verlag, Grabenberg 2 Postfach 343, 8700 Wuerzburg Germany. Tel 0931/51157. Ed H M Biedermann. Ind/Abst New Testam. Abstr., Relig. Index One, Period., Hist. Abstr., Am. Hist. Life, Hist. Abstr., Part A, Mod. Hist. Abstr., Hist. Abst., Part B, Twent. Century Abstr. LC BX100. DD 281.5. bk rev. adv acc. Circ 620. (ctrl). Eastern churches studies, bibliography, articles and reviews.

PRAVOSLAVLJE. (No. -19). Periodical. YU. Serbo-Croatian -C. sm. Jugoslavanska Knjica, PO Box 36, Beograd Yugoslavia. LC BX710.

PRAVOSLAVNAJA ZIZN. (PRAVOSLAVNAIA ZHIZN). VFOAT Orthodox Life. V. 1- Jan. 1950-. 0032-6992. Periodical. US. Russian. bm. $10.00. Holy Trinity Manastery, PO Box 36, Jordanville NY 13361. Tel (315)858-0940. Ed Bishop Hilarion. LC BX460. DD 281.93. bk rev. Circ 1,600. Othodox life publishes articles of a wide variety-all concerning the orthodox church. Frequent topics include lives of saints, liturgics, church history, the tenor is solid and sober.

PRAVOSLAVNOE OBOZRENIE. (PRAVOSLAVNOE OBOZRIENIE). VFOAT Orthodox Observer. Began publication in 1953?. 0225-0292. Periodical. CN. Russian. bm. Orthodox Observer, 8011 Champagneur Avenue, Montreal Quebec H3N 2K4 Canada. DD 281.905.

PROCHE-ORIENT CHRETIEN. V. 1- 1951-. 0032-9622. Periodical. IS. French. qt. $14.00. Sainte-Anne, PO Box 19079, Jerusalem Israel. Tel (02)28 32 85. Ed Frans Bouwen. Ind/Abst Relig. Index One, Period. LC BR1070. bk rev. Circ 800. Research and information periodical on Eastern Christian churches and ecumenism in dialogue with the other monotheistic religions in the Middle-East.

ROMANIAN ORTHODOX CHURCH NEWS QUARTERLY BULLETIN. Year 1, No. 1 (1971)-. Periodical. English. qt. Department of Foreign Relations of the Romanian Patriarchate, Bucharest - Str. Antim Nr. 29 - Sector 5 Romania. LC BX690. DD 281.93.

THE RUSSIAN ORTHODOX JOURNAL. Vol. 1- May 1927-. 0036-0317. Periodical. US. English. ir. $10.00. Federated Russian Orthodox, 10 Downs Drive Plains, Wilkes Barre PA 18705. Tel (717)825-3158. Ed John Behuniak. LC BX496.A1. DD 281.973. bk rev. adv acc. Circ 3,500. (ctrl). Fraternal activities of federated Russian Orthodox clubs including religious, cultural, sports, and educational topics.

RUSSKOE VOZROZHDENIE. VFOAT Renaissance Russe, Russian Renascence. Began in 1978. 0222-1543. Periodical. US. Russian. qt. $24.00. 1000 Anniversary Committee, 322 West 108 Street, New York NY 10025. Tel (212)663-9093. DD 947. Topics dealing with the upcoming milenium of Orthodox Christianity in Russia.

SOBORNOST. V. 1- 1979-. 0144-8722. Periodical. UK. English. sa. $7.66. Fellowship of St Alban and Sergius, St Basil House, 52 Ladbrove Grove, London W11 England. Tel (01)727-7713. Ed Sergei Hackel. Ind/Abst Relig. Index One, Period. LC BX100. DD 281.905. bk rev. adv acc. Circ 2,300. Articles on Eastern Christian churches and east-west ecumenism; reports, news items, book reviews, and fellowship affairs. *Sobornost, 0144-8722; Eastern Churches Review.*

SOURCES CHRETIENNES. No. 1- 1941-. Monographic Series. FR. French. ir. Editions Du Cerf, 29 Boulevard La Tour Maubourg, 75340 Paris Cedex 07 France. Tel 16/78/37/08. Ind/Abst MLA Int. Bibliogr. Books Artic. Mod. Lang. Lit. bk rev. adv acc. Circ 2,500. (ctrl). Ancient manuscripts for the modern reader. The 1st text of christian culture I-XII Century.

STIMME DER ORTHODOXIE. VFOAT Golos Pravoslaviia. 0562-0694. Periodical. German. ir. 1.30 Each Issue. Wildensteiner Strasse 10, 1157 Berlin East Germany. LC BX460.

STUDI E RICERCHE SULL'ORIENTE CRISTIANO. Year 1- Jan./April 1978-. Periodical. IT. Italian. ir. 7000. C C Postale N 64082001, Intestato a Studi E Ricerche Sull Oriente Cristiano, Roma Italy. LC BX100.

Religion, Mythology, Rationalism—Islam, Bahaism, Theosophy

TRAIT D'UNION. V. 1- March 1964-. 0701-0486. Periodical. CN. French (text in English). qt. $5.00. Paroisse St-Saveur, G Coriaty, CP 578 Succursale C, Montreal Quebec H2L 4K4 Canada. **DD** 281.9714281.

TROITSKII PRAVOSLAVNYI RUSSKII KALENDAR. 1945-. US. Russian. an. **LC** BX496.A5. *Troitskii Kalendar.*

UKRAINIAN ORTHODOX WORD. 0147-1015. Periodical. US. English. bm. $3.00. Ukrainian Orthodox Church of the USA, Box 495, South Bound Brook NJ 08880. **LC** BX738.U4. **DD** 281.973.

VIRA J KULTURA. (VIRA I KULTURA). VFOAT Faith and Culture. Began publication in 1974. 0701-2675. Periodical. CN. Ukrainian. 9 Saint John's Avenue, Winnipeg Manitoba R2W 1G8 Canada. **DD** 281.9305.

YEARBOOK AND CHURCH DIRECTORY OF THE ORTHODOX CHURCH IN AMERICA. *See* Yearbooks, Almanacs, Directories.

ZHURNAL MOSKOVSKOI PATRIARKHII. Main/Corp Russkaia Pravoslavnaia Tserkov. Moskovskaia Patriarkhiia. 1931-. 0044-4553. Periodical. UR. Russian. mo. Moscow Patriarchate, Novodevichii Pr1, Moscow G-435 USSR. **Ind/Abst** Am. Hist. Life, Hist. Abstr., Part A, Mod. Hist. Abstr., Hist. Abst., Part B, Twent. Century Abstr., Chem. Abstr. **LC** BX460.

ISLAM, BAHAISM, THEOSOPHY

15-21. VFOAT Khamis Ashar-Al-Wahid Wa-Al-Ishrun. No. 1 (November 1982-). Periodical. Arabic. mo. 160.00. 3 Nahj Al-Hijab, S B 1024, Tunis Tunisia. **LC** BP1.

ABRAXAS (HOLLYWOOD, LOS ANGELES, CALIF.). (ABRAXAS). 8755-1780. Periodical. US. English. an. $4.00. The Gnostic Society, P O Box 3993, Hollywood CA 90078. **LC** BP600. **DD** 299.93205.

ABSTRACTS (CENTRE FOR THE STUDY OF ISLAM AND CHRISTIAN-MUSLIM RELATIONS (BIRMINGHAM, WEST MIDLANDS, ENGLAND)). *See* Indexes/Abstracts.

AFRICA ISMAILI. Periodical. English or Gujarati. ir. $0.60 US. Shia Imami Ismaila Association for Kenya, PO Box 30606, Nairobi Kenya. **LC** BP195.I8. **DD** 297.82205.

AHMADIYYA GAZETTE. (AHMADIYYA GAZETTE (CANADA)). Jan. 1978-. 0229-5644. Periodical. CN. English (text also in Urdu). mo. Free. Ahmadiyyah Gazette, 15 Thorncliffe Park Drive/Suite 311, Toronto Ontario M4H 1H6 Canada. **DD** 297.8605. (ctrl).

AL-ALAM AL-ISLAMI. Periodical. Arabic. ir. Al-Muassasah Al-Misriyah Lil-Nashr Wa-Al-Ilan, 51 Shari Najib, Al-Rihani, PO Box 126, Al-FAjjala, Al-Qahirah United Arab Republic (Egypt). **LC** BP1.

AL-ATASH. VFOAT Atash, Communicating the Uncommunicated. V. 1- Dec. 1977-. Periodical. English (Urdu). ir. Taha Turabi, PO Box 8976, Karachi Pakistan. **LC** BP193.5. **DD** 297.8205.

AL-BALAGH. Periodical. in Urdu. mo. 40.00. Muhammad Taqi Usmani, Al-Balagh Darallum, 14, Karaci Pakistan. **Tel** 311217. Ed Muhammad Taqi Usmani. **LC** BP1. **Circ** 3,000. (ctrl). Journal to Propogali Islamic teachings and to publish recent researches on the current Islamic studies.

AL-BALAGH. Periodical. Arabic. ir. Muassasat Al-Balagh Lil-Sihafah Wa-Al-Tibaah, Shari Al-Matar Al-Dawli, PO Box 4558, Al-Kuwayt Kuwait. **LC** BP1.

AL-BASHIR. V. 1- Mar./Apr. 1972-. Periodical. Urdu. ir. Mir Najaf Ali, 288 Khamosh Kalony Tard Chaurangi (1), Karachi Pakistan. **LC** BP1.

AL-BATH AL-ISLAMI. VFOAT Albaas-El-Islami. Periodical. Arabic. mo. **LC** BP1.

AL-BAYAN. Arabic. ir. 0.10. PO Box 1458, Al-Khartum Sudan. **LC** BP1.

AL-DAWAH. Periodical. Arabic. ir. 1.5 Per Issue. 18 Ibn Khaldoon Street, Al-Riyad Saudi Arabia. **LC** BP1.

AL-DAWAH. Periodical. Arabic. ir. $18.00. PO Box 1636, Al-Qahirah United Arab Republic. **LC** BP1.

AL-FATH AL-ISLAMI. VFOAT Al-Fateh Al-Islami. Periodical. Arabic. ir. S B 41/1636, Tihran Iran. **LC** BP1.F39.

AL-ILM WA-AL-IMAN. Periodical. Arabic. ir. 2 Td (Single Issue), Tunis Tunisia. **LC** BP190.5.S3.

AL-IRSHAD. VFOAT Irchad. Periodical. Arabic (French). ir. 30.00. Al-Mamlakah Al-Maghribiyah Mudiriyat Al-Shuun Al-Islamiyah Al-Tabiah Li-Wizarat Al-Awqaf Wa-Al-Shuun Al-Islamiyah, Al Irchad, C C P 37-50, Al-Rabat Morocco. **LC** BP1.

AL-ITISAM. Periodical. Arabic. ir. PO Box 1707, Al-Qahirah United Arab Republic. **LC** BP1.

AL-ITTIHAD CEASED. Vol. 1 (1964)-. US. English. an. $16.00. Muslim Students Association, PO Box 38, Plainsfield IN 46168. **Tel** (317)839-8157.

AL-MARJI. V. 1, No. 1 (April 1982)-. Periodical. Arabic. ir. 5.00. 9 Najk Al-Jaz Irah Tunis, Al-Tabiq Al-Thani, S B 277 Tunis. **LC** BP1.

AL-MUKHTAR AL-ISLAMI. V. 1- October 1979. Periodical. Arabic. ir. 5.00. Dar Al-Salam, Tariq Misr/Hilwan Al-Zirai, Al-Qahirah United Arab Republic (Egypt). **LC** BP1.

AL-MUNTALAQ. Periodical. Arabic. ir. 13.00 Single Issue. P O Box 25105, Al-Ghubayri Lubnan. **LC** BP1.

AL-MUSHIR. VFOAT The Counselor. Began with issue for Jan. 1959. Periodical. PK. English (Urdu). ir. $12.00. Christian Study Centre, 126-B Murree Road, Rawalpindi Cantt Pakistan. Ed Yusuf Zalil. bk rev. **Circ** 700. The study of local culture, particularly, to study and interpret the faiths of Muslims and Christians, their relationships, both past and present.

AL-MUSLIH. July 1- August 23, 1973-. Periodical. Urdu. ir. 12.00. Mirza Abdurrahim Beg, Ahmadia Mall MagazineLane, Karachi Pakistan. **LC** BP195.A5.

AL-MUSLIM AL-MUASIR. VFOAT Majallat Al-Muslim Al-Muasir, Contemporary Muslim. Periodical. LE. Arabic. qt. 15.00. PO Box 119429, Beirut Lebanon. **LC** BP1.

AL-NAHDAH. Vol. 1, No. 1 (Mar. 1981)-. 0127-2284. Periodical. English. qt. 7.00 Malaysia, Singapore, Brurei, 12.00 Australia/ Middle East, North Africa, 14.00 Europe, North, South, and Central America. Al Nahdah, 250D Jalan Ipoh, Kuala Lumpur 13-03 Malaysia. **Tel** 2988166. Ed Fudlullah Wilmot. **LC** BP1. **DD** 297.05. bk rev. adv acc. **Circ** 5,000. General information on activities and problems of Muslims in the sea and Pacific region as well as articles by contemporary Muslim thinkers.

AL-RAID. Arabic. ir. Islamisches Zentrum, Al-Raid, Prof Pirletstr 20, 5100 Aachen West Germany. **LC** BP1.

AL-RISALAH AL-ISLAMIYAH. Periodical. Arabic. ir. 1.50 Single Issue. PO Box 155063, Bayrut Liberia. **LC** BP1.

AL-RISALAH AL-ISLAMIYAH. Arabic. ir. 6. Kurnish Al-Azamiayh, Qurb Al-Mathaf Al-Harbi, Baghdad Iraq. **LC** BP1.

AL-TAQRIR AL-ISLAMI. No. 1- 10 AB 1979-. Periodical. Arabic. ir. 1.00 Single Issue. Al-Markaz Al-Islami Lil-Tarbiyah Bayrut Lubnan, PO Box 14/53, Bayrut Lebanon. **LC** BP63.L4.

AL-TARBIYAH AL-ISLAMIYAH. Periodical. Arabic. ir. 1.25. PO Box 34, Baghdad Lebanon. **LC** BP1.

AL-TASAWWUF AL-ISLAMI : SHARIAH WA-TARIQAH WA-HAQIQAH. VFOAT Majallat Al-Tasawwuf Al-Islami, Midan Al-Husayn, 1 Shari Umm Al-Ghulam, PO Box 992, Cairo Egypt. **LC** BP188.45.

AL-TAWHID. Periodical. Arabic. ir. Jamaat Ansar Al-Sunnah Al-Muhammadiyah, 8 Shari Qawlah Abdin, Al-Qahirah United Arab Republic (Egypt). **LC** BP1.

AL-YASAR AL-ISLAMI. Jan. 1, 1981-. Periodical. UA. Arabic. ir. 1.00 Single Issue. S B 34 Hilyubulis, Al-Qahirah Egypt. **LC** BP1.

ALMANAK MUHAMMADIYAH. *See* Yearbooks, Almanacs, Directories.

A.M. JOURNAL. (A.M. JOURNAL : AMERICAN MUSLIM JOURNAL). VFOAT American Muslim Journal. VAT A.M. Journal. Vol. 7, No. 31 (May 21, 1982)-. 0744-7639. Periodical. US. English. wk. American Muslim Journal, 7801 South Cottage Grove Avenue, Chicago IL 60601. **Tel** (312)651-7600. Ed Wali Akbar Muhammad. bk rev. adv acc. **Circ** 40,000. Islamically oriented third world publication championing the rights of developing nations. Health and family oriented. *A.M. News,* 0744-7647.

THE AMERICAN THEOSOPHIST. 0003-1402. Periodical. US. English. mo. Theosophical Society of America, Box 270, Wheaton IL 60187.

ANNALES ISLAMOLOGIQUES. Periodical. UA. French (Arabic). ir. $67.00. Leila Bookshop, 17 Gawad Hosni Street, PO Box 2353, Cairo Egypt. **Tel** 42802. **LC** BP1. Ideas in the areas of Islamic arts, architecture, and archeology. *Melanges Islamologiques.*

AYANDAH-I SAZAN : URGAN-I ITTIHADIYAH-I ANJUMANHA-YI ISLAMI-I DANISH-I AMUZAN. Periodical. Persian, Modern. ir. 40.00 Single Issue. **LC** BP192.7.I68.

BAHAI NEWS. 0195-9212. Periodical. US. English. mo. $8.00. National Spiritual Assembly of the Bahais of the United States, 112 Linden Avenue, Wilmette IL 60091. **LC** BP300. **DD** 297.8905.

BAHAI STUDIES NOTEBOOK. 1, No. 1 (Dec. 1980)-. 0228-7013. Periodical. CN. English (text also in French). ir. Bahai Studies Notebook, 224 4th Avenue, Ottawa Ontario K1S 2L8 Canada. **DD** 297.8905.

BASIR. VFOAT Baseer. Periodical. in Urdu. ir. 10.00. Zafar Hamid, Hamid Manzil Basir Istrit Nazim Abad No 2, Karachi Pakistan. **LC** BP1.

BULLETIN ON ISLAM AND CHRISTIAN-MUSLIM RELATIONS IN AFRICA. VFOAT B.I.C.M.U.R.A. Vol. 1, No. 1 (Jan. 1983)-. 0264-1356. Periodical. UK. English. qt. 7.50. Centre for the Study of Islam and Christian-Muslim Relations, Selly Oak Colleges, Birmingham B29 6LE England. **LC** BP64.A1. **DD** 297.197205.

CANADIAN MUSLIM. (THE CANADIAN MUSLIM). V. 1- July 1977-. 0707-2945. Periodical. CN. English (Arabic). ir. Free. Ottawa Muslim Association, PO Box 2952 Station D, Ottawa Ontario K1P 5W9 Canada. **DD** 297.65. (ctrl).

CANADIAN THEOSOPHIST. (THE CANADIAN THEOSOPHIST). V. 1- Mar., 1920-. 0045-544X. Periodical. CN. English. bm. Theosophical Society in Canada, 2307 Sovereign Crescent SW, Calgary Alberta T3C 2M3 Canada.

CONCEPT (ISLAMABAD, PAKISTAN). *See* History (General) - History of Asia.

DAKWAH. Periodical. MY. Malay. ir. $1.00 Single Issue. Yayasan Dakwah Islamiah Malaysia, Tingkat 11 Wisma Batik Jalan Tun Perak, Kuala Lumpur Malaysia. **LC** BP1.

DARSHAI AZ MAKTAB-I ISLAM. VFOAT Maktab-I Islam. Periodical. Persian, Modern. mo. 1000.00. Khiyaban-I Iram, Qom Iran.

DIES NATALIS IAIN. Main/Corp Institut Agama Islam Negeri Syarif Hidayatullah. Indonesian. ir. Institut Agama Islam Negeri Syarif Hidayatullah, Jl Indramaya 14, Jakarta Indonesia. **LC** BP1.

DIN O DANISH. VFOAT Din-W-Danish Quarterly. 1970-. Periodical. Urdu or English. ir.

ETUDES MUSULMANES. Vol. 1 1954-. 0531-1888. Monographic Series. FR. French. ir. Librairie Philosophique Vrin, 6 Place de la Sorbonne, 75005 Paris France. **Tel** (1)43 54 03 47. We publish without periodicity, new titles in this area: Islamic philosophy, agreed by the director's collection.

FAIZULISLAM. VFOAT Faiz-Ul-Islam. Periodical. Urdu. ir. 30.00. Anjuman-I Faizulislam, Monthly Faiz-Ul-Islam, Rawalpindi Pakistan. **Tel** 72909. Ed Muhammad Fazil. **LC** BP1. bk rev. adv acc. **Circ** 3,000. (ctrl). Short articles and literature on Islam biographical subjects Anjuman Faizul Islam's activities and monthly accounts of donations received for Anjumanis Orphanage.

FAJAR ISLAM. 0046-3183. Malay. qt. Majlis Ugama Islam Singapore, c/o Ministry of Social Affairs, Singapore 6 Singapore. **LC** BP1.

GEGENWART. Vol. 1-. 0016-5867. Periodical. SZ. German. bm. Troxler Verlag, Friedheimweg 11, 3007 Bern Switzerland. **Ind/Abst** Am. Hist. Life, Hist. Abstr. **LC** BP595.

HADY AL-ISLAM. Periodical. Arabic. ir. **LC** BP1. Index in last issue of volume - attached.

HAMDARD ISLAMICUS. (HAMDARD ISLAMICUS : QUARTERLY JOURNAL OF THE HAMDARD NATIONAL FOUNDATION, PAKISTAN). Vol. 1, No. 1 (Summer 1978)-. 0250-7196. Periodical. English. qt. $15.00. Hamdard Foundation, Nazimabad, Karachi 18 Pakistan. **Tel** 616001. Ed Hakim Mohammed Said. **Ind/Abst** Am. Hist. Life, Hist. Abstr., Relig. Index One, Period. **LC** BP1. **DD** 297.05. bk rev. adv acc. **Circ** 2,000. (ctrl). Seeks to build a bridge between Islam and the West. Publishes articles on

Religion, Mythology, Rationalism—Islam, Bahaism, Theosophy

every branch of Islamic sciences such as Quran, Hadith, jurisprudence and law, etc.

HUDA (JAMIYAT JAMAAT AL-DAWAH AL-ISLAMIYAH (MOROCCO)). (AL-HUDA). Periodical. Arabic. ir. 75. 11329 P Al-Rabat Morocco. LC BP1.

INDEX ISLAMICUS (LONDON, ENGLAND : 1983). *See* Indexes/Abstracts.

IQBAL REVIEW. 1960. 0021-0773. Periodical. PK. Published alternately in English and Urdu. qt. $15.00. Iqbal Academy Pakistan, 116-McLeod Road, Lahore Pakistan. **Tel** 57214. **Ed** Muhammad Munawwar. **Ind/Abst** MLA Int. Bibliogr. Books Artic. Mod. Lang. Lit. **LC** BP80.16. bk rev. adv acc. **Circ** 500. Studies in Iqbal's life, poetry and thought, Islamic studies, philosophy, history, comparative religion, art and literature.

IRSHAD (SANA, YEMEN). (AL-IRSHAD). Periodical. Arabic. mo. 20.00. Maktab Al-Tawjih Wa-Al-Irshad Al-Amm Al-Wizarat Al-Awqaf Bi-Al-Jumhuriyah Al-Arabiyah Al-Yamaniyah, S B 852, Sana Yemen. LC BP1.

AL ISLAM. Periodical. Malay. ir. $1.00 Single Issue. Kumpulan Syari Kat Utusan Melayu (M) Bhd, No 46M Jalan Lima Jaland Chan Sow Lin, Kuala Lumpur Malaysia. LC BP1.

ISLAM. VFOAT Islam Journal. No. 1-. Periodical. UK. English. qt. $12.00. Diwan Press, The Annex Wood Dalling Hall, Norwich NR11 6SG Norfolk England.

ISLAM AND THE MODERN AGE. V. 1- May 1970-. 0021-1826. Periodical. II. English. qt. $16.00. Zakir Hussain, Institute of Islamic Studies Jamia Millia Islamia Jamianager, 110025 New Delhi India. **Tel** 630258. **Ed** Ziya Ul Hasan Farugi. **LC** D199.3. **Circ** 1,500. Articles on Islam and other religions are published in this journal. Moreover, historical and philosophical aspects of religions are also studied through articles.

ISLAM AND THE MODERN WORLD. V. 1- Mar. 1977-. Periodical. BG. English. qt. $8.00. GPO Box 351 16-A Larmini, Dacca Bangladesh. LC BP1. DD 297.05.

ISLAM TETKIKLERI ENSTITUS DERGISI. **Main/Corp** Istanbul. Universite. Islam Tetkikleri Enstitusu. VFOAT Review of the Institute of Islamic Studies. Vol. 1- (Cuz 1-). TU. chiefly in Turkish. qt. Ayniyat Burosu, Istanbul Univ-Fac of Letters, Istanbul Turkey. **Ind/Abst** Am. Hist. Life, Hist. Abstr., Part A, Mod. Hist. Abstr., Hist. Abst., Part B, Twent. Century Abstr., Hist. Abstr. LC BP20.

ISLAMIC AFFAIRS. 0748-0482. Periodical. US. English. mo. $15.00. Islamic Affairs, POB 5132, Falls Church VA 22044. **Tel** (703)379-7493. **Ed** Yasin T Aljibouri. bk rev. adv acc. **Circ** 6,000. Covers non-sectarian, non-political Islamic information.

ISLAMIC AND COMPARATIVE LAW QUARTERLY. Vol. 1, No. 1 (Jan./Mar. 1981)-. Periodical. II. English. qt. 60.00. Head Department of Law of the Indian Institute of Islamic Studies, Hamdard Nagar PO Pushpa Bhavan, New Delhi 110062 India.

ISLAMIC HERALD. V. 1- May 1975-. English. bm. $0.63. Islamic Herald, 250 D Tingkat 2, Jalan Ipoh Kuala Lumpur Malaysia. LC BP1. DD 297.05.

ISLAMIC ORDER. V. 1- Jan. 1979-. Periodical. English. ir. $20.00. Ismail, Ahmad Minai 218, Bahadurabad Karachi Pakistan. LC BP1. DD 297.05.

ISLAMIC PERSPECTIVES. V. 1- Mar. 1971-. Periodical. English. ir. LC BP1. DD 297.05.

ISLAMIC REVIEW (AHMADIYYA ANJUMAN ISHAAT ISLAM, LAHORE). (THE ISLAMIC REVIEW). Vol. 1, No. 1 (Oct. 1980)-. 0735-3758. Periodical. US. English. ir. $12.00. Ahmadiyya Anjuman Ishaat Islam Lashore Inc, 36911 Walnut Street, Newark CA 94560. **Tel** (415)791-6449.

ISLAMIC REVOLUTION. Vol. 1 Apr. 1979-. 0730-613X. Periodical. US. English. mo. $12.00 Domestic, $14.00 Canada. Research and Publication, PO Box 2556, Falls Church VA 22042.

ISLAMIC STUDIES. V. 1- Mar. 1962-. 0578-8072. Periodical. PK. English. qt. 15.00. Islamic Research Institute, PO Box 1035, Islamabad Pakistan. **Tel** 854560. **Ed** Muhammad Khalid Masud. LC BP1. DD 297.05. bk rev. **Circ** 700. Publishes articles on Islamic history, law, jurisprudence, politics, economics, literature, culture, science, religion, and other Islamic subjects.

ISMAILI MIRROR. Periodical. English (Gujarati). ir. Gardem Jamatkhana, Garden East, Karachi Pakistan. LC BP195.18. DD 297.822095491.

JAWHAR AL-ISLAM. VFOAT Jaoqhar el Islam. Periodical. Arabic or French. ir. 28 Jamal Abdul Nasser Street, Tunis Tunisia. LC BP1.

JERNAL JIHAD. VFOAT Jihad. V. 1- 1972/73-. Malay. ir. Persatuan Mahasiswa Fakulti Pengajian Islam, Jalan University, Petaling Jaya Malaysia. LC BP1.

THE JOURNAL OF MUSLIM WORLD LEAGUE. **Main/Corp** Rabitat Al-Alam AL-Islami. VFOAT Journal of Rabitatul Aalami Islami. V. 1- Oct. 1973-. SU. Arabic and English. mo. $9.45. Muslim World League, PO Box 537 and 538, Mecca Saudi Arabia. LC BP1. DD 297.

KAYHAN-I FARHANGI. 1 (63, I.E. March/April 1984)-. Periodical. Persian, Modern. mo. Khiyaban-I Firdawsi, Kuchah-I Atabak, Muassasah-I Kayhan, Daftar-I Kayhan-I Farhang I. LC BP193.5.

KUTUB ISLAMIYAH. V. 1- (No. 1)-. Periodical. UA. Arabic. mo. LC BP20.

LAPORAN TAHUNAN DIREKTORAT PENDIDIKAN AGAMA ISLAM. **Main/Corp** Indonesia. Direktorat Pendidikan Agama Islam. Indonesian. ir. Direktorat Pendidikan Agama Islam, Jl M H Thamrin No 6, Jakarta Indonesia. LC BP10.I5. *Laporan Tahunan - Direktorat Pendidikan Agama, Direktorat Jenderal Bimbingan Masyarakat Islam.*

LIGHT. (THE LIGHT). Vol. 1, No. 1 (1978)-. 0229-5636. Periodical. CN. English. ir. The Light, Suite 505/39 Thorncliffe Park Drive, Toronto Ontario M4H 1J1 Canada. DD 297.8605.

MAAS JOURNAL OF ISLAMIC SCIENCE. VFOAT Journal of Islamic Science. Vol. 1, No. 1 (Jan. 1985)-. Periodical. English. ir.

MAHJUBAH. Periodical. English. ir. $2.00 Single Issue. Box 314/1947, Tehran Islamic Republic of Iran. LC BP193.5. DD 297.05.

MAJALAH HAJI. Periodical. IO. Indonesian. ir. Direktorat Jenderal Bimas Islam dan Urusan Haji, Departemen Agama RI, JI Jaksa No 24, Jakarta Indonesia. LC BP187.3.

MAJALLAH-I NUR-I ILM : NASHRIYAH-I JAMIAH-I MUDARRISIN-I HAWZAH-I ILMIYAH-I QUM. Periodical. Persian, Modern. ir. LC BP193.5.

MAJALLAT ABHATH AL-IQTISAD AL-ISLAMI. VFOAT Journal of Research in Islamic Economics. Journal 1, No. 1, (Sayf 1983)-. Periodical. Arabic (English). ir. International Centre for Research in Islamic Economics, King Abdulaziz University, PO Box 16711, Jeddah 21474 Saudi Arabia. LC BP173.75.

MAJALLAT AL-AZHAR CEASED. **Main/Corp** Jami Al-Azhar. VFOAT Azhar Review, Azhar Magazine, Magallatul-Azhar. Journal 7- (Two Times 1-) Forbidden 1355 March 1936. Ceased publication in Feb. Periodical. UA. Arabic (English). **Ed** M F Wajdi. LC BP1. Index in last issue of volume - attached. *Nur Al-Islam.*

MAJALLAT AL-FIKR AL-ISLAMI. V. 1, No. 1, (September 1983)-. Periodical. SJ. Arabic. qt. $2.00 single issue. Slkritir Tahrir Majallat, Al-Fikr Al-Islami, PO Box 2469 Al-Khartum Sudan.

MAJALLAT RABITAT AL-ALAM AL-ISLAMI. **Main/Corp** Muslim World League. Periodical. Arabic. ir. $3.00. PO Box 538, Makkah Saudi Arabia. LC BP1. *Rabitat Al-Alam Al-Islami.*

MAKARIM AL-AKHLAQ AL-ISLAMIYAH. Began in 1900. Periodical. Arabic. ir. Jamiyat Makarim Al-Akhlaq Al-Islamiyah, 61 Shari Jazirat Badran Shubra, Al-Qahirah United Arab Republic (Egypt). LC BP1.

MANAR AL-ISLAM. V. 1- Jan. 1976-. Periodical. Arabic. ir. PO Box 2922, Abu Zaby Trucial States. LC BP1.

THE MINARET. VFOAT Minaret Monthly International. Began with 1964 issue. CF NST. 0026-4415. Periodical. English. ir. LC BP1.

MINBAR AL-ISLAM. Vol. 1 (July 1961)-. Periodical. UA. English. mo. Miss Linda Fawzi, 3 Kobessi Str Fagallah, Cairo Egypt.

MIZAN (JAKARTA, INDONESIA). (MIZAN : INDONESIAN FORUM FOR ISLAMIC AND SOCIAL STUDIES). VFOAT Indonesian Forum for Islamic and Social Studies. Vol. 1, No. 1 (Jan. 1984)-. Periodical. English. qt. $4.50 Each Issue. LC BP63.I5. DD 297.09598.

AL MOMIN. VFOAT Mumin. Began in 1980. Periodical. in English. ir. Jamia Mosque Railway Landhies and Islamia Primary School Association, P O Box 72624, Nairobi Kenya. LC BP1. DD 297.05.

AL MUNTAKA. VFOAT Muntaqa. No. 1-. Periodical. FR. Arabic (English, and French). qt. Al Muntaka, 23 Rue Jean Giraudoux, 75116 Paris France. **Tel** 77891232. bk rev. **Circ** 1,000. A review for the dissemination of muslim writings. It contains articles in Arabic, English and French in addition to summaries and a bibliography of articles dealing with Islam.

MUSLIM EDUCATION QUARTERLY. Vol. 1, No. 1 (Autumn 1983)-. 0263-6247. Periodical. UK. English. ir.

MUSLIM (JAMAAH AL-ISLAMIYAH (LIBIYA)). (AL-MUSLIM). Periodical. Arabic. ir. $15.00. Al-Muslim, PO Box 1147, Port of Spain Trinidad West Indies. LC DS35.3.

THE MUSLIM WORLD. V. 38- Jan. 1948-. 0027-4909. Periodical. US. English. qt. $20.00. Hartford Seminary, 77 Sherman Street, Hartford CT 06105. **Tel** (203)232-4451. **Ed** W Bijleveld, Y Haddad and W Haddad. **Ind/Abst** Am. Hist. Life, Hist. Abstr., Part A, Mod. Hist. Abstr., Hist. Abst., Part B, Twent. Century Abstr., MLA Int. Bibliogr. Books Artic. Mod. Lang. Lit., Hist. Abstr., Humanit. Index, Relig. Index One, Period., Years Work Eng. Stud. (cum index). bk rev. adv acc. **Circ** 1,400. Study of Islam and Christian-Muslim relations. *Moslem World*, 0362-4641.

THE MUSLIM WORLD BOOK REVIEW. Vol. 1, No. 1 (Autumn 1980)-. 0260-3063. Periodical. UK. English. qt. $22.98. Islamic Foundation Publishing Unit, Unit 9 Old Dunlop Facty 9 Evington Valley Road, Leicester England. **Tel** (0533) 734860. **Ed** Khurram Murad and Manazir Ahsan. LC DS35.3. DD 909.097671. bk rev. adv acc. **Circ** 1,000. Aspires both to inform and stimulate the lay readers as well as the scholars through in-depth reviews, short introductions and select bibliographies.

THE MUSLIM WORLD LEAGUE JOURNAL. VFOAT M.W.L. Journal. Periodical. English. mo. 20.00. Muslim World League, PO Box 537, Makkah Al-Mukkarramah Saudi Arabia. LC BP1. DD 2997.05. *Journal of Muslim World League.*

NADWAT AL-MUHADARAT. Arabic. ir. LC BP1.

NASHR-I DANISH. V. 1, (1359 I.E. Nov./Dec. 1980)-. Periodical. IR. Persian, Modern. bm. 850.00. Nasrollah Pourjavady, 85 Park Avenue, Tehran Islamic Republic of Iran. LC DS266.

NASHRAH AL-IKHBARIYAH (RESEARCH CENTRE FOR ISLAMIC HISTORY, ART, AND CULTURE). (AL-NASHRAH AL-IKHBARIYAH). TU. Arabic. ir. PO Box 24, Besiktas Istanbul Turkey.

NASHRAT MAHAD SHUUN AL-AQALLIYAT AL-MUSLIMAH, JAMIAT AL-MALIK ABD AL-AZIZ BI-JIDDAH. **Main/Corp** Jamiat Al-Malik Abd Al-Aziz. Mahad Shuun Al-Aqalliyat Al-Muslimah. VFOAT Bulletin - Institute of Muslim Minority Affairs (IMMA), King Abdul Aziz University, Jeddah. Arabic (English). ir. Mahad Shuun Al-Aqallitay Al-Muslimah Bi-Jamiat, Al-Malik Abd Al-Aziz, PO Box 1540, Jiddah AL-Mimlakah Al-Arabiyah Al-Saudiyah, Jiddah Sudan. LC BP52.5.

NEWS OF MUSLIMS IN EUROPE. Began with: Mar. 7, 1980. 0143-9774. Periodical. UK. English. bm. The Centre Selly Oak Colleges, Birmingham B29 6LE United Kingdom.

NIDA AL-ISLAM. VFOAT Mawsuat Nida Al-Islam. Periodical. Arabic. ir. 0.60 Single Issue. Dar Al-Fikr Lil-Nashr Wa-Al-Ilam, 58 Shari 26 Yuliyu, Al-Qahirah United Arab Republic (Egypt). LC BP1.

NUR-I HAYAT. VFOAT Noor-E-Hyat. Periodical. Urdu. ir. 8.00. Markazi Anjiman-I Mahdviyyah Building, Chancalguda, Haidrabad India. LC BP193.5.

NURADEEN. 8756-4637. Periodical. US. English. qt. $16.00. Zahra Publications, PO Box 730, Blanco TX 78606. DD 297.

Religion, Mythology, Rationalism—Judaism

RESEARCH PAPERS (CENTRE FOR THE STUDY OF ISLAM AND CHRISITAN-MUSLIM RELATIONS (BIRMINGHAM, WEST MIDLANDS, ENGLAND)). (RESEARCH PAPERS : MUSLIMS IN EUROPE). VFOAT Muslims in Europe. Began with Mar. 1979. 0260-3772. Periodical. UK. English. qt. The Centre Selly Oak Colleges, Birmingham B29 6LE United Kingdom.

REVISTA DEL INSTITUTO DE ESTUDIOS ISLAMICOS EN MADRID. Vol. 5 (1957)-16 (1971). Periodical. SP. Spanish (text in Arabic). an. Institut Francisco de Asia Mendz, Casariego 10-Matias Montero 14, Madrid 2 Spain. Ind/Abst Am. Hist. Life, Hist. Abstr. *Revista del Instituto Egipcio de Estudios Islamicos.*

REVUE DES ETUDES ISLAMIQUES. V. 1-. 0336-156X. Periodical. FR. French. sa. Libraries Paul Geuthner, 12 rue Vavin, Paris 6E France. Ed L Massignon. Ind/Abst MLA Int. Bibliogr. Books Artic. Mod. Lang. Lit. LC BP1. DD 297.05. *Revue du Monde Musulman.*

RISALAH - PROYEK PENERANGAN BIMBINGAN DAN DAWAH/ KHOTBAH AGAMA ISLAM (PUSAT). Main/Corp Indonesia. Proyek Penerangan Bimbingan Dan Daway/Khotbah Agama Islam (Pusat). Periodical. Indonesian. ir. LC BP1.

RISALAH (RABAT, MOROCCO). (AL-RISALAH). VFOAT Arrisala. Periodical. Arabic. sm. 1.00 Single Issue. B P 356, Rabat Morroco. LC BP1.

RISALAT AL-AZHAR. No. 1- (July 3, 1981). Periodical. UA. Arabic. wk. Idarat Al-Azhar Bi-Al-Qahirah Egypt, Majma Al-Buhuth, Al-Islamiyah Bi-Al-Azhar, Al-Qahirah Egypt. LC BP1.

RISALAT AL-ISLAM (CAIRO, EGYPT : 1983). (RISALAT AL-ISLAM). No. 1, (December 1983)-. Periodical. Arabic. mo. 0.25 Single Issue. 12 Shari Ramsis, Al-Qahirah Egypt. LC BP1.

RISALAT AL-JIHAD. (RISALAT AL-JIHAD). VFOAT Rissalat Al-Jihad. Periodical. in English. mo. $1.00 Single Issue. PO Box 2682, Tripoli Libya. LC BP1. DD 297.05.

RISALAT AL-MAAHID AL-ILMIYAH. VFOAT Message Magazine. Periodical. Arabic. ir. Al-Batha Mahad Al-Riyad Al-Ilmi, Al-Riyad Saudi Arabia. LC BP1.

RISALAT AL-THAWRAH AL-ISLAMIYAH : MAJALLAT HARAS AL-THAWRAH AL-ISLAMIYAH. No. 1, (June 1981)-. Periodical. IR. Arabic. ir. Al-Jumhuriyah Al-Islamiyah Al-Iraniyah, Mintaqat 14, SB 41/1588, Tehran Iran. LC BP63.I68.

SINAR DARUSSALAM. Vol. 1.- (No. 1-). Periodical. English or Indonesian. ir. 100 Each Issue. Kopelma Darussalam, Kotak Pos 29, Banda ACEH Indonesia. LC BP1.

SINAR ISLAM. Began with Sept. 1932 issue. Periodical. Indonesian. ir. 150 Each Issue. Jemaat Ahmadiyah Indonesia, Jl Tawakkal Ujung Raya 7, Jakarta Barat, Jakarta Indonesia. LC BP195.A5.

STATISTIK KEAGAMAAN. See Statistics.

STUDIA ISLAMICA. 1.-. 0585-5292. Periodical. FR. French (English). sa. Editions GP Maisonneuve & Larose, 11 rue Victor Cousin, Paris 5E France. Ed R Brunschvig and J Schacht. Ind/Abst Am. Hist. Life, Hist. Abstr., Part A, Mod. Hist. Abstr., Hist. Abst., Part B, Twent. Century Abstr., MLA Int. Bibliogr. Books Artic. Mod. Lang. Lit., Hist. Abstr. LC BP1. (cum index).

STUDIES IN ISLAM. Vol. 1, No. 1 (Jan. 1964)-V. 10 (Jan. 1974). 0039-3711. Periodical. II. English. qt. 12.00. Indian Institute of Islamic Studies, Tughlaqabad PO Madangir, New Delhi 110062 India. Tel 6439685. Ed Hakim Abdul Hamid. LC BP1. bk rev. adv acc. Circ 1,000. Promotes interest in Islamic studies-particularly those aspects that are obscure by allowing in its pages a healthy discussion between Muslim thinkers and non-Muslim scholars, about Muslim arts, sciences, history and literature.

SUARA TAQWA. Vol. 1- Oct. 1976-. Periodical. MY. Malay. ir. $13.80. D/A Johan Security Sdn Bhd, Tingkat 4 Bangunan Bakti No 91 Jl Campbell, Kuala Lumpur Malaysia. LC BP1.

TAHQIQAT-I ISLAMI. Periodical. Urdu. qt. 20.00. Idarah-Yi Tahqiq Va Tasnif-I, Islami Panvali Kothi, Dudhpur Aligarh 202001. LC BP1.

TAWHID (TEHRAN, IRAN). (AL-TAWHID). Vol. 1, No. 1 (Muharram 1404 Oct. 1983)-. Periodical. English. qt. $16.00. Islamic Propagation Organization/International Relations Department, P O Box 41-2959, Tehran Iran. LC BP1. DD 297.05.

THAQAFAH (DEOBAND, INDIA). (AL-THAQAFAH). VFOAT Saqafah. Periodical. Arabic. mo. $10.00. LC BP1.

THE THEOSOPHICAL MOVEMENT. V. 1- Nov. 1930-. 0040-5884. Periodical. II. English. mo. 21.00. Theosophy Company India Private Ltd, Theo Hall, 40 New Marine Lines, Bombay 400-020 India. Tel 299024. Ed M Dastur. LC BP500. DD 212. Circ 320. (ctrl). Devoted to the living of the higher life.

UHUD. VFOAT Ohad. Periodical. Urdu. ir. 6.50. Ilyas Husain Arzu, Bazaria Fath Ali, Rampur India. Ed Ilyas Husain Arzu. LC BP1.

UMMAH (DAWHAH, QATAR). (AL-UMMAH). V. 1, No. 1, (Nov. 1980)-. QA. Arabic. mo. $16.00. S B 893, Al-Dawhah Qatar. LC BP1.

THE UNIVERSAL MESSAGE. V. 1- June 1979-. Periodical. PK. English. mo. 11.00 Pounds, $21.00. Islamic Research Acadmey, C-163/10 Mansoora, Karachi 3805 Pakistan. Tel 681157. Ed Syed Wajahat Ali. LC BP1. DD 909.097671. bk rev. adv acc. Circ 750. Discussing social, historical, political and economic subjects as enunciated by Islam.

URWAH AL-WUTHQA (GENEVA, SWITZERLAND). (FIRMEST BOND). VFOAT Le Lien Indeliable. Periodical. SW. English (Arabic). qt. $40.00. Al-Urwa Al-Wathqa, PO Box 1894, CH-1218 Geneva Switzerland. LC BP1. DD 297.05.

THE VOICE OF ISLAM. 0042-8132. Periodical. English. mo $7.00. Voice of Islam, Box 7141, Karachi 3 Pakistan. LC BP1.

WAHYU. Ed. 1.- Oct. 1978-. Periodical. Indonesian. mo. 400 Single Issue. Yayasan Wahyu, Jl Kebon Dacang 30 No 9, Jakarta Indonesia. LC BP63.I5.

WELT DES ISLAMS. (DIE WELT DES ISLAMS). VFOAT The World of Islam, Le Monde de l'Islam. V. 1 (1913)-V. 25 (1943). 0043-2539. NE. German (articles in English and French). sa. 72.-. E J Brill, PO Box 9000, 2300 PA Leiden The Netherlands. Tel (071)312624. Ed S Wilde and W Ende. Ind/Abst MLA Int. Bibliogr. Books Artic. Mod. Lang. Lit., Am. Hist. Life, Hist. Abstr., Part A, Mod. Hist. Abstr., Hist. Abst., Part B, Twent. Century Abstr., Hist. Abstr. LC DS36. (cum index). bk review. Circ 500. Focuses on the history and culture of the peoples of Islam from the end of the 18th Century. Special attention is given to literature.

JUDAISM

ACTUALITE JUIVE. VFOAT Canadian Jewish Digest. VAT Canadian Jewish Digest (1978). V. 19, No. 4-. 0711-2092. Periodical. CN. English (French). sa. $1.00. Canadian Jewish Digest, 6750 Wesbury Avenue, Montreal Quebec H3W 2X6 Canada. DD 971.004924. *Selections de Canadian Jewish Digest, 0711-2084.*

AGADA. VFOAT Agadah. Vol. 1 No. 1 (Summer 1981)-. 0740-2392. Periodical. US. English. ty. $10.00. Agada, 2020 Essex Street, Berkeley CA 94703. LC BM1. DD 296.05.

AJL NEWSLETTER. See Library and Information Science.

AJS REVIEW. Main/Corp Association for Jewish Studies. VAT Association for Jewish Studies Review. V. 1- 1976-. 0364-0094. US. English (German or Hebrew). sa. KTAV Publishing House, 900 Jefferson Street #6249, Hoboken NJ 07030. Tel (201)963-9524. Ed Robert Chazin. Ind/Abst Am. Hist. Life, Hist. Abstr., Part A, Mod. Hist. Abstr., Hist. Abst., Part B, Twent. Century Abstr. LC BM1. DD 296. bk rev. Circ 500. Scholarly studies of any subject relating to Jews and Judaism.

ALON LA-MADRIKH. Main/Corp Erza, Irgun Ha-Noar Ha-Haredi Be-Erets Yisrael. Mahleket Ha-Hadrakhah. Hebrew. ir. 114 Allenby Road, PO Box 114, Tel-Avia Israel. LC BM100.

THE AMERICAN JEWISH WORLD. 1912. 0002-9084. Periodical. US. English. wk. $14.75. World Publishing Inc, 4509 Minnetonka Boulevard, Minneapolis MN 55416. Tel (612)920-7000. Ed Stacey R Bush. bk rev. adv acc. Circ 7,000. Newspaper publishing international, national and local news of Jewish interest.

AMERICAN JEWISH YEAR BOOK. See Yearbooks, Almanacs, Directories.

THE AMIT WOMAN. V. 56, N. 3 (Dec. 1983/Jan. 1984)-. 0747-0258. Periodical. US. English. bm. $15.00 Membership. Amit Women, 817 Broadway, New York NY 10003. LC DS150.R3. DD 956.9400105. *American Mizrachi Woman, 0161-3952.*

ANGLO-JEWISH MEDIA LIST. 0198-7151. US. English. R K Communications Inc, 98-15 65th Road, Rego Park NY 11374. LC Z6367, DS101. DD 016.0713089924.

ANNUAL PUBLICATION - JEWISH HISTORICAL SOCIETY OF WESTERN CANADA. Main/Corp Jewish Historical Society of Western Canada. 1st- June 1970-. 0317-1655. Periodical. CN. English (text in summaries in Yiddish). an. 365 Hargrave Street/Room 406, Manitoba R3B 2K3 Canada. LC F1035.J5. DD 917.106924.

ANNUAL REPORT - HEBREW UNION COLLEGE-JEWISH INSTITUTE OF RELIGION. Main/Corp Hebrew Union College-Jewish Institute of Religion. US. English. an. KTAV Publishing House Inc, 75 Varick Street, New York NY 10013. LC BM90.H44. DD 296.07103.

ANNUAL - SOCIAL CULTURAL AND EDUCATIONAL ASSOCIATION OF THE JEWS IN THE PEOPLE'S REPUBLIC OF BULGARIA. CENTRAL BOARD. Main/Corp Social Cultural and Educational Association of the Jews In the People's Republic of Bulgaria. Central Board. VFOAT Godishnik. V. 1- 1966-. Periodical. Bulgarian (added title pages, contents and summaries in English, French, German, Russian and Spanish). ir. LC DS135.B8.

ARCHE (1957). (L'ARCHE). Began with: Jan. 1957 issue. 0518-2840. Periodical. FR. French. ir. $23.95. L'Arche, 14 rue Georges Berger, 75017 Paris France. LC DS101. *Revue du F.S.J.U.*

ATERET ZEKENIM. 1-. US. Hebrew. Simcha-Graphic Associates, 4914 13th Avenue, Brooklyn NY 11219. LC BM520.

AVOTAYNU. See Genealogy and Heraldry.

BALTIMORE JEWISH TIMES. 0005-450X. Periodical. US. English. wk. Baltimore Jewish Times Weekly, 2104 North Charles Street, Baltimore MD 21218. Tel (301)752-3504.

BARKAI (JERUSALEM). (BARKAI). Hebrew. ir. LC BM520.

BE-IKVE HA-TSON. VFOAT Bikvy Hatzon. Vol. 1. (December 1980)-. Periodical. US. Hebrew (Yiddish). mo. $0.50 Per Issue. Rabbi Mayer Simon, PO Box 628, Monreo NY 10950. LC BM1.

BE-OR HA-TORAH (JERUSALEM). (BE-OR HA-TORAH). VFOAT Bor Hatorah. Vol. 1 (1982)-. Periodical. English (Hebrew). sa. $9.00. Bor Hatorah c/o Dr Yaacov Hanoka, 107 York Terrace, Brookline MA 02146. LC BM1. DD 296.83205.

BET MIKRA : KETAV-ET SHEL HA-HEVRAH LE-HEKER HA-MIKRA BE-YISRAEL. VFOAT Beth Mikra. Vol. 1 (Mar. 1956)-. 0005-979X. Periodical. IS. Hebrew. qt. 15.00. World Jewish Bible Society, Box 7024, Jerusalem Israel. Tel 02-245751. Ed Ben-Zion Luria. Ind/Abst Old Testam. Abstr. LC BS410. bk rev. Circ 1,300. (ctrl). The only Hebrew-language, dedicated entirely to Bible studies. Covers articles based on Jewish Bible, language, geography, history, Jewish belief and archaeology.

BIULETYN ZYDOWSKIEGO INSTYTUTU HISTORYCZNEGO. Began publication with No. 1 (Jan./June 1951). Periodical. PL. Polish. qt. ARS Polona, Krakowskie Przedmiescie 7, 00-068 Warsaw Poland. (cum index).

THE B'NAI B'RITH INTERNATIONAL JEWISH MONTHLY. VFOAT Jewish Monthly. Vol. 96, No. 1 (Aug.-Sept. 1981)-. 0279-3415. Periodical. US. English. ir. $8.00. B'Nai B'Rith Inc, 1640 Rhode Island Avenue Northwest, Washington DC 20036. Tel (202)857-6645. Ed Marc Silver. Ind/Abst Index Jew. Period. LC HS2228.B4. DD 369. bk rev. adv acc. Circ 180,000. A Jewish family publication that covers Israel, politics, religion, current events, history, culture and lifestyles. *National Jewish Monthly, 0027-9552.*

Religion, Mythology, Rationalism—Judaism

BROWN JUDAIC STUDIES. No. 1-. 0147-927X. Monographic Series. US. English. Scholars Press, PO Box 1608, Decatur GA 30029. Tel (404)329-6950. Ed Jacob Neusner. LC UNC. Studies in Jewish history and culture, including all epochs from ancient to contemporary.

BULLETIN OF THE INTERNATIONAL ORGANIZATION FOR SEPTUAGINT AND COGNATE STUDIES. Main/Corp International Organization for Septuagint and Cognate Studies. VFOAT Bulletin IOCOS. No. 1- June 1968-. 0145-3890. US. Multilingual (English, French, and German). an. $3.00. Cleveland State University, Department of Religious Studies, Cleveland OH 44115. Ind/Abst New Testam. Abstr., Old Testam. Abstr., Relig. Index One, Period.

BULLETIN OF THE JEWISH HISTORICAL SOCIETY OF ENGLAND. Main/Corp Jewish Historical Society of England. 1981-2-. UK. English. an. Honorable Secretary, 33 Seymour Place, London W1H 5AP England. LC DS135.E5. DD 942.004924006. *Annual Report and Accounts for the Session, 0306-7998.*

CAHIERS BERNARD LAZARE. 1957. Periodical. FR. French. ir. $19.96. Cahiers Bernard Lazare, 10 rue St Claude, 75003 Paris France. Ed Cercle Bernard Lasar. bk rev. adv acc. Circ 2,000. Information, articles on Israel, Jewish diaspora and left wing ideas.

CANADIAN ZIONIST. (THE CANADIAN ZIONIST). 0008-5383. Periodical. CN. English (includes some text in Hebrew). bm. $3.86. Canadian Zionist Federation, 1310 Green Aveune/Suite 822, B Brodwin, Montreal Quebec H3Z 2B2 Canada. Tel (514)034-0804.

CENTRAL AFRICAN ZIONIST DIGEST. V. 1- April 1958-. Periodical. English. ir. Central Africa Zionist Organization, PO Box 1162, Bulawayo Rhodesia. LC DS149.A1. DD 956.94001.

CENTRAL CONFERENCE OF AMERICAN RABBIS ANNUAL CONVENTION. See Yearbooks, Almanacs, Directories.

CHALLENGE: SUPPLEMENT OF BA-MAARAKHAH. V. 1, No. 2/3-. Periodical. IS. English. qt. $10.00. Sephardic Council of Jerusalem, PO Box 10, Jerusalem Israel.

CHRISTIAN JEWISH RELATIONS. No. 70-81, Mar. 1980-Dec. 1982. 0144-2902. Periodical. UK. English. qt. $25.00. Institute of Jewish Affairs, 11 Hartford Street, London W1Y 7DX England. Tel 01-491 3517. LC BM535. DD 261.2. A documentary survey of the more important statements and publications relevant to the churches' new approach. *Christian Attitudes on Jews and Judaism.*

CHRISTIANS, JEWS TODAY. VFOAT Chretiens, Juifs Aujourd'Hui. VAT Chretiens, Juifs Aujourd'Hui (Edition Anglaise). V. 6, No. 1- Oct. 1979-. 0225-5375. Periodical. CN. French. ir. Ligue pur les Droits de l'Homme des Bnai Brith, Bureau 200/7881 Boulevard Decarie, Montreal Quebec H4P 2H2 Canada. DD 296.3872. *Chretiens et Juifs Aujourd'Hui.*

COLUMBIA UNIVERSITY STUDIES IN JEWISH HISTORY, CULTURE, AND INSTITUTIONS. Main/Corp Columbia University. Center of Israel and Jewish Studies. No. 1- 1971-. 0069-6366. US. English. ir. Columbia University Press, 136 South Broadway, Irvington-On-Hudson NY 10533.

COMMENTARY. V. 1- Nov. 1945-. 0010-2601. Periodical. US. English. mo. Commentary, 165 East 56th Street, New York NY 10022. Tel (212)751-4000. Ind/Abst Book Rev. Index, MLA Int. Bibliogr. Books Artic. Mod. Lang. Lit., Pop. Mag. Rev., Film Lit. Index, Media Rev. Dig., Read. Guide Period. Lit., Index Jew. Period., ABC Pol Sci, Funk Scott Index Corp. Ind., Hist. Abst., Part B, Twent. Century Abstr., Am. Hist. Life, Infobank, Energy Res. Abstr., Humanit. Index, Abstr. Soc. Work., Book Rev. Digest, Soc. Sci. Citation Index, Mag. Index, Sociol. Abstr., Guide Soc. Sci. Relig. Period. Lit. LC DS101. DD 296.05. *Contemporary Jewish Record, 0363-6909.*

COMMON GROUND. Vol. 1-30A, No. 3. 0010-325X. Periodical. UK. English. qt. $7.66. Council of Christians and Jews, 1 Pennington Park Road, London NW6 1AX England. Tel 01-794-8178. Ed I Levy. bk rev. Circ 2,500. Features articles and reviews on Christianity and Judaism and relations between these two religions. *Christians and Jews.*

CONSERVATIVE JUDAISM. Vol. 1, No. 1- Jan. 1945-. 0010-6542. Periodical. US. English. qt. The Rabbinical Assembly, 3080 Broadway, New York NY 10027. Tel (212)243-6000. LC BM197.5. DD 296.834205.

CURRENT DIALOGUE. No. 1 (Winter 1980/81)-. Periodical. SZ. English (French and German). ir. Newsletter DFI, 150 Route de Ferney, 1211 Geneva 20 Switzerland. *Church and the Jewish People.*

DAAT/A JOURNAL OF JEWISH PHILOSOPHY & KABBALAH. V. 1- Winter 738 1978-. 0334-2336. Periodical. IS. English (Hebrew). ir. $8.00. Universitat Bar-Ilan, Department of Philosophy, Bar-Ilan University, Ramat-Gan Israel. LC B154. DD 296.

DAPE YIUTS VE-HADRAKHAH. 1-. Hebrew. ir. LC BM100.

DIRECTORY OF JEWISH RESIDENT SUMMER CAMPS. See Yearbooks, Almanacs, Directories.

DOR LE-DOR. VFOAT Dor le Dor. V. 1- 1- Fall 1972-. 0334-2166. Periodical. IS. English. qt. 12.00. World Jewish Bible Society, PO Box 7024, Jerusalem Israel. Tel 02-245751. Ed Louis Katzoff. Ind/Abst Old Testam. Abstr. LC BS410. DD 221.605. bk rev. Circ 1,300. (ctrl). A journal of Jewish Bible studies, on popular and academic levels of Jewish scripture. Intended for rabbis, laymen, universities, theologians, students, and libraries.

EMUNA/ISRAEL FORUM. 1976. Periodical. GW. German. bm. 18.00. Verlag Israel-Forum, Postfach 69, D8802 Rothenburg West Germany. LC BM535. *Emuna, Israel/Forum.*

ENCOUNTER TODAY CEASED. VFOAT Judaism and Christianity in the Contemporary World. V. 1-14. 0013-709X. Periodical. FR. English. ir. 71 rue Notre-Dame-des-Champs, 75006 Paris France. *Jews and Ourselves.*

ESTUDIOS SEFARDIES. VFOAT ESEF. No. 1 (1978)-. 0210-9077. Periodical. SP. English (Spanish). $7.85. C.S.I.C, Vitrubio 15, Servicio de Distribution, Madrid 8 Spain. Ind/Abst MLA Int. Bibliogr. Books Artic. Mod. Lang. Lit.

ETHIOPIAN JEWRY REPORT. Vol.1, No. 1 (Spring 1982)-. 0827-8687. Periodical. CN. English. ir. Free. Canadian Association for Ethiopian Jews, 788 Marlee Avenue, Toronto Ontario Canada. DD 963.004924. (ctrl).

EUROPEAN JUDAISM. V. 1- 1966-. 0014-3006. Periodical. UK. English. sa. $9.00. European Judaism, Kent House Rutland Gardens, London SW7 1BX England. Tel (01)584-2754. Ed Albert M Friedlander. (cum index). bk rev. Circ 500. Serves as a link between European Jewish communities which survived the holocaust and a focal point for American and Israeli influences, etc.

EVREI I EVREISKII NAROD. VFOAT Jews and the Jewish People. V. 1, No. 1 (ZA Period 1.1. 1960-30.6.1960)-. Periodical. UK. Russian. ir. Hebrew University of Jerusalem, Ctr Docum East European Jewry, Jerusalem Israel. Tel 01-58271. Ed Jacob Ingerman. bk rev. Circ 300. The collection has systematic information about attitudes to Jews, state of Israel and Zionism, which are reflected in the Soviet Press. Includes material about religion, history, and culture of Soviet Jewry from Soviet sources.

GENERATIONS. V. 1- Dec.1978-. 0191-6939. Periodical. US. English. sa. $4.50. Jewish Historical Society of Maryland, 15 Lloyd Street, Baltimore, MD 21202. Tel (301)732-6400. Ed Mary Sue Greisman. LC F190.J5. DD 975.2004924. Circ 1,400. (ctrl). Articles, oral histories, and other studies relating to the history, development and character of Jewish communities in Maryland.

GENUZOT. Sefer 1, 1-. Hebrew. ir. Ed M Hershler. LC BM1.

GESHER (NEW YORK, N.Y.). (GESHER). Periodical. US. English. ir. $5.00. Gesher, 500 West 185 Street, New York NY 10033. LC BM1. DD 296.05.

GREATER PHOENIX JEWISH NEWS. 0747-444X. Periodical. US. English. wk. $18.00. Greater Phoenix Jewish News, PO Box 26590, Phoenix AZ 85068. Tel (602)870-9470. Ed Flo Eckstein. bk rev. adv acc. Circ 6,000. News and feature stories of special interest to Jewish readers including local and world events, social milestones, politics, and community business news. *Phoenix Jewish News, 0747-444X.*

GUIA ANUAL ISRAELITA. AG. Spanish. an. Editorial Promocion, Pueyrredon 468 40 Piso Of 16, Buenos Aires Argentina. LC F3001.9.J5.

HA-DOAR. VFOAT Hadoar. Began in July 1922. 0017-6524. Periodical. US. Hebrew. ir. $25.00. Hadoar Association Inc, 1841 Broadway, New York NY 10023. Tel (212)581-5151. Ed Shlomo Shamir and Yael Feldman. LC DS101. bk rev. adv acc. Hebrew articles about Jews and Judaism with concentration on United States and Israel. Scholarly and literary works are included.

HA-EMEQ. (HA-EMEK). VFOAT Torah Journal Ho'Ameck. No. 1- April 1971-. 0303-1497. Hebrew. ir. Kolel Yire Ha-Shem, 8 Baal Hatanye Street, PO Box 5181, Yerushalagim Israel. LC BM520.

HA-MAOR. VFOAT Hamaor. Periodical. US. Hebrew. bm. $7.00 Domestic, $9.00 Foreign. Hamaor, 5002 18th Avenue, Brooklyn NY 11204. LC BM520.

HA-METIVTA. 0094-9701. US. Hebrew. 452 East 9th Street, Brooklyn NY 11218. LC BM520.

HA-OHEL. Year 1- 715 1954-. Periodical. Hebrew. ir. LC BM496.A1.

HA-PARDES. VFOAT Hapardes. V. 1- April 1927-. Periodical. US. Hebrew. mo. $8.00. S Elberg, 135 East Broadway, New York NY 11106. Ed S A Pardes. LC BM520. *Pardes.*

HADASSAH MAGAZINE. Began with Apr. 1961 issue. 0017-6516. Periodical. US. English. mo. $15.00. Womens Zionist Organization of America, 50 West 58th Street, New York NY 10019. Tel (212)303-8017. Ed Alan Tigay. LC DS101. DD 956.94005. bk rev. adv acc. Circ 370,000. (ctrl). Articles on Jewish life in Israel, American and around the world. *Hadassah Newsletter.*

HARVARD JUDAIC MONOGRAPHS. 1-. Monographic Series. US. English. ir. Harvard University Press, 79 Garden Street, Cambridge MA 02138.

THE HEBREW CHRISTIAN. V. 1- 1928-. 0017-9477. Periodical. UK. English. qt. $2.00. Shalom, Brockenhurst Road, Ramsgate England. Tel 0843 592669. Ed Ronald Lewis. LC BV2619. DD 296. bk rev. Circ 5,000. Hebrew Christianity and the spiritual and temporal help of Hebrew Christians.

HEBREW STUDIES. V. 17- 1976-. 0146-4094. US. English or Hebrew. an. $20.00. University of Wisconsin, c/o K N Schoville, 1220 Linden Drive/1346 Van Hise, Madison WI 53706. Tel (608)262-9785. Ed Keith N Schocille. Ind/Abst Relig. Index One, Period., Old Testam. Abstr. LC PJ4501. DD 492.405. bk rev. adv acc. Circ 600. A journal devoted to Hebrew language, literature, the Bible and related areas of scholarship. *Hebrew Abstracts, 0438-895X.*

HEBREW UNION COLLEGE ANNUAL. V. 1- 1924-. 0360-9049. US. English (some articles in German, Hebrew, and French). an. $20.00. Hebrew Union College, 3101 Clifton Avenue, Cincinnati OH 45220. Tel (513)221-1875. Ed Sheldon H Blank. Ind/Abst Am. Hist. Life, Hist. Abstr., Part A, Mod. Hist. Abstr., Hist. Abst., Part B, Twent. Century Abstr., New Testam. Abstr., Old Testam. Abstr., Relig. Index One, Period., Hist. Abstr. LC BM11. DD 296.05. (cum index). Circ 2,500. Scholarly essays in the several areas of Jewish and Congnate studies, ancient and modern: Bible, rabbinies, language and literature, history, philosophy, religion. *Journal of Jewish Lore and Philosophy, 0190-4361.*

HEBREW UNION COLLEGE ANNUAL SUPPLEMENTS. (HEBREW UNION COLLEGE ANNUAL. SUPPLEMENTS). No. 1-. 0275-9993. Monographic Series. US. English (German, or Portuguese). ir. $20.00. Hebrew Union College, 3101 Clifton Avenue, Cincinnati OH 45220. Tel (513)221-1875. Ed Shelton H Blank. Circ 2,400. Scholarly essays in Jewish and Cognate studies ancient and modern: Bible, rabbinies, language and literature, history, philosophy and religion.

HERITAGE SOUTHWEST JEWISH PRESS MICROFORM. VFOAT Heritage. 0018-0726. Periodical. US. English. wk. $20.00. Heritage Publishing Company, 2130 South Vermount Avenue, Los Angeles CA 90007.

HUMANISTIC JUDAISM. Began publication in 1967. 0441-4195. Periodical. US. English. qt. $15.00. Society for Humanistic Judaism, 28611 West 12 Mile Road, Farmington Hill MI 48018. Tel (313)478-7610. Ed M Bonnie Cousens and Ruth Duskin Feldman. bk rev. Circ 1,400. Contains philosophical, informational, educational, creative,

Religion, Mythology, Rationalism—Judaism

and celebratory materials that reflect the philosophy of humanistic Judaism. A reasoned, secular, and humanistic approach directed at contemporary issues and concerns.

ICJC NEWSLETTER. Main/Corp International Council of Jews from Czechoslovakia. VFOAT Newsletter. VAT International Council of Jews from Czechoslovakia Newsletter. V. 4- Feb. 1973-. Periodical. UK. English. bm. International Council of Jews from Czechoslovakia, 30 Craven Street, London WC2N 5NT England. LC DS135.C95. DD 301.4519240437. *Newsletter (Council of Jews from Czechoslovakia).*

IMMANUEL. (IMANUEL). No. 1- Summer 1972-. 0302-8127. IS. English. sa. $3.00. POB 249, Jerusalem Israel. Ind/Abst Old Testam. Abstr. LC BM1. DD 296.05.

ISRAEL HORIZONS. VFOAT Israel Horizons and Labour Israel. V. 1- Nov. 1952-. 0021-2083. Periodical. US. English. ir. $10.00. Americans Progressive Israel, 150 5th Avenue/Suite 911, New York NY 10011. Tel (212)255-8760. Ed Richard Yaffe. Ind/Abst Public Aff. Inf. Serv. Bull. LC DS101. DD 915.694005. bk rev. adv acc. Circ 3,500. Socialist Zionist exploration of the Jewish world—Israel, United States, and other communities. *Labour Israel.*

ISRAEL LAW REVIEW. See Law.

ISRAEL SCENE. Feb. 1980-. 0199-7424. Periodical. US. English. mo. World Zionist Organization, American Section, 515 Park Avenue, New York NY 10022. LC DS101. DD 956.94005. *Israel Digest. American Edition, 0021-2024.*

ISSUES OF THE AMERICAN COUNCIL FOR JUDAISM. VFOAT Issues. Autumn 1979-. 0741-465X. Periodical. US. English. qt. Free. American Council for Judaism, 307 Fifth Avenue, New York NY 10016. *Brief, 0006-9922.*

JEWISH AFFAIRS. V. 1- June 1946-. Periodical. SA. English. mo. 10.00. Jewish Affairs, PO Box 1180, Johannesburg South Africa. Tel 331-0331. Ed Hadassah Sacks. LC DS101. DD 296. bk rev adv acc. A cultural magazine with articles of Jewish interest in the fields of literature, art, history, and Judaism and reflecting the contemporary Jewish situation in South Africa and worldwide.

JEWISH BOOK NEWS. 8755-299X. US. English. bm. Free. Jewish Book Club, 230 Livingston Street, Northvale NJ 07647. Tel (201)767-4093. Ed Arthur Kurzweil. LC DS101. DD 909.04924. bk rev. Circ 15,000. (ctrl) A 64 page journal devoted to current books of judaica; sent to members of the Jewish Book Club.

JEWISH CURRENT EVENTS. 0021-6380. Periodical. US. English. bw. Jewish Current Events, 430 Keller Avenue, Elmont NY 11003. Ed Samuel Deutsch. bk rev. Jewish current events for children ages nine to fifteen, adolescents and of interest to priests, rabbis, ministers and schools.

JEWISH CURRENTS. V. 12- Nov. 1957-. 0021-6399. Periodical. US. English. mo. $12.00. Association Promo Jewish Secularism 22 East 17th Street, New York NY 10003. Tel (212)924-5740. Ed Morris U Schappes. bk rev. adv acc. Circ 3,800. (ctrl). Independent progressive secular Jewish-covers Jewish life at home and abroad-proIsrael nonzionis-stress Jewish culture, in all languages, also black-Jewish relations.

JEWISH DIALOGUE. (JEWISH DIALOG). VFOAT Dialog. Spring 1970-. 0315-2685. Periodical. CN. English. qt. D J Publishing Company, 1498 Young Street/Suite 7, Toronto Ontario M4T 1Z6 Canada. LC AP92. DD 050.

JEWISH DIGEST. (THE JEWISH DIGEST). V. 1- Oct. 1955-. 0021-6410. Periodical. US. English. mo. $14.00 Domestic, $15.00 Foreign. Jewish Digest, 1363 Fairfield Avenue, Bridgeport CT 0605. Ed B Postal. Ind/Abst Index Jew. Period. LC DS101.

JEWISH EDUCATION DIRECTORY. See Yearbooks, Almanacs, Directories.

JEWISH EXPONENT. (THE JEWISH EXPONENT). 0021-6437. Periodical. US. English. wk. $22.00. Federation of Jewish Agencies of Greater Pennsylvania, 226 16th Street, Philadelphia PA 19102.

JEWISH FOLKLORE AND ETHNOLOGY NEWSLETTER. See Folklore.

THE JEWISH JOURNAL OF SOCIOLOGY. See Sociology: General Works, Theory.

THE JEWISH LEDGER. 0021-6550. Periodical. US. English. wk. $11.50. Jewish Ledger, 1427 Monroe Avenue, Rochester NY 14618.

THE JEWISH MONITOR. 0021-6593. Periodical. US. English. mo. Jewish Monitor, PO Box 9155, Birmingham AL 35213.

JEWISH NEWS (RICHMOND, VA.). (THE JEWISH NEWS). 0744-6632. Periodical. US. English. wk. $18.00. The Jewish News of Michigan, 2300 Civic Center Drive/Suite 240, Southfield MI 48075. Tel (313)354-6060.

THE JEWISH OBSERVER. V. 1- Sept. 1963-. 0021-6615. Periodical. US. English. ir. $10.00. Agudath Israel of America, 5 Beekman Street, New York NY 10038. Tel (212)791-1800. Ed Nisson Wolpin. LC BM1. bk rev. adv acc. Circ 15,000. (ctrl). Comments on contemporary issues and events from a religious Jewish perspective, biographical sketches, book reviews, essays on Jewish festivals, interviews, and letters to the editor.

JEWISH POST AND OPINION. 0021-6658. Periodical. US. English. wk. $55.00. Jewish Post and Opinion, PO Box 1308, EG Fort Lee NJ 07024.

THE JEWISH PRESS. 1961. 0021-6674. Periodical. US. English. wk. $30.00. Jewish Press, 338 Third Avenue, Brooklyn NY 11215. Tel (718)330-1100. Ed Judah Schwartz. bk rev. adv acc. Circ 170,000. News items pertaining to Jewish views and news from Isreal. Columns and stories with a Jewish viewpoint. Classified magazine section and childrens section.

JEWISH QUARTERLY. Vol. 1, No. 1 (Spring 1953)-. 0449-010X. Periodical. UK. English. qt. $15.00. Jewish Quarterly, 344 East Finchley Road, Ruth Sonntag, London NW3 7AJ England. Tel 01-431-2225. Ind/Abst Abstr. Engl. Stud.

THE JEWISH QUARTERLY REVIEW. New Ser., V. 1 (July 1910)-. 0021-6682. Periodical. US. English. qt. $35.00. Dropsie College, 250 North Highland Avenue, Merion Station PA 19066. Tel (215)667-1830. Ed Russell Johnson. Ind/Abst Relig. Theol. Abstr., Relig. Index One, Period., Hist. Abstr., Am. Hist. Life, MLA Int. Bibliogr. Books Artic. Mod. Lang. Lit., Hist. Abstr., Part A, Mod. Hist. Abstr., Hist. Abstr., Part B, Twent. Century Abstr., New Testam. Abstr., Old Testam. Abstr. LC DS101. DD 296.05. (cum index). bk rev acc. Circ 1,00. (ctrl). Publishes ancient and medieval texts, articles on the history of Jewish language and culture, and critical reviews of relevant books. *Jewish Quarterly Review, 0021-6682.*

JEWISH SOCIAL STUDIES. Vol. 1, No. 1 (Jan. 1939)-. 0021-6704. Periodical. US. English. qt. $30.00. Conference of Jewish Social Studies, 211 Broadway/Room 206, New York NY 10023. Tel (212)724-5336. Ed Tobey B Gitelle. Ind/Abst Am. Hist. Life, Hist. Abstr., Part A, Mod. Hist. Abstr., Hist. Abstr., Part B, Twent. Century Abstr., Sociol. Abstr., Soc. Welf. Soc. Plan./Policy Soc. Dev., Writ. Am. Hist., Ref. Source, Soc. Sci. Index, Book Rev. Index, Public Aff. Inf. Serv. Bull., Soc. Sci. Citation Index, Sociol. Abstr., Lang. Lang. Behav. Abstr., Hist. Abstr., Recent Publ. Artic. LC DS101. DD 909.04924. (cum index). bk rev. Circ 1,300. Devoted to contemporary and historical aspects of Jewish life. Scholarly articles on Jewish topics in social science.

JEWISH SPECTATOR. (JEWISH SPECTATOR). V. 1- Nov./Dec. 1935-. 0021-6720. Periodical. US. English. qt. $15.00 Domestic, $18.00 Foreign. Jewish Spectator, PO Box 2016, Santa Monica CA 90406. Tel (213)393-9063. Ed Trude Weiss Rosmarin. Ind/Abst Guide Soc. Sci. Relig. Period. Lit. LC AP92. DD 052. bk rev. adv acc. Circ 8,000. Journal of Jewish and world affairs with a liberal orientation. *News from the School of the Jewish Woman.*

THE JEWISH STANDARD. Began publication in 1930?. 0021-6739. Periodical. CN. English. sm. Julius Hayman, Colborne Street, Toronto Ontario Canada.

JEWISH STAR. See Ethnic.

JEWISH TIMES. (THE JEWISH TIMES). V. 1- Feb. 14, 1975-. 0382-0254. Periodical. CN. English. bw. $5. North American Press, 365A Wilson Avenue/Suite 7, Downsview Ontario M3H 1T3 Canada. DD 301.451924.

THE JEWISH TIMES. (JEWISH TIMES). 0021-6771. Newspaper. US. English. ir. $12.00. Jewish Times, Box 35/Wareham Street Box 18427, Boston MA 02118. Tel (617)357-8636. Ed Sten B Lukin. bk rev. adv acc. Circ 7,000. The interpretation of international, national and local events as seen through the eyes of identifying American Jews.

THE JEWISH VOICE. 0021-6828. Periodical. US. English. sm. $5.00. Jewish Federation of Delaware, 101 Garden of Eden Road, Wilmington DE 19803. Tel (302)654-4527. Ed Karen Moss. bk rev adv acc. Circ 3,000. Local, national and international articles concerning American and worldwide Jewry.

JEWISH WESTERN BULLETIN. V. 1, No. 31- Oct. 9, 1930-. 0021-6879. CN. English. ir. $19.16. Jewish Western Bulletin, 3268 Heather Street, Vancouver British Columbia V5Z 3K5 Canada. Tel (604)879-6575. Ed Samuel Kaplan. bk rev. adv acc. Circ 2,400. (ctrl). News and features on Jewish themes, religious as well as secular, book reviews, cultural and educational, Israel-Diaspora communities' news. *Jewish Centre News.*

THE JEWISH WOMAN'S OUTLOOK. VFOAT Outlook. No. 1 (May-June 1980)-. Periodical. English. bm. LC BM729.W6. DD 296.088042.

JONATHAN (MONTREAL, QUEBEC). (JONATHAN). No.1 (Oct. 1981)-. 0711-026X. Periodical. CN. French. ir. $9.67. Jonathan, 1310 Avenue Green/Suite 710, Montreal Quebec H3Z 2B2 Canada. Tel (514)934-0772. Ed Victor Teboul. DD 305.89240714. bk rev. adv acc. Circ 5,000. Jewish, French language, cultural magazine dealing with French Canada, USA, Europe, and Israel.

JOURNAL FOR THE STUDY OF JUDAISM IN THE PERSIAN, HELLENISTIC AND ROMAN PERIODS. Periodical. NE. Multilingual (English, French, and German). sa. E J Brill, P O Box 9000, 2300 PA Leiden The Netherlands. Ind/Abst Relig. Index One, Period. An international forum of scholarly discussions on the history, literature and religious ideas of Judaism.

JOURNAL OF AGING AND JUDAISM. See Senior Citizens.

JOURNAL OF HALACHA AND CONTEMPORARY SOCIETY. VFOAT Journal of Halacha. Vol. 1, No. 1 (Spring 1981)-. 0730-2614. Periodical. US. English. sa. $10.00. Rabbi Jacob Joseph School, 3495 Richmond Road, Staten Island NY 10306. Tel (212)979-6333. Ed Alfred Cohen. LC BM520. DD 296.1805. bk rev. Circ 2,500. (ctrl). Concerns modern life issues and problems analyzed in terms of Jewish Law.

JOURNAL OF JEWISH MUSIC AND LITURGY. See Music.

JOURNAL OF JEWISH STUDIES. 0022-2097. Periodical. UK. English. sa. $30.00. Oriental Institute, Pusey Lane, Oxford OX1 2LE England. Tel 59272. Ed Geza Vermes. Ind/Abst Am. Hist. Life, Hist. Abstr., Relig. Index One, Period. bk rev. adv acc. Circ 1,000. A periodical concerned with Jewish civilization, in particular in the second temple and the Mishnaic-Talmudic eras. Full bibliographical coverage.

JOURNAL OF PSYCHOLOGY AND JUDAISM. See Psychology.

JOURNAL OF REFORM JUDAISM. V. 25, No. 2- (No. 101-). 0149-712X. Periodical. US. English. qt. $12.00. Journal of Reform Judaism, 21 East 40th Street, New York NY 10016. Tel (212)684-4990. Ed Samuel M Stahl. LC BM197.A1. DD 296.8346. bk rev. adv acc. Circ 1,500. Publication containing articles of contemporary interest by leading members of the rabbinic, scholarly and lay communities. *CCAR Journal, 0007-7976.*

JOURNAL OF SYNAGOGUE MUSIC. See Music.

JTA DAILY NEWS BULLETIN. 0021-3772. Periodical. US. English. da. $150.00. Jewish Telegraph Agency, 165 West 46th Street, New York NY 10036. Tel (212)575-9370. Ed Murray Zuckoff. LC DS101. DD 296. bk rev. Circ 2,500. News of Jewish concern and interest from international news agency.

JTA WEEKLY NEWS DIGEST. Main/Corp Jewish Telegraphic Agency. VFOAT Weekly News Digest. VAT Jewish Telegraphic Agency Weekly News Digest. 0021-6763. Periodical. US. English. wk. $30.00. Jewish Telegraphic Agency, 165 West 46th Street, New York NY 10036. Tel (212)575-9370. Circ

Religion, Mythology, Rationalism—Judaism

5,000. (ctrl). Summary of major stories and events from international Jewish news agency.

JUDAICA. Vol. 1-. 0022-572X. Periodical. SZ. German. qt. $30.00. Redaktion der Judaica, Etzelstrasse 19, CH-8038 Zurich Switzerland. Ed K Hruby and Mastin Cunt. **Ind/Abst** Am. Hist. Life, Hist. Abstr., Part A, Mod. Hist. Abstr., Hist. Abst., Part B, Twent. Century Abstr., Old Testam. Abstr., Hist. Abstr. **LC** DS101. bk rev. adv acc. **Circ** 1,000. Information and research on Jewish-Christian subjects; Bible, dialogue, book reviews.

JUDAICA BOOK NEWS. V. 1- Fall 1970-. 0022-5754. Periodical. US. English. sa. $8.00. Book News Periodicals Inc, 303 West 10th Street, New York NY 10024. **Tel** (212)691-3817. Ed Ernest Weiss. **LC** Z6367. **DD** 016.91003924. bk rev. adv acc. Articles, critical book reviews, picture stories, comprehensive bibliography of news and forthcoming English language books of Jewish interest.

JUDAISM. V. 1- Jan. 1952-. 0022-5765. Periodical. US. English. qt. $12.00. American Jewish Congress, 15 East 84th Street, New York NY 10028. **Tel** (212)879-4500. Ed Robert Gordis. **Ind/Abst** MLA Int. Bibliogr. Books Artic. Mod. Lang. Lit., Relig. Index One, Period., Guide Soc. Sci. Relig. Period. Lit., New Testam. Abstr., Abstr. Engl. Stud. **LC** BM1. **DD** 296.05. bk rev. adv acc. **Circ** 5,000. Creative discussion and exposition of the religious, moral and philosophical concepts of Judaism and their relevance to the problems of modern society.

THE KASHRUS NEWSLETTER. 0882-3898. Periodical. US. English. bm. $10.00. Kashrus Customer Service Department, POB 17305, Milwaukee WI 53217. **DD** 296.

KEFAR HABAD : SHEVUON TSEIRE AGUDAT HABAD BE-E. HA-K. Periodical. US. Hebrew. wk. $68.00. Kfar Chabad Weekly Magazine, 648 Lefferts Avenue, Brooklyn NY 11203. **LC** BM1.

KIRYAT SEFER = QIRYAT SEPR. (KIRYAT SEFER : RIVON BIBLIYOGRAFI SHEL BET HA-SEFARIM HA-LEUMI VEHA-UNIVERSITAI BI-YERUSHALAYIM). **VFOAT** Kiryat Sefer. Began with: Vol. 1 (Apr. 1924). 0023-1851. Periodical. IS. Hebrew (English). qt. 50.00. Jewish National and University Library, PO Box 503, Jerusalem 91-000 Israel. **Tel** (02)585039. Ed Avigdor Shinan. **LC** Z6367, DS102.5. **DD** 016.8924. **NLM** Z 7070 K58. Index published separately - free - automatically sent. (cum index). bk rev. **Circ** 1,000. (ctrl). Contains a complete list of new Israeli publications and books related to Jewish studies published outside Israel in different languages.

KIVUNIM. No. 1- Nov. 1978-. Periodical. Hebrew. qt. $15.00. World Zionist Organization, PO Box 92, Department of Education and Culture, Jerusalem Israel. **LC** BM1. *Bi-Tefutsot Ha-Golah.*

KOL YAAKOV. Published since Sept. 1979?. 0228-2577. Periodical. CN. French. bm. Free. Rabbinat Sepharade du Quebec, Kol Yaakov, 4735 Cote Sainte-Catherine, Montreal Quebec H3W 1M1 Canada. **DD** 296.09714281.

KOL YISRAEL. **VFOAT** Kol Israel Jerusalem. Periodical. IS. Hebrew. ir. 3.00 Single Issue. Kol Israel, P O B 513, Jerusalem Israel. **LC** BM390.

KOVETS BE-OHOLE YAAKOV. **VFOAT** Be-Ohole Yaakov. Periodical. US. Hebrew. Boholei Yakov, 11 Adams Lane, New Square NY 10977. **LC** BM520.

KOVETS HIDUSHE TORAH PERI TEMARIM. **VFOAT** Peri Temarim. Periodical. US. Hebrew. **LC** BM520.

KOVETS KEREM SHELOMOH. **VFOAT** Kerem Shelomoh. Vol. 1, No. 1, (Nov. 1977)-. Periodical. US. Hebrew. mo. $15.00. Kerem Shlomo M E CH of Bobov, 1577 48th Street, Brooklyn NY 11219. **Tel** (718)871-6623. Ed Shmerel Zitronenbaum. **LC** BM520. **Circ** 2,000. Commentary and sermons on the Bible and talmud historical documents regarding rabbinical society and hasidim.

KOVETS YAGDIL TORAH (BROOKLYN, NEW YORK, N.Y. : 1976). (KOVETS YAGDIL TORAH). **VFOAT** Yagdil Torah. V. 1-, No. 1-. Periodical. US. Hebrew. bm. Yagdil Torah, 770 Eastern Parkway, Brooklyn NY 11213. **LC** BM520.

LA-MISHPAHAH. LAMISHPAHA. **VFOAT** Lamishpaha. Began publication in 1962. Periodical. US. Hebrew (English). mo. $7.00. Histadruth Ivrit of America, 1841 Broadway, New York NY 10023. **Tel** (212)581-5151. **LC** PJ4569. bk rev. adv acc. A magazine, in simple Hebrew, for students of Hebrew, youngsters as well as adults.

LAPIDE ESH DAT. V. 1- Feb. 1977-. Periodical. US. Hebrew. 3921 13th Avenue, Brooklyn NY 11218. **LC** BM1.

LE-TORAH VE-HORA AH. 0094-5625. US. Hebrew. 145 East Braodway, New York NY 10002. **LC** BM520.

LEOM, LEOM U-MASORET. **VFOAT** Leom U-Masoret. 1- Jan. 727- 1966-. Periodical. Hebrew. bm. $2.50. Adhut Yisrael Be-Erets Yisrael, Tel-Hai Street 9, Tel-Aviv Israel. **LC** BM390.

LILITH (NEW YORK, N.Y.). (LILITH). Vol. 1, No. 1 (Fall 1976)-. 0146-2334. Periodical. US. English. ir. $48.00. Lilith Magazine, 250 West 57th Street, New York NY 10019. **Tel** (212)757-0818. Ed Susan Weidman Schneider. **Ind/Abst** Women Stud. Abstr. **LC** BM729.W6. **DD** 296.387834405. bk rev. adv acc. **Circ** 10,000. Focus on Jewish women issues all over the world.

MABUE HA-NAHAL. Year 1- (1-). Periodical. IS. Hebrew. mo. $2.00 single issue. Mabue Ha-Nahal, PO Box 5404, Jerusalem ISRAEL. **LC** BM198.

MADRIKH LA-KASHRUT. **VFOAT** Madrich Lakashrus. Periodical. US. English, Hebrew or Yiddish. bm. $4.00. Vaad Hakashrus, PO Box 56, Brooklyn NY 11228. **LC** BM710.

MAHASHEVET. Periodical. IS. Hebrew. ir. 35.00. Mahashevet, PO Box 363, Bene Berak Israel. **LC** BM1.

MAHLKHIM. V. 1- March 1969-. Periodical. Hebrew. ir. **LC** BM1. *Hadash Yitkadesh Veha-Kadosh Yithadesh.*

MEHKERE YERUSHALAYIM BE-MAHASHEVET YISRAEL. **VFOAT** Jerusalem Studies in Jewish Thought. 1-. 0333-7081. Periodical. IS. Hebrew. ir. Magnes Press, The Hebrew University, Jerusalem 91904 Israel. **LC** BM1.

THE MELTON JOURNAL. *See* Education (General).

MEOROT : RIVON HA-RABANUT HA-RASHIT LE-YISRAEL LE-INYENE HALAKHAH, AGADAH, MUSAR, VE-YAHADUT. Periodical. Hebrew. qt. **LC** BM1.

MICHIGAN JEWISH HISTORY. V. 1- Mar. 1960-. 0543-9833. US. English. sa. $10.00. Michigan Jewish History, 1036 David Whitney Boulevard, Detroit MI 48226. **Ind/Abst** Hist. Abstr., Part A, Mod. Hist. Abstr., Hist. Abst., Part B, Twent. Century Abstr., Writ. Am. Hist., Am. Hist. Life, Hist. Abstr. **LC** F575.J5. **DD** 977.4004924.

MIDSTREAM; A MONTHLY JEWISH REVIEW. V. 1- Autumn 1955-. 0026-332X. Periodical. US. English. mo. Midstream Magazine, 515 Park Avenue, New York NY 10022. **Tel** (212)752-0600. Ed Joel Carmichael. **Ind/Abst** Film Lit. Index, Index Book Rev. Humanit., Index Jew. Period., Public Aff. Inf. Serv. Bull., Hist. Abstr., Writ. Am. Hist., Am. Hist. Life, Hist. Abstr., Part A, Mod. Hist. Abstr., Hist. Abst., Part B, Twent. Century Abstr., Guide Soc. Sci. Relig. Period. Lit., Recent Publ. Artic. **LC** DS149. **DD** 296.05. bk rev. adv acc. **Circ** 10,000. Concerned with Judaism in contemporary life and culture and clarification of the central issues of our times. Contains stories and articles by prominent library figures.

MITSPEH. **VFOAT** Mizpeh. V. 1- Spring 1974-. English. ir. Mercaz Olami of Mizrachi and Hapoel Hamizrachi Information Department, PO Box 588, Jerusalem Israel. **LC** DS150.R3. **DD** 296.3877.

AL MITZPE HAHINUCH. V. 1- Nov. 1972-. 0316-5256. Periodical. CN. English (text also in Hebrew, each with special title page). Free. Canadian Zionist Federation, Bureau of Education and Culture, 1310 Green Avenue, Montreal Que H3Z 2B2 Canada. **DD** 377.960971.

MODERN JUDAISM. Vol. 1, No. 1 (May 1981)-. 0276-1114. Periodical. US. English. ty. $31.00. Johns Hopkins University Press Journals Division, 701 West 40th Street/Suite 275, Baltimore MD 21211. **Tel** (301)338-6987. Ed Steven T Katz. **Ind/Abst** Am. Hist. Life, Hist. Abstr., Relig. Index One, Period. **LC** BM195. **DD** 296.0903. bk rev. adv acc. **Circ** 957. Provides a forum for the discussion of all aspects of the modern Jewish experience since the Haskalah, the Jewish enlightenment.

MOMENT. V. 1- May/June 1975-. 0099-0280. Periodical. US. English. $45.00. Jewish Educational Ventures, 462 Boylston Street, Boston MA 02116, (subscription address: Fulfillment Associates Incorp 155 Allen Boulevard Farmingdale NY 11735). **Tel** (617)536-6252. Ed Leonard Fein. **Ind/Abst** Index Jew. Period. **LC** DS101. **DD** 909.0492408. bk rev. adv acc. **Circ** 25,000. (ctrl). A contemporary, independent, Jewish magazine containing pieces on Israel, Judaism, politics-American and Israeli, fiction and sociology. America's leading independent Jewish magazine.

MONOGRAPHS OF THE HEBREW UNION COLLEGE. **Main/Corp** Hebrew Union College. No. 1-. 0190-5627. Monographic Series. US. English. ir. KTAV Publishing House, 900 Jefferson Street #6249, Hoboken NY 07030-7205. **Tel** (513)221-1875. Ed Abraham Peck and Jacob Reader Marcus. Scholarly studies of any subject relating to Jews or Judaism, including but not limited to history, theology, philosophy, art, literature, etc.

MORIYAH. **VFOAT** Moriah. Began in 1968. Periodical. Hebrew. mo. **LC** BM520. (cum index).

MUSICA JUDAICA. *See* Music.

THE NATIONAL JEWISH MONTHLY CEASED. Began publication in 1908. 0027-9552. Periodical. US. English. mo. National Jewish Monthly, 1640 Rhode Island Avenue NW, Washington DC 20036. **LC** HS2228.B4. **DD** 296.05.

NEW TRADITIONS. Spring 1984-. 0882-4851. Periodical. US. English. ir. $18.00. National Havurah Committee, 270 West 89th Street, New York NY 10024. Ed William Novak. **DD** 296. **Circ** 3,000. (ctrl). Essays, literature and poetry. Each edition contains an interview with a prominent Jewish figure. Emphasis on Judaism in the modern world.

THE NEW YORK JEWISH WEEK. **VFOAT** Jewish Week. Vol. 195, No. 10 (July 30, 1982)-. 0745-5356. Periodical. US. English. wk. $16.00 NY, Long Island, and Westchester, $19.00 Others. Jewish Week, 1 Park Avenue, New York NY 10016. **LC** DS101. **DD** 909.04924005. *New York Jewish Week and the American Examiner*, 0737-352X.

NEWS OF THE YIVO. **VFOAT** Yedies Fun YIVO. Began in 1945. 0028-9302. Periodical. US. English (Yiddish). qt. $15.00. YIVO Institute Jewish Research, 1048 5th Avenue, New York NY 10028. **Tel** (212)535-6700.

NEWSLETTER - ASSOCIATION FOR JEWISH STUDIES. (NEWSLETTER). **Main/Corp** Association for Jewish Studies. 0278-4033. US. English. sa. Association for Jewish Studies, Widener Library M, Harvard University, Cambridge MA 02138. **LC** BM21. **DD** 296.05.

NEWSLETTER - CENTER FOR HOLOCAUST STUDIES (BROOKLYN, NEW YORK, N.Y.). *See* History (General) - History of Europe.

NEWSLETTER - CENTRAL ARCHIVES FOR THE HISTORY OF THE JEWISH PEOPLE. *See* Genealogy and Heraldry - Archives.

NORTHERN CALIFORNIA JEWISH BULLETIN. 0745-0664. Periodical. US. English. wk. $15.00. San Francisco Jewish Community Publication Inc, 870 Market Street/Suite 954, San Francisco CA 94102. *San Francisco Jewish Bulletin*, 0021-6364.

LES NOUVEAUX CAHIERS. 1. - Year. (No. 1-). 0550-1350. Periodical. FR. French. ir. 140. Alliance Isrealite Universelle, 45 Rue de la Bruyere, Paris 9E France. **Tel** (1) 42 80 35 00. **LC** DS101. Jewish and Isreali literature, poetry, human rights, sociology, books movies and exhibitions review, zionism, and judeo-christian relations.

OLAMENU. *See* Education (General) - Special Aspects of Education.

OLSCHWANGER JOURNAL. *See* Genealogy and Heraldry.

OPTIONS. 0362-2770. Periodical. US. English. mo. $15.00. Options Publishing Company, Box 311, Wayne NJ 07470. **Tel** (201)694-2327. Ed Betty J Singer. (ctrl). Clearinghouse of American Jewish resources.

OR-TORAH. V. 1- June/July? 1968-. Periodical. Hebrew. bm. $5.00. Or Torah, PO Box 18, Ashkelon Israel.

Religion, Mythology, Rationalism—Judaism

ORAITA. Periodical. IS. Hebrew. ir. 12.00. Orayta, PO Box 245, Netanya Israel. **Tel** (053)44864. Ed Robbi Amihud Levin. **LC** BM520. bk rev. **Circ** 2,500. (ctrl). Rabbinical publication for Jewish thought and Halacha.

OTSROT YERUSHALAYIM. Helek 1- 715 1955-. Periodical. Hebrew. ir. Ed Z Moskovitz. **LC** BM520.

PEER MORDEKHAI. 1- Feb. 1969-. US. Hebrew. an. 28400 Euclid Avenue, Viklif OH 44092. **LC** BM504.2.

PERI HA-ARETS. Vol. 1 (Nov. 1980)-. Periodical. Hebrew. ir. **LC** BM520.

PIONEER WOMAN. (THE PIONEER WOMAN). **VFOAT** Pionern Froy. Began with Feb. 1926 issue. 0032-0021. Periodical. US. English (Yiddish). ir. $5.00. Pioneer Women, 200 Madison Avenue, New York NY 10016. **Tel** (212)725-8010. Ed Judith A Sokoloff. **LC** DS150.L3. bk rev. adv acc. **Circ** 30,000. Covers a wide spectrum of topics of interest to Jewish community - Jewish culture, Israel, Zionism and social, political and women's issues.

POLYDOXY. V. 1- Autumn 1975-. 0146-888X. Periodical. US. English. ty. $25.00. Polydoxy, PO Box 2044, Cincinnatti OH 45220. **LC** BM1. **DD** 296.834605.

PROCEEDINGS - AMERICAN ACADEMY FOR JEWISH RESEARCH. **Main/Corp** American Academy for Jewish Research. **VFOAT** Proceedings of the American Academy for Jewish Research. Vol.1- 1928/30-. 0065-6798. US. English (Hebrew). $10.00. H Kraus, 16 East 46th Street, New York NY 10017. **LC** DS101. **DD** 296. Index in last issue of volume - attached.

PROCEEDINGS OF THE ANNUAL CONVENTION OF THE NATIONAL ASSOCIATION OF SYNAGOGUE ADMINISTRATORS. **Main/Corp** National Association of Synagogue Administrators. 0145-4366. US. English. an. National Association of Synagogue Administrators, 3080 Broadway, New York NY 10027. **LC** BM653. **DD** 296.60973.

PROCEEDINGS OF THE ASSOCIATIONS OF ORTHODOX JEWISH SCIENTISTS. **Main/Corp** Association of Orthodox Jewish Scientists. V. 1- 1966-. 0571-6489. Periodical. US. English (Hebrew). ir. $5.00. Association of Orthodox Jewish Scientists, 45 West 36th Street, New York NY 10016. **LC** BM1. **DD** 215.

PROOFTEXTS. See Literature.

LA RASSEGNA MENSILE DI ISRAEL. V. 1- Oct. 1925-. 0033-9792. Periodical. IT. Italian. mo. Unione delle Comun Israel Ita, Lungotevere Sanzio 9, 00153 Roma Italy. **Ind/Abst** MLA Int. Bibliogr. Books Artic. Mod. Lang. Lit. **LC** DS101. (cum index).

RECONSTRUCTIONIST. Began in 1935. 0034-1495. Periodical. US. English. ir. $20.00. Reconstructionist, 270 West 89th Street, New York NY 10024. **Tel** (212)496-2960. Ed Jacob Staub. **Ind/Abst** Index Jew. Period., Public Aff. Inf. Serv. Bull. **LC** DS133. **DD** 296. bk rev. adv acc. **Circ** 8,500. (ctrl). A review of the contemporary Jewish world—its cultural expression, religious and social issues, middle east, philosophy, synagogue life, and ritual observance.

REFORM JUDAISM. V. 1- Sept. 1972-. 0482-0819. Periodical. US. English. qt. $10.00. Union of American Hebrew Congregation, 838 Fifth Avenue, New York NY 10021. **Tel** (212)249-0100. Ed Aron Hirt-Manheimer. bk rev. adv acc. **Circ** 276,000. (ctrl). In-depth articles about current issues of interest to the Jewish community and articles about the reform Jewish movement.

THE RELIGION & SOCIETY REPORT. **VFOAT** Religion and Society Report. Vol. 1, No. 1 (June 1984)-. 0742-6984. Periodical. US. English. mo. $24.00. Rockford Institute, 934 North Main Street, Rockford IL 61103. **Tel** (815)964-5811. Ed Richard John Neuhaus. **DD** 261. **Circ** 5,000. Reports on the intersection of religion and society and serves to reinvigorate religious sensibilities in "The Public Square" by exemplifying Hebraic and Christian traditions.

REPORT TO SOUTH AFRICAN JEWRY. **Main/Corp** South African Jewish Board of Deputies. SA. English. ir. South African Jewish Board of Deputies, 29 Kruis Street, PO Box 1180, Johannesburg South Africa. **LC** DS135.S6. **DD** 968.004924. Report of the Executive Council.

RESEARCH REPORT (INSTITUTE OF JEWISH AFFAIRS). (RESEARCH REPORT). **VFOAT** IJA Research Reports. Began with Dec. 1968 issues. UK. English. ir. **Tel** 491-3517. **Circ** 1,000. Background surveys and analyses of topical political, social, economic, and legal issues particularly relevant to world Jewry.

RESPONSE; A CONTEMPORARY JEWISH REVIEW. 1- Summer 1967-. 0034-5709. Periodical. US. English. qt. $8.00. Response, 523 West 113 Street, New York NY 10014. **LC** BM1. Available on microfilm from University Microfilms International.

REVUE DE QUMRAN. V. 1- (No. 1-). 0035-1725. Periodical. FR. English (articles in French, German, Italian, or Latin). sa. $51.00. Editions Gabalda, 90 rue Bonaparte, 75006 Paris France. **Tel** 326 53 SS. Ed Cabbe Carmiquec. **Ind/Abst** Old Testam. Abstr., New Testam. Abstr., Relig. Index One, Period. **LC** BM487.A62. **DD** 296.155. bk rev. Articles about the Dead Sea Scrolls and proof of the Grottos of Qumran.

REVUE DES ETUDES JUIVES. Vol. 134-Jan./June 1975-. Periodical. BE. French. qt. 2500. Editions Peeters SA, Bondgenotenlaan 153 Box 41, B-3000 Leuven Belgium. **Ind/Abst** Sociol. Abstr., Am. Hist. Life, Hist. Abstr., Lang. Lang. Behav. Abstr. **LC** DS 101. adv acc. (ctrl).

ROCKY MOUNTAIN JEWISH HISTORICAL NOTES. V. 1- Oct. 1977-. Periodical. US. English. qt. Rocky Mountain Jewish Historical Society, University of Denver, Denver CO 80208.

SAFRA. Vol. 1, No. 1 (Fall 1980)-. 0733-9062. Periodical. US. English. sa. $3.00 Domestic, $4.50 Canada. Jewish Education Service of North America, 114 Fifth Avenue, New York NY 10011. **LC** BM100. **DD** 377.960973.

SERIDIM. No. 1 (October 1981)-. Periodical. English (French, and Hebrew). sa. 5.00. Sridim, PO Box 5324, Jerusalem 91052 Israel. **Tel** (02)812859. Ed Moshe Rosee. **LC** BM520. **Circ** 600. (ctrl). Essays, lectures, and response on rabbinic themes.

SERMON MANUAL. **Main/Corp** Rabbinical Council of America. **VFOAT** Rabbinical Council Sermon Manual. V. 27- 1969-. 0099-2488. US. English. an. Rabbinical Council Press, 1250 Broadway/8th Floor, New York NY 10001. **LC** BM735. **DD** 296.42. Manual of Holiday and Sabbath Sermons.

SHALOM. 1974-. Periodical. UK. English. qt. Churchs Ministry Among Jews, Vincent House, Vincent Square, London SW1P 2PX England. CMJ Quarterly.

SHEVILEY HA-HINNUKH. 0037-3656. Periodical. US. Hebrew (English). qt. $10.00. Council for Jewish Education, 114 Fifth Avenue, New York NY 10011. **Ind/Abst** Relig. Index One, Period.

SHIRIM : A JEWISH POETRY JOURNAL. See Literature - Poetry.

SHMA YISRAEL. V. 1- Summer 1974-. Periodical. English. ir. $3.00. College Youth for Torah, 116 East 27th Street, New York NY 10016. **LC** BM1. **DD** 296.83205.

SHOFAR (MELVILLE, N.Y.). See Children and Youth Interests.

SHOFAR (WASHINGTON, D.C.). (THE SHOFAR). 0745-9327. Periodical. US. English. bm. B'nai B'rith Youth Organization, Circulation Manager, 1640 Rhode Island Avenue NW, Washington DC 20036. **DD** 296.

SHOFAR (WEST LAFAYETTE, IND.). (SHOFAR). Vol. 1, No. 1 (Fall 1982)-. 0882-8539. Periodical. US. English. qt. $10.00 Domestic, $15.00 Foreign. Shofar, Recitation 222 Purdue University, West Lafayette IN 47907. **Ind/Abst** Old Testam. Abstr. **DD** 296.

SINAI. V. 1- (Vol. 1-). Periodical. IS. Hebrew. bm. $15.00. Sinai, PO Box 642, Jerusalem Israel. Ed Yitzchale Raphael. **LC** BM1. (cum index). bk rev. **Circ** 1,000. (ctrl). Studies in Jewish religious life, history and literature.

SIYYON. (ZION). Vol. 1 1949-. 0044-4758. IS. English. qt. Historical Society of Isreal, PO Box 4179, Jerusaleum Isreal. **Ind/Abst** Am. Hist. Life, Hist. Abstr., Part A, Mod. Hist. Abstr., Hist. Abstr., Part B, Twent. Century Abstr., Hist. Abstr. New Judea.

THE SOUTHERN ISRAELITE. 1925. 0038-4224. Periodical. US. English. wk. $15.00. Southern Newspaper Enterprises, PO Box 77388, Atlanta GA 30357. **Tel** (404)876-8248. Ed Vida Goldgar. bk rev. adv acc. **Circ** 7,000. (ctrl). General coverage of items of Jewish interest.

SOVIET JEWISH AFFAIRS. No. 1 (June 1971)-No. 3 (May 1972). 0038-545X. Periodical. UK. English. ty. $25.00. Institute of Jewish Affairs, 11 Hertford Street, London W1Y 7DX England. **Tel** (01)491-3517. Ed Lukasz Hirszowicz. **Ind/Abst** Am. Hist. Life, Hist. Abstr., Part A, Mod. Hist. Abstr., Hist. Abst., Part B, Twent. Century Abstr., Artbibliogr. Mod., Hist. Abstr. **LC** DS135.R92. **DD** 301.451924047. bk rev. adv acc. **Circ** 1,500. (ctrl). An interdisciplinary journal on Jewish and related issues in the USSR and Eastern Europe. Bulletin on Soviet and East European Jewish Affairs, 0525-1559.

SPECIAL INTEREST REPORT - AMERICAN COUNCIL FOR JUDAISM. (SPECIAL INTEREST REPORT). **Main/Corp** American Council for Judaism. 0740-8528. Periodical. US. English. mo. American Council for Judaism, 309 Fifth Avenue, New York NY 10016.

STUDIA JUDAICA; FORSCHUNGEN ZUR WISSENSCHAFT DES JUDENTUMS. Vol. 1- 1961-. 0585-5306. Monographic Series. German or English. ir. Walter de Gruyter Inc, 200 Saw Mill River Road, Hawthorne NY 10532. **Tel** (914)747-0110.

STUDIA ROSENTHALIANA. V. 1- Jan. 1967-. 0039-3347. Periodical. NE. chiefly Dutch, with some English, French and German articles; English summaries. sa. 77.50. Van Gorcum & Company BV, PO Box 43, 9400 AA Assen Netherlands. **Tel** (05920)46846. Ed A K Offenberg. **Ind/Abst** Am. Hist. Life, Hist. Abstr., Part A, Mod. Hist. Abstr., Hist. Abst., Part B, Twent. Century Abstr., Hist. Abstr. **LC** DS135.N4. **DD** 914.92. bk rev. adv acc. **Circ** 400. (ctrl). The periodical is devoted to Jewish literature and history and aims to stimulate studies in this field.

STUDIES IN BIBLIOGRAPHY AND BOOKLORE. See Bibliographies.

STUDIES IN JUDAISM AND CHRISTIANITY IN ANTIQUITY. No. 1- 1975-. Monographic Series. US. English. ir. University of Notre Dame, Box 91, Notre Dame IN 46556.

STUDIES IN ZIONISM. 4 (Autumn 1981)-. Periodical. US. English. sa. $28.00. Johns Hopkins University Press, 701 West 40th Street, Suite 275, Baltimore MD 21211. **Tel** (301)338-6987. Ed Ronald W Zweig. **Ind/Abst** Am. Hist. Life, Hist. Abstr., Part A, Mod. Hist. Abstr., Hist. Abst., Part B, Twent. Century Abstr. **LC** DS149.A1. **DD** 956.9400105. bk rev. adv acc. **Circ** 305. Publishes articles on the history of the Zionist movement and the Jewish community in Palestine.

STUDIES ON THE TEXTS OF THE DESERT OF JUDAH. V. 1- 1957-. 0585-7457. Monographic Series. US. English, French, and German. ir. EJ Brill, POB 9000, 2300 PA Leiden The Netherlands.

SVET (BROOKLYN, NEW YORK, N.Y.). (SVET). 1 (Oct. 1981)-. 0731-3993. Periodical. UR. Russian. mo. $18.00. Svet, 1383 President Street, Brooklyn NY 11213. **LC** BM1.

TEHUMIN. **VFOAT** Techumin. 1 (Winter 740 1979/80)-. Periodical. Hebrew. an. **LC** BM520.

TELEM. Periodical. IS. Hebrew. ir. Tenuah Le-Yahadut Mitkademet Be-Yisrael, Rehov David Ha-Melekh 13, Jerusalem Israel. **LC** BM197.

TORAH EDUCATION. V. 1- Sept. 1969-. US. English. ir. World Zionist Organization, 515 Park Avenue, New York NY 10022. **LC** BM100. **DD** 377.9605.

TORAT HA-ADAM. **VFOAT** Torath Haadam. Periodical. US. Hebrew. 1467 48th Street, Brooklyn NY 11219. **LC** BJ1279.

TRADITION. V. 1- Fall 1958-. 0041-0608. Periodical. US. English. qt. $28.00. Rabbinical Council of America, 1250 Broadway, New York NY 10001. **Tel** (212)243-6000. **Ind/Abst** MLA Int. Bibliogr. Books Artic. Mod. Lang. Lit., New Testam. Abstr., Arts Humanit. Citation Index, Index Jew. Period. **LC** BM1. **CODEN** TRADD2. (cum index).

TSOFAR. Periodical. IS. Hebrew. ir. $40.00. Hotsat Hadshabat, Tsofer, POB 5430, Jerusalem Israel. **LC** BM1.

VOIX SEFARAD. (LA VOIX SEFARAD). **VFOAT** Voix Sepharade. June 1977-Sept./Oct. 1981. 0704-5352. Periodical. CN. French (text also in Hebrew). bm. 25.00. Voix Sepharade, 4735 Chemin Cote Ste Catherine, Montreal Quebec H3W 1M1 Canada. **Tel** (514)733-4998. **DD** 301.4519240714. bk rev. adv acc. **Circ** 6,000. Preservation of Sephardic Jewish traditions in Canada. Community services and activities coordination. *Presence, 0380-2396.*

VOZROZHDENIE. HA-TEHIYAH. **VFOAT** Ha-Tehiyah. 1-. IS. Russian, English, and Hebrew. ir. Vozrozhdenie, c/o B Haskelewitvh, 701 Empire Boulevard/Apt 1-A, Brooklyn NY 11213. **LC** BM1.

DE VRIJDAGAVOND. 1.-9. Vol. Dutch. ir. **LC** DS101.

WASHINGTON JEWISH WEEK. Began with Nov. 3, 1983 issue. 0746-9373. Periodical. US. English. wk. $18.00. Washington Jewish Week, PO Box 848, Gaithersburg MD 20877. **Tel** (301)948-1500. **Ed** Renee Matalion. bk rev. adv acc. **Circ** 15,000. A paper concerned with the Jewish community and anything relating to Judaism. *Jewish Week (Washington, D.C. : 1975), 0272-7781.*

WESTERN STATES JEWISH HISTORICAL QUARTERLY *CEASED.* V. 1-15. 0043-4221. Periodical. US. English. qt. $10.00 Domestic, $12.00 Foreign. Norton B Stern, Western States Jewish Historical Quarterly, 2429 23rd Street, Santa Monica CA 90405. **Ind/Abst** Writ. Am. Hist. **LC** F591. **DD** 301.451924078. (cum index).

WOMEN'S LEAGUE OUTLOOK. **VFOAT** Outlook. 1930. 0043-7557. Periodical. US. English. qt. $4.00. Womens League for Conservative Judaism, 48 East 74th Street, New York NY 10021. **Tel** (212)628-1600. **Ed** Yvette Rosenberg. bk rev. adv acc. **Circ** 145,000. A publication of the Women's arm of conservative synagogues functioning all over the US, Canada and overseas.

WORLD OF LUBAVITCH. (THE WORLD OF LUBAVITCH : PUBLICATION OF THE LUBAVITCH YOUTH ORGANIZATION, TORONTO). Vol. 1, No. 1 (Jan. 1980)-. 0824-7420. Periodical. CN. English. bm. Free. Chabad-Lubavitch, 770 Chabad Gate, Thornhill Ontario L4J 3V9 Canada. **Tel** (416)731-7000. **Ed** J Gansburg. **DD** 296.833. adv acc. **Circ** 5,000. (ctrl). Jewish religion, Hasidic viewpoint, and community affairs.

YAHADUT. Periodical. Hebrew. ir. Mekhon Yisrael Sava, PO Box 11 Kiryath Sanz, Netanyah Israel. **LC** BM1.

YALE JUDAICA SERIES. Vol. 1-. 0084-3369. Monographic Series. US. English. ir. Yale University Press, 92A Yale Station, New Haven CT 06520. **Tel** (203)436-7583.

YEARBOOK (WORLD CONFEDERATION OF JEWISH COMMUNITY CENTERS). *See* Yearbooks, Almanacs, Directories.

YIDDISHER KEMFER. *See* Economics - Labor.

YONTEV BLETER. **VFOAT** Yomtov Bletter. SA. English (Yiddish). ir. $6.00. PO Box 7690, Johannesburg 2000 Yohanesburg South Africa. **LC** BM690.

YOUNG ISRAEL VIEWPOINT. (THE YOUNG ISRAEL VIEWPOINT). 1937. 0044-0809. Periodical. US. English. mo. $5.00. Young Israel Viewpoint, 3 West 16th Street, New York NY 10011. **Ed** Yaakov Kornreich. bk rev. adv acc. **Circ** 40,000. (ctrl). Articles of interest to religious Jews and news of the Young Israel Synagogue movement around the world.

YOUNG JUDAEAN. (THE YOUNG JUDAEAN). 0044-0817. Periodical. US. English. ir. National Young Judaea, 50 West 58th Street, New York NY 10019. **LC** AP222.

ZIONIST RECORD AND SA JEWISH CHRONICLE. **VAT** Zionist Record and South African Jewish Chronicle. Aug. 14, 1959-. Periodical. English. ir. 10.00. 84 de Villiers Street, PO Box 150, Jahannesburg South Africa. **LC** DS133. **DD** 968.004924. *Zionist Record SA Jewish Chronicle.*

ZIONIST YEAR BOOK. *See* Yearbooks, Almanacs, Directories.

PROTESTANTISM

20TH CENTURY CHRISTIAN. **VAT** Twentieth Century Christian. 0162-6418. Periodical. US. English. mo. $7.50. 20th Century Christian, 2809 Granny White Pike, Nashville TN 37204.

A-CROSS. V. 1- Advent 1976-. Periodical. US. English. qt. Ann Knight, Box 1615, Iowa City IA 52240. **Tel** (319)354-5721.

ACCENT ON ARTS. (ACCENT ON ARTS : NEWS HIGHLIGHTS FROM ADVENTIST RADIO TELEVISION SERVICES). **VAT** Accent on Adventist Radio Television Services. 0821-0209. Periodical. CN. English. qt. Free. Adventist Radio Television Services, Unit N/500 Dufferin Street, Downsview Ontario M3H 5T5 Canada. **DD** 269.2. (ctrl).

ACCION. 0731-2687. US. Spanish. qt. $2.50. Sunday School Board of SBC, 127 Ninth Avenue North, Nashville TN 37234.

ACCORD (NEW YORK, N.Y.). (ACCORD). Vol. 1, No. 1 (Dec. 1984)-. 0883-8933. Periodical. US. English. mo. $28.00 Domestic, $35.00 Canada. Accord Inc, Midtown Station Box 655, New York NY 10018. **LC** BX9750. **DD** 289.9.

ACTS AND PROCEEDINGS OF THE GENERAL ASSEMBLY OF THE PRESBYTERIAN CHURCH IN CANADA. (THE ACTS AND PROCEEDINGS OF THE GENERAL ASSEMBLY OF THE PRESBYTERIAN CHURCH IN CANADA). **Main/Corp** Presbyterian Church in Canada. General Assembly. Began publication in 1875?. 0079-4996. Periodical. CN. English. an. 9.00. Presbyterian Church in Canada, 50 Wynford Drive, Don Mills Ontario M3C 1J7 Canada. **Tel** 441-1111. **Ed** E F Roberts. **DD** 285.271. **Circ** 5,000. (ctrl). Yearbook containing reports, statistics and minutes of the meeting of the general assembly.

ADELANTE (EL PASO, TEX.). (ADELANTE). 0731-2733. Periodical. US. Spanish. qt. $2.75. The Sunday School Board of SBC, 127 Ninth Avenue North, Nashville TN 37234.

ADVENT CHRISTIAN WITNESS (1983). (THE ADVENT CHRISTIAN WITNESS). Apr. 1983-. 0741-4307. Periodical. US. English. $11.00. Advent Christian Witness Publications, Box 23152, Charlotte NC 28212. **Tel** (704)545-6161. **Ed** Robert J Mayer. bk rev. **Circ** 5,000. A magazine that serves members and friends of the Advent Christian Church. *Advent Christian Witness to the World, 0274-9289.*

ADVENTIST HERITAGE. V. 1- Jan. 1974-. 0360-389X. Periodical. US. English. sa. Adventist Heritage, Loma Linda University, Box 1844, Loma Linda CA 92515. **Tel** (714)785-2435. **Ind/Abst** Am. Hist. Life, Hist. Abstr., Part A, Mod. Hist. Abstr., Hist. Abst., Part B, Twent. Century Abstr., Writ. Am. Hist., Hist. Abstr. **LC** BX6101. **DD** 286.709.

ADVENTIST REVIEW. V. 155- Jan 5, 1978-. 0161-1119. Periodical. US. English. wk. $34.95. Review & Herald Publishing Association, 6856 Eastern Avenue Takoma Park South, Washington DC 20012. **Tel** (202)722-6966. **Ed** William G Johnson. **LC** BX6101. **DD** 286.73. adv acc. **Circ** 78,000. The general magazine for the Seventh-day Adventist Church membership. A variety of topics are covered that inform and inspire the church members. Covers both new and general articles. *Advent Review and Sabbath Herald, 0095-2397.*

ADVENTIST REVIEW. 0163-8866. Periodical. US. English. mo. $11.95. Manager Periodical Department, Review and Herald, 6856 Eastern Avenue NW, Washington DC 20012.

ADVENTIST REVIEW. (ADVENTIST REVIEW : GENERAL ORGAN OF THE SEVENTH-DAY ADVENTIST CHURCH). 0745-6441. Periodical. US. English. wk. $34.95. Review and Herald Publishing Association, 6856 Eastern Avenue Northwest, Washington DC 20012. **Tel** (301)791-7000. **DD** 286.73205. adv acc.

ADVENTURE. 0001-8783. Periodical. US. English. mo. $8.00. Materials Services Department, 127 9th Avenue North, Nashville TN 37234. **Tel** (615)251-2000.

AFRICAN CHRISTIAN. V. 1, No. 1 (Mar. 16, 1981)-. Periodical. English. ir. $13.24. Africa Church Information Service, PO Box 14205, Nairobi Kenya.

AGLOW. No. 1 (Nov. 1969)-. 0748-6677. Periodical. US. English. bm. $6.00. Women's Aglow Fellowship International, P O Box I, Lynnwood WA 98046-1557. **Ed** L Carpenter. **Ind/Abst** Christ. Period. Index.

AGLOW NEWSLETTER (MELVILLE, SASK.). (AGLOW NEWSLETTER). 0823-0315. Periodical. CN. English. mo. Free. Women's Aglow Fellowship, P O Box 2675, Melville Saskatchewan S0A 2P0 Canada. **DD** 248.405. (ctrl).

AHORA (EL PASO, TEX.). (AHORA). 0731-2679. US. Spanish. qt. $2.50. The Sunday School Board of the Southern Baptist Convention, 127 9th Avenue North, Nashville TN 37234.

AL-MASHAL. **VFOAT** Arabic Baptist Church Bulletin, Washington D.C. Periodical. US. Arabic. Free. 4605 Massachusetts Avenue NW, Washington DC 20016. **LC** BX6480.W3.

ALABAMA BAPTIST. Periodical. US. English. wk. The Alabama Baptist, 3310 Independence Drive, Birmingham AL 35209. **Tel** (205)870-4720. **LC** Microfilm 04409 BX, BX6201.

THE ALABAMA BAPTIST HISTORIAN. V. 1, No. 1 Nov. 1964-. 0002-4147. Periodical. US. English. sa. Alabama Baptist Historian, Samford University, Birmingham Al 35209. **Tel** (205)870-2749. **Ed** F Wilbur Helmbold. **Ind/Abst** Am. Hist. Life, Hist. Abstr., Part A, Mod. Hist. Abstr., Hist. Abst., Part B, Twent. Century Abstr. bk rev. **Circ** 200. (ctrl). Alabama Baptist history.

ALASKA BAPTIST MESSENGER. 0194-7834. Periodical. US. English. mo. Alaska Baptist Convention, Star Route A Box 1791, Anchorage AK 99507.

ALASKAN EPIPHANY. V. 1- April 1980-. 0742-7735. Periodical. US. English. qt. $7.00. Reverend Scott Fisher, Box 441, Fairbanks AK 99701. **Tel** (907)452-3040. **Ed** David Skidmore. bk rev. **Circ** 3,000. The activities, past and present, of the Episcopal state of Alaska-coverage of Alaskan native, rural, urban, statewide, and national issues. *Alaskan Churchman, Epiphany.*

ALCUIN. 1973/74-. UK. English. an. Alcuin Club, 5 St Andrew Street, London EC4A 3AB England. **LC** BX5141.A1. **DD** 264.03005. *Report.*

ALIVE. 0002-5461. Periodical. US. English. mo. $14.50. Christian Board of Publication, Beaumont & Pine Boulevard, Box 179, St Louis MO 63166. **Tel** (314)371-6900. **Ed** Michael Dixon. bk rev. **Circ** 10,000. Mainline protestant magazine for and by young adolescents (12-16) distributed mainly through church schools and military chapels.

ALIVE NOW. Periodical. US. English. bm. $6.00. Upper Room, 1908 Grand Avenue, Nashville TN 37203. **Tel** (615)327-2700.

THE A.M.E. ZION QUARTERLY REVIEW. **Main/Corp** African Methodist Episcopal Zion Church. **VAT** African Methodist Episcopal Zion Quarterly Review. 0360-3717. Periodical. US. English. qt. $2.50. AME Zion Quarterly Review, PO Box 146, Bedford PA 15522. **Ind/Abst** Relig. Index One, Period. **LC** BX8450. **DD** 287.9. *Church Quarterly.*

AMERICAN BAPTIST QUARTERLY. Vol. 1, No. 1 (Oct. 1982)-. 0745-3698. Periodical. US. English. qt. $17.00 Domestic, $20.00 Foreign. American Baptist Historical Society, PO Box 851, Valley Forge PA 19482. **Tel** (215)768-2373. **Ed** William Millar. **Ind/Abst** Hist. Abstr., Relig. Theol. Abstr., Am. Hist. Life, Relig. Index One, Period., Recent Publ. Artic. **LC** BX6201. **DD** 286.05. bk rev. **Circ** 1,000. Matters of interest to Baptists, biblical, historical and theological. Organized around themes of archival resources; cultural mythologies; social-scientific study of the Bible; last century Baptists and today's minister, etc. *Foundations, 0015-8992.*

AMERICAN HOLINESS JOURNAL. 1944. Periodical. US. English. mo. $3.00. American Holiness Journal, West Publishing Company, Apollo PA 15613. **Tel** (412)727-7256. **Ed** A J West. adv acc. Religious, conservative, holiness.

AMTSBLATT DER EVANGELISCHEN LANDESKIRCHE IN WURTTEMBERG. Periodical. GW. German. wk. Evang Oberkirchenrat, Gansheidestrasse 2-4, 7000 Stuttgart 1 West Germany.

ANALISIS. Yearly V. 1- (No. - 2). English. ir. $50 Single Issue. Academia de Humanismo Cristiano, Ismael Valdes Vergara 348, Oficina 202, Santiago Chile. **LC** AS81.A1. *Academia.*

ANGLICAN. (THE ANGLICAN). V. 1- Easter 1958-. 0517-7731. CN. English. mo. 4.00. Anglican Diocese of Toronto, 135 Adelaide Street East, Toronto Ontario M5C 1L8 Canada. **Ed** Debbie Dimmick. bk rev. adv acc. **Circ** 44,000. Serves the clergy and laity of the Anglican Diocese of Toronto. Includes national publication 'Canadian Churchman'.

ANGLICAN MESSENGER (EDMONTON, ALTA.). (ANGLICAN MESSENGER). Vol. 53, No. 1 (Jan. 1984)-. 0823-8308. CN. English. Anglican Church of Canada, Diocese of Edmonton, 1003 84 Avenue, Edmonton Alberta T6E 2G6 Canada. **DD** 283.71231. *Peace Messenger, Edmonton Anglican, 0229-1800.*

ANNUAL BIBLIOGRAPHY OF CHRISTIANITY IN INDIA. *See* Bibliographies.

Religion, Mythology, Rationalism—Protestantism

ANNUAL MESSAGE OF THE PRESIDENT OF THE LIBERIA BAPTIST MISSIONARY AND EDUCATIONAL CONVENTION DELIVERED AT THE SESSION OF THE CONVENTION. Main/Corp Liberia Baptist Missionary and Educational Convention. English. ir. LC BX6322.L5. DD 286.16662.

ANNUAL REPORT - SOCIETY OF FRIENDS, AMERICAN FRIENDS SERVICE COMMITTEE. Main/Corp American Friends Service Committee. US. English. ir. American Friends Service Committee, 1300 5th Avenue, Pittsburgh PA 15219. LC BX7635.A1.

APPEL DU SACRE-COEUR. (L'APPEL DU SACRE-COEUR). Published since Jan. 1948. 0705-9590. Periodical. CN. French. ir. $4.65. Montmartre Canadien, 1679 Ch St Louis, Quebec Province of Quebec G1S 1G5 Canada. *Message du Coeur de Jesus, 0704-0105.*

L'ARALDO DELLA SCIENZA CRISTIANA. VFOAT The Herald of Christian Science. New Series V. 9- Jan./March 1959-. 0145-7519. Periodical. US. Italian (parallel text in English). qt. $7.00. Christian Science Publishing Society, 1 Norway Street, Boston MA 02115. LC BX6901. *Herald of Christian Science. Spanish-Portuguese-Italian Edition.*

O ARAUTO DA CIECIA CRISTA. VFOAT The Herald of Christian Science. 0145-7489. Periodical. US. Portuguese (parallel text in English). mo. $7.00. Christian Science Publishing Society, 1 Norway Street, Boston MA 02115. LC BX6901.

O ARAUTO DA SANTIDADE. Vol. 1, No. 1 (Aug. 1972)-. 8750-4723. Periodical. US. Portuguese. sm. $4.00. Casa Nazarena de Publicacoes, PO Box 527, Kansas City MO 64141. DD 289.

ARC (MONTREAL, QUEBEC). (ARC). 0229-2807. Periodical. CN. English. sa. Faculty of Religious Studies, McGill University/3520 University Street, Montreal Quebec H3A 2A7 Canada. DD 205.

ARCHIV FUR SCHLESISCHE KIRCHENGESCHICHTE. See Genealogy and Heraldry - Archives.

ARCHIVUM HISTORIAE PONTIFICIAE. See Genealogy and Heraldry - Archives.

THE ARIZONA NEWS OF THE EPISCOPAL CHURCH. VFOAT Arizona News. Vol. 1, No. 1 (Feb. 1981)-. 0279-0475. Periodical. US. English. mo. The Arizona News, PO Box 15565, Phoenix AZ 85060.

ARKANSAS BAPTIST NEWSMAGAZINE. VFOAT Arkansas Baptist. 0004-1734. Periodical. US. English. wk. Arkansas Baptist State Convention, PO Box 552, Little Rock AR 72203. Tel (501)376-4791.

ASIA LUTHERAN NEWS : ALN. VFOAT ALN. Periodical. English. mo $12.00. Asia Lutheran News, 29A Melder Place, Nugegoda Sri Lanka.

THE ASSOCIATE REFORMED PRESBYTERIAN. V. 1- Jan. 1976-. 0362-0816. Periodical. US. English. mo. $12.00. Associate Reformed Presbyterian Center, One Cleveland Street, Greenville SC 29601. Tel (803)232-8297. Ed Ben Johnston. bk rev. adv acc. Circ 5,860. Official publication of the Associate Reformed Presbyterian Church, reflecting the special programs and emphasis of all arms of the domination. *Associate Reformed Presbyterian, 0362-0816; Associate Reformed Presbyterian Synodical Journal.*

ATLANTIC BAPTIST. (THE ATLANTIC BAPTIST). V. 1- Jan. 1, 1965-. 0004-6752. Periodical. CN. English. mo. $9.28. Atlantic Baptist, PO Box 756, Kentville Nova Scotia B4N 3X9 Canada. Tel (902)678-6868. Ed Michael A Lipe. bk rev. adv acc. Circ 9,000. (ctrl). News and features of interest to all ages of persons. Directed specifically to members of churches in the United Baptist Convention of the Atlantic Provinces of Canada. *Maritime Baptist, 0315-4084.*

AURORE. (L'AURORE). 0381-5897. Periodical. CN. French. bm. l'Aurore Publishing Co Ltd, 1174 rue Duvernay, St Bruno Quebec J3V 2T2 Canada. Tel (514)766-3403. DD 248.05.

AURORE. TRAITE. (L'AURORE. TRAITE). No. 1- . -. 0228-9148. Periodical. CN. French. L'Aurore, 1174 rue Duvernay, St-Bruno Quebec J3V 2T2 Canada. DD 284.09714.

AUSTIN SEMINARY BULLETIN. Main/Corp Austin Presbyterian Theological Seminary, Austin, Texas. 0191-8613. Periodical. US. English. $2.00. Austin Presbyterian Theological Seminary, 100 East 27th Street, Austin TX 78705. Tel (512)472-6736. Ed Robert Paul. Ind/Abst Relig. Index One, Period. DD 285. Circ 12,000. (ctrl). Background and progress in thinking concerning worship, evangelism, beliefs and the practice of ministry in the Christian church, with an emphasis on the Presbyterian viewpoint.

AUSTRALIAN BAPTIST. 0004-8739. Periodical. US. English. sm. $10.14. Australian Baptist Publ House, PO Box 228 Broadway, Sydney New South Wales 2007 Australia.

AUSTRALIAN PRESBYTERIAN LIFE. Feb. 5, 1966-. Periodical. AT. English. mo. $8.85. Australian Presbyterian Life, PO Box 100 GPO, Sydney Australia 2001. Tel 0011 61 2 292 804. Ed Bob Thomas. bk rev. adv acc. Circ 6,500. (ctrl). News and features to aid Christian growth. *Presbyterian Life.*

BANNER (GRAND RAPIDS, MICH.). (THE BANNER). V. 1- 1907-. 0005-5557. Periodical. US. English. ir. $16.00. Christian Reformed Publishing House, 2850 Kalamazoo Avenue SE, Grand Rapids MI 49560. Ind/Abst Guide Soc. Sci. Relig. Period. Lit. *Banner of Truth, 0731-6089.*

BAPTIST BIBLE TRIBUNE. Began in 1950. 0745-5836. Periodical. US. English. bw. $7.00. Baptist Bible Tribune, PO Box 309 HSJ, Springfield MO 65801. Tel (417)831-3996. Ed James O Combs. bk rev. adv acc. Circ 35,000. (ctrl). Baptist Bible fellowship church news, sermons, book reviews, and family articles of interest to conservative Christians.

THE BAPTIST BULLETIN. VFOAT Baptist Bulletin for Bible-Believing Baptists. Began with June/July 1935. 0005-5689. Periodical. US. English. mo. $5.50. Regular Baptist Press, 1300 North Meacham Road Box 95500, Schaumburg IL 60195. Tel (312)843-1600. Ed Merle R Hull. Ind/Abst Guide Soc. Sci. Relig. Period. Lit. bk rev. adv acc. Circ 43,000. Official organ of the General Association of Regular Baptist Churches.

THE BAPTIST CHALLENGE. VFOAT Challenge. 8756-9612. Periodical. US. English. mo. Free. Central Baptist Church, 5722 West 12th Street, Little Rock AR 72204. Tel (501)664-3225. Ed M L Moser Jr. bk rev. adv acc. Circ 5,000. (ctrl).

BAPTIST COURIER. 0744-6985. Periodical. US. English. wk. Baptist Courier, PO Box 2168/ 100 Manly Street, Greenville SC 29602. Tel (803)232-8736. *Working Christian.*

THE BAPTIST HERALD. 0005-5700. Periodical. US. English. mo. $8.00 Domestic, $10.50 Canada. North American Baptists Inc, 1 South 255 Summitt Avenue, Oakbrook Terrace IL 60181. Tel (312)495-2000. Ed Barbara J Binder. adv acc. Circ 8,000.

BAPTIST HERALD (MAYFIELD, KY.). (THE BAPTIST HERALD). V. 1, No. 1 (Jan. 1950). 8750-1422. Periodical. US. English. mo. $2.50. Mid-Continent Baptist Bible College, Route 2, Mayfield KY 42066.

BAPTIST HERITAGE IN ATLANTIC CANADA. V. 1-. Monographic Series. CN. English. Lancelot Press, PO Box 425, Hantsport Nova Scotia B0N 2T0 Canada.

BAPTIST HISTORY AND HERITAGE. V. 1- Aug. 1965-. 0005-5719. Periodical. US. English. sa. $22.95. Historical Commission of the Southern Baptist Convention, 901 Commerce/Suite 400, Nashville TN 37203-3620. Tel (615)244-0344. Ed Lynn E May. Ind/Abst Am. Hist. Life, Hist. Abstr., Part A, Mod. Hist. Abstr., Hist. Abst., Part B, Twent. Century Abstr., Hist. Abstr., Writ. Am. Hist., Relig. Index One, Period., Recent Publ. Artic. LC BX6207. bk rev. Circ 2,000. (ctrl). Presents articles which interpret Baptist history and heritage.

BAPTIST MESSAGE. 0740-2104. Periodical. US. English. wk. $6.75. Baptist Message, PO Box 311, Alexandria LA 71301. *Baptist Chronicle.*

BAPTIST MESSENGER. 0744-9518. Periodical. US. English. wk. $4.00. Bapt General Convention-Okla, 1141 No Robinson, Oklahoma City OK 73101. Tel (405)236-4341. Ed Richard T McCartney. adv acc. Circ 121,000. (ctrl). Information of interest to or about Oklahoma Southern Baptists.

BAPTIST PEACEMAKER. Vol. 1, No. 1 (Dec. 1980)-. 0735-5815. Periodical. US. English. qt. Free. Baptist Peacemaker, 1733 Bardstrom Road, Louisville KY 40205. Tel (502)451-7220. Ed Glen Hinson and Carman Sharp. bk rev. Circ 26,000. Biblical studies, articles on peacemaking, editorials, and book reviews.

THE BAPTIST PROGRAM. Began in 1927. 0005-5743. Periodical. US. English. mo. Executive Committee of the Southern Baptist Convention, 460 J Robertson Parkway, Nashville TN 37219. LC BX6207. DD 286.13205.

THE BAPTIST PROGRESS. (BAPTIST PROGRESS). 1866. 0005-5751. Periodical. US. English. wk. $9.50. Baptist Progress, 403 West 12th/ PO Box 4205, Dallas TX 75208. Tel (214)942-0606. Ed Danny W Pope. bk rev. adv acc. Circ 15,500. (ctrl). Promote interest in missions, evangelism, benevolence and christian education among the churches of the Baptist Missionary Association of Texas.

BAPTIST PROGRESS. 0164-7423. Periodical. US. English. bm. $2.00. Baptist Progress, 712-714 Quincy Street, Brooklyn NY 11221.

THE BAPTIST QUARTERLY. New Ser., V. 1- Jan. 1922-. 0005-576X. Periodical. UK. English. qt. $16.85. Baptist Historical Society, 148 Greenvale Road, London SE9 1PQ England. Tel (01)850-5732. Ed Y H Y Briggs. Ind/Abst Am. Hist. Life, Hist. Abstr., Part A, Mod. Hist. Abstr., Hist. Abstr., Part B, Twent. Century Abstr., Br. Humanit. Index, Relig. Theol. Abstr., Relig. Index One, Period., Hist. Abstr., Recent Publ. Artic. LC BX6276.A1. bk rev. Circ 650. (ctrl). Baptist history and theology. *Transactions of the Baptist Historical Society.*

THE BAPTIST RECORD. 1877. 0005-5778. Periodical. US. English. wk. Mississippi Baptist Convention, Box 530, Jackson MS 39205. Tel (601)968-3800. Ed Donald T McGregor. bk rev. adv acc. Circ 124,000.

BAPTIST STANDARD. 1888. Periodical. US. English. wk. $6.60. Baptist Standard Publishing Company, Box 660267, Dallas TX 75266-0267. Tel (214)630-4571. Ed Presnall H Wood. bk rev. adv acc. Circ 355,000. Newsmagazine for the Baptists of Texas dealing primarily with Baptist news in the state of Texas and the Southern Baptist Convention.

BAPTIST TIMES. Began with No. 4583, Sept. 1925. 0005-5786. Periodical. UK. English. wk. $24.30. Baptist Times Ltd/Baptist Church House/4 Southhampton Row, London WC1B 4AB England. Ed G Docks. bk rev. adv acc. Baptist and other news for British readers. *Baptist Times and Freeman.*

BAPTIST TRUE UNION. VFOAT True Union. Vol. 68, No. 14 (Apr. 4, 1985)-. 0883-7864. Periodical. US. English. wk. $4.75. Baptist True Union, 1313 York Road PO Box 1003, Lutherville MD 21093. Tel (301)321-7900. Ed W Fletcher Allen. adv acc. Circ 17,000. We are the official newsjournal for Southern Baptists in Maryland and Delaware. News is about our convention and related Christian topics. *Maryland Baptist, 0025-4169.*

BAPTIST UNION DIRECTORY. See Yearbooks, Almanacs, Directories.

BAPTIST WORLD. V. 1- 1954-. 0005-5808. Periodical. US. English. qt. Baptist World Alliance, 1628 16th Street NW, Washington DC 20009. Ed Reinhold J Kerstan. Circ 5,000. Provides news of baptists in 142 countries of the world.

B.C. AREA ANNUAL DOCKET. (B. C. AREA ANNUAL DOCKET). Main/Corp Baptist Union of Western Canada. B.C. Area. Assembly. VAT British Columbia Area Annual Docket, Annual Docket of the B.C. Area. Began publication in 1975 or 1976. 0227-2962. CN. English. an. Free. Baptist Union of Western Canada B C Area, 8411 Rosebank Crescent, Richmond British Columbia V7A 2K8 Canada. DD 286.1711. (ctrl). *Annual Assembly of the B.C. Area, 0227-2954.*

BEREAN AMBASSADOR. (THE BEREAN AMBASSADOR). No. 1-. 0227-5554. Periodical. CN. English. mo. Free. Reverend J R Boyd, PO Box 232, Sudbury Ontario P3E 4N5 Canada. DD 286.05. (ctrl).

BERICHT UBER DIE VERHANDLUNGEN DER ORDENTLICHEN SYNODE DE NORDELBISCHEN EV.-LUTH. KIRCHE. Main/Corp Nordelbische Evangelisch-Lutherische Kirche. Synod. German. ir. Nordelisch-Lutherische Kirche, Danische Strasse 21/35, 2300 Kiel 1 West Germany. Tel (0431)991250. LC BX8022.N67. The report on the session of the Northelbian Evangelical Lutheran Church.

BIBLE PRESBYTERIAN REVIEW CEASED. -Mar. 1983. Periodical. US. English. mo.

BIBLICAL RECORDER. 1833. 0279-8182. Periodical. US. English. wk. $7.21. Biblical Recorder, Box 26568/ 301 Hillsboro Street, Raleigh NC 27611.

Religion, Mythology, Rationalism—Protestantism

Ed R G Puckett. adv acc. Religious publication of the Baptist State Convention of North Carolina.

BIBLIOGRAPHY IN CHRISTIAN EDUCATION FOR SEMINARY AND COLLEGE LIBRARIES. ADDENDA . . . . See Bibliographies.

BOLETIN. No. 6-. Periodical. CK. Spanish. ir. Secretaria Ejecutiva, Apartado 20439, Bogota Colombia. LC BR600. DD 278.005. *Boletin Informativo (Comision de Estudios de Historia de la Iglesia en Latinoamerica).*

BOLLETTINO DELLA SOCIETA DI STUDI VALDESI. Main/Corp Societa di Studi Valdesi. 54th Yr. (N. 64)- Sept. 1935-. 0037-8739. Periodical. IT. Italian (text in English and French). sm. 20.000 Domestic, 23.000 Foreign. Via Roberto D'Azeglio 2, 10066 Torre Pellice Italy. Tel (0121)932179. Ind/Abst Am. Hist. Life, Hist. Abstr., Relig. Index One, Period., Hist. Abstr., Part A, Mod. Hist. Abstr., Hist. Abst., Part B, Twent. Century Abstr. Circ 850. History of the Waldensians and of the Protestantism in Italy. *Bollettino Della Societa di Storia Valdese.*

BOND (MINNEAPOLIS, MINN.). (BOND). VFOAT Lutheran Brotherhood Bond. 0279-9111. Periodical. US. English. qt. Free to Members, $1.00 Non-Members. Lutheran Brotherhood, 625 4th Avenue South, Minneapolis MN 55415. LC BX8001. DD 284.105. *Lutheran Brotherhood Bond.*

BONNE NOUVELLE DE L'ALLIANCE. First issue in 1974. 0701-0648. Periodical. CN. French. ir. Free. Bonne Nouvelle de l'Alliance, 7505 Boulevard Parent, Trois-Rivieres Quebec G9A 5E1 Canada. DD 234.105.

BORN-AGAIN CHRISTIAN DIRECTORY-CATALOG. See Yearbooks, Almanacs, Directories.

BRATSKII VESTNIK. Periodical. UR. Russian. Union Evangelical Christians, Foreign Trade Bank of USSR, Moscow USSR. LC BX6310.R9.

BRETHREN IN CHRIST HISTORY AND LIFE. VFOAT History and Life. Vol. 1, No. 1 (June 1978)-. Periodical. US. English. sa. $5.00. Brethren in Christ Historical Society, Messiah College, Grantham PA 17027. Tel (717)766-2511. Ed E Morris Sider. bk rev. Circ 500. Church history, with a focus on Anabaptist related groups.

BULLETIN - COMMITTEE ON ARCHIVES AND HISTORY OF THE UNITED CHURCH OF CANADA. (THE BULLETIN). No. 28 (1979)-. 0824-5843. CN. English. an. United Church of Canada, Committee on Archives and History, Victoria University, Toronto Ontario M5S 1K7 Canada. Ind/Abst Am. Hist. Life, Hist. Abstr., Part A, Mod. Hist. Abstr., Hist. Abst., Part B, Twent. Century Abstr. DD 2879205. *Bulletin, 0082-786X.*

THE BULLETIN - COMMITTEE ON ARCHIVES OF THE UNITED CHURCH OF CANADA. See Genealogy and Heraldry - Archives.

BULLETIN DE LA SOCIETE DE L'HISTOIRE DU PROTESTANTISME FRANCAIS (1981). (BULLETIN DE LA SOCIETE DE L'HISTOIRE DU PROTESTANTISME FRANCAIS). VFOAT Bulletin Historique et Litteraire de la Societe de l'Histoire du Protestantisme Francais. V. 127 (Jan./March 1981)-. 0037-9050. Periodical. FR. French. qt. 54 rue des Saints-Peres, Paris France 75007. Ind/Abst Am. Hist. Life, Hist. Abstr., Part A, Mod. Hist. Abstr., Hist. Abst., Part B, Twent. Century Abstr. *Bulletin (Societe de l'Histoire du Protestantisme Francais (France)).*

BULLETIN DU CENTRE PROTESTANT D'ETUDES. Main/Corp Centre Protestant d'Etudes. No. 1- Oct. 1948-. Periodical. French. ir. 20.00. Centre Protestant d'Etudes, 7 rue Tabazan, 1204 Geneva Switzerland. Ind/Abst Old Testam. Abstr., New Testam. Abstr.

BULLETIN DU CENTRE PROTESTANT D'ETUDES ET DE DOCUMENTATION. VFOAT Bulletin du C.P.E.D. No. 230 (April 1978)-. 0181-7671. Periodical. FR. French. ir. Centre Protestand d'Etudes et de Documentation, 46 rue de Vaugirard, 75006 Paris France. Tel (1)663-77-24. *Centre Protestand d'Etudes et de Documentation.*

BULLETIN - LUTHERAN THEOLOGICAL SEMINARY, GETTYSBURG. Main/Corp Lutheran Theological Seminary, Gettysburg. VFOAT Gettysburg Seminary Bulletin. V. 20- Nov. 1941-. 0362-0581. Periodical. US. English. qt. Lutheran Theological Seminary, Business Office, The Bulletin, Gettysburg PA 17325. Tel (717)334-6286. Ind/Abst Relig. Index One, Period. *Gettysburg Seminary Bulletin, 0016-9366.*

BULLETIN (SOCIETE DE L'HISTOIRE DU PROTESTANTISME FRANCAIS). (BULLETIN). VFOAT Bulletin Historique et Litteraire de la Societe de L'Histoire du Protestantisme Francais. 52nd (Jan./Feb. 1903)-. 0037-9050. Periodical. FR. French. qt. 27.94. Societe Histoire du Protestantisme Francais, 54 rue de Saints-Peres, 75007 Paris France. Tel (1) 548 62 07. bk rev. *Bulletin Historique et Litteraire.*

BULLETIN - SOCIETE D'HISTOIRE DU PROTESTANTISME BELGE. Main/Corp Societe d'Histoire du Protestantisme Belge. Ser. 6, Issue 4- Jan./Mar. 1975-. Periodical. BE. French. ir. $9.88. rue Leys 52, 1040 Bruxelles Belgium. *Annales.*

THE BULWARK. 1851. 0045-3536. Periodical. UK. English. bm. $3.07. Scottish Reformation Society, 17 George IV Bridge, Edinburgh EH1 1EE Scotland. Tel 031 225 1836. Ed A Sinclair Horne. bk rev. Circ 5,000. Traditional, biblical Protestant witness emphasizing reformed theology and history of reformation. *Bulwark, or, Reformation Journal in Defence of the True Interests of Man and of Society, especially in Reference to the Religious, Social and Political Bearings of Popery.*

THE CALIFORNIA SOUTHERN BAPTIST. 1941. 0008-1558. Periodical. US. English. wk. $7.95. Southern Baptist General Convention of California, PO Box 5168, Fresno CA 93755. Tel (209)229-9533. Ed Herb V Hollinger. bk rev. adv acc. Circ 22,500. News for and about Southern Baptist churches and state, national and international news affecting them. Promotion of denominational work locally, nationally and internationally.

CALVINIST CONTACT. 3rd- Year (No. 26-). 0410-3882. Periodical. CN. text in English and Dutch. wk. $22.50. Calvinist-Contact, 99 Niagara Street, St Catharines Ontario LLR 4L3 Canada. Tel (416)682-8311. Ed Bert Witvoet. bk rev. adv acc. Circ 7,500. (ctrl). News, idea and contact paper distributed weekly to the reformed community in Canada and USA. *Contact, 0382-5949.*

CANADIAN ADVENTIST MESSENGER. V. 46, No. 13- July 7, 1977-. 0702-5084. Periodical. CN. English. sm. $2.00. Seventh-Day Adventist Church in Canada, Canadian Adventist Messenger, 1148 King Street East, Oshawa Ont L1H 1 Canada. Tel (416)433-0011. Ed G E Maxson. DD 286.771. adv acc. Circ 13,400. (ctrl). This is our church journal beamed at sharing with out members what is happening in our denomination across Canada and questions that might affect them or the church. *Canadian Union Messenger, 0383-252X.*

CANADIAN BAPTIST. (THE CANADIAN BAPTIST). V. 7- 1860-. 0008-2988. Periodical. CN. English. mo. $8.00. Canadian Baptist, 217 St George Street, Toronto Ontario M5R 2M2 Canada. Tel (416)922-5163. Ed William H Jones. bk rev. adv acc. Circ 18,000. A platform for discussion regarding Canadian Baptist beliefs. *Christian Messenger, Western Baptist.*

CANADIAN FREE METHODIST HERALD CEASED. (THE CANADIAN FREE METHODIST HERALD). V. 60, No. 7-. 0383-0136. Periodical. English. ir.

C&C : CHRISTIANITY AND CRISIS. VFOAT Christianity and Crisis. Vol. 32, No. 1 (Feb. 7, 1972)-. 0009-5745. Periodical. US. English. bw. $24.00. Christianity and Crisis, PO Box 1308-C, Fort Lee NJ 07024. Tel (212) 662-5907. Ed Leoh Howell. Ind/Abst Sociol. Abstr., Soc. Welf. Soc. Plan./Policy Soc. Dev., Public Aff. Inf. Serv. Bull., Relig. Index One, Period., Humanit. Index, Guide Soc. Sci. Relig. Period. Lit., Am. Hist. Life, Hist. Abstr., Lang. Lang. Behav. Abstr. bk rev. adv acc. Circ 13,000,000. (ctrl). Protestant liberal journal of opinion with ecumenical outlook. *Christianity and Crisis, 0009-5745.*

CAPITAL BAPTIST. 1954. 0528-0559. Periodical. US. English. bw. $12.00. District of Columbia Baptist, 1628 16th Street NW, Washington DC 20009. Tel (202)265-1526. Ed James A Langley. bk rev. adv acc. Circ 8,500. (ctrl). News of American Baptist Churches USA, Southern Baptist Convention, District of Columbia Baptist Convention, religion in general, and articles on theology and inspiration.

CAREE COMMUNICATOR. 0732-9245. US. English. ir. Free with Membership. CAREE Communicator, c/o Dr Paul Mojzes Rosemont College, Rosemont PA 19010. *CAREE Newsletter.*

CARREFOUR CHRETIEN. (CARREFOUR CHRETIEN : JOURNAL CATHOLIQUE D'INFORMATION ET DE SPIRITUALITE). 0227-6135. Periodical. CN. French. mo. $5,00. Carrefour Chretien, 346 Ouest rue des Frenes, Quebec Quebec G1L 1G8 Canada. DD 248.482005. *Sourire.*

CCA NEWS. VFOAT Christian Conference of Asia CCA News. VAT Christian Conference of Asia News. 0129-9891. Periodical. SI. English. mo. $8.00 Australia, New Zealand, Europe, Africa and the Americas. Christian Conference of Asia, 480 Lorong 2, TOA Payoh/Singapore 12 Republic of Singapore.

CCPD ACTIVITY REPORT. Main/Corp World Council of Churches. Commission on the Churches' Participation in Development. English. ir. Commission on the Churches' Participation in Development World Council of Churches, 150 Route de Ferney, 1211 Geneva 20 Switzerland. LC BR115.U6. DD 261.8.

CCSA ANNUAL REPORT. Main/Corp Christian Concern for Southern Africa. VAT Christian Concern for Southern Africa Annual Report. UK. English. an. Christian Concern for Southern Africa, 1 Cambridge Terrace Regents Park, London NW1 4TJ England. LC HG5851.A2. DD 332.6730968.

CENTER JOURNAL. Vol. 1, No. 1 (Winter 1981)-. 0730-0069. Periodical. US. English. qt. $50.00. Center for Christian Studies, PO Box A, Notre Dame IN 46556. Tel (219)287-9636. Ed Kerry J Koller. Ind/Abst Relig. Index One, Period. LC BR121.2. DD 209.04. adv acc. Circ 600. Dedicated to the investigation of the many issues which arise out of the interaction of Christianity and Modernity.

CENTRAL CANADA LUTHERAN. V. 17, No. 3- May/June 1978-. 0708-7969. Periodical. CN. English. Central Canada Synod, Lutheran Church in America, Suite 211, 2281 Portage Avenue, Winnipeg Manitoba R3J 0M1 Canada. DD 284.17124. *Central Canada Lutheran Circle 'N Dot, 0705-8926.*

CENTRAL CHRISTIAN ADVOCATE. Periodical. US. English.

THE CHALLENGE OF CONSERVATIVE BAPTIST HOME MISSIONS. VFOAT Challenge. 0745-2918. Periodical. US. English. qt. Conservative Baptist Home Mission Society, 25W560 Geneva Road, Wheaton IL 60187. Tel (312)653-4900. Ed Jack Estep. Circ 95,000. Provides information about conservative Baptist missionary activity in North and Central America.

CHAN LY. (CHAN LY : NGUYET-SAN CUA HOI-THANH TIN-LANH VIET-NAM). VAT Chanly. V. 1 (April, 1976)-. 0821-7688. Periodical. CN. Vietnamese. mo. Chanly c/o Vietnamese Alliance Church, 11 West 10th Avenue, Vancouver British Columbia V5Y 1R5 Canada. DD 248.489905.

CHARISMA. 0279-0424. Periodical. US. English. mo. $16.97. Charisma, 190 North Westmonte Drive, Alto Monte Springs FL 32714. Tel (305)869-5005. Ed Stephen Strang. bk rev. adv acc. Circ 150,000. The magazine about spirit-led living. Provides balanced teaching and inspiration from a spirit-filled perspective.

CHARITY & CHILDREN. See Sociology: General Works, Theory - Social Pathology, Welfare, Criminology.

CHECKPOINT. 1972. US. English. bm. Church Missionary Society of Australia, 93 Bathurst Street, Sydney New South Wales 2000 Australia. Tel (02)267-3711. Ed Betty Durham. bk rev. Circ 7,500. (ctrl). Content mainly on Christian mission, both overseas and in North Australia. Articles, news items, and pictures.

THE CHRISTIAN ACTIVIST. (THE CHRISTIAN ACTIVIST : A SCHAEFFER V PRODUCTIONS NEWSLETTER). Vol. 1, No. 1 (Spring 1984)-. 8756-9930. Periodical. US. English. qt. Free. Schaeffer V Productions, PO Box 909, Los Gatos CA 95031. DD 261.

THE CHRISTIAN ADVENTURER. (CHRISTIAN ADVENTURER). 0009-5214. Periodical. US. English. qt. The Christian Adventurer, PO Box 850, Joplin MO 64801. Tel (417)624-7050.

CHRISTIAN ADVERTISING FORUM. See Business - Advertising & Public Relations.

CHRISTIAN AIRMAN. See Transportation.

CHRISTIAN BEACON. V. 1- Feb. 13, 1936-. 0009-5265. Periodical. US. English. wk. $12.00. Christian Beacon, 756 Haddon Avenue, Collingswood NJ 08108. Tel (609)858-0700. Ed C McIntire.

Religion, Mythology, Rationalism—Protestantism

CHRISTIAN BOOKSELLER & LIBRARIAN. See Publishing - Books and Bookmaking.

CHRISTIAN BOOKSELLER (WHEATON, ILL. : 1983). See Publishing - Books and Bookmaking.

CHRISTIAN BUS DRIVER. See Transportation.

THE CHRISTIAN CHALLENGE. Periodical. US. English. mo. $15.00. Foundation of Christian Theology, PO Box 2624, Victoria TX 77901.

THE CHRISTIAN COMMUNITY. V. 1- 1949-. 0145-3297. Periodical. US. English. ir. $10.00. National Council of Community Churches, 900 Ridge Road, Homewood IL 60430. Tel (312)798-2254.

CHRISTIAN DIRECTORY. See Yearbooks, Almanacs, Directories.

CHRISTIAN EDUCATORS JOURNAL. See Education (General) - Theory, Practice of Education.

CHRISTIAN ENTERTAINMENT GUIDE. 8756-2421. Periodical. US. English. bm. $7.50. Christian Entertainment Publications, 1008 Tenth Street, Sacramento CA 95814.

CHRISTIAN HERALD. See Biographies.

THE CHRISTIAN HOME. V. 1- Sept. 1968-. 0009-5370. Periodical. US. English. qt. $6.25. Graded Press, United Methodist Publishing House, 201 Eighth Avenue South, Nashville TN 37202. Ind/Abst United Methodist Period. Index. LC BV4485. DD 249.05. Christian Home.

THE CHRISTIAN INDEX. See Indexes/Abstracts.

THE CHRISTIAN INDEX. See Indexes/Abstracts.

CHRISTIAN INFO COMMUNIGRAM. V. 1, No. 1 (Jan./Feb. 1981)-. 0229-0219. CN. English. $2.00. Christian Info Communigram, 1623-3rd Street North West, Calgary Alberta T2M 2X9 Canada. DD 277.1233082.

CHRISTIAN INFO DIRECTORY. See Yearbooks, Almanacs, Directories.

CHRISTIAN INQUIRER. VFOAT Inquirer. National Ed. May 1972-. 0315-6532. Periodical. CN. English. mo. $3. Christian Inquirer, PO Box 339, Ridgeway Ontario L0S 1N0 Canada. DD 269.205. Enquirer. National Ed., 0315-6516.

CHRISTIAN INQUIRER. VFOAT Inquirer. May 1972-. 0315-6559. Periodical. CN. English. mo. $3. Christian Inquirer, PO Box 339, Ridgeway Ontario L0S 1N0 Canada. DD 269.205. Enquirer. Toronto Ed., 0315-6540.

CHRISTIAN INQUIRER. CANADIAN EDITION. (CHRISTIAN INQUIRER). Began with April 1976? issue. 0383-8773. Periodical. CN. English. ir. $18.00. Christian Inquirer, 2002 Main Street, Niagara Falls NY 14305. Tel (716)284-5194. Ed Ron Marr. DD 261.8097. bk rev. adv acc. Circ 90,000. Comprehensive news summary for the conservative christian. Learn how to protect your families and freedoms. Christian Inquirer. National Ed., 0315-6532; Christian Inquirer. Toronto Ed., 0315-6559.

CHRISTIAN JOURNAL. (CHRISTIAN JOURNAL MICROFORM). 0821-0977. Periodical. CN. English. DD 287.471.

CHRISTIAN LEADER. 1937. 0009-5419. Periodical. US. English. bw. $12.00. Mennonite Brethren Publishing House, Box L, Hillsboro KS 67063. Ed Wally Kroeker. bk rev. adv acc. Circ 9,500. (ctrl). Devoted to the interests of the Mennonite Brethren Conference and the cause of Christ in general.

THE CHRISTIAN LIBRARIAN : THE JOURNAL OF THE ASSOCIATION OF CHRISTIAN LIBRARIANS. See Library and Information Science.

CHRISTIAN LIVING. 0162-9255. US. English. qt. $4.25. David C Cook Publishing Co, 850 North Grove Avenue, Elgin IL 60120.

CHRISTIAN MESSENGER. 1960-. 0009-5478. Periodical. English (English and Twi). mo. 540.00. Presbyterian Book Depot, Box 195, Accra Ghana. Tel 662415. Ed G B K Owusu. bk rev. adv acc. Circ 40,000. (ctrl). Has a circulation of 40,000 and it is patronized by Christians from different denominations.

CHRISTIAN MONTHLY. 0009-5494. Periodical. US. English. mo. $5.00. Apostolic Luteran Bk Concern, Route 2 Box 197, New York Mills MN 56567. Tel (218)385-2970. Ed Alvav Helmes. Circ 900. A publications of religious news from our church federation. Articles and notices of meetings are sent in by various members and pastors. We do not have any advertisements just news items.

CHRISTIAN NEWS. V. 1- Jan. 1, 1968-. 0009-5516. Periodical. US. English. wk. $15.00. Lutheran News, Box 168, New Haven MO 63068. Tel (314)237-3110. Ed Herman Otten. bk rev. Circ 13,000. Independent. Theologically conservative. Anti-communist. Includes church news for members of all denominations. Lutheran News.

CHRISTIAN OUTREACH. 0701-0451. Periodical. CN. English. mo. $3.50. Dellcraft Publishing Co, 111 Broadway East, Vancouver British Columbia V5T 1W1 Canada. DD 205.

CHRISTIAN PERIODICAL INDEX. See Indexes/Abstracts.

CHRISTIAN RENEWAL. Vol. 1, No. 1 (Oct. 11, 1982)-. 0820-7593. Periodical. CN. English. ir. $17.00. Christian Renewal, PO Box 777, Jordan Station Ontario L0R 1S0 Canada. DD 248.05.

THE CHRISTIAN SCIENCE JOURNAL. V. 1- April 14, 1883-. 0009-5613. Periodical. US. English. mo. $12.00. The Christian Science Publishing Society, 1 Norway Street, Boston MA 02115. LC BX6901.

CHRISTIAN SCIENCE QUARTERLY. 0009-5621. Periodical. US. English. qt. Christian Science Publishing Society, One Norway Street, Boston MA 02115. Tel (800)225-7090.

CHRISTIAN SCIENCE SENTINEL. V. 1- Sept. 1898-. 0009-563X. Periodical. US. English. wk. $28.00. Christian Science Publishing Society, One Norway Street, Boston MA 02115. Tel (800)225-7090. LC BX6901.

CHRISTIAN SINGLE. V. 1- April 1979-. 0191-4294. Periodical. US. English. mo. $14.25. Materials Services Department, 127 Ninth Avenue North, Nashville TN 37234. Tel (615)251-2000. LC BV4596.S5. DD 248.48613204.

THE CHRISTIAN VERDICT. VFOAT Verdict. Essay 1, 1983-. Periodical. US. English. ir. $18.00. Verdict Publications, PO Box 1311, Fallbrook CA 92028. Verdict.

LE CHRISTIANISME AU VINGTIEME SIECLE. VFOAT Christianisme au 20eme Siecle, Christianisme au XXE Siecle. Began in 1872. 0009-5729. Periodical. FR. French. wk. 100. 8 Villa du Parc Montsouris, 75014 Paris France.

CHRISTIANISME AU XXE SIECLE (1984). (LE CHRISTIANISME AU XXE SIECLE). N. 1 (Jan. 2, 1984)-. Periodical. French. wk. 8 Villa du Parc Montsouris, 75014 Paris France. Christianisme au 20eme Siecle.

CHUGAN KIDOKKYO. Periodical. KO. Korean. wk. 4,800. Chugan Kidokkyo, 319-7 Sinsa-Dong, Kangnam-Ku, Seoul South Korea. LC BR1320.

CHURCH HISTORY. V. 1- Mar. 1932-. 0009-6407. Periodical. US. English. qt. $25.00. American Society of Church History, 305 East Country Club Lane, Wallingford PA 19086. Tel (215)566-7126. Ed Jerold C Braver, Robert Grant, and Martin E Marty. Ind/Abst Am. Hist. Life, Hist. Abstr., Part A, Mod. Hist. Abstr., Hist. Abst., Part B, Twent. Century Abstr., Sociol. Abstr., Soc. Welf. Soc. Plan./Policy Soc. Dev., Old Testam. Abstr., Women Stud. Abstr., Annu. Bibliogr. Engl. Lang. Lit., Writ. Am. Hist., Ref. Source, Soc. Work Res. Abstr., Book Rev. Index, Christ. Period. Index, Humanit. Index, Relig. Index One, Period., Repert. Int. Litt. Art, Lang. Lang. Behav. Abstr., Recent Publ. Artic. LC BR140. DD 270.05. (cum index). bk rev. adv acc. Circ 2,950. Vols. for 1932-48 available on microfilm from Alta Board of Microtext. Seeks to advance and deepen historical knowledge of Christianity in all periods and places, in every aspect of its expression: institutional, religious, and intellectual.

THE CHURCH MUSICIAN. See Music.

THE CIRCUIT RIDER. V. 1- Oct. 1976-. 0146-9924. Periodical. US. English. ir. $6.00. United Methodist Publishing House, PO Box 801, Nashville TN 37202. Tel (615)749-6488. LC BX8382.2.A1. DD 287.673.

CITHARA. V. 1- Nov. 1961-. 0009-7527. Periodical. US. English. sa. $5.00. Editor of Cithara, PO Box BC, St Bonaventure NY 14778. Ind/Abst Abstr. Engl. Stud., MLA Int. Bibliogr. Books Artic. Mod. Lang. Lit., Writ. Am. Hist., Cathol. Period. Lit. Index, Am. Hist. Life, Hist. Abstr., Part A, Mod. Hist. Abstr., Hist. Abst., Part B, Twent. Century Abstr., Years Work Eng. Stud. DD 205. Available on microfilm from University Microfilms International.

CLEVELAND LUTHERAN MESSENGER. V. 1- 1911-. 0745-435X. Newspaper. US. English. mo. $4.50. Cleveland Lutheran Messenger, 2031 West 30th Street, Cleveland OH 44113. Tel (216)281-8116. Ed Marion R Rengstorf. adv acc. Circ 12,000. (ctrl). News of Cleveland Lutheran community.

CMBC ALUMNI BULLETIN. VAT Canadian Mennonite Bible College Alumni Bulletin (1978). V. 17, No. 1 (March 1978)-. 0823-2725. Periodical. CN. English. qt. Canadian Mannonite Bible College Alumni Association, 600 Shaftesbury Boulevard, Winnipeg Manitoba R3P 0M4 Canada. DD 207.71274. Alumni Bulletin, 0823-2733.

COCK-A-DOODLE WAKE UP WORLD. 0735-8628. Periodical. US. English. mo. $15.00. Rhema Christian Center, 4915 Sargent Road NE, Washington DC 20017.

COLLECTION ESSAIS SUR L'HISTOIRE DU PROTESTANTISME FRANCAIS. V. 1- 1963-. 0530-7848. Periodical. BE. French. ir. Belge rue Leys 52, 1040 Bruxelles Belgium.

COMMON GROUND. See Religion, Mythology, Rationalism - Judaism.

COMMUNICARE. Vol. 56, No. 1 (May 1981)-. 0279-1196. Periodical. US. English. bm. Christian Communications Inc, PO Box 1601, Wichita KS 67201. Defender Magazine.

COMPASS (HAMILTON, ONT.). (COMPASS). 0821-574X. Periodical. CN. English. ir. Free. Compass Christadelphian Publishing Society, PO Box 6145 Station F, Hamilton Ontario L9C 5S2 Canada. DD 289.9.

CONCORDIA HISTORICAL INSTITUTE QUARTERLY. Vol. 1- 1928-. 0010-5260. Periodical. US. English. qt. $15.00. Concordia Historical Institute, Department of Archaeology and History, 801 de Mun Avenue, St Louis MO 63105. Tel (314)721-5934. Ed Hilton C Oswald. Ind/Abst Am. Hist. Life, Hist. Abstr., Part A, Mod. Hist. Abstr., Hist. Abst., Part B, Twent. Century Abstr., Writ. Am. Hist., Relig. Index One, Period., Recent Publ. Artic. LC BX8001. DD 284.105. (cum index). bk rev. adv acc. Circ 2,000. (ctrl). The oldest journal published in America which is devoted to the study of Lutheranism in our country.

THE CONGREGATION. V. 1- Jan./Feb. 1972-. 0361-8862. Periodical. US. English. bm. Free. Lutheran Church in America, 2900 Queen Lane, Philadelphia PA 19129.

CONGREGATIONAL JOURNAL. V. 1- Sept. 1975-. 0361-2376. Periodical. US. English. ty. $4.00. Hollywood Congregational Center, 7065 Hollywood Boulevard, Hollywood CA 90028.

CONQUISTADORES. ALUMNOS. (CONQUISTADORES). 0731-2717. Periodical. US. Spanish. qt. $2.50. The Sunday School Board of Southern Baptist Convention, 127 Ninth Avenue North, Nashville TN 37234.

CONQUISTADORES. MAESTROS. (CONQUISTADORES). 0731-2725. US. Spanish. qt. $4.50. Sunday School Board of the Southern Baptist Convention, 127 Ninth Avenue North, Nashville TN 37234.

CONTACT. Series/Conf Paris. VFOAT Institute for Church Management News. Periodical. US. English. mo. Free Anglican Church in America, 24017 Narbonne Avenue 2002, Lomita CA 90717.

CORNERSTONE. 0275-2743. Periodical. US. English. bm. $6.00. Jesus People USA, 4707 North Malden, Chicago IL 60640. Tel (312)989-6333. Ed Dawn Herrin. bk rev. adv acc. Circ 90,000. Presents Christian worldview. Geared to youth.

CORPUS CATHOLICORUM. No. 1- 1919-. GW. German. ir. Aschendorffsche Verlagsbuchhan Dlung, Postfach 1124, 4400 Munster West Germany. Tel 251/6901. Ed Erwin Iserlott. Works of Catholic authors during the reformation. Monograph series on the issues and theologians and important personalities of that era, arguments, interpretations, and protestant reform.

COVENANT COMPANION. V. 48- 1959-. 0011-0671. Periodical. US. English. mo. $16.00. Covenant Companion, 5101 North Francisco Avenue,

Religion, Mythology, Rationalism—Protestantism

Chicago IL 60625. **Ed** James R Hawkinson. bk rev. adv acc. **Circ** 27,500. The official organ of the Evangelical Covenant Church. Seeks to stimulate, gather, and build up the church it serves, as well as put it in touch with the wider Christian world. *Covenant Weekly.*

THE CRESSET. V. 1- Nov. 1937-. 0011-1198. Periodical. US. English. $13.00. Cresset, Valparaiso University, Val Paraiso IN 46383. **Tel** (219)464-5274. **Ed** James Nuechterlein. **Ind/Abst** Book Rev. Index. bk rev. **Circ** 3,900. A journal of ideas: a review of literature, the arts, and public affairs from a Lutheran Christian perspective.

CRISTIANESIMO NELLA STORIA. Vol. 1, issue 1 (Apr. 1980)-. Periodical. IT. Italian (summaries in English). bm. 25.00. Centro Editoriale Dehoniano, Via Nosadella 6, 40123 Bologna Italy. **Tel** 051/23-95-32. **Ed** Giuseppe Alberigo. **Ind/Abst** Old Testam. Abstr., New Testam. Abstr. **LC** BR140. **DD** 270.05. bk rev. **Circ** 1,000. (ctrl). The journal publishes critical essays on the history of Christianity from the judaic origins to the present age, and researches of Istituto Scienze Religiose.

CRITERION. V. 1- 1962-. 0590-0980. Periodical. US. English. bm. $5.00. University of Chicago, The Divinity School, Chicago IL 60637. **Tel** (312)962-8200. **Ed** Richard Rosengarten. **Ind/Abst** Relig. Index One, Period. **LC** BR1. **Circ** 5,000. (ctrl). Articles reflecting the life of the faculty, students, and alumni of The Divinity School of The University of Chicago. *Divinity School News.*

CROITRE. (CROITRE—). Vol. 1 No. 1-. 0712-2292. Periodical. CN. French. ir. Free. Oasis Maison Rivat, Cap-Rouge Quebec G0A 1K0 Canada. **DD** 248.05.

CROSS TALK. 0090-3949. Periodical. US. English. qt. $3.90. Graded Press, 201-8th Avenue, Nashville TN 37202. **LC** BX8225.A1. **DD** 268.87673. *Christian Action.*

CRUSADER. V. 1- Oct. 1970-. 0011-2151. Periodical. US. English. mo. $8.76. Baptist Brotherhood Commission, 1548 Poplar Avenue, Memphis TN 38104. **Tel** (901)272-2461. **Ed** James D Warren. bk rev. **Circ** 120,000. (ctrl). Microfilm copies of back issues of Crusader are available from the Southern Baptist Historical Commission. Missions education for boys grades 1-6 in Southern Baptist Churches.

CULTURA E FE. Yearly V. 1, (No. 1-). Periodical. BL. Portuguese. ir. $15.00. Caixa Postal 702, Porto Alegre Brasil. **LC** BR115.C8. **DD** 261.05.

THE CUMBERLAND PRESBYTERIAN. (CUMBERLAND PRESBYTERIAN). 1874. 0011-2976. Periodical. US. English. sm. $9.00. Cumberland Presbyterian, 1978 Union, Memphis TN 38104. **Tel** (901)276-4572. **Ed** J Richard Magrill Jr. bk rev. adv acc. **Circ** 7,400.

CURRICULUM PLANS. 0160-0885. US. English. an. $3.00. Curriculum Resources Committee, United Methodist Church, 201-8th Avenue South, Nashville TN 37202. **LC** BX8225.A1. **DD** 268.6.

DE WACHTER. (DE WACHTER : TWEE-WEKELIJKS BLAD VAND CHRISTIAN REFORMED CHURCH). 0745-4511. Periodical. US. Dutch. bw. $11.25 Domestic, $13.60 Canada. Christian Reformed Church, 2850 Kalamazoo Avenue, Grand Rapids MI 49508.

DESERET NEWS CHURCH ALMANAC. See Yearbooks, Almanacs, Directories.

DEVOTIONAL SPEECHES OF THE YEAR. 0160-6654. US. English. $4.95. Brigham Young University Press, Provo UT 84602. **LC** BX8639.A1. **DD** 252.0933.

DIACONAL QUARTERLY. 0273-0855. Periodical. US. English. qt. $3.00 US, $5.00 Foreign. Diaconal Quarterly, Bishops' Committee on the Permanent Diaconate, 1312 Massachusetts Avenue NW, Washington DC 20005.

DIAKONIA MAS TES BASILEIAS. (E DIAKONIA MAS TES BASILEIAS). V. 19, No. 7- July 1976-. 0382-7933. Periodical. CN. Greek, Modern. mo. Watch Tower Bible and Tract Society Canadian Branch, 150 Bridgeland Avenue, Toronto Ontario M6H 1Z5 Canada. **DD** 289.9. *E Yperesia Mas Tes Basileias, 0382-7925.*

DIAKONIA TES BASILEIAS. V. 17, No. 6- June 1974-. 0316-6864. Periodical. CN. Greek, Modern. mo. Free. Watch Tower Bible and Tract Society, 150 Bridgeland Avenue, Toronto Ontario M6A 1Z5 Canada. **DD** 289.9.

DIALOGUE. V. 1- Spring 1966-. 0012-2157. Periodical. US. English. qt. **Tel** (801)355-9492. **Ind/Abst** Ref. Source, Am. Hist. Life, Hist. Abstr., Part A, Mod. Hist. Abstr. **LC** BX8601. **DD** 289.305. bk rev. **Circ** 300. An independent journal established to express Mormon culture and examine the relevance of religion to secular life.

DIOCESE. (DIOCESE : NEWS OF THE EPISCOPAL CHURCH IN THE DIOCESE OF ATLANTA). 0417-5077. Periodical. US. English. mo. Diocese of Atlanta, 122 North Broad Street, Monroe GA 30655.

DIRECTORY : LUTHERAN CHURCHES IN CANADA. See Yearbooks, Almanacs, Directories.

DIRECTORY. LUTHERAN CHURCHES IN CANADA. See Yearbooks, Almanacs, Directories.

DIRECTORY OF SOUTHERN BAPTIST CHURCHES. See Yearbooks, Almanacs, Directories.

DIRECTORY OF THE AMERICAN BAPTIST CHURCHES IN THE U.S.A. See Yearbooks, Almanacs, Directories.

DIRECTORY (UNITARIAN UNIVERSALIST ASSOCIATION : 1965). See Yearbooks, Almanacs, Directories.

DISCIPLE. (THE DISCIPLE). Began with Jan. 6, 1974 issue. 0092-8372. Periodical. US. English. mo. $8.95. Christian Board of Publication, PO Box 179, St Louis MO 63166. **LC** BX7301. **DD** 286.63. *Christian, World Call.*

DOCUMENTATION ET INFORMATION PROTESTANTES : DIP. VFOAT DIP. Periodical. English. mo. $25.00. Eglise du Christ Au Zaire, BP 4938, Kinshasha-Gombe Republic of Zaire.

DOMINION. (THE DOMINION). Vol. 1, No. 1 (Fall 1982)-. 0827-2395. Periodical. CN. English. sa. Free. Maranatha Christian Fellowship, PO Box 664 Station P, Toronto Ontario M5S 2Y4 Canada. **DD** 289.9.

DRUM MAJOR. Began with Aug. 1, 1971. Periodical. US. English. ir. Southern Christian Leadership, 334 Auburn Avenue NE, Atlanta GA 30303. **Tel** (404)522-1420.

EL EXPOSITOR BIBLICO. MAESTROS DE ADOLESCENTES-JOVENES-ADULTOS. (EL EXPOSITOR BIBLICO). 0014-5238. US. Spanish. qt. $5.75. The Sunday School Board of SBC, 127 Ninth Avenue North, Nashville TN 37234.

ENCOUNTER. V. 1- Winter 1971/72-. 0315-0097. Periodical. CN. English. qt. Ken Campbell c/o Evangelistic Association, PO Box 100, Milton Ontario L9T 2Y3 Canada.

ENSIGN. (ENSIGN : THE ENSIGN OF THE CHURCH OF JESUS CHRIST OF LATTER-DAY SAINTS). Periodical. US. English. mo. $9.00. Ensign, 50 East North Temple Street, Salt Lake City UT 84150.

ENSIGN OF THE CHURCH OF JESUS CHRIST OF LATTER-DAY SAINTS CEASED. **Main/Corp** Church of Jesus Christ of Latter-Day Saints. VFOAT Ensign. V. 1- Jan. 1971-. 0013-8606. Periodical. US. English. mo. $9.00. Ensign, 50 East North Temple, Salt Lake City UT 84111. **LC** BX8601. **DD** 289.305. *Improvement Era.*

THE EPISCOPAL CHURCH ANNUAL. 1953-. 0071-1012. US. English. an. Morehouse Barlow Co, 78 Danbury Road, Wilton CT 06897. **Tel** (203)762-0721. *Living Church Annual.*

THE EPISCOPAL NEWS. 0195-0681. Periodical. US. English. mo. $5.00. Diocese of Los Angeles, PO Box 2164, Los Angeles CA 90054. **Tel** (213)482-2040. **Ed** Ruth Nicastro. bk rev. adv acc. **Circ** 35,000. (ctrl). News of the Diocese of Los Angeles, the Episcopal Church in the USA, the worldwide Anglican Communion, and the larger Christian Church, for diocesan members.

EPISCOPAL RECORDER. 0013-9610. Periodical. US. English. mo. Episcopal Recorder, Box 152, Pipersville PA 18947. **Ind/Abst** Guide Soc. Sci. Relig. Period. Lit. *Philadelphia Recorder.*

THE EPISCOPAL WOMEN'S HISTORY PROJECT. (THE EPISCOPAL WOMEN'S HISTORY PROJECT : NEWSLETTER). Vol. 1, No. 1 (Fall 1981)-. 0749-9574. Periodical. US. English. qt. $35.00. Episcopal Women's History Project, General Theological Seminary, 175 Ninth Avenue, New York NY 10011. **DD** 283. Research and oral history notes, photos and primary source material documenting work of women in Episcopal Church, project news and plans.

THE EPISCOPALIAN. V. 125, No. 4- Apr. 1960-. 0013-9629. Periodical. US. English. mo. Episcopalian Inc, 1930 Chestnut Street, Philadelphia PA 19103. *Forth.*

EPWORTH REVIEW. 0308-0382. Periodical. UK. English. ty. 0.25 Single Issue. Methodist Publishing House, Wellington Road, Wimbledon London SW19 8EU England. **Ind/Abst** Old Testam. Abstr., New Testam. Abstr. **LC** BR1. **DD** 230.705.

ESSAYS AND REPORTS - LUTHERAN HISTORICAL CONFERENCE. Main/Conf Lutheran Historical Conference. Began with 1962/64 issue. 0090-3817. US. English. be. Lutheran Historical Conference, 801 Del Mar Avenue, St Louis MO 63105. **Tel** (314)721-5934. **Ind/Abst** Relig. Index One, Period. **LC** BX8011.A1.

ETOILE BRILLANTE DU MATIN. (L'ETOILE BRILLANTE DU MATIN). 5-6. 0825-5954. Periodical. CN. French. mo. Free. M Labossiere, #7-6301 Arthur-Chevrier, Montreal-Nord Quebec H1G 1S1 Canada. **DD** 242.505. *Etoile du Matin (Montreal-Nord, Quebec), 0824-0582.*

EVANGELICAL BAPTIST. V. 10- Nov. 1962-. 0014-3324. Periodical. CN. English. mo. $4.26. Fellowship Evangelical Baptist Churches of Canada, 74 Sheppard Avenue, Willowdale Ontario M2N 1M3 Canada. *Fellowship Baptist.*

EVANGELICAL FRIEND. 0014-3340. Periodical. US. English. ir. $7.00. Barclay Press, 600-3rd Street, PO Box 232, Newburg OR 97132. **Tel** (503)538-9419. **Ed** Jack L Willcuts. bk rev. adv acc. **Circ** 12,000. (ctrl). General denominational magazine covering a variety of themes and of friends denomination (Quaker).

THE EVANGELICAL METHODIST. (THE EVANGELICAL METHODIST : VOICE OF BIBLE-BELIEVING METHODISM). 0745-8495. Periodical. US. English. mo. $3.00. The Evangelical Methodist, Street MD 21154.

EVANGELISCHE KOMMENTARE. Vol. 1-. 0300-4236. Periodical. GW. German. mo. 86.-. Kreuz-Verlag Zeitschriften GMBH, Breitwiesenstr 30, D7000 Stuttgart West Germany. **Tel** (0711)7800281-83. **Ind/Abst** Energy Res. Abstr. bk rev. adv acc. **Circ** 10,500. Magazine with analysis, reports, notes, commentaries, interviews, and documentations to the contemporary history in church and society. *Evangelische Welt, Kirche in Der Zeit; Evangelischer Literaturbeobachter.*

EXCHANGE. V. 1- Nov. 1976-. 0700-7949. Periodical. CN. English. ty. United Church of Canada, Division of Mission in Canada, 85 St Clair Avenue East, Toronto Ontario M4T 1M8 Canada. **DD** 287.9205.

EXPLORING 1 FOR LEADERS. VFOAT Exploring One for Leaders. 0745-0346. Periodical. US. English. qt. Sunday School Board of the Southern Baptist Convention, 127 Ninth Avenue North, Nashville TN 37234. *Exploring A for Leaders, 0162-4423.*

EXPLORING B. V. 1- 1969-. 0162-4431. Periodical. US. English. qt. $3.50. Sunday School Board of the Southern Baptist Convention, Material Services Department, 127 Ninth Avenue, Nashville TN 37234. **Tel** (615)251-2884. **Ed** Neal C Buchanan. **Circ** 140,000. (ctrl). Religious education material for children who are in grades four, five, and six.

FAITH AND FELLOWSHIP. VFOAT Faith & Fellowship. 1934. Periodical. US. English. ir. $8.00. Faith and Fellowship, Box 655, Fergus Falls MN 56537. **Tel** (218)736-7357. **Ed** David R Rinden. bk rev. **Circ** 5,000. (ctrl). A publication of the Lutheran Brethren synod which provides news and articles of current interest within the denomination.

FAITH-LIFE. V. 1- 1928-. 0360-9065. Periodical. US. English. bm. $6.00. Protestant Conference, c/o M Meier, 1023 Colan Boulevard, Rice Lake WI 54868. **Tel** (715)234-4164.

FE Y VIDA. 0745-8215. Periodical. US. Spanish. qt. Fe Y Vida, American Baptist Churches, Valley Forge PA 19481.

FINANCIELE GEGEVENS KERKGENOOTSCHAPPEN. VFOAT Financial Data of Religious Denominations. NE. Dutch (summaries in English). ir. 7.15. Centraal Bureau Voor De Statistiek, Prinses Beatrixlaan 428 Postbus 959,

Religion, Mythology, Rationalism—Protestantism

2270 AZ Voorburg Netherlands. **LC** BR903. **DD** 338.432809492.

FIRM FOUNDATION. Periodical. US. English. wk. $12.00. Firm Foundation, 3110 Guadalupe Street, Austin TX 78705. **Tel** (904)433-4262. **LC** BX7094.C95.

FLORIDA BAPTIST WITNESS. Feb. 1883-. Periodical. US. English. ir. $5.25. Florida Baptist Witness, 1230 Hendricks Avenue, Jacksonville FL 32207. **Tel** (904)396-2351. **Ed** Jack E Brymer Sr. bk rev. adv acc. **Circ** 95,000. (ctrl). News and information concerning the work of the Florida and Southern Baptist conventions, featuring outstanding contributions of people, churches in ministry.

FOCAL POINT. Vol. 1, No. 1 (Jan.-Mar. 1981)-. 0279-8840. Periodical. US. English. qt. Free. Denver Conservative Baptist Seminar, PO Box 10000, Denver CO 80210. **Tel** (303)761-2482. **Ed** Alice Mathews. bk rev. **Circ** 33,000. Focal point provides practical, immediately usable articles for effective daily living. *Conservative Seminarian.*

FOLIO (LOUISVILLE, KY.). (FOLIO : A NEWSLETTER FOR SOUTHERN BAPTIST WOMEN IN MINISTRY). Vol. 1, No. 1 (June 1983)-. 0741-1537. Periodical. US. English. qt. $3.00. Folio, PO Box 875, Louisville KY 40280. **LC** BX6345. **DD** 262.14632088042.

FREE METHODIST HERALD. (THE FREE METHODIST HERALD). Vol. 60, No. 8 (Sept. 1982)-. 0823-4590. Periodical. CN. English. mo. $6.75. Fred Methodist Church of Canada, Jurisdictional Conference, 371 Delaware Avenue, Toronto Ontario M6H 2T7 Canada. **DD** 287.9705. *Canadian Free Methodist Herald, 0383-0136.*

FRIEND (LONDON, ENGLAND). (THE FRIEND). Began with: Jan. 1843. 0016-1268. Periodical. UK. English. wk. 36.00 Domestic, 40.00 US, 50.00 Canada. Headley Brothers Ltd, Invicta Press, Ashford Kent England. **LC** BX7601. **DD** 289.605.

FRIENDLY WOMAN. See Women.

FRIENDS WORLD NEWS : NEWS BULLETIN OF THE FRIENDS WORLD COMMITTEE FOR CONSULTATION. No. 3 (July 1940)-. 0016-1365. Periodical. UK. English. sa. $2.00. Friends World Committee, 1506 Race Street, Philadelphia PA 19102. **Tel** (215)241-7250. Newsletter for members and interested others, worldwide, Religious Society of Friends (Quakers). *News Bulletin (Friends World Committee for Consultation).*

DIE FROHE BOTSCHAFT. V. 17, Doppelfolge 11/12 (Nov./Dec. 1962). Periodical. GW. German. wk. $7.15. Vandenhoeck & Ruprecht, Postfach 3753, Theaterstr 13, D-3400 Goettingen West Germany. **Tel** 0551/65061.

FULL GOSPEL BUSINESS MEN'S VOICE. VFOAT FGBMFI Voice. 1953. 0042-8264. Periodical. US. English. mo. $4.35. Full Gospel-Businessmens, PO Box 5050, Costa Mesa CA 92628. **Tel** (714)754-1400. **Ed** Jerry Jensen. **Circ** 700,000. Men's Christian testimony magazine.

THE GAY LUTHERAN. No. 1- July/Aug. 1974-. 0360-571X. Periodical. US. English. ir. Lutherans Concerned, PO Box 19114A, Los Angeles CA 90019. **Tel** (213)663-7816.

GEMEINDE UNTERWEGS. V. 1, 1 (Jan. 1974)-. Periodical. GW. German. mo. $20.29. Gemeinde Unterwegs, c/o Hermann Schmitt, 6748 Deutschhof 2 West Germany. *Gemeindeblatt des Verbandes.*

GENERAL MINUTES OF THE ANNUAL CONFERENCES OF THE UNITED METHODIST CHURCH. Main/Corp Methodist Church (U.S.). 1968-. 0503-3551. US. English. an. Section of Records and Statistics, 1200 Davis Street, Evanston Il 60201. **LC** BX8382.2.A1. **DD** 287.673. *General Minutes of the Annual Conferences of the Methodist Church in the United States, Territories, and Cuba.*

GEREFORMEERD THEOLOGISCH TIJDSCHRIFT. Vol. 13-. 0016-8610. Periodical. NE. Dutch. qt. 41 Domestic, 13.95. J H Kok, Gildestraat 5, 8263 AH Kampen The Netherlands. **Tel** 05202-13545. **Ind/Abst** Old Testam. Abstr., New Testam. Abstr. bk rev. **Circ** 5,000. Theological articles. *Gereformeerd Tijdschrift.*

GLAUBE UND HEIMAT. 0323-8202. Periodical. SZ. German. wk. Kunst & Wissen Erich Bieber, Dufourstrasse 51, CH-8008 Zurich Switzerland. **LC** BX9798.U5. **DD** 284.1432205.

GOOD NEWS. V. 1- Winter 1967-. 0436-1563. Periodical. US. English. ir. $9.00. Good News, 308 East Main Street, Wilmore KY 40390. **Tel** (606)858-4661. **Ed** James V Heidinger II. bk rev. adv acc. **Circ** 18,500. Forum for scriptural renewal within the UM Church.

GOOD NEWS FROM NARAMATA CENTRE. 0229-091X. Periodical. CN. English. qt. Free. Naramate Centre, PO Box 68, Naramata British Columbia V0H 1N0 Canada. **DD** 267.1. (ctrl)

GOSPEL TIDINGS (OMAHA, NEB.). (GOSPEL TIDINGS). 0745-7618. Periodical. US. English. mo. $6.75. Evangelical Mennonite Brethren, Conference Central Office, 5800 South 14th Street, Omaha NE 68107. **Tel** (402)731-4780. **Ed** Lyle Wahl. bk rev. (ctrl). Educational inspirational content, directed to members in our fellowship of churches.

THE HANDBOOK OF THE UNITED FREE CHURCH OF SCOTLAND. Main/Corp United Free Church of Scotland. Began with the 1931 issue. 0082-7908. UK. English. an. United Free Church of Scotland, 11 Newton Place, Glasgow G3 7PR Scotland. **LC** BX9089. **DD** 285.241.

HANGUK KIDIKKYO CHANGNOHOE HOEBO. VFOAT The Presbyterian Life. Periodical. KO. Korean. mo. Hanguk Kidokkyo Changnohoe, Chonghoe 136-46 Yonji-dong Chongno-ku, Seoul Korea. **LC** BX9151.K6.

THE HARVEST. Periodical. US. English. qt. Baptist Mid-Missions, 4205 Chester Avenue, Cleveland OH 44103. **Tel** (216)432-2200. **Ed** Bernice Inman. **Circ** 80,000. Report to churches and individuals on activity of fundamental Baptist Missionaries around the world.

HAWKEYE METHODIST. -V. 12, No. 7. 0438-8364. Periodical. US. English. mo. Iowa Methodist Information, 1019 Chestnut Street, Des Moines IA 50309. **Tel** (515)283-1991.

EL HERALDO DE LA CIENCIA CRISTIANA. VFOAT The Herald of Christian Science. New Series V. 9- Jan./March 1959-. 0439-0148. Periodical. US. Spanish (parallel text in English). mo. $7.00. Christian Science Publishing Society, 1 Norway Street, Boston MA 02115. **LC** BX6901. *Herald of Christian Science. Spanish-Portuguese-Italian Edition.*

LE HERAUT DE LA SCIENCE CHRETIENNE. VFOAT Herald of Christian Science. 0145-7470. Periodical. US. French (parallel text in English). mo. $7.00. Christian Science Publishing Society, 1 Norway Street, Boston MA 02115. **LC** BX6901. **DD** 289.505.

DE HERAUT VAN DE CHRISTELIJKE WETENSCHAP. VFOAT The Herald of Christian Science. 0145-756X. Periodical. US. Dutch (parallel text in English). qt. Christian Science Publishing Society, 1 Norway Street, Boston MA 02115. **LC** BX6901. **DD** 289.505.

DER HEROLD DER CHRISTLICHEN WISSENSCHAFT. VFOAT The Herald of Christian Science. V. 1-. 0145-7578. Periodical. US. German (parallel text in English). mo. Christian Science Publishing Society, 1 Norway Street, Boston MA 02115. **LC** BX6901. **DD** 289.505.

DIE HERVORMER. Began with Vol. for 1909/10. Periodical. SA. Afrikaans. ir. Nederduitsch Hervormde Weeshuispers, Posbus 18061 Hercules, Pretoria South Africa.

HICALL. VAT Hi Call. 0018-120X. Periodical. US. English. qt. Gospel Publishing House, 1445 Booneville Avenue, Springfield MO 65802.

HIS. See Education (General) - Higher Education.

HISTORICAL INTELLIGENCER. (HISTORICAL INTELLIGENCER : HISTORICAL JOURNAL OF THE UNITED CHURCH OF CHRIST). Vol. 1, No. 1 (Fall 1980)-. 0270-4919. Periodical. US. English. an. $20.00. Historical Council, United Church of Christ, 297 Park Avenue South, New York NY 10010. **LC** BX9884. **DD** 285.834.

HISTORICAL MAGAZINE OF THE PROTESTANT EPISCOPAL CHURCH. V. 1- Mar. 1932-. 0018-2486. Periodical. US. English. qt. $13.50. Historical Society of the Episcopal Church, 606 Rathervue Place, PO Box 2247, Austin TX 78768. **Tel** (512)472-6816. **Ed** John F Woolverton. **Ind/Abst** Hist. Abstr., Part A, Mod. Hist. Abstr., Hist. Abst., Part B, Twent. Century Abstr., Hist. Abstr., Am. Hist. Life, Relig. Index One, Period., Writ. Am. Hist., Recent Publ. Artic. **LC** BX5800. **DD** 283.73. bk rev. adv acc. **Circ** 1,400. Available on microfilm from University Microfilms International. Serves a growing number of church people who seek to learn about their heritage. Articles on women in church world missions, church music, minorities and theology.

THE HISTORIOGRAPHER. V. 1- Whitsuntide 1938-. US. English. an. Church Historical Society, PO Box 2247, Austin TX 78767. **LC** BX5810. **DD** 283.73.

THE HISTORIOGRAPHER OF THE EPISCOPAL DIOCESE OF CONNECTICUT. No. 1- June 1952-. 0018-2591. Periodical. US. English. ir. $10.00. Archivist/Diocesan House, 1335 Asylum Avenue, Hartford CT 06105. **LC** BX5917.C8. **DD** 283.746.

HRVATSKA KRSCANSKA BIBLIOGRAFIJA. See Bibliographies.

IEVANHELSKYI RANOK. VFOAT Evangelical Morning. US. chiefly in Ukrainian. mo. Evangelical Morning, Mr M Kozak, PO Box 185 Postal Station E, Toronto 4 Ontario Canada. **LC** BX4800. *Kanadiiskyi Ranok.*

THE ILIFF REVIEW. V. 1- Winter 1944-. 0019-1795. Periodical. US. English. ty. $4.00. The Iliff School of Theology, 2201 South University Boulevard, Boulder CO 80210. **Tel** (303)744-1287. **Ed** Charles S Milligan. **Ind/Abst** MLA Int. Bibliogr. Books Artic. Mod. Lang. Lit., Old Testam. Abstr., Relig. Index One, Period. **LC** BR1. **DD** 205. bk rev. **Circ** 500. (ctrl). Religious studies including standard academic areas in the field.

ILLINOIS BAPTIST. 0019-1868. Periodical. US. English. wk. $6.00. Illinois Baptist State Association, Box 3486, Springfield IL 62708.

IMPACT. VFOAT Conservative Baptist Impact. Vol. 26- Jan. 1969-. 0019-2821. Periodical. US. English. bm. $3.00. Conservation Baptist for Mission, PO Box 5, Wheaton IL 60187. *Conservative Baptist Impact.*

INDEPENDENT BAPTIST MISSIONARY MESSENGER. (THE INDEPENDENT BAPTIST MISSIONARY MESSENGER). VAT Independant Baptist Missionary Messenger, Missionary Messenger (Qualicum Beach 1981). Vol. 9, No. 5 (May 1981)-. 0711-334X. Periodical. CN. English. mo. Independent Baptist Missionary Messenger, PO Box 1030, Qualicum Beach British Columbia V0Z 2T0 Canada. **DD** 230.605. *Missionary Messenger, 0381-0763.*

THE INDEPENDENT METHODIST BULLETIN. Vol. 2, No. 10 & 11 (Oct./Nov. 1980)-. 0744-4087. Periodical. US. English. bm. The Independent Methodist, PO Box 4274, Jackson MS 39216. *Independent Methodist.*

INDIANA APOSTOLIC TRUMPET. (INDIANA APOSTOLIC TRUMPET : OFFICIAL PUBLICATION, INDIANA DISTRICT, UNITED PENTECOSTAL CHURCH). 8750-8176. Periodical. US. English. mo. $4.00. Indiana Apostolic Trumpet, c/o S Young, PO Box 2125, Terre Haute IN 47802.

INFORMATION BULLETIN - CHRISTIAN SOCIAL ASSOCIATION. Main/Corp Christian Social Association. VFOAT Ches Information Bulletin. Periodical. PL. English. mo. ARS Polona, Karakowskie Przedmieschie 7, 00-068 Warsaw Poland.

INFORMATION - LUTHERAN WORLD FEDERATION NEWS SERVICE. Main/Corp Lutheran World Federation. News Service. VFOAT LWF Information. Periodical. ir. $30.00. Lutheran World Federation, PO Box 66, Route de Ferney 150, 1211 Geneva 20 Switzerland. **Tel** (4122)91 63 54. **Ed** Roger Kahle. bk rev. **Circ** 3,000. (ctrl). International news service covering Lutheranism in particular and relief/development issues and ecumenism in general. Noted for coverage of Southern Africa and anitapartheid movement. *Press Service - News Bureau, Lutheran World Federation.*

INFORMATION NATIONALE - SOCIETE SAINT-JEAN-BAPTISTE DE MONTREAL. (L'INFORMATION NATIONALE - SOCIETE SAINT-JEAN-BAPTISTE DE MONTREAL). Main/Corp Societe Saint-Jean-Baptiste de Montreal. V. 10, No. 8/9- Jan./Feb. 1962-. 0537-6211. Periodical. CN. French. mo. Information Nationale, 82 Quest rue Sherbrooke, Montreal Quebec H2X 1X3 Canada.

INFORMER. (THE INFORMER). VFOAT Christian Informer. June 1979-. 0227-5406. Periodical. CN. English. qt. Free. Christian Informer, 223A-10 Street

Religion, Mythology, Rationalism—Protestantism

North West, Calgary Alberta T2N 1V5 Canada. **DD** 267.1.

INSIGHTS INTO CHRISTIAN EDUCATION. **VFOAT** Insights. 8756-3347. Periodical. US. English. qt. $13.00. Parish Ministries Resource, PO Box 321, Drundee IL 60118. **Tel** (312)428-8341. Ed Thomas Couser. **DD** 377. bk rev. **Circ** 400. An independent journal serving educators of the Lutheran Church.

INTEGRITY FORUM. Vol. 3, No. 8 (June-July 1977)-. 0095-2184. Periodical. US. English. bm. Integrity Forum, PO Box 891, Oak Park IL 60303. *Integrity (Fort Valley, Ga.)*, 0095-2184.

INTERCOM. V. 1- Oct. 1968-. 0383-6061. Periodical. CN. English. Fellowship of Evangelical Baptist Churches in Canada, 74 Sheppard Avenue West, Willowdale Ontario M2N 1M3 Canada.

THE INTERNATIONAL PENTECOSTAL HOLINESS ADVOCATE. V. 59, No. 20- Feb. 8, 1976-. 0145-6970. Periodical. US. English. sm. $4.00. International Penestecostal Holiness Church, Advocate Press, Box 98, Franklin Springs GA 30639. **Tel** (404)245-7272. **LC** BX8795.P25. **DD** 289.9. *Pentecostal Holiness Advocate.*

THE INTERPRETER. V. 13- Jan. 1969-. 0020-9678. Periodical. US. English. mo. $6.00. The Interpreter, 810 12th Avenue South, Nashville TN 37203. Available on microfilm from University Microfilms. *Methodist Story-Spotlight.*

IRISH BAPTIST. 1900. Periodical. IE. English. mo. $12.00. Baptist Union of Ireland, 3 Fitzwilliam Street, Belfast BT9 6AW Ireland. Ed N A Shields. bk rev. adv acc. **Circ** 2,500. News of local churches, missions, home and abroad. Devotional articles, contraversial subjects, etc.

IRISH BAPTIST HISTORICAL SOCIETY JOURNAL. V. 1- 1968/69-. 0021-1060. Periodical. UK. English. an. Baptist Union of Ireland, 3 Fitzwilliam Street, Belfast BT9 6AW Ireland. **LC** BX6281.A1. **DD** 286.1415.

JAARBOEK VAN DIE CHRISTELIJKE GEREFORMEERDE KERKEN IN NEDERLAND. See Yearbooks, Almanacs, Directories.

JD. See Law.

JED SHARE. Main/Corp Joint Educational Development. **VFOAT** Share. **VAT** Joint Educational Development Share. V. 1, No. 3- Nov. 1972-. 0199-6843. Periodical. US. English. qt. $18.50. United Church Press, 132 West 31st Street, New York NY 10001. **Tel** (212)239-8700. Ed Norma E Koenig. **Ind/Abst** Media Rev. Dig. bk rev. **Circ** 6,500. A journal for church teachers and leaders- articles on A-V resources, novel teaching techniques, teacher-to-teacher exchange of ideas, Christmas and other seasonal items. *Share.*

JEDNOTA. V. 1- 1957-. Periodical. PL. Polish. mo. ARS Polona, Krakowskie Przedmieschie 7, 00-068 Warsaw Poland. **LC** BX9480.P7.

JEDNOTA BRATRSKA. Periodical. CS. Czech. mo. Artia, PO Box 79, Praha 1 Czechoslovakia. **LC** BX4922.

THE JOHN WHITMER HISTORICAL ASSOCIATION JOURNAL. **VFOAT** Journal. Vol. 1 (1981)-. 0739-7852. Periodical. US. English. an. $7.50. Graceland College, c/o Betty Winholtz, Lamoni IA 50140. **Tel** (515)784-5171. Ed William Russell. bk rev. **Circ** 600. Publication dealing with Latter Day Saint history as a means of encouraging serious research and exchange of various scholarly viewpoints.

JOURNAL OF CHRISTIAN EDUCATION. See Education (General).

JOURNAL OF MORMON HISTORY. V. 1- 1974-. 0094-7342. US. English. an. $10.00. Mormon History Association, PO Box 7010/University Station, Provo UT 84602. **LC** BX8601. **DD** 289.309.

JOURNAL OF PRESBYTERIAN HISTORY. V. 1- May 1901-. 0022-3883. Periodical. US. English. qt. $10.00. Editor/Journal of Presbyterian History, 425 Lombard Street, Philadelphia PA 19147. **LC** BX8905.P7. (cum index). Available on microfilm.

JOURNAL OF PROCEEDINGS - ANGLICAN CHURCH OF CANADA GENERAL SYNOD CEASED. (JOURNAL OF PROCEEDINGS - ANGLICAN CHURCH OF CANADA, GENERAL SYNOD). **Main/Corp** Anglican Church of Canada. General Synod. 19th-29th Session. 0380-2469. CN. English. te. General Synod, Anglican Church of Canada, 600 Jarvis Street, Toronto Ontario M4Y 2J6 Canada. **DD** 283.71. *Journal of Proceedings.*

THE JOURNAL OF PSYCHOLOGY AND CHRISTIANITY. (JOURNAL OF PSYCHOLOGY AND CHRISTIANITY). **VFOAT** J.P.C. Vol. 1, No. 1-. 0733-4273. Periodical. US. English. qt. $55.00. Christian Association for Psychological Studies, 26075 Farmington Road, Farmington Hills MI 48018. **Tel** (313)477-1350. Ed J Harold Ellens. **Ind/Abst** Psychol. Abstr. **LC** BR110. **DD** 150.190882. bk rev. adv acc. **Circ** 2,500. (ctrl). Addresses the interface of religion and social sciences and the cutting edge issues of all related subjects. *Bulletin*, 0147-7978.

JOURNAL OF RELIGIOUS EDUCATION OF THE AFRICAN METHODIST EPISCOPAL CHURCH. (JOURNAL OF RELIGIOUS EDUCATION OF THE AFRICAN METHODIST EPISCOPAL CHURCH). Vol. 40, No. 4 (July, Aug, Sept. 1980)-. 0276-0770. Periodical. US. English. qt. $6.50. Division of Christian Education, 500 8th Avenue South, Nashville TN 37203. *Journal of Religious Education*, 0022-4219.

JOURNAL OF THE ANNUAL CONVENTION - EPISCOPAL CHURCH. DIOCESE OF BETHLEHEM. (JOURNAL OF THE . . . ANNUAL CONVENTION). **Main/Corp** Episcopal Church. Diocese of Bethlehem. 0730-6938. US. English. an. The Episcopal Diocese of Bethleham, 826 Delaware Avenue, Bethlehem PA 18015. **LC** BX5918.B5. **DD** 283.748205. *Journal of the Proceedings of the . . . Annual Convention of the Protestant Episcopal Church in the Diocese of Bethlehem.*

JOURNAL OF THE FRIENDS' HISTORICAL SOCIETY. (THE JOURNAL OF THE FRIENDS' HISTORICAL SOCIETY). **Main/Corp** Friends' Historical Society. V. 1- 1903-. 0071-9587. Periodical. UK. English. ir. $4.00. Friends Historical Society, Euston Road, London NW1 2BJ England. **Ind/Abst** Am. Hist. Life, Hist. Abstr., Part A, Mod. Hist. Abstr., Hist. Abst., Part B, Twent. Century Abstr. **LC** BX7676.A1.

JOURNAL OF THE GENERAL CONVENTION OF THE NEW JERUSALEM. **Main/Corp** General Convention of the New Jerusalem in the United States of America. 1817-. US. English. an. General Convention of the New Jerusalem in the United States of America, 48 Sargent Street, Newton MA 02158. **LC** BX8705.

JOURNAL OF THE . . . GENERAL SYNOD - ANGLICAN CHURCH OF CANADA. (JOURNAL OF THE . . . GENERAL SYNOD). **Main/Corp** Anglican Church of Canada. General Synod. 30th-. 0826-3205. CN. English. te. Free to Qualified Subscribers. Anglican Church of Canada, 600 Jarvis Street, Toronto Ontario M4Y 2J6 Canada. **DD** 283.71. (ctrl). *Journal of Proceedings - Anglican Church of Canada, General Synod.*

JOURNAL OF THE NORTH MISSISSIPPI CONFERENCE OF THE UNITED METHODIST CHURCH . . . SESSION SINCE MERGER OF THE UPPER MISSISSIPPI CONFERENCE (ORGANIZED IN 1891) AND THE NORTH MISSISSIPPI CONFERENCE (ORGANIZED IN 1870). **Main/Corp** United Methodist Church (U.S.). North Mississippi Conference. **VFOAT** Journal, North Mississippi Conference of the United Methodist Church. 3rd (1975)-. US. English. an. *Journal of the New North Mississippi Conference.*

JOURNAL OF THE SOUTH CAROLINA BAPTIST HISTORICAL SOCIETY. **Main/Corp** South Carolina Baptist Historical Society. V. 1- Nov. 1975-. 0146-0196. US. English. an. $3.00. Baptist Historical Collection, Furman University Library, Greenville SC 29613. **Tel** (803)294-2194. Ed J Glenwood Clayton. **LC** BX6248.S6. **DD** 285.1757. **Circ** 150. Articles about South Carolina Baptist history. We reprint some original documents.

JOURNAL OF THE UNITED REFORMED CHURCH HISTORY SOCIETY. (JOURNAL - UNITED REFORMED CHURCH HISTORY SOCIETY). **Main/Corp** United Reformed Church History Society. V. 1-May 1973-. 0049-5433. Periodical. UK. English. sa. 6.49. United Reformed Church Historical Society, 86 Tavistock Place/Church House, London WC1H 9RT England. **Tel** (01)837-7661. Ed Clyde Binfield. **Ind/Abst** Am. Hist. Life, Hist. Abstr., Part A, Mod. Hist. Abstr., Hist. Abst., Part B, Twent. Century Abstr., Recent Publ. Artic. **LC** BX9890.U25. **DD** 285.2. bk rev. Historical material relating to congregational and presbyterian worthies, practices and theological teaching. *Journal - Presbyterian Historical Society of England*, 0079-5011.

KHAOUA. V. 1- Nov. 1967-. 0700-9496. Periodical. CN. French. qt. $7.74. Service Preparation A La Vie, 10215 rue Sacre Coeur, Montreal Quebec H2C 2S6 Canada. **Tel** (514)387-6475. **DD** 248.405.

KIDOKKYO SASANG. Periodical. KO. Korean. ir. 5.000. Taehan Kidokkyo Sohoe, 84-8 2-Ka Chongno, Seoul South Korea. **LC** BR9.K6.

THE KINGDOM BUILDER. **VFOAT** B.T.U. Young People's Quarterly. The Kingdom Builder. 0746-6889. Periodical. US. English. qt. National Baptist Publications Inc, 7145 Centennial Boulevard, Nashville TN 37209. *Baptist Training Union Young People's Quarterly.*

KIRCHE IM OSTEN. MONOGRAPHIENREIHE. V. 1- 1959-. 0453-9281. Monographic Series. German. ir.

KIRCHE IM SOZIALISMUS. Nov. 1973-. Periodical. German. ir. Bachstrasse 1-2, 1000 Berlin 21 East Germany. **LC** BX4844.

KIRCHENBLATT FUR DIE REFORMIERTE SCHWEIZ. Began with V. 1, in 1845. 0023-1797. Periodical. SZ. German. ir. Verlag Friedrich Reinhardt AG, Missionstrasse 36, CH-4012 Basel Switzerland.

KIRCHLICHES AMTSBLATT DER EVANGELISCHEN KIRCHE IM RHEINLAND. **Main/Corp** Evangelsche Kirche Im Rheinland. Periodical. German. ir. 7.50 Quarterly. Landeskirchenamt, Verlag: Landeskirchenamt, Hans-Bockler-Strasse 7, 4000 Dusseldorf West Germany. **LC** BX7567.A1.

KIRCHLICHES JAHRBUCH FUR DIE EVANGELISCHE KIRCHE IN DEUTSCHLAND. See Yearbooks, Almanacs, Directories.

LANCASTER CONFERENCE NEWS. Began in 1984?. 0747-2706. Periodical. US. English. sm. $4.00. Lancaster Conference News, PO Box 128, Salunga PA 17538-0628. *Lancaster Mennonite Conference News*, 0273-981X.

LAPORAN TAHUNAN DIREKTORAT JENDERAL BIMBINGAN MASYARAKAT KRISTEN/PROSTESTAN DEPARTAMEN AGAMA R. I. Main/Corp Indonesia. Direktorat Jenderal Bimbingan Masyarakat Kristen/Prostestan. Indonesian. ir. Departamen Agama R I, Direktorat Jendral Bimbingan, Jl Moh Husni Thamrin, Jakarta Indonesia. **LC** BR1220.

LATIN AMERICA EVANGELIST. See History (General) - History of North, South, and Central America.

LATVIJAS EV.-LUT. BAZNICAS GADA GRAMATA UN KALENDARS. **VFOAT** Baznicas Gada Gramata. 1973-. US. Latvian. an. 425 Elm Street, Glenview IL 60025. *Latvijas Ev.-Lut. Baznicas Kalendars.*

LCA PARTNERS. **VFOAT** L.C.A. Partners. **VAT** Lutheran Church in America Partners. Vol. 1, No. 2 (Apr. 1979)-. Periodical. US. English. bm. $7.00. Lutheran Church in America, 2900 Queen Lane, Philadelphia PA 19129. **Tel** (215)849-5800. Ed Richard E Koenig. adv acc. **Circ** 11,000. (ctrl). A professional leadership journal that stands at the intersection of Lutheran theology and parish practice. *Partners (Philadelphia, Pa.).*

LETTRE DE L'ABBE GRAVEL. (LA LETTRE DE L'ABBE GRAVEL). No. 41-. 0380-0946. Periodical. CN. French. ir. l'Abbe Pierre Gravel, Presbytere de Boischatel, Boischatel Quebec G0A 1H0 Canada. **DD** 205. *Lettre de Michelle de St. - Antoine.*

LIBERTY. V. 1- Apr. 1906-. 0024-2055. Periodical. US. English. bm. Review & Herald Publishing Company, 6856 Eastern Avenue NW, Tokoma Park, Washington DC 20012. **Tel** (202)723-3700. **LC** BX6101. **DD** 286.73.

LIFE AND WORK. New Ser., No. 1- Jan. 1930-. 0024-306X. Periodical. UK. English. mo. $7.35. Church of Scotland, 121 George Street, Edinburgh

EH2 4YN Scotland. **Tel** 031-225-5722. **Ed** Robert D Kernohan. bk rev. adv acc. **Circ** 110,000. News magazine and review of the church of Scotland (Presbyterian). *Church of Scotland Home and Foreign Mission Record, Record of the Church of Scotland.*

LIGHT AND LIFE. 1868. 0024-3299. Periodical. US. English. mo. $28.00. Free Methodist Church of North America, 901 College Avenue, Wiona Lake IN 46590. **Tel** (219)267-7656. **Ed** Lyn Cryderman. bk rev. adv acc. **Circ** 46,000. All articles are devoted to helping persons live as Christians in a secular world.

LIGHT 'N' HEAVY. **VAT** Light and Heavy. V. 52, No. 3- Spring 1979-. Periodical. US. English. qt. $5.00. General Council for Assembles of God, 1445 Boonville Avenue, Springfield MO 65802. *Youth Alive, 0009-5826.*

LIGHTBEARER. **VFOAT** Light Bearer. V. 1- 1905-. Periodical. UK. English. bm. 3.00. Sudan United Mission, 75 Granville Road, Sidcup Kent England. **Tel** 01 300 1109. **Ed** D Calcott. **Circ** 5,000. (ctrl). A missionary magazine of the SUM fellowship. Covers missionary work in the Sudan and northern Nigeria. The mission is Protestant Evangelical.

LIVING THE WORD. LEVEL 2. LEADER'S GUIDE. (LIVING THE WORD. LEVEL 2). **VFOAT** Living the Word. 0745-8266. Periodical. US. English. qt. Leader's Guide Level 2, CTW American Baptist Churches, Valley Forge PA 19481.

LIVING WITH PRESCHOOLERS. 0162-4350. Periodical. US. English. qt. $8.75. Materials Services Department, 127-9th Avenue North, Nashville TN 37234. **Tel** (615)251-2000.

LOGOS. *See* Philosophy.

LOOK INSIDE (PENTECOSTAL ASSEMBLIES OF CANADA. YOUTH DEPT. WESTERN ONTARIO DISTRICT). (LOOK INSIDE). Vol. 1, No. 1 (Winter 1975)-. 0226-9848. Periodical. CN. English. qt. Free. Look Inside, 3419 Mainway, Burlington Ontario L7M 1A9 Canada. **DD** 259.2. (ctrl).

LOVE (TORONTO, ONT. : 1984). (LOVE). Aug. 1984-. 0825-1959. Periodical. CN. English. mo. Free. Love, PO Box 476 Station C, Toronto Ontario M6J 3P5 Canada. **Tel** (416)364-2697. **Ed** Anthony Ing. **DD** 248.405. bk rev. (ctrl).

LUTHER. Vol. 1-. 0340-6210. Periodical. GW. German. ty. $11.64. Vandenhoeck & Ruprecht, Postfach 3753, Theaterstr 13, D 3400 Goettingen West Germany. **Tel** 0551/65061. **Ind/Abst** MLA Int. Bibliogr. Books Artic. Mod. Lang. Lit. **LC** BR323.5.

THE LUTHERAN. V. 1- Jan. 2, 1963-. 0024-743X. Periodical. US. English. ir. $6.00. The Lutheran Church in America, 2900 Queen Lane, Philadelphia PA 19129. **Tel** (215)438-6580. **Ed** Edgar R Trexler. **Ind/Abst** Guide Soc. Sci. Relig. Period. Lit. **LC** BX8001. **DD** 284.133. bk rev. adv acc. **Circ** 532,000. Feature and news content about the people and congregations of the Lutheran Church in American and key news about the world of religion. *Lutheran.*

THE LUTHERAN. V. 1- Jan. 21, 1967-. Periodical. AT. English. ir. $12.55. Lutheran Publishing House, Box 1368, Government Printing Office, Adelaide 5001 Australia. **Ed** E W Wiebusch. adv acc. (ctrl). Reports and information concerning the running of the Lutheran Church of Australia, including reports from overseas missions. *Lutheran Herald, Australian Lutheran.*

THE LUTHERAN AMBASSADOR. Began in 1963. 0746-3413. Periodical. US. English. bw. The Lutheran Ambassador, 3110 East Medicine Lake Boulevard, Minneapolis MN 55441.

LUTHERAN CHURCH DIRECTORY FOR THE UNITED STATES. *See* Yearbooks, Almanacs, Directories.

THE LUTHERAN; CONVENTION DAILY. V. 5, No. 1- Oct. 13, 1932-. Periodical. US. English. ir. $3.00. Milwaukee Lutheran, PO Box 18011, Milwaukee WI 53214. *Daily Lutheran.*

LUTHERAN COUNCIL IN THE U.S.A. NEWS BUREAU. (NEWS RELEASES - NEWS BUREAU, LUTHERAN COUNCIL IN THE USA). V. 1- 1914-. 0361-8757. US. English. News Bureau, Lutheran Council in the USA, 315 Park Avenue South, New York NY 10010.

THE LUTHERAN DIGEST. V. 1- Summer 1953-. 0458-497X. Periodical. US. English. ir. $10.00. Lutheran Digest, PO Box 23009, Minneapolis MN 55423. **LC** BR1. **DD** 205.

LUTHERAN EDUCATION. Began in 1947. 0024-7448. Periodical. US. English. ir. $7.50. Concordia Teachers College, 7400 Augusta, River Forest IL 60305. **Tel** (312)771-8300. **Ed** M L Radke. **Ind/Abst** Educ. Index. **LC** LC573. **DD** 377.84173. bk rev. adv acc. **Circ** 4,000. (ctrl). Available on microfilm from University Microfilms. A journal designed for/by teachers of elementary schools especially those in Lutheran schools. *Lutheran School Journal, 0362-465X.*

LUTHERAN EDUCATOR. Periodical. US. English. ir.

LUTHERAN FORUM. V. 1- Jan. 1967-. 0024-7456. Periodical. US. English. qt. $10.00. American Lutheran Publicity Bureau, 155 East 22nd Street, New York NY 10010. **LC** BX8001. *American Lutheran.*

THE LUTHERAN JOURNAL. 0360-6945. Periodical. US. English. qt. $4.00. Outlook Publications, 7317 Cahill Road, Edina MN 55435. **Tel** (612)941-6830. **Ed** Armin U Deye. **LC** BX8001. **DD** 284.105. bk rev. adv acc. **Circ** 136,000. (ctrl). Wholesome and inspirational material for the enjoyment and enrichment of Lutherans. *Northwest Lutheran Journal.*

THE LUTHERAN LAYMAN. 1929. 0024-7464. Periodical. US. English. ir. $3.00. Lutheran Layman, 2185 Hampton Avenue, St Louis MO 63139. **Tel** (314)647-4900. **Ed** Walter E Cranor. bk rev. **Circ** 98,000. Official publication of the Lutheran layman's league. Gives information about the League's media ministries and stories about laymen serving Christ in the Church and the League.

LUTHERAN LIBRARIES. *See* Library and Information Science.

LUTHERAN PERSPECTIVE. Vol. 9, No. 1 (Oct. 19, 1981)-. 0279-4462. Periodical. US. English. bw. The Lutheran Perspective, 6337 Clayton Road, St Louis MO 63117. issued also in microform by University Microfilms International. *Missouri in Perspective, 0194-9705.*

LUTHERAN SENTINEL. V. 1- 1918-. 0024-7510. Periodical. US. English. mo. $4.00. Lutheran Sentinel, 204 North Second Avenue West, Lake Mills IA 50450. **Tel** (218)596-8761. **Ed** Paul G Madson. **Circ** 5,200. (ctrl). The official church organ of the evangelical Lutheran synod with articles of a devotional and doctrinal nature, others of church news and information.

LUTHERAN SPOKESMAN. V. 1- 1958-. 0024-7537. Periodical. US. English. mo. $5.00. Lutheran Spokesman, Bus Manager, 2750 North Oxford Street, Roseville MN 55113. **Tel** (612)484-4043. **Ed** Paul Fleischer. bk rev. **Circ** 2,700. (ctrl). Official organ of the church of the Lutheran confession, religious articles, bible study, book reviews, devotions, and current events.

LUTHERAN STANDARD. (THE LUTHERAN STANDARD). V. 1- Jan. 3, 1961-. 0024-7545. Periodical. US. English. bw. $8.00. Augsburg Publishing House, Box 1209, 426 South Fifth Street, Minneapolis MN 55440. **Tel** (612)330-3300. **Ed** Lowell G Almen. **Ind/Abst** Guide Soc. Sci. Relig. Period. Lit. **LC** BX8001. bk rev. adv acc. **Circ** 580,000. Available on tape for the blind. General national magazine of American Lutheran Church. Includes church news, analysis of theological and social issues, and inspirational studies. *Ansgar Lutheran, 0272-944X; Lutheran Herald; Lutheran Standard.*

LUTHERAN VISTAS. Periodical. US. English. qt. $3.50. Lutheran Vistas, 16105 Elmwood Station, Minneapolis MN 55416. **Tel** (612)926-5949. **Ed** P A Engfer. adv acc. **Circ** 45,000. (ctrl). Religious articles by nationally known authors.

LUTHERAN WITNESS (CLEVELAND, OHIO). (THE LUTHERAN WITNESS). Began with: Vol. 1 (May 21, 1882). 0024-757X. Periodical. US. English. mo. $6.50. Concordia Publishing House, Order Services Department, 3558 South Jefferson Avenue, St Louis MO 63118. **Tel** (314)965-9000. **Ed** David L Mahsman. **LC** BX8001. adv acc. **Circ** 480,000. Available on microfilm from Xerox University Microfilms. Provides reflective articles related to the church's mission and issues of the day, features on people, places, news and opinion columns.

LUTHERAN WITNESS REPORTER. 1882. 0024-7588. US. English. mo. $6.50. Concordia Publishing House, 3558 South Jefferson Avenue, St Louis MO 63118. **Tel** (314)664-7000. **Ed** Robin Mueller. **Ind/Abst** Guide Soc. Sci. Relig. Period. Lit. adv acc. **Circ** 400,000. Religious articles on missions, doctrine, people and places, current issues, letters, opinions, and editorials.

LUTHERAN WOMEN. V. 1- Jan. 1963-. 0024-7596. Periodical. US. English. $4.50. Lutheran Church Women, 2900 Queen Lane, Philadelphia PA 19129. **Tel** (215)438-2200. **Ed** Terry Schute. **LC** BX8001. bk rev. **Circ** 35,000. Articles describing work of church and church women, essays advocating and supporting equality of women in church and society, short stories, poetry, Bible studies and book reviews.

LUTHERANS ALERT, NATIONAL. (LUTHERANS ALERT). V. 1- 1966-. 0361-2392. Periodical. US. English. mo. Lutherans-Alert-National, PO Box 7186, Tacoma Washington 98407.

LUTHERISCHE KIRCHE. V. 1-. Periodical. GW. German. mo. Lutherische Kirche, Dietesheimer Str 139, 6052 Muehlheim West Germany. *Kirchenblatt der Evangelisch-Lutherischen (Altluth.) Kirche Mit Amtlichen Mitteilungen, Lutheraner; Unter der Kreuze.*

LUTHERSK KIRKETIDENDE. V. 1-12 July 5, 1863-27. June 1869. 0332-5431. Periodical. NO. Norwegian. sm. Lutherstiftelsen Sog Forlag, Akerscate 47, Oslo 1 Norway.

LWF REPORT. **VFOAT** L.W.F. Report. Began with issue for Sept. 1978. 0174-1764. Monographic Series. GW. English (German). qt. Kreuz Verlag Erich Breitsohl GMBH, 7000 Stuttgart 80 West Germany. **Ind/Abst** Relig. Index One, Period. **LC** BX8001. **DD** 284.105. *Lutheran World.*

THE MAGAZINE FOR CHRISTIAN YOUTH. 8756-4564. Periodical. US. English. mo. $15.00. PO Box 801, Nashville TN 37202. **Tel** (615)749-6463. **Ed** Sidney D Fowler. adv acc. The purpose of Youth is to help teens develop Christian identity and live the Christian faith in their contemporary culture. The articles and fiction support this purpose.

THE MAINE UNITED METHODIST. 0745-0273. Periodical. US. English. bm. Maine Annual Conference Council on Ministries, POB 277, Winthrop ME 04364-0277. **Tel** (207)377-2912. **Ed** Beverly J Abbott. bk rev. **Circ** 5,200. (ctrl).

MANNAM. **VFOAT** The Monthly Young Nak. Periodical. Korean. mo. Yongnak Kyohoe Hongbo Chulpanbu, 69 Cho-dong 2-ka Chung-ku, Seoul Korea. **LC** BX9215.S4.

MARANATHA NEWS. (THE MARANATHA NEWS). Vol. 1, No. 1-. 0823-1427. Periodical. CN. English. Free. Maranatha Christian Centre, 3540-6TH Avenue, Regina Saskatechewan S4T 0N5 Canada. **DD** 289.9.

MARCH OF FAITH. 0461-0636. Periodical. US. English. qt. Wings of Healing Inc, 110 South Garfield Avenue, Montebello CA 90604. **DD** 289.

MARYLAND BAPTIST (BALTIMORE, MD. : 1934) *CEASED.* (THE MARYLAND BAPTIST). Vol. 17, No. 10 (Oct. 1934)-. 0025-4169. Periodical. US. English. Maryland Baptist, 1313 York Road, Baptist Building, Lutherville MD 21093. *Maryland Baptist Church Life.*

MATURE CHRISTIAN. Vol. 1, No. 1 (Mar.-Apr. 1985)-. 8750-9725. Periodical. US. English. bm. $12.00. Mature Christian, PO Box 1505, Murfreesboro TN 37133-1505.

MENNOGESPRACH. Vol. 1, No. 1 (Mar. 1983)-. 0824-5673. Periodical. CN. English. sa. 10.00 Domestic and US. Mennonite Historical Society of Ontario, Conrad Grebel College, Waterloo Ontario N2L 3G6 Canada. **Tel** (519)885-0220. **Ed** Samuel Steiner. **DD** 289.771309. bk rev. **Circ** 150. Devoted to history and genealogy of Mennonites and Amish in Ontario, Canada.

DER MENNONIT. Vols. 1-26-. Periodical. German. mo. Der Mennonit, 75 Karlsruhe 41, Thomashof-Deutschland Germany.

THE MENNONITE. 1885. 0025-9330. Periodical. US. English. bm. General Conference Mennonite, 722 Main Street, PO Box 347, Newton KS 67114. **Tel** (316)283-5100. **Ed** Bernie Wiebe. **Ind/Abst** Guide Soc. Sci. Relig. Period. Lit. bk rev. adv acc. **Circ** 13,000. Features articles that teach Christian discipleship from a Mennonite perspective and news about the Christian world, particularly about the General Conference Mennonite Church. *Christian Evangel.*

MENNONITE HISTORICAL BULLETIN. V. 1- Apr. 1940-. 0025-9357. Periodical. US. English. qt. $5.00. Leonard Gross, 1700 South Main Street, Goshen IN 46526. **Tel** (219)533-3161. **Ed** Leonard Gross. **Ind/Abst** Am. Hist. Life, Hist. Abst., Part B,

Religion, Mythology, Rationalism—Protestantism

Twent. Century Abstr., Writ. Am. Hist., Hist. Abstr., Part A, Mod. Hist. Abstr. **LC** BX8101. (cum index). bk rev. **Circ** 350. Microfilms of Vols. 1-34 are available from University Microfilms. A publication which covers all aspects of Mennonite and baptist history including book reviews, recent publications, interpretive and descriptive articles.

MENNONITE LIFE. V. 1- Jan. 1946-. 0025-9365. Periodical. US. English. qt. Bethel College, Historical Library and Archives, North Newton KS 67117. **Tel** (316)283-2500. Ed David A Haury. **Ind/Abst** Am. Hist. Life, Hist. Abstr., Part A, Mod. Hist. Abstr., Hist. Abstr., Part B, Twent. Century Abstr., Artbiliogr. Mod., Writ. Am. Hist., Relig. Index One, Period., Hist. Abstr. **LC** BX8101. **DD** 289.705. (cum index). bk rev. **Circ** 1,000. (ctrl). Illustrated articles related to Mennonite/Anabaptist history, faith, life and culture.

MENNONITE WORLD HANDBOOK. 0163-3503. US. English. an. Mennonite World Conference, 528 East Madison Street, Lombard IL. **LC** BX8107. **DD** 289.7.

MENNONITE YEARBOOK AND DIRECTORY. See Yearbooks, Almanacs, Directories.

MENNONITISCHE GESCHICHTSBLATTER. Vol. 1-. 0342-1171. German. mo. $10.65. Menonitischen Geschichtsvere, Birmesstrasse 41, 4150 Krefeld 1 West Germany. **Ind/Abst** Recent Publ. Artic. **LC** BX8101.

DIE MENNONITISCHE POST. V. 1- April 21, 1977-. 0705-4041. Newspaper. CN. German. sm. Die Mennonitische Post, PO Box 1926, Steinbach Manitoba R0A 2A0 Canada. **Tel** (204)326-6790. **DD** 289.705.

LE MESSAGER EVANGELIQUE. Feb. 22, 1970-. Periodical. French (German). ir. 30.00. Messager Evangelique, 19 rue des Francs-Bourgeois, Strasbourg France. Messager Evangelique de l'Eglise de la Confession d'Augsbourg d'Alsace et de Lorraine.

THE METHODIST CHURCHMAN. V. 149- Jan. 1971-. Periodical. US. English. ir. New England United Methodist, 581 Boylston Street, Boston MA 02116. **LC** BX8201. **DD** 287.674.

METHODIST HISTORY. V. 1- Oct. 1962-. 0026-1238. Periodical. US. English. qt. $10.00. General Commission on Archives and History, The United Methodist Church, PO Box 127, Madison NJ 07940. **Tel** (201)822-2787. Ed Charles Yrigoyen. **Ind/Abst** Hist. Abstr., Part A, Mod. Hist. Abstr., Hist. Abstr., Part B, Twent. Century Abstr., Writ. Am. Hist., Relig. Index One, Period., United Methodist Period. Index, Relig. Theol. Abstr., Am. Hist. Life, Index Relig. Period. Lit., Hist. Abstr. **LC** BX8235. **DD** 287.05. (cum index). bk rev. adv acc. **Circ** 825. (ctrl). Articles, book reviews and news on the history of the United Methodist Church and its antecedent bodies and the Wesleyan-Methodist heritage. World Parish.

METHODIST PERIODICAL INDEX. See Indexes/Abstracts.

METHODIST RECORDER. No. 1- Apr. 4, 1861-. Periodical. UK. English. wk. $42.14 Canada. Methodist Newspaper Company Ltd, 122 Golden Lane, London EC1Y 0TL England. **Tel** 01-251 8414. Ed Michael Taylor. bk rev. adv acc. **Circ** 29,865. Available on microfilm from World Microfilm Publications Ltd., London. British and world methodist church news with articles on religious and social issues. Also general church interest features and advertising.

METODISTKYRKANS I SVERIGE ARSBOK. See Yearbooks, Almanacs, Directories.

MINISTERE DU ROYAUME POUR LE CANADA. (LE MINISTERE DU ROYAUME POUR LE CANADA). Vol. 25, No. 1 (Jan. 1982)-. 0823-2555. Periodical. CN. French. mo. Temoins de Jehova, Canadian Branch, C P 4100, Georgetown Ontario L7G 4Y4 Canada. **DD** 289.9205. Service du Royaume, 0710-1473.

MINISTERO DEL REGNO PER IL CANADA. (IL MINISTERO DEL REGNO PER IL CANADA). Vol. 25, No. 1 (Jan. 1982)-. 0823-2571. Periodical. CN. Italian. mo. Watch Tower Bible And Tract Society, Canadian Branch, PO Box 4100, Georgetown Ontario L7G 4Y4 Canada. **DD** 289.9205. Servizio del Regno, 0382-4802.

MINUTES. **Main/Corp** United Church of Christ. General Synod. 2nd (1959)-. US. English. be. $3.00. Office of the Secretary UCC, 105 Madison Avenue, New York NY 10016. Minutes.

MINUTES - ANNUAL CONVENTION OF THE EASTERN CANADA SYNOD, LUTHERAN CHURCH IN AMERICA. **Main/Corp** Lutheran Church in America. Eastern Canada Synod. Convention. **VAT** Minutes - Eastern Canada Synod, Minutes. Annual Convention - Eastern Canada Synod, Lutheran Church in America. 1st- 1962-. 0317-9583. CN. English. an. Eastern Canada Synod of the Lutheran Church in America, 251 King Street West, Kitchener Ontario N2G 1B5 Canada. **DD** 284.171.

MINUTES OF THE ANNUAL CONVENTION - MINNESOTA SYNOD OF THE LUTHERAN CHURCH IN AMERICA. **Main/Corp** Lutheran Church in America Minnesota Synod. 1st- 1962-. US. English. an. Minnesota Synod of the Lutheran Church in America, 122 West Franklin Avenue, Minneapolis MN 55404.

MINUTES OF THE ANNUAL CONVENTION OF THE WESTERN CANADA SYNOD OF THE LUTHERAN CHURCH IN AMERICA. **Main/Corp** Lutheran Church in America. Western Canada Synod. Convention. 1st- 1962-. 0460-024X. CN. English. an. Lutheran Church in America Western Canada Synod, 9901-107 Street, Edmonton Alberta T5K 1G4 Canada. **DD** 284.1712.

MINUTES OF THE GENERAL ASSEMBLY OF THE PRESBYTERIAN CHURCH IN THE UNITED STATES OF AMERICA. US. English. an. $5.00. Materials Distribution Center, 341 Ponce de Leon Avenue NE, Atlanta GA 30308.

MINUTES - UNITED PRESBYTERIAN CHURCH IN THE U.S.A. **Main/Corp** United Presbyterian Church in the U.S.A. General Assembly. New Ser. V. 1-23, 1870-1900. 0082-8548. US. English. an. United Presbyterian Church in US, 475 Riverside Drive/Room 1244, New York NY 10027. **LC** BX895L. **DD** 285.1. Minutes of the General Assembly of the Presbyterian Church in the U.S.A.

MISSION HANDBOOK. NORTH AMERICAN PROTESTANT MINISTRIES OVERSEAS. (MISSION HANDBOOK : NORTH AMERICAN PROTESTANT MINISTRIES OVERSEAS). **VFOAT** North American Protestant Ministries Overseas. 10th- Ed. 0093-8130. US. English. ir. Missions Advanced Research and Communication Center(MARC), 919 West Huntington Drive, Monrovia CA 91016. **Tel** (818)574-9018. **LC** BV2050. **DD** 266.023. adv acc. **Circ** 15,000. A convenient reference to descriptive and statistical data on all North American Protestant overseas ministries or related agencies with overseas operations. North American Protestant Ministries Overseas.

MISSIONARY HERALD (LONDON, ENGLAND : 1921). (MISSIONARY HERALD : THE MONTHLY MAGAZINE OF THE BAPTIST MISSIONARY SOCIETY). Began with V. 103, Jan. 1921. Periodical. UK. English. mo. Baptist Missionary Society, 93-97 Gloucester Place, London W1H 4AA England. **Tel** 01-935-1482. Ed David Pountain. bk rev. adv acc. **Circ** 20,000. Baptist world mission third world issues including agriculture, rural development, education, preventive medicine, health education, and relations with churches overseas. Herald (Baptist Missionary Society).

MITTEILUNGSBLATT DES BUNDES DER EVANGELISCHEN KIRCHEN IN DER DEUTSCHEN DEMOKRATISCHEN REPUBLIK. **Main/Corp** Bund der Evangelischen Kirchen in der DDR. German. ir. 6.00. Verlag Evangelische Verlagsanstalt GMBH, Auguststrasse 80, 1040 Berlin East German Democratic Republic. **Tel** 2886-242. **LC** BX8018. **DD** 284.1431. **Circ** 2,800. Official statements, laws and orders of the Protestant church in East Germany.

THE MONTHLY RECORD OF THE FREE CHURCH OF SCOTLAND. **Main/Corp** Free Church of Scotland. Began in 1901. Periodical. UK. English. mo. $7.66. Treasurer, Free Church Offices, The Mound, Edinburgh EH1 2LS Scotland. Free Church of Scotland Monthly.

MOTIF. See Music.

MUKYOKAISHUGI NO JIKO TENKEN. No. 1-. JA. Japanese. ir. c/o Okawara Reizo, 5-16 Higashi Gotanda 5, Shinagawa-Ku 141, Tokyo Japan. **LC** BX8699.M8.

MUSTARD SEED. (THE MUSTARD SEED). 0711-1843. Periodical. CN. English. mo. Diocese of Brandon, 341 13th Street, Brandon Manitoba R7A 4P8 Canada. **DD** 283.7127305.

NAE WASHINGTON INSIGHT. **VFOAT** Washington Insight. **VAT** National Association of Evangelicals Washington Insight. 0199-3038. Periodical. US. English. mo. $15.00. National Association of Evangelicals, Box 28, Wheaton IL 60187. **Tel** (312)665-0500. Ed Robert Dugan. **Circ** 65,000. (ctrl). Informs evangelical Christians about important issues and bills in Washington; also encourages evangelicals to be concerned about political activities.

NAPJAINK (WEST-HILL, ONT.). (NAPJAINK). **VFOAT** Our Days. **VAT** Our Days (West-Hill). Nov. 1974-. 0821-5995. Periodical. CN. Hungarian. bm. 0.25. Napjaink, PO Box 67, West Hill Ontario M1E 4R4 Canada. **DD** 289.9.

NATIONAL LUTHERAN. (THE NATIONAL LUTHERAN). V. 1- Sept. 1975-. 0319-695X. Periodical. CN. English. The National Lutheran, 212 Wiggins Avenue North, Saskatoon Saskatchewan S7N 1K4 Canada. **DD** 284.171.

NEBRASKA LUTHERAN. 0745-2705. Periodical. US. English. bm. Business Manager, Nebraska Lutheran, Waterloo NE 68069.

THE NEVADA BAPTIST. 0279-4535. Periodical. US. English. mo. $3.00. Nevada Baptist, Box 6538, Reno NV 89513.

NEW CHURCH LIFE. V. 1- Jan. 1881-. 0275-0805. Periodical. US. English. mo. $12.00. General Church of the New Jerusalem, Bryn Athyn PA 19009. **Tel** (215)947-2317. Ed Donald L Rose. **LC** BX8701. **DD** 289.405. Index in last issue of volume - attached. (cum index). bk rev. **Circ** 2,000. The religious works of Emanuel Swedenborg. Has for more than a hundred years been the focus in this journal, also the new church founded thereon.

NEW CREATION. V. 1- Fall 1968-. Periodical. US. English. qt. $3.35. 201 Eighth Avenue South, Nashville TN 37203. **Ind/Abst** United Methodist Period. Index. **LC** BX8201. **UD** 287/.05.

THE NEW DISCIPLES TEACHER. Vol. 1, No. 1 (1st Quarter, Jan./Feb./Mar. 1984)-. 0746-7702. Periodical. US. English. qt. National Baptist Publishing Board, 7145 Centinnial Boulevard, Nashville TN 37209.

NEW LITURGY. BULLETIN OF THE NATIONAL SECRETARIAT, IRISH EPISCOPAL COMMISSION FOR LITURGY. Periodical. IE. English. qt. 4.50 Domestic, $5.50 Foreign. Irish Institute of Pastoral Liturgy, College Street, Carlow Ireland. **Tel** (0503)42942. Ed Sean Swayne. bk rev. **Circ** 3,000. Contains articles of practical and pastoral interest.

THE NEW PILGRIM. Vol. 67, No. 1 (Spring 1980)-. 0735-2786. Periodical. US. English. qt. $2.00. Maine Conference, United Church of Christ, 53 Baxter Boulevard, Portland ME 04101. **LC** BX7101. **DD** 285.8741. Maine Christian Pilgrim (Portland, ME. : 1951).

NEWS-GRAM - CHRISTIAN BUSINESS MEN OF CANADA. (NEWS-GRAM). Vol. 1, No. 1 (Jan. 1974)-. 0710-5770. Periodical. CN. English. ir. Free. Christian Business Men of Canada, 960 Portage Avenue, Winnipeg Manitoba R3G 0R4 Canada. **DD** 267.230971.

NEWSPEACE. May 1971-. 0048-0304. Periodical. UK. English. mo. 4.00. Fellowship of Reconciliation, 9 Coombe Rd New Maiden, Surrey KT3 4QA England. **Tel** 01 942 6521. Ed Gordon Slater. **Circ** 1,000. Reconciliation (New Malden, Surrey).

NIAGARA ANGLICAN. (THE NIAGARA ANGLICAN). V. 1- Jan. 1955-. 0703-5888. Periodical. CN. English. mo. $1. Synod Office, Diocese of Niagara, 67 Victoria Avenue South, Hamilton Ontario L8N 2S8 Canada. **DD** 283.71352.

NORTH STAR BAPTIST. Began with V. 1, No. 2, 1916. 0744-0278. Periodical. US. English. bm. $4.00. Minnesota Baptist Association, 5000 Golden Valley Road, Minneapolis MN 55422. **Tel** (612)588-2755. Ed Richard L Paige Jr. bk rev. **Circ** 1,800. (ctrl). Spiritual challenge and message news for fundamental Christians, and reports from the churches of our fellowship along with missionary reports. Minnesota Baptist.

THE NORTHEASTERN CHRISTIAN CEASED. V. 1-24, No. 2. 0468-6756. Periodical. US. English. qt.

NORTHWEST BAPTIST WITNESS. 0745-2195. Periodical. US. English. sm. $12.00. Northwest Baptist Witness, 1633 Northeast 6th Avenue, Portland OR 97232. **Tel** (503)238-4545.

THE NORTHWESTERN LUTHERAN. V. 1- 1914-. 0029-3512. Periodical. US. English. ir. $6.00. Northwestern Publishing House, PO Box 26975, Milwaukee WI 53226-0975. **Tel** (414)475 6600.

NOSSO MINISTERIO DO REINO PARA O CANADA. Vol. 25, N. 1 (Jan. 1982)-. 0823-2598. Periodical. CN. Portuguese. mo. Watch Tower Bible and Tract Society/Canadian Branch, PO Box 4100, Georgetown Ontario L7G 4Y4 Canada. **DD** 289.9205.

NOTRE SEMAINE COMMUNAUTAIRE. V. 2, No. 2- Dec. 6/12, 1970-. 0384-0530. Periodical. CN. French. wk. $5. Notre Semaine Communautaire, 5750 Boulevard Rosemont, Montreal Quebec H1T 2H2 Canada. **DD** 248.05. *Vie Paroissiale, 0384-0522.*

NUESTRO MINISTERIO DEL REINO PARA EL CANADA. V. 25, No. 1 (Jan. 1982)-. 0823-258X. Periodical. CN. Spanish. mo. Watch Tower Bible And Tract Society Canadian Branch, PO Box 4100, Georgetown Ontario L7G 4Y4 Canada. **DD** 289.9205.

OFFICIAL REPORT OF THE . . . CONGRESS. Main/Conf Baptist World Congress. **VFOAT** Truth That Makes Men Free. 11th (1965)-. US. English. ir. Baptist World Alliance, 1628 16th Street NW, Washington DC 20009. **Tel** (202)265-5027. *Official Report.*

OHIO CHRISTIAN NEWS. 0030-0845. Periodical. US. English. mo. Ohio Council of Churches, 89 East Wilson Bridge Road, Columbus OH 43085.

THE ORTHODOX HERALD. 0744-1495. Periodical. US. English. mo. $2.00. The Orthodox Herald, PO Box 9, Hunlock Creek PA 18621.

OUR KINGDOM SERVICE *CEASED.* V. 19-24, No. 12. 0382-4837. Periodical. CN. English. mo. Free. Watch Tower Bible and Tract Society, Canadian Branch, 150 Bridgeland Avenue, Toronto Ontario M6A 1Z5 Canada. **DD** 289.9. (ctrl). *Kingdom Ministry, 0316-6945.*

OUTLOOK (GRAND RAPIDS, MICH.). (THE OUTLOOK). Vol. 21, No. 6 (June 1971)-. 8750-5754. Periodical. US. English. mo. $7.50. Reformed Fellowship Inc, 4855 Starr Street SE, Grand Rapids MI 49506. **Ed** Peter de Jong. **DD** 200. bk rev. **Circ** 4,500. (ctrl). Gives sharpened expression to the reformed faith, to promote the spiritual welfare and purity of the Christian Reformed Church in particular. *Christian Reformed Outlook, 0732-5177.*

PACIFIC THEOLOGICAL REVIEW. V. 6, No. 2- 1974-. 0360-1897. Periodical. US. English. San Francisco Theological Seminary, 2 Kensington Road, San Anselmo CA 94960. **Tel** (415)453-2280. **Ed** Robert B Coote. bk rev. **Circ** 7,500. (ctrl). Articles on biblical studies, theology, postoral ministry, and church history. *Action, Reaction, 0001-7485.*

PAPERS - CANADIAN METHODIST HISTORICAL SOCIETY. (PAPERS). **Main/Corp** Canadian Methodist Historical Society. 0826-0877. Periodical. CN. English. ir. Canadian Methodist Historical Society c/o United Church Archives/Victoria University, 73 Queen's Park Crescent, Toronto Ontario M5S 1K7 Canada. **DD** 287.0971.

PATRISTICS. V. 1- April 1972-. 0360-652X. Periodical. US. English. sa. $15.00. North American Patristics Society, F W Norris Emmanuel School of Religion, Johnson City TN 37601. **Tel** (615)926-1186. **Ed** Frederick W Norris. bk rev. **Circ** 350. Review of early Christianity, 1st-7th centuries: book reviews and conference news, international coverage: English, French, German volumes; reviews in English, French, or Spanish.

PENN JERSEY BAPTIST. 1970. 0195-1815. Periodical. US. English. mo. $5.00. Penn-Jersey Baptist, 4620 Fritchey Street, Harrisburg PA 17109. **Tel** (717)652-5856. **Ed** Ellis M Bush. **Circ** 6,500. Articles pertaining to life and work of Southern Baptists and around the world.

PENSION BOARDS. (PENSION BOARDS - UNITED CHURCH OF CHRIST). **Main/Corp** United Church of Christ. 1967-. 0360-9782. US. English. an. United Church of Christ, 287 Park Avenue South, New York NY 10010. **LC** BX7245.5. **DD** 658.3253.

THE PENTECOSTAL EVANGEL. (PENTECOSTAL EVANGEL). 6381-4897. Periodical. US. English. wk. $9.00. Gospel Publishing House, 14445 Boonville Avenue, Springfield MO 65802. **Tel** (417)862-2781. **Ed** Richard Champion. **Ind/Abst** Guide Soc. Sci. Relig. Period. Lit. **LC** BX6198.A7. **DD** 289.9. **Circ** 275,000.

THE PENTECOSTAL FREE WILL BAPTIST MESSENGER. (PENTECOSTAL FREE-WILL BAPTIST MESSENGER). **VFOAT** Messenger. V. 1- 1938-. 0745-2330. Periodical. US. English. mo. $4.20. PO Box 1568, Dunn NC 28334. **Ed** Herbert Carter.

PEOPLE OF DESTINY MAGAZINE. VFOAT People of Destiny. 8750-8346. Periodical. US. English. bm. $12.95. People of Destiny Magazine, PO Box 2335, Wheaton MD 20902. **Tel** (301)946-4486. **Ed** John Loftness. **DD** 289. bk rev. adv acc. **Circ** 12,000. This magazine speaks to the church concerning restoration of New Testament Christianity. It is a practical guide to maturity, commitment, and ministry.

PIELGRZYM POLSKI. Began in 1926. Periodical. PL. Polish. mo. ARS Polona, Krakowskie Przedmiescie 7, 00-068 Warsaw Poland. **LC** BX8201.

THE PLOUGH. (THE PLOUGH : PUBLICATION OF THE BRUDERHOF COMMUNITIES). No. 1 (Nov. 1983)-. 0740-9125. Periodical. US. English. bm. The Plough, Woodcrest Service Committee, Rifton NY 12471. *Plough (1953), 0740-9125.*

POSITIONS LUTHERIENNES. 1.- Year. 0032-5228. Periodical. FR. French. qt. $19.96. Positions Lutheriennes, 16 rue Chauchat, 75009 Paris France. **Tel** (1) 47-70-80-30. bk rev. Religious sciences - church history, ethics, ecumenicism, explanation and critical interpretations of text, musicology.

PRAYER BOOK STUDIES. Main/Corp Protestant Episcopal Church in The United States of America Turgical Commission. 0478-6076. US. English. ir. Church Hymnal Corporation, 800 Second Avenue, New York NY 10017.

PRESBYTERIAN COMMENT *CEASED.* V. 1-18, No. 1. 0383-7645. CN. English. bm. Editor, P3-120 Edinburgh Road South, Guelph Ontario N1H 5P7 Canada.

THE PRESBYTERIAN JOURNAL. V. 1- May 1942-. 0032-7549. Periodical. US. English. ir. $12.00. Presbyterian Journal, PO Box 2330, Asheville NC 28802. **Tel** (704)254-4015. **Ed** Will Barker. **Ind/Abst** Guide Soc. Sci. Relig. Period. Lit. **LC** BX8901. **DD** 285.175. bk rev. adv acc. **Circ** 15,000. (ctrl). Religious news and commentary on current and ecclesiastical issues from a biblical perspective, intended for lay people and clergy, particularly in conservative presbyterian and reformed circles.

THE PRESBYTERIAN KEY. V. 1- 1945-. 0361-2724. Periodical. US. English. ir. Presbyterian Historical Society, 425 Lombard Street, Philadelphia PA 19147.

THE PRESBYTERIAN LAYMAN. V. 1- Jan. 1968-. 0555-0572. Periodical. US. English. bm. Presbyterian Layman, 1245 North Providence Road, Media PA 19063. **Tel** (215)565-4764. **Ed** George M Booker. **Circ** 435,000. (ctrl). Presbyterian church (USA) related, independent, evangelical, advocacy publication.

PRESBYTERIAN OUTLOOK. 0032-7565. Periodical. US. English. ir. Outlook Publishers Inc, 512 East Main Street, Richmond VA 23219. **Tel** (804)649-1371. *Presbyterian of the South and the Presbyterian Standard, Presbyterian Tribune.*

PRESBYTERIAN RECORD. (THE PRESBYTERIAN RECORD). **VFOAT** Record. Began with: Vol. 25, No. 1 (Jan. 1899)?. 0032-7573. Periodical. CN. English. mo. $7.50. Presbyterian Record, 50 Wynford Drive, Don Mills Ontario M3C 1J7 Canada. **Tel** (416)441-1111. **Ed** James Ross Dickey. **LC** BX8901. **DD** 285.171. bk rev. adv acc. **Circ** 76,000. The national magazine of the Presbyterian church in Canada. Unsubsidized, independent editorial policy. Pays contributors. *Record (Presbyterian Church in Canada).*

PRESBYTERIAN SURVEY. V. 1- Nov. 1911-. 0032-759X. Periodical. US. English. mo. $8.50. Presbyterian Survey, 341 Ponce de Leon Avenue NE, Atlanta GA 30308. **Tel** (404)873-1549. **Ed** Vic Jameson. **LC** BV2570.A1. **DD** 266.51. bk rev. adv acc. **Circ** 192,000. Articles/columns on faith and action for Presbyterians. *Missionary, 0362-9007; Home Mission Herald.*

PRESBYTERION. V. 1- Spring 1975-. 0193-6212. Periodical. US. English. sa. $6.00. Covenant Theological Seminary, 12330 Conway Road, St Louis MO 63141. **Tel** (314)434-4044. **Ind/Abst** New Testam. Abstr., Old Testam. Abstr., Christ. Period. Index, New Testam. Abstr., Relig. Index One, Period.

PRESUPUESTO - IGLESIA EVANGELICA ESPANOLA. Main/Corp Iglesia Evangelica Espanola. English and French. ir. Iglesia Evangelica Espanola, Raimundo Lulio 2, Madrid Spain. **LC** BX7990.I45.

PRIMITIVE BAPTIST YEARBOOK. *See* Yearbooks, Almanacs, Directories.

PROBLEMES D'HISTOIRE DU CHRISTIANISME. 1- 1970/71-. BE. French. an. Editions de Universite Bruxelles, Avenue Paul Heger 26, B 1050 Bruxelles Belgium. **Tel** 021642 37 93. **LC** BR140. **DD** 209. **Circ** 1,000. Publication devoted to an objective study of questions of christianism history recording four orientations of research: antiquity, middle ages, modern times and contemporary times.

PROCEEDINGS OF THE . . . GENERAL SYNOD, OFFICIAL REPORT. Main/Corp Anglican Church of Australia, General Synod. 6th (1981)-. English. an. General Synod Office, St Andrews House, Sydney Square New South Wales 2000 Australia. **LC** BX5703. **DD** 283.94. *Proceedings of the General Synod, Official Report.*

THE PROCEEDINGS OF THE UNITARIAN UNIVERSALIST HISTORICAL SOCIETY. Vol. 19, Pt. 1 (1980-1981)-. 0731-4078. US. English. ir. Prof C Wright, Harvard Divinity School, Cambridge MA 02138. **Ed** Richard Myers. bk rev. **Circ** 350. Scholarly articles on unitarianism, universalism, and related movements in liberal religion. *Proceedings of the Unitarian Historical Society, 0082-7819.*

PROCEEDINGS OF THE WESLEY HISTORICAL SOCIETY. Main/Corp Wesley Historical Society. Vol. 1, Pt. 1-. 0043-2873. Periodical. UK. English. ty. 6.00 Domestic, $12.00 US. Bognor Regis, 87 Marshall Avenue, West Sussex PO21 2TW England. **Ed** E A Rose. **Ind/Abst** Am. Hist. Life, Hist. Abstr., Part A, Mod. Hist. Abstr., Hist. Abst., Part B, Twent. Century Abstr. (cum index). bk rev. adv acc. **Circ** 1,000. (ctrl). Denominational history.

PROMISE. (THE PROMISE). Vol. 1, Issue 1 (June 1983)-. 0826-533X. Periodical. CN. English. qt. Promise, c/o Barbara Thompson St Luke's Anglican Church 3233 Argyle Road, Regina Saskatchewan S4S 2B5 Canada. **DD** 283.71244.

PROTESTANT TELEGRAPH. Periodical. US. English. Puritan Printing Company Ltd, 71 Ravenhill Road, Belfast BT6 8DQ Ireland. **LC** Microfilm 05483 DA, DA990.U45.

PROTESTANTESIMO. 0033-1767. Periodical. IT. Italian. qt. 20.000. Facolta Valdese di Teologia, Via Pietro Cossa 42, 00193 Rome Italy. **Tel** 631585. **Ind/Abst** Relig. Index One, Period., Hist. Abstr., Hist. Abst., Part B, Twent. Century Abstr., Am. Hist. Life. **LC** BR5. Index in last issue of volume - attached. bk rev. adv acc. **Circ** 1,000. (ctrl). The magazine tends to put the readers in contact with the thought-world issued from the reformation and with the leading motifs of the ecumenical movement.

QUAKER CONCERN. Vol. 2, No. 3 (Nov./Dec. 1976)-. 0229-1916. Periodical. CN. English. ir. Quaker Concern, Canadian Friends Service Committee, 60 Lowther Avenue, Toronto Ontario M5R 1C7 Canada. **DD** 289.671. *Quaker Service Report, 0703-9425.*

QUAKER RELIGIOUS THOUGHT. VFOAT QRT. V. 1- Spring 1959-. 0033-5088. Periodical. US. English. ir. Quaker Theological Discipline Group, Route 1 Box 549, Alburtis PA 18011. **Tel** (215)682-7332. **Ed** Dean Freiday. **LC** BX7601. bk rev. **Circ** 500. Historical and theological studies of Quakerism and its relevance to contemporary life.

QUARTERLY - CHRISTIAN LEGAL SOCIETY. *See* Law.

RADIX. V. 8- July/Aug. 1976-. 0275-0147. Periodical. US. English. bm. $10.00. Radix, Box 4307, Berkeley CA 94703. **Tel** (415)548-5329. **Ed** Sharon Gallagher. bk rev. adv acc. **Circ** 5,000. Interacts with the ideas, events, and people who shape our culture from a Christian perspective and offers Christian alternatives. *Right On.*

REAPER; NEW ZEALAND'S EVANGELICAL MONTHLY. 0034-107X. Periodical. NZ. English. mo. 12. Bible College of New Zealand, 221 Lincoln Road, Henderson Auckland 8 New Zealand. **Tel** (089)837-0675. **Ed** D G Stewart and S J Sands. bk rev. adv acc. **Circ** 6,500. Official publication of Bible College of New Zealand. Evangelical, Protestant; topical and devotional articles. Also, news of the Bible College and graduates.

RECONCILIATION QUARTERLY (NEW MALDEN, SURREY). (RECONCILIATION QUARTERLY : RQ). **VFOAT** RQ. No. 1(Oct. 1967-) No. 10 I.E. 13- (Dec. 1970). 0034-1479. Periodical. UK. English. qt. $6.89. Fellowship of Reconciliation, 9

Coombe Road, New Malden KT3 4QR Surrey England. **Tel** 01 942 6521. **Ed** Elnora and John Ferguson. bk rev. adv acc. **Circ** 1,000. *Reconciliation (London, England : 1947).*

RECORD OF PROCEEDINGS - GENERAL COUNCIL. UNITED CHURCH OF CANADA. (RECORD OF PROCEEDINGS - UNITED CHURCH OF CANADA, GENERAL COUNCIL. COMPTE RENDU). **Main/Corp** United Church of Canada. General Council. **VFOAT** Compte Rendu. 1st- 1925-. 0082-7878. Periodical. CN. English. be. United Church of Canada, General Council Office, 85 St Clair Avenue East, Toronto Ontario M4T 1L8 Canada. **DD** 287.92.

REFORM. Nov. 1972-. 0306-7262. Periodical. UK. English. mo. $8.81. United Reformed Church, 86 Tavistock Place, London WC1H 9RT England. **Tel** 01-837-7661. **Ed** Norman Hart. bk rev. adv acc. **Circ** 20,000. Magazine of the United Reformed Church for the exchange of news and ideas. *Congregational Monthly, Outlook; Enterprise.*

REFORMATIO. V. 1- 1952-. 0034-3021. Periodical. SZ. German. mo. 50.00. Administration Benteli AG, 3018 Bern Switzerland. **Tel** (0041)31 55 44 33. **Ed** Verein Reformatio. **Ind/Abst** Relig. Index One, Period. **LC** BR4. bk rev. **Circ** 1,800. Protestant publication for culture, politics and church.

REFORMATUS EGYHAZ. Began in 1949. Periodical. HU. Hungarian. mo. Akademiai Kiado, POB 24, 1363 Budapest Hungary.

REFORMATUSOK LAPJA. V. 1, No. 1, (March 31, 1957)-. Periodical. HU. Hungarian. wk. 400.- Domestic, $8.00 Foreign. Budapest 62, PO Box 424, 1395 Hungary. **Tel** 1/176-809. **Ed** Attila P Komlos. bk rev. adv acc. **Circ** 35,000. For Presbyterian church-related people, dealing with question of religion, church-policy, ecumenism and social activity of believers, dialog between christians and marxists.

REFORMED LITURGY & MUSIC. **VFOAT** Reformed Liturgy and Music. Began with Winter 1981 issue. 0362-0476. Periodical. US. English. qt. $12.50. Reformed Liturgy and Music, 1044 Alta Vista Road, Louisville KY 40205. **Tel** (502)895-2441. **Ed** Peter C Bower. **Ind/Abst** Relig. Index One, Period. **LC** BX9185. **DD** 264.051. bk rev. **Circ** 3,000. (ctrl). Historical, theological and practical articles - journal is thematic - contains book book reviews, news columns of what is happening in worship - music, lectionary aids, viewpoint - pastor, musicians. *Reformed Liturgy and Music, 0362-0476.*

REFORMED WORLD. V. 31, No. 5- Mar. 1971-. 0034-3056. Periodical. English. qt. $4.00. World Alliance of Reformed Churches, 150 Route de Ferney, 1211 Geneva 20 Switzerland. **Tel** 022/ 98 94 00. **Ind/Abst** Relig. Index One, Period. **LC** BX8901. All issues of Reformed World and Predecessors since 1879 are available from University Microfilms, Ann Arbor. *Bulletin of the Department of Theology of the World Alliance of Reformed Churches, Reformed and Presbyterian World.*

REMONSTRANTS WEEKBLAD : RW. **VFOAT** RW. Periodical. NE. Dutch. sm. Stichting Centraal Service Bureau, Neuwe Gracht 27, 3512 Lc Utrecht Netherlands.

REPORT VOLUME OF THE BAPTIST FEDERATION OF CANADA. **Main/Corp** Baptist Federation of Canada. Assembly. 1967/70-. 0317-767X. CN. English. te. Baptist Federation of Canada, 91 Queen Street, Box 1289, Brantford Ontario N3T 5T6 Canada. **LC** BX6251. **DD** 286.106271. *Proceedings and Minutes of the Assembly of the Baptist Federation of Canada, 0317-7661.*

RESPONSE. V. 1- Jan. 1969-. 0034-5725. Periodical. US. English. ir. $7.00. Magazine Circulation, 7820 Reading Road, Cincinnati OH 45237. *Methodist Woman, World Evangel.*

RESPUESTA. Periodical. MX. Spanish. ir. Filipinas 205-101 A, Mexico 13 DF Mexico. **Ed** MA Teresa Romero.

RESPUESTA. 0744-0251. Periodical. US. Spanish. qt. $4.25. The Sunday School Board of SBC, 127 Ninth Avenue North, Nashville TN 37234.

RESTORATION (BOUNTIFUL, UTAH). (RESTORATION). Vol. 1, No. 1 (Jan. 1982)-. 0730-2185. Periodical. US. English. qt. $8.00 Domestic, $10.00 Canada, $16.00 All other countries. PO Box 547, Bountiful UT 84010. **LC** BX8601. **DD** 289.305. News, views and history of the Latter Day Saint (Mormon) movement.

RESTORATION HERALD. 1925. 0034-5830. Periodical. US. English. mo. $6.00. Christian Restoration Association, 5664 Cheviot Road, Cincinnati OH 45247. **Tel** (513)385-0461. **Ed** H Sherwood Evans. **Circ** 7,000. (ctrl). Features, submitted articles and news related to Biblical teachings and the activities of Christian churches and churches of Christ.

RESTORATION QUARTERLY. V. 1- 1957-. 0486-5642. Periodical. US. English. qt. $11.00. Abilene Christian College, Box 8227, Abilene TX 79601. **Tel** (915)672-8196. **Ed** Thomas H Olbricht. **Ind/Abst** Old Testam. Abstr., New Testam. Abstr., Relig. Index One, Period. bk rev. adv acc. **Circ** 1,200. Biblical studies and history of the restoration movement.

REVUE D'HISTOIRE DE L'EGLISE DE FRANCE. Vol. 1- (No. 1-). 0300-9505. FR. French. sa. $31.26. Office General du Livre, 14 Bis rue Jean-Ferrandi, 75006 Paris France. **Ind/Abst** Am. Hist. Life, Hist. Abstr., Part A, Mod. Hist. Abstr., Hist. Abst., Part B, Twent. Century Abstr., Hist. Abstr. **LC** BR840. **DD** 274.4. (cum index).

LA REVUE REFORMEE. Began with Apr. 1950 issue. 0035-3884. Periodical. FR. French. qt. Fac Libre Theologie Reformee, 33 Avenue Jules Ferry, 13100 Aix en Provece France. **Ind/Abst** Old Testam. Abstr., New Testam. Abstr. **LC** BX9401. **DD** 284.205. (cum index).

RISK BOOK SERIES. No. 1-. Monographic Series. SZ. English. ir. $14.00. World Council of Churches, 150 Route de Ferney, 1211 Geneva 20 Switzerland. **Tel** 022/91 61 11. **Ind/Abst** Relig. Index One, Period. **Circ** 4,000. Deals with issues which are of crucial importance to Christians, providing provocative perspectives on emerging themes and concerns in the ecumenical movement.

ROCKY MOUNTAIN AMERICAN BAPTIST. 0745-3884. Periodical. US. English. bm. Rocky Mountain American Baptist, 1344 Pennsylvania Street, Denver CO 80203. *Colorado Baptist, Wyoming Baptist News.*

ROCKY MOUNTAIN BAPTIST. 1955. 0485-294X. Periodical. US. English. wk. Colorado Baptist General Convention, 7393 South Alton Way, Englewood CO 80112. **Tel** (303)771-2480. **Ed** Don L Turner. adv acc. **Circ** 8,500. News of local state churches, national news of interest to southern Baptists, Sunday school lesson, editorials, pictures, letters, and columns of specialties.

ROUNDTABLE - LUTHERAN COUNCIL IN CANADA. **VFOAT** Roundtable. V. 1- Jan. 1968-. Periodical. CN. English. Lutheran Council in Canada, 500-365 Hargrave Street, Winnipeg Manitoba 2 Canada.

ROYAL SERVICE. 0035-9084. Periodical. US. English. mo. $4.00 Domestic, $5.50 Foreign. Woman's Missionary Union, Auxiliary to Southern Baptist Convention, 600 North 20th Street, Birmingham AL 35203. **LC** BV2520.A1. **DD** 266.61. *Our Mission Fields.*

RUPERT'S LAND NEWS. 0228-8095. Periodical. CN. English. mo. Anglican Centre, 935 Nesbitt Bay, Winnipeg Manitoba R3T 1W6 Canada. **DD** 283.71274.

RURAL GLEANINGS. V. 1- Fall 1974-. 0700-3897. Periodical. CN. English. qt. Free. Christian Rural Research and Resource Service, R R 1, Debert Nova Scotia B0M 1G0 Canada. **DD** 254.2405. (ctrl).

THE SABBATH RECORDER. (SABBATH RECORDER, A SEVENTH-DAY BAPTIST WEEKLY). 0036-214X. Periodical. US. English. mo. $6.00 Domestic, $6.50 Foreign. The Sabbath Recorder, PO Box 868, Plainfield NJ 07061.

ST. MARK'S REVIEW. **VAT** Saint Mark's Review. Began in 1955. 0036-3103. Periodical. AT. English. qt. 10 Domestic, 12.50 Foreign. St Marks Library, PO Box E67 Queen Victoria Terrace, Canberra Australian Capital Territory 2600 Australia. **Tel** 062/731573. **Ed** Peter Mendham. **Ind/Abst** Relig. Index One, Period., Aust. Public Aff. Inf. Serv. bk rev. adv acc. **Circ** 1,300. Available on microfilm from Xerox University Microfilms. Journal for general, scholarly but non-technical discussion of issues of importance to Christians in Australia and in the world-wide community.

ST. PAUL'S CHILDREN'S MAGAZINE. *See* Children and Youth Interests.

SAINTS HERALD. **VFOAT** Herald. V. 1- 1860-. 0036-3251. Periodical. US. English. mo. $11.00. Herald House, PO Box HH, Independence MO 64055. **DD** 289. *Vision, A Magazine for Youth, True Latter-Day Saints' Herald.*

SALAM. (SALAM : BULLETIN MISSIONNAIRE DE SAINTE-CROIX). 0710-023X. Periodical. CN. French. ir. $1.00. Salam, 3744 rue Jean-Brillant, Montreal Quebec H3T 1P1 Canada. **DD** 266.205. *Bulletin Missionnaire des Freres de Sainte-Croix.*

SASKATCHEWAN ANGLICAN. Began publication in 1972?. 0703-9433. Periodical. CN. English. mo. Free. Saskatchewan Anglican, 1501 College Avenue, Regina Saskatchewan S4P 1B8 Canada. **DD** 283.7124.

THE SCHWENKFELDIAN. 0036-8032. Periodical. US. English. ty. $4.00. Gen Con Schwenkfelder Chrch, 1 Seminary Street, Pennsburg PA 18073. **Tel** (215)584-4480. **Ed** Nancy MacQueen Byron. **LC** UNC. bk rev. **Circ** 2,600. (ctrl). Report of the activities, events, and scholarship of the Schwenkfelder Churches of America.

SCLC. (SCLC : THE SOUTHERN CHRISTIAN LEADERSHIP CONFERENCE NATIONAL MAGAZINE). **VFOAT** Southern Christian Leadership Conference National Magazine. **VAT** Southern Christian Leadership Conference. 0735-7443. Periodical. US. English. bm. $12.00. Southern Christian Leadership, 334 Auburn Avenue Northeast, Atlanta GA 30303. **Tel** (404)522-1420. **Ed** Quentin Bradford. adv acc. **Circ** 600,000. News of Southern Christian Leadership Conference activities, programs, and events that are of interest to black and poor people.

SCOTTISH BAPTIST MAGAZINE. 0036-9136. Periodical. UK. English. 3.05. Baptist Union of Scotland, 14 Aytoun Road, Glasgow G41 5RT Scotland. **Tel** 041 423 6169. **Ed** Robert M Armstrong. bk rev. adv acc. **Circ** 3,500. Features and news of interest and relating to Baptists in Scotland. Nider church science and Christian involvement in and comment on social and moral issues.

SEARCH. 0048-9913. Periodical. US. English. qt. $11.50. Materials Service Department, 127 9th Avenue North, Nashville TN 37234. **Tel** (615)251-2074. **Ed** Judith Slayden Hayes. **Ind/Abst** Funk Scott Index Corp. Ind. bk rev. **Circ** 11,500. Professional journal for Southern Baptist Ministers. Contemporary issues: theology, education, music, administration.

THE SECOND CENTURY. Vol. 1, No. 1 (Spring 1981)-. 0276-7899. Periodical. US. English. qt. $10.00. The Second Century Journal Inc, Box 8227/ Station ACU, Abilene TX 79699. **Tel** (915)674-2382. **Ed** Everett Ferguson. **Ind/Abst** New Testam. Abstr., Relig. Index One, Period. bk rev. adv acc. **Circ** 650. A journal of early christian studies.

THE SEMINARY REVIEW. V. 1- Oct. 1954-. 0197-4122. Periodical. US. English. qt. $4.00. Seminary Reviews, 2700 Glenway Avenue, Cincinnati OH 45204. **Tel** (513)244-8171. **Ed** James B North and W W Winter. **LC** BR1. **DD** 230.05. bk rev. **Circ** 1,600. (ctrl). A scholarly religious journal, aimed at ministers, college alumni, and seminary libraries.

SENTINEL. (THE SENTINEL). V. 1- Nov. 1966-. 0037-2307. Periodical. CN. English (includes some text in French). ir. $3.86. Provincial Association of Protestant, 84 J Brunswick Avenue, Dollard Ormeaux H9B 2C5 Canada. **Tel** (514)683-9330.

SENTINEL. (THE SENTINEL). V. 82- Oct. 1957-. 0049-0202. Periodical. CN. English. bm. $4.65. British America Publishing Company Limited, 94 Sheppard Avenue West, Willowdale Ontario M2N 1M5 Canada. **Tel** (416)223-1690. **Ed** Norman R Ritchie. bk rev. adv acc. **Circ** 9,400. (ctrl). Religious news, patriotic items, and lodge events. The official publication of the Loyal Orange Association. *Sentinel and Orange and Protestant Advocate, 0381-5358.*

SERVANT. (THE SERVANT). V. 1- Nov./Dec. 1977-. 0705-6338. Periodical. CN. English. bm. Free. Steinbach Bible Institute, Box 1420, Steinbach Manitoba R0A 2A0 Canada. **DD** 207.71274. *S B I Bulletin, 0705-632X.*

SERVIZIO DEL REGNO *CEASED.* (IL SERVIZIO DEL REGNO). V. 19, No. 3 Vol. 24 No. 12. 0382-4802. Periodical. CN. Italian. mo. Free. Watch Tower Bible and Tract Society, Canadian Branch, 150 Avenue Bridgeland, Toronto Ontario M6A 1Z5 Canada. **DD** 289.9. (ctrl). *Ministero del Regno, 0382-4799.*

SEVENTH-DAY ADVENTIST PERIODICAL INDEX. *See* Indexes/Abstracts.

SHIN-AKI. 1st Year, 3d Issue- June 1975-. 0384-1510. Periodical. CN. English. ir. Ahimsa House, 63 Beaty Avenue, Toronto Ontario M6K 3B5 Canada. **DD** 248.062713541. *Unicorn Hunter's Guide, 0384-1502.*

SIGNS OF THE TIMES. Began in 1874. 0037-5047. Periodical. US. English. mo. $6.99. Pacific Press Publishing Association, PO Box 7000, Boise ID 83707-1000. **Tel** (208)465-2577. **Ed** Kenneth J Holland. **LC** BX6101. **Circ** 375,000. Practical christianity showing that Bible principles are relevant today. *These Times, 0040-6058.*

SINGLE I. **VFOAT** Single Eye. Began publication with: Vol. 1 (Nov. 1973). 0737-2078. Periodical. US. English. mo. $15.00. Single I, PO Box 11394, Kansas City MO 64112. **Tel** (816)763-9401. **Ed** Don Davidson. bk rev. (ctrl). A national newsletter for leaders of Christian singles groups and ministries.

SOCIAL WORK AND CHRISTIANITY. *See* Sociology: General Works, Theory - Social Pathology, Welfare, Criminology.

SOURCE (MONTREAL, QUEBEC). (SOURCE). 0704-6324. Periodical. CN. English (French). Church of Scientology of Montreal, 4489 Papineau, Montreal Quebec H2H 1T7 Canada. **DD** 299.93605. *Source, 0704-6324.*

THE SOUTHERN BAPTIST EDUCATOR. 1919. 0038-3848. Periodical. US. English. mo. $14.50. Southern Baptist Convention, 460 James Robertson Parkway, Nashville TN 37219. **Ed** Lonnie H Wilkey. **Circ** 8,700. News and feature articles related to Southern Baptist educational institutions.

SOUTHERN BAPTIST JOURNAL. 0199-8269. Periodical. US. English. mo. $9.00. Southern Baptist Journal, PO Box 468, c/o Bill Powell, Buchanan GA 30113. **Tel** (404)646-3856.

SOUTHERN BAPTIST PERIODICAL INDEX. *See* Indexes/Abstracts.

THE SOUTHERN FRIEND. (THE SOUTHERN FRIEND : JOURNAL OF THE NORTH CAROLINA FRIENDS HISTORICAL SOCIETY). Vol. 1, No. 1 (Spring 1979)-. 0743-7439. Periodical. US. English. sa. $10.00. North Carolina Friends, Historical Society, Box 8502, Greensboro NC 27410. **Tel** (919)292-5511. **Ed** Damon D Hickey and Herbert Poole. **LC** BX7648.N8. **DD** 289.6756. bk rev. **Circ** 400. (ctrl). History of friends (Quakers) in the Southeastern United States.

SPICILEGIUM FRIBURGENSE. Vol. 1- 1957-. 0561-6158. Monographic Series. SZ. German. ir. Universitatsverlag Freiburg, Perolles 36, 1700 Fribourg Switzerland. **Tel** 037-24 68 12. Furnishes tools for the research, identification, and study of texts informative of the history of the Christian life.

AS THE SPIRIT MOVES. 0227-499X. Periodical. CN. English. mo. Free. As the Spirit Moves, 60 McNaughton Avenue, Regina Saskatchewan S4M 4M3 Canada. **DD** 269.40971.

THE STANDARD - BAPTIST GENERAL CONFERENCE. **Main/Corp** Baptist General Conference. 1911. 0038-9382. Periodical. US. English. mo. $10.35. Baptist General Conference, 2002 South Arlington Heights Road, Arlington Heights IL 60005. **Tel** (312)228-0200. **Ed** Donald E Anderson. **DD** 286. **Circ** 23,000. Promotion for the Baptist General Conference (BGC), information and inspiration for members of BGC churches.

THE STUDENT. V. 1- 1922-. 0039-2685. Periodical. US. English. mo. $16.00. Materials Service Department, 127 9th Avenue North, Nashville TN 37234. **Tel** (615)251-2777. **LC** BX6205.B27. **DD** 248.83.

STUDIES IN THE HISTORY OF CHRISTIAN THOUGHT. V. 1- 1966-. 0081-8607. Monographic Series. NE. German, French and English. ir. E J Brill, PO Box 9000, 2300 PA Leiden The Netherlands.

SUCCESS (DENVER, COLO.). (SUCCESS). Vol. 10, Nos. 3-4 (Summer-Fall 1959)-Ceased in 1985. Periodical. US. English. qt. $8.00. Accent Publications, 12100 West 6th Avenue, Box 15337, Denver CO 80215. **Tel** (303)988-5300. *Baptist Outlook.*

SUNSTONE REVIEW (SALT LAKE CITY, UTAH). (THE SUNSTONE REVIEW). Vol. 1, No. 1 (July/August 1981)-. 0731-6518. Periodical. US. English. mo. Sunstone Review, PO Box 2272, Salt Lake City UT 84110. **LC** BX8601. **DD** 289.33205.

SUPPLEMENTARY DIRECTORY OF THE AMERICAN BAPTIST CHURCHES IN THE U.S.A. *See* Yearbooks, Almanacs, Directories.

TCNN RESEARCH BULLETIN. **VFOAT** T.C.N.N. Research Bulletin. No. 1 (July 1978)-. Periodical. English. ir. 1.00. Theological College of Northern Nigeria, PO Box 64, Bukuru Plateau State Nigeria Africa. **LC** BR1463.N5. **DD** 276.69005.

TEXAS BAPTIST HISTORY. (TEXAS BAPTIST HISTORY : JOURNAL OF THE TEXAS BAPTIST HISTORICAL SOCIETY). Vol. 1 (1981)-. 0732-4324. Periodical. US. English. an. $5.00. Texas Baptist Historical Society, Box 22000-2E, Fort Worth TX 76122. **Tel** (817)294-7142. **Ed** Ellen Brown. **LC** BX6248.T4. **DD** 286.176405. bk rev. **Circ** 200. Devoted to the study of baptists in Texas.

TEXTE ZUR KIRCHEN- UND THEOLOGIEGESCHICHTE. No. 1- 1966-. 0082-3597. Monographic Series. GW. German. ir. Guetersloher Verlagshaus, Postfach 1343/ Koenigstrasse 23-25, 4830 Guetersloh West Germany. **Tel** 5241-6620. **Ed** Wolfgang Wischmeyer, Gerhard Ruhbach, Gustav A Benrath, Heinz Scheible and Kurt V Selge. Monograph series on Protestantism in Germany.

THIRD WAY. Began with V. 1 in 1977?. 0309-3492. Periodical. UK. English. mo. $25.66. Elm House Christian Communications Ltd, 37 Elm Road, New Malden Surrey KT3 3HB England. **Tel** 01-942 9761. **Ed** Tim Dean. bk rev. adv acc. **Circ** 2,600. Christian perspectives on social, political and cultural issues, in the contemporary world.

THIS PEOPLE. 0273-6527. Periodical. US. English. ir. $12.00. This People Publishing Company, PO Box 21116, Salt Lake City UT 84121. **Tel** (801)263-3577. **LC** BX8601. **DD** 289.33.

THIS WEEK IN THE PRESBYTERIAN CHURCH IN THE UNITED STATES. 1972. Periodical. US. English. wk. $7.50. Presbyterian Church, 341 Ponce de Leon Avenue NE, Atlanta GA 30308. **Tel** (404)873-1531. **Ed** Marj Carpenter. **Circ** 3,600. (ctrl). News on Presbyterian Church (USA) covers meetings of general assembly, synods, Presbyteries seminaries, colleges and other mission activities.

THOUGHT. V. 1- (No. 1-). 0040-6457. Periodical. US. English. qt. $20.00. Fordham University Press, Box L, Fordham University, Bronx NY 10458. **Tel** (212)579-2320. **Ind/Abst** Am. Hist. Life, Hist. Abstr., Part A, Mod. Hist. Abstr., Hist. Abst., Part B, Twent. Century Abstr., MLA Int. Bibliogr. Books Artic. Mod. Lang. Lit., Old Testam. Abstr., New Testam. Abstr., Book Rev. Index, Ref. Source, Index Book Rev. Humanit., Cathol. Period. Lit. Index, Soc. Sci. Index, Humanit. Index, Philos. Index, Hist. Abstr. **LC** AP2. **DD** 051. Index in last issue of volume - attached. (cum index). adv acc. **Circ** 1,500. Available on microfilm from University Microfilms International. Articles on timely, contemporary issues in philosophy, theology, literature and the arts within the context of the Judeo-Christian tradition.

TOPIC (ANGLICAN CHURCH OF CANADA. DIOCESE OF NEW WESTMINSTER). (TOPIC). 0710-2135. Periodical. CN. English. mo. $2.00. Topic, 692 Burrard Street, Vancouver British Columbia V6L 2L1 Canada. **DD** 283.71133.

TRANSACTIONS OF THE MORAVIAN HISTORICAL SOCIETY. **Main/Corp** Moravian Historical Society. 1857/1858-. 0886-1730. US. English. ir. $500.00. Moravian Historical Society Inc, Whitfield House, 214 East Center, Nazareth PA 18064. **Ind/Abst** Am. Hist. Life, Hist. Abstr., Writ. Am. Hist. **LC** BX8553. **DD** 284.6.

TRANSACTIONS OF THE UNITARIAN HISTORICAL SOCIETY. **Main/Corp** Unitarian Historical Society, London. V. 1- 1916/18-. 0082-7800. UK. English. an. 5.00. Unitarian Historical Society, 6 Ventnor Terrace, Edinburgh EH9 2BL Scotland. **Tel** (031)667-4360. **Ed** J McLachlan. **Ind/Abst** Am. Hist. Life, Hist. Abstr., Part A, Mod. Hist. Abstr., Hist. Abst., Part B, Twent. Century Abstr. **LC** BX9803. **DD** 288. bk rev. adv acc. **Circ** 350. History of Unitarianism and related traditions primarily in the British Isles but also in the British commonwealth. Concerned with Unitarian churches, societies, individuals and Unitarian thought.

TRINITY WORLD FORUM. Periodical. US. English. ty. $2.00. Trinity Evangelical Divinity School, 2065 Half Day Road, Deerfield IL 60090. **Tel** (312)945-8800. bk rev. **Circ** 3,500. Seeks to relate important and current issues in mission and evangelism to the missionary, pastor, and the mission-minded layman.

TRUST FUNDS. **Main/Corp** Protestant Episcopal Church in the U.S.A. Committee on Trust Funds. 0149-6468. US. English. Protestant Episcopal Church in the USA, 815 Second Avenue, New York NY 10017. **LC** BX5961. **DD** 254.8.

TWENTIETH CENTURY WATCH. Vol. 1, No. 1 (May-June 1980)-. 0276-6604. Periodical. US. English. bm. $7.50. Twentieth Century Watch Subscriber Services Department, Box 2530, Tyler TX 75710. **LC** BX6178. **DD** 289.9.

THE TWIN CITIES CHRISTIAN. (TWIN CITIES CHRISTIAN). V. 1- Sept. 1978-. 0745-8606. Periodical. US. English. bw. $11.00. Twin Cities Christian, 1619 Portland Avenue South, Minneapolis MN 55404. **Tel** (612)339-9579. **Ed** Doug Trouten. bk rev. adv acc. **Circ** 6,000. (ctrl). Independent Christian newspaper serving Christian community in the St. Paul/Minneapolis area.

UNITARIAN QUEST. 1961-. Periodical. AT. English. qt. 4. Austria and New Zealand Unitarian Association, P O Box 355, Darlinghurst New South Wales 2010 Australia. **Tel** (02)33 4863. **Ed** Geoffrey R Usher. bk rev. **Circ** 170. Aspects of liberal religion, ethics, social responsibility, Unitarian church organisation and news, especially in Australia and New Zealand. *Unitarian, Quest.*

UNITARIAN UNIVERSALISM. 1985-. 0882-4029. Periodical. US. English. an. Unitarian Universalist Ministers Association, 25 Beacon Street, Boston MA 02108. **DD** 082.

THE UNITARIAN UNIVERSALIST CHRISTIAN. V. 25- Spring 1969-. 0362-0492. Periodical. US. English. qt. $10.00. Unitarian Universalist, 110 Arlington Street, Boston MA 02116. **Tel** (617)482-2957. **Ed** Thomas D Wintle. **Ind/Abst** Relig. Index One, Period. **LC** BX9801. **DD** 288.3205. bk rev. adv acc. **Circ** 1,000. Journal of liberal christian thought and opinion, with attention to theology, worship, spirituality, history and ecumenical developments; book reviews, poetry. *Unitarian Christian, 0364-3506.*

UNITARIAN UNIVERSALIST WORLD. (UNITARIAN UNIVERSALIST WORLD : THE JOURNAL OF THE UNITARIAN UNIVERSALIST ASSOCIATION). **VFOAT** UU World. Began with issue for March 1, 1970. 0041-7122. Periodical. US. English. mo. $5.00. Unitarian Universalist Association, 25 Beacon Street, Boston MA 02108. **Tel** (617)742-2100. **Ed** David B Parke. **LC** BX9801. **DD** 288.3205. bk rev. adv acc. **Circ** 100,000. (ctrl). Liberal religious values. *UUA Now.*

UNITAS FRATRUM. Began in 1978. 0344-9254. Periodical. GW. German (summaries in English). sa. $15.00. Moravian College, Reeves Library, Bethlehem PA 18018. **Tel** (215)861-1540. **Ind/Abst** Relig. Index One, Period. bk rev. adv acc. **Circ** 300. Journal devoted to the history, present life and work of the Moravian church.

UNITED CHURCH NEWS. 0882-7214. Periodical. US. English. mo. $8.00. United Church of Christ, Office of Communication/105 Madison Avenue, New York NY 10016-7451. **Tel** (212)683-5656. **Ed** W Evan Golder. adv acc. **Circ** 105,000. National publication for United Church of Christ clergy and laity. News and features on significant issues for church members and friends.

UNITED EVANGELICAL. 0041-7262. Periodical. US. English. mo. $7.00. Church Center Press, Myerstown PA 17067. **Tel** (717)866-7581. bk rev. adv acc. **Circ** 2,800. (ctrl). Religious articles and news about the E. C. Churches.

UNITED EVANGELICAL ACTION. **VFOAT** Action. V. 1- Aug. 1, 1942-. 0041-7270. Periodical. US. English. bm. $10.00. National Association of Evangelicals, PO Box 28, Wheaton IL 60187. **Tel** (312)665-0500. **Ed** Donald R Brown. adv acc. **Circ** 8,500. (ctrl). Presents issues of interest to evangelical Christians.

THE UNITED METHODIST CHRISTIAN ADVOCATE. **VFOAT** Christian Advocate. 8750-7668. Periodical. US. English. bw. $7.50. The United Methodist Christian Advocate, 909 Ninth Avenue West, Birmingham AL 35204.

Religion, Mythology, Rationalism—Roman Catholic Church

THE UNITED METHODIST PERIODICAL INDEX. See Indexes/Abstracts.

UNITED METHODIST REPORTER (SOUTHERN NEW ENGLAND CONFERENCE EDITION). (THE UNITED METHODIST REPORTER). VFOAT Southern New England Reporter. -V. 9, No. 49 (Nov. 13, 1981). Periodical. US. English. wk. United Methodist Reporter, PO Box 221076, Dallas TX 75222. Tel (214)630-6495. Southern New England Reporter.

VAN ALPHEN'S NIEUW KERKELIJK HANDBOEK. VFOAT Nieuw Kerkelijk Handboek. Dutch. ir. LC BR901. DD 280.409492. Nieuw Kerkelijk Handboek.

VAR LOSEN. V. 1-. Periodical. Swedish. ir. Box 68, S193 00 Sigtuna Sweden. LC BX8001.

VIE CHRETIENNE. (LA VIE CHRETIENNE). Began publication in 1951. 0382-0181. Periodical. CN. French. mo. Periodica Inc, PO Box 444, 1155 Ducharme, Outremont Quebec H2V 4R6 Canada. Tel (514)274-5468.

VIE CHRETIENNE A L'ECOLE. (VIE CHRETIENNE A LECOLE : BULLETIN D'INFORMATION DU SERVICE DE PASTORALE A L'ELEMENTAIRE). Nov. 15,/Dec. 15, June 1970/'74 No. 1, (Sept. '74)-. 0712-3574. Periodical. CN. French. bm. Free. Office Diocesain d'Education, 114 East rue Jacques-Cartier, Chicoutimi Quebec G7H 1Y3 Canada. DD 268.432. (ctrl).

VIE CHRETIENNE (NIMES, FRANCE). (LA VIE CHRETIENNE). 1 Yearly Vol., 1 half-year (July 1884 Jan. 1885)-. Periodical. FR. French. ir. Vie Chretienne, 14 rue d'Assas, 75006 Paris France. Tel (01)45485251.

VIEWPOINTS : GEORGIA BAPTIST HISTORY. Main/Corp Georgia Baptist Historical Society. V. 1- 1967?-. Periodical. US. English. be. Ind/Abst Am. Hist. Life, Hist. Abstr., Part A, Mod. Hist. Abstr.

VIP - LUTHERAN WOMEN'S MISSIONARY LEAGUE. WYOMING DISTRICT. (VIP : LUTHERAN WOMEN'S MISSIONARY LEAGUE, WYOMING DISTRICT). VFOAT V.I.P. VAT Very Important Publication. 0745-2020. Periodical. US. English. qt. Lutheran Women's Missionary League, 1212 East 8th Street, Kimball NE 69145.

VIRGINIA ADVOCATE. 0042-6458. Periodical. US. English. bw. $7.50. Virginia Advocate, PO Box 11367, Richmond VA 23230. Tel (804)359-9451. Ed James D Righter. bk rev. adv acc. Circ 17,000. (ctrl). Methodist-related stories and ads.

VIRGINIA BAPTIST REGISTER. 1962. 0083-6311. Periodical. US. English. an. $4.50. Virginia Baptist Historic Society, University of Richmond, Box 348, Richmond VA 23173. Tel (804)285-6324. Ed John S Moore Jr. Ind/Abst Am. Hist. Life, Hist. Abstr. bk rev. Circ 750. (ctrl). Includes previously unpublished articles, diaries, journals, documents especially related to early baptist history in Virginia.

VOICE OF MISSIONS. V. 1- Jan. 1893-. 0042-8175. Periodical. US. English. mo. African Methodist Episcopal Church, 475 Riverside Drive/Room 1926, New York NY 10115. Tel (212)864-2471. Ed Frederick C Harrison. bk rev. Circ 4,100. News from 29 countries which the African Methodist Episcopal Church serves. Mission trends and activities plus promotional material in missions.

THE WAR CRY OF THE SALVATION ARMY. VFOAT War Cry. 1880. 0744-5040. Periodical. US. English. wk. $7.50. The Salvation Army, 799 Bloomfield Avenue, Verona NJ 07044. Tel (201)239-0606. Ed Henry Gariepy. bk rev. Circ 300,000. (ctrl). Inspiration evangelism, information on programs, policies, and personnel of the salvation army. War Cry, 0043-0234.

THE WATCHTOWER. VFOAT Watchtower Announcing Jehovah's Kingdom. 0043-1087. Periodical. CN. English. sm. $2.50 US, $3.00 Others. Watchtower, 150 Bridgeland Avenue, Toronto Ontario M6A 1Z5 Canada. Tel (718)625-3600. Ed F W Franz. Circ 11,150,000. Announces Jehovah God's heavenly kingdom. It is the principal publication of Jehovah's Witnesses. Discusses prophecy; gives counsel.

WEE WISDOM; YOUNG FOLKS MAGAZINE DEVOTED TO PRACTICAL CHRISTIANITY. 1894. 0043-1710. Periodical. US. English. ir. Unity School of Christianity, Unity Village MO 64065. Tel (816)524-3550. Ed Colleen Zuch. Ind/Abst Child. Mag. Guide. Character-building magazine for children.

WELLWOMAN. (WELL WOMAN). June 1978-. 0275-6528. Periodical. US. English. qt. Lutheran Women's Caucus, 1124 South Ashland Avenue, Chicago IL 60607. Adam's Rib.

THE WESLEYAN ADVOCATE. V. 127- July 15, 1968-. 0043-289X. Periodical. US. English. sm. $5.00. Wesleyan Publishing House, Box 2000, Marion IN 46952. Wesleyan Methodist, 0190-6100; Pilgrim Holiness Advocate.

WESLEYAN CHRISTIAN ADVOCATE. V. 1- 1836-. 0190-6097. Periodical. US. English. wk. $10.00. Wesleyan Christian Advocate, 159 Ralph McGill Boulevard NE, Atlanta GA 30308. Tel (404)659-0002. Ed William M Holt. bk rev. adv acc. Circ 31,500. Newspaper of the United Methodist Church in Georgia.

WHITE WING MESSENGER. 0043-5007. Periodical. US. English. bw. $7.50. White Wing Publishing, PO Box 3000, Cleveland TX 37311. Tel (615)476-8536.

WORLDWIDE CHALLENGE. Began with Aug. 1970 issue. Periodical. US. English. mo. $9.95. Campus Crusade for Christ International, Arrowhead Springs, San Bernardino CA 92414. Tel (714)886-5224. LC BV4501.2. DD 248.05.

WORT IN DER WELT (AUSGABE FUR DIE EVANGELISCH-LUTHERISCHE MISSION). (DAS WORT IN DER WELT). Began Apr. 1973. Ceased 1982, No. 6 (Dec). Periodical. German. bm. Nachrichten aus dem Missionswerk der Evang.-Luth. Kirche in Bayern.

YEARBOOK - BAPTIST CONVENTION OF ONTARIO AND QUEBEC. See Yearbooks, Almanacs, Directories.

YEARBOOK - BAPTIST UNION OF WESTERN CANADA. See Yearbooks, Almanacs, Directories.

YEARBOOK - CONFERENCE OF MENNONITES IN CANADA. See Yearbooks, Almanacs, Directories.

YEARBOOK OF TESTIMONY. See Yearbooks, Almanacs, Directories.

YEARBOOK OF THE AMERICAN BAPTIST CHURCHES IN THE U.S.A. See Yearbooks, Almanacs, Directories.

YEARBOOK OF THE AMERICAN LUTHERAN CHURCH. See Yearbooks, Almanacs, Directories.

YEARBOOK OF THE UNITED BAPTIST CONVENTION OF THE ATLANTIC PROVINCES. See Yearbooks, Almanacs, Directories.

YEARBOOK. PROCEEDINGS AND APPOINTMENTS. NEW YORK YEARLY MEETING, RELIGIOUS SOCIETY OF FRIENDS. See Yearbooks, Almanacs, Directories.

YEARBOOK - UNITED CHURCH OF CANADA. See Yearbooks, Almanacs, Directories.

YMCA YEAR BOOK AND OFFICIAL ROSTERS. See Yearbooks, Almanacs, Directories.

ZEITSCHRIFT FUR BAYERISCHE KIRCHENGESCHICHTE. V. 1- 1926-. GW. German. an. $8.11. Zeitschrift fur Bayerische Kirchengeschichte, Veilhofstrasse 28, D-8500 Nurnburg West Germany. Tel 0911/550269. Ed Horst Weigelt. LC BR857.B37. bk rev. Circ 700. (ctrl). Ecclesiastical history of Bavaria, and history of Protestantism in Bavaria. Beitrage zur Bayerischen Kirchengeschichte.

ZEITSCHRIFT FUR EVANGELISCHES KIRCHENRECHT. Vol. 1-. 0044-2690. Periodical. GW. German. qt. JCB Mohr/Paul Siebeck, Postfach 2040, 7400 Tuebingen West Germany. Tel (070)26064.

ZION'S HERALD. V. 153, No. 6- June/July 1975-. 0098-9282. Periodical. US. English. wk. $7.00. Zions Herald, 581 Boylston Street, Boston MA 02116. Tel (617)266-9038. Ed Ann Greene Whiting. LC BX8201. DD 287.674. bk rev. adv acc. Circ 6,000. (ctrl). Focuses on news and features about New England United Methodists. Methodist Churchman.

ROMAN CATHOLIC CHURCH

THE ABRIDGED CATHOLIC PERIODICAL AND LITERATURE INDEX. See Indexes/Abstracts.

ABSIDE. 0515-0981. Periodical. SP. Spanish. ir. Ona Espana, Facultad de Tecologia, San Cugat Del Valles, Barcelona Spain. LC BX805. DD 282.05.

ACTA APOSTOLICA SEDIS, COMMENTARIUM OFFICIALE. (ACTA APOSTOLICAE SEDIS). Main/Corp Catholic Church. Pope. V. 1- 1 Jan. 1909-. 0001-5199. Periodical. IT. Latin (English, French, German, Italian, and Polish). mo. $40.00. Liberia Editrice Vaticana, Citta del Vaticano, Rome Italy. Ind/Abst Cathol. Period. Lit. Index. LC BX850. Index published separately - free - upon request. Acta Santae Sedis.

ACTA NUNTIATURAE GALLICAE. 1-. 0065-1443. Monographic Series. French. ir. Universita Gregoriana Editrice, Piazza Della Piotta 4, 00187 Rome Italy. LC BX1528.

ACTA ORDINIS FRATRUM MINORUM. V. 1- 1982-. 0001-6411. Periodical. IT. Latin. bm. Curia Generalis OfM, Via South Maria Mediatrice 25, 00165 Roma Italy. (cum index).

ACTUALIDAD PASTORAL. Periodical. Spanish. ir. $10.50. Bonum, Maipu 859, Buenos Aires Argentina. LC BX1425.A1.

ALBANIAN CATHOLIC BULLETIN. VFOAT Buletini Katholik Shqiptar. V. 1-. 0272-7250. Periodical. US. English (some Albanian). ir. $10.00 Donation. Albanian Catholic Information Center, PO Box 1217, Santa Clara CA 95053. Tel (415)387-2020. Ed Gjon Sinishta. bk rev. Circ 1,500. Promoting religious freedom and information about historical and cultural heritage of Albanian people.

ALBERTA CATHOLIC DIRECTORY. See Yearbooks, Almanacs, Directories.

ALMANACH POPULAIRE CATHOLIQUE. See Yearbooks, Almanacs, Directories.

THE AMERICAN BENEDICTINE ACADEMY NEWSLETTER. VFOAT Newsletter. Periodical. US. English. PO Box 2128, Saint Leo FL 33574.

THE AMERICAN CATHOLIC FAMILY. V. 1, No. 1 (July/Aug. 1982)-. 0733-1363. Periodical. US. English. mo. $35.00 US, Canada, Mexico, $45.00 Others. National Center for Family Studies, St John's Hall/Suite 200, Catholic University of America, Washington DC 20064.

AMERICAN CATHOLIC STUDIES NEWSLETTER. Vol. 1, No. 1 (April 1975)-. Periodical. US. English. sa. $3.00. Cushwa Center for Studies of American Catholic, University of Notre Dame 614 Memorial Library, Notre Dame IN 46556. Tel (219)239-5441. Circ 800.

THE AMPLEFORTH JOURNAL. Began with V. 1 in July 1895. 0003-2018. Periodical. UK. English. sa. 5.20. Ampleforth Journal, Ampleforth College, York YO6 4EN England. Tel 04393.225. Ed Felix Stephens. bk rev. adv acc. Circ 3,000. (ctrl). Activities of Ampleforth College and Ampleforth Abbey news.

ANALECTA AUGUSTINIANA. V. 1- 1905-. IT. Italian. an. 40,000. Curia Gen Agostiniana Econ Gen, Via S Uffizio 25, 00193 Roma Italy. Tel 6542040. bk rev. Circ 600. Publication of original documentation and studies on the history of the Augustinian order.

ANALECTA CALASANCTIANA. Began publication in 1959. 0569-9789. Periodical. SP. English. sa. 18. Orden De Las Escuelas Pias, Apartado 206, 37080 Salamanca Spain. Tel (923) 243861. Circ 400. (ctrl). Theological research, historical literary research, and general research on the Scuole Pie (history of the order, spirituality, etc.).

ANALECTA CISTERCIENSIA. Vol. 21- 1965-. 0003-2476. Periodical. IT. English (French, German and Latin). ir. 55,000. Edizioni Cisterciensi, Piazza Tempio di Diana 14, 1-00153 Rome Italy. Tel (06)57 551 10. Ed Polycarp Zakar O Cist. Ind/Abst MLA Int. Bibliogr. Books Artic. Mod. Lang. Lit. Index in last issue of volume - attached. (cum index). bk rev. Circ 400. History, law, liturgy, art, faith, etc. of the Cistercian order. Analecta Sacri Ordinis Cisterciensis.

ANALECTA GREGORIANA. Issue 1- 1930-. 0066-1376. Monographic Series. IT. English, Spanish, or Italian. ir. Pontificio Istituto Biblico, Piazza Della Pilotta 35, 00187 Rome Italy. Tel 06/678 1567.

ANGLICAN CHURCH OF CANADA. JOURNAL OF PROCEEDINGS OF THE INCORPORATED SYNOD OF THE DIOCESE OF OTTAWA. (JOURNAL OF PROCEEDINGS OF THE INCORPORATED SYNOD OF THE DIOCESE OF OTTAWA). VFOAT

Religion, Mythology, Rationalism—Roman Catholic Church

Diocese of Ottawa-Journal of Synod. Began publication with 1955 issue?. 0317-3003. Periodical. CN. English. Anglican Book Centre, 600 Jarvis Street, Toronto Ontario M4Y 2J6 Canada. **DD** 283.71384. *Journal of Proceedings.*

ANGLICAN NEWS (ANGLICAN CATHOLIC CHURCH OF CANADA). (ANGLICAN NEWS). Vol. 1, No. 1 (Feb. 15, 1979)-. 0710-1139. Periodical. CN. English. mo. Free. Anglican Catholic Church of Canada, 295 King Street West, Cobourg Ontario K9A 2N4 Canada. **DD** 283.71.

ANNEXE A L'ANNUAIRE DIOCESAIN (SAINTE-ANNE-DE-LA-POCATIERE). *See* Yearbooks, Almanacs, Directories.

ANNUAIRE - ARCHIDIOCESE DE SHERBROOKE. *See* Yearbooks, Almanacs, Directories.

ANNUAIRE CATHOLIQUE DE FRANCE. *See* Yearbooks, Almanacs, Directories.

ANNUAIRE - CONFERENCE DES EVEQUES CATHOLIQUES DU CANADA. *See* Yearbooks, Almanacs, Directories.

ANNUAIRE DE L'ASSOCIATION CANADIENNE DES PERIODIQUES CATHOLIQUES. *See* Yearbooks, Almanacs, Directories.

ANNUAIRE DE L'EGLISE CATHOLIQUE AU CANADA. *See* Yearbooks, Almanacs, Directories.

ANNUAIRE DE L'EGLISE CATHOLIQUE EN TERRE SAINTE. *See* Yearbooks, Almanacs, Directories.

ANNUAIRE DE L'EGLISE DU QUEBEC. *See* Yearbooks, Almanacs, Directories.

ANNUAIRE DIOCESAIN - DIOCESE DE SAINT-JEROME. *See* Yearbooks, Almanacs, Directories.

ANNUAIRE DIOCESAIN - EGLISE DE JOLIETTE. *See* Yearbooks, Almanacs, Directories.

ANNUAIRE - EGLISE DE MONTREAL. *See* Yearbooks, Almanacs, Directories.

ANNUAIRE MUNICIPAL DE ST. I.E. SAINT DENIS. *See* Yearbooks, Almanacs, Directories.

ANNUAL SURVEY - NATIONAL CONFERENCE OF CATHOLIC CHARITIES. **Main/Conf** National Conference of Catholic Charities. 0161-4894. US. English. an. National Conference of Catholic Charities, 1346 Connecticut Avenue Northwest, Washington DC 20036. **LC** HV530. **DD** 361.75.

ANNUARIO PONTIFICIO PER L'ANNO . . . . *See* Yearbooks, Almanacs, Directories.

ARCHIEF VOOR DE GESCHIEDENIS VAN DE KATHOLIEKE KERK IN NEDERLAND. Vol. 1-. 0003-8326. Periodical. NE. Dutch. sa. 52.50. Van Gorcum & Company BV, PO Box 43, 9400 AA Assen Netherlands. **Tel** 080-232765. **Ed** T H J Clemens. **Ind/Abst** Am. Hist. Life, Hist. Abstr., Part A, Mod. Hist. Abstr., Hist. Abst., Part B, Twent. Century Abstr., Recent Publ. Artic. adv acc. **Circ** 750. (ctrl). The journals leading objective is the furtherance in learning about the past of the Roman Catholic Church in the Netherlands. *Archief voor de Geschiedenis van het Aartsbisdom Utrecht and Haarlemse Bijdragen.*

ARCHIV FUR KATHOLISCHES KIRCHENRECHT. *See* Genealogy and Heraldry - Archives.

ARCHIV FUR KIRCHENGESCHICHTE VON BOHMEN-MAHREN-SCHLESLEN. *See* Genealogy and Heraldry - Archives.

ARCHIV FUR LITURGIEWISSENSCHAFT. *See* Genealogy and Heraldry - Archives.

ARCHIVES DE L'EGLISE D'ALSACE. *See* Genealogy and Heraldry - Archives.

ARCHIVO TEOLOGICO GRANADINO. *See* Genealogy and Heraldry - Archives.

ARCHIVUM FRANCISCANUM HISTORICUM. *See* Genealogy and Heraldry - Archives.

ARCHIVUM HISTORICUM SOCIETATIS IESU. *See* Genealogy and Heraldry - Archives.

ARLINGTON CATHOLIC HERALD. **VFOAT** ARH, Arlington Catholic Herald. V. 1- Jan. 8, 1976-. 0361-3712. Periodical. US. English. wk. $10.00. 200 North Glebe Road/Suite 614, Arlington VA 22203. **Tel** (703)841-2590. **Ed** Charles W Carruth. **LC** BX801. **DD** 282.755295. bk rev. adv acc. **Circ** 30,000. (ctrl). Local, national, and international news of interest to Catholics. Supports Orthodox Roman Catholic teaching, the Pope, and the Magisterium. Focus is on the positive, not the negative.

ASSEMBLY. V. 4, No. 4- Feb. 1978-. Periodical. US. English. ir. $6.00 Domestic, $7.00 Canada, $8.00 Foreign. Notre Dame Center for Pastoral Liturgy, 1224 Memorial Library, Notre Dame IN 46556. **Tel** (219)239-5435. **Ed** Barbara Schmich. **Circ** 1,500. Aims to promote genuine liturgical renewal, explore the liturgical tradition, and make the links between the mysteries we celebrate and the mystery of life. Hucusque.

ATENEUM KAPANSKIE. **VFOAT** Revue Theologique. Began publication in 1909. Periodical. PL. Polish (tables of contents also in French). bm. ARS Polona, Krakowskie Przedmiescie 7, 00-068 Warsaw Poland. **LC** BX801.

AUGUSTINUS. 1- (1-). 0004-802X. Periodical. SP. Spanish. qt. $30.00. Augustinus, General Davila 5 Bajo D, 28003 Madrid Spain. **Tel** 2342070. **Ed** Padres Agustinos Recoletos. **Ind/Abst** MLA Int. Bibliogr. Books Artic. Mod. Lang. Lit., Philos. Index. bk rev **Circ** 700. Studies on life, doctrine, thought, spirituality, influence of St Augustine and his relation with other authors. The history of his age. Augustine, founder of religious order and monachism.

AVE MARIA. 0746-3499. Periodical. US. in Slovenian. mo. Franciscan Fathers, PO Box 608, Lemont IL 60439. **LC** BX806.S5.

AVEC LE CHRIST ET LE SAINT-PERE. V. 1- Oct. 1979-. 0228-2747. Periodical. CN. French. 15 Per No. Avec le Christ et le St-Pere, CP 5185, Beauport Quebec G1E 6B5 Canada. **DD** 282.714.

BASILIAN ANNALS. (THE BASILIAN ANNALS). V. 1- (No. 1-). 0316-9030. Periodical. CN. English. an. Basilian Fathers, 20 Humewood Drive, Toronto Ontario M6C 2W2 Canada. **DD** 255.79.

B.C. CATHOLIC. (THE B. C. CATHOLIC). 0007-0483. Periodical. CN. English. ir. $9.28. British Columbia Catholic, 150 Robson Street, Vancouver British Columbia V6B 2A7 Canada. **Tel** (604)683-0281.

BEITRAGE ZUR GESCHICHTE DER REICHSKIRCHE IN DER NEUZEIT. No. 1-. Monographic Series. GW. German. ir. Franz Stiener Verlag GMBH, Postfach 347, D7000 Stuttgart 1 West Germany. **Tel** (0711) 2582229. **Ed** R Reimhard. Monographs dedicated to the history of the Roman Catholic Church in Germany since 1500.

BENEDICTINA. Vol. 1- Jan./June 1947-. Periodical. IT. Italian. sa. 35.000. Benedictina, Via Ostiense 186, 00146 Roma Italy. **Tel** (06)5410341. **Ind/Abst** New Testam. Abstr. bk rev. **Circ** 2,000. Monasticism studies and researches in Mondastic field and related topics.

BIBLICA ET ORIENTALIA. No. 1-. Monographic Series. IT. Italian. ir. Biblical Institute Press, Piazza Della Pilotta 35, I-00187 Rome Italy.

BOLETIM INFORMATIVO - CONFERENCIA NACIONAL DOS BISPOS DO BRASIL, SECRETARIADO REGIONAL LESTE 2. **Main/Corp** Conferencia Nacional dos Bispos do Brasil. Secretariado Regional Leste 2. Periodical. Portuguese. ir. Conferencia Nacional Bispos do Brasil, Secretariado Regional Leste, Kavenida Brasil 2079, Minas Gerais, Belo Horizonte Brazil.

BOLETIN OFICIAL DE LA JURISDICCION ECLESIASTICA CASTRENSE. **Main/Corp** Catholic Church. Vicariato General Castrense. Periodical. Spanish. ir. Vicatiato General Castrense, Nuncio 13, Madrid Spain. **LC** BX1583.A1.

BOLIVIA : GUIA ECLESIASTICA. **VFOAT** Guis Eclesiastica de Bolivia. 1977-. Spanish. ir. Secretario General de la CEB, Casilla 2309, La Paz Bolivia. **LC** BX1464.A1. *Guia de la Iglesia.*

BOLLETTINO DELL'ARCHIVIO PER LA STORIA DEL MOVIMENTO SOCIALE CATTOLICO IN ITALIA. *See* Genealogy and Heraldry - Archives.

BONJOUR. V. 1- April 1979-. 0226-7152. Periodical. CN. French. qt. Free. Journal Bonjour Paroisse, Sainte-Catherine-de-Sienne, Trois Rivieres Ouest Quebec G9A 4N6 Canada. **DD** 282.71445.

BOTTIN. EGLISE DE MONTREAL. *CEASED.* (BOTTIN, EGLISE DE MONTREAL). **Main/Corp** Eglise Catholique. Archidiocese de Montreal. **VFOAT** Eglise de Montreal. -1983. 0317-8463. Periodical. CN. French. an. La Chancellerie Archeveche de Montreal, 2000 Ouest rue Sherbrooke, Montreal Quebec H3H 1G4 Canada. **DD** 282.025714281.

BUCHREIHE DER CUSANUS-GESELLSCHAFT. **Main/Corp** Cusanus-Gesellschaft, Vereinigung zur Forderung der Cusanusforschung. Vol. 1-. 0070-2234. Monographic Series. GW. German. ir. Aschendorff, Postfach 1124, 4400 Munster West Germany. **LC** BX4705.N58.

BUKU PETUNJUK GEREJA KATOLIK INDONESIA. Indonesian. ir. Bagian Dokumentasi-Penerangan, Kantor Waligereja Indonesia, Taman Cut Mutiah 10, Jakarta Indonesia. **LC** BX1653.A3.

BULLETIN DE LITTERATURE ECCLESIASTIQUE. V. 1- Jan. 1899-. 0007-4322. Periodical. FR. French. qt. 195. Institut Catholique de Toulouse, 31 rue de la Fonderie, Toulouse France. **Tel** 61/52 6235. **Ind/Abst** MLA Int. Bibliogr. Books Artic. Mod. Lang. Lit., Old Testam. Abstr., New Testam. Abstr., Bull. Signal. (cum index). bk rev. **Circ** 700. Articles concerning the history of theology and religious literature in the epochs of the two testaments, the patristic and the scholastic with some more speculative articles of theology or philosophy. *Bulletin Theologique, Scientifique et Litteraire de l'Institut Catholique de Toulouse.*

BULLETIN OF MEDIEVAL CANON LAW. New Series, Vol. 1, 1971-. 0146-2989. US. English. an. $10.00. Institute of Medieval Canon Law, University of California, Boalt Hall, Berkeley CA 94720. **Tel** (415)642-5094. **Ed** Stephan Kuttner. **Circ** 600. Articles concerning the history of Canon law and its impact on the law and institutions of medieval Europe with an emphasis on manuscript research, annotated bibliography.

BULLETIN OF THE NATIONAL GUILD OF CATHOLIC PSYCHIATRISTS. (THE BULLETIN OF THE NATIONAL GUILD OF CATHOLIC PSYCHIATRISTS, INC). **Main/Corp** National Guild of Catholic Psychiatrists. V. 15, No. 3- July 1968-. 0547-7115. US. English. an. $12.00. National Guild of Catholic Psychiatrists, 120 Hill Street, Whitinsville MA 01588. **Tel** (617)234-6266. **Ed** Anna Polcino. **Ind/Abst** Cathol. Period. Lit. Index. **LC** RC321. **DD** 261.832205. bk rev. adv acc. **Circ** 250. Topics are on the theological reflections on the practice of psychiatry and psychology and/or ethics. It is geared to psychiatrists, psychologists and other mental health professionals. *Bulletin of the Guild of Catholic Psychiatrists, 0275-0775.*

BULLETIN - SECRETARIATUS PRO NON CHRISTIANIS. **Main/Corp** Catholic Church. Secretariatus Pro Non-Christianis. 1st Year- (1-). Periodical. IT. English (French). ty. $15.00. Via Della Erba 1, Vatican City Italy. **Ind/Abst** Recent Publ. Artic.

CAHIERS DE JOSEPHOLOGIE. Vol. 1, No. 1 (Jan-June 1953). 0007-9774. Periodical. CN. French (summaries in English). sa. $15.00. Centre de Recherche, 3800 Chemin Reine-Marie, Montreal H3V 1H6 Canada. **Tel** (514)733-8211. **Ind/Abst** Old Testam. Abstr., New Testam. Abstr. **LC** BT690. bk rev. **Circ** 800. Everything in relation with the theology of St Joseph and the history of the devotion to St Joseph.

CANADA ECCLESIASTIQUE. (LE CANADA ECCLESIASTIQUE). **VFOAT** Catholic Directory of Canada. 1st- Ed. 0315-6710. Periodical. CN. English (before 1967, published only in French). an. Librarie Beauchemin, 450 Beaumont, Montreal 303 Quebec Canada. **DD** 282.02571.

CANADIAN CATHOLIC REVIEW. (THE CANADIAN CATHOLIC REVIEW). Vol. 1, No. 1 (Jan. 1983)-. 0714-7724. Periodical. CN. English. ir. $25.00. Canadian Catholic Review, 1437 College Drive, Saskatoon Saskatchewan S7N 0W6 Canada. **Tel** (306)966-8900. **Ed** Daniel Callam. **DD** 282.05. bk rev. adv acc. **Circ** 2,000. Contains gospel of Jesus, articles on Saints, scholars and founders of spiritual insights, justice, community, church in other countries, scripture, liturgy, columns on movies, television, American notes, and Eastern church.

CARA SEMINARY FORUM. Vol. 1, No. 1 (March 1972)-. Periodical. US. English. qt. $7.00 Domestic, $10.00 Foreign. Center for Applied Research, 3700 Oak View Terrace NE, Washington

Religion, Mythology, Rationalism—Roman Catholic Church

DC 20017. **Tel** (202)832-2300. Ed Adrian Ruerst. **Circ** 800. Analyzes and seeks solutions to major concerns of Roman Catholic seminaries and presents annual commentary on enrollment statistics.

THE CARDINAL YEARBOOK. See Yearbooks, Almanacs, Directories.

CARITAS (MADRID, SPAIN). (CARITAS : REVISTA MENSUAL DE CARITAS ESPANOLA). Periodical. Spanish. mo. **LC** BX1583.A1. **DD** 261.80946.

CATECHIST. 1966. 0008-7726. Periodical. US. English. ir. $15.95. The Catechist, 2451 East River Road/Suite 200, Dayton OH 45439. **Tel** 294-5785. Ed Patricia Fischer. **Ind/Abst** Cathol. Period. Lit. Index, Media Rev. Dig. bk rev. adv acc. **Circ** 42,000. Religious education, background ideas and teaching suggestions.

CATEQUESIS LATINOAMERICANO. Began 1969?. Periodical. Spanish. ir.

CATEQUETICA. No. 4- (513-). Periodical. Spanish. ty. $7.00. Editorial Sal Terrae, Guevara 20 Apt 77, Santander Spain. **Tel** 212617. (cum index). Religious celebrations, solutions for difficulties, religious instructions, informal expositions on scripture for Baptisms, first communion, weddings, funerals, etc. Admonitions to the faithful and instructions from the Pope. Sal Terrae. Parte Catequetica.

THE CATHOLIC ACCENT. Began in 1961. 0745-399X. Periodical. US. English. wk. Catholic Accent, PO Box 850, Greensburg PA 15601.

CATHOLIC ADVANCE. 1901. 0008-7904. Periodical. US. English. wk. $13.00 state. Catholic Advance, 424 North Broadway, Wichita KS 67202. **Tel** (316)263-8191. Ed M Cecilia Bush. bk rev. adv acc. **Circ** 18,000. Publishes news of Catholic and religious interest of the Diocese of Wichita, national and international scenes to inform and inspire.

CATHOLIC ALMANAC. See Yearbooks, Almanacs, Directories.

CATHOLIC ARCHIVES. See Genealogy and Heraldry - Archives.

THE CATHOLIC BIBLICAL QUARTERLY. V. 1- Jan. 1939-. 0008-7912. Periodical. US. English. qt. $15.00. Catholic Biblical Association, Catholic University of America, Washington DC 20064. **Tel** (202)635-5519. Ed W S Reilly. **Ind/Abst** Old Testam. Abstr., New Testam. Abstr., Ref. Source, Cathol. Period. Lit. Index, Humanit. Index, Relig. Index One, Period. **LC** BS410. (cum index).

CATHOLIC BIBLICAL QUARTERLY. MONOGRAPH SERIES. V. 1- 1971-. Monographic Series. US. English. ir. Catholic Biblical Association, Catholic University of America, Washington DC 20064. **Tel** (202)635-5519.

CATHOLIC BULLETIN. Newspaper. US. English. wk. $69.00. Catholic Bulletin Publishing Company, 244 Dayton Avenue, St Paul MN 55102. **Tel** (612)291-4444.

THE CATHOLIC CHALLENGE. 8756-7482. Periodical. US. English. qt. $15.00. Sanderleaf Publishing Inc, 182 109th Avenue, Elmont NY 11003.

THE CATHOLIC CHRONICLE. 0008-7971. Periodical. US. English. wk. $13.00. Catholic Chronicle, 1933 Spielbush Avenue, Toledo OH 43624. **Tel** (419)243-4178. Ed Daniel J McCarthy. bk rev. adv acc. **Circ** 46,000. (ctrl) News and instructional material involving and affecting Catholics.

THE CATHOLIC COMMENTATOR. 0746-0511. Periodical. US. English. wk. Catholic Diocese of Baton Rouge, 1800 South Acadian Thruway, Baton Rouge LA 70808.

CATHOLIC DIGEST. (THE CATHOLIC DIGEST). V. 1- 1936-. 0008-7998. Periodical. US. English. mo. $6.97. Catholic Digest, PO Box 1812, Des Moines IA 50306. **Tel** (515)284-2194. **Ind/Abst** Cathol. Period. Lit. Index. **LC** BX801. **UD** 282.05.

CATHOLIC DIRECTORY. See Yearbooks, Almanacs, Directories.

CATHOLIC DIRECTORY FOR SCOTLAND. See Yearbooks, Almanacs, Directories.

THE CATHOLIC DIRECTORY OF ENGLAND AND WALES. See Yearbooks, Almanacs, Directories.

THE CATHOLIC EXPONENT. 0162-7031. Periodical. US. English. wk. Catholic Press Union, 1027 Superior Avenue, Cleveland OH 44114.

CATHOLIC FALCON. VFOAT Katolicky Sokol. 0745-1571. Periodical. US. English (Slovak). bw. Slovak Catholic Sokol, PO Box 899, 205 Madison Street, Passaic NJ 07055. **LC** AP58.

CATHOLIC FAMILY FARMER CEASED. (THE CATHOLIC FAMILY FARMER). No. 1, June/July 1974. Ceased with No. 17. 0382-5515. Periodical. CN. English (includes some text in French). bm. $100. St Joseph Farm, Rural Route 2, Ripon Quebec J0V 1V0 Canada. **DD** 248.05.

THE CATHOLIC FREE PRESS. 0008-8056. Periodical. US. English. wk. $8.00. Catholic Free Press, 47 Elm Street, Worcester MA 01692. **Tel** (617)757-6387. Ed Owen J Murphy. bk rev. adv acc. **Circ** 25,942.

CATHOLIC GAZETTE. Began in 1910. 0008-8064. Periodical. UK. English. mo. Catholic Missionary Society, Mission House, 114 West Heath Road, London NW4 England.

CATHOLIC HEALTH WORLD. Vol. 1, No. 1 (Feb. 15, 1985)-. 8756-4068. Periodical. US. English. sm. $20.00 Domestic, $24.00 Foreign. Catholic Health World, 4455 Woodson Road, St Louis MO 63134. **DD** 362.

CATHOLIC HERALD. Began publication in 1894. 0008-8072. Periodical. UK. English. wk. $30.65. Catholic Herald/England, Herald House, Lamb Pass, Bunhill Row, London EC1Y 8TQ England. **Tel** (01)588-3101. Ed Terence J Sheehy. bk rev. adv acc. **Circ** 24,000. Serious weekly religious journal of opinion giving also news from at home and abroad. A page of book reviews. Weekly Herald, South Coast Catholic Herald.

THE CATHOLIC HISTORICAL REVIEW. V. 1- April 1915-. 0008-8080. Periodical. US. English. qt. $20.00. Catholic University of America Press, 620 Michigan Avenue NE, Washington DC 20064. **Tel** (202)635-5052. Ed Robert Trisco. **Ind/Abst** Hist. Abstr., Part A, Mod. Hist. Abstr., Hist. Abst./Part B, Twent. Century Abstr., Old Testam. Abstr., Annu. Bibliogr. Engl. Lang. Lit., Hist. Abstr., Writ. Am. Hist., Book Rev. Index, Ref. Source, Cathol. Period. Lit. Index, Soc. Sci. Index, Hist. Abstr., Am. Hist. Life, Relig. Theol. Abstr., Index Book Rev. Humanit., Humanit. Index, Recent Publ. Artic. **LC** BX1404. **DD** 282.73. (cum index). bk rev. adv acc. **Circ** 2,200. Original, scholarly articles on history of Catholic church broadly defined, book reviews on history of Christianity, both in all ages and places, professional news, lists of current periodical literature, etc.

CATHOLIC INSTITUTIONAL GUIDE OF CANADA. 2nd-5th Issue. 0316-5507. CN. English. an. $7., $5. For clergy, religious orders, school boards. Paul A Joncas, 250 Faillon Street West, Montreal Quebec H2R 2V7 Canada. **DD** 282.02571. Institutions.

CATHOLIC JOURNALIST. See Journalism.

THE CATHOLIC LAWYER. See Law.

CATHOLIC LIBRARY WORLD. See Library and Information Science.

CATHOLIC LIFE. 0008-8218. Periodical. US. English. bm. $5.00. Catholic Life, 35760 Moravian Drive, Fraser MI 48026. Available on microfilm from Xerox University Microfilms.

CATHOLIC LIFE IN POLAND; THE PRESS SURVEY. Periodical. PL. English. mo. Ars Polona, Krakowskie Przedmiescie 7, 00-068 Warsaw Poland. **LC** BX1564.A1. **DD** 282.438.

THE CATHOLIC LIGHT. 0164-9418. Newspaper. US. English. bw. Catholic Light, PO Box 708, Scranton PA 18501. **Tel** (717)346-8915.

CATHOLIC MEDICAL QUARTERLY : JOURNAL OF THE GUILD OF CATHOLIC DOCTORS. See Medicine.

CATHOLIC MIND CEASED. (THE CATHOLIC MIND). Began publication in 1903. Ceased April 1982. 0008-8242. Periodical. US. English. mo. $7.00. 106 West 56th Street, New York NY 10019. **Ind/Abst** Cathol. Period. Lit. Index. **LC** BX801. **DD** 282.

THE CATHOLIC MIRROR. (THE CATHOLIC MIRROR : OFFICIAL NEWSPAPER OF THE DES MOINES DIOCESE). 0279-1528. Periodical. US. English. wk. Catholic Mirror, 200 Jewett Building, Des Moines IA 50309.

CATHOLIC NEAR EAST MAGAZINE. V. 1- Winter 1974-. 0164-0674. Periodical. US. English. qt. $3.00. Catholic Near East Welfare Association, 1011 First Avenue, New York NY 10022. **LC** BX1617. **DD** 282.56.

CATHOLIC NEW TIMES. V. 1- Jan. 16, 1977-. 0701-0788. Periodical. CN. English. bw. $20.90. New Catholic Times, 80 Sackville Street, Toronto Ontario M5A 3E5 Canada. **Tel** (416)361-0761. Ed Mary Jo Leddy. **DD** 282.71. bk rev. adv acc. **Circ** 12,000. Independent, national catholic newspaper, with emphasis on social and economic justice world news, original reports and analysis, reviews of books and media, etc.

CATHOLIC NEW YORK. V. 1, No. 1 (Sept. 27, 1981)-. 0278-1174. Periodical. US. English (some Spanish). wk. $15.00. Catholic New York, PO Box 5133, New York NY 10150. **Tel** (212)688-2399.

THE CATHOLIC PERIODICAL AND LITERATURE INDEX (CUMULATION). See Indexes/Abstracts.

THE CATHOLIC PERIODICAL INDEX. See Indexes/Abstracts.

CATHOLIC PRESS DIRECTORY. See Yearbooks, Almanacs, Directories.

CATHOLIC REGISTER. (THE CATHOLIC REGISTER). April 15, 1972-. 0383-1620. Periodical. CN. English. wk. 15.50 Domestic, 26.50 Foreign. Catholic Register, 67 Bond Street, Toronto Ontario M5B 1X6 Canada. **Tel** (416)362-6822. Ed Larry Henderson. bk rev. adv acc. **Circ** 45,000. (ctrl). This is a Catholic newspaper giving news and features of the Catholic church and its challenges in the modern world. Canadian Register National Ed., 0008-4913.

CATHOLIC RESOURCE NEWSLETTER. 8756-9698. Periodical. US. English. $15.00 Domestic, $18.00 Canada. Thalassa Resources, Box 273575, Boca Raton FL 33427-3575. **DD** 261.

THE CATHOLIC REVIEW. 0008-8315. Periodical. US. English. wk. $10.00. Catholic Review, 320 Cathedral Street, Box 777, Baltimore MD 21203.

CATHOLIC RURAL LIFE. V. 1- 1952-. 0008-8331. Periodical. US. English. mo. $75.00. National Catholic Rural Life Conference, 4625 Northwest Beaver Drive, Des Moines IA 50322.

CATHOLIC STANDARD. V. 1-. US. English. wk. $15.00. The Catholic Standard, 5001 Eastern Avenue, PO Box 4464, Washington DC 20017. **Tel** (301)853-4563. **LC** BX801.

THE CATHOLIC SUN. VFOAT Sun. 1892. 0744-267X. Periodical. US. English. wk. $15.00. Catholic Sun, 257 East Onondaga Street, Syracuse NY 13202. **Tel** (315)422-8153. Ed Wesley J Brush. bk rev. adv acc. **Circ** 46,000. (ctrl). News and features relating activities, policies and teachings of Roman Catholic Diocese of Syracuse in Central New York.

CATHOLIC TELEGRAPH. Periodical. US. English. wk. $12.00. Catholic Telegraph, 100 East 8th Street, Cincinnati OH 45202. **Tel** (513)421-3139. Ed James Stackpoole. bk rev. adv acc. **Circ** 45,000. Catholic paper for the archdiocese of Cincinnati.

CATHOLIC TELEPHONE GUIDE. 0147-5959. US. English. an. $15.00. The Catholic News, 68 West Broad Street Fleetwood, Mt Vernon NY 10552.

CATHOLIC TIMES. (THE CATHOLIC TIMES). V. 1- Dec. 1976-. 0703-1521. Periodical. CN. English. mo. 5.00. Catholic Times, 2005 St Mark Street West, Montreal Quebec H3H 2G8 Canada. **Tel** (514)937-2301. Ed Eric Durocher. **DD** 282.714281005. bk rev. adv acc. **Circ** 12,000. (ctrl) An English language newspaper for Roman Catholics of the Archdioceses of Montreal and surrounding area.

CATHOLIC TIMES (COLUMBUS, OHIO). (THE CATHOLIC TIMES). 0745-6050. Periodical. US. English. wk. $13.00. Catholic Times Inc, PO Box 636, Columbus OH 43216. **Tel** (614)224-5195.

CATHOLIC TRENDS. Periodical. US. English. bw. $29.00. NC News Service, 1312 Massachusetts Avenue Northwest, Washington DC 20005. **Tel** (202)659-6742. Ed David Gibson.

CATHOLIC TWIN CIRCLE. 0273-6136. Periodical. US. English. wk. Twin Circle Publishing Co, 1901 Avenue of the Stars, Suite 1511, Los Angeles CA 90067. Twin Circle, 0041-4654.

Religion, Mythology, Rationalism—Roman Catholic Church

CATHOLIC UNIVERSITY LAW REVIEW (1975). *See* Law.

THE CATHOLIC VIRGINIAN. (CATHOLIC VIRGINIAN). 0008-8404. Periodical. US. English. bw. $12.50. Catholic Virginian Press Inc, PO Box 26843, Richmond VA 23261.

CATHOLIC VOICE (OAKLAND, CALIF.). (THE CATHOLIC VOICE). 0279-0645. Periodical. US. English. ir. $6.00. Catholic Voice, 2918 Lakeshore Avenue, Oakland CA 94610.

THE CATHOLIC WORKER. V. 1- May 1933-. 0008-8463. Periodical. US. English. bm. Catholic Worker, 36 East First Street, New York NY 10003. **Ind/Abst** Cathol. Period. Lit. Index. LC BX801. DD 282.05.

CATHOLIC YOUTH MINISTRY. 0277-8165. Periodical. US. English. mo. $19.50. Growth Associates, 22 Willow Street, Mystic CT 06355. Tel (203)536-0705.

CATHOLIC YOUTH WORK ANNUAL. 0093-1187. US. English. an. National CYO Association, 1321 Massachusetts Avenue Northwest, Washington DC 20005. LC BV4470. DD 261.8343105.

CATHOLICA. Vol. 1-. 0008-8501. Periodical. GW. German. qt. $29.87. Aschendorffsche Verlagsbuchhan Dlung, Postfach 1124, 4400 Muenster West Germany. Tel 0251/6901. **Ind/Abst** New Testam. Abstr., Relig. Index One, Period. adv acc. **Circ** 800. Journal for ecumenical theology. Helps to further understanding among different faiths, unity of the church and open theological discussions.

CHA GUIDEBOOK. Main/Corp Catholic Health Association of the United States. **VAT** Catholic Health Association of the United States Guidebook. 0270-7470. US. English. an. The Catholic Health Association of the United States, 1438 South Grand Boulevard, St Louis MO 63104. LC RA977. DD 362.1102573.

CHAC INFO. (CHAC INFO : QUARTERLY NEWSLETTER OF THE CATHOLIC HEALTH ASSOCIATION OF CANADA). **VFOAT** Info Accs. **VAT** Catholic Health Association of Canada Info, Info Association Catholique Canadienne de la Sante. Vol. 1, No. 1 (Mar. 1983)-. 0822-8426. Periodical. CN. English (text also in French with French text on inverted pages). qt. $8.00. Catholic Health Association of Canada, 312 Daly Avenue, Ottawa Ontario K1N 6G7 Canada. DD 362.106071. *C.H.A.C. Review, 0226-5923.*

CHARISMATIQUE DE L'ATLANTIQUE. **VFOAT** Atlantic Charismatic. **VAT** Atlantic Charismatic (1983). Vol. 3, No. 1 (Jan./Feb. 1983)-. 0821-6460. Periodical. CN. English (includes some text in French). mo. 10.00. Charismatique de l'Atlantique, PO Box 225, Amherst Nova Scotia B4H 3N6 Canada. Tel (902)667-7179. Ed Rick Hartnett. DD 270.8205. bk rev. **Circ** 3,500. (ctrl). English/French language news items, teachings, and explanations of the charismatic renewal in the Catholic Church in the Atlantic provinces. *Atlantic Charismatic, 0821-6479.*

CHEVRON. (LE CHEVRON). Vol. 1, No. 1 (Oct. 1979)-. 0712-3337. Periodical. CN. French. ir. Free. Le Chevron, Office Diocesain des Communications Sociales, 54 Nord Place Bourget, Joliette Quebec J6E 5E4 Canada. DD 282.71442.

THE CHICAGO CATHOLIC. V. 85, No. 35- Sept. 2, 1977-. 0149-970X. Periodical. US. English. wk. $12.00. Chicago Catholic, PO Box 11181, Chicago IL 60611. Tel (312)751-8317. Ed Robert L Johnson. LC BX801. DD 282.77311. bk rev. adv acc. **Circ** 100,000. Providing Catholics of primarily Cook and Lake counties in Illinois religious education, news, features, columns, commentaries, and texts of pastoral documents. *New World, 0028-7016.*

CHICAGO STUDIES. V. 1- Spring 1962-. 0009-3718. Periodical. US. English. ir. Chicago Studies, Box 665, Mundelein IL 60060. Tel (312)566-1462. Ed George J Dyer. **Ind/Abst** Old Testam. Abstr., Cathol. Period. Lit. Index, New Testam. Abstr. LC BX801. DD 230.205. **Circ** 15,000. Available on microfilm from University Microfilms. A theological journal that addresses itself to priests, religious educators and other Catholics who wish to hear the voice of scholarship without the "impediments" of the trade.

CHRONICLE OF THE CATHOLIC CHURCH IN LITHUANIA. No. 12-. 0197-0348. Monographic Series. US. English (Lithuanian). Lithuanian Catholic Religious Aid Inc,
351 Highland Boulevard, Brooklyn NY 11207. LC BX1559.L5. DD 282.475.

CHRZESCIJANIE. Began in 1974. Periodical. Polish. ir. 460.00. Akademia Teologii Katolickiej, Ul Dewajtis 3, 01-653 Warsawa Poland. LC BX4690.P6.

CHRZESCIJANIN W SWIECIE. Began in 1969. Periodical. PL. Polish. mo. Ars Polona, Krakowskie Przedmiescie 7, 00-068 Warsaw Poland. LC BX806.P6.

CISTERCIAN FATHERS SERIES. No. 1- 1970-. Periodical. US. English. ir. Cistercian Publications, 1749 West Michigan, Kalamazoo MI 49008.

CISTERCIAN STUDIES. V. 1-. 0578-3224. Monographic Series. US. English. qt. $12.00. Kevin White, St Joseph's Abbey, Spencer MA 01562. **Ind/Abst** Cathol. Period. Lit. Index. LC BX3401. DD 271.12005.

CISTERCIAN STUDIES SERIES. V. 1- 1969-. Monographic Series. US. English. qt. St Josephs Abbey, c/o Brother Kevin White, Spencer MA 01562.

CITEAUX; COMMENTARII CISTERCIENSES. V. 1- 1950-. Periodical. BE. French (also in German and English). sa. 750.-. Commentarii Cistercienses, Cistercien Abbey, B-3590 Hamont-Archel Belgium. **Ind/Abst** Am. Hist. Life, Hist. Abstr. bk rev. (ctrl). Cistercian monastic history: general history, spirituality, arts, economics, and bibliography.

THE CLERGY REVIEW. V. 1- 1931. 0009-8736. Periodical. UK. English. mo. 16.30. Tablet Publishing Company, 48 Great Peter Street, London SW1 England. Tel 222-7462. Ed Bernard Bickers. **Ind/Abst** Old Testam. Abstr., New Testam. Abstr., Cathol. Period. Lit. Index, Relig. Theol. Abstr. adv acc. **Circ** 18,000. Available on microfilm from Xerox University Microfilms. A ready source of information on theology, scripture, philosophy, history, law, psychology, sociology and pastoral studies.

COLLECTANEA CISTERCIENSIA. **VFOAT** Nova et Vetera. Began with V. 27 (1965). Periodical. BE. French (some contributions in Dutch, English and German). ty. St Josephs Abbey, c/o Brother Kevin White, Spencer MA 01562. *Collectanea Ordinis Cisterciensium Reformatorum.*

COLLECTANEA THEOLOGICA. Began in 1920. 0137-6985. Periodical. Polish (Latin). ir. **Ind/Abst** Old Testam. Abstr., New Testam. Abstr. LC BX880.

COLUMBAN MISSION. 1918. 0095-4438. Periodical. US. English. mo. $3.00. Columban Missions, Columban Fathers Street, Columbans NE 68056. Tel (402)291-1920. Ed Richard Steinhilber. LC BV3410. DD 266.205. bk rev. **Circ** 230,000. (ctrl). To educate, inform, and inspire our readers about the missionary work of the Catholic church in today's world and specifically about the work of the Columban Fathers. *Columban Fathers Missions.*

COLUMBIA. V. 1- Aug. 1921-. 0010-1869. Periodical. US. English. mo. $6.00. Knights of Columbus, PO Drawer 1670, New Haven CT 06507. Ed Elmer Vonfeldt. **Ind/Abst** Cathol. Period. Lit. Index. LC AP2. bk rev. adv acc. **Circ** 1,370,000. Covers current events, social problems, apostolic activities, education, rearing a family, patriotic endeavors, and profiles of triumph over handicaps.

COMUNICADO MENSAL DA CONFERENCIA NACIONAL DOS BISPOS DO BRASIL. Main/Corp Catholic Church. Conferencia Nacional dos Bispos do Brasil. BL. Portuguese. ir. rua do Russell 76, CP 16085, Rio de Janeiro Brazil. LC BX805.

CONCILIUM. Periodical. Polish (Multilingual). ir. Pallottinum, Ul Przebyszewskiego 30, Poznan Poland. LC BX806.P6.

CONCILIUM (PARIS, FRANCE). (CONCILIUM : REVUE INTERNATIONALE DE THEOLOGIE). Periodical. FR. French. bm. 200.00 Domestic, 260.00 Foreign. Beauchesne Editeur, 72 rue des Saints-Peres, 75007 Paris France. Tel 5488028. Covers latest research in religious science and thought, problems of contemporary church and discrimination within the church and society.

CONTRE-REFORME CATHOLIQUE AU 20E SIECLE. (LA CONTRE-REFORME CATHOLIQUE AU XXE SIECLE). **VAT** CRC Canada. No. 1- Jan. 1975-. 0704-724X. Periodical. CN. French. sa. $3.00. Contre-Reforme Catholique Canada, CP
511, Trois-Rivieres Quebec G9A 5H7 Canada. DD 282.0904.

CONVERGENCE (FRIBOURG, SWITZERLAND : ENGLISH EDITION). (CONVERGENCE). 1968, 2-. 0010-8154. Periodical. English. ir. $10.00. Pax Romana, BT 1062, CH-1701 Fribourg Switzerland. Tel (037)262649. Ed R J Rajkumar. LC BX801. DD 282.05. **Circ** 2,500. (ctrl). Intellectual review on themes, women and development, spirituality, human rights, socio-cultural affairs, development, and theology. *Pax Romana Journal.*

THE CORD; A FRANCISCAN SPIRITUAL REVIEW. 1951. 0010-8685. Periodical. US. English. mo. $11.00. Franciscan Institute, St Bonaventure New York 14778. Tel (716)375-2105. Ed Michael Meilach. bk rev. **Circ** 1,500. Monthly review of Franciscan topics scriptural and doctrinal topics also biographical and factual accounts of movements affecting day to day spirituality.

COUNSELING AND VALUES. V. 16- Fall 1971-. 0160-7960. Periodical. US. English. $11.00. American Association of Counseling Development, 5999 Stevenson Avenue, Alexandria VA 22304. Tel (703)823-9800. Ed Nicholas Colangelo. **Ind/Abst** Cathol. Period. Lit. Index, Curr. Index J. Educ., Psychol. Abstr. LC LC461. DD 371.405. CODEN COVADQ. adv acc. **Circ** 458. (ctrl). Articles on morals and values development, clarification, religious and spiritual issues. *National Catholic Guidance Conference Journal.*

COURIER-JOURNAL (PALMYRA, N.Y.). (COURIER-JOURNAL). **VFOAT** Courier Journal. Vol. 43, No. 34 (Sept. 29, 1971)-. Newspaper. US. English. wk. $15.00. Courier Journal, 114 South Union Street, Rochester NY 14607. Tel (716)454-7050. Ed Karen M Franz. bk rev. adv acc. **Circ** 51,000. (ctrl). Also available in microfilm from Biels Microfilm. Community newspaper of the Catholic diocese of Rochester, New York. Emphasis on events, and issues relevant to Catholic Church; particularly parish news. *Palmyra Courier-Journal (1943).*

COURRIER MARGUERITE BOURGEOYS. (COURRIER MARGUERITE BOURGEOYS). No. 1 (1971)-. 0823-7808. Periodical. CN. English. ir. Free. Centre Marguerite-Bourgeoys, 3040 Sherbrooke Street West, Montreal Quebec H3Z 1A4 Canada. DD 282.0924.

CROIRE AUJOURD'HUI. Began in 1971. 0223-4734. Periodical. FR. French. ir. $23.95. Croire Aujourd'Hui, Surface 12 rue d'Assas, 75006 Paris France.

DAN CHUA. SO MAT- Feb. 15, 1977-. 0747-2315. Periodical. US. Vietnamese. mo. $28.00. Nguyet San Cong Giap, PO Box 13455, New Orleans LA 70185. LC BX806.V5.

THE DEAF CATHOLIC. 0045-978X. Periodical. US. English. qt. The Deaf Catholic, 814 Thayer Avenue, Silver Springs MD 20910.

DECISIONES SEU SENTENTIAE. Main/Corp Catholic Church. Rota Romana. Tribunal Apostolicum. V. 1- 1909-. IT. Latin. ir. Liberria Editrice Vaticano, Citta del Vaticano Italy.

DEUTSCHE KATHOLIK IN KANADA. (DER DEUTSCHE KATHOLIK IN KANADA). Began publication in May 1964. 0381-8950. Periodical. CN. German. ir. Catholic in Canada, der 131 McCaul Street, Toronto Ontario 130 Canada. DD 282.05.

DIAKONIA (BRONX, NEW YORK, N.Y.). (DIAKONIA). Began with V. 1, No. 1966. Ceased V. 19, 1984. 0012-1959. Periodical. US. English. ty. $7.00. Diakonia John XXIII Center, Fordham University, Bronx NY 10458. **Ind/Abst** Cathol. Period. Lit. Index.

DIALOGUE DIOCESAIN. Vol. 12, No. 4 (Jan./Feb. 1982)-. 0821-3151. Periodical. CN. French. mo. Office de Communications Sociales, 49 Ouest rue St-Jean Baptiste, Rimouski Quebec G5L 4J2 Canada. DD 282.71477105. *En 4 Pages, 0821-316X.*

DIRETORIO LITURGICO. *See* Yearbooks, Almanacs, Directories.

IL DIRITTO ECCLESIASTICO E RASSEGNA DI DIRITTO MATRIMONIALE. *See* Law.

DOCTOR COMMUNIS. Year 1- Jan./April 1948-. 0012-4443. Periodical. IT. Italian (French, Latin or Spanish). ir. $24.00. Doctor Communis, Palazzo

Cononici, 00120 Vatican City Italy. **Ind/Abst** New Testam. Abstr., Philos. Index. *Acta Pont. Academiae Romanae S. Thomae AQ. et Religionis Catholicae.*

LA DOCUMENTATION CATHOLIQUE. Vol. 1- (No. 1-). 0012-4613. Periodical. FR. French. sm. 96.00. La Documentation Catholique, Bayard Presse, 5 rue Bayard, 75380 Paris 8E France. **Ind/Abst** Cathol. Period. Lit. Index. **LC** BX802. *Questions Actuelles.*

DOCUMENTS PRESENTS. V. 1. 0701-046X. Periodical. CN. French. Eglise de Gloire, CP 304 Succursale R, Montreal Quebec H2S 3K9 Canada. **DD** 282.05.

THE DOWNSIDE REVIEW. V. 1- July 1880-. 0012-5806. Periodical. UK. English. ir. Downside Review-Downside Abbey, Stratton on the Fosse, Bath BA3 4RH England. **Ind/Abst** New Testam. Abstr., Years Work Eng. Stud., Cathol. Period. Lit. Index, Relig. Theol. Abstr., Relig. Index One, Period., MLA Int. Bibliogr. Books Artic. Mod. Lang. Lit., Recent Publ. Artic. **LC** BX801. (cum index).

ECCLESIASTICAL PROVINCE OF NEWFOUNDLAND DIRECTORY. *See* Yearbooks, Almanacs, Directories.

EGLISE DE CHICOUTIMI. ANNUAIRE DIOCESAIN. *See* Yearbooks, Almanacs, Directories.

EGLISE DE ROUYN-NORANDA. (L'EGLISE DE ROUYN-NORANDA). V. 1- April 1974-. 0226-7942. Periodical. CN. French. mo. Free. l'Eglise de Rouyn-Noranda, CP 1060, Rouyn Quebec J8X 5C8 Canada. **DD** 282.714212. (ctrl).

EGLISE DE TROIS—RIVIERES. (EGLISE DE TROIS-RIVIERES : BULLETIN). 0227-6364. Periodical. CN. French. mo. Free. Eglise de Trois-Rivieres, CP 1480, Trois-Rivieres Quebec G9A 5L6 Canada. **DD** 282.71445. *Bulletin d'Information Pastorale, 0227-6356.*

EGLISE DE TROIS-RIVIERES. DOCUMENT. (EGLISE DE TROIS-RIVIERES : BULLETIN. DOCUMENT). 1 (2 Oct. 1977)-. 0227-6372. Periodical. CN. French. bw. Free. Eglise de Trois-Rivieres, CP 1480, Trois-Rivieres Quebec G9A 5L6 Canada. **DD** 282.71445. *Eglise de Trois-Rivieres : Bulletin, 0227-6364.*

EGLISE ICI ET LA. (L'EGLISE ICI ET LA). V. 1-Jan. 1977-. 0705-8659. Periodical. CN. French. bw. Service d'Animation Pastorale, 435 de la Madone, Mont-Laurier Quebec J9L 1S1 Canada. **DD** 282.714225. *Information, 0317-9397.*

ENVOY. 0013-9408. Periodical. US. English. bm. $6.00. Institute of Formative Spirituality, Duquesne University, Pittsburgh PA 15282. **Tel** (412)434-6029. **Ed** Adrian van Kaam. **Ind/Abst** Cathol. Period. Lit. Index. **Circ** 2,000. A journal of reflective reading bringing the word of God into one's everyday life through inspirational articles, poetry and spiritual reading of scripture and the masters.

EPHEMERIDES IURIS CANONICI. V. 1-. 0013-9491. Periodical. IT. English (French, Italian, Latin, and Spanish). sa. $35.00. Catholic Book Agency, Via dei Lucchesi 20, 00187 Roma Italy. (cum index).

ERBE UND AUFTRAG. 35.Yearly Vol (1959). 0013-9963. Periodical. GW. German. mo. 33.-. Beuroner Kunstverlag, Erzabtei St Martin, D-7792 Beuron West Germany. **Tel** 7466-263. **Ed** Benedikt Schwank. **Ind/Abst** New Testam. Abstr., Old Testam. Abstr. bk rev. adv acc. **Circ** 2,000. (ctrl). *Benediktinische Monatsschrift zur Pflege Religiosen und Geistigen Lebens.*

ESKIMO; COUNTRY, INHABITANTS, CATHOLIC MISSION. V. 1-84, Oct. 1944-1970. 0318-7551. Periodical. CN. English. sa. $1.55. Oblate Fathers of Hudson Bay, Vicareate PO 10, Churchill Manitoba Canada.

ESSEX RECUSANT. V. 1- Apr. 1959-. 0423-4456. Periodical. UK. English. ty. (cum index).

ESTATISTICA DO CULTO CATOLICO. Began in 1956. BL. Portuguese. ir. $0.20. Ministerio da Justica, Esplanada dos Ministerios, Ed Sede do MJ-Bloco, 10 Brasilia DF CEP 70064 Brazil. **LC** BX1466.A1.

ESTUDIOS ECLESIASTICOS. V. 1- (No. 1-). 0210-1610. Periodical. SP. Spanish. qt. 39.00. Centro Loyola, Pablo Aranda 3, E-28006 Madrid Spain. **Tel** (91)2624930. **Ed** A Vargas-Machuca. **Ind/Abst** Am. Hist. Life, Hist. Abstr., Part A, Mod. Hist. Abstr., Hist. Abst., Part B, Twent. Century Abstr., Old Testam. Abstr., New Testam. Abstr., Hist. Abstr. bk rev. adv acc. **Circ** 700. Investigation and information on all subjects of theology, especially on Catholic theology and Bible.

FAITH & REASON. VAT Faith and Reason. V. 1- Spring 1975-. 0098-5449. Periodical. US. English. qt. $15.00. Christendom College, Route 3 Box 87, Front Royal VA 22630. **Tel** (703)636-2908. **Ed** Timothy O'Donnell. **Ind/Abst** Cathol. Period. Lit. Index. **LC** BR1. **DD** 230.05. bk rev. **Circ** 1,000. An academic journal with articles by Catholic scholars in fields such as theology, philosophy, politics, literature, history and philosophy of science.

FILIPINO CATHOLIC. 0273-7280. Periodical. US. English. sm. $20.00. Filipino Catholic, 1725 Silverlake Boulevard, Los Angeles CA 90026. **Tel** (213)667-3465. **Ed** Ping Bayani. adv acc. **Circ** 10,000. *Filipino Catholic News-Magazine, 0199-6355.*

FILM-KORRESPONDENZ. Periodical. GW. German. mo. Katholisches Institut fur Medieninformation, Postfach 101088, 5000 Koln 1 West Germany.

THE FLORIDA GOOD NEWS. Periodical. US. English. mo. $117.00. Sunday Publications Inc, PO Box 9501, Lake Worth FL 33466. **Tel** (305)533-0990.

THE FRANCISCAN. 1959. Periodical. UK. English. ty. The Friary, Little Portion, Mt Sinai, Long Island NY 11766. bk rev. adv acc. **Circ** 5,000. (ctrl). News of the Society of St. Francis and comments, reflections and thoughts on issues affecting the Church today.

FRANCISCAN MISSIONARY. VFOAT Reporter. Fall 1972-. 0319-6739. Periodical. CN. English. qt. Franciscan Missionary Union, PO Box 220, Lumsden Saskatchewan S0G 3C0 Canada. **DD** 266.285. *Franciscan Missionary Reporter, 0319-6720.*

FRANCISCAN STUDIES. V. 1-21, Jan. 1924-40. 0080-5459. Periodical. US. English. an. $7.00. Franciscan Institute, St Bonaventure University, St Bonaventure NY 14778. **Ind/Abst** MLA Int. Bibliogr. Books Artic. Mod. Lang. Lit., Philos. Index, Cathol. Period. Lit. Index. **LC** BX3601. **DD** 255.3. (cum index).

FRANZISKANISCHE STUDIEN. Vol. 1-. 5396-0067. Periodical. GW. German (English and French). qt. $19.08. Dietrich Coelde Verlag AG, Postfach 2060, 4760 Werl West Germany. **Ind/Abst** MLA Int. Bibliogr. Books Artic. Mod. Lang. Lit., Recent Publ. Artic. **LC** BX3601. (cum index). Franciscan philosophy and theology.

FREEING THE SPIRIT *CEASED.* V. 1-7, No. 1. 0360-5701. Periodical. US. English. qt. $10.00. Department of Culture and Worship, National Office for Black Catholics, 1234 Massachusetts Avenue NW/ Suite 1004, Washington DC 20005. **LC** BX1407.N4. **DD** 282.73.

FURROW. (THE FURROW). V. 1- Feb. 1950-. 0016-3120. Periodical. IE. English. mo. $26.00. Saint Patricks College, Maynooth County, Kildare Ireland. **Tel** (01)286215. **Ed** Ronan Drury. **Ind/Abst** Old Testam. Abstr., New Testam. Abstr., Cathol. Period. Lit. Index, Index Free Period. (cum index). bk rev. adv acc. **Circ** 8,000. Available on microfilm from Xerox University Microfilms. A pastoral review dealing with the religions concerns in the Roman Catholic Church especially the various ministries within it and its wider outreach to the churches and the arts.

GERMANIA SACRA. Vols. 1-3, 1924-41. Monographic Series. GW. German. ir. Walter de Gruyter, Genthiner Strasse 13, 1 Berlin 30 West Germany. **Tel** 030/26005-0. **LC** BX1534.A1.

GUIA ECLESIASTICA LATINOAMERICANA. CK. Spanish. ir. Secretariado General del Celam, Calle 78 No 11-17, Apartado Aereo, 51086 Bogota Columbia. **LC** BX1425.A4.

GUIDE DES INSTITUTIONS CATHOLIQUES DU CANADA. VFOAT Guide des Institutions. Institutional Guide. 34th Ed.-. 0316-5485. Periodical. CN. text in English and French. an. Paul A Joncas Inc, 250 Ouest rue Faillon, Montreal Quebec H2R 2V7 Canada. **DD** 282.02571. *Catholic Institutional Guide of Canada, 0316-5507; Guide des Institutions Catholiques du Canada, 0316-5485.*

GUIDELINES FOR PASTORAL LITURGY. **Main/Corp** Catholic Church. Canadian Conference of Catholic Bishops. National Liturgical Office. **VFOAT** Liturgical Calendar. 1977-. 0317-7203. CN. English. an. National Liturgical Office, Canadian Conference of Catholic Bishops, 90 Parent Avenue, Ottawa Ontario K1N 7B1 Canada. **DD** 264.021. *Guidelines for Pastoral Liturgy, 0317-7203.*

HERALD OF HOLINESS. Began with Apr. 17, 1912 issue. 0018-0513. Periodical. US. English. bw. Nazarene Publishing House, PO Box 527, Kansas City MO 64141. **Ind/Abst** Guide Soc. Sci. Relig. Period. Lit. **LC** BX8699.N3. **DD** 289.9.

HERDER-KORRESPONDENZ. VFOAT Herder Korrespondenz. Vol. 1-. 0018-0645. Periodical. GW. German. mo. Verlag Herder Freiburg, Hermann-Herder Strasse 4, D-7800 Freiburg West Germany. **Ind/Abst** Energy Res. Abstr. **LC** BX803.

HIDUP. Vol. 24, No. 25- July 5, 1970-. 0377-9610. Periodical. Indonesian. wk. $24.00. Yayasan Hidup Katolik, Kotakpos 2197, Jakarta 10001 Indonesia. **Tel** 365307/372170. **Ed** Subroto Widjojo. **LC** BX1653.A1. bk rev. adv acc. **Circ** 50,000. (ctrl). Deepens and broadens the Christian faith and vision among the Catholics in Indonesia; it commits itself to evangelization, inculturation and ocumenism. *Hidup Katolik, 0376-6330.*

HISTORY COLLECTION. CANADIAN CATHOLIC CHURCH *CEASED.* (HISTORY COLLECTION : CANADIAN CATHOLIC CHURCH). **Main/Corp** St. Thomas More College, Saskatoon, Sask. Library. **VFOAT** Collection d'Histoire: l'Eglise Catholique Canadienne. No. 1- 1971. Ceased with. 0315-3371. CN. entries in English and French: some copies issued with introduction in English. ir. St Thomas More College, 1437 College Drive, Saskatoon Saskatchewan S7N 0W6 Canada. **Ed** A de Valk. **DD** 016.28271.

THE HOMILETIC & PASTORAL REVIEW. Vol. 71, No. 7 (April 1971)-. 0018-4268. Periodical. US. English. ir. $20.00. Catholic Polls Inc, 86 Riverside Drive, New York NY 10024. **Tel** (212)799-2600. **Ed** Kenneth Baker. **Ind/Abst** New Testam. Abstr., Old Testam. Abstr., Cathol. Period. Lit. Index. bk rev. adv acc. **Circ** 15,000. Microfilm available from University Microfilms International. *Homiletic and Pastoral Review.*

HOMILETICA. No. 20- (No. 513-). 0439-4208. Periodical. Spanish. ty. $7.00. Editorial Sal Terrae, Guevara 20 Apartado 77, Santander Spain. **Tel** 212617. Contains informal exposition of scripture for each Sunday and holiday for the Roman Catholic Church. *Sal Terrae. Parte Practica.*

HUMANITAS (BRESCIA, ITALY). *See* Philosophy.

ICI, INFORMATIONS CATHOLIQUES INTERNATIONALES. No. 375- 1 Jan. 1971-. Periodical. FR. French. ir. $15.69. Dawson-France, B P 40, 91 Palaiseau France. **Tel** 009-0122. **Ind/Abst** Point Repere. *Informations Catholiques Internationales.*

ICLA BOLETIN. VFOAT Boletin Informativo Catolico Latinoamericano. **VAT** Informativo Catolico Latinoamericano Boletin. No. 1-. Periodical. PE. Spanish. ir. Secretariado Latinoamericano Pax Romana Miec-Jeci Centro de Documentation, Apartado 3564, Lima 100 Peru.

IDEA INK. 8755-6871. Periodical. US. English. qt. $5.95. Idea Inc, PO Box 4010, Madison WI 53711. **Tel** (608)273-0330. **Ed** Charles Fiore. **DD** 261. adv acc. **Circ** 70,000. An authentically Catholic opinion quarterly, with emphasis on the family and personal morality, spirituality, social issues, and matters of current public concern.

IGLESIA DE SANTIAGO. Periodical. Spanish. ir. $25.00. Arzabispado de Santiago de Chile, Erasmo Escala 1822 Oficina 503, Santiago Chile. **LC** BX1468.A1. **DD** 282.833.

IN CHRISTO : A QUARTERLY FOR RELIGIOUS. Periodical. English. qt. $5.00. The Manager in Christo, Xavier Publications Ranchi, PO Box 8, Ranchi-834001 India. **LC** BX2400. **DD** 255.005.

INFORMATEUR CATHOLIQUE. (L'INFORMATEUR CATHOLIQUE). **VFOAT** Informateur. **VAT** Informateur (Montreal. 1982). V. 1, No. 1, (Dec. 20, 81/Jan. 9, 82)-V. 2, No. 15, (July 2/ 20 1983). 0712-3973. Periodical. CN. French. sm. $32.50. l'Informateur Catholique, 1915 East Boulevard Gouin, Montreal Province of Quebec, H2B 1W7 Canada. **DD** 261.8309714. *Esprit-Vivant, 0382-0394.*

INFORMATIONS - EGLISE DE SAINT-JEROME. (INFORMATIONS—). 0712-6999. Periodical. CN. French (text in English). mo. Free. Diocese de Saint-Jerome, CP 580, Saint-Jerome Quebec J72 5A9 Canada. **DD** 262.027142405. (ctrl).

Religion, Mythology, Rationalism—Roman Catholic Church

INTERNATIONALE KATHOLISCHE ZEITSCHRIFT. VFOAT Internationale Katholische Zeitschrift Communio. Vol. 1-. 0341-8693. Periodical. GW. German. bm. 50.00. Verlag Bonifatius-Druckerei, Liboristarbe 1-3, D4790 Paderborn West Germany. Tel (0221)392913. Ed Franz Greiner. **Ind/Abst** Old Testam. Abstr., New Testam. Abstr., Relig. Index One, Period., Recent Publ. Artic. LC BX803. **Circ** 3,000.

JAARBOEK VAN HET KATHOLIEK DOCUMENTATIE CENTRUM. See Yearbooks, Almanacs, Directories.

JETA KATHOLKE SHQIPTARE. VFOAT Albanian Catholic Life. Vjeti 1- 1966-. Periodical. US. Albanian. ir. 4221 Park Avenue, Bronx NY 10457. LC BX1404.J47.

JOLIET CATHOLIC EXPLORER. VFOAT Explorer. 0273-6217. Periodical. US. English. wk. $10.00. Joliet Chatolic Explorer, Route 53 and Airport Road, Romeoville IL 60441. Tel (815)838-6475.

JOURNAL OF THE AUSTRALIAN CATHOLIC HISTORICAL SOCIETY. Periodical. English. an. 5.00. Australian Catholic Historical Society, 13 Mitchell Street/2nd Floor, Glebe 2037 New South Wales Australia. Tel 660-2407. Ed A E Cahill. **Ind/Abst** Am. Hist. Life, Hist. Abstr., Aust. Public Aff. Inf. Serv. bk rev. adv acc. **Circ** 400. Contains papers on the history of the Roman Catholic Church in Australia.

THE JURIST. V. 1- Jan. 1941-. Periodical. US. English. ir. $12.00. Reverend Thomas J Green JCD Business Manager of the Jurist, The Catholic University of America, Washington DC 20064. LC Microfilm (O).

JURIST (WASHINGTON, D.C.). (THE JURIST). Vol. 1, No. 1 (Jan. 1941)-. 0022-6858. Periodical. US. English. sa. $20.00. Catholic University of America, School of Canon Law, Washington DC 20064. Tel (202)635-5718. Ed James Provost. **Ind/Abst** Cathol. Period. Lit. Index, Index Leg. Period., Curr. Law Index, Leg. Resour. Index. Index in last issue of volume - attached. (cum index). bk rev. **Circ** 3,000. (ctrl). The only journal published in the United States devoted to the study and promotion of Canon Law.

KALENDAR GOLOSU SPASYTELJA. See Yearbooks, Almanacs, Directories.

KALENDAR SVITLA. VFOAT Light Almanac. Began publication in 1951?. 0380-0962. CN. Ukrainian. an. Basilian Press, 286 Lisgar Street, Toronto Ontario M6J 3G9 Canada. DD 282.05.

KALENDAR SVITLA. THE LIGHT ALMANAC. See Yearbooks, Almanacs, Directories.

KARYA-KARYA GEREJA KATOLIK INDONESIA. Indonesian. ir. Bagian Dokumentasi Penerangan, Kantor Waligeneja Indonesia, Taman Cut Mutiah 10, Jakarta Indonesia. LC BX1653.A1.

DIE KATHOLISCHEN MISSIONEN. VFOAT KM. Periodical. GW. German. bm. Verlag Herder Freiburg, Hermann-Herder Strasse 4, D-7800 Freiburg West Germany. (cum index). *Katholischen Missionen, Illustrierte Monatsschrift des Vereins der Glaubenverbreitung in den Landern Deutscher Zunge Mit den Zentralen Aachen, Munchen, Wien und Teplitz-Schonau,* 0022-9407.

KATHOLISCHES LEBEN UND KIRCHENREFORM IN ZEITALTER DER GLAUBENSSPALTUNG. Monographic Series. GW. German. ir. Aschendorffsche Verlagsbuchhandlung, Postfach 1124, 4400 Muenster West Germany. Tel 251/6901. Ed Erwin Iserlah. Monograph series on Catholic life and church reform during the period of reformation and counter-reformation, Martin Luther and the Pope, theologians and important personalities of that era. *Katholisches Leben und Kampfen in Zeitalter Der Glaubensspaltung.*

KATOLICKE NOVINY. Began publication in 1949. Periodical. CS. Czech. wk. Artia, PO Box 790, Praha 1 Czechoslovakia. LC BX806.C9.

KATORIKKU KENKYU. VFOAT Catholic Studies. Japanese (summaries in English). ir. Jochi Daigaku Shingakukai, 710 Kami Shakujii 1 Nerima-Ku (600), Fukuoka Japan. **Ind/Abst** Old Testam. Abstr. LC BX806.J36.

KENT RECUSANT HISTORY. No. 1 (Spring 1979)-. Periodical. UK. English. 2.50. Kent Recusant History Society, 2 Sea Street, Whitstable Kent England. LC BX1494.K46. DD 282.4223.

KYOHOESA YON'GU. VFOAT Research Journal of Korean Church History. V. 1- Series. Periodical. French (Korean). ir. 2.000 Single Issue. Hanguk Kyohoesa Yonguso, 367-27 Hapchong-Dong, Mapo-Ku 121, Seoul South Korea. LC BX1670.5. DD 282.519.

KYONGHYANG CHAPCHI. Periodical. KO. Korean. ir. 3.000. Hanguk Chonjugyo Chungang Hyobuihoe, C P O Box 16, Seoul South Korea. LC BX806.K67.

LAURENTIANUM. Began publication in 1960. 0023-902X. Periodical. IT. Latin. ty. 13.50. Collegio S Lorenzo, G R A Km 68800, 00163 Rome Aurelio Italy. Tel (06)1958. **Ind/Abst** MLA Int. Bibliogr. Books Artic. Mod. Lang. Lit., Old Testam. Abstr., New Testam. Abstr. bk rev. **Circ** 500. (ctrl). Theology, philosophy, Canon law, history, Bible, spirituality, Franciscan history, and spirituality.

LET'S PRAY TOGETHER. (LET'S PRAY TOGETHER : A PUBLICATION OF FAMILIES FOR PRAYER). VFOAT Together. 0740-9613. Periodical. US. English. wk $7.00. Families for Prayer, 775 Madison Avenue, Albany NY 12208. Tel (518)462-6458. Ed Theresa Bronner. **Circ** 70,000. (ctrl). A publication to foster, encourage and facilitate prayer in the home.

LETTRES MANUSCRITES OU COMMUNIQUES PUBLIES DANS L'ARCHIDIOCESE D'OTTAWA. Main/Corp Eglise Catholique. Archidiocese d'Ottawa. Archeveque (1967- : Plourde). Vol. 1, No. 1 (1967)-. 0820-6945. CN. French. an. *Lettres Manuscrites ou Communiques Publies dans l'Archidiocese d'Ottawa,* c/o l'Archidiocese d'Ottawa, 256 rue King Edward, Ottawa Ontario K1N 7M1 Canada. DD 262.027138405.

LIBERAL CATHOLIC. V. 1- 1921-. 0024-1792. Periodical. UK. English. ty. $10.19. Liberal Catholic Church, 30 Gordon Street, London WC1H 0BE England.

LIETUVOS KATALIKU BAZNYCIOS KRONIKA. (THE CHRONICLE OF THE CATHOLIC CHURCH IN LITHUANIA). No. 1-. 0730-7349. Periodical. US. English (Lithuanian). Loyola University Press, 3441 North Ashland, Chicago IL 60657. LC BX1559.L5. DD 282.475.

LIFE FORUM. Vol. 14, No. 1-. Periodical. English. qt. 28.00. Life Forum, Room 6/Caritas Manila Otis Cor Santiago, Pandacan Manila Phillippines. LC BX1912. *Philippine Priests' Forum.*

LIGUORIAN. 0024-3450. Periodical. US. English. mo. $12.00. Liguorian, One Liguori Drive, Liguori MO 63057. Tel (314)464-2500. Ed Norman J Muckerman. **Ind/Abst** Cathol. Period. Lit. Index. LC BX4020.A1. DD 271.6. bk rev. **Circ** 50,000. Leading Catholic family magazine. Ideas mixed with ideals, informative and inspiring.

THE LIVING LIGHT. V. 1, No. 1- Spring 1964-. 0024-5275. Periodical. US. English. qt. $38.00. W H Sadlier Inc, 11 Park Place, New York NY 10007. Tel (202)365-5705. **Ind/Abst** Old Testam. Abstr., Cathol. Period. Lit. Index. LC BX923.

LOGOS CEASED. (LOHOS; BOHOSLOVSKYI KRARTALNYK). VAT Lohos (Yorkton). V. 1- Jan./Sept. 1950. Ceased with V. 33, No. 4, 1982. 0024-5895. CN. Ukranian. qt. Lohos, 165 Catherine Street, PO Box 220, Yorkton Saskatchewan Canada. **Ind/Abst** MLA Int. Bibliogr. Books Artic. Mod. Lang. Lit. LC BX4711.74. DD 281.5.

LA MAISON-DIEU. No. 1- Jan. 1945-. 0025-0937. Periodical. FR. French. qt. $24.88. Editions du Cerf, 29 Boulevard la Tour Maubourg, 75340 Paris Cedex 07 France. **Ind/Abst** New Testam. Abstr. (cum index).

MAJALAH BIMAS KATOLIK. Main/Corp Indonesia. Direktorat Jenderal Bimas Katolik. VAT Majalah Bimbingan Masyarakat Katolik. Indonesian. ir. Direktorat Jenderal Bimas Katolik, Jln Moh Husni Thamrin 6, Jakarta Indonesia. LC BX1653.A1. *Madjalah.*

MANUSCRIPT LETTERS OR COMMUNIQUES PUBLISHED IN THE ARCHDIOCESE OF OTTAWA. Main/Corp Catholic Church. Archdiocese of Ottawa. Archbishop (1967- : Plourde). 0820-6937. CN. English. an. *Manuscript Letters or Communiques Published in the Archdiocese of Ottawa,* c/o the Archdiocese of Ottawa, 256 King Edward Street, Ottawa Ontario K1N 7M1 Canada. DD 262.027138405.

MARYKNOLL. V. 33, No. 5- May 1939-. 0025-4142. Periodical. US. English. ir. $1.00. Catholic Foreign Mission Society, Maryknoll NY 10545. *Field Afar,* 0271-7204.

MEDELLIN. V. 1- March 1975-. Periodical. CK. Spanish. qt. Instituto Teologico Pastoral, Apartado Aereo 1931, Medellin Colombia. Tel 57-94 238-70-35. Ed Alfred Morin. LC BX1751.2. bk rev. **Circ** 2,000. Concerns pastoral studies, Bible, theology, spirituality, catechetics, social studies, and philosophy.

MESSENGER (TORONTO, ONT. : 1980). (MESSENGER). VFOAT Canadian Messenger of the Sacred Heart. Canadian Messenger of the Sacred Heart (1980). Vol. 90, No. 12 (Dec. 1980)-. 0706-6619. Periodical. CN. English. mo. $3.86. Canadian Messenger of the Sacred Heart, 661 Greenwood Avenue, Toronto Ontario M4J 4B3 Canada. Tel (416)466-1195. Ed F J Power. DD 282.05. adv acc. **Circ** 18,000. Ideas on prayer and living a Christian life. *Messenger of the Sacred Heart of Jesus (Toronto, Ont.),* 0708-3203.

THE MICHIGAN CATHOLIC. New Ser., V.1-. Newspaper. US. English. wk. $27.00. Michigan Catholic, 2701 Chicago Boulevard, Detroit MI 48206. Tel (313)865-1100.

MILITANT CHRETIEN INTERNATIONAL. (LE MILITANT CHRETIEN INTERNATIONAL). VFOAT Le Militant Catholique International. VAT Militant Catholique International (1980). No. 14- May 1980-. 0228-1171. Periodical. CN. French. qt. 0.25 Per No. Le Militant Cretien International, CP 5130 Succursale Beauport, Quebec Quebec G1E 6B5 Canada. DD 248.05. *Militant Catholique International,* 0701-0613.

THE MINDSZENTY REPORT. 0026-4474. Periodical. US. English. mo. $8.00 Domestic, $12.00 Foreign. Cardinal Mindszenty Foundation, PO Box 11321, St Louis MO 63150. Tel (314)991-2939. Ed John Boland. Education for faith, freedom, and family against militant atheism.

MINUTES OF THE SEMI-ANNUAL MEETING OF THE BOARD OF DIRECTORS OF THE FIRST CATHOLIC SLOVAK UNION OF THE UNITED STATES AND CANADA. Main/Corp First Catholic Slovak Union of America. Board of Directors. 0275-6250. US. English. sa. 3298 East 55th Street, Cleveland OH 44127. LC E184.S64. DD 973.049187.

MISCELLANEA BAVARICA MONACENSIA. No. 1- 1967-. 0581-0124. Monographic Series. German. ir. R Wolfle, Amalienstrafe 65, 8000 Muenchen 40 Germany.

MISCELLANEA FRANCESCANA. Began with Vol. 36. Periodical. IT. Italian. qt. $11.88. Miscellanea Francescana, Via del Serafico 1, 00142 Rome Italy. **Ind/Abst** MLA Int. Bibliogr. Books Artic. Mod. Lang. Lit. *Miscellanea Francescana di Storia, di Lettere, di Arti.*

MISSIONALIA HISPANICA. Vol. 1- (No. 1/2-). 0211-5492. Periodical. SP. Spanish. ty. Consejo Super Invest Cientific, Vitruvio 8, Apartado 14 458, 28006 Madrid Spain. **Ind/Abst** Hist. Abstr., Am. Hist. Life. LC BV2130. DD 266.2.

MISSIONNAIRES CATHOLIQUES CANADIENS. STATISTIQUES. See Statistics.

MONASTIC STUDIES. 0026-9190. CN. French. an. 12.50. Benedictine Priory, 1475 Pine Avenue West, Montreal Quebec H3G 1B3 Canada. Tel (514)849-2728. Ed Laurence Freeman. LC BX2400. DD 255.0105. bk rev. **Circ** 2,000. (ctrl). A journal of topics on monasticism, monastic history, theology, and monastic spirituality. *Cistercian Studies.*

MONDO E MISSIONE. IT. Italian. ir. 20.000. Pontificio Istituto Missioni Estere, c/o N. 3-704, Milano Italy. Tel (02)7980741. LC BV2130. DD 266.205. bk rev. adv acc. **Circ** 50,000. International third world missionary and churches information. Social and political problems, economics and dialogue with other religions. *Missioni Cattoliche.*

MONITOR ECCLESIASTICUS. Series 7- (V. 74-). 0026-976X. Periodical. IT. Italian (Latin). qt. 13.46. Monitor Ecclesiasticus c/o E Colagiovanni, Via Enrico Besta 30/4, 00167 Rome Italy. Tel 06-62-25-387. Index in last issue of volume - attached. bk rev. adv acc. Church's law (mostly Roman Catholic) in its relationship with the state law in the world-studies of scholars in canonical and civil law- jurisprudence of Catholic tribunals especially in marriage cases. *Monitore Ecclesiastico.*

THE MONTANA CATHOLIC. Vol. 1, No. 1 (Apr. 17, 1985)-. 0883-7899. Periodical. US. English. bw. The Montana Catholic, 515 North Ewing, Helena MT 59620. *Westmont Word,* 8750-4715.

Religion, Mythology, Rationalism—Roman Catholic Church

MONUMENTA HISTORICA SOCIETATIS IESU. Monographic Series. IT. Latin. ir. Institutum Historicum Societatis Iesu, via dei Penitenzieri 20, 00193 Rome Italy.

MONUMENTA IURIS CANONICI. SERIES A : CORPUS GLOSSATORUM. V. 1- 1969-. Periodical. US. English. ir. Biblioteca Apostolica Vatican, 00120 Culta del Vaticano, Roma Italy.

MUNCHENER THEOLOGISCHE ZEITSCHRIFT CEASED. Began with issue for Jan. 1950-Vol. 35, No. 4. 0580-1400. Periodical. GW. German. qt. Paul Pattloch Verlag GMBH & Co KG, Postfach 549, Golderbacher Strasse 6/X, 8750 Aschaffenburg West Germany. **Ind/Abst** MLA Int. Bibliogr. Books Artic. Mod. Lang. Lit., New Testam. Abstr. **LC** BR4.

MUSICAE SACRAE MINISTERIUM (ROME). See Music.

MY FRIEND. See Children and Youth Interests.

NAROD POLSKI. 0027-7894. Periodical. Polish. sm. $10.00. Polish Roman Catholic Union, 984 Milwaukee Avenue G, Chicago IL 60622. **Tel** (312)278-3210. Ed Joseph W Zurawski. bk rev. **Circ** 31,000. (ctrl). Polish-American journal describing official activities of the Polish Roman Catholic Union of America: fraternal, religious, sports, cultural, historical, literary and social.

NATIONAL CATHOLIC REGISTER. Vol. 46, No. 40 (Aug. 30, 1970)-. 0027-8920. Periodical. US. English. wk. $23.00. Twin Circle Publishing Company, PO Box 25986, Los Angeles CA 90025. **Tel** (213)553-4911. **Ind/Abst** Cathol. Period. Lit. Index. *National Register*.

THE NATIONAL CATHOLIC REPORTER. V. 1- Oct. 28, 1964-. Periodical. US. English. ir. National Catholic Reporter Publishing Company, PO Box 281/115 East Armour Boulevard, Kansas City MO 64141. **Tel** (816)531-0538. **LC** Microfilm 02591BX,BX801.

NATIONAL DIRECTORY OF CATHOLIC HIGHER EDUCATION. See Yearbooks, Almanacs, Directories.

NATURALEZA Y GRACIA. Vol. 1-. 0470-3790. Periodical. Spanish. ty.

DIE NEUE ORDNUNG IN KIRCHE, STAAT, GESELLSCHAFT, KULTUR. 0028-3304. Periodical. GU. German. bm. 27.30. IFG Verlagsgesellschaft MBH, Simrockstrasse 19, 5300 Bonn 1 West Germany. **Tel** (0228)216852. **Ed** Heinrich Basilius. **Ind/Abst** Foreign Lang. Index, PAIS Foreign Lang. Index. bk rev. adv acc. **Circ** 2,000. (ctrl). Essays on church, public, social and cultural problems. *Neue Ordnung (Heidelberg)*.

NEW CATHOLIC WORLD. V. 215- (No. 1282-). 0363-5066. Periodical. US. English. bm. New Catholic World, 997 MacArthur Boulevard, Mahwah NJ 07430. **Tel** (201)825-7300. Ed Laurie Felknor. **Ind/Abst** Annu. Bibliogr. Engl. Lang. Lit., Book Rev. Index, Cathol. Period. Lit. Index, Read. Guide Period. Lit., Mag. Index, Access, Guide Soc. Sci. Relig. Period. Lit., Am. Hist. Life, Hist. Abstr., Hist. Abstr., Part A, Mod. Hist. Abstr., Hist. Abst., Part B, Twent. Century Abstr. **LC** AP2. **DD** 282.05. bk rev. **Circ** 9,000. Available on microfilm from University Microfilms. A journal with a pastoral focus. It is concerned with the confusion brought on by the profound social and religious changes of our times. *Catholic World*.

NEW COVENANT. Began in July 1971. 0744-8589. Periodical. US. English. mo. New Covenant, PO Box 7009, Ann Arbor MI 48107. **Tel** (313)761-8505. **Ind/Abst** Cathol. Period. Lit. Index. **LC** BX2350.57. **DD** 248.48205. *Pastoral Review*.

NEW OXFORD REVIEW. V. 44, No. 2- Feb. 1977-. 0149-4244. Periodical. US. English. $19.00. New Oxford Review Inc, 1069 Kains Avenue, Berkeley CA 94706. **Tel** (415)526-5374. Ed Dale Vree. bk rev. adv acc. **Circ** 6,500. Available on microfilm from University Microfilms. Journal of ideas. Ecumenical Christian monthly edited by Lay Roman Catholics, interested in doctrinal orthodoxy, morality, evangelism, social justice, peace, and family life. *American Church News*.

NEWSLETTER - CATHOLICS UNITED FOR THE FAITH. CANADA. (NEWSLETTER - CATHOLICS UNITED FOR THE FAITH/CANADA). **Main/Corp** Catholics United for the Faith/Canada. **VFOAT** Bulletin - Catholiques Unis pour la Foi/Canada. **VAT** Bulletin - Catholiques Unis pour la Foi. Canada (English Edition). March/April 1974-. 0705-1638. Periodical. CN. English. bm. Free. Catholics United for the Faith, PO Box 6361, Edmonton Alberta T5B 4 Canada. **DD** 267.18271.

NOEUD. (LE NOEUD : LAMORANDIERE SIC & LAC CASTAGNIER). 0227-0021. Periodical. CN. French. mo. Free. Le Noeud, c/o RR No 1, Rochebeaucourt Quebec J0Y 2J0 Canada. **DD** 282.71413. (ctrl).

NORTHERN CATHOLIC HISTORY. Spring 1975-. Periodical. UK. English. sa. North East Catholic History Society, 4 Oaklands Gosforth, New Castle NE 34YQ UK. **LC** BX1491.A1. **DD** 282..428.

NOS ECOLES (OTTAWA, ONT.). (NOS ECOLES). Vol. 1, No. 1 (June 1974)-. 0229-110X. Periodical. CN. French. Conseil des Ecoles Separes Catholique d'Ottawa, 140 rue Cumberland, Ottawa Ontario K1N 7G9 Canada. **DD** 371.9711407138405.

NOTITIAE. V. 1- 1965-. 0029-4306. Periodical. VC. Latin (French, German, Italian and Spanish with summaries in English, French, German, and Spanish). mo. $22.00. Libreria Editrice Vaticana, Citta del Vaticano, Rome Italy. **Ind/Abst** Cathol. Period. Lit. Index. Index in last issue of volume - attached.

NOTRE-DAME DU CAP. **VFOAT** Annales de Notre-Dame du Cap. Jan. 1945-. 0700-6500. CN. French. ir. Oblate Fathers of Mary Immaculate, Cap de la Madelaine, Quebec Canada. *Annales de Notre-Dame du Cap, 0700-6497*.

NOTRES. (LES NOTRES). No. 5- Feb. 1962-. 0029-4578. Periodical. CN. French. qt. Procure des Missions, 665 Church Street, Dorval Lachine Quebec Canada. *Bulletin Missionnaire Montfortain, 0383-2716*.

NUESTRO TIEMPO. No.1- Jul. 1949-. MX. Spanish. mo. C Editorial Don Bosco SA, Apartado 920, Mexico 1 DF Mexico. **Tel** 5 12 11 01. **Ind/Abst** Am. Hist. Life, Hist. Abstr. **LC** DP1. bk rev. adv acc. **Circ** 5,000. General information on Catholic news for parents and youth.

NUNTIA. 1 (1975)-. Periodical. Latin. sa. $16.00. Liberia Editrice Vaticana, Citta del Vaticano, Rome Italy.

ONS GEESTELIJK ERF. Periodical. BE. Dutch. qt. 1050.00. Ruusbroecgenootschap, Prinsstraat 17, 2000 Antwerpen Belgium. **Tel** (03)232-3711. **Ind/Abst** MLA Int. Bibliogr. Books Artic. Mod. Lang. Lit. **LC** BX806.D8. (cum index). bk rev. **Circ** 450. Historical study of the spirituality of the Low Countries (before 1800).

ONTARIO CATHOLIC DIRECTORY. See Yearbooks, Almanacs, Directories.

A ORDEM. 1.- 1921-. Periodical. Portuguese. ty. **LC** BX805.

ORDO. **Main/Corp** Eglise Catholique. Conference des Eveques Catholiques du Canada. Office National de Liturgie. **VFOAT** Notes Pastorales, Calendrier pour l'Annee Liturgique. 1971-. 0708-711X. CN. French. an. Office National de Liturgie, Conference des Eveques Catholiques du Canada, 90 Av Parent, Ottawa Ontario K1N 7B1 Canada. **DD** 264.021. *Notes Pastorales, Calendrier Liturgique, Supplements, Diocesains, 0317-722X*.

ORIGINS. V. 1- May 24, 1971-. 0093-609X. Periodical. US. English. National Catholic News Service, 1312 Massachusetts Avenue NW, Washington DC 20005. **Tel** (202)659-6742. Ed David Gibson. **Ind/Abst** Cathol. Period. Lit. Index. **LC** BX801. **DD** 282.73. Religious.

OUR DIOCESE (GRAND FALLS, NFLD.). (OUR DIOCESE). V. 1, No. 1 (Oct. 1982)-. 0823-7069. Periodical. CN. English. bm. Free to Members. Our Diocese c/o V Blackmore, Chancery Office, PO Box 397, Grand Falls Newfoundland A2A 2J8 Canada. **DD** 282.71805.

OUR SCHOOLS (OTTAWA, ONT.). (OUR SCHOOLS). 0229-1096. Periodical. CN. English. Ottawa Roman Catholic Separate School Board, 140 Cumberland Street, Ottawa Ontario K1N 7G9 Canada. **DD** 377.8271384.

L'OUVROIR LITURGIQUE. V. -2, No. 13, -1948. Periodical. French. ir. **LC** BX1970.A1.

OVERVIEW. Began publication in Oct. 1966. 0030-7564. 2,000. US. English. mo. $10.95. Thomas More Association, 223 West Erie, Chicago IL 60601. **Tel** (800)835-8965. Ed Edward C Herr. (ctrl). A continuing survey of issues, events, trends, and opinions affecting catholics, as reported in journals and newspapers from around the world.

PACT. PROVINCIAL ASSOCIATION OF CATHOLIC TEACHERS. (PACT). **Main/Corp** Provincial Association of Catholic Teachers of Quebec. V. 1- Sept. 1970-. 0384-1006. Periodical. CN. English. mo. Provincial Association of Catholic Teachers du Quebec, 5767 Monkland Avenue, Montreal Quebec H4A 1E8 Canada. *P A C T Magazine, 0552-6736*.

PASAULIO LIETUVIU KATALIKU ZINYNAS. See Yearbooks, Almanacs, Directories.

PASTORALE-QUEBEC. V. 83- Jan. 14, 1971-. 0383-2236. Periodical. CN. French. ir. $15.48. Romain de Quebec, 1073 Ouest Boulevard Saint Cyrille, Sillery Quebec G1S 4R5 Canada. **Tel** (418)688-1211. *Eglise de Quebec*.

LA PENSEE CATHOLIQUE. 1-. 0031-4781. Periodical. FR. French. bm. $46.57. Led Editions du Cedre, 13 rue Mazarine Paris 6E France. **LC** BX802. **DD** 282.05. (cum index). bk rev. History, theology, philosophy, literature, etc.

PERABA. Vol. 19, No. 15- June 1968-. Periodical. Multilingual. ir. 150 Per Month. Yayasan Badan Penerbit Peraba, Bintaran Kidul 5, Jogjakarta Indonesia. **LC** BX1653.A1. *Praba*.

PERSONNEL ECCLESIASTIQUE. **Main/Corp** Catholic Church. Archdiocese of Kinshasa (Zaire). French. ir. Secretariat et Chancellerie Archidiocese de Kinshasa, B P 8431, Kinshasa 1 Zaire. **LC** BX1682.C6. **DD** 282.675114025.

PERSPECTIVAS DE DIALOGO. Periodical. UY. Spanish. ir. $6.00. Centro Pedro Fabro Cerrito, 400 Montevideo Uruguay. **LC** BX805. **DD** 282.05.

PERSPECTIVE (MUNICH, GERMANY). (PERSPECTIVE). Year 1- July/Oct. 1978-. Periodical. Romanian. ir. Rumanisch-Katolische Mission in Deutschland, Kreittmayrstr 28, 8000 Munchen 2 Germany.

PHASE. Began in 1961. Periodical. SP. Spanish. bm. $22.00. Centre de Pastoral Liturgica, Rivadeneyra 6 7, 08002 Barcelona Spain. **Tel** (93)302 22 35. bk rev. adv acc. **Circ** 2,000. All the subjects related with the liturgy of the Roman Catholic Church.

PICENUM SERAPHICUM. Italian. ir. 3.500. Biblioteca Francescana, Conto Corrente Postale 15/27009, 60015 Falconara Italy. **LC** BX3601.

PIERRES VIVANTES. April 1974-. 0226-3572. CN. French. an. Free. Comite des Fondateur de L Eglise du Canada, Pierres Bibantes, 1085 Rue de la Cathedrale, Montreal Quebec H3B 2V4 Canada. **DD** 261.70971. (ctrl).

PITTSBURGH CATHOLIC. Began in 1844. 0032-0323. Periodical. US. English. wk. $8.00. Pittsburgh Catholic Associates, 110 Third Avenue, Pittsburgh PA 15222.

PNCC STUDIES. **VFOAT** P.N.C.C. Studies. **VAT** Polish National Catholic Church Studies. 1980-. 0734-4570. Periodical. US. English. an. $5.00 Single Issue. Polish National Catholic Church, Commission of History and Archives, 1004 Pittston Avenue, Scranton PA 18505. **LC** BX4795.P64. **DD** 284.8.

THE POPE SPEAKS. V. 1- 1st Quarter 1954-. 0032-4353. Periodical. US. English. qt. $36.00. Our Sunday Visitor, PO Box 920, Huntington IN 46750. **Tel** (800)348-2440. Ed Rev Vincent J Giese. **Ind/Abst** Cathol. Period. Lit. Index. **LC** BX850. **DD** 282.05. Index in last issue of volume - attached. **Circ** 5,900. Quarterly journal of recent papal letters, addresses, and other major church documents.

THE POPE TEACHES. V. 1- Oct./Dec. 1978-. Periodical. UK. English. mo. $24.52. Catholic Truth Society, PO Box 422, London SW1V 1PO England. **LC** BX801.

POSOL. 1/2- Jan./Feb. 1974-. 0701-0192. Periodical. CN. Slovak (includes some text in English). mo. $5.00. Posol, PO Box 600, 147 Elgin Street North, Cambridge Ontario N1R 5W3 Canada. **DD** 282.71.

PRAIRIE MESSENGER. 0032-664X. CN. English. wk. $21.67. Prairie Messenger, Box 190, Muenster Saskatchewan S0K 2Y0 Canada. **Tel** (306)682-5215. Ed Andrew M Britz. bk rev. adv acc. **Circ** 14,300. Also available in microfilm format. Catholic diocesan weekly, strong ecumenical and social justice thrust deals with N-S issues, militarism, uranium mining and distribution, ecology and family agricultural issues.

Religion, Mythology, Rationalism—Roman Catholic Church

PRAYER GROUP DIRECTORY. See Yearbooks, Almanacs, Directories.

PRESENCE. ARCHDIOCESE OF OTTAWA CEASED. (PRESENCE; ARCHDIOCESE OF OTTAWA). V. 1-7, No. 8. 0382-8875. Periodical. CN. English. mo. Diocesan Communications Service, Archdiocese of Ottawa, 256 King Edward Avenue, Ottawa Ontario K1N 7M1 Canada. DD 282.71384005.

PRESENCE. L'EGLISE D'OTTAWA CEASED. (PRESENCE; L'EGLISE D'OTTAWA). V. 1-7, No. 8. 0382-8743. Periodical. CN. French. Free. Centre Diocesain, Office des Communications Sociales, 256 Av King Edward, Ottawa Ontario K1N 7M1 Canada. DD 282.71384.

PRO MUNDI VITA DOSSIERS. AFRICA (ENGLISH EDITION). (PRO MUNDI VITA DOSSIERS. AFRICA DOSSIER). VFOAT Africa Dossier. 1 (Mar. 1976)-. 0378-3413. Periodical. BE. English. qt. Pro Mundi Vita, rue de la Limite 6, B-1030 Brussels Belgium. Ind/Abst Relig. Index One, Period. LC BX809.P76. DD 282.605. Special Note (Pro Mundi Vita Society).

PRO MUNDI VITA DOSSIERS. ASIA-AUSTRALASIA. (PRO MUNDI VITA DOSSIERS. ASIA-AUSTRALASIA DOSSIER). VFOAT Asia-Australasia Dossier. 1 (Jan. 1976)-. 0379-3427. Periodical. BE. English. mo. Pro Mundi Vita, rue de la Limite 6, B-1030 Brussels Belgium. Ind/Abst Relig. Index One, Period. LC BX809.P76. DD 282.505. Special Note (Pro Mundi Vita Society).

PRO MUNDI VITA DOSSIERS. EUROPE-NORTH AMERICA. (PRO MUNDI VITA DOSSIERS. EUROPE/NORTH AMERICA). VFOAT Europe/North America. 1- Nov. 1976-. 0379-4113. Monographic Series. BE. English. ir. Pro Mundi Vita, rue de la Limite 6, B-1030 Brussels Belgium. Ind/Abst Relig. Index One, Period. LC BX809.P76. DD 280. Special Note - Pro Mundi Vita, 0079-5593.

PROCEEDINGS OF THE AMERICAN CATHOLIC PHILOSOPHICAL ASSOCIATION. See Philosophy.

PROCEEDINGS OF THE ANNUAL CONVENTION - CANON LAW SOCIETY OF AMERICA. (PROCEEDINGS OF THE . . . ANNUAL CONVENTION). Main/Conf Canon Law Society of America. Convention. 0277-9889. US. English. ir. Canon Law Society of America Proceedings, Catholic University/Room 431, Washington DC 20064. Ind/Abst Cathol. Period. Lit. Index. DD 262.9.

PROGRESS (SEATTLE, WASH.). (THE PROGRESS). 0739-6023. Periodical. US. English. wk. $14.00. The Progress, 910 Marion Street, Seattle WA 98104. Catholic Northwest Progress.

PRZEWODNIK KATOLICKI. Began in 1895. Periodical. PL. Polish. wk. ARS Polona, Krakowskie Przedmiescie 7, 00-068 Warsaw Poland. LC BX806.P6.

PUBLICATIONS - LOUVAIN. UNIVERSITE CATHOLIQUE. SECTION D'ARCHEOLOGIE ET D'HISTORIE DE L'ART. Main/Corp Louvain. Universite Catholique. Section d'Archeologie et d'Historie de l'Art. 1- 1970-. BE. French. ir. Universite Catholique de Louvain, Collige Erasme, 1348 Louvain la Neuve Belgium.

PUBLICATIONS. (MONOGRAPH SERIES). Main/Corp Catholic Record Society, London. Vol. 1 1968-. 0576-9515. Monographic Series. UK. English. 20.00. Mr L Gooch, 12 Melbourne Place, Wolsingham Company, Durham DL13 3EH England. Ed J A Williams. Circ 1,000. Postreformation of English Catholic history.

LES QUATRE FLEUVES. 1-. Monographic Series. FR. French. sa. 120. Beauchesne Editeur, 72 rue des Saints Peres, 75006 Paris France. Tel 45 48 80 28.

QUEST CEASED. Periodical. English. ir. $2.00. Aquinas University College, Columbo-8 Ceylon Sri Lanka. LC BX1646. DD 282.5493.

R N D. REVUE NOTRE DAME. (R N D REVUE NOTRE DAME). 1970-. 0035-3795. Periodical. CN. French. mo $6.00. Revue Notre Dame, CP 400, Sillery Quebec G1T 2R7 Canada. Tel (418)681-3581. Ed Yvon Labbe. Ind/Abst Point Repere. DD 248.05. Circ 150,000. A Catholic magazine for social and religious formation. R N D Revue Notre-Dame du Sacre-Coeur, 0382-6961.

REB. REVISTA ECLESIASTICA BRASILEIRA. (REVISTA ECLESIASTICA BRASILEIRA). VFOAT REB. V. 1-. 0101-8434. Periodical. BL. Portuguese. qt. $60.00. Editora Vozes Ltda, R Frei Luis, 100-C P 90023, 25600 Petropolis RJ Brazil. Tel (0242)43-5112. Ind/Abst Old Testam. Abstr., New Testam. Abstr., Cathol. Period. Lit. Index. LC BX805. DD 282.05. bk rev. Circ 4,000. Catholic theology, pastoral work in a country where the majority of population is Christian but oppressed by poverty.

RECHERCHES ACTUELLES - INSTITUT CATHOLIQUE DE PARIS. Main/Corp Institut Catholique de Paris. 1-. FR. French. ir. Beauchesne, 72 rue de Saint Peres, Paris France 75007. LC BR45. DD 230.08 S.

RECORDS OF THE AMERICAN CATHOLIC HISTORICAL SOCIETY OF PHILADELPHIA. V. 1- 1884/86-. 0002-7790. Periodical. US. English. qt. $10.00. American Catholic Historical Society of Philadelphia, 263 South 4th Street, Box 84, Philadelphia PA 19105. Tel (215)925-5752. Ed 900. Ind/Abst Am. Hist. Life, Hist. Abstr., Part A, Mod. Hist. Abstr., Hist. Abstr., Part B, Twent. Century Abstr., Cathol. Period. Lit. Index, Hist. Abstr. LC E184.C3. Index in last issue of volume - attached. (cum index). bk rev. Circ 900. Founded for the purpose of collecting and preserving materials relating to American history and the contributions of Catholics to the building of the Americas, as well as the Catholic church in the United States. American Catholic Historical Researches.

RECUEIL DES HISTORIENS DE LA FRANCE. POUILLES. Main/Corp Academie des Inscriptions et Belles-Lettres, Paris. FR. French. ir. Diffusion de Boccard, 11 rue de Medicia, 75006 Paris France. LC BX1528.A1.

REFORMATIONSGESCHICHTLICHE STUDIEN UND TEXTE. No. 1-. 0080-0473. Monographic Series. GW. German. ir. Aschendorffsche Verlagsbuchhndlung, Postfach 1124, 4400 Munster West Germany. Tel 251/6901. Ed Erwin Iserloh. History of the reformation of the Roman Catholic Church, texts and important monograph series, theologians and important personalities of that era, counter-reformation, state and church reform.

REIGN OF THE SACRED HEART. 0048-7155. Periodical. US. English. mo. Reign of the Sacred Heart, 6889 South Lovers Lane, Hales Corner WI 53130.

RELATIONS. Vol. 1- (No. 1-). 0034-3781. Periodical. CN. French. mo. $10.00. Relations, 8100 Boul Saint-Laurent, Montreal Quebec H2P 2L9 Canada. Ind/Abst Can. Period. Index, Point Repere. LC BX802. DD 282.05. Available on microfilm from University Microfilms.

REPERTOIRE - DIOCESE DE CHICOUTIMI CEASED. Main/Corp Eglise Catholique. Diocese de Chicoutimi. Published since 1975?. 0381-6710. CN. French. an. Eveche de Chicoutimi, C P 278, Chicoutimi Quebec G7H 5C3 Canada. DD 282.02571416. Annuaire Diocesain, 0380-0504.

RERUM ECCLESIASTICARUM DOCUMENTA. SERIES MAIOR : FONTES. 1- 1956-. 0484-4823. Latin. ir. Herder Editrice E Liberia, Piazza Montecitorio 121, Rome Italy.

RESTORATION. Periodical. CN. English. mo. $1.55. Restoration, Combermere Ontario K0J 1L0 Canada. Tel (613)756-3713. Ed Catherine Doherty. bk rev. Circ 11,000.

REVIEW FOR RELIGIOUS. V. 1- Jan. 1942-. 0034-639X. Periodical. US. English. bm. $11.00. Review for Religious-Catholics, PO Box 6070, Duluth MN 55802. Tel (314)535-3048. Ed Daniel F X Meenan. Ind/Abst New Testam. Abstr., Book Rev. Index, Cathol. Period. Lit. Index. LC BX2400. DD 271.05. Index in last issue of volume - attached. bk rev. Circ 18,500. Available on microfilm from University Microfilms International. Intended for Roman Catholic priests, brothers and sisters, it deals with their personal lives and vowed commitments.

REVISTA DE ESPIRITUALIDAD. No. 1- Oct./Dec. 1941-. 0034-8147. Periodical. SP. Spanish. qt. $18.00. Revista de Espiritualidad, Triana 9, Madrid 16 Spain. Ind/Abst New Testam. Abstr. LC BX805.

REVISTA DE INVESTIGACION. Main/Corp Universidad Nacional de San Agustin. V. 1- Dec. 1970-. Spanish. ir. Direccion Universitaria de Investigacion, Casilla 23, Arequipa Peru. LC AS88.U55.

REVUE DE L'UNIVERSITE D'OTTAWA. Main/Corp University of Ottawa. V. 1- Jan./Mar. 1931-. 0041-9206. Periodical. CN. contributions in French and English. qt $15.48. University of Ottawa Press, 603 Cumberland Avenue, Ottawa Ontario K1N 6N5 Canada. Tel (613)231-2270. Ind/Abst Am. Hist. Life, Hist. Abstr., Part A, Mod. Hist. Abstr., Hist. Abstr., Part B, Twent. Century Abstr., MLA Int. Bibliogr. Books Artic. Mod. Lang. Lit., Can. Period. Index, Cathol. Period. Lit. Index, Philos. Index, Point Repere, Years Work Eng. Stud., Hist. Abstr. LC BX802. DD 205. Proceedings of the Annual Symposium of the Ottawa-Carleton Medieval Renaissance Club, 0319-1753.

REVUE SCOLAIRE CEASED. (LA REVUE SCOLAIRE). Began in 1948. Ceased with Vol. 30, No. 6. 0035-4104. Periodical. CN. French. ir. Federation des Commissions Scolaires Catholiques du Quebec, CP 490, Saint-Foy Quebec G1V 4C7 Canada.

RICERCHE STORICHE SALESIANE. Yearly V. 1, No. 1, (July/Dec. 1982)-. Periodical. IT. Italian. sa. 18.000. Piazza dell'Ateneo Salesiano 1, 00139 Roma Italy. LC BX4045.A1. DD 255.79.

RIVISTA LITURGICA. 0035-6956. Periodical. IT. Italian. bm. 19,000.00 Domestic, 25,000.00 Foreign. Editrice Elle di Ci, Corso Francia 214, 10096 Leumann Torino Italy. Tel (011)959.10.91. bk rev. Circ 4,800. Devoted to a bibliographical bulletin which is unique in Italy.

ROZE MARYI. 0745-3299. Periodical. US. Polish. mo. Congregation of Marian, Stockbridge MA 01262.

RSCJ: A JOURNAL OF REFLECTION. V. 1- Apr. 1979-. 0272-0418. Periodical. US. English. sa. $3.00 US and Canada, $4.00 Others. Sacred Heart Higher Education Association, Religious of the Sacred Heart, 4535 Maryland Avenue, St Louis MO 63108. LC BX4435. DD 255.93005.

SAEBYOK (CATHOLIC CHURCH. ARCHDIOCESE OF SEOUL (KOREA). HANGBOGUK). (SAEBYOK). Periodical. KO. Korean. mo. Chonjugyo Soul Tae Kyogu Hongboguk, 1 2-Ka Myong-Dong Chung-ku, Seoul Korea. LC BX1670.7.S46.

ST. ANTHONY MESSENGER. (SAINT ANTHONY MESSENGER). Began with V. 1 in 1892. 0036-276X. Periodical. US. English. mo. $34.00. Saint Anthony Messenger, 1615 Republic Street, Cincinnati OH 45210. Tel (513)241-5615. Ed Norman Perry. Ind/Abst Cathol. Period. Lit. Index. bk rev. adv acc. Circ 430,000. A family oriented, general-interest Catholic magazine. Helps readers better understand the teachings of the gospel and Catholic church and how they apply to life.

ST. LOUIS REVIEW. VAT Saint Louis Review. 1941-. 0036-3022. Periodical. US. English. wk. $10.00. St Louis Review, 462 North Taylor Avenue, St Louis MO 63108. Tel (314)531-9700. Ed Edward J Sudekum. bk rev. adv acc. Circ 96,500. Catholic news, views and features of interest in the St. Louis area, nationally and internationally.

SALESIANUM. Vol. 1, 1939-. 0036-3502. Periodical. IT. French (German, Italian, Latin or Spanish, with summaries in these languages including English). qt. 35.000 Domestic, 45.000 Foreign, $25.00. Libreria Ateno Salesiano, Piazza dell Ateneo Salesiano 1, 00139 Rome Italy. Tel (06)8132041. Ind/Abst MLA Int. Bibliogr. Books Artic. Mod. Lang. Lit., New Testam. Abstr. LC BX800.A1. (cum index). bk rev. Circ 700.

SALMANTICENSIS. V. 1- Jan. 1954-. 0036-3537. Periodical. SP. Spanish. ir. $32.00. Revista Univ Pontificia, Compania 1, Salamanca Spain. Ed JRE Ramin Trevijuno. Ind/Abst Am. Hist. Life, Hist. Abstr., Part A, Mod. Hist. Abstr., Hist. Abstr., Part B, Twent. Century Abstr., New Testam. Abstr., Hist. Abstr. bk rev. Circ 600.

SAMARITANO. (IL SAMARITANO). Vol. 1- 25 Jan. 1975-. 0318-0514. CN. Italian. wk. Italmedia Services, 100 Ouest Avenue Lawrence/Bureau 100, Toronto Ontario M6A 1P2 Canada. DD 282.05.

LA SCUOLA CATTOLICA. Began with 4. Ser., V. 1, Jan. 1902. 0036-9810. Periodical. IT. Italian. bm. 15,000. Seminario Arcivescovile di Milano, La Tipografica Varese Via Tonale 49, Milano Italy. Ind/Abst New Testam. Abstr. Scuola Cattolica e la Scienza Italiana.

SEMINARIUM. Began with V. 1 in 1950. 0582-6314. Periodical. IT. French (German, Italian, Latin and Spanish with contents page in English,

Religion, Mythology, Rationalism—Roman Catholic Church

French, German, Italian, Portuguese and Spanish). qt. $25.00. Liberze Editrize Vaticana, Citta del Vaticano, Rome Italy. **Ind/Abst** Cathol. Period. Lit. Index. Index in last issue of volume - attached.

SERVICO DE DOCUMENTACAO. BL. Portuguese. ir. Editora Vozes Ltda, R Frei Luis 100 CP 90023, 25600 Pertopolis RJ Brazil. **LC** BX805.

SHROUD SPECTRUM INTERNATIONAL. V. 1, No. 1-. 0738-6524. Periodical. US. English. qt. Indiana Center for Shroud Studies, Route 3 Box 557, Nashville IN 47448.

SINHAK CHONMANG. Series/Titl Kyooi Sinhak. **VFOAT** Theological Perspective. Periodical. Korean. ir. **LC** BX1751.2.A1.

SISTERS TODAY. 0037-590X. Periodical. US. English. $12.00. Liturgical Press, Collegeville MN 56321. **Ind/Abst** Cathol. Period. Lit. Index. *Sponsa Regis.*

SOCIAL JUSTICE REVIEW. V. 33- Apr. 1940-. 0037-7767. Periodical. US. English (Vols. 33-38 German). bm. $12.00 Domestic, $15.00 Foreign. Catholic Central Union of America, 3835 Westminster Place, St Louis MO 63108. **Tel** (314)371-1653. Ed Harvey J Johnson. **Ind/Abst** Cathol. Period. Lit. Index. bk rev. adv acc. **Circ** 1,050. Primary aim is Catholic social action, stressing the Roman Catholic viewpoint in social, economic, religious, intellectual and political problems affecting contemporary society. *Central-Blatt and Social Justice.*

SOUNDS OF TRUTH AND TRADITION. 0038-187X. Periodical. US. English. qt. Catholic Traditionalist Movement, Suite 303, East Pan Am Building, 200 Park Avenue, New York NY 10017. **LC** BX1752. **DD** 282.05.

SOUTHERN CROSS (SAN DIEGO, CALIF.). (SOUTHERN CROSS). 0745-0257. Periodical. US. English. ir. $15.00. Southern Cross, PO Box 81869, San Diego CA 92138. **Tel** (619)574-6393. Ed Louis Copestake. bk rev. adv acc. **Circ** 20,000. (ctrl). We are a newspaper of the Roman Catholic Diocese of San Diego.

SPIRITUALITY TODAY. V. 30- Mar. 1978-. 0162-6760. Periodical. US. English. qt. Spirituality Today, 1909 South Ashland Avenue, Chicago IL 60608. **Tel** (212)226-0074. **Ind/Abst** Old Testam. Abstr., Cathol. Period. Lit. Index. **LC** BX2350.A1. **DD** 205. Available on microfilm. *Cross and Crown, 0011-1910.*

STATISTIQUES DE L'ENSEIGNEMENT PRIMAIRE ET SECONDAIRE. See Education (General) - Special Aspects of Education.

STROMATA. Yearly V. 21, No. 3/4- Jul/Dec 1965-. 0049-2353. Periodical. AG. Spanish. qt. 20. Universidad del Salvador, Av Mitre 3226, 1663 San Miguel Argentina. **Tel** 667-1992. Ed Jorge Seibold. **Ind/Abst** Old Testam. Abstr., New Testam. Abstr., Philos. Index. **LC** BX805. bk rev. adv acc. **Circ** 1,000. *Ciencia y Fe.*

STUDI CATTOLICI. Year 1- (No. 1-). 0039-2901. Periodical. IT. Italian. mo. Studi Cattolici, Via A Stradivari N7, Milano Italy. **Tel** (02)20-92-02. Ed Cesare Cavalleri. **LC** BX804. bk rev. adv acc. Topics include theology, literature, arts, sociology, philosophy, history, and actuality.

STUDI E RICERCHE FRANCESCANE. Year 1- 1972-. Periodical. IT. Italian. ir. $11.88. Studi e Ricerche Francescane, Piazza S Efra, P Vecchio 21, 1-80137 Napoli Italy.

STUDI STORICI DELL'ORDINE DEI SERVI DI MARIA. 0039-3045. Periodical. English (Italian, and Spanish). sa. $15.00. Viale Trenta Aprile 6, 00153 Roma Italy. **LC** BX4055.A1. **DD** 271.47005. *Studi Storici Sull'Ordine dei Servi di Maria.*

STUDIA CANONICA. V. 1- 1967-. 0039-310X. Periodical. CN. English (text in French). sa. $24.76. Saint Paul University Faculty of Canon Law, 223 Main Street, Ottawa Ontario K1S 1C4 Canada. **Tel** (613)236-1393. Ed Francis J Morrisey. **Ind/Abst** Cathol. Period. Lit. Index. **LC** K23. **DD** 262.905. bk rev. **Circ** 1,300. Only one of the canonical series in North America, one of the few in the world. Bilingual (English-French). Contains selected judgments from matrimonial courts.

STUDIA ET DOCUMENTA IURIS CANONICI. 1 (1970)-. Monographic Series. IT. Italian. ir. Catholic Book Agency, Via dei Lucchesi 20, 00187 Roma Italy.

STUDIA GRATIANA. V 1- 1953-. IT. Latin (English, Italian, German). ir. Libreria Ateneo Salesiano, Piazza Dell Ateneo Salesian0 1, 00139 Rome Italy. **Tel** (06)813.21.40. Ed Alphons Kerd Stickler. adv acc. **Circ** 1,000. History of church-law in the Middle Ages.

STUDIA MISSIONALIA. Vol. 1 (1943)-. 0080-3987. IT. Italian (English, French, German, and Latin). an. $40.00. Pontificio Instituto, Piazza Della Pilotta 35, 00187 Rome Italy. **Ind/Abst** New Testam. Abstr., Cathol. Period. Lit. Index, Relig. Index One, Period. **LC** UNC. **DD** 266.205.

STUDIA PATRISTICA CEASED. GE. German. ir. Akademie Verlag, Leipziger Strasse 3/4/PF 1233, DDR 1086 Berlin East Germany.

STUDIA Z HISTORII KOSCIOA W POLSCE. Vol. 1-. Monographic Series. Polish (summaries in French, German, or Latin). ir. **LC** BX1564.

STUDIEN UND MITTEILUNGEN ZUR GESCHICHTE DES BENEDIKTINER-ORDENS UND SEINER ZWEIGE. 1.- Vol., 1880-. Periodical. GW. German. ir. EOS Verlag, Erzabtei St Ottilien, D-8917 St Ottilien West Germany.

STUDIES IN FORMATIVE SPIRITUALITY. V. 1- Feb. 1980-. 0193-2748. Periodical. US. English. ty. $16.00. Institute of Formative Spirituality, Duquesne University, Pittsburgh PA 15282. **Tel** (412)434-6029. Ed Adrian van Kaam. **Ind/Abst** Humanit. Index, Cathol. Period. Lit. Index. bk rev. **Circ** 2,000. A discipline-related approach to the issues of formation and human experience designed to integrate the transcendent, functional, vital and socio-historical dimensions of life. *Humanitas, 0018-7496.*

STUDY SESSIONS - CANADIAN CATHOLIC HISTORICAL ASSOCIATION. Main/Corp Canadian Catholic Historical Association. **VFOAT** Sessions d'Etude. Vol. 33- 1966-. 0318-6156. CN. English (French. Divided in 2 sections, one for each language. Each with separate title page and paging. Sessions d'Etude). an. 20.00. Reverend Edward Jackman OP, 355 Church Street, Toronto Ontario M5B 1Z8 Canada. **Tel** (416)977-1500. Ed Alphonse de Valk. **DD** 282'.71. **Circ** 300. A series of articles on the history of the Catholic church in English and French Canada respectively. *Report - Canadian Catholic Historical Association, 0318-6148.*

SUBSIDIA HAGIOGRAPHICA. 1- 1886-. Monographic Series. BE. French. sa. Societe Des Bollandistes, 24 Boulevard Saint-Michel, B-1040 Bruxelles Belgium. A collection of studies.

SUPPLEMENT - DIOCESE DE SAINTE-ANNE-DE-LA-POCATIERE. (SUPPLEMENT). **Main/Corp** Eglise Catholique. Diocese de Sainte-Anne-de-la-Pocatiere. 1982/83-. 0820-9669. CN. French. an. Eveche de Sainte-Anne, C P 430, La Pocatiere Quebec G0R 1Z0 Canada. **DD** 282.02571475. *Annexe a l'Annuaire Diocesain, 0820-9650.*

SYLLOGE EXCERPTORUM E DISSERTATIONIBUS AD GRADUM DOCTORIS IN SACRA THEOLOGIA VEL IN IURE CANONICO CONSEQUENDUM CONSCRIPTIS. **Main/Corp** Louvain. Universite Catholique. Vol. 1- 1932/33-. Periodical. BE. texts in Latin or French. ir. University Catholique de Louvain, Collige Erasme, 1348 Louvain la Neuve Belgium. **LC** BX1751.A1. **DD** 208.2.

SZOLGALAT. 1.- Sz. Monographic Series. Hungarian. ir. Pruug Verlag, Osterreich, 7000 Eisenstadt Austria. **LC** BX880.

THE TABLET. Began in 1908. Periodical. US. English. wk. $36.00. The Tablet, 1 Hanson Place, Brooklyn NY 11217. **Tel** (212)789-1500. Ed Don Zirkel. **LC** BX801. bk rev. adv acc. **Circ** 93,000. Catholic weekly newspaper.

TAG DES HERRN. 0492-1283. Periodical. GE. German. bw. 4.80. Deutscher Buch Export-Import, Leninstrasse 16, DDR-701 Leipzig East Germany. **Tel** 44 161. **Circ** 100,000. (ctrl). Bulletin of the Catholic Church in East Germany. Pastoral and cathecistic concepts and information concerning the world church and the Catholic church in East Germany.

TALKS OF POPE JOHN PAUL II. V. 14, No. 5- Mar. 1979-. Periodical. US. English. ir. $10.00. Pro Ecclesia, 663 Fifth Avenue, New York NY 10022. **Tel** (212)673-7447. Ed Timothy A Mitchell. bk rev adv acc. **Circ** 1,500. (ctrl). Reproduces talks of our Holy Father. *Talks of the Pope.*

THEOLOGISCHE REVUE. Vol. 1-. 0040-568X. Periodical. GW. German. bm. $38.23. Aschendorffsche Verlagsbuchhan, Postfach 1124, 4400 Muenster West Germany. **Tel** 251/6901. **Ind/Abst** New Testam. Abstr. **LC** BR4. **DD** 230.05. bk rev. adv acc. **Circ** 900. Critical reviews of theological literature especially Roman Catholic church, current bibliography of important theological publications, international discussions of new works.

TIDINGS. 0040-6791. Periodical. US. English. wk. $12.00. Tidings Publishing Company, 1530 West 9th Street, Los Angeles CA 90015. **Tel** (213)251-3360. Ed Al Antczak. bk rev. adv acc. **Circ** 47,000. Official publication of the Roman Catholic Archdiocese of Los Angeles.

TODAY'S CATHOLIC. (TODAY'S CATHOLIC : OFFICIAL PUBLICATION OF THE ARCHDIOCESE OF SAN ANTONIO AND THE DIOCESE OF VICTORIA). Began in 1972. 0745-3612. US. English (Spanish). bw. $10.00. Today's Catholic, PO Box 28410, San Antonio TX 78228. **Tel** (512)734-2620. Ed Martha Brinkmann. bk rev. adv acc. **Circ** 33,000. Available in microform. A paper published for catholics which offers information on all phases of life. *Alamo Messenger.*

TODAY'S MISSAL. 0199-8803. Periodical. US. English. bm. $1.98. Today's Missal, PO Box 14809, Portland OR 97214-0809. **Tel** (503)281-1191. Ed Randall DeBruyn. Providing liturgy and music for Catholic worship, including 7 seasonal missals and a music issue/hymnal.

TSERKOVNYI VISNYK. V. 4, No. 57 (Jan. 24, 1971)-. Periodical. US. Ukrainian. bw. $7.00. Cerkovnyi Visnyk, 2247 West Chicago Avenue, Chicago IL 60622. **LC** BX4711.736.C5. *Visnyk Ukrainskoi Katolytskoi Parafii Sviatykh Volodymyra I Olhy V Chikago.*

UJ EMBER. Periodical. US. Hungarian. wk. **LC** BX2348.A1.

UNIREA. ALMANAC. See Yearbooks, Almanacs, Directories.

U.S. CATHOLIC. V. 37- Jan. 1972-. 0041-7548. Periodical. US. English. mo. Claretian Publishing, 221 West Madison Street, Chicago IL 60606. **Tel** (312)236-7782. Ed Mark J Brummel. **Ind/Abst** Pop. Mag. Rev., Cathol. Period. Lit. Index, Read. Guide Period. Lit., Mag. Index, Guide Soc. Sci. Relig. Period. Lit. **LC** BX801. **DD** 282.73. bk rev. adv acc. **Circ** 68,000. A format for discussion of ideas affecting modern Catholics. *U.S. Catholic and Jubilee.*

U.S. CATHOLIC HISTORIAN. **VFOAT** US Catholic Historian. Vol. 1, No. 1 (Fall 1980)-. 0735-8318. Periodical. US. English. qt. $10.00 Members. US Catholic Historical Society, c/o St Joseph's Seminary, Dunwoodie Yonkers NY 10704. **LC** BX1404. **DD** 282.0973.

THE UNIVERSE. Periodical. US. English. wk. Association of Catholic Newspapers, 1 Marsh Lane Bootle, Merseyside L20 4HZ England. **LC** ABX1491. *Universe and Catholic Times.*

UPDATE (WILMINGTON, N.C.). (UPDATE). Series/Titl Official Catholic Teachings. **VFOAT** Official Catholic Teachings. 1977-. 0731-4809. US. English. an. McGrath Publishing Company, PO Box 9001, Wilmington NC 28402. **LC** BX850. **DD** 262.91. (cum index).

THE UPPER PENINSULA CATHOLIC. (THE UPPER PENINSULA CATHOLIC : THE NEWSPAPER OF THE DIOCESE OF MARQUETTE). **VFOAT** U.P. Catholic. 0747-1440. Periodical. US. English. bw. U P Catholic, PO Box 548, Marquette MI 49855.

VERMONT CATHOLIC TRIBUNE. **VFOAT** Catholic Tribune. 0042-4145. Periodical. US. English. ir. $7.00 Domestic, $8.00 Foreign. Vermont Catholic Tribune, 351 North Avenue, Burlington VT 05401.

VICARIA DE LA SOLIDARIDAD. Main/Corp Catholic Church. Archdiocese of Santiago (Chile). Vicaria de la Solidaridad. Began with: Yearly V. (Jan. '77. CL. Spanish. an. Plaza de Armas 444 Casilla 30 D, Santiago de Chile.

VIDA Y PENSAMIENTO. V. 1, No. 1 (Jan./June 1981)-. Periodical. Spanish. sa. $8.00. Seminario Biblico Latinoamericano, Departamento de Publicaciones, Apartado 901, 1000 San Jose Costa Rica.

Religion, Mythology, Rationalism—Theology

VIDYAJYOTI. V. 39- Jan. 1975-. Periodical. II. English. mo. $10.00. Catholic Press, PB 8, Ranchi 834001 Bihar India. **Ind/Abst** New Testam. Abstr. Index in last issue of volume - attached. *Clergy Monthly.*

VIE CONSACREE. Yearly V. 38, Jan./Feb. 1966-. Periodical. BE. French. bm. $6.92. Vie Consacree, rue de Bruxelles 61, B 5000 Namur Belgium. **Tel** 081/22.90.61. **Ed** Andre De Jaer, SJ. bk rev. **Circ** 6,500. Addressed to religious men and women, to help them fulfill their consecration by theoretical and practical papers. *Revue des Communautes Religieuses.*

VIE OBLATE. VFOAT Oblate Life. V. 33, No. 1- March 1974-. 0318-9392. CN. text in French and English. ty. $7.74. Vie Oblate Life, 175 Main Street, Ottawa Ontario K1S 1C3 Canada. **Tel** (613)237-0580. **DD** 255.76005. bk rev. **Circ** 500. (ctrl) Mostly on oblate of Mary Immaculate (Order): founder, spirituality of the order, history of the order and their works in all parts of the world. *Etudes Oblates, 0318-9384.*

VIGILIA. Vol. 1- (No. 1-). Periodical. Spanish. ir. $20.00. Editorial Vaitea Teatinos, 371 Santiago de Chile, Casilla 6140-Correo 22, Santiago Chile. **LC** BX1793.

VIGILIA. 0042-6024. Periodical. HU. Hungarian. mo. Akademiai Kiado, POB 24, 1363 Budapest Hungary. **LC** BX806.H8.

VINCENTIAN HERITAGE. Vol. 1 (1980)-. 0277-2205. Periodical. US. English. an. $15.00. St Joseph's Provincial House, 333 South Seton Avenue, Emmitsburg MD 21727. **Tel** (301)447-3121. **Ed** John W Carven. **LC** BX3770.A1. **DD** 255.77005. **Circ** 1,200. History of communities founded by St. Vincent de Paul, both worldwide and American.

VITA SOCIALE. 0042-7365. Periodical. IT. Italian. bm. Edizioni Vita Sociale, Vita Sociale Piazza S Domenico, 1 Pistoia Italy.

VOX BENEDICTINA. Vol. 1, No. 1 (Jan. 1984)-. 0715-8726. Periodical. CN. English. qt. 25.00. 409 Garrison Crescent, Saskatoon Saskatchewan S7H 2Z9 Canada. **Ed** Margot H King. **DD** 282.088042. bk rev. adv acc. **Circ** 385. Articles about and translations of the lives and writings of women whose lives have been informed by monastic spirituality.

THE WANDERER. V. 1-V. 37, No. 42, 1931-Oct. 19, 1967. Periodical. US. English. wk. $25.00. Eanderer Printing Company, 201 Ohio Street, St Paul MN 55107-9984. **Tel** (612)224-5733. **Ed** A J Matt Jr. bk rev. adv acc. **Circ** 36,500. Publishes news, reviews, and commentary on history, philosophy, theology, politics, religions, and other topics as they affect the Roman Catholic.

WESTERN CATHOLIC REPORTER. V. 1- Sept. 9, 1965-. 0512-5235. CN. English. wk. 18. Western Catholic Reporter, 10562 109th Street, Edmonton Alberta T5H 3B2 Canada. **Tel** (403)420-1330. **Ed** Shirley Pfister. bk rev. adv acc. **Circ** 37,000. A newspaper dealing with what's going on in the Catholic church everywhere, but principally in Alberta. *Western Catholic, 0384-7551.*

THE WYOMING CATHOLIC REGISTER. 0746-5580. Periodical. US. English. wk. $7.50. Business Office, Box 1308, Cheyenne WO 82001.

ZA RIDNU CERKVU. (ZA RIDNU TSERKVU). VFOAT Bulletin Za Ridnu Cerkvu. Vol. 1- July 1966-. 0318-1642. Periodical. CN. Ukrainian. $3.00. Bulletin Za Ridnu Cerkvu, PO Box 874 Terminal A, Toronto Ontario M5W 1G3 Canada. **DD** 282.71.

ZEITSCHRIFT FUR DIE NEUTESTAMENTLICHE WISSENSCHAFT UND DIE KUNDE DER ALTEREN KIRCHE. BEIHEFTE. No. 1-. Monographic Series. German. ir. Walter de Gruyter Inc, 200 Sawmill River Road, Hawthorne NY 10532. **Tel** (914)747-0110.

ZEITSCHRIFT FUR KATHOLISCHE THEOLOGIE. Vol. 1-. 0044-2895. Periodical. AU. German. qt. 68.00. Verlag Herder Wollzeile, 33 Postfach 248, A-1011 Wien Austria. **Ind/Abst** Old Testam. Abstr., New Testam. Abstr. **LC** BX803. **DD** 230.205. (cum index).

ZUPNI VJESNIK NASE GOSPE KRALJICE HRVATA, TORONTO, HRVATSKIH MUCENIKA, MISSISSAUGA. VFOAT Zupski Vjesnik. No. 33 (13 Edition 1978)-. 0820-6449. Periodical. CN. Serbo-Croatian(R) (Croatian). wk. Free. Zupni Vjesnik, 7 Awde Street, Toronto Ontario M6H 1K8 Canada. **Tel** (416)536-3669. **Ed** Josip D Gjuran. **DD** 282.05. adv acc. **Circ** 2,000. (ctrl). Journal of Catholic religion in Canada. *Zupski Vjesnik Nase Gospe Kraljice Hrvata, Toronto, Hrvatskih Mucenika, 0820-6430.*

THEOLOGY

14TH CENTURY ENGLISH MYSTICS NEWSLETTER. VFOAT Fourteenth Century English Mystics Newsletter. Vol. 1, No. 3 (Sept. 1975)-. 0737-5840. Periodical. US. English. qt. $10.00. University of Iowa, Publications Order Department GSB, Iowa City IA 52242. **Tel** (319)353-4171. **Ed** Valerie Lagorio and Ritamary Bradley. **Ind/Abst** MLA Int. Bibliogr. Books Artic. Mod. Lang. Lit. **LC** BV5077.G7. **DD** 248.220942. bk rev. adv acc. **Circ** 500. A scholarly and informative international journal devoted to the study of medieval English and continental mystics. *Newsletter, Fourteenth-Century English Mystics.*

ABBA. (ABBA, A JOURNAL OF PRAYER). V. 1- Easter 1976-. 0361-686X. Periodical. US. English. ir. $8.00. Eutychus Peterson, PO Box 8516, Austin TX 78712. **LC** BV210.2. **DD** 248.305.

ACCENT/REVIEWS. VFOAT Accent. VAT Accent Reviews. 1-. 0277-9102. Periodical. US. English. bm. $25.00. Accent/Reviews, PO Box 4463, Washington DC 20017. **Tel** (202)635-5916. **Ed** William E Hartgen Jr. bk rev. adv acc. **Circ** 6,300. Reviews and resources for local church ministry cross-cultural and cross-confessional.

ACTA THEOLOGICA DANICA. V. 1- 1958-. 0065-1672. Monographic Series. NE. Latin. ir. E J Brill, POB 9000, 2300 Pa Leiden The Netherlands. **Tel** 01 63 87 68. **Ed** Edward Nielsen. **Circ** 1,000. A series of theological dissertations, dealing with bible of religion, philosophy, and church history or dogmatic issues.

ACTION. (L'ACTION). V. 1, No. 8- Dec. 1979-. 0227-2040. Periodical. CN. French. $1.00 Per No. without Supplement, $2.50 Per No. with Supplement. Centre Unev l'Action, CP 97, Limoilou Quebec G1N 2N9 Canada. **DD** 261.8309714. *Action Sociale Catholique, 0707-8005.*

ACTION INFORMATION. VFOAT Alban Institute Action Information. V. 1- 1975-. Periodical. US. English. ir. $150.00. Alban Institute, Mt St Alban, Washington DC 20016. **Tel** (202)244-7320. **Ed** Celia Allison Hahn. bk rev. **Circ** 7,000. (ctrl). Practical aid to ministers and lay leaders to help dynamics of congregational life.

ACTIVITY REPORT - KOREA THEOLOGICAL STUDY INSTITUTE. Main/Corp Hanguk Sinhak Yonguso. VFOAT Report of the Activities. 1973/75-. English. ir. Korea Theological Study Institute, Room 201 Hyangrin Building 164-11 2KA Ulchi-ro Chung-ku, Seoul Korea. **LC** BR1320. **DD** 230.05.

ADULT LIFE AND WORK LESSON ANNUAL. 0732-3573. US. English. an. Editor/ Sunday School Board, 127 Ninth Avenue North, Nashville TN 37234. **LC** BX6225. **DD** 230.61. *Life and Work Lesson Annual.*

THE ADVENTURER CEASED. V. 1-2 (No. 1-140) Nov. 7, 1752-Mar. 9, 1754. 0001-8821. Periodical. US. English. ir. United Society for Propagation of the Gospel, 15 Tufton Street, London SW1 England.

AFFIRMATIONS. V. 1- Jan. 1974-. 0162-8038. Periodical. US. English. mo. Affirmations, Women's Theological Coalition, 210 Herrick Road, Newton Centre MA 02159. *Sisterhood.*

AFRICA. May/June 1967-. 0706-8581. Periodical. CN. French. bm. $2.00. Soeurs Missionnaires de Notre-Dame d'Afrique, 34 rue Fraser, Levis Quebec G6V 3R7 Canada. **DD** 266.26. *Soeurs Blanches, 0706-8573.*

AFRICA INLAND MISSION, CANADA. (AFRICA INLAND MISSION (CANADA) : LETTER). 0824-3166. Periodical. CN. English. bm. Free. Africa Inland Mission (Canada). **DD** 266.0096.

AFRICA NOW (CEDAR GROVE, N.J.). (AFRICA NOW). -No. 117 (Nov/Dec 1981). 0044-6513. Periodical. US. English. bm. Sudan Interior Mission, Cedar Grove NJ 07009. **LC** BV3500. **DD** 266.023096.

AFRICA PULSE CEASED. VFOAT Pulse. 0739-0556. Periodical. US. English. sa. $25.00. Evangelical Missions, Information Service, 25 West 560 Geneva Road, Box 794, Wheaton IL 60189.

ALASKA MISSION OUTREACH. VFOAT Outreach. Vol., No. 1 (Fall 1979)-. Periodical. US. English. qt. 1134 South 8th Street, Minneapolis MN 55404. *Norsk Ungdom.*

ALERTE. V. 1, No. 6- Jan. 1976-. 0383-896X. Periodical. CN. French. mo. $5. Canada, $8. Others. Publications Alberte Envr, 25 Avenue Royale, Ste-Petronille Quebec G0A 4C0 Canada. **DD** 248.05. *Alerte au Quebec, 0319-6984.*

ALMANACH FUR LITERATUR UND THEOLOGIE. See Yearbooks, Almanacs, Directories.

ALPEC. ANIMATION ET LITURGIE PAR L'EXPRESSION ET LA COMMUNICATION. (ALPEC : ANIMATION ET LITURGIE PAR L'EXPRESSION ET LA COMMUNICATION). VFOAT ALPEC : Animation et Liturgie Par l'Expression et la Communication. Vol. 1, No. 1 (Nov. 1980)-. 0228-5320. Periodical. CN. French. ty. Free to Members. ALPEC, CP 10.000, Ste-Foy Quebec G1V 4C6 Canada. **DD** 264.02005.

AMERICAN REVIEW OF EASTERN ORTHODOXY CEASED. VFOAT AREO. V. 1-26, No. 6. 0003-0791. Periodical. US. English. bm. $5.50. 20204 Gulf Boulevard, Indian Shores FL 33535. *AREO Quarterly.*

AMERICAN UNIVERSITY STUDIES. SERIES VII, THEOLOGY AND RELIGION. VFOAT Theology and Religion. 0740-0446. Monographic Series. US. English. ir. Peter Lang Publishing Inc, 34 East 39th Street, New York NY 10016. **LC** UNC.

AMICI DEL BURUNDI. Periodical. Italian. ir. Via S Gimignano 19, Milano 20146 Italy. **LC** BV3625.B8.

AMIS DE JESUS. (LES AMIS DE JESUS). No. 1, (Dec. 1980)-. 0823-6178. Periodical. CN. French. ir. Free. Association des Amis de Jesus, C P 5185, Beauport Quebec G1E 6B5 Canada. **DD** 248.8205. (ctrl).

ANALES DE LA FACULTAD PONTIFICIA DE TEOLOGIA. See Yearbooks, Almanacs, Directories.

ANALES VALENTINOS. See Yearbooks, Almanacs, Directories.

ANARSIS BLUE. V.1, No. 1 (Aug./Sept. 1982)-. 0826-4333. Periodical. CN. English. bm. Free. Liturgical Arts Guild, 7 Fraser Crescent, Saskatoon Saskatchewan S7H 3G9 Canada. **DD** 264.005. (ctrl).

ANDREWS UNIVERSITY SEMINARY STUDIES. Main/Corp Andrews University. Seventh-Day Adventist Theological Seminary. V. 1- 1963-. 0003-2980. Periodical. US. English. ty. $15.00. Andrews University, Seminary Studies, Berrien Springs MI 49104. **Tel** (616) 471-6023. **Ed** Kenneth Strand. **Ind/Abst** Old Testam. Abstr., Elenchus Bibliogr. Bibicus, Int. Bibliogr. Hist. Relig., Int. Zeitschriftenschan Bibelwissenschaft Grenzgeb., New Testam. Abstr., Relig. Theol. Abstr., Relig. Index One, Period., Index Relig. Period. bk rev. **Circ** 1,000. (ctrl). Biblical linguistics, theology, archeology, geography, history of religions, church, ancient world: textual criticism, exegesis, philosophy of religion, ethics, missiology, ministry, and religious education.

ANGELOS. Main/Corp Atlantic School of Theology. VFOAT Angelos : A Bulletin of Atlantic School of Theology. Vol. 1, No. 1 (Summer 1981)-. 0710-0612. Periodical. CN. English. ir. $5.00. Angelos, c/o Atlantic School of Theology, 640 Francklyn Street, Halifax Nova Scotia B3H 3B5 Canada. **DD** 207.71622.

ANGLICAN THEOLOGICAL REVIEW. V. 1- May 1918-. 0003-3286. Periodical. US. English. $35.00. Anglican Theological Review, 600 Haven Street, Evanston IL 60201. **Ind/Abst** Old Testam. Abstr., Hist. Abstr., Ref. Source, Relig. Index One, Period., Int. Bibliogr. Zeitschriftenliteratur aller Gebieten Wissens, Relig. Theol. Abstr., New Testam. Abstr., Am. Hist. Life, Recent Publ. Artic., Hist. Abstr., Part A, Mod. Hist. Abstr., Hist. Abstr., Part B, Twent. Century Abstr. **LC** BR1. (cum index). adv acc. **Circ** 2,000. Available on microfilm from University Microfilms International. General theological journal which seeks to promote discussion of basic contemporary issues to increase understanding of the role of the church in a society.

ANGLICAN THEOLOGICAL REVIEW. SUPPLEMENTARY SERIES. Began with No. 1 (July 1973). 0097-4951. Periodical. US. English. Anglican Theological Review, 600 Haven Street, Evanston IL 60201. **DD** 230.305.

Religion, Mythology, Rationalism—Theology

L'ANNEE CANONIQUE; RECUEIL D'ETUDES ET D'INFORMATIONS. V. 1- 1952-. 0570-1953. FR. French (English, Italian and Spanish). an. Office General du Liure, 14 Bis rue Jean Ferrandi, 75006 Paris France.

ANNEE SAINTE AVEC PAUL VI. 1- Feb. 1974-. 0319-7166. Periodical. CN. French. bm. 60 Per No. Cahiers d'Animation Spirituelle, 850 Sault St-Louis, La Prairie Quebec J5R 1E1 Canada. **DD** 242.05.

ANNUAL CONFERENCE - NATIONAL ASSOCIATION OF CHURCH BUSINESS ADMINISTRATORS. CONFERENCE. (ANNUAL CONFERENCE). **Main/Conf** National Association of Church Business Administrators. 0730-1561. US. English. an. National Association of Church Business Administrators, PO Box 7181, Kansas City MO 64113. **LC** BV652.A1. **DD** 254.005. *Proceedings of the . . . Annual Conference of the National Association of Church Business Administrators, 0730-1553.*

ANNUAL REPORT - HAWAIIAN MISSION CHILDREN'S SOCIETY. **Main/Corp** Hawaiian Mission Children's Society. 86th (1938)-. US. English. an. 553 South King Street, Honolulu HI 96813. **LC** BV3680.H2. *Annual Report of the Hawaiian Mission Children's Society . . . .*

ANNUAL REPORT - WORLD ALLIANCE OF YOUNG MEN'S CHRISTIAN ASSOCIATIONS. **Main/Corp** World Alliance of YMCAS. English. ir. World Alliance of Young Men's Christian Associations, 37. Quai Wilson, 1201 Geneva Switzerland. **LC** BV1032. **DD** 267.3305.

ARBEITEN ZUR GESCHICHTE DES PIETISMUS. Vol. 1- 1967-. Monographic Series. GW. German. ir. Vandenhoeck & Ruprecht, Postfach 3753, Theaterstr 13, D 3400 Goettingen West Germany. **Tel** (0551)65061. adv acc.

ARCHIVES D'HISTOIRE DOCTRINALE ET LITTERAIRE DU MOYEN AGE. *See* Genealogy and Heraldry - Archives.

ARCHIVO TEOLOGICO GRANADINO. *See* Genealogy and Heraldry - Archives.

ARSBOK FOR KRISTEN HUMANISM. *See* Yearbooks, Almanacs, Directories.

THE ASBURY SEMINARIAN. V. 1- Spring 1946-. 0004-4253. Periodical. US. English. sa. $7.00. Asbury Theological Seminary, Wilmore KY 40390. **Tel** (606)858-3581. **Ind/Abst** Christ. Period. Index. **LC** BX8001. **DD** 287.05. bk rev. **Circ** 1,000. Material of interest because of its intrinsic value in the ongoing discussion of theological issues.

ASIA PULSE *CEASED.* VFOAT Pulse. 0739-0548. Periodical. US. English. sa. $25.00. Evangelical Missions Information Service, Box 794, Wheaton IL 60189.

ASIA THEOLOGICAL NEWS. V. 1- June 1975-. Periodical. CN. English. qt. $5.00. Asia Theological Association, PO Box 1477, Taichung Roc 400 Taiwan. **Ed** Bong Rin Ro. bk rev. adv acc. **Circ** 2,000. (ctrl). Intended to upgrade the quality of evangelical Christian education in Asia and to build up church leaders.

ASSEMBLIES OF GOD HOME MISSIONS. VFOAT Home Missions. 0162-2234. Periodical. US. English. bm. Gospel Publishing House, 1445 Boonville, Springfield MO 65802. **Tel** (417)862-2781.

ASSOCIATION DE MESSES DES MISSIONNAIRES DES SAINTS-APOTRES. (L'ASSOCIATION DE MESSES DES MISSIONNAIRES DES SAINTS-APOTRES). No. 1-. 0820-7836. Periodical. CN. French. ir. Free. Fondation Pere Eusebe Menard, 65 Ouest rue de Castelnau, Montreal Quebec H2R 2W3 Canada. **DD** 264.02036. *Missionnaires des Saints-Apotres (Bulletin), 0820-7828.*

ATLA BIBLIOGRAPHY SERIES. *See* Bibliographies.

ATLA MONOGRAPH SERIES. *See* Library and Information Science.

AU COEUR DE L'AFRIQUE. V. 9- Jan. 1969-. Periodical. French. bm. $16.50. Conference des Ordinaires du, BP 1390, Bujumbura Burndi. **LC** BX1682.R8. **DD** 282.6757. *Theologie et Pastorale au Rwanda et au Burundi.*

AUGUSTINIANUM. Vol. 1- Apr. 1961-. 0004-8011. Periodical. IT. Multilingual (English, French, German, Italian, Latin, and Spanish). ty. 40,000. Curia Gen Agostiniana, Via S Uffizio 25, 00193 Roma Italy. **Tel** 654-2040. **Ind/Abst** MLA Int. Bibliogr. Books Artic. Mod. Lang. Lit., Old Testam. Abstr., New Testam. Abstr. bk rev. **Circ** 1,000. Research in the area of the literature of Christian antiquity and the thought of the fathers of the Church.

AUPRES DU CHRIST, PAIN ROMPU. 1-. 0823-5449. Periodical. CN. French. mo. Congregation du T S Sacrement, 4450 Rue St-Hubert, Montreal Quebec H2J 2W9 Canada. **DD** 234.16305.

AUSTRALASIAN CATHOLIC RECORD. (THE AUSTRALASIAN CATHOLIC RECORD). V. 1- Jan. 1924-. Periodical. AT. English. qt. $14.75. Saint Patricks College, Manly New South Wales 2095 Australia. **Tel** (02)798 6657. **Ind/Abst** New Testam. Abstr. Index in last issue of volume - attached. (cum index). bk rev. adv acc. **Circ** 2,500. Contains Catholic theology and Australian church history.

BANGALORE THEOLOGICAL FORUM. V. 1- Jan. 1967-. 0253-9365. Periodical. II. English. ty. $10.00. United Theological College, 17 Millers Road, Bangalore 560046 Karnataka India. **Tel** 55844. **Ind/Abst** New Testam. Abstr., Relig. Index One, Period.

THE BANNER OF TRUTH. No. 1- Sept. 1955-. 0408-4748. Periodical. UK. English. mo. $11.00. Banner of Truth-Pennsylvania, PO Box 621, Carlisle PA 17013. **Tel** (717)249-5747. **Ed** Iain Murray. bk rev. **Circ** 5,000. (ctrl). A periodical with articles dealing with doctrinal and practical issues related to Christian life. Also book reviews and items of correspondence.

BAOBAB. 1967-. 0381-9795. Periodical. CN. French. ir. $3. Missionnaires Comboniens, 7025 Boul Comboni, Brossard Quebec J4Y 1E9 Canada. **DD** 266.205.

BASLER UND BERNER STUDIEN ZUR HISTORISCHEN UND SYSTEMATISCHEN THEOLOGIE. V. 23-. Monographic Series. SZ. German. ir. Peter Lang, Jupiterstrasse 15, PO Box 277, CH-3000 Bern 15 Switzerland. *Basler Studien zur Historischen und Systematischen Theologie.*

BEAR & COMPANY. VFOAT Bear and Company. Began in 1981. 0275-6587. Periodical. US. English. mo. $15.00 Domestic, $17.00 Foreign. Bear & Company Inc, 6 Vista Grande Court, Santa Fe NM 87501.

BEGINNER TEACHER. 0190-3950. Periodical. S. English. qt. Gospel Publishing House, 1445 Boonville Avenue, Springfield MO 65802.

BEITRAGE ZUR ALTBAYERISCHEN KIRCHENGESCHICHTE. VFOAT Deutingers Beitrage. V. 1- 1850-. Periodical. German. ir. **LC** BR857.B37.

BEITRAGE ZUR GESCHICHTE DER PHILOSOPHIE UND THEOLOGIE DES MITTELALTERS. *See* Philosophy.

BEITRAGE ZUR HISTORISCHEN THEOLOGIE. 1- 1929-. Monographic Series. GW. German. ir. JCB Mohr/Paul Siebeck, Postfach 2040, 7400 Tuebingen West Germany.

BEITRAGE ZUR OKUMENISCHEN THEOLOGIE. V. 1-. 0067-5172. Monographic Series. GW. German. ir. Ferdinand Schoeningh Verlag, Postfach 2540, Juehenplatz Rathaus, D4790 Paderborn West Germany.

BELL (SAINT PAUL, MINN.) *CEASED.* (THE BELL). VFOAT Bell of Northwestern Lutheran Theological Seminary. Began with V. 1, No. 1, (Jan. Ed. 1975). Ceased with V. 6, No. 2 (May Ed. 1980). Periodical. US. English. qt.

BIBEL UND LITURGIE. *See* Religion, Mythology, Rationalism - Bible.

THE BIBLICAL EVANGELIST. 1- 1966-. 0740-7998. Periodical. US. English. bw. Biblical Evangelism, PO Box 1513, Murfreesboro TN 37133-1515. **Tel** (615)890-3495. **Ed** Robert L Sumner. bk rev. adv acc. **Circ** 18,200. (ctrl). Promoting Biblical Christianity through Bible studies, sermons, music, trends in religion, family life, book reviews and evagelism from a fundamentalist.

BIBLICAL MISSIONS. 1935. 0006-0909. Periodical. US. English. bm. Independent Board for Presbyterian Foreign Missions, 246 Walnut Lane, Philadelphia PA 19144. **Ed** Earle R White. (ctrl). Presentation of foreign missions and work of Independent Board for Presbyterian Foreign Missions.

BIBLICUM. *See* Religion, Mythology, Rationalism - Bible.

BIBLIOTHECA FRANCISCANA SCHOLASTICA MEDII AEVI. 1- 1903-. Periodical. ir. International College of St Bonaventure, 00046 Grottaferrata Rome Italy. **Tel** (06)945.82.48. **Ed** Jacques Guy Bougerol. **Circ** 900. (ctrl). Edition of unpublished texts of Franciscan medieval masters; theological or philosophical.

BIBLIOTHECA SACRA. V. 33- (No. 129-). 0006-1921. Periodical. US. English. qt. $8.00. Dallas Theological Seminary, 3909 Swiss Avenue, Dallas TX 75204. **Tel** (214)824-3094. **Ed** Roy B Zuck. **Ind/Abst** Relig. Index One, Period., Christ. Period. Index. bk rev. **Circ** 8,500. (ctrl). Available on microfilm. A theological journal that seeks to provide continuing biblical and theological instruction to biblical scholars, alumni, pastors, teachers, and serious lay Bible students. *Bibliotheca Sacra and Theological Eclectic, Christian Faith and Life.*

BIBLISCH-THEOLOGISCHE STUDIEN. *See* Religion, Mythology, Rationalism - Bible.

BIJDRAGEN TIJDSCHRIFT VOOR FILOSOFIE EN THEOLOGIE. *See* Philosophy.

BOGOSLOVNI VESTNIK. Began in 1920. 0006-5722. Periodical. Serbo-Croatian -R (Latin, with some summaries in French or German). ir. **LC** BR9.S5.

BREAD OF LIFE. (THE BREAD OF LIFE). Vol. 1, No. 1 (Nov. 1977)-. 0821-168X. Periodical. CN. English. bm. 7.00. Bread of Life, 437 Wilson Street East, Ancaster Ontario L9G 3K4 Canada. **DD** 269405.

BRESIL-MALI-SENEGAL. (BRESIL, MALI, SENEGAL). Vol. 9, No 1 (Autumn 1976)-. 0228-4707. Periodical. CN. French. qt. Centre Cor Jesu, Mont-Sacre-Coeur, CP 32, Granby Quebec J2G 8E3 Canada. **DD** 266.281. *Bresil, Senegal, 0227-4736.*

BRETHREN LIFE AND THOUGHT. V. 1- Autumn 1955-. 0006-9663. Periodical. US. English. qt. $12.00. Business and Subscription Office, PO Box 833J, Wheaton IL 60189-0833. **Tel** (312)851-0709. **Ed** Warren S Kissinger. **Ind/Abst** Book Rev. Mon., Relig. Theol. Abstr., Relig. Index One, Period. **LC** BX7801. bk rev. **Circ** 850. Available on microfilm from University Microfilms. Religious/theological issues relating to "Peace" churches. Historical as well as current happenings. Special emphasis on Church of the Brethren and Bethany Theological Seminary reporting.

THE BRIDE OF CHRIST. 1977. 0197-3045. Periodical. US. English. qt. $8.00. Lutheran Liturgical Renewal, Box 2931, Lehigh Valley PA 18001. **Tel** (215)868-5229. **Ed** Aubrey Boucher. **LC** BX8067.A1. **DD** 264.041. bk rev. adv acc. **Circ** 1,000. Liturgy, liturgiology, theology-primarily, but not exclusively Lutheran. Subscription includes membership in Lutheran Liturgical Renewal, Inc.

BRIERCREST ECHO. Vol. 41, No. 2 (Sept. 1982)-. 0821-5839. Periodical. CN. English. qt. Briercrest Bible College, Caronport Saskatchewan S0H 0S0 Canada. **Tel** (306)756-2321. **Ed** Paul E Magnus. **DD** 207.71244. **Circ** 21,000. (ctrl). A thematic topical approach to current issues within the evangelical Christian world. Primarily deals with biblical and theological topics. *Echo (Caronport, Sask.), 0824-9288.*

B.T.I. NEWSLETTER. **Main/Corp** Boston Theological Institute. **VAT** Boston Theological Institute Newsletter. V. 1- Oct. 1968-. 0145-7934. Periodical. US. English. wk. Free. Boston Theological Institute, 210 Herrick Road, Newton Centre MA 02159.

BULLETIN DE L'ENTRAIDE MISSIONNAIRE. **Main/Corp** Entraide Missionnaire, Inc. V. 1- 1954-. 0382-9472. Periodical. CN. French. qt. $4.65. Bulletin de l'Entraidemission, 15 Quest de Castelnau, Montreal Quebec H1R 2W3 Canada. **Tel** (514)270-6089. bk rev. **Circ** 600. Topics include missionary work, politics, health, etc. Also, includes book reviews.

BULLETIN DE THEOLOGIE AFRICAINE. (BULLETIN DE THEOLOGIE AFRICAINE : ORGANE DE L'ASSOCIATION OECUMENIQUE DES THEOLOGIENS AFRICAINS). 0253-9969. Periodical. French (English or Portuguese). ir. Bulletin de Theologie Africaine, c/o

Religion, Mythology, Rationalism—Theology

Secretary, BP BP 823, Kinshasa XI Republique de Zaire. Ind/Abst Relig. Index One, Period.

BULLETIN FROM THE HILL. Vol. 54, No. 1 (Dec. 1981)-. 8755-450X. Periodical. US. English. ty. 1100 South Goodman Street, Rochester NY 14620. LC BV4070.C66. DD 207.74789. *Bulletin - Colgate-Rochester Divinity School, Bexley Hall, Crozer Theological Seminary.*

THE BULLETIN - MORAVIAN THEOLOGICAL SEMINARY. Main/Corp Moravian Theological Seminary. 0540-8644. US. English. ir. Moravian Theological Seminary, Bethlehem PA 18018. Tel (215)865-0741. Ind/Abst Relig. Index One, Period.

BULLETIN - NORTHWESTERN SEMINARY. (NORTHWESTERN SEMINARY BULLETIN). Main/Corp Northwestern Lutheran Theological Seminary, St. Paul. V. 1- 1925-. 0362-0573. Periodical. US. English. sa. Free upon request. Northwestern Lutheran Theological Seminary, c/o Rev John J Zeigler, 1501 Fulham Street, St Paul MN 55108. *Northwestern Lutheran (Minneapolis).*

BULLETIN OF THE GENERAL THEOLOGICAL LIBRARY. *See* Library and Information Science.

BULLETIN OZANAM. March 1983-. 0823-7883. Periodical. CN. French. bm. Free. Societe de Saint-Vincent de Paul Hull et Gatineau, 102 rue Eddy, Hull Quebec J8X 2W4 Canada. DD 267.24271422105. (ctrl).

BULLETIN SIGNALETIQUE. 527, HISTOIRE ET SCIENCES DES RELIGIONS. VFOAT Histoire et Sciences des Religions. Vol. 33, No. 1-. 0180-9296. French. qt. 295.00. 54M Boulevard Raspail, BP 140, 75260 Paris Cedex 06 France. Tel 544.38.49. LC Z7751, BR1.A1. DD 016.2. *Bulletin Signaletique. 527: Sciences Religieuses, 0007-5620.*

CA NEWSERVICE. VFOAT CA News Service. VAT Churches Alive Newservice. Periodical. US. English. qt. Churches Alive, PO Box 3800, San Bernardino CA 92413.

CAHIERS D'ANIMATION MISSIONNAIRE. V. 1, No. 1, (Aug./Sept. 1973)-. 0381-7652. Periodical. CN. French. qt. $5.00. Cahiers d'Animation Missionnaire, CP 220, Limoilou Quebec G1L 4V7 Canada. DD 266.205. *Messages, 0381-7628.*

CAHIERS D'ANIMATION SPIRITUELLE. No. 1 (Feb. 15, 1971)-. 0227-5988. Periodical. CN. French. qt. $5.00. Cahiers d'Animation Spirituelle, c/o Bureau Regional des Freres de l'Instruction Chretienne, 1293 Est Boulevard St-Jospeh, Montreal Quebec H2J 1L9 Canada. DD 260.5.

CAHIERS DE LA REVUE DE THEOLOGIE ET DE PHILOSOPHIE. 1-. Monographic Series. French. ir. Librarie Drox SA, 11 rue Massot, 1211 Geneva Switzerland. Ind/Abst Relig. Index One, Period. Circ 600. Religion philosophy.

CAHIERS DE RECHERCHES EN SCIENCES DE LA RELIGION. (LES CAHIERS DE RECHERCHES EN SCIENCES DE LA RELIGION). VFOAT Cahiers du C.R.S.R. Vol. 4 (1982)-. 0821-459X. Periodical. CN. French. an. Editions Bellarmin, 8100 Boul Saint-Laurent, Montreal Quebec H2P 2L9 Canada. Tel (514)387-2541. Ed Jean-Paul Rouleau. LC BT738. DD 200.5. Circ 1,000. *Cahiers du CRSR.*

CAHIERS D'ETUDES CATHARES. Yearly V. 1- 1949-. 0008-0063. Periodical. FR. French. qt. $15.96. Societe du Souvenir et Etudes, 23 Avenue President-Kennedy, 11100 Narbonne France. Tel 63/74 03 53.

CAHIERS DU TEMOIGNAGE CHRETIEN. VFOAT Temoignage Chretien. 1 (Nov. 1941)-28/29 (July 1944). Periodical. FR. French. wk. $77.16. ETC, 49 rue du fg Poissonniere, 75009 Paris France. Tel 246.37.50.

CALGARY Y F C FOCUS. Main/Corp Calgary Youth for Christ. Sept./Oct. 1970-. 0319-3829. Periodical. CN. English. ir. Calgary Youth for Christ, PO Box 6151/Station D, Calgary Alberta T2P 2C8 Canada. DD 269.

CANADIAN ECUMENICAL NEWS. VFOAT B.C. Ecumenical News. V. 5, No. 1- Feb. 1980-. 0227-8782. Periodical. CN. English. ir. $5. Canadian Ecumenical Action, 1811 West 16th Avenue, Vancouver British Columbia V6J 2M3 Canada. DD 262.0011. *Ecumenical News, 0227-8243.*

CAPUCHINS CANADIENS. (CAPUCHINS CANADIENS : BULLETIN DU CENTRE MISSIONNAIRE STE-THERESE). 0821-6355. Periodical. CN. French. ty. Centre Missionnaire Ste-Therese, 4387 Av Esplanade, Montreal Quebec H2W 1T3 Canada. DD 266.27105.

CENTERING. V. 1, No. 1 (June 1983)-. Periodical. US. English. ir. Center Ministry Laity, 210 Herrick Road, Newton Centre MA 02159. Tel 964-1100. Ed David Specht. adv acc. Circ 2,500. (ctrl). This publication is filled with articles by and for people who risk living their whole lives, work, recreation and relationship, as expression of their faith.

THE CHICAGO THEOLOGICAL SEMINARY REGISTER. V. 1- Mar. 1908-. 0739-5124. Periodical. US. English. ty. The Register, 5757 South University Avenue, Chicago IL 60637. Ind/Abst Relig. Index One, Period. LC BV4070. DD 207.773.

CHRIST TO THE WORLD. V. 1- 1955-. 0011-1465. Periodical. English. ir. 16.00. Christ to the World, Via di Propaganda 1-C, Rome 00187 Italy. Ed Basil Mary Arthadeva. Ind/Abst Cathol. Period. Lit. Index. Index in last issue of volume - attached. bk rev. Circ 5,000. Directives of the Pope on the appropriate experiences of mission and parish, and work problems of current doctrinal errors.

DIE CHRISTENLEHRE. V. 1, No. 1, (April 1948)-. 0009-5192. Periodical. SZ. German. mo. $13.46. Kunst & Wissen Erich Bieber, Dufourstrasse 51, CH-8008 Zurich Switzerland. Tel 01/69 44 20.

CHRISTIAN. V. 1- Easter 1973-. Periodical. UK. English. $9.00. Institute of Christian Studies, 7 Margaret Street, W1 London England. LC BR1. DD 205.

CHRISTIAN BOOKSELLER. Began in 1955. Ceased with V. 28, No. 9, Sept. 1982. 0009-5273. US. English. mo. $6.00. LC BV2369. DD 381.450705.

CHRISTIAN BRETHREN REVIEW : THE JOURNAL OF THE CHRISTIAN BRETHREN RESEARCH FELLOWSHIP. VFOAT Christian Brethren Review Journal. Nos. 31, 32 (Feb. 1982)-. 0306-7467. Periodical. UK. English. ir. 5.00. Paternoster Press Ltd, 3 Mount Radford Crescent, Exeter EX2 4J United Kingdom. LC BX8799. DD 289.9. *Journal of the Christian Brethren Research Fellowship.*

CHRISTIAN CENTURY (CHICAGO, ILL. : 1902). (THE CHRISTIAN CENTURY). Vol. 19, No. 1 (Jan. 2, 1902)-. 0009-5281. Periodical. US. English. wk. $12.00 Domestic, $13.00 Canada. Christian Century, 5616 West Cermak Road, Cicero IL 60650. Tel (312)427-5380. Ind/Abst Mag. Index, Pop. Mag. Rev., Annu. Bibliogr. Engl. Lang. Lit., Film Lit. Index, Book Rev. Index, Index Am. Period. Verse, Read. Guide Period. Lit., Media Rev. Dig., Relig. Index One, Period., Book Rev. Digest, Am. Hist. Life, Hist. Abstr., Guide Soc. Sci. Relig. Period. Lit., Hist. Abstr., Part A, Mod. Hist. Abstr., Hist. Abstr., Part B, Twent. Century Abstr. LC BR1. Available on microfilm and microfiche from University Microfilms International., Available on microfiche from Microcard Editions. *Christian Century of the Disciples of Christ, Christian Work (New York, N.Y. : 1914); Baptist; World Tomorrow, 0364-8583; New Christian.*

CHRISTIAN COMMUNICATIONS. V. 1- Dec. 1962-. 0009-5303. Periodical. CN. English. qt. $2.00. St Paul Society, 223 Main Street, Ottawa 1, Sherbrooke Quebec Canada. Also available in microfilm format.

CHRISTIAN CRUSADE. 0195-265X. Periodical. US. English. bm.

CHRISTIAN EDUCATION JOURNAL. Vol. 3, No. 2 (Jan. 1983)-. 0739-8913. Periodical. US. English. sa. $7.00. Scripture Press Ministries, PO Box 513, Glen Ellyn IL 60137. LC BV1460. DD 207. *Journal of Christian Education.*

CHRISTIAN EDUCATOR. V. 1- May 1973-. 0091-2867. Periodical. US. English. qt. $7.50. Christian Warriors for Christian Education(CWCE), Drawer C, Cape Canaveral FL 32920. LC BV1460. DD 207.73.

CHRISTIAN HI-TECH REVIEW. Vol. 1, No. 1 (March 1984)-. 0824-1511. Periodical. CN. English. bm. $1.00 Per No. Christian Hi-Tech Review, No 7, 1319 45th Avenue Northeast, Calgary Alberta T2E 2P3 Canada. DD 268.635.

THE CHRISTIAN HOME CEASED. V. 1-27. 0009-5370. Periodical. US. English. mo. $8.00. The Upper Room, 1908 Grand Avenue, PO Box 189, Nashville TN 37202. Tel (615)327-2700. Ed David I Bradley. LC BV4485. DD 249.05. bk rev. Circ 50,000. (ctrl). For concerned Christian families interested in improving their relationships with one another and growing in their knowledge of God. *Christian Home, 0009-5370; First Steps in Christian Nurture.*

THE CHRISTIAN MINISTRY. V. 1- Nov. 1969-. 0033-4138. Periodical. US. English. bm. The Christian Century, 5615 West Cermak Road, Cicero IL 60650. Tel (312)427-5380. Ind/Abst Relig. Index One, Period., Guide Soc. Sci. Relig. Period. Lit. LC BV4000. DD 250.5. *Pulpit, 0362-4617.*

CHRISTIAN MISSIONS IN MANY LANDS CEASED. July/Aug. 1972-July/Aug. 1980. 0316-2990. Periodical. CN. English. *Fields Canadian Ed., 0316-0025.*

CHRISTIAN MISSIONS IN MANY LANDS. VFOAT Missions. 0744-4052. Periodical. US. English. mo. Christian Missions in Many Lands Inc, PO Box 13, Spring Lake NJ 07762. DD 266.005. *Christian Missions in Many Lands. Canadian Ed., 0316-2990.*

CHRISTIAN NEWS FROM ISRAEL. VFOAT Nouvelles Chretiennes d'Israel. V. 1- Aug. 1949-. 0009-5532. Periodical. IS. English (text of V. 6 (1955) also in French). qt. $4.00. POB 11627, 23 Shomo Hameleh, Jerusalem Israel. Ind/Abst Old Testam. Abstr., New Testam. Abstr. LC BR1110. (cum index).

CHRISTIAN ORDER. Began with Jan. 1960 issue. 0009-5559. Periodical. UK. English. mo. $3.00. Christian Order of England, 65 Belgrave Road, London SW1 England. LC BT738.

CHRISTIAN SCHOLAR'S REVIEW. V. 1-. 0017-2251. Periodical. US. English. qt. $15.00. Christian Scholars Review, 955 la Paz Road, Santa Barbara CA 93108. Tel (616)957-6112. Ind/Abst Am. Hist. Life, Hist. Abstr., Part A, Mod. Hist. Abstr., Hist. Abst., Part B, Twent. Century Abstr., Abstr. Engl. Stud., MLA Int. Bibliogr. Books Artic. Mod. Lang. Lit., Old Testam. Abstr., Relig. Index One, Period., Guide Soc. Sci. Relig. Period. Lit., Christ. Period. Index, Abstr. Engl. Stud., Hist. Abstr., Years Work Eng. Stud. LC BR1. DD 230.05. bk rev. adv acc. Circ 4,200. *Gordon Review, 0436-1644.*

CHRISTIAN THEOLOGICAL SEMINARY BULLETIN. (BULLETIN - CHRISTIAN THEOLOGICAL SEMINARY). V. 1- 1960-. 0529-472X. Periodical. US. English. bm. Christian Theological Seminary, 1000 West 42nd Street, Indianapolis IN 46208.

CHRISTIAN WRITER (LAKELAND, FLA.). (THE CHRISTIAN WRITER). Began Jan. 1982?. 0734-6824. Periodical. US. English. mo. $18.00. Christian Writer, PO Box 5650, Lakeland FL 33807. Tel (813)644-3548. Ed Thomas A Noton. LC BR44. DD 808.0662. bk rev. adv acc. Circ 15,000. Education and encouragement in the craft of writing as it applies to the Christian life.

CHRISTIANITY TODAY. V. 1- Oct. 15, 1956-. 0009-5753. Periodical. US. English. ir. $19.50. Christianity Today, PO Box 1915, Marion OH 43305. Tel (312)260-6200. Ed Terry Muck. Ind/Abst Mag. Index, Pop. Mag. Rev., New Testam. Abstr., Read. Guide Period. Lit., Christ. Period. Index, Relig. Index One, Period., Energy Inf. Abstr., Environ. Abstr., Guide Soc. Sci. Relig. Period. Lit., Book Rev. Digest. LC BR1. DD 230.05. bk rev. adv acc. Circ 180,000. News and information about issues facing evangelical Christians.

CHRISTIANITY TODAY. V. 1- Oct. 15, 1956-. Periodical. US. English. sm. $15.48. Christianity Today, PO Box 3800, Greenwich CT 06830. Ind/Abst Read. Guide Period. Lit., Christ. Period. Index, Relig. Index One, Period.

CHRISTIANS AGAINST TERRORISM. March 1974-. 0317-0772. Periodical. CN. English. Christians Against Terrorism, PO Box 332, Rexdale Ontario M9W 5L3 Canada. DD 261.87.

CHRISTIANS, JEWS TODAY. VFOAT Chretiens, Juifs Aujourd'hui. VAT Chretiens, Juifs Auhourd'Hui (Edition Anglaise). V. 6, No. 2- Oct. 1979-. 0225-5367. Periodical. CN. English. ir. League for Human Rights of Bnai Brith, Suite 200/7881

Decarie Boulevard, Montreal Quebec H4P 2H2 Canada. **DD** 296.3872. *Christians and Jews Today.*

CHRISTUS. V. 1- (No. 1-). 0009-5834. Periodical. FR. French. qt. $16.63. Assas Editions, 14 rue d Assas, 75006 Paris France. **Tel** 45 48 52 51. **Ed** Bernard Merdilous. adv acc. **Circ** 5,000. Spirituality and action according to the Jesuits.

CHRISTUS (MEXICO CITY, MEXICO). (CHRISTUS). Periodical. MX. Spanish. mo. $35.30. R P Xavier Garibay SJ, Auguste Redin No 355, Mexico 19 DF Mexico. **LC** BR7. **DD** 230.2.

CHUIL HAKKYO KYOSA UI POT. **VFOAT** Sunday School Teacher. Periodical. KO. Korean. mo. 7,700. Hanguk Kidokkyo Kyoyuk, Yonguwon 35-14 Tongja-dong, Yongsan-ku Seoul Korea. **LC** BV1500.

CHURCH ADVOCATE (FINDLAY, OHIO). (THE CHURCH ADVOCATE). 1835. 0009-630X. Periodical. US. English. mo. $8.15. Churches of God Publications, PO Box 926, Findlay OH 45839. **Tel** (419)424-1961. **Ed** Linda M Draper. bk rev. **Circ** 7,800. A denominational publication intended to encourage and inform people to live as the Church.

CHURCH AND SOCIETY. V. 60, No. 3- Jan./Feb. 1970-. 0037-7805. Periodical. US. English. bm. $7.50. United Presbyterian Church-USA, 475 Riverside Drive/Room 1244, New York NY 10115. **Tel** (212)870-2040. **Ed** Gaspar Langella. **Ind/Abst** Relig. Index One, Period. **Circ** 3,000. (ctrl). A Presbyterian publication that provides a forum for the church on subjects of social concerns for Christians: reflective comment, models and resources for individuals and groups. *Social Progress.*

CHURCH DIVINITY. **Series/Titl** Church Divinity Monograph Series. 1981-. 0737-4690. US. English. an. $10.00. Graduate Theological Foundation, PO Box 661, Notre Dame IN 46556. **Tel** (219)848-7920. **Ed** John H Morgan. **Circ** 250. Essays in theology by doctral students.

CHURCH TRAINING. 0162-4601. Periodical. US. English. $10.50. Materials Services Department, 127 Ninth Avenue North, Nashville TN 37234. **Tel** (615)251-2843. **Ed** Richard B Sims. **Circ** 30,000. Publication for all workers with the church training program of local churches. Contains both doctrinal and practical articles to train church members, new Christians and church leaders.

THE CHURCHMAN. V. 23- Jan. 5, 1867-. 0009-6628. Periodical. US. English. $10.00. The Churchman, 1074 23rd Avenue North, St Petersburg FL 33713. **Tel** (813)894-0097. **Ed** Edna Ruth Johnson. **Ind/Abst** Am. Hist. Life, Hist. Abstr., Part A, Mod. Hist. Abstr., Hist. Abst., Part B, Twent. Century Abstr. **LC** BX5800. bk rev. **Circ** 10,000. (ctrl). Available on microfilm from American Theological Library Association, Board of Microtext, Princeton, NJ. An independent journal of religious humanism, edited in the conviction that religious journalism must provide a free exchange of ideas. *Connecticut Churchman, American Churchman; Churchman Magazine.*

CHURCHMAN. V. 1-14, Oct. 1879-Sept. 1886. 0009-661X. Periodical. UK. English. qt. 10.00. Church Society, 186 Kennington Park Road, London SE11 4BT England. **Tel** 01 582-0132. **Ed** Gerald Bray. **Ind/Abst** Old Testam. Abstr., New Testam. Abstr., Relig. Index One, Period., Am. Hist. Life, Hist. Abstr., Christ. Period. Index. **LC** BX5011. bk rev. adv acc. **Circ** 1,200. The leading Anglican theological journal written from a conservative evangelical standpoint. Deals in-depth with issues facing the church of England and the Anglican communion. Extensive book reviews.

CIENCIA TOMISTA. No. 1- (Vol. 1-). 0210-0398. Periodical. SP. Spanish. qt. $20.00. Ciencia Tomista, Convento de San Esteban, Apt 17, 37080 Salamanca Spain. **Tel** (923)21 50 00. **Ind/Abst** MLA Int. Bibliogr. Books Artic. Mod. Lang. Lit., Cathol. Period. Lit. Index. **LC** BX805. bk rev. **Circ** 700. Journal for research and critique of theology published for the Dominican Monks of St Esteban.

CIENCIAS DA RELIGIAO. Yearly V. 1, No. 1, (June 1983)-. Periodical. Portuguese. sa. **LC** HN39.B8. **DD** 261.830981.

CIRCULAIRE AUX PRETRES ET AUTRES AGENTS DE PASTORALE. (CIRCULAIRE AUX PRETRES ET AUTRES AGENTS DE PASTORALE : PRINCIPAUX DOCUMENTS PUBLIES EN . . .). **Main/Corp** Eglise Catholique. Diocese de Trois-Rivieres. Eveque (1975- : Noel). **Series/Titl** Mandements des Eveques de Trois-Rivieres. No. 1 (1975/76)-. 0227-552X. CN. French. an. Free to Priests and Pastors. l'Eveche de Trois-Rivieres, 362 rue Bonaventure, Trois-Rivieres Quebec G9A 5J9 Canada. **DD** 262.027144505. *Circulaires au Clerge.*

CITTA DI VITA. Began with Vol. 1 in 1946. 0009-7632. Periodical. IT. Italian. bm. Citta di Vita, Piazza Santa Croce 16, 50122 Firenze Italy. **Ind/Abst** MLA Int. Bibliogr. Books Artic. Mod. Lang. Lit.

CITY OF GOD (INDIANAPOLIS, IND. : 1979). (THE CITY OF GOD). Vol. 1, No. 1 (Winter 1979)-. 0590-8418. Periodical. US. English. ty. City of God, 4545 Northwestern Avenue, I Hughes, Indianapolis IN 46200. **Tel** (317)925-9095. **LC** BV637. **DD** 253. *City of God (Indianapolis, Ind. : 1968), 0590-8418.*

CLINS D'OEIL DE DIEU. 0823-9614. Periodical. CN. French. ir. Free. Guides du Canada Guides Catholiques du Canada Secteur Francaise, 3827 rue St-Hubert, Montreal Quebec H2L 4A4 Canada. **DD** 248.482.

CMS NEWS-LETTER. **Main/Corp** Church Missionary Society. Periodical. UK. English. ir. $4.50. Church Missionary Society, 157 Waterloo Road, London SE1 8VV England. **Ed** Simon Barrington Ward. **Circ** 5,000. (ctrl). Theological commentary.

COLLEGIATE QUARTERLY. **VFOAT** Collegiate Quarterly. 0744-2939. Periodical. US. English. qt. Pacific Press Publishing Association, 1350 North Kings Road, Nampa ID 83653. **DD** 268.

THE COMING REVOLUTION. V. 1- Summer 1980-. 0270-4307. Periodical. US. English. qt. $7.50. Coming Revolution, PO Box 28761, San Diego CA 92128. **Tel** (213)991-4751.

COMMUNAUTE *CEASED.* V. 4-10. 0316-7291. CN. French. $5. **DD** 262.001. *Koinonia, 0316-7259.*

COMMUNAUTES ET LITURGIES. V. 57-1975-. Periodical. BE. French. bm. 722.00. Communautes et Liturgies, 1 Allee de Clerlande, B-1340 Ottignies Belgium. **Tel** 32 10 417461. **Ind/Abst** Old Testam. Abstr. **DD** 282. One of the oldest liturgical review articles about celebration, prayers. liturgists and theologians. Special liturgy for the church holidays, including a bibliography. *Paroisse et Liturgie, 0031-2347.*

COMMUNICANTES. (COMMUNICANTES : LE BULLETIN DU PRIEURE). Vol. 2, No. 1 (March 1978)-. 0706-3644. Periodical. CN. French. ir. Fraternite Saint-Pie X Canada, CP 1190, Shawinigan-Sud Quebec G9P 4E8 Canada. **DD** 269.609714465. *Bulletin du Prieure, 0706-3636.*

COMMUNICATE. 0384-661X. CN. English. ir. $5.42. Evangelistic Enterprises, PO Box 600, Beaverlodge Alberta T0H 0C0 Canada. **Tel** (403)345-2818. *Bible Evangelism.*

COMMUNICATIO SOCIALIS YEARBOOK. *See* Yearbooks, Almanacs, Directories.

COMMUNIO. **VFOAT** International Catholic Review. V. 1- Spring 1974-. 0094-2065. Periodical. US. English. qt. Communio, PO Box 1046, Notre Dame IN 46556. **Tel** (219)239-5723. **Ed** David L Schindler. **Ind/Abst** Old Testam. Abstr., New Testam. Abstr., Cathol. Period. Lit. Index, Relig. Index One, Period. **LC** BX801. **DD** 282.05. **Circ** 2,300. (ctrl). A journal of theological and cultural reflections from a Catholic perspective by noted theologians, philosophers, historians and scientists.

COMPASS. (COMPASS : A JESUIT JOURNAL). Vol. 1, No. 1 (1983)-. 0715-8777. Periodical. CN. English. qt. Free. Society of Jesus/Upper Canada Province, Suite 206/1709 Bloor Street West, Toronto Ontario M6P 1B2 Canada. **DD** 248.482005. (ctrl).

CONCILIUM. **VFOAT** Concilium Theology in the Age of Renewal. 1-. 0010-5236. Monographic Series. UK. English. mo. Seabury Press, 815 Second Avenue, New York NY 10017. **Ind/Abst** New Testam. Abstr.

CONCORDIA JOURNAL. 1974. 0145-7233. Periodical. US. English. bm. $10.00. Concordia Seminary, 801 de Mun Avenue, St Louis MO 63105. **Tel** (314)721-5934. **Ed** Quentin F Wesselschmidt. **Ind/Abst** Old Testam. Abstr., Int. Zeitschriftenschan Bibelwissenschaft Grenzgeb., New Testam. Abstr., Relig. Theol. Abstr., Repert. Bibliogr. Inst. Chret., Relig. Index One, Period., Christ. Period. Index. **LC** BX8001. **DD** 230.4173. bk rev. **Circ** 9,000. Publishes scholarly and practical articles dealing with exegetical, historical, practical, and systematic theology. It also contains editorials, homiletical helps, and book reviews. *CTM, 0090-9823.*

CONCORDIA THEOLOGICAL QUARTERLY. **VFOAT** CTQ Quarterly. V. 41- Jan. 1977-. 0038-8610. Periodical. US. English. qt. $5.00. Concordia Theological Seminary, 6600 North Clinton, Ft Wayne IN 46825. **Tel** (219)482-9611. **Ed** David P Scaer. **Ind/Abst** Old Testam. Abstr., New Testam. Abstr., Relig. Index One, Period. **DD** 284. bk rev. adv acc. **Circ** 10,000. Articles on theology, also homiletical studies designed to aid the busy parish pastor. *Springfielder, 0884-2825.*

CONGRES - ENTRAIDE MISSIONNAIRE. (CONGRES). **Main/Corp** Entraide Missionnaire, Inc. Congres. 82-. 0821-1752. CN. French. an. Entraide Missionnaire, 2295 rue Chambly, Montreal Quebec H1W 3J6 Canada. **DD** 261.805. *Dossier du Congres, 0821-1744.*

CONOSCENZA RELIGIOSA. No. 1- Jan./March 1960-. Periodical. IT. Italian. qt. Nouva Italia Editrice, Via Ernesto Codignola, 50018 Scandicci Fl Italy.

THE CONRAD GREBEL REVIEW. Vol. 1, No. 1 (Winter 1983)-. Periodical. CN. English. ty. 21.00. Nelson Scheifele, Conrad Grebel College, Waterloo Ontario N2L 3G6 Canada. **Tel** (519)885-0220. **Ed** Walter Klaassen. bk rev. **Circ** 400. (ctrl). Interdisciplinary journal of Christian inquiry exploring contemporary issues in light of Christian faith. Includes book reviews of interest to academics and professionals.

CONSENSUS. V. 1- Jan. 1975-. 0317-1493. CN. English. qt. $5.42. Lutheran Council in Canada, 500-365 Hargrave Street, Winnipeg Manitoba R3B 2K3 Canada. **Tel** (204)942-0096. **Ind/Abst** Relig. Index One, Period. **DD** 230.4171.

CONSOLATA MISSIONARIES. No. 8 (March/April 1981)-. 0826-7499. Periodical. CN. English. bm. $2.00. Consolata Missionaries of Canada, 214 Heath Street, Toronto Ontario M4V 1V5 Canada. **DD** 266.205. *Consolata, 0226-8957.*

CONTACTS. **VFOAT** Revue Francaise de l'Othrodoxie. V. 1- 1949-. 0045-8325. Periodical. FR. French. qt. $34.00. Revue Orthodoxe Theologie et Spiritualite, 43 rue fer a Moulin, 75005 Paris France. **Tel** 45 35 80 98. **Ed** S Balzon & Revault d'Allonnes. bk rev. **Circ** 2,000. Orthodox theology and spirituality.

CONTEMPLATIVE REVIEW. V. 1- 1968-. 0193-8452. Periodical. US. English. qt. $8.00. Contemplative Review, Beckley Hill, Rural Route 2 Box 4784, Barre VT 05641. **Tel** (802)476-8362. **Ed** Mary Roman. **Ind/Abst** Cathol. Period. Lit. Index. bk rev. **Circ** 5,800. (ctrl). Articles, book reviews, and meditations to help people understand the Christian tradition of meditation, mysticism and contemplation and to practise contemplative prayer.

CONTINENTAL REFLECTIONS. Vol. 1, No. 1 (May 1980)-. 0226-8949. Periodical. CN. English. bm. Free. Continental Reflections, PO Box 98, Thompson Manitoba R8N 1M9 Canada. **DD** 226.009719.

COQUILLE. (LA COQUILLE). V. 1- 1972-. 0318-4374. CN. French. qt. La Coquille, 61 Promenade Riverside, Saint-Lambert Quebec Canada. **DD** 267.182.

CORPUS SCRIPTORUM ECCLESIASTICORUM LATINORUM. V. 1- 1866-. Monographic Series. Latin. ir. Holder Pichler Tempsky, Frankgasse 4, 1096 Wien Austria. **LC** BR60.

COURRIER DE ST-JOSEPH. (LE COURRIER DE ST-JOSEPH : REVUE DU CENTRE DE RECHERCHE ET DE DIFFUSION DE L'OUEST, C.R.E.D.O). No. 4 (May/Oct. 1984)-. 0828-7546. Periodical. CN. French. ir. Free. C.R.E.D.O., C P 220, Cookshire Quebec J0B 1M0 Canada. **DD** 231.8. *Courrier de Joseph, 0828-7538.*

THE COVENANT QUARTERLY. V. 1- 1941-. 0361-0934. Periodical. US. English. qt. $6.00. Covenant Press, 3200 West Foster Avenue, Chicago IL 60625. **Tel** (312)784-3000. **Ed** Wayne Weld. **Ind/Abst** Relig. Index One, Period. bk rev. **Circ** 1,800. The theological journal of the Evangelical Covenant Church, aimed at ministers, missionaries, and interested laypeople.

CROSS CURRENTS. V. 1- Fall 1950-. 0011-1953. Periodical. US. English. qt. $33.00. Cross Currents Corporation, Mercy College, Dobbs Ferry NY 10522. **Tel** (914)358-4898. **Ind/Abst** Annu. Bibliogr.

Religion, Mythology, Rationalism—Theology

Engl. Lang. Lit., Cathol. Period. Lit. Index, MLA Int. Bibliogr. Books Artic. Mod. Lang. Lit., Old Testam. Abstr., Humanit. Index, Guide Soc. Sci. Relig. Period. Lit. **LC** BR1. **DD** 205. bk rev. **Circ** 4,600. available on microfilm from University Microfilm to subscribers only. A review to explore the implications of Christianity for our times. It is international, ecumenical and interdisciplinary.

CRUCIBLE. 1963-. 0011-2100. Periodical. UK. English. qt. 5.60. Crucible-British, Church House/Deans Yard, London SW10 3NQ England. **Tel** 01-222 9011. Ed Michael Atkinson. **LC** HN30. **DD** 261. bk rev. adv acc. **Circ** 2,000. Christian comment on current issues: international affairs, faith and morals, social problems and politics.

CRUX. V. 1-. 0011-2186. Periodical. CN. English. Editor Crux, Scarborough College University of Toronto, West Hill Ontario M1C 1A4 Canada.

CRUX OF THE NEWS. V. 1- Aug. 18, 1980-. 0591-2296. Periodical. US. English. wk. $34.50. Clarity Publ Inc, 75 Champlain Street, Albany NY 12204. **Tel** (518)465-4591. Crux of the News, 0591-2296.

CUADERNOS DE TEOLOGIA. Yearly V. 1-. Periodical. AG. Spanish. ir. $15.00. Instituto Superior Evangelico, Camacua 282, 1406 Buenos Aires Argentina. **Tel** 631-1882. bk rev. Organ of the protestant institute for higher theological studies with articles related to ecclesiastical and historical subjects. Ekklesia, Cuadernos Teologicos.

THE CUMBERLAND SEMINARIAN. V. 1- Fall 1953-. 0590-3386. Periodical. US. English. ty. Free. 168 East Parkway South, Memphis TN 38104. **Ind/Abst** Relig. Index One, Period.

CURRENT CHRISTIAN BOOKS. See Indexes/Abstracts.

CURRENTS IN THEOLOGY AND MISSION. V. 1- Aug. 1974-. 0098-2113. Periodical. US. English. bm. $26.00. Currents in Theology and Mission, 1100 East 55th Street, Chicago IL 60615. **Tel** (312)753-0763. Ed Klein. **Ind/Abst** Old Testam. Abstr., New Testam. Abstr., Ref. Source, Relig. Index One, Period. bk rev. adv acc. **Circ** 4,000. Essays and reviews aimed at pastors and laypersons dealing with questions of belief and ministry.

DAILY BREAD. 0092-7147. US. English. bm. Royal National Institute for the Blind, 224 Great Portland Street, London W1N 6AA England. **LC** BV4810. **DD** 242.2.

DAILY GUIDEPOSTS. Began with 1977 Vol. 0190-5457. US. English. am. $4.95. Guideposts, Carmel NY 10512. **LC** BV4810. **DD** 242.105.

DANSK TEOLOGISK TIDSSKRIFT. Began with Vol. 1 in 1938. 0105-3191. Periodical. DK. Danish. qt. $15.31. G E C Gads Forlab, Vimmelskaftet 32, 1161 Kobenhavnk Denmark. **Tel** (01)150558. **Ind/Abst** Old Testam. Abstr., New Testam. Abstr., Relig. Index One, Period. (cum index).

DECISION. Began in 1963. 0751-6274. Periodical. French. bm. $5.00. Decision, 1300 Harmon Place, Minneapolis MN 55403. **Tel** (612)338-0500. Ed Roger C Palms. **Circ** 2,000,000. To present Gospel of Jesus Christ and to encourage, teach and strengthen Christians.

DESERT CALL. Periodical. US. English. qt. $8.00. Spiritual Life Institute, Nada Hermitage, Crestone CO 81131. **Tel** (303)256-4778. Ed Tessa Bielecki. bk rev. **Circ** 2,300. Fosters contemplation as the way to lead an integrated, God-centered life.

DESTINY. V. 1- May 1979-. 0225-9796. Periodical. CN. English. mo. $7.95 Domestic. $8.95 Others. Paradise Publishers Company, Destiny Magazine, Suite 606, 3 Church Avenue, Toronto Ontario M5E 1M2 Canada. **DD** 248.05.

DIAKONIA. V. 3-. 0341-9592. Periodical. German. ir. 54.00. Grunewald Verlag, D-65 Mainz Bischofsplatz 6, Matthhias-Grunewald-Verlag, Mainz West Germany. **Ind/Abst** New Testam. Abstr. **LC** BX1913. Daikonia. Der Seelsorger.

DIALOG. V. 1- Winter 1962-. 0012-2033. Periodical. US. English. qt. Dialog, 2375 Como Avenue, St Paul MN 55108. **Ind/Abst** New Testam. Abstr., Old Testam. Abstr., Relig. Index One, Period. **LC** BR1. **DD** 230.05. (cum index).

DIALOGO ECUMENICO. V. 1- (No. 1-). 0210-2870. Periodical. SP. Spanish. ir. 20.00. University Pontificia Salamanca, Calle Compania 5E-37008, Salamanca Spain. **Tel** (923)238235. Ed Adolfo Gonzalez Montes. bk rev. adv acc. **Circ** 500. A theological journal which focuses on the fundamental issues of ecumenical thinking in the Roman Catholic Church, Eastern Christian Churches and Protestantism.

DIALOGO TEOLOGICO. Began in 1973. Periodical. US. Spanish. sa. Box 5671, El Paso TX 79914. **LC** BX6201. **DD** 230.6105.

DIDASKALIA. V. 1- 1971-. 0253-1674. English (French, German, Latin, Portuguese or Spanish). ir. $4.10. Didaskalia, Palma de Cima, Lisboa 4 Portugal. **Ind/Abst** Old Testam. Abstr., New Testam. Abstr. **LC** BR7.

DIMANCHE ET FETE. No. 1- Jan. 1975-. 0317-2198. CN. French. ir. $3. Dimanche et Fete, 2715 Chemin de la Cote Ste-Catherine, Montreal Quebec H3T 1B6 Canada. **DD** 264.02005.

DIRECTION. V. 1- Jan. 1972-. 0384-8515. Periodical. CN. English. sa. $8.50. Mennonite Brethren Biblical Seminar, 4824 East Butler at Chestnut, Fresno CA 93727-5097. Ed Allen Guenther. **Ind/Abst** New Testam. Abstr. bk rev. **Circ** 500. Seeks to serve its consistiuency by addressing biblical, theological and church-related issues. Church and conference leaders, pastors, educators, and informed church members are the intended audience. Voice, 0384-8507; Journal of Church & Society.

DIRECTORY - ASSOCIATION OF THEOLOGICAL SCHOOLS IN THE UNITED STATES AND CANADA. See Yearbooks, Almanacs, Directories.

DIRECTORY OF MEMBERS - ACADEMY OF PARISH CLERGY. See Yearbooks, Almanacs, Directories.

DIRECTORY OF RELIGIOUS BROADCASTING (MORRISTOWN, N. J. : 1982). See Yearbooks, Almanacs, Directories.

THE DISCIPLES THEOLOGICAL DIGEST. Vol. 1, No. 1 (1986)-. 0888-8111. Periodical. US. English. an. $10.00. Division of Higher Education, 11780 Borman Drive/Suite 100, St Louis MO 63146. **DD** 286.

DISCOVERY (UPPER DARBY, PA.). (DISCOVERY). 8750-4456. Periodical. US. English. bm. $12.00. Discovery c/o Scripture Union, 7000 Ludlow Street, Upper Darby PA 19082. **DD** 230.

DIVINE LOVE. Began in 1958. 0417-7320. Periodical. US. English. qt. Apostolate of Christian Action, PO Box 24, Fresno CA 93707.

DIVINITAS. Vol. 1- Apr. 1957-. 0012-4222. Periodical. VC. English (French, German, Italian. Latin and Spanish). ty. $24.00. Mons Antonio Piolanti, Direttore di Divinitas, Palazzo Canonici, 00120 Citta del Vaticano. **Ind/Abst** New Testam. Abstr. **LC** BR1.A1. (cum index).

DIVUS THOMAS; COMMENTARIUM DE PHILOSOPHIA ET THEOLOGIA. Vol. 1-6. 0012-4257. Periodical. IT. Italian (English). qt. Editrice Divus Thomas, Coll Alberonavi Emilia Parmense, 29100 Piacenza Italy. **Ind/Abst** MLA Int. Bibliogr. Books Artic. Mod. Lang. Lit.

LE DOCTRINAIRE. 0709-583X. Periodical. CN. French. ir. $8.00. Le Doctrinaire, CP 421, Sainte-Therese Quebec J7E 4J7 Canada. **DD** 230.205.

DOCTRINE AND LIFE. Began with Feb./Mar. 1951 issue. 0012-446X. Periodical. English. mo. $18.00. Dominican Publications, St Saviors, Dominick Street, Dublin 1 Ireland. **Ind/Abst** Old Testam. Abstr., New Testam. Abstr. Available on microfilm from Xerox University Microfilms.

DOXOLOGY. (DOXOLOGY : JOURNAL OF THE ORDER OF ST. LUKE IN THE UNITED METHODIST CHURCH). Vol. 1 (1984)-. 0748-4682. US. English. an. $5.00. PO Box 429, Hackettstown NJ 07840. **DD** 242.

THE DREW GATEWAY. V. 1- 1930-. 0012-6152. Periodical. US. English. ty. $9.00. Drew University, Theological School, Madison NJ 07940. **Tel** (201)377-3000. Ed Edward Leroy Long Jr. **Ind/Abst** Relig. Index One, Period., Index Relig. Period. Lit. **LC** BX8201. **DD** 287.673. (cum index) bk rev. **Circ** 600. (ctrl). Available on microfilm from University Microfilms. Theological and ethical ideas related to the practice of ministry.

DUQUESNE STUDIES. THEOLOGICAL SERIES. Vol. 1 1963-. 0070-7734. US. English. ir. Humanities Press, Atlantic Highlands NJ 07716. **Tel** (201)872-1441.

THE EAST ASIA JOURNAL OF THEOLOGY. Vol. 1, No. 1-. 0217-3859. Periodical. Sl. English. sa. $14.82. East Asia Journal of Theology, 4 Mount Sophia, Singapore 0922 Singapore. **Tel** 3386613. Ed Yeow Choo Lak. **Ind/Abst** New Testam. Abstr., Relig. Index One, Period. **LC** BR1.A1. **DD** 230.095. bk rev. **Circ** 1,200. (ctrl). Encourages Asian Biblical scholarship and theological thinking; relates the gospel to our cultural, historical and religious situtation in East Asia. South East Asia Journal of Theology, Northeast Asia Journal of Theology, 0549-8899.

EAST ASIAN PASTORAL REVIEW. V. 16 No. 4-. 0040-0564. Periodical. PH. English. qt. $12.00. East Asian Pastoral Institute, Box 1815, Manila Philippines. **Tel** 983182. Ed Felipe Gomez. **Ind/Abst** Cathol. Period. Lit. Index. bk rev. **Circ** 1,500. (ctrl). Addresses practical issues concerning the church in Asia and the Pacific, putting the emphasis on inculturation and theological, catechetical and liturgical updating. Teaching All Nations, Good Tidings.

ECO DE AFRICA Y DE OTROS CONTINENTES. Periodical. SP. Spanish. ir. Instituto de San Pedro Claver, Travesia del Cano 10, Aravaca, Madrid 23 Spain. **LC** BV2130. **DD** 266.26.

ECUMENICAL DIRECTORY OF RETREAT AND CONFERENCE CENTERS. See Yearbooks, Almanacs, Directories.

EDIFIEZ-VOUS SUR VOTRE TRES SAINTE FOI. VAT Edifiez-Vous. 0823-6569. Periodical. CN. French. mo. $5,00. Edifiez-Vous c/o Samuel Coppieters, 159 Viens St-Alphonse-De-Granby, Quebec J0E 2A0 Canada. **DD** 269.205.

EGLISE ET THEOLOGIE. 1- Jan. 1970-. 0013-2349. Periodical. CN. French (English). ty. 30.00 Domestic. St Paul University, 223 Main Street, Ottawa 1 Canada K1S 1C4. **Tel** (613)236-1393. Ed Leo Laberge. **Ind/Abst** New Testam. Abstr., Old Testam. Abstr., Relig. Index One, Period. bk rev. **Circ** 500. Doctrinal and practical theology, Bible, history of ideas: Christianity and church history/problems of culture.

EICHSTATTER STUDIEN. 1- 1936-. Monographic Series. German. ir.

ENCOUNTER. V. 17- Winter 1956-. 0013-7081. Periodical. US. English. qt. $12.00. Christian Theological Seminary, Box 88267, Indianapolis IN 46208. **Tel** (317)924-1331. Ed Clark M Williamson. **Ind/Abst** Old Testam. Abstr., Writ. Am. Hist., Relig. Index One, Period., Relig. Theol. Abstr., New Testam. Abstr., Int. Zeitschriftenschan Bibelwissenschaft Grenzgeb. **LC** BR1. **UD** 205. bk rev. adv acc. **Circ** 550. (ctrl). Available on microfilm from University Microfilms. Creative discussion among Christians of various communions throughout the world: among theologians and other scholars, among believers in Christ and people of other faiths. Shane Quarterly, 0362-4609.

END-TIME NEWS. July 6, 1970-. 0702-844X. Periodical. CN. English. Solbrekken Evangelistic Association, PO Box 2424, Edmonton Alberta T5J 2R4 Canada. **DD** 269.205. News, 0702-8458.

ENTRE NOUS. VFOAT Revue de Notre-Dame du Cap. June 1974-. 0316-7364. CN. French. qt. $3.00 for two years. Bureau de la Revue Notre-Dame-du-Cap, 270 Boulevard Loranger, Cap-de-la-Madeleine Quebec Canada. **DD** 263.042714465. Ensemble, 0316-7356.

ENTRETIENS D'ORAISON. VFOAT Oraison. V. 1- Sept./Oct. 1974-. Periodical. CN. French. bm. Free. Entretiens d'Oraison, 4120 Avenue de Vendome, Montreal Quebec H4A Canada. **DD** 248.305.

EP NEWS SERVICE. (EP NEWS SERVICE : OFFICIAL WEEKLY NEWS SERVICE OF THE EVANGELICAL PRESS ASSOCIATION). VFOAT News Service. VAT Evangelical Press News Service. 8750-7064. Periodical. US. English. wk. EP News Service, 1619 Portland Avenue South, Minneapolis MN 55404.

EPHEMERIDES CARMELITICAE. Vol. 1- May 1947-. Periodical. IT. English (French, German, Italian, Latin or Spanish). sa. 30.000 Domestic. Ephemerides Carmeliticae, Piazza San Pancrazio 5A, Rome Italy 00152. **Tel** (06)582.362. **Ind/Abst** Old Testam. Abstr. **LC** BX800.A1. **DD** 282.05. bk rev. **Circ** 800. (ctrl). We publish all articles dealing with religious and Christian spirituality.

Religion, Mythology, Rationalism—Theology

EPHEMERIDES MARIOLOGICAE. V. 1- Jan./Mar. 1951-. 0425-1466. Periodical. SP. Spanish (French, English, German or Italian). qt. 20.00. Ephemerides Mariologicae, Buen Suceso 22, Madrid Spain. **Tel** 248601. **Ind/Abst** New Testam. Abstr. **LC** BT595. bk rev. **Circ** 800. Christology and mariology.

EPHEMERIDES THEOLOGICAE LOVANIENSES. Vol. 1- Jan. 1924-. 0013-9513. Periodical. BE. French (English and Latin). qt. 39.52. Editions Peeters Sa, Bondgenotenlaan 153 Box 41, B 3000 Leuven Belgium. **Ind/Abst** Old Testam. Abstr., New Testam. Abstr., Relig. Index One, Period. Index in last issue of volume - attached. adv acc. (ctrl)

EPIPHANY (SAN FRANCISCO, CALIF.). (EPIPHANY). Vol. 1, No. 1 (Fall 1980)-. 0273-6969. Periodical. US. English. qt. Epiphany Journal, PO Box 14727, San Francisco CA 94114. **Tel** (415)431-1917. **Ed** Philip Tolbert. **Ind/Abst** Relig. Index One, Period. **LC** BV4485. **DD** 230.05. bk rev. **Circ** 1,000. Brings an orthodox Christian hierarchy of values and world view to bear on crucial issues facing the church today. Patristic spirituality confronts modernization. *Sonflowers Discipleship Journal, 0194-9179.*

ESCRITOS DEL VEDAT. V. 1- 1971-. 0210-3133. Periodical. SP. Spanish. an. $17.00 US. Seccion PP Dominicos, Facultad Teologia San Vicente, Torrente Valencia Spain. **Tel** (96)3517750. **Ed** Martin Gelabert. **Ind/Abst** New Testam. Abstr. **LC** BR45. adv acc. (ctrl). Scientific research in history, the Bible, theology, morality, canon law and philosophy.

ESPRIT-VIVANT CEASED. V. 1-6, No. 9. 0382-0394. Periodical. CN. French. ir. Esprit-Vivant, 2531 Frontenac, Montreal Quebec H2K 3A2 Canada. **DD** 248.05.

ESTUDIOS MARIANOS. Began publication in 1942. SP. Spanish. an. $11.00. Editorial de Espiritualidad, Sociedad Mariologica Espanola, Triana 9/Madrid 16 Spain. **LC** BT596.

ESTUDOS TEOLOGICOS. (ESTUDOS TEOLOGICOS : ORGAO DA FACULDADE DE TEOLOGIA). New Ser. 1st Year, No. 1 (3. Quarter, 1961)-. 0101-3130. Periodical. BL. Portuguese (German). ty. Faculdade de Teologia Comisso de Publicoes, Caixa Postal 14 BR 93000 Sao Leopoldo RS Brazil. **Ind/Abst** Old Testam. Abstr., Relig. Index One, Period. *Estudos Teologicos - Studien und Berichte.*

ETERNITY. VFOAT Eternity Magazine. V. 1- Apr. 1950-. 0014-1682. Periodical. US. English. mo. Evangelical Ministries, 1716 Spruce Street, Philadelphia PA 19103. **Tel** (215)546-3696. **Ind/Abst** Guide Soc. Sci. Relig. Period. Lit., Christ. Period. Index. **LC** BR1. **DD** 261.05. *Revelation.*

ETM REVIEW. VFOAT Review. Periodical. US. English.

ETOILE POLAIRE. (L'ETOILE POLAIRE). No. 1-. 0820-7445. Periodical. CN. French. qt. Free to Members. Association des Eclaireurs Baden-Powell, 70 rue Lahaie, Laval Quebec H7G 3A8 Canada. **DD** 248.4820305.

ETUDES PASTORALES. Published since 1971?. 0316-1080. Periodical. CN. French. an. La Librairie de d'Universite de Montreal, C.P. 6128, Montreal Quebec H3C 3J7 Canada. **DD** 253.05.

EUNTES DOCETE. Vol. 1- 1948-. Periodical. IT. Italian (English, French, Latin, and Spanish). ty. $30.00. Urbaniana University Press, Vatican City, 00120 Roma Italy. **Tel** 06/655992. **Ind/Abst** New Testam. Abstr. Index in last issue of volume - attached. bk rev. adv acc. **Circ** 1,000. (ctrl). Missionary, law, missionology, and psychology.

EUROPE PULSE CEASED. VFOAT Pulse. 0739-0521. Periodical. US. English. sa. $25.00. Evangelical Missions Information Service, Box 794, Wheaton IL 60189.

EVALUATION DES PRODUCTIONS AUDIOVISUELLES. VAT Audiovisuelles (Montreal). 1-. 0229-060X. Periodical. CN. French. ir. $6.00. Office des Communications Sociales, 4635 Avenida de Lorimer, Montreal Quebec H2H 2B4 Canada. **DD** 268.63505.

EVANGELICAL MISSIONS QUARTERLY. V. 1- Fall 1964-. 0014-3359. Periodical. US. English. qt. $10.95. Evangelical Missions Information, Box 794, Wheaton IL 60189. **Tel** (312)653-2158. **Ed** Jim Reapsome. **Ind/Abst** Christ. Period. Index, Relig. Index One, Period. **LC** BV2350.

DD 266.005. bk rev. adv acc. **Circ** 7,000. Professional journal for missionaries, teachers, students and clergymen, emphasizing evangelical missionary life, thought, and practice.

EVANGELICAL NEWSLETTER. V. 1- Nov. 5, 1973-. 0744-8783. Periodical. US. English. bw. Eternity Subscriber Services, PO Box 611, Holmes PA 19043. **Tel** (215)546-3696.

EVANGELICAL QUARTERLY. (THE EVANGELICAL QUARTERLY). Began in 1929. 0014-3367. Periodical. UK. English. qt. $17.55 US and Canada. Paternoster Press Limited, PO Box 11127, Birmingham AL 35202. **Tel** (205)991-6925. **Ed** I Howard Marshall. **Ind/Abst** Old Testam. Abstr., New Testam. Abstr., Relig. Index One, Period., Christ. Period. Index. **LC** BR1. **DD** 230.05. bk rev. Committed to the historic Christian faith, it promotes a theology based on scripture, yet it is sensitive to practical contemporary issues.

EVANGELICAL REVIEW OF THEOLOGY. V. 1- Oct. 1977-. 0144-8153. Periodical. US. English. sa. $16.20 US and Canada. Paternoster Press, PO Box 11127, Birmingham AL 35202. **Tel** (205)991-6925. **Ed** Bruce J Nicholls. bk rev. Offers the thinking Christian top articles and reviews from international publication, covering the spectrum of evangelical thought.

THE EVANGELICAL SUNDAY SCHOOL TEACHER'S GUIDE. 1982-83-. 0731-0463. US. English. an. $5.95. Fleming H Revell Company, 184 Central Avenue, Old Tappan NJ 07675.

EVANGELIET TIL VERDEN. 1966-. Periodical. DK. Danish. an. DMS-Forlag, Strandagervej 24, 2900 Hellerup Denmark. **LC** WMLC L 83/157. Each issue contains an index to its own contents - no vol index - loose. *Danske Missionsselskabs Arbog.*

DER EVANGELISCHE ERZIEHER. Began in 1949. 0014-3413. Periodical. GW. German. bm. $14.61. Moritz Diesterweg, Postfach 110651, D-6 Frankfurt 11 West Germany.

EVANGELISCHE INFORMATION : NACHRICHTENSPIEGEL DES EVANGELISCHEN PRESSEDIENSTES. Began in Jan. 1977. Periodical. GW. German. wk. Evagelisher Press, Friedrichster 34, D6000 Frankfurt 4 West Germany. *Nachrichtenspiegel des Evangelischen Pressedienstes.*

EVANGELISCHE THEOLOGIE. Vol. 1-. 0014-3502. Periodical. GW. German. bm. Kaiser Verlag, Isabellastrasse 20, Postfach 509, D8000 Munchen 43 West Germany. **Tel** (089)3712097. **Ind/Abst** Old Testam. Abstr., New Testam. Abstr., Energy Res. Abstr., Relig. Index One, Period. **LC** BR4. (cum index). bk rev. adv acc. **Circ** 3,300. Evangelical theology. *Blatter zur Kirchlichen Lage, Zwischen den Zeiten.*

EVANGELIST. (EVANGELIST MICROFORM). VAT Evangelist (Toronto). Vol. 1, No. 1 (Jan. 1848)-. 0821-0985. Periodical. CN. English. **DD** 287.471.

EVANGELIUM. VFOAT Gospel, Euaggelion. Began publication in 1974. Periodical. GW. German (text in English in parallel columns). bm. Die Lutherische Stunde, Postfach 10 35 46, 2800 Bremen 1 West Germany. *Verkungdigung.*

EVANGELIZE. V. 1- May 1945-. 0745-4074. Periodical. US. English. mo. Lutheran Evangelical Movement, 333-2nd Avenue South, Minneapolis MN 55402. **Tel** (612)332-5677.

EXPLOR. V. 1- Spring 1975-. 0362-0867. Periodical. US. English. ty. Garrett Evangelical Theological Seminary, c/o Kenneth I Clawson, 2121 Sheridan Road, Evanston IL 60201. **Ind/Abst** Old Testam. Abstr., Relig. Index One, Period. **LC** BR1. **DD** 230.

THE EXPOSITORY TIMES. See Religion, Mythology, Rationalism - Bible.

FACULTY STUDIES. Began in 1965?. 0734-1539. Periodical. US. English. an. Carson-Newman College, Box 1898, Jefferson City TN 37760. **LC** BX6201. **DD** 286.13205.

FAITH ALIVE. Vol. 1, No. 1 (1983)-. 0822-5087. Periodical. CN. English. qt. $2.75 Per No., $8.00 Per Year. Evangelical Fellowship of Canada, PO Box 8800 Station B, Willowdale Ontario M2K 2R6 Canada. **DD** 269.205. *Thrust, 0318-7381.*

FAITH AND THOUGHT : JOURNAL OF THE VICTORIA INSTITUTE. Vol. 90, No. 1 (Spring 1958)-. 0014-7028. Periodical. UK. English. ir. $34.20. The Paternoster Press Ltd, PO Box 11127, Birmingham AL 35202. **Tel** (205)991-6925. **Ed** A B Robins. bk rev. **Circ** 600. (ctrl). Committed to relating new insights to the Christian faith, this journal takes account of developments not only in natural sciences, but also in archeology, history, philosophy, and sociology. *Journal of the Transactions of the Victoria Institute, or Philosophical Society of Great Britain.*

FAITH AND THOUGHT (MONTCLAIR, N.J.). (FAITH AND THOUGHT). Vol. 1, No. 1 (Spring 1983)-. Periodical. US. English. ir. $8.00. First Baptist Church of Mt Clair, Church Street & Trinity Place, Montclair NJ 07042. **Tel** (210)744-1033. **Ed** Robert M Price. bk rev. **Circ** 300. Issues in religious life and theology, studies of major religious thinkers, reviews, interviews and columns.

FAITH FOR THE FAMILY. V. 1- Mar./Apr. 1973-. 0099-1759. Periodical. US. English. mo. $5.00. Bob Jones University, Greenville SC 29614. **Tel** (614)242-5100. **Ed** Bob Jones. **Ind/Abst** Guide Soc. Sci. Relig. Period. Lit. **LC** BT82.2. **DD** 248.405. bk rev. **Circ** 60,000. Offers Christian family reading-newsworthy issues in the Christian world, non-fiction, fiction and other interesting reading material for the family.

FEUILLET SPIRITUEL DE L'OEUVRE DU PELERINAGE DES MALADES. (LE FEUILLET SPIRITUEL DE L'OEUVRE DU PELERINAGE DES MALADES). Vol. 1, No. 1 (Mar. 1980)-. 0824-1546. Periodical. CN. French. bm. $1.00. l'Oeuvre du Pelerinage des Malades de l'Oratoire Saint-Joseph, 3800 Ch Reine-Marie, Montreal Quebec H3V 1H6 Canada. **DD** 232.93205.

FIDES ET HISTORIA. V. 1- Fall 1968-. 0884-5379. Periodical. US. English. sa $40.00. Conference on Faith & History, Department of History, Indiana State University, Terre Haute IN 47809. **Tel** (812)232-6311. **Ind/Abst** Am. Hist. Life, Hist. Abstr., Part A, Mod. Hist. Abstr., Hist. Abstr., Part B, Twent. Century Abstr., Old Testam. Abstr., Writ. Am. Hist., Relig. Index One, Period., Christ. Period. Index, Recent Publ. Artic. **DD** 261.

FLASHLIGHT. VFOAT VOCA Flashlight. 0274-6522. Periodical. US. English. mo. VOCA, PO Box 15-M, Pasadena CA 91102. **DD** 266.

FLOODTIDE. Began with V. 1, Mar./Apr. 1948. Periodical. US. English. qt. $1.00. Christian Literature Crusade, PO Box 1449, Fort Washington PA 19034. **Tel** (215)542-1242. **Ed** Deborah Meroff. bk rev. **Circ** 2,000. News and ideas in Christian literature distribution.

FOCUS ON MISSIONS. 1970. Periodical. US. English. ir. Free. Fellowship of Missions, 4205 Chester Avenue, Cleveland OH 44103. **Tel** (216)432-2200. **Ed** Bernice Inman. bk rev. **Circ** 25,000. (ctrl). A conservative fundamental news supplement for missionaries.

FOCUS ON YOUTH FOR CHRIST CALGARY. (FOCUS). 0319-3837. Periodical. CN. English. qt. Youth for Christ, PO Box 6151 Station D, Calgary Alberta T2P 2C8 Canada. **DD** 267.610971233. *Focus on Youth for Christ Calgary, 0319-3837.*

FORSCHUNGEN ZUR SYSTEMATISCHEN UND OKUMENISCHEN THEOLOGIE. V. 1-. 0429-162X. Monographic Series. GW. German. ir. Vandenhoeck & Ruprecht, Postfach 3753, Theaterstr 13, D 3400 Goettingen West Germany. **Tel** (0551)65061. adv acc.

FORUM KATHOLISCHE THEOLOGIE. Vol. 1, No. 1-. 0178-1626. Periodical. German. qt. *Munchener Theologische Zeitschrift.*

FOUNDATIONS CEASED. V. 1-25, (No. 2). 0015-8992. Periodical. US. English. qt. $12.00 Domestic, $20.00 Foreign. American Baptist Historical Society, 1106 South Goodman Street, Rochester NY 14620. **Ind/Abst** Relig. Index One, Period., Hist. Abstr., Relig. Theol. Abstr., Writ. Am. Hist. **LC** BX6201. Available on microfilm from University Microfilms. *Chronicle, 0360-5779.*

FRAGMENTS (SCARBOROUGH, ONT.). (FRAGMENTS). No. 2 (Mar. 1977)-. 0711-2211. Periodical. CN. English. ir. Toronto Pastoral Centre for Liturgy, 2661 Kingston Road, Scarborough Ontario M1M 1M3 Canada. **DD** 264.02. *Untitled Publication (Toronto Pastoral Center for Liturgy), 0711-2203.*

Religion, Mythology, Rationalism—Theology

FREIBURGER THEOLOGISCHE STUDIEN. Vol. 1-. Monographic Series. GW. German. ir. Verlag Herder Freiburg, Hermann-Herder Strasse 4, D-7800 Freiburg West Germany. **Tel** 00497612717230. **Ed** Gerbert Brunner. **Circ** 500. Covers Catholic theology, dogmatic theology, and development of doctrine. Includes history of dogmas, history of theology, theology and philosophy, Biblical theology and history of moral theology.

FREIBURGER ZEITSCHRIFT FUR PHILOSOPHIE UND THEOLOGIE. See Philosophy.

FRESH PERSPECTIVES. Began in 1984. 8756-7784. Periodical. US. English. mo. $24.00 Domestic, $42.00 Foreign. Fresh Perspectives, 3301 Clinton Parkway, Court #1, Lawrence KS 66046. **DD** 248. Datadigest, 9742-9401.

THE FRIEND. (FRIEND). 0009-4102. Periodical. US. English. mo. $7.00. LDS Church Magazines, 50 East Temple/24th Floor, Salt Lake City UT 84150. **Tel** (801)531-2947. Children's Friend.

FUNDAMENTALIST JOURNAL. Vol. 1, No. 1 (Sept. 1982)-. 0736-1963. Periodical. US. English. mo. $14.95 Domestic, $17.95 Foreign. Fundamentalist Journal, Lynchburg VA 24514. **LC** BT82.2. **DD** 280.4.

FUTURE IS TODAY. (THE FUTURE IS TODAY). Vol. 1, No. 1 (Apr./May/June 1982)-. 0712-8320. Periodical. CN. English. qt $7.50. Future is Today, 566 21st Avenue, Hanover Ontario N4N 3H4 Canada. **DD** 248.405.

G + K, GOTTESDIENST UND KIRCHENMUSIK. VFOAT G + K. Jan./Feb. 1969-. Periodical. GW. German. bm. $6.08. Freimund-Verlag, PO Box 48, D-8806 H Neuenedettelsau West Germany. Gottesdienst und Kirchenmusik.

G T M S. GLAD TIDINGS MISSIONARY SOCIETY CEASED. (G T M S, GLAD TIDINGS MISSIONARY SOCIETY). **Main/Corp** Glad Tidings Missionary Society. Began with V. 28, No. 6. Oct. 1974. Ceased with summer 1981 issue. 0380-1136. Periodical. CN. English. mo. $2.00. Glad Tidings Missionary Society, PO Box 2480, Vancouver British Columbia V6B 3W7 Canada. **DD** 266.99. Harvest Time, 0380-1144.

GLENMARY'S CHALLENGE. 0017-1182. Periodical. US. English. qt Glenmary's Challenge, PO Box 46404, Cincinnati OH 45246.

THE GOOD NEWS. Began with 1- 1951-. 0432-0816. Periodical. US. English. mo. Free. Worldwide Church of God, 300 West Green Street, Pasadena CA 91129. **Tel** (818)304-6000. **Ed** Herbert W Armstrong. **Circ** 700,000. Practical articles on Christian living and Bible prophecy.

GOOD NEWS OF TOMORROW'S WORLD. (THE GOOD NEWS OF TOMORROW'S WORLD). VFOAT Tomorrow's World. V. 1- June 1969-. 0093-5026. Periodical. US. English. ir. 300 West Green, Pasadena CA 91105. **LC** BR1. **DD** 248.4899.

GOSPEL. 0740-123X. Periodical. US. English. bm. Bronze Co, 1904 North 25th Street, Richmond VA 23223.

THE GOSPEL ADVOCATE. July, 1885-. English. ir.

GOSPEL HERALD AND THE SUNDAY SCHOOL TIMES. Vol. 1, No. 1 (Spring Quarter 1983)-. 0746-0880. Periodical. US. English. qt. $5.00 Domestic, $5.75 Foreign. Gospel Worker Society, Union Gospel Press Division, 2000 Brookpark Road, Cleveland OH 44109. Sunday School Times and Gospel Herald.

THE GOSPEL MESSAGE. Began publication with April 1892 issue. 0744-5814. Periodical. US. English. qt. Gospel Message, Gospel Missionary Union, Smithville MO 64089. **LC** BV2350. **DD** 266.005.

GOTTINGER THEOLOGISCHE ARBEITEN. Vol. 1-. Monographic Series. GW. German. ir. Vandenhoeck & Ruprecht, Postfach 3753/Theaterstr 13, D-3400 Goettingen West Germany. **Ed** George Strecker. This is a series of monographs.

GRACE THEOLOGICAL JOURNAL. Vol. 1, No. 1 (Spring 1980)-. 0198-666X. Periodical. US. English. sa. $11.50. Grace Theological Journal, 200 Seminary Drive, Winona Lake IN 46590. **Tel** (219)372-5123. **Ed** John C Whitcomb. **Ind/Abst** Old Testam. Abstr., New Testam. Abstr., Relig. Index One, Period. bk rev. **Circ** 2,500. Deals with many areas of Christian scholarship, including Bible, theology, biblical languages and backgrounds, Church history, hermeneutics, philosophy, and Christian ministry.

GREGORIANUM. Vol. 1- 1920-. 0017-4114. Periodical. IT. English (French, German, Italian, Latin and Spanish). qt. $20.00. Pontificia Universita Gregorianum, 4 Piazza della Pilotta, Roma I-00187 Italy. **Ind/Abst** Old Testam. Abstr., Cathol. Period. Lit. Index, New Testam. Abstr., Philos. Index, Relig. Index One, Period., Recent Publ. Artic. **LC** BX800.A1. (cum index).

GREGORIOS HO PALAMAS. Periodical. Greek, Modern. ir. Hiera Metropolis Thessalonikes, Thessaly Greece. **Ind/Abst** MLA Int. Bibliogr. Books Artic. Mod. Lang. Lit. **LC** BX610.

GROUP. 1974. 0163-8971. Periodical. US. English. ir. $19.50. Group, PO Box 481, Loveland CO 80539. **Tel** (303)669-3836. **Ed** Gary Richardson. bk rev. adv acc. **Circ** 65,000. The magazine for leaders of Christian youth groups.

HARVARD DIVINITY BULLETIN. V. 24-30, 1959-67. 0017-8047. Periodical. US. English. mo. Harvard Divinity School, 45 Francis Avenue, Cambridge MA 02138. **Ind/Abst** Relig. Index One, Period. **LC** BV4070. Harvard Divinity School Bulletin, 0362-5117.

HARVARD THEOLOGICAL REVIEW. (THE HARVARD THEOLOGICAL REVIEW). **VFOAT** HTR. V. 1- Jan. 1908-. 0017-8160. Periodical. US. English. qt $40.00. Harvard Theological Review, 45 Francis Avenue, c/o P Chance, Cambridge MA 02138. **Tel** (617)495-5786. **Ed** Helmut Koester. **Ind/Abst** Humanit. Index, Abstr. Engl. Stud., Am. Hist. Life, Hist. Abstr., Part A, Mod. Hist. Abstr., Hist. Abstr., Part B, Twent. Century Abstr., MLA Int. Bibliogr. Books Artic. Mod. Lang. Lit., Old Testam. Abstr., Annu. Bibliogr. Engl. Lang. Lit., New Testam. Abstr., Writ. Am. Hist., Relig. Index One, Period., Years Work Eng. Stud., Hist. Abstr., Recent Publ. Artic. **LC** BR1. **DD** 205. adv acc. **Circ** 2,000. Investigations, discussions and essays in the various areas of religious studies that contribute to enlargement of knowledge and scholarship.

HARVARD THEOLOGICAL STUDIES. No. 1-. 0073-0726. Monographic Series. US. English. ir. Fortress Press, 2900 Queen Lane, Philadelphia PA 19129. **Tel** (215)848-6800. **LC** UNC.

HARVEST FIELD. V. 1- Aug. 1976-. 0702-7117. Periodical. CN. English. mo. $5. Harvest Field, PO Box 1145, South Porcupine Ontario P0N 1H0 Canada. **DD** 266.0220971.

THE HARVESTER. 0017-8217. Periodical. UK. English. mo. $18.90 US and Canada. The Paternoster Press Ltd, PO Box 11127, Birmingham AL 35202. **Tel** (205)991-6925. **Ed** Jonathan Lamb. bk rev adv acc. With an emphasis on Bible study, this journal seeks to inform readers of current worldwide issues. Provides an excellent book review service.

HELLENIKE THEOLOGIKE VIVLIOGRAPHIA. Began with 1977 Volume. Greek, Modern. an. Ioannou Generadiou 14, Athenai 140 Greece. **LC** Z7842.A3, BX320.2.

HENCEFORTH. Vol. 1, No. 1 (Fall 1972)-. Periodical. US. English. ir. $7.00. Berkshire Christian College, 200 Stockbridge Rd, Lenox MA 01240. **Tel** (413)637-0838. **Ed** Freeman Barton. bk rev adv acc. **Circ** 400. A journal by the faculty of Berkshire Christian College particularly for Advent Christian ministers.

HERITAGE BOOK. (THE HERITAGE BOOK). 1st Ed. (1977)-. 0711-4737. CN. English. an. $4.50 Per Volume. The Heritage Book, c/o Collier MacMillan, 1125 B Leslie Street, Don Mills Ontario M3C 2K2 Canada. **LC** BV4810. **DD** 242.2.

HERMES (SANTA BARBARA, CALIF.). (HERMES). Vol. 1, No. 1 (Jan. 4, 1975)-. 0736-0940. Periodical. US. English. mo. Hermes, PO Box 959, Santa Barbara CA 93102. **Tel** (805)966-3941.

HEROLD DER WAHRHEIT. Began in 1912. 0300-8851. Periodical. US. English or German. mo. Herold der Wahr Heit, Kalona IA 52247.

HEYTHROP JOURNAL. V. 1- Jan. 1960-. 0018-1196. Periodical. UK. English. qt. $30.00. Heythrop Journal, 11 Cavendish Square, London W1M 0AN England. **Tel** (01)491 7596. **Ed** J A Munitiz. **Ind/Abst** Old Testam. Abstr., Philos. Index, New Testam. Abstr., Ref. Source, Cathol. Period. Lit. Index, Recent Publ. Artic. **LC** BX801. bk rev acc. **Circ** 900. Articles and book reviews on religious dogma, history, philosophy and related topics, broad Catholic ecumenical slant. University research level.

HIGLEY COMMENTARY; INTERNATIONAL UNIFORM SUNDAY SCHOOL LESSONS. VFOAT International Uniform Sunday School Lessons. US. English. an. **LC** BV1560.

HOLY CROSS. V. 1-. Periodical. US. English. qt. Order of the Holy Cross, West Park NY 12493. Holy Cross.

HOME MISSIONS (TORONTO, ONT.). (HOME MISSIONS). Sept. 1982-. 0823-8464. Periodical. CN. English. qt $2.00 Per Year. Catholic Church Extension Society of Canada, 67 Bond Street, Toronto Ontario M5B 1X5 Canada. **DD** 266.27105.

HOMILETIC SERVICE. Began publication in 1961. 0381-7466. Periodical. CN. English. bm. Npvalis, Box 9700 Terminal, Ottawa Ontario K1G 4B4 Canada.

HOMILY HINTS FOR CONTEMPORARY PREACHING. 0227-0676. Periodical. CN. English. bw. $77.38. Capsulized Communications Ltd, Box 968, Vernon British Columbia V1T 6N2 Canada. **Tel** (604)545-8632. **Ed** R G Fitzpatrick. **DD** 251.0205. Christian message presented in today's terms with a life event, deepened by relating to the gospel and integrated into the personal life of the listener.

HORIZONS. V. 1- Fall 1974-. 0360-9669. Periodical. US. English. sa. $16.00. Wilfrid Laurier University Press, Wilfrid Laurier University, Waterloo Ontario N26 3C5 Canada. **Tel** (215)645-7302. **Ed** Walter E Conn. **Ind/Abst** Old Testam. Abstr., Cathol. Period. Lit. Index, Guide Soc. Sci. Relig. Period. Lit., Relig. Index One, Period., New Testam. Abstr., Soc. Sci. Citation Index. **LC** BR1. **DD** 230.205. bk rev adv acc. **Circ** 1,450. A journal exploring developments in Catholic theology, the total Christian tradition, human religious experience, and the concerns of creative teaching from the college and university environment.

HORIZONS IN BIBLICAL THEOLOGY. See Religion, Mythology, Rationalism - Bible.

HORIZONS (OAKVILLE, ONT.). (HORIZONS). Jan. 1981-. 0712-6077. Periodical. CN. English. ir. Horizons, c/o Salvation Army, Editorial Department, 455 North Service Road East, Oakville Ontario L6H 1A5 Canada. **DD** 267.1505. Officer Bulletin.

HOSANNA. 0276-3729. Periodical. US. English. Free. Hosanna, c/o North American Liturgy Resources, 2110 West Peoria Avenue, Phoenix AZ 85029.

HUMAN DEVELOPMENT (NEW YORK, N.Y. : 1980). See Psychology.

THE HYMN. See Music.

HYONDAE MOKHOE. Periodical. Korean. mo. 19.000. Chu, Hyondae Mokhoe, PO Box 144, Youido Ucheguk Seoul 150. **LC** BV4000.

HYONDAE SAJO. VFOAT The Current Thoughts. V. 1- Dec. 1971-. Periodical. Korean (Korean). ir. 5.000. Kidokkyo Sajosa, 22 2-ka Namsan-dong, Chung-ku Seoul South Korea. **LC** BV4485. **DD** 248.405.

IMSS NEWSLETTER. VAT Inter Mennonite Student Services Newsletter. Vol. 1, No. 1 (Nov. 1982)-. 0823-8812. Periodical. CN. English. ty. Free to Young Ontario Mennonites. IMSS Newsletter, University Community Centre/Room 4, University of Western Ontario, London Ontario N6A 3K7 Canada. **DD** 259.2409713.

THE INDIAN JOURNAL OF THEOLOGY. Began publication in 1952. 0019-5685. Periodical. II. English. qt. $5.20. Bishops College, 224 Lower Circular Road, Calcutta 700017 India. **Ind/Abst** New Testam. Abstr., Relig. Index One, Period. **LC** BR1.

INDIAN THEOLOGICAL STUDIES. Vol. 14, No. 1 (Mar. 1977)-. Periodical. II. English. qt. $10.00. Indian Theological Studies, St Peters Seminary, Bangalore 560 055 India. **Ind/Abst** Old Testam. Abstr., New Testam. Abstr. Indian Ecclesiastical Studies.

INFORMATEUR. (L'INFORMATEUR). V. 2, No. 16/17 Aug. 21/ Sept. 3, 1983)-. 0824-4111. Periodical. CN. French. bm. $25.00 Per Year. Informateur, 1915 East Boulevard Gouin, Montreal Quebec H2B 1W7 Canada. **DD** 261.8309714. Informateur Catholique, 0712-3973.

Religion, Mythology, Rationalism—Theology

INLAND AFRICA CEASED. Began in 1917. 0020-1464. Periodical. US. English. qt. **DD** 266. Hearing and Doing.

INTENTION MISSIONNAIRE. (INTENTION MISSIONNAIRE : COMMENTAIRE MENSUEL DE L'INTENTION PONTIFICALE). V. 15, No. 1 (Jan. 1980)-. 0228-6971. Periodical. CN. French. mo. $1.50. Intention Missionnaire, CP 220, Limoilou Quebec G1L 4V7 Canada. **DD** 266.205. Feuillet Missionnaire, 0700-9291.

INTERCHANGE : PAPERS ON BIBLICAL AND CURRENT QUESTIONS. No. 14-. Periodical. English. ir. Interchange, Second Floor/SU House, 129 York Street, Sydney 2000 Australia.

INTERNATIONAL BULLETIN OF MISSIONARY RESEARCH. VFOAT International Bulletin. Vol. 5, No. 1 (Jan. 1981)-. 0272-6122. Periodical. US. English. qt. Hochman Associates, 120 East 56th Street, New York NY 10022. **Tel** (212)371-4932. **Ed** Gerald Anderson. **Ind/Abst** Bibliogr. Mission., Christ. Period. Index, Guide Soc. Sci. Relig. Period. Lit., Missionalia, Relig. Index One, Period., Relig. Theol. Abstr. **LC** BV2350. **DD** 266.005. bk rev. adv acc. Christian missionary magazine about the ministry throughout the world. Occasional Bulletin of Missionary Research, 0364-2178.

INTERNATIONAL JOURNAL OF FRONTIER MISSIONS. Vol. 1, No. 1-. 0743-2429. Periodical. US. English. qt $15.00. International Student Leaders Coalition for Frontier Missions, PO Box 40628, Pasadena CA 91104-7638. **Tel** (818)797-1111. **Ed** Bradley A Gill. **DD** 266. bk rev. adv acc. **Circ** 375. A professional journal of evangelical persuasion, focusing on missionary endeavor in societies presently without Christian chruches.

INTERNATIONALE KIRCHLICHE ZEITSCHRIFT. VFOAT Revue Internationale Ecclesiatique, International Church Review. Began with Vol. 1 in 1911. 0020-9252. Periodical. SZ. German. qt. $23.75. Staempfli & Cie SA, Hallerstrasse 7-9, Postfach 2728, CH-3001 Berne Switzerland. **Ed** Adolk Thurlings. **Ind/Abst** Old Testam. Abstr., New Testam. Abstr. (cum index) Revue Internationale de Theologie.

INTERPRETATION. V. 1- Jan. 1947-. 0020-9643. Periodical. US. English. qt. $12.00 Domestic, $13.50 Foreign. Union Theological Seminary, 3401 Brook Road, Richmond VA 23227. **Tel** (804)355-0671. **Ed** Paul J Achtemeier. **Ind/Abst** Book Rev. Index, Old Testam. Abstr., Soc. Sci. Index, Int. Zeitschriftenschan Bibelwissenschaft Grenzgeb., Relig. Index One, Period., New Testam. Abstr., Christ. Period. Index, Relig. Theol. Abstr., Humanit. Index, Ref. Source, Guide Soc. Sci. Relig. Period. Lit., Index Relig. Period. Lit. **LC** BR1. **DD** 205. (cum index). bk rev. adv acc. **Circ** 12,000. (ctrl). Articles and essays of "biblical and theological interpretation in the community of faith" for scholars, clergy, and laity of all denominational backgrounds. Union Seminary Review, 0362-904X.

ISSUE. 1- June 1973-. 0316-7550. CN. English. ir. Free. United Church of Canada, Division of Mission in Canada, 85 St Clair Avenue East, Toronto Ontario M4T 1M8 Canada. **DD** 261.8.

ISTINA. 1 - Volume. 0021-2423. Periodical. FR. French. qt. $30.59. Centre d'Etudes Istina, 45 rue de la Glaciere, F 75013 Paris France. **Tel** 45 35 3704. **Ind/Abst** New Testam. Abstr., Relig. Index One, Period. **LC** BX1781. bk rev. Ecumenical journal; theological dialogue between Christian churches, Jewish Christian dialogue, religious liberty and human rights in East-European countries. Russie et Chretiente.

JAHRBUCH FUR LITURGIK UND HYMNOLOGIE. See Yearbooks, Almanacs, Directories.

JESUS, MARIE ET NOTRE TEMPS. VFOAT Notre Temps. V. 4, No. 2- Jan. 1974-. 0383-2635. Periodical. CN. French. mo. **DD** 232.9105. Marie et Notre Temps, 0383-2627; Annoncer Jesis-Christ.

JESUS, TON AMI, TE PARLE ET T'ECOUTE. Published since 1979?. 0226-7381. Periodical. CN. French. qt. Assemblee Canadienne Francophone du Renouveau, Charismatique Catholique, CP 207, Chambly Quebec J3L 4B3 Canada. **DD** 248.8205.

JEUNESSE FRANCOIS D'ASSISE. (JEUNESSE FRANCOIS D'ASSISE : BULLETIN). **VAT** Bulletin - Jeunesse Francois d'Assiee. 0822-5559. Periodical. CN. French. bm. Free. Jeunesse Francois d'Assise, C P 5185, Beauport Quebec G1E 6B5 Canada. **DD** 248.8305.

JOUR DU SEIGNEUR. (LE JOUR DU SEIGNEUR). Vol. 1, No. 1 (Sept./Oct./Nov. 1984)-. 0828-4717. Periodical. CN. French. $1.00 Per No. Jour du Seigneur, c/o Editions Fides, 5710 Av DeCelles, Montreal Quebec H3S 2C5 Canada. **DD** 264.02305.

JOURNAL OF CHRISTIAN COUNSELING. V. 1- Winter 1977-. 0146-0366. Periodical. US. English. qt $12.00. PO Box 548, Mt Pleasant MI 48858. **LC** BV4012. **DD** 253.505.

JOURNAL OF CHRISTIAN JURISPRUDENCE. See Law.

JOURNAL OF CHRISTIAN NURSING. See Medicine - Nursing.

THE JOURNAL OF CHRISTIAN RECONSTRUCTION. V. 1- Summer 1974-. 0360-1420. Periodical. US. English. ir. Chalcedon, PO Box 158, Vallecito CA 95251. **Tel** (209)736-4365. **Ed** R J Rushdoony. **Ind/Abst** Christ. Period. Index. **LC** BR1. **DD** 230.05. bk rev. **Circ** 1,500. A compendium of original monographs and reviews applying Christian principles of analyses to contemporary and historical situations, persons, and trends.

JOURNAL OF CURRENT SOCIAL ISSUES. V. 9, No. 5- Spring 1971-. 0041-7211. Periodical. US. English. qt. $3.00. United Church of Christ, Division of Higher Education, Office of Publication, Todd Hill Road, Lakeside CT 06758. **Ind/Abst** Public Aff. Inf. Serv. Bull. **LC** BX9884.A1. **DD** 261.8305. Journal - United Church of Christ, Division of Higher Education.

THE JOURNAL OF PASTORAL CARE. V. 1- Sept. 1947-. 0022-3409. Periodical. US. English. qt. $5.00. Association for Clinical Pastoral Education, Business Office, 475 Riverside Drive/Suite 450, New York NY 10027. **Ind/Abst** Relig. Index One, Period., Hospit. Lit. Index, Psychol. Abstr., Theol. Relig. Index, Soc. Work Res. Abstr. **LC** BV4000. **DD** 250.5. **NLM** W1 JO828. **CODEN** JPACA. Journal of Clinical Pastoral Work.

THE JOURNAL OF PASTORAL COUNSELING. Began with V. 1 in 1966. 0449-508X. Periodical. US. English. sa. $6.00. Iona College, 715 North Avenue, New Rochelle NY 10801. **Tel** (914)633-2418. **Ed** Samuel M Natale. **Ind/Abst** Relig. Index One, Period. **DD** 253. bk rev. adv acc. **Circ** 1,000. Counseling and religious values. Iona Journal of Pastoral Counseling.

JOURNAL OF PSYCHOLOGY AND THEOLOGY. See Psychology.

JOURNAL OF RELIGIOUS EDUCATION : JRE CEASED. VFOAT JRE. Ceased with Vol. 40, No. 3 (April/June 1980). 0022-4219. Periodical. US. English. qt. Journal of Religious Education, 414 8th Avenue South, Nashville TN 37203.

JOURNAL OF SUPERVISION AND TRAINING IN MINISTRY. V. 1- Winter 1978-. 0160-7774. US. English. ir. $8.00. Journal of Supervision and Training in Ministry, PO Box 6777, Chicago IL 60680. **Tel** (312)942-5572. **Ed** George Fitchett. **Ind/Abst** Relig. Index One, Period. **LC** BV4012. **DD** 207.73. bk rev. adv acc. Only publication devoted exclusively to consideration of practice-based aspects of education for religious leadership, both theoretical and applied aspects.

JOURNAL OF THE EVANGELICAL THEOLOGICAL SOCIETY. Main/Corp Evangelical Theological Society. V. 12- Winter 1969-. 0360-8808. Periodical. US. English. qt. $5.00. Vernon Grounds Conservative Baptist Theological Seminary, University Park Station, PO Box 10000, Denver CO 80210. **Ind/Abst** Old Testam. Abstr., New Testam. Abstr., Christ. Period. Index, Relig. Theol. Abstr., Bibliogr. Repert. Christ. Inst., Relig. Index One, Period. **LC** BR21. **DD** 205. Bulletin of the Evangelical Theological Society, 0361-5138.

THE JOURNAL OF THE FAITH THEOLOGICAL SEMINARY ALUMNI ASSOCIATION. Main/Corp Faith Theological Seminary. Alumni Association. Periodical. US. English. qt. Journal of the Faith Theological Seminary Alumni Association, 723 West 7th Street, Chester PA 19013.

JOURNAL OF THE INTERDENOMINATIONAL THEOLOGICAL CENTER. (THE JOURNAL OF THE INTERDENOMINATIONAL THEOLOGICAL CENTER). Main/Corp Interdenominational Theological Center, Atlanta. V. 1- Fall 1973-. 0092-6558. Periodical. US. English. sa. $8.00. Journal of Interdenominational Theological Center, 671 Beckwith Street SW, Atlanta GA 30314. **Tel** (404)522-1772. **Ed** John C Diamond. **Ind/Abst** New Testam. Abstr., Relig. Index One, Period. **LC** BR1. **DD** 230.05. bk rev. **Circ** 1,000. A theological interpretation to social, ethical, economical, and religious issues from the perspective of worldwide scholars.

JOURNAL OF THEOLOGICAL STUDIES. V. 1-50 (No. 1-199/200) Oct. 1899-July/Oct. 1949. 0022-5185. Periodical. UK. English. sa. $80.00. Oxford University Press, Walton Street, Oxford OX2 6DP England. **Tel** 0865 56767. **Ed** H Chadwick, M Hooker and M Wiles. **Ind/Abst** Old Testam. Abstr., New Testam. Abstr., MLA Int. Bibliogr. Books Artic. Mod. Lang. Lit., Ref. Source, Relig. Index One, Period. **LC** BR1. **DD** 230.05. adv acc. **Circ** 507. Available on microfilm from University Microfilms International. Includes all areas of academic study of Christian theology, old and new testaments, church history, philosophy of religion and ethics with both ancient and modern texts and documents.

JOURNAL OF THEOLOGY. 1961. 0361-1906. Periodical. US. English. qt. $5.00. Church of the Lutheran Confession, Immanuel Lutheran College, Eau Claire WI 54701. **Tel** (715)834-3301. **Ed** C M Gullerud. bk rev. **Circ** 300. Professional journal of confessional Lutheran theology for pastors and teachers.

JOURNAL OF THEOLOGY FOR SOUTHERN AFRICA. No. 1- Dec. 1972-. 0047-2867. Periodical. SA. English. qt. 25-00. Journal Theology Southern Africa, University Cape Town, Religious Studies, Rondebosch 7700 South Africa. **Ed** John W de Gruchy. **Ind/Abst** Old Testam. Abstr., New Testam. Abstr., Relig. Index One, Period. **LC** BR1. **DD** 230.0968. bk rev. adv acc. **Circ** 850. Journal of theology for Southern Africa.

JOURNAL OF THETA ALPHA KAPPA. VFOAT JTAK. 8756-4785. Periodical. US. English. sa. $1.50. Editor JTAK, Theology Department, St John's University, Jamaica NY 11439. **DD** 207.

THE JOYFUL WOMAN. 0164-4882. Periodical. US. English. mo. $9.50. Joyful Woman, PO Box 3227, Chattanooga TN 37404. **Tel** (615)893-7961. **DD** 248.

JUSTICE. No. 1- May 1971-. Periodical. JM. English. ir. Social Action Centre, 8 Oliver Road, Kingston 8 Jamaica West Indies. **LC** HN39.J28. **DD** 261.83097292.

KAEHYOK SINANG. VFOAT Refromed Faith. Periodical. KO. Korean. mo. Kaehyok Sinangsa, 34 Amnam-dong So-ku, Pusan Korea. **LC** BV4485.

KATOLSK ARSSKRIFT. Swedish. ir. 40.00. Katolska Teologforeningen, Hogbergsgatan 67 116 20, Stockholm Sweden. **LC** BR50.

KERK EN THEOLOGIE. 1st Volume-. 0450-1489. Periodical. NE. Dutch. qt. Boekencentrum Nieuws, Scheveningseweg 72, 2517 KX Den Haag Netherlands. Onder Eigen Vaandel.

KERYGMA. V. 1- 1967-. 0023-0693. Periodical. CN. French (English). sa. 12.00. Institute of Mission Studies, St Paul University, 233 Main Street, Ottawa K1S 1C4 Canada. **Tel** (613)236-1393. **Ed** Achiel Peelman. **Circ** 220. (ctrl). Communication medium between missionaries and researchers for discussion on contemporary issues: inculturation traditional religions and Christianity faith-cultures social challenges.

KERYGMA UND DOGMA. Vol. 1-. 0023-0707. Periodical. GW. German. qt. $28.40. Vandenhoeck & Ruprecht, Postfach 3753/Theaterstr 13, D 3400 Goettingen West Germany. **Tel** 0551/65061. **Ind/Abst** Old Testam. Abstr., New Testam. Abstr., Relig. Index One, Period. **LC** BR4.

KERYGMA UND DOGMA. BEIHEFT. VFOAT Beiheft Zu Kerygma und Dogma. 1-. 0453-7726. Monographic Series. German. ir. Verlag Vandenhoeck & Ruprecht, Postfach 77, 3400 Gottingen West Germany.

KEY TO CHRISTIAN EDUCATION. VFOAT Key. V. 1- Oct./Dec. 1962-. 0023-0839. Periodical. US. English. qt. $4.00. Standard Publishers Company, 8121 Hamilton Avenue, Cincinnati OH 45231. **Tel** (800)543-1301. **Ed** Virginia

Religion, Mythology, Rationalism—Theology

Beddow. LC BV1500. **Circ** 65,000. Ideas that are working in the field of Christian education.

KINDERGARTEN TEACHER. 0745-8258. Periodical. US. English. qt. Kindergarten Teacher, American Baptist Churches, Valley Forge PA 19481.

KLERONOMIA : PERIODIKON DEMOSIEUMA TOU PATRIARCHIKOU HIDRYMATOS PATERIKON MELETON. V. 1, (Jan. 1969)-. Periodical. GR. English (chiefly Greek, with occasional articles in French, German and Italian). sa. $32.00. Patriarchikon Hidryma Pateriko, 64 Eptapyrigiou St Moni Vladtad Thessalonike Greece. **Tel** (031)202 301. LC BR66.

KNOW YOUR MISSIONARIES. No. 1-. 0229-0537. Periodical. CN. English. mo. Free. Know Your Missionaries, Everyday Publications, Suite 1915/43 Thorncliffe Park Drive, Toronto Ontario M4C 3T4 Canada. **DD** 266.005. (ctrl).

KRISTET FORUM. Feb. 1954-. 0452-716X. Periodical. SW. Swedish. ir. $8.00. Forbundet for Kristen Humanism Och Samnallssyn/Kristna Studentrorelsen i Svenge, Box 2044, S-750 02 Uppsala Sweden. **Tel** 018-108648. **Ed** Erik Lindberg. LC LH5.S9. bk rev. adv acc. **Circ** 2,700. Christian bookpublishing, migration, mission, freedom, sabotage in Nicaragua, preachers on film, rich and poor, feminist theology, and devotion to the devil in the "heavy metal-music". *Frikyrklig Ungdom, Kristendom Och Samhalle.*

LATIN AMERICAN PULSE CEASED. VFOAT Pulse. 0739-0513. Periodical. US. English. sa. $25.00. Evangelical Missions Information Service, Box 794, Wheaton IL 60189. *Pulse.*

LAVAL THEOLOGIQUE ET PHILOSOPHIQUE. VFOAT Laval Theologique Philosophique. VAT Laval Theologique Philosophique. V. 1- 1945-. 0023-9054. Periodical. CN. French (English). ir. 15.00. Faculte de Philosophie, Universite Laval, Pavillon Felix-Antoine-Savard, Ste-Foy Quebec Canada G1K 7P4. **Tel** (418)656-7612. **Ed** Yvan Pelletier. **Ind/Abst** New Testam. Abstr., Cathol. Period. Lit. Index, Old Testam. Abstr., Philos. Index, Point Repere, MLA Int. Bibliogr. Books Artic. Mod. Lang. Lit. LC BX802. DD 282.05. Index in last issue of volume - attached. (cum index). bk rev. adv acc. **Circ** 1,000. Available on microfilm or microfiche from Bibliotheque National du Quebec, Micromedia Limited, or University Microfilms International. A Quebec journal to promote research and discussion in all fields of theological and philosophical thinking.

LEADER GUIDEBOOK. V. 68, No. 4- Oct./Dec. 1967-. 0023-9623. Periodical. US. English. qt. $3.80. D C Cook Publishing Co, 850 North Grove Avenue, Elgin IL 60120. LC BV1500. **DD** 268.05. *Leader.*

LEADERSHIP 100. VAT Leadership One Hundred. Vol. 1, No. 1 (Mar.-Apr. 1982)-. Periodical. US. English. qt. $18.00. Leadership 100, Subscription Department, PO Box 1916, Marion OH 43305. **Tel** (312)260-6200. **Ed** Terry C Muck. bk rev. adv acc. **Circ** 80,000. (ctrl). Articles to meet the everyday needs and problems of ministry for pastors, Sunday school leaders, elders, deacons and leaders in the church.

LEADERSHIP (CAROL STREAM). (LEADERSHIP : A PUBLICATION OF CHRISTIANITY TODAY, INC): Vol. 1, No. 1 (Winter 1980)-. 0199-7661. Periodical. US. English. qt. $16.00. Leadership Subscription Services, PO Box 1105, Dover NJ 07801. LC BV4000. **DD** 253.05.

LECCIONES CRISTIANAS. 0149-8363. Periodical. US. Spanish. qt. $3.75. Graded Press, United Methodist Publishing House, 201 8th Avenue South, Nashville TN 37202.

LECCIONES DE LA ESCUELA SABATICA. VFOAT Sabbath School Lessons. 8750-4448. Periodical. US. Spanish. qt. $3.40. Lecciones de la Escuela Sabatica, PO Box 7000, Boise ID 83707. **DD** 242.

LECTERN RESOURCE. Vol. 1, No. 1 (Jan./Feb./Mar. 1984)-. 0746-763X. Periodical. US. English. qt. $12.00 Domestic, $13.00 Canada. Pulpit Resource Inc, 5016 Double Point Way, Byron CA 94514-9321. **Tel** (808)373-4410. **Circ** 1,500. Aid for planning worship, scriptural resource material, word for children intercession and includes international focus.

LEGAL SHOCK. VFOAT Legal Shock - Without Prejudice - A Search for Justice Under God. V. 1- Jan. 1980-. 0225-5391. Periodical. CN. English. mo. $12.00. Legal Shock, PO Box 284 Station G, Toronto Ontario M4M 3G7 Canada. **DD** 261.5.

LELKIPASZTOR. Periodical. HU. Hungarian. mo. Akademiai Kiado, POB 24, 1363 Budapest Hungary. LC BV4000.

LETTER FROM TAIZE. Began with No. 1 published May 1970 issue. Periodical. US. English. mo. $9.00. Letter from Taize, 2150 Almaden Road, 114 San Jose CA 95123. LC BV4408.A1.

LEXINGTON THEOLOGICAL QUARTERLY. V. 1- Jan. 1966-. 0024-1628. Periodical. US. English. qt. Lexington Theological Seminary, 631 South Limestone Street, Lexington KY 40508. **Tel** (606)252-0361. **Ed** Richard Harrison. **Ind/Abst** Old Testam. Abstr., New Testam. Abstr., Relig. Index One, Period. LC BR1. bk rev. **Circ** 2,500. (ctrl). For ministers and professors of religion, it includes scholarly articles on Bible, theology, church history, ethics, sermons and sermon preparation, Christian unity, and pastoral care. *College of the Bible Quarterly, 0160-8770.*

LIBERATION. No. 1- Jan. 1979-. 0227-2687. Periodical. CN. English. Renaissance International, PO Box 100, Milton Ontario L9T 2Y3 Canada. **DD** 269.20971.

THE LITTLE LAMP. 0460-1297. Periodical. US. English. qt. $8.00. Blue Mountain Center of Meditation, Box 477, Petaluma CA 94953. **Tel** (707)878-2369. **Ed** Christine Easwaran. LC BL624. **DD** 294.54405. **Circ** 2,000. A journal for leading the spiritual life in the home and the community. *Newsletter (Blue Mountain Center of Meditation).*

LITURGIEWISSENSCHAFTLICHE QUELLEN UND FORSCHUNGEN. Vol. 32- 1957-. 0076-0048. Monographic Series. German. ir. **Tel** 251/6901. LC BV170. Research and documentation on doctrinal theology, from the beginnings of Christianity through the middle ages and the reformation. *Liturgiegeschichtliche Quellen und Forschungen.*

LITURGISCHES JAHRBUCH. See Yearbooks, Almanacs, Directories.

LITURGY CEASED. Began with Mar. 1956 issue. Ceased with Mar./Apr. 1980 issue. 0458-063X. Periodical. US. English. mo. LC BV169. **DD** 264.005.

LITURGY DOCUMENTARY SERIES. 1-. Monographic Series. US. English. Office of Publishing Services, United States Catholic Conference, 1312 Massachusetts Avenue NW, Washington DC 20005.

LIVING THE WORD. LEVEL 8, GRADES TEN-TWELVE STUDENT'S RESOURCE. (LIVING THE WORD. LEVEL 8, GRADES TEN-TWELVE). VFOAT Living the Word. 0883-7236. Periodical. US. English. qt. United Church Press, 132 West 31st Street, New York NY 10001. **DD** 268.

LIVING WORSHIP CEASED. 0360-6244. Periodical. US. English. mo. $4.00. 1330 Massachusetts Avenue, Washington DC 20005. LC BV169. **DD** 264.005.

LOAVES & FISHES (TORONTO, ONT.). (LOAVES & FISHES). VAT Loaves and Fishes. Vol. 1 (Fall 1978)-. 0714-7880. Periodical. CN. English. sa. $10.00. Canec Publishing and Supply House, 85 St Clair Avenue East, Toronto Ontario M4T 1M8 Canada. **DD** 268.432.

LONERGAN STUDIES NEWSLETTER. Vol. 1, No. 1 (Jan. 1980)-. Periodical. CN. English. qt. $5.00. Marist College/Religious Studies, Michael O'Callaghan, Poughkeepsie NY 12601. **Tel** (914)471-3240. **Ed** Michael C O'Callaghan. bk rev. **Circ** 350. International quarterly presenting and reviewing scholarship related to the methodology proposed by Bernard Lonergan for contemporary philosophy and theology.

LONERGAN WORKSHOP. V. 1-. 0148-2009. Periodical. US. English. an. Scholars Press, University of Montana, Missoula MT 59801. LC BX4705.L7133. **DD** 230.05.

LOUVAIN STUDIES. Vol. 1, No. 1 (Fall 1966)-. 0024-6964. Periodical. BE. English. sa. $8.00. Louvain Studies, University of Louvain, Faculty of Theology, Naamsestraat 100, B-3000 Leuven Belgium. **Ed** Raymond F Collins. **Ind/Abst** New Testam. Abstr., Cathol. Period. Lit. Index. LC BX801. bk rev. **Circ** 1,500. Available on microfilm from University Microfilms International. Presents current scholarship in Roman Catholic theology.

LUCRURI NOI SI VECHI. Began in 1984. 8756-8012. Periodical. US. Romanian (Rumanian, with occasional articles in English). mo. $25.00. Motz Publications, 9304 Annapolis Court, Fairfax VA 22032. **Ed** Dorin ('Doru") Motz. **DD** 947. bk rev. adv acc. **Circ** 2,900. (ctrl). Non-denominational Christian publication with many additional subjects geared for preservation of Romanian language in its best form. Also many articles on English language.

LUMEN VITAE. 0024-7324. BE. English. qt. $27.50. Lumen Vitae, International Review of Religious Education, 186 rue Washington, B-1050 Bruxelles Belgium. **Tel** 02/344 18 82. **Ed** P Mourlon Beernaert. **Ind/Abst** Educ. Index, Cathol. Period. Lit. Index. bk rev. adv acc. **Circ** 1,500. Religious education, faith formation, and pastoral theology.

LUMIERE ET VIE (SAINT-ALBAN-LEYSSE, FRANCE). (LUMIERE ET VIE). Began with: No 1 (Dec. 1951). 0024-7359. Periodical. FR. French. ir. 160.00. Lumiere Et Vie, 2 Place Gailleton, Lyon F-69002 France. **Tel** 33-7842 6683. **Ind/Abst** New Testam. Abstr., Cathol. Period. Lit. Index. (cum index). bk rev. adv acc. **Circ** 3,000. Journal dealing with theological structure and reflection.

THE LUTHERAN SYNOD QUARTERLY. V. 1-20, 1940-60. 0360-9685. Periodical. US. English. qt. $10.00. Bethany Lutheran Seminary, 447 North Division, Mankato MN 56001. **Tel** (507)625-2977. **Ed** Wilhelm W Petersen. bk rev. **Circ** 300. Microfilm. Articles on theological issues of the day, and on our doctrinal heritage based on the Lutheran reformation.

LUTHERAN THEOLOGICAL JOURNAL. V. 1-. 0024-7553. Periodical. AT. English. ty. $7.75. Lutheran Publishing House, Box 1368, GPO Adelaide 5001 Australia. **Ed** Hamann. **Ind/Abst** Old Testam. Abstr., New Testam. Abstr., Relig. Index One, Period. bk rev. (ctrl). Theological articles. *Australasian Theological Review.*

LUTHERAN WOMEN'S MISSIONARY LEAGUE QUARTERLY ECHO. VFOAT Quarterly Echo. 8750-5207. Periodical. US. English. qt. LWML Quarterly, Echo Rt 1/Box 60, Pleasanton NE 68866.

LUTHERISCHE THEOLOGIE UND KIRCHE. Feb. 1977-. Periodical. GW. German. ir. 25. Lutherische Theologie und Altkonigstrasse, 150, 6370 Oberursel West Germany. bk rev. Essays concerning Lutheran theology, including doctrinal and practical theology.

MC : THE MODERN CHURCHMAN. New Ser., V. 25, No. 1 (1982)-. Periodical. UK. English. qt. $10.73. Modern Churchmens Union, School House Leysters Leominis, Herefordshire HR6 OHS England. **Tel** 056 887 271. **Ed** A O Dyson. **Ind/Abst** New Testam. Abstr. bk rev. **Circ** 1,200. Informed Christian thinking and a questioning approach to issues of theology and the ethical, pastoral, spiritual and socio-political aspects of contemporary life. *Modern Churchman, 0026-7597.*

MANDATE. V. 10, No. 7- Oct. 1979-. 0225-7068. Periodical. CN. English. ir. $4. per year. Mandate, Canec Publishing and Supply House, 47 Coldwater Road, Don Mills Ontario M3B 1Y9 Canada. **DD** 266.79205. *Mandate Newsletter, 0383-1493.*

MARBURGER THEOLOGISCHE STUDIEN. Began publication in 1963. 0542-657X. Monographic Series. GW. German. ir. N G Elwert Verlag, Postfach 1128, Reitgasse 7+9, D-3550 Marburg West Germany.

MEDIA & VALUES. Began in 1977. 0149-6980. Periodical. US. English. qt. $12.00. Media Action Research Center, 1962 South Shenandoah, Los Angeles CA 90034. **Tel** (213)559-2944. **Ed** Elizabeth Thoman. bk rev. **Circ** 2,500. An interfaith media education magazine prompting social analysis and practical local action on issues of contemporary media and new technology.

MEDIA DEVELOPMENT. See Communication.

MEGIDDO MESSAGE; DEVOTED TO THE CAUSE OF CHRIST. See Religion, Mythology, Rationalism - Bible.

MELANESIAN JOURNAL OF THEOLOGY. Vol. 1, No. 1 (Apr. 1985)-. Periodical. English. sa. $6.00. Martin Luther Seminary, Rev Kasek Kautil, PO Box 80, Lae Morobe Province, Paupua New Guinea.

MELITA THEOLOGICA : THE REVIEW OF THE ROYAL UNIVERSITY STUDENTS' THEOLOGICAL ASSOCIATION, MALTA. Began publication in 1947. Periodical. MM. English (French or Italian). sa. $8.00. Theology Students' Association, Faculty of Theology, Tal-Virtu, Rabat Malta. **Tel** 675497/8. **Ed** Carmelo Sant. **Ind/Abst** Old Testam. Abstr., New Testam. Abstr. **LC** BX804. **DD** 282.05. bk rev. adv acc. **Circ** 1,000.

MEMBERSHIP DIRECTORY - ASSOCIATION FOR CREATIVE CHANGE WITHIN RELIGIOUS AND OTHER SOCIAL SYSTEMS (U.S.). *See* Yearbooks, Almanacs, Directories.

MEMBERSHIP DIRECTORY - NATIONAL ASSOCIATION OF CHURCH BUSINESS ADMINISTRATION (U.S.). *See* Yearbooks, Almanacs, Directories.

MEMORIE DOMENICANE (PISTOIA : 1970). *See* History (General) - History of Europe.

METHOD (LOS ANGELES, CALIF.). *See* Philosophy.

MIC MISSION NEWS. (M I C MISSION NEWS). **Main/Corp** Missionary Sisters of the Immaculate Conception. V. 1- Jan./Feb. 1974-. 0315-9655. Periodical. CN. English. bm. Missionary Sisters of the Immaculate Conception, PO Box 157 Laval Branch PO, Laval Quebec H7N 424 Canada. **DD** 266.2. *Precursor, 0315-9663.*

MICHAEL FIGHTING. 0227-0978. CN. English. Pilgrims of Saint Michael, Rougement Quebec Canada. **DD** 261.805.

MID-AMERICA THEOLOGICAL JOURNAL. 1977. 0734-9882. Periodical. US. English. sa. $12.00. Mid American Baptist Theological Seminary, PO Box 3624, Memphis TN 38173. **Tel** (901)726-9171. **Ed** Jimmy A Millikin. **LC** BR1. **DD** 230.613205. bk rev. **Circ** 500. Studies on biblical and theological themes from both A practical and technical perspective.

MID-STREAM. V. 1- Nov. 1961-. 0544-0653. Periodical. US. English. qt. $15.00. Council on Christian Unity, 222 South Downey Avenue, PO Box 1986, Indianapolis IN 46206. **Tel** (317)353-1491. **Ed** Paul A Crow Jr. **Ind/Abst** Abstr. Engl. Stud., Relig. Index One, Period., Am. Hist. Life, Hist. Abstr. **LC** BX1. **DD** 262.001. bk rev. **Circ** 1,000. A journal bringing together articles, documentation, and book reviews on the direction and history of the ecumenical movement in the United States and internationally. *Digest of the Proceedings of the Meeting of the Consultation on Church Union, 0589-4867.*

MILLTOWN STUDIES. 1977. 0332-1428. Periodical. IE. English. sa. 7.00. Institute of Theology and Philosophy, Milltown Park, Dublin 6 Ireland. **Tel** (01)697257. **Ed** Wilfrid Harrington. **Ind/Abst** Old Testam. Abstr., New Testam. Abstr. bk rev. adv acc. **Circ** 300. Theological and philosophical reviews.

MINISTRIES (WINTER PARK, FLA.). (MINISTRIES). Vol. 1, No. 1 (Winter 1983)-. 0739-3997. Periodical. US. English. $20.00 Domestic and US Possessions, $22.00 Canada. Ministries Magazine, Box 1161, Dover NJ 07801. **LC** BV4000. **DD** 253.05.

MINISTRY (WASHINGTON, D.C. : 1981). (MINISTRY). 0026-5314. Periodical. US. English. mo. $19.95. 6840 Eastern Avenue Northwest, Washington DC 20012. **Tel** (202)722-6506. **Ed** J Robert Spangler. **LC** BX 6101. **DD** 253.05. bk rev. Ministerial journal for Seventh-Day Adventist pastors and clergy of other faiths.

MINUTES OF THE . . . MEETING. **Main/Corp** World Council of Churches. Central Committee. Began with 27th (1974). English. an. World Council of Churches, 150 Route de Ferney, 1211 Geneva 20 Switzerland. **LC** BX6.W773. **DD** 270.82. *Minutes and Reports of the Meeting.*

MISCELANEA COMILLAS. **Main/Corp** Universidad Pontificia de Comillas. V. 3-. 0210-9522. Periodical. Spanish. sa. **Ind/Abst** New Testam. Abstr. **LC** BX880. **DD** 230.2. *Miscelanea de Colaboracion Cientifica de los Antiguos Alumnos de la Universidad Pontificia de Comillas.*

MISION (BUENOS AIRES, ARGENTINA). (MISION). Vol. 1, No. 1 (Mar.-Jun. 1982)-. Periodical. Spanish. qt. Orientacion Cristiana, PO Box 140385, Miami FL 33114. **Ed** C Renepadilla.

MISIONES EXTRANJERAS. Periodical. Spanish. ir. $8.00. Seminario Nacional de Misiones, Garcia Morato 76 - 1, Madrid Spain. **LC** BV2130.

MISSIOLOGY. V. 1- Jan. 1973-. 0091-8296. Periodical. US. English. qt. $20.00. American Society of Missiology, 616 Walnut Avenue, Scottdale PA 15683. **Tel** (412)887-8500. **Ed** Ralph Covell. **Ind/Abst** Christ. Period. Index, Relig. Theol. Abstr., Relig. Index One, Period., Sociol. Abstr., Am. Hist. Life, Hist. Abstr., Lang. Lang. Behav. Abstr. **LC** BV2000. **DD** 266.007. bk rev. adv acc. **Circ** 2,000. (ctrl). Official journal of the American Society of Missiology. *Practical Anthropology, 0032-633X.*

MISSION. V. 72, No. 4- July/Aug. 1976-. 0708-9813. Periodical. CN. French. ir. $10.83. Mission, 1640 St-Hubert, Montreal Province of Quebec, H2L 4K3 Canada. **Tel** (514)849-1169. **Ed** Yvon Lavoie. **DD** 266.205. bk rev. **Circ** 48,000. (ctrl). Roman Catholic missionary work in Africa. *Missions d'Afrique, 0708-9805.*

MISSION FOCUS. (MISSION-FOCUS). V. 1- Sept. 1972-. 0164-4696. Periodical. US. English. qt. $5.00. Mennonite Board of Missions, 500 South Main Street, Box 370, Elkhart IN 46515. **Tel** (219)294-7523. **Ed** Wilbert R Shenk. bk rev. **Circ** 1,700. To provide an inter-Mennonite tool, review missionary experience and practice from a believers' free church perspective and stimulate serious reflection on the mission of the church.

MISSION HAND BOOK. **Main/Corp** United States Catholic Mission Council. 0095-2036. US. English. 1325 Massachusetts Avenue NW/Room 500, Washington DC 20005. **LC** BV2190. **DD** 266.205.

MISSION INTERCOM. 1971. Periodical. US. English. ir. $5.00. US Catholic Mission Council, 1233 Lawrence Street NE, Washington DC 20017. **Tel** (202)785-9450. **Ed** Anne Pope. **Circ** 843. A newsletter published ten times a year containing items of mission interest gleaned from a broad spectrum of publications.

MISSION MAGAZINE. V. 1- June 1977-. 0706-5590. Periodical. CN. English. sa. Free to Subscribers of Mandate Newsletter. Division of Communication of United Church of Canada, 85 St Clair Avenue East, Toronto Ontario M4T 1M8 Canada. **DD** 266.792.

MISSION NEWS. First issue in 1968. 0318-9872. CN. Italian. ir. Free. Verona Fathers, 7025 Boulevard Comboni, Brossard Quebec J4Y 1E9 Canada. **DD** 266.205.

EN MISSION (ST-LAMBERT, QUEBEC). (EN MISSION). Vol. 1, No. 1 (Mar. 1984)-. 0822-837X. Periodical. CN. French. mo. $15,00. Amis du Pere Jean-Marie Labonte, CP 241, St-Lambert Quebec J4P 3N8 Canada. **DD** 266.272945.

MISSION STUDIES (LEIDEN, NETHERLANDS). (MISSION STUDIES : JOURNAL OF THE INTERNATIONAL ASSOCIATION FOR MISSION STUDIES). Nr. 1-. Periodical. English. sa. $12.00. IAMS Secretariat, c/o Department of Missiology IIMO, Rapenburg 61, NL-2311 GJ Leiden Netherlands. **Tel** 7071/144248. **Ed** F J Verstrelen. **Ind/Abst** Relig. Index One, Period. bk rev. adv acc. **Circ** 1,000. A forum for the scholarly study of theological, historical, and practical questions related to mission. The journal is multi-denominational and multi-cultural. *IAMS News Letter.*

MISSIONALIA. Vol. 1, No. 1 (Apr. 1973)-. Periodical. SA. English. ir. $12.00. Journal of South African Missiological Society, 31 14th Street, Menlo Park, Pretoria South Africa. **Tel** (012)440-2322. **Ed** David J Bosch. **Ind/Abst** Relig. Index One, Period. bk rev. **Circ** 1,400. Publishes scholarly articles on Christian misson and annually about 1,000 abstracts of articles on missiological themes appearing in theological journals on all continents. *Lux Mundi (Pretoria, South Africa), Missionaria.*

MISSIONARY EVANGEL. 0273-6780. Periodical. US. English. qt. Missionary Evangel, Route 1, Box 404, Salem OR 97305.

MISSIONARY MESSENGER *CEASED.* (THE MISSIONARY MESSENGER). V. 1-9, No. 4. 0381-0763. Periodical. CN. English. Box 40 Station J, Calgary Alberta T2A 4X4 Canada.

MISSIONARY MONTHLY. 1896. 0161-7133. Periodical. US. English (Dutch). ir. $21.00. Missionary Monthly, PO Box 6181, Grand Rapids MI 49506. **Tel** (616)458-0404. **Ed** Dick L Van Halsema. bk rev. adv acc. **Circ** 4,000. Devoted to the worldwide evangelistic and missionary outreach of Christian reformed and reformed churches of North America. *Missionary Monthly Reformed Review.*

MISSIONARY TIDINGS (WINONA LAKE, IND.). (THE MISSIONARY TIDINGS). Periodical. US. English. mo. Missionary Tidings, 901 College Avenue, Winona Lake IN 46590.

MISSIONETTES SPONSORS MESSAGE. 0190-4426. Periodical. US. English. bm. Women's Ministries Department, Assemblies of God, 1445 Boonville Avenue, Springfield MO 65802.

MISSIONS DES FRANCISCAINS. 0700-4192. Periodical. CN. French. Missions des Franciscains, 2080 Ouest Boulevard Dorchester, Montreal Quebec H3H 1R6 Canada. **DD** 266.285.

MISSIONS DES ILES. 0229-0928. Periodical. CN. French. qt. $2.00. Missions des Iles, Missions Maristes, 2315 Chemin St-Louis, Sillery Quebec G1T 1R5 Canada. **DD** 266.29.

MISSIONS ETRANGERES. 0026-6116. Periodical. CN. French. bm. $2.00 Canada, $3.00 Foreign. Societe des Missions Etrangeres, C P 69, L D R Pont-Viau, Ville de Laval Quebec H7N 4Z2 Canada. **DD** 266.205. *Missions-Etrangeres du Quebec, 0706-845X.*

MISSIONS USA. **VAT** Missions United States of America. 0279-5345. Periodical. US. English. mo. $10.50. Southern Baptist Convention, 1350 Spring NW, Atlanta GA 30309. **Tel** (404)873-4041. **LC** BV2520.A1. **DD** 266.6173. *Home Missions, 0018-408X.*

DIE MITARBEIT. Vol. 1-. 0026-6779. Periodical. GW. German. ir. 44.00. Verlag und Buchdruckerei Otto Schwartz and Company, Annastrasse 7, 3400 Gottingen West Germany. **Ind/Abst** Foreign Lang. Index. **LC** H5. **DD** 261.05. *Arbeiterbrief.*

MODERN CHURCHMAN. (THE MODERN CHURCHMAN). V. 1-46, Apr. 1911-Dec. 1956. 0026-7597. Periodical. UK. English. qt. 6.50. FE Compton, The School House Leysters Leominster, Herfordshire HR6 OHB Leysters England. **Tel** (056)887-271. **Ed** A O Dyson. **Ind/Abst** New Testam. Abstr., Relig. Index One, Period. **LC** BX5011. **DD** 283.3. (cum index). bk rev. adv acc. **Circ** 1,100. A journal with a questioning approach to the ethical, pastoral theological aspects of contemporary living, bringing together theory and practice, knowledge and faith.

MODERN LITURGY. Began with May/July 1976 issue. 0363-504X. Periodical. US. English. ir. $36.00. Resource Publications, 160 East Virginia Street #290, San Jose CA 95112. **Tel** (408)286-8505. **Ind/Abst** Cathol. Period. Lit. Index, Music Artic. Guide, Music Index. **LC** BV169. **DD** 264.005. bk rev. adv acc. **Circ** 11,000. (ctrl). The creative idea journal for worship leaders and religious educators. *Folk Mass and Modern Liturgy Magazine, 0094-775X.*

A MONTHLY LETTER ABOUT EVANGELISM. **VFOAT** Monatlicher Informationsbrief uber Evangelisation, Lettre Mensuelle sur l'Evangelisation. Jan. 1956-. 0540-8059. Periodical. English. ir. $5.93. World Council of Churches, 150 Route de Ferney, 1211 Geneva 20 Switzerland. **Tel** (022)91.61.11. **Ed** Raymong Fung. **Circ** 8,000. (ctrl). An ongoing reflection on communicating the Christian faith.

MONTHLY NEWSLETTER - AMERICAN ASSOCIATION OF THEOLOGICAL SCHOOLS. **Main/Corp** American Association of Theological Schools. V. 1- Sept. 1970-. Periodical. US. English. mo. 534 Third National Building, Dayton OH 45402. *Highlights.*

MONUMENTA HISPANIAE SACRA. SERIE LITURGICA. **VFOAT** Serie Liturgica. Vol. 1-. SP. Spanish. ir. Consejo Super Invest Cientific Vitruvio 8, Apartado 14 458, 28006 Madrid Spain. **Tel** 2612833.

MOUNTAIN MOVERS. V. 21- Jan. 1979-. 0164-7253. Periodical. US. English. mo. Assembly of God-Foreign Missions, 1445 Boonville Avenue, Springfield MO 65802. *Good News Crusades, 0017-2162.*

MY BROTHER AND I. V. 1- Oct. 1968-. 0316-8913. Periodical. CN. English. qt. Missionary Association of Mary Immaculate Oblate Missionary Center, PO Box 721, Winnipeg Manitoba R3C 2K3 Canada. **DD** 266.2.

MY DEVOTIONS. 0027-5387. Periodical. US. English. mo. Concordia Publishing House, 3558 South Jefferson Avenue, St Louis MO 63118.

NATIONAL CATHOLIC FORESTER. 0745-5127. Periodical. US. English. qt. National Catholic Forester, 35 E Wacker Drive, Chicago IL 60601. **Tel** (312)939-5750.

NED. GEREF. TEOLOGIESE TYDSKRIF. VAT Nederduitse Gereformeerde Teologiese Tydskrif. V. 1- Dec. 1959-. 0028-2006. Periodical. SA. Afrikaans (English). ir. 5.50. Nederduitse Gereformeerde Kerk Uitgewers, Box 4539, Cape Town South Africa. **Ind/Abst** Old Testam. Abstr., New Testam. Abstr. **LC** BR9.A34.

NEDERLANDS THEOLOGISCH TIJDSCHRIFT. Vol. 1-. 0028-212X. Periodical. NE. Dutch. qt. 66.00. Boekencentrum BV, Postbus 84176, 2508 AD Den Haag Holland Netherlands. **Ind/Abst** New Testam. Abstr., Relig. Index One, Period., Recent Publ. Artic. *Nieuwe Theologische Studien.*

NEUE ZEITSCHRIFT FUR SYSTEMATISCHE THEOLOGIE UND RELIGIONSPHILOSOPHIE. 5.- Vol.-. 0028-3517. Periodical. German. ty. Walter de Gruyter and Company, 200 Sawmill River Road, Hawthorne NY 10532. **Tel** (914)747-0110. **Ind/Abst** Relig. Index One, Period. *Neue Zeitschrift fur Systematische Theologie.*

NEUES LEBEN. 1.-. Periodical. UR. German. mo. $18.00. Victor Kamkin Inc (50084), 12224 Parklawn Drive, Rockville MD 20852. **Tel** (301)881-5973. **LC** AP205. **DD** 053.

NEVERWERBUNGEN THEOLOGIE UND ALLGEMEINE RELIGIONSWISSENSCHAFT. **Main/Corp** Universitat Tubingen. Universitatsbibliothek. Theologische Abteilung. No. 1-. 0720-3772. German (English, French, Italian, and Spanish). mo. Universitatsbibliothek Theologische Abteilung, Postfach 2670, D-7400 Tubingen 1 West Germany. *Mitteilungen und Neueuwerbungen.*

NEW BLACKFRIARS. V. 46- (No. 532-). 0028-4289. Periodical. UK. English. mo. 10.00 Domestic, 23.00 Foreign. New Blackfriars, Blackfriars, St Giles Oxford England. **Tel** 0865-57607. **Ed** John Ormemills. **Ind/Abst** New Testam. Abstr., Cathol. Period. Lit. Index. bk rev. adv acc. **Circ** 1,300. A critical review surveying the field of theology, philosophy, sociology and the arts from the standpoint of Christian principles in the modern world. *Blackfriars, Life of the Spirit.*

NEW CONVERSATIONS. V. 1- Spring/ Summer 1975-. 0360-0181. Periodical. US. English. ty. $10.00. United Church Board for Homeland Ministries, 287 Park Avenue South, New York NY 10010. **Tel** (212)239-8700. **Ed** William Mckinney. bk rev. **Circ** 1,500. A journal exploring mission issues facing churches in the US, with special attention to the United Church of Christ.

NEW WORLD OUTLOOK. V. 60, No. 2- Feb. 1970-. 0043-8812. Periodical. US. English. mo. New World Outlook, 475 Riverside Drive/Room 1351, New York NY 10115. **Tel** (212)870-3758. **Ed** Arthur J Moore. **LC** BV2550. bk rev. adv acc. **Circ** 35,000. A principal but not exclusive concern, is to inform our church audience about work and issues of the United Methodist Church. *New, World Outlook.*

NEWSLETTER - AMERICAN ASSOCIATION OF BIBLE COLLEGES. (NEWSLETTER). 0736-2595. Periodical. US. English. ir. American Association of Bible College, PO Box 1523, Fayetteville AR 72701. **Tel** (501)521-8164. **LC** BV4019. *AABC Newsletter, 0094-260X.*

NEWSLETTER (ENABLEMENT INFORMATION SERVICE (BOSTON, MASS.)). (NEWSLETTER). Periodical. US. English. mo. Enablement Inc, 14 Beacon Street, Room 715, Boston MA 02108. **Ed** James L Lowery Jr. **Circ** 600. Tested new alternatives in clergy ministry development. Special sections on tentmakers, clergy associations and the clergy career spectrum.

NEWSLETTER OF THE CENTER FOR PROCESS STUDIES. **Main/Corp** Center for Process Studies. V. 1- Spring 1975-. 0360-618X. Periodical. US. English. qt. $5.00. Center for Process Studies, 1325 North College Avenue, Claremont CA 91711. **Tel** (714)626-3521. **Ed** Jeff Graves. **Circ** 550. (ctrl). News of conferences, publications, and personalities involved in the center for process studies or of interest to students of process thought.

NIHON NO SHINGAKU. VFOAT Theological Study in Japan. (1962)-. Japanese (English). an. $10.00. Nihon Kiristokyo Gakkai Hatsubaimoto Kyobunkan Tokyo, c/o I C U, 10-2 Osawa 3-Chome, Mitaka Tokyo 181 Japan. **LC** BR9.J3.

NORDISK MISSIONS-TIDSSKRIFT. 1.-81. Year, Number 2. 0029-1447. Periodical. Norwegian. qt. 75.00. Dansk Missionsrad, Norrebrogade 56, DK-2200 Copenhagen N Denmark. **Tel** (01)355911. **LC** BV2540. (ctrl). Informs about Christian mission around the world as well as it tells about movements and growth in younger churches and revivals.

NORSK TEOLOGISK TIDSSKRIFT. **VFOAT** Norsk Theologisk Tidsskrift. Vol. 1-. 0029-2176. Periodical. NO. Norwegian. qt. $31.00. Universitetsforlaget, PO Box 2959-Toyen, Oslo 6 Norway. **Tel** 02-276 0 60. **Ind/Abst** Am. Hist. Life, Hist. Abstr., Part A, Mod. Hist. Abstr., Hist. Abst., Part B, Twent. Century Abstr., Old Testam. Abstr., New Testam. Abstr., Relig. Index One, Period., Hist. Abstr. (cum index). Theological research.

THE NORTHEAST ASIA JOURNAL OF THEOLOGY *CEASED.* Began with No. 1-28/29. Ceased with No. 28/29, Mar./Sept. 1982. 0549-8899. Periodical. JA. English. sa. $10.00 US and Canada. Northeast Asia Journal of Theology, c/o Japan Lutheran Theological Seminary, 3-10-20 Osawa Mitaka-Shi, Tokyo 181 Japan. **LC** BR1.A1. **DD** 205.

NOTICIAS CRISTIANAS DE ISRAEL. Began with Aug. 1949 issue?. Periodical. Spanish. ir. **LC** BR1110.

NOTRE PAIN QUOTIDIEN (CAP-DE-LA-MADELEINE, QUEBEC). (NOTRE PAIN QUOTIDIEN). Jan./Feb./Mar.-. 0820-7526. Periodical. CN. French. qt. Free. Notre Pain Quotidien, c/o Publications Chretiennes, 230 Lupien, Cap-De-La-Madeleine Quebec G8T 6W4 Canada. **DD** 242.205.

NOUVELLE REVUE THEOLOGIQUE. V. 1-. 0029-4845. Periodical. BE. French. bm. $33.00. Casterman S A, 28 rue des Soeurs Noires, 7500 Tournai Belgium. **Ind/Abst** Cathol. Period. Lit. Index, Relig. Theol. Abstr. **LC** BX802. **DD** 282.05. (cum index). bk rev. adv acc. Periodical concerned with theological subjects in a broad meaning, at a high but not strictly specialized level. The book review section is especially esteemed. *Revue Theologique.*

OBRA. (LA OBRA : THE WORK OF THE MISSIONARIES OF THE HOLY APOSTLES). **VFOAT** Work of the Missionaries of the Holy Apostle. Vol. 1, No. 1 (Easter 1981)-. 0821-2686. Periodical. CN. English (French version on verso, each with separate title page). ty. Free. La Obra c/o Fondation Pere Eusebe Menard, 65 Castelneau Street West, Montreal Quebec Canada. **DD** 266.28.

OCCASIONAL ESSAYS. **Main/Corp** Latin American Evangelical Center for Pastoral Studies. V. 4- Jan. 1977-. Periodical. CR. English. sa. $7.00. Centro Evangelico Latinoamerica, Apartado Postal 1307, 1000 San Jose Costa Rica. **Tel** 22-50-38. **Ed** Guillermo Cook and James Dekker. bk rev. adv acc. **Circ** 2,000. (ctrl). Explores issues of missiology, theology and social ethics particularly as they pertain to Latin America or, by natural extension to the Two-Thirds World. *Occasional Essays.*

OKUMENISCHE RUNDSCHAU. Vol. 1-. 0029-8654. Periodical. GW. German. qt. Verlag Otto Lembeck, Leerbachstrasse 42, D6000 Frankfurt 1 West Germany. **Tel** 069/720376. (cum index). bk rev. adv acc. Available on microfilm from Microfilm Service & Sales, Dallas, TX. Library of Church Unity Periodicals.

OMS OUTREACH. **Main/Corp** OMS International, Inc. **VFOAT** Outreach. **VAT** Oriental Missionary Society Outreach. Vol. 72, No. 4 (Apr. 1973) -. 0274-9459. Periodical. US. Newari. bm. $5.00. OMS International, Box A, Greenwood IN 46142. *Missionary Standard, 0738-4521.*

THE ORB. V. 1- 1972/73-. 0361-5472. Periodical. US. English. qt. First Unitarian Church of Harvard, Harvard MA 01451.

ORDER OF DIVINE SERVICE. **Main/Corp** Anglican Church of Canada. 1958/59-. 0319-2679. CN. English. an. Church Supplies and Book Department, Society of Saint John the Evangelist, PO Box 660, Bracebridge Ontario P0B 1C0 Canada. **DD** 264.035. *Liturgical and Devotional Order of Divine Service, 0319-2687.*

ORIENTASI. Indonesian. ir. **LC** BR9.I53.

ORIENTIERUNG. 11.- Year-. 0030-5502. Periodical. SZ. German. sm. Apologetisches Inst, Scheideggstr 45, CH 8002 Zurich Switzerland. **Ind/Abst** Ephemer. Theologicae Lovanienses, New Testam. Abstr. *Apologetische Blatter.*

THE OTHER SIDE. 1965. 0145-7675. Periodical. US. English. mo. $16.50. The Other Side, 300 West Apsley Street, Philadelphia PA 19144. **Tel** (215)849-2178. **Ed** Mark Olson. **Ind/Abst** Relig. Index One, Period. bk rev. adv acc. **Circ** 13,000. (ctrl). Contains provocative opinions, biblical analyses, and personal experiences which provide help and encouragement for Christians who care about peace and justice.

PACIFIC THEOLOGICAL REVIEW. *See* Religion, Mythology, Rationalism - Protestantism.

PADRES' TRAIL. 0030-9222. Periodical. US. English. qt. $2.00. Franciscan Friars, St Michael Mission, St Michael AZ 86511.

PADRI CAPPUCCINI. (I PADRI CAPPUCCINI : BOLLETINO DEL CENTRO MISSIONARIO DI S. TERESA). Fall 1981-. 0821-6347. Periodical. CN. Italian. ty. Free to Italian Patrons. Saint Theresa Missionary Center, 4387 Avenue Esplanade, Montreal Quebec H2W 1T3 Canada. **DD** 266.27105.

PAGINAS (CENTRO DE ESTUDIOS Y PUBLICACIONES). (PAGINAS). Periodical. PE. Spanish. ir. $30.00. Centro de Estudios y Publicaciones, Apartado 6118, Lima Peru. **LC** HN30. **DD** 261.83098.

PALAN. (LE PALAN). V. 1- June 1976-. 0705-0879. Periodical. CN. French. qt. Free to Members. Mouvement des Cursillos du Secteur des Laurentides, c/o J G Gilles, Charron 181, 6E Avenue, Boisbriand Quebec J7G 1Y5 Canada. **DD** 248.05.

PAPE NOUS PARLE. (LE PAPE NOUS PARLE). 0823-9800. Periodical. CN. French. wk. Free. Le Pape Nous Parle, 5055 rue St-Dominique, Montreal Quebec H2T 1V1 Canada. **DD** 262.9105.

PARISH TEACHER. V. 1- Sept. 1977-. 0738-7962. Periodical. US. English. mo. $4.25 Regular, $3.75 Two or More at One Address. Augsburg Publishing House, 426 South 5th Street, Minneapolis MN 55415. *Learning with: Everyone in the Congregation.*

PAROLE DE L'ORIENT. V. 1-. Periodical. LE. French (some articles in English, 1970-). sa. **LC** BR3. **DD** 201.1. *Orient Syrien, Melto.*

PAROLE (LONGUEUIL, QUEBEC). (PAROLE). **VFOAT** Revue Parole. V. 1, No. 1, (Christmas 1979)-. 0709-9533. Periodical. CN. French. qt. $1.75 Per No. Revue Parole, 1190 rue Maple, Longueuil Quebec J4J 4N6 Canada. **DD** 230.05.

PASS IT ON (TORONTO, ONT.). (PASS IT ON). 0713-3685. Periodical. CN. English. ir. Free. United Church of Canada, 85 St Clair Avenue East, Toronto Ontario M4T 1L8 Canada. **DD** 267.6279205.

PASTORAL LIFE. Began with V. 1, Nov./Dec. 1952. 0031-2762. Periodical. US. English. ir. $12.00. Pastoral Life, Route 224, Canfield OH 44406. **Tel** (216)533-5503. **Ed** Jeffrey Mickler. bk rev. adv acc. **Circ** 6,000. Available on microfilm from University Microfilms. Pastoral life ministers to priests, sisters, brothers, deacons, and anyone interested in or involved with today's ministry.

PASTORAL PSYCHOLOGY. V. 1- (No. 1-). 0031-2789. Periodical. US. English. qt. Human Sciences Press, 72 5th Avenue, New York NY 10011. **Tel** (212)243-6000. **Ind/Abst** Psychol. Abstr., Relig. Index One, Period., Abstr. Res. Pastor. Care Couns., Guide Soc. Sci. Relig. Period. Lit. **LC** BV4012. **DD** 253.5. **NLM** W1 PA874H.

PASTORAL SCIENCES. Vol. 1 (1982)-. 0713-3383. CN. English (French). an. 12.00. Ecclesiastical Book-Store, St Paul University, 223 Main Street, Ottawa Ontario K1S 1C4 Canada. **Tel** (613)236-1393. **Ed** Maureen Slattery. **DD** 253.05. adv acc. **Circ** 500. Forum for dialogue among researchers, trainers and practitioners in the area of pastoral studies. Aims to contribute to the integration of theology and the human sciences in an ecumenical framework.

PASTOR'S BULLETIN. V. 1- Feb. 1980-. 0226-5001. Periodical. CN. English. Canadian Home Bible League, PO Box 524 Station A, Weston Ontario M9N 3N3 Canada. **DD** 266.

THE PASTOR'S STORY FILE. 0882-3545. Periodical. US. English. mo. $24.95. Saratoga Press, 14200 Victor Place, Saratoga CA 95070. **DD** 252.

PAX REGIS. 0031-3335. CN. English. sa. Westminster Abbey & Seminary of Christ of the King, Mission City British Columbia Canada.

PENINJAU. V. 1- 1974-. Periodical. Indonesian. ir. 900. Lembaga Penelitan dan Studi-Dewan, Gereja-Gereja, Jalan Salemba Raya 10, Jakarta Indonesia. **LC** BR1220.

THE PENTECOSTAL MESSENGER. 1926. 0031-4919. Periodical. US. English. mo. $14.00. Messenger Publishing House, PO Box 850, Joplin MO

Religion, Mythology, Rationalism—Theology

64802. **Tel** (417)624-7050. Ed Don Allen. bk rev. adv acc. **Circ** 9,000. (ctrl). Inspirational and devotional articles and reports. For ministers and adult church members.

PENTECOSTES. V. 1- (1-). Periodical. Spanish. qt. $5.00. Instituto Superior de Ciencias Morales, Felix Boix 13, Madrid Spain. LC BX1751.2. DD 230.205.

THE PERE MARQUETTE THEOLOGY LECTURE. Monographic Series. US. English. an. The Marquette University Press, 1324 West, Winconsin Avenue, Milwaukee WI 53233. **Tel** (414)224-1564. Ed Paul McInerny. Composed of annual public lectures by distinguished theologians of international fame. No. 16 in the series, 1985 publication is Orsy: from vision to legislation.

PERSPECTIVA TEOLOGICA. Periodical. BL. Portuguese. ty. Universidade do Vale, Praca Tiradentes 35, 93000 Sao Leopoldors Brazil.

PEUPLES DU MONDE. Began with May 1967 Issue. Periodical. FR. French. mo. $16.63. Peuples du Monde, 8 rue Francois Villon, 75015 Paris France. **Tel** 531 1300. LC BV2130. DD 266.2.

PITTSBURGH THEOLOGICAL MONOGRAPH SERIES. 1-. Monographic Series. US. English. ir. Pickwick Press, 5001 Baum Boulevard, Pittsburgh PA 15213.

PMC. PRACTICE OF MINISTRY IN CANADA. (PMC : THE PRACTICE OF MINISTRY IN CANADA). VFOAT Practice of Ministry in Canada. Vol. 1, No. 1 (Mar. 1984)-. 0825-0391. Periodical. CN. English. qt $15.00. PMC, c/o Wood Lake Books Inc Box 700, Winfield British Columbia V0H 2C0 Canada. DD 253.05.

PNEUMA. V. 1- Spring 1979-. 0272-0965. Periodical. US. English. sa. $18.00. Society for Pentecostal Studies, Attention R Spittle 135 North Oakland Avenue, Pasadena CA 91182-1110. **Tel** (818)449-1745. Ed Cecil M Robeck Jr. **Ind/Abst** Relig. Index One, Period. LC BR1644. DD 270.82. bk rev. adv acc. **Circ** 600. Biblical, theological, historical, and sociological studies related to the Pentecostal and Charismatic movements.

LE POINT THEOLOGIQUE. 1-. Monographic Series. FR. French. ir. Beauchesne Editeur, 72 rue des Saints Peres, 75007 Paris France. **Tel** 5488028. bk rev. adv acc. Publishes practical theology of today, accomplishments in research groups, theological schools, or Christian communities.

POOR KONRAD. No. 1 (Dec. 1982)-. 0741-1588. Periodical. US. English. sm. $6.00. Second Coming, PO Box 4770, Berkeley CA 94704. *Second Coming (Berkeley, Calif.), 0741-1596.*

PRAIRIE HARVESTER. (THE PRAIRIE HARVESTER). Vol. 1 (Winter issue 1982)-. 0383-7653. Periodical. CN. English. qt. Prairie Bible Institute, Three Hills Alberta T0M 2A0 Canada. DD 207.71233. *Prairie Harvesters, 0383-7653.*

PRAKTISCHE THEOLOGIE. 1.-Yearly volume. Periodical. Dutch. ir. 66.-. Uitgeverij Waanders, Postbus 1129, Zwolle Netherlands. **Tel** 038-217106. bk rev. adv acc. **Circ** 3,000. Periodical for practical theology. *Ministerium Theologie en Pastoraat, Tijdschrift voor Pastorale Psychologie.*

THE PREACHER'S MAGAZINE. Began with Jan. 1926 issue. 0162-3982. Periodical. US. English. qt. $3.50. Nazarene Publishing House, PO Box 527, Kansas City MO 64141. **Tel** (816)333-7000. Ed Wesley Tracy. **Ind/Abst** Guide Soc. Sci. Relig. Period. Lit. bk rev. **Circ** 20,000. (ctrl). Practical helps for clergy to assist them in ministry and in their own personal growth.

PREACHING HELPS. V. 1- 1974-. 0098-2156. Periodical. US. English. bm. $5.00. Currents in Theology & Mission, 1100 East 55th Street, Chicago IL 60615. **Tel** (312)753-0763. Ed George Hoyer. bk rev. adv acc. **Circ** 3,400. Sermon studies based on the three year lectionary.

PREACHING (JACKSONVILLE, FLA.). (PREACHING). 0882-7036. Periodical. US. English. bm. $15.00. Preaching Resources Inc, 1529 Cesery Boulevard, Jacksonville FL 32211. **Tel** (904)743-5994. bk rev. adv acc. **Circ** 5,000. (ctrl). An interdenominational, evangelical publication offering information and inspiration in the area of preaching through articles, sermons, features, and homiletical helps.

PRETRE ET PASTEUR. Began with V. 74, Jan. 1971. 0383-8307. Periodical. CN. French. mo. 20.00. Pretre et Pasteur, 4450 St Hubert, Montreal Quebec H2J 2W9 Canada. **Tel** (514)355-1168. bk rev. adv acc. **Circ** 2,200. (ctrl). A review concerned with up-to-date pastoral theology and liturgical renewal. *Revue Eucharistique du Clerge, 0383-8293.*

THE PRIEST. V. 1- Jan. 1945-. 0032-8200. Periodical. US. English. ir. $16.50. Our Sunday Visitor, PO Box 920, Huntington IN 46750. **Tel** (800)348-2440. Ed Vincent J Giese. **Ind/Abst** Cathol. Period. Lit. Index. LC BX803. DD 250.5. Index in last issue of volume - attached. (cum index). bk rev. adv acc. **Circ** 10,606. Monthly magazine written for and about the priestly vocation. Includes homily backgrounds, showcase and more. *Acolyte.*

THE PRINCETON SEMINARY BULLETIN. **Main/Corp** Princeton Theological Seminary. V. 1-68, No. 3, May 1907-Winter 1976. 0032-8413. Periodical. US. English. ty. Free to alumni. Princeton Seminary Bulletin, Princeton, NJ 08540. **Ind/Abst** Old Testam. Abstr., New Testam. Abstr., Relig. Index One, Period. LC BV4070. DD 230.05.

PROBE (CHICAGO, ILL.). (PROBE). Vol. 1, No. 1 (Sept. 1970)-. Periodical. US. English. ir. $100.00. National Assembly of Womens Religious, 1307 South Wabash/Room 206, Chicago IL 60605. **Tel** (312)663-1980. Ed Marjorie Tuite. **Circ** 3,000. Bimonthly national publication of theological reflection, social analysis and steps for feminist women of faith in justice ministry.

PROCEEDINGS - COLLEGE THEOLOGY SOCIETY. **Main/Corp** College Theology Society. 0069-5750. US. English. an. $12.00. Watson E Mills, Mercer University, Macon GA 31207. **Tel** (912)744-2880.

PROCESS STUDIES. See Philosophy.

PROCLAIM. 0162-4326. Periodical. US. English. qt. $9.50. Materials Services Department, 127 9th Avenue North, Nashville TN 37234. **Tel** (615)251-2072. Ed James Hightower. bk rev. **Circ** 18,000. A preaching journal for the Southern Baptist Convention.

PROFILES OF ADVANCED CANDIDATES IN THEOLOGICAL STUDIES CEASED. Began with 1973 issue. 0382-7283. CN. English. an. Institute of Christian Thought, University of St Michael's College, 50 St Joseph Street, Toronto Ontario M5S 1J4 Canada. DD 207.713541.

PROGRAM-CURRICULUM PLANS. **Main/Corp** United Methodist Church (United States). Program-Curriculum Committe. 0147-3336. US. English. PO Box 801, Nashville TN 37202. LC BV1559. DD 208.

PULPIT DIGEST (LOUISVILLE, KY). (PULPIT DIGEST). Began with issue for Jan./Feb. 1978. 0160-838X. Periodical. US. English. bm $58.00. Pulpit Digest Inc, PO Box 6405, Louisville KY 40206. **Tel** (502)423-0221. Ed David A Farmer. bk rev. adv acc. **Circ** 6,500. (ctrl). An ecumenical preaching journal presenting sermons and feature material by contemporary preachers for enhancing the preacher's creativity in the pulpit ministry and for devotional purposes. *New Pulpit Digest, 0145-7969.*

QUAESTIONES DISPUTATAE. Vol. 1 1958. 0481-1216. Periodical. GW. German. ir. Verlag Herder Freiburg, Auslands-Vertrief 282, Hermann Herder Strasse 4, D-7800 Freiburg West Germany. **Tel** 0761/2717 1. Ed Verlag Herder Freiburg.

QUARTERLY REVIEW - UNITED METHODIST BOARD OF HIGHER EDUCATION AND MINISTRY (U.S.). (QUARTERLY REVIEW : QR). VFOAT QR. Vol. 1, No. 1 (Fall 1980)-. 0270-9287. Periodical. US. English. qt. $15.00. United Methodist Publishing House, PO Box 801, Nashville TN 37202. **Ind/Abst** Relig. Index One, Period. LC BX8201. DD 287.605. *Religion in Life, 0034-3986.*

RASSEGNA DI TEOLOGIA. Began in 1960. 0033-9644. Periodical. IT. Italian. bm $13.06. Editrice a VE, via Aurelia 48, 1-00165 Roma Italy. **Ind/Abst** New Testam. Abstr.

RECHERCHES DE THEOLOGIE ANCIENNE ET MEDIEVALE. V. 1- 1929-. 0034-1266. Periodical. BE. French (English, or German). an. $25.00. d'Recherches de Theologie Ancienne et Medievale, Mechelse Straat 202, B3000 Leuven Belgium. **Ind/Abst** MLA Int. Bibliogr. Books Artic. Mod. Lang. Lit., New Testam. Abstr. LC BX800.A1.

THE REFORMED JOURNAL. V. 1- 1951-. 0486-252X. Periodical. US. English. mo. $10.00. The Reformed Journal, 255 Jefferson Avenue SE, Grand Rapids MI 49502. **Tel** (616)459-4591. Ed Jan Pott. **Ind/Abst** Relig. Index One, Period. LC BX9401. bk rev. adv acc. **Circ** 2,500. (ctrl). Intened for a well-educated readership-both clergy and laity-among both evangelical and mainline Christians.

REFORMED LITURGY AND MUSIC CEASED. V. 6, No. 2-V. 15, No. 4. 0362-0476. Periodical. US. English. qt. $10.00. DD 260. *Reformed Liturgics, 0486-2538.*

REFORMED LITURGY & MUSIC. See Religion, Mythology, Rationalism - Protestantism.

REFORMED REVIEW. (THE REFORMED REVIEW). 0034-3064. Periodical. US. English. ir. Western Theological Seminary, 86 East 12th Street, Holland MI 49423. **Tel** (616)392-8555. **Ind/Abst** New Testam. Abstr., Relig. Index One, Period. *Western Seminary Bulletin, 0361-5480.*

REFORMED THEOLOGICAL REVIEW. (THE REFORMED THEOLOGICAL REVIEW). V. 1- 1941-. 0034-3072. Periodical. AT. English. ty. $5.31. Reformed Theological Review, PO Box 2587, Elizabeth Street, Melbourne Victoria 3001 Australia. **Tel** (03)211-1846. Ed D W B Robinson and R Swanbon. **Ind/Abst** New Testam. Abstr., Relig. Index One, Period. Biblical and theological articles and book reviews.

RELIGIAO E SOCIEDADE. No. 1- May 1977-. Periodical. BL. Portuguese. sa. Editora de Humanismo, Ciencia e Technologia, Almeda Jau 404, Sao Paulo Brazil. LC HN39.L3. DD 261.83098.

RELIGIOUS HUMANISM. V. 1- Winter 1967-. 0034-4095. Periodical. US. English. qt. $10.00. Fellowships Religious Humanists, Box 278, Yellow Spring OH 45387. **Tel** (513)324-8130. Ed Paul H Beattie. **Ind/Abst** Philos. Index, Relig. Index One, Period., Guide Soc. Sci. Relig. Period. Lit. LC BL2747.6. bk rev. adv acc. **Circ** 1,500. To promote and encourage the religious, ethical and philosophical thought.

RELIGIOUS MEDIA TODAY CEASED. 0145-5427. Periodical. US. English. qt. $8.00. Christian Interfaith Media Evaluation Center, 432 Park Avenue, New York NY 10016. LC BV652.95. DD 207.2.

RELIGIOUS STUDIES AND THEOLOGY. VFOAT RS&T. Vol. 5, No. 1 (Jan. 1985)-. 0829-2922. Periodical. CN. English. ty. 12.00. Religious Studies and Theology, c/o University of Alberta, Edmonton Alberta T6G 2E5 Canada. **Tel** 432-2174. Ed P J Cahill. 60.75. bk rev. adv acc. **Circ** 600. Wide scope, major focus on contemporary issues across the field of religious studies and theology. Also addresses the traditional issues, interdisciplinary, and international. *Religious Studies Bulletin (Calgary, Alta.), 0710-0655.*

RELIGIOUS STUDIES NEWS. VFOAT RSN. Sept. 1985-. 0885-0372. Periodical. US. English. bm. Religious Studies Newsletter, PO Box 1608, Decatur GA 30031. *Bulletin - Council on the Study of Religion, 0002-7170.*

RENEWALS. V. 1- Mar. 1978-. 0160-7138. Periodical. US. English. bm. $3.00. Boston Theological Institute, Library Development Program, 45 Francis Avenue, Cambridge MA 02138.

REPERTOIRE BIBLIOGRAPHIQUE DES INSTITUTIONS CHRETIENNES. See Bibliographies.

REPORT AND RESOLUTIONS OF THE . . . MEETING OF THE EXECUTIVE COMMITTEE. **Main/Corp** World Alliance of YMCAS. Executive Committee. VFOAT Report and Resolutions of the Executive Committee. English. ir. World Alliance of YMCAS, 37 Quai Wilson, 1201 Geneva Switzerland. LC BV1032. DD 267.3305.

REPORT OF THE ANNUAL CONVENTION - RELIGION-LABOUR COUNCIL OF CANADA. **Main/Corp** Religion-Labour Council of Canada. Convention. 1960-. 0700-530X. Periodical. CN. English. an. Religion-Labour Council of Canada, Corbett House, 21 Sultan Street, Toronto Ontario M5S 1L8 Canada. DD 261.8506271.

REPORT TO THE PEOPLE - YOUTH FOR CHRIST, HAMILTON AREA. (REPORT TO THE PEOPLE). 0821-7238. Periodical. CN. English. bm. Free. Youth for Christ/Hamilton

Area, PO Box 4582 Station D, Hamilton Ontario L8V 4S7 Canada. **DD** 267610971352. (ctrl).

REPORT TO THE PEOPLE - YOUTH FOR CHRIST/VANCOUVER. (REPORT TO THE PEOPLE). Vol. 1, No. 1 (March 1979)-. 0228-8044. Periodical. CN. English. mo. Free. Youth for Christ Vancouver, PO Box 80267, Burnaby British Columbia V5H 3X5 Canada. **DD** 267.610971133.

REPORTS & FINANCIAL STATEMENTS. **Main/Corp** all Africa Conference of Churches. Refugee Dept. **VAT** Reports and Financial Statements. Periodical. English. ir. **LC** BV4470. **DD** 259.

RESOURCES FOR YOUTH MINISTRY. *See* Children and Youth Interests.

THE RETREAT DIRECTORY. *See* Yearbooks, Almanacs, Directories.

REVIEW AND EXPOSITOR. V. 1- Apr. 1904-. 0034-6373. Periodical. US. English. qt. $23.00. Theological Seminary/Fac SO BA, 2825 Lexington Road, Louisville KY 40280. **Tel** (502)897-4408. **Ed** Alan Culpepper. **Ind/Abst** Index Relig. Period. Lit., South. Baptist Period. Index, Int. Zeitschriftenschan Bibelwissenschaft Grenzgeb., New Testam. Abstr. **LC** BX6201. **DD** 286.105. bk rev. adv acc. **Circ** 6,000. Scholarly investigation of biblical and theological subjects and issues.

REVISTA CATALANA DE TEOLOGIA. 1/1 (1976)-. 0210-5551. Periodical. SP. Catalan (Spanish or French; summaries in English). sa. $25.00. Barcelona Facultat Teologia, Barcelona/ Diputacion 231, Barcelona 7 Spain. **Tel** 93 2541600. **Ind/Abst** Old Testam. Abstr., New Testam. Abstr.

REVISTA ESPANOLA DE DERECHO CANONICO. V. 1- (No. 1-). 0034-9372. Periodical. Spanish (summaries in English and Latin). ir. 1,200. Index in last issue of volume - attached. (cum index).

REVISTA ESPANOLA DE TEOLOGIA. Vol. 1, No. 1-. 0210-7112. Periodical. SP. Spanish. qt. $9.81. Consejo Super Invest Cientific, Vitruvio 8, Apartado 14 458, 28006 Madrid Spain. **Ind/Abst** MLA Int. Bibliogr. Books Artic. Mod. Lang. Lit. **LC** BR7. **DD** 205.

REVISTA LATINOAMERICANA DE TEOLOGIA. Vol. 1, 1 (Jan./April 1984)-. Periodical. Spanish. ty. **LC** BT30.L37. **DD** 230.098.

REVISTA TEOLOGICA LIMENSE. Periodical. PE. Spanish. ty. 20. Revista Teologica Limense, Apartado 1838, Lima Peru. **Tel** 62 07 32. **LC** BX1751.2. bk rev. **Circ** 500. Articles are always about theology with some articles on philosophy. *Revista Teologica.*

REVUE AFRICAINE DE THEOLOGIE. No. 1, (April 1977)-. Periodical. CG. French. sa. $20.00. Faculte Theologie Catholique, Kinshasa/B P 1534, Kinshasa Limete Zaire. **Ind/Abst** New Testam. Abstr., Recent Publ. Artic. **LC** BR3. **DD** 230.2605. bk rev. **Circ** 7,000. Covers theology, philosophy, and religions.

REVUE BENEDICTINE. Vol. 7- Jan. 1890-. 0035-0393. Periodical. BE. French. sa. $45.00. Revue Benedictine, Abbaye de Maredsous, B 5198 Denee Belgium. **Tel** 32/82-69.91.55. **Ind/Abst** MLA Int. Bibliogr. Books Artic. Mod. Lang. Lit., Old Testam. Abstr., New Testam. Abstr. Index in last issue of volume - attached. (cum index). bk rev. **Circ** 1,000. Church history with special interest for monasticism. *Messager des Fideles.*

REVUE DE DROIT CANONIQUE. V. 1- March 1951-. 0556-7378. Periodical. FR. French. ir. $25.28. Revue de Droit Canonique, CCP 1829 18J, 2 rue des Freres, 67081 Strasbourg Cedex France. **LC** K21. **DD** 262.905.

REVUE DES ETUDES AUGUSTINIENNES. 1-. 0035-2012. Periodical. FR. French (English, German, Italian, or Spanish). sa. $37.92. Etudes Augustiniennes, 3 rue de l'Abbaye, 75006 Paris France. **Tel** 43 54 80 25. **Ind/Abst** MLA Int. Bibliogr. Books Artic. Mod. Lang. Lit., New Testam. Abstr., Philos. Index. **LC** BX2901. **DD** 270.2. bk rev. Learned studies about history, literature, philosophy, theology from the middle ages to our age. *Annee Theologique Augustinienne.*

REVUE DES SCIENCES PHILOSOPHIQUES ET THEOLOGIQUES (PARIS : 1947). *See* Philosophy.

REVUE DES SCIENCES RELIGIEUSES. Vol. 1-. 0035-2217. Periodical. FR. French. qt. $16.63. Palais Universite, Assoc des Publ, Pres les Universite Strasbourg, 67084 Strasbourg Cedex France. **Ind/Abst** New Testam. Abstr., Relig. Index One, Period. **LC** BX802. (cum index). *Bulletin d'Ancienne Litterature et d'Archeologie Chretiennes.*

REVUE D'HISTOIRE ET DE PHILOSOPHIE RELIGIEUSES. V. 1- Yearly. 0035-2403. Periodical. FR. French. qt. 150 Domestic, $16.67. Presses Universitaires France, 12 rue Jean-de-Beauvais, 75005 Paris France. **Tel** (1)326-2216. **Ed** Marc Philonenko. **Ind/Abst** Am. Hist. Life, Hist. Abstr., Part A, Mod. Hist. Abstr., Hist. Abst., Part B, Twent. Century Abstr., New Testam. Abstr., Relig. Index One, Period., Hist. Abstr. **LC** BR3. **DD** 230.05. (cum index). Concentrating on Protestant Theology, this journal is also open to all religious and philosophical currents. The scientific objective is the study of problems inherited in Christian Theology and its relationship with non-Christian thought.

REVUE DU CLERGE AFRICAIN. V. 1, No. 1- Jan. 1946-. Periodical. French. ir. $5.00. J de Cock Mayidi, BP 6, Inkisi Congo. **LC** BX802. **DD** 230.205.

REVUE THEOLOGIQUE DE LOUVAIN. Vol. 1-. 0080-2654. Periodical. BE. French. qt. 950 Domestic, $22.00 Foreign. College Albert Descamps, Grand Place 45, 1348 Louvain-la-Neive Belgium. **Tel** (010)434592. **Ind/Abst** New Testam. Abstr., Cathol. Period. Lit. Index. bk rev. **Circ** 1,200. Review dealing with various topics of the theological field.

REVUE THOMISTE; REVUE DOCTRINALE DE THEOLOGIE ET DE PHILOSOPHIE. Vol. 1-. 0035-4295. Periodical. FR. French. qt. Desclee de Brower, 83 rue Hoche/ 92240 Malakoff, 92240 Paris France. **Tel** 1/ 656 26 93. **Ind/Abst** New Testam. Abstr., Philos. Index, MLA Int. Bibliogr. Books Artic. Mod. Lang. Lit. **LC** BX802. adv acc. Only thorist science.

RIC; REPERTOIRE BIBLIOGRAPHIQUE DES INSTITUTIONS CHRETIENNES. *See* Bibliographies.

RITE IDEAS. Vol. 1, No. 1 (Dec. 1984)-. F11544380. Periodical. US. English. mo. Rite Ideas, 628 South Main Street, Lima OH 45804. **DD** 264. *In the Worship Workshop with Avery & Marsh.*

RIVISTA DI TEOLOGIA MORALE. Yearly V. 1- Jan./March 1969-. Periodical. IT. Italian. qt. $13.67. Centro Editoriale Dehoniano, Via Nosadella 6, 40123 Bologna Italy. **LC** BJ1188.5. **DD** 241.05.

ROCZNIKI TEOLOGICZNO-KANONINCZNE. **VFOAT** Annales Theologico-Canonicae, Annales de Theologie et du Droit Canon, Annals of Theology and Canon Law. V. 1-. 0035-7723. Periodical. PL. Polish (summaries in English, French, German or Latin; table of contents also in Latin). bm. ARS Polona, Krakowskie Przedmiescie 7, 00-068 Warsaw Poland. **Ind/Abst** New Testam. Abstr. **LC** BX806.P6.

THE SABBATH WATCHMAN. 0098-9517. Periodical. US. English. bm. $8.00. Religious Liberty Publishing Association, 1151 Xenia Street, Denver CO 80220. **Tel** (303)363-9853. **Ed** L Watts. **LC** BX6101. **DD** 286.73. **Circ** 500. (ctrl). The official organ of the International Missionary Society, Seventh-Day Adventist Church, reform movement, and American union.

SACRA DOCTRINA. Vol. 1- (Issue 1-). 0036-2190. Periodical. IT. Italian. bm. $20.79. Studio Domenicano, Piazza S Domenico 13, 40124 Bologna Italy. **Ind/Abst** New Testam. Abstr. Index in last issue of volume - attached.

THE SAINT LUKE'S JOURNAL OF THEOLOGY. **VFOAT** Saint Luke's Journal. V. 1- St. Luke's Day 1957-. 0036-309X. Periodical. US. English. qt. $15.00. University of the South, School of Theology, Sewanee TN 37375. **Tel** (615)598-5931. **Ed** John M Gessell. **Ind/Abst** Old Testam. Abstr., Relig. Index One, Period., Index Relig. Period. Lit. **LC** BR1. bk rev. adv acc. **Circ** 2,700. Available on microfilm from University Microfilms. A journal of religious thought for clergy and laity who wish to relate theological studies to contemporary issues.

ST. VLADIMIR'S THEOLOGICAL QUARTERLY. V. 13-. 0036-3227. Periodical. US. English. qt. St Vladimirs Orthodox Theological Seminary, 575 Scarsdale Road, Crestwood, Tuckahoe NY 10707. **Ind/Abst** Old Testam. Abstr., New Testam. Abstr., Relig. Index One, Period. **LC** BX460. **DD** 230.193. *St. Vladimir's Seminary Quarterly, 0360-6481.*

SAL TERRAE. V. 52- Jan. 1964-. Periodical. Spanish. mo. $23.00. Editorial Sal Terrae, Guevara 20 Apt 77, Santander Spain. **Tel** 212617. Journal on the Latin-American priesthood and pastoral theology. Largest journal of its kind in the Spanish-speaking countries. *Sal Terrae. Parte Teorica.*

SALT (CHICAGO, ILL.). (SALT). Began with: Vol. 1, No. 1, published in Jan. 1981. 0883-2587. Periodical. US. English. mo. $10.00. Salt, 221 West Madison, Chicago IL 60606. **Tel** (312)236-7782. **Ed** Kevin H Axe. **DD** 261. bk rev. **Circ** 13,711. Social justice issues in the US, ways in which Christians can live the principles of the Gospel by helping others around them. Contains personality profiles, features, and columns.

SAMA. SOCIETE D'AIDE MISSIONNAIRE ANTIPODE. (SAMA : BULLETIN D'INFORMATION DE LA SAMA). **VAT** Societe d'Aide Missionnaire Antipode. Vol. 1, No. 1 (Oct./Nov.)-. 0225-3313. Periodical. CN. French. bm. Free. SAMA, 7596 Av Rolland, Charlesbourg Quebec G1H 6C3 Canada. **DD** 266.02371401724. (ctrl).

SAMETA. First issue in 1966. 0705-0518. Periodical. CN. French. qt. Sameta, 3719 Est Boul Gouin, Montreal Province of Quebec H1H 5L8 Canada. **Tel** (514)322-0560. **DD** 266.023096711.

SAPIENZA. *See* Philosophy.

SAVING HEALTH. V. 1- Mar. 1962-. 0036-5106. Periodical. UK. English. qt. 2.50. Medical Missionary Association, 6 & 7 Canonbury Place, London N 1 England. **Tel** UK 01-359-1313. **Ed** P F Green. bk rev. **Circ** 1,000. Articles written by doctors and nurses serving as missionaries overseas about their work in Third World Countries. *Conquest by Healing.*

SCARBORO MISSIONS. 1919. 0700-6802. CN. English. mo. Scarboro Foreign Mission Society, 2685 Kingston Road, Scarborough Ontario M1M 1M4 Canada. **Tel** (416)261-7135. **Ed** J Lynch. **Circ** 40,000. Publication of Mission Society covering religious missiology development.

SCHOLAR'S CHOICE : SIGNIFICANT CURRENT THEOLOGICAL LITERATURE FROM ABROAD. **Main/Corp** Richmond. Union Theological Seminary. 1960-. Periodical. US. English. $4.00. Union Theological Seminary, 3401 Brook Road, Richmond VA 23227. **Tel** (804)355-0671. **Ed** John B Trotti. **Circ** 200. (ctrl). A bibliography of current titles in religion published abroad and selected by our panel of scholars for American theological libraries.

SCIENCE ET ESPRIT. *See* Philosophy.

SCOTTISH JOURNAL OF THEOLOGY. V. 1- June 1948-. 0036-9306. Periodical. UK. English. qt. 65.00. Scottish Academic Press Ltd, 33 Montgomery Street, Edinburgh EH7 5JX Scotland. **Tel** (031)556-2796. **Ed** A I C Heron and J Houston. **Ind/Abst** New Testam. Abstr., Ref. Source, Relig. Index One, Period. **LC** BR1. **DD** 200.5. bk rev. adv acc. **Circ** 1,200. Publishes contributions of major theological and philosophical interest from the worlds leading scholars also articles on Biblical and applied theology.

SCOTTISH JOURNAL OF THEOLOGY. MONOGRAPH SUPPLEMENT. V. 1-. Monographic Series. UK. English. ir. Cambridge University Press, Shaftesbury Road, Edinburgh Building, Cambridge CB2 2RU England.

SCP NEWSLETTER. Began Feb./Mar. 1980 (Per Publ.). 0883-1319. Periodical. US. English. qt. Spiritual Counterfeits Projects Inc, PO Box 4308, Berkeley CA 94704. **DD** 239. *Newsletter - Spiritual Counterfeits Project.*

SCRIPTA THEOLOGICA. 0036-9764. Spanish. ir. $33.00. Universidad de Navarra, Ronda de Baranain 1-10 B, Pomplona Spain. **Tel** (948)252700. **Ed** Pedro Rodriguez. **Ind/Abst** Old Testam. Abstr., New Testam. Abstr. **LC** BR7. bk rev. adv acc. **Circ** 1,000. (ctrl). Aims to provide the reader with comprehensive studies on the most important theological subjects of discussion within the Catholic Church.

SEARCH. V. 1- Spring 1978-. Periodical. IE. English. sa. 4.00. Religious Education Resource Centre, Mount Argus Road, Dublin 6 Ireland. **Tel** 972821. **Ed** E Ferrar. **Ind/Abst** New Testam. Abstr. bk rev. **Circ** 600. Contains information about: liberation theology, old testament convenant, the Huguenots,

Religion, Mythology, Rationalism—Theology

music in worship, book reviews, books for teachers, the Catholic Church and education. *New Divinity, Resources.*

SELECCIONES DE TEOLOGIA. Vol. 1, No. 1 (Feb. 1962)-. 0037-119X. SP. Spanish. qt. $10.00. Selecciones de Teologia, Roger de Lluria 13, 08010 Barcelona 8 Spain. LC WMLC L 82/396. adv acc. **Circ** 5,000. Abstracts of the best articles of theology published in the world.

SELF-REALIZATION. V. 43- Winter 1971-. 0037-1564. Periodical. US. English. qt. $7.00. Self-Realization Fellowship, 3880 San Rafael Avenue, Los Angeles CA 90065. **Tel** (213)225-2471. **Ed** Jane Brush. **Circ** 22,000. Practical application of spiritual principles for healing of body, removing mental inharmonies by concentration and positive thinking, freeing the soul from ignorance by yoga. *Self-Realization Magazine.*

SELON SA PAROLE. V. 3- Jan. 1977-. 0701-4260. Periodical. CN. French. mo. $4.00. Service du Renouveau Charismatique, 2140 Chemin St-Louis, Sillery Quebec G1T 1P8 Canada. **DD** 269. *Bulletin de Liaison des Groupes de Prieres du Diocese de Quebec, 0384-6164.*

SEMINARY QUARTERLY. V. 1- Fall 1959-. Periodical. US. English. ty. Ministers Life & Casualty Union, 3100 West Lake Street, Minneapolis MN 55416.

SENTINEL. (THE SENTINEL). Jan. 1977-. 0225-512X. Periodical. CN. English. Canadian Council for National Righteousness, PO Box 339, Ridgeway Ontario L0S 1N0 Canada. **DD** 248.25.

THE SERMON BUILDER. Periodical. US. English. mo. $7.00. Church Extension Service Inc, PO Box 552, Golden CO 80401. **Tel** (303)279-1011. *New Sermon Builder.*

SERVICE TO REFUGEES; PROGRESS REPORT. **Main/Corp** All Africa Conference of Churches. Refugee Dept. English. ir. All Africa Conference of Churches, PO Box 20301, Nairobi Kenya. LC BV4470. **DD** 259.

SERVICE TO REFUGEES : PROJECTS BOOK. **Main/Conf** All Africa Conference of Churches. Refugee Dept. English. ir. Refugee Department, All Africa Conference of Churches, Waiyaki Way, PO Box 14205, Nairobi Kenya. LC BV4470. **DD** 362.87096. *Service to Refugees.*

SHARING THE PRACTICE. V. 1- Jan./Feb. 1978-. 0193-8274. Periodical. US. English. qt. $20.00. Academy of Parish Clergy Inc, 12604 Britton Drive, Cleveland OH 44120. **Tel** (216)791-4005. **Ed** Robert E Lair Jr. bk rev. adv acc. **Circ** 600. (ctrl). Articles on the practice of ministry by ministers. Reviews of books covering the practice of ministry. News about members. *News and Views - Academy of Parish Clergy, 0361-2406.*

SIC. **Main/Corp** Seminario Interdiocesano de Caracas. Periodical. Spanish. ir. LC BX805. **DD** 282.05. (cum index).

SIM NOW. **VAT** Sudan Interior Mission Now. No. 1 (Jan./Feb. 1982)-. 0711-6683. Periodical. US. English. bm. Free. Sudan Interior Mission, Cedar Grove NJ 07009. **DD** 266.02306. *Africa Now (Cedar Grove, (N.J.), 0044-6513.*

SIMPOSIO. Vol. 1 No. 1 (May 1968)-. Periodical. BL. Portuguese. ir. Aste Rua Rego Freitas, 530 Conj F 13, Sao Paulo Brazil. **Ind/Abst** Relig. Index One, Period. LC BR7. **DD** 230.05.

SINANGGYE. Periodical. KO. Korean. mo. 8,000. Sinanggye, 1-20 Yoido-dong Yongdungpo-ku, Seoul 150 Korea. LC BV4485.

SINHAK KWA SONKYO. **VFOAT** Theology and Mission. Periodical. KO. English (Korean). ir. 1,000. Soul Sinhak Taehak, 101 Sosa-dong, Puchon-si Korea. LC BR9.K6.

SLAVNA NADEJE. **VFOAT** Glorious Hope. V. 1- Oct. 1974-. 0700-5202. Periodical. CN. Czech. qt. Slavna Nadeje, PO Box 1271, Windsor Ontario N9A 6R3 Canada. **DD** 266.27.

SOCIAL ACTION NEWS LETTER. **VFOAT** Social Action Newsletter. V. 1- Jan. 1938-. 0199-7033. Periodical. US. English. ir. Free. Department of Church In Society Division of Homeland, Ministries Box 1986, Indianapolis IN 46206. Available in microform from American Theological Library Association Board of Microtext.

SOCIAL QUESTIONS BULLETIN. Vol. 71, No. 6 (Nov.-Dec. 1981)-. 0731-0234. Periodical. US. English. bm. $10.00. Methodist Federation for Social Action, 76 Clinton Avenue, Staten Island NY 10301. **Tel** (718)273-4941. **Ed** George D McClain. bk rev. **Circ** 1,700. We provide issue analyses and social action suggestions for religious activists (especially Methodists) on key national and international questions. *SQB, 0274-5208.*

SOCIAL THOUGHT. V. 1- Spring 1975-. 0099-183X. Periodical. US. English. qt. $12.00. National Conference of Catholic Charities, 1346 Connecticut Avenue #307, Washington DC 20036. **Ind/Abst** Sociol. Abstr., Cathol. Period. Lit. Index, Soc. Work Res. Abstr., Public Aff. Inf. Serv. Bull. LC HN30. **DD** 261.830973.

SOLIDARITES. V. 1- Oct. 1976-. 0383-6711. Periodical. CN. French. bm. Organisation Catholique Canadienne Pour le Developpment et la Paix, 2111 rue Centre, Montreal Quebec H3K 1J5 Canada. **DD** 266.205.

THE SOUTH EAST ASIA JOURNAL OF THEOLOGY CEASED. -V. 23. Periodical. English. ir. $3.00. Association of Theological Schools in South East Asia, R L Turner, RD 3 East, Stroudsburg PA 18301. LC BR1. **DD** 230.095. (cum index). Available on microfilm from University Microfilms International. *S.E. Asia Journal of Theology.*

THE SOUTH INDIA CHURCHMAN. Feb. 1948-. Periodical. II. English. mo. $4.00. Synod Office, Cathedral PO, Madras 7 South India. **Tel** 811266. Available on microfilm from the American Theological Library Association. Microtext Project. *Madras Diocesan Magazine.*

SOUTHWESTERN JOURNAL OF THEOLOGY. V. 1- Oct. 1958-. 0038-4828. Periodical. US. English. ty. $12.00 Domestic, $14.00 Foreign. Southwestern Journal of Theology, Box 22000 E2, Fort Worth TX 76122. **Tel** (817)923-1921. **Ed** Dan G Kent. **Ind/Abst** Old Testam. Abstr., New Testam. Abstr., Relig. Index One, Period., Christ. Period. Index. LC BX6201. **DD** 286.105. bk rev. adv acc. **Circ** 3,500. Fall issue is a Biblical book, Spring and Summer issues rotate among various theological disciplines.

SPIRIT. V. 1-. 0160-7367. Periodical. US. English. ty. $3.00. J S Tinney, PO Box 386, Howard University, Washington DC 20059. LC BR1644. **DD** 269.

SPIRIT & LIFE. **VAT** Spirit and Life (Clyde, MO.). 0038-7592. Periodical. US. English. bm. $5.00. Benedictine Convent of Perpetual Adoration, 8300 Morganford Road, St Louis MO 63123. **Tel** (314)638-6427. Practical, simple, pithy articles inspiring readers to live out their Christian lives prayerfully on a day-to-day basis.

SPIRITUS. 1- May 1959-. 0038-7665. Periodical. FR. French. qt. 100. S P E S, 9110 Avenue Papineau, Montreal Quebec H2M 2C8 Canada. **Tel** (1) 288 8264. (cum index). **Circ** 2,000. (ctrl). Tri-mester magazine of studies in experience and missionaries reflections in the Catholic Church.

STUDI FRANCESCANI. Year 1- 1903-. Periodical. PL. Italian. ir.

STUDIA ANSELMIANA; PHILOSOPHICA, THEOLOGICA. See Philosophy.

STUDIA BIBLICA ET THEOLOGICA. 0094-2022. Periodical. US. English. sa. Fuller Theological Seminary, 135 North Oakland Avenue, Pasadena CA 91101. **Tel** (203)453-9674. **Ind/Abst** Elenchus Bibliogr. Bibicus, Int. Zeitschriftenschan Bibelwissenschaft Grenzgeb., Old Testam. Abstr. LC BR1. **DD** 205.

STUDIA EKUMENICZNE. Vol. 1-. Periodical. Polish (summaries in English, French, and Italian). ir. Dzia Administracyjno-Gospodarczy, Akademii Teologii Katolickiej, Dewajtis 3, 01-653 Warszawa UL Poland. LC BX1.

STUDIA MISSIONALIA UPSALIENSIA. 1- 1956-. 0585-5373. Monographic Series. SW. English, Swedish or German. ir. Liber International, S-205 10 Malmo Sweden.

STUDIA PATAVINA. Vol. 1- Jan./Apr. 1954-. 0039-3304. Periodical. IT. Italian. ty. 24.000 Domestic, 35.000 Foreign, $22.00. Rivista di Science Religiose, Via del Seminario 29, 35122 Padova Italy. **Tel** (049)657099. **Ind/Abst** New Testam. Abstr., MLA Int. Bibliogr. Books Artic. Mod. Lang. Lit. bk rev. **Circ** 600.

Official publication of the School of Divinity of Northern Italy with seat in Padova. Deals with theology in general and related areas with religious thoughts and experiences especially in Christianity.

STUDIA THEOLOGICA. **VFOAT** Scandinavian Journal of Theology. V. 1- 1947-. 0039-338X. Periodical. NO. English, French or German. sa. 27.00. Universitetsforlaget, PO Box 2959-Toyen, Oslo 6 Norway. **Tel** (45)-2-27 60 60. **Ed** Jacob Jervell and Arvid S Kapelrud. **Ind/Abst** MLA Int. Bibliogr. Books Artic. Mod. Lang. Lit., New Testam. Abstr., Relig. Index One, Period. LC BR1. **DD** 230.05. (cum index). adv acc. **Circ** 600. Aims to present Scandinavian contributions to the field of international theology in the major languages.

STUDIA THEOLOGICA VARSAVIENSIA. Began with Vol. 1 in 1963?. 0585-5594. Periodical. PL. Polish (with summaries in English, French, German or Latin). sa. ARS Polona, Krakowskie Przedmiescie 7, 00-068 Warsaw Poland. **Ind/Abst** New Testam. Abstr. LC BR9.P6.

STUDIEN UND ARBEITEN DER THEOLOGISCHEN FAKULTAT. **Main/Corp** Innsbruck. Universitat. Theologische Fakultat. 1968-. 0579-7780. Monographic Series. AU. German. ir. University of Innsbruck, Faculty of Theology, Innsbruck Austria. **Tel** 05222-724-9396. **Ed** Hans Bernhard Meyer. **Circ** 800. (ctrl). Studies on philosophical and theological subjects.

STUDIEN ZUR GESCHICHTE DER KATH. MORALTHEOLOGIE. Vol. 1-. 0081-7295. Monographic Series. GW. German. ir. Verlag Friedrich Pustet, Postfach 339, 8400 Regensburg 11 West Germany.

STUDIES IN HISTORICAL THEOLOGY (STILL RIVER, MASS.). (STUDIES IN HISTORICAL THEOLOGY). Vol. 1-. Monographic Series. US. English. St Bede's Publications, PO Box 132, Still River MA 01467.

STUDIES IN THE REFORMATION. 1- 1977-. Periodical. US. Multilingual. ir. **DD** 230.3.

STUDIES IN THE SPIRITUALITY OF JESUITS. Vol. 1, No. 1 (Sept. 1969)-. Periodical. US. English. ir. $4.50. The American Assistancy Seminar Fusz Memorial, 3700 West Pine Boulevard, St Louis MO 63108. **Tel** (314)652-5737. **Ed** George E Ganss SJ. **Circ** 7,500. Five issues a year, published by the American Assistancy Seminar on Jesuit Spirituality especially but not exclusively for Jesuits and their updating in accordance with the spirit of Vatican Council II.

STUDII TEOLOGICE. **VFOAT** Etudes Theologiques. Periodical. RM. Romanian. ir. Ilexim Press Department, PO Box 1-136-1-137, Bucharest Romania. **Ind/Abst** MLA Int. Bibliogr. Books Artic. Mod. Lang. Lit. LC BX690.

SUNDAY SCHOOL YOUTH TEACHER. Vol. 13, No. 2 (Jan./Feb./Mar. 1984)-. 0736-9174. Periodical. US. English. qt. Sunday School Board of the Southern Baptist Convention, 127 Ninth Avenue North, Nashville TN 37234. *Youth Teacher, 0162-4865.*

SUNDIAL. (THE SUNDIAL). Mar./Apr. 1984-. 0827-312X. Periodical. CN. English. qt. Free. Evangelical Fellowship of Canada, PO Box 8800 Station B, Willowdale Ontario M2K 2R6 Canada. **DD** 269.2. (ctrl).

SUPPLEMENT TO DOCTRINE AND LIFE CEASED. **VFOAT** Doctrine and Life. Began with No. 1, Jan./Feb. 1963. Ceased No. 87, Nov./Dec. 1980. 0419-5078. Periodical. IE. English. ir. $7.60 US, $9.00 Canada. Dominican Publications, c/o The Manager Saint Saviour's, Dublin 1 Ireland.

SVENSK TEOLOGISK KVARTALSKRIFT. (STK, SVENSK TEOLOGISK KVARTALSKRIFT). Vol. 47-. Periodical. SW. Swedish. qt. 100. Liber International, S-205 10, S-205 10 Malmo Sweden. **Tel** 46-40-70650. **Ind/Abst** New Testam. Abstr., Old Testam. Abstr., Relig. Index One, Period. (cum index). bk rev. **Circ** 1,000. Contains articles on actual theological and religious questions. *Svensk Teologisk Kvartalskrift.*

SYNAXIS. 0710-1627. CN. English. an. Synaxis Press, PO Box 404, Chilliwach British Columbia V2P 6J7 Canada. **DD** 230.193.

SYNTHESIS. Vol. 1, No. 1 (Mar. 1981)-. 0279-781X. Periodical. US. English. mo. $19.50. Growth Associates, PO Box 215, Weston VT 05161-0215. **Tel** (802)824-3440. **Ed** William V Coleman. bk rev. **Circ** 600. Abstracts of current literature of interest to church leaders plus, weekly liturgy aids.

TAIWAN SHENXUE LUNKAN. (TAI-WAN SHEN HSUEH LUN KAN). **VFOAT** Taiwan Journal of Theology. Vol. 1, No. 1 (March 1979)-. 0251-4788. Periodical. CH. Chinese (English). ir. $4.00. Taiwan Theological College, 20 Lane 2 Section 2 Yang Teh Ta Road, Shihlin Taipei Taiwan China. **Ind/Abst** Relig. Index One, Period. **LC** BR118. **DD** 230.05.

TANTUR NEWSLETTER. No. 6- June 1974-. Periodical. English. ir. Ecumenical Institute, POB 19556, Jerusalem Israel. *Newsletter - Ecumenical Institute for Advanced Theological Studies.*

TEAM HORIZONS. **Main/Corp** Evangelical Alliance Mission. **VAT** The Evangelical Alliance Mission Horizons. V. 54, No. 3- May/June 1978-. 0163-3422. Periodical. US. English. bm. $2.00. Evangelical Alliance Mission, PO Box 969, Wheaton IL 60187. **Tel** (312)653-5300. **LC** BV2350. **DD** 266.005. *Horizons.*

TELEMA : LEVE-TOI ET MARCHE. Yearly V. 5- (No. 17-). Periodical. CG. French. qt. Telema, BP 3277, Kinshasa Gombe Zaire. **Ind/Abst** Old Testam. Abstr., New Testam. Abstr. **LC** BR3. **DD** 230.2. bk rev. adv acc. Christian (Ecumerical) reflections and creativity in Africa. *Telema.*

TEOCOMUNICACAO. Portuguese. ir. Diretorio Academico Instituto de Teologia, Caxia Postal 1429, Av Ipiranga, 6681 Porto Alegre Brazil. **LC** BX805. **DD** 301.58.

TEOLOGIA (BUDAPEST, HUNGARY). (TEOLOGIA). Vol. 1, 1. Sz. (1967. Oct.)-. Periodical. HU. Hungarian. qt. 40 Domestic, $10.50. Akademiai Kiado, POB 24, 1363 Budapest Hungary. **Tel** 36-1-174-533. **Ed** Szennay Andras. **Circ** 4,000. (ctrl). In its thematic issues it is publishing the authentic teachings of the Catholic theology. It is giving help to the pastoral work. It is reviewing the activity and works of the Hungarian and foreign personalities of theology.

TEOLOGIA Y VIDA. V. 1- Jan./March 1960-. 0049-3449. Periodical. CL. Spanish. qt. 27.00. Facultad de Theologia UC, Casilla Postal 114 D, Santiago Chile. **Tel** 744041. **Ind/Abst** New Testam. Abstr., Cathol. Period. Lit. Index. bk rev. adv acc. **Circ** 700. Theological reflection for the world of today. Studies, reflections, church documents and reviews of books, and international and Latin-American journals.

TEOLOGINEN AIKAKAUSKIRJA. TEOLOGISK TIDSKRIFT. **VFOAT** Teologisk Tidskrift. Vol. 1-. 0040-3555. Periodical. FI. Finnish (Swedish). bm. 140.00. Teologinen Aikakauskirja, Neitsytpolku 1 B, SF-00140 Helsinki Finland. **Tel** 90-661791/267. **Ed** Euro Huovinen. **LC** BR9.F5. bk rev. adv acc. **Circ** 2,800. A scientifical, theological journal.

TFP INFORME. **VFOAT** Tradition, Famille, Propriete. **VAT** Tradition, Famille Propriete Informe. No. 1 (1980)-. 0229-964X. Periodical. CN. French. ty. Free. Jeunes Canadiens pour une Civilisation Chretienne, CP 566 Succurslae Youville, Montreal Quebec H2P 2W1 Canada. **DD** 248.405.

TFP NEWSLETTER. **VFOAT** Tradition, Family, Property. **VAT** Tradition, Family, Property Newsletter. No.1 (1980)-. 0229-9631. Periodical. CN. English. ty. Free. Young Canadians for a Christian Civilization, PO Box 566 Youville Station, Montreal Quebec H2P 2W1 Canada. **DD** 248.405.

THEMELIOS. V. 1-11, No. 2. 0307-8388. Periodical. UK. English. ty. $6.00. TSF Subscriptions, 233 Langdon, Madison WI 53703. **Tel** (608)257-1103. **Ed** David Wenham. **Ind/Abst** Relig. Index One, Period., New Testam. Abstr., Old Testam. Abstr. **DD** 201.105. bk rev. **Circ** 1,000. An international journal for theological students, expounding and defending the historic Christian faith. *TSF Bulletin.*

THEMEN DER PRAKTISCHEN THEOLOGIE — THEOLOGIA PRACTICA. **VFOAT** Theologia Practica. Vol. 16, No. 1/2-. 0720-9525. Periodical. GW. German. sa. Kaiser Verlag, Postfach 509, Isabellastrasse 20, D-8000 Munchen 43 West Germany. *Theologia Practica, 0049-3643.*

THEODOLITE. V. 5, No. 3- Nov./Dec. 1979-. 0225-7270. Periodical. CN. English. sa. $2.32. McMaster Divinity College, Hamilton Ontario L8S 4K1 Canada. **Tel** (416)525-9140. **Ed** T R Hobbs. **DD** 230.05. **Circ** 1,000. Seeks to provide pastors, educators and interested laypersons with the fruits of modern theology and biblical studies in a readable form. *Theological Bulletin, 0381-9310.*

THEOLOGIA 21. **VAT** Theologia Twenty-One. V. 6- Jan. 1976-. 0362-0085. Periodical. US. English. ir. $15.00. Dominion Press, PO Box 37, San Marcos CA 92609. **Tel** (619)746-9430. **Ed** A S Otto. **Circ** 100. Microform. Alternative interpretation of Christianity but completely Bible based. A theology for the 21st century. *Immortality Newsletter, 0019-2783.*

THEOLOGIA EVANGELICA. Began with issue for Apr. 1968. Periodical. SA. Afrikaans (English). ty. $4.05. University of South Africa, Room 4-2 Box 392, Pretoria 0001 South Africa. **Ind/Abst** Old Testam. Abstr., New Testam. Abstr., Relig. Index One, Period. **LC** BR9.A34. **DD** 230.05.

THEOLOGIA PRACTICA. Vol. 1-. 0049-3643. Periodical. German. qt. Furche Verlag, Bielefeld 1 Postfach 3020, Hamburg West Germany. **LC** BV1.

THEOLOGIA REFORMATA. Began with Vol. 1 in 1957. 0040-5612. Periodical. NE. Dutch. $16.17. Oosterbaan & Le Cointre B V, Westwal 45, 4461 CM Goes Netherlands. (cum index).

THEOLOGIA VIATORUM (BERLIN, GERMANY). *See* Yearbooks, Almanacs, Directories.

THEOLOGIA VIATORUM (PIETERSBURG, SOUTH AFRICA). (THEOLOGIA VIATORUM). Vol. 1, No. 1 (Nov. 1973)-. Periodical. SA. English (Afrikaans). sa. $0.62. Private Bag X1102, Sovenga Transvaal, Republic of South Africa.

THEOLOGIAI SZEMLE. V. 1, No. 1 (1925 Easter)-1, Newsletter (1948). Periodical. HU. Hungarian. mo. Akademiai Kiado, POB 24, 1363 Budapest Hungary. **Ind/Abst** Am. Hist. Life, Hist. Abstr., Part A, Mod. Hist. Abstr., Hist. Abst., Part B, Twent. Century Abstr.

THEOLOGICA XAVERIANA. Yearly 25-. Periodical. CK. Spanish. qt. $25.00. Universidad Javeriana, Carrera 10 #65-48, Bogoto 2 Columbia. **Tel** 211-78-11. **Ed** Alberto Parra. bk rev. adv acc. **Circ** 1,300. (ctrl). Doctrinal and practical theology in the Roman Catholic Church especially in Latin America; Biblical, pastoral and moral subjects. *Ecclesiastica Xaveriana.*

THEOLOGICAL AND RELIGIOUS INDEX. *See* Indexes/Abstracts.

THEOLOGICAL EDUCATION. V. 1- Autumn 1964-. 0040-5620. Periodical. US. English. sa. $5.00. Association of Theological Schools, PO Box 130, Vandalia OH 45377. **Tel** (513)898-4654. **Ed** David Schuller. **Ind/Abst** Index Relig. Period. Lit., Curr. Contents Educ., Relig. Index One, Period. **LC** BV4019. **DD** 207.73. **Circ** 3,200. Only periodical in North America dealing with major issues of theological education.

THE THEOLOGICAL EDUCATOR. 1967. 0198-6856. Periodical. US. English. sa. $4.00. New Orleans Baptist Theological Seminary, 3939 Gentilly Boulevard, New Orleans LA 70126. **Tel** (504)282-4455. **Ed** Fisher Humphreys. **LC** BR1. **DD** 230.05. bk rev. **Circ** 3,000. A journal of theology and ministry includes book reviews.

THEOLOGICAL SOUNDINGS. Vol. 1, No. 1 (July 1984)-. 0748-1772. Periodical. US. English. qt. $12.00. Theological Soundings, Oldham House 62 South Swan Street, Albany NY 12210. **DD** 230.

THEOLOGICAL STUDIES. V. 1- Feb. 1940-. 0040-5639. Periodical. US. English. qt. Theological Studies, PO Box 64002, Baltimore MD 21264. **Tel** (301)528-4105. **Ind/Abst** Old Testam. Abstr., New Testam. Abstr., Ref. Source, Cathol. Period. Lit. Index, Relig. Index One, Period., Humanit. Index. **LC** BX801. **DD** 230.05.

THEOLOGICKA REVUE CIRKVE CESKOSLOVENSKE HUSITSKE. **Main/Corp** Cirkev Ceskoslovenske Husitske. Began with Vol. 5 in 1972. 0139-7702. Periodical. CS. Czech. bm. 30.-. Artia, PO Box 790, Praha 1 Czechoslovakia. **Tel** 320569. bk rev. **Circ** 900. Doctrinal, Biblical, practical and social theological studies, history, and spiritual contributions. *Theologica Revue Ceskoslovenske Cirkve.*

THEOLOGIE DER GEGENWART. 3. Vol., 1 (Winter 1960)-. Periodical. GW. German. qt. 32.-. Verlag Regensberg, Postfach 6748, Daimlerweg 58, D-4400 Muenster West Germany. **Tel** (0251)717061. (cum index). bk rev. adv acc. (ctrl). International informations about the actuality of theology. *Theologischer Digest.*

THEOLOGIE HISTORIQUE. 1- 1963-. 0563-4253. Monographic Series. FR. French. ir. Beauchesne Editeur, 72 rue des Saints Peres, 75007 Paris France. **Tel** 5433028. History of Christianity in France-Roman Catholic Church, Reformation, Protestatism.

THEOLOGIE UND GLAUBE. Vol. 1-. 0049-366X. GW. German. qt. $20.94. Ferdinand Schoeningh Verlag, Postfach 2540 Juehenplatz-Rathaus, D-4790 Paderborn West Germany. **Ind/Abst** Old Testam. Abstr., New Testam. Abstr. **LC** BR4. (ctrl).

THEOLOGIE UND PHILOSOPHIE. Vol. 41-. Periodical. GW. German. qt. Verlag Herder Freiburg, Hermann Herder Strasse 4, D7800 Freiburg West Germany. **Ind/Abst** New Testam. Abstr., Philos. Index. *Scholastik.*

THEOLOGISCH-PRAKTISCHE QUARTALSCHRIFT. 1- Yearly volume. 0040-5663. Periodical. AU. German. qt. Oberosterreichischer Landesvlg, Landstrasse 41/ Postfach 50, A-4020 Linz Austria. **Tel** 0732/27 81 21/ 240. **Ind/Abst** New Testam. Abstr. **LC** BX803. (cum index). bk rev. adv acc. **Circ** 2,500. (ctrl). Gives information on the various topics of Roman Catholic Theology for both students, ministers and others interested in theology.

THEOLOGISCHE ARBEITEN. Vol. 1- 1955-. 0495-4505. Monographic Series. GE. German. ir. Evangelische Verlagsgesellschaft, Leninstrasse 16, DDR-701 Leipzig East Germany. **Tel** 2700521. **Circ** 1,300. Theology, works of young and unknown authors, studies, actual theological discussion, etc.

THEOLOGISCHE BUCHEREI. V. 1- 1953-. 0563-430X. Monographic Series. GW. German. ir. Kaiser Verlag, Postfach 509, Isabellastrasse 20, D8000 Munchen 43 West Germany.

THEOLOGISCHE EXISTENZ HEUTE. No. 1-77, 1933-41. Monographic Series. GW. German. ir. Kaiser Verlag, Postfach 509, Isabellastrasse 20, D8000 Munchen 43 West Germany. (cum index).

THEOLOGISCHE LITERATURZEITUNG. V. 1-. 0040-5671. Periodical. GE. German. ir. Evangelische Verlangsanstalt, Krautstr 52, DDR 1017 East Berlin. **Ind/Abst** New Testam. Abstr., Relig. Index One, Period. **LC** Z7753. *Theologisches Literaturblatt.*

THEOLOGISCHE QUARTALSCHRIFT. **VFOAT** Tubingen Quartalschrift. 1.-Yearly Volume. 0342-1430. Periodical. GW. German. qt. $21.11. Erich Wewel Verlag, Anzinger Strasse 1, D-8000 Munchen 80 West Germany. **Tel** 0049 89/403037. **Ind/Abst** Old Testam. Abstr., New Testam. Abstr., Relig. Index One, Period. **LC** BR4. (cum index). bk rev. adv acc. Deals with the subject of theologie.

THEOLOGISCHE RUNDSCHAU. 1.-20. Vol., 1897-Dec. 1917. 0040-5698. Periodical. GW. German. qt. 98.-. JCB Mohr and Paul Siebeck, Postfach 2040, 7400 Tuebingen West Germany. **Tel** (07071)26064. **Ed** Jorg Baur and Lothar Perlitt. **Ind/Abst** Old Testam. Abstr., New Testam. Abstr., Relig. Index One, Period., Recent Publ. Artic. **LC** BR4. **DD** 230.05. (cum index). bk rev. adv acc. Aims to inform everybody interested in theological work by collective reports and sporadically by single reviews of important results and present problems in all theological fields.

THEOLOGISCHE ZEITSCHRIFT. 1.- Year. 0040-5701. Periodical. SZ. qt. 92.—. Verlag Friedrich Reinhardt Ag, Missionsstrasse 36, CH-4012 Basel Switzerland. **Tel** 061/ 25 33 90. **Ed** K Seybold. **Ind/Abst** Old Testam. Abstr., New Testam. Abstr., Relig. Index One, Period. **LC** BR4. **DD** 230.05. bk rev. adv acc. **Circ** 800. Lectures and articles on theological subjects.

THEOLOGY. Began in 1920. 0040-571X. Periodical. UK. English. bm. $19.98. Society to Promote Christian Knowledge, Holy Trinity Church, Marylebone Road, London NW1 4DU England. **Tel** (01)387-5282. **Ed** Peter Coleman, John Durry and Leslie Houlden. **Ind/Abst** New Testam. Abstr., Index Relig. Period. Lit., Ref. Source, Relig. Index One, Period. **LC** BR1. bk rev. adv acc. **Circ** 5,000. A forum for all people who think about their faith and its relation to current theological study and everyday life.

THEOLOGY ANNUAL. Periodical. Chinese (English). an. $2.50. Holy Spirit Seminary College, 6 Welfare Road Theology Division, Aberdeen Hong

Kong. **Tel** (5)530266. **Ed** Sean O Cearbhallain, SJ. **Circ** 500. Articles in English and Chinese in the general areas of Catholic Theology (Dogmatics, moral, scripture) and philosophy, written by members of our faculty and students.

THEOLOGY DIGEST. V. 1- Winter 1953-. 0040-5728. Periodical. US. English. qt. $17.00. Theology Digest, 3634 Lindell Boulevard, St Louis MO 63108. **Tel** (314)658-2857. **Ed** Bernhard A Asen. **Ind/Abst** Old Testam. Abstr., Cathol. Period. Lit. Index. **LC** BX801. **DD** 230.2. (cum index). bk rev. adv acc. **Circ** 5,000. Available on microfilm from University Microfilms. Offers translations and condensations of articles selected from over 400 theology journals from around the world on scripture, morality, ecumenism, history, and systematics.

THEOLOGY NEWS & NOTES. **VFOAT** Theology News and Notes. **VAT** Theology News and Notes. Began in Apr. 1954. Periodical. US. English. qt. 135 North Oakland Avenue, Pasadena CA 91101.

THEOLOGY TODAY. V. 1- Apr. 1944-. 0040-5736. Periodical. US. English. qt. $14.00. Theology Today, PO Box 29, Princeton NJ 08542. **Tel** (609)921-8300. **Ed** Hugh T Kerr. **Ind/Abst** Book Rev. Index, Book Rev. Mon., Guide Soc. Sci. Relig. Period. Lit., Humanit. Index, Relig. Index One, Period., New Testam. Abstr., Old Testam. Abstr., Relig. Theol. Abstr., Subj. Index Sel. Period. Lit. **LC** BR1. **DD** 205. (cum index). bk rev. adv acc. **Circ** 12,000. Microtext reprints available through the American Theological Library Association., Available on microfilm from University Microfilms. A non-denominational journal of religious opinion on Biblical, theological and social issues.

THE THOMIST. *See* Philosophy.

THRUST. V. 1-15, No. 1. 0318-7381. Periodical. CN. English. mo. $7.00. Evangelical Thrust, PO Box 3627, Manila Phillipines. **Tel** 35-03-88. **DD** 269.205.

TIDSSKRIFT FOR TEOLOGI OG KIRKE. Began in 1930. 0040-7194. Periodical. NO. Norwegian. qt. $31.00. Universitetsforlaget, PO Box 2959-Toyen, Oslo 6 Norway. **Tel** 02-276-0-60. **Ind/Abst** Old Testam. Abstr., New Testam. Abstr. **LC** BX8001. Theological and ecclesiastical problems in Norway and internationally.

TIJDSCHRIFT VOOR THEOLOGIE. 1.- Vol. 0563-5357. Periodical. NE. Dutch. qt. $23.71. Tijdschrift Voor Theologie, Postbus 9009, 6500 GK Mijmegen Netherlands. **Tel** 080 229844. **Ed** T M Schoof. **Ind/Abst** New Testam. Abstr. bk rev. adv acc. **Circ** 2,000. Treats actual religious problems on theological level. *Studia Catholica.*

TJURUNGA: AN AUSTRALASIAN BENEDICTINE REVIEW. No. 1- Sept. 1971-. Periodical. AT. English. sa. 12.00 Domestic, 14.00 Foreign. St Benedict's Monastery, Arcadia New South Wales 2159 Australia. **Tel** 02-653-1159. **Ed** BR Terence Kavenagh. (cum index). bk rev. adv acc. **Circ** 240. Studies on the rule of St Benedict and its present relevance, on monastic spirituality and history in general.

TODAY'S CHRISTIAN WOMAN. Fall/Winter 1978/79-. 0163-1799. Periodical. US. English. bm. $13.95. Today's Christian Woman, PO Box 1918, Marion OH 43302. **Tel** (201)768-8060. **LC** BV4527. **DD** 248.84305.

TODAY'S MINISTRY *CEASED.* Sept. 1965-. 0563-637X. Periodical. US. English. Andover Newton Theological School, 210 Herrick Road, Newton Centre MA 02159.

TORONTO STUDIES IN THEOLOGY. BONHOEFFER SERIES. **VFOAT** Bonhoeffer Series. Monographic Series. US. English. $199.80. The Edwin Mellen Press, PO Box 450, Lewiston NY 14092. **Tel** (716)754-8566. **Ed** H Richardson. **Circ** 1,000. (ctrl). Monographs on contemporary theology, ethics, and philosophy of religion.

TOUCHSTONE (WINNIPEG, MAN.). (TOUCHSTONE). **VFOAT** Touchstone, Heritage and Theology in a New Age. Vol. 1, No. 1 (Jan. 1983)-. 0827-3200. Periodical. CN. English. ty. 15.00. Touchstone, University of Winnipeg, c/o Faculty of Theology, Winnipeg Manitoba R3B 2E9 Canada. **Tel** (204)786-9855. **Ed** Mac Watts. **Ind/Abst** Relig. Index One, Period. **DD** 230.79205. bk rev. **Circ** 2,000. (ctrl). To bring the heritage of theology and faith to bear on present life and witness, to engage the issues of our day in the light of the biblical message and Christian tradition.

TRAI TIM DU'C ME. **VFOAT** Immaculate Heart of Mary Magazine. 0744-6128. Periodical. US. Vietnamese. mo. $20.00. Trai Tim Duc Me, PO Box 836, Carthage MO 64836. **Tel** (417)358-8296.

TRAIT D'UNION JEUNESSE. (LE TRAIT D'UNION JEUNESSE). V. 2- Sept. 1979-. 0225-7416. Periodical. CN. French. ir. $2.00. Communaute R3 du Diocese de Valleyfield, Secretariat R3, 31 rue Fabrique, Valleyfield Quebec J6T 4G9 Canada. **DD** 248.05. *Trait d'Union R P3 S, 0225-7408.*

TRANSPORTEUR. (LE TRANSPORTEUR). No. 15 (Oct./Dec. 1980)-. 0229-4362. Periodical. CN. French. ir. Free. Le Transporteur, Christian Transportation Inc, 512 rue Yonge, Toronto Ontario M4Y 1X9 Canada. **DD** 248.88. *Bonne Nouvelle pour le Transporteur, 0229-4354.*

TRIERER THEOLOGISCHE STUDIEN. V. 1-. Monographic Series. GW. German. ir. Paulinus Verlag, Fleischstr 61-65 Postfach 30-40, D-5500 Trier West Germany.

TRIERER THEOLOGISCHE ZEITSCHRIFT. 56.- Vol. 0041-2945. Periodical. GW. German. qt. Paulinus Verlag, Fleischstr 61-65, Pstfch 30-40, D-5500 Trier West Germany. **Ind/Abst** Old Testam. Abstr., New Testam. Abstr. **LC** BR4. **DD** 230.205. *Theologie und Seelsorge.*

TRINITY JOURNAL. V.1 (NS), No.1-. 0360-3032. Periodical. US. English. sa. $7.50. Trinity Evangelical Divinity School, 2065 Half Day Road, Bannockburn, Deerfield IL 60015. **Tel** (312)945-8800. **Ed** D A Carson. **Ind/Abst** New Testam. Abstr., Relig. Index One, Period. **Circ** 900. Issues in relation to Biblical, theological, historical, philosophical, and educational concerns of the Christian community. *Trinity Journal, 0360-3032.*

TRINITY SEMINARY REVIEW. Vol. 1, No. 1 (Spring 1979)-. 0270-2533. Periodical. US. English. sa. Free. Trinity Lutheran Seminary, 2199 East Main Street, Columbus OH 43209. **Tel** (614)235-4136. **Ed** Walter F Taylor Jr. **Ind/Abst** Relig. Index One, Period. bk rev. **Circ** 6,000. Forum for interaction between theological disciplines and practice of ministry.

TSF BULLETIN (MADISON, WIS.). (TSF BULLETIN). **VFOAT** T.S.F. Bulletin. **VAT** Theological Students Fellowship Bulletin (Madison). Vol. 4, No. 1 (Oct. 1980)-. 0272-3913. Periodical. US. English. bm. $40.00. Inter-Varsity Fellowship, 233 Langton, Madison WI 53703. **Tel** (608)257-1103. **Ed** Vernon C Grounds. **Ind/Abst** Relig. Index One, Period. bk rev. adv acc. **Circ** 1,500. Journal of evangelical thought making available to theology students the scholarly and practical resources of classical Christianity. *TSF News and Reviews, 0272-040X.*

UNDER AFRIKAS SOL. **Main/Corp** Dansk Forenet Sudan Mission. Danish. ir. (Forlag Suvanne), Box 30, 6070 Christiansfeld Denmark. **LC** BV3500.

UNDERGROUND EVANGELISM MAGAZINE. 0097-6784. Periodical. US. English. Underground Evangelism, PO Box 250, Glendale CA 91209. **Tel** (213)254-4371. **LC** BV3777.C62. **DD** 269.2091717.

UNITE CHRETIENNE. **VFOAT** Pages Documentaires Unitas. No 19- Aug. 1970-. Periodical. FR. French. qt. 60 Domestic, 70 Foreign. Unite Chretienne, 2 rue Jean Carries, 69005 Lyon France. **Tel** 78 42 11 67. **Ed** Pere Pierre Michalon. bk rev. **Circ** 2,000. Two or three basic articles on the subject matter of each issue. Book reviews and ecumenical news. *Unitas, Pages Documentaires.*

UNIVERSITAS CANONICA. V. 1, Year 1, (Oct. 1980)-. Periodical. CK. Spanish. sa. Pontificia Universidad Javeriana, Cra. 7 No. 40-62, Oficina B - 441, Bogota Columbia. **LC** K25. **DD** 262.905.

USPG IN ACTION, ANNUAL REPORT. **Main/Corp** United Society for the Propagation of the Gospel. UK. English. an. United Society for the Propagation of the Gospel, 15 Tufton Street, London SW1P 3QQ England. **LC** BV2361. **DD** 266.3.

USQR, UNION SEMINARY QUARTERLY REVIEW. (UNION SEMINARY QUARTERLY REVIEW). **VFOAT** USQR. V. 1- Nov. 1945-. 0362-1545. Periodical. US. English. qt. $35.00. Union Seminary Quarterly Review, 3041 Broadway at 20th Street, New York NY 10027. **Tel** (212)662-7100. **Ed** Alex Coe and Earl Kooper Kamp. **Ind/Abst** Old Testam. Abstr., New Testam. Abstr., Relig. Index One, Period. **LC** BV4070. **DD** 205. bk rev. adv acc. **Circ** 1,400. Vols. 1-30 available from University Microfilms. A journal dedicated to general issues of theology and culture. *Union Review, Alumni Bulletin - Union Theological Seminary.*

THE UTAH EVANGEL. Periodical. US. English. mo.

VAINQUEUR. (LE VAINQUEUR). Vol. 9, No. 5 (June 1984)-. 0824-1678. Periodical. CN. French. mo. $7.00. Vainqueur, C P 22, St-Hubert Quebec J3Y 5S9 Canada. **DD** 248.05. *Revue le Vainqueur, 0824-166X.*

VAN. (LE VAN). 0824-0388. Periodical. CN. French. mo. $2.95 Each Number. Le Van, CP 214 Succursale B, Longueuil Quebec J4L 4G7 Canada. **DD** 261.805.

VANGUARD. V. 1- Jan./Feb. 1954-. 0042-2568. Periodical. US. English. mo. Lutheran Human Relations Association of America, 2703 North Sherman Boulevard, Milwaukee WI 53210. **LC** BT734. **DD** 261.83.

VENTURE INWARD. Vol. 1, No. 1 (Sept./Oct. 1984)-. 0748-3406. Periodical. US. English. bm. Free to Members. Association for Research and Enlightenment, PO Box 595, Virginia Beach VA 23451. *A.R.E. Journal, A.R.E. News.*

VERKUNDIGUNG UND FORSCHUNG. Yearly V. 1-. 0342-2410. Periodical. GW. German. sa. $13.55. Kaiser-Verlag, Postfach 509, Isabellastrasse 20, D8000 Munchen 43 West Germany. **Ind/Abst** New Testam. Abstr. **LC** BR4. bk rev. adv acc. **Circ** 2,700. Evangelical theology.

VERONA MISSIONS. 0164-4211. Periodical. US. English. bm. Verona Missions, 2104 St Michael Street, Cincinnati OH 45204. **Tel** (513)921-4400. *Verona Father Missions, 0042-4234.*

VERS DEMAIN PELERIN. No. 2, (April/June 1974)-. 0227-471X. Periodical. CN. French. qt. $5.00 for 2 Years. Vers Demain Pelerin, c/o Journal Vers Demain 1101 rue Principale, Rougemont Quebec J0L 1M0 Canada. **DD** 261.805. *Vers Demain.*

VIATEURS EN MISSION. No. 203- Dec. 1979-. 0226-7861. Periodical. CN. French. Missions Saint-Viateur, 450 Av Querbes, Montreal Quebec H2V 3W5 Canada. **DD** 266.205. *Missions Saint-Viateur, 0226-7888.*

VICTORY (SAN DIEGO, CALIF.). (VICTORY). Vol. 1, No. 1 (Apr. 1983)-. 0745-9173. Periodical. US. English. bm. $6.00. World Evangelism Inc, PO Box 700, San Diego CA 92138. **DD** 266. *Deeper Life.*

VICTORY (SAN DIEGO, CALIF.). (VICTORIA). 8750-2534. Periodical. US. Spanish. qt. $6.00. Victoria, PO Box 700, San Diego CA 92138. **DD** 266.

VIE LITURGIQUE. First issue in 1968?. 0380-8254. Periodical. CN. French. ir. $15.48. Vie Liturgique, 1073 St Cyrille Ouest, Sillery Quebec G1S 4R5 Canada. **Tel** (418)688-1211. **DD** 264.02005.

VIE LITURGIQUE CHEZ NOUS *CEASED.* (LA VIE LITURGIQUE CHEZ NOUS). V. 1-14, No. 4. 0381-9221. Periodical. CN. French. bm. Office Diocensain de Liturgie, 679 rue Chabanel, Chicoutimi Quebec G7H 3S5 Canada. **DD** 264.0200971416.

VIRTUE. V. 1- Sept./Oct. 1978-. 0164-7288. Periodical. US. English. bm. Virtue, PO Box 850, Sisters OR 97759. **Tel** (503)549-8261. **Ed** Becky Durost. **LC** BJ1610. **DD** 248.84305. bk rev. adv acc. **Circ** 110,000. The Christian magazine for women.

VIVRE. **VFOAT** Revue Vocationnelle. V. 1- Nov./Dec. 1978-. 0226-7772. Periodical. CN. French. ir. Free. Centre Projet de Vie, CP 32, Granby Quebec J2G 8E3 Canada. **DD** 248.05. *Grandir.*

VOICE. 0049-6669. Periodical. US. English. bm. $4.50. Independent Fund Churches of America, 1860 South Mannheim Road Box 250, Westchester IL 60153. **Tel** (312)562-0234. **Ed** Paul J Dollaske. bk rev. adv acc. **Circ** 9,000. (ctrl). An in-house publication for member churches and men, with contributed articles, news of interest to same, some other subscribers, specialized articles included.

THE VOICE OF EVANGELICAL METHODISM. 0164-3606. Periodical. US. English. mo. $5.00. The Voice of Evangelical Methodism, 3036 North Meridian, Wichita KS 67024.

VOICE OF TRIUMPH. Vol. 1, No. 1 (Jan. 1975)-. 8750-572X. Periodical. US. English. bm. Voice of Triumph Ministries, 9201 SE 162nd Avenue, Portland OR 97236. **DD** 248.

VOIX DU SANCTUAIRE. **Main/Corp** Sanctuaire de Notre-Dame de Lourdes, Rigaud, Quebec. V. 1- 1957-. 0700-9313. CN. French. an. Pere

Directeur Sanctuaire de Norte-Dame-de-Lourdes, Rigaud Quebec J0P 1P0 Canada. **DD** 263.042714263.

VOX PATRUM. Periodical. Polish. sa. Miedzuwudziaowy Zakad Badan Nad Antykiem, Chrzescijanskim Kul Ul Chopina 29/5A, 20-023 Lubin Poland. **LC** BR162.2.

WEGE ZUM MENSCHEN. Vol. 6- 1954-. 0043-2040. Periodical. GW. German. ir. Vandenhoeck & Ruprecht, Postfach 3753, Theaterstr 13, D 3400 Goettingen West Germany. **Tel** (0551)65061. *Weg Zur Seele.*

WELTMISSION (EVANGELISCHES MISSIONSWERK IN DER BUNDESREPUBLIK DEUTSCHLAND UND BERLIN WEST). (DIE WELTMISSION). Vol. 53, No. 1 (Feb. 1983)-. 0341-082X. Periodical. German. bm. 9.00. Missionshilfe Verlag, Mittelweg 143, 2000 Hamburg 13 West Germany. **LC** BV2354. **DD** 266.005. *Wort in der Welt (Deutsche Evangelische Missions-Rat Germany).*

WENDING. 1. Volume, No. 1 (March 1946)-. 0043-2695. Periodical. NE. Dutch. mo. Boekencentrum B V, Scheveningsweg 72, 2517 KX The Hague Netherlands. **LC** BR2. *Algemeen Weekblad voor Kerk en Christendom, Kouter.*

WESLEYAN THEOLOGICAL JOURNAL. 1966. 0092-4245. US. English. sa. $6.00. Wesleyan Theological Society, c/o Dr Caldwell, 215 East 43rd Street, Marion IN 46952. **Tel** (317)674-7810. **Ed** Alex R G Deasley. **Ind/Abst** Relig. Index One, Period., Christ. Period. Index. **LC** BR1. **DD** 287.1. bk rev adv acc. **Circ** 1,600. (ctrl) Historical theological biblical topics in the Wesleyan Arminian interpretation and tradition.

THE WESTMINSTER THEOLOGICAL JOURNAL. V. 1- Nov. 1938-. 0043-4388. Periodical. US. English. ty. $20.00. Westminster Theological Seminary, Chestnut Hill, PO Box 27009, Philadelphia PA 19118. **Tel** (215)887-5511. **Ed** Moises Silva. **Ind/Abst** Old Testam. Abstr., Recent Publ. Artic., New Testam. Abstr., Elenchus Bibliogr. Bibicus, Christ. Period. Index, Int. Zeitschriftenschau Bibelwissenschaft Grenzgeb., Relig. Theol. Abstr. **LC** BR1. **DD** 205. (cum index). bk rev. **Circ** 1,200. Available on microfilm from University Microfilms. A journal with articles and book reviews in the areas of Biblical studies, theology, church history, apologitics and practical theology.

WIENER BEITRAGE ZUR THEOLOGIE. Vol. 1- 1963-. Monographic Series. AU. German. ir. Wiener Dom-Verlag, Strozzigasse 8, A-1080 Vienna Austria.

WISCONSIN LUTHERAN QUARTERLY. V. 57- 1960-. 0362-5648. Periodical. US. English. qt. $15.00. Northwestern Publishing House, 3624 West North Avenue, Milwaukee WI 53208. **Tel** (414)242-7200. **Ed** Edward C French. bk rev. **Circ** 1,450. Serves as a testimony of its theological convictions and a public witness to the Bible's truths. *Quartalschrift.*

WISSENSCHAFT UND WEISHEIT. 1.-Volume. 0043-678X. Periodical. GW. German. ty. $24.35. Verlag B Kuhlen KG, Bettrather Str 79, 405 Moenchengladbach West Germany. **Ind/Abst** Old Testam. Abstr., New Testam. Abstr., Philos. Index. **LC** BR4. **DD** 230.205.

THE WITNESS. 0197-8896. Periodical. US. English. mo. $25.00. The Witness, PO Box 359/119 East Butler Pike, Ambler PA 19002. **Tel** (215)643-7067. **Ed** Mary Lou Suhor. **Ind/Abst** Relig. Index One, Period. **LC** BX5800. **Circ** 5,500. (ctrl). A journal of social concern dedicated to systemic change, confronting issues of racism, sexism, classism and imperialism, and examining the Christian response.

WOLGAN MOKHOE. VFOAT The Pastoral Monthly. Began in 1976. Periodical. KO. Korean. mo. 33,000. Wolgan Mokhoesa, 1-1325 2-ka Yongsan-dong Yongsan-ku, Seoul 140 Korea. **LC** BV4000.

THE WOMAN'S PULPIT. V. 1- 1922-. 0043-7379. Periodical. US. English. qt. $50.00. International Association of Women Ministers, 579 Main Street, Stroudsburg PA 18360. **Tel** (717)421-7701. **LC** BV676. **DD** 262.14.

THE WORD AMONG US. 1981. 0742-4639. Periodical. US. English. mo. $25.00. The Word Among Us, PO Box 3646, Washington DC 20037. **Tel** (301)977-2500. **Ed** Joseph Difato. **Circ** 50,000. A practical guide to living the Christian life designed to help Catholics draw closer to Jesus Christ through daily personal prayer and scripture reading.

WORD AND SPIRIT. VFOAT Word & Spirit. 1-. 0193-9211. Periodical. US. English. an. $7.00. St Bede's Publications, Box 132, Still River MA 01467. **Tel** (617)456-8138. **Ed** Mary Joseph. **Ind/Abst** Old Testam. Abstr. **LC** BX801. **DD** 282. **Circ** 250. A monastic journal which deals with a different theme each year focusing on topics of monastic, theological, or spiritual interest or celebrating an anniversary of some (religious or church-oriented) historical event.

WORD & WITNESS. VAT Word and Witness. Began in 1976. Periodical. US. English. bm. $30.00. Sunday Publications, 1937 10th Avenue North Box 9501, Lake Worth FL 33466. **Tel** (305)533-0990. Index in first issue of next volume - loose - unpaged.

WORD & WORLD. VFOAT Word and World. Vol. 1, No. 1 (Winter 1981)-. 0275-5270. Periodical. US. English. qt. Word and World, 2481 Como Avenue, St Paul MN 55108. **Tel** (612)641-3482. **Ind/Abst** New Testam., Old Testam. Abstr., Relig. Index One, Period., Relig. Theol. Abstr. **LC** BR1. **DD** 230.41.

WORD IN THE WORLD. (THE WORD IN THE WORLD). 0097-8310. US. English. Divine Word Missionaries Etc, Techny IL 60082. **LC** BV2130. **DD** 266.205.

WORLD MISSION JOURNAL. Periodical. US. English. mo. Baptist Brotherhood Commission, 1548 Poplar Avenue, Memphis TN 38104. **Tel** (901)272-2461.

WORLD PENTECOST. 1- 1971-. Periodical. UK. English. qt. $5.00. Reverend Jakob Zopfi, PO Box 44, CH-6376 Emetten Switzerland. **Tel** 0041 41 64 25 55. **Ed** Jakob Zopfi. **LC** BX8762.A1. **DD** 289.9. bk rev. **Circ** 1,500. Publishes reports from Pentecostal churches all over the world. There is as well doctrinal teaching, reports from conferences and book reviews.

WORLD RELIEF CANADA. Issue 1 (1983)-. 0824-5088. Periodical. CN. English. qt. Free. WRC, P O Box 874 Station B, Willowdale Ontario M2K 2R1 Canada. **DD** 266.02371.

WORLD VIEW (TORONTO, ONT.). (WORLD VIEW). VFOAT Worldview. Vol. 1, No. 1 (July 1982)-. 0713-3391. CN. English. an. $1.00. Canec, 85 Street Clair Avenue East, Toronto Ontario M4T 1M8 Canada. **DD** 266.02305.

WORLDMISSION. V. 1- Sept. 1950-. 0043-9282. Periodical. US. English. qt. $5.00. National Office of the Society for the Propagation of Faith of the United States, 366 Fifth Avenue, New York NY 10001. **LC** BV2130. **DD** 266.205. *Mission Studies.*

WORLDWIDE MISSIONS. VAT World Wide Missions. 0199-0292. Periodical. US. English. mo. World-Wide Missions, Box G, Pasadena CA 91109.

WORSHIP AND ARTS. 1956. Periodical. US. English. bm. Worship and Arts, 11392 Wallingsford Road, Los Alamitos CA 90720. **Ed** E J Mero. bk rev. adv acc. **Circ** 1,000. Non-denominational publication promoting worship arts in the church. Reviews of new music for adult, youth and childrens choirs and of organ music, books and records.

WORT IN DER WELT (DEUTSCHE EVANGELISCHE MISSIONS-RAT (GERMANY). (DAS WORT IN DER WELT). Vol. 62- No. 6 (Dec. 1982). 0341-082X. Periodical. GW. German. bm. Deutsche Evange, Miss Hilfe, Mittelweg 143, 2000 Hamburg 13 West Germany. **LC** BV2354. **DD** 266.005. *Allgemeine Missions-Nachrichten.*

YOUR EDMUNDITE MISSIONS NEWS LETTER. VFOAT Edmundite Missions. 0044-1015. Periodical. US. English. bm. Edmundite Mission, 1428 Broad Street, Selma AL 36701.

YOUTH & ADULTS TOGETHER. 0713-3634. Periodical. CN. English. ir. Free. Division Of Mission In Canada, United Church Of Canada, 85 St Clair Avenue East, Toronto Ontario M4T 1M8 Canada. **DD** 268.43305.

THE YOUTH LEADER. 0190-4566. Periodical. US. English. mo. $12.00. The Youth Leader, 1445 Boonville, Springfield MO 65802. **Tel** (417)862-2781.

ZEAL. 0514-2482. Periodical. US. English. qt. Zeal, St Elizabeth Mission Society, Allegheny NY 14706.

ZEICHEN DER ZEIT (BERLIN, GERMANY). (DIE ZEICHEN DER ZEIT). Began with 1, Vol. (1947). 0044-2038. Periodical. SZ. German. mo. $13.46. Kunst & Wissen Erich Bieber, Dufourstrasse 51, CH-8008 Zurich Switzerland. **Tel** 011-41-1-69 44 20. **LC** BR4. **DD** 230.05.

ZEITSCHRIFT FUR BAYERISCHE KIRCHENGESCHICHTE. *See* Religion, Mythology, Rationalism - Protestantism.

ZEITSCHRIFT FUR DIE ALTTESTAMENTLICHE WISSENSCHAFT. Vol. 1- 0044-2526. Periodical. German. ir. 146. Walter de Gruyter Company, Genthiner Strasse 13, 100 Berlin 30 West Germany. **Tel** 030/26005-0. **Ed** Otto Kaises. **Ind/Abst** New Testam. Abstr., Old Testam. Abstr., Relig. Index One, Period., Recent Publ. Artic. **LC** BS410. **DD** 221.605. (cum index). bk rev. adv acc. **Circ** 1,600.

ZEITSCHRIFT FUR KIRCHENGESCHICHTE. Vol. 1- Mar. 1876-. 0044-2925. Periodical. GW. German. ir. 172.-. W Kohlhammer, Kessbruhlstrasse 69, Postfach 800430, 7000 Stuttgart 80 West Germany. **Tel** (0711)7863-1. **Ed** Faulenbach. bk rev. adv acc. (ctrl). Non-denominational publication includes summarized descriptions of large complex of questions on miscelleneous subjects. Texts as well as reviews of important publications on church history from Germany and abroad.

ZEITSCHRIFT FUR MISSIONSWISSENSCHAFT UND RELIGIONSWISSENSCHAFT. 1.- Yearly, 1911-. 0044-3123. Periodical. GW. German. qt. $18.51. Aschendorffsche Verlagsbuchhan Dlung, Postfach 1124, 4400 Muenster West Germany. **Tel** 251/6901. **Ind/Abst** Relig. Index One, Period. (cum index). adv acc. **Circ** 850. Journal for mission work as an application of the Christian faith, with view towards the world church and interdenominational dialog.

ZEITSCHRIFT FUR THEOLOGIE UND KIRCHE. 1.-27. Vol., 1891-1917. 0513-9147. Periodical. GW. German. qt. 66.-. JCB Mohr and Paul Siebeck, Postfach 2040, 7400 Tuebingen West Germany. **Tel** (07071)26064. **Ed** Eberhard Jungel. **Ind/Abst** Old Testam. Abstr., New Testam. Abstr., Relig. Index One, Period., Recent Publ. Artic. **LC** BR4. **DD** 230.05. (cum index). bk rev adv acc. A scholarly journal devoted to all areas of theological research and the teachings of the Church.

ZEITSCHRIFTENINHALTSDIENST THEOLOGIE. VAT Zeitschriften Inhaltsdienst Theologie. 1975-. 0340-8361. Periodical. GW. German. mo. $18.26. Univ-Bibliothek Tubingen Theol Orientabteilung, Postfach 2620, D7400 Tubingen 1 West Germany. **Tel** (07071)296499. **Circ** 930. Theology.

RESTAURANTS

ALBERTA GASTRONOMIC. 2nd- Ed. 0709-6747. CN. English. an. $3.95. Apogee Enterprises, PO Box 48525 Station Bentall, Vancouver British Columbia V7X 1A2 Canada. **DD** 642.5602571233.

THE . . . ANALYSIS OF IMPULSE SNACK BAR OPERATIONS : A STUDY PRESENTED TO THE GOLD MEDAL PRODUCTS COMPANY OF CINCINNATI, OHIO. VFOAT Biennial Analysis of Impulse Snack Bar Operations. US. English. be. Gold Medal Products Company, 1825 Freeman Avenue, Cincinnati OH 45214. **LC** TX945. **DD** 338.476479573.

THE ANNUAL DIRECTORY OF VEGETARIAN RESTAURANTS. *See* Yearbooks, Almanacs, Directories.

ANNUAL TABLESERVICE RESTAURANT OPERATIONS REPORT . . . FOR THE UNITED STATES. 1st- 1976-. US. English. an. National Restaurant Association, 311 1st NW, Washington DC 20001.

ATLANTIC CONTROL STATES BEVERAGE JOURNAL. 0044-9881. Periodical. US. English. mo. $6.00. Arnold Lazarus, 3 Twelfth Street, Wheeling WV 26003. **Tel** (304)232-7620. **Ed** Arnold Lazarus. bk rev. adv acc. **Circ** 15,500. (ctrl). We are a trade journal serving the food/drink service industry.

Restaurants

BALTIMORE EPICURE. US. English. Peanut Butter Publishing, 911 Western Avenue/Suite 401, Seattle WA 98104. **Tel** (206)628-6200. **Circ** 250,000. Reproduction of the menus from 75 of the best and most popular restaurants in major cities across the country. Series of 20 epicures.

BHRCA OFFICIAL GUIDE TO HOTELS AND RESTAURANTS IN GREAT BRITAIN, IRELAND AND OVERSEAS. See Hotels/Motels.

BIBLIOGRAPHY OF HOTEL AND RESTAURANT ADMINISTRATION. See Bibliographies.

THE BOSTON RESTAURANT GUIDE. (THE ... BOSTON RESTAURANT GUIDE). 1980-. 0731-1923. US. English. an. $3.95. Jubilee Publications Inc, 227 Statler Office Building, Boston MA 02116.

CAFES ET RESTAURANTS CHOUETTES. VAT Restaurants Chouettes (1981). 1981-. 0711-6322. CN. French. an. $2.50 Per Number. Cafes et Restaurants Chouettes, 1026 East rue Mont-Royal, Montreal Quebec H2J 1X2 Canada. **DD** 647.95714281. *Restaurants Chouettes de Montreal, 0711-6314.*

CAMERON'S FOODSERVICE PROMOTIONS REPORTER. See Hotels/Motels.

CANADIAN HOTEL & RESTAURANT. See Hotels/Motels.

CANADIAN HOTEL & RESTAURANT. SOURCES DIRECTORY. See Yearbooks, Almanacs, Directories.

CAPITAL FEASTS. 1970-. 0148-4516. US. English. an. $4.50. Rock Creek Publishing Company, PO Box 19273, Washington DC 20036. **LC** TX907. **DD** 647.95753.

COOKING FOR PROFIT. 1932. 0091-861X. Periodical. US. English. mo. $30.00. Cooking for Profit, 131 South Main Street, PO Box 267, Fond du Lac WI 54935. **Tel** (414)923-3700. **Ed** Bill Dittrich. **DD** 338. adv acc. **Circ** 21,000. Practical food service operations information for industry personnel.

THE CORNELL HOTEL AND RESTAURANT ADMINISTRATION QUARTERLY. See Hotels/Motels.

DIRECTORY OF CHAIN RESTAURANT OPERATORS. See Yearbooks, Almanacs, Directories.

DIRECTORY OF RESTAURANT AND FAST FOOD CHAINS IN CANADA. See Yearbooks, Almanacs, Directories.

DOWNTOWN AND SUBURBAN OFFICE BUILDING EXPERIENCE EXCHANGE REPORT. 56th- 1976-. 0196-982X. US. English. an. Building Owners & Manager Association, 1250 Eye Street NW/Suite 200, Washington DC 20005. **Tel** (202)289-7000. **LC** TX980. **DD** 338.476479623. *Office Building Experience Exchange Report.*

DYNAMICS OF THE CHAIN RESTAURANT MARKET. VFOAT Chain Restaurant Market. US. English. an. $825.00. International Foodservice Manufactoring Association, 875 N Michigan Avenue/Suite 3460, Chicago IL 60611. **Tel** (312)944-3838. The most comprehensive source of current information for marketers to the chain restaurant foodservice market, includes executive summary, and available on data disk.

EDITION QUEBECOISE. V. 2- Jan. 1977-. 0704-5999. Periodical. CN. French. mo. $2. le No. Infhotel Presse, CP 6053, Montreal 101 Quebec H3C 3A7 Canada. **DD** 641.57209714. *Special Canada, 0700-799X.*

EGON RONAY'S TWA GUIDE TO GOOD RESTAURANTS IN 35 EUROPEAN BUSINESS CITIES. (EGON RONAY'S TWA GUIDE . . . TO GOOD RESTAURANTS IN 35 EUROPEAN BUSINESS CITIES). VFOAT TWA Guide . . . to Good Restaurants in 35 European Business Cities. 1983-. 0882-0376. US. English. an. $6.95. Harmony Books, One Park Avenue, New York NY 10016. **LC** TX910.A1. **DD** 647.954.

ENERGACTION HOSPITALITY. Vol. 1, No. 1 (Spring 1984)-. 0826-4309. Periodical. CN. English. qt. Free. Energaction Hospitality, 1016-130 Albert Street, Ottawa Ontario K1P 5G4 Canada. **DD** 647.94. (ctrl).

ESPANA (MADRID, SPAIN : 1981). (ESPANA). VFOAT Guia del Viajero. 1981-. Spanish. an. **LC** TX910.S7. **DD** 647.9546.

FAST SERVICE CEASED. V. 35, No. 5-V. 40, No. 10. 0363-5120. Periodical. US. English. mo. $10.00. 757 Third Avenue, New York NY 10017. **LC** TX901. **DD** 642.5605. *Drive-in Fast Service.*

FIELDING'S FAVORITES. HOTELS & INNS, EUROPE. VAT Fielding's Favorites. Hotels and Inns, Europe. 1978-. 0191-0329. US. English. an. $4.95. Fielding Publications, 105 Madison Avenue, New York NY 10016. **LC** TX910.A1. **DD** 647.944. *Fielding's Selected Favorites. Hotels & Inns. Europe, 0092-9506.*

FIESTA (MCALLEN, TEX.). (FIESTA). VFOAT Fiesta Magazine. 0738-7822. Periodical. US. English. mo. $12.00. Fiesta Publications, 709 Jackson Avenue, McAllen TX 78501. **Tel** (512)682-8371. **Ed** Gretchen L Sammons. adv acc. **Circ** 9,000. (ctrl). Visitors and resident guide to restaurants, lodging, entertainment, sight-seeing, special events, travel, living and services in South Texas and Mexico.

FLORIDA RESTAURATEUR. 0192-348X. Periodical. US. English. mo. $15.00. Florida Restauranteur, 1065 NE 125 Street North, Miami FL 33161. **Tel** (305)891-1852. **Ed** Angela Pyke. adv acc. **Circ** 7,000. (ctrl). Service articles and news for Florida foodservice operators. Covers business ideas, new products and developments, and changes in the restaurant and hospitality industry.

FLORIDA RESTAURATEUR & PURVEYOR NEWS. 1956-. 0046-418X. Periodical. US. English. ir. $15.00. Florida Restaurateur, 1065 Northeast 125 Street, North Miami FL 33161. **Tel** (305)891-1852. **Ed** Angela Pyke. **DD** 642.5. adv acc. **Circ** 7,000. (ctrl). Service articles and news for Florida foodservice operators. New products, changes in industry, employee relations, trends, energy, food, economics, alcohol, and wages.

FOODSERVICE & HOSPITALITY. V. 6, No. 1- Jan. 1973-. 0007-8972. Periodical. CN. English. mo. $18.58. Foodservice Hospitality, 980 Yonge Street/Suite 400, Toronto Ontario M4W 2J8 Canada. **Tel** (416)923-8888. **Ed** Steven and Sherwood. **Ind**/**Abst** Can. Bus. Index. bk rev. adv acc. **Circ** 30,000. (ctrl). *Foodservice/Hospitality Canada, 0317-5162.*

FOODSERVICE & HOSPITALITY NEWS. V. 1- Sept. 17, 1979-. 0225-4050. Periodical. CN. English. bw. 824 Domestic. Foodservice & Hospitality, 980 Yonge Street/Suite 400, Toronto Ontario M4W 2H8 Canada. **Tel** (416)923-8888. **Ed** Steven Isherwood. **DD** 338.476479471. bk rev. adv acc. **Circ** 30,000. (ctrl).

FOODSERVICE DIRECTORY. See Yearbooks, Almanacs, Directories.

FOODSERVICE EQUIPMENT SPECIALIST. 0148-4958. Periodical. US. English. ir. $40.00 Domestic, $50.00 Canada/Mexico, $65.00 Others. Cahners Publishers, 270 Saint Paul Street, Denver CO 80206. **Tel** (312)635-8800. **Ed** Robin Ashton. adv acc. **Circ** 16,600. (ctrl). The standard journal of the foodservice equipment industry in intended for buyers specifiers, and distributors of foodservice equipment for commercial and institutional use. *Foodservice Equipment Dealer, 0015-671X.*

THE GALLUP MONTHLY REPORT ON EATING OUT. 0739-9502. Periodical. US. English. mo. $120.00. The Gallup Organization Inc, 53 Bank Street, Princeton NJ 08540. **Tel** (609)924-9600. **Ed** Valerie Sinclair. **Circ** 1,000. (ctrl). Market research measuring the incidence of eating out, consumer's attitudes toward pricing, menu items beverages; information on take-out food and other relevant restaurant data. *Gallup Monthly Report on Eating Out Attitudes and Behavior.*

GITE. See Hotels/Motels.

GOURMERTOUR. VFOAT Guia Gastronomica y Turistica de Espana. Began in 1979. Spanish. an. **LC** TX910.S7. **DD** 647.9446.

GROSS- UND EINZELHANDEL, GASTGEWERBE, REISEVERKEHR. REIHE 7 : GASTGEWERBE. **Main**/**Corp** Germany (West). Statistisches Bundesamt. VFOAT Gastgewerbe. German. ir. 10.00. **LC** JX910.G4. *Gross- und Einzelhandel, Gastgewerbe, Fremdenverkehr. Reihe 7: Gastgewerbe.*

GUIDE FRANCE . . . . VFOAT Gault Millau Guide France. FR. French. an. 55.00. Societe Anonyme Jour-Azur, 4 rue de Presbourg, 75116 Paris France. **LC** TX907. **DD** 647.944405.

GUIDE SCHWEIZ. See Hotels/Motels.

GUIDE TO FOODSERVICE - ONTARIO RESTAURANT AND FOODSERVICES ASSOCIATION. (A GUIDE TO FOODSERVICE). **Main**/**Corp** Ontario Restaurant and Foodservices Association. VFOAT Foodservice Guide. VAT Membership Directory and Buyers' Guide - Ontario Restaurant and Foodservices Association, Foodservice Quide - Ontario Restaurant and Foodservices Association. 0822-8272. CN. English. an. Ontario Restaurant and Foodservices Association, Park Plaza Hotel/Suite 302, 170 Bloor Street West, Toronto Ontario M5S 1T9 Canada. **DD** 381.456425025713.

HANDEL, GASTGEWERBE, REISEVERKEHR. REIHE 4 : BESCHAFTIGTE UND UMSATZ IM GASTGEWERBE, MESSZAHLEN. **Main**/**Corp** Germany (West). Statistisches Bundesamt. VAT Handel, Gastgewerbe, Reiseverkehr. Reihe Vier: Beschaftogte und Umsatz im Gastgewerbe, Messzahlen. 1976-. GW. German. an. 1.10. **LC** TX910.G4. *Gross- und Einzelhandel, Gastgewerbe, Reiseverkehr. Reihe 7: Gastgewerbe.*

HOSPITALITE. (L'HOSPITALITE). V. 1- Mar. 1977-. 0704-6359. Periodical. CN. French. bm. $30.18. MacLean Hunter, PO Box 100 Station A, Toronto Ontario M5W 1A7 Canada. **Tel** (416)596-5970. **DD** 647.95714.

HOSPITALITY EDUCATION AND RESARCH JOURNAL. See Hotels/Motels.

HOTEL & CATERING REVIEW (BLACKROCK, DUBLIN). See Hotels/Motels.

HOTEL AND RESTAURANT GUIDE INDIA. See Hotels/Motels.

HOTEL- EN RESTAURANTGIDS NEDERLAND. See Hotels/Motels.

HOTELLERIE RESTAURATION. See Hotels/Motels.

HOTELS & RESTAURANTS IN BRITAIN. See Hotels/Motels.

HOTELS & RESTAURANTS INTERNATIONAL. See Hotels/Motels.

HOTELS, RESTAURANTS. SCHWEIZ. See Hotels/Motels.

HOUSTON MONTHLY. (HOUSTON MONTHLY'S RESTAURANT & ENTERTAINMENT GUIDE). VFOAT Restaurant & Entertainment Guide. VAT Houston Monthly's Restaurant and Entertainment Guide. 0272-6602. US. English. an. Party Line Publishing Company, 6603 Rookin, Houston TX 77074.

ILLINOIS FOODSERVICE NEWS. (ILLINOIS FOODSERVICE NEWS : THE MAGAZINE OF THE ILLINOIS RESTAURANT ASSOCIATION). Vol. 69, No. 3 (Apr. 1981)-. 0279-9618. Periodical. US. English. mo. Illinois Restaurant Association, 20 North Wacker Drive/Suite 1130, Chicago IL 60606. *Cirashoppe 0191-6769.*

INDEPENDENT RESTAURANTS. Vol. 45, No. 7 (July 1983)-. 0746-1887. Periodical. US. English. mo. $24.00 Domestic and Possessions, $75.00 Foreign. EIP Inc, 2132 Fordem Avenue, Madison WI 53704. *Foodservice Marketing for Independent Restaurants, 0738-4254.*

INDUSTRY NEWS (RICHMOND, VA.). (INDUSTRY NEWS). 8750-5525. Periodical. US. English. mo. $15.00. VRA, 2101 Libbie Avenue, Richmond VA 23230. **Tel** (804)288-3065. **Ed** Elizabeth Parchoc. adv acc. **Circ** 1,400. (ctrl). Articles and features on foodservice topics and foodservice people and places. *VRA News, 0745-3876.*

INSTITUTIONAL DISTRIBUTION. VFOAT ID. Institutional Distribution. V. 1- Jan. 1965-. 0020-3572. Periodical. US. English. mo. $50.00. Bill Publishing Company, 633 3rd Avenue, New York NY 10017. **Tel** (212)986-4800. **Ed** Robert Ciuin. **Ind**/**Abst** Trade Ind. Index. bk rev. adv acc. **Circ** 32,000. (ctrl). Serves the field of foodservice distributors, foodservice brokers and foodservice equipment distributors who sell to the away-from-home eating market.

INSTITUTIONS; MAGAZINE OF THE SERVICE WORLD. See Hotels/Motels.

THE INTERNATIONAL GUILD GUIDE. 0361-4220. US. English. $6.00. Guild Book Service, PO Box 14064, Norfolk VA 23518. **LC** TX950.53. **DD** 647.95.

Restaurants

INVENTARISASI AKOMODASI PROPINSI MALUKU. Main/Corp Maluku, Indonesia. Kantor Sensus Dan Statistik. Series/Titl Akomodasi. Indonesian. ir. Kantor Sensus and Statistik Propinsi Maluku, Jl Pattimora, Ambon Indonesia. LC TX910.I6.

ISLAND GASTRONOMIC. (THE ISLAND GASTRONOMIC). VFOAT Vancouver Island Gastronomic. 1st Ed. 0714-8348. CN. English. an. $3.95 Per Volume. Island Gastronomic, c/o Apogee Enterprises, PO Box 48525, Station Bentall, Vancouver British Columbia V7X 1A2 Canada. DD 642.502571134.

JOURNAL OF FOOD SERVICE SYSTEMS. (JOURNAL OF FOODSERVICE SYSTEMS). Vol. 1, No. 1 (Summer 1980)- . 0196-4283. Periodical. US. English. qt. $60.00. Food & Nutrition Press, 155 Post Road East/PO Box 71, Westport CT 06881. Tel (203)227-6596. Ed O P Snyder Jr. Ind/Abst Bibliogr. Agric. bk rev. adv acc. Designed to keep all professionals in food service informed of new developments and trends.

JUST A BITE. 1979-. UK. English. an. 1.50 Domestic, $3.95 US. Egon Ronay Organisation, Greencoat House, Francis Street, London SWIP 1 England. LC TX910.G7. DD 647.9541.

KANSAS RESTAURANT. 0022-8753. Periodical. US. English. mo. $6.00. Kansas Restaurant, 359 South Hydraulic, Wichita KS 67211. Tel (316)267-8383. Ed George Puckett. bk rev. adv acc. Circ 1,200. (ctrl). Trade publication for members of the Kansas Restaurant Association.

KANTINEN-ANZEIGER : GEMEINSCHAFTSVERPFLEGUNG UND CATERING, GV + C. VFOAT Kantinen-Anzeiger. 1977, No. 1/2- 1977-. Periodical. German. ir.

KITCHEN PLANNING CEASED. V. -18. 0300-7952. Periodical. US. English. bm. LC TX943.

LAYOUT & DESIGN. VFOAT Foodservice Equipment Dealer. No. 1- Mar. 1972-. US. English. LC TX945. DD 658.23.

MAJOITUSLIIKKEIDEN KAPASITEETTI. VFOAT Harbargeringsstallenas Kapacitet, Capacity of Accommodation Facilities. 1977-. English, Finnish, and Swedish. ir. Tilastokeskus Jakagai: Vation Dainatuskus, Annankatu 44, 00100 10 Helsinki Finland. LC TX901. Majoitustilasto, Majoitusliikkeiden Kapasiteetti.

MANHATTAN MENUS. 0197-5099. US. English. an. $11.45. Manhattan Menus, 149 Madison Avenue, New York NY 10017. Tel (212)679-3555. LC TX907. DD 647.95747105.

MEMBERSHIP/COMMITTEE DIRECTORY - NATIONAL ASSOCIATION OF MEAT PURVEYORS (U.S.). See Yearbooks, Almanacs, Directories.

MENUS OF THE VALLEY'S FINEST RESTAURANTS. 0148-4133. US. English. an. Quail Run Publications Inc, 5221 Quail Run Place, Paradise Valley AZ 85253. Tel (602)955-5953. Ed John V Long. Circ 10,000. (ctrl). Restaurant menus as they actually appear from select dining establishments in the Phoenix Arizona metro area, cross referenced by location and food classification.

METRO FOODSERVICE NEWS. VFOAT Metropolitan Restaurant News. 0744-0065. Periodical. US. English. mo. Metropolitan Restaurant News Inc, 1225 Broadway, New York NY 10001. Metropolitan Restaurant News, 0026-1564.

MICHELIN GREAT BRITAIN AND IRELAND. See Travel.

MICHELIN GREATER LONDON. See Hotels/Motels.

MONTHLY SUPPLY LETTER. Main/Corp United Fresh Fruit and Vegetable Association. Began publication in 1946?. 0194-0848. Periodical. US. English. mo $10.00. United Fresh Fruit & Vegetable Association, 727 North Washington Street, Alexandria VA 22314. Tel (703)836-3410. Ed Charles Magoon. Circ 500. Particularly helpful to menu planners, this newsletter estimates availability of 60 or so fresh fruits and vegetables for the coming month. Green Grocery Monthly Supply Letter.

MONTREAL CUISINE. VFOAT Cuisine de Montreal. 0823-2857. CN. English (French). an. 9.95. Montreal Cuisine, PO Box 1471 Place Bonaventure, Montreal Quebec H5A 1H5 Canada. DD 647.95714281.

MYRA WALDO'S RESTAURANT GUIDE TO NEW YORK CITY AND VICINITY. VFOAT Restaurant Guide to New York City and Vicinity. 0196-0032. US. English. $5.95 per copy. MacMillan Publishing Company, 866 Third Avenue, New York NY 10022. LC TX907. DD 647.957471.

NATION'S RESTAURANT NEWS. 0028-0518. Periodical. US. English. bw. $16.00. Lebhar-Friedman Publishing, 99 Park Avenue, New York NY 10016. Ind/Abst Trade Ind. Index, Predicasts, Infobank, Funk Scott Index Corp. Ind. DD 642. National Restaurant News.

NEW JERSEY MONTHLY. V. 1- Nov. 1976-. 0273-270X. Periodical. US. English. mo. $18.00. New Jersey Monthly, PO Box 806, Martinsville NJ 08836. Tel (201)539-8230. Ed Larry Marcheck. LC F131. DD 974.904305. adv acc. Circ 95,000. Mission is to inform, educate, persuade, and entertain through articles that address vital statewide issues, explore changing lifestyles, offer self-help information, and provide the best in cultural and leisure activities.

NRA NEWS (WASHINGTON, D.C. : 1981). (NRA NEWS). VFOAT N.R.A. News. VAT National Restaurant Association News. Vol. 1, No. 1 (Oct. 1981)- . 0465-7004. Periodical. US. English. mo. $125.00. National Restaurant Association, 311-1st Northwest, Washington DC 20001. Tel (202)638-6100. Ed Sylvia Rivchum. Ind/Abst Predicasts. LC TX901. DD 647.9505. bk rev. Circ 23,000. Restaurant industry trade press featuring articles, studies, research on industry trends. Foodservice Trends, NRA News (Washington, D.C. : 1985); Washington Report (National Restaurant Association (U.S.)), 0274-6387.

NRA WASHINGTON WEEKLY. VFOAT Washington Weekly. VAT National Restaurant Association Washington Weekly. Vol. 1, No. 1 (Sept. 11, 1981)- . 0279-3350. Periodical. US. English. wk. National Restaurant Association, 311 First Street NW, Washington DC 20001. Tel (202)638-6100. Ed Jay Morris. Circ 8,500. Reports on activities of congress, Reg. agencies and courts affecting restaurants as well as economic and demographic trends, agriculture, nutrition, etc. Washington Report, 0274-6387.

OBSHCHESTVENNOE PITANIE. Began with Aug. 1933 issue. Periodical. UR. Russian. mo $20.00. Victor Kamkin Inc (70660), 12224 Parklawn Drive, Rockville MD 20852. Tel (301)881-5973. LC TX1.

OFFICERS' REPORT & DAILY CONVENTION PROCEEDINGS. See Hotels/Motels.

THE OFFICIAL GUIDE, HOTELS AND RESTAURANTS IN GREAT BRITAIN AND IRELAND. See Hotels/Motels.

THE OFFICIAL GUIDE TO FOOD SERVICE AND HOSPITALITY MANAGEMENT CAREERS. VFOAT Food Service. 1st ed-. 8755-0431. US. English. bm. Foodservice Careers International Publishing Company, 665 Lavilla Drive, Miami Springs FL 33166. Tel (305)887-1701. Ed Pat Morrissey-Havlin. DD 658. Why choose and career in the foodservice industry? Job classifications throughout the industry. Careers ladders in restaurants and fast food, and career ladders in hotels.

OTTAWA-HULL GASTRONOMIC. VFOAT Gastronomique d'Ottawa-Hull. 1st Ed. 0714-8232. CN. English (French). an. $3.95 Each Volume. Ottawa-Hull Gastronomic, c/o Apogee Enterprises, PO Box 48525 Station Bentall, Vancouver British Columbia V7X 1A2 Canada. DD 642.502571384.

PAKISTAN HOTEL & RESTAURANT GUIDE. See Hotels/Motels.

PARIS AND ENVIRONS : HOTELS AND RESTAURANTS. See Hotels/Motels.

PARIS ET SA BANLIEUE : HOTELS ET RESTAURANTS. See Hotels/Motels.

PASSEPORT GASTRONOMIQUE. LE QUEBEC. VFOAT Gourmet Passport. Le Quebec. 1981-. 0824-779X. CN. English (French). an. $6.95. France-Amerique, 170 Benjamin-Hudon Street, Montreal Quebec H4N 1H8 Canada. DD 647.9571427.

PASSEPORT GASTRONOMIQUE. MONTREAL ET ALENTOURS. VFOAT Gourmet Passport. Montreal and Vicinity. 1980-. 0226-7292. CN. English (French). an. DD 647.95714281.

PASSEPORT GASTRONOMIQUE. QUEBEC ET ALENTOURS. VFOAT Gourmet Passport. Quebec and Vicinity. 1982-. 0710-040X. CN. English (French). an. Gourmet Passport, 2401 de la Province, Longueuil Quebec J4G 1G3 Canada. DD 647.9571447.

LA PETITE BIBLE DES RESTAURANTS PARISIENS. Series/Titl Les Petites Bibles de Roland Escaig. Began with Vol. for 1979. FR. French. an. Editions Roland Escaig and Company, 41 rue Ybry, 92200 Neuilly France. LC TX910.F8. DD 647.954436.

PROFESSOR DIVINSKY'S SELECT RESTAURANT GUIDE. 4th- Ed. 0704-6561. CN. English. an. $2.00 Each Number. N Divinsky, 2909-1733 Comox Street, Vancouver British Columbia V6G 1P6 Canada. DD 647.9571133. Professor Divinsky's Guide to Good Food in Metro Vancouver, 0315-3592.

RESTAURANT AND HOTEL DESIGN. VFOAT R. & H.D., R. and H.D. R & HD. 0745-4929. Periodical. US. English. ir. $32.00 Domestic, $40.00 Canada. Restaurant Business Inc, 633 Third Avenue, New York NY 10017. Ind/Abst Trade Ind. Index. LC NA7800. DD 725.710973. Restaurant Design, 0191-345X.

RESTAURANT BUSINESS. V. 73, No. 4- Apr. 1974-. 0097-8043. Periodical. US. English. ir. $63.00. Bill Brothers Publishing Company, 633 3rd Avenue, New York NY 10017. Tel (212)986-4800. Ind/Abst Bibliogr. Agric., Predicasts, Bus. Period. Index, Funk Scott Index Corp. Ind. LC TP628. DD 642.5. Fast Food.

RESTAURANT BUSINESS. (RESTAURANT BUSINESS : ID, INSTITUTIONAL DISTRIBUTION). VFOAT ID, Institutional Distribution. 0360-117X. US. English. mo. $3.00. Restaurant Business, 633 Third Avenue, New York NY 10017. Ind/Abst Bus. Period. Index. LC TX901. DD 642.5605.

RESTAURANT BUYERS GUIDE. See Business - Purchasing.

RESTAURANT, CATERER AND TAVERN STATISTICS. See Statistics.

RESTAURANT EXECUTIVE. 0095-5159. Periodical. US. English. mo. $25.00. Morken/Greve Communications Inc, 645 North Michigan Avenue, Chicago IL 60611. LC TX945. DD 647.9505. Quickservice Operations Management.

RESTAURANT HOSPITALITY. V. 61- Jan. 1977-. 0147-9989. Periodical. US. English. mo. Penton/IPC, PO Box 95759, Cleveland OH 44101. Tel (216)696-7000. Ind/Abst Trade Ind. Index, Predicasts, Account. Index. Suppl., Funk Scott Index Corp. Ind. LC TX901. DD 642.5605. Hospitality, Restaurant, 0098-3292.

RESTAURANT INDUSTRY OPERATIONS REPORT FOR THE UNITED STATES. (RESTAURANT INDUSTRY OPERATIONS REPORT . . . FOR THE UNITED STATES). VFOAT Restaurant Industry Operations Report. Began with 1979 issue. 0739-1439. US. English. an. National Restaurant Association, 311 First Street NW, Washington DC 20001. LC TX909.A1. DD 338.436479573. Restaurant Operations, 0190-9452.

RESTAURANTS & INSTITUTIONS. VFOAT Restaurants and Institutions. VAT Restaurants and Institutions (Chicago, Ill.). Vol. 88, No. 1 (Jan. 1, 1981)- . 0273-5520. Periodical. US. English. bw. $80.00. Cahners Publications, 270 St Paul Street, Denver CO 80206. Tel (312)635-8800. Ed Howard Schlossberg. Ind/Abst Hospit. Lit. Index, Predicasts. LC TX1. DD 642.505. adv acc. Circ 130,000. (ctrl). Serving management in the food preparation industries. Features news, product reviews and updates, profiles of successful operations and the ingredients that made them successful. Institutions (Chicago, Ill.).

RESTAURANTS, CATERERS AND TAVERNS INDUSTRY SURVEY. SERVICES. VFOAT Enquete sur l'Industrie des Restaurants, Traiteurs et Tavernes. Services. 1977-. 0713-746X. CN. French (English). an. Statistics of Canada, Publications Distribution, Ottawa Ontario K1A 0T6 Canada. DD 338.4764795710212. Food and Beverage Industry Survey, 0713-7451.

RESTAURATEUR. (LE RESTAURATEUR : REVUE DE L'ASSOCIATION DES RESTAURATEURS DU QUEBEC). Vol. 1, No 1 (Sept. 1982)- . 0821-2775. Periodical. CN. French. ir. Free. Les Publications Parade Inc, C P 249, Saint-Etienne-de-Lauzon Quebec G0S 2L0 Canada. DD 647.9571405. (ctrl).

Romance and Adventure

ROBERT FINIGAN'S PRIVATE GUIDE TO RESTAURANTS. VFOAT Private Guide to Restaurants. 1967. 0162-1319. Periodical. US. English. mo. $24.00. Walnuts & Wine Inc, 724 Pine Street, San Francisco CA 94108. **Tel** (415)956-1314. Ed Robert Finigan. **Circ** 3,500. Criticism of northern California restaurants and others in major U.S. cities and abroad.

ROSTER - RESTAURANT & FOODSERVICES ASSOCIATION OF BRITISH COLUMBIA. (ROSTER). **Main/Corp** Restaurant & Foodservices Association of British Columbia. 0714-315X. CN. English. an. Free to Members. Restaurant & Foodservices of British Columbia Roster, c/o Naylor Communications, 1494 Regent Street, West Winnipeg Manitoba R2C 3A8 Canada. **DD** 642.5025711.

SEYMOUR BRITCHKY'S RESTAURANT LETTER. No. 1- Mar. 1980-. 0196-5220. Periodical. US. English. mo. $24.00. Seymour Britchkys Restaurant, PO Box 155, New York NY 10003. Ed Seymour Britchky. A private guide to New York's newest restaurants and an ongoing review of established ones, in the form of detailed, literate reviews.

STATISTIK RESTORAN : HASIL PELAKSANAAN SURVEI KHUSUS RESTORAN DI 12 PROPINSI. See Statistics.

SURVEY OF WHOLESALE & RETAIL TRADE & RESTAURANTS. VFOAT Survey of Wholesale and Retail Trade and Restaurants. 1975-76-. English. an. **LC** HF5429.6.P3. **DD** 381.095491.

TEXAS FOOD & SERVICE NEWS. (TEXAS FOOD & SERVICE NEWS : PUBLICATION OF THE TEXAS RESTAURANT ASSOCIATION). VFOAT Texas Food and Service News. Vol. 44, No. 2 (Sept. 1983)-. 0746-5211. Periodical. US. English. mo. Texas Restaurant Association, PO Box 1429, Austin TX 78767. Chuck Wagon, 0009-6210.

TORONTO GASTRONOMIC. 0714-833X. CN. English. an. $4.95 Each Volume. Toronto Gastronomic c/o H B Fenn & Company, 2421 Drew Road, Mississauga Ontario L5S 1A1 Canada. **DD** 642.5025713541.

VANCOUVER GASTRONOMIC. 1976/77-. 0706-5302. CN. English. an. 4.99. Apogee Enterprises Ltd, PO Box 48525 Station Bentall, Vancouver British Columbia V7X 1A2 Canada. **DD** 642.5602571133.

VITRIINI. See Hotels/Motels.

VRA ECONOMIC DIGEST. VFOAT V.R.A. Economic Digest. **VAT** Virginia Restaurant Association Economic Digest. 0747-7996. US. English. an. Virginia Restaurant Association, 2102 Libbie Avenue, Richmond VA 23230. **LC** TX945. **DD** 338.4764795755.

WHERE TO EAT IN CANADA. 1971/72-. 0315-3088. Periodical. CN. English. an. $9.95. Oberon Press, 401 A ln of the Provinces, Ottawa, Ontario Canada. Ed Anne Hardy. **DD** 647.9571. **Circ** 5,000. A guide to Canadian restaurants from coast to coast with over 500 listings in every part of Canada. It's the only one of its kind on the market today.

THE WISCONSIN RESTAURATEUR. 1933. 0274-7472. Periodical. US. English. mo. $15.00. Wisconsin Restaurant Association, 122 West Washington Avenue, Madison WI 53703. **Tel** (608)251-3663. Ed Jan La Rue. bk rev. adv acc. **Circ** 3,600. (ctrl). Educational, promotional, informational vehicle. A trade publication for the promotion, protection and improvement of Wisconsin's food service industry.

ROMANCE AND ADVENTURE

5 GREAT ROMANCES. VFOAT Five Great Romances. Began in 1983. 0738-0941. Periodical. US. English. mo. $10.87. Digest Publishing Inc, 333 Sylvan Avenue, Englewood Cliffs NJ 07632.

ALFRED HITCHCOCK'S MYSTERY MAGAZINE. 0002-5224. Periodical. US. English. ir. $19.50. Davis Publications, 380 Lexington Avenue, New York NY 10017, (subscription address: Fulfillment Corp of America Box 1932 Marion OH 43305). **Tel** (212)557-9100. Ed Cathleen Jordan. bk rev. adv acc. **Circ** 200,000. Over 150 pages of mystery stories all with that special twist plus book and movie reviews, articles and more in every issue.

ANTITHESIS. Began with Jan. 1978?. 0732-8923. Periodical. US. English. qt. $18.00. Triad Publications, 687 East Market Street, Marietta PA 17547.

ARES. SPECIAL ED. (ARES). VFOAT Ares Magazine. No. 1 (Summer 1983)-. 0737-6545. Periodical. US. English. sa. $24.00 Domestic, $32.40 Canada. Dragon Publishing, PO Box 110, Lake Geneva WI 53147.

AURORA. 0275-3715. Periodical. US. English. qt. $6.00. Aurora/WI/, c/o SF 3, Box 1624, Madison WI 53701. Janus, 0197-775X.

CLASSIC MYSTERIES MAGAZINE. VFOAT Classic Mysteries. 0882-2263. Periodical. US. English. ir. $3.00 Single Issue. International Trends Publications, PO Box 724198, Atlanta GA 30339.

CONTRIBUTIONS TO THE STUDY OF SCIENCE FICTION AND FANTASY. No. 1-. 0193-6875. Monographic Series. US. English. ir. Greenwood Press, 88 Post Road West, Westport CT 06881. **Tel** (203)226-3571. Ed Marshall B Tymn.

DAREDEVIL. See Recreation, Leisure - Games & Amusements.

ELLERY QUEEN'S PRIME CRIMES. VFOAT Prime Crimes. Winter 1983-. 0748-1101. Periodical. US. English. an. $2.95. Davis Publications, 380 Lexington Avenue, New York NY 10017. **LC** PR1309.D4. **DD** 823.087208.

ESPIONAGE MAGAZINE. VFOAT Espionage. 8756-8535. Periodical. US. English. bm. $15.00. Espionage Magazine, PO Box 48000, Bergenfield NJ 0707621. **Tel** (201)569-4072. Ed Jackie Lewis. bk rev. adv acc. **Circ** 60,000. (ctrl). Espionage stories on international intrigue, suspense, blackmail. Fiction and non-fiction. Issue contains biographies, short stories, humor, games, movie and book reviews, and interviews of spy authors.

FANFARE. Jan. 1978-. 0705-7954. Periodical. CN. English. sa. $2 Per No. C Odell, Fanfare Magazine, PO Box 1542, Victoria British Columbia V8W 2X7 Canada. **DD** 791.4309091.

FANTASIAE; MONTHLY NEWSLETTER OF THE FANTASY ASSOCIATION. V. 1- Apr. 1973-. 0094-2375. Periodical. US. English. mo. $10.00. Fantasy Association, PO Box 24560, Los Angeles CA 90024.

FANTASY BOOK. See Literature.

FRONT PAGE DETECTIVE. 0016-2043. Periodical. US. English. mo. $15.00. RGH Publishing Corporation, PO Box 1159, Dover NJ 07801. **Tel** (201)361-5135.

THE FURTHER ADVENTURES OF INDIANA JONES. VFOAT Indiana Jones. No. 1 (Jan. 1983)-. 8750-4324. Periodical. US. English. mo. Marvel Comics Group, 387 Park Avenue South, New York NY 10016.

HARD BOILED DICKS. VFOAT Durs a Cuire. Periodical. French. ir. 19. 23-25 rue Juliette Dodu, Paris 10 EME France. **LC** PS374.D4. **DD** 813.087209.

HARLEQUIN. V. 3, No. 5- 1975-. 0319-0595. Periodical. CN. English. mo. $9.00. Harlequin Reader Service, 649 Ontario Street, Stratford Ontario N5A 3J6 Canada. **DD** 823.085. Harlequin's Woman, 0319-0587.

INSIDE DETECTIVE. 0020-1847. Periodical. US. English. mo. $15.00. RGH Publishing Corporation, PO Box 1159, Dover NJ 07801. **Tel** (201)361-5135.

LOST TREASURE. 0195-2692. Periodical. US. English. mo. $12.00. National Reporter Publications, 15115 S 76th East Avenue, Bixby OK 74008. **Tel** (918)366-4441. Ed Jim Watts. **Ind/Abst** GeoRef, Bibliogr. Index Geol. **LC** G521. **DD** 973.05. bk rev. adv acc. **Circ** 40,000. The treasure hunter's guide to adventure and fortune.

LUNA. No. 64- Summer 1976-. Periodical. US. English. ir. $3.00. 655 Orchard Street, Oradell NJ 07649. Luna Monthly, 0024-7375 Luna.

MIKE SHAYNE MYSTERY MAGAZINE. 1936. 0026-3621. Periodical. US. English. mo. $18.00. Renown Publications, PO Box 18060, Reseda CA 91335. **Tel** (818)343-2992. Ed Charles Fritch. bk rev. adv acc.

MS. TREE. VFOAT Max Collins and Terry Beatty's Ms. Tree. Began with No. 4, (Oct. 1983). 0826-2586. Periodical. CN. English. mo. $24.00. Renegade Press, 10408 Oxnard Street, North Hollywood CA 91606. **Tel** (818)763-4806. **DD** 741.5971. adv acc. **Circ** 12,000. (ctrl). Fictional account of female detective's search for her husband's killer in a modern setting. Told in graphic art format. Contains some violence adult material. Ms. Tree's Thrilling Detective Adventure.

OFFICIAL DETECTIVE STORIES. 0030-0306. Periodical. US. English. mo. RGH Publishing Corporation, PO Box 1159, Dover NJ 07801. **Tel** (201)361-5135.

PERSONAL ROMANCES. 0031-5613. Periodical. US. English. bm. $12.00. Dynasty Media Publishing Corporation, PO Box 5000 HA, Ridgefield NJ 07657. **Tel** (212)371-4932.

ROMANCE. V. 1- 1980-. 0228-0205. Periodical. CN. French. 4.50 Domestic Per No.; $1.25 Per No. U.S. Les Productions Amerique Francaise, Bureau 203, 4920 Ouest Boul. de Maisonneuve, Westmount Quebec H3Z 1N1 Canada. **DD** 843.08505.

ROMANTIC TIMES. (ROMANTIC TIMES : FOR READERS OF ROMANTIC FICTION). Began with: Vol. 1, No. 1 (July/Aug. 1981)-. 0747-3370. Periodical. US. English. bm. $15.95. Romantic Times, 163 Joralemon Street, 1234 Brooklyn Heights NY 11201. **Tel** (718)237-1097. Ed Kathryn Falk. bk rev. adv acc. **Circ** 70,000. (ctrl). Includes book reviews of all romance titles in advance of publication, author profiles, and writing tips.

SHOSETSU GENDAI. VFOAT Shosetugendai Magazine. Vol. 1, No. 1-. 0559-9202. Periodical. Japanese. mo. $63.00. Kinokuniya Book Stores, 1581 Webster Street, San Francisco CA 94115. **Tel** (415)567-7625.

STARTLING DETECTIVE. 0038-996X. Periodical. US. English. bm. $11.00. Globe Communications Corporation, 1440 St Catherine West, Montreal Quebec 107 Canada. **Tel** (514)866-7744.

TRUE DETECTIVE. 0041-350X. Periodical. US. English. mo. RGH Publishing Corporation, PO Box 1159, Dover NJ 07801. **Tel** (201)361-5135.

WEIRDBOOK. VFOAT Weird Book. 8755-7452. Periodical. US. English. ir. $22.50. W Paul Ganley, Box 149 Amherst Branch, Buffalo NY 14226-0149. **Tel** (716)839-2415. Ed W Paul Ganley. **DD** 813. bk rev. adv acc. **Circ** 900. Fantasy/horror fiction for the aficionado.

YADAM KWA SIRHWA. See Literature.

RUBBER

ANNUAL REPORT - RUBBER RESEARCH INSTITUTE OF MALAYSIA. **Main/Corp** Rubber Research Institute of Malaysia. 1973-. 0126-8279. English. an. $16.00. Rubber Research Institute of Malaysia, PO Box 150, Kuala Lumpur Malaysia. **LC** SB290. **DD** 633.895209595. Annual Report (1953).

AUSTRALIAN PLASTICS & RUBBER. See Plastics.

BLUE BOOK (NEW YORK, N.Y.). (BLUE BOOK : MATERIALS, COMPOUNDING INGREDIENTS, AND MACHINERY FOR RUBBER). VFOAT Rubber World Blue Book. 1981-. US. English. an. Bill Communications Inc, 633 Third Avenue, New York NY 10017. **LC** TS1893. **DD** 678.210294. Materials, Compounding Ingredients and Machinery for the Rubber Industry.

BP&R BRITISH PLASTICS AND RUBBER. See Plastics.

BUKU MAKLUMAT PERANGKAAN GETAH BAGI MALAYSIA. See Statistics.

Rubber

C R C CRITICAL REVIEWS IN CLINICAL LABORATORY SCIENCES. 0590-8191. Periodical. US. English. ir. CRC Press Inc, 2000 Corporate Boulevard NW, Boca Raton FL 33431. **Tel** (305)994-0555. **Ind/Abst** Sci. Cit. Index, Abr. Ed., Index Med., Chem. Abstr.

CAOUTCHOUCS & PLASTIQUES. VFOAT Revue Generale des Caoutchoucs & Plastiques. No. 597 (Jan./Feb. 1980)-. 0035-3175. Periodical. FR. French (summaries in English and German). ir. 506. 5 Rue Jules Lefebvre, 75009 Paris France. **Ind/Abst** Art Archaeol. Tech. Abstr., Chem. Abstr., CIS Abstr., Energy Res. Abstr., Eng. Index Annu., Eng. Index Bioeng. Abstr., Eng. Index Mon., Predicasts. **LC** TS1870. **DD** 668.905. **CODEN** RCPLA5. Revue Generale des Caoutchoucs & Plastiques.

CAUCHO. Began with Jan./Feb. 1958 issue. 0528-3280. Periodical. SP. Spanish. ir. Federacion Argentina de la Industria del Caucho, Cordoba 890 - 6 Piso, Buenos Aires Argentina. **Ind/Abst** Chem. Abstr. **LC** TS1870. **CODEN** CAUCDV.

CONSUMPTION, PRODUCTION AND INVENTORIES OF RUBBER. VFOAT Consommation, Production et Stocks de Caoutchouc. V. 26- Jan. 1972-. 0008-2651. Periodical. CN. English (French). mo. $3.00. **LC** HD9161.C2. **DD** 338.4767820971. Monthly Report on Consumption, Production and Inventories of Rubber, 0829-9412.

CURRENT INDUSTRIAL REPORTS. MA-30B, RUBBER AND PLASTICS HOSE AND BELTING. VFOAT Rubber and Plastics Hose and Belting. Began with 1973 issue. US. English. an. $1.00. Data User Services Division, Customer Services Publication, Bureau of the Census, Washington DC 20233. **Tel** (301)763-4100. Presents timely data on the production, inventories, and orders of approximately 5,000 products, which represents 40 percent of all US manufacturing.

DEVELOPMENTS IN RUBBER AND RUBBER COMPOSITES. Series/Titl Developments Series. Began in 1980. 0262-1592. UK. English. Elsevier Science Publishing Co Inc, 52 Vanderbilt Avenue, New York NY 10017. **LC** TS1870. **DD** 678.205. **CODEN** DRRCDA.

DEVELOPMENTS IN RUBBER TECHNOLOGY. Series/Titl Developments Series. 1-. 0262-1584. Monographic Series. UK. English. Elsevier Science Publ Co, 52 Vanderbilt Avenue, New York NY 10017. **Ind/Abst** Chem. Abstr. **LC** TS1870. **DD** 678.205. **CODEN** DERTD4.

ELASTOMERICS. V. 109- Jan. 1977-. 0146-0706. Periodical. US. English. mo. $26.00. Communication Channels Inc, 6255 Barfield Road, Atlanta GA 30328. **Tel** (404)256-9800. **Ind/Abst** Eng. Index Mon., Eng. Index Bioeng., Eng. Index Energy Abstr., Predicasts, Excerpta Med., Coal Abstr., Appl. Sci. Technol. Index, Chem. Abstr., Eng. Index Annu., Eng. Index, Energy Ind. Abstr., Environ. Abstr., Funk Scott Index Corp. Ind., Sci. Cit. Index, Abr. Ed. **LC** TS1870. **DD** 338.47678205. **CODEN** ELASDA. Available on microfilm from University Microfilms. Rubber Age, 0035-9440.

ELASTOMERICS NEWS-LOG. (NEWS LOG). V. 1, No. 8- Jan. 1977-. 0146-0714. Periodical. US. English. mo. Palmerton Publishing Company, 461 Eighth Avenue, New York NY 10001. **Ind/Abst** Chem. Abstr. **LC** TS1870. **DD** 338.47678205. **CODEN** ENLODX. Rubber Age News-Log, 0363-8650.

ELASTOMEROS. 0048-0894. Periodical. BL. Portuguese. bm. Editora Technica, Caixa Postal 18.811, 01000 Sao Paulo Brazil. **Ind/Abst** Predicasts, Bibliogr. Agric., Funk Scott Index Corp. Ind. **LC** TS1870.

ELASTOMERS. See Plastics.

ELASTOMERS NOTEBOOK. No.1- 1938-. US. English. qt. Elastomers Notebook, Room 7523A Nemours Building, Wilmington DE 19898.

EUROPEAN RUBBER DIRECTORY. See Yearbooks, Almanacs, Directories.

EUROPEAN RUBBER JOURNAL (LONDON, ENGLAND : 1982). (EUROPEAN RUBBER JOURNAL). Vol. 164, No. 1 (Feb. 1982)-. 0260-5317. Periodical. UK. English (French, German and Italian). ir. 27.00. Crain Communications Ltd, Subscription Services Department, 120-126 Lavender Avenue, Mitcham Surrey CR4 3HP England. **Tel** (01)831-9511. Ed Robert C Grace. **Ind/Abst** Fluidex, Predicasts, Eng. Index Annu., Eng. Index Mon., Eng. Index Bioeng. Abstr., Eng. Index Energy Abstr., Chem. Abstr. **LC** TS1870. **DD** 338.476782094. **CODEN** ERJODH. bk rev adv acc. **Circ** 8,000. (ctrl). Back copies are available on microfilm. Provides news and analyses of technical and commercial developments in the rubber and related end-user industries. Also, details new equipment materials, processes and applications. European Rubber Journal + Urethanes Today, 0260-5317.

GOODYEAR CHEMICAL REVIEW. Vol. 1-. 0432-0905. US. English. ir. Goodyear Tire & Rubber Company, 1144 East Market Street, Akron OH 44316.

GOSEI GOMU. VFOAT The Synthetic Rubber. Began in 1959. Periodical. JA. Japanese. sa. Maruzen Company Ltd, PO Box 5050, 100-31 Tokyo Japan. **Ind/Abst** Chem. Abstr. **CODEN** GOGOD3. (ctrl).

GUMMI, ASBEST, KUNSTSTOFFE CEASED. (GUMMI, ASBEST, KUNSTSTOFFE : GAK). VFOAT G.A.K. Vol. 30, 1 (Jan. 1977)-Vol. 36, 12 (Dec. 1983). 0017-5595. Periodical. GE. German. mo. AW Gentner Verlag, Postfach 688 Forststr 131, 7000 Stuttgart 1 West Germany. Ed Heinz B P Gupta. **Ind/Abst** Predicasts, Chem. Abstr., Energy Res. Abstr., Excerpta Med., Coal Abstr. **CODEN** GGAKD7. bk rev. adv acc. **Circ** 7,800. Rubber, plastics and fibre processing. Machines for these activities. Raw materials testing and products. Gummi, Asbest, + I.E. und Kunststoffe.

GUMMI BEREIFUNG. 1- 1921-. Periodical. GW. German. mo. $51.13. Bielefelder Verlagsanstalt KG, Postfach 1140/Niederwall 33, D4800 Bielefeld 1 West Germany. **Ind/Abst** CIS Abstr.

GUMMI, FASERN, KUNSTSTOFFE. Vol. 37, 1 (Jan. 1984)-. 0017-5595. Periodical. German. mo. 177.60. AW Gentner Verlag, Postfach 688, Forststr 131, 7000 Stuttgart 1 West Germany. **Tel** 0711/63 83 56. Ed No. **Ind/Abst** Excerpta Med., Fluidex, Predicasts, Coal Abstr. **LC** TS1870. **DD** 678.205. **CODEN** GAKSA2. bk rev adv acc. **Circ** 8,275. Processing and application of rubber, plastics, and fibers. Gummi, Asbest, Kunststoffe, 0017-5595.

INTERNATIONAL RUBBER DIGEST. Periodical. UK. English. mo $23.00 Domestic, $28.00 Foreign. International Rubber Study Group, Brettenham House 5-6 Lancaster Place, London WC2E 7ET England. **Tel** 836-6811. Ed J D Carr. **Circ** 500. Summary of topical items on rubber matters from various journals including a report on the natural rubber market and a statistical update on the world supply/demand of natural and synthetic rubber.

JOURNAL OF ELASTOMERS AND PLASTICS. See Plastics.

JOURNAL OF THE RUBBER RESEARCH INSTITUTE OF MALAYSIA. Main/Corp Rubber Research Institute of Malaysia. V. 24- 1974/75-. 0035-953X. MY. English. ir. $19.00. Journal of the Rubber Research, PO Box 150, Kuala Lumpur Malaysia. **Ind/Abst** Life Sci. Collect., Excerpta Med., Biol. Abstr., Chem. Abstr. **LC** SB290. **DD** 633.895205. **CODEN** JRRIAN.

JURNAL SAINS PUSAT PENYELIDIKAN GETAH MALAYSIA. Main/Corp Rubber Research Institute of Malaysia. V. 1-. 0126-6136. Periodical. Malay (summaries in English). ir. **Ind/Abst** Chem. Abstr. **LC** SB291.H4. **CODEN** JSPMDZ.

KAUCHUK I REZINA. Began in 1949. UR. Russian. mo. $33.50. Victor Kamkin Inc (70429), 12224 Parklawn Drive, Rockville MD 20852. **Tel** (301)881-5973. **Ind/Abst** Coal Abstr., Energy Res. Abstr. **LC** TS1870.

KAUTSCHUK UND GUMMI. See Plastics.

KOMU KONGHAKHOE CHI. Main/Corp Han'Guk Komu Konghakhoe. VFOAT Journal of the Korean Institute of Rubber Industry. Periodical. KO. Korean. ir. Hanguk Komu Konghakhoe, Ipchong-dong Chung-ku, Seoul South Korea. **LC** TS1870.

KUNSTSTOF EN RUBBER. Vol. 36, No. 4 (Apr. 1983)-. 0167-9597. Periodical. Dutch. ir. Tijl Tijdschriften BV, Postbus 9943, 1006 AP Amsterdam Netherlands. **Ind/Abst** Chem. Abstr., Predicasts. **CODEN** KRUBDV. Plastica.

LAPURAN TAHUNAN - MAJLIS PENGELUAR-PENGELUAR GETAH MALAYSIA. Main/Corp Majlis Pengeluar-Pengeluar Getah Malaysia. VFOAT Annual Report - Rubber Producers' Council of Malaysia. 1973-. 0126-8309. MY. Malay and English. ir. Majlis Pengelluar-Pengellur Getah Malaysia, Peti Surat 272, Kuala Lumpur Malaysia. **LC** HD9161.M32. Laporan Tahunan - Majlis Pengeluar P2 S Getah Tanah Melayu.

MAJALAH RISDA. Main/Corp Malaysia. Pihak Berkuasa Kemajuan Pekebun Kecil Perusahaan Getah. Vol. 1- Apr. 1973-. Periodical. MY. Malay. qt. Bangunan Getah Asli, Petit Surat 1067 Jalan Ampang, Kuala Lumpur Malaysia. **LC** HD9161.M32.

MATERIALS, COMPOUNDING INGREDIENTS, AND MACHINERY FOR RUBBER. VFOAT Blue Book. 1977-. 0196-5697. US. English. an. $66.00. Rubber World, PO Box CS 528, Baldwin NY 11510. **Tel** (216)864-2122. **LC** TS1893. **DD** 678.210216. Each issue contains an index to its own contents - no vol index - loose. Materials and Compounding Ingredients for Rubber, 0196-5689.

MONTHLY STATISTICAL BULLETIN (MAJLIS PENGELUAR-PENGELUAR GETAH MALAYSIA). See Statistics.

NATURAL RUBBER NEWS. Began publication with the Jan./Feb. 1951 issue. 0028-0755. Periodical. US. English. mo. Malaysian Rubber Bureau, 1925 K Street NW, Washington DC 20006. **Ind/Abst** Fluidex, Predicasts, Bibliogr. Agric., Funk Scott Index Corp. Ind. **LC** HD9161.A1.

NTDRA DEALER NEWS. Main/Corp National Tire Dealers and Retreaders Association. 0027-7045. Periodical. US. English. ir. $18.00. National Tire Dealers & Retreaders Association, 1250 I Street NW/Suite 400, Washington DC 20005. **Tel** (202)789-2300.

NTDRA MEMBERGRAM. VFOAT N.T.D.R.A. Membergram. VAT National Tire Dealers and Retreaders Association Membergram. Vol. 1, No. 1 (Mar. 1982)-. 0744-5679. Periodical. US. English. mo. $6.00. National Tire Dealers and Retreaders Association, 1343 L Street NW, Washington DC 20005.

N.T.D.T.A. TIRE DEALERS SURVEY. (NTDRA TIRE DEALERS SURVEY). 0077-5886. US. English. $3.00. National Tire Dealers & Retreaders Association, 1343 L Street NW, Washington DC 20005. **LC** HD9161.U5. **DD** 380.1456783202573.

THE PLANTER. See Agriculture.

PLANTERS' BULLETIN (RUBBER RESEARCH INSTITUTE OF MALAYSIA). (PLANTERS' BULLETIN). VFOAT Plrs' Bull. Rubb. Res. Inst. Malaysia. 0032-096X. Periodical. English. qt. $9.00. Rubber Research Institut of Malaysia, PO Box 150, Kuala Lumpur Malaysia. **LC** SB290. **DD** 633.895205. Planters' Bulletin of the Rubber Research Institute of Malaysia.

PLASTICOS & I.E. E BORRACHA. See Plastics.

PLASTICS AND RUBBER INTERNATIONAL. See Plastics.

PLASTICS AND RUBBER PROCESSING AND APPLICATIONS. See Plastics.

PLASTICS & RUBBER WEEKLY. See Plastics.

POLYMER TESTING. See Plastics.

PROCEEDINGS OF THE ... ASSEMBLY OF THE INTERNATIONAL RUBBER STUDY GROUP. Main/Corp International Rubber Study Group. UK. English. **LC** HD9161.A2. **DD** 338.476782.

PROCEEDINGS OF THE CALIFORNIA CONFERENCE ON RUBBER-TOUGHENED PLASTICS. See Plastics.

RAPRA NEW TRADE NAMES. VFOAT R.A.P.R.A. New Trade Names. 0747-4954. US. English. an. Pergamon Press, Maxwell House Fairview Park, Elmsford NY 10523. New Trade Names in the Rubber and Plastics Industries.

RETREADER'S JOURNAL. See Business.

RMA MONTHLY TIRE REPORT. See Manufacturing.

RUBBER & PLASTICS NEWS. VAT Rubber and Plastics News. Began publication in 1971. 0300-6123. Periodical. US. English. bw. $28.00. Crain Communications, Comand Building, 34 North Hawkins Avenue, Akron OH 44313. **Tel** (216)836-9180. Ed E H Zielasko. **Ind/Abst** Predicasts, Funk Scott Index Corp. Ind. bk rev. adv acc. **Circ** 15,000.

Sanitation, Environmental Technology

Available in microform from University Microfilms. Publishes news for and about the rubber industry.

RUBBER & PLASTICS NEWS II. VAT Rubber and Plastics News Two. V. 1- Oct. 8, 1979-. 0197-2219. Periodical. US. English. bw. $20.00. Circulation Department, Rubber & Plastics News, 740 North Rush Street, Chicago IL 60611. **Ind/Abst** Predicasts.

RUBBER BOARD BULLETIN. Main/Corp India (Republic). Rubber Board. VFOAT Bulletin. V. 1- Jan./Mar. 1951-. 0537-0507. Periodical. II. English. qt. 10 Domestic, 35 Foreign. The Rubber Board, PB No 280, Sastri Road, Kottayam, 686001 Kerala State India. **Tel** 3232 Kottayam. Ed PK Narayanan. **Ind/Abst** Chem. Abstr. LC SB290. bk rev. adv acc. **Circ** 1,000. Promotion of rubber cultivation and rubber research on various aspects of cultivation.

RUBBER CHEMISTRY AND TECHNOLOGY. V. 1- Apr. 1928-. 0035-9475. Periodical. US. English. $75.00. American Chemical Society, The University of Akron, Akron OH 44325. **Tel** (216)375-7814. Ed Gary Hamed. **Ind/Abst** Eng. Index Mon., Eng. Index Bioeng. Abstr., Eng. Index Energy Abstr., Fluidex, Int. Aerosp. Abstr., Art Archaeol. Tech. Abstr., Chem. Abstr., Eng. Index Annu., Eng. Index, Nuci. Sci. Abstr., Appl. Sci. Technol. Index, Sci. Cit. Index, Abr. Ed. LC TS1870. CODEN RCTEA4. (cum index). bk rev. adv acc. **Circ** 5,500. Publishes major technical papers relating to rubber and polymer chemistry published anywhere in the world.

RUBBER INDIA. V. 1- Jan. 1949-. 0035-9491. Periodical. II. English. mo. $30.00. All India Rubber Industry Association, Lamington Road Building 3, Bombay 8 India. **Tel** 395032/892174. Ed Peter Philip. **Ind/Abst** Chem. Abstr. LC TS1885.I5. DD 678.05. CODEN RUIDA4. bk rev. adv acc. **Circ** 1,000. (ctrl). Intended to serve technical and non-technical information needs of the Indian rubber industry and to act as a spokesman for the Indian rubber industry.

THE RUBBER INDUSTRY STATISTICAL REPORT, AND, CHANGING MARKETS AND MANUFACTURING PATTERNS IN THE SYNTHETIC RUBBER INDUSTRY. See Statistics.

RUBBER MANUFACTURERS ASSOCIATION INDUSTRY RUBBER REPORT. See Manufacturing.

RUBBER, PRODUCTION, SHIPMENTS, AND STOCKS. (CURRENT INDUSTRIAL REPORTS. MA-30A, RUBBER, PRODUCTION, SHIPMENTS, AND STOCKS). 1980-. 0738-033X. US. English. an. $1.50. Data User Services Division, Customer Services Publication, Bureau of the Census, Washington DC 20233. **Tel** (301)763-4478. Ed Robert Marske. LC HD9161.U5. DD 338.4767820973. **Circ** 500. Reports on manufacturers production of synthetic rubber elastomers, by type of elastomer. Current Industrial Reports. MA-30A, Rubber, Production, Consumption, and Stocks, 0278-9310.

RUBBER PRODUCTS GUIDE. US. English. ir. Rubber Products Guide, 33-61 190th Street, Flushing NY 11358. LC TS1877. DD 338.47678202573.

RUBBER STATISTICAL BULLETIN. See Statistics.

RUBBER TRENDS. 0035-9564. Periodical. UK. English. qt. 310.00. Economist Intelligence Unit, 40 Duke Street, London W1M 5DG England. **Tel** 01-493 6711. Ed Arthur Way. **Ind/Abst** Predicasts. LC HD9161.A1. Analysis and evaluation of market and industrial trends in both natural and synthetic rubber.

RUBBER WORLD. V. 1- Oct. 15, 1889-. 0035-9572. Periodical. US. English. mo. $14.00. Rubber, Automotive Division of Hartman Communications, 633 Third Avenue, New York NY 10017. **Ind/Abst** Chem. Abstr., Eng. Index Annu. LC TS1870. DD 338.47678205. CODEN RUBWAQ.

RUBBER WORLD. Began in 1954. 0035-9572. Periodical. US. English. mo. Rubber World, PO Box CS 528, Baldwin NY 11510. **Tel** (216)864-2122. **Ind/Abst** Fluidex, Predicasts, Coal Abstr., Energy Res. Abstr., Chem. Abstr., Eng. Index, Energy Inf. Abstr., Environ. Abstr. CODEN RUBWAQ. Also available on microfilm from University Microfilms. Indian Rubber World, 0096-5790.

RUBBERVERWERKENDE INDUSTRIE. See Manufacturing.

RUSSKII GOLOS. VFOAT Russian Voice, Russky Golos. Began Feb. 1, 1917. 0036-0406. Newspaper. US. Russian. wk. Russky Golos Publishing Corporation, 130 East 16th Street, New York NY 10003.

STATISTIK INDUSTRI KARET REMAH (CRUMB RUBBER). See Statistics.

SUMMARY OF PROCEEDINGS OF THE . . . ASSEMBLY. Main/Corp International Rubber Study Group. English. ir. International Rubber Study Group, Brettenham House 5-6 Lancaster, London WC2 England. **Tel** (01)836-6811. Ed J D Carr. LC HD9161.A2. DD 338.476782. Collection of papers on worldwide trends in rubber production/consumption and transport given at International Rubber Study Group Assembly. Summary of Proceedings of the Meeting.

TIRE REPAIR JOURNAL. See Business.

TIRE REVIEW (AKRON, OHIO : 1966). (TIRE REVIEW). Began with: June 1966. 0040-8085. Periodical. US. English. mo. Babcox Business Publications, Babcox Building, 11 Forge Street, Akron OH 44304. **Tel** (216)535-6117. LC TS1870. DD 381.4567832068. Tire and TBA Review.

ULASAN GETAH MALAYSIA. VFOAT Malaysian Rubber Review. V. 1- July 1976-. 0126-9089. MY. English (summaries in Malaysian). ir. $26.00. Malaysian Rubber Research Development Board, PO Box 10508, Kuala Lumpur 01-02 Malaysia. **Tel** (03)484422. Ed Ahmad Farouk, Bin Haji and S M Ishak. **Ind/Abst** Predicasts. LC TS1870. DD 338.173895209595. **Circ** 1,500. (ctrl). A general assesment of the rubber industry in Malaysia and the world with emphasis on current economic and technical information.

URW. UNITED RUBBER WORKER. Main/Corp United Rubber, Cork, Linoleum and Plastic Workers of America. VFOAT United Rubber Worker. 1935. 0162-3869. Periodical. US. English. bm. United Rubber Cork Linoleum and Plastic Workers, 87 South High Street, Akron OH 44308. **Tel** (216)376-6181. Ed Milan Stone. (ctrl). United Rubber Worker, 0041-7475.

THE WING FOOT CLAN. VFOAT Wingfoot Clan. 0043-5872. Periodical. US. English. wk. Free. Goodyear Tire & Rubber Co, Akron OH 44316. **Tel** (216)796-4143. Ed Dotti Eitel. **Circ** 21,000. (ctrl). Company policy and procedure information, economic information, subjects impacting rubber industry and general interest employee stories.

SANITATION, ENVIRONMENTAL TECHNOLOGY

102 MONITOR. See Conservation & Natural Resources.

305 (B) TECHNICAL REPORT FOR OKLAHOMA. VFOAT Three Hundred Five (B) Technical Report for Oklahoma. 6740-9923. US. English. be. 1000 Northeast 10th, Oklahoma City OK 73152. LC TD224.O5. DD 363.7394209766.

ABATEMENT AND POLLUTION CONTROL TRAINING AND EDUCATIONAL PROGRAMS PRESENTED BY THE UNITED STATES ENVIROMENTAL PROTECTION AGENCY. (ABATEMENT AND POLLUTION CONTROL TRAINING AND EDUCATIONAL PROGRAMS). Main/Corp United States. Environmental Protection Agency. Office of Education and Manpower Planning. 0093-1616. US. English. be. Environmental Protection Agency, Office of Education and Manpower Planning, 401 M Street, Washington DC 20460. LC TD171. DD 628.50973.

ABSTRACTS - ANNUAL SYMPOSIUM ON RECENT ADVANCES IN THE ANALYTICAL CHEMISTRY OF POLLUTANTS. See Indexes/Abstracts.

ABSTRACTS ON HEALTH EFFECTS OF ENVIRONMENTAL POLLUTANTS. See Indexes/Abstracts.

ABWASSERTECHNIK. Vol. 1-. 0001-3706. Periodical. GW. German. bm. 110,50. Bauverlag GMBH, Wittelsbacher Strasse 10, D6200 Wiesbaden West Germany. **Tel** 06121/791-0. Ed M Schirmer. **Ind/Abst** Chem. Abstr., Bibliogr. Agric. CODEN ABWTA6. bk rev. adv acc. **Circ** 5,000. Contains reports on the treatment of sewage and industrial effluents and wastes, water purification, environmental protection, recycling, research, current practice, innovations, and new developments.

ACID PRECIPITATION. Doe/Apc-83/1 (Oct. 30, 1983)-. 0741-5230. Periodical. US. English. sm. $40.00. National Technical Information Service, 5285 Port Royal Road, Springfield VA 22161.

ACID RAIN. V. 1, N. 1-. Periodical. US. English. bm.

ACID RAIN ABSTRACTS. See Indexes/Abstracts.

ACID RAIN ESSENTIALS. Vol. 1, No. 1 (Sept/Oct 1984)-. 0883-3435. Periodical. US. English. bm. $232.00 Domestic, $240.00 Foreign. Acid Rain Essentials, PO Box 321, Narberth PA 19072. DD 363.

ACID RAIN NOTES. Vol. 1, No. 1 (Sept. 1982)-. 0824-5096. CN. English. an. Free. District Municipality of Muskoka, 10 Pine Street PO Box 1720, Bracebridge Ontario P0B 1C0 Canada. DD 363.73920971316.

ACQUA ARIA. 0391-5557. Periodical. Italian. ir. **Ind/Abst** Chem. Abstr., Bibliogr. Agric. CODEN AQARDW. Ecologia Acqua E Aria Suolo.

ACTION BULLETIN (ARLINGTON, VA.). (ACTION BULLETIN). 0749-3959. Periodical. US. English. $25.00 Nonmembers. Citizens Clearinghouse for Hazardous Wastes, PO Box 926, Arlington VA 22216. **Tel** (703)276-7070. bk rev. **Circ** 7,500. News, resources and timely information on current events in hazardous waste management aimed at the average citizen concerned about the environment.

ACTIVE RESEARCH PROJECTS REPORT. Main/Corp National Environmental Research Center, Cincinnati. 1971/72-. 0095-070X. US. English. LC TD157.5. DD 301.31072073.

ACTIVE RESEARCH TASKS REPORT. Main/Corp National Environmental Research Center, Cincinnati. 0092-9891. US. English. National Environmental Research Center, Cincinnati OH 45268. LC TD169. DD 363.6.

ADMINISTRATION OF THE PESTICIDE PROGRAMS. Main/Corp United States. Environmental Protection Agency. Office of Pesticide Programs. 0277-2329. US. English. an. US Environmental Protection Agency, Office of Pesticide Programs, Washington DC 20460. LC SB97-0.4.U5. DD 632.950973.

ADVANCES IN ENVIRONMENTAL SCIENCE AND ENGINEERING. V. 1- 1979-. 0141-8106. US. English. ir. Gordon & Breach, 1 Bedford Street, London WC2E 9HD England. **Tel** 01 836 5125. **Ind/Abst** Chem. Abstr. LC TD169. DD 363.700973. CODEN AESEDX.

ADVANCES IN ENVIRONMENTAL SCIENCE AND TECHNOLOGY. V. 2- 1971-. 0065-2563. US. English. ir. John Wiley & Sons Inc, 1 Wiley Drive, Somerset NJ 08873. **Ind/Abst** Life Sci. Collect., Comput. Control Abstr., Electr. Electron. Abstr., Sci. Abstr. Sect. A. Phys. Abstr., Bibliogr. Agric., Energy Res. Abstr., Phys. Abstr. LC TD180. DD 628.05. NLM W1 AD552T. CODEN AESTC9. Advances in Environmental Sciences, 0095-4535.

ADVANCES IN MODERN ENVIRONMENTAL TOXICOLOGY. Vol. 1-. 0276-5063. Monographic Series. US. English. ir. Princeton Scientific Publisher, PO Box 2155, Princeton NJ 08540. **Tel** (609)683-4750. Ed M A Mehlman. **Ind/Abst** Chem. Abstr. LC UNC. NLM W1. CODEN AETODY. **Circ** 1,500. This is a series of volumes dealing with topics of interest to professional biological chemists, toxicologists, pharmacologists, occupational physicians, industrial hygienists, and scientists working in related disciplines.

AFRICAN ENVIRONMENT. V. 1, No. 2- Apr. 1975-. Periodical. English. qt. $60.00. Enda T M, B P 3370, Dakar Senegal Africa. **Ind/Abst** Energy Inf. Abstr., Environ. Abstr. LC QH194. DD 301.31096. Environment in Africa.

AFVALSTOFFEN, BEDRIJFSAFVALSTOFFEN. Series/Titl Milieustatistieken. VFOAT Waste, Industrial Waste. 1978-. Dutch (summaries in English). ir. LC TD897.8.N4. DD 363.72.

Sanitation, Environmental Technology

AGENCY PUBLICATION - TEXAS WATER QUALITY BOARD. See Law.

AN AGREEMENT BETWEEN THE STATE OF CALIFORNIA AND THE U.S. ENVIRONMENTAL PROTECTION AGENCY, REGION IX, ON THE DEVELOPMENT AND IMPLEMENTATION OF THE CALIFORNIA STATE WATER QUALITY MANAGEMENT PROGRAM. Main/Corp California. State Water Resources Control Board. VFOAT State-EPA Agreement. US. English. an. State Water Resources Control Board, Sacramento CA 95808. LC TD224.C3. DD 363.73945609794.

AGRICULTURE AND ENVIRONMENT. See Agriculture.

AGRICULTURE, ECOSYSTEMS & ENVIRONMENT. See Agriculture.

AICHI-KEN KOGAI CHOSA SENTA SHOHO. VFOAT Bulletin of the Aichi Environmental Research Center. 1- No. JA. Japanese. ir. Aichi-Ken Kogai Chosa Senta, 7-ban 6-go Aza nagare Tsujicho, Nagoya Japan. Ind/Abst Chem. Abstr. LC TD178.7.J3. CODEN AKCSD3.

AIR CONSERVATION. Periodical. English (Polish). ir. Foreign Scientific Publications, Department of the National Center for Scientific Technical and Economic Information, Springfield VA 22151. LC TD881. DD 614.7105.

AIR POLLUTION CONTROL. Series/Titl Environmental Science and Technology. Pt. 1-. 0161-3901. US. English. ir. John Wiley & Sons Inc, 1 Wiley Drive, Somerset NJ 08873. Ind/Abst Bibliogr. Agric., Chem. Abstr. CODEN APLCCY.

AIR POLLUTION CONTROL. Apr. 2, 1980-. 0196-7150. Periodical. US. English. bw. $316.00. Bureau of National Affairs Inc, 1231 25th Street NW, Washington DC 20037. Tel (301)258-1033.

AIR POLLUTION TITLES. Began with Jan./Feb. 1966 issue. 0002-2497. Periodical. US. English. bm. $95.00. Pennsylvania State University, 226 Fenske Laboratory, University Park PA 16802. Tel (814)865-1415. Ed Elizabeth J Carroll. LC Z5862.2A4 TD883. DD 016.3636. Circ 90. Survey of current air pollution literature, listing titles on air environment, effects of air pollution on plants and people, control of air pollution monitoring and analysis of air pollution.

AIR QUALITY ABSTRACTS. See Indexes/Abstracts.

AIR QUALITY CONTROL DIGEST. Periodical. US. English. bm. $81.00. University of Digest Services, PO Box 343, Troy MI 48084.

AIR QUALITY CONTROL FOR ARIZONA. 8755-6243. US. English. an. LC TD883.5.A6. DD 363.7392609791.

AIR QUALITY DATA. Main/Corp United States. Environmental Protection Agency. Office of Air Quality Planning and Standards. 0093-8165. US. English. an. Air Pollution Technical Information Center, US Environmental Protection Agency, Office of Air Quality and Planning, Durham NC 27711. LC TD883.2. DD 363.6. Air Quality Data.

AIR QUALITY DATA - STATISTICS. See Statistics.

AIR QUALITY IN MINNESOTA. Main/Corp Minnesota. Air Quality Division. Technical Services Section. 1973-. 0361-5650. US. English. an. 1935 West County Road/B2, St Paul MN 55113. LC TD883.5.M5. DD 363.6.

AIR QUALITY IN SELECTED URBAN AREAS. Series/Titl Who Offset Publication. Began with: 1973-74. English. be. NLM W1.

AIR QUALITY MONOGRAPHS. No. 69-1- 1969-. 0568-3653. Monographic Series. US. English. ir. American Petroleum Institute, 1220 L Street NW, Washington DC 20005. Tel (214)741-6791.

AIR QUALITY. NORTHWESTERN ONTARIO. ANNUAL REPORT. (AIR QUALITY, NORTHWESTERN ONTARIO : ANNUAL REPORT . . .). 1980-. 0713-9330. CN. English. an. Ontario Ministry of the Environment, 135 St Clair Avenue West/Suite 100, Toronto Ontario M4V 1P5 Canada. DD 363.739220971311. Air Quality, Atikokan, Kenora, Red Rock, 0713-1941; Air Quality, Balmerton, 0704-3279; Air Quality, Dryden, 0704-3309; Air Quality, Fort Frances, 0704-3287; Air Quality, Marathon, 0704-3317.

AIR RESEARCH SUMMARY. Main/Corp Oregon. State University, Corvallis. Air Resources Center. VFOAT Air: Air Research Summary. 1971-. 0094-8160. US. English. be. LC TD883.15. DD 363.6.

AIR-WATER POLLUTION REPORT. (AIR/WATER POLLUTION REPORT). 0002-2608. Periodical. US. English. wk. $175.00. Business Publishers Inc, PO Box 1067, Silver Spring MD 20910. Air and Water News, 0002-2187.

AIR WAVES. V. 1- Aug. 1979-. Periodical. US. English. mo. National Commission for Air Quality, 499 South Capitol Street Southwest 2nd Floor, Washington DC 20003.

ALAM SEKITAR. V. 1- July/Aug. 1976-. 0126-7280. Periodical. English (Malay). ir. $1.20 Single Issue. P S 382 Jln Sultan, Petaling Jaya Selangor Malaysia. LC TD171.5.M4. DD 363.7009595.

ALASKA LITTER REDUCTION/RECYCLING PROGRAM . . . ANNUAL REPORT. Main/Corp Alaska. Dept. of Environmental Conservation. 1st (Apr. 1981)-. US. English. an. Department of Environmental Conservation, Pouch O, Juneau AK 99811. LC TD788.4.A4. DD 363.728.

ALGEMENE MILIEUSTATISTIEK. See Statistics.

ALI-ABA COURSE OF STUDY. ENVIRONMENTAL LAW : MATERIALS. See Law.

ALI-ABA COURSE OF STUDY. ENVIRONMENTAL LITIGATION : MATERIALS. See Law.

ALI-ABA COURSE OF STUDY. WATER AND AIR POLLUTION : MATERIALS. See Law.

ALTANLAGEN-REPORT. German. an. Unweltbundesamt, Bismarckplatz 1, 1000 Berlin 33 West Germany. LC TD897.8.G3. DD 363.739220943.

AMBIENT AIR QUALITY DATA. ANNUAL REPORT. (AMBIENT AIR QUALITY DATA : ANNUAL REPORT). Main/Corp Virginia. State Air Pollution Control Board. Monitoring Division. 0146-3195. US. English. an. State Air Pollution Control Board, Monitoring Division, 1005 West Cary Street, Richmond VA 23220. LC TD883.5.V8. DD 363.6.

AMBIO. Vol. 1, No. 1 (Feb. 1972)-. 0044-7447. Periodical. in English. bm. $85.00. Pergamon Press, 395 Sawmill River Road, Elmsford NY 10523. Tel (914)592-7700. Ind/Abst Electron. Commun. Abstr. J., ISMEC Bull., Can. Environ., Life Sci. Collect., Coal Abstr., Excerpta Med., Energy Inf. Abstr., Environ. Abstr., Int. Aerosp. Abstr., GeoRef, CIS Abstr., Sel. Water Resour. Abstr., Biol. Abstr., Chem. Abstr., Eng. Index Annu., Eng. Index Mon., Eng. Index Bioeng. Abstr., Energy Res. Abstr., Nuci. Sci. Abstr., Sci. Cit. Index, Abr. Ed., Pollut. Abstr. Indexes, Ocean. Abstr., Eng. Index. LC QH540. DD 301.3105. NLM W1 AM103K. CODEN AMBOCX.

AMCA NEWSLETTER. Main/Corp American Mosquito Control Association. VAT American Mosquito Control Association Newsletter. Began with issue for June 1975. 0195-4180. Periodical. US. English. qt.

ANALYTICAL STUDIES FOR THE U.S. ENVIRONMENTAL PROTECTION AGENCY. VAT Analytical Studies for the United States Environmental Protection Agency. V. 1-. 0270-0697. Monographic Series. US. English. Printing and Publishing Office National Academy of Sciences, 2101 Constitution Avenue, Washington DC 20418. LC UNC.

ANNUAIRE QUALITE DES EAUX (QUEBEC). See Yearbooks, Almanacs, Directories.

ANNUAL AIR QUALITY REPORT (DES MOINES, IOWA). (ANNUAL AIR QUALITY REPORT). 1982-. 0882-7796. US. English. an. Program Development Division, Iowa Department of Water Air and Waste Management, Henry A Wallace Building, 900 East Grand Avenue, Des Moines IA 50319. Iowa Air Quality Report, 0882-780X.

ANNUAL DATA SUMMARY FOR AIR QUALITY CONTROL REGIONS 1, 2, 3, 4, 6, 8, 9, 11, AND 12. Main/Corp Texas. Air Control Board. VAT Annual Data Summary for Air Quality Control Regions One, Two, Three, Four, Six, Eight, Nine, Eleven, and Twelve. 0148-0774. US. English. an. LC TD883.5.T4. DD 363.6.

ANNUAL ENVIRONMENTAL MONITORING REPORT - MOUND FACILITY. Main/Corp Mound Facility. 1977-. US. English. an. US Department of Energy, Office of the Assistant Secretary for Defense Programs, Mound Facility, 5285 Port Royal Road, Springfield VA 22161. Annual Environmental Monitoring Report.

ANNUAL EVALUATION - NEW MEXICO. ENVIRONMENTAL IMPROVEMENT DIVISION. (ANNUAL EVALUATION). Main/Corp New Mexico. Environmental Improvement Division. VFOAT E.I.D. Annual Evaluation. 0742-8022. US. English. an. New Mexico Environmental Improvement Division, PO Box 968, Santa Fe NM 87503. LC TD171.3.N49. DD 363.7009789.

ANNUAL LIST OF PUBLICATIONS - DEPARTMENT OF THE ENVIRONMENT. DEPARTMENT OF TRANSPORT. LIBRARY SERVICES. See Bibliographies.

ANNUAL PROCEEDINGS - ARIZONA WATER SYMPOSIUM. (ANNUAL PROCEEDINGS). Main/Conf Arizona Water Symposium. VAT Arizona Water Symposium Annual Proceedings. 22nd-. 0731-874X. US. English. an. LC TD224.A7. Proceedings, 0571-0162.

ANNUAL PROGRESS REPORT TO THE INTERNATIONAL JOINT COMMISSION FROM THE INTERNATIONAL REFERENCE GROUP ON GREAT LAKES POLLUTION FROM LAND USE ACTIVITIES (PLUARG). Main/Corp International Reference Group On Great Lakes Pollution From Land Use Activities. 1975-. CN. English. an. International Joint Commission, Great Lakes Regional Office, 100 Ouelette Avenue, Windsor Ontario N9A 6T3 Canada. LC TD223.3. DD 363.61. Vols. for 1975- distributed to Depository Libraries in microfiche.

ANNUAL REPORT - AIR POLLUTION CONTROL COMMISSION. Main/Corp West Virginia. Air Pollution Control Commission. 0161-3855. US. English. an. 4104-A MacCorkle Avenue SE, Charleston WV 25304. LC TD883.5.W4. DD 353.9754008232.

ANNUAL REPORT AND ACCOUNTS - BRITISH STEEL CORPORATION. Main/Corp British Steel Corporation. 1st (1967/68)-. 0068-2586. UK. English. an. Thames Water Authority, New River Head Roseberry Avenue, London EC1R4TP England. LC WMLC L 82/144.

ANNUAL REPORT AND ACCOUNTS - NATIONAL WATER COUNCIL. Main/Corp Great Britain. National Water Council. 1974/75-. UK. English. an. 1.75. National Water Council, 1 Queen Anne's Gate, London SW1 9BT England. LC TD257. DD 354.41008232.

ANNUAL REPORT AND ACCOUNTS - WATER RESEARCH CENTRE. See Water Resources.

ANNUAL REPORT AND AUDITED FINANCIAL STATEMENTS - NORTHEAST MARYLAND WASTE DISPOSAL AUTHORITY. Main/Corp Northeast Maryland Waste Disposal Authority. US. English. an. Northeast Maryland Waste Disposal Authority, 131 East Redwood Street/Suite 503, Baltimore MD 21202-1275. LC HD4484.M3. DD 352.63097527.

ANNUAL REPORT - BUREAU OF AIR POLLUTION CONTROL. STATE OF NEW JERSEY. DEPARTMENT OF ENVIRONMENTAL PROTECTION. (ANNUAL REPORT). Main/Corp New Jersey. Bureau of Air Pollution Control. 0090-5429. US. English. an. State of New Jersey, Bureau of Air Pollution Control, Trenton NJ 08625. LC TD883.5.N5. DD 353.9749008232.

ANNUAL REPORT - CENTRE FOR ENVIRONMENTAL STUDIES. Main/Corp Centre For Environmental Studies (Great Britain). Periodical. UK. English. an. Centre for Environmental Studies, 62 Chandos Place, London WC2N 4HH England.

ANNUAL REPORT - DEPARTMENT OF ENVIRONMENTAL PLANNING AND ENERGY (SOUTH AFRICA). Main/Corp South Africa. Dept. of Environmental Planning and Energy. VFOAT Jaarverslag - Departement Van Omgewingsbeplanning en Energie. SA. Afrikaans (English). ir. 6.50. Government Printer, Private Bag X85, Pretoria 0001 South Africa. LC HC905.Z9. DD 354.680082306.

ANNUAL REPORT - DEPARTMENT OF PLANNING AND THE ENVIRONMENT (SOUTH AFRICA). See Housing and Urban Development.

Sanitation, Environmental Technology

ANNUAL REPORT - DESPLAINES VALLEY MOSQUITO ABATEMENT DISTRICT (LYONS, ILL.). Main/Corp Desplaines Valley Mosquito Abatement District (Lyons, Ill). 1939-. US. English. an. *A Report upon Mosquito Control Activities.*

ANNUAL REPORT - ENVIRONMENT CANADA. (ANNUAL REPORT). Main/Corp Canada. Environment Canada. VFOAT Rapport Annuel. 1979/1980-. 0711-1320. CN. English (French). an. Information Directorate, Department of the Environment, Ottawa Ontario K1A 0H3 Canada. LC HC120.E5. DD 354.7100823206. *Annual Report, 0706-2583.*

ANNUAL REPORT - ENVIRONMENT COUNCIL OF ALBERTA. SCIENCE ADVISORY COMMITTEE. Main/Corp Environment Council of Alberta. Science Advisory Committee. 0710-829X. CN. English. an. Free. Environment Council of Alberta, 2100 College Plaza/ Tower 3, 8215-112 Street, Edmonton Alberta T6G 2M4 Canada. DD 354.71230082321. *Annual Report, 0710-829X.*

ANNUAL REPORT - ENVIRONMENTAL CONTROL COUNCIL (NOVA SCOTIA). Main/Corp Nova Scotia. Environmental Control Council. 1973-. 0317-3526. CN. English. an. Howe Building/PO Box 2107, Halifax B3J 3B7 Nova Scotia. LC HC120.E5. DD 354.7160077.

ANNUAL REPORT - ENVIRONMENTAL DEFENSE FUND. (ANNUAL REPORT). Main/ Corp Environmental Defense Fund. 0091-9837. US. English. an. Environmental Defense Fund, 162 Old Town Road, East Setauket NY 11733. LC HC110.E5. DD 301.310973.

ANNUAL REPORT - ENVIRONMENTAL EDUCATION ADVISORY COUNCIL. Main/Corp United States. Advisory Council on Environmental Education. 1975-. 0148-9313. US. English. an. LC GF27. DD 353.008232.

ANNUAL REPORT - ENVIRONMENTAL QUALITY COUNCIL (MONTANA). (ANNUAL REPORT). Main/Corp Montana Environmental Quality Council. 1st- 1971/72-. 0091-0457. US. English. an. State of Montana, Environmental Quality Control, State Capital, Helena MT 59601. LC GF504.M9. DD 301.3109786.

ANNUAL REPORT - ERIE COUNTY DEPARTMENT OF HEALTH. AIR POLLUTION CONTROL DIVISION. (ANNUAL REPORT). Main/Corp Erie Co., N.Y. Air Pollution Control Division. 0090-6212. US. English. an. Erie County NY, Pollution Control Division, Edward A Rath County Office Building, Buffalo NY 14260. LC TD883.5.N7. DD 363.

ANNUAL REPORT - GREAT LAKES SCIENCE ADVISORY BOARD. (ANNUAL REPORT : REPORT TO THE INTERNATIONAL JOINT COMMISSION). Main/Corp Great Lakes Science Advisory Board. 1980-. 0710-8702. CN. English. an. International Joint Commission, Great Lakes Science Advisory Board, 100 Ouellette Avenue/ 8th Floor, Windsor Ontario N9A 6T3 Canada. LC TD223.3. DD 363.73940977. Vols. for 1980- distributed to depository libraries in microfiche.

ANNUAL REPORT - GREATER LONDON COUNCIL. DEPT. OF PUBLIC HEALTH ENGINEERING. Main/Corp Greater London Council. Dept. of Public Health Engineering. Series Corp Greater London Council Publication. UK. English. an. Greater London Council Department of Public Health Engineering, 10 Great George Street, SW1P 3AB London England. LC TD64.L8. DD 352.409421.

ANNUAL REPORT - ILLINOIS ENVIRONMENTAL FACILITIES FINANCING AUTHORITY. Main/Corp Illinois Environmental Facilities Financing Authority. US. English. an. Illinois Environmental Facilities Financing Authority, 100 North LaSalle Street/Room 1903, Chicago IL 60602. LC HC107.I33. DD 353.9773008232206.

ANNUAL REPORT - ILLINOIS INDUSTRIAL POLLUTION CONTROL FINANCING AUTHORITY. Main/Corp Illinois Industrial Pollution Control Financing Authority. US. English. an. Illinois Industrial Pollution Control Financing Authority, 100 North LaSalle Street/Suite 814, Chicago IL 60602. LC TD897.75.I3. DD 353.9773008232.

ANNUAL REPORT - ILLINOIS INSTITUTE FOR ENVIRONMENTAL QUALITY. (ANNUAL REPORT). Main/Corp Illinois Institute for Environmental Quality. 0090-8967. US. English. an. Institute for Environmental Quality, 309 West Washington, Chicago IL 60606. LC TD171.3.I45. DD 333.7209773.

ANNUAL REPORT - INDIA. DEPT. OF ENVIRONMENT. Main/Corp India. Dept. of Environment. 1980-81-. English. an. LC HC79.E5. DD 354.54008232106.

ANNUAL REPORT - INDUSTRIAL ENVIRONMENTAL RESEARCH LABORATORY. (ANNUAL REPORT). Began with 1975. 0364-3964. US. English. an. Technical Information Service, Mail Drop 64, Industrial Environmental Research Laboratory, Environmental Protection Agency, Research Triangle Park NC 27711. LC TD157.5. DD 628.5.

ANNUAL REPORT - IOWA. DEPT. OF WATER, AIR, AND WASTE MANAGEMENT. Main/Corp Iowa. Dept. of Water, Air, and Waste Management. 1982/83-. US. English. an. Iowa Department of Water Air and Waste Management, Henry A Wallace Building, 900 East Grand Avenue, Des Moines IA 50319. *Annual Report.*

ANNUAL REPORT - IOWA ENVIRONMENTAL QUALITY COMMISSION. Main/Corp Iowa Environmental Quality Commission. 1st (1981)-. US. English. an. Full Depository, 707 Savings and Loan Building, Des Moines IA 50309. *Annual Report, 0196-5794.*

ANNUAL REPORT - KUCHING WATER BOARD. Main/Corp Kuching Water Board. English. ir. Government Printing Office, Kuching Water Board, PO Box 483, Singapore Malaysia. LC TD313.S32. DD 354.595400871.

ANNUAL REPORT MADE TO THE SECRETARY OF STATE FOR THE ENVIRONMENT, SECRETARY OF STATE FOR SCOTLAND, SECRETARY OF STATE FOR WALES. Main/Corp Great Britain. Radioactive Waste Management Advisory Committee. 1st- 1980-. UK. English. an. 2.75. LC TD898. DD 363.728.

ANNUAL REPORT - MANITOBA ENVIRONMENTAL COUNCIL. Main/ Corp Manitoba. Environmental Council. 1- 1972/73-. 0380-9803. CN. English. an. Free. Manitoba Environmental Council, Box 139, 139 Tuxedo Avenue, Winnipeg Manitoba R3N 0H6 Canada. LC TD171.5.C2. DD 354.7127008232.

ANNUAL REPORT - METROPOLITAN WATER BOARD. Main/Corp Metropolitan Water Board. AT. English. ir. Government Printer, GPO Box 307C, Hobart 7000 Tasmania Australia. LC TD322.T38. DD 354.94600871.

ANNUAL REPORT - MINISTRY OF ENVIRONMENT (BRITISH COLUMBIA). Main/Corp British Columbia. Ministry of Environment. 1978-. 0227-7506. CN. English. an. Ministry of Environment, Parliament Buildings, Victoria British Columbia V8V 1X5 Canada. Tel (604)387-1161. LC TD171.5.C2. DD 354.7110682321. Report for British Columbia the Ministry of Environment. *Report of the Ministry of the Environment, 0704-3200 Annual Report (Ministry of Recreation and Conservation).*

ANNUAL REPORT - MISSISSIPPI AIR AND WATER POLLUTION CONTROL COMMISSION. Main/Corp Mississippi. Air & Water Pollution Control Commission. 0193-158X. US. English. an. Mississippi Air & Water Pollution Control Commission, PO Box 827, Jackson MS 39205. LC TD171.3.M7. DD 614.709762.

ANNUAL REPORT - NATIONAL ADVISORY ENVIRONMENTAL HEALTH SCIENCES COUNCIL, NATIONAL INSTITUTES OF HEALTH. Main/Corp National Advisory Environmental Health Sciences Council. US. English. an. National Advisory Environmental Health Sciences Council, National Institutes of Health, 9000 Rockville Pike, Bethesda MD 20014.

ANNUAL REPORT - NATIONAL CENTER FOR RESOURCE RECOVERY. Main/Corp National Center for Resource Recovery. US. English. an. National Center for Resource Recovery, 1211 Connecticut Avenue Northwest, Washington DC 20036. LC TD794.5. DD 354.5990083.

ANNUAL REPORT - NATIONAL ENVIRONMENTAL RESEARCH CENTER. Main/Corp National Environmental Research Center, Cincinnati. 0093-9021. US. English. National Environmental Research Center, Cincinnati OH 45268. LC TD171. DD 628.106173.

ANNUAL REPORT - NATIONAL ENVIRONMENTAL RESEARCH CENTER. (ANNUAL REPORT). Main/Corp United States. National Environmental Research Center (Research Triangle Park, N.C.). 1971/72-. 0098-5341. US. English. an. National Environmental Research Center, Research Triangle Park, Durham NC 27711. LC TD178.8.U52. DD 363.6. NLM W2 A N155A.

ANNUAL REPORT OF ACTIVITIES OF THE EFFLUENT STANDARDS AND WATER QUALITY INFORMATION ADVISORY COMMITTEE. Main/Corp United States. Effluent Standards and Water Quality Information Advisory Committee. -3rd (1975-1976). 0096-9923. US. English. an. Environmental Protection Agency ESWQIAC, Washington DC 20460. LC TD223. DD 363.6.

ANNUAL REPORT OF ENVIRONMENTAL RADIATION IN PENNSYLVANIA. Main/Corp Pennsylvania. Division of Environmental Radiation. July-Dec. 1979-. US. English. an. LC TD196.R3. DD 353.97480082323.

ANNUAL REPORT OF THE ABANDONED MINE LAND SECTION. Main/Corp Missouri. Land Reclamation Commission. Abandoned Mine Land Section. VFOAT AML Section Annual Report. 1981-. 0734-0532. US. English. an. Abandoned Mine Land Section, PO Box 1368, Jefferson City MO 65101. LC TD195.C58. DD 353.97780082326.

ANNUAL REPORT OF THE EASTERN ENVIRONMENTAL RADIATION FACILITY, U. S. ENVIRONMENTAL PROTECTION AGENCY. Main/Corp Eastern Environmental Radiation Facility (U.S.). VAT Annual Report of the Eastern Environmental Radiation Facility, United States Environmental Protection Agency. 0361-9087. US. English. an. PO Box 3009, Montgomery AL 36109. LC TD196.R3. DD 353.0077.

ANNUAL REPORT - OHIO AIR QUALITY DEVELOPMENT AUTHORITY. Main/Corp Ohio Air Quality Development Authority. 0162-797X. US. English. an. 1901 Leveque Tower, 50 West Broad Street, Columbus OH 43215. LC TD883.5.O5. DD 353.9771008235.

ANNUAL REPORT ON AIR QUALITY IN THE STATE OF MAINE. Main/Corp Maine. Division of Air Quality Services. 0738-0356. US. English. an. LC TD883.5.M2. DD 363.7392209741.

ANNUAL REPORT ON MICHIGAN-ONTARIO AIR POLLUTION. Main/Corp International Joint Commission. CN. English. an. LC TD883.5.M47. DD 363.739263097743.

ANNUAL REPORT ON THE QUALITY OF THE AIR IN WASHINGTON, D. C. Main/Corp District of Columbia. Air & Water Monitoring Division. 0093-4135. US. English. an. LC TD883.5.D6. DD 363.6.

ANNUAL REPORT ON THE QUALITY OF THE ENVIRONMENT (MINNESOTA). VFOAT Report On the Quality of the Environment. 1st- 1974-. 0094-1697. US. English. an. Centennial Office Building, St Paul MN 55155. LC GF504.M6. DD 301.3109776.

ANNUAL REPORT - OREGON. SOLID WASTE DIVISION. (ANNUAL REPORT). Main/Corp Oregon. Solid Waste Division. VFOAT Solid Waste Annual Report. 0883-3222. US. English. an. Oregon Department of Environmental Quality, PO Box 1760, Portland OR 97207.

ANNUAL REPORT - PRINCE EDWARD ISLAND. ENVIRONMENTAL CONTROL COMMISSION. Main/Corp Prince Edward Island. Environmental Control Commission. 1971/72-. CN. English. an. LC TD27.P7. DD 354.717008232.

ANNUAL REPORT, PUBLIC WATER SUPPLIES FOR THE STATE OF OKLAHOMA, NORTHWEST DISTRICT. Main/Corp State Water Quality Laboratory (Okla.). VFOAT Public Water Supply Report, Northwest District. 0272-4529. US. English.

Sanitation, Environmental Technology

an. State Water Quality Laboratory, 1000 NE 10th, Oklahoma City OK 73152. **LC** TD224.O5. **DD** 363.61.

ANNUAL REPORT, PUBLIC WATER SUPPLIES FOR THE STATE OF OKLAHOMA, SOUTH CENTRAL DISTRICT. VFOAT Public Water Supplies for the State of Oklahoma, South Central District. 0276-4539. US. English. an. State Water Quality Laboratory / Oklahoma State Department of Health, 1000 NE Tenth, Oklahoma City OK 73152. **LC** TD224.O5. **DD** 363.61.

ANNUAL REPORT - RESEARCH AND RESOURCE SERVICES, ST. JOHN'S, NEWFOUNDLAND. (ANNUAL REPORT . . .). **Main/Corp** Canada. Fisheries and Marine Service. Newfoundland Region. Research and Resource Services. 1975-. 0713-6412. CN. English (includes some text in French). an. Environment Canada, 131 Greber Boulevard, Point Gatineau Quebec J8T 3R1 Canada. **DD** 354.71008232809718. *Annual Report, 0713-6404.*

ANNUAL REPORT, RESULTS OF AMBIENT AIR MONITORING. Series/Titl Air Quality Data Analysis. VFOAT Results of Ambient Air Monitoring. US. English. an. T.A.B.C., 6330 Highway 290 East, Austin TX 78723. **LC** TD883.5.T4. **DD** 363.7392209764.

ANNUAL REPORT - SASKATCHEWAN ENVIRONMENT. (ANNUAL REPORT). **Main/Corp** Saskatchewan. Saskatchewan Environment. 1977/78-. 0710-6718. CN. English. **LC** HC117.S3. **DD** 354.7124008232106, 354. 7124068232. *Annual Report, 0317-4611.*

ANNUAL REPORT - STATE ENVIRONMENTAL IMPROVEMENT AUTHORITY. **Main/Corp** State Environmental Improvement Authority. 0190-3934. US. English. an. State Environmental Improvement Authority, 330 East High Street, Jefferson City MO 65101. **LC** TD171.3.M8. **DD** 614.7.

ANNUAL REPORT - STATE OF CONNECTICUT, COUNCIL ON ENVIRONMENTAL QUALITY. **Main/Corp** Connecticut. Council on Environmental Quality. 0095-4624. US. English. an. State Office Building, Hartford CT 06115. **LC** TD171.3.C6. **DD** 363.6.

ANNUAL REPORT TO THE LEGISLATIVE COMMITTEE ON TRADE AND ECONOMIC DEVELOPMENT - OREGON. AIR QUALITY DIVISION. **Main/Corp** Oregon. Air Quality Division. VFOAT Field Burning Report. 0272-653X. US. English. an. Oregon Department of Environmental Quality/Field Burning Office, 16 Oakway Mall, Eugene OR 97401. **LC** TD883.5.O72. **DD** 363.7392.

ANNUAL REPORT - TOKYO-TO KOGAI KENKYUJO. **Main/Corp** Tokyo-To Kogai Kenkyujo. Began in 1970. English. an. 5 Yurakucho 2-chome Chiyoda-ku, Tokyo Japan. **Ind/Abst** Chem. Abstr. **LC** TD169. **DD** 301.310952. **CODEN** TKKNDX.

ANNUAL REPORT - VICTORIA, AUSTRALIA. ENVIRONMENT PROTECTION AUTHORITY. **Main/Corp** Victoria, Australia. Environment Protection Authority. 1st- 1971/72-. AT. English. ir. Melbourne Government Printer, 232 Victoria Parade, East Melbourne 3002 Australia. **DD** 354.945008232.

ANNUAL REPORT - VIRGINIA. COUNCIL ON THE ENVIRONMENT. (ANNUAL REPORT). **Main/Corp** Virginia. Council on the Environment. 0197-7415. US. English. Council on the Environment, 6th Street North/Suite 301, Richmond VA 23219. **LC** HC107.V83. **DD** 363.7056109755. *Annual Report of the Council on the Environment, 0097-0447.*

ANNUAL REPORT - VIRGINIA ENVIRONMENTAL ENDOWMENT. **Main/Corp** Virginia Environmental Endowment. 1977-. 0191-4049. US. English. an. Virginia Environmental Endowment, PO Box 790, Richmond VA 23206. **LC** TD171.3.V8. **DD** 333.7.

ANNUAL REPORT - WASTEWATER TECHNOLOGY CENTRE. CENTRE FOR INLAND WATERS. (ANNUAL REPORT - WASTEWATER TECHNOLOGY CENTRE). **Main/Corp** Wastewater Technology Centre (Canada). Began publication in 1972?. 0317-7890. Periodical. CN. English. ir. Eastman Kodak Company, 343 State Street, Department 940, Rochester NY 14650. **Tel** (716)724-4000. **LC** TD526.A1. **DD** 628.2.

ANNUAL REPORT - WATER QUALITY COUNCIL OF QUEENSLAND. (ANNUAL REPORT - THE WATER QUALITY COUNCIL OF QUEENSLAND). **Main/Corp** Water Quality Council of Queensland. 1st- 1972/73-. 0311-2101. AT. English. an. Water Quality Council of Queensland Commission, GPO Box 2454, Brisbane Queensland 4001 Australia. **LC** TD321.Q8. **DD** 354.94300871.

ANNUAL REPORT - WATER RESEARCH CENTRE. **Main/Corp** Water Research Centre. 1973/74-. 0143-2443. UK. English. an. Water Research Centre, Stevenage Laboratory/ Elder Way, Herts SG1 1TH England. **LC** TD201. **DD** 628.1072042579. **NLM** W1 WA692AC. *Annual Report - The Water Research Association, Water Pollution Research.*

ANNUAL STATE STRATEGY - CALIFORNIA. STATE WATER RESOURCES CONTROL BOARD. **Main/Corp** California. State Water Resources Control Board. 0361-4506. Periodical. US. English. an. State Water Resources Control Board, PO Box 100, Sacramento CA 95801. **LC** TD224.C3. **DD** 363.6109794.

ANNUAL STATUS REPORT ON THE INACTIVE URANIUM MILL TAILINGS SITES REMEDIAL ACTION PROGRAM. **Main/Corp** United States. Dept. of Energy. Division of Environmental Control Technology. 1979-. 0271-9754. US. English. an. $9.25. National Technical Information Service/US Department of Commerce, 5285 Port Royal Road, Springfield VA 22161. **LC** TD899.U73. **DD** 363.728.

ANNUAL STATUS REPORT ON THE URANIUM MILL TAILINGS REMEDIAL ACTION PROGRAM. 0277-0504. US. English. an. National Technical Information Service, US Department of Commerce, 5285 Port Royal Road, Springfield VA 22161.

ANNUAL STATUS REPORT. SAFETY OF NUCLEAR MATERIALS. Series/Titl EUR. VFOAT Safety of Nuclear Materials. English. an. **LC** TD898. **DD** 363.728.

ANNUAL TENNESSEE AIR QUALITY REPORT, STATE & LOCAL. US. English. an. **LC** TD883.5.T2. **DD** 363.7392209768.

AOMORI-KEN KOGAI SENTA SHOHO. 1 No. Japanese. an. 1-131 Oaza Kawaragi Aza Kitanuma (031), Hachinoe Japan. **Ind/Abst** Chem. Abstr. **LC** TD187.5.J32. **CODEN** AKSSDF.

APC. AIR POLLUTION CONTROL. (APC - AIR POLLUTION CONTROL BRANCH). VAT Air Pollution Control. 0826-6425. Monographic Series. CN. English. Department of the Environment, Air Pollution Control Branch, Saskatchewan Power Building, Regina Saskatchewan S4P 0R9 Canada.

A.P.C.A. DIRECTORY AND RESOURCE BOOK. See Yearbooks, Almanacs, Directories.

API HAZARDOUS WASTE ENFORCEMENT REPORT. VFOAT A.P.I. Hazardous Waste Enforcement Report. No. 1 (June 1, 1983)-. 0747-7457. Periodical. US. English. mo. American Petroleum Institute Litigation Support Center, 2101 L Street NW, Washington DC 20037. **LC** KF3946.A15. **DD** 344.730462202648, 347. 304462202648.

APPROVED LIST, SANITARY INSPECTED FISH ESTABLISHMENTS. See Fish Culture and Fisheries.

APTD. (PUBLICATION APTD). **Main/Corp** United States. Environmental Protection Agency. Office of Air Quality Planning and Standards. 0361-2945. US. English. US Environmental Protection Agency, Office of Air Quality and Planning, Durham NC 27711. **Ind/Abst** Chem. Abstr. **LC** TD883.2. **DD** 628.530973. **CODEN** XETDAD. *Publication APTD.*

ARCHIVES OF ENVIRONMENTAL CONTAMINATION AND TOXICOLOGY. See Genealogy and Heraldry - Archives.

ARCHIVES OF ENVIRONMENTAL HEALTH : OFFICIAL PUBLICATION FOR THE AMERICAN ACADEMY OF OCCUPATIONAL MEDICINE. See Genealogy and Heraldry - Archives.

ATMOSPHERIC ENVIRONMENT. V. 1- Jan. 1967-. 0004-6981. Periodical. UK. English. mo. Pergamon Press, 395 Sawmill River Road, Elmsford NY 10523. **Tel** (914)592-7700. **Ind/Abst** Pollut. Abstr. Indexes, GeoRef, Eng. Index Mon., Eng. Index Bioeng. Abstr., Eng. Index Energy Abstr., Life Sci. Collect., Can. Environ., Sel. Water Resour. Abstr., Coal Abstr., Excerpta Med., Energy Inf. Abstr., Environ. Abstr., Fluidex, Int. Aerosp. Abstr., Index Med., Biol. Abstr., Chem. Abstr., Energy Res. Abstr., Appl. Sci. Technol. Index, Comput. Control Abstr., Electr. Electron. Abstr., Sci. Abstr. Sect. A. Phys. Abstr., Sci. Cit. Index, Abr. Ed., Appl. Mech. Rev., CIS Abstr., Phys. Abstr. **LC** TD881. **DD** 628.5305. **NLM** W1 AT57. **CODEN** ATENBP. Available on microfilm from Microforms International Marketing Corp. (MIMC). *Air and Water Pollution, 0568-3408.*

AUSGEWAHLTE DATEN AUS DER WASSERWIRTSCHAFT. German. ir. **LC** TD273.3. **DD** 363.610943.

AVAILABLE INFORMATION MATERIALS ON SOLID WASTE MANAGEMENT. **Main/Corp** United States. Environmental Protection Agency. 1966/1979-. US. English. be. US Environment Protection Agency, Office of Solid Waste Management, Washington DC 20460. **Tel** (202)755-7985.

BAYER AGROCHEM COURIER. (1976, No. 1-). Periodical. English. ir.

BEE, BULLETIN OF ENVIRONMENTAL EDUCATION. VFOAT Bulletin of Environmental Education. 1- May 1971-. 0045-1266. Periodical. UK. English. ir. 17.00. Streetwork/Notting Dale Urban Studies Center, 189 Frston Road, London W10 6Th England. **Tel** 441 968 5440. **Ind/Abst** Archit. Period. Index. bk rev. adv acc. **Circ** 1,250. Articles describe projects in environmental education, research reports or urban and community issues.

BEITRAGE ZUR UMWELTGESTALTUNG. Monographic Series. GW. German. ir. Erich Schmidt Verlag GMBH, POB 7330 Viktoriastr 44-A, D4800 Bielefeld 1 West Germany. **Tel** 0521/66061. Studies on environment, pollution, environmental law, and environmental policies.

BELGIUM ENVIRONMENTAL RESEARCH INDEX. See Indexes/Abstracts.

BERICHTE (GERMANY (WEST). UMWELTBUNDESAMT)). (BERICHTE - UMWELTBUNDESAMT). 0171-1911. Monographic Series. German. ir. E Schmidt, Umweltbundesamt, 1000 Berlin 33, Bismarckplatz 1, Berlin East Germany. **Ind/Abst** Chem. Abstr. **LC** TD186.5.G3. **DD** 363.700943. **CODEN** BEUMDA.

BIBLIOGRAPHY OF SMALL WASTEWATER FLOWS. See Bibliographies.

BIENNIAL REPORT - CALIFORNIA WASTE MANAGEMENT BOARD. (BIENNIAL REPORT). **Main/Corp** California Waste Management Board. 1982/1983-. 0882-8407. US. English. be. California Waste Management Board, 1020 Ninth Street/Suite 300, Sacramento CA 95814. *Annual Report.*

BIENNIAL REPORT - LAND RECLAMATION COMMISSION. **Main/Corp** Missouri. Land Reclamation Commission. 1st- 1972/73-. US. English. be. Land Reclamation Commission, PO Box 1368, Jefferson City MO 65101. **LC** TD195.S75. **DD** 353.9778008232.

BIENNIAL REPORT OF EXAMINING AND LICENSING BOARDS - MINNESOTA. ENVIRONMENTAL HEALTH SPECIALIST/SANITARIAN ADVISORY COUNCIL. **Main/Corp** Minnesota. Environmental Health Specialist/ Sanitarian Advisory Council. US. English. be. Environmental Health Specialist/Sanitarian Advisory Council, 717 Delaware Street SE, Minneapolis MN 55440.

BIENNIAL REPORT PREPARED IN ACCORDANCE WITH THE OZONE PROTECTION PROVISION, SECTION 153 (G), OF THE CLEAN AIR ACT AMMENDMENTS OF 1977. (BIENNIAL REPORT PREPARED IN ACCORDANCE WITH THE STRATOSPHERIC OZONE PROTECTION PROVISION, SECTION 153(G), OF THE CLEAN AIR ACT AMENDMENT OF 1977). **Main/Corp** High Altitude Pollution Program (U.S.). 0270-1596. US. English. be. National Technical Information Service, 5285 Port Royal Road, Springfield VA 22161. **LC** TD886.7. **DD** 353.0082324.

Sanitation, Environmental Technology

BIENNIAL REPORT - TEXAS AIR CONTROL BOARD. Main/Corp Texas. Air Control Board. 0360-9499. US. English. be. 8520 Shoal Creek Boulevard, Austin TX 78758. LC TD883.5.T4. DD 353.9764008232.

BIOCYCLE. Vol. 22, No. 1 (Jan./Feb. 1981)-. 0276-5055. Periodical. US. English. ir. $43.00. The JG Press Inc, Box 351, Emmaus PA 18049. Tel (215)967-4135. Ed Jerome Goldstein. Ind/Abst Eng. Index Annu., Eng. Index Mon., Eng. Index Bioeng. Abstr., Eng. Index Energy Abstr., Life Sci. Collect., Sel. Water Resour. Abstr., Coal Abstr., Excerpta Med., Energy Inf. Abstr., Environ. Abstr., Biol. Abstr., Met. Abstr., World Alum. Abstr., Chem. Abstr., Bibliogr. Agric. LC S661. DD 628.4458. CODEN BCYCDK. bk rev. adv acc. Circ 8,000. Specializes in new solutions for managing city and industry wastes. Reports (technical and operations) on composting, recycling, and land application. *Compost Science/Land Utilization, 0160-7413.*

BOLETIM TECNICO DA SECRETARIA DO SANEAMENTO, HABITACAO E OBRAS. Main/Corp Pernambuco, Brazil (State). Secretaria do Saneamento, Habitacao e Obras. Portuguese. ir. Secrataria do Saneamento, Av Cruz Cabuga 1111, Recife Brazil. LC TD41.P47.

BOLETIN DE PLAGUICIDAS. Spanish. ir.

BULLETIN - BRITISH ECOLOGICAL SOCIETY. (BULLETIN). 1, 1 (June 1970)-. 0306-8307. Periodical. UK. English. qt. Expediters of the Printed Word, 527 Madison Avenue, New York NY 10022.

BULLETIN - CALIFORNIA WATER POLLUTION CONTROL ASSOCIATION. Main/Corp California Water Pollution Control Association. V. 1- July 1964-. 0008-1620. Periodical. US. English. qt. $20.00. California Water Pollution Control Association, P O Box 575, Lafayette CA 94549-0575. Tel (415)284-1778. Ed Kirt Brooks. Ind/Abst Int. Aerosp. Abstr. adv acc. Circ 4,000. Publication distributed to members, wastewater engineers, operators, designers regulators and academics.

BULLETIN DE DOCUMENTATION - MINISTERE DE LA QUALITE DE LA VIE (FRANCE). Main/Corp France. Ministere de la Qualite de la Vie. FR. French. ir. Documentation Francaise, 29-31 Quai Voltaire, 75340 Paris Cedex 07 France. LC Z5863.P6, HC280.E5. DD 016.6147.

BULLETIN DES PUBLICATIONS - ENVIRONNEMENT CANADA. Main/Corp Canada. Environment Canada. VFOAT Notice of Publications - Environment Canada. Began with June/Dec. 1979? issue. 0225-6983. Periodical. CN. English (includes English and French publications). Environment Canada, Inquiry Center, Ottawa Ontario K1A 0H3 Canada. Ind/Abst Abstr. Bull. Inst. Paper Chem. DD 015.710534. *Bulletin des Publications, 0225-6983.*

BULLETIN - ENVIRONMENT COUNCIL OF ALBERTA. Main/Corp Environment Council of Alberta. No. 1-. 0227-3462. Periodical. CN. English. Environment Council of Alberta, 2100 College Plaza Tower 3, 8215 - 112 Street, Edmonton Alberta T6G 2M4 Canada. DD 363.70097123.

BULLETIN MENSUEL : POLLUTION ATMOSPHERIC, FUMEE ET SO2. MAANDBERICHT: LUCHTVERONTREINIGING, ROOK EN SO2. Main/Corp Brussels. Institut Royal Meteorologique de Belgique. VFOAT Maandbericht. 0524-7802. Periodical. BE. French. mo. Free. Instutut Hygiene en Epidemiologie, Bibliotheek/J Wijtsmanstraat 4, 1050 Bruxelles Belgium. Tel 642-5111. Circ 200. Daily value and monthly average of smoke and SO2 in more than 100 points of measuring in Belgium and Luxembourg.

BULLETIN SIGNALETIQUE. 885 : NUISANCES. V. 34- 1973-. 0301-3499. Periodical. FR. French. ir. Centre National de la Recherche Scientifique, Centre de Documentation, 23 rue du Maroc, 75019 Paris France. LC Z5853.S22. DD 016.6268. *Bulletin Signaletique. 885: Eau et Assinissement, Pollution Atmospherique.*

BUNKYO-KU NO KOGAI. Main/Corp Bunkyo-ku, Tokyo. Kenchiku Kogaibu. Kogaika. Japanese. ir. LC HC463.B77.

BUSINESS MONITOR. REPORT ON THE CENSUS OF PRODUCTION: FORMULATED PESTICIDES, ETC. *See Business.*

BUYER'S GUIDE TO ENVIRONMENTAL MEDIA. VFOAT Energy. No. 1- 1973-. US. English. New York Environmental Information Center, 292 Madison Avenue, New York NY 10017.

CA SELECTS. ENVIRONMENTAL POLLUTION. (CA SELECTS : ENVIRONMENTAL POLLUTION). VFOAT Environmental Pollution. VAT Chemical Abstracts Selects. Environmental Pollution. July 10, 1978-. 0160-9041. US. English. bw. $90.00. Chemical Abstracts Service, PO Box 3012, Columbus OH 43210. Tel (614)421-3600. Ed David W Weisgerber. CODEN CSPODW. Covers pollution of the environment by gaseous, liquid, solid and radioactive wastes, oil spills, nuclear fallout, runoff containing fertilizers from agricultural lands, and eutrophication of bodies of water.

CA SELECTS. WATER TREATMENT. *See Indexes/Abstracts.*

CALIDAD DEL AGUA - GUATEMALA. INSTITUTO GEOGRAFICO NACIONAL. Main/Corp Guatemala. Instituto Geografico Nacional. VFOAT Programa de Investigacion de Los Recursos de Agua de la Republica de Guatemala. No. 1-. GT. Spanish. ir. Av Las Americas 5 76 Zona 13, Guatemala Guatemala. LC TD231.G8. DD 363.61.

CALIFORNIA AIR QUALITY DATA. V. 8- 1976-. US. English. an. Air Resources Board, Technical Services Division, PO Box 2815, Sacramento CA 95812. LC TD883.5.C2. DD 553.9. NLM W1 CA285K.

CARBON DIOXIDE EFFECTS RESEARCH AND ASSESSMENT PROGRAM. CARBON DIOXIDE RESEARCH PROGRESS REPORT. Main/Corp United States. Dept. of Energy. Office of Health and Environmental Research. VFOAT Carbon Dioxide Effects Research Progress Report. 1978/79-. US. English. an. National Technical Information Service, 5285 Port Royal Road, Springfield VA 22161.

CATALOG OF INFORMATION ON WATER DATA. (CATALOG OF INFORMATION ON WATER DATA. INDEX TO WATER-DATA ACQUISITION). 0362-1928. US. English. an. US Geological Survey, Office of Water Data Coordination, 417 National Center, Reston VA 22092. LC TD223. DD 551.480974. *Catalog of Information on Water Data. Index to Water Quality Stations, Catalog of Information on Water Data. Index to Surface Water Stations.*

CATALOG OF RESEARCH PROJECTS - UNITED STATES DEPARTMENT OF THE INTERIOR OFFICE OF SALINE WATER. (CATALOG OF RESEARCH PROJECTS). Main/Corp United States. Office of Saline Water. Series/Titl Research and Development Report. 0093-3945. US. English. Office of Saline Water, Superintendent of Documents, US Government Printing Office, Washington DC 20402. LC TD478.3. DD 628.167072073.

CATALOGO NACIONAL DAS INSTITUICOES QUE ATUAM NA AREA DO MEIO AMBIENTE. 1981/82-. Portuguese. an. LC HC190.E5. DD 354.810082321025. *Cadastro Nacional das Instituicoes Que Atuam na Area do Meio Ambiente.*

CATALYST FOR ENVIRONMENT/ENERGY CEASED. VFOAT Catalyst. VAT Catalyst for Environment Energy. V. 6, No. 4- V. 7, No. 4. 0194-1445. Periodical. US. English. ir. Catalyst, 274 Madison Avenue, Room 1804, New York NY 10016. Tel (212)685-8310. Ind/Abst Energy Inf. Abstr., Environ. Abstr. LC TD172. DD 333.720973. *Catalyst for Environmental Quality, 0008-7688.*

CBS LUCHTVERONTREINIGING, METINGEN BUITENLUCHT. Series/Titl Milieustatistieken. VFOAT C.B.S. Luchtvereiniging, Metingen Buitenlucht. Dutch (summaries in English). an. 21.50. Staatsuitgeverij, The Hague Netherlands. LC TD883.7.N4.

CELA NEWSLETTER. *See Law.*

CHARACTERISTICS OF WASTES AND SOILS AFFECTING TRANSPORT OF RADIONUCLIDES THROUGH THE SOIL AND THEIR RELATIONSHIP TO WASTE MANAGEMENT. 1979-. US. English. an. Governemt Printing Office, Divison of Technical Information and Document Control, US Regulatory Commission, Washington DC 20555.

CHEMICAL ACTIVITIES STATUS REPORT. Series/Titl Toxics Integration Information Series. VFOAT CASR Toxics Integration Information Series. US. English. NLM WA 39. *EPA Chemical Activities Status Report.*

CHEMICAL AND PHYSICAL CHARACTERISTICS OF WATER IN ESTUARIES OF TEXAS. Began with Sept. 1967/Sept. 1968. 0748-0075. US. English. an. Texas Department of Water Resources, Box 13087, Austin TX 78711. LC TD224.T4. DD 333.91009764, 363.7394.

CHEMICAL & RADIATION WASTE LITIGATION REPORTER. VFOAT Chemical and Radiation Waste Litigation Reporter. Vol. 1, No. 1 (Dec. 1980)-. 0731-8839. Periodical. US. English. mo. $975.00. Chemical and Radiation Waste, 1519 Connecticut Avenue NW/Suite 200, Washington DC 20036. Tel (202)462-5755. Ed Neil J Cohen. LC KF3945.A59. DD 344.730462, 347.304462. bk rev. A publication of ISO pages including articles, decisions, developments and documents in all aspects of hazardous waste litigation. Indexed every 6 months.

CHIBA-KEN KANKYO HAKUSHO. Main/Corp Chiba-Ken (Japan). Kankyobu. 1974-. Japanese. ir. Chibe-ken Kankyobu 1-1, Ichibacho, Chiba 280 Japan. LC TD187.5J32. *Chiba-Ken Kogai Hakusho.*

CHIBA-KEN KOGAI KENKYUJO KENKYU HOKOKU. VFOAT Bulletin of Chiba Prefecutural Research Institute for Environmental Pollution. Japanese (summaries in English). ir. Chiba-ken Kogai Kenkyujo, 254 Iwasaki (290), Ichihara Japan. Ind/Abst Chem. Abstr. LC TD187.5.J32. CODEN CKHUDM.

CHUNG-KUO HUAN CHING KO HSUEH. VFOAT Zhongguo Huanjing Kexue. First published in 1981. Periodical. CH. Chinese. bm. 0.45. Post Office Peking, Peking China. LC TD4. DD 620.805. NLM W1.

CITIZENS' BULLETIN. 0229-1401. Periodical. CN. English. bm. Free. Citizens Bulletin/Information Directorate Environment Canada, 10th Floor/Fontaine Building, 200 Sacre Coeur Boulevard, Hull Quebec K1A 0H3 Canada. DD 363.700971.

CIVIC PUBLIC WORKS. VFOAT Public Works Reference Manual & Buyers Guide. Vol. 30, No. 5 (May 1978)-. 0829-772X. Periodical. CN. English. mo. Tel (416)596-5953. Ind/Abst Can. Bus. Index. DD 352.00720971. adv acc. Circ 13,500. (ctrl). Covers every aspect of the environment, including water supply, sewage treatment, with comprehensive and informative articles on highways, transportation, solid waste management, parks, public safety, public utilities, office equipment and systems. *Wastes Handling, 0315-1921; Civic, 0315-1972.*

CLEAN AIR. V. 1- Spring 1971-. 0300-5143. Periodical. UK. English. qt. $18.33. National Society for Clean Air, 136 North Street, Brighton BN1 1RG England. Tel 26313. Ed Jane Dunmore. Ind/Abst Excerpta Med., Coal Abstr., Int. Aerosp. Abstr., Biol. Abstr., Chem. Abstr., Bibliogr. Agric., Meteorol. Geoastrophys. Abstr., Pollut. Abstr. Indexes. LC TD881. DD 628.5305. NLM W1 CL122K. CODEN CLNABV. bk rev. adv acc. Circ 2,500. Contains feature articles, scientific and technical data, pollution abstracts, industrial news, book reviews, and international news. *Smokeless Air.*

CLEAN AIR CONFERENCE. 0077-5746. UK. English. 9.25. National Society for Clean Air, 136 North Street, Brighton Sussex, London BN1 1RG England. Tel (0273)26313. Ed Jane Dunmore. Ind/Abst Chem. Abstr. LC TD883.7.G7. DD 363.6. CODEN NSCAA9. bk rev. adv acc. Circ 500. Pollution control and related legal, policy, science and technology issues.

CLEAN WATER REPORT. V. 1- Jan. 1964-. 0009-8620. Periodical. US. English. bw. Business Publishers Inc, 951 Pershing Drive, Silver Spring MD 20910. Tel (301)587-6300. Ed Jaime Steve. NLM W1 CL123H. Report focusing on safe drinking water, water resources projects, water quality and effluent standards on national and local level.

CLEAN WATER; REPORT TO CONGRESS. Main/Corp United States. Environmental Protection Agency. 1973-. 0092-9433. US. English. Environmental Protection Agency, 401 M Street, Washington DC 20460. Ind/Abst GeoRef. LC TD223. DD 363.61. NLM W1 A E4C.

CLEANING MANAGEMENT MAGAZINE. 1964. Periodical. US. English. mo. $15.00. Harris Communications, 17911 C Sky Park Boulevard, Irvine CA 92714. Tel (714)770-5008. Ed R

Sanitation, Environmental Technology

Daniel Harris Jr and Teri Fivecoat-Wilhelm. adv acc. Circ 34,000. (ctrl). Edited for end-user managers and supervisors who are directly responsible for building maintenance and housekeeping operations in all types of buildings and institutions.

CLEAR AIR ACT. ANNUAL REPORT CEASED. (THE CLEAN AIR ACT; ANNUAL REPORT). Main/Corp Canada. Air Pollution Control Directorate. VFOAT Loi sur la Lutte Contre la Pollution Atmospherique, Rapport Annuel . . . Sur les Operations Relatives a la loi sur la Lutte contre la Pollution Atmospherique. VAT Rapport Annuel sur les Operations Relatives a la Loi sur la Lutte Contre la Pollution Atmospherique. 1972/73-. 0381-3177. CN. English (French). an. Free. Department of the Environment, Place Vincent Massey/Twelth Floor, Ottawa Ontario K1A 0H3 Canada. LC Law. DD 344.710463.

COASTAL OCEAN POLLUTION ASSESSMENT NEWS. (COASTAL OCEAN POLLUTION ASSESSMENT NEWS : MAN AND THE MARINE ENVIRONMENT). VFOAT C.O.P.A.S. Vol. 1, No. 1 (Fall 1980)-. 0738-2472. Periodical. US. English. ir. Marine Sciences Research Center, State University of New York, Stony Brook NY 11794. Ind/Abst GeoRef.

COLLECTION ECOLOGIE APPLIQUEE ET SCIENCES DE L'ENVIRONNEMENT. VFOAT Ecologie Appliquee et Sciences de Lenvironnement. Monographic Series. French. ir.

COLORADO AIR QUALITY DATA REPORT. 1978-. US. English. an. LC TD883.5.C6. DD 363.7392209788. Report to the Public, 0097-9996.

COMMON SENSE. No. 1- Sept. 1978-. 0709-4191. Periodical. CN. English. bm. $8.00. Common Sense, PO Box 446, New Denve British Columbia V0G 1S0 Canada. Tel (604)358-7764. DD 301.3105.

COMMON SENSE PEST CONTROL QUARTERLY. Vol. 1, No. 1 (Fall 1984)-. 8756-7881. Periodical. US. English. qt. $45.00. Bio Integral Resource Center, PO Box 7414, Berkeley CA 94707. Tel (415)524-2567. Ed William Olkowski, Helga Olkowski and Sheila Daar. DD 648. bk rev. Circ 500. Describes least-toxic methods for managing insect, weed, disease and rodent pests; written for non-technical readers.

THE COMMUNITIES R & D PROGRAMME : RADIOACTIVE WASTE MANAGEMENT AND STORAGE, ANNUAL PROGRESS REPORT. Main/Corp Commission of the European Communities. Directorate-General for Research, Science, and Education. VFOAT Nuclear Science and Technology. 1st- 1977-. English. ir. European Community Information Service, 2100 M Street/Suite 707, Washington DC 20037. LC TD898. DD 363.6.

COMPOST SCIENCE-LAND UTILIZATION. V. 19- Jan./Feb. 1978-. 0160-7413. Periodical. US. English. bm. Compost Science, 0010-4388.

COMPREHENSIVE ENVIRONMENT, HEALTH, AND SAFETY PROGRAM REPORT. Main/Corp United States. Dept. of Energy. Assistant Secretary for Environment. Office of Program Coordination. 0192-270X. US. English. an. $5.25. National Technical Information Service, US Department of Commerce, 5285 Port Royal Road, Springfield VA 22161. LC TD195.E49. DD 614.7.

COMPUTERS IN THE ENVIRONMENTAL SCIENCES. 1971-. 0300-0842. UK. English. an $2.00. School of Environmental Science University of East Anglia, Geo Abstracts, Norwich NOR88C England. Ed J R Tarrant. LC TD1. DD 620.80285425. NLM Q 223 C738. Computers in Geography.

CONNECTICUT AIR QUALITY SUMMARY. Main/Corp Connecticut. Dept. of Environmental Protection. 0147-3557. US. English. an. Connecticut Department of Environmental Protection, State Office Building, Hartford CT 06106. LC TD883.5.C8. DD 363.6.

CONNIE DATA SUMMMARIES. Main/Corp Texas. Air Control Board. 0145-5907. US. English. an. 8520 Shoal Creek Boulevard, Austin TX 78758. LC TD883.5.T4. DD 363.6.

CONTAMINACION AMBIENTAL. Year 1- (No. 1-). Periodical. CK. Spanish. sa. University Pontificia Bolivariana Centro, De Invest le Desarrollo Integ Cidi, Medellin Colombia.

CONTROL OF WASTE AND WATER POLLUTION FROM COAL-FIRED POWER PLANTS. 2nd- 1978-. US. English. an. Environmental Protection Agency, Office of Research and Development, Office of Energy Minerals and Industry, Industrial Environmental Research Laboratory, Springfield VA 22161. Control of Waste and Water Pollution from Power Plant Flue Gas Cleaning Systems.

CONTROL OF WASTE AND WATER POLLUTION FROM POWER PLANT FLUE GAS CLEANING SYSTEMS. 1976-. Periodical. US. English. an. Environmental Protection Agency, Office of Research and Development, Office of Energy, Minerals and Industry, Industrial Environmental Research Laboratory, Springfield VA 22161.

THE COST OF CLEAN AIR AND CLEAN WATER. Main/Corp United States. Environmental Protection Agency. 1979-. 0275-0384. US. English. an. Superintendent of Documents, US Government Printing Office, Washington DC 20402. LC HC110.P55. DD 338.43363730973. Cost of Clean Air, Economics of Clean Water.

COURSE ANNOUNCEMENT - DIVISION OF TRAINING. NATIONAL INSTITUTE FOR OCCUPATIONAL SAFETY AND HEALTH. See Yearbooks, Almanacs, Directories.

CUMULATIVE INDEX OF THE JOURNAL OF THE AIR POLLUTION CONTROL ASSOCIATION. See Indexes/Abstracts.

DAIRY AND FOOD SANITATION. See Agriculture - Dairy & Related Technologies.

DAMMING THE SOLID WASTE STREAM, THE BEGINNING OF SOURCE REDUCTION IN MINNESOTA. (DAMMING THE SOLID WASTE STREAM : THE BEGINNING OF SOURCE REDUCTION IN MINNESOTA). Main/Corp Minnesota. Pollution Control Agency. 1st- 1975-. 0361-3569. US. English. an. 1935 West County Road/B2, St Paul MN 55113. LC TD788.4.M5. DD 363.6.

DATEN ZUR UMWELT. See Statistics.

DEPARTMENT OF THE ENVIRONMENT REPORT. Main/Corp Ireland. Dept. of the Environment. VFOAT An Roinn Comhshaoil Tuarascail. 1977-. IE. English. an. 1.20. Government Publications Sale Office, Government Printing Office Arcade, Dublin 1 Ireland. LC HD4150.3. DD 354.417008232106. Tuarascail.

DESERTIFICATION CONTROL. 0379-2455. Periodical. English. sa. LC GB611. DD 333.73. Desertification Control Bulletin.

DETAILED SURFACE WATER QUALITY DATA. NORTHWEST TERRITORIES. VFOAT Donnees Detaillees sur la Qualite des eaux de Surface. Territoires du Nord-Ouest. 1974/1976-. 0823-4833. CN. English (prefatory material in French). be. LC TD227.N58. DD 363.73942097192.

DETAILED TECHNICAL PLAN FOR THE GREAT LAKES ENVIRONMENTAL RESEARCH LABORATORY. Main/Corp Great Lakes Environmental Research Laboratory. VFOAT Detailed Technical Plan for Glerl. US. English. an. 2300 Washtenaw Avenue, Ann Arbor MI 48104.

DEVELOPMENTS IN ENVIRONMENTAL MODELLING. 1-. 0167-8892. Monographic Series. US. English. ir. Elsevier Scientific Publishing Company, 52 Vanderbilt Avenue, New York NY 10017. Ind/Abst Chem. Abstr. CODEN DEMODW.

DICTAMEN DEL PRESUPUESTO DEL SERVICIO AUTONOMO NACIONAL DE ACUEDUCTOS Y ALCANTARILLADOS. Spanish. ir. LC HD4465.H7. DD 354.728300871.

DIGEST OF ENVIRONMENTAL POLLUTION AND WATER STATISTICS. See Statistics.

THE DIGESTER, OVER THE SPILLWAY. Periodical. US. English. Illinois Environmental Agency, Operator Certification Section, 2200 Churchill Road, Springfield IL 62706. LC TD524.I3. Digester, 0362-8795; Over the Spillway.

DIRECTORY OF CANADIAN ENVIRONMENTAL EXPERTS. See Yearbooks, Almanacs, Directories.

DIRECTORY OF ENVIRONMENTAL CONSULTANTS. See Yearbooks, Almanacs, Directories.

DIRECTORY OF PUBLISHED PROCEEDINGS. SERIES PCE - POLLUTION CONTROL - ECOLOGY. See Yearbooks, Almanacs, Directories.

DIVISION OF ENVIRONMENTAL CONTROL TECHNOLOGY PROGRAM. Began with 1976/77. 0197-2731. US. English. an. National Technical Information Service, 5285 Port Royal Road, Springfield VA 22161. LC TD195.E49. DD 353.0082321.

EAST END ENVIRONMENT. Periodical. US. English.

EAU DU QUEBEC CEASED. V. 1-16, No 2. 0315-2081. Periodical. CN. French. qt. Association Quebecoise des Techniques de l'Eau, 6075 Quest rue Sherbrooke, Montreal Quebec H4A 1Y2 Canada. Ind/Abst Life Sci. Collect., Excerpta Med., Point Repere, GeoRef, Biol. Abstr., Chem. Abstr. CODEN EAQUDJ.

ECO 3. VFOAT Eco Trois. No. 96 (Feb. 1981)-. 0247-8277. Periodical. FR. French. mo. 182.00. Editions de Presse, d'Information Economique, 20 rue Richer, 75441 Paris Cedex 09 France. Ind/Abst Predicasts, Excerpta Med., Energy Res. Abstr. NLM W1 EC909D. Nuisances & Environnement.

ECO/LOG WEEK. Began publication in 1972. 0315-0380. Periodical. CN. English. wk. 347.00. Corpus Information Service Ltd, 1450 Don Mills Road, Don Mills Ontario M3B 2X7 Canada. Tel (416)445-6641. Ed William M Glenn. bk rev. Newsletter covering waste management and industrial pollution control technology, environmental concerns, toxic chemicals, acid rain, health and safety.

ECOLOGY USA. See Biology.

ECONOMIC AND TECHNICAL REPORT EPS 3-AP CEASED. (ECONOMIC AND TECHNICAL REVIEW REPORT). Main/Corp Canada. Air Pollution Control Directorate. VAT Technical Appraisal. Air Pollution Control Directorate, Technical Appraisal Report EPS 3-AP, Revision Economique et Technique. Rapport EPS 3-AP. Began publication in 1972. Ceased in 1982/83. 0706-4489. Monographic Series. CN. English (includes some Nos. in French). Technical Appraisal Report, 0706-4489.

ECONOMIC IMPACT ANALYSIS PROGRAM, THE ANNUAL REPORT. (ECONOMIC IMPACT ANALYSIS PROGRAM, THE . . . ANNUAL REPORT). 8755-7053. US. English. an. Illinois Institute of Natural Resources, 309 West Washington, Chicago IL 60606. Ed Niels Herlevsen. LC TD194.6. DD 330.9773043. Economic Impact Studies, the . . . Year in Review, 8755-7045.

ECOS. No. 1- Aug. 1974-. 0311-4546. Periodical. AT. English. qt. $5.17. R Hill & Son Limited, 117 Wellington Street, Windsor Victoria 3181 Australia. Tel 03/51 1531. Ind/Abst Coal Abstr.

EDF LETTER. See Conservation & Natural Resources.

EFFECTS OF POLLUTION ABATEMENT ON INTERNATIONAL TRADE. (THE EFFECTS OF POLLUTION ABATEMENT ON INTERNATIONAL TRADE). Main/Corp United States. Dept. of Commerce. 1st- 1973-. 0093-9692. US. English. an. Superintendent of Documents, US Government Printing Office, Washington DC 20402. LC HC110.E5. DD 382. NLM W1 EF33.

EIS. (EIS. DIGESTS OF ENVIRONMENTAL IMPACT STATEMENTS). VFOAT Digests of Environmental Impact Statements. VAT Environmental Impact Statements. V. 3, No. 7- July 1979-. 0364-1074. Periodical. US. English. mo. $200.00. Cambridge Scientific Abstracts, 5161 River Road, Washington DC 20016. Tel (301)951-1400. Ed Roberta Gorinson. Ind/Abst Energy Res. Abstr., Coal Abstr. NLM ZWA 670 E105. CODEN EEISDZ. Abstracts environmental impact statements from the environmental protection agency including both positive and negative impacts. EIS, 0364-1074.

EIS ANNUAL REVIEW. VAT Environmental Impact Statement Annual Review. V. 1- 1978-. 0190-471X. Periodical. US. English. an. 2100 M Street NW, Washington DC 20037. LC TD194.6. DD 333.7.

EIS CUMULATIVE. VFOAT EIS. VAT Environmental Impact Statements Cumulative. 1977-. 0190-0250. US. English. an. Information Resources Press, 2100 M Street Northwest/Suite 316,

Sanitation, Environmental Technology

Washington DC 20037. **LC** TD194.6. **DD** 333.7. Available on Computer-Searchable Tape.

ELSNERS HANDBUCH FUR STADTISCHEN INGENIEURBAU. **VFOAT** Handbuch fur Stadtischen Ingenieurbau. 1973-. German. ir. O Elsner Verlagsgesellschaft, Schofferstrasse 15, 6100 Darmstadt West Germany. **LC** TD159.A1.

END OF YEAR REPORT. REGIONAL PLANS ASSESSMENT. See Public Administration.

ENERGY AND ENVIRONMENT ANNUAL REPORT. See Energy.

ENERGY AND THE ENVIRONMENT (OAK RIDGE, TENN.). See Energy.

ENFO. 1974-. 0276-9956. Periodical. US. English. bm. $25.00. Environmental Info Center, 1203 Orange Avenue, Winter Park FL 32789. **Tel** (305)644-5377. **Ed** Gerald Grow. bk rev. adv acc. **Circ** 1,200. Environmental studies and issues affecting Florida. *Enfo Newsletter.*

ENGINEERING, HYDROLOGY, AND WATER QUALITY ANALYSIS OF DETENTION/RETENTION SITES. July 1979-. US. English. an. South Florida Water Management District, 3301 Gun Club Road, West Palm Beach FL 33406. **LC** TD224.F6. **DD** 353.97590082325.

ENVIROLINE USER'S MANUAL. 0270-0751. US. English. an. $45.00. Eic, 48 West 38th Street, New York NY 10018. **Tel** (212)944-8500. Manual giving search strategies and keyterm lists to aid in use of Enviorline.

ENVIRONMENT. V. 11- Jan./Feb. 1969-. 0013-9157. Periodical. US. English. mo. $6.00. H D Reid Educational Foundation, 4000 Albemarle Street NW, Washington DC 20016. **Ind/Abst** Book Rev. Index, Can. Environ., Excerpta Med., Coal Abstr., GeoRef, Int. Aerosp. Abstr., Abr. Read. Guide, Bibliogr. Agric., Biol. Abstr., Chem. Abstr., Sel. Water Resour. Abstr., Energy Res. Abstr., Gen. Sci. Index, Nucl. Sci. Abstr., Energy Inf. Abstr., Environ. Abstr., Pop. Mag. Rev., Read. Guide Period. Lit., Curr. Index J. Educ. **LC** UF767. **DD** 301.31. **CODEN** ENVTAR. *Scientist and Citizen.*

ENVIRONMENT. **VFOAT** Annual Editions: Environment. 2nd- Ed. 0272-9008. Periodical. US. English. an. $8.95. Dushkin Publishing Group Inc, Sluice Dock, Guilford CT 06437. **Tel** (203)453-4351. **Ed** John Allan. **LC** TD172. **DD** 304.2. An updated collection of public press articles covering current issues in environment. Includes topic guide and complete index. *Readings in Environment, 0196-4542.*

ENVIRONMENT ABSTRACTS ANNUAL. See Indexes/Abstracts.

ENVIRONMENT BULLETIN (SASKATCHEWAN). Main/Corp Saskatchewan. Saskatchewan Environment. Public Information and Education Branch. **VAT** Environment Bulletin (Regina). May 1981-. 0714-8410. Periodical. CN. English. ir. Saskatchewan Department of Environment, 5th Floor/1855 Victoria Avenue, Regina Saskatchewan 54P 3V5 Canada. **DD** 363.70097124. *Saskatchewan Environment Bulletin, 0711-3080.*

ENVIRONMENT FILM REVIEW. (THE ENVIRONMENT FILM REVIEW). V. 1- , 1972-. Periodical. US. English. an. $20.00. Environment Information Center, Film Reference Department, 48 West 38th Street, New York NY 10018. **LC** GF1. **DD** 301.31.

ENVIRONMENT INDEX. See Indexes/Abstracts.

ENVIRONMENT INTERNATIONAL. Began in 1978. 0160-4120. Periodical. UK. English. bm. Pergamon Press, 395 Sawmill River Road, Elmsford NY 10523. **Ind/Abst** Electron. Commun. Abstr. J., ISMEC Bull., Eng. Index, Life Sci. Collect., Can. Environ., Sel. Water Resour. Abstr., Excerpta Med., Coal Abstr., Energy Inf. Abstr., Environ. Abstr., GeoRef, Biol. Abstr., Chem. Abstr., Energy Res. Abstr. **LC** TD169. **DD** 363.7005. **NLM** W1 EN98NV. **CODEN** ENVIDV.

ENVIRONMENT MIDWEST CEASED. Ceased with Dec. 14, 1981. 0364-2151. Periodical. US. English. mo. US Environmental Protection Agency, Office of Public Affairs, 230 South Dearborn, Chicago IL 60604. **Ind/Abst** Energy Inf. Abstr., Environ. Abstr. *Region Five, Public Report.*

THE ENVIRONMENT MONTHLY. June 1969-. 0013-919X. Periodical. US. English. mo. $35.00. Environment League Inc, 284 Alexander Avenue, Bronx NY 10454. **NLM** W1 EN98P. Available on microfilm from University Microfilms International.

ENVIRONMENT NEWS (BOSTON, MASS.). (ENVIRONMENT NEWS). 0364-1317. Periodical. US. English. mo. Enviromental Protection Agency, JFK Federal Building Road 2203, Boston MA 02203.

ENVIRONMENT PROBE. No. 55- June 1975-. 0381-646X. Periodical. CN. English. Free to Members, Membership $5.00. Saskatoon Environmental Society, PO Box 1372, Saskatoon Saskatchewan S7K 3N9 Canada. **DD** 301.31097124. *Probe, 0316-0033.*

ENVIRONMENT PROTECTION BOARD GAS PIPELINE NEWSLETTER. **VFOAT** Gas Pipeline Newsletter. Feb. 1971-. 0384-8140. Periodical. CN. English. ir. Environment Protection Board, 528 St James Street South, Winnipeg Manitoba R3G 3J4 Canada. **DD** 333.82.

ENVIRONMENT PROTECTION ENGINEERING. V. 1- 1975-. 0324-8828. English (summaries in German, Polish, and Russian). qt. Wrocaw Technical University, Wydrz Wyspianskiego 27, Wrocaw Poland. **Tel** 20-37-38. **Ed** Tomasz Z Winnicki and Alicja M Mika. **Ind/Abst** Coal Abstr., GeoRef, Chem. Abstr., Excerpta Med. **LC** TD169. **DD** 628.505. **CODEN** EPEND9. bk rev. (ctrl). Covers water purification, wastewater treatment, emission abatement, dedusting processes, systems of air and water pollution control, ecological problems and environmental economy.

ENVIRONMENT REPORT. V. 1- May 7, 1970-. 0013-9203. Periodical. US. English. sm. $390.00. Trends Publishing Inc, 233 National Press Building, Washington DC 20045. **Tel** (202)393-0031. **Ed** A Kranish. bk rev. (ctrl). General environmental topics - water pollution, air pollution, pesticides etc. Also book reports and upcoming items of interests.

ENVIRONMENT REPORTER. 0013-9211. Periodical. US. English. wk. Bureau of National Affairs Inc, 1231-25th Street NW, Washington DC 20037. **Tel** (301)258-1033.

ENVIRONMENT, SAFETY, HEALTH AT DOE FACILITIES. Main/Corp United States. Dept. of Energy. Assistant Secretary for Environmental Protection Safety, and Emergency Preparedness. **VFOAT** Environment, Safety, Health at D.O.E. Facilities. **VAT** Environment, Safety, Health at Department of Energy Facilities. Fiscal Year-1980-. 0738-3746. US. English. an. National Technical Information Service, US Department of Commerce, 5285 Port Royal Road, Springfield VA 22161. *Operational Accidents & Radiation Exposures at DOE Facilities, 0276-7880.*

ENVIRONMENT VIEWS. V. 1- Apr./May 1978-. 0701-9637. Periodical. CN. English. bm. Department of the Environment, 9820-106th Street, Edmonton Alberta T5K 2J6 Canada. **Tel** (403)427-6310. **Ind/Abst** Can. Environ., Energy Inf. Abstr., Environ. Abstr. *Environment News, 0701-6840.*

ENVIRONMENTAL ACTION. V. 1- Feb. 19, 1970-. 0013-922X. Periodical. US. English. bm. $20.00. Environmental Action, 1525 New Hampshire Avenue NE, Washington DC 20036. **Tel** (202)745-4870. **Ed** Rose Avdette, and Jeff Johnson. **Ind/Abst** Coal Abstr., Energy Inf. Abstr., Environ. Abstr., Altern. Press Index, Public Aff. Inf. Serv. Bull., Environ. Period. Bibliogr., Environ. Index. **LC** HC110.E5. **DD** 301.310973. bk rev. adv acc. **Circ** 20,000. News journal on environmental issues, including toxics, energy, nuclear weapons, pollution, politics, agriculture, urban, transportation, etc. *Rodale's Environment Action Bulletin, 0048-850X.*

ENVIRONMENTAL ASSESSMENT. ELECTRIC HYBRID VEHICLE RESEARCH, DEVELOPMENT AND DEMONSTRATION PROGRAM. Main/Corp United States. Dept. of Energy. Office of Conservation and Solar Applications. **VFOAT** Electric Hybrid Vehicle Research, Development and Demonstration Program. 0197-1956. US. English. an. NTIS, US Department of Commerce, 5285 Port Royal Road, Springfield VA 22161. Available on microfiche from NTIS.

ENVIRONMENTAL ASSESSMENT OF THE ALASKAN CONTINENTAL SHELF. ANNUAL REPORTS OF PRINCIPAL INVESTIGATORS. (ENVIRONMENTAL ASSESSMENT OF THE ALASKAN CONTINENTAL SHELF. ANNUAL REPORTS OF PRINCIPAL INVESTIGATORS FOR THE YEAR ENDING . . .). **VFOAT** Annual Reports of Principal Investigators for the Year Ending . . . . Began with 1976. 0748-1527. US. English. an. United States Department of Commerce, National Oceanic and Atmospheric Administration, Office of Marine Pollution Assessment, Rockville MD 20852. **LC** TD194.6. **DD** 333.918. Vols. for (1980, V. 7-) distributed to depository libraries in microfiche.

ENVIRONMENTAL ASSESSMENT OF THE ALASKAN CONTINENTAL SHELF. EXECUTIVE SUMMARY. **VFOAT** Executive Summary. Began with Apr. 1976-Mar. 1977. 0748-1519. US. English. an. US Department of Commerce, National Oceanic and Atmospheric Administration, Boulder CO 80302. **LC** GC85.2.A4. **DD** 333.8231509798.

ENVIRONMENTAL BIOLOGY; REPORT. See Biology.

ENVIRONMENTAL CONTROL NEWS FOR SOUTHERN INDUSTRY. **VFOAT** Southern Pollution Control Newsletter. 1971. 0013-9238. Periodical. US. English. mo. $24.00. Williams and Associates, 3637 Park Avenue, Suite 224, Memphis TN 38111. **Tel** (901)458-4696. **Ed** E F Williams. bk rev. adv acc. **Circ** 300. (ctrl). Industrial pollution control newsletter reporting regulatory, legislative, and technical developments plus activities of environmentalists within the South.

ENVIRONMENTAL CONTROL TECHNOLOGY ACTIVITIES OF THE DEPARTMENT OF ENERGY. 1976/77-. 0192-8856. US. English. an. $6.25. National Technical Information Center Service, US Department of Commerce, 5285 Port Royal Road, Springfield VA 22161. **LC** HC110.E5. **DD** 301.310973.

ENVIRONMENTAL DEVELOPMENT PLAN. BIOMASS ENERGY SYSTEMS. See Energy.

ENVIRONMENTAL DEVELOPMENT PLAN. COAL LIQUEFACTION. Main/Corp United States. Office of the Assistant Secretary for Fossil Energy. **VFOAT** Coal Liquefaction. Aug. 1980-. US. English. US Department of Energy, Office of the Assistant Secretary for Fossil Energy, 5285 Port Royal Road, Springfield VA 22161. *Environmental Development Plan (EDP). Coal Liquefaction Program.*

ENVIRONMENTAL DEVELOPMENT PLAN. DECONTAMINATION AND DECOMMISSIONING. Main/Corp United States. Dept. of Energy. Office of the Assistant Secretary for Environment. **VFOAT** Decontamination and Decommissioning. July 1979-. Periodical. US. English. US Department of Energy, Office of the Assistant Secretary for the Environment, 5285 Port Royal Road, Springfield VA 22161. *Environmental Development Plan (EDP). Decontamination Decommissioning.*

ENVIRONMENTAL DEVELOPMENT PLAN. URANIUM MINING, MILLING, AND CONVERSION. Main/Corp United States. Dept. of Energy. Office of the Assistant Secretary for Environment. **VFOAT** Uranium Mining, Milling, and Conversion. US. English. US Department of Energy, Office of the Assistant Secretary for the Environment, 5285 Port Royal Road, Springfield VA 22161.

ENVIRONMENTAL EDUCATION. UK. English. Heinemann Educational Books Ltd, 22 Bedford Square, London WC1B 3HH England. **LC** GF28.G7. **DD** 301.31071042.

ENVIRONMENTAL EDUCATION AND INFORMATION. See Education (General).

ENVIRONMENTAL EFFECTS OF DREDGING : INFORMATION EXCHANGE BULLETIN. Vol. D-83-2 (May 1983)-. Periodical. US. English. qt. **Ind/Abst** Fluidex.

ENVIRONMENTAL ENGINEERING & POLLUTION CONTROL. (ENVIRONMENTAL ENGINEERING & POLLUTION CONTROL MICROFORM). **VFOAT** Environmental Engineering and Pollution Control. Vol. 1, No. 1-. 0732-7188. Monographic Series. US. English. ir. $600.00. Comtex, 850 3rd Avenue, New York NY 10022.

ENVIRONMENTAL ENGINEERING NEWSLETTER CEASED. Began with Vol. 1, Sept. 1971. Ceased with Vol. 10, No. 12. 0315-0011. Periodical. CN. English. mo. $30.00. Canadian Engineering Publications, 46 St Clair Avenue East, Toronto Ontario M4T 1N2 Canada.

Sanitation, Environmental Technology

ENVIRONMENTAL ETHICS. See Ethics.

ENVIRONMENTAL FINANCE. See Business - Public Finance.

ENVIRONMENTAL FORUM (WASHINGTON, D.C.). (THE ENVIRONMENTAL FORUM). Vol. 1, No. 1 (May 1982)-. 0731-5732. Periodical. US. English. mo. $48.00. Environmental Law Institute, 1616 P Street NW/Suite 200, Washington DC 20036. **Tel** (202)328-5150. **Ed** Morris A Ward. **LC** KF3775.A15. **DD** 363.700973. bk rev. **Circ** 2,000. Feature and analysis coverage of timely environmental pollution control, and natural resources public policies, for professionals in the field (lawyers, engineers, public administrators, etc).

ENVIRONMENTAL HEALTH CRITERIA. 1-. 0250-863X. Monographic Series. SZ. English. ir. World Health Organization, 49 Sheridan Avenue, Albany NY 12210. **Tel** (518)436-9686. **Ind/Abst** Excerpta Med., Chem. Abstr. NLM W1 EN983. **CODEN** EHCRDN.

ENVIRONMENTAL HEALTH PERSPECTIVES. Periodical. US. English. bm. Government Printing Office, Washington DC 20402. **Tel** (202)783-3238. **Ind/Abst** Index Med., Pollut. Abstr. Indexes, Sci. Cit. Index, Abr. Ed., Index U.S. Gov. Period., Hospit. Lit. Index.

ENVIRONMENTAL HEALTH REVIEW. V. 15- Spring 1971-. 0319-6771. Periodical. CN. English. qt. $7.74. Canadian Institute of Public Health Inspectors, Box 1280 Postal Station B, Burlington Ontario LTP 359 Canada. **Ed** D Stronach and R Hart. NLM W1 EN984AC. bk rev. adv acc. **Circ** 1,000. Topics of public health concerns; includes disease control, pollution, food poisoning, swimming pools, water and wastewater and occupational health. Canadian Sanitarian, 0527-9747.

ENVIRONMENTAL IMPACT ASSESSMENT REVIEW. VFOAT EIA Review. V. 1- Mar. 1980-. 0195-9255. Periodical. US. English. qt. $80.00. Elsevier Science Publishing Company Inc, 52 Vanderbilt Avenue, New York 10017. **Tel** (212)916-1050. **Ind/Abst** Electron. Commun. Abstr. J., ISMEC Bull., Pollut. Abstr. Indexes, Saf. Sci. Abstr. J., Excerpta Med., Energy Inf. Abstr., Environ. Abstr., Ecol. Abstr., Geophys. Abstr., Ref. Z., Eng. Index, Energy Res. Abstr. **LC** TD194.6. **DD** 333.710973. NLM W1 EN984Q. **CODEN** EIARDK.

ENVIRONMENTAL IMPACT NEWS. V. 1- Jan. 1975-. 0148-8317. Periodical. US. English. mo. $35.00. Technomic Publishing Co Inc, 265 Post Road West, Westport CT 06880. **Ind/Abst** Energy Res. Abstr.

ENVIRONMENTAL INFORMATION SYSTEMS DIRECTORY. See Yearbooks, Almanacs, Directories.

ENVIRONMENTAL LAW AND PRACTICE. See Law.

ENVIRONMENTAL LAW HANDBOOK. See Law.

ENVIRONMENTAL LAW (NORTHWESTERN SCHOOL OF LAW). See Law.

ENVIRONMENTAL LAW REPORTER. See Law.

ENVIRONMENTAL LEGISLATION. See Law.

ENVIRONMENTAL MANAGEMENT. See Conservation & Natural Resources.

ENVIRONMENTAL MEDICINE : ANNUAL REPORT OF THE RESEARCH INSTITUTE OF ENVIRONMENTAL MEDICINE, NAGOYA UNIVERSITY. See Medicine.

ENVIRONMENTAL MONITORING AND ECOLOGICAL STUDIES PROGRAM. Main/Corp Northern States Power Company. Engineering Vice Presidential Staff Dept. VFOAT Annual Report of the Environmental Monitoring and Ecological Studies Program. 1970-. Periodical. US. English. ir. **LC** TD877.5. **DD** 628.

ENVIRONMENTAL MONITORING AT MAJOR U.S. ENERGY RESEARCH & DEVELOPMENT ADMINISTRATION CONTRACTOR SITES. Main/Corp United States. Energy Research and Development Administration. Division of Safety, Standards, & Compliance. 0148-6004. US. English. an. $18.75. National Technical Information Service, 5285 Port Royal Road, Springfield VA 22161. **LC** TD195.E4. **DD** 363.6.

ENVIRONMENTAL MONITORING OF THE SPRUCE BUDWORM SPRAY PROGRAM IN NEWFOUNDLAND. VFOAT Environmental Monitoring. VAT Final Report - Environmental Monitoring Committee, Final Report of the Environmental Monitoring Committee. 0713-1690. Periodical. CN. English. an. Department of Consumer Affairs and Environment, 95 Bonaventure Avenue, St Johns Newfoundland A1C 5T7 Canada. **DD** 354.7180082328.

ENVIRONMENTAL MONITORING REPORT, UNITED STATES DEPARTMENT OF ENERGY, PADUCAH GASEOUS DIFFUSION PLANT. See Energy.

ENVIRONMENTAL MUTAGENESIS. 0192-2521. Periodical. US. English. bm. Alan R Liss Inc, 41 East 11th Street, New York NY 10003. **Tel** (212)741-2515. **Ind/Abst** Life Sci. Collect., Excerpta Med., Coal Abstr., Index Med., Biol. Abstr., Chem. Abstr., Bibliogr. Agric., Energy Res. Abstr., Sci. Cit. Index, Abr. Ed. **LC** QH465.C5. **DD** 575.292. NLM W1 EN984UN. **CODEN** ENMUDM.

ENVIRONMENTAL NEWS. Periodical. English. ir.

ENVIRONMENTAL NOTICE BULLETIN. 0740-5847. Periodical. US. English. wk. $12.00. Environmental Notice Bulletin, Department of Environmental Conservation, Albany NY 12233.

ENVIRONMENTAL PERIODICALS BIBLIOGRAPHY : INDEXED ARTICLE TITLES. See Indexes/Abstracts.

ENVIRONMENTAL POLLUTION & CONTROL. VAT Environmental Pollution and Control. 0364-4936. Periodical. US. English. wk. National Technical Information Service, 5285 Port Royal Road, Springfield VA 22161. **Ind/Abst** Bull. Inst. Paper Chem.

ENVIRONMENTAL POLLUTION. SERIES A. ECOLOGICAL AND BIOLOGICAL. (ENVIRONMENTAL POLLUTION. SERIES A, ECOLOGICAL AND BIOLOGICAL). Began with Jan. 1980 issue. 0143-1471. Periodical. UK. English. mo. 202.00 Domestic, 225.00 Foreign. Elseiver Applied Science Publishers, Crown House, Linton Road, Barking Essex IG11 8JU England. **Tel** 01 594 7272. **Ind/Abst** Eng. Index Annu., Eng. Index Mon., Eng. Index Bioeng. Abstr., Life Sci. Collect., Excerpta Med., Coal Abstr., Energy Inf. Abstr., Environ. Abstr., Biol. Abstr., Chem. Abstr., Energy Res. Abstr., Biol. Agric. Index, Sel. Water Resour. Abstr., Sci. Cit. Index, Abr. Ed., Pet. Abstr., Eng. Index. **LC** QP82.2.P6. **DD** 574.5222. NLM W1 EN984XFB. **CODEN** EPEBD7. bk rev. adv acc. Concerned with the biological effects of pollution and includes research papers on ecological effects on all types of environmental pollution and pollution control. Environmental Pollution.

ENVIRONMENTAL POLLUTION. SERIES B. CHEMICAL AND PHYSICAL. (ENVIRONMENTAL POLLUTION. SERIES B, CHEMICAL AND PHYSICAL). VFOAT Chemical and Physical. Began with Vol. 1, No. 1 (Jan./March 1980). 0143-148X. Periodical. UK. English. ir. 135.00 Domestic, 150.00 Foreign. Elsevier Applied Science Publishers, Crown House, Linton Road, Barking Essex IG11 8JU England. **Tel** 01 594 7272. **Ed** Kenneth Mellonby. **Ind/Abst** Eng. Index Annu., Eng. Index Mon., Eng. Index, Eng. Index Bioeng. Abstr., Eng. Index Energy Abstr., Life Sci. Collect., Excerpta Med., Coal Abstr., GeoRef, Int. Aerosp. Abstr., Biol. Abstr., Chem. Abstr., Energy Res. Abstr., Sel. Water Resour. Abstr., Pollut. Abstr. Indexes, Sci. Cit. Index, Abr. Ed. NLM W1 EN984XG. **CODEN** EPSPDH. bk rev. adv acc. Concerned with the chemical and physical aspects of pollution and includes research papers on the distribution of pollutants, and new techniques for their study and measurement. Environmental Pollution.

ENVIRONMENTAL PROGRAM ADMINISTRATORS. Main/Corp United States. Environmental Protection Agency. Office of Regional and Intergovernmental Operations. 0099-2275. US. English. an. Environmental Protection Agency, Regional and Intergovernmental Operations, 401 M Street, Washington DC 20460. **LC** TD12. **DD** 353.008232.

ENVIRONMENTAL PROGRESS. Vol. 1, No. 1 (Feb. 1982)-. 0278-4491. Periodical. US. English. qt. $50.00. American Institute of Chemical Engineers, 345 East 47 Street, New York NY 10017. **Tel** (212)705-7338. **Ed** Gary F Bennett. **Ind/Abst** Eng. Index Mon., Eng. Index Bioeng. Abstr., Eng. Index Energy Abstr., Coal Abstr., Chem. Abstr., Eng. Index Annu. **LC** TD1. **DD** 628.54605. **CODEN** ENVPDI. adv acc. **Circ** 3,084. Reports advances of interest to the chemical and environmental engineer concerning pollution as related to water, atmosphere, liquid and solid wastes.

ENVIRONMENTAL PROTECTION AGENCY HEADQUARTERS VIDEOTAPE CATALOG. Main/Corp United States. Environmental Protection Agency. Office of Public Affairs. VFOAT Videotape Catalog. 0747-6523. US. English. **LC** TD171. **DD** 016.363700973.

ENVIRONMENTAL PROTECTION AGENCY PLANNING AND BUDGETING GUIDANCE. Main/Corp United States. Environmental Protection Agency. VFOAT Budgeting and Planning Guidance. US. English. an. Environmental Protection Agency, 401 M Street, Washington DC 20460.

ENVIRONMENTAL PROTECTION REPORT. 0739-7887. Periodical. US. English. mo. $35.00. National Association of Attonerys General, 444 North Capitol Street, Washington DC 20001. **Tel** (202)628-0435. **Ed** Phillip B Rarick. **Circ** 500. (ctrl). Covers state environment litigation: hazardous waste, air pollution, water pollution, nuclear waste, land use, right to know, energy litigation, etc.

ENVIRONMENTAL PROTECTION SURVEY. Periodical. UK. English. 2.00. 30 Calderwood Street, London SE18 6QH England. **LC** TD169. **DD** 363.6.

ENVIRONMENTAL QUALITY. (ENVIRONMENTAL QUALITY : THE . . . ANNUAL REPORT OF THE COUNCIL ON ENVIRONMENTAL QUALITY). Began with 1970. 0095-2044. US. English. an. Superintendent of Documents, US Government Printing Office, Washington DC 20402. **Ind/Abst** Life Sci. Collect., Energy Res. Abstr. **LC** TD169. **DD** 301.31. NLM W2 A C93E.

ENVIRONMENTAL QUALITY ABSTRACTS. See Indexes/Abstracts.

ENVIRONMENTAL QUALITY AND SAFETY. VFOAT EQS, Environmental Quality and Safety. V. 1- 1972-. 0300-824X. GW. English, French, or German. ir. G Thieme, Postfach 732 Herdweg 63, D7000 Stuttgart 1 West Germany. **Ind/Abst** Life Sci. Collect., Chem. Abstr., Biol. Abstr., Bibliogr. Agric. **LC** QH545.A1. **DD** 615.90205. NLM W1 EN984XK. **CODEN** EQSFAP.

ENVIRONMENTAL QUALITY CONTROL. GOVERNMENTAL FINANCES. Series/Titl State and Local Government Special Studies. Began with 1974/75. US. English. an. Customer Services Section Publications, Data User Services Division, Bureau of the Census, Washington DC 20233. Environmental Quality Control. Governmental Finances and Employment, 0146-325X.

ENVIRONMENTAL QUALITY SERIES. No. 1-. Monographic Series. US. English. ir. Institute of Government & Public Affairs, University of California, Los Angeles CA 90024.

ENVIRONMENTAL RADIATION SURVEILLANCE IN WASHINGTON STATE. Main/Corp Washington (State). Dept. of Social and Health Services. Health Services Division. 0509-769X. US. English. an. Health Services Division, PO Box 1788, Olympia Airport, Olympia WA 98504. **Tel** (202)754-3303. **Ind/Abst** Chem. Abstr. **LC** RA569. **DD** 363.6. NLM W2 AW2 D34E. **CODEN** ERSSD6. **Circ** 400. (ctrl). Pertains to environmental radiation surveillance in Washington state. 0509-769X.

ENVIRONMENTAL RADIOACTIVITY ANNUAL REPORT. 0110-9944. English. an. NLM W2 KN4 N27F. Environmental Radioactivity in New Zealand.

ENVIRONMENTAL RADIOACTIVITY IN DENMARK. Series/Titl Ris Report. 0106-407X. Periodical. DK. English. ir. NLM W1 RI285H No.23 etc. Environmental Radioactivity at Riso, 0416-9840.

ENVIRONMENTAL REPORT. 0731-7751. Periodical. US. English. Environment Measurements Laboratory, US Department of Energy, New York NY 10014. **Ind/Abst** Chem. Abstr. **CODEN** EREMDK.

ENVIRONMENTAL RESEARCH. V. 1- June 1967-. 0013-9351. Periodical. US. English. bm. Academic Press, 4805 Sand Lake Road, Orlando FL

Sanitation, Environmental Technology

32819. **Tel** (305)345-4100. **Ind/Abst** Life Sci. Collect., Can. Environ., Excerpta Med., Coal Abstr., GeoRef, Int. Aerosp. Abstr., CIS Abstr., Chem. Abstr., Biol. Abstr., Meteorol. Geoastrophys. Abstr., Nucl. Sci. Abstr., Sel. Water Resour. Abstr., Bibliogr. Agric., Index Med., Appl. Sci. Technol. Index, Energy Res. Abstr., Energy Inf. Abstr., Environ. Abstr., Sci. Cit. Index, Abr. Ed., Bibliogr. Index Geol., Pollut. Abstr. Indexes, Ocean. Abstr., Hospit. Lit. Index, Humanit. Index. **LC** RA565. **NLM** W1 EN985J. **CODEN** ENVRAL.

ENVIRONMENTAL RESEARCH. English. ir. Smidesvagen, 5 Fack, S-171 Solna 1 Sweden. **LC** QH540. **DD** 333.720720485.

ENVIRONMENTAL RESEARCH MONOGRAPH. Periodical. CN. English.

ENVIRONMENTAL RESEARCH OUTLOOK CEASED. **Main/Corp** United States. Environmental Protection Agency. Office of Research and Development. 1976/80-1977/81. 0147-4456. US. English. an. **DD** 363.700973.

ENVIRONMENTAL RIGHTS AND REMEDIES. CUMULATIVE SUPPLEMENT. See Law.

ENVIRONMENTAL SCIENCE & TECHNOLOGY. (ES&T, ENVIRONMENTAL SCIENCE & TECHNOLOGY). **VAT** Environmental Science and Technology. V. 12- Jan. 1978-. 0013-936X. Periodical. US. English. mo. $164.00. American Chemical Society, PO Box 57136 West End Station, Washington DC 20037. **Tel** (202)872-4600. **Ed** Russell F Christman. **Ind/Abst** Excerpta Med., CIS Abstr., Eng. Index, Abstr. Bull. Inst. Paper Chem., Can. Environ., World Surf. Coat. Abstr., GeoRef, Int. Aerosp. Abstr., Comput. Control Abstr., Electr. Electron. Abstr., Sci. Abstr., Predicasts, Chem. Abstr., Sel. Water Resour. Abstr., Energy Res. Abstr., Biol. Abstr., Microbiol. Abstr., World Alum. Abstr., Met. Abstr., Gen. Sci. Index. **NLM** W1 EN985S. **CODEN** ESTHAG. bk rev. adv acc. **Circ** 13,018. Serves environmental engineers and scientists with legislative action, emerging technology, industrial activity, contributed technical articles, news, new products and new literature section, and a reader service department. *Environmental Science & Technology, 0013-936X.*

ENVIRONMENTAL SCIENCE AND TECHNOLOGY. 0194-0287. Monographic Series. US. English. ir. John Wiley & Sons Inc, 1 Wiley Drive, Somerset NJ 08873. **Ind/Abst** Int. Aerosp. Abstr.

ENVIRONMENTAL SCIENCE AND TECHNOLOGY SERIES. V. 1-. Monographic Series. US. English. ir. Marcel Dekker, 270 Madison Avenue, New York NY 10016. **Tel** (212)696-9000. **Ed** J Carrell Morris. **Ind/Abst** Int. Aerosp. Abstr. This is an ongoing series each title in the series has a different subject.

ENVIRONMENTAL SCIENCE RESEARCH. V. 1-. 0090-0427. Monographic Series. US. English. ir. Plenum Press, 227 West 17th Street, New York NY 10011. **Ind/Abst** GeoRef, Chem. Abstr., Bibliogr. Agric. **LC** UNC. **NLM** W1 EN986F. **CODEN** EVSRBT.

ENVIRONMENTAL SOURCEBOOK. Sept. 1981-. 0823-7360. CN. English. an. Ontario Environmental Non-Governmental Organizations Network, 730 Bathurst Street, Toronto Ontario M5S 2R4 Canada. **DD** 016.3637009713.

ENVIRONMENTAL SPECTRUM. 0013-9386. Periodical. US. bm. Free. Rutgers University, Cook College, Box 231, New Brunswick NJ 08903. **Tel** (201)932-9444. **Ed** Joseph J Soporowski. **Ind/Abst** Electron. Commun. Abstr. J., ISMEC Bull., Pollut. Abstr. Indexes, Saf. Sci. Abstr. J. bk rev. **Circ** 7,000. (ctrl) Current information for the continuing education of those involved or interested in the enviromental sciences.

ENVIRONMENTAL SURVEILLANCE AT LOS ALAMOS DURING . . . . US. English. an. Los Alamos Scientific Laboratory, Environmental Surveillance Group, PO Box 1663, Los Alamos NM 87645.

ENVIRONMENTAL SURVEILLANCE REPORT FOR THE INEL RADIOACTIVE WASTE MANAGEMENT COMPLEX. **VAT** Environmental Surveillance Report for the Idaho National Engineering Laboratory Radioactive Waste Management Complex. US. English. an. National Technical Information Service, US Department of Commerce, 5285 Port Royal Road, Springfield VA 22161.

ENVIRONMENTAL TECHNOLOGY & ECONOMICS. (ENVIRONMENTAL TECHNOLOGY AND ECONOMICS). **VFOAT** E.T. & E. V. 1- Sept. 1966-. 0046-2330. Periodical. US. English. sm. $100.00 US and Canada, $135.00 all other countries. Chem Tech Services Inc, PO Box 5005, Mt Carmel CT 06518. **Tel** (203)272-3101. **DD** 363. An environmental newsletter presenting the technical and economic view of the environmental news and keeping its readers abreast of the latest developments.

ENVIRONMENTAL TECHNOLOGY LETTERS. Vol. 1, No. 1 (Jan. 1980)-. 0143-2060. Periodical. UK. English (French or German). mo. Science and Technology Letters, 12 Clarence Road, Surrey KEW England. **Ind/Abst** Electron. Commun. Abstr. J., ISMEC Bull., Pollut. Abstr. Indexes, Saf. Sci. Abstr. J., Life Sci. Collect., Excerpta Med., Coal Abstr., Energy Inf. Abstr., Environ. Abstr., Biol. Abstr., Met. Abstr., World Alum. Abstr., Chem. Abstr., Energy Res. Abstr. **LC** TD1. **DD** 628.05. **CODEN** ETLEDB.

ENVIRONMENTAL TOXICOLOGY AND CHEMISTRY. Vol. 1, No. 1-. 0730-7268. Periodical. US. English. bm. Pergamon Press, Attn Cashier, 395 Sawmill River Road, Elmsford NY 10523. **Tel** (914)592-7700. **Ind/Abst** Life Sci. Collect., Pestdoc, Ringdoc, Vetdoc, Biol. Abstr., Chem. Abstr. **LC** QH545.A1. **DD** 574.24. **NLM** W1 **CODEN** ETOCDK.

ENVIRONMENTAL UPDATE. See Law.

ENVIRONNEMENT. (L'ENVIRONNEMENT). V. 6, No. 3- May 1979-. 0709-8847. Periodical. CN. French. ir. $11.61. Environnement, CP 65 Place d'Armes, Montreal Quebec H2Y 3E9 Canada. **DD** 301.310971. *Journal l'Environnement, 0382-7828.*

ENVIRONNEMENT PLUS. **VFOAT** Revue Environnement Plus. Summer 1981. 0711-5806. Periodical. CN. French. qt. $1.50 Per Number, $6.00 Per Issue. Environnement Plus, 57-B Bellevue, Drummondville Quebec J2B 6V1 Canada. **DD** 574.509714.

ENVIROSOUTH. **VFOAT** Environmental Periscope. V. 1- Spring 1977-. 0272-1120. Periodical. US. English. qt. $20.00. Envirosouth, Box 11468, Montgomery AL 36111. **Tel** (205)277-7050. **LC** QH104.5.S59. **DD** 333.950975.

EPA AND THE ACADEMIC COMMUNITY, PARTNERS IN RESEARCH SOLICITATION FOR GRANT PROPOSALS. **Main/Corp** United States. Environmental Protection Agency. **VAT** Environmental Protection Agency and the Academic Community, Partners in Research, Solicitation for Grant Proposals. US. English. Center for Environmental Protection Agency, Cincinnati OH 45268.

EPA CHEMICAL ACTIVITIES STATUS REPORT. Series/Titl Toxics Integration Information Series. **VAT** Environmental Protection Agency Chemical Activities Status Report. 1st- Ed. 0271-9541. US. English. ir. **NLM** W1 E412.

EPA COMPENDIUM OF REGISTERED PESTICIDES. VOLUME 1. HERBICIDES AND PLANT REGULATORS. **Main/Corp** United States. Environmental Protection Agency. **VFOAT** Herbicides and Plant Regulators. 1973-. Periodical. US. English. ir. US Environmental Protection Agency, Office of Pesticide Programs, Technical Services Division, Washington DC 20402.

EPA COMPENDIUM OF REGISTERED PESTICIDES. VOLUME 2. FUNGICIDES AND NEMATICIDES. **Main/Corp** United States. Environmental Protection Agency. **VFOAT** Fungicides and Nematicides. 1973-. Periodical. US. English. ir. US Environmental Protection Agency, Office of Pesticide Programs, Technical Services Division, Washington DC 20402.

EPA COMPENDIUM OF REGISTERED PESTICIDES. VOLUME 3. INSECTICIDES, ACARICIDES, MOLLUSCICIDES AND ANTIFOULING COMPOUNDS. **Main/Corp** United States. Environmental Protection Agency. **VFOAT** Insecticides, Acaricides, Molluscicides and Antifouling Compounds. 1972-. Periodical. US. English. ir. US Environmental Protection Agency, Office of Pesticide Programs, Technical Services Division, Washington DC 20402.

EPA COMPENDIUM OF REGISTERED PESTICIDES. VOLUME 4. RODENTICIDES AND MAMMAL, BIRD AND FISH TOXICANTS. **Main/Corp** United States. Environmental Protection Agency. **VFOAT** Rodenticides and Mammal, Bird and Fish Toxicants. 1972-. Periodical. US. English. ir. US Environmental Protection Agency, Office of Pesticide Programs, Technical Services Division, Washington DC 20402.

EPA COMPENDIUM OF REGISTERED PESTICIDES. VOLUME 5. DISINFECTANTS. **Main/Corp** United States. Environmental Protection Agency. **VFOAT** Disinfectants. 1973-. Periodical. US. English. ir. US Environmental Protection Agency, Office of Pesticide Programs, Technical Services Division, Washington DC 20402.

EPA JOURNAL. **VAT** Environmental Protection Agency Journal. Began with: Vol. 1, No. 1 (Jan. 1975). 0145-1189. Periodical. US. English. $25.00. US Government Printing Office, Washington DC 20402. **Tel** (202)783-3238. **Ind/Abst** Excerpta Med., Energy Inf. Abstr., Environ. Abstr., Abstr. Bull. Inst. Paper Chem., GeoRef, Index U.S. Gov. Period., Bibliogr. Agric., Public Aff. Inf. Serv. Bull., Curr. Index J. Educ., Soc. Sci. Index, Gen. Sci. Index, Pollut. Abstr. Indexes, Bibliogr. Index Geol. **LC** TD169. **DD** 363.6.

EPA PROGRAM STATUS REPORT: OIL SHALE. (EPA PROGRAM STATUS REPORT, OIL SHALE). **VFOAT** E.P.A. Program Status Report, Oil Shale. **VAT** Environmental Protection Agency Program Status Report: Oil Shale. Began with vol. for 1978. 0732-8257. US. English. Environmental Protection Agency, Minerals and Industry, National Technical Information Service, 5285 Port Royal Road, Springfield VA 22161. **LC** TD195.O4. **DD** 363.701.

EPA PUBLICATIONS. (PUBLICATIONS- A QUARTERLY GUIDE). 0192-5008. Periodical. US. English. ir. US Environmental Protection Agency, Printing Management, Washington DC 20460. **LC** Z5863.P7, TD170. **DD** 016.61470973. Each issue contains an index to its own contents - no vol index - loose.

EQB MONITOR (MINNESOTA). **Main/Corp** Minnesota. Environmental Quality Board. V. 1- 1976-. Periodical. US. English. wk. $8.00. MN Environmental Quality Board, 550 Cedar Street 100 Capital Square, St Paul MN 55101. **Tel** (612)296-8542.

EQL REPORT. **Main/Corp** California Institute of Technology, Pasadena. Environmental Quality Laboratory. **VAT** Environmental Quality Laboratory Report. 0149-3094. Monographic Series. US. English. Environmental Quality Laboratory, California Institute of Technology, Pasadena CA 91125. **Ind/Abst** GeoRef. **CODEN** CEQLAT.

E.S.E. PUBLICATION (NORTH CAROLINA). **Main/Corp** North Carolina. University. Dept. of Environmental Sciences and Engineering. **VAT** Environmental Sciences and Engineering Publication. 0090-2837. US. English. University of North Carolina, Department of Environmental Sciences & Engineering, Chapel Hill NC 27514. **LC** TD7. **DD** 628.08 S. *Publication.*

ESTADISTICA - OSE. See Statistics.

ETAT DE L'ENVIRONNEMENT (PARIS, FRANCE). (L'ETAT DE L'ENVIRONNEMENT). Began with 1976/77 Vol. FR. French. ir. Documentation Francaise, 124 rue Henri Barbusse, 93308 Aubervilliers Cedex France. **Tel** 834-92-75. **LC** HC280.E5. **DD** 333.70944.

ETUDES DE POLLUTION ATMOSPHERIQUE A PARIS ET DANS LES DEPARTEMENTS PERIPHERIQUES. **Main/Corp** Laboratoire Central. French. ir. **LC** TD883.7.F7. **DD** 363. *Etudes de Pollution Atmospherique dans le Departement de la Seine.*

EUROPEAN APPLIED RESEARCH REPORTS. ENVIRONMENT AND NATURAL RESOURCES SECTION. Vol. 1, No. 1 (Nov. 1980)-. 0272-4626. Periodical. UK. English. ir. $89.50/Vol. Harwood Academic, PO Box 786 Cooper Station, New York NY 10026. **Ed** Edward Phillips. **Ind/Abst** Eng. Index Annu., Eng. Index Mon., Eng. Index Bioeng. Abstr., Eng. Index Energy Abstr., Chem. Abstr. **LC** TD1. **DD** 628.505. **CODEN** EAPRD5. bk rev. adv acc.

Sanitation, Environmental Technology

EVERYONE'S BACKYARD. VFOAT
Everyone's Back Yard. Vol. 1, No. 1 (Fall 1982)-. 0749-3940. Periodical. US. English. $25.00. Citizen's Clearinghouse for Hazardous Wastes, PO Box 926, Arlington VA 22216. **Tel** (703)276-7070. **Ed** Will Collette. **DD** 363. bk rev. **Circ** 7,500. (ctrl). Looks at controversial hazardous waste issues, in depth, from a grassroots perspective.

EXCERPTA MEDICA. SECTION 46, ENVIRONMENTAL HEALTH AND POLLUTION CONTROL. VFOAT
Environmental Health and Pollution Control. Vol. 17, Issue 1- – Abstracts No. 1-240-. Periodical. ir. Elsevier Science Publishers, PO Box 211, 1000 AE Amsterdam Netherlands. NLM ZW 1. *Environmental Health and Pollution Control, 0300-5194.*

FEAT LETTER. (FEAT LETTER : A PUBLICATION FOR MEMBERS OF THE FLINT ENVIRONMENTAL ACTION TEAM AND FEAT FOUNDATION). VFOAT F.E.A.T. Letter. Aug. 1982-. 0733-6578. Periodical. US. English. bm. FEAT Foundation, 936 Mott Foundation Building, Flint MI 48502.

THE FEAT MAGAZINE. VFOAT F.E.A.T. Magazine. VAT Flint Environmental Action Team Magazine. 0732-8044. Periodical. US. English. qt. Feat Foundation, 936 Mott Foundation Building, Flint MI 48502.

FIELD BURNING IN THE WILLAMETTE VALLEY. Main/Corp Oregon. Air Quality Control Division. 1969-. 0095-3598. US. English. an. 1400 SW Fifth Avenue, Portland OR 97201. LC TD883.5.O7. **DD** 363.6. *Operational Control of Field Burning in the Willamette Valley.*

FINAL WATER POLLUTION CONTROL PROGRAM PLAN. Main/Corp Illinois. Environmental Protection Agency. Federal Fiscal Year 1980-. US. English. an. Illinois Environment Protection Agency, 2200 Churchill Road, Springfield IL 62706. LC TD224.I3. **DD** 363.73945609773. *Water Pollution Control Plan.*

FISH KILLS CAUSED BY POLLUTION. VFOAT Fish Kills. 10th- 1969-. 0071-5506. US. English. an. US Environmental Protection Agency, Office of Water Planning and Standards, Room 3101/401 M Street SW, Washington DC 20460. LC TD223. **DD** 628.168. *Pollution Caused Fish Kills: Annual Report.*

FISH KILLS CAUSED BY POLLUTION. See Fish Culture and Fisheries.

FLORIDA AIR QUALITY STATISTICAL REPORT. See Statistics.

FLUORVERONTREINIGING DOOR STEENBAKKERIJEN. Main/Corp Institut d'Hygiene et d'epidemiologie (Belgium). BE. Dutch. ir. Instituut voor Hygiene en Epidemiologie, Juliette Wytsmanstraat 14, 1050 Brussel Belgium. LC TD887.F63.

FOCUS ON GREAT LAKES WATER QUALITY. VFOAT Focus. Vol. 7, Issue No. 2-. 0711-0855. Periodical. CN. English. qt. International Joint Commission, 100 Ouellette Avenue, Windstor Ontario N9A 6T3 Canada. **Tel** (313)963-9041. **Ind/Abst** Energy Inf. Abstr., Environ. Abstr. **DD** 363.73940977. *Great Lakes Focus on Water Quality, 0708-4218.*

FORTSCHRITTE DER WASSERCHEMIE UND IHRER GRENZGEBIETE. Vol. 1-. 0071-7983. German. ir. Akademie-Verlag, Leipziger Strasse 3-4 Postfach 1233, DDR-1080 Berlin East Germany. LC TD430. NLM W1 FO895. (cum index).

FORUM STADTE-HYGIENE. (FORUM, STADTE, HYGIENE). V. 28-. 0342-202X. Periodical. GW. German. bm. Patzer Verlag, Koenigsallee 65, D-1000 Berlin 33 West Germany. **Ind/Abst** Excerpta Med., Chem. Abstr., Energy Res. Abstr. LC TD3. NLM W1 FO958I. **CODEN** FSHYDL. *Forum Umwelt-Hygiene, 0340-2290.*

FROM THE STATE CAPITALS. ENVIRONMENTAL HEALTH. Jan. 1984-. 0741-3580. Periodical. US. English. mo. Wakeman/Walworth Inc, Box 1939, New Haven Ct 06509.

FROM THE STATE CAPITALS. WASTE DISPOSAL AND POLLUTION CONTROL. VFOAT Waste Disposal and Pollution Control. 0749-2758. Periodical. US. English. mo. $75.00. Wakeman/Walworth Inc, PO Box 1939, New Haven CT 06509. *From the State Capitals. Waste Disposal and Pollution Control, 0734-0923; From the State Capitals. Environmental Health, 0741-3580.*

FUKUOKA-SHI EISEI SHIKENJOHO. (FUKUOKA-SHI EISEI SHIKENJO HO). VFOAT Annual Report of Fukuoka City Hygienic Laboratory. 0388-6166. JA. Japanese. an. Fukuoka City Institute of Public Health, 2-5-10 Maizuru Chuo-ku, Fukuoka-shi 810 Japan. **Ind/Abst** Chem. Abstr. **CODEN** FESHDT.

GARBAGE COALITION. V. 1- May 1973-. 0382-6015. Periodical. CN. English. bm. Ontario Garbage Coalition, c/o 43 Queen's Park Crescent East, Toronto Ontario M5S 2C3 Canada. **DD** 628.4409713.

GAZ, WODA I TECHNIKA SANITARNA. VFOAT Gaz, Woda, Technika Sanitarna. Began 1921. 0016-5352. Periodical. Polish (summaries in English, French, and Russian). mo. ARS Polona, Krakowskie Przedmiescie 7, 00-068 Warsaw Poland. **Ind/Abst** Excerpta Med., Coal Abstr., CIS Abstr., Chem. Abstr. **CODEN** GWTSAV.

GEOCHEMISTRY AND THE ENVIRONMENT. V. 1-. 0271-664X. US. English. ir. **Ind/Abst** GeoRef. LC RA565. **DD** 612'.01524'08. NLM QU130 .G341 1972.

GESUIDO ROPPO (JAPAN). JA. Japanese. ir. 3300. 17 Saneicho, c/o Kinen Building, Shijuku-ku (160), Tokyo Japan.

GESUNDHEITSTECHNIK. 0435-852X. Periodical. SZ. German. mo. Umweltschutz Brunner Verlag AG, Stauffacherstrasse 5, CH-8004 Zurich Switzerland. **Ind/Abst** Chem. Abstr. **CODEN** GESUB9.

GLOBAL ATMOSPHERIC BACKGROUND MONITORING FOR SELECTED ENVIRONMENTAL PARAMETERS. BAPMON DATA. (GLOBAL ATMOSPHERIC BACKGROUND MONITORING FOR SELECTED ENVIRONMENTAL PARAMETERS BAPMON DATA FOR . . .). VAT Global Atmospheric Background Monitoring for Selected Environmental Parameters. Background Air Pollution Monitoring Network Data. 1978-. 0278-9132. US. English. an. National Climatic Center, Federal Building, Asheville NC 28801. LC QC976.T8. **DD** 628.53028. *Global Monitoring of the Environment for Selected Atmospheric Constituents, 0270-0018.*

THE GOULD LEAGUER. VFOAT New South Wales Gould Leaguer. V. 1, No. 1 Feb. 1969-. Periodical. AT. English. ir. 4.00. Gould League of New South Wales, Mary Street/Beecroft 2119, New South Wales Australia. **Tel** 846235. **Circ** 70,000. (ctrl). Environmental education resource materials for teachers and pupils, interdisciplinary approaches are largely adopted in published materials.

THE GOVERNOR'S REPORT ON ENVIRONMENTAL QUALITY. Main/Corp Minnesota. Governor. 1979-. US. English. an. Minnesota State Planning Agency, Room 101/Capitol Square Building, 550 Cedar Street, St Paul MN 55103. LC GF504.M6. **DD** 333.7209776. *Annual Report on the Quality of the Environment, 0094-1697.*

HABITAT INTERNATIONAL. Vol. 2, No. 5/6-. 0197-3975. Periodical. UK. English. bm. Pergamon Press, 395 Sawmill River Road, Elmsford NY 10523. **Ind/Abst** Energy Inf. Abstr., Life Sci. Collect., Int. Labour Doc., Excerpta Med., Energy Res. Abstr., Environ. Abstr. *Habitat, 0361-3690.*

HANDBUCH DER GEFAHRLICHEN GUTER. 0172-9578. German. ir. Springer Verlag-New York Inc, Subscription Department, 175 5th Avenue, New York NY 10010. **Tel** (212)460-1500.

HAZARD ASSESSMENT OF CHEMICALS. Vol. 1-. 0730-5427. US. English. an. Academic Press Inc, 4805 Sand Lake Road, Orlando FL 32819. **Ind/Abst** Chem. Abstr. LC QH545.A1. **DD** 363.7384. **CODEN** HACCDU.

HAZARDOUS MATERIALS & WASTE MANAGEMENT. VFOAT Hazardous Materials and Waste Management. Vol. 1, No. 1 (Jan./Feb. 1983)-. 0739-6295. Periodical. US. English. bm. $18.00. Hazardous Materials & Waste Management, 243 West Main Street, Kutztown PA 19503. **Tel** (215)683-5098. **Ed** Margaret M Nemec. LC TD811.5. **DD** 363.72805. bk rev. adv acc. **Circ** 22,000. (ctrl). Clarifies the interface between the Department of Transportation, the Environmental Protection Agency, and the Occupational Safety and Health Administration agencies that regulate the hazardous materials, chemicals and waste management industry.

HAZARDOUS MATERIALS INTELLIGENCE REPORT. 1980. 0272-9628. Periodical. US. English. wk. $325.00. World Information Systems, PO Box 535 Harvard Square, Cambridge MA 02238. **Tel** (617)491-5100. **Ed** Richard S Golob. adv acc. **Circ** 550. (ctrl). An international weekly newsletter that focuses on a wide range of hazardous materials and hazardous waste issues.

HAZARDOUS SUBSTANCES ADVISOR. VFOAT HS Advisor. V. 1- Jan. 1980-. 0196-3767. Periodical. US. English. mo. $126.00. J J Keller & Associates Inc, 145 West Wisconsin Avenue, Neenah WI 54956. **Tel** (800)558-5011. **Ed** Linda Werely. LC KF3945.A15. **DD** 344.730472. Monthly information report on federal congressional and regulatory activity to control, monitor and eliminate hazards caused by hazardous and toxic substances.

HAZARDOUS WASTE CEASED. Vol. 1, No. 1-Vol. 1, No. 4 (Winter 1984). 0738-6168. Periodical. US. English. qt. $80.00. Mary Ann Liebert Inc Publishers, 157 East 86th Street, New York NY 10028. **Ind/Abst** Life Sci. Collect. NLM W1.

HAZARDOUS WASTE & HAZARDOUS MATERIALS. VFOAT Hazardous Waste and Hazardous Materials. Vol. 2, No. 1 (Spring 1985)-. 0882-5696. Periodical. US. English. qt. $80.00 Domestic, $108.00 Foreign. Mary Ann Liebert Inc, 157 East 86th Street, New York NY 10028. **Ind/Abst** Chem. Abstr. LC TD811.5. **DD** 628.5. NLM W1. **CODEN** HWHME2. *Hazardous Waste, 0738-6168.*

HAZARDOUS WASTE & POLLUTION COMPLIANCE GUIDELINES. VFOAT Hazardous Waste and Pollution Compliance. 0737-8963. Periodical. US. English. mo. Bureau of Business Practice, 24 Rope Ferry Road, Waterford CT 06386.

THE HAZARDOUS WASTE CONSULTANT. (THE HAZARDOUS WASTE CONSULTANT : A BIOMONTHLY PUBLICATION). Vol. 1, No. 1 (July 1983)-. 0738-0232. Periodical. US. English. bm. $350.00. McCoy and Associates, 13131 West Cedar Drive, Lakewood CO 80228. LC TD811.5. **DD** 363.728.

HAZARDOUS WASTE LITIGATION. See Law.

HAZARDOUS WASTE LITIGATION REPORTER. See Law.

HAZARDOUS WASTE MANAGEMENT HANDBOOK. VFOAT Eco/Log Hazardous Waste Management Handbook. 1982-. 0711-7140. CN. English. an. $167.00. Hazardous Waste Management Handbook, Corpus Information Services, 1450 Don Mills Road, Don Mills Ontario M3B 2X7 Canada. **DD** 363.7280971.

HAZARDOUS WASTE MANAGEMENT IN MASSACHUSETTS. 0743-7331. US. English. an. LC TD811.5. **DD** 363.728.

HAZARDOUS WASTE NEWS. (HAZARDOUS WASTE NEWS INCLUDING NUCLEAR WASTE BULLETIN). Vol. 1, No. 1 (Aug. 6, 1979)- V. 3, No. 6 (Feb. 9, 1981). 0275-374X. Periodical. US. English. # $297.00. Business Publishers Inc, 951 Pershing Drive, Silver Spring MD 20910. **Tel** (301)587-6300. **Ed** Charlotte Garvey. Report on hazardous waste collection, transportation, storage, and disposal. Information on federal, state, and local laws as well as new technologies and products.

HAZARDOUS WASTE NEWS. Vol. 3, No. 7 (Feb. 16, 1981)-. 0275-374X. Periodical. US. English. wk. $195.00. Business Publishers Inc, 951 Pershing Drive, Silver Spring MD 20910. Plugs you into new opportunities for research grants, service contracts, and equipment sales throughout the country. *Hazardous Waste News including Nuclear Waste Bulletin, 0275-374X.*

HAZARDOUS WASTE REPORT. Vol. 1, No. 1 (Aug. 13, 1979)-. 0271-2601. Periodical. US. English. bw. Aspen Systems Corporation, 1600 Research Boulevard, Rockville MD 20850. **Tel** (301)251-5000. LC KF3945.A15. **DD** 363.728.

THE HAZARDOUS WASTE TRAINING BULLETIN FOR SUPERVISORS. 0744-4168. Periodical. US. English. mo. J F Brady, 114 Manhattan Street, Box 1274, Stanford CT 06904. **Tel** (203)245-7448. **Ed** John F Brady. **Circ** 2,100. Up-to-date information gives supervisors time to plan. Actual cases shows ways to solve problems, special features gives practical solutions.

Sanitation, Environmental Technology

HEALTH AND ENVIRONMENTAL EFFECTS RESEARCH PROGRAM ABSTRACTS. See Indexes/Abstracts.

HEALTH AND SAFETY INDUSTRIAL AIR POLLUTION. Main/Corp Great Britain. Health and Safety Executive. UK. English. Her Majestys Stationery Office, 49 Holborn, London WC1V 6HB England. LC TD883.7.G7. DD 363.6.

HIROSHIMA-KEN KANKYO SENTA KENKYU HOKOKU. VFOAT Bulletin of Hiroshima Prefectural Research Center for Environmental Sciences. No. 1-. 0389-0082. Periodical. JA. Japanese (some summaries in English). ir. Hiroshima-Ken Kankyo Senta, 6-29 Minamimashi 1-chome, Hiroshima-shi 734 Japan. Ind/Abst Chem. Abstr. CODEN HIHODB.

HOKKAIDO KOGAI BOSHI KENKYUJO HO. VFOAT Report of Hokkaido Research Institute for Environmental Pollution. No. 1-. JA. Japanese (summaries in English or Japanese). ir. Nishi 12-chome Kita 19-jo, Kita-ku Sapporo Japan. Ind/Abst Chem. Abstr. LC TD172. CODEN HKBKDH.

HOME, YARD, AND GARDEN PEST NEWSLETTER. No. 1- 1978-. US. English. ir. $10.50. Agricultural Newsletter Services, University of Illinois/120 Munford Hall, Urbana IL 61801. Tel (217)333-1000.

HUAN CHING KO HSUEH. HUANJING KEXUE. VFOAT Huanjing Kexue. 0250-3301. Periodical. CC. Chinese. bm. $14.31. China Publication Centre, PO Box 2820, Beijing China. Ind/Abst Chem. Abstr. LC TD4. CODEN HCKHDV.

HUAN CHING KO HSUEH TSA CHIH. VFOAT Huan Ching Ko Hsueh. V. 1-. Periodical. CH. Chinese. ir. $160.00. Tung Hai Ta Hsuen Huan Ching Ko Hsuen Yen Chiu Chung Hsin, PO Box 915, Tai-Chung Shih Taiwan. LC TD4. DD 620.805.

HUANJING HUAXUE. (HUAN CHING HUA HSUEH). VFOAT Environmental Chemistry. Began in 1982. 0254-6108. Periodical. CH. Chinese. bm. 0.50. Chung-Kuo Kuo Chi Shu Tien, PO Box 2820, Pei-Ching China. LC QD1. DD 540.

HUANJING KEXUE XUEBAO. (HUAN CHING KO HSUEH HSUEH PAO). VFOAT Acta Scientiae Circumstantiae. Began in 1981. 0253-2468. Periodical. CH. Chinese (English). qt. $15.48. China Publication Centre, PO Box 2820, Beijing China. Ind/Abst Chem. Abstr. LC TD4. DD 620.805. CODEN HKXUDL.

HWANGYONG KWA KONGHAE. VFOAT Environment and Pollution. Periodical. KO. Korean. mo. Hyondae Hwangyong Kwalliso, 991-2 Taerim-dong Yongdungpo-ku, Seoul Korea. Ind/Abst Energy Res. Abstr. LC TD172.

HWANGYONG POJON. VFOAT Journal of the Korea Environmental Preservation Association. Periodical. Korean (summaries in English). ir. Hwangyong Pojon Hyophoe, 111 Sogong-dong Chung-ku, Seoul Korea. LC TD187.5.K6.

HWANGYONG YONGU = ENVIRONMENTAL STUDIES. VFOAT Environmental Studies. Periodical. English (Korean). an. Soul Taehakkyo Hwangyong, Taehagwon Wonuhoe San 156-1 Sillim-dong, Kwanak-ku Seoul Korea. LC HC470.E5.

THE IAO INSPECTOR. VFOAT Inspecteur Du Gta. VAT Insurers' Advisory Organization Inspector, Inspecteur du Gta, Inspecteur du Groupememt Technique des Asseurers du Canada. Vol. 11, No. 2 (Summer 1974)-. 0226-2460. Periodical. CN. English (text in French with text on inverted pages 1974/75). qt. Free. Insurers' Advisory Organization of Canada, 180 Dundas Street West, Toronto Ontario M5G 1Z9 Canada. DD 628.922. CUA Inspector, 0821-7149.

IBARAKI-KEN NI OKERU HOSHANO CHOSA. Japanese. ir. Ibarnki-ken Kogai Gijutsu Senta, 4043 Ishikawa 1-chome 310, Mita Japan. LC TD196.R3.

ILLINOIS AIR QUALITY REPORT CEASED. Main/Corp Illinois. Ambient Air Monitoring Section. VFOAT Annual Air Quality Report. 0360-9162. US. English. an. Illinois Environmental Protection Agency, Ambient Air Monitoring, 2200 Churchill Road, Springfield IL 62706. LC TD883.5.I45. DD 363.6.

ILLINOIS WATER QUALITY INVENTORY REPORT. Main/Corp Illinois. Environmental Protection Agency. 0360-7755. US. English. Illinois Environmental Protection Agency, 2200 Church Hill Road, Springfield IL 62706. LC TD224.I3. DD 363.61.

ILLUSTRATED WHITE PAPER ON THE ENVIRONMENT IN JAPAN. Main/Corp Japan. Kankyocho. English. an. LC TD187.5.J3. DD 363.700952.

IMPLEMENTATION OF LITTLE BLUE RIVER BASIN WATER QUALITY MANAGEMENT PLAN. Main/Corp Nebraska. Natural Resources Commission. 1976/77-. US. English. be. Nebraska Natural Resources Commission, 301 Centennial Mall South, Lincoln NE 68508. LC TD225.L627. DD 363.739456097823.

INDEX OF CURRENT GOVERNMENT AND GOVERNMENTAL-SUPPORTED RESEARCH IN ENVIRONMENTAL POLLUTION IN GREAT BRITAIN. See Indexes/Abstracts.

INDIAN JOURNAL OF ENVIRONMENTAL HEALTH. V. 13, No. 3-. 0367-827X. Periodical. II. English. qt. $25.00. National Environmental Engineering Research Institute, Nehru Marg, Nagpur 440 020 India. Tel 26071. Ind/Abst Eng. Index Annu., Eng. Index Mon., Eng. Index Bioeng. Abstr., Eng. Index Energy Abstr., Sel. Water Resour. Abstr., Excerpta Med., Coal Abstr., Biol. Abstr., Chem. Abstr., Nuci. Sci. Abstr., Pollut. Abstr. Indexes, Eng. Index. LC RA565.A1. DD 628.05. NLM W1 IN208N. CODEN IJEHBP. Circ 1,600. (ctrl). Covers all aspects of environmental engineering and sciences including air, water, wastewater, industrial and solid wastes, ecology, ecosystems and instrumentation. Environmental Health.

INDIVIDUAL ONSITE WASTEWATER SYSTEMS. Main/Conf National Conference on Individual Onsite Wastewater Systems. 1st- 1974-. 0160-6662. US. English. an. Ann Arbor Science Publishers, PO Box 1425, Ann Arbor MI 48106. Ind/Abst Chem. Abstr., GeoRef. LC TD523. DD 628.74. CODEN IOWSDF.

INDUSTRIAL POLLUTION CONTROL YEARBOOK. See Yearbooks, Almanacs, Directories.

INDUSTRIAL WASTES (CHICAGO, ILL. : 1971). (INDUSTRIAL WASTES). Began in 1971. 0046-9262. Periodical. US. English. bm. $10.00 Domestic, $13.00 Foreign. Scranton Gillette Communications Inc, 380 NW Highway, Des Plaines IL 60016. Ind/Abst Eng. Index Annu., Eng. Index Mon., Eng. Index Bioeng. Abstr., Eng. Index Energy Abstr., Excerpta Med., Sel. Water Resour. Abstr., Coal Abstr., Energy Inf. Abstr., Environ. Abstr., Chem. Abstr., Appl. Sci. Technol. Index, Energy Res. Abstr. LC TD896. DD 628.4. CODEN INWABK.

INDUSTRIEABWASSER. 1958-. 0073-7755. GW. German. an. Deutscher Kommunal Verlag, Roseggerstrasse 5 A, Dusseldorf West Germany. Ind/Abst Chem. Abstr.

INFORM. See Conservation & Natural Resources.

INFORMATION EAUX. 20.- Vol. (No. 193). 0012-9003. Periodical. FR. French. mo. Assoc Francaise Etude des Eaux, 21 23 rue de Madrid, 75008 Paris France. Tel (33)45221467. Ind/Abst GeoRef. NLM W1 IN4203. Covers water, hydrology, hydrogeology, water quality, drinking water, water and wastewater treatment, seawater, sludge treatment, corrosion, irrigation and drainage. Eaux et Industries.

INFORMATION SERIES - COLORADO STATE UNIVERSITY, ENVIRONMENTAL RESOURCES CENTER. (INFORMATION SERIES - ENVIRONMENTAL RESOURCES CENTER). Main/Corp Colorado State University. Environmental Resources Center. No. 1- Jan. 1971-. 0147-5061. US. English. ir. Colorado State University, Environmental Resources Center, Ft Collins CO 80521. Ind/Abst Chem. Abstr. DD 628. CODEN ICERD8.

INFORUM. ENVIRONMENTAL REPORT DATA SYSTEM. (INFORUM : ENVIRONMENTAL REPORT DATA SYSTEM). VFOAT Environmental Report Data System. V. 1- Aug. 1975-. 0360-4985. US. English. ir. $300.00. 1747 Pennsylvania Avenue NW/Suite 1150, Washington DC 20006. LC TD195.E4. DD 016.3337.

INQUINAMENTO. ACQUA, ARIA, SUOLO. (INQUINAMENTO). Vol. 12, No. 1 (March 1970)-. 0567-7149. Periodical. IT. Italian. $41.58. Etas Kompass Periodici Tecnici, Via Mantegna 6, 20154 Milano Italy. Ind/Abst Sel. Water Resour. Abstr., Coal Abstr., Int. Aerosp. Abstr., Chem. Abstr., Bibliogr. Agric. CODEN IQAAAW. Acquq Industriale Inquinamento.

INSECT AND DISEASE CONTROL IN THE HOME GARDEN. 1977/1978-. 0713-1313. CN. English. be. $0.50. Ministry of Agriculture and Food, 801 Bay Street, Toronto Ontario M7A 1B3 Canada. DD 635.04909713. Insect, Disease and Weed Control in the Home Garden, 0713-1305.

INSIDE CANADA. V. 1- 1970-. 0382-8174. CN. English. an. Ed B Vass.

INSIDE E.P.A. WEEKLY REPORT. VFOAT Inside E.P.A. VAT Inside Environmental Protection Agency Weekly Report. 0270-8965. Periodical. US. English. wk. $593.25. Inside Washington Publishers, PO Box 7167/Benjamin Franklin, Washington DC 20044. Tel (800)424-9068.

INSPECTEUR DE GTA. (L'INSPECTEUR DU GTA). VAT Inspecteur de Groupement Technique des Assureurs du Canada (1975). 0226-2452. Periodical. CN. English (text in French). qt. Free. Insurers' Advisory Organization of Canada, 180 Dunas Street West, Toronto Ontario M5G 1Z9 Canada. DD 628.922. IAO Inspector, 0226-2460.

INSTRUMENTATION FOR ENVIRONMENTAL MONITORING. Main/Corp Lawrence Berkeley Laboratory. Environmental Instrumentation Group. Vol. 1- May 1972-. Periodical. US. English. ir. University of California, Lawrence Berkeley Laboratory, Berkeley CA 94720. Tel (415)843-2740.

INTER-NOISE; PROCEEDINGS. Main/Conf International Conference on Noise Control Engineering. 1972-. 0105-175X. US. English. ir. Institute of Noise Control Engineering, PO Box 3206/Arlington Branch, Poughkeepsie NY 12603 12603. Ind/Abst Eng. Index Annu., Eng. Index Mon., Eng. Index Bioeng. Abstr., Eng. Index Energy Abstr. LC TD891. DD 620.23. CODEN PICEDA. Each issue contains an index to its own contents - no vol index - loose.

INTERAFRICAN PHYTOSANITARY BULLETIN. See Horticulture and Plant Culture.

INTERNATIONAL CONFERENCE ON ENVIRONMENTAL PROBLEMS OF THE EXTRACTIVE INDUSTRIES. 0270-2584. US. English. ir. Wright Company, 1436 Adirondack Trail, Dayton OH 45409. Ind/Abst Chem. Abstr. CODEN ICEIDF.

INTERNATIONAL ENVIRONMENT & SAFETY. VAT International Environment and Safety. 1978. 0141-4836. Periodical. UK. English. qt. $60.00. Labmate Ltd, New Gate/Dandpit Lane, St Alban Herts AL4 0BS England. Tel 0727 31337. Ed M H Pattison. Ind/Abst Chem. Abstr. bk rev. adv acc. Circ 13,000. (ctrl). Analysis and control of pollutants together with personal protective equipment and instruments.

INTERNATIONAL ENVIRONMENT REPORTER. CURRENT REPORT. V. 1- Jan. 1978-. 0149-8738. Periodical. US. English. mo. Bureau of National Affairs Inc, 1231 25th Street NW, Washington DC 20037. Tel (301)258-1033. LC TD169. DD 614.705.

INTERNATIONAL JOURNAL OF ENVIRONMENTAL STUDIES. (THE INTERNATIONAL JOURNAL OF ENVIRONMENTAL STUDIES). VFOAT Environmental Studies. V. 1- Oct. 1970-. 0020-7233. Periodical. US. English. ir. $312.00. Gordon & Breach, PO Box 197, London WC2E 9PX England. Ed J Rose. Ind/Abst Public Aff. Inf. Serv. Bull., Energy Res. Abstr., Eng. Index Annu., Eng. Index Mon., Eng. Index Bioeng. Abstr., Life Sci. Collect., Can. Environ., Pestdoc, Ringdoc, Vetdoc, Excerpta Med., Coal Abstr., Energy Inf. Abstr., Environ. Abstr., Int. Aerosp. Abstr., GeoRef, Eng. Index, ABI/Inform, Ref. Source, Chem. Abstr., Biol. Abstr., Nuci. Sci. Abstr., Sel. Water Resour. Abstr., Bibliogr. Agric., Bibliogr. Index Geol., Sci. Cit. Index, Abr. Ed., Pollut. Abstr. Indexes. LC HC79.E5. DD 301.3105. NLM W1 IN766H. CODEN IJEVAW. bk rev. adv acc.

INTERNATIONAL WATER REPORT. VFOAT WIC International Water Report. 1977. Periodical. US. English. qt. $27.00. Water Information Center, 6800 Jericho Turnpike, North Shore Atrium, Syosset NY 11791. Tel (516)921-7690. Ed Judith Schoeck Corcoran. bk rev. Water supply and

Sanitation, Environmental Technology

treatment, pollution and waste control, legislation, new products, research and developments.

INVENTORY OF INTERSTATE CARRIER WATER SUPPLY SYSTEMS BY STATES AND ENVIRONMENTAL PROTECTION AGENCY REGIONS. Main/Corp United States. Environmental Protection Agency. Water Supply Division. VFOAT Inventory of Interstate Carrier Water Supply Systems. 0094-0569. US. English. Environmental Protection Agency, Water Supply Division, 401 M Street, Washington DC 20460. LC TD223. DD 363.61.

INVENTORY OF WASTE WATER PRODUCTION AND WASTE WATER RECLAMATION PRACTICES IN CALIFORNIA. Main/Corp California. Dept. of Water Resources. Series Corp Its Bulletin. 0092-9158. US. English. an. $1.50. Department of Water Resources, PO Box 388, Sacramento CA 95802. LC TD524.C2. DD 333.91009794.

THE INVESTIGATION OF AIR POLLUTION. Main/Corp Stevenage, Eng. Warren Spring Laboratory. VFOAT National Survey, Smoke and Sulphur Dioxide. UK. English. Warren Spring Library, PO Box 20/Gunnels Wood Road, Hartfordshire SG1 2BX England. LC TD883.7.G7. DD 628.53.

IRPTC BULLETIN. Began with Vol. 1, No. 1 (Jan. 1979). 0250-4227. Periodical. English. ir. Ind/Abst Life Sci. Collect. NLM W1. (cum index).

ISRAEL ENVIRONMENT BULLETIN. V. 1- Mar. 1974-. 0334-3804. Periodical. IS. English. ir. Free. Environmental Protection Service, Ministry of the Interior, PO Box 6158, Jerusalem Israel. Tel 660151. Ed Shoshana Gabbay. Ind/Abst Energy Inf. Abstr., Environ. Abstr. bk rev. Circ 2,000. Survey of environmental protection activities in Israel including air and water quality, noise, environmental education, legislation, energy, environmental impact statements, cleanliness, etc.

IVL. B. (INSTITUTET FOR VATTEN- OCH LUFTVARDS FORSKNING. B : IVL : PUBLIKATION). VFOAT IVL. 0347-8696. Monographic Series. SW. Swedish (English). ir. IVL Box 21060, 100 31 Stockholm Sweden. Ind/Abst Chem. Abstr. CODEN IVLBDQ.

IVL BULLETIN. VFOAT I.V.L. Bulletin. VAT Instituter for Vatten- Och Luftvardsforkining Bulletin. Vol. 1, No. 1-. Periodical. English. sa. Ind/Abst Bull. Inst. Paper Chem.

JAHRBUCH FUR UMWELTSCHUTZ. See Yearbooks, Almanacs, Directories.

JAHRESBERICHT DER HAUPTABTEILUNG STADTENTWASSERUNG. Main/Corp Hamburg. Amt. fur Ingineurwesen 3. Hauptabteilung Stadtentwasser. German. ir. LC TD574.H35. DD 628.30943.

JAHRESBERICHT (GERMANY (WEST). UMWELTBUNDESAMT). (JAHRESBERICHT). German. an. Unweltbundesamt, Bismarckplatz 1, D-1000 Berlin 33 West Germany. LC TD171.5.G3. DD 354.43008232106.

JAHRESBERICHT - GROSSER ERFTVERBAND. Main/Corp Grosser Erftverband. German. an. Grosser Erftverband, Paffendorfer Weg 42, Postfach 1320, 5010 Bergheim West Germany. LC TD273.7. DD 363.61. Bericht Uber die Verbandtatigkeit - Grosser Erftverband.

JAVNI VODOVOD I KANALIZACIJA U NASELJIMA SR SRBIJE. Main/Corp Republicki Zavod za Statistiku sr Srbije. Series Corp Its Bulletin. 1970-. Serbo-Croatian(R). ir. LC HA1651, TD295.S5.

JOURNAL - AMERICAN WATER WORKS ASSOCIATION CEASED. (JOURNAL OF THE AMERICAN WATER WORKS ASSOCIATION). Vol. 1, No. 1 (March 1914)-V. 39, No. 12 (Dec. 1947). 0003-150X. Periodical. US. English. mo. $50.00. American Water Works Association, 6666 West Quincy Avenue, Denver CO 80235. Tel (303)794-7711. Ed Nancy M Zeillg. Ind/Abst Appl. Sci. Technol. Index, Abstr. Bull. Inst. Paper Chem., Biol. Abstr., Can. Environ., Chem. Abstr., Coal Abstr., Eng. Index Bioeng. Abstr., Eng. Index Energy Abstr., Fluidex, Excerpta Med., Energy Res. Abstr., Life Sci. Collect., GeoRef, Int. Aerosp. Abstr., Ref. Source, Eng. Index Annu., Sel. Water Resour. Abstr., Energy Inf. Abstr., Environ. Abstr., Eng. Index Mon., Nucl. Sci. Abstr. LC TD201. CODEN JAWWA5. (cum index). bk rev. adv acc. Circ 40,000. Available on microfilm from University Microfilms. Articles oriented toward water-supply management, technical developments, and research, as well as news pertinent to the water-supply field. Proceedings of the Annual Convention of the American Water Works Association, 0097-2630.

JOURNAL - AMERICAN WATER WORKS ASSOCIATION. V. 1- Mar. 1914-. 0003-150X. Periodical. US. English. mo. American Water Works Association, 6666 West Quincy Avenue, Denver CO 80325. Available on microfilm from University Microfilms. Proceedings of the Annual Convention of the American Water Works Association, 0097-2630.

JOURNAL L'ENJEU. (JOURNAL L'ENJEU : ORGANE OFFICIEL D'INFORMATION DE:ENJEU ET ENVIRONNEMENT JEUNESSE INC). Vol. 1, No. 1-. 0712-2128. Periodical. CN. French. bm. Free to Members. Journal L'Enjeu, Bureau 2 26, 1415 East rue Jarry, Montreal Quebec H2E 2Z7 Canada. DD 363.7058060714.

JOURNAL - MAINE WATER UTITLITES ASSOCIATION. Main/Corp Maine Water Utilities Association. Began in 1924. US. English. bm. Maine Water Utilities Association, 225 Douglas Street, Portland ME 04104. LC TD201. DD 628.1062741.

JOURNAL OF ENVIRONMENTAL BIOLOGY. Began with: Vol. 1 (1980). 0254-8704. Periodical. English. qt. $80.00. Journal of Environmental Biology, 567/5, Civil Lines South, Muzaffarnagar 251 001 India. Ind/Abst Electron. Commun. Abstr. J., ISMEC Bull., Pollut. Abstr. Indexes, Saf. Sci. Abstr. J., Life Sci. Collect., Energy Inf. Abstr., Environ. Abstr., Chem. Abstr. NLM W1 JO644AP. CODEN JEBIDP.

JOURNAL OF ENVIRONMENTAL ECONOMICS AND MANAGEMENT. V. 1- May 1974-. 0095-0696. Periodical. US. English. qt. Academic Press, 4805 Sand Lake Road, Orlando FL 32819. Tel (305)345-4100. Ind/Abst Manage. Contents, GeoRef, Eng. Index, Can. Environ., Life Sci. Collect., Sel. Water Resour. Abstr., Excerpta Med., Coal Abstr., Energy Inf. Abstr., Environ. Abstr., Index Econ. Artic. J. Collect. Vol., ABI/Inform, Int. Aerosp. Abstr., Biol. Abstr., Bibliogr. Abstr., Public Aff. Inf. Serv. Bull., Ocean. Abstr., Soc. Sci. Citation Index, Sci. Cit. Index, Abr. Ed., Pollut. Abstr. Indexes, Bibliogr. Index Geol., Energy Res. Abstr., Eng. Index Annu., Eng. Index Mon., Eng. Index Energy Abstr. LC HC79.P55. DD 301.3105. CODEN JEEMDI.

JOURNAL OF ENVIRONMENTAL ENGINEERING (NEW YORK, N.Y.). (JOURNAL OF ENVIRONMENTAL ENGINEERING). VFOAT A.S.C.E. Environmental Engineering. Vol. 109, No. 1 (Feb. 1983)-. 0733-9372. Periodical. US. English. bm. $80.00. American Society of Civil Engineers, 345 East 47th Street, New York NY 10017. Tel (212)705-7275. Ind/Abst ASCE Annu. Comb. Index, ASCE Publ. Inf., Trans. Am. Soc. Civ. Eng., Appl. Sci. Technol. Index, Fluidex, Can. Environ., Life Sci. Collect., Excerpta Med., Abstr. Bull. Inst. Paper Chem., Coal Abstr., GeoRef, Energy Res. Abstr., Sel. Water Resour. Abstr. LC TD1. DD 628.05. CODEN JOEEDU. Circ 5,900. Concerned with provision of safe, ample water supply and proper disposal and/or recycling of wastewater and solid wastes and all areas of sanitation and pollution. Journal of the Environmental Engineering Division, 0090-3914.

JOURNAL OF ENVIRONMENTAL HEALTH. V. 26, No. 2- Sept./Oct. 1963-. 0022-0892. Periodical. US. English. bm. $90.00. National Enviornmental Health Association, 720 South Colorado Boulevard/Suite 970, Denver CO 80222. Tel (303)756-9090. Ed Ida Frances Marshall. Ind/Abst Life Sci. Collect., Excerpta Med., Coal Abstr., Energy Inf. Abstr., Environ. Abstr., CIS Abstr., Bibliogr. Agric., Biol. Abstr., Chem. Abstr., Environ. Period. Bibliogr., Hospit. Lit. Index, Sel. Water Resour. Abstr., Curr. Index J. Educ., Appl. Sci. Technol. Index, Gen. Sci. Index, Sci. Cit. Index, Abr. Ed., Pollut. Abstr. Indexes. NLM W1 JO644B. CODEN JEVHAH. bk rev. adv acc. Circ 5,000. Protection of human health through prevention and control of the environment. Sanitarian's Journal of Environmental Health, 0092-6957.

JOURNAL OF ENVIRONMENTAL MANAGEMENT. V. 1- Jan. 1973-. 0301-4797. Periodical. UK. English. qt. Academic Press, 4805 Sand Lake Road, Orlando FL 32819. Tel (305)345-4100. Ind/Abst Electron. Commun. Abstr. J., ISMEC Bull., Pollut. Abstr. Indexes, Saf. Sci. Abstr. J., Can. Environ., Life Sci. Collect., Sel. Water Resour. Abstr., Excerpta Med., Coal Abstr., Energy Inf. Abstr., Environ. Abstr., Biol. Abstr., GeoRef, Bibliogr. Agric., Energy Res. Abstr., Sci. Cit. Index, Abr. Ed., Soc. Sci. Citation Index, Ocean. Abstr. LC HC79.E5. DD 301.31. NLM W1 JO644BD. CODEN JEVMAW.

JOURNAL OF ENVIRONMENTAL QUALITY. Periodical. US. English. qt. $24.00. American Society of Agronomy, 677 South Segoe Road, Madison WI 53711. Tel (608)274-1212. Ind/Abst Biol. Agric. Index, Eng. Index, Sci. Cit. Index, Abr. Ed., Int. Aerosp. Abstr., Pollut. Abstr. Indexes, Chem. Abstr., Bibliogr. Index Geol.

JOURNAL OF ENVIRONMENTAL QUALITY. VFOAT Environmental Quality. V. 1- Jan./Mar. 1972-. 0047-2425. Periodical. US. English. qt. $7.00 US Member, $8.00 Foreign Member, $12.00 US Nonmember, $13.50 Foreign Nonmember. Executive Vice President, American Society of Agronomy, 677 South Segoe Road, Madison WI 53711. Ind/Abst Can. Environ., Life Sci. Collect., Pestdoc, Ringdoc, Vetdoc, Excerpta Med., Coal Abstr., Energy Inf. Abstr., Environ. Abstr., Int. Aerosp. Abstr., GeoRef, Biol. Abstr., Chem. Abstr., Nucl. Sci. Abstr., Sel. Water Resour. Abstr., Bibliogr. Agric., Biol. Agric. Index, Energy Res. Abstr., Eng. Index Annu., Eng. Index Mon. LC S1. DD 631. NLM W1 JO644BG. CODEN JEVQAA.

JOURNAL OF ENVIRONMENTAL SCIENCE AND HEALTH. PART A, ENVIRONMENTAL SCIENCE AND ENGINEERING. (JOURNAL OF ENVIRONMENTAL SCIENCE AND HEALTH. PART A : ENVIRONMENTAL SCIENCE AND ENGINEERING). VFOAT Environmental Science and Engineering. 0360-1226. Periodical. US. English. $210.00. Marcel Dekker Journals, PO Box 11305/Church Street Station, New York NY 10249. Ed James W Robinson. Ind/Abst GeoRef, Air Pollut. Titles, Anal. Abstr., INIS Atomindex, Biol. Abstr., Can. Environ., Chem. Abstr., Curr. Adv. Plant Sci., Curr. Contents, Agric. Biol. Environ. Sci., Ecol. Abstr., Energy Res. Abstr., Eng. Index, Environ. Abstr., Environ. Period. Bibliogr., Excerpta Med., Index Med., Phys. Briefs, Sci. Cit. Index, Abr. Ed., Sel. Water Resour. Abstr., Autom. Subj. Citation Alert. LC TD1. DD 620.85. NLM W1 JO644BH. CODEN JESEDU. bk rev. adv acc. Environmental Letters, 0013-9300.

JOURNAL OF ENVIRONMENTAL SCIENCE AND HEALTH : PART B, PESTICIDES, FOOD CONTAMINANTS, AND AGRICULTURAL WASTES. VFOAT Pesticides, Food Contaminants, and Agricultural Wastes. V. B11- 1976-. 0360-1234. Periodical. US. English. bm. $195.00. Marcel Dekker, PO Box 11305, Church Street Station, New York NY 10249. Ed Shahamat U Khan. Ind/Abst Eng. Index Annu., Eng. Index Mon., Eng. Index Bioeng. Abstr., Eng. Index Energy Abstr., Can. Environ., Life Sci. Collect., Excerpta Med., Coal Abstr., Energy Inf. Abstr., Environ. Abstr., Index Med., Biol. Abstr., Chem. Abstr., Energy Res. Abstr., Sel. Water Resour. Abstr. LC QH545.A1. DD 574.24. NLM W1 JO644BI. CODEN JPFCD2. bk rev. adv acc. Environmental Letters, 0013-9300.

JOURNAL OF ENVIRONMENTAL SCIENCE AND HEALTH. PART C, ENVIRONMENTAL CARCINOGENESIS REVIEWS. VFOAT Environmental Carcinogenesis Reviews. Vol. C1, No. 1-. 0736-3001. Periodical. US. English. sa. $75.00. Marcel Dekker Inc, PO Box 11305/Church Street Station, New York NY 10249. Ed Joseph C Arcos. Ind/Abst Energy Res. Abstr., Excerpta Med., Life Sci. Collect., Sel. Water Resour. Abstr. LC RC268.5. DD 616.99407105. NLM W1. CODEN JECREO. bk rev. adv acc. Journal of Environmental Science and Health. Part C. Environmental Health Sciences, 0360-1242.

JOURNAL OF ENVIRONMENTAL SYSTEMS. VFOAT Environmental Systems. V. 1- Mar. 1971-. 0047-2433. Periodical. US. English. qt. $64.00. Baywood Publishing Company Inc, 120 Marine Street/PO Box D, Farmingdale NY 11735. Tel (516)269-2464. Ed Paul R Decicco. Ind/Abst Eng. Index, Soc. Sci. Citation Index, Sci. Cit. Index, Abr. Ed., GeoRef, Eng. Index Annu., Eng. Index Mon., Eng. Index Bioeng. Abstr., Eng. Index Energy Abstr., Can. Environ., Life Sci. Collect., Sel. Water Resour. Abstr., Excerpta Med., Energy Inf. Abstr., Environ. Abstr., Biol. Abstr., Bibliogr. Agric., Pollut. Abstr.

Sanitation, Environmental Technology

Indexes. LC TD1. DD 620.8. A journal addressed to the professional concerned with the analysis, design and management of our environment offering solutions to problems relating to system complexes.

JOURNAL OF LIGHT & VISUAL ENVIRONMENT. VFOAT Journal of Light and Visual Environment. Vol. 1-. 0387-8805. Periodical. English. sa. $59.00. Illuminating Engineering Institute of Japan, 7-1 Yurakucho 1-chome Chiyoda-ku, Tokyo 100 Japan. Ind/Abst Chem. Abstr. CODEN JLEVDQ.

JOURNAL OF THE AIR POLLUTION CONTROL ASSOCIATION. Main/Corp Air Pollution Control Association. V. 5- May 1955-. 0002-2470. Periodical. US. English. mo. Air Pollution Control Association, PO Box 2861, Pittsburgh PA 15230. Tel (412)621-1090. Ind/Abst Appl. Mech. Rev., Life Sci. Collect., Excerpta Med., Coal Abstr., Abstr. Bull. Inst. Paper Chem., Int. Aerosp. Abstr., CIS Abstr., Comput. Control Abstr., Electr. Electron. Abstr., Sci. Abstr., Ref. Source, Pollut. Abstr. Indexes, Environ. Abstr., Minproc, Bibliogr. Agric., Biol. Abstr., Chem. Abstr., Hospit. Lit. Index, Eng. Index, Sci. Cit. Index, Abr. Ed., Nucl. Sci. Abstr., Index Med., Sel. Water Resour. Abstr., Appl. Sci. Technol. Index, Energy Res. Abstr., Phys. Abstr., Fluidex, Energy Inf. Abstr. NLM W1 JO907F. CODEN JPCAAC. Available on microfilm from University Microfilms International. *Air Repari, 0096-6665; APCA News.*

JOURNAL OF THE AMERICAN MOSQUITO CONTROL ASSOCIATION. VFOAT Mosquito News. Vol. 1, No. 1 (Mar. 1985)-. 8756-971X. Periodical. US. English. qt. $35.00. American Mosquito Control Association, 5545 East Shields Avenue, Fresno CA 93727. DD 363. Index in first issue of next volume - attached. *Mosquito News, 0027-142X.*

JOURNAL OF THE ENVIRONMENTAL ENGINEERING DIVISION CEASED. Main/Corp American Society of Civil Engineers. Environmental Engineering Division. V. 99-108. 0090-3914. Periodical. US. English. bm. $10.00. American Society of Civil Engineers, 345 East 47th Street, New York NY 10017. Ind/Abst ASCE Annu. Comb. Index, Eng. Index Mon., Eng. Index Bioeng. Abstr., Eng. Index Energy Abstr., Excerpta Med., Coal Abstr., Energy Inf. Abstr., Environ. Abstr., Int. Aerosp. Abstr., Chem. Abstr., Eng. Index Annu., Sel. Water Resour. Abstr., GeoRef, Bibliogr. Agric., Energy Res. Abstr. LC TD1. DD 628.05. CODEN JEEGAV. *Journal of the Sanitary Engineering Division.*

JOURNAL OF THE FLORIDA ANTI-MOSQUITO ASSOCIATION. 0743-1554. Periodical. US. English. Florida Anti-Mosquito Association, PO Box 06005, Fort Myers FL 33906. *Proceedings of the Florida Anti-Mosquito Association, 0194-0066.*

THE JOURNAL OF THE INSTITUTION OF ENGINEERS (INDIA). Main/Corp Institution of Engineers (India). Environmental Engineering Division. V. 56, No. 2- Feb. 1976-. Periodical. II. English. ir. $8.00. Institution of Engineers, 8 Gokhale Road, Calcutta 700 020 India. Tel 44-8347. Ed B D Varma. Ind/Abst Coal Abstr., GeoRef, Energy Res. Abstr., Eng. Index Annu., Eng. Index Mon., Eng. Index Bioeng. Abstr., Eng. Index Energy Abstr. LC TA1. DD 620.6254. NLM W1 JO931Q. adv acc. Circ 6,000. Contains original research papers on environmental engineering subjects. *Journal of the Institution of Engineers (India). Part PH, 0020-3416.*

JOURNAL OF THE MISSOURI WATER AND SEWERAGE CONFERENCE. Main/Conf Missouri Water and Sewerage Conference. VFOAT Missouri Water & Sewage Conference Journal. Vol. 12- Jan. 1941-. 0096-4255. Periodical. US. English. qt. $5.00. Missouri Water and Sewerage, PO Box 774, Jefferson City MO 65102. Tel (314)635-3365. Ed Robert S Miller. LC TD1. adv acc. Circ 1,200. (ctrl). Water and wastewater operations. *Report of the . . . Annual Missouri Water and Sewerage Conference.*

JOURNAL OF THE NEW ENGLAND WATER POLLUTION CONTROL ASSOCIATION. Main/Corp New England Water Pollution Control Association. 0548-4502. Periodical. US. English. sa. $16.00. Journal of New England Water, Box 8714, Boston MA 02114. Ind/Abst Eng. Index Annu., Eng. Index Mon., Eng. Index Bioeng. Abstr., Eng. Index Energy Abstr. LC TD201. CODEN NEWJB5.

JOURNAL - SOUTHEASTERN SECTION, AMERICAN WATER WORKS ASSOCIATION. Main/Corp American Water Works Association. Southeastern Section. V. 1-. 0097-2614. Periodical. US. English. ir. American Water Works Association, 6666 West Quincy Avenue, Denver CO 80235. Ind/Abst Chem. Abstr. LC TD201. DD 628.106273. CODEN JSWWAT.

JOURNAL - WATER POLLUTION CONTROL FEDERATION. Main/Corp Water Pollution Control Federation. VFOAT Journal of the Water Pollution Control Federation. V. 32, No. 2- Feb. 1960-. 0043-1303. Periodical. US. English. ir. $120.00. Water Pollution Control Federation, 2626 Pennsylvania Avenue NW, Washington DC 20037. Tel (202)3372500. Ind/Abst Pestdoc, Abstr. Bull. Inst. Paper Chem., Can. Environ., Coal Abstr., Int. Aerosp. Abstr., GeoRef, Comput. Control Abstr., Electr. Electron. Abstr., Sci. Abstr. Sect. A. Phys. Abstr., Pap. Board Abstr., Sel. Water Resour. Abstr., Nuci. Sci. Abstr., Biol. Abstr., Chem. Abstr., Eng. Index Mon., Pet. Abstr., Pollut. Abstr. Indexes, Ocean. Abstr., Bibliogr. Agric., Index Med., Appl. Sci. Technol. Index, Energy Res. Abstr., Sci. Cit. Index, Abr. Ed., Hospit. Lit. Index, Appl. Mech. Rev. NLM W1 JO99D. CODEN JWPFA5. *Sewage and Industrial Wastes, 0096-364X.*

JOURNAL - WATER POLLUTION CONTROL FEDERATION. Main/Corp Water Pollution Control Federation. V. 1- Oct. 1928-. Periodical. US. English. ir. LC TD511. DD 628.205.

JUMIN KATSUDO. No. 1- 1972 12. Periodical. JA. Japanese. ir. 250 Single Issue. Shinseikatsu Undo Kyokai, 1-3 Hibiya Koen Chiyoda-ku, Tokyo Japan. LC HC465.E5. *Shinseikatsu Tokushin.*

KANAGAWA-KEN KOGAI SENTA NEMPO. Began with the Report for 1968. JA. Japanese. an. 87-1 Futamatagawa 1-chome Asahi-ku, Yokohama Japan. Ind/Abst Chem. Abstr. LC TD187.5.J32. CODEN KKNPDN.

KANKYO HAKUSHO. Main/Corp Tochigi, Japan (Prefecture) Eisei Kankyobu. 1974-. Japanese. ir. 1-20 Haniwada 1 (320), Utsunomiya Japan. LC TD187.5.J32. *Kogai No Jokyo ni Kansuru Nenji Hokoku.*

KANKYO HAKUSHO. Main/Corp Nagasaki (Prefecture). Japanese. ir. LC TD187.5.J32.

KANKYO HAKUSHO. Main/Corp Shiga, Japan. Seikatsu Kankyobu. Kankyo Hozenka. 1975-. Japanese. ir. Shiga-ken, 1-1 Kyomachi 4-chome, Otsu 520 Japan. LC HC463.S45. *Kogai Hakusho.*

KANKYO HAKUSHO. Main/Corp Kagoshima, Japan (Prefecture). 1975-. Japanese. ir. Kagoshima-ken, 14-50 Yamashitacho 892, Kagoshima Japan. LC TD187.5.J32.

KANKYO HAKUSHO. 1972-. Japanese. ir. NLM W1 KA47C.

KANKYO HAKUSHO. Main/Corp Yamaguchi, Japan (Prefecture). Japanese. ir. LC TD187.5.J32. *Kogai Hakusho.*

KANKYO HAKUSHO. Main/Corp Gifu-Ken (Japan). Kankyobu. Japanese. ir. LC TD187.5.J32. *Kankyo Hakusho.*

KANKYO HAKUSHO. Main/Corp Saitama, Japan. Kankyobu Kankyo Kanrika. JA. Japanese. ir. Saitama-Ken Kankyobu Kankyo, Kanrika 15-1, Takasago 3 Urawa. LC TD187.5.J32.

KANKYO HAKUSHO. Main/Corp Miyagi, Japan (Prefecture). Seikatsu Kankyobu. VFOAT Mayagi-Ken Kankyo Hakusho. 1977-. Periodical. JA. Japanese. ir. Miyagi-ken Seikatsu Kankyobu, 8-1 Honcho 3-chome Sendai Japan. LC TD187.5.J32. *Kogai Hakusho.*

KANKYO HAKUSHO (AOMORI-KEN, JAPAN). (KANKYO HAKUSHO). 1979-. Japanese. an. LC TD187.5.J32. *Kogai Hakusho (Aomori-Ken, Japan).*

KANKYO HAKUSHO (EHIME-KEN, JAPAN). (KANKYO HAKUSHO). Japanese. ir. Ehime-ken 4-2 Ichiban-cho 4-chome, Matsuyama-shi 790 Japan. LC TD187.5.J3.

KANKYO HAKUSHO (FUKUSHIMA-KEN, JAPAN. KOGAI KISEIKA). (KANKYO HAKUSHO). JA. Japanese. an. Sukushima-ken, 2-6 Sugitsumacho, Fukushima-shi 960 Japan. LC TD187.5.J32. *Kogai Hakusho (Fukushima-ken, Japan).*

KANKYO HAKUSHO (SHIZUOKA-KEN, JAPAN). (KANKYO HAKUSHO). Japanese. ir. LC TD187.5.J32.

KANKYO HOZEN NO GENKYO TO TAISAKU. Main/Corp Oita, Japan (Prefecture) Kankyo Hokenbu. 1976-77-. JA. Japanese. ir. Oita-ken Kankyo Hokenbu, 1-1 Otemachi 3-chome 870, Oita Japan. LC TD187.5.J32.

KANKYO KAGAKU : HOKKAIDO DAIGAKU KANKYO KAGAKU KENKYUKA KIYO. VFOAT Environmental Science, Hokkaido. 0386-8788. Periodical. English (Japanese). ir. Hokkaido Daigaku Kankyo Kagaku Kenkyuka, Nishi 5-chome Kita 10-jo Kita-ku, Sapporo-shi Japan. LC TD169. DD 333.705.

KANKYO KAGAKU KENKYUKA NEMPO. Main/Corp Tsukuba Daigaku. Kankyo Kagaku Kenkyuka. VFOAT Annual Report of the Graduate School of Environmental Sciences. JA. Japanese. an. Tsukuba Daigaku Kankyo Kagaku Kenkyuka, 1-1-1 Tennodai Sakuramura Niihari-gun, Ibaraki-ken Japan.

KANKYO KOGAI BUNKENSHU. See Bibliographies.

KANKYO KOGAI NENKAN. JA. Japanese. ir. 950. Gakyuo Shobo, 1-7-5 Fujimi Chiyoda-ku, Tokyo Japan.

KANSAS ENVIRONMENT. Summer 1980-. 0279-5078. Periodical. US. English. qt. Department of Health and Environment (Depository), Topeka KS 66613. *Waterwatch.*

KEGAI, HAKUSHO. Main/Corp Itami, Japan. Japanese. ir. Itami-Shi, 1 Senzo 1, Itami 664 Japan. LC TD187.5.J32.

KENKYU HOKOKU (KINKI DAIGAKU. KANKYO KAGAKU KENKYUJO). (KENKYU HOKOKU). VFOAT Report of the Environmental Science Research Institute, Kinki University. Began in 1981. 0287-5071. Periodical. JA. Japanese. an. Kinki Daigaku Kogakubu, Shinaki Yasunaga Hiro-machi Kure, Hiroshima-ken 737-01 Japan. Ind/Abst Chem. Abstr. CODEN KKKDE7. *Kogai Kenkyujo Kenkyu Hokoku (Kinki Daigaku).*

KENTUCKY CONVERSATION NEWS. See Conservation & Natural Resources.

KHIMIIA I TEKHNOLOGIIA VODY. (SOVIET JOURNAL OF WATER CHEMISTRY AND TECHNOLOGY). Vol. 3, No. 1-. 0734-1679. Periodical. US. English (cover-to-cover translation from Russian). bm. $325.00. Allerton Press, 150 Fifth Avenue, New York NY 10011. Ind/Abst Excerpta Med., Coal Abstr., GeoRef. LC TD204. DD 628.305.

KOGAI BOSHI GIJUTSU RISUTO. JA. Japanese. ir. Chusho Kigyo Joho Senta, c/o Senkaido Building, 9-13 Akasaka 1, Minato-ku 107 Tokyo Japan. LC TD187.5.J3.

KOGAI HAKUSHO. Main/Corp Yamaguchi, Japan (Prefecture). Japanese. ir. LC TD187.5.J32.

KOGAI HAKUSHO. Main/Corp Kanagama, Japan (Prefecture). Japanese. ir. LC TD187.5.J32.

KOGAI HAKUSHO (NAGANO-SHI, JAPAN) CEASED. (KOGAI HAKUSHO). 1973-1981. Japanese. ir. LC HC463.N28.

KOGAI KANKEI TOSHO MOKUROKU. TSUIROKU. Main/Corp Zenkoku Shiyu Bukken Saigai Kyosaikai. Bosai Semmon Toshokan. 1- 1969-. JA. Japanese. ir. 2-4-1 Hirakawacho Chiyoda-ku, Tokyo Japan. LC Z5862, TD174.

KOGAI KANKEI ZASSHI KIJI SAKUIN. 1973-. JA. Japanese. ir. Osaka Shiritsu Chuo Toshokan, 1 Kita Horie Mikedori 5-Chome Nishi-Ku, Osaka Japan. LC TD172.

KOGAI KENKYU NEMPO. Main/Corp Tolyi-to Kogai Kenkyujo. Japanese. ir. Tokyo Daigaku Shuppankei, Todai Konai Hongo Bunkyo-ku (113), Tokyo Japan. LC TD172.

KOGAI NO ARAMASHI. Main/Corp Tokyo. Kogaikyoku. Somubu. Sodanka. JA. Japanese. ir. Tokyo-To Kogaikyoku Somubu Sodanka, 7-1 Yurakucho 1-Chome, Chiyoda-Ku 100, Tokyo Japan. LC TD187.5.J32.

KOGAI SHIGEN KENKYUJO YORAN. VFOAT National Research Institute for Pollution and Resources. Japanese and English. ir. LC TD178.8.J33.

KOGAI SHIGENKEN NYUSU. JA. Japanese. ir. Kogyo Gijutsuin Kogai, Shigen Kenkyujo 1-1, Kawagushi 3 Kawaguchi Japan. Ind/Abst Coal Abstr. LC TD178.8.J33.

KORNYEZETSTATISZTIKAI ADATGYUJTEMENY. See Statistics.

KUNG YEH WU JAN FANG CHIH. 1-. Periodical. CH. Chinese. ir. Ching Chi Pu Kung Yeh Wu Jan Fang Chih Chi Shu Fu Tao Hsiao, TSU 109 Han-Kou St 1 Sect, Taipei Taiwan China. LC TD172. DD 363.7.

Sanitation, Environmental Technology

KUNNALLISTEKNIIKKA. VFOAT Kommunalteknik. Began publication in 1949. Periodical. Finnish (summaries in English). ir. LC TD4.

LAKE ERIE WASTEWATER MANAGEMENT STUDY PUBLIC INFORMATION FACT SHEET. VFOAT Public Information Fact Sheet. Began with unnumbered issues for Oct. 1977. Periodical. US. English. ir. Department of Defense and Department of the Army, 1776 Niagara Street, Buffalo NY 14207.

LAKE MICHIGAN WATER QUALITY REPORT. Main/Corp Illinois. Environmental Protection Agency. 0361-8188. US. English. an. Illinois Environmental Protection Agency, 2200 Churchill Road, Springfield IL 62706. Ind/Abst Chem. Abstr. LC TD223.3. DD 551.48209774. CODEN LMWRDV.

LAST GASP. (LAST GASP : NEWSLETTER OF THE ENVIRONMENTAL WORKING GROUP). VFOAT Etouffes, Les Etouffes : Nouvelles du Groupe d'Etude sur le Milieu de Travail. No. 1 (May 22, 1981)-. 0710-6920. Periodical. CN. English (French). ir. Free. Environmental Working Group, PO Box 2150 Station B, Place du Portage, Hull Quebec J8X 3Z4 Canada. DD 620.8509714221. (ctrl).

LEGACY. VFOAT Environment Ontario Legacy. V. 1- Apr./May 1972-. 0382-2788. Periodical. CN. English. bm. Ministry of the Environment, 135 St Clair Avenue West/Suite 100, Toronto Ontario M4V 1P5 Canada. Tel (416)965-7117. Watertalk, 0512-5057.

LIMPEZA PUBLICA. Portuguese. ir. Associacao Brasileira de Residuos Solidos e Limpeza Publica, Viaduto Dona Paulina 80-80 Andar, CEP 01361 Sao Paulo Brazil. LC TD785.

LITERATURBERICHTE UBER WASSER, ABWASSER, LUFT UND FESTE ABFALLSTOFFE. V. 16- 1968-. 0340-4900. GW. German. bm. $168.00. VCH Publishers Inc, 303 NW 12th Avenue, Deerfield Beach FL 33442. Tel (305)428-5566. LC Z6673, TD1. NLM ZWA 675 L776. Literaturberichte Uber Wasser, Abwasser, Luft und Boden.

LJUSKULTUR. Began publication in 1929. Periodical. SW. Swedish. bm. $13.97. Ljuskultur, PO Box 5512, South 114-85 Stockholm Sweden. Ind/Abst Comput. Control Abstr., Electr. Electron. Abstr., Sci. Abstr. Sect. A. Phys. Abstr. LC TH7700. CODEN LJUSAY.

MAINE WATER QUALITY STATUS. 0147-4596. US. English. Department of Environmental Protection, State House, Augusta ME 04333. LC TD224.M2. DD 363.61.

MAINTENANCE SUPPLIES. V. 6, No. 11- Nov. 1961-. 0025-0929. Periodical. US. English. mo. $22.00. Mac Nair Dorland Company, 101 West 31st Street, New York NY 10001. Tel (212)279-4455. Ed Dominic Mariani. bk rev. adv acc. Circ 10,000. (ctrl). A magazine for distributors of sanitary supplies and equipment. Maintenance-Sanitary Supplies.

THE MANAGEMENT OF WORLD WASTES. VFOAT World Wastes. Vol. 26, No. 3 (Mar. 1983)-. 0745-6921. Periodical. US. English. mo. $23.00 Domestic, $26.00 Canada. Management of World Wastes, 6255 Barfield Road, Atlanta GA 30328. Ind/Abst Can. Environ., Predicasts, Appl. Sci. Technol. Index, Energy Inf. Abstr., Environ. Abstr. LC TD791. DD 363.72005. Solid Wastes Management, 0886-1579.

MANAGING SOLID WASTE IN OREGON. (MANAGING SOLID WASTE IN OREGON : ANNUAL REPORT). Began with 1980 Vol. 0737-2957. US. English. an. Oregon Department of Environmental Quality, 522 Southwest 5th Avenue, Portland OR 97207. LC TD788.4.O7. DD 363.728.

MARINE ENVIRONMENTAL RESEARCH. Vol. 1, No. 1 (July 1978)-. 0141-1136. Periodical. UK. English. mo. 221.00 Domestic, 245.00 Foreign. Elsevier Applied Science Publishing, Crown House/Linton Road, Barking Essex IG11 8JU England. Tel 01 594 7272. Ed G W Heath. Ind/Abst Can. Environ., Eng. Index Annu., Eng. Index Mon., Eng. Index Bioeng. Abstr., Eng. Index Energy Abstr., Life Sci. Collect., Excerpta Med., Sel. Water Resour. Abstr., Energy Inf. Abstr., Environ. Abstr., Biol. Abstr., GeoRef, Chem. Abstr. LC QH545.W3. DD 574.5263605. CODEN MERSDW. bk rev. adv acc. Deals with relevant research on all aspects of the marine environment in the fields of biology, chemistry, oceanography, pollution and marine monitoring methods.

MARINE POLLUTION RESEARCH TITLES. UK. English. mo. $105.00. Marine Biological Association of the United Kingdom, Citadel Hill, Plymouth PLI 2PB England. Tel 0752-221761. Ed D S Moulder. LC Z5862.2.M3, GC1085. DD 016.6281686162. Circ 220. Marine and estuarine pollution references including detection, analysis, levels, effects, and removal.

MARYLAND STATE YEARLY AIR QUALITY DATA REPORT. Main/Corp Maryland. Bureau of Air Quality Control. VFOAT Maryland Air Quality Data Report. 1977-. 0191-2194. US. English. an. Maryland Department of Health and Mental Hygiene, Environmental Health Administration, 201 West Preston Street, Baltimore MD 21201. LC TD883.5.M3. DD 553.9. Maryland State Yearly Air Quality Data Report, 0191-2194.

MEMBERS DIRECTORY - INSTITUTION OF ENVIRONMENTAL HEALTH OFFICERS. See Yearbooks, Almanacs, Directories.

MEMBERSHIP DIRECTORY - NATIONAL ASSOCIATION OF RECYCLING INDUSTRIES. See Yearbooks, Almanacs, Directories.

MEMBERSHIP DIRECTORY - WATER POLLUTION CONTROL FEDERATION. See Yearbooks, Almanacs, Directories.

METHODS FOR THE EXAMINATION OF WATERS AND ASSOCIATED MATERIALS. 0141-075X. Monographic Series. UK. English. ir. Ind/Abst Chem. Abstr. CODEN MEWMD5. Analysis of Raw, Potable and Waste Waters.

METINGEN VAN XENOBIOTISCHE STOFFEN IN HET BIOLOGISCH MILIEU IN NEDERLAND. Main/Corp Netherlands (Kingdom, 1815-) Coordinatie Commissie voor de Metingen van Radioactiviteit en Xenobiotische Stoffen. VFOAT Measurements of Xenobiotic Substances in the Biological Environment in the Netherlands. 1975-. NE. Dutch (summaries in English). ir. Ministerie van Volksgezondheiden Milieuhygiene, Dokter Reijersstrat 10, Leidschendam Netherlands. LC TD186.5.N47. DD 363.6.

MICHIGAN ANNUAL AIR QUALITY REPORT. (MICHIGAN . . . ANNUAL AIR QUALITY REPORT). VFOAT Air Quality Report. 0275-2840. US. English. an. Air Quality Division, PO Box 30028, Lansing MI 48909. LC TD883.5.M47. DD 363.7392209774.

MICHIGAN CRITICAL MATERIALS REGISTER. Main/Corp Michigan. Environmental Protection Bureau. Environmental Services Division. VFOAT Critical Materials Register. 0270-4579. US. English. an. Michigan Department of Natural Resources, Environmental Protection, Bureau of Environmental Services Division, PO Box 30028, Lansing MI 48909. LC TD224.M5. DD 363.73809774. Critical Materials Register.

MIDDLE EAST WATER & SEWAGE. See Water Resources.

MILJSTATISTIKK. See Statistics.

MINERALS AND THE ENVIRONMENT. See Earth Sciences - Mineralogy.

MINNESOTA WATER QUALITY WORK PLAN FY . . . . Main/Corp Minnesota Pollution Control Agency. 1980-1-. US. English. an. 1935 West County Road B-2, Roseville MN 55113. LC TD224.M6. DD 363.73945609776. State of Minnesota Water Quality Work Plan, 0278-0100.

MINUTES OF ANNUAL SOUTHERN FOREST INSECT WORK CONFERENCE. Main/Conf Southern Forest Insect Work Conference. 1956?-. 0584-4460. US. English. an.

MINUTES OF PROCEEDINGS AND EVIDENCE OF THE SUB- COMMITTEE ON ACID RAIN OF THE STANDING COMMITTEE ON FISHERIES AND FORESTRY. Main/ Corp Canada. Parliament. House of Commons. Sub- Committee on Acid Rain. VFOAT Proces-Verbaux et Temoignages du Sous-Comite sur les Pluies Acides du Comite Permanent des Peches et des Forets. CN. English (French). Canadian Government Publishing Center, Supply & Services Canada, Hull Quebec K1A 0S9 Canada. LC TD196.A25. DD 363.7860971.

MIYAGI-KEN GENSHIRYOKU SENTA NENPO. VFOAT Annual Report of Environmental Radioactivity Research Institute of Miyagi. 1st (1982)-. Japanese. Miyagi-ken Genshiryoku Senta, 12-2 Onagawahama AZA Ise Onagawa-cho Oshika-gun, Miyagi-ken 986-22 Japan.

MONITOR (STOCKHOLM, SWEDEN). (MONITOR). Series/Titl Statens Naturvardsverk Meddelande. SW. Swedish. an. Liber Distribution, Forlagsorder 162 89, Stockholm Sweden. LC QH545.A1. DD 363.7309485.

MONOGRAPH. VFOAT Center for Technology, Environment, and Development Monograph Series. No. 1-. 0275-2751. Monographic Series. US. English. ir. Publication Office, The Center for Technology Environment and Development Clark University, 950 Main Street, Worcester MA 01610.

MONTANA AIR QUALITY DATA AND INFORMATION SUMMARY. (MONTANA AIR QUALITY DATA AND INFORMATION SUMMARY FOR . . .). VFOAT Montana Air Quality Data & Information Summary for . . . . 0732-2801. US. English. be. Air Quality Bureau, Helena MT 59620. LC TD883.5.M6. DD 363.7392209786. Annual Air Quality Data Summary for Montana, 0161-1666.

MONTANA ENVIRONMENTAL SCIENCES. 0193-8126. US. English. an. Department of Health & Environmental Sciences, Board of Health Building, Helena MT 59601. LC TD171.3.M9. DD 614.709786.

MONTANA NETWORK REVIEW. (MONTANA . . . NETWORK REVIEW). 0883-4458. US. English. an. Air Quality Bureau, Department of Health and Environmental Sciences, Helena MT 59620. Tel (406)444-3454.

MONTANA WATER POLLUTION CONTROL PROGRAM PLAN. 0149-8509. US. English. an. LC TD224.M9. DD 363.6109786.

MONTANA WATER SUPPLY OUTLOOK. See Water Resources.

MONTHLY AWARDS FOR CONSTRUCTION GRANTS FOR WASTEWATER TREATMENT WORKS. Jan. 1978-. 0276-3826. Periodical. US. English. mo. Superintendent of Documents, US Government Printing Office, Washington DC 20402. Tel (202)783-3238. LC TD746. DD 363.728. Monthly Listing of Awards for Construction Grants for Wastewater Treatment Works.

MOSQUITO NEWS CEASED. Began in Mar. 1941. Ceased V. 44, No. 4 Dec. 1984. 0027-142X. Periodical. US. English. qt. Ind/Abst Life Sci. Collect., Pestdoc, Ringdoc, Vetdoc, Energy Inf. Abstr., Environ. Abstr., Biol. Abstr., Chem. Abstr., Nuci. Sci. Abstr., Sel. Water Resour. Abstr. DD 363. NLM W1 MO94. CODEN MOSQAU. (cum index).

MOSQUITO SYSTEMATICS. V. 4- Mar. 1972-. 0091-3669. Periodical. US. English. qt. $20.00. American Mosquito Control Association, 5545 East Shields Avenue, Fresno CA 93727. Tel (209)292-5329. Ed Lewis T Neilsen. Ind/Abst Biol. Abstr., Bibliogr. Agric. LC QL536. DD 595.771. CODEN MSQSAK. bk rev. Circ 400. (ctrl). Devoted to the improvement and support of mosquito taxonomy as a vital service to sound mosquito control activities. Mosquito Systematics Newsletter, 0091-3677.

THE MUNICIPAL ENGINEERS JOURNAL. V. 1- May 1915-. 0027-3465. Periodical. US. English. ty. $8.00. Municipal Engineers of the City of New York, 51 Chamber Street, New York NY 10007. Ind/Abst Eng. Index Annu. LC TD1. DD 628.105. CODEN MUEJAF. (cum index).

MUNICIPAL JOURNAL (LONDON, ENGLAND : 1970). (MUNICIPAL JOURNAL). V. 78, No. 25- June 19, 1970-. 0143-4187. Periodical. UK. English. wk. Municipal Journal, 178-202 Great Portland Street, London W1N 6NH England. Ind/Abst Libr. Inf. Sci. Abstr. LC TD1. DD 352.041. Municipal and Public Services Journal, Municipal Engineering.

NATIONAL AIR POLLUTION SURVEILLANCE. VFOAT Surveillance Nationale de la Pollution Atmospherique, Air Surveillance Atmospherique. Began in 1970. 0381-2995. CN. English (French). an. Air Pollution Control Directorate of Environmental Protection Service, Department of the Environment, Ottawa Ontario K1A 0H3 Canada. LC TD883.7.C2. DD 363.6.

NATIONAL EMISSIONS REPORT. Main/ Corp United States. Environmental Protection Agency. National Air Data Branch. 0094-8748. US. English. National Technical Information Service, 5285 Port Royal Road, Springfield VA 22161. LC TD883.2. DD 363.6.

NATIONAL ENVIRONMENTAL IMPACT PROJECTION. No. 1-. 0195-9794. US. English. an. NLM W1 NA405.

Sanitation, Environmental Technology

NATIONAL MARINE POLLUTION PROGRAM PLAN, FEDERAL PLAN FOR OCEAN POLLUTION RESEARCH, DEVELOPMENT & MONITORING. Main/Corp United States. National Marine Pollution Program Office. VFOAT Federal Plan for Ocean Pollution Research, Development & Monitoring. Fiscal Years 1981-1985-. US. English. be. NOAA/National Marine Program, Pollution Office, Washington DC 20230. *Federal Plan for Ocean Pollution Research, Development, and Monitoring.*

THE NATIONAL UTILITY CONTRACTOR. See Building and Construction.

NATIONAL WASTE NEWS. V. 1- Sept. 1978-. 0190-7808. Periodical. US. English. mo. Free to Members, $12.00 Others. NWN, 4001 Westerly Place/PO Box W, Newport Beach CA 92663. Ind/Abst Energy Inf. Abstr., Environ. Abstr. LC TD785. DD 614.760973. *Solid Waste Systems*, 0094-5358.

NATUR UND LAND. See Conservation & Natural Resources.

N.C. . . . ANNUAL REPORT OF HAZARDOUS WASTE GENERATED, STORED, TREATED OR DISPOSED. VFOAT NC . . . Annual Report of Hazardous Waste Generated, Stored, Treated, or Disposed. US. English. an. North Carolina Solid and Hazardous Waste Management Branch, Division of Health Services, Box 2091, Raleigh NC 27602. Tel (919)733-2178. LC TD811.5. DD 363.728. Circ 1,000. A report of waste, generation and handling.

N.C.A.P NEWS. Main/Corp Northwest Coalition for Alternatives to Pesticides. VAT Northwest Coalition for Alternatives to Pesticides News. V. 1- Spring 1979-. 0194-5939. Periodical. US. English. qt. NCAP, Box 375, Eugene OR 97440. Tel (503)344-5044. Ed Mary H O'Brien. bk rev. Circ 2,500. Articles on the scientific, economic, political and legal issues surrounding pesticide use and abuse, alternatives to pesticides and community organizing for pesticide reform. Mckenzie Enterprise.

NCRR BULLETIN. Main/Corp National Center for Resource Recovery. VAT National Center for Resource Recovery Bulletin. Began with V. 1, 1971. 0099-1821. Periodical. US. English. qt. $12.00. National Center for Resource Recovery, 1211 Connecticut Avenue NW, Washington DC 20036. Tel (202)223-6154. Ind/Abst Coal Abstr., Energy Inf. Abstr., Environ. Abstr. LC TD785. DD 628.445.

NEERI ANNUAL REPORT. Main/Corp National Environmental Engineering Research Institute. VFOAT Annual Report - National Environmental Engineering Research Institute. 1974-. ll. English. ir. National Environmental Engineering Research Institute, Nehro Mara, Nagpur 3 India. LC TD4. DD 363.6. *Report.*

NEIWPCC AQUA NEWS CEASED. (NEIWPCC AQUA NEWS : NEWSLETTER OF THE NEW ENGLAND INTERSTATE WATER POLLUTION CONTROL COMMISSION). VFOAT Aqua News. VAT New England Interstate Water Pollution Control Commission Aqua News. Began June 1968. Ceased with V. 11, No. 3 June 1980. 8755-2426. Periodical. US. English. bm. DD 363. *News Letter (New England Interstate Water Pollution Control Commission).*

NEW ENGLAND ENVIRONMENTAL NETWORK NEWS. 0198-8476. Periodical. US. English. qt. $6.00. New England Environmental, NWK Tufts University, Medford MA 02155. Tel (617)381-3451.

THE NEW JERSEY HAZARDOUS WASTE NEWS. (NEW JERSEY HAZARDOUS WASTE NEWS). VFOAT Hazardous Waste News. Vol. 1, No. 1 (Jan. 1981)-. 0885-9833. Periodical. US. English. bm. Association of New Jersey Environmental Commissions, PO Box 157, Mendham NY 07945. DD 363.

NEW JERSEY/USEPA REGION II WATER RESOURCES MANAGEMENT AGREEMENT. Main/Corp New Jersey. Division of Water Resources. VFOAT Water Resources Management Agreement. VAT New Jersey, United States Environmental Protection Agency Region Two Water Resources Management Agreement. Began with 1979-80. 0730-6369. US. English. an. United States Environmental Protection Agency, Region II, 26 Federal Plaza, New York NY 10007. LC TD224.N5. DD 363.73945609749.

NEW YORK STATE ENVIRONMENT. VFOAT NYS Environment. V. 1- July 1971-. 0048-0053. Periodical. US. English. ir. Department of Environmental Conservation, 50 Wolf Road, Albany NY 12233. Ind/Abst Energy Inf. Abstr., Environ. Abstr.

NEWSLETTER - BUREAU OF LABORATORIES. Main/Corp South Carolina. Dept. of Health and Environmental Control. Bureau of Laboratories. 19 -. US. English. ir. 2600 Bull Street, Columbia SC 29201.

NEWSLETTER - PLANETARY ASSOCIATION FOR CLEAN ENERGY. Main/Corp Planetary Association for Clean Energy. V. 1- May 1979-. 0708-918X. Periodical. CN. English. ir. $27.86. Planetary Association for Clean Energy, 77 Metcalfe Street/Suite 212, Ottawa Ontario K1P 5L6 Canada. Tel (613)236-6268. Ed Monique Michaud. Ind/Abst Energy Res. Abstr. DD 363.6. bk rev. adv acc. Circ 2,500. Forum for advanced scientific thinking merging latest conventional research with unconventional approaches for a clean technology.

NEWSLETTER, SOLID WASTE NEWS BRIEF. Main/Corp Municipal Environmental Research Laboratory. VFOAT Solid Waste News Brief. US. English. Environmental Protection Agency, Office of Research and Development, Cincinnati OH 45268.

NEWSROOM DIRECTORY & GUIDE TO THE ILLINOIS ENVIRONMENTAL PROTECTION AGENCY. See Yearbooks, Almanacs, Directories.

NOISE & VIBRATION CONTROL WORLDWIDE. Vol. 11- Jan. 1980-. 0143-6481. Periodical. UK. English. ir. $64.36. Trade and Technical Press Ltd, Crown House Morden, Surrey SM4 5EW England. Tel 01-540-3897. Ind/Abst Eng. Index, Excerpta Med., Fluidex, Coal Abstr., Comput. Control Abstr., Electr. Electron. Abstr., Sci. Abstr., Pap. Board Abstr., Ship Abstr. LC TD891. DD 620.2305. CODEN NVCWDV. *Noise Control Vibration Isolation.*

NOISE-CON PROCEEDINGS. Main/Conf National Conference on Noise Control Engineering. VFOAT Noise CON Proceedings, Proceedings of Noise-CON. Began in 1973. 0736-2935. US. English. be. $42.00. Noise Control Foundation, PO Box 3469, Arlington Branch, Poughkeepsie NY 12603. Ind/Abst Eng. Index Annu., Eng. Index Bioeng. Abstr., Eng. Index Energy Abstr., Eng. Index Mon. LC TD891. DD 620.2305.

NOISE CONTROL DIRECTORY. See Yearbooks, Almanacs, Directories.

NOISE CONTROL ENGINEERING CEASED. V. 1-19, NO. 1. 0093-9978. Periodical. US. English. bm. $30.00. 9 Saddle Road, Cedar Knolls NJ 07927. Ind/Abst Electron. Commun. Abstr. J., ISMEC Bull., Pollut. Abstr. Indexes, Saf. Sci. Abstr. J., Eng. Index Annu., Eng. Index Mon., Eng. Index Bioeng. Abstr., Eng. Index Energy Abstr., Coal Abstr., Energy Inf. Abstr., Environ. Abstr., Int. Aerosp. Abstr., CIS Abstr., Ref. Source, Ship Abstr., Comput. Control Abstr., Electr. Electron. Abstr. LC TD891. DD 620.23. CODEN NCEGAR.

NOISE CONTROL REPORT. V. 1- 1972-. 0146-4817. Periodical. US. English. bw. Business Publishers Inc, 951 Pershing Drive, Silver Spring MD 20910. Tel (301)587-6300. Ed Ginny Gibbons. LC TD891. DD 620.2305. A report on noise control policy and problems at federal, state and local levels, plus information on the industry, new products, grants and contracts.

NOISE-NEWS. (NOISE NEWS). 0146-4809. Periodical. US. English. bm. $21.00 Domestic, $26.00 Others. Institute of Noise Control Engineering, PO Box 3469/Arlington Branch, Poughkeepsie NY 12603. Tel (914)691-7271. Ed G Maling. bk rev. adv acc. Information on technical meetings, government reports, book reviews and other news items.

NOISE POLLUTION PUBLICATIONS ABSTRACTS. See Indexes/Abstracts.

NORSK INSTITUTT FOR VANNFORSKNING. 1958/67-. 0333-3280. NO. Norwegian. an. Postboks 260 Blindern, Oslo 3 Norway. Ind/Abst Chem. Abstr. LC TD281.A1. CODEN NIVAD3.

NORTH CAROLINA'S ENVIRONMENT. . . REPORT. 1981-. US. English. an. Department of Natural Resources Community Development, PO Box 27687, Raleigh NC 27611. LC TD171.3.N8. DD 333.7209756.

NORTHEASTERN ENVIRONMENTAL SCIENCE. Vol. 1, No.1-. 0730-630X. Periodical. US. English. qt. $35.00. Northeastern Science Fnd Inc, PO Box 746, Troy NY 12181. Tel (518)273-3247. Ed Steve Scholle. Ind/Abst Energy Inf. Abstr., Environ. Abstr., Biol. Abstr., GeoRef, Chem. Abstr. LC TD171.3.N65. DD 363.700974. CODEN NOESDE. adv acc. Circ 150. (ctrl). Intended to address environmental concerns vital to the NE United States and Canadian coastal areas, farms, lakes, and forests.

NOVOSTI TEKHNICHESKOI LITERATURY. STROITELSTVO I ARKHITEKTURA. RAZDEL A. SERIIA X : SANITARNAIA TEKHNIKA, INZHENERNOE OBORUDOVANIE ZDANII. VFOAT Stroitelstvo I Arkhitektura. 1974-. UR. Multilingual (Russian). mo. A-47 Ul Corkogo Dom 38, Moskva 125047 Russia. LC Z5853.S22, TD145. *Novosti Tekhnicheskoi Literatury. Stroitelstvo I Arkhitektura. Razdel A. Seriia XII: Sanitarnaia Tekniika, Inzhernerneo Oborudovsnie Zdanii.*

NSCA MEMBERS' HANDBOOK. See Industrial Health & Safety.

NSWMA REPORTS FOR THE WASTE MANAGEMENT INDUSTRY. VFOAT N.S.W.M.A. Reports for the Waste Management Industry. VAT National Solid Wastes Management Association Reports For the Waste Management Industry. Began with: Vol. 12, No. 6 (June 1977). Periodical. US. English. mo. National Solid Wastes Management Association, Suite 930/1120 Connecticut Avenue NW, Washington DC 20036. *NSWMA Washington Report.*

NUCLEAR AND CHEMICAL WASTE MANAGEMENT. V. 1-. 0191-815X. Periodical. US. English. qt. $125.00. Pergamon Press, 395 Sawmill River Road, Elmsford NY 10523. Ind/Abst Electron. Commun. Abstr. J., ISMEC Bull., Pollut. Abstr. Indexes, Saf. Sci. Abstr. J., Eng. Index Annu., Eng. Index Mon., Eng. Index, Eng. Index Bioeng. Abstr., Eng. Index Energy Abstr., Excerpta Med., Energy Inf. Abstr., Environ. Abstr., Energy Res. Abstr., Chem. Abstr., GeoRef, Appl. Sci. Technol. Index, Bibliogr. Index Geol. LC TD811.5. DD 621.483805. CODEN NCWMD2.

NUCLEAR WASTE MANAGEMENT PROGRAM SUMMARY DOCUMENT. Main/Corp United States. Dept. of Energy. Office of Nuclear Waste Management. 0196-772X. US. English. National Technical Information Service, US Department of Commerce, 5285 Port Royal Road, Springfield VA 22161. LC TD898. DD 363.728.

NUNG YEH HUAN CHING PAO HU. VFOAT Nongye Huanjing Baohu. Periodical. CC. Chinese. bm. 0.25. Post Office, Tien-Chin Shih China. LC S589.75. DD 363.731.

NVB. NOISE & VIBRATION BULLETIN. VFOAT Noise & Vibration Bulletin. VAT NVB. Noise and Vibration Bulletin. Jan. 1971-. 0144-7785. Periodical. UK. English. mo. $90.00. Multi Science Publ Co Ltd, 42/45 New Broad Street, London ECEM 1QY England. NLM ZWD 735 N107. *Noise & Vibration Bulletin.*

NYEN. NEW YORK ENVIRONMENTAL NEWS. (NEW YORK ENVIRONMENTAL NEWS : NYEN). VFOAT NYEN. 0273-6438. Periodical. US. English. sm. Free. NYEN New York Environmental News, Atmospheric Sciences Research Center Suny-Albany, Albany NY 12222.

OCCASIONAL PAPER. Main/Corp Johannesburg. University of the Witwatersrand. Dept. of Geography and Environmental Studies. VFOAT Environmental Studies. No. 1-. Monographic Series. English. ir. Ind/Abst GeoRef. CODEN PWGEDQ.

OCCASIONAL PAPER - ENVIRONMENT CANADA. Main/Corp Canada. Environment Canada. No. 1- 1972-. CN. English and French. Environment Canada, Lands Directorate EN Ward, Ottawa Ontario K1A 0E7 Canada. LC TD171.5.C2. DD 363.6.

OCCASIONAL PAPER - FACULTY OF ENVIRONMENTAL STUDIES. UNIVERSITY OF WATERLOO. (OCCASIONAL PAPER - UNIVERSITY OF WATERLOO, FACULTY OF ENVIRONMENTAL STUDIES). Main/Corp University of Waterloo. Faculty of Environmental Studies. No. 4- Nov. 1972-. 0317-8641. Monographic Series. CN. English. University of Waterloo, Faculty of Environmental

Sanitation, Environmental Technology

Studies, Waterloo Ontario N2L 3G1 Canada. **DD** 301.31.

OCHRONA SRODOWISKA I GOSPODARKA WODNA.... Series/Titl Statystyka Polski. Seria Materiay Statystyczne. 1981-. Polish. an. 150.00. Ksiegarnia Naukowa Im, Bolesawa Prusa Ul Krakowskie Przedmiescie 7, 00-068 Warzawa Poland. **LC** TD171.5.P6.

OFFALY RESOURCES FOR ENVIRONMENTAL STUDIES. VFOAT Resources for Environmental Studies. 1-. 0332-4397. Monographic Series. English. ir. **Ind/Abst** GeoRef. **LC** UNC.

OFFENTLICHE ABFALLBESEITIGUNG. Series/Titl Statistik Niedersachsen. **GW**. German. ir. 7.50. Niedersachsisches Landesverwaltungsamt Statistik, Postfach 107, 3000 Hannover 1 West Germany. **LC** TD789.G42. **DD** 363.7280943.

OFFICE OF AIR AND WATER PROGRAMS PUBLICATION. Main/Corp United States. Environmental Protection Agency. Office of Air and Water Programs. US. English. National Technical Information Service, 5285 Port Royal Road, Springfield VA 22161. **LC** TD883.2. **DD** 363.6. *Publication APTD.*

OFFICE OF ENVIRONMENT STATEMENT OF PROGRAMS. Main/Corp United States. Dept. of Energy. Office of the Assistant Secretary for Environment. 1978/79-. US. English. an. US Department of Energy, Office of the Assistant, Secretary for Environment, Office of Planning Coordination, Washington DC 20402.

OFFICE OF WATER OPERATING GUIDANCE AND ACCOUNTABILITY SYSTEM. APPENDIX. *See Law.*

OFFICIAL PROCEEDINGS - INTERNATIONAL WATER CONFERENCE. (OFFICIAL PROCEEDINGS). Main/Conf International Water Conference. **VFOAT** Proceedings, International Water Conference. 41st (1980)-. 0739-4977. US. English. an. $30.00. Pennsylvania Sheraton Hotel, Pittsburgh PA 15230. **Ind/Abst** Eng. Index Annu., Eng. Index Mon., Eng. Index Bioeng. Abstr., Eng. Index Energy Abstr. **LC** TD201. **DD** 628.105. *International Water Conference Annual Meeting, 0074-9575.*

OHIO EPA ANNUAL REPORT SUMMARY. VFOAT Summary Annual Report. **VAT** Ohio Environmental Protection Agency Annual Report Summary. 0147-3182. US. English. an. Ohio Environmental Protection Agency, Columbus OH 42212. **LC** TD171.3.O35. **DD** 353.008232.

OHIO LITTER CONTROL PROGRAM . . . ANNUAL REPORT. Main/Corp Ohio. Office of Litter Control. US. English. an. **LC** TD818.O3. **DD** 363.729.

OIL & PETROCHEMICAL POLLUTION. *See Petroleum and Natural Gas.*

OITA-KEN KOGAI EISEI SENTA NENPO. VFOAT Annual Report of Institute of Environmental Pollution and Public Health, Oita Prefecture. Japanese. an. Oita-Ken Kogai Eisei Senta, Aza Yoshikawara Danchi, Oaza Magari, Oita-shi 870 Japan. **LC** TD187.5.J32.

OKLAHOMA'S WATER QUALITY STANDARDS. 8756-8322. US. English. **LC** TD224.O5. **DD** 363.73946209766.

ONDERZOEK NAAR MILIEU EN NATUUR IN NEDERLAND. Main/Corp Studie- en Informatiecentrum Tno voor Milieu-Onderzoek. **NE**. Dutch. ir. Studie-en Informatiecentrum Tno voor Milieu-Onderzoek, Schoemakerstraat 97, Postbus 186, 2600 Ad Delft, S-Gravenhage Netherlands. **LC** TD178.7.N4.

ONTARIO RECYCLING UPDATE. *See Conservation & Natural Resources.*

ONTARIO SOCIETY FOR ENVIRONMENTAL MANAGEMENT. (O. S. E. M. NEWSLETTER). V. 1, No. 3- Sept. 1977-. 0705-9523. Periodical. CN. English. qt. Ontario Society for Environmental Management, 1735 Bayview Avenue, Toronto Ontario M4G 3C1 Canada. **Tel** (416)488-5116. **DD** 620.8062713. *Newsletter, 0705-8666.*

OREGON AIR QUALITY ANNUAL REPORT. 0147-2941. US. English. an. Air Quality Control Division, 1234 SW Morrison Street, Portland OR 97205. **LC** TD883.5.O7. **DD** 363.6.

ORSANCO. Main/Corp Ohio River Valley Water Sanitation Commission. **VFOAT** O.R.S.A.N.C.O. **VAT** Ohio River Valley Water Sanitation Commission. 1981-. 0734-4724. US. English. an. ORSANCO, 414 Walnut Street, Cincinnati Ohio 45202. *Riverscape.*

OUTLOOK (BOULDER, COLO.). (OUTLOOK). No. 1 (Winter 1970)-. Periodical. US. English. qt. Mt View Publishing Company, 2929 6th Street, Boulder CO 80302. **Tel** (303)443-7278.

OWMC EXCHANGE. (THE OWMC EXCHANGE). Main/Corp Ontario Waste Management Corporation. **VFOAT** Exchange. **VAT** Ontario Waste Management Corporation Exchange, (Toronto 1982). Vol. 1, No. 1 (Summer 1982)-. 0715-0237. Periodical. CN. English. qt. Free. Ontario Waste Management Corp, 2 Bloor Street West/11th Floor, Toronto Ontario M4W 3E2 Canada. **DD** 363.17609713.

PACIFIC NORTHWEST REGION ENVIRONMENTAL QUALITY PROFILE. US. English. an. US Environmental Protection Agency Region 10, 1200 Sixth Avenue, Seattle WA 98101. **LC** TD171.3.N67. **DD** 363.70209795.

PAPERS PRESENTED AT THE ANNUAL CONVENTION. Main/Corp Western Canada Water and Sewage Conference. 0083-8799. Periodical. CN. English. ir. Western Canada Water & Sewage, PO Box 6070, Saskatoon Saskatchewan S7K 4E5 Canada. **LC** TD201. **DD** 628.

PEST CONTROL. V. 17, No. 8- Aug. 1949-. 0031-6121. Periodical. US. English. mo. Pest Control, 1 East 1st Street, Duluth MN 55802. **Tel** (218)723-9200. **Ind/Abst** Excerpta Med., Pestdoc, Ringdoc, Vetdoc, Energy Inf. Abstr., Environ. Abstr., Bibliogr. Agric., Biol. Abstr., Chem. Abstr., Nucl. Sci. Abstr. **LC** TX325. **DD** 648.705. **NLM** W1 PE925. **CODEN** PCONAI. Available on microfilm from University Microfilms. *Pests and Their Control, 0096-2147.*

PEST CONTROL LETTER. Began with: V. 1, in 1975. Periodical. US. English. mo. $53.00. Research Endeavors Company, PO Box 26, San Bruno CA 94066. **Tel** (415)593-9311.

PEST CONTROL TECHNOLOGY. 0730-7608. Periodical. US. English. mo. $15.00 US, $20.00 Canada. Gie Inc Publishers, 2803 Bridge Avenue, Cleveland OH 44113. **LC** SB950.A1. **DD** 632.905. *PCT, Pest Control Technology, 0091-6692.*

PEST MANAGEMENT. Vol. 1, No. 1 (Nov. 1981)-. 0744-6357. Periodical. US. English. mo. $35.00. National Pest Control Association, PO Box 377/8100 Oak Street, Dunn Loring VA 22027. **Tel** (703)573-8330. **Ed** Kathleen H Bova. bk rev. adv acc. **Circ** 5,500. (ctrl). Trade journal geared to the pest control operator amd technician. Contains technical articles concerning new chemicals on the market and ways to treat a pest problem.

PEST MANAGEMENT PAPERS. No. 1- 1975-. 0703-7643. Monographic Series. CN. English. ir. Simon Fraser University, Bookstore, Burnaby British Columbia V5A 1S6 Canada.

PESTICIDE & TOXIC CHEMICAL NEWS. VAT Pesticide and Toxic Chemical News. V.5- Dec. 1, 1976-. 0146-0501. Periodical. US. English. wk. Food Chemical News, 1101 Pennsylvania Avenue SE, Washington DC 20003. **Tel** (202)544-1980. *Pesticide Chemical News.*

PESTICIDE SCIENCE. V. 1- 1970-. 0031-613X. Periodical. UK. English. bm. $150.00. Blackwell Scientific Publisher, PO Box 88, Oxford OX2 OEL England. **Ind/Abst** Life Sci. Collect., Excerpta Med., Sel. Water Resour. Abstr., Pestdoc, Ringdoc, Vetdoc, Energy Inf. Abstr., Environ. Abstr., Biol. Abstr., Chem. Abstr., Biol. Agric. Index, Sci. Cit. Index, Abr. Ed., Pollut. Abstr. Indexes. **NLM** W1 PE923N. **CODEN** PSSCBG.

PESTICIDE USE REPORT BY COMMODITY. Main/Corp California. Dept. of Food and Agriculture. Agricultural Chemicals and Feed. 1972-. US. English. an. *Pesticide Use Report by Commodity.*

PESTICIDES. V. 1- Sept. 1967-. 0031-6148. Periodical. II. English. mo. 50.00. Colour Publications Pvt Ltd, 126 A Dhuruwadi/Dr Nariman Road, Bombay 40025 India. **Tel** 430 9610/9318/6319. **Ed** R V Raghavan. **Ind/Abst** Chem. Abstr., Predicasts, Pestdoc, Ringdoc, Vetdoc. **LC** SB951. **DD** 632.9505. **CODEN** PSTDAN. bk rev. adv acc. **Circ** 4,876. Technical articles, special columns and news reports pertaining to the pesticides industry and pest control.

PESTICIDES ABSTRACTS. *See Indexes/Abstracts.*

PESTICIDES & TOXIC SUBSTANCES MONITORING REPORT. VAT Pesticides and Toxic Substances Monitoring Report. Vol. 1, No. 1 (July 1980)-. 0273-348X. US. English. Environmental Protection Agency, Office of Pesticides and Toxic Substances, Survey and Analysis Division, Washington DC 20460. **NLM** W1 PE931T. *Pesticide Monitoring Semi-Annual Report.*

PESTICIDES IN THE ENVIRONMENT. V. 1- 1971-. Periodical. US. English. ir. Marcel Dekker/Continuation Department, 270 Madison Avenue, New York NY 10016. **Ed** Robert White and Stevens. This is an ongoing series. Each title has a different subject.

PESTICIDES MONITORING JOURNAL CEASED. Vol. 1, No. 1 (June 1967)-V. 15, No. 3 (Dec. 1981). 0031-6156. Periodical. US. English. qt. Superintendent of Documents, U S Government Printing Office, Washington DC 20402. **Ind/Abst** Am. Stat. Index, Bibliogr. Agric., Can. Environ., Energy Inf. Abstr., Environ. Abstr., Pestdoc, Ringdoc, Sel. Water Resour. Abstr., Vetdoc, Biol. Abstr., Chem. Abstr., Index Med. **LC** QH545.P4. **NLM** W1 PE932. **CODEN** PEMJAA.

PESTICIDES REVIEW. No. 10- Mar. 1974-. English. ir. Australian Government Publication Service, PO Box 100, Woden Australian Capital Territory 2606 Canberra Australia. **LC** RA1270.P4. **DD** 632.9505. *Pesticides Review.*

PLAN FOR ENVIRONMENTAL RADIATION SURVEILLANCE IN NORTH CAROLINA. Main/Corp North Carolina. Radiation Protection Branch. 0148-8120. US. English. PO Box 12200, Raleigh NC 27605. **LC** TD890. **DD** 363.6.

PM NEWSLETTER (WADHURST, EAST SUSSEX). (PM NEWSLETTER). **VFOAT** P.M. Newsletter. 0264-1771. UK. English. mo. 45.00. Wealden Press Ltd, South Park Lodge Mayfield Lane, Wadhurst East Sussex TN5 6JE England. **Ind/Abst** Ref. Source. **LC** TD172. **DD** 363.7005. *Pollution, Energy & Safety Monitor.*

POLICY AND PLANNING (CANADA. ENVIRONMENTAL IMPACT CONTROL DIRECTORATE) CEASED. (POLICY AND PLANNING - ENVIRONMENT IMPACT CONTROL DIRECTORATE). Ceased 1982?. Monographic Series. CN. English.

POLITIQUE ET PLANIFICATION (CANADA. DIRECTION GENERALE DU CONTROLE DES INCIDENCES ENVIRONNEMENTALES) CEASED. (POLITIQUE ET PLANIFICATION - DIRECTION GENERALE DU CONTROLE DES INCIDENCES ENVIRONNEMENTALES). No longer published after 1982?. Monographic Series. CN. French.

POLLUSTOP. VFOAT Pollu Stop. 0300-3574. Periodical. FR. French. mo. Editions Edidam, 4 Avenue de la Porte-Villiers, 17 EME Paris France. **LC** HC280.E5. **DD** 301.310944.

POLLUTING INCIDENTS IN AND AROUND U.S. WATERS. Series/Titl Comdtinst. **VAT** Polluting Incidents in and Around United States Waters. 0092-0320. US. English. an. G-WEP-1/73, US Coast Guard, Washington DC 20590. **LC** TD223. **DD** 614.7720973. *Polluting Spills in U.S. Waters.*

POLLUTION ABATEMENT COSTS AND EXPENDITURES. (CURRENT INDUSTRIAL REPORTS. MA-200, POLLUTION ABATEMENT COSTS AND EXPENDITURES). Began with 1973. 0149-4449. US. English. an. Data User Services Division, Customer Services Publication, Bureau of the Census, Washington DC 20233. **Tel** (301)763-4100. **LC** HC110.P55. **DD** 338.43. Presents timely data on the production, inventories, and orders of approximately 5,000 products, which represents 40 percent of all US manufacturing.

POLLUTION ABSTRACTS. ANNUAL INDEX. *See Indexes/Abstracts.*

POLLUTION ABSTRACTS WITH INDEXES. *See Indexes/Abstracts.*

POLLUTION AND WATER RESOURCES, COLUMBIA UNIVERSITY SEMINAR SERIES. *See Water Resources.*

Sanitation, Environmental Technology

POLLUTION ATMOSPHERIQUE. 1- Yearly V. No. 1-. 0032-3632. Periodical. FR. French. qt. $50.56. Soc Revue Pollution Atmospher, 58 rue du Rocher, 75008 Paris France. Tel (1) 293 62 07. LC TD881. NLM W1 PO254J. CODEN POATBH. bk rev. adv acc. Circ 2,800. Articles about atmospheric pollution, international information, legislation, rules, manifestations and conferences, communiques and bibliographies.

POLLUTION (BOCA RATON, FLA.). (POLLUTION). Series/Titl Social Issues Resources Series. Vol. 1, Article 1-. 0273-253X. US. English. an. Social Issues Resources Series Inc, PO Box 2507, Boca Raton FL 33432. Ed E C Goldstein. LC TD172. DD 363.7305.

THE POLLUTION CONTROL AGENCY'S . . . BIENNIAL REPORT. VFOAT Biennial Report to the Legislature. US. English. be. Minnesota Pollution Control Agency, 1935 West County Road 82, Roseville MN 55113. LC TD180. DD 353.9776008232206.

POLLUTION CONTROL GUIDE. Main/Corp Commerce Clearing House. 0162-1238. Periodical. US. English. wk. $790.00. Commerce Clearing House, 4025 West Peterson Avenue, Chicago IL 60646. LC KF3775.A6. Reports federal, state laws relating to water and air pollution, land use and environmental impact procedures; spans federal rules for solid waste, noise, pesticides, radiation, toxic substances, etc.

POLLUTION CONTROL JOURNAL. 0095-6074. Periodical. US. English. qt. $4.00. L Thomas, PO Box 533, Denver CO 80202. LC TD169. DD 363.6.

POLLUTION ENGINEERING. V. 1- Oct./Nov. 1969-. 0032-3640. Periodical. US. English. mo. $12.00. Pudvan Publishing Company, 1935 Shermer Road, Northbrook IL 60062. Ed Richard A Young. Ind/Abst Eng. Index Mon., Eng. Index Bioeng. Abstr., Eng. Index Energy Abstr., Can. Environ., Excerpta Med., Coal Abstr., Energy Inf. Abstr., Environ. Abstr., Comput. Control Abstr., Electr. Electron. Abstr., Sci. Abstr. Sect. A. Phys. Abstr., Energy Res. Abstr., Chem. Abstr., Eng. Index Annu., Sel. Water Resour. Abstr., Bibliogr. Agric., Appl. Sci. Technol. Index, Pollut. Abstr. Indexes, Comput. Control Abstr., Eng. Index, Phys. Abstr., Phys. Abstr. LC TD172. DD 628.505. CODEN PLENBW. adv acc. Circ 55,000. (ctrl). Leading monthly environmental magazine for municipal and industrial engineers and managers of air/water pollution and hazardous wastes.

POLLUTION ENGINEERING AND TECHNOLOGY. V. 1-. 0148-4435. Monographic Series. US. English. ir. Marcel Dekker, 270 Madison Avenue, New York NY 10016. Ind/Abst Comput. Control Abstr., Electr. Electron. Abstr., Sci. Abstr. Sect. A. Phys. Abstr., Chem. Abstr. LC UNC. CODEN PEGTDD.

POLLUTION EQUIPMENT NEWS. Dec. 1968-. 0032-3659. Periodical. US. English. bm. Pollution Equipment News, 8550 Babcock Boulevard, Pittsburgh PA 15237. LC TD1. DD 628.05.

POLLUTION SURVEY REPORT. No. 1- 19 -. 0468-5520. Periodical. US. English. ir. North Carolina State Stream Sanitation Committee, Raleigh NC 27687. DD 333.9.

POLLUTION TECHNOLOGY REVIEW. 0090-516X. Monographic Series. US. English. ir. Noyes Data Corporation, Mill Road at Grand Avenue, Park Ridge NJ 07656. Tel (201)391-8484. Ed J Paul. Ind/Abst Eng. Index Mon., Eng. Index Bioeng. Abstr., Eng. Index Energy Abstr., GeoRef, Eng. Index Annu., Bibliogr. Index Geol. CODEN PTERDY. Environmental engineering technology. *Pollution Control Review, 0079-3116.*

POPULATION DOSE COMMITMENTS DUE TO RADIOACTIVE RELEASES FROM NUCLEAR POWER PLANT SITES IN . . . . Began with 1975. US. English. an. NRC/GPO Sales Program, US Nuclear Regulatory Commission, Washington DC 20555. Vols. for (1978-) distributed to depository libraries in microfiche.

PROBE. (THE PROBE). Began with Feb. 1971 issue. 0380-7916. Periodical. CN. English. Pollution Probe London, Urban Resource Centre, 322 Queens Avenue, London Ontario Canada.

PROBLEMY KONTROLIA I ZASHCHITA ATMOSFERY OT ZAGRIAZNENIIA. Periodical. UR. Russian. 1.50. Izdatelstvo Naukova Dumka, 252601 Kiev, Gsp Repina 3, Kiev Ukrainian USSR. Ind/Abst Chem. Abstr. LC TD881. CODEN PKZZDW.

PROCEEDINGS AND PAPERS OF THE ANNUAL CONFERENCE OF THE CALIFORNIA MOSQUITO AND VECTOR CONTROL ASSOCIATION, INC. (PROCEEDINGS AND PAPERS OF THE ANNUAL CONFERENCE OF THE CALIFORNIA MOSQUITO AND VECTOR CONTROL ASSOCIATION). Main/Corp California Mosquito and Vector Control Association. V. 45- 1977-. 0160-6751. US. English. an. $10.00. California Mosquito Vector Control Association, 197 Otto Circle, Sacramento CA 95822. Tel (916)393-7216. Ed John C Combs. Ind/Abst Chem. Abstr., Bibliogr. Agric. NLM W1 PR583. CODEN PCMVDZ. Circ 600. Mosquito research papers presented at the California Mosquito and Vector Control Association, Inc Annual Conference. *Proceedings and Papers of the Annual Conference of the California Mosquito Control Association, Inc., 0091-6501.*

PROCEEDINGS, ANNUAL MEETING - NEW JERSEY MOSQUITO CONTROL ASSOCIATION, INC. Main/Corp New Jersey Mosquito Control Association. 62nd- 1975-. 0198-7267. US. English. an. New Jersey Mosquito Control Association, 200 Parsonage Road, Edison NJ 08817. Tel (201)549-0665. CODEN PMNADD. *Proceedings of the Annual Meeting - New Jersey Mosquito Extermination Association, 0096-5596.*

PROCEEDINGS, ANNUAL TECHNICAL MEETING - INSTITUTE OF ENVIRONMENTAL SCIENCES. Main/Corp Institute of Environmental Sciences. 1960. 0361-2007. US. English. an. Institute of Environmental Science, 940 East Northwest Highway, Mt Prospect IL 60056. Tel (312)255-1561. Ed Janet Ehmann. Ind/Abst Eng. Index Annu., Eng. Index Mon., Eng. Index Bioeng. Abstr., Eng. Index Energy Abstr., GeoRef, Biol. Abstr., Chem. Abstr., Bibliogr. Agric. CODEN IESPAF. Circ 2,000. Contains papers presented at meetings dealing with contamination, control, energy, waste, disposal, etc.

PROCEEDINGS - ATLANTIC WORKSHOP. (PROCEEDINGS). Main/Conf Atlantic Workshop. VFOAT Atlantic Workshop Proceedings. 1st-. 0738-0135. US. English. an. $13.45 Members, $16.80 Nonmembers. American Water Works Association, 6666 West Quincy Avenue, Denver CO 80235. LC TD426. DD 628.1.

PROCEEDINGS, AWWA ANNUAL CONFERENCE. (PROCEEDINGS AWWA ANNUAL CONFERENCE). Main/Corp American Water Works Association. VFOAT Annual Conference Proceedings. VAT Proceedings, American Water Works Association Annual Conference, Proceedings American Water Works Annual Conference. 95th- 1975-. 0360-814X. US. English. an. $20.00 Members, $40.00 Nonmembers. The American Water Works Association, 6666 West Quincy Avenue, Denver CO 80235. Tel (303)794-7711. Ind/Abst Chem. Abstr., GeoRef. LC TD201. DD 363.61. CODEN PWACDO. Circ 500. Scientific and management papers pertaining to water-supply and water quality issues and innovations.

PROCEEDINGS - AWWA WATER QUALITY TECHNOLOGY CONFERENCE. Main/Conf AWWA Water Quality Technology Conference. VFOAT Technology Conference Proceedings. 0164-0755. US. English. an. American Water Works Association, 6666 West Quincy Avenue, Denver CO 80235. Tel (303)794-7711. Ind/Abst Chem. Abstr. CODEN PWQCD2.

PROCEEDINGS - INTERNATIONAL WATER CONFERENCE. See Water Resources.

PROCEEDINGS - NORTH AMERICAN MOTOR VEHICLE EMISSIONS CONTROL CONFERENCE. (PROCEEDINGS). Main/Conf North American Motor Vehicle Emissions Control Conference. 0278-5986. US. English. an. LC TD886.5. DD 363.7392.

PROCEEDINGS OF NATIONAL WASTE PROCESSING CONFERENCE, INCLUDING DISCUSSIONS. Main/Conf National Waste Processing Conference. VFOAT Energy Conservation Through Waste Utilization. 8th- 1978-. 0195-8291. Periodical. US. English. be. American Society of Mechanical Engineers, United Engineering Center, 345 East 47th Street, New York NY 10017. Ind/Abst Chem. Abstr., Eng. Index Annu., Eng. Index Bioeng. Abstr., Eng. Index Energy Abstr., Eng. Index Mon. LC TD796. DD 628.44505. *Proceedings of National Waste Processing Conference, 0145-4781; Discussions - National Incinerator Conference.*

PROCEEDINGS OF THE ANNUAL CONFERENCE - NORTH AMERICAN LAKE MANAGEMENT SOCIETY. CONFERENCE. (PROCEEDINGS OF THE . . . ANNUAL CONFERENCE). Main/Corp North American Lake Management Society., Conference. 0743-8141. US. English. an. US EPA, Office of Water Regulations and Standards, Washington DC 20460.

PROCEEDINGS OF THE ANNUAL MEETING OF THE UTAH MOSQUITO ABATEMENT ASSOCIATION. (PROCEEDINGS AND PAPERS OF THE ANNUAL MEETING OF THE UTAH MOSQUITO ABATEMENT ASSOCIATION). Main/Corp Utah Mosquito Abatement Association. VFOAT Proceedings of the Annual Meeting of the Utah Mosquito Abatement Association. 1st- 1948-. 0502-8701. US. English. an. Ind/Abst Biol. Abstr. LC RA640. DD 628.96. NLM W1 UT146. CODEN PAMUBG.

PROCEEDINGS OF THE . . . ANNUAL MEETING - UTAH MOSQUITO ABATEMENT ASSOCIATION. Main/Corp Utah Mosquito Abatement Association. 0502-8701. Periodical. US. English. an. Ind/Abst Bibliogr. Agric. *Abstracts and Proceedings of the . . . Annual Meeting.*

PROCEEDINGS OF THE ANNUAL NORTHEASTERN FOREST INSECT WORK CONFERENCE. Main/Conf Northeastern Forest Insect Work Conference. 1968-. 0160-2950. US. English. an. Department of Agriculture Forest Service, Northeastern Forest Experiment Station 6816 Market Street, Upper Darby PA 19082.

PROCEEDINGS OF THE BRITISH INSECTICIDE AND FUNGICIDE CONFERENCE. Main/Conf British Insecticide and Fungicide Conference. 0524-613X. UK. English. ir. BCPC Publications Sales, Bear Farm, Binfield Bracknell, Berks RG12 5QE England. Tel 0734 343527. Ind/Abst Chem. Abstr. CODEN PBICDJ.

PROCEEDINGS OF THE DOE NUCLEAR AIR CLEANING CONFERENCE. Main/Conf DOE Nuclear Air Cleaning Conference. VAT Proceedings of the Department of Energy Nuclear Air Cleaning Conference. 15th- 1978-. 0193-9408. Periodical. US. English. sa. Ed M W First. Ind/Abst Chem. Abstr. NLM W3 D101. CODEN PDNCDO. *Proceedings of the ERDA Air Cleaning Conference, 0160-8088.*

PROCEEDINGS OF THE INDUSTRIAL WASTE, ADVANCED WATER AND SOLID WASTE CONFERENCE. Main/Conf Industrial Waste, Advanced Water and Solid Waste Conference. 0163-2345. US. English. LC TD896. DD 628.4.

PROCEEDINGS OF THE INTERNATIONAL SYMPOSIUM ON REMOTE SENSING OF ENVIRONMENT. Main/Conf International Symposium on Remote Sensing of Environment. 6th- Oct. 1969-. 0275-5505. US. English. an. Environment Research Institute of Michigan, PO Box 8518, Ann Arbor MI 48109. Tel (313)994-1200. Ed Jerald J Cook. Ind/Abst Eng. Index, Coal Abstr., GeoRef. LC QC808.5. DD 681. CODEN PISEDM. Circ 1,000. Continuing series on remote sensing of environment research development application throughout earth sciences. 200 to 500 technical papers annually. *Proceedings of the Symposium on Remote Sensing of Environment.*

PROCEEDINGS OF THE MEETING OF THE EXPERT PANEL ON AIR POLLUTION MODELING. Main/Corp North Atlantic Treaty Organization. Expert Panel on Air Pollution Modeling. Series/Titl Air Pollution. 0377-7669. English. ir. North Atlantic Treaty Organization, 1110 Brussels Belgium. LC TD881. DD 628.530184.

PROCEEDINGS OF THE TECHNICAL PROGRAM. Main/Conf National Noise and Vibration Control Conference. VFOAT Noisexpo Proceedings. 1973-. 0149-3019. US. English. an. Ind/Abst Eng. Index Annu., Eng. Index Mon., Eng. Index Bioeng. Abstr., Eng. Index Energy Abstr. LC TD891. DD 363.6. NLM W3 NO372. CODEN PTPCDA.

PROFILE OF ENVIRONMENTAL QUALITY. REGION 8, COLORADO, MONTANA, NORTH DAKOTA, SOUTH DAKOTA, UTAH, WYOMING. VAT Profile of Environmental Quality. Region Eight: Colorado, Montana, North Dakota, South Dakota, Utah, Wyoming. Began with 1978. 0193-1652. US.

Sanitation, Environmental Technology

English. US Environmental Protection Agency, Region 8, 1860 Lincoln Street, Denver CO 80295. LC TD181.M54. DD 614.7.0978.

PROGRAM AND PROJECT ACCOMPLISHMENTS; ANNUAL PROGRESS REPORT. Main/Corp Louisiana. Air Control Commission. 0093-8106. US. English. an. Air Control Commission, PO Box 60630, New Orleans LA 70160. LC TD883.5.L8. DD 363.6.

PROGRAM REQUIREMENTS MEMORANDA FOR FISCAL YEAR . . . : MUNICIPAL WASTEWATER TREATMENT WORKS CONSTRUCTION GRANTS PROGRAM. Main/Corp United States. Environmental Protection Agency. Office of Water Program Operations. US. English. an. United States Environmental Protection Agency, Office of Water Program Operations WH-547, Washington DC 20460.

PROGRESS IN AIR POLLUTION CONTROL. Main/Corp Wayne Co., Mich. Air Pollution Control Division. 0098-0463. US. English. Wayne County Health Department/Air Pollution Countrol Division, 1311 East Jefferson, Detroit MI 48207. LC TD883.5.M47. DD 363.6. *Air Pollution Control Progress Report.*

PROGRESS IN HAZARDOUS CHEMICALS HANDLING AND DISPOSAL. See Engineering - Chemical Engineering.

PROGRESS IN RESOURCE MANAGEMENT AND ENVIRONMENTAL PLANNING. V. 1-. 0271-7395. UK. English. ir. John Wiley & Sons Company, 605 Third Avenue, New York NY 10158. Tel (212)850-6000. Ed T O'Riordan and R C D'Arge. LC HN18. DD 361.61.

PROGRESS IN THE IMPLEMENTATION OF MOTOR VEHICLE EMMISSION STANDARDS. (PROGRESS IN THE IMPLEMENTATION OF MOTOR VEHICLE EMISSION STANDARDS : REPORT TO CONGRESS). Main/Corp United States. Environmental Protection Agency. 0098-7069. US. English. US Environmental Protection Agency, Office of Public Affairs, Washington DC 20460. LC TD886.5. DD 363.6.

PROGRESS IN THE PREVENTION AND CONTROL OF AIR POLLUTION. (PROGRESS IN THE PREVENTION AND CONTROL OF AIR POLLUTION IN . . . : ANNUAL REPORTS OF THE ADMINISTRATOR OF THE ENVIRONMENTAL PROTECTION AGENCY TO THE CONGRESS OF THE UNITED STATES IN COMPLIANCE WITH SECTION 127(D), 202, 306(E), AND 313 OF PUBLIC LAW 91-604, AND THE CLEAN AIR ACT, THE CLEAN AIR ACT, AS AMENDED). 0735-6633. US. English. an. LC TD883.2. DD 363.739260973. NLM W2 A E4P.

PROGRESS REPORT - STATE WATER CONTROL BOARD, COMMONWEALTH OF VIRGINIA. Main/Corp Virginia. State Water Control Board. 1975/76-. 0194-3375. US. English. be. VSCWB, Information Office, PO Box 11143, Richmond VA 23230. LC TD224.V8. DD 353.9755008232. *Annual Report of the Virginia State Water Control Board, 0095-1978.*

PROJECT REPORT - PULP AND PAPER POLLUTION ABATEMENT. Main/Corp Canada. Forestry Service. Cooperative Pollution Abatement Research Program. VFOAT Pulp and Paper Pollution Abatement. (1972/73). Periodical. CN. English. an.

PROPERTIES OF RADIOACTIVE WASTES AND WASTE CONTAINERS, PROGRESS REPORT. US. English. qt. National Technical Information Service, 5285 Port Royal Road, Springfield VA 22161.

PROPOSED FISCAL YEAR . . . PROGRAM. FINAL ENVIRONMENTAL IMPACT STATEMENT. Main/Corp United States. Bonneville Power Administration. VFOAT Final Environmental Impact Statement. US. English. an. National Technical Information Service, United States Department of Commerce, 5285 Port Royal Boulevard, Springfield VA 22161. *Final Environmental Statement.*

PUBLIC HEALTH ENGINEER. (THE PUBLIC HEALTH ENGINEER). No. 1- Jan. 1973-. 0300-5925. Periodical. UK. English. qt. Sterling Professional Publishers Ltd, PO Box 839-86-88, Edgware Road, London W2 2YW England. Ind/Abst Excerpta Med., Chem. Abstr., Pollut. Abstr. Indexes. LC TD1. DD 628.05. NLM W1 PU458H. CODEN PHEEDD. *Journal of the Institution of Public Health Engineers, 0020-3513.*

PUBLIC WATER SUPPLY REPORT. 1982-. US. English. ty. Oklahoma State Department of Health, Environmental Health Services, State Environmental Laboratory, 1000 NE Tenth, Oklahoma City OK 73152. LC TD224.O5. DD 363.61.

PUBLICATION - CORNELL UNIVERSITY WATER RESOURCES AND MARINE SCIENCES CENTER. See Water Resources.

PUBLICATIONS ABSTRACTS. See Indexes/Abstracts.

PUBLICATIONS AND FINAL REPORTS ON CONTRACTS AND GRANTS. Series/Titl Nooa Technical Memorandum Ness. US. English. an. Environmental Science Information Center OA/D812, National Oceanic and Atmospheric Administration, United States Department of Commerce, Rockville MD 20852.

PUBLIKATION - CHALMERS TEKNISKA HOGSKOLA, GOTEBORG. INSTITUTIONEN FOR VATTENFORSORJNINGS- OCH AVLOPPSTEKNIK. (PUBLIKATION). Began in 1982. 0280-4026. Monographic Series. SW. Swedish. ir. Institutionen for Vattenforsorjnings- och Avloppsteknik, Chalmers Tekniska Hogskola 412 96, Goteborg Sweden. Ind/Abst Chem. Abstr. CODEN PCTHET. *Publikation A (Chalmers Tekniska Hogskola. Institutionen for Va-Teknik), Publikation B (Chalmers Tekniska Hogskola. Institutionen Publikation C (Chalmers Tekniska Hogskola. Institutionen.*

QIYYUM. (KIYUM). Vol. 1- Sept. 1971-. 0303-139X. English (Hebrew). ir. Rehov Ha-Universitah 26, Ramat Aviv, Tel Aviv Israel. LC TD883.7.I75.

QUARTERLY SUMMARY. Main/Corp United States. Southeast Environmental Research Laboratory, Athens, Ga. VFOAT Southeast Environmental Research Laboratory Quarterly Summary. Periodical. US. English. qt. US Environmental Protection Agency, Southeast Environmental Research Laboratory, College Station Road, Athens GA 30601.

RADIATION PROTECTION ACTIVITIES. Main/Corp United States. Environmental Protection Agency. Office of Radiation Programs. 1976-. 0161-7796. US. English. an. Environmental Protection Agency, Office of Radiation Programs, 401 M Street, Washington DC 20460. LC TD196.R3. DD 614.8390973. NLM W2 A O35A. *Radiation Protection.*

RADIOACTIVE WASTE MANAGEMENT. DOE/RWM-81/1 (Jan. 15, 1981)-. 0275-3707. US. English. sm. National Technical Information Service, 5285 Port Royal Road, Springfield VA 22161. Tel (703)487-4630.

RADIOACTIVE WASTE MANAGEMENT. 0275-7273. Monographic Series. UK. English. ir. $132.00. Harwood Academic Publishers, PO Box 197, London WC2E 9PX England. Tel (212)242-4464. Ed R D Anderson. Ind/Abst Comput. Control Abstr., Electr. Electron. Abstr., Sci. Abstr. Sect. A. Phys. Abstr., Chem. Abstr. CODEN RAWMDW. bk rev. adv acc.

RADIOACTIVE WASTE MANAGEMENT AND THE NUCLEAR FUEL CYCLE. Vol. 3, No. 1 (Sept. 1982)-. 0739-5876. Periodical. US. English. ir. Harwood Academic Publishers, PO Box 786 Cooper Station, New York NY 10276. Ind/Abst Comput. Control Abstr., Electr. Electron. Abstr., Sci. Abstr. Sect. A. Phys. Abstr., Chem. Abstr., Energy Inf. Abstr., Energy Res. Abstr., Eng. Index Annu., Eng. Index Bioeng. Abstr., Eng. Index Energy Abstr., Eng. Index Mon., Environ. Abstr., Excerpta Med., Life Sci. Collect. LC TD812. DD 621.483805. CODEN RWMCD4. *Radioactive Waste Management (Chur, Switzerland : 1980), 0142-2405.*

RAPPORT ANNUEL - CONSEIL CONSULTATIF DE L'ENVIRONNEMENT. Main/Corp Quebec (Province). Conseil Consultatif de l'Environnement. 1973/74-. 0383-5308. Periodical. CN. French. an. EOQ, Montreal Quebec Canada.

RAPPORT ANNUEL - GROUPE INTERMINISTERIEL D'EVALUATION DE L'ENVIRONNEMENT. Main/Corp France. Groupe Interministeriel d'Evaluation de l'Environnement. FR. French. ir. La Documentation Francaise, 29-31 Quai Voltaire, 75340 Paris Cedex 07 France. LC HC280.E5.

RAPPORT INZAKE DE TOESTAND VAN DE OPPERVLAKTEWATEREN IN DE PROVINCIE LIMBURG. Main/Corp Limburg (Netherlands). Provinciale Waterstaat. VFOAT Toestand Oppervlaktewater in Limburg. Dutch. ir. Provinciale Waterstaat in Limburg, Stadhuisstraat 4, Limburg Netherlands. LC TD277.L45.

RAPPORTO ANNUALE SULLA RADIOATTIVITA AMBIENTALE IN ITALIA. VOL. II, RETI LOCALI. VFOAT Reti Locali. Italian. an. LC TD196.R3. DD 363.179.

RAPPORTO ANNUALE SULLA RADIOATTIVITA AMBIENTALE IN ITALIA.VOL. I., RETI NAZIONALI. VFOAT Reti Nazionali. Italian. an. LC TD887.R3.

RAT EN MUIS. No. 2- July, 1961-. 0481-8024. Periodical. Dutch. ir.

RECLAMATION INDUSTRIES INTERNATIONAL. No. 1- May/June 1973-. 0306-3658. UK. English (summaries in English, French and German). 5.50. PO Box 109, Davi House/ 69 77 High Street, Croydon CR9 10H England. LC TD794.5. DD 338.4.

RECOUP. V. 1- Mar. 1978-. 0709-6402. Periodical. CN. English. mo. $67.32. Venture Publications Ltd, 223A McLeod Street, Ottawa Ontario K2P 0Z8 Canada. Tel (613)725-1178. Ed Thomas J Daigneault. DD 338.476046. bk rev. adv acc. (ctrl). Resource recovery news and market trends for recyclable commodities across North America. Industrial and scientific perspectives.

RECYCLING TODAY; SECONDARY RAW MATERIALS. 1963-. Periodical. US. English. mo. $19.00. Market News Publishing Corporation, 156 Fifth Avenue, New York NY 10010. Tel (212)255-2277. Ed Anthony J Abitante. Ind/Abst Met. Abstr., World Alum. Abstr. adv acc. Circ 5,400. Covers recycling industry. Recycling of secondary materials in the form of all metallics, waste, paper and textiles. Also covers heavy equipment to process above materials. Offers market reviews and prices.

REDUCTION IN WATER CONSUMPTION AND FLOW OF SEWAGE. Main/Corp United States. Environmental Protection Agency. 0095-4357. US. English. an. Environmental Protection Agency, 401 M Street, Washington DC 20460. LC TD388.A1. DD 363.6.

REGISTER OF RESEARCH. Main/Corp Great Britain. Dept. of the Environment. 1975-. UK. English. Headquarters Library, Department of the Environment etc, 2 Marsham Street, London SW1P 3EB England. LC TD171.5.G7. DD 304.28072041.

REGISTERED PESTICIDES. Main/Corp New Mexico. Dept. of Agriculture. Division of Pesticide Control. VFOAT Pesticides Registered by the New Mexico Department of Agriculture. 1973-. Periodical. US. English. an. *Annual Economic Poisons Report.*

REGULATORY REPORTER (WASHINGTON, D.C.). (REGULATORY REPORTER). Began with V. 1, Apr. 1979. 0194-0376. US. English. sa. US Environmental Protection Agency, Regulatory Development Work Group, 401 M Street SW, Washington DC 20460. LC KF3958. DD 344.73047205. NLM QV 33 AA1 R344.

RELATORIO ANUAL DA DIRETORIA - CETESB. See Yearbooks, Almanacs, Directories.

RELATORIO - COMPANHIA DE SANEAMENTO DE MINAS GERAIS. Main/Corp Companhia de Saneamento de Minas Gerais. BL. Portuguese. ir. Copasa Mg, rua Sergipe 580, 30.000 Belo Horizonte Brazil. LC TD41.M56.

RELATORIO DA DIRETORIA - CORSAN. Main/Corp Corsan. Portuguese. ir. rua Caldas Junio 120 - 17.18, 19 Andares, Porto Alegre Brazil. LC TD241.R5.

REPORT - ALBERTA ENVIRONMENT. RESEARCH SECRETARIAT. (REPORT). 1978/1-. 0707-9079. Monographic Series. CN. English. Alberta Environment Research Secretariat, Oxbridge Place 9820-106 St, Edmonton Alberta T5K 2J6 Canada. DD 363.7'0097123.

REPORT - CENTRE FOR OVERSEAS PEST RESEARCH. (REPORT). Main/Corp Great Britain. Centre for Overseas Pest Research. 1971/72-. 0307-9082. UK. English. Centre for

Sanitation, Environmental Technology

Overseas Pest Research, Wrights Lane, London W8 5SJ England. **Ind/Abst** Life Sci. Collect. LC SB950.A1. DD 354.42134008233.

REPORT - DIVISION OF ENVIRONMENTAL MECHANICS. CSIRO. (REPORT FOR . . .). **Main/Corp** Commonwealth Scientific and Industrial Research Organization (Australia). Division of Environmental Mechanics. 1971/72-. 0312-567X. AT. English. be. CSIRO, PO Box 821, Canberra Australian Capital Territory 2601 Australia. LC Z5363.P7, TD170. DD 016.6285.

REPORT (INSTITUTE OF GEOLOGICAL SCIENCES (GREAT BRITAIN). ENVIRONMENTAL PROTECTION UNIT). (REPORT). Monographic Series. UK. English. ir. Environmental Protection Unit, Building 151, Harwell Laboratory, Oxfordshire OX11 ORA England. **Ind/Abst** Life Sci. Collect., GeoRef.

REPORT - INTERMOUNTAIN REGION AND METHODS APPLICATION GROUP, FOREST INSECT AND DISEASE MANAGEMENT. Main/Corp United States. Forest Insect and Disease Management. Intermountain Region and Methods Application Group. Monographic Series. US. English.

REPORT - NEW ENGLAND INTERSTATE WATER POLLUTION CONTROL COMMISSION. Main/Corp New England Interstate Water Pollution Control Commission. US. English. an. LC TD223.15.N4.

REPORT NO. D.O.T.-T.S.T. See Transportation.

REPORT NO. T.E.S. (REPORT NO. TES). **Main/Corp** United States. Dept. of Transportation. Office of Hazardous Materials. 0093-8947. US. English. Us Department of Transportation, Office of Hazardous Materials, Washington DC 20590. LC HE199.5.D3. DD 604.7.

REPORT OF ACTIVITIES. MINNESOTA ENVIRONMENTAL QUALITY BOARD. Main/Corp Minnesota Environmental Quality Board. US. English. be. Power Plant Siting Staff, Minnesota Envitonmental Quality Board, Capitol Square Building/500 Cedar Street, St Paul MN 55101. LC TD195.E4. DD 363.62.

REPORT OF PROGRESS BY THE ILLINOIS ENVIRONMENTAL PROTECTION AGENCY. (REPORT OF PROGRESS). **Main/Corp** Illinois Environmental Protection Agency. VFOAT Our Shared Environment. 0092-0770. US. English. an. Illinois Environmental Protection Agency, 2200 Churchill Road, Springfield IL 62706. LC TD171.3.I45. DD 353.97730084.

REPORT OF PROGRESS - MERL. Main/Corp Municipal Environmental Research Laboratory. VAT Report of Progress - Municipal Environmental Research Laboratory. 0193-3310. US. English. an. Municipal Environmental Research Laboratory, Office of Research and Development, US Environmental Protection Agency, Cincinnati OH 45268. LC TD178.8.U53. DD 628.4072073.

REPORT OF THE AQUATIC ECOSYSTEM OBJECTIVES COMMITTEE. Main/Corp Great Lakes Science Advisory Board. Aquatic Ecosystem Objectives Committee. Periodical. CN. English. 100 Ouellette Avenue/8th Floor, Windsor Ontario Canada N9A 6T3.

REPORT OF THE ENVIRONMENTAL MONITORING AND SUPPORT LABORATORY, LAS VEGAS. Main/Corp Environmental Monitoring and Support Laboratory, Las Vegas, Nev. Jan./Mar. 1976-. Periodical. US. English. qt. Environmental Protection Agency, PO Box 15027, Las Vegas NV 89114. *Report of the National Environmental Research Center, Las Vegas.*

REPORT OF THE INTERAGENCY TOXIC SUBSTANCES DATA COMMITTEE. 1st-. US. English. Environmental Protection Administration, Office of Pesticides and Toxic Substances, Office of Toxics Integration TS-777, Office of Network Administration, 401 M Street South West, Washington DC 20460.

A REPORT OF THE PROCEEDINGS - NATIONAL CENTER FOR A BARRIER FREE ENVIRONMENT. Main/Corp National Center for a Barrier Free Environment. 0270-9376. US. English. National Center for a Barrier Free Environment, Suite 1006/1140 Conn Avenue, Washington DC 20024.

REPORT OF THE WORKING PARTY ON PESTICIDE RESIDUES. Main/Corp Great Britain. Working Party of Pesticide Residues. Series/Titl Food Surveillance Paper. 1977-1981-. UK. English. LC TX571.P4. DD 363.1922.

REPORT ON ENVIRONMENTAL RADIATION SURVEILLANCE IN NORTH CAROLINA. See Physics - Light, Optics, Radiation.

REPORT ON GREAT LAKES WATER QUALITY : REPORT TO THE INTERNATIONAL JOINT COMMISSION. Main/Corp Great Lakes Water Quality Board. 1980-. CN. English. an. International Joint Commission, Great Lakes Regional Office, 100 Ouellette Avenue/Eighth Floor, Windsor Ontario N9A 6T3 Canada. LC TD223.3. DD 363.73940977. Vols. for (1981-) distributed to depository libraries in microfiche. *Great Lakes Water Quality . . . Annual Report to the International Joint Commission, 0706-1013.*

REPORT - SPECIAL STUDIES SECTION, FIELD OPERATIONS DIVISION, TEXAS WATER QUALITY BOARD. Main/Corp Texas. Water Quality Board. Field Operations Division. Special Studies Section. 0145-2215. US. English. Texas Water Quality Board, PO Box 13246 Capitol Station, Austin TX 78711. LC TD224.T4. DD 363.6109764.

REPORT TO CONGRESS ON ADMINISTRATION OF OCEAN DUMPING ACTIVITIES. PUBLIC LAW 92-532, MARINE PROTECTION, RESEARCH, AND SANCTUARIES ACT OF 1972. Main/Corp United States. Army. Corps of Engineers. 1976-. 0163-4755. US. English. LC TD763. DD 614.76.

REPORT TO THE COLORADO WATER QUALITY CONTROL COMMISSION. Main/Corp Colorado. Dept. of Health. Water Quality Control Division. VFOAT Water Quality Control Division's . . . Annual Report to the Colorado Water Quality Control Commission. 0733-3633. US. English. an. Water Quality Control Division, 4210 East 11th Avenue, Denver CO 80220. LC TD224.C7. DD 353.97880082325.

A REPORT TO THE HONORABLE . . . GOVERNOR OF THE STATE OF ALABAMA AND MEMBERS OF THE ALABAMA LEGISLATURE. Main/Corp Alabama. Water Improvement Commission. VFOAT Report of Progress. 1980-. US. English. an. Public Health Services Building, Montgomery AL 36130. LC TD224.A2. DD 353.97610082325. *Annual Report of the Alabama Water Improvement Commission.*

REPORT TO THE PRESIDENT AND TO THE COUNCIL ON ENVIRONMENTAL QUALITY. Main/Corp United States. Citizens' Advisory Committee on Environmental Quality. 1973-. 0148-0596. US. English. an. Citizens' Advisory Committee on Environmental Quality, 1700 Pennsylvania Avenue NW, Washington DC 20006. *Annual Report to the President and to the Council on Environmental Quality.*

REPORT TO THE PUBLIC - COLORADO. AIR QUALITY CONTROL COMMISSION. (REPORT TO THE PUBLIC). **Main/Corp** Colorado. Air Quality Control Commisson. 1979-. 0733-3706. US. English. an. Colorado Department of Health, 4210 East 11th Avenue, Denver CO 80220. LC TD883.5.C6. DD 353.9788008232406. *Report to the Public, 0097-9996.*

REPORT - WORKING PARTY ON SEWERS AND WATER MAINS. Main/Corp Great Britain. Working Party on Sewers and Water Mains. 1st- 1975-. UK. English. be. Her Majesty's Stationery Office, PO Box 276, London SW8 5DT England. LC TD511. DD 628.24.

RESEARCH BULLETIN - ALABAMA AGRICULTURAL AND MECHANICAL UNIVERSITY, SCHOOL OF AGRICULTURE AND ENVIRONMENTAL SCIENCE. See Agriculture.

RESEARCH HIGHLIGHTS. Main/Corp United States. Environmental Protection Agency. Office of Research and Development. 1977-. 0192-9852. US. English. an. LC TD178.6. DD 628.5.

RESEARCH ISSUES AND SUPPORTING RESEARCH OF THE NATIONAL PROGRAM ON CARBON DIOXIDE, ENVIRONMENT AND SOCIETY. Fiscal Year 1980-. US. English. National Technical Information Service, US Department of Commerce, 5285 Port Royal Road, Springfield VA 22161.

RESEARCH NEEDS : GREAT LAKES WATER QUALITY. Main/Corp Great Lakes Research Advisory Board. Sept. 1973-. Periodical. CN. English. sa. Great Lakes Research Advisory Board, International Joint Commission, 880 Ouellette Avenue/Suite 803, Windsor Ontario N9A 1C7 Canada. LC TD223.3. DD 363.61.

RESEARCH PROGRAMS - NATIONAL INSTITUTE OF ENVIRONMENTAL HEALTH SCIENCES. (RESEARCH PROGRAMS). **Main/Corp** National Institute of Environmental Health Sciences. 0148-5547. US. English. Superintendent of Documents, US Government Printing Office, Washington DC 20402. LC RA566.3. DD 614.7072073. NLM W 20.5 R434.

RESEARCH REVIEW - INDUSTRIAL ENVIRONMENTAL RESEARCH LABORATORY. Main/Corp United States. Industrial Environmental Research Laboratory (Research Triangle Park, N.C.). Periodical. US. English. an. Office of Research and Development, Office of Environmental Engineering and Technology, Industrial Environmental Research Laboratory, Research Triangle Park NC 27711.

RESIDUE REVIEWS. VFOAT Ruckstands-Berichte. V. 1-. 0080-181X. Periodical. US. English (French, and German with summaries in all three languages). ir. Springer Verlag-New York Inc, 175 5th Avenue, New York NY 10010. **Tel** (212)460-1500. **Ind/Abst** Energy Res. Abstr., Excerpta Med., Bibliogr. Agric., Biol. Abstr., Chem. Abstr., Index Med., Life Sci. Collect., Nuci. Sci. Abstr., Sel. Water Resour. Abstr., Biol. Agric. Index, Pestdoc, Ringdoc, Vetdoc, Energy Inf. Abstr., Environ. Abstr., Sci. Cit. Index, Agric. LC TX501. DD 628.5. NLM W1 RE246. CODEN RREVAH. Contains articles on residues of pesticides and other contaminants in the environment.

RESOURCE RECOVERY REPORT. See Energy.

RESOURCE RECYCLING. Vol. 1, No. 1 (Mar./Apr. 1982). 0744-4710. Periodical. US. English. bm. $18.00. Resource Recycling, PO Box 10540, Portland OR 97210. **Tel** (503)227-1319. Ed Jerry Powell. **Ind/Abst** Public Aff. Inf. Serv. Bull. bk rev. adv acc. **Circ** 2,500. Comprehensive journal of solid waste recycling from community collection to industrial use of material.

RESSOURCES EN EAU DE TUNISIE. 0330-0005. French. ir. **Ind/Abst** GeoRef. LC TD319.T85. DD 551.578109611.

RESULTS OF ENVIRONMENTAL RADIOACTIVITY MEASUREMENTS IN THE MEMBER STATES OF THE EUROPEAN COMMUNITY FOR AIR, DEPOSITION, WATER, MILK. Series/Titl Radiological Protection** EUR. VFOAT Resultats des Mesures des Niveaux de Radioactivite dans l'Environnement des Etats Membres de la Communaute Europeene pour Air, Retombees, Eaux, Lait. 1973-1974-. English (text also in Danish, Dutch, French, German and Italian). an. NLM W1. *Radioactivite Ambiante dans les Pays de la Communaute.*

RESULTS OF RESEARCH RELATED TO STRATOSPHERIC OZONE PROTECTION. VFOAT Research and Development, Results of Research Related to Stratospheric Ozone Protection. Oct. 1980-. US. English. be. US Environmental Protection Agency, Center for Environmental Research Information, Cincinnati OH 45268. *Results of Research Related to Stratospheric Ozone Protection, Report to Congress.*

RESULTS OF WATER QUALITY MONITORING IN RAYMOND BASIN. 0743-0965. US. English. an. $2.00. State of California, Department of Water Resources, PO Box 6598, Los Angeles CA 90055. LC TD224.C3. DD 363.7394209794. *Results of Areawide Water Quality Monitoring Program for the Raymond Basin, July 1 . . . to June 30 . . . .*

REVIEWS IN ENVIRONMENTAL TOXICOLOGY. See Medicine - Toxicology.

Sanitation, Environmental Technology

REVIEWS ON ENVIRONMENTAL HEALTH. V. 1- 1972-. 0048-7554. Periodical. IS. English. qt. Freund Publishing House Ltd, PO Box 35010, Tel Aviv Israel. **Ind/Abst** Life Sci. Collect., Excerpta Med., Index Med., Energy Res. Abstr., Chem. Abstr. **LC** RA565.A1. **DD** 614.705. **NLM** W1 RE257CH. **CODEN** REVHA3.

REVUE PRATIQUE DU FROID ET DU CONDITIONNEMENT DE L'AIR. See Heating, Plumbing, & Refrigeration.

RIVER QUALITY REPORT. 1981-. 0742-4426. US. English. an. Metropolitan Waste Control Commission, 350 Metro Square Building, St Paul MN 55101. **LC** TD225.M6. **DD** 363.739420977657. *Water Quality Report of River Water Quality in the Minneapolis-St. Paul Metropolitan Area*, 0734-323X.

SACRAMENTO-SAN JOAQUIN DELTA WATER QUALITY SURVEILLANCE PROGRAM : MONITORING RESULTS PURSUANT TO CONDITIONS SET FORTH IN DELTA WATER RIGHTS DECISION. . . . VFOAT Water Quality Surveillance Program. 1975-. US. English. an. **LC** TD224.C3. **DD** 363.7342097945.

SAFETY AND ENVIRONMENTAL PROTECTION DIVISION PROGRESS REPORT. Main/Corp United States. Brookhaven National Laboratory, Upton, N.Y. Safety and Environmental Protection Division. 0160-8290. US. English. an. $4.50. National Technical Information Service, 5285 Port Royal Road, Springfield VA 22161. **LC** TD196.R3. **DD** 628.5.

SALINE WATER CONVERSION SUMMARY REPORT. Main/Corp United States. Office of Saline Water. 1971/72-. 0098-3012. US. English. an. $1.55. Superintendent of Documents, US Government Printing Office, Washington DC 20402. **LC** TD478.3. **DD** 628.167. *Saline Water Conversion Report*, 0083-291X.

SANGYO KAGAKU KENKYUJO SHOHO. Main/Corp Tokai Daigaku. Sangyo Kagaku Kenkyujo. VFOAT Sanken Report. No. 1-. JA. Japanese. ir. Tokai Daigaku, Sangyo Kagaku Kenkyujo, 1117 Kita-Kaneme Hiratsuka Japan.

SANGYO KOGAI BOSHI NO GIJUTSU. 1973-. JA. Japanese. ir. Tokyo Toritsu Kogyo Gijutsu Senta, 13-10 Nishigaoka 3 Kita-ku (115), Tokyo Japan. **LC** TD187.5.J32.

SANITARY ENGINEERING PAPERS. No. 1- June 1966-. 0069-6129. Monographic Series. US. English. ir. Colorado State University, Fort Collins CO 80523. **Tel** (303)491-8652. Ed D Hendricks. **LC** TD1. **DD** 628. Circ 50. (ctrl) Sanitary engineer thesis and dissertations summary reports.

SANITARY LANDFILLS; A BIBLIOGRAPHY. See Bibliographies.

SANITARY MAINTENANCE. 0036-4436. Periodical. US. English. mo. $30.00. Trade Press Publishing Company, PO Box 694, Milwaukee WI 53202. **Tel** (414)228-7701. **LC** HD9999.S383. **DD** 338.476485.

SANITARY SERVICES IN TENNESSEE. Main/Corp Tennessee. State Planning Office. 0162-6256. US. English. be. 660 Capitol Hill Building, Nashville TN 37219. **LC** HC107.T3. **DD** 309.2509768 S, 338.437. *Sanitary Services in Tennessee*, 0162-6256.

SANITATION INDUSTRY YEARBOOK. See Yearbooks, Almanacs, Directories.

SAVANNAH RIVER LABORATORY QUARTERLY REPORT, WASTE MANAGEMENT. VFOAT Waste Management. US. English. qt. US Department of Energy, Savannah River Laboratory, Aiken SC 29801.

SCHRIFTTUMSUBERSICHT LARMMINDERUNG. See Bibliographies.

SCIENCE AND ENVIRONMENT. See Science (General).

SCIENCE OF THE TOTAL ENVIRONMENT. (THE SCIENCE OF THE TOTAL ENVIRONMENT). V. 1 - May 1972-. 0048-9697. Periodical. NE. English (French and German). mo. 1701.00 Domestic, $549.00 US. Elsevier Science Publishers, PO Box 1991, 1000 AH Amsterdam Netherlands. **Tel** 5862911. Ed Eric I Hamilton. **Ind/Abst** Can. Environ., Environ., Excerpta Med., Pestdoc, Ringdoc, Vetdoc, Coal Abstr., Sel. Water Resour. Abstr., Energy Inf. Abstr., Environ. Abstr., Index Med., Int. Aerosp. Abstr., GeoRef, Biol. Abstr., Chem. Abstr., Nucl. Sci. Abstr., Sci. Cit. Index, Abr. Ed., Ocean. Abstr., Eng. Index, Pollut. Abstr. Indexes. **LC** RA565. **DD** 614.705. **NLM** W1 SC751N. **CODEN** STENDL. bk rev. adv acc. An international journal for scientific research into the environment and its relationship with man. Particular emphasis is placed on applied environmental chemistry.

SCIENTIFIC AND TECHNICAL PUBLICATIONS OF THE ENVIRONMENTAL RESEARCH LABORATORIES. See Earth Sciences - Meteorology.

SCOPE MISCELLANEOUS PUBLICATION. Main/Corp International Council of Scientific Unions. Scientific Committee on Problems of the Environment. VAT Scientific Committee on Problems of the Environment Miscellaneous Publication. No. 1-. 0275-7389. Monographic Series. US. English. Scope Secretariat, 51 Boulevard de Montmorency, Paris 75016 France. **LC** UNC.

SCRAP AGE. See Metals & Metallurgy.

SEAWATER AND DESALTING. Vol. 1-. 0720-0773. English. be. **LC** TD478. **DD** 628.16705.

SEISO GIHO. Main/Corp Tokyo. Seisokyoku. VFOAT Technical Report - Bureau of Public Cleansing, Tokyo Metropolitan Government. V. 1-. 0385-1907. JA. Japanese. ir. Tokyo-to Seisokyoku, 5-1 Marunouchi 3-chome Chiyoda-ku (100), Tokyo Japan. **Ind/Abst** Chem. Abstr. **LC** TD785. **CODEN** SIGHD4.

SELECTED PAPERS ON THE ENVIRONMENT IN ISRAEL. No. 1- 1974-. 0334-2050. IS. English. ir. Environmental Protection Service, Ministry of the Interior, POB 6158, Jerusalem Israel. **Ind/Abst** Life Sci. Collect., Chem. Abstr. **LC** TD171.5.I75. **DD** 363. **CODEN** SPEIDC.

SELECTED URBAN STORM WATER RUNOFF ABSTRACTS. See Indexes/Abstracts.

SEMIANNUAL REPORT - DIVISION OF AIR POLLUTION CONTROL. Main/Corp Illinois. Division of Air Pollution Control. US. English. sa. **LC** TD883.5.I45. **DD** 363.6.

SERIE MEIO AMBIENTE. No. 1- 1975-. Monographic Series. Portuguese. ir.

SEWAGE TREATMENT CONSTRUCTION GRANTS MANUAL. 0149-5879. Periodical. US. English. mo. $284.00. Bureau of National Affairs Inc, 1231 25th Street NW, Washington DC 20037. **Tel** (301)258-1033.

SHENG HUO YU HUAN CHING. First published in Oct. 1981. Periodical. CH. Chinese. mo. $400.00. Lien Feng Shu Pao She, Tai Pei Taiwan. **LC** TD169.

SLAMS ANNUAL REPORT FOR TEXAS. Main/Corp Texas Air Control Board. VFOAT S.L.A.M.S. Annual Report for Texas. US. English. an. **LC** TD883.5.T4. **DD** 363.7392209764.

SLUDGE. 0148-4125. Periodical. US. English. bw. Business Publishers Inc, 951 Pershing Drive, Silver Spring MD 20910. **Tel** (301)587-6300. Ed Susan Darcey Bartlett. **Ind/Abst** Energy Inf. Abstr., Environ. Abstr. A report on pollution control residuals management: generation, collection storage treatment and ultimate disposal. Also covers legislation, research, and product development.

SOLID WASTE REPORT. V. 1- Oct. 19, 1970-. 0038-1128. Periodical. US. English. bw. Business Publishers Inc, 951 Pershing Drive, Silver Spring MD 20910. **Tel** (301)587-6300. Ed Susan Darcey-Bartlett. **LC** TD795. Report on solid waste collection, processing, recovery, recycling, and ultimate disposal.

SOLID WASTES. Main/Corp American Chemical Society. 1898. 0094-0828. US. English. mo. 22.00 Domestic, 26.00 Foreign. Institute of Wastes Management, 3 Albion Place, Northampton NN1 1UD England. **Tel** (0604)20426. Ed D Taylor. **Ind/Abst** Pollut. Abstr. Indexes. **LC** TD791. **DD** 363.6. bk rev. adv acc. Circ 3,000. The science and practice of wastes management.

SOURCE. (LA SOURCE). Vol. 1, No 1 (Oct.)-. 0712-3361. Periodical. CN. French. mo. Free. Conseil Regional de l'Environnement de l'East du Quebec, CP 1119, Rimouski Quebec G5L 1A8 Canada. **DD** 363.700607147.

SOUTHWEST & TEXAS WATER WORKS JOURNAL. VFOAT Southwest and Texas Water Works Journal. Vol. 61, No. 7 (Oct. 1979)-. 0196-0717. Periodical. US. English. mo. $10.00. American Water Works Association, 306 East Adams Avenue, Temple TX 76501. **Tel** (817)778-1313. **Ind/Abst** Sel. Water Resour. Abstr., Chem. Abstr. **LC** TD201. **DD** 628.10976. **CODEN** STWJDV. Deals with areas of water in regards to sewerage, purification, wastewater, engineering, and related fields. *Water (Temple, Tex.)*, 0099-8729.

SPECTRUM. Feb. 1974-. 0318-6369. Periodical. CN. English. bm. Society for Pollution and Environmental Control, 2007 West 4th Avenue, Vancouver British Columbia V6J 1N3 Canada. **DD** 301.31. *Perspective*, 0315-0372.

SPEER'S DIGEST OF TOXIC SUBSTANCES STATE LAW. See Law.

SPENT FUEL AND RADIOACTIVE WASTE INVENTORIES, PROJECTIONS, AND CHARACTERISTICS. Oct. 1982-. US. English. an. National Technical Information Service, US Department of Commerce, 5285 Port Royal Road, Springfield VA 22161. Vols. for 1982- distributed to depository libraries in microfiche. *Spent Fuel and Radioactive Waste Inventories and Projections as of . . . .*

SPILL TECHNOLOGY NEWSLETTER. V. 1- 1976-. 0381-4459. Periodical. CN. English. an. **Ind/Abst** Can. Environ., Energy Inf. Abstr., Environ. Abstr., ASTIS Curr. Aware. Bull. **LC** TD427.P4. **DD** 628.1683305.

SRW. Main/Corp West Virginia. Plant Pest Control Division. VFOAT West Virginia Cooperative Federal-State Stem Rust Control Program. (1972-). Periodical. US. English. an.

STACK SAMPLING NEWS. 0148-8309. Periodical. US. English. mo. $80.00. Technomic Publishing Company, 851 New Holland Avenue Box 3535, Lancaster PA 17604. **Tel** (717)291-5609. Ed Paul N Cheremisinoff. bk rev. Circ 150. Information for air pollution control professionals on techniques for monitoring, sampling and analysis; on new findings on sources and emissions; on new equipment, instruments, and systems.

STADS- OG HAVNEINGENIREN. Periodical. DK. Danish. mo. $29.83. Danish Technical Press, Skelbaekgade 4, Copenhagen V Denmark. **LC** TD4.

STANDARD METHODS FOR THE EXAMINATION OF WATER AND WASTEWATER. Main/Corp American Public Health Association. 1st- Ed. US. English. ir. American Public Health Association, 1015 15th Street NW, Washington DC 20005. **Tel** (202)789-5600. **LC** QD142. **DD** 543.3.

STANDARD METHODS FOR THE EXAMINATION OF WATER AND WASTEWATER. (STANDARD METHODS FOR THE EXAMINATION OF WATER AND WASTEWATER : INCLUDING BOTTOM SEDIMENTS AND SLUDGES). VFOAT Standard Methods. Began with 11th Ed., 1960-. 8755-3546. US. English. ir. Water Pollution Control Federation, 2626 Pennsylvania Avenue NW, Washington DC 20037. **Tel** (202)337-2500. **DD** 543. *Standard Methods for the Examination of Water, Sewage, and Industrial Wastes*.

STANFORD ENVIRONMENTAL LAW ANNUAL. See Law.

STATE AIR POLLUTION IMPLEMENTATION PLAN PROGRESS REPORT. Main/Corp United States. Environmental Protection Agency. Office of Air and Water Programs. Jan./June 1973-. 0094-2871. US. English. sa. US Environmental Protection Agency, Office of Air Quality and Planning, Durham NC 27111. **LC** TD883.2. **DD** 363.6.

STATE OF THE ENVIRONMENT. Main/Corp Commission of the European Communities. 1st- 1977-. English (issued also in Danish, Dutch, French, German and Italian). ir. European Community Information Service, 2100 M Street NW/Suite 707, Washington DC 20037. **LC** HC240.9.E5. **DD** 363.70094.

STATE OF WASHINGTON ENVIRONMENTAL RADIATION PROGRAM . . . ANNUAL REPORT. See Physics - Light, Optics, Radiation.

Sanitation, Environmental Technology

STATE REGULATION REPORT, TOXIC SUBSTANCES & HAZARDOUS WASTE. VAT State Regulation Report, Toxic Substances and Hazardous Waste. Began with vol. 1, no. 1 (Jan. 22, 1981). 0276-2870. Periodical. US. English. bm. Business Publishers Inc, 951 Pershing Drive, Silver Spring MD 20910. Ed Joan Murphy. Report on state legislative and regulatory initiatives on toxic substances and hazardous wastes plus updates on federal legislation and regulation affecting businesses, especially chemical manufacturers.

STATUS OF WATER QUALITY IN COLORADO. 0731-8936. US. English. be. Water Quality Control Division, Colorado Department of Health, 4210 East 11th Avenue, Denver CO 80220. Tel (303)320-8333. An assessment of water quality in the state of Colorado.

STAUB, REINHALTUNG DER LUFT. 0039-0771. Periodical. German (summaries in English and French). ir. 130.00 Foreign. VDI-Verlag, Graf-Recke-Strasse 84 4 1, Dusseldorf West Germany. Tel (0211)6214-1. Ind/Abst CIS Abstr., Eng. Index Mon., Eng. Index Bioeng. Abstr., Eng. Index Energy Abstr., Excerpta Med., Coal Abstr., Int. Aerosp. Abstr., Energy Res. Abstr., Nucl. Sci. Abstr., Chem. Abstr., Eng. Index Annu., Energy Inf. Abstr. NLM W1 ST431. CODEN STRHAV. bk rev. adv acc. Circ s,256. (ctrl). Dust-cleanliness. Staub.

STH-BERICHTE. (STH BERICHTE). VAT Strahlenhygiene Berichte. 0172-0198. Monographic Series. German. ir. Ind/Abst Chem. Abstr. NLM W1 S668. CODEN STBEDD.

STROJARSTVO. Began in 1959?. 0562-1887. Periodical. Serbo-Croatian. bm. Strojarstvo, Berislaviceva 6, 41000 Zagreb Yugoslavia. Ind/Abst Electron. Commun. Abstr. J., ISMEC Bull., Met. Abstr., Pollut. Abstr. Indexes, Saf. Sci. Abstr. J., Ship Abstr., Fluidex, World Text Abstr., Energy Inf. Abstr., Environ. Abstr., World Alum. Abstr., Chem. Abstr. CODEN STJSAO.

STUDENT-ORIGINATED STUDIES PROJECTS. ABSTRACT REPORTS. See Indexes/Abstracts.

STUDI ALIMENTARI CU APA. Main/Corp Institutul de Studii, Cercetari Si Proiectari Pentru Gospodarirea Apelor. 0521-3479. English, French, or Romanian. ir. Splaiul Independentei 294, Bucharest 17 Romania. Ind/Abst Chem. Abstr. LC TD204. CODEN SDAABI. Studii de Alimentari Cu Apa.

STUDII DE EPURAREA APELOR. Main/Corp Institutul de Studii, Cercetari Si Proiectari Pentru Gospodarirea Apelor. Romanian (summaries in English, French, and Russian). ir. Ind/Abst Sel. Water Resour. Abstr. LC TD511.

SUISHITSU ODAKU KENKYU. VFOAT Japan Journal of Water Pollution Research. Began in 1978. 0387-2025. Periodical. Japanese (summaries in English). bm. 7640. Kogai Taisaku Gijutsu Doyukai, 1-244 Akasaka 9 Shinjuku-ku, Tokyo-to 162 Japan. Ind/Abst Chem. Abstr. LC TD424.5. CODEN SOKEDN.

SUISHITSU SHIKEN SEISEKI NARABINI CHOSA HOKOKU. JA. Japanese. an. Suishitsu Shikenjo, 2714 Shimomizo, Sagamihara-shi, Kanagawa-ken Japan. LC TD305.K35.

SUJI DE MIRU KOGAI. Series/Tlti Kogai Kenkyujo Shiryo. 1970-. Japanese. ir. Tokyo-to Kogaki Kenkyujo, 7-1 Yurakucho 2 Chiyoda-ku, Tokyo Japan. LC TD187.5.J32.

SUMMARIES OF FOREIGN GOVERNMENT ENVIRONMENTAL REPORTS. VFOAT Foreign Documents Announcements. 0094-3142. Periodical. US. English. mo. $35.00 Domestic, $45.00 Foreign. Environmental Protection Agency, 401 M Street, Washington DC 20460. LC TD172. DD 363.6.

SUMMARY OF WATER QUALITY. Main/Corp Massachusetts. Water Quality and Research Section. US. English. an. LC TD224.M4. DD 363.7394209744.

SURVEYOR. 0039-6303. Periodical. UK. English. wk. $113.80. Business Press International Ltd, Perrymount Road, Haywards Heath West Sussex RH163BR England. Ind/Abst Coal Abstr., Excerpta Med., Life Sci. Collect. LC TD1. DD 620.005. Surveyor and Municipal Engineer.

TAEHAN HWANGYONG KONGHAKHOE CHI. VFOAT Journal of Korean Society of Environmental Engineers. Periodical. KO. Korean (summaries in English). ir. Taehan Hwangyong Konghakhoe, 56-3 Supyo-dong, Chung-ku, Seoul South Korea. LC TD169. DD 620.8.

TAI-WAN SHUI LI. VFOAT Taiwan Water Conservancy. Began with June 1953 issue. Periodical. CH. Chinese (English). qt. 160.00 Domestic, $45.00. Tai-Wan Shui Li Chu Pan Wei Yuan Hui, 11 Tsun Hsien St 5th Floor, Tai-Chung Shih Taiwan China. Tel (04)2260781-3. LC TD302.5.A1. DD 333.91160951249. bk rev. adv acc. Circ 700.

TAIKI OSEN NYUSU. VFOAT Air Pollution News Report. Japanese. ir. Taiki Osen Kenkyu Zenkoku Kyogikai, 6-1 Shirokanedai 4-chome Minato-ku (108), Tokyo Japan. LC TD881. NLM W1 TA41R.

T.E.C. (TRANSPORT, ENVIRONNEMENT, CIRCULATION). VFOAT TEC. No. 1 (1973)-. 0397-6513. Periodical. FR. French (summaries in English and German). bm. $33.26. A T E C, Place Adolphe Cherioux 11, 75015 Paris France. Ind/Abst Excerpta Med., Comput. Control Abstr., Electr. Electron. Abstr., Sci. Abstr. Sect. A. Phys. Abstr. Index published separately - free - automatically sent.

TECHNICAL BULLETIN (CANADA. INLAND WATERS DIRECTORATE). (TECHNICAL BULLETIN - INLAND WATERS DIRECTORATE). VAT IWD Technical Bulletin, Inland Waters Directorate Technical Bulletin. No. 65-. 0318-5842. Monographic Series. CN. English (some no. include abstract in French). ir. Enviroment Canada, 74 Place Vincent Massey, Hull Quebec Canada K1A 0E7. Tel (613)997-2601. Ind/Abst Eng. Index Annu., Eng. Index Mon., Eng. Index Bioeng. Abstr., Eng. Index Energy Abstr., GeoRef, ASTIS Bibliogr., ASTIS Curr. Aware. Bull., Chem. Abstr. CODEN CIWDDW. Technical Bulletin, 0576-2499.

TECHNICAL PAPER - HUDSON RIVER BASIN STUDY GROUP, NEW YORK STATE DEPARTMENT OF ENVIRONMENTAL CONSERVATION. See Water Resources.

TECHNICAL PROGRESS REPORT - BATTELLE MEMORIAL INSTITUTE. OFFICE OF NUCLEAR WASTE ISOLATION. (TECHNICAL PROGRESS REPORT FOR THE QUARTER . . .). Main/Corp Battelle Memorial Institute. Office of Nuclear Waste Isolation. 0742-2156. Periodical. US. English. qt. Battelle Memorial Institute, 505 King Avenue, Columbus OH 43201.

TECHNICAL RELEASE - NATIONAL PEST CONTROL ASSOCIATION. Main/Corp National Pest Control Association. Periodical. US. English. ir. $35.00. National Pest Control Association, PO Box 377, 8100 Oak Street, Dunn Loring VA 22027. Tel (703)573-8330.

TECHNICAL REPORT - TEXAS WATER RESOURCES INSTITUTE. See Water Resources.

TECHNIQUES ET SCIENCES MUNICIPALES. (TECHNIQUES & I.E. ET SCIENCES MUNICIPALES). Yearly V. 66, No. 11- Nov. 1971-. 0151-6973. FR. French. ir. Association Generale des Hygienistes et Techniciens, 9 rue de Phalsbourg, Paris 75017 France. Ind/Abst Electron. Commun. Abstr. J., ISMEC Bull., Pollut. Abstr. Indexes, Saf. Sci. Abstr. J., Life Sci. Collect., Excerpta Med., CIS Abstr., Coal Abstr., Sel. Water Resour. Abstr., Energy Res. Abstr., Energy Inf. Abstr., Environ. Abstr. LC TD2. DD 628.405. NLM W1. Techniques et Sciences Municipales et Revue l'Eau.

TECHNIQUES ET SCIENCES MUNICIPALES. L'EAU. VFOAT EAU. 0151-6973. Periodical. FR. French. ir. 430.00. Association Generale des Hygienists Techniciens Municipaux, 9 rue de Phalsbourg, 75854 Paris Cedex 17 France. Tel (1)227-3891. Ind/Abst Fluidex, Pollut. Abstr. Indexes, Bibliogr. Index Geol. CODEN TSCMA9. Publication of the general association of municipal hygienists and technicians of Paris. Technology and science as it applies to cities, also water supply. Technologie Sanitaire, EAU.

TECHNOLOGY. (E A UPDATE SUMMARY). Main/Corp Ontario. Environmental Approvals Branch. Jan. 1979-. 0708-7292. CN. English. an. Environmental Approvals Branch, 135 Saint Clair Avenue West, Toronto Ontario M4V 1P5 Canada.

TEKHNICHESKIE USLOVIIA NA METODY OPREDELENIIA VREDNYKH VESHCHESTV V VOZDUKHE. Vol. 1- 1960-. UR. Russian. NLM W1 TE296K.

TELKWA FOUNDATION NEWSLETTER. 0710-6432. Periodical. CN. English. ir. Telkwa Foundation, PO Box 100, Telkwa British Columbia V0J 2X0 Canada. DD 330.971132.

TEXAS FOREST PEST ACTIVITY AND FOREST PEST CONTROL SECTION BIENNIAL REPORT. 0148-3455. US. English. Texas Forest Service, 200 East Ohio Street, Chicago IL 60611. LC SB763.T4. DD 634.96909764.

TEXAS HERBICIDE REGULATION. See Agriculture.

THEORETICAL AND APPLIED ENVIRONMENTAL REVIEW. 0197-839X. Periodical. US. English. ir. Harwood Academic Publishers, PO Box 786, Cooper Station, New York NY 10276. Tel (212)689-0360.

TOPICS IN ENVIRONMENTAL HEALTH. See Public Health and Safety.

TOPICS IN ENVIRONMENTAL PHYSIOLOGY AND MEDICINE. Began In 1974. 0172-6048. Monographic Series. US. English. ir. Springer Verlag-New York Inc, 175 5th Avenue, New York NY 10010. Tel (212)460-1584. Contains articles on man and animal and health and the environment.

TOWN & COUNTRY PLANNING. See Public Administration.

TOXIC AND HAZARDOUS WASTE DISPOSAL. V. 1-. 0271-9371. Monographic Series. US. English. ir. Ann Arbor Science Publishers, PO Box 1425, Ann Arbor MI 48106. Ed Robert B Pojasek. Ind/Abst Chem. Abstr., Bibliogr. Agric. CODEN THWDD8.

TOXIC MATERIALS TRANSPORT. See Transportation.

TOXIC SUBSTANCES REPORTER. Vol. 1, No. 1 (Nov. 10, 1980)-. 0270-675X. Periodical. US. English. mo. $244.00. Aspens System Corporation, 1600 Research Boulevard, Rockville MD 20550.

TOXIC SUBSTANCES SOURCEBOOK. V. 1-. 0147-5118. US. English. an. Environment Information Center Inc Toxic Substances Reference Department, 292 Madison Avenue, New York NY 10017. LC T55.3.H3. DD 615.9. NLM ZQV 600 T756.

TRANSPORTATION NOISE BULLETIN. See Transportation.

TRAVAUX. Yearly V. 17-. 0041-1906. Periodical. FR. French. ir. 600. Editions Science et Industrie, 6 Avenue Pierre 1 de Serbie, Paris France 75116. Tel 723 61.54. Ed Christine Coville. Ind/Abst Eng. Index Annu., Eng. Index Mon., Eng. Index Bioeng. Abstr., Eng. Index Energy Abstr., Excerpta Med., Coal Abstr., Nuci. Sci. Abstr. LC TA2. DD 620.5. CODEN TRAVAJ. adv acc. Circ 5,000. Public works and associated disciplines. Mostly water drainage, special foundations, materials structure and industrial equipment, pipelaying, roads and aerodromes, earthworks, underground and railways. Science et Industrie.

LA TRIBUNE DU CEBEDEAU. Main/Corp Centre Belge d'Etude et de Documentation de l'Eau, de l'Air et de l'Environnement. V. 30- (No. 398-). Periodical. English (French). ir. $82.99. Cebedoc Sprl, rue Armand Stevart 2, B-4000 Liege Belgium. Ind/Abst Eng. Index. LC TD202. DD 628.05. Tribune.

TRIBUNE DU CEBEDEAU (CENTRE D'ETUDE ET DE DOCUMENTATION DE L'ENVIRONNEMENT (BELGIUM)). (LA TRIBUNE DU CEBEDEAU). Vol. 32, Nos. 422-423 (Jan./Feb. 1979)-. Periodical. FR. French (summaries in English). mo. 3.500. Editions Cebedoc, 2 rue Armand Stevart, B-4000 Liege Belgium. LC TD202. DD 628.05. Tribune du Cebedeau (Centre Belge d'Etude et de Documentation de l'Eau, de l'Air et de l'Environnement).

TSCA STATUS REPORT FOR EXISTING CHEMICALS. See Medicine - Toxicology.

TUNG CHI NIEN PAO - TAI-PEI TZU LAI SHUI CHANG CHU CHI SHIH. Main/Corp Tai-Pei Tzu Lai Shui Chang. Chu Chi Shih. VFOAT Tai-Pei Tzu Lai Shui Chang Tung Chi Nien Pao. Chinese. ir. LC TD302.6.T3.

UCLA JOURNAL OF ENVIRONMENTAL LAW & POLICY. VFOAT U.C.L.A. Journal of Environmental Law & Policy. VAT UCLA Journal of Environmental Law and Policy, University of California, Los Angeles Journal of Environmental Law and Policy. Vol. 1, No. 1 (Fall 1980)-. 0733-401X. Periodical. US. English. sa. $15.00. University of California at Los Angeles, 405 Hilgard Avenue, Los Angeles CA 90024. Tel (213)829-5296. Ed Roy Ogden. Ind/Abst Public Aff. Inf. Serv. Bull. LC

Sanitation, Environmental Technology

K25. **DD** 344.7304605, 347.3044605. **Circ** 300. Supply forum for scholarly discussion concerning the environment and other related topics.

ULTRAPURE WATER. Vol. 1, No. 1 (July/Aug. 1984). 0747-8291. Periodical. US. English. bm. $18.00. Tall Oaks Publishing Inc, 1507 Evesham Road, Voorhees NJ 08043. **DD** 628.

UMWELT. See Engineering.

UMWELTDATEN. **Main/Corp** Osterreichisches Statistisches Zentralamt. **Series/Titl** Beitrage zur Osterreichischen Statistik. 1978-. Periodical. German. ir. **LC** HA1173, TD186.5. A9.

UMWELTFORSCHUNGSKATALOG. **VFOAT** Umplis, Informations und Dokumentations-System zur Umweltplanung, Ufokat. GW. German. an. E Schmidt Verlag, Bismarckplatz 1, D-1 Berlin West Germany. **LC** TD171.5.G3. **DD** 363.70072.

UMWELTHYGIENE. (UMWELTHYGIENE : JAHRESBERICHT). **VFOAT** Jahresbericht (Medizinisches Institut fur Umwelthygiene (Universitat Dusselforf)). V. 12 (1979)-. 0174-3244. German (with some English). an. **Ind/Abst** Chem. Abstr. **NLM** W1. **CODEN** UMHYD8. *Lufthygiene und Silikoseforschung.*

UNEP-ASIA REPORT. Began with Vol. for 1977. English. an. UNEP Regional Office for Asia & the Pacific, United Nations Building/10th Floor Rajdamnern Avenue, Bangkok 2 Thailand. **LC** TD171.5. **DD** 363.70095.

UNEP STUDIES. **Main/Corp** United Nations Environment Programme. V. 1-. Monographic Series. UK. English. ir. Pergamon Press, 395 Sawmill River Road, Elmsford NY 10523. **Tel** (914)592-7700. **LC** UNC.

U.S. ENVIRONMENTAL PROTECTION AGENCY LIBRARY SYSTEM BOOK CATALOG. See Library and Information Science.

U.S. IBP ANALYSES OF ECOSYSTEMS PROGRAM INTERBIOME ABSTRACTS. See Indexes/Abstracts.

UNSERE UMWELT. See Conservation & Natural Resources.

UPDATE - INTERPRETATION CANADA. See Education (General).

UPPER ATMOSPHERIC PROGRAMS, BULLETIN. 0276-5411. Periodical. US. English. bm. Office of Environment and Energy of the Federal Aviation Administration, 800 Independence Avenue Southwest, Washington DC 20591.

URANIUM MILL TAILINGS MANAGEMENT. (URANIUM MILL TAILINGS MANAGEMENT : PROCEEDINGS OF A SYMPOSIUM . . .). 1st (Nov. 20, 21, 1978)-. 0742-8502. US. English. an. **Ind/Abst** GeoRef. **LC** TD899.U73. **DD** 622.34932.

URBAN ENVIRONMENT STUDY; PUBLICATION. **Main/Corp** Detroit. Metropolitan Area Regional Planning Commission. Began with No. 1, 1953. 0417-1233. Periodical. US. English. Metro Area Regional Planning Committee, 800 Cadillac Square Building, Detroit MI 48201.

VANN. V. 1-. 0042-2592. Periodical. NO. Norwegian. ir. Norwegian Water Cons & Hyg Association, Kronpininsensgt 17, Oslo 1 Norway. **Ind/Abst** Energy Res. Abstr. **LC** TD204.

VERSLAG ONDERZOEK KWALITEIT OPPERVLAKTEWATER IN ZEELAND. **Main/Corp** Zealand. Provincicale Waterstaatsdienst. NE. Dutch. an. Rouaansekaai 43, Middelburg Netherlands. **LC** TD278.Z4.

VIRUSES IN WASTE, RENOVATED, AND OTHER WATERS. 1969-. 0736-6647. US. English. an. US Environmental Protection Agency, Center for Environmental Research Information, Cincinnati OH 45268. **NLM** ZQW 80 V82. Each issue contains an index to its own contents - no vol index - loose.

VIZGAZDALKODAS ES KORNYEZETVEDELEM. **VFOAT** Vizgazdalkodas. Hungarian. ir. Orszagos Vizugyi Foigazgatosag, VII Kazinczy U. 3/B, Budapest Hungary. **LC** TD265.5.

VIZMINOSEGI ES VIZTECHNOLOGIAI KUTATASI EREDMENYEK. **Main/Corp** Vizgazdalkodasi Tudomanyos Kutato Intezet Vizminosegi es Viztechnologiai Foosztaly. **VFOAT** Research in Water Quality and Water Technology. 1958/68-. English or Hungarian (1958/68, Hungarian only). ir. **LC** TD365.

VOLUNTEER LAKE MONITORING. US. English. Illinois Environmental Protection Agency, Division of Water Pollution Control, 2200 Churchhill Road, Springfield IL 62706. **LC** TD224.I3. **DD** 363.7394.

VOM WASSER. V. 1-. 0083-6915. German. ir. VCH Publishers Inc, 303 NW 12th Avenue, Deerfield Beach FL 33442. **Tel** (305)428-5566. **Ind/Abst** Excerpta Med., Sel. Water Resour. Abstr., Biol. Abstr., Chem. Abstr., Eng. Index, Eng. Index Mon., Nuci. Sci. Abstr., Energy Res. Abstr. **LC** TD203. **DD** 628.105. **NLM** W1 VO604. **CODEN** VJWWAU. (cum index).

WASHINGTON ENVIRONMENTAL QUALITY PROFILE. Began with 1977. US. English. an. US Environmental Protection Agency Region 10, 1200 Sixth Avenue, Seattle WA 98101.

WASSER, LUFT UND BETRIEB. WLB-HANDBUCH UMWELTTECHNIK. **VFOAT** W.L.B.-Handbuch Umwelttechnik, WLB-Handbuch Umwelttechnik. GW. German. an. 28.00. Vereinigte Fachverlage, Lessingstrasse 12, D-6500 Mainz West Germany. **Tel** (06131)609-0. **Ed** Hans Joadiun Schmitz. **LC** TD3. **DD** 628.05. adv acc. **Circ** 8,000. (ctrl).

WASTE AGE. V. 1- Apr. 1970-. 0043-1001. Periodical. US. English. mo. $27.00. Waste Age, 1730 Rhode Island Avenue NW/Suite 1000, Washington DC 20036. **Tel** (202)861-0708. **Ind/Abst** Electron. Commun. Abstr. J., ISMEC Bull., Pollut. Abstr. Indexes, Saf. Sci. Abstr. J., Excerpta Med., Can. Environ., Predicasts, Energy Inf. Abstr., Environ. Abstr., Int. Aerosp. Abstr., Ocean. Abstr., Energy Res. Abstr., Funk Scott Index Corp. Inc.

WASTE DISPOSAL STATISTICS BASED ON ESTIMATES. See Statistics.

WASTE DISPOSAL STATISTICS . . . ESTIMATES. See Statistics.

WASTE MANAGEMENT & RESEARCH. (WASTE MANAGEMENT & RESEARCH : THE JOURNAL OF THE INTERNATIONAL SOLID WASTES AND PUBLIC CLEANSING ASSOCIATION, ISWA). **VFOAT** Waste Management and Research. Vol. 1, No. 1 (Mar. 1983)-. 0734-242X. Periodical. UK. English. qt. Academic Press, 4805 Sand Lake Road, Orlando FL 32819. **Tel** (305)345-4100. **Ind/Abst** Chem. Abstr. **LC** TD896. **DD** 628.405.

WASTE MANAGEMENT RESEARCH ABSTRACTS : INFORMATION ON RESEARCH IN PROGRESS. See Indexes/Abstracts.

WASTE TREATMENT TECHNOLOGY NEWS. Vol. 1, No. 1 (Sept. 1985)-. 0885-0003. Periodical. US. English. mo. $200.00. Business Communications Company, PO Box 2070C, Stamford CT 06906. **DD** 604.

WASTES MANAGEMENT. Vol. 72, No. 1 (Jan. 1982)-. Periodical. UK. English. mo. $33.71. Institute of Wastes Management, 3 Albion Place, Northampton NN1 1UD England. **Tel** (0604) 20426. **Ed** D Taylor. adv acc. **Circ** 3,000. Professional institute journal dealing with all aspects of wastes management. *Solid Wastes.*

WATER, AIR, AND SOIL POLLUTION. V. 1- Nov. 1971-. 0049-6979. Periodical. NE. English. ir. 470.00. Kluwer Academic Publishers Group, PO Box 322, 3300 AH Dordrecht Netherlands. **Tel** (31)78-334911. **Ed** Billy M McCormac. **Ind/Abst** Life Sci. Collect., Excerpta Med., Can. Environ., Pestdoc, Ringdoc, Vetdoc, Coal Abstr., Energy Inf. Abstr., Environ. Abstr., GeoRef, Int. Aerosp. Abstr., Comput. Control Abstr., Electr. Electron. Abstr., Sci. Abstr. Sect. A. Phys. Abstr., Biol. Abstr., Chem. Abstr., Eng. Index Annu., Eng. Index Mon., Meteorol. Geoastrophys. Abstr., Sel. Water Resour. Abstr., Bibliogr. Agric., Energy Res. Abstr., Fluidex, Phys. Abstr., Pollut. Abstr. Indexes, Ocean. Abstr., Sci. Cit. Index, Abr. Ed., Eng. Index. **LC** TD172. **DD** 628.505. **NLM** W1 WA69D. **CODEN** WAPLAC. bk rev. adv acc. **Circ** 1,100. Physical and biological processes affecting flora, air, water, and solid earth in relation to environmental pollution.

WATER & POLLUTION CONTROL. V. 103, No. 8- Aug. 1965-. 0043-1117. Periodical. CN. English. mo. $12.00. Southam Business Publications Ltd, 1450 Don Mills Road, Don Mills Ontario M3B 2X7 Canada. **Ind/Abst** Electron. Commun. Abstr. J., ISMEC Bull., Pollut. Abstr. Indexes, Saf. Sci. Abstr. J., Eng. Index Annu., Eng. Index Mon., Eng. Index Bioeng. Abstr., Eng. Index Energy Abstr., Life Sci. Collect., Excerpta Med., Can. Environ., Energy Inf. Abstr., Environ. Abstr., Sel. Water Resour. Abstr., Abstr. Bull. Inst. Paper Chem., Mintec, Min. Technol. Abstr., Minproc, Can. Bus. Index, Appl. Sci. Technol. Index. **LC** TA1. **DD** 363.6105. **CODEN** WPCOAR. *Canadian Municipal Utilities, 0366-7197.*

WATER & SEWAGE WORKS. **VAT** Water and Sewage Works. Began in 1890. 0043-1125. Periodical. US. English. mo. $10.00. Scranton Publishing Company, 434 South Wabash, Chicago IL 60605. **LC** TD1. **DD** 628.05. **CODEN** WSIWAY. *Water Works, Industrial Water & Wastes.*

WATER AND SEWER PROGRAMS FOR OHIO. See Water Resources.

WATER & WASTE TREATMENT. **VAT** Water and Waste Treatment. V. 9-24. 0043-1133. Periodical. UK. English. mo. $38.31. Quadrant Subscription Services Ltd, Oakfield House, Perrymount Road, Haywards Heath Sussex England. **Tel** 0684 4082. **Ed** John Lambert. **Ind/Abst** Life Sci. Collect., World Text Abstr., Coal Abstr., Ship Abstr., World Surf. Coat. Abstr., Energy Res. Abstr., Excerpta Med., Pap. Board Abstr., Sel. Water Resour. Abstr. adv acc. (ctrl). Water treatment, pollution, waste disposal and industrial Effluent Treatment. *Water & Waste Treatment Journal (1957).*

WATER & WASTES DIGEST. (WATER AND WASTES DIGEST). V. 1- 1961-. 0043-1141. Periodical. US. English. bm. Scranton Gillette Publishing, 380 North West Highway, Des Plaines IL 60016. **Tel** (312)298-6622. **Ed** Dawn Meyers. **Ind/Abst** Electron. Commun. Abstr. J., ISMEC Bull., Pollut. Abstr. Indexes, Saf. Sci. Abstr. J., Energy Inf. Abstr., Environ. Abstr., Abstr. Bull. Inst. Paper Chem. adv acc. **Circ** 99,518. (ctrl).

WATER AND WASTES ENGINEERING CEASED. (WATER & WASTES ENGINEERING). V. 3-17. 0043-115X. Periodical. US. English. mo. **Ind/Abst** Coal Abstr., Excerpta Med., GeoRef, Int. Aerosp. Abstr., Life Sci. Collect., Sel. Water Resour. Abstr. **CODEN** WWAEA2. *Waterworks and Wastes Engineering, 0096-6320; Water Wastes Engineering/Industrial.*

WATER & WASTEWATER DIGEST. **VFOAT** Water and Wastewater Digest. Oct. 1981-. 0748-2612. Periodical. US. English. mo. Missouri Department of Natural Resources, Division of Environmental Quality, PO Box 1368, Jefferson City MO 65102. **LC** TD224.M8. **DD** 363.6109778. *Missouri Water & Wastewater Digest, 0731-2903.*

WATER NEWSLETTER; WATER SUPPLY, WASTE DISPOSAL, CONSERVATION. V. 1- Feb. 17, 1959-. 0043-1273. Periodical. US. English. sm. $97.00. Water Information Center Inc, 6800 Jericho Turnpike, Syosset NY 11791. **Tel** (516)921-7690. **Ed** Judith Schoeck Corcoran. bk rev. Water supply; waste disposal; conservation; legislation; new products; research and developments.

WATER POLLUTION ABSTRACTS. See Indexes/Abstracts.

WATER POLLUTION CONTROL. 1901-. 0043-129X. Periodical. UK. English. qt. 42.00. Inst Water Pollution Control, Ledson House 53 London Road, Maidstone Kent England ME16 8JH. **Tel** (0622)62034. **Ed** I M Lamont. **Ind/Abst** Eng. Index, Pollut. Abstr. Indexes. (cum index). adv acc. **Circ** 3,200. (ctrl). Wastewater and industrial effluent treatment and disposal. Sewage and sludge treatment and disposal. Design and operation of wastewater treatment works.

WATER POLLUTION CONTROL. 0194-0147. Periodical. US. English. bw. $315.00. Bureau of National Affairs Inc, 1231 25th Street NW, Washington DC 20037.

WATER POLLUTION CONTROL ASSOCIATION OF PENNSYLVANIA MAGAZINE. Vol. 1, No. 1 (Mar.-Apr. 1968)-. Periodical. US. English. bm. $12.00. Water Pollution Control Association, PO Box 20, Locust Grove VA 22508. **Ind/Abst** Electron. Commun. Abstr. J., ISMEC Bull., Pollut. Abstr. Indexes, Saf. Sci. Abstr. J., Chem. Abstr.

WATER POLLUTION CONTROL PLAN. **Main/Corp** Illinois. Environmental Protection Agency. 0091-4541. US. English. IL Environmental Protection Agency, 2200 Churchill Road, Springfield IL 62706. **LC** TD224.I3. **DD** 363.6.

WATER POLLUTION CONTROL PROGRAM PLAN. 0192-4605. US. English. an. Department of Environmental Conservation, Pouch O, Juneau AK 99811. **LC** TD224.A25. **DD** 614.77209798.

Science (General)

WATER POLLUTION REPORT. Vl. English. ir. Virgin Island of the US, Division of Environmental Health, St Thomas Virgin Islands. LC TD233.V5. DD 628.16808 S.

WATER POLLUTION RESEARCH. Main/ Corp Great Britain. Dept. of the Environment. 1972-. UK. English. an. 1.10. Her Majesty's Stationery Office, Great Britain Department of the Environment, 49 High Holborn, London WC1V 6HB England. LC TD420. DD 628.168. *Water Pollution Research the Report of the Water Pollution Research Board with the Report of the Director of the Water Pollution Research Laboratory.*

WATER POLLUTION RESEARCH JOURNAL OF CANADA. New Ser., V. 15, No. 1-. 0197-9140. Periodical. US. English (some text and abstracts in French). qt. $60.00. Pergamon Press Inc, Maxwell House, Fairview Park, Elmsford NY 10523. **Ind/Abst** Excerpta Med., Can. Environ., GeoRef, Biol. Abstr., Comput. Control Abstr., Electr. Electron. Abstr., Sci. Abstr. Sect. A. Phys. Abstr., Chem. Abstr., Energy Inf. Abstr., Environ. Abstr. DD 363.73940971. **CODEN** WRJCD9. *Water Pollution Research in Canada,* 0705-288X.

WATER POLLUTION RESEARCH. SUMMARY OF CURRENT LITERATURE... ABSTRACTS.... *See* Indexes/Abstracts.

WATER POLLUTION SURVEILLANCE SYSTEM. ANNUAL COMPILATION OF DATA. (WATER POLLUTION SURVEILLANCE SYSTEM : ANNUAL COMPILATION OF DATA). **Main/ Corp** United States. Division of Water Supply and Pollution Control. **VFOAT** PHS Water Pollution Surveillance System. 6th- 1962/63-. 0502-0395. Periodical. US. English. an. US Division of Water Supply and Pollution Control, Washington DC 20017. LC GB701. DD 614. *National Water Quality Network: Annual Compilation of Data.*

WATER QUALITY AND POLLUTION CONTROL IN MICHIGAN. US. English. an. Michigan Department of Natural Resources, Environmental Services Division PO Box 30028, Lansing MI 48909. LC TD224.M5. DD 363.739409774.

WATER QUALITY AND WATER POLLUTION CONTROL IN NEW MEXICO. 0741-1375. US. English. be. PO Box 968, Santa Fe NM 87504-0968. LC TD224.N6. DD 363.73945609789.

WATER QUALITY ASSOCIATION NEWSLETTER. 0745-1512. Periodical. US. English. bw. $150.00. Water Quality Association, 4151 Naperville Road, Lisle IL 60532. DD 363.

WATER QUALITY CONTROL DIGEST. 1- 1969-. 0043-1346. US. English. bm. $88.00. University Digest Service, PO Box 343, Troy MI 48084. LC Z7173.W3. DD 016.628168.

WATER QUALITY INSTRUMENTATION. V. 1- 1972-. 0096-6304. US. English. Instrument Society of America, PO Box 3561, Durham NC 27702. Ed J Scales. LC TD423. DD 628.16108.

WATER QUALITY INVENTORY 305 (B) REPORT, VIRGINIA. Main/Corp Virginia. State Water Control Board. **VAT** Water Quality Inventory Three Hundred Five (B) Report, Virginia. 0149-8266. US. English. an. 211 North Hamilton Street, PO Box 11143, Richmond VA 23230. LC TD224.V8. DD 363.6109755.

WATER QUALITY MANAGEMENT DIRECTORY. *See* Yearbooks, Almanacs, Directories.

WATER QUALITY MANAGEMENT PROGRAM SUPPLEMENTAL GUIDANCE FOR FY.... Main/Corp United States. Environmental Protection Agency. Water Planning Division. 81-. US. English. an. US Environmental Protection Agency, Office of Water Program Operations, Washington DC 20460. *Supplemental Water Quality Management Program Guidance for FY....*

WATER QUALITY MONITORING DATA FOR GEORGIA STREAMS. Main/Corp Georgia. Environmental Protection Division. 0097-7519. US. English. an. Environmental Protection Protection, Department of Natural Resources, 47 Trinity Avenue SW, Atlanta GA 30334. **Ind/Abst** GeoRef. LC TD224.G4. DD 363.6109758.

WATER-RELATED DISEASE OUTBREAKS SURVEILLANCE. ANNUAL SUMMARY. (WATER-RELATED DISEASE OUTBREAKS SURVEILLANCE). Annual summary 1978-. 0275-7249. US. English. an. US Department of Health and Human Services, Public Health Service, Centers for Disease Control, Atlanta GA 30333. LC RC143. DD 614.4. **NLM** W2 A C2FB. Vols. for (1983-) distributed to depository libraries in microfiche. *Foodborne & Waterborne Disease Surveillance,* 0737-1241.

WATER RESEARCH TOPICS. V. 1-. 0730-9619. Periodical. UK. English. Halsted Press, John Wiley & Sons, 605 Third Avenue, New York NY 10016. **Ind/Abst** Chem. Abstr. LC TD201. DD 628.1. **CODEN** WRTODR.

WATER S. A. VAT Water South Africa. V. 1- Apr. 1975-. 0378-4738. Periodical. SA. English. qt. Water Research Commission, 705 Van der Suite, Box 824 179 Pretorius Street, Pretoria 0001 South Africa. **Ind/ Abst** Electron. Commun. Abstr. J., ISMEC Bull., Pollut. Abstr. Indexes, Saf. Sci. Abstr. J., Eng. Index Annu., Eng. Index Mon., Eng. Index Bioeng. Abstr., Eng. Index Energy Abstr., Life Sci. Collect., Excerpta Med., Coal Abstr., Sel. Water Resour. Abstr., Abstr. Bull. Inst. Paper Chem., Biol. Abstr., Chem. Abstr., Energy Inf. Abstr., Environ. Abstr. LC TD201. DD 628.1. **CODEN** WASADV.

WATER SCIENCE AND TECHNOLOGY. (WATER SCIENCE AND TECHNOLOGY : A JOURNAL OF THE INTERNATIONAL ASSOCIATION ON WATER POLLUTION RESEARCH). Vol. 13, No. 1-. 0273-1223. Periodical. UK. English. mo. $836.00. Pergamon Press, 395 Sawmill River Road, Elmsford NY 10523. **Ind/Abst** Eng. Index Annu., Eng. Index Mon., Fluidex, Life Sci. Collect., Excerpta Med., Can. Environ., Pestdoc, Ringdoc, Vetdoc, Coal Abstr., Energy Inf. Abstr., Environ. Abstr., Sel. Water Resour. Abstr., GeoRef, Biol. Abstr., Chem. Abstr. LC TD419. DD 628.16805. **CODEN** WSTED4. *Progress in Water Technology,* 0306-6746.

WATER SERVICES. Vol. 78, No. 935 (Jan. 1974)-. 0301-7028. Periodical. UK. English. mo. 45.00. Industrial & Marine Publishing Ltd, Queensway House, 2 Queensway, Redhill Surrey RH1 1QS England. Tel 0737 68611. Ed Victor H French. **Ind/ Abst** Electron. Commun. Abstr. J., ISMEC Bull., Pollut. Abstr. Indexes, Saf. Sci. Abstr. J., Eng. Index Annu., Eng. Index Mon., Eng. Index Bioeng. Abstr., Eng. Index Energy Abstr., Fluidex, Excerpta Med., Coal Abstr., Energy Inf. Abstr., Environ. Abstr., Sel. Water Resour. Abstr., Chem. Abstr., Eng. Index. LC TD201. DD 628.105. **CODEN** WTSVAK. bk rev. adv acc. **Circ** 2,500. Water supply and treatment, distribution, sewage treatment, effluent reuse, sludge disposal. *Water and Water Engineering,* 0043-1168.

WATER TECHNOLOGY. 0192-3633. Periodical. US. English. ir. $29.00. National Trade Publications, 8 Stanley Circle, Latham NY 12110. **Tel** (518)783-1281. Ed Susan Mayer. adv acc. **Circ** 10,500. (ctrl). Provides technical sales and marketing information to water treatment dealers, bottled water dealers, professional and specifying engineers and water treatment consultants.

WATER, WASTEWATER-CHEMICAL AND RADIOLOGICAL ANALYSES : TABULATION. 0192-3374. US. English. an. Department of Social Services, 44 Medical Drive, Salt Lake City UT 84115. LC TD224.U8. DD 553.709792.

WATERWORLD NEWS. VFOAT Water World News. Vol. 1, No. 1 (Jan./Feb. 1985)-. 0747-9735. Periodical. US. English. bm. $10.00. American Water Works Association, 666 West Quincy Avenue, Denver CO 80235. DD 628.

WISCONSIN WATER QUALITY, REPORT TO CONGRESS. (WISCONSIN WATER QUALITY... REPORT TO CONGRESS). **Main/Corp** Wisconsin. Dept. of Natural Resources. **VFOAT** Wisconsin Water Quality. 1982-. 0740-4700. US. English. an. Wisconsin Department of Natural Resources, Box 7921, Madison WI 53707. LC TD224.W6. DD 363.7394209775. *Wisconsin... Water Quality Inventory Report to Congress,* 0191-3190.

WORLD BANK STUDIES IN WATER SUPPLY AND SANITATION. *See* Water Resources.

THE WORLD ENVIRONMENT HANDBOOK. 1st Ed.-. 0749-1069. US. English. be. World Environment Center, 605 3rd Avenue 17th Floor, New York NY 10158. DD 333.

WORLD ENVIRONMENT REPORT. V. 1- Feb. 3, 1975-. 0098-8235. US. English. sm. $179.00. Business Publishers Inc, 951 Pershing Drive, Silver Spring MD 20910. **Ind/Abst** Energy Inf. Abstr., Environ. Abstr. **NLM** W1 WO856. Offers unparalleled coverage of international air and water pollution control, waste management and toxic substances, energy and natural resources and other environmental protection issues.

WORLD WATER. *See* Water Resources.

WORLDWIDE REPORT. ENVIRONMENTAL QUALITY (FOUO). VFOAT Environmental Quality (FOUO). Began in 1979-. Periodical. US. English. *Translations on Environmental Quality (FOUO).*

WYOMING STATE PLAN. Main/Corp Wyoming. Water Quality Division. 0098-0846. US. English. Wyoming Department of Environmental Quality Water Division, Cheyenne WY 82002. LC HC107.W93. DD 333.91009787.

WYOMING WATER POLLUTION CONTROL PROGRAM PLAN. Main/Corp Wyoming. Water Quality Division. 0147-4197. US. English. an. Water Qualithy Division, Hathaway Building, Cheyenne WY 82002. LC TD224.W8. DD 363.6109787.

YAMAGUCHI-KEN KOGAI SENTA NENPO. VFOAT Annual Report of Yamaguchi Prefectural Environmental Pollution Research Center. JA. Japanese. ir. Yamaguchi-Ken Kogai Senta, 535 Aza Hiruta, Oaza Asada, Yamaguchi 75 Japan. **Ind/ Abst** Chem. Abstr. LC TD187.5.J32. **CODEN** YKSNDQ.

YEARBOOK. *See* Yearbooks, Almanacs, Directories.

YOKOHAMA SHIRITSU DAIGAKU SOGO KENKYU. VFOAT Kankyo Kanri No Kenkyu. Vol. 1- (March 2, 1982)-. JA. Japanese. ir. Yokohama Shiritsu Daigaku Kankyo Kanri Keikaku, Kankyukai 22-2 Seto Kanazawa-ku, Yokohama-shi 236 Japan. LC TD169.

YOSUI TO HAISUI. VFOAT Journal of Water and Waste. Began in 1959. 0513-5907. Periodical. JA. Japanese. mo. 95.00. Maruzen Company Ltd, PO Box 5050, 100-31 Tokyo Japan. **Tel** (03)354-0150. Ed Fiusako Yamane. **Ind/Abst** Chem. Abstr. **CODEN** YOHAAP. adv acc. **Circ** 28,000. (ctrl). The journal of environmental integrity about water.

YOUR GOVERNMENT AND THE ENVIRONMENT. V. 1- 1971-. US. English. an. Output Systems Corporation, 2300 9th Street South, Arlington VA 22204. LC HC110.E5. DD 301.31.

ZEITSCHRIFT FUR LARMBEKAMPFUNG. 0174-1098. Periodical. German. bm. Springer Verlag-New York Inc, 175 5th Avenue, New York NY 10010. **Tel** (212)460-1500. Ed G Jansen. **Ind/Abst** Excerpta Med. LC TD891. Only German-language journal for noise control. Original articles on physical and psychological and social consequences of noise. Answers technical questions on noise levels and their control. *Kampf Dem Larm.*

ZEITSCHRIFT FUR UMWELTPOLITIK. VFOAT Journal of Environmental Policy. Vol. 1, (May 1978)-. 0343-7167. Periodical. GW. English (French and German). qt. 155.50. Deutscher Fachverlag GMBH, Postfach 2625, 6000 Frankfurt 1 West Germany. **Ind/Abst** Energy Res. Abstr. LC HC79.E5. DD 363.7052505.

ZEITSCHRIFT FUR WASSER- UND ABWASSER FORSCHUNG. VFOAT Journal for Water and Waste Water Research. 1.- Yearly Volume. 0044-3727. Periodical. GW. German (English). bm. Grossohaus Wegner & Company, PO Box 10 25 40, D-2000 Hamburg 1 West Germany. **Ind/Abst** Life Sci. Collect., Excerpta Med., Energy Inf. Abstr., Environ. Abstr., Coal Abstr., Sel. Water Resour. Abstr., GeoRef, Chem. Abstr., Energy Res. Abstr., Sci. Cit. Index, Abr. Ed. LC TD203. DD 628.05. **CODEN** ZWABAQ.

SCIENCE (GENERAL)

THE 5-YEAR OUTLOOK ON SCIENCE AND TECHNOLOGY. VFOAT Five Year Outlook on Science and Technology. 1981-. 0736-2242. US. English. an. Superintendent of

Science (General)

Documents, US Government Printing Office, Washington DC 20402. LC Q127.U6. DD 306.450973. *Five-Year Outlook.*

AAAS ANNUAL MEETING PROGRAM. Series/Titl AAAS Publication. Began with 149th. US. English. an. *Program of the . . . National Meeting.*

AAAS PUBLICATION. VAT American Association for the Advancement of Science Publication. 0271-2229. Monographic Series. US. English. ir. American Association for the Advancement of Science, 1515 Massachusetts Avenue NW, Washington DC 20005. Ind/Abst GeoRef. LC Q181.A1. DD 508.1. *AAAS Miscellaneous Publication.*

AAAS SELECTED SYMPOSIUM. VFOAT A.A.A.S. Selected Symposium. VAT American Association for the Advancement of Science Selected Symposia Series. 1-. 0164-0429. Monographic Series. US. English. ir. Westview Press, 5500 Central Avenue, Boulder CO 80301. Tel (303)444-3541. Ind/Abst Chem. Abstr., GeoRef, Bibliogr. Index Geol., Math. Rev. LC UNC. NLM W3 A101S. CODEN ASSYDL.

AARDE & KOSMOS. (AARDE & I.E. EN KOSMOS). 0166-4786. Periodical. NE. Dutch. mo. Stichting Mens en Wetenschap, Postbus 108, 1270 AC Huizen Netherlands. Ind/Abst Excerpta Med. LC Q4.

ABHANDLUNGEN DER AKADEMIE DER WISSENSCHAFTEN DER DDR. (ABHANDLUNGEN). Main/Corp Akademie der Wissenschaften der DDR. 0302-8054. GE. German. ir. Akademie-Verlag, Leipziger Str 3-4, 108 Berlin East Germany. Ind/Abst Life Sci. Collect. LC Q49.

ABHANDLUNGEN DER BRAUNSCHWEIGISCHEN WISSENSCHAFTLICHEN GESELLSCHAFT. Main/Corp Braunschweigische Wissenschaftliche Gesellschaft. V. 1- 1949-. 0068-0737. GW. German. ir. Verlag Erich Goltze KG, Stresemannstrasse 28, PF 360, 34 Gottingen West Germany. Ind/Abst GeoRef, Chem. Abstr., Int. Aerosp. Abstr., Math. Rev., Bibliogr. Index Geol. CODEN ABWGAZ.

ABHANDLUNGEN DER MATHEMATISCH-NATURWISSENSCHAFTLICHEN KLASSE - AKADEMIE DER WISSENSCHAFTEN UND DER LITERATUR. (ABHANDLUNGEN DER MATHEMATISCH- NATURWISSENSCHAFTLICHEN KLASSE). Main/Corp Akademie der Wissenschaften und der Literatur, (Germany). 1950-. 0002-2993. Monographic Series. GW. German. ir. Franz Steiner Verlag GMBH, Postfach 347, D7000 Stuttgart 1 West Germany. Tel (0711) 2582229. Ind/Abst Math. Rev., Life Sci. Collect., GeoRef. NLM W1 AK324. CODEN AWLMA9. Mostly short monographs dedicated to all natural sciences, medicine, and mathematics.

ABHANDLUNGEN DER SACHSISCHEN AKADEMIE DER WISSENSCHAFTEN ZU LEIPZIG. Main/Corp Sachsische Akademie der Wissenschaften Zu Leipzig. 0365-6470. GE. German. ir. Deutscher Buch Export-Import, Leninstrasse 16, DDR-701 Leipzig East Germany. Ind/Abst Math. Rev., Chem. Abstr., GeoRef. CODEN ASAWAO. *Abhandlungen der Mathematisch-Physikalen Klasse der Sachsischen Akademie der Wissenschaften.*

ABSTRACTS OF PAPERS OF THE NATIONAL MEETING - AMERICAN ASSOCIATION FOR THE ADVANCEMENT OF SCIENCE. *See* Indexes/Abstracts.

ABSTRACTS OF PUBLICATIONS - NATIONAL SCIENCE FOUNDATION U.S. *See* Indexes/Abstracts.

ABSTRACTS OF ROMANIAN SCIENTIFIC AND TECHNICAL LITERATURE. *See* Indexes/Abstracts.

ABSTRACTS OF SCIENTIFIC AND TECHNICAL PAPERS PUBLISHED IN U. A. R. *See* Indexes/Abstracts.

ABSTRACTS OF UPPSALA DISSERTATIONS FROM THE FACULTY OF SCIENCE. *See* Indexes/Abstracts.

ACADEMIC SCIENCE, SCIENTISTS AND ENGINEERS. DETAILED STATISTICAL TABLES. *See* Statistics.

ACADEMIE ROYALE DES SCIENCES D'OUTRE-MER. CLASSE DES SCIENCES TECHNIQUES. *See* Education (General).

ACCELERATOR CEASED. V. 1-14, No. 2. 0001-446X. Periodical. CN. English. ir. Free to Member. Saskatchewan Science Teachers' Society, PO Box 1108, Saskatoon Saskatchewan. Ind/Abst Can. Educ. Index.

ACCELERATOR NEWSLETTER. VFOAT Science into the 80'S. Vol. 5, No. 5 (Nov. 1980)-. 0712-1377. Periodical. CN. English. ir. Saskatchewan Teachers' Federation, 2317 Arlington Avenue, Saskatoon Saskatchewan S7J 2H8 Canada. DD 507. *Newsletter,* 0712-1369.

ACCESS (OTTAWA, ONT.). (ACCESS). Vol. 1, No. 1-. 0824-2399. Periodical. CN. English. bm. Association for the Advancement of Science in Canada, 805-151 Slater Street, Ottawa Ontario K1P 5H3 Canada. DD 303.4830971.

ACHIEVEMENTS OF CZECHOSLOVAK SCIENCE AND TECHNOLOGY WHICH WERE AWARDED STATE PRIZES CEASED. Main/Corp Ustredi Vedeckych, Technickych A Ekonomickych Informaci. English. ir. Central Office of Scientific Technical and Economic Information, 113 57 Praha 1 Konviktska 5, Prague Czechoslovakia. LC Q127.C9. DD 509.437.

ACTA BOREALIA. A: SCIENTIA. (ACTA BOREALIA. A. SCIENTIA). No. 1-30. 0065-1109. Monographic Series. No. English (Norwegian). ir. Universitetsforlaget, PO Box 2959-Toyen, Oslo 6 Norway. Ind/Abst GeoRef, Biol. Abstr., Chem. Abstr. LC Q111. DD 505. CODEN ABOAAB. *Troms Museums Arshefter.*

ACTA CIENTIFICA VENEZOLANA - ASOCIACION VENEZOLANA PARA EL AVANCE DE LA CIENCIA. V. 1- May/June 1950-. 0001-5504. Periodical. VE. Spanish. bm. $100.00. Acta Cientifica Venezolana, Apartado Postal 47286, Caracas 1041 Venezuela. Tel (02)752-1002. Ed V Rodriguez Lemoine. Ind/Abst Index Med., Math. Rev., Chem. Abstr. bk rev. adv acc. Circ 21,000. Covers biology, mathematics, physical sciences, natural sciences, social sciences, medicine, engineering, etc.

ACTA HISTORICA SCIENTIARIUM NATURALIUM ET MEDICINALIUM. Began in 1942. 0065-1311. Monographic Series. DK. English (Danish, French, or German). ir. C A Reitzel Booksellers, Norregade 4, DK-1165 Copenhagen K Denmark. Ind/Abst Index Med., Bibliogr. Index Geol., GeoRef. NLM W1 AC81G. CODEN AHSMA7.

ACTA MANILANA. No. 1 (Aug. 1965)-No. 4 (June 1967). 0065-1370. Monographic Series. English. ir. 3.00. Research Center, University of Tomas, Manila Philippines. Tel 731-4031. Ed Ciriaco Pedrosa. Ind/Abst Phys. Abstr., Comput. Control Abstr., Electr. Electron. Abstr. Circ 500. Natural and applied science.

ACTES. Main/Conf International Congress on the History of Science. English, French, German and Russian. ir. $29.27. Actes, 1 rue des Fosses Strasse Jacques, 75005 Paris France. Tel (1)341 37 16. LC Q101. DD 509.

ACTIVITIES OF THE FEDERAL COUNCIL FOR SCIENCE AND TECHNOLOGY AND THE FEDERAL COORDINATING COUNCIL FOR SCIENCE, ENGINEERING AND TECHNOLOGY. Main/Corp United States. Federal Coordinating Council For Science, Engineering and Technology. 1975/76-. 0149-2829. US. English. Executive Office of the President, Office of Science and Technology, Washington DC 20402. *Activities of the Federal Council For Science and Technology.*

ACTIVITIES OF THE LABORATORIES - NATIONAL RESEARCH COUNCIL CANADA CEASED. Main/Corp National Research Council of Canada. VFOAT Activites des Laboratoires - Conseil National de Recherches Canada. VAT Activities of the Laboratories - National Research Council of Canada., NRCL. Activities of the Laboratories, National Research Council Laboratories. Activities of the Laboratories. 1971-. 0384-3033. CN. English (French, 1973-). an. National Research Council of Canada, Montreal Road, Ottawa Ontario K1A 0R6 Canada. DD 507.2071. *Review of the Activities of the Laboratories,* 0373-5753.

ACTUALITES SCIENTIFIQUES ET INDUSTRIELLES. Began with 31?. 0365-6861. French. ir. Hermann Editeurs Sciences Arts, 293 rue Lecourbe, 75015 Paris France. Ind/Abst Math. Rev. *Conferences d'Actualites Scientifiques et Industrielles.*

ADVANCEMENT OF SCIENCE. (THE ADVANCEMENT OF SCIENCE). V. 1-27 No. 1-134. 0001-866X. UK. English. ir. W W Norton & Company, 500 Fifth Avenue, New York NY 10110. Tel (212)354-5500. Ind/Abst GeoRef, Bibliogr. Index Geol. LC Q41. DD 505. NLM W1 AD423. CODEN ADSCAH. Index in last issue of volume - loose - separately paged.

AETS YEARBOOK. *See* Yearbooks, Almanacs, Directories.

AGENDA. V. 1- Aug. 1978-. 0706-2613. Periodical. CN. English (text in French, each with special title page and separate paging. French text on inverted pages). qt. Science Council of Canada, 150 Kent Street, Ottawa Ontario K1P 5P4 Canada.

AGROCHEMOPHYSICA CEASED. VFOAT Agrochemophysica Ground-, Chemiese en Fisiese Wetenskappe. Soil, Chemical and Physical Sciences, Ground-, Chemiese en Fisiese Wetenskappe, Soil, Chemical and Physical Sciences. Vols. 1-13. 0302-7112. Periodical. SA. Afrikaans (articles also in English, with summaries in English, Afrikaans or French). ir. Ind/Abst Life Sci. Collect., Pestdoc, Ringdoc, Vetdoc, Excerpta Med., Sel. Water Resour. Abstr., Biol. Abstr., Chem. Abstr., Nuci. Sci. Abstr. CODEN AGPYAL. *Suid-Afrikaanse Tydskrif Vir Landbouwetenskap.*

A.I.D. EVALUATION SPECIAL STUDY. VFOAT Aid Evaluation Special Study. No. 1-. 0735-1488. Monographic Series. US. English. ir. Bureau for Science and Technology, Agency for International Development, Washington DC 20523. LC UNC.

A'IN SHAMS SCIENCE BULLETIN. VFOAT Nashra Al-Ilmiyah Li-Jamiat Ayn Shams. No.1- 1956-. Periodical. English. ir. LC Q1.

AKHBAR AL-AKADIMIYAH. Periodical. Arabic. mo. Akadimiyat Al-Bahth Al-Ilmi Wa-Al-Tiknulujiya, 101 Shari Qasr Al-Ini, Cairo United Arab Republic Egypt. LC Q180.E3.

AL-ILM. Periodical. Arabic. mo. $6.00. Sharikat Al-Tawzi Al-Muttahidah, 21 Shari Qasr Al-Nil, Al-Qahirah United Arab Republic. LC Q4.

AL-ILM WA-AL-HAYAH. Periodical. Arabic. ir. LC Q4.

AL-SHABAB WA-ULUM AL-MUSTAQBAL. VFOAT Youth, Science & Future. V. 1- August 1977-. Periodical. UA. Arabic (English). $15.00. Al Ahram, Al Galaa St, Cairo UAR Egypt. LC Q4.

AL-TURATH AL-ILMI AL-ARABI. V. 1-. Periodical. IQ. Arabic. ir. 0.15 Single Issue. Riasat Markaz Ihya Al-Turath Al-Ilmi Al-Arabi Al-Waziriyah, Shari Al-Sahib Bin Abbad, Baghdad Iraq. LC Q127.A5.

LOS ALAMOS SCIENCE. Vol. 1, No. 1 (Summer 1980)- V. 3, No. 3 (Fall 1982). 0273-7116. Periodical. US. English. ir. Los Alamos Science, Los Alamos MN 87544. Ind/Abst Math. Rev., GeoRef, Chem. Abstr. LC Q11. DD 505. CODEN LASCDI.

ALBERTA SCIENCE EDUCATION. V. 12, No. 2-14, No. 2. 0317-8730. Periodical. CN. English. ir. $20.00. Alberta Teachers' Association, 11010 - 142 Street, Edmonton Alberta T5N 2R1 Canada. Tel 753-2411. Ed Gary Gay. DD 507. bk rev. Circ 800. (ctrl). The journal contains articles of interest to science teachers interested in expanding their knowledge and in improving their practices. *S C A T Bulletin,* 0036-1100.

ALBERTA SCIENCE EDUCATION JOURNAL. V. 14, No. 3- Aug. 1976-. 0701-1024. Periodical. CN. English. Alberta Teachers' Association, 11010 - 142 Street, Edmonton Alberta T5N 2R4 Canada. Ind/Abst Can. Educ. Index. DD 507. *Alberta Science Education,* 0317-8730.

ALBERTA SCIENCE TEACHER. (THE ALBERTA SCIENCE TEACHER). Vol. 1, No. 1 (Dec. 1980)-. 0229-3099. Periodical. CN. English. qt. $20.00. Alberta Teachers' Association, 11010-142 Street, Edmonton Alberta T2N 2R1 Canada. DD 507. *Science Newsletter,* 0384-1847.

ALS LIFE LINES. VFOAT Life Lines. VAT Assembly of Life Sciences Life Lines. V. 1- June 1975-. 0190-0765. Periodical. US. English. qt. National Research Council, 2101 Constitution Avenue, Washington DC 20418. NLM W1 A117P.

AMERICAN JOURNAL OF SCIENCE. V. 119- Jan. 1880-. 0002-9599. Periodical. US. English. ir. Kline Geology Laboratory, PO Box 6666, New

Science (General)

Haven CT 06511. **Tel** (203)432-4658. **Ind/Abst** Eng. Index Annu., Eng. Index Mon., Eng. Index, Eng. Index Bioeng. Abstr., Eng. Index Energy Abstr., Coal Abstr., Excerpta Med., Energy Inf. Abstr., Environ. Abstr., Int. Aerosp. Abstr., GeoRef, Chem. Abstr., Energy Res. Abstr., Appl. Sci. Technol. Index, Comput. Control Abstr., Electr. Electron. Abstr., Sci. Abstr. Sect. A. Phys. Abstr., Gen. Sci. Index, Phys. Abstr., Sci. Cit. Index, Abr. Ed., Pet. Abstr., Bibliogr. Index Geol. **DD** 505. **NLM** W1 AM522D. **CODEN** AJSCAP. (cum index). Available on microfilm. *American Journal of Science and Arts, 0099-5363*.

AMERICAN MEN AND WOMEN OF SCIENCE. CONSULTANTS. (AMERICAN MEN AND WOMEN OF SCIENCE : CONSULTANTS). 0146-0064. US. English. Bowker, 1180 Avenue of the Americas, New York NY 10036. **LC** Q141. **DD** 509.22.

AMERICAN MEN & WOMEN OF SCIENCE : PHYSICAL AND BIOLOGICAL SCIENCES. 14th Ed.-. 0192-8570. US. English. ir. R R Bowker, Box 1807, Ann Arbor MI 48106. **Tel** (800)521-0600. **LC** Q141. **DD** 509.22, B. *American Men and Women of Science. Physical and Biological Sciences, 0192-8570*.

AMERICAN MEN AND WOMEN OF SCIENCE. PHYSICS, ASTRONOMY, MATHEMATICS, STATISTICS, AND COMPUTER SCIENCE. (AMERICAN MEN AND WOMEN OF SCIENCE : PHYSICS, ASTRONOMY, MATHEMATICS, STATISTICS, AND COMPUTER SCIENCE). 0146-003X. US. English. Bowker, 1180 Avenue of the Americas, New York NY 10036. **LC** Q141. **DD** 509.22, B.

THE AMERICAN MIDLAND NATURALIST. MONOGRAPH. No. 1-. 0065-9436. Monographic Series. US. English. ir. American Midland Naturalist, University of Notre Dame, Nortre Dame IN 46556. **Tel** (219)239-7481. **Ed** R P McIntosh.

AMERICAN SCIENTIST. *See* Education (General) - Higher Education.

ANAIS DA ACADEMIA BRASILEIRA DE CIENCIAS. Vol. 13, No. 3 (Sept. 30, 1941-). 0001-3765. Periodical. BL. English (Portuguese). qt. Academia Brasileira Ciencias, Caxis Postal 229, Rio de Janeiro Brazil. **Ind/Abst** Life Sci. Collect., GeoRef, Art Archaeol. Tech. Abstr., Biol. Abstr., Chem. Abstr., Nuci. Sci. Abstr., Index Med., Bibliogr. Agric., Math. Rev., Comput. Control Abstr., Electr. Electron. Abstr., Sci. Abstr. Sect. A. Phys. Abstr., Sci. Cit. Index, Abr. Ed., Bibliogr. Index Geol., Phys. Abstr. **LC** Q33. **DD** 506-281. **NLM** W1 AN108B. **CODEN** AABCAD. *Annaes da Academia Brasileira de Sciencias*.

ANAIS DA FACULDADE DE CIENCIAS. **Main/Corp** Oporto, Portugal. Universidade. Instituto de Zoologia. V. 1- 1905/06-. Periodical. Portuguese. ir. **Ed** Francisco Gomes Teixeira. **LC** Q65. **CODEN** AFPOAI. *Jornal de Sciencias Mathematicas e Astronomicas*.

ANAIS DA REUNIAO BRASILEIRA DE CIENCIA DA INFORMACAO. **Main/Conf** Reuniao Brasileira de Ciencia da Informacao. 1- 1975-. Portuguese. ir. **LC** Q224.3.B6.

ANALES. CIENCIAS - UNIVERSIDAD DE MURCIA. *See* Yearbooks, Almanacs, Directories.

ANALES CIENTIFICOS - UNIVERSIDAD NACIONAL DEL CENTRO DEL PERU. *See* Yearbooks, Almanacs, Directories.

ANALES DE LA SOCIEDAD CIENTIFICA ARGENTINA. *See* Yearbooks, Almanacs, Directories.

ANALES DE L'ACADEMIA NACIONAL DE CIENCIAS EXACTAS, FISICAS Y NATURALES, BUENOS AIRES. *See* Yearbooks, Almanacs, Directories.

ANALYTICAL INSTRUMENTATION. Vol. 13, No. 1-. 0743-5797. Periodical. US. English. qt. $80.00. Marcel Dekker, Journals Department, 270 Madison Avenue, New York NY 10016. **Ind/Abst** Air Pollut. Titles, Chem. Abstr., Curr. Contents, Eng. Index, Energy Res. Abstr., Sci. Cit. Index, Abr. Ed., Abstr. Bull. Inst. Paper Chem., Excerpta Med. **DD** 542. **CODEN** ANINE6. *Chemical, Biomedical, and Environmental Instrumentation, 0190-4094*.

ANEKA KEGIATAN LIPI. **VFOAT** Aneka Kegiatan L.I.P.I. 0126-2009. IO. Indonesian. ir. Biro Hubungan Masyarakat Lipi, Jl Teuku Tjik Di Tiro 43, Jakarta Indonesia. **LC** Q80.I5.

ANNALES DE L'A C F A S. **Main/Corp** Association Canadienne-Francaise pour l'Avancement des Sciences. **VFOAT** Resumes des Communications. V. 1- 1935-. 0066-8842. Periodical. CN. French. qt. 7.74. Assn Canadienne Francaise, Avancement Sciences/C P 6060, Montreal Quebec Canada H3C 3A7. **Tel** (514)342-1411. **DD** 016.0841. bk rev. adv acc. **Circ** 6,000. (ctrl). General information concerning Canadian research.

ANNALES DE LA FACULTE DES SCIENCES DE YAOUNDE. **Main/Corp** University of Yaounde. Faculte des Sciences. 1975-. 0251-4192. French. ir. Bibliotheque Universitaire Diffusion des Annales Sciences, B P 1312, Yaounde Cameroon. **Ind/Abst** GeoRef. **LC** Q2. **DD** 505.

ANNALES DE LA FACULTE DES SCIENCES, UNIVERSITE DE DAKAR. (ANNALES DE LA FACULTE DES SCIENCES). **Main/Corp** Universite de Dakar. Faculte des Sciences. V. 4- 1959-. 0418-2952. SG. French. ir. Universite de Dakar, Faculte des Sciences, Dakar Fann Senegal. **Ind/Abst** GeoRef, Bibliogr. Agric. **CODEN** AFSDAY. *Annales de l'Ecole Superieure des Sciences, Institut des Hautes Etudes de Dakar*.

ANNALI DELL'ISTITUTO E MUSEO DI STORIA DELLA SCIENZA DI FIRENZE. Began in 1976. Periodical. IT. Italian (English, with summaries in French and German). sa. $40.00. Istituto e Museo di Storia della Scienza di Firenze, Piazza dei Giudici 1, Firenze Italy. **Tel** (055)293493. **Ed** Paolo Galluzzi. **Ind/Abst** Am. Hist. Life, Hist. Abstr., Part A, Mod. Hist. Abstr., Hist. Abstr., Part B, Twent. Century Abstr. **LC** Q127.I8. **DD** 509. **NLM** W1 AN486BM. bk rev. adv acc. **Circ** 500. Articles on the history of science.

ANNALS - JAPAN ASSOCIATION FOR PHILOSOPHY OF SCIENCE. **Main/Corp** Japan Association for Philosophy of Science. V. 1- 1956-. Periodical. JA. English. an. 2400. Japan Association for Philosophy of Science, c/o Keio University, 2-15-45 Minta Minato-ku, Tokyo 108 Japan. **Tel** (03)453-4511. **Ed** Hiroshi Kurosaki. Logic, philosophy of mathematics, foundational studies on natural and social sciences, philosophy of science.

ANNALS OF SCIENCE. V. 1- Jan. 1936-. 0003-3790. Periodical. UK. English. bm. $260.00. Taylor & Francis Ltd, 242 Cherry Street, Philadelphia PA 19106. **Tel** (215)238-0939. **Ed** G L E Turner. **Ind/Abst** Am. Hist. Life, Hist. Abstr., Part A, Mod. Hist. Abstr., Hist. Abstr., Part B, Twent. Century Abstr., Energy Inf. Abstr., Environ. Abstr., GeoRef, Biol. Abstr., Chem. Abstr., Math. Rev., Comput. Control Abstr., Electr. Electron. Abstr., Sci. Abstr. Sect. A. Phys. Abstr., Soc. Sci. Citation Index, Phys. Abstr., Sci. Cit. Index, Abr. Ed., Bibliogr. Index Geol., Hist. Abstr., Sci. Cit. Index, Abr. Ed. **LC** Q1. **DD** 509. **NLM** W1 AN625. **CODEN** ANNSA8. (cum index). Deals with the development of modern science, from its beginning in the Renaissance down to its extraordinary advances in recent times.

ANNALS OF THE NEW YORK ACADEMY OF SCIENCES. V. 1- July 1877-. 0077-8923. Monographic Series. US. English. bw. Editorial Department/New York Academy of Sciences, 2 East 63rd Street, New York NY 10021. **Ind/Abst** Energy Inf. Abstr., Index Med., Int. Aerosp. Abstr., GeoRef, CIS Abstr., Biol. Abstr., Chem. Abstr., Psychol. Abstr., Math. Rev., Bibliogr. Agric., Energy Res. Abstr., Ringdoc, Pestdoc. **LC** Q11. **DD** 500. **NLM** W1 AN626YL. **CODEN** ANYAA9. *Annals of the Lyceum of Natural History of New York*.

ANNALS OF THE SOUTH AFRICAN MUSEUM. *See* Museums.

ANNALS OF TROPICAL RESEARCH. (ANNALS OF TROPICAL RESEARCH : TECHNICAL JOURNAL OF THE VISAYAS STATE COLLEGE OF AGRICULTURE). Vol. 1, No. 1 (July-Sept. 1979)-. Periodical. PH. English. qt. 30.00. Science Journal of Visayas State College of Agriculture, Visca Leyte 7127-A Philippines. **Ed** Rolinda L Talatala. **Ind/Abst** Biol. Abstr. **CODEN** ATREDV. **Circ** 500. (ctrl). Research results covering the biological-both plant and animal, physical and social sciences.

ANNUAIRE - ACADEMIE DES SCIENCES. *See* Yearbooks, Almanacs, Directories.

ANNUAIRE DES LOISIRS SCIENTIFIQUES. *See* Yearbooks, Almanacs, Directories.

ANNUAIRE INFORMATIQUE-PHYSIQUE. *See* Yearbooks, Almanacs, Directories.

ANNUAL NUMBER - NATIONAL ACADEMY OF SCIENCES, INDIA. (ANNUAL NUMBER). **Main/Corp** National Academy of Sciences, India. 0469-6786. II. English. an $8.00. Generay Secretary/National Academy of Sciences India, 5 Lajpatrai Road, Allahabad 211002 India. **Tel** 55224. **Ed** U S Srivastava. **Ind/Abst** Chem. Abstr. **CODEN** NASAAV. **Circ** 800. Publishes presidential addresses of physical and biological sciences and abstract of research papers presented at the annual session of the Academy in Physical and Biological Sciences.

ANNUAL PROCEEDINGS - ASSOCIATED SCIENTIFIC AND TECHNICAL SOCIETIES OF SOUTH AFRICA. (THE ANNUAL PROCEEDINGS). 0373-4250. English. an. The Associated Scientific and Technical Societies of South Africa. **Ind/Abst** Electr. Electron. Abstr., Comput. Control Abstr., Sci. Abstr. Sect. A. Phys. Abstr. **CODEN** ATSAAL.

ANNUAL REPORT - ALBERTA RESEARCH COUNCIL. (ANNUAL REPORT). **Main/Corp** Alberta Research Council. **VAT** Annual Report - Alberta Research. 1972-. 0701-5151. CN. English. an. Alberta Research Council, 250 Karl Clark Road, Edmonton Alberta T6N 1E4 Canada. **Tel** (403)438-1666. **Ed** Peter Roaf. **Ind/Abst** GeoRef. **CODEN** AALRA6. **Circ** 5,000. (ctrl). Review of research and development programs in energy, agriculture, advanced technologies, industrial engineering and environment. *Annual Report, 0080-1526*.

ANNUAL REPORT - AUCKLAND INSTITUTE AND MUSEUM. **Main/Corp** Auckland Institute and Museum. 1967/68-. English. an. Auckland Institute & Museum, N Gardner, 6 Tuj Glen Road, Birkenhd Auckland 10 New Zealand. **LC** Q93. **DD** 069.0993122. *Annual Report of the Auckland Institute and Museum*.

ANNUAL REPORT - BATTELLE MEMORIAL INSTITUTE. (ANNUAL REPORT). **Main/Corp** Battelle Memorial Institute. 1981-. 0736-6159. US. English. an. Battelle Memorial Institute, 505 King Avenue, Columbus OH 43201. **LC** Q11. **DD** 506.077157. *President's Report and Annual Review, 0163-0814*.

ANNUAL REPORT - BRITISH COLUMBIA RESEARCH COUNCIL. **Main/Corp** British Columbia Research Council. 0068-1652. CN. English. an. 3650 Wesbrook Crescent 8, Vancouver British Columbia Canada. **LC** Q41.B92. **DD** 354.71100855.

ANNUAL REPORT - CALIFORNIA ACADEMY OF SCIENCES. **Main/Corp** California Academy of Sciences. 0161-3634. US. English. an. California Academy of Sciences, San Francisco CA 94118. **CODEN** CASRDW.

ANNUAL REPORT - CANADA INSTITUTE FOR SCIENTIFIC AND TECHNICAL INFORMATION. **Main/Corp** Canada Institute For Scientific and Technical Information. **VFOAT** Rapport Annuel. CN. English (text in French). qt. Free. Canadian Institute for Scientific and Technical Information, Montreal Road, Ottawa Ontario K1A 0S2 Canada. **Tel** (613)993-3736. **Circ** 3,100. Newsletter giving up-to-date information on CISTI's activities and services to users of scientific and technical information. *Report*.

ANNUAL REPORT - COMMITTEE ON SCIENTIFIC FREEDOM AND RESPONSIBILITY. *See* Political Science - Civil Rights.

ANNUAL REPORT - COUNCIL FOR SCIENTIFIC AND INDUSTRIAL RESEARCH. **Main/Corp** South African Council for Scientific and Industrial Research. **VFOAT** CSIR Annual Report. 17th- 1961-. 0081-2382. Periodical. SA. English. ir. Council for Scientific & Industrial Research, PO Box 395, Pretoria 0001 South Africa. **LC** Q180.A55. *Annual Report - South African Council for Scientific and Industrial Research*.

ANNUAL REPORT - CRANBROOK INSTITUTE OF SCIENCE. **Main/Corp** Cranbrook Institute of Science, Bloomfield Hills, Mich. 1st- 1930/31-. 0197-0534. US. English. an. Cranbrook Institute of Science, Cranbrook Educational Community, Bloomfield Hills MI 48013. **LC** Q11.

ANNUAL REPORT - DEPARTMENT OF EDUCATION AND SCIENCE (GREAT BRITAIN). *See* Education (General).

Science (General)

ANNUAL REPORT - EUROPEAN SCIENCE FOUNDATION. Main/Corp European Science Foundation. English. an. 1 Quai Lezay-Marnesia, 67000 Strasbourg France. LC Q180.E9. DD 001.4094.

ANNUAL REPORT - EUROPEAN SCIENCE FOUNDATION. Main/Corp European Science Foundation. FR. English. an. European Science Foundation, 1 Quai Lezay-Marnesia, 67000 Strasbourg France.

ANNUAL REPORT FOR THE FISCAL YEAR - INSTITUTE FOR ADVANCED STUDY (PRINCETON, N.J.). Main/Corp Institute For Advanced Study (Princeton, N.J.). VFOAT Annual Report. US. English. an. The Institute for Advanced Study, Olden Lane, Princeton NJ 08540. LC Q180.U5. DD 001.40974967.

ANNUAL REPORT - GREAT BRITAIN. ADVISORY COUNCIL ON SCIENTIFIC POLICY. Main/Corp Great Britain. Advisory Council On Scientific Policy. Series Corp Great Britain. Parliament. Papers By Command. 1st- 1947/48-. UK. English. ir. Her Majestys Stationery Office, PO Box 276, SW8 5DT England. LC Q127.G4. DD 507.2.

ANNUAL REPORT - INDONESIAN NATIONAL SCIENTIFIC DOCUMENTATION CENTER. Main/Corp Pusat Dokumentasi Ilmiah Nasional. English. ir. Indonesian National Scientific Documentation Center, Jl Jenderal Gatot Subroto, Jakarta Indonesia. LC Q224.3.I5. DD 354.5980081. NLM W2 LI4 P9A.

ANNUAL REPORT - NANTUCKET MARIA MITCHELL ASSOCIATION. Main/Corp Nantucket Maria Mitchell Association. US. English. an. Nantucket Maria Mitchell Association, Vestal Street, Nantucket MA 02554. LC Q11.

ANNUAL REPORT - NATIONAL PHYSICAL LABORATORY (GREAT BRITAIN). Main/Corp National Physical Laboratory (Great Britain). UK. English. an. National Physical Laboratory, Teddington Middlesex TW11 0LW England.

ANNUAL REPORT - NATIONAL SCIENCE FOUNDATION. (ANNUAL REPORT FOR FISCAL YEAR . . .). VFOAT N.S.F. Annual Report. Began with 4th, 1974. 0083-2332. US. English. an. Superintendent of Documents, US Government Printing Office, Washington DC 20402. Ind/Abst Biol. Abstr. LC Q11. DD 353.00855. NLM W2 A N37A. CODEN NSFAAO. Annual Report of National Science Foundation.

ANNUAL REPORT - NATIONAL SCIENCE FOUNDATION. (ANNUAL REPORT OF THE NATIONAL SCIENCE FOUNDATION). Main/Corp National Science Foundation (U.S.). 1st- 1951-. Periodical. US. English. an. Superintendent of Documents, US Government Printing Office, Washington DC 20402. Ind/Abst Biol. Abstr.

ANNUAL REPORT - NATIONAL SCIENCE FOUNDATION. (PROGRAM REPORT). Began with March 1977. 0195-6132. Monographic Series. US. English. Superintendent of Documents, US Government Printing Office, Washington DC 20402. Ind/Abst GeoRef. LC Q180.U5. DD 505. NLM W2 A N37P.

ANNUAL REPORT - NATIONAL SCIENCE FOUNDATION, OFFICE OF NATIONAL R&D ASSESSMENT. Main/Corp United States. National Science Foundation. Office of National R&D Assessment. 0362-1944. US. English. an. National Science Foundation, 1800 G Street NW, Washington DC 20550. LC Q180.U5. DD 353.0082.

ANNUAL REPORT OF THE ALASKA COUNCIL ON SCIENCE AND TECHNOLOGY. Main/Corp Alaska Council on Science and Technology. 0737-4259. US. English. an. Alaska Council on Science and Technology, Pouch CV, Juneau AK 99801. LC Q127.U6. DD 353.97980085506.

ANNUAL REPORT OF THE NATIONAL SCIENCE BOARD. Main/Corp United States. National Science Foundation. National Science Board. 1969-. Periodical. US. English. an. Superintendent of Documents, US Government Printing Office, Washington DC 20402.

ANNUAL REPORT - SCIENCE COUNCIL OF CANADA. Main/Corp Science Council of Canada. 1st- 1966/67-. 0080-7478. CN. English. an. Science Council of Canada, 100 Metcalfe Street, Ottawa Ontario K1P 5M1 Canada. Tel (613)992-1142. Ed Jane Whitney. LC Q21. DD 506.171. Circ 3,000. Annual report of the Science Council of Canada-includes information on research program, mandate, members and budget.

ANNUAL REPORT - SRI INTERNATIONAL. Main/Corp SRI International. 1977-. 0191-2852. US. English. an. SRI International, 333 Ravenswood Avenue, Menlo Park CA 94025. Tel (415)326-6200. NLM W1 S601.

ANNUAL REVIEW - SCIENCE COUNCIL OF CANADA. (ANNUAL REVIEW . . .). Main/Corp Science Council of Canada. VFOAT Expose Annuel . . . . 1980-. 0228-6246. Periodical. CN. English (French). an. Science Council of Canada, 100 Metcalfe, Ottawa Ontario K1P 5M1 Canada. DD 354.7100855. Annual Report.

ANNUAL SCIENCE AND TECHNOLOGY REPORT TO THE CONGRESS. Main/Corp National Science Foundation (U.S.). 1980-. 0734-5526. US. English. an. Superintendent of Documents, US Government Printing Office, Washington DC 20402. Ind/Abst Am. Stat. Index. LC Q180.U5. DD 353.00855. Vol. for 1981 distributed to depository libraries in microfiche. Science and Technology Report, 0163-6421.

ANUARIO CIENTIFICO (BARRANQUILLA, COLOMBIA). See Yearbooks, Almanacs, Directories.

ANUDANOM KI MANGEM (INDIA. DEPT. OF SCIENCE AND TECHNOLOGY). Main/Corp India (Republic). Dept. of Science and Technology. VFOAT Demands For Grants. 1971/72-. II. Hindi and English. ir. Government of India Press, Minto Road, New Delhi India. LC Q127.I4.

ANZEIGER DER OSTERREICHISCHE AKADEMIE DER WISSENSCHAFTEN, MATHEMATISCH-NATURWISSENSCHAFTLICHE KLASSE. (ANZEIGER). V. 84 No. 1 Bis 15 (1947)-. 0376-1606. German. ir. Springer Verlag-New York Inc, 175 5th Avenue, New York NY 10010. Tel (212)460-1500. Ind/Abst Math. Rev., Life Sci. Collect., GeoRef, Energy Res. Abstr. LC AS142. DD 505. CODEN OSAWA8. Anzeiger (Akademie der Wissenschaften in Wein).

APIMONDIA SCIENTIFIC BULLETIN. VFOAT Scientific Bulletin. 1972-. English. ir. Apimondia, Pitar Mos 20, Bucharest 1 Romania.

APPLIED SCIENCE & TECHNOLOGY INDEX. See Indexes/Abstracts.

APPLIED SCIENTIFIC RESEARCH. See Engineering.

APPRAISAL. See Education (General) - Theory, Practice of Education.

ARAB GULF JOURNAL OF SCIENTIFIC RESEARCH. VFOAT Majallat Al-Khalij Al-Arabi Lil-Buhuth Al-Ilmiyah. Vol. 1, No. 1-. Periodical. English (summaries in Arabic). sa. $30.00. Arab Bureau of Education for the Gulf States, PO Box 3908, Riyadh 11481 Saudi Arabia. Ind/Abst Math. Rev., Life Sci. Collect. LC Q1. DD 505.

ARABIAN JOURNAL FOR SCIENCE AND ENGINEERING. See Engineering.

ARBOK FOR UNIVERSITETET I BERGEN, MATEMATISK-NATURVITENSKAPELIG SERIE. See Yearbooks, Almanacs, Directories.

ARCHITECTURAL, ENGINEERING, AND SCIENTIFIC SERVICES. VFOAT Bireaux d'Architectes, d'Ingenieurs-Conseils et de Services Scientifiques. CN. English (French). ir. $7.75 Domestic, $9.30 Foreign. Statistics Canada, Publication Sales and Services, Ottawa Ontario K1A 0T6 Canada.

ARCHIVE FOR HISTORY OF EXACT SCIENCES. See Genealogy and Heraldry - Archives.

ARCHIVES DES SCIENCES. See Genealogy and Heraldry - Archives.

ARCHIVNI ZPRAVY. See Genealogy and Heraldry - Archives.

ARCTIC AND ALPINE RESEARCH. V. 1- Winter 1969-. 0004-0851. Periodical. US. English. qt. $55.00 Domestic, $58.00 Foreign. Institute of Artic and Alpine Research, University of Colorado/Campus Box 450, Boulder CO 80309. Tel (303)492-6387. Ed Kathleen A Salzberg. Ind/Abst Electron. Commun. Abstr. J., ISMEC Bull., Pollut. Abstr. Indexes, Saf. Sci. Abstr. J., Life Sci. Collect., Can. Environ., Sel. Water Resour. Abstr., Energy Inf. Abstr., Environ. Abstr., Int. Aerosp. Abstr., GeoRef, Biol. Abstr., ASTIS Bibliogr., ASTIS Curr. Aware. Bull., Chem. Abstr., Curr. Contents, Agric. Biol. Environ. Sci. LC GB395. DD 500.10998. CODEN ATLPAV. bk rev. Circ 950. Available on microfilm from University Microfilms. Original research papers and notes on scientific and cultural aspects of cold environments and related paleoenvironments.

ARGENTINIEN, FORSCHUNGSPOLITIK UND FORSCHUNGSPRAXIS. Series/Titl Marktinformation. German. an. 3.00. Bundesstelle fur Aussenhandelsinformation, Blaubach 13 Postfach 10 80 07, D-5000 Koln 1 West Germany. LC Q180.A7. DD 001.40982.

ARSREDOGORELSE - STATENS NATURVETENSKAPLIGA FORSKNINGSRAD. Main/Corp Statens Naturvetenskapliga Forskningsrad (Sweden). VFOAT Annual Report - Swedish Natural Science Research Council. English and Swedish. ir. Statens Naturvetenskapliga Forskningsrad, Wenner-Gren Center, Box 23136, Stockholm S-10435 Sweden. LC Q180.S8. Redogorelse.

ASPECTS DE LA POLITIQUE SCIENTIFIQUE DU CANADA CEASED. Began with 1, Sept. 1974. Ceased with Vol. for July 1976. 0318-532X. Periodical. CN. French. $1.00. Conseil des Sciences du Canada, Kent-Albert Building, 150 Kent Street, Ottawa Ontario K1P 5P4 Canada. LC Q127.C2. DD 338.4750971.

ASTMS JOURNAL. VAT Association of Scientific, Technical, and Managerial Staffs Journal. 1968-. Periodical. UK. English. bm. ASCW Journal, Asset Journal.

ATTI DELLA ACCADEMIA DELLE SCIENZE DI TORINO. CLASSE DI SCIENZE FISICHE, MATEMATICHE E NATURALI. (ATTI DELLA ACCADEMIA DELLE SCIENZE DI TORINO. TOMO I, CLASSE DI SCIENZE FISICHE, MATEMATICHE E NATURALI). 0001-4419. Periodical. IT. Italian. ir. F Casanova & Company, Via Cesare Battisti 7, Torino Italy. Ind/Abst Math. Rev., Life Sci. Collect., Biol. Abstr., Chem. Abstr., Comput. Control Abstr., Electr. Electron. Abstr., Sci. Abstr. Sect. A. Phys. Abstr. CODEN AATFAA. Atti della Reale Accademia delle Scienze di Torino.

ATTI DELLA ACCADEMIA LIGURE DI SCIENZE E LETTERE. Began in 1941. 0392-2219. Italian (includes summaries in English or French). an. Atti della Accademia Ligure di Scienze e Lettere, Via Balbi 10, 16126 Genova Italy. Ind/Abst Math. Rev., GeoRef, Bibliogr. Agric., Comput. Control Abstr., Electr. Electron. Abstr., Sci. Abstr. Sect. A. Phys. Abstr. CODEN AALGA7. Atti della Societa di Scienze e Lettere di Genova.

ATTI DELLA SOCIETA PELORITANA DI SCIENZE FISICHE, MATEMATICHE E NATURALI. Main/Corp Societa Peloritana di Scienze Fisiche, Matematichee Naturali. V. 1- 1955-. 0037-8860. Periodical. IT. Italian. qt. Universita de Messina, Messina Italy. Ind/Abst Math. Rev., Chem. Abstr., Comput. Control Abstr., Electr. Electron. Abstr., Sci. Abstr. Sect. A. Phys. Abstr. LC Q4. CODEN ASPSAJ.

ATTI - INSTITUTO VENETO DI SCIENZE, LETTRE ED ARTI. CLASSE DI SCIENZE FISICHE, MATEMATICHE E NATURALI. (ATTI. CLASSE DI SCIENZE FISICHE, MATEMATICHE E NATURALI). Vol. 137-141- School Year (1978-79). 0392-6680. Italian. an. Ind/Abst Chem. Abstr. NLM W1 AT752H. CODEN AIVNDZ. Atti. Classe di Scienze Matematice e Naturali, 0373-255X.

AUDIOTAPES REPRINTS PUBLICATIONS. Main/Corp American Association for the Advancement of Science. 0363-2547. US. English. American Association for the Advancement of Science, 1515 Massachusetts

Science (General)

Avenue Northwest, Washington DC 20005. **LC** Q197. **DD** 016.5.

AUSTRALIAN SCIENCE INDEX. *See* Indexes/Abstracts.

AUSTRALIAN SCIENCE TEACHERS' JOURNAL. *See* Education (General) - Theory, Practice of Education.

AWIS NEWSLETTER. Main/Corp Association for Women in Science. **VAT** Association for Women in Science Newsletter. 0160-256X. Periodical. US. English. bm. $35.00. Association for Women in Science Inc, 1346 Connecticut Avenue SW, Washington DC 20036. **Tel** (202)833-1998. **LC** Q149.U5. **DD** 331.48150973. bk rev. adv acc. **Circ** 3,500. (ctrl). Articles, interviews and book reviews on topics of pertinence to the professional careers and personal lives of women scientists. *AWIS Newsletter of the Association of Women in Science, 0098-6267.*

BANGLADESH JOURNAL OF SCIENTIFIC AND INDUSTRIAL RESEARCH. V. 8- Jan./Oct. 1973-. 0304-9809. Periodical. BG. English. qt. Bangladesh Council of Scientific & Industrial Research, Dlaumondi Mirpur Road, Dacca 5 Bangladesh. **Ind/Abst** Chem. Abstr., Comput. Control Abstr., Electr. Electron. Abstr., Sci. Abstr. Sect. A. Phys. Abstr., Phys. Abstr. **LC** Q1. **DD** 505. **NLM** W1 BA643. **CODEN** BJSIBL. *Scientific Researches.*

BANGLADESH SCIENCE AND TECHNOLOGY INDEX. *See* Indexes/Abstracts.

BASE (BERKELEY, CALIF.). (BASE). Vol. 1, No. 1 (Oct. 1982)-. 0732-7706. Periodical. US. English. sa. Alin Foundation Press, 2107 Dwight Way, Berkeley CA 94704. **Tel** (415)845-4907.

BC SCIENCE TEACHER. (THE B C SCIENCE TEACHER). V. 14- Sept. 1972-. 0381-6036. Periodical. CN. English. mo. British Columbia Science Teachers' Association, 2235 Burrard Street, Vancouver British Columbia V6J 3H9 Canada. **Ind/Abst** Can. Educ. Index. *S T A News, 0048-9719.*

BEITRAGE ZUR GESCHICHTE DER WISSENSCHAFT UND DER TECHNIK. Vol. 1-. 0522-6570. Periodical. GW. German. ir. Franz Steiner Verlag GMBH, Postfach 347, D 7000 Stuttgart 1 West Germany. **Tel** (0711)2582229. *Mitteilungen zur Geschichte der Medizin, der Naturwissenschaften und der Tecknik.*

BERICHT DER BUNDESREGIERUNG AN DEN NATIONALRAT. Main/Corp Austria. Bundesministerium fur Wissenschaft und Forschung. German. ir. *Bericht der Bundesregierung an den Nationalrat.*

BERICHT - STIFTERVERBAND FUR DIE DEUTSCHE WISSENSCHAFT. Main/Corp Stifterverband Fur die Deutsche Wissenschaft. GW. German. an. Stifterverband fur die Deutsche Wissenschaft, Brucker Holt 56-60 Postfach 23 03 60, 4300 Essen 1 West Germany. **LC** AZ664. **DD** 063.56. *Tatigkeitsbericht.*

BERICHTE ZUR WISSENSCHAFTSGESCHICHTE. V. 1- 1978-. 0170-6233. Periodical. German. ir. $48.00. VCH Publishers Inc, 303 Northwest 12th Avenue, Deerfield Beach FL 33442. **Tel** (305)428-5566. **Ind/Abst** Math. Rev., Chem. Abstr. **NLM** W1 BE653. **CODEN** BEWID8.

BERITA ILMU PENGETAHUAN DAN TEKNOLOGI. Periodical. Indonesian. ir. Lembaga Ilmu Pengetahuan Indonesia, Biro Publikasi Ilmiah Lipi, Medan Merdeka Selatan No 11, Jakarta Indonesia. **LC** Q4. *Berita L.I.P.I.*

BERKELEY PAPERS IN HISTORY OF SCIENCE. 1-. 0145-0379. Monographic Series. US. English. ir. Office for History of Science and Technology, University of California, Berkeley CA 94720. **Tel** (415)642-4581. Ed J L Heilbron. **Ind/Abst** Math. Rev. **LC** UNC. Bibliographical sources for historians of science.

BIBLIOGRAFIA BRASILEIRA DE POLITICA CIENTIFICA E TECNOLOGICA. *See* Bibliographies.

BIBLIOGRAPHIA SCIENTIAE NATURALIS HELVETICA. *See* Bibliographies.

BIBLIOGRAPHY OF SCIENCE COURSES OF STUDY AND TEXTBOOKS FOR GRADES K-12. *See* Bibliographies.

BIENNIAL REPORT - APPLIED SCIENTIFIC RESEARCH CORPORATION OF THAILAND. Main/Corp Applied Scientific Research Corporation of Thailand. 1972/73-. Periodical. English. ir. *Annual Report.*

BIENNIAL REPORT OF THE NEW YORK STATE SCIENCE SERVICE. Main/Corp New York (State). State Science Service. US. English. be. New York State Science Service, The State Education Department, Albany NY 12230. **LC** Q224.3.U62. **DD** 353.974700855.

BIENNIAL REPORT - UNITED STATES-ISRAEL BINATIONAL SCIENCE FOUNDATION. Main/Corp United States-Israel Binational Science Foundation. 1979/1980-. Periodical. US. English. be. National Science Foundation, Division of International Programs, Washington DC 20550.

BIOGRAPHICAL MEMOIRS OF FELLOWS OF THE INDIAN NATIONAL SCIENCE ACADEMY. *See* Biographies.

BIOLOGICAL CYBERNETICS. *See* Biology.

BIOLOGICAL SCIENCE TEXTS. 0272-054X. UK. English. ir. John Wiley and Sons Inc, 605 Third Avenue, New York NY 10158.

BIOLOGICAL SCIENCE (TOKYO). *See* Biology.

BIOTECHNOLOGY INVESTMENT OPPORTUNITIES. Sept. 1981-. 0277-9773. Periodical. US. English. ir. $195.00. High Tech Publishing Company, PO Box 266, Brattleboro VT 05301. **Tel** (802)869-2833. Ed Philip T Diperi. bk rev. Identifies/analyzes emerging investment opportunities in genetic engineering. Follows trends/conditions having significant impact on development applications.

BIOTECHNOLOGY (NEW YORK, N.Y.: 1983). (BIOTECHNOLOGY). 0275-7559. Periodical. US. English. mo. $78.00. Bio/Technology, PO Box 596, Martinsville NJ 08836. **Tel** (212)477-9600. Ed Douglas McCormich. bk rev. adv acc. **Circ** 15,000. Industrial biology, news research products and techniques from start to full scale processes profiles on films and personalities.

BIULLETEN MEZHDUNARODNYKH NAUCHNYKH SEZDOV, KONFERENTSII, KONGRESSOV, VYSTAVOK. 1977-. Periodical. UR. Russian. bm. $17.00. Victor Kamkin Inc, 12224 Parklawn Drive, Rockville MD 20852. **Tel** (301)881-5973. *Biulleten Mezhdunarodnykh Nauchnykh Sezdov, Konferentsii I Kongressov.*

BMBW-FORDERUNGSKATALOG. Main/Corp Germany (West). Bundesministerium fur Bildung und Wissenschaft. GW. German. ir. Bundesministerium fur Bilduna und Wissenschaft, 53 Bonn Bad Godesberg Goethestrasse 54, Bonn West Germany. **LC** Q180.G4. **DD** 001.430943.

BOLETIN - ACADEMIA DE CIENCIAS DE CUBA. Main/Corp Academia de Ciencias de Cuba. Instituto de Documentacion e Informacion Cientifica y Tecnica. Began in 1963. CU. Spanish. ir. **LC** Z7401.

BOLETIN DE LA ACADEMIA DE CIENCIAS DEL INSTITUTO DE CHILE. Vol. 1, No. 1 (1968)-. Spanish. an. **LC** Q33. **DD** 505.

BOLETIN INFORMATIVO - SISTEMA NACIONAL DE INFORMACION CIENTIFICA Y TECNOLOGICA. Main/Corp Venezuela. Sistema Nacional de Informacion Cientifica y Tecnologica. Periodical. VE. Spanish. ir. Coordinacion de Sistema Nacional de Informacion Cientifica y Technologica, Caracas Venezuela.

BOLETIN - OFICINA REGIONAL DE CIENCIA Y TECNOLOGIA DE LA UNESCO PARA AMERICA LATINA Y EL CARIBE. Main/Corp United Nations Educational, Scientific, and Cultural Organization. Oficina Regional de Ciencia y Tecnologia Para America Latina y el Caribe. **VAT** Boltein - Oficina Regional de Ciencia y Tecnologia, de la Organizacion de las Naciones Unidas Para la Educacion, la Ciencia y la Cultura, Para America Latina y el Caribe. No. 9- July/Dec. 1974-. Periodical. UY. Spanish. sa.

UNESCO, 1320 Bulevar Artigas, Montebiedo Uruguay. **LC** Q33.

BOLETIN ROSTLAC. No. 21-. Periodical. UY. Spanish (English). ir. Oficina Regional de Ciencia y Tecnologia Para America, Latina y el Caribe Bulevar Aulevar Artigas 1320-24 Casilla de Correo 859, Montevideo Uruguay. **LC** Q33. **DD** 509.8.

BOLETIN TECNICO. Main/Corp Inter-American Institute of Agricultural Sciences. 1- 1949-. 0574-203X. Periodical. CR. Spanish. ir. Inter-American Institute of Science, Oficina de Dist de Publ, Turrialba Costa Rica.

BOLETIN - UNIVERSIDAD LIBRE, SECCIONAL DE PEREIRA, CENTRO DE INVESTIGACIONES. Main/Corp Colombia. Universidad Libre, Pereira. Centro de Investigaciones. Periodical. Spanish. ir. Universidad Libre Seccional de Pereira, Centro de Investigaciones, Apartado Aereo 1330, Pereira Colombia.

BOSTID DEVELOPMENTS. Vol. 1, No. 1 (Mar. 1981)-. 0278-4076. Periodical. US. English. qt. Bostid Developments Board on Science and Technology, Commission on Internaton Relations, National Research Council, 2101 Constitution Avenue NW, Washington DC 20418.

BOSTON STUDIES IN THE PHILOSOPHY OF SCIENCE. V. 1-. US. English. ir. Kluwer Boston Inc, 190 Old Derby Street, Hingham MA 02043. **Tel** (201)872-1441. **Ind/Abst** Math. Rev. **LC** Q175.

BOTTIN - CONSEIL DE LA JEUNESSE SCIENTIFIQUE. Main/Corp Conseil de la Jeunesse Scientifique. Began 1977?. 0705-8292. CN. French. an. $1 Domestic. Conseil de la Jeunesse Scientifique, 1415 East rue Jarry, Montreal Quebec H2E 2Z7 Canada. **DD** 506.2714.

BRASILIEN, FORSCHUNGSPOLITIK UND FORSCHUNGSPRAXIS. Series/Titl Marktinformation. German. an. 3.00. Bundesstelle fur Aussenhandelsinformation, Blaubach 13 Postfach 10 80 07, D-5000 Koln 1 West Germany. **LC** Q180.B7. **DD** 507.2081.

BRITISH JOURNAL FOR THE HISTORY OF SCIENCE. (THE BRITISH JOURNAL FOR THE HISTORY OF SCIENCE). V. 1- June 1962-. 0007-0874. Periodical. UK. English. ty. 30.00 Domestic, $52.00 Foreign. British Society of History of Science, H-PNY Frze, Mill Lane Chalfont, S-Giles Buckhmshre HP8 4NR England. **Tel** (0865)240201. Ed D M Knight. **Ind/Abst** Am. Hist. Life, Hist. Abstr., Part A, Mod. Hist. Abstr., Hist. Abst., Part B, Twent. Century Abstr., Life Sci. Collect., GeoRef, Math. Rev., Biol. Abstr., Chem. Abstr., Humanit. Index, Comput. Control Abstr., Electr. Electron. Abstr., Sci. Abstr. Sect. A. Phys. Abstr., Soc. Sci. Citation Index, Bibliogr. Index Geol., Sci. Cit. Index, Abr. Ed., Phys. Abstr., Hist. Abstr. **LC** Q125. **NLM** W1 BR472. **CODEN** BJHSAT. bk rev. adv acc. **Circ** 1,400. The journal contains articles and reviews encompassing social and economic history, the philosophy and sociology of science, the history of technology and the relations between science and theology. *Bulletin of the British Society for the History of Science.*

BRITISH JOURNAL FOR THE PHILOSOPHY OF SCIENCE. (THE BRITISH JOURNAL FOR THE PHILOSOPHY OF SCIENCE). Vol. 1, No. 1 (May 1950)-. 0007-0882. Periodical. UK. English. qt. 27.00. Aberdeen University Press, Farmers Hall, Aberdeen AB9 2XT Scotland. **Tel** 0224-630724. **Ind/Abst** Math. Rev., Life Sci. Collect., Philos. Index, Index Book Rev. Humanit., Comput. Control Abstr., Electr. Electron. Abstr., Sci. Abstr. Sect. A. Phys. Abstr., Humanit. Index, Soc. Sci. Citation Index, Sci. Cit. Index, Abr. Ed., Phys. Abstr. **LC** Q175. **DD** 501. **NLM** W1 BR475. **CODEN** BJPIA5. Index published separately - free - automatically sent. (cum index).

EL BUHUTH. VFOAT Periodical Review. V. 1-. English. ir. National Council for Research, PO Box 321, Khartoum Sudan. **LC** Q91.S73. **DD** 505.

BULETIN I SHKENCAVET TE NATYRES. V. 26, No. 1/2- 1972-. Periodical. Albanian. ir. Universiteti I Tiranes Fakulteti I Shkencave te Netyres, Bulevard Stalin, Tirane Albania. **Ind/Abst** GeoRef, Chem. Abstr. **LC** Q4. **CODEN** BSNUAQ. *Buletin. Seria Shkencat Natyrore.*

BULETINUL STIINTIFIC - INSTITUTUL DE CONSTRUCTII BUCURESTI. (BULETINUL STIINTIFIC). Main/Corp Institutul de Constructii (Bucharest, Romania). 0524-8159.

Science (General)

Periodical. RM. Romanian (summaries in Russian, French, English or German). an. Ilexim Press Department, PO Box 1-136-1-137, Bucharest-Romania. Ind/Abst Eng. Index Annu., Eng. Index Mon., Eng. Index Bioeng. Abstr., Eng. Index Energy Abstr., GeoRef. CODEN BUICAT.

BULETINUL UNIVERSITATII DIN BRASOV. SERIA C : MATEMATICA, FIZICA, CHIMIE, STIINTE NATURALE. Main/Corp Universitatea Din Brasov. RM. English, French or Romanian. an. $35.00. Ilexim Press Department, PO Box 1-136-1-137, Bucharest-Romania. Ind/Abst Math. Rev., Chem. Abstr. LC Q49. DD 505. CODEN BUBCDV.

BULLETIN - ALBERTA RESEARCH COUNCIL. (BULLETIN). VFOAT Alberta Research Council Bulletin. 31-. 0383-5359. Monographic Series. CN. English. Alberta Research Council, 11315-87 Avenue, Edmonton Alberta T6G 2C2 Canada. Ind/Abst GeoRef. LC Q180.C2. DD 557.123. CODEN BARCD5. *Bulletin, 0034-5172.*

BULLETIN - AMERICAN ASSOCIATION OF BASIC SCIENCE BOARDS. Main/Corp American Association of Basic Science Boards. Began with Dec. 1949 issue. Periodical. US. English. American Association, Basic Science Boards, Omaha NE 68107. LC Q181.A1. DD 610.7.

BULLETIN - CRANBROOK INSTITUTE OF SCIENCE. No. 1-. 0070-1416. Monographic Series. US. English. ir $15.00. Cranbrook Institute of Science, PO Box 801, Bloomfield Hills MI 48013. Tel (313)645-3255. Ed Christine E Bartz. Ind/Abst Biol. Abstr. LC Q11. DD 505. A monographic series for both a scholarly and popular audience. Topics covered focus on the natural sciences and archaeology of the Great Lakes region.

BULLETIN DE LA CLASSE DES SCIENCES. ACADEMIE ROYALE DE BELGIQUE. (BULLETIN DE LA CLASSE DES SCIENCES). VFOAT Bulletins de la Classe des Sciences. 4. Series, 1899-1910. 0001-4141. Periodical. French. ir. Tel 512 73 23. Ind/Abst Biol. Abstr., Int. Aerosp. Abstr., Math. Rev. LC AS242. NLM W1 AC443D. CODEN BCSAAF. Index in last issue of volume - attached. (cum index). Circ 500. (ctrl). *Bulletins de l'Academie Royale des Sciences, des Lettres et des Beaux-Arts de Belgique.*

BULLETIN DE LA SOCIETE ROYALE DES SCIENCES DE LIEGE. Main/Corp Societe Royale des Sciences de Liege. V. 1-. 0037-9565. Periodical. BE. French. ir. $41.50. Societe Royale des Sciences de Liege, 15 Avenue des Tilleuls, B 4000 Leige Belgium. Ed J Godeaux. Ind/Abst Math. Rev., Int. Aerosp. Abstr., GeoRef, Comput. Control Abstr., Electr. Electron. Abstr., Sci. Abstr. Sect. A. Phys. Abstr., Chem. Abstr., Energy Res. Abstr. LC Q56. NLM W1 BU523. CODEN BSRSA6. Circ 750. University research papers in mathematics, physics, chemistry and the natural sciences.

BULLETIN DE L'ACADEMIE DES SCIENCES ET LETTRES DE MONTPELLIER. Main/Corp Academie des Sciences et Lettres de Montpellier. V. 1- 1909-. Periodical. FR. French. ir. l'Academie des Sciences, 4 rue Ecole-Mage, 34060 Montpellier Cedex France. LC AS162.

BULLETIN DE L'ACADEMIE POLONAISE DES SCIENCES. SERIE DES SCIENCES TECHNIQUES. Main/Corp Polska Akademia Nauk. V. 1-30. 0001-4125. PL. French (English, German or Russian). mo. $87.00. ARS Polona, Krakowskie Przedmiescie 7, 00-068 Warsaw Poland. Ind/Abst Appl. Mech. Rev., Chem. Abstr., Eng. Index, Keyword Index Intern. Med., Wildl. Rev., Met. Abstr., Sci. Abstr., Math. Rev., Electr. Electron. Abstr., Comput. Control Abstr., Phys. Abstr. CODEN BAPTA9.

BULLETIN DE L'ACFAS. (BULLETIN DE L'A C F A S). Main/Corp Association Canadienne-Francaise pour l'Avancement des Sciences. VAT Bulletin de l'Association Canadienne-Francaise pour l'Avancement des Sciences. Began with V. 1-6, No. 3, Jun. 1959-Oct. 1965. 0066-8850. Periodical. CN. French. qt. Free. ACFAS, C P 6060, Montreal Quebec H3C 3A7 Canada. DD 507.20714.

BULLETIN DE LIAISON DU CONSEIL DE LA JEUNESSE SCIENTIFIQUE. Main/Corp Conseil de la Jeunesse Scientifique. V. 1- Mar. 1971-. 0317-9273. CN. French. ir. Free. Conseil de la Jeunesse Scientifique, 230 Est Boulevard Henri-Bourassa Bureau 14, Montreal Quebec H3L 1B8 Canada. DD 505.

BULLETIN DE L'INSTITUT FONDAMENTAL D'AFRIQUE NOIRE. SERIE A. SCIENCES NATURELLES. (BULLETIN DE L'INSTITUT FONDAMENTAL D'AFRIQUE NOIRE. SERIE A : SCIENCES NATURELLES). VFOAT Sciences Naturelles. Vol. 28, No. 2- April 1966-. 0018-9634. Periodical. SG. English (text in French with some summaries in both languages). ir. Institut Fondamental Afrique Noire, Boite Postale 206, Dakar Senegal Africa. Ind/Abst Life Sci. Collect., GeoRef, Biol. Abstr., Bibliogr. Index Geol., Bibliogr. Index. NLM W1 BU539A. CODEN BASNB7. *Bulletin de l'Institut Francais d'Afrique Noire. Serie A: Sciences Naturelles.*

BULLETIN DE L'INSTITUT FONDAMENTAL D'AFRIQUE NOIRE. SERIE B : SCIENCES HUMAINES. V. 28- Jan./April 1966-. 0018-9642. Periodical. SG. French. qt. $32.73. Institut Fondamental d'Afrique Noire, Boite Postale 206, Dakar Senegal. Ind/Abst Am. Hist. Life, Hist. Abstr., Part A, Mod. Hist. Abstr., Hist. Abst., Part B, Twent. Century Abstr., MLA Int. Bibliogr. Books Artic. Mod. Lang. Lit., Bibliogr. Index, Hist. Abstr. NLM W1 BU539B. *Bulletin de l'Institut Francais d'Afrique Noire. Serie B : Sciences Humaines.*

BULLETIN DE L'INSTITUT PASTEUR. Main/Corp Paris. Institut Pasteur. V. 1- 1903-. 0020-2452. Periodical. FR. French (English). qt. $67.00. Edition Scientifiques Elsevier, 91 rue de Rennes, 75006 Paris France. Ind/Abst Life Sci. Collect., Chem. Abstr., Curr. Contents, Biol. Abstr., Bull. Signal., Energy Res. Abstr., Sci. Cit. Index, Abr. Ed. LC R108. DD 610.82. NLM W1 BU541D. CODEN BIPAA8.

BULLETIN DES SEANCES - ACADEMIE ROYALE DES SCIENCES D'OUTRE-MER. Main/Corp Academie Royale des Sciences d'Outre-Mer. VFOAT Mededelingen der Zittingen. V. 1-20, 1955-74. Periodical. BE. French. ir. 2500. Academie Royale des Sciences d'Outre-Mer, rue Defacqz 1, 1050 Bruxelles Belgique. Tel (02)538.02.11. Ind/Abst Am. Hist. Life, Hist. Abstr. *Bulletin des Seances.*

BULLETIN - INDONESIAN INSTITUTE OF SCIENCES. Main/Corp Lembaga Ilmu Pengetahuan Indonesia. English. ir. Djalan Raden Saleh 43, Djakarta Indonesia. LC AS522.M3. *Bulletin - Indonesian Institute of Science.*

BULLETIN MENSUEL DE LA SOCIETE LINNEENNE DE LYON. Main/Corp Societe Linneenne de Lyon. V. 1-. 0366-1326. Periodical. FR. French. mo. $14.00. Societe Linneene de Lyon, 33 rue Bossuet, 69006 Lyon France. Ind/Abst Life Sci. Collect., GeoRef, Biol. Abstr., Bibliogr. Agric. CODEN BMSLAG. *Bulletin Bi-Mensuel de la Societe Linneenne de Lyon et des Societes Botanique de Lyon, d'Anthropologie et de Biologie de Lyon, Reunies.*

BULLETIN - NATIONAL SCIENCE FOUNDATION. (BULLETIN). VFOAT NSF Bulletin. 0145-0670. Periodical. US. English. ir. National Science Foundation, 1800 G Street NW, Washington DC 20550. Tel (202)632-5722.

THE BULLETIN - NEW JERSEY ACADEMY OF SCIENCE. Main/Corp New Jersey Academy of Science. V. 1- May 1955-. 0028-5455. Periodical. US. English. sa. $20.00. New Jersey Academy of Science, Rutgers University, PO Box B, Hill Center/Room 213, New Brunswick NJ 08903. Tel (201)463-0511. Ed William Sebetich. Ind/Abst Biol. Abstr., Excerpta Med., Int. Aerosp. Abstr., GeoRef, Chem. Abstr., Bibliogr. Index Geol. DD 505. CODEN BJASAS. Circ 600. Peer-reviewed scientific research journal reporting results of fundamental study, chiefly in the areas of biology and earth sciences, reflecting efforts of university and college faculty.

BULLETIN OF LAW, SCIENCE & TECHNOLOGY. See Law.

BULLETIN OF MATERIALS SCIENCE. 0250-4707. Periodical. English. ir. $125.00. J C Baltzer, Wettsteinplatz 10, CH-4058 Basel Switzerland. Tel 61 26 8925. Ind/Abst Met. Abstr., World Alum. Abstr., Chem. Abstr., Comput. Control Abstr., Electr. Electron. Abstr., Sci. Abstr. Sect. A. Phys. Abstr. CODEN BUMSDW.

BULLETIN OF SCIENCE, TECHNOLOGY & SOCIETY. VFOAT BULLETIN OF SCIENCE, TECHNOLOGY AND SOCIETY. Vol. 1, No. 1/2-. 0270-4676. Periodical. US. English. ir. $85.00. STS Press, Materials Research Laboratory, University Park PA 16802. Tel (814)865-1137. Ind/Abst Sociol. Abstr., Soc. Welf. Soc. Plan./Policy Soc. Dev., Excerpta Med. LC Q175.4. DD 303.48305. CODEN BSTSDJ.

BULLETIN OF THE CHICAGO ACADEMY OF SCIENCES. Main/Corp Chicago Academy of Sciences. VFOAT Chicago Academy of Sciences Bulletin. V. 1-. 0009-3491. Monographic Series. US. English. ir. Chicago Academy of Sciences, 2001 North Clark Street, Chicago IL 60614. LC Q11. DD 574.05.

BULLETIN OF THE INSTITUTE OF JAMAICA. SCIENCE SERIES. Main/Corp Institute of Jamaica. No. 1- 1940-. Monographic Series. JM. English. ir.

BULLETIN OF THE KOREAN CHEMICAL SOCIETY. See Chemistry.

BULLETIN OF THE UNESCO REGIONAL OFFICE OF SCIENCE AND TECHNOLOGY FOR AFRICA. Main/Corp United Nations Educational, Scientific, and Cultural Organization. Regional Office of Science and Technology for Africa. V. 9- Jan./Mar. 1974-. 0304-9590. Periodical. English. ir. UNESCO Regional Office of Science and Technology for Africa, PO Box 30592, Nairobi Kenya. LC Q10. DD 509.6. *Bulletin.*

BULLETIN - ROCHESTER ACADEMY OF SCIENCE. Main/Corp Rochester Academy of Science, Rochester, N.Y. 0360-7879. Periodical. US. English. mo. Rochester Academy of Science, PO Box 1742, Rochester NY 14603.

BULLETIN - ROYAL SOCIETY OF NEW ZEALAND. Main/Corp Royal Society of New Zealand. No. 4- 1954-. 0370-6559. NZ. English. ir. Royal Society of New Zealand, Private Bag, Wellington New Zealand. Tel Wellington 727-421. Ind/Abst GeoRef. CODEN RNZBAY. Circ 300. Monographs or any work of science that is too large for publication in the society's journal. *Bulletin.*

BULLETIN - SCIENCE COUNCIL OF THE ALBERTA TEACHERS' ASSOCIATION. (BULLETIN). 0820-7941. Periodical. CN. English. Alberta Teachers' Association, 11010-142 Street, Edmonton Alberta T5N 2R1 Canada. DD 507.107123.

BULLETIN SIGNALETIQUE 522 : HISTOIRE DES SCIENCES ET DES TECHNIQUES. See Bibliographies.

BULLETIN - SOUTHERN CALIFORNIA ACADEMY OF SCIENCES. (BULLETIN). VFOAT Bulletin of the Southern California Academy of Sciences. V. 1- Jan. 1902-. 0038-3872. Periodical. US. English. ty. Southern California Academy of Sciences, 900 West Exposition Boulevard, Los Angeles CA 90007. Tel (213)744-3384. Ed Jon E Keeley and Gretchen Sibley. Ind/Abst Bibliogr. Agric., Biol. Abstr., Bibliogr. Index Geol., Ocean. Abstr. CODEN BCASAD. Circ 600. Scientific journal; manuscripts considered in all categories of the natural and social sciences. *Bulletin of the Southern California Academy of Sciences.*

BULLETIN - SOUTHERN RESEARCH INSTITUTE (BIRMINGHAM, ALA.). (BULLETIN). Vol. 16, No. 1 (Spring 1963)-. 0038-4518. Periodical. US. English. sa. Southern Research Institute, PO Box 55305, Birmingham AL 35255. Ind/Abst Electron. Commun. Abstr. J., ISMEC Bull., Pollut. Abstr. Indexes, Saf. Sci. Abstr. J., World Text Abstr., Energy Res. Abstr. *Bulletin of Southern Research Institute, 0038-4518.*

BUNDESBERICHT FORSCHUNG - GERMANY (FEDERAL REPUBLIC, 1949-). BUNDESMINISTERIUM FUR BILDUNG UND WISSENSCHAFT. (FORSCHUNGSBERICHT DER BUNDESREGIERUNG). 0300-2047. German. ir. Bundesminister fur Bildung und Wissenschaft, 53 Bonn-Bad Godesberg Goethestrasse 54, Bonn Germany. LC Q180.G4.

C. S. I. R. REFERENCE NO. R/BOU. Main/Corp South African Council for Scientific and Industrial Research. National Building Research Institute. English. ir.

CADERNOS DE TECNOLOGIA E CIENCIA. See Technology (General).

CAHIERS D'HISTOIRE ET DE PHILOSOPHIE DES SCIENCES. No 1- 1977-. 0221-3664. Monographic Series. FR. French. ir. 200. Editions Belin, 8 rue Ferou, 75006 Paris France. Tel 40745070. Ind/Abst Math. Rev. adv acc. Circ 500.

Science (General)

To give commentaries on essential texts in the sciences in an historical and epistemological perspective.

CAHIERS DU CENTRE SCIENTIFIQUE ET TECHNIQUE DU BATIMENT. Main/Corp Centre Scientifique et Technique du Batiment (France). No. 1- (Nos. 1-). 0008-9850. Periodical. FR. French. ir. $138.35. Centre Sci Technique Batiment, 4 Avenue Recteur Poincare, 75782 Paris Cedex 16 France. **Ind/Abst** CIS Abstr. (cum index).

CANADIAN INDEX TO GEOSCIENCE DATA. MANITOBA. *See* Indexes/Abstracts.

CANADIAN JOURNAL OF STATISTICS. *See* Statistics.

CANADIAN RESEARCH. Began with July/Aug. 1975. 0319-1974. Periodical. CN. English. bm. $30.18. MacLean Hunter, PO Box 100 Station A, Toronto Ontario M5W 1A7 Canada. **Ind/Abst** Can. Environ., Predicasts, Coal Abstr., Excerpta Med., Can. Bus. Index, Chem. Abstr. **LC** Q180.C2. **DD** 507.2071. **CODEN** CAREDM. *Canadian Research and Development, 0008-493X.*

CANADIAN TECHNICAL & SCIENTIFIC INFORMATION NEWS JOURNAL. VAT Canadian Technical and Scientific Information News Journal. Vol. 1, No. 1 (June 1982)-. 0715-5492. Periodical. CN. English (includes some text in French). mo. Canadian Technical and Scientific Information News Journal, 4650 Suite/Catherine Street West, Westmount Quebec H3Z 1S5 Canada. **DD** 505.

CARIBBEAN JOURNAL OF SCIENCE. V. 1- Feb. 1961-. 0008-6452. Periodical. PR. English (Spanish or French). sa. $13.00. University of Puerto Rico, College of Arts and Sciences, Mayaguez Puerto Rico 00708. **Tel** (809)834-4040. **Ed** Allen Lewis. **Ind/Abst** Life Sci. Collect., GeoRef, Bibliogr. Agric., Biol. Abstr., Chem. Abstr., Sel. Water Resour. Abstr., Bibliogr. Index Geol. **LC** QC1. **CODEN** CRJSA4. **Circ** 1,000. (ctrl). Publishes papers relating to all fields of natural science in the Caribbean.

THE CARIBBEAN JOURNAL OF SCIENCE AND MATHEMATICS. V. 1- May 1968-. 0008-6460. Periodical. US. English. ir. Western Carolina University Press, Western Carolina University, Callowhie NC 28723. **Ind/Abst** Math. Rev., Chem. Abstr. **LC** Q1. **DD** 505. **CODEN** CJSCAD.

CAROLINA TIPS. V. 1- 1938-. 0045-5865. Periodical. US. English. mo. Carolina Biological Supply Co, 2700 York Road, Burlington NC 27215. **Tel** (919)584-0381. **Ed** Barbara Kuyper. **Circ** 125,000. Articles for science teachers.

CATALOGUE COLLECTIF DES LIVRES FRANCAIS DE SCIENCES ET TECHNIQUES. VFOAT Catalogue Collectif des Livres Francais de Sciences & Techniques. Began publication with 1965/66 issue. FR. French. ir. Cercle de la Librairie, 117 Boulevard St Germain, Paris 6 France.

CATALOGUE DU SERVICE DU FILM DE RECHERCHE SCIENTIFIQUE. Main/Corp Centre National de Documentation Pedagogique (France). Service du Film de Recherche Scientifique. VFOAT Catalogue du SFRS. FR. French. te. Le Service, 96 Boulevard Raspail, 75272 Paris Cedex 06 France. **LC** Q192. **DD** 016.5.

CEDECKE PRACE OVOCNARSKE. VFOAT Scientific Studies on Pomology. Began in 1960?. Periodical. Czech (summaries in English, German, and Russian) ir. Obarovy Podnik Sempra, Prague Czechoslovakia. **Ind/Abst** Chem. Abstr. **CODEN** VPOVAT.

CESKOSLOVENSKE VYZKUMNE ZPRAVY A DISERTACE. Czech. ir. 260.-. Ustredi Vedeckych Technickych A Ekonomickych Informaci, 113 57 Praha 1, Konviktska 5, Praha Czechoslovakia. **Tel** 265721. **LC** Z7403, Q158.5. **Circ** 660. (ctrl). List of Czechoslovakian research reports and dissertation.

CHAEMI KWAGIHYOP HOEBO. VFOAT K.S.E.A. Letters, KSEA Letters. Periodical. English (Korean). bm. Korean Scientists and Engineers Association in America Inc, 6261 Executive Boulevard, Rockville MD 20852. **LC** AS36.C338.

CHAOS. V. 1- Aug. 1978-. 0706-5337. Periodical. CN. English. ir. $15.00. Res Bureaux, PO Box 1598, Kingston Ontario K7L 5C8 Canada. **DD** 001.905.

CHARACTERISTICS OF DOCTORAL SCIENTISTS AND ENGINEERS IN THE UNITED STATES. Series/Titl Surveys of Science Resource Series. 1973-. 0741-7640. US. English. be. **LC** Q149.U5. **DD** 331.125150973.

CHARACTERISTICS OF DOCTORAL SCIENTISTS AND ENGINEERS IN THE UNITED STATES. DETAILED STATISTICAL TABLES. *See* Statistics.

CHAYON KWAHAK YONGU. VFOAT Natural Science Research. Periodical. KO. Korean (summaries in English). ir. Choson Taehakkyo Chayon, Kwahak Yonguso 17 Pullo-dong, Tong-ku Kwangju-si Korea. **Ind/Abst** Energy Res. Abstr. **LC** Q80.K6.

CHAYON KWAHAK YONGUSO HAKSUL NONMUNJIP. VFOAT Haksul Nonmunjip, Journal of the Natural Science Research Institute. Periodical. English (Korean). ir. Yonse Taehakkyo Chayon Kwahak Yonguso, 134 Sinchon-dong Sodaemun-ku, Seoul 120 Korea. **Ind/Abst** Energy Res. Abstr. **LC** Q4.

CHIAO HSUEH TUNG HSUN. LI KO PAN. VFOAT Jiaoxuetongxun. Periodical. CH. Chinese. mo. 0.36. Post Office, Cheng-chou Shih, Cheng-chou Shih China. **LC** Q183.4.C5. **DD** 507.1251.

CHIAO HSUEH YUEH KAN. CHUNG HSUEH LI KO PAN. VFOAT Jiaoxueyuekan, Jiaoyuyuekan i.e. Jiaoxueyuekan. Periodical. CH. Chinese. mo. 0.30. Post Office Hang-chou Shih, Hang-chou Shih China. **LC** Q181.A1. **DD** 607.12.

CHINA SCIENCE & TECHNOLOGY ABSTRACTS. SERIES I, MATHEMATICS, ASTRONOMY, PHYSICS. *See* Indexes/Abstracts.

CHINA SCIENCE & TECHNOLOGY ABSTRACTS. SERIES II, CHEMISTRY, EARTH SCIENCE, ENERGY SOURCES. *See* Indexes/Abstracts.

CHINESE SCIENCE. V. 1- May 1975-. 0361-9001. US. English. ir. $1.50 Single Issue. Technology Studies Program, Room 20D-212 Massachusetts Institute of Technology, Cambridge MA 02139. **Ed** N Sivin. **LC** Q145. **DD** 509.51. **NLM** Q 145 C539.

CHINESE SCIENCE ABSTRACTS. PART A. *See* Indexes/Abstracts.

CHINESE SCIENCE ABSTRACTS. PART B. *See* Indexes/Abstracts.

CHINESE SCIENCE AND TECHNOLOGY. V. 1- Summer 1979-. 0192-981X. Periodical. US. English (Chinese). qt. $50.00. M E Sharpe Inc, 901 North Broadway, White Plains NY 10603. **LC** Q127.C5. **DD** 509.51. **NLM** W1 CH792L.

CHISPA. *See* Children and Youth Interests.

CHONGUK TAEHAKSAENG HAKSUL YONGU PALPYO NONMUNJIP : KICHO KWAHAK PUNYA. KO. Korean (English). ir. Sogang Taehakkyo Hakto Hoguktan, 1 Sinsu-dong, Mapo-ku Seoul Korea. **LC** Q4. **DD** 505.

CHUNG HSUEH LI KO CHIAO HSUEH. VFOAT Zhongxue Like Jiaoxue. First published in April 1978-. Periodical. Chinese. ir. $0.15. **LC** Q183.4.C5.

CHUNG-HUA KO HSUEH HUA PAO. VFOAT Chung Hwa Popular Science. V. 1, (March 1954)-. Periodical. CC. Chinese. bm. $4.86. China Publication Centre, PO Box 2820, Beijing China.

CHUNG-KUO KO CHI SHIH LIAO. VFOAT China Historical Materials of Science and Technology. Periodical. CH. Chinese. qt. 0.70. Post Office Peking, Peking China. **LC** Q127.C5. **DD** 505.

CHUNG-KUO KO HSUEH. VFOAT Scientia Sinica. Series A, Mathematical, Physical, Astronomical & Technical Sciences. Vol. 25, No. 1 (Jan. 1982)-. 0253-5831. Periodical. bi-mo. China Publication Centre, PO Box 2820, Beijing China. **Ind/Abst** Bibliogr. Agric., Coal Abstr., Int. Aerosp. Abstr., Math. Rev., Met. Abstr., World Alum. Abstr., World Text Abstr. **NLM** W1 SC822A. *Scientia Sinica.*

CHUNGNAM KWAHAK YONGUJI. VFOAT Chungnam Journal of Sciences. Periodical. English (Korean). sa. **LC** Q4. **CODEN** CJOSDA.

CHUO DAIGAKU RIKOGAKUBU KIYO. VFOAT Bulletin of the Faculty of Science and Engineering, Chuo University. JA. summaries and some articles in English. ir. 1-13-27 Kasuga Bunkyo-ku, Tokyo Japan. **Ind/Abst** Chem. Abstr. **LC** Q1.A1. **CODEN** CDSEAB.

CICLO DE CONFERENCIAS. Main/Corp Sociedad Cientifica Argentina, Buenos Aires. Spanish. ir. Comision de Cursos y Confereneias, Av Santa Fe 1145, Buenos Aires Argentina. **LC** Q33.

CIECIA Y DESARROLLO. (CIENCIA Y DESARROLLO). No. 1- March/April 1975-. 0185-0008. Periodical. MX. Spanish. bm. 1000.00 Domestic, $33.00 Foreign. Consejo Nac Ciencia y Tecn, Apartado 20 033, 04515 Mexico DF Mexico. **Tel** 655-6366. **Ed** Mauricio Fortes. **Ind/Abst** Chem. Abstr. **LC** Q4. **CODEN** CIDED8. bk rev. adv acc. **Circ** 50,000. Bridging the gap between basic science and technology and the layman. Forum for establishing official scientific planning.

CIENCIA AL DIA. Began in 1961. 0529-7281. Periodical. Spanish. qt. 12.00. Sociedad Venezolane de Ciencias Naturales, Apartado Postal 62.173, Caracas Venezuela. **LC** Q4.

CIENCIA E INVESTIGACION. V. 1- Jan. 1945-. 0009-6733. Periodical. AG. Spanish. ir. Associacion Argent Progreso, Avenida Rogue Saenz Pena, 555 Buenos Aires Argentina. **Ind/Abst** Biol. Abstr., Chem. Abstr. **LC** Q4. **NLM** W1 CI223. **CODEN** CIBAAH.

CIENCIA HOJE : REVISTA DE DIVULGACAO CIENTIFICA DA SOCIEDADE BRASILEIRA PARA O PROGRESSO DA CIENCIA. Yearly V. 1, No. 1, (July/Aug. 1982)-. 0101-8515. Periodical. Portuguese. bm. $2400. Av Venceslau Braz, 71 Fundos Casa 27, Rio de Janeiro RJ CEP 222 Brazil. **LC** Q4. **DD** 505.

CIENCIA INTERAMERICANA. V. 1- Jan./Feb. 1960-. 0009-675X. Periodical. US. Spanish. qt. Organization of American States, 17th and Constitution Avenue Northwest, Washington DC 20006. **Ind/Abst** GeoRef, Chem. Abstr., Bibliogr. Agric. **NLM** W1 CI223J. **CODEN** CIIABJ.

CIENCIA (MEXICO CITY, MEXICO). (CIENCIA : REVISTA HISPANO-AMERICANA DE CIENCIAS PURAS Y APLICADAS). V. 1, (March 1940)-. 0185-075X. Periodical. MX. Spanish (summaries and added table of contents in English). ir. 25.00. Academia de la Inve Cientifica, Apartado Postal 690692, Mexico 21 DF Mexico. **Tel** 548-6957. **Ed** Fernando del Rio. **Ind/Abst** Biol. Abstr., Comput. Control Abstr., Electr. Electron. Abstr., Sci. Abstr. Sect. A. Phys. Abstr., Chem. Abstr. **LC** Q4. **DD** 505. **NLM** W1 CI226L. **CODEN** CIENA3. (cum index). bk rev. adv acc. **Circ** 2,000. (ctrl). Review articles in all scientific fields.

CIENCIA Y NATURALEZA. V. 1- June 1957-. 0009-6768. Periodical. EC. Spanish. an. Universidad Centre, Instituto de Cien Cias Naturales, POB 633, Quito Canje Ecuador. **Ind/Abst** GeoRef, Biol. Abstr. **CODEN** CINQAN. *Boletin del Instituto de Ciencias Naturales.*

CIENCIA Y TECNOLOGIA DE VENEZUELA. V. 1- (No. 1-). Periodical. Spanish (English summaries). ir. Conicit, Apartado de Correos, 70617 Caracas Venezuela.

CIRCULAR - NEW YORK STATE MUSEUM AND SCIENCE SERVICE. (CIRCULAR). No. 39-. 0271-4213. Monographic Series. US. English. ir. State Science Service, New York State Museum, 3140 Cultural Education Center, Albany NY 12230. **Ind/Abst** Biol. Abstr., GeoRef. **LC** Q11. **DD** 508.747. **CODEN** NYMSCL. *Circular (New York State Museum).*

CLEARINGHOUSE REPORT ON SCIENCE AND HUMAN RIGHTS. VFOAT AAAS Clearinghouse Report on Science and Human Rights. 0734-4171. Periodical. US. English. qt. AAAS, 1515 Massachusetts Avenue Northwest, Washington DC 20005.

CNPQ BOLETIM. Main/Corp Conselho Nacional de Desenvolvimento Cientifico e Tecnologico. Portuguese. ir. Praia do Flamengo 200, Rio de Janiero Brazil. **LC** Q180.B7. **DD** 507.2081.

CODATA BULLETIN. Main/Corp CODATA. VAT Committee on Data for Science and Technology Bulletin. 1- Oct. 1969-. 0366-757X. UK. English. bm. Pergamon Press, 395 Sawmill River Road, Elmsford NY 10523. **Tel** (914)592-7700. **Ind/Abst** Life Sci.

Science (General)

Collect., Int. Aerosp. Abstr., GeoRef, Chem. Abstr., Energy Res. Abstr., Bibliogr. Index Geol. LC Q183.9. DD 502.854. NLM W1 C542X. CODEN CODBA4.

COGEODATA NEWSLETTER. See Earth Sciences - Geology.

COLLEGE OF SCIENCE ALUMNI DIRECTORY, THE PENNSYLVANIA STATE UNIVERSITY. See Yearbooks, Almanacs, Directories.

COLOMBIA, CIENCIA Y TECNOLOGIA. VFOAT Ciencia y Tecnologia. 0120-4335. Periodical. Spanish. qt. Colciencias, Transversal 9A No 133-28, Bogota Colombia. LC Q33. DD 509.861. Ciencia y Tecnologia (Bogota, Columbia).

COMMENTATIONES PHYSICO-MATHEMATICAE, SOCIETAS SCIENTIARUM FENNICA. (COMMENTATIONES PHYSICO-MATHEMATICAE). Vol. 1-. 0069-6609. Periodical. Fl. English (German and Swedish). qt. Akakeeminen-Kirjakuppa, PO Box 128, 00101 Helsinki Finland. Ind/Abst Math. Rev., GeoRef, Comput. Control Abstr., Electr. Electron. Abstr., Sci. Abstr. Sect. A. Phys. Abstr., Energy Res. Abstr., Sci. Cit. Index, Abr. Ed., Phys. Abstr. LC Q60. CODEN CPHMAU. Ofversigt af Finska Vetenskaps-Sociatetens Forhandlingar.

COMMUNICATIONS - ROYAL SOCIETY OF EDINBURGH. PHYSICAL SCIENCES CEASED. (THE ROYAL SOCIETY OF EDINBURGH COMMUNICATIONS, PHYSICAL SCIENCES). VFOAT Communications, Physical Sciences, Communications to the Royal Society of Edinburgh, Physical Sciences. 1-19. 0308-129X. UK. English. Royal Society of Edinburgh, 22 George Street, Edinburgh EH2 2PQ England. Ind/Abst Math. Rev., Int. Aerosp. Abstr., Comput. Control Abstr., Electr. Electron. Abstr., Sci. Abstr. Sect. A. Phys. Abstr. LC Q41.R895. DD 500.205. CODEN CRYSAB. Proceedings. Section A, Mathematical and Physical Sciences.

COMMUNIQUE - CONSEIL DE LA JEUNESSE SCIENTIFIQUE. Main/Corp Conseil de la Jeunesse Scientifique. VFOAT C J S-Communique. No. 1- Nov. 1973-. 0317-8803. CN. French. mo. Secretariat du Conseil de la Jeunesse Scientifique Bureau, 14 230 Est Boulevard Henri-Bourassa, Montreal Quebec H3L 1B8 Canada. DD 506.2714.

COMPARISON OF COMPENSATION PAID SCIENTISTS AND ENGINEERS IN RESEARCH AND DEVELOPMENT. See Economics - Labor.

COMPOSITES SCIENCE AND TECHNOLOGY. See Engineering.

COMPTES RENDUS DE L'ACADEMIE DES SCIENCES. SERIE II, MECANIQUE, PHYSIQUE, CHIMIE, SCIENCES DE L'UNIVERS, SCIENCES DE LA TERRE. VFOAT Mecanique, Physique, Chimie, Sciences de l'Univers, Sciences de la Terre. V. 298, Series II, No. 1 (Jan. 1984)-. Periodical. French (summaries in English). ir. 1570. Gauthier-Villars CDR, Centrale de Revue, BP No 119, 93104 Montreuil Cedex France. Ind/Abst Chem. Abstr., Curr. Contents, Pestdoc, Ringdoc, Vetdoc, Met. Abstr., World Alum. Abstr. Comptes Rendus des Seances de l'Academie des Sciences. Serie II, Mecanique, Physique, Chimie, Sciences de l'Univers, Sciences de la Terre, 0249-6305.

COMPTES RENDUS DE L'ACADEMIE DES SCIENCES. SERIE III, SCIENCES DE LA VIE. VFOAT Sciences de la Vie. V. 298, No. 1 (Jan. 7, 1984)-. Periodical. French (summaries in English). ir. 1570. Gauthier-Villars CDR, Centrale des Revues, 11 rue Gossin, 92543 Montrouge Cedex France. Ind/Abst Excerpta Med., Curr. Contents, Chem. Abstr., Life Sci. Collect., Pestdoc, Ringdoc, Vetdoc. Comptes Rendus des Seances de l'Academie des Sciences. Serie III, Sciences de la Vie, 0249-6313.

COMPTES RENDUS DES SEANCES DE L'ACADEMIE DES SCIENCES. VIE ACADEMIQUE. VFOAT Vie Acadmeique. Jan. 1979-. FR. French. mo. Gauthier-Villars CDR, Centrale des Revues, BP No 119, 93104 Montreuil Cedex France. Ind/Abst Chem. Abstr. LC Q2. DD 505. CODEN CRSAAT. Comptes Rendus Hebdomadaires des Seances de l'Academie des Sciences. Vie Academique.

COMPTES RENDUS HEBDOMADAIRES DES SEANCES DE L'ACADEMIE DES SCIENCES. VIE ACADEMIQUE. V. 262 (1966)-V. 291 (1980). Periodical. French (summaries in English). ir.

COMPTES RENDUS MENSUELS DES SEANCES DE L'ACADEMIE DES SCIENCES D'OUTRE-MER CEASED. Main/Corp Academie des Sciences d'Outre-Mer. V. 17, No. 5- V. 30. FR. French. ir. Academie des Sciences d'Outre-Mer, 15 rue La Perouse, Paris 75116 France. Comptes Rendus Mensuels des Seances de l'Academie des Sciences Coloniales.

COMPUTERS IN LIFE SCIENCE EDUCATION. See Computers and Computer Science.

COMPUTING REPORT IN SCIENCE AND ENGINEERING. See Computers and Computer Science.

CONFERENCE PAPERS ANNUAL INDEX. See Indexes/Abstracts.

CONTRIBUCION - INSTITUTO ECUATORIANO DE CIENCIAS NATURALES. (CONTRIBUCION - QUITO. INSTITUTO ECUATORIANO DE CIENCIAS NATURALES). Main/Corp Instituto Ecuatoriano de Ciencias Naturales. No. 1-. 0480-8029. EC. Spanish. ir. Instituto Ecuatoriano de Ciencias Naturales, Quito Ecuador. Ind/Abst GeoRef. CODEN IECCAW.

CONTRIBUCIONES CIENTIFICAS Y TECNOLOGICAS. 0716-0127. Periodical. Spanish. bm. $30.00. Universidad d Santiago d Chile, Avd Eduador 3469 Dept Investmt, Correo 2 Santiago Chile. Tel 761011. Ed Bernd J Schulz. Ind/Abst Chem. Abstr. CODEN CCTEDC. Circ 1,000. Research results in science and technology done in the University in chemistry, mathematics, physics, engineering, metallurgy, electrical geoscience and mechanical chemicals.

CONTRIBUTIONS A L'ETUDE DES SCIENCES DE L'HOMME. 1- 1952-. 0589-5820. Periodical. CN. French (English). ir. Centre de Recherches en Relations Humaine, 2715 Cote St Catherine, Montreal Quebec H3T 1B6 Canada.

LE COURRIER DU CNRS. 0153-985X. Periodical. FR. French. ir. 84. Centrale des Revues, 11 rue Gossin, 92543 Montrouge Cedex France. Ed G Delacote. Ind/Abst Life Sci. Collect., GeoRef, Energy Res. Abstr. LC Q180.F7. DD 505. Journal of general interest to scientists. Courrier.

CPST; COMPUTER PROGRAMS IN SCIENCE AND TECHNOLOGY. VFOAT Computer Programs in Science and Technology. V. 1- July 1971-. Periodical. US. English. qt. Science Associates International Inc, 1841 Broadway, New York NY 10023. LC T1. DD 502.85425.

CREATION RESEARCH SOCIETY QUARTERLY. See Religion, Mythology, Rationalism.

CRUCIBLE. (THE CRUCIBLE). Began publication in 1964. 0381-8047. Periodical. CN. English. ir. $27.00. S T A of Ontario, Box 975 Postal Station A, Scarborough Ontario M1K 5E4 Canada. Ed Gary Forsyth. Ind/Abst Can. Educ. Index, Met. Abstr., World Alum. Abstr. DD 507. bk rev. adv acc. Circ 1,600. (ctrl). Science teaching - all levels.

CRUSTACEANA. SUPPLEMENT. V. 1-. 0590-1391. Monographic Series. NE. English (French and German). ir. EJ Brill, POB 9000, 2300 PA Leiden The Netherlands. Ind/Abst Life Sci. Collect. CODEN CRUSBQ.

CRYO-LETTERS. (CRYO LETTERS). V. 1- Oct. 1979-. 0143-2044. Periodical. UK. English. bm. $150.00. Cryoletters, 7 Wooton Way, Cambridge CB3 9LX England. Ed Felix Franks. Ind/Abst Biol. Abstr., Chem. Abstr. CODEN CRLED9. bk rev. adv acc. Circ 200. Low temperature sciences, technology, physics chemistry, biology, medicine and agriculture.

CSHPS COMMUNIQUE. (C S H P S COMMUNIQUE). Main/Corp Canadian Society for the History and Philosophy of Science. VFOAT Communique de la Schps. VAT Canadian Society for the History and Philosophy of Science Communique. V. 1- May 1979-. 0226-8698. Periodical. CN. English (includes some text in French). ir. Free to Members. Michel Paradis, Canadian Society for the History and Philosophy of Science, Secretary-Treasurer, Department of Linguistics, 1007 Sherbrooke Street West, Montreal Quebec H3A 1G5 Canada. DD 506.071.

CSIR ANNUAL REPORT. Main/Corp South African Council for Scientific and Industrial Research. 17th- 1961-. SA. English. ir. South African Council for Scientific and Industrial Research, PO Box 395, Pretoria 0001 South Africa. LC Q85.S46. DD 507.2068. Jaarverslag.

CSIR HANDBOOK. Main/Corp Council of Scientific & Industrial Research (India). VFOAT C.S.I.R. Handbook. English. ir. Council of Scientific & Industrial Research, Publications & Information Director Hillside Road, New Delhi 110001 India. LC Q73. DD 507.2054. Handbook.

CSIRO INDEX. See Indexes/Abstracts.

CURRENT CONTENTS. CLINICAL PRACTICE. (CURRENT CONTENTS : CLINICAL PRACTICE). VFOAT Clinical Practice. V. 1- Jan. 3, 1973-. 0091-1704. Periodical. US. English. wk. $325.00. Institute for Scientific Information, 3501 Market Street, University City Science, Philadelphia PA 19104. Tel (800)523-1850. Ind/Abst Soc. Sci. Citation Index, Sci. Cit. Index, Abr. Ed. NLM ZW 1 C95. CODEN CCPCDK.

CURRENT CONTENTS : ENGINEERING, TECHNOLOGY & APPLIED SCIENCES. VFOAT Current Contents. V. 6- Jan. 6, 1975-. 0095-7917. Periodical. US. English. wk. $325.00. Institute for Scientific Information, 325 Chestnut Street, Philadelphia PA 19106. Tel (800)523-1850. Ind/Abst Abstr. Bull. Inst. Paper Chem., Sci. Cit. Index, Abr. Ed., Soc. Sci. Citation Index. NLM Z 7911 C976. CODEN CCETA. Current Contents: Engineering & Technology, 0011-3395.

CURRENT CONTENTS. LIFE SCIENCES. Began with Vol. 10, 1967. 0011-3409. Periodical. US. English. wk. Institution for Scientific Information, 3501 Market Street, University City of Science, Philadelphia PA 19104. Tel (800)523-1850. Ind/Abst Abstr. Bull. Inst. Paper Chem., Soc. Sci. Citation Index, Sci. Cit. Index, Abr. Ed., Life Sci. Collect. LC Z5321, QH301. DD 016.574. NLM ZW 1 C959. Current Contents. Your Weekly Guide to the Chemical, Pharmaco-Medical & Life Sciences, 0272-1503.

CURRENT CONTROVERSY. (CURRENT CONTROVERSY : A PUBLICATION OF THE INSTITUTE FOR SCIENTIFIC INFORMATION). Vol. 1, No. 1-. 0278-3525. Periodical. US. English. mo. Institute for Scientific Information, 3501 Market Street, Philadelphia PA 19104. Tel (800)523-1850. DD 505.

CURRENT JOURNALS IN THE SCIENCES. 1st- Ed. 0190-034X. US. English. ir. Harvard University Press, 79 Garden Street, Cambridge MA 02138. NLM ZQ 1 C971.

CURRENT LITERATURE ON SCIENCE OF SCIENCE. V. 1- Jan. 1972-. Periodical. II. English. mo. $30.00. Publications & Information Directorate, Hillside Road, New Delhi 110012 India. Tel 586301. LC Z7405.R4. DD 016.301248. Index to Literature on Science of Science.

CURRENT RESEARCH IN THE NETHERLANDS : MATHEMATICS, PHYSICS, GEOLOGY, ASTRONOMY. English. ir. Netherlands Organization for the Advancement of Pure Research, Juliana Van Stolberglaan, PO Box 2138, The Hague The Netherlands. LC Q180.N35. DD 507.20492.

CURRENT SCIENCE. V. 1- July 1932-. 0011-3891. Periodical. II. English. sm. $165.00. J C Baltzer, Wettsteinplatz 10, CH-4058 Basel Switzerland. Tel 61 26 8925. Ind/Abst Life Sci. Collect., Pestdoc, Excerpta Med., Ringdoc, Int. Aerosp. Abstr., Vetdoc, GeoRef, Biol. Abstr., Comput. Control Abstr., Electr. Electron. Abstr., Sci. Abstr. Sect. A. Phys. Abstr., Curr. Contents, Chem. Abstr., Phys. Abstr. LC Q1. NLM W1 CU81. CODEN CUSCAM.

CURRENT SCIENCE. 0011-3905. Periodical. US. English. ir. $5.25. Xerox Education Publ, PO Box 16626, Columbus OH 43216. Tel (203)638-2697. Ed Vincent J Marteka. Ind/Abst Child. Mag. Guide, Energy Inf. Abstr., Environ. Abstr. Circ 350,000. Also available in braille. Published 18 times during school year, covers stories in all areas of science and health curriculums. Lavish use of 4-color illustrations. Has skills component.

CURRENT TITLES IN TURKISH SCIENCE. Main/Corp Turkiye Bilimsel Ve Teknik Dokumantasyon Merkezi. V. 3- 1976-. 0378-4681. English. mo. Ataturk Bulvari, 221 Kavaklidere, Ankara

Science (General)

Turkey. **Ind/Abst** Fluidex. **LC** Z7401, Q158.5. **DD** 016.5. **NLM** ZQ 1 M789. *Monthly Current Awareness Service on Scientific Publications. Series B. Foreign Edition, 0377-9769.*

CURRENT TRENDS IN LIFE SCIENCES. **VFOAT** Current Trends in Life Science. Began in 1977. 0378-7540. II. English. ir. 195.00 Domestic, $39.00 Foreign. Today & Tomorrows Printers & Publishers, 24-5/B Deshbandhu Gupta Road, New Delhi 110005 India. Ed S K Chauhan, V P Singh, P S Dubey, D Amritphale and S K Billore. **Ind/Abst** Chem. Abstr. **LC** UNC. **NLM** W3 CU613. **CODEN** CTSCDI. Encourages individual initiative for the acquisition and dissemination of knowledge as well as the discovery of new knowledge.

CYCLES. V. 1- June 1950-. 0011-4294. Periodical. US. English. mo. $175.00. Foundation for Study of Cycles, 124 South Highland Avenue, Pittsburgh PA 15206. **Tel** (412)441-1666. Ed Gertrude F Shirk. **Ind/Abst** Coal Abstr., Public Aff. Inf. Serv. Bull. **LC** Q176. **DD** 501. bk rev. **Circ** 1,500. Articles on fluctuations (cycles) in all disciplines from animal abundance to zinc production, with history and extrapolations. Also on methodology and computer techniques.

DAEDALUS : PROCEEDINGS OF THE AMERICAN ACADEMY OF ARTS AND SCIENCES. V. 86- May 1955-. 0011-5266. Periodical. US. English. qt. Daedalus, PO Box 515, Canton MA 02021. **Tel** (617)828-8450. **Ind/Abst** Am. Hist. Life, Hist. Abstr., Part A, Mod. Hist. Abstr., Hist. Abstr., Part B, Twent. Century Abstr., Repert. Int. Litt. Art, Sociol. Abstr., ABC Pol Sci, Biol. Abstr., Book Rev. Index, Chem. Abstr., GeoRef, Humanit. Index, Soc. Work Res. Abstr., Sci. Abstr., Public Aff. Inf. Serv. Bull., Soc. Sci. Index, Humanit. Index, Psychol. Abstr., Energy Res. Abstr., Hospit. Lit. Index, Soc. Welf. Soc. Plan./Policy Soc. Dev. **NLM** W1 DA229. **CODEN** DAEDAU. *Proceedings of the American Academy of Arts and Sciences, 0199-9818.*

DEJINY VED A TECHNIKY. (DVT, DEJINY VED A TECHNIKY). **VFOAT** Dejiny Ved a Techniky. Vol. 1- 1968-. 0300-4414. Periodical. CS. Czech (summaries in French, English and German). qt. Kubon & Sagner, Postfach 34 01 08, 8 Munchen 34 West Germany. **Tel** (089)52 20 27. **Ind/Abst** Math. Rev. **CODEN** DVTDAE. Deals with the history of the natural sciences, medicine, and technology as well as with the history of scientific institutions and their activities.

DENKSCHRIFTEN DER SCHWEIZERISCHEN NATURFORSCHENDEN GESELLSCHAFT. **Main/Corp** Schweizerische Naturforschende Gesellschaft. **VFOAT** Memoires de la Societe Helvetique des Sciences Naturelles. Vol. 55-. Monographic Series. SZ. German. ir. Gebruder Fretz, Nuhlebach Strq 54, Zurich Switzerland. **Ind/Abst** Life Sci. Collect., GeoRef, Biol. Abstr. **CODEN** DSNGA6. *Neue Denkschriften der Schweizerischen Naturforschenden Gesellschaft.*

DEPONIROVANNYE RUKOPISI. *See* Bibliographies.

DEUTSCHER FORSCHUNGSDIENST : DF. **VFOAT** DF, German Research Service. Began with Vol. 1, No. 1 (April 1962). 0072-1476. Periodical. GW. English. ir. Forschungsdienst GMBH, Ahrstrasse 45, Wissenschaftszentrum Postfach 20 50 06, D-5300 Bonn 2 West Germany.

DEVELOPMENTS IN CHROMATOGRAPHY. 1-. 0260-4221. UK. English. ir. Elsevier Applied Science Publications, Crown House, Linton Road, Barking Essex IG11 8JU England. **Ind/Abst** Chem. Abstr. **CODEN** DECHDT.

DEVELOPMENTS IN PRESSURE VESSEL TECHNOLOGY. Series/Titl Developments Series. 1-. 0266-156X. Periodical. UK. English. ir. Elsevier Science Publ Co, 52 Vanderbilt Avenue, New York NY 10017.

LA DIDATTICA SCIENTIFICA. Vol. 1- Feb. 1971-. Periodical. Italian. ir. 3.000. Instituto Italiano Edizioni, Via Crescenzi 88, 24100 Bergamo Italy. **LC** Q4.

DIFFUSION OF INNOVATIONS, COAST-HINTERLAND-CONTINUUM. PRELIMINARY REPORT. (DIFFUSION OF INNOVATION, COAST-HINTERLAND-CONTINUUM). **Main/Corp** Heidelberg. Universitat. Sudasien-Institut. Thailand Research Project. Monographic Series. English. ir.

DIJALEKTIKA. **VFOAT** Dialectics. V. 1- 1966-. 0419-1439. Periodical. YU. Serbo-Croatian -C (Russian, with English, French, or Russian summaries). ir. Univerzitet U Beogradu, Pravni Fakultet, Belgrade Stud TRG1 Yugoslavia. **LC** Q175.

DIRECTORY OF AAAS FELLOWS. *See* Yearbooks, Almanacs, Directories.

DIRECTORY OF CHINESE OFFICIALS. SCIENTIFIC AND EDUCATIONAL ORGANIZATIONS. *See* Yearbooks, Almanacs, Directories.

DIRECTORY OF COMPUTERIZED INFORMATION IN SCIENCE AND TECHNOLOGY. *See* Yearbooks, Almanacs, Directories.

DIRECTORY OF JAPANESE SCIENTIFIC PERIODICALS. *See* Yearbooks, Almanacs, Directories.

DIRECTORY OF NATIONAL SCIENCE FOUNDATION PROGRAMS AND GUIDELINES. *See* Yearbooks, Almanacs, Directories.

DIRECTORY OF PUBLISHED PROCEEDINGS. SERIES SEMT- SCIENCE-ENGINEERING- MEDICINE-TECHNOLOGY. *See* Yearbooks, Almanacs, Directories.

DIRECTORY OF SCIENTIFIC AND TECHNICAL PERSONNEL OF SRI LANKA. *See* Yearbooks, Almanacs, Directories.

DIRECTORY OF SCIENTIFIC AND TECHNICAL SOCIETIES IN SOUTH AFRICA. *See* Yearbooks, Almanacs, Directories.

THE DIRECTORY OF SCIENTIFIC RESEARCH INSTITUTIONS IN INDIA. *See* Yearbooks, Almanacs, Directories.

DIRECTORY OF SCIENTIFIC RESEARCH INSTITUTIONS IN THE CENTO REGION. *See* Yearbooks, Almanacs, Directories.

DIRECTORY OF SCIENTIFIC RESEARCH ORGANIZATIONS IN SOUTH AFRICA. *See* Yearbooks, Almanacs, Directories.

DIRECTORY OF SOVIET OFFICIALS. SCIENCE AND EDUCATION. *See* Yearbooks, Almanacs, Directories.

DIRECTORY OF THE RESEARCH ESTABLISHMENTS IN PAKISTAN. *See* Yearbooks, Almanacs, Directories.

DISCOVER. V. 1- Oct. 1980-. 0274-7529. Periodical. US. English. mo. Time Inc, 301 East Ohio Street, Chicago IL 60611. **Ind/Abst** Abr. Read. Guide, GeoRef, Pop. Mag. Rev., Read. Guide Period. Lit., Predicasts, Energy Inf. Abstr., Environ. Abstr., Gen. Sci. Index. **LC** Q1. **DD** 505.

DISCUSSION PAPER. **VFOAT** DSIR Discussion Paper. **VAT** Department of Scientific and Industrial Research Discussion Paper. No. 1 (1978)-. 0110-5221. Monographic Series. English. ir. **Tel** 858 939. **Circ** 2,000. Analyses problems and opportunities for New Zealand research within areas of concerns and gives recommendations on preferred options.

DISSERTATIONEN DER UNIVERSITAT WIEN. 0419-4225. Periodical. AU. German. ir. Verband Wissen Gesellschaften, Osterreichs- Lindengasse 37, A 1070 Wien Austria. **Tel** 93 47 56. **Ind/Abst** MLA Int. Bibliogr. Books Artic. Mod. Lang. Lit. **Circ** 200. Each volume is a single doctoral dissertation. The subjects cover many sciences and humanities.

DOKLADY BOLGARSKOJ AKADEMIJA NAUK. (DOKLADY BOLGARSKOI AKADEMII NAUK). **Main/Corp** Bulgarska Akademiia na Naukite. **VFOAT** Comptes Rendus de Lacademie Bulgare des Sciences. Vol. 1- 1948-. 0366-8681. Periodical. BU. Bulgarian, French, English and German. mo. $70.00. Hemus, 6 Boulevard Rusky, Sofia Bulgaria. **Ind/Abst** Bibliogr. Agric., Biol. Abstr., Chem. Abstr., Coal Abstr., Comput. Control Abstr., Electr. Electron. Abstr., Energy Res. Abstr., GeoRef, Int. Aerosp. Abstr., Life Sci. Collect., Math. Rev., Met. Abstr., Sci. Abstr. Sect. A. Phys. Abstr., World Alum. Abstr. **LC** Q69. **NLM** W1 DO64BT. **CODEN** DBANAD.

DONG GOP. 1- No. 7, 1977-. 0705-1492. Periodical. CN. Vietnamese. qt. $9. Union of Vietnamese in Canada, Box 220 Station G, Montreal Quebec H2W 2M9 Canada. **DD** 509.597.

DOPOVIDI AKADEMII NAUK UKRAINSKOI RSP. SERIJA B: GEOLOGICNI, HIMICNI TA BIOLOGICNI NAUKI. (DOPOVIDI AKADEMII NAUK UKRAINSKOI RSR. SERIA B : HEOLOHICHNI, KHIMICHNI TA BIOLOHICHNI NAUKI). **Main/Corp** Akademiia Nauk Ukrainskoi RSR. Jan. 1976-. 0377-9785. Periodical. UR. Ukrainian (summaries in English). mo. 0.40. Dumka, Repina 3, Kiev Ukrainian SSR. **Ind/Abst** Chem. Abstr., Life Sci. Collect., Math. Rev. **LC** Q4. **NLM** W1 DO736UA. **CODEN** DANND6. *Dopovidi. Seria B: Heolohia, Heofizika, Khimiia Ta Biolohiia, 0002-3523.*

DOSHISHA DAIGAKU RIKOGAKU KENKYU HOKOKU. (THE SCIENCE AND ENGINEERING REVIEW OF DOSHISHA UNIVERSITY). V. 1-, March 1960-. 0036-8172. Periodical. JA. English (Japanese with English summaries). qt. $27.50. Japan Publishers Trading Co Ltd, PO Box 5030 Tokyo International, Tokyo 100-31 Japan. **Ind/Abst** Fluidex, GeoRef, Comput. Control Abstr., Electr. Electron. Abstr., Sci. Abstr. Sect. A. Phys. Abstr., Chem. Abstr., Met. Abstr., World Alum. Abstr., Phys. Abstr. **CODEN** DDRKAZ. *Doshisha Kogaku Kaishi.*

DSIR BULLETIN. **VFOAT** D.S.I.R. Bulletin. 0077-961X. Monographic Series. NZ. English. bm. Science Information Publishing Center, Box 9741, Wellington New Zealand. **Tel** 858-939. **Ind/Abst** Comput. Control Abstr., Electr. Electron. Abstr., Life Sci. Collect., Sci. Abstr. Sect. A. Phys. Abstr., Biol. Abstr. **CODEN** NEZSAC. Monograph series covering various physical, chemical and biological sciences. *Bulletin (New Zealand. Dept. of Scientific and Industrial Research).*

DSIR INFORMATION SERIES. VAT Department of Scientific and Industrial Research Information Series. Began with: No. 127, published in 1977. 0077-9636. Monographic Series. English. ir. Science Information Publishing Center, Box 9741, Wellington New Zealand. **Tel** 838 939. **Ind/Abst** GeoRef, Chem. Abstr., Life Sci. Collect. **LC** UNC. **CODEN** NZIBAN. Informative books for general reader or student on wide range of science topics. Well illustrated. *Information Series (New Zealand. Dept. of Scientific and Industrial Research).*

EAST EUROPE REPORT. SCIENTIFIC AFFAIRS. **VFOAT** Scientific Affairs. No. 635- July 2, 1979-. Periodical. US. English (Multilingual). ir. Executive Office of the President, Foreign Broadcast Information Service, Joint Publications Research Service, 5285 Port Royal Road, Springfield VA 22161. *Translations on Eastern Europe. Scientific Affairs.*

EDUCATION IN SCIENCE : THE BULLETIN OF THE ASSOCIATION FOR SCIENCE EDUCATION. VFOAT Bulletin of the Association for Science Education. 0013-1377. Periodical. UK. English. ir. $13.80. Association for Science Education, College Lane, Hatfield Herts England. **Tel** Hatfield 67411. **Ind/Abst** Energy Inf. Abstr., Environ. Abstr., Curr. Index J. Educ.

EHIME DAIGAKU KYOIKU GAKUBU KIYO. DAI 3-BU, SHIZEN KAGAKU. VFOAT Memoirs of the Faculty of Education, Ehime University. V. 1-. English (Japanese). ir. Ehime Daigaku Kyoiku Gakubu, 3-ban Bunkyo-cho, Matsuyama-shi 790 Japan. **LC** Q4.

EKTHESIS PEPRAGMENON - HYPOURGEION POLITISMOU KAI EPISTEMON, HYPERESIA EPISTEMONIKES EREUNES KAI ANAPTYXEOS. **Main/Corp** Greece. Hypourgeion Politismou kai Epistemon. Hyperesia Epistemonikes Ereunes Kai Anaptyxeos. 1971/72-. Greek, Modern. ir. **LC** Q180.G8.

ENCOUNTERS. (ENCOUNTERS). Vol. 1, No. 1 (Mar. 1978)-. 0273-5717. Periodical. US. English. bm. $6.50. Science Museum of Minnesota, 30 East 10th Street, St Paul MN 55101. **Tel** (612)221-9451. Ed Susan Wichmann. bk rev. adv acc. **Circ** 24,000. Membership magazine of the Science Museum of Minnesota. Articles include coverage of anthropology, biology, archaeology, paleontology, and technology.

ENCYCLIA. V. 54-. 0196-9110. Periodical. US. English. an. $12.00. Brigham Young University, 3146 JKHB, c/o J A Waterstradt, Provo UT 84602. **Tel**

Science (General)

(801)378-3385. **Ed** Jean Anne Waterstradt. **Ind/Abst** Math. Rev., MLA Int. Bibliogr. Books Artic. Mod. Lang. Lit., Life Sci. Collect., GeoRef, Chem. Abstr. **LC** Q11. **DD** 081. **CODEN** ENCYDI. **Circ** 1,000. (ctrl). Scholarly papers on miscellaneous subjects in sciences, social sciences, letters and arts. *Proceedings of the Utah Academy of Sciences, Arts, and Letters, 0083-4823.*

ENDEAVOUR. V. 1-. 0160-9327. Periodical. UK. English. qt. Pergamon Press, Attn: Cashier 395 Sawmill River Road, Elmsford NY 10523. **Ind/Abst** Art Archaeol. Tech. Abstr., Bibliogr. Agric., CIS Abstr., Coal Abstr., Comput. Control Abstr., Electr. Electron. Abstr., Energy Inf. Abstr., Energy Res. Abstr., Environ. Abstr., Excerpta Med., Gen. Sci. Index, GeoRef, Int. Aerosp. Abstr., Life Sci. Collect., Met. Abstr., Sci. Abstr. Sect. A. Phys. Abstr., Ref. Source, Ship Abstr., World Alum. Abstr., Biol. Abstr. **NLM** W1 EN358. **CODEN** ENDEAS. Available on microfilm and microfiche. *Endeavour.*

ENGINEERING & SCIENCE. See Engineering.

ERGONOMICS ABSTRACTS (1959). See Indexes/Abstracts.

ERZIEHUNG UND WISSENSCHAFT. See Education (General).

ESTIMATES. PART III, MINISTRY OF STATE, SCIENCE AND TECHNOLOGY CANADA. **Main/Corp** Canada. **VFOAT** Budget des Depenses. **CN.** English (French). $3.00 Domestic, $3.60 Foreign. Canadian Government Publishing Centre, Supply and Services Canada, Ottawa Ontario K1A 0S9 Canada. **LC** Q127.C2. **DD** 3547100855.

ESTIMATES. PART III, NATURAL SCIENCES AND ENGINEERING RESEARCH COUNCIL OF CANADA. **VFOAT** Budget des Depenses. **CN.** English (French). $6.00 Domestic, $7.20 Foreign. Canadian Government Publishing Centre, Supply and Services Canada, Ottawa Ontario K1A 0S9 Canada. **LC** Q127.C2. **DD** 354.710085.5.

ESTIMATES. PART III, SCIENCE COUNCIL OF CANADA. **VFOAT** Budget des Depenses. **CN.** English (French). $3.00 Domestic, $3.60 Foreign. Canadian Government Publishing Centre, Supply and Services Canada, Ottawa Ontario K1A 0S9 Canada. **LC** Q127.C2. **DD** 354.7100855.

ESTUDIOS INTERDISCIPLINARIOS. Yearly V. 1- August 1973-. Periodical. Spanish. ir. Argentina CEP, San Nicolas 66, Cordoba Argentina. **LC** AS78.A1.

ETTORE MAJORANA INTERNATIONAL SCIENCE SERIES. PHYSICAL SCIENCE. (ETTORE MAJORANA INTERNATIONAL SCIENCE SERIES : PHYSICAL SCIENCE). V. 1-. 0270-188X. Monographic Series. US. English. ir. Plenum Press, 233 Spring Street, New York NY 10013. **Tel** (212)620-8000. **Ind/Abst** Chem. Abstr. **CODEN** EISSDB.

ETUDE DE DOCUMENTATION POUR LE CONSEIL DES SCIENCES DU CANADA CEASED. No. 30-43. 0705-4777. Monographic Series. **CN.** French. *Etude Speciale, 0586-4232.*

EURO ABSTRACTS : SCIENTIFIC AND TECHNICAL PUBLICATIONS AND PATENTS. See Indexes/Abstracts.

EUROPEAN JOURNAL OF SCIENCE EDUCATION. V. 1- Jan./Mar. 1979-. 0140-5284. Periodical. UK. English (French or German). qt. $96.00. Taylor & Francis Ltd, 242 Cherry Street, Philadelphia PA 19106. **Tel** (215)238-0939. **Ed** Karl Frey. **Ind/Abst** Excerpta Med., Biol. Abstr., Comput. Control Abstr., Electr. Electron. Abstr., Sci. Abstr. Sect. A. Phys. Abstr., Curr. Index J. Educ., Phys. Abstr., Soc. Sci. Citation Index. **CODEN** EJSEDA. Bridges the gap between research and practice, providing information, ideas and opinion, serving as a medium for the publication of definitive research findings, and setting these in the context of the classroom.

EUROPEAN SPECTROSCOPY NEWS. V. 1- July 1975-. 0307-0026. Periodical. UK. English. bm. 30.00 Domestic, $55.00 Foreign. John Wiley & Sons Ltd, Baffins Lane, Chichester Sussex PO19 1UD England. **Tel** 0243 784531. **Ed** Ian Michael. **Ind/Abst** Excerpta Med., World Surf. Coat. Abstr., Ref. Source, Chem. Abstr. **CODEN** ESNEDE. bk rev. adv acc. **Circ** 11,000. (ctrl). Articles, news items, book reviews, product news, diary and reports from exhibitions and meetings. Designed to be a club magazine to keep the spectroscopic community informed. *British Bulletin of Spectroscopy, 0007-0378.*

EXAKT. 0340-0220. Periodical. German. ir. 42.00. Deutsche Verlags-Anstalt, Neckarstrasse 121-125, 7 Stuttgart 1 West Germany. **LC** Q3. *Ideen des Exakten Wissens, 0019-1426.*

EXPERIENTIA. Vol. 1, No. 1 (Apr. 15, 1945)-. 0014-4754. Periodical. SZ. French (text in English, German and Italian). mo. $265.00. Birkhauser Boston Inc, 380 Green Street, PO Box 3005, Cambridge MA 02139. **Tel** (617)576-6638. **Ind/Abst** Pestdoc, Ringdoc, Vetdoc, Excerpta Med., Coal Abstr., Energy Inf. Abstr., Environ. Abstr., Index Med., GeoRef, Biol. Abstr., Chem. Abstr., Bibliogr. Agric., Energy Res. Abstr., Life Sci. Collect., Sci. Cit. Index, Abr. Ed. **LC** Q1.A1. **DD** 505. **NLM** W1 EX223. **CODEN** EXPEAM.

EXPERIENTIA. SUPPLEMENTUM. **VFOAT** Supplementum. Began with 1 in 1953. 0071-335X. US. German (text in French, Italian or English). ir. Birkhauser Boston Inc, 380 Green Street, PO Box 3005, Cambridge MA 02139. **Tel** (617)876-2333. **Ind/Abst** Index Med., Chem. Abstr. **NLM** W1 EX23. **CODEN** EXPSAU.

EXPLORERS JOURNAL. V. 1- Nov. 1921. 0014-5025. Periodical. US. English. qt. $15.00. The Explorers Club, 46 East 70th Street, New York NY 10021. **Tel** (212)628-8383. **Ed** Henry S Evans. **Ind/Abst** GeoRef, ASTIS Bibliogr., ASTIS Curr. Aware. Bull., Ref. Source, Biol. Abstr., Bibliogr. Index Geol. **LC** G1. **DD** 910.5. **CODEN** EXJOAM. (cum index). bk rev. adv acc. Exploration reports, anthropology, zoology, archeology, earth sciences, physics, navigation, and aviation.

EXTRAORDINARY SESSION; GENERAL INFORMATION. **Main/Corp** United Nations Educational, Scientific and Cultural Organization. General Conference. **VFOAT** General Information. Periodical. English (French). ir.

FACSIMILE REPRINTS IN THE HISTORY OF SCIENCE. 1- , 1959-. 0429-9809. US. English. ir. University of Illinois, History of Science Society, Urbana IL 61802.

THE FACTS ON FILE SCIENTIFIC YEARBOOK. See Yearbooks, Almanacs, Directories.

F.A.S. PUBLIC INTEREST REPORT. See Political Science - International Relations.

FEDERAL FUNDS FOR RESEARCH AND DEVELOPMENT. See Public Administration.

FEDERAL FUNDS FOR RESEARCH, DEVELOPMENT, AND OTHER SCIENTIFIC ACTIVITIES. DETAILED STATISTICAL TABLES. APPENDICES C AND D. See Statistics.

FEDERAL R & D FUNDING BY BUDGET FUNCTION. **VFOAT** Federal R and D Funding by Budget Function. **VAT** Federal Research and Development Funding by Budget Function. Fiscal years 1978-80-. 0747-5616. US. English. an. Division of Science Resources Studies, National Science Foundation, Washington DC 20550. **LC** Q180.U5. **DD** 338.9730205. Vols. for 1978/80- Distributed to depository libraries in microfiche. *Analysis of Federal R & D Funding by Function, 0145-4625.*

FEDERAL SCIENTIFIC ACTIVITIES. 1984/1985-. 0824-0310. **CN.** English. an. $7.75 Domestic, $9.30 Foreign. Publication Sales and Services, Statistics Canada, Ottawa Ontario K1A 0T6 Canada. **LC** Q180.C2. **DD** 354.7100819. *Federal Science Activities, 0706-2206.*

FEDERAL SCIENTIFIC AND TECHNICAL COMMUNICATION ACTIVITIES, PROGRESS REPORT. (FEDERAL SCIENTIFIC AND TECHNICAL COMMUNICATION ACTIVITIES : PROGRESS REPORT). **Main/Corp** United States. National Science Foundation. Division of Science Information. 0145-2282. US. English. an. US National Science Foundation, Division of Science Resources Studies, 1800 G Street NW, Washington DC 20550. **LC** T10.63.A1. **DD** 507. **NLM** Z 699 F295. *Federal Scientific and Technical Communication Activities, Progress Report, 0145-2282.*

FERNBANK QUARTERLY. Began with issue for Spring 1975. 0742-650X. Periodical. US. English. qt. Free to Members. Fernbank Science Center, 156 Heaton Park Drive NE, Atlanta GA 30307.

FIBER SCIENCE SERIES. V. 1- 1970-. 0071-4682. Monographic Series. US. English. ir. Marcel Dekker Continuation Department, 270 Madison Avenue, New York NY 10016. **Tel** (212)696-9000. **Ed** Rebenfeld. **Ind/Abst** Chem. Abstr. **CODEN** FSCSDC. This is an ongoing series. Each title has a different subject.

THE FILIPINAS JOURNAL OF SCIENCE AND CULTURE. Vol. 1-. Periodical. PH. English. sa. Filipinas Foundation Inc, Makati Stock Exchange Building, 303 Ayala Avenue/ Room 303, Makati Metro Manila Philippines. **LC** Q76. **DD** 505.

FLORIDA SCIENTIST. V. 36- Winter 1973-. 0098-4590. Periodical. US. English. qt. $20.00. Florida Academy of Sciences, Orlando Science Center, 810 East Rollins Street, Orlando FL 32803-1221. **Tel** (305)896-7151. **Ed** Dean F Martin. **Ind/Abst** Life Sci. Collect., Sel. Water Resour. Abstr., Excerpta Med., GeoRef, Biol. Abstr., Chem. Abstr., Bibliogr. Index Geol. **LC** Q11. **DD** 509.759. **CODEN** FLSCAQ. bk rev. **Circ** 1,050. A scientific and educational journal covering many categories of science for a highly diversified professional, non-professional, student and concerned citizen membership. *Quarterly Journal of the Florida Academy of Sciences, 0015-3850.*

FOCUS ON RESEARCH. Periodical. SA. English (Afrikaans). ir. Research and Publication Committee, University of Zululand, Private Bag, KWA-Dlangezwa 3886, Empangeni South Africa. **LC** Q127.S693. **DD** 001.40968491.

FOLIA FACULTATIS SCIENTIARUM NATURALIUM UNIVERSITATIS PURKYNIANAE BRUNENSIS. GEOLOGIA. **VFOAT** Geologia. 1-. 0323-0139. Monographic Series. **CS.** Czech (summaries in Russian, and English or German). ir. Univ J E Purkyne V Brne, Janackovo Nam 2A, Brno Czechoslovakia. **LC** Q1.

FORHANDLINGER - KONGELIGE NORSKE VIDENSKABERS SELSKAB. (FORHANDLINGER - DET KONGELIGE NORSKE VIDENSKABERS SELSKAB). **Main/Corp** Norske Videnskabers Selskab, Trondheim. V. 1- 1926/28-. 0368-6302. NO. Norwegian. an. Kongelige Worske Videnskabers, Erling Skakkes GT 47, Tronoheim 7000 Norway. **Ind/Abst** Math. Rev., GeoRef, Comput. Control Abstr., Electr. Electron. Abstr., Sci. Abstr. Sect. A. Phys. Abstr., Phys. Abstr. **LC** AS283. **DD** 506.2481. **CODEN** KNSFA2. *Arsberetning.*

LES FORMATIONS DE RECHERCHE. **Main/Corp** Centre National de la Recherche Scientifique (France). FR. French. ir. Centre National de la Recherche Scientifique, 15 Quai Anatole, Paris France. **LC** Q180.F7. **DD** 001.430944.

FORSCHUNG : MITTEILUNGEN DER DFG. **VAT** Forschung Mitteilungen der Deutsche Forschungsgemeinschaft. 79/1-. Periodical. GW. German. mo. Deutsche Forschungsgemeinschaft, Kennedyallee 40, 5300 Bonn 2 West Germany. **Ind/Abst** Sociol. Abstr., GeoRef, Energy Res. Abstr. **LC** Q180.G4. **DD** 505. *Mitteilungen (Deutsche Forschungsgemeinschaft).*

FORSCHUNGSBERICHT. (FORSCHUNGSBERICHT). German. ir. **LC** Q180.G4. **DD** 507.204355.

FORSCHUNGSBERICHT - UNIVERSITAT ULM. **Main/Corp** Ulm. Universitat. German. ir. Universitat Ulm, Oberer Eselsberg Postfach 4066, 79 Ulm West Germany. **LC** Q49.

FORSCHUNGSBERICHTE AUS TECHNIK UND NATURWISSENSCHAFTEN. **VFOAT** Reports in the Fields of Science and Technology. 0343-5520. Periodical. US. English (German). qt. $170.00. Verlag Chemie International Inc, Plaza Centre/Suite E, 1020 NW 6th Street, Deerfield Beach FL 33441.

FORSCHUNGSFORDERUNGEN UND FORSCHUNGSAUFTRAGE. See Public Administration.

FORSCHUNGSPOLITISCHE ZIELVORSTELLUNGEN. 1980-. German. ir. Schweizerischer Wissenschaftsrat Wildhainweg, 9 Postfach 2732, 3001 Bern Switzerland. **Tel** (031)619666. **LC** Q180.S9. **DD** 338.9494. **Circ** 4,000. (ctrl). Swiss research policy: its beginnings and ends.

FORSKNINGSNYTT. **VFOAT** Forskningsnytt FRA Norges Almenvitenskapelige Forskningsrad. 0015-7945. Periodical. NO. Norwegian. ir.

Science (General)

Universitetsforlaget, PO Box 2959-Toyen, Oslo 6 Norway. Tel 02-276-060. **Ind/Abst** Energy Res. Abstr.

FORUM PENDIDIKAN SCIENCE DAN MATEMATIKA. Periodical. indonesian. ir. IKIP Jogjakarta, Kampus IKIP Karangmalang, Jogjakarta Indonesia. **LC** Q183.4.I53.

FRANKREICH, FORSCHUNGSPOLITIK UND FORSCHUNGSPRAXIS. Series/Titl Marktinformation. GW. German. ir. 3.00. Bundesstelle fur Aussenhandelsinformation, Blaubach 13 Postfach 10 80 07, D-5000 Koln 1 West Germany. **LC** Q180.55.G3. **DD** 001.40943.

FRENCH SCIENCE NEWS. Began in 1957. 0532-6826. Periodical. FR. English. ir. Association pour la Diffusion de la Pensee Francaise, 11 rue Georges Pitard, 75 Paris 1SE France. **DD** 500.

FU JEN STUDIES : NATURAL SCIENCES. No. 6- 1973-. Periodical. ir. $1.50. Dr H Hesselfeld, College of Natural Sciences/242, Hsin Chuang China. **LC** Q72.5. *Fu Jen Studies, Fu Jen Studies: Natural Sciences & Foreign Languages.*

FUKUI DAIGAKU KOGAKUBU SENI KINOSEI ZAIRYO KENKYU SHISETSU HOKOKU. VFOAT Bulletin of the Research Institute for Material Science and Engineering, Faculty of Engineering, Fukui University, Fukui, Japan. Periodical. JA. Japanese (summaries in English). ir. Fukui Daigaku Kogakubu Seni Kinosei Zairyo Kenkyu Shisetsu, 9-1 Bunkyo 3-chome, Fukui-shi 910 Japan. *Seni Kinasei Zairyo Kenkyu Shisetsu Hokoku.*

FUKUOKA DAIGAKU KENKYUJO HO : SHIZEN KAGAKU HEN. VFOAT Bulletin of the Institute for Advanced Research of Fukuoka University: Natural Sciences. No. 1-. English (Japanese). ir. Fukuoka Daigaku Kenkyujo, 11 Nanakuma Nishi-ku, Fukuoka Japan. **LC** Q4.

FUNDAMENTA SCIENTIAE. Vol. 1, No. 1 (1980)-. 0160-7847. Periodical. UK. English (French, German, Italian, and Spanish). qt. $75.00. Pergamon Press, 395 Sawmill River Road, Elmsford NY 10523. Tel (914)592-7700. **Ind/Abst** Math. Rev. **LC** Q172. **DD** 505. **NLM** W1 FU537K. **CODEN** FUSCDO.

FUTURES RESEARCH QUARTERLY. *See* Technology (General).

GAKKAI SENTA NEWS. Periodical. JA. Japanese. mo. 1,000. Gakkaishi Kanko Senta, 4-16 Yayoi 2, Bunkyo-ku 113, Tokyo Japan. Tel (03)817-5825. Ed Tadahiro Ohmi. **LC** AS541. bk rev. adv acc. Circ 3,000. Gives academic (scientific) meeting information and related topics mainly domestic societies and associations of Japan.

GAKUJUTSU ZASSHI SOGO MOKUROKU. OBUN HEN. HOIBAN. *See* Bibliographies.

GALAKSIJA. 0350-123X. Periodical. Serbo-Croatian -R. ir. $7.00. Duga, Vlajkoviceva 8, Beograd Yugoslavia. **LC** Q4.

GARYOUNIS SCIENTIFIC BULLETIN. Vol. 1, No. 1 (Feb. 1979)-. 0253-634X. Periodical. English. ir. Director of Research Center, Garyounis University, PO Box 9521, Benghazi Libya. **Ind/Abst** Math. Rev., Chem. Abstr. **CODEN** GSBUDO.

GEC JOURNAL OF SCIENCE & TECHNOLOGY CEASED. VFOAT G.E.C. Journal of Science & Technology, GEC Journal of Science and Technology, General Electric Company Journal of Science. Began with V. 39, No. 2. Ceased with V. 49, No. 1. 0302-2587. Periodical. UK. ty. **Ind/Abst** Eng. Index Annu., Eng. Index Mon., Eng. Index Bioeng. Abstr., Eng. Index Energy Abstr., World Text Abstr., Coal Abstr., Ship Abstr., Int. Aerosp. Abstr., Comput. Control Abstr., Electr. Electron. Abstr., Sci. Abstr. Sect. A. Phys. Abstr., Energy Res. Abstr., Electron. Pub. Abstr., Met. Abstr., World Alum. Abstr. **CODEN** GJSTA6. *Journal of Science & Technology.*

GENDAI KAGAKU RONSO. VFOAT Gendaikagaku Ronso. No. 1- (1967)-. 0389-956X. Periodical. JA. Japanese (some text in English). an. Gendai Kagaku Kenkyukai, c/o Chiba Keiai Gakuen, 5-21 Anagawa 1-chome, Chiba-shi 260 Japan.

GENERAL INFORMATION PROGRAMME - UNISIST NEWSLETTER. Main/Corp UNESCO. General Information Programme. VFOAT Unisist Newsletter. V. 7-. 0379-2218. Periodical. FR. English. ir. c/o C Coudert-Schklowski, General Information Programme, UNESCO, Place Fontenoy, 75700 Paris France. **LC** Q223. **DD** 025.04. **NLM** Z 1007 G326. *Bibliography, Documentation, Terminology,* 0523-2821 UNISIST Newsletter.

GENERAL SCIENCE INDEX. *See* Indexes/Abstracts.

GEORGIA JOURNAL OF SCIENCE. (GEORGIA JOURNAL OF SCIENCE). V. 35, No. 1-. 0147-9369. Periodical. US. English. qt. Georgia Academy of Science, Mercer University, Physics Department, Macon GA 31207. Tel (404)542-1555. Ed G L Plummer. **Ind/Abst** Coal Abstr., Biol. Abstr., GeoRef, Chem. Abstr., Bibliogr. Agric., Energy Res. Abstr. **CODEN** GJSCDQ. bk rev. adv acc. Circ 1,000. Results of studies and investigations. *Bulletin of the Georgia Academy of Science.*

GEOSCIENCE AND MAN. 0072-1395. Monographic Series. US. English. ir. Geoscience Publications, 238 Geology Building-Louisiana State University, Baton Rouge LA 70803. Tel (504)388-6245. **Ind/Abst** GeoRef, Bibliogr. Index Geol., Pollut. Abstr. Indexes, Ocean. Abstr. **CODEN** GSCMA2. Scholarly papers published in one volume on subjects in geography, anthropology, or archaeology; not a journal, but a series of publications.

GHANA JOURNAL OF SCIENCE. (GHANA JOURNAL OF SCIENCE: A JOINT PUBLICATION OF THE COUNCIL FOR SCIENTIFIC AND INDUSTRIAL RESEARCH AND THE GHANA SCIENCE ASSOCIATION). V. 1- Oct. 1961-. 0016-9544. Periodical. GH. English. qt. Ghana Science Association, University of Ghana, Legon Ghana. **Ind/Abst** Life Sci. Collect., Sociol. Abstr., Soc. Welf. Soc. Plan./Policy Soc. Dev., GeoRef, Bibliogr. Agric., Biol. Abstr., Chem. Abstr., Bibliogr. Index Geol. **NLM** W1 GH373. **CODEN** GHJSAC.

GMRMLN UPDATE. VFOAT G.M.R.M.L.N. Update. VAT Greater Midwest Regional Medical Library Network Update. No. 1 (Apr. 1984)-. 0743-9008. Periodical. US. English. ir. $2.00 Members, $2.50 Non-members. GMRMLN Management Office, Library of Health Sciences, Health Sciences Center, University of Illinois at Chicago, PO Box 7509, Chicago IL 60680. **DD** 500. *MHSLN Update,* 0277-9994.

GNSI NEWSLETTER. Main/Corp Guild of Natural Science Illustrators. VAT Guild of Natural Science Illustrators Newsletter. 0199-5464. Periodical. US. English. mo. Free to Members. Guild of Natural Science Illustrators Inc, PO Box 652, Ben Franklin Station, Washington DC 20044.

GOTTINGISCHE GELEHRTE ANZEIGEN. Vol. 1-. 0017-1549. Periodical. GW. German. sa. Vandenhoeck & Ruprecht, Postfach 3753, Theaterstr 13, D 3400 Goettingen West Germany. Tel 0551/65061. **LC** AS182. (cum index). adv acc.

GOVERNMENT R & D REPORT. VAT Government Research and Development Report. V. 1- Feb. 1, 1974-. 0161-1127. Periodical. US. English. sm. $80.00. MIT Station, PO Box 284, Cambridge MA 02139. **LC** Q180.U5. **DD** 353.0081.

GOVERNMENT REPORTS ANNUAL INDEX. *See* Indexes/Abstracts.

GOVERNMENT RESEARCH CENTERS DIRECTORY. *See* Yearbooks, Almanacs, Directories.

GRADUATE SCIENCE EDUCATION STUDENT SUPPORT AND POSTDOCTORALS. Main/Corp National Science Foundation (U.S.). **Series/Titl** Surveys of Science Resources Series. 1972-. 0094-7881. US. English. an. Superintendent of Documents, US Government Printing Office, Washington DC 20402. **LC** Q183.3.A1. **DD** 507.173. *Graduate Student Support and Manpower Resources in Graduate Science Education,* 0092-6604.

GRANTS AND AWARDS. (GRANTS AND AWARDS FOR FISCAL YEAR . . .). **Main/Corp** National Science Foundation (U.S.). Began with 1963/64. 0565-825X. US. English. an. Superintendent of Documents, US Government Printing Office, Washington DC 20402. **LC** Q180.U5. **DD** 507. **NLM** Q 180.U5 G764. Vols. for (1983-) distributed to depository libraries in microfiche.

GUIA DE REUNIONES CIENTIFICAS Y TECNICAS EN ARGENTINA. 0301-7567. AG. Spanish. ir. **LC** Q101.

GUIDE BOOK FOR FIRST YEAR STUDENTS IN THE SCHOOL OF NATURAL SCIENCES. Main/Corp University of Zambia. School of Natural Sciences. English. ir. University of Zambia, PO Box 2379, Lusaka Zambia. **LC** Q183.4.Z33. **DD** 507.116894.

GUIDE TO INTERNATIONAL DATA EXCHANGE THROUGH THE WORLD DATA CENTRES. Main/Corp International Council of Scientific Unions. Panel on World Data Centres (Geophysical and Solar). 1st- 1957-. US. English.

GUIDE TO PROGRAMS. Main/Corp National Science Foundation (U.S.). US. English. an. US Government Printing Office, Superintendent of Documents, Washington DC 20402. Tel (202)783-3238. **LC** Q180.U5. **DD** 507.2073. **NLM** Q 181.A1 N279G.

GUIDE TO RUSSION SCIENTIFIC PERIODICAL LITERATURE. Main/Corp Brookhaven National Laboratory. V. 1- 1948-. Periodical. English. ir. **LC** Z7403.

GUIDE TO SCIENTIFIC INSTRUMENTS. Began with Vol. for 1963. 0533-5426. US. English. an. American Association for the Advancement of Science, 1515 Massachusetts Avenue NW, Washington DC 20005. **LC** Q184. **DD** 681.75029473. **NLM** Q 185 G946.

GUIDE TO SCIENTIFIC INSTRUMENTS. 1978/79-. 0533-5426. US. English. an. $10.00. American Association for the Advancement of Science, 1333 H Street NW, Washington DC 20005. Tel (202)326 6400. *Guide to Scientific Instruments,* 0533-5426.

GUIDES TO INFORMATION SOURCES IN SCIENCE AND TECHNOLOGY. *See* Bibliographies.

GUNMA DAIGAKU KYOIKU GAKUBU KIYO : SHIZEN KAGAKU HEN. VFOAT Science Reports of the Faculty of Education, Gunma University. V. 15-. 0017-5668. English (Esperanto, or Japanese). an. Gumma Daigaku Kyoikugakubu, 1375 Aramakicho, Maebashi 371 Japan. **Ind/Abst** Chem. Abstr. **LC** Q4. **CODEN** GDSHAU. *Gumma Daigaku Kiyo: Shizen Kagaku Hen.*

HAKUSHI GAKUI ROMBUN NO GAIYO OYOBI SHINSA NO YOSHI. Main/Corp Tokai Daigaku. Rigakubu. Japanese. ir. Tokai Daigaku Rigakubu, Kaname Hiratsuke, Hiratsuka Japan. **LC** Q4.

HANDBOOK - AMERICAN ASSOCIATION FOR THE ADVANCEMENT OF SCIENCE. Main/Corp American Association for the Advancement of Science. 0361-7874. US. English. an. American Association for the Advancement of Science, 1515 Massachusetts Avenue Northwest, Washington DC 20005.

HANDBOOK - MAKERERE UNIVERSITY. SCIENCE FACULTY. Main/Corp Makerere University. Science Faculty. English. ir. Makerere University/Science Faculty, PO Box 7062, Kampala Uganda. **LC** Q183.4.U35. **DD** 507.116761.

HANDBUCH DER GROSSFORSCHUNG. Main/Corp Arbeitsgemeinschaft der Grossforschungseinrichtungen (Germany). 1985/86-. 0174-5026. GW. German. ir. Arbeitsgemeinschaft der Grossforschungseinrichtungen, Ahr-Strasse 45, Wissenschaftszentrum, 5300 Bonn-Bad Godesberg West Germany. **LC** 0180.3. **DD** 506.043.

HANGUK KWAHAK KISULWON HAGWI NONMUN CHOROKCHIP. *See* Indexes/Abstracts.

HANGZHOU DAXUE XUEBAO. ZIRAN KEXUE BAN. (HANG-CHOU TA HSUEH HSUEH PAO. TZU JAN KO HSUEH PAN). VFOAT Journal of Hangzhou University. Natural Science Edition. 0253-3618. Periodical. CC. Chinese. qt. $4.50. China Publication Centre, PO Box 2820, Beijing China. **Ind/Abst** Math. Rev., Chem. Abstr. **LC** Q4. **DD** 505. **CODEN** HHHPD7.

HARVARD CASE HISTORIES IN EXPERIMENTAL SCIENCE. US. English. ir. Harvard University Press, 79 Garden Street, Cambridge MA 02138.

HARVARD MONOGRAPHS IN APPLIED SCIENCE. No. 1-. Monographic Series. US. English. ir. Harvard University Press, 79 Garden Street, Cambridge MA 02138. Tel (617)661-3761.

HARVARD MONOGRAPHS IN THE HISTORY OF SCIENCE. Monographic Series. US. English. ir. Harvard University Press, 79 Garden Street, Cambridge MA 02138. Tel (617)661-3761.

Science (General)

HEBDO SCIENCE. (HEBDO-SCIENCE). 0711-3463. Periodical. CN. French. wk. $300.00 Particuliers. $125.00 Bibliotheques, $60.00 Media. Hebdo-Science, Service d'Information, Hebdo-Science, 1415 East rue Jarry, Montreal Quebec H2E 2Z7 Canada. **DD** 505.

HEIDELBERG SCIENCE LIBRARY. V. 1-. 0073-1595. Monographic Series. US. English. ir. Springer Verlag-New York Inc, 175 5th Avenue, New York NY 10010. **Tel** (212)460-1584. **Ind/Abst** Biol. Abstr. **CODEN** HSCLAA. Studies on molecular and genetic counseling.

HEIDELBERGER JAHRBUCHER. See Yearbooks, Almanacs, Directories.

HELICTITE. 1962. 0017-9973. Periodical. AT. English. sa. 12.00. Helictite, PO Box 183, Broadway NSW Australia 2007. Ed J James and G Cox. **Ind/Abst** GeoRef, Bibliogr. Index Geol. **CODEN** HELIBH. bk rev. adv acc. **Circ** 170. (ctrl). Scientific aspects of speleology, biology, chemistry, geography, geomorphology, history, hydrology, meteorology, photography, and caving techniques.

HERCYNIA. Vol. 1- 1963-. 0018-0637. Periodical. SZ. German. qt $21.47. Kunst & Wissen Erich Bieber, Dufourstrasse 51, CH-8008 Zurich Switzerland. **Tel** 011-41-1-69 44 20. **Ind/Abst** Biol. Abstr., GeoRef, Chem. Abstr. **CODEN** HERCAS. Index published separately - free - automatically sent. Hercynia.

HIROSHIMA DAIGAKU SOGO KAGAKUBU KIYO. 3, JOHO KODO KAGAKU KENKYU. **VFOAT** Joho Kodo Kagaky Kenkyu. Periodical. JA. English (Japanese). an. Hiroshima Daigaku Sogo Kagakubu, 1089 Higashi Sendacho 1-chome, Naka 730, Hiroshima-shi Japan. **LC** Q4.

HISTORIA SCIENTIARUM. (HISTORIA SCIENTIARUM : INTERNATIONAL JOURNAL OF THE HISTORY OF SCIENCE SOCIETY OF JAPAN). No. 19 (Sept. 1980)-. 0285-4821. JA. English (French or German). an. $48.50. Japan Publishing Trading Company Ltd, PO Box 5030, Tokyo International, Tokyo 100-31 Japan. **Ind/Abst** Math. Rev., Am. Hist. Life, Hist. Abstr., Part A, Mod. Hist. Abstr., Hist. Abst., Part B, Twent. Century Abstr. **LC** Q124.6. **DD** 509. **NLM** W1 HI79M. Japanese Studies in the History of Science, 0090-0176.

HISTORICAL STUDIES IN THE PHYSICAL SCIENCES. V. 1- 1969-. 0073-2672. Periodical. US. English. sa. $25.00. University of California Press, 2120 Berkeley Way, Berkeley CA 94720. **Tel** (415)642-4191. Ed John Heilbron. **Ind/Abst** Am. Hist. Life, Hist. Abstr., Part A, Mod. Hist. Abstr., Hist. Abst., Part B, Twent. Century Abstr., Chem. Abstr., Writ. Am. Hist., Hist. Abstr., Recent Publ. Artic. **LC** QC7. **DD** 530.09. **NLM** W1 HI81. **CODEN** HSPSAS. adv acc. **Circ** 500. Articles on the history of the physical sciences. Chymia, 0095-9367.

HISTORY OF SCIENCE. V. 1- 1962-. 0073-2753. Periodical. UK. English. qt. 81.00. Science History Publications, Mill Lane Chalfont, St Giles Bucks HP8 4NR England. **Tel** (02407)2509. Ed R S Porter. **Ind/Abst** Math. Rev., Am. Hist. Life, Hist. Abstr., Part A, Mod. Hist. Abstr., Hist. Abst., Part B, Twent. Century Abstr., Ref. Source, GeoRef, Hist. Abstr. **LC** Q125. **NLM** W1 HI88. **CODEN** HISCAR. bk rev. adv acc. **Circ** 750. Discussion articles on the history of science.

HOJA INFORMATIVA DE LA SECCION DE HISTORIA DE LA CIENCIA Y LA TECNOLOGIA DEL INSTITUTO DE INVESTIGACIONES HISTORICAS, UNIVERSIDAD NACIONAL AUTONOMA DE MEXICO. No. 1 (Oct. 1980)-. MX. Spanish. ir. La Seccion, Comerico y Administracion 35, Mexico 21 DF Mexico.

HOKKAIDO KYOIKU DAIGAKU KIYO. DAI 2-BU, A SUGAKU, BUTSURIGAKU, KAGAKU, KOGAKU-HEN. (HOKKAIDO KYOIKU DAIGAKU KIYO. DAI 2-BU). **VFOAT** Journal of Hokkaido University of Education. 0367-5939. JA. Japanese (English). ir. Hokkaido Kyoiku Daigaku, Nishi 13-chome Minami 24-jo, Chuo-ku Sapporo 064 Japan. **Ind/Abst** Math. Rev., GeoRef. **LC** Q77. **DD** 505. **CODEN** HKDSAE.

THE HOWARD UNIVERSITY JOURNAL OF SCIENCE. V. 1, No. 4- Winter 1973-. US. English. Howard University Journal of Science, PO Box 701, Howard University, Washington DC 20001. Howard University Reviews of Science, 0093-6057.

HOWARD UNIVERSITY REVIEWS OF SCIENCE. (THE HOWARD UNIVERSITY REVIEWS OF SCIENCE). V. 1, No. 3- Nov. 1972-. 0093-6057. US. English. Howard University, Physics Department, Washington DC 20001. **LC** Q1. **DD** 505. Howard University Reviews of Science.

HSIA-MEN TA HSUEH HSUEH PAO. TZU JAN KO HSUEH PAN. **VFOAT** Journal of Xiamen University. Natural Science. 0438-0479. Periodical. Chinese (abstracts in English). qt. Chung-Kuo Kuo Chi Shu Tien, PO Box 2820, Pei-Ching China. **Ind/Abst** Math. Rev. **LC** Q4. **DD** 605.

HSING CHENG YUAN KUO CHIA KO HSUEH WEI YUAN HUI NIEN PAO. 1977-. CH. Chinese. an. Hsing Cheng Yuan Kuo Chia Ko Hsueh Wei Yuan Hui, #2 Kuang-chou Street, Tai-Pei Taiwan. **LC** Q72. **DD** 354.5124900855. Kua Chia Ko Hsueh Wei Yuan Hui Nien Pao.

HSTC BULLETIN. **VAT** History of Science and Technology of Canada Bulletin, Historie des Sciences et Technologie Canadiennes. Bulletin. 0228-0086. Periodical. CN. English (articles in French). ty. $10.00. **NLM** W1 HS883M.

HUA-KANG LI KO HSUEH PAO. **VFOAT** Hwa Kang Journal of Sciences. V. 1, (June 1981)-. Periodical. CH. Chinese (English). an. College of Sciences, Chinese Culture University, Hwa Kang Yang Ming Shan Taipei Republic of China. **LC** Q4. **DD** 505.

THE HUDSON INSTITUTE REPORT TO THE MEMBERS. 0073-3776. US. English. an. Hudson Institute, Croton-on-Hudson NY 10520. **LC** Q180.U5. **DD** 001.43.

IBARAKI DAIGAKU KYOIKUGAKUBU KIYO : SHIZEN KAGAKU. **VFOAT** Bulletin of the Faculty of Education, Ibaraki University : Natural Science. No. 1-. JA. Japanese (abstracts in English). ir. Ibaraki Daigaku, 1-1 Bunkyo, Mito 310 Japan. **LC** Q4. Ibaraki Daigaku Kyoikugakubu Kiyo.

IBERICA. ACTUALIDAD CIENTIFICA. Periodical. SP. Spanish. mo. $25.00. Iberica, Apartado 23095, Barcelona Spain.

ICR ACTS & FACTS. Main/Corp Institute for Creation Research. **VFOAT** Acts & Facts. **VAT** Institute for Creation Research Acts and Facts. 0196-8068. Periodical. US. English. mo. Free. Institute for Creation Research, 2716 Madison Avenue, San Diego CA 92116.

IIASA PUBLICATIONS. Main/Corp International Institute for Applied Systems Analysis. Began in 1974. Periodical. AU. English. 150.00. International Institute Applied System Analysis, Publication Department, A-2361 Laxenburg Australia. **Tel** (02236)71521/483. Publishes publications dealing with all aspects of systems analysis and cooperates with other publishers on specific ventures.

ILLINOIS HEALTH SCIENCES LIBRARIES SERIAL HOLDINGS LIST. See Library and Information Science.

IMAGING SCIENCE. 0732-6726. Periodical. US. English. qt. $86.00. Crane Russak, 3 East 47th Street, New York NY 10017.

IMPACT OF SCIENCE ON SOCIETY. V. 1- April/June 1950-. 0019-2872. Periodical. English. qt. $22.00. UNIPUB, PO Box 1222, Ann Arbor MI 48106. **Tel** (800)521-8110. **Ind/Abst** Sociol. Abstr., Soc. Welf. Soc. Plan./Policy Soc. Dev., Coal Abstr., Energy Inf. Abstr., Environ. Abstr., Int. Aerosp. Abstr., GeoRef, Chem. Abstr., Biol. Abstr., Nuci. Sci. Abstr., Public Aff. Inf. Serv. Bull., Curr. Index J. Educ., Soc. Sci. Index, Soc. Sci. Citation Index, Lang. Lang. Behav. Abstr., Bibliogr. Index Geol., Sci. Cit. Index, Abr. Ed. **LC** Q1. **DD** 505. **NLM** W1 IM595. **CODEN** ISSOA8. The continuing impact of science and technology on the quality of life and the interdependence of science and human developments.

IMPACT OF SCIENCE ON SOCIETY. (AL-ILM WA-AL-MUJTAMA). Periodical. Arabic. qt. 0.25 Single Issue. Markaz Matabuat Al-Yunisku, 1 Shari Talat Harb Midan Al-Tahrir, Al-Qahirah Egypt. **LC** Q1.

IMPACT OF SCIENCE ON SOCIETY. (KWAHAK KWA SAHOE). **VFOAT** Impact of Science on Society. Vol. 1- (1984, 7)-. Periodical. KO. Korean (translation of: Impact of Science on Society). qt. 6.000. Yunesuko Hanguk Wiwonhoe, 50-16 Myong-dong Chung-ku, Seoul Korea. **LC** Q175.4.

IMPACT, SCIENCE ET SOCIETE. 0304-2944. Periodical. French. qt. $10.64. UNESCO, 7 Place de Fontenoy, 75700 Paris France. **Ind/Abst** Point Repere, Energy Res. Abstr. **LC** Q124.6. **DD** 301.243.

IN TOUCH. Main/Corp Science Council of Canada. **VFOAT** Resonances. Vol. 1, No. 1 (Oct./Nov. 1983)-. 0826-0648. Periodical. CN. English (text in French with French text on inverted pages). bm. Science Council of Canada, 100 Metcalf Street, Ottawa Ontario K1P 5M1 Canada. **DD** 509.71.

INDEX TO RESEARCH FRONTS IN ISI/GEOSCITECH. See Indexes/Abstracts.

INDEX TO SCIENTIFIC & TECHNICAL PROCEEDINGS. See Indexes/Abstracts.

INDEX TO SCIENTIFIC REVIEWS. See Indexes/Abstracts.

AN INDEX TO STANDARD INTEREST PROFILES IN SCIENCE AND TECHNOLOGY. See Indexes/Abstracts.

INDIAN GEOSCIENCE ABSTRACTS. See Indexes/Abstracts.

INDIAN JOURNAL OF HISTORY OF SCIENCE. **VFOAT** I.J.H.S. Vol. 1, No. 1 (May 1966)-. 0019-5235. Periodical. II. English. sa. $100.00. Asia Books & Periodicals Company, 11/3 Darya Genj Ansari Road, New Delhi 110002 India. **Ind/Abst** Math. Rev., GeoRef, Art Archaeol. Tech. Abstr., Chem. Abstr., Bibliogr. Index Geol. **LC** Q125. **DD** 509. **NLM** W1 IN209C. **CODEN** IJHSA4.

INDIAN SCIENCE ABSTRACTS. See Indexes/Abstracts.

INDIAN SCIENCE INDEX. See Indexes/Abstracts.

INDIANA UNIVERSITY PUBLICATIONS. SCIENCE SERIES. **VFOAT** Science Series. No. 1-. Monographic Series. US. English. ir. Indiana University Press, 10 and Morton Street, Bloomington IN 47405.

INDICE ESPANOL DE CIENCIA Y TECNOLOGIA. See Indexes/Abstracts.

INDUSTRY AND SCIENTIFIC RESEARCH MEMORANDA. Main/Corp Great Britain. Parliament. House of Commons. Select Committee on Science and Technology. Science Sub-Committee. **VFOAT** Memoranda Submitted to the Select Committee on Science and Technology (Science Sub-Committee). UK. English. Her Majesty's Stationery Office, PO Box 276, London SW8 5DT England. **LC** Q41. **DD** 338.941.

INFO JOURNAL. 0019-0144. Periodical. US. English. ir. $10.00. Info Journal, PO Box 367, Arlington VA 22210. **Tel** (703)522-9232. Ed Raymond D Manners. bk rev. adv acc. **Circ** 850. Microform. Publishes papers, notes and comments on anomalous events that are unexplainable within the context of conventional science.

INFORMACION CIENTIFICA Y TECNOLOGICA. V. 1- (NO. 1-). Periodical. Spanish. sm. Censejo Nacional de Ciencia y Tecnologia, Insurgentes Sur 1814 - 60 Piso, Mexico City Mexico.

INFORMATIK. 16. Volume. Periodical. SZ. German. bm. $28.01. Kunst & Wissen Erich Bieber, Dufourstrasse 51, CH-8008 Zurich Switzerland. **Tel** 011-41-1-69 44 20. **Ind/Abst** Comput. Control Abstr., Energy Res. Abstr., Electr. Electron. Abstr., Libr. Inf. Sci. Abstr., Sci. Abstr. Sect. A. Phys. Abstr., Phys. Abstr. **LC** Q224.3.G3. Ziid Zeitschrift.

INFORMATION AND CONTROL. V. 1- Sept. 1957-. 0019-9958. Periodical. US. English. mo. Academic Press, 4805 Sand Lake Road, Orlando FL 32819. **Tel** (305)345-4100. **Ind/Abst** Comput. Control Abstr., Electr. Electron. Abstr., Sci. Abstr. Sect. A. Phys. Abstr., Eng. Index, Bioeng. Abstr., Eng. Index Energy Abstr., MLA Int. Bibliogr. Books Artic. Mod. Lang. Lit., Sci. Cit. Index, Abr. Ed., Eng. Index Annu., Int. Aerosp. Abstr., Eng. Index Mon., Math. Rev., Nuci. Sci. Abstr., Comput. Abstr., Phys. Abstr., Comput. Rev., Eng. Index. **LC** Q350. **DD** 006.05. **NLM** Q 180 I43. **CODEN** IFCNA4.

INFORMATION RESEARCH AND RESOURCE REPORTS. Vol. 1-. Monographic Series. US. English. ir. Elsevier Science Publishing Company Inc, 52 Vanderbilt Avenue, New York NY 10017. **Ind/Abst** Comput. Control Abstr., Electr. Electron. Abstr., Sci. Abstr. Sect. A. Phys. Abstr.

Science (General)

L'INFORMATION SCIENTIFIQUE. Yearly V. 3-. Periodical. FR. French. ir. J B Brailliere et Fils, 10 rue Thenard, 75005 Paris France. *Information des Sciences Physiques.*

INFORMATIONEN. Main/Corp Universitat Bielefeld. German. ir. Universitat Bielefeld, Wellenberg 5, Postfach 8640, 48 Bielefeld West Germany. LC Q180.G4.

INFORMATIONSBLATT FUR DEUTSCHE WISSENSCHAFTLER IM AUSLAND. GW. German. ir. W E Saarbach GMBH, Postfach 101610, D-5000 Koeln 1 West Germany. Tel 02 21-23 46 31. LC Q49. DD 509.43.

INFORMATIVO - SNI. Main/Corp Sistema Nacional de Informacion. VAT Informativo - Sistema Nacional de Informacion. V. 1- May 1972-. 0302-4830. Spanish. ir. Sistana Nacionel de Informacion, Calle 13 No 7-46, Officina 203 Apartado Aereo, Bogota Columbia. LC Q224.3.C7.

INFORMATSIONNYI UKAZATEL BIBLIOGRAFICHESKIKH RABOT, VYPOLNENNYKH BIBLIOTEKAMI I NAUCHNYMI UCHREZHDENIIAMI SISTEMY AN USSR V . . . GODU. See Indexes/Abstracts.

INFORME CIENCIA E ARTE. BOLETIM. (INFORME CIENCIA E ARTE : BOLETIM). V. 1- Sept./Oct. 1973-. 0100-0365. Portuguese. ir. Universidade Federal de Sao Carlos, KM 235 Caica Postal 384, Sao Carlos Brazil. LC AS80.U55.

INFORME - UNIVERSIDAD CENTRAL DE VENEZUELA, FACULTAD DE INGENIERIA, ESCUELA DE GEOLOGIA Y MINAS, LABORATORIO DE PETROGRAFIA Y GEOQUIMICA. Main/Corp Venezuela. Universidad Central, Caracas. Escuela de Geologia y Minas. 0378-1836. Monographic Series. VE. Multilingual (English and Spanish). ir. Universidad Central Caracas, Apartado 50926, Caracas 105 Venezuela. Ind/Abst Chem. Abstr., GeoRef. CODEN IUCGDN.

INSIDE R & D. See Technology (General).

INSTRUCTIONAL SCIENCE. See Education (General).

INSTRUMENT ABSTRACTS. See Indexes/Abstracts.

INTER-SOCIETY COLOR COUNCIL NEWSLETTER. 0300-7588. Periodical. US. English. bm. $35.00. Inter-Society Color Council Inc, 1100 East-West Highway, Silver Springs MD 20910. Tel (301)589-4747. Ed Mary Ellen. Information on color as it relates to the scientists, artist and teacher.

INTERCIENCIA. V. 1-May/June 1976-. 0378-1844. Periodical. VE. English, Portuguese, and Spanish. bm. 76.00. Interciencia, Apartado de Correo 51842, Caracas 1050A Venezuela. Tel (582)92-32-24. Ed Marcel Roche. Ind/Abst Coal Abstr., Int. Aerosp. Abstr., Biol. Abstr., GeoRef, Chem. Abstr., Energy Res. Abstr., Energy Inf. Abstr., Environ. Abstr., Life Sci. Collect., Sci. Cit. Index, Abr. Ed., Bibliogr. Index Geol. LC Q4. DD 505. NLM W1 IN671. CODEN ITRCDB. bk rev. adv acc. Circ 1,500. Problems related to development with Latin America: amazonia, nutrition, energy, health and population, arid land, marine and earth sciences, tropical agriculture and environmental problems, science policy, etc.

INTERFACE. (INTERFACE : LA REVUE DE L'ACFAS). 0826-4864. Periodical. CN. French. bm. Association Canadienne-Francaise pour l'Avancement des Science, 2730 Cote Ste-Catherine, Montreal Quebec H3T 1B7 Canada. DD 507.20714. *Bulletin de l'A C F A S, 0066-8850.*

INTERNATIONAL ANNUAL JOURNAL OF ARTS, SCIENCES, ENGINEERING, AGRICULTURE, AND TECHNOLOGY. 0749-0682. Periodical. US. English. an. $200.00. Siveast Consultants, 410 South State Street, Dover DE 19901. Ed C V Ramasastry. bk rev. adv acc. Aims to provide link between research and practice between researchers, university professors, consultants from various specializations, tries bringing together new ideas and research findings.

INTERNATIONAL GUIDE TO PERIODICALS & REFERENCE WORKS. Main/Corp Maxwell Scientific International. VFOAT International Guide to Periodicals and Reference Works. 1984/85-. 0742-3985. US. English. be. Free. Maxwell Scientific International, Fairview Park, Elmsford NJ 10523. *Guide to Collections of International Periodicals, 0197-6605.*

INTERNATIONAL JOURNAL OF CONTROL. V. 1- Jan. 1965-. 0020-7179. Periodical. UK. English. mo. $690.00. Taylor & Francis Ltd, 242 Cherry Street, Philadelphia PA 19106. Tel (215)238-0939. Ed A G J MacFarlane. Ind/Abst Electron. Commun. Abstr. J., ISMEC Bull., Pollut. Abstr. Indexes, Saf. Sci. Abstr. J., Eng. Index Mon., Eng. Index Bioeng. Abstr., Eng. Index Energy Abstr., Energy Inf. Abstr., Environ. Abstr., Comput. Control Abstr., Electr. Electron. Abstr., Sci. Abstr. Sect. A. Phys. Abstr., Chem. Abstr., Eng. Index Annu., Eng. Index Mon., Int. Aerosp. Abstr., Math. Rev., Nuci. Sci. Abstr., Sci. Cit. Index, Abr. Ed., Eng. Index, Phys. Abstr. CODEN IJCOAZ. Attracts articles reporting on the major problems of modern control theory and its applications that arise in a broad range of generalized systems. *Journal of Electronics and Control.*

INTERNATIONAL JOURNAL OF MODELLING & SIMULATION. (INTERNATIONAL JOURNAL OF MODELLING & SIMULATION : A JOURNAL OF THE INTERNATIONAL ASSOCIATION OF SCIENCE AND TECHNOLOGY FOR DEVELOPMENT, IASTED). VFOAT International Journal of Modelling and Simulation. Vol. 1, No. 1-. 0228-6203. Periodical. US. English (French or German). qt. $80.00 Libraries, Government Departments and Establishments. ACTA Press, PO Box 2482, Anaheim CA 92804. LC TA342. DD 001.434.

INTERNATIONAL JOURNAL OF SYSTEMS SCIENCE. VFOAT Systems Science. Began with July 1970 issue. 0020-7721. Periodical. UK. English. mo. $560.00. Taylor & Francis Ltd, 242 Cherry Street, Philadelphia PA 19106. Tel (215)238-0939. Ed B Porter. Ind/Abst Electron. Commun. Abstr. J., ISMEC Bull., Pollut. Abstr. Indexes, Saf. Sci. Abstr. J., Eng. Index Annu., Eng. Index Mon., Eng. Index Bioeng. Abstr., Eng. Index Energy Abstr., Life Sci. Collect., Excerpta Med., Int. Aerosp. Abstr., Comput. Control Abstr., Electr. Electron. Abstr., Sci. Abstr. Sect. A. Phys. Abstr., Biol. Abstr., Math. Rev., Phys. Abstr., Sci. Cit. Index, Abr. Ed., Appl. Mech. Rev., Eng. Index. LC QA402. DD 001.6105. NLM W1 1N791M. CODEN IJSYA9. Publishes original contributions on the theory and practice of mathematical modelling, simulation, optimization and control.

INTERNATIONAL SCIENCE REVIEW SERIES. VFOAT ISRS. V. 1-. 0074-7866. Monographic Series. US. English. ir. Gordon & Breach Science Publishing, 50 West 23rd Street, New York NY 10010. Tel (212)206-8900.

INTERNATIONAL SERIES IN THE SCIENCE OF THE SOLID STATE. 0146-5589. Monographic Series. UK. English. ir. Pergamon Press, 395 Sawmill River Road, Elmsford NY 10523. Ind/Abst Comput. Control Abstr., Electr. Electron. Abstr., Sci. Abstr. Sect. A. Phys. Abstr., Chem. Abstr. CODEN ISSTDQ. *International Series of Monographs in the Science of the Solid State, 0146-5570.*

INVENTORIES OF APPARATUS AND MATERIALS FOR TEACHING SCIENCE. Main/Corp Unesco. English. ir. LC Q181. DD 507.8.

INVESTIGATIONS IN SCIENCE EDUCATION. V. 1- Autumn 1974-. Periodical. US. English. qt. $8.00. SMEAC Information Reference Center, 1200 Chambers Road/Room 310, Columbus OH 43212. Tel (614)422-6717. Ed Patricia Blosser. Circ 800. Contains critical reviews and abstracts to research in science education, k-college.

IOWA SCIENCE TEACHERS' JOURNAL. See Education (General) - Theory, Practice of Education.

IOWA STATE JOURNAL OF RESEARCH. VFOAT Journal of Research. 1926. 0092-6345. Periodical. US. English. qt. $20.00. Iowa State University Press, 2121 South State Avenue, Ames IA 50010. Tel (515)294-5280. Ed Duane Isely. Ind/Abst Abstr. Engl. Stud., Life Sci. Collect., Excerpta Med., Biol. Abstr., Chem. Abstr., Sel. Water Resour. Abstr., Bibliogr. Agric., Years Work Eng. Stud. LC Q1. DD 505. CODEN ISJRA6. adv acc. Circ 675. Available on microfiche from University Microfilms International. Research on various topics. *Iowa State Journal of Science, 0021-0684.*

IPSU CHAPCHI MONGNOK. Main/Corp Hanguk Sanop Kyongje Kisul Yonguwon. English (Korean). ir. LC Z7403, Q1.A1.

IRISH JOURNAL OF FOOD SCIENCE AND TECHNOLOGY. See Food & Drink.

ISI ALERT. Main/Corp Institute for Scientific Information. VFOAT Alert. V. 1, No. 1- May 1977-. Periodical. US. English. Institute for Scientific Information, 3501 Market Street, University City, Philadelphia PA 19104. Tel (215)923-3300.

ISIS GUIDE TO THE HISTORY OF SCIENCE. 1st- Ed. US. English. ir. $10.00. University of Pennsylvania ISIS Editorial Office, E F Smith Hall/215 South 34th Street, Philadelphia PA 19104. Tel (215)898-5575. Ed Arnold Thackray. adv acc. Circ 4,500. Official guide to the history of science. A listing with descriptions of the discipline's societies, organizations, publications, scholars, graduate and research programs.

ISOTOPE GEOSCIENCE. V. 1, No. 1 (Mar. 1983)-. 0167-6695. Periodical. English (French, German). ir. $6.75 Institutions, $46.50 Individuals. Elsevier Science Publishers, B V Journals Department, PO Box 211, 1000 AE Amsterdam The Netherlands.

ISR, INDEX TO SCIENTIFIC REVIEWS. See Indexes/Abstracts.

ISR, INTERDISCIPLINARY SCIENCE REVIEWS. (ISR. INTERDISCIPLINARY SCIENCE REVIEWS). VFOAT ISR. V. 1- March 1976-. 0308-0188. Periodical. UK. English. qt. $90.00. J W Arrowsmith Ltd, 71 Winterstroke Road, Bristol BS3 2N England. Tel (0272)667545. Ed A R Michaelis. Ind/Abst Math. Rev., Life Sci. Collect., Excerpta Med., Int. Aerosp. Abstr., GeoRef, Comput. Control Abstr., Electr. Electron. Abstr., Sci. Abstr. Sect. A. Phys. Abstr., Chem. Abstr., Energy Res. Abstr., Sci. Cit. Index, Abr. Ed., Bibliogr. Index Geol. NLM W1 I35D. CODEN ISCRD8. bk rev. adv acc. Circ 800. Interdisciplinary reviews by eminent scientists of current and historic scientific and technological achievements.

ISSUES AND STUDIES - NATIONAL RESEARCH COUNCIL (U.S.). (ISSUES AND STUDIES). Main/Corp National Research Council (U.S.). 1981-1982-. 0733-9046. US. English. an. Office of Information, National Academy of Science, 2101 Constitution Avenue, Washington DC 20418. Ind/Abst Excerpta Med., Chem. Abstr. LC Q180.U5. DD 505. NLM W1 NA628AA. CODEN ISNCDI. *Issues and Current Studies.*

ISSUES IN CANADIAN SCIENCE POLICY CEASED. Began with Vol. 1- Sept. 1974. Ceased with issue for July 1976?. 0318-5311. Periodical. CN. English. ir. $0.93. Receiver General for Canada, Supply and Services Canada, Ottawa Ontario K1A 0S9 Canada. Tel (819)997-2560. LC Q127.C2. DD 338.4750971.

ISSUES IN SCIENCE AND TECHNOLOGY. Vol. 1, No. 1 (Fall 1984)-. 0748-5492. Periodical. US. English. qt. $36.00. Issues in Science and Technology, Reader Services, 2101 Constitution Avenue, Washington DC 20418. Tel (202)334-3318. Ed Allen L Hammond. DD 306. bk rev. adv acc. Circ 15,000. Providing a forum where today's most critical problems can be explored and debated by the nation's best minds.

IZVESTIIA. V. 1- 1957-. 0525-0870. Periodical. BU. Bulgarian. ir. Bulgarski Academiia Naukite Inst, Nauchen Arkhiv, Sofia Bulgaria.

IZVESTIIA. Main/Corp Bulgarska Akademiia Na Naukite, Sofia. Tsentralna Khelmintologichna Laboratoriia. VFOAT Bulletin. 1- 1955-. 0068-371X. Periodical. BU. Bulgarian (summaries in Russian and German, French, or English). ir. Bulgarski Academiia Naukite Institute, Tsentralna Khelmintologichna Laboratoriia, Sofia Bulgaria.

IZVESTIJA AKADEMII NAUK ARMJANSKOJ SSSR. SERIJA TEHNICESKIH NAUK. (IZVESTIIA AKADEMII NAUK ARMIANSKOI SSR. SERIIA TEKHNICHESKIKH NAUK). VFOAT Seriia Tekhnicheskikh Nauk. V. 10, 1 (1957)-. 0002-306X. Periodical. UR. Russian. mo. $10.00. Victor Kamkin Inc, 12224 Parklawn Drive, Rockville MD 20852. Tel (301)881-5973. Ind/Abst Math. Rev., Int. Aerosp. Abstr., Comput. Control Abstr., Electr. Electron. Abstr., Sci. Abstr. Sect. A. Phys. Abstr., Chem. Abstr. CODEN IATNAK. Index in last issue of volume - attached. *Izvestiia Akademii Nauk Armianskoi SSR.*

Fiziko-Matematicheskie, Estestvennye i Tekhnicheskie Nauki.

IZVESTIJA AKADEMII NAUK BELORUSSKOJ SOVETSKOJ SOCIALISTICESKOJ RESPUBLIKI. (DOKLADY AKADEMII NAUK BSSR). **Main/Corp** Akademiia Navuk Belaruskai SSR. V. 1- July 1956-. 0002-354X. Periodical. UR. Russian (table of contents also in English). mo. $33.50. Victor Kamkin Inc (74875), 12224 Parklawn Drive, Rockville MD 20852. **Tel** (301)881-5973. **Ind/Abst** Math. Rev., Coal Abstr., Abstr. Bull. Inst. Paper Chem., GeoRef, Int. Aerosp. Abstr., Art Archaeol. Tech. Abstr., Met. Abstr., World Alum. Abstr., Chem. Abstr., Bibliogr. Agric. **LC** Q60. **NLM** W1 DO64AD. **CODEN** DBLRAC.

IZVESTIJA AKADEMII NAUK KIRGIZSKOJ SSR *CEASED.* (IZVESTIIA AKADEMII NAUK KIRGIZSKOI SSR). Began 1955-, Ceased 1958?. 0002-3221. Periodical. UR. Russian (added table of contents in Kirghiz and English). bm. **Ind/Abst** Math. Rev., Int. Aerosp. Abstr., GeoRef, Chem. Abstr. **NLM** W1 IZ652L. **CODEN** INKSAD.

IZVESTIJA AKADEMII NAUK KIRGIZSKOJ SSR. (IZVESTIIA AKADEMII NAUK KIRGIZSKOI SSR). **VFOAT** Kyrgyz SSR Ilimder Akademiiasynyn Kabarlary. Began in July 1966. 0002-3221. Periodical. UR. Russian. bm. **Tel** (301)881-5973. **Ind/Abst** Abstr. Bull. Inst. Paper Chem., Int. Aerosp. Abstr. Index in last issue of volume - attached. *Izvestiia Akademii Nauk Kirgizskoi SSR. Seriia Biologicheskikh Nauk, Izvestiia Akademii Nauk Kirgizskoi SSR. Seriia Estestvennykh i Tekhnicheskikh Nauk; Izvestiia Akademii Nauk Kirgizskoi SSR. Seriia Obshchestvennykh Nauk.*

IZVESTIJA AKADEMII NAUK LATVIJSKOJ SSR. SERIJA HIMICESKAJA. (LATVIJAS PSR ZINATNU AKADEMIJAS VESTIS. KIMIJAS SERIJA). **VFOAT** Kimijas Serija, Izvestiia Akademii nauk Latviiskoi SSR. Seriia Khimicheskaia. No. 1 (1961)-. 0002-3248. Periodical. UR. Russian. bm. Victor Kamkin Inc, 12224 Parklawn Drive, Rockville MD 20852. **Tel** (301)881-5973. **Ind/Abst** Abstr. Bull. Inst. Paper Chem., Met. Abstr., World Alum. Abstr., Chem. Abstr. **CODEN** LZAKAM.

IZVESTIJA AKADEMII NAUK TADZIKSKOJ SSR. OTDELENIE FIZIKO-MATEMATICESKIH I GEOLOGICESKO-HIMICESKIH NAUK. (AKHBOROTI AKADEMIIAI FANHOI RSS TOJIKISTON : SHUBAI FANHOI FIZIKAIU MATEMATIKA VA GEOLOGIIAIU KHIMIIA). **VFOAT** Izvestiia Akademii Nauk Tadzhikskoi SSR, Otdelenie Fiziko-Matematicheskikh I Geologichesko-Khimicheskikh Nauk. No. 1 (1959)-. 0002-3485. Periodical. Russian (summaries in Tajik). qt. Victor Kamkin Inc, 12224 Parklawn Drive, Rockville MD 20852. **Tel** (301)881-5973. *Izvestiia.*

JAARVERSLAG. **Main/Corp** South African Council for Scientific and Industrial Research. **VFOAT** Annual Report. 1st- 1945/46-. English. an. **LC** Q180.A55. **DD** 507.2.

JAHRBUCH (SCHWEIZERISCHE NATURFORSCHENDE GESELLSCHAFT. *See* Yearbooks, Almanacs, Directories.

JANYEN GWAHAG DAIHAG NONMUNJIB. (CHAYON KWAHAK TAEHAK NONMUNJIP). **VFOAT** Proceedings of the College of Natural Sciences. 0253-6277. Periodical. KO. Korean (English). ir. College of Natural Sciences, Seoul National University, 56 Shinlim Dong, Kwanak Ku 151, Seoul South Korea. **Ind/Abst** Math. Rev., Chem. Abstr. **LC** Q4. **CODEN** CKTNDR.

JAYNE LECTURES. 1961-. Monographic Series. US. English. an. American Philosophical Society, Independence Square, Philadelphia PA 19106. **LC** Q11. **DD** 081. *Jayne Memorial Lecture.*

JE ME PETITDERBROUILLE. (JE ME PETITDEBROUILLE : JOURNAL DU CLUB DES PETITS DEBROUILLARDS). No. 1 (Jan. 1982)-. 0714-4067. Periodical. CN. French. ir. $5.42. Club des Petits Debrouillards, 1415 East rue Jarry, Montreal Quebec H2E 2Z7 Canada. **Tel** (514)374-0173. **DD** 500.

JEUNES SCIENTIFIQUES *CEASED.* Oct. 1975-May? 1980. 0319-4779. Periodical. CN. French. ir. Conseil de la Jeunesse Scientifique, 1415 East rue Jarry, Montreal Quebec H2E 2Z7 Canada. **DD** 505.

JORNAL SUL-AMERICANO DE BIOCIENCIAS. **VFOAT** South American Journal of Bio-Sciences. Began with: 2 (2-4), published 1980. 0100-7319. Periodical. Portuguese. ir. $20.00. **Ind/Abst** Excerpta Med. **NLM** W1. *Jornal Sul-Americano de Medicina.*

JOURNAL AND PROCEEDINGS OF THE ROYAL SOCIETY OF NEW SOUTH WALES. **Main/Corp** Royal Society of New South Wales, Sydney. V. 1- 1867-. 0035-9173. AT. English. sa. $19.18. Royal Society of New South Wales, PO Box N112 Grosvenor Street, New South Wales 2000 Australia. **Ed** M Krysko. **Ind/Abst** Bibliogr. Agric., Chem. Abstr., Nuci. Sci. Abstr. **CODEN** JPRSA5. **Circ** 900. Research papers on all branches of science, earth sciences, biology, astronomy, chemistry, physics, mathematics and agriculture, as well as invited lectures on science.

JOURNAL - ANDHRA PRADESH AKADEMI OF SCIENCES. **Main/Corp** Andhra Pradesh Akademi of Sciences. II. English. ir. Andhra Pradesh Akademi of Sciences, c/o Osmania University Campus, Hyderabad-7 India. **LC** Q1. **DD** 505.

JOURNAL CHICOBI. SECTION INFORMATION. **Main/Corp** Camp-Ecole Chicobi. First issue in Nov. 1972?. 0318-4218. CN. French. qt. $1. Camp-Ecole Chicobi Guyenne, Abitibi-Ouest, Quebec J0Y 1L0 Canada. **DD** 500.1071071413.

JOURNAL FOR THE HISTORY OF ARABIC SCIENCE. **VFOAT** Majallat Tarikh Al-Ulum Al-Arabiyah. V. 1- May 1977-. 0379-2927. Periodical. English (Arabic, French or German). sa. $10.00. **Tel** (21)236130. **Ind/Abst** Math. Rev. **LC** Q127.A5. **DD** 509.17671. **NLM** W1 JO399P. adv acc. An international review devoted exclusively to the history of Arabic-Islamic science: exact sciences, technology, applied sciences and medical sciences.

JOURNAL - FORENSIC SCIENCE. (JOURNAL - THE FORENSIC SCIENCE SOCIETY). **Main/Corp** Forensic Science Society. V. 1- 1960-. 0015-7368. Periodical. UK. English. bm. $135.00. Forensic Science Society, PO Box 40 Harrogate, North Yorkshire HG1 1QL England. **Tel** (0423)56068. **Ed** W J Tilstone. **Ind/Abst** Index Med., Chem. Abstr., Sci. Cit. Index, Abr. Ed., Leg. Resour. Index, Curr. Law Index. **NLM** WI JO42. **CODEN** FSSJAS. bk rev. adv acc. **Circ** 2,500. The application of science to the investigation of crime.

JOURNAL OF BANGLADESH ACADEMY OF SCIENCES. **Main/Corp** Bangladesh Academy of Sciences. V. 1-. 0378-8121. Periodical. BG. English. ir. $20.00. Editor, Journal of Bangladesh Academy of Sciences, Department of Chemistry, Dacca University, Dacca 2 Bangladesh. **Tel** 315991 500010. **Ed** S Z Haider. **Ind/Abst** Comput. Control Abstr., Electr. Electron. Abstr., Sci. Abstr. Sect. A. Phys. Abstr., Chem. Abstr. **LC** Q80.B3. **DD** 505. **CODEN** JBACDF. **Circ** 500. (ctrl). Covers chemistry, biochemistry, biological sciences, mathematics, electronics, physics, botany, earth sciences, engineering, medical sciences, and energy.

JOURNAL OF CEREAL SCIENCE. Vol. 1, No. 1 (Jan. 1983)-. 0733-5210. Periodical. UK. English. qt. $98.00. Academic Press, 4805 Sand Lake Road, Orlando FL 32819. **Tel** (305)345-4100.

JOURNAL OF CHEMICAL TECHNOLOGY AND BIOTECHNOLOGY. BIOTECHNOLOGY. **VFOAT** Biotechnology. Vol. 33B, No. 1 (Mar. 1983)-. 0264-3421. Periodical. UK. English. mo. 70.00 Domestic, $157.00. Blackwell Scientific Publications, PO Box 88, Osney Mead, Oxford OX2 OEL England. **Tel** (0865)240201. **Ed** J Pirt. **Ind/Abst** Excerpta Med., Life Sci. Collect., Pestdoc, Ringdoc, Vetdoc, Sel. Water Resour. Abstr., Minproc, Coal Abstr. **LC** TP248.2. **DD** 620.805. **NLM** W1. **CODEN** JTBBD7. adv acc. **Circ** 1,150. Publishes in-depth review articles and research papers on the various aspects of chemical technology and biotechnology, emphasising interactions of science, technology and economics. *Journal of Chemical Technology and Biotechnology, 0142-0356.*

JOURNAL OF COLLEGE SCIENCE TEACHING. **VFOAT** College Science Teaching. V. 1- Oct. 1971-. 0047-231X. Periodical. US. English. bm. $25.00. National Science Teachers Association, 1742 Connecticut Avenue NE, Washington DC 20009. **Ind/Abst** Educ. Index, Ref. Source, Chem. Abstr., Curr. Index J. Educ., Media Rev. Dig., Biol. Abstr. **LC** Q183.U6. **DD** 507.1173. **CODEN** JSCTBN.

JOURNAL OF FOOD SCIENCE AND TECHNOLOGY. *See* Nutrition and Dietetics.

JOURNAL OF NATURAL SCIENCES AND MATHEMATICS. 0022-2941. Periodical. PK. English. sa. $15.00. Government College Lahore, c/o Professor Shaftav Aftab, MG Education and Physics Department, Lohore Pakistan. **Ind/Abst** Chem. Abstr., Math. Rev., Nuci. Sci. Abstr. **LC** Q1. **DD** 505. **CODEN** JNSMAC.

THE JOURNAL OF NEUROSCIENCE. *See* Medicine - Neurology.

THE JOURNAL OF PHOTOGRAPHIC SCIENCE. *See* Photography & Photographs.

JOURNAL OF PHYSICAL AND CHEMICAL REFERENCE DATA. V. 1- 1972-. 0047-2689. US. English. qt. $25.00 Members, $75.00 Nonmembers. American Chemical Society, 1155 165th Street NW, Washington DC 20056. **Ind/Abst** Comput. Control Abstr., Electr. Electron. Abstr., Sci. Abstr. Sect. A. Phys. Abstr., Spin, Chem. Abstr., Curr. Phys. Index, Nuci. Sci. Abstr., Appl. Sci. Technol. Index, Energy Res. Abstr. **LC** Q199. **DD** 530.0212. **NLM** W1 JO832K. **CODEN** JPCRBU. (cum index).

JOURNAL OF POLYMER SCIENCE. Periodical. US. English. mo. John Wiley & Sons Inc, 605 Third Avenue, New York NY 10158. **Tel** (800)526-5368. **Ind/Abst** Appl. Mech. Rev., Chem. Abstr., Sci. Cit. Index, Abr. Ed., Int. Aerosp. Abstr., Electr. Electron. Abstr., Phys. Abstr., Comput. Control Abstr., Eng. Index.

JOURNAL OF PURE AND APPLIED SCIENCES. *See* Engineering.

JOURNAL OF RESEARCH IN SCIENCE TEACHING. V. 1- Mar. 1963-. 0022-4308. Periodical. US. English. ir. John Wiley and Sons Inc, 605 Third Avenue, New York NY 10158. **Tel** (212)850-6000. **Ind/Abst** Educ. Index, Psychol. Abstr., Bibliogr. Index, Soc. Sci. Citation Index, Curr. Index J. Educ., Chem. Abstr. **LC** Q181.A1. **DD** 507. **CODEN** JRSTAR.

JOURNAL OF SCIENCE AND MATHEMATICS EDUCATION IN SOUTHEAST ASIA. *See* Education (General).

JOURNAL OF SCIENCE AND TECHNOLOGY. V. 1- Jan. 1977-. 0250-5339. Periodical. PK. English. ir. $10.00. University of Peshawar, Peshawar Pakistan. **Ind/Abst** Chem. Abstr. **LC** Q80.P3. **DD** 505. **CODEN** JSTPDU.

JOURNAL OF SCIENTIFIC & INDUSTRIAL RESEARCH. **VFOAT** Journal of Scientific and Industrial Research. V. 1- Oct. 1942-. 0022-4456. Periodical. II. English. mo. 120.00 Domestic, 23.00 England, $40.00 US. Indian Books and Periodicals Syndicate, B-5/62 Dev Nagar P L Road Karol Bagh, New Delhi 110005 India. **Ed** S P Ambasta and S S Saksena. **LC** T1. **CODEN** JSIRAC. Index published separately - free - automatically sent. bk rev. adv acc. **Circ** 1,100. The journal is one of India's leading general science periodicals carrying critical review articles on topics of current interest in various disciplines of science and technology.

JOURNAL OF THE ARIZONA-NEVADA ACADEMY OF SCIENCE. **VAT** Journal of the Arizona Nevada Academy of Science. Began in Feb. 1978. 0193-8509. Periodical. US. English. sa. $20.00. Arizona-Nevada Academy of Science, Laboratory of Climatology, Arizona Street, Temple AZ 85281. **Tel** (602)965-6265. **Ed** W Linn Montgomery and David K Elliott. **Ind/Abst** Biol. Abstr., Chem. Abstr., Excerpta Med., Sel. Water Resour. Abstr. **LC** Q11.A72. **DD** 505. **CODEN** JAASDM. bk rev. adv acc. **Circ** 800. Research in environmental and social sciences in the American Southwest and Mexico. *Journal of the Arizona Academy of Science, 0004-1378.*

JOURNAL OF THE COLLEGE OF SCIENCE, KING SAUD UNIVERSITY. **VFOAT** Majallat Kulliyat Al-Ulum, Jamiat Al-Malik Saud. 0735-9799. Periodical. SU. English (summaries in Arabic). sa. $10.00. King Saud University, University Libraries, PO Box 2454, Riyadh Saudi Arabia. **Ind/Abst** Life Sci. Collect. **NLM** W1. *Journal of the College of Science, University of Riyadh.*

THE JOURNAL OF THE COLORADO-WYOMING ACADEMY OF SCIENCE. **Main/Corp** Colorado-Wyoming Academy of Science. Vol. 1, No. 1 (Apr. 1929)-. 0096-2279. US. English. an. University of Northern Colorado, c/o Ronald Plakke, Department of Biology, Greeley CO 80639. **Ind/Abst** GeoRef, Biol. Abstr., Chem. Abstr. **LC** AS36. **DD** 505. **CODEN** JCOQAT.

JOURNAL OF THE FRANKLIN INSTITUTE. V. 5- 1828-. 0016-0032. Periodical. US. English. mo. Pergamon Press, 395 Sawmill River Road, Elmsford NY 10523. **Tel** (914)592-7700. **Ind/**

Abst Electron. Commun. Abstr. J., ISMEC Bull., Pollut. Abstr. Indexes, Saf. Sci. Abstr. J., Eng. Index, Pet. Abstr., Phys. Abstr., Appl. Mech. Rev., Comput. Rev., Eng. Index Energy Abstr., World Surf. Coat. Abstr., GeoRef, Comput. Control Abstr., Electr. Electron. Abstr., Sci. Abstr. Sect. A. Phys. Abstr., Chem. Abstr., Eng. Index Mon., Int. Aerosp. Abstr., Math. Rev., Nuci. Sci. Abstr., Sel. Water Resour. Abstr., Comput. Abstr., Sci. Cit. Index, Abr. Ed. **NLM** W1 J0923. **CODEN** JFINAB. (cum index). *Franklin Journal and American Mechanics' Magazine, 0093-7029.*

JOURNAL OF THE IDAHO ACADEMY OF SCIENCE. **Main/Corp** Idaho Academy of Science. V. 1- 1960-. 0536-3012. Periodical. US. English. sa. $4.00. Lorents Pearson Ricks College, Rexburg ID 83440. **Tel** (208)885-7014. **Ed** Duane Letourneau. bk rev. **Circ** 400. Articles on research in all scientific fields, particularly as pertaining to Idaho.

JOURNAL OF THE INDIAN ACADEMY OF FORENSIC SCIENCES. **Main/Corp** Indian Academy of Forensic Sciences. 0579-4749. Periodical. II. English. sa. $15.00. Journal of Indian Academy of Forensic Sciences, 30 Gora Chand Road, Calcutta 14 India. **Ind/Abst** Chem. Abstr., Nuci. Sci. Abstr. **NLM** W1 JO93N. **CODEN** JIFSAW.

JOURNAL OF THE INDIAN INSTITUTE OF SCIENCE. **Main/Corp** Indian Institute of Science, Bangalore. V. 1- Feb. 1914-. 0019-4964. Periodical. II. English. mo. $40.00. Indian Institute of Science, c/o IISC Library, Bangalore 560012 India. **Tel** 364411-407. **Ed** S Soundranayagam. **Ind/Abst** Bibliogr. Agric., Chem. Abstr., Comput. Control Abstr., Electr. Electron. Abstr., Life Sci. Collect., Math. Rev., Met. Abstr., Pestdoc, Sci. Abstr. Sect. A. Phys. Abstr., Ringdoc, Vetdoc, World Alum. Abstr., Phys. Abstr., Appl. Mech. Rev., Int. Aerosp. Abstr., Biol. Abstr. **LC** Q1. **CODEN** JIISAD. (cum index). bk rev. adv acc. **Circ** 600. Publishes original and review papers in many branches of science and engineering.

JOURNAL OF THE KARNATAK UNIVERSITY. SCIENCE. **Main/Corp** Karnatak University, Dharwar, India. V. 4- 1959-. 0075-5168. English. an. Karnatak University, Dhawar 580003, Karnatak India. **Ind/Abst** Math. Rev., GeoRef, Chem. Abstr. **LC** Q1. **DD** 505. **CODEN** KUJSAB.

JOURNAL OF THE MADRAS UNIVERSITY. SECTION B: CONTRIBUTIONS IN MATHEMATICS, PHYSICAL AND BIOLOGICAL SCIENCES. (JOURNAL OF THE MADRAS UNIVERSITY. SECTION B, SCIENCE). Began in 1943. 0368-3184. Periodical. II. English. ir. University of Madras-Registrar, University Buildings/Chepauk, Madras 600 005 India. **Ind/Abst** Chem. Abstr., Math. Rev. **LC** AS472. **DD** 505. **CODEN** JMUBAG. *Journal of the Madras University.*

JOURNAL OF THE MINNESOTA ACADEMY OF SCIENCE. V. 32- 1964-. 0026-539X. Periodical. US. English. ir. Minnesota Academy of Science, Pioneer Building/Room 410, St Paul MN 55101. **Tel** (613)227-6361. **Ind/Abst** Excerpta Med., GeoRef, Biol. Abstr., Chem. Abstr., Sel. Water Resour. Abstr., Bibliogr. Agric., Bibliogr. Index Geol. **NLM** W1 JO94K. **CODEN** JMNAAC. *Proceedings of the Minnesota Academy of Science.*

JOURNAL OF THE NATIONAL SCIENCE COUNCIL OF SRI LANKA. **Main/Corp** National Science Council of Sri Lanka. V. 1- Aug. 1973-. 0300-9254. Periodical. English. sa. $27.00. Natural Resources Energy and Science Authority of Sri Lanka, 47/5 Maitland Place, Colombo 7 Sri Lanka. **Tel** 596771-3. **Ed** Nimala R Amarasuriya. **Ind/Abst** Biol. Abstr., Chem. Abstr., Bibliogr. Agric. **LC** Q4. **DD** 505. **NLM** W1 JO941PK. **CODEN** JNSCBH. **Circ** 300. Includes research and review papers and short communications in all fields of science and technology mainly by Sri Lankan scientists.

JOURNAL OF THE ROYAL SOCIETY OF WESTERN AUSTRALIA. Began publication with Vol. 11 (1924/1925). 0035-922X. Periodical. AT. English. ir. $11.80. Royal Society of Western Australia, Western Australian Museum, Beafort Street, Perth WA 6000 Australia. **Ed** B Dell. **Ind/Abst** Life Sci. Collect., Biol. Abstr., GeoRef, Chem. Abstr., Bibliogr. Agric. **CODEN** JRSUAU. **Circ** 600. Individual papers on western Australian natural history or other sciences including agriculture and forestry. *Journal and Proceedings of the Royal Society of Western Australia.*

JOURNAL OF THE SCIENCE SOCIETY OF THAILAND. V. 1- Mar. 1975-. 0303-8122. Periodical. English. ir. **Ind/Abst** Energy Inf. Abstr., Environ. Abstr., Comput. Control Abstr., Electr. Electron. Abstr., Sci. Abstr. Sect. A. Phys. Abstr., Chem. Abstr. **NLM** W1 JO954FS. **CODEN** VKSTDB.

JOURNAL OF THE SINGAPORE NATIONAL ACADEMY OF SCIENCE. **Main/Corp** Singapore National Academy of Science. V. 1- 1969-. 0129-3729. Periodical. SI. English. ir. $20.00. 11 Napier Road, Singapore 10 Singapore. **Ind/Abst** Math. Rev., Comput. Control Abstr., Electr. Electron. Abstr., Sci. Abstr. Sect. A. Phys. Abstr., Chem. Abstr. **LC** Q80.S5. **DD** 505. **CODEN** JSNABL.

JOURNAL OF THE SOCIETY OF RESEARCH ADMINISTRATORS. *See* Business - General Management.

JOURNAL OF THE TENNESSEE ACADEMY OF SCIENCE. **Main/Corp** Tennessee Academy of Science. V. 1-. 0040-313X. Periodical. US. English. qt. $15.00. Tennessee Technological University, c/o Dr R Fletcher Jr, PO Box 5044, Cookeville TN 38505. **Tel** (615)528-3853. **Ed** Gus Tomlinson. **Ind/Abst** Life Sci. Collect., Excerpta Med., Coal Abstr., GeoRef, Bibliogr. Agric., Biol. Abstr., Chem. Abstr., Nuci. Sci. Abstr., Sel. Water Resour. Abstr., Sci. Cit. Index, Abr. Ed., Energy Res. Abstr., Bibliogr. Index Geol. **LC** Q11. **DD** 505. **NLM** W1 TE415P. **CODEN** JTASAG. **Circ** 750. (ctrl). Scientific research from all areas of science with more articles in biology. *Transactions of the Tennessee Academy of Science.*

JOURNAL OF THE UNIVERSITY OF KUWAIT. SCIENCE. (THE JOURNAL OF THE UNIVERSITY OF KUWAIT, SCIENCE). **Main/Corp** Jamiat Al-Kuwayt. Kulliyat Al-Ulum. **VFOAT** Majallat Jamiat Al-Kuwayt, Al-Ulum. V. 1- 1974-. 0376-4818. Periodical. English (summaries in Arabic). ir. **Ind/Abst** Math. Rev., Life Sci. Collect., Excerpta Med., Biol. Abstr., Comput. Control Abstr., Electr. Electron. Abstr., Sci. Abstr. Sect. A. Phys. Abstr., Chem. Abstr., Energy Res. Abstr. **LC** Q80.K9. **DD** 505. **CODEN** JUKSD8.

JOURNAL OF THE WASHINGTON ACADEMY OF SCIENCES. **Main/Corp** Washington Academy of Sciences, Washington, D.C. V. 1- July 19, 1911-. 0043-0439. Periodical. US. English. qt. Washington Academy of Science, 1101 North Highland Street, Arlington VA 22201. **Tel** (703)527-4800. **Ind/Abst** Life Sci. Collect., GeoRef, Bibliogr. Agric., Biol. Abstr., Chem. Abstr., Nuci. Sci. Abstr., Sel. Water Resour. Abstr., Bibliogr. Index Geol. **LC** Q11. **DD** 506.2753. **NLM** W1 WA57. **CODEN** JWASA3. *Proceedings of the Washington Academy of Sciences, 0363-1095.*

JOURNAL : SCIENCE. **Main/Corp** Nagpur, India (City). University. V. 1- 1970-. English. ir. 10.00. University, Nagpur-1, Nagpur India. **LC** Q1. **DD** 505.

JOURNAL: SCIENCE, TECHNOLOGY & MEDICINE. **Main/Corp** Jiwaju University. V. 1- Jan. 1973-. English. ir. **Ind/Abst** Math. Rev. **LC** Q73. **DD** 505.

JOURNAL - THAILAND NATIONAL RESEARCH COUNCIL. **Main/Corp** Thailand. National Research Council. Vol. 1 (Nov. 1960)-. English (Thai). sa. 3.00. National Research Council, 196 Phahonyothin Road, Bangkok Thailand. **Tel** 5792285. **Ed** Choompol Swaskiyakorn. (ctrl). The content is divided into 2 parts: natural science and social science including: engineering and industrial research, sociology, physical science, mathematics, philosophy, medical science, law, chemical and pharmaceutical sciences, etc.

JOURNEES SCIENTIFIQUES. **Main/Corp** France. Centre National de Coordination des Etudes et Recherches sur la Nutrition et l'Alimentation. 0532-3606. Periodical. FR. French. ir. Centre National de Coordination des Etudes et Recherches, BP 119 93104 Montreal, Paris Cedex France.

JSPS ANNUAL REPORT. **Main/Corp** Nippon Gakujutsu Shinkokai. English. an. Japan Society for the Promotion of Science, Nihon Gakujutsu Shinkokai Yamato Building 5-3-1 Kojimachi Chiyoda-Ku, Tokyo 102 Japan. **LC** Q77. **DD** 506.052.

KAGAKU GIJUTSU KENKYU CHOSA HOKOKU. **VFOAT** Report on the Survey of Research and Development in Japan. Began in 1960. Japanese (English). an. **LC** Q180.J3. **DD** 001.40952. *Kenkyu Kikan Kihan Tokei Chosa Kekka Hokoku.*

KAGAKU SHINBUN. **VFOAT** Science News. Periodical. JA. Japanese. ir. 5000. Kagaku Shinbunsha, 8-1 Hamamatsu-cho 1 Minato-ku, Tokyo-to Japan. **LC** Q4.

KAGAKUSHI KENKYU. **VFOAT** Kagakusi Kenkyu. 0022-7692. Periodical. JA. Japanese (added table of contents in English). qt. Japan Publishing Trading Company Ltd, PO Box 5030, Tokyo International 100-31 Japan.

KANAZAWA KAIGAKU KYOIKUGAKUBU KIYO. SHIZEN KAGAKU-HEN. *See* Education (General) - Higher Education.

KENYA JOURNAL OF SCIENCE AND TECHNOLOGY. SERIES A. PHYSICAL AND CHEMICAL SCIENCES. (KENYA JOURNAL OF SCIENCE AND TECHNOLOGY. SERIES A, PHYSICAL AND CHEMICAL SCIENCES). **VFOAT** Physical and Chemical Sciences. Vol. 1, No. 1-. 0250-8265. Periodical. English. sa. Free. Kenya National Academy, PO Box 47288, Nairobi Kenya. **Tel** 721138. **Ed** J K A Mati. **Ind/Abst** Chem. Abstr. **CODEN** KJSSDG. bk rev. adv acc. **Circ** 4,000. For promotion of science and technology.

KEXUE TONGBAO. (KO HSUEH TUNG PAO). **VFOAT** Science Bulletin, Kexue Tongbao. Vol. 25, No. 1-2 (Jan. 1980)-. 0250-7862. Periodical. UK. English. mo. $150.50. Scientific and Technical Book, PO Box 197, London WC2N 4DE England. **Tel** (415)282-2994. **Ind/Abst** Math. Rev., Life Sci. Collect., Comput. Control Abstr., Electr. Electron. Abstr., Sci. Abstr. Sect. A. Phys. Abstr., GeoRef, Bibliogr. Agric. **CODEN** KHTPBU.

KEXUE TONGBAO, SCIENTIA. (KEXUE TONGBAO (SCIENTIA)). July 1974-. 0097-7411. Periodical. US. English. mo. $90.00 (Six Issues). Plenum/China Program, 227 West 17th Street, New York NY 10011. **Ind/Abst** Chem. Abstr. **LC** Q1. **DD** 505. **NLM** W1 KE765. **CODEN** KETOD8.

KEY TO TURKISH SCIENCE: MATHEMATICS & PHYSICAL SCIENCES. English. ir. Bayindir Sakak 33, Yenisehir Ankara Turkey. **LC** Q1. **DD** 508.

KEY TO TURKISH SCIENCE: PHYSICAL SCIENCES. V. 1- Aug. 1969-. 0023-0936. English. ir. Bayindir Sokak 33, Yenisehir Ankara Turkey. **LC** Q1. **DD** 500.208.

KICHO KWAHAK YONGU. **VFOAT** Journal of Natural Sciences. V. 1-. Periodical. KO. English (Korean). ir. Yongham Taehakkyo Pusol, Kicho Kwahak Yonguso 241-1, Tae-dong Kyongsan-up Kyongbul Korea 632. **Ind/Abst** Energy Res. Abstr. **LC** Q4.

KIELER MEERESFORSCHUNGEN. V. 1-31, No. 2. 0023-1339. Periodical. GW. German (summaries in English). sa. Walter G Muhlau, Holtenauer Strasse 116, D-2300 Kiel West Germany. **Ind/Abst** GeoRef, Chem. Abstr., Bibliogr. Index Geol., Sel. Water Resour. Abstr. **LC** Q49. **CODEN** KMEEAO. *Wissenschaftliche Meeresuntersuchungen. Abt. Kiel.*

KINKI DAIGAKU RIKOGAKUBU KENKYU HOKOKU. **VFOAT** Journal of the Faculty of Science and Technology, Kinki University. Began in 1966. 0386-4928. Periodical. JA. Japanese. an. Free. Kinki Daigaku Rikogakubu, 4-1 Kowakae 3 Higashosaka-shi Osaka-F Japan. **Tel** (06)721-2332. **Ed** Yoshihide Honda. **Ind/Abst** Chem. Abstr. **LC** Q77. **CODEN** KDRKBB. **Circ** 1,000. (ctrl). Our journal contains the contributions from over eleven departments in the Faculty of Science and Technology, Kinki University.

KIRTLANDIA. Began with No. 1 in 1967. 0075-6245. US. English. sa. $17.50. Cleveland Museum of History, Wade Oval-University Circle, Cleveland OH 44106. **Tel** (216)231-4600. **Ind/Abst** Life Sci. Collect., GeoRef, Biol. Abstr., Bibliogr. Index Geol., Zool. Rec. **LC** QH1. **DD** 508. **CODEN** KIRTA4. **Circ** 500. (ctrl). Contains: natural history and sciences.

KO HSUEH HSUEH YU KO HSUEH CHI SHU KUAN LI. **VFOAT** Scientology and Management of S. & T. Began in 1980. Periodical. Chinese. ir. 0.39. Post Office, Tien-chin Shih China. **LC** Q179.9.K6. **DD** 507.2.

KO HSUEH HUA PAO. **VFOAT** Science Pictorial. Began with Jan. 1937 issue. Periodical. CC. Chinese. ir. 0.26. Chung-kuo Kuo Chi Shu Tien, PO Box 399, Peking China Mainland. **LC** Q4. **DD** 505.

KO HSUEH SHIH TAI. **VFOAT** Age of Science. Periodical. CH. Chinese. ir. 0.38. Chung-Kuo Kuo Chi Shu Tien, PO Box 2820, Pei-Ching China. **LC** Q4. **DD** 505.

KO HSUEH SHIH YEN. **VFOAT** Ke Xue Shi Yan. 1971-. Periodical. Chinese. ir. **LC** Q4.

KOCHI DAIGAKU KYOIKU GAKUBU KENKYU HOKOKU. DAI 3-BU. **VFOAT** Bulletin of the Faculty of Education, Kochi University. Began with No. 19, published in 1967 CF. Gakujutsu

Science (General)

Zasshi Sog. 0389-0449. English (Japanese). an. Kochi Daigaku Kyoiku Gakubu, 5-ban 1-go Akebono-cho 2-chome, Kochi-shi Japan. **Ind/Abst** Chem. Abstr. **LC** Q77. **CODEN** KDKDDP. *Kochi Daigaku Kyoiku Gakubu Kenkyu Hokoku.*

KOGAI SHIGEN KENKYUJO IHO. VFOAT Bulletin of the National Research Institute for Pollution. V. 1- Dec. 1971-. Periodical. Multilingual (Japanese and English). ir. 188 Kotobukicho, Kawaguchi Japan. **Ind/Abst** Coal Abstr., Chem. Abstr. **LC** Q4. **NLM** W1 KO289G. **CODEN** KSKID9.

KOKURITSU KAGAKU HAKUBUTSUKAN NYUSU. Periodical. JA. Japanese. ir. 30 Single Issue. 7-20 Ueno Koen Taito-ku (110), Tokyo Japan. **LC** Q4.

KOKURITSU KYOKUCHI KENKYUJO YORAN. JA. Japanese. ir. 9-10 Kaga, 1 Itabasjo-ku Tokyo Japan. **LC** Q77.

KOKYO SHIKEN KENKYU KIKAN ANNAI : RIKOGAKU TEMA HEN. JA. Japanese. ir. Nihon Kagaku Gijutsu Joho Senta, 5-2 Nagatacho 2-chome, Chiyoda-ku 100, Tokyo Japan. **LC** Z7403, Q158.5.

KONGLIGA SVENSKA VETENSKAPS-AKADEMIENS HANDLINGAR. VFOAT Handlingar. SW. Swedish. mo. Almqvist & Wiskell, 108 Drottinggatan, PO Box 45150, S-104 30 Stockholm Sweden. **Tel** 85413160.

KOREAN SCIENTIFIC ABSTRACTS. *See* Indexes/Abstracts.

KOSMOS. Vol. 1- Jan. 1904-. 0023-4230. Periodical. GW. German. mo. 73.80. Franckh Sche Verlagshandlung, 1 Pfizerstrasse 5 7, D7000 Stuttgart 1 West Germany. **Tel** (0711)2191313. Ed Jaus. **Ind/Abst** Excerpta Med., GeoRef, Energy Res. Abstr. **CODEN** KSMSAC. (cum index). bk rev. adv acc. **Circ** 100,000. (ctrl). Popular magazine about natural history, and science. *Tier & Naturfotografie.*

KUNI NO SHIKEN KENKYU GYOMU KEIKAKU. JA. Japanese. ir. 10000. Nihon Kagaku Gijutsu Joho Senta, 5-2 Nagatacho 2-chome, Chiyoda-ku 100 Tokyo Japan. **LC** Q180.J3.

KYBERNETIKA. Vol. 1- 1965-. 0023-5954. Periodical. GW. chiefly in Czech, English, or German. bm. Kubon and Sagner, Postfach 34 01 08, D-8000 Munchen 34 West Germany. **Tel** (089)52 20 27. **Ind/Abst** Math. Rev., Eng. Index Annu., Eng. Index Mon., Eng. Index Bioeng. Abstr., Eng. Index Energy Abstr., Sociol. Abstr., Comput. Control Abstr., Electr. Electron. Abstr., Sci. Abstr. Sect. A. Phys. Abstr., Lang. Lang. Behav. Abstr., Comput. Rev., Phys. Abstr., Sci. Cit. Index, Abr. Ed., Eng. Index, Sociol. Abstr. **LC** Q300. **CODEN** KYBNAI. An international journal of cybernetic theory, publishing discussions on the problems of cybernetics, information theory, automatic control, abstract languages and applied cybernetics in biology, medicine and linguistics.

KYOIKUGAKUBU KENKYU HOKOKU. SHIZEN KAGAKU. (GIFU DAIGAKU KYOIKUGAKUBU KENKYU HOKOKU. SHIZEN KAGAKU). VFOAT Science Report of the Faculty of Education, Gifu University. Natural Science. V. 3, No. 5, (1966)-. 0533-9529. English (Japanese). an. **Ind/Abst** Math. Rev., Chem. Abstr. **LC** Q4. **CODEN** GDGKAD. *Gifu Daigaku Gakugei Gakubu Kenkyu Hokoku. Shizen Kagaku,* 0434-0078.

KYOKUCHIKEN NYUSU. Main/Corp Kokuritsu Kyokuchi Kenkyujo. VAT Kokuritsu Kyokuchi Kenkyujo NYUSU. 1- August 1974-. Periodical. JA. Japanese. ir. Kokuritsu Kyokuchi Kenkyujo, 9-10 Kaga 1-chome Itabashi-ku (173), Tokyo Japan. **LC** Q77.

KYUSHU TOKAI DAIGAKU KIYO. VFOAT Proceedings of Kyushu Tokai University. No. 1-. Japanese (summaries in English). ir. Kyushu Tokai Daigaku, 223 Toroku Oemachi, Kumamoto Japan. **LC** Q4.

LABDEV. PART A, PHYSICAL SCIENCES. VFOAT Physical Sciences. Vol. 6-A, No. 1 (Jan. 1968)-. 0368-7430. Periodical. English. ir. **Ind/Abst** Math. Rev. **CODEN** LAPSBF. *Labdev.*

LABORATORY BUYERS GUIDE. 1975/76-. 0381-6729. Periodical. CN. English. $35.00. Southam Communications Ltd, 1450 Don Mills Road, Don Mills Ontario M3B 1X2 Canada. **Tel** (416)445-6641. Ed Rita Tate. **DD** 338.475028. adv acc. **Circ** 20,000. (ctrl). Comprehensive directory of instruments, equipment, materials and chemicals for every type of laboratory. All products are linked to their manufacturers and/or distributors. *Laboratory Guide,* 0381-6737.

LABORATORY DIRECTORY, ARTICLES OF INCORPORATION, BY-LAWS, STATEMENTS OF COMPETENCE. *See* Yearbooks, Almanacs, Directories.

LABORATORY EQUIPMENT. 0023-6810. Periodical. US. English. mo. $12.00. Gordon Publications Inc, Box 1952, 13 Emory Avenue, Dover NJ 07801-0952. **Tel** (201)361-9060.

LABORATORY EQUIPMENT DIGEST. Began with Feb. 1963 issue. 0023-6829. Periodical. UK. English. mo. 32 Domestic, 80 Europe, 110 Others. Morgan Grampian, 30 Calderwood Street, London SE18 6QH England. **Tel** 855-7777. Ed M Spear. **Ind/Abst** Life Sci. Collect., World Text Abstr., Excerpta Med., World Surf. Coat. Abstr., CIS Abstr., Comput. Control Abstr., Electr. Electron. Abstr., Sci. Abstr. Sect. A. Phys. Abstr., Chem. Abstr., Phys. Abstr. **LC** Q185. **DD** 681.7505. **CODEN** LEQDA2. bk rev. adv acc. **Circ** 15,548. (ctrl). Laboratory products and applied technology covering industrial, medical, research, educational and governmental sectors.

LABORATORY EQUIPMENT DIRECTORY. *See* Yearbooks, Almanacs, Directories.

LABORATORY EQUIPMENT DIRECTORY & BUYERS GUIDE. *See* Yearbooks, Almanacs, Directories.

LABORATORY MANAGEMENT. V. 1- March/May 1963-. 0023-6845. Periodical. US. English. mo. $22.00. Media Horizons Inc, 50 West 23rd Street, New York NY 10010. **Tel** (212)645-1000. Ed Kenneth W Lane. **Ind/Abst** Biol. Abstr. **LC** Q183. **DD** 658.9161. **NLM** W1 LA219. **CODEN** LABMAS. bk rev. adv acc. **Circ** 55,000. (ctrl). Technical articles on disease diagnosis for pathologists and other scientists in clinical medical laboratories.

LABORATORY POSTURE REPORT. Main/Corp U.S. Army Human Engineering Laboratories. VFOAT Annual Posture Report. 0161-7281. US. English. an. US Army Human Engineering Laboratory, Aberdeen Proving Ground MD 21005. **LC** UB393.5. **DD** 623.

LABORATORY PRACTICE. V. 1- Apr. 1952-. 0023-6853. Periodical. UK. English. mo. United Trade Press Ltd, 33-35 Bowling Green Lane, London EC1R 0DA England. **Tel** 01-837-1212. **Ind/Abst** Fluidex, Life Sci. Collect., Excerpta Med., World Surf. Coat. Abstr., Int. Aerosp. Abstr., Comput. Control Abstr., Electr. Electron. Abstr., Sci. Abstr. Sect. A. Phys. Abstr., Met. Abstr., World Alum. Abstr., Ref. Source, Biol. Abstr., Chem. Abstr., Nuci. Sci. Abstr., Index Med., Sel. Water Resour. Abstr., Bibliogr. Agric., Phys. Abstr. **LC** Q183. **NLM** W1 LA231. **CODEN** LABPA3. (cum index).

LABORATORY PRODUCT NEWS. V. 1- Mar. 1971-. 0047-3855. Periodical. CN. English. bm. 30.00. Southam Communications Ltd, 1450 Don Mills Road, Don Mills Ontario M3B 2X7 Canada. **Tel** (416)445-6641. Ed Rita Tate. adv acc. **Circ** 19,100. (ctrl). Instruments, equipment, chemicals and materials for every type of research, clinical testing and industrial quality control, laboratory. *Laboratory Guide,* 0075-7500.

LABORATORY REGULATION MANUAL. *See* Law.

LABORATORY WORKLOAD RECORDING METHOD. US. English. an. $18.00. College American Pathologists, 7400 North Skokie Boulevard, Skokie IL 60077. *Workload Recording Method for Clinical Laboratories.*

LAND RESOURCES LABORATORY SERIES. *See* Conservation & Natural Resources.

LANZHOU DAXUE XUEBAO. ZIRAN ZIRAN KEXUE BAN. (LAN-CHOU TA HSUEH HSUEH PAO. TZU JAN KO HSUEH PAN). VFOAT Journal of Lanzhou University. Began with Aug. 1957 issue. 0455-2059. Periodical. CN. Chinese (abstracts in English). qt. 0.60. Chung-Kuo Kuo Chi Shu Tien, PO Box 2820, Peking China. **Ind/Abst** Math. Rev., Chem. Abstr. **LC** Q4. **DD** 505. **CODEN** LCTHAF.

LARGE SCALE SYSTEMS : THEORY AND APPLICATIONS. 0167-420X. Periodical. English. bm. Elsevier Science Publishers, PO Box 211, 1000 AE Amsterdam Netherlands. **Tel** (020)5803.911. **Ind/Abst** Math. Rev., Comput. Control Abstr., Electr. Electron. Abstr., Sci. Abstr. Sect. A. Phys. Abstr. **CODEN** LSSAD2.

LAURENTIAN UNIVERSITY REVIEW. VFOAT Revue de l'Universite Laurentienne. V. 1- June 1968-. 0023-9011. Periodical. CN. English (French). sa. $11.61. Laurentian University of Sudbury, Chemin du Lac Ramsey, Sudbury Ontario P3E2C6 Canada. **Tel** (705)675-1151. **LC** AS42.L38. **DD** 054.1. **Circ** 125. A bilingual journal of the sciences, arts and humanities. Welcomes articles from social sciences, literary scholars, historians, philosophers and physical scientists.

LC SCIENCE TRACER BULLET. *See* Bibliographies.

LEBENDE SPRACHEN. *See* Linguistics.

LEITUNG UND PLANUNG VON WISSENSCHAFT UND TECHNIK. Periodical. SZ. German or Russian. mo. Kunst & Wissen Erich Bieber, Dufourstrasse 51, CH-8008 Zurich Switzerland. **LC** Z7403, Q158.5.

LEOPOLDINA. Year 1- 1955-. Periodical. German. ir. **Ind/Abst** GeoRef, Bibliogr. Agric. **LC** Q49. **DD** 505. **CODEN** LEOPAS.

LIBYAN JOURNAL OF SCIENCE. (THE LIBYAN JOURNAL OF SCIENCE). V. 1- May 1971-. 0368-7481. English (summaries in Arabic). an. University of Libya, PO Box 656, Tripoli Libya. **Ind/Abst** Math. Rev., Life Sci. Collect., GeoRef, Chem. Abstr., Pet. Abstr., Bibliogr. Index Geol. **LC** Q1. **CODEN** LBJSAP.

LIFE SCIENCES AND SPACE RESEARCH CEASED. Main/Conf International Space Science Symposium. Began with 3rd, 1962. Ceased after V. 18, 1980. 0075-9422. English, French, or Russian. ir. **NLM** W3 LI44.

LIFE SCIENCES (NEW YORK, N.Y. : 1973). (LIFE SCIENCES). V. 13- July 1, 1973-. 0024-3205. Periodical. UK. English. wk. Pergamon Press, Maxwell House, Fairview Park, Elmsford NY 10523. **Ind/Abst** Life Sci. Collect., Excerpta Med., Pestdoc, Ringdoc, Vetdoc, Energy Res. Abstr., Sel. Water Resour. Abstr., Chem. Abstr., Biol. Abstr., Bibliogr. Agric., Index Med., Int. Aerosp. Abstr., Nuci. Sci. Abstr., Psychol. Abstr. **NLM** W1 LI4067. **CODEN** LIFSAK. *Life Sciences. Part I, Physiology and Pharmacology,* 0300-9653; *Life Sciences. Part II, Biochemistry, General and Molecular Biology,* 0300-9637.

LIFE SCIENCES RESEARCH REPORT. 1- 1976-. 0340-8132. Monographic Series. GW. English. ir. **Ind/Abst** Chem. Abstr. **NLM** W1 LI4067R. **CODEN** LSRPD8.

LINDA HALL LIBRARY MISCELLANY. *See* Library and Information Science.

LINDE REPORTS ON SCIENCE AND TECHNOLOGY. 1-. 0024-3736. Periodical. English (German). Linde AG, Lincolnstrasse 21, Wiesbaden West Germany. **Ind/Abst** Fluidex, Eng. Index Annu., Eng. Index Mon., Eng. Index Bioeng. Abstr., Eng. Index Energy Abstr., Coal Abstr., Comput. Control Abstr., Electr. Electron. Abstr., Sci. Abstr. Sect. A. Phys. Abstr., Energy Res. Abstr., Phys. Abstr., Eng. Index. **LC** T1. **CODEN** LRSTAF.

LISTE BIBLIOGRAPHIQUE DES TRAVAUX. *See* Bibliographies.

LISTE DES BENEFICIAIRES D'UNE SUBVENTION DU FONDS NATIONAL DE LA RECHERCHE SCIENTIFIQUE OU D'UN DES TROIS FONDS ASSOCIES AVEC INDICATION DES RECHERCHES POURSUIVIES ET DE L'INSTITUTION D'ACCUEIL. Main/Corp Fonds National de la Recherche Scientifique (Belgium). VFOAT Lijst der Kredietgenieters van Het Nationaal Fonds Voor Wetenschappelijk Onderzoek en van de Geassocieerde Fondsen, Met Opgave van Hun Programma en Onthaalinstelling. BE. English, Flemish or French. ir. rue d'Egmont 5, 1050 Bruxelles Belgium. **LC** Q180.B4.

LISTING OF PEER REVIEWERS USED BY NSF DIVISIONS. Main/Corp United States. National Science Foundation. 1975/76-. 0146-6968. US. English. an. $8.60. Superintendent of Documents, US Government Printing Office, Washington DC 20402. **LC** Q149.U5. **DD** 502.573.

LOGOS (ARGONNE, ILL.). (LOGOS). 0748-2116. Periodical. US. English. ty. Free. Argonne National Laboratory, 9700 South Cass Avenue, Argonne IL 60439. **Tel** (312)972-5584. Ed David Baurac. **LC** QC789.2.U62. **DD** 605. **Circ** 10,000. (ctrl). Updated reports on selected programs at Argonne National Laboratory.

LOISIR-SCIENCE. (LOISIR SCIENCE). First issue in Sept. 1975. 0705-4378. Periodical. CN. French. qt. 5. Conseil de Dev du Loisir Science, 1415

Science (General)

Jarry Est, Montreal Quebec H2E 2Z7 Canada. **Tel** (514)252-3027. **DD** 506.2714. bk rev. adv acc. **Circ** 4,000. (ctrl). Promotional magazine of scientific leisure covering natural, physical and human sciences.

LONDON PAPERS IN REGIONAL SCIENCE. 1- 1969-. 0076-0633. UK. English. ir. Academic Press, 4805 Sand Lake Road, Orlando FL 32819. **Tel** (305)345-4100.

LYCHNOS : LARDOMSHISTORISKA SAMFUNDETS ARSBOK. See Yearbooks, Almanacs, Directories.

M T P INTERNATIONAL REVIEW OF SCIENCE. Monographic Series. UK. English. ir. University Park Press, 300 North Charles Street, Baltimore MD 21201. **Tel** (800)638-7511.

MCGRAW-HILL DICTIONARY OF SCIENTIFIC AND TECHNICAL TERMS. See Encyclopedias & General Reference Books.

MCGRAW-HILL ENCYCLOPEDIA OF SCIENCE & TECHNOLOGY. See Encyclopedias & General Reference Books.

MCGRAW-HILL YEARBOOK OF SCIENCE AND TECHNOLOGY. See Yearbooks, Almanacs, Directories.

MAGYAR TUDOMANY. (MAGYAR TUDOMANY : A MAGYAR TUDONANYOS AKADEMIA ERTESITOJE). Began in 1956. 0025-0325. Periodical. HU. Hungarian. mo. Akademiai Kiado, PO Box 24, 1363 Budapest Hungary. **Tel** 382-344. Ed F B Straub. **Ind/Abst** Am. Hist. Life, Hist. Abstr., Part A, Mod. Hist. Abstr., Hist. Abst., Part B, Twent. Century Abstr. **NLM** W1 MA431. bk rev. adv acc. **Circ** 3,400. Science management, sociology of science. Akademiai Ertesito.

MAJALLAT AL-INMA AL-ARABI LIL-ULUM WA-AL-TAQNIYAH. VFOAT Arab Development Journal for Science and Technology. V. 1- March 1978-. Periodical. Arabic (English articles have summaries in Arabic). ir. Mahad Al-Inmaal-Arabi, PO Box 8004, Tarabulus Libiya. **LC** Q80.L75.

MALAWI JOURNAL OF SCIENCE. V. 1- 1972-. English. ir. Association for the Advancement of Science of Malawi, Chancellor College, PO Box 280, Zomba Malawi. **LC** Q91.M3. **DD** 505.

MALAYAN SCIENTIST. 1- 1963/64-. 0542-3449. Periodical. MY. English. ir. University of Malaya, Kuala Lumpar 22 11 Malaysia. **Ind/Abst** GeoRef. **LC** Q1. **DD** 505. **CODEN** MALSA5.

MALAYSIAN JOURNAL OF SCIENCE. VFOAT Jernel Sains Malaysia. V. 1- 1972-. 0301-0554. English. ir. Kedaibuku Koperatif Univ Malay Univ Malaya-Lembah Pantai, Kuala Lumpur 22-11 Malaysia. **Ind/Abst** GeoRef, Chem. Abstr. **LC** Q1. **DD** 505. **NLM** W1 MA5247K. **CODEN** MLJSA4.

MANITOBA SCIENCE TEACHER. See Education (General) - Theory, Practice of Education.

MASCA JOURNAL. See Museums.

MASTERS THESES IN THE PURE AND APPLIED SCIENCES ACCEPTED BY COLLEGES AND UNIVERSITIES OF THE UNITED STATES AND CANADA. (MASTERS THESES IN THE PURE AND APPLIED SCIENCES ACCEPTED BY COLLEGES AND UNIVERSITIES OF THE UNITED STATES AND CANADA : A PUBLICATION OF THE CENTER FOR INFORMATION AND NUMERICAL DATA ANALYSIS AND SYNTHESIS). VFOAT Masters Theses in the Pure and Applied Sciences. Vol. 18 (1973)-. 0736-7910. US. English. an. Plenum Press, 233 Spring Street, New York NY 10013. **Tel** (212)620-8000. Ed Wade H Shafer. **DD** 016.5. **NLM** Z 7401 M423. Masters Theses in the Pure and Applied Sciences Accepted by Colleges and Universities of the United States.

MATERIALS SCIENCE RESEARCH. V. 1-. 0076-5201. Monographic Series. US. English. ir. Plenum Publishing Company, 233 Spring Street, New York NY 10013. **Tel** (212)620-8000. **Ind/Abst** Eng. Index Annu., Eng. Index Mon., Eng. Index Bioeng. Abstr., Eng. Index Energy Abstr., Comput. Control Abstr., Electr. Electron. Abstr., Sci. Abstr. Sect. A. Phys. Abstr., Chem. Abstr., Phys. Abstr., Eng. Index. **LC** UNC. **CODEN** MTSRAY.

MEDDELELSER OM GRNLAND CEASED. Vol. 1-206, No. 6. 0025-6676. Monographic Series. DK. English (contributions in German, French, Russian or Danish). ir. **Ind/Abst** GeoRef, Life Sci. Collect. **LC** Q115. **NLM** W1 ME11K. **CODEN** MGROAV.

MEDDELELSER OM GRNLAND. BIOSCIENCE. See Biology.

MEMBRANE SCIENCE AND DESALINATION. Periodical. NE. English. ir. $772.76. Elsevier Science Publishers, PO Box 211, 1000 AE Amsterdam Netherlands. **Tel** (02)5803.911.

MEMOIRES DE LA CLASSE DES SCIENCES. ACADEMIE ROYALE DE BELGIQUE. COLLECTION IN 8. (MEMOIRES DE LA CLASSE DES SCIENCES : COLLECTION IN OCTAVO. 2E SER). 2E. Ser. Vol. 1. (1904)-. 0365-0936. BE. French. ir. Office Intl des Periodiques, Avenue Louise 485, B-1050 Bruxelies Belgium. **Tel** (02)513-66-75. **Ind/Abst** Biol. Abstr., Math. Rev. **LC** Q56. **NLM** W1 ME8947H. **CODEN** ABSCA3.

MEMOIRES DE LA SOCIETE VAUDOISE DES SCIENCES NATURELLES. Main/Corp Societe Vaudoise des Sciences Naturelles, Lausanne. V. 1- (No. 1-). 0037-9611. Monographic Series. SZ. English (French or German). ir. SASN, Palasis de Rumine, 1005 Lausanne Switzerland. **Ind/Abst** Life Sci. Collect., GeoRef, Biol. Abstr., Chem. Abstr. **LC** Q67. **DD** 505. **CODEN** MSVNAU.

MEMOIRS OF THE FACULTY OF SCIENCE, SHIMANE UNIVERSITY. VFOAT Shimane Daigaku Rigakubu Kiyo. Began in 1978. 0387-9925. Periodical. English. ir. Shimane Daigaku Rigakubu, Nishikawazu-cho, Matsue-shi Japan. **Ind/Abst** Math. Rev., Chem. Abstr. **LC** Q1. **DD** 505. **CODEN** SDRKDX. Memoirs. Natural Sciences.

MEMOIRS OF THE INSTITUTE OF SCIENTIFIC AND INDUSTRIAL RESEARCH OSAKA UNIVERSITY. (MEMOIRS OF THE INSTITUTE OF SCIENTIFIC AND INDUSTRIAL RESEARCH, OSAKA UNIVERSITY). Main/Corp Osaka Daigaku. Sangyo Kagaku Kenkyujo. V. 6- 1948-. 0369-0369. JA. English. an. Osaka Daigaku Sangyo Kagaku Kenkyujo, Oaza Yamadakami, Suita 565 Japan. **Ind/Abst** Chem. Abstr. **LC** Q180.J3. **DD** 505. **CODEN** MISIAW.

MEMORIA - CONSEJO SUPERIOR DE INVESTIGACIONES CIENTIFICAS. Main/Corp Consejo Superior de Investigaciones Cientificas (Spain). 1940/41-. SP. Spanish. ir. Consejo Superior de, Egupciacas 15, Barcelona Spain. **LC** AS302. **DD** 066.

MEMORIA - SOCIEDAD DE CIENCIAS NATURALES LA SALLE. Main/Corp Sociedad de Ciencias Naturales la Salle, Caracas. VFOAT Memoria de la S. C. N.-La Salle. No. 1- July 1941-. VE. Spanish. ir. Sociedad de Ciencias Naturales la Salle, Apartado 1930, Caracas 1010-A Venezuela. **CODEN** SCNSAR.

MEMORIE. Main/Corp Accademia Nazionale dei Lincei. Classe di Scienze Fisiche, Matematiche e Naturali. Series/Titl Atti Atti della Accademia Nazionale dei Lincei. Ser. 8, V. 1-. Monographic Series. IT. Italian. ir. $18.90. Accademi Nazionale dei Lincei, via Della Lingara 10, 00165 Rome Italy. Memorie Della Classe di Scienze Fisiche, Matematiche e Naturali.

MEMORIILE SECTIILOR STIINTIFICE - ACADEMIA REPUBLICII SOCIALISTE ROMANIA. (MEMORIILE SECTIILOR STIINTIFICE). VFOAT Memoirs of the Scientific Sections of the Academy of the Socialist Republic of Romania. 0254-8607. Periodical. RM. English (French, German, and Romanian). ir. 23,50. Editura Academiei Republicii Socialiste Romania, Calea Victoriei 125, 79 717 Bucuresti Romania. **Ind/Abst** Chem. Abstr. **LC** Q1.A1. **DD** 505. **CODEN** MSARD8.

METHODICUM CHIMICUM : A CRITICAL SURVEY OF PROVEN METHODS AND THEIR APPLICATION IN CHEMISTRY, NATURAL SCIENCE, AND MEDICINE. See Chemistry.

METROPOLITAN DETROIT SCIENCE REVIEW. V. 1-40. 0096-9087. Periodical. US. English. qt. $12.00. Metropolitan Detroit Science, Room 932/Schools Center Building, Woodward Detroit MI 48202. **Tel** (313)494-1613. **LC** Q1. **DD** 505.

MICHIGAN SCIENCE IN ACTION. VFOAT Science in Action. -No. 46 (Fall 1981). 0076-809X. Periodical. US. English. ir. Agricultural Experiment Station, Michigan State University, Room 101/ Agricultural Hall, East Lansing MI 48824. **Ind/Abst** Bibliogr. Agric.

MICRO-SCOPE (WATERLOO, ONT.). (MICRO-SCOPE). VFOAT Microscope. Vol. 1, No. 1 (Oct. 31, 1979)-. 0229-4710. Periodical. CN. English. Free to Members. Micro-Scope, Waterloo University Science Society, c/o The University, Waterloo Ontario M2L 3C5 Canada. **DD** 505.

MIDIST BULLETIN D'INFORMATION. VFOAT M.I.D.I.S.T. Bulletin d'Information. VAT Mission Interministerielle de l'Information Scientifique et Technique Bulletin d'Information. Periodical. FR. French. ir. Ministere de l'Industrie et de l'Information de la Recherche/Mission Interministerielle de l'Information et de la Recherche, 280 Bd Saint-Germain, 75007 Paris France. **Ind/Abst** Libr. Inf. Sci. Abstr.

MINERVA. V. 1- Autumn 1962-. 0026-4695. Periodical. UK. English. qt. $45.98. International Association for Cultural Freedom, 59 St Martins Lane, London WC2 N4JS England. **Tel** (01)836-4194. Ed Edward Shils. **Ind/Abst** Sociol. Abstr., Public Aff. Inf. Serv. Bull., Am. Hist. Life, Hist. Abstr., Part A, Mod. Hist. Abstr., Hist. Abst., Part B, Twent. Century Abstr., Soc. Sci. Citation Index, Sociol. Abstr., Lang. Lang. Behav. Abstr. **LC** AS121. **DD** 052. **NLM** W1 MI629. Index published separately - free - automatically sent. bk rev. adv acc. **Circ** 1,500. A quarterly review of science, learning and policy.

MINNESOTA SCIENCE. V. 23- Sept. 1966-. 0026-5675. Periodical. US. English. qt. University of Minnesota, 448 Coffey Hall, University of Minnesota, St Paul MN 55108. **Tel** (612)373-0751. Minnesota Farm and Home Science, 0096-655X.

MINNESOTA STUDIES IN THE PHILOSOPHY OF SCIENCE. Vol. 1-. 0076-9258. US. English. ir. **LC** Q175. **DD** 501.

MISCELLANEOUS PUBLICATION. See Education (General) - Higher Education.

MOKSLAS IR GYVENIMAS. 176- Geg. 1972-. Periodical. UR. Lithuanian. mo. $17.00. Victor Kamkin Inc (76725), 12224 Parklawn Drive, Rockville MD 20852. **Tel** (301)881-5973. **LC** Q4. MG, Mokslas Ir Gyvenimas.

MONOGRAPH (ACADEMY OF NATURAL SCIENCES OF PHILADELPHIA). (MONOGRAPH). 15-. Monographic Series. US. English. Academy of Natural Sciences of Philadelphia, 19th and the Parkway, Philadelphia PA 19103. **Ind/Abst** GeoRef. **CODEN** MGAPAH. Monographs of the Academy of Natural Sciences of Philadelphia.

MONOGRAPH - INDIANA ACADEMY OF SCIENCE. Main/Corp Indiana Academy of Science. No. 1- 1969-. Monographic Series. US. English. ir. Indiana Academy of Sciences, Indiana State Library, 140 North Senate Avenue, Indianapolis IN 46204. **Tel** (317)232-3686. Ed William R Eberly. (ctrl).

MONOGRAPH SERIES - REGIONAL SCIENCE RESEARCH INSTITUTE. Main/Corp Regional Science Research Institute. 0080-0627. Monographic Series. US. English. ir. Regional Science Research Institute, 256 North Pleasant Street, Wentworth Bl, Amherst MA 01002. **LC** UNC.

MONOGRAPHS AND TEXTBOOKS IN MATERIAL SCIENCE. 0077-0744. Monographic Series. US. English. ir. Marcel Dekker, PO Box 11305, Church Street Station, New York NY 10249. **Ind/Abst** Chem. Abstr. **CODEN** MTMSDA.

MOSAIC (WASHINGTON, D.C.). (MOSAIC). Vol. 1, No. 1 (Winter 1970)-. 0027-1284. Periodical. US. English. qt. Superintendent of Documents, US Government Printing Office, Washington DC 20402. **Tel** (202)783-3238. **Ind/Abst** Sociol. Abstr., GeoRef, Met. Abstr., World Alum. Abstr., Index U.S. Gov. Period., Energy Inf. Abstr., Environ. Abstr., Gen. Sci. Index, Access, Women Stud. Abstr., Lang. Lang. Behav. Abstr., Bibliogr. Index Geol. **LC** Q11. **NLM** W1 MO917F. **CODEN** MOSAAG. Available on microfilm from University Microfilms International.

MPG SPIEGEL. VFOAT M.P.G. Spiegel. 0341-7727. Periodical. German. ir. Max-Planck-Gesellschaft zur Forderung der Wissenschaften, Residenzstrasse 1 A, 8000 Munchen 2 West Germany. **Ind/Abst** Energy Res. Abstr. **LC** Q49. **DD** 505.

Science (General)

MUHIBBAH. Periodical. chiefly Indonesian. ir. 150 Each Issue. Universitas Islam Indonesia, Jl Cik Di Tiro, Yogyakarta Indonesia. LC Q183.4.I5.

MULTI-INDUSTRY R&D VOLUME. (MULTI-INDUSTRY R & D VOLUME). Main/Corp Government Data Publications (Firm). VFOAT Multi-Industry R and D Volume. VAT Multi-Industry Research and Development Volume. 0887-4093. US. English. sa. Government Data Publications, 1661 McDonald Avenue, Brooklyn NY 11230. Tel (718)627-0819. DD 650. Describes research and developments over a twelve-month period in all fields of industrial and scientific endeavor. Minutely indexed by activities, organizations, processes, inventions, etc. *Aerospace R & D Volume.*

MULTIPHASE SCIENCE AND TECHNOLOGY. Vol. 1-. 0276-1459. Periodical. US. English. ir. Hemisphere Publishing Corporation, 1010 Vermont Avenue NW/Suite 612, Washington DC 20005. Ind/Abst Chem. Abstr. CODEN MSTEDU.

NATIONAL ACADEMY OF SCIENCES PUBLICATION. Monographic Series. US. English. ir.

NATIONAL ACADEMY SCIENCE LETTERS. V. 1- Jan. 1978-. 0250-541X. Periodical. II. English. mo. $30.00. National Academy of Sciences India, 5 Lajpatrai Road, Allahabad 211002 India. Tel 55224. Ind/Abst Biol. Abstr., Comput. Control Abstr., Electr. Electron. Abstr., Sci. Abstr. Sect. A. Phys. Abstr., Chem. Abstr. LC Q73. DD 505. CODEN NASLDX. bk rev. Circ 200. This journal publishes short original research papers breaking fresh ground in all branches of science, medicine and engineering.

NATIONAL PATTERNS OF R. & D. RESOURCES. (NATIONAL PATTERNS OF R & D RESOURCES). Main/Corp National Science Foundation (U.S.). 1953/68-. 0093-8572. US. English. an. Superintendent of Documents, Printing Office, Washington DC 20402. LC Q180.U5. DD 507.2073. NLM W2 A N37N.

NATIONAL PATTERNS OF SCIENCE AND TECHNOLOGY RESOURCES. 1980-. US. English. National Science Foundation, Washington DC 20550. LC Q180.U5. DD 507.2073. NLM W2 A N37NA.

NATIONAL SURVEY OF SCIENTIFIC MANPOWER. *See* Economics - Labor.

NATO ADVANCED SCIENCE INSTITUTES SERIES. SERIES A, LIFE SCIENCES. VFOAT Life Sciences. Vol. 53-. Monographic Series. US. English. Plenum Publishing Corporation, 233 Spring Street, New York NY 10013. Tel (212)620-8000. Ind/Abst Chem. Abstr. CODEN NALSDJ. *NATO Advanced Study Institutes Series. Series A, Life Sciences.*

NATO ASI SERIES. SERIES E, APPLIED SCIENCE. VFOAT N.A.T.O. A.S.I. Series. VAT North Atlantic Treaty Organization Advanced Science Institutes Series. Sereis E, Applied Science. Monographic Series. US. English. ir. Sijthoff & Noordhoff Intl Publ, 20010 Century Boulevard, Germantown MD 20767. Ind/Abst Chem. Abstr. CODEN NAESDI.

NATO CONFERENCE SERIES. VI. MATERIALS SCIENCE. (NATO CONFERENCE SERIES : VI, MATERIALS SCIENCE). V. 1-. 0197-5145. Monographic Series. US. English. ir. Plenum Press, 233 Spring Street, New York NY 10013. Tel (212)620-8000. Ind/Abst Eng. Index Annu., Eng. Index Mon., Eng. Index, Eng. Index Bioeng. Abstr., Eng. Index Energy Abstr., Chem. Abstr. CODEN NCSSDY.

NATO SCIENCE COMMITTEE YEAR BOOK. *See* Yearbooks, Almanacs, Directories.

NATUR UND MUSEUM (FRANKFURT AM MAIN : 1962). (NATUR UND MUSEUM). Vol. 92, No. 1 (Jan. 1962)-. 0028-1301. Periodical. GW. German. mo $8.11. Senckenberg Naturforsche Gesellschaft, D-6000 Frankfurt West Germany. Ind/Abst Life Sci. Collect., GeoRef, Bibliogr. Index Geol. CODEN NAMUAR. Index in last issue of volume - attached. *Natur und Volk.*

NATURAL SCIENCE CENTERS; DIRECTORY. 1975/76-. US. English. Natural Science for Youth Foundation, 11 Wildwood Valley NE, Atlanta GA 30338. *Natural Science Centers for Youth.*

NATURAL SCIENCES. V. 1- Apr. 1979-. 0253-830X. Periodical. English. ir. $35.00. Ind/Abst Chem. Abstr. NLM W1 NA805T. CODEN NASIDO.

NATURE. V. 229- Jan. 1, 1971-. 0028-0836. Periodical. English. wk. $240.00. Nature, PO Box 1502, Neptune NJ 07753. Tel (800)524-0384. Ed John Maddox. bk rev. adv acc. Circ 30,000. (ctrl). International journal of the scientific community publishing the most up-to-date data on astronomy to zoology. *Nature.*

NATUREN. Began in 1881. NO. Norwegian. ir. $12.00. Universitetsforlaget, Postboks 7508 Skillebekk, Oslo 2 Norway. LC Q4.

NATUREN; ILLUSTRERET MAANEDSSKRIFT FOR POPULAER NATURVIDENSKAB. Vol. 1- 1877-. 0028-0887. Periodical. NO. Norwegian. bm $22.00. Universitetsforlaget, PO Box 2959 Toyen, Oslo 6 Norway. Tel 02-276-0-60. Ind/Abst GeoRef, Energy Res. Abstr., Chem. Abstr. CODEN NTUNA9. Popular scientific journal of natural science.

NATURVETENSKAPLIGA FORSKNINGSRADETS ARSBOK. *See* Yearbooks, Almanacs, Directories.

NATURWISSENSCHAFTEN. (DIE NATURWISSENSCHAFTEN). Vol. 1-. 0028-1042. Periodical. WB. German (some articles in English). mo. Springer-Verlag New York, 175 Fifth Avenue, New York NY 10010. Ind/Abst Biol. Abstr., Comput. Control Abstr., Electr. Electron. Abstr., Sci. Abstr. Sect. A. Phys. Abstr., GeoRef, Art Archaeol. Tech. Abstr., Energy Res. Abstr., Chem. Abstr., Bibliogr. Agric., Index Med. LC Q3. DD 574.05. NLM W1 NA924. CODEN NATWAY. (cum index). Available on microfilm from University Microfilms. *Naturwissenschaftliche Rundschau.*

NAUCNI I STRUCNI SKUPOVI U JUGOSLAVIJI I U INOSTRANSTVU. VFOAT Scientific and Professional Meetings in Yugoslavia and Foreign Countries. Began in 1975. Serbo-Croatian-R (issues for (Jan./June 1976-) lack title in English). ir. 800.00. Jugoslovenski Centar za Tehnicku I Naucnu Dokumentaciju, Slobodana Penezica Krcuna, 29-31 Postfach 724, Beograd South Africa. LC Q101.

NAUKA I ZHIZN. V. 1- Oct. 1934-. 0028-1263. Periodical. UR. Russian. mo. $29.00. Victor Kamkin Inc (70601), 12224 Parklawn Drive, Rockville MD 20852. Tel (301)881-5973. Ind/Abst Int. Aerosp. Abstr. LC Q4. DD 505. NLM W1 NA985.

NAUKA POLSKA. R. 1- (Nr. 1-). 0028-1271. Periodical. PL. Polish (tables of contents also in English and Russian). bm. ARS Polona, Krakowskie Prezedmiescie 7, 00-068 Warsaw Poland. Ind/Abst Am. Hist. Life, Hist. Abstr., Part A, Mod. Hist. Abstr., Hist. Abstr., Part B, Twent. Century Abstr., Coal Abstr., Bibliogr. Agric., Hist. Abstr. LC AS261. NLM W1 NA9857. *Sprawozdania Z Czynnosci I Prac.*

NAUKA SEGODNIA. Began with Vol. for 1973. UR. Russian. an. 0.59 Single Issue. Znanie, 101835 Tsentr Proezd Serova D 3/4, Moskva USSR. LC Q9.

NAUKA V SSSR. No. 1 (1981)-. 0203-4425. Periodical. UR. Russian. 1.10. Izdatelstvo Nauka, 117049 Moskva, Maronovskii Pereulok 26, Moskva Russian SFSR. Ind/Abst Chem. Abstr. LC Q60. DD 509.47. CODEN NASRDH.

NAVORSINGSBULLETIN - SUID-AFRIKAANSE RAAD VIR GEESTESWETENSKAPLIKE NAVORSING, INSTITUUT VIR NAVORSINGSONTWIKKELING. Main/Corp Human Sciences Research Council. Institute for Research Development. VFOAT Research Bulletin - South African Human Sciences Research Council, Institute for Research Development. V. 1- 1971-. SA. Afrikaans or English. ir. Private Bag X41, Pretoria 0001 South Africa. LC AZ821.S65. DD 916.80072. *Register of Research in the Human Sciences in South Africa.*

NCSR/TR/. No. 1-. Monographic Series. English. ir. National Council for Scientific Research, Lusaka Zambia. LC Q91.Z33. DD 508.1.

NEUJAHRSBLATT. (NEUJAHRSBLATT, HRSG. VON DER NATURFORSCHENDEN GESELLSCHAFT IN ZURICH). Main/Corp Naturforschende Gesellschaft in Zurich. VFOAT Zurcherische Jugend. Vol. 1-. Monographic Series. German. ir. LC Q67. (cum index).

NEW MEXICO JOURNAL OF SCIENCE. V. 18, No. 2- Dec. 1978-. 0270-3017. Periodical. US. English. sa. $15.00. New Mexico Academy of Science Journal, New Mexico Highland University, Dr Jos A Schufle, Las Vegas NM 87701. Ind/Abst Chem. Abstr. CODEN NMJSDP. *Bulletin - New Mexico Academy of Science, 0028-6133.*

NEW RESEARCH CENTERS. 2nd Ed. Issue No. 1- May 1965-. 0028-6591. US. English. ir. $210.00. Gale Research Center, Book Tower, Detroit MI 48226. Tel (800)521-0707. Ed M Watkins and J Ruffner. LC AS25. NLM Q 180.U5 D598N. (cum index). Periodical supplements to RCD.

NEW SCIENTIST (1971). (NEW SCIENTIST). Began with Vol. 52, No. 772 (Dec. 2, 1971) issue. 0262-4079. Periodical. UK. English. wk. New Science Publications, 128 Long Acre, London WC2E 9QH England. Ind/Abst Excerpta Med., Predicasts, Coal Abstr., Ship Abstr., Energy Inf. Abstr., Environ. Abstr., Abstr. Bull. Inst. Paper Chem., Int. Aerosp. Abstr., CIS Abstr., Comput. Control Abstr., Electr. Electron. Abstr., Fluidex, Sci. Abstr. Sect. A. Phys. Abstr., GeoRef, Int. Packag. Abstr., Sel. Water Resour. Abstr., Ref. Source, Met. Abstr., World Alum. Abstr., Pap. Board Abstr., Chem. Abstr., Print. Abstr., Electron. Pub. Abstr., Gen. Sci. Index, Recent Publ. Artic. LC Q1. DD 505. NLM W1 NE494. CODEN NWSCAL. *New Scientist and Science Journal, 0369-5808.*

NEW SERIAL HOLDINGS. Main/Corp United States. National Bureau of Standards. Library Division. VFOAT NBS Serial Holdings. VAT National Bureau of Standards Serial Holdings. 1977-. US. English. Department of Commerce, National Bureau of Standards, Gaithersburg MD 20760. *Library List of Serials.*

NEW TRENDS IN INTEGRATED SCIENCE TEACHING. VFOAT Tendances Nouvelles de L'Integration des Enseignements Scientifiques. V. 1- 1969/70-. Periodical. English (French, 1969/70). ir. UNIPUB Inc, PO Box 1222, Ann Arbor MI 48106. Tel (212)764-2791/(800)521-8110. LC Q181.A1. DD 507.1.

NEW ZEALAND SCIENCE REVIEW. V. 1- Dec. 1942-. 0028-8667. Periodical. NZ. English. bm. $8.44. New Zealand Association of Scientist, PO Box 1874, Wellington New Zealand. Ed F B Shorland. (cum index). bk rev. adv acc. Circ 400. (ctrl). Concerns science policy, science and society and scientist and ethics.

NEWS REVIEW ON SCIENCE AND TECHNOLOGY. Main/Corp Institute for Defence Studies and Analyses. Feb. 1972-. Periodical. II. English. mo. $5.46. Institute for Defence Studies and Analyses, Sapru House, Barakhamba Road, New Delhi 110 001 India. *News Review on Science, Technology and Other Major Developments.*

NEWSLETTER - CALIFORNIA ACADEMY OF SCIENCES. Main/Corp California Academy of Sciences, San Francisco. No. 409- Jan. 1974-. 0271-020X. Periodical. US. English. mo. California Academy of Sciences, Golden Gate Park, San Francisco CA 94118. LC Q1. DD 506.079461. *Academy News Letter.*

NEWSLETTER FROM THE COMMISSION FOR SCIENTIFIC RESEARCH IN GREENLAND. No. 1- Apr. 1979-. 0106-1372. Periodical. English. ir. Free. Kommissionen for Videnskabelige Undersgelser I Grnland Ster Volgade 10 Tr G St, DK-1350 Copenhagen K Denmark. Tel 451113666. Ed Gregers E Andersen. Circ 1,400. Forthcoming scientific research activities in Greenland, abstracts of Meddelelser Om Gronland Publications, general information about arctic scientific research.

NEWSLETTER - SCIENCE CURRICULUM IMPROVEMENT STUDY. Main/Corp Science Curriculum Improvement Study. 0036-8288. Periodical. US. English. ir. Union of California, Department of Physics, Berkeley CA 94720. LC LB1585.

NEWSLETTER - STATISTICAL SOCIETY OF CANADA. *See* Statistics.

NEWSLETTER VERMONT INSTITUTE OF NATURAL SCIENCE. Main/Corp Vermont Institute of Natural Science. Periodical. US. English. mo.

NIEUWE NEDERLANDSE BIJDRAGEN TOT DE GESCHIEDENIS DER GENEESKUNDE EN DER NATUURWETENSCHAPPEN. No. 4-. Monographic Series. Dutch (English). ir. LC UNC. DD 505. NLM W1. *Nieuwe Nederlandse Bijdragen Tot de Geschiedenis de Geneeskunde, 0167-4404.*

Science (General)

NIGERIAN JOURNAL OF SCIENCE. V. 1- Mar. 1966-. 0029-0114. Periodical. NR. English (articles in French, or German). sa. $8.60. Science Association of Nigeria, Box 4039, University of Ibadan, Ibadan Nigeria. **Ind/Abst** Math. Rev., Life Sci. Collect., Chem. Abstr. **LC** Q1. **CODEN** NJSCAW. *Proceedings of the Science Association of Nigeria.*

NIHON NO KAGAKUSHA. VFOAT Journal of Japanese Scientists. Began in 1966. Periodical. JA. Japanese. mo. Nihon Kagakusha Kaigi, 9-16 Yushima-1 Bunkyo-ku, Tokyo-to 113 Japan.

NIPPON NAIBUNPI GAKKAI ZASSHI. (NIHON NAIBUNPI GAKKAI ZASSHI). Began in 1925. 0029-0661. Periodical. JA. Japanese (English). mo. Japan Publications Trading Co, PO Box 5030 Tokyo International, Tokyo 100-31 Japan. **Ind/Abst** Life Sci. Collect., Excerpta Med., Index Med., Biol. Abstr. **CODEN** NNGZAZ. Index in last issue of volume - attached.

NOESIS (BUCHAREST, ROMANIA). (NOESIS : TRAVAUX DU COMITE ROUMAIN D'HISTOIRE ET DE PHILOSOPHIE DES SCIENCES). VFOAT Travaux du Comite Roumain d'Histoire et de Philosophie des Sciences. Began in 1972. Periodical. BU. English (French, German, and Russian). ir. 11 Single Issue. Calea Victoriei 125, 79717 Bucuresti Romania. **LC** Q127.R6. **DD** 509.498.

NONDESTRUCTIVE TESTING COMMUNICATIONS. Vol. 1, No. 1-. 0278-0895. Periodical. US. English. ir. $278.00. Gordon & Breach, PO Box 197, London WC2E 9PX England. Ed Jack Blitz. **Ind/Abst** Met. Abstr., World Alum. Abstr. bk rev. adv acc.

NORTH AUSTRALIA RESEARCH DIRECTORY. See Yearbooks, Almanacs, Directories.

NORTHWEST SCIENCE. V. 1- Mar. 1927-. 0029-344X. Periodical. US. English. qt. $25.00. Northwest Science of Washington, Washington State University, Pullma WA 99164-5910. Tel (509)335-3518. Ed Fred Bohm. **Ind/Abst** Life Sci. Collect., Excerpta Med., Int. Aerosp. Abstr., GeoRef, Bibliogr. Agric., Biol. Abstr., Chem. Abstr., Nuci. Sci. Abstr., Sel. Water Resour. Abstr., Sci. Cit. Index, Abr. Ed. **CODEN** NOSCAX. bk rev. Circ 1,200. Publishes articles in the basic, applied, and social sciences that deal with the Pacific Northwest.

NOTES AND RECORDS OF THE ROYAL SOCIETY OF LONDON. Main/Corp Royal Society (Great Britain). V. 1- Apr. 1938-. 0035-9149. Periodical. UK. English. ir. 17.50. Royal Society, 6 Carlton House Terrace, London SW1Y 5AG England. Tel (01)839-5561. Ed R V Jones, and William Paton. **Ind/Abst** Math. Rev., Am. Hist. Life, Hist. Abstr., Part A, Mod. Hist. Abstr., Hist. Abstr., Part B, Twent. Century Abstr. **LC** Q41. **DD** 506.242. **NLM** W1 NO739D. **CODEN** NOREAY. (cum index). Circ 1,400. Definitive papers on the history of science, medicine and technology. *Occasional Notices of the Royal Society of London.*

NOTULAE NATURAE OF THE ACADEMY OF NATURAL SCIENCES OF PHILADELPHIA. Main/Corp Academy of Natural Sciences of Philadelphia. VFOAT Notulae Naturae. No. 1-. 0029-4608. Monographic Series. US. English. ir. $26.00. Proceedings of the Academy of Natural Sciences, 19th and The Parkway, Philadelphia PA 19103. Tel (215)299-1050. Ed K Elaine Hoogland. **Ind/Abst** Life Sci. Collect., GeoRef, Bibliogr. Agric., Bibliogr. Index Geol. **LC** Q111. **CODEN** NONAA2. Index published separately - free - automatically sent. Circ 250. (ctrl). Original research in systematics, evolution, ecology, taxonomy, biogeography. Most articles contain analyses of new data, but succinct reviews and speculative or theoretical works that make major contributions may also appear.

LES NOUVELLES DE L'ACADEMIE. Main/Corp Academie des Sciences (France). Jan. 1984-. Periodical. FR. French. mo. Academie des Sciences, 23 Quai de Conti, 75006 Paris France. *Comptes Rendus des Seances de l'Academie des Sciences. Vie Academique.*

NOVA ACTA LEOPOLDINA. 0369-5034. Monographic Series. GE. German. ir. Deutscher Buch Export-Import, Leninstrasse 16, DDR-701 Leipzig East Germany. Tel 70131. Ed J H Scharf. **Ind/Abst** Math. Rev., Life Sci. Collect., Int. Aerosp. Abstr., Biol. Abstr., GeoRef, Energy Res. Abstr., Chem. Abstr., Bibliogr. Agric., Bibliogr. Index Geol. **CODEN** NOALA4. Composes all branches of natural sciences from pure mathematics to applied biology. *Nova Acta.*

NOVAIA INOSTRANNAIA LITERATURA PO OBSHCHESTVENNYM NAUKAM : NAUKOVEDENIE. 1976-. UR. Multilingual (Russian). mo. 0.35 Single Issue. Akademiia Nauk SSSR, Ul Krasikova 28/45, Moskva Russia. **LC** Z7403, Q158.5. *Novaia Literatura O Nauke I Nauchno-Issledovatelskoi Rabote za Rubezhom.*

NOVAIA SOVETSKAIA LITERATURA PO OBSHCHESTVENNYM NAUKAM : NAUKOVEDENIE. 1976-. Periodical. UR. Russian. mo. 0.40 Single Issue. Akademiia Nauk SSR, UL Krasikova 28/45, Moskva Russia. **LC** Z5055.R78, Q4. *Novaia Sovetskaia Literatura O Nauke I Nauchno-Issledovatelskoi Rabote V SSSR.*

NOVYE KNIGI ZA RUBEZHOM : SERIIA A. ATEMATIKA, MEKHANIKA, ASTRONOMIIA, FIZIKA, GEOFIZIKA, KHIMIIA, GEOLOGIIA. V. 10- Jan. 1957-. Periodical. UR. Russian. mo. $58.50. Victor Kamkin Inc, 12224 Parklawn Drive, Rockville MD 20852. Tel (301)881-5973. **LC** Z7403. *Novye Knigi za Rubezhom.*

NRCP RESEARCH BULLETIN. Main/Corp National Research Council of the Philippines. VAT National Research Council of the Philippines Research Bulletin. English. ir. **LC** Q180.P45. **DD** 505.

NSF GRANT POLICY MANUAL. Main/Corp National Science Foundation (U.S.). VFOAT Grant Policy Manual. Oct. 1977-. US. English. ir. Superintendent of Documents, Atten SSO, Government Printing Office, Washington DC 20402. Tel (202)783-3238. *NSF Grant Administration Manual.*

N.T.M. (NTM). VAT Naturwissenschaften, Technik und Medizin. Yearly V. 1-. 0036-6978. Periodical. SZ. German. ir. $14.44. Kunst & Wissen Erich Bieber, Dufourstrasse 51, CH-8008 Zurich Switzerland. Tel 011-41-1-69 44 20. Ed G Harig, A Mette and others. **Ind/Abst** Math. Rev., Energy Res. Abstr. **LC** Q125. **NLM** W1 N69.

OBSHCHESTVENNYE NAUKI ZA RUBEZHOM. SERIIA 8 : NAUKOVEDENIE. VFOAT Naukovedenie. VAT Obshchestvennye Nauki za Rubezhom. Seriia Vosem : Naukovedenie. Began in 1973. Periodical. UR. Russian. qt. Akademii Nauk SSSR, Ul Krasikova D 28/45, Moskva USSR. **LC** Q4.

OCCASIONAL NOTES. Main/Corp University of Colorado. Libraries. No. 1- Jan. 1963-. 0531-1624. Periodical. US. English. Institute of Arctic and Alpine Research, University of Colorado Campus Box 450, Boulder CO 80309. Tel (303)492-6387. Ed Kathleen A Salzberg. Circ 200. Monographs of work done by Institute personnel and associates.

OCCASIONAL PAPER - MISSOURI ACADEMY OF SCIENCE. Main/Corp Missouri Academy of Science. No. 3-. 0148-0944. Periodical. US. English. ir. $3.50. Missouri Academy of Science, NMSU Science Division, PO Box 828, Kirksville MO 63501. Tel (816)785-4635. **Ind/Abst** Chem. Abstr. **CODEN** OPMSD4. Circ 1,000. (ctrl). Publications which contain the complete work of a specific subject and are published as needed. They are referred publications containing archival material. *Bulletin of the Missouri Academy of Science. Supplement, 0093-853X.*

OCCASIONAL PAPERS OF THE BUFFALO SOCIETY OF NATURAL SCIENCES. No. 1 (1976)-. Monographic Series. US. English. ir. Buffalo Society of Natural Sciences, Buffalo NY 14211.

DE OFFENTLIGE BEVILLINGER TIL FORSKNING OG UDVIKLINGSARBEJDE + OFFENTILICHE AUFWENDUNGEN FUR FORSCHUNG UND ENTWICKLUNG. Main/Corp Statistical Office of the European Communities. VFOAT Government Financing of Research and Development. LU. Danish (Dutch, English, French, German, and Italian). ir. $8.00. European Community Information Service, 2100 M Street NW/Suite 707, Washington DC 20037. **LC** Q180.E9.

THE OHIO JOURNAL OF SCIENCE. 1900. 0030-0950. Periodical. US. English. ir. $25.00 Domestic, $30.00 Foreign. Ohio Academy of Science, 445 King Avenue, Columbus OH 43201. Tel (614)424-6045. Ed Tim Berra. **Ind/Abst** Bibliogr. Agric., Biol. Abstr., Chem. Abstr., Nuci. Sci. Abstr., Sel. Water Resour. Abstr., Sci. Cit. Index, Abr. Ed., Bibliogr. Index Geol. **CODEN** OJSCA9. (cum index). bk rev. adv acc. Circ 2,200. Original peer reviewed papers in all science fields.

OKAYAMA RIKA DAIGAKU KIY . A, SHIZEN KAGAKU. VFOAT Bulletin of the Okayama University of Science. No. 17 (1981)-. 0285-7685. Periodical. Japanese (English). an. Okayama Rika Daigaku 1, Ridaicho Okayama-Shi 700 Japan. **CODEN** ORDKDH. *Oakyama Rika Daigaku Kiyo.*

ONOMASTICKY ZPRAVODAJ CSAV. VFOAT Onomasticheskii Biulleten Chekhoslovatskoi Akademii Nauk. V. 24, No. 1-2-. Periodical. Czech. ir. Onomasticky Usek Ujc Csav, Krakovska 10, 110 00 Praha 1 Czechoslovakia. *Zpravodaj Mistopisne Komise Csav.*

OR-SPEKTRUM. (OR SPEKTRUM : ORGAN DER DEUTSCHEN GESELLSCHAFT FUR OPERATIONS RESEARCH). VFOAT O.R. Spektrum. Vol. 1, No. 1-. 0171-6468. Periodical. US. German (English). qt. Springer Verlag-New York Inc, 175 th Avenue, New York NY 10010. Tel (212)460-1500. Ed G Fandel. **Ind/Abst** Math. Rev., Excerpta Med., Comput. Control Abstr., Electr. Electron. Abstr., Sci. Abstr. Sect. A. Phys. Abstr. **CODEN** ORSPD5. Research contributions in model building: solution and implementation process, specializing in the construction of models and their practical application. Also development of mathematical solutions.

ORGANIZATIONAL DIRECTORY - NATIONAL SCIENCE FOUNDATION (U.S.). See Yearbooks, Almanacs, Directories.

ORGANON. No. 1- 1964-. 0078-6500. PL. French or English. an. Ars Polona, Krakowskie Przediescie 7, 00-068 Warsaw Poland. **Ind/Abst** Math. Rev. **LC** Q9. **NLM** W1 OR663S. *Organon, International Review.*

ORION NATURE QUARTERLY. See Conservation & Natural Resources.

OR/MS TODAY. VFOAT OR MS Today. V. 1- Jan.1974-. Periodical. US. English. bm. $6.00. Operations Research Society of America, Circulation Department, PO Box 64237, Baltimore MD 21264. Tel (301)528-4146.

ORSA/TIMS MEMBERSHIP DIRECTORY. See Yearbooks, Almanacs, Directories.

OSAKA DENKI TSUSHIN DAIGAKU KENKYU RONSHU. SHIZEN KAGAKU HEN. VFOAT Reports of Osaka Electro-Communication University. No. 1 (1965)-. 0386-4987. Periodical. English (Japanese). ir. Osaka Denki Tsushin Daigaku, 18-bam 8-go Hatsu-cho, Neyagawa-shi 572 Japan. **LC** Q4.

OSU QUEST. See Education (General) - Higher Education.

OTTAWA R & D REPORT. May 1970-. 0380-6251. Periodical. CN. English. mo. $38.69. CCH Capital Communications Ltd, 77 Metcalfe Street/Suite 306, Ottawa Ontario K1P 5L6 Canada. Tel (613)235-9183. Ed B Wrangham. Circ 150. Canadian research and development news. Federal provincial governments, industry and university.

OUTLOOK ON SCIENCE POLICY. VFOAT Outlook: Science Policy. V. 1- June 1978-. 0165-0262. UK. English. mo. $110.00. Beech Tree Publishing, 10 Watford Close, Guildford Surrey GU1 2EP England. Tel (0483)67497. Ed Maurice Goldsmith. **NLM** W1 OU553H. Circ 350. News on science and technology policies, and reports internationally.

PACIFIC DISCOVERY. See Natural History.

PACIFIC SCIENCE. V. 1- Jan. 1947-. 0030-8870. Periodical. US. English. qt. $31.00. University of Hawaii Press, 2840 Kolawalu Street, Honolulu HI 96822. Tel (808)948-8697. Ed Charles H Lamoureux. **Ind/Abst** Life Sci. Collect., Energy Inf. Abstr., Environ. Abstr., Int. Aerosp. Abstr., GeoRef, Bibliogr. Agric., Biol. Abstr., Chem. Abstr., Nuci. Sci. Abstr., Sel. Water Resour. Abstr., Sci. Cit. Index, Abr. Ed., Bibliogr. Index Geol., Pollut. Abstr. Indexes, Ocean. Abstr. **LC** QH1. **DD** 574.05. **CODEN** PASCAP. adv acc. Circ 780. Multidisciplinary journal devoted to reporting research in biological and physical sciences, with a focus in the Pacific basin.

PAKISTAN JOURNAL OF SCIENCE. Series Corp Pakistan Association for the Advancement of Science. Miscellaneous Publication. V. 1- Jan. 1949-. 0030-9877. Periodical. PK. English. qt. $25.00. Pakistan Association for Government Science, 6-B Gulberg II, Lahore Pakistan. Tel 883882.

Ed M I D Chughtai. **Ind/Abst** Life Sci. Collect., GeoRef, Comput. Control Abstr., Electr. Electron. Abstr., Sci. Abstr. Sect. A. Phys. Abstr., Biol. Abstr., Chem. Abstr., Meteorol. Geoastrophys. Abstr., Nuci. Sci. Abstr., Bibliogr. Agric., Bibliogr. Index Geol., Phys. Abstr. **LC** Q73. **DD** 506.254. **NLM** W1 PA357. **CODEN** PAJSAS. (cum index). adv acc. **Circ** 850. (ctrl). A research journal devoted to general scientific articles and dissemination of scientific information.

PAKISTAN JOURNAL OF SCIENTIFIC AND INDUSTRIAL RESEARCH. V. 1- Jan. 1958-. 0030-9885. Periodical. English. bm. 34.00. Pakistan Council of Scientific and Industrial Research, 39 Garden Road Saddar, Karachi 0310 Pakistan. **Ed** Azmat Ali Khan. **Ind/Abst** Life Sci. Collect., Excerpta Med., GeoRef, Comput. Control Abstr., Electr. Electron. Abstr., Sci. Abstr. Sect. A. Phys. Abstr., Biol. Abstr., Chem. Abstr., Nuci. Sci. Abstr., Sel. Water Resour. Abstr., Bibliogr. Agric., Bibliogr. Index Geol., Phys. Abstr. **LC** Q180.A1. **DD** 507.2. **NLM** W1 PA357R. **CODEN** PSIRAA. bk rev. **Circ** 1,000. (ctrl). Available on microfilm from Xerox University Microfilms.

PANTNAGAR JOURNAL OF RESEARCH. V. 1- Jan. 1976-. 0377-9386. Periodical. English. ir. 10. Business Manager of the University Book Depot, Govind Ballabh Pant University of Agriculture and Technology, Pantnagar 263145 District Naini Tal Uttar Pradesh India. **Ind/Abst** Chem. Abstr. **CODEN** PJREDO.

PAPERS AND PROCEEDINGS OF THE ROYAL SOCIETY OF TASMANIA. **Main/Corp** Royal Society of Tasmania, Hobart. V. 1- 1863-. 0080-4703. AT. English. an. $8.38. Royal Society of Tasmania, Government Printing Office, Box 1166M, Hobart Tasmania 7001 Australia. **Ind/Abst** Math. Rev., Life Sci. Collect., Biol. Abstr., GeoRef, Art Archaeol. Tech. Abstr., Bibliogr. Index Geol. **LC** Q93. **CODEN** PPRTA6. *Papers and Proceedings of The Royal Society of Van Diemen's Land.*

PAPERS OF THE REGIONAL SCIENCE ASSOCIATION. **Main/Corp** Regional Science Association. V. 1- 1954-. 0486-2902. US. English. sa. Regional Science Association, PO Box 8077, Philadelphia PA 19101. **Tel** (215)387-0681. **Ind/Abst** Soc. Sci. Citation Index.

PATTERN RECOGNITION. V. 1- July 1968-. 0031-3203. Periodical. UK. English. bm. Pergamon Press, 395 Sawmill River Road, Elmsford NY 10523. **Tel** (914)592-7700. **Ind/Abst** Electron. Commun. Abstr. J., ISMEC Bull., Pollut. Abstr. Indexes, Saf. Sci. Abstr. J., Eng. Index Bioeng. Abstr., Eng. Index, Eng. Index Energy Abstr., Life Sci. Collect., Excerpta Med., Int. Aerosp. Abstr., Comput. Control Abstr., Electr. Electron. Abstr., Sci. Abstr. Sect. A. Phys. Abstr., Biol. Abstr., Eng. Index Annu., Eng. Index Mon., Math. Rev., Electron. Pub. Abstr., Phys. Abstr., Sci. Cit. Index, Abr. Ed., Comput. Rev., Math. Rev. **LC** Q327. **DD** 001.533. **NLM** Z 699.A1 P316. **CODEN** PTNRA8. Available on Microfilm from Microforms International Marketing Corporation.

PB - U.S. CLEARINGHOUSE FOR FEDERAL SCIENTIFIC AND TECHNICAL INFORMATION. **Main/Corp** Clearinghouse for Federal Scientific and Technical Information (U.S.). No. 164496-190196(?). Periodical. US. English. ir. *PB.*

PENSEE. Began with Feb. 1971 issue. 0098-776X. Periodical. US. English. qt. $10.00. Student Academic Freedom Forum, PO Box 414, Portland OR 97207. **Ind/Abst** Int. Aerosp. Abstr., GeoRef. **LC** Q1. **DD** 505. **CODEN** PNSEAK.

PERIODICA. Vol. 1, No. 1-2 (Jan.-June 1978)-. 0185-1004. Spanish. qt. $160.00. Periodica, Cich-Unam Apartado Postal 20-281, Mexico 20 DF Mexico. **Tel** 5 48 08 58. **LC** Z7403, Q158.5. **DD** 016.5. bk rev. **Circ** 300. Citations about articles published in science (general) in Latin American journals.

PERIODICALS SCANNED AND ABSTRACTED. LIFE SCIENCE COLLECTION. *See* Indexes/Abstracts.

PERIODICOS BRASILEIROS DE CIENCIA E TECNOLOGIA. BL. Protuguese. an. Ibict, Scrn Q 708/709-Bloco B Loja 18, 70740 Brasilia DF Brazil. **LC** Q4.

THE PHILIPPINE SCIENTIST. Began with Vol. for 1967. 0079-1466. Periodical. PH. English. an. $8.00 US. University of San Carlos, San Carlos Publications, Cebu City J217 Philippines. **Tel** 7-08-74. **Ed** Joseph Baumgartner. **Ind/Abst** Chem. Abstr., Biol. Abstr. **CODEN** PHISB5. **Circ** 100. Annual publication offering contributions on various fields of botany, zoology and biology with emphasis on marine biology and entomology. *Junior Philippine Scientist, 0115-2750.*

PHILOSOPHICAL MEMOIRS OF SCIENCES & MATHS. V. 1- 1974-. CN. English. $2.80 Single Issue. Institute of Sciences & Maths, PO Box 1374, Guelph Ontario N1H 6N7 Canada. **LC** Q174. **DD** 501.

PHILOSOPHY IN SCIENCE. 1-. 0277-2434. Periodical. US. English. ir. $28.00. Pachart Publishing House, Box 35549, Tucson AZ 85740. **Tel** (602)297-4797. **Ed** M Heller, W R Stoeger, S J Zycinski, and J M Zycinski. **LC** Q174. **DD** 501. bk rev. Aims to foster the development and understanding of philosophical questions as they are encountered within the sciences and seeks to promote mutually enriching dialog at the professional level among scientists, philosophers and philosophers of science.

PHILOSOPHY OF SCIENCE. V. 1- Jan. 1934-. 0031-8248. Periodical. US. English. qt. $45.00 Domestic, $46.00 Foreign. Philosophy of Science Association, 18 Morrill Hall, Department of Philosophy, East Lansing MI 48824. **Tel** (517)353-9392. **Ed** Robert E Butts. **Ind/Abst** Sociol. Abstr., Comput. Control Abstr., Electr. Electron. Abstr., Sci. Abstr. Sect. A. Phys. Abstr., Index Book Rev. Humanit., Biol. Abstr., Math. Rev., Humanit. Index, Philos. Index. **LC** Q1. **DD** 505. **NLM** W1 PH619. **CODEN** PHSCA6. bk rev. adv acc. **Circ** 2,200. (ctrl). Carries essays, discussion articles, and book reviews in the general area of philosophy of science.

PHILOSOPHY OF SCIENCE ASSOCIATION NEWSLETTER. 0163-0881. Periodical. US. English. ir. $10.00 Domestic, $12.00 Foreign. Michigan State University, Philosophy Department, East Lansing MI 48823. **Tel** (517)353-9392. **Ed** Peter D Asquith. **Circ** 850. (ctrl). Provides a channel for communication of such information as grants, conferences, new periodicals and bibliographic notes.

PHONE TES PROODOU. Periodical. Greek, Modern. ir. 5.00. D Kounousos, Kratinou 7, Athenai Greece. **LC** Q4.

PHYSIS. Yearly V. 1- 1959-. 0031-9414. Periodical. IT. Italian. qt. $38.61. Casa Editrice Leo S Olschki, Casella Postale PO Box 66, CCP 5/1020 50100 Firenze Italy. **Tel** 055/687444/5. **Ind/Abst** Math. Rev., Am. Hist. Life, Hist. Abstr., Part A, Mod. Hist. Abstr., Hist. Abst., Part B, Twent. Century Abstr. **LC** Q54. **NLM** W1 PH986H. **CODEN** PYSSA3.

POKROKY MATEMATIKY, FYSIKY ASTRONOMIE. (POKROKY MATEMATIKY, FYSIKY A ASTRONOMIE). Vol. 1- 1956-. 0032-2423. Periodical. GW. Czech. bm. Kubon and Sagner, Postfach 34 01 08, D8 Munchen 34 West Germany. **Tel** (089)52 20 27. **Ind/Abst** Math. Rev., Int. Aerosp. Abstr., Chem. Abstr. **LC** Q44.J3. **CODEN** PMFAA4. Publishes articles on advances in the above named scientific fields, modern trends in the teaching of mathematics and physics.

POLISH POLAR RESEARCH. VFOAT Polskie Badania Polarne. Vol. 1, No. 1-. 0138-0338. Periodical. PL. English (summaries in English, Polish, and Russian). qt. 400. Polish Academy of Sciences, Nowy Swiat, Warsaw Poland. **Tel** 26-84-10. **Ind/Abst** Life Sci. Collect. **LC** G575. **DD** 919.8005. bk rev. adv acc. **Circ** 650. (ctrl). Theory, practice, collection, elaboration, and finding classification of scientific information, library science, librarianship, and languages of information.

POPULAR SCIENCE DO-IT-YOURSELF YEARBOOK. *See* Yearbooks, Almanacs, Directories.

POPULAR SCIENCE (NEW YORK, N.Y. : 1969). (POPULAR SCIENCE). VFOAT Popular Science Monthly. Vol. 195, No. 1 (July 1969)-. Periodical. US. English. mo. Times Mirror, 380 Madison Avenue, New York NY 10017, (subscription address: Neodata PO Box 2606 Boulder CO 80322). **Tel** (303)447-9330. *Popular Science Monthly (New York, N.Y. : 1950).*

POPULAR SCIENCE SERIES. V. 1-. 0360-0297. Monographic Series. US. English. ir. Illinois State Museum Society, Spring & Edwards Street, Springfield IL 62706. **Ind/Abst** GeoRef, Bibliogr. Index Geol. **DD** 500.

POPYURA SAIENSU. VFOAT Popular Science. Periodical. JA. Japanese. mo. 710 Each Issue. Daiyamondosha 4-2 Kasumigaseki 1 Chiyoda-ku, Tokyo-to 100 Japan. **LC** Q4.

PORTUGAL, FORSCHUNGSPOLITIK UND FORSCHUNGSPRAXIS. **Series/Titl** Marktinformation. GW. German. ir. 3.00. Bundesstelle fur Aussenhandelsinformation, Blaubach 13 Postfach 10 80 07, D-5000 Koln 1 West Germany. **LC** Q180.P6. **DD** 507.20469.

POST. KENYA. (POST, KENYA). **VAT** Promotion of Science and Technology Kenya. V. 1- Jan. 1973-. 0253-5963. Periodical. English. ir. Free. Kenya National Academy of Sciences, PO Box 47288, Nairobi Kenya. **Tel** 721138. **Ed** J K G Mati. **Ind/Abst** Chem. Abstr. **LC** Q225. **DD** 509.6762. **CODEN** POKEDO. bk rev. adv acc. **Circ** 4,000. A magazine for promoting science and technology through young people by inculcating scientific attitudes.

PRACE NAUKOZNAWCZE I PROGNOSTYCZNE. No. 7- 1972-. PL. Polish (summaries in English and Russian). qt. ARS Poloand, Krakowskie Przedmiescie 7, 00-068 Warsaw Poland. **LC** Q158.5. *Prace Naukoznawcze.*

PRACE POPULARNONAUKOWE. **Main/Corp** Bydgoskie Towarzystwo Naukowe. 1- 1965-. 0525-3187. Periodical. PL. Polish. ir. ARS Polona, Krakowskie Przedmiescie 7, 00 068 Warsaw Poland.

PRAKRUTI. Periodical. II. English. sa. Utkal University, Vani Vihar, Bhubaneswar Orissa 75104 India. **LC** Q73. **DD** 505.

PRIRODA. 1912-. 0032-874X. Periodical. UR. Russian (tables of contents also in English). mo. $41.50. Victor Kamkin Inc (70707), 12224 Parklawn Drive, Rockville MD 20852. **Tel** (301)881-5973. **Ind/Abst** Int. Aerosp. Abstr., GeoRef, Comput. Control Abstr., Electr. Electron. Abstr., Sci. Abstr. Sect. A. Phys. Abstr., Art Archaeol. Tech. Abstr., Chem. Abstr., Bibliogr. Agric., Bibliogr. Index Geol., Phys. Abstr. **LC** Q4. **NLM** W1 PR525E. **CODEN** PRIRA3.

PRIRODA. Vol. 1- Jan./Feb. 1952-. 0032-8731. Periodical. BU. Bulgarian. bm. $28.00. Hemus, 6 Boulevard Rusky, Sofia Bulgaria. **Ind/Abst** Chem. Abstr., Bibliogr. Agric. **CODEN** PRIRB4.

PRIRODNI VEDY. **Series/Titl** Sbornik Praci Pedagogicke Fakulty V Ostrave. 1971-. 0139-6544. Periodical. Czech (German). ir. **Ind/Abst** Chem. Abstr. **LC** Q4. **CODEN** SPOEBE.

PRIRODNI VEDY VE SKOLE. Began in 1951. Periodical. CS. Czech. ir. Artia, PO Box 790, Praha 1 Czechoslovakia. **LC** Q181.A1.

PROBE POST. *See* Conservation & Natural Resources.

PROBLEMI ATTUALI DI SCIENZA E DI CULTURA. No. 1-. 0369-8408. Monographic Series. IT. Italian. ir. Bardi Editore, Salita de Crescenzi 16, 00186 Rome Italy. **Ind/Abst** GeoRef. **LC** AS222. **DD** 055.1.

PROBLEMS OF CONTROL AND INFORMATION THEORY. VFOAT Problemy Upravleniia I Teorii Informatsii. V. 1- 1972-. 0370-2529. Periodical. HU. Multilingual (summaries in English and Russian). qt. $304.00. Pergamon Press, 395 Sawmill River Road, Elmsford NY 10523. **Ind/Abst** Math. Rev., Electron. Commun. Abstr. J., ISMEC Bull., Pollut. Abstr. indexes, Saf. Sci. Abstr. J., Eng. Index Annu., Eng. Index Mon., Eng. Index Bioeng. Abstr., Eng. Index Energy Abstr., Int. Aerosp. Abstr., Comput. Control Abstr., Electr. Electron. Abstr., Sci. Abstr. Sect. A. Phys. Abstr., Phys. Abstr., Eng. Index. **LC** Q350. **CODEN** PUTIAI.

PROBLEMS OF THE SCIENCE OF SCIENCE. 1st- 1970-. Periodical. PL. English or French. ir. ARS Polona, WarsZaua Vl Kiakowski, Warsaw Poland. **Ind/Abst** Lang. Lang. Behav. Abstr., Sociol. Abstr.

PROBLEMY PEREDACI INFORMACII. (PROBLEMY PEREDACHI INFORMATSII). 0555-2923. Periodical. UR. Russian. qt. $25.00. Victor Kamkin Inc (70741), 12224 Parklawn Drive, Rockville MD 20852. **Tel** (301)881-5973. **Ind/Abst** Math. Rev., Comput. Control Abstr., Electr. Electron. Abstr., Sci. Abstr. Sect. A. Phys. Abstr., Phys. Abstr. **LC** Q350. **CODEN** PPDIA5. (cum index). *Problemy Peredachi Informatsii.*

PROCEEDINGS - ARKANSAS ACADEMY OF SCIENCE. (PROCEEDINGS OF THE ARKANSAS ACADEMY OF SCIENCE). **Main/Corp** Arkansas Academy of Science. V. 1- 1941-. 0097-4374. US. English. an. $10.50. Arkansas Academy of Science, Hendrix College c/o A Johnson Conway AR 72032. **Tel** (501)450-1377. **Ed** V Rick McDaniel. **Ind/Abst** Excerpta Med., GeoRef, Biol. Abstr., Chem. Abstr., Bibliogr. Agric., Bibliogr. Index Geol. **LC** AS36. **DD** 061.67. **CODEN** AKASAO. **Circ**

450. (ctrl). A publication of the papers presented at the annual meeting of the Arkansas Academy of Science covering all fields of science.

THE PROCEEDINGS, DIRECTORY AND HANDBOOK OF THE NATIONAL ASSOCIATION OF ACADEMIES OF SCIENCE. *See* Yearbooks, Almanacs, Directories.

PROCEEDINGS - INDIAN ACADEMY OF SCIENCES. **Main/Corp** Indian Academy of Sciences. V. 89- March 1980-. Periodical. English. ir. $762.92. J C Baltzer, Wettsteinplatz 10, CH-4058 Basle Switzerland. **Tel** 61-268925. *Proceedings. Part I: Chemical Sciences, Proceedings. Part II: Earth and Planetary III: Mathematical Sciences.*

PROCEEDINGS - INSTITUT TEKNOLOGI BANDUNG. **Main/Corp** Institut Teknologi Bandung. V. 4- 1967-. 0522-2133. English (Indonesian). ir. Jl Surapati 1, Bandung Indonesia. **Ind/Abst** GeoRef. **LC** Q75. **CODEN** PITBBG. *Madjalah - Institut Teknologi Bandung. Proceedings - Institut Teknologi Bandung.*

PROCEEDINGS - NEBRASKA ACADEMY OF SCIENCES AND AFFILIATED SOCIETIES. (PROCEEDINGS - THE NEBRASKA ACADEMY OF SCIENCES AND AFFILIATED SOCIETIES). **Main/Corp** Nebraska Academy of Sciences. 79th- 1969-. 0077-6343. US. English. an. Nebraska Academy of Sciences, 306 Morriee Hall, 14th Street and U Street, Lincoln NE 68588. **Ind/Abst** Biol. Abstr., Bibliogr. Agric. **LC** Q11. **DD** 505. **CODEN** PNBAAP. *Proceedings of the Annual Meeting - Nebraska Academy of Sciences and Affiliated Societies, 0191-2755.*

PROCEEDINGS OF THE . . . ANNUAL BANGLADESH SCIENCE CONFERENCE. **Main/Conf** Bangladesh Science Conference. English. an. **LC** Q101. **DD** 505.

PROCEEDINGS OF THE ARAB SCHOOL ON SCIENCE AND TECHNOLOGY. **Main/Conf** Arab School on Science and Technology. 1st-. 0730-7845. Monographic Series. US. English. ir. Hemisphere Publishing Corporation, 19 West 44 Street, New York NY 10036.

PROCEEDINGS OF THE FULL BOARD MEETING - ISCU AB. (PROCEEDINGS OF THE FULL BOARD MEETING). **VFOAT** Proceedings of the General Assembly Meeting. 1970-. 0303-1136. FR. English. ir. ICSU AB, 17 rue Mirabeau, 75016 Paris France. **NLM** W1.

PROCEEDINGS OF THE INDIAN NATIONAL SCIENCE ACADEMY, PART A: PHYSICAL SCIENCES. (PROCEEDINGS OF THE INDIAN NATIONAL SCIENCE ACADEMY. PART A, PHYSICAL SCIENCES). **Main/Corp** Indian National Science Academy. **VFOAT** Physical Sciences. Vol. 36, No. 1 (Jan. 1970)-. 0370-0046. II. English. bm. $20.00. Indian National Science Academy, 1 Bahadur Shah Zafar Marg, New Delhi-110 002 India. **Ind/Abst** Math. Rev., GeoRef, Comput. Control Abstr., Electr. Electron. Abstr., Sci. Abstr. Sect. A. Phys. Abstr., Met. Abstr., World Alum. Abstr., Chem. Abstr. **LC** Q73. **DD** 500.205. **NLM** W1 PR585W. **CODEN** PIPSBD.

PROCEEDINGS OF THE INDIAN SCIENCE CONGRESS. **Main/Conf** Indian Science Congress Association. 1st- 1914-. 0373-0786. II. English. ir. $15.00. Indian Books and Periodical, 3341 Christian Colony-Pyarey Lal Road, New Delhi India 110005. **Ind/Abst** GeoRef, Chem. Abstr., Bibliogr. Index Geol. **CODEN** PISCAD.

PROCEEDINGS OF THE INDIANA ACADEMY OF SCIENCE. **Main/Corp** Indiana Academy of Science. V. 1- 1891-. 0073-6767. US. English. an. Indiana Academy of Science, 140 North Senate Avenue, Indianapolis IN 46204. **Ind/Abst** GeoRef, Life Sci. Collect., Chem. Abstr., Biol. Abstr., Nuci. Sci. Abstr. **LC** Q11. **DD** 500. **NLM** W1 PR585Y. **CODEN** PIACAP. (cum index). (ctrl). Series of scientific papers presented at the annual fall meeting of the Academy.

PROCEEDINGS OF THE INTERNATIONAL CONFERENCE ON CYBERNETICS AND SOCIETY (1972) *CEASED.* (PROCEEDINGS OF THE INTERNATIONAL CONFERENCE ON CYBERNETICS AND SOCIETY). **Main/Conf** International Conference on Cybernetics and Society. 1972-1973. 0360-8913. US. English. an. Institute of Electrical and Electronic Engineers, 345 East 47th Street, New York NY 10017. **Ind/Abst** Index IEEE Publ., Eng. Index Annu., Eng. Index Mon., Eng. Index Bioeng. Abstr., Eng. Index Energy Abstr. **LC** Q300. **DD** 001.53. **NLM** W3 IN597J. **CODEN** PCCSDA.

THE PROCEEDINGS OF THE IOWA ACADEMY OF SCIENCE. **Main/Corp** Iowa Academy of Science. V. 1- 1887-. 0085-2236. Periodical. US. English. qt. $20.00. Iowa Academy of Science, University of Northern Iowa, PO Box 868, Cedar Falls IA 50613. **Tel** (319)273-2022. **Ed** Roger and Marilyn Bachmann. **Ind/Abst** Excerpta Med., Coal Abstr., GeoRef, Comput. Control Abstr., Electr. Electron. Abstr., Sci. Abstr. Sect. A. Phys. Abstr., Biol. Abstr., Chem. Abstr., Nuci. Sci. Abstr., Sel. Water Resour. Abstr., Math. Rev., Bibliogr. Agric., Bibliogr. Index Geol., Phys. Abstr. **LC** Q11. **DD** 505. **NLM** W1 IO225. **CODEN** PIAIA9. (cum index). bk rev. adv acc. A refereed scientific journal publishing articles in all areas of biological and physical science.

PROCEEDINGS OF THE LOUISIANA ACADEMY OF SCIENCES. (THE PROCEEDINGS OF THE LOUISIANA ACADEMY OF SCIENCES). **Main/Corp** Louisiana Academy of Sciences. V. 1- 1932-. 0096-9192. US. English. an. Louisiana State University, Department of Entomology, Baton Rouge LA 70803. **Ind/Abst** Energy Res. Abstr., Bibliogr. Agric., Biol. Abstr., Chem. Abstr., Nuci. Sci. Abstr. **LC** Q11. **CODEN** PLAAA6.

PROCEEDINGS OF THE MONTANA ACADEMY OF SCIENCES. **Main/Corp** Montana Academy of Sciences. V. 1- 1940-. 0096-9206. US. English. an. $10.00. Montana Academy of Sciences, 341 Beverly Avenue, Missoula MT 59801. **Tel** (406)243-0211. **Ind/Abst** GeoRef, Biol. Abstr., Chem. Abstr., Bibliogr. Agric., Bibliogr. Index Geol. **LC** Q11. **DD** 506.2786. **CODEN** PMASAX. **Circ** 500. Papers and abstracts of papers presented at the annual meeting of the Montana Academy of Sciences, plus a few additional selected scientific papers.

PROCEEDINGS OF THE NATIONAL ACADEMY OF SCIENCES OF THE UNITED STATES OF AMERICA. (PROCEEDINGS). 0744-2831. Periodical. US. English. sm. $215.00 Domestic, $250.00 Foreign. National Academy of Sciences, 2101 Constitution Avenue NW, Washington DC 20418. **Tel** (201)334-2525. **Ed** Maxine F Singer. **Circ** 9,500. (ctrl). Reports that describe the results of original theoretical or experimental research of exceptional importance and broad interest to diverse groups of scientists.

PROCEEDINGS OF THE NATIONAL ASSOCIATION OF ACADEMIES OF SCIENCE. **Main/Corp** National Association of Academies of Science. **VFOAT** Proceedings of the Association of Academies of Science. 1978/79-. US. English. an. Ohio Academy of Sciences, Archivist, 445 King Avenue, Columbus OH 43201. *Proceedings of the Association of Academies of Science.*

PROCEEDINGS OF THE NATIONAL SCIENCE COUNCIL, REPUBLIC OF CHINA *CEASED.* **Main/Corp** Kuo Chia Ko Hsueh Wei Yuan Hui. Vol. 1, No. 1-V. 4. CH. English (some articles in Chinese). qt. National Science Council, 214 Roosevelt Road, Section 3, Taipei Taiwan. **LC** Q1. *Proceedings of the National Council on Science Development.*

PROCEEDINGS OF THE NATIONAL SCIENCE COUNCIL, REPUBLIC OF CHINA. PART A, PHYSICAL SCIENCE AND ENGINEERING. **VFOAT** Physical Science and Engineering. Vol. 8, No. 1 (Jan. 1984)-. Periodical. English (summaries in Chinese). qt. National Science Council, Republic of China, 2 Canton Street, Taipei Taiwan Republic of China. **Ind/Abst** Chem. Abstr. **CODEN** PNAEE2. *Proceedings of the National Science Council, Republic of China. Part A, Applied Sciences, 0253-8415.*

PROCEEDINGS OF THE NATIONAL SCIENCE COUNCIL, REPUBLIC OF CHINA. PART B, LIFE SCIENCES. **VFOAT** Life Sciences. Vol. 8, No. 1 (Jan. 1984)-. Periodical. English. qt. $8.00. National Science Council, Republic of China, 2 Canton Street, Taipei Taiwan Republic of China. **Ind/Abst** Chem. Abstr., Index Med. **NLM** W1. **CODEN** PNBSEF. *Proceedings of the National Science Council, Republic of China. Part B, Basic Science, 0253-6870.*

PROCEEDINGS OF THE NORTH DAKOTA ACADEMY OF SCIENCE. **Main/Corp** North Dakota Academy of Science. V. 1- 1947-. 0096-9214. US. English. an. $5.00. North Dakota Academy of Science, PO Box 8123 University Station, Grand Forks ND 58202. **Tel** (701)777-2786. **Ed** A William Johnson. **Ind/Abst** GeoRef, Biol. Abstr., Bibliogr. Index Geol. **LC** Q11. **DD** 506.2784. **NLM** W1 PR586EN. **CODEN** PNDAAZ. **Circ** 750. (ctrl). Symposia and contributed papers on research done by or of interest to North Dakota scientists.

PROCEEDINGS OF THE NOVA SCOTIAN INSTITUTE OF SCIENCE. **Main/Corp** Nova Scotian Institute of Science. V.1- 1863/66-. CN. English. ir. **LC** Q21. (cum index).

PROCEEDINGS OF THE NOVA SCOTIAN INSTITUTE OF SCIENCE. **Main/Corp** Nova Scotian Institute of Science. V. 18, Pt. 1- 1930/31-. 0078-2521. Periodical. CN. English. 15.00. Nova Scotian Institute of Science, c/o Dalhousie University, Science Library, Halifax Nova Scotia B3H 4J3 Canada. **Tel** 424-2331. **Ed** Gary Hicks. **Ind/Abst** GeoRef, Chem. Abstr., Bibliogr. Agric. **LC** Q21. **CODEN** PNSIAW. **Circ** 50. (ctrl). Proceedings of the Institute of Science; regional original articles and review articles in the physical and natural sciences. *The Proceedings and Transactions of the Nova Scotian Institute of Science.*

PROCEEDINGS OF THE OREGON ACADEMY OF SCIENCE. **Main/Corp** Oregon Academy of Science. Vol. 1 (1943-1947)-. 0370-1093. US. English. an. $8.00. Oregon State University, Science-Technology Division-Library, Corvalis OR 97331. **Tel** (503)754-4594. **Ed** Claude Curran. **Ind/Abst** GeoRef. **LC** Q11. **DD** 506.2795. **CODEN** PORSAU. **Circ** 150. Consists of abstracts of papers given at the annual meetings of the academy. Selected papers are published in full.

PROCEEDINGS OF THE PAKISTAN ACADEMY OF SCIENCES. (PROCEEDINGS). **Main/Corp** Pakistan Academy of Sciences. 0377-2969. PK. English. ir. Pakistan Academy of Sciences, PO Box 1090, Islamabad Pakistan. **Ind/Abst** Math. Rev., Biol. Abstr., Chem. Abstr. **LC** Q1. **DD** 505. **CODEN** PKSPAW.

PROCEEDINGS OF THE PENNSYLVANIA ACADEMY OF SCIENCE. **Main/Corp** Pennsylvania Academy of Science. V. 1- 1924/26-. 0096-9222. US. English. sa. $25.00. P A S Treasurer, c/o S S Hendrix, Gettysburg College, Gettysburg PA 17325. **Tel** (717)749-3111. **Ed** Daniel Klemm. **Ind/Abst** Excerpta Med., Int. Aerosp. Abstr., GeoRef, Bibliogr. Agric., Biol. Abstr., Chem. Abstr., Bibliogr. Index Geol. **LC** Q11. **DD** 506. **NLM** W1 PR586RN. **CODEN** PPASAK. (cum index). **Circ** 600. General science journal open to all branches of science. The subject matter is not limited geographically to Pennsylvania.

PROCEEDINGS OF THE ROCHESTER ACADEMY OF SCIENCE. **Main/Corp** Rochester Academy of Science, Rochester, N.Y. V. 1- Jan. 1889-. 0096-4166. US. English. ir. University of Rochester, Rochester Academy of Science, Rochester NY 14627. **Tel** (716)275-4485. **Ind/Abst** GeoRef, Bibliogr. Index Geol. **LC** Q11. **DD** 505. **NLM** W1 PR586ST. **CODEN** PROSA2.

PROCEEDINGS OF THE ROYAL SOCIETY OF NEW ZEALAND. **Main/Corp** Royal Society of New Zealand. V. 85- May 1957-. 0557-4161. NZ. English. an. $22.00. Royal Society of New Zealand, Private Bag, Wellington New Zealand. **Tel** 727-421. **Ind/Abst** GeoRef, Bibliogr. Index Geol. **CODEN** PSNZAP. Each issue contains an index to its own contents - no vol index - loose. **Circ** 770. The report of the Royal Society of New Zealand, the concerns and activities of its staff and fellows.

PROCEEDINGS OF THE ROYAL SOCIETY OF QUEENSLAND. **Main/Corp** Royal Society of Queensland, Brisbane. V. 1-. 0080-469X. AT. English. an. 15 Australia. Royal Society of Queensland, Chemical Department, University of Queensland, St Lucia Queensland 4067 Australia. **Tel** 07-377-3483. **Ed** E D McKenzie. **Ind/Abst** GeoRef, Biol. Abstr., Chem. Abstr., Index Med., Bibliogr. Index Geol. **LC** Q93. **CODEN** PRSQAG. (cum index). **Circ** 2,000. (ctrl). Refereed scientific papers in any specialized area of science and some important review lectures.

PROCEEDINGS OF THE ROYAL SOCIETY OF VICTORIA. **Main/Corp** Royal Society of Victoria (Melbourne, Vic.). N.S. V. 1- June 1889-. 0035-9211. Periodical. AT. English. sa. $25.08. Royal Society of Victoria, 9 Victoria Street, Melbourne 3000 Australia. **Tel** (03)663 5259. **Ed** G F Watson. **Ind/Abst** Biol. Abstr., GeoRef, Comput. Control Abstr., Electr. Electron. Abstr., Sci. Abstr. Sect. A.

Science (General)

Phys. Abstr., Bibliogr. Index Geol., Phys. Abstr. LC Q93. NLM W1 PR5861G. CODEN PRSVAV. Index in last issue of volume - attached. (cum index). Circ 1,000. (ctrl). Papers on scientific research, projects on geology, zoology, biology, botany, agriculture, meteorology, paleontology and social sciences. Transactions and Proceedings of the Royal Society of Victoria.

PROCEEDINGS OF THE SOUTH DAKOTA ACADEMY OF SCIENCE. Main/Corp South Dakota Academy of Science. V. 1- 1916-. 0096-378X. US. English. an. $13.75. South Dakota Academy of Science, Department of Math, Augustana College, Sioux Falls SD 57107. Tel (605)336-4825. Ed Carroll Hanten. Ind/Abst GeoRef, Biol. Abstr., Chem. Abstr., Bibliogr. Index Geol. LC Q11. NLM W1 PR5868. CODEN PSDAA2. Circ 350. (ctrl). Research by South Dakota scientists in all areas of biological, physical, and mathematical sciences.

PROCEEDINGS OF THE SPECIAL COMMITTEE OF THE SENATE ON SCIENCE POLICY. Main/Corp Canada. Parliament. Senate. Special Committee on Science Policy. VFOAT Deliberations du Comite Special du Senat sur la Politique Scientifique. Dec. 3, 1975-. CN. English (French). LC Q180.C2. DD 338.4750971. Deliberations du Comite Special du Senat sur la Politique Scientifique.

PROCEEDINGS OF THE SPECIAL COMMITTEE OF THE SENATE ON SCIENCE POLICY. Main/Corp Canada. Parliament. Senate. Special Committee on Science Policy. VFOAT Deliberations du Comite Special du Senat sur la Politique Scientifique. CN. English and French. Deliberations du Comite, Ottawa Ontario K1A 0S9 Canada. LC Q180.C2. DD 338.971.

PROCEEDINGS, THE . . . INTERNATIONAL SYMPOSIA. Main/Corp Taehan Minguk Haksurwon. English. an. LC Q1. DD 505. Proceedings, the . . . International Symposium.

PROGRAM OF THE NATIONAL MEETING - AMERICAN ASSOCIATION FOR THE ADVANCEMENT OF SCIENCE. (PROGRAM OF THE . . . NATIONAL MEETING). Main/Corp American Association for the Advancement of Science. Series/Titl AAAS Publication. VFOAT Annual Meeting Program, AAAS Annual Meeting. 142nd (18-24 Feb. 1976)-148th (3-8 Jan. 1982). 0272-4189. US. English. an. $6.00. American Association for the Advancement of Science, 1333 H Street NW, Washington DC 20005. Tel (202)326-6400. Ind/Abst GeoRef. Annual Meeting.

PROGRAMS AND PLANS - ENVIRONMENTAL RESEARCH LABORATORIES. (PROGRAMS AND PLANS). Main/Corp Environmental Research Laboratories (U.S.). VFOAT Programs & Plans. 0149-6034. US. English. an. Environmental Research Laboratories, University of Colorado, Boulder CO 80309. LC Q180.U5. DD 353.00855. Vols. for (1982, 1983-) distributed to depository libraries in microfiche.

PROGRESS IN PATTERN RECOGNITION. Vol. 1-. US. English. ir. Elsevier North-Holland Inc, 52 Vanderbilt Avenue, New York NY 10017. LC Q327. DD 001.534. NLM W1 PR677D.

PROGRESS REPORT - NATIONAL SCIENCE COUNCIL (IRELAND). Main/Corp National Science Council (Ireland). IE. English. ir. Stationery Office, St Martins House, Waterloo Road, Dublin 4 Ireland. LC Q127.I73. DD 354.4150085505.

PROGRESS REPORTS. Main/Corp Statens Naturvetenskapliga Forskningsrad (Sweden). 1970/71-. English. ir. Box 23136, S-10435 Stockholm 23 Sweden. LC Q180.S8.

PROJECT SUMMARIES - NATIONAL SCIENCE FOUNDATION (U.S.). DIVISION OF SCIENCE RESOURCES STUDIES. (PROJECT SUMMARIES). Main/Corp National Science Foundation (U.S.). Division of Science Resources Studies. 1980/81-. 0748-2701. US. English. an. National Science Foundation, Washington DC 20550. LC Q11. DD 338.97306.

PROVISIONAL VERBATIM RECORD, PLENARY MEETING. Main/Corp United Nations Educational, Scientific and Cultural Organization. General Conference. VFOAT VR. Periodical. English. ir. United Nations Publications, Sales Section/Room A-3315, New York NY 10017.

PRZEGLAD INFORMACJI O NAUKOZNAWSTWIE. Periodical. PL. Polish. qt. ARS Polona, Krakowskie Przedmiescie 7, 00-068 Warsaw Poland. LC Q4.

PSA. Main/Corp Philosophy of Science Association. VAT Philosophy of Science Association. Began with 1970. 0270-8647. US. English. be. Department of Local Government Affairs, Office of Financial Affairs, 303 East Monroe Street, Springfield IL 62706. LC Q174. DD 501. NLM W1 PH619E.

PUBLIC SCIENCE NEWSLETTER. V. 4- Jan. 1973-. 0091-1720. Periodical. US. English. mo. $30.00. Massachusetts Institute of Technology, Room E53-450, Cambridge MA 02142. LC Q127.U6. NLM W1 PU638. SPPSG Newsletter.

PUBLICACIONES. Main/Corp Guatemala (City) Universidad de San Carlos. Instituto de Investigaciones Cientificas. Spanish. ir. LC Q25.

PUBLICATIONS - ENGLISH DIALECT SOCIETY. Main/Corp English Dialect Society. UK. English. ir. Elsevier Scientific Publishers of Ireland Ltd, PO Box 85, Limerick Ireland. Ind/Abst Index Med., Sci. Cit. Index, Abr. Ed., Chem. Abstr.

PUBLICATIONS OF LASL RESEARCH. Main/Corp Los Alamos Scientific Laboratory. US. English. LC Z7405.R4.

PUBLICATIONS OF THE NATIONAL RESEARCH COUNCIL OF CANADA. VFOAT Publications du Conseil National de Recherches du Canada. 1918/38-. 0077-5584. Periodical. CN. English. ir. Ind/Abst Excerpta Med., GeoRef. NLM Z 7401 P975. CODEN NTCPAR.

PUBLIKATIONEN - INSTITUT FUR DIE PADAGOGIK DER NATURWISSENSCHAFTEN AN DER. Main/Corp C. German. ir. Olshausenstrasse 40-60, D-2300 Kiel West Germany. LC Z5818.S3, Q183.4.G29.

PUBLISHED SEARCHES. (PUBLISHED SEARCHES : MASTER CATALOG). VFOAT NTIS Published Searches. 1982-. 0743-6955. US. English. an. N T I S, 2585 Port Royal Road, Springfield VA 22161. LC Z7403, Q158.5. DD 016.5. Vols. for 1982- distributed to depository libraries in microfiche. Current Published Searches.

PUCE A L'ORIELLE. See Children and Youth Interests.

PURSUIT. 0033-4685. Periodical. US. English. qt. $12.00. Society for Investigating Unexplained, Box 265, Little Silver NJ 07739. Tel (201)542-2000. Ind/Abst GeoRef.

PUSAN SUSAN TAEHAK YON'GU POGO : CHAYON KWAHAK. VFOAT Chayon Kwahakpyon, Bulletin of National Fisheries University of Pusan : Natural Sciences. V. 1- Dec. 1956-. Periodical. Korean (with summaries in English). ir. Hanguk Susan Hakhoe, National Fisheries University of Pusan, Pusan 608 Korea. Ind/Abst Biol. Abstr., Energy Res. Abstr. LC Q4. DD 505. CODEN PSCKAR.

QUEBEC SCIENCE. VFOAT Magazine Quebec. V. 8, No. 3- Jan. 1970-. 0021-6127. Periodical. CN. French. mo. Le Magazine Quebec Science, CP 220 Ville Mont Royal, Quebec H3P 3C4 Canada. Tel (418)657-3551. Ind/Abst Environ., Point Repere. DD 505. bk rev. adv acc. Scientific popularization. Jeune Scientifique, 0317-400X.

R & D ACTIVITIES IN STATE GOVERNMENT AGENCIES. Series Corp Surveys of Science Resources Series. 1964/65-. 0565-8284. Periodical. US. English. ir. National Science Foundation, 1800 G Street NW Washington DC 20550. LC Q180.U5. DD 600, 500.

R & D MANAGEMENT DIGEST. VAT Research and Development Management Digest. 0361-753X. Periodical. US. English. mo. $48.00 Domestic, $58.00 Foreign. Lomond Systems Incorporated, Po Box 88, Mt Airy MD 21771. Tel (301)829-1496. Ed Lowell H Hattery. bk rev. A summary of literature, events, and opportunities for R&D managers and persons interested in science/technology policy.

RADICAL SCIENCE. 14 (1984)-. Periodical. UK. English. sa. 18.00 Three Issues. Radical Science, 26 Freegrove Road, London N7 9RQ England. LC Q175.4. DD 306.4505. Radical Science Journal, 0305-0963.

RADICAL SCIENCE JOURNAL CEASED. No. 1- Jan. 1974-. 0305-0963. Periodical. UK. English. ty. $27.58. Radical Science Journal, 26 Freegrove Road, London N7 9RQ England. Tel 609-5646. Ind/Abst Sociol. Abstr., Soc. Welf. Soc. Plan./Policy Soc. Dev., Altern. Press Index, Soc. Sci. Citation Index. LC Q175.4. DD 301.24305. bk rev. Circ 2,000. Extended analyses of the ideology and practice of science, technology and medicine from a radical political perspective.

RADIOISOTOPES. Began 1952. 0033-8303. Periodical. JA. English (Japanese). mo. $46.51. Japan Radioisotopes Association, 28-45 Honkomagome 2 Chome, Bunkyo-Ku Tokyo 113-91 Japan. Tel 03-946-7111. Ed Hisao Yamashita. Ind/Abst Excerpta Med., Index Med., Biol. Abstr., Comput. Control Abstr., Electr. Electron. Abstr., Sci. Abstr. Sect. A. Phys. Abstr., Energy Res. Abstr., Chem. Abstr., Phys. Abstr. NLM W1 RA265. CODEN RAISAB. adv acc. Circ 6,000. Papers in the fields of physics, biochemistry, medical science, pharmacology and engineering by using radioisotopes.

RAINGAN PRACHAM PI. Main/Corp Sathaban Wichai Witthayasat Prayuk Haeng Prathet Thai. VFOAT Report. 1st- 1964-. Thai. ir.

RAND PAPER SERIES. (THE RAND PAPER SERIES). P-1- 1947-. 0092-2803. US. English. Rand Corporation, 1700 Main Street, Santa Monica CA 90406. Ind/Abst Popul. Index. LC AS36. DD 081. CODEN RCOPAC.

R&D CONTRACTS MONTHLY. See Technology (General).

R&D REVIEW. (R & D REVIEW). Main/Corp Mississippi Research and Development Center. VFOAT R and D Review. 0735-0872. US. English. Mississippi Research and Development Center, PO Drawer 2470, 3825 Ridgewood Road, Jackson MS 39205. LC Q180.U5. DD 353.97620082.

RANGE SCIENCE SERIES. No. 1- Oct. 1972-. 0190-5511. Monographic Series. US. English. ir. Society for Range Management, 2760 West Fifth Avenue, Denver CO 80204. Tel (303)571-0174. Ind/Abst GeoRef. LC UNC. CODEN SRMTBT.

RAPPORT ANNUEL - CONSEIL DES SCIENCES DU CANADA. Main/Corp Science Council of Canada. 1- 1966/67-. 0582-2017. CN. French. an. Conseil des Sciences du Canada, 100 Metcalfe Street, Ottawa Ontario K1P 5M1 Canada. LC Q21. DD 354.7100855.

RAPPORT ANNUEL - FONDS F.C.A.C. POUR L'AIDE ET LE SOUTIEN A LA RECHERCHE. (RAPPORT ANNUEL). Main/Corp Quebec (Province). Fonds F.C.A.C. pour l'Aide et le Soutien a la Recherche. 1980-1981-. 0711-5237. CN. French. an. LC Q180.C2. DD 001.4409714.

RAPPORT D'ACTIVITE - CENTRE NATIONAL DE DOCUMENTATION SCIENTIFIQUE ET TECHNIQUE. See Technology (General).

RAPPORT D'ACTIVITE DE LA MIDIST. Main/Corp France. Mission Interministerielle de l'Information Scientifique et Technique. VFOAT Rapport M.I.D.I.S.T. FR. French. ir. Ministere de l'Industrie et de l' Recherche Mission Interministerielle de l'Information et de la Recherche, 280 Bd Saint-Germain, 75007 Paris France. LC Q223.

RAPPORT NATIONAL DE CONJONCTURE SCIENTIFIQUE : RAPPORT DE SYNTHESE. Main/Corp France. Centre National de la Recherche Scientifique. Comite National de la Recherche Scientifique. French. ir. 15 Quai Anatole, Paris France 75700. LC Q46. DD 505.

RAPPORTS ET PROCES-VERBAUX DES REUNIONS. Main/Corp International Council for the Exploration of the Sea. V. 1- July. 1902/July. 1903-. Monographic Series. DK. English (French or German). ir. C A Reitzel Forlag AS, Norregade 20, DK-1165 Copenhagen K Denmark. Tel (01)12 24 00. Ind/Abst Ocean. Abstr.

RARE EARTH BULLETIN. 0307-8531. Periodical. UK. English. bm. Multi Science Publishing Company Ltd, 42/45 New Broad Street, London EC2M 1QY England. Ind/Abst GeoRef, Bibliogr. Index Geol. LC QD172.R2. DD 505.

RCUH ANNUAL REPORT. Main/Corp Research Corporation of the University of Hawaii. VAT Research Corporation of the University of Hawaii Annual Report. 0273-2211. US. English. an. Research

Science (General)

Corporation of the University of Hawaii, Honolulu HI 96822. **LC** Q180.U5. **DD** 574.0720969.

REACTION (SCIENCE TEACHERS' ASSOCIATION OF ONTARIO). (REACTION). 0715-562X. Periodical. CN. English. qt. Free to Members. Science Teachers' Association Of Ontario, Box 975 Postal Station A, Scarborough Ontario M1K 5E4 Canada. **DD** 507.

RECAPITULATIF MENSUEL DES SIGNALEMENTS D'ORIGINE CEDOCAR. **Main/Corp** Centre de Documentation de l'Armement. **VFOAT** Nouveautes Scientifiques et Techniques. **VAT** Recapitulatif Mensuel des Signalements d'Origine Centre de Documentation de l'Armement. No 1- Jan. 1976-. Multilingual (English, French, German, Italian, and Russian). ir. 85. 2 Bd Victor, 75996 Paris France. **LC** Z7403, Q158.5. **DD** 016.623. *Bulletin Signaletique*.

RECHERCHE. (LA RECHERCHE). No. 1- May 1970-. 0029-5671. Periodical. FR. French. mo. $66.39. Societe Editions Scientifiques, 57 rue de Sein, 75280 Paris 06 France. **Tel** (1) 354 32 84. **Ed** Claude Cherki. **Ind/Abst** Environ., Excerpta Med., Sociol. Abstr., Soc. Welf. Soc. Plan./Policy Soc. Dev., Life Sci. Collect., Coal Abstr., Energy Inf. Abstr., Environ. Abstr., Point Repere, GeoRef, Int. Aerosp. Abstr., Energy Res. Abstr., Met. Abstr., World Alum. Abstr., Chem. Abstr., Avery Index Archit. Period., Comput. Control Abstr., Sci. Cit. Index, Abr. Ed., Lang. Lang. Behav. Abstr., Bibliogr. Index Geol., Phys. Abstr., Electr. Electron. Abstr. **LC** Q2. **NLM** W1 RE107N. **CODEN** RCCHBV. bk rev. adv acc. **Circ** 88,505. (ctrl.) A multi-disciplinary magazine for readers with a scientific background, which covers all modern scientific and technical developments. The articles are written by French and foreign writers. *Atomes, Nucleus; Science Progres d'Ecouverte*.

RECORDS OF THE AUSTRALIAN ACADEMY OF SCIENCE CEASED. **Main/Corp** Australian Academy of Science. V. 1-4, No. 3. 0067-155X. AT. English. ir. **LC** Q93. **DD** 509.94. **NLM** W1 AU46K.

REGISTER OF RESEARCH IN FIJI. English. ir. University of the South Pacific, Library, PO Box 1168, Suva Fiji. **LC** Q180.F4. **DD** 001.43099611.

REHOVOT. V. 5, No. 1- Summer 1968-. US. English. ir. American Committee Weizmann Institute, 515 Park Avenue, New York NY 10022. **LC** Q1. **DD** 505. **NLM** W1 RE177K. *Rehovoth*.

RELATORIO - FUNDACAO BRASILERIA PARA O DESENVOLVIMENTO DO ENSINO DE CIENCIAS. **Main/Corp** Fundacao Brasileira Para o Desenvolvimento do Ensino de Ciencias. BL. Portuguese. ir. Cidade Universitaria, Caixa Postal 2089, Sao Paulo Brasil. **LC** Q183.4.B6. **DD** 507.1081.

RELATORIOS E COMUNICOES - INSTITUTO DE INVESTIGACAO CIENTIFICA DE ANGOLA. (RELATORIOS E COMUNICOES). **Main/Corp** Luanda. Instituto de Investigacao Cientifica de Angola. 1-. 0003-343X. Monographic Series. Portuguese. ir. **Ind/Abst** GeoRef. **LC** Q180.A58. **DD** 508.1. **CODEN** RCIAA5.

REMOTE SENSING IN CANADA. VFOAT Teledetection au Canada. No. 1- July 1972-. Periodical. CN. English (French). ir. Free. Canadian Centre for Remote Sensing, 2464 Sheffield Road, Department of E M & R, Ottawa Ontario K1A 0Y7 Canada. **Tel** (613)990-5878. **Ed** Cameron Wade. **Ind/Abst** GeoRef. **CODEN** RSCADM. **Circ** 2,000. (ctrl). Newsletter designed to keep users abreast of research and applications of remotely sensed data, chiefly images obtained by satellite or aerial photography.

RENSSELAER ENGINEER. *See* Engineering.

REPERTORIO DEL FILM INDUSTRIALE. *See* Technology (General).

REPORT - ASSEMBLY OF LIFE SCIENCES, NATIONAL RESEARCH COUNCIL. **Main/Corp** Assembly of Life Sciences (U.S.). 1973/75-1979/80. 0194-0872. US. English. an. National Academy of Sciences, 2101 Constitution Avenue NW, Washington DC 20418. **NLM** W2 A A7R. *Annual Report, Annual Report - Division of Medical Sciences, 0193-9386*.

REPORT - AUSTRALIAN ACADEMY OF SCIENCE CEASED. **Main/Corp** Australian Academy of Science. 0067-1568. Monographic Series. AT. English. ir. Australian Academy of Science, PO Box 783, Canberra City 2601 Australia. **Tel** 062 47 5335. **Ind/Abst** Chem. Abstr. **CODEN** RAASD8.

REPORT - AUSTRALIAN RESEARCH GRANTS COMMITTEE. **Main/Corp** Australian Research Grants Committee. AT. English. ir. $0.80. Commonwealth Government Printing Office, PO Box 84, Canberra Australian Capital Territory 2600 Australia. **LC** J905, Q180.A8. **DD** 328.9401 S, 507.2094.

REPORT - BRITISH SCHOOLS EXPLORING SOCIETY. **Main/Corp** British Schools Exploring Society. **VFOAT** BSES Report. 0521-1573. UK. English. an. 75/-. British Schools Exploring Society, 175 Temple Chamber, Temple Avenue, London EC44 England. **LC** Q41.B927. **DD** 508.305. *Annual Report - British Schools Exploring Society, 0306-3399*.

REPORT - DEPARTMENT OF SCIENCE, ANTARCTIC DIVISION. **Main/Corp** Australia. Dept. of Science. Antarctic Division. AT. English. ir. $0.50. Government Printer, PO Box 84, Canberra Australian Capital Territory 2600 Australia. **LC** J905, Q180.A6. **DD** 328.9401 S, 507.20989.

REPORT - INDIA (REPUBLIC). DEPT. OF SCIENCE AND TECHNOLOGY. **Main/Corp** India (Republic). Dept. of Science and Technology. 1971/72-. II. English. ir. Government of India Press, Department of Science & Technology, Minto Road, New Delhi India. **LC** Q127.I4. **DD** 354.540085505.

REPORT - NATIONAL RESEARCH COUNCIL OF CANADA. **Main/Corp** National Research Council of Canada. 1918-. Monographic Series. English. ir. **LC** Q180.C2.

REPORT OF ACTIVITIES. SCIENCE MUSEUM OF VICTORIA. **Main/Corp** Science Museum of Victoria. English. ir. Science Museum of Victoria, 304-328 Swanston Street, 3000 Melbourne Australia. **LC** Q105. **DD** 507.409945. *Report of Activities*.

REPORT OF PROCEEDINGS - FLORIDA-COLOMBIA ALLIANCE CONFERENCE. **Main/Conf** Florida-Columbia Alliance Conference. 1st- 1966-. 0532-9957. US. English. ir. Florida Secretary of State, Tallahassee FL 32301.

REPORT OF THE DEPARTMENT OF SCIENTIFIC AND INDUSTRIAL RESEARCH. **Main/Corp** New Zealand. Dept. of Scientific and Industrial Research. 1957/58-. NZ. English. an. 3.75. New Zealand Department Scientific & Industrial Research, Box 9741, Wellington New Zealand. **Tel** 858 939. **Ed** Ruscoe. **Circ** 1,600. A report to the New Zealand parliament of activities of Department of Scientific and Industrial Research. *Annual Report of the Department of Scientific and Industrial Research, 0077-9601*.

REPORT OF THE NATIONAL SCIENCE BOARD. **VFOAT** Annual Report of the National Science Board. 1968-. 0197-4319. US. English. an. Superintendent of Documents, U S GPO, Washington DC 20402. **LC** T14.5. **DD** 301.5. **NLM** W1 RE209VH.

REPORT OF THE PRESIDENT - NATIONAL RESEARCH COUNCIL CANADA. (REPORT OF THE PRESIDENT). **Main/Corp** National Research Council Canada. **VFOAT** rapport du President. **VAT** Report of the President - National Research Council of Canada, Rapport du President - Conseil National de Recherches du Canada. 1972/1973-1979/1980. 0373-904X. CN. English (French). an. Free. National Research Council of Canada, Canada Institute of Scientific Technology, Ottawa Ontario K1A 0R6 Canada. **Tel** 993-9101. **Ed** Joan Powers Rickerd. **DD** 354.7100855. **NLM** W2 DC2 N2RC. **Circ** 10,000. (ctrl). Report of the president of the National Research Council of Canada to the responsible minister. Covers scientific and industrial research at the council during the past year. *Report of the President, 0373-904X*.

REPORT OF THE TREASURER FOR THE FISCAL YEAR ENDED JUNE 30 - NATIONAL ACADEMY OF SCIENCES (U.S.). **Main/Corp** National Academy of Sciences (U.S.). US. English. an. National Academy of Sciences, 2101 Constitution Avenue NW, Washington DC 20418. **LC** Q11. **DD** 506.073.

REPORT - ROYAL SOCIETY (GREAT BRITAIN). **Main/Corp** Royal Society (Great Britain). Council. **VFOAT** Annual Report. 1979-. UK. English. an. The Royal Society, 6 Carlton House Terrace, London SW1Y 5AG England. **LC** Q41. **DD** 506.0421.

REPORT - SCIENCE AND ENGINEERING RESEARCH COUNCIL. GREAT BRITAIN. **Main/Corp** Science and Engineering Research Council (Great Britain). **VFOAT** Report of the Science and Engineering Research Council for the Year .... 1980-1981-. 0261-7005. UK. English. an. 4.00. Science & Engineering Research Council, Central Office, North Star Avenue, Swindon SN2 1ET England. **LC** Q180.G7. **DD** 507.2041. *Report of the Council for the Year ....*

REPORT - SCIENCE COUNCIL OF CANADA. **Main/Corp** Science Council of Canada. No. 1-30. 0080-7486. Monographic Series. CN. English. ir. Science Council of Canada, 100 Metcalfe Street, Ottawa Ontario K1P 5M1 Canada. **Tel** (819)997-2560. **DD** 509.71.

REPORTS OF THE DEPARTMENT OF GEODETIC SCIENCE AND SURVEYING. 0733-1983. Monographic Series. US. English. ir. Ohio State University, Research Foundation, Columbus OH 43212. *Reports of the Department of Geodetic Science, 0275-1097*.

RESEARCH ACTIVITIES - AUTHORITY FOR RESEARCH AND DEVELOPMENT. **Main/Corp** Universitah Ha-Ivrit Bi-Yerushalayim. Rashut Le-Mehkar Ule-Fituah. 1978-. English. ir. **LC** Q180.I78. **DD** 001.40956944. *Research Report. Volume I: Science, Agriculture, Research Report. Volume II: Medicine, Pharmacy, Dental Medicine; Research Report. Volume III: Humanities, Social Sciences, Law, Education, Social Work, Library*.

RESEARCH & CREATIVE ACTIVITY. **VAT** Research and Creative Activity. Began with Nov. 1977 issue. 0731-4981. Periodical. US. English. qt. $6.00. Office of Research and Graduate Development, Indiana University, Bryan 104, Bloomington IN 47405. **LC** Q180.U5. **DD** 001.409772.

RESEARCH AND DEVELOPMENT BULLETIN. (RESEARCH AND DEVELOPMENT BULLETIN - SUPPLY AND SERVICES CANADA). **Main/Corp** Canada. Dept. of Supply and Services. **VFOAT** Bulletin Recherche et Developpement. **VAT** Bulletin. Recherche et Developpement, Bulletin R. et D., R&D Bulletin. No. 1-39. 0707-8730. Periodical. CN. English (text in French, each with special t.p. and separate paging. French text on inverted pages). Free. Receiver General for Canada, Supply & Services, Ottawa Ontario K1A 0S9 Canada. **Tel** (819)997-7676. **Ed** Jane Regan. **Circ** 12,000. (ctrl). Federal science procurement activities and opportunities.

RESEARCH & DEVELOPMENT DIRECTORY. *See* Yearbooks, Almanacs, Directories.

RESEARCH AND DEVELOPMENT IN THE FEDERAL BUDGET CEASED. Series/Titl AAAS Publication. 1976/77-1977/78. 0147-6289. US. English. ir. American Association for the Advancement of Science, 1515 Massachusetts Avenue, Washington DC 20005. **Tel** (202)326-6400. **LC** Q181.A1, HJ2052. **DD** 508.1 S, 353.00722. *Research and Development: AAAS Report*.

RESEARCH BULLETIN. SCIENCE SECTION. **Main/Corp** Panjab University. V. 1-9 (No. 1-156), 1950-58. Periodical. English. ir. **LC** Q180.I5.

RESEARCH FRONTS IN ISI/BIOMED. 0732-5606. Periodical. US. English. an. ISI Institute for Scientific Information, 3501 Market Street, University City Science Center, Philadelphia PA 19104.

RESEARCH IN NORWAY. English. an. Norwegian Research Council Science/Humanities, Munthesgt 29, Oslo 2 Norway. **LC** Q180.N6. **DD** 001.4309481.

RESEARCH IN PROGRESS. PHYSICS, CHEMISTRY, BIOLOGICAL SCIENCES, MATHEMATICS, ENGINEERING SCIENCES, METALLURGY AND MATERIALS SCIENCE, GEOSCIENCES, ELECTRONICS, EUROPEAN RESEARCH PROGRAM. **VFOAT** Physics, Chemistry, Biological Sciences, Mathematics, Engineering Sciences, Metallurgy and Materials Science, Geosciences, Electronics, European Research Program. 1982-. US. English. an. US Army Research Office, PO Box 12211, Research Triangle

Park NC 27709. *Research in Progress. Chemistry, Biological Sciences, Engineering Sciences, Metallurgy and Materials Science, European Research Program, Research in Progress. Physics, Electronics, Mathematics, Geosciences, European Research Program.*

RESEARCH NEWS. **Main/Corp** Michigan. University. Division of Research Development and Administration. V. 24, No.1/2- July/Aug. 1973-. Periodical. US. English. bm. University of Michigan, 241 West Engineering, Ann Arbor MI 48109. **Tel** (313)763-5587. **Ed** Lee Katterman. **LC** Q1. **DD** 505. **Circ** 11,000. Reports on research and scholarship at the University of Michigan in language that the non-specialist can understand. *Research News.*

RESEARCH NEWS - DIVISION OF RESEARCH DEVELOPMENT AND ADMINISTRATION. **Main/Corp** Michigan. University. Division of Research Development and Administration. V. 24- July/Aug. 1973-. 0093-7991. Periodical. US. English. ir. Michigan University, Division of Research and Development, Ann Arbor MI 48105. **Ind/Abst** Index Free Period., Biol. Abstr. **LC** Q1. **DD** 505. **CODEN** RNWSD5. *Research News.*

RESEARCH POLICY. V. 1- Nov. 1971-. 0048-7333. Periodical. NE. English (summaries in French and German). bm. Elsevier Science Publishers, PO Box 211, 1000 AE Amsterdam Netherlands. **Tel** (020)5803.911. **Ind/Abst** Manage. Contents, ABI/Inform, Energy Inf. Abstr., Environ. Abstr., Ship Abstr., Soc. Sci. Citation Index. **LC** Q180.A1. **DD** 658.5705. **NLM** W1 RE233B. **CODEN** REPYBP. Each issue contains an index to its own contents - no vol index - loose.

RESEARCH SERVICES DIRECTORY. *See* Yearbooks, Almanacs, Directories.

RESEARCH STUDIES - WASHINGTON STATE UNIVERSITY *CEASED.* (RESEARCH STUDIES : A QUARTERLY PUBLICATION OF WASHINGTON STATE UNIVERSITY). V. 27, No. 3 (Sept. 1959)-V. 51 i.e. 51, No 3/4 (Sept./Dec. 19-). 0043-0838. Periodical. US. English. qt. Washington State University Press, Pullman WA 99164. **Tel** (509)335-3518. **Ind/Abst** Abstr. Engl. Stud., Annu. Bibliogr. Engl. Lang. Lit., MLA Int. Bibliogr. Books Artic. Mod. Lang. Lit., Public Aff. Inf. Serv. Bull., Soc. Welf. Soc. Plan./Policy Soc. Dev., Sociol. Abstr., Am. Hist. Life, Hist. Abstr., Lang. Lang. Behav. Abstr., Years Work Eng. Stud. (cum index). *Research Studies of the State College of Washington, 0363-3829.*

RESEARCHER'S GUIDE TO WASHINGTON EXPERTS. 5th Ed. (1981)-. 0740-087X. US. English. an. Washington Researchers, 2612 P Street NW, Washington DC 20007. **Tel** (202)333-3499. **Ed** Michael Glennon. **NLM** JK 6 R432. *Researcher's Guide to Washington, 0195-4229.*

RESEAU. V. 1- 15/29 Oct. 1969-. 0700-6004. CN. French. Universite du Quebec, 2875 BD Laurier, Ste Foye Quebec G1V 2M3 Canada. **Tel** (418)657-3551.

RETE. Vol. 1- 1971-. Periodical. English or German with summaries in the other language. ir. 16 Single Issue. Verlag Dr H A Gerstenberg, Rathausstrasse 20, 32 Hildeshein West Germany. **LC** Q4. **NLM** W1 R11K.

REVIEW OF SCIENTIFIC INSTRUMENTS. V. 1- Jan. 1930-. 0034-6748. Periodical. US. English. mo. $12.00 Members, $35.00 Nonmembers. American Institute of Physics, 335 East 45th Street, Lancaster PA 10017. **Ind/Abst** Abstr. Bull. Inst. Paper Chem., Coal Abstr., GeoRef, Comput. Control Abstr., Energy Res. Abstr., Met. Abstr., World Alum. Abstr., Ref. Source, Spin, Appl. Sci. Technol. Index, Biol. Abstr., Chem. Abstr., Curr. Phys. Index, Eng. Index Annu., Eng. Index Mon., Index Med., Int. Aerosp. Abstr., Nuci. Sci. Abstr., Sel. Water Resour. Abstr. **LC** Q184. **NLM** W1 RE255. **CODEN** RSINAK. Available on microfilm from American Institute of Physics. *Journal of the Optical Society of America and Review of Scientific Instruments, 0093-4119.*

THE REVIEW OF THE POLISH ACADEMY OF SCIENCES *CEASED.* **Main/Corp** Polska Akademia Nauk. Began with V. 1, No. 1. Ceased with V. 25, No. 4, 1980. 0032-2776. Periodical. PL. English. qt. **Ind/Abst** GeoRef, Bibliogr. Agric. **LC** AS262. **DD** 506.1438. **CODEN** RPASA8.

REVIEWS IN RURAL SCIENCE. Periodical. AT. English. ir. $18.45. Review in Rural Science, University of New England Publishing Unit, Armidale NSW 2351 Australia. **Tel** (067)73-2898. **Ind/Abst** Chem. Abstr.

REVIEWS OF DATA ON SCIENCE RESOURCES. Began with No. 1, Dec. 1964. US. English. US Government Printing Office, Superintendent of Documents, Washington DC 20402. *Reviews of Data on Research and Development, Scientific Manpower Bulletin.*

REVISTA DA FACULDADE DE CIENCIAS. **Main/Corp** Coimbra. Universidade. Faculdade de Ciencias. V.1- 1931-. PO. Portuguese. ir. Imprensa da Universidade, Lisboa 2 Portugal. **LC** Q4. **DD** 505. (cum index).

REVISTA DE INFORMACION CIENTIFICA Y TECNICA CUBANA. CU. Spanish. ir. **LC** Q4. *Boletin de Informacion Cientificia y Tecnica Cubana.*

REVISTA DE LA SOCIEDAD CIENTIFICA DEL PARAGUAY. **Main/Corp** Sociedad Cientifica del Paraguay. Began in June 1921. 0379-9123. Periodical. Spanish. ir. **Ind/Abst** GeoRef, Energy Res. Abstr. **LC** Q33. **DD** 506.289. **CODEN** SCPGB2.

REVISTA DO MUSEU PAULISTA. *See* Museums.

REVUE DE L'UNIVERSITE NATIONALE DU ZAIRE, CAMPUS DE LUBUMBASHI. SERIE B: SCIENCES. **Main/Corp** Universite Nationale du Zaire, CAmpus de Lubumbashi. CG. French. ir. Universite Nationale du Zaire, Campus de Lubumbashi, Service des Publications et des Echanges, BP 2896, Lubumbashi Zaire. **LC** Q91.C6. **DD** 505.

REVUE DES QUESTIONS SCIENTIFIQUES. V. 1- Jan. 1877-. 0035-2160. Periodical. BE. French. qt. 145. Secretariat de la Societe Scientifique, 61 rue de Bruxelles, 5000 Namur Belique. **Tel** 081 229001. **Ed** C Courtoy. **Ind/Abst** Math. Rev., Excerpta Med., GeoRef, Chem. Abstr. **LC** Q2. **DD** 505. **CODEN** RQSCAN. (cum index). bk rev. adv acc. **Circ** 800. Information on sciences with emphasis on critical reflexion and history.

REVUE D'HISTOIRE DES SCIENCES. V. 24- 1971-. 0151-4105. Periodical. French (summaries in English). qt. **Tel** (1)326-22-16. **NLM** W1 RE831E. bk rev. Of importance to all who are interested in the development of scientific ideas and techniques. Includes original work on great scientists of the past. *Revue d'Histoire des Sciences et de Leurs Applications.*

REVUE DU PALAIS DE LA DECOUVERTE. (REVUE). **Main/Corp** Paris. Palais de la Decouverte. 0339-7521. Periodical. French. ir. 35.00. Avenue Franklin-Roosevelt, Paris France 75008. **Ind/Abst** Math. Rev., Int. Aerosp. Abstr., Energy Res. Abstr. **LC** Q46. **DD** 505.

REVUE ROUMAINE DES SCIENCES TECHNIQUES. SERIE ELECTROTECHNIQUE ET ENERGETIQUE. 1964-. 0035-4066. Periodical. French (articles in English, German or Russian with summaries in various languages). qt. $58.00. Ilexim Press Department, PO Box 1-136-1-137, Bucharest Romania. **Ind/Abst** Math. Rev., Eng. Index Annu., Eng. Index Mon., Eng. Index Bioeng. Abstr., Eng. Index Energy Abstr., Coal Abstr., Int. Aerosp. Abstr., Comput. Control Abstr., Electr. Electron. Abstr., Sci. Abstr. Sect. A. Phys. Abstr., Energy Res. Abstr., Chem. Abstr. **CODEN** RTEEAE *Revue d'Electrotechnique et d'Energetique, Serie A: Electrotechnique, Electroenergetique et Energetique Generale, Revue d'Electrotechnique et d'Energetique, Serie B: Thermoenergetique et Utilisation Energetique des Combustibles.*

RINTISAINS. Malay. ir. $0.80 Single Issue. Dewan Bahasa Dan Pustaka, Peti Surat 803, Kuala Lumpur Malaysia. **LC** Q4.

RISALAT MAHAD AL-TURATH AL-ILMI AL-ARABI. **Main/Corp** Jamiat Halab. Mahad Al-Turath Al-Ilmi Al-Arabi. **VFOAT** Institute for the History of Arabic Science Newsletter. Periodical. Arabic (English). qt. Free. Institute for the History of Arabic Science, University of Aleppo, Allepo Syria. **Tel** (21)236130. **LC** Q127.A5. adv acc. (ctrl). Gives up-to-date news of the Institute for the History of Arabic Science activities and other institutions activities concerning the study of Arabic-Islamic science and civilization.

ROBOTICA. Vol. 1, Pt. 1 (Jan. 1983)-. 0263-5747. Periodical. UK. English. qt. $120.00. Cambridge University Press, 32 East 57th Street, New York NY 10022. **Tel** (212)688-8888. **Ed** J Rose. **Ind/Abst** Electron. Commun. Abstr. J., ISMEC Bull., Pollut. Abstr. Indexes, Saf. Sci. Abstr. J. **LC** TJ210.2. **DD** 629.89205. bk rev. adv acc. **Circ** 400. An international forum for the multi-disciplinary subject of robotics devised to encourage developments in the important field of automation.

ROMANIAN SCIENTIFIC ABSTRACTS (RED COVER EDITION). *See* Indexes/ Abstracts.

THE ROYAL INSTITUTION LIST OF MEMBERS AND SUBSCRIBERS. UK. English. Royal Institute of Great Britain, 21 Albemarle Street, London W1X 4BS England. **LC** Q41. **DD** 506.241.

ROZPRAVY. RADA MATEMATICKYCH A PRIRODNICH VED. **Main/Corp** Ceskoslovenska Akademie Ved. Vol. 63- 1953-. 0069-228X. Periodical. CS. Czech. ir. Academia - Export Department, Vodickova 40, Praha 1 Czechoslovakia. **LC** Q44. Pertains to mathematics, chemistry, biology and physics. *Rozpravy.*

RSRI ABSTRACTS. *See* Indexes/Abstracts.

RSRI DISCUSSION PAPER SERIES. **Main/Corp** Regional Science Research Institute. **VAT** Regional Science Research Institute Discussion Paper Series. Began in 1963. 0485-8255. Monographic Series. US. English. ty. $19.00. Regional Science Research Institute, 256 North Pleasant Street, Amherst MA 01002. **Tel** (413)256-8526. **Ind/Abst** GeoRef.

SAGA DAIGAKU RIKOGAKUBU SHUHO. **VFOAT** Reports of the Faculty of Science and Engineering, Saga University. No. 1-. 0385-6186. Japanese (English). ir. 1 Honjomachi, Saga 830 Japan. **Ind/Abst** Chem. Abstr. **LC** Q4. **CODEN** RFSSDV.

SAINS MALAYSIANA. Vol. 1- July 1972-. 0126-6039. Periodical. MY. English or Malay. an. Perpustzkaan, PO Box 1124, Kuala Lumpur Malaysia. **Ind/Abst** GeoRef, Energy Res. Abstr., Chem. Abstr., Bibliogr. Index Geol. **LC** Q1. **CODEN** SAMADP.

SAIONSU. **VFOAT** News Magazine of Science. V. 1- (1982/5)-. Periodical. KO. Korean. mo. 29,000. Saionsu SA 79-1 Pangsan-Dong, Chung-ku Seoul Korea. **LC** Q4.

SALARY SURVEY. *See* Economics - Labor.

SCHOLASTIC SCIENCE WORLD. **VFOAT** Science World. Began with Vol. 29, No. 1, Sept. 19, 1974. 0162-8399. Periodical. US. English. bw. Science World, 902 Sylvan Avenue, Englewood Cliffs NJ 07632. **Ind/Abst** Child. Mag. Guide. **LC** Q1. **DD** 505. *Science World.*

SCHOOL SCIENCE. V. 1- 1962-. 0036-679X. Periodical. II. English. qt. National Council of Educational Research, Sri Aurobindo Marg-Publishing Unit, New Delhi 16 India.

SCI NEWS. *See* Indexes/Abstracts.

SCIENCE. V. 1-23, Feb. 9, 1883-Mar. 23, 1894. 0036-8075. Periodical. US. English. AAAS, 1515 Massachusetts Avenue Northwest, Washington DC 20005. **Ind/Abst** Read. Guide Period. Lit., Gen. Sci. Index, Curr. Index J. Educ., Energy Res. Abstr., Biol. Abstr., Chem. Abstr., Index Med., Int. Aerosp. Abstr., Psychol. Abstr., Sel. Water Resour. Abstr., Infobank, Bibliogr. Agric., Met. Abstr., World Alum. Abstr., Appl. Sci. Technol. Index, Nuci. Sci. Abstr., Meteorol. Geoastrophys. Abstr., Ind. Arts Index. **LC** Q1. **DD** 505. **NLM** W1 SC653. **CODEN** SCIEAS. (cum index). *Science, 0036-8075.*

SCIENCE. V. 1- Nov./Dec. 1979-. 0193-4511. Periodical. US. English. ir. American Association for the Advancement of Science, PO Box 10789, Des Moines IA 50340. **Tel** (800)247-5470. **Ind/Abst** Pop. Mag. Rev., GeoRef, Abr. Read. Guide, Energy Res. Abstr., Chem. Abstr., Appl. Sci. Technol. Index, Read. Guide Period. Lit., Energy Inf. Abstr., Environ. Abstr., Gen. Sci. Index, Mag. Index. **LC** Q1. **DD** 505. **NLM** W1 SC653B. **CODEN** SCEHDK.

SCIENCE ABSTRACTS. *See* Indexes/ Abstracts.

SCIENCE ACTIVITIES. V. 1- June 1969-. 0036-8121. Periodical. US. English. qt. Heldref Publishers, 4000 Albemarle Street NW/Suite 100, Washington DC 20016. **Tel** (202)362-6445. **Ed** Dale Saul. **Ind/Abst** Educ. Index, Curr. Index J. Educ., Media Rev. Dig. **LC** Q181.A1. **DD** 507. bk rev. adv acc. **Circ** 1,330. Available on microfilm from University Microfilms. A one-step source of experiments, explorations, and projects in the biological, physical, and behavioral sciences. Features include news notes, computer news, and new products for the classroom.

SCIENCE AND CHILDREN. *See* Education (General).

SCIENCE & ENGINEERING. **VAT** Science and Engineering. V. 1- July 1948-. Periodical. II. English. mo. $10.00. India Society of Engineers, 12B

Science (General)

Netaji Subhas Road, Calcutta 1 India. **Ind/Abst** Met. Abstr., World Alum. Abstr. **LC** T1. **DD** 605. *Journal.*

SCIENCE AND ENGINEERING PERSONNEL : A NATIONAL OVERVIEW. 1980-. US. English. be.

SCIENCE AND ENVIRONMENT. Periodical. English. sa. $22.00. **LC** Q1. **DD** 505.

SCIENCE & GOVERNMENT REPORT. **VAT** Science and Government Report. V. 1- Feb. 1, 1971-. 0048-9581. Periodical. US. English. sm. $185.00. Science & Government Report, PO Box 6226, Washington DC 20015. **Tel** (202)244-4135. **Ed** Daniel S Greenberg. **Ind/Abst** Energy Inf. Abstr., Environ. Abstr. **LC** Q127.U6. **DD** 353.0085505. **NLM** W1 SC668M. **Circ** 1,000. Reporting, analysis, and grant-contract information regarding science politics at the federal and international levels.

SCIENCE & GOVERNMENT REPORT INTERNATIONAL ALMANAC. See Yearbooks, Almanacs, Directories.

SCIENCE AND INDUSTRY. **VFOAT** Philips: Science and Industry. New Series 3- 1975-. 0036-8180. Periodical. NE. English. ir. NV Philips/S&I Division, Building TQIII-2, 5600 MD Eindhoven Netherlands. **Ind/Abst** Art Archaeol. Tech. Abstr., Pap. Board Abstr., Met. Abstr., World Alum. Abstr. *Serving Science and Industry.*

SCIENCE & LIVING TOMORROW. **VAT** Science and Living Tomorrow. V. 1- June 1980-. 0272-4510. Periodical. US. English. mo. $18.00 Domestic, $24.00 Foreign. Science & Living Tomorrow, Box 1604 Grand Central Station, New York NY 10017. **LC** Q1. **DD** 505.

SCIENCE AND NATURE. See Philosophy.

SCIENCE AND PUBLIC AFFAIRS BULLETIN OF THE ATOMIC SCIENTISTS. 26,1970-. US. English. mo. $65.00. Educational Foundation for Nuclear Science, 5801 South Kenwood Avenue, Chicago IL 60637. **Tel** (312)363-5225. **Ed** Len Ackland. **Ind/Abst** Book Rev. Digest, Read. Guide Period. Lit., Mag. Index, Sociol. Abstr., Gen. Sci. Index, Infobank, Book Rev. Index, ABC Pol Sci, Lang. Lang. Behav. Abstr., Sci. Cit. Index, Abr. Ed., Hist. Abstr., Am. Hist. Life. bk rev adv acc. **Circ** 22,000. A magazine of science and world affairs.

SCIENCE & PUBLIC POLICY. See Public Administration.

SCIENCE & TECHNOLOGIE. Vol. 1, No 1 (Feb. 1982)-. 0711-7566. Periodical. CN. French. bm. $15.48. Science & Technologie, CP 1800 Succ Cote-des-Neiges, Montreal Quebec H3S 2R1 Canada. **Tel** 288-1373. **Ind/Abst** Point Repere. **DD** 505. bk rev adv acc. **Circ** 35,000. (ctrl). The only publication devoted to the technological results of scientific research.

SCIENCE AND TECHNOLOGY. V. 15, No 5- Mar. 1978-. 0156-1464. Periodical. English. ir. $12.00. Research Publications, 418 Canterbury Road, Victoria 3127 Australia. **Ind/Abst** Energy Res. Abstr., Chem. Abstr. **LC** T1. **DD** 605. **CODEN** STGYB5. *Science and Australian Technology, 0036-875X.*

SCIENCE AND TECHNOLOGY : A PURCHASE GUIDE FOR BRANCH AND PUBLIC LIBRARY. See Library and Information Science.

SCIENCE AND TECHNOLOGY : ANNUAL REPORT TO THE CONGRESS. Main/Corp National Science Foundation. 1978-. Periodical. US. English. an.

SCIENCE AND TECHNOLOGY FOR THE EXECUTIVE. **VFOAT** Science and Technology. Began in 1984?. 0747-2714. Periodical. US. English. mo. $36.00. Science and Technology for the Executive, 111 Radio Circle, Mt Kisco NY 10549. *High Technology for the Executive, 0747-1254.*

SCIENCE & TECHNOLOGY IN JAPAN. **VFOAT** Science and Technology in Japan. Vol. 1, No. 1 (Jan. 1982)-. 0286-0406. Periodical. JA. English. qt. 880. Three I Publications Ltd, Kamakuracho Parking Building, 5-16 Uchikanda 1-chome, Chiyoda-ku 101, Tokyo Japan. **LC** Q127.J3. **DD** 609.52.

SCIENCE AND TECHNOLOGY PLAN. 1984-. NZ. English. an. National Research Advisory Council, Box 12240, Wellington New Zealand. **LC** Q127.N2. **DD** 338.47509931.

SCIENCE & TECHNOLOGY QUARTERLY. **VFOAT** Science and Technology Quarterly. Vol. 1, No. 1 (July 1980)-. Periodical. SI. English. qt. $40.00. Science Council of Singapore, 63 Blk 1, Science Park Drive, Singapore 0511 Republic of Singapore.

SCIENCE AND TECHNOLOGY RESEARCH IN PROGRESS. 1972/73-. US. English. $895.00. 32 Lincoln Avenue, Orange NJ 07050. **LC** Z7401. **DD** 016.5.

SCIENCE AND TECHNOLOGY YEARBOOK. See Yearbooks, Almanacs, Directories.

SCIENCE AND TECHNOLOY INDICATORS. **VFOAT** Indicateurs de l'Activite Scientifique et Technologique. 1984-. 0825-5717. CN. English (French). an. $11.10 Domestic, $13.50 Foreign. Publication Sales and Services, Statistics Canada, Ottawa Ontario K1A 0T6 Canada. **DD** 509.71. *Canadian Science Indicators, 0823-0641.*

SCIENCE BOOKS & FILMS. **VAT** AAAS Science Books & Films, Science Books and Films. V. 11- May 1975-. 0098-342X. US. English. ir. $20.00. Science Books & Films, PO Box 465, Hanover PA 17331. **Tel** (202)326-6464. **Ed** Kathleen S Johnston. **Ind/Abst** Book Rev. Index, Ref. Source, Media Rev. Dig. **LC** Z7403, Q158.5. **DD** 016.5. **NLM** Z 7401 A11. bk rev. adv acc. **Circ** 4,000. Review journal of books and audio-visual media in the sciences and mathematics for all ages; pre-school to kindergarten to junior-high to college undergraduate to teaching professional. *AAAS Science Books, 0036-8253.*

SCIENCE BUDGET. 1980-. 0332-1126. IE. English. an. 5.50. National Board for Science and Technology, Shelbourne House Shelbourne Road, Dublin 4 Ireland. **Tel** (01)683311. **Ed** John Colgan. **LC** Q127.I73. **DD** 354.4170085506. **Circ** 1,700. Inventory of publicly funded science and technology in Ireland, program descriptions and commentary on national policy for statistics and technology.

SCIENCE CHALLENGE. Vol. 4, No. 7 (Mar. 1982)-. 0744-4419. Periodical. US. English. mo. Current Innovations, 3500 Western Avenue, Highland Park IL 60035. **Tel** (312)432-2700. *Current Energy & Ecology, 0194-5572.*

SCIENCE CITATION INDEX. ABRIDGED EDITION. See Indexes/Abstracts.

SCIENCE COUNCIL OF CANADA BACKGROUND STUDY. (BACKGROUND STUDY). 43-. 0705-4769. Periodical. CN. English. ir. Science Council of Canada, 100 Metcalfe Street, Ottawa Ontario K1P 5M1 Canada. **DD** 354.7100855. *0705-4769.*

SCIENCE DIGEST (HEARST CORPORATION : 1980). (SCIENCE DIGEST). Nov./Dec. 1980-. 0036-8296. Periodical. US. English. mo $14.00 Domestic, $17.60 Foreign. Hearst Corporation, 224 West 57th Street, New York NY 10019 (subscription address: Communication Data Services 110 Tenth Street Des Moines IA 50309). **Tel** (800)247-5470. **Ind/Abst** Read. Guide Period. Lit., Abr. Read. Guide, Hospit. Lit. Index, Energy Inf. Abstr., Environ. Abstr., Pop. Mag. Rev., GeoRef, Gen. Sci. Index. **LC** Q1. **DD** 505.

SCIENCE DIMENSION. V. 1- Apr. 1969-. 0036-830X. Periodical. CN. English (text in French on opposite pages, 1969-1982). bm. Free. National Research Council of Canada, Ottawa Ontario Canada. **Ind/Abst** Can. Period. Index, Comput. Control Abstr., Electr. Electron. Abstr., Index Free Period., Sci. Abstr. Sect. A. Phys. Abstr. **LC** Q2. **DD** 509.71. **CODEN** NRSDAN. *N R C Research News, 0382-3962.*

SCIENCE EDITOR TRANSCRIPT. 0276-0789. US. English. wk. University of California, 131 University Hall, Berkeley CA 94720.

SCIENCE EDUCATION. V. 13, No. 4- May 1929-. 0036-8326. Periodical. US. English. ir. John Wiley and Sons Inc, 605 Third Avenue, New York NY 10158. **Tel** (800)526-5368. **Ind/Abst** Curr. Index J. Educ., Educ. Index, Res. High. Educ. Abstr., Bibliogr. Index, Soc. Sci. Citation Index. **NLM** W1 SC693. **CODEN** SEDUAV. *General Science Quarterly, 0097-0352.*

SCIENCE EDUCATION IN THE REGION. See Education (General) - Higher Education.

SCIENCE, ENGINEERING, AND HUMANITIES DOCTORATES IN THE UNITED STATES. Began with Vol. for 1977. 0732-5924. US. English. be. **LC** Q149.U5. **DD** 510.71173. *Doctoral Scientists and Engineers in the United States, 0095-0750.*

SCIENCE ET FRANCOPHONIE. 0825-9879. Periodical. CN. French. ir. Free to Members, $25.00 Per Year Others. Lingue Internationale des Scientifiques pour l'Usage de la Langue Francaise, 1200 rue Latour, St-Laurent Quebec H4L 4S4 Canada. **DD** 501.41.

SCIENCE ET RECHERCHE. Began in 1980. Periodical. FR. French. an. CEA Department des Relations Publiques et de la Communication, 31-33 rue de la Federation, 75752 Paris Cedex 15 France. **Ind/Abst** Chem. Abstr. **CODEN** SCRHDH.

SCIENCE ET VIE, MAGAZINE DES SCIENCES ET DE LEURS APPLICATIONS A LA VIE MODERNE. Vol. 1- Apr. 1913-. 0036-8369. Periodical. FR. French. mo. $37.25. Excelsior, 5 rue de la Baume, 75008 Paris France. **Tel** 563 01 02.

SCIENCE FILM. Periodical. English or French. ir. International Scientific Film Association, 38 Avenue des Ternes 17, Paris France. **LC** Q192. **DD** 502.8.

SCIENCE FOR PEOPLE. Began in 1972. 0144-8447. Periodical. UK. English. qt. British Society for Social Responsibility in Science, 9 Poland Street, London W1V 3DG England. **Ind/Abst** Altern. Press Index. *BSSRS News Sheet.*

SCIENCE FOR THE PEOPLE. V. 2, No 2- Mar./Apr. 1970-. 0048-9662. Periodical. US. English. bm. $24.00. Science for the People, 897 Main Street, Cambridge MA 02139. **Tel** (617)547-0370. **Ed** Leslie Fraser. **Ind/Abst** Energy Inf. Abstr., Environ. Abstr., Women Stud. Abstr., Altern. Press Index. **LC** Q175.52.U5. **DD** 301.243. bk rev. adv acc. **Circ** 5,000. Available on microfilm from Xerox University Microfilms. Explores the social and political impact of science and technology. *Newsletter.*

SCIENCE IN NEW GUINEA. V. 1, No. 1- Nov. 1972-. 0310-4303. Periodical. PP. English. qt. $7.63. University of Papua in New Guinea, Biology Department, Box 320 University Post Office, Papua New Guinea. **Tel** 25-3900. **Ed** P O Osborne. **Ind/Abst** GeoRef, Bibliogr. Agric. bk rev. **Circ** 350. Material in following fields: agriculture, botany, chemistry, conservation, fisheries, forestry, geology, geophysics, physical geography, mathematics, physics, science teaching, zoology, archaeology.

SCIENCE IN THE USSR. Periodical. UR. English. bm. **LC** Q127.S696. **DD** 509.47. *Science in USSR.*

SCIENCE IN USSR CEASED. **VFOAT** Science in U.S.S.R. 1981, No. 1-. 0203-4638. Periodical. UR. English. bm. $27.00. Science in USSR, 33/12 Arbot, Moscow 121002 USSR. **Ind/Abst** GeoRef. **LC** Q127.S696. **DD** 505.

SCIENCE INDICATORS. 1972-. 0092-315X. US. English. be. US Government Printing Office, Superintendent of Documents, Washington DC 20402. **LC** T14.5, Q172.5.S34 S34. **DD** 338.973. **NLM** W2 A N371R. Vol. for 1980 distributed to depository libraries in microfiche.

SCIENCE-LOISIR. Vol. 2, No 2 (April 1983)-. 0823-2342. Periodical. CN. French. ir. 5. Conseil de Developpement du Losir Scientifique, 1415 Jarry Est, Montreal Quebec H2E 2Z7 Canada. **Tel** (514)252-3027. **DD** 502.3714. bk rev adv acc. **Circ** 4,000. (ctrl). Promotional magazine of scientific leisure in natural, physic, and human sciences. *Science Express, 0712-435X.*

SCIENCE MONOGRAPH. Main/Corp Wyoming Agricultural Experiment Station. 1- 1966-. 0084-3156. Monographic Series. US. English. University of Wyoming, Agricultural Experiment Station, Laramie WY 82071. **Ind/Abst** Bibliogr. Agric.

SCIENCE NEWS (WASHINGTON, D.C.). (SCIENCE NEWS). Vol. 89, No. 11 (Mar. 12, 1966)-. 0036-8423. Periodical. US. English. wk. $27.50 Domestic, $30.50 Canada. Science News, 231 West Center Street, Marion OH 43302. **Ind/Abst** Pop. Mag. Rev., GeoRef, Chem. Abstr., Curr. Index J. Educ., Read. Guide Period. Lit., Abr. Read. Guide, Gen. Sci. Index, Predicasts, Energy Inf. Abstr., Environ. Abstr. **LC** Q1. **DD** 505. **NLM** W1 SC75. **CODEN** SCNEBK. Available from University Microfilms. *Science News Letter, 0096-4018.*

SCIENCE NEWSLETTER CEASED. V. 4, NO. 2-V. 15. 0384-1847. Periodical. CN. English. ir. Alberta Teachers' Association, 11010 - 142 Street, Edmonton Alberta T5N 2R1 Canada. **DD** 507. *Newsletter, 0384-1855.*

SCIENCE NOTES. US. English. New Jersey State Museum, PO Box 1868, Trenton NJ 08607. **LC** Q11. **DD** 505.

SCIENCE OF SCIENCE. Vol. 1, No. 1-. 0138-0532. Periodical. PL. English (summaries In French, German, and Russian). qt. Kluwer Academic Publisher Group, PO Box 322, 3300 AH Dordrecht Netherlands. **Tel** (31)78-334911. **Ed** Ignacy Malecki. **Ind/Abst** Sociol. Abstr., Soc. Welf. Soc. Plan./Policy Soc. Dev. **LC** Q180.A1. **DD** 505. bk rev. adv acc. **Circ** 500. Theory and methodology of research and design; science, technology and society; sociology of sciences; creativity in science; organization of scientific activity; and science policy studies. *Problems of the Science of Science, 0302-9476.*

SCIENCE POLICY STUDIES AND DOCUMENTS. No. 1- 1965-. Monographic Series. US. English (French). ir. UNIPUB, PO Box 1222, Ann Arbor MI 48106. **Tel** (800)521-8110.

SCIENCE PROGRESS; A REVIEW JOURNAL OF CURRENT SCIENTIFIC ADVANCE. **VFOAT** Science Progress in the Twentieth Century. V. 11- (No. 41-). 0036-8504. Periodical. UK. English. qt. 32 Domestic, 38.50 Foreign, $85.00 North America. Blackwell Scientific Publishing Ltd, PO Box 88, Oxford England. **Tel** 0865-240201. **Ed** J M Ziman and P J B Slater. **Ind/Abst** Life Sci. Collect., Excerpta Med., Energy Inf. Abstr., Environ. Abstr., Index Med., Int. Aerosp. Abstr., GeoRef, Comput. Control Abstr., Electr. Electron. Abstr., Sci. Abstr. Sect. A. Phys. Abstr., Chem. Abstr., Bibliogr. Agric., Biol. Abstr., Sci. Abstr. **NLM** W1 SC756. **CODEN** SCPRAY. adv acc. Reviews of a particular region of research. *Science Progress in the Twentieth Century, 0302-1785.*

SCIENCE QUEST. V. 1- Jan. 1973-. 0090-9378. Periodical. US. English. bm. $4.50. Science Quest, Box 384, Downers Grove IL 60515. **LC** Q175.4. **DD** 301.24305.

SCIENCE REPORTER. V. 1- Jan. 1964-. 0036-8512. Periodical. English. mo. $5.00. Publishing & Information Directorate, Chief Editor, Hillside Road, New Delhi 110012 India. **Ind/Abst** Chem. Abstr. **LC** Q1. **DD** 505. **CODEN** SCRPA4.

THE SCIENCE REPORTS OF SAITAMA UNIVERSITY. SERIES A. MATHEMATICS, PHYSICS, CHEMISTRY AND BIOCHEMISTRY *CEASED.* **Main/Corp** Saitama Daigaku. V. 6-10. English. ir. *Science Reports of Saitama University. Series A. Mathematics, Physics and Chemistry.*

SCIENCE REPORTS OF THE HIROSAKI UNIVERSITY. (HIROSAKI DAIGAKU RIKA HOKOKU). **VFOAT** The Science Reports of the Hirosaki University. 0367-6439. JA. English (Japanese). ir. Hirosaki Daigaku Rigakubu, 3 Bunkyo-cho, Hirosaki Shi 036 Japan. **Ind/Abst** Math. Rev., Life Sci. Collect., Chem. Abstr. **LC** Q4. **CODEN** HUSRAK.

SCIENCE REPORTS OF THE YOKOHAMA NATIONAL UNIVERSITY. SECTION I : MATHEMATICS, PHYSICS, CHEMISTRY. **Main/Corp** Yokohama Kokuritsu Daigaku. Kyoikugakubu. **VFOAT** Yokohama Kokuritsu Daigaku Rika Kiyo. No. 4- 1955-. English. ir. Yokohama National University, 41 Shimizugaoka Minami-ku, Yokohama Japan. **LC** Q77. **DD** 500.205. *Science Reports of the Yokohama National University. Section I. Mathematics, Physics.*

SCIENCE REPORTS OF TOKYO WOMAN'S CHRISTIAN UNIVERSITY. **VFOAT** Tokyo Joshi Daigaku Kiyo Ronshu. 0386-4006. Periodical. English (Japanese). an. Tokyo Woman's Christian University, Zempukuji Suginami, Tokyo Japan. **Ind/Abst** Math. Rev., Chem. Abstr. **CODEN** SRTUDZ. *Science Reports of Tokyo Woman's Christian College.*

SCIENCE REPORTS - OSAKA UNIVERSITY. COLLEGE OF GENERAL EDUCATION. (SCIENCE REPORTS). **Main/Corp** Osaka Daigaku. Kyoyobu. Began in 1953. 0474-781X. Periodical. JA. English. ir. Osaka University, College of General Education, Machikaneyama, Osaka T565 Japan. **Ind/Abst** Math. Rev., Biol. Abstr., GeoRef, Comput. Control Abstr., Electr. Electron. Abstr., Sci. Abstr. Sect. A. Phys. Abstr., Chem. Abstr. **LC** Q1.A1. **DD** 505. **CODEN** SREOA7.

SCIENCE RESEARCH ANNUAL. 1980-. US. English. an. Illinois Legislative Council, 107 Stratton Building, Springfield IL 62706.

SCIENCE RESOURCES STUDIES HIGHLIGHTS. 0566-9995. Periodical. US. English. National Science Foundation, 1800 G Street NW, Washington DC 20550. **LC** Q180.U5. **DD** 509.73.

SCIENCE REVIEW (INDIAN SCIENCE NEWS ASSOCIATION). (SCIENCE REVIEW). Vol. 1-. 0253-6684. Periodical. English. ir. Indian Science News, Association 92, Acharya Prafulla Chandra Road, Calcutta 700 009 India. **Ind/Abst** Chem. Abstr. **CODEN** SCRVDP.

SCIENCE STATISTICS. **VFOAT** Statistique des Sciences. V. 1- Aug. 1977-. 0706-0793. Periodical. CN. French (English with French in parallel columns). mo. 60.00 Domestic, 70.00 Foreign. Receiver General for Canada, Statistics Canada Publications, Ottawa Ontario K1A 0T6 Canada. **Tel** (800)268-1151. **DD** 509.71. Contains summary statistics from recently completed surveys and studies, descriptions of current surveys and notices of available statistical tabulation. *Service Bulletin (Statistique Canada. Division de l'Education, des Sciences et de la Culture), 0317-5383.*

THE SCIENCE TEACHER. V. 1- Feb. 1934-. 0036-8555. Periodical. US. English. ir. $25.00 Libraries, $26.26 Canada, $18.00 Individuals with Secondary Membership in NSTA. National Science Teachers Association (NSTA), 1742 Connecticut Avenue NW, Washington DC 20009. **Tel** (202)328-5800. **Ind/Abst** Int. Aerosp. Abstr., Curr. Index J. Educ., Educ. Index, Int. Index Multi Media Inf., Media Rev. Dig. **LC** Q181. **DD** 507. (cum index). Also available on microfilm from University Microfilms. *Illinois Chemistry Teacher.*

SCIENCE TECHNOLOGY AND DEVELOPMENT. Vol. 1, No. 1 (Jan. 1982)-. Periodical. English. bm. **LC** Q127.P26. **DD** 338.95491.

SCIENCE, TECHNOLOGY & SOCIETY. (SCIENCE, TECHNOLOGY & SOCIETY : CURRICULUM NEWSLETTER OF THE LEHIGH UNIVERSITY STS PROGRAM). **VAT** Science, Technology and Society. 1977. 0275-8075. Periodical. US. English. bm. $6.00. Lehigh University, 327 Maginnes Hall/#9, STS Program, Bethlehem PA 18015. **Tel** (215)861-3350. **Ed** Stephen H Cutcliffe. bk rev. **Circ** 500. Curriculum oriented material with respect to the relationship between science, technology and society oriented issues (syllabi, articles, reviews, bibliography, etc.).

SCIENCE TRENDS. V. 31, No. 11- Dec. 1973-. 0043-0749. Periodical. US. English. wk. $390.00. Trends Publishing Inc, 233 National Press Building, Washington DC 20045. **Tel** (202)393-0031. **Ed** A Kranish. bk rev. (ctrl). General science and technology research and development. *Washington Science Trends.*

SCIENCE UPDATE. 0163-4720. US. English. an. **Ed** T G Aylesworth and S Klein. **LC** Q1. **DD** 505.

SCIENCE WORLD. 0036-8601. Periodical. US. English. ir. Scholastic Magazines, PO Box 644, Lyndhurst NJ 07071. **Tel** (800)631-1586.

SCIENCE YEAR; THE WORLD BOOK SCIENCE ANNUAL. **VFOAT** World Book Science Annual. 0080-7621. US. English. an. World Book Encyclopedia Inc, PO Box 3564, Chicago IL 60654. **LC** Q9.

SCIENCELAND. 0147-3654. Periodical. US. English. ir. $11.95. Scienceland, 501 Fifth Avenue/ Suite 2102, New York NY 10017. **Tel** (212)490-2180. **Ind/Abst** Child. Mag. Guide.

THE SCIENCES. V. 1- June 1961-. 0036-861X. Periodical. US. English. bm. $27.00. New York Academy of Sciences, 2 East 63rd Street, New York NY 10021. **Tel** (212)838-0230. **Ed** Paul Libassi. **Ind/Abst** Excerpta Med., Sociol. Abstr., Soc. Welf. Soc. Plan./Policy Soc. Dev., Int. Aerosp. Abstr., GeoRef, Life Sci. Collect., Bibliogr. Agric., Biol. Abstr., Nuci. Sci. Abstr., Gen. Sci. Index, Energy Inf. Abstr., Environ. Abstr., Access, Sci. Cit. Index, Abr. Ed., Abstr. Anthropol., Lang. Lang. Behav. Abstr. **LC** Q1. **DD** 505. **NLM** W1 SC787. **CODEN** SCNCAD. adv acc. **Circ** 65,000. A non-technical general interest magazine. Beautifully illustrated and written by distinquished scientists.

SCIENCES A L'AFFICHE. 0706-8603. Periodical. CN. French. ir. Ontario Science Centre, 770 rue Don Mills, Don Mills Ontario M3C 1T3 Canada. **DD** 505.

SCIENCES DE LA VIE. LEXIQUE. 0154-0319. FR. French. ir. Informascience, Centre de Documentation Scientifique et Technique Service des Abonnements, 26 rue Boyer, 75971 Paris Cedex 20 France.

SCIENCES DE L'INGENIEUR. LEXIQUE. 0154-0351. FR. French. ir. Informascience, Centre de Documentation Scientifique et Technique Service des Abonnements, 26 rue Boyer, 75971 Paris Cedex 20 France.

SCIENCES ET AVENIR. No. 1- May 19, 1947-. 0036-8636. Periodical. FR. French. mo. $33.26. Sciences et Avenir, 99 rue d'Amsterdam, 75008 Paris France. **Tel** 280 68 55. **Ed** G Lefevrve. **Ind/Abst** Excerpta Med., Coal Abstr., GeoRef, Energy Res. Abstr. **LC** Q2. *Terre, Air, Mer, Avenir.*

SCIENCES ET TECHNIQUES. 0036-8652. Periodical. French. **Tel** (1) 874 83 56. **Ind/Abst** Excerpta Med., Coal Abstr., CIS Abstr., Energy Res. Abstr., Appl. Mech. Rev., Met. Abstr., World Alum. Abstr. **LC** TA2. adv acc. Expert writings in all fields of science and technology. *Memoires.*

SCIENCES ET TECHNIQUES EN PERSPECTIVE. Vol. 1 (Year 1981-1982)-. 0294-0264. Periodical. English (French). an. 110.00. Institut de Mathematiques Universite de Nantes, 2 Chemin de la Houssiniere, 44072 Nantes Cedex France. **Tel** (40)745070. **Ed** J Thombres. **LC** Q46. **DD** 505. bk rev. adv acc. **Circ** 500. A series about science and its surroundings in the Eighteenth and Nineteenth century with an emphasis on mathematisation of the sciences.

SCIENCES, TECHNIQUES, INFORMATIONS CRIAC. **Main/Corp** Centre de Recherches Industrielles en Afrique Centrale. **VAT** Sciences, Techniques, Informations Centre de Recherches Industrielles en Afrique Centrale. No. 1- 1974-. 0377-5135. Periodical. CG. French. ir. Centre de Recherches Industrielles en Afrique Centrale, BP 54 Av du President Ileo, Lubumbashi Congo Zaire. **Ind/Abst** Chem. Abstr. **LC** T175. **CODEN** STICD8. *Bulletin d'Information - Centre de Recherches Industrielles en Afrique Centrale.*

SCIENCETECH BULLETIN. *See* Technology (General).

SCIENTIA. V. 1- (Year 1-). 0036-8687. Periodical. IT. Italian, French, English and German. ty. 40.000 Domestic, 45.000 Europe and $60.00 US. Scientia, Via Guastalla 9, 20122 Milano Italy. **Tel** (02)780 669. **Ed** N Bonetti. **LC** Q4. bk rev. adv acc. Publication aims at being a means of communication between specialists in various disciplines that can promote a synthetic vision and a critical examination of the problems of science.

SCIENTIA CANADENSIS. **VFOAT** Journal of the History of Canadian Science, Technology and Medicine. Vol. 8, No. 1 (June 1984)- – Whole No. 26-. 0829-2507. Periodical. CN. English (includes some text in French). qt. **DD** 509.71. *HSTC Bulletin, 0228-0086.*

SCIENTIA SINICA. **VFOAT** Chung-kuo Ko Hsueh. V. 1- Oct. 1952-. 0582-236X. Periodical. UK. English (Russian). mo. $150.00. Scientific & Technical Book SR, PO Box 197, London WC2N 4DE England. **Ind/Abst** Bibliogr. Index Geol. **LC** Q1.

SCIENTIA SINICA. SERIES B: CHEMICAL, BIOLOGICAL, AGRICULTURAL, MEDICAL & EARTH SCIENCES. (SCIENTIA SINICA. SERIES B, CHEMICAL, BIOLOGICAL, AGRICULTURAL, MEDICAL & EARTH SCIENCES). **VFOAT** Chung-Kuo ko Hsueh. Vol. 25, No. 1 (Jan. 1982)-. 0253-5823. Periodical. CC. English. mo. China Publication Centre, PO Box 2820, Beijing China. **Ind/Abst** Bibliogr. Agric., Biol. Abstr., Chem. Abstr., Coal Abstr., Excerpta Med., Index Med., Math. Rev., Met. Abstr., World Alum. Abstr., World Text Abstr. **NLM** W1 SC822B. **CODEN** SSBSEF. *Scientia Sinica, 0250-7870.*

SCIENTIAE. Periodical. Indonesian. ir. 350. PO Box 82, Bandung Indonesia. **LC** T4.

SCIENTIARUM HISTORIA. Vol. 1- 1959-. 0036-8725. Periodical. BE. Dutch. qt. Scientiarum Historia, Prinsstraat 5, Antwerp Belgium. **Ed** P Bockstaele. **Ind/Abst** Math. Rev. **LC** Q125. **NLM** W1 SC832.

SCIENTIFIC ACTIVITIES : FEDERAL GOVERNMENT COSTS AND EXPENDITURES. **Main/Corp** Canada. Ministry of State, Science and Technology. **VFOAT** Activites Scientifiques: Couts et Depenses Supportes par le Gouvernment Federal. CN. English and French. an. Information Canada/Receiver General Canada, Statistics Publications Canada, Ottawa Ontario K1A 0T6 Canada. **LC** Q180.C2. **DD** 354.71008.

SCIENTIFIC ACTIVITIES OF THE POLISH ACADEMY OF SCIENCES, INSTITUTE OF FUNDAMENTAL TECHNOLOGICAL RESEARCH. **Main/Corp** Instytut Podstawowych Problemow Techniki (Polska Akademia Nauk). PL. Polish (English,

Science (General)

Russian). ir. Panstwowe Wydawn Naukowe, Miodowa 10 PO Box 391, 00 251 Warsaw Poland. **LC** T4. **DD** 607.2438.

SCIENTIFIC AMERICAN. V. 1-14, Aug. 28, 1845-June 25, 1859. 0036-8733. Periodical. US. English. mo. $18.00. Scientific American Inc, 415 Madison Avenue, New York NY 10017. **Tel** (212)754-0550. **Ind/Abst** Int. Packag. Abstr., Ref. Source, Appl. Sci. Technol. Index, Biogr. Index, Ind. Arts Index, Read. Guide Period. Lit., Bibliogr. Agric., Chem. Abstr., Print. Abstr., Index Med., Int. Aerosp. Abstr., Math. Rev., Nucl. Sci. Abstr., Psychol. Abstr., Electron. Pub. Abstr., Curr. Index J. Educ., Met. Abstr., World Alum. Abstr., Abr. Read. Guide, Gen. Sci. Index, Infobanks. **LC** T1. **DD** 505. **NLM** W1 SC833. **CODEN** SCAMAC. (cum index). Microform. *People's Journal, Scientific American Monthly, 0740-6495.*

SCIENTIFIC AND TECHNICAL BOOKS AND SERIALS IN PRINT. VFOAT Sci-Tech Books and Serials in Print. 1978-. 0000-054X. US. English. an. $149.95. R R Bowker, PO Box 1807, Ann Arbor MI 48106. **Tel** (212)916-1600. **LC** Z7401, Q158.5. **DD** 016.5. **NLM** Z 7401 S414. Provides bibliographic information on all U.S. scientific and technical books in print, plus serials. *Scientific and Technical Books in Print, 0000-0248.*

SCIENTIFIC AND TECHNICAL INFORMATION PROCESSING. 1974-. 0147-6882. Periodical. US. English (Russian). bm. Allerton Press, 150 Fifth Avenue, New York NY 10011. **Tel** (212)924-3950. **Ind/Abst** Excerpta Med., Biol. Abstr., Chem. Abstr. **LC** Z699.A1. **DD** 029.95. **CODEN** STIPDD.

SCIENTIFIC AND TECHNICAL SOCIETIES OF CANADA. VFOAT Societes Scientifiques et Techniques du Canada. 1st- Ed. 0586-7746. Periodical. CN. English (French). ir. Canada Institute of Science Technology Info, National Research Council of Canada, Ottawa Ontario K1A 0S2 Canada. **Tel** (613)993-3736. **LC** AS40. **DD** 506.271. **NLM** Q 21 C212S. *Scientific and Technical Societies of the United States and Canada.*

SCIENTIFIC AWAKENING IN THE RESTORATION. 0882-2034. Periodical. US. English. AMS Press, 56 East 13th Street, New York NY 10003.

SCIENTIFIC BULLETIN (SAN FRANCISCO, CALIF.). (SCIENTIFIC BULLETIN). **Series/Titl** NAVSO P. **VFOAT** ONR Tokyo Scientific Bulletin, ONR Far East Scientific Bulletin, ONRFE. Vol. 1, No. 1 (June to Sept. 1976)-. 0271-7077. Periodical. US. English. qt. US Department of the Navy, Office of Naval Research, Arlington VA 22217. **Ind/Abst** Index U.S. Gov. Period., GeoRef. **LC** Q1. **DD** 505. **CODEN** SBULD3.

SCIENTIFIC DIRECTORY . . . ANNUAL BIBLIOGRAPHY . . . . See Yearbooks, Almanacs, Directories.

SCIENTIFIC, ENGINEERING, AND MEDICAL SOCIETIES PUBLICATIONS IN PRINT. 1976-1977-. 0277-7355. US. English. ir. R R Bowker, PO Box 1807, Ann Arbor MI 48106. **Tel** (800)521-0600. **LC** Z7911, T45. **DD** 016.5. **NLM** Z 7911 S416. *Scientific, Technical, and Engineering Societies Publications in Print, 0730-1820.*

SCIENTIFIC, ENGINEERING, TECHNICAL MANPOWER COMMENTS. VFOAT Manpower Comments, SET Manpower Comments. V. 1- Nov. 1964-. 0036-8768. Periodical. US. English. mo. $35.00. Scientific Manpower Commission, 1500 Massachusetts Avenue Northwest/Suite 831, Washington DC 20005. **Tel** (202)223-6995. Ed Betty M Vetter and Eleanor L Babco. **Ind/Abst** Abstr. Bull. Inst. Paper Chem. **LC** TA157. **NLM** W1 SC842. **Circ** 1,200. Available on microform from University Microfilms. Human resources in science and engineering.

SCIENTIFIC HONEYWELLER. Vol. 1, No. 1 (Mar. 1980)-. 0196-8440. Periodical. US. English. qt. Honeywell Inc, Honeywell Plaza, Minneapolis MN 55408. **LC** T1. **DD** 605.

SCIENTIFIC INFORMATION NOTES. V. 1- 1969-. 0036-8784. Periodical. US. English. qt. $110.00. Trends Publications Inc, 233 National Press Building, Washington DC 20045. **Tel** (202)393-0031. Ed A Karnish. **Ind/Abst** Predicasts. **LC** Q1. **DD** 505. **NLM** W1 SC848G. bk rev. (ctrl). Database and information, sciences information, also book reviews.

SCIENTIFIC MANPOWER. Main/Corp National Science Foundation (U.S.). 1956-. 0565-8306. US. English. an. US Government Printing Office, Superintendent of Documents, Washington DC 20402. **LC** Q147. **DD** 500.

SCIENTIFIC MAPS AND ATLASES AND OTHER RELATED PUBLICATIONS. See Geography.

SCIENTIFIC MEETINGS. V. 21- Jan. 1977-. 0487-8965. Periodical. US. English. qt. Scientific Meetings Publishing, PO Box 81662, San Diego CA 92138. **Tel** (619)270-2910. Ed R Holleman. **LC** Q101. **DD** 506. **NLM** W 3.5 S426. **Circ** 1,500. Directory describing future meetings of technical, scientific, medical and management organizations. *Scientific Meetings, 0487-8965.*

SCIENTIFIC PAPERS OF THE COLLEGE OF ARTS AND SCIENCES, THE UNIVERSITY OF TOKYO. VFOAT Tokyo Daigaku Kyoyobu Shizen Kagaku Kiyo. Vol. 33, No. 1 (June 1983)-. 0040-8964. Periodical. JA. English. sa. Chairman of Scientific Papers, The College of Arts and Sciences, Kyoyo Gakubu 113, Tokyo Japan. **Ind/Abst** Chem. Abstr., Comput. Control Abstr., Electr. Electron. Abstr., Sci. Abstr., Math. Rev. **LC** Q1. **DD** 505. **CODEN** SPCTDZ. *Scientific Papers of the College of General Education, 0040-8964.*

SCIENTIFIC PAPERS OF THE INSTITUTE OF PHYSICAL AND CHEMICAL RESEARCH. Main/Corp Rikagaku Kenkyujo. V. 52- (No. 1492-). 0020-3092. Periodical. JA. English (French or German). qt. $35.50. Japan Publishing Trading, PO Box 5030, Tokyo International, Tokyo 100-31 Japan. **Ind/Abst** Eng. Index Annu., Eng. Index Mon., Eng. Index, Eng. Index Bioeng. Abstr., Eng. Index Energy Abstr., Int. Aerosp. Abstr., GeoRef, Comput. Control Abstr., Electr. Electron. Abstr., Sci. Abstr. Sect. A. Phys. Abstr., Chem. Abstr., Met. Abstr., World Alum. Abstr., Appl. Mech. Rev. **CODEN** SPIPAG. *Journal of the Scientific Research Institute.*

SCIENTIFIC POLICY, RESEARCH AND DEVELOPMENT IN CANADA. Main/Corp Canada Institute for Scientific and Technical Information. **VFOAT** La Politique des Sciences, la Recherche et le Developpement au Canada. 1972/75-. 0703-9492. Periodical. CN. English (French). National Research Council Canada, Canada Scientific and Technical Information, Ottawa Ontario K1A 0S2 Canada. **DD** 016.3547100855. *Scientific Policy, Research and Development in Canada.*

THE SCIENTIFIC PROCEEDINGS OF THE ROYAL DUBLIN SOCIETY. SERIES A CEASED. Main/Corp Royal Dublin Society. V. 1-6, No. 15. 0080-4339. Monographic Series. English. ir. **ind/Abst** Life Sci. Collect., GeoRef, Met. Abstr., World Alum. Abstr. **CODEN** SPDAAE. Index published separately - free - automatically sent. *Scientific Proceedings of The Royal Dublin Society.*

SCIENTIFIC PROGRESS. VFOAT Wetenskaplike Vordering. 0036-8814. Periodical. SA. Afrikaans and English. ir. The Editor Scientific Progress, PO Box 395, Pretoria South Africa. **Ind/Abst** Energy Res. Abstr. **LC** Q85. **DD** 509.68. **NLM** W1 SC863.

SCIENTIFIC PUBLICATIONS OF THE SCIENCE MUSEUM OF MINNESOTA. Main/Corp Science Museum of Minnesota. New Series V. 2-. 0161-4452. Monographic Series. US. English. ir. Science Museum of Minnesota, 30 East 10th Street, Saint Paul MN 55101. **Tel** (612)222-6303. **Ind/Abst** GeoRef, Bibliogr. Index Geol. **LC** Q11. **DD** 500. **CODEN** SCSPBA. *Scientific Publications of the Science Museum.*

SCIENTIFIC RESEARCH. V. 1- Jan. 1966-. Periodical. US. English. mo. McGraw Hill, 1221 Avenue of the Americas, New York NY 10020. **Ind/Abst** CIS Abstr. **LC** Q180.A1. **DD** 507.2. **NLM** W1 SC865S.

SCIENTIFIC RESEARCH ABSTRACTS IN REPUBLIC OF CHINA. See Indexes/Abstracts.

SCIENTIFIC, TECHNICAL, AND RELATED SOCIETIES OF THE UNITED STATES. 9th- Ed. 0085-5995. US. English. National Academy of Sciences, 2101 Constitution Avenue, Washington DC 20418. **LC** Q11. **DD** 506.273. *Scientific and Technical Societies of the United States.*

SCIENTOMETRICS. V. 1- Sept. 1978-. Periodical. English. bm. 468.00. Elsevier Science Publishers, PO Box 330, 1000 AH Amsterdam Netherlands. **Tel** 5862911. Ed T Braun. **Ind/Abst** Electr. Electron. Abstr., Phys. Abstr., Comput. Control Abstr., Soc. Sci. Citation Index, Sci. Cit. Index, Abr. Ed., Bibliogr. Index Geol., Sociol. Abstr., Soc. Welf. Soc. Plan./Policy Soc. Dev., Biol. Abstr., Libr. Inf. Sci. Abstr., Chem. Abstr., Life Sci. Collect., Electron. Pub. Abstr. **LC** Q1. **DD** 505. **NLM** W1 SC8705. **CODEN** SCNTDX. bk rev. An international journal for all quantitative aspects of the science of science, communication in science and science policy.

SCIS NEWSLETTER. Main/Corp Science Curriculum Improvement Study. VAT Science Curriculum Improvement Study Newsletter. 0036-8288. Periodical. US. English. ir. Science Curriculum Improvement Study, Lawrence Hall of Science, University of California, Berkeley CA 94720. *Newsletter - Science Curriculum Improvement Study.*

SCITECH BOOK NEWS. VAT Sci Tech Book News. 1977. 0196-6006. Periodical. US. English. mo. $28.00. Scitech Books, 5600 Northeast Hassalo, Portland OR 97213-3640. **Tel** (503)281-9230. Ed Mary Hart. bk rev. adv acc. **Circ** 5,400. Speedy compact reviews of very high-level books in science, technology, medicine, agriculture, engineering and the bibliography of all.

SEARCH. V. 1- July 1970-. 0004-9549. Periodical. AT. English. bm. 60.00. Anzaas/Search Inc, PO Box 873, GPO Sydney New South Wales 2001 Australia. **Tel** (02)231-4827. Ed B Walby. **Ind/Abst** Biol. Abstr., GeoRef, Chem. Abstr., Excerpta Med., Bibliogr. Agric., Bibliogr. Index Geol., Sci. Cit. Index, Abr. Ed. **LC** Q1. **DD** 505. **NLM** W1 SE162. **CODEN** SRCHAA. bk rev. adv acc. Multidisciplinary science and technology journal published by the Australian and New Zealand Association for the Advancement of Science. *Australian Journal of Science.*

SEARCH AT THE STATE UNIVERSITY OF NEW YORK. (SEARCH). V. 1- Fall 1975-. 0360-8476. Periodical. US. English. qt. State University of New York, New York NY 12234. **LC** Q11. **DD** 051.

SEMI-ANNUAL REPORT. Main/Corp UNESCO. Regional Office for Science and Technology for Southeast Asia. English. sa. United Nations Building, Jalan Thamrin No 14, Tromolpos 273/JKT, Jakarta Indonesia.

SENCKENBERG-BUCH. Monographic Series. German. ir. **LC** UNC.

SERIAL TITLES IN THE PURE AND APPLIED SCIENCES(WINDSON). See Bibliographies.

SERIES IN FOOD MATERIAL SCIENCE. See Food & Drink.

SERIES IN SCIENCE. OCCASIONAL PAPER. No. 1- 1973-. Newspaper. English. ir. *Occasional Paper.*

SERIES IN THERMAL AND TRANSPORT SCIENCES. 0276-9662. Monographic Series. US. English. ir. John Wiley and Sons Inc, 605 Third Avenue, New York NY 10158.

SHANGHAI JIAOTONG DAXUE XUEBAO. (SHANG-HAI CHIAO-TUNG TA HSUEH HSUEH PAO). VFOAT Journal of Shanghai Jiaotong University. 0253-9942. Periodical. CC. Chinese (abstracts in English). bm. China Publication Centre, PO Box 2820, Beijing China. **Ind/Abst** Math. Rev., Comput. Control Abstr., Electr. Electron. Abstr., Sci. Abstr. Sect. A. Phys. Abstr., Chem. Abstr. **LC** Q4. **DD** 505. **CODEN** SCTPDH.

SHANXI DAXUE XUEBAO. ZIRAN KEXUE BAN. (SHAN-HSI TA HSUEH HSUEH PAO. TZU JAN KO HSUEH PAN). VFOAT Shanxi University Journal. Began in 1979. 0253-2395. Periodical. CH. Chinese. qt. 0.45. Post Office, Tai-Yuan China. **Ind/Abst** Chem. Abstr. **LC** Q4. **DD** 505. **CODEN** SDXKDT.

SHAO NIEN KO CHI. SHAO NIAN KE JI. VFOAT Shao Nian Ke Ji. 1- April 1977-. Periodical. Chinese. ir. $0.19 Per Copy. **LC** Q163.

SHAO NIEN KO HSUEH. VFOAT Shaonian Kexue. 1 (1977)-. Periodical. CC. Chinese. mo. $5.13. China Publication Centre, PO Box 2820, Beijing China. **LC** Q163. **DD** 505.

SHAO NIEN TAN SO CHE. Periodical. CH. Chinese. ir. 0.22. Kuang-Tung Sheng Hsin Hua Shu Tien, Canton China. **LC** Q163. **DD** 500.

Science (General)

SHEN PIEN TI KO HSUEH. VFOAT Shenbian de Kexue. Periodical. CH. Chinese. qt. 0.28. Nei Meng-Ku Hsin Hua Shu Tien China. **LC** Q4. **DD** 505.

SHIH SUI. V. 1-. Periodical. CH. Chinese. mo. $17.15. CMC Taipei Liaison Office, PO Box 22048, Taipei Taiwan 100 China. **Tel** 996-2-752-9244. **Ed** Editorial Committee of Shih-Sui. adv acc. **Circ** 1,000. Translations of Western-language articles on science, with some music, short stories, etc.

SHIMA MARINRANDO KENKYU HOKOKU. VFOAT Science Report of Shima Marineland. Began Publication with No. 1 July 1972. 0385-1109. Periodical. JA. Japanese (English). ir. Shima Marineland Kashikojima, Ago-cho Shima-gun, Mie Prefecture 517-05 Japan.

SHIZUOKA DAIGAKU KYOYOBU KENKYU HOKOKU. SHIZEN KAGAKU HEN. VFOAT Reports of the Department for Liberal Arts. Periodical. JA. English (Japanese). an. Shizuoka Daigaku Kyoyobu, 836 Banchi, Otani, Shizuoka-Shi Japan. **LC** Q4. *Shizuoka Daigaku Kyoyobu Kenkyu Hokoku.*

SHKENCA DHE JETA. Periodical. AA. Albanian. bm. $4.45. Book Distribution Enterprise, Rue Konference E Pezes, Tirana Albania. **LC** Q4.

SIGNIFICANT ADVANCES IN SCIENCES. 0145-7683. Periodical. US. English. mo. Royal M Frye, Box 65, Royalston MA 01368.

SILLIMAN JOURNAL. V. 1- Jan. 1954-. 0037-5284. Periodical. PH. English. qt. Silliman University, Dumaguete City 6501 Philippines. **Ind/Abst** MLA Int. Bibliogr. Books Artic. Mod. Lang. Lit. **LC** AS540. **DD** 068.9914. (cum index).

SISTEMY AVTOMATIZATSII NAUCHNYKH ISSLEDOVANII CEASED. Began in 1975. Periodical. UR. Russian. 0.75. Izd-Vo Zinatne, Ul Turgeneva 19, Riga USSR. **Ind/Abst** Comput. Control Abstr., Electr. Electron. Abstr., Sci. Abstr. Sect. A. Phys. Abstr. **LC** Q180.55.E4. **CODEN** SIISDD.

SITZUNGSBERICHTE DER HEIDELBERGER AKADEMIE DER WISSENSCHAFTEN,. **Main/Corp** Heidelberger Akademie der Wissenschaften. 0371-0165. Periodical. GW. German. qt. Springer Verlag-New York Inc, 175 5th Avenue, New York NY 10010. **Tel** (212)460-1584. **Ind/Abst** Math. Rev., Int. Aerosp. Abstr., GeoRef. **LC** AS182. **CODEN** SHWMAL.

SITZUNGSBERICHTE DES PLENUMS UND DER KLASSEN DER AKADEMIE DER WISSENSCHAFTEN DER DDR. No. 1-. 0138-2608. Monographic Series. GE. German. ir. Deutscher Buch Export-Import, Leninstrasse 16, DDR-701 Leipzig East Germany. **Ind/Abst** Chem. Abstr. **NLM** W1 SI766. **CODEN** SPKWBE. *Sitzungsberichte des Plenums und der Problemgebunden Klassen der Deutschen Akademie der Wissenschaften zur Berlin, 0300-0699.*

SKRIFTER (KONGELIGE NORSKE VIDENSKABERS SELSKAB). (SKRIFTER). 1970. No. 1-. NO. Norwegian. ir. Universitetsforlaget, PO Box 2959-Toyen, Oslo 6 Norway. **Ind/Abst** Biol. Abstr., Math. Rev., GeoRef, Comput. Control Abstr., Electr. Electron. Abstr., Sci. Abstr. Sect. A. Phys. Abstr., Energy Res. Abstr. **CODEN** KNSSA7. *KGL. Norske Videnskabers Selskabs Skrifter.*

SKRIFTER - NORSK POLARINSTITUTT. **Main/Corp** Norsk Polarinstitutt. Vol. 90-. 0369-5417. NO. English (French or German). ir. Universitetsforlaget, PO Box 2959-Toyen, Oslo 6 Norway. **Ind/Abst** Life Sci. Collect., Biol. Abstr., GeoRef, ASTIS Bibliogr., ASTIS Curr. Aware. Bull. **LC** Q115. **DD** 508.98. **CODEN** NPOSAY. *Skrifter - Norges Svalbard- og Ishavs-Underskelser.*

THE SMITHSONIAN TORCH CEASED. No.-80-6 (June 1980). 0037-7341. Periodical. US. English. mo. Smithsonian Institution, Office of Public Affairs, Washington DC 20560. **LC** Q11.S8.

SMITHSONIAN YEAR. (SMITHSONIAN YEAR : ANNUAL REPORT OF THE SMITHSONIAN INSTITUTION). **Main/Corp** Smithsonian Institution. Began with 1978/79. 0273-4982. US. English. an. Superintendent of Documents, US Government Printing Office, Washington DC 20402. **Ind/Abst** Life Sci. Collect. **LC** Q11. **DD** 353.00853. *Programs and Activities, 0190-714X.*

SOCIETY AND SCIENCE : JOURNAL OF NEHRU CENTRE. Periodical. II. English. qt. $7.00. Nehru Centre, Administrative Office, 7th Floor/Sterling Centre, Dr Annie Besant Road, Worli Bombay -400 018 India. **LC** Q175.52.I4. **DD** 303.483.

SOCIOLOGY OF THE SCIENCES. V. 1- 1977-. 0167-2320. Monographic Series. English. an. Kluwer Boston Inc, 190 Old Derby Street, Hingham MA 02043. **NLM** W1 SO879NM.

SOLUTIONS. (SOLUTIONS : THE NEWSLETTER OF THE SCIENCE COUNCIL OF THE NEW BRUNSWICK TEACHERS' ASSOCIATION). 0710-779X. Periodical. CN. English. ty. Free. New Brunswick Teachers' Association, PO Box 752, Fredericton New Brunswick E3B 5R6 Canada. **Ind/Abst** Can. Educ. Index. **DD** 507.12715. (ctrl).

SOSHIKI KAGAKU. VFOAT Organization Science. 0286-9713. Periodical. JA. Japanese. qt. $24.00. Maruzen Company Ltd, Import & Export Department, PO Box 5050 Tokyo International, Tokyo 100-31 Japan. **LC** HD28.

SOURCES IN THE HISTORY OF MATHEMATICS AND PHYSICAL SCIENCES. See Mathematics.

SOUTH AFRICAN JOURNAL OF SCIENCE. VFOAT Suid-Afrikaanse Joernaal van Wetenskap. Began with V. 6, Aug. 1909. 0038-2353. Periodical. SA. English. ir. $13.63. South African Association for the Advancement of Science, PO Box 61019, Marshalltown 2107 Transvaal South Africa. **Tel** 832-2177. **Ind/Abst** Excerpta Med., Sel. Water Resour. Abstr., Energy Inf. Abstr., Environ. Abstr., Int. Aerosp. Abstr., Biol. Abstr., GeoRef, Chem. Abstr., Bibliogr. Agric., Met. Abstr., World Alum. Abstr. **NLM** W1 SO905T. **CODEN** SAJSAR. *Report of the South African Association for the Advancement of Science, South African Science.*

SOUTH AMERICAN EXPLORER. See Travel.

SOUTH PACIFIC RESEARCH REGISTER. 1982-. English. ir. University of the South Pacific Library, Pacific Information Centre, PO Box 1168, Suva Fiji. **Tel** 313900. **LC** Paf. **Circ** 150. Lists researchers whose interests are related directly to the South Pacific. Only those who have replied to a questionnaire are included. Includes a detailed subject index.

SOUTHERN RESEARCH. (SOUTHERN RESEARCH : A QUARTERLY BULLETIN OF SOUTHERN RESEARCH INSTITUTE). Vol. 35, No. 1 (Summer 1983)-. 8756-9868. Periodical. US. English. qt. Southern Research Institute, 2000 Ninth Avenue South, PO Box 55305, Birmingham AL 35255-5305. **Ind/Abst** World Text Abstr. **LC** Q180.U5. **DD** 605. *Bulletin (Southern Research Institute (Birmingham, Ala.)), 0038-4518.*

SOVIET ANTARCTIC EXPEDITION; INFORMATION BULLETIN. **Main/Corp** Sovetskaia Antarkticheskaia Ekspeditskia, 1955-. V. 1-. 0038-5271. US. English (Russian). American Geophysical Union, 2000 Florida Avenue NW, Washington DC 20009. **Ind/Abst** GeoRef. **LC** Q115. **DD** 508.99. **CODEN** SAEBAJ.

SOVIET LIFE. Jan. 1965-. 0038-5549. Periodical. US. English. mo. Soviet Life, 1706 Eighteenth Street NW, Washington DC 20009. **Tel** (202)628-9691. **Ind/Abst** Mag. Index, Int. Aerosp. Abstr. **DD** 508680. *USSR (Soviet Union. Posolstvo (U.S.)).*

SOVIET SCIENTIFIC REVIEWS. SECTION D, PHYSICOCHEMICAL BIOLOGY REVIEWS. VFOAT Physicochemical Biology Reviews. 0734-9351. English (language translations of papers originally written in Russia). an. Harwood Academic Publishers, PO Box 786, Cooper Station, New York NY 10276. **DD** 574. *Soviet Scientific Reviews. Section D, Biology Reviews, 0143-0424.*

SPACE SCIENCE INSTRUMENTATION. See Aeronautics, Astronautics.

SPECIAL PUBLICATION - ACADEMY OF NATURAL SCIENCES OF PHILADELPHIA. (SPECIAL PUBLICATION - THE ACADEMY OF NATURAL SCIENCES OF PHILADELPHIA). No. 1-. 0097-3254. Monographic Series. US. English. ir. Scientific Publications, Academy of Natural Sciences, 19 and Parkway, Philadelphia PA 19103. **Tel** (215)299-1050. **Ed** K Elaine Hoagland. **Ind/Abst** GeoRef, Biol. Abstr. **LC** UNC. **CODEN** AYSPAX. **Circ** 1,000. Occasional symposia, catalogs or other works relating to natural sciences, biogeography, systematics, evolution and ecology.

SPECTRUM. Vol. 10-. 0049-1861. Periodical. German. ir. Akademie der Wissenschaften Der DDR, 108 Berlin, Otto-Nuschke Strasse 22/23, Berlin East Germany. **Ind/Abst** Chem. Abstr., Met. Abstr., World Alum. Abstr., Energy Res. Abstr. **LC** Q49. **DD** 505. **CODEN** SPEKDI. *Spektrum.*

SPECULATIONS IN SCIENCE AND TECHNOLOGY. V. 1- Apr. 1978-. 0155-7785. Periodical. UK. English. ir. $123.00. Science and Technology Letters, Royal Society of Chemistry, Burlington House, London W1V 0BN England. **Ed** Alan L Mackay. **Ind/Abst** Eng. Index Annu., Eng. Index Mon., Eng. Index Bioeng. Abstr., Eng. Index Energy Abstr., Life Sci. Collect., Excerpta Med., Sociol. Abstr., Soc. Welf. Soc. Plan./Policy Soc. Dev., Int. Aerosp. Abstr., Biol. Abstr., GeoRef, Comput. Control Abstr., Energy Inf. Abstr., Environ. Abstr., Electr. Electron. Abstr., Sci. Abstr. Sect. A. Phys. Abstr., Chem. Abstr., Met. Abstr., World Alum. Abstr. **LC** Q1. **DD** 505. **NLM** W1 SP325I. **CODEN** SPSTDD. bk rev. adv acc. **Circ** 800. Logically argued contributions which go beyond the realm of conventional journals of science and technology to serve the international scientific community as the focus of intellectual debate.

SPEKTRA. Periodical. Malay. ir. $7.20. Selangor/Sharikat Spektra, Peti Surat 1113 No 12, Jalan 14/54C Malaysia. **LC** Q4.

SPEUR- EN ONTWIKKELINGSWERK IN NEDERLAND. VFOAT Research and Development in the Netherlands. Began in 1959. Dutch. an. 22.00. Centraal Bureau voor de Statistiek, Prinses Beatrixlaan 428, Postbus 959, 2270 Az Voorburg Netherlands. **LC** Q180.N35. **DD** 001.409492.

SPRINGER SERIES IN SOLID-STATE SCIENCES. V. 1-. 0171-1873. Monographic Series. English. ir. Springer Verlag-New York Inc, 175 5th Avenue, New York NY 10010. **Tel** (212)460-1584. **Ind/Abst** Comput. Control Abstr., Electr. Electron. Abstr., Sci. Abstr. Sect. A. Phys. Abstr., Chem. Abstr. **CODEN** SSSSDV. Contains articles on heterostructures and superlattices, magnetic excitations, and fluctuations.

SSIE SCIENCE NEWSLETTER CEASED. **Main/Corp** Smithsonian Science Information Exchange. **VAT** Smithsonian Science Information Exchange Science Newsletter. V. 1- Oct. 1971-. 0094-7024. Periodical. US. English. mo. Room 300/1730 M Street NW, 20036.

SSIE SUBJECT TERMS AND SYNONYMS. **Main/Corp** Smithsonian Science Information Exchange. 1975-. US. English. $50.00. Smithsonian Science Information Exchange Inc, 1730 M Street NW, Room 300, Washington DC 20036. **Tel** (202)634-3933.

SSRS NEWSLETTER. **Main/Corp** Society for Social Responsibility in Science. **VAT** Society for Social Responsibility in Science Newsletter. 0036-1917. Periodical. US. English. mo. Dr Herbert Hayward, 420 East 72nd Street, New York NY 10021. **LC** Q175.4. **DD** 174.950973.

STATEMENT BY THE SECRETARY - SMITHSONIAN INSTITUTION. (STATEMENT BY THE SECRETARY). **Main/Corp** Smithsonian Institution. VFOAT Years Ahead. Began with 1977. 0147-2925. US. English. an. Smithsonian Institution, Office of the Secretary, 1000 Jefferson Drive SW, Washington DC 20560. **LC** Q11. **DD** 353.00853. *Smithsonian Year (1965), 0096-8404.*

STATUS OF SCIENCE REVIEWS. 0737-013X. US. English. an. National Science Foundation, National Science Board, Washington DC 20550. **LC** Q127.U6. **DD** 509.73.

STUDI TRENTINI DI SCIENZE NATURALI. SEZIONE B. BIOLOGICA. 0585-5616. Periodical. Italian. ir. 20000 Domestic, 40000 Foreign. Edizioni del Museo Tridentino di Scienze Naturali Trento, Via Rosmini 39, Trento Italy. **Tel** (0461)983334. **Ind/Abst** GeoRef, Chem. Abstr. **CODEN** SSNBBL. **Circ** 1,000. Covers geology, quaternary, applied geology, palaeontology, petrography, hydrology, physical geography, sedimentology, mine, zoology, entomology, arachnology, mammals, ornithology, lymnology, sociobiology. *Studi Trentini di Scienze Naturali.*

Science (General)

STUDIA I MATERIAY Z DZIEJOW NAUKI POLSKIEJ. SERIA C : HISTORIA NAUK MATEMATYCZNYCH, FIZYKO-CHEMICZNYCH I GEOLOGICZNO-GEOGRAFICZNYCH. VFOAT Historia Nauk Matematycznych, Fizyko-Chemicznyi Geologiczno-Geograficznych. Vol. 1- 1957-. 0081-6590. Polish (summaries in Russian and English). ir. *Studia I Materiay Z Dziejow Nauki Polskiej.*

STUDIEN ZUR WISSENSCHAFTSTHEORIE CEASED. Vol. 1- 1968-. Monographic Series. GW. German. ir. Anthenaum Verlag GMBH, Adelheidstrabe 2, 6240 Konigstein/TS West Germany. Tel 067 53/ 24 88.

STUDIES IN HISTORY AND PHILOSOPHY OF SCIENCE. V. 1- May 1970-. 0039-3681. Periodical. UK. English. qt. $171.00. Pergamon Press, 395 Sawmill River Road, Elmsford NY 10523. Tel (0865)64881. Ind/Abst Math. Rev., Am. Hist. Life, Hist. Abstr., Part A, Mod. Hist. Abstr., Hist. Abst., Part B, Twent. Century Abstr., Life Sci. Collect., Biol. Abstr., Comput. Control Abstr., Electr. Electron. Abstr., GeoRef, Humanit. Index, Sci. Abstr. Sect. A. Phys. Abstr., Recent Publ. Artic., Soc. Sci. Citation Index, Sci. Cit. Index, Abr. Ed., Phys. Abstr., Bibliogr. Index Geol., Hist. Abstr. LC Q125. DD 509. NLM W1 ST92L. CODEN SHPSB5.

STUDIES IN MANAGEMENT SCIENCE AND SYSTEMS. V. 1-. Monographic Series. English. ir. Elsevier Science Publishing Company Inc, PO Box 1663, Grand Central Station, New NY 10163. Ind/Abst Math. Rev., Comput. Control Abstr., Electr. Electron. Abstr., Sci. Abstr. Sect. A. Phys. Abstr.

STUDIES IN SCIENCE EDUCATION. V. 1- 1974-. 0305-7267. Periodical. UK. English. an. $12.00. Nafferton Books, 2 Railway Cottages Wansford Road, Driffield Yorks England. Ed David Layton. Ind/Abst Curr. Index J. Educ. bk rev. adv acc. Circ 800. All aspects of science education.

STUDIES IN SURFACE SCIENCE AND CATALYSIS. 0167-2991. Monographic Series. US. English. ir. Elsevier North Holland Inc, 52 Vanderbilt Avenue, New York NY 10017. Ind/Abst Eng. Index Annu., Eng. Index Mon., Eng. Index Bioeng. Abstr., Eng. Index Energy Abstr., Comput. Control Abstr., Electr. Electron. Abstr., Sci. Abstr. Sect. A. Phys. Abstr., Chem. Abstr. CODEN SSCTDM.

STUDIES IN THE HISTORY OF MODERN SCIENCE. V. 1- 1977-. Periodical. US. English. ir. D Reidel Publishing Company, 160 Old Derby Street, Hingham MA 02043. Ed Robert S Cohen, Erwin N Hiebert, and Everett I Mendelsohn. Ind/Abst Math. Rev.

SUDAN JOURNAL OF FOOD SCIENCE AND TECHNOLOGY. See Food & Drink.

SUDAN NOTES AND RECORDS. See Humanities.

SUID-AFRIKAANSE TYDSKRIF VIR NATUURWETENSKAP EN TEGNOLOGIE. VFOAT Natuurwetenskap en Tegnologie. 0254-3486. Periodical. SA. Afrikaans. ir. Suid-Afrikaanse Akademie vir Wetenskap en Kuns Posbus 538, Pretoria 0001 South Africa. Ind/Abst Chem. Abstr., Energy Res. Abstr., Life Sci. Collect., Math. Rev. CODEN SATTDF. *Tydskrif vir NAtuurwetenskappe.*

SUMMARIES OF PROJECTS COMPLETED. (SUMMARIES OF PROJECTS COMPLETED IN FISCAL YEAR . . .). Began with 1976/77. 0161-4169. US. English. an. National Science Foundation, 1800 G Street NW, Washington DC 20550. LC Q180.U5. DD 505. Vols. for 1980- distributed to depository libraries in microfiche.

SUMMARY OF AWARDS. 1975/76-. US. English. an. National Science Foundation, Computer Science Section, Washington DC 20550. LC Q224.3.U6. DD 507. Vols. for 1976, 1980, 1982- distributed to depository libraries in microfiche.

A SUMMARY OF RESEARCH IN SCIENCE EDUCATION CEASED. 1973-76. 0360-2907. US. English. an. John Wiley & Sons Inc, 605 Third Avenue, New York NY 10158. Tel (212)850-6000. LC Q181.A1. DD 507.

SURFACE SCIENCE LETTERS. Jan. 1980-. 0167-2584. Periodical. English. mo. Elsevier Science Publishers, PO Box 211, 1000 AE Amsterdam Netherlands. Tel (020)5803.911.

SURFACE SCIENCE REPORTS. Vol. 1, No. 1 (June 1981)-. 0167-5729. Monographic Series. English. ir. Elsevier Science Publishers, PO Box 211, 1000 AE Amsterdam Netherlands. Tel (020)5803.911. Ind/Abst Comput. Control Abstr., Electr. Electron. Abstr., Sci. Abstr. Sect. A. Phys. Abstr., Chem. Abstr., Met. Abstr., World Alum. Abstr. CODEN SSREDI.

SURVEY OF SCIENTIFIC SALARIES. See Economics - Labor.

SVODNYI KATALOG BIBLIOGRAFICHESKIKH RABOT, VYPOLNENNYKH V SOVETSKOM SOIUZE : ESTESTVENNYE I FIZIKO-MATEMATICHESKIE NAUKI. See Bibliographies.

SYLLOGEUS - NATIONAL MUSEUM OF NATURAL SCIENCES. See Museums.

SYMPOSIUM OF THE CONFERENCE ON SCIENCE, PHILOSOPHY AND RELIGION. Main/Conf Conference on Science, Philosophy and Religion in their Relation to the Democratic Way of Life. 12th-15th. Monographic Series. US. English. ir. Conference on Science, 3080 Broadway, New York NY 10027. *Symposium.*

SYNTHESIS CEASED. V. 1-5, No. 2. 0090-6883. Periodical. US. English. qt. Synthesis, 838 Holyoke Center, Cambridge MA 02138. Ind/Abst Life Sci. Collect. LC Q124.6. DD 509. NLM W1 SY66F.

SYSTEMS RESEARCH. (SYSTEMS RESEARCH : THE OFFICIAL JOURNAL OF THE INTERNATIONAL FEDERATION FOR SYSTEMS RESEARCH). Vol. 1, No. 1-. 0731-7239. Periodical. UK. English. qt. Free to Members, $30.00 Individuals of Institution with Subscription, $60.00 Others. Pergamon Press, Maxwell House Fairview Park, Elmsford NY 10523. LC Q295. DD 003. CODEN SYREER.

TADRIS AL-ULUM WA-AL-RIYADIYAT. Main/Corp Al-Munazzamah Al-Arabiyah Lil-Tarbiyah Wa-Al-Thaqafah Wa-Al-Ulum. VFOAT Science and Mathematics Education. Vol. 1-. Periodical. Arabic or English. ir. 109 Tahreer Street, Al-Qahirah United Arab Republic (Egypt) LC Q183.4.A65.

TAP CHI KHOA HOC KY THUAT. See Technology (General).

TASKS FOR VEGETATION SCIENCE. See Agriculture.

TATIGKEITSBERICHT DER OSTERREICHISCHEN AKADEMIE DER WISSENSCHAFTEN. Main/Corp Osterreichische Akademie der Wissenschaften. 1978-79-. AU. German. ir. Osterreichischen Akad Wissenschaften/Dr Inez-Spiel-Pltz 2, A-1010 Wien Austria. Ind/Abst GeoRef. LC AS142. DD 505. *Almanach (Osterreichische Akademie der Wissenschaften).*

TEACHING SCIENCE. Vol. 1, No. 1 (Spring 1983)-. 0028-0763. Periodical. UK. English. ty. 8.00. School Natural Science Society, 9 Killington Dr Mr A R Nicholls, Kendal Cumbria LA9 7NY. Ed E R Smith. bk rev. adv acc. Circ 900. (ctrl). Microform. Articles on science and technology teaching and conservation to children up to about 13 years. Teaching aids, background information, news, research reports and book reviews. *Natural Science in Schools.*

TECHNICAL BOOK REVIEW INDEX. See Indexes/Abstracts.

TECHNICAL REPORT - MARINE SCIENCES RESEARCH CENTER, STATE UNIVERSITY OF NEW YORK. Main/Corp State University of New York at Stony Brook. Marine Sciences Research Center. VFOAT Technical Report Series. 0362-2886. Monographic Series. US. English. ir. Marine Sciences Research Center, State University of New York, Stony Brook NY 11794. Ind/Abst GeoRef, Biol. Abstr. CODEN NYTRAH.

TECHNICAL REPORT SERIES P. PHYSICAL SCIENCES PUBLICATION. VFOAT Physical Sciences Publication. No. 1- 1966-. 0077-796X. Monographic Series. US. English. ir. University of Nevada, Desert Institute, 3700 Stead Campus, Reno NV 89507. DD 500. *Technical Report - Desert Research Institute.*

TECHNICAL TRANSLATION - NATIONAL RESEARCH COUNCIL OF CANADA CEASED. (TECHNICAL TRANSLATION - CANADA INSTITUTE FOR SCIENTIFIC AND TECHNICAL INFORMATION). VFOAT Traduction Technique - Institut Canadien de l'Information Scientifique et Technique. VAT Traduction Technique - National Research Council of Canada. Ceased publication with NRC/CNR TT-2082 (1984). 0077-5606. Monographic Series. CN. English (prefatory material in French). Canada Institute for Scientific & Technical Information, Montreal Road, Ottawa Ontario K1A 0S2 Canada. DD 500. *Technical Translation (National Research Council Canada), 0825-1940.*

TECHNICAL TRANSLATIONS. V. 1-18. 0497-0497. Periodical. US. English. sm. LC Z7401. DD 016.5. (cum index). *Translation Monthly, 0584-8210.*

TECHNISCH-WISSENSCHAFTLICHE ABHANDLUNGEN DER OSRAM-GESELLSCHAFT. 0371-5264. German. ir. Springer Verlag-New York Inc, 175 5th Avenue, New York NY 10010. Tel (212)460-1584. Ind/Abst Energy Res. Abstr. *Technisch-Wissenschaftliche Abhandlungen.*

TEORIE ROZVOJE VEDY. VFOAT Teoriia Razvitiia Nauki, Theory of Science Development. 1-. Periodical. CS. Czech (English or German with summaries in Russian). ir. LC Q174. DD 505. *Teorie a Metoda.*

TERMESZET VILAGA. V. 12, No. 1- Jan. 1968-. Periodical. Hungarian. ir.

TESTI E CONTESTI. 1-. Periodical. IT. Italian (summaries in English). ty. 11000. Conto Corrente N 53392205, Intestato A Clup, P.ZA Leonardo da Vinci 32, Milano Italy. LC Q124.6. DD 509.

THE TEXAS JOURNAL OF SCIENCE. V. 1- Mar. 1949-. 0040-4403. Periodical. US. English. qt. $45.00. Texas Acad of Sciences, PO Drawer H6, c/o Fred S Hendricks, College Station TX 77844. Tel (409)845-5704. Ed J Knox Jones. Ind/Abst Math. Rev., Life Sci. Collect., Excerpta Med., Energy Inf. Abstr., Environ. Abstr., Int. Aerosp. Abstr., GeoRef, Comput. Control Abstr., Electr. Electron. Abstr., Sci. Abstr. Sect. A. Phys. Abstr., Bibliogr. Agric., Biol. Abstr., Chem. Abstr., Nuci. Sci. Abstr., Sel. Water Resour. Abstr., Phys. Abstr., Bibliogr. Index Geol. LC Q1. DD 505. NLM W1 TE774. CODEN TJSCAU. bk rev. Circ 1,100. (ctrl). Science in any specific area by Texas scientists or concerning science in Texas.

THAI ABSTRACTS. SERIES A : SCIENCE AND TECHNOLOGY. See Indexes/Abstracts.

TIANJIN DAXUE XUEBAO. (TIEN-CHIN TA HSUEH HSUEH PAO). VFOAT Journal of Tianjin University. 0493-2137. Periodical. Chinese (abstracts in English). qt. $4.14. China Publication Centre, PO Box 2820, Beijing China. Ind/Abst Eng. Index Annu., Eng. Index Mon., Eng. Index Bioeng. Abstr., Eng. Index Energy Abstr., Chem. Abstr. LC Q4. DD 505. CODEN TCHHA9.

TJS SPEC. PUBL. VAT Texas Journal of Science Spacial Publication. No. 1-. 0145-0123. Monographic Series. US. English. $20.00 Single Issue. Texas Journal of Science, Po Box 10979 Asu Station, San Angelo TX 76901. Ind/Abst Chem. Abstr. CODEN TJSPD4.

TOKYO-TO SHIKEN KENKYU KIKAN NO KENKYU KEIKAKU. JA. Japanese. ir. Tokyo-To Somukyoku, 5-1 Marunouchi 3, Chiyoda-Ku, Tokyo Japan. LC Q180.J3.

TOYAMA DAIGAKU KYOIKU GAKUBU KIYO. B, RIKA-KEI. (TOYAMA DAIGAKU KYOIKU GAKUBU KIYO. B, RIKAKEI). VFOAT Memoirs of the Faculty of Education, Toyama University. Began in 1978. 0285-9610. English (Japanese). ir. Toyama Daigaku Kyoiku Gakubu, 3190 Gofuku, Toyama-Shi 930 Japan. Ind/Abst Chem. Abstr. LC Q4. CODEN TDKBDG.

TRANSACTIONS OF THE DELAWARE ACADEMY OF SCIENCE. (TRANSACTIONS). Main/Corp Delaware Academy of Science. V. 1/2- 1970/71-. 0093-6456. US. English. an. Delaware Academy of Science, Old Baltimore Pike Road 2, Newark DE 19711. LC Q11. DD 505.

TRANSACTIONS OF THE ILLINOIS STATE ACADEMY OF SCIENCE. Main/Corp Illinois State Academy of Science. V. 1- 1908-. 0019-2252. US. English. qt. $20.00. Illinois State Museum Society, Spring and Edwards Street, Springfield IL 62706. Tel (217)782-6436. Ind/Abst Math. Rev., Excerpta Med., GeoRef, Abstr. North Am. Geol., Bibliogr. Agric., Biol. Abstr., Chem. Abstr., Nuci. Sci. Abstr., Sel. Water Resour. Abstr., Bibliogr. Index Geol. LC Q11. DD 505. CODEN TISAAH. (cum index). adv acc. Circ 1,300.

Science (General)

TRANSACTIONS OF THE KENTUCKY ACADEMY OF SCIENCE. Main/Corp Kentucky Academy of Science. V. 1- 1914/23-. 0023-0081. US. English. sa. $30.00. Eastern Kentucky University, Department Biology/Dr Robert Creek, Richmond KY 40475. **Tel** (606)622-1537. **Ed** Branley Branson. **Ind/Abst** Excerpta Med., GeoRef, Bibliogr. Agric., Sci. Cit. Index, Abr. Ed., Biol. Abstr., Chem. Abstr., Sel. Water Resour. Abstr., Bibliogr. Index Geol. **LC** Q11. **CODEN** TKASAT. **Circ** 800. (ctrl). The official publication of the academy and publishes original papers based on research in any field of science.

TRANSACTIONS OF THE MISSOURI ACADEMY OF SCIENCE. Main/Corp Missouri Academy of Science. V. 1- 1967-. 0544-540X. US. English. an. $10.00. Missouri Academy of Science, PO Box 828, Kirksville MO 63501. **Tel** (816)785-4635. **Ed** John R Jones. **Ind/Abst** Excerpta Med., Int. Aerosp. Abstr., GeoRef, Biol. Abstr., Chem. Abstr. **LC** Q11. **DD** 505. **CODEN** MISTBW. **Circ** 1,300. (ctrl). The official technical publication of the Academy, contains referred works in areas of scientific interest, which includes twenty-four sections.

TRANSACTIONS OF THE NEBRASKA ACADEMY OF SCIENCES AND AFFILIATED SOCIETIES. Main/Corp Nebraska Academy of Sciences. Began with Vol. 4 (1977) issue. 0163-9013. US. English. Nebraska Academy of Sciences Inc, 306 Morrill Hall, 14th and U Streets, Lincoln NB 68588-0339. **Ind/Abst** GeoRef, Chem. Abstr. **LC** Q1. **DD** 505. **CODEN** TNASDJ. *Transactions of the Nebraska Academy of Sciences, 0077-6351.*

TRANSACTIONS OF THE NEW YORK ACADEMY OF SCIENCES. Main/Corp New York Academy of Sciences. V. 1-16, Oct. 1881-Dec. 1897. 0028-7113. Periodical. US. English. ir. New York Academy of Sciences, 2 East 63rd Street, New York NY 10021. **Tel** (212)838-0230. **Ind/Abst** GeoRef, Biol. Abstr., Chem. Abstr., Index Med., Int. Aerosp. Abstr., Math. Rev., Nucl. Sci. Abstr., Energy Res. Abstr., Bibliogr. Index Geol. **LC** Q11. **DD** 505. **NLM** W1 TR226T. **CODEN** TNYAAE. (cum index).

TRANSACTIONS OF THE RHODESIA SCIENTIFIC ASSOCIATION CEASED. Main/Corp Rhodesia Scientific Association. Vol. 56, No. 1 (Nov. 1974)-V. 59, No. 7 (Jan. 1980). 0379-9638. Monographic Series. English. ir. **CODEN** TRSADF. *Proceedings and Transactions (Rhodesia Scientific Association), 0370-2294.*

TRANSACTIONS OF THE SAEST. VFOAT Transactions of SAEST. Vol. 4, No. 1 (Jan./Mar. 1969). 0036-0678. Periodical. English. qt. $12.00. Society for Advancement of Electrochemical Science and Technology, Karaikudi 623 006 India. **Tel** 2368. **Ed** P V Vasudeva Rao. **Ind/Abst** Eng. Index Annu., Eng. Index Mon., Eng. Index Bioeng. Abstr., Eng. Index Energy Abstr., Met. Abstr., Chem. Abstr., World Alum. Abstr. **CODEN** TSETA6. bk rev. adv acc. **Circ** 1,150. (ctrl). Original research papers and authoritative reviews accepted. Brief communications on power sources, electrometallurgy, corrosion, engineering, electroplating, and metal finishing, electrochemicals, material science, solid state electrochemistry and basic electrochemistry. *Transactions of the Society for Advancement of Electrochemical Science and Technology.*

TRANSATIONS OF THE KANSAS ACADEMY OF SCIENCE (1903). (TRANSACTIONS OF THE KANSAS ACADEMY OF SCIENCE). VFOAT Transactions. Vol. 18-. 0022-8443. Periodical. US. English. sa. $20.00. Kansas Academy of Science, Emporia State University, c/o Neufeld, Emporia KS 66801. **Tel** (316)343-1200. **Ed** J Robert Berg. **Ind/Abst** Life Sci. Collect., GeoRef, Biol. Abstr., Chem. Abstr., Index Med., Nucl. Sci. Abstr., Energy Res. Abstr., Bibliogr. Index Geol. **LC** Q11. **NLM** W1 TR226G. **CODEN** TSASAH. (cum index). **Circ** 500. Papers describing the results of research in the natural and behavioral sciences. *Transactions of the ... Annual Meetings of the Kansas Academy of Science.*

TRUDY AKADEMII NAUK LITOVSKOI SSR. SERIIA B, KHIMIIA, TEKHNIKA, FIZICHESKAIA GEOGRAFIIA. VFOAT Lietuvos TSR Mokslu Akademijos Darbai. 1970, 3 (62)-. 0132-2729. Periodical. UR. Russian. bm. $59.50. Victor Kamkin Inc, 12224 Parklawn Drive, Rockville MD 20852. **Tel** (301)881-5973. **Ind/Abst** Math. Rev., Met. Abstr., World Alum. Abstr. Index in last issue of volume - attached. *Trudy Akademii Nauk Litovskoi SSR. Seriia B, Khimiia, Tekhnika, Geografiia.*

TRUDY SEVERO-VOSTOCHNOGO KOMPLEKSNOGO NAUCHNO-ISSLEDOVATELSKOGO INSTITUTA. Main/Corp Severo-Vostochnyi Kompleksnyi Nauchno-Issledovatelskii Institut (Akademiia Nauk SSSR). UR. Russian. 0.90 Each Issue. Nauka, Magazin Akademkniga 76, Krasnyi Prospekt 51, 630076 Navosibirsk USSR. **LC** Q60.

TZU JAN KO HSUEH NIEN CHIEN. See Yearbooks, Almanacs, Directories.

TA TZU JAN TAN SO. VFOAT Exploration of Nature. V. 1, 1982. Periodical. CH. Chinese. qt. 1.20. Hsin Hua Shu Tien, Chuang-Ching Fa Hsing So, Chuang-Ching China. **Ind/Abst** Math. Rev. **LC** Q4. **DD** 505.

U. L. SCIENCE MAGAZINE. Main/Corp Monrovia, Liberia. University of Liberia. Division of Science. V. 1- July 1972-. Periodical. English. ir. $2.00. University of Liberia, Division of Science, Editor-In-Chief, Monrovia Liberia. **LC** Q1. **DD** 505. *Liberian Naturalist.*

UCMP QUARTERLY. VFOAT UCMP. VAT Union Catalog of Medical Periodicals Quarterly. Apr. 1973-. 0276-7570. US. English. qt. $150.00. Medical Library Center of New York, 17 East 102nd Street, New York NY 10029. **Tel** (212)427-1630. **Ed** Robert Dempsey. **NLM** ZW 1 U42A. Union List (microfiche) of serials for health science libraries.

AS UFONOTAS. Portuguese. ir. $6.00. Centro de Estudos Ufologicos, Jean Alencar, Caixa Postal 689, 60.000 Fortaleza Ceara Brazil. **Tel** 55-085-239.24.29. **Ed** Jose Jean Pereira de Alencar. adv acc. **Circ** 300. (ctrl). Our bulletin divulges theories, studies, facts and research about, the UFO phenomena in all its aspects.

UIR-RESEARCH NEWSLETTER CEASED. (UIR/RESEARCH NEWSLETTER). V. 1-15. 0041-512X. Periodical. US. English. **LC** Q179.9. **DD** 500. **NLM** W1 U43.

UMSCHAU (FRANKFURT AM MAIN, GERMANY : 1982). (DIE UMSCHAU). V. 82, No. 1, (Jan. 8, 1982)-. 0722-8562. Periodical. GW. German (summaries in English). mo. Umschau Verlag Breidenstein Kg Stuttgrtr Str 18-24/Postfach 10262, 6000 Frankfurt 1 West Germany. **Tel** 069/2 60 01. **Ind/Abst** Electron. Commun. Abstr. J., ISMEC Bull., Pollut. Abstr. Indexes, Saf. Sci. Abstr. J., Excerpta Med., Coal Abstr., Comput. Control Abstr., Electr. Electron. Abstr., Sci. Abstr. Sect. A. Phys. Abstr., Chem. Abstr., Energy Res. Abstr. **CODEN** UMSCDV. *Umschau in Wissenschaft und Technik.*

UNDERCURRENTS. Periodical. UK. English. qt. $2.50. 34 Cholmley Gardens Aldred Road, London NW6 England. **LC** Q162. **DD** 505.

UNITED STATES-JAPAN COOPERATIVE SCIENCE PROGRAM : STATUS REPORT. Main/Corp National Science Foundation (U.S.). 1977/78-. English. an. **LC** Q172.5.I5. **DD** 507.2052.

U.S. / R&D. See Technology (General).

U.S. SCIENTISTS AND ENGINEERS. Series/Titl Surveys of Science Resources Series. VAT United States Scientists and Engineers. 1974-. 0163-2302. US. English. be. **LC** Q149.U5. **DD** 331.11. **NLM** W2 A N37U.

UNIVERSITY OF ALASKA RESEARCH ANNUAL REPORT. 0161-8865. US. English. an. University of Alaska, Fairbanks AK 99701. **LC** Q180.U5. **DD** 507.20798.

THE UNIVERSITY OF KANSAS SCIENCE BULLETIN. Series Corp Its Bulletin of the University of Kansas. Its University of Kansas Publications. VFOAT Science Bulletin. V. 1- Feb. 1902-. 0022-8850. US. English. ir. University of Kansas Libraries, Exchange & Gift Department, Lawrence KA 66044. **Ind/Abst** Biol. Abstr., Chem. Abstr., Nucl. Sci. Abstr., Bibliogr. Index Geol. **LC** Q1. **DD** 508. **NLM** W1 SC69. **CODEN** UKSBAB. *Kansas University Quarterly, 0885-4068.*

URANIA. V. 1-. 0049-562X. Periodical. SZ. German. mo. Kunst & Wissen Erich Bieber, Dufourstrasse 51, CH-8008 Zurich Switzerland. **Ind/Abst** Chem. Abstr. **LC** Q3. **CODEN** URAAAZ.

USSR REPORT. LIFE SCIENCES. EFFECTS OF NONIONIZING ELECTROMAGNETIC RADIATION (PUBLIC ED.). (USSR REPORT. LIFE SCIENCES. EFFECTS OF NONIONIZING ELECTROMAGNETIC RADIATION). VFOAT U.S.S.R. REPORT. VAT Union of Soviet Socialist Republics Report. Life Sciences. Effects of Nonionizing Electromagnetic Radiation. No. 1 (Apr. 17, 1980)-. 0733-9151. US. English. **NLM** W1 US918M. Available in microform. *USSR Report. Biomedical and Behavioral Sciences. Public Ed.*

VAIJNANIKA. Hindi. ir. 1.00 Single Issue. 85 Bambai India. **LC** Q4.

VAN NOSTRAND'S SCIENTIFIC ENCYCLOPEDIA. See Encyclopedias & General Reference Books.

VEDA A LIDSTVO. Periodical. Czech (Slovak). an. 40.00 Paper Cover, 49.00 Clothbound. **LC** Q180.C9.

VEDA A ZIVOT. 1935-. Periodical. CS. Czech. mo. ARTIA, PO Box 790, Praha 1 Czechoslovakia.

VENEZUELA AHORA : CIENCIA. Periodical. VE. Spanish. ir. Ministerio de Informacion Y Turismo, Apartado de Correos1 192, Caracas Venezuela.

VENTURE PRODUCT NEWS. See Technology (General).

VENTURES IN RESEARCH. Ser. 1- 1972-. 0092-556X. US. English. an. $4.95. Long Island University, CW Post Center, Northern Boulevard, Greenvale NY 11548. **Tel** (516)299-2957. **Ed** Donald K Frank. **LC** AS36.P864. **DD** 081. bk rev. (ctrl). Lectures by the faculty of C. W. Post Campus of Long Island University.

VERHANDELINGEN DER KONINKLIJKE NEDERLANDSE AKADEMIE VAN WETENSCHAPPEN, AFDELING NATUURKUNDE. EERSTE SECTIE. (VERHANDELINGEN DER KONINKLIJKE NEDERLANDSE AKADEMIE VAN WETENSCHAPPEN, AFD. NATUURKUNDE. EERSTE REEKS). Began in 1892. 0065-5503. Monographic Series. NE. Dutch (English, French, and German). ir. **Ind/Abst** GeoRef. **LC** Q57. **DD** 505. **CODEN** VNANAN. Index published separately - free - automatically sent. *Verhandelingen (Koninklijke Nederlandse Akademie van Wetenschappen. Afdeling Natuurkunde).*

VERHANDELINGEN VAN DE KONINKLIJKE ACADEMIE VOOR WETENSCHAPPEN, LETTEREN EN SCHONE KUNSTEN VAN BELGIE, KLASSE DER WETENSCHAPPEN. Main/Corp Academie Voor Wetenschappen, Letteren en Schone Kunsten Van Belgie. Klasse der Wetenschappen. Vol. 34- (No. 122-). 0372-6916. Monographic Series. BE. Dutch. ir. Academie Voor Wetenschappen Letteren En Schone Kunsten Van Belgie, Paleis der Academien Hertogsstraat 1, B-1000 Brussel Belgium. **Ind/Abst** Math. Rev., Biol. Abstr. **LC** Q56. **CODEN** VKKWAB. *Verhandelingen.*

VERHANDLUNGEN DER NATURFORSCHENDEN GESELLSCHAFT IN BASEL. Vol. 1- 1854/57-. 0077-6122. Periodical. German (French, with summaries in English). ir. Birkhauser Boston Inc, 380 Green Street, PO Box 3005, Cambridge MA 02139. **Tel** (617)876-2333. **Ind/Abst** Life Sci. Collect., Biol. Abstr., GeoRef, Bibliogr. Index Geol. **NLM** W1 VE483Z. **CODEN** VNGBAH. Index published separately - free - automatically sent. (cum index). *Bericht Uber die Verhandlungen der Naturforschenden Gesellschaft in Basel.*

VERHANDLUNGEN DER SCHWEIZERISCHEN NATURFORSCHENDEN GESELLSCHAFT. Main/Corp Schweizerische Naturforschende Gesellschaft. VFOAT Actes de la Societe Helvetique des Sciences Naturelles. 1909-1959. SZ. German. an. 60. Birkhauser Verlag, PO Box 133, CH 4010 Basel Switzerland. **Tel** 061 735300. **Ind/Abst** GeoRef. **CODEN** VSNGAY. Official journal of the Swiss Academy of Natural Sciences. Publishes the proceedings of the annual meetings. *Verhandlungen.*

VESTNIK AKADEMII NAUK SSSR. Main/Corp Akademiia Nauk SSSR. V. 1- 1931-. 0002-3442. Periodical. UR. Russian. mo. $64.00. Victor Kamkin Inc (70115), 12224 Parklawn Drive, Rockville MD 20852. **Tel** (301)881-5973. **Ind/Abst** Math. Rev., Am. Hist. Life, Hist. Abstr., Part A, Mod. Hist. Abstr., Hist. Abst., Part B, Twent. Century Abstr., Sociol. Abstr., Soc. Welf. Soc. Plan./Policy Soc. Dev., Lang. Lang. Behav. Abstr., Int. Aerosp. Abstr., GeoRef, Chem. Abstr., Energy Res. Abstr., Sci. Cit. Index, Abr. Ed. **LC** AS262. **NLM** W1 VE818. **CODEN** VANSAC.

VESTNIK - CESKOSLOVENSKA AKADEMIE VED. Main/Corp Ceslpslovenska Akademie Ved. Vol. 1- Oct. 1891-. 0009-0492. Periodical. CS. Czech. bm. $66.55. Kubon Sagner,

Science (General)

Postfach 34 01 08, D 8 Muenchen 34 West Germany. Tel 0811 52 20 27. (cum index).

VESTNIK LENINGRADSKOGO UNIVERSITETA. MATEMATIKA, MEKHANIKA, ASTRONOMIJA. (VESTNIK LENINGRADSKOGO UNIVERSITETA. MATEMATIKA, MEKHANIKA, ASTRONOMIIA). Vol. 1, 1967-. 0024-0850. Periodical. UR. Russian (has also tables of contents and summaries in English). qt. Victor Kamkin Inc, 12224 Parklawn Drive, Rockville MD 20852. Tel 33813501-5973. Ind/Abst Energy Res. Abstr., Math. Rev., GeoRef, Int. Aerosp. Abstr., Comput. Control Abstr., Electr. Electron. Abstr., Sci. Abstr. Sect. A. Phys. Abstr., Chem. Abstr. CODEN VMMAA3. *Vestnik Leningradskogo Universiteta. Seriia Matematiki, Mekhaniki I Astronomii.*

VESTNIK MOSKOVSKOGO UNIVERSITETA. SERIIA II, KHIMIIA. See Chemistry.

VETENSKAPSAKADEMIEN. Main/Corp Kungliga Svenska Vetenskapsakademien. Swedish. ir. 104, 05 Stockholm Sweden. LC Q64.

VIRGINIA JOURNAL OF SCIENCE. V. 1- Jan. 1940-. 0042-658X. Periodical. US. English. qt. $27.50. J S Reynolds Community College, Department of Biology, c/o Dr J H Martin, Richmond VA 23241. Tel (804)264-3064. Ed James H Martin FREER. Ind/Abst Math. Rev., Life Sci. Collect., Excerpta Med., Int. Aerosp. Abstr., Biol. Abstr., GeoRef, Chem. Abstr., Bibliogr. Agric., Bibliogr. Index Geol. LC Q1. DD 505. NLM W1 VI799. CODEN VJSCAI. adv acc. Circ 1,500. Original articles in science and engineering or dealing with advancements in science and technology and the impact on man and society. *Claytonia.*

VOPROSY ISTORII ESTESTVOZNANIIA I TEKHNIKI CEASED. Vol. 1-67-68. 0507-3367. Periodical. UR. Russian. ir.

VOPROSY ISTORII ESTESTVOZNANIJA I TEHNIKI. (VOPROSY ISTORII ESTESTVOZNANIIA I TEKHNIKI). 1980, 1-. UR. Russian (summaries in English). qt. $48.00. Victor Kamkin Inc (70143), 12224 Parklawn Drive, Rockville MD 20852. Tel (301)881-5973. Ind/Abst Math. Rev., Am. Hist. Life, Hist. Abstr., Part A, Mod. Hist. Abstr., Hist. Abst., Part B, Twent. Century Abstr. LC Q124.6. *Voprosy Istorii Estestvoznaniia I Tekhniki.*

VORTRAGE - RHEINISCH-WESTFALISCHE AKADEMIE DER WISSENSCHAFTEN, N, NATUR-, INGENIEUR- UND WIRTSCHAFTSWISSENSCHAFTEN. (NATUR-, INGENIEUR- UND WIRTSCHAFTSWISSENSCHAFTEN). Main/Corp Rheinisch-Westfalische Akademie der Wissenschaften. 0066-5754. Monographic Series. GW. German. ir. Westdeutscher Verlag GMBH, Postfach 5829, S6200 Wiesbaden 1 West Germany. Ind/Abst Biol. Abstr., Chem. Abstr., GeoRef, Life Sci. Collect. LC Q49.C95. DD 508.1. CODEN RWAVAW. *Natur-, Ingenieur- Und Gesellschaftswissenschaften.*

WASEDA JINBUN SHIZEN KAGAKU KENKYU. VFOAT Waseda Journal of General Sciences. Began in 1967. 0286-1275. Periodical. JA. Japanese. ir. Waseda Daigaku Shakai Kagakubu Gakkai, c/o Waseda Daigaku Shakai Kagakubu 6-1 Nishi Waseda 1 Shinjuku-Ku, Tokyo-To Japan. LC AS552.W37.

WASHINGTON REMOTE SENSING LETTER. VFOAT RSL. 1981. Periodical. US. English. ir. $210.00 Foreign. Washington Remote Sensing, PO Box 2075, Washington DC 20013. Tel (202)393-3640. Ed Murray Felsher. bk rev. Reports on all aspects of US and foreign applications of surveillance and photography of the earth from space. Reconnaissance, etc.

WEST EUROPE REPORT. SCIENCE AND TECHNOLOGY. VFOAT Science and Technology. No. 1 (1 Nov. 1979)-. Periodical. US. English (Multilingual). ir. National Technical Information Service, Foreign Broadcast Information Service, Joint Publications Research Service, 5285 Port Royal Road, Springfield VA 22161. Available in microform also.

THE WESTERN AUSTRALIAN NATURALIST. V. 1- 1947-. 0508-4865. Periodical. AT. English. ir. Western Australian Naturalist Club, PO Box 156, 65 Merriwa Street, Nedland WA Australia 6009. Ind/Abst Biol. Abstr. CODEN WAUNA9.

WILHELM ROUX'S ARCHIVES OF DEVELOPMENTAL BIOLOGY. See Genealogy and Heraldry - Archives.

WINDOWS (COLLEGE STATION, TEX.). (WINDOWS). Vol. 1, No. 1 (Spring 1982)-. 0745-0729. Periodical. US. English. qt. Free. Tees Information Service, 323 ERC Texas A & M University, College Station TX 77843-3134. Tel (409)845-5510. Ed Debbie Reddin and Laura Colunga. bk review. Circ 5,000. (ctrl). Science and technology research performed at Texas universities and non-profit research institutions.

WISSENSCHAFT AKTUELL. No. 1 (Dec. 1979)-. Periodical. German. ir. $5.25. Dr Ekkehard Schultze, Porzellangasse 2/2/34, 1090 Wien Austria. LC Q3. DD 505.

WISSENSCHAFT UND FORTSCHRITT. Began in May 1951. 0510-6966. Periodical. German. mo. Kunst & Wissen Erich Bieber, Dufourstrasse 51, CH-8008 Zurich Switzerland. Tel 011-41-1-69 44 20. Ind/Abst Coal Abstr., Chem. Abstr., Bibliogr. Agric. LC Q3. CODEN WIFOAR.

WISSENSCHAFT UND GEGENWART. GEISTESWISSENCHAFTLICHE REIHE. No. 45- 1969-. Periodical. GW. German. ir. Vittorio Klostermann, Postfach 900701 Frauenlobstrasse 22, 6000 Frankfurt 90 West Germany. Tel (611)774011. *Wissenschaft und Gegenwart.*

WISSENSCHAFTEN IN DER DDR. Series/Titl ABG. 1975-. German. an. 7.00. Institut fur Gesellschaft und Wissenschaft, Aussere Brucker Str 33, Postfach 1409, 8520 Erlangen-Nurnberg West Germany. LC H5, Q127. *Jahresbericht zur Wissenschaftsentwicklung und Wissenschaftspolitik in der DDR.*

WISSENSCHAFTLICHE NORMUNG. 0084-0947. Monographic Series. German. ir. Springer Verlag-New York Inc, 175 5th Avenue, New York NY 10010. Tel (212)460-1584.

WISSENSCHAFTLICHE ZEITSCHRIFT. Main/Corp Wilhelm-Peick-Universitat Rostock. Vol 1- 1951/52-. 0043-6933. Periodical. some summaries in English, French, and Russian. ir. Ind/Abst Math. Rev. LC Q3. NLM W1 WI983.

WISSENSCHAFTLICHE ZEITSCHRIFT DER HUMBOLDT-UNIVERSITAT ZU BERLIN. See Social Sciences (General).

WISSENSCHAFTLICHE ZEITSCHRIFT DER MARTIN-LUTHER-UNIVERSITAT HALLE-WITTENBERG. Vol. 1, Issue 1/2 (1951/52)-Vol.14, Issue 7. 0440-128X. Periodical. GE. German. bm. Deutscher Duch Export-Import, Leninstrasse 16, DDR-701 Leipzig East Germany. Ind/Abst Lang. Lang. Behav. Abstr., Math. Rev., Sociol. Abstr. LC Q49. NLM W1 WI984H.

WISSENSCHAFTLICHE ZEITSCHRIFT DER WILHELM-PIECK-UNIVERSITAT ROSTOCK. NATURWISSENSCHAFTLICHE REIHE. VFOAT WZ Rostock. Vol. 31, No. 1-. 0323-4681. Periodical. German (summaries in English, French, and Russian). ir. Wilhelm-Pieck-Universitat Rostock, Vogelsang 13/1, DDR-2500 Rostock East Germany. Ind/Abst Chem. Abstr., Excerpta Med. *Wissenschaftliche Zeitschrift der Wilhelm-Pieck-Universitat Rostock.*

WISSENSCHAFTLICHE ZEITSCHRIFT. MATHEMATISCH-NATURWISSENSCHAFTLICHE REIHE. Main/Corp Karl-Marx-Universitat Leipzig. Vol. 1- 1951/52. 0043-6860. Periodical. GE. German. bm. Ind/Abst Life Sci. Collect., Excerpta Med., GeoRef, Biol. Abstr., Comput. Control Abstr., Electr. Electron. Abstr., Sci. Abstr. Sect. A. Phys. Abstr., Chem. Abstr., Energy Res. Abstr. LC Q49. NLM W1 WI981K. CODEN WZMNA8. Index published separately - free - automatically sent.

WISSENSCHAFTLICHER ERGEBNISBERICHT ... DES ZENTRALINSTITUTS FUR ISOTOPEN- UND STRAHLENFORSCHUNG DER ADW DER DDR. Series/Titl ZFI-Mitteilingen. 0323-8776. German. an. Akademie der Wissenschaften der DDR Zentralinstitut fur Isotopen- und Strahlenforschung (RIS0903).

WNNR JAARVERSLAG. Main/Corp South African Council for Scientific and Industrial Research. SA. Afrikaans. ir. South African Council for Scientific and Industrial Research, PO Box 395, Pretoria 0001 South Africa. LC Q180.S6. *Jaarverslag.*

WO MEN AI KO HSUEH. VFOAT Women Ai Kexue. Vol. 17 (March 1978) – 1-. Periodical. CC. Chinese. mo. $5.13. China Publication Centre, PO Box 2820, Beijing China. LC Q163. DD 505. *Shao Nien Ko Chi.*

WOLGAN KWAHAK. VFOAT Newton Graphic Science Magazine. Changgan Chonho-. Periodical. Korean. mo. 42,000. Kyemongsa, PO Box 83-HO, Mapo Ucheguk, Seoul Korea. LC Q4.

WOMEN AND MINORITIES IN SCIENCE AND ENGINEERING. Jan. 1982-. 0739-666X. US. English. be. National Science Foundation, Washington DC 20550. LC Q130. DD 331.48150973.

WORLD MEETINGS, UNITED STATES AND CANADA. (WORLD MEETINGS : OUTSIDE UNITED STATES AND CANADA). 19 -. Periodical. US. English. qt. $165.00. MacMillan Publishing Company, 866 3rd Avenue, New York NY 10022. Tel (800)257-8247. Ed Clark Hansen. Circ 1,000. A two-year registry of all important future medical, scientific, and technical meetings to be held outside the United States and Canada. Revised and updated quarterly.

WORLD TRANSINDEX. See Indexes/Abstracts.

XIBEI SHIFAN XUEYUAN XUEBAO. ZIRAN KEXUE BAN. (HSI PEI SHIH FAN HSUEH YUAN HSUEH PAO. TZU JAN KO HSUEH PAN). VFOAT Journal of the Northwestern Teachers College. 0254-6167. Periodical. CH. Chinese. qt. 0.50. Post Office, Lan-Chou Shih China. Ind/Abst Chem. Abstr. LC Q4. DD 505. CODEN XSXKDJ.

XIN GINGNIAN KEXUE. (HSIN CHING NIEN KO HSUEH). First published in May 1972-. 0303-089X. Chinese. ir. $0.30 Single Issue. 111-E Jalan Satu, Singapore 14 Singapore. LC Q111.

YALE SCIENTIFIC. VFOAT Yale Scientific Magazine. V. 33- Oct. 1958-. 0091-0287. Periodical. US. English. qt. $6.50 Domestic, $12.00 Foreign. Yale Scientific Magazine, 244-A Yale Station, New Haven CT 06520. Tel (203)436-3222. Ed Howard Rubin. Ind/Abst Int. Aerosp. Abstr. NLM W1 YA459. bk rev. adv acc. Circ 7,000. (ctrl). Reports in-depth the new and exciting research going on at Yale, as well as general interest topics in science, to the layman. *Yale Scientific Magazine,* 0044-0140.

YAMAGATA DAIGAKU KIYO : KYOIKU KAGAKU. VFOAT Bulletin of the Yamagata University: Educational Science. Vol. 1- 1927 March 1952-. Japanese (summaries in English). ir. LC L67. DD 370.952.

YAMAGATA DAIGAKU KIYO, SHIZEN KAGAKU. (YAMAGATA DAIGAKU KIYO: SHIZEN KAGAKU). VFOAT Bulletin of the Yamagata University: Natural Science. Vol. 1- 1925- March 1950-. 0513-4692. Japanese (English). ir. Ind/Abst Math. Rev., Comput. Control Abstr., Electr. Electron. Abstr., Sci. Abstr. Sect. A. Phys. Abstr., Chem. Abstr. LC Q4. CODEN YDKSAH.

YEAR BOOK - ANDHRA PRADESH AKADEMI OF SCIENCES. See Yearbooks, Almanacs, Directories.

YEAR BOOK - CARNEGIE INSTITUTION OF WASHINGTON. See Yearbooks, Almanacs, Directories.

YEAR BOOK OF THE INDIAN NATIONAL SCIENCE ACADEMY. See Yearbooks, Almanacs, Directories.

THE YEAR BOOK OF THE INTERNATIONAL COUNCIL OF SCIENTIFIC UNIONS. See Yearbooks, Almanacs, Directories.

YEAR BOOK OF THE ROYAL SOCIETY OF EDINBURGH. See Yearbooks, Almanacs, Directories.

YEARBOOK OF SCIENCE AND THE FUTURE. See Yearbooks, Almanacs, Directories.

YEARBOOK OF THE NATIONAL SCIENCE TEACHERS ASSOCIATION. See Yearbooks, Almanacs, Directories.

YIQI YIBIAO XUEBAO. VFOAT Chinese Journal of Scientific Instrument. 0254-3087. Periodical. CH. Chinese. qt. China Publication Centre, PO Box 2820, Beijing China. **Ind/Abst** Comput. Control Abstr., Electr. Electron. Abstr., Sci. Abstr. Sect. A. Phys. Abstr.

YMCHWIL, CYMRU, CYNTAF. Main/Corp Great Britain. Welsh Office. VFOAT Research, Wales, Report. 1st- 1973/74-. UK. English and Welsh. an. 0.45. H M Stationery Office, PO Box 276, London 5W8 5DT England. **LC** Q180.G7. **DD** 350.8109429.

YONSE NONCHONG. CHAYON KWAHAK PYON. VFOAT Yonsei Nonchong. Periodical. KO. English (Korean). an. Yonse Taehakkyo Taehagwon, 134 Sinchon-Dong, Sodaemun-Ku, Seoul South Korea. **Ind/Abst** Energy Res. Abstr. **LC** Q4.

ZAGADNIENIA NAUKOZNAWSTWA. Vol. 1- (No. 1-). 0044-1619. Periodical. PL. Polish. qt. ARS Polona, Krakowskie Przedmiescie 7, 00-068 Warsaw Poland. **LC** Q4.

ZAMBIA JOURNAL OF SCIENCE AND TECHNOLOGY. V. 1- Jan. 1976-. 0378-8857. Periodical. ZA. English. ir. 15.00. National Council for Scientific Research, PO Box CH 158 Chelston, Lusaka Zambia. **Ind/Abst** GeoRef, Chem. Abstr. **LC** Q91.Z33. **DD** 505. **NLM** W1 ZA756. **CODEN** ZJSTDE.

ZEITSCHRIFT FUR ALLGEMEINE WISSENSCHAFTSTHEORIE. VFOAT Journal for General Philosophy of Science. Vol. 1- 1970-. 0044-2216. Periodical. GW. German. sa. 120. Franz Steiner Verlag GMBH, Postfach 347, D7000 Stuttgart 1 West Germany. **Tel** (0711)2582229. **Ed** A Diemer, L Geldsetzer and G Koenig. **Ind/Abst** Math. Rev., Philos. Index, Comput. Control Abstr., Electr. Electron. Abstr., Sci. Abstr. Sect. A. Phys. Abstr., Index Book Rev. Humanit., Phys. Abstr. **LC** Q3. **CODEN** ZAWTA2. **adv acc. Circ** 700. Matter concerns the general philosophy of science.

ZEITSCHRIFT FUR NATURFORSCHUNG. B. ANORGANISCHE, ORGANISCHE UND BIOLOGISCHE CHEMIE, BOTANIK, ZOOLOGIE UND VERWANDTE GEBIETE. VFOAT Anorganische, Organische und Biologische Chemie, Botanik, Zoologie und Verwandte Gebiete. Vol. 2B, No. 1/2 (Jan./Feb. 1947)- Vol. 2B, No 11/12 (Nov. Dec. 1947). Periodical. GW. German. mo. Zeitschrift fur Naturforschung Uhlander 11, 7400 Tuebingen West Germany. **LC** QD1. **DD** 505. Zeitschrift fur Naturforschung.

ZEITSCHRIFT FUR SEMIOTIK. Vol. 1- 1979-. 0170-6241. Periodical. GW. German. qt. $31.65. Gunter Narr Verlag, Dischingerweg 5, 7400 Tuebingen 5 West Germany. **Tel** 00071-78091. **Ed** Roland Posner. bk rev. adv acc. **Circ** 1,200. Theoretical bases of semiotics historical bases of semiotics, semiotic bases of sciences, semiotics of everyday life and aesthetic experience and problems of application.

ZESZYTY NAUKOWE AKADEMII GORNICZO-HUTNICZEJ IM. STANISAWA STASZICA. MATEMATYKA, FIZYKA, CHEMIA. (MATEMATYKA, FIZYKA, CHEMIA). Series/Titl Zeszyty Naukowe Akademii Gorniczo-Hutnicza Im. S. Staszica. VFOAT Mathematics, Physics, Chemistry. No. 1- 0372-8838. Monographic Series. Polish (summaries in English and Russian). ir. **Ind/Abst** Math. Rev.

ZHONGGUO KEXUE JISHU DAXUE XUEBAO. (CHUNG-KUO KO HSUEH CHI SHU TA HSUEH HSUEH PAO). VFOAT Journal of the China University of Science and Technology. Began publication in 1965. 0253-2778. Periodical. CH. Chinese. qt. $6.66. China Publication Centre, PO Box 2820, Beijing China. **Ind/Abst** Math. Rev., Int. Aerosp. Abstr., Chem. Abstr. **CODEN** CKHPD7.

THE ZIMBABWE SCIENCE NEWS. V. 14, No 4/5- Apr./May 1980-. Periodical. English. mo. Zimbabwe Scientific Association, PO Box 8351, Causeway Salisbury. **Ind/Abst** Life Sci. Collect., Biol. Abstr. **CODEN** ZSNED7. Zimbabwe Rhodesia Science News, 0253-049X.

ZIRAN ZAZHI. (TZU JAN TSA CHIH. ZIRAN ZAZHI). Began in 1978. 0253-9608. Periodical. CC. Chinese. mo. $17.82. China Publication Centre, PO Box 2820, Beijing China. **Ind/Abst** Chem. Abstr. **LC** Q4. **CODEN** TJTCD4.

ZNANSTVENOISTRAZIVACKE I RAZVOJNE ORGANIZACIJE. Main/Corp Republicki Zavod Za Statistiku Sr Hrvatske. Serbo-Croatian(R). ir. Republicki Zavod Za Statistiku SRH, Ilica 3, Zagreb Yugoslavia. **LC** Q180.Y8.

ZUGAKU KENKYU. VFOAT Journal of Graphic Science of Japan. 0387-5512. Periodical. Japanese (with summaries in English). ir. Nihon Zugakkai c/o Tokyo Daigaku Kyoyo Gakubu Zugaku Kyoshitsu, 8-1 Komaba Meguro-Ku Tokyo-To 153 Japan.

ZWO : PLAATS EN PERSPECTIEF. Main/Corp Netherlands (Kingdom, 1815-). Nederlandse Organisatie voor Zuiver-Wetenschappelijk Onderzoek. NE. Dutch. ir. Nederlandse Organisatie voor Zuiver-Wetenschappelijk Onderzoek, Juliana van Stolberglaan 148, S-Gravenhage Netherlands. **LC** Q180.N35.

SENIOR CITIZENS

50 PLUS. VAT Fifty Plus. V. 18, No.9- Sept. 1978-. 0163-2027. Periodical. US. English. mo. $10.95. Retirement Living Publishing Co, 850 Third Avenue, New York NY 10022. **Ind/Abst** Abr. Read. Guide, Read. Guide Period. Lit., Pop. Mag. Rev. **LC** HQ1060. **DD** 301.43505. Retirement Living, 0090-4910.

AARP NEWS BULLETIN. VAT American Association of Retired Persons News Bulletin. V. 10- Nov. 1968-. 0010-0200. Periodical. US. English. mo. $5.00. American Association of Retired Persons, 1909 K Street Northwest, Washington DC 20049. **Tel** (202)662-4842. **Ed** C Joseph Dooley. adv acc. **Circ** 10,000,000. Newspaper informing subscribers of the latest legislative and social issues relating to the 50 and over population. News Bulletin.

ACA NEWS (ALBERTA COUNCIL ON AGING). (ACA NEWS). Vol. 16, No. 1 (Jan. 1984)-. 0826-497X. Periodical. CN. English. mo. Free. Alberta Council on Aging, 10010-105 Street, Edmonton Alberta T5J 1C4 Canada. **DD** 305.26097123. (ctrl). News, 0383-7998.

AGE D'OR HEBDO. V. 1-3, No. 50. 0704-710X. Periodical. CN. French. wk. Charles Desmarteau Inc, 414 Marie Victorin, Boucherville Que J4B 1L6 Canada. **DD** 362.609714.

AGE D'OR, VIE NOUVELLE. VFOAT Vie Nouvelle. V. 1- Oct. 1978-. 0226-6121. Periodical. CN. French. bm. $4. Members, $6. Others. Age D Ore Vie Nouvelle, Publications F.A.D.O.Q., 1415 East Rue Jarry, Montreal Quebec H2E 2Z7 Canada. **DD** 362.609714.

AGED CARE & SERVICES REVIEW. See Sociology: General Works, Theory - Social Pathology, Welfare, Criminology.

AGING (BOCA RATON, FLA.). (AGING). Series/Titl Social Issues Resources Series. Vol. 1, Article 1-. 0273-2467. US. English. an. Social Issues Resources Series Inc, P O Box 2507, Boca Raton FL 33432. **Ed** Eleanor C Goldstein. **LC** HQ1064.U5. **DD** 305.2605.

AGING PROGRAM LETTER. Vol. 1, No. 1 (May 1984)-. 0742-3438. Periodical. US. English. mo. $84.00. Omni Reports, P O Box 34031, Bethesda MD 20817. **DD** 362.

AGING SERVICES NEWS. 0197-4025. Periodical. US. English. bw. Business Publishers Inc, 951 Pershing Drive, Silver Springs MD 20910. **Tel** (301)587-6300. **Ed** Nancy Aidrich. Report on federal programs affecting the elderly nationwide- health, social services, social security, housing, transportation, etc. Including grant opportunities for local area agencies on aging. Supportive Services.

A.I.M., AGING IN MICHIGAN. VFOAT Aging in Michigan. V. 1-4, No. 9. 0360-3644. Periodical. US. English. ir. Office Services to the Aging, PO Box 30026, Lansing MI 48909. **Tel** (517)373-8230. Aging in Michigan, 0515-667X.

ANNUAL REPORT. Main/Corp Kansas. Advisory Council on Aging. 1978/1979-. Periodical. US. English. an. Kansas Advisory Council on Aging, State Capitol, Topeka KS 66612.

Senior Citizens

ANNUAL REPORT - CENTRE FOR POLICY ON AGING (LONDON, ENGLAND). Main/Corp Centre for Policy on Aging (London, England). UK. English. an. Centre for Policy on Aging, Nuffield Lodge Studio, Regents Park, London NWI 4RS England. Annual Report for the Year Ended 30th September . . . .

ANNUAL REPORT - GOVERNOR'S CITIZENS' COUNCIL ON AGING (MINNESOTA). See Sociology: General Works, Theory - Social Pathology, Welfare, Criminology.

ANNUAL REPORT - NATIONAL INSTITUTE ON AGING. Main/Corp National Institute on Aging. VFOAT NIA Annual Report. Oct. 1, 1979 through Sept. 30, 1980-. US. English. an. National Institutes on Aging, National Institutes of Health, Bethesda MD 20205. **LC** HV1457. **DD** 353.0084606. **NLM** W2. National Institute on Aging. NIA Annual Report, 0192-7744.

ANNUAL REPORT OF THE ONTARIO ADVISORY COUNCIL ON SENIOR CITIZENS. (ANNUAL REPORT - ONTARIO ADVISORY COUNCIL ON SENIOR CITIZENS). Main/Corp Ontario Advisory Council On Senior Citizens. VFOAT Rapport Annuel. 1974/75-. 0704-2663. CN. English. an. Ontario Advisory Council Senior Citizens, 2505 Lakeshohre Boulevard West, Toronto Ontario M8W 1NS Canada. **LC** HV1475.O5. **DD** 354.71300846.

ANNUAL REPORT - THE NEBRASKA COMMISSION ON AGING. Main/Corp Nebraska. Commission for Aging. US. English. ir. The Nebraska Commission On Aging, PO Box 95044 Centennial Mall South, Lincoln NE 68509. **LC** HQ1064.U6. **DD** 353.978200846.

ANNUAL REVIEW - SENIOR CITIZENS' PROVINCIAL COUNCIL OF SASKATCHEWAN. Main/Corp Saskatchewan. Senior Citizens' Provincial Council. 1st- 1977-. 0704-9048. CN. English. an. **LC** HV1475.S35. **DD** 362.60627124.

THE ARIZONA SENIOR WORLD. VFOAT Senior World of Arizona. V. 1- Mar. 1979-. 0270-0425. Periodical. US. English. mo. $9.00. Arizona Senior World, 818 East Osborn Road Suite 203, Phoenix AZ 85014. **Tel** (602)279-4490. **Ed** Kathy Wilson. bk rev. adv acc. **Circ** 130,000. (ctrl). Newspaper targetted to the 50 year and over market.

AUDIT REPORT - COMMISSION ON AGING. (AUDIT REPORT, COMMISSION ON AGING). Main/Corp Tennessee. Division of State Audit. 0147-8117. US. English. Tennessee Comptroller of the Treasury, Division of the State Audit, Nashville TN 37219.

BEST YEARS. V. 1, No. 1 (Spring 1977 Ed.)-. 0730-1065. Periodical. US. English. bm. National Association for Mature People, 2212 NW 50th Street, Oklahoma City OK 73126. **Tel** (405)848-1832. **Ed** Ann Cade. **LC** HQ1064.U5. **DD** 305.260973. bk rev. adv acc. **Circ** 250,000. (ctrl). An educational and informative magazine. Also includes light, fun articles. Each issue contains articles on food, travel, money management, and special features on retirement planning.

BULLETIN DE L'AGE D'OR. (LE BULLETIN DE L'AGE D'OR). Vol. 1, No. 1-. 0229-866X. Periodical. CN. French. qt. Free. Boucher Marois, Boucher et Associes 10, 887 Boulevard, Pie 1X Montreal-Nord Quebec H1H 4B2 Canada. **DD** 305.2609714. (ctrl).

CALIFORNIA SENIOR CITIZEN. 0748-5727. Periodical. US. English. mo. $2.00. Osmon Publications, 4805 Alta Canyada Road, Lacanada CA 91011. **Tel** (818)790-0651. **Ed** Carol Osmon. adv acc. **Circ** 55,500. (ctrl). Opportunities and services available for senior citizens. 0008-1531.

CENTRE ON AGING NEWS. Vol. 1, No. 1 (Summer 82)- 0826-4694. Periodical. CN. English. ir. Free. University of Manitoba Centre on Aging, 338 Ibster Building, Winnipeg Manitoba R3T 2N2 Canada. **DD** 612.6706071274.

CURRENT LITERATURE ON AGING. Main/Corp National Council on the Aging. V. 1- 1957-. 0011-3662. Periodical. US. English. qt. $24.00 Domestic, $30.00 Foreign. National Council on the Aging, 600 Maryland Avenue SW West Wing 100, Washington DC 20024. **Tel** (202)479-1200. **Ed** Carol Forney. **Circ** 5,200. (ctrl). Annotated bibliography of current books and journal articles in the field of social gerontology.

Senior Citizens

DECEMBER ROSE. 0748-1195. Periodical. US. English. qt. $10.00. December Rose Association, 255 South Hill Street, Los Angeles CA 90012. **Tel** (213)617-7002. Ed Don Jarman. bk rev. adv acc. **Circ** 80,000. (ctrl). Seeks to be a showcase for the creativity of older people. It publishes material written by or about seniors.

DEVELOPMENT IN AGING. (DEVELOPMENTS IN AGING : A REPORT OF THE SPECIAL COMMITTEE ON AGING, UNITED STATES SENATE). **Main/Corp** United States. Congress. Senate. Special Committee on Aging. 0734-3213. US. English. an. Superintendent of Documents, US Government Printing Office, Washington DC 20402. LC HQ1064.U5. **DD** 305.260973. **NLM** W2 A C84D. Vols. for (1981-) distributed to some depository libraries in microfiche.

DIRECT LOAN PROGRAM FOR THE ELDERLY OR HANDICAPPED. See Sociology: General Works, Theory - Social Pathology, Welfare, Criminology.

DIRECTORY OF RESOURCES FOR SENIOR CITIZENS OF OTTAWA-CARLETON. See Yearbooks, Almanacs, Directories.

DIRECTORY OF SENIOR CENTERS AND CLUBS. See Yearbooks, Almanacs, Directories.

DISCOVERY (TORONTO, ONT.). (DISCOVERY). **VFOAT** Discovery For Seniors. Mar./Apr. 1980-. 0710-0957. Periodical. CN. English. mo. 10.00 Domestic, $14.00 Foreign. Terrace Publication Ltd, 302 Merton Street, Toronto M4S 1A9 Canada. **Tel** (416)484-1771. Ed Mary Schmieder. **DD** 646.7909713541. bk rev. adv acc. **Circ** 15,000. A lifestyle magazine for the pre- and post retirement Canadian.

DISTRICT OF COLUMBIA PLAN ON AGING. FY 1982-1984-. US. English. LC HQ1064.U6. **DD** 352.94409753. *District of Columbia Plan on Aging for Fiscal Years . . . .*

DYNAMIC YEARS. V. 12, No. 4, (July/Aug. 1977)-. 0148-799X. Periodical. US. English. bm. AIM Membership Processing Department, PO Box 199, Long Beach CA 90801. **Ind/Abst** Mag. Index, Pop. Mag. Rev., Consum. Index Prod. Eval. Inf. Source. LC HQ1060. **DD** 301.435. *Dynamic Maturity,* 0012-7388.

EIJINGU. **VFOAT** Aging. V. 1, No. 1, (1983-6)-. 0288-3619. Periodical. JA. Japanese. bm. 4440. Chuo Hoki Shuppan Kabushiki Kaisha 27-4, Yoyogi 2 Shibuya-ku, Tokyo-to 151 Japan. LC HQ1060. *Kikan Rojin Mondai.*

FOCUS, LIBRARY SERVICE TO OLDER ADULTS, PEOPLE WITH DISABILITIES. See Library and Information Science.

FORESIGHT (EDMONTON, ALTA.). (FORESIGHT). **VAT** Foresight Magazine. Vol. 1, No. 1 (Sept. 1981)-. 0711-3927. Periodical. CN. English. bm. $8.51. Alberta Council on Aging, 24 10010 105 Street, Edmonton Alberta T5J 1C4 Canada. **Tel** (403)423-7782. Ed Sheila Smith. **DD** 646.7905. bk rev. adv acc. **Circ** 6,000. Pre-Retirement Planning.

GERIATRIC & RESIDENTIAL CARE NEWS MONTHLY. **VAT** Geriatric and Residential Care News Monthly. 1975. 0163-0717. Periodical. US. English. mo. $59.00. HRS Geriatric Publishing Corporation, 451 Greenwich Street, New York NY 10013. **Tel** (206)232-9689. Ed Frances Greer. NLM W1 GE455M. bk rev. adv acc. **Circ** 1,000. Essential research and reference tool covers programs and events affecting the elderly, medicaid, medicare, social security legislation. Invaluable for professionals in health and social sciences.

GERONTOPHILE. (LE GERONTOPHILE : BULLETIN DE L'ASSOCIATION QUEBECOISE DE GERONTOLOGIE). Vol. 1, No. 1 (Mar. 1979)-. 0225-4271. Periodical. CN. French. ir. Free to Members, $25.00 Others. Le Gerontophile Chambre, 2467 Pavillon de Koninck Universite, Laval Quebec G1K 7P4 Canada. **DD** 305.2605.

THE GOLDEN YEARS SENIOR NEWS INC. SPACE COAST EDITION. (THE GOLDEN YEARS SENIOR NEWS INC). **VFOAT** Golden Years. 0733-0529. Periodical. US. English. mo. Golden Years Senior News Inc, PO Box 537, 460 South Harbor City Boulevard, Melbourne FL 32901. **Tel** (305)725-4882.

GROWING OLDER. No. 1 1976-. Periodical. US. English. an. Rational Island Publishers, 719 2nd Avenue North, Seattle WA 98109.

INFORMATION STATEMENT FOR APPLICANTS AND GRANTEES MODEL PROJECTS ON AGING. **Main/Corp** United States. Administration on Aging. US. English. United States Department of Health Education and Welfare, Office of Human Resources Services, Administration on Aging, Room 4273/Hew Building North, Washington DC 20201.

JOURNAL DE L'AGE D'OR. See Sociology: General Works, Theory - Social Pathology, Welfare, Criminology.

JOURNAL OF AGING AND JUDAISM. 0884-8688. Periodical. US. English. sa. $40.00. Human Sciences Press, 72 5th Avenue, New York NY 10011.

JOURNAL OF GERONTOLOGY. V. 1- Jan. 1946-. 0022-1422. Periodical. US. English. bm. $55.00 Domestic, $65.00 Foreign. Gerontological Society Inc, 1411 K Street NW/Suite 300, Washington DC 20005. **Tel** (202)393-1411. Ed Martha Storandt. **Ind/Abst** Hospit. Lit. Index, Life Sci. Collect., Excerpta Med., Women Stud. Abstr., Int. Aerosp. Abstr., Biol. Abstr., Chem. Abstr., Psychol. Abstr., Nuci. Sci. Abstr., Index Med., Public Aff. Inf. Serv. Bull., Curr. Index J. Educ., Energy Res. Abstr., Soc. Sci. Index, Abstr. Anthropol., Soc. Sci. Citation Index, Sci. Cit. Index, Abr. Ed., Chem. Abstr., Abstr. Soc. Work. LC HQ1060. **DD** 301.435. NLM W1 JO669P. **CODEN** JOGEA3. bk rev. adv acc. **Circ** 8,733. (ctrl). Available on microfilm from University Microfilms. Reports original research in the biological, medical, psychological, and social sciences.

THE JOURNAL OF MINORITY AGING. V. 3, No. 6- Aug. 1978-. 0742-6291. Periodical. US. English. sa. $30.00. Black Aging, PO Box 8813, Durham NC 27707. **Tel** (919)489-2563. Ed Jacquelyne J Jackson. LC HQ1064.U5. **DD** 362.60973. **Circ** 750. Research about aging of older minorities in the United States. Emphasizing public policies, services, and age changes. *Black Aging.*

JOURNAL OF NUTRITION FOR THE ELDERLY. See Nutrition and Dietetics.

KOREIKA SHAKAI NENKAN. '84-. Periodical. JA. Japanese. an. 7000. Shin Jidaisha, 2 Kanda Jinbo-Cho Chiyoda-Ku, Tokyo-To Japan. LC HQ1064.J3.

LIFE LINES. V. 1- Oct 1974- (No. 1-). 0744-0677. Periodical. US. English. bm. Lincoln Area Agency on Aging, Life Lines Magazine, 129 North 10th Street/Room 241, Lincoln NB 68508-356.

MAIN DE L'AGE D'OR. (LA MAIN DE L'AGE D'OR). Vol. 1, No. 1 (Winter 1984)-. 0824-1503. Periodical. CN. French. qt. Free. La Main de l'Age d'Or, C P 421, Drummondville Quebec J2B 6W3 Canada. **DD** 305.2605. (ctrl).

MATURE LIVING. 0162-427X. Periodical. US. English. mo. $11.25. Materials Service Department, 127 9th Avenue North, Nashville TN 37234. **Tel** (615)251-2191. Ed Jack Gulledge. **Circ** 306,000. A leisure-reading magazine in large print for older adults, sixty plus with a christian-orientation.

MATURE OUTLOOK. Vol. 1, No. 1 (Winter 1984)-. 0742-0935. Periodical. US. English. bm. $8.00. Allstate Enterprises, 3701 West Lake Street, Glenview IL 60025-8205. **Tel** (312)291-4738. Ed Mary Kelly Selober. adv acc. **Circ** 900,000. A lifestyle publication edited for people age 50 and over. It features personalities, travel information, money management and other topics of interest to this age group.

MATURE OUTLOOK NEWSLETTER. Began with Vol. 1, No. 1 in 1984. 0748-4003. Periodical. US. English. bm. $6.00. Allstate Enterprises, 3701 West Lake Street, Glenview IL 60025-8205. **Tel** (312)291-5416. Ed Nancy Goode. adv acc. **Circ** 900,000. A guide to money management, healthcare and fitness, and travel. Designed to appeal to the special interests and concerns of people age 50 and older.

MINIMUM MONTHLY BUDGET FOR RETIRED COUPLE. See Business - Public Finance.

MINIMUM MONTHLY BUDGETS FOR ELDERLY PERSONS LIVING ALONE. See Business - Public Finance.

MODERN MATURITY. (MODERN MATURITY : PUBLICATION OF THE AMERICAN ASSOCIATION OF RETIRED PERSONS). Vol. 25, No. 1 (Feb.-Mar. 1982)-. 0747-6302. Periodical. US. English. bm. AARP, 215 Long Beach Boulevard, Long Beach CA 90801. *NRTA Journal,* 0027-6979.

NAT'L PENSIONERS, SENIOR CITIZENS NEWS. V. 1- Jan. 1969-. 0380-0989. Periodical. CN. English (French). qt. 3.00. National Pensioners & Senior Citizens Federation, 3033 Lakeshore Place West, Toronto Ontario M8V 1Y5 Canada. **Tel** (416)251-7042. **Circ** 5,000. Serving senior citizens across Canada.

NENKIN FUKUSHI JIGYODAN NEMPO. See Insurance.

NENKIN KENKYU NENPO. See Insurance.

NEW ENGLAND SENIOR CITIZEN. 1970. 0163-2248. Periodical. US. English. mo. $20.00. R A De Vito, 470 Boston Post Road, Weston MA 02193. **Tel** (617)899-2702. Ed Shirely Copithorne. bk rev. adv acc. **Circ** 50,000. (ctrl). Upbeat tabloid newspaper. Covers entertainment and travel for those over 50.

NEWS FOR SENIORS. 0710-958X. Periodical. CN. English. mo. Society for the Retired and Semi-Retired, 10004-105th Street, Edmonton Alberta P5J 1C3 Canada. **DD** 362.60971233.

NEWSCENE CEASED. **VFOAT** AAHA Newscene. **VAT** American Association of Homes for the Aging Newscene. Periodical. US. English. qt. American Association of Homes for the Aging, 1050 Seventeenth Street Northwest, Washington DC 20036.

NEWSLETTER - CANADIAN ASSOCIATION ON GERONTOLOGY. (NEWSLETTER). **Main/Corp** Canadian Association on Gerontology. **VFOAT** Bulletin d'Information. 0712-676X. Periodical. CN. English (French text on inverted pages). qt. Canadian Association on Gerontology, PO Box 1859, Winnipeg Manitoba R3C 3R1 Canada. **DD** 305.260971.

NSCLC WASHINGTON WEEKLY. See Law.

OLDER AMERICAN REPORTS. V. 1- Nov. 22. 1976-. 0146-3640. Periodical. US. English. ir. $197.00. Capitol Publications Inc, 1300 North 17th Street, Arlington VA 22209. **Tel** (703)528-5400. **NLM** W1 OL34.

OLDTIMERS' SPORTS NEWS. See Recreation, Leisure - Sports.

OUR AGE (ARLINGTON, VA.). (OUR AGE). 0739-2362. Periodical. US. English. bm. $6.00. National Alliance of Senior Citizens Inc, 2525 Wilson Boulevard, Arlington VA 22201. **Tel** (703)528-4380. Ed C C Clinkscales III. bk rev. adv acc. **Circ** 150,000. (ctrl). National membership publication of the National Alliance of Senior Citizens. Deals in issues of concern and light topics of interest to the senior community.

PEEL SENIORS REGIONAL NEWS. No. 1- May 1974-. 0319-0196. Periodical. CN. English. ir. Peel Seniors Regional News, c/o Mrs M Thrower, 2515 Shepard Avenue, Mississauga Ontario L5A 2H7 Canada. **DD** 362.6309713535.

PRIME TIME. Jan. 1980-. 0194-2611. Periodical. US. English. mo. $8.85. Herald & Weekly Times, 44-74 Flinders Street, Melbourne 3000 Australia. **Tel** 63 0211. Ed Russ Gleeson. LC WMLC L 83/132. bk rev. adv acc. Generally deals with retired persons and their needs when retired.

PRIME TIME MAGAZINE. Vol. 1, No. 1 (Aug. 1983)-. 0824-5479. Periodical. CN. English. mo. $1.00 Each Number. Prime Time Magazine, 975 Alston Street, Victoria British Columbia V9A 3S5 Canada. **DD** 051.

PRIME TIMES. V. 1- Spring 1979-. 0195-5934. Periodical. US. English. qt. National Association for Retired Credit Union People, PO Box 391, Madison WI 53701. **Tel** (608)238-4286. Ed Steven A Goldberg. bk rev. adv acc. **Circ** 55,000. Consumer information, investigative reporting, personal profiles, humor and fiction to help people redefine retirement and help them take a fresh, active approach to growing older.

PROCEEDINGS - JOINT CONFERENCE ON THE PROBLEM OF MAKING A LIVING WHILE GROWING OLD. **Main/Conf** Joint Conference on the Problem of Making a Living While Growing Old. **VFOAT** Age Barriers to Employment. US. English.

Sewing and Needlework

REPORT ON THE ACTIVITIES IN THE CONGRESS OF THE SELECT COMMITTEE ON AGING, U.S. HOUSE OF REPRESENTATIVES. See Public Administration.

RETIREMENT LETTER. 0093-5352. Periodical. US. English. mo. $48.00. Phillips Publishing Inc, 7811 Montrose Road, Potomac MD 20854. **Tel** (301)986-0666.

ROJIN MONDAI CHIIKI KAIGI HOKOKUSHO. Japanese. ir. LC HQ1064.J3.

ROJIN MONDAI KENKYU. VFOAT Journal for the Study of Gerontology. Vol. 1 (1981)-. 0286-8539. Periodical. Japanese. ir. Osaka Furitsu Rojin Sogo Senta, 3-ban 1-go Yamada-kita, Suita-shi 565 Japan. LC HQ1064.J3.

THE SANTA BARBARA SENIOR WORLD. VFOAT Senior World/Santa Barbara. 0276-0800. Periodical. US. English. mo. $24.00. Senior World Publications, PO Drawer 1565, El Cajon CA 92022. **Tel** (619)442-4404.

SASCH NEWSLETTER. Vol. 1, issue 1 (1983)-. 0826-1962. Periodical. CN. English. ir. Free. Saskatchewan Association of Special Care Homes, 2-1540 Albert Street, Regina Saskatchewan S4P 2S4 Canada. **Tel** (306)565-0744. **Ed** John F Carter. **DD** 362.160607124. bk rev. adv acc. **Circ** 1,000. (ctrl). An in-house publication keeping members and interested persons informed on issues related to long term care in this province. *Saskatchewan Care, 0048-9166.*

SENIOR AMERICAN NEWS. 0163-2256. Periodical. US. English. mo. $20.00. R A de Vito, 470 Boston Post Road, Weston MA 02193. **Tel** (617)899-2702. **Ed** Shirley Copithorne. bk rev. adv acc. **Circ** 30,000. (ctrl). Upbeat tabloid newspaper. Covers entertainment and travel for those over 50.

SENIOR CITIZENS ADVOCATE AND ASPECTS OF AGING. VFOAT Senior Citizens Advocate. 0882-9403. Periodical. US. English. bm. Senior Citizens Advocate, 40 West 68th Street, New York NY 10023. **Tel** (212)724-3200. **Ed** Mirian Koren. **Circ** 56,000. (ctrl). An action newspaper covering legislation and government programs for older adults and how to preserve and improve them.

SENIOR CITIZENS' CONSULTANTS OF ST. CATHARINES INC. (SENIOR CITIZENS' CONSULTANTS OF ST. CATHARINES : NEWSLETTER). Vol. 4, No. 1 (Jan. 1982)-. 0714-5756. Periodical. CN. English. mo. Senior Citizens' Consultants Newsletter, 355 St Paul Street, St Catharines Ontario L2R 3N2 Canada. **DD** 362.60971351. *Senior Citizens' Advisory Council (Newsletter), 0229-2785.*

SENIOR CITIZENS NEWS. 0559-4677. Periodical. US. English. mo. $8.00. National Council of Senior Citizens, 925 15th Street NW, Washington DC 20005. **Tel** (202)232-6570.

SENIOR CITIZENS TODAY. 0049-0199. Periodical. US. English. mo. $8.00. Senior Citizens Today, PO Box 160274, Sacramento CA 95816. **Tel** (916)447-8885.

THE SENIOR GUARDIAN. 1975. 0730-577X. Periodical. US. English. mo. $15.00. National Alliance Senior Citizen, PO Box 28008, Washington DC 20005. **Ed** C C Clinkscales III. **Circ** 34,000. Senior citizen issue periodical dealing with state and federal legislation from a moderate and conservative point-of-view.

SENIOR SCENE. (THE SENIOR SCENE). 0714-5624. Periodical. CN. English. ir. Free. Senior Scene Newspaper Inc, 1200 Atwater Avenue/Room 2, Montreal Quebec H3A 2A8 Canada. **DD** 305.2609714281.

THE SENIOR TRIBUNE. 0149-7413. Periodical. US. English. mo. $3.00. Senior Tribune Subscriptions, PO Box 28285, Atlanta GA 30328.

SENIOR WORLD QUARTERLY. Vol. 1, No. 1 (Spring 1981)-. 0714-8798. Periodical. CN. English. qt. $3.86. Senior World, PO Box 6098/Station A, St John New Brunswick E2L 4R5 Canada. **Tel** (506)657-8671. **Ed** Louise Adler. **DD** 362.60971. bk rev. adv acc. **Circ** 30,000. Among topics included are maintaining health, financial security, and full living. Intended for Canadians of 55 years or older.

SENIORS' REPORT. Began publication in 1977 or 1978. 0225-1566. Periodical. CN. English. mo. Free. **DD** 305.260971233.

SENIORS TODAY. Vol. 1, No. 1 (Feb. 24, 1982)-. 0715-4046. Periodical. CN. English. wk. $15.00. L & M Publications Ltd, 1443 Arlington Street, Winnipeg Manitoba R2X 1T2 Canada. **DD** 362.60971274.

SHAKAI-RONENGAKU. VFOAT Social Gerontology. No. 1- 1974-NEN 3-GATSU. Periodical. Japanese or English. ir. Tokyo-to Rojin Sogo Kenkujo, 35-2 Sakaecho, Itabaski-ku 173 Tokyo Japan. LC HQ1060.

SUCCESSFUL MARKETING TO SENIOR CITIZENS. See Business - Marketing.

TEMPS DE VIVRE. (LE TEMPS DE VIVRE). V. 1- Feb./March 1979-. 0708-7632. Periodical. CN. French. mo. 18.00. Les Temps de Vivre, 8050 Metropoloitain Boulevard East, Montreal Quebec H1K 1A1 Canada. **Tel** (514)353-7660. **DD** 301.43509714. adv acc. **Circ** 40,000. A magazine regarding the needs and informatives for (50 plus persons) senior citizens.

TOP GENERATION NEWSLETTER. (TOP GENERATION NEWSLETTER : A NEWSLETTER FOR SENIOR CITIZENS). 0229-2602. Periodical. CN. English (includes some text in French). ir. $2.00 Members, $2.50 Nonmembers. c/o C Dean, 1984 Cannaught Avenue, Halifax Nova Scotia B3N 1S6 Canada. **DD** 305.2609716.

TRAINING AND MANPOWER DEVELOPMENT ACTIVITIES. See Sociology: General Works, Theory - Social Pathology, Welfare, Criminology.

TYOELAKEJARJESTELMAN TILASTOLLINEN VUOSIKIRJA. OSA I, TILASTOTIETOJA TYOELAKKEEN SAAJISTA. See Statistics.

UNITED RETIREMENT BULLETIN. Began with: V. 3, No. 7 (July 1977). Periodical. US. English. mo. $21.00. United Business Service Company, 210 Newbury Street, Boston MA 02116. **Tel** (617)267-8855. **Ed** Carol Finnegan. **Circ** 10,000. Provides helpful information on retirement planning and living. *United Retirement Newsletter.*

VIEIL ART. (LE VIEIL ART). V. 1- Sept./Oct. 1977-. 0228-2623. Periodical. CN. French. bm. $2.00. Les Ateliers Vieil Art, 1014 rue Jogues, Drummondville-Sud Quebec J2B 4X6 Canada. **DD** 305.2605.

VIVRE +. V. 1, No. 1, (April 1973)- V. 4, No. 2, (Dec. 1976). 0228-5517. Periodical. CN. French. mo. Vivre +, 233 Av Murray, Ottawa Ontario K1N 5M9 Canada. **DD** 305.2609713.

VOICE OF UNITED SENIOR CITIZENS OF ONTARIO, INC. (THE VOICE OF UNITED SENIOR CITIZENS OF ONTARIO, INC). **Main/Corp** United Senior Citizens of Ontario. V. 1- Sept. 1969-. 0382-0068. Periodical. CN. English. mo. $3.86. United Senior Citizens Ontario, 3505 Lakeshore Boulevard West, Toronto Ontario M8W 1N5 Canada. **Tel** (519)252-2021. **Ed** Ellis Blair. adv acc. **Circ** 2,500.

WOODALL'S RETIREMENT DIRECTORY. See Yearbooks, Almanacs, Directories.

ZIKNA. V. 1- Fall 1972-. English. sa. POB 11243, Tel Aviv Israel. LC HQ1060.

SEWING AND NEEDLEWORK

100'S OF NEEDLEWORK & CRAFT IDEAS. Series/Titl Better Homes and Gardens Creative Ideas. VFOAT Hundreds of Needlework and Craft Ideas. 0278-7504. Periodical. US. English. sa. $2.25. Special Interest Publications, 1716 Locust Street, Des Moines IA 50336. LC TT740. **DD** 746.405.

ANNUAL REPORT - NEEDLEWORK GUILD OF AMERICA, INC. (ANNUAL REPORT - NEEDLEWORK GUILD OF AMERICA). **Main/Corp** Needlework Guild of America. 0360-1102. US. English. an. Needleword Guild of America, 1736 Pine Street, Philadelphia PA 19103. LC HV696.C5. **DD** 362.5. *Report of the Meeting and Reports of the Chairmen and the Branches.*

ANNUARIO . . . DELL'INDUSTRIA ITALIANA DELLA MAGLIERIA E DELLA CALZETTERIA. See Yearbooks, Almanacs, Directories.

BEST OF MCCALL'S NEEDLEWORK & CRAFTS. (THE BEST OF MCCALL'S NEEDLEWORK & CRAFTS). VAT The Best of McCall's Needlework and Crafts. V. 1- 1975-. 0098-9290. US. English. $1.65. McCall Pattern Co, 230 Park Avenue, New York NY 10017. LC TT740. **DD** 746.4.

BULLETIN - INTERNATIONAL OLD LACERS. Main/Corp International Old Lacers. VFOAT Bi-Monthly Bulletin for Members. 1952. US. English. bm. $8.00. International Old Lacers Inc, PO Box 1029, Westminister CO 80030. **Tel** (303)429-3258. **Ed** Robert C Ridell. bk rev. adv acc. **Circ** 2,100. (ctrl). Lace articles, patterns, pictures of lace exhibits, club activities, advertising of lace related materials, and information on the yearly convention. *International Old Lacers Inc., Bulletin, 0740-6746.*

THE BULLETIN OF THE NEEDLE AND BOBBIN CLUB. Main/Corp Needle and Bobbin Club, New York. V. 1-. 0273-0197. Periodical. US. English. an. $15.00. Needle & Bobbin Club, 1225 Park Avenue 7-A, New York NY 10028. **Tel** (212)876-8372. **Ed** Ann Hecht. LC NK9100. **DD** 746.05. bk rev. adv acc.

BUTTERICK. Periodical. US. English. Butterick Fashion Marketing Company, 161 6th Avenue, New York NY 10013. adv acc. **Circ** 20,000. The latest in design for fashion conscious dressmakers together with helpful hints and tips.

BUTTERICK SEWING WORLD. Periodical. US. English. qt. $11.00. Butterick Sewing World, PO Box 569, Altoona PA 16603. *Butterick Home Catalog, 0007-7305.*

CALIFORNIA ASSOCIATION OF MACHINE EMBROIDERY. Issue 1 (Jan. 1985)-. 0882-2697. Periodical. US. English. bm. $30.00 Membership. Gloria Waterman, 7207 Pomelo Drive, Canoga Park CA 91307.

CANADA QUILTS. Began publication in Dec. 1973. 0381-7369. Periodical. CN. English. ir. 14.50. Canada Quilts c/o Marilyn Holowachuk, 13 Pinewood Avenue, Grimsby Ontario L3M 1W2 Canada. **Tel** (416)945-9290. **Ed** Marilyn Holowachuk. **DD** 746.460971. bk rev. adv acc. **Circ** 3,500. (ctrl). A magazine for quilters containing new ideas, color photos of quilts, patterns and instructions.

CANADIAN LACEMAKER GAZETTE. Vol. 1 (Spring)-. 0824-1856. Periodical. CN. English. qt. 16.00. Canadian Lacemaker Gazette, c/o K Russell R R #3 Site 388 C #22, Courtenay British Columbia V9N 5M8 Canada. **Ed** Jeannie M Martin. **DD** 746.220971. bk rev. adv acc. **Circ** 300. Bobbin lacemaking lessons patterns, hints and news. regular honiton and pointground columns as well as tatting and some needlelace. Related advertising.

CAREFREE PATTERNS FROM MCCALL'S. US. English. 230 Park Avenue, New York NY 10017. LC TT520. **DD** 646.4.

CEGMENTS. VAT Canadian Embroiderers' Guildments. Autumn 1975-. 0712-9076. Periodical. CN. English. sa. Free. **DD** 746.4406071.

COUNTED THREAD. V. 6- March 1979-. 0164-3406. Periodical. US. English. qt. $9.00. Counted Thread Society of America, 3305 South Newport Street, Denver CO 80224. **Tel** (303)733-0196. **Ed** Elizabeth Stears and Joan McBride. bk rev. adv acc. **Circ** 8,000. (ctrl). We publish articles and charts on counted cross stitch, blackwork, pulled thread, ethnic counted embroideries, and other wonderful information about counted thread embroidery.

CRAFT & NEEDLEWORK AGE/ WORLD OF MINIATURES. VFOAT Craft and Needlework Age, World of Miniatures. Vol. 36, No. 443 (Jan. 1982-). 0744-2319. Periodical. US. English. mo. $15.00. Hobby Publ Inc, Box 420, Englishtown NJ 07726. **Tel** (201)972-1022. **Ed** Jennifer Jones. LC TT159. **DD** 688. bk rev. adv acc. **Circ** 24,000. (ctrl). Trade publication serving the craft and needlework industry with quarterly features on quilting, yarns and notionsat all levels. *Craft, Model & Hobby Industry, 0011-0752.*

CROCHET WORLD. V. 1- March/April 1978-. 0164-7962. Periodical. US. English. bm. $21.00. House of White Birches-Tower Press, PO Box 377, Seabrook NH 03874. **Tel** (603)474-2404. adv acc.

Sewing and Needlework

(ctrl). For all those with crochet in their hearts, each issue bursting with thrilling crochet delights.

CROCHET WORLD OMNIBOOK. VFOAT Omnibook. V. 1- Summer 1979-. 0199-0993. Periodical. US. English. qt. $6.00. Crochet World, PO Box 337, Seabrook NH 03874. Tel (603)474-2404. Ed Susan Hankins Andrews. adv acc. (ctrl). At least 100 crochet patterns published during the year. Crochet patterns, designs, exchanges, gossip, news, contest, photos, features, articles, etc.

DANISH HANDCRAFT GUILD. Began publication with 1, 1961. 0416-6817. Periodical. DK. English. ir. 38 Vimmelskaftet, Copenhagen K Denmark.

EMBROIDERY. V. 1-7, 1932-1939. 0013-6611. Periodical. UK. English. qt. 10.00 Domestic, 20.00 US, 30.00 Canada, 25.00 Australia. E G Enterprises Ltd, PO Box 62B, East Molesey Surrey KT8 9BB England. Tel 01 943 1229. Ed Christine Blacham. Ind/Abst Artbibliogr. Mod. bk rev. adv acc. Circ 11,500. A magazine for the professional amateur, the teacher and the historian. All aspects of the craft are regularly covered.

THE FASHION/SEWING NEWSLETTER. VAT Fashion Sewing Newsletter. 0738-7083. Periodical. US. English. mo. $15.00. Rosalie Lemontree, 320 East 54th Street, New York NY 10022.

FIBERARTS. See Textiles.

FIBERSCOPE. See Textiles.

THE FLYING NEEDLE. 0270-2959. Periodical. US. English. qt. $15.00 Domestic, $17.00 Canada. National Standards Council of American Embroiderers, c/o Barbara B Rowland, 6290 East Pinchot, Scottsdale AZ 85251. LC TT740. DD 746.4405.

HANDMADE. Vol. 1, No. 1 (Apr.-June 1981)-. 0275-9640. Periodical. US. English. bm. $26.97. Lark Communications, 50 College Street, Asheville NC 28801. Tel (704)253-0468. Ed Rob Pulleyn. LC WMLC L 83/33. bk rev. adv acc. Circ 100,000. Sewing, knitting, needlework, weaving and crafts, lively, exciting and challenging projects and articles.

HANDWOVEN. See Textiles.

HARPER'S BAZAAR. See Clothing and Fashion.

INTERNATIONAL QUILT GUILD DIRECTORY. See Yearbooks, Almanacs, Directories.

JARDIN DES MODES. Aug. 1922-Sept. 1971. 0021-5457. Periodical. French. mo. $37.25. Editions du Hennin, Borte Postale 22, 77301 St Farquea Ponth France. l'Illustration, Chic et Practique.

JUST CROSSSTITCH. VFOAT Just Cross Stitch. Vol. 1, No. 1 (May-June 1983)-. 0883-0797. Periodical. US. English. bm. $15.00. Just Crossstitch, PO Box 36987, Birmingham AL 35236. Tel (205)967-8402. Ed Phyllis Hoffman. adv acc. Circ 100,000. Articles on cross stitch shops, graphs for cross-stitching, instructions for cross-stitching, pictures of each finished product for which graphs are included.

KNIT & CHAT. V. 1, No. 1-. 0711-639X. Periodical. CN. English. ir. $18.58. Knit & Chat, PO Box 363, Lancaster Ontario K0C 1N0 Canada. Tel (514)626-9478. Ed May MacLean. DD 746.4. bk rev. adv acc. Circ 20m. (ctrl). Concerns the homecrafts, craft using yarn/thread and needle(s) as a medium, icludes knitting, sewing, needlework, crochet, talting, quilting, etc., also includes book reviews, historical features, etc.

KNIT AND CROCHET FOR THE HOME. 1981-. Periodical. US. English. LC WMLC L 83/110.

KNIT SANOP. VFOAT Knitting Industry. Periodical. Korean. qt. Taehan Meriyasu Kongop Hyoptong Chohap Yonhaphoe, 48 1-Ka Sinmunno Chongno-Ku, Seoul Korea. LC HD9969.K5.

KNITTERS. Vol. 1, No. 1-. 0747-9026. Periodical. US. English. sa. $7.00 US, $8.59 Canada. Golden Fleece Publications, 126 South Phillips Avenue, Sioux Falls SD 57102. DD D46.

KNITTER'S JOURNAL. V. 1- May/June 1973-. 0090-8215. Periodical. US. English. bm. $7.00. Handweaver and Craftsman Inc, 220 Fifth Avenue, New York NY 10001. LC TT820. DD 746.43.

KNITTING ELEGANCE. 8750-9768. Periodical. US. English. bm. $21.00. All American Crafts Inc, 70 Sparta Avenue, Sparta NJ 07871.

KNITTING TECHNIQUE. Vol. 7, No. 1 (Jan. 1985)-. 0177-4875. Periodical. English. bm. WST Knitting Technic, 0173-4415.

KNITTING TIMES. VFOAT Knitting Times Newsweekly, Apparel World. V. 39, No. 33- Aug. 10, 1970-. 0023-2300. Periodical. US. English. $30.00 Domestic, $50.00 Foreign. Knitting Times, 386 Park Avenue South, New York NY 10016. Ind/Abst World Text Abstr. LC TT679. DD 677.66105. Knitted Outerwear Times.

KNITTING TIMES BUYERS' GUIDE DIRECTORY. See Yearbooks, Almanacs, Directories.

KNITTING WORLD. 0194-8083. Periodical. US. English. bm. $17.00. House of White Birches-Tower Press, PO Box 337, Seabrook NH 03874. Tel (603)474-2404. Ind/Abst Predicasts, Funk Scott Index Corp. Ind. adv acc. (ctrl). Has been in publication for over 5 years. It is the lowest price in it's field, as a knitter you owe it to yourself to see a copy.

LADY'S CIRCLE KNITTING & CROCHET CREATIVE IDEAS. VFOAT Lady's Circle Knitting and Crochet Creative Ideas. 0732-9504. Periodical. US. English. qt. $9.00 Domestic, $11.00 Foreign. Mailing Department, Lopez Publications Inc, 23 West 26th Street, New York NY 10010. Lady's Circle Knitting & Crochet Guide, 0731-9975.

LADY'S CIRCLE PATCHWORK QUILTS. VFOAT Patchwork Quilts. 0731-9916. Periodical. US. English. bm. $12.95. Lopez Publishing Corporation, 602 Mongomery Street, Alexandria VA 22314. Tel (212)689-3933. Ed Carter Houck. bk rev. adv acc. Circ 70,000. Shows all aspects of quilting techniques along with ready-to-use patterns for piecing and applique, and brilliant color photos.

LAPEL PIN POTPOURRI. No. 1 (Fall 1982)-. 0738-2936. Periodical. US. English. sa. $5.50. Lapel Pin Potpourri, Rural Route 1 Box 28, Charlotte Hall MD 20622. Tel (301)884-4823. Ed Roberta J Kieliger. Circ 500. For crochet lapel pin enthusiasts to share their ideas, containing designs with monthly themes, birthday ideas, and accompanying verses for nursing home residents, hospital patients and meals-on-wheels recipients.

LIST OF ART NEEDLEWORK, YARN KNITTING STORES. VFOAT Art Needlework, Yarn Knitting Shops. 0161-6218. US. English. Leads-Prospects Inc, 234 Fifth Avenue, New York NY 10001. LC TT751. DD 338.47746402573.

MCCALL'S. 0198-2478. US. English. mo. McCall's Pattern Company, 230 Park Avenue, New York NY 10017. LC TT500. DD 646.407.

MCCALL'S CHRISTMAS KNIT & CROCHET. 0276-6671. US. English. $2.95. ABC Needlework and Crafts Magazines Inc, 825 7th Avenue, New York NY 10019. LC TT820. DD 746.43041.

MCCALL'S NEEDLEWORK & CRAFTS. VAT McCall's Needlework and Crafts. 0024-8924. Periodical. US. English. bm. $11.97. ABC Needlework & Crafts, 825 7th Avenue, New York NY 10019, (subscription address: Communication Data Services 112 Tenth Street Des Moines IA 50309). Tel (212)887-8404.

MCCALL'S PATTERNS. 0198-6457. Periodical. US. English. qt. McCall Pattern Company, 230 Park Avenue, New York NY 10017. LC TT500. DD 646.4304.

MCCALL'S STITCHERY. APPLIQUE. (MCCALL'S STITCHERY : APPLIQUE). V. 2. 0364-8192. US. English. $1.35. McCall Pattern Company, 230 Park Avenue, New York NY 10017. LC TT779. DD 746.44.

MERIYASU KONGOP YONBO. See Textiles.

MUSCLE WEST. Vol. 1, No. 1 (Summer 1983)-. 0824-4480. Periodical. CN. English. qt. $6.00. Muscle West, Suite 1/246 East Broadway, Vancouver British Columbia V5T 1W3 Canada. DD 646.75.

NEEDLE & THREAD. Vol. 1, No. 1 (Mar./Apr. 1981)-. 0279-876X. Periodical. US. English. bm. $32.00. Charter Date Service, 112 Tenth Street, Des Moines IA 50309. Tel (817)732-7494.

NEEDLEPOINT NEWS. 1973. 0145-8256. Periodical. US. English. bm. $9.00. Needlepoint News, Box 668, Evanston IL 60204. Tel (206)842-5222. Ed Carol Labianche. DD 746. bk rev. adv acc. Circ 15,000. Includes graphs, charts, books, letters, questions, answers and everything there is to know about needlepoint.

OLDE TIME NEEDLEWORK PATTERNS AND DESIGNS. VFOAT Olde Time Needlework. V. 1- Feb./Mar. 1973-. 0199-0233. Periodical. US. English. bm. $4.00 Domestic, $5.00 Foreign. Olde Time Needlework, Box 428, Seabrook NH 03874. LC TT753. DD 746.4.

PATTERN MAKERS' JOURNAL. 0031-319X. Periodical. US. English. qt. $1.00. Pattern Makers League of North America, 1925 North Lynn Street/Suite 304, Arlington VA 22209. Tel (202)296-3790.

THE QUILT DIGEST. 1st ed. (1983)-. 0740-4093. US. English. an. $9.95. The Quilt Digest Press, 955 14th Street, San Francisco CA 94114. Tel (415)431-1222. Ed Michael M Kile. LC WMLC L 83/142. The leading series on antique and contemporary quilts. Profuse color illustrations. Leading authorities on a wide variety of quilt and quilt-related subjects.

QUILT WORLD. V. 1- Mar./Apr. 1976-. 0149-8045. Periodical. US. English. bm. $8.00. House of White Birches-Tower Press, PO Box 377, Seabrook NH 03874. Tel (603)474-2404. LC TT835. DD 746.97. adv acc. (ctrl). Featuring: quilt designs, quilt features, quilt talk, quilt pictures, quilt news, quilt exchanges, quilt letters, quilt columnists, etc.

QUILT WORLD OMNIBOOK. Vol. 1, No. 1 (Summer 1979)-. 0199-0985. Periodical. US. English. qt. $14.00. House of White Birches-Tower Press, PO Box 377, Seabrook NH 03874. Tel (603)474-2404. LC TT835. DD 746.9705. adv acc. (ctrl). Contains at least 100 exciting quilt patterns during the year, at a cost of just 5 cents per pattern.

QUILTER'S NEWSLETTER MAGAZINE. VFOAT QN. 0274-712X. Periodical. US. English. ir. $13.95. Leman Publications Inc, Box 394, Wheatridge CO 80033. Tel (303)420-4272. Ed Bonnie Leman. LC TT835. DD 746.4605. bk rev. adv acc. Circ 134,000. Articles on design, technique, history, new and old quilt patterns, trends, museum quilts, and current events in quilting. Exhibitions, quilt shows, quiltmaking lessons, and quilt competitions.

QUILTING AND RELATED NEEDLEWORK. V. 1- (Issue 1-). 0190-0935. Periodical. US. English. qt. $5.00. Ruth Briggs Quilts, PO Box 403, Rancho Santa Fe CA 92067.

SEW IT BEGINS. Issue No. 1 (June 1983)-. 0821-4247. Periodical. CN. English. ir. 12.50. F Wershler, Box 263 Station A, Winnipeg Manitoba R3K 2A1 Canada. Tel 832-0123. Ed Frances A Wershler. DD 646.205. bk rev. Circ 300. Canadian sewing newsletter for people who sew crafts, clothing and home decorating items. Discusses sewing techniques, notions and equipment with ideas and patterns for projects.

SIMPLICITY FASHIONS. 0091-1879. US. English. ty. $2.00. Simplicity Pattern Company, 200 Madison Avenue, New York NY 10016. LC TT500. DD 646.43005. Simplicity.

SIMPLICITY TODAY. V. 13, No. 2- Summer 1979-. 0198-7100. Periodical. US. English. ty. $3.75 Domestic, $5.25 Foreign. Subscription Department of Simplicity Pattern Company, 901 Wayne Street, Niles MI 49121. Simplicity Home Catalog, 0364-1732.

SOMETHING SPECIAL PATTERN CLUB. VFOAT Something Special Pattern Club Newsletter. 0883-3710. Periodical. US. English. bm. $10.00. Something Special Inc, Department A/919 Maple Drive, Medford OR 97501. Tel (503)773-6876. Ed June Blanchard. adv acc. Circ 1,500. (ctrl). A 32 page full color needlecraft pattern booklet on sewing, crochet, needlepoint etc. Full size pattern sheet. Articles, contests and more.

SPIN-OFF. See Textiles.

STITCH 'N SEW. VAT Stitch and Sew. 0195-2595. Periodical. US. English. qt. $10.50. House of White Birches-Tower Press, PO Box 337, Seabrook NH 03874. Tel (603)474-2404. adv acc. (ctrl). Each issue contains unusual interesting, unique patterns, designs, columns, and features on every phrase of needlework. Also addresses, sewing problems, wants and exchanges.

Sexual Life

STITCH 'N SEW QUILTS. VFOAT Stitch and Sew Quilts. Vol. 1, No. 1 (Jan./Feb. 1982)-. 0744-1649. Periodical. US. English. bm. $14.00. House of White Birches Tower Press, PO Box 337, Seabrook NH 03874. Tel (603)474-2404. adv acc. (ctrl). At least 100 companies exciting quilting patterns are published in this magazine annually. (This comes to just 6 cents per pattern.).

STOF & SAKS. VAT Stof Og Saks. Periodical. DK. Danish. ir. Dansk Beklaedings- OG, Textilarbejderforbund, Postbox 16, 4550 Asnaes Denmark.

SUPER SCRAPS. Vol. 1, No. 1 (Summer, 1982)-. 0744-5768. Periodical. US. English. qt. $6.00. House of White Birches-Tower Press, PO Box 377, Seabrook NH 03874. Tel (603)474-2404. adv acc. (ctrl). Shows many fascinating things to make out of all kinds of fabric leftover bits and pieces.

SWEATERS AND AFGHANS. Series/Titl Better Homes and Gardens Creative Ideas. 0278-7466. Periodical. US. English. an. $2.00. Special Interest Publications, 1716 Locust Street, Des Moines IA 50336. LC TT825. DD 746.92.

TRICOT (MONTREAL, QUEBEC). (TRICOT). VAT Condense Pratique Presente Tricot. V. 1 No. 1 (21 Feb. 1980)-V. 1, No. 25 (7 March 1981). 0228-8338. Periodical. CN. French. sm. $1,25 for Four Numbers. Tircot, a/s Les Condeses Pratiques, 2170 Rue Charland, Montreal Quebec H1Z 1B1 Canada. DD 746.43205.

UNCOVERINGS. (UNCOVERINGS : THE . . . RESEARCH PAPERS OF THE AMERICAN QUILT STUDY GROUP). 1980-. 0277-0628. Periodical. US. English. an. $7.00 Members, $8.50 Nonmembers. American Quilt Study Group, 105 Molino Avenue, Mill Valley CA 94941. LC TT835. DD 746.970973.

VOGUE KNITTING. Vol. 1, No. 1 (Fall/Winter 1982)-. Periodical. US. English. sa. 5.00. Vogue Knitting, New Lane, Havant Hants P09 2N0 England. Tel 0705 486221. Ed Wendy Rawlins. adv acc. Circ 40,000. Over 40 international knitting designs with full instructions helpful articles and knitting techniques.

VOGUE PATTERNS. V. 46, No. 6- June/July 1972-. 0095-2788. Periodical. US. English. bm. $6.00. Vogue Patterns, Subscription Department, Greenwich CT 06830. LC TT500. DD 646.40405. *International Vogue Pattern Book.*

VOGUE PATTERNS. 0142-338X. Periodical. UK. English. bm. 6.30. Vogue Patterns Service, New Lane Havant, Hants PO9 2ND England. Tel 0705 486221. Ed Wendy Rawlins. adv acc. Circ 49,659. (ctrl). International designer fashion, very easy very vogue designs for all occasions. Tips, articles on dressmaking skills.

VOTRE BEAUTE, VOTRE SANTE. SPECIAL HAUTE COUTURE. VFOAT Special Haute Couture. No. 1 (Autumn-Winter 82-83)-. Periodical. FR. French. sa. 25 Single Issue. 38 rue Jean-Mermoz, 75008 Paris France. LC TT500. DD 646.3405.

WOMEN'S HOUSEHOLD CROCHET. Vol. 1, No. 4 (Winter 1982)-. 0745-0575. Periodical. US. English. an. $10.50. House of White Birches Tower Press, PO Box 337, Seabrook NH 03874. Tel (603)474-2404. adv acc. (ctrl). At least 60 to 80 wonderful, exciting patterns published annually. Patterns come to just pennies in cost when you subscribe to this magazine. The ideal way to buy. You save. *Crochet for Women Only, 0744-1665.*

YARNCRAFT. VFOAT Yarn Craft. VAT YARN CRAFT. No. 1-. 0730-7640. Periodical. US. English. bm. $11.70. Yarncraft, PO Box 238, West Hempstead NY 11552.

SEXUAL LIFE

5TH FREEDOM. VAT Fifth Freedom. V. 1- 1971-. 0197-033X. Periodical. US. English. mo. $3.50. 5th Freedom, 975 Ellicott Station, Buffalo NY 14205.

AFTER STONEWALL. No. 1-11. 0707-5138. Periodical. CN. English. qt. Grassroots c/o Gay Saskatchewan, P O Box 7508, Saskatoon Sask S7K 4R5 Canada. Tel (204)475-1670. DD 301.415705.

ANGLES (VANCOUVER, B.C.). (ANGLES). 1st Issue (Dec. 1983)-. 0824-2100. Periodical. CN. English. mo. $0.75 Per No. Vancouver Gay Community Centre, PO Box 2259 Main Post Office, Vancouver British Columbia V6B 3W2 Canada. DD 306.76609711. *Vancouver Gay Community Centre News.*

ANNUAL EDITIONS. READINGS IN HUMAN SEXUALITY. (ANNUAL EDITIONS : READINGS IN HUMAN SEXUALITY). VFOAT Readings in Human Sexuality. 0163-836X. US. English. an. Dushkin Publishing Group, Sluice Dock, Guilford CT 06437. Tel (203)453-4351. LC HQ21. DD 301.41. *Focus. Human Sexuality, 0147-0655.*

ARCHIVES OF SEXUAL BEHAVIOR. See Genealogy and Heraldry - Archives.

ATTITUDE (MONTREAL, QUEBEC). (ATTITUDE). 0712-1954. Periodical. CN. French. mo. $2.75 Per No. Attitude, CP 115 Succursale H, Montreal Quebec H3G 2K5 Canada. DD 306.766209714281.

AUSTRALIAN JOURNAL OF SEX, MARRIAGE & FAMILY. VFOAT Australian Journal of Sex, Marriage and Family. Vol. 1, No. 1 (Feb. 1980)-. 0159-1487. Periodical. AN. English. qt. $22.13. Australian Journal of Sex, PO Box 143, Concord NSW 2137 Australia. Tel (02)736 2838. Ed Bruce H Peterson. Ind/Abst APAIS, Aust. Public Aff. Inf. Serv. bk rev. adv acc. Circ 600. Academic and research writings on sexual, marital and family issues, mainly but not exclusively of Australian authorship.

BLAGUES DE SEXE. Vol. 3, No. 1 (18 Feb. 1980)-. 0712-2039. Periodical. CN. French. ir. $1.25 Per Issue. Blagues de Sexe, c/o Publications Joyeueses, CP 145 Succursale H, Montreal Quebec H3G 2K5 Canada. DD 741.505. *Blagues Magazine, 0226-3645.*

BODY POLITIC. (THE BODY POLITIC). No. 1- Nov./Dec. 1971-. 0315-3606. Periodical. CN. English. bm. $24.95. Body Politic, Box 7289 Station A, Toronto Ontario M5W 1X9 Canada. Tel (416)364-6320. Ind/Abst Altern. Press Index. bk rev. adv acc. Circ 6,500. Canada's national gay liberation journal. *Our Image, 0703-1467.*

BODY POLITIC XTRA. No., 1 (Mar. 3, 1984)-. 0826-0508. Periodical. CN. English. bw. Free. Xtra, PO Box 7289 Station A, Toronto Ontario M5W 1X9 Canada. Tel 364-6320. Ed Ken Popert. DD 306.76609713541. adv acc. Circ 10,000. A guide to entertainment and local events in the city of Toronto. We accept display and classified ads. Published by the Body Politic Collective and is coordinated by Ken Popert.

CANADIAN KEY. (THE CANADIAN KEY). VFOAT Key. Vol. 16, No. 2-. 0823-1559. Periodical. CN. English. bm. $25.00. The Canadian Key, PO Box 68 Station L, Toronto Ontario M6E 4Y4 Canada. DD 306.705. *All New Key, 0823-1540; Canadian Connection (Toronto, Ont.), 0826-1938.*

CHRISTOPHER STREET. V. 1- July 1976-. 0146-7921. Periodical. US. English. mo. $27.00. That New Magazine Inc, 249 West Broadway, New York NY 10013. Tel (212)925-8021. Ed Tom Steele. LC HQ75. DD 301.415705. bk rev. adv acc. Circ 20,000. Gay literary magazine including interviews, essays, art, film and book reviews, plus excerpts from upcoming fiction and non-fiction books.

COEUR ATOUT. VFOAT Coeur A Tout. Vol. 1, No. 1-. 0712-6042. Periodical. CN. French. ir. $1,00 Per No. Coeur Atout a/s Publications Domaine Ltee, 4270 Avenue Papineau, Montreal Quebec H2H 1S9 Canada. DD 306.705.

CONFIDENCES. First issue in 197-. 0317-3607. CN. French. wk. 50. Per No. Confidences, CP 368, Montreal Quebec H4A 3P7 Canada. DD 301.41705. *Le Nouveau Confidences, 0316-7453.*

CONFIDENTIEL COUPLE EPANOUI. V. 1, No. 1, (Dec. 1982)-. 0823-6259. Periodical. CN. French. mo. $25.00. Confidential Couple Epanoui, CP 186, Gatineau Quebec J8P 6J2 Canada. DD 306.705.

CONTACT. V. 1- Dec. 15, 1976-. 0701-0818. Periodical. CN. French. wk. 50. Per No. Contact, Bureau 406/180 Est Boulevard Dorechester, Montreal Quebec H2X 1N6 Canada. DD 301.41705.

CONTACT (MONTREAL, QUEBEC : CA 1981). (CONTACT). 0712-6050. Periodical. CN. French. ir. $1,25 Per No. Contact a/s Publications Domaine Ltee, 4270 Avenue Papineau, Montreal Quebec H2H 1S9 Canada. DD 306.766305.

CURRENT RESEARCH UPDATES IN HUMAN SEXUALITY. Began with issue for Jan. 1984?. 0748-0679. Periodical. US. English. mo. $48.00 Domestic, $63.00 Foreign. Current Research Updates in Human Sexuality, PO Box 2577, Bellingham WA 98227. DD 306.

DIGNITY. V. 1- Feb. 1970-. 0147-1139. Periodical. US. English. mo. $15.00 with Membership. Dignity Inc, 755 Boylston Street/Room 412, Boston MA 02116.

EXCLUSIF. (L'EXCLUSIF). 0712-8401. Periodical. CN. French. mo. $2.00 Per No. l'Exclusif, CP 98, Ahuntsic, Montreal Quebec H3L 3N7 Canada. DD 306.705.

EXTRA PLUS. Vol. 1, No. 1-. 0712-600X. Periodical. CN. French. ir. $7.75 Each Number. Extra Plus c/o Publications Domaine Ltee, 4270 Av Papineau, Montreal Quebec H2H 1S9 Canada. DD 306.766305.

FIRST HAND. VFOAT Firsthand. 0744-6349. Periodical. US. English. mo. $33.00. Jackie Lewis, PO Box 1314, Teaneck NJ 07666. Tel (201)836-9177. Ed Jack Veasey. bk rev. adv acc. Circ 70,000. Gay men's first hand sexual experiences. Includes letters from readers and erotic fiction.

FORUM. V. 7, No. 3- Dec. 1977-. 0160-2195. Periodical. US. English. mo. $12.00. Forum, 155 Allen Boulevard, Framingdale NY 11735. LC HQ1. DD 301.41705. *Penthouse Forum.*

FORUM. VAT Forum de la CCDLG, Forum de la Coalition Canadienne pour les Droits des Lesbiennes et des Gais. V. 3, No. 3- Summer 1978-. 0708-2584. Periodical. CN. French. qt. $2.00. Forum de la Coalition Canadienne pour les Droits des Lesbiennes et des Gias, CP 36 Succursale C, Montreal Quebec H2L 4J7 Canada. DD 323.4. *Forum de la C N D H, 0704-0598.*

FORUM. VAT CLGRC Forum, Canadian Lesbian and Gay Rights Forum. V. 3, No. 3- Summer 1978-. 0708-2576. Periodical. CN. English. qt. $2.00. NGRC Forum, PO Box 36 Station C, Montreal Quebec H2L 4J7 Canada. DD 323.4. *N G R C Forum, 0704-0598.*

G B B. (GAY BOOKS BULLETIN). VFOAT G.B.B. V. 1- Spring 1979-. 0731-1648. Periodical. US. English. ir. $15.00. Gay Academic Union, Box 480, Lenox Hill, New York NY 10021. Tel (212)242-7276. Ind/Abst MLA Int. Bibliogr. Books Artic. Mod. Lang. Lit. *Gay Academic Union Journal.*

GAIBECOIS. (LE GAIBECOIS). V. 1- Aug. 1977-. 0703-9778. Periodical. CN. French. ir. Free to Members of C H A L, $3.00 all others. Le Gaibecois C H A L, CP 596 Haute-Ville, Quebec Quebec G1R Canada. DD 301.415709714.

GALA REVIEW. See Religion, Mythology, Rationalism.

GAY ARCHIVIST. See Genealogy and Heraldry - Archives.

GAY CALGARY (1982). (GAY CALGARY). Mar.-. 0820-8220. Periodical. CN. English. mo. Gay Information and Resources Calgary, PO Box 2715/Station M, Calgary Alberta T2P 3C1 Canada. DD 306.7660971233. *Gay Horizons, 0709-9061.*

GAY CHRISTIAN WITNESS. (GAY CHRISTIAN WITNESS : AN OCCASIONAL PUBLICATION OF THE COUNCIL ON HOMOSEXUALITY AND RELIGION). No. 1 (Mar. 1980)-. 0226-0441. Periodical. CN. English. ir. Gay Christian Witness, PO Box 1912, Winnipeg Manitoba R3C 3R2 Canada. DD 261.83576.

GAY COMMUNITY NEWS. VFOAT GCN. 1973. 0147-0728. Periodical. US. English. wk. Gay Community News, 167 Tremont Street/5th Floor, Boston MA 02111. Tel (617)426-4469. Ed Gordon Gottleib. Ind/Abst Altern. Press Index. bk rev. adv acc. Circ 25,000. Available on microform. News and analysis of gay liberation movement. Monthly book review supplement. Litigation and legislation affecting rights of lesbians and gay men.

THE GAY LUTHERAN. See Religion, Mythology, Rationalism - Protestantism.

GAY MONTREAL. V. 1- April 27, 1976-. 0381-6931. Periodical. CN. French. wk. .50 Per Number. Le Journal Gay Montreal, CP 568/Station Youville, Montreal Quebec H2P 2W1 Canada. DD 301.415709714281.

GAY NEWS. No. 1- 1972-. Periodical. UK. English. bw.

Sexual Life

GAY RISING. V. 1- Mar. 1975-. 0700-3536. Periodical. CN. English. ir. Gay Alliance Toward Equality, 193 Carlton Street, Toronto Ontario M5A 2K7 Canada. **DD** 301.41570971.

GAY SUNSHINE CEASED. Began with No. 1, 1970. Ceased with No. 46. 0046-550X. Periodical. US. English.

GAYELLOW PAGES. **VAT** Gay Yellow Pages. 1- 1979-. US. English. an. $10.00. Renaissance House, Box 292 Village Station, New York City NY 10014. **Tel** (212)674-0120. Ed Frances Green. adv acc. **Circ** 50,000. Directory of services and businesses for the gay and lesbian community in USA and Canada.

GAY/LESBIAN MEDIA DIRECTORY WORLDWIDE. See Yearbooks, Almanacs, Directories.

GAYSWEEK. **VAT** Gays Week. Feb. 28, 1977-. 0145-9104. Periodical. US. English. wk. Gaysweek, 216 West 18th Street, New York NY 10014. **Tel** (212)929-7720.

GENOS. (GENOS : A GENDER-GENOCIDE). 0712-3221. Periodical. CN. English. mo. Genos, c/o Project Lambda, 299 Kennedy Street, Winnipeg Manitoba R3B 2M7 Canada. **DD** 051.

GPU NEWS. **Main/Corp** Gay Peoples Union. **VAT** Gay Peoples Union News. 0145-5400. Periodical. US. English. mo $6.00. Liberation Publications, PO Box 92203, Milwaukee WI 53202.

HUMAN SEXUALITY. Began with 1980/85 Ed. Periodical. US. English. an. $8.95. Dushkin Publishing Group Inc, Sluice Dock, Guilford CT 06437. **Tel** (203)453-4351. Ed Ollie Pocs. Annually updated collection of public press articles covering current issues in human sexuality. Includes topic guide and complete index. Readings in Human Sexuality Annual Editions.

HUSTLER HUMOR. 0199-5405. Periodical. US. English. bm. $14.00. F S C Inc, PO Box 67068, Los Angeles CA 90067. **Tel** (213)556-9200.

IMPACT. Vol. 1- Oct. 1978-. 0163-8262. Periodical. US. English. an. Institute for Family Research and Education of Syracuse University, 760 Ostrom Avenue, Syracuse NY 13210. **LC** HQ57. **DD** 306.705.

INTEGRITY FORUM. See Religion, Mythology, Rationalism - Protestantism.

INTERDIT (MONTREAL, QUEBEC : 1981). (INTERDIT). No. 1-. 0712-8339. Periodical. CN. French. mo $1.25 Per No. Interdit, c/o Distributeurs Associes du Quebec, 3600 Boulevard du Tricentenaire, Montreal Quebec H1B 5M8 Canada. **DD** 306.705.

JOKER DU SEXE. (LE JOKER DU SEXE : LE MAGAZINE DE BLAGUES LES PLUS SEXEES AU QUEBEC). **VAT** Joker (1980), Joker de Sexe. V. 3, No 6. (May 26, 1980)-. 0228-6882. Periodical. CN. French. mo. $0.75 LE NO. **DD** 306.705. Joker, 0227-1257.

JOURNAL OF HOMOSEXUALITY. V. 1- Fall 1974-. 0091-8369. US. English. qt. $30.00. Haworth Press/Business Office, 149 Fifth Avenue, New York NY 10010. **Ind/Abst** Soc. Welf. Soc. Plan./Policy Soc. Dev., Excerpta Med., Index Med., Biol. Abstr., Writ. Am. Hist., Psychol. Abstr., Bull. Signal., Sociol. Abstr., Abstr. Anthropol., Coll. Stud. Pers. Abstr., Abstr. Soc. Work., Psychol. Read. Guide, Chicago Psychoanal. Lit. Index, Women Stud. Abstr., Crime Delinq. Lit., Index Period. Artic. Relat. Law, Pastor. Care Couns. Abstr., Public Aff. Inf. Serv. Bull. **LC** HQ75. **DD** 301.415705. **NLM** W1 JO672H. **CODEN** JOHOD7.

JOURNAL OF SEX & MARITAL THERAPY. See Medicine - Psychiatry, Psychopathology.

JOURNAL OF SEX EDUCATION & THERAPY. US. English. sa. $8.00. American Association of Sex Education Council and Therapy, 11 Dupont Circle NW/Suite 220, Washington DC 20036. **Tel** (202)462-1171. Ed Gary Kelly. **NLM** W1 JO876P. bk rev. adv acc. **Circ** 4,500. A non-profit education association dedicated to the highest standard of sex education training research ethics and patient care in the field of human sexuality. Journal of Sex Education and Therapy, 0161-4576.

THE JOURNAL OF SEX RESEARCH. V. 1- Mar. 1965-. 0022-4499. Periodical. US. English. qt. $40.00. Society for Scientific Study of Sex, PO Box 29795, Philadelphia PA 19117. **Tel** (215)782-1430. Ed Clive M Davis. **Ind/Abst** Sociol. Abstr., Soc. Welf. Soc. Plan./Policy Soc. Dev., Excerpta Med., Women Stud. Abstr., Psychol. Abstr., Lang. Lang. Behav. Abstr., Soc. Sci. Citation Index. **LC** HQ5. **DD** 612.60072. **NLM** W1 JO876R. **CODEN** JSXRAJ. bk rev. adv acc. **Circ** 1,500. Scholarly research on psychological, sociological and medical issues in human sexuality. Advances in Sex Research.

KALOS. (KALOS : ON GREEK LOVE). V. 1- Spring 1976-. 0145-2398. Periodical. US. English. ty. $8.50. Comita, PO Box 7071, Arlington VA 22207. **LC** HQ75. **DD** 301.415705.

LESBIAN CONTRADICTION. VFOAT Lescon. Periodical. US. English. qt. Lesbian Contradiction, 584 Castro Street/Suite 263, San Francisco CA 94114.

LESBIAN ETHICS. See Ethics.

THE LESBIAN NEWS. (LESBIAN NEWS). No. 1- Aug. 1975-. 0739-1803. Periodical. US. English. mo. $10.00. Lesbian News, 6507 Franrivers Avenue, Canoga Park CA 91307.

THE LESBIAN READER. 1st- Ed. 0361-5928. Periodical. US. English. qt. $4.50. Amazon Press, 395 60th Street, Oakland CA 94618. **LC** HQ75. **DD** 301.4157.

LESBIAN/GAY LAW NOTES. See Law.

LESBO (MONTREAL, QUEBEC). (LESBO). 0712-8398. Periodical. CN. French. $1.25 Per No. Lesbo, c/o Distributeurs Associes du Quebec, 3600 Boulevard du Tricentenaire, Montreal Qeubec H1B 5M8 Canada. **DD** 306.766305.

LIFESTYLES (NEW YORK, N.Y.). (LIFESTYLES). **VFOAT** Life Styles. Vol. 7, No. 1 (Fall 1984)-. 0882-3391. Periodical. US. English. qt. Human Sciences Press, 72 Fifth Avenue, New York NY 10011. **Ind/Abst** Psychol. Abstr., Abstr. Soc. Work., Except. Child Educ. Abstr., Curr. Contents, Soc. Sci. Citation Index, Prev. Hum. Serv., Sage Fam. Stud. Abstr., Chicorel Abstr. Read. Learn. Disabil., Educ. Index. **DD** 301. **NLM** W1. Alternative Lifestyles, 0161-570X.

LONG TIME COMING. Began with July 1973 issue. 0382-5868. Periodical. CN. English. Long Time Coming, Box 128 Station G, Montreal Quebec H2W 2M9 Canada. **DD** 301.41570971.

LUI ET LUI. 0712-5992. Periodical. CN. French. ir. $3.95 Each Number. Lui Et Lui c/o Publications Domaine Ltee, 4270 Av Papineau, Montreal Quebec H2H 1S9 Canada. **DD** 306.766209714.

LUZ. 1953. 0271-0846. Periodical. US. Spanish. mo. $15.00. Luz Magazine, 313 West 53rd Street, New York NY 10019. **Tel** (305)592-1760. Sex education.

MAKING WAVES CEASED. (MAKING WAVES : AN ATLANTIC QUARTERLY FOR LESBIANS & GAY MEN). No. 1 (Spring 1981)-. 0228-7579. Periodical. CN. English (includes some text in French). qt. $1.00 Per Number, $4.00 Per Year. Making Waves, PO Box 8953, Station A, Halifax NS B3K 5M6 Canada. **DD** 306.7609715.

MEDICAL ASPECTS OF HUMAN SEXUALITY. Periodical. US. English. mo. $75.00. Hospital Publications Inc, 90 Park Avenue, New York NY 10016. **Tel** (212)682-5430.

MON SEXE. (MON SEXE. . .ET CELUI DES AUTRES). First issue in 1976?. 0383-6185. Periodical. CN. French. wk. Messageries Dynamiques Inc, 775 Boulevard Lebeau, Saint-Laurent Quebec H4N 1S5 Canada. **DD** 301.4105.

MONOGRAPH (ASSOCIATION OF SEXOLOGISTS). (MONOGRAPH). 1-. Monographic Series. US. English. The Association of Sexologists, 1523 Franklin Street, San Francisco CA 94109.

MOVIE X. See Motion Picture.

MYSTIQUE (TORONTO, ONT.). (MYSTIQUE). 0710-1988. Periodical. CN. English. ir. 4.00 per issue. Mystique, PO Box 561 Station Q, Toronto Ontario M4T 1L0 Canada. **DD** 306.73.

NEW YORK NATIVE. 1980. 0744-060X. Periodical. US. English. bw. $29.00. That New Magazine Inc, 249 West Broadway, New York NY 10013. **Tel** (212)925-8021. Ed Patrick Merla. bk rev. adv acc. **Circ** 26,000. Newspaper dealing with current gay news events plus film, theatre, art and book reviews.

NISSO ONDERZOEKSRAPPORT. **Main/Corp** Nederlands Institut Voor Sociaal Sexuologisch Onderzoek. **VAT** Nederlands Institut Voor Sociaal Sexuologisch Onderzoek Onderzoeksrapport. DUTCH. ir. **LC** HQ18.N45. RAPPORT.

NOUVELLES DES SWINGERS. VFOAT Swingers. V. 1- Aug. 1969-. 0226-5958. Periodical. CN. French. mo. Les Publications Joyeuses, CP 145 Succursale H, Montreal Quebec H3G 2K5 Canada. **DD** 306.705.

ORGASME. Vol. 1, No. 1-. 0712-6018. Periodical. CN. French. mo. Orgasme a/s Publications Domaine Ltee, 4270 Av Papineau, Montreal Qyebec H2H 1S9 Canada. **DD** 306.705.

OUI. 0090-2047. Periodical. US. English. mo. $9.00. Playboy Enterprises, 919 North Michigan Avenue, Chicago IL 60611. **Ind/Abst** Media Rev. Dig. **LC** AP2. **DD** 051.

OUI ALBUM. 0146-4183. US. English. mo. Oui Magazine, 300 West 43rd Street, New York NY 10036. **Tel** (914)469-2102. **LC** TR676. **DD** 779.28.

OUT & ABOUT. Issue No. 1- Feb. 1978-. 0228-247X. Periodical. CN. English. mo. $4. Project Lambda, PO Box 3742, Station B, Winnipeg Manitoba R2W 3R6 Canada. **DD** 306.760971274.

OUT HEALTH. See Public Health and Safety.

PENTHOUSE. V. 1- Sept. 1969-. 0090-2020. Periodical. US. English. mo. $36.00. Penthouse International LTD, 909 3rd Avenue, New York NY 10022, (subscription address: Communication Data Services 80 New Bridge Road Bergenfield NJ 07621). **Tel** (212)496-6100. **Ind/Abst** Pop. Mag. Rev., Film Lit. Index, Mag. Index, Access. **LC** AP2. **DD** 051.

PENTHOUSE FORUM. V. 2, No. 11- Aug. 1973-. Periodical. US. English. mo. $18.00. Penthouse International Ltd, 909 3rd Avenue, New York NY 10022. **Tel** (212)593-3301. **LC** HQ1. **DD** 301.41705. Forum.

PENTHOUSE VARIATIONS. VFOAT Variations. 0274-5143. Periodical. US. English. mo. $20.00. Penthouse International Ltd, 909 Third Avenue, New York NY 10022.

PETIT BERDACHE. (LE PETIT BERDACHE). No. 1-. 0826-2500. Periodical. CN. French. bm. Free. Association pour les Droits des Gais et Lesbiennes du Quebec, C P 36 Succursale C, Montreal Quebec H2L 4J7 Canada. **DD** 306.76606714. Berdache, 0227-1168.

PLACES OF INTEREST. (PLACES OF INTEREST : GAY MAP GUIDE USA & CANADA). VFOAT Map Guide USA and Canada. 1982-. 0731-096X. US. English (French, German and Spanish). an. $7.00 Domestic, $8.50 Canada. Ferrari Publications, PO Box 16054, Phoenix AZ 85011.

PLAYBOY. V. 1- Dec. 1953-. 0032-1478. Periodical. US. English. mo. HMH Publishing Company, 919 North Michigan Avenue, Chicago IL 60611, (subscription address: Neodata PO Box 2606 Boulder CO 80322). **Ind/Abst** Pop. Mag. Rev., Film Lit. Index, Index Am. Period. Verse, Media Rev. Dig. **LC** AP2. **DD** 051. (cum index).

PLAYBOY COLLECTORS GUIDE & PRICE LIST. (THE PLAYBOY COLLECTORS GUIDE & PRICE LIST). **VAT** Playboy Collectors Guide & Pricelist. 5Th Ed. (1982/1983)-. 0228-7226. CN. English. be. $10.95 Per Vol. Budget Enterprises, PO Box 592 Snowdon Station, Montreal Quebec H3X 3T7 Canada. **DD** 051. Collector's Guide and Price List of Playboy Back Issues, 0315-3177.

THE PLAYBOY INDEX. See Indexes/Abstracts.

PLAYGIRL. 0032-1494. Periodical. US. English. mo. $20.00. Playgirl Enterprises Inc, I Epstein, 3420 Ocean Park Boulevard, Santa Monica CA 90405. **Tel** (213)450-0900. Ed Thomasine Lewis. adv acc. **Circ** 1,500,000. Published for the spirited woman of today. Featuring exclusive interviews, fiction, beauty, health, and of course our men.

PROGRAMS AND PROJECTS OF THE COUNCIL ON HOMOSEXUALITY AND RELIGION. **Main/Corp** Council on Homosexuality and Religion. 1978-. 0705-8764. CN. English. an. Free. Council on Homosexuality and Religion, Box 1912, Winnipeg Manitoba R3C 3R2 Canada. **DD** 301.415706271274.

QUEBEC G. **VAT** Quebec Gai (1984). Summer 1984-. 0824-0965. Periodical. CN. French. mo. $2.50 Per No. Quebec G, a/s Productions Visuelles Tym, C P 941 Succursale Desjardins, Montreal Quebec H5B 1C1 Canada. **DD** 306.766209714. QG : Quebec Gai, 0824-0957.

Social Sciences (General)

RENCONTRES GAIES. Vol. 1, No. 1 Jan. 1982-. 0712-838X. Periodical. CN. French. $1.50 Per Number. Rencontres Gaies, CP 245, Succursale N, Montreal Quebec H2X 3M4 Canada. **DD** 306.766209714.

RESEARCH ON HOMOSEXUALITY. Monographic Series. US. English. **NLM** W1 JO672H V.6 No.4 Etc. (P).

REVUE QUEBECOISE DE SEXOLOGIE. V. 1- July/Aug./Sept. 1979-. 0707-9516. Periodical. CN. French. qt. $3.50 Per No.; $12.00 Per Year Domestic; $15.00 Per Year Foreign. Collectif d'Informations Sexuelles et Sexologique, 6109 Av Durocher, Outremont Quebec H2V 3Y7 Canada. **DD** 301.4105.

RFD. **VAT** Recruiting Feminist Drakes (Wolf Creek). 1974. 0149-709X. Periodical. US. English. qt. $23.00. RFD, Route 1 Box 127-E, Bakersville NC 28705. **Tel** (704)688-2447. Ed Ron Lambe. **Ind/Abst** Altern. Press Index. bk rev. adv acc. **Circ** 2,200. (ctrl). Country journal for gay men everywhere. Focuses on country living and alternative lifestyles exploring environmental concerns and gay men's experiences.

RITES FOR LESBIAN AND GAY LIBERATION. Vol. 1, No. 1 (May 1984)-. 0828-5802. Periodical. CN. English. mo. $1.75 Per No. Rites, P O Box 65 Station F, Toronto Ontario M4Y 2L4 Canada. **DD** 306.7660971.

SCANDALE (MONTREAL, QUEBEC). (SCANDALE). 0712-6026. Periodical. CN. French. ir. $1.25 Per No. Publications Domaine Ltd, 4270 Av Papineau, Montreal Quebec H2H 1S9 Canada. **DD** 306.705.

SENSASS. Vol. 1, No. 1-. 0712-8347. Periodical. CN. French. mo. $2.25 Per No. Sensass, c/o Distributeurs Associes du Quebec, 3600 Boulevard du Tricentenaire, Montreal Quebec H1B 5M8 Canada. **DD** 306.705.

SEXE EXTRA. **VFOAT** Sexe. Vol. 1, No. 1-. 0712-8371. Periodical. CN. French. mo. $1.25 Per No. Sexe Extra, c/o Distributeurs Associes du Quebec, 360 Boulevard du Tricentenaire, Montreal Quebec H1B 5M8 Canada. **DD** 306.705.

SEXE PLUS. 0712-6034. Periodical. CN. French. ir. $1.25 Per No. Sexe Plus a/s Publications Domaine Ltee, 4270 Av Papineau, Montreal Quebec H2H 1S9 Canada. **DD** 306.705.

SEXO GAGS. V. 1- 1973-. 0701-1466. Periodical. CN. French. bm. $0.25 Per No. Editions Publiitee, CP 71 Succursale R, Montreal Quebec H2S Canada. **DD** 301.410207.

SEXUAL BEHAVIOR (MARCEL DEKKER, INC.). (SEXUAL BEHAVIOR). 1-. 0739-7321. Monographic Series. US. English. Marcel Dekkar, 270 Madison Avenue, New York NY 10016. Ed Richard C Friedman. **LC** UNC. **NLM** W1 SE99E.

SEXUAL FREEDOM. Began in 1969. US. English. ir. $3.00 5 Issues. San Francisco Sexual Freedom League, PO Box 14034, San Francisco CA 94114. **LC** HQ1. **DD** 301.41705.

SEXUAL HEALTH AND RELATIONSHIPS. **VFOAT** SHAR. V. 1- Jan. 1978-. 0148-7914. Periodical. US. English. mo. $9.50. SHAR, PO Box 627, Northampton MA 01060.

SEXUAL WELL-BEING. 0749-7997. Periodical. US. English. mo. $36.00. Sexual Well-Being, PO Box 60332, Palo Alto CA 94306. **DD** 613.

SEXUALITY. **VFOAT** Sussualita. Year 1- 1975-. Periodical. English and Italian. ir. $25.00. Bulzoni, Via dei Liburni 14, Roma 00185 Italy. **LC** HQ1. **DD** 301.4105. **NLM** W1 SE86V.

SEXUALITY AND DISABILITY. V. 1- Spring 1978-. 0146-1044. Periodical. US. English. qt. Human Sciences Press, 72 5th Avenue, New York NY 10011. **Tel** (212)243-6000. **Ind/Abst** Electron. Commun. Abstr. J., ISMEC Bull., Pollut. Abstr. Indexes, Saf. Sci. Abstr. J., Excerpta Med., Soc. Welf. Soc. Plan./Policy Soc. Dev., Cumul. Index Nurs. Allied Health Lit., Saf. Sci. Abstr. J., Psychol. Abstr., Sociol. Abstr. **LC** HQ30.5. **DD** 613.95. **NLM** W1 SE99J. **CODEN** SDISCD.

SEXUALITY (BOCA RATON). (SEXUALITY). Series/Titl Social Issues Resources Series. V. 1, Article 1-. 0273-2564. US. English. an. Social Issues Resources Series Inc, PO Box 2507, Boca Raton FL 33432. Ed Eleanor C Goldstein. **LC** HQ18.U5. **DD** 306.70973.

SEXUALITY TODAY. 0148-883X. Periodical. US. English. ir. $82.00. Atcom Company, 2315 Broadway, New York NY 10024. **Tel** (212)873-5900. Ed Suzanne Prescod. **Circ** 952. (ctrl). A newsletter for professionals working in the sensitive area of human sexuality.

SEXUALLY TRANSMITTED DISEASE (STD) STATISTICAL LETTER. See Statistics.

SEXUALLY TRANSMITTED DISEASES. See Public Health and Safety.

SIECUS REPORT. **Main/Corp** Sex Information and Education Council of the U.S. **VAT** Sex Information and Education Council of the United States Report. V. 1- Sept. 1972-. 0091-3995. Periodical. US. English. bm. $40.00. Sex Information & Education Council of the United States, 80 5th Avenue Street 801, New York NY 10011. **Tel** (212)929-2300. Ed Sharon Edwards. **Ind/Abst** Educ. Index, Media Rev. Dig. **LC** HQ1. **DD** 301.41705. **NLM** W1 S355N. bk rev. adv acc. **Circ** 3,000. Also available on microfilm from University Microfilms. All aspects of human sexuality. Siecus Newsletter, 0036-150X.

SORTIE (MONTREAL, QUEBEC). (SORTIE). No. 1 (Oct. 1982)-. 0714-7376. Periodical. CN. French. ir. $12.50 for 10 Number. Sortie, C P 232 Succursale C, Montreal Quebec H2L 4K1 Canada. **DD** 306.76605.

STANDOUT MAGAZINE. **VFOAT** Standout. Sept. 1978-. 0708-109X. Periodical. CN. English. mo. $10.00 Domestic, $12.00 Foreign. Outstanding Productions, PO Box 5071 Station A, Toronto Ontario M5W Canada. **DD** 301.415705.

SUPER SEXE. 0712-5984. Periodical. CN. French. ir. $1.25 Each Number. Super Sexe a/s Publications Domaine Ltee, 4270 Av Papineau, Montreal Quebec H2H 1S9 Canada. **DD** 306.705.

SWINGTIME NEWS. **VFOAT** Confidentially Yours, Swingtime News. 0227-6836. Periodical. CN. English. $3.00 Each Number. Swingtime News, PO Box 2410, New Westminister British Columbia V3L 5B6 Canada. **DD** 306.73.

TURNABOUT. No. 1- June 1963-. 0148-7388. Periodical. US. English. qt. $3.00 Each Issue. Abbe de Choisy Press, PO Box 4053 Grand Central Station, New York NY 10017. **LC** HQ77. **DD** 362.19.

VIVRE EN AMOUR. 1-. 0711-6306. Periodical. CN. French. wk. $1.75 Per No. Vivre en Amour, c/o F Boisvert, 385 Boulevard Lebeau, Saint-Laurent Quebec H4N 1S2 Canada. **DD** 613.9605.

WILDE TIMES. Oct. 1980-. 0712-4279. Periodical. CN. English. mo. Free. The Society, Wilde Times, c/o O W M S, Box 221, Winnipeg Manitoba R3C 3R5 Canada. **DD** 306.76605.

SOCIAL SCIENCES (GENERAL)

4S REVIEW. (4S REVIEW : JOURNAL OF THE SOCIETY FOR SOCIAL STUDIES OF SCIENCE). **VFOAT** 4 S Review. Vol. 1, No. 1 (Spring 1983)-. 0738-0526. Periodical. US. English. qt. $25.00. Lowell Hargens 4S, Department of Sociology, Indiana University, Bloomington IN 47405. **LC** Q175.4. **DD** 303.48305. *4S. Society for Social Studies of Science, 0146-1435.*

ABASS NEWSLETTER. **Main/Corp** National Research Council (U.S.) Assembly of Behavioral and Social Sciences. **VAT** Assembly of Behavioral and Social Sciences Newsletter. No. 1-12. 0361-9222. US. English. sa. Assembly Behavioral & Social Science, 2101 Constitution Avenue NW, Washington DC 20418.

ABG. **VFOAT** Analysen und Berichte aus Gesellschaft und Wissenschaft. GW. German. ir. Insitut fur Gesellschaft und Wissenschaft, Schuhstrasse 44, 8520 Erlangen West Germany. **LC** AM **DD** 300.5, 943.10072. *Analysen und Berichte aus Gesellschaftswissenschaften, 0572-3287.*

ABHANDLUNGEN - SACHSISCHE AKADEMIE DER WISSENSCHAFTEN, LEIPZIG. PHILOGOGISCHE-HISTORISCHE KLASSE. **Main/Corp** Sachsische Akademie der Wissenschaften, Leipzig. Philogogische-Historische Klasse. 1- Vol. 0080-5297. GE. German. ir. Deutscher Buch Export-Import, Leninstrasse 16, DDR-701 Leipzig East Germany. Index published separately - free - automatically sent.

ABHANDLUNGEN ZUR HANDELS-UND SOZIALGESCHICHTE. Vol. 1- 1958-. Periodical. GE. German. ir. Deutscher Buch Export-Import, Leninstrasse 16, DDR-701 Leipzig East Germany.

ABS. AMERICAN BEHAVIORAL SCIENTIST. (ABS, AMERICAN BEHAVIORAL SCIENTIST). **VFOAT** American Behavioral Scientist. V. 10- Sept. 1966-. 0002-7642. Periodical. US. English. bm. Sage Publishing Inc, 275 South Beverly Drive, Beverly Hills CA 90212. **Tel** (213)274-8003. **Ind/Abst** ABC Pol Sci, Curr. Index J. Educ., Soc. Sci. Index, Psychol. Abstr., Public Aff. Inf. Serv. Bull., Women Stud. Abstr., Writ. Am. Hist., Am. Hist. Life, Hist. Abstr., Part A, Mod. Hist. Abstr., Hist. Abstr., Part B, Twent. Century Abstr. **NLM** W1 AM281L. Available on microfilm.

ABSTRACTS OF ARI RESEARCH PUBLICATIONS. See Indexes/Abstracts.

ABSTRACTS OF BULGARIAN SCIENTIFIC LITERATURE. SCIENTIFIC COMMUNISM, PHILOSOPHY, SOCIOLOGY, SCIENCE OF SCIENCE AND SCIENTIFIC INFORMATION. See Indexes/Abstracts.

ACQUISITIONS - METROPOLITAN TORONTO LIBRARY. SOCIAL SCIENCES DEPARTMENT. See Bibliographies.

ACTA MEXICANA DE CIENCIAS SOCIALES. V. 1- (No. 1-). Periodical. MX. Spanish. ir. $10.00. Instituto Politecnico Nacional, Escuela Superior de Medicina, Apartado Postales 42-161, Mexico 17 DF Mexico. **LC** H8.

ADMINISTRATION IN SOCIAL WORK. V. 1- Spring 1977-. 0364-3107. Periodical. US. English. qt. $102.00. Haworth Press, 28 East 22nd Street, New York NY 10010. **Tel** (212)228-2800. Ed Simon Slavin. **Ind/Abst** Hospit. Lit. Index, Sociol. Abstr., Soc. Welf. Soc. Plan./Policy Soc. Dev., Soc. Work Res. Abstr. **LC** HV1. **DD** 658.91361005. **NLM** W1 AD339S. **CODEN** ASWODB. bk rev. adv acc. **Circ** 1,446. The source for authoritative and pertinent material of vital interest to administrators, supervisors, managers, and sub-executives in social work and related human services fields.

ADMINISTRATIVE DIRECTIVE - DEPARTMENT OF SOCIAL SERVICES. **Main/Corp** New York (State). Dept. of Social Services. 1977-. Periodical. US. English. 40 North Pearl Street, Albany NY 12243. *Administrative Letter - Department of Social Services.*

ADMINISTRATIVE SCIENCE QUARTERLY. V. 1- June 1956-. 0001-8392. Periodical. US. English. qt. $62.00. Administrative Science Quarterly, Malott Hall/Cornell University, Ithaca NY 14850. **Tel** (607)256-5117. Ed John H Freeman. **Ind/Abst** Am. Hist. Life, Hist. Abstr., Part A, Mod. Hist. Abstr., Lang. Lang. Behav. Abstr., Manage. Contents, Hospit. Lit. Index, Sociol. Abstr., Soc. Welf. Soc. Plan./Policy Soc. Dev., Cumul. Index Nurs. Allied Health Lit., Account. Index. Suppl., ABC Pol Sci, Int. Aerosp. Abstr., ABI/Inform, Manage. Market. Abstr., Writ. Am. Hist., Soc. Work Res. Abstr., Public Aff. Inf. Serv. Bull., Psychol. Abstr., Curr. Index J. Educ., Bus. Period. Index, Soc. Sci. Index. **LC** HD28. **DD** 658.05. **NLM** W1 AD347. **CODEN** ASCQAG. (cum index). bk rev. adv acc. **Circ** 5,500. Empirical and theoretical articles that contribute to knowledge of business, governmental, military, health, and other organizations.

ADOLESCENCE. See Children and Youth Interests.

ADVANCES IN MEDICAL SOCIAL SCIENCE. Vol. 1 (1983)-. 0275-5742. US. English. an. Gordon and Breach Science Publishers Inc, 1 Park Avenue, New York NY 10016. Ed Julio L Ruffini. **DD** 362. **NLM** W1.

AFFARI SOCIALI INTERNAZIONALI. Yearly V. 1- Mar. 1973-. 0390-1181. Periodical. IT. Italian. qt. $35.64. Franco Angeli Editore Riviste, Via le Monza 106, 20127 Milano Italy. **Tel** (02)28.27.651/2/3/. **Ind/Abst** Int. Labour Doc. **LC** H7.

AFRICA DEVELOPMENT. **VFOAT** Afrique et Developpement. V. 1- May 1976-. 0378-3006. Periodical. English (May 1976- English or French, (July/Sept. 1977-)). qt. 32.00 Domestic $35.00

Social Sciences (General)

Foreign. Codesria, BP 3304, Dakar Senegal Africa. **Tel** 23 02 11. **Ed** A S Bujra. **Ind/Abst** Recent Publ. Artic. **LC** HC501. **DD** 330.966003. bk rev. adv acc. **Circ** 1,000. (ctrl) A critical analysis of the socio-economic development of Africa.

AFRICA INSIGHT. Vol. 10, No. 1-. Periodical. SA. English. qt. 16. Africa Institute of South Africa, PO Box 630, Pretoria South Africa. **Ed** Madeline Munnick. **Ind/Abst** Recent Publ. Artic. **LC** HC501. **DD** 960.05. bk rev. adv acc. **Circ** 5,000. A politically independent journal which promotes understanding of the process of change in Africa. *South African Journal of African Affairs.*

AFRICA SEMINAR : COLLECTED PAPERS. **Main/Corp** University of Cape Town. Centre For African Studies. **VFOAT** Africa Seminar. V. 1-. SA. English. ir. 5.00. University of Cape Town, Centre for African Studies, 7700 Rondebosch South AFrica. **Tel** 698531. **LC** DT751. **DD** 968. **Circ** 300. Collection of seminar papers in African studies, University of Cape Town, concerning history, ecology, sociology, anthropology, linguistics, archaeology, and geography.

AFRICAN SOCIAL RESEARCH. No. 1- June 1966-. 0002-0168. Periodical. UK. English. sa. $18.00. University of Zambia, PO Box 32379, Lusaka Zambia. **Ind/Abst** Am. Hist. Life, Hist. Abstr., Part A, Mod. Hist. Abstr., Hist. Abst., Part B, Twent. Century Abstr., Sociol. Abstr., Recent Publ. Artic., Psychol. Abstr., Soc. Sci. Citation Index. **LC** HN771. **DD** 309.16. **NLM** W1 AF56. **CODEN** ASREDO. *Rhodes-Livingstone Journal.*

AFRICAN STUDIES BY SOVIET SCHOLARS. No. 1-. Monographic Series. English. ir. 8. Social Sciences Today Editorial Board, USSR Academy of Sciences, 33/12 Arbat, Moscow 121002 USSR. **Tel** 241-09-06. **Ed** Iosiph R Grigulevich. bk rev. adv acc. **Circ** 3,000. (ctrl).

AFRICAN URBAN STUDIES (MICHIGAN STATE UNIVERSITY. AFRICAN STUDIES CENTER). (AFRICAN URBAN STUDIES). Began with new Ser. No. 1, Spring 1978. 0736-6760. Periodical. US. English. ty. $18.00. African Studies Center, 100 International Center/Michigan State University, East Lansing MI 48824-1035. **Tel** (517)353-1700. **Ed** Ruth Simms Hamilton. **Ind/Abst** Am. Hist. Life, Hist. Abstr., Part A, Mod. Hist. Abstr., Hist. Abst., Part B, Twent. Century Abstr., Recent Publ. Artic. **LC** HT148.A2. **DD** 307.76096. bk rev. adv acc. **Circ** 205. Scholarly journal concerning urban society, urbanization, and cities in the world's fastest urbanizing continent. *African Urban Notes.*

AGEING AND SOCIETY. Vol. 1, Pt. 1 (Mar. 1981)-. 0144-686X. Periodical. UK. English. ir. $65.00. Cambridge University Press, 510 North Avenue, New Rochelle NY 10801. **Tel** (914)235-0300. **Ed** Malcolm L Johnson. **Ind/Abst** Sociol. Abstr., Soc. Welf. Soc. Plan./Policy Soc. Dev. **LC** HQ1060. **DD** 305.2605. **NLM** W1 AG343T. bk rev. International journal devoted to publishing contributions to the understanding of human ageing, particularly from the social and behavioral sciences and humanities.

AGENDA (NATIONAL COUNCIL OF LA RAZA) CEASED. (AGENDA). Began with June 1971 issue. 0146-020X. Periodical. US. English (Spanish). bm. $15.00. Agenda, National Council of La Raza, 1725 Eye Street NW/2nd Floor, Washington DC 20006. **Ind/Abst** Curr. Index J. Educ. **LC** E184.S75. **DD** 305.8687207305.

AKHBOROTY AKADEMIIAI FANHOI RSS TOJIKISTON, SHUBAI FANHOI JAMIIATI. IZVESTIIA AKADEMII NAUK TADZHIKSKOI SSR, OTDELENIE OBSHCHESTVENNYKH NAUK. **Main/Corp** Akademiia Nauk Tadzhikskoi SSR, Dushanbe. Otdelenie Obshchestvennykh Nauk. **VFOAT** Izvestiia Akademii Nauk Tadzhikskoi SSR, Otdelenie Obshchestvennykh Nauk. 21- 1959-. 0568-689X. Periodical. UR. Russian (Tajik). qt. Victor Kamkin Inc, 12224 Parklawn Drive, Rockville MD 20852. **Tel** (301)881-5973. *Izvestiia Otdeleniia Obshchestvennykh Nauk.*

AL-BUHUTH. Periodical. Arabic. ir. PO Box 2402, Al-Khartum Sudan. **LC** Q180.S73.

AMERICA INDIGENA. See Anthropology.

AMERICA MERIDIONAL : REVISTA DE LA SOCIEDAD REGIONAL DE CIENCIAS HUMANAS. 1-. Periodical. Spanish. sa. Manuel Errazquin, 2351 Punta Carretas.

AMERICAN COMMUNITIES TOMORROW. V. 1-. 0192-5903. Periodical. US. English. sa. $25.00. Social Science Services & Resources, P O Box 241, Aurora IL 60507.

AMERICAN MEN AND WOMEN OF SCIENCE. SOCIAL AND BEHAVIORAL SCIENCES. (AMERICAN MEN AND WOMEN OF SCIENCE : THE SOCIAL AND BEHAVIORAL SCIENCES). **VFOAT** Social and Behavioral Sciences. 12th Ed.-. 0065-9363. US. English. ir. $125.00. R R Bowker, PO Box 1807, Ann Arbor MI 48106. **Tel** (212)916-1600. **LC** H50. **DD** 300.922, B. (ctrl). An index of 297,000 scientists, alphabetically by name. *American Men of Science, 0192-7647.*

AMERICAN QUARTERLY. V. 1- Spring 1949-. 0003-0678. Periodical. US. English. $30.00 Domestic, $35.00 Foreign. University of Pennsylvania, 307 College Hall, Philadelphia PA 19104-6303. **Tel** (215)898-6252. **Ed** Janice Radway. **Ind/Abst** Abstr. Engl. Stud., MLA Int. Bibliogr. Books Artic. Mod. Lang. Lit., Women Stud. Abstr., Annu. Bibliogr. Engl. Lang. Lit., Recent Publ. Artic., Writ. Am. Hist., Int. Index, Soc. Sci. Index, Humanit. Index, Am. Hist. Life, Hist. Abstr., Relig. Index One, Period. **LC** AP2. **DD** 051. bk rev. adv acc. **Circ** 4,500. (ctrl). Scholarly articles with an interdisciplinary approach which provides an insight into the nature of American culture.

AMERICAN REVIEW OF ART AND SCIENCE. See The Arts (General).

ANALELE UNIVERSITATII DIN TIMISOARA. STIINTE SOCIALE SI ECONOMICE. **VFOAT** Stiinte Sociale Si Economice. Vol. 1 (1982)-. Periodical. English (French, German, and Romanian). an. Universitatea Din Timisoara Facultatea de Stiinte Economice Bul Vasile Parvan, NR 4, 1900 Timisoara Romania. *Analele Universitatii Din Timisoara. Stiinte Economice, Analele Universitatii Din Timisoara. Stiinte Sociale.*

ANALISE PSICOLOGICA. See Psychology.

ANALISIS. No. 1- Jan./March 1977-. Periodical. PE. Spanish. ir. Apartado 11093, Correo Santa Beatriz, Lima Peru. **LC** H8.

ANALYSE & KRITIK. **VFOAT** Analyse und Kritik. 0171-5860. Periodical. GW. German (English). sa. $25.00. Westdeutscher Verlag GMBH, Postfach 5829, D6200 Wiesbaden 1 West Germany. **LC** H1. **DD** 300.5.

ANNALES DE L'EST. See History (General).

ANNALI DELL'ISTITUTO ALCIDE CERVI. **VFOAT** Annali. 1 (1979)-. Periodical. IT. Italian. ir. Societa Editrice Il Mulino, Via Santo Stefano 6, 40125 Bologna Italy. **LC** HD1536.I8. **DD** 305.563.

THE ANNALS OF THE AMERICAN ACADEMY OF POLITICAL AND SOCIAL SCIENCE. See Political Science.

L'ANNEE SOCIALE. 1960-. 0066-2380. BE. French. ty. $24.23. Editions Universite de Bruxelles, Avenue Paul Heger 26, B1050 Bruxelles Belgium. **Tel** 021 642 37 93. adv acc. **Circ** 1,200. A synthesis of Belgian social life.

ANNUAIRE CNRS SCIENCES DE L'HOMME. See Yearbooks, Almanacs, Directories.

ANNUAIRE DU TIERS MONDE. See Yearbooks, Almanacs, Directories.

ANNUAIRE SCIENCES DE L'HOMME. See Yearbooks, Almanacs, Directories.

ANNUAL GUIDE TO PUBLIC POLICY EXPERTS. (THE ANNUAL GUIDE TO PUBLIC POLICY EXPERTS). 1982-. 0731-339X. US. English. an. $4.00. The Heritage Foundation, 513 C Street Northeast, Washington DC 20002. **LC** H50. **DD** 361.6102573.

ANNUAL REPORT - AMERICAN ENTERPRISE INSTITUTE FOR PUBLIC POLICY RESEARCH. **Main/Corp** American Enterprise Institute for Public Policy Research. 0748-626X. US. English. an. American Enterprise Institute, 1150 17th Street NW, Washington DC 20036. **LC** H62.5.U5. **DD** 300.6073.

ANNUAL REPORT - CARIBBEAN RESEARCH INSTITUTE. **Main/Corp** Caribbean Research Institute. 1965-. 0069-0503. VI. English. an. College of Virgin Island, Caribbean Research Institute, St Thomas VI West Indies. **LC** H67.C28.

ANNUAL REPORT - ECONOMIC AND SOCIAL COMMISSION FOR ASIA AND THE PACIFIC. **Main/Corp** United Nations. Economic and Social Commission for Asia and the Pacific. US. English. an. United Nations, 866 United Nations Plaza, New York NY 10017. **LC** JX1977, HC411. **DD** 300.8 S, 341.759.

ANNUAL REPORT - INSTITUTE FOR POLICY ANALYSIS. UNIVERSITY OF TORONTO. (ANNUAL REPORT - INSTITUTE FOR POLICY ANALYSIS, UNIVERSITY OF TORONTO). **Main/Corp** University of Toronto. Institute for the Quantitative Analysis of Social and Economic Policy. 1976-. 0703-6949. CN. English. an. Institute for Policy Analysis, 150 Sainte George Street, Toronto Ontario M5S 1A1 Canada. **LC** H67.T65. **DD** 330.0720713541. *Newletter.*

ANNUAL REPORT - INSTITUTE FOR SOCIAL AND ECONOMIC RESEARCH. **Main/Corp** University of Durban-Westville. Institute for Social and Economic Research. English. ir. Private Bag X54001, South Africa. **LC** H64.U55. **DD** 300.711684.

ANNUAL REPORT - INSTITUTE OF DEVELOPMENT STUDIES AT THE UNIVERSITY OF SUSSEX. **Main/Corp** University of Sussex Institute of Development Studies. 3rd-. Periodical. UK. English. an. Free. Institute of Development Studies, University of Sussex, Brighton BN1 9R3E England. **Tel** 0273 606261. **Ed** Ann Segrave. **Circ** 6,000. An account of research, teaching, and consultancy at the 105 - a post-doctoral research institute working on Third World problems from an interdisciplinary social science perspective.

ANNUAL REPORT - INTERNATIONAL INSTITUTE OF SOCIAL HISTORY. **Main/Corp** International Institute for Social History. 0304-713X. English. ir. International Institute of Social History, Herengracht 262-266, Amsterdam Netherlands. **LC** H67.A655. **DD** 309.0621.

ANNUAL REPORT - INTERNATIONAL SECRETARIAT FOR VOLUNTEER SERVICE. **Main/Corp** International Secretariat for Volunteer Service. [nglish. ir. International Secretariat for Volunteer Service, 10-12 CH. Surville 1213-Petit, Geneva Switzerland. **LC** HC60. **DD** 309.2235.

ANNUAL REPORT - JAPAN-UNITED STATES FRIENDSHIP COMMISSION. (ANNUAL REPORT). **Main/Corp** Japan-United States Friendship Commission. Began with 1977. 0163-5557. US. English. an. Japan United States Friendship Commission, 1875 Connecticut Avenue Northwest/ Suite 910, Washington DC 20009. **LC** E183.8.J3. **DD** 301.2973052.

ANNUAL REPORT - NEW JERSEY. DEPT. OF COMMUNITY AFFAIRS. **Main/Corp** New Jersey. Dept. of Community Affairs. 1st (Fiscal Year 1968)-. US. English. an. New Jersey Department of Community Affairs, Office of Public Information, 363 West State Street, PO Box 2768, Trenton NJ 08625. **LC** HN79.N333. **DD** 353.97490084.

ANNUAL REPORT - NORTH CAROLINA HUMAN RELATIONS COMMISSION. (ANNUAL REPORT). **Main/Corp** North Carolina. Human Relations Commission. Human Relations Commission. 0093-5085. US. English. an. North Carolina Human Relations Commission, PO Box 12525, Raleigh NC 27605. **LC** F251. **DD** 353.97560084.

ANNUAL REPORT OF THE EXECUTIVE DIRECTOR - UNITED NATIONS. INDUSTRIAL DEVELOPMENT BOARD. **Main/Corp** United Nations. Industrial Development Board. AU. English. ir. United Nations Industrial Development Board, PO Box 300, 1400 Vienna Austria. **DD** 300.8.

ANNUAL REPORT OF THE INSTITUTE OF SOCIAL SCIENCES, MEIJI UNIVERSITY. **Main/Corp** Meiji Daigaku, Tokyo. Shakai Kagaku Kenkyujo. **VFOAT** Meiji Daigaku Shakai Kagaku Kenkyujo Nempo. 1st No. JA. in Japanese. ir. 1 Kanda Surugadai 1 Chiyoda-ku, Tokyo Japan. **LC** H8.

ANNUAL REPORT - SOCIAL SCIENCE RESEARCH COUNCIL. **Main/Corp** Social Science Research Council (U.S.). 0361-462X. US. English. an. Social Science Research Council, 605 3rd Avenue, New York NY 10158. **LC** H11. **DD** 300.6273. **NLM** W1 SO128.

Social Sciences (General)

ANNUAL REPORT - SOCIAL SCIENCES AND HUMANITIES RESEARCH COUNCIL OF CANADA. (ANNUAL REPORT). Main/Corp Social Sciences and Humanities Research Council of Canada. VFOAT Rapport Annuel. 1978/79-. 0225-2384. CN. English (French). an. Receiver General for Canada, Statistics Canada Publications, Ottawa Ontario K1A 0T6 Canada. LC H62.5.C22. DD 354.710085406.

ANNUAL REPORT - SOLICITOR GENERAL CANADA. (ANNUAL REPORT). Main/Corp Canada. Solicitor General Canada. VFOAT Rapport Annuel. VAT Rapport Annuel - Solliciteur General Canada, Rapport Annuel du Solliciteur General du Canada, Rapport Annuel - Solliciteur General du Canada, Annual Report of the Solicitor General of Canada. 1976/1977-. 0576-4076. CN. English (French text on inverted pages). an. Free. Solicitor General Canada, 340 Laurier Avenue West, Ottawa Ontario K1A 0P8 Canada. Tel (613)991-2810. LC HV9660.C2. DD 354.710674. Circ 6,400. Secretariat, Royal Canadian Mounted Police, National Parole Board, the Correctional Service of Canada. Annual Report, 0576-4076.

ANNUAL REPORT - UNIVERSITY OF ZAMBIA. SCHOOL OF HUMANITIES & SOCIAL SCIENCES. See Humanities.

ANNUARIO - INSTITUTO GIAPPONESE DI CULTURA IN ROMA. See Yearbooks, Almanacs, Directories.

ANTHROPINES SHESEIS. (ANTHROPINES SCHESEIS). V. 1- 1972-. 0302-1122. Greek, Modern. ir. $10.00. Voukourestiou 4, Athenai Greece. LC H8.

ANUARIO COLOMBIANO DE HISTORIA SOCIAL Y DE LA CULTURA. See Yearbooks, Almanacs, Directories.

AOYAMA SHAKAI KAGAKU KIYO. VFOAT Aoyama Journal of Social Sciences. 1 No. Periodical. JA. Japanese. ir. Aoyama Gakuin Daigoku Daigakuin, 4-4-25 Shibuya Shibuya-Ku, Tokyo Japan. LC H8.

APUNTES. Yearly V. 1- 1973-. Spanish. ir. 0.50. Universidad Del Pacifico Centro De Investigacion, Avenida Salaverry 2020 Jesus Maria, Lima Peru. LC H8. DD 300.5.

ARCHIV FUR RECHTS- UND SOZIALPHILOSOPHIE. See Genealogy and Heraldry - Archives.

ARCHIVES DE SCIENCES SOCIALES DE LA COOPERATION ET DU DEVELOPPEMENT. See Genealogy and Heraldry - Archives.

ARCHIVES DE SCIENCES SOCIALES DES RELIGIONS. See Genealogy and Heraldry - Archives.

ARETE. 1969. 0363-2903. Periodical. US. English. sa. $12.00. University of South Carolina, Graduate School of Social Work, Columbus SC 29208. Tel (803)777-5291. Ed Deborah Valentine. Ind/Abst Soc. Work Res. Abstr., Abstr. Soc. Work. LC PN6099.6. DD 811.5405. Circ 750. Includes articles concerned with social problems, new developments, issues in health care, social work, and social work education. Includes a special section on educational innovation.

DAS ARGUMENT; BERLINER HEFTE FUR PROBLEME DER GESELLSCHAFT. See Philosophy.

THE ARKANSAS SOCIAL STUDIES TEACHER. V. 1- 1975-. 0196-8122. Periodical. US. English. an. $2.00. Dr Jerry Long, Box 33, State University AR 72467. LC H62. DD 300.71073.

ARSBERETNING - ROSKILDE UNIVERSITETSCENTER. INSTITUT FOR GEOGRAFI, SAMFUNDSANALYSE OG DATALOGI. Main/Corp Roskilde Universitetscenter. Institut For Geografi, Samfundsanalyse Og Datalogi. Series/Titl Publikationer Fra Institut For Geografi, Samfundsanalyse Og Datalogi. 0106-2778. Danish. an. Roskilde Universitetscenter Institut for Geografi Samfundsanalyse Og Datalogi, Postbox 260, 4000 Roskilde Denmark. LC H67.R744.

ASIAN SOCIAL SCIENCE BIBLIOGRAPHY WITH ANNOTATIONS AND ABSTRACTS. See Indexes/Abstracts.

ASIS SPECIAL INTEREST GROUP IN THE BEHAVIORAL AND SOCIAL SCIENCES NEWSLETTER. See Psychology.

ATLANTIDA. Spanish. ir. Universidad Simon Bolivar, Valle de Sartenejas, Caracas Venezuela. LC H8.

ATTI - ACCADEMIA DELLE SCIENZE DI TORINO. CLASSE DI SCIENZE MORALI, STORICHE E FILOLOGICHE. Main/Corp Accademia delle Scienze di Torino. Classe di Scienze Morali, Storiche e Filologiche. V. 42- 1906/07-. Periodical. IT. Italian. ir. Bottega d'Erasmo, Via Gaud Ferrari 9, 10124 Torino Italy.

BALLENA PRESS PUBLICATIONS IN ARCHAEOLOGY, ETHNOLOGY AND HISTORY. VFOAT Publications in Archaeology, Ethnology and History. No. 1-. Monographic Series. US. English. ir. Ballena Press, 381 First Street/Suite 5033, Los Altos CA 94022.

BC. VFOAT BC Politico, Economico E Financeiro. Periodical. English. ir. $360. Empresa Jornalistica e Editora Boletim Cambial, Treze de Maio, 44-A/90 Andar, Rio de Janeiro Brazil. LC H8.

B.C.S.S.T.A. NEWS BULLETIN. VAT British Columbia Social Studies Teachers' Association News Bulletin. May 1984-. 0824-054X. Periodical. CN. English. ir. Free to members. British Columbia Social Studies Teachers' Federation, 105-2235 Burrard Street, Vancouver British Columbia V6J 3H9 Canada. DD 300.70711.

BEHAVIOR SCIENCE RESEARCH. V. 9- 1974-. 0094-3673. Periodical. US. English. qt. $3.00. Human Relations Area Files, Box 2015, New Haven CT 06521. Ind/Abst Psychol. Abstr. LC H1. DD 300.5. NLM W1 BE128B. Behavior Science Notes, 0005-7886.

BETWEEN OUR SELVES. Vol. 1, No. 1 (Winter 1985)-. 0882-4355. Periodical. US. English. qt. $15.00. B O S, PO Box 1939, Washington DC 20013. DD 305.

BETWEEN THE ISSUES. No. 1-. 0715-4259. Periodical. CN. English. bm. Free to Members. Ecology Action Centre Forest Building, Dalhousie University, Halifax Nova Scotia B3H 3J5 Canada. DD 304.20971.

BEVOLKINGSSTATISTIEKEN - NATIONAAL INSTITUUT VOOR DE STATISTIEK. See Statistics.

BIBLIOGRAFIE VAN REGIONALE ONDERZOEKINGEN OP SOCIAAL-WETENSCHAPPELIJK TERREIN. See Bibliographies.

BIBLIOGRAPHIE COURANTE D'ARTICLES DE PERIODIQUES POSTERIEURS A 1944 SUR LES PROBLEMES POLITIQUES, ECONOMIQUES, ET SOCIAUX. SUPPLEMENT. See Bibliographies.

BIBLIOGRAPHIE DE L'AFRIQUE SUD-SAHARIENNE, SCIENCES HUMAINES ET SOCIALES. See Bibliographies.

BIBLIOGRAPHIE DES TRAVAUX EN LANGUE FRANCAISE SUR L'AFRIQUE AU SUD DU SAHARA, SCIENCES HUMAINES ET SOCIALES. See Bibliographies.

BIBLIOGRAPHY OF NOISE. See Bibliographies.

BIBLIOGRAPHY : PUBLICATIONS RESULTING FROM COUNCIL SUPPORT. See Bibliographies.

BIBLIOGRAPHY SERIES - CENTRE FOR DEVELOPING-AREA STUDIES. MCGILL UNIVERSITY. See Bibliographies.

BIBLIOTEKETS FORTEGNELSE OVER NYERHVERVELSER. SUPPLEMENT. See Bibliographies.

BIULLETEN REGISTRATSII NIR. OBSHCHESTVENNYE NAUKI. SERIIA 1. UR. Russian. qt. 125493 Moskva, Smolnaia 14, Vsesoiuznyi Nauchno-Tekhnicheskii Informatsionnyi Tsentr, Moskva Russian SFSR. LC H62.A1. Biulleten Registratsii. Obshchestvennye Nauki. Seriia 1, Marksizm-Leninizm, Filosofiia, Sotsiologiia, Psikhologiia.

BLACFAX. Vol. 1, No. 1 (Winter 1982)-. 0882-6595. Periodical. US. English. qt. $5.00. R Edward Lee, 214 West 138th Street, New York NY 10030. DD 305.

BLATTER DES IZ3W. Main/Corp Informationszentrum Dritte Welt. Periodical. GW. German. ir. 18.00. Informationszentrum Dritte Welt, Postfach 5328, D-78 Freiburg West Germany. LC HC59.7. DD 309.11724.

THE BLESSINGS OF LIBERTY. V. 1- July 1956-. 0006-4696. Periodical. US. English. qt. $3.00. Charles W Lowry, PO Box 1829, Pinehurst NC 28374. Tel (919)692-6726. Ed Charles W Lowry. LC HN39.U6. Circ 1,100. Features articles dealing with national and world affairs against an historical background and from a theological perspective.

BOGAZICI UNIVERSITESI DERGISI. SOSYAL BILIMLER. VFOAT Bogazici University Journal. Social Sciences. V. 1- 1973-. Periodical. TU. Multilingual. an. Bogazici University, Public Relations Office, Harbiye-Istanbul Turkey.

BOLETIM TECNICO INFORMATIVO. Main/Corp Universidade do Amazonas. Centro de Pesquisas Socio-Economicas. Portuguese. ir. Divisuo de Documentacao, Rua Jose Paranagua 200/Caixa Postal 378, Manaus Brazil. LC H67.U55.

BOLETIN. Main/Corp Instituto de Estudios Sociales-Ormeu. Periodical. Spanish. ir. LC H8.

BOLETIN CLACSO CEASED. Main/Corp Consejo Latinoamericano de Ciencias Sociales. Secretaria Ejecutiva. Periodical. AG. Spanish. sa. $23.00. Consejo Latinamericana de Ciencias Sociales, Callao 875, 3E Buenos Aires Argentina. Tel (44)8459. LC H62.5.L3. Boletin.

BOLETIN DE CIENCIAS ECONOMICAS Y SOCIALES. See Economics.

BOLETIN DE ESTUDIOS LATINOAMERICANOS Y DEL CARIBE. VFOAT Journal of Latin American and Caribbean Studies. No. 16- June 1974-. 0304-2634. Periodical. NE. English, French, Portuguese, or Spanish. sa. $21.56. Cedla, Keizersgracht 395-397, 1016 EK Amsterdam Netherlands. Tel (020)-5252521. Ed Peter Mason. Ind/Abst Am. Hist. Life, Hist. Abstr., Part A, Mod. Hist. Abstr., Hist. Abst., Part B, Twent. Century Abstr., Int. Labour Doc., Foreign Lang. Index, Public Aff. Inf. Serv. Bull., Hist. Abstr., PAIS Foreign Lang. Index. LC F1401. DD 980.005. bk rev. adv acc. Circ 1,600. Interpretative and comparative studies in social sciences of Latin America and the Caribbean (including anthropology, archaeology, economics, geography, history, and political science). Boletin de Estudios Latinoamericanos, 0006-6397.

BOLLETTINO DELLA DOXA. See Statistics.

BOOK REVIEW INDEX TO SOCIAL SCIENCE PERIODICALS. See Indexes/Abstracts.

BOTENJEU. (BOTENJEU : REPERTOIRE DES ORGANISMES IMPLIQUES AUPRES DES JEUNES). 1983-. 0828-6612. CN. French. an. Fondation pour l'Enfance et la Jeunesse Saguenay-Lac-St-Jean-Chibou Gamau, 711 rue Jacques-Cartier, Chicoutimi Quebec G7H 5B7 Canada. DD 305.2302571410.

BRIAR PATCH. Began publication 1970. 0703-8968. Periodical. CN. English. mo. $34.05. Briarpatch, Huston House/2138 McIntyre Street, Regina Saskatchewan S4P 2R7 Canada. Tel (306)525-2949. Ed Elizabeth Smillie. Ind/Abst Altern. Press Index. DD 330.97124. bk rev. adv acc. Circ 1,400. (ctrl). Alternative news and analysis on regional, national and international issues. Covers a broad range of issues including social policy, labor, women, environment, agriculture, third world, culture, peace, all from a progressive perspective.

BROOKINGS BULLETIN (WASHINGTON, D.C. : 1962) CEASED. (THE BROOKINGS BULLETIN). Began with spring 1962 issue. Ceased with V. 18, No. 3 and 4, winter-spring 1982. 0007-229X. Periodical. US. English. qt. Ind/Abst Predicasts, Index Free Period., Public Aff. Inf. Serv. Bull. LC H1. DD 300.5.

THE BROOKINGS REVIEW. Vol. 1, No. 1 (Fall 1982)-. 0745-1253. Periodical. US. English. qt. Brookings Institution, 1775 Massachusetts Avenue NW, Washington DC 20036. Ind/Abst Hospit. Lit. Index, Predicasts, ABI/Inform, Public Aff. Inf. Serv.

Social Sciences (General)

Bull., Energy Res. Abstr. LC H1. DD 300.5. *Brookings Bulletin (Washington, D.C. : 1962).*

BULLETIN ANALYTIQUE DE DOCUMENTATION POLITIQUE, ECONOMIQUE ET SOCIALE CONTEMPORAINE. Yearly Vol. 1- (May 1946)-. 0007-4071. Periodical. FR. French. mo. $38.58. Presses Foundation, National des Sciences Politiques, 27 rue Saint Guillaume, 75341 Paris Cedex 07 France. Tel 260-3960. Ind/Abst Popul. Index, Foreign Lang. Index, PAIS Foreign Lang. Index. LC Z7163. DD 016.3.

BULLETIN - CANADIAN COMMISSION FOR UNESCO. Main/Corp Canadian Commission for UNESCO. VFOAT Bulletin - Commission Canadienne pour l'UNESCO. V. 11, No. 2- Dec. 1968-. 0008-4557. CN. English (French). ir. Free. Canadian Commission for UNESCO, 99 Metcalfe Street/PO Box 1047, Ottawa Ontario Canada K1P 6L7. Tel (613)237-3400. Ed Olga Jurgens and Carmelia Quinn. LC AS4.U825. Circ 5,000. (ctrl). Covers activities of the Canadian Commission for UNESCO and UNESCO news of particular interest to Canadians.

BULLETIN - CONSEIL DU CIVISME DE MONTREAL. (BULLETIN). No. 1 (March 1978)-. 0229-4001. Periodical. CN. English (text in French). Free. Montreal Citizenship Council, 10025 Boulevard de l'Acadie, Montreal Quebec H4n 1L6 Canada. DD 305.800971.

BULLETIN D'ANALYSES DE LA LITTERATURE SCIENTIFIQUE BULGARE. CULTURE. VFOAT Culture. Vol. 25, No. 1-. Periodical. French. qt. Centre d'Information Scientifique, Pres l'Academie Bulgare des Sciences, 1 rue 7 Noemvri, Sofia Bulgaria. LC DR91. DD 306.094977. *Bulletin d'Analyses de la Litterature Scientifique Bulgare. Arts et Culture, 0205-0684.*

BULLETIN - DATA CLEARING HOUSE FOR THE SOCIAL SCIENCES CEASED. Main/Corp Data Clearing House for the Social Sciences. Nov. 1975-Spring 1978. 0383-140X. Periodical. CN. English (French). ir. Data Clearing House for the Social Sciences, 151 Slater Street, Ottawa K1P 5N1 Canada. DD 029.93005.

BULLETIN DE LIAISON DE DEMOGRAPHIE AFRICAINE. VFOAT Demographie Africaine. No. 29- Mar./April 1979-. Periodical. English (French). ir. Institut de Formation et de Recherche Demographiques, Service des Publications, B P 1556, Yaounde Cameroun. Ind/Abst Popul. Index. LC HB3661.A3. DD 304.6096. *Demographie Africaine.*

BULLETIN DE LIAISON : INVENTAIRE DESCRIPTIF DES UNITES DE RECHERCHE ET DE FORMATION EN SCIENCES SOCIALES, AMERIQUE LATINE. See Yearbooks, Almanacs, Directories.

BULLETIN - MADRAS INSTITUTE OF DEVELOPMENT STUDIES. Main/Corp Madras Institute of Development Studies. Periodical. II. English. ir. 74 Second Main Road, Gandhinagar Adyar Madras 20 India. LC HC431. DD 309.15405.

BULLETIN OF THE INSTITUTE OF TRADITIONAL CULTURES. Main/Corp Institute of Traditional Cultures. 1957-. 0541-7562. Periodical. II. English. sa. 20.00. University of Madras, Registrar, University Buildings, Chepauk Madras 600 005 India. LC AS472.M13. adv acc. Circ 250. Covers anthropology, dance, education (general), folklore, literature music, religion, sociology and history (general).

BUNKAGAKU NENPO (KOBE DAIGAKU. BUNKAGAKU KENKYUKA). See Humanities.

CAHIERS DE L'I.S.E.A. : SERIE M. Main/Corp Institut de Science Economique Appliquee. Series/Titl Economies et Societes. VFOAT Philosophie et Sciences de l'Homme. French. ir. Institut de Science Economique Appliquee, 11 Boulevard de Sebastopol, Paris France 75001. LC H31. DD 300.8. *Cahiers. Serie M: Recherches et Dialogue Philosophiques et Economiques.*

CAHIERS DE L'OBSERVATION DU CHANGEMENT SOCIAL. Vol. 1-. FR. French. ir. Editions du Centre National de la Recherche Scientifique, 15 Quai Anatole France, 75700 Paris France. LC HN421. DD 303.40944.

CAHIERS DES NATURALISTES. (CAHIERS DES NATURALISTES : BULLETIN DES NATURALISTES PARISIENS). N. S. V. 8, No. 1/2-. 0008-0039. Periodical. FR. French. qt. $22.62. Librairie du Museum Sarl, 36 rue Geoffery St Hilaire, 75005 Paris France. Ind/Abst GeoRef, Biol. Abstr. CODEN CNBNAN.

LES CAHIERS DU CEDAF. Main/Corp Centre d'Etude et de Documentation Africaines. 0008-9753. Periodical. BE. French. 2000. Centre d'Etude et de Documentation Africaines, Place Royale 7, 1000 Brussels Belgium. Tel (02)5129212. Ed Verhaegen Benoit. Ind/Abst Int. Labour Doc. LC DT1. Central and North Africa, social sciences, economics, education, and history of Africa.

CAHIERS VILFREDO PARETO. V. 1- 1963-. 0008-0497. Periodical. SZ. French. ir. Librarie Droz SA, 11 rue Massot, 1211 Geneva Switzerland. Ind/Abst Soc. Sci. Citation Index, Foreign Lang. Index, Lang. Lang. Behav. Abstr., Sociol. Abstr., PAIS Foreign Lang. Index. Circ 600. Social sciences.

CAIRO PAPERS IN SOCIAL SCIENCE. VFOAT Buhuth Al-Qahirah Fi Al-Ulum Al-Ijtima Iyah. V. 1- (Monograph 1-). Periodical. UA. English. ir. $25.00. American University of Cairo Press, 113 Sharia Dasr el Aini, Cario Egypt. Tel 3542969. Ed Nicholas S Hopkins. adv acc. Circ 300. Publishes results of indigenous research on social, economic, and political developments in the Middle East.

CAKRAWALA. No. 4- July/Aug. 1971-. Periodical. chiefly Indonesian. ir. 500. Lembaga Penelitian Ilmul-Ilmu Sosial, Universitas/Ikip Kristen Satya Wacana, Jalan P Diponegoro 54-58, Salatiga Indonesia. LC H62.5.I6. *Warta.*

THE CALIFORNIA POLL. 0195-4520. US. English. ir. $250.00. The Field Institute, 234 Front Street, San Francisco CA 94111. Tel (415)781-4921. Ed Mark DiCamillo. Circ 900. (ctrl). Regular statewide public opinion reports in California on political, social, economic and other topics.

CANADIAN JOURNAL OF BEHAVIORAL SCIENCE. See Psychology.

CANADIAN JOURNAL OF REGIONAL SCIENCE. (THE CANADIAN JOURNAL OF REGIONAL SCIENCE). VFOAT La Revue Canadienne des Sciences Regionales. V. 1- Spring 1978-. 0705-4580. Periodical. CN. English. sa. $23.21. Institute of Public Affairs, Dalhousie University, Halifax Nova Scotia B3H 3J5 Canada. Tel (902)424-2526. Ed William Coffey and Mario Polese. Ind/Abst Soc. Sci. Citation Index. DD 309.1715. bk rev. adv acc. Circ 500. Canadian regional development policy, policy and methods of regional analysis.

CANADIAN MEDIA DIRECTORS COUNCIL MEDIA DIGEST. (MEDIA DIGEST). VAT Media Digest - Canadian Media Directors Council. Began with V. for 1971/72?. 0829-1888. CN. English. an. $5.00 Per Volume. Canadian Media Directors Council, 481 University Avenue, Toronto Ontario M5W 1A7 Canada. DD 302.2340971.

CANADIAN SOCIAL SCIENCE DATA CATALOG. 1st- Ed. CN. English. ir. York University/Institute for Behavioral Research, 4700 Keele Street, Downsview Ontario M3J 2R6 Canada. Tel (416)667-3026.

EL CARABO. No. 1-. Periodical. Spanish. ir. 1,000. Secisa, Apartado 1315, Madrid Spain. LC H8.

CARINDEX, SOCIAL SCIENCES CEASED. V. 1- Jan. 1977-. TR. English. sa. $45.00. Carindes, c/o The Library, University of West Indies, St Augustine Trinidad. Ed Shirley Evelyn. LC Z7163. DD 016.3009729. Circ 100. Index to journals and newspapers published in the Englsih speaking Caribbean.

CARITAS. ZEITSCHRIFT FUR DIE WERKE DER NACHSTENLIEBE IM KATHOLISCHEN DEUTSCHLAND. 1910-. Periodical. GW. German. bm. Lambertus Verlag, Postfach 1026, D78 Freiburg West Germany. Ind/Abst Soc. Sci. Citation Index.

CASE ANALYSIS IN SOCIAL SCIENCE N SOCIAL THERAPY. VFOAT Case Analysis. V. 1- Fall/Winter 1977/78-. 0149-6948. Periodical. US. English. ir. $25.00. Progressive Publisher, 401 East 32 #1002, Chicago IL 60618. Tel (312)225-9181. Ed Kenneth Ives. Ind/Abst Sociol. Abstr., Psychol. Abstr. LC HM1. DD 301.072. bk rev. Circ 100. Case studies from various fields, thoroughly analyzed. Factors and frameworks for case comparisons, inductive methods for developing theory from data.

CASOPIS MORAVSKEHO MUZEA V BRNE. VEDY SPOLECENSK. VFOAT Acta Musei Moraviae. Scientiae Sociales. 37 (1952)-61 (1976). 0521-2367. Periodical. CS. Czech (some material in English or German with some summaries in French or Russian). an. $29.40. Artia, PO Box 790, Ve-Smeckach 30, Praha 1 Czechoslovakia. Ind/Abst GeoRef, Life Sci. Collect. *Casopis Moravskeho Musea V Brne. Vedy Spolecenske.*

CATALOGO COLETIVO DE PUBLICACOES PERIODICAS EM CIENCIAS SOCIAIS E HUMANIDADES. Portuguese. ir. LC Z7161, H1. DD 016.3005.

THE CATO JOURNAL. Vol. 1, No. 1 (Soring 1981)-. 0273-3072. Periodical. US. English. ty. $18.00. Cato Institute, 224 Second Street SE, Washington DC 20003. Tel (202)546-0200. Ind/Abst Am. Hist. Life, Hist. Abstr., Energy Inf. Abstr., Environ. Abstr., ABC Pol Sci, ABI/Inform, Curr. Contents, Soc. Behav. Sci., Soc. Sci. Citation Index, Public Aff. Inf. Serv. Bull., Energy Res. Abstr. LC H1. DD 361.6105. Issued also in microform by University Microfilms International.

CENTER FOR POLICY RESEARCH MONOGRAPH SERIES. Vol. 1 (1980)-. 0731-809X. Monographic Series. US. English. ir. Human Sciences Press, 72 Fifth Avenue, New York NY 10011.

THE CENTER MAGAZINE. V. 1- Oct./Nov. 1967-. 0008-9125. Periodical. US. English. bm. $15.00 Members. The Center, University of California, Box 4068, Santa Barbara CA 93103. Ind/Abst Am. Hist. Life, Hist. Abstr., Part A, Mod. Hist. Abstr., Hist. Abst., Part B, Twent. Century Abstr., Pop. Mag. Rev., Public Aff. Inf. Serv. Bull., Read. Guide Period. Lit., Soc. Sci. Index, Women Stud. Abstr., Writ. Am. Hist., Energy Inf. Abstr., Environ. Abstr. LC H11. Available on microform. *Center Diary, 0577-0165.*

CENTERPOINT. V. 1- Spring 1974-. 0098-924X. Periodical. US. English. qt. $10.00. Centerpoint, Room 427/Graduate School University Center of the City University of New York, 33 West 42nd Street, New York NY 10036. Ind/Abst MLA Int. Bibliogr. Books Artic. Mod. Lang. Lit., Psychol. Abstr., Sociol. Abstr., Soc. Welf. Soc. Plan./Policy Soc. Dev., Music Index, Recent Publ. Artic., Am. Hist. Life, Hist. Abstr., Part A, Mod. Hist. Abstr., Hist. Abst., Part B, Twent. Century Abstr. LC AP2. DD 051.

THE CENTRE FOR DEVELOPMENT RESEARCH AND OTHER SOCIAL SCIENCE DEVELOPMENT RESEARCH IN DENMARK. See Economics.

CEPAL REVIEW. See Economics.

LE C.E.S.A.O. AUJOURD'HUI. Main/Corp Centre d'Etudes Economiques et Sociales d'Afrique Occidentale. French. ir. Centre d'Etudes Economiques et Sociales d'Afrique Occidentale, B P 305, Bobo-Dioulasso Upper Volta. LC H62.5.A343. DD 309.223266.

CHAYU AKADEMI YON'GU NONCHONG. VFOAT Journal of Freedom Academy. V. 1- Series. Periodical. KO. Korean. ir. Chayu Akademi, San 1 Sokkwan-dong Songbuk-ku, Seoul Korea. LC H8.

CHE-CHIANG HSUEH KAN. VFOAT Zhejiangxuekan. Periodical. CH. Chinese. bm. 4.80. Post Office, Hang-chou Shih China. LC AS451. DD 089.951. bk rev. adv acc. Circ 3,000. A comprehensive academic and theoretical magazine directed by Provincial Academy of Social Sciences of Zhejiang. Facing to whole China, it reflects the subjects with local characteristics of Zhejiang as well.

CHIANG-HSI SHE HUI KO HSUEH. VFOAT Jiangxi Shehui Kexue. Periodical. CH. Chinese. bm. 0.35. Post Office, Nan-chang Shih China. LC H8.C47. DD 300.5.

CHICOREL INDEX TO ABSTRACTING AND INDEXING SERVICES. PERIODICALS IN HUMANITIES AND THE SOCIAL SCIENCES. See Indexes/Abstracts.

CHILD DEVELOPMENT ABSTRACTS AND BIBLIOGRAPHY. See Indexes/Abstracts.

Social Sciences (General)

CHINA AND US. 0191-3166. US. English. bm. China-US-China Friendship Association, 41 North Union Square West/Room 1228, New York NY 10003. Tel (212)255-4727. LC E183.8.C5. DD 301.2973051.

CHINA EXCHANGE NEWS. V. 8, No. 1- Feb. 1980-. 0272-0086. Periodical. US. English. qt. CSCPRC, National Academy of Sciences, 2101 Constitution Avenue, Washington DC 20418. Ind/Abst GeoRef. LC E183.8.C5. DD 303.482. *China Exchange Newsletter, 0145-6318.*

CHO'N-TRO'I. VFOAT Horizon. VAT Horizon (Sherbrooke). April 4, 1982-. 0713-4002. Periodical. CN. French (Vietnamese). $0.50 Per Number. Chon-Tro'l, c/o 4345 rue Brunalt, Sherbrooke Quebec J1L 1S7 Canada. DD 305.89592071.

CHON'GUK TAEHAKSAENG HAKSUL YON'GU PALPYO NONMUNJIP : SAHOE KWAHAK PUNYA. KO. Korean. ir. Songagungwan Taehakkyo Hakto Hoguktan, 53-3-ka Myongnyun-dong, Chongno-u Seoul South Korea. LC H8.

CHRISTIAN PEACE CONFERENCE. *See* Religion, Mythology, Rationalism.

CHUGOKU KENKYU GEPPO. May 1960-. Periodical. JA. Japanese. mo. $96.00 US. Maruzen Company Ltd, PO Box 5050, 100-31 Tokyo Japan. (ctrl). Study of China. *Chugoku Shiryo Geppo.*

CHUNG-KUO SHE HUI KO HSUEH. VFOAT Zhongguo Shehui Kexue. Periodical. CC. Chinese. bm. 1.10. Chung-Kuo Kuo Chi Shu Tien, PO Box 2820, Peking China Mainland. LC H8.C47. DD 300.5.

CIENCIA (MEXICO CITY, MEXICO). *See* Science (General).

CIENCIAS HUMANAS. V. 1- April/July 1977-. Periodical. Portuguese. ir. $8.00. Universidade Gama Filho, rua Manoek Vitorino, 625 Piedade Brazil. LC AP66.

CIRES, CAHIERS IVOIRIENS DE RECHERCHE ECONOMIQUE ET SOCIALE. Main/Corp Abidjan, Ivory Coast. Universite. VFOAT Cahiers Ivoiriens de Recherche Economique et Sociale. VAT Cahiers Ivoiriens de Recherche Economique et Sociale, Cahiers Ivoiriens de Recherche Economique et Sociale. No. 1- 1970-. IV. French. qt. Univ Nationale Cote Ivoire Ctr, Ivoiriensrech Econ Social, BOV 34, Abidjan Ivory Coast. Ind/Abst Int. Labour Doc., Foreign Lang. Index. LC HC501. DD 309.1600305.

CLASE. *See* Indexes/Abstracts.

COLECCION CIENCIAS SOCIALES. Main/Corp Universidad Central de Venezuela. V. 1- 1961-. 0505-172X. VE. Spanish. ir. Editions de la Bibleteca, Universidad of Central Venezuela, Caracas Venzuela.

COLECCION ESTUDIOS CIEPLAN. *See* Economics.

COLLAGE MAGAZINE. VAT Collage (Calgary). Vol. 1, Issue 1 (Feb. 1984)-. 0828-4016. Periodical. CN. English. mo. Free(Calgary). Collage Magazine, 9848 Oakhill Drive Southwest, Calgary Alberta T2V 3X Canada. DD 305.800971233. (ctrl).

COLLECTION SCIENCES SOCIALES DU TRAVAIL. VFOAT Sciences Sociales du Travail. 1-. 0588-2478. Monographic Series. FR. French. ir. Librairie Armand Colin, 103 Bd St Michel, 75005 Paris Cedex 5 France.

COLORADO PROSPECTOR. *See* History (General) - History of North, South, and Central America.

COLUMBIA JOURNAL OF LAW AND SOCIAL PROBLEMS. *See* Law.

COMMUNITY DEVELOPMENT JOURNAL. V. 1- Jan. 1966-. 0010-3802. Periodical. UK. English. qt. $38. Oxford University Press, Walton Street, Oxford OX2 6DP England. Tel 0632 367142. Ed Gary Craig. Ind/Abst Int. Labour Doc., Sociol. Abstr., Soc. Welf. Soc. Plan./Policy Soc. Dev., Soc. Work Res. Abstr., Public Aff. Inf. Serv. Bull., Curr. Index J. Educ., Lang. Lang. Behav. Abstr., Soc. Sci. Citation Index. LC HN1. bk rev. adv acc. Circ 1,500. (ctrl). An international forum for community development linking theory and practice. *Community Development Bulletin.*

COMMUNITY HEALTH STUDIES. *See* Public Health and Safety.

COMMUNITY REVIEW. (COMMUNITY REVIEW : CR). 0163-8475. Periodical. US. English. sa. $6.50. Transaction Periodicals Consortium, Rutgers University, Department 2000, New Brunswick NJ 08903. Tel (201)932-2280. Ed Kenneth Peeples Jr. LC AS30. DD 051. bk rev. adv acc. Circ 2,000. Provides a wide range of topics including specialized sections on experimental programs, curriculum, population, conference news, and book reviews. *La Guardia Review.*

COMPANIONS OF THE TERRY FOX CANADIAN YOUTH CENTRE. VFOAT Compagnons du Centre Terry Fox de la Jeunesse Canadienne. 1 (June 1983)-. 0823-0455. Periodical. CN. English (French). sa. Free. Terry Fox Canadian Youth Centre, PO Box 7279, Ottawa Ontario K1L 8E3 Canada. DD 305.2306071. (ctrl).

COMPARATIVE POLITICS (GUILFORD, CONN.). *See* Political Science.

COMPARATIVE STUDIES IN SOCIETY AND HISTORY. V. 1- Oct. 1958-. 0010-4175. Periodical. UK. English. qt $57.00. Cambridge University Press, 510 North Avenue, New Rochelle NY 10801. Tel (914)235-0300. Ed Raymond Grew and Eric R Wolf. Ind/Abst Am. Hist. Life, Hist. Abstr., Part A, Mod. Hist. Abstr., Hist. Abstr., Part B, Twent. Century Abstr., ABC Pol Sci, Humanit. Index, Soc. Sci. Citation Index, Soc. Welf. Soc. Plan./Policy Soc. Dev., Sociol. Abstr., Writ. Am. Hist., Recent Publ. Artic., Lang. Lang. Behav. Abstr. LC H1. DD 305. (cum index). bk rev. Publishes the work of authors from throughout the world in many disciplines-including history, sociology, anthropology, political science, law, economics, and the humanities.

COMPUTERS AND THE SOCIAL SCIENCES. VFOAT CASS. 0748-9269. Periodical. US. English. qt. $75.00. Paradigm Press, PO Box 1057, Osprey FL 33559-1057. Tel (813)922-7666. Ed Ronald E Anderson. bk rev. adv acc. Creative applications of computers among social scientists, research into the impact of computers on society. Reviews of software, hardware and books.

CONFRONTATION/CHANGE LITERARY REVIEW. VFOAT Confrontation/Change Review. V. 1- Fall/Winter 1976-. 0363-9460. Periodical. US. English. qt. $10.00. Confrontation/Change Review, 1107 Lexington Avenue, Dayton OH 45407-1608. Tel (513)275-6879. Ed F M Finney. bk rev. adv acc. Circ 2,000. A journal of social and applied economics, political science fiction and book reviews. Focus on blacks and Third World international affairs.

CONTEMPORARY SOCIAL SCIENCES. V. 1- Jan./March 1972-. Periodical. II. English. ir. A 14 Green Park Extension, New Delhi 16 India. LC H8. DD 300.

CONTRAPONTO. Yearly V. 1- Nov. 1976-. Portuguese. ir. Centro de Estudos Noel Nutels, rua Aurelino Leal 38 30 Andar Caixa Postal, Niteroi Brazil. LC H8. DD 300.5.

CONTRIBUTIONS A L'HISTOIRE ECONOMIQUE ET SOCIALE. Main/Corp Brussels. Universite Libre. Centre d'Historie Economique et Sociale. V.1- 1962-. 0524-7926. BE. French. ir. Editions de Univ, Bruxelles Avenue Paul Heger 26 B, 1050 Bruxelles Belgium.

CONVERSATIONS. *See* Sociology: General Works, Theory - Social Pathology, Welfare, Criminology.

THE CORNELL JOURNAL OF SOCIAL RELATIONS. V. 1- Spring 1966-. 0010-8820. Periodical. US. English. sa. $2.00. Cornell University/Uris Hall, Department of Sociology, Ithaca NY 14853. Ind/Abst Sociol. Abstr., Soc. Welf. Soc. Plan./Policy Soc. Dev., Psychol. Abstr., Lang. Lang. Behav. Abstr. LC H1. DD 300.5. CODEN CJSRAO.

COSSA WASHINGTON UPDATE. VFOAT C.O.S.S.A. Washington Update. VAT Consortium of Social Science Associations Washington Update. 0749-4394. Periodical. US. English. bm. $90.00. Consortium of Social Science Associations, 1200 Seventeenth Street NW/Suite 520, Washington DC 20036. DD 300.

COUNCIL UPDATE. Main/Corp Social Sciences and Humanities Research Council of Canada. VFOAT Quoi de Neuf au Conseil?. Began publication in 1979?. 0225-1787. Periodical. CN. English (French). Free. Social Sciences and Humanities Research Council of Canada, Office of the Director of Information, 255 Albert Street, PO Box 1610, Ottawa Ontario K1P 6G4 Canada. DD 354.710085.

COURRIER ROUMAIN. (LE COURRIER ROUMAIN). 0827-4045. Periodical. CN. French (text in French and Romanian). ir. Federation des Associations Roumaines du Canada, 3500 rue Fullum, Montreal Quebec H2K 3P6 Canada. DD 305.859071.

CRIMINAL JUSTICE. *See* Law Enforcement.

CRIMINAL LAW MONTHLY (HOUSTON, TEX.). *See* Law.

CRITICA & I.E. Y UTOPIA LATINOAMERICANA DE CIENCIAS SOCIALES. VFOAT Critica & I.E. Y Utopia. 1-. Periodical. AG. Spanish. ir. Critica and Utopia, Alsina 500-2O Piso, 1087 Buenos Aires Argentina. LC H8.S7.

CRUCIBLE. *See* Religion, Mythology, Rationalism - Theology.

CSSSC MONOGRAPH. VFOAT C.S.S.S.C. Monograph. 1-. Monographic Series. II. English. ir. Registrar, Centre for Studies in Social Sciences Calcutta, 10 Lake Terrace, Calcutta 700 029 India.

CUADERNOS DE COMUNICACION & INFORMACION. *See* Literature.

CUADERNOS POLITICOS. No. 1- July/Sept. 1974-. Periodical. MX. Spanish. qt. $18.00. Ediciones Era, Apartado Postal 74-092, Avena 102, 09810 Mexico DF Mexico. Tel 581-77-44. LC F1414.2. adv acc. Circ 3,000. Journal for political and social analyses especially for the Latin American countries.

CULTURA LUDENS. I:1-. 0882-3049. Monographic Series. US. English. John Benjamins North America Inc, One Buttonwood Square, Philadelphia PA 19130. Tel (215)564-6379. Ed Mihai Spariosu. DD 306. Focuses on interrelationship of play and initiation in western culture, treating them as broad cultural phenomena and key concepts in the direction of our civilization.

CULTURAL CRITIQUE. No. 1 (Fall 1985)-. 0882-4371. Periodical. US. English. ty. $30.00. Telos Press, 431 East 12th Street, New York NY 10009. DD 306.

CULTURES AU ZAIRE ET EN AFRIQUE. 1973-. 0302-5640. Periodical. CG. French. qt. $16.00. Office National de la Recherche et du Development, BP 16706, 1 Kinshasa Congo Zaire. LC DT641. DD 916.7510305. *Dombi.*

CURRENT CONTENTS OF ACADEMIC JOURNALS IN JAPAN. HUMANITIES AND SOCIAL SCIENCES. *See* Humanities.

CURRENT CONTENTS. SOCIAL & BEHAVIORAL SCIENCES. VFOAT Social & Behavioral Sciences. VAT Current Contents. Social and Behavioral Sciences. V. 6, No. 2- Jan. 2, 1974-. 0092-6361. US. English. wk. $325.00. Institute for Scientific Information, 3501 Market Street, University City of Science, Philadelphia PA 19184. Tel (800)523-1850. Ind/Abst Popul. Index, Sci. Cit. Index, Abr. Ed., Soc. Sci. Citation Index. NLM Z 7161 C976. *Current Contents. Behavioral, Social & Educational Sciences, 0011-3387.*

CURRENT DEVELOPMENTS IN THE SOVIET UNION AND EASTERN EUROPE. BUSINESS ROUNDTABLES . . . . *See* Business - Commerce.

CURRENT ISSUES. *See* Political Science.

CURRENT RESEARCH PROJECTS. Main/Corp Industriens Utredningsinstitutet, Stockholm. English. ir. Industriens Utredningsinstitut, Grevgatan 34 Box 5037, S-102 41 Stockholm Sweden. LC H62.5.S8. DD 330.0720485.

CURRENT WORLD LEADERS. *See* Political Science - International Relations.

DATA BOOK OF SOCIAL STUDIES MATERIALS AND RESOURCES. Began with: Vol. 5, 1980. 0747-4857. US. English. an. $10.00. Social Science Education Consortium, 855 Broadway, Boulder CO 80302. Tel (303)492-8154. Ed Ann M Williams. LC HG1. DD 300.7. Circ 400. Vol. (8-) distributed to depository libraries in microfiche. Analyses of elementary and secondary social studies, social science textbooks, teacher resources, supplementary materials, non-print materials and ERIC documents. *Social Studies Materials and Resources Data Book.*

Social Sciences (General)

DDR-PUBLIKATIONEN ZUR IMPERIALISMUSFORSCHUNG, AUSWAHLBIBLIOGRAPHIE. See Bibliographies.

DEBATE & I.E. E CRITICA. No. 1- July/Dec. 1973-. Portuguese. ir. Editora de Humanismo Ciencia e Tecnologia Hucitec, rua Conde de Sarzedas 38, Sao Paulo Brazil. LC H8. DD 300.5.

DERECHO Y CIENCIAS SOCIALES (UNIVERSIDAD AUTONOMA DE NUEVO LEON. FACULTAD DE DERECHO Y CIENCIAS SOCIALES). See Law.

DESARROLLO ECONOMICO. V. 1- (No. 1-). 0046-001X. Periodical. AG. Spanish. qt. $44.00. Instituto de Desarrollo Economico, Guemes 3950, 1425 Buenos Aires Argentina. Ind/Abst Am. Hist. Life, Hist. Abstr., Int. Labour Doc., Sociol. Abstr., Soc. Welf. Soc. Plan./Policy Soc. Dev., Foreign Lang. Index, Lang. Lang. Behav. Abstr., Hist. Abstr., Part A, Mod. Hist. Abstr., Hist. Abst., Part B, Twent. Century Abstr. LC HD85.S7. (cum index). bk rev. adv acc. Circ 2,000. (ctrl). Covers social sciences, economics, political science, history and social anthropology.

DEUTSCHE JUGEND. Year 1- Apr. 1953-. 0012-0332. Periodical. GW. German. mo. 55.00. Juventa Verlag GMBH, Boecklinstrasse 34, 8000 Muenchen 19 West Germany. Tel 02161/551535. Ed Gerd Brenner. bk rev. adv acc. Circ 4,000. (ctrl). Youth, social work, problems of adolescence, sociology and psychology of adolescence, politics concerning adolescents. A practical guide to social work.

DEVELOPMENT AND CHANGE. V. 1, No. 1- 1969-. 0012-155X. Periodical. US. English. ty. $59.76. Sage Publications Inc, 28 Banner Street, London EC1Y 8QE England. Tel 01-253-1516. Ind/Abst Curr. Contents, Am. Hist. Life, Hist. Abstr., Part A, Mod. Hist. Abstr., Hist. Abst., Part B, Twent. Century Abstr., Int. Labour Doc., Energy Inf. Abstr., Environ. Abstr., ABC Pol Sci, Recent Publ. Artic., Bibliogr. Agric., Soc. Sci. Citation Index, Hist. Abstr. LC HD82. DD 309.205.

THE DILIMAN REVIEW. See Journalism.

DIMENSIONS ECONOMIQUES DE LA BOURGOGNE. See Statistics.

DIRECTORIO INTERAMERICANO DE INSTITUCIONES DE INVESTIGACION Y DESARROLLO. See Yearbooks, Almanacs, Directories.

DIRECTORY OF CROSS-CULTURAL RESEARCH AND RESEARCHERS. See Yearbooks, Almanacs, Directories.

DISCOVERY (SANTA FE, N.M.). (DISCOVERY). 0277-4542. US. English. an. School of American Research, PO Box 2188, Santa Fe NM 87501. LC E78.S7. DD 306.0899707905.

DISSERTATIES MAATSCHAPPIJWETENSCHAPPEN. Main/Corp Sociaal-Wetenschappelijk Informatie- en Documentatiecentrum (Koninklijke Nederlandse Akademie van Wetenschappen). 1972/73-. NE. Dutch an. 10.00. Noord-Hollandsche Uitgevers Maatschappij, Keizersgracht 569-571, Amsterdam Netherlands. LC H62.A1. *Dissertaties Maatschappijwetenschappen*.

DOKUMENTATIONSDIENST LATEINAMERIKA. See Bibliographies.

DOKUMENTE; ZEITSCHRIFT FUR UBERNATIONALE ZUSAMMENARBEIT. Vol. 1-. 0012-5172. Periodical. German. qt. Ind/Abst Foreign Lang. Index. LC H5.

DROIT POPULAIRE. (LE DROIT POPULAIRE). V. 1- July 1972-. 0384-6008. Periodical. CN. French. mo. Free. Association pour la Defense des Droits Sociaux du Montreal Metropolitan, 1850 Est rue Ontario, Montreal Quebec H2K 1T7 Canada. DD 309.1714281.

ECONOMIA Y CIENCIAS SOCIALES. Began with Sept. 1958 issue. (Sept. 1958). 0505-1797. Periodical. VE. Spanish. ir. University Central de Venezuela, Faculty Economia Institute de Inves, Caracas Venezuela. Ind/Abst Am. Hist. Life, Hist. Abstr., Part A, Mod. Hist. Abstr., Hist. Abst., Part B, Twent. Century Abstr., Lang. Lang. Behav. Abstr., Sociol. Abstr., Hist. Abstr. LC H8.S7. DD 300.5.

THE ECONOMIC AND SOCIAL REVIEW. V. 1- Oct. 1969-. 0012-9984. Periodical. IE. English. qt. $32.00. Economic & Social Studies, 4 Burlington Road, Dublin 4 Ireland. Tel 760115. Ed D Conniffee, T Garvin and B M Marsh. Ind/Abst Am. Hist. Life, Hist. Abstr., Part A, Mod. Hist. Abstr., Hist. Abst., Part B, Twent. Century Abstr., Manage. Contents, Index Econ. Artic. J. Collect. Vol., Public Aff. Inf. Serv. Bull., Soc. Sci. Citation Index, Hist. Abstr. LC HC257.16. DD 309.1415. bk rev. Circ 300. A journal of the social sciences with topics including economics, sociology, demography, politics, social geography, statistics and psychology.

ECONOMIC AND SOCIAL STUDIES. No. 1-. Monographic Series. UK. English. ir. Cambridge University Press, 510 North Avenue, New Rochelle NY 10801.

ECONOMY AND SOCIETY. V. 1- Feb. 1972-. 0308-5147. Periodical. UK. English. qt. 30.00 UK and World, 55.00 US. Routledge & Kegal Paul Inc, Broadway House/Newtown Road, Henley-on-Thames England RG9 1EN England. Tel 0491578321. Ed HM Gane. Ind/Abst Sociol. Abstr., Soc. Welf. Soc. Plan./Policy Soc. Dev., Soc. Sci. Citation Index, Lang. Lang. Behav. Abstr. LC H1. DD 300.5. bk rev. adv acc. Circ 1,000. A journal for Marxist scholarships and analysis of the social sciences, with particular emphasis on philosophical and political debate.

EDITORIAL RESEARCH REPORTS. 0013-0958. Periodical. US. English. wk. Congressional Quarterly Inc, 1414-22nd Street NW, Washington DC 20037. Tel (202)887-8500. Ind/Abst Coal Abstr., Public Aff. Inf. Serv. Bull., Nexis, Energy Res. Abstr. LC H35.

EDUCATION & SOCIAL SCIENCE. See Education (General).

EIDOS. (EIDOS : THE JOURNAL OF AWARD-WINNING ESSAYS IN THE FACULTY OF SOCIAL SCIENCE). Vol. 1 (Sept. 1983)-. 0824-6645. CN. English. an. $5.00. Social Science Students' Union, Room 3255 University of Western Ontario, London Ontario N6A 5C2 Canada. DD 300.5.

DIE EINHEIT DER GESELLSCHAFTSWISSENSCHAFTEN. V. 1- 1964-. 0424-6985. Monographic Series. GW. German. ir. JCB Mohr, Paul Siebeck, Postfach 2040, 7400 Tuebingen West Germany.

EMPIRISCHE SOZIALFORSCHUNG. VFOAT Empirical Social Research. 1968-. GW. German. ir. K G Saur Verlag, Postfach 711009, Possenbacherstr 2B, D8000 Muenchen 71 West Germany. Tel (089) 798901.

EN. EVALUATION NEWS. VFOAT Evaluation News. 0191-8036. Periodical. US. English. qt. Sage Publications, 275 South Beverly Drive, Beverly Hills CA 90212. Tel (213)836-5172.

ENCYCLIA. See Science (General).

ENSAYOS. VFOAT Coleccion Ensayos. 1-. Periodical. Spanish. ir. Editora Debates, Simon Bolivar, 5870 - K Santiago Chile. LC H8.

ENTRE NOUS. First issue in 1975?. 0705-0631. Periodical. CN. French. ir. Free. CRD-04, 1617 rue Royale, Trois-Rivieres G9A 4K2 Canada. DD 309.250971445.

ENVIRONMENT AND PLANNING. D, SOCIETY & SPACE. VFOAT Society & Space. Vol. 1, No. 1 (Mar. 1983)-. 0263-7758. Periodical. UK. English. qt. 90.00. Pion Ltd, 207 Brondesbury Park, London NW2 5JN England. Tel (01)459-0066. Ed M Dear. LC H1. DD 300.5. bk rev. adv acc. Development of social theory in the explanation of time-space relationships. Covers topics such as the state, deindustrialisation, uneven development, labor markets, social welfare, housing, and planning.

EPITHEORESE TON EUROPAIKON KOINOTETON. VFOAT Revue des Communautes Europeennes. Periodical. Greek, Modern (summaries in French). qt. $75.00. Europublishing Ltd, 6 rue Kriezotou, Athenes 134 Greece. LC H8.G74.

EPITHEORESIS KOINONIKON EREUNON. 1- July/Sept. 1969-. Periodical. GR. Greek, Modern. ir. $2.50. EKD Ethnikou Kentrou Koinikon Ereunon, Veranzerou 23A, Athens (102) Greece. Ind/Abst Sociol. Abstr. LC H8.

ESPANA, PANORAMICA SOCIAL. Main/Corp Spain. Instituto Nacional de Estadistica. 1974-. SP. Spanish. ir. Instituto Nacional de Estadistica, AVDA Generalismo 91, Madria 16 Spain. LC HN584. DD 309.146082.

ESTIMATES. PART III, SOCIAL SCIENCES AND HUMANITIES RESEARCH COUNCIL (CANADA). VFOAT Budget des Depenses. CN. English (French). $6.00 Domestic, $7.20 Foreign. Canadian Government Publishing Centre, Supply and Services Canada, Ottawa Ontario K1A 0S9 Canada.

ESTUDIOS CEDES. VAT Estudios Centro de Estudios de Estado y Sociedad. V. 1-. Monographic Series. AG. Spanish. ir. Centro de Estudios de Estado y Sociedad, Av Pueyrredon 510-7, 1032 Buenos Aires Argentina. Tel 87-2496. Circ 2,000. (ctrl). Dissemination of results of research carried out in CEDES in the following areas: social sciences, politics, economics, history and public administration.

ESTUDIOS DE ASIA Y AFRICA. V. 10- 1975-. 0185-0164. Periodical. MX. Spanish. qt. $26.00. Colegio de Mexico, Camino Al, Ajusco 20 Pedregal Sta Teresa, 10740 Mexico D F Mexico. Tel 568-60-33. Ed Flora Botton. Ind/Abst Am. Hist. Life, Hist. Abstr., Part A, Mod. Hist. Abstr., Hist. Abst., Part B, Twent. Century Abstr., MLA Int. Bibliogr. Books Artic. Mod. Lang. Lit., Hist. Abstr. LC DS1. DD 950.05. bk rev. Circ 1,500. Social sciences and literature of Asia (Far East, Near East) and Africa. *Estudios Orientales*, 0185-0156.

ESTUDIOS DE HISTORIA DE LAS INSTITUCIONES POLITICAS Y SOCIALES. No. 1- Yearly V. 1966-. 0425-3558. CL. Spanish. ir. Av R Lyon Casilla 4256, Santiago Chile. LC JL2603. DD 309.18308.

ESTUDIOS SOCIALES CENTROAMERICANOS. Vol. 1- Jan./Apr. 1972-. 0303-9676. Periodical. CR. Spanish. ty. $23.00. Secretaria de la Revista, Apartado 37, Ciudad University, Rodrigo Jac, San Jose Costa Rica. Ind/Abst Am. Hist. Life, Hist. Abstr., Part A, Mod. Hist. Abstr., Hist. Abst., Part B, Twent. Century Abstr., Int. Labour Doc., Foreign Lang. Index, Soc. Sci. Citation Index, Hist. Abstr., PAIS Foreign Lang. Index. LC HN121.

ESTUDIOS SOCIALES (SANTIAGO, CHILE). (ESTUDIOS SOCIALES). Began in Mar. 1973. 1696-0321. Periodical. CL. Spanish. qt. $28.00. Corporacion de Promocion, Universitaria Avenida Miguel Claro, 1460 Santiago Chile.

ETHNIKE ANASYNKROTESIS. Greek, Modern. ir. 10.00. Leoph Panepistemiou 34 & Hippokratous 1, Athenai Greece. LC H8.

ETUDES & I.E. ET EXPANSION CEASED. VAT Etudes et Expansion. 75.-79. Year (No 269-286). Periodical. French. ir. 12 Avenue Rogier, 4000 Belgium. LC H3. DD 300.5. *Revue de la Societe d'Etudes et d'Expansion*.

ETUDES RURALES. No. 57 (Jan./Mar. 1975)-. 0014-2182. Periodical. French. qt. 274.50 Domestic, 346.50 Foreign. Europeriodiques SA, B P 104, 78191 Trappes Cedex France. Tel (1)30 62 93 86. Ind/Abst Int. Labour Doc., Sociol. Abstr., Soc. Welf. Soc. Plan./Policy Soc. Dev., Soc. Sci. Citation Index, Am. Hist. Life, Hist. Abstr., Lang. Lang. Behav. Abstr. LC HN1. *Etudes Rurales*.

EVALUATION AND PROGRAM PLANNING. VFOAT Journal of Evaluation and Program Planning. V. 1- Jan. 1978-. 0149-7189. Periodical. US. English. qt. Pergamon Press, 395 Sawmill River Road, Elmsford NY 10523. Ind/Abst Hospit. Lit. Index, Sociol. Abstr., Soc. Welf. Soc. Plan./Policy Soc. Dev., Excerpta Med., Cumul. Index Nurs. Allied Health Lit., Psychol. Abstr., Curr. Index J. Educ. LC H62.A1. DD 300.72. NLM W1 EV13G. Available on microfilm and microfiche from Pergamon Press and its division, Microforms International Marketing Company.

EVALUATION STUDIES REVIEW ANNUAL. V. 1- 1976-. 0364-7390. US. English. an. Sage Publicatons, 275 South Beverly Drive, Beverly Hills CA 90212. LC H1. DD SOCIOLOGY. NLM W1 EV131J.

EXECUTIVE MEMORANDUM - HERITAGE FOUNDATION (WASHINGTON D.C.). (EXECUTIVE MEMORANDUM). No. 1 (7/19/82)-. 8755-433X. Periodical. US. English. The Heritage Foundation, 513 C Street NE, Washington DC 20002. DD 300.

FLORIDA ENVIRONMENTAL AND URBAN ISSUES. V. 1- 1973-. 0145-5885. Periodical. US. English. qt. Free. Editor Florida Environmental & Urban Issues, Fau Fiu Joint Central,

Social Sciences (General)

1515 West Commerce Boulevard, Ft Lauderdale FL 33309. **Tel** (305)776-1240. **Ed** W DeHaven-Smith. **Ind/Abst** Public Aff. Inf. Serv. Bull. **LC** HC107.F63. **DD** 333.709759. bk rev. **Circ** 1,400. Presents articles that contribute to the understanding and solution of problems relating to growth, the environment and urbanization. *Florida Planning and Development, 0015-4210.*

FOCUS. V. 1- June 1977-. Periodical. English. ir. 36.00. Collective, 26 Clifford Avenue, Colombo Sri Lanka. **LC** H1. **DD** 300.5.

FOCUS (NEW BRUNSWICK TEACHERS' ASSOCIATION. SOCIAL STUDIES COUNCIL). (FOCUS). Vol. 7, No. 2 (Jan. 1977)-. 0710-7692. Periodical. CN. English. ty. Free. New Brunswick Teachers' Association, PO Box 752, Fredericton New Brunswick E3B 5R6 Canada. **Ind/Abst** Can. Educ. Index. **DD** 300.70715. (ctrl) *Social Studies News, 0710-7684.*

FOHN. Periodical. German. ir. 30.00 Single Issue. Gruppe Fohn, Adolf-Pichler-Platz 6, 6020 Innsbruck Austria. **LC** HQ799.G53. **DD** 305.23509431.

FOREIGN AND COMPARATIVE STUDIES : LATIN AMERICAN SERIES. VFOAT Latin American Series. 1-5. Monographic Series. English. ir. **Tel** (315)423-2552. Scholarly monographs: political science, history, economics, linguistics, anthropology, literature, texts and editions.

FORSCHUNGSPOLITISCHE DOKUMENTATION. 1968/71-. German. ir. **LC** Z7164.S68.

FORUM. 0376-5687. Indonesian. ir. Universitas Diponegoro Fakultas Sosial & Politik, Jl Imam Barjo S H, Semarang Indonesia. **LC** H8.

FRANKFURTER WIRTSCHAFTS- UND SOZIALWISSENSCHAFTLICHEN STUDIEN. (FRANKFURTER WIRTSCHAFTS- UND SOZIALWISSENSCHAFTLICHE STUDIEN). Issue 1- 1975-. 0532-6028. Monographic Series. German. ir. Duncker und Humbolt Verlag, Dietrich-Schafer-Weg 9, 1000 Berlin 41 West Germany.

THE FRANKLIN LECTURES IN THE SCIENCES AND HUMANITIES. 1st Ser.- 1970-. 0533-0130. Monographic Series. US. English. ir. University of Alabama, Drawer 2877, University AL 35486.

FUTURABLE. Yearly V. 1- May 1979-. Periodical. English (Spanish). ir. $8.00. Fundacion Argentina Ano 2000, Leandro N Slem 36, 110 Piso, 1003 Buenos Aires Argentina. **LC** H8.

FUTURE FOCUS. Vol. 1, No. 1 (Fall 1980)-. 0226-921X. Periodical. CN. English. qt. $7.00 Canada. Pedowie Publishing, 632 Queen Street West, Toronto Ontario M6J 1E4 Canada. **DD** 303.405.

FUTURE PLANNER. Vol. 1, No. 1 (Mar. 1983)-. 0821-4808. Periodical. CN. English. qt. $15.00. Future Planner, 118 Thomas Street, Oakville Ontario L6J 3A8 Canada. **DD** 307.12.

FUTURE SURVEY. Vol. 1, No. 1 (Jan. 1979)-. 0190-3241. Periodical. US. English. mo. $130.00. World Future Society, 4916 Elmo Avenue, Bethesda MD 20814. **Tel** (301)677-9278. **Ed** Michael Marien. **LC** HM24. bk rev. **Circ** 2,500. Abstracts of current books and articles dealing with future trends and alternatives: subject areas include; communications, defence, economics, energy, food, government health, science, technology, etc. *Public Policy Book Forecast, 0197-9035.*

THE FUTURIST. V. 1- Feb. 1967-. 0016-3317. Periodical. US. English. bm. $29.00. World Future Society, 4916 St Elmo Avenue, Bethesda MD 20814. **Tel** (301)656-8274. **Ed** Edward Cornish. **Ind/Abst** Manage. Contents, Mag. Index, Int. Labour Doc., Sociol. Abstr., Soc. Welf. Soc. Plan./Policy Soc. Dev., Predicasts, Energy Inf. Abstr., Environ. Abstr., Pop. Mag. Rev., ABI/Inform, Book Rev. Index, Bibliogr. Agric., Curr. Index J. Educ., Read. Guide Period. Lit., Energy Res. Abstr., Soc. Sci. Index, Soc. Sci. Citation Index, Funk Scott Index Corp. Ind. **LC** CB158. **DD** 905. **CODEN** FUTUAC. (cum index). bk rev. adv acc. **Circ** 25,000. A journal of forecasts, trends, and ideas about the future.

GARLAND REFERENCE LIBRARY OF SOCIAL SCIENCE. DEVELOPMENTAL DISABILITIES. *See* Library and Information Science.

GAZDASAG ES JOGTUDOMANY. V. 1-. Periodical. Hungarian. ir. 40.00. Magyar Tudomanyos Akademia Gazdesag- Es Jogtudomanyi Osztalya, 1051 Budapest V Munnich F U 7 Hungary. **LC** H8. *Magyar Tudomanyos Akademia Gazdesag- es Jogtudomanyok Osztalyanak Kozlemenyei.*

GDI IMPULS. V. 1, No. 4, (Oct. 1982)-. Periodical. German. qt. 120.00. Gottlieb Duttweiler-Institut, CH-8803 Ruschlikon Switzerland. **LC** H5. **DD** 300.5.

GENDAI TO SHISO. No. 1- Oct. 1970-. Periodical. JA. Japanese. ir. 2400. Aoki Shoten, 60 Kanda Jimbocho Chiyoda-Ku, Tokyo Japan. **Ind/Abst** Am. Hist. Life, Hist. Abstr., Part A, Mod. Hist. Abstr., Hist. Abstr., Part B, Twent. Century Abstr. **LC** H8.

GENERAL SYSTEMS. V. 1- 1956-. 0072-0798. US. English. an. $36.00. Social Sciences for General Systems Resources, University of Louisville, Louisville KY 40208. **LC** H9. **DD** 006.

GENEVE-AFRIQUE. VFOAT Geneva-Africa. VAT Geneve Afrique. V. 1- 1962-. 0016-6774. Periodical. SZ. French (English and French). sa. $12.87. Institut Universite d'Etudes du Developpement et Societe, Suisse d'Etudes Africaines, 24 rue Rothschild, 1211 Geneva 21 Switzerland. **Tel** (022)31 59 40. **Ind/Abst** Am. Hist. Life, Hist. Abstr., MLA Int. Bibliogr. Books Artic. Mod. Lang. Lit., ABC Pol Sci, Hist. Abstr., Part A, Mod. Hist. Abstr., Hist. Abstr., Part B, Twent. Century Abstr. **LC** DT1. bk rev. **Circ** 1,500. (ctrl). Aims to promote dialogue and scientific exchanges between Africa and Switzerland on an interdisciplinary basis.

GESCHICHTE UND GESELLSCHAFT. Vol. 1-. 0340-613X. Periodical. GW. German. qt. $27.60. Vandenhoeck & Ruprecht, Postfach 3753, Theaterstr 13, D-3400 Goettingen West Germany. **Tel** (0551)65061. **Ind/Abst** Am. Hist. Life, Hist. Abstr., Part A, Mod. Hist. Abstr., Hist. Abstr., Part B, Twent. Century Abstr., Energy Res. Abstr., Soc. Sci. Citation Index, Writ. Am. Hist., Recent Publ. Artic. **LC** H5.

GESELLSCHAFTSWISSENSCHAFTLICHE INFORMATIONEN. V. 1-. Periodical. German. ir. **LC** H5.

GHANA SOCIAL SCIENCE JOURNAL. V. 1- May 1971-. 0046-5925. Periodical. GH. English. sa. $9.80. Ghana Social Science Journal, c/o Faculty of Social Science, PO Box 72, Legon Accra Ghana. **LC** H1. **DD** 300.5.

GLOBAL VILLAGE VOICE. (THE GLOBAL VILLAGE VOICE). V. 1- Oct. 1976-. 0383-6703. Periodical. CN. English. ir. Canadian Catholic Organization for Development and Peace, 67 Bond Street/Suite 305, Toronto Ontario M5B 1X5 Canada. **Tel** (416)868-0540. **DD** 309.223571. *News Views, 0382-8646.*

GRANT LIST. Fiscal year 1979-. US. English. an. National Science Foundation, Washington DC 20550. **LC** H62.5.U5. **DD** 338.4330072073. *Division of Social Sciences Grant List.*

GRANTEE PERFORMANCE REPORT FOR THE COMMUNITY DEVELOPMENT BLOCK GRANT PROGRAM. US. English. **LC** HN80.W3. **DD** 307.7609753.

THE GREATER LLANO ESTACADO SOUTHWEST HERITAGE. *See* History (General).

GRITO DEL SOL CEASED. Year 1, Bk. 1, (Jan./March 1976)- Year 7, Bk. 3 and 4 (1982). 0278-727X. Periodical. US. English (Spanish). an. $10.00. Tonatiuh International, 2150 Shattuck Avenue, Berkeley CA 94704. **LC** E184.M5. **DD** 306.0896872073.

GUAMAN-POMA. VFOAT Guaman Poma. 1-. Periodical. PE. Spanish. ir. Biblioteca Central Uncp, Ferrocarril 489, Huancayo Peru. **LC** AS88.A1. **DD** 300.5.

GUIDE TO SOCIAL SCIENCE AND RELIGION IN PERIODICAL LITERATURE. *See* Bibliographies.

GUIDE TO SOCIAL SCIENCE AND RELIGION IN PERIODICAL LITERATURE. *See* Bibliographies.

GUIDE TO SOCIAL SCIENCE AND RELIGION IN PERIODICAL LITERATURE. *See* Bibliographies.

HA-SHILTH-SA. *See* Political Science.

HARVEST QUARTERLY. No. 1- Mar. 1976-. 0146-5414. Periodical. US. English. qt. $5.00. Harvest Publications, 907 Santa Barbara Street, Santa Barbara CA 93101. **LC** HN1. **DD** 301.2405.

HIKONE RONSO: GAIDANSU TOKUSHU. VFOAT Hikone Ronso: Special Edition for Guidance. No. 1-. JA. Japanese. ir. Shiga Daigaku Keizaigakkai, 1-1 Baba 1, Hikon Japan. **LC** H8.

HISTOIRE, ECONOMIE ET SOCIETE. 1 (1st Spring 1982)-. Periodical. FR. French. qt. $46.00. 88 Bd St-Germain, F 75005 Paris France. **LC** H3. **DD** 300.5.

HISTORICAL METHODS. *See* History (General).

HISTORISCHE SOZIALFORSCHUNG. Series/Titl H. VFOAT Historical Social Research. 1979-. German. an. **LC** H62.5.G4. **DD** 300.72043. *Quantum Dokumentation.*

HISTORY AND SOCIAL SCIENCE TEACHER. (THE HISTORY AND SOCIAL SCIENCE TEACHER). V. 10- Fall 1974-. 0316-4969. Periodical. CN. English. qt. $18.00. Grolier Limited, 16 Overlea Road, Toronto Ontario M4H 1A6 Canada. **Tel** (416)425-1924. **Ed** Christopher Moore. **Ind/Abst** Can. Educ. Index, Curr. Index J. Educ. **LC** D16.4.C3. **DD** 907.1071. bk rev. adv acc. **Circ** 2,100. Special attention is given to issues and ideas related to the social studies curriculum and to class-tested strategies and practical resources. *Canadian Journal of History and Social Science, 0316-4977.*

HITOTSUBASHI JOURNAL OF SOCIAL STUDIES. Began in Aug. 1960. 0073-280X. JA. English (French, German, and Russian). ir. Japan Publishing Trading Company, PO Box 5030 Tokyo International, Tokyo 100-31 Japan. **Ind/Abst** Public Aff. Inf. Serv. Bull. **LC** H1. **DD** 300.5. *Annals of the Hitotsubashi Academy, 0439-2841.*

HOKEI RONSO (IWATE KENRITSU MORIOKA TANKI DAIGAKU). (HOKEI RONSO). VFOAT Journal of Law and Economics. Began publication with Dec. 1980 issue. 0389-6498. English (Japanese). ir. Iwate Kenritsu Morioka Tanki Daigaku, 1-ban 48-go Sumiyoshi-cho, Morioka-shi 020 Japan. **Ind/Abst** ABC Pol Sci. **LC** H8.J3. *Morioka Tanki Daigaku Kenkyu Hokoku. Horitsu Keizai Hen.*

HOM-INFO. (HOM-INFO : BULLETIN). 0712-9645. Periodical. CN. French. ir. $5.00. Hom-Info, 1710 rue Amherst, Montreal Quebec H2L 3L5 Canada. **DD** 305.3205.

HORS D'ORDRE. Vol. 1, No. 1 (Jan./Feb.1983)-. 0823-6119. Periodical. CN. French. bm. $5.00 Per Year. IMAJ, 85 C P 106, Montreal Quebec H2E 2Z7 Canada. **DD** 305.23509714.

HRAF NEWSLETTER. Main/Corp Human Relations Area Files, Inc. VAT Human Relations Area Files Newsletter. V. 1- Nov. 1975-. 0195-3869. Periodical. US. English. qt. Human Relations Area File Inc, PO Box 2054 Yale Station, New Haven CT 06520.

HSDP-SCA SERIES. 0379-5772. Monographic Series. JA. English. ir. United Nations University, 29th Floor/Toho Seimei Building 15-1 Shibuya 2-chome Shibuya-ku Tokyo 150 Japan.

HSIA-MEN TA HSUEH HSUEH PAO. CHE HSUEH SHE HUI KO HSUEH PAN. *See* Philosophy.

HSUEH LI LUN. VFOAT Xuelilun. Periodical. CC. Chinese. mo. 0.20. Post Office, Ha-Erh-Pin Shih China. **LC** AP95.C4. **DD** 300.951.

HSUEH PAO. CHE HSUEH SHE HUI KO HSUEH PAN. VFOAT Xinan Shifan Xueyuan Xuebao. Periodical. CC. Chinese. qt. 2000. Post Office, Chung-Ching Shih China. **Tel** 3578. **Ed** Ji Ping. **LC** AS452.C5914. bk rev. **Circ** 4,000. A comprehensive academic theoretical magazine, publishing the latest achievements in the research and study of literature, history, philosophy, economics and education.

HUA-CHUNG SHIH YUAN HSUEH PAO. CHE HSUEH SHE HUI KO HSUEH PAN. *See* Philosophy.

HUA-KANG SHE HUI KO HSUEH PAO. VFOAT Hwa Kang Journal of Social Sciences. V. 1, (June 1981)-. Periodical. Chinese (English). ir. Chung-Kuo Wen Hua Ta Hsueh She Hui Ko Hsueh Yuan, Hua-Kang Ta Cheng Kuan Yang-Ming-Shan, Taipei Taiwan. **LC** H8.C47. **DD** 300.5.

HUMAN AFFAIRS. Vol. 1, No. 1 (Fall 1981)-. 0714-4873. Periodical. CN. English. sa. $10.00 Per Year. Human Affairs, PO Box 32/Station A, Kingston Ontario K7M 6P9 Canada. **DD** 300.5.

HUMAN ECOLOGY FORUM. V. 1- 1970/71-. 0018-7178. Periodical. US. English. qt. $10.00. Cornell University, 1150 Academic II, Ithaca NY 14853. **Tel** (607)256-3126. **Ed** James Titus. **Ind/Abst** Environ. Period. Bibliogr., Public Aff. Inf. Serv. Bull., Energy Res. Abstr., Soc. Sci. Index. **LC** HM206. **DD** 301.3105. bk rev. **Circ** 5,000. Research reports of college of

Social Sciences (General)

human ecology; commentaries on critical social problems by faculty and outside experts; summaries of public policy studies.

HUMAN MOSAIC. 1967. 0018-7240. Periodical. US. English. sa. $6.00. Tulane Uiversity, Department of Anthropology, New Orleans LA 70118. **Tel** (504)865-5336. Ed Ann E Smith. **Ind/Abst** Sociol. Abstr., Soc. Welf. Soc. Plan./Policy Soc. Dev., Lang. Lang. Behav. Abstr. **LC** GN1. **DD** 300.5. **Circ** 125. Social science-related articles of original research, contributed by undergraduates, graduate students, and other academically-oriented scholars. Mosaic.

HUMAN RELATIONS. V. 1- June 1947-. 0018-7267. Periodical. US. English. mo. $215.00. Plenum Press, 233 Spring Street, New York NY 10013. **Tel** (212)620-8000. Ed Michael Foster. **Ind/Abst** Int. Labour Doc., Sociol. Abstr., Soc. Welf. Soc. Plan./Policy Soc. Dev., ABI/Inform, Soc. Work Res. Abstr., Psychol. Abstr., Women Stud. Abstr., Soc. Sci. Index, Cumul. Index Nurs. Allied Health Lit., Soc. Sci. Citation Index, Abstr. Anthropol., Abstr. Soc. Work. **LC** H1. **DD** 305. **NLM** W1 HU461. **CODEN** HUREAA. bk rev. adv acc. Founded on the belief that social scientists in all fields should work toward integration in their attempts to understand the complexities of human problems.

HUMBOLDT JOURNAL OF SOCIAL RELATIONS. V. 1- Fall 1973-. 0160-4341. Periodical. US. English. sa. $40.00. The Humbolt Journal, 211 Administration Building Humbolt Street University, Arcata CA 95521. **Tel** (707)826-4771. Ed James W Carroll. **Ind/Abst** Sociol. Abstr., Soc. Welf. Soc. Plan./Policy Soc. Dev., Psychol. Abstr., Lang. Lang. Behav. Abstr. **LC** HN65. **DD** 300.5. **CODEN** HJSRAB. bk rev. adv acc. **Circ** 400. An interdisciplinary social science journal which publishes original research critical essays, and book reviews in the areas of sociology, anthropology, social welfare, geography, political science, economics.

HUXLEY INSTITUTE, CSF NEWSLETTER. See Biology.

ICMC NEWSLETTER. Main/Corp International Catholic Migration Commission. **VAT** International Catholic Migration Commission Newsletter. V. 1-. Periodical. English. qt. International Catholic Migration Commission, 37-39 rue de Vermont CP 96 1211 Geneva Switzerland. **Tel** (022)33 41 50. Ed Dennis Clagett. Articles and information on ICMC activities on behalf of refugees and migrants in the world.

ICSSR JOURNAL OF ABSTRACTS AND REVIEWS. See Indexes/Abstracts.

ICSSR JOURNAL OF ABSTRACTS AND REVIEWS. SOCIOLOGY AND SOCIAL ANTHROPOLOGY. See Indexes/Abstracts.

ICSSR NEWSLETTER. Main/Corp Indian Council of Social Science Research. V. 1- Nov. 1969-. 0018-9049. Periodical. English. ir. **LC** H62.5.I5. **DD** 300.5.

IDEAS EN CIENCIAS SOCIALES. V. 1, No. 1, (Jan./Mar. 1984)-. 0326-386X. Periodical. Spanish. qt. $48.00. Universidad de Belgrano, Teodoro Garcia 2090, (1426 Buenos Aires). **LC** H8.S7. **DD** 300.5.

IDEES. Periodical. Greek, Modern. ir. Voulis 24, Athens Greece. **LC** H8.

IDEES ET PRATIQUES ALTERNATIVES. VFOAT Alternatives. V. 1, No. 1, (Fall 1983)-. 0823-5724. Periodical. CN. French. qt. $2.50 Per No. Productions Reseau, C P 580 Succursale North, Montreal Quebec H2X Canada. **DD** 304.2805.

IDS BULLETIN CEASED. Vol. 7, No. 1 (Apr. 1975)-V. 10, No. 4 (June 1979). 0308-5872. Periodical. UK. English. qt $19.00. Institute of Development Studies, University of Sussex, Brighton BN1 9R3E England. **Tel** (0273)606261. **Ind/Abst** Int. Labour Doc., Soc. Sci. Citation Index. Publishes brief, direct articles on development problems, and communicates research results.

IKEN TO ISHIKI NO HYAKKA JITEN. Began with 1972 issue. Japanese. ir. 2500. Sankei Maketingu, c/o Sankei Building, 7-2 Otemachi 1 Chiyoda-ku (100), Tokyo Japan. **LC** HN730.Z9.

ILMU MASYARAKAT : TERBITAN PERSATUAN SAINS SOSIAL MALAYSIA. VFOAT Malaysian Social Science Association Publication. 1 (Jan.-Mar. 1983)-. Periodical. English (text in Malay). qt. $16.00 Overseas, Surface Mail, $68.00 Airmail, US. ILMU Masyarakat d/a Jabatan Antropologi dan Sosiologi, Universiti Malaya, Kuala Lumpur Malaysia. **LC** H1. **DD** 300.9595.

IMPULSE. Vol. 1- Fall 1971-. 0315-3649. Periodical. CN. English. ir. $19.35. Impulse of Canada, PO Box 370/Station B, Toronto Ontario M5T 2W2 Canada. **Tel** (416)368-7511. Ed Judith Doyle, Eldon Garnet, Gerald Owen and Carolyn White. adv acc. **Circ** 5,000. Primary post-modern cultural material produced specifically for the magazine by visual artists and writers of fiction, poetry, social, cultural, and political analysis.

IN SUMMARY. Vol. 1 Oct. 1979-. 0228-2518. Periodical. CN. English. ty. Free. Population Research Laboratory, Department of Sociology, University of Alberta, Edmonton Alberta T6G 2E1 Canada. **DD** 300.720712. (ctrl).

IN THESE TIMES. See Political Science.

INDEX TO SOCIAL SCIENCES & HUMANITIES PROCEEDINGS. See Indexes/Abstracts.

INDIAN BEHAVIOURAL SCIENCES ABSTRACTS. See Indexes/Abstracts.

INDIAN DISSERTATION ABSTRACTS. See Indexes/Abstracts.

INDIAN JOURNAL OF SOCIAL SCIENCES. V. 1- Sept. 1971-. 0376-9879. Periodical. II. English. ir. $5.00. Society for the Study of Social Sciences, Department of Sociology/ Osmania University, Hyderabad 500007 India. **LC** H1. **DD** 300.954.

INDICADORES SOCIAIS DE SERGIPE. No. 1 (1979)-. Portuguese. an. Secretaria do Planejamento do Estado de Sergipe, Coordenacao de Planejamento e Estatistica, Praca Fausto Cardoso, s/no Ed Walter Franco, 5 O Andar, 49 000 Aracaju Sergipe. **LC** HN284. **DD** 306.098141.

INDICADORES SOCIAIS (MARANHAO (BRAZIL : STATE)). FUNDACAO INSTITUTO DE PESQUISAS ECONOMICAS E SOCIAIS). (INDICADORES SOCIAIS). Began with 1978 Vol. Portuguese. an. **LC** HN284.

INDICADORES SOCIAIS RS. Main/Corp Rio Grande do sul, Brazil (State). Secretaria de Coordenacao e Planejamento. Superintendencia de Planejamento Global. No. 1- Nov. 1973-. Portuguese. ir. Rua Siqueira de Campos No 1044, Porto Alegre Brazil. **LC** HN290.R48. **DD** 309.1816.

INDICADORES SOCIO-ECONOMICOS DEL CAMPO ESPANOL. Main/Corp Confederacion Espanola de Cajas de Ahorros. **Series Corp** Para la Investigacion Economica y Social. Publicaciones. Vol. 1970-. Spanish. ir. Alcala 29, Madrid Spain. **LC** HN583.5.

INDICE ESPANOL DE CIENCIAS SOCIALES. See Indexes/Abstracts.

INDIKATOR SOSIAL PROPINSI MALUKU. VFOAT Indikator Sosial. 1980-. Indonesian. ir. **LC** HN704.

THE INDIVIDUAL AND THE FUTURE OF ORGANIZATIONS. Main/Corp Franklin Foundation. V. 7- 1976/77-. 0161-4177. US. English. an. University Plaza, Atlanta GA 30303. **LC** H1. **DD** 300.5. Man and the Future of Organizations, 0097-6261.

INDUSTRIELLE WELT. V. 1-. 0537-5762. GW. German. ir. W E Saarbach GMBH, Postfach 101610, D5000 Koeln 1 West Germany. **LC** HN5.

INFORMATION LETTER (LUTHERAN WORLD FEDERATION. DEPT. OF STUDIES). (INFORMATION LETTER). No. 1 (Sept. 1972)-. Periodical. English. ir. Lutheran World Federation, Department of Studies, PO Box 66, Route de Fernay 150, 1211 Geneva Switzerland.

INFORMATIONS SOCIALES. Began in 1947. 0046-9459. FR. French. mo. $11.31. Caisse National Allocation Familia, 23 rue Daviel, 75634 Paris Cedex 13 France. **Ind/Abst** Int. Labour Doc. **LC** HN421.

INFORME DE LABORES DE LA SECRETARIA EJECTIVA DEL CONVENIO ANDRES BELLO. Main/Corp Secretaria Ejecutiva Permanente del Convenio Andres Bello. Spanish. ir. Carrera 21, No 33 A-64, AP Aereo, Bogota Columbia. **LC** H19.

INTERNATIONAL AND COMPARATIVE PUBLIC POLICY CEASED. V. 1-3/4. 0364-8303. Periodical. US. English. ir. $12.00. 156 Fifth Avenue, Office 1223, New York NY 10010. **LC** H1. **DD** 300.5.

INTERNATIONAL BEHAVIOURAL SCIENTIST. V. 1- Mar. 1969-. 0020-613X. Periodical. English. ir. **LC** H1. **DD** 300.5.

INTERNATIONAL DEVELOPMENT ABSTRACTS. See Indexes/Abstracts.

INTERNATIONAL DIRECTORY OF BEHAVIOR AND DESIGN RESEARCH. See Yearbooks, Almanacs, Directories.

INTERNATIONAL DIRECTORY OF SOCIAL SCIENCE ORGANIZATIONS. See Yearbooks, Almanacs, Directories.

INTERNATIONAL JOURNAL OF POLICY ANALYSIS AND INFORMATION SYSTEMS. V. 4- Mar. 1980-. 0195-9301. Periodical. US. English. qt. $60.00 Domestic, $68.00 Foreign. Plenum Publishing Corporation, 227 West 17th Street, New York NY 10011. **Ind/Abst** Math. Rev., Eng. Index Annu., Eng. Index Mon., Eng. Index Bioeng. Abstr., Eng. Index Energy Abstr., Coal Abstr., Energy Inf. Abstr., Environ. Abstr., Comput. Control Abstr., Electr. Electron. Abstr., Sci. Abstr. Sect. A. Phys. Abstr., Energy Res. Abstr. **LC** H1. **DD** 361.6105. **CODEN** IPASDE. Policy Analysis and Information Systems, 0193-7189.

INTERNATIONAL JOURNAL OF SMALL GROUP RESEARCH. VFOAT IJSGR. Vol. 1, No. 1 (Mar. 1985)-. 8756-0275. Periodical. US. English. sa. $30.00. Richard B Polley, Department of Management and Policy, University of Arizona, Tucson AZ 85721. **Tel** (612)621-5857. Ed Richard B Polley. **DD** 302. **Circ** 200. Systematic research into small groups-observation, analysis, feedback-theory, empirical studies, and applications of small group research.

INTERNATIONAL JOURNAL OF SOCIAL ECONOMICS. See Economics.

INTERNATIONAL JOURNAL ON POLICY AND INFORMATION. VFOAT Policy and Information. 0251-1266. Periodical. US. English. sa. $42.00. Knowledge Systems Institute, PO Box 41, Glencoe IL 60022. **Tel** (312)567-3401. Ed Chang Shi-Kuo. **Ind/Abst** Eng. Index Annu., Eng. Index Mon., Eng. Index Bioeng. Abstr., Eng. Index Energy Abstr., Comput. Control Abstr., Electr. Electron. Abstr., Sci. Abstr. Sect. A. Phys. Abstr. **LC** H1. **DD** 361.6105. **CODEN** IJPIDH. bk rev. adv acc. **Circ** 800. (ctrl). The application of information science theory and technology to decision making and policy analysis in management, business, economics, regional planning and social sciences. Policy Analysis and Information Systems.

INTERNATIONAL REVIEW OF SOCIAL HISTORY. Vol. 1 (1956)-. 0020-8590. Periodical. NE. English. ty. 80,-. Van Gorcum & Company BV, PO Box 43, 9400 AA Assen Netherlands. **Tel** 05920-46846. Ed Van Woerden. **Ind/Abst** Am. Hist. Life, Hist. Abstr., Part A, Mod. Hist. Abstr., Hist. Abst., Part B, Twent. Century Abstr., Hist. Abstr., Soc. Work Res. Abstr., Soc. Sci. Index, Soc. Sci. Citation Index, Recent Publ. Artic. **LC** HN1. **DD** 309. bk rev. adv acc. **Circ** 1,400. (ctrl). A journal which functions as a forum for exchanges of views and which contributes to the further development of social history. Bulletin of the International Institute for Social History, Amsterdam.

INTERNATIONAL SOCIAL SCIENCE COUNCIL : DIRECTORY. See Yearbooks, Almanacs, Directories.

INTERNATIONAL SOCIAL SCIENCE JOURNAL. Began with Vol. 11, No. 1, published in 1959. 0020-8701. Periodical. FR. English. qt. 285.00. UNESCO, 7 Place de Fontenoy, 75700 Paris France. **Tel** (1)45 68 37 98. Ed Ali Kazancigil. **Ind/Abst** Sociol. Abstr., Soc. Sci. Index, Am. Hist. Life, Hist. Abstr., Part A, Mod. Hist. Abstr., Hist. Abst., Part B, Twent. Century Abstr., MLA Int. Bibliogr. Books Artic. Mod. Lang. Lit., Int. Labour Doc., Soc. Welf. Soc. Plan./Policy Soc. Dev., Index Econ. Artic. J. Collect. Vol., ABC Pol Sci, Women Stud. Abstr., GeoRef, Soc. Work Res. Abstr., Public Aff. Inf. Serv. Bull., Curr. Index J. Educ. **LC** H1. **DD** 305. **NLM** W1 IN841N. adv acc. **Circ** 4,000. (ctrl). Available on microfilm from University Microfilms International. International and multidisciplinary with thematic issues on all social science disciplines and study areas. International Social Science Bulletin.

INTERNATIONAL SOCIAL SCIENCE REVIEW. Vol. 57, No. 1 (Winter 1982)-. 0278-2308. Periodical. US. English. qt. $10.00. Pi Gamma Mu, 1717 Ames, Winfield KS 67156. **Tel**

(316)221-3128. **Ed** Panos D Bardis. **Ind/Abst** Am. Hist. Life, Hist. Abstr., Int. Polit. Sci. Abstr., Sociol. Abstr. **LC** H1. **DD** 300.5. bk rev. **Circ** 4,400. (ctrl). Scholarly articles from single social science disciplines (economics, history, international relations, political science, sociology/anthropology) or interdisciplinary treatments of social science subjects. *Social Science (Winfield, Kan.), 0037-7848.*

INTERPRETIVE SERIES - E.R.I.C. CLEARINGHOUSE FOR SOCIAL STUDIES-SOCIAL SCIENCE EDUCATION. (INTERPRETIVE SERIES). **Main/Corp** ERIC Clearinghouse for Social Studies/Social Science Education. 0091-4339. US. English. Superintendent of Documents, US Government Printing Office, Washington DC 20402. **LC** H62.5.U5. **DD** 300.71073.

IREX OCCASIONAL PAPERS. **Main/Corp** International Research and Exchanges Board. **VAT** International Research and Exchanges Board Occasional Papers. 0198-8875. Monographic Series. US. English. International Research and Exchanges Board, 655 3rd Avenue, New York NY 10017. **LC** H31, HF1411. **DD** 300.

IRSS TECHNICAL PAPERS. No. 1-. Monographic Series. US. English. ir. Institute Research of Social Science, Manning Hall/026A, University of North Carolina, Chapel Hill NC 27514.

ISEGR REPORT. **Main/Corp** University of Alaska, Fairbanks. Institute of Social, Economic and Government Research. **Series/Titl** State Constitutional Convention Studies. **VAT** Institute of Social, Economic and Government Research Report. Monographic Series. US. English. ir. University of Alaska Press, GEO Physical Institute, Fairbanks AK 99701. **LC** HC107.A45. **DD** 309.1798. *ISEGR Report.*

ISR NEWSLETTER. **Main/Corp** University of Michigan. Institute for Social Research. **VAT** Institute for Social Research Newsletter. Winter 1969-. 0020-2622. Periodical. US. English. ir. Institute for Social Research, 426 Thompson Street, Ann Arbor MI 48104.

ISRALEFT BI-WEEKLY NEWS SERVICE. Periodical. IS. English. bw. 40. Israleft News Service, PO Box 9013, Jerusalem Israel 91090. News usually buried or minimized by Israeli establishment; counter source of reliable information on activities and thinking of peace forces and left-opposition in Israel.

ISSQ. INDIANA SOCIAL STUDIES QUARTERLY. **VFOAT** Indiana Social Studies Quarterly. Vol. 15, No. 1 (Spring 1962)-. Periodical. US. English. ir. Ball State University, c/o Richard Wires, Muncie IN 47306. **Ind/Abst** Curr. Index J. Educ., Hist. Abstr., Part A, Mod. Hist. Abstr., Hist. Abst., Part B, Twent. Century Abstr., Am. Hist. Life. (cum index). Available on microfilm from University Microfilms. *Indiana Social Studies Quarterly.*

ITEMS - SOCIAL SCIENCE RESEARCH COUNCIL. **Main/Corp** Social Science Research Council (U.S.). V. 1- Mar. 1947-. 0049-0903. Periodical. US. English. qt. Social Science Research Council, 605 Third Avenue, New York NY 10158. **Ind/Abst** Am. Hist. Life, Hist. Abstr., Part A, Mod. Hist. Abstr. **LC** H62. **DD** 307.2. **NLM** W1 IT57K. (cum index).

IUSTITIA. *See* Philosophy.

IZTAPALAPA. V. 1- (No. 1-). Periodical. MX. Spanish. ir. $100.00. Uam Unidad Iztapalapa, Division de Ciencias, Sociales y Humanidades Michoacan y Michoacan y la Purisima, Iztapalapr DF Mexico. **LC** H8.S7. **DD** 300.5.

IZVESTIIA. SERIIA OBSHCHESTVENNYKH NAUK. **Main/Corp** Akademiia Nauk Kazakhskoi SSR, Alma-Ata. V. 12- 1974-. 0568-4927. Periodical. US. text and summaries in Russian or Kazakh. bm. $33.50. Victor Kamkin Inc, 12224 Parklawn Drive, Rockville MD 20852. **Tel** (301)881-5973. **Ind/Abst** Chem. Abstr. *Izvestiia. Seriia Obshchestvennaia.*

IZVESTIIA SIBIRSKOGO OTDELENIIA AKADEMII NAUK SSSF. SERIIA OBSHCHESTVENNYKH NAUK *CEASED.* **Main/Corp** Akademiia Nauk SSSR. Sibirskoe Otdelenie. 1963-1983. 0568-6555. Periodical. UR. Russian. ty. **Ind/Abst** Sociol. Abstr., Soc. Welf. Soc. Plan./Policy Soc. Dev., Lang. Lang. Behav. Abstr., Am. Hist. Life, Hist. Abstr., Part A, Mod. Hist. Abstr. **DD** 300. *Izvestiia Sibirskogo Otdeleniia Akademii Nauk SSSR.*

JAHRBUCH FUR SOZIALWISSENSCHAFT. *See* Yearbooks, Almanacs, Directories.

JAHRESBERICHT (GERMANY (WEST). BUNDESMINISTERIUM FUR INNERDEUTSCHE BEZIEHUNGEN). (JAHRESBERICHT). German. an. Bundesministerium fur Innerdeutsche Beziehungen, Postfach 16 40, 5300 Bonn 1 West Germany. **LC** DD259.4. **DD** 303.482430431.

JAHRESBERICHT - OSTEUROPA-INSTITUT. **Main/Corp** Munich. Osteuropa-Institut. German. an. Free. Osteuropa-Institut, 8000 Munchen 80, Scheinerstrasse 11, Munchen West Germany. **Tel** (89)983821. **LC** H62.5.G4. adv acc. **Circ** 250. (ctrl). Report on the work of the institute and published working papers and book series.

JAHRESHERICHT - RHEINLAND PFALZ, MINISTERIUM FUR SOZIALES, GESUNDHEIT UND SPORT. **Main/Corp** Rhineland-Palatinate. Ministerium fur Soziales, Gesundheit und Sport. German. ir. Ministerium fur Soziales Gesundheit und Sport, Bauhofstrasse 4 65, Mainz West Germany. **LC** HN458.R53.

JAPAN INTERPRETER. V. 6- Spring 1970-. Periodical. JA. English. sa. $10.00. Center for Japanese Social and Political Studies, 4-12-24 Higashi Shibuya-Ku, Tokyo Japan. **Ind/Abst** MLA Int. Bibliogr. Books Artic. Mod. Lang. Lit. **LC** H1. **DD** 300.5. *Journal of Social and Political Ideas in Japan, 0388-0478.*

JASA SHARE. **VFOAT** Jasa-Share. 1-. 0882-9411. Periodical. US. English (Russian). Jasa-Share, 40 West 68th Street, New York NY 10023. **DD** 305.

JEN KOU YU CHING CHI. **VFOAT** Renkou Yu Jingji. Periodical. CH. Chinese. bm. 0.35. Pei-Ching Pao Kan Fa Housing, Chu Peking China. **LC** HB3654.A3. **DD** 304.60951.

JEWISH SOCIAL STUDIES. *See* Religion, Mythology, Rationalism - Judaism.

JIMBUNGAKU RONSHU. **VFOAT** Journal of Humanistic Studies. JA. Japanese. ir. Bukkyo Daigaku Bungakubu Gakkai, 9-6 Murasakino Kita Hananobocho, Kita-Ku, Kyoto Japan. **LC** AS552.B84.

THE JOHNS HOPKINS UNIVERSITY STUDIES IN HISTORICAL AND POLITICAL SCIENCE. **VFOAT** Studies in Historical and Political Science. Ser. 1- 1882/83-. 0075-3904. US. English. ir. Johns Hopkins University Press, 615 North Wolfe Street, Baltimore MD 21218. **LC** H31. **DD** 300.5.

JORNADAS. *See* Humanities.

THE JOURNAL OF APPLIED BEHAVIORAL SCIENCE. V. 1- Jan./Mar. 1965-. 0021-8863. Periodical. US. English. qt. $33.00. JAI Press Inc, PO Box 1678/36 Sherwood Place, Greenwich CT 06836. **Tel** (203)661-7602. **Ed** Lewis Zurcher. **Ind/Abst** Manage. Contents, Hospit. Lit. Index, Sociol. Abstr., Soc. Welf. Soc. Plan./Policy Soc. Dev., Cumul. Index Nurs. Allied Health Lit., ABC Pol Sci, ABI/Inform, Soc. Work Res. Abstr., Psychol. Abstr., Soc. Sci. Index, Hospit. Lit. Index, Lang. Lang. Behav. Abstr., Soc. Sci. Citation Index, Educ. Index, Bibliogr. Index, Abstr. Soc. Work. **LC** H1. **DD** 305. **NLM** W1 JO539S. **CODEN** JABHAP. bk rev. adv acc. **Circ** 3,000.

JOURNAL OF APPLIED COMMUNICATIONS RESEARCH. *See* Communication.

THE JOURNAL OF APPLIED SOCIAL SCIENCES. 0146-4310. Periodical. US. English. sa. $7.50. School of Applied Social Science Case, Western Reserve University, 2035 Abington Road, Cleveland OH 44106. **Tel** (216)368-2134. **Ind/Abst** Psychol. Abstr. **LC** HV1. **DD** 361.005.

JOURNAL OF AREA STUDIES. No. 1 (Spring 1980)-. 0261-3530. Periodical. UK. English. sa. 5.00. Portsmouth Polytechnic School, Languages Department, Hampshire Terrace, Portsmouth P01 2BU England. **Tel** 0705-827681. **Ind/Abst** Am. Hist. Life, Hist. Abstr., ABC Pol Sci. bk rev. adv acc. **Circ** 250. Theory and methodology of area studies. Comparative and cross-area research mainly in social science. Oriented towards current public issues.

JOURNAL OF ASIAN-PACIFIC & WORLD PERSPECTIVES. **VAT** Journal of Asian-Pacific and World Perspectives. V. 1- Summer 1977-. 0148-611X. Periodical. US. English. sm. $3.00. Asian-Pacific Services Institute, 3583 Waialae Avenue, Honolulu HI 96816. **Ind/Abst** Soc. Work Res. Abstr. **LC** H1. **DD** 300.5.

THE JOURNAL OF BARD. **VFOAT** Journal of the Bangladesh Academy for Rural Development. Vol. 11, No. 1 092 (July 1981 & Jan. 1982)-. Periodical. English. sa. **LC** HN690.6.Z9. **DD** 307.72095492. *Journal of the Bangladesh Academy for Rural Development, Comilla.*

JOURNAL OF BIOSOCIAL SCIENCE. SUPPLEMENT. No. 1- July 1969-. 0300-9645. Periodical. UK. English. Biochemical Society, PO Box 32, Commerce Way, Colchester C02 8HP England. **Ind/Abst** Index Med., Chem. Abstr. **NLM** W1 JO568A. **CODEN** JBSCBZ.

THE JOURNAL OF DEVELOPING AREAS. V. 1- Oct. 1966-. 0022-037X. Periodical. US. English. qt. $22.00. Journal of Developing Areas, West Illinois University, 900 West Adams Street, Macomb IL 61455. **Tel** (309)298-1108. **Ed** Nicholas C Pano. **Ind/Abst** ABI/Inform, Bus. Period. Index, Manage. Contents, Trade Ind. Index, Soc. Welf. Soc. Plan./Policy Soc. Dev., Electron. Commun. Abstr. J., ISMEC Bull., Pollut. Abstr. Indexes, Saf. Sci. Abstr. J., Am. Hist. Life, Soc. Sci. Citation Index, Hist. Abstr., Women Stud. Abstr., Recent Publ. Artic., Int. Labour Doc., Sociol. Abstr., Energy Inf. Abstr., Environ. Abstr., Index Econ. Artic. J. Collect. Vol., ABC Pol Sci. **LC** HC59.7. **DD** 338.911724. **CODEN** JDARB4. bk rev. adv acc. **Circ** 1,500. (ctrl). Main interest focuses on political, economic, social, cultural, historical, and comparative studies of the Third World and the development process.

JOURNAL OF EASTERN AFRICAN RESEARCH AND DEVELOPMENT. (JOURNAL OF EASTERN AFRICAN RESEARCH & DEVELOPMENT). **VFOAT** Eastern African Research and Development. V. 1- 1971-. 0251-0405. Periodical. KE. English (articles published in Swahili). an. $28.00. Editor/Professor Gideon S Were, PO Box 10622, Nairobi Kenya Africa. **Tel** 331135. **Ed** Gideon S Were. **Ind/Abst** Recent Publ. Artic. **LC** DT365.A2. **DD** 916.70305. bk rev. adv acc. **Circ** 200. Caters for history, sociology, economics, anthropology, languages, religion, political science, musicology, literature and culture.

JOURNAL OF FORECASTING. **VFOAT** Forecasting. Vol. 1, No. 1 (Jan.-Mar. 1982)-. 0277-6693. Periodical. UK. English. qt. John Wiley & Sons, Baffins Lane, Chichester Sussex PO19 1UD England. **Ind/Abst** Manage. Contents, Sociol. Abstr., ABI/Inform, Met. Abstr., World Alum. Abstr., Public Aff. Inf. Serv. Bull. **LC** H61.4. **DD** 003.205. **CODEN** JOFODV.

JOURNAL OF INDO-EUROPEAN STUDIES : MONOGRAPH. No. 1-. Monographic Series. US. English. ir. Institute for the Study of Man, 1133 13th Street NW/Suite Comm 2, Washington DC 20005. **Tel** (202)789-0231. **Ed** Roger Pearson. **Circ** 400. Scholarly research in area of Indo-European studies including mythology and social organization interdisciplinary.

JOURNAL OF INDUSTRIAL RELATIONS. (THE JOURNAL OF INDUSTRIAL RELATIONS). **VFOAT** JIR. V. 1- April 1959-. 0022-1856. Periodical. AT. English. qt. 32.00 Domestic, 38.00 Foreign. Industrial Relations Society of New South Wales, GPO Box 4479, Sydney New South Wales 2001 Australia. **Tel** (02)235-8662. **Ed** J Niland. **Ind/Abst** Int. Labour Doc., Sociol. Abstr., Soc. Welf. Soc. Plan./Policy Soc. Dev., APAIS, Aust. Public Aff. Inf. Serv., Lang. Lang. Behav. Abstr. **LC** HD4811. bk rev. **Circ** 4,000. Articles and book reviews on industrial relations and related subjects from contributors in management, trade unions, government services, professions and specialists in academic disciplines.

JOURNAL OF INTERCULTURAL STUDIES. *See* Ethnic.

THE JOURNAL OF KARNATAK UNIVERSITY. SOCIAL SCIENCES. **Main/Corp** Karnatak University, Dharwar, India. V. 1- 1965-. 0075-5176. Periodical. II. English. Karnatak University, Dhawar 580003, Karnatak India. **LC** HN681. **DD** 309.154.

JOURNAL OF LATIN AMERICAN STUDIES. 0022-216X. Periodical. UK. English. sa. $70.00. Cambridge University Press, 510 North Avenue, New Rochelle NY 10801. **Tel** (914)235-0300. **Ed** Harold Blakemore and Alan Angell. **Ind/Abst** Soc. Sci. Index, Sociol. Abstr., Soc. Sci. Citation Index, Lang. Lang. Behav. Abstr., Hist. Abstr., Am. Hist. Life, ABC Pol Sci, Abstr. Anthropol. bk rev. Considers Latin America from the standpoint of the social sciences, including anthropology, archaeology, economics, geography, history, international relations, politics and sociology.

JOURNAL OF POLICY MODELING. V. 1- Jan. 1979-. 0161-8938. Periodical. US. English. qt. $103.00. Elsevier Science Publishers Company Inc,

Social Sciences (General)

PO Box 1663 Grand Central Station, New York NY 10163. **Tel** (212)370-5520. **Ind/Abst** Manage. Contents, Sociol. Abstr., Soc. Welf. Soc. Plan./Policy Soc. Dev., ABI/Inform, Energy Res. Abstr., Recent Publ. Artic. LC H1. DD 300.151. CODEN JPMOD5.

JOURNAL OF PUBLIC AND INTERNATIONAL AFFAIRS. V. 1- Spring 1979-. 0195-6000. US. English. sa. $15.00. Graduate School of Public and International Affairs, University of Pittsburgh/Editorial Office, Pittsburgh PA 15260. **Ind/Abst** Public Aff. Inf. Serv. Bull. LC H1. DD 300.5.

JOURNAL OF SOCIAL AND BEHAVIORAL SCIENCES. Periodical. US. English. ir. $20.00. Association of Social and Behavioral Scientists, Box 1515, South Carolina College, Orangeburg SC 29117. LC H1. DD 300.5. *Journal of Social Science Teachers.*

JOURNAL OF SOCIAL PHILOSOPHY. 0047-2786. Periodical. US. English. ty. $12.00 Domestic, $13.00 Foreign. Villanova University, c/o Dr Joseph Betz, Villanova PA 19085. **Tel** (215)645-4708. Ed Joseph Betz. **Ind/Abst** Philos. Index, Relig. Index One, Period. LC H1. DD 300.5. bk rev. **Circ** 300. Philosophical studies of important issues in society, politics, law, and morality.

JOURNAL OF SOCIAL POLICY. 0047-2794. Periodical. UK. English. qt. $98.00. Cambridge University Press, 510 North Avenue, New Rochelle NY 10801. **Tel** (212)688-8888. Ed K Judge. **Ind/Abst** Public Aff. Inf. Serv. Bull., Soc. Sci. Citation Index, Sociol. Abstr., ABC Pol Sci, Hospit. Lit. Index, Soc. Sci. Index, Lang. Lang. Behav. Abstr., Int. Labour Doc., Soc. Welf. Soc. Plan./Policy Soc. Dev., Recent Publ. Artic. LC HV1. DD 361.2505. NLM W1 JO88M. bk rev. adv acc. **Circ** 2,000. Contains scholarly papers which analyze any aspect of social policy and administration. Seeks to encourage contributions which integrate conceptual or theoretical issues with the use of empirical evidence.

THE JOURNAL OF SOCIAL, POLITICAL AND ECONOMIC STUDIES. Vol. 6, No. 1 (Spring 1981)-. 0278-839X. Periodical. US. English. qt. Journal of Social Political and Economic Studies, 1133 13th Street NW/Suite C2, Washington DC 20005. **Tel** (202)232-1040. Ed Roger Pearson. **Ind/Abst** ABC Pol Sci, Public Aff. Inf. Serv. Bull., Recent Publ. Artic. LC H1. DD 300.5. bk rev. adv acc. Contemporary policy issues of international, social, political, and economic significance. *Journal of Social and Political Studies, 0193-5941.*

JOURNAL OF SOCIAL RECONSTRUCTION. V. 1- Jan./Mar. 1980-. 0196-2000. Periodical. US. English. qt. $39.50. Coleman, White Gates, West Mount Airy Road, Croton-on-Hudson NY 10510. LC HN51. DD 361.610973.

JOURNAL OF SOCIAL SCIENCE. Vol. 1- 1972-. MW. English. an. $10.00. Journal of Social Science, Chancellor College, PO Box 5200, Limbe Malawi. LC H1. DD 300.5.

THE JOURNAL OF SOCIAL STUDIES. V. 1- Jan. 1978-. English. ir. Centre for Social Studies, Department of Political Science, Room 1107/Arts Building/University of Dacca, Dacca-2 Belgium. LC H1. DD 300.5.

JOURNAL OF SOCIAL STUDIES RESEARCH. *See* Sociology: General Works, Theory.

THE JOURNAL OF SOCIAL TRANSFORMATION. V. 1- June 1977-. Periodical. II. English. ir. 8.00. Sanjivayya Institute of Socio-Economic Studies, Bapu Bhawan sat Nagar Karol Bagh, New Delhi 110005 India. LC HN681. DD 309.15405.

JOURNAL OF THE AMERICAN PLANNING ASSOCIATION. *See* Housing and Urban Development.

JOURNAL OF THE ARIZONA-NEVADA ACADEMY OF SCIENCE. *See* Science (General).

JOURNAL OF THE HUMANITIES AND SOCIAL SCIENCES. *See* Humanities.

THE JOURNAL OF THE NEW ALCHEMISTS. 1-. 0162-833X. Periodical. US. English. $6.00. New Alchemy Institute, PO Box 432, Woods Hole MA 02543. LC GF50. DD 301.3105.

THE JOURNAL OF THE NORTH-EAST INDIA COUNCIL FOR SOCIAL SCIENCE RESEARCH. **Main/Corp** North-East India Council for Social Science Research. Periodical. English. ir. $18.00 US. North-East India Council for Social Science Research, B T Hostel, Shillong 793003 India 793003. **Tel** Shillong 24501. Ed B Pakem, J B Bhattacharjee, I J S Jaswal, S Sen, and B Dattaray. LC HN681. bk rev. adv acc. **Circ** 1,000. Our focus is on North-East India. Economic, social and political aspects.

JOURNAL OF THE SOUTH SEAS SOCIETY. *See* History (General) - History of Asia.

JOURNAL OF URBAN AFFAIRS. Vol. 3, No. 4 (Fall 1981)-. 0735-2166. Periodical. US. English. qt. $25.00 $40.00. Virginia Tech, Division of Environmental and Urban System, Blacksburg VA 24060. **Tel** (703)961-5177. Ed John R Gist. **Ind/Abst** Public Aff. Inf. Serv. Bull. bk rev. adv acc. **Circ** 450. A multidisciplinary journal of urban research which addresses contemporary urban issues of interest to scholars, practitioners, policy makers, and students. *Urban Interests, 0192-4974; Urban Affairs Papers, 0735-2158.*

JOURNAL POPULAIRE. (LE JOURNAL POPULAIRE). V. 1- May 1974-. 0319-5791. CN. French. mo. Journal Populaire, 18 rue Charlevoix, Hull Quebec J8X 1N8 Canada. DD 309.1714221.

JOURNAL - THAILAND NATIONAL RESEARCH COUNCIL. *See* Science (General).

JPS, JURNAL PENELITIAN SOSIAL. VFOAT Jurnal Penelitian Sosial. Vol. 1- Jan. 1976-. Periodical. Indonesian. ir. 1500. Fakultas Ilmu-Ilmu Sosial, Universitas Indonesia, Perpustaan Kampus U I, Jl Pemuda Rawamangun, Jakarta Indonesia. LC H62.A1.

JUDICATURE. *See* Law.

JUNIOR EAGLE. 1979-. 0193-6131. US. English. ir. World Eagle, 64 Washburn Street, Wellesley MA 02181.

KAGOSHIMA DAIGAKU SHAKAI KAGAKU ZASSHI. VFOAT Shakai Kagaku Zasshi. No. 1-. Periodical. Japanese. ir. LC H8.

KEGIATAN L.S.D. SELURUH INDONESIA. **Main/Corp** Indonesia. Direktorat Jenderal Pembangunan Masyarakat Desa. VAT Kegiatan Lembaga Sosial Desa Seluruh Indonesia. Vol. 1- 1974-. IO. Indonesian. ir. Departemen Dalam Negeri, JL Pasar Minggu Pejatan, Jakarta Selatan Indonesia. LC HN710.Z9.

KENKYU NENPO. DAI 1-GO, SHAKAI KAGAKU KEI. VFOAT Annals of Takushoku University. 1981-. Periodical. JA. Japanese. an. Takushoku Daigau Kenkyujo, 4-14 Kohinata 3 Bunkyo-ku, Tokyo-to Japan. LC H8.J3.

KETTERING REPORT. **Main/Corp** Charles F Kettering Foundation. 1981/1982-. 0743-8478. US. English. sa. Kettering Foundation, 5335 Far Hills Avenue, Dayton OH 45429. **Tel** (513)298-0392. Ed Robert E Daley. LC AS911.C46. DD 300.5. **Circ** 10,000. (ctrl). A report of a research foundation concerned with basic problems in education, government, and science. *Annual Report - Charles F Kettering Foundation.*

KIHO NIRA. **Main/Corp** Sogo Kenkyu Kaihatsu Kiko. VFOAT NIRA. VAT Kiho National Institute for Research Advancement I.E. Sogo Kenkyu Kaihatsu Kiko. 1974 Ed. Yearly Issue. Japanese. ir. Sogo Kenkyu Kaitatsu Kiko, c/o Mitsui Building, 1-1 Nishi Shinjuku, 2-chome Shinjuku-ku (160), Tokyo Japan. LC H62.5.J3.

KITAKYUSHU DAIGAKU SHOKEI RONSHU. VFOAT Kitakyushu-Daigaku Sho-Kei-Ronshu. JA. Japanese. ir. Kitakyushu Daigaku Shokei, Gakkai Kitagata Kokura Minami-Ku, Kitakyushu Japan. LC H8.

KNOWLEDGE. V. 1- Sept. 1979-. 0164-0259. Periodical. US. English. qt. $33.00 Domestic, $34.00 Foreign. Sage Publications, 275 South Beverly Drive, Beverly Hills CA 90212. LC H62. DD 300.72. NLM W1 KN735M.

KOSMAS. (KOSMAS : JOURNAL OF THE CZECHOSLOVAK SOCIETY OF ARTS AND SCIENCES (SVU)). Vol. 1, No. 1 (Summer 1982)-. 0731-5430. Periodical. US. English. sa. $15.00. Czechoslovak Society of Arts and Science, 30 Bellevue Avenue, Cambridge MA 02140. **Tel** (412)782-5864. Ed Zdenek L Suda. **Ind/Abst** Recent Publ. Artic. LC D1. DD 943.0005. bk rev. adv acc. **Circ** 1,000. Scholarly essays and studies concerning contemporary social life, politics, and economics, as well as history and arts of Czechoslovakia and the Central European region.

KOSMOS + OEKUMENE. *See* Religion, Mythology, Rationalism.

KRISTET FORUM. *See* Religion, Mythology, Rationalism - Tneology.

KUEI-CHOU SHE HUI KO HSUEH. Periodical. CH. Chinese. bm. $4.86. China Publication Centre, PO Box 2820, Beijing China.

KULFOLDI TARSADALOMTUDOMANYI KEZIKONYVEK. *See* Bibliographies.

KULTURJAHRBUCH. 1 (1982/83)-. Periodical. AU. German. an. Verlag fur Gesellschaftskritik Langegasse 42, 1080 Wien Austria. LC HM101. DD 306.1.

KYKLOS. V. 1- 1947-. Periodical. Articles in German, French or English. qt. 70.-. Kyklos Verlag, Postfach 524, 4002 Basel Switzerland. **Tel** (01141)61 25 26 05. Ed R L Frey and B S Frey. **Ind/Abst** Soc. Sci. Index, Soc. Sci. Citation Index, Public Aff. Inf. Serv. Bull., Sociol. Abstr., Am. Hist. Life, Lang. Lang. Behav. Abstr., Hist. Abstr. LC H1. bk rev. adv acc. **Circ** 2,500. International review for social sciences.

KYODO KENKYU KATSUDO HOKOKUSHO. **Main/Corp** Momoyama Gakuin Daigaku. Sogo Kenkyujo. VFOAT Momoyama Gakuin Daigaku Kyodo Kenkyu Katsudo Hokokusho. V. 1, 1975-1980-. Japanese. ir. Momoyama Gakuin Daigaku Sogo Kenkyujo, 237-1 Nishino Sakai-shi, Osaka-fu 588 Japan. **Tel** 0722-36-1181. LC AZ188.J3. **Circ** 550. Activity reports of collaborative research in the Research Institute including their lists of members and publications.

LADOC. *See* Religion, Mythology, Rationalism.

LAN-CHOU TA HSUEH HSUEH PAO. SHE HUI KO HSUEH PAN. VFOAT Journal of Lanzhou University. Social Sciences, Lanzhoudaxue Xuebao. Periodical. CC. Chinese. qt. 0.40. Chung-Kuo Kuo Chi Shu Tien, PO Box 2820, Peking China. LC H8.C47. DD 300.5.

LAND AND HUMAN SETTLEMENTS. *See* Economics - Economics: Land.

LAPORAN TAHUNAN - PROYEK PENGEMBANGAN PUSAT DOKUMENTASI DAN INFORMASI BIDANG ILMU-ILMU SOSIAL DAN KEMANUSIAAN. **Main/Corp** Proyek Pengembangan Pusat Dokumentasi dan Informasi Bidang Ilmu-Ilmu Sosial dan Kemanusiaan. Began with 1974/75 Vol. Indonesian. ir. d/a Pusat Dokumentasi Ilmiah, Nasional - Lipi, Jalan Jenderal Gatot Subroto, PO Box 3065/JKT, Jakarta Indonesia. LC H62.5.I6.

LATIN AMERICAN PERSPECTIVES. V. 1- (Issue 1-). 0094-582X. Periodical. US. English. qt. Latin American Perspectives, PO Box 5703, Riverside CA 92517. **Tel** (213)274-8003. **Ind/Abst** Am. Hist. Life, Hist. Abstr., Part A, Mod. Hist. Abstr., Hist. Abst., Part B, Twent. Century Abstr., Int. Labour Doc., ABC Pol Sci, Soc. Sci. Citation Index, Altern. Press Index, Public Aff. Inf. Serv. Bull., Abstr. Anthropol., Recent Publ. Artic., Hist. Abstr. LC F1401. DD 320.98003.

LATIN AMERICAN RESEARCH REVIEW. V. 1- Fall 1965-. 0023-8791. Periodical. US. English. ir. $18.00. Latin American Research Review, Latin American Institute, University of New Mexico, Albuquerque NM 87131. **Tel** (505)277-5985. Ed Gilbert W Merkx. **Ind/Abst** Am. Hist. Life, Hist. Abstr., Part A, Mod. Hist. Abstr., Hist. Abstr., Part B, Twent. Century Abstr., Int. Labour Doc., ABC Pol Sci, Public Aff. Inf. Serv. Bull., Soc. Sci. Index, Soc. Sci. Citation Index, Abstr. Anthropol., Hist. Abstr. LC F1401. (cum index). bk rev. adv acc. **Circ** 4,000. (ctrl). Articles, research notes, and book reviews and essays of an interdisciplinary nature relating to Latin America.

LATIN AMERICAN STUDIES IN THE UNIVERSITIES OF THE UNITED KINGDOM: STAFF RESEARCH IN PROGRESS OR RECENTLY COMPLETED IN THE HUMANITIES AND THE SOCIAL SCIENCES. *See* Bibliographies.

Social Sciences (General)

LEISURE SCIENCES. See Recreation, Leisure.

LEISURE STUDIES. (LEISURE STUDIES : THE JOURNAL OF THE LEISURE STUDIES ASSOCIATION). Vol. 1, No. 1 (Jan. 1982)-. 0261-4367. Periodical. UK. English. ty. Associated Book Publishers, North Way Andover, Hampshire SP10 5BE England. **Tel** (0264)62141. **Ed** John Roberts. **Ind/Abst** Psychol. Abstr. bk rev. adv acc. Publishes papers on leisure behaviour from a wide range of disciplinary bases including sociology, psychology, planning and economics as well as leisure professionals.

LETTERS & PAPERS ON THE SOCIAL SCIENCES; AN UNDERGRADUATE REVIEW. V. 1- Fall 1973-. 0092-718X. Periodical. US. English. sa. $4.00. Johns Hopkins University, Box 1310, Baltimore MD 21218. **Tel** (301)243-9530. **LC** H1. **DD** 300.5.

LIBRE POLITIQUE, ANTHROPOLOGIE, PHILOSOPHIE. 1-. French. ir. Editions Payot, 106 BD Saint Germain, Paris France 75006. **LC** H3.

LISTE DES PERIODIQUES REGULIEREMENT RECUS - UNIVERSITE DE MONTREAL. BIBLIOTHEQUE DES SCIENCES HUMAINES ET SOCIAL. See Bibliographies.

LITERATURWISSENSCHAFT, GESELLSCHAFTSWISSENSCHAFT. VFOAT LGW. 1-. Monographic Series. GW. German. ir. W E Saarbach GMBH, Postfach 101610, D5000 Koeln 1 West Germany.

A LONDON BIBLIOGRAPHY OF THE SOCIAL SCIENCES. See Bibliographies.

THE LONDON RISING TIDE. VFOAT Rising Tide. UK. English. 4.50. Federation for World Peace & Unification, Rowland Farmhouse, Dumsden Reading RG4 9PT England. **LC** HN30. **DD** 261.830441.

LUCHA STRUGGLE. Vol. 4, No. 3 (June 1980)-. Periodical. US. English. bm. $20.00. New York Circus Inc, PO Box 37 Times Square Station, New York NY 10108. **Tel** (212)316-0040. **Ind/Abst** Altern. Press Index. bk rev. adv acc. (ctrl). Journal of Christian reflection on struggles for liberation. Focus on social change and the popular church in Latin America. New York Circus.

MCGILL STUDIES IN INTERNATIONAL DEVELOPMENT. VFOAT Etudes de McGill sur le Developpement International. 0821-6452. Monographic Series. CN. English (includes abstracts in French). ir. 2.50 Per Issue. Publications Centre for Developing-Area Studies, McGill University, 3715 Peel Street, Montreal Quebec H3A 1X1 Canada. **Tel** (514)392-5327. **Ed** Rosalind Boyd. **DD** 330.91724. **Circ** 2,000. Contemporary problems in developing countries from socio-economic perspectives. Working Paper Series (McGill University. Center for Developing-Area Studies), 0824-6041.

MACHIKANEYAMA RONSO: SHIGAKUHEN. See Humanities.

MAIEUTICS. V. 1, No. 1 (Spring 1980)-. 0226-2428. Periodical. CN. English. sa. $30.00 per year. Centre for Theory in the Humanities and Social Sciences, S436 Ross Building/York University, 4700 Keele Street, Downsview Ontario M3J 1P3 Canada. **DD** 300.1.

MAJALAH ILMIAH FAKULTAS ILMU SOSIAL UNIVERSITAS AIRLANGGA. Vol. 1 No. 1 (Apr.-June 1981)-. Periodical. IO. Indonesian. qt. Dampus Fakultas Ilmu Sosial Unair, Jl Airlangga, Surabaya Indonesia. **LC** H8.I5.

MAJALLAT AL-ULUM AL-IJTIMAIYAH. (JOURNAL OF THE SOCIAL SCIENCES : A PUBLICATION OF KUWAIT UNIVERSITY). VFOAT JSS. Periodical. English. ir. $40.00. **Ind/Abst** Sociol. Abstr. **LC** H1. **DD** 300.5.

MANITOBA SOCIAL SCIENCES TEACHER CEASED. (THE MANITOBA SOCIAL SCIENCES TEACHER). V. 1-5, No. 1. 0316-6473. Periodical. CN. English. Free to Members. Manitoba Teachers Society, 191 Harcourt Street, Winnipeg Manitoba R3J 3H2 Canada. **Ind/Abst** Can. Educ. Index. **DD** 372.8305. Manitoba Geography Teachers, 0316-6471.

MASTER'S THESES IN THE ARTS AND SOCIAL SCIENCES. VFOAT Master's Theses in the Arts and Social Sciences in the United States and Canada. No. 1- 1976-. 0160-8797. US. English. an. $25.00. Research Publications, Box 92, Cedar Falls IA 50613. **Tel** (319)273-6412. **Ed** H M Silvey. **LC** Z5055.U5, LB2385. **DD** 013.375. (ctrl).

MASYARAKAT INDONESIA. V. 1- Aug. 1974-. Periodical. English (or Indonesian with summaries in the other language). sa. 800. Lembaga ILMU Pengetahuan Indonesia, Jakarta Indonesia. **LC** H8.

MASYARAKAT KITA. Vol. 1- Oct. 1976-. Periodical. English (Indonesian). ir. Pusat Pengkajian Ilmu-Ilmu Sosial, Jalan Merbau No 38A, Medan Indonesia. **LC** H35.

MATHEMATICAL SOCIAL SCIENCES. Vol. 1, No. 1 (Sept. 1980)-. 0165-4896. Periodical. English. bm. Elsevier Science Publishers, PO Box 211, 1000 AE Amsterdam Netherlands. **Tel** (020)5803.911. **Ind/Abst** Math. Rev., Sociol. Abstr., Soc. Welf. Soc. Plan./Policy Soc. Dev., Index Econ. Artic. J. Collect. Vol., Comput. Control Abstr., Electr. Electron. Abstr., Sci. Abstr. Sect. A. Phys. Abstr. **CODEN** MSOSDD.

A MATTER OF FACT : A DIGEST OF CURRENT FACTS WITH CITATIONS TO SOURCES. VFOAT Digest of Current Facts, with Citations to Sources. 1 (1984)-. US. English. **Ed** C Edward Wall.

MAWAZO. V. 1-. 0047-6293. Periodical. UG. English. sa. Makerere Institute of Social Research, PO Box 16022, Kampala Uganda. **Ind/Abst** Am. Hist. Life, Hist. Abstr., Part A, Mod. Hist. Abstr., Hist. Abst., Part B, Twent. Century Abstr., MLA Int. Bibliogr. Books Artic. Mod. Lang. Lit. **LC** DT1. Makerere Journal.

MAXWELL REVIEW. V. 1- 1965-. 0025-6110. Periodical. US. English. sa. $1.50 Students, $4.00 Others. Maxwell Review, 502 Maxwell Hall, Syracuse University, Syracuse NY 13210. **Ind/Abst** Public Aff. Inf. Serv. Bull. **LC** H1. **DD** 300.5. Available on microfilm from University microfilms.

MEDEDELINGEN VAN DE KONINKLIJKE ACADEMIE VOOR WETENSCHAPPEN, LETTEREN EN SCHONE KUNSTEN VAN BELGIE, KLASSE DER LETTEREN. Main/Corp Vlaamse Academie voor Wetenschappen, Letteren en Schone Kusten van Belgie. Klasse der Letteren. Vol. 1- 1939-. Dutch. ir. Konunklijke Academie voor Wetenschappen, Hertogsstraat 1, D-1000 Brussels Belgium. **Tel** 02/511 26 23. **Ed** G Verbeke. **Ind/Abst** Comput. Control Abstr., Electr. Electron. Abstr., Sci. Abstr. Sect. A. Phys. Abstr. **Circ** 800. (ctrl). Proceedings of the humanities section of the Academy, containing articles related to history, philosophy, legal sciences, psychology, linguistics, theology, etc.

MEDIUM. See Communication.

MEIJI DAIGAKU SHAKAI KAGAKU KENKYUJO KIYO. VFOAT Memoirs of the Institute of Social Sciences, Meiji University. No. 1-. JA. Japanese (with summaries in English). ir. Meiji Daigaku, 1 Kanda Surugadai 1 Chiyoda-ku, Tokyo Japan. **LC** H8.

MELBURNER BLETER. VFOAT Melbourne Chronicle. No. 1- Dec. 1975-. Periodical. English or Yiddish. ir. $12.00. Cystralye Kadimah, 7 Selwyn Street Elsternwick, Victoria 3185, Melbourne Australia. **Tel** 523-9817. **Ed** Yvonne Fein. **LC** DS101. bk rev. adv acc. **Circ** 1,000. Independent cultural social periodical, promoting various aspects of Jewish culture with special emphasis on Yiddish language.

MEMOIRS OF THE CONNECTICUT ACADEMY OF ARTS AND SCIENCES. See Humanities.

MEMORIA - DESCO. Main/Corp Desco. Spanish. ir. Desco, Leon Velarde 1226 Lince, Lima Peru. **LC** H62.5.P45.

MEMORIAS DE LA REAL ACADEMIA DE CIENCIAS NATURALES Y ARTES DE BARCELONA. See The Arts (General).

METHODOLOGY AND SCIENCE. See Philosophy.

METHODS AND MODELS IN THE SOCIAL SCIENCES. V. 1- 1971-. 0076-6828. Monographic Series. GW. English. ir. Walter de Gruyter, Genthiner Strasse 13, 1 Berlin 30 West Germany. **Tel** 030/26005-0.

MICHIGAN SOCIAL STUDIES TEXTBOOK STUDY. See Education (General) - Theory, Practice of Education.

THE MIDDLE EAST. ABSTRACTS AND INDEX. See Indexes/Abstracts.

MIGRATION NEWS. V. 5- Jan./Feb. 1956-. 0026-3583. Periodical. SZ. English. $10.- US. International Catholic Migration Commission, 37-39 rue de Vermont CP 96, 1211 Geneva 20 CIC Switzerland. **Tel** (022)33 41 50. **Ed** Dennis Clagett. Articles on migration and refugee affairs aimed both at professional and interested layman. News.

THE MISSISSIPPI QUARTERLY. See Humanities.

MISSOURI OVERALL PROGRAM DESIGN AND ANNUAL WORK PROGRAM. Main/Corp Missouri. Division of Budget and Planning. VFOAT Missouri Overall Program Design and Annual Work Program Fiscal Year. 1977-. 0149-9610. US. English. an. Division of Budget and Planning, B-9 Capitol Building, Jefferson City MO 65101. **LC** HT393.M8. **DD** 309.2509778. Missouri Overall Program Design, 0360-9634.

MONDES NOUVEAUX. V. 1- Feb. 1975-. 0318-8280. Periodical. CN. French. qt. Organisation Catholique Canadienne pour le Developpement et la Paix, 1452 rue Drummond, Montreal Quebec H3G 1W2 Canada. **DD** 309.11724.

MONITORING THE FUTURE. 1975-. 0190-9185. US. English. an. University of Michigan, PO Box 1248, Institution Social Research, Ann Arbor 48106. **Tel** (313)763-5043. **LC** HQ796. **DD** 305.230973.

MONOGRAPH - INSTITUTE OF APPLIED SOCIAL AND ECONOMIC RESEARCH. Main/Corp Institute of Applied Social and Economic Research. 1-. Periodical. English. ir. Institute of Applied Social & Economic Research, PO Box 5853, Boroko Papua New Guinea. **Tel** 25-3200. **Ed** E Makis. **Circ** 200. Scholarly writings based on research on the social, economic and political problems of Papau, New Guinea with practical applications for government planning and policy making.

MONOGRAPHS. SOCIAL SCIENCES - UNIVERSITY OF FLORIDA. Main/Corp University of Florida. No. 1- 1959-). Monographic Series. US. English. ir. University of Florida Press, 15 NW 15th Street, Gainesville FL 32601. **Tel** (904)392-1351. **Ed** George Pozzetta. **Circ** 750. Various topics in the social sciences. Each volume by a single author on a single topic.

MONTCLAIR JOURNAL OF SOCIAL SCIENCES AND HUMANITIES. (THE MONTCLAIR JOURNAL OF SOCIAL SCIENCES AND HUMANITIES). 0093-5778. Periodical. US. English. sa. $3.00. Montclair NJ 07043. **LC** H1. **DD** 300.5.

MONTHLY REPORT - ALLIANCE QUEBEC. (THE MONTHLY REPORT). Vol. 1, No. 1 (Nov. 1ST, 1982)-. 0821-6266. Periodical. CN. English. mo. Free. Alliance Quebec, Suite 501/ 1411 Crescent, Montreal Quebec H3G 2B8 Canada. **DD** 305.7210714. (ctrl).

MORALIA. V. 1- 1979-. Periodical. SP. Spanish. qt. 1.400 Spain/Portugal, $21.00 US. Moralia, Felix Boix 13, 28036 Madrid Spain. **Tel** (91)457 96 12. **Circ** 1,000. Covers ethics—moral, Bible, Christianity, practical theology, social sciences, anthropology, psychology, and philosophy.

MOUVEMENT SOCIAL. See History (General) - History of Europe.

MU KARA SANI NOUVELLE FORMULE : BULLETIN D'INFORMATION ET DE LIAISON DE L'INSTITUT DE RECHERCHES EN SCIENCES HUMAINES L'UNIVERSITE DE NIAMEY. V. 1, No. 1, (Year 1982)-. Periodical. French. ir. Institut de Recherches en Sciences Humaines, BP 318, Niamey Niger. **LC** Revpar. MU Kaara Sani.

MUSLIM SCIENTIST. 0148-0995. US. English. qt. $35.00 US and Canada, $40.00 Foreign. Association of Muslim Social Scientists, PO Box 38, Plainfield IN 46148. **Tel** (317)839-8157. **Ed** Sulayman Nyang. **Ind/Abst** Chem. Abstr. **CODEN** MUSCDX. bk rev. adv acc. **Circ** 1,500. (ctrl). To facilitate the collection, distribution and dissemination of social sciences information within an Islamic framework through well written scholarly articles.

NACHRICHTEN ZUR WIRTSCHAFTS- UND SOZIALPOLITIK. Began with Nov. 1971 issue. 0047-8598. Periodical. German. mo. **LC** H5. **DD** 300.5. Nachrichten: Informationen und Kommentare zur Wirtschafts- und Sozialpolitik.

Social Sciences (General)

NACLA REPORT ON THE AMERICAS. Main/Corp North American Congress on Latin America. VAT North American Congress on Latin America Report on the Americas. V. 11, No. 7- Sept./Oct. 1977-. 0149-1598. Periodical. US. English. bm. $29.00. North American Congress on Latin America, 151 West 19th Street, New York NY 10011. Tel (212)989-8890. Ed George Black. Ind/Abst Altern. Press Index. LC F1401. DD 309.18003. bk rev. adv acc. Circ 10,000. Principal objectives are to examine the forces which shape existing US governmental and business operations in Latin America and to analyze political and economic development. *N.A.C.L.A.'S Latin America & Empire Report*, 0095-5930.

NANZAN REVIEW OF AMERICAN STUDIES : A JOURNAL OF CENTER FOR AMERICAN STUDIES, NANZAN UNIVERSITY. Vol. 1 (1979)-. Periodical. JA. English. an. $6.00. Center for American Studies at Nanzan University, 18 Yamazato-cho Showo-ku, Nagoya 466 Japan. Tel (052)832-311. LC E169.1. DD 973.05. bk rev. Circ 500. (ctrl). Monographs in American studies in the field of social sciences such as history, sociology, economics, and political science, etc. US-Japan relationship is also emphasized.

NASIONALE REGISTER VAN NAVORSINGSPROJEKTE : NATUUR-EN GEESTESWETENSKAPPE. VFOAT National Register of Research Projects. Afrikaans and English. ir. Prime Minister, Private Bag X420, Pretoria 0001 South Africa. LC H62.5.A342. NLM Q 179.98 N254. *Nasionale Register Van Navorsingsprojekte: Natuurwetenskappe.*

NATIONAL ISSUES-OUTLOOK. See Public Administration.

NDVP VOLUNTEER JOURNAL. Main/Corp National Development Volunteer Programme. Research and Development Cell. VAT National Development Volunteer Programme Volunteer Journal. V. 1- Mar. 1975-. Periodical. English. ir. 1.00 Single Issue. National Development Volunteer Programme, 6th Floor/P I D C House, Karachi Pakistan. LC LC191. DD 309.23.

NEGACIONES. No. 1- Oct. 1976-. Periodical. Spanish. ir. 8000. Editorial Ayuso, San Bernardo 34, Madrid Spain. LC H8.

NEI MENG-KU FU NU. Periodical. CH. Chinese. ir. 0.20. Post Office, Hu-Ho-Hao-T E China. LC HQ1769.I56. DD 305.4095177.

NEPAL DOCUMENTATION. See Bibliographies.

NEUE POLITISCHE LITERATUR. 1.- Vol. 0028-3320. Periodical. GW. German. qt. 88. Franz Steiner Verlag GMBH, Postfach 347, D7000 Stuttgart 1 West Germany. Tel (0711)2582229. Ed W Michaeka. Ind/Abst Am. Hist. Life, Hist. Abstr., Part A, Mod. Hist. Abstr., Hist. Abst., Part B, Twent. Century Abstr., Foreign Lang. Index, PAIS Foreign Lang. Index, Hist. Abstr. LC H5. DD 300.5. bk rev. adv acc. Circ 1,000. Reviews in the fields of contemporary history and political science. *Politische Literatur.*

NEW APPROACHES TO SOCIAL SCIENCE HISTORY. Vol. 1-. Monographic Series. US. English. Sage Publications Inc, 275 South Beverly Drive, Beverly Hills CA 90212.

NEW DIRECTIONS FOR METHODOLOGY OF SOCIAL AND BEHAVIORAL SCIENCE. Began with: No. 3 (1980). 0271-1249. Monographic Series. US. English. qt. $30.00. Jossey-Bass Inc, 433 California Street, San Francisco CA 94104. Ed D W Fiske. Ind/Abst Psychol. Abstr. LC UNC. DD 300.18. NLM W1 NE374ES. *New Directions for Methodology of Behavioral Science*, 0271-0552.

NEW DIRECTIONS FOR PROGRAM EVALUATION. No. 1 (Spring 1978)-. 0164-7989. Monographic Series. US. English. qt. $40.00. Jossey-Bass Inc, 433 California Street, San Francisco CA 94104. Tel (415)433-1767. Ed Mark W Lipsey. Ind/Abst Educ. Index, Curr. Index J. Educ. LC UNC. DD 379.154. NLM W1 NE374ET. Circ 600. Outlines techniques and procedures for conducting useful evaluation studies of all types of programs, from educational curricular to welfare projects.

NEW EDITION. (THE NEW EDITION). Vol. 1, No. 1 (June 1984)-. 0824-1813. Periodical. CN. English. ir. Free. National Council of Jewish Women of Canada, Suite 401/1111 Finch Avenue, Downsview Ontario M3J 2E5 Canada. DD 305.488924071. (ctrl). *Keeping You Posted*, 0317-719X.

NEW ENGLAND JOURNAL OF BLACK STUDIES. See Ethnic.

THE NEW ENGLAND SOCIAL STUDIES BULLETIN. V. 1- Feb. 1944-. 0028-4912. Periodical. US. English. ty. New England History Teachers Association, Bentley College, Home Office, Waltham MA 02154. Tel (617)891-214. Ind/Abst Am. Hist. Life, Hist. Abstr., Part A, Mod. Hist. Abstr., Hist. Abst., Part B, Twent. Century Abstr., Curr. Index J. Educ., Hist. Abstr. LC H1. DD 305.

THE NEW SCHOLAR. V. 1- Apr. 1969-. 0028-6613. Periodical. US. English. sa. $10.00. The New Scholar, University of California, San Diego B-001, La Jolla CA 92093. Ind/Abst Am. Hist. Life, Hist. Abstr., Part A, Mod. Hist. Abstr., Hist. Abstr., Part B, Twent. Century Abstr., MLA Int. Bibliogr. Books Artic. Mod. Lang. Lit., Sociol. Abstr., Recent Publ. Artic., ABC Pol Sci, Altern. Press Index, Am. Hist. Life, Hist. Abstr., Psychol. Abstr., Educ. Resour. Inf. Cent. CLGH. LC H1. DD 300.5. CODEN NESCDY. Available on microfilm from University Microfilms.

THE NEW SCHOOL OBSERVER. June 1979-. 0883-6248. US. English. ir. New School for Social Research, 66 West 21st Street, New York NY 10013.

NEW SOCIETY. Began with issue for Oct. 4, 1962. 0028-6729. Periodical. UK. English. wk. $92.50. Statesman & Nation Publishing Co Ltd, 14-16 Farringdon Lane, London EC1R 3AU England. Tel (01)253-2001. Ind/Abst Sociol. Abstr., Soc. Welf. Soc. Plan./Policy Soc. Dev., Energy Inf. Abstr., Environ. Abstr., Women Stud. Abstr., CIS Abstr., Soc. Sci. Citation Index, Lang. Lang. Behav. Abstr. LC H1. DD 300.5.

NEW YORK AFFAIRS. V. 1- Summer 1973-. 0090-9920. Periodical. US. English. qt. $24.00. Urban Periodicals Inc, 25 West 45th Street, New York NY 10036. Ind/Abst Am. Hist. Life, Hist. Abstr., Part A, Mod. Hist. Abstr., Hist. Abst., Part B, Twent. Century Abstr., Avery Index Archit. Period. Second Ed. Revis. Enlarged Suppl., Public Aff. Inf. Serv. Bull. LC HN80.N5. DD 309.17471.

NEW YORK CITY SOCIAL REPORT. Mar. 1980-. 0736-5608. US. English. qt. Human Resources Administration, Office of Policy and Economic Research, 71 Worth Street/4th Floor, New York NY 10013. LC HN80.N5. DD 361.97471.

NEW ZEALAND JOURNAL OF INDUSTRIAL RELATIONS. V. 1- May 1976-. 0110-0637. Periodical. NZ. English. ty. 19.92. Industrial Relations Centre, Victoria University Private Bag, Wellington New Zealand. Tel 0064. Ed David Smith. Ind/Abst Int. Labour Doc., Public Aff. Inf. Serv. Bull. bk rev. adv acc. Circ 375. New Zealand industrial relations.

NEWFOUNDLAND SOCIAL AND ECONOMIC PAPERS. No. 1- 1968-. 0078-0332. Monographic Series. CN. English. ir. Institute of Social Economic Research, University of Newfoundland, St John Newfoundland Canada A1C 5S7. Tel (709)737-8000.

NEWSLETTER (AFRICAN SOCIAL STUDIES PROGRAMME). (NEWSLETTER). Periodical. KE. English. ir. African Social Studies Programme, PO Box 44777, Nairobi Kenya. LC H62.5.A34. DD 300.706.

NEWSLETTER - ASIAN BUREAU AUSTRALIA. See Political Science - International Relations.

NEWSLETTER - ECONOMIC AND SOCIAL RESEARCH COUNCIL. (ESRC NEWSLETTER). VFOAT E.S.R.C. Newsletter. 51 (Mar. 1984)-. 0266-2639. Periodical. UK. English. School Government Publishing Co, Darby House Bletchingley Road, Merstham Redhill RH1 3DN England. Ind/Abst World Text List. LC H62.5.G7. DD 300.72. Functions are to carry news on ESRC developments; to record all new awards; reports and publications arising from earlier awards, and to illustrate the achievements of UK social science. *SSRC Newsletter.*

NEWSLETTER - INTERNATIONAL CENTRE. CITIZENSHIP COUNCIL OF MANITOBA. (NEWSLETTER). VAT International Centre Newsletter (Winnipeg Manitoba). 0822-7659. Periodical. CN. English. bm. International Centre of Winnipeg, 700 Elgin Avenue, Winnipeg Manitoba R3E Canada. DD 304.87127.

NEWSLETTER - N. K. BOSE MEMORIAL FOUNDATION. Main/Corp NK Bose Memorial Foundation. No. 1- Dec. 1978-. Periodical. English. ir. 0.15 Non-members. LC H53.I5. DD 300.954.

NEWSLETTER - NATIONAL ASSOCIATION OF SOCIAL WORKERS. WASHINGTON STATE CHAPTER. See Sociology: General Works, Theory.

NEWSLETTER - SOCIAL SCIENCE COMPUTING LABORATORY. (NEWSLETTER). Main/Corp University of Western Ontario. Social Science Computing Laboratory. VFOAT SSCL Newsletter. VAT Social Science Computing Laboratory Newsletter. Vol. 1, No. 1 (Sept. 1982)-. 0714-6647. Periodical. CN. English. Free. Social Science Computing Laboratory, University of Western Ontario, London Ontario N6A 5C2 Canada. DD 025.06300971326.

NEWSLETTER (SOUTHWESTERN ANTHROPOLOGICAL ASSOCIATION). See Anthropology.

THE NIGERIAN JOURNAL OF ECONOMIC AND SOCIAL STUDIES. See Economics.

NIRA SOGO KENKYU KAIHATSU KIKO . . . NENJI HKOKUSHO. Main/Corp Sogo Kenkyu Kaihatsu Kiko. VAT National Institute for Research Advancement I.E. Sogo Kenkyu Kaihatsu Kiko. 1974-. Japanese. ir. c/o Shinjuku Mitsui Building, 37-kai 1-1 Nishi Shinjuku 2-chome, Shinjuku-ku (160) Tokyo Japan. LC H62.5.J3.

THE NORTH AMERICAN MENTOR MAGAZINE. See Literature.

NORTHERN SOCIAL SCIENCE REVIEW. 0196-1063. Periodical. US. English. an. Free. Editor NSSR, Social Science Department of Northern State College, Aberdeen SD 57401. Tel (605)622-2601. Ed Tracey Gladstone, Robert Stahl and Hillar Neumann. LC H1. DD 300.5. Circ 300. (ctrl). An inter-disciplinary journal of the social sciences regularly publishing articles in the fields of history, sociology, political science, economics and psychology.

NOVA HRVATSKA. Periodical. UK. Serbo-Croatian -R. bw. $70.00. Nova Hrvatska Ltd, 30 Fleet Street, London EC4Y 1AJ England. Tel (01)947-0498. Ed J Kusan. LC DB361. bk rev. Circ 15,000. A fornightly review in the Croatian language; critically appraising contemporary Yugoslav political, economic, social, cultural and religious life.

NOVAIA SOVETSKAIA I INOSTRANNAIA LITERATURA PO KULTURE I ISKUSSTVU : KULTURNO-PROSVETITELNAIA RABOTA I NARODNOE TVORCHESTVO. VFOAT Novaia Sovetskaia l Inostrannaia Literatura Po Kulturno-Prsovetitelnoi Rabote. No. Dec./Jan. 1974-. UR. Mutlilingual (Russian). mo. $18.60. Victor Kamkin Inc, 12224 Parklawn Drive, Rockville MD 20852. Tel (301)881-5973. LC Z2517.C55, AZ710. *Novaiia Sovetskaai I Inostrannaia Literatura po Kulturno-Prosvetitelnoi Rabote.*

NOVAIA SOVETSKAIA I INOSTRANNAIA LITERATURA PO OBSHCHESTVENNYM NAUKAM : EVROPEISKIE SOTSIALISTICHESKIE STRANY, OBSHCHIE PROBLEMY. VFOAT Evropeiskie Sotsialisticheskie Strany, Obshchie Problemy. 1976-. Periodical. UR. Russian (Multilingual). mo. 0.25 Single Issue. Vestnik Moskovskogo Universiteta, 103009 Ul Gertsena 5/7, Moskva Russian SFSR. AZ2483, H53.E83. *Novaia Literatura po Obshchim Problemam Evropeiskikh Sotsialisticheskikh Stran.*

NOVINKY LITERATURY. VFOAT Spolecenske Vedy. Rada III : Stat a Pravo. 1964-70. Periodical. CS. Czech. qt. Artia, PO Box 790, Praha 1 Czechoslovakia. LC Z7161. *Novinky Literatury. Spolecenske Vedy. Rada I.*

NOVINKY LITERATURY. POLITIKA. VFOAT Politika. V. 1/2- 1971-. Czech. ir. LC Z7161.A15. *Novinky Literatury. Spolecenske Vedy. Rada V, Politika.*

NOVYE KNIGI ZA RUBEZHOM PO OBSHCHESTVENNYM NAUKAM. V. 1- 1958-. Periodical. UR. Russian. mo. $18.00. Victor Kamkin Inc, 12224 Parklawn Drive, Rockville MD 20852. Tel (301)881-5973. LC H91.

NOWE DROGI. Vol. 1- (No. 1-). 0029-5388. Periodical. PL. Polish. mo. ARS Polona, Krakowskie Przedmiescie 7, 00-068 Warsaw Poland. **Ind/Abst** Am. Hist. Life, Hist. Abstr., Part A, Mod. Hist. Abstr., Hist. Abst., Part B, Twent. Century Abstr., Hist. Abstr. **LC** H8. **DD** 300.5.

NUSANTARA. Bilangan 1- Jan. 1972-. Periodical. English or Malay. ir. $6.50 Single Issue. Dewan Bahasa Dan Pustaka, PO Box 803, Kuala Lumpur Malaysia. **LC** H8.

OBSHCHESTVENNYE NAUKI. Began in 1976. Periodical. UR. Russian. bm. $23.00. Victor Kamkin Inc (70677), 12224 Parklawn Drive, Rockville MD 20852. **Tel** (301)881-5973. **LC** H8.

OBSHCHESTVENNYE NAUKI V SSSR. SERIIA 1 : PROBLEMY NAUCHNOGO KOMMUNIZMA. **VFOAT** Problemy Nauchnogo Kommunizma. **VAT** Obshchestvennye Nauki V SSSR. Seriia Odin : Problemy Nauchnogo Kommunizma. Began in 1973. 0202-2036. Periodical. UR. Russian. bm. Akademiia Nauk SSR, G-19 Ul Krasikova 28/45, Moskva USSR. **LC** H8.

OBSHCHESTVENNYE NAUKI V TADZHIKISTANE; UKAZATEL LITERATURY. *See* Indexes/Abstracts.

OCCASIONAL PAPER - INSTITUTE OF PUBLIC AFFAIRS. DALHOUSIE UNIVERSITY. (OCCASIONAL PAPER - THE INSTITUTE OF PUBLIC AFFAIRS, DALHOUSIE UNIVERSITY). **Main/Corp** Dalhousie University. Institute of Public Affairs. No. 1-. 0381-7024. Periodical. CN. English. ir. Institute of Public Affairs, Dalhousie University, Halifax Nova Scotia B3H 3J5 Canada. **DD** 300.

OCCASIONAL PAPERS. *See* Economics.

OEGUK CHAPCHI CHUYO KISA SAEGIN. **VFOAT** Foreign Periodicals Index. Chinese (English, Japanese, Korean, and Russian). ir. **LC** Z7163, H1. *Haeoe Chonggi Kanhaengmul Kisa Saegin.*

OIKOS. V. 1- 1949-. 0030-1299. Periodical. DK. English (some in French and German with summaries in Russian). bm. $112.67. Munksgaard Ltd, 35 Norre Sogade, DK-1370 Copenhagen K Denmark. **Tel** 1 12 70 30. **Ed** Per Brinck. **Ind/Abst** Excerpta Med., Sel. Water Resour. Abstr., Energy Inf. Abstr., Environ. Abstr., GeoRef, ASTIS Bibliogr., ASTIS Curr. Aware. Bull., Energy Res. Abstr., Biol. Abstr., Chem. Abstr., Sci. Cit. Index, Abr. Ed., Bibliogr. Agric., Excerpta Med., Sel. Water Resour. Abstr., Energy Inf. Abstr., Environ. Abstr., GeoRef, ASTIS Bibliogr., ASTIS Curr. Aware. Bull., Energy Res. Abstr., Biol. Abstr., Chem. Abstr., Sci. Cit. Index, Abr. Ed., Bibliogr. Agric., Bibliogr. Index Geol. **LC** QH540. **CODEN** OIKSAA. (cum index). adv acc. **Circ** 1,000. Ecology.

OKINAWA KOKUSAI DAIGAKU BUNGAKUBU KIYO: *SHAKAIGAKKA-HEN. **VFOAT** Bulletin of the Department of Sociology, Okinawa Kokusai University. Japanese. ir. 276-2 Ginowan, Ginowan Japan. **LC** H8.

O.P.T. (OPT, THE MAGAZINE ON PEOPLE AND THINGS). V. 6- May 1974-. 0095-5868. Periodical. US. English. sm. $3.80. Xerox Education Center, 1250 Fairwood Avenue, Columbus OH 43216. **LC** LH1. **DD** 051. *Issues Today.*

ORGANIZATION STUDIES. 1, Issue 1-. 0170-8406. Periodical. English. $49.95. Walter Gruyter Inc, 200 Saw Mill River Road, Hawthorne NY 10532. **Tel** (914)747-0110. **Ed** David J Hickson. **Ind/Abst** Electron. Commun. Abstr. J., ISMEC Bull., Pollut. Abstr. Indexes, Saf. Sci. Abstr. J., Sociol. Abstr., Manage. Contents, Soc. Welf. Soc. Plan./Policy Soc. Dev., Cumul. Index Nurs. Allied Health Lit., ABI/Inform, Psychol. Abstr. bk rev. adv acc. **Circ** 1,000. Aims to promote the understanding of organizations and the social relevance of that understanding.

OSMANIA JOURNAL OF SOCIAL SCIENCES : BI-ANNUAL JOURNAL OF THE FACULTY OF SOCIAL SCIENCES. Vol. 1, No. 1 (June 1981)-. English. sa. $15.00 Foreign. Editor/Osmania Journal of Social Sciences, Office of the Dean Faculty of Social Sciences, Osmania University, Hyderabad 50007 India. **Ind/Abst** Public Aff. Inf. Serv. Bull. **LC** HC431. **DD** 300.5.

PAN AFRICAN SOCIAL SCIENCE REVIEW. (PAN AFRICAN SOCIAL SCIENCE REVIEW : PASSR). 8755-7436. Periodical. US. English. an. Victor Manfredi, c/o Wooden Shoe Printing Co, 241 5th Street, Cambridge MA 02139.

PAPERS IN THE SOCIAL SCIENCES. (PAPERS IN THE SOCIAL SCIENCES : A JOURNAL OF THE COLLEGE OF LIBERAL AND FINE ARTS, UNIVERSITY OF THE DISTRICT OF COLUMBIA). Vol. 2 (1982)-. 0732-1082. US. English. an. $5.00. Editor of Papers in the Social Sciences, University of the District of Columbia College of Liberal and Fine Arts 4200 Connecticut Avenue Northwest, Washington DC 20008. **Ind/Abst** Psychol. Abstr. **LC** H1. **DD** 300.5. *Working Papers in the Social Sciences.*

PARLEMENTAIRE DOCUMENTATIE. **Main/Corp** Belgium. Parlement. **VFOAT** Documentation Parlementaire. Dutch (French). ir. **LC** Z7166, H8.D8. *Documentation Parlementaire.*

PARTICIPONS. V. 1-5, No. 9. 0701-1148. Periodical. CN. French. mo. La Chambre de Commerce de Sainte-Foy, CP 9426, Sainte-Foy Quebec G1V 4B8 Canada. **DD** 309.171447. *Commerce Sainte-Foy, 0317-2414.*

PEI-CHING SHIH FAN TA HSUEH HSUEH PAO : SHE HUI KO HSUEH PAN. BEIJING SHIFAN DAXUE XUEBAO. **VFOAT** Beijing Shifan Daxue Xuebao. Vol. 1, No. 1 (Sept 1956)-. Periodical. Chinese. qt. China Publication Centre, PO Box 2820, Beijing China. **Ind/Abst** Chem. Abstr. **LC** AS452.P25. **DD** 300.5. *Pei-Ching Shih Ta Hsueh Pao: She Hui Ko Hsueh Pan.*

PENYELIDIK. V. 1- Oct. 1972-. Malay. ir. $2.50 (Single Issue). Persatuan Pelajar-Pelajar Lupusan Sekolah Alam Shah, Jalan Cheras, Kuala Lumpur Malaysia. **LC** H62.A1.

PEOPLE AND PROJECTS. Periodical. English. ir. Ministry of Education, Private Bag 7724, Causeway Salisbury Rhodesia. **LC** HN800.R64. **DD** 309.263096891. *Projects and People.*

PERSPECTIVES. V. 8- Fall 1972-. 0316-3334. Periodical. CN. English. qt. $7.74. Saskatchewan Council of Social Studies Teachers, c/o Dr John Schaller, University of Regina, Regina Saskatchewan S4S 0A2 Canada. **Tel** (306)584-4625. **Ed** John Schaller. **Ind/Abst** Can. Educ. Index. bk rev. adv acc. **Circ** 205. (ctrl). The journal for social studies teachers in elementary and secondary schools of Saskatchewan Canada. It is a subject council publication of the Teacher's Federation. *Social Sciences for the Seventies, 0316-3644; Social Science Teachers Newsletter, 0316-3318.*

PERSPECTIVES - NIAGARA INSTITUTE. (PERSPECTIVES). **Main/Corp** Niagara Institute. Vol. 1, No. 1 (Spring 1981)-. 0711-4931. Periodical. CN. English. ty. Free. Niagara Institute, Box 1041, Niagara-on-the-Lake Ontario L0S 1J0 Canada. **DD** 303.3406071351. (ctrl).

PEUPLES MEDITERRANEENS. **VFOAT** Mediterranean Peoples. No. 1- Oct./Dec. 1977-. 0399-1253. Periodical. FR. French (English or French, with summaries in other language). qt. 255. Inst d'Etudes Mediterraneenes, BP 1907, 75327 Paris Cedex 07 France. **Tel** 45 67 01 41. **Ind/Abst** Am. Hist. Life, Hist. Abstr., Part A, Mod. Hist. Abstr., Hist. Abst., Part B, Twent. Century Abstr., Sociol. Abstr., Soc. Welf. Soc. Plan./Policy Soc. Dev., Recent Publ. Artic. **LC** DE1. **DD** 909.09822. adv acc. **Circ** 2,000. Organ of free speech, in its pages, world specialists on the Inland Sea bring critical thought to bear upon contemporary societies and renew scientific debate concerning past and present social formations in the region.

PHILOSOPHY & PUBLIC AFFAIRS. Vol. 1 (Fall 1971)-. 0048-3915. Periodical. US. English. qt. $22.50. Princeton University Press, 3175 Princeton Pike, Lawrenceville NJ 08648. **Tel** (609)452-5173 **Ed** Kathy Astrue. **Ind/Abst** Sociol. Abstr., Soc. Welf. Soc. Plan./Policy Soc. Dev., Energy Inf. Abstr., Environ. Abstr., ABC Pol Sci, Women Stud. Abstr., Philos. Index, Humanit. Index. **LC** H1. **DD** 300.5. bk rev. adv acc. **Circ** 3,000. Discussions of public concern in law, political science, economics, sociology, and ethics.

PHILOSOPHY OF THE SOCIAL SCIENCES. **VFOAT** Philosophie des Sciences Sociales. V. 1- Jan. 1971-. 0048-3931. Periodical. CN. English (French). qt. 27.00. Wilfred Laurier University Press, 75 University Avenue West, Waterloo Ontario Canada. **Tel** (416)667-2582. **Ed** I C Jarvie. **Ind/Abst** Sociol. Abstr., Philos. Index, Index Book Rev. Humanit., Soc. Sci. Citation Index, Lang. Lang. Behav. Abstr. bk rev. adv acc. **Circ** 900. Concerned with issues of general methodology in all the social sciences.

PHYLON. V. 21- Spring 1960-. 0031-8906. Periodical. US. English. qt. $24.00 Domestic, $26.00 Foreign. Atlanta University, 223 James P Brawley Drive, Atlanta GA 30314. **Tel** (404)681-0251. **Ed** Wilbur Watson. **Ind/Abst** MLA Int. Bibliogr. Books Artic. Mod. Lang. Lit., Soc. Welf. Soc. Plan./Policy Soc. Dev., Women Stud. Abstr., Hist. Abstr., Writ. Am. Hist., Book Rev. Index, Int. Index, Am. Hist. Life, Hist. Abstr., Part A, Mod. Hist. Abstr., Psychol. Abstr., Curr. Index J. Educ., Soc. Sci. Citation Index, Lang. Lang. Behav. Abstr., Guide Soc. Sci. Relig. Period. Lit. **LC** E185.5. bk rev. adv acc. **Circ** 2,000. (ctrl). Available in microfilm from University Microfilms. Examines issues of race and culture as they relate to social and political behaviors and literary analysis. *Phylon Quarterly, 0885-6826.*

POLICY ANALYSIS *CEASED.* V. 1-7, No. 2. 0098-2067. US. English. qt. $12.00. 2607 Hearst Avenue, Berkeley CA 94720. **Ind/Abst** Sociol. Abstr., Soc. Welf. Soc. Plan./Policy Soc. Dev., Bibliogr. Agric., Public Aff. Inf. Serv. Bull., Index Econ. Artic. J. Collect. Vol. **LC** H1. **DD** 300.5. **NLM** W1 PO211L. Index in last issue of volume - attached.

POLICY AND RESEARCH REPORT. **VFOAT** Urban Institute Policy and Research Report. Vol. 9, No. 1 (Fall 1979)-. 0741-8485. Periodical. US. English. sa. Free. Urban Institute, 2100 M Street NW Washington DC 20037. **Tel** (202)857-8702. **Ed** K Storck. **Circ** 8,500. Social and economic problems that confront the nation and government policies and programs designed to alleviate such problems. *Search, 0582-3552.*

POLICY PUBLISHERS AND ASSOCIATIONS DIRECTORY. *See* Yearbooks, Almanacs, Directories.

POLICY RESEARCH CENTERS DIRECTORY. *See* Yearbooks, Almanacs, Directories.

POLICY REVIEW. 1- Summer 1977-. 0146-5945. Periodical. US. English. qt. $38.00. Heritage Foundation, 214 Massachusetts Avenue NE, Washington DC 20002. **Tel** (202)546-4400. **Ind/Abst** Sociol. Abstr., Soc. Welf. Soc. Plan./Policy Soc. Dev., Predicasts, Index Econ. Artic. J. Collect. Vol., ABC Pol Sci, Book Rev. Index, Public Aff. Inf. Serv. Bull., Soc. Sci. Index. **LC** H1. **DD** 300.5.

THE POLICY STUDIES DIRECTORY. *See* Yearbooks, Almanacs, Directories.

POLICY STUDIES PERSONNEL DIRECTORY. *See* Yearbooks, Almanacs, Directories.

POLICY STUDIES REVIEW ANNUAL. V.1- 1977-. 0163-108X. US. English. an. Transaction Books & Periodical, Rutgers University, New Brunswick NJ 08903. **Tel** (201)932-2280. **Ed** S S Nagel. **LC** H1. **DD** 300.5.

DIE POLITISCHE MEINUNG. Vol. 1-. 0032-3446. Periodical. GW. German. bm. Verlag A Fromm GMBH, Postfach 1048, Briet Gang 11-14, D-4500 Osnabruck West Germany. **Ed** K W Beer. **Ind/Abst** Energy Res. Abstr., PAIS Foreign Lang. Index, Foreign Lang. Index. **LC** H5. **DD** 300.5.

POTOMAC REVIEW. (THE POTOMAC REVIEW). V. 6-8, No. 2, 1973-Fall 1979/Winter 1980. 0091-2573. Periodical. US. English. ir. Potomac Review Inc, PO Box 378, Dunn Loring VA 22027. **Ed** Charles K White. **Ind/Abst** Am. Hist. Life, Hist. Abstr., Part A, Mod. Hist. Abstr., Hist. Abst., Part B, Twent. Century Abstr., ABC Pol Sci, Public Aff. Inf. Serv. Bull., Hist. Abstr. **LC** AS30. **DD** 300.5. bk rev. adv acc. **Circ** 500. Graduate research in history, politics and the social sciences. *Journal of International & Comparative Studies, 0022-1988.*

POWER AND ELITES. Vol. 1, No. 1 (Fall 1984)-. 0743-9253. Periodical. US. English. sa. $14.00. Associated Faculty Press Inc, 90 South Bayles Avenue, Port Washington KY 11050. **DD** 305.

PRACE Z NAUK SPOECZNYCH. **Main/Corp** Uniwersytet Slaski W Katowicach. **Series/Titl** Prace Naukowe Uniwersytetu Slaskiego W Katowicach. 1- 1975-. Polish (summaries in English and Russian). ir. 13.00 Single Issue. Uniwersytet Shaski, Ksiegarnia Naukowa Nr 4 Dom, Ksiazki Ul Warszawska 11/40-009, Katowice Poland. **LC** H8.

PROBLEMES POLITIQUES ET SOCIAUX. 0015-9743. Periodical. FR. French. sm. 308.00 Domestic, 333.00 Foreign. La Documentation Francaise, 29-31 Quai Voltaire, 75007 Paris France. **Tel** 834-9275. **LC** H3. *Articles et Documents.*

PROBLEMES SOCIAUX ZAIROIS *CEASED.* No. 96/97-No. 126/127. Periodical. CG. French. qt. Centre d'Execution des Programmes Sociaux et Economiques, 208 Av Kasavubu, Boite PN

Social Sciences (General)

1873, Lubumbashi Republic of Zaire. **LC** DT641. **DD** 309.1675103. *Problemes Sociaux Congolais.*

PROBLEMI DI CIVILTA. Yearly V. 1- 1978-. Periodical. IT. Italian (with summaries in English, French, German, and Spanish). ir. 20000. Societa Ed Napoletana, Corso Umberto I 34, 80138 Napoli Italy. **LC** H1.

PROCEEDINGS - INDIANA ACADEMY OF THE SOCIAL SCIENCES. Main/Corp Indiana Academy of the Social Sciences. New Ser., V. 3 (1958)-New Ser. V. 10 (1965). US. English. an. **Tel** (219)980-6698. **Circ** 300. *Proceedings of the Annual Meeting.*

PROMETEO (MILAN, ITALY). (PROMETEO). Year 1, No.1 (Feb./Apr. 1983)-. Periodical. IT. Italian. qt. 18.77. Mondadori Editore, via Bianca di Savoia 20, 20122 Milano Italy. **Tel** 02/75421. Ed Andreina Vanni. bk rev. adv acc. **Circ** 10,000. A review concerning history, anthropology, biology semiology, philosophy, archaeology, ethnology, ethno history, new technologies.

PSSC SOCIAL SCIENCE INFORMATION. Main/Corp Philippine Social Science Council. V. 1- May 1973-. Periodical. PH. English. qt. $8.00. PSSC Central Subscription Service, PO Box 655 Greenhills, Metro Manila 3113 Philippines. **Tel** 922-9621. Ed Olivia Caoili. **LC** H62.5.P47. **DD** 300.9599. bk rev. adv acc. **Circ** 1,000. Contains articles relative to the status and growth of political science in the Philippines.

PSYCHOANALYTIC STUDY OF SOCIETY. V. 1-. 0079-7294. US. English. ir. Analytic Press Inc, 365 Broadway, Hillsdale NJ 07642. **LC** H9. **DD** 305.8. **NLM** W1 PS452. *Psychoanalysis and the Social Sciences.*

PUBLIC AFFAIRS INFORMATION SERVICE BULLETIN (ANNUAL). (PUBLIC AFFAIRS INFORMATION SERVICE BULLETIN). **VFOAT** Bulletin. 54th Annual cumulation (1968)-62nd Annual Cumulation (1976). 0033-3409. US. English. an. Public Affairs Information Service Inc, 11 West 40th Street, New York NY 10018. **Ind/Abst** Popul. Index. **NLM** Z 7163. (cum index). *Bulletin of the Public Affairs Information Service, 0731-0110.*

THE PUBLIC INTEREST. No. 1- Fall 1965-. 0033-3557. Periodical. US. English. qt. National Affairs Inc, 10 East 53rd Street, New York NY 10022. **Tel** (212)593-7123. **Ind/Abst** Am. Hist. Life, Avery Index Archit. Period., Hist. Abstr., Abstr. Soc. Work., Hist. Abstr., Part A, Mod. Hist. Abstr., Hist. Abst., Part B, Twent. Century Abstr., Manage. Contents, Sociol. Abstr., Soc. Welf. Soc. Plan./Policy Soc. Dev., Hospit. Lit. Index, ABC Pol Sci, ABI/Inform, Public Aff. Inf. Serv. Bull., Energy Inf. Abstr., Environ. Abstr., Curr. Index J. Educ., Bus. Period. Index, Soc. Sci. Index, Soc. Sci. Citation Index, Soc. Work Res. Abstr. **LC** H1. **DD** 300.5. **CODEN** PUBIBV.

PUBLIC POLICY STUDIES IN THE SOUTH. 1975-. US. English. an. $5.00. Clark College, Southern Center for Studies in Public Policy, Atlanta GA 30314. **LC** H62.5.U5. **DD** 300.2575.

PUBLICATIONS OF THE INSTITUTE OF SOCIAL STUDIES. PAPERBACK SERIES. Main/Corp Institute of Social Studies (Netherlands). 1- 1970-). Monographic Series. US. English. ir. Walter de Gruyter Inc, 200 Saw Mill River Road, Hawthorne NY 10532. **Tel** (914)747-0110.

QQ. (QQ : REPORT FROM THE CENTER FOR PHILOSOPHY & PUBLIC POLICY). **VFOAT** Report from the Center for Philosophy & Public Policy. Vol. 1, No. 1 (Winter 1981)-. 0735-8555. Periodical. US. English. qt. Center for Philosophy and Public Policy, Rm 0123 Woods Hall/University of Maryland, College Park MD 20742. **Tel** (301)454-4103. Ed Claudia Mills. **LC** H1. **DD** 361.6105. bk rev. **Circ** 9,500. Features articles on the concepts and values that underlie various policy issues such as: nuclear deterrence, equal opportunity, environmental protection, regulation of risk, and the role of the media in a democracy.

QUANTITATIVE APPLICATIONS IN THE SOCIAL SCIENCES. 1-. 0149-192X. US. English. ir. Sage Publications, 275 South Beverly Drive, Beverly Hills CA 90212.

QUARTERLY SUMMARY OF TITLE XX SERVICES AND EXPENDITURES IN NORTH CAROLINA. Vols. 1, No. 1 (Oct./Dec. 1977)-. Periodical. US. Enlgish. qt. NC Department of Human Resources, Division of Plans and Operations, Title XX Reports Unit, 325 North Salisbury Street, Raleigh NC 27611. **LC** HV98.N8. **DD** 361.609756.

A QUESTAO SOCIAL NO BRASIL. 1-. Monographic Series. BL. Portuguese. ir. Lech Livraria Editora Ciencias Humanas, rua 7 de Abril 264 Subsolo B Sala 5, CEP 01044 Sao Paulo Brazil.

QUESTIONS DE CULTURE. No. 1-. 0229-6829. Monographic Series. CN. French. Institut Quebecois de Recherche sur la Culture, 93 rue Saint-Pierre, Quebec Quebec G1K 4A3 Canada. **Tel** (418)643-9107. **DD** 306.05.

RAISON PRESENTE. No. 1- 4E Quarterly 1966-. 0033-9075. Periodical. FR. French. qt. 180. Raison Presente, 16 rue de Lecole Polytechnique, Paris 5E France. **Tel** 46330350. **Ind/Abst** Sociol. Abstr., Lang. Lang. Behav. Abstr. bk rev. **Circ** 1,200. Essays on various subjects such as education, physics, psychology, history, politics, etc.

RAIZ & I.E. E UTOPIA. VAT Raiz e Utopia. No. 1- Primavera 1977-. Periodical. PO. Portuguese. ir. 350.00. Raiz and Utopia, rua Antonio Maria Cardoso, 68 No 1, Lisboa Portugal. **LC** H8.

RAPPORT ANNUEL - INSTITUT ECONOMIQUE ET SOCIAL DES CLASSES MOYENNES (BELGIUM). Main/Corp Institut Economique et Social des Classes Moyennes (Belgium). BE. French. an. Institut Economique et Social des Classes Moyennes, rue du Congres 33, 1000 Bruxelles Belgium.

RAPPORT SUR LES FEMMES. Sept. 1982-. 0824-3883. Periodical. CN. French. ir. Free. Rapport sur les Femmes, c/o Parti Nouveau Democratique, Chambre des Communes, Ottawa Ontario K1A 0A6 Canada. **DD** 305.420971.

READINGS IN THE SOCIAL SCIENCES. Main/Corp Scientific American Resource Library. US. English. ir. $47.90. W H Freeman & Publications, 660 Market Street, San Francisco CA 94104.

REASON. Began with Spring 1968 issue. 0048-6906. Periodical. US. English. ir. $16.00. Reason Foundation, PO Box 40105, Santa Barbara CA 93103. **Tel** (805)963-5993. Ed Marty Zupan. **Ind/Abst** Am. Hist. Life, Hist. Abstr., Part A, Mod. Hist. Abstr., Hist. Abst., Part B, Twent. Century Abstr., Public Aff. Inf. Serv. Bull., Energy Inf. Abstr., Environ. Abstr., Hist. Abstr. **LC** H1. **DD** 300.5. bk rev adv acc. **Circ** 38,000. Vols. 1-4 available on microfilm from University of Southern California Library micrographics department. Analysis and commentary on current affairs and issues, from a libertarian (individualist, free-market) perspective.

REASON PAPERS. Began with Fall 1974 issue. 0363-1893. US. English. $4.00. 14063. **Ind/Abst** Philos. Index. **LC** H1. **DD** 300.5.

RECHERCHE ET DOCUMENTATION - COMITE DE DIRECTION SCIENTIFIQUE DU C D S H. (RECHERCHE ET DOCUMENTATION - COMITE DE DIRECTION SCIENTIFIQUE, CENTRE DE DOCUMENTATION EN SCIENCES HUMAINES, UNIVERSITE DU QUEBEC A MONTREAL). **Main/Corp** Universite du Quebec a Montreal. Centre de Documentation en Sciences Humaines. Comite de Direction Scientifique. No. 1, 1974. 0701-0699. Periodical. CN. French. an. Centre de Documentation en Sciences, Humaines rue Pavillon, Local 9345, Montreal Quebec Canada. **DD** 016.3005.

RECUEILS DE LA SOCIETE JEAN BODIN POUR L'HISTOIRE COMPARATIVE DES INSTITUTIONS. Main/Corp Societe Jean Bodin pour l'Histoire Comparative des Institutions. 1- 1936-. Monographic Series. French. ir. **LC** H13.

REFERENCE SOURCES FOR THE SOCIAL SCIENCES AND HUMANITIES. No. 1-. 0730-3335. Monographic Series. US. English. ir. Greenwood Press, 88 Post Road West, PO Box 5007, Westport CT 06881. **Tel** (203)226-3571. Ed Raymond G McInnis.

REGIONAL STUDIES. V. 1- May 1967-. 0034-3404. Periodical. UK. English. $130.00. Cambridge University Press, 510 North Avenue, New Rochelle NY 10801. Ed W I Morrison, Peter Damesick and G L Clark. **Ind/Abst** Avery Index Archit. Period., Soc. Sci. Citation Index, Int. Labour Doc., Excerpta Med., Sociol. Abstr., Soc. Welf. Soc. Plan./Policy Soc. Dev., Index Econ. Artic. J. Collect. Vol., Popul. Index, Public Aff. Inf. Serv. Bull., Writ. Am. Hist. **LC** HT390. **CODEN** REGSAT. bk rev. Available on microfilm. Research on such topics as industrial, retail and office location, labor markets, housing, migration, recreation, transport, communications and the evaluation of public policy.

REGISTER VAN SOCIAAL-WETENSCHAPPELIJK ONDERZOEK. VFOAT Register of Social Science Research in the Netherlands. 1970/72-. NE. Dutch. ir. Koninklijke Nederlandse Akademi Van Wetenschapen, Sociaal-Wetenschappelijk Informatie en Documentatiecentrum, Amsterdam Netherlands. **LC** H62.A1. *Register van Lopend Onderzoek in de Sociale Wetenschappen.*

RELATORIO GERAL, RELATORIO DAS UNIDADES, PRESTACAO DE CONTAS. Main/Corp Fundacao Getulio Vargas. BL. Portuguese. ir. Funda Caogetulio Vargas, Caixa Postal 9052, Rio de Janeiro Brazil. **LC** H67.F9. **DD** 300.71081. *Relatorio e Prestacao de Contas.*

RENAISSANCE UNIVERSAL JOURNAL. 0712-4767. Periodical. US. English. qt. 30.00. Renaissance Universal, 904 Sanford Drive, Bulington Ontario L7T 3G6 Canada. **Tel** (416)632-5602. Ed Dhanjoo N Ghista. **LC** HN1. **DD** 301.24. bk rev. adv acc. **Circ** 1,000. Global distributive injustices and cruelties arising out of lack of means for self-direction and concept of a progressive society, constitute the thesis of this area.

REPERTOIRE DES THESES AFRICANISTES FRANCAISES. 1977-. FR. French. an. Sec des Publ du Cea Cardan, 54 Bd Raspail, 75006 Paris France. **Tel** (1)544 3979. **LC** Z3501, DT3. **DD** 016.96. Publication examines doctoral theses written during the year in France dealing with social sciences, law, political science, economic science of continental Africa and its islands.

REPORT OF ACTIVITIES - CEDES. Main/Corp Centro de Estudios de Estado y Sociedad. English. ir. Centro de Estudios de Estado y Sociedad, Hipolito Yrigoyen 1156, 1086 Buenos Aires Argentina. **LC** H62.A1. **DD** 300.72082.

A REPORT ON THE BACKGROUND, CURRENT PROGRAMMES AND PLANNED DEVELOPMENT OF THE BANGLADESH INSTITUTE OF DEVELOPMENT STUDIES. Main/Corp Bangladesh Institute of Development Studies. 1975-. English. ir. Bangladesh Institute of Development Studies, Adamjee Court Motijheel Commercial Area, Dacca Bangladesh. **LC** H62.5.B35. **DD** 338.95492.

REPORT ON THE DEVELOPMENT OF THE SOCIAL SITUATION IN THE COMMUNITIES. Main/Corp Commission of the European Communities. **VFOAT** Social Rep. English. ir. $5.80. **LC** HN380.5. **DD** 309.14055.

REPORT - PUERTO RICO. UNIVERSITY. SOCIAL SCIENCE RESEARCH CENTER. Main/Corp Puerto Rico. University. Social Science Research Center. 1946/47-. PR. English. ir. Universidad de Puerto Rico, Facultad de Ciencias Sociales, Rio Piedras Puerto Rico 00931. **LC** HC157.P8. **DD** 307.2.

REPORTS AND PAPERS IN THE SOCIAL SCIENCES. Main/Corp United Nations Educational, Scientific and Cultural Organization. Social Science Clearing House. **Series Corp** United Nations Educational, Scientific and Cultural Organization. Document. No. 1- 1955-. 0080-1348. English (No. 8 has title also in French). ir. Unipub, Po Box 1222, Ann Arbor MI 48106. **Tel** (800)521-8110. **LC** AS4.U8.

REPORTS OF INVESTIGATIONS - SOUTHERN METHODIST UNIVERSITY. INSTITUTE FOR THE STUDY OF EARTH AND MAN. (REPORTS OF INVESTIGATIONS). **Main/Corp** Southern Methodist University. Institute for the Study of Earth and Man. N. No. 1- 1975-. US. English. ir. Southern Methodist University, Dallas TX 75275. **Ind/Abst** GeoRef. **CODEN** RISMDY.

REPORTS. SS. (REPORTS : SS). **Main/Conf** Inter-African Conference. Social Sciences. **VFOAT** Reports: Social Sciences. 1- 1955-. 0414-0524. Periodical. UK. English. ir. Europa Publications Ltd, 18 Bedford Square, London WC1B 3JN England. **DD** 338.9.

REPRINT SERIES - INSTITUTE FOR RESEARCH ON POVERTY CEASED. (REPRINT). **Main/Corp** University of Wisconsin. Institute for Research on Poverty. 1- 1966-.

0084-0769. Monographic Series. US. English. $20.00. Institute of Research on Poverty, 1180 Observatory Road University of Wisconsin, Madison WI 53706. **Tel** (608) 262-6358. **Circ** 200. (ctrl). Professional journal, articles published by Institute Staff, disseminating research findings and addressing public policy issues.

RESEARCH ABSTRACTS AND NEWSLETTER. *See* Indexes/Abstracts.

RESEARCH & INNOVATION BULLETIN. **VFOAT** Research and Innovation Bulletin. Began in 1972. 0155-1051. Periodical. AT. English. sa. 32.00. Research & Advisory Service, PO Box 188, Churchill Victoria 3842 Australia. **Tel** (051)221552. **Ed** Lenore Cox. Each issue contains an index to its own contents - no vol index - loose. **Circ** 200. Research from all colleges of advanced education in Australia. Subject areas cover education, engineering, paramedical, science and social science.

RESEARCH AND PUBLICATIONS. *See* Economics.

RESEARCH IN BRITISH UNIVERSITIES, POLYTECHNICS AND COLLEGES. **VFOAT** RBUPC. 1979-. 0142-2472. UK. English. ir. British Library, Bibliographic Service Division, 2 Sheraton Street, London W1V 4BH England. **Tel** (01)636-1544. **LC** Q180.G7. **DD** 001.40941. **NLM** Q 180.G5 5416. *Scientific Research in British Universities and Colleges, 0080-7745.*

RESEARCH IN PUBLIC POLICY ANALYSIS AND MANAGEMENT. (RESEARCH IN PUBLIC POLICY ANALYSIS AND MANAGEMENT : OFFICIAL PUBLICATION OF THE ASSOCIATION FOR PUBLIC POLICY ANALYSIS AND MANAGEMENT). Vol. 1-. 0732-1317. Periodical. US. English. ir. $49.50. JAI Press, PO Box 1678, Greenwich CT 06836. **Tel** (203)661-7602. **Ed** John P Crecine. **LC** H97. **DD** 361.6105. **NLM** W1 RE227KM.

RESEARCH SUPPORTED BY THE SOCIAL SCIENCE RESEARCH COUNCIL. **Main/Corp** Social Science Research Council (Great Britain). UK. English. an. Social Science Research Council, 1 Temple Avenue, London EC4Y OBD England. **Tel** (01)637-1499. **Ed** David Wainwright and Ian Miller. **LC** H62.5.G7. **DD** 300.72041. **Circ** 1,500. Lists research projects in the fields of economic affairs, education and human development, environment and planning, government and law, industry and employment and social affairs.

REVIEW JOURNAL OF PHILOSOPHY & SOCIAL SCIENCE. **VFOAT** Review Journal of Philosophy and Social Science. V. 1-. Periodical. II. English. sa. 10.00. Anu Books, Shivaji Road, Meerut 250001 India. **Ed** Michael Belok. **Ind/Abst** Philos. Index. **LC** H1. **DD** 300.5. bk rev. adv acc. **Circ** 500. (ctrl). History of education, such as educational policy studies, philosophy of education, education and social sciences are included.

THE REVIEW OF ANTI-SEMITISM IN CANADA. **VFOAT** Rapport Annuel sur l'Antisemitisme au Canada. 1983-. CN. English (text in French on inverted pages). an. $5.00 Per No. League for Human Rights of B'Nai Brith Canada, 15 Hove Street, Downsview Ontario M3H 4Y8 Canada. **DD** 305.8924071. *Rapport Annuel sur l'Antisemitisme au Canada, 0828-6167.*

REVIEW OF PUBLIC DATA USE. Began with Dec. 1972 issue. 0092-2846. US. English. qt. **Ind/Abst** Hospit. Lit. Index, Popul. Index, Women Stud. Abstr., Public Aff. Inf. Serv. Bull., Sociol. Abstr., Soc. Welf. Soc. Plan./Policy Soc. Dev. **LC** H62.A1. **DD** 300.72073.

REVISTA ANDINA. Year 1, V. 1 (Sept. 1983)-. Periodical. PE. Spanish. sa. $30.00. Centro Las Casas, Apartado 477, Cusco Peru. **Tel** 233472. **LC** F2212. **DD** 980.005. bk rev. adv acc. **Circ** 1,000. (ctrl). A specialized journal on Andean matters (collaborations by experts in economics, history, linguistics, anthropology, archaeology and sociology), aiming to stimulate debate within the journal itself.

REVISTA DE CIENCIAS HUMANAS. Vol. 1, No. 1 (Jan. 1982)-. Periodical. Portuguese. sa. 700.00. Editora da UFSC, Caixa Postal 476, 88.000 Florianopolis SC Brazil. **LC** H8.P8. **DD** 300.5.

REVISTA DE CIENCIAS SOCIALES. No. 4- 1959-. 0482-5276. Periodical. PR. Spanish. ir. 15.00. Editorial University of Costa Rica, Ciudad University R Facio, Aprido 75, San Jose Costa Rica. **Tel** 25/63/25. **Ed** Daniel Camacho. **Ind/Abst** Int. Labour Doc., Foreign Lang. Index, Sociol. Abstr., Psychol. Abstr., Lang. Lang. Behav. Abstr. **LC** K19. bk rev. **Circ** 3,000. (ctrl). Anthropology, archaeology, economics, ethnic, geography, history, journalism, political sciences, psychology, agricultural production, union workers, etc. *Revista de Ciencias Juridico-Sociales.*

REVISTA DE CIENCIAS SOCIALES (UNIVERSIDAD DE VALPARAISO. FACULTAD DE CIENCIAS JURIDICAS, ECONOMICAS Y SOCIALES). (REVISTA DE CIENCIAS SOCIALES : PUBLICACION DE LA FACULTAD DE CIENCIAS JURIDICAS, ECONOMICAS Y SOCIALES). No. 17 (Second Semester, 1980)-. Periodical. Spanish. sa. Casilla 211-V, Valparaiso Chile. **LC** K19. **DD** 300.5. *Revista de Ciencias Sociales (Universidad de Chile. Sede Valparaiso. Facultad de Ciencias Juridicas, Economicas, y Sociales).*

REVISTA DE LA UNIVERSIDAD NACIONAL DE RIO CUARTO. Vol. 1, No. 1-. 0325-9587. Periodical. Spanish (summaries in English). sa. Enlace Rutas 8 Y 36 Km 603, 5800 Rio Cuarto Argentina. **LC** Q33. **DD** 086.1.

REVISTA INTERAMERICANA DE BIBLIOGRAFIA : ORGANO DE ESTUDIOS HUMANISTICOS. *See* Bibliographies.

REVISTA INTERNACIONAL DE CIENCIAS ADMINISTRATIVAS. Periodical. BE. Spanish (Articles in French or English, summaries in Spanish). qt. $48.00. Intl Inst of Adm Science, 25 rue de la Charite, 1040 Brussels Belgium.

REVISTA MEXICANA DE CIENCIAS POLITICAS Y SOCIALES. New Series, V. 21- (81-). Periodical. MX. Spanish. qt. $150.00. Universidad Nacional Autonoma de Mexico Servi-Libros, Apartado Postal 25-328, Mexico City Mexico. **Ind/Abst** Am. Hist. Life, Hist. Abstr., Part A, Mod. Hist. Abstr., Hist. Abst., Part B, Twent. Century Abstr., Sociol. Abstr., Soc. Welf. Soc. Plan./Policy Soc. Dev., ABC Pol Sci, Foreign Lang. Index. **LC** JA5. *Revista Mexicana de Ciencia Politica.*

REVISTA PARAGUAYA DE SOCIOLOGIA. Year 1- (No. 1-) Sept.Dec. 1964-. 0035-0354. Periodical. PY. Spanish. ty. $30.00. Centro Paraguayo Est Sociologi Eligio Ayala 973/ Casilla de Correo 2157, Asuncion Paraguay. **Tel** 43-734. **Ed** Grazziella Corvalan. **Ind/Abst** Sociol. Abstr., Soc. Welf. Soc. Plan./Policy Soc. Dev., Foreign Lang. Index, Lang. Lang. Behav. Abstr., PAIS Foreign Lang. Index. **LC** HM7. (cum index). bk rev. Deals with social sciences in general.

REVISTA URUGUAYA DE CIENCIAS SOCIALES. V. 1- April/June 1972-. Periodical. UY. Spanish. ir. Libreria Anticuaria Americana, Juan Carlos Gomez, 1418 Montevideo Uraguay. **LC** H8.

REVISTA/REVIEW INTERAMERICANA. **VFOAT** Review Interamericana. **VAT** Revista Review Interamericana. V. 6- Spring 1976-. 0360-7917. Periodical. PR. English (Spanish). qt. $26.00. Centro de Publicaciones, Universidad Interamericana de Puerto Rico, Call Box 5100, San German Puerto Rico 00753. **Tel** (809)892-1095. **Ed** Sonia Iris Garcia. **Ind/Abst** Abstr. Engl. Stud., Am. Hist. Life, Hist. Abstr., MLA Int. Bibliogr. Books Artic. Mod. Lang. Lit., Index Am. Period. Verse. **LC** AS74.A1. **DD** 050. bk rev. adv acc. **Circ** 800. Multidisciplinary, bilingual, scholarly journal in the social sciences and humanities, belle letres, on topics concerning Puerto Rico, the Caribbean, Latin America and on the Interamerican and Hispanic themes and subjects. *Revista Interamericana.*

REVUE DE L'INSTITUT DE SOCIOLOGIE. **Main/Corp** Brussels. Universite Libre. Institut de Sociologie Solvay. Vol. 1- July 1920-. 0770-0962. Periodical. BE. French. qt. $27.96. Editions University Bruxelles, Avenue Paul Heger 26, B1050 Bruxelles Belgium. **Tel** 021642 32 93. **Ind/Abst** Soc. Sci. Citation Index, Sociol. Abstr., Am. Hist. Life, Hist. Abstr., Lang. Lang. Behav. Abstr. **LC** H13. **DD** 306.2493. bk rev. **Circ** 7,200. The publication is devoted to the social sciences: political science, political economy, social economy, general sociology, and sociology of work.

REVUE DES SCIENCES SOCIALES DE LA FRANCE DE L'EST. Began with 1972 issue. 0336-1578. FR. French. an. 69.00. Universite des Sciences Humaines de Strasbourg, 22 rue Descartes, 67084 Strasbourg Cedex France. **Tel** (88)61-39-39. adv acc. Dedicated to problems of cultural, economic, demographic and social nature of the eastern part of France.

REVUE INTERNATIONALE D'ACTION COMMUNAUTAIRE. **VFOAT** International Review of Community Development. 1- (41-). 0707-9699. Periodical. CN. French (text in English). sa. Ecole de Service Social, Universite de Montreal, Montreal Quebec H3C 3J7 Canada. **Ind/Abst** Point Repere, Sociol. Abstr., Soc. Welf. Soc. Plan./Policy Soc. Dev., Abstr. Soc. Work. **DD** 309.2605. *Community Development, 0020-854X.*

REVUE ROUMAINE DES SCIENCES SOCIALES. SERIE DE SCIENCES JURIDIQUES. V. 8- 1964-. 0035-4023. Periodical. RM. French (English, German or Russian). sa. $45.00. Rompresfilatelia, PO Box 1362137, Bucharest Romania. **Ind/Abst** Foreign Lang. Index, Public Aff. Inf. Serv. Bull., PAIS Foreign Lang. Index. *Revue des Sciences Sociales.*

RISSHO DAIGAKU JIMBUN KAGAKU KENKYUJO NEMPO. **VFOAT** Annual Report of the Institute of Cultural Sciences, Rissho University. JA. Japanese. ir. Rissho Daigaku, 2 Osaki 4-chome Shinagawa-ku, Tokyo Japan. **LC** AS552.R56.

RIVISTA INTERNAZIONALE DI SCIENZE SOCIALI. Began pubication with yearly V. 42 in 1934?. 0035-676X. Periodical. IT. Italian. qt. Soc Edit Vita e Pensiero, Largo Agostino Gemelli 1, 20102 Milano Italy. **Ind/Abst** Sociol. Abstr., Foreign Lang. Index. *Rivista Internazionale di Scienze Sociali e Discipline Ausiliare.*

RIV'ON LE-MEHKAR HEVRATI. **VFOAT** Social Research Review. 1- 1972-. Periodical. IS. Hebrew. ir. Zalman Aranne Workers College, 5 Nehardea Street, Tel Aviv Isreal. **Tel** (03)240277. **Ed** Avraham Wolfensohn. bk rev. adv acc. **Circ** 200. Each issue gives a number of articles- surveys of researchers - in the social sciences(general). Anthropology and methodology of social sciences.

ROCZNIKI NAUK SPOECZNYCH. **VFOAT** Annales des Sciences Sociales. French, German, or Polish. ir. 70.00. **LC** H9.

ROTUNDA. *See* Humanities.

ROUND TABLE. *See* Political Science.

ROYAL AUSTRALIAN PLANNING INSTITUTE JOURNAL : APIJ *CEASED.* **VFOAT** APIJ, RAPIJ, R.A.P.I.J., A.P.I.J. Began with V. 8, No. 3, (July 1970). Ceased with V. 19, No. 4 (Nov. 1981). 0004-9999. Periodical. AT. English. qt. **LC** H1169.A8. **DD** 307.120994.

RSA 2000. **VFOAT** R.S.A. 2000. **VAT** Republic of South Africa Two Thousand. Periodical. Afrikaans (English). sa. Suid-Afrikaanse Road Vir Geestewetenskaphke Navorsing, Institut Vir Navorsingsontwikkeling, Private Bag X41, Pretoria South Africa. **LC** HN800.S59. **DD** 309.105.

RUCH PRAWNICZY, EKONOMICZNY I SOCJOLOGICZNY. V. 24- 1962-. 0035-9629. Periodical. PL. Polish (summaries in English and French). qt. ARS Polona, Krakowskie Przedmiescie 7, 00-068 Warsaw Poland. *Ruch Prawniczy I Ekonomiczny.*

RURAL DEVELOPMENT PROGRESS. **Main/Corp** United States. Dept. of Agriculture. Office of the Secretary. 4th- 1976-. 0161-7273. US. English. an. Department of Agriculture, Office of the Secretary, Washington DC 20250. **LC** HN56. **DD** 309.2630973. *Rural Development Goals, 0145-4102.*

SAGE LIBRARY OF SOCIAL RESEARCH. V. 1- 1973-. Monographic Series. US. English. ir. Sage Publications, PO Box 776, Beverly Hills CA 90210.

SAHOE KWAHAK KWA CHONGCHAEK YONGU. **VFOAT** Social Science and Policy Research. Periodical. English (Korean). ir. **LC** H8.K6.

SAHOE KWAHAK NONCHONG. **VFOAT** Journal of the Social Science. V. 1- Series-. Periodical. KO. Korean. ir. Kukche Taehak Sahoe Kwahak Yonguso, 2-2-2 Chungjong-no Sodaemun-ku, Seoul South Korea. **LC** H8.K6.

SAHOE KWAHAK NONMUNJIP (MYONGJI TAEHAKKYO. SAHOE KWAHAK YONGUSO). (SAHOE KWAHAK NONMUNJIP). **VFOAT** Journal of Social Science. Periodical. English (Korean). ir. Not for Sale. Myongji Taehak Chulpanbu, 50-3 Nam Kajwa-dong Sodaemun-ku, Seoul Korea. **LC** H8.K6.

SAHOE KWAHAK (YONGNAM TAEHAKKYO. SAHOE KWAHAK YONGUSO). (SAHOE KWAHAK). **VFOAT** Social Science. Periodical. KO. English (German, and Korean). ir. Yongnam Taehakkyo Sahoe Kwahak Yonguso, Taegu Korea. **LC** H8.K6. **DD** 300.5.

Social Sciences (General)

SAHOE KWAHAK YONGU. VFOAT Social Science Research. Periodical. KO. Korean. ir. Choson Taehakkyo Sahoe Kwahak Yonguso, 17 Pullo-dong Tung-ku, Kwangju-si Korea. LC H31.S24.

SAHOE KWAHAK YONGU (YONGNAM TAEHAKKYO. SAHOE KWAHAK YONGUSO). (SAHOE KWAHAK YONGU). VFOAT Journal of Social Science. V. 1- Series, No. 1.2- (August 1981)-. Periodical. English (German and Korean). ir. Institute of Social Science, Yeungnam University, Gyongsan Korea. LC H8.K6.

SALT. See Journalism.

SAMAJ VIGYAN JAGAT. VFOAT Samaja Vijnana Jagata. Vol. 1, Nos. 1 & 2 (June/Dec. 1978)-. Periodical. II. English (Hindi). sa. 30.00. Scientific Publishers, Man Bhawan Ratanada Road, Jodhpur 342 India. LC H53.I5. DD 300.954.

SAMHALLSVETENSKAPLIGA STUDIER. Monographic Series. SW. Swedish. ir. Gleerup Bokforlag, Box 1205, 22105 Lund Sweden.

SAMLET KATALOG FOR TIDSSKRIFTER. Main/Corp Council of the European Communities. Libraries-Documentation. VFOAT Gesamtkatalog der Zeitschriften, General Catalogue of Periodicals. Danish (Multilingual). ir. LC Z7161, H1.

SANGKHOM MANUTSAT. Periodical. Thai. ir.

SASKATCHEWAN COUNCIL OF SOCIAL STUDIES TEACHER. (SASKATCHEWAN COUNCIL OF SOCIAL STUDIES TEACHERS : NEWSLETTER). Nov. 3, 1976-. 0711-3021. Periodical. CN. English. ir. Saskatchewan Teachers' Federation, PO Box 1108, Saskatoon Saskatchewan S7K 3N3 Canada. DD 300.707124. Social Studies Teachers Newsletter, 0711-3013.

SCHRIFTEN ZUR WIRTSCHAFTS- UND SOZIALGESCHICHTE. V. 1- 1966-. 0582-0588. Monographic Series. GW. German. ir. Duncker and Humblot Verlag, Dietrich-Schaefer-Weg 9, 1000 Berlin 41 West Germany.

SCIENCE AND CULTURE. (SCIENCE & CULTURE). Vol. 35, No. 4 (Apr. 1969)-. 0036-8156. Periodical. II. English. mo. $20.00. Indian Science News Association, 92 Acharya prafulla Chandra Road, Calcutta 9 India. Ind/Abst Art Archaeol. Tech. Abstr. Science and Culture.

SCIENCE & SOCIETY. VAT Science and Society. V. 1- Fall 1936-. 0036-8237. Periodical. US. English. qt $15.00. Science & Society, John Jay College, 445 West 59th Street/Room 4331, New York NY 10019. Tel (212)757-3556. Ind/Abst Altern. Press Index, Book Rev. Index, Energy Inf. Abstr., Environ. Abstr., Am. Hist. Life, Soc. Sci. Citation Index, Hist. Abstr., Lang. Lang. Behav. Abstr., Index Econ. Artic. J. Collect. Vol., Int. Labour Doc., Public Aff. Inf. Serv. Bull., Humanit. Index, Book Rev. Index, Soc. Welf. Soc. Plan./Policy Soc. Dev., Sociol. Abstr., Women Stud. Abstr., Soc. Sci. Index, ABC Pol Sci, Int. Polit. Sci. Abstr., Recent Publ. Artic. LC H1. DD 305. NLM W1 SC686. (cum index). Available on microfilm from University Microfilms.

SCIENCE, TECHNOLOGY, & HUMAN VALUES. (SCIENCE, TECHNOLOGY & HUMAN VALUES). VFOAT Science, Technology and Human Values. Began with No. 25 (Fall 1978) issue. 0162-2439. Periodical. US. English. qt. $52.00. John Wiley & Sons, 605 Third Avenue, New York NY 10158. Tel (800)526-5368. Ind/Abst Sociol. Abstr., Soc. Welf. Soc. Plan./Policy Soc. Dev., Energy Inf. Abstr., Environ. Abstr., Philos. Index, Public Aff. Inf. Serv. Bull. LC Q175.4. DD 303.483. Newsletter on Science, Technology, & Human Values, 0738-2618.

SCIENCES HUMAINES (MONTREAL, QUEBEC). (SCIENCES HUMAINES). Vol. 1, No. 1 (Sept. 1980)-. 0714-4040. Periodical. CN. French. mo. $0.50 Per No. Sciences Humaines, 3688 rue Fleury East, Montreal-Nord Quebec H1H Canada. DD 372.83076.

SCIENCES SOCIALES PANORAMA : REVUE TRIMESTRIELLE EDITEE SOUS L'EGIDE DU MINISTERE DE L'ENSEIGNEMENT SUPERIEUR ET DE LA RECHERCHE SCIENTIFIQUE, O.N.R.S. VFOAT Ulum Al-Ijtimaiyah. No. 1 (Sept. 1979)-. Periodical. Arabic (French). ir. 150.00 Francs. Sciences Sociales, Panorama 51 rue Didouche Mourad, Alger Algeria. LC H1. DD 300.5.

SCIENTIA ET PRAXIS. No. 1-. 0559-1414. Spanish (English). ir. Grafica Panamericana, Av Javier Prado S/N Monterrico, Lima Peru. LC H8.

SCOTTISH ECONOMIC & SOCIAL HISTORY. VFOAT Scottish Economic and Social History. Vol. 1, No. 1-. UK. English. an. 4.00 Domestic, 5.00 Foreign. Business Manager/Scottish Economic And Social History, Department of Scottish History, University of Glasgow, Glasgow G12 8QH Scotland. Ed R M Mitchison and H W Fraser. bk rev. Circ 650. Articles, surveys, and reviews on all aspects of Scottish economic social history.

THE SECOL REVIEW. See Linguistics.

SELECTIONS FROM THE ANNALES, ECONOMIES, SOCIETES, CIVILISATIONS. See History (General).

SERIAL TITLES IN THE HUMANITIES AND SOCIAL SCIENCES (WINDSOR). See Bibliographies.

SERIE COSTA CENTRAL. No. 1-. Monographic Series. PE. Spanish. ir. Taller de Estudios Andinos, Department de Ciencias Humanas, University Nacional Agraria, Apartado 456, la Molina Lima Peru.

SERIE U.R.S.S. Series/Titl Problemes Politiques et Sociaux. VAT Serie Union des Republiques Socialistes Sovietiques. FR. French. ir. 20.00. La Documentation Francaise, 31 Quai Voltaire, 75340 Paris Cedex 07 France. LC H3. DD 300.8 S, 309.147.

SERVICIO DE DOCUMENTACION SOCIAL. Periodical. UY. Spanish. qt. Instituo de Estudios Socials Consejo Uruguays de Bienestar Social, Pza Independencia 838 P 5 Esc 31, Montevideo Uruguay. Servicio de Documentacion (Montevideo, Uruguay).

SHAKAI BUNKA KENKYU. VFOAT Studies in Social Sciences. V. 1-. JA. Japanese. ir. Hiroshima Daigaku Sogo Kagakubu, 1-89 Higashi Sendacho 1-chome, Hiroshima 730 Japan. LC H8.

SHAKAI KAGAKU KENKYU. VFOAT Journal of Social Science. V. 1- 1948-. 0387-3307. Periodical. English. ir. Ind/Abst Am. Hist. Life, Hist. Abstr., Part A, Mod. Hist. Abstr., Hist. Abst., Part B, Twent. Century Abstr.

SHAKAI KAGAKU RON SHU. VFOAT Shakaikagaku Ronshu, Report of Studies, Kochi Junior College. JA. Japanese. ir. Kochi Tanki Daigaku Shakai Kagakukai, 5-ban 15-go Eikokujicho, Kochi Japan. LC H8.

SHAKAI KAGAKU TOKYU. VFOAT Social Science Review. V. 1- No. (1-)-. Periodical. JA. Japanese or English. ir. Waseda Daigaku Shakai Kagaku Kenkyujo, 1-647 Totsukamachi, Shinjuku-ku 160 Tokyo Japan. Ind/Abst Am. Hist. Life, Hist. Abstr., Part A, Mod. Hist. Abstr., Hist. Abst., Part B, Twent. Century Abstr. LC H8.

SHAKAI SHISO SHI KENKYU. VFOAT Annals of the Society for the History of Social Thought. Edition- 1977-. Japanese. ir. 1500. Minaruva Shobo, 1 Hioka Tsutsumigayacho, Yamashina-ku 607 Kyoto Japan. LC H8.

SHAKAIGAKU KENKYUJO KIYO. VFOAT Bulletin of Sociological Studies. 0285-4015. JA. Japanese. ir. Bukkyo Daigaku Shakaigaku Kenkyujo, 96 Murasakino Kita, Hananobo-cho, Kita-ku 603, Kyoto-shi Japan. LC H8.J3.

SHAKAIKA KYOIKU KENKYU. VFOAT Journal of Social Studies. Began in 1953. JA. Japanese. ir. Nihon Shakaika Kyoiku Gakkai c/o Tokyo Gakugei Daigaku Shakaika Kyoiku Kenkyushitsu Nukui Kita-Machi 4-chome, Koganei-shi Tokyo-to 184 Japan. LC H62.5.J3.

SHAKAIKA KYOIKU RONSO : NIHON SHAKAIKA KYOIKU KENKYUKAI NENPO. VFOAT Nihon Shakaika Kyoiku Kenkyukai Nenpo. JA. Japanese. an. Nihon Shakaika Kyoiku Kenkyukai, c/o Hiroshima Daigaku Kyoiku Gakabu, Higashi Senda-cho, Naka-ku, Hiroshima-shi Japan. LC H62.5.J3.

SHAN-HSI SHIH TA HSUEH PAO. CHE HSUEH SHE HUI KO HSUEH PAN. Periodical. CH. Chinese. qt 0.30. Chung-Kuo Kuo Chi Shu Tien, P O Box 2820, Peking China. LC H8.C47. DD 059.951.

SHAN-HSI TA HSUEH HSUEH PAO. CHE HSUEH SHE HUI KO HSUEH PAN. Periodical. CH. Chinese. qt. 0.35. Post Office, Shan-Hsi China. LC AS452.T38. DD 300.5.

SHE HUI CHIH PIAO TUNG CHI. VFOAT Social Indicators of the Republic of China. 1979-. CH. Chinese (English). an. LC HN747.7. DD 310.072051249.

SHE HUI KO HSUEH. VFOAT Shehui Kexue. Periodical. CC. Chinese. mo. 0.35. Chung-Kuo Kuo Chi Shu Tien, PO Box 2820, Peking China Mainland. LC AS451. DD 300.5.

SHE HUI KO HSUEH CHI KAN (LIAO-NING SHE HUI KO HSUEH YUAN). (SHE HUI KO HSUEH CHI KAN). VFOAT Shehuikexuejikan. Periodical. CC. Chinese. bm. 0.60. Chung-Kuo Kuo Chi Shu Tien, PO Box 2820, Peking China. LC H8.C47. DD 300.5.

SHE HUI KO HSUEH (LAN-CHOU SHIH, CHINA). (SHE HUI KO HSUEH). VFOAT Social Science. Periodical. CH. Chinese. bm. 0.30. Post Office Lan-Chou Shih, Lan-Chou Shih China. LC AS452.L37. DD 300.5.

SHIH HUO. See History (General) - History of Asia.

SIGSOC BULLETIN CEASED. VFOAT S.I.G.S.O.C Bulletin. VAT Special Interest Group on the Social and Behavioral Science of Computing Bulletin. Began in 1970. 0163-5794. Periodical. US. English. qt. Association for Computing Machinery, 1133 Avenue of the Americas, New York NY 10036. LC H61.3. DD 300.2854. CODEN SGBLDB.

SIMULATION & GAMES. VAT Simulation and Games. V. 1- Mar. 1970-. 0037-5500. Periodical. US. English. qt. Sage Publications, 275 South Beverly Drive, Beverly Hills CA 90212. Ind/Abst Electron. Commun. Abstr. J., ISMEC Bull., Pollut. Abstr. Indexes, Saf. Sci. Abstr. J., Sociol. Abstr., ABC Pol Sci, Comput. Control Abstr., Electr. Electron. Abstr., Sci. Abstr. Sect. A. Phys. Abstr., Curr. Index J. Educ., Media Rev. Dig., Psychol. Abstr., Soc. Sci. Index. LC H62. CODEN SMUGA.

SINTESE. New No., V. 1- (No. 1-). Portuguese. ir. $25.00. Centro Joao XXIII (RJ) e Grupo de Reflexao, Belo Horizonte. Tel (031)4410233. LC H8. bk rev. adv acc. Circ 500. Sintese Politicia, Economica, Social.

SINTOMAS EN LA CIENCIA, LA CULTURA, Y LA TECNICA. No. 1 (Nov. 1980)-. Periodical. Spanish. sa. Pedro Goyena, 301 Poste Restante Sucursal 24, 1424 Capital Federal, Buenos Aires Argentina.

SISTEMA. No. 1- Jan. 1973-. 0210-0223. Periodical. Spanish. ir. 600. Apartado Num 502 FD, Madrid Spain. LC H8.

THE SMALL CITY AND REGIONAL COMMUNITY. V. 1- 1978-. 0194-2735. US. English. an. Foundation Press, University of Wisconsin-Stevens Point, Stevens Point WI 54481. Tel (715)346-2708. Ed Robert Wolensky and Edward J Miller. LC HT123. DD 307.760973. Circ 500. (ctrl). Proceedings on the conferences of the small city and regional community.

SMITHSONIAN FOLKLIFE STUDIES. VFOAT Folklife Studies. No. 1-. Monographic Series. US. English. Superintendent of Documents, US Government Printing Office, Washington DC 20402. DD 306.

SOCIAL ACTION. Began in 1951. 0037-7627. Periodical. II. English. bm. 10.00. Indian Social Institute, Lodi Road, New Delhi 110003 India. Tel 622379. Ed Walter Fernandes. Ind/Abst Asian Soc. Sci. Bibliogr. Annot. Abstr., Sociol. Educ. Abstr., Book Rev. Index, Relig. Index One, Period. LC HN681. DD 309.154. bk rev. adv acc. Circ 1,000. Available on Microfilm from University Microfilms. Each issue is on a special theme. The new issues will be on the scheduled casts: labor and employment and an economic policy for the weaker sections.

SOCIAL ACTION & THE LAW. VAT Social Action and The Law. V. 1- Mar. 1973-. 0272-765X. Periodical. US. English. qt. $30.00. Center for Responsive Psychology, Brooklyn College, Brooklyn New York NY 11210. Tel (718)780-5960. Ed Allen Lichtenstein. Ind/Abst Leg. Resour. Index, Sociol. Abstr. LC K23. DD 349.7305, 347.3005. bk rev. adv acc. Circ 1,000. A journal presenting social science findings to law professionals.

SOCIAL ANALYSIS (ADELAIDE, S. AUST.). (SOCIAL ANALYSIS). No. 1 (Feb. 1979)-. 0155-977X. Periodical. AT. English. sa. $11.07. University of Adelaide, GPO Box 498, Department Anthropology, Adelaide South Australia 5001. Ed Micheal Roberts. Ind/Abst APAIS, Aust. Public Aff. Inf. Serv. Publishes articles of a combined theoretical and substantive nature which addresses critical issues and problems in cultural and social studies.

SOCIAL AND BEHAVIORAL SCIENCES. US. English. an. **LC** H1. **DD** 300.5.

SOCIAL AND CULTURAL REPORT. **Main/Corp** Sociaal en Cultureel Planbureau. Began with 1974 issue. English (Dutch). ir. J C Van Markenlaan 3, Rijswijk Netherlands. **LC** HN511. **DD** 309.149207.

SOCIAL AND ECONOMIC STUDIES. Vol. 1-Feb. 1953-. 0037-7651. Periodical. JM. English. qt. $40.00. Institute of Social and Economic Research, University of the West Indies, Mona Kingston 7 Jamaica. **Tel** 92 76661-9. **Ed** Wentworth Bonen. **Ind/Abst** Am. Hist. Life, Hist. Abstr., Part A, Mod. Hist. Abstr., Hist. Abst., Part B, Twent. Century Abstr., Int. Labour Doc., Sociol. Abstr., Soc. Welf. Soc. Plan./Policy Soc. Dev., Index Econ. Artic. J. Collect. Vol., Popul. Index, Public Aff. Inf. Serv. Bull., Soc. Sci. Index, Soc. Sci. Citation Index, Lang. Lang. Behav. Abstr., Hist. Abstr. **LC** HN244. **DD** 972.9. Index published separately - free - automatically sent. bk rev. adv acc. **Circ** 2,000. (ctrl). Theoretical and applied issues of development in Third World countries especially the Caribbean.

SOCIAL DEVELOPMENT ACTIVITIES IN LATIN AMERICA PROMOTED BY THE INTER-AMERICAN FOUNDATION. *See* Economics.

SOCIAL EDUCATION. V. 1- Jan. 1937-. 0037-7724. Periodical. US. English. ir. National Council of Social Studies, 3501 Newark Street NW, Washington DC 20016. **Tel** (202)966-7840. **Ind/Abst** Am. Hist. Life, Hist. Abstr., Part A, Mod. Hist. Abstr., Hist. Abst., Part B, Twent. Century Abstr., Women Stud. Abstr., Book Rev. Index, Educ. Index, Curr. Index J. Educ., Media Rev. Dig., Hist. Abstr. **LC** H62.A1. **DD** 307.

SOCIAL FORECASTING : DOCUMENTATION. English. ir. Irades Edizione Previsionali, Via Paisiello 6, 00198 Roma Italy. **LC** CB158. **DD** 309.025.

SOCIAL INDICATORS FOR FIJI. **Main/Corp** Fiji. Bureau of Statistics. English. ir. PO Box 2221, Suva Fiji. **LC** HN936.A8. **DD** 309.1961105. Industrial health and safety, economics, education, and statistics.

SOCIAL INDICATORS NETWORK NEWS. (SOCIAL INDICATORS NETWORK NEWS : SINET). **VFOAT** Sinet. Periodical. US. English. PO Box 24064, Emory University Station, Atlanta GA 30322. *Social Indicators Newsletter, 0363-3195.*

SOCIAL INDICATORS RESEARCH. V. 1- May 1974-. 0303-8300. Periodical. NE. English. qt. 69. Kluwer Academic Publishers Group, PO Box 322, 3300 AH Dordrecht Netherlands. **Tel** (31)78-334911. **Ed** Alex C Michalos. **Ind/Abst** Sociol. Abstr., Soc. Welf. Soc. Plan./Policy Soc. Dev., Philos. Index, Writ. Am. Hist., Public Aff. Inf. Serv. Bull., Bibliogr. Index, Soc. Sci. Citation Index. **LC** HN25. **DD** 309.072. **NLM** W1 SO115. bk rev. adv acc. Health, population, shelter, transportation, natural environment, social customs and morality, mental health, law enforcement, politics, education, religion, the media and the arts, etc.

SOCIAL MARKETING UPDATE. SPANISH. (ACTUALIDADES SOBRE MERCADEO SOCIAL). 0882-3529. Periodical. US. Spanish (summaries in English). qt. Free. The Futures Group, 1029 Vermont Avenue NW, Washington DC 20005. **DD** 363.

THE SOCIAL MIRROR. V. 1- Jan./Feb. 1977-. Periodical. English. ir. 10.00. AFM Golam Kibria on Behalf of the Socio-Economic Research Centre, 181 Zafrabad Road No 24, Dhamondi r/a North of K D H Laboraori, Dacca Bangladesh. **LC** HN690.6. **DD** 309.1549205.

SOCIAL POLICY & ADMINISTRATION. *See* Public Administration.

SOCIAL POLICY RESEARCH MONOGRAPHS SERIES. 1-. 0276-9654. Monographic Series. UK. English. ir. John Wiley & Sons, 605 Third Avenue, New York NY 10158.

SOCIAL PRACTICE. Fall 1978-. 0192-8686. Periodical. US. English. qt. $6.00. Inter-University Consortium for Ethics and Aesthetics, PO Box 211, Winfield IL 60190. **LC** HN1. **DD** 300.5.

SOCIAL PROBLEMS. V. 1- June 1953-. 0037-7791. US. English. ir. $40.00. State University College of Buffalo, HB 208 1300 Elmwood Drive, Buffalo NY 14222. **Tel** (716)878-6935. **Ed** James D Orcutt. **Ind/Abst** Am. Hist. Life, Hist. Abstr., Part A, Mod. Hist. Abstr., Hist. Abst., Part B, Twent. Century Abstr., Excerpta Med., Sociol. Abstr., Soc. Welf. Soc. Plan./Policy Soc. Dev., Public Aff. Inf. Serv. Bull., Humanit. Index, Bibliogr. Agric., Curr. Index J. Educ., Psychol. Abstr., Soc. Sci. Index, Women Stud. Abstr., Soc. Work Res. Abstr., Soc. Sci. Citation Index, Hospit. Lit. Index, Lang. Lang. Behav. Abstr., Abstr. Soc. Work., Hist. Abstr. **LC** HN1. **DD** 301.153, 301.46. **NLM** W1 SO123. **CODEN** SOPRAG. (cum index). adv acc. **Circ** 4,000. Articles cover a broad range of social phenomena. Recent articles deal with health and illness, crime and deviance, corporate power, sexual and racial discrimination, migrant and immigrant workers.

SOCIAL PROBLEMS. *See* Sociology: General Works, Theory.

SOCIAL PROCESS IN HAWAII (1979). (SOCIAL PROCESS IN HAWAII). Vol. 27 (1979)-. 0737-6871. Periodical. US. English. an. Univeristy Press of Hawaii, 2840 Kolowalu Street, Honolulu HI 96822. **Tel** (808)948-8255. Current issues reflect both the traditional social science image of Hawaii as a social laboratory and the state's image as a microcosm of the modern world. *Social Process.*

SOCIAL RESEARCH. V. 1- Feb. 1934-. 0037-783X. Periodical. US. English. qt. $40.00. New School for Social Research, 66 West Twelfth Street, New York NY 10011. **Tel** (212)741-5776. **Ed** Arien Mack. **Ind/Abst** Am. Hist. Life, Hist. Abstr., Part A, Mod. Hist. Abstr., Hist. Abst., Part B, Twent. Century Abstr., ABC Pol Sci, Sociol. Abstr., Soc. Welf. Soc. Plan./Policy Soc. Dev., Index Econ. Artic. J. Collect. Vol., Public Aff. Inf. Serv. Bull., Soc. Sci. Index, Soc. Sci. Citation Index, Lang. Lang. Behav. Abstr., Hist. Abstr. **LC** H1. **DD** 305. **NLM** W1 SO125. **Circ** 2,300.

SOCIAL RESOURCES INVENTORY. CALGARY REGION. 1980-. 0228-1279. Periodical. CN. English. Alberta Social Resources Inventory #3, 12227-107 Avenue, Edmonton Alberta T5M 1Y9 Canada. **LC** HV110.C34. **DD** 361.002571233.

SOCIAL RESOURCES INVENTORY, EDMONTON REGION. (SOCIAL RESOURCES INVENTORY. EDMONTON REGION). 1983-. 0228-1333. CN. English. $10.00. Alberta Social Services and Community Health, 10030-107 Street, Edmonton Alberta T5J 3E4 Canada. **LC** HV109.A5. **DD** 361.80257123.

SOCIAL RESOURCES INVENTORY, NORTHEASTERN REGION. (SOCIAL RESOURCES INVENTORY. NORTHEASTERN REGION). **VFOAT** Northeastern Region. 1st Ed. (Nov. 1982)-. 0228-1325. CN. English. Alberta Social Resources Inventory, 10030-197 Street, Edmonton Alberta T5J 3E4 Canada. **LC** HV109.A5. **DD** 361.002571232.

SOCIAL RESOURCES INVENTORY. SOUTH REGION. **VFOAT** South Region. 1984-. 0715-9625. CN. English. $9.50. Alberta Social Resources, Inventory Planning Secretariat Alberta Social Services and Community Health, 10030-107 Street, Edmonton Alberta T5J 3E4 Canada. **LC** HV109.A5. **DD** 362.02571234.

SOCIAL SCIENCE *CEASED.* V. 1-56. 0037-7848. Periodical. US. English. qt. $4.00. Pi Gamma Mu, c/o Ina Turner Gray, Winfield KS 67156. **Ind/Abst** Soc. Welf. Soc. Plan./Policy Soc. Dev., Hist. Abstr., Int. Polit. Sci. Abstr., Sociol. Abstr., Public Aff. Inf. Serv. Bull. **LC** H1. **NLM** W1 SO127. (cum index).

SOCIAL SCIENCE & MEDICINE (1982). (SOCIAL SCIENCE & MEDICINE). **VFOAT** Social Science and Medicine. Vol. 16, No. 1 (1982)-. 0277-9536. Periodical. US. English. sm. $1045.00. Pergamon Press, 395 Sawmill River Road, Elmsford NY 10523. **Tel** (914)592-7700. **Ind/Abst** Sociol. Abstr., Soc. Welf. Soc. Plan./Policy Soc. Dev., Excerpta Med., Index Med., Cumul. Index Nurs. Allied Health Lit., Popul. Index, Biol. Abstr., Hospit. Lit. Index, Psychol. Abstr., Soc. Sci. Index, Recent Publ. Artic. **LC** RA418. **DD** 362.105. **NLM** W1 SO127G. **CODEN** SSMDEP. Issued also in microform. *Social Science & Medicine. Part A, 0271-7123; Social Science & Medicine. Part B, 0160-7987; Social Science & Medicine. Part C, 0160-7995; Social Science & Medicine. Part D, 0160-8002; Social Science & Medicine. Part E, 0271-5384; Social Science & Medicine. Part F, 0271-539.*

SOCIAL SCIENCE (CHAPEL HILL, N.C.). (SOCIAL SCIENCE). Vol. 71, No. 1 (Spring 1986)-. 0886-280X. Periodical. US. English. qt. $25.00. Institute for Research in Social Science, Manning Hall/ University of North Carolina, Chapel Hill NC 27514. **DD** 300. *Social Science News Letter, 0743-8974.*

SOCIAL SCIENCE HISTORY. V. 1- Fall 1976-. 0145-5532. Periodical. US. English. qt. $50.00. Duke University Press, PO Box 6697 College Station, Durham NC 27708. **Tel** (919)684-2173. **Ed** James Q Graham Jr and Robert P Swierenga. **Ind/Abst** Am. Hist. Life, Hist. Abstr., Part A, Mod. Hist. Abstr., Hist. Abst., Part B, Twent. Century Abstr., Sociol. Abstr., Soc. Welf. Soc. Plan./Policy Soc. Dev., Writ. Am. Hist., Soc. Sci. Citation Index, Soc. Work Res. Abstr., Recent Publ. Artic., Hist. Abstr. **LC** H1. **DD** 300.5. bk rev. adv acc. **Circ** 900. Presents innovative research by historians, sociologists, anthropologists, political scientists, and demographers, providing an interdisciplinary forum for longitudinal analyses and studies with consciously theoretical orientations.

SOCIAL SCIENCE INFORMATION. **VFOAT** Information sur les Sciences Sociales. Vol. 6, No. 1 (Feb. 1967)-. 0539-0184. Periodical. UK. English (French). bm. Sage Publications, 28 Banner Street, London EC1Y 8QE England. **Tel** (01)253-1516. **Ind/Abst** Am. Hist. Life, Hist. Abstr., Part A, Mod. Hist. Abstr., Hist. Abst., Part B, Twent. Century Abstr., MLA Int. Bibliogr. Books Artic. Mod. Lang. Lit., Sociol. Abstr., Soc. Welf. Soc. Plan./Policy Soc. Dev., ABC Pol Sci, Soc. Sci. Citation Index, Curr. Contents, Hum. Resour. Abstr., Sage Public Adm. Abstr., Psychol. Abstr., Lang. Lang. Behav. Abstr., Recent Publ. Artic. **NLM** W1 SO129. **CODEN** SSCIBL. *Social Sciences Information, 0539-0184.*

SOCIAL SCIENCE INFORMATION STUDIES. (SOCIAL SCIENCE INFORMATION STUDIES : SSIS). **VFOAT** SSIS. Vol. 1, No. 1 (Oct. 1980)-. 0143-6236. Periodical. UK. English. qt. $101.00. Butterworth Scientific Limited, PO Box 63 Westbury House Bury Street, Guildford GU2 5BH England. **Tel** 0483 31261. **Ed** T D Wilson. **Ind/Abst** Comput. Control Abstr., Electr. Electron. Abstr., Sci. Abstr. Sect. A. Phys. Abstr., Libr. Inf. Sci. Abstr., Public Aff. Inf. Serv. Bull. **LC** H61.9. **DD** 025.063. **CODEN** SOSSD3. bk rev. Also available in microfiche. Publishes, in addition to major original articles, book reviews and essay reviews, the latter covering a number of related documents or books as considered by a specialist in the field.

SOCIAL SCIENCE JOURNAL. 1973-. KO. English. an. $5.00. Korean National Commission, PO Box Central 64, Seoul Korea. **Ind/Abst** Lang. Lang. Behav. Abstr., Sociol. Abstr., Public Aff. Inf. Serv. Bull. **LC** HN730.5. **DD** 309.151904.

THE SOCIAL SCIENCE JOURNAL. V. 12, No. 3/V. 13, No. 1- Oct. 1975/Jan. 1976-. 0362-3319. Periodical. US. English. qt. $15.00. Editor Social Science Journal, Social Science Building, Colorado State University, Fort Collins CO 80523. **Ind/Abst** Am. Hist. Life, Hist. Abstr., Part A, Mod. Hist. Abstr., Hist. Abst., Part B, Twent. Century Abstr., Soc. Sci. Index, Sociol. Abstr., Soc. Welf. Soc. Plan./Policy Soc. Dev., Public Aff. Inf. Serv. Bull. **LC** H1. **DD** 300.5. *Rocky Mountain Social Science Journal, 0035-7634.*

SOCIAL SCIENCE MICRO REVIEW *CEASED.* **VFOAT** SSMR. Vol. 2, issues 1 & 2 (Fall 1983)-. 8755-3031. Periodical. US. English. qt. $40.00. North Carolina State University, 106 Link Building, Raleigh NC 27650. **DD** 001. *Political Science Micro Review.*

SOCIAL SCIENCE MICROCOMPUTER REVIEW. Vol. 3, No. 1 (Spring 1985)-. 0885-0011. Periodical. US. English. qt. Duke University Press, Periodicals Department, 6697 College Station, Durham NC 27695. **Tel** (919)684-2173. bk rev. adv acc. **Circ** 550. Each issue includes comprehensive reports on new microcomputing products related to the social sciences, a tutorials section for beginning users, and more. *Social Science Micro Review, 8755-3031.*

SOCIAL SCIENCE MONITOR. 1979. 0195-7791. Periodical. US. English. mo. $83.00. Communication Research Associates, 7100 Baltimore Boulevard/Suite 500, College Park MD 20740. **Tel** (301)927-3998. **Ed** Ray E Hiebert. **Circ** 400. Abstracts the latest research pertinent to public relations and applies social science to the work of informing and persuading the public.

SOCIAL SCIENCE NEWS LETTER. Vol. 68, No. 1-2 (Jan./Apr. 1983)-. 0743-8974. Periodical. US. English. qt. $15.00. Institute for Research in

Social Sciences (General)

Social Science, University of North Carolina at Chapel Hill, Chapel Hill NC 27514. **LC** F251. **DD** 300.5. *University of North Carolina News Letter, 0886-2621.*

SOCIAL SCIENCE RECORD. V. 1- Spring 1964-. 0037-7872. Periodical. US. English. sa. $20.00. New York State Council for the Social Studies, PO Box 131, Glen Head NY 11545. **Tel** (516)759-9532. **Ed** Gloria Sesso. **Ind/Abst** Curr. Index J. Educ. **LC** H62.5.U5. **DD** 300.71273. bk rev. adv acc. **Circ** 2,000. (ctrl). A journal of theoretical and practical articles dealing with social studies education.

SOCIAL SCIENCE RESEARCH. V. 1- Apr. 1972-. 0049-089X. Periodical. US. English. qt. Academic Press, 4805 Sand Lake Road, Orlando FL 32819. **Tel** (305)345-4100. **Ind/Abst** Am. Hist. Life, Hist. Abstr., Part A, Mod. Hist. Abstr., Hist. Abstr., Part B, Twent. Century Abstr., Sociol. Abstr., Soc. Welf. Soc. Plan./Policy Soc. Dev., ABC Pol Sci, Psychol. Abstr., Soc. Sci. Index, Bibliogr. Index Geol., Lang. Lang. Behav. Abstr., Soc. Sci. Citation Index, Bibliogr. Index. **LC** H1. **DD** 300.72. **NLM** W1 SO127N. **CODEN** SSREBG.

SOCIAL SCIENCE RESEARCH NEWSLETTER. V. 1- Spring 1976-. 0383-7580. Periodical. CN. English. qt. Free. United Way of Greater Vancouver, 1625 West 8th Avenue, Vancouver British Columbia V6J 1T9 Canada. **DD** 360.971134.

SOCIAL SCIENCE REVIEW. VFOAT Review of Social Science. V. 1- Mar. 1976-. Periodical. English. ir. Social Science Association Press, PO Box 5/84, Bangkok 5 Thailand. **LC** H1. **DD** 300.9593. *Journal of Social Science Review.*

SOCIAL SCIENCE REVIEW (SOCIAL SCIENTISTS ASSOCIATION OF SRI LANKA). (SOCIAL SCIENCE REVIEW : JOURNAL OF THE SOCIAL SCIENTISTS ASSOCIATION OF SRI LANKA). No. 1 (Sept. 1979)-. Periodical. English. qt. $15.00. Editor Social Science Review, c/o SLAAS 120/10 Wijerama Mawatha, Colombo Sri Lanka.

SOCIAL SCIENCE REVIEW (VILLANOVA, PA.). (THE SOCIAL SCIENCE REVIEW). Vol. 5, No. 1 (Fall 1983)-. 0737-4410. Periodical. US. English. sa. $20.00. Villanova University, Social Science Review, Villanova PA 19085. **DD** 300. *Social Science Forum, 0146-8847.*

SOCIAL SCIENCES. V. 1- (No. 1-). 0134-5486. Periodical. UR. English. qt. USSR Academy of Sciences, Section of Social Sciences, 33/12 Arbat, Moscow 121002 USSR. **Ind/Abst** Am. Hist. Life, Hist. Abstr., Part A, Mod. Hist. Abstr., Hist. Abstr., Part B, Twent. Century Abstr., Int. Aerosp. Abstr., Lang. Lang. Behav. Abstr., Sociol. Abstr. **LC** H1. **DD** 300.5.

SOCIAL SCIENCES CITATION INDEX. See Indexes/Abstracts.

SOCIAL SCIENCES IN CANADA. VFOAT Sciences Sociales au Canada. V. 1- 1971-. 0049-092X. Periodical. CN. English (French). qt. $13.93. Social Science Federation of Canada, 151 Slater Street, Suite 415, Ottawa Ontario K1P 5H3 Canada. **Tel** (613)238-6112. **Ed** Michelle Albagli. **Ind/Abst** Sociol. Abstr., Soc. Welf. Soc. Plan./Policy Soc. Dev., Sociol. Abstr., Lang. Lang. Behav. Abstr. adv acc. **Circ** 12,000. (ctrl). Information of general interest to the social science community, i.e. government legislation in Canada and elsewhere, research funding, conferences, publications, awards, sources of funding, etc.

SOCIAL SCIENCES IN CHINA. V. 1-. 0252-9203. Periodical. CC. English. bm. China Publication Centre, PO Box 2820, Beijing China. **Ind/Abst** Int. Labour Doc., Public Aff. Inf. Serv. Bull. **LC** HC426. **DD** 300.951.

SOCIAL SCIENCES INDEX. See Indexes/Abstracts.

SOCIAL SCIENCES RESEARCH JOURNAL. Began with issue for April/June 1976. Periodical. II. English. ty. 30.00 Domestic, $6.00. Panjan University Campus, Chief Editor, Social Sciences Research, Journal Arts Block No 3, Chandigarh 160014 India. **LC** H1. **DD** 300.5.

SOCIAL SCIENTIST. V. 1- Aug. 1972-. Periodical. II. English. mo. $30.00. Indian School of Social Science, Trivandrum-1 Kerala India. **Ind/Abst** Int. Labour Doc. **LC** HN681. **DD** 309.154.

SOCIAL SERVICE DELIVERY SYSTEMS. V. 1-. 0271-4086. Monographic Series. US. English. an. Sage Publications Inc, 275 South Beverly Drive, Beverly Hills CA 90212. **Ed** M I Teicher. **LC** UNC. **NLM** W1 SO1322.

SOCIAL SERVICES. Main/Corp United States. Superintendent of Documents. 0363-9584. US. English. **LC** Z1223, Z7165. U5U73A. **DD** 016.361973.

THE SOCIAL STUDIES. V. 1- Sept. 1909-. 0037-7996. Periodical. US. English. bm. $28.00. Heldref Publications, 4000 Albemarle Street NW/Suite 302, Washington DC 20016. **Tel** (202)362-6445. **Ed** Helen Kress. **Ind/Abst** Educ. Index, Book Rev. Index, Public Aff. Inf. Serv. Bull., Am. Hist. Life, Hist. Abstr., Women Stud. Abstr., Book Rev. Digest, Curr. Index J. Educ. adv acc. **Circ** 2,663. A lively, independent forum for teachers of social studies. Provides in-depth resource material in one convenient source, the journal has periodic special issues.

SOCIAL STUDIES OF SCIENCE. V. 5- Feb. 1975-. 0306-3127. Periodical. UK. English. qt. 60.00. Sage Publications Inc, 28 Banner Street, London EC1Y 8QE England. **Tel** (01)253-1516. **Ed** David Edge and Roy McLeod. **Ind/Abst** Am. Hist. Life, Hist. Abstr., Part A, Mod. Hist. Abstr., Hist. Abstr., Part B, Twent. Century Abstr., Life Sci. Collect., Excerpta Med., Sociol. Abstr., Soc. Welf. Soc. Plan./Policy Soc. Dev., Energy Res. Abstr., ABC Pol Sci, Sci. Cit. Index, Abr. Ed., Soc. Sci. Citation Index, Lang. Lang. Behav. Abstr., Hist. Abstr., Sociol. Abstr. **LC** Q1. **DD** 301.24305. **NLM** W1 SO133K. adv acc. *Science Studies, 0036-8539.*

THE SOCIAL STUDIES PROFESSIONAL. (THE SOCIAL STUDIES PROFESSIONAL : A NEWSLETTER FROM THE NATIONAL COUNCIL FOR THE SOCIAL STUDIES). No. 1- 1969-. 0586-6235. Periodical. US. English. bm. $2.50. National Council for the Social Studies, 3501 Newark Street, Washington DC 20016.

SOCIAL STUDIES REVIEW. V. 13- Fall 1973-. Periodical. US. English. ir. **Tel** (916)786-6056. **Ind/Abst** Curr. Index J. Educ. bk rev. adv acc. **Circ** 1,500. (ctrl). Available on microfilm from University Microfilms International. Educational publication with various subjects relating to social studies and articles of interest to social studies educators. *Review.*

SOCIAL TRENDS. See Statistics.

SOCIETAS CEASED. V. 1-8, No. 3. 0037-8879. Periodical. US. English. qt. $10.00. Societas Inc, PO Box 1293, Oshkosh WI 54901. **Ind/Abst** Soc. Work Res. Abstr., Am. Hist. Life, Hist. Abstr., Part A, Mod. Hist. Abstr. **LC** H1. **DD** 901.9.

SOCIETY. V. 9, No. 4- (No. 74-). 0147-2011. Periodical. US. English. bm. $35.00. Transaction Inc, Rutgers University, New Brunswick NJ 08903. **Tel** (201)932-2280. **Ed** Irving Louis Horowitz. **Ind/Abst** Abr. Read. Guide, ABC Pol Sci, Am. Hist. Life, Hist. Abstr., Part A, Mod. Hist. Abstr., Book Rev. Index, Excerpta Med., Sociol. Abstr., Soc. Welf. Soc. Plan./Policy Soc. Dev., Pop. Mag. Rev., Energy Inf. Abstr., Public Aff. Inf. Serv. Bull., Curr. Index J. Educ., Film Lit. Index, Women Stud. Abstr., Med. Socioecon. Res. Source, U.S. Polit. Sci. Doc. **LC** H1. **DD** 309.173092. **NLM** W1 SO85. bk rev. adv acc. **Circ** 25,000. Available on microfilm and microfiche from Bell and Howell and Johnson Associates. The periodical of record in the social sciences and public policy. *Trans-Action, 0041-1035.*

SOCIETY. See Sociology: General Works, Theory.

SOUTHEAST ASIAN JOURNAL OF SOCIAL SCIENCE. V. 1- 1973-. Periodical. SI. English. sa. $19.50. Singapore University Press, National University of Singapore, Kent Ridge 0511 Singapore. **Tel** 7761148. **Ed** Rosalind Chan. **LC** HN661. **DD** 301.0959. bk rev. **Circ** 500. Comprehensive analyses of the process of social change and development in Southeast Asian societies. *Southeast Asian Journal of Sociology, Southeast Asian Journal of Economic Development and Social Change; Southeast Asia Ethnicity and Development Newsletter.*

SOUTHERN NEIGHBORHOODS. (SOUTHERN NEIGHBORHOODS : THE BIMONTHLY PUBLICATION OF THE COMMUNITY CONTROL MOVEMENT IN THE SOUTH). 0735-8644. Periodical. US. English. bm. $6.00. Southern Neighborhoods, 2406-A Albion Street, Nashville TN 37208. **Tel** (616)320-5757. **Ed** Rebecca Marnhout. **DD** 307. bk rev. adv acc. **Circ** 400. Focuses on community organizing efforts of all types. Major emphasis are on the South. Also covers important regional political, civil rights, and economic issues.

SOUTHERN SOCIAL STUDIES QUARTERLY. (SOUTHERN SOCIAL STUDIES QUARTERLY : OFFICIAL PUBLICATION OF THE KENTUCKY COUNCIL FOR THE SOCIAL STUDIES). Vol. 1, No. 1 (Summer 1975)-. 0741-143X. Periodical. US. English. sa. $7.00. Morehead State University, UPO 738, Morehead KY 40351. **Tel** (606)783-2590. **Ed** Charles Hold and Kent Freeland. bk rev. **Circ** 300. Official publication of Kentucky Council for the Social Sciences. Publishes articles for and by people interested in social studies. Emphasis is on practical teaching strategies.

SOUTHWESTERN JOURNAL OF SOCIAL EDUCATION. V.L- Fall 1970-. 0049-1683. Periodical. US. English. sa. $5.00. North Texas State University, PO Box 5427, Denton TX 76201. **Ind/Abst** Curr. Index J. Educ.

SOVETSKAIA LITERATURA PO OBSHCHIM PROBLEMAM KULTURNO-PROSVETITELNOI RABOTY I KLUBOVEDENIIU. UR. Russian. 0.34. Informatsionnyi Tsentr Po Problemamskultury I Iskusst, Prospekt Kalinina 3, Moskva USSR. **LC** Z7164.C84, HN46.R9.

SOVIET JEWISH AFFAIRS. See Religion, Mythology, Rationalism - Judaism.

SOWJETWISSENSCHAFT. (SOWJETWISSENSCHAFT). Yearly Volume 1956, No. 1-. 0038-6006. Periodical. GE. German. bm. Verlag Volk und Welt, Glinkastr 13-15, 108 Berlin East Germany. **Ind/Abst** Philos. Index, Foreign Lang. Index. **LC** H5. *Sowjetwissenschaft.*

SOZIALE BEWEGUNGEN : ANALYSE UND DOKUMENTATION DES IMSF. See Economics - Labor.

SOZIALER FORTSCHRITT. Volume 1- 1952-. 0038-609X. Periodical. GW. German. mo. Dunker & Humbolt, Dietrich Schaefer Weg 9, 1 Berlin 41 West Germany. **Ind/Abst** Int. Labour Doc., Foreign Lang. Index, PAIS Foreign Lang. Index.

SOZIALPOLITISCHE SCHRIFTEN. Began publication in 1956. 0584-5998. Monographic Series. GW. German. ir. Duncker und Humblot Verlag, Dietrich-Schafer-Weg 9, 1 Berlin 41 West Germany.

THE SPECIALISED NATIONAL COUNCILS' MAGAZINE. Main/Corp Egypt. Al-Majalis Al-Qawmiyah Al-Mutakhassisah. Al-Amanah Al-Ammah. 1- June 1976-. Periodical. English. ir. Arab Socialist Union Building, Nile Corniche, Cairo Egypt. **Ind/Abst** Public Aff. Inf. Serv. Bull. **LC** HN786. **DD** 309.162.

SPECTRUM. (SPECTRUM). Vol. 1, No. 1 (Jan. 1981)-. 0228-8982. Periodical. CN. English (text in French). ir. Free. Council of Quebec Minorities, Suite 2/3437 Peel Street, Montreal Quebec H3A 1W7 Canada. **DD** 305.060714. *Interaction (Montreal, Quebec).*

SRI LANKA JOURNAL OF SOCIAL SCIENCES. V. 1- June 1978-. Periodical. CE. English. sa. $8.50. Natl Resources Energy & Science Authority, 47 Maitland Place, Colombo 7 Sri Lanka. **Tel** 596771. **LC** H1. **DD** 300.5. **Circ** 500. Incorporates research sponsored by the Natural Resources Energy and Science Authority on social sciences and those written by researchers working independently.

SRM ABSTRACTS. See Indexes/Abstracts.

SSRC NEWSLETTER. Main/Corp Social Science Research Council (Great Britain). Nov. 1967-. Periodical. UK. English. ty. **Ind/Abst** World Text Abstr. **LC** H62.5.G7. **DD** 300.72.

SSRC STUDENTSHIP HANDBOOK. POSTGRADUATE STUDENTSHIPS IN THE SOCIAL SCIENCES. Main/Corp Social Science Research Council (Gt. Brit.) Postgraduate Training Division. UK. English. Social Science Research Council, Postgraduate Training Division, 1 Temple Avenue, London EC4Y 0BD England. **LC** H62.5.G7. **DD** 300.71141. *Postgraduate Studentships in the Social Sciences.*

SSU YU YEN. See Humanities.

STATE, CULTURE AND SOCIETY. Vol. 1, No. 1 (Fall 1984)-. 0743-9245. Periodical. US. English. ty. $27.00. Associated Faculty Press Inc, 19 West 36th Street 12th Floor, New York NY 10018-7909. **Tel** (914)762-2200. **Ed** Arthur J Vidich and Stanford M Lyman. **DD** 300. adv acc. **Circ** 200. Provides a forum for discussion, dialogue and debate on points of tension between state and civil society, between nations and global institutions.

STATISTICAL INFORMATION SERVICE : PERSONAL SOCIAL SERVICES STATISTICS ACTUALS. See Statistics.

STATISTICAL JOURNAL OF THE UNITED NATIONS ECONOMIC COMMISSION FOR EUROPE. See Statistics.

Social Sciences (General)

STATISTICAL POCKET BOOK OF THE DEMOCRATIC SOCIALIST REPUBLIC OF SRI LANKA. See Statistics.

STATISTICHE SOCIALI. See Statistics.

STATISTISCH-PROGNOSTISCHER BERICHT. See Statistics.

STATISTISCHE HEFTE. See Statistics.

STUDENT DISCUSSION PAPER. Main/Corp York University (Toronto, Ont.) Faculty of Environmental Studies. No. 1- Nov. 1975-. 0383-9990. Monographic Series. CN. English. Faculty of Environmental Studies Resources Centre, York University, 4700 Keele Street, Downsview Ontario M3J 1P3 Canada. **DD** 301.31.

STUDIA SOCJOLOGICZNE. Vol. 1- (No. 1-). 0039-3371. Periodical. PL. Polish (tables of contents also in Russian and English). qt. ARS Polona, Krakowskie Przedmiescie 7, 00-068 Warsaw Poland. **Ind/Abst** Sociol. Abstr., Soc. Welf. Soc. Plan./Policy Soc. Dev., Psychol. Abstr., Lang. Lang. Behav. Abstr. **LC** H8. **CODEN** STSOCP.

STUDIES. V. 1- (No. 1-). 0039-3495. Periodical. IE. English. qt. $16.00. Studies, c/o PO Connell 35, Lower Leeson Street, Dublin 2 Ireland. **Tel** (01) 766785. Ed Brian D Lennon. **Ind/Abst** Annu. Bibliogr. Engl. Lang. Lit., Am. Hist. Life, Hist. Abstr., Part A, Mod. Hist. Abstr., Hist. Abst., Part B, Twent. Century Abstr., Abstr. Engl. Stud., MLA Int. Bibliogr. Books Artic. Mod. Lang. Lit., Cathol. Period. Lit. Index. **LC** AP4. **DD** 052. (cum index). adv acc. **Circ** 3,000. Founded in 1912, it analyses social, political, economic, historical, literary and religious questions in modern Ireland and abroad.

STUDIES IN COMPARATIVE INTERNATIONAL DEVELOPMENT. V. 1- 1965-. 0039-3606. Periodical. US. English. qt. $79.00. Transaction Books and Periodicals, Rutgers University, New Brunswick NJ 08903. **Tel** (201)932-2280. Ed Jay Weinstein. **Ind/Abst** Am. Hist. Life, Hist. Abstr., Part A, Mod. Hist. Abstr., Hist. Abst., Part B, Twent. Century Abstr., Int. Labour Doc., ABC Pol Sci, Recent Publ. Artic., Sociol. Abstr., Soc. Welf. Soc. Plan./Policy Soc. Dev., Soc. Sci. Citation Index, Lang. Lang. Behav. Abstr. **LC** H31. **DD** 300.5. bk rev. adv acc. **Circ** 1,000. A interdisciplinary social science journal exploring current issues in development theory and practice.

STUDIES IN HISTORY AND SOCIAL SCIENCES. See History (General).

STUDIES IN SOCIAL LIFE. 1- 1953-. 0081-8518. Monographic Series. English. ir. Martinus Nihhoff Publishers, PO Box 163, Spulboulevard 50, 3300AD Dordrecht Nethelands.

STUDIES IN SOCIETY. 1-. Monographic Series. English. ir. Allen and Unwin Sydney, PO Box 978, Edison NJ 08817. **Tel** (617)729-0830.

STUDIES IN THE SOCIAL SCIENCES. Main/Corp West Georgia College. Vol. 1 May 1962-. 0081-8682. US. English. ir. $4.00. West Georgia College, Stanford Hall, Carrollton GA 30118-0001. **Tel** (404)834-1405. Ed Robert H Claxton. **Ind/Abst** Am. Hist. Life, Hist. Abstr., Part A, Mod. Hist. Abstr., Hist. Abst., Part B, Twent. Century Abstr., Hist. Abstr. **DD** 300. **Circ** 500. This work will interest sociologists, historians, physical education instructors, and all observers of the women's liberation movement.

STUDIES ON DEVELOPMENT PROBLEMS IN COUNTRIES OF WESTERN ASIA. Main/Corp United Nations. Economic Commission for Western Asia. 1974-. US. English. an. United Nations Publications, Sales Section/Room A-3315, New York NY 10017. **LC** JX1977, HC410.7. **DD** 300.8 S, 338.956. Studies on Development Problems in Selected Countries of the Middle East.

SUDAN JOURNAL OF ECONOMIC AND SOCIAL STUDIES. See Economics.

SUDOST EUROPA : MONATSSCHRIFT DER ABTEILUNG GEGENWARTSFORSCHUNG DES SUDOST-INSTITUTS. VFOAT Sudosteuropa. Vol. 31, No. 1 (Jan. 1982)-. 0043-695X. Periodical. GW. German. mo. 48.00. Sudost-Institut Munchen Abteilung Gegenwartsforschung, Gulstr 7, 8000 Munchen West Germany. **LC** H5. **DD** 947.0005. Wissenschaftlicher Dienst Sudosteuropa.

SUMMARY OF ACTIVITIES - SOCIAL PLANNING AND RESEARCH COUNCIL OF HAMILTON AND DISTRICT. Main/Corp Social Planning and Research Council of Hamilton and District. 1974/75-. 0706-8301. CN. English. an. Free. Social Planning and Research Council of Hamilton and District, 153 1/2 King Street East, Hamilton Ontario L8N 1B1 Canada. **DD** 309.26206271352.

SUMMARY OF ACTIVITIES - UNIVERSITY OF CALIFORNIA, LOS ANGELES. CHICANO STUDIES RESEARCH CENTER. (SUMMARY OF ACTIVITIES). Main/Corp University of California, Los Angeles. Chicano Studies Research Center. 8755-8807. US. English. an. University of California, Chicano Studies Research Center, Center Publications, 405 Hilgard Avenue, Los Angeles CA 90024. **DD** 305.

SUNBURST. 7184-9181. Periodical. US. English. qt. $10.00. California Council of Social Studies, 616 Juanita Way, Roseville CA 95678. **Tel** (916)786-6056. Ed Bill Smiley. **Circ** 1,500. (ctrl). This publication is a composite of all local council news in the State, as well as announcements of upcoming workshops, conferences and meetings.

SUNG LIAO HSUEH KAN. SHE HUI KO HSUEH PAN. VFOAT Songliao Journal. Phylosophy i.e. Philosophy and Social Science, Song Liao Xue Kan. Began in 1983. Periodical. CC. Chinese. qt. 0.40. Post Office, SSU-Ping Shih China. **LC** AS452.S787. **DD** 059.951. SSU-Ping Shih Yuan Hsueh Pao.

SUPPLEMENT BIJ DE SOCIAAL-ECONOMISCHE MAANDSTATISTIEK. See Statistics.

SURVEY METHODOLOGY. VFOAT Techniques d'Enquete. Vol. 1, No. 1 (June 1975)-. 0714-0045. Periodical. CN. English (French, English only, Vol. 1, No. 1 (June 1975)-Vol. 2, No. 1 (June 1976)). sa. Receiver General for Canada, Statistics Canada Publications, Ottawa Ontario K1A 0T6 Canada. **Tel** (800)268-1511. **DD** 001.42205.

SURVEY SARAJEVO. VFOAT Survey. 1-. 0350-0144. Periodical. English. ir. $3.00. University of Sarajevo, Editorial Offices Obla 7/III, Room 202 POB 265, 71.000 Sarajevo Yugoslavia. **LC** H1. **DD** 3005.

SVODNYI BIULLETEN NOVYKH INOSTRANNYKH KNIG, POSTUPIVSHIKH V BIBLIOTEKI SSSR : OBSHCHESTVENNYE NAUKI. VAT Svodnyi Biulleten Novykh Inostrannykh Knig, Postupivshikh V Biblioteki Soiuza Sovetskikh Sotosialisticheskikh Respublik: Obshchestvennye Nauki. 1977-. UR. Multilingual (Russian). bm. 1.30. IZD-VO Kniga, K-9 UI Nezhdanovoi 8/10, Moskva Russian SFSR. **LC** Z7161, H62. Svodnyi Biulleten Novykh Inostrannykh Knig, Postupivshikh V Krupneishie Biblioteki SSSR. Seriia B. Obshchestvennye Nauki.

SWEDISH BEHAVIORAL SCIENCE RESEARCH REPORTS. Main/Corp Statens Psykologisk-Pedagogiska Bibliotek. VFOAT Beteendevetenskapliga Rapporter. English. ir. National Library for Psychology and Education, Box 23 099 S-104 35, Stockholm Sweden. **LC** H62.5.S8. **DD** 300.720485.

SYNTEZA. V. 1- No. 1- June 1968-. 0322-9386. Periodical. CS. Czech (summaries and/or contents lists in English and Russian). ir. Ceskoslovensky Vyskumny Ustav Prace a Socialnych, Veci Bezrucova 8, Bratislava Czechoslavakia. **Ind/Abst** Psychol. Abstr. **CODEN** SYNZAW.

TARSADALOMTUDOMANYI KOZLEMENYEK. Periodical. HU. Hungarian (summaries in English and Russian). qt. Akademiai Kiado, POB 24, 1363 Budapest Hungary. **LC** H8.

TECHNICAL PAPER - ARCTIC INSTITUTE OF NORTH AMERICA CEASED. (TECHNICAL PAPER). Began with No. 1, 1956. 0066-698X. Monographic Series. US. English. ir. $50.00. Arctic Institute of North America, University of Calgary, 2500 University Drive NW, Calgary Alberta T2N 1N4 Canada. **Tel** (403)284-7515. Ed Gordon W Hodgson. **Ind/Abst** GeoRef, Biol. Abstr., Bibliogr. Index Geol. **CODEN** AIATAD. bk rev. **Circ** 2,800. (ctrl). Scholarly, original treatment of aspects of the polar and sub-polar regions of the world, particularly those pertaining to the physical, biological, social and engineering sciences.

TECHNOCRACY DIGEST. 0040-1587. Periodical. CN. English. qt. $5.00. Technocracy Digest, 3642 Kingway, Vancouver V2V 4H9 BC Canada. **Tel** (604)434-1134. Ed Ed McBurnie. Science in the social field.

TELOS. No. 1- Spring 1968. 0090-6514. Periodical. US. English. qt. $50.00. Telos, 431 East 12th Street, New York NY 10009. **Tel** (212)228-6479. Ed Paul Picconi. **Ind/Abst** Sociol. Abstr., Philos. Index, Altern. Press Index, Lang. Lang. Behav. Abstr. **LC** H1. **DD** 300.5. (cum index). bk rev. adv acc. **Circ** 2,500. (ctrl). Back issues available in microform from University Microfilms. A scholarly journal of social and political theory. Each issue includes notes and commentary as well as a review section. Translations from foreign publications are also often included.

THEORY AND DECISION. See Philosophy.

THEORY AND RESEARCH IN SOCIAL EDUCATION. VFOAT TRSE. V. 1- Oct. 1973-. 0093-3104. Periodical. US. English. qt. $35.00. University of Georgia, Dr G Larking, Social Science Education, Athens GA 30602. **Tel** (201)932-7106. **Ind/Abst** Curr. Index J. Educ., Psychol. Abstr. **LC** H1. **DD** 300.7.

THIRD WAY. See Religion, Mythology, Rationalism - Protestantism.

TIJDSCHRIFT VOOR SOCIALE WETENSCHAPPEN. See Sociology: General Works, Theory.

THE TOCQUEVILLE REVIEW. (THE TOCQUEVILLE REVIEW). Main/Corp Tocqueville Society. VFOAT Revue Tocqueville. V. 1- Fall 1979-. 0730-479X. Periodical. US. English (French). sa. $10.00 Members, $16.00 Nonmembers, $24.00 Institutions and Libraries. Office Manager, The Tocqueville Society, 543 Cabell Hall, University of Virginia, Charlottesville VA 22901. **Ind/Abst** Writ. Am. Hist. **LC** H1. **DD** 300.5.

TOWNSHIPS CROSSROADS. No. 1 (July 4, 1980)-. 0228-6858. Periodical. CN. English. qt. Free to Members. Townships Crossroads c/o Townshipers Association, Room 310/31 King West, Sherbrooke Quebec J1H 1N5 Canada. **DD** 305.72107146.

TRANSICION. V. 1- Oct. 1978-. Periodical. SP. Spanish. ir. 1.000. Inciativas Editoriales, Ramblas 130 4, Barcelona - 2 Spain. **LC** H8.S7.

TRAVAUX ET MEMOIRES DE L'INSTITUT D'ETHNOLOGIE. Main/Corp Paris. Universite. Institut d'Ethnologie. 1926-. Monographic Series. FR. French. ir. Institut d'Ethnologie, Place du Trocadero, F-75116 Paris France. **Tel** 4553 82 15. Volumes of ethnology, archaeology, linguistics, monographies, ethnohistoric studies, codex, oral literature, both urban and European.

TROPICAL ABSTRACTS. See Indexes/Abstracts.

TUNG CHI YEN CHIU. Periodical. CH. Chinese. ir. 1.00. Hsin Hua Shu Tien, Pei-Ching fa Hsing So, Peking China. **LC** HA1. **DD** 300.72.

TUNG HAI SHE HUI KO HSUEH HSUEH PAO. VFOAT Tunghai Journal of Social Sciences. V. 1-. Periodical. CH. Chinese (English). ir. Tunghai Journal of Social Sciences, PO Box 938, Tunghai University Taichung Taiwan 400 Republic of China. **LC** H8.C47. **DD** 300.5.

TUNG WU CHENG CHIH SHE HUI HSUEH PAO. VFOAT Soochow Journal of Social & Political Sciences. V. 1-. CH. Chinese (English). ir. Soochow University Shih Lin Taipei, 111 Taipei Taiwan. **LC** H8.C47.

TVI JOURNAL. VFOAT Terrorism, Violence, Insurgency Journal. VAT Terrorism, Violence and Insurgency Journal. V. 1-. 0195-8003. Periodical. US. English. qt. $60.00. Terrorism Violence Insurgency, PO Box 1055, Beverly Hills CA 90213. **Tel** (213)276-3378. Ed Brian M Jenkins. bk rev. adv acc. **Circ** 2,000. Studies contemporary terrorism and related forms of criminal violence.

UKEIRE TOSHO MOKUROKU : WASHO NO BU. Main/Corp Nihon Yushutsunyu Ginko. Kaigai Toshi Kenkyujo. Tosho Shiryoshitsu. Japanese. ir. **LC** Z7166, H83.

UNION LIST OF SERIALS IN THE SOCIAL SCIENCES AND HUMANITIES HELD BY CANADIAN LIBRARIES. See Bibliographies.

UNIVERSITIES QUARTERLY. (UNIVERSITIES QUARTERLY : CULTURE, EDUCATION & SOCIETY). Vol. 37, No. 1 (Winter 1982/83)-. 0263-9769. Periodical. UK. English. qt. $61.00 US. Basil Blackwell, Journals Department, 108 Cowley Road, Oxford OX4 1JF England. **Tel** 0865-722146. Ed Boris Ford. **Ind/Abst** Index Book Rev. Humanit., Public Aff. Inf. Serv. Bull., Curr. Index J. Educ. **LC**

Societies and Clubs

LA630. **DD** 370.941. adv acc. Informed and wide ranging discussion of contemporary culture and society. *New Universities Quarterly, 0307-8612.*

UNSERE JUGEND. *See* Education (General).

URAL-ALTAISCHE JAHRBUCHER (BLOOMINGTON, IND.). *See* Yearbooks, Almanacs, Directories.

THE URBAN & SOCIAL CHANGE REVIEW. VAT Urban and Social Change Review. V. 3- Fall 1969-. 0042-0832. Periodical. US. English. sa. $8.00. Urban & Social Change Review, McGuinn Hall Boston College, Chestnut Hill MA 02167. **Tel** (617)552-4038. **Ed** Robert M Moroney and Karen Wolk Feinstein. **Ind/Abst** Am. Hist. Life, Hist. Abstr., Part A, Mod. Hist. Abstr., Hist. Abstr., Part B, Twent. Century Abstr., Sociol. Abstr., Soc. Welf. Soc. Plan./Policy Soc. Dev., ABC Pol Sci, Soc. Work Res. Abstr., Soc. Sci. Citation Index, Lang. Lang. Behav. Abstr., Avery Index Archit. Period., Hist. Abstr. **LC** HT101. bk rev. adv acc. **Circ** 1,500. (ctrl). Interdisciplinary action-oriented journal focusing on urban and social problems. Articles on human services plus information clearinghouse included.

URBAN ECOLOGY. V. 1- June 1975-. 0304-4009. Periodical. NE. English. qt. Elsevier Science Publishers, PO Box 211, 1000 AE Amsterdam Netherlands. **Tel** (020)5803911. **Ind/Abst** Electron. Commun. Abstr. J., ISMEC Bull., Pollut. Abstr. Indexes, Saf. Sci. Abstr. J., Life Sci. Collect., Excerpta Med., Energy Inf. Abstr., Environ. Abstr., Biol. Abstr., Energy Res. Abstr., Sci. Cit. Index, Abr. Ed., Soc. Sci. Citation Index. **LC** GF125. **DD** 304.2091732. **CODEN** URECDU.

URBAN GEOGRAPHY. *See* Geography.

URBAN STUDIES. V. 1- May 1964-. 0042-0980. Periodical. UK. English. bm. 64.00. Longman Group Ltd, Fourth Avenue, Harlow Essex CM19 5AA England. **Tel** 0279 442601. **Ed** W Lever, U Money and G Wood. **Ind/Abst** Am. Hist. Life, Hist. Abstr., Archit. Period. Index, Life Sci. Collect., Excerpta Med., Sociol. Abstr., Soc. Welf. Soc. Plan./Policy Soc. Dev., Avery Index Archit. Period., Index Econ. Artic. J. Collect. Vol., Ref. Source, Public Aff. Inf. Serv. Bull., Soc. Sci. Index, Lang. Lang. Behav. Abstr., Soc. Sci. Citation Index, Hist. Abstr., Part A, Mod. Hist. Abstr., Hist. Abstr., Part B, Twent. Century Abstr., Avery Index Archit. Period. **LC** HT103. **DD** 307.12. (cum index). bk rev. adv acc. International forum for discussion on urban affairs and regional planning.

UTAFITI. V. 1- 1976-. Periodical. KE. English. sa. $5.20. PO Box 30022, Nairobi Kenya Africa. **LC** H1. **DD** 300.5.

VERSTANDLICHE WISSENSCHAFT. *See* History (General).

VIE OUVRIERE (MONTREAL, QUEBEC). *See* Economics - Labor.

VIE SOCIALE. No. 1- Jan. 1964-. 0042-5605. Periodical. French. ir. **LC** H3. **NLM** W1 VI227. *Cahiers du Musee Social.*

VILLAGE NEPAL. Vol. 1, No. 1 (Nov. 1980)-. English. sa. $3.00. Village Nepal, 1/138 GA Pulchowk, Lalitpur Nepal. **LC** HN670.9.Z9.

VIRGINIA SOCIAL SCIENCE JOURNAL. VFOAT VSSJ. V. 1- Apr. 1966-. 0507-1305. Periodical. US. English. sa. $12.00. Thomas Bertsch Management & Marketing Department, James Madison University, Harrisburg VA 22807. **Tel** (203)434-4362. **Ed** Thomas Bertsch. **Ind/Abst** Public Aff. Inf. Serv. Bull. **LC** H1. **Circ** 300. Social science research issues of interest and concern to Virginians.

WASEDA SHAKAI KAGAKU KENKYU. VFOAT Waseda Journal of Social Sciences. Began in 1967. 0286-1283. Periodical. JA. Japanese. ir. Waseda Daigaku Shakai Kagakubu Gakkai, c/o Waseda Daigaku Shakai, Kagakubu 6-1, Nishi Waseda 1, Shinjuku-Ku Tokyo-to Japan. **LC** H8.J3.

THE WASHINGTON MONTHLY. *See* Political Science.

WESTERN CIVILIZATION. *See* History (General).

WESTERN GEOGRAPHICAL SERIES. *See* Geography.

THE WESTERN JOURNAL OF BLACK STUDIES. *See* Ethnic.

THE WILSON QUARTERLY. V. 1- Autumn 1976-. 0363-3276. Periodical. US. English. Woodrow Wilson International Center for Scholars, Smithsonian Institution Building, Washington DC 20560, (subscription address: Neodata PO Box 2606 Boulder CO 80322). **Tel** (212)490-1840. **Ed** Peter Braestrup. **Ind/Abst** Am. Hist. Life, Hist. Abstr., Part A, Mod. Hist. Abstr., Hist. Abstr., Part B, Twent. Century Abstr., Book Rev. Index, Public Aff. Inf. Serv. Bull., Writ. Am. Hist., Soc. Sci. Index, Recent Publ. Artic., Hist. Abstr. **LC** AS36.W79. **DD** 051. bk rev. adv acc. **Circ** 110,000. This Smithsonian newsmagazine summarizes developments in research on politics, environment, foreign affairs, history environment, the arts, television, the press, economics and science.

WISCONSIN ACADEMY REVIEW. *See* Humanities.

WISSENSCHAFTLICHE ZEITSCHRIFT DER ERNST-MORITZ-ARNDT-UNIVERSITAT, GREIFSWALD. GESSELSCHAFTS- UND SPRACHWISSENSCHAFTLICHE REIHE CEASED. Year- 4-15. Periodical. GE. German. qt. Deutscher Buch Export-Import, Leninstrasse 16, DDR-701 Leipzig East Germany. **Ind/Abst** Artbibliogr. Mod., Repert. Int. Litt. Art. *Wissenschaftliche Zeitschrift der Universitat Greifswald. Gesellschafts- und Sprachwissenschaftliche Reihe.*

WISSENSCHAFTLICHE ZEITSCHRIFT DER HUMBOLDT-UNIVERSITAT ZU BERLIN. 32, 1-. 0522-9855. Periodical. GE. German (text in English, French, or Russian). ir. 237.50. Deutscher Buchexport Import, Postfach 160, 7010 Leipzig East Germany. **Tel** 20932627. **Ind/Abst** MLA Int. Bibliogr. Books Artic. Mod. Lang. Lit., Writ. Am. Hist. Publishes original papers of all fields represented in the university. The individual issues are restricted to one or two topics. *Wissenschaft Zietschrift. Gesellschafts-und Sprachwissenschaftliche Reihe.*

WISSENSCHAFTLICHE ZEITSCHRIFT DER MARTIN-LUTHER-UNIVERSITAT HALLE-WITTENBERG. GESELLSCHAFTS- UND SPRACHWISSENSCHAFTLICHE REIHE. Vol. 1, No. (1951)-Vol. 14, No. 7 (1965). Periodical. German. bm. Kunst & Wissen Erich Bieber, Dufourstrasse 51, CH-8008 Zurich Switzerland. **Tel** 011-41-1-69 44 20.

WISSENSCHAFTLICHER DIENST SUDOSTEUROPA. Vol. 1- Oct. 1952-. 0463-9642. Periodical. GW. German. mo. Suedost-Institut, Gullstrasse 7, 8 Muenchen 2 West Germany. **Ind/Abst** Foreign Lang. Index. **LC** H5. **DD** 300.5.

WORKERS EDUCATION. *See* Economics - Labor.

WORKING PAPER SERIES - UNIVERSITY OF ARIZONA. MEXICAN AMERICAN STUDIES AND RESEARCH CENTER. (WORKING PAPER SERIES). 1-. 0732-7749. Monographic Series. US. English. tw. University of Arizona, Mexican American Studies and Research Center, Modern Languages Room 209, Tucson AZ 85721. **Tel** (602)621-7551. **Ed** John A Garcia. **LC** UNC. (ctrl). Policy areas of economics, education, acculturation of Hispanics in the US and expressive culture.

WORKING PAPERS FOR A NEW SOCIETY CEASED. V. 1-8, No. 3. 0091-1615. Periodical. US. English. bm. $8.00. 123 Mt Auburn Street 02138. **Ind/Abst** Sociol. Abstr., Soc. Welf. Soc. Plan./Policy Soc. Dev., Public Aff. Inf. Serv. Bull. **LC** H1. **DD** 300.5.

WORKING PAPERS IN METHODOLOGY. No. 1-10. Monographic Series. US. English. ir. Institute Research Social Science, Manning Hall 026A University North Carolina, Chapel Hill NC 27514. **DD** 301.018.

WORKING PAPERS MAGAZINE. VFOAT Working Papers. Vol. 8, No. 4 (July/Aug. 1981)-. 0744-9836. Periodical. US. English. ir. Monash University, Centre for Southeast Asian Studies, Clayton Victoria 3168 Australia. **Ind/Abst** Altern. Press Index. *Working Papers for a New Society, 0091-1615.*

YAGL-AMBU. V. 1- Mar. 1974-. Periodical. PP. English. qt. $15.91. University of Papua New Guinea, University PO Box 320, Papua New Guinea. **Tel** 245443. **Ed** Desh Gupta. bk rev. **Circ** 300. (ctrl). Examines issues concerned with Papua New Guinea's social and economic developments.

YEAR-BOOK OF WORLD PROBLEMS AND HUMAN POTENTIAL. *See* Yearbooks, Almanacs, Directories.

YEARBOOK - NATIONAL COUNCIL FOR THE SOCIAL STUDIES. *See* Yearbooks, Almanacs, Directories.

THE YENCHING JOURNAL OF SOCIAL STUDIES. V. 1- June, 1938-. Periodical. CH. English. ir. Yenching University, Peking Peoples Republic of China. **LC** H1. **DD** 305.

YOUTH (BOCA RATON, FLA.). (YOUTH). Series/Titl Social Issues Resources Series. Vol. 1, Article 1-. 0273-2610. US. English. an. Social Issues Resources Series Inc, PO Box 2507, Boca Raton FL 33432. **Ed** Eleanor C Goldstein. **LC** HQ796. **DD** 305.2350973.

ZONA ABIERTA. No. 1- Oct. 1974-. Periodical. SP. Spanish. qt. 900. Argueso 8, Madrid Spain. **LC** H8.

SOCIETIES AND CLUBS

ADDRESSES - EMPIRE CLUB OF CANADA. Main/Corp Empire Club of Canada. VFOAT Empire Club Speeches. Began with 9th, 1911/12 issue?. 0316-0548. Periodical. CN. English. an. Empire Club, Royal York Hotel, 100 Front Street, Toronto Ontario M5J 1E3 Canada. **DD** 081. *Empire Club Speeches, 0316-0580.*

ADVANCES IN INSTRUMENTATION : PROCEEDINGS OF THE . . . ANNUAL ISA CONFERENCE. VFOAT Proceedings of the . . . Annual ISA Conference. Vol. 23 (1968)-. 0065-2814. US. English. an. Instrument Society of America, PO Box 3561, Durham NC 27702. **Tel** (412)281-3171. **Ind/Abst** Eng. Index, Chem. Abstr. **CODEN** AVINBP. *Annual I.S.A. Conference Proceedings, 0097-675X.*

AICHI KYOIKU DAIGAKU KENKYU HOKOKU. GEIJUTSU, HOKEN TAIIKU, KASEI, GIJUTSU KAGAKU. 0388-7367. Periodical. JA. Japanese. ir. Aichi Kyoiku Daigaku, Hirosawa 1 Igaya-cho, Kariya-shi 448 Japan. **LC** AS552.K343.

AL-MAJALLAH AL-THAQAFIYAH. No. 1, (April 1983)-. Arabic. qt. Al-Jamiah Al-Urduniyah, Amman Al-Urdun. **LC** AS593.A934.

ALLIANCE. (L'ALLIANCE : BULLETIN MENSUEL DES FRANCS-MACONS DE MTL). 1 (May 1983)-. 0822-4285. Periodical. CN. French. mo. Ecole du Vendredi des Francs-Macons, 7459A rue Millet, St-Leonard Quebec H1S 2N1 Canada. **DD** 366.105.

ALPHA DELTA KAPPAN. VFOAT Kappan. 1933. 0002-6387. Periodical. US. English. sa. $3.00. Alpha Delta Kappan, Honorary Society for Women Educators, 1615 West 92nd Street, Kansas City MO 64114. **Tel** (816)363-5525. **Ed** Florence Barrett. **Circ** 55,000. (ctrl). Deals with educational developments and classroom projects, professional accomplishments of members, and membership directory.

THE AMERICAN HOSTA SOCIETY NEWSLETTER. No. 1 (1968)-. Periodical. US. English. ir. American Hosta Society, 980 Stanton Avenue, Baldwin NY 11510.

AMERICAN KING CLUB BULLETIN. 0164-9361. Periodical. US. English. qt. American King Club, 7914 East Hubbell Street, Scottsdale AZ 85257.

AMERICAN MENSA REGISTER. 0738-5218. US. English. American Mensa Ltd, 1701 West 3rd Street/Suite 1 R, Brooklyn NY 11223. **LC** BF431. **DD** 367.

ANNALS OF THE ISRAEL PHYSICAL SOCIETY. V. 1-. 0309-8710. Monographic Series. UK. English. ir. American Institute of Physics, 335 East 45th Street, New York NY 10017. **Tel** (516)349-7800. **Ind/Abst** Chem. Abstr., Comput. Control Abstr., Electr. Electron. Abstr., Sci. Abstr. Sect. A. Phys. Abstr. **CODEN** AIPSDK.

Societies and Clubs

ANNUAL REPORT - ASIATIC SOCIETY. Main/Corp Asiatic Society (Calcutta, India). 0403-4457. English. ir. The Asiatic Society, 1 Park Street, Calcutta 16 India. LC AS472.A85. DD 068.5414.

ANNUAL REPORT - CAMP FIRE, INC. (ANNUAL REPORT). Main/Corp Camp Fire, Inc. US. English. an. Camp Fire Inc, 4601 Madison Avenue, Kansas City MO 64112.

ANNUAL REPORT - CHAMPLAIN SOCIETY. Main/Corp Champlain Society. 1st-. 0069-2646. CN. English. Champlain Society, Royal York Hotel/100 Front Street West, Toronto Ontario M5J 1E3 Canada.

ANNUAL REPORT - DANFORTH FOUNDATION. Main/Corp Danforth Foundation, St. Louis, MO. 0070-2706. US. English. an. Danfourth Foundation, 222 South Central Avenue, St Louis MO 63105.

ANNUAL REPORT - HERITAGE FOUNDATION. (ANNUAL REPORT). Main/Corp Heritage Foundation (Washington, D.C.). 0732-975X. US. English. an. The Heritage Foundation, 513 C Street Northeast, Washington DC 20002. LC AS36.W285. DD 061.3.

ANNUAL REPORT - MOUNT VERNON LADIES' ASSOCIATION OF THE UNION. (ANNUAL REPORT - THE MOUNT VERNON LADIES' ASSOCIATION OF THE UNION). Main/Corp Mount Vernon Ladies' Association of the Union. 1896-. 0276-9484. US. English. an. Mount Vernon Ladies' Association of the Union, Mount Vernon VA 22121.

ANNUAL REPORT OF THE HENRY BRADSHAW SOCIETY. Main/Corp Henry Bradshaw Society. UK. English. an.

ANNUAL REPORT - TWENTIETH CENTURY FUND. Main/Corp Twentieth Century Fund. 0363-3047. US. English. an. Twentieth Century Fund, 41 East 70th Street, New York NY 10021. LC AS25.

ANUARIO VERITAS. See Yearbooks, Almanacs, Directories.

ASAHI GURAFU BESSATSU. JA. Japanese. ir. 980. Asahi Shimbun Sha, 6-1 Yurakucho, Chiyoda-ku 100 Tokyo Japan. LC AS551.

ASIA (NEW YORK, N.Y. : 1984). (ASIA : NEWSLETTER OF THE ASIA SOCIETY). Periodical. US. English. bm. Asia.

ASPP NEWSLETTER (NEW YORK, N.Y.). (ASPP NEWSLETTER). VFOAT A.S.P.P. Newsletter. VAT American Society of Picture Professionals Newsletter. 0740-4115. Periodical. US. English. ir. $30.00. American Society of Picture Professionals, POB 5283, Grand Central Station, New York NY 10017.

ASSOCIATIONS OF DELAWARE VALLEY. 0161-0023. US. English. Greater Philadelphia Chamber of Commerce, 1528 Walnut Street, Philadelphia PA 19102. LC HS61.D3. DD 366.0025749.

ASSOCIATIONS, OTTAWA & AREA. VFOAT Associations d'Ottawa et de la Region. 0714-4946. CN. English (French). be. $15.00 Per Volume. Assistant Director's Office, Ottawa Public Library, 120 Metcalfe Street, Ottawa Ontario K1P 5MS Canada. LC AS40.A7. DD 061.1384.

ASU NO KADAI. First issue No. 1. JA. Japanese. ir. 4800. c/o Toranomon Jitsugyo Kaikan, 8 Shiba Toronoman, Minato-ku 105 Tokyo Japan. LC AS551.

THE ATO PALM. VFOAT A.T.O. Palm. Periodical. US. English. qt. Alpha Tau Omega, 107 East Green Street, Champaign IL 61820. LC LJ75. DD 378.19855.

AUTREMENT. Began with Spring 1975 issue. Periodical. FR. French. ir. Editions Autrement, 4 rue d'Enghien, 75010 Paris France. Tel 770 1250. LC AS161. DD 054.1. Preuves.

AWARDS, HONORS & PRIZES. VFOAT Awards, Honors, and Prizes. 4th Ed.-. 0196-6316. US. English. Ed P Wasserman and J McLean. LC AS8. DD 001.44. Alphabetical directory of organizations in the US and Canada that sponsor awards in virtually every field of human endeavor, from academic awards to prizes in sports. Awards, Honors, and Prizes, 0196-6316.

BARDY. (LE BARDY). 1st Yearly V.- Jan. 1966-. 0381-6982. Periodical. CN. English. mo. $15.48. Societe St Jean Baptiste du Quebec, 555 Chemin Ste-Foy, Quebec Quebec G1S 2J9 Canada. Tel (418)525-4501. Chez-Nous.

BERICHT - STIFTUNG VOLKSWAGENWERK. Main/Corp Stiftung Volkswagenwerk. German. ir. Vandenhoeck and Ruprecht, Postfach 81 05 09, Katanienalles 35, D-3000 Hannover 81 West Germany. LC AS182.S79.

BIC. BULLETIN D'INFORMATION AUX CADRES. (BIC : BULLETIN D'INFORMATION AUX CADRES). VAT Bulletin d'Information Aux Cadres. No. 1 (Oct. 1981)-. 0714-7546. Periodical. CN. French. ir. Free. Federation Quebecoise du Guidisme et du Scoutisme, 1415 Est rue Jarry, Montreal Quebec H2E 2Z7 Canada. DD 369.43060714. Guide-Express, Mini-Scoutbec, 0713-5505.

BIENNIAL REPORT - THE ACCOKEEK FOUNDATION. Main/Corp Accokeek Foundation. 1st- 1958/59-. US. English. ir. Accokeek Foundation, 525 School Street SW, Washington DC 20024.

BIVOUAC. (BIVOUAC : MAGAZINE DES SCOUTS DU QUEBEC). 0228-4448. Periodical. CN. French. ir. $2,00. Bivouac, Federation des Scouts du Quebec, 1415 Est rue Jarry, Montreal Quebec H2E 2Z7 Canada. DD 369.4309714.

BOLETIM - CONSELHO FEDERAL DE CULTURA. Main/Corp Conselho Federal de Cultura (Brazil). Yearly V.- 1 Jan/March 1971-. Periodical. Portuguese. ir. Conselho Federal de Cultura, rua de Imprensa 16-70 Andar, Rio de Janeiro Brazil. LC AS80.C65.

BOLETIN OFICIAL. Main/Corp Scottish Rite (Masonic Order). Grande Oriente do Rio Grande Do Sul. Portuguese. sa. LC HS779.B62. DD 366.1.

THE BOOK OF THE OLD EDINBURGH CLUB. Main/Corp Old Edinburgh Club. V. 1- 1908-. UK. English. ir. 5.00. Old Edinburgh, 10 Broomhall Loan, Edinburgh EH12 7PY Scotland United Kingdom. Tel 031-334 5762. LC DA7890.E2. (cum index). Circ 500. (ctrl). Publication of articles and documents relating to the history, culture and development of Edinburgh.

THE BOXWOOD BULLETIN. V. 1- Oct. 1961-. 0006-8535. Periodical. US. English. qt. American Boxwood Society, Blandy Experiment Farm-Box 85, Boyce VA 22620. (cum index).

THE BRASILIANS (PORTUGUESE EDITION). (THE BRASILIANS). Portuguese. mo. 20 West 46th Street, New York NY 10036.

BRATSTVO. VFOAT Fraternity. V. 1- 1954-. 0006-9264. Periodical. CN. Serbo-Croatian(R). mo. 345 Dovercourt Road, Toronto Ontario M6J 3E4 Canada.

BROTHERHOOD ACTION. 0300-4678. Periodical. AT. English. bm. $1.48. Brotherhood of St Laurence, 67 Brunswick Street, Fitzroy Victoria 3065 Australia. DD 03-4197055.

BULLETIN AUX CADRES - GUIDES CATHOLIQUES DU CANADA. (BULLETIN AUX CADRES). Main/Corp Guides Catholiques du Canada (Secteur Francais). Vol. 1, No. 1-. 0228-457X. Periodical. CN. French. mo. Guides Catholiques du Canada, Secteur Francais, 3827 rue St-Hubert, Montreal Quebec H2L 4A4 Canada. DD 369.46305.

BULLETIN - COSMOS CLUB. Main/Corp Cosmos Club (Washington, D.C.). VFOAT Cosmos Club Bulletin. V. 1- Nov. 1947-. Periodical. US. English. mo. Cosmos Club, 2121 Massachusetts Avenue NW, Washington DC 20008. LC HS2725.W3.

BULLETIN DE LA SOCIETE DES AMIS DE MONTAIGNE. Periodical. FR. French. sa. Amis de Montaigne, BP 92, F 94104 St Maur Cedex France. Bulletin des Amis de Montaigne.

BULLETIN DE L'ANIMATEUR. (LE BULLETIN DE L'ANIMATEUR). No. 25- Jan. 1980-. 0228-1503. Periodical. CN. French. bm. $4.00. Federation des Scouts du Quebec, 1415 Est rue Jarry, Montreal Quebec H2E 2Z7 Canada. DD 369.4305. Fiches de l'Animateur, 0228-149X.

BULLETIN - HOLLY SOCIETY OF AMERICA, INC. (BULLETIN - HOLLY SOCIETY OF AMERICA). Main/Corp Holly Society of America. No. 1- 1947-. 0273-0448. Monographic Series. US. English. ir. Holly Society of America, 304 Northwind Road, Baltimore MD 21204.

THE BULLETIN OF TAU BETA PI. Vol. 58, No. 2 (Dec. 1984)-. 8755-5670. Periodical. US. English. ty. Tau Beta Pi Association, PO Box 8840 University Station, Knoxville TN 37996-4800. DD 620. Council Bulletin of Tau Beta Pi, 0161-8814.

BUMMEI JIHYO. Japanese. ir. 200. Nihon Bunka Rengokai, 1312-255 Uchikoshicho 192, Hachioji Japan. Tel 0426-35-8451. Ed Noboru Komiyama. LC AS551. bk rev. Circ 2,000. Promotion of Japanese cultural development for the good of mankind thru academic association giving the true meaning of arts and sciences to the world.

DIE BUNDESREPUBLIK DEUTSCHLAND STAATSHANDBUCH. TEILAUSGABE, VERBANDE, VEREINIGUNGEN, WISSENSCHAFTLICHE EINRICHTUNGEN, JURISTISCHE PERSONEN DES ÖFFENTLICHEN RECHTS. VFOAT Teilausgabe, Verbande, Vereinigungen, Wissenschaftliche Einrichtungen, Juristische Personen des Offentlichen Rechts. German. ir. LC AS178. DD 063. Bundesrepublik Deutschland Staatshandbuch. Teilausgabe, Verbande, Vereinigungen, Wissenschaftliche Einrichtungen, Zusammenschlusse des Offentlichen Lebens.

BUNKA. VFOAT Culture. March 1974 Edition-. JA. Japanese. ir. Komazawa Daigaku Bungakubu Bunkagaku Kyoshitsu, 23 Komazawa 1-chome Setagaya-ku, Tokyo Japan. LC AS552.K67.

THE CAMELLIA REVIEW. V. 12- Oct. 1950-. Periodical. US. English. bm. Southern California Camellia Society Bulletin.

CAMP FIRE LEADERSHIP. 0092-1289. Periodical. US. English. ty. $8.00. Camp Fire Inc, 4601 Madison Avenue, Kansas City MO 64112. Tel (816)756-1950. Ed Julie Mierau. LC HS3353.C3. DD 369.4705. Circ 45,000. (ctrl). Articles appropriate to adults who work with Camp Fire youth members, including project descriptions, activity ideas and social issues that involve youth. Camp Fire Girl, 0008-2287.

CANADIAN GIDEON. (THE CANADIAN GIDEON). V. 12- Feb. 1955-. 0316-2907. Periodical. CN. Multilingual. bm. $4.65. Gideons International Canada, 501 Imperial Road, Guelph Ontario N1H 7A2 Canada. Tel (519)823-1140. Torch and Trumpet, 0316-2915.

CANADIAN IRIS SOCIETY NEWSLETTER. 0715-3775. Periodical. CN. English. qt. Free to Members. Canadian Iris Society News, c/o Royal Botanical Gardens, Box 399/Station A, Hamilton Ontario 20 Canada. DD 635.9342405.

CAPITAL COGS. Main/Corp Rotary Club of Albany. V. 1- 1921-. Periodical. US. English. wk. Rotary Club of Albany, Best Western Thurway House/1375 Washington Avenue, Albany NY 12206.

CEESSA BULLETIN. VAT Central and East European Studies Society of Alberta Bulletin. Vol. 3, No. 2-. 0826-7545. Periodical. CN. English. ir. Central and East European Studies Society of Alberta, #7 8540-109th Street, Edmonton Alberta T6G 1E6 Canada. DD 947.000707123. CEESSA News, 0821-2759.

CHENG MING (NAN-CHANG SHIH, CHINA). (CHENG MING). VFOAT Zheng Ming. Periodical. CH. Chinese. qt. 0.35. Chiang-hsi Sheng She Lien Cheng Mind Pien Chi Shih, Nan-ching Shi China. LC AS451. DD 089.951.

CHI NO KOKOGAKU. April/May 1975 Edition-. JA. Japanese. ir. 2880. Shakai Shiso Sha, 25-21 Hongo, 1-chome Bunkyo-ku (113) Tokyo Japan. LC AS551.

CHIANG HAI HSUEH KAN (1982). (CHIANG HAI HSUEH KAN). VFOAT Jianghai Xuekan. Periodical. CH. Chinese. bm. 0.40. Chung-kuo Kuo Chi Shu Tien, PO Box 2820, Pei-ching China Mainland. LC AS452.N38. DD 089.951. Chun Chun Lun Tsung.

CHIANG-HSI SHIH YUAN HSUEH PAO. CHE HSUEH SHE HUI KO HSUEH PAN. VFOAT Jiangxi Shiyuan Xuebao. Periodical. Chinese. qt. 0.35. Post Office, Nan-Chang Shih China. LC AS452.N352. DD 089.951.

Societies and Clubs

CHIANG-HSI TA HSUEH HSUEH PAO. SHE HUI KO HSUEH PAN. VFOAT Jiangxidaxuexuebao. Periodical. Chinese. qt. 0.40. Post Office Nan-chang Shih, Nan-chang Shih China. LC AS452. DD 089.951.

CHUNG-CHING TA HSUEH HSUEH PAO. VFOAT Chongqing Daxue Xueba. 0253-3626. Periodical. CC. Chinese. qt. $5.76. China Publication Centre, PO Box 2820, Beijing China. **Ind/Abst** Chem. Abstr. LC AS451. DD 089.951. CODEN CPAOD4.

CHUNG-CHOU HSUEH KAN. VFOAT Zhongzhouxuekan. Periodical. CH. Chinese. bm. 0.45. Post Office Cheng-chou Shih, Cheng-chou Shih China. LC AS452.C4614. DD 089.951.

CLUB BOOK OF THE KNICKERBOCKER CLUB. (CLUB BOOK OF THE KNICKERBOCKER CLUB, INC). **Main/Corp** Knickerbocker Club, New York. 0362-5168. US. English. an. Knickerbocker Club, New York NY 10022. LC HS2725.N5. DD 367.97471.

THE CLUB MAC NEWS. 0882-875X. Periodical. US. English. mo. Club Mac, 735 Walnut, Boulder CO 80302. **Tel** (303)449-5533. DD 001.

CLUBS & ORGANIZATIONS. DARTMOUTH & HALIFAX CEASED. (CLUBS & ORGANIZATIONS; DARTMOUTH & HALIFAX). VFOAT Halifax and Dartmouth Clubs & Organizations. 1973-1981/82. 0383-1744. CN. English. an. Dartmouth Regional Library, 100 Wyse Road, Dartmouth Nova Scotia B3A 1M1 Canada. DD 061.1622.

CLUBS & ORGANIZATIONS. INDUSTRIAL CAPE BRETON. (CLUBS AND ORGANIZATIONS, INDUSTRIAL CAPE BRETON). VFOAT Industrial Cape Breton, Clubs and Organizations. 0227-6682. CN. English. an. Cape Breton Regional Library, 110 Townsend Street, Sydney Nova Scotia B1P 5E1 Canada. DD 061.169.

CLUBS IN TOWN AND COUNTRY. Began in 1953. 0438-6256. US. English. an. Free. Pannell Kerr Forster, 420 Lexington Avenue, New York NY 10170. **Tel** (713)999-5134. **Ed** D Walker. LC HS2507. DD 367.97305. **Circ** 16,000. Statistical review of financial data on private clubs for both city and country clubs. Designed as a reference and management or operational aid for clubs and club managers.

COLOMBIEN. (LE COLOMBIEN). Periodical. CN. French. mo. $4.65. Chevaliers du Columb du Quebec, 3565 Berri, Montreal Quebec H2L 4G5 Canada. **Tel** (203)772-2130.

THE COMMUNICATOR OF PHI DELTA CHI FRATERNITY. **Main/Corp** Phi Delta Chi Fraternity. VFOAT Who's Who in Phi Delta Chi. Began publication in 1909. 0746-3979. Periodical. US. English. qt. $12.00. Executive Director, Phi Delta Chi, PO Box 140887, Dallas TX 75214.

COMMUNIQUE - SOCIETY FOR INTERCULTURAL EDUCATION, TRAINING AND RESEARCH. (COMMUNIQUE). 1970. 0276-1386. Periodical. US. English. ir. Society for Intercultural Education Training and Research, 1414 22nd Street NW, Washington DC 20037. **Tel** (202)296-4710. **Ed** Diane Zeller. bk rev. adv acc. **Circ** 1,600. (ctrl). Activities of the society and happenings in the intercultural field.

COMPTES RENDUS DES SEANCES - ACADEMIE DES INSCRIPTIONS & BELLES-LETTRES. **Main/Corp** Academie des Inscriptions & Belles-Lettres (France). 1857-. 0065-0536. Periodical. French. qt. Editions Klincksieck, 11 rue de Lille, 75007 Paris France. **Ind/Abst** Repert. Int. Litt. Art. LC AS162. DD 054.1. (cum index).

LA COMUNE. Vol. 1- May 1971-. Periodical. Italian. ir. 1000 Single Issue. Laboratorio Teatrale, Via Lago di Varano 67, 58100 Grosseto Italy. LC AS221.

CONFEDERATE VETERAN (MURFREESBORO, TENN.). (CONFEDERATE VETERAN). VFOAT Confederate Veteran Magazine. Vol. 32, No. 6 (Sept. 1984)-. Periodical. US. English. bm. Confederate Veteran, Sons of Confederate Veterans PO Box 1641, Murfreesboro TN 37130. LC E482. DD 369.17.

CONSENSUS. V. 1- Winter 1972-. 0090-0842. Periodical. US. English. wk. $365.00. Consensus, 30 West Pershing Road, Kansas City MO 64108. **Tel** (816)471-3862. **Ind/Abst** Relig. Index One, Period. LC HS2501. DD 367.05.

CORPUS ALMANAC & CANADIAN SOURCEBOOK. See Yearbooks, Almanacs, Directories.

COURRIER SPCA CEASED. **Main/Corp** Canadian Society for the Prevention of Cruelty to Animals. VFOAT SPCA Courier. V. 1-11, No. 2. 0382-4497. Periodical. CN. English (French). qt. 5215 Jean Talon Street West, Montreal Quebec H4P 1X4 Canada. Animal News, 0382-442X.

CROSS CULTURE : KORYO JOSHI TANKI DAIGAKU KENKYU KIYO. VFOAT Koryo Joshi Tanki Daigaku Kenkyu Kiyo. 1 (1983)-. Periodical. English (Japanese). ir. Koryo Joshi Tanki Daigaku Mitsugamine, Nisshin-cho Aichi-gun, Aichi-ken 470-01 Japan. LC AS552.N5274.

THE CSA JOURNAL CEASED. (CSA JOURNAL). **Main/Corp** Czechoslovak Society of America. VAT Czechoslovak Society of America Journal. 0195-9050. Periodical. US. Czech (English). ir. $7.20. CSA Journal, CSA Plaza, 2701 South Harlem Avenue, Berwyn IL 60402. LC E184.B67. *Official Journal.*

DELTA EPSILON SIGMA JOURNAL. VFOAT Journal. Vol. 27, No. 2 (May 1982)-. 0745-0958. Periodical. US. English. qt. Delta Sigma Epsilon Journal, Union-Hoermann Press, 2175 Kerper Boulevard, PO Box 916, Dubuque IA 52001. **Ind/Abst** Cathol. Period. Lit. Index. *Delta Epsilon Sigma Bulletin, 0011-8028.*

DELTA PI EPSILON RAPID READER. No. 1-. 0160-3949. Monographic Series. US. English. ir. Delta Pi Epsilon, Gustavus Adolphus College, St Peter MN 56082. **Tel** (507)931-4184.

DELTA PI EPSILON SERVICE BULLETIN. VFOAT Service Bulletin. No. 1-. 0160-3957. Monographic Series. US. English. ir. Delta Pi Epsilon National Office, Gustavus Adolphus College, St Peter MN 56082. LC UNC.

DIRECTORY OF CLUB OFFICERS - HARVARD ALUMNI ASSOCIATION. See Yearbooks, Almanacs, Directories.

THE DIVINE LIFE : MONTHLY JOURNAL OF THE DIVINE LIFE SOCIETY. Began in Sept. 1938. Periodical. II. English. mo. Divine Life Society Press, PO Sivanada Nagar, Rishikash Himalayas India.

DOC ITALIA. Began with 1978 Vol. Italian. ir. Editoriale Italiana, Via Viglienea 10, 00192 Roma Italy. LC AS218. DD 065. *DOC.*

DIE DRITTE WELT. Volume 1- 1972-. 0340-160X. Periodical. GW. English (German with French and Spanish summaries). ir. Verlag Anton Hain Meisenheim, Postfach 180, D-6554 Meisenheim West Germany. **Tel** (067)532488. **Ind/Abst** Sociol. Abstr., Soc. Welf. Soc. Plan./Policy Soc. Dev., Bibliogr. Agric., Lang. Lang. Behav. Abstr. LC AS181.

ECONOMETRIC SOCIETY PUBLICATION. No. 1-. Monographic Series. UK. English. Cambridge University Press, 32 East 57th Street, New York NY 10022.

THE ELGAR SOCIETY JOURNAL. V. 1- Jan. 1979-. Periodical. UK. English. 15.00. Elgar Society, 104 Crescent Road, New Barnet Herts EN4 9RJ England. **Tel** (01)440-2651. **Ed** Ronald Taylor. LC ML410.E41. DD 780.924, B. bk rev. **Circ** 1,200. (ctrl). Articles, news and reviews of books and records on the music and life of the composer Sir Edward Elgar and his times. *Newsletter - Elgar Society.*

THE ELIZABETHAN CLUB SERIES. Monographic Series. US. English. ir. Yale University Press, 92A Yale Station, New Haven CT 06520. **Tel** (203)436-7583.

THE ELKS MAGAZINE. V. 1- June 1922-. 0013-6263. Periodical. US. English. Elks Magazine, 425 West Diversey Parkway, Chicago IL 60614. LC HS1510.E4. DD 366.

EMPIRE STATE MASON. V. 1- Oct. 1952-. 0013-6794. Periodical. US. English. qt. Grand Lodge FTAM State of New York, 71 West 23rd Street, New York NY 10010. **Tel** (212)741-4500. bk rev. adv acc. **Circ** 150,000. (ctrl). The official publication of the Grand Lodge of Free and Accepted Masons of the state of New York. Edited for members of the Masonic fraternity and their families.

THE EVENSONGS. VFOAT Yeh Ko. Periodical. Chinese or English. ir. The Evensongs Association of English Department, Evening School/TamKang College No 5 Lane 199 Kinghua Street, Taipei China. LC AS455.A1. DD 052.

EXCHANGITE. (THE EXCHANGITE). V. 1- Dec. 1921-. 0014-4487. Periodical. US. English. ir. $4.00. National Exchange Club, 3050 Central Avenue, Toledo OH 43606. **Tel** (419)535-3232. **Ed** Philip A Flis. **Circ** 44,000. (ctrl). News and features relative to the functioning and fund raising, motivation, and service programs of exchange clubs and the education of its members.

FERNALD CLUB YEARBOOK. See Yearbooks, Almanacs, Directories.

FIELDS WITHIN FIELDS WITHIN FIELDS. VFOAT Fields within Fields. No. 1- Spring 1968-. 0015-0770. Periodical. US. English. qt. World Institute Council, 777 United Nations Plaza, New York NY 10017. LC AS4. Available on microfilm and microfiche from University Microfilms.

FORD FOUNDATION ANNUAL REPORT. 1951-. 0071-7274. US. English. an. Ford Foundation, 320 East 43rd Street, New York NY 10017. **Tel** (212)573-5000. LC AS911.F6. DD 061. NLM W1 FO558C. *Preliminary Report.*

FORUM (BONNER, MONT.). (FORUM). VFOAT Foundations & Facets Forum. 0883-4970. Periodical. US. English. qt. $30.00. Forum, c/o Robert W Funk, Riverbend Drive, SR 68, Bonner MT 59823. DD 232.

FORUM - CANADIAN COUNCIL ON 4-H CLUBS. (FORUM). VAT Forum - Canadian 4-H Foundation, Forum - Conseil Canadien des Cercles 4-H, Forum - Fondation des 4-H du Canada, Forum - National 4-H Office. 0715-5301. Periodical. CN. English (includes some text in French). qt. Canadian Council on 4-H Clubs, 323 Chapel Street, Ottawa Ontario K1N 7Z2 Canada. DD 630.6071.

FRATERNAL HERALD. VFOAT Bratrsky Vestnik. V. 60- Jan. 1957-. 0006-9256. Periodical. US. English (Czech). mo. $3.00. Fraternal Herald, 1900 1st Avenue NE, Cedar Rapids IA 52402. **Tel** (319)363-2653. **Ed** Diane S Nolan. bk rev. **Circ** 24,000. (ctrl). Official organ of Czech fraternal benefit society describing/reporting lodge activities, insurance products and Czech activities and history. *Bratrsky Vestnik.*

FRATERNITY NEWS - FRATERNITY FOR CANADIAN ASTROLOGERS. (THE FRATERNITY NEWS). Vol. 2, Issue No. 1 (Winter 1979)-. 0710-510X. Periodical. CN. English (includes some text in French). qt. Free. Fraternity for Canadian Astrologers, Box 4924/Station E, Ottawa Ontario K1S 5J1 Canada. DD 133.505. (ctrl). *Fraternity Newsletter.*

FUKUOKA UNESCO. JA. Japanese or English. ir. Fukuoka Yunesuko Kyokai, 13-51 Yakuin 4-chome Chuo-ku 810, Fukuoka Japan. LC AS4.U84.

LA GACETA DEL FONDO DE CULTURA ECONOMICA. Series/Conf Gaceta (Mexico City, Mexico : 1954). VFOAT Gaceta del Fondo de Cultura Economica. Began with Vol. 1, No. 1. 0531-9919. Periodical. MX. Spanish. mo. La Gaceta, Avenida de la Universidad 975, Mexico 12 DF Mexico. LC AS63.F6.

GAKUJUTSU KENKYU NEMPO. VFOAT Annual Reports of Studies. Began in 1950. 0418-0038. English (Japanese). an. 500. Doshisha Joshi Daigaku, 602 Gembucho, Imadegawadori Teramachi Nishi Iru, Kamigyo-ku 602, Kyoto-shi Japan. **Ind/Abst** MLA Int. Bibliogr. Books Artic. Mod. Lang. Lit., Chem. Abstr. LC AS552.D64. DD 050. CODEN DOJDAH.

THE GARNET AND WHITE. V. 1- 1900-. 0746-7079. Periodical. US. English. qt. Alpha Chi Rho, 109 Oxford Way, Neptune NJ 07753.

THE GATOR GREEK. V. 1- Nov. 11, 1960-. 143230091. Periodical. US. English. ir. University of Florida, Interfraternity Council, Gainesville FL 32601.

GIRL SCOUT LEADER. Dec. 1923-. 0017-0577. Periodical. US. English. qt. $4.00. Girl Scouts of the USA, 830 Third Avenue, New York NY 10022. **Tel** (212)940-7500. **Ed** Carolyn Caggine. bk rev. **Circ** 560,000. Designed to provide current information on activities and ideas of interest to adults in Girl Scouting. Includes program ideas, and trends which affects the interest of girls and women. *Field News.*

GIRL SCOUTS AROUND NEW YORK. 0747-508X. Periodical. US. English. bm. Girl Scout Council of Greater New York, 335 East 46th Street, New York NY 10017.

Societies and Clubs

GODISNJAK ZA . . . . Main/Corp Vojvoanska Akademija Nauka i Umetnosti. 1 (1980 / 1981)-. Serbo-Croatian -R. an. Vojvoanska Akademija Nauka i Umetnosti, Svetozara Markovica 6, Novi Sad Yugoslavia. LC AS346.N67.

THE GOLD STAR MOTHER. Periodical. US. English. bm. American Gold Star Mothers National Headquarters, 2128 Leroy Place, Washington DC 20008.

THE GRAINGER SOCIETY JOURNAL. Periodical. UK. English. Barry Peter Ould, 69 Felbrigge Road Seven Kings, Guilford Essex IG3 8DP United Kingdom. *Grainger Journal, 0141-5085.*

GRAND LODGE BULLETIN. Main/Corp Freemasons. Iowa. Grand Lodge. V. 1- Jan. 1898-. Periodical. US. English. mo. LC HS537.I8. *Occasional Bulletin.*

GREAT MASTERS OF THE PAST. Vol. 1 1955-. 0434-5797. US. English. ir. New York Graphic Society, 140 Greenwich Avenue, Greenwich CT 06830.

GROUP HQ DIRECTORY. See Yearbooks, Almanacs, Directories.

GROUPES ET SOCIETES D'AFRIQUE NOIRE. Yearly V. 20- (No. 440-). Periodical. French. sm. $179.60. Ediafric Documentation African, 57 Ave d'Iena, 75783 Paris Cedex 16 France. *Hommes et Organisations d'Afrique Noire.*

GUIDE TO PROFESSIONAL BODIES IN MALAWI. English. an. 20. Centraf Associates Ltd, PO Box 30462, Chichiri Blantyre 3 Malawi. LC AS621.A1. DD 068.6897.

HALIFAX AND DARTMOUTH CLUBS AND ORGANIZATIONS. 1982/83-. 0826-0095. CN. English. an. DD 061.1622. *Clubs and Organizations.*

THE HEATHER SOCIETY BULLETIN. Vol. 2, No. 16 (Spring 1979)-. Periodical. UK. English. ty. *Bulletin (Heather Society).*

HELICON. V. 1- Spring 1979-. 0196-6820. Periodical. US. English. $2.50 single issue. Connecticut College, New London CT 06320. Ed J A Newman. LC AS30. DD 051.

HIBARINO : TOYOHASHI GIJUTSU KAGAKU DAIGAKU JIMBUN KAGAKUKEI KIYO. VFOAT Lark Hill. No. 1- (1979)-. Periodical. JA. English (Japanese with some summaries in English and German). an. Toyohashi Gijutsu Kagaku Daigaku, 1-1 Hibarigaoka Tempakucho, Toyohashi-shi 440 Japan. LC AS552.T724. DD 080.

HIBOUCOU CEASED. (L'HIBOUCOU). V. 1-9, No. 4. 0316-666X. Periodical. CN. French. $1.00. Guides Catholiques du Canada Quartier General, 3827 rue St Hubert, Montreal Quebec H2L 4A4 Canada. DD 369.46305.

HO-NAN SHIH TA HSUEH PAO. SHE HUI KO HSUEH PAN. VFOAT Enanshidaxuebao. Periodical. CH. Chinese. bm. 0.40. Chung-Kuo Kuo Chi Shu Tien, PO Box 399, Pei-Ching China. LC AS452.K34. DD 059.951.

HO-PEI HSUEH KAN. VFOAT hebei Xuekan. Periodical. CH. Chinese. qt. 0.60. Post Office, China. LC AS451. DD 089.951.

HOLLY SOCIETY JOURNAL. Vol. 1, No. 1 (Spring 1983)-. 0738-2421. Periodical. US. English. qt. Free to Members. Holly Society of America, c/o Mrs C F Richardson/Secretary, 304 North Wind Road, Baltimore MD 21204. *Holly Letter, 0046-774X.*

HOMMES ET ORGANISATIONS D'AFRIQUE NOIRE. V. 1-20 (No. 1-439). 0018-4373. Periodical. FR. French. ir. Ediafric Documentation African, Avenue D Iena, 75783 Paris Cedix 16 France.

HSI PEI SHIH YUAN HSUEH PAO. VFOAT Xibei Shiyuan Xuebao. Periodical. CH. Chinese. qt. $3.24. China Publication Centre, PO Box 2820, Beinjing China. LC AS451. DD 059.951.

HSU-CHOU SHIH FAN HSUEH YUAN HSUEH PAO. CHE HSUEH SHE HUI KO HSUEH PAN. VFOAT Xuzhou Shifan Xueyuan Xuebao. Periodical. CH. qt 0.40. Post Office, Hsu-chou Shih China. LC AS452.H87. DD 059.951.

HSUEH HSI YU SSU KAO. VFOAT Xuexi Yu Sikao, Study and Reflection. Began publication in Jan. 1980. Periodical. CH. Chinese. bm. $5.67. China Publication Centre, PO Box 2820, Beijing China. LC AS452.P443. DD 059.951.

HSUEH LIN MAN LU. Periodical. CH. Chinese. ir. 0.63. Hsin Hua Shu Tien, Pei-ching Fa Hsing So, Peking China. LC AS451. DD 089.951.

HUMANIDADES (BRASILIA, BRAZIL). (HUMANIDADES). Vol. 1, No. 1 (Oct./Dec. 1982 1982)-. Periodical. Portuguese. qt. Editora Universidade de Brasilia, CX Postal 153001 Campus Universitario, 7910 Brasilia DF Brazil. LC AS80.A1. DD 056.9.

IBARAKI DAIGAKU IZURA BIJUTSU BUNKA KENKYUJO HO. JA. Japanese. ir. Ibaraki Daigaku Izura Bijutsu Bunka Kenkyujo, Ho 2-1-1 Bunkyo, Mito Japan. LC AS552.I215.

IDEAS CONCRETAS. VFOAT IC. June/July 1972-. Periodical. Spanish. ir. Avenida Libertador-Esquina las Acacias-Edificio las Vegas, 58 Piso-ofinina 5-B, Caracas Venezuela. LC AS90.A1.

THE INDIANA FREEMASON. 1923. 0019-6622. Periodical. US. English. mo. $8.00. Indiana Freemason, Box 38, Franklin IN 46131-0038. Tel (317)736-5741. Ed Dwight L Smith. adv acc. Circ 9,000. (ctrl) Fraternal history and lodge news.

INFORMACNI PRIRUCKA - CESKOSLOVENSKA AKADEMIE VED. (CESKOSLOVENSKA AKADEMIE VED). VFOAT Slovenska Akademie Ved. 1972-. 0231-5386. Czech (Slovak). ir. LC AS142. NLM AS 142.C4 C421.

INTER-ACAO. V. 1- Nov. 1975-. Portuguese. ir. Faculdade de Educacao da Universidade Federal de Goias, Praca Universitaria S/N, 70 000 Golaria Brazil. LC AS80.A1.

INTERFACE. V. 1- Summer/Fall 1973-. 0094-5838. US. English. University System of Georgia/Board of Regents, 244 Washington Street SW, Atlanta GA 30334. LC AS36.U6. DD 051.

JAHRBUCH DER AKADEMIE DER WISSENSCHAFTEN DER DDR. See Yearbooks, Almanacs, Directories.

JALONS. V. 1- Dec. 15, 1973-. 0383-672X. Periodical. CN. French. ir. Federation des Eclaireurs du Quebec, Secretariat National, 217 de l'Etoile, Laval Quebec H7N 4T4 Canada. DD 369.4309714.

JCI WORLD. Main/Corp Jaycees International. VAT Jaycees International World. 0021-3578. Periodical. US. English. ir. $2.00. Junior Chamber International, 400 University Drive, Coral Gables FL 33134. Tel 446-7608. *Future and JCI World.*

JINBUN RONSHU (WASEDA DAIGAKU. HOGAKKAI). (JINBUN RONSHU). Began in 1963. 0441-4225. French (Japanese). ir. Waseda Daigaku Hogakubu, c/o Waseda Daigaku, Shinjuku-ku Tokyo-to Japan. LC AS552.W37.

JOHN & MARY'S JOURNAL. VAT John and Mary's Journal. No. 2- Spring 1976-. 0364-6572. US. English. $5.00. Dickinson College Friends of the Library, Mary C Slotten Secretary, Carlisle PA 17013. LC AS36.D53. DD 051.

JOURNAL OF THE ACOUSTICAL SOCIETY OF JAPAN. E. (THE JOURNAL OF THE ACOUSTICAL SOCIETY OF JAPAN (E)). Vol. 1, No. 1 (Jan. 1980)-. 0388-2861. Periodical. JA. English. qt. Maruzen Company Ltd, PO Box 5050/Tokyo International, Tokyo 100-31 Japan. Tel 03/278 9224. Ind/Abst Excerpta Med., Comput. Control Abstr., Electr. Electron. Abstr., Sci. Abstr. Sect. A. Phys. Abstr. NLM W1 JO907E. CODEN JASED2.

JOURNAL OF THE AMERICAN BAMBOO SOCIETY. Main/Corp American Bamboo Society. V. 1- Feb. 1980-. 0197-3789. Periodical. US. English. qt. $20.00. American Bamboo Society, 1101 San Leon Court, Solana Beach CA 92075.

JOURNAL OF THE ASIATIC SOCIETY OF BANGLADESH. Main/Corp Asiatic Society of Bangladesh. V. 16- Dec. 1971-. 0377-0540. BG. English. ty. $10.00. Asiatic Society of Bangladesh, Dacca Museum Building, Dacca Bangladesh. Ind/Abst Am. Hist. Life, Hist. Abstr., Part A, Mod. Hist. Abstr., Hist. Abstr., Part B, Twent. Century Abstr. AS599.A8. DD 052. *Journal of the Asiatic Society of Pakistan.*

JOURNAL OF THE ASIATIC SOCIETY OF BOMBAY. Main/Corp Asiatic Society of Bombay. V. 1-26, July 1841-1923. 0004-9709. II. English. ir. Hindustan Book Agency, 17 UB Jawahar Nagar, Delhi 7 India. Ind/Abst MLA Int. Bibliogr. Books Artic. Mod. Lang. Lit. LC AS472.

JOURNAL OF THE CHINA SOCIETY. Main/Corp Chung-Kuo Hsuen Hui, T'ai-Pei. V. 1- 1961-. 0578-154X. Periodical. CH. English. ir. PO Box 1321, Taipei Taiwan Republic China.

JOURNAL OF THE HONG KONG BRANCH OF THE ROYAL ASIATIC SOCIETY. V. 1- 1960-61-. 0085-5774. HK. English. an. $3.39. Royal Asiatic Society, Hong Kong Branch, PO Box 3864, Hong Kong. Ind/Abst Am. Hist. Life, Hist. Abstr., Part A, Mod. Hist. Abstr., Hist. Abstr., Part B, Twent. Century Abstr., Hist. Abstr.

THE JOURNAL OF THE OPERATIONAL RESEARCH SOCIETY. (OR; THE JOURNAL OF THE OPERATIONAL RESEARCH SOCIETY). V. 29- Jan. 1978-. 0160-5682. Periodical. US. English. mo. Pergamon Press, Attn Cashier, 395 Sawmill River Road, Elmsford NY 10523. *Operational Research Quarterly.*

JOURNAL - ROYAL BRITISH LEGION. (JOURNAL). Main/Corp Royal British Legion. 0308-4949. Periodical. UK. English. mo. 5 Per Copy. National Executive Council Royal British Legion, Pall Mall, London SW1Y 5JY England. LC D546.A11. DD 369.242. *British Legion Journal.*

KAGAKU/NINGEN. JA. Japanese. ir. Kanto Gakuin Daigaky Kegakubu Kyoyo Gakkai, 4834 Rokuuramachi, Kanazawa-ku, Yokohama-shi Japan. LC AS552.K33.

KANAZAWA DAIGAKU BUNGAKUBU RONSHU. KODO KAGAKUKA HEN. VFOAT Studies and Essays. 1980-. Periodical. JA. Japanese. ir. Kanazawa Daigaku Bungakubu, 1-1 Marunouchi, Kanazawa-shi 920 Japan. LC AS552.K26.

KANSAS JOURNAL. VFOAT Kansas 4-H Journal. Vol. 1, No. 1 (Feb 1955)-. Periodical. US. English. mo.

THE KAPPA ALPHA JOURNAL. Periodical. US. English. bm. LC LJ75.

KAPPA DELTA PI RECORD. V. 1- Oct. 1964-. 0022-8958. Periodical. US. English. qt. $5.00. Kappa Delta Pi, Box A, West Lafayette IN 47906. Tel (317)743-1705. Ed Gerald Ponder. Ind/Abst Except. Child Educ. Resour., Curr. Index J. Educ. LC LJ75. bk rev. Circ 46,000. A journal of educational thought directed to the practitioner. *Educational Forum.*

KEGON. Periodical. JA. Japanese. ir. 6000. Kokon Hyoronsa, 22-2 Hommachi 6, Shibuya-ku, Tokyo Japan. LC AS551.

KENKYU KIYO - RISSHO JOSHI DAIGAKU TANKI DAIGAKUBU. Main/Corp Rissho Joshi Daigaku. Tanki Daigakubu. VFOAT Annual Reports of Studies. Multilingual (English and Japanese). ir. Rissho Joshi Daigaku Tanki Daigakubu, 2-17 Hatanodai 3 Shinagawa-ku (141), Tokyo Japan. LC AS552.R57.

KENKYU NENPO. DAI 2-GO, JINBUN SHIZEN KAGAKU KEI. VFOAT Annals of Takushoku University. 1981-. Periodical. JA. Japanese. an. Takushoku Daigau Kenkyujo 4-14, Kohinata 3 Bunkyo-ku, Tokyo-to Japan. LC AS552.T7155.

THE KENTUCKY CLUBWOMAN. (THE KENTUCKY CLUBWOMAN : OFFICIAL PUBLICATION OF G.F.W.C./KENTUCKY FEDERATION OF WOMEN'S CLUBS). VFOAT Kentucky Club Woman. 0740-6185. Periodical. US. English. qt. Kentucky Federation Woman's Clubs, 1228 Cherokee Road, Louisville KY 40204. Tel (502)451-8435. adv acc. Circ 8,000. News and feature articles pertaining to club work.

KIKAN AKADEMI. VFOAT Akademi, Quarterly Academy. Jan. 1976 Edition-. JA. Japanese. ir. 2000. Sekai Heiwa Kyoju Akademi, Bunka Sogoo Shuppan 3-10 Hongo 2-chome Bunkyo-ku (113), Tokyo Japan. LC AS551.

KISARAZU KOGYO KOTO SEMMON GAKKO KIYO. VFOAT Bulletin of Kisarazu Technical College. Japanese (summaries in English). ir. Kisarazu Kogyo Koto Semmon Gakko, 834 Gion 292, Kisarazu Japan. Ind/Abst Chem. Abstr. LC AS552.K42. CODEN KKSKDX.

KIYO - CHUO DAIGAKU BUNGAKUBU. Main/Corp Chuo Daigaku, Tokyo Bungakubu. VFOAT Journal of the Faculty of Literature. Began with Dec. 1954 issue. Japanese. ir.

Societies and Clubs

Chuo Daigaku Bugakubu, 9on Kanda Surugadai 3 Chiyoda-ku, Tokyo Japan. **LC** AS552.C5.

KIYO - HIROSAKI DAIGAKU IRYO GIJUTSU TANKI DAIGAKUBU. Main/Corp Hirosaki Daigaku. Iryo Gijutsu Tanki Daigakubu. **VFOAT** Hirosaki Daigaku Iryo Gijutsu Tanki Daigakubu Kiyo. No. 1-. JA. Japanese. ir. Hirosaki Daigaku Iryo Gijutsu Tanki Daigakubu, 201-9 Shinderacho, Hirosaki 036 Japan. **LC** AS552.H53.

KOGAKKAN DAIGAKU KIYO. **VFOAT** Bulletin of Kogakkan University. Began with 1963 issue. Japanese. ir. Kogakkan Daigaku, Kuratayama 516, Ise Japan. **LC** AS552.K53.

KOKUSAI JIJO. No. 1- 1970-. JA. Japanese. ir. Nagasaki Gaikokugo Tanki Diagaku Kobusai Jijo Kenjujo, 243 Izumimachi, Nagasaki Japan. **LC** AS551.

KOMSOMOLSKAIA ZHIZN. 0452-4071. Periodical. UR. Russian. sm. $17.00. Victor Kamkin Inc (70442), 12224 Parklawn Drive, Rockville MD 20852. **Tel** (301)881-5973.

KUEI SUAN YEN HSUEH PAO. **VFOAT** Guisuanyan Xuebao, Journal of the Chinese Silicate Society. Began in 1962. 0454-5648. Periodical. CH. Chinese. qt. $13.86. China Publication Centre, PO Box 2820, Beijing China. **Ind/Abst** Chem. Abstr., Art Archaeol. Tech. Abstr. **CODEN** KSYHA5.

KUEI-YANG SHIH YUAN HSUEH PAO. SHE HUI KO HSUEH PAN. **VFOAT** Guiyang Shiyuan Xuebao. Periodical. CH. Chinese. qt. 1.20. Post Office Kuei-Yang, Kuei-Yang China. **LC** AS452.K78.

KUKCHE HAKSUL KANGYONHOE NONMUNJIP. Periodical. KO. Korean. ir. Haksurwon, 1 Sejongno Chongno-Ku, Seoul South Korea. **LC** AS559.A1.

KULTURA ES KOZOSSEG. 0133-2597. Periodical. HU. Hungarian (contents page also in English and Russian). bm. Akademiai Kiado, POB 24, 1363 Budapest Hungary. **LC** AS205.A1.

KYOYUK NONCHONG (TONGGUK TAEHAKKYO. KYOYUK TAEHAGWON). (KYOYUK NONCHONG). V. 1-. Periodical. KO. Korean. ir. Tongguk Taehakkyo Kyoyuk Taehagwon, 26 3-ka Pil-dong, Chung-ku, Seoul South Korea. **LC** AS559.S62.

LA MAISON DE MARIE-CLAIRE. (LA MAISON DE MARIE CLAIRE). Began in 1967. 0542-1594. Periodical. FR. French. mo. $27.54. Societe Marie Claire, 1 Avenue Descartes, 92358 Plessis Robinson France.

LAN-CHOU HSUEH KAN. **VFOAT** Lan Zhou Xue Kan. Periodical. CC. Chinese. qt. 0.30. Post Office, Lan-chou Shih China. **Tel** 26492. **LC** AS451. **DD** 089.951. adv acc. **Circ** 3,500.

LATVIJAS PSR ZINATNU AKADEMIJAS VESTIS. **VFOAT** Izvestiia Akademii Nauk Latviiskoi SSR. Began in 1947. 0023-8929. Periodical. US. Latvian (Lettish and Russian). mo. $56.50. Victor Kamkin Inc, 12224 Parklawn Drive, Rockville MD 20852. **Tel** (301)881-5973. **Ind/Abst** Math. Rev., MLA Int. Bibliogr. Books Artic. Mod. Lang. Lit., Biol. Abstr., Comput. Control Abstr., Electr. Electron. Abstr., Sci. Abstr. Sect. A. Phys. Abstr., Chem. Abstr., Appl. Mech. Rev. **LC** AS262. **CODEN** LZAVAL.

LIMOI. Mar. 1975-. 0704-0318. Periodical. CN. French. ir. Guides Catholiques du Canada, Diocese d'Ottawa, 353 rue Friel, Ottawa Ontario K1N 7W7 Canada. **DD** 369.463097138.

LINNEAN SOCIETY SYMPOSIUM SERIES. No. 1-. 0161-6366. Monographic Series. UK. English. Academic Press, 4805 Sand Lake Road, Orlando FL 32819. **Ind/Abst** GeoRef, Chem. Abstr. **CODEN** LSSSDM.

THE LION. Began publication in 1918. 0024-4163. Periodical. US. English. mo. $3.00. Lions International, York and Cermak Roads, Oak Brook IL 60521. **Tel** (312)986-1700. **Ed** Robert Kleinfelder. **LC** HS2705.L5. adv acc. **Circ** 640,000. (ctrl). The official publication of lions clubs international. Our content deals primarily with activities of lions clubs and articles of interest to service-oriented individuals.

LIST OF CULTURAL ORGANISATIONS IN QUEENSLAND AND MAJOR NATIONAL AND STATE ORGANISATIONS OUTSIDE QUEENSLAND. English. an. Office of the Director of Cultural Activities for Queensland, PO Box 155, North Quay Queensland 4000 Australia.

LOGOS. Yearly V. 1- (No. 1-). Portuguese. ir. Faculdade de Filosofia, Ciencias e Letras de Divinopolis, Av 21 de Abril 645 35 500, Divinopolis Brazil. **LC** AS80.F32. *Dialogo.*

THE LUTE : THE JOURNAL OF THE LUTE SOCIETY. Vol. 22-. Periodical. UK. English. an. Francesca McManus, 71 Priory Road/Kew Gardens, Richmond Surrey England. *Journal, Newsletter.*

THE MCCONNAUGHEY BULLETIN (MCCONNAUGHEY AND VARIANTS). Main/Corp McConnaughey Society of America. **VFOAT** Annual Bulletin - McConnaughey Society of America. No. 1- 1963-. 0196-2078. US. English. an. $12.00. The McConnaughey Society of America, PO Box 27051, Indianapolis IN 46227.

THE MACE. (THE MACE : OFFICIAL JOURNAL OF THE SNODGRASS CLAN SOCIETY). 0740-5057. Periodical. US. English. qt. The Snodgrass Clan Inc, 2444 Lafayette Road, Indianapolis IN 46222.

MACHIKANEYAMA RONSO: SHINRIGAKU, SHAKAIGAKU, KYOIKUGAKU HEN. **VFOAT** Machikaneyama Ronso. No. 6-. JA. some articles in English. ir. Osaka Daigaku Bungakubu, 1-1 Machikaneyamacho, Toyonaka Osaka Japan. **LC** AS551. *Machikaneyama Ronso: Kyoikugakuhen.*

MAGNOLIA. V. 16, No. 1- Spring/Summer 1980-. 0738-3053. Periodical. US. English. sa. $12.00. American Magnolia Society, PO Box 129, Manuet NY 10954. *Newsletter of the American Magnolia Society, 0730-5737.*

MAITRISE. 0383-8595. Periodical. CN. French. bm. Association des Eclaireurs, Baden Powell Inc, Secretariat National, 217 l'Etoile, Laval Quebec H7N 4T4 Canada. **DD** 369.4309714. *Jalons, 0383-672X.*

MAJALLAT KULLIYAT AL-ADAB WA-AL-ULUM AL-INSANIYAH BI-AL-RABAT. Main/Corp Jamiat Muhammad V. Kulliyat Al-Adab. No. 1-. Periodical. Arabic. ir. 3 rue Ibn Battouta, Al-Rabat Morocco. **LC** AS697.

MAKING WAVES. (MAKING WAVES : SURFRIDER FOUNDATION NEWSLETTER). **VFOAT** Surfrider Foundation Newsletter. Spring 1985-. 0883-5616. Periodical. US. English. $25.00 Membership. Surfrider Foundation, PO Box 60582, Pasadena CA 91106.

MANAR (JIDDAH, SAUDI ARABIA). (AL-MANAR). Periodical. Arabic. mo. Jamiat Al-Malik ABD Al-Aziz S B 1540, Jiddah Majallat, Al-Manar Al-Lajnah Al-thaqafiyah Al-Ammah. **LC** AS587.J524.

MANUAL - UNITED NATIONS EDUCATIONAL, SCIENTIFIC AND CULTURAL ORGANIZATION. GENERAL CONFERENCE. Main/Corp United Nations Educational, Scientific and Cultural Organization. General Conference. Series Corp UNESCO. UNESCO Publication, No. 689. 1950-. English. ir. UNIPUB, 345 Park Avenue South, New York NY 10010. **LC** AS4.U82. **DD** 060.

MATERIALS EVALUATION. 0025-5327. Periodical. US. English. mo. $50.00. American Society Nondestruct Testing, 4153 Arlingate Plaza Caller #28518, Columbus OH 43228. **Tel** (614)274-6003. **Ind/Abst** Appl. Sci. Technol. Index, Appl. Mech. Rev., Eng. Index, Int. Aerosp. Abstr., Pet. Abstr., Sci. Cit. Index, Abr. Ed., Electr. Electron. Abstr., Phys. Abstr., Comput. Control Abstr.

MATERIALS RESEARCH SOCIETY SYMPOSIA PROCEEDINGS. **VFOAT** Symposia Proceedings. Vol. 1-. 0272-9172. US. English. ir. Elsevier North Holland Inc, 52 Vanderbilt Avenue, New York NY 10017. **Ind/Abst** Eng. Index Annu., Eng. Index Mon., Eng. Index Bioeng. Abstr., Eng. Index Energy Abstr., Comput. Control Abstr., Electr. Electron. Abstr., Sci. Abstr. Sect. A. Phys. Abstr., Chem. Abstr. **DD** 620. **CODEN** MRSPDH.

MAZAMA. Began publication May 1, 1896. 0275-6226. Periodical. US. English. mo. $3.50. Mazamas Club, 909 NW 19th Avenue, Portland OR 97209. **Ind/Abst** GeoRef.

MEETINGS CANADA. Apr. 1980-. 0226-7500. Periodical. CN. English. ir. $22.50 Domestic, $30.00 US, $45.00 Other Countries. Sovereign Publications, 67 Yonge Street, Toronto Ontario M6B 1J8 Canada. **DD** 061.105.

MEMBERSHIP LIST - AMERICAN MENSA LIMITED. Main/Corp American Mensa Limited. 0363-3616. US. English. an. 1701 West 3rd Street, Brooklyn NY 11223. **LC** BF431. **DD** 367.973.

MEMOIRES DE L'ACADEMIE ROYALE DES SCIENCES, DES LETTRES ET DES BEAUX-ARTS DE BELGIQUE. Began with: V. 20. BE. French. ir. Office Intl de Librairie, 30 Ave Marnix, Brussels 5 Belgium. **LC** AS242. **DD** 068.493. *Nouveaux Memoires de l'Academie Royale des Sciences, et Belles-Lettres de Belgique.*

MEMORIAS DA ACADEMIA DAS CIENCIAS DE LISBOA. CLASSE DE LETRAS. Main/Corp Academia das Ciencias de Lisboa. Classe de Letras. V. 1-. 0378-116X. PO. Portuguese. ir. Academia das Ciencias de Lisboa, R Academia das Ciencia 19 1200, Lisboa Portugal. **Ind/Abst** MLA Int. Bibliogr. Books Artic. Mod. Lang. Lit. **LC** AS304. **DD** 066.9. *Historia E Memorias. Nova Serie.*

MENSA BULLETIN. 105- Nov. 1967-. 0025-9543. Periodical. US. English. ir. $12.00. American Mensa Committee, 1701 West Third Street, Brooklyn NY 11223. **Tel** (212)376-1925. **Ed** Katherine M Dewitt Jr. **LC** AS36.A4868. **DD** 051. bk rev. adv acc. **Circ** 50,000. (ctrl). Basically a house organ for the members of Mensa, the high I.Q. society. Articles on intelligence, education of the gifted, humor, puzzles and letters. *Intelligence.*

MENSA CANADA COMMUNICATIONS (1978). (MENSA CANADA COMMUNICATIONS). **VFOAT** MCP2S i.e. Squared. **VAT** MCP2S (1978). Vol. 11, No. 6 (July/Aug. 1978)-. 0229-5342. Periodical. CN. English (includes some text in French). Free to Members. Mensa Canada Communications, 361 Yonge Street, Toronto Ontario M5B 1S1 Canada. **DD** 367.971. *MCP2S i.e. Squared, 0380-5344.*

MERIWETHER CONNECTIONS. Began with V. 1, No. 1 (Jan. 1982). Periodical. US. English. qt. Meriwether Society, 6536 Green Gables Avenue, San Diego CA 92119.

MINERVA : INTERNATIONALES VERZEICHNIS WISSENSCHAFTLICHER INSTITUTIONEN. WISSENSCHAFTLICHE GESELLSCHAFTEN. 33- Edition (Yearly Volume). German. ir. Walter de Gruyter, 220 Sawmill River Road, Hawthorne NY 10532. **LC** AS2. **DD** 060.25. *Minerva.*

MISSISSIPPI LEGION'AIRE. **VFOAT** Mississippi Legionaire. 0026-6299. Periodical. US. English. mo. Mississippi Legionaire, PO Box 688, Jackson MS 39205.

MONOGRAPH. Main/Corp George Eastman House. Vol. 1 1960-. 0435-4419. US. English. ir. George Eastman House, 900 East Avenue, Rochester NY 14607. **Tel** (716)271-3361. **Ed** Barbara Hall. (ctrl). Covers exhibit information fundraising, special programs-films, receptions, trips; annual report-finance, and goals.

MS DIRECTORY. *See* Yearbooks, Almanacs, Directories.

NAN-CHING SHIH YUAN HSUEH PAO. CHE HSUEH SHE HUI KO HSUEH PAN. Periodical. CH. Chinese. qt. 0.35. Post Office, Nan-Ching China. **LC** AS452.N385. **DD** 089.951.

NATIONAL 4-H NEWS CEASED. **VAT** National Four-H News. V. 25, No. 4- Apr. 1947-. 0027-9285. Periodical. US. English. $3.00. National 4-H Council, 7100 Connecticut Avenue, Chevy Chase MD 20815. **Tel** (301)656-9000. **DD** 369. *National 4-H Club News.*

THE NATIONAL GLEANER FORUM. Periodical. US. English. mo.

NATIONAL NEWS - AMERICAN LEGION AUXILIARY. Main/Corp American Legion. Auxiliary. Periodical. US. English. bm. $3.00. American Legion Auxillary, 777 North Meridian Street, Indianapolis IN 46204. **Tel** (317)635-6291.

NEUVE EGLISE. V. 1- Mar. 1979-. 0228-2585. Periodical. CN. French. ir. Association des Scouts du Canada, 3055 Av Lacombe, Montreal Quebec H3T 1L5 Canada. **DD** 248.83205.

THE NEW AGE. **VFOAT** New Age Magazine. Periodical. US. English. mo. $4.00. New Age Magazine, 1733 16th Street NW, Washington DC 20009. **Tel** (202)232-3579. **Ed** Aemil Pouler. **Circ** 650,000. (ctrl). Articles relating to Masonry, patriotism, public education, Masonic charities and human interests.

THE NEW JERSEY CLUB WOMAN AND EVEN'TIDE. 0028-5587. Periodical. US. English. qt. $3.00. New Jersey Federal Womens Club, 55 Clifton Avenue, New Brunswick NJ 08901.

Societies and Clubs

NEW YORK SHELL CLUB NOTES. 0545-6347. Periodical. US. English. mo. LC QL401. DD 594.047105. *NYSC Notes.*

NEWS FROM THE CANADA-JAPAN SOCIETY OF VANCOUVER. (NEWS FROM CANADA-JAPAN SOCIETY OF VANCOUVER). Main/Corp Canada-Japan Society of Vancouver. Began publication in 1971?. 0382-8417. CN. English. ir. Canada-Japan Society of Vancouver, 207 West Hastings Street, Vancouver Victoria V6B 1H7 Canada. DD 301.2971052.

THE NEWS - GARDEN CLUB FEDERATION OF PENNSYLVANIA. Main/Corp Garden Club Federation of Pennsylvania. 0195-0991. Periodical. US. English. bm. $2.00. Garden Club Federation of Pennsylvania, 540 Carter Avenue, Indiana PA 15701.

NEWS-LETTER - NATIONAL SOCIETY OF UNITED STATES DAUGHTERS OF 1812. Main/Corp National Society of United States Daughters of 1812. VAT News-Letter - National Society of United States Daughters of Eighteen Hundred Twelve. 0271-7522. Periodical. US. English. ty. National Society of United States, Daughters of 1812, 1612 California Street, Omaha NE 68102. LC E351.6.

NEWS LETTER OF THE ST. ANDREW'S SOCIETY OF TORONTO. Main/Corp St. Andrew's Society of Toronto. No. 2 (Oct. 1983)-. 0822-2401. Periodical. CN. English. qt. Free. St Andrew's Society of Toronto, 35 Austin Terrace, Toronto Ontario M5R 1Y2 Canada. DD 369.2713541. *St. Andrew's Society of Toronto Quarterly Newsletter, 0822-8337.*

NEWS - ONTARIO COUNCIL OF RABBIT CLUBS. Main/Corp Ontario Council of Rabbit Clubs. Jan. 1977-. 0703-783X. Periodical. CN. English. mo. Ontario Council of Rabbit Clubs, B Schmidt Secretary, Searchmont Ontario P0S 1J0 Canada. DD 636.932209713.

NEWSLETTER - BYRON SOCIETY. (NEWSLETTER - THE BYRON SOCIETY). Main/Corp Byron Society. American Committee. VFOAT Byron Society Newsletter. V. 1- 1973-. 0196-8998. US. English. an. Free to Members. The American Committee, The Byron Society, 205 West End Avenue #1-B, New York NY 10023.

NEWSLETTER - CANADIAN SOCIETY FOR COLOUR IN ART, INDUSTRY AND SCIENCE. Main/Corp Canadian Society for Colour. V. 1- Mar. 1973-. 0317-1825. CN. English. ir. Free to Members. Canadian Society for Colour, c/o Sherwin-Williams Company, PO Box 489, Montreal Quebec H3C 2T4 Canada. DD 535.606271.

NEWSLETTER - JOHN HOWARD SOCIETY OF ONTARIO. Main/Corp John Howard Society of Ontario. July 1957-. 0449-0827. Periodical. CN. English. sa. John Howard Society of Ontario, 168 Isabella Street, Toronto Ontario M4Y 1P6 Canada.

NEWSLETTER - JOHN MACMURRAY SOCIETY. (NEWSLETTER - THE JOHN MACMURRAY SOCIETY). Main/Corp John MacMurray Society. V. 1- Spring 1976-. 0705-1611. Periodical. CN. English. ir. Free. John MacMurray Society, 265 Scott Road, Toronto Ontario M6M 3V3 Canada. DD 192.

NEWSLETTER - LUTE SOCIETY OF AMERICA. (NEWSLETTER). 0882-0155. Periodical. US. English. qt. Lute Society of America, 1930 Cameron Court, Concord CA 94518. DD 787.

NGUYET SAN MINH DUC. So 1/2- Thang 6/7, 1972-. VM. Vietnamese. Truong Dai-Hoc Nhan-Van Va Nghe-Thuat, 245/5 Pham-Hong-Thai, Saigon Viet Nam. LC AS496.V53.

NIHON JOZO KYOKAI ZASSHI. VFOAT Journal of the Brewing Society of Japan. Began in 1906. 0369-416X. Periodical. JA. Japanese. mo. Kyowa Book Company Inc, 1-38 Kanda Jinbocho/Chiyoda-Ku, Tokyo 101 Japan. Tel 293-0727. Ind/Abst Chem. Abstr. CODEN NIJKA4. Index in last issue of volume - attached.

NIHON REOROJI GAKKAI SHI. VFOAT Journal of the Society of Rheology, Japan. No. 1-. 0387-1533. Periodical. Japanese (with summaries in English). qt. Nihon Reoroji Gakkai, 1-Banchi No 101 Yoshida Izumiden-Cho Sakyo-Ku, Kyoto-Shi 606 Japan. Ind/Abst Chem. Abstr. CODEN NRGADP.

NING-HSIA SHE HUI KO HSUEH. Periodical. CH. Chinese. qt. 0.40. Post Office, Yin-Chuan Shih, China. LC AS452.Y55. DD 089.951.

NN&Q. NEWS, NOTES, AND QUOTES. VFOAT News, Notes, and Quotes. 0028-923X. Periodical. US. English. qt. Phi Delta Kappa, 8th & Union Avenue, Box 789, Bloomington IN 47402. Tel (812)339-1156. Ed Derek L Burleson. Circ 126,000. (ctrl). Contains news of fraternity and information about programs of Phi Delta Kappa.

NUOVA STOA. Yearly V. 1- Jan./April 1974-. Periodical. Italian. ir. 7.000. Dielle S P A, C/C Postale N 3/8052, Milano Italy. LC AS222.P39.

NUUSBRIEF. Main/Corp Suid-Afrikaanse Akademie Vir Wetenskap en Kuns. Vol. 1-. Periodical. SA. Afrikaans. qt. 7.00. Suid Afrikakao Wetens Kuns, Box 53 8, Pretoria South Africa. Tel (012)285082. Ed D J C Geldenhuys. adv acc. Circ 2,000. General news regarding the activities of the SA Akademie vir Wetenskap en Kuns and its members.

OCCASIONAL PAPERS - DUGDALE SOCIETY. Main/Corp Dugdale Society. No. 1- 1924-. Monographic Series. UK. English. ir.

OCCASIONAL PAPERS OF THE AMERICAN SOCIETY FOR REFORMATION RESEARCH. Main/Corp American Society for Reformation Research. V. 1- 1977-. 0198-9979. US. English. ir. American Society Reformation Research, 6477 Bonita Avenue, St Louis MO 63105. Tel (314)727-6655. LC BR300. DD 270.6.

OFFICERS, COMMITTEES, CONSTITUTION AND BY-LAWS, MEMBERS. Main/Corp Grolier Club. US. English. an. Grolier Club, 47th East 60th Street, New York NY 10022. LC Z1008.G886. DD 070.5. *Officers, Committees, Members (1931), Officers, Committees, Members.*

OFFICERS, COMMITTEES, CONSTITUTION AND BY-LAWS, MEMBERS, REPORTS OF OFFICERS AND COMMITTEES. Main/Corp Grolier Club. 1884-. 0362-8019. US. English. an. LC Z1008.

THE OFFICIAL PRICE GUIDE TO SCOUTING COLLECTIBLES. VFOAT Scouting Collectibles. 1st Ed. (1983)-. 0747-5055. US. English. an. House of Collectibles Inc, Orlando Central Park, 1900 Premier Row, Orlando FL 32809. LC HS3313.A4. DD 343.409730075.

OFICIALA JARLIBRO DE LA ESPERANTO-MOVADO. See Yearbooks, Almanacs, Directories.

ONKO SOSHI. Fukkan No. 1-. Periodical. JA. Japanese. ir. Onko Gakkai, 9-1 Higashi 2 Shibuya-ku, Tokyo 150 Japan. LC AS552.T7152.

OPTIMIST HOTLINE. VFOAT Hotline. 0744-9755. Periodical. US. English (articles in French). mo. $2.00 Members, $3.00 Others. Optimist International, 4494 Lindell Boulevard, St Louis MO 63108.

THE OPTIMIST MAGAZINE. 0744-4672. Periodical. US. English (French). mo. Optimist International, 4494 Lindell Boulevard, St Louis MO 63108. *Optimist International.*

ORGANIZATION TRENDS. Vol. 1, No. 1 (July 1984)-. 0882-5769. Periodical. US. English. mo. Organization Trends, 1612 K Street Northwest/Suite 605, Washington DC 20006. DD 060.

OSAKA DAIGAKU NINGEN-KAGAKUBU KIYO. Main/Corp Osaka Daigaku. Ningen-Kagakubu. VFOAT Bulletin. V. 1-. Japanese or English. ir. 286-1 Ogawa Oaza Yamada (565), Suita Japan. LC AS552.O76.

OUTLOOK. (THE OUTLOOK). Dec. 1973-. 0700-4176. CN. English. Boy Scouts of Canada, 719 West 16th Avenue, Vancouver British Columbia V5Z 1S8 Canada.

PA. JAYCEES FUTURE. (PA. JAYCEES FUTURE : OFFICIAL PUBLICATION OF THE PENNSYLVANIA JAYCEES). VFOAT Pennsylvania Jaycees Future. 0744-8392. Periodical. US. English. qt. Pennsylvania Jaycees, 200 Richardson Drive, Lancaster PA 17603.

PALMETTO STAR NEWS. 0199-0861. Periodical. US. English. mo. $3.00. Grand Chapter of South Carolina Order of the Eastern Star, PO Box 228, Swansea SC 29160.

PANHELLENICALLY SPEAKING...THE RUSHEE'S HANDBOOK. Main/Corp Florida. University. Gainesville. Panhellenic Association. VFOAT A Key to the Greeks. English. ir.

PAPERS READ AT THE MEETING OF GRAND DRAGONS, KNIGHTS OF THE KU KLUX KLAN. Main/Corp Ku Klux Klan (1915-). Series/Titl Anti-Movements in America. 1st- 1923-. US. English. Arno Press, 330 Madison Avenue, New York NY 10017. LC HS2330.K6. DD 322.420973.

THE PENNSYLVANIA ANTI-MASONIC ALMANAC. See Yearbooks, Almanacs, Directories.

THE P.E.O. RECORD. (P. E. O. RECORD). Began with issue for Jan. 1889. 0746-5130. Periodical. US. English. mo. P E O Record, 3700 Grand Avenue, Des Moines IA 50712. LC HQ1903.P2. DD 371.856.

THE PEREGRINE FUND NEWSLETTER. VFOAT Newsletter. Began with: No. 1 in Aug. 1973. US. English. an. Peregrin Fund, 159 Sapsucker Woods, Ithaca NY 14850. Tel (607)256-4414.

PERSPECTIVE. V. 1- Feb. 1975-. 0745-3027. Periodical. US. English. ir. $10.00. Association of Professional Directors of YMCA'S, C 40 West Long Street, Columbus OH 43215.

THE PHI GAMMA DELTA. Periodical. US. English. qt. LC LJ75. *Phi Gamma Delta Quarterly.*

PHI KAPPA PHI NEWSLETTER. No. 15- Aug. 1973-. 0093-5328. Periodical. US. English. qt. *Journal.*

PIONYRSKA STAFETA. Vol. 1-. Periodical. CS. Czech. mo. Artia, PO Box 790, Praha 1 Czechoslovakia. LC HS3325.C9.

PLUS (ST-HYACINTHE, QUEBEC). (PLUS). 0710-1716. Periodical. CN. French. ir. DD 369.40607145.

POLICY ORGANIZATION AND RULES - GIRL GUIDES OF CANADA. (POLICY, ORGANIZATION AND RULES - GIRL GUIDES OF CANADA). Main/Corp Girl Guides of Canada. 0316-8158. Periodical. CN. English. an. Girl Guides of Canada, 50 Merton Street, Toronto Ontario M4S 1A3 Canada. DD 3694630971.

POLISH RESEARCH GUIDE. 0554-4955. PL. English. ir. ARS Polona, Krakowskie Przedmiescie 7, 00 068 Warsaw Poland. LC AS248.

PRASSI E TEORIA. Periodical. IT. Italian. qt. $29.70. Franco Angeli Editore Riviste, Via le Monza 106, 20127 Milano Italy. LC AS221.

PRESENTATION - SOCIETE ROYALE DU CANADA. Main/Corp Societe Royale du Canada. VFOAT Reception. No. 1- 1943/44-. 0317-0179. Periodical. CN. French. an. Societe Royale du Canada, 395 rue Wellington, Ottawa Ontario K1A 0N4 Canada. DD 061.1.

THE PRESIDENTS REPORT - COLONIAL WILLIAMSBURG FOUNDATION. Main/Corp Colonial Williamsburg Foundation. 1971-. 0270-3467. US. English. an. *Annual Report - Colonial Williamsburg Foundation, 0270-3475.*

PROCEEDINGS - AMERICAN SOCIETY FOR TESTING AND MATERIALS. Main/Corp American Society for Testing and Materials. V. 45- 1945-. 0066-0515. US. English. an. American Society for Testing and Materials, 1916 Race Street, Philadelphia PA 19103. Tel (215)299-5451. Ind/Abst Fluidex. CODEN ASTEAV. *Proceedings of the Annual Meeting - American Society for Testing Materials.*

PROCEEDINGS AND TRANSACTIONS OF THE ROYAL SOCIETY OF CANADA. Main/Conf Royal Society of Canada. VFOAT Deliberations et Memoires de la Societe Royale du Canada. Ser. 1, V. 1-23, 1882/83-1894. 0316-4616. Periodical. CN. English (French). an. 26.25. Royal Society of Canada, 395 Wellington Street, Ottawa Ontario K1A 0N4 Canada. Tel (613)992-3468. Ed John M Robson. Ind/Abst MLA Int. Bibliogr. Books Artic. Mod. Lang. Lit., Can. Period. Index, Bibliogr. Index Geol. LC AS42. DD 061.1. (cum index). Circ 1,500.

PROCEEDINGS OF THE LINNAEAN SOCIETY OF NEW YORK. Main/Corp Linnaean Society of New York. No. 45/46 (1933/34)-. 0075-9694. US. English. ir. American Museum of Natural History, Central Park West at 79th Street, New York NY 10024. *Abstract of the Proceedings of the Linnaean Society of New York.*

PROCEEDINGS OF THE ROYAL SOCIETY OF CANADA. Main/Corp Royal Society of Canada. VFOAT Deliberations de la Societe Royale du Canada. Ser. 1 V. 1-12, 1882/83-1894. CN. English (French). an. Royal Society of Canada, 344 Wellington, Ottawa Ontario K1A 0N4 Canada. (cum index).

Societies and Clubs

PROCEEDINGS OF THE VIRGIL SOCIETY. Main/Corp Virgil Society. No. 1- 1961/62-. 0083-629X. UK. English. an. University of Reading, Whiteknights Reading, Berkshire RG6 2AH England.

PROCES-VERBAL DU CONGRES GENERAL ANNUEL - SOCIETE SAINT-JEAN-BAPTISTE DE QUEBEC. Main/Corp Societe Saint-Jean-Baptiste de Quebec. First issue in 1936. 0384-7357. Periodical. CN. French. Free. Societe Saint-Jean-Baptiste de Quebec, 430 Chemin Sainte-Foy, Quebec Quebec G1S 2J5 Canada. DD 369.2714471. (ctrl).

PROGRAMME UND PROJEKTE. Main/Corp Deutsche Forschungsgemeinschaft. Series/Titl Jahresbericht der DFG. 1970-. GW. German. an. Kenndyalle 40, Postfach 2050004, 5300 Bonn 2, Goldesberg West Germany. LC AS182.D39. DD 053.1. Bericht, 0418-8411.

PROSVETA. Newspaper. US. Slovak. wk. $14.00. Slovene National Benefit Society, 166 Shore Drive, Burr Ridge IL 60521. Tel (312)887-7660. Ed Ted Pogacar. Circ 25,000. Fraternal and lodge information based on reports and members. Contains information and news of interest and educational reading.

PUBLICATIONS - BRISTOL RECORD SOCIETY. Main/Corp Bristol Record Society. V. 1- 1930-. 0305-8727. Monographic Series. UK. English. ir. $10.73. Bristol Record Office, c/o M E Williams/Council House, Bristol BS1 5TR England.

PUBLICATIONS IN OPERATIONS RESEARCH. Main/Corp Operations Research Society of America. US. English. ir. John Wiley & Sons Inc, 1 Wiley Drive, Somerset NJ 08873.

PUBLICATIONS OF THE CHAMPLAIN SOCIETY. ONTARIO SERIES. (THE PUBLICATIONS OF THE CHAMPLAIN SOCIETY : ONTARIO SERIES). Main/Corp Champlain Society. Vol. 1 1957-. 0078-5091. CN. English. ir. University of Toronto Press, Front Campus, Toronto Ontario M5S 1A6 Canada.

PUBLICATIONS OF THE GENERAL SOCIETY OF COLONIAL WARS. 0882-2336. Monographic Series. US. English. ir. Society of Colonial Wars, Office of the Secretary General, 840 Woodbine Avenue, Glendale OH 45246. DD 369.

PUBLICATIONS OF THE HARLEIAN SOCIETY. NEW SERIES. Main/Corp Harleian Society (London). Vol. 1- 1979-. Monographic Series. UK. English. an.

THE PUBLICATIONS OF THE PIPE ROLL SOCIETY. Monographic Series. UK. English. ir. Society Public Record Office, Chancery Lane, London WC2A 1LR England.

PUBLICATIONS OF THE THORESBY SOCIETY. Main/Corp Thoresby Society. V. 1-. 0082-4232. Monographic Series. UK. English. ir. LC DA670.Y59. DD 942.819. (cum index).

A QUARTERLY NEWS JOURNAL OF THE CROSBY ARBORETUM. 1.1 (Winter 83)-. 0741-9635. Periodical. US. English. qt. The Crosby Arboretum Foundation, 3702 Hardy Street, Hattiesburg MS 39401.

THE RAMON MAGSAYSAY AWARDS. 1958-1962-. PH. English. ir. Ramon Magsaysay Award Foundation, Ramon Magsaysay Center, 1680 Roxas Boulevard, Manila Philippines. LC AS911.R39. DD 001.44.

RAND. 0162-8704. US. English. an. Rand Corporation, 1700 Main Street, Santa Monica CA 90406. LC AS36.R344. DD 081.

REFLECTIONS. Vol. 1-. 0885-8144. Periodical. US. English. qt. Sigma Theta Tau, 610 Barnhill Drive, Indianapolis IN 46223. Ind/Abst Cumul. Index Nurs. Allied Health Lit. DD 610.

REGISTRE-ANNUAIRE - MENSA CANADA. See Yearbooks, Almanacs, Directories.

THE REPORTER. 0149-8754. Periodical. US. English. ir. Phi Alpha Delta, 10722 White Oak Avenue, Grenade Hills CA 91344. Tel (703)860-0213. LC UNC.

REPORTS OF OFFICERS AND PROCEEDINGS OF THE SUPREME LODGE OF THE ANCIENT ORDER OF UNITED WORKMEN. (REPORT OF OFFICERS AND PROCEEDINGS). Main/Corp Ancient Order of United Workmen. Supreme Lodge. 0090-8010. US. English. Ancient Order of United Workmen, PO Box 98830, Seattle WA 98188. LC HS1510.A58. DD 366.

REPORTS OF THE PRESIDENT AND THE TREASURER - JOHN SIMON GUGGENHEIM MEMORIAL FOUNDATION. Main/Corp John Simon Guggenheim Memorial Foundation. 1961/62-. 0190-227X. US. English. an. John Simon Guggenheim Memorial Foundation, 90 Park Avenue, New York NY 10016. LC AS911. DD 061.3. NLM AS 911 J6. Reports of the Secretary General and of the Treasurer.

REVISTA DE INFORMACION DE LA COMISION NACIONAL ESPANOLA DE COOPERACION CON LA UNESCO. Main/Corp Spain. Comision Nacional Espanola de Cooperacion Con la UNESCO. No. 2- April/June 1975-. Periodical. Spanish. ir. Seibunsha, Ciudad Universitaria, Tokyo Japan. LC AS4.U825. Revista de Informacion de la UNESCO.

REVISTA DE LA UNIVERSIDAD COMPLUTENSE. Main/Corp Universidad Complutense de Madrid. V. 21- (No. 83-). 0210-7872. SP. Spanish. ir. $9.81. Universidad de Madrid, Madrid Spain. Ind/Abst Am. Hist. Life, Hist. Abstr., Part A, Mod. Hist. Abstr., Hist. Abst., Part B, Twent. Century Abstr., GeoRef, Hist. Abstr. LC AS302. CODEN RUCMAZ. Revista.

REVISTA ROTARIA. Began in 1933. 0035-0443. Periodical. US. Spanish. mo. $8.00. Rotary International, 1600 Ridge Avenue, Evanston IL 60201. Tel (312)328-0100. Ed Alfonso Rubiano-Groot. adv acc. Circ 32,000. (ctrl). News about the rotary world, general interest articles, international understanding, vocational and human relationships, etc.

REVUE - LA COMMISSION NATIONALE DE LA REPUBLIQUE SOCIALISTE DE ROUMANIE. Main/Corp Romania. Comisia Nationala a Republicii Socialiste Romania Pentru UNESCO. VFOAT Journal - The National Commission of the Socialist Republic of Romania. English (French). ir. Journal - The National, 47 Chaussee Kisseleff, R-71268 Bucarest Romania. LC AS4.U825. DD 082. Bulletin de la Commission Nationale de la Republique Socialiste de Roumanie pour l'UNESCO.

RICARDIAN. (THE RICARDIAN : JOURNAL OF THE RICHARD III SOCIETY). 0048-8267. Periodical. UK. English. qt. Free to Members, 6.00 Non-Members. The Editor, 17 Enfield Cloisters, Fanshaw Street, London N1 6LD England. Ind/Abst Am. Hist. Life, Hist. Abstr., Part A, Mod. Hist. Abstr., Hist. Abst., Part B, Twent. Century Abstr.

ROCKEFELLER BROTHERS FUND ANNUAL REPORT. Main/Corp Rockefeller Brothers Fund. 1972-. 0485-2826. US. English. an. Rockefeller Brothers Fund Inc, 1290 Avenue of the Americas, New York NY 10104. LC AS911.R6. DD 061.471.

THE ROYAL NEIGHBOR. 0035-905X. Periodical. US. English. mo. The Royal Neighbor Magazine, 230 Sixteenth Street, Rock Island IL 61201. LC HS1510.R895.

SAHOE MUNHWA YONGU. VFOAT Journal of Sociocultural Studies. V. 1-Series. Periodical. Korean (summaries in English and German). ir. Hansa Taehak, Sahoe Munhwa Yonguso, 2288 Taemyong-Dong Nam-ku Taegu Korea. LC AS559.H37.

SAITAMA DAIGAKU KIYO. SOGO HEN. VFOAT Sogo Hen. V. 1-. Periodical. Japanese. ir. Saitama Daigaku, 255 Shimookubo, Urawa-shi Japan. LC AS552.U727.

SAMOUPRAVNE INTERESNE ZAJEDNICE. See Statistics.

SAN DIEGO SOURCE BOOK. VFOAT Source Book. 1st.- Ed. 0196-8564. US. English. an. $75.00. Bernardo Press, 16496 Bernardo Center Drive, Rancho Bernardo CA 92128. Tel (619)451-3790. Ed Jack Mayo. Circ 500. (ctrl). Directory of business, trade and professional groups, civic, social and fraternal clubs, special interest groups, hobbies and athletic clubs of San Diego county.

SANTIAGO. VFOAT Revista Santiago. Year 1, No. 1 (Dec. 1970)-. 0581-653X. Periodical. CU. Spanish. qt. $11.45. Empresa Ediciones Cubanas, Sub-Direccion Exportacion, Oreilly 407 Ciudad, Habana Cuba. Ind/Abst Am. Hist. Life, Hist. Abstr., Part A, Mod. Hist. Abstr., Hist. Abst., Part B, Twent. Century Abstr., Bibliogr. Index Geol., Hist. Abstr. LC AS71.A1. DD 056.1. Revista (Universidad de Oriente (Santiago de Cuba, Cuba)).

THE SAR MAGAZINE. Main/Corp Sons of the American Revolution. VAT The Sons of the American Revolution Magazine. Began in 1967. 0161-0511. Periodical. US. English. qt. $5.00. National Society of the Sons of the American Revolution, 1000 South Street, Louisville KY 40203. Tel (502)589-1776. Ed Winston C Williams. LC E202.3. DD 369.13. adv acc. Patriotic and educational publication. Sons of the American Revolution Magazine.

SCOTTISH RITE JOURNAL. V. 1- June 1921-. 0279-7011. Periodical. US. English. qt. Scottish Rite Journal, c/o R Larson, 200 East Plato Boulevard, St Paul MN 55107.

SCOUTING. V. 1- Apr. 15, 1913-. 0036-9500. Periodical. US. English. bm. Boy Scouts of America, PO Box 61030, Dallas TX 75261. Ind/Abst Mag. Index. LC HS3313.B7. DD 369.430973.

SCOUTING NEWS. Spring Issue 1975-. 0318-3521. Periodical. CN. English. PO Box 533, Charlottetown Prince Edward Island C1A 7L1 Canada. DD 369.4305. Scouting in Prince Edward Island, 0318-3513.

SCOUTS & GUIDES AUJOURD'HUI. VFOAT Aujourd'Hui. VAT Scouts et Guides Aujourd'Hui. Vol. 1, No. 1 (Oct. 1984)-. 0826-6786. Periodical. CN. French. ir. $2.00 Per No. Association des Scouts du Canada, 9907 rue Parthenais, Montreal Quebec H2B 2L3 Canada. DD 369.430971. Defis (Montreal, Quebec : Edition Nationale), 0821-0292.

SEIJO BUNGEI. JA. Japanese. ir. Seijo Kaigaku Bungeigakubu Kenkyushitsu, 1-20 Seijo 6, Setagaya-ku 157, Tokyo Japan. LC AS552.S44.

SEINAN GAKUIN DAIGAKU BUNRI RON SHU. VFOAT Studies in Literature and Science of Seinan Gakuin University. Began with June 1960 issue. JA. Japanese or English. ir. Seinan Gakuin Daigaku Gakujutsu Kenkyujo, 2-6 Nishijin 6-chome Nishi-ku 814, Fukuoka Japan. LC AS552.S444.

SEM. Main/Corp Societe des Ecrivains Canadiens. Section de Montreal. V. 1- Jan./Feb. 1975-. 0318-5508. Periodical. CN. French. bw. $6.00 Domestic, $8.00 Foreign. La Revue Sem, Bureau 502/ 2767 Boil Edouard-Montpetit, Montreal Quebec H3T 1J6 Canada. DD 054.1.

SHAKESPEAREAN AUTHORSHIP REVIEW. No. 1-29. Periodical. UK. English. sa. Shakespearean Authorship Society, 25 Montagu Square, London W1H 1RE England. Shakespeare Fellowship Newsletter.

SHE HUI KO HSUEH YEN CHIU (CHENG-TU, CHINA). (SHE HUI KO HSUEH YEN CHIU). VFOAT Shehui Kexue Yanjiu. Began in 1979. Periodical. CC. Chinese. bm. 0.50. Post Office, Cheng-Tu China. LC AS452.C46165. DD 059.951.

SHEN-YANG SHIH FAN HSUEH YUAN HSUEH PAO. CHE HSUEH SHE HUI KO HSUEH PAN. VFOAT Shenyangshifanxueyuanxuebao. Periodical. CC. Chinese. qt. 0.35. Post Office, Shen-Yang Shih China. LC AS452.S54. DD 089.951.

SHO TO KIROKU NO JIMMEI JITEN. 1973-. JA. Japanese. ir. 920. Jiyu Kokumin Sha, c/o Daiichi Seimei Bunkan 8 Kyobashi-2 Chuo-ku, Tokyo Japan. LC AS548.

SIGNE DE PISTE. VFOAT Amis du Signe de Piste. VAT Amis du Signe de Piste (1980). No. 41 (Oct. 1980)-. 0820-0424. Periodical. CN. French. ir. $12.00. Signe De Piste, No 12 7154 rue Hamilton, Ville Eymard Montreal Quebec H4E 3E1 Canada. DD 369.4305. Amis du Signe de Piste, 0709-5147.

SITZUNGBERICHTE. Main/Corp Akademie der Wissenschaften, Vienna. Vol. 1 1848-. Periodical. German. ir. Deutscher Buch Export-Import, Leninstrasse 16, DDR-701 Leipzig East Germany. (cum index). Available also on microfilm.

SOIS PRET. V. 2, No 1- Dec. 1976/Jan. 1977-. 0383-8587. Periodical. CN. French. bm. Free to Members, $5.00 Domestic, $8.00 Foreign. Revue Sois Pret, 217 de Letoile Laval (L-D-R), Quebec H7H 4T4 Canada. DD 369.4305. Scout du Canada, 0319-1702.

SON OF THE STARS. 1st- Ed. US. English. George Banta Publishing Company, 450 Ahnaip Street, Menasha WI 54952. LC LJ75.B54. DD 371.855.

SOONER JAYCEE. (SOONER JAYCEE : THE OFFICIAL PUBLICATION OF THE OKLAHOMA JAYCEES). Main/Corp Oklahoma Jaycees. Vol. 1, No.

Sociology: General Works, Theory

1 (Sept. issue 1982)-. 0279-2451. Periodical. US. English. bm. Oklahoma Jaycees, State Headquarters, PO Box 348, 109 South Cleveland, Cushing OK 74023. *Sooner Jaycee, 0279-2451.*

SOUTHAMPTON RECORDS SERIES. 1- 1951-. 0584-4029. Monographic Series. UK. English. ir. University of Southampton, c/o G L Felix, Southampton SO9 5NH England. *Publications of the Southampton Record Society.*

STATISTIQUES DES SOCIETES. See Statistics.

STUDIA VARIA. Main/Corp Royal Society of Canada. 1957-. 0080-4533. Monographic Series. CN. English (includes some text in French). ir. University of Toronto Press, Front Campus, Toronto Ontario M5S 1A6 Canada.

STUDIUM. Italian. ir. 6.500. Via Della Conciliazione 4/D, Rome Italy. LC AS221.

TAKAMATSU KOGYO KOTO SENMON GAKKO KENKYU KIYO. (KENKYU KIYO). VFOAT Takamatsu Kogyo Koto Semmon Gakko Kenkyu Kiyo. No. 1-. 0389-9268. JA. Japanese (some articles and summaries in English). ir. No 355 Chokushicho, Takamatsu Japan. Ind/Abst Chem. Abstr. LC AS552. CODEN TAKYDU.

IL TAMBURO DI LATTA. 1- 1971-. Italian. ir. P Tolsca (Nuovi Quaderni), Via de Gusperi 3 CAS Post 243, Parma Italy. LC AS221.

TEMAS EM FOCO. No. 1- 1970-. Periodical. Portuguese. ir. Rua Monsenhor Coutinho 224, Manaus Brazil. LC AS80.U53.

TORCH (INDIANAPOLIS, IND.). (TORCH). Fall 1983-. 8755-3600. Periodical. US. English. sa. Sigma Delta Tau National Office, 9202 North Meridian Street/Suite 305, Indianapolis IN 46260. LC LJ145.S52. DD 378.1985605. *Torch of Sigma Delta Tau, 0495-8837.*

TRACKS (LANSING, MICH.). (TRACKS). 0738-8810. Periodical. US. English. mo. $5.00. Michigan United Conservation Clubs, PO Box 30235, Lansing MI 48909.

TRANSACTIONS OF THE HUGUENOT SOCIETY OF SOUTH CAROLINA. Main/Corp Huguenot Society of South Carolina. No. 1-. 0363-3152. US. English. an. $5.00. Huguenot Society of South Carolina, 25 Charles Street, Charleston SC 29401. LC F280.H8.

TRANSACTIONS OF THE ROYAL SOCIETY OF SOUTH AUSTRALIA, INCORPORATED. Vol. 62(1938)-. Periodical. AT. English. ir. Royal Society of South Australia Inc, State Library Building, North Terrace, Adelaide South Australia 5000. Tel (08)223-5360. Ed M Davies. Circ 800. (ctrl). Original papers in natural sciences: botany, zoology, earth sciences, and anthropology. *Transactions and Proceedings of the Royal Society of Australia.*

TRANSITION. V. 1- Dec. 1972-. 0382-0750. Periodical. CN. English. Transition Society, 123 20th Street West, Saskatoon Saskatchewan Canada.

THE TRIDENT OF DELTA DELTA DELTA. Main/Corp Delta Delta Delta. Began in 1891. Periodical. US. English. qt. LC LJ145.D17. DD 371.856.

THE TRUTH. 1902. 0041-3690. Periodical. US. English. mo. $3.50. Russian Brotherhood Organ USA, 1733 Spring Garden Street, Philadelphia PA 19130. Tel (215)563-2537. Ed Stephen P Kopestonsky. bk rev. Circ 4,000. A family-oriented fraternal paper.

TUMBLEWEED. Sept. 1975-. 0380-1667. Periodical. CN. English. mo. Girl Guides of Canada Alberta Council, Room 202/10169-104th Street, Edmonton Alberta T5J 1A5 Canada. DD 369.46305. *Newsletter, 0380-1675.*

TUNG-PEI SHIH TA HSUEH PAO. CHE HSUEH SHE HUI KO HSUEH PAN. VFOAT Dongbei Shida Xuebao. Periodical. CH. Chinese. bm. 0.40. Chung-Kuo Kuo Chi Shu Tien, PO Box 2820, Pei-Ching China. LC AS451. DD 089.951.

TYDSKRIF VIR GEESTESWETENSKAPPE. 1st Year March 1961-. 0041-4751. Periodical. SA. Afrikaans (summaries in English or German). qt. Suidafrik Akadwetens Kuns, Box 538, Pretoria South Africa. Ind/Abst MLA Int. Bibliogr. Books Artic. Mod. Lang. Lit. LC AS611. *Tydskrif vir Wetenskap en Kuns.*

UMBRA. Vol. 1, No. 1 (Winter 1963)-. 0016-6618. Periodical. US. English. ir. Society of Umbra, Box 4338, Sather Gate, Berkeley CA 94704.

UNESCO CHRONICLE CEASED. Vol. 1, No. 1 (July 1955)-Vol. 26, No. 1 (Jan./Feb. 1980). 0041-526X. Periodical. FR. English. bm. Ind/Abst Women Stud. Abstr., Public Aff. Inf. Serv. Bull. DD 060. NLM W1 U575P. *UNESCO Bulletin, UNESCO Newsletter.*

UNESCO FEATURES : A FORTNIGHTLY PRESS SERVICE. No. 1 July 15, 1949-. Periodical. English. bm. UNESCO, 7 Place de Fontenoy, 75700 Paris France. LC AS4.U8. DD 060. *UNESCO Newsletter.*

UNESCO NEWS CEASED. English. ir. Australian National Commission for UNESCO, Australian Government Publishing Service, PO Box 84, Canberra Australia. LC AS4.U825. DD 052.

THE UNIVERSAL FREEMASON. V. 1- June 1908-. Periodical. US. English. mo. LC HS901.

VICTORIANS INSTITUTE JOURNAL. No. 1- July 1972-. Periodical. US. English. an. $7.00. Victorians Institute Journal, East Carolina University, English Department, Greenville NC 27834. Tel (919)757-6041. Ind/Abst MLA Int. Bibliogr. Books Artic. Mod. Lang. Lit. LC AS36. DD 051.

VIGENCIA. V. 1- Sept./Oct. 1968-. Periodical. Spanish. mo. MacMillan, 866 Third Avenue, New York NY 10022. LC AS78. DD 056.1.

VOICE OF THE TURTLE. (VOICE OF THE TURTLE : THE MONTHLY NEWSLETTER OF THE SAN DIEGO TURTLE AND TORTOISE SOCIETY). 0739-9324. Periodical. US. English. mo. Free to Domestic Members, $8.00 Foreign Members. The San Diego Turtle and Tortoise Society, 6957 Tanglewood Road, San Diego CA 92111.

VYTIS. 0042-9384. Periodical. US. English (Lithuanian). mo. Knights of Lithuania, 2524 West 45th Street, Chicago IL 60632. LC HS2008.L49.

WARTA UNIVERSITAS RIAU. Main/Corp Universitas Riau. Periodical. chiefly Indonesian. ir. Hupenmas Universitas Riau, Jalan Ronggowarsito, Pekanbaru Indonesia. LC AS522.U54.

WERKEN UITGEGEVEN DOOR DE LINSCHOTEN-VEREENIGING. 1-. Monographic Series. NE. Dutch. ir. Martinus Nijhoff Publishers, PO Box 163, Spul Boulevard 50, 3300 AD Dordrecht Netherlands. (cum index).

WISCONSIN DIALOGUE : A FACULTY JOURNAL FOR THE UNIVERSITY OF WISCONSIN-EAU CLAIRE. No. 1 (Fall 1980)-. Periodical. US. English. an. University of Wisconsin-Eau Claire, 234 Schofield, Eau Claire WI 54701. LC AS30. DD 051.

WISSENSCHAFTLICHE ZEITSCHRIFT DER HUMBOLDT-UNIVERSITAT ZU BERLIN. GESELLSCHAFTS-UND SPRACHWISSENSCHAFTLICHE REIHE CEASED. VFOAT Gesellschafts-und Sprachwissenschaftliche Reihe. Began with: Vol. 1 (1951/52). 0522-9855. Periodical. GE. German (summaries in English, French, German, and Russian). bm. Ind/Abst Sociol. Abstr., Lang. Lang. Behav. Abstr., Writ. Am. Hist. LC AS182. DD 053.1. (cum index).

WISSENSCHAFTLICHE ZEITSCHRIFT DER WILHELM-PIECK-UNIVERSITAT ROSTOCK. VFOAT WZ Rostock. Year 31, Issue 1/2-. Periodical. German (summaries in English, French and Russian). ir. Wilhelm-Pieck-Universitat Rostock, Vogelsang 13/1, DDR-2500 Rostock East Germany. Ind/Abst MLA Int. Bibliogr. Books Artic. Mod. Lang. Lit., Comput. Control Abstr., Electr. Electron. Abstr., Sci. Abstr. LC AS182. DD 063. *Wissenschaftliche Zeitschrift der Wilhelm-Pieck-Universitat Rostock. Gesellschafts- und Sprachwissenschaftliche Reihe.*

WORCESTERSHIRE HISTORICAL SOCIETY. (PUBLICATIONS). Main/Corp Society. New Series 1- 1928-. 0141-4577. Monographic Series. UK. English. ir.

WORK REPORTS - EARLY SITES RESEARCH SOCIETY. Main/Corp Early Sites Research Society. V. 1- (No.1/10-). Periodical. US. English. ir. Early Sites Research Society, Long Hill, Rowley MA 01969. Tel (617)948-2410.

WORLD FUTURE SOCIETY. (WORLD FUTURE SOCIETY : NEWSLETTER). 0732-7676. Periodical. US. English. mo. World Future Society, Washington DC Chapter, 4916 St Elmo Avenue, Bethesda MD 20814.

WORLD SCOUTING. VFOAT Scoutisme Mondial. V. 1- Jan./Feb. 1965-. 0043-8995. Periodical. English (French). qt. PO Box 78, 1211 Geneva 4 Switzerland. LC HS3312. *World Scouting Bulletin, 0510-9426.*

YENI UFUKLAR. Turkish. ir. 100.00. Can Yaknlar, PK 1034 Karakoy, Istanbul Turkey. LC AS348.A1.

YON'GU NONJIP - IHWA YOJA TAEHAKKYO, TAEHAGWON. Main/Corp Ihwa Yoja Taehakkyo, Seoul, Korea. Taehagwon. Periodical. KO. Korean. ir. 11-1 Taehyon-Dong, Sodaemun-Ku Seoul. LC AS559.A1. DD 059.957. (ctrl).

YON'GU NONMUNJIP - TAEPYONGYANG CHANGHAK MUNHWA CHAEDAN. Main/Corp Taepyongyang Changhak Munhwa Chaedan. Vol.1 -. Periodical. KO. English (Korean). ir. 181 2-ka, Hangangno Yongsan-Ku Seoul. LC AS559.A1. (ctrl).

YORK GEORGIAN SOCIETY ANNUAL REPORT. VFOAT Annual Report - York Georgian Society. UK. English. an. 1.05. York Georgian Society, Kings Manor, York Y01 2EW England. Ind/Abst Avery Index Archit. Period. Second Ed. Revis. Enlarged Suppl. LC NA12. DD 720.6242843.

YOUNG FABIAN PAMPHLET. 0513-5982. Monographic Series. UK. English. Fabian Society, 11 Dartmouth Street, London SWIH 9BN England.

ZEITSCHRIFT FUR GANZHEITSFORSCHUNG. Periodical. German. ir. $4.40. 1191 Franz-Klein-Gasse 1, Wien Australia. LC AS141.

ZESZYTY NAUKOWE KATOLICKIEGO UNIWERSYTETU LUBELSKIEGO. Vol. 1, No. 1-. 0044-4405. Periodical. PL. Polish. qt. ARS Polona, Krakowskie Przedmiescie 7, 00-068 Warsaw Poland. LC AS262.L84. (cum index).

SOCIOLOGY: GENERAL WORKS, THEORY

ACCION. VFOAT Revista Paraguaya de Educacion y del Hogar. 2. Ser., No. 1- Apr. 1964-. Periodical. PY. Spanish. bm $10.00. Accion Revista de Reflexion, Colon 1301 C Correo 1072, Asuncion Paraguay. Tel 33962. Ed Antonio Guasch. bk rev. adv acc. Circ 1,000. Reflections on Paraguay and Latin America in its various aspects: political, social, religious, human rights, art, and literature; also includes documents.

ACTA SOCIOLOGICA. V. 1-. 0001-6993. Periodical. NO. English (text in Danish, French, German, Norwegian and Swedish). qt. 50.-. Universitetsforlaget, PO Box 2959-Toyen, Oslo 6 Norway. Tel (45)-2-27 60 60. Ed Raimo Blom, Markku Kivinen and Harri Melin. Ind/Abst Sociol. Abstr., ABC Pol Sci, Soc. Welf. Soc. Plan./Policy Soc. Dev., Public Aff. Inf. Serv. Bull., Soc. Sci. Index, Am. Hist. Life, Hist. Abstr., Part A, Mod. Hist. Abstr., Hist. Abst., Part B, Twent. Century Abstr., Soc. Sci. Citation Index, Lang. Lang. Behav. Abstr., Hist. Abstr. LC HM1.A1. DD 301. NLM W1 AC949JM. (cum index). bk rev. adv acc. Circ 2,600. Presents research results that fulfill international standards within the field of sociology and social research.

ACTES DE LA RECHERCHE EN SCIENCES SOCIALES. Began in 1975. 0335-5322. Periodical. FR. French (summaries in English and German). bm. 121.00 Domestic, 170.00 Foreign. CDR Gauthier-Villars, 11 rue Gossin, 92543 Montrouge Cedex France. Tel 656 52 66. Ed Pierre Bourdieu. Ind/Abst Am. Hist. Life, Hist. Abstr., Part A, Mod. Hist. Abstr., Hist. Abst., Part B, Twent. Century Abstr., Sociol. Abstr., Soc. Sci. Citation Index. LC H3. DD 300.944. Circ 2,500. Publishes results of leading research in sociology, ethnology, social psychology, psychology, social history, sociolinguistics, the economics of consumption, etc.

Sociology: General Works, Theory

ACTION AGENDAS. (ACTION AGENDAS : A PUBLICATION OF THE UNITED CHURCH OF CANADA). Fall '82-. 0824-4103. Periodical. CN. English. ir. $5.00. United Church of Canada/Working Unit on Social Issues and Justice, 85 St Clair Avenue East, Toronto Ontario M4T 1M8 Canada. **DD** 361.26.

L'ACTIVITE SCIENTIFIQUE DU CENTRE DE SOCIOLOGIE URBAINE. **Main/Corp** Centre de Sociologie Urbaine (France). 1978-1981-. FR. French. ir. 118 rue de la Tombe Issoire, 75014 Paris France. **LC** HT135. **DD** 307.7606044361.

ADVANCES IN EXPERIMENTAL SOCIAL PSYCHOLOGY. VFOAT Experimental Social Psychology. V. 1-. 0065-2601. Monographic Series. US. English. ir. Academic Press, 4805 Sand Lake Road, Orlando FL 32819. Ed L Berkowitz. **Ind/Abst** Biol. Abstr., Soc. Sci. Citation Index. **LC** HM251. **DD** 301.105. **NLM** W1 AD561. **CODEN** AXSPAQ.

ADVANCES IN GROUP PROCESSES. Vol. 1 (1984)-. 0882-6145. US. English. an. $56.50. Jai Press Inc, 36 Sherwood Place, Greenwich CT 06836. **Tel** (203)661-7602. Ed Edward J Lawler.

AFRICAN JOURNAL OF SOCIOLOGY. V. 1, No. 1 and 2 (May 1981)-. Periodical. English. sa. African Journal of Sociology, Department of Sociology, University of Nairobi, PO Box 30197, Nairobi Kenya. **Ind/Abst** Sociol. Abstr., Soc. Welf. Soc. Plan./Policy Soc. Dev. **LC** HM22.A4. **DD** 301.096.

AFRICAN NOTES. V. 1- Oct. 1963-. 0002-0087. Periodical. NR. English. ir. Institute of African Studies, University of Ibadan/Ms Purisch, Ibadan Nigeria. **Tel** (022)400550-614. Ed Mabel Segun. **Ind/Abst** Am. Hist. Life, Hist. Abstr., Part A, Mod. Hist. Abstr., Hist. Abst., Part B, Twent. Century Abstr., MLA Int. Bibliogr. Books Artic. Mod. Lang. Lit., Hist. Abstr. bk rev. adv acc. **Circ** 500. African agriculture, anthropology, archaeology, arts, folklore, history, linguistics, literature, traditional medicine, and sociology.

AID BULLETIN. VAT Addiction Intervention with the Disabled Bulletin (Kent, Ohio). Vol. 1, No. 1 (Fall 1980)-. 0275-6692. Periodical. US. English. qt. $6.00. Kent State University, Department of Sociology, Kent OH 44242. **Tel** (216)672-2440.

AIM, RACIAL HARMONY & PEACE. VFOAT Racial Harmony & Peace. VAT Aim, Racial Harmony and Peace. V. 3- Jan./Feb. 1976-. 0194-2069. Periodical. US. English. qt. $6.00. Aim-Quarterly, PO Box 20554, Chicago IL 60620. **Tel** (312)874-6184. Ed Ruth Apilado. **LC** E184.A1. **DD** 301.450973. bk rev. adv acc. **Circ** 10,000. Articles, short stories promoting racial harmony and peace. We strive to eliminate racism from the human bloodstream. Want to be vehicle for promising new writers. Aim for Racial Harmony, 0194-2077.

ALBERTA SERIES REPORT CEASED. No. 1- 1973-. 0317-3119. Monographic Series. CN. English. Population Research Laboratory, Department of Sociology, Tory Building, University of Alberta, Edmonton Alberta Canada. **DD** 301.3297123.

ALLENSBACHER JAHRBUCH DER DEMOSKOPIE. See Yearbooks, Almanacs, Directories.

ALTERNATE ROUTES. V. 1- 1977-. 0702-8865. CN. English. an. $1.00 Per No. Alternate Routes, Department of Sociology and Anthropology, Carleton University, Ottawa Ontario K1S 5B6 Canada. **Ind/Abst** Sociol. Abstr. **DD** 301.05.

ALTERNATIVES. V. 1- Summer 1971-. 0002-6638. Periodical. CN. English. qt. $8.00. Alternatives Resource Center, 1124 Main Street, PO Box 1707, Forest Park GA 30050. **Tel** (404)361-5823. **Ind/Abst** Can. Environ., Can. Period. Index, Altern. Press Index, Curr. Index J. Educ. **LC** HC79.E5. **DD** 301.3105. **NLM** W1 AL987K. Also available in microfilm format. Conserver Society Notes, 1980, 0709-5791.

AMERASIA JOURNAL. V. 1- Mar. 1971-. 0044-7471. US. English. sa. $14.00. Regents University of California, 3232 Campbell, Asian American Study, Los Angeles CA 90024. Ed Russell C Leong. **Ind/Abst** Am. Hist. Life, Hist. Abstr., Part A, Mod. Hist. Abstr., Hist. Abst., Part B, Twent. Century Abstr., Writ. Am. Hist. **LC** E184.O6. **DD** 917.3069505. bk rev. adv acc. **Circ** 1,500. Interdisciplinary analysis of Asian Americans, social historical, literary aspects; especially race and class, immigration, and community history.

THE AMERICAN CITY & COUNTY. VFOAT American City. VAT American City and County. V. 90, No. 9- Sept. 1975-. 0149-337X. Periodical. US. English. mo. $39.00. Communication Channels Inc, 6255 Barfield Road, Atlanta GA 30328. **Tel** (404)256-9800. **Ind/Abst** Electron. Commun. Abstr. J., ISMEC Bull., Pollut. Abstr. Indexes, Saf. Sci. Abstr. J., Trade Ind. Index, Mag. Index, Eng. Index Mon., Eng. Index Bioeng. Abstr., Eng. Index Energy Abstr., Sel. Water Resour. Abstr., Excerpta Med., Book Rev. Index, Appl. Sci. Technol. Index, Eng. Index, Read. Guide Period. Lit., Avery Index Archit. Period., Eng. Index Annu. **LC** HT101. **DD** 301.360973. **CODEN** ACCOD3. Available in microform from Xerox University Microfilms. American City, 0002-7936.

THE AMERICAN EAGLE. (AMERICAN EAGLE). V. 1- 1906-. 0742-8197. Periodical. US. English. wk. $2.00. Koreshan Unity, PO Box 97, Estero FL 33928. **Tel** (813)992-2184. Ed Jo Bigelow. **Circ** 650. Devoted to the preservation of and education about the Koreshan Unity Communal Colony from 1870's through 1982. Founded by Dr Cyrus Teed-Koresh.

THE AMERICAN JOURNAL OF ECONOMICS AND SOCIOLOGY. See Economics.

AMERICAN JOURNAL OF SOCIOLOGY. (THE AMERICAN JOURNAL OF SOCIOLOGY). VFOAT AJS. V. 1- July 1895-. 0002-9602. Periodical. US. English. bm. $24.00. University of Chicago at the University of Chicago Press, 5801 Ellis Avenue, Chicago IL 60637. **Ind/Abst** Sociol. Abstr., Soc. Sci. Index, ABC Pol Sci, Am. Hist. Life, Book Rev. Index, Soc. Sci. Index, Index Med., Guide Soc. Sci. Relig. Period. Lit., Int. Labour Doc., Popul. Index, Psychol. Abstr., Soc. Welf. Soc. Plan./ Policy Soc. Dev., Soc. Work Res. Abstr., Women Stud. Abstr., Pooles Index Period. Lit., Humanit. Index, Soc. Sci. Citation Index, Lang. Lang. Behav. Abstr., Curr. Index J. Educ., Hist. Abstr., Part A, Mod. Hist. Abstr. **LC** HM1. (cum index).

AMERICAN MAN. V. 1- Winter 1980-. 0271-9487. Periodical. US. English. ir. $5.00. American Man, Box 693, Columbia MD 21045. **Tel** (301)338-2009. Ed Richard Haddad. bk rev. adv acc. **Circ** 500. Focus on the male gender role and the male experience through articles, fiction, poetry, and satire. The only periodical of its type in the US.

AMERICAN PUBLIC OPINION DATA. (AMERICAN PUBLIC OPINION DATA. MICROFORM). 1981-. 0885-6893. US. English. an. Opinion Research Service, PO Box 70205, Louisville KY 40270. **DD** 303.

AMERICAN PUBLIC OPINION INDEX. See Indexes/Abstracts.

AMERICAN ROMANIAN REVIEW. V. 1- May 1977-. 0193-8118. Periodical. US. English (in Romanian). ir. $10.00. American Romanian Review, 17313 Puritas Avenue, Cleveland OH 44135. **Tel** (216)265-3532. Ed T Andrica. **LC** E184.R8. **DD** 301.4515907305. **Circ** 600. Gives information about cultural and historic background of American Romanians.

THE AMERICAN SOCIOLOGIST CEASED. V. 1-17. 0003-1232. Periodical. US. English. qt. American Sociological Association, 1722 North Street NW, Washington DC 20036. **Ind/Abst** Soc. Sci. Index. **LC** HM9. **NLM** W1 AM808K.

ANALELE UNIVERSITATII BUCURESTI. SOCIOLOGIE. (ANALELE UNIVERSITATII BUCURESTI: SOCIOLOGIE). **Main/Corp** Universitatea Din Bucuresti. 0068-3302. RM. Romanian (with summaries in English and French). ir. Universitetea din Bucaresti, B-Dul Gh Gheorghiu-Dej Nr 64, Bucuresti Romania. **LC** HN15.

ANALISE SOCIAL. V.1- Jan.1963-. 0003-2573. Periodical. PO. Portuguese (summaries in French and English). ir. $30.00. Instituto de Ciencias Sociais, Universite de Lisboa, Rua Miguel LUP I18, 1200 Lisboa Portugal. **Ind/Abst** Int. Labour Doc., Sociol. Abstr., Soc. Welf. Soc. Plan./Policy Soc. Dev., Lang. Lang. Behav. Abstr.

I & C. VFOAT I and C. No. 6 (Autumn 1979)-. 0309-9156. Periodical. UK. English. sa. $12.26. Ideology and Consciousness, Westminster College, North Hinksey, Oxford OX2 9AT England. **Ind/Abst** Sociol. Abstr., Altern. Press Index. Ideology & Consciousness.

LES ANNALES DE LA RECHERCHE URBAINE. No 1 Oct. 1978-. Periodical. FR. French (summaries in English and Spanish). qt. 382. Centrale des Revues, 11 rue Gossin, 92543 Montrouge Cedex France. **Tel** (1)43201550. Ed Anne Querrien. **Ind/Abst** Am. Hist. Life, Hist. Abstr., Part A, Mod. Hist. Abstr., Hist. Abst., Part B, Twent. Century Abstr., Hist. Abstr. bk rev. adv acc. **Circ** 1,150. Results of research in urban problems theory and practice, social movements, town planning, land management, and social practices in cities; improvement of the environment. Annales / Centre de Recherche d'Urbanisme.

ANNALES UNIVERSITATIS SCIENTIARUM BUDAPESTINENSIS DE ROLANDO EOTVOS NOMINATAE. SECTIO PHILOSOPHICA ET SOCIOLOGICA. See Philosophy.

ANNEE SOCIOLOGIQUE. (L'ANNEE SOCIOLOGIQUE). 3rd Ser., 1940/1948-. 0066-2399. French. an. **Tel** (1)326-22-16. **Ind/Abst** Sociol. Abstr., Soc. Welf. Soc. Plan./Policy Soc. Dev. bk rev. A collection of reports on important sociological studies and on sociological research in progress during the year. Annales Sociologiques.

ANNUAL EDITIONS. READINGS IN SOCIOLOGY. (ANNUAL EDITIONS : READINGS IN SOCIOLOGY). VFOAT Readings in Sociology. 1972/73-. 0090-4236. US. English. an. Dushkin Publishing Group, Sluice Dock, Guilford CT 06437. **Tel** (203)453-4351. **LC** HM1. **DD** 301.05.

ANNUAL OF POWER AND CONFLICT. 1971-. UK. English. an. $16.50. Institute for the Study of Conflict 17, Northumberland Avenue, London WC2N 5BJ England. **LC** D839. **DD** 301.63305.

ANNUAL PROCEEDINGS - AMERICAN SOCIOLOGICAL ASSOCIATION. **Main/Corp** American Sociological Association. VFOAT Proceedings - American Sociological Association. US. English. an. $2.50. American Sociological Association, 1722 N Street Northwest, Washington DC 20036. **Tel** (202)833-3410. **Circ** 3,500. Abstracts of papers presented at the Annual Meeting of the American Sociological Association. Distributed at meeting and by request.

ANNUAL REPORT - AQUATIC ECOSYSTEM OBJECTIVES COMMITTEE. (ANNUAL REPORT : REPORT OF THE AQUATIC ECOSYSTEM OBJECTIVES COMMITTEE). **Main/Corp** Great Lakes Science Advisory Board. Aquatic Ecosystem Objectives Committee. VFOAT Report of the Aquatic Ecosystem Objectives Committee. Nov. 1983-. 0826-6611. CN. English. an. International Joint Commission Great Lakes Regional Office, 100 Ouellette Avenue, Windsor Ontario N9A 6T3 Canada. **DD** 363.73940977. Report of the Aquatic Ecosystem Objectives Committee, 0826-6603.

ANNUAL REPORT - CANADIAN COUNCIL ON SOCIAL DEVELOPMENT. **Main/Corp** Canadian Council on Social Development. 51st- 1970/71-. CN. English. an. Canadian Council on Social Development, 55 Parkdale Avenue, Box 3505 Station C, Ottawa Ontario K1Y 4G1 Canada. Annual Report.

ANNUAL REPORT - CHRISTIAN COMMISSION FOR DEVELOPMENT IN BANGLADESH. **Main/Corp** Christian Commission for Development in Bangladesh. English. an. 616 Dhanmondi Residential Area, Road No 18, Dacca Bangladesh. **LC** HN690.6.Z9. **DD** 307.72095492.

ANNUAL REPORT - FIELD FOUNDATION OF ILLINOIS. (ANNUAL REPORT FOR THE YEAR ENDED APRIL 30 . . .). **Main/Corp** Field Foundation of Illinois. 0743-5118. US. English. an. Field Foundation of Illinois Inc, 135 South LaSalle Street, Chicago IL 60603. **LC** AS36.C425. **DD** 361.7632.

ANNUAL REPORT FOR THE PERIOD - CAMEROON. MINISTRY OF INFORMATION AND CULTURE. **Main/Corp** Cameroon. Ministry of Information and Culture. Provincial Delegation for the South West. English. an. **LC** HN819.S68. **DD** 354.67110085.

ANNUAL REPORT - INTEGRATED RURAL DEVELOPMENT PROGRAMME (ZAMBIA). NORTHERN PROVINCE. **Main/Corp** Integrated Rural Development Programme (Zambia). Northern Province. English. an. **LC** HN803.N67. **DD** 307.14096894.

Sociology: General Works, Theory

ANNUAL REPORT - NETHERLANDS-AMERICA COMMUNITY ASSOCIATION. Main/Corp Netherlands-America Community Association. US. English. an. Netherlands-America Community Association Inc, One Rockefeller Plaza, New York NY 10020. LC E184.D9. DD 361.77.

ANNUAL REPORT OF THE INSTITUTE OF RACE RELATIONS. (ANNUAL REPORT). Main/Corp Institute of Race Relations. 0307-9740. UK. English. an. Institute of Race Relations, 11 Nelson Road Greenwich, London SE 10 England. LC HT1503.A3. DD 301.451042.

ANNUAL REPORT - TUSKEGEE INSTITUTE. HUMAN RESOURCES DEVELOPMENT CENTER. Main/Corp Tuskegee Institute. Human Resources Development Center. 0739-7127. US. English. an. LC HN79.A43. DD 307.1409761.

ANNUAL REPORT - UNIVERSITY OF ZAMBIA. RURAL DEVELOPMENT STUDIES BUREAU. Main/Corp University of Zambia. Rural Development Studies Bureau. English. an. LC HN803.Z9. DD 307.72096894.

ANNUAL REVIEW OF SOCIOLOGY. V. 1- 1975-. 0360-0572. US. English. an. $31.00 Domestic, $34.00 Foreign. Annual Reviews Incorporated, 4139 El Camino Way, Palo Alto CA 94306. Tel (415)493-4400. Ed Ralph H Turner. Ind/Abst Sociol. Abstr., Soc. Welf. Soc. Plan./Policy Soc. Dev., Biol. Abstr., Psychol. Abstr., Soc. Sci. Index, Soc. Sci. Citation Index. LC HM1. DD 301.05. NLM W1 AN7798. CODEN ARVSDB. Comprehensive, thorough articles that review the coverage of latest advances in sociology, written by acknowledged experts in the field. Extensive literature citations included.

ANUARIO DE LA SOCIOLOGIA ESPANOLA. See Yearbooks, Almanacs, Directories.

APPLIED SOCIAL PSYCHOLOGY ANNUAL. V. 1- 1980-. 0196-4151. US. English. an. Sage Publications Inc, 275 South Beverly Drive, Beverly Hills CA 90212. Ind/Abst Psychol. Abstr. LC HM251. DD 302. NLM W1 AP528W.

ARAB DAWN. VFOAT Aube Arabe. V. 4-6. 0383-087X. Periodical. CN. English (includes some text in French and Arabic). ir. Canadian Arab Federation, PO Box 416 Station K, Toronto Ontario M4P 2G7 Canada. DD 301.451927071005. Aube Arabe, 0383-0861.

ARCHIVES EUROPEENNES DE SOCIOLOGIE. See Genealogy and Heraldry - Archives.

ARCHIVES INTERNATIONALES DE SOCIOLOGIE DE LA COOPERATION ET DU DEVELOPPEMENT. See Genealogy and Heraldry - Archives.

THE ARMENIAN REVIEW. V. 1- (No. 1-). 0004-2366. Periodical. US. English. qt. $25.00 Domestic, $30.00 Foreign. 80 Bigelow Avenue, Watertown MA 02172-2012. Tel (617)926-4037. Ed Gerard J Libaidian. Ind/Abst Hist. Abstr., Part A, Mod. Hist. Abstr., Hist. Abst., Part B, Twent. Century Abstr., Artbibliogr. Mod., Writ. Am. Hist., Am. Hist. Life, Hist. Abstr. LC AP2. DD 052. (cum index). bk rev. adv acc. Circ 1,100. Available on microfilm from Xerox University Microfilms. Scholarly, interdisciplinary research in Armenian studies, contemporary near East and Soviet studies, Armenian Diaspora and Soviet Armenian, humanities, social sciences and arts.

ASA FOOTNOTES. Main/Corp American Sociological Association. VFOAT Footnotes. V. 1- 1973-. Periodical. US. English. mo. $18.00 Domestic, $20.00 Foreign. American Sociological Association, 1722 N Street Northwest, Washington DC 20036. Tel (202)833-3410. Ed William V D'Antonio. adv acc. Circ 13,000. Published nine times a year, this newsletter contains departmental news, activities of the association, the Washington office, news of the profession, plus the association's official reports and proceedings. American Sociologist.

ASIAN THOUGHT & SOCIETY. VAT Asian Thought and Society. V. 1- Apr. 1976-. 0361-3968. Periodical. US. English. ty. $40.00. Asian Thought and Society, University of New York, Department of Political Science, Oneonta NY 13820. Tel (607)431-3550. Ed Ignatius J H Tsao. Ind/Abst Am. Hist. Life, Hist. Abstr., Part A, Mod. Hist. Abstr., Hist. Abst., Part B, Twent. Century Abstr., ABC Pol Sci, Recent Publ. Artic., Hist. Abstr. LC DS1. DD 950.05. bk rev. adv acc. Intellectual development and societal structures and changes in East, South and Southeast Asia.

ASIANADIAN. (THE ASIANADIAN). V. 1- Spring 1978-. 0705-8861. Periodical. CN. English. qt. $14.70. Asianadian Resource Workshop, PO Box 1256, Station Q, Toronto Ontario M4T 2P4 Canada. Tel (416) 591-1625. Ed Mina Wong. DD 301.45195071. bk rev. adv acc. Circ 500. Provides an Asian-Canadian perspective on Canadian life and society by providing a forum for Asian artists and writers.

ASIAWEEK. VAT Asia Week. Dec. 19, 1975-. Periodical. HK. English. wk. $82.50. Asiaweek Ltd, 22 Westlands Road, Toppan Building/7th Floor, Quarry Bay Hong Kong. Tel (5) 630232. Ed Michael O'Neill. LC DS1. DD 950.05. bk rev. adv acc. Circ 60,200. Report accurately and fairly the affairs of Asia and her people in all spheres of activity and the world beyond Asia from an Asian perspective.

ATLANTEAN ERA. Dec. 1979-. 0225-5421. Periodical. CN. English. wk. $0.35 Per No. Atlantean Era, PO Box 1223, Belleville Ontario K8N 5E9 Canada. DD 051.

AUSTRALIAN AND NEW ZEALAND JOURNAL OF SOCIOLOGY. (THE AUSTRALIAN AND NEW ZEALAND JOURNAL OF SOCIOLOGY). VFOAT Journal of Sociology. V. 1- April 1965-. 0004-8690. Periodical. AT. English. ty. 42.25 Domestic, 53.75 Foreign. La Trobe University Bookshop, La Trobe University, Bundoora Victoria 3083 Australia. Tel 377-2740. Ind/Abst Sociol. Abstr., APAIS, Aust. Public Aff. Inf. Serv., Am. Hist. Life, Hist. Abstr., Part A, Mod. Hist. Abstr., Hist. Abst., Part B, Twent. Century Abstr., Psychol. Abstr., Soc. Welf. Soc. Plan./Policy Soc. Dev., Curr. Contents Behav. Soc. Educ. Sci., Soc. Sci. Citation Index, Bibliogr. Index, Lang. Lang. Behav. Abstr., Hist. Abstr. LC HM1. DD 301.05. NLM W1 AU498K. (cum index). Available on microfilm from Xerox University Microforms.

AUSTRALIAN JOURNAL OF CULTURAL STUDIES. Vol. 1, No. 1 (May 1983)-. 0810-9648. Periodical. English. sa. Western Australian Institute of Technology, School of English, Bentley WA 6102 Australia. Ind/Abst MLA Int. Bibliogr. Books Artic. Mod. Lang. Lit.

AUSTRALIAN SOCIAL WORK. V.24, No.3/4- Sept./Dec. 1971-. 0312-407X. Periodical. AT. English. qt. 40.00. Australian Association of Social Workers, Box 258, Civic Square, Canberra Australian Capital Territory 2600 Australia. Tel 062 473253. Ed Elizabeth Rabbitts. Ind/Abst Soc. Work Res. Abstr., APAIS, Aust. Public Aff. Inf. Serv., Abstr. Soc. Work. bk rev. adv acc. Circ 2,500. The theory and practice of social work. Australian Journal of Social Work, 0004-9565.

AUSTRALIAN SOCIETY. Vol. 1, No. 1 (1 Oct. 1982)-. 0729-8595. Periodical. English. ir. $30.00. David Scott/Australian Society, PO Box 274, Fitzroy Victoria 3065 Australia. LC HN841. DD 301.0994.

AWR BULLETIN. (A.W.R. BULLETIN). Main/Corp Association for the Study of the World Refugee Problem. V. 1- 1963-. 0001-2947. Periodical. AU. English (in French, German, and Italian). qt. 320.00. Braumuller Univers Buchhandl, Servitengasse 5, A 1092 Vienna Austria. Tel 02 22-34 81 24. Ed Wilhelm Braumuller. bk rev. adv acc. Circ 1,000. Quarterly on refugee problems.

BEHAVIOR & SOCIETY. VAT Behavior and Society. 0145-0034. US. English. wk. $84.00. National Technical Information Service, 5285 Port Royal Road, Springfield VA 22161. Tel (703)487-4650.

BEITRAGE ZUR GESCHICHTE DER FDJ. No. 1-. Periodical. German. ir. Wilhelm-Pieck-Universitat Rostock, DDR 25 Rostock Vogelsand 13/14, Rostock West Germany. LC HQ799.G5. DD 301.431506243.

BEITRAGE ZUR WISENSSOZIOLOGIE, BEITRAGE ZUR RELIGIONS-SOZIOLOGIE. Series/Titl Internationales Jahrbuch fur Wissens-Und Religions-Soziologie. VFOAT Beitrage zur Religions-Soziologie, Contributions to the Sociology of Knowledge, Contributions to the Sociology of Religion. English (French or German with summaries in English or German). ir. Westdeutscher Verlag, Postfach 5829, D 6200 Wiesbaden 1 West Germany. LC BD175. DD 301.21.

BERKELEY JOURNAL OF SOCIOLOGY. V. 5, No 1-. US. English. an. $12.00. University of California, 410 Barrows Hall, Department of Sociology, Berkeley CA 94720. Tel (415)642-2771. Ind/Abst Sociol. Abstr., Altern. Press Index, Lang. Lang. Behav. Abstr. bk rev. adv acc. Circ 1,100. Articles of a critical nature—whether critical of mainstream sociology or other forms of social control. Berkeley Publications in Society and Institutions.

BHARATA VARSHA. (THE BHARATA VARSHA). V. 1- April 1973-. 0304-9116. Periodical. II. English. qt. $4.00. Mr Ramahari Mishra Honorary Executive Director, Indian Institute for National Integration, Cuttack India. LC HN681. DD 309.15404.

BIBLIOGRAPHIES AND INDEXES IN SOCIOLOGY. See Indexes/Abstracts.

BIENNIAL REPORT OF THE SOCIAL SERVICE BOARD OF NORTH DAKOTA. Main/Corp North Dakota. Social Service Board. VFOAT Social Services in North Dakota. 1970/72-. 0094-1220. US. English. be. North Dakota Department of Human Services, Judicial Wing, State Capitol, Bismarck ND 58505. Tel (701)224-2310. Circ 600. (ctrl). Report describes function, evaluation, program inventory and cost analysis summary of the Department of Human Services.

BIORESEARCH TODAY. HUMAN ECOLOGY. VFOAT Human Ecology. 0149-0931. US. English. mo. $100.00. Bioscience Information Service, 2100 Arch Street, Philadelphia PA 19103. Tel (215)587-4800. Current awareness journal covering human ecology.

BLACK MALE/FEMALE RELATIONSHIPS. VAT Black Male Female Relationships. V. 1, No. 1 (June/July 1979)-. 0740-2163. Periodical. US. English. ir. $6.00. Black Think Tank Inc, 1801 Bush Street Suite 118, San Francisco CA 94105. Tel (415)929-0204. Ed Nathan Hare. bk rev. adv acc. Circ 3,000. Studies in black male/female relationships and how these are shaped by and interface with social, political and situational factors.

BLACK PULSE. Bulletin No. 1 (Aug. 1980)-. 0731-1192. US. English. National Urban League Research Department, 733-15th Street NW/Suite 1020, Washington DC 20005. LC E185.86. DD 305.896073073.

THE BLACK SOCIOLOGIST. 0160-3566. Periodical. US. English. qt. $10.00. Professor Howard Taylor, Department of Sociology, Princeton University, Princeton NJ 08540. Ind/Abst Sociol. Abstr., Soc. Welf. Soc. Plan./Policy Soc. Dev. LC HM1. DD 301.05.

BOLETIN INFORMATIVO - CENTRO DE INVESTIGACION PARA LA INTEGRACION SOCIAL. Main/Corp Centro de Investigacion Para la Integracion Social. No. 1-. MX. Spanish. ir. Centro de Investigacion Para la Integracion Social, Plaza del Carmen No 7, San Angel Mexico 20 DF Mexico.

BOLETIN URUGUAYO DE SOCIOLOGIA. V. 1- June 1961-. 0006-6508. Periodical. UY. Spanish. ir. Calle Juncal 1395, Piso 2 Escritorio 5, Montevideo Uruguay. Ind/Abst Sociol. Abstr., Lang. Lang. Behav. Abstr.

BOLGARSKII SOTSIOLOGICHESKII ZHURNAL. V. 1- 1978-. Periodical. UR. Russian. an. Khemus, Bulvar Russkii, 6, Sofiia Bulgaria. LC HM7.

BONNER BEITRAGE ZUR SOZIOLOGIE. Began publication with No. 1 in 1964. 0068-0044. Monographic Series. GW. German. ir. Ferdinand Enke Verlag, Postfach 1304, D7 Stuttgart 1 West Germany. Tel (0711)8931-0. Ed G Eisermann. LC HM15.

THE BRITISH JOURNAL OF SOCIOLOGY. Began with: Vol. 1 in March 1950. 0007-1315. Periodical. UK. English. qt. 27.50. Routledge & Kegan Paul Ltd, Broadway House/Newtown Road, Henley-Thames RG9 1EN England. Tel 0491578321. Ed Cohen (Rencys). Ind/Abst Am. Hist. Life, Hist. Abstr., Part A, Mod. Hist. Abstr., Hist. Abst., Part B, Twent. Century Abstr., Int. Labour Doc., Sociol. Abstr., Soc. Welf. Soc. Plan./Policy Soc. Dev., Index Med., Women Stud. Abstr., Soc. Work Res. Abstr., Psychol. Abstr., Soc. Sci. Index, Soc. Work Res. Abstr., Lang. Lang. Behav. Abstr., Soc. Sci. Citation Index, Soc. Sci. Index, Abstr. Soc. Work., Hist. Abstr., Recent Publ. Artic. LC HM1. DD 301.05. NLM W1 BR637D. (cum index). bk rev. adv acc. Circ 2,600. The leading British journal in its field, providing a medium for the publication of original papers in sociology and related subjects.

BUDGET PROPOSAL . . . AND PROGRESS REPORT. **Main/Corp** Integrated Rural Development Programme (Zambia). Northern Province. English. an. **LC** HN803.N67. **DD** 307.72096894.

BULGARIAN JOURNAL OF SOCIOLOGY. V. 1- 1978-. Periodical. BU. English. ir. $8.00. Hemus, Foreign Trade Company for Import and Export of Literature, Works Fine Arts and Culture, Sofia 6 Rousky Boulevard, Sophia Bulgaria. **LC** HM1. **DD** 301.094977.

BULLETIN SIGNALETIQUE. 521, SOCIOLOGIE, ETHNOLOGIE. **VFOAT** Sociologie, Ethnologie. Vol. 24, No. 1 (1970)-. Periodical. FR. French. qt. $54.28. Centre Documentation Science Humaines, 54 Boulevard Raspail, 75260 Paris Cedex 06 France. **Tel** 260.034. *Bulletin Signaletique. 521. Sociologie, Ethnologie, Prehistoire et Archeologie.*

BULLETIN SIGNALETIQUE. SECTION 521 : SOCIOLOGIE, ETHNOLOGIE. **VFOAT** Sociologie, Ethnologie. V. 23- 1969-. 0007-5566. Periodical. French. ir. **LC** Z1007. *Bulletin Signaletique. Section 19-24: Sciences Humaines.*

BULLETIN SOCIALE GEOGRAFIE ONTWIKKELINGSLANDEN; SERIE 2 (UTRECHT). **Main/Corp** Utrecht. Rijksuniversiteit. Geografisch Instituut. No. 1- March 1971-. Dutch. ir. Heidelberglaan 2, Utrecht Netherlands. **LC** HN980. **DD** 309.11724.

BUNKAGAKU NEMPO. **VFOAT** Annual Report of Cultural Studies. Began in 1950. French (Japanese). ir. 500. Doshisha Kaigaku Bunkagakkai, c/o Doshisha Daigaku Bungakubu Bunka Gakka Kenkyushitsu, Karasumaru Imadegawa, Kyoto Japan. **LC** AS552.D58.

CAHIERS DE CLIO. Began in 1965. 0575-0598. Periodical. BE. French. qt. Maggy Hodeige, rue Saint-Gilles 343 - Bte 054, B4000 Liege Belgium. **Ind/Abst** Am. Hist. Life, Hist. Abstr., Part A, Mod. Hist. Abstr., Hist. Abst., Part B, Twent. Century Abstr. **LC** AS241. **DD** 301.05.

LES CAHIERS DE LA CULTURE & DE L'ENVIRONNEMENT. **VFOAT** Cahiers de la Culture et de l'Environnement. No. 1 (Oct. 77!)-. 0154-2680. Periodical. FR. French. ir. Documentation Francaise, 124 rue Henri Barbusse, 93308 Aubervilliers Cedex France. **Tel** 834-9275.

LES CAHIERS DE LA WALLONIE ET DE BRUXELLES. Yearly V. 8, No. 37, (Oct. 1982)-. Periodical. BE. French. qt. 600.00. Groupe de Sociologie Wallonne, Universite Catholique de Louvain, 1 Place Montesquieu, 1348 Louvain-la-Neuve Belgium.

CAHIERS DES ETUDES RURALES. Periodical. French. ir. Walter de Gruyter Inc, 200 Sawmill River Road, Hawthorne NY 10532. **Tel** (914)747-0110.

CAHIERS D'ETUDE DE SOCIOLOGIE CULTURELLE. 1- 1971-. Periodical. FR. French. ir. Psychologie des Peuplos 56 rue Analole, 76600 Le Havre France.

CAHIERS INTERNATIONAUX DE SOCIOLOGIE. Vol. 1-. 0008-0276. Periodical. FR. French. sa. 180 Domestic, $20.00 Foreign. Presses Universitaires France, 12 rue Jean-de-Beauvais, 75005 Paris France. **Tel** (1)326-2216. **Ed** Georges Balandier. **Ind/Abst** Sociol. Abstr., Soc. Welf. Soc. Plan./Policy Soc. Dev., Point Repere, Soc. Sci. Citation Index, Lang. Lang. Behav. Abstr. **LC** HM3. **DD** 301.05. **NLM** W1 CA145. Applies a contemporary sociological orientation to various analyses of reality, including psychology, demography and ethnological studies. Also of interest to historians and geographers.

CALIFORNIA SOCIOLOGIST. V. 1- Winter 1978-. 0162-8712. Periodical. US. English. sa. $12.00. California State University at Los Angeles, 5151 State University Drive, Los Angeles CA 90032. **Tel** (213)224-3837. **Ed** Terry Kandal. **Ind/Abst** Sociol. Abstr., Soc. Welf. Soc. Plan./Policy Soc. Dev. **LC** HM1. **DD** 301.05. adv acc. **Circ** 200. A journal for sociologist and social workers. It publishes original research and theoretical articles. Special issues are published periodically.

CAMBRIDGE STUDIES IN ORAL AND LITERATE CULTURE. **VFOAT** Studies in Oral and Literate Culture. No. 1-. Monographic Series. UK. English. Cambridge University Press, 32 East 57th Street, New York NY 10022.

CAMBRIDGE STUDIES IN SOCIOLOGY. Vol. 1 1968-. Periodical. UK. English. ir. Cambridge University Press, 510 North Avenue, New Rochelle NY 10801.

CANADIAN JOURNAL OF POLITICAL AND SOCIAL THEORY. **VFOAT** Revue Canadienne de Theorie Politique et Sociale. Began with issue for Winter 1977. 0380-9420. Periodical. CN. English. ty. $28.00. Dr A Kroker, Corcordia University, Political Science Department/Room CH300-3, Montreal Quebec H4B 1M8 Canada. **Tel** 525-0501. **Ed** Arthur Kroker. **Ind/Abst** Sociol. Abstr., Soc. Welf. Soc. Plan./Policy Soc. Dev., ABC Pol Sci, Altern. Press Index, Can. Period. Index. **LC** JA4. **DD** 320.05. bk rev. adv acc. **Circ** 1,500. From its first issue in 1977, it has developed a reputation as a creative and highly original forum of political and social thought, "A window on the world" as one critic noted.

CANADIAN JOURNAL OF SOCIOLOGY. **VFOAT** Cahiers Canadiens de Sociologie. Began with issue for Spring 1975. 0318-6431. CN. English (includes abstracts in French). qt. 50.00. University of Alberta, Department of Sociology, Edmonton Alberta T6G 2E1 Canada. **Tel** 432-5941. **Ed** Richard Ericson and Nico Stehr. **Ind/Abst** Sociol. Abstr., Soc. Welf. Soc. Plan./Policy Soc. Dev., Soc. Sci. Citation Index, Lang. Lang. Behav. Abstr. **LC** HM1. **DD** 301.05. bk rev. adv acc. General sociology with one special issue per year devoted to more focused interest e.g. family or criminology. Emphasis on but not restricted to Canadian content.

CANADIAN MOSAICO. **VFOAT** Mosaico. Yearly V. 1- Nov. 1974. 0316-6988. CN. Multilingual (text in English and Italian). mo. Free (Italian Households in Canada.). Canadian Mosaico, Itcan Media Inc, 2400 Finch Avenue West, Weston Ont M9M 2C3 Canada. **DD** 301.45151071. (ctrl).

CANADIAN REVIEW OF SOCIOLOGY AND ANTHROPOLOGY. (THE CANADIAN REVIEW OF SOCIOLOGY AND ANTHROPOLOGY). **VFOAT** Revue Canadienne de Sociologie et d'Anthropologie. V. 1- Feb. 1964-. 0008-4948. Periodical. CN. English (some text and summaries in French). qt. 55.00. CSAA, Concordia University, 1455 Boulevard de Maisonneuve West, Montreal Quebec H3G 1M8 Canada. **Tel** (514)848-8980. **Ed** Peta Tancred-Sheriff. **Ind/Abst** Am. Hist. Life, Hist. Abstr., Part A, Mod. Hist. Abstr., Hist. Abst., Part B, Twent. Century Abstr., Sociol. Abstr., Soc. Welf. Soc. Plan./Policy Soc. Dev., Women Stud. Abstr., Can. Period. Index, ASTIS Bibliogr., ASTIS Curr. Aware. Bull., Soc. Sci. Index, Soc. Sci. Citation Index, Lang. Lang. Behav. Abstr., Hist. Abstr. **LC** GN1. **DD** 301.05. **NLM** W1 CA66. (cum index). bk rev. adv acc. **Circ** 1,800. Articles and book reviews.

CDS. CONSEIL DE DEVELOPPEMENT SOCIAL DU MONTREAL METROPOLITAIN. (LE CDS). **Main/Corp** Conseil de Developpement Social du Montreal Metropolitain. V. 1- April 1974-. 0316-5175. Periodical. CN. French. bm. $3.00. Le Conseil de Developpement Social du Montreal Metropolitain, 445 rue St-Francois-Xavier, Montreal Quebec H2Y 2T1 Canada. **DD** 309.1714281.

CHANGE. (CHANGE : NEWSLETTER OF THE NATIONAL SUPPORT CENTER FOR FAMILIES OF THE AGING). 1-. 0749-0194. Periodical. US. English. ir. National Support Center for Families of the Aging, PO Box 245, Swarthmore PA 19081.

CHARACTER II. **VFOAT** Character 2. **VAT** Character Two. Vol. 1, No. 1 (Jan./Feb. 1982). 0883-1718. Periodical. US. English. bm. $18.00. Character Incorporated, ARL Services Incorporated, PO Box 88, Posen IL 60469. **Tel** (312)597-0121. **Ed** Edward A Wynne. bk rev. **Circ** 4,500. A newsletter about the public and private policies affecting youth character. *Character, 0162-8933.*

CHASQUI. **VFOAT** Revista de Ciespal. Periodical. EC. Spanish. qt. $35.00. Ciespal, Apartado 584, Quito Ecuador. **Ind/Abst** MLA Int. Bibliogr. Books Artic. Mod. Lang. Lit. **LC** HM258. **DD** 301.14098.

CHINESE SOCIOLOGY AND ANTHROPOLOGY. V. 1- Fall 1968-. 0009-4625. Periodical. US. English (Chinese). qt. $70.00. M E Sharpe, 901 North Broadway, White Plains NY 10603. **Ind/Abst** Sociol. Abstr., Recent Publ. Artic., Curr. Contents, Soc. Behav. Sci., Curr. Contents Behav. Soc. Educ. Sci. **LC** HM1.

CHONGHWA. Periodical. KO. Korean. mo. Sahoe Chonghwa Wiwonhoe, 32-3 3-ka Namsan-dong, Chung-ku, Seoul South Korea. **LC** HN730.5.Z9.

CHOSON NONGMIN. Periodical. KO. Korean. ir. 7,000. Posongsa, 33-16 6-Ka Pomun-Dong, Songpuk-Ku Seoul Korea. **LC** HN730.5.

CHRONOS (WALTHAM, MASS.). (CHRONOS). No. 1 (Fall 1981)-. 0733-6470. US. English. an. $3.00. History Department, Brandeis University, Waltham MA 02254. **LC** HN1. **DD** 301.09.

CHUNG-HUA MIN KUO MIN I TSE YEN HUI PIEN. **VFOAT** Public Opinion in China. Chinese. ir. **LC** HM261.

CIVILISATIONS. V. 1- Jan. 1951-. 0009-8140. Periodical. BE. English (French). sa. 1000 Domestic, $20.00 Foreign. Universite Libre de Bruxelles, CP 124 Avenue Jeanne 44, B-1050 Brussels Belgium. **Tel** 02/649-00-30. **Ind/Abst** Am. Hist. Life, Hist. Abstr., Part A, Mod. Hist. Abstr., Hist. Abst., Part B, Twent. Century Abstr., ABC Pol Sci, Foreign Lang. Index, Public Aff. Inf. Serv. Bull., Hist. Abstr. **LC** AP1. **DD** 054. bk rev. adv acc. Non-western civilizations. Covers anthropology, ethnology, sociology, political science, economic problems.

CIVITAS; JAHRBUCH FUR SOZIALWISSENSCHAFTEN. *See* Yearbooks, Almanacs, Directories.

CLINICAL SOCIOLOGY REVIEW. Vol. 1 (1982)-. 0730-840X. Periodical. US. English. an. $22.50. Brunner/Mazel Inc, 19 Union Square West, New York NY 10003. **Tel** (212)924-3344. **Ed** David S Kallen. **Ind/Abst** Sociol. Abstr., Soc. Welf. Soc. Plan./Policy Soc. Dev., Psychol. Abstr. **LC** RC455. **DD** 616.8914. bk rev. adv acc. **Circ** 1,500. Theory and practice of the methods of clinical sociology.

COMENTARIO SOCIOLOGICO. **Main/Corp** Confederacion Espanola de Cajas de Ahorros. Direccion de Estudios Sociales. **VFOAT** Estructura Social de Espana. SP. Spanish. ir. Direccion de Estudios Sociales de la Confederation Espanola de Cajas de Ahorros, Alcala 27, Madrid 14 Spain. **LC** HN581. **DD** 946.08305. *Comentario Sociologico.*

COMMUNAL SOCIETIES. Vol. 1 (Autumn 1981)-. 0739-1250. Periodical. US. English. an. $15.00. Center for Communal Studies, Indiana State University at Evansville, Evansville IN 47712. **Tel** (812)464-1719. **Ed** Mario S DePillis. **Ind/Abst** Writ. Am. Hist. **LC** HX653. **DD** 335.973. bk rev. **Circ** 1,000. (ctrl). Interdisciplinary monographs and book reviews concerning historic and current communal societies worldwide.

COMMUNIQUE - INTERMET. **Main/Corp** Intermet. V. 1- Jan. 1970-. 0315-5900. Periodical. CN. English only, 1970-Jan. 1975. ir. $12. Intermet, Suite 1200/130 Bloor Street West, Toronto Ontario M4W 1A2 Canada. **DD** 301.364072. *Communique. Ed. Francaise, 0315-5919.*

COMMUNITY SERVICE BUSINESS. **VFOAT** CSB. Vol. 5, No. 1 (July 1984)-. 0747-6086. Periodical. US. English. mo. $30.00. MLP Enterprises, 236 East Durham Street, Philadelphia PA 19119. **DD** 361. *CBO Management Report, 0272-6300.*

COMPARATIVE SOCIAL RESEARCH. V. 2- 1979-. 0195-6310. US. English. ir. $49.50. JAI Press, PO Box 1678, Greenwich CT 06836. **Tel** (203)661-7602. **Ed** Richard F Tomasson. **Ind/Abst** Sociol. Abstr., Soc. Welf. Soc. Plan./Policy Soc. Dev. **LC** HM1. **DD** 301.05. **NLM** W1 CO437H. *Comparative Studies in Sociology, 0164-1247.*

COMPARATIVE URBAN RESEARCH. V. 1- Spring 1972-. 0090-3892. Periodical. US. English. ty. $25.00. Transaction Books Inc, Rutgers University, New Brunswick NJ 08903. **Tel** (201)932-2280. **Ed** William John Hanna. **Ind/Abst** Energy Inf. Abstr., Environ. Abstr., Avery Index Archit. Period., ABC Pol Sci. **LC** HT101. **DD** 301.36072. bk rev. adv acc. **Circ** 1,000. An international interdisciplinary journal of information and ideas on the comparative study of urban areas, urban systems, and urbanization throughout the world, with special emphasis on Third World urbanization.

COMPRENDRE. No. 1- 1950-. 0010-4418. Periodical. IT. French. ir. Societe Europeenne de Culture, San Marco 2516, I 30124 Venezia Italy. **Tel** 5230210. **Ed** Norberto Bobbio. **LC** AY832. bk rev. **Circ** 2,000. (ctrl). Theoretical and practical organ of politics of culture.

COMPUTERS IN HUMAN SERVICES. *See* Computers and Computer Science.

COMUNICACION. 1-. Periodical. Spanish. ir. $11.00. Centro de Comunicacion Social Jesus Maria Pellin, Apartado 20133, Caracas Venezuela. **LC** HM258. **DD** 301.14.

CONNECTIONS. (CONNECTIONS : BULLETIN OF THE INTERNATIONAL NETWORK FOR SOCIAL NETWORK ANALYSIS). Vol. 1, No. 1 (Summer 1977)-. 0226-1766. Periodical. CN. English. ty. $16.00. INSNA, c/o Structural Analysis Programme, Department of Sociology, University of Toronto, 563 Spadina Avenue, Toronto Ontario M5S 1A1 Canada. **Ind/Abst** Sociol. Abstr., Soc. Welf. Soc. Plan./Policy Soc. Dev. **DD** 302.072.

CONNEXIONS. V. 3, No. 5- Sept. 1978-. 0708-9422. Periodical. CN. English. qt. $23.21. 427 Bloor Street West, Toronto Ontario M5S 1X7 Canada. **Tel** (416)960-3903. **Ed** Ulli Diemer. **DD** 309.171064. bk rev. adv acc. **Circ** 1,100. (ctrl). Summarizes the work of social change organizations and publications to enable people facing common situations and problems to communicate with and learn from each other's ideas and experiences. *C I S S, 0708-9414.*

CONSOMMATION, REVUE DE SOCIO-ECONOMIE. No. 1 (Jan./March 1983)-. 0010-6593. Periodical. FR. French (summaries in English). qt. 390. DUNOD, Centrale des Revues, 11 rue Gossin, 92543 Montrouge Cedex France. **Tel** (1)43 20 15 50. **Ed** Catherine Blum-Girardeau. **Ind/Abst** Foreign Lang. Index, Index Econ. Artic. J. Collect. Vol. adv acc. **Circ** 1,200. Surveys on the living conditions of the French population - results of statistical, economic and sociological research.

CONSTRUCTIVE CITIZEN PARTICIPATION. V. 1- June 1973-. 0319-2385. Periodical. CN. English. qt. $11.61. Development Press, 5096 Catalina Terrace, Victoria British Columbia V8Y 2A5 Canada. **Tel** (604)658-1323. **Ed** Desmond M Connor. bk rev. **Circ** 200. Happenings in the field of citizen participation across Canada and the US through news items, book reviews, case materials and articles on rising issues and practical techniques.

CONTEMPORARY SOCIOLOGY. V. 1- Jan. 1972-. 0094-3061. Periodical. US. English. bm. $27.00. American Sociological Association, 1722 N Street NW, Washington DC 20036. **Tel** (202)833-3410. **Ed** Barbara Laslett. **Ind/Abst** Sociol. Abstr., Soc. Welf. Soc. Plan./Policy Soc. Dev., Women Stud. Abstr., Book Rev. Index, Ref. Source, Soc. Sci. Citation Index, Book Rev. Digest, Lang. Lang. Behav. Abstr. **LC** HM1. **DD** 30L.05. **NLM** Z 7164.S68 C761. bk rev. adv acc. **Circ** 9,000. Publishes reviews and critical discussions of recent works in sociology and related disciplines which merit the attention of sociologists. Selection reflects important issues and trends.

CONTRIBUTIONS IN SOCIOLOGY. Began in 1970. 0084-9278. Monographic Series. US. English. ir. Greenwood Press Inc, 88 Post Road West, Box 5007, Westport CT 06881. **Tel** (203)226-3571. **Ed** Don Martindale. **LC** UNC.

CONTRIBUTIONS TO HUMAN DEVELOPMENT. V. 1- 1974-. 0301-4193. Periodical. English. ir. S Karger AG, PO Box, CH-4009 Basel Switzerland. **Tel** 061-39 08 80. **Ed** J A Meacham. **Ind/Abst** Biol. Abstr., Psychol. Abstr. **NLM** W1 CO778S. **CODEN** CHDEDZ. This series features original articles concerned with behavioral growth and development in individuals throughout the life span. *Bibliotheca Vita Humana, 0523-4867.*

CONTRIBUTIONS TO INDIAN SOCIOLOGY. NEW SERIES. No. 1- Dec. 1967-. 0069-9667. Periodical. US. English. sa. Sage Publishing Inc, 275 South Beverly Drive, Beverly Hills CA 90212. **LC** HN681. **DD** 309.154. *Contributions to Indian Sociology.*

CONTRIBUTIONS TO THE STUDY OF POPULAR CULTURE. No. 1-. 0198-9871. Monographic Series. US. English. ir. Greenwood Press, 88 Post Road West, Westport CT 06881. **Tel** (203)226-3571. An interdisciplinary series which examines popular culture topics and theory throughout the world.

CRITICA. (CRITICA : A JOURNAL OF CRITICAL ESSAYS). Vol. 1, No. 1 (Spring 1984)-. 8755-3325. Periodical. US. English (text in Spanish). sa. $10.00. Chicano Studies, D-009 USCD, La Jolla CA 92093. **DD** 305.

CRITICA SOCIOLOGICA. (LA CRITICA SOCIOLOGICA). 1.- Spring 1967-. 0011-1546. Periodical. IT. Italian. ir. La Critica Sociologica, Via Appennini 42-00198, Roma Italy. **Ind/Abst** Sociol. Abstr., Soc. Welf. Soc. Plan./Policy Soc. Dev. **LC** HM7. **DD** 301.05.

CUADERNOS HISPANOAMERICANOS. Vol. 1 (Jan.-Feb. 1948)-. 0011-250X. Periodical. SP. Spanish. mo. $60.00. Institute de Cultura Hispanica, Avda Delos Reyes Catolicos, Madrid Spain. **Ind/Abst** Am. Hist. Life, Hist. Abstr., Part A, Mod. Hist. Abstr., Hist. Abst., Part B, Twent. Century Abstr., MLA Int. Bibliogr. Books Artic. Mod. Lang. Lit., Artbibliogr. Mod., Hist. Abstr., Recent Publ. Artic. **LC** AP63. **DD** 056. Index in last issue of volume - attached. (cum index).

CULTIC STUDIES JOURNAL. Vol. 1, No. 1 (May 84)-. 0748-6499. Periodical. US. English. sa. $10.00. American Family Foundation, PO Box 336, Weston MA 02193. **DD** 305. *Cultic Studies Newsletter.*

CULTURES CANADA : NEWSLETTER OF THE CANADIAN CONSULTATIVE COUNCIL ON MULTICULTURALISM. **VFOAT** Canada Multiculturel. Vol. 1, No. 1 (Jan. 1980)-. 0710-8559. Periodical. CN. English (French, inverted with respect to each other). ir. Multiculturalism Directorate, Secretary of State, Ottawa Ontario K1A 0M5 Canada.

CURRENT OPINION. V. 1- Aug. 1972-. 0090-824X. Periodical. US. English. mo. Roper Public Opinion Research Center/Williams College, PO Box 633, Williamstown MA 01267. **LC** HM261. **DD** 301.154205.

CURRENT PERSPECTIVES IN SOCIAL THEORY. Vol. 1 (1980)-. 0278-1204. Periodical. US. English. an. $49.50. JAI Press Inc, PO Box 1678 36 Sherwood Place, Greenwich CT 06836. **Tel** (203)661-7602. **Ed** Scott McNall. **Ind/Abst** Sociol. Abstr., Soc. Welf. Soc. Plan./Policy Soc. Dev. **LC** HM1. **DD** 301.018.

CURRENT RESEARCH IN SOCIAL SECURITY. **VFOAT** Recherches en Securite Sociale, Forschungen in der Sozialen Sicherheit, Investigaciones en la Seguridad Social. 1- 1978-. 0379-0290. Periodical. English (text in French, German and Spanish). sa. International Social Security Association, Casle Postal 1, CH-1211 Geneva 22 Switzerland. *Lists of Research Reports.*

CURRENT SOCIOLOGY. **VFOAT** Sociologie Contemporaine, La Sociologie Contemporaine. V. 1- 1952-. 0011-3921. Periodical. UK. English (French). ty. 43.00. Sage Publications Inc, 28 Banner Street, London EC1Y 8QE England. **Tel** (01)253-1516. **Ed** James A Beckford. **Ind/Abst** Curr. Contents, Sociol. Abstr., Int. Labour Doc., Public Aff. Inf. Serv. Bull., Soc. Sci. Index, ABC Pol Sci, Lang. Lang. Behav. Abstr., Soc. Sci. Citation Index. **LC** Z7161. **DD** 150.151. **NLM** W1 CU81N. bk rev. adv acc. Publishes new research in sociology and research methodology.

CURRENTS (TORONTO, ONT.). (CURRENTS). Vol. 1, No. 1 (Winter 1983)-. 0715-7045. Periodical. CN. English. qt. 15.00. 229 College Street/ Suite 302, Toronto Ontario M5G 1R4 Canada. **Tel** (416)598-0111. **Ed** Tim Rees. **DD** 305.800971. bk rev. adv acc. **Circ** 1,000. Contains readings in race relations. Analyses of research, initiatives, and ideas in race relations of particular interest to public, academic, and voluntary sectors.

CUSSNEWS. **Main/Corp** Canadian Institute of International Affairs. Advisory Committee on Canada-United States Studies. V. 1- Feb. 1974-. 0316-6791. CN. English. ty. $4.25. Canadian Institute of International Affairs, 31 Wellesley Street East, Toronto Ontario M4Y 1H1 Canada. **DD** 301.2971073.

DANISH DATA GUIDE UPDATE. 1982-. English. ir. DDA University of Odense, Campusvej 55, DK-5230 Odense M Denmark. **LC** HN543. **DD** 306.0720489.

DAVANTAGE. V. 1- May 1978-. 0705-7032. Periodical. CN. French. mo. 60. Per No. Club STEP International, 400 Route 2-20, Point-Claire Quebec H9S 3X7 Canada. **DD** 301.431509714.

DEPARTMENTAL WORKING PAPER - CARLETON UNIVERSITY. DEPARTMENT OF SOCIOLOGY AND ANTHROPOLOGY. *See* Anthropology.

DER VEKER. (DER VEKER : TSVEY HADOSHIM SHRIFT FUN YIDISHN SOTSYALISTISHN FARBAND). **VFOAT** Der Wecker. Began publication in 1921. 8750-8478. Periodical. US. Yiddish. bm. $10.00. Der Wecker, 45 East 33rd Street, New York NY 10016. **Tel** (212)686-1536. **Ed** Elias Sehulruan. **DD** 301. bk rev. **Circ** 1,000.

DIALOGO SOCIAL. No. 86-87 (Feb./March 1977)-. 0046-0206. Periodical. PN. Spanish. mo. $20.00. Centro de Capacitacion Social, Apartado 9A - 192, Panama R P Panama. **LC** HN1. **DD** 909.82. *DS: Dialogo Social.*

DIALOGUE ORIENTAL GAZETTE. **VAT** Dialogue Oriental. V. 1- Apr. 1974-. 0703-2145. Periodical. CN. English (French). ir. Centre de Culture Dialogue Oriental, Suite 5/5336 Queen Mary Road, Montreal Quebec H3K 1T8 Canada. **DD** 301.4511920714281.

DIGEST OF SELECTED REPORTS - UNITED WAY OF AMERICA. (DIGEST OF SELECTED REPORTS). **Main/Corp** United Way of America. Information Center. V. 2, No. 2- Oct. 1973-. 0146-9088. US. English. sa. $10.00. United Way of America, 701 North Fairfax Street, Alexandria VA 22314. **Tel** (703)836-7100. **Ed** Barbara L Owen. **LC** HV91. **DD** 361.973. **Circ** 2,500. Abstracts local United Way Organization reports in planning, allocations, research and social welfare. *Digest of Current Reports & Publications Catalog.*

DIRECTORY OF HEALTH, WELFARE AND RECREATION SERVICES FOR GREATER DALLAS. *See* Yearbooks, Almanacs, Directories.

DIRECTORY OF HEALTH, WELFARE, VOCATIONAL AND RECREATIONAL SERVICES IN LOS ANGELES CITY AND COUNTY. *See* Yearbooks, Almanacs, Directories.

DIRECTORY OF MEMBERS - AMERICAN SOCIOLOGICAL ASSOCIATION. *See* Yearbooks, Almanacs, Directories.

DIRECTORY OF SOCIAL SERVICES. OTTAWA-CARLETON. *See* Yearbooks, Almanacs, Directories.

THE DITCHLEY JOURNAL *CEASED.* V. 1-8, No. 1. 0305-4322. Periodical. UK. English. sa. $5.00. 39 East 51st Street, New York NY 10022. **Ind/Abst** Public Aff. Inf. Serv. Bull. **LC** HN1. **DD** 309.104.

DROIT DE PAROLE. V. 1- Sept. 1974-. 0315-9574. Periodical. CN. French. mo. Droit de Parole, 570 du Roi, Quebec Quebec G1K 2X4 Canada. **DD** 309.1714471.

ECONOMIES ET SOCIETES. *See* Economics.

ECOTROPIE. **Main/Corp** Auberge des Trois Soleils. 0710-8621. CN. French. an. Auberge des Trois Soleils, 39 Rang Jean-Baptiste, St-Urbain-De-Charlevoix Quebec G0A 4K0 Canada. **DD** 307.7740971449.

EDUCATION AND SOCIETY. *See* Education (General).

EMERGING PATTERNS OF WORK AND COMMUNICATIONS IN AN INFORMATION AGE. 0882-3316. Monographic Series. US. English. ir. Greenwood Press, 88 Past Road West, Westport CT 06881. **Tel** (203)226-3571. **LC** UNC.

EMERGING SOCIOLOGY. Vol. 1, No. 1 (Jan. 1979)-. Periodical. English. an. $6.00. Sociology Workers Sangam, 53 Mohanpuri Colony, Meerut 2500 01 India. **Ind/Abst** Sociol. Abstr., Soc. Welf. Soc. Plan./Policy Soc. Dev.

ENVIRONMENT AND BEHAVIOR. **VFOAT** EB. Environment and Behavior. V. 1- June 1969-. 0013-9165. Periodical. US. English. bm. Sage Publications, 275 South Beverly Drive, Beverly Hills CA 90212. **Ind/Abst** Electron. Commun. Abstr. J., ISMEC Bull., Pollut. Abstr. Indexes, Saf. Sci. Abstr. J., Life Sci. Collect., Can. Environ., Sociol. Abstr., Soc. Welf. Soc. Plan./Policy Soc. Dev., Excerpta Med., Energy Inf. Abstr., Environ. Abstr., Avery Index Archit. Period., Curr. Contents, Environ. Period. Bibliogr., Soc. Sci. Citation Index, Public Aff. Inf. Serv. Bull., Psychol. Abstr., Curr. Index J. Educ., Soc. Sci. Index, Energy Res. Abstr., Lang. Lang. Behav. Abstr. **LC** HM206. **DD** 301.3. **NLM** W1 EN98NK. **CODEN** EVBHAF.

ENVIRONMENTAL REVIEW. (ENVIRONMENTAL REVIEW : ER). **VFOAT** ER. No. 1-6, 1976-1978. 0147-2496. Periodical. US. English. qt. $63.00. Environmental Review, University of Denver, Department of Philosophy, Denver CO 80208-0195. **Tel** (503)754-3421. **Ed** William G Robbins. **Ind/Abst** Energy Inf. Abstr., Environ. Abstr., GeoRef, Am. Hist. Life, Hist. Abstr., Part A, Mod. Hist. Abstr., Hist. Abst., Part B, Twent. Century Abstr., Hist. Abstr. **LC** GF1. **DD** 301.3105. (cum index). bk rev. adv acc. **Circ** 500. (ctrl). An international journal that seeks understanding of human ecology through the perspectives of history and the humanities.

EPOCH. V. 1- Autumn 1972-. 0301-0643. Periodical. UK. English. qt. $3.07. Howey Foundation, 2 A Lebannon Road, Croydon Surrey CRO 6UR England. **LC** GF1. **DD** 301.3105. **NLM** W1 EP465.

ESTADISTICA DEL SUICIDIO EN ESPANA. *See* Statistics.

ETHNIC AND RACIAL STUDIES. *See* Ethnic.

ETHNIC GROUPS. V. 1- June 1976-. 0308-6860. Periodical. US. English. ir. $130.00. Gordon & Breach, PO Box 197, London WC2E 9PX England. **Tel** (01)836-5125. **Ed** A La Ruffa. **Ind/Abst** Am. Hist. Life, Hist. Abstr., Part A, Mod. Hist. Abstr., Hist. Abst., Part B, Twent. Century Abstr., Sociol. Abstr., Soc. Welf. Soc. Plan./Policy Soc. Dev., Soc. Sci. Index. **LC** GN495.4. **DD** 301.45105. bk rev. adv acc. *Afro-American Studies.*

EUROPEAN JOURNAL OF SOCIAL PSYCHOLOGY. V. 1- 1971-. 0046-2772. Periodical. UK. English (summaries in French, German, and occasionally Russian). qt. John Wiley & Sons Ltd, Baffins Lane, Chichester Sussex PO19 1UD England. **Ind/Abst** Sociol. Abstr., Psychol. Abstr., Soc. Sci. Citation Index, Lang. Lang. Behav. Abstr. **LC** HM251. **DD** 301.105. **NLM** W1 EU72EK. **CODEN** EJSPA6.

EVALUATION NEWS. No. 1- 197?-. Periodical. US. English. qt. $25.00. Evaluation Network, West Michigan University, Kalamazoo MI 49008. **Tel** (202)626-9240. **Ed** Barbara Davis.

EVALUATION REVIEW. V. 4- Feb. 1980-. 0193-841X. Periodical. US. English. bm. Sage Publications, 275 South Beverly Drive, Beverly Hills CA 90212. **Ind/Abst** Leg. Resour. Index, Sociol. Abstr., Soc. Welf. Soc. Plan./Policy Soc. Dev., Public Aff. Inf. Serv. Bull., Psychol. Abstr., Curr. Index J. Educ., Soc. Sci. Citation Index, Curr. Law Index. **LC** HM1. **DD** 300.72. **NLM** W1 EV131HC. *Evaluation Quarterly, 0145-4692.*

EXCERPTA BOTANICA. SECTIO B. SOCIOLOGICA. Vol. 1- 1959-. 0014-4045. Periodical. German, English or French. ir. $89.00. VCH Publishers Inc, 303 NW 12th Avenue, Deerfield Beach FL 33442. **Tel** (305)428-5566.

EXPLORATIONS IN SOCIOLOGY. No. 1- 1970-. Periodical. UK. English. ir. British Sociological Association, 10 Portugal Street, London WC2A 2HU England. **Tel** 0252 331551.

FABIAN TRACT. **Main/Corp** Fabian Society (Great Britain). No. 1- 1884-. 0307-7535. Monographic Series. UK. English. mo. $22.98. Fabian Society, 11 Dartmouth Street, London SW1H 9BN England. **Tel** 01-222-8877. **Ed** Pauline Bryan. **LC** HX11. **DD** 335.106242. (cum index). bk rev. adv acc. **Circ** 4,000. (ctrl). Social policy and general political theory and practice.

FACTS ABOUT TVA OPERATIONS. **Main/Corp** Tennessee Valley Authority. Periodical. US. English. ir. TVA, 400 Commerce Avenue, Knoxville TN 37902. **LC** HN79.A135.

FAIRSHARE. *See* Law.

FIGHT BACK. V. 1-. Periodical. US. English. mo. Revolutionary Student Brigade, PO Box A3423, Chicago IL 60690. **Tel** (312)252-5780.

FIRST READING. Vol. 1, No. 1 (Oct. 1982)-. 0824-197X. Periodical. CN. English. mo. Free. Edmonton Social Planning Council, No 418 10010-105th Street, Edmonton Alberta T5J 1C4 Canada. **Tel** (403)432-2031. **Ed** Joseph Miller. **DD** 361.61097123. bk rev. **Circ** 1,000. Analysis and discussion of social policy issues.

FOCUS - JOINT CENTER FOR POLITICAL STUDIES. *See* Ethnic.

FOCUS. UNEXPLORED DEVIANCE. (FOCUS : UNEXPLORED DEVIANCE). **VFOAT** Unexplored Deviance. 1st- Ed. 0160-9807. Periodical. US. English. be. Dushkin Publishing Group, Sluice Dock, Guilford CT 06437. **Tel** (203)453-4351. **LC** HM291. **DD** 301.62.

FOOTNOTES (WASHINGTON, D.C.). (FOOTNOTES). **VFOAT** Foot Notes. Began in 1973. Periodical. US. English. mo. $28.00. American Sociological Association, 1722 N Street Northwest, Washington DC 20036. **Tel** (202)833-3410. **Ed** William V d'Antonio. **Ind/Abst** Sociol. Abstr., Ref. Source. **LC** HM1. **DD** 301.05. adv acc. **Circ** 15,000. Professional work of sociologists and association business.

FREE INQUIRY IN CREATIVE SOCIOLOGY. V. 7- May 1979-. 0736-9182. Periodical. US. English. sa. $10.00 Domestic, $13.00 Foreign. Free Inquiry in Creative Sociology, University of Oklahoma, c/o Editor, Department of Sociology, Norman OK 73019. **Tel** (405)325-3482. **Ed** Marilyn Affleck. **Ind/Abst** Sociol. Abstr., Soc. Welf. Soc. Plan./Policy Soc. Dev. **LC** HM1. **DD** 301.05. **Circ** 450. Articles from all areas of sociology. Cross cultural studies and studies of timely and controversial social issues are welcome. A variety of viewpoints of interest to the lay reader included. *Free Inquiry, 0886-1749.*

FRENCH POLITICS AND SOCIETY. *See* Political Science.

FU NU SHENG HUO (CHENG-CHOU SHIH, CHINA). (FU NU SHENG HUO). **VFOAT** Funu Sheng Huo. Periodical. CC. Chinese. ir. 0.25. Post Office, Cheng-Chou China. **LC** AP95.C4. **DD** 305.40951.

FUTURIBLES (PARIS : 1981). (FUTURIBLES). No. 40 (Jan. 1981)-. 0337-307X. Periodical. FR. French. mo. $54.54. Association Internationale Futuribles, 55 rue de Varenne, 75007 Paris France. **Tel** 924 54 79/766 59 46. **Ind/Abst** Sociol. Abstr., Soc. Welf. Soc. Plan./Policy Soc. Dev., Int. Labour Doc., ABC Pol Sci, Foreign Lang. Index. *Futuribles 2000 i.e. Deux Mille, 0337-307X.*

GALLUP REPORT (PRINCETON, N.J. : 1981). (THE GALLUP REPORT). Report No. 185 (Feb. 1981)-. 0731-6143. Periodical. US. English. mo. $75.00. Gallup Poll, PO Box 628, Princeton NJ 08540. **Tel** (609)924-9600. **Ind/Abst** Public Aff. Inf. Serv. Bull., Predicasts. **LC** HM261.A1. **DD** 303.38. *Gallup Opinion Index, 0016-4194.*

THE GARTH ANALYSIS. Vol. 1, No. 1 (June 1982)-. 0745-6468. Periodical. US. English. bm. $295.00. The Garth Analysis, 1501 3rd Avenue, New York NY 10028. **LC** HN90.P8. **DD** 303.380973.

THE GERONTOLOGIST. V. 1- Mar. 1961-. 0016-9013. Periodical. US. English. bm. $45.00 Domestic, $55.00 Foreign. Gerontological Society, 1411 K Street NW/Suite 300, Washington DC 20005. **Tel** (202)393-1411. **Ed** Sheldon Tobin. **Ind/Abst** Life Sci. Collect., Hospit. Lit. Index, Excerpta Med., Cumul. Index Nurs. Allied Health Lit., Index Med., Women Stud. Abstr., Psychol. Abstr., Soc. Work Res. Abstr., Abstr. Soc. Work., Energy Res. Abstr., Soc. Sci. Index, Lang. Lang. Behav. Abstr., Soc. Sci. Citation Index, Sociol. Abstr., Curr. Index J. Educ. **LC** HQ1060. **DD** 305.2605. **NLM** W1 GE583. **CODEN** GRNTA3. bk rev. adv acc. **Circ** 9,771. (ctrl). Available on microfilm from University Microfilms. Practical and clinical aspects of management in medical and behavioral care of the aging population.

GHANA JOURNAL OF SOCIOLOGY. V. 1- 1965-. 0435-9380. Periodical. GH. English. sa. University of Ghana, Department of Sociology, Legon Ghana West Africa. **Ind/Abst** Sociol. Abstr., Lang. Lang. Behav. Abstr.

GOTTINGER ABHANDLUNGEN ZUR SOZIOLOGIE. V. 1- 1957-. 0072-4874. Monographic Series. GW. German. ir. Ferdinand Enke Verlag, Rudigerstr 14, Postfach 1304, 7000 Stuttgart 1 BRD West Germany. **Tel** (0711)8931-0. **Ed** H Plessner and H P Bahrdt.

GOUT DE VIVRE. (LE GOUT DE VIVRE). First issue in 1972. 0383-6738. Periodical. CN. French. mo. 5.00. Le Gout de Vivre, Claudette Paquin-Brown CP 58, Penetanguishene Ontario L0K 1P0 Canada. **Tel** (705)533-2400. **Ed** Claudette Paquin. **DD** 054.1. bk rev. adv acc. **Circ** 1,200. Newspaper representing the Franco-Ontarian community in all of its aspects, a minority group interested in cultural, social, traditional and education as well as political events.

GREEN REVOLUTION. 0017-3983. Periodical. US. English. qt. $12.00. Green Revolution School of Living, Route 7 Box 888, York PA 17402. **Tel** (717)755-2666. **Ed** George Yamada. **Ind/Abst** Altern. Press Index, Energy Inf. Abstr., Environ. Abstr., New Period. Index. **DD** 051. bk rev. **Circ** 1,200. Cooperative alternatives to the present economy, such as land trusts and local money systems. Decentralization of government and industry. Self reliant nutritional gardening and global peace plans.

GROUP & ORGANIZATION STUDIES. **VAT** Group and Organization Studies. V. 1- Mar. 1976-. 0364-1082. Periodical. US. English. qt. Sage Publications, 275 South Beverly Drive, Beverly Hills CA 90212. **Tel** (714)578-5900. **Ind/Abst** Manage. Contents, Sociol. Abstr., Soc. Welf. Soc. Plan./Policy Soc. Dev., Cumul. Index Nurs. Allied Health Lit., ABI/Inform, Curr. Index J. Educ., Psychol. Abstr. **LC** HM134. **CODEN** GOSTDA.

GUIDE TO DEPARTMENTS OF SOCIOLOGY, ANTHROPOLOGY, AND ARCHAEOLOGY IN UNIVERSITIES AND MUSEUMS IN CANADA. *See* Yearbooks, Almanacs, Directories.

GUIDE TO GRADUATE DEPARTMENTS OF SOCIOLOGY. **VFOAT** Graduate Departments of Sociology. 0091-7052. US. English. an. $10.00. American Sociological Association, 1722 North Street Northwest, Washington DC 20036. **Tel** (202)833-3410. **Ed** Karen Gray Edwards. **Circ** 2,200. Listing of 250 graduate departments of sociology. Includes information on special programs/specialties, faculty, financial aid, tuition, enrollment and degrees offered and awarded.

GUIDE TO THE LITERATURE OF SOCIAL CHANGE. V. 1-. 0161-4134. US. English. sa. Urban Information Interpreters, Box A-H, College Park MD 20740. **Tel** (301)864-7628. **Ed** M L Bundy. **LC** Z7164.S66, HM101. **DD** 016.3012405.

GURU NANAK JOURNAL OF SOCIOLOGY. Vol. 1, No. 1-2 (Apr.-Oct. 1980)-. Periodical. II. English. sa. 40 Domestic, $15.00. Guru Nanak Dev University, Sociology Department, Amritsar 143005 India. **Tel** 47785. **Ed** Jaspal Singh. **Ind/Abst** Sociol. Abstr., Soc. Welf. Soc. Plan./Policy Soc. Dev. **LC** HN681. bk rev. adv acc. **Circ** 500. Publishes articles on a broad range of topics in sociology.

GUYANA JOURNAL OF SOCIOLOGY. Periodical. English. ir. $5.00. **LC** HM1. **DD** 301.05.

HABARI KIJIJI. **VFOAT** Village News. 0700-8074. Periodical. CN. English. National Black Coalition of Canada, 8130 Place Vaujours, Ville d'Anjou, Montreal Quebec H1K 1H4 Canada. **DD** 301.45196071.

HANGUK SAHOE YONGU. 1 (1983, 6)-. Periodical. KO. Korean. ir. 4,000. Hangilsa 101-21 5-ka Anam-dong Songbuk-ku, Seoul 132 Korea. **LC** HN730.5.

HAN'GUK SAHOEHAK YON'GU. **VFOAT** Korean Sociological Review. V. 1- Series. Korean. ir. **LC** HM7.

HANSARD, OFFICIAL REPORT OF DEBATES - LEGISLATIVE ASSEMBLY OF ONTARIO. STANDING COMMITTEE ON SOCIAL DEVELOPMENT. (HANSARD, OFFICAL REPORT OF DEBATES). **Main/Corp** Ontario. Legislative Assembly. Standing Committee on Social Development. No. S-1 (May 16, 1983)-. 0822-126X. CN. English. tw. $15.00 Per Session. Sessional Subscription Service, Information Services Branch, Ministry of Government Services, 5th Floor/880 Bay Street, Toronto Ontario M7A 1N8 Canada. **LC** HN110.O5. **DD** 361.6109713. *Legislature of Ontario Debates, Official Report (Hansard).*

HAQQ. (AL-HAQQ). **VFOAT** Verite. **VAT** Truth (St-Leonard), Verite (St-Leonard). Ad. (Jan. 1983)-. 0821-3186. Periodical. CN. French (text in Arabic and English). mo. $15.00. Maison d'Edition la Verite, CP 395 Jean-Talon, Saint-Leonard Quebec H1S 2Z3 Canada. **DD** 305.89320714281.

THE HARRIS SURVEY YEARBOOK OF PUBLIC OPINION. *See* Yearbooks, Almanacs, Directories.

HDS TELEPHONE DIRECTORY. *See* Yearbooks, Almanacs, Directories.

HEIDELBERGER SOCIOLOGICA. 1- 1962-. 0073-1676. Monographic Series. GW. German. ir. JCB Mohr/Paul Siebeck, Postfach 2040, 7400 Tuebingen West Germany. **LC** HM15.

HISTOIRE ET SOCIOLOGIE DE LA CULTURE. 1- 1971-). Monographic Series. CN. French. ir. Presses de l'Universite Laval CP 2447/ Avenue de la Medecine, Ste-Foy Quebec G1K 7R4 Canada. **Tel** (418)656-5106.

HISTOIRE SOCIALE. **VFOAT** Social History. V. 1- April 1968-. 0018-2257. Periodical. CN. English (French). sa. $15.48. University of Ottawa Press, 603 Cumberland Avenue, Ottawa Ontario K1N 6N5 Canada. **Tel** (613)231-2270. **Ind/Abst** Am. Hist. Life, Hist. Abstr., Part A, Mod. Hist. Abstr., Hist. Abst., Part B, Twent. Century Abstr., Point Repere, Soc. Sci. Citation Index, Hist. Abstr. **LC** HN1.

HISTORICAL SOCIAL RESEARCH (QUANTUM (ASSOCIATION) : 1979). (HISTORICAL SOCIAL RESEARCH). **VFOAT** Historische Sozialforschung. No. 12 (Oct. 1979)-. 0172-6404. Periodical. GW. English (German). qt. Quantum Greinstrasse 2, D-5000 Koln 41 West Germany. **Ind/Abst** Am. Hist. Life, Hist. Abstr., Part A, Mod. Hist. Abstr., Hist. Abst., Part B, Twent. Century Abstr., Sociol. Abstr. **LC** HM1. **DD** 301.07.

Sociology: General Works, Theory

L'HOMME ET L'HUMANITE. Periodical. FR. French. ir. 40.00. F R H, 16250 N Banque Jordaan, 3 rue Saint-Georges, 75009 Paris France. LC CB197. DD 309.05. *Bulletin.*

HOMMES ET MIGRATIONS. DOCUMENTS. VFOAT Documents. 0018-4365. Periodical. FR. French. ir. Hommes et Migrations, 40 rue de la Duee, 75020 Paris France.

HOMO (TOULOUSE, FRANCE). (HOMO). Began with 1952/53 Vol. FR. French (summaries in English). an. 17.00. Universite de Toulouse-le Mirail, Service des Publications, 56 rue du Taur, 31000 Toulouse France. LC HM3. DD 301.05.

HOW. Periodical. II. English. ir. $25.00. Circulation Manager How, Post Box 653/Dr Rajendra Prasad Road, New Delhi 110001 India. LC HN690.Z9. DD 307.720954.

HUMAN COMMUNICATION RESEARCH. V. 1- Fall 1974-. 0360-3989. Periodical. US. English. qt. Sage Publications, 275 South Beverly Drive, Beverly Hills CA 90212. Tel (213)274-8003. Ind/Abst Sociol. Abstr., Soc. Welf. Soc. Plan./Policy Soc. Dev., Lang. Lang. Behav. Abstr., Film Lit. Index, Curr. Index J. Educ., Psychol. Abstr., Soc. Sci. Citation Index. LC P91.3. DD 301.21. NLM W1 HU445H.

HUMAN ECOLOGY. V. 1- Mar. 1972-. 0300-7839. Periodical. US. English. qt. $125.00 Domesitc, $140.00 Foreign. Plenum Press, 233 Spring Street, New York NY 10013. Tel (212)620-8000. Ed Susan H Lees and Daniel G Bates. Ind/Abst Electron. Commun. Abstr. J., Soc. Sci. Citation Index, Lang. Lang. Behav. Abstr., Eng. Index Energy Abstr., Life Sci. Collect., Sociol. Abstr., Soc. Welf. Soc. Plan./ Policy Soc. Dev., Energy Inf. Abstr., Environ. Abstr., Women Stud. Abstr., Recent Publ. Artic., Anthropol. Index, Biol. Abstr., Curr. Contents, Saf. Sci. Abstr. J., Eng. Index, Excerpta Med., Bibliogr. Agric., Energy Res. Abstr., Soc. Sci. Index. LC GF1. DD 301.3105. NLM W1 HU446DE. CODEN HMECAJ. bk rev. adv acc. Provides a forum for papers concerned with the varied systems of interaction between people and their environment.

HUMAN SERVICES MONOGRAPH SERIES. No. 1- 1976-. Monographic Series. US. English. ir. Project Share, PO Box 2309, Rockville MD 20852.

HUMANITAS (PRETORIA, SOUTH AFRICA) CEASED. (HUMANITAS). Began in 1971. 0046-8258. Periodical. SA. Afrikaans (English). qt. South African Human Sciences, Private Bag X41, Pretoria South Africa. Ind/Abst Sociol. Abstr., Soc. Welf. Soc. Plan./Policy Soc. Dev., Philos. Index, Lang. Lang. Behav. Abstr. *Journal for Social Research.*

HUMANITY & SOCIETY. VAT Humanity and Society. V. 1- Summer 1977-. 0160-5976. Periodical. US. English. qt. $28.00. Drew University, Department of Sociology, c/o Susan Mason, Madison NJ 07940. Tel (301)320-4034. Ind/Abst Sociol. Abstr., Soc. Welf. Soc. Plan./Policy Soc. Dev. LC HM1. DD 301.05.

IMAGE. V. 1- June 1972-. 0319-3012. Periodical. CN. English. mo. Image Publications, Rural Route 5, Fenwick Ontario L02 1C0 Canada. DD 301.43150971338.

IN REVIEW. VFOAT B M R in Review. Spring 1975-. 0700-3854. Periodical. CN. English. qt. Bureau of Municipal Research, 73 Richmond Street West, Toronto Ontario M5H 1Z4 Canada. Ind/Abst Libr. Inf. Sci. Abstr. DD 301.360710713.

INCHIESTA. Periodical. Italian. qt. 45.000. Edizioni Dedalo Spa, Casella Postale 362, 70100 Bari Italy. Tel (080)371025. bk rev. adv acc. Circ 14,000.

INDIAN JOURNAL OF COMPARATIVE SOCIOLOGY. V. 1- Aug. 1974-. Periodical. English. ir. 20.00. Forum for Sociologists, L S Ainapur Secretary Dhanvantri Building T C Road, Dharwar India. LC HM1. DD 301.05.

INDIAN RECORD. Began in 1957. 0019-6282. Periodical. CN. English. qt. 5.42. Indian Record, 480 Aulneau Street/Apartment 503, Winnipeg Manitoba R2H 2V2 Canada. Tel (204)233-6430. Ed Gontran Laviolette. bk rev. adv acc. Circ 2,100. Available on microfilm: Indian Record (Winnipeg), Toronto, Micromedia, 1977-. Political, cultural, religious, literary, and historical news; analysis and comment. Government for Canadian Indians and social workers, educators, and church personnel. *Indian Missionary Record, 0380-3910.*

INDIAN SOCIO-LEGAL JOURNAL. *See* Law.

INDICADORES SOCIAIS (SALVADOR, BRAZIL). (INDICADORES SOCIAIS). Began with 1977 V. 0102-1265. Portuguese. an. LC HN290.B3. DD 306.09814.

INDIKATOR KESEJAHTERAAN RAKYAT. VFOAT Welfare Indicators. 1979-. IO. English (Indonesian). an. $4.00. Bagian Statistik Tahunan dan Penerbitan, Biro Pusat Statistik JI Dr Sutoma No 8, PO Box 3, Jakarta Indonesia. Tel 372808. LC HN704. DD 305.09598. bk rev. adv acc. (ctrl). *Indikator Sosial.*

INDIKATOR SOSIAL. Main/Corp Indonesia. Biro Pusat Statistik. VFOAT Social Indicators. Began with Vol. for 1971. English and Indonesian. ir. Biro Pusat Statistik, JI Dr Sutomo No 8, Jakarta Indonesia. LC HN704.

INDO-KOREAN FRIENDSHIP. Periodical. II. English. ir. 0.60 Single Issue. All India Indo-Korean Friendship Association, Delhi-6 India. LC DS450.K7. DD 301.295193054.

INFORMATIVE BULLETIN (SAVEZNI ZAVOD ZA MEUNARODNU NAUCNU, PROSVJETNO-KULTURNU I TEHNICKU SARADNJU (YUGOSLAVIA)). (INFORMATIVE BULLETIN). English. ir. Federal Administration for International Scientific Educational/Cultural and Technical Cooperation, Belgrade Yugoslavia. LC DR1303. DD 303.482497.

INNSBRUCKER BEITRAGE ZUR KULTURWISSENSCHAFT. Vol. 1- 1953-. 0537-7250. Monographic Series. AU. German. ir. Institute fur Sprachwissenschaft, Universitat Innsbruck, Innsbruck Innrain 30 Austria. Ind/Abst Lang. Lang. Behav. Abstr., Sociol. Abstr.

THE INSURGENT SOCIOLOGIST. Began in 1971. 0047-0384. Periodical. US. English. qt. $20.00. University of Oregon, Department of Sociology, Eugene OR 97403. Tel (503)686-5039. Ed Al Szymanski. Ind/Abst Sociol. Abstr., Soc. Welf. Soc. Plan./Policy Soc. Dev., Altern. Press Index, Lang. Lang. Behav. Abstr. LC HM1. DD 301.05. bk rev. adv acc. Circ 1,000. Leading leftist journal of sociology with special interests in labor, socialism, race, imperialism, Marxist theory, women's struggles, third world, radical analysis, political economy.

INTERCONTINENTAL PRESS COMBINED WITH INPRECOR. *See* Political Science.

INTERNATIONAL CANADA CEASED. V. 1-13, No. 2. 0027-0512. Periodical. CN. English. mo. Canadian Institute of International Affairs, 31 Wellesley Street East, Toronto Ontario M4Y 1G9 Canada. LC F1029. DD 301.2971. *C.I.I.A. Monthly Report on Canadian External Relations, 0574-9492.*

INTERNATIONAL JOURNAL OF AGING & HUMAN DEVELOPMENT. (THE INTERNATIONAL JOURNAL OF AGING & HUMAN DEVELOPMENT). VAT International Journal of Aging and Human Development. V. 4- Winter 1973-. 0091-4150. Periodical. US. English. ir. $96.00. Baywood Publishing Company, 120 Marine Street/PO Box D, Farmingdale NY 11735. Tel (516)249-2464. Ed Robert T Kastenbaum. Ind/Abst Sociol. Abstr., Soc. Welf. Soc. Plan./Policy Soc. Dev., Excerpta Med., Cumul. Index Nurs. Allied Health Lit., Index Med., Biol. Abstr., Soc. Work Res. Abstr., Curr. Index J. Educ., Energy Res. Abstr., Soc. Sci. Index, Soc. Sci. Citation Index, Hospit. Lit. Index, Lang. Lang. Behav. Abstr., Psychol. Abstr., Abstr. Soc. Work. LC HQ1060. DD 301.43505. NLM W1 IN7652V. CODEN IJADDT. bk rev. Psychological and social studies of aging and the aged, with research that illuminates the human side of gerontology. *Aging & Human Development, 0002-0974.*

INTERNATIONAL JOURNAL OF COMPARATIVE SOCIOLOGY. Vol. 1 (Mar. 1960)-. 0020-7152. Periodical. NE. English. qt. E J Brill, PO Box 9000, 2300 PA Leiden The Netherlands. Ind/Abst Sociol. Abstr., Soc. Welf. Soc. Plan./Policy Soc. Dev., ABC Pol Sci, Soc. Sci. Index, Am. Hist. Life, Hist. Abstr., Hist. Abstr., Part A, Mod. Hist. Abstr., Hist. Abst., Part B, Twent. Century Abstr. NLM W1 IN766E. Focuses on problems of sociological documentation and analyses, specifically in a comparative perspective.

INTERNATIONAL JOURNAL OF CONTEMPORARY SOCIOLOGY. Began with Vol. 8 in 1971. 0019-6398. Periodical. US. English. qt. $25.00. International Journal of Contemporary Sociology, Rakesh Marq Pili Kothi Gt Road, Ghaziabad India. Ind/Abst Am. Hist. Life, Hist. Abstr., Part A, Mod. Hist. Abstr., Hist. Abst., Part B, Twent. Century Abstr., Sociol. Abstr., Soc. Welf. Soc. Plan./Policy Soc. Dev. *Indian Sociological Bulletin.*

INTERNATIONAL JOURNAL OF GROUP TENSIONS. V. 1- Jan./Mar. 1971-. 0047-0732. Periodical. US. English. qt. $28.00. International Organization for the Study of Group Tensions, 10 West 66th Street, New York NY 10023. Ind/Abst Psychol. Abstr. LC HN1. DD 301.6305. NLM W1 IN766R. CODEN IJGTB3.

THE INTERNATIONAL JOURNAL OF HUMAN RELATIONS. V. 1- 1976-. 0148-1169. Periodical. US. English. an. Human Relations Association, PO Box 2039, Norman OK 73069. LC HM1. DD 301.105.

INTERNATIONAL JOURNAL OF INTERCULTURAL RELATIONS. Periodical. US. English. ir. Pergamon Press, c/o Cashier, 395 Sawmill River Road, Elmsford NY 10523. Tel (914)592-7700. Ind/Abst Psychol. Abstr. 0147-1767.

INTERNATIONAL JOURNAL OF ORAL HISTORY. *See* History (General).

INTERNATIONAL JOURNAL OF SOCIOLOGY. V. 1- Spring 1971-. 0020-7659. Periodical. US. English. qt. $178.50. M E Sharpe Inc, 80 Business Park Drive, Armonk NY 10504. Tel (914)273-1800. Ed Patricia A Kolb. Ind/Abst Sociol. Abstr., Soc. Welf. Soc. Plan./Policy Soc. Dev., Public Aff. Inf. Serv. Bull., Lang. Lang. Behav. Abstr. LC HM1. DD 301.05. NLM W1 IN7889. adv acc. Circ 350. Translations of major studies in all areas of sociology from sources throughout the world. *Eastern European Studies in Sociology and Anthropology.*

INTERNATIONAL JOURNAL OF SOCIOLOGY AND SOCIAL POLICY. (THE INTERNATIONAL JOURNAL OF SOCIOLOGY AND SOCIAL POLICY). Vol. 1, No. 1-. 0144-333X. Periodical. UK. English. qt. MCB University Press Ltd, PO Box 10812, Birmingham AL 35202. Tel (205)991-6925. Ed Ron Pansler. Ind/Abst Sociol. Abstr., Soc. Welf. Soc. Plan./Policy Soc. Dev. LC HM1. DD 301.05. bk rev. adv acc. Publishes a wide variety of articles outlining the latest developments internationally within the fields of sociology and social policy. *Scottish Journal of Sociology, 0309-4006.*

INTERNATIONAL JOURNAL OF SOCIOLOGY OF THE FAMILY. Began with Mar. 1971 issue. 0020-7667. Periodical. US. English. sa. $7.50. Asia Books and Periodicals Company, 11 Darya Ganj, New Delhi 110002 India. Ed Mansingh Dass. Ind/Abst Sociol. Abstr., Soc. Welf. Soc. Plan./Policy Soc. Dev., Popul. Index. LC HQ1. DD 301.4205. NLM W1 IN789H.

INTERNATIONAL PROBLEMS. *See* Political Science - International Relations.

INTERNATIONAL REVIEW OF MODERN SOCIOLOGY. Began with Mar. 1972 issue. Periodical. II. English. sa. $14.00. Vikas Publishing House, 5 Ansari Road, New Delhi 110002 India. Ind/Abst Sociol. Abstr., Soc. Welf. Soc. Plan./ Policy Soc. Dev. LC HM1. DD 301.05. *International Review of Sociology.*

INTERNATIONAL REVIEW OF MODERN SOCIOLOGY. V. 2- 1972-. Periodical. II. English. sa. Asia Books and Periodicals Company, 11 Darya Ganj, New Delhi 110002 India. Ed Mansingh Dass. *International Review of Sociology.*

INTERNATIONAL STUDIES IN SOCIOLOGY AND SOCIAL ANTHROPOLOGY. V. 1- 1963-. 0074-8684. Monographic Series. NE. English. EJ Brill, POB 9000, 2300 PA Leiden The Netherlands.

INTERSECTIONS. 1974. 0095-6945. US. English. an. $3.00. Center Urban and Environmental Studies, Rensselaer Polytechnic Institute, Troy NY 12181. Tel (518)270-6565. Ed Robert Huneau. Ind/ Abst Avery Index Archit. Period. LC HC79.E5. DD 301.3105. Circ 500. Subjects related to any facet of urban or environmental related research, public policy, or historical analysis.

IRDP ANNUAL REPORT. Main/Corp Integrated Rural Development Programme (Zambia). VFOAT I.R.D.P. Annual Report. English. an. Ministry of Agriculture And Water Development, PO Box 50197, Lusaka Zambia. LC HN803.Z9. DD 307.72096894.

IRISH STUDIES. *See* Ethnic.

ISTMO. No. 1- Jan./Feb. 1959-. 0021-261X. Periodical. MX. Spanish. bm. $25.00. Editora de Revistas SA, Coya 73-102 Mizcoac, Mexico 19 DF

Mexico. **Tel** 563-19-63. **LC** AP63. (cum index). bk rev. adv acc. **Circ** 12,000. (ctrl). Journal for cultural information. Fundamentally structured by subject: philosopy, education, heads of companies complemented with studies and commentaries on sociology art and religion.

JAHRBUCH FUR SOZIOLOGIE UND SOZIALPOLITIK. *See* Yearbooks, Almanacs, Directories.

JAHRESBERICHT (INSTITUT FUR EMPIRISCHE SOZIOLOGIE EMPIRISCHE SOZIOLOGISCHE FORSCHUNG)). (JAHRESBERICHT). GW. German. an. Institut fur Empirische Soziologie, Marienstrasse 2/IV, 8500 Nurnberg 1 West Germany. LC HM5. **DD** 301.01.

THE JEWISH JOURNAL OF SOCIOLOGY. V. 1- Apr. 1959-. 0141-6534. Periodical. UK. English. sa. $18.00. Jewish Journal of Sociology, 187 Glouchester Place, London NW1 6BU England. **Tel** 262-8939. **Ed** Judith Freedman. **Ind/Abst** Sociol. Abstr., Soc. Welf. Soc. Plan./Policy Soc. Dev., Public Aff. Inf. Serv. Bull., Lang. Lang. Behav. Abstr., Soc. Sci. Citation Index, Recent Publ. Artic. **LC** DS101. bk rev. adv acc. Articles on Jewish social affairs, reviews of books on Judaism and on sociology, research notes, and a chronicle.

THE JEWISH SOCIAL WORK FORUM. V. 1- Fall 1963-. 0021-6712. US. English. an. $4.00. Jewish Social Work Forum, Yeshiva University, 55 5th Avenue, New York NY 10003. **Tel** (212)960-0841. **Ed** Norman Linzer. **Ind/Abst** Sociol. Abstr. **LC** HV3190. **DD** 362.84924. bk rev. adv acc. **Circ** 800. The focus is on issues pertaining to social work, social welfare, social work education, the organized Jewish community and Jewish communal service.

JIKKEN SHAKAI SHINRIGAKU KENKYU. VFOAT Japanese Journal of Experimental Social Psychology. 0387-7973. Periodical. Japanese (summaries in English). ir. Nihon Gurupu Dainamikkusu Gakkai, Nishinippon Shinbun Kaikan, 14-F Shudan Rikigaku Kenkyujo 4-ban 1-go Tenjin 1-chome Chuo-ku, Fukuoka-shi 810 Japan. **Ind/Abst** Psychol. Abstr. **LC** HM251.

JOURNAL FOR THE THEORY OF SOCIAL BEHAVIOUR. *See* Philosophy.

JOURNAL OF APPLIED SOCIAL PSYCHOLOGY. *See* Psychology.

JOURNAL OF APPLIED SOCIOLOGY - SOCIETY FOR APPLIED SOCIOLOGY (U.S.). (JOURNAL OF APPLIED SOCIOLOGY). Vol. 1, No. 1-. 0749-0232. Periodical. US. English. sa. $7.50. c/o J Miller Keystone, University Research Corporation, 434 West 8th Street, Erie 16502. **Tel** (814)453-4713. **Ed** Joyce Miller Iutcovich. **DD** 361. bk rev. adv acc. **Circ** 300. Articles on the application of sociological knowledge and methods, practice oriented articles, book reviews, works in progress.

JOURNAL OF BIOSOCIAL SCIENCE. V. 1- Jan. 1969-. 0021-9320. Periodical. UK. English. qt. 37 Domestic, $70.00 Foreign. Biochemical Society, PO Box 32/Commerce Way, Colchester C02 8HP England. **Tel** (0206) 46351. **Ed** D F Roberts. **Ind/Abst** Sociol. Abstr., Soc. Welf. Soc. Plan./Policy Soc. Dev., Excerpta Med., Energy Inf. Abstr., Environ. Abstr., Index Med., Women Stud. Abstr., Popul. Index, Sociol. Abstr., Chem. Abstr., Bibliogr. Agric., Psychol. Abstr., Lang. Lang. Behav. Abstr., Hospit. Lit. Index, Sci. Cit. Index, Abr. Ed., Soc. Sci. Citation Index, Recent Publ. Artic. **LC** HQ750.A1. **NLM** W1 JO568. **CODEN** JBSLAR. bk rev. adv acc. **Circ** 570. Contains original papers, lectures and reviews on social aspects of human biology and biosocial aspects of demography. Interdisciplinary material preferred. *Eugenics Review.*

THE JOURNAL OF COMMUNITY COMMUNICATION. *See* Communication.

THE JOURNAL OF COMPARATIVE CULTURES. V. 1- Fall 1972-. 0363-6666. Periodical. US. English. qt. $10.00. National Bilingual Education Association, 8332 Vista Bonita, Cypress CA 90630.

JOURNAL OF COMPARATIVE SOCIOLOGY AND RELIGION. VFOAT Bulletin de Sociologie et de Religion Comparees. Vol. 6 and 7 (1979 and 1980). 0709-3519. Periodical. CN. English (includes some text in French). an. $38.69. Canadian Sociological Research Center, PO Box 7305, Ottawa Ontario K1L 8E4 Canada. **Ed** A S Sethi. **LC** BL60. **DD** 306.6. bk rev. adv acc. Variety of sociological and religious issues including women issues, technological issues, religious differences and similarities, stress and related topics. *Journal of Comparative Sociology, 0382-5469.*

JOURNAL OF DEVELOPMENT STUDIES. *See* Economics.

JOURNAL OF EXPERIMENTAL SOCIAL PSYCHOLOGY. V. 1- Jan. 1965-. 0022-1031. Periodical. US. English. bm. Academic Press, 4805 Sand Lake Road, Orlando FL 32819. **Tel** (305)345-4100. **Ind/Abst** Sociol. Abstr., Women Stud. Abstr., Biol. Abstr., Psychol. Abstr., Soc. Sci. Index, Soc. Sci. Citation Index, Lang. Lang. Behav. Abstr. **LC** HM251. **DD** 301. **NLM** W1 JO644X. **CODEN** JESPAQ. Index in last issue of volume - attached.

THE JOURNAL OF FAMILY AND CULTURE. Vol. 1, No. 1 (Spring 1985)-. Periodical. US. English. qt. $10.00. **NLM** W1.

JOURNAL OF GERONTOLOGICAL SOCIAL WORK. V. 1- Fall 1978-. 0163-4372. Periodical. US. English. qt. Haworth Press, 28 East 22nd Street, New York NY 10010. **Tel** (212)228-2800. **Ed** Rose Dobrof. **Ind/Abst** Sociol. Abstr., Soc. Welf. Soc. Plan./Policy Soc. Dev., Excerpta Med., Cumul. Index Nurs. Allied Health Lit., Soc. Work Res. Abstr., Psychol. Abstr. **LC** HV1451. **DD** 362.60973. **NLM** W1 JO669NS. Index in last issue of volume - attached. bk rev. adv acc. **Circ** 2,051. The journal is devoted exclusively to social work practice, theory, administration, and consultation in the field of aging.

JOURNAL OF HEALTH AND HUMAN RESOURCES ADMINISTRATION. V. 1- Aug. 1978-. 0160-4198. Periodical. US. English. qt. $32.00. Journal of Health and Human Resources Administration, Department of Government, Auburn University at Montgomery, Montgomery AL 36193. **Tel** (205)271-9696. **Ed** Jack Rabin and Thomas Vacino. **Ind/Abst** Manage. Contents, Hospit. Lit. Index, Excerpta Med., Cumul. Index Nurs. Allied Health Lit. **LC** RA1. **DD** 362.105. **NLM** W1 JO6694H. bk rev. **Circ** 800. Focuses on administrative and policy issues faced by health and human service professionals and academics.

JOURNAL OF HEALTH AND SOCIAL BEHAVIOR. V. 8- Mar. 1967-. 0022-1465. Periodical. US. English. qt. $48.00 Domestic, $51.00 Foreign. American Sociological Association, 1722 North Street Northwest, Washington DC 20036. **Tel** (202)833-3410. **Ed** Eugene Gallagher. **Ind/Abst** Hospit. Lit. Index, Sociol. Abstr., Soc. Welf. Soc. Plan./Policy Soc. Dev., Excerpta Med., Cumul. Index Nurs. Allied Health Lit., Women Stud. Abstr., Soc. Work Res. Abstr., Biol. Abstr., Psychol. Abstr., Index Med., Soc. Sci. Index, Soc. Sci. Citation Index, Lang. Lang. Behav. Abstr. **NLM** W1 JO67BG. **CODEN** JHSBA5. adv acc. **Circ** 4,000. The publication reports of empirical studies, theoretical analyses and synthesizing reviews that employ a sociological perspective to clarify aspects of social life bearing on human health and illness, both physical and mental. *Journal of Health and Human Behavior, 0095-9006.*

JOURNAL OF INTERGROUP RELATIONS. V. 1- Fall 1970-. 0047-2492. Periodical. US. English. bm. $17.50. Michigan Department of Civil Rights, c/o Jeffrey Jenks, 1200 6th Street/7th Floor, Detroit MI 48226. **Tel** (313)256-2622. **Ed** Jeff Jenks and Mary Davidson. **Ind/Abst** Am. Hist. Life, Hist. Abstr., Part A, Mod. Hist. Abstr., Hist. Abst., Part B, Twent. Century Abstr., Curr. Index J. Educ. **DD** 305. **NLM** W1 JO716MA. bk rev. adv acc. **Circ** 600. Professional journal covering civil rights, race relations, women's issues, affirmative action, housing, law enforcement, and education. Twenty-sixth year of publication. *Journal of Intergroup Relations, 0047-2492.*

JOURNAL OF JEWISH COMMUNAL SERVICE. V. 32, No. 3- Spring 1956-. 0022-2089. Periodical. US. English. qt. $18.00. Conference of Jewish Communal Service, 111 Prospect Street, East Orange NJ 07017. **Tel** (201)676-6070. **Ed** Sanford N Sherman. **Ind/Abst** Ref. Source, Soc. Work Res. Abstr., Public Aff. Inf. Serv. Bull., Abstr. Soc. Work. **NLM** W1 JO732N. bk rev. adv acc. **Circ** 3,600. (ctrl). Covers professional trends and developments in all fields of Jewish communal service. *Jewish Social Service Quarterly.*

JOURNAL OF LAW AND SOCIETY. *See* Law.

THE JOURNAL OF MATHEMATICAL SOCIOLOGY. V. 1- Jan. 1971-. 0022-250X. Periodical. US. English. qt. $278.00. Gordon & Breach, PO Box 197, London WC2E 9PX England. **Ed** Patrick Doreian. **Ind/Abst** Sociol. Abstr., Math. Rev., Comput. Control Abstr., Electr. Electron. Abstr., Sci. Abstr. Sect. A. Phys. Abstr., Psychol. Abstr., Soc. Sci. Citation Index, Phys. Abstr., Lang. Lang. Behav. Abstr. **LC** HM1. **DD** 301.0151. bk rev. adv acc.

JOURNAL OF OCCUPATIONAL BEHAVIOUR. Began in Jan. 1980. 0142-2774. Periodical. UK. English. qt. John Wiley & Sons Ltd, Baffins Lane Chichester, Sussex PO19 1UD England. **Ind/Abst** Electron. Commun. Abstr. J., ISMEC Bull., Pollut. Abstr. Indexes, Saf. Sci. Abstr. J., Manage. Contents, Int. Labour Doc., Life Sci. Collect., Sociol. Abstr., Soc. Welf. Soc. Plan./Policy Soc. Dev., Psychol. Abstr., Soc. Sci. Citation Index. **LC** HD6951. **DD** 158.705. **NLM** W1 JO801R. **CODEN** JOBEDF.

JOURNAL OF OFFENDER COUNSELING, SERVICES & REHABILITATION. VAT Journal of Offender Counseling, Services and Rehabilitation. V. 4- Fall 1979-. 0195-6116. Periodical. US. English. qt. Haworth Press, 28 East 22nd Street, New York NY 10010. **Tel** (212)228-2800. **Ed** Sol Cheneles. **Ind/Abst** Sociol. Abstr., Soc. Welf. Soc. Plan./Policy Soc. Dev., Curr. Index J. Educ., Psychol. Abstr. **LC** HV9261. **DD** 365.66. **NLM** W1 JO802R. adv acc. **Circ** 505. The journal publishes scholarly articles relevant to rehabilitation research and programs. *Offender Rehabilitation, 0364-3093.*

THE JOURNAL OF PEASANT STUDIES. V. 1- Oct. 1973-. 0306-6150. Periodical. UK. English. qt. 55.00. Frank Cass & Company Ltd, 11 Gainsborough Road, London E11 1RS England. **Tel** (01)530-4226. **Ed** T J Byres and Henry Bernstein. **Ind/Abst** Am. Hist. Life, Hist. Abstr., Part A, Mod. Hist. Abstr., Hist. Abst., Part B, Twent. Century Abstr., Int. Labour Doc., Sociol. Abstr., Soc. Welf. Soc. Plan./Policy Soc. Dev., Public Aff. Inf. Serv. Bull., Soc. Sci. Citation Index, Recent Publ. Artic., Hist. Abstr. **LC** HD1513.A3. **DD** 301.444305. bk rev. adv acc. **Circ** 927. A multi-disciplinary journal which provides a forum for peasant studies, based on the premise that studies of the peasantries within the broader systems and historical situations is the only way to achieve a true understanding of the role of peasants.

JOURNAL OF SOCIAL AND PERSONAL RELATIONSHIPS. Vol. 1, No. 1 (Mar. 1984)-. 0265-4075. Periodical. UK. English. qt. 45.00. Sage Publications Inc, 28 Banner Street, London EC1Y 8QE England. **Tel** (01)253-1516. **Ed** Steve Duck. bk rev. adv acc.

THE JOURNAL OF SOCIAL ISSUES. V. 1- Feb. 1945-. 0022-4537. Periodical. US. English. qt. $95.00 Domestic, $107.00 Foreign. Plenum Publishing Corporation, Journals Order Department, 233 Spring Street, New York NY 10013. **Tel** (212)620-8000. **Ed** George Levnger. **Ind/Abst** Psychol. Abstr., Soc. Work Res. Abstr., Soc. Sci. Citation Index, Soc. Sci. Index, Sociol. Abstr., Am. Hist. Life, Hist. Abstr., Lang. Lang. Behav. Abstr., Hospit. Lit. Index, Women Stud. Abstr., ABC Pol Sci, Abstr. Soc. Work., ABC Pol Sci, Soc. Welf. Soc. Plan./Policy Soc. Dev., Public Aff. Inf. Serv. Bull., Curr. Index J. Educ. **LC** HN51. **DD** 305. **NLM** W1 JO88I. **CODEN** JSISAF. adv acc. This journal is sponsored by the SPSSI who all share a concern with research on the phychological aspects of important social issues. Seeks to bring theory and practice into focus on human problems.

JOURNAL OF SOCIAL STUDIES RESEARCH. V. 1- Winter 1977-. 0885-985X. Periodical. US. English. sa. $5.00. Journal of Social Studies, University of Georgia, 104 Dudley Hall, Athens GA 30602. **Tel** (404)542-7265. **Ind/Abst** Curr. Index J. Educ. **DD** 300.

THE JOURNAL OF SOCIOLOGICAL STUDIES. Vol. 1, No. 1 (Jan. 1982)-. Periodical. English. an. 25.00. Kirti Khanna, Department of Sociology, University of Jodhpur, Rajasthan India. **Tel** 22306. **Ed** Sheo Kumarlal. **LC** HN681. **DD** 301.05. bk rev. adv acc. **Circ** 100.

JOURNAL OF SOCIOLOGY. Main/Corp Case Western Reserve University. Began in 1967. 0069-0864. Periodical. US. English. an. Case Western Reserve University, Department of Sociology, University Circle, Cleveland OH 44106. **LC** HM1. **DD** 301.05.

JOURNAL OF SPORT AND SOCIAL ISSUES. V. 1-. 0193-7235. Periodical. US. English. ir. Institute of Sport and Social Analysis, 360 Huntington, c/o J Gebre-Medhin, Boston MA 02115. **Tel** (617)437-3148. **Ed** Jordan Gebre-Medhin. **Ind/Abst** Soc. Welf. Soc. Plan./Policy Soc. Dev., Leis. Recreat. Tour. Abstr., Phys. Educ. Index, Sociol.

Sociology: General Works, Theory

Abstr., Sociol. Leis. Sport Abstr. **LC** GV561. **DD** 796.05. bk rev. adv acc. **Circ** 500. Purpose is the study and research of impact of sport on society.

JOURNAL OF THE COMMUNITY DEVELOPMENT SOCIETY. Began in 1970. 0010-3829. Periodical. US. English. sa. $35.00. Community Development Society, c/o John D Rohrer, Ohio State University, 2120 Fyffe Road, Columbus OH 43210. **Tel** (614)422-8436. Ed Douglas C Bachtel. **Ind/Abst** Sociol. Abstr., Soc. Welf. Soc. Plan./Policy Soc. Dev., Curr. Index J. Educ., Soc. Work Res. Abstr. **LC** HN1. **DD** 301.3405. **Circ** 1,000. The official journal of the Community Development Society concerning the full range of social and economic issues for persons working and interested in community development.

THE JOURNAL OF THE DELTA SOCIETY. *See* Medicine.

THE JOURNAL OF THE HISTORY OF SOCIOLOGY CEASED. **VFOAT** JHS. Began with Vol. 1, Fall 1978 Ceased with Vol. 5, No. 1. 0190-2067. Periodical. US. English. sa. $16.50 Domestic, $18.00 Foreign. The Journal of the History of Sociology, 42 Englewood Avenue, Brookline MA 02146. **Ind/Abst** Sociol. Abstr., Writ. Am. Hist., Am. Hist. Life, Hist. Abstr., Part A, Mod. Hist. Abstr., Hist. Abst., Part B, Twent. Century Abstr. **LC** HM1. **DD** 301.09.

THE JOURNAL OF THE INSTITUTE FOR SOCIOECONOMIC STUDIES CEASED. **Main/Corp** Institute for Socioeconomic Studies. V. 1- Summer 1976-. 0364-0779. Periodical. US. English. qt. $15.00. Institute for Socioeconomic Studies, Airport Road, White Plains NY 10604. **Tel** (914)428-7400. Ed B A Rittersporn Jr. **Ind/Abst** Manage. Contents, ABI/Inform, Public Aff. Inf. Serv. Bull., Energy Res. Abstr. **LC** HV95. **DD** 362. **CODEN** JISSDW. **Circ** 17,500. Economic development, social motivation, poverty, urban regeneration, and the quality of life of the elderly.

JOURNAL OF THE INSTITUTE FOR THE NEW MAN. Vol. 1, No. 1- 0743-8532. Periodical. US. English. Institute for the New Man, PO Box 2919, Littleton CO 80161. **DD** 303.

JOURNAL OF VOLUNTARY ACTION RESEARCH. V. 1- Jan. 1972-. 0094-0607. Periodical. US. English. qt. $55.00. Association of Voluntary Action Scholars, S126 Human Development Building/Penn State University, University Park PA 16802. **Tel** (814)863-2944. Ed Jon Van Til. **Ind/Abst** Sociol. Abstr., Soc. Welf. Soc. Plan./Policy Soc. Dev., Soc. Sci. Citation Index. **LC** HV1. **DD** 361.7072. bk rev. adv acc. **Circ** 400. Professional and scholarly association for those concerned with better understanding of citizen involvement and volunteer participation.

JOURNAL OF YOUTH AND ADOLESCENCE. V. 1- Mar. 1972-. 0047-2891. Periodical. US. English. bm. $170.00 Domestic, $190.00 Foreign. Plenum Publishing Company, 233 Spring Street, New York NY 10013. **Tel** (212)620-8000. Ed Daniel Offer. **Ind/Abst** Soc. Welf. Soc. Plan./Policy Soc. Dev., Women Stud. Abstr., Biol. Abstr., Educ. Index, Except. Child Educ. Resour., Excerpta Med., Curr. Contents, Psychol. Abstr., Sage Urban Stud. Abstr., Sociol. Abstr., Abstr. Criminol. Penol., Curr. Index J. Educ., Lang. Lang. Behav. Abstr., Soc. Sci. Citation Index, Bibliogr. Index. **LC** HQ796. **DD** 301.43105. **NLM** W1 JO974G. **CODEN** JYADA. bk rev. adv acc. Provides a single high-level medium of communication for psychiatrists, psychologists, biologists, sociologists, educators and professionals who address themselves to the subject of youth and adolescence.

JPMS. JOURNAL OF THE POLITICAL & MILITARY SOCIOLOGY. (JPMS). **VFOAT** Journal of Political & Military Sociology. V. 1- Spring 1973-. 0047-2697. Periodical. US. English. sa. $8.50. Social Science Research Institute, Northern Illinois University, DeKalb IL 60115. **Ind/Abst** Sociol. Abstr., Public Aff. Inf. Serv. Bull., Int. Polit. Sci. Abstr., Soc. Sci. Citation Index, Hist. Abstr., Am. Hist. Life, Hist. Abstr., Part A, Mod. Hist. Abstr., Hist. Abst., Part B, Twent. Century Abstr., Soc. Welf. Soc. Plan./Policy Soc. Dev., Predicasts, ABC Pol Sci, Writ. Am. Hist., Recent Publ. Artic. **LC** HM1. **DD** 301.5905. Available on Microfilm from Xerox University Microfilms.

KAIHO NO HI O MOYASE. **Main/Conf** Buraku Kaiho Shogakusei Zenkoku Shukai. JA. Japanese. ir. 650. Buraku Kaiho Domei Chus Shuppankyoku, 1247 Kuboyoshicho Naniwa-ku, Osaka Japan. **LC** HT725.J3.

KALOS. *See* Sexual Life.

KATALOG BINA DESA. IO. Indonesian. ir. Sekretariat Pembinaan Sumber Daya Manusiawi Pedesaan, Jl Gunung Sahari III/7, Jakarta Pusat Indonesia. **LC** HN710.Z9.

KEEPING YOU POSTED CEASED. **Main/Corp** National Council of Jewish Women of Canada. **VFOAT** National Newsletter. Began publication 1977?. 0317-719X. Periodical. CN. English. Keeping You Posted, Apartment # 2/300 A Wilson Avenue, Downsview Ontario M3H 1S8 Canada. **DD** 301.451924.

KENKYUSHITSU IHO. **Main/Corp** Hokkaido Daigaku, Sapporo, Japan. Shakaigaku Kenkyushitsu. No. 1-. JA. Japanese. ir. Hokkaido Daigaku Bungakubu Shakaigaku Kenkyushitsu, Kita 10-jo, Nishi 7-chome, Kita-ku 060, Sapporo Japan. **LC** HM7.

KERALA SOCIOLOGIST. Periodical. English. ir. Kerala Sociological Society, c/o Department of Sociology, University of Kerala, Karyavattom Trivandrum 695581. **LC** HM1. **DD** 301.05.

KEY CEASED. (THE KEY). Began Publication in 1967?. 0381-968X. Periodical. CN. English. bm. $2. Per No. The Key Social Services, Box 68/Station L, Toronto Ontario M6E 4 Canada. **DD** 301.4105.

KIRISUTOKYO SHAKAI MONDAI KENKYU. **VFOAT** Study of Christianity and Social Problems. Began with Apr. 1958 issue. 0450-3139. Japanese. ir. **Ind/Abst** Am. Hist. Life, Hist. Abstr., Part A, Mod. Hist. Abstr., Hist. Abst., Part B, Twent. Century Abstr. **LC** HN30.

KNOWLEDGE AND SOCIETY: STUDIES IN THE SOCIOLOGY OF CULTURE PAST AND PRESENT. (KNOWLEDGE AND SOCIETY, STUDIES IN THE SOCIOLOGY OF CULTURE PAST AND PRESENT). Vol. 3 (1981)-. 0278-1557. US. English. an. JAI Press Inc, 165 West Putnam Avenue, Greenwich CT 06830. **Ind/Abst** Sociol. Abstr. **LC** BD175. **DD** 306.4. *Research in Sociology of Knowledge, Sciences and Art*, 0163-0180.

KOLNER BEITRAGE ZUR SOZIALFORSCHUNG UND ANGEWANDTEN SOZIOLOGIE CEASED. Vol. 1- 1966-. 0454-1286. Monographic Series. GW. German. ir. Anthenaum Verlag GMBH, Adelhidstrabe 2, 6240 Koningstein/TS West Germany. **Tel** 067 53/24 88.

KOLNER ZEITSCHRIFT FUR SOZIOLOGIE UND SOZIALPSYCHOLOGIE. Vol. 1-. 0023-2653. Periodical. GW. German. qt. 49.35. Westdeutscher Verlag Gmbh, Postfach 5829, D6200 Wiesbaden 1 West Germany. **Tel** (06121)5341. Ed Rene Konig. **Ind/Abst** Psychol. Abstr., Sociol. Abstr., Soc. Sci. Citation Index, Foreign Lang. Index, Philos. Index, Bibliogr. Index, Lang. Lang. Behav. Abstr. (cum index). bk rev. adv acc. **Circ** 3,400.

DIE KULTURPFLANZE : BERICHTE UND MITTEILUNGEN AUS DEM INSTITUT FUR KULTURPFLANZENFORSCHUNG DER DEUTSCHEN AKADEMIE DER WISSENSCHAFTEN ZU BERLIN IN GATERSLEBEN KRS. ASCHERLEBEN. BEIHEFT. 1-. 0454-6032. Monographic Series. GW. German (English). ir. Akademie-Verlag, Leipziger Str 3-4 PF 1233, DDR 1080 Berlin West Germany.

KUMTUKS REVIEW. 1974-. 0318-2894. Periodical. CN. English. an. University of Victoria British Columbia, Department of Anthropology, PO Box 1700, Victoria British Columbia V8W 2Y2 Canada. **DD** 301.205. *Journal of Student Papers in Anthropology and Sociology*, 0318-2886.

KUNGMIN SAENGHWAL SIGAN CHOSA. 1981-. KO. Korean. ir. 48.000. Hanguk Pansong Kongsa, 1 Youido-dong Yongdungpo-ku, Seoul 15 Korea. **LC** HN730.5.Z9.

KURUKSHETRA. V. 1- Aug. 1952-. 0023-5660. Periodical. II. English. sm. $14.78. Ministry of Information Broadcasting, Government of India, Patiala House, New Delhi 110001 India. **Ind/Abst** Sociol. Abstr., Lang. Lang. Behav. Abstr. **LC** HN681.

LAPORAN KEGIATAN DEPARTEMEN SOSIAL. **Main/Corp** Indonesia. Departemen Sosial. Indonesian. ir. Departemen Sosial R I, Jln Ir H Juanda No 36, Jakarta Indonesia. **LC** HN702.5.

LAPORAN KERJA UNIT SEKRETARIAT JENDERAL, DEPARTEMEN SOSIAL. **Main/Corp** Indonesia. Departemen Sosial. Sekretariat Jenderal. Indonesian. ir. Sekretariat Jenderal Departemen Sosial, Jlh Ir H Juanda No 3, Jakarta Indonesia. **LC** HN702.5.

THE LEAVES OF TWIN OAKS. V.1-. 0023-9836. Periodical. US. English. qt $6.00. Leaves of Twin Oaks, Rt 4 Box 169, Louisa VA 23093. **Tel** (703)894-2126. Ed Kat Kinkade. **Circ** 700. A newsletter describing events, ideas, issues and attitudes of the Twin Oaks community.

LEISURE NEWSLETTER. Began publication in 1973?. 0701-1334. Periodical. CN. English (French). G Pronovost, University of Quebec at Trois-Rivieres, PO Box 500, Trois-Rivieres Quebec G9A 5H7 Canada. **DD** 301.57072.

THE LEO M. FRANKLIN LECTURES IN HUMAN RELATIONS. **VFOAT** Franklin Memorial Lectures. 0459-0996. Monographic Series. US. English. ir. Wayne State University Press, 5959 Woodward Avenue, Detroit MI 48202.

LEVIATHAN. 1973-. 0340-0425. Periodical. GW. German. qt. 68.00. Westdeutscher Verlag GMBH, Postfach 5829, D6200 Wiesbaden 1 West Germany. **Tel** (06121)5341. **Ind/Abst** Energy Res. Abstr., Foreign Lang. Index. **LC** H5. **DD** 300.5. bk rev adv acc. **Circ** 2,000.

LEVNADSFORHALLANDEN ARSBOK. *See* Yearbooks, Almanacs, Directories.

LIGNE DIRECTE MILITANTE. V. 1- Feb. 1976-. 0701-0559. CN. French. ir. Centrale de l'Enseignement du Quebec, 2336 Chemin Ste-Foy, Quebec G1V 1S5 Canada. **DD** 301.41205.

LIVABILITY DIGEST. **VFOAT** Digest. Vol. 1, No. 1 (Fall 1981)-. 0278-9485. Periodical. US. English. qt. $15.00. Partners for Livable Places, 1429-21st Street North West, Washington DC 20036. **LC** HN90.C6. **DD** 307.140973.

LOSS, GRIEF & CARE. **VFOAT** Loss, Grief and Care. 8756-4610. Periodical. US. English. qt. Haworth Press Inc, 75 Griswold Street, Binghamton NY 13904.

LA LUZ. V. 1, No. 1- Apr. 1972-. Periodical. US. Spanish. mo. La Luz Publications Inc, 1000 Logan Street, Denver CO 80203. **LC** E184.S75. **DD** 301.45168073.

MA BERICHTSBAND. **Main/Corp** Arbeitsgemeinschaft Media-Analyse (Germany). **VAT** Media Analyse Berichtsband. 1972-. German. ir. **LC** HN460.M3. *Berichtsband - Arbeitsgemeinschaft Leseranalyse*.

MCFARLAND COMMUNITY LIFE. **VFOAT** Community Life. V. 1, No. 1 (Aug. 18, 1966)-. 0883-6566. Newspaper. US. English. wk. McFarland Community Life, 6041 Monona Drive, Monona WI 53716. Ed Peg Zaemisch. Available on microfilm from the State Historical Society of Wisconsin.

MAJALAH ILMU-ILMU SASTRA INDONESIA = INDONESIAN JOURNAL OF CULTURAL STUDIES. V. 1- April 1963-. 0541-721X. IO. chiefly in Indonesian with some articles in English. ir. $15.00. Mrs Haryati Soebadio, JL Kyai Maja 2A/Kebayoran Baru, Jakarta Selatan Indonesia.

MAN TO MAN. (MAN TO MAN : NEWSLETTER OF THE OTTAWA-HULL MEN'S FORUM). V. 1, No. 1 (Summer 1984)-. 0825-3498. Periodical. CN. English. ty. Free. Ottawa-Hull Men's Forum, PO Box 177 Station B, Ottawa Ontario Canada. **DD** 305.32. (ctrl).

MANAS. 0025-1976. US. English. Manas Publishing Company, PO Box 32112 El Sereno Station, Los Angeles CA 90032. **Ind/Abst** Psychol. Abstr. **CODEN** MJSPDT.

MANNHEIMER SOZIALWISSENSCHAFTLICHE STUDIEN. Vol. 1- 1970-). Monographic Series. GW. German. ir. Verlag Anton Hain Meisenheim, Postfach 1220, D-6240 Koenigstein/TS West Germany. **Tel** 06174/3021. Ed Hans Albert, Martin Irle, M M Rainer Lepsius, Erich Matthias, Wolfgang Hirsch-Weber, Hermann Weber, Rudolf Wildenmann, Wolfgang Zapf and Axel Rutters. adv acc. **Circ** 600. Studies in sociology.

MAZINGIRA. No. 1-. 0250-6858. Periodical. UK. English. qt. $25.00. UNIPUB, PO Box 1222, Ann Arbor MI 48106. **Tel** (313)761-4700. **Ind/Abst** GeoRef, Energy Res. Abstr., Excerpta Med., Energy Inf. Abstr., Environ. Abstr. **LC** GF1. **DD** 301.305. Available on microfilm.

MEDIA, CULTURE & SOCIETY. **VFOAT** Media, Culture, and Society. Vol. 1, No. 1 (Jan. 1979)-. 0163-4437. Periodical. UK. English. qt. 3.00.

Sociology: General Works, Theory

Sage Publications, 28 Bonner Street, London EC1 8QE England. **Tel** (01)253-1516. **Ed** Richard Collins and James Curran. **LC** HM258. **DD** 302.23405. bk rev. adv acc.

MEDIA WEST. V. 1- Mar. 1, 1980-. 0228-1554. Periodical. **CN.** English. bw. Pacific Rim Publications, 601-510 West Hastings Street, Vancouver British Columbia V6B 1L8 Canada. **DD** 302.2309712.

MEETING - INTER-AFRICAN CONFERENCE ON RURAL WELFARE. Main/Conf Inter-African Conference on Rural Welfare. First conference held in 1953. 0538-2793. English. ir. **LC** HN772.A1. **DD** 301.35.

MEMBERSHIP ROSTER - SOCIETY FOR HOSPITAL PLANNING (U.S.). (MEMBERSHIP ROSTER). **Main/Corp** Society for Hospital Planning (U.S.). Began with Dec. 1979. 0749-2405. US. English. an. The Society for Hospital Planning of the American Hospital Association, 840 North Lake Shore Drive, Chicago IL 60611. **DD** 362. **NLM** WX 22 AA1 S678M.

MEMO FROM PROBE. Began publication in May? 1976. 0708-0735. Periodical. **CN.** English. qt. Free. Pollution Probe-Ottawa, 53 Queen Street, Ottawa Ontario K1P 5C5 Canada. **DD** 301.3106271384. (ctrl). *Prober-O, 0319-2105.*

MENS EN MAATSCHAPPIJ. Began in 1947?. 0025-9454. Periodical. NE. Dutch. qt. Libresso BV, Postbus 878, 7400 AW Deventer Netherlands. **Ind/Abst** Sociol. Abstr., Soc. Welf. Soc. Plan./Policy Soc. Dev., Soc. Welf. Soc. Plan./Policy Soc. Dev., Recent Publ. Artic. *Mensch en Maatschappij.*

MICHI. V. 1- Spring 1978-. Periodical. JA. English (Japanese). ir. 1800. Yamaguchi Shoten, 72 Ichijoji Tsukidacho, Sakyo-ku 606, Kyoto Japan. **LC** HM258.

MID-AMERICAN REVIEW OF SOCIOLOGY. Vol. 1, No. 1 (Spring 1976)-. 0732-913X. Periodical. US. English. sa. $20.00. University of Kansas, Department of Sociology, Lawrence KS 66045. **Tel** (913)864-4111. **Ed** Robert John. **Ind/Abst** Sociol. Abstr., Soc. Welf. Soc. Plan./ Policy Soc. Dev., Soc. Sci. Citation Index. **LC** HM1. **DD** 301.05. **Circ** 400. Publishes articles on historical and contemporary issues in a wide range of subdisciplines within sociology. *Kansas Journal of Sociology, 0022-8648.*

MIN I TSA CHIH. **VFOAT** Public Opinion Review. Periodical. CH. Chinese. ir. Min i Tsa Chih She, Chin Shn Chieh Taipei Taiwan. **LC** HM261.

MONITORING TINGKAT PERKEMBANGAN DESA SWADAYA- SWAKARYA-SWASEMBADA DAERAH ISTIMEWA ACEH. Indonesian. an. **LC** HN710.Z9.

MONOGRAPH SERIES - WISCONSIN UNIVERSITY INSTITUTE FOR RESEARCH ON POVERTY. *See* Sociology: General Works, Theory - Social Pathology, Welfare, Criminology.

THE MOTHER EARTH NEWS. No. 1- Jan. 1970-. 0027-1535. Periodical. US. English. bm. Mother Earth News, PO Box 70, Hendersonville NC 28739, (subscription address: Communication Data Services 110 Tenth Street Des Moines IA 50309). **Tel** (704)693-0211 or (800)247-5470. **Ind/Abst** Pop. Mag. Rev., Energy Res. Abstr., Consum. Index Prod. Eval. Inf. Source, Read. Guide Period. Lit., Mag. Index, New Period. Index, Consum. Index Prod. Eval. Inf. Source. **LC** AP2. **DD** 051.

MULTICULTURALISM. V. 1- 1977-. 0701-2586. Periodical. **CN.** English. qt $7.74. University of Toronto, Guidance Centre, 1000 Yonge Street, Toronto Ontario M4W 2K8 Canada. **Tel** (416)978-3210. **Ind/Abst** Can. Educ. Index. **DD** 301.4510971.

NAPO NEWS. **VFOAT** Echo de l'Onap. **VAT** National Anti-Poverty Organization News, Echo de l'Organisation Nationale Anti-Pauvrete. No. 1 (Winter 1983)-. 0820-7364. Periodical. **CN.** English (French). qt. 10.00. National Anti-Poverty Organization, 456 Rideau Street, Ottawa Ontario K1N 5Z1 Canada. **Tel** (613)234-3332. **Ed** Patrick Johnston. **DD** 362.50971. **Circ** 1,000. (ctrl). Newsletter concerning issues of relevance to low income Canadians; includes national news and regional reports. *NAPO Info News, 0225-7130.*

NATIONAL BANG. (THE NATIONAL BANG). No. 1- Nov. 10, 1974-. 0316-5604. Periodical. **CN.** English. ir. 12.75. MIM Publications Group Ltd, PO Box 24 Snowdon Station, Montreal Quebec Canada. **DD** 301.417.

NATIONAL DIRECTORY OF PRIVATE SOCIAL AGENCIES. *See* Yearbooks, Almanacs, Directories.

NATIONAL MINORITY DIGEST. English. ir. **LC** E184.A1. **DD** 301.450973.

NATIONAL OPINION POLL. V. 1- Jan. 1978-. 0148-8449. Periodical. US. English. mo. $36.00. National Opinion Poll Corporation, 30 North San Pedro Road, San Rafael CA 94903. **LC** HN90.P8. **DD** 301.1540973.

NATIONAL VANGUARD. No. 59- April 1978-. Periodical. US. English. ir. $12.00. National Alliance, PO Box 3535, Washington DC 20007. **Tel** (703)979-1886. **Ed** William Pierce. bk rev. **Circ** 4,000. Also available on microfilm from the State Historical Society of Wisconsin. History, culture and mores of the European peoples, from a racial viewpoint; analysis and extrapolation of current social/political trends; exposition of radical alternatives.

NATURAL HAZARD RESEARCH. WORKING PAPER. (NATURAL HAZARD RESEARCH WORKING PAPER). No. 1-. 0082-5166. Monographic Series. US. English. ir. University of Colorado, Campus Box 482/IBS #6, Boulder CO 80309. **Tel** (303)492-6818. **Ed** Nathe and Butler. **Ind/Abst** GeoRef, Bibliogr. Index Geol. **LC** UNC. **Circ** 200. (ctrl). Research on natural hazards and human response.

NETHERLANDS JOURNAL OF SOCIOLOGY. (THE NETHERLANDS JOURNAL OF SOCIOLOGY). **VFOAT** Sociologia Neerlandica. Began in July 1976. 0038-0172. Periodical. NE. English. sa. 80,-. Van Gorcum and Company BV, PO Box 43, 9400 AA Assen Netherlands. **Tel** 05940-46846. **Ed** B Van Heerikhuizen. **Ind/Abst** Soc. Welf. Soc. Plan./Policy Soc. Dev., Bibliogr. Index, Sociol. Abstr., Sociol. Educ. Abstr., Curr. Contents, Soc. Sci. Citation Index, Recent Publ. Artic. **LC** HM1. **DD** 301.05. **NLM** W1 NE229P. adv acc. **Circ** 2,500. (ctrl). The journal primarily aims toward selected studies that have previously appeared in the Netherlands. *Sociologia Neerlandica.*

NEUVE-FRANCE. V. 4, No. 2- June 1979-. 0226-5362. Periodical. **CN.** French. qt. $25.00. Neuve-France Association Quebec-France, 9 Place Royale, Quebec Quebec G1K 4G2 Canada. **DD** 303.482. *Quebec-France, 0700-3951.*

NEW COMMUNITY. *See* Ethnic.

NEW DAWN. Began with April 1970 issue. Periodical. English. ir. New South Wales Department of Child Welfare and Social Welfare, Box K718/PO Haymarket, 2000 Sydney Australia. **LC** GN667.N5. **DD** 301.4519910944.

NEW DIRECTIONS. No. 15- Sept. 1976-. 0384-9147. Periodical. **CN.** English. mo. $10.00. New Directions, 1962 West 4th Avenue, Vancouver British Columbia V6J 1M5 Canada. **DD** 301.3105. *New Age Community, 0384-9139.*

NEW FRONTIERS. Summer 1974-. 0095-5248. Periodical. US. English. sa. $3.00 Single Issue. Council of Executive Directors, 105-14th Avenue, Seattle WA 98122. **LC** E185.5. **DD** 301.45196073.

NEW QUEST. No. 1- May 1977-. Periodical. II. English. bm. 10.00. New Quest, 850/8A Shivajinagar, Pune 411004 India. **Tel** 55744. **Ed** M P Rege, M V Namfoshi and M L Raina. **Ind/Abst** MLA Int. Bibliogr. Books Artic. Mod. Lang. Lit. **LC** AP8. **DD** 052. bk rev. adv acc. **Circ** 700. A journal of ideas and critical inquiry into social and political institutions. Also deals with philosophy and moral issues in human context. *Quest.*

NEWS - ALBERTA COUNCIL ON AGING CEASED. **Main/Corp** Alberta Council on Aging. Began publication in 1968? Ceased with V. 15, No. 10 Dec. 1983. 0383-7998. Periodical. **CN.** English. mo. Alberta Council on Aging, 360-10012 Jasper Avenue, Edmonton Alberta T5J 1R7 Canada. **DD** 301.435097123. *Horizons, 0018-4985.*

THE NEWS CIRCLE. *See* Ethnic.

NEWSBANK : WELFARE AND POVERTY. 1970-. Periodical. US. English. mo. **LC** HV91. (cum index).

NEWSLETTER - CANADIAN ASSOCIATION IN SUPPORT OF THE NATIVE PEOPLES CEASED. **Main/Corp** Canadian Association in Support of the Native Peoples. No. 1-19. 0319-7514. **CN.** English. Free. Canadian Association in Support of the Native Peoples, 251 Laurier Avenue West/Suite 901, Ottawa Ontario K2P 5J6 Canada. **DD** 301.45197071. (ctrl).

NEWSLETTER FOR AMERICAN- GERMAN CULTURAL STUDIES IN THE SOUTHEAST. No. 1 (Jan. 1983)-. US. English. an. Duke University, Center for International Studies, 2122 Campus Drive, Durham NC 27706. **Ed** L R Phelps.

NEWSLETTER - NATIONAL ASSOCIATION OF SOCIAL WORKERS. WASHINGTON STATE CHAPTER. (NEWSLETTER). **Main/Corp** National Association of Social Workers. Washington State Chapter. **VFOAT** NASW Newsletter, Washington State Chapter. 0745-3531. Periodical. US. English. qt. $15.00. National Association of Social Workers Inc, 7981 Eastern Avenue, Silver Spring MD 20910. **Tel** (301)565-0333. **Ed** Lucy Norman de Sanchez. adv acc. **Circ** 100,000. The official newspaper of NASW, is a compendium of current events in social work and related fields.

NEWSLETTER OF THE C A F. **Main/Corp** Canadian Arab Federation. 1976-. 0700-9798. Periodical. **CN.** English. Canadian Arab Federation, PO Box 416 Station K, Toronto Ontario M4P 2G8 Canada. **DD** 301.451927071005. *Arab Dawn, 0383-087X.*

NEWSLETTER - SOCIAL WORK ALUMNI ASSOCIATION, UNIVERSITY OF TORONTO. (NEWSLETTER). 0711-723X. Periodical. **CN.** English. ir. Free. Alumni House, University of Toronto, 47 Willcocks Street, Toronto Ontario M5S 1A1 Canada. **DD** 378.713541. (ctrl).

NEWSLINE. 0198-9316. Periodical. US. English. bm. Rural Sociological Society, Iowa State University, 318 East Hall, Ames IA 50011. **LC** HT401. **DD** 307.7205.

NICARAUAC : REVISTA BIMESTRAL DEL MINISTERIO DE CULTURA. **VFOAT** Revista Cultural Nicarauac. Yearly V. 1, No. 1, (May/June 1980)-. Periodical. NR. Spanish. Revista Nicarauac, Apartado 3269, Managua Nicaragua.

NIEUWE WEST-INDISCHE GIDS. Vol. 40- (July 1960)-. 0028-9930. Periodical. NE. Dutch (English). qt. 95.- Domestic, $37.50. Foris Publications, PO Box 509, 3300 AM The Netherlands. **Tel** (078)510454. **Ed** H Hoetink. **Ind/Abst** Am. Hist. Life, Hist. Abstr., Part A, Mod. Hist. Abstr., Hist. Abst., Part B, Twent. Century Abstr., Hist. Abstr. bk rev adv acc. Publishes articles and book reviews relating to the Caribbean region in the social sciences and humanities. *West-Indische Gids, Christoffel; Vox Guyane.*

NOGET OM SOCIALE FORHOLD, ADMINISTRATION OG POLITISKE INSTITUTIONER. Danish. an. Aalborg Universitetsforlag, Postbox 159, 9100 Aalborg Denmark. **LC** HN547.

NOI DONNE. Year 1- 1944-. Periodical. IT. Italian. wk. 87.000. Cooperative Libera Stampa, Via Trinita dei Pellegrini 12, 00186 Rome Italy. **Tel** 6564562-6564387. bk rev. adv acc. (ctrl). The world seen through social, political, sentimental, family problems, women's faces in Italy and in the world.

NONGOCHON KAEBAL = AFDC REVIEW. Periodical. Korean. ir. Nongochon Kaebal Kongsa, 13-8 Noryangjin-dong, Kwanak-ku, Seoul Korea. **LC** HN730.5.

NORTH AMERICAN CULTURE. Vol. 1 (1984)-. 0882-1968. Periodical. US. English. an. Department of Geography, Okland State University, Stillwater OK 74078. **DD** 306.

NOTORU DAMU SEISHIN JOSHI DAIGAKU KIYO : BUNKAGAKU HEN. **VFOAT** Notre Damu Seishin University Kiyo: Cultural Studies. V. 1- (Tsukan No. 12-). JA. Japanese (with summaries in English). ir. Notoru Damu Seishin Joshi Daigaku, 16-9 Ifukucho, 700 Okayama Japan. **LC** AS552.N6. **DD** 059.956. *Kiyo.*

NOUVELLES MONCHANIN CEASED. **VFOAT** Monchanin News Letter. **VAT** Nouvelles Monchanin (English Ed.). 0822-5583. Periodical. **CN.** English. qt. $3.00. Monchanin Crosscultural Center, 4917 St Urbain, Montreal Quebec H2T 2W1 Canada. **DD** 306.060714281.

NUOVO MONDO. Yearly V. 1- Nov. 1977-. 0705-7202. Periodical. **CN.** Italian. mo. $0.25 Per No. Nuovo Mondo Publisher Co, 2924A Dufferin Street, Toronto Ontario M6B 3S8 Canada. **DD** 301.45151071.

Sociology: General Works, Theory

OCCASIONAL PAPERS OF THE MCMASTER UNIVERSITY SOCIOLOGY OF WOMEN PROGRAMME. Main/Corp McMaster University. Sociology of Women Programme. V. 1. 0384-8841. Periodical. CN. English. ir. McMaster University, Department of Sociology, Kenneth Taylor Hall/Room 628, Hamilton Ontario L8N 4M4 Canada. DD 305.4'2.

ON TEACHING UNDERGRADUATE SOCIOLOGY, NEWSLETTER. VFOAT ASA on Teaching Undergraduate Sociology. -V. 4, No. 3 (Feb. 1979). Periodical. US. English. bm. $10.00. American Sociological Association, 1722 N Street NW, Washington DC 20036. Tel (202)833-3410.

ORAL HISTORY. 0143-0955. Periodical. UK. English. sa. University of Essex, Oral History Society, Sociology Department, Colchester CO4 3SQ England. Tel 862286. Ed Paul Thompson and Joanna Bornat. Ind/Abst MLA Int. Bibliogr. Books Artic. Mod. Lang. Lit. LC D16.14. DD 907.2. bk rev. adv acc. Circ 1,000. Provides regular news, reviews, guides to research important articles on wide-ranging topics.

ORGANIZACIJE I ZAJEDNICE. Began with Vol. for 1976. Serbo-Croatian. ir. 15.00. Savezni Zabod za Statistiku, Kneza Milosa BR 20, Beograd Yugoslavia.

OZS, OSTERREICHISCHE ZEITSCHRIFT FUR SOZIOLOGIE. VFOAT Osterreichische Zeitschrift fur Soziologie. 1976-. Periodical. German. ir. 300.00. Osterreichische Gesellschaft fur Soziologie, Postfach 2 Ogs, 1016 Wien Austria. Ind/Abst Sociol. Abstr., Soc. Welf. Soc. Plan./Policy Soc. Dev. LC HM5.

PACIFIC SOCIOLOGICAL REVIEW CEASED. V. 1-25. 0030-8919. Periodical. US. English. qt. $22.50. 275 South Beverly Drive, Beverly Hills CA 90212. Ind/Abst Sociol. Abstr., Soc. Welf. Soc. Plan./Policy Soc. Dev., Women Stud. Abstr. LC HM1. DD 301.05. NLM W1 PA208R. (cum index).

PAROLE + I.E. ET SOCIETE. VFOAT Parole et Societe. New Series, Yearly V. 80-. Periodical. FR. French. bm. $26.61. Parole & Societe, 49 rue de la Glaciere, 75013 Paris France. LC HN30. Christianisme Social, 0009-5737.

PEACEWORK (CAMBRIDGE, MASS.). See Political Science.

PEASANT STUDIES. See History (General).

PEOPLE AND COMMUNICATION. See Communication.

PERSONA Y DERECHO. V. 1- 1974-. SP. Spanish (English, French, German and Italian, with summaries in English or Spanish). an. $33.00. Ediciones Universidad de Navar, Apartado 396, 31080 Pamplona Spain. Tel (48)25 68 50. Ed Javier Hervada. Circ 250. Offers studies on a wide variety of topics dealing with the philosophy of law and contributions to the diffusion of human values in society.

PERSPECTIVA SOCIAL. 1- 1973-. Periodical. Catalan, French or Spanish. sa. 250. Institut Catolic d'Estudis Socials de Barcelona, Rivadeneyra 6, 3 ER Barcelona Spain. LC HN1. DD 309.1.

PERSPECTIVES CANADA. 3-. 0710-4669. CN. English. $9.50 Canada, $11.95 Other Countries. Printing and Publishing, Supply and Services Canada, Ottawa Ontario K1A 0S9 Canada. LC HN104. DD 301.0723, 309.173. Perspective Canada, 0710-4650.

PERSPECTIVES IN SOCIAL WORK. 0079-1040. Monographic Series. US. English. ir. Adelphi University, School of Social Work, Garden City NY 11530.

PHAT-TRIEN XA-HOI. So 1- April 9, 1971-. Periodical. VM. Vietnamese. qt. $4.50. Hoi Khoa Hoc Xa Hoi Viet Nam, 33 Dng Vinh Vien Chln, Saigon Vietnam. LC HN700.V5.

PHENOMENOLOGY AND THE HUMAN SCIENCES. 1981-. Periodical. US. English. an. LC HM1. DD 300.1. Annals of Phenomenological Sociology, 0363-647X.

PHILIPPINE BRIEFINGS. 1-. English. ir. Department of Public Information, Tuason Building Solana, Intramuros, Manila Philippines. LC HN711. DD 309.159904.

PHILIPPINE QUARTERLY OF CULTURE AND SOCIETY. VFOAT San Carlos Publications. V. 1- Mar. 1973-. 0115-0243. Periodical. PH. English. qt. $15.00. University of San Carlos, San Carlos Publications, Cebu City J217 Philippines. Tel 7-08-74. Ed Joseph Baumgartner. Ind/Abst MLA Int. Bibliogr. Books Artic. Mod. Lang. Lit., Writ. Am. Hist. LC DS651. DD 959.9005. bk rev. adv acc. Circ 360. All subjects throwing light on Philippine culture and society, both in the past and at present, with emphasis on cultural minorities. San Carlos Publications. Series E: Miscellaneous Contributions in the Humanities.

PHILIPPINE SOCIOLOGICAL REVIEW. Began with Aug. 1953 issue. 0031-7810. Periodical. PH. English. qt. $20.00. PSSC Central Subscription Service, PO Box 655, Greenhills, Metro Manila 3113 Philippines. Tel 922-9621. Ed Ricardo G Abad. Ind/Abst MLA Int. Bibliogr. Books Artic. Mod. Lang. Lit., Sociol. Abstr., Soc. Welf. Soc. Plan./Policy Soc. Dev., Lang. Lang. Behav. Abstr. LC HM1. (cum index). bk rev. adv acc. Circ 1,000. Publishes original studies and papers on sociology, anthropology, and demography.

PHILOSOPHY AND SOCIAL ACTION. V. 1- Jan. 1975-. 0377-2772. II. English. qt. $35.00. Institute of Socio-Political Dynamics, M-120 Greater Kailash 1, New Delhi 110048 India. Tel 641-5365. Ed Dhirendra Sharma. Ind/Abst Sociol. Abstr., Soc. Welf. Soc. Plan./Policy Soc. Dev., Philos. Index. LC HN681. DD 309.15405. bk rev. adv acc. Circ 1,000. Covers development science policy, Third World issues, human rights, and world peace.

PHILOSOPHY & SOCIAL CRITICISM. VFOAT Philosophy and Social Criticism. V. 5- Jan. 1978-. 0191-4537. Periodical. US. English. qt $46.00 Vol 1, $50.00 Vol 2. Philosophy & Social Criticism, Dept of Philosophy, Boston College, Chestnut Hill MA 02167. Tel (617)552-3860. Ed David M Rasmussen. Ind/Abst Sociol. Abstr., Soc. Welf. Soc. Plan./Policy Soc. Dev., Index Book Rev. Humanit., Philos. Index. LC AS30. DD 301. bk rev. adv acc. Circ 700. To foster a critical attitude in philosophy and politics, philosophy and social theory, socio-economic thought, critique of science, theory and praxis. Cultural Hermeneutics.

THE PINK SHEET ON THE LEFT CEASED. Issue 1-265. 0048-4180. Periodical. US. English. bw. $39.00. 8401 Connecticut Avenue, Washington DC 20015. LC HN90.R3. DD 322.420973.

PLANTATION SOCIETY IN THE AMERICAS. V. 1- Feb. 1979-. 0192-5059. Periodical. US. English. ty. Plantation Society in the Americas Department of History, University of New Orleans, New Orleans LA 70122. Ed T Fiehrer and M Lodwick. Ind/Abst Am. Hist. Life, Hist. Abstr., Part A, Mod. Hist. Abstr., Hist. Abst., Part B, Twent. Century Abstr. LC HN50. DD 909.09812.

PLURAL SOCIETIES. V. 1- 1970-. 0048-4482. Periodical. NE. English. ir. 90-. E J Brill, PO Box 9000, 2300 PA Leiden The Netherlands. Tel (071)312-624. Ed W A Veenhoven. Ind/Abst Am. Hist. Life, Hist. Abstr., ABC Pol Sci. LC HM73. DD 301.1. bk rev. adv acc. Circ 800. An independent international forum for scholarly discussion on the interaction between coexisting human communities. Includes case studies.

THE POLISH SOCIOLOGY OF LAW NEWSLETTER. See Law.

POLITICAL POWER AND SOCIAL THEORY. See Political Science.

POLITICS & SOCIETY. See Political Science.

PONTE. (IL PONTE). VFOAT Bridge. Vol. 1- Sept. 1973-. 0316-7232. CN. Italian and English. Il Ponte, 650 East Avenue Sheppard, Willowdale Ontario M2X 1B7 Canada. DD 301.451510713541.

PORTUGIESISCHE FORSCHUNGEN. Main/Corp Gorres Gesellschaft zur Pflege der Wissenschaft im Katholischen Deutschland. German. ir. Tel 0251/6901. Covers Portuguese culture and history. Also, can help to promote cultural relations between Portugal or Brazil and the German-speaking countries.

POVERTY IN TEXAS. Main/Corp Texas. Office of Economic Opportunity. 1972-. 0097-7950. US. English. an. Free. Office of Economic Opportunity, 611 South Congress Avenue, PO Box 13166 Capitol Station, Austin TX 78711. Tel (512)834-6217. Ed Deborah Amberson. LC HC107.T43. DD 301.441. Circ 1,100. (ctrl). Technical newsletter designed for nonprofits serving elderly, handicapped, and poor persons. Topic of main concern is poverty and related issues. Monitors state/federal regulations affecting the poor.

PREZENTACJE. No. 290- July 1978-. Periodical. PL. Polish. ir. Prasa-Ksiazka-Ruch, Centrala Kolportazu Prasy I Wydawnictw Ruch Warszawa, Ul Towarowa 28, Warszawa Poland. LC AS261. Zeszyty Teoretyczno-Polityczne.

PROBLEMS OF CULTURE. Began with Vol. for 1978. 0204-8620. Periodical. BU. English. ir. 4.20. Problems of Culture, 1000 Sofia, 4 Sofiiska Komuna Str PR, 1000 Sofia Bulgaria. Ed Elite Nicholov. LC HM101. DD 306. bk rev. Circ 5,000. Covers cultural problems and history, aesthetic training, education, management and social developments, arts and the mass media, creative personality problems, etc.

PROGRAM ON TECHNOLOGY, ENVIRONMENT AND MAN MONOGRAPH. (PROGRAM ON TECHNOLOGY, ENVIRONMENT, AND MAN). -Monograph #34. 0145-9961. Monographic Series. US. English. ir. Kate Preston, University of Colorado, Institute of Behavior, Boulder CO 80309. Tel (303)492-8147. Ind/Abst GeoRef. LC UNC.

PROGRAMMA DRASTERIOTETOS. Main/Corp Ethnikon Kentron Koinonikon Ereunon. VFOAT Program of Activities. summaries in English. ir. Sophokleous 1, Athens Greece. LC HM48.

PROGRESS IN APPLIED SOCIAL PSYCHOLOGY. Series/Titl Wiley Series on Progress in Applied Social Psychology. Vol. 1-. 0740-297X. UK. English. ir. John Wiley & Sons Inc, 1 Wiley Drive, Somerset NJ 08873. LC HM251. DD 302.

PROGRESS IN INTER-GROUP AND RACE RELATIONS. Main/Corp South Africa. Dept. of Information. SA. English. ir. Department of Information, Private Bag X152, Pretoria South Africa. LC DT763. DD 305.800968.

PROGRESS IN SOCIAL PSYCHOLOGY. See Psychology.

PROGRESS REPORT - NATIONAL URBAN LEAGUE. Main/Corp National Urban League. 0098-7735. US. English. National Urban League, 55 East 52nd Street, New York NY 10022. LC E185.5. DD 301.3606273.

PRZEGLAD SOCJOLOGICZNY. VFOAT Sociological Review. Began in 1930. 0033-2356. PL. Polish (summaries in English). an. Zakad Narodowy Im Ossolinskich We Wrocawiu, Krakowskie Przedmiescie 7, 00 068 Warsaw Poland. Ind/Abst Am. Hist. Life, Hist. Abstr., Part A, Mod. Hist. Abstr., Hist. Abst., Part B, Twent. Century Abstr., Sociol. Abstr., Soc. Welf. Soc. Plan./Policy Soc. Dev. LC HM7. DD 301.05.

PSYCHOLOGY & SOCIAL THEORY. See Psychology.

PSYCHOLOGY AND SOCIOLOGY OF SPORT. See Psychology.

PUBLIC OPINION. V. 1- March/Apr. 1978-. 0149-9157. Periodical. US. English. bm. $26.00. American Enterprise Institute, 1150 17th Street NW, Department 260, Washington DC 20036. Tel (202)862-5931. Ind/Abst Energy Res. Abstr., Infobank, Public Aff. Inf. Serv. Bull., Soc. Sci. Index. LC HN90.P8. DD 301.1540973.

PUBLIC OPINION QUARTERLY. V. 1- Jan. 1937-. 0033-362X. Periodical. US. English. qt. $20.00 Domestic, $23.00 Foreign. Elsevier Science Publishing Company, 52 Vanderbilt Avenue, New York NY 10017. Ed D C Poole. Ind/Abst Hospit. Lit. Index, Sociol. Abstr., Soc. Welf. Soc. Plan./Policy Soc. Dev., ABC Pol Sci, Account. Index, Appl. Suppl., ABI/Inform, Book Rev. Index, Public Aff. Inf. Serv. Bull., Soc. Sci. Index, Humanit. Index, U.S. Polit. Sci. Doc., Infobank, Psychol. Abstr. LC HM261.A1. DD 301.15. NLM W1 PU627. CODEN POPQAE. (cum index).

PUBLIC TECHNOLOGY. 0882-1445. Periodical. US. English. mo. $35.00. Public Technology Inc, 1301 Pennsylvania Avenue NW, Washington DC 20004. DD 303.

QUADERNI DI CULTURA FRANCESE. Vol. 1 1959-. 0481-097X. Monographic Series. IT. Italian. ir. Edizioni di Storia e Letteratura, Via Lancellotti 18, Rome Italy.

QUALITATIVE SOCIOLOGY. V. 1- May 1978-. 0162-0436. Periodical. US. English. qt. $38.00. Human Sciences Press, 72 Fifth Avenue, New York NY 10011. Ind/Abst Sociol. Abstr., Soc. Welf. Soc. Plan./Policy Soc. Dev. LC HM1. DD 301.05.

QUALITY & QUANTITY. VAT Quality and Quantity. V. 1- Jan. 1967-. 0033-5177. Periodical. NE. English (text in French). bm. $88.00. Kluwer Academic Publishers Group, Spui Boulevard 50, PO Box 989, 3300 AZ Dordrecht Netherlands. Tel

Sociology: General Works, Theory

(020)5803.911. **Ind/Abst** Sociol. Abstr., Soc. Welf. Soc. Plan./Policy Soc. Dev., Soc. Sci. Citation Index, Lang. Lang. Behav. Abstr. **LC** H61. **NLM** W1 QU158K.

QUARTERLY JOURNAL OF IDEOLOGY. (QUARTERLY JOURNAL OF IDEOLOGY : QJI). **VFOAT** Journal of Ideology. Began with Vol. 1, Fall 1976. 0738-9752. Periodical. US. English. qt. $12.00 Libraries, $9.00 Faculty, $5.00 Students. QJI Publications, 406 Greenwood Drive, Tahlequah OK 74464. **Ind/Abst** Sociol. Abstr., Soc. Welf. Soc. Plan./Policy Soc. Dev.

QUARTERLY OF THE CULTURAL TRIANGLE. Vol. 1 (Dec. 1983)-. Periodical. CE. English. qt. Central Cultural Fund Office, 212 Bauddhaloka Mawatha, Colombo Sri Lanka.

R N D. REVUE NOTRE DAME. *See* Religion, Mythology, Rationalism - Roman Catholic Church.

RACE RELATIONS SURVEY. Vol. 38 (1984)-. English. ir. South African Institute of Race Relations, PO Box 97, Johannesburg 2000 South Africa. **Tel** 724-4441. **Circ** 4,000. Segregation, population, economy, business, employment, labour relations, urbanization, housing, transport, homeland affairs, education, welfare, politics and international research. *Survey of Race Relations in South Africa.*

RACE TODAY. Began with Vol. 1, in May 1969. 0033-7358. Periodical. UK. English. bm. $5.50. Institute of Race Relations Research Publications II, Nelson Road, Greenwich London SE 10 England. **LC** HT1501. *News Letter.*

RAPPORT ANNUEL - CIPACC. (RAPPORT ANNUEL). **Main/Corp** Quebec (Province). Comite d'Implantation du Plan d'Action a l'Intention des Communautes Culturelles. 1981-1982-. 0715-9102. CN. French. an. Secretariat du CIPACC, 515 rue Sainte-Catherine Ouest Bureau 400, Montreal Quebec H3B 1B4 Canada.

RAPPORT NATIONAL DE CONJONCTURE SCIENTIFIQUE : SCIENCES DE L'HOMME. **Main/Corp** France. Centre National de la Recherche Scientifique. Comite National de la Recherche Scientifique. French. ir. 15 Quai Anatole, Paris France 75700. **LC** HM101. **DD** 301.2.

RAPPORTO SULLA SITUAZIONE SOCIALE DEL PAESE. **Main/Corp** Centro Studi Investimenti Sociali. Began in 1967. IT. Italian. an. $7.12. Franco Angeli, Viale Monza, 106 - 20127 Milano Italy. **LC** HN471.

RASSEGNA ITALIANA DI SOCIOLOGIA. Vol. 1- Jan./Mar. 1960-. 0079-9734. Periodical. IT. Italian. qt. 100.000 Domestic, 130.000 Foreign. Societa Editrice Il Mulino Spa, Via Santo Stefano 6, 40125 Bologna Italy. **Tel** (051)23 34 15. **Ind/Abst** Lang. Lang. Behav. Abstr., Hist. Abstr., Am. Hist. Life, Sociol. Abstr., Psychol. Abstr.

RASY I NARODY. 1.- 1971-. UR. Russian (table of contents also in English). an. **LC** HT1521.

RECHERCHE SOCIALE. No. 1- Sept./Oct. 1965-. 0034-124X. Periodical. FR. French summaries in French and (English). qt. 170 Domestic, 200 Foreign. Foundation pour Recherche Sociale, 14 rue Saint Benoit, Paris 6E France. **Ind/Abst** Am. Hist. Life, Hist. Abstr., Part A, Mod. Hist. Abstr., Hist. Abst., Part B, Twent. Century Abstr., ABC Pol Sci, Foreign Lang. Index, Hist. Abstr., PAIS Foreign Lang. Index. Especially directed to students and teachers in higher education as well as social workers. Addresses problems of economic development and changes of lifestyles in the modern society. *Etudes et Documents.*

RECHERCHES SOCIOGRAPHIQUES. V. 1- 1960-. 0034-1282. Periodical. CN. French. ir. Universite Laval, Faculte des Sciences Sociales, Quebec Quebec G1K 7P4 Canada. **Tel** (418)656-2438. **Ind/Abst** Sociol. Abstr., Point Repere, Am. Hist. Life, Foreign Lang. Index, Int. Labour Doc., Soc. Welf. Soc. Plan./Policy Soc. Dev., Lang. Lang. Behav. Abstr., Hist. Abstr., Part A, Mod. Hist. Abstr., Hist. Abstr., Hist. Abst., Part B, Twent. Century Abstr. (ctrl). Includes research in sociology, articles on the society of Quebec-crossroads of human sciences, research, monographs, critical essays, and balances.

RECHERCHES SOCIOLOGIQUES. V. 1- June 1970-. 0303-9625. Periodical. BE. French. ir. 900 Domestic, $17.00. Centre Recherches Sociologique, Place Montesquieu One Box 70, 1348 Louvain la Neuve Belgium. **Tel** 010/434204. **Ind/Abst** Am. Hist. Life, Hist. Abstr., Part A, Mod. Hist. Abstr., Hist. Abst. Part B, Twent. Century Abstr., Sociol. Abstr., Soc. Welf. Soc. Plan./Policy Soc. Dev., Foreign Lang. Index, Lang. Lang. Behav. Abstr., PAIS Foreign Lang. Index, Hist. Abstr. **LC** HM3. **DD** 301.05. adv acc. **Circ** 300. (ctrl). Orientations and problems of the Actual Society, education, ethnicity, and migrants' life, individualism, new ways of living, job sharing, family everyday life, and methodology.

REGIONAL JOURNAL OF SOCIAL ISSUES. 1977. 0158-7102. Periodical. AT. English. ir. Warrnambook Institute of Advanced Education, PO Box 423, Warrnambook Victoria 3280 Australia. **Tel** 055/640111. **Ind/Abst** APAIS, Aust. Public Aff. Inf. Serv. adv acc. **Circ** 250. Social issues arising in Australian society. Focuses on regional questions from multidisciplinary perspectives.

REGIONAL PROFILES. **Main/Corp** Massachusetts. Dept. of Community Affairs. Bureau of Regional Planning. 0362-3718. US. English. an. Department of Community Affairs/Bureau of Regional Planning, 141 Milk Street, Boston MA 02109. **LC** HT393.M4. **DD** 309.2509744.

REGISTRY OF MEMBERS - CLINICAL SOCIOLOGY ASSOCIATION. (REGISTRY OF MEMBERS : A BIENNIAL PUBLICATION OF THE CLINICAL SOCIOLOGY ASSOCIATION). **Main/Corp** Clinical Sociology Association. **VFOAT** CSA Registry. 1st ed. (1981)-. 0733-0251. US. English. be. $5.00. John Glass, 4242 Wilkinson Avenue, Studio City CA 91604. **Tel** (914)469-4187. **Ed** Elizabeth T Clark. **LC** HM9.C54. **DD** 301.0601. bk rev. adv acc. **Circ** 600. (ctrl). Directory of the National Clinical Sociology Association. Listing of 500 clinical sociologists by alphabetical, geograhic area, specialty areas.

REKAMAN PERISTIWA . . . . '82-. Indonesian. an. Penerbit Sinar Harapan, JL Dewi Sartika 136D Cawang, Jakarta Timur Indonesia. **Tel** 803208. **Ed** Umar Nur Zain and Apul D Maharaja. **LC** AP95.I5. adv acc. **Circ** 10,000. (ctrl). Chronological notes and details on affairs during the year.

RELATORIO - BAHIA (BRAZIL). SECRETARIO DE TRABALHO E BEW ESTAR SOCIAL. **Main/Corp** Bahia (Brazil : State). Secretaria do Trabalho e Bem Estar Social. Portuguese. ir. **LC** HN290.B3. **DD** 361.610981.

REPORT OF THE ECONOMIC AND SOCIAL COUNCIL (UNITED NATIONS). *See* Economics.

REPORT ON COMMUNITY DEVELOPMENT WEEK. **Main/Corp** India (Republic). Dept. of Community Development. 1970-. II. English. ir. Government of India Press, Simla India. **LC** HN690.Z9. **DD** 309.230954.

REPORT ON THE WORLD SOCIAL SITUATION. **Main/Corp** United Nations. Dept. of International Economic and Social Affairs. **VFOAT** World Social Situation. 1978-. US. English. ir. $17.50. United Nations Publications, Sales Section Room A-3315, New York NY 10017. **Tel** (212)754-8302. **Ind/Abst** Bibliogr. Index Geol. Basic aim of the report is to explore the design and delivery of social services and to assess their capacity to enhance the quality of living. *Report on the World Social Situation.*

REPORT - TAVISTOCK INSTITUTE OF HUMAN RELATIONS, LONDON. **Main/Corp** Tavistock Institute of Human Relations, London. UK. English. an. Tavistock Center, Belsize Lane, London NW3 5BA England. **LC** HM47.G72. **DD** 362.9421.

REPRESENTATIVE RESEARCH IN SOCIAL PSYCHOLOGY. Began in 1970. 0034-4907. Periodical. US. English. sa. $15.00 Domestic, $17.00 Canada and Mexico. Representative Research in Social Psychology, Department of Psychology, Davie Hall, University of North Carolina, Chapel Hill NC 27514. **Ind/Abst** Psychol. Abstr. **LC** HM251. **DD** 302.05. **CODEN** RRSPD4. (cum index).

RESEARCH IN ECONOMIC ANTHROPOLOGY. V. 1- 1978-. 0190-1281. US. English. ir. $49.50. JAI Press, PO Box 1678, Greenwich CT 06836. **Tel** (203)661-7602. **Ed** Barry Issac. **LC** GN448. **DD** 301.51.

RESEARCH IN LAW, DEVIANCE, AND SOCIAL CONTROL. Vol. 4 (1982)-. 0737-1136. US. English. $49.50. JAI Press, PO Box 1678, Greenwich CT 06836. **Tel** (203)661-7602. **Ed** Steven Spitzer and Andrew T Scull. **Ind/Abst** Leg. Resour. Index, Sociol. Abstr. **LC** K18. **DD** 340.115072. (cum index). *Research in Law and Sociology, 0163-6588.*

RESEARCH IN ORGANIZATIONAL BEHAVIOR. V. 1- 1979-. 0191-3085. Periodical. US. English. ir. $57.50. JAI Press, PO Box 1678, Greenwich CT 06836. **Tel** (203)661-7602. **Ed** Barry M Staw and L L Cummings. **Ind/Abst** Psychol. Abstr., Soc. Sci. Citation Index. **LC** HD28. **DD** 301.183205.

RESEARCH IN RACE AND ETHNIC RELATIONS. V. 1- 1979-. 0195-7449. US. English. ir. $49.50. JAI Press, PO Box 1678, Greenwich CT 06836. **Tel** (203)661-7602. **Ed** Cora Bagley Marrett and Cheryl B Leggon. **Ind/Abst** Sociol. Abstr., Soc. Welf. Soc. Plan./Policy Soc. Dev., Psychol. Abstr. **LC** GN495.4. **DD** 305.8005.

RESEARCH IN RURAL SOCIOLOGY AND DEVELOPMENT. Vol. 1 (1984)-. Monographic Series. US. English. an. JAI Press Inc, 36 Sherwood Place, PO Box 1678, Greenwich CT 06836. **Tel** (203)661-7602. **LC** HT401. **DD** 307.7205.

RESEARCH IN SOCIAL MOVEMENTS, CONFLICTS AND CHANGE. V. 1- 1978-. 0163-786X. US. English. ir. $49.50. JAI Press, PO Box 1678, Greenwich CT 06836. **Tel** (203)661-7602. **Ed** Louis Kreisberg. **Ind/Abst** Sociol. Abstr., Soc. Welf. Soc. Plan./Policy Soc. Dev. **LC** HN1. **DD** 301.24205.

RESEARCH IN SOCIAL PROBLEMS AND PUBLIC POLICY. V. 1- 1979-. 0196-1152. US. English. ir. $49.50. JAI Press, PO Box 1678, Greenwich CT 06836. **Tel** (203)661-7602. **Ed** Michael Lewis and Joann L Miller. **Ind/Abst** Sociol. Abstr., Soc. Welf. Soc. Plan./Policy Soc. Dev., Psychol. Abstr. **LC** HM1. **DD** 301.072. **NLM** W1 RE227N.

RESEARCH IN SOCIAL STRATIFICATION AND MOBILITY. Vol. 1 (1981)-. 0276-5624. US. English. ir. $49.50. JAI Press, PO Box 1678, Greenwich CT 06836. **Tel** (203)661-7602. **Ed** Robert V Robinson. **Ind/Abst** Sociol. Abstr., Soc. Welf. Soc. Plan./Policy Soc. Dev. **LC** HT601. **DD** 305.5072.

RESEARCH IN SOCIOLOGY OF EDUCATION AND SOCIALIZATION. V. 1- 1980-. 0197-5080. US. English. an. $49.50. JAI Press, PO Box 1678, Greenwich CT 06836. **Tel** (203)661-7602. **Ed** Alan C Kerckhoff. **Ind/Abst** Sociol. Abstr., Soc. Welf. Soc. Plan./Policy Soc. Dev. **LC** LC189.8. **DD** 370.190973.

RESEARCH IN THE INTERWEAVE OF SOCIAL ROLES. V. 1- 1980-. 0272-2801. US. English. ir. $49.50. JAI Press, PO Box 1678, Greenwich CT 06836. **Tel** (203)661-7602. **Ed** Helena Z Lopata. **Ind/Abst** Sociol. Abstr., Psychol. Abstr. **LC** HQ1075. **DD** 305.3. **NLM** W1 RE227NI.

RESEARCH IN THE SOCIOLOGY OF HEALTH CARE. Vol. 1 (1980)-. 0275-4959. US. English. an. $52.50. JAI Press, PO Box 1678, Greenwich CT 06836. **Tel** (203)661-7602. **Ed** Julius Roth. **Ind/Abst** Sociol. Abstr. **LC** RA418. **DD** 362.1042. **NLM** W1 RE227Q.

RESEARCH IN THE SOCIOLOGY OF ORGANIZATIONS. Vol. 1 (1982)-. 0733-558X. US. English. an. $49.50. JAI Press, 36 Sherwood Place, PO Box 1678, Greenwich CT 06836. **Tel** (203)661-7602. **Ed** Sam Bachanach. **Ind/Abst** Sociol. Abstr., Soc. Welf. Soc. Plan./Policy Soc. Dev. **LC** HM131. **DD** 302.35.

RESEARCH IN THE SOCIOLOGY OF WORK. Vol. 1 (1981)-. 0277-2833. US. English. an. $49.50. JAI Press, PO Box 1678, Greenwich CT 06836. **Tel** (203)661-7602. **Ed** Ida Harper Simpson. **Ind/Abst** Sociol. Abstr. **LC** HD6951. **DD** 306.3.

RESEARCH PROJECT. *See* Psychology.

RESEARCH REPORT - INSTITUTE FOR RESEARCH ON POVERTY. (RESEARCH REPORT). **Main/Corp** Wisconsin. University—Madison. Institute for Research on Poverty. 0092-847X. US. English. sa. University of Wisconsin-Madison, Institute for Research on Poverty, 1180 Observatory Drive, Madison WI 53706. **LC** HC110.P6. **DD** 301.441.

RESEARCH REPORT - YORK UNIVERSITY. SOCIAL PSYCHOLOGY RESEARCH PROGRAMME. INSTITUTE FOR BEHAVIOURAL RESEARCH. (RESEARCH REPORT - YORK UNIVERSITY, INSTITUTE FOR BEHAVIOURAL RESEARCH, SOCIAL PSYCHOLOGY RESEARCH PROGRAMME). **Main/**

Sociology: General Works, Theory

Corp York University (Toronto, Ont.). Institute for Behavioural Research. Social Psychology Research Programme. Began publication 1969?. 0316-070X. Monographic Series. CN. English. Institute for Behavioural Research, York University, 4700 Keele Street, Downsview Ontario M3J 1P3 Canada. **DD** 301.1. *Research Report - York University, Institute for Behavioural Research, Psychosocial Research Programme, 0316-067X.*

REVIEW OF PERSONALITY AND SOCIAL PSYCHOLOGY. *See* Psychology.

REVISTA COLOMBIANA DE SOCIOLOGIA. V. 1, No. 1 (Dec. 1979)-. 0120-159X. Periodical. Spanish. ir. El Departamento, Apartado Aereo 058443, Bogota Colombia.

REVISTA ESPANOLA DE INVESTIGACIONES SOCIOLOGICAS. (REIS). No. 1 (Jan./March 1978)-. 0210-5233. Periodical. SP. Spanish. qt. $22.00. Itaca S A Distribuciones Editoriales, Calle l'Opez de Hoyos 141, Madrid 2 Spain. **Ind/Abst** Am. Hist. Life, Hist. Abstr., Part A, Mod. Hist. Abstr., Hist. Abst., Part B, Twent. Century Abstr., Sociol. Abstr., Soc. Welf. Soc. Plan./Policy Soc. Dev. **LC** HM7. **DD** 301.05.

REVISTA ESPANOLA DE LA OPINION PUBLICA. No. 1-50. 0034-9429. Periodical. SP. Spanish. qt. Editora Nacional, c/o Torregalindo 10, Madrid 16 Spain. **Ind/Abst** Foreign Lang. Index, Am. Hist. Life, Hist. Abstr., Lang. Lang. Behav. Abstr., Sociol. Abstr., Hist. Abstr., Part A, Mod. Hist. Abstr., Hist. Abst., Part B, Twent. Century Abstr. **LC** HM261.A1.

REVISTA INTERAMERICANA DE SOCIOLOGIA. V. 1- 1966-. 0557-8558. Periodical. MX. Spanish. ir. Associacion Mexicana Socio, Providencia 330 Col del Valle, Mexico 12 DF Mexico. **Ind/Abst** Foreign Lang. Index.

REVISTA MEXICANA DE SOCIOLOGIA. Yearly V. 1- March/April 1939-. 0035-0087. Periodical. MX. Spanish. ir. 43.00. Torre de Humanidades, Ciudad Universitaria, Coyoacan 20 Mexico DF Mexico. **Tel** 550-5214 (29-48). **Ed** Marvan L Ignacio. **Ind/Abst** Int. Labour Doc., Sociol. Abstr., Soc. Welf. Soc. Plan./Policy Soc. Dev., Foreign Lang. Index, Am. Hist. Life, Hist. Abstr., Lang. Lang. Behav. Abstr., Hist. Abstr., Part A, Mod. Hist. Abstr., Hist. Abst., Part B, Twent. Century Abstr. **LC** H8. **DD** 300.5. (cum index). adv acc. **Circ** 3,000. (ctrl). Works concerning social problems of Mexico and Latin America. Reflections of contemporary social theories and historical analyses.

REVUE FRANCAISE DE SOCIOLOGIE. Vol. 1 No. 1 (Jan./March 1960)-. 0035-2969. Periodical. FR. French (summaries in English, German, Russian and Spanish). qt. 286. Centrale des Revues, 11 rue Gossin, 92543 Montrouge Cedex France. **Tel** 656-52-66. **Ed** J Stoetzel. **Ind/Abst** Int. Labour Doc., Sociol. Abstr., Soc. Welf. Soc. Plan./Policy Soc. Dev., Point Repere, Women Stud. Abstr., Foreign Lang. Index, Lang. Lang. Behav. Abstr., Soc. Sci. Citation Index, Bibliogr. Index. **LC** HM3. **DD** 301.05. **NLM** W1 RE848. (cum index). bk rev. Theoretical and methodological articles recording fundamental research: trends and developments, research notes, debates, critical notes, and reviews.

REVUE INTERNATIONALE DE SOCIOLOGIE. Vol. 1 (1893)- Vol. 1 (1939). Periodical. French. ir. **Ind/Abst** Sociol. Abstr., Soc. Welf. Soc. Plan./Policy Soc. Dev., Psychol. Abstr. **LC** HM3. **CODEN** RISOD6. (cum index).

REVUE ROUMAINE DES SCIENCES SOCIALES. SERIE DE SOCIOLOGIE. V. 10/11- 1966/67-. 0080-2646. RM. French, English or Russian. sa. $45.00. Rompresfilatelia, PO Box 1362137, Bucharest Romania. *Revue Roumaine des Sciences Sociales.*

ROCZNIK DOLNOSLASKI. Vol. 1- 1972-. PL. Polish. sm. ARS Polona, Krakowskie Prezedmiescie 7, 00-068 Warsaw Poland. **LC** HC287.S5.

ROPER REPORTS. 0196-3589. Periodical. US. English. mo. $20000.00. Roper Organization Inc, 205 East 42nd Street, New York NY 10017. **Tel** (212)599-0700. **LC** HN90.P8. **DD** 301.1540973.

RS. CUADERNOS DE REALIDADES SOCIALES. VFOAT Cuadernos de Realidades Sociales. **VAT** Realidades Sociales. Cuadernos de Realidades Sociales. 0302-7724. Periodical. Spanish. ir. 400. Instituto de Sociologia Aplicada, Claudio Coello 141, 6 Madrid Spain. **Ind/Abst** Sociol. Abstr., Soc. Welf. Soc. Plan./Policy Soc. Dev. **LC** HN1.

RURAL AFRICANA. No. 1-31. 0085-5839. Monographic Series. US. English. ir. $18.00. Michigan State University, African Studies Center, East Lansing MI 48824. **Tel** (517)353-1700. **Ed** Assefa Mehretu and David Wiley. **Ind/Abst** Am. Hist. Life, Hist. Abstr., Part A, Mod. Hist. Abstr., Hist. Abst., Part B, Twent. Century Abstr., Int. Labour Doc., Public Aff. Inf. Serv. Bull., Recent Publ. Artic. **LC** HC501. **DD** 301.350967. bk rev. adv acc. **Circ** 200. Journal of multidisciplinary research on rural Africa, rural development, and agricultural issues.

RURAL INDIA. V. 1- Nov. 1938-. 0036-0058. Periodical. II. English (Hindi). mo. $13.00. Asia Books & Periodicals Company, 11 Darya Ganj, New Delhi 110002 India. **Tel** 268645. **Ed** G K Puranik. **Ind/Abst** Bibliogr. Agric. **LC** HN681. **DD** 307.720954.

THE RURAL SOCIOLOGIST. (THE RURAL SOCIOLOGIST : A PUBLICATION OF THE RURAL SOCIOLOGICAL SOCIETY). Vol. 1, No. 1 (Jan. 1981)-. 0279-5957. Periodical. US. English. bm. $18.00. Rural Sociologist, Iowa State University 318 East Hall, Ames IA 50011. **Tel** (406)994-5248. **Ed** Robert C Bealer. **LC** HT401. **DD** 307.720973. **Circ** 1,000. (ctrl). Forum for exchange of views on matters of concern to the profession of rural sociology.

RURAL SOCIOLOGY. Vol. 1, No. 1 (Mar. 1936)-. 0036-0112. Periodical. US. English. qt. $48.00. Rural Sociology Society, 325 Morgan Hall, University of Tennessee, Knoxville TN 37916. **Tel** (406)994-5248. **Ed** William W Falk. **Ind/Abst** Am. Hist. Life, Abstr. Soc. Work., Hist. Abstr., Hist. Abst., Part B, Twent. Century Abstr., Int. Labour Doc., Sociol. Abstr., Soc. Welf. Soc. Plan./Policy Soc. Dev., Energy Inf. Abstr., Environ. Abstr., Popul. Index, Women Stud. Abstr., Curr. Index J. Educ., Soc. Sci. Index, Agric. Index, Bibliogr. Agric., Sci. Cit. Index, Abr. Ed., Public Aff. Inf. Serv. Bull., Psychol. Abstr., Soc. Sci. Citation Index, Abstr. Anthropol., Abstr. Soc. Work. **LC** HT401. **NLM** W1 RU714. **CODEN** RUSCA. bk rev. **Circ** 2,400. Publishes theoretical and research articles and book reviews on topics relevant to all aspects of rural society.

I S A BULLETIN. **Main/Corp** International Sociological Association. VFOAT I S A Newsletter. 9- Autumn 1975-. 0383-8501. Periodical. CN. English (includes some text in French). International Sociological Association, PO Box 719/Station A, Montreal Quebec H3C 2V2 Canada. **DD** 301.0621. *I S A Newsletter, 0318-7292.*

SAE MAUL, CHIYOK KAEBAL YONGU. Periodical. Korean (summaries in English). ir. **LC** HN730.5.Z9.

SAE MAUL UNDONG YONGU. VFOAT Saemaul Undong Research Review. V. 1- Series (1981)-. Periodical. Korean. ir. **LC** HN730.5.Z9.

SAE MAUL UNDONG YONGU NONMUNJIP. Periodical. Korean. ir. **LC** HN730.5.Z9.

SAE MAUL YONGU (CHONNAM TAEHAKKYO. SAE MAUL YONGUSO). (SAE MAUL YONGU). VFOAT Saemaul Review. Periodical. KO. Korean. ir. Chonnam Taehakkyo Sae Maul Yonguso Yongbong-dong, Puk-ku, Kwangju-si Korea. **LC** HN730.5.Z9.

SAGE RACE RELATIONS ABSTRACTS. *See* Indexes/Abstracts.

SAGE STUDIES IN INTERNATIONAL SOCIOLOGY. 1-. Monographic Series. UK. English. ir. Sage Publications, 275 South Beverly Drive, Beverly Hills CA 90212.

SAHOE YON'GU. VFOAT Social Research. V. 1- Series. Periodical. KO. Korean. ir. Not for Sale. Hanguk Sahoe Kwahak Yonguso, PO Box 122, Young Deung Po, Seoul South Korea. **LC** HM7.

SAKSHARATA SANDESA. Periodical. Mewari. mo. 9.00. Seva Mandir, Fatehpura Udaipur 313001 India. **LC** HN690.R3.

LE SAUVAGE. VFOAT Nouvel Observateur/Ecologie. No. 1- April/May 1973-. Periodical. FR. French. ir. 53.00. C.C.P. 3 143-54, Paris France. **LC** HC79.E5. **DD** 301.3105.

SCHRIFTEN - GESELLSCHAFT FUR SOZIALEN FORTSCHRITT. **Main/Corp** Gesellschaft fur Sozialen Fortschritt. Vol. 1- 1951-. 0435-8287. GW. German. ir. Duncker and Humblot Verlag, Dietrich-Schaefer-Weg 9, 1000 Berlin 41 West Germany. **Tel** 030/7912026. **Ed** Dunckere Humblot. **LC** HN5.

SCHRIFTENREIHE DES INSTITUTES FUR SOZIOLOGIE AN DER UNIVERSITAT GRAZ. **Main/Corp** Graz. Universitat. Institut fur Soziologie. 1- 1967-. 0436-3426. Monographic Series. German. ir.

SCHWEIZERISCHE ZEITSCHRIFT FUR SOZIOLOGIE. VFOAT Revue Suisse de Sociologie. 0379-3664. Periodical. SZ. French (German). ty. $68.00. Schweizerische Zeitschrift fur Soziologie, 8 rue du 31-Decembre, 1207 Geneva Switzerland. **Ind/Abst** Sociol. Abstr., Soc. Welf. Soc. Plan./Policy Soc. Dev. **LC** HM5.

SEIKATSU-GAKU. No. 1- Satsu. Japanese. ir. Domesu Shuppan, 35-2 Komagome 1-chome Toshima-ku, Tokyo Japan. **LC** HN721.

SELF-HELP GROUP DIRECTORY. *See* Yearbooks, Almanacs, Directories.

SERIA SOCJOLOGIA. No. 1- 1964-. 0554-8225. Monographic Series. Polish. ir. **LC** HM9.P6.

SERIES 2. RESEARCH REPORT - CENTER FOR SETTLEMENT STUDIES. UNIVERSITY OF MANITOBA. (SERIES 2 : RESEARCH REPORTS - CENTER FOR SETTLEMENT STUDIES, UNIVERSITY OF MANITOBA). **Main/Corp** University of Manitoba. Center for Settlement Studies. No. 1- 1969-. 0076-3934. Monographic Series. CN. English. University of Manitoba, Center for Settlement Studies, Winnipeg Manitoba R3T 2N2 Canada. **DD** 301.340971.

SERIES IN SOCIAL STUDIES : OCCASIONAL PAPER. No. 1-. Monographic Series. RH. English. an. University Rhodesia, Department of Sociology, PO Box HP 45, Mt Pleasant Rhodesia.

SERIES ON THE DEVELOPMENT OF SOCIETIES. V. 1-. Monographic Series. NE. English. Martinus Nijhoff Publishers, PO BOX 163, Spulboulevard 50, 3300-AD Dordrecht Netherlands.

SERON CHOSA NENKAN. ZENKOKU SERON CHOSA NO GENKYO. **Main/Corp** Japan. Sorifu. Naikaku Sori Daijin Kambo. VFOAT Zenkoku Seron Chosa No Genkyo. JA. Japanese. an. $34.27. Sorifu, Prime Minister's Office, 1-1-1 Nagata Cho, Chiyoda-ku Tokyo 100 Japan. **LC** HM261.

SEX ROLES. V.1- Mar. 1975-. 0360-0025. Periodical. US. English. sm. $275.00 Domestic, $315.00 Foreign. Plenum Publishing Corporation, 233 Spring Street, New York NY 10013. **Tel** (212)620-8000. **Ed** Phyllis A Katz. **Ind/Abst** Excerpta Med., Soc. Sci. Index, Sociol. Abstr., Soc. Welf. Soc. Plan./Policy Soc. Dev., Women Stud. Abstr., Ref. Source, Curr. Index J. Educ., Psychol. Abstr., Soc. Sci. Citation Index. **LC** HQ768. **DD** 301.4105. **NLM** W1 SE987. **CODEN** SROLDH. bk rev. adv acc. A forum that will publish original research articles and theoretical manuscripts concerned with the basic processes underlying gender role socialization in children and its consequences.

SHAKAIGAKU HYORON. VFOAT Japanese Sociological Review. V. 1- 1950-. 0021-5414. Periodical. Japanese. ir. **Ind/Abst** Sociol. Abstr., Soc. Welf. Soc. Plan./Policy Soc. Dev. (cum index).

SHAKAIGAKU NENSHI. VFOAT Annuals of Sociology. Began in 1956. Periodical. JA. Japanese. ir. Waseda Daigaku Shakaigakkai c/o Waseda Daigaku Bungakubu, Tokyo Japan. **LC** HM7.

SHAKAISHI KENKYU. 1 (Oct. 1982)-. Periodical. JA. Japanese. sa. 1800 Single Issue. Nihon Edita Sukuru Shuppanbu, 6 Ichigaya Tamachi 1, Shinjuku-ku Tokyo 162 Japan. **LC** HN1.

SHEHUI YU SIXIANG. (SHE HUI YU SSU HSIANG). VFOAT Society and Thought. V. 1, 1983-. 0740-1051. Periodical. US. Chinese (English). ty. $10.00 Institutions, $7.50 Individuals. Society & Thought Institute, Department of Philosophy, Boston College, Chestnut Hill MA 02167. **LC** HM7. **DD** 301.05.

SHIMPO. Began in Sept. 1978. Periodical. JA. Japanese. ir. 500. c/o Daini Watanabe, Building 17-1 Kamiyamacho, Shibuya-ku Tokyo 150. **LC** HN723.5.

SIECUS REPORT. *See* Sexual Life.

SINGA. No. 1 (Dec. 1980)-. 0129-9387. Periodical. SI. English. sa. $4.00. Singa, Cultural Affairs Division Ministry of Culture 3rd Floor City Hall, Singapore 0617 Singapore.

SINGLE. V. 1- Aug. 1973-. 0091-8652. Periodical. US. English. mo. $12.00. Steirman Communications Inc, 545 Madison Avenue, New York NY 10022. **LC** HQ800. **DD** 301.4.

SINGLE (TAMPA, FLA.). (SINGLE). **VFOAT** Single Magazine. Began in 1984. 0747-3184. Periodical. US. English. mo. $14.00. Single Life Inc, 7821 North Dale Mabry/Suite 204, Tampa FL 33614. *Single Life, 0746-9667.*

SINO-WESTERN WEEKLY POST. **VFOAT** Chung Hsi Chou Pao. 1- Oct. 24, 1975-. 0382-4845. Periodical. CN. Chinese (includes some text in English). wk. Sino-Western Cultural Enterprises, 111-193 East Hastings Street, Vancouver British Columbia V6A 1N Canada. **DD** 301.451951071133.

SLEZSKY SBORNIK. Began publication in 1878. 0037-6833. Periodical. GW. Tables of Contents also in Russian and German. qt. Kubon and Sagner, Postfach 34 01 08, D8 Munchen 34 West Germany. **Tel** (089)52 20 27. **Ind/Abst** Am. Hist. Life, Hist. Abstr. **LC** DD491.S4. Concerned with the mutual Czech-Polish relations with respect to the Silesian border region and Ostrava industrial district. Articles appear on the history, contemporary social life, cultural affairs and economic-political questions concerning the region.

SMALL GROUP BEHAVIOR. V. 4- Feb. 1973-. 0090-5526. Periodical. US. English. qt. Sage Publishers Inc, 275 South Beverly Drive, Beverly Hills CA 90212. **Tel** (213)274-8003. **Ind/Abst** Sociol. Abstr., Soc. Welf. Soc. Plan./Policy Soc. Dev., Women Stud. Abstr., Curr. Index J. Educ., Psychol. Abstr., Soc. Sci. Citation Index, Lang. Lang. Behav. Abstr. **LC** HM133. **DD** 301.18505. **NLM** W1 SM21. **CODEN** SGBEDO. *Comparative Group Studies, 0010-4108.*

SMITH COLLEGE STUDIES IN SOCIAL WORK. V. 1- Sept. 1930-. 0037-7317. Periodical. US. English. ir. $8.50 Domestic, $10.00 Foreign. Smith College School for Social Work, Lilly Hall, Northampton MA 01063. **Tel** (413)584-2700. **Ed** Roger R Miller. **Ind/Abst** Sociol. Abstr., Soc. Welf. Soc. Plan./Policy Soc. Dev., Women Stud. Abstr., Soc. Work Res. Abstr., Psychol. Abstr., Soc. Sci. Citation Index, Am. Hist. Life, Hist. Abstr., Lang. Lang. Behav. Abstr., Abstr. Soc. Work., Hist. Abstr., Part A, Mod. Hist. Abstr., Hist. Abst., Part B, Twent. Century Abstr. **LC** HV1. **DD** 360.5. **NLM** W1 SM401. **CODEN** SMSWAW. bk rev. **Circ** 1,350. Psychoanalytic, psychological scholarship and research in mental health and clinical social work issues.

SOCIAAL BESTEK. Vol. 31-. Periodical. NE. Dutch. bw. 82.50. YUGA Uitgeverij BV, Zeestraat 65, Postbus 16400, 2500 BK's Gravenhage The Netherlands. **Tel** 070-614011. **Ed** E Velthuizen. bk rev. adv acc. **Circ** 3,000. Official periodical for directors and staff of social work administration and finance. *Sociale Zorg.*

SOCIAAL-CULTUREEL KWARTAALBERICHT. No. 1 (1979)-. NE. Dutch. qt. 42.00. Centraal Bureau voor de Statistiek, Staatsuitgeverij, The Hague Netherlands. **LC** HN514.

SOCIAAL EN CULTUREEL RAPPORT. **Main/Corp** Netherlands. Sociaal en Cultureel Planbureau. 1974-. Dutch. ir. Sociaal en Cultureel Planbureau, J C Van Markelaan 3, Rijswijk Netherlands. **LC** HN511.

SOCIAL ALTERNATIVES. Began with Spring 1977 issue. 0155-0306. Periodical. AT. English. qt. $14.75. University of Queensland, Department of External Studies, St Lucia Queensland 4067 Australia. **Tel** 377 2324. **Ind/Abst** Sociol. Abstr., Soc. Welf. Soc. Plan./Policy Soc. Dev., Energy Res. Abstr., Soc. Sci. Citation Index. **LC** HN841. **DD** 306.0994. bk rev. adv acc. **Circ** 3,500. Provides a forum for the analysis of social, cultural and economic oppression and focuses on the development or alternative proposals to greater freedom and democracy.

SOCIAL BEHAVIOR AND PERSONALITY. V. 1- 1973-. 0301-2212. Periodical. NZ. English. sa. $24.00. Editorial Services Ltd, PO Box 108, Featherston New Zealand. **Tel** 313 900/224. **Ed** Robert A C Stewart. **Ind/Abst** Sociol. Abstr., Soc. Welf. Soc. Plan./Policy Soc. Dev., Biol. Abstr., Curr. Index J. Educ., Psychol. Abstr., Soc. Sci. Citation Index, Lang. Lang. Behav. Abstr. **LC** HM1. **DD** 301.105. **NLM** W1 SO104I. **CODEN** SBHPAF. bk rev. adv acc. Publishes research and theoretical papers on all aspects of social psychology and personality. Circulates in over 40 countries.

SOCIAL BIOLOGY AND HUMAN AFFAIRS. Vol. 45, No. 1-. 0143-5051. Periodical. UK. English. sa. British Social Biology Council, 69 Eccleston Square, London WC1 Enland. **Ind/Abst** Biol. Abstr. **NLM** W1 SO104M. **CODEN** SBHAD7. *Biology and Human Affairs, 0006-3355.*

SOCIAL CHANGE. 0308-0005. Periodical. US. English. ir. Gordon & Breach, 1 Bedford Street, London WC2E 9HD England.

SOCIAL COGNITION. Vol. 1, No. 1-. 0278-016X. Periodical. US. English. qt. $45.00 Domestic, $55.00 Foreign. Guilford Publications Inc, 200 Park Avenue South, New York NY 10003. **Ind/Abst** Psychol. Abstr. **LC** BF311. **DD** 153. **NLM** W1 SO104M.

SOCIAL DEVELOPMENT *CEASED.* **VFOAT** Developpement Social. Began with V. 1-, Jan. 1972-. Ceased 1982. 0316-313X. Periodical. CN. English (only, except when the English and French editions are combined in one). ir. 55 Parkdale Avenue, Ottawa Ontario K1Y 1E5 Canada. **DD** 361.971. *Developpement Social.*

SOCIAL DEVELOPMENT ISSUES. V. 1- Spring 1977-. 0147-1473. Periodical. US. English. ir. $20.00. University of Iowa, Department GSB, Iowa City IA 52242. **Tel** (319)353-4171. **Ind/Abst** Sociol. Abstr., Soc. Welf. Soc. Plan./Policy Soc. Dev., Soc. Work Res. Abstr. **LC** HV1. **DD** 361.005. **Circ** 400. (ctrl). To promote the consideration of issues that impact upon social justice and the development and well-being of individuals and their communities. *Iowa Journal of Social Work.*

SOCIAL DEVELOPMENT NEWSLETTER. No. 1 (Sept. 1980)-. Periodical. TH. English. Economic and Social Commission for Asia and the Pacific, United Nations Building, Rajdamnern Avenue, Bangkok 2 Thailand. *Social Work Education and Development Newsletter.*

SOCIAL DEVELOPMENT OVERVIEW. **VFOAT** Overview. **VAT** Overview - Canadian Council on Social Development. Vol. 1, No. 1-. 0822-711X. Periodical. CN. English. ir. Free to Members. Canadian Council on Social Development, 55 Parkdale Avenue, Ottawa Ontario K1Y 4G1 Canada. **DD** 361.971. *Social Development, 0316-313X.*

SOCIAL FORCES. Vol. 4, No. 1 (Sept. 1925)-. 0037-7732. Periodical. US. English. an. $30.00. University of North Carolina Press, PO Box 2288, Chapel Hill NC 27514. **Tel** (919)966-3561. **Ind/Abst** Am. Hist. Life, Hist. Abstr., Sociol. Abstr., Soc. Welf. Soc. Plan./Policy Soc. Dev., ABC Pol Sci, Women Stud. Abstr., Writ. Am. Hist., Book Rev. Index, Ref. Source, Int. Index, Humanit. Index, Psychol. Abstr., Soc. Sci. Index, Soc. Sci. Citation Index, Hospit. Lit. Index, Lang. Lang. Behav. Abstr., Pollut. Abstr. Indexes. **LC** MICROFILM 07515 (MICRORR). **NLM** W1 SO104R. **CODEN** SOFOAP. Index in last issue of volume - attached. (cum index). bk rev. adv acc. **Circ** 5,000. (ctrl). Highlights sociological inquiry and explores realms shared with social psychology, anthropology, political science, history, and economics. *Journal of Social Forces.*

SOCIAL IMPACT ASSESSMENT. 1- 19 -. 0741-5761. Periodical. US. English. bm. $20.00. C P Wolf, Box 587, Canal Street Station, New York NY 10013. **Tel** (212)966-2708.

SOCIAL INDICATORS NEWSLETTER *CEASED.* No. 1- Mar. 1973-. 0363-3195. Periodical. US. English. ir. Social Science Research Council, 1755 Massachusetts Avenue Northwest, Washington DC 20036.

SOCIAL NETWORKS. Began with Vol. 1 (Aug. 3, 1978) issue. 0378-8733. Periodical. English. qt. Elsevier Science Publishers, PO Box 211, 1000 AE Amsterdam Netherlands. **Tel** (020)5803.911. **Ed** L C Freeman. **Ind/Abst** Math. Rev., Psychol. Abstr., Sociol. Abstr., Soc. Welf. Soc. Plan./Policy Soc. Dev. **LC** HM73. **DD** 305.05. **NLM** W1 SO121.

SOCIAL POLICY. May/June 1970-. 0037-7783. Periodical. US. English. qt. $20.00. Social Policy, 33 West 42nd Street/Room 1212, New York NY 10036. **Ed** Frank Riessman. **Ind/Abst** Soc. Sci. Index, Am. Hist. Life, Hist. Abstr., Part A, Mod. Hist. Abstr., Hist. Abst., Part B, Twent. Century Abstr., Hospit. Lit. Index, Int. Labour Doc., ABC Pol Sci, Women Stud. Abstr., Sociol. Abstr., Film Lit. Index, Curr. Index J. Educ., Soc. Welf. Soc. Plan./Policy Soc. Dev., Altern. Press Index, Soc. Sci. Citation Index, Med. Socioecon. Res. Source, Hist. Abstr., Abstr. Soc. Work., Soc. Sci. Index, Lang. Lang. Behav. Abstr. **LC** HN51. **DD** 309.173. **NLM** W1 SO122P. bk rev. adv acc. **Circ** 3,000. Available on microfilm from University Microfilms. Emphasizes human service policy issues: education, health, mental health, self help, consumerism, neighborhood organizing, employment for social action leaders, academics, social welfare practitioners, etc.

SOCIAL PROBLEMS. **VFOAT** Annual Editions, Social Problems. 0272-4464. US. English. an. $8.95. Dushkin Publishing Group Inc, Sluice Dock, Guilford CT 06437. **Tel** (203)453-4351. **Ed** Leroy W Barnes. **LC** HN51. **DD** 362.0420973. Collection of public press articles covering current issues in social problems. Includes topic guide and complete index. *Annual Editions. Readings in Social Problems, 0094-9183.*

SOCIAL RESEARCH (SHILLONG, INDIA). (SOCIAL RESEARCH : JOURNAL OF INSTITUTE OF SOCIAL RESEARCH). Vol. 1, No. 1 (Jan. 1981)-. Periodical. II. English. qt. $15.00. Dr M Kar Director, Institute of Social Reserch, Dev Lodge Road, Shillong 793003 India. **LC** DS401. **DD** 306.0954.

SOCIAL SECURITY PROGRAMS THROUGHOUT THE WORLD. **Main/Corp** United States. Social Security Administration. Division of Research. 1958-. US. English. Superintendent of Documents, US Government Printing Office, Washington DC 20402.

SOCIAL SURVEY. Began in 1952. Periodical. AT. English. mo. $3.91. Institute of Social Order, 12 Stackville Street, New Victoria 3101 Australia. **LC** HN30.

SOCIAL TEXT. V. 1- Winter 1979-. 0164-2472. Periodical. US. English. ir. $26.00. Social Text, 3041 Broadway, New York NY 10027. **Tel** (212)663-5642. **Ed** David Wildman. **Ind/Abst** Sociol. Abstr., Soc. Welf. Soc. Plan./Policy Soc. Dev. **LC** HN1. **DD** 303.48405. adv acc. **Circ** 1,200. A journal on theory, culture, and ideology.

SOCIALNI POLITIKA. SOCIALNA POLITIKA. **VFOAT** Socialna Politika. 1977-. Periodical. Czech (Slovak). ir. 24.00. Vydavatelstvo Obzor, 593 34 Bratislava Cs Armady 35, Bratislava Czechoslovakia. **LC** HN420.3. *Socialna Politika.*

SOCIETY. **VFOAT** Societe. **VAT** Societe (Montreal). Began publication in 1977?. 0381-1794. Periodical. CN. English (French). ty. $3.86. CSAA/Concordia University, 1455 Boulevard de Maisonneuve West, Montreal Quebec H3G 1M8 Canada. **Tel** (514)848-8980. **Ed** Neil Guppy. **Ind/Abst** Sociol. Abstr. **DD** 301.06271. adv acc. **Circ** 1,300. Newsletter, internal communications, and official policies. *Bulletin, 0008-5049.*

SOCIETY IN SOUTHERN AFRICA. **Main/Conf** Association for Sociologists in Southern Africa. SA. English. ir. Witwatersrand University Press, 1 Jan Smuts Avenue, Johannesburg 2001 South Africa. **LC** HN800.A7. **DD** 301.

SOCIJALNA PSIHIJATRIJA. *See* Medicine - Psychiatry, Psychopathology.

SOCIOECONOMIC ISSUES OF HEALTH. *See* Public Health and Safety.

THE SOCIOECONOMIC NEWSLETTER. *See* Economics.

SOCIOLINGUISTICS NEWSLETTER *CEASED.* V. 1-13. 0049-1217. Periodical. US. English. sa. $22.00. Erasmus University, PB 1738, 3000 DR Rotterdam Netherlands. **Tel** 010-634100. **Ed** Tony Hak. **Ind/Abst** Sociol. Abstr., Lang. Lang. Behav. Abstr., MLA Int. Bibliogr. Books Artic. Mod. Lang. Lit., Lang. Teach. **LC** P40. **DD** 301.21. bk rev. **Circ** 600. Overviews and reviews in the field of sociolinguistics in the broadest sense.

SOCIOLOGIA. V.1- March 1939-. Periodical. Portuguese. ir. **Ed** Romano Barreto and Emilio Willems. **LC** HM7. **DD** 301.

SOCIOLOGIA. Vol. 1-. Periodical. Czech. bm. Kubon and Sagner, Postfach 34 01 08, D8 Munchen 34 West Germany. **Tel** (089)52 20 27. **LC** HM7. Analysis of sociological theories, sociological problems of our civilization and its perspectives. Theoretical and empirical results achieved in the various sections of sociological research.

SOCIOLOGIA DEL LAVORO. Year 1, N. 1 (Mar. 1978)-. 0392-5048. Periodical. IT. Italian (summaries in English and French). ty. 52.000 Domestic, 65.000 Foreign. Franco Angeli Editore, Via le Monza 106, 20127 Milano Italy. **Tel** (051)233380. **Ind/Abst** Int. Labour Doc., Sociol. Abstr., Foreign Lang. Index. **LC** HD6951. **DD** 306.3605. adv acc. **Circ** 1,500. (ctrl).

SOCIOLOGIA DELL'ORGANIZZAZIONE. Year 1- Jan./June 1973-. 0390-4229. Italian. ir. $12.00. Marsilio, Piazza de Gasperi 41, 35100 Padova Italy. **Ind/Abst** Sociol. Abstr. **LC** HM131.

SOCIOLOGIA E RICERCA SOCIALE. VFOAT SRS. Year 1, No. 1 (June 1980)-. Periodical. Italian (summaries in English). ty. 48.000. La Goliardica Editrice Universitaria di Roma, Via Domenico de Dominicis 15, 00159 Roma Italy.

SOCIOLOGIA INDICA. V. 1- May 1977-. Periodical. II. English. ir. 30.00. Indian Institute of Sociology, Room 23 Bidhan Sarani, Calcutta-700006 India. **LC** HN681. **DD** 301.05.

SOCIOLOGIA INTERNATIONALIS. 0038-0164. Periodical. GW. English (French, German, or Spanish). sa. Duncker & Humblot, Dietrich Schafer Weg 9, 1 Berlin 41 West Germany. **Tel** (030)7912026. **Ed** H Winkmann. **Ind/Abst** Sociol. Abstr., Soc. Welf. Soc. Plan./Policy Soc. Dev. **LC** HM1.A1. **DD** 301.05. Index published separately - free - automatically sent. bk rev. adv acc. **Circ** 600. International journal for sociology and social psychology.

SOCIOLOGIA RURALIS. V. 1- Spring 1960-. 0038-0199. Periodical. NE. English (French and German). qt. 85.00. Can Gorcum & Company BV, PO Box 43, 9400 AA Assen Netherlands. **Tel** 05920/46846. **Ed** Anton J Jansen. **Ind/Abst** Int. Labour Doc., Sociol. Abstr., Soc. Welf. Soc. Plan./Policy Soc. Dev., Recent Publ. Artic., Bibliogr. Agric., Foreign Lang. Index, Public Aff. Inf. Serv. Bull., Lang. Lang. Behav. Abstr., Soc. Sci. Citation Index, PAIS Foreign Lang. Index. **LC** HT401. **NLM** W1 SO878S. bk rev. adv acc. **Circ** 1,000. (ctrl). The journal is mainly concerned with theoretical and empirical contributions from the social sciences to rural problems in Europe and the developing countries.

SOCIOLOGIA URBANA E RURALE (UNIVERSITA DI BOLOGNA. (SOCIOLOGIA URBANA E RURALE). 0392-4939. Periodical. IT. Italian. ty. 45.000. V Le Monza 106, 20127 Milano Italy. Centro Studi Sui Problemi Della Citta e del Territorio).

SOCIOLOGICAL ABSTRACTS. *See* Indexes/Abstracts.

SOCIOLOGICAL BULLETIN. Began in 1952. 0038-0229. Periodical. II. English. sa. 10.00. Indian Sociological Society, Department of Sociology, University of Poona, Pune 411007 India. **Tel** 5510400. **Ed** S B Chitnis. **Ind/Abst** Am. Hist. Life, Hist. Abstr., Part A, Mod. Hist. Abstr., Hist. Abst., Part B, Twent. Century Abstr., Sociol. Abstr., Soc. Welf. Soc. Plan./Policy Soc. Dev., Lang. Lang. Behav. Abstr. **LC** HN681. bk rev. (ctrl). Consists of articles by Indian and foreign authors on a wide range of sociological themes, book reviews, and news about sociology in India.

SOCIOLOGICAL CONTRIBUTIONS FROM FLANDERS. Periodical. English. ir. Belguim Etc, Transtraat 5 2900, Londerzeel Belgium. **LC** HM1.

SOCIOLOGICAL FOCUS. V. 1- Fall 1967-. 0038-0237. Periodical. US. English. qt. Kent State University, Department of Sociology, Kent OH 44242. **Tel** (216)672-2749. **Ed** Bebe Lavin and Elizabeth I Mullins. **Ind/Abst** Energy Inf. Abstr., Environ. Abstr., Sociol. Abstr., Soc. Welf. Soc. Plan./Policy Soc. Dev., Soc. Sci. Citation Index, Women Stud. Abstr., Lang. Lang. Behav. Abstr. **LC** HM1. **Circ** 1,000. Regional journal of North Central Sociological Association for publication of research in the field of sociology and related areas. *Ohio Valley Sociologist.*

SOCIOLOGICAL INQUIRY. V. 31- 1961-. 0038-0245. Periodical. CN. English. qt. $26.00. University of Texas Press, Box 7819 Journals Department, Austin TX 78712. **Tel** (512)471-4531. **Ed** James K Skipper. **Ind/Abst** Sociol. Abstr., Soc. Welf. Soc. Plan./Policy Soc. Dev., Am. Hist. Life, Hist. Abstr., Part A, Mod. Hist. Abstr., ABC Pol Sci, Soc. Sci. Index, Soc. Sci. Citation Index, Bibliogr. Index, Lang. Lang. Behav. Abstr., Abstr. Soc. Work., Hist. Abstr., Hist. Abst., Part B, Twent. Century Abstr. **LC** HM1. adv acc. **Circ** 2,500. (ctrl). Maintains a general perspective to cater to the interests and needs of sociologists and other social scientists with differing theoretical and methodological backgrounds. *Alpha Kappa Deltan.*

SOCIOLOGICAL METHODS & RESEARCH. VAT Sociological Methods and Research. V. 1- Aug. 1972-. 0049-1241. Periodical. US. English. qt. Sage Publications Inc, 275 South Beverly Drive, Beverly Hills CA 90212. **Tel** (213)836-5172. **Ind/Abst** Soc. Welf. Soc. Plan./Policy Soc. Dev., Sociol. Abstr., Hum. Resour. Abstr., Sociol. Educ. Abstr., Sage Urban Stud. Abstr., Soc. Sci. Citation Index, Public Aff. Inf. Serv. Bull., Lang. Lang. Behav. Abstr. **LC** HM1. **DD** 301.072.

SOCIOLOGICAL OBSERVATIONS. V. 1-. 0149-4872. Monographic Series. US. English. ir. Sage Publications, PO Box 776, Beverly Hills CA 90213. **LC** UNC.

SOCIOLOGICAL PERSPECTIVES. Vol. 26, No. 1 (Jan. 1983)-. 0731-1214. Periodical. US. English. qt. Free to Members, $48.00 Domestic, $52.00 Foreign. Sage Publications Inc, 275 South Beverly Drive, Beverly Hills CA 90212. **Tel** (213)274-8003. **Ind/Abst** Am. Hist. Life, Hist. Abstr., ABC Pol Sci, Sage Urban Stud. Abstr., Abstr. Criminol. Penol., Sociol. Educ. Abstr., Hum. Resour. Abstr., Sage Fam. Stud. Abstr., Curr. Contents, U.S. Polit. Sci. Doc., Soc. Sci. Citation Index. **LC** HM1. **DD** 301.05. **NLM** W1 SO879BH. Available on microfilm from University Microfilms. *Pacific Sociological Review, 0030-8919.*

SOCIOLOGICAL PRACTICE. V. 3- Spring 1979-. 0163-8505. Periodical. US. English. sa. $30.00. Progressive Publisher, 401 East 31 #10021, Chicago IL 60616. **Tel** (312)225-9181. **Ed** Kenneth Ives. **Ind/Abst** Soc. Welf. Soc. Plan./Policy Soc. Dev., Sociol. Abstr., Curr. Contents, Soc. Behav. Sci. **LC** HM1. **DD** 301.05. bk rev. **Circ** 200. Applied sociology in various fields-function, problems, training needed. Problems and examples of research for applied and policy uses. *SP, Sociological Practice, 0360-845X.*

SOCIOLOGICAL QUARTERLY. VFOAT SQ. V. 1- Jan. 1960-. 0038-0253. Periodical. US. English. qt. $65.00. JAI Press Inc, PO Box 1678, 36 Sherwood Place, Greenwich CT 06836. **Tel** (203)661-7602. **Ed** Gary Albrecht. **Ind/Abst** Hist. Abst., Part B, Twent. Century Abstr., Soc. Welf. Soc. Plan./Policy Soc. Dev., ABC Pol Sci, Women Stud. Abstr., Soc. Work Res. Abstr., Sociol. Abstr., Psychol. Abstr., Abstr. Soc. Work., Hist. Abstr., Part A, Mod. Hist. Abstr., Am. Hist. Life, Soc. Sci. Index, Lang. Lang. Behav. Abstr., Soc. Sci. Citation Index, Psychol. Abstr., Soc. Work Res. Abstr., Hist. Abstr. **LC** HM1. **DD** 300.5. **NLM** W1 SO879C. **CODEN** SOLQAR. adv acc. **Circ** 2,800. *Midwest Sociologist.*

SOCIOLOGICAL REVIEW. (THE SOCIOLOGICAL REVIEW). New Series V. 10, No. 1 (Mar. 1962)-. 0038-0261. Periodical. UK. English. qt. 37.50. Routledge & Kegan Paul Ltd, Broadway House Newtown Road, Henley-on-Thames Oxon RG9 1EN England. **Tel** 0491578321. **Ed** G Fyfe. **Ind/Abst** Sociol. Abstr., Soc. Welf. Soc. Plan./Policy Soc. Dev., Book Rev. Index, Soc. Sci. Index, Am. Hist. Life, Hist. Abstr., Part A, Mod. Hist. Abstr., Hist. Abst., Part B, Twent. Century Abstr. **NLM** W1 SO879E. bk rev. adv acc. **Circ** 1,600. One of the oldest sociological journals, it will continue its policy of publishing articles on a wide range of sociological topics, and critical comments on previous articles. *Sociological Review (University College of North Staffordshire).*

SOCIOLOGICAL REVIEW MONOGRAPH. (THE SOCIOLOGICAL REVIEW MONOGRAPH). No. 1- 1958-. 0081-1769. Monographic Series. UK. English. ir. 40.00. University of Keele, Keele Staffordshire England. **Tel** (0782)621111. **Ed** John Eggleston, Ronald Frankenberg, and Gordon Fyfe. **Ind/Abst** Sociol. Abstr., Soc. Welf. Soc. Plan./Policy Soc. Dev., Index Med. **LC** HM15. **NLM** W1 S0879F. bk rev. adv acc. **Circ** 170. Usually six articles plus extended review plus reviews and list of books received.

SOCIOLOGICAL SPECTRUM. (SOCIOLOGICAL SPECTRUM : THE OFFICIAL JOURNAL OF THE MID-SOUTH SOCIOLOGICAL ASSOCIATION). Vol. 1, No. 1 (Jan./Mar. 1981). 0273-2173. Periodical. US. English. qt. $59.95. Hemisphere Publishing Corp, 79 Madison Avenue #1110, New York NY 10016. **Tel** (202)783-3958. **Ed** J J Salomone and H D Allen. **Ind/Abst** Sociol. Abstr., Soc. Welf. Soc. Plan./Policy Soc. Dev. **LC** HM1. **DD** 301.05. **CODEN** SOSPDS. bk rev. adv acc. **Circ** 880. Refereed interdisciplinary social science journal publishing theoretical methodological, and applied research articles in sociology, education, anthropology, political science. *Sociological Symposium, 0038-027X; Sociological Forum, 0160-3469.*

SOCIOLOGICAL STUDIES. No. 1- Jan./Mar. 1977-. Periodical. US. English (Russian). qt. National Technical Information Service, Joint Publications Research Service, 5285 Port Royal Road, Springfield VA 22161.

SOCIOLOGICAL SYMPOSIUM *CEASED.* No. 1-31. 0038-027X. Periodical. US. English. qt. $8.00. Department of Sociology, Virginia Polytechnic, Institute and State University, Blacksburg VA 24061. **LC** HM1.

SOCIOLOGICAL THEORY. **Series/Titl** Jossey-Bass Social and Behavioral Science Series. 1983-. 0735-2751. Periodical. US. English. an. Jossey-Bass Inc, 433 California Street, San Francisco CA 94104. **Ind/Abst** Sociol. Abstr. **LC** HM24. **DD** 301.01.

SOCIOLOGICKY CASOPIS. Vol. 1- 1965-. 0038-0288. Periodical. CS. Czech (summaries in English). bm. Praha Czechoslovakia. **Tel** (089)52 20 27. **Ind/Abst** Sociol. Abstr., Soc. Welf. Soc. Plan./Policy Soc. Dev., Psychol. Abstr., Soc. Sci. Citation Index, Lang. Lang. Behav. Abstr. **LC** HM7. **CODEN** SLCSB2. Studies in general sociology and the specialized sociological branches. Publishes information from Czechoslovakia and from abroad in various social subjects and the methodology of analysis and interpretation.

SOCIOLOGIE DU TRAVAIL. 1.- Year. 0038-0296. Periodical. FR. French. qt. Centrale des Revues, 11 rue Gossin, 92543 Montrouge Cedex France. **Tel** (1)43 20 15 50. **Ed** Odile Benoit Guilbot. **Ind/Abst** Int. Labour Doc., Excerpta Med., Sociol. Abstr., Soc. Welf. Soc. Plan./Policy Soc. Dev., Foreign Lang. Index, Soc. Sci. Citation Index, PAIS Foreign Lang. Index. **LC** HD4807. (cum index). bk rev. adv acc. **Circ** 2,400. Covers factory work, social work, office work, professional and social groups, companies, public offices, labor movement, trade unions, and work relations.

SOCIOLOGIE ET SOCIETES. V. 1- May 1969-. 0038-030X. Periodical. CN. French (summaries in French, English, and Spanish). sa. $24.76. Presses de L'Universite, University of Montreal, CP 6128, Montreal Quebec H3C 3J7 Canada. **Tel** (514)343-6321. **Ed** Robert Sevigny. **Ind/Abst** Sociol. Abstr., Soc. Welf. Soc. Plan./Policy Soc. Dev., Foreign Lang. Index, Point Repere, Psychol. Abstr. **LC** HM3. bk rev. adv acc. **Circ** 1,500. A thematic periodical dealing with sociological research inside and outside Quebec; the fruit of collaboration between Quebec sociologists and those of the United States, Europe and Latin America.

SOCIOLOGIJA. V. 1- 1959-. 0038-0318. Periodical. Serbo-Croatian -R. ir. **Ind/Abst** Sociol. Abstr., Soc. Welf. Soc. Plan./Policy Soc. Dev.

SOCIOLOGIJA SELA. Began with July/Sept. 1963 issue. 0038-0326. Periodical. YU. Serbo-Croatian -R (summaries in English and Russian). qt. $40.00. Centar Drustvena Istrazivanja Sveucil Zagrebu, Zagreb 41000, Amruseva 8 LLL Yugoslavia. **Tel** 430-675. **Ind/Abst** Sociol. Abstr., Soc. Welf. Soc. Plan./Policy Soc. Dev., Lang. Lang. Behav. Abstr. **LC** HT401. bk rev. **Circ** 1,000. Theoretical and empirical papers on rural sociology, agricultural economics, and social anthropology issues of current development.

SOCIOLOGISCHE GIDS. TIJDSCHRIFT VOOR SOCIOLOGIE EN SOCIAAL ONDERZOEK. 0038-0334. Periodical. NE. Dutch (with summaries in English). bm. $31.44. Boom en Zoom, Postbus 58, Meppel Netherlands. **Ed** H M Huttner. **Ind/Abst** Sociol. Abstr., Soc. Welf. Soc. Plan./Policy Soc. Dev., Lang. Lang. Behav. Abstr. (cum index). bk rev. adv acc. **Circ** 1,000. A journal for sociology and social research.

SOCIOLOGISKE MEDDELELSER. Ser. 1-. 0038-0350. DK. Danish (English). sa. Sociologisk Institut-Kobenhavn, Rosenborgade 15, Copenhagen Denmark. **Ind/Abst** Am. Hist. Life, Hist. Abstr., Part A, Mod. Hist. Abstr., Hist. Abst., Part B, Twent. Century Abstr., Sociol. Abstr., Soc. Welf. Soc. Plan./Policy Soc. Dev., Lang. Lang. Behav. Abstr., Hist. Abstr. **LC** HM7.

SOCIOLOGUS. VFOAT Journal for Empirical Ethno-Sociology and Ethno-Psychology. 1.-9 Yearly Vol. 1925-1933. 0038-0377. Periodical. GW. German. sa. Duncker & Humblot, Dietrich Shafer Weg 9, Postfach 330, 1 Berlin 41 West Germany. **Tel** (030)7912026. **Ed** W Rudolph. **Ind/Abst** Foreign Lang. Index, PAIS Foreign Lang. Index. **LC** HM5. adv acc. **Circ** 500. Journal for empirical ethno-sociology and ethno-psychology. *Archiv fur Anthropologie Volkerforschung und Kolonialen Kulturwandel.*

SOCIOLOGY. V. 1- Jan. 1967-. 0038-0385. Periodical. UK. English. qt. 37.80. British Sociological Association, 351 Station Road Solihull, West Midlands

B93 8EY England. **Tel** 44 5645 2402. **Ed** Jennifer Platt. **Ind/Abst** Am. Hist. Life, Hist. Abstr., Part A, Mod. Hist. Abstr., Hist. Abst., Part B, Twent. Century Abstr., Sociol. Abstr., Soc. Sci. Index, Soc. Welf. Soc. Plan./Policy Soc. Dev., Soc. Sci. Citation Index, Lang. Lang. Behav. Abstr., Hist. Abstr. **LC** HM1. **DD** 301.05. **NLM** W1 SO879J. bk rev. adv acc. **Circ** 2,700. Articles on all aspects of sociology, book reviews, debates, and reports on work in progress.

SOCIOLOGY *CEASED.* V. 1-10. 0094-1638. US. English. qt. $20.00. 4000 Albemarle Street NW/Suite 302, Washington DC 20016. **Ind/Abst** Sociol. Abstr., Soc. Welf. Soc. Plan./Policy Soc. Dev., Book Rev. Index. **LC** HM1. **DD** 301.05.

SOCIOLOGY AND SOCIAL RESEARCH. V. 12- Sept./Oct. 1927-. 0038-0393. Periodical. US. English. qt. Sociology & Social Research, University of South California, University Park, Los Angeles CA 90089. **Ind/Abst** Sociol. Abstr., Am. Hist. Life, Hist. Abstr., Part A, Mod. Hist. Abstr., Hist. Abst., Part B, Twent. Century Abstr., Soc. Welf. Soc. Plan./Policy Soc. Dev., Popul. Index, Women Stud. Abstr., Curr. Index J. Educ., Psychol. Abstr., Soc. Sci. Index, Soc. Sci. Citation Index, Hist. Abstr., Lang. Lang. Behav. Abstr. **NLM** W1 SO879K. **CODEN** SSORA5. (cum index). *Journal of Applied Sociology, Bulletin of Social Research.*

SOCIOLOGY (DUSHKIN PUBLISHING GROUP). (SOCIOLOGY). **VFOAT** Annual Editions. 0277-9315. US. English. an. $8.95. Dushkin Publishing Group Inc, Sluice Dock, Guilford CT 06437. **Tel** (203)453-4351. **Ed** Kurt Finsterbusch. **LC** HM1. **DD** 301.05. Collection of public press articles covering current issues in sociology. Includes topic guide and complete index. *Annual Editions. Readings in Sociology, 0090-4236.*

SOCIOLOGY OF HEALTH & ILLNESS. **VFOAT** Sociology of Health and Illness. Vol. 1, No. 1 (June 1979)-. 0141-9889. Periodical. UK. English. ty. 30.00 Domestic, 37.50 Foreign, $60.00. Basil Blackwell, 108 Cowley Road, Oxford OX4 1JF England. **Tel** (0865)722146. **Ed** Anne Murcott. **Ind/Abst** Excerpta Med., Hospit. Lit. Index, Sociol. Abstr., Soc. Welf. Soc. Plan./Policy Soc. Dev., Psychol. Abstr., Soc. Sci. Citation Index, Recent Publ. Artic. **LC** RA418. **DD** 306.46. **NLM** W1 SO879NE. bk rev. adv acc. **Circ** 750. An international journal publishing sociological articles on all aspects of health, illness and medicine-both theoretical and practical.

SOCIOMETRY. *See* Psychology.

EL SOL HOUSTON. 1965. Periodical. US. English. wk. $20.00. El Sol, PO Box 3795, Houston TX 77001. **Tel** (713)224-0616. **Ed** James L Novarro. bk rev. **Circ** 37,000. (ctrl). Cultural development; linguistic bridge of communication; local, national, international information and bridge of goodwill.

SOTSIOLOGICHESKI PROBLEMI. Vol. 1- 1969-. 0038-1683. Periodical. BU. Bulgarian (summaries in English and Russian). bm. Hemus, 6 Boulevard RuskY, Sofia Bulgaria. **Ind/Abst** Lang. Lang. Behav. Abstr., Sociol. Abstr. **LC** HM7.

SOTSIOLOGICHESKIE ISSLEDOVANIIA. July/Sept. 1974-. 0132-1625. Periodical. UR. Russian. qt. $39.00. Victor Kamkin Inc (70934), 12224 Parklawn Drive, Rockville MD 20852. **Tel** (301)881-5973. **Ind/Abst** Lang. Lang. Behav. Abstr., Sociol. Abstr., Soc. Sci. Citation Index. **LC** HM7.

SOUTHERN EXPOSURE. V. 1- Spring 1973-. 0146-809X. Periodical. US. English. bm. $20.00. Institute Southern Studies, PO Box 531, Durham NC 27702. **Tel** (919)688-8167. **Ed** Marc Miller. **Ind/Abst** Am. Hist. Life, Hist. Abstr., Part A, Mod. Hist. Abstr., Hist. Abst., Part B, Twent. Century Abstr., Sociol. Abstr., Energy Res. Abstr., Altern. Press Index, Humanit. Index, Energy Inf. Abstr., Environ. Abstr., Access, Hist. Abstr. **LC** F206. **DD** 975.005. bk rev. adv acc. **Circ** 9,000. Regional political affairs and reform efforts, people and organizations taking positive steps to make the South a better place to call home.

SOUTHERN STRUGGLE. V. 35- Jan. 1977-. 0199-8668. Periodical. US. English. ir. $5.00. Southern Struggle, PO Box 10797, Atlanta GA 30310. **LC** HN79.A2. **DD** 309.175. *Southern Patriot, 0038-4402.*

SOVIET SOCIOLOGY. V. 1- Summer 1962-. 0038-5824. Periodical. US. English (Russian). ir. $178.50. M E Sharpe Inc, 80 Business Park Drive, Armonk NY 10504. **Tel** (914)273-1800. **Ed** Stephen P Dunn. **Ind/Abst** Popul. Index, Public Aff. Inf. Serv. Bull., Sociol. Abstr., Lang. Lang. Behav. Abstr. **LC** HX542. adv acc. This journal contains unabridged translations intended to reflect developments in Soviet sociology and to be of interest to those professionally concerned with this field.

SOZIALE WELT. Began with Oct. 1949 issue. 0038-6073. Periodical. GW. German. qt. Verlag Otto Schwartz & Company, Annastrasse 7, D-3400 Gottingen West Germany. **Ind/Abst** Sociol. Abstr., Soc. Welf. Soc. Plan./Policy Soc. Dev., Philos. Index, Foreign Lang. Index, Bibliogr. Index, Lang. Lang. Behav. Abstr., PAIS Foreign Lang. Index. **LC** H5. **DD** 300.5. (cum index). bk rev. adv acc.

SOZIALPADAGOGIK. Vol. 1-. Periodical. German. bm. **LC** HN30.

SOZIALWISSENSCHAFT UND MEDIZIN. Vol. 1-. 0175-8209. Monographic Series. German. ir. **Ed** H Weber-Falkensammer. **NLM** W1 SO999W.

SOZIOLOGISCHE ABHANDLUNGEN. No. 1- 1961-. 0584-6048. Monographic Series. GW. German. ir. Duncker und Humblot Verlag, Dietrich-Schafer-Weg 9, 1 Berlin 41 West Germany.

SOZIOLOGISCHE REVUE. Vol. 1- Jan. 1978-. 0343-4109. Periodical. GW. German. qt. 106.-. R Oldenbourg Verlag, Postfach 801360, D 8000 Munchen 80 West Germany. **Tel** (089)4112-0. **Ed** Johannes Weiss. bk rev. adv acc. **Circ** 1,500. Critical essays, reviews and discussions on books concerning all aspects of sociology published especially in Germany.

SPINNER (NEW BEDFORD, MASS.). *See* History (General) - History of North, South, and Central America.

SPOECZENSTWO STAROPOLSKIE. V. 1-. Polish (summaries in French). ir. **LC** HN537.

SRPSKA BORBA. *See* Ethnic.

STATE AND MIND. V. 5, No. 3- July/Sept. 1976-. 0161-1089. Periodical. US. English. bm. $6.00. RT Inc, PO Box 89, W Somerville MA 02144. **LC** HN1. **DD** 362.04205. *RT, A Journal of Radical Therapy, 0360-4713.*

STATISTIQUES SOCIALES. *See* Statistics.

STOP PRESS (1980). (STOP PRESS). **VFOAT** SOS Montreal. Vol. 5, No. 3 (Fall 1980)-. Periodical. CN. English (French, 1980- French text on inverted pages, 1980-Summer 1982). qt. **DD** 363.7309714281. *S O S Montreal, 0383-6347.*

STUDI DI SOCIOLOGIA. Year 1- Jan./March 1963-. 0039-291X. Periodical. IT. Italian. qt. Universita Cattolica del Sacro Cuore, Largo Agostino Gemelli 1, 20102 Milano Italy. **Ind/Abst** Sociol. Abstr. **LC** HM7. **DD** 301.05. (cum index).

STUDIA MEDIEWISTYCZNE. *See* Philosophy.

STUDIA SOCJOLOGICZNE. *See* Social Sciences (General).

STUDIES IN SYMBOLIC INTERACTION. V. 1- 1978-. 0163-2396. US. English. sa. $30.00. JAI Press Inc, PO Box 1678, 36 Sherwood Place, Greenwich CT 06836. **Tel** (203)661-7602. **Ed** Norman K Denzin. **Ind/Abst** Sociol. Abstr., Psychol. Abstr. **LC** HM1. **DD** 301.1.

STUDIES OF ISRAELI SOCIETY. **Series/Titl** Publication Series of the Israel Sociological Society. Vol. 1-. 0734-4937. Monographic Series. US. English. Transcation Books, Rutgers-The State University, New Brunswick NJ 08903.

THE SUBTERRANEAN SOCIOLOGY NEWSLETTER. Began with Vol. 1 (July 1967). 0039-4394. Periodical. US. English. an. $3.00. c/o Marcello Truzzi, Subterranean Sociology, Department of Sociology, Eastern Michigan University, Ypsilani MI 48197. **Ed** Marcello Truzzi.

SUICIDE & LIFE-THREATENING BEHAVIOR. **VFOAT** Suicide and Life-Threatening Behavior, Suicide and Life Threatening Behavior. V. 6- Spring 1976-. 0363-0234. Periodical. US. English. qt. $80.00. The Guilford Press, 200 Park Avenue, New York NY 10003. **Tel** (212)243-6000. **Ed** Ronald Maris. **Ind/Abst** Electron. Commun. Abstr. J., ISMEC Bull., Pollut. Abstr. Indexes, Saf. Sci. Abstr. J., Excerpta Med., Sociol. Abstr., Soc. Welf. Soc. Plan./Policy Soc. Dev., Index Med., Soc. Sci. Citation Index, Abstr. Criminol. Penol., Curr. Contents, Curr. Index J. Educ., Lang. Lang. Behav. Abstr., Hospit. Lit. Index, Psychol. Abstr. **LC** RC569. **DD** 616.85844. **NLM** W1 SU283L. **CODEN** SLBEDP. bk rev. adv acc. **Circ** 1,000. Devoted to emergent approaches in theory and practice to life-threatening behaviors. Multi-disciplinary topics: suicide, suicide prevention, accidents, sub-intentional destruction, etc. *Suicide, 0360-1390.*

DIE SUID-AFRIKAANSE TYDSKRIF VIR SOSIOLOGIE. THE SOUTH AFRICAN JOURNAL OF SOCIOLOGY. **VFOAT** South African Journal of Sociology. No. 1- Nov. 1970-. Periodical. SA. Afrikaans (English). ir. **Ind/Abst** Sociol. Abstr., Soc. Welf. Soc. Plan./Policy Soc. Dev. **LC** HM1.

SUMMATION *CEASED.* Began in 1968. Ceased with V. 7, No. 1, Fall/Winter 1980/81. 0300-8657. Periodical. US. English. sa.

A SURVEY OF RACE RELATIONS IN SOUTH AFRICA. Began publication with 1951/52. 0081-9778. SA. English. an. South African Institute of Race Relations, PO Box 97, Johannesburg South Africa. **LC** DT763.

SURVIVAL TOMORROW. Vol. 1, No. 1 (Mar. 1981)-. 0273-2017. Periodical. US. English. mo. Kephart Communications, 901 North Washington Street/Suite 605, Alexandria VA 22314.

SYMBOLIC INTERACTION. V. 1- Fall 1977-. 0195-6086. Periodical. US. English. sa. Institute for the Study of Science and Society Press, 720 Washington Avenue SE, Minneapolis MN 55414. **Ind/Abst** Sociol. Abstr., Soc. Welf. Soc. Plan./Policy Soc. Dev., Psychol. Abstr. **LC** HM1. **DD** 302.

SZOCIOLOGIA. 1972-. 0133-3461. Periodical. HU. Hungarian. qt. Akademiai Kiado, POB 24, 1363 Budapest Hungary. **Ind/Abst** Sociol. Abstr., Soc. Welf. Soc. Plan./Policy Soc. Dev. **LC** HM7.

TAAWUN (KUWAIT, KUWAIT). (AL-TAAWUN). Periodical. Arabic. mo. 2.5. Ittihad Al-Jamiyat Al-Taawuniyah Al-Istihlakiyah SB 1836, Al-Safah Al-Kuwayt. **LC** HN669.

TAB INTERNATIONAL. V. 10, No. 8- July 1965-. 0380-2604. Periodical. CN. English. .35 Each Number. Tab Publishing, 43 Victoria Street, Toronto Ontario M5C 2A3 Canada. **DD** 301.4105. *Tab Confidential, 0380-2612.*

TALK. 0164-8535. Periodical. US. English. mo. Donovan Communications, 100 Park Avenue, New York NY 10017. **LC** AP2. **DD** 305.405.

TALKING DRUMS. V. 1- Dec. 17, 1975-. 0383-9192. Periodical. CN. English. ir. .25 Each Number. Talking Drums Magazine/Suite 301 Triller Avenue, Toronto Ontario M6K 3B7 Canada. **DD** 301.451960713541.

TEACHING NEWSLETTER. V. 4, No. 4- Apr. 1979-. Periodical. US. English. bm. $10.00. American Sociological Association, 1722 N Street NW, Washington DC 20036. *On Teaching Undergraduate Sociology Newsletter.*

TEACHING SOCIOLOGY. V. 1- Oct. 1973-. 0092-055X. Periodical. US. English. qt. $48.00 Domestic, $51.00 Foreign. American Sociological Association, 1722 N Street Northwest, Washington DC 20036. **Tel** (202)833-3410. **Ed** Theodore C Wagenaar. **Ind/Abst** Sociol. Abstr., Soc. Welf. Soc. Plan./Policy Soc. Dev., Educ. Index, Curr. Index J. Educ., Soc. Sci. Citation Index, Lang. Lang. Behav. Abstr. **LC** HM1. **DD** 301.07. adv acc. **Circ** 2,000. This journal publishes research articles, teaching tips and reports on teaching sociology in particular. Also includes the shorter reports of class projects and innovations previously published in the Teaching Newsletter.

TELEVISION & CHILDREN *CEASED.* **VFOAT** Television and Children. **VAT** Television and Children. Vol. 3, No. 2 (Summer 1980)-V. 7, No. 3 & 4 (Summer/Fall 1984). 0276-7309. Periodical. US. English. qt. National Council of Families and Television, 20 Nassau Street/Suite 200, Princeton NJ 08542. **Ed** Nicholas B Van Dyck. **Ind/Abst** Curr. Index J. Educ. **LC** HQ784.T4. **DD** 305.23. bk rev. (ctrl). Articles about television and its effects on children and families. *NCCT Forum.*

TERRORISM (MINNEAPOLIS, MINN.) *CEASED.* (TERRORISM). Vol. 1 (1982)-. 0278-663X. US. English. an. $36.00. J L Scherer, 4900 18th Avenue South, Minneapolis MN 55417. **LC** HV6431. **DD** 303.62505.

THE TEXAS OBSERVER. *See* Political Science.

THANATOS. V. 1- Sept. 1975-. 0160-8681. Periodical. US. English. qt. $15.00. Florida Consumer Information Bureau, PO Box 6009, Tallahassee FL

32314. **Tel** (904)224-1969. **Ed** Jan Scheff. **LC** BD444. **DD** 128.5. bk rev. **Circ** 2,500. Personal experiences with dying, death and bereavement. Also profiles of organizations or individiuals with the same.

THEORIES OF CONTEMPORARY CULTURE. Began publication with V. 1, 1977. Monographic Series. US. English. Coda Press, 700 West Badger Road, Madison WI 53713.

THEORY. (THE POLISH SOCIOLOGICAL BULLETIN). No. 1/2-. 0032-2997. Periodical. PL. English. qt. ARS Polona, Krakowskie Przedmiescie 7, 00-068 Warsaw Poland. **Ind/Abst** Int. Labour Doc., Soc. Sci. Citation Index, Sociol. Abstr., Lang. Lang. Behav. Abstr. **LC** HM1. **DD** 301.05.

THEORY AND SOCIETY. V. 1- 1974-. 0304-2421. Periodical. NE. English. bm. $88.00. Kluwer Academic Publishers Group, Spui Boulevard 50, PO Box 989, 3300 AZ Dordrecht Netherlands. **Tel** (020)5803.911. **Ind/Abst** Sociol. Abstr., Soc. Welf. Soc. Plan./Policy Soc. Dev., Public Aff. Inf. Serv. Bull., Soc. Sci. Citation Index, Lang. Lang. Behav. Abstr. **LC** HM1. **DD** 301.05.

THESIS ELEVEN. **VFOAT** Thesis 11. No. 1-. 0725-5136. Periodical. AT. English. ty. $26.57. Thesis Eleven, Phillip Institute of Technology, c/o Sociology Department, Bundoora 3083 Australia. **Ed** John Murphy. **Ind/Abst** Altern. Press Index. bk rev. adv acc. **Circ** 1,500. A scholarly journal of socialist theory; special interest: critical political theory, Eastern Europe, cultural analysis, class and feminism and questions of modernity.

TIDS NOG. Swedish. ir. Konsumentverket, Box 503, 162 15 Vallingby Sweden. **LC** HN580.Z9.

TIDSSKRIFT FOR SAMFUNNSFORSKNING. 0040-716X. Periodical. No. Norwegian (summaries in English). bm. $46.00. Universitetsforlaget, PO Box 2959-Toyen, Oslo 6 Norway. **Tel** 02-276 0 60. **Ind/Abst** Soc. Welf. Soc. Plan./Policy Soc. Dev., Sociol. Abstr., Am. Hist. Life, Soc. Sci. Citation Index, Lang. Lang. Behav. Abstr., Hist. Abstr., Part A, Mod. Hist. Abstr., Hist. Abst., Part B, Twent. Century Abstr. (cum index). Social research including sociology, social anthropology, social psychology and political science.

TIETOJA KAUPUNGEISTA, KAUPPALOISTA JA KAUPUNKILIITOSTA. **Main/Corp** Suomen Kaupunkiliitto. **VFOAT** Uppgifter Om Staderna, Kopingarna Och Stadsforbundet. Finnish and Swedish. ir. Suomen Kaupunkiliitto, Riksdagsgatan 4 00100 10, Helsinki Finland. **LC** HT145.F5.

TIJDSCHRIFT VOOR SOCIALE WETENSCHAPPEN. 1.- Volume. 0040-7615. Periodical. BE. Dutch. qt. $29.64. Seminarie Voor Sociologie, Universiteitstraat 8, Gent B-9000 Belgium. **Tel** (091)257651. **Ed** G Van Parys. **Ind/Abst** Sociol. Abstr., Soc. Welf. Soc. Plan./Policy Soc. Dev., Recent Publ. Artic., Lang. Lang. Behav. Abstr. **LC** H8. **DD** 330.5. bk rev. **Circ** 600. Articles on sociology, social sciences, criminology, psychology and economy.

TOKYO-TO ROJIN SOGO KENKYUJO NEMPO. JA. Japanese. ir. Free. Tokyo-To Rojin Sogo Kenkyujo, 35-2 Sakaecho, Itabashi-Ku 173 Tokyo Japan. **Tel** 03(964)1131. **Ed** Imahori Kazutomo. **LC** RC952. (ctrl). This is the report of Tokyo Metropolitan Institute of Gerontology which is conducting basic research on aging in the sphere from biomedical to sociological aspects.

TOURBILLON. V. 1-. 0704-6332. Periodical. CN. French. bm. **DD** 301.41'7'05.

TRADICION, FAMILIA, PROPIEDAD. V. 1- (No. 1-)-. Periodical. Spanish. ir. $22.00. Sociedad Argentina de Defensa de la Tradicion Familia y Propiedad, Avda Figueroa Alcorta 3260, Buenos Aires Argentina. **LC** HN30. **DD** 261.83. *Cruzada.*

TRANSMARGE. No. O (Fall 1984)-. 0823-9274. Periodical. CN. French. ir. $8.00 Each Number. Galeries d'Idees Dialyse, CP 745 Succursale C, Montreal Quebec H2L 4L5 Canada. **DD** 306.1.

TRAVAUX DE DROIT, D'ECONOMIE, DE SOCIOLOGIE ET DE SCIENCES POLITIQUES. *See* Economics.

UNIVERSAL MAN. V. 10 May 1974-. 0318-9821. CN. English. Earth City Foundation, 6902 Cote des Neiges, Montreal Quebec H3S 2B6 Canada. **DD** 301.3105. *Ecology Canada, 0318-983X.*

UNSCHEDULED EVENTS. V. 1- Spring 1967-. 0042-0468. Periodical. US. English. ir. $22.00. Research Committee Disasters, PO Box 513, S-751 20 Uppsala Sweden. **Tel** 45-18-155400. **Ed** Jan E Trost. bk rev. adv acc. **Circ** 300. News in the field of disasters and mass emergenices (mainly for members of the Committee of Disaster Research).

URBAN AFFAIRS ANNUAL REVIEWS. V. 1- 1967-. 0083-4688. Monographic Series. US. English. an. Sage Publication, 275 South Beverly Drive, Beverly Hills CA 90212. **LC** HT108. **DD** 301.3.

URBAN ANTHROPOLOGY. V. 1- Spring 1972-. 0363-2024. Periodical. US. English. qt. $50.00. Plenum Publishing Corporation, 227 West 17th Street, New York NY 10011. **Ind/Abst** Sociol. Abstr., Soc. Welf. Soc. Plan./Policy Soc. Dev., Recent Publ. Artic., Curr. Index J. Educ., Soc. Sci. Index. **LC** HT101. **DD** 301.36. **CODEN** URAND9. (cum index). *Urban Anthropology Newsletter.*

USSR REPORT. HUMAN RESOURCES. **VFOAT** Human Resources. Began in 1980-. US. English (translated from Russian). Available in microform. *USSR Report. Trade and Services.*

VIDEOSOCIOLOGY. V. 1- May 1972-. 0099-1384. US. English. $7.00. Boston University Graduate School, Walden Street, Newton Centre, Boston MA 02159. **LC** H62.A1. **DD** 301.07.

VIETNAM YOUTH. *See* Children and Youth Interests.

VIITORUL SOCIAL. Vol. 1- 1972-. 0379-3745. Periodical. RM. Romanian. qt. Ilexim Press Department, PO Box 1-136-1-137, Bucharest Romania. **Ind/Abst** Sociol. Abstr., Lang. Lang. Behav. Abstr. **LC** HM7.

VOILA. Periodical. German. ir. 41.50. Morgartenstrasse 29, CH8021 Zurich Switzerland. **LC** HQ1229. **DD** 305.40943.

VORT FOLK. Periodical. Danish. wk. **LC** HN30.

WAR & SOCIETY. **VFOAT** War and Society. Vol. 1, No. 1 (May 1983)-. 0729-2473. Periodical. English. sa. 15.00. Joint Editors War & Society, Department of History, University of New South Wales, Duntroon New South Wales 2600 Australia. **Tel** (062)688867. **Ed** P J Dennis and R C Thompson. **LC** HM36.5. **DD** 303.6605. adv acc. **Circ** 300. Journal is designed to provide a forum for the discussion of the history of war and its impact on society. Publishes scholarly articles on causes, experiences, and impact of war in all periods of history.

WEST AFRICAN JOURNAL OF SOCIOLOGY AND POLITICAL SCIENCE. (THE WEST AFRICAN JOURNAL OF SOCIOLOGY AND POLITICAL SCIENCE). **VFOAT** The West African Journal of Sociology & Political Science. Vol. 1, No. 1 (Oct. 1975)-. 0308-4450. Periodical. UK. English. qt. $30.00. University of Ibadan, Sociology Department, c/o Dr J Labinjoh, Ibadan Nigeria. **Ind/Abst** Sociol. Abstr., Soc. Welf. Soc. Plan./Policy Soc. Dev.

WIES WSPOCZESNA; PISMO RUCHU LUDOWEGO. Vol. 1- 1957-. 0511-9375. Periodical. PL. Polish (issues accompanied by tables of contents and summaries in English and Russian). mo. ARS Polona, Krakowskie Przedmiescie 7, 00-068 Warsaw Poland. **LC** HN536.

THE WISCONSIN SOCIOLOGIST. New Ser., V. 1- Spring 1962-. 0043-6666. Periodical. US. English. qt. $13.50. C S Green, University of Wisconsin, Department of Sociology, Whitewater WI 53190-1790. **Tel** (414)472-1125. **Ed** Charles S Green III. **Ind/Abst** Sociol. Abstr., Soc. Welf. Soc. Plan./Policy Soc. Dev., Lang. Lang. Behav. Abstr. **LC** HM1. **DD** 301.05. **CODEN** WSSCA. bk rev. adv acc. **Circ** 500. (ctrl). Research papers of general interest to the discipline; papers on social and public policy issues pertinent to the state and region; book reviews.

WOMEN'S STUDIES. *See* Women.

WORKING PAPER. **Main/Corp** Wisconsin Research and Development Center for Cognitive Learning. NO. Monographic Series. US. English. University of Wisconsin, 4412 Social Science Building, Demo Ecol, 1180 Observatory Drive, Madison WI 53706. **Tel** (608)262-2182. **Circ** 700. Demographic research articles.

WORKING PAPER SERIES - STRUCTURAL ANALYSIS PROGRAMME. DEPARTMENT OF SOCIOLOGY. UNIVERSITY OF TORONTO. (WORKING PAPER SERIES). **VAT** Working Paper - Structural Analysis Programme. Department of Sociology. University of Toronto. No. 6 (Dec. 1979)-. 0226-1774. Monographic Series. CN. English. Structural Analysis Programme, University of Toronto, Department of Sociology, 563 Spadina Avenue, Toronto Ontario M5S 1A1 Canada. **DD** 301. *Research Paper (University of Toronto. Structural Analysis Programme), 0825-3773.*

WORKING PAPERS IN CULTURAL STUDIES. **Main/Corp** University of Birmingham. Centre for Contemporary Cultural Studies. **VFOAT** Cultural Studies. 1- Spring 1971-. 0049-7991. UK. English. sa. Hutchinson Publishers, 3 Fitzroy Square, London WIP 6JD England. **Ind/Abst** Sociol. Abstr., Soc. Welf. Soc. Plan./Policy Soc. Dev., Lang. Lang. Behav. Abstr., Years Work Eng. Stud. **LC** AS122.B53. **DD** 082.

WORLD MEETINGS. SOCIAL & BEHAVIORAL SCIENCES, HUMAN SERVICES & MANAGEMENT. **VFOAT** Social & Behavioral Sciences, Human Services & Management, Social and Behavioral Sciences, Human Services and Management. Vol. 7, No. 2 (Apr. 1977)-. 0194-6161. Periodical. US. English. qt. $150.00. MacMillan Publishing Company, 866 3rd Avenue, New York NY 10022. **Tel** (800)257-8247. **Ed** Clark Hansen. **NLM** W 3.5 W926. **CODEN** WMSMPF. **Circ** 400. A two year registry of future meetings in the areas of social science, management, computer science, education, environment and energy as well as other subject areas. *World Meetings. Social & Behavioral Sciences, Education & Management, 0043-8685.*

WORLD OPINION UPDATE. V. 1- Sept. 1977-. 0193-3329. Periodical. US. English. mo. $48.00. Survey Research Consultants International Inc, PO Box 25, Williamstown MA 01267. **Tel** (413)458-4414. **Ed** Elizabeth H Hastings. **LC** D839. **DD** 309.1047. **Circ** 500. Opinion data worldwide on social, political, economic issues. Data is drawn from 100 survey organizations in 60 countries.

WSR, WESTERN SOCIOLOGICAL REVIEW. **VFOAT** Western Sociological Review. **VAT** Western Sociological Review, Western Sociological Review. 0097-8868. US. English. an. Utah State University, Department of Sociology, Logan UT 84322. **Ind/Abst** Sociol. Abstr., Soc. Welf. Soc. Plan./Policy Soc. Dev. **LC** HM1. **DD** 301.05. *Utah State Journal of Sociology.*

X-RAY. Periodical. UK. English. mo. Africa Bureau, 48 Grafton Way, London W1 England. **LC** DT737. **DD** 3014510968.

YEAR BOOK (LEO BAECK INSTITUTE). *See* Yearbooks, Almanacs, Directories.

YOUTH & SOCIETY. **VAT** Youth and Society. V. 1- Sept. 1969-. 0044-118X. Periodical. US. English. qt. Sage Publishers Inc, 275 South Beverly Drive, Beverly Hills CA 90212. **Tel** (213)274-8003. **Ind/Abst** Am. Hist. Life, Hist. Abstr., Part A, Mod. Hist. Abstr., Hist. Abst., Part B, Twent. Century Abstr., Sociol. Abstr., Soc. Welf. Soc. Plan./Policy Soc. Dev., Soc. Work Res. Abstr., Curr. Index J. Educ., Soc. Sci. Citation Index, Lang. Lang. Behav. Abstr., Hist. Abstr. **LC** HQ793. **DD** 301.431505. **NLM** W1 YO99N.

ZEITSCHRIFT FUR SOZIALPSYCHOLOGIE. Vol. 1., Issue 1 (1970)-. 0044-3514. Periodical. SZ. German. qt. Verlag Hans Huber AG, Laenggasstrasse 76 POB, CH-3000 Bern 9 Switzerland. **Tel** (031)242533. **Ed** H Feger, C F Graumann, K Holzkamp and M Ir. **Ind/Abst** Sociol. Abstr., Philos. Index, Psychol. Abstr., Soc. Sci. Citation Index. **LC** HM251. **CODEN** ZSPSDP.

ZIONIST IDEAS. **VFOAT** Mahashavot Tsiyoniyot. Monographic Series. English. sa. 10. Department of Development and Services, World Zionist Organization, P O B 92, Jerusalem 91920 Israel. **Tel** (02)635733. **Ed** Geoffrey Wigoder. bk rev. **Circ** 7,000.

ZYCIE OTTAWY. V. 1- May 7, 1978-. 0707-3976. Periodical. CN. Polish (text in English). bw. $7.00. Zycie Ottawy, Box 203 Station A, Ottawa Ontario K1P 6C4 Canada. **DD** 301.4519185071384.

MANNERS AND CUSTOMS

AKWESASNE NOTES. Began in 1969. 0002-3949. Periodical. US. English. bm. $10.00. Mohawk Nation, PO Box 196, Rooseveltown NY 13683-0196. **Tel** (518)358-9531. **Ed** Peter Blue Cloud. **Ind/Abst** Altern. Press Index. bk rev. **Circ** 15,000. (ctrl). Native American journal for native and natural people, selfsufficiency, native philosophy, issues as

Sociology: General Works, Theory—Manners and Customs

natives view it, includes North, South and Central America- poetry, art and book reviews.

ALCOHOL IN HISTORY. No. 9 (Spring 1984)-. 0749-7989. Periodical. US. English. sa. $5.00. David M Fahery, Department of History Miami University, Miami OH 45056. DD 394. *Alcohol and Temperance History Group Newsletter.*

AMERICAN POPULAR CULTURE. 0193-6859. Monographic Series. US. English. ir. Greenwood Press Inc, 51 Riverside Avenue, Westport CT 06880.

ANNUAL OWEN SOUND SUMMERFOLK FESTIVAL. VAT Program - Owen Sound Summerfolk Festival. 7th (1982)-. 0821-2813. CN. English. an. $0.50 Per No. Georgian Bay Folk Society, PO Box 521, Owen Sound Ontario N4K 5R1 Canada. DD 780.7971315. *Summerfolk (Owen Sound, Ont.), 0821-2805.*

ANNUAL REPORT - HAWAII BICENTENNIAL COMMISSION. (ANNUAL REPORT). Main/Corp Hawaii Bicentennial Commission. VFOAT Count Down to 1976. 0093-9080. US. English. an. Hawaii Bicentennial Commission, PO Box 2359, Honolulu HI 96804. LC E285.4.H3. DD 791.

BULITIN PERANGKAAN SOSIAL MALAYSIA. See Statistics.

THE BULLETIN OF THE CENTER FOR THE STUDY OF SOUTHERN CULTURE AND RELIGION. Main/Corp Florida State University. Center for the Study of Southern Culture and Religion. V. 1- Summer 1977-. 0272-023X. Periodical. US. English. ty. The Bulletin, Florida State University, Center for the Study of Southern Culture and Religion, 236 Williams Building, Tallahassee FL 32306.

CAHIERS NEPALAIS. No. 1- 1969-. Periodical. FR. French. ir. Editions du CNRS, 15 Quai Anatole France, F-75700 Paris France. Studies of history and customs of Nepal, Tibet and the Himalayans.

CALENDAR OF FESTIVALS. Began in 1977. 0271-9096. US. English. $3.25 Single Issue. National Council for the Traditional Arts, 1346 Connecticut Avenue/No 1118, Washington DC 20036. LC GT4802. DD 394.26973. *Calendar of Folk Festivals & Related Events, 0360-3334.*

CALGARY WEDDING. Vol. 1, No. 1 (Fall/ Winter 1983). 0821-1884. Periodical. CN. English. sa. $1.00 Per Number. Calgary Wedding, 815 4th Avenue SW/Suite 1802, Calgary Alberta T2P 3G Canada. DD 392.50971233.

CHANOYU QUARTERLY (KYOTO, JAPAN : 1976). (CHANOYU QUARTERLY). VFOAT Chanoyu. No. 13-. 0009-1537. Periodical. JA. English. qt. $20.00 US. Urasenke Foundation, Ogawa Teranouchi Agaru, Kamikyo-Ku Kyoto Japan 602. Tel (075)431-3111. Ed Gretchen Mittwer. LC GT2910. DD 394.15. bk rev. Circ 2,000. Beautifully illustrated articles, many original translations, on Japanese aesthetics, fine and applied arts, history, literature, philosophy, and religion in relation to the way of tea. *Chanoyu.*

CHASE'S ANNUAL EVENTS. VFOAT Annual Events. 1984-. 0740-5286. US. English. an. $12.95. Contemporary Books, 100 North Michigan Avenue, Chicago IL 60601. Ed William D and Helen M Chase. LC GT4803. DD 394.2605. *Chases' Calendar of Annual Events.*

CHRISTMAS : AN AMERICAN ANNUAL OF CHRISTMAS LITERATURE AND ART. Began publication with V. 1, 1931. US. English. an. Augsburg Publishing House, 57 East Main, Columbus OH 43215. Tel (614)221-7411. Ed R E Haugan.

CHRISTMAS IDEALS. US. English. an. Ideals Publishing Co, 11315 West Watertown Plank Road, Milwaukee WI 53226. LC GT4985. DD 394.268.

CHRISTMAS TREE TALK. 1- April 1969-. 0578-0284. Periodical. US. English. qt. 611 East Wells Street, Milwaukee WI 53202.

CIDOC CUADERNO. Main/Corp Centro Intercultural de Documentacion. 0577-2966. Periodical. MX. Spanish (contains articles in Portuguese, French, German and English). ir. Centro Intercultural Documentacion, Apartado 479, Cuernauaca Mexico.

CIVILISATIONS ET SOCIETES. 1- 1965-. 0069-4290. Monographic Series. French. ir. Walter de Gruyter Inc, 200 Sawmill River Road, Hawthorne NY 10532.

CIVILIZACION (MEXICO CITY, MEXICO). (CIVILIZACION : CONFIGURACIONES DE LA DIVERSIDAD). 1-. Periodical. MX. Spanish. ir. Ceestem Corl Porfirio Diaz, No 50 San Jeronimo l'Idice, 10200 Mexico DF Mexico.

CIVILTA VENEZIANA. SAGGI. 11- 1962-. 0069-4371. Periodical. IT. Italian. ir. Casa Editrece Leo S Olschki, Casella Postale PO Box 66, 50100 Firenze Italy. *Saggi Historici, Saggi Storici.*

THE DIGEST - UNIVERSITY OF PENNSYLVANIA. DEPT. OF FOLKLORE AND FOLKLIFE. (THE DIGEST). Vol. 1, No. 1 (Nov. 1977)-. f737-7703. Periodical. US. English. ty. $9.00. Subscription Manager of The Digest, Department of Folklore/ Folklife 415 Logan Hall/CN University of Pennsylvania, Philadelphia PA 19104. Tel (215)898-7352. Ed Kathy Neustadt. LC GT2850. DD 394.105. bk rev. Circ 200. A clearinghouse for people interested in the study of food and culture, from diverse points of view, anthropological, historical, gastronomic, etc.

EIGHTEENTH-CENTURY LIFE. V. 1- Sept. 1974-. 0098-2601. Periodical. US. English. ty. c/o English Department, College of William & Mary, Williamsburg VA 23185. Tel (804)253-4468. Ind/Abst Abstr. Engl. Stud., Am. Hist. Life, Hist. Abstr., Part A, Mod. Hist. Abstr., Hist. Abst., Part B, Twent. Century Abstr., MLA Int. Bibliogr. Books Artic. Mod. Lang. Lit., Recent Publ. Artic., Hist. Abstr. LC HN1. DD 309.103.

FAT TUESDAY. V. 1, No. 1-. 0276-2072. Periodical. US. English. sa. $5.00. Fat Tuesday Publications, 7215 Hillside #6, Los Angeles CA 90046.

FILM A DOBA; MESICNIK PRO FILMOVOU KULTURU. 19 -. Periodical. CS. Czech. mo. Artia, V E Smecky 30, Praha 1 Czechoslovakia. Ind/Abst Film Lit. Index.

THE FOLK DIRECTORY. See Yearbooks, Almanacs, Directories.

GYOJI SAMBYAKU-ROKUJUGONICHI. 1972-. JA. Japanese. ir. 1300. Mainichi Shimbun Sha, 1-1 Hitotsubashi Chiyoda-Ku, Tokyo 100 Japan. LC GT4884.A2. *Gyoji Saijiki.*

HEIMATLEBEN = COSTUMES ET COUTUMES. V. 49-. Periodical. French (German). ir. 12.00. Schweizerische Trachtenvereinigung, Postfach 8023, Zurich Switzerland. LC GT1240. DD 391.009494. *Heimatleben, Costumes et Coutumes.*

INTRODUCTION TO AFRICAN CULTURE. VFOAT Introduction A la Culture Africaine. 1-. Monographic Series. FR. English (French). ir. United Nations Educational Scientific and Cultural Organization, 7 Place de Fontenoy, 75700 Paris France.

IPADE ALAGBARA. 0883-6620. Periodical. US. English. mo $10.50. IPADE Alagbara, Kameleon Publications, PO Box 1534 Los Angeles CA 90028. Tel (213)468-9165. Ed Taivina Songobunmi. DD 305. bk rev. adv acc. Circ 3,000. (ctrl). An international journal of African traditional arts and lifestyles of Afrikans in the new world. Features healing, herbology, divination, astrology, dance, music, rituals. Total traditional arts.

KOBE ZEIKAN. Main/Corp Japan. Zeikan, Kobe. VFOAT Kobe Customs. Japanese (English). ir. Kobe Zeikan, Kanocho 6-Chome Ikuta-Ku (650), Kobe Japan. LC HJ7276.Z7.

LC FOLK ARCHIVE FINDING AID. See Genealogy and Heraldry - Archives.

LC FOLK ARCHIVE REFERENCE AID. See Genealogy and Heraldry - Archives.

MARIPOSA FOLK FESTIVAL. (MARIPOSA FOLK FESTIVAL : PROGRAMME). VFOAT Mariposa. 0712-6263. CN. English. an. 16.00. Mariposa Folk Foundation, 525 Adelaide Street East, Toronto Ontario M5A 2R2 Canada. Tel (416)363-4009. Ed Joan Smith. DD 780.79713541. bk rev. adv acc. Circ 25,000. Newsletter providing information regarding the folk arts, including articles on dance, singing-songwriting, crafts, instrument making, etc. Also interviews with artists, folk calendar and reviews.

NAYER DOR. (DER NAYER DOR). VAT Nouvelle Generation (Montreal), New Generation (Montreal). Spring 1978-. 0705-7822. Periodical. CN. Yiddish. D Botwinik, 5775 Wentworth Cote St-Luc, Montreal Quebec H4W 2S3 Canada. Tel (514)488-4469. Ed Leon Botwinik. DD 437.947. Circ 1,000. (ctrl). Yiddish cultural and educational magazine promoting the widespread use of Yiddish as a spoken language. Stories, humour, music, articles, children's section, and a computer science section.

NEWSLETTER - MEMORIAL SOCIETY OF EDMONTON AND DISTRICT. Main/ Corp Memorial Society of Edmonton and District. Oct. 1975-. 0703-9069. Periodical. CN. English. Memorial Society of Edmonton and District, 5326 Ada Boulevard, Edmonton Alberta T5W 4N7 Canada. DD 393.06271233. *Newsletter, 0703-9050.*

NOTEBOOKS IN CULTURAL ANALYSIS. 1-. 8756-9051. Periodical. US. English. an. Duke University Press, Box 6697 College Station, Durham NC 27708. DD 306.4.

OBSHCHIE PROBLEMY KULTURY I KULTURNOGO STROITELSTVA. See Ethnic.

THE OFFICIAL INTERNATIONAL DIRECTORY OF SPECIAL EVENTS & FESTIVALS. See Yearbooks, Almanacs, Directories.

THE OFFICIAL SOUVENIR PROGRAM OF SPOLETO FESTIVAL U.S.A. See Music.

PALESTINE EXPLORTION QUARTERLY. Jan./March 1869-. 0031-0328. Periodical. UK. English. sa. Palestine Exploration Fund, 2 Hinde Mews Marylebone Lane, London W1M 5RH England. Tel (01)935-5379. Ed P R Ackroyo. bk rev. adv acc. Circ 1,000. Covers manners and customs of ancient and modern Syria (Syria, Lebanon, Jordan, and Israel) and their inhabitants.

PIONEER AMERICA, THE JOURNAL OF HISTORIC AMERICAN MATERIAL CULTURE. V. 1- 1969-. Periodical. US. English. sa.

PROSPETTIVE CULTURALI. Yearly V. 1, No. 1 (Sept./Oct. 1979)-. Periodical. IT. Italian. qt. Societe Editrice Napoletana, Corso Umberto 34, 80138 Naples Italy. LC AP37. DD 055.1.

PUBLICATIONS - GYPSY LORE SOCIETY, NORTH AMERICAN CHAPTER. (PUBLICATIONS). Began with: No. 1, published in 1981. 8756-7245. US. English. ir. Gypsy Lore Society, North American Chapter, c/o Joann Grumet, 250 Riverside Drive, New York NY 10025. DD 390.

RAPPORT D'ACTIVITE - INSTITUT AFRICAIN POUR LE DEVELOPPEMENT ECONOMIQUE ET SOCIAL. See Economics - Economics: Land.

RESEARCH PAPER - RESEARCH GROUP ON LEISURE AND CULTURAL DEVELOPMENT, UNIVERSITY OF WATERLOO. (RESEARCH PAPER). VFOAT Research Papers on Leisure and Cultural Development. No. 1-. 0821-1299. Monographic Series. CN. English. Research Group on Leisure and Cultural Development, Department of Recreation/University of Waterloo, Waterloo Ontario N2L 3G1 Canada. DD 306.

REVUE DE PRESSE - FESTIVAL D'ETE DE QUEBEC. (LA REVUE DE PRESSE DU . . . FESTIVAL D'ETE DE QUEBEC). Main/Corp Festival d'Ete de Quebec. 16E (7/17 July 1983)-. 0822-8701. CN. French. an. Festival d'Ete de Quebec, C P 24/Station B, Quebec Quebec G1K 7A1 Canada. DD 394.2509714471. *Revue de Presse, 0822-8701.*

TAM TI DELAM. (TAM TI DELAM : BULLETIN DE LA SOCIETE DES FESTIVALS POPULAIRES DU QUEBEC). 0705-3428. Periodical. CN. French. ir. Free. Societe des Festivals Populaires, 1415 Est rue Jarry, Montreal Quebec H2E 2Z7 Canada. DD 394.25060714.

TAWON. V. 1-. Periodical. KO. Korean. mo. 30,000. Tawon, 49-40 2-Ka, Namsan-Dong Chung-Ku Seoul Korea. LC GT2907.K6.

TIRE-PIPE. (LE TIRE-PIPE). Vol. 1, No. 1 (1982)-. 0821-6894. Periodical. CN. French. qt. Free to Members. Club des Fumeurs de Pipes du Quebec, C

Sociology: General Works, Theory—Social Pathology, Welfare, Criminology

P 117, l'Assomption Quebec J0K 1G0 Canada. **DD** 394.14.

UNTERSUCHUNGEN UBER GRUPPEN UND VERBANDE. V. 1 1964-. 0566-2753. Monographic Series. German. ir. Duncker und Humbolt Verlag, Dietrich-Schafer-Weg 9, 1 Berlin 41 West Germany.

WEN WU. VFOAT Cultural Relics. 1950-. 0511-4772. Periodical. CC. Chinese. mo. China Publication Centre, PO Box 2820, Beijing China. **Ind/Abst** Am. Hist. Life, Hist. Abstr.

WESTERN FRONTIER LIBRARY. See History (General) - History of North, South, and Central America.

WORLD CALENDAR OF HOLIDAYS CEASED. 1977-81. 0161-0066. US. English. an. 23 Wall Street, New York NY 10015. **LC** GT3930. **DD** 394.268. Bank and Public Holidays.

YASURAGI. 1st 1- Vol. Periodical. JA. Japanese. ir. 400. Geijutsu Bunkasha, c/o Daini Tanko Building, Horikawadori Kuramaguchi Noboru, Kita-ku (603), Kyoto Japan. **LC** GT2910.

SOCIAL PATHOLOGY, WELFARE, CRIMINOLOGY

4TH QUARTER STATISTICAL REPORT & ANNUAL REPORT. See Statistics.

65 A L'HEURE. V. 1- Oct. 1972-. Periodical. CN. French. mo. 3. Ministere des Affaires, Edifice Parlementaire 1005 Chemin Ste-Foy, Quebec Que G1A 1C3 Canada. **LC** HV109.Q44. **DD** 362.9714.

ABSTRACTS FOR SOCIAL WORKERS. CEASED. V. 1-13, No. 1. 0001-3412. Periodical. US. English. qt. $20.00. 2 Park Avenue, New York NY 10016. **LC** HV1. **DD** 361.008. **NLM** Z 7164.C4 A164.

ABSTRACTS ON CRIME AND JUVENILE DELINQUENCY: AN INDEX TO THE MICROFORM COLLECTION. See Indexes/Abstracts.

ABSTRACTS ON CRIMINOLOGY AND PENOLOGY CEASED. VFOAT Criminology and Penology. V. 9-19. 0001-3684. English. ir. **LC** HV6001. **DD** 364.08. **NLM** Z 5118.C9 E96. Excerpta Criminologica.

ABSTRACTS. STATE APPALACHIAN DEVELOPMENT PLANS AND INVESTMENT PROGRAMS. See Indexes/Abstracts.

ACQUISITIONS LIST - CENTRE OF CRIMINOLOGY LIBRARY. UNIVERSITY OF TORONTO. See Library and Information Science.

ACTION - CANADIAN COUNCIL ON CHILDREN AND YOUTH. (ACTION FOR CANADA'S CHILDREN). VFOAT Action pour les Enfants du Canada. Vol. 1, No. 1-. 0229-2653. Periodical. CN. English (with French text on inverted pages, 1980-Spring 1983). qt. 4.00 Members, 5.00 Non-members. Canadian Council on Children and Youth, 323 Chapel Street, Ottawa Ontario K1N 7X2 Canada. **DD** 649.10971.

L'ACTION SOCIALE DES CAISSES D'ALLOCATIONS FAMILIALES. Main/Corp Caisse Nationale des Allocations Familiales. VFOAT Statistiques Concernant l'Action Sociale des Caisses d'Allocations Familiales. 1971-. French. ir. Caisse d'Allocations Familiales, 63 Bd Haussmann, 8 Paris France. **LC** HD4925.5.F8. **DD** 362.5. Statistiques Concernant l'Activite des Caisses et Services Particuliers d'Allocations Familiales.

ACTIVITE. (ACTIVITE - MINISTERE DE LA SANTE). Main/Corp Nouveau-Brunswick. Ministere de la Sante. Published since July 1978?. 0706-1803. Periodical. CN. French. ir. Ministere de la Sante, CP 690 Moncton, Fredericton NB E1C 8M7 Canada. **DD** 362.6109715.

ADAMIS ANNUAL REPORT. Fiscal Year 1983-. US. English. an. State of Missouri/Department of Mental Health, 2002 Missouri Boulevard PO Box 687, Jefferson City MO 65102.

ADDITIONS TO STATE MENTAL HEALTH FACILITIES, FISCAL YEAR . . . . 1978/79-. US. English. an. Mis and Data Services Division/Department of Mental Health Retardation, PO Box 1797, Richmond VA 23214. **LC** RA790.65.V54. **DD** 362.209755.

ADMISSIONS TO JUVENILE INSTITUTIONS. 1970-. US. English. an. Wisconsin Division of Corrections, Office of Information Management and Operations, Madison WI 53707. **LC** HV9105.W6. **DD** 365.4209775. Juveniles Admitted to Division of Corrections' Juvenile Institutions.

ADOPTION & FOSTERING. VAT Adoption and Fostering. 84- 1976-. 0308-5759. Periodical. UK. English. qt. $22.22. British Agencies for Adoption & Fostering, 11 Southwark St, London SE1 1RQ England. Tel 01.407-8800. Ed Sarah Curtis. **Ind/Abst** Psychol. Abstr. **LC** HV875. **DD** 362.7330941. bk rev. adv acc. Circ 4,400. Social work, legal and medical issues concerning children and public care and provide security if care is necessary. Child Adoption.

ADOPTIONS - STATE OF VERMONT, DEPARTMENT OF SOCIAL AND REHABILITATION SERVICES. Main/Corp Vermont. Dept. of Social and Rehabilitation Services. US. English. 81 River Street, Montpelier VT 05602. **LC** HV883.V5. **DD** 362.73409743. Vermont Adoptions.

ADULT COUNTY JAIL AND DETENTION FACILITY REPORT. Series/Titl Statistical Bulletin C. 1980-. US. English. an. Wisconsin Division of Corrections, PO Box 7925, Madison WI 53707. **LC** HV7299. **DD** 365.34. County Jail and Detention Facility Report.

ADULT CRIMINAL DETENTION. (ADULT CRIMINAL DETENTION : REFERENCE TABLES). Main/Corp California. Bureau of Criminal Statistics. 0092-2080. US. English. an. 3301 C Street, PO Box 13427, Sacramento CA 95813. **LC** HV7254. **DD** 365.609794.

ADULT OFFENDERS. Series/Titl Statistical Report. US. English. an. **LC** HV7277. **DD** 364.309782.

ADULT PROBATION. Main/Corp Texas Adult Probation Commission. US. English. an. **LC** HV9305.T4. **DD** 353.976400849306. Available on microfiche from Texas State Library.

ADULT PROBATION ADMISSIONS. Main/Corp Wisconsin. Division of Corrections. Office of Systems and Evaluation. Series/Titl Statistical Bulletin, C. 1976-. 0095-4004. US. English. an. Division of Corrections, Office of Systems and Evaluation, PO Box 669, Madison WI 53701. **LC** HV7299. **DD** 364.6309775. Adult Probation Admissions, 0095-4004.

ADULT PROSECUTION: REFERENCE TABLES. VFOAT Adult Prosecution : Reference Tables. Periodical. US. English. an. 3301 C Street/PO Box 13427, Sacramento CA 95813.

ADULTS UNDER COMMUNITY SUPERVISION. Fiscal year 1981-. US. English. an. Virginia Department of Corrections/Division of Program Development and Evaluation Research and Reporting Unit, PO Box 26963, Richmond VA 23261. **LC** HV9305.V8. **DD** 364.6309755. Adults and Children Under Community Supervision.

ADVIES INZAKE PRIJSREGELEN BEJAARDENOORDEN. Main/Corp Netherlands (Kingdom, 1815-). Centrale Commissie Voor de Bejaardenoorden. Dutch. ir. **LC** HV1481.N4.

AFDC QUALITY CONTROL CORRECTIVE ACTION PLAN. VFOAT Aid to Families with Dependent Children Quality Control Corrective Action Plan. Apr. 1983-Mar. 1984-. US. English. an. **LC** HV742.C2. **DD** 353.9794008482. California AFDC Quality Control Corrective Action Plan.

AFRICAN SOCIAL SECURITY DOCUMENTATION. Main/Corp International Social Security Association. General Secretariat. No. 2-. English. ir. 12.00. International Social Security Association, Casle Postale 1, CH-1211 Geneva 22 Switzerland. Tel (022) 99.61.11. **LC** HD7237. **DD** 368.40096. Circ 500. Studies of various aspects or problems of social protection in African countries.

AFTERWORDS. 8756-3010. Periodical. US. English. qt. $5.00. Afterwords, 5124 Grove Street, Minneapolis MN 55436. **DD** 361.

AGED CARE & SERVICES REVIEW. VAT Aged Care and Services Review. V. 1- Jan./Feb. 1978-. 0161-1151. Periodical. US. English. qt. $42.00 US(Libraries), $38.00 Other Institutions US, $47.00 Canada(Libraries), $38.00 Other Institutions Canada. Haworth Press, 149 Fifth Avenue, New York NY 10010. **Ind/Abst** Sociol. Abstr., Soc. Welf. Soc. Plan./Policy Soc. Dev., Psychol. Abstr. **NLM** ZWT 100.3 A26. CODEN ACSRDO.

AGENCY CATALOG. US. English. **LC** RA790.65.M5. **DD** 362.2025774.

AGENCY DIRECTORY - AMERICAN HUMANE ASSOCIATION. See Yearbooks, Almanacs, Directories.

AGGRESSION AND ANTI-SOCIAL BEHAVIOR IN CHILDHOOD AND ADOLESCENCE. 1st- Ed. UK. English. Pergamon Press Ltd, Headington Hill Hall, Oxford OX3 0BW England. **LC** RJ506.A35. **DD** 305.23.

AGING (UNITED STATES ADMINISTRATION ON AGING). (AGING). Began with Oct. 1965. 0002-0966. Periodical. US. English. bm. $13.00 Domestic, $16.25 Foreign. Superintendent of Documents, US Government Printing Office, Washington DC 20402. **Ind/Abst** Book Rev. Index, Hospit. Lit. Index, Life Sci. Collect., Pop. Mag. Rev., Ref. Source, Read. Guide Period. Lit., Public Aff. Inf. Serv. Bull., Index U.S. Gov. Period. **LC** HV1457. **NLM** W1 AG342. Available on microfilm. Aging (United States Office of Aging), 0002-0966.

AICHI-KEN CHIIKI BOSAI KEIKAKU. FUSUIGAI TO SAIGAI TAISAKU KEIKAKU. Main/Corp Aichi Bosai Kaigi. 1963. JA. Japanese. ir. Aichi Bosai Kaigi, 1-Ban 2-Go Sannomaru, 3-Chome Naka-Ku, Nagoya Japan. **LC** HV555.J3.

AICHI-KEN CHIIKI BOSAI KEIKAKU. FUZOKU SHIRYO. 1963-. JA. Japanese. ir. Aichi Bosai Kaigi Jimukyoku 1-2 Sannomaru 3-Chome Naka-Ku, Nagoya-Shi Japan. **LC** HV555.J3.

AICHI-KEN CHIIKU BOSAI KEIKAKU. JISHIN SAIGAI TAISAKU KEIKAKU. Main/Corp Aichi-Ken Bosai Kaigi. 1965. Japanese. ir. **LC** HV555.J3.

AICHI KENRITSU DAIGAKU BUNGAKUBU RON SHU : SHAKAI-FUKUSHIGAKUKA HEN. VFOAT Bulletin of the Faculty of Literature, Aichi Prefectural University. No. 21- May. JA. Japanese. ir. 3-28 Takadacho Mizuho-Ku, Nagoyo Japan. **LC** HV4. Aichi Kenritsu Daigaku Bungakubu Ron Shu: Jimbun, Shakai, Shizen.

AID TO FAMILIES WITH DEPENDENT CHILDREN. US. English. be. Department of Public Welfare, St Paul MN 55101. **LC** HV699. **DD** 326.8209776. Minnesota Aid to Families with Dependent Children for Fiscal Year.

AJL NEWSLINE. (AJL NEWSLINE : NEWS ABOUT VOLUNTEERING, VOLUNTEERS, & THE ASSOCIATION OF JUNIOR LEAGUES). VAT Association of Junior Leagues Newsletter. Vol. 1, No. 1 (Feb. 1981)-. 0279-6929. Periodical. US. English. bm. Association of Junior Leagues Inc, 825 Third Avenue, New York NY 10022.

ALABAMA SOCIAL WELFARE. Began with issue for Oct./Nov./Dec. 1936. 0002-4368. US. English. bm. Alabama State Department of Pensions & Securities, 64 North Union Street, Montgomery AL 36104. **LC** HV86. **DD** 360.9761. **NLM** W2 AA4 S73AA.

ALBANY BULLETIN ON HEALTH AND WELFARE LEGISLATION OF THE STATE COMMUNITIES AID ASSOCIATION : BULLETIN. See Public Health and Safety.

ALBERTA HEALTH AND SOCIAL SERVICE TRAINING PROGRAM INVENTORY. Academic Years 1974-1975, 1975-1976, 1976-1977, 1977-1978-. 0709-9517. CN. English. an. Health and Social Service Programs Branch, Alberta Advanced Education and Manpower, 7th Floor Devonian Building, 11160 Jasper Avenue, Edmonton Alta T5K 0L1 Canada. **DD** 360.7117123.

ALBERTA PERSPECTIVE. Vol. 1, No. 1 (Fall 1981)-. 0713-8067. Periodical. CN. English. qt. $6.19. Alberta Association of the Mentally Handicapped, 11728 Kingsway Avenue, Edmonton Alberta TSG 0X5 Canada. Tel (403)451-3055. Ed Carol M Peters. **DD** 362.3097123. bk rev. Circ 1,200. (ctrl). Articles of interest to the mentally handicapped, their families and support people. Current and upcoming events. New Horizon, 0028-5366.

ALL THE WORLD. A QUARTERLY REVIEW OF THE WORLD-WIDE WORK OF THE SALVATION ARMY. V. 1-49, 1884-1929. 0002-5623. Periodical. UK. English. qt. 1.60. Salvationist Publishing & Supplies, 117-121 Judd St-Kings Cross, London WCI England. Tel 01 387 1656. Ed William Burrows. **LC** BX9701. **DD**

Sociology: General Works, Theory—Social Pathology, Welfare, Criminology

267.1505. **Circ** 20,000. Articles describing remedical work undertaken in all classes of homes, institutions, and hospitals by the Salvation Army world-wide.

ALTERNATIVE CHILD CARE PROGRAMS. Main/Corp California. State Dept. of Education. Office of Child Development. US. English. an. California State Department of Education, 721 Capitol Mall, Sacramento CA 95814.

AMERICAN REHABILITATION. (AMERICAN REHABILITATION : AR). Began with V. 1, No. 1 (Sept/Oct 1975)-. 0362-4048. Periodical. US. English. qt. Superintendent of Documents, US Government Printing Office, Washington DC 20402. **Ind/Abst** Index U.S. Gov. Period. **LC** HD7255.A2. **DD** 362.85. **NLM** W1 AM7435.

ANALES DE CIENCIAS HUMANAS. See Yearbooks, Almanacs, Directories.

ANALISIS (SAN JUAN, P.R.). (ANALISIS). V. 1, No. 1 (Jan./June 1982)-. Periodical. English (Spanish). sa. $9.00. Analisis, Revista de Planificacion, Apartado 8085, Santurce Puerto Rico 00910. **LC** H97. **DD** 361.61097295.

ANALYSE DE LA CAMPAGNE. Main/Corp United Way of Canada. **VFOAT** Campaign Analysis. 1978-. 0228-6610. **CN**. English (French). an. Free. United Way of Canada, 915-112 Kent, Ottawa Ontario K1P 5P2 Canada. **DD** 361.70971. Information and Statistics, 0383-9826.

AN ANALYSIS OF COUNTY REFERRAL CASES - CALIFORNIA YOUTH AUTHORITY. Main/Corp California Youth Authority. 0094-6419. US. English. **LC** HV9105.C2. **DD** 364.6.

ANALYSIS OF CRIME IN OREGON. 1980-. US. English. an. Oregon Law Enforcement Council, 2001 Front Street NE, Salem OR 97310. **LC** HV7287. **DD** 364.9795. State of Oregon Analysis of Criminal Offenses and Arrests, 0145-6903.

ANAPERIKON VEMA. Periodical. GR. Greek, Modern. ir. Pankyprios Organoses Ap Anaperon, Penetlis 50 Strovolos/Nicosia, Leukosia Greece. **LC** HV1551.

THE ANGOLITE. (ANGOLITE). V. 1- Dec. 1952-. 0402-4249. Periodical. US. English. bm. $12.00. Angolite, Louisiana State Penitentiary, Angola LA 70712. **Tel** (504)655-4411. Ed Wilbert Rideau and Billy Sinclair. bk rev. **Circ** 4,000. News coverage of life in the Louisiana State Penitentiary and coverage of issues and events affecting the criminal justice system.

ANNALES DE VAUCRESSON. No. 1- 1963-. Periodical. FR. French. an. $3.99. Centre de Formation et de Recherche de l'Education Surveillee, 54 rue de Garches, 92 Vaucresson France. **LC** HV9051. **DD** 364.3605.

ANNALES INTERNATIONALES DE CRIMINOLOGIE. See Yearbooks, Almanacs, Directories.

ANNUAIRE STATISTIQUE DE LA JUSTICE. See Yearbooks, Almanacs, Directories.

ANNUAL ACTION PLAN - UTAH COUNCIL ON CRIMINAL JUSTICE ADMINISTRATION. Main/Corp Utah. Council on Criminal Justice Administration. **VFOAT** Plan - Utah Council on Criminal Justice Administration. US. English. an. Utah Council on Criminal Justice Administration, 255 South 3rd East, Salt Lake City UT 84111. **LC** HV7294. **DD** 364.9792.

THE ANNUAL ACTION PROGRAM TO PREVENT & CONTROL CRIME (WEST VIRGINIA). Main/Corp West Virginia. Governor's Committee on Crime, Delinquency and Corrections. **VFOAT** Synopsis, Criminal Justice Programs in the State of West Virginia. **VAT** Annual Action Program to Prevent and Control Crime. 0145-6962. US. English. an. **LC** HV7298. **DD** 364.09754.

ANNUAL ACTION PROGRAMS - MONTANA. BOARD OF CRIME COUNCIL. Main/Corp Montana. Board of Crime Council. US. English. an. Montana Board of Crime Control, 303 North Roberts, Helena MT 59601. **LC** HV7276. **DD** 364.9786.

ANNUAL ADMINISTRATION REPORT, FAMILY WELFARE PROGRAMME (INDIA). Main/Corp Gujarat (India : State). Demographic & Evaluation Cell. 1978-79-. English. an. **LC** HQ766.5.I5. **DD** 354.548500815. Annual Administration Report on Family Planning Programme.

ANNUAL ADMINISTRATION REPORT OF THE SOCIAL WELFARE DEPARTMENT (INDIA). Main/Corp Andhra Pradesh (India). Dept. of Social Welfare. 1974/75-. English. an. **LC** HV394.A5. **DD** 354.5484008406.

ANNUAL ADOPTION REPORT - MISSOURI. DIVISION OF FAMILY SERVICES. Main/Corp Missouri. Division of Family Services. **VFOAT** Missouri Adoptions. 1979-. US. English. an. **LC** HV883.M625. **DD** 362.73409778. Missouri Adoptions.

ANNUAL BRIEF SUBMITTED BY THE QUEBEC ASSOCIATION FOR THE MENTALLY RETARDED TO THE GOVERNMENT OF QUEBEC. Main/Corp Quebec Association for the Mentally Retarded. Nov. 1976-. 0713-8555. **CN**. English. an. $1.25 Per Vol. Quebec Association for the Mentally Retarded, Suite 15/5890 Monkland Avenue, Montreal Quebec H4A 1G2 Canada. **DD** 362.309714.

ANNUAL CATALOGUE OF JUSTICE RESEARCH AND POLICY STUDIES IN B.C. VAT Annual Catalogue of Justice Research and Policy Studies in British Columbia. Vol. 2-. 0710-4332. **CN**. English. an. Free. **LC** HV9509.B6. **DD** 364.9711, 347.7110072. Annual Review of Criminal Justice Research in B.C.

ANNUAL CAUSES & CONDITIONS OF POVERTY IN SOUTH DAKOTA. Main/Corp South Dakota. State Economic Opportunity Office. 0091-0724. US. English. an. State Economic Opportunity Office, Capital Building, Pierre SD 57501. **LC** HC107.S83. **DD** 301.441.

ANNUAL CONFERENCE PROCEEDINGS - CONFERENCE FOR THE ADVANCEMENT OF PRIVATE PRACTICE IN SOCIAL WORK. Main/Conf Conference for the Advancement of Private Practice in Social Work. 1- 1962-. 0069-8385. US. English. an. **LC** HV41.

ANNUAL FINANCIAL AND STATISTICAL REPORT - OHIO. DEPT. OF MENTAL RETARDATION AND DEVELOPMENTAL DISABILITIES. See Statistics.

ANNUAL FINANCIAL REPORT - BROWNWOOD STATE SCHOOL. Main/Corp Brownwood State School. US. English. an. Brownwood State School, PO Box 1267, Brownwood TX 76801. **LC** HV9105.T45. **DD** 353.9764007232.

ANNUAL FINANCIAL REPORT, CENTRAL OFFICE OF THE TEXAS YOUTH COUNCIL. Main/Corp Texas Youth Council. Central Office. US. English. an. Texas Youth Council, 8900 Shoal Creek Boulevard PO Box 9999, Austin TX 78766. **LC** HV1435.T4. **DD** 353.9764007232.

ANNUAL FINANCIAL REPORT - COMMISSION ON JAIL STANDARDS. Main/Corp Texas. Commission on Jail Standards. US. English. an. Texas Commission on Jail Standards, 1414 Colorado Street/Suite 500, PO Box 12985, Austin TX 78711. **LC** HV7293. **DD** 353.9764007232.

ANNUAL FINANCIAL REPORT - CORSICANA STATE HOME. Main/Corp Corsicana State Home. US. English. an. Corsicana State Home, PO Box 610, Corsicana TX 75110. **LC** HV995.C752. **DD** 353.9764007231.

ANNUAL FINANCIAL REPORT - DISTRICT OF COLUMBIA. DEPT. OF HUMAN SERVICES. Main/Corp District of Columbia. Dept. of Human Services. US. English. an. Department of Human Services/ Office of the Controller, 801 North Capitol Street NE, Washington DC 20002. **LC** HV99.W29. **DD** 352.94409753.

ANNUAL FINANCIAL REPORT - WEST TEXAS CHILDREN'S HOME. Main/Corp West Texas Children's Home. US. English. an. West Texas Children's Home, PO Box 415, Pyote TX 79777. **LC** HV9105.T45. **DD** 353.9764008495.

ANNUAL GOVERNOR'S REPORT - NEBRASKA LIQUOR CONTROL COMMISSION. Main/Corp Nebraska. Liquor Control Commission. US. English. an. Nebraska Liquor Control Commission, Lincoln NE 68508. **LC** HV5079.N2. **DD** 353.97820076106. Annual Report.

ANNUAL JOURNAL - PETER W. RODINO INSTITUTE OF CRIMINAL JUSTICE. (ANNUAL JOURNAL). Vol. 1, No. 1 (1979)-. 0276-8151. Periodical. US. English. an. Peter W Rodino Institute of Criminal Justice, 2039 Kennedy Boulevard, Jersey City NJ 07305. **LC** HV8143. **DD** 364.9749.

ANNUAL JUVENILE STATISTICAL REPORT - SUPERIOR COURT OF THE DISTRICT OF COLUMBIA. WASHINGTON, D.C. See Statistics.

ANNUAL MANAGEMENT/ ADMINISTRATIVE STATISTICS REPORT ON THE CRIMINAL JUSTICE SYSTEM. See Statistics.

ANNUAL PLAN OF THE ILLINOIS DEPARTMENT OF MENTAL HEALTH AND DEVELOPMENTAL DISABILITIES. (ANNUAL PLAN . . . OF THE ILLINOIS DEPARTMENT OF MENTAL HEALTH AND DEVELOPMENTAL DISABILITIES). **Main/Corp** Illinois. Dept. of Mental Health and Developmental Disabilities. 1979, 1980, 1981, 1982-. 0276-6922. US. English. an. Illinois Department of Mental Health and Developmental Disabilities, 160 North LaSalle Street, Chicago IL 60601. **LC** RA790.65.I4. **DD** 362.209773. **NLM** W2 AI3 D37A.

ANNUAL PLAN OF WORK - DEPARTMENT OF HUMAN RESOURCES. (ANNUAL PLAN OF WORK). **Main/Corp** North Carolina. Dept. of Human Resources. 0095-4942. US. English. an. Department of Human Resources, 325 North Salisbury Street, Raleigh NC 27611. **LC** HV86. **DD** 361.6209756.

ANNUAL PRIVACY AND SECURITY AUDIT REPORT ON THE PROCEDURES, POLICIES, AND PRACTICES OF THE DEPARTMENT OF LAW ENFORCEMENT FOR MAINTAINING CRIMINAL HISTORY RECORD INFORMATION FOR THE PERIOD ENDING . . . . US. English. an. Illinois Criminal Justice, Information Council, 120 South Riverside Place, Chicago IL 60606. **LC** HV9305.I3. **DD** 353.97730074.

ANNUAL REPORT - ADDIS ABABA UNIVERSITY, SCHOOL OF SOCIAL WORK. Main/Corp Addis Ababa University. School of Social Work. English. ir. Addis Ababa University, School of Social Work, Addis Ababa Ethiopia. **LC** HV11. **DD** 361.00711633. Annual Report - School of Social Work.

ANNUAL REPORT - ALABAMA. ALCOHOLIC BEVERAGE CONTROL BOARD. (ANNUAL REPORT). **Main/Corp** Alabama. Alcoholic Beverage Control Board. Began with 1st issue in 1937. 0733-2874. US. English. an. Alcohol Beverage Control Board, State of Alabama, Montgomery AL 36104. **LC** HV5079.A3. **DD** 178.409761.

ANNUAL REPORT - ALBERTA DISASTER SERVICES. Main/Corp Alberta. Disaster Services Agency. **VFOAT** Report of the Alberta Disaster Services Agency. **VAT** Report of the Alberta Disaster Services Agency. 0703-0797. **CN**. English. an. Alberta Disaster Services Agency, 10320 146th Street, Edmonton Alberta T5N 1Y8 Canada. **LC** HV555.C3. **DD** 354.71230084.

ANNUAL REPORT - ALBERTA SOLICITOR GENERAL. See Public Administration.

ANNUAL REPORT - AMERICAN NATIONAL RED CROSS. (ANNUAL REPORT - THE AMERICAN NATIONAL RED CROSS). **Main/Corp** American National Red Cross. 0080-0384. US. English. an. American National Red Cross, Washington DC 20006. **LC** HV575. **DD** 361.77. **NLM** W1 RE1579U. Annual Report of the American National Red Cross.

ANNUAL REPORT AND STATEMENT OF ACCOUNTS - BRITISH ASSOCIATION OF SOCIAL WORKERS. Main/Corp British Association of Social Workers. 1st- 1970/71-. UK. English. an. British Association of Social Workers, 42 Bedford Square, WC1B 3DP London England. **LC** HV244. **DD** 361.006242.

ANNUAL REPORT - ARIZONA. DEPT. OF CORRECTIONS. Main/Corp Arizona. Dept. of Corrections. 1978-1979-. 8756-7997. US. English. an. Arizona Department of Corrections, 321

Sociology: General Works, Theory—Social Pathology, Welfare, Criminology

West Indian School Road, Phoenix AZ 85013. DD 353.

ANNUAL REPORT - ARKANSAS. DEPT. OF CORRECTION. Main/Corp Arkansas. Dept. of Correction. US. English. an. Department of Correction, PO Box 8707, Pine Bluff AR 71611. *Annual Report of the Arkansas Department of Correction.*

ANNUAL REPORT - ARKANSAS. DEPT. OF HUMAN SERVICES. DIVISION OF YOUTH SERVICES. Main/Corp Arkansas. Dept. of Human Services. Division of Youth Services. 1979-. US. English. an. LC HV1435.A8. DD 353.97670084706.

ANNUAL REPORT - ARKANSAS SOCIAL SERVICES. Main/Corp Arkansas. Arkansas Social Services. 1971/72-. US. English. an. Arkansas Social Services, Little Rock AR 72201.

ANNUAL REPORT - BRITISH COLUMBIA. LIQUOR DISTRIBUTION BRANCH. Main/Corp British Columbia. Liquor Distribution Branch. 0710-8648. CN. English. an. Province of British Columbia, Liquor Distribution Branch, Head Office & Distribution Centre, 3200 East Broadway, Vancouver British Columbia V5M 1Z6 Canada. LC HV5087.C2. DD 354.7110076106. *Liquor Distribution Branch and Liquor Control and Licensing Branch: Annual Report.*

ANNUAL REPORT - CALIFORNIA. OFFICE OF EMERGENCY SERVICES. Main/Corp California. Office of Emergency Services. US. English. an. California Office of Emergency Services, 2800 Meadowview Road, Sacramento CA 95832. LC HV555.U62. DD 353.97940075406.

ANNUAL REPORT - CBF WORLD JEWISH RELIEF (ORGANIZATION). Main/Corp CBF World Jewish Relief (Organization). UK. English. an. CBF World Jewish Relief, Woburn House, Upper Woburn Place, London WC1H 0AB England. LC HV640.5.J4. DD 362.84924. *Annual Report.*

ANNUAL REPORT - CHILD WELFARE LEAGUE OF AMERICA, INC. Main/Corp Child Welfare League of America. 0412-1058. US. English. an. Child Welfare League of America, 440 First Street Northwest, Washington DC 20001. Tel (202)638-2952. LC HV741. DD 362.706073. Circ 2,500. Annual report.

ANNUAL REPORT - COLORADO. DEPT. OF CORRECTIONS. Main/Corp Colorado. Dept. of Corrections. US. English. an. LC HV7255. DD 353.97880084906. Available on microfiche at Colorado State depositories.

ANNUAL REPORT - COMMONWEALTH OF MASSACHUSETTS, DEPARTMENT OF PUBLIC WELFARE, STATE ADVISORY BOARD. (ANNUAL REPORT - DEPARTMENT OF PUBLIC WELFARE, STATE ADVISORY BOARD). Main/Corp Massachusetts. Dept. of Public Welfare. State Advisory Board. 0095-4020. US. English. an. LC HV86. DD 353.97440084.

ANNUAL REPORT - CONNECTICUT ADOPTION RESOURCE EXCHANGE. Main/Corp Connecticut Adoption Resource Exchange. Jan. 1, 1980-Dec. 31, 1980-. US. English. an. Department of Children & Youth Services, Division of Policy and Licensing, 170 Sigourney Street, Hartford CT 06105. LC HV880. DD 362.8.

ANNUAL REPORT - CONNECTICUT DEPARTMENT OF INCOME MAINTENANCE. Main/Corp Connecticut. Dept. of Income Maintenance. 1978/79-. US. English. an. Connecticut Department of Income, Maintenance Central Office, 110 Bartholomew Avenue, Hartford CT 06115. LC HV86. DD 353.974600845.

ANNUAL REPORT - CONNECTICUT JUSTICE COMMISSION. Main/Corp Connecticut Justice Commission. US. English. an. Connecticut Justice Commission, 75 Elm Street, Hartford CT 06115. LC HV7256. DD 364.9746.

ANNUAL REPORT - CORE SERVICES ADMINISTRATION. Main/Corp Saskatchewan. Core Services Administration. 1973/74-. CN. English. an. 2240 Albert Street, Regina Saskatchewan S4P 2Y3 Canada. LC HV3008.C3. DD 354 .712400843.

ANNUAL REPORT - CRIMINAL INJURIES COMPENSATION COMMISSION. Main/Corp Hawaii. Criminal Injuries Compensation Commission. 0098-5708. US. English. an. PO Box 339, Honolulu HI 96809. LC HV8688. DD 353.9969008488.

ANNUAL REPORT - CRIMINAL INVESTIGATION BUREAU. Main/Corp Alaska. Criminal Investigation Bureau. 0362-7284. US. English. an. PO Box 6188, Anchorage AK 99502. LC HV7251. DD 353.97980074.

ANNUAL REPORT - CRIMINAL JUSTICE TRAINING AND STANDARDS COUNCIL. (ANNUAL REPORT - NORTH CAROLINA, CRIMINAL TRAINING AND STANDARDS COUNCIL). Main/Corp North Carolina. Criminal Justice Training and Standards Council. 1973-. 0095-179X. US. English. an. PO Box 149, Raleigh NC 27602. LC HV7283. DD 364.

ANNUAL REPORT - CRIMINOLOGY RESEARCH COUNCIL. Main/Corp Criminology Research Council. English. ir. Criminology Research Council, 10-16 Colbee Court, Phillip 2606 Australia. LC HV6024.5. DD 364.072094.

ANNUAL REPORT - DEPARTMENT FOR COMMUNITY WELFARE. WESTERN AUSTRALIA. (ANNUAL REPORT - WESTERN AUSTRALIA DEPARTMENT FOR COMMUNITY WELFARE). Main/Corp Western Australia. Dept. for Community Welfare. 1972/73-. 0311-4341. AT. English. ir. LC HV511. DD 354.9410084. NLM W2 KA8 D2A.

ANNUAL REPORT - DEPARTMENT OF CORRECTIONS (VIRGINIA). Main/Corp Virginia. Dept. of Corrections. 1974/75-. 0364-1457. US. English. an. Department of Corrections, 22 East Cary Street, Richmond VA 23219. LC HV7296. DD 353.975500849. *Annual Report - Department of Welfare and Institutions, 0362-3355.*

ANNUAL REPORT - DEPARTMENT OF HEALTH AND HUMAN RESOURCES (LOUISIANA). Main/Corp Louisiana. Dept. of Health and Human Resources. 0740-8153. US. English. an. Department of Health and Human Resources, 755 Riverdale North, PO Box 3776, Baton Rouge LA 70821. LC HV86. DD 353.9763008406.

ANNUAL REPORT - DEPARTMENT OF HEALTH AND SOCIAL SERVICES. Main/Corp Delaware. Dept. of Health and Social Service. 0095-6422. US. English. an. Deparment of Health and Social Services, Dover DE 19901. LC HV86. DD 353.97510084. NLM W2 AD4 D3A.

ANNUAL REPORT - DEPARTMENT OF HEALTH & WELFARE. Main/Corp Idaho. Dept. of Health and Welfare. US. English. an. Statehouse, Boise ID 83720. LC HV86. DD 353.9796008405.

ANNUAL REPORT - DEPARTMENT OF HUMAN RESOURCES. Main/Corp Maryland. Dept. of Human Resources. 0146-5767. US. English. an. Department of Human Resources, Office of the Secretary, 1100 North Eutaw Street, Baltimore MD 21201. LC HV86. DD 353.9752008406.

ANNUAL REPORT - DEPARTMENT OF HUMAN RESOURCES (D.C.). Main/Corp District of Columbia. Dept. of Human Resources. 1976/77-. 0197-9132. US. English. an. NLM W2 AD6 D3A.

ANNUAL REPORT - DEPARTMENT OF HUMAN RESOURCES (MARYLAND). (REPORT TO THE GOVERNOR). Main/Corp Maryland. Dept. of Human Resources. VFOAT Annual Report, Department of Human Resources. 0146-2466. US. English. an. Department of Human Resources, Office of the Secretary, 1100 North Eutaw Street, Baltimore MD 21201. LC HV86. DD 353.97520084.

ANNUAL REPORT - DEPARTMENT OF SOCIAL AND REHABILITATION SERVICES (KANSAS). See Public Administration.

ANNUAL REPORT - DEPARTMENT OF SOCIAL SERVICES, DIVSION OF DATA PROCESSING (MISSOURI). Main/Corp Missouri. Dept. of Social Services. Division of Data Processing. 1977-. US. English. an. Department of Social Services, Division of Data Processing, Broadway State Office Building, Jefferson City MO 65101. LC HV98.M8. DD 353.9778008402854.

ANNUAL REPORT - DEPARTMENT OF SOCIAL SERVICES (NOVA SCOTIA). Main/Corp Nova Scotia. Dept. of Social Services. 1974-. 0383-4808. CN. English. an. Department of Social Sciences, PO Box 696, Johnston Building, Prince Street, Halifax Nova Scotia B3J 2T7 Canada. LC HV109.N9. DD 354.716008405. *Annual Report, 0550-1776.*

ANNUAL REPORT - DEPARTMENT ON AGING (CONNECTICUT). Main/Corp Connecticut. Dept. on Aging. US. English. an. State of Connecticut, Department on Aging, 80 Washington Street, Hartford CT 06115. LC HV1468.C8. DD 353.97460084606. *Report to the Governor and General Assembly - Department on Aging, 0090-6077.*

ANNUAL REPORT - DIVISION OF APPALACHIAN DEVELOPMENT, STATE OF MISSISSIPPI (MISSISSIPPI). Main/Corp Mississippi. Division of Appalachian Development. US. English. an. Office of the Governor, PO Box 1606, Tupelo MS 38801. LC HV86. DD 353.97620084.

ANNUAL REPORT - DIVISION OF FAMILY AND CHILDREN SERVICES (ALASKA). (ANNUAL REPORT). Main/Corp Alaska. Division of Family and Children Services. 0094-1174. US. English. an. LC HV86. DD 353.97980084.

ANNUAL REPORT - FLORIDA DEPARTMENT OF CORRECTIONS. Main/Corp Florida. Dept. of Corrections. 1977/78-. US. English. an. Department of Corrections, 1311 Winewood Boulevard, Tallahassee FL 32301. LC HV7259. DD 353.97590084906.

ANNUAL REPORT FOR DIVISION OF SOCIAL WELFARE. Main/Corp South Dakota. Dept. of Social Services. Program Analysis Unit. VFOAT Annual Statistical Report for Division of Social Welfare. 0145-2827. US. English. an. Capitol Lake Plaza, Pierre SD 57501. LC HV86. DD 362.9783.

ANNUAL REPORT FOR FISCAL YEAR - ALABAMA. DEPT. OF CORRECTIONS. Main/Corp Alabama. Dept. of Corrections. US. English. an. Department of Corrections, State Capitol Building, Montgomery AL 36130. LC HV7250. DD 353.97610084906. *Annual Report for Fiscal Year . . . .*

ANNUAL REPORT FOR THE PROVISION OF CHILD PROTECTIVE SERVICES IN NEW YORK STATE. Main/Corp New York (State). Dept. of Social Services. 1st- 1973-. 0360-5515. US. English. an. State Department of Social Services, 40 North Pearl Street, Albany NY 12243. LC HV86, HV742.N7. DD 361.9747 S, 353.974700847.

ANNUAL REPORT FOR THE YEAR ENDED AUGUST 31 - TEXAS. DEPT. OF MENTAL HEALTH AND MENTAL RETARDATION. CENTRAL OFFICE. Main/Corp Texas. Dept. of Mental Health and Mental Retardation. Central Office. US. English. an. LC RA790.65.T4. DD 353.976400842.

ANNUAL REPORT - GEORGIA ORGANIZED CRIME PREVENTION COUNCIL. Main/Corp Georgia. Organized Crime Prevention Council. 0362-9996. US. English. an. Georgia Organized Crime Prevention Council, 1430 West Peachtree Street Suite 318, Atlanta GA 30309. LC HV7260. DD 353.975800756.

ANNUAL REPORT - GOVERNOR'S ADVISORY COMMITTEE ON CHILD DEVELOPMENT PROGRAMS (CALIFORNIA). Main/Corp California. Governor's Advisory Committee on Child Development Programs. 0147-9830. US. English. Governor's Advisory Committee on Child Development Programs, 1500 Fifth Street, Sacramento CA 95814. LC HV742.C2. DD 362.709794.

ANNUAL REPORT - GOVERNOR'S CITIZENS' COUNCIL ON AGING (MINNESOTA). Main/Corp Minnesota. Governor's Citizens Council on Aging. 0145-6709. US. English. an. 204 Metro Square, 7th & Robert, St Paul MN 55101. LC HV1468.M6. DD 362.609776.

ANNUAL REPORT - GOVERNOR'S COMMITTEE ON CRIME, DELINQUENCY AND CORRECTIONS (WEST VIRGINIA). Main/Corp West Virginia. Governor's Committee on Crime, Delinquency, and Corrections. 0094-4238. US. English. an. 1524

Sociology: General Works, Theory—Social Pathology, Welfare, Criminology

Kanawha Boulevard East, Charleston WV 25305. **LC** HV7298. **DD** 353.97540074.

ANNUAL REPORT - HAWAII. EXECUTIVE OFFICE ON AGING. (ANNUAL REPORT). **Main/Corp** Hawaii. Executive Office on Aging. 0275-9551. US. English. an. Executive Office on Aging, Office of the Governor, 1149 Bethel Street, Room 307, Honolulu HI 96813. **LC** HV1468.H3. **DD** 353.99690084606.

ANNUAL REPORT - HAWAII. STATE INTAKE SERVICE CENTER. Main/Corp Hawaii. State Intake Service Center. US. English. an. State Intake Service Center, 2199 Kamchameha Highway, Honolulu HI 96819. **LC** HV7260.5. **DD** 353.9969007406.

ANNUAL REPORT - ILLINOIS. DEPARTMENT OF PUBLIC AID. (ANNUAL REPORT). **Main/Corp** Illinois. Dept. of Public Aid. 0091-6099. US. English. an. Illinois Department of Public Aid, 222 South College Street, Springfield IL 62704. **LC** HV86.

ANNUAL REPORT - ILLINOIS. GANG CRIMES STUDY COMMISSION. Main/Corp Illinois. Gang Crimes Study Commission. 1983-. US. English. an. Gang Crimes Study Commission, State of Illinois, 318 State of Illinois Building, 160 North Lasalle, Chicago IL 60601.

ANNUAL REPORT - ILLINOIS JUVENILE OFFICERS INFORMATION FILE. Main/Corp Illinois Juvenile Officers Information File. 0536-4752. US. English. an. 3600 Kirchoff Road, Rolling Meadows IL 60008. **LC** HV9105.I3. **DD** 352.2.

ANNUAL REPORT - ILLINOIS. PRISONER REVIEW BOARD. Main/Corp Illinois. Prisoner Review Board. 1st (Feb. 1, 1978 to Jan. 31, 1979)-. US. English. an. Prisoner Review Board, 534 South Fourth Street, Springfield IL 62706. **LC** HV9278. **DD** 353.977300849306.

ANNUAL REPORT - ILLINOIS TITLE XX CITIZENS' ADVISORY COUNCIL. Main/Corp Illinois Title XX Citizens' Advisory Council. US. English. an. Bureau of Title XX Administration, 528 South Fifth Street, Springfield IL 62762. **LC** HV98.I152. **DD** 353.9773008406.

ANNUAL REPORT - INDIA. MINISTRY OF HEALTH AND FAMILY WELFARE. Main/Corp India. Ministry of Health and Family Welfare. English. an. **LC** RA311. **DD** 354.540084106. *Report.*

ANNUAL REPORT - INDIANA. DIVISION OF PROBATION. Main/Corp Indiana. Division of Probation. US. English. an. Department of Correction, 804 State Office Building, 101 North Senate Avenue, Indianapolis IN 46204. **LC** HV9305.I6. **DD** 353.977200849306.

ANNUAL REPORT - INDIANA ORGANIZED CRIME PREVENTION COUNCIL. Main/Corp Indiana. Organized Crime Prevention Council. US. English. an. I.O.C.P.C. Ista Building Suite 400/150 West Market Street, Indianapolis IN 46204. **LC** HV6793.I6. **DD** 364.40456060772.

ANNUAL REPORT - IOWA. COMMISSION ON THE AGING. Main/Corp Iowa. Commission on the Aging. US. English. an. Commission on the Aging, 415 10th Street, Des Moines IA 50319. **LC** HV1468.I8. **DD** 353.97770084606.

ANNUAL REPORT - KENTUCKY. DEPT. OF CHILD WELFARE. Main/Corp Kentucky. Dept. of Child Welfare. US. English. an. State of Kentucky, Department of Child Welfare, Frankfort KY 40601. **LC** HV742.K4. **DD** 362.709769.

ANNUAL REPORT - LOS ANGELES COUNTY AREA AGENCY ON AGING, ADVISORY COUNCIL. Main/Corp Los Angeles Co., Calif. Area Agency on Aging. Advisory Council. 1974/79-. US. English. an. Area Agency on Aging, 601 South Kingsley Drive, Los Angeles CA 90005. **LC** HV1471.L72. **DD** 352.94460979493.

ANNUAL REPORT - LOUISIANA HEALTH AND HUMAN RESOURCES ADMINISTRATION. Main/Corp Louisiana. Health and Human Resources Administration. 0149-4112. US. English. an. Health and Human Resources Administration, 150 Riverside Mall/PO Box 44215, Baton Rouge LA 70804. **LC** HV86. **DD** 353.97630084105.

ANNUAL REPORT - LOUISIANA. STATE DEPT. OF CORRECTIONS. Main/Corp Louisiana. State Dept. of Corrections. US. English. an. Louisiana State Department of Corrections, Baton Rouge LA 70804. **LC** HV9305.L8. **DD** 365.9763.

ANNUAL REPORT - LYNCHBURG TRAINING SCHOOL AND HOSPITAL. (ANNUAL REPORT). **Main/Corp** Lynchburg Training School and Hospital. 0736-816X. US. English. an. Lynchburg Training School and Hospital, PO Box 1098, Lynchburg VA 24505. **LC** HV3006.V72. **DD** 362.38509755496.

ANNUAL REPORT - MAINE HUMAN SERVICES COUNCIL. Main/Corp Maine. Human Services Council. US. English. an. Maine Human Services Council, State House, Augusta ME 04333. **LC** HV98.M2. **DD** 353.9741008406.

ANNUAL REPORT - MARCH OF DIMES BIRTH DEFECTS FOUNDATION. (ANNUAL REPORT). **Main/Corp** March of Dimes Birth Defects Foundation. 1980-. 0730-1286. US. English. an. March of Dimes, 1275 Mamaroneck Avenue, White Plains NY 10605. **NLM** W1 MA643. *Annual Report, 0735-0163.*

ANNUAL REPORT - MARYLAND. FOSTER CARE REVIEW BOARD. Main/Corp Maryland. Foster Care Review Board. US. English. an. Maryland Citizen Board for Review of Foster Care of Children, 101 West Read Street/Suite 621, Baltimore MD 21201. **LC** HV883.M3. **DD** 362.73309752.

ANNUAL REPORT - MASSACHUSETTS. DEPT. OF SOCIAL SERVICES. Main/Corp Massachusetts. Dept. of Social Services. 1983-. US. English. an. Massachusetts Department of Social Services, 150 Causeway Street, Boston MA 02114.

ANNUAL REPORT - MASSACHUSETTS PAROLE BOARD. Main/Corp Massachusetts Parole Board. 1937-. US. English. an. **LC** HV9305.M4. **DD** 353.974400849306.

ANNUAL REPORT - MICHIGAN. OFFICE OF SERVICES TO THE AGING. Main/Corp Michigan. Office of Services to the Aging. US. English. an. Michigan Office of Services to the Aging, 300 East Michigan Avenue, Lansing MI 48909. **LC** HV1468.M5. **DD** 353.97740084606.

ANNUAL REPORT - MINNESOTA PROGRAM FOR VICTIMS OF SEXUAL ASSAULT. Main/Corp Minnesota Program for Victims of Sexual Assault. US. English. an. Minnesota Department of Corrections, 430 Metro Square Building, 7th & Robert Streets, St Paul MN 55150. **LC** HV6250.3.U5. **DD** 362.88.

ANNUAL REPORT - MISSISSIPPI. DEPT. OF YOUTH SERVICES. Main/Corp Mississippi. Dept. of Youth Services. US. English. an. **LC** HV9105.M. **DD** 353.9762008495.

ANNUAL REPORT - MISSISSIPPI STATE DEPARTMENT OF PUBLIC WELFARE. (ANNUAL REPORT - MISSISSIPPI, STATE DEPARTMENT OF PUBLIC WELFARE). **Main/Corp** Mississippi. State Dept. of Public Welfare. 0098-5120. US. English. an. State Department of Public Welfare, PO Box 4321 Fondren Station, Jackson MS 49503. **LC** HV86. **DD** 353.97620084.

ANNUAL REPORT - MISSISSIPPI VOCATIONAL REHABILITATION FOR THE BLIND. Main/Corp Mississippi Vocational Rehabilitation for the Blind. 1975-. US. English. an. Mississippi Vocational Rehabilitation for the Blind, 5455 Executive Place 1-5 N, PO Box 4872, Fondren Station, Jackson MS 39216. **LC** HV1796.M7. **DD** 362.4184. *Report for the Fiscal Year.*

ANNUAL REPORT - MISSOURI DEPARTMENT OF SOCIAL SERVICES. Main/Corp Missouri. Dept. of Social Services. US. English. an. Missouri Department of Social Services, Broadway State Office Building, Jefferson City MO 65101. **LC** HV86. **DD** 353.9778008405.

ANNUAL REPORT—MISSOURI DIVISION OF FAMILY SERVICES. Main/Corp Missouri. Division of Family Services. 1st-1974/75. Periodical. US. English. an. **LC** HV86. **DD** 353.977884.

ANNUAL REPORT - MISSOURI STATE DIVISION OF YOUTH SERVICES. (ANNUAL REPORT - MISSOURI, STATE DIVISION OF YOUTH SERVICES). **Main/Corp** Missouri. State Division of Youth Services. 0098-0110. US. English. an. State Division of Youth Services, 402 Dix Road, PO Box 447, Jefferson City MO 65101. **LC** HV1435.M8. **DD** 353.977800847.

ANNUAL REPORT - MONTANA. FIRE MARSHAL BUREAU. (ANNUAL REPORT). **Main/Corp** Montana. Fire Marshal Bureau. 0732-9148. US. English. an. Fire Marshal Bureau, 1409 Helena Avenue, Helena MT 59601. **LC** HV8079.A7. **DD** 353.97860078206.

ANNUAL REPORT - MYSORE. PRISONS DEPT. Main/Corp Mysore. Prisons Dept. English. ir. **LC** HV8451.M75. **DD** 354.548700849. *Annual Administration Report.*

ANNUAL REPORT - NATIONAL COUNCIL, NICRO. Main/Corp National Institute for Crime Prevention and Rehabilitation of Offenders. National Council. 1970/71-. English (Afrikaans, the latter inverted with titls: Jaarverslag). ir. **LC** HV9421.S6. **DD** 354.6800849.

ANNUAL REPORT - NATIONAL SAFETY COUNCIL OF WESTERN AUSTRALIA. Main/Corp National Safety Council of Western Australia. AT. English. an. National Safety Council of Western Australia, Safety Instructional Centre, PO Box 42, Mount Lawley 6050 Western Australia. **LC** HV677.A8. **DD** 363.1060941.

ANNUAL REPORT - NEW BRUNSWICK SOCIAL SERVICES (NEW BRUNSWICK). Main/Corp New Brunswick. Dept. of Social Services. **VFOAT** Rapport Annuel - Services Sociaux Nouveau-Brunswick, Rapport Annuel. **VAT** Rapport Annuel - Ministere des Services Sociaux (Fredericton), Rapport Annuel - Services Sociaux. Nouveau-Brunswick, Annual Report - Social Services (Fredericton). 1971/72-. 0708-4242. Periodical. CN. English (text also in French). an. **LC** HV109.N38. **DD** 354.715008405.

ANNUAL REPORT - NEW JERSEY CASINO CONTROL COMMISSION. Main/Corp New Jersey. Casino Control Commission. 1978/79-. US. English. an. New Jersey Casino Control Commission, 379 West State Street, Trenton NJ 08625. **LC** HV6721.N48. **DD** 353.97490076.

ANNUAL REPORT - NEW JERSEY, STATE PAROLE BOARD. Main/Corp New Jersey. State Parole Board. US. English. an. State Parole Board, PO Box 7387, Trenton NJ 08628. **LC** HV9305.N48. **DD** 353.974900849306.

ANNUAL REPORT - NEW MEXICO COMMITTEE ON CHILDREN AND YOUTH. (ANNUAL REPORT). **Main/Corp** New Mexico. Committee on Children and Youth. **VFOAT** Where Are the Youth of New Mexico?. 0092-329X. US. English. an. Committee on Children and Youth, PO Box 6223, Albuquerque NM 87107. **LC** HV742.N6. **DD** 362.709789.

ANNUAL REPORT - NEW MEXICO. DEPT. OF HUMAN SERVICES. Main/Corp New Mexico. Dept. of Human Services. US. English. an. PO Box 2348, Santa Fe NM 87503. **LC** HV98.N6. **DD** 353.9789008406.

ANNUAL REPORT - NEW MEXICO. GOVERNOR'S COMMITTEE ON CONCERNS OF THE HANDICAPPED. Main/Corp New Mexico. Governor's Committee on Concerns of the Handicapped. 1982-. US. English. an. State of New Mexico Governor's Committee on Concerns of the Handicapped, Bataan Memorial Building/Room 309, Santa Fe NM 87503. **LC** HV1555.N6. **DD** 353.97890084406.

ANNUAL REPORT - NEW YORK STATE DIVISION FOR YOUTH. Main/Corp New York (State). Division for Youth. **VFOAT** Report. 1961-. 0545-4891. US. English. an. New York State Division for Youth, 84 Holland Avenue, Albany NY 12208. **LC** HV9105.N7. **DD** 353.97470084706.

ANNUAL REPORT - NEW YORK (STATE). LEGISLATURE. ASSEMBLY. COMMITTEE ON SOCIAL SERVICES. Main/Corp New York (State). Legislature. Assembly. Committee on Social Services. US. English. an. New York State Assembly, Albany Office, Room 844/Legislative Office Building, Albany NY 12248. **LC** KFN5600. **DD** 342.747052, 347.470252.

Sociology: General Works, Theory—Social Pathology, Welfare, Criminology

ANNUAL REPORT - NORTH CAROLINA DEPARTMENT OF HUMAN RESOURCES. (ANNUAL REPORT - NORTH CAROLINA, DEPARTMENT OF HUMAN RESOURCES). Main/Corp North Carolina. Dept. of Human Resources. 0362-0301. US. English. an. 325 North Salisbury Street, Raleigh NC 27611. LC HV86. DD 353.97560084.

ANNUAL REPORT - NOVA SCOTIA YOUTH AGENCY. Main/Corp Nova Scotia. Youth Agency. 0381-2006. CN. English. an. Nova Scotia Youth Agency, 5867 Spring Garden Road, Nova Scotia Canada. LC HV745.N6. DD 354.71600847.

ANNUAL REPORT OF AGENCY TRAINING ACTIVITIES. Main/Corp Oregon. Children's Services Division. Staff Development Unit. 0098-8723. US. English. an. LC HV742.O7. DD 353.979500847. *Annual Report of Agency Training Activities, 0098-8723.*

ANNUAL REPORT OF BEANO. Main/Corp Massachusetts. State Lottery Commission. 1st- 1973/74-. 0147-4081. US. English. an. Massachusetts State Lottery Commission, 15 Rockdale Street, Braintree MA 02184. LC HV6721.M35. DD 353.974400762.

ANNUAL REPORT OF DEPARTMENT OF SOCIAL SERVICES (PRINCE EDWARD ISLAND) CEASED. (ANNUAL REPORT - DEPARTMENT OF SOCIAL SERVICES). Main/Corp Prince Edward Island. Dept. of Social Services. VAT Annual Report - Department of Social Services (Charlottetown). 1st-8th. 0701-5291. CN. English. an. Prince Edward Island Department of Social Services, Box 2000, Charlottetown Prince Edward Island Australia. LC HV109.P7. DD 354.717008405. *Annual Report.*

ANNUAL REPORT OF FELONS AND RECIDIVISTS COMMITTED AND CONFINED. VFOAT Felons and Recidivists. Fiscal year 1980-. US. English. an. Virginia Department of Corrections, PO Box 26963, Richmond VA 23261. LC HV7296. DD 364.309755. *Annual Statistical Report of Felons and Misdemeanants Committed to the Virginia State Correctional System and Felons Confined in the Correctional System including Felon Recidivists Committed and Confined.*

ANNUAL REPORT OF HAWAII CRIME COMMISSION. Main/Corp Hawaii Crime Commission. US. English. an. Hawaii Crime Commission, State Capitol, Honolulu HI 96813. LC HV7260.5. DD 353.99690075.

ANNUAL REPORT OF NIJJDP. Main/Corp National Institute for Juvenile Justice and Delinquency Prevention. VAT Annual Report of National Institute for Juvenile Justice and Delinquency Prevention. 0193-483X. US. English. an. US Department of Justice/Office of Juvenile Justice and Delinquency Prevention, Washington DC 20531. LC HV9104. DD 364.360973.

ANNUAL REPORT OF OPERATIONS. Main/Corp Ohio. Dept. of Mental Retardation and Developmental Disabilities. July 1, 1982-June 30, 1983-. US. English. an. LC HV3006.O3. DD 353.977100841.

ANNUAL REPORT OF THE BOARD OF VISITORS AND SUPERINTENDENT OF THE NEW YORK STATE SCHOOL FOR THE BLIND. Main/Corp New York State School for the Blind. VFOAT Annual Report of the Board of Visitors and Superintendent, New York State School for the Blind. 59th (1926/27)-. US. English. an. LC HV1796. NLM HV 1796.N7 N573A. *Annual Report of the Board of Managers and Superintendent of the New York State School for the Blind.*

ANNUAL REPORT OF THE BUSINESS DONE IN PURSUANCE OF THE PUBLIC SERVICE BENEFIT PLANS ACT. See Business.

ANNUAL REPORT OF THE CHAIRMAN - ONTARIO. MINISTRY OF COMMUNITY AND SOCIAL SERVICES. BOARD OF REVIEW. Main/Corp Ontario. Ministry of Community and Social Services. Board of Review. CN. English. an. LC HV109.O6. DD 362.9713.

ANNUAL REPORT OF THE CHAIRMAN - UTAH COUNCIL FOR HANDICAPPED AND DEVELOPMENTALLY DISABLED PERSONS. Main/Corp Utah Council for Handicapped and Developmentally Disabled Persons. US. English. an. Utah Council for Handicapped and Developmentally Disabled Persons, PO Box 11356, Salt Lake City UT 84147. LC HV1555.U8. DD 353.979200844.

ANNUAL REPORT OF THE CHILDREN'S FOSTER CARE REVIEW BOARD SYSTEM OF THE STATE OF SOUTH CAROLINA. Main/Corp South Carolina. Children's Foster Care Review Board System. 1981-. US. English. an. Children's Foster Care Review Board System, 2221 Devine Street, Suite 418, Columbia SC 29205. LC HV883.S6. DD 353.975700847.

ANNUAL REPORT OF THE COMMITTEE TO CONDUCT CONTINUING STUDIES OF PUBLIC AND PRIVATE SERVICES PROGRAMS AND FACILITIES FOR THE AGING (SOUTH CAROLINA). Main/Corp South Carolina. General Assembly. Study Committee on Aging. US. English. an. Director of Research and Administration/Joint Legislative Study Committee on Aging, PO Box 142/305 Gressette Building, Columbia SC 29202. LC HQ1064.U6. DD 362.609757.

ANNUAL REPORT OF THE CORRECTIONAL INVESTIGATOR. Main/Corp Canada. Correctional Investigator. VFOAT Rapport Annuel de l'Enqueteur Correctionnel. 1973/74-. 0383-4379. Periodical. CN. text in English and French, each with special t.p. and separate paging. French text on inverted pages. an. Correctional Investigator, PO Box 950, Station B, Ottawa Ontario K1P 5R1 Canada. LC HV7315. DD 354.7100849.

ANNUAL REPORT OF THE CRIME VICTIMS REPARATIONS BOARD OF MINNESOTA. Main/Corp Minnesota. Crime Victims Reparations Board. 1976/77. US. English. an. Crime Victims Reparations Board, 702 American Center Building, 160 East Kellogg Boulevard, St Paul MN 55101. LC KFM5600. DD 345.7760405, 347.7605405.

ANNUAL REPORT OF THE CRIMINAL HISTORY SYSTEMS BOARD - MASSACHUSETTS. Main/Corp Massachusetts. Criminal History Systems Board. 1st- 1972/74-. 0098-5112. US. English. an. Criminal History Systems Board, 80 Boylston Street Room 740, Boston MA 02116. LC HV7271. DD 353.9744008.

ANNUAL REPORT OF THE DEPT. OF HUMAN RESOURCES (BRITISH COLUMBIA). Main/Corp British Columbia. Dept. of Human Resources. VFOAT Services For People. CN. English. an.

ANNUAL REPORT OF THE DEPARTMENT OF SOCIAL AND REHABILITATION SERVICES TO THE GOVERNOR OF MONTANA. (ANNUAL REPORT). Main/Corp Montana. Dept. of Social and Rehabilitation Services. 1971/72-. 0091-0996. US. English. an. Department of Social and Rehabilitation Service, State Capitol, Helena MT 59601. LC HV86. DD 353.97860084.

ANNUAL REPORT OF THE DIVISION OF SOCIAL SERVICES OF THE DEPARTMENT OF HEALTH AND SOCIAL SERVICES - DELAWARE. (ANNUAL REPORT). Main/Corp Delaware. Division of Social Services. 1970-. 0090-3051. US. English. an. Delaware Division of Social Sciences, PO Box 309, Wilmington DE 19899. LC HV86. DD 353.9751008405.

ANNUAL REPORT OF THE DIVISION OF YOUTH AND FAMILY SERVICES, DEPARTMENT OF INSTITUTIONS AND AGENCIES (NEW JERSEY). (ANNUAL REPORT OF THE DIVISION OF YOUTH AND FAMILY SERVICES). Main/Corp New Jersey. Division of Youth and Family Services. 1st- 1972/73-. 0095-3393. US. English. an. One South Montgomery Street, Trenton NJ 08625. LC HV742.N5. DD 353.974900847.

ANNUAL REPORT OF THE GOVERNOR'S INTER-AGENCY COMMITTEE ON MENTAL RETARDATION (NEBRASKA). Main/Corp Nebraska. Governor's Inter-Agency Committee on Mental Retardation. 0470-5378. US. English. an. LC HV3006.N2.

ANNUAL REPORT OF THE JUSTICE SYSTEM IMPROVEMENT ACT AGENCIES. 1st (Fiscal Year 1980)-. 0278-0526. US. English. an. US Department of Justice, Washington DC 20531. LC HV7245. DD 353.008806. *Annual Report.*

ANNUAL REPORT OF THE MENTAL HEALTH AUTHORITY, VICTORIA. Main/Corp Victoria. Mental Health Authority. 1977-. 0725-4865. English. an. NLM W2 KA8.1 V6D54R.

ANNUAL REPORT OF THE NATIONAL COUNCIL ON CRIME AND DELINQUENCY. Main/Corp National Council of Crime and Delinquency. US. English. an. National Council of Crime and Delinquency, 44 East 23rd Street, New York NY 10010.

ANNUAL REPORT OF THE NEW YORK STATE COMMISSION OF CORRECTION. Main/Corp New York (State). State Commission of Correction. 1926/27-. 0275-8806. US. English. an. New York State Commission of Correction, Albany NY 12203. LC HV8352. DD 353.7470084906. *Annual Report of the State Commission of Prisons.*

ANNUAL REPORT OF THE OLD AGE, SURVIVORS, DISABILITY AND HEALTH INSURANCE PROGRAM. VFOAT Old Age, Survivors, Disability, and Health Insurance Program. 1977-. US. English. an. Office of Administration, Jefferson City MO 65102. LC HD7126.M8. DD 353.9778008256.

ANNUAL REPORT OF THE REHABILITATION SERVICES ADMINISTRATION TO THE PRESIDENT AND THE CONGRESS ON FEDERAL ACTIVITIES RELATED TO THE ADMINISTRATION OF THE REHABILITATION ACT OF 1973, AS AMENDED. VFOAT Annual Report to the President and the Congress . . . on Federal Activities Related to the Administration of the Rehabilitation Act of 1973, as Amended. VAT Annual Report of the Rehabilitation Services Administration to the President and the Congress on Federal Activities Related to the Administration of the Rehabilitation Act of Nineteen Seventy Three, as Amended. Began with fiscal year 1979. 0272-8753. US. English. an. US Department of Education, Office of Special Education & Rehabilitative Services, Rehabilitation Services Administration, Washington DC 20202. LC HV1553. DD 362.0425. NLM W2 A R3A. *Annual Report of the U.S. Department of Health, Education, and Welfare to the President and to the Congress on Federal Activities Related to the Administration of the Rehabilitation Act, 0098-4930.*

ANNUAL REPORT OF THE STATE BOARD OF JUVENILE PLACEMENT AND AFTERCARE (SOUTH CAROLINA). Main/Corp South Carolina. State Board of Juvenile Placement and Aftercare. 1st- 1969/70-. US. English. an. 1001 Main Street Room 203, Columbia SC 29201. LC HV9105.S6. DD 364.3609757.

ANNUAL REPORT OF THE STATE DEPARTMENT OF YOUTH SERVICES FOR THE PERIOD BEGINNING JULY 1 . . . AND ENDING JUNE 30 . . . (SOUTH CAROLINA). Main/Corp South Carolina. Dept. of Youth Services. 1981/1982-. US. English. an. LC HV9105.S6. DD 353.975700849088055. *Report to the People about the South Carolina Department of Youth Services, 0145-1553.*

ANNUAL REPORT OF THE TEXAS COMMISSION ON SERVICES TO CHILDREN & YOUTH. Main/Corp Texas. Commission on Services to Children and Youth. VAT Annual Report of the Texas Commission on Services to Children and Youth. 0149-7049. US. English. an. Texas Department of Community Affairs, 210 Barton Springs Road, Austin TX 78704. LC HV742.T4. DD 353.976400847.

ANNUAL REPORT OF THE U.S. DEPARTMENT OF HEALTH AND HUMAN SERVICES TO THE CONGRESS OF THE UNITED STATES ON SERVICES PROVIDED TO HANDICAPPED CHILDREN IN PROJECT HEAD START. VFOAT Status of Handicapped Children in Head Start Programs. 0882-5203. US. English. an. Department of Health & Human Services/Administration for Children Youth and Families, Head Start Bureau/400 Sixth Street SW, Washington DC 20201.

ANNUAL REPORT OF THE UTAH LIQUOR CONTROL COMMISSION. See Public Administration.

Sociology: General Works, Theory—Social Pathology, Welfare, Criminology

ANNUAL REPORT OF THE VIOLENT CRIMES COMPENSATION BOARD (NEW JERSEY). (ANNUAL REPORT). Main/Corp New Jersey. Violent Crimes Compensation Board. 1st- 1971/73-. 0092-3079. US. English. an. Violent Crime Compensation Board, 1100 Raymond Boulevard, Newark NJ 07102. LC HV8691.U5. DD 353.9749008488.

ANNUAL REPORT OF THE VIRGINIA STATE CRIME COMMISSION. See Public Administration.

ANNUAL REPORT - OHIO COMMISSION ON AGING CEASED. Main/Corp Ohio. Commission on Aging. 0363-9207. US. English. an. 34 North High Street, Columbus OH 43215. LC HV1468.O3. DD 353.977100846.

ANNUAL REPORT - OHIO PEACE OFFICER TRAINING COUNCIL. Main/Corp Ohio Peace Officer Training Council. US. English. an. Ohio Peace Officer Training Council, State Office Tower, 30 East Broad Street, Columbus OH 43215. LC HV8145.O3. DD 353.977100740683.

ANNUAL REPORT - OKLAHOMA. DEPT. OF CHARITIES AND CORRECTIONS. Main/Corp Oklahoma. Dept. of Charities and Corrections. US. English. an. Oklahoma Department of Charities and Corrections, Guthrie OK 73044. Ind/Abst Eng. Index.

ANNUAL REPORT - OKLAHOMA. DEPT. OF HUMAN SERVICES. (ANNUAL REPORT). Main/Corp Oklahoma. Dept. of Human Services. Fiscal Year '80-. 0277-8289. US. English. Oklahoma Department of Human Services, PO Box 25352, Oklahoma City OK 73125. LC HV86. DD 353.9766008406. *Annual Report, 0270-6008.*

ANNUAL REPORT - OKLAHOMA POLICE PENSION & RETIREMENT BOARD. Main/Corp Oklahoma Police Pension & Retirement Board. US. English. an. Oklahoma Police Pension and Retirement Board, 4001 North Lincoln Boulevard/Suite 300, Oklahoma City OK 73105. LC HV8145.O5. DD 353.97660074.

ANNUAL REPORT ON PUBLICLY SUBSIDIZED CHILD CARE SERVICES (CALIFORNIA). Main/Corp California. State Dept. of Education. Office of Child Development. 0197-744X. US. English. an. $2.50. Publications Sales/California State Department of Education, PO Box 271, Sacramento CA 95802. LC HV857.C2. DD 362.71209794.

ANNUAL REPORT ON THE ACTIVITIES OF THE NEW EUROPEAN SOCIAL FUND. (THE ANNUAL REPORT ON THE ACTIVITIES OF THE NEW EUROPEAN SOCIAL FUND). Main/Corp European Social Fund. Began with vol. for 1972. 0304-8039. English. ir. Office for Official Publications of the European Communities, Boite Postale 1003, Luxembourg Luxembourg. LC HD5715.5.E8. DD 362.85.

ANNUAL REPORT ON THE ADMINISTRATION OF PRISONS IN KENYA. Main/Corp Kenya. Ministry of Home Affairs. English. ir. Government Printer Kenya, PO Box 30128, Nairobi Kenya. LC HV9849.K4. DD 365.96762.

THE ANNUAL REPORT ON THE FINDINGS AND RECOMMENDATIONS ON THE DEAF AND HEARING IMPAIRED OF OKLAHOMA. (ANNUAL REPORT ON THE FINDINGS AND RECOMMENDATIONS ON THE DEAF AND HEARING IMPAIRED OF OKLAHOMA). Main/Corp Oklahoma. Commission On the Deaf and Hearing Impaired. 1st- 1973/74-. 0362-8256. US. English. an. PO Box 25352 State Capitol Station, Oklahoma City OK 73105. LC HV2561.O5. DD 362.4209766.

ANNUAL REPORT ON THE PROVISION OF CHILD WELFARE SERVICES IN NEW YORK STATE. Main/Corp New York (State). Dept. of Social Services. 1974/75-. 0363-9673. US. English. an. Department of Social Services, 1450 Western Avenue, Albany NY 12243. LC HV86, HV742.N7. DD 361.9747 S, 362.709747.

AN ANNUAL REPORT ON THE STATUS OF POVERTY IN CALIFORNIA. VFOAT California's Poor. 0749-9337. US. English. an. Office of Economic Opportunity, 1600 9th Street/Suite 340, Sacramento CA 95814. DD 362.

ANNUAL REPORT - PENNSYLVANIA. BUREAU OF CORRECTION. Main/Corp Pennsylvania. Bureau of Correction. US. English. an. Pennsylvania Bureau of Correction, PO Box 598, Camp Hill PA 17011.

ANNUAL REPORT - PRISONS DEPARTMENT (INDIA). Main/Corp Karnataka, India. Dept. of Prisons. 1975/76-. II. English. ir. Prisons Department, Inspector General of Prisons, Bangalore India. LC HV7371.K373. DD 365.95487. *Administration Report of the Prisons Department.*

ANNUAL REPORT - PRISONS DEPARTMENT (SINGAPORE). Main/Corp Singapore. Prisons Dept. English. ir.

ANNUAL REPORT - PROVINCIAL SENIOR CITIZENS ADVISORY COUNCIL (ALTA.). Main/Corp Provincial Senior Citizens Advisory Council (Alta.). Dec. 1981-. 0823-583X. CN. English. an. LC HV1475.A5. DD 362.6097123.

ANNUAL REPORT - QUEENSLAND. COMPTROLLER-GENERAL OF PRISONS. Main/Corp Queensland. Comptroller-General of Prisons. English. ir. LC HV8473.

ANNUAL REPORT - REGIONAL INSTITUTE OF SOCIAL WELFARE RESEARCH. (ANNUAL REPORT). Main/Corp Regional Institute of Social Welfare Research. 0091-2859. US. English. an. Regional Institute of Social Welfare Research, 1260-80 South Lumpkin Street, Athens GA 30601. LC HV98.G5. DD 361.00720758.

ANNUAL REPORT - REPUBLIC OF KENYA, DEPARTMENT OF SOCIAL SERVICES, COAST PROVINCE. Main/Corp Kenya. Dept. of Social Services, Coast Province. English. ir. Department of Social Services, PO Box 82573, Mombasa Kenya. LC HV449.K43. DD 354.6762008405.

ANNUAL REPORT - RHODE ISLAND GOVERNOR'S COUNCIL ON MENTAL HEALTH. Main/Corp Rhode Island. Governor's Council On Mental Health. 0556-8471. US. English. an. Governor's Council on Mental Health, 333 Grotto Avenue, Providence RI 02906. LC RA790.65.R4. DD 353.974500842.

ANNUAL REPORT - RUSSELL SAGE FOUNDATION. Main/Corp Russell Sage Foundation. US. English. an. Russell Sage Foundation, 230 Park Avenue, New York NY 10017. LC HV97.R8. DD 061. NLM HV 97 R968A.

ANNUAL REPORT - SAMUEL H. KRESS FOUNDATION. (ANNUAL REPORT). Main/Corp Samuel H. Kress Foundation. 0581-4766. US. English. an. Samuel H Kress Foundation, 221 West 57th Street, New York NY 10019. LC HV97.S25. DD 361.76.

ANNUAL REPORT - SARAH SCAIFE FOUNDATION. Main/Corp Sarah Scaife Foundation. 1974-. 0149-5143. US. English. an. Sarah Scaife Foundation, 1114 Oliver Building, Pittsburgh PA 15222. LC HV97.S27. DD 361.760973.

ANNUAL REPORT - SINGAPORE ANTI-NARCOTICS ASSOCIATION. Main/Corp Singapore Anti-Narcotics Association. SI. English. ir. Sana House, 46 Scotts Road, Singapore 0922 Singapore. LC HV5840.S55. DD 362.293860605957.

ANNUAL REPORT - SINGAPORE RED CROSS SOCIETY. Main/Corp Singapore Red Cross Society. SI. English. ir. Singapore Red Cross Society, 15 Penang Lane, Singapore 9. LC HV580.S53. DD 361.77.

ANNUAL REPORT - SOCIAL SERVICES AND COMMUNITY HEALTH. Main/Corp Alberta. Alberta Social Services and Community Health. 1974/75-. 0700-2688. CN. English. an. Department of Social Services and Community Health, Legislative Building, Edmonton Alberta T5K 2B6 Canada. LC HV109.A5. DD 354.71230084. NLM W2 DC2.1 A3D36A. *Annual Report, 0702-9527.*

ANNUAL REPORT - SOCIAL SERVICES AND HOUSING DEPARTMENT. Main/Corp Mombasa, Kenya. Social Services and Housing Dept. English. ir. Mombosa Kenya 90440. LC HV447.K44. DD 352.9440967623.

ANNUAL REPORT - SOUTH CAROLINA. CHILDREN'S RESOLUTION COMMITTEE. Main/Corp South Carolina. Children's Case Resolution Committee. 1983-. US. English. an. LC HV889.S6. DD 353.75700844088054.

ANNUAL REPORT - SOUTH CAROLINA COMMISSION ON AGING. Main/Corp South Carolina. Commission On Aging. 0362-756X. US. English. an. 915 Main Street, Columbia SC 29201. LC HV1468.S6. DD 353.975700846.

ANNUAL REPORT - STATE BOARD OF INSTITUTIONAL TRUSTEES (NEW JERSEY). (ANNUAL REPORT). Main/Corp New Jersey. State Board of Institutional Trustees. 1st-. 0092-2714. US. English. an. LC HV86. DD 353.97490084.

ANNUAL REPORT - STATE COMMISSION ON AGING (HAWAII). (ANNUAL REPORT). Main/Corp Hawaii. Commission on Aging. 0092-8356. US. English. an. LC HV1468.H3. DD 353.996900846.

ANNUAL REPORT - STATE OF ALASKA, DIVISION OF SOCIAL SERVICES. Main/Corp Alaska. Division of Social Services. US. English. an. Division of Social Services, Pouch H-05, Juneau AK 99811. LC HV86. DD 361.6209798.

ANNUAL REPORT - STATE OF CONNECTICUT, CRIMINAL INJURIES COMPENSATION BOARD. Main/Corp Connecticut. Criminal Injuries Compensation Board. 1st- 1979-. US. English. an. Criminal Injuries Compensation Board, 101 Lafayette Street, Hartford CT 06106. LC HV8691.U5. DD 353.974600848806.

ANNUAL REPORT - STATE OF FLORIDA, ORGANIZED CRIME CONTROL COUNCIL. Main/Corp Florida. Organized Crime Control Council. 0149-8789. US. English. an. PO Box 1489, Tallahassee FL 32302. LC HV7259. DD 364.1060759.

ANNUAL REPORT - STATE OF MARYLAND. CRIMINAL INJURIES COMPENSATION BOARD. (ANNUAL REPORT). Main/Corp Maryland. Criminal Injuries Compensation Board. 1st- 1969/70-. 0092-6051. US. English. an. Criminal Injuries Compensation Board, 601 Jackson Towers, Baltimore MD 21201. LC HV7270. DD 353.9752008488.

ANNUAL REPORT - STATE OF NEBRASKA, DEPARTMENT OF CORRECTIONAL SERVICES. Main/Corp Nebraska. Dept. of Correctional Services. 0362-8485. US. English. an. Department of Correctional Service, PO Box 94661 Statehouse Station, Lincoln NE 68509. LC HV7277. DD 353.97820084.

ANNUAL REPORT - STATE OF NEW MEXICO, GOVERNOR'S ORGANIZED CRIME PREVENTION COMMISSION. Main/Corp New Mexico. Governor's Organized Crime Prevention Commission. 1975-. US. English. an. Governors Organized Crime Prevention Commission, PO Box 1807, Albuquerque NM 87103. LC HV7281. DD 364.978905. *Annual Report and Guidelines for a Comprehensive Plan, 0098-0536.*

ANNUAL REPORT - STATE OF SOUTH DAKOTA, OFFICE OF CORRECTIONAL SERVICES. Main/Corp South Dakota. Office of Correctional Services. 1977/78-. US. English. an. Board of Charities & Corrections, Office of Correctional Services, Pierre SD 57501. LC HV9305.S8. DD 353.97830084906.

ANNUAL REPORT - TEXAS BOARD OF PRIVATE INVESTIGATORS AND PRIVATE SECURITY AGENCIES. Main/Corp Texas. Board of Private Investigators and Private Security Agencies. US. English. an. Texas Board of Private Investigators and Private Security Agencies, Box 13509, Austin TX 78711. LC HV8096.T4. DD 353.97640074.

ANNUAL REPORT - TEXAS VETERANS AGENT ORANGE ASSISTANCE PROGRAMS. Main/Corp Texas Veterans Agent Orange Assistance Program. US. English. an. Texas Department of Health, 1100 West 49th Street, Austin TX 78756.

Sociology: General Works, Theory—Social Pathology, Welfare, Criminology

ANNUAL REPORT - THE MISSISSIPPI CRIMINAL JUSTICE PLANNING DIVISION. Main/Corp Mississippi. Criminal Justice Planning Division. US. English. an. Office of the Governor, Mississippi Criminal Justice Planning Div, Jackson MS 39205. LC HV7274. DD 353.97620074.

ANNUAL REPORT - THE RAINER FOUNDATION. Main/Corp Rainer Foundation. UK. English. an. The Rainer Foundation, 89A Blackheath Hill, London SE10 8TJ England. LC HV9148.L8. DD 362.7062421.

ANNUAL REPORT TO CONGRESS ON TITLE XX OF THE SOCIAL SECURITY ACT. (ANNUAL REPORT TO THE CONGRESS ON TITLE XX OF THE SOCIAL SECURITY ACT). VAT Annual Report to Congress on Title Twenty of the Social Security Act. Began with 1978/79. 0160-9262. US. English. an. US Department of Health and Human Services, Office of Human Development Services, Washington DC 20201. LC HV85. DD 338.4336160973. NLM W2 A 0227A. *Annual Report to Congress on Title XX of the Social Security Act, 0160-9262.*

ANNUAL REPORT TO CONGRESS - URBAN INITIATIVES ANTI-CRIME PROGRAM. Main/Corp United States. Urban Initiatives Anti-Crime Program. 1st- 1980-. 0272-8974. Periodical. US. English. an. US Department of Housing & Urban Development, Room 2118/ 451 7th Street, Washington DC 20410. LC HV7245. DD 353.007406.

ANNUAL REPORT TO THE BOARD OF HEALTH AND SOCIAL SERVICES (LINCOLN BOYS SCHOOL). Main/Corp Lincoln Boys School. US. English. an. Division of Corrections, PO Box 96, Irma WI 54442. LC HV9105.W7. DD 353.977500849.

ANNUAL REPORT TO THE CITIZENS' ADVISORY BOARD ON CORRECTIONS (KANSAS). Main/Corp Kansas. Office of the Ombudsman For Corrections. 1st- 1975/76-. US. English. an. Office of the Ombudsman for Corrections, 503 Kansas Avenue/Suite 539, Topeka KS 66603. LC HV7266.

ANNUAL REPORT TO THE CITIZEN'S ADVISORY BOARD ON CORRECTIONS (KANSAS). Main/Corp Kansas. Office of the Ombudsman of Correctional Institutions. 1975/76-. Periodical. US. English. ir. Office of the Ombudsman of Correctional Institutions, 503 Kansas Avenue/Suite 539, Topeka KS 66603.

ANNUAL REPORT TO THE CONGRESS ON THE STATUS AND ACCOMPLISHMENTS OF THE CENTERS FUNDED UNDER THE RUNAWAY AND HOMELESS YOUTH ACT. 0742-9525. US. English. an. LC HV1431. DD 362.74.

ANNUAL REPORT TO THE GOVERNOR AND THE LEGISLATURE - CALIFORNIA. JUDICIAL CRIMINAL JUSTICE PLANNING COMMITTEE. Main/Corp California. Judicial Criminal Justice Planning Committee. US. English. an. Judicial Criminal Justice Planning Committee, 333 Golden Gate Avenue, San Francisco CA 94102. LC HV7254. DD 353.97940074.

ANNUAL REPORT TO THE GOVERNOR AND THE OHIO GENERAL ASSEMBLY - OHIO COMMISSION FOR CHILDREN. Main/Corp Ohio Commission For Children. 1st- 1978/79-. US. English. an. Ohio Commission For Children, 65 South Front Street/Suite 508, Columbus OH 43215. LC HV742.O3. DD 353.97710084706.

ANNUAL REPORT TO THE GOVERNOR AND WASHINGTON STATE LEGISLATURE - WASHINGTON (STATE). GAMBLING COMMISSION. Main/Corp Washington State Gambling Commisssion. VFOAT Report to the Governor and Legislature. US. English. an. State of Washington, Gambling Commission, Olympia WA 98504. LC HV6708. DD 353.97970076205.

ANNUAL REPORT TO THE GOVERNOR - CALIFORNIA. STATE AND CONSUMER SERVICES AGENCY. Main/Corp California. State and Consumer Services Agency. US. English. an. LC HV1555.C2. DD 362.4045609794.

ANNUAL REPORT TO THE GOVERNOR - DEPARTMENT OF CORRECTION, STATE OF DELAWARE. (ANNUAL REPORT TO THE GOVERNOR). Main/Corp Delaware. Dept. of Correction. 0147-4073. US. English. an. Department of Correction, R D #1 Box 245-A, Smyrna DE 19977. LC HV8327. DD 353.975100849. *Report to the Governor.*

THE ANNUAL REPORT TO THE GOVERNOR, LEGISLATURE, AND GENERAL PUBLIC - MISSISSIPPI SCHOOL FOR THE BLIND. Main/Corp Mississippi School for the Blind. 1978-1979-. US. English. an. LC HV1796.M72. DD 371.91109762. *Annual Report of the Mississippi School for the Blind....*

ANNUAL REPORT TO THE GOVERNOR, LIEUTENANT GOVERNOR, AND SPEAKER OF THE HOUSE OF REPRESENTATIVES OF TEXAS. Main/Corp Texas. Commission On Jail Standards. 1978-. US. English. an. Texas Commission on Jail Standards, 1414 Colorado Street/Suite 500, PO Box 12985, Austin TX 78711. LC HV7293. DD 353.9764008495.

ANNUAL REPORT TO THE MISSISSIPPI LEGISLATURE - MISSISSIPPI COUNCIL ON AGING. Main/Corp Mississippi Council On Aging. US. English. an. Mississippi Council on Aging, 510 George Street, PO Box 5136, Jackson MS 39216. LC HV1468.M65. DD 353.97620084605.

THE ANNUAL REPORT TO THE STATE BOARD OF HEALTH AND SOCIAL SERVICES - WISCONSIN. Main/Corp Wisconsin. Child Center and Annex, Sparta. 0098-5201. US. English. an. LC HV743.S62. DD 353.977500847.

ANNUAL REPORT .... - UNITED ISRAEL APPEAL. Main/Corp United Israel Appeal. 1978-. US. English. an. United Israel Appeal, 515 Park Avenue, New York NY 10022. LC HV3191. DD 361.763. *Report to the Annual Meeting of the Board of Trustees ....*

ANNUAL REPORT - UNITED SOUTH AND EASTERN TRIBES, INC. (ANNUAL REPORT). Main/Corp United South and Eastern Tribes, Inc. 0741-4153. US. English. an. 1101 Kermit Drive/Suite 800, Nashville TN 37217. LC E78.S65. DD 362.8.497073.

ANNUAL REPORT - UNITED STATES. NATIONAL ADVISORY COMMITTEE FOR JUVENILE JUSTICE AND DELINQUENCY PREVENTION. (ANNUAL REPORT). Main/Corp United States. National Advisory Committee for Juvenile Justice and Delinquency Prevention. 0273-5245. US. English. an. United States Department of Justice, Office of Juvenile Justice and Delinquency Prevention, 633 Indiana Avenue NW, Washington DC 20531. LC HV9103. DD 353.0075.

ANNUAL REPORT - UNIVERSITY OF NORTH CAROLINA AT CHARLOTTE, CRIMINAL JUSTICE PROGRAM. Main/Corp University of North Carolina at Charlotte. Criminal Justice Program. US. English. an. LC HV7923. DD 364.071175676.

ANNUAL REPORT - UTAH JUVENILE COURT. Main/Corp Utah. Juvenile Court. 0566-4152. US. English. an. 339 South 6th East, Salt Lake City UT 84102. LC HV9093.U8. DD 345.79208.

ANNUAL REPORT - VERMONT OFFICE ON AGING. Main/Corp Vermont. Office on Aging. US. English. an. Vermont Office on Aging, 103 South Main Street, Waterbury VT 05676. LC HV1468.V4. DD 353.97430084606.

ANNUAL REPORT - VICTORIA. HOSPITAL AND CHARITIES COMMISSION. Main/Corp Victoria. Hospital and Charities Commission. AT. English. an. Victoria Hospital & Charities Commission, Melbourne Victoria Australia. LC HV506. DD 360.994. NLM W2 KA8.1 V6H8A.

ANNUAL REPORT - VIRGINIA ASSOCIATION OF COMMUNITY SERVICES BOARDS. Main/Corp Virginia Association of Community Services Boards. US. English. an. Virginia Association of Community Services Boards Inc, PO Box 9416, Richmond VA 23228.

ANNUAL REPORT - VIRGINIA. DEPT. OF REHABILITATIVE SERVICES. OFFICE OF PUBLIC RELATIONS *CEASED.* Main/Corp Virginia. Dept. of Rehabilitative Services. Office of Public Relations. 1980-. US. English. an. Virginia Department of Rehabilitative Services, PO Box 11045, Richmond VA 23230. LC HV1555.V8. DD 353.97550084406. *Annual Report.*

ANNUAL REPORT - VIRGINIA. OFFICE OF EMERGENCY AND ENERGY SERVICES. Main/Corp Virginia. Office of Emergency and Energy Services. 1978-. US. English. an. Commonwealth of Virginia, Office of Emergency & Energy Services, Richmond VA 23219. LC HV555.U62. DD 353.97550075406.

ANNUAL REPORT - VIRGINIA STATE OFFICE ON VOLUNTEERISM. Main/Corp Virginia. State Office on Volunteerism. 1976/77-. US. English. an. Virginia State Office on Volumteerism, Fourth Street Office Building/205 North 4th Street, Richmond VA 23219. LC HV86. DD 353.97550084.

ANNUAL REPORT - WASHINGTON STATE COMMISSION FOR THE BLIND. Main/Corp Washington. State Commission For the Blind. 1st- 1977/78-. US. English. an. Commission For the Blind, 3411 South Alaska Street PO Box 18379, Seattle WA 98118. LC HV1796.W2. DD 353.979700844.

ANNUAL REPORT - WAYNE COUNTY DEPARTMENT OF SOCIAL SERVICES. (ANNUAL REPORT). Main/Corp Wayne Co., Mich. Dept. of Social Services. **Series Corp** Its DSS Publication. 0093-7665. US. English. an. Wayne County Department of Social Services, 640 Temple, Detroit MI 48201. LC HV86.M58. DD 362.977473.

ANNUAL REPORT - WILLIAM T. GRANT FOUNDATION. Main/Corp William T. Grant Foundation. 1975/76-. 0160-7200. US. English. an. William T Grant Foundation, 130 East 59th Street, New York NY 10022. LC HV97. DD 362.70973. NLM W1 WI549J. *Annual Report - Grant Foundation, 0147-4138.*

ANNUAL REPORT - WISCONSIN DEPARTMENT OF JUSTICE, DIVISION OF CRIMINAL INVESTIGATION, ARSON BUREAU. (ANNUAL REPORT - ARSON BUREAU). Main/Corp Wisconsin. Arson Bureau. 0098-4183. US. English. an. Arson Bureau, 123 West Washington Avenue, Madison WI 53702. LC HV6638. DD 353.977500782.

ANNUAL RESEARCH REVIEW - CALIFORNIA DEPARTMENT OF CORRECTIONS. Main/Corp California. Dept. of Corrections. 0196-7746. US. English. an. California Department of Corrections, 714 P Street/Room 740, Sacramento CA 95814. LC HV8324. DD 365.9794.

ANNUAL REVIEW - BRITISH AGENCIES FOR ADOPTION AND FOSTERING. Main/Corp British Agencies For Adoption and Fostering. 1980-81-. UK. English. an. British Agencies for Adoption and Fostering, 11 Southwark Street, London SE1 1RQ England. LC HV875. DD 362.73306041.

ANNUAL REVIEW - BRITISH RED CROSS SOCIETY. Main/Corp British Red Cross Society. 1983-. UK. English. an. 9 Grosvenor Crescent, London SW1X 7EJ England. *Annual Review of the British Red Cross Society.*

ANNUAL REVIEW - NATIONAL CHILDREN'S BUREAU. Main/Corp National Children's Bureau. UK. English. an. National Childrens Bureau, 8 Wakley Street, Islington EC, London England. LC HV751.A255. DD 362.70942.

ANNUAL REVIEW OF CHILD ABUSE AND NEGLECT RESEARCH. 1978-. 0192-5644. US. English. an. US Department of Health, Education and Welfare, Office of Human Development Services, Administration for Children, Youth and Families, Children's Bureau, Washington DC 20402. LC HV741. DD 362.71. NLM WA 22 AA1 A7.

ANNUAL REVIEW OF REHABILITATION. V. 1- 1980-. 0197-2251. US. English. an. Springer Publishing Company, 536 Broadway, New York NY 10012. Tel (212)4431-4370. Ed Elizabeth Pan. Ind/Abst Index Med., Psychol. Abstr. LC HD7255.A2. DD 362.0425. NLM W1

Sociology: General Works, Theory—Social Pathology, Welfare, Criminology

AN7797. bk rev. Resource for the practitioner highlighting developments in rapidly changing field of rehabilitation.

ANNUAL SALARY STUDY AND SURVEY OF SELECTED PERSONNEL ISSUES. See Economics - Labor.

ANNUAL SERVICES PLAN - DEPARTMENT OF SOCIAL SERVICES. Main/Corp South Dakota. Dept. of Social Services. US. English. an. Department of Social Services, State Office Building, Illinois Street, Pierre SD 57501. LC HV98.S8. DD 361.6209783.

ANNUAL STATE PLAN FOR DEVELOPMENTAL DISABILITIES, SUMMARY (NEW JERSEY). Main/Corp New Jersey. Developmental Disabilities Council. 1978-. US. English. an. New Jersey Developmental Disabilities Council, 169 West Hanover Street, PO Box 1237, Trenton NJ. LC HV3006.N5. DD 362.309749.

ANNUAL STATEMENT OF OPERATIONS - NEW HAMPSHIRE. STATE LIQUOR COMMISSION. Main/Corp New Hampshire. State Liquor Commission. US. English. an. LC HV5297.N4.

ANNUAL STATISTICAL REPORT - BOARD OF PARDONS AND PAROLES. See Statistics.

ANNUAL STATISTICAL REPORT (COLORADO. DEPT. OF CORRECTIONS). See Statistics.

ANNUAL STATISTICAL REPORT - DEPARTMENT OF CORRECTIONS. See Statistics.

ANNUAL STATISTICAL REPORT - DIVISION OF FAMILY SERVICES. See Statistics.

ANNUAL STATISTICAL REPORT - MARYLAND. JUVENILE SERVICES ADMINISTRATION. See Statistics.

ANNUAL STATISTICAL REPORT OF FELONS AND MISDEMEANANTS COMMITTED TO THE VIRGINIA STATE CORRECTIONAL SYSTEM AND FELONS CONFINED IN THE CORRECTIONAL SYSTEM INCLUDING FELON RECIDIVISTS COMMITTED AND CONFINED. See Statistics.

ANNUAL STATISTICAL REPORT OF PENNSYLVANIA COUNTY PRISONS AND JAILS. See Statistics.

ANNUAL STATISTICAL REPORT - PENNSYLVANIA DEPT. OF JUSTICE. See Statistics.

ANNUAL STATISTICAL REPORT - SOUTH DAKOTA DEPARTMENT OF SOCIAL SERVICES. See Statistics.

ANNUAL STATISTICAL REPORT - STATE OF NEW MEXICO, HEALTH AND SOCIAL SERVICES DEPARTMENT, STATE WELFARE AGENCY. See Statistics.

ANNUAL SYMPOSIUM REPORT - BRITISH COLUMBIA ASSOCIATION OF JUSTICE COUNCILS. Main/Corp British Columbia Association of Justice Councils. VFOAT Symposium: Community Justice Exchange. CN. English. LC KEB570.A13. DD 364.9711.

ANUARIO ESTATISTICO - SERVICO SOCIAL DO COMERCIO, ADMINISTRACAO REGIONAL EM MINAS GERAIS. See Statistics.

APEX. 0141-2205. Periodical. UK. English. qt. NLM W1 AP115B.

APPEALS NEWS. Winter 1977/78-. Periodical. US. English. qt. Massachusetts Department of Education/Bureau of Special Education Appeals, 31 St James Avenue, Boston MA 02116. LC KFM2795.9.H3. DD 344.744079105.

ARCHIV FUR KRIMINOLOGIE. See Genealogy and Heraldry - Archives.

ARGUS-JOURNAL. VFOAT Argus-Journal. V. 1- Aug. 1966-. 0004-1211. Periodical. CN. text in English and French with French text on inverted pages. Public Service Alliance Canada, 233 Gilmour Street, Ottawa Ontario K2P 0P1 Canada. *Argus, 0570-8907; CSAC Journal, 0381-5773.*

ARIZONA COMPREHENSIVE BEHAVIORAL HEALTH PLAN. 1977/82-. 0162-6922. Periodical. US. English. NLM W2 AA7 D6A. *Mental Health Plan, State Alcohol and Drug Abuse Plan.*

ARIZONA CRIMINAL JUSTICE EXPENDITURES. Main/Corp Arizona. State Justice Planning Agency. Statistical Analysis Center. US. English. an. Arizona State Justice Planning Agency, Statistical Analysis Center, 5119 North 19th Avenue, Phoenix AZ 85015. LC HV7252. DD 338.43.

ARIZONA STATE PLAN FOR CONSTRUCTION OF MENTAL HEALTH CENTERS. Main/Corp Arizona. State Dept. of Health. Division of Mental Health and Mental Retardation. US. English. an. Arizona State Department of Health, 1624 West Adams Street, Phoenix AZ 85007. LC RA790.65.A6. DD 353979100842.

ARIZONA SUICIDE STATISTICS. See Statistics.

ARKANSAS MENTAL HEALTH SERVICES BIENNIAL REPORT. US. English. be. Department of Social and Rehabilitation Services, 4313 West Markham Street, Little Rock AR 72201. LC RA790.65.A8. DD 353.976700842. NLM W2 AA8 M4A.

ARKANSAS SOCIAL SERVICES ANNUAL REPORT. (ANNUAL REPORT). Main/Corp Arkansas. Social Services. Research and Statistics. 0092-0215. US. English. an. Welfare Employment Security Building, State Capitol Mall, Little Rock AR 72203. LC HV86. DD 362.9767.

ASSISTANCE PAYMENTS STATISTICS. See Statistics.

L'ASSISTENZA SOCIALE. Yearly V. 1, Jan. 1947-. 0392-1026. Periodical. IT. Italian. bm. $17.82. Ediesse, Corso d'Italia 25, 00146 Roma Italy. Ind/Abst CIS Abstr., Foreign Lang. Index. LC HV4. DD 360.5.

ASSOCIATION FOR RETARDED CHILDREN OF BRITISH COLUMBIA. ANNUAL CONFERENCE (MINUTES). (ANNUAL CONFERENCE). Began publication with 1958 issue. 0316-9332. Periodical. CN. English. an. British Columbia Association for the Mentally Retarded, 221 119th West Pender Street, Vancouver British Columbia V6B 1S5 Canada. DD 362.3062711.

ASWEA: JOURNAL FOR SOCIAL WORK EDUCATION IN AFRICA. Main/Corp Association For Social Work Education in Africa. VFOAT Journal For Social Work Education in Africa. V. 1- June 1974-. English. ir. PO Box 1176, Addis Ababa Ethopia. LC HV11. DD 361.007116.

ATTICA NEWS SERVICE. V. 1- Mar. 1973-. Periodical. US. English. ir.

AUDIT GUIDE AND STANDARDS FOR COMMUNITY DEVELOPMENT BLOCK GRANT RECIPIENTS. US. English. ir. Department of Housing and Urban Development, 451 Seventh Street Southwest, Washington DC 20401.

AUDIT REPORT. DEPARTMENT OF JUDICIAL, STATE PROSECUTIONS. (AUDIT REPORT, DEPARTMENT OF JUDICIAL, STATE PROSECUTIONS). Main/Corp Tennessee. Division of State Audit. 0148-3854. US. English. Tennessee Comptroller of the Treasury, Nashville TN 37202. LC KFT562. DD 353.97680088.

AUGUST VOLLMER CRIMINALISTIC SERIES. 0067-0561. Monographic Series. English. ir. Charles C Thomas Publ, 301-327 East Lawrence Avenue, Springfield IL 62717.

AUSTRALIAN & NEW ZEALAND JOURNAL OF CRIMINOLOGY. (THE AUSTRALIAN & NEW ZEALAND JOURNAL OF CRIMINOLOGY). V. 1- March 1968-. 0004-8658. Periodical. English. qt. Gaunt & Sons, 3011 Gulf Drive, Holmes Beach FL 33510. Ind/Abst Leg. Resour. Index, APAIS, Aust. Public Aff. Inf. Serv. LC HV6001. DD 364.05.

AUSTRALIAN CITIZEN LIMITED. 0313-6620. AT. English. ir. $2.00. PO Box 91, Brighton South Australia 5048. Ind/Abst Except. Child Educ. Resour. LC HV901.A8. DD 362.7830994. NLM W1 AU5185. *Australian Children Limited, 0004-8844.*

THE AUSTRALIAN JOURNAL OF SOCIAL ISSUES. V. 1- Spring 1961-. 0004-9557. Periodical. AT. English. qt. 32.00. Australian Council of Social Services, 147-149 Castlereagh Street, Sydney 2000 New South Wales Australia. Tel 2648188. Ed Sheina Shaver. Ind/Abst Int. Labour Doc., Sociol. Abstr., Soc. Welf. Soc. Plan./Policy Soc. Dev., Ref. Source, Soc. Work Res. Abstr., Lang. Lang. Behav. Abstr., Soc. Sci. Citation Index. LC HN841. (cum index). bk rev. adv acc. Circ 1,000. (ctrl). A forum for discussion to stimulate debate and action on significant and controversial social issues currently of public concern.

AWARE CEASED. Main/Corp Virginia. Commission For Children and Youth. V. 1-3, No. 6. Periodical. US. English. mo. Virginia Division For Children, 805 East Broad Street, Richmond VA 23219. Tel (804)786-5507.

B. C. CORRECTIONS COURIER. V. 8, No. 4- Dec. 1971-. 0318-4080. CN. English. qt. British Columbia Corrections Association, #302 2515 Burrard Street, Vancouver British Columbia V6J 3J6 Canada. DD 365.05. *The Courier, 0045-8864.*

B R I C NEWS. Main/Corp Black Resources & Information Centre. V. 1- May 1976-. 0703-7112. Periodical. CN. English. mo. $10.00. Black Resources & Information Centre, Suite 101/167 Church Street, Toronto Ontario M5B 1Y4 Canada. DD 362.84.

BAN THONG TIN - HOI GIUP NGTY NAN NANAIMO. (BAN THONG TIN). 15/6/81-. 0824-5193. Periodical. CN. Vietnamese. bm. $0.50 Per No. Nanaimo Refugee Co-Ordination Society, Suite 225/228 Community Services Facility, 285 Prideaux Street, Nanaimo British Columbia V9R 2N2 Canada. DD 362.870971. *Ban Thong Tin Cua Hoi Gip Ngi Ty Nan Tai Nanaimo, 0824-5215.*

BAPTIST HOSPITAL FUND BULLETIN. V. 7, No. 4 (Sept./Oct. 1963)-. 8750-2151. Periodical. US. English. bm. Baptist Hospital Fund Inc, 1700 University Avenue, St Paul MN 55104. DD 362. *Baptist Hospital Bulletin.*

BARNOMSORGEN I SIFFROR. Series/Titl Barnomsorgsplanering. Began with 1977-81. Swedish. an. LC HV790.

BASIC FACTS ABOUT CORRECTIONS IN CANADA. VFOAT Recueil de Donnees Concernant les Services Correctionnels Canadiens. 1982-. 0821-0594. CN. English (text also in French with French text on inverted pages). an. Communications Branch Correctional Service Of Canada, 340 Laurier Avenue, West Ottawa Ontario K1A O9P Canada. DD 365.971.

BCMHP NEWS. (BCMHP NEWS : THE NEWSLETTER OF BRITISH COLUMBIANS FOR MENTALLY HANDICAPPED PEOPLE). VFOAT Newsletter of British Columbians for Mentally Handicapped People. VAT British Columbians for Mentally Handicapped People News. Vol. 1, No. 3 (Fall 1983)-. 0827-2344. Periodical. CN. English. qt. Free. British Columbians for Mentally Handicapped People, #155-1200 West 73rd Avenue, Vancouver British Columbia V6P 6G5 Canada. DD 362.3060711. *BCAMR News, 0827-2336.*

BERETNING - SOCIAL- OG SUNDHEDSFORVALTNINGEN I KBENHAVN. Main/Corp Copenhagen. Social-Og Sundhedsforvaltningen. 1976-. DK. Danish. ir. Planlaegningsafdelingen, Svendborggade 5, 2100 Kbenhavn Denmark. LC HV325.C6.

BIBLIOGRAFIA ANALITICA EM BEM-ESTAR SOCIAL. 1- 1974-. Portuguese. ir. Secretaria de Benn-Estar Social, rua Pedro de Toledo 1529, 04039 Sao Paulo Brazil. LC Z7164.C4, HV40.

BIENNIAL BUDGET REQUEST - WISCONSIN DEPARTMENT OF HEALTH AND SOCIAL SERVICES. Main/Corp Wisconsin. Dept. of Health and Social Services. 0147-3492. US. English. be. Department of Health and Social Sciences, 1 East Wilson Street, Madison WI 53702. LC HV86. DD 353.97750084.

BIENNIAL REPORT - GOVERNOR'S ADVOCACY COMMITTEE FOR CHILDREN AND YOUTH. Main/Corp Wisconsin. Governor's Advocacy Committee for Children and Youth. 0146-2423. US. English. be. Governor's Advocacy Committee for Children and Youth, 106 East Doty Street/Suite 208, Madison WI 53703. LC HV742.W5. DD 362.709775.

BIENNIAL REPORT - KANSAS ADULT AUTHORITY. Main/Corp Kansas. Adult Authority. 1974/76-. 0149-340X. US. English. be. Kansas Adult Authority, KPL Towers/Suite 600, 818

Sociology: General Works, Theory—Social Pathology, Welfare, Criminology

Kansas Avenue, Topeka KS 66612. **LC** HV7266. **DD** 353.978100849. *Biennial Report - Kansas Board of Probation and Parole, 0149-3396.*

BIENNIAL REPORT - LEAGUE OF RED CROSS SOCIETIES. **Main/Corp** League of Red Cross Societies. 1977/78-. 0253-0406. **SZ.** English. be. League of Red Cross Societies, Case Postale 276, 1211 Geneva 19 Switzerland. **LC** HV560. **DD** 361.77. **NLM** W1 LE264C. *Annual Report - League of Red Cross Societies.*

BIENNIAL REPORT - MINNESOTA. DEPT. OF CORRECTIONS. **Main/Corp** Minnesota. Dept. of Corrections. 1979-80-. US. English. be. Minnesota Department of Correction, 430 Metro Square Building, 7th & Robert Street, St Paul MN 55101. *Update - Minnesota Department of Corrections, 0195-6507.*

BIENNIAL REPORT - MISSOURI DIVISION OF CORRECTIONS. **Main/Corp** Missouri. Division of Corrections. US. English. be. Missouri Division of Corrections/Donald R Jenkins Director, PO Box 236, Jefferson City MO 65102. **LC** HV7275. **DD** 353.97780084906. *Report.*

BIENNIAL REPORT - NEVADA GIRLS TRAINING CENTER. **Main/Corp** Nevada Girls Training Center. 0099-2216. US. English. be. PO Box 427, Caliente NV 89008. **LC** HV9105.N32. **DD** 365.66.

BIENNIAL REPORT - NORTH CAROLINA. DIVISION OF YOUTH SERVICES. **Main/Corp** North Carolina. Division of Youth Services. US. English. be. North Carolina Department of Human Resources/Division of Youth Services, 401 Glenwood Avenue, Raleigh NC 27603. **LC** HV9105.N9. **DD** 364.6088055.

BIENNIAL REPORT - NORTH CAROLINA. STATE DEPARTMENT OF SOCIAL SERVICES OF THE DEPARTMENT OF HUMAN RESOURCES. (BIENNIAL REPORT). **Main/Corp** North Carolina. Dept. of Social Services. 0093-3988. US. English. be. North Carolina Department of Social Services, 325 North Salisbury Street, Raleigh NC 27611. **LC** HV86. **DD** 353.97560084.

BIENNIAL REPORT - TEXAS ADULT PROBATION COMMISSION. **Main/Corp** Texas Adult Probation Commission. 1977/79-. US. English. be. Texas Adult Probation Commission, 812 San Antonio Street/Suite 4000 PO Box 12427, Austin TX 78711. **LC** HV9305.T4. **DD** 353.976400849306.

BIENNIAL REPORT TO THE GOVERNOR - TEXAS PLANNING COUNCIL FOR DEVELOPMENTAL DISABILITIES. **Main/Corp** Texas Planning Council for Developmental Disabilities. US. English. be. **LC** HV1555.T4. **DD** 362.1968. Available on microfiche from Texas State Library.

BILDUNG UND REHABILITATION SEHGESCHADIGTER. See Physically Impaired.

BIMONTHLY REPORTS. No. 1- Dec. 1977-. 0705-8772. Periodical. CN. English. bm. $46.43. John Whitelaw's Bimonthly, PO Box 731 Station A, Toronto Ontario M5W 1G2 Canada. **Tel** (416)469-0778. **DD** 364.1630971.

BJULETEN SUSPILNOJI SLUZLY KANADY. (BIULETEN SUSPILNOI SLUZHBY UKRAINTSIV KANADY). **VFOAT** Bulletin, Ukrainian Canadian Social Services. Began publication in 197-. 0700-8198. Periodical. CN. Ukrainian. sa. Ukrainian Canadian Social Services, 2445 Bloor Street West, Toronto Ontario M6S 1P7 Canada. **DD** 361.706271. *Biuleten Ukrainskoi Kanadskoi Suspilnoi Sluzhby, 0700-818X.*

THE BLACK CHILD ADVOCATE. V. 1- 1972-. Periodical. US. English. qt. National Black Children's Development Institution Inc, 1463 Rhode Island Avenue, Washington DC 20005. **Tel** 202/387-1281. **Ed** Merlene Alicia Vassall. **Circ** 1,500. Issues affecting black children and families in education, child care, child welfare, health, and public policy.

BLOOD ALCOHOL TESTING FOR MOTOR VEHICLE DEATHS, WISCONSIN. Began in 1968. 0731-2393. US. English. an. Wisconsin Division of Health/ Bureau of Health Statistics, PO Box 309, Madison WI 53701. **LC** HE5614.3.W5. **DD** 363.1251. **NLM** W2 AW6 D53B.

BOLETIM BIBLIOGRAFICO. See Bibliographies.

BOLETIN DE ESTUDIOS Y DOCUMENTACION DE SERVICIOS SOCIALES. No. 1 (Jan./March 1980)-. 0211-0334. Periodical. SP. Spanish. ir. Inserso Gabinete Tecnico, Maria De Guzman 52, Madrid 3 Spain. **LC** HV4. **DD** 361.005.

BOLETIN DEL INSTITUTO INTERAMERICANO DEL NINO. **Main/Corp** Interamerican Children's Institute. V. 31, No. 3- (No. 122-). 0020-4056. Periodical. UY. English, French, or Spanish. sa. Instituto Interamer del Nino, Avenida 8 de-Octubre, 2882 Montevideo Uruquay. **Ind/Abst** Foreign Lang. Index. **NLM** W1 BO291. *Boletin del Instituto Internacional Americano de Proteccion A la Infancia.*

BOLETIN ESTADISTICO - ASIGNACIONES FAMILIARES. **Main/Corp** Asignaciones Familiares (Uruguay). No. 1- July 1976-. UY. Spanish. ir. Asignaciones Familiares Oficina Central, San Jose 1132, Montevideo Uruguay. **LC** HV700.U7. **DD** 362.828209895.

BOMB SUMMARY. Began with 1973. 0360-3245. US. English. an. US Department of Justice, Federal Bureau of Investigation, Washington DC 20535. **LC** HV8059. **DD** 364.164.

BOOMERANG. (THE BOOMERANG). **VFOAT** Maritime Penitentiary News. V. 1- June 1979-. 0228-2321. Periodical. CN. English. mo. $5.00. The Boomerang, PO Box A, Dorchester New Brunswick EOA 1MO Canada. **DD** 365.971523.

BOSAI ROPPO. **Main/Corp** Japan. Japanese. ir. 2500. Zenkoku Kajo Horei Shuppan, c/o Zenkoku Building, 17 Saneicho Shinjuku-ku, Tokyo 160 Japan.

BRA APROPA. SW. Swedish. qt. Brottsforebyggande Radet, Box 12070, 120 22 Stockholm Sweden. **LC** HV7037. **DD** 364.9485.

BREAKING THE SILENCE (OTTAWA, ONT.). See Women.

BRISE DE L'EST. (LA BRISE DE L'EST). First issue in Sept. 1971. 0384-9058. Periodical. CN. French. ir. $2. Les Retraites a l'Action, c/o M Gertrude Genest, 337 rue Moreault, Rimouski Quebec G5L 1P4 Canada. **DD** 362.630971477.

BRITISH COLUMBIA ASSOCIATION FOR THE MENTALLY RETARDED. ANNUAL CONFERENCE. (ANNUAL CONFERENCE). 14th- 1971-. 0316-9324. Periodical. CN. English. an. British Columbia Association for the Mentally Retarded, 221-119 West Pender Street, Vancouver British Columbia V6B 1S5 Canada. **DD** 362.3062711. *Annual Conference: Minutes, 0316-9332.*

THE BRITISH JOURNAL OF CRIMINOLOGY, DELINQUENCY AND DEVIANT SOCIAL BEHAVIOR. (THE BRITISH JOURNAL OF CRIMINOLOGY). Vol. 1, No. 1 (July 1960)-. 0007-0955. Periodical. UK. English. qt. $42.50. Fred B Rothman and Company, 10368 West Centennial Road, Littletown CO 80127. **Tel** (303)979-5657. **Ind/Abst** Leg. Resour. Index, Sociol. Abstr., Soc. Welf. Soc. Plan./Policy Soc. Dev., Psychol. Abstr., Soc. Sci. Index, Lang. Lang. Behav. Abstr., Curr. Law Index, Soc. Sci. Citation Index. **LC** HV6001. **DD** 364.05. **NLM** W1 BR521. **CODEN** BJCDAR. (cum index). adv acc. A British journal of criminology involving delinquency and deviant social behavior. *British Journal of Delinquency.*

THE BRITISH JOURNAL OF SOCIAL WORK. Vol. 1, No. 1 (Apr. 1971)-. 0045-3102. Periodical. UK. English. bm. $93.50. Academic Press, 4805 Sand Lake Road, Orlando FL 32819. **Tel** (305)345-4100. **Ind/Abst** Psychol. Abstr., Soc. Sci. Citation Index, Soc. Work Res. Abstr., Abstr. Soc. Work. **LC** HV1. **DD** 361.005. **NLM** W1 BR636. **CODEN** BJSWAS. *British Journal of Psychiatric Social Work, Social Work.*

BUDGET RECOMMENDATIONS. EXECUTIVE SUMMARY. **Main/Corp** Massachusetts. Executive Office of Human Services. **VFOAT** Executive Summary. US. English. **LC** HV86. **DD** 353.9744007222.

BULLDOZER. 0821-0357. Periodical. CN. English. sa. Bulldozer, PO Box 5052 Station A, Toronto Ontario M5W 1W4 Canada. **Ind/Abst** Altern. Press Index. **DD** 365.70971.

BULLETIN - BRITISH COLUMBIA POLICE COMMISSION CEASED. **Main/Corp** British Columbia Police Commission. No. 1-7. 0380-1063. Periodical. CN. English. an. **LC** HV7642.B7. **DD** 363.209711.

BULLETIN DE L'ADMINISTRATION PENITENTIAIRE (BELGIUM. MINISTERE DE LA JUSTICE). (BULLETIN DE L'ADMINISTRATION PENITENTIAIRE). French. qt. Direc Etudes et Affaire Gen Minist de Justic, 4 PL Poelaert, Brussels 1 Belgium. *Bulletin de l'Administration des Prisons.*

BULLETIN DE L'A.I.F.A. **VAT** Bulletin de l'Association Internationale Francophone des Aines. Vol. 1, No. 1 (Winter 1983)-. 0822-5656. Periodical. CN. French. qt. Free to Members. Association Internationale Francophone des Aines, 1415 Est rue Jarry, Montreal Quebec H2E 2Z7 Canada. **DD** 362.60601.

BULLETIN DE L'AQDR. (LE BULLETIN DE L'AQDR). 0226-9880. Periodical. CN. French. bm. Free. Association Quebecoise pour la Defense des Retraites et Pre-Retraites, 1850 rue Bercy Bureau/Suite 115, Montreal Quebec H2K 2V2 Canada. **DD** 362.6060714.

BULLETIN DE L'INSTITUT DE READAPTATION DE MONTREAL. (LE BULLETIN DE L'INSTITUT DE READAPTATION DE MONTREAL). V. 27, No. 1, (Aug. 1983)-. 0316-4454. Periodical. CN. English (French). Rehabilitation Institute of Montreal, 6300 Darlington Avenue, Montreal Quebec H3S 2J4 Canada. **DD** 362.4060714. *Bulletin.*

BULLETIN DE NOUVELLES - DES TRAVAILLEURS SOCIAUX DU QUEBEC. (BULLETIN DE NOUVELLES). No. 1, (April 1982)-. 0713-4290. Periodical. CN. French (English). bm. Bulletin de Nouvelles, c/o Corporation Professionnelle des Travailleurs Sociaux du Quebec, 5757 Avenue Descelles, Montreal Quebec H3S 2C3 Canada. **DD** 361.0060714. *Bulletin, 0318-9627.*

BULLETIN DES CENTRES CANADIENS CONTRE LE VIOL. (LE BULLETIN DES CENTRES CANADIENS CONTRE LE VIOL). June 1980- . -. 0228-5509. Periodical. CN. French. Centres Canadiens Contre le Viol, A/S 4-45 Kingsway, Vancouver British Columbia V5T 3H7 Canada. **DD** 364.15320971.

BULLETIN - FEDERATION DES EQUIPES LOCORDAIRES ET DES CARREFOUR DE SOBRIETE DU QUEBEC. See Drug Abuse and Alcoholism.

BULLETIN NATIONAL DU CCA. **VFOAT** Bulletin National CCA. **VAT** Bulletin National du Conseil Canadien des Aveugles, Bulletin National - Conseil Canadien des Aveugles. 0822-9309. Periodical. CN. French. ir. Conseil Canadien des Aveugles, Bureau 610/220 rue Dundas, London Ontario N6A 1H3 Canada. **DD** 362.4106071. *Bulletin de Nouvelles National du CCA, Communis, 0826-2551.*

BULLETIN OF THE BIHAR TRIBAL WELFARE RESEARCH INSTITUTE. **Main/Corp** Bihar Tribal Welfare Research Institute. V. 7- 1965-. Periodical. in. **LC** DS485.B51. **DD** 362.84095412. *Bulletin.*

BULLETIN OF THE CRIMINOLOGICAL RESEARCH DEPARTMENT. **Main/Corp** Homu Sogo Kenkyujo. JA. English. ir. Research & Training Institute, Ministry of Justice, Homu Sogo Kenkyujo, 1-1-1 Kasumigaseki Chiyoda-ku, Tokyo Japan. **LC** HV6024.5. **DD** 364.30952.

THE BULLETIN OF THE NATIONAL ASSOCIATION OF SCHOOL SOCIAL WORKERS. **Main/Corp** National Association of School Social Workers. -V. 31, No. 1 (Sept. 1955). Periodical. US. English. National Association of Social Workers, 7981 East Avenue, Silver Springs MD 20910. **Tel** (301)565-0333. *Bulletin.*

BULLETIN ORGANISMES PROVINCIAUX. **VAT** B.O.P. Bulletin Organismes Provinciaux. Vol. 1, No. 1 (Jan. 1983)-. 0823-9320. Periodical. CN. French. bm. $8.00 Non-Profit Institutions, $10.00 Others. Table de Concertation des Organismes Provinciaux de Promotion des Droits et Interets des Personnes Handicappees du Quebec, Bureau 420 Est rue Ste-Catherine, Montreal Quebec H2L 2G3 Canada. **DD** 362.4048060714.

BULLETIN - SASKATCHEWAN COUNCIL FOR CRIPPLED CHILDREN AND ADULTS. (BULLETIN). **Main/Corp** Saskatchewan Council for Crippled Children and Adults. Vol. 8, No. 3 (Fall 1980)-. 0820-9847. Periodical. CN. English. qt. Saskatchewan Council for Crippled Children and Adults, 1410

Sociology: General Works, Theory—Social Pathology, Welfare, Criminology

Kilburn Avenue, Saskatoon Saskatchewan S7M 0J8 Canada. DD 362.43097124. *Council Bulletin, 0701-1903.*

BULLETIN SSQ SUR LES LOIS SOCIALES. FRANCAIS. (BULLETIN SSQ SUR LES LOIS SOCIALES). VAT Bulletin Services de Sante du Quebec sur les Lois Sociales. Vol. 9, No. 1 (Jan. 1980)-. 0713-8431. CN. French. an. Mutuelle S S Q, 2525 Boulevard Laurier, CP 10500, Sainte-Foy Quebec G1V 4H6 Canada. DD 344.71402. *Bulletin SSQ, 0713-0120.*

BULLETIN STATISTIK DEPARTEMEN SOSIAL (INDONESIA). Main/Corp Indonesia. Departemen Sosial. Indonesian. ir. D/A Biro Perencanaan & Evaluasi, Jl Ir H Juanda No 36, Jakarta Indonesia. LC HV401.

BULLETIN - UNITED STATES. BUREAU OF JUSTICE STATISTICS. (BULLETIN). VFOAT Bureau of Justics Statistics Bulletin. Feb. 1981-. 0742-7271. Periodical. US. English. mo. US Department of Justice, Bureau of Justice Statistics, Washington DC 20531. Ind/Abst Index U.S. Gov. Period. LC HV9278.

CADASTRO DAS EMPRESAS ESTATAIS. Sept. 1981-. BL. Portuguese. ir. Secretatia de Planejamento da Presidencia da Republica, Secretaria de Controle de Empresas Estatais, Esplanada dos Ministerios, Bloco K, 6O Andar, 70.063 Brasilia Brazil. LC HD4091. DD 363.0981.

CADEC-ARC ANNUAL REPORT. Main/Corp Christian Action for Development in the Caribbean. VFOAT C.A.D.E.C.-A.R.C. Annual Report. VAT CADEC ARC Annual Report. 1981-. English. an. LC HN195.2.C6. DD 361.7509729. *Annual Report.*

CAHIERS DE DEFENSE SOCIALE. French. ir. Centro Nazionale di Prevenzione e Difesa Sociale, 3 Piazza Castello, 20121 Milano Italy. LC HV6002. DD 364.05. *Bulletin de la Societe Internationale de Defense Sociale.*

CALA NEWSLETTER CEASED. VAT Community Action on Latin America Newsletter. V. 1, No. 1-V. 9, No. 1. Periodical. US. English. ir.

CALGARY COMMUNITY SERVICES DIRECTORY. See Yearbooks, Almanacs, Directories.

CALIFORNIA CAREER CRIMINAL APPREHENSION PROGRAM. ANNUAL REPORT TO THE LEGISLATURE. Main/Corp California. Office of Criminal Justice Planning. US. English. an. LC HV7254. DD 353.97640074.

CALIFORNIA CHILDREN SERVICES INFORMATION AND STATISTICS FOR FISCAL YEARS . . . . See Statistics.

CALIFORNIA COMMUNITY CRIME RESISTANCE PROGRAM : ANNUAL REPORT TO THE LEGISLATURE. 1st (1982)-. US. English. an. LC HV9475.C2. DD 364.4045809794.

CALIFORNIA CORRECTIONAL NEWS. VFOAT Correctional News. V. 1- Jan. 1947-. 0194-1682. Periodical. US. English. mo. $18.00. California Probation, Parole and Correction Association, 1722 J Street/Suite 18, Sacramento CA 95814. Tel (916)442-4721. Ed Susan B Cohen. bk rev. adv acc. Circ 2,400. (ctrl). Professional journal for criminal justice and corrections professionals and others interested in the field.

CALIFORNIA CRIPPLED CHILDREN SERVICES STATISTICAL REPORT. See Statistics.

CALIFORNIA LAWS RELATING TO YOUTHFUL OFFENDERS, *INCLUDING THE YOUTH AUTHORITY ACT, THE JUVENILE COURT LAW, . . . LEGISLATIVE CHANGES. See Law.

THE CALIFORNIA PRISONER. 1971. Periodical. US. English. bm. $25.00. Prisioners Union, 1315 18th Street, San Francisco CA 94107. Tel (415)648-2880. Ed Paula Norbert and Patricia Horn. Ind/Abst Altern. Press Index. bk rev. adv acc. Circ 9,000. (ctrl). A newspaper which deals with a variety of prison issues in the state of California.

CALIFORNIA STATE PLAN FOR REHABILITATION FACILITIES. Main/Corp California. Dept. of Rehabilitation. Community Resources Development Section. US. English. an. State of California/ Department of Rehabilitation, 830 K Street Mall, Sacramento CA 95814. LC HD7256.U6. DD 362.0425.

CALIFORNIA'S PROBATION SUBSIDY PROGRAM. Main/Corp California Youth Authority. US. English. California Youth Authority, 4241 Williams Bourgh Drive, Sacramento CA 95823. LC HV7254. DD 364.63.09794.

CAMBRIDGE STUDIES IN CRIMINOLOGY. V. 1- 1940-. Periodical. UK. English. mo.

CANADIAN BOOK OF CHARITIES. (THE CANADIAN BOOK OF CHARITIES). VFOAT Le Volume Canadien des Oeuvres de Charite. 1st- Ed. 0226-0409. CN. English (includes some test in French, 1982-). an. Free. Mavora Publications, Canadian Book of Charities, 124 Westwood Lane, Thornhill Ontario L4S 1R1 Canada. DD 361.002571. (ctrl).

CANADIAN CRIMINOLOGY FORUM. VFOAT Le Forum Canadien de Criminologie. V. 1- Spring 1979-. 0708-3165. Periodical. CN. English (French). sa. $11.61. Canadian Criminology Forum, 130 St George Street/Room 8001, Toronto Ontario M5S 1A1 Canada. Tel (416)978-7124. Ed Gail Kellough, Dany LaCombe. DD 364.05. bk rev. adv acc. Circ 200. Interdisciplinary journal which publishes theoretical and substantive articles relevent to criminology in Canada.

CANADIAN JOURNAL OF COMMUNITY MENTAL HEALTH. Vol. 1, No. 1 (March 1982)-. 0713-3936. Periodical. CN. English (includes some text in French). sa. $30.00. Canadian Journal of Community Mental Health, 1364 McTavish Road RR #2, Sidney British Columbia V8L 3S1 Canada. DD 362.20971.

CANADIAN JOURNAL OF CRIMINOLOGY. VFOAT Revue Canadienne de Criminologie. VAT Revue Canadienne de Criminologie (1978). V. 20, No. 1- Jan. 1978-. 0704-9722. Periodical. CN. English (includes some text in French). qt. $23.21. Canadian Criminal Justice Association, 55 Parkdale, Ottawa Ontario K1Y 1E5 Canada. Tel (613)725-3715. Ed Marc LeBlanc. Ind/Abst Leg. Resour. Index, Can. Period. Index, Soc. Work Res. Abstr., Psychol. Abstr. LC HV6001. DD 364.97105. bk rev. adv acc. Circ 1,200. Also available in microfiche format. Journal concerned with theoretical and scientific aspects of the study of crime and with practical problems of law enforcement, administration of justice, and treatment of offenders. *Canadian Journal of Criminology and Corrections.*

CANADIAN JOURNAL OF SOCIAL WORK EDUCATION CEASED. VFOAT Revue Canadienne d'Education en Service Social. V. 1-8, No. 3. 0316-8565. Periodical. CN. English (includes some text and resumes in French). ty. $14.00. Canadian Journal of Social Work Education, Canadian Association of Schools of Social Work, 151 Slater Street, Ottawa Ontario K2P 5H3 Canada. Ind/Abst Soc. Work Res. Abstr. DD 361.00711.

CANADIAN JOURNAL ON MENTAL RETARDATION. (THE CANADIAN JOURNAL ON MENTAL RETARDATION). VFOAT Mental Retardation. Vol. 33, No. 3 (Summer 1983)-. 0826-4082. Periodical. CN. English. qt. Canadian Journal of Mental Retardation, Kinsmen Building, York University, 4700 Keele Street, Downsview Ontario M3J 1P3 Canada. DD 362.30971. *Mental Retardation (Downsview, Ont.), 0710-0698.*

CANADIAN SOCIAL WORK REVIEW. VFOAT Revue Canadienne de Service Social. 1983-. 0820-909X. Periodical. CN. English (French). an. 18.00 Domestic, 22.00 US. Canadian Social Work Review, 151 Slater Street, Ottawa Ontario K1P 5N1 Canada. Tel (613)563-1217. Ed Shan Kar Yelaia and Robert Mayer. DD 361.005. bk rev. adv acc. Circ 350. Provides knowledge regarding issues, trends and inquiries relevant to Canadian social work theory, practice, policy, administration and education. *Canadian Journal of Social Work Education, 0316-8565.*

CANADIAN SUICIDE RATIOS BY LOCAL AREAS AND BY URBAN CENTRES. Main/Corp Canada. Statistics Canada. Vital Statistics Section. VFOAT Taux de Suicide du Canada, par Localite et par Centre Urbain. 1970/72-. CN. English (French in parallel columns). ir. $0.70. Information Canada, 171 Slater Street, Ottawa Onario K1A 059 Canada. LC HV6548.C3. DD 312.276.

CAPITAL PUNISHMENT. Main/Corp United States. Bureau of Justice Statistics. Series/Titl National Prisoner Statistics Bulletin. 1979-. US. English. an. Free. US Department of Justice, Bureau of Justice Statistics, Washington DC 20531. Tel (202)724-6100. Ed Marilyn Marbrook. LC HV86.99.U5. DD 364.660973. Circ 7,000. (ctrl). Statistical data on the death-row population of the United States and on the status of state and federal death penalty laws. *Capital Punishment.*

CAPITULO CRIMINOLOGICO. Began with Vol. for 1973. Spanish. ir. 15.00. LC HV6005. DD 364.05.

CARING. V. 1- Fall 1975-. 0735-5696. Periodical. US. English. qt. $20.00. NCPCA Subscription Service, 332 South Michigan Avenue/Suite 1250, Chicago IL 60604-4357.

CARP NEWS. VAT Canadian Association of Rehabilitation Personnel News. 0821-0128. Periodical. CN. English (includes some text in French). qt. Canadian Association of Rehabilitation Personnel, 160 Eglington Avenue East/Suite 305, Toronto Ontario M4P 1G3 Canada. DD 362.406071.

CARREFOUR DES AFFAIRES SOCIALES. V. 1- Nov. 1978-. 0226-6849. Periodical. CN. French. qt. $3.09. Publications du Quebec, Ministere des Comm, CP 1005, Quebec Quebec G1K 7B5 Canada. Tel (418)643-5150. Ind/Abst Point Repere. DD 361.9714.

CATALOGO DE RECURSOS SOCIAIS DOS MUNICIPIOS DA REGIAO METROPOLITANA DE PORTO ALEGRE, RS. Portuguese. ir. LC HV195.P6. DD 361.00258165.

CATALYST (NEW YORK : 1978). (CATALYST). Vol. 1, No. 1 (1978)-. 0191-040X. Periodical. US. English. qt $35.00. Institute Social Service Alternatives, Box 1144, Cathedral Station, New York NY 10025. Ind/Abst Sociol. Abstr., Soc. Welf. Soc. Plan./Policy Soc. Dev., Altern. Press Index. LC HV1. DD 362.05. bk rev. adv acc. Circ 600. Committed to developing a socialist theory of social services, organization of human service workers on the job and in the political arena. Stimulating debate about policy, practice and social change.

CAUSE & FUNCTION. VFOAT Cause and Function. Vol. 1, No. 1 (Fall 1980)-. 0731-7433. Periodical. US. English. sa. 525 West Redwood Street, Box 598, Baltimore MD 21201. LC HV1. DD 361.005.

CCB OUTLOOK. See Physically Impaired.

CDF REPORTS. VAT Children's Defense Fund Reports. 1982. 0276-6531. Periodical. US. English. mo. $29.95. Childrens Defense Fund, 122 C Street Northwest, Washington DC 20001. Tel (202)628-8787. Ed Virginia Witt. Circ 4,000. Comprehensive news on education, child care, child health and mental health, foster care and adoption, child abuse and neglect, child nutrition, and child poverty.

CENSUS OF REQUESTS FOR CHILD WELFARE SERVICES. Main/Corp Child Welfare League of America. Research Center. 0362-0778. US. English. Child Welfare League of America, 67 Irving Place, New York NY 10003. LC HV741. DD 362.70973.

CENTRACARENEWS. Main/Corp Centracare Saint John. V. 1, No. 1 (Jan./March 1981)-. 0821-2678. Periodical. CN. English. qt. Free. Centracare Saint John Inc, 281 Lancaster Avenue, Saint John New Brunswick E2M Canada. DD 362.210971532.

DET CENTRALE HANDICAPRADS VIRKSOMHED I . . . . Main/Corp Centrale Handicaprad (Denmark). VFOAT Arsberetning. 1980-. DK. Danish. an. Socialstyrelsen, Kristineberg 6 Postboks 2555, 2100 Kbenhavn Denmark. LC HV1559.D4.

CENTRE - CONSEIL DE LA SANTE DES SERVICES SOCIAUX, REGION SAGUENAY-LAC-ST-JEAN (QUEBEC). (LE CENTRE). Main/Corp Conseil de la Sante et des Services Sociaux, Region Saguenay-Lac-St-Jean (Quebec). V. 1- Aug./Sept. 1974-. 0381-8152. Periodical. CN. French. bm. Conseil de la Sante et des Services Sociaux, Region Saguenay-Lac-St-Jean, 930 Est rue J-Cartier, Chicoutimi Quebec G7H 2B1 Canada. DD 362.971416.

CENTRE SCOPE. 0715-5700. Periodical. CN. English. mo. Free. Centrescope, Health Sciences Centre, 800 Sherbrook Street, Winnipeg Manitoba R23A 1M4 Canada. DD 362.110971274.

Sociology: General Works, Theory—Social Pathology, Welfare, Criminology

CERCLE. (LE CERCLE). Sept. 1973-. 0319-4795. Periodical. CN. French. $1.00. Societe Canadienne de la Croix-Rouge, 95 Est rue Wellesley, Toronto Ontario M4Y 1H6 Canada.

CHAEHWAL YONGU. *See* Physically Impaired.

CHAIRMAN'S REPORT - NEW MEXICO, GOVERNOR'S COMMITTEE ON EMPLOYMENT OF THE HANDICAPPED. *See* Economics - Labor.

THE CHALLENGE. V. 1- May 1957-. 0528-7928. Periodical. US. English. bm. LC HV98.P4. NLM W2 AP4 D7C.

CHARACTERISTICS OF CHILDREN COMMITTED TO THE VIRGINIA DEPARTMENT OF CORRECTIONS. VFOAT Children Committed. 0148-4222. US. English. an. Department of Corrections, Research & Reporting Unit, 22 East Cary Street, Richmond VA 23219. LC HV9105.V7. DD 364.2409755.

CHARACTERISTICS OF INMATES DISCHARGED. VFOAT Characteristics of Inmates Discharged From New York State Department of Correctional Services Facilities. US. English. an.

CHARACTERISTICS OF INSTITUTIONAL POPULATIONS (MINNESOTA). Main/Corp Minnesota. Dept. of Corrections. Research Section. US. English. an. LC HV7273. DD 364.309776. *Characteristics of Populations under Supervision of the Institutions and Field Services, 0092-1033.*

CHARACTERISTICS OF NEW COMMITMENTS (NEW YORK (STATE)). Main/Corp New York (State). Dept. of Correctional Services. Office of Program Planning, Evaluation, and Research. 0098-4892. US. English. Department of Correctional Services, State Office Building Campus, Albany NY 12226. LC HV7282. DD 365.609747. *Characteristics of New Commitments.*

CHARACTERISTICS OF PERSONS ENTERING PAROLE. (CHARACTERISTICS OF PERSONS ENTERING PAROLE DURING . . . AND . . .). **Series/Titl** Uniform Parole Reports. 1978/79-. 0749-3347. US. English. be. National Criminal Justice Reference Service, Box 6000, Rockville MD 20850. LC HV9304. DD 364.30973. *Characteristics of the Parole Population, 0749-3339.*

CHARACTERISTICS OF STATE PLANS FOR AID TO FAMILIES WITH DEPENDENT CHILDREN UNDER THE SOCIAL SECURITY ACT, TITLE IV-A. (CHARACTERISTICS OF STATE PLANS FOR AID TO FAMILIES WITH DEPENDENT CHILDREN UNDER THE SOCIAL SECURITY ACT, TITLE IV-A, AND FOR GUAM, PUERTO RICO, & VIRGIN ISLANDS). VFOAT Aid to Families with Dependent Children, Characteristics of State Plans for AFDC. VAT Characteristics of State Plans for Aid to Families with Dependent Children Under the Social Security Act, Title Four-A. 0149-1792. US. English. an. Social Security Administration, Office of Family Assistance, Washington DC 20201. LC HV95. DD 362.71. *Aid to Families with Dependent Children, 0363-5686.*

CHARITABLE TRUST DIRECTORY, OFFICE OF ATTORNEY GENERAL (WASHINGTON (STATE)). *See* Yearbooks, Almanacs, Directories.

CHARITIES DIGEST. 0590-9783. Periodical. UK. English. an. Family Welfare Association, Warner House Folkstone, Kent CT19 6PH England. NLM HV 245.A2 A615. *Annual Charities Digest.*

CHARITIES - NORTHERN IRELAND. DEPT. OF FINANCE. Main/Corp Northern Ireland. Dept. of Finance. UK. English. 30. Her Majesty's Stationery Office, 80 Chichester Street, Belfast BT1 4JY Northern Ireland. LC HV247.5. DD 354.4160084.

CHARITIES USA. VAT Charities United States of America. V. 1- Sept./Oct. 1974-. 0364-0760. Periodical. US. English. mo. $20.00. National Conference of Catholic Charities, 1346 Connecticut Avenue NW/Suite 307, Washington DC 20036. Tel (202)785-2757. Ed Elizabeth Johnson. LC HV530. DD 360.6. adv acc. Circ 6,000. (ctrl) Monthly journal for professionals in Catholic social services, parishes and outreach ministries in United States and Canada. *Aging News Notes, Catholic Charities Newsletter.*

CHARITY & CHILDREN. (CHARITY AND CHILDREN). 0009-1723. Periodical. US. English. sm. $2.00. Baptist Childrens Home of North Carolina, 515 Watson Avenue, Box 338, Thomasville NC 27360. Tel (919)476-6183. Ed Marianna Boucher. Circ 58,000. Focuses on family issues and information about Baptist children's homes of NC. Includes editorials, and opinion poll, alumni news and a children's page.

CHARITY STATISTICS. *See* Statistics.

CHART BOOK - OKLAHOMA DEPARTMENT OF INSTITUTIONS, SOCIAL AND REHABILITATIVE SERVICES. (CHART BOOK - OKLAHOMA, DEPARTMENT OF INSTITUTIONS, SOCIAL AND REHABILITATIVE SERVICES). Main/Corp Oklahoma. Dept. of Institutions, Social and Rehabilitative Services. 0098-8715. US. English. an. PO Box 25352, Oklahoma City OK 73125. LC HV86. DD 353.766008405.

CHARTBOOK OF FEDERAL PROGRAMS IN AGING. VFOAT Chartbook on Aging. VAT Chart Book of Federal Programs in Aging. 1980-. 0197-0429. US. English. sa. $29.00. Business Publishers, 951 Pershing Drive, Silver Spring MD 20910. Tel (301)320-2110. Ed Irma Schechter. LC HV1457. DD 362.6. An authoritative and practical compilation of federal aging programs and contacts. Provides services for our aging population.

CHECKPOINTS FOR CHILDREN. Vol. 1, No. 1 (Spring 1976)-. Periodical. US. English. bm. $20.00. Regional Institute of Social Welfare Research, Box 152, Athens GA 30603. Tel (404)542-7614.

CHILD ABUSE & NEGLECT. V. 1- 1977-. 0145-2134. Periodical. US. English (French). qt. $145.00. Pergamon Press, 395 Sawmill River Road, Elmsford NY 10523. Ind/Abst Sociol. Abstr., Soc. Welf. Soc. Plan./Policy Soc. Dev., Index Med., Except. Child Educ. Resour., Psychol. Abstr., Curr. Index J. Educ. LC HV713. DD 362.71. NLM W1 CH642N. Issued in microfiche simultaneously with the paper edition and in microfilm at at the end of the subscription year.

CHILD ABUSE AND NEGLECT AUDIOVISUAL MATERIALS. 8755-0733. US. English. Superintendent of Documents, US Government Printing Office, Washington DC 20402. DD 362.

CHILD ABUSE AND NEGLECT GRANTS PROGRAM. Main/Corp United States. Administration for Children, Youth, and Families. 0195-8836. US. English. an. Department of Health/Education and Welfare, Office of Human Development Services, Administration for Children Youth and Families, Washington DC 20201. LC HV741. DD 362.71.

CHILD ABUSE AND NEGLECT PROGRAMS. June 1976-. 0146-9665. Periodical. US. English. sa. $11.00. National Technical Information Service, 5285 Port Royal Road, Springfield VA 22161. LC HV741. DD 362.73. NLM WA 22 AA1 C4.

CHILD ABUSE AND NEGLECT RESEARCH. (CHILD ABUSE AND NEGLECT RESEARCH : PROJECTS AND PUBLICATIONS). May 1976-. 0145-3025. US. English. sa. $25.00. National Technical Information Service, 5285 Port Royal Road, Springfield VA 22161. LC HV741. DD 362.710973. NLM ZWA 320 C536.

CHILD ABUSE AND NEGLECT STATISTICS. *See* Statistics.

CHILD ABUSE REPORT (HARRISBURG, PA.). (CHILD ABUSE REPORT). 1976-. 0148-5061. US. English. an. Commonwealth of Pennsylvania, Department of Public Welfare, Harrisburg PA 17120. LC HV742.P4. DD 362.71.

CHILD & ADOLESCENT SOCIAL WORK JOURNAL. (CHILD & ADOLESCENT SOCIAL WORK JOURNAL : C & A). VFOAT Child and Adolescent Social Work Journal. Vol. 1, No. 1 (Spring 1984)-. 0738-0151. Periodical. US. English. qt. $58.00. Human Sciences Press Inc, 72 Fifth Avenue, New York NY 10011. NLM W1.

CHILD & YOUTH SERVICES. VAT Child and Youth Services. V. 1-. 0145-935X. Periodical. US. English. qt. $24.00 US, $29.00 Canada. Haworth Press, 149 Fifth Avenue, New York NY 10010. Ind/Abst Sociol. Abstr., Except. Child Educ. Resour., Psychol. Abstr., Curr. Index J. Educ. LC HV701. DD 362.705. NLM W1 CH644. CODEN CYSEDP.

CHILD CARE. (CHILD CARE : A COMPREHENSIVE GUIDE). V. 1-. 0164-1549. Monographic Series. US. English. ir. Human Sciences Press, 72 Fifth Avenue, New York NY 10011. Tel (212)243-6000. Ed S Auerbach and J A Rivaldo. NLM W1 CH646DB.

CHILD CARE ARRANGEMENT OF A.F.D.C. RECIPIENTS UNDER THE WORK INCENTIVE PROGRAM. (CHILD CARE ARRANGEMENTS OF AFDC RECIPIENTS UNDER THE WORK INCENTIVE PROGRAM). Main/Corp National Center for Social Statistics. Series Corp Its NCSS Report. VAT Child Care Arrangements of Aid to Families with Dependent Children Recipients Under the Work Incentive Program. 0091-813X. US. English. qt. US Department of Health Education & Welfare, Social Rehabilitation Service, Center for Special Services, Washington DC 20201. LC HV854. DD 362.71.

CHILD CARE INFORMATION EXCHANGE. 1978. 0164-8527. Periodical. US. English. bm. $25.00. Child Care Information, PO Box 2890, Redmond WA 98052. Tel (206)883-9394. Ed Roger Neugebauer. Ind/Abst Educ. Index. adv acc. Circ 10,800. (ctrl). Management magazine providing directors of child care centers, ideas on managing staff, money, marketing, and evaluation.

CHILD CARE QUARTERLY. V. 1- Fall 1971-. 0045-6632. Periodical. US. English. qt. Human Sciences Press, 72 Fifth Avenue, New York NY 10011. Tel (212)243-6000. Ind/Abst Educ. Index, Except. Child Educ. Resour., Soc. Work Res. Abstr., Psychol. Abstr., Curr. Contents Behav. Soc. Educ. Sci., Soc. Sci. Citation Index, Curr. Index J. Educ. LC HV701. DD 362.710973. NLM W1 CH646F. CODEN CCQYAK.

CHILD CARE WORK. (CHILD CARE WORK : A QUARTERLY PUBLICATION OF THE NATIONAL ORGANIZATION OF CHILD CARE WORKER ASSOCIATIONS, INC). Began in 1983. 0741-2398. Periodical. US. English. qt. $10.00. Noccwa Publications Office, PO Box 28170, Wadesboro NC 28170.

CHILD DEVELOPMENT STATE PLAN (PENNSYLVANIA). Main/Corp Pennsylvania. Commonwealth Child Development Committee. 0093-8009. US. English. Commonwealth Child Development Committee, 512 Finance Building, Harrisburg PA 17120. LC HV742.P4. DD 362.709748.

CHILD PROTECTIVE SERVICES ANNUAL REPORT (VIRGINIA). Main/Corp Virginia. Unit of Child Protective Services. US. English. an. Commonwealth of Virginia, Department of Social Services, Blair Building, 8007 Discovery Drive, Richmond VA 23288. LC HV742.V8. DD 353.975500847.

CHILD PROTECTIVE SERVICES IN NEW YORK STATE . . . ANNUAL REPORT. Main/Corp New York (State). Dept. of Social Services. US. English. an. LC HV98.N7. DD 353.974700847.

CHILD REFERENCE BULLETIN. (CHILD REFERENCE BULLETIN : A UNITED NATIONS CHILDREN'S FUND PUBLICATION ON ACTION FOR CHILDREN). No. 1 (May 1981)-. 0251-5547. Periodical. US. English. qt. Child Reference Bulletin, UNICEF UNited Nations, New York NY 10017.

CHILD WELFARE. V. 27, No. 7- July 1948-. 0009-4021. Periodical. US. English. bm. $35.00. Child Welfare League of America, c/o Transaction Journals Rutgers University, New Brunswick NJ 08903. Tel (201)932-2280. Ed Carl Schoenberg. Ind/Abst Sociol. Abstr., Soc. Welf. Soc. Plan./Policy Soc. Dev., Index Med., Except. Child Educ. Resour., Soc. Work Res. Abstr., Educ. Index, Public Aff. Inf. Serv. Bull., Abstr. Soc. Work., Child Dev. Abstr. Bibliogr., Except. Child Educ. Abstr., Pover. Hum. Resour. Abstr., Psychol. Abstr., Women Stud. Abstr., Curr. Index J. Educ., Soc. Sci. Index. NLM W1 CH692. CODEN CHWFA. Index in last issue of volume - attached. bk rev. adv acc. Circ 7,548. The foremost professional journal focusing on the needs of people who provide child welfare services in both public and voluntary agencies.

CHILD WELFARE PLANNING NOTES. V. 1, No. 1/2- March 8, 1976-. 0738-5986. Periodical. US. English. mo. CWLA Editorial Office, 1346 Connecticut Avenue NW, Washington DC 20036.

CHILD WELFARE SERVICES TRAINING GRANTS. Main/Corp United States. Children's Bureau. Training and Technical Assistance Division. 0198-6538. US. English. Department of Health Education & Welfare, Office of Human Development, Washington DC 20201. LC HV741. DD 362.7071173.

Sociology: General Works, Theory—Social Pathology, Welfare, Criminology

CHILDREN & TEENS TODAY. VFOAT Children and Teens Today. Vol. 5, No. 9 (May 1985)-. 0882-942X. Periodical. US. English. mo. Atcom Inc, 2315 Broadway, New York NY 10024. **Tel** (212)873-5900. Ed Suzanne Prescod. DD 305. bk rev. **Circ** 2,500. A newsletter for professionals in the fields of child welfare and child advocacy. *Children & Teens in Crisis, 0732-7420.*

CHILDREN AND YOUTH SERVICES REVIEW. V. 1- Spring 1979-. 0190-7409. Periodical. US. English. qt. $30.00 Individual, $50.00 Others. Pergamon Press, Maxwell House Fairview Park, Elmsford NY 10523. **Ind/Abst** Sociol. Abstr., Soc. Welf. Soc. Plan./Policy Soc. Dev., Excerpta Med., Psychol. Abstr. LC HV701. DD 362.705. NLM W1 CH694Q.

CHILDREN FOR WHOM ADOPTION PETITIONS WERE GRANTED IN SOUTH DAKOTA, BY RELATIONSHIP OF PETITIONER AND TYPE OF PLACEMENT. Main/Corp South Dakota. Dept. of Social Services. **Series/Titl** Program Analysis Report. 1973-. 0094-0941. US. English. South Dakota Department of Social Services, Office Building No 1, Pierre SD 57501. LC HV875. DD 362.73409783.

CHILDREN IN CARE IN ENGLAND AND WALES. Main/Corp Great Britain. Dept. of Health and Social Security. 0307-675X. UK. English. an. Her Majestys Stationery Office, PO Box 276, London SW8 5DT England. LC HV751. DD 362.730942. *Children in the Care of Local Authorities in England and Wales.*

CHILDREN IN CARE OR UNDER SUPERVISION ORDERS IN WALES. Year ended March 31st 1980-. 0263-2667. English. an. 2. Economic And Statistical Services Division, Welsh Office, New Crown Building, Cathays Park Cardiff CF1 3NQ Wales England. **Tel** (0222)825087. Ed E Swires-Hennessy. LC HV1149.W34. DD 362.73209429. **Circ** 450. Contains statistical information on children in care of local authority social services departments or under supervision orders. *Children in Care of Local Authorities in Wales.*

CHILDREN IN CUSTODY. Main/Corp United States. National Criminal Justice Information and Statistics Service. 0147-9881. US. English. US Department of Justice, 1405 Eye Street NW, Washington DC 20537. LC HV7245. DD 365.420973.

THE CHILDREN OF THE STATE (NEW YORK (STATE)). Main/Corp New York (State)., Temporary State Commission on Child Welfare. Began in 1975. US. English. an. Temporary State Commission on Child Welfare, Rockefeller Empire State Plaza, Agency Building, No 1 11th Floor, Albany NY 12223. LC HV742.N7. DD 362.79509747.

CHILDREN TODAY. Series/Titl DHHS Publications. Began with V. 1, No. 1, Jan./Feb. 1972. 0361-4336. Periodical. US. English. bm. Superintendent of Documents, US Government Printing Office, Washington DC 20402. **Ind/Abst** Read. Guide Period. Lit., Cumul. Index Nurs. Allied Health Lit., Curr. Index J. Educ., Educ. Index, Ref. Source, Soc. Work Res. Abstr., Consum. Index Prod. Eval. Inf. Source, Book Rev. Index, Except. Child Educ. Resour., Women Stud. Abstr., Hospit. Lit. Index, Index U.S. Gov. Period. LC HV741. DD 362.705. NLM W1 CH694V. CODEN CHTDA. *Children (Washington, D.C.).*

CHILDREN UNDER COMMUNITY SUPERVISION. Fiscal Year 1981-. US. English. an. Virginia Department of Corrections, Division of Program Development and Evaluation Research and Reporting Unit, PO Box 26963, Richmond VA 23261. LC HV9105.V7. DD 364.63088055. *Adults and Children Under Community Supervision.*

CHILDREN'S CASES DISPOSED OF BY THE JUVENILE COURTS. Main/Corp Virginia. Dept. of Corrections. Bureau of Management Information. 0507-0619. US. English. Department of Correction, PO Box 26963, Richmond VA 23261. LC KFV2471.55. DD 345.75508.

A CHILDREN'S DEFENSE BUDGET. 1st Ed.-. 0736-6701. US. English. an. $10.00. Children's Defense Fund, 122 C Street NW, Washington DC 20001. LC HV741. DD 362.7950973.

CHILDREN'S SERVICES NEEDS ASSESSMENT. US. English. an. Massachusetts Office for Children, 120 Bolyston Street, Boston MA 02116. LC HV742.M4. DD 362.709744.

CHIU CHI NIEN PAO. Main/Corp Chung-Kuo Ta Lu Tsai Pa Chiu Chi Tsung Hui. Chinese. ir. LC HV640.5.C5.

CHONGSONYON POMJOE YONGU. VFOAT Studies in Juvenile Delinquency. V. 1- Series (1983)-. Periodical. KO. Korean. ir. LC HV9208. (ctrl).

CHUNG-HUA MIN KUO TAI-WAN SHENG SHE HUI SHIH YEH TUNG CHI. VFOAT Republic of China Social Affairs Statistics of Taiwan. Chinese and English. ir. LC HV390.5.

CIENCIA PENAL. 1- 1973-. BL. Portuguese. ir. J Bushatsky, rua Senador Feijo 176-90 Andar, Sao Paulo Brazil. LC HV7239.

CITEPHILE. (CITEPHILE : JOURNAL DES ADEPTES DE LA CITE DE LA SANTE DE LAVAL). V. 1, No. 1, (Aug. 1981)-. 0823-616X. Periodical. CN. French. ir. Cite de la Sante de Laval, 1755 Boulevard, Rene-Laennec Laval, Quebec H7M 3L9 Canada. DD 362.1109714271.

CIVIC. (THE CIVIC). VFOAT Civique. VAT Civique (Ottawa). Fall 1979-. 0229-706X. Periodical. CN. English (French text on inverted pages). qt. Ottawa Civic Hospital, 1053 Carling Avenue, Ottawa Ontario K1Y 4E9 Canada. DD 362.110971384.

CJ INTERNATIONAL. VFOAT C.J. International. Winter 1985-. 0882-0252. Periodical. US. English. qt. $12.00. Center for Research in Law and Justice, University of Illinois at Chicago, Chicago IL 60680. DD 364.

CLEARINGHOUSE TRANSFER. Main/Corp National Clearinghouse for Criminal Justice Planning and Architecture. VFOAT Transfer. US. English. University of Illinois at Urbana-Champaign, Department of Agriculture, 505 East Green Street/Suite 200, Champaign IL 61820.

CLIN D'OEIL - CENTRE HOSPITALIER DES BOIS-FRANCS. (CLIN D'OEIL). 0821-2252. Periodical. CN. French. qt. Centre Hospitalier des Bois-Francs, 61 Avenue de L-Ermitage, Victoriaville Quebec G6P 6X4 Canada. DD 362.16. *Etincelle (Victoriaville, Quebec).*

CLINICAL PROGRAMS FOR MENTALLY RETARDED CHILDREN. See Medicine - Pediatrics.

CLINICAL SOCIAL WORK JOURNAL. V. 1- Spring 1973-. 0091-1674. Periodical. US. English. qt. Behavioral Publications, 2852 Broadway-Morningside Heights, New York NY 10025. **Tel** (212)243-6000. **Ind/Abst** Sociol. Abstr., Soc. Welf. Soc. Plan./Policy Soc. Dev., Soc. Work Res. Abstr., Psychol. Abstr., Soc. Sci. Citation Index, Abstr. Soc. Work. LC HV1. DD 361.305. NLM W1 CL784K. CODEN CSWJBG.

CMHA FOCUS. VAT Canadian Mental Health Association Focus, Focus - Canadian Mental Health Association. Vol. 1, No. 1 (April 1982)-. 0715-5654. Periodical. CN. English. ir. $10.00. CMHA Focus, 207-4921 49th Street, Red Deer Alberta T4N 1V4 Canada. DD 362.20971233.

C/O : JOURNAL OF ALTERNATIVE HUMAN SERVICES. VFOAT Journal of Alternative Human Services. V. 1- Aug. 1973-. 0192-0618. Periodical. US. English. qt. $12.00. Community Congress of San Diego, 1172 Morena Boulevard, San Diego CA 92110. LC HV89. DD 361.005.

CODES DE LA SANTE PUBLIQUE DE LA FAMILLE ET DE L'AIDE SOCIALE - (FRANCE). French. ir. Dalloz, 11 rue Soufflot, Paris France 75240.

COLLINS BAY CON. T.A.C.T. (COLLINS BAY CON. T. A. C. T). VFOAT Collins Bay CONTACT. VAT Collins Bay Convict Together Against Cruel Times. Oct./Nov. 1978-. 0225-0535. Periodical. CN. English. mo. $4. Contact, PO Box 190, Kingston Ontario K7L 4V9 Canada. DD 365.971372. *Avatar, 0382-7240.*

COMMITMENTS AND RELEASES : ANNUAL STATISTICAL REPORT. See Statistics.

COMMITMENTS TO COUNTY & CITY JAILS AND CITY JAIL FARMS. Main/Corp Virginia. Dept. of Corrections. Bureau of Management Information. VFOAT Commitments to Jails. 54th (1970)-. US. English. an. Department of Corrections, 22 East Cary Street, Richmond VA 23219. LC HV7296. DD 365.9755. *Annual Report.*

COMMONWEALTH OF VIRGINIA COMPREHENSIVE ANNUAL PLAN FOR SOCIAL SERVICES UNDER TITLE XX OF THE NATIONAL SOCIAL SECURITY ACT. Main/Corp Virginia. Dept. of Welfare. VAT Commonwealth of Virginia Comprehensive Annual Plan for Social Services Under Title Twenty of the National Social Security Act. 0148-6780. US. English. Virginia Department of Welfare, Office of Communications, 8007 Discovery Drive, Richmond VA 23288. LC HV86. DD 362.9755.

COMMUNICATIONS - AMNISTIE INTERNATIONALE. SECTION CANADIENNE. (COMMUNICATIONS - AMNISTIE INTERNATIONALE, SECTION CANADIENNE). Main/Corp Amnesty International Canada. VFOAT Bulletin Mensuel. V. 1- Oct. 1979-. 0226-3556. Periodical. CN. French. mo. Amnistie Internationale, Section Canadienne, 1800 Ouest Boulevard Dorchester, Montreal Quebec H3H 2H2 Canada. DD 364.1305.

COMMUNICATOR. (THE COMMUNICATOR). Began publication in 1973?. 0381-095X. Periodical. CN. English. ir. Communicator/Nova Scotia, PO Box 2140, Springhill Nova Scotia Canada. **Tel** (902)597-3755. DD 365.971611.

COMMUNIQUE - CHILDREN'S AID SOCIETY OF OTTAWA. Main/Corp Children's Aid Society of Ottawa. Mar. 1974-. 0319-7468. Periodical. CN. English (text in French). Children's Aid Society of Ottawa, 1370 Bank Street, Ottawa Ontario K1H 7Y3 Canada. *The CAS Record, 0045-6675.*

COMMUNIQUE - CHILDREN'S AID SOCIETY OF OTTAWA. (COMMUNIQUE - SOCIETE DE L'AIDE A L'ENFANCE D'OTTAWA). Main/Corp Societe de l'Aide a l'Enfance d'Ottawa. March 1974-. 0319-7468. Periodical. CN. English and French. 1370 rue Bank, Ottawa Ontario K1H 7Y3 Canada. *The CAS Record, 0045-6675.*

COMMUNITY (ALEXANDRIA, VA. : 1982). (COMMUNITY). 0736-2099. Periodical. US. English. bm. United Way of America, United Way Plaza, Alexandria VA 22314. **Tel** (703)836-7100. Ed Roberta A Lindsay. LC HV88. DD 361.973. **Circ** 5,500. (ctrl). Ideas in the area of health and human services, voluntarism and the nonprofit sector. *Community Focus.*

COMMUNITY CARE. Main/Corp Illinois. Dept. on Aging. Sept. 1982-. US. English. an. State of Illinois, Department of Aging, 421 East Capitol Avenue, Springfield IL 62706. LC HV1468.I3. DD 362.6042. *Community Care for the Elderly.*

COMMUNITY MENTAL HEALTH CLIENT AND SERVICES SUMMARY. VFOAT Community Mental Health Client & Services Summary. Fiscal Year 1979. US. English. an. State of Alaska Department of Health and Social Services Office of the Commissioner, Office of Information Systems Pouch H-01G, Juneau AK 99811. LC RA790.65.A4. DD 362.2209798.

COMMUNITY MENTAL HEALTH JOURNAL. V. 1- Spring 1965-. 0010-3853. Periodical. US. English. qt. Human Sciences Press, 72 Fifth Avenue, New York NY 10011. **Tel** (212)243-6000. **Ind/Abst** Electron. Commun. Abstr. J., ISMEC Bull., Pollut. Abstr. Indexes, Saf. Sci. Abstr. J., Life Sci. Collect., Hospit. Lit. Index, Sociol. Abstr., Soc. Welf. Soc. Plan./Policy Soc. Dev., Excerpta Med., Index Med., Cumul. Index Nurs. Allied Health Lit., Abstr. Soc. Work., Soc. Sci. Citation Index, Soc. Sci. Index, Psychol. Abstr., Coll. Stud. Pers. Abstr., Ment. Retard. Abstr., Lang. Lang. Behav. Abstr., Occup. Ment. Health Notes, Hum. Resour. Abstr., Media Rev. Dig. LC RA790.A1. DD 614.5805. NLM W1 CO429N. CODEN CMHJAY.

COMMUNITY MENTAL HEALTH JOURNAL. MONOGRAPH SERIES. No. 1-. 0069-7850. Monographic Series. US. English. ir. Human Sciences Press, 72 Fifth Avenue, New York NY 10011. **Tel** (212)243-6000.

COMMUNITY MENTAL HEALTH REVIEW CEASED. V. 1-5. 0363-1605. US. English. bm. $30.00 Domestic, $35.00 Canada. Haworth Press, 149 Fifth Avenue, New York NY 10010. **Ind/Abst** Sociol. Abstr. LC RA790.A1. DD 362.205. NLM W1 CO429RN. (cum index).

COMMUNITY SERVICE ORDERS IN ENGLAND AND WALES. Main/Corp Great Britain. Probation and After-Care Dept. UK. English. ir. LC HV7343. DD 364.68.

Sociology: General Works, Theory—Social Pathology, Welfare, Criminology

COMMUNITY SERVICES DIRECTORY. See Yearbooks, Almanacs, Directories.

COMMUNITY SOCIAL SERVICES ACT ... EFFECTIVENESS REPORT. 1980-. US. English. an. State of Minnesota, Department of Public Welfare, Centennial Office Building, St Paul MN 55155. **LC** HV98.M65. **DD** 353.97760084.

COMMUNITY WORK. V. 1- 1974-. 0307-6067. UK. English. ir. Routledge & Kegan Paul, Broadway House, Newtown Road, Henley-Thames RG9 1EN England. **Tel** (617)742-5863. **LC** HN400.C6. **DD** 309.260941.

A COMPARISON OF ADMISSION CHARACTERISTICS OF YOUTH AUTHORITY WARDS. US. English. an. **LC** HV9105.C2. **DD** 364.3609794.

A COMPARISON OF CHARACTERISTICS OF YOUTH AUTHORITY WARDS IN INSTITUTIONS AND ON PAROLE. **Main/Corp** California Youth Authority. US. English. an. California Youth Authority, Department of Youth Authority, Sacramento CA 95834. **LC** HV9105.C2. **DD** 364.3609794.

COMPENSATION & BENEFITS REPORT. See Economics - Labor.

THE COMPREHENSIVE ANNUAL SERVICES PLAN FOR ILLINOIS. TITLE 20, SOCIAL SECURITY ACT CEASED. (THE COMPREHENSIVE ANNUAL SERVICES PLAN FOR ILLINOIS : TITLE 20, SOCIAL SECURITY ACT). **Main/Corp** Illinois. Dept. of Public Aid. 1975/77-1980/81. 0363-0544. US. English. an. 624 South Michigan Avenue, Chicago IL 60605. **LC** HV86. **DD** 362.9773.

COMPREHENSIVE ANNUAL SERVICES PROGRAM PLAN - (ARKANSAS). **Main/Corp** Arkansas. Office of Title XX Service. 1978/79-. US. English. an. Office of Title XX Service, Blue Cross/Blue Shield Building, PO Box 1437, Little Rock AR 72203. **LC** HV86. **DD** 361.6209767. Comprehensive Annual Servises Program Plan.

COMPREHENSIVE ANNUAL SERVICES PROGRAM PLAN FOR SOCIAL SERVICES UNDER TITLE 20. (COMPREHENSIVE ANNUAL SERVICES PROGRAM PLAN FOR SOCIAL SERVICES UNDER TITLE XX - (LOUISIANA)). **Main/Corp** Louisiana. Health and Human Resources Administration. 0362-8868. US. English. an. Louisiana Health and Human Resources Administration, PO Box 3318, Baton Rouge LA 70821. **LC** HV86. **DD** 361.609763.

COMPREHENSIVE ANNUAL SERVICES PROGRAM PLAN - (NEVADA). **Main/Corp** Nevada. Dept. of Human Resources. Welfare Division. US. English. an. Department of Human Resources, Welfare Division, 251 Jeanell Drive, Capital Complex, Carson City NV 89701. **LC** HV86. **DD** 361.609793.

COMPREHENSIVE CRIMINAL JUSTICE PLAN, CRIMINAL JUSTICE PROGRAMS - (MASSACHUSETTS). **Main/Corp** Massachusetts. Committee on Criminal Justice. 0098-5740. US. English. Committee on Criminal Justice, 80 Boylston Street, Boston MA 02116. **LC** KFM2962. **DD** 364.

COMPREHENSIVE CRIMINAL JUSTICE PLAN - (SOUTH CAROLINA). **Main/Corp** South Carolina. Office of Criminal Justice Programs. 0364-3271. US. English. an. Office of Criminal Justice, Edgar A Brown Building, 1205 Pendelton Street, Columbia SC 29201. **LC** HV7290. **DD** 364.09757. South Carolina Comprehensive Plan for Criminal Justice.

COMPREHENSIVE GUIDE OF ORGANIZATIONS OFFERING SERVICES FOR DRUG RELATED PROBLEMS - (MARYLAND). See Drug Abuse and Alcoholism.

COMPREHENSIVE PLAN FOR CRIMINAL JUSTICE - (CALIFORNIA). **Main/Corp** California. Office of Criminal Justice Planning. 1974-. 0093-8912. US. English. Office of Criminal Justice Plan, PO Box 61047, Sacramento CA 95860. **LC** KFC1102. **DD** 364. Comprehensive Plan for Criminal Justice.

COMPREHENSIVE PLAN - GOVERNOR'S COMMISSION ON LAW ENFORCEMENT AND THE ADMINISTRATION OF JUSTICE - (MARYLAND). See Law Enforcement.

COMPREHENSIVE SERVICES PROGRAM PLAN. Program year July 1, 1981-June 30, 1983-. US. English. be. Department of Human Resources, Welfare Division, 251 Jeanell Drive, Capitol Complex, Carson City NV 89701. **LC** HV86. **DD** 361.609793. Comprehensive Annual Services Program Plan.

COMPTE GENERAL DE L'ADMINISTRATION DE LA JUSTICE PENALE - FRANCE. MINISTERE DE LA JUSTICE. **Main/Corp** France. Ministere de la Justice. FR. French. ir. 150. 29-31 Quai Voltaire, 75340 Paris Cedex 07 France. **LC** HV7348. **DD** 364.9440212.

COMPTE-RENDU D'ACTIVITES. **Main/Corp** Comite Departemental de Defense Contre l'Alcoolisme de la Reunion. French. an. Boite Postale 1047, 9010 S I D R Camelias, 97481 Saint-Denis CE France. **LC** HV5670.6. **DD** 362.29256096891.

COMSERVANT. (THE COMSERVANT). Issue 1- Sept. 1973-. 0319-4523. Periodical. CN. English. qt. Saskatchewan Association for the Mentally Retarded, 103-219 22nd Street East, Saskatoon Saskatchewan S7K 0G4 Canada. **DD** 362.1097124.

COMUNIDADE : SUMARIO DE EXPERIENCIAS. **Main/Corp** Legiao Brasileira de Assistencia. BL. Portuguese. ir. **LC** HV700.B7.

CONCERNING YOU. Dec. 1983-. 0823-8545. Periodical. CN. English. ir. Free to students and faculty of the University of Western Ontario. Student Centre for Public Issues, Room 203G/University Community Centre, University of Western Ontario, London Ontario N6A 3K7 Canada. **DD** 361.105. Newsletter (University of Western Ontario. Student Centre for Public Issues), 0822-5060.

CONCERTACTION. VFOAT Concert Action. V. 1- March 1979-. 0226-5729. Periodical. CN. French. mo. FRee. Conseil Regional de la Sante et des Services Sociaux de la Region Sud de Montreal, Concertaction Secretariat, General/Communications, CRSS 6-C 125 Boulevard Ste-Foy, Longueuil Quebec J4J 1W7 Canada. **DD** 361.97143. (ctrl).

CONJUNTURA SOCIAL. Periodical. BL. Portuguese. ir. MPAS, rua Pedro Lessa 36 12 Andar, Rio de Janeiro Brazil. **LC** HV193. **DD** 361.60981.

CONNECTICUT COMPREHENSIVE TITLE XX SOCIAL SERVICES PROGRAM PLAN, PROPOSED PLAN. **Main/Corp** Connecticut. Dept. of Human Resources. VFOAT Connecticut Social Services. US. English (summaries in Spanish). an. Department of Human Resources, PO Box 786, 1175 Main Street, Hartford CT 06101. **LC** HV86. **DD** 361.609746.

CONNECTICUT TITLE XX COMPREHENSIVE ANNUAL SERVICES PROGRAM PLAN. **Main/Corp** Connecticut. Dept. of Human Resources. VFOAT Connecticut Human Resource Department Annual Services Plan. 1980/81-. US. English. an. State of Connecticut, Department of Human Resources, PO Box 786, 1179 Main Street, Hartford CT 06101. **LC** HV86. **DD** 353.9746008405. Connecticut Comprehensive Title XX Social Services Program Plan.

CONSTABULARY LIST AND DIRECTORY. See Yearbooks, Almanacs, Directories.

CONSULTATION (LOS ANGELES, CALIF.). (CONSULTATION). Vol. 1, No. 1 (Fall 1981)-. 8756-6508. Periodical. US. English. ty. Human Interaction Research Institute, 10889 Wilshire Boulevard/Suite 1120, Los Angeles CA 90024. **DD** 362.

CONTACT - COMITE NATIONAL MIXTE DE L'ACCP & SCF. (CONTACT). VAT Contact - Comite National Mixte de l'Association Canadienne des Chefs de Police et des Services Correctionnels Federaus. Vol. 1, No. 1 (Summer 1982)-. 0822-2592. Periodical. CN. French. qt. Free. Comite National Mixte de l'ACCP & SCF, 2E Etage 340 Ouest Av Laurier, Ontario K1A 0P9 Canada. **DD** 365.06071.

CONTACT - NATIONAL JOINT COMMITTEE OF THE CACP & FCS. (CONTACT). VAT Contact - National Joint Committee of the Canadian Association of Chiefs of Police and the Federal Correctional Services. Vol. 1, No. 1 (Summer 1982)-. 0823-681X. Periodical. English. qt. Free. National Joint Committee of the CACP & FCS, 2nd Floor/340 Laurier Avenue, West Ottawa Ontario K1A 0R9 Canada. **DD** 365.0607.

CONTACT - RED CROSS YOUTH, CANADIAN RED CROSS SOCIETY, BRITISH COLUMBIA/YUKON. (CONTACT). 0713-3979. Periodical. CN. English. ir. Free. Red Cross Youth, British Columbia Yukon Division, 4750 Oak Street, Vancouver British Columbia V6H 2N9 Canada. **DD** 361.763405. (ctrl).

CONTEMPORARY CRISES. See Political Science.

CONTEMPORARY LONGTERM CARE. VFOAT Contemporary Longtermcare. Began in 1985. 8750-9652. Periodical. US. English. mo. $19.00. Sunbelt Fulfillment Services, PO Box 41094, Nashville TN 37204. **DD** 362. Contemporary Administrator for Long-Term Care, 0745-2837.

CONTEMPORARY SOCIAL WORK EDUCATION. See Education (General) - Special Aspects of Education.

CONTRIBUTIONS IN CRIMINOLOGY AND PENOLOGY. No. 1-. 0732-4464. Monographic Series. US. English. ir. Greenwood Press, 88 Post Road West, Box 5007, Westport CT 06881. **Tel** (203)226-3571. This series examines the issues on criminology and penology throughout the world Historical as well as contemporary concerns are analyzed.

CONTROLLED SUBSTANCES SEIZED IN CALIFORNIA. **Main/Corp** California. Bureau of Criminal Statistics and Special Services. US. English. an. State of California, Department of Justice, 77 Cadillac Drive, PO Box 13427, Sacramento CA 95813. **LC** HV5831.C2. **DD** 363.4509794.

CONVERSATIONS. **Main/Corp** Child Welfare League of America. 1- 1971-. Periodical. US. English. ir. $30.00. Child Welfare League of America, 67 Irving Place, New York NY 10003. **Tel** (212)254-7410. Ed Carl Schoenberg. bk rev. adv acc. **Circ** 7,000.

COPY. **Main/Corp** Community Service Society of New York. Dept. of Public Affairs. VFOAT Release. US. English. 105 East 22nd Street, New York NY 10010.

CORD. (THE CORD). V. 1- Nov. 1977-. 0225-7033. Periodical. CN. English. qt. Free. Regional Association of Co-Ordinators of Volunteers, c/o Editor, 541 Mohawk Road West, Hamilton Ontario L9C 1X5 Canada. **DD** 361.3706071352. (ctrl).

CORPORATE COMMENTARY. Vol. 1, No. 1 (June 1984)-. 0749-4335. Periodical. US. English. qt. $29.00. Washington Business Group on Health, 922 Pennsylvania Avenue SE, Washington DC 20003. **DD** 362. **NLM** W1.

CORRECTIONAL COMPASS; OFFICIAL NEWSLETTER. **Main/Corp** Florida. Division of Corrections. V. 1- Sept. 1, 1961-. Periodical. English. ir.

CORRECTIONAL LITERATURE PUBLISHED IN CANADA. VFOAT Ouvrages de Criminologie Publies au Canada. 1968-. 0070-0509. Periodical. CN. French (text in English). an. Le Conseil Canadien de Developpement Social, 55 Parkdale CP 3505 Succursale C, Ottawa Ontario K1Y 4G1 Canada. **DD** 016.364.

CORRECTIONAL SERVICES NEWS. V. 1- Jan. 1976-. 0196-2353. Periodical. US. English. mo. New York State Department of Correctional Services, State Office Building, Campus Building 2, Albany NY 12206.

CORRECTIONS COMPENDIUM. 0738-8144. Periodical. US. English. mo. $48.00 Domestic, $51.00 Foreign. Contact Incorporated, PO Box 81826, Lincoln NE 68501.

CORRECTIONS MAGAZINE CEASED. V. 1-9, No. 3. 0095-4594. Periodical. US. English. bm. $17.97, $12.50 Inmates & Students. 801 Second Avenue, New York NY 10017. **Ind/Abst** Public Aff. Inf. Serv. Bull., Soc. Sci. Index. **LC** HV9261. **DD** 364.60973.

CORRECTIONS, STATE OF RHODE ISLAND. **Main/Corp** Rhode Island. Dept. of Corrections. 1972/73-. 0364-1716. US. English. Department of Corrections, 75 Howard Avenue, Cranston MA 02920. **LC** HV7289. **DD** 364.609745.

CORRECTIONS TODAY. V. 41- Jan./Feb. 1979-. 0190-2563. Periodical. US. English. bm. $25.00. American Correctional Association, 4321 Hartwick Road/Suite L-208, College Park MD 20740. **Tel** (301)699-7600. Ed Patricia L Millard. **Ind/Abst** Soc. Sci. Index. **LC** HV7231. **DD** 364.605. bk rev. adv acc. **Circ** 14,300. Each issue provides an in-depth

Sociology: General Works, Theory—Social Pathology, Welfare, Criminology

examination of major issues in corrections. Serves as a forum for presenting and discussing important issues in corrections. *American Journal of Correction, 0002-9203.*

THE COST OF SOCIAL SECURITY. **Main/Corp** International Labour Office. **VFOAT** Cout de la Securite Sociale, Le Cout de la Securite Sociale, El Costo de la Seguridad Social. 1951-. 0538-8295. US. English (Vols. for 1954- also have title and text in French and Spanish). ir. ILO Publications, International Labour Office, CH-1211 Geneva 22 Switzerland. **Tel** (241)060-003. **LC** HD7091. **DD** 368.4. A world-wide comparison of social security expenditures.

COUNSELING AND HUMAN DEVELOPMENT. Vol. 10, No. 1 (Sept. 1977)-. 0193-7375. Periodical. US. English. Love Publishing Company, 1777 South Bellaire Street, Denver CO 80222. **Tel** (303)757-2579. **Ed** Stanley F Love. **Circ** 2,000. Available in microform from University Microfilms International. For counselors and those engaged in human services. *Focus on Guidance.*

COUNTY JAIL INSPECTIONS. US. English. an. **LC** HV8339.

COURRIER - CENTRE INTERNATIONAL DE L'ENFANCE. (COURRIER). **Main/Corp** International Children's Centre. V. 1- Nov. 1950-. 0538-5482. Periodical. English (French). bm. **LC** HV703. **NLM** ZWS 100 C858.

CRADO 4-1. (CRADO 4-1 : JOURNAL DE L'AGE D'OR, CENTRE DU QUEBEC 4-1). **VAT** Journal de l'Age d'Or, Centre du Quebec 4-1, Conseil Regional de l'Age d'Or 4-1. 0227-0048. Periodical. CN. French. qt. Conseil Regional de l'Age Dor, 682 Mgr Courchesne, CP 848, Nicolet Quebec J0G 1E0 Canada. **DD** 362.60971445.

CRIME AND DELINQUENCY. **VFOAT** Crime & Delinquency. Vol. 6, No. 3 (July 1960)-. 0011-1287. Periodical. US. English. qt. National Council on Crime and Delinquency, Continental Plaza 411, Hackensack NJ 07601. **Ind/Abst** Leg. Resour. Index, Sociol. Abstr., Soc. Welf. Soc. Plan./Policy Soc. Dev., Excerpta Med., Curr. Index J. Educ., Psychol. Abstr., Soc. Sci. Index. **LC** HV6001. **DD** 364.05. **NLM** W1 CR194. **CODEN** CRDLAL. *NPPA Journal, NCCD News, 0027-6235.*

CRIME AND DELIQUENCY ABSTRACTS CEASED. Series/Titl DHEW Publication. **VFOAT** Crime and Delinquency Abstracts and Current Projects. V. 4-8. 0045-902X. US. English. bm. **LC** Z5118 .C9. **NLM** Z 5118.C9 I51. *International Bibliography on Crime and Delinquency.*

CRIME AND JUSTICE. V. 1-. 0192-3234. US. English. an. University of Chicago Press, Thomas Fischer, 5801 Ellis Avenue, Chicago IL 60637. **Ind/Abst** Essay Gen. Lit. Index. **LC** HV6001. **DD** 364.05.

CRIME AND JUVENILE DELINQUENCY : A BIBLIOGRAPHIC GUIDE TO THE DOCUMENTS UPDATE. See Bibliographies.

CRIME AND SOCIAL JUSTICE. 1- Spring/Summer 1974-. 0094-7571. US. English. sa. $35.00. Crime and Social Justice, PO Box 4373, Berkeley CA 94704. **Tel** (415)550-1284. **Ind/Abst** Sociol. Abstr., Soc. Welf. Soc. Plan./Policy Soc. Dev., Altern. Press Index, Public Aff. Inf. Serv. Bull., Lang. Lang. Behav. Abstr. **LC** HV6001. **DD** 364.05. (cum index). bk rev. adv acc. **Circ** 3,000. Offers new directions for criminology drawing upon history, economics and political theory to address social policy issues. *Issues in Criminology, 0021-2385.*

CRIME ET JUSTICE. **VFOAT** Crime and Justice. V. 4, No. 1- May 1976-. 0381-1557. Periodical. CN. English (French). qt. 15.00. University of Ottawa Press, University of Ottawa, Ottawa Ontario K1N 6N5 Canada. **Ind/Abst** Psychol. Abstr. **LC** HV6002. **DD** 364.05. *Criminologie Made in Canada, 0381-1549.*

CRIME IN ALABAMA. Began in 1976. US. English. an. **LC** HV7250.

CRIME IN ARKANSAS. Series/Titl A Research and Statistics Division Report. Began in 1974. US. English. an. Arkansas Crime Information Center, One Capitol Mall, Little Rock AR 72201. **LC** HV6793.A8. **DD** 364.9767.

CRIME IN COLORADO. Began in 1976. US. English. an. 2002 South Colorado Boulevard, Denver CO 80222. **LC** HV6793.C6. **DD** 364.9788.

CRIME IN CONNECTICUT. US. English. an. State of Connecticut, Department of Public Safety, Division of State Police, Uniform Crime Reporting Program, 294 Cology Street, Meridan CT 06450. **LC** HV7936.C88. **DD** 364.974605.

CRIME IN HAWAII. **Main/Corp** Hawaii Criminal Justice Statistical Analysis Center. Uniform Crime Reporting Division. 1975-. 0146-9029. US. English. an. PO Box 2560, Honolulu HI 96804. **LC** HV7260.5. **DD** 364.9969.

CRIME IN LOUISIANA. **Main/Corp** Louisiana. Criminal Justice Information System Division. US. English. an. Louisiana Criminal Justice, Information System Division, 1885 Wooddale Boulevard, Room 502, Baton Rouge LA 70806. **LC** HV7268. **DD** 364.9763.

CRIME IN MAINE. 1975-. 0148-6292. Periodical. US. English. an. Maine Department of Public Safety, 36 Hospital Street, Augusta ME 04330. **LC** HV6793.M3. **DD** 364.9741.

CRIME IN MASSACHUSETTS. **Main/Corp** Massachusetts. Crime Reporting Unit. 1977-. US. English. an. Commonwealth of Massachusetts, Department of Public Safety, Uniform Crime Report, 1010 Commonwealth Avenue, Boston MA 02215. **LC** HV7271. **DD** 364.97440212.

CRIME IN MONTANA. **Main/Corp** Montana. Criminal Justice Data Center. 1974-. 0160-7103. US. English. an. Montana Board of Crime and Control, 1336 Helena Avenue, Helena Montana 59601. **LC** HV7276. **DD** 364.9786. *Montana: Arrests, Offenses, 0361-414X.*

CRIME IN NEVADA. **Main/Corp** Nevada. Dept. of Law Enforcement Assistance. US. English. an. **LC** HV7278. **DD** 364.9793.

CRIME IN NORTH DAKOTA. 1980-. US. English. an. **LC** HV6793.N9. **DD** 364.97840212.

CRIME IN SOUTH CAROLINA. US. English. an. PO Box 21398, Columbia SC 29211. **LC** HV7290. **DD** 364.9757.

CRIME IN TEXAS. **Main/Corp** Texas. Dept. of Public Safety. US. English. Texas Department of Public Safety, PO Box 50805 North Lamar Boulevard, Austin TX 78773. **LC** HV7293. **DD** 364.109764.

CRIME IN WISCONSIN COMPARISON WITH OTHER STATES AND THE NATION. **Main/Corp** Wisconsin. Crime Information Bureau. **VFOAT** Crime in Wisconsin Comparison with Nation. US. English. **LC** HV7299. **DD** 364.9775.

CRIME IN WYOMING. US. English. an. **LC** HV6793.W8. **DD** 364.04209787.

CRIME LABORATORY DIGEST. 0743-1872. Periodical. US. English. qt. Crime Laboratory Digest, Forensic Science Research and Training Center, FBI Academy, Quantico VA 22135. **LC** HV8073. **DD** 363.2560973.

CRIME PREVENTION REVIEW. Began with Oct. 1973 issue. 0093-044X. Periodical. US. English. qt. Attorney General Office, 217 West First Street/Room 203, Los Angeles CA 90012. **LC** HV7431. **DD** 364.9794.

CRIMES AGAINST BUSINESS. Jan. 1977/ June 1978-. 0192-706X. US. English. Arno Press, 3 Park Avenue, New York NY 10016. **LC** HV6768. **DD** 364.16805.

CRIMES COMPENSATION BOARD ANNUAL REPORT. (THE CRIMES COMPENSATION BOARD ANNUAL REPORT). **Main/Corp** Alberta. Crimes Compensation Board. **VFOAT** Annual Report. 0826-9440. CN. English. an. Crimes Compensation Board, 4th Floor Bowker Building, 9833 -109th Street, Edmonton Alberta T5K 2E8 Canada. **LC** HV8688. **DD** 354.712300849.

CRIMINAL DIVISION. See Law.

CRIMINAL JUSTICE ABSTRACTS. See Indexes/Abstracts.

CRIMINAL JUSTICE AND BEHAVIOR. V. 1- Mar. 1974-. 0093-8548. Periodical. US. English. qt. Sage Publications, 275 South Beverly Drive, Beverly Hills CA 90212. **Tel** (213)274-8003. **Ind/Abst** Leg. Resour. Index, Excerpta Med., Women Stud. Abstr., Curr. Index J. Educ., Psychol. Abstr., Soc. Sci. Index, Soc. Sci. Citation Index, Biol. Abstr., Contents Curr. Leg. Period., Curr. Law Index, Lang. Lang. Behav. Abstr. **LC** HV9261. **DD** 364.6019. **NLM** W1 CR194J. **CODEN** CJBHAB. *Correctional Psychologist, 0589-8218.*

CRIMINAL JUSTICE AND THE PUBLIC. 0160-9688. Periodical. US. English. mo. $32.00. Crafton Publications Inc, 667 Madison Avenue, New York NY 10021. *Delinquency and Rehabilitation Report, 0094-2340.*

CRIMINAL JUSTICE COMPREHENSIVE PLAN. **Main/Corp** Nebraska Commission on Law Enforcement and Criminal Justice. 0091-9128. US. English. Natural Resources Commission, PO Box 94725 State Capitol Building, Lincoln NE 68509. **LC** HV7277. **DD** 364.

CRIMINAL JUSTICE ETHICS. See Ethics.

CRIMINAL JUSTICE EXPENDITURE AND EMPLOYMENT. **VFOAT** Criminal Justice Information System. 1980-. Periodical. US. English. an. Depository. **LC** HV9475.K3. **DD** 350.7409781. *Employment and Expenditures for Criminal Justical Activities by Kansas Local Governments.*

CRIMINAL JUSTICE HIGHLIGHTS. 1967?-. Periodical. US. English. mo. Criminal Justice Highlights, 411 West 13th Street, Austin TX 78701. **Tel** (512)475-4101.

CRIMINAL JUSTICE HISTORY. Vol. 1 (1980)-. 0194-0953. US. English (French). an. $49.50. Meckler Publishing, 11 Ferry Lane West, Westport CT 06880. **Tel** (203)226-6967. **Ind/Abst** Am. Hist. Life, Hist. Abstr., Part A, Mod. Hist. Abstr., Hist. Abst., Part B, Twent. Century Abstr., Writ. Am. Hist. **LC** HV7921. **DD** 364.9. bk rev. **Circ** 450. Publishes papers and articles on the history of crime and criminal justice.

CRIMINAL JUSTICE JOURNAL. See Law.

CRIMINAL JUSTICE LITERATURE. See Literature.

CRIMINAL JUSTICE MONOGRAPH. Monographic Series. US. English. Criminal Justice Monograph, Huntsville TX 77340.

CRIMINAL JUSTICE NEWSLETTER. Vol. 1 1969?-. 0590-0859. Periodical. US. English. Pace Publications, PO Box 2972, Grand Central Station, New York NY 10163.

CRIMINAL JUSTICE NEWSLETTER. **VFOAT** CJN. V. 1- June 1970-. 0045-9038. Periodical. US. English. bw. $159.00. Pace Publications, PO Box 2972 Grand Central Station, New York NY 10163. **Tel** (212)685-5450. **Ind/Abst** Curr. Law Index, Leg. Resour. Index. **LC** K3. **DD** 345.730505.

CRIMINAL JUSTICE NEWSLETTER. 0095-7496. US. English. mo. 400 East Seventh Street, Bloomington IN 47401. **LC** KFI3562.A73. **DD** 364.

CRIMINAL JUSTICE NEWSLETTER. 0098-7670. US. English. Illinois State Bar Association, Illinois Bar Center, Springfield IL 62701. **LC** KFI1762.A15. **DD** 345.77305. *Criminal Law Newsletter.*

THE CRIMINAL JUSTICE PERIODICAL INDEX. See Indexes/Abstracts.

CRIMINAL JUSTICE PLAN. **Main/Corp** Virginia. Division of Justice and Crime Prevention. **VFOAT** Virginia Criminal Justice Plan. 0362-8353. US. English. Division of Justice and Crime, 8501 Mayland Drive, Richmond VA 23229. **LC** HV7296. **DD** 364.

CRIMINAL JUSTICE PLAN FOR NEW JERSEY. APPLICANTS GUIDE. **Main/Corp** New Jersey. State Law Enforcement Planning Agency. Series/Titl Dissemination Document. 1978-. US. English. an. 3535 Quaker Bridge Road, Trenton NJ 08625. **LC** HV7280. **DD** 364.9749. *New Jersey Plan for Criminal Justice, 0092-4652; Applicants Guide.*

CRIMINAL JUSTICE PLAN FOR TEXAS. **Main/Corp** Texas. Criminal Justice Division. 1975-. 0360-3229. US. English. Criminal Justice Division, 610 Brazos/Box 1828, Austin TX 78757. **LC** HV7293. **DD** 364. *Criminal Justice Plan for Texas.*

CRIMINAL JUSTICE PROFILE. ALAMEDA COUNTY. **VFOAT** Alameda County. 1976-. US. English. an. Bureau of Criminal Statistics, 77 Cadillac Drive PO Box 13427, Sacramento CA 95813.

CRIMINAL JUSTICE PROFILE. ALPINE COUNTY. **VFOAT** Alpine County. 1976-. US. English. an. Bureau of Criminal Statistics, 77 Cadillac Drive, PO Box 13427, Sacramento CA 95813.

Sociology: General Works, Theory—Social Pathology, Welfare, Criminology

CRIMINAL JUSTICE PROFILE; STATEWIDE. Main/Corp California. Bureau of Criminal Statistics and Special Services. 1978-. US. English. an. LC HV7254. DD 364.9794. *Criminal Justice Profile.*

CRIMINAL JUSTICE RESEARCH. Fiscal Year 1979-. 0736-2382. US. English. be. US Department of Justice, National Institute of Justice, Washington DC 20531. LC HV9471. DD 364.97305. *Annual Report.*

CRIMINAL JUSTICE RESEARCH. ANNUAL REPORT. Main/Corp National Institute of Justice (U.S.). Nov. 1980-. US. English. be. US Department of Justice, National Institute of Justice, Washington DC 20531. *Annual Report.*

CRIMINAL JUSTICE REVIEW. V. 1- Spring 1976-. 0734-0168. Periodical. US. English. sa. $20.00. Department of Criminal Justice, Georgia State University, Atlanta GA 30303-3091. Tel (404)658-3500. Ed Robert E Croom. Ind/Abst Public Aff. Inf. Serv. Bull. LC K3. DD 364. bk rev. adv acc. Circ 1,000. International and systemwide in scope and focuses on trends, problems and research in criminalization, criminology, administration, law enforcement, courts, juvenile services, and corrections.

CRIMINAL STATISTICS, ENGLAND AND WALES. SUPPLEMENTARY TABLES. VOL. 1, PROCEEDINGS IN MAGISTRATES' COURTS. See Statistics.

CRIMINAL STATISTICS, ENGLAND AND WALES. SUPPLEMENTARY TABLES. VOL. 3, TABLES BY POLICE FORCE AREAS AND SOME COURT AREAS. See Statistics.

CRIMINAL STATISTICS. SCOTLAND. See Statistics.

CRIMINAL VICTIMIZATION IN THE UNITED STATES. Jan./June 1973-. 0095-5833. US. English. an. US Department of Justice, Bureau of Justice Statistics, Washington DC 20531. LC HV7245. DD 362.880973.

CRIMINALIDAD EN . . . . VFOAT Estadistica de Criminalidad. Spanish. an. LC HV6903. DD 364.04209861.

LA CRIMINALITE EN FRANCE EN . EN. . . D'APRES LES STATISTIQUES DE POLICE JUDICIAIRE. See Statistics.

CRIMINOLOGIE. V. 8- 1975-. 0316-0041. Periodical. CN. French (summaries in English). sa. $9.28. Presses de l'Universite, University of Montreal, CP 6128, Montreal Quebec H3C 3J7 Canada. Tel (514)343-6321. Ed Denis Szabo. Ind/Abst Point Repere, Foreign Lang. Index, PAIS Foreign Lang. Index. LC HV6002. DD 364'.05. adv acc. Circ 700. Of interest to professionals, articles include research data, commentaries on recent publications, proposed legislation, actual experiences. *Acta Criminologica, 0065-1168.*

CRIMINOLOGIE MADE IN CANADA CEASED. VFOAT Criminology Made in Canada. First issue in 1973. Ceased Vol. 3, No. 2. 0381-1549. Periodical. CN. French (English). $7.50. Criminologie Made in Canada, PO Box 142, North Montreal Quebec H1H 5L2 Canada. DD 364.05.

THE CRIMINOLOGIST. 0164-0240. Periodical. US. English. qt. American Society of Criminology, 1314 Kinnear Road, Columbus OH 43212. Tel (614)422-9207.

CRIMINOLOGY. V. 8, No. 1- May 1970-. 0011-1384. Periodical. US. English. qt. American Society of Criminology, 1314 Kinnear Road/Suite 212, Columbus OH 43212. Tel (213)274-8003. Ind/Abst Excerpta Med., Women Stud. Abstr., Soc. Work Res. Abstr., Public Aff. Inf. Serv. Bull., Psychol. Abstr., Soc. Sci. Index, Soc. Sci. Citation Index, Sociol. Abstr., Curr. Law Index, Leg. Resour. Index, Lang. Lang. Behav. Abstr., Abstr. Soc. Work. LC HV6001. DD 364.05. NLM W1 CR196K. CODEN CRINYA. *Criminologica.*

CRIMINOLOGY & PENOLOGY ABSTRACTS. See Indexes/Abstracts.

CRITICA SOCIAL. No. 1- Dec. 1974-. Portuguese. ir. Escola de Servicio Social da Universidade Catolica de Minas gerais, Av Dom Jose Gaspar 500, Belo Horizonte 30.000 Brazil. LC HV4.

CROIX-ROUGE AU QUEBEC. (LA CROIX-ROUGE AU QUEBEC). VFOAT Red Cross in Quebec. 0226-9872. Periodical. CN. English (French). ir. Canadian Red Cross Society, Quebec Division/2170 Dorchester Boulevard West, Montreal Quebec H3H 1R6 Canada. DD 363.14.

CROSSWORLD. V. 5, No. 2- Apr. 1979-. 0225-3992. Periodical. CN. English (includes some text in French). ir. Free. Canadian Crossroads International, 361 Windermere Road, London Ontario N6G 2K3 Canada. DD 361.26. (ctrl) *Newsletter, 0225-3984.*

CRSSS 09. (CRSSS 09 : BULLETIN D'INFORMATION). VAT Bulletin d'Information - CRSSS 09, Conseil Regional de la Sante et des Services Sociaux 09. Vol. 1, No. 1 (31 Jan. 1978)-. 0701-8967. Periodical. CN. French. Free. CRSSS 09, 896 rue de Puyjalon, Hauterive Quebec G5C 1N1 Canada. DD 361.971417. (ctrl)

CSALADI LAP. Periodical. HU. Hungarian. mo. Akademiai Kiado, POB 24, 1363 Budapest Hungary. LC Microfilm 05512HV, HV580.

CUADERNO (INSTITUTO URUGUAYO DE DERECHO PENAL). (CUADERNO). VFOAT Cuaderno del Instituto Uruguayp de Derecho Penal. No. 1-. Periodical. UY. Spanish. ir. Editorial Amalio M Fernandez, 25 de Mayo 477 P Baja, Ofic 11, Montevideo Uruguay. DD 345.895, 348.9505.

CURRENT INTERESTS OF THE FORD FOUNDATION. Main/Corp Ford Foundation. 1974/75-. 0162-5780. US. English. be. Office of Reports, 320 East 43rd Street, New York NY 10017. LC HV97.F62. DD 361.760973.

CWLA DIRECTORY OF MEMBER AND ASSOCIATE AGENCIES. See Yearbooks, Almanacs, Directories.

DATA ON FEMALE VETERANS. 8755-710X. US. English. Veterans Administration Office of Management and Statistics, 810 Vermont Avenue Northwest, Washington DC 20420. LC UB357. DD 362.86088042.

DAY CARE. No. 1- Jan. 1970-. 0384-1537. Periodical. CN. English. ir. Free. Action Committee on Day Care, Ontario Welfare Council, 1240 Bay Street/Suite 404, Toronto Ontario M5R 2A7 Canada. DD 362.71.

DAY CARE AND EARLY EDUCATION. V. 1- Sept. 1973-. 0092-4199. Periodical. US. English. qt. Human Sciences Press, 72-5th Avenue, New York NY 10011. Tel (212)243-6000. Ind/Abst Soc. Work Res. Abstr., Chicorel Abstr. Read. Learn. Disabil., Curr. Index J. Educ., Educ. Index, Except. Child Educ. Resour., Media Rev. Dig., Soc. Work Res. Abstr., Bibliogr. Agric., Abstr. Soc. Work. LC HV854. DD 362.71.

DAY CARE CENTRES AND NURSERY SCHOOLS HAMILTON-WENTWORTH. 1981-. 0711-7930. Periodical. CN. English. Free. Day Care Centres and Nursery Schools Hamilton-Wentworth, Community Information Service, Hamilton-Wentworth/6th Floor, 155 James Street South, Hamilton Ontario L8P 3A4 Canada. DD 362.71202571352. *Day Care Directory, 0382-0645.*

DAY CARE FOR CHILDREN (KITCHENER, ONT.). (DAY CARE FOR CHILDREN). 1982/83-. 0821-4360. CN. English. an. $0.50 Per No. Community Information Centre, 18 Queen Street North, Kitchener Ontario N2H 2G8 Canada. DD 362.71202571344.

DAY CARE IN METROPOLITAN TORONTO. 1983/84-. 0822-9422. CN. English. an. $12.00. Community Information Centre of Metropolitan Toronto, 3rd Floor/34 King Street East, Toronto Ontario M5C 1E5 Canada. DD 362.712025713541. *Day Care, Nursery Schools, 0714-8712.*

DAY CARE JOURNAL. (DAY CARE JOURNAL : VOICE OF THE DAY CARE COUNCIL OF AMERICA). Vol. 1, No. 1 (Summer 1982)-. 0732-7889. Periodical. US. English. bm. $24.00. Day Care Council of America, 1602-17th Street NW, Washington DC 20009. LC HV854. DD 362.7120973.

DELIKT EN DELINKWENT. See Law.

DEI DELITTI E DELLE PENE. Yearly V. 1, No. 1, (Jan./April 1983)-. Periodical. Italian. ty. 50.000. Lungomare Nazario Sauro 25, 70121 Bari Italy.

DEPARTMENT OF HEALTH AND SOCIAL SERVICES QUARTERLY MAGAZINE. Main/Corp Alaska. Dept. of Health and Social Services. VFOAT Alaska Health and Social Services Quarterly. Periodical. US. English. qt. Pouch H-81, Juneau AK 99811. LC HV86. DD 361.9798. *HSS Quarterly.*

DETAILED DEMAND FOR GRANTS OF HOME DEPARTMENT. See Public Administration.

DETAILED DEMAND FOR GRANTS OF LABOUR AND SOCIAL WELFARE DEPARTMENT. See Economics - Labor.

DEUTSCHES ROTES KREUZ DER DEUTSCHEN DEMOKRATISCHEN REPUBLIK. Main/Corp Red Cross. Germany (Democratic Republic) Deutsches Rotes Kreuz. Periodical. SZ. German. mo. Kunst & Wissen, Erich Bieber, Dufourstrasse 51, CH-8008 Zurich Switzerland. LC HV580.G3. DD 361.770943.

DEVELOPMENTAL DISABILITIES STATE PLAN. Main/Corp Minnesota. Developmental Disabilities Planning Office. US. English. Developmental Disabilities Planning Office of the State Planning Agency, 200 Capitol Square Building, 550 Cedar Street, St Paul MN 55101. LC HV3006.M58. DD 362.309776.

DEVELOPMENTS IN HUMAN SERVICES. V. 1- 1973-. 0092-5470. US. English. ir. Human Sciences Press, 72-5th Avenue, New York NY 10011. LC HV13. DD 361.005. NLM W1 DE997W.

DEVELOPPEMENT SOCIAL CEASED. VFOAT Social Development. Began with V. 1- Jan. 1972. 0316-3148. Periodical. CN. French (text in French exclusively except when the French and English editions are published in soley one issue). ir. Conseil Canadien de Developpement Social, 55 Avenue Parkdale, Ottawa Ontario K1Y 1E5 Canada. DD 361.971.

DEVELOPPEMENT SOCIAL EN PERSPECTIVES. VFOAT Perspectives. VAT Perspectives - Conseil Canadien de Developpement Social. Vol. 1, No. 1-. 0822-7128. Periodical. CN. French. ir. Free to Members Only. Conseil Canadien de Developpement Social, 55 Av Parkdale, Ottawa Ontario K1Y 4G1 Canada. DD 361.971. (ctrl) *Social Development, 0316-313X.*

DEVIANCE ET SOCIETE. V. 1- May 1977-. 0378-7931. Periodical. French. qt. 15.00 Domestic, $31.00 Foreign. Editions Medecine & Hygiene, Case Postale 229, CH-1211 Geneve 4 Switzerland. Tel (022)469355. LC HM291. DD 301.6205. adv acc. Circ 750.

DHARMA WARTA. Indonesian. ir. Badan Koordinasi Pelaksana Instruksi Presiden, Jalan Senopati 1/No 51, Jakarta Indonesia. LC HV7102.

DIABETIC DIARY. Vol. 1, issue 1 (Nov./Dec. 1984)-. 8755-8858. Periodical. US. English. bm. $15.00. Diabetic Diary, PO Box 836, Enfield CT 06012. DD 362.

DIALECT. V. 1- Feb. 1, 1976-. 0383-8528. Periodical. CN. English. mo. Saskatchewan Association for the Mentally Retarded, 103 Central Chambers, Saskatoon Saskatchewan S7K 0G4 Canada. DD 362.30627124.

DIFFERENT STROKES. Began publication in Fall 1979. 0226-0468. Periodical. CN. English. Royal Life Saving Society, 13 Mission Avenue, St Albert Alberta T8N 1H Canada. DD 363.1.

DIGEST OF CALIFORNIA CRIMINAL CASES. V. 1- July/Dec. 1976-. US. English. California Continuing Education of the Bar, 2300 Shatluck Avenue, Berkeley CA 94704. LC KFC1100.A53. DD 345.794002648.

DIGEST OF CURRENT REPORTS. Main/Corp United Way of America. Information Center. 0090-3191. Periodical. US. English. qt. United Way of America, 801 North Fairfax Street, Alexandria VA 22314. LC HV40. DD 361.008. *Bibliography of Reports and Manuals.*

DIMENSIONS . . . . Main/Corp Michigan. State Dept. of Corrections. 1976-. US. English. an. State Department of Corrections, Stevens T Mason Building, PO Box 30003, Lansing MI 48909. LC HV7272. DD 353.977400849. *MDC, Michigan Department of Corrections Annual Report, 0363-9630.*

DIMENSIONS OF THE INDEPENDENT SECTOR. 1st Ed.-. US. English. an.

DIRECT LOAN PROGRAM FOR THE ELDERLY OR HANDICAPPED. US. English. ir. Department of Housing and Urban Development, 451 Seventh Street Southwest, Washington DC 20401.

DIRECTIONS. VFOAT Human Resources Directory of San Diego-Imperial Counties & Tijuana. V. 1- Spring 1974-. Periodical. US. English. be. United

Sociology: General Works, Theory—Social Pathology, Welfare, Criminology

Way of San Diego County, PO Box 17720, San Diego CA 92117. **Tel** (714)/292-4777. *Directory of Organizations Meeting Human Needs in San Diego County.*

DIRECTORY. DIOCESAN AGENCIES OF CATHOLIC CHARITIES. UNITED STATES, PUERTO RICO AND CANADA. See Yearbooks, Almanacs, Directories.

DIRECTORY : JEWISH FEDERATIONS, WELFARE FUNDS AND COMMUNITY COUNCILS. See Yearbooks, Almanacs, Directories.

DIRECTORY : JUVENILE AND ADULT CORRECTIONAL DEPARTMENTS, INSTITUTIONS, AGENCIES AND PAROLING AUTHORITIES, UNITED STATES AND CANADA. See Yearbooks, Almanacs, Directories.

DIRECTORY OF AGENCIES : U.S. VOLUNTARY, INTERNATIONAL VOLUNTARY, INTERGOVERNMENTAL. See Yearbooks, Almanacs, Directories.

DIRECTORY OF CALIFORNIA JUSTICE AGENCIES SERVING JUVENILES AND ADULTS. See Yearbooks, Almanacs, Directories.

DIRECTORY OF CANADIAN HUMAN SERVICES. See Yearbooks, Almanacs, Directories.

DIRECTORY OF CHILD CARE CENTERS. See Yearbooks, Almanacs, Directories.

DIRECTORY OF COMMUNITY-BASED MENTAL RETARDATION SERVICES. See Yearbooks, Almanacs, Directories.

DIRECTORY OF COMMUNITY SERVICE ORGANIZATIONS IN THE WASHINGTON METROPOLITAN AREA. See Yearbooks, Almanacs, Directories.

DIRECTORY OF COMMUNITY SERVICES. See Yearbooks, Almanacs, Directories.

DIRECTORY OF COMMUNITY SERVICES. See Yearbooks, Almanacs, Directories.

DIRECTORY OF COMMUNITY SERVICES. See Yearbooks, Almanacs, Directories.

DIRECTORY OF COMMUNITY SERVICES. See Yearbooks, Almanacs, Directories.

DIRECTORY OF COMMUNITY SERVICES FOR EDMONTON & DISTRICT. See Yearbooks, Almanacs, Directories.

DIRECTORY OF COMMUNITY SERVICES FOR GREATER WINDSOR. See Yearbooks, Almanacs, Directories.

DIRECTORY OF COMMUNITY SERVICES FOR WATERLOO REGION. See Yearbooks, Almanacs, Directories.

DIRECTORY OF COMMUNITY SERVICES IN MARYLAND. See Yearbooks, Almanacs, Directories.

DIRECTORY OF COMMUNITY SERVICES IN REGIONAL NIAGARA. See Yearbooks, Almanacs, Directories.

DIRECTORY OF COMMUNITY SERVICES (LONDON, ONT.). See Yearbooks, Almanacs, Directories.

DIRECTORY OF COMMUNITY SERVICES (NEW YORK PUBLIC LIBRARY). See Yearbooks, Almanacs, Directories.

DIRECTORY OF COMMUNITY SERVICES. OTTAWA-CARLETON. See Yearbooks, Almanacs, Directories.

DIRECTORY OF COMMUNITY SERVICES - THUNDER BAY. See Yearbooks, Almanacs, Directories.

DIRECTORY OF CRIMINAL JUSTICE AGENCIES IN ARIZONA. See Yearbooks, Almanacs, Directories.

DIRECTORY OF CRIMINAL JUSTICE INFORMATION SOURCES. See Yearbooks, Almanacs, Directories.

DIRECTORY OF HUMAN SERVICE AGENCIES IN RHODE ISLAND. See Yearbooks, Almanacs, Directories.

DIRECTORY OF HUMAN SERVICE ORGANIZATIONS. See Yearbooks, Almanacs, Directories.

DIRECTORY OF HUMAN SERVICES. See Yearbooks, Almanacs, Directories.

DIRECTORY OF HUMAN SERVICES IN SASKATCHEWAN. See Yearbooks, Almanacs, Directories.

DIRECTORY OF HUMAN SERVICES IN THE KALAMAZOO AREA. See Yearbooks, Almanacs, Directories.

DIRECTORY OF INFORMATION AND REFERRAL SERVICES IN THE UNITED STATES AND CANADA. See Yearbooks, Almanacs, Directories.

THE DIRECTORY OF INTERPRETERS FOR THE DEAF. See Yearbooks, Almanacs, Directories.

DIRECTORY OF JEWISH FAMILY & CHILDREN'S AGENCIES. See Yearbooks, Almanacs, Directories.

DIRECTORY OF MEMBERS - UNITED WAY OF CANADA. See Yearbooks, Almanacs, Directories.

DIRECTORY OF MINNESOTA'S AREA MENTAL HEALTH-MENTAL RETARDATION-INEBRIETY PROGRAMS. See Yearbooks, Almanacs, Directories.

DIRECTORY OF OREGON CRIMINAL JUSTICE AGENCIES. See Yearbooks, Almanacs, Directories.

DIRECTORY OF PROGRAMS AND SERVICES FOR OLDER ADULTS. STATE OF OREGON BY COUNTIES. See Yearbooks, Almanacs, Directories.

DIRECTORY OF REGIONAL SOCIAL WELFARE ACTIVITIES. See Yearbooks, Almanacs, Directories.

DIRECTORY OF RESIDENTIAL PROGRAMS FOR COURT-INVOLVED YOUTH. See Yearbooks, Almanacs, Directories.

DIRECTORY OF RESOURCES FOR OLDER PEOPLE IN NEW HAMPSHIRE. See Yearbooks, Almanacs, Directories.

DIRECTORY OF SERVICES, ARKANSAS MENTAL HEALTH SERVICES. See Yearbooks, Almanacs, Directories.

DIRECTORY OF SERVICES FOR GREATER VANCOUVER. See Yearbooks, Almanacs, Directories.

DIRECTORY OF SOCIAL SERVICE ADMINISTRATORS OF LOCAL MUNICIPALITIES. See Yearbooks, Almanacs, Directories.

DIRECTORY OF SOCIAL WELFARE ACTIVITIES IN AFRICA. See Yearbooks, Almanacs, Directories.

DIRECTORY OF VOLUNTARY AGENCIES. See Yearbooks, Almanacs, Directories.

DIREKTORAT JENDERAL BANTUAN SOSIAL DALAM ANGKA. Main/Corp Indonesia. Direktorat Jenderal Bantuan Sosial. Indonesian. ir. **LC** HV401.

DISASTER INFORMATION. June 1978-July 1979. Periodical. US. English. ir. Federal Emergency Management, Agency Disaster Response and Recovery, Washington DC 20472.

DISASTER PREPAREDNESS IN THE AMERICAS. 0251-4494. Periodical. US. English. qt. Free. Disaster Preparedness in the Americas, Organization of American States 525-23rd Street Northwest, Washington DC 20037.

DISASTERS. V. 1- 1977-. 0361-3666. Periodical. UK. English. qt. $76.63. International Disaster Institute, 85 Marylebone High Street, Lonoon W1M 3DE England. **Tel** (01)935-0756. Ed Charles Melville. **Ind/Abst** Sociol. Abstr., Soc. Welf. Soc. Plan./Policy Soc. Dev., Excerpta Med., GeoRef, Soc. Sci. Citation Index. **LC** HV553. **DD** 361.505. **NLM** W1 DI742T. bk rev. adv acc. **Circ** 700. Multi-disciplinary journal covering all aspects of disasters-including sudden onset disasters, food emergencies, refugees, disasters and developments.

DISCUS FACTS BOOK. Main/Corp Distilled Spirits Council of the U.S. **VAT** Distilled Spirits Council of the United States Facts Book. 1975-. 0160-1504. US. English. an. Distilled Spirits Council of the US, 425-13th Street Northwest, Washington DC 20004. **LC** HV5285. **DD** 338.4766310973. *Facts Book.*

DISCUSSION PAPER - SPECIAL COMMITTEE ON CRIMINAL JUSTICE. Main/Corp Association of the Bar of the City of New York. Special Committee on Criminal Justice. No. 1- Jan. 1978-. Periodical. US. English. 42 West 44th Street, New York NY 10036.

DISCUSSION PAPERS (UNIVERSITY OF WISCONSIN—MADISON. INSTITUTE FOR RESEARCH ON POVERTY) CEASED. (DISCUSSION PAPERS). US. English. ir. $25.00. Institute for Research on Poverty, University of Wisconsin, 1180 Observatory Drive, Madison WI 53706. **Tel** (608)262-6358. Ed E Evanson L Uhr. **Circ** 200. (ctrl). Professional journal articles disseminating research findings. Includes technical treatments of research in progress. Addresses public policy issues. *Discussion Papers (University of Wisconsin. Institute for Research on Poverty).*

DOCUMENT RETRIEVAL INDEX. See Indexes/Abstracts.

DOCUMENTATION SERVICE BULLETIN. 0376-8651. English. an. Government of India, Department of Social Welfare, Shastri Bhavan, New Delhi India. **LC** Z7163. **DD** 016.30915404.

DOMESTIC VIOLENCE AND SEXUAL ASSAULT PROGRAMS IN ALASKA, FISCAL YEAR . . . : AN ANNUAL REPORT . . . BY THE COUNCIL ON DOMESTIC VIOLENCE AND SEXUAL ASSAULT. Main/Corp Alaska. Council on Domestic Violence and Sexual Assault. US. English. an. Council on Domestic Violence and Sexual Assault, Pouch N Room 312 Goldstein Building, Juneau AK 99811. **LC** HQ809.3.U5. **DD** 362.83809798.

DPI YELLOW PAGES. Main/Corp Nebraska. Dept. of Public Institutions. **VAT** Department of Public Institutions Yellow Pages. 0360-4357. US. English. an. Department of Public Institutions, PO Box 94728, Lincoln NE 68509. **LC** HV86. **DD** 362.025782.

DRIVERS LICENSE GUIDE. 0276-1696. US. English. an. $12.95. Drivers License Guide Company, 1492 Oddstad Drive, Redwood City CA 94063. **LC** HV8074. **DD** 658.47.

DROIT DE PASSAGE. (DROIT DE PASSAGE : MAGAZINE DE CONVERGENCE POUR UNE VISION GLOBALE DE LA REALITE-JEUNESSE). Vol. 4, No. 3 (Mar. 1984)-. 0826-5062. Periodical. CN. French. ir. $19,00. Droit de Passage, Suite 201/355 Ste-Catherine Ouest, Montreal Quebec H3B 1A4 Canada. **DD** 362.709714. *Convergence (Montreal, Quebec), 0228-9180.*

DYNAMO (MONTREAL, QUEBEC). (DYNAMO). Vol. 1, No. 1 (May 1982)-. 0821-2597. Periodical. CN. French (text in English). mo. $1.25 Per Number. Dynamo, c/o Bureau 106/1370 Est rue Henri-Bourassa, Montreal Quebec H2C 1G9 Canada. **DD** 362.409714.

EARLY CHILDHOOD DEVELOPMENT IN TEXAS. Main/Corp Texas. Office of Early Childhood Development. 1972-. 0092-7368. US. English. an. PO Box 13166, Capital Station, Austin TX 78711. **LC** HV742.T4. **DD** 362.709764.

EARLY CHILDHOOD EDUCATION AND CHILD CARE CENTRES, WESTERN AUSTRALIA. See Education (General).

ECHO. Nov. 1972-. 0382-7194. Periodical. CN. text in English and French. Hopital pour Enfants de l'Est de l'Ontario, 401 Chemin Smyth, Ottawa Ontario K1H 8L1 Canada. **DD** 362.78110971384.

Sociology: General Works, Theory—Social Pathology, Welfare, Criminology

ECHO. Jan. 1978-. 0705-1123. Periodical. CN. English (French). Children's Aid Society of Ottawa-Carleton, 1370 Bank Street, Ottawa Ontario K1H 7Y3 Canada. **DD** 362.70971384. *Information Bulletin, 0709-0706.*

ECONOMIC CRIME DIGEST. 0362-0697. Periodical. US. English. National District Attorneys Association, 1033 North Fairfax Street/Suite 200, Alexandria VA 22314. **LC** HV6693. **DD** 364.1630973. *Economic Crime Project Newsletter.*

ECONOMIC CRIME PROJECT. ANNUAL REPORT. (ECONOMIC CRIME PROJECT ANNUAL REPORT). 1st- 1973/74-. 0097-9643. US. English. an. Economic Crime Project Center, 1900 L Street NW/Suite 601, Washington DC 20036. **LC** HV6693. **DD** 364.16.

ECONOMIC WELFARE (FREDERICTON, N.B.). (ECONOMIC WELFARE). Vol. 1, No. 1 (Jan. 1974)-. 0711-4958. Periodical. CN. English. ir. Free. New Brunswick Teachers' Federation, PO Box 1535, Fredericton New Brunswick E3B 5G3 Canada. **DD** 331.20413711. (ctrl).

EDUCATION SERIES. Book 1-. 0459-1798. US. English. **LC** HV2353.

EFFECTIFS DES TRAVAILLEURS ASSUJETTIS A LA SECURITE SOCIALE. See Insurance.

ELATUSTUKI. Main/Corp Finland. Sosiaalihallitus. Suunnittelu- Ja Tilastotoimisto. **VFOAT** Underhallsstod. Fl. Finnish (Swedish). ir. Tilastokeskus, Valtion Painatuskeskus, PI 516, 00101 Helsinki 10 Finland. **LC** HV700.F5.

EMERGENCY MANAGEMENT TODAY. (EMERGENCY MANAGEMENT TODAY : AN INFORMATION SERVICE OF EMERGENCY MANAGEMENT INFORMATION SERVICES). Began in 1983. 0747-9085. Periodical. US. English. bw. $90.00. Emergency Management Information Services, 25 McLean Place, Indianapolis IN 46202. **DD** 363.

EMPLOYMENT DEVELOPMENT DEPARTMENT WELFARE EMPLOYMENT PROGRAMS REPORT TO THE LEGISLATURE (CALIFORNIA). Main/Corp California. Employment Development Dept. **VFOAT** Welfare Employment Programs Report to the Legislature. 1981-82-. Periodical. US. English. **LC** HV98.C3. **DD** 362.0425.

EMPLOYMENT OPPORTUNITIES - UNITED STATES. ENVIRONMENTAL PROTECTION AGENCY. PERSONNEL MANAGEMENT DIVISION. (EMPLOYMENT OPPORTUNITIES). **Main/Corp** United States. Environmental Protection Agency. Personnel Management Division. 0747-8186. US. English. an. U S Environmental Protection Agency, Personnel Management Division (PM 212), Washington DC 20460. **LC** TD180. **DD** 363.7002373.

ENCYCLOPEDIA OF SOCIAL WORK. 1st- Issue. 0071-0237. US. English. National Association of Social Workers, 2 Park Avenue, New York NY 10017. **LC** HV35. **DD** 361.003.

ENERGY CREDIT PROGRAM. Series/Titl Table H-2. 1980-81 Heating Season-. US. English. an. Department of Taxation, Research and Statistics Section, PO Box 530, Columbus OH 43216. **LC** HV1468.O3. **DD** 363.58. *Residential Heating Bill Discount and Cash Payment Program.*

ENTRAIDE SOCIALE. (L'ENTRAIDE SOCIALE). Vol. 1 (Sept./Oct. 1981)-. 0711-4567. Newspaper. CN. French. mo. $20.00 Per Issue. L'Entraide Sociale, Suite 104/72 Laval, Hull Quebec J8X 3H3 Canada. **DD** 361.97142.

ENVIRONMENT UPDATE (CANADA. ENVIRONMENT CANADA). (ENVIRONMENT UPDATE). **VFOAT** Environnement A la Une. 0714-9263. Periodical. CN. English (text in French with French text on inverted pages). ir. Free. Environment Canada, 10 rue Wellington/27th Floor, Hull Quebec K1A 0H3 Canada. **Ind/Abst** Abstr. Bull. Inst. Paper Chem. **DD** 363.700971.

ESTADISTICA DE CRIMINALIDAD. See Statistics.

ESTADISTICA PANAMENA. SITUACION POLITICA, ADMINISTRATIVA Y JUSTICIA, SECCION 631 : JUSTICIA. See Statistics.

ESTATISTICAS DA ORGANIZACAO CORPORATIVA E PREVIDENCIA : CONTINENTE E ILHAS ADJACENTES. VFOAT Statistiques de l'Organisation Corporative et Prevoyance : Continent et Iles Adjacentes. Began with 1966 Vol. PO. French and Portuguese. ir. Instituto Nacional Estatistica, AV antonio Jose de Almeida, 1078 Lisboa Codex Portugal. **LC** HV346. **DD** *Statiistica da Organizacao Corporativa E Previdencia Social.*

ESTIMATES. PART III, CORRECTIONAL SERVICE CANADA. VFOAT Budget des Depenses. CN. English (French). $9.00 Domestic, $10.80 Foreign. Canadian Government Publishing Centre, Supply and Services Canada, Ottawa Ontario K1A 0S9 Canada. **LC** HV9506. **DD** 354.7100849.

ESTIMATES. PART III, HEALTH AND WELFARE CANADA, HEALTH AND SOCIAL SERVICES PROGRAM, INCOME SECURITY PROGRAM, FITNESS AND AMATEUR SPORT PROGRAM. VFOAT Budget des Depenses. CN. English (French). $12.00 Domestic, $14.40 Foreign. Canadian Government Publishing Centre, Supply and Services Canada, Ottawa Ontario K1A 0S9 Canada. **LC** HD7102.C2. **DD** 354.7100841.

ESTIMATES. PART III, NATIONAL PAROLE BOARD (CANADA). VFOAT Budget des Depenses. CN. English (French). $6.00 Domestic, $7.20 Foreign. Canadian Government Publishing Centre, Supply and   rvices Canada, Ottawa Ontario K1A 0S9 Canada. **LC** HV9278. **DD** 354.71008493.

ETINCELLE. (L'ETINCELLE). Vol. 1, No. 1 Mar. 1981-. 0226-9783. Periodical. CN. French. ir. $7.00. l'Etincelle, 3165 Circle de Paris, Laval Quebec H7E 3E7 Canada. **DD** 362.8286.

THE EVALUATION OF JUVENILE DIVERSION PROGRAMS; ANNUAL REPORT. Main/Corp California Youth Authority. 1st- 1975-. US. English. an. **LC** HV7254. **DD** 364.3609794.

EXCERPTA CRIMINOLOGICA *CEASED.* V. 1-8. Periodical. English. ir. **LC** HV6001.

EXPENDITURES FOR PUBLIC ASSISTANCE PROGRAMS. (EXPENDITURES FOR PUBLIC ASSISTANCE PROGRAMS : (APPROVED UNDER TITLES I, IV-A, IV-B, X, XIV, XVI, XIX, AND XX OF THE SOCIAL SECURITY ACT)). 0271-3071. US. English. Superintendent of Documents, US Government Printing Office, Washington DC 20402. **LC** HV85. **DD** 338.4336160973. **NLM** W2 A S63E. *State Expenditures for Public Assistance Programs Approved under Titles I, IV-A, X, XIV, XVI, XIX, XX of the Social Security Act, 0147-4170.*

EXPLOSIVES INCIDENTS. Series/Titl ATF P. 0273-5032. US. English. an. Department of the Treasury, Bureau of Alcohol, Tobacco and Firearms, 1200 Pennsylvania Avenue NW, Washington DC 20226. **LC** HV6635. **DD** 364.164. Vols. for 1980-1981 distributed to depository libraries in microfiche.

EXTRA TO THE ONTARIO WELFARE REPORTER. (EXTRA TO THE ONTARIO WELFARE REPORTER : A NEWS BULLETIN TO UPDATE AND PREVIEW THE BI-MONTHLY ISSUES). 0821-3356. Periodical. CN. English. Ontario Welfare Council, Suite 404/1240 Bay Street, Toronto Ontario M5R 2A7 Canada. **DD** 361.609713.

EYE SPY. No. 1- Mar. 1976-. 0381-7423. Periodical. CN. English. Eye Spy Publications, Box 3250 Station B, Calgary Alberta T2M 4L9 Canada. **DD** 365.971233.

FACT SHEET BOOKLET. (STATE VOCATIONAL REHABILITATION AGENCY : FACT SHEET BOOKLET). **Main/Corp** United States. Rehabilitation Services Administration. 0098-7964. US. English. an. Rehabilitation Services Administration, 330 Independence Avenue SW, Washington DC 20201. **LC** HD7256.U5. **DD** 362.85. **NLM** W2 A R3S.

FAENGSELSVASENET. Main/Corp Denmark. Direktoratet for Kriminalforsorgen. **VFOAT** Prison Department. Danish (summaries in English). ir. Justitsministeriet, Klareboderne L, Kbenhavn 1115 K Denmark. **LC** HV8485.D4.

FAMILY SERVICE HIGHLIGHTS. V. 1- June 1974-. 0046-323X. Periodical. US. English. mo. Family Service Association of America, 44 East 23rd Street, New York NY 10010. **LC** HV88. **DD** 362.820973. *Family Service Highlights.*

FAMILY SERVICES IN UTAH. (FAMILY SERVICES IN UTAH : ANNUAL REPORT). **Main/Corp** Utah. Dept. of Social Services. Division of Family Services. 0361-4158. US. English. an. Department of Social Services, 333 South 2nd East, Salt Lake City UT 84111. **LC** HV86. **DD** 362.8209792.

FANON CENTER JOURNAL. Main/Corp Fanon Research and Development Center. V. 1- May 1980-. 0273-3366. Periodical. US. English. sa. $12.00. Fanon Research & Development Center, 12714 S Avalon Boulevard/Suite 301, Los Angeles CA 90061. **Tel** (213)603-3121. **LC** RC451.5.N4. **DD** 362.208996073.

FARM FATALITY REPORTS. 1978-. 0821-3879. CN. English. an. Farm Safety Association, Suite 22-23/340 Woodlawn Road West, Guelph Ontario N1H 7K9 Canada. **DD** 363.1196309713. *Fatality Reports, 0821-3860.*

FEDE EXPRESS. V. 2, No 2- Feb. 1979-. 0225-1124. Periodical. CN. French. bm. Federation des C L S C du Quebec, Bureau 410/7333 Place des Roseraies, Anjou Quebec H1M 2X6 Canada. **DD** 362.9714. *Information, 0705-8098.*

FEDERAL ASSISTANCE FOR PROGRAMS SERVING THE HANDICAPPED. Began with 1976. 0198-9367. US. English. an. Superintendent of Documents, US Government Printing Office, Washington DC 20402. **LC** HV3001.A2. **DD** 362.404560973.

THE FEDERAL EMPLOYMENT INFORMATION DIRECTORY. See Yearbooks, Almanacs, Directories.

FEDERAL PROBATION. Began with issue for May/June 1937. 0014-9128. Periodical. US. English. qt. $11.00 Domestic, $13.75 Foreign. Administrative Office of the United States Courts, Probation Division, Washington DC 20544. **Tel** (202)633-6226. **Ed** Lorene Lake. **Ind/Abst** Excerpta Med., Index U.S. Gov. Period., Public Aff. Inf. Serv. Bull., Soc. Sci. Index. **LC** HV9261, W1 FE234. **DD** 364.6305, 364. **CODEN** FDEPA. (cum index). bk rev. **Circ** 4,300. Also available on microfiche. Articles, reviews (books and journals), and columns on topics concerning preventative and correctional activities in delinquency and crime.

FELONS PAROLED AND DISCHARGED FROM THE STATE PENAL SYSTEM. Main/Corp Virginia. Dept. of Corrections. Bureau of Research, Reporting and Evaluation. Reporting Section. 0148-4540. US. English. Department of Corrections, Bureau of Research Reporting and Evaluation, Reporting Section, 22 East Cary Street, Richmond VA 23219. **LC** HV7296. **DD** 365.64709755.

FEMA NEWSLETTER. See Public Administration.

FINAL ANNUAL TITLE 20 SERVICE PLAN. (FINAL ANNUAL TITLE XX SERVICES PLAN). **Main/Corp** Tennessee. Dept. of Human Services. **VAT** Final Annual Title Twenty Services Plan. Began with Vol. for 1975/76. 0145-6733. US. English. an. Department of Human Services, Andrew Jackson State Office Building, Nashville TN 37219. **LC** HV86. **DD** 362.9768.

FINAL COMPREHENSIVE ANNUAL SERVICE PLAN FOR THE COMMONWEALTH OF MASSACHUSETTS UNDER TITLE XX OF THE SOCIAL SECURITY ACT. VFOAT Title XX, Final Comprehensive Annual Service Plan . . . . July 1, 1980 to June 30, 1981-. US. English. an. Massachusetts Office of Policy and Program, Department of Social Services, 150 Causeway Street, Boston MA 02114. **LC** J87, HV98. M39. **DD** 300.9744, 362.9744. *Comprehensive Annual Social Service Plan under Title XX of the Social Security Act for the Commonwealth of Massachusetts, 0738-4416.*

FINAL COMPREHENSIVE ANNUAL SERVICES PROGRAM PLAN FOR TITLE XX - SOCIAL SECURITY ACT. Main/Corp Florida. Dept. of Health and Rehabilitative Services. Office of the Assistant Secretary for Program Planning and Development. **VFOAT** State of Florida Final Comprehensive Annual Services Program Plan for Social Security Act Title XX. US. English. an. State of Florida Department of Health and Rehabilitative Services, Office of the Assistant

Sociology: General Works, Theory—Social Pathology, Welfare, Criminology

Secretary for Program Planning and Development, Tallahassee FL 32304. **LC** HV86. **DD** 361.609759.

FINAL COMPREHENSIVE ANNUAL SOCIAL SERVICE PROGRAM PLAN. Main/Corp Missouri. Division of Family Services. 1975/76-. US. English. an. Missouri Division of Family Service, Broadway State Office Building, Jefferson City MO 65101. **LC** HV86. **DD** 361.9778.

FINAL NEBRASKA COMPREHENSIVE ANNUAL SERVICES PLAN. Main/Corp Nebraska. Dept. of Public Welfare. **VFOAT** Title XX Nebraska Comprehensive Social Services Plan. US. English. Department of Public Welfare, PO Box 95026, Lincoln NE 68509. **LC** HV86. **DD** 362.9782. *Title XX Comprehensive Annual Services Program Plan, 0362-7616.*

FINAL STATE BIENNIAL COMMUNITY SOCIAL SERVICES PLAN. Main/Corp Minnesota. Dept. of Public Welfare. US. English. be. **LC** HV98.M65. **DD** 362.9776.

FINAL TITLE XX COMPREHENSIVE ANNUAL SERVICES PLAN FOR NORTH CAROLINA. Main/Corp North Carolina. Dept. of Human Resources. Title XX Branch. **VFOAT** Final Title 20 Comprehensive Annual Services Plan for North Carolina. US. English. an. Department of Human Resources, 325 North Salisbury Street, Raleigh NC 27611. **LC** HV86. **DD** 361.609756. *Final Comprehensive Annual Services Plan for North Carolina Pursuant to Title XX of the Federal Social Security Act.*

FINANCIAL REPORT ON REGISTERED CHARITABLE ORGANIZATIONS. Main/Corp Wisconsin. Dept. of Regulation and Licensing. 0147-8508. Periodical. US. English. sa. Wisconsin Department of Regulation and Licensing, PO Box 7969, Madison WI 53707. **LC** HV86. **DD** 338.43.

THE FIRE AND ARSON INVESTIGATOR. See Fire Prevention.

FISCAL YEAR REPORT. Main/Corp Pennsylvania. Dept. of Aging. **VFOAT** Pennsylvania Department of Aging Fiscal Year Report. 1979-80-. US. English. an. **LC** HV1468.P4. **DD** 353.97480084606. *Annual Report.*

FISCAL YEAR SUMMARY REPORT OF POPULATION MOVEMENT. Series/Titl Statistical Bulletin. 0362-7322. US. English. an. Wisconsin Division of Corrections, PO Box 7925, Madison WI 53707. **LC** HV7299. **DD** 365.609775.

FISH DIRECTORY. See Yearbooks, Almanacs, Directories.

FLORIDA CRIME AND DELINQUENCY. (FLORIDA CRIME AND DELINQUENCY : OFFICIAL ORGAN OF THE FLORIDA COUNCIL ON CRIME AND DELINQUENCY). **VFOAT** Crime and Delinquency. Vol. 1, No. 1 (Fall 1977)-. 0733-804X. Periodical. US. English. qt. Florida Crime and Delinquency Editor, 3715 SW 5th Place, Gainesville FL 32607.

THE FLORIDA SCHOOL HERALD. 1885. 0015-4288. Periodical. US. English. qt. $5.00. Florida School for Deaf & Blind, 207 North San Marco Avenue, St Augustine FL 32084. **Tel** (904)824-1654. Ed Cindy K Donovan. **LC** HV1796. **NLM** W1 FL852K. **Circ** 2,200. (ctrl). Stories about students and activities at the Florida School for the Deaf and Blind.

FLUTE. (LA FLUTE). V. 32, No. 1- Oct. 1976-. 0703-4725. Periodical. CN. French. mo. Free. Fraternite des Policiers de la Cum, 480 Gilford, Montreal Quebec H2J 1N3 Canada. **DD** 363.20971428. *Police, 0380-8548.*

FOCUS ON AGING (TORONTO, ONT.). (FOCUS ON AGING). Vol. 1, No. 1 (Feb. 1980)-. 0822-3637. Periodical. CN. English. qt. Free. Programme on Gerontology, University of Toronto, 455 Spadina Avenue, Toronto Ontario M5S 1A1 Canada. **DD** 362.60420720713. (ctrl).

FOOD STAMP PROGRAM. (THE FOOD STAMP PROGRAM). Main/Corp Detroit. Dept. of Public Welfare. 0091-777X. US. English. an. Department of Public Welfare, Food Stamp Program, Detroit MI 48226. **LC** HV696.F6. **DD** 362.5.

FOOD STAMP PROGRAM. STATISTICAL SUMMARY OF OPERATIONS. See Statistics.

FORT WAYNE STATE HOSPITAL AND TRAINING CENTER. 1974/75-. 0272-9350. US. English. an. Fort Wayne State Hospital and Training Center, 4900 St Joe Road, Fort Wayne IN 46815. **LC** HV897.I6. **DD** 362.3850977274. *Annual Report - Fort Wayne State Hospital and Training Center, 0537-300X.*

FORTUNE NEWS. 0015-8275. Periodical. US. English. bm. $10.00. Fortune Society, 39 West 19th Street, New York NY 10011. **Tel** (212)206-7070. Ed Daniel Rothenberg. bk rev. adv acc. **Circ** 35,000. (ctrl). Covers information about nationwide prison conditions, programs and related issues of criminal justice, especially, prison, parole, probation and alternatives to incarceration. Book reviews, interviews and operations of Fortune are also highlighted.

FORUM - CANADIAN SOCIETY FOR INDUSTRIAL SECURITY. (FORUM). **VFOAT** CSIS Forum. **VAT** Forum - Societe Canadienne de la Surete Industrielle. Jan. 1983-. 0823-0382. Periodical. CN. English (includes some text in French). ir. Free to Members, $15.00 Nonmembers. Canadian Society For Industrial Security, 55 York Street/Suite 512, Toronto Ontario M5J 1S2 Canada. **DD** 363.289. *CSIS Forum, 0229-3226.*

FORUM (JOHN HOWARD SOCIETY OF METROPOLITAN TORONTO). (FORUM). Vol. 1 (Winter 1980)-. 0229-9526. Periodical. CN. English. qt. Forum, John Howard Society of Metropolitan Toronto, 168 Isabella Street, Toronto Ontario M4Y 1P6 Canada. **DD** 365.6605.

FOSTER PARENT. See Family and Marriage.

FOUNDATION 500. **VAT** Foundation Five Hundred. 0145-6067. US. English. an. Douglas M Lawson Associates, Foundation Research Service, 39 East 51st Street, New York NY 10022. **Tel** (212)759-5660. **LC** HV97.F66. **DD** 361.702573.

FOUNDATION GRANTS INDEX (1982). See Indexes/Abstracts.

FRIENDS (COBOURG, ONT.). (FRIENDS). 0823-0250. Periodical. CN. English. qt. Free. Horizons of Friendship, PO Box 402, Cobourg Ontario K9A 4L1 Canada. **DD** 361.7630971.

FRIENDSHIP FORUM. Began with July 1978 issue?. 0709-6259. Periodical. CN. English. ir. Free. Big Sister Association of Guelph, 107 Quebec Street/Suite 2, Guelph Ontario N1H 2T5 Canada. **DD** 362.7. (ctrl). *Newsletter, 0709-6267.*

FROM THE STATE CAPITALS. JUVENILE DELINQUENCY & FAMILY RELATIONS. (FROM THE STATE CAPITALS. JUVENILE DELINQUENCY AND FAMILY RELATIONS). **VFOAT** Juvenile Delinquency and Family Relations. 1946-Jan. 9, 1984. 0016-1764. Periodical. US. English. wk. $175.00. Wakeman/Walworth Inc, PO Box 1939, New Haven CT 06509. **Tel** (203)562-8518. Projects a national perspective on developments in family law and juvenile justice, including laws affecting marital rights, child support, adoption, abuse centers, counseling and shelter programs.

FROM THE STATE CAPITALS. PUBLIC ASSISTANCE & WELFARE TRENDS. **VFOAT** Public Assistance & Welfare Trends. 0734-1601. Periodical. US. English. wk. $175.00. Wakeman/Walworth Inc, PO Box 1939, New Haven CT 06509. Reviews the administration and financing of public aid programs in states across the country. Includes welfare, aid to families with dependent children and services for the elderly and disabled. *From the State Capitals. Public Assistance.*

FRONTIERS OF HEALTH SERVICES MANAGEMENT. Vol. 1, No. 1 (Sept. 1984)-. 0748-8157. Periodical. US. English. qt. $50.00. Health Administration Press, 1021 East Huron Street, Ann Arbor MI 48104. **DD** 362.

FUND RAISING EVENT REPORT. Vol. 1, No. 1 (Sept. 1980)-. 0228-3891. Periodical. CN. English. mo. $75.00. Fundraising Event Report, 287 Macpherson Avenue, Toronto Ontario M4V 1A4 Canada. **DD** 361.7.

FUND RAISING REVIEW. Feb. 1982-. 0735-8873. Periodical. US. English. bm. $49.50. American Association of Fund-Raising Counsel Inc, 25 West 43rd Street, New York NY 10036. **Tel** (212)354-5799. Ed Fred Schnaue. **LC** HV41. **DD** 361.70973. **Circ** 3,200. (ctrl). A summary of articles, speeches, and trends on philanthropy. *Giving USA Bulletin, 0731-5678.*

FUNDING REPORT - CONNECTICUT JUSTICE COMMISSSION. Main/Corp Connecticut Justice Commission. 1976-. 0148-9291. US. English. an. 75 Elm Street, Hartford CT 06115. **LC** HV7256. **DD** 364.9746. *Funding Report - Connecticut Planning Committee on Criminal Administration, 0363-9649.*

GAZETTE DE LA BUTTE. (LA GAZETTE DE LA BUTTE). V. 1, No. 1, (Dec. 23, 1968)-. 0711-3528. Periodical. CN. French. ir. Hotel-Dieu d'Alma, 300 Boulevard Champlain, Alma Quebec G8B 5W3 Canada. **DD** 362.1106071414.

G.C.B. BULLETIN. Main/Corp Nevada. State Gaming Control Board. 0095-196X. US. English. 515 E Musser Street, Carson City NV 89701. **LC** HV6721.N45. **DD** 353.979300762.

GEMA PEKERJAAN SOSIAL. Periodical. Indonesian. ir. Jln Tanjung Ria Base-G Kotak Pos 43, Jayapura Indonesia. **LC** HV404.I75.

GENERAL ASSISTANCE STANDARDS. US. English. an. **LC** HV98. **DD** 361.609776.

GEVANGENISSTATISTIEK. Main/Corp Netherlands (Kingdom, 1815-). Centraal Bureau voor de Statistiek. Dutch. ir. **LC** HV8434. *Crimineele Statistiek, Gevangenisstatistiek en Statistiek van de Toepassing der Kinderwetten.*

GOAL ATTAINMENT REVIEW. 0147-7811. US. English. an. Program Evaluation Resource Center, 501 Park Avenue South, Minneapolis MN 55415. **LC** RA790.A1. **DD** 362.2.

GOELAND. (LE GOELAND). Fall 1982-. 0820-7518. Periodical. CN. French. qt. $12.00. Le Goeland, 860 Est rue Sauve, Montreal Quebec H2C 1Z2 Canada. **DD** 362.409714.

GOVERNMENT REPORT FOR NONPROFITS. FEDERAL. (GOVERNMENT REPORT FOR NONPROFITS). V. 1- Sept. 1979-. 0709-9134. Periodical. CN. English. sm. $37.50 Individuals and Non-Profit Organizations, $75. Corporations. A R Gabel, Editor, Government Report for Nonprofits, 287 MacPherson Avenue, Toronto Ontario M4V 1A4 Canada. **DD** 361.7630971.

GOVERNMENT REPORT FOR NONPROFITS. ONTARIO. (GOVERNMENT REPORT FOR NONPROFITS). V. 1- Sept. 1979-. 0709-9142. Periodical. CN. English. sm. $37.50 Individuals and Non-Profit Organizations, $75. Corporations. A R Gabel, Editor, 287 MacPherson Avenue, Toronto Ontario M4V 1A4 Canada. **DD** 361.76309713.

GOVERNOR'S YOUTH CONFERENCE. US. English. an. Nevada Advisory Council on Children and Youth, Reno NV 89501. **LC** HQ796. **DD** 362.704209793.

GRANTS - U.S. DEPARTMENT OF HEALTH, EDUCATION, AND WELFARE. OFFICE OF HUMAN DEVELOPMENT. OFFICE OF YOUTH DEVELOPMENT. (GRANTS). Main/Corp United States. Office of Youth Development. 0094-1387. US. English. Office of Youth Development, Commissioner US Department of Health Education and Welfare, Washington DC 20201. **LC** HV9103. **DD** 364.360973.

A GRAPHIC OVERVIEW OF INDIANA'S PUBLIC WELFARE PROGRAMS FOR FISCAL YEAR . . . . US. English. an. State of Indiana, Department of Public Welfare, 701 State Office Building, Indianapolis IN 46204. **LC** HV98.I2. **DD** 362.9772.

THE GREEN PAGES REHAB SOURCEBOOK. **VFOAT** Green Pages. **VAT** Green Pages Rehab Source Book. Began in 1976. 0196-9870. US. English. an. $20.00. Sourcebook Publications Inc, Box 1586, Winter Park FL 32790. **LC** RD755. **DD** 362.404802573.

GRIT. (GRIT : THE OFFICIAL PUBLICATION OF DELTA THETA TAU SORORITY, INC). 0883-6876. Periodical. US. English. qt. Grit, 201 Third Street, Cayuga IN 47928. **DD** 361.

GUIDE TO ACCREDITATION OF CANADIAN MENTAL HEALTH SERVICES. 1975-. 0383-2457. Periodical. CN. English. Canadian Council on Hospital Accreditation, 25 Imperial Street, Toronto Ontario M5P 1P1 Canada. **DD** 362.20971. *Standards for Accreditation of Canadian Mental Hospitals, 0383-2465.*

GUIDE TO CALIFORNIA FOUNDATIONS. Began in 1976. 0163-4623. US. English. ir. $6.00. PO Box 5646, San Francisco CA. **LC** HV98.C3. **DD** 361.76025794.

Sociology: General Works, Theory—Social Pathology, Welfare, Criminology

HACTION. Vol. 2, No. 6 (June 1982)-. 0714-7066. Periodical. CN. English. mo. Free, $5.00 Mailed Subscriptions. Handicapped Action Committee, 521-620 View Street, Victoria British Columbia V8W 1J6 Canada. **DD** 362.40971134. *H.A.C.-ing Away, 0715-3163.*

HANGUK UI WONHO CHONGCHAEK. **Main/Corp** Korea (South). Wonhocho. Korean. ir. **LC** HV415.5.

HANZAI HAKUSHO. Began in 1960. JA. Japanese. an. **LC** HV7112.

HANZAI-SHINRIGAKU KENKYU. VFOAT Japanese Journal of Criminal Psychology. V. 1-. JA. Japanese (some summaries in English). ir. Nihon Hanzai-Shinrigakkai, 11-7 2-chome Hikwawadai Nerima-ku, Tokyo Japan. **Ind/Abst** Psychol. Abstr. **LC** HV6080. **NLM** W1 HA542.

HARVEST. No. 1- Sept./Oct. 1979-. 0226-1499. Periodical. CN. English. bm. $12. Domestic, $18. US. Headway Copy Company, PO Box 4490 Station South Edmonton, Edmonton Alberta T6E 4T7 Canada. **DD** 363.45.

HASIL PENENELITIAN I.E. PENELITIAN KESEJAHTERAAN SOSIAL ANAK. VFOAT Hasil Penelitian Kesejahteraan Sosial Anak. IO. Indonesian. ir. Biro Pusat Statistik/Kantor Statistik Propinsi D K I Jakarta, JL Merdeka Selatan 8 9, Jakarta Indonesia. **LC** HV800.I56.

HAZARDOUS SUBSTANCES. Began in 1985. 0885-1751. Periodical. US. English. mo. $240.00. Executive Enterprises Publications Company, 33 West 60th Street/9th Floor, New York NY 10023-9988. **DD** 363.

HEAD START NEWSLETTER. **Main/Corp** Project Head Start (U.S.). **Series/Titl** DHEW Publication. 0017-8721. Periodical. US. English. Project Head Start, Office of Economic Opportunity, Washington DC 20506.

HEALTH AND PERSONAL SOCIAL SERVICES STATISTICS FOR WALES. *See* Statistics.

HEALTH AND SOCIAL SERVICE JOURNAL. *See* Public Health and Safety.

HEALTH & SOCIAL WORK. VFOAT Health and Social Work. V. 1- Feb. 1976-. 0360-7283. Periodical. US. English. qt. $57.00. National Association of Social Workers, 7981 Eastern Avenue, Silver Spring MD 20910. Tel (800)638-8799. Ed Barbara Berkman. **Ind/Abst** Index Med., Psychol. Abstr., Cumul. Index Nurs. Allied Health Lit., Hospit. Lit. Index, Soc. Work Res. Abstr., Abstr. Soc. Work. **LC** HV687.5.U5. **DD** 362.10425. **NLM** W1 HE266S. bk rev. adv acc. Circ 5,000. A scholarly journal for professionals who work in health and mental health care settings.

HEALTH DEVICES INSPECTION AND PREVENTIVE MAINTENANCE SYSTEM. 1st Ed., Apr. 1984-. 8756-8713. US. English. an. $75.00. ECRI, 5200 Butler Pike, Plymouth Meeting PA 19462. **DD** 362.

HEALTH FOR ALL SERIES. No. 1-. Monographic Series. English. ir. **DD** 362.1. **NLM** W1 HE3365M.

HEALTH INFORMATION RESOURCES IN THE FEDERAL GOVERNMENT. **Main/Corp** National Health Information Clearinghouse (U.S.). **Series/Titl** DHHS (PHS) Publication. 1984-. Periodical. US. English. ir. **NLM** W 22. *Health Information Resources in the Department of Health and Human Services.*

HEALTH NEWS DIGEST (HEALTH LEAGUE OF CANADA). (HEALTH NEWS DIGEST). V. 1, No. 1 (Feb. 1982)-. 0714-7392. Periodical. CN. English. bm. Free to Members. Membership $10.00 per year. Health News Digest, Health League of Canada, Suite 304/1560 Bayview Avenue, Toronto Ontario M4G 3B9 Canada. **DD** 362.105. *Health, 0017-8837.*

HEALTH SERVICES DIRECTORY. *See* Yearbooks, Almanacs, Directories.

HEARINGS IN PUBLIC ASSISTANCE. **Main/Corp** National Center For Social Statistics. **Series Corp** Its NCSS Report. Jan./June 1976-. 0161-2417. Periodical. US. English. sa. Department of Health Education and Welfare, National Center for Social Statistics, Washington DC 20201. **LC** HV91.N25B. **DD** 361.620973. *Fair Hearings in Public Assistance, 0145-9422.*

HELPER (AMERICAN SOCIAL HEALTH ASSOCIATION). *See* Public Health and Safety.

THE HELPING PERSON IN THE GROUP. V. 1- 1965/66-. US. English. ir. Ed M Casper. **LC** Z7164.C4. **DD** 016.3614.

HELPING THE EXOFFENDER. *See* Yearbooks, Almanacs, Directories.

HEVRAH U-REVAHAH. VFOAT Society and Welfare. V. 1- March 1978-. Periodical. IS. Hebrew (summaries in English). ir. 40.00. Misrad Ha-Avodah, Veha-Revahah, 11 King David Road, Jerusalem Israel. **LC** HV378.5. **DD** 361.9569405. *SAAD.*

THE HHS FELLOWS PROGRAM. **Main/Corp** United States. Dept. of Health and Human Services. VAT Health and Human Services Fellows Program. 1981-82-. US. English. an. The Director, HHS Fellows Program, 330 Independence Avenue SW, Washington DC 20201. *HEW Fellows Program.*

HIBAKUSHA. No. 1 ('82-12)-. Periodical. JA. Japanese. ir. 500 Single Issue. Genbaku Higaisha Sodanin No 0 Kai, 11 Hatchobori 7 Naku-ku, Hiroshima-shi 730 Japan. **LC** HV639.

HIGHWAY PATROLMENS FUND, STATEMENT TO EMPLOYEES. **Main/Corp** Minnesota State Retirement System. Began in 1973. US. English. an. Minnesota State Retirement System, 529 Jackson at 10th Street, St Paul MN 55101. **LC** HV8145.M6. **DD** 353.97760074.

HIHOGOSHA SEIKATSU JITTAI CHOSA KEKKA HOKOKU. **Main/Corp** Japan. Koseisho. Shakaikyoku. Hogoka. Japanese. ir. **LC** HV411.

HOIKU HAKUSHO. 1976-. Japanese. ir. 900. Sodo Bunka, 10-6 Gobancho Chiyoda-ku (102), Tokyo Japan. **LC** HV861.J3.

HOME CARE SERVICES, DAY CARE ESTABLISHMENTS, DAY SERVICES, SCOTLAND. UK. English. an. Social Work Services Group, Statistics Branch, 43 Jeffrey Street/Room 424, Edinburgh EHL 1DN Scotland. **LC** HV861.G62. **DD** 362.0425.

HOME SERVICES AND TRANSPORTATION. VFOAT Home Services and Transportation in Metropolitan Toronto. -1981. 0711-4192. CN. English. be. Community Information Centre of Metropolitan Toronto, 3rd Floor/34 King Street, Toronto Ontario M5C 1E5 Canada. **DD** 362.40483.

HOME SUPPORT SERVICES IN METROPOLITAN TORONTO. 1983-. 0822-9406. CN. English. be. Community Information Centre of Metropolitan Toronto, 3rd Floor/34 King Street East, Toronto Ontario M5C 1E5 Canada. **DD** 362.40483. *Home Services and Transportation, 0711-4192.*

HOMECARE (LOS ANGELES, CALIF.). (HOMECARE). VFOAT Home Care. 0882-2700. Periodical. US. English. mo. Free to Qualified Professionals, $25.00 Domestic, $45.00 Foreign. Miramar Publishing Company, 2048 Cotner Avenue, Los Angeles CA 90025. **DD** 362. *Homecare Rental/Sales, 0192-1673.*

HOMICIDE IN CALIFORNIA. **Main/Corp** California. Bureau of Criminal Statistics and Special Services. 1978-. US. English. California Bureau of Criminal Statistics and Special Services, 77 Cadillac Drive, Sacramento CA 95813. **LC** HV6533.C2. **DD** 312.27609794. *Homicide in California, 0098-8537.*

HOMICIDE IN CANADA, A STATISTICAL PERSPECTIVE. *See* Statistics.

HOMICIDE IN LOUISIANA. **Main/Corp** Louisiana. Criminal Justice Information System Division. 1978-. US. English. an. Louisiana Commission on Law Enforcement, Louisiana Criminal Justice Information System Division, 1885 Wooddale Boulevard/Room 502, Baton Rouge LA 70806. **LC** HV7268.A17A SUPPL. **DD** 364.15209763.

HOMICIDE STATISTICS (STATISTICS CANADA). *See* Statistics.

HOMICIDE SURVEILLANCE. (CENTERS FOR DISEASE CONTROL HOMICIDE SURVEILLANCE). 1970-1978-. 0749-2286. US. English. US Department of Health and Human Services, Public Health Service Center for Disease Control, Center for Health Promotion and Education, Atlanta GA 30333. **LC** HV6528. **DD** 364.15230973.

HOMU SOGO KENKYUJO KENKYUBU KIYO. VFOAT Bulletin of the Criminological Research Department. JA. Japanese (some summaries in English). ir. 1-1-1 Kasumigaseki Chiyoda-ku, Tokyo Japan. **LC** HV7111.

HORBUCHVERZEICHNIS. *See* Bibliographies.

HORIZON D'OR. First issue in Jan. 1972. 0701-1490. Periodical. CN. French. ir. 25 Per No. Conseil de Lage D'Or Region, Sud-Ouest du Quebec, 50 Avenue Grand-Ile, Salaberry de Valleyfield Quebec J6S 3L8 Canada. **DD** 362.63.

HORIZONS. Began with Nov. 1970 issue. 0380-4046. Periodical. CN. English. qt. Free. Horizons, 350 Rumsey Road, Toronto Ontario M4G 1R8 Canada. **DD** 362.43. (ctrl).

HOTLINE. Vol. 1, No. 1 (Spring 1981)-. 0273-5946. Periodical. US. English. qt. Illinois Department of Children and Family Services, 1 North Old State Capital Place, Springfield IL 62706. Tel (217)785-2670. *Together, 0199-1841.*

HOUSING FOR SENIORS. 1982/83-. 0823-6003. CN. English. an. $0.50 Per No. Housing for Seniors, c/o Community Information Centre, 18 Queen Street North, Kitchener Ontario N2H 2G8 Canada. **DD** 363.59.

HOW FEDERAL AGENCIES HAVE SERVED THE HANDICAPPED. *See* Physically Impaired.

HOW TO GET HELP FOR KIDS. 1980-. 0275-4819. US. English. be. Ed B Zang. **NLM** WA 22 AA1 H9.

HOWARD JOURNAL OF PENOLOGY AND AND CRIME PREVENTION CEASED. (THE HOWARD JOURNAL OF PENOLOGY AND CRIME PREVENTION). VFOAT Howard Journal of Penology & Crime Prevention. Vol. 11, No. 4 (1965)-V. 22, No. 3. 0073-3741. Periodical. UK. English. ty. **Ind/Abst** Sociol. Abstr., Soc. Welf. Soc. Plan./Policy Soc. Dev. **LC** HV8995.A1. (cum index). *Howard Journal.*

HSA/NENY NEWS. **Main/Corp** Health Systems Agency of Northeastern New York. VFOAT H.S.A./N.E.N.Y. VAT Health Systems Agency of Northeastern New York News. 8755-1241. Periodical. US. English. Health Systems Agency of Northeastern New York, 75 New Scotland Avenue, Albany NY 12208. **DD** 362.

HUBER LAW SURVEY. **Main/Corp** Wisconsin. Division of Corrections. Bureau of Planning, Development, and Research. 0094-0763. US. English. Division of Corrections/Bureau of Planning, Development and Research, Madison WI 53701. **LC** HV9305.W6. **DD** 365.6.

HUERFANO. V. 1- 1973-. Periodical. US. English. sa. Daran Inc, Box 49155, Tucson AZ 85717. Tel (602)887-9622.

HUMAN RESOURCES ABSTRACTS. *See* Indexes/Abstracts.

HUMAN RESOURCES AND SERVICES, DIRECTORY. US. English. Office of Planning and Programing, Lincoln NE 94601. **LC** HV98.N2. **DD** 362.025782.

HUMAN SERVICES DIRECTORY. *See* Yearbooks, Almanacs, Directories.

HUMAN SERVICES DIRECTORY (SAINT JOHN, N.B.). *See* Yearbooks, Almanacs, Directories.

HUMAN SERVICES IN NORTH DAKOTA. **Main/Corp** North Dakota. Dept. of Human Services. 1983-. 8755-1659. Periodical. US. English. be. North Dakota Department of Human Services, State Capitol, Bismarck ND 58505. **LC** HV98.N9. **DD** 353.9784008406. **NLM** W2. *Social Services of the Social Service Board.*

HUMAN SERVICES IN THE RURAL ENVIRONMENT. 0193-9009. Periodical. US. English. qt. University of Tennessee, 1838 Terrace Avenue, Knoxville TN 37916. Tel (615)974-6015. **Ind/Abst** Soc. Work Res. Abstr., Curr. Index J. Educ.

HUMAN SERVICES NEWS. Periodical. US. English. bm. Lincoln Action Program Public Affairs Office, 2202 South 11th Street, Lincoln NE 68502.

HUMAN SERVICES REGISTER. **Main/Corp** New Mexico. Dept. of Human Services. VFOAT State of New Mexico Human Services Register. Vol. 2, No. 31 (Sept. 19, 1979)-. 0276-9131. US. English. **LC** KFN3949.A39. **DD** 344.78903, 347.89043. *State of New Mexico Human Services Register.*

HUMAN SERVICES (WOODHAVEN, N.Y.). (HUMAN SERVICES). 0745-2616. Periodical. US. English. bw. $15.00. Human Services, 80-34 Jamaica Avenue, Woodhaven NY 11421. Tel (212)296-2860.

Sociology: General Works, Theory—Social Pathology, Welfare, Criminology

THE HUMANE SOCIETY OF THE UNITED STATES NEWS. Periodical. US. English. qt. Humane Society of the United States, 2100 L Street Northwest, Washington DC 20037. **LC** HV4702. **DD** 636.083.

HUMANISME. No. 54- Nov./Dec. 1965-. Periodical. FR. French. bm. Assoc Anciens Eleves Villiers, 77 rue de Villiers, 92523 Neully Cedex France. **Tel** 747-60-26. **LC** HS355. **DD** 366.105. *Bulletin.*

HUMANITE. (HUMANITE : ORGANE OFFICIEL DE L'ASSOCIATION NATIONALE D'AIDE AUX HANDICAPES). Vol. 1, No. 1-. 0712-2780. Periodical. CN. French. ir. Humanite, Bureau 404, 140 Ouest Place Cremazie, Montreal Quebec H2P 1C3 Canada. **DD** 362.4060714.

HUMBER HIGHLIGHTS. 0821-2465. Periodical. CN. English. qt. Free. Humber Highlights/ Humber Memorial Hospital, 200 Church Street, Weston Ontario M9N 1N8 Canada. **DD** 362.1109713541. (ctrl).

THE HUNGER PROJECT PAPERS. No. 1 (May 1984)-. 0743-6416. Monographic Series. US. English. ir. Hunger Project, 2015 Steiner Street, San Francisco CA 94115. **LC** UNC.

HUOLTOAPU. Main/Corp Finland. Sosiaalihallitus. Suunnittelu- Ja Tilastotoimisto. **Series/Titl** Suomen Virallinen Tilasto. **VFOAT** Socialhjalp, Social Assistance. Began with Vol. for 1969. 0355-4759. Fl. Finnish (Swedish with summaries in English). ir. Valtion Painatuskeskus, Annankatu 44, 00100 Helsinki 10 Finland. **LC** HA1448, HV315.5. **NLM** W2 GF5 S86H. *Huoltotilasto.*

IASSW DIRECTORY; MEMBER SCHOOLS AND ASSOCIATIONS. See Yearbooks, Almanacs, Directories.

IHSA MUNSHAAT AL-RIAYAH AL-IJTIMAIYAH. Arabic. ir. **LC** HV443.

ILLINOIS HOME ENERGY ASSISTANCE PROGRAM FY ... ANNUAL REPORT. 82-. US. English. an. State of Illinois, Department of Commerce and Community Affairs, 222 South College Street, Springfield IL 62706. **LC** HC107.I33. **DD** 362.582.

ILLINOIS HUMAN SERVICES PLAN. VFOAT Human Services Plan. Began with 1978-80. 0191-5797. Monographic Series. US. English. an. **LC** HV98.I15. **DD** 362.9773. **NLM** W2 AI3 D25I. *Illinois Welfare and Rehabilitation Services Plan.*

ILLINOIS INSIGHTS. Vol. 1, 1976-. 0275-4096. Periodical. US. English (Vietnamese). Governor's Information Center for Asian Assistance, 160 North Lasalle Street/Room 2006, Chicago IL 60601.

ILLINOIS STATE PLAN: DEVELOPMENTAL DISABILITIES SERVICES AND FACILITIES CONSTRUCTION ACT OF 1970, P. L. 91-517. Main/Corp Illinois. Dept. of Mental Health. **VFOAT** Developmental Disabilities Services and Facilities Construction Act of 1970, P. L. 91-517. US. English. Illinois Department of Mental Health, 401 State Office Building, Springfield IL 62706. **LC** HV3006.I3. **DD** 362.309773.

ILLINOIS UNIFORM CRIME REPORTS USER'S GUIDE UPDATE. (ILLINOIS UNIFORM CRIME REPORTS USER'S GUIDE UPDATE FOR . . . DATA). 0732-9849. US. English. an. Statistical Analysis Center, Illinois Law Enforcement Commission, 120 South Riverside Plaza, Chicago IL 60606. **LC** HV6793.I3. **DD** 364.109773.

IN. See The Arts (General).

IN A NUTSHELL. Vol. 1 No. 2- May 1971-. 0380-2892. Periodical. CN. English. ir. Mental Patients Association, 2146 Yew Street, Vancouver British Columbia V6K 3G7 Canada. **DD** 362.205. *M. P. A. News, 0380-2906.*

INCIDENTS OF SUSPECTED CHILD ABUSE IN MARYLAND. Main/Corp Maryland. Social Services Administration. 0092-0169. US. English. Social Services Administration, 1315 St Paul Street, Baltimore MD 21202. **LC** HV742.M3. **DD** 362.7109752.

INCOME ASSISTANCE, COMMUNITY SOCIAL SERVICES, AND MEDICAL ASSISTANCE. Periodical. US. English. mo. Division of Administration, MS OB-34F, Olympia WA 98504. **LC** HV86. **DD** 361.609797. *Income Maintenance, Community Social Services, and Medical Assistance.*

INCOME SECURITY PROGRAMS. VFOAT Income Security. 0707-3283. CN. English. Government Services, Publications and Statutes, 11510 Kingsway Avenue, Edmonton Alberta TG5 2Y5 Canada. **LC** HV109.A5. **DD** 361.6097123. *Social Services, Income Security Programs.*

INDEX TO PERIODICAL LITERATURE ON AGING. See Indexes/Abstracts.

INDIAN ECONOMIC EMPLOYMENT ASSISTANCE PROGRAM, PROGRESS REPORT. Main/Corp Washington (State). Indian Assistance Division. US. English. be. Indian Assistance Division, 400 Capitol Center Building, Olympia WA 98504. **LC** E78.W3. **DD** 362.5.

INDIAN JOURNAL OF CRIMINOLOGY. V. 1- July 1973-. 0376-9844. Periodical. II. English. sa. $14.00. Indian Society of Criminology, 2 Temple Lane, Alagappa Nagar, Madras 600 005 India. **Ed** N Pitchandi. **Ind/Abst** Chem. Abstr. **LC** HV6201. **DD** 364.0954. **CODEN** IJOCDS. bk rev. **Circ** 750. (ctrl). Covers all aspects of criminology, criminological sciences (criminal biology, psychology, and sociology, and penology) and subsidiary sciences.

THE INDIAN JOURNAL OF CRIMINOLOGY & CRIMINALISTICS. VFOAT Indian Journal of Criminology and Criminalistics. Vol. 1, No. 1 (Mar. 1981)-. Periodical. II. English. qt. $30.00. Institute of Criminology and Forensic Science, 4-E Jhandewalan Extension Rani Jhansi Road, New Delhi 110055 India. **Ind/Abst** Excerpta Med. **LC** HV7093. **DD** 364.954. **NLM** W1 IN207D.

INDIAN JOURNAL OF MENTAL RETARDATION. V. 1-. 0019-5375. Periodical. II. English. sa. $15.00. K G Agrawal, AB 6 Safdarjang Enclave, New Delhi 110 016 India. **LC** HV3004. **DD** 362.305.

INDIAN JOURNAL OF PSYCHIATRIC SOCIAL WORK. Vol. 1- July 1972-. 0302-1610. English. ir. Hospital for Mental Diseases, Kanke 6, Ranchi India. **LC** HV689. **DD** 362.20954.

THE INDIAN JOURNAL OF SOCIAL WORK. V. 1- June 1940-. 0019-5634. Periodical. II. English. qt. 10.00 South Asian Countries, 15.00 Southeast Asian Countries, 20.00 US, Canada and Europe. Tata Institute of Social Sciences, Sion Trombay Road Deonar, Bombay 400 088 India. **Tel** 551-0400. **Ed** Armaity Desai. **Ind/Abst** Women Stud. Abstr., Soc. Work Res. Abstr., Soc. Sci. Citation Index, Sociol. Abstr., Public Aff. Inf. Serv. Bull., Psychol. Abstr., Soc. Sci. Citation Index, Lang. Lang. Behav. Abstr., Soc. Welf. Soc. Plan./Policy Soc. Dev., Abstr. Soc. Work. **LC** HV1. **DD** 360.5. **NLM** W1 IN234S. **CODEN** IJSWA3. Index published separately - free - automatically sent. bk rev. adv acc. **Circ** 900. Articles are based on especially social work, welfare development, and personnel management, industrial relations, and organisational behavior.

THE INDIANA OFFICE OF COMMUNITY SERVICES ADMINISTRATION ANNUAL REPORT. Main/Corp Indiana Office of Community Services Administration. 1976-. 0148-9232. US. English. an. 26 North Meridian Street/ Suite 212, Indianapolis IN 46204. **LC** HV86.

INDOPOP NONCHONG. VFOAT Korean Journal of Humanitarian Law. V. 1-. Periodical. KO. English (Korean). ir. Taehan Choksipcha S A, 523-1 Majang-dong Songdong-ku, Seoul Korea. **LC** HV640.

INDUSTRIAL SECURITY TIMES. Began publication with July/Sept. 1964 issue. 0537-5479. Periodical. English. ir. **LC** HV8290.

INEDIT. (L'INEDIT : JOURNAL DU PERSONNEL DU C.S.S.M.M). V. 1, No. 1, (April 1982)-. 0713-3855. Periodical. CN. French. ir. Centre de Services Sociaux du Montreal Metropolitain, 1001 East Boulevard de Maisonneuve, Montreal Quebec H2L 4R5 Canada. **DD** 361.971427.

INFO 9. 0228-2453. Periodical. CN. French. wk. $.080 Per No. CSSM Service de l'Information, 1001 Boulevard Maisonneuve East, Montreal Quebec H4L 2R5 Canada. **DD** 361.9714281. *Information 9.*

INFO-ACTUALITE, 3E AGE. No. 1-. 0711-7779. Periodical. CN. French. ir. Free. Information et Communication, 3E Age, CP 267, Succursale Delorimier, Montreal Quebec H2H 2N6 Canada. **DD** 362.609714281.

INFO-R.A.A.Q. (INFO-R.A.A.Q). **VAT** Info-Regroupement des Aveugles et Amblyopes du Quebec. Vol. 1, No. 1 (Mar. 1980). 0820-7429. Periodical. CN. French. mo. Free. Info R A A Q, 2ME Etage 3740 rue Berri, Montreal Quebec H2L 4 Canada. **DD** 362.4109714.

INFORMACCUEIL. (L'INFORMACCUEIL). V. 1, No. 2 (May 1978)-. 0229-4338. Periodical. CN. French. ir. Free. Federation des Familles d'Accueil du Quebec Edifice, Blouin Ville-Vanier Quebec G1M 1E3 Canada. **DD** 362.73309714. (ctrl). *Federation des Familles d'Accueil du Quebec : Journal, 0229-432X.*

INFORMATION - ARCAD. (INFORMATION - A R C A D). **Main/Corp** Association des Rencontres Culturelles Avec Les Detenus. V. 1- May 1973-. 0702-875X. Periodical. CN. French. ir. Association des Rencontres Culturelles Avec les Detenus, Arcad 750, Croissant Frontenac, Duvernay-Laval Quebec H7G 4N5 Canada. **DD** 365.609714.

INFORMATION BULLETIN OF AUSTRALIAN CRIMINOLOGY. Periodical. AT. English. qt. Australian Institute of Criminology, 10-18 Colbee Court, Philipp Australian Capital Territory 2066 Australia. **LC** HV7171. **DD** 364.994. *Information Bulletin (Australian Institute of Criminology).*

INFORMATION - CANADIAN ASSOCIATION OF SOCIAL WORKERS. Main/Corp Canadian Association of Social Workers. V. 1- Mar. 1971-. 0315-3150. Periodical. CN. English (French). 23.00 Domestic, 27.50 Foreign. Canadian Association of Social Workers, 55 Parkdale Avenue, Ottawa Ontario K1Y Canada. **Tel** 728-1865. **Ed** Sherri Resin Torjman. bk rev. adv acc. **Circ** 10,000. (ctrl). Contains articles of interest to professional social workers and information on conferences and developments in the social welfare field.

INFORMATION - FEDERATION DES C.L.S.C. DU QUEBEC. SUPPLEMENT. (L'INFORMATION - FEDERATION DES C. L. S. C. DU QUEBEC. SUPPLEMENT). **Main/Corp** Federation des Centres Locaux de Services Communautaires du Quebec. **VAT** Information - Federation des Centres Locaux de Services Communautaires du Quebec. Supplement. No. 1- Sept. 1977-. 0705-8101. Periodical. CN. French. Federation des C L S C du Quebec, Bureau 410, 7333 Place des Roseraies, Anjou Quebec H1M 2X6 Canada. **DD** 362.9714.

INFORMATION FOR SENIORS. Began publication in 1973?. 0228-3123. CN. English. be. Free. Community Information Centre of Metropolitan Toronto, 34 King Street East, Toronto Ontario M5C 1E5 Canada. **DD** 362.609713541.

INFORMATION - HOPITAL LOUIS-H LOUIS-H LAFONTAINE. Main/Corp Hopital Louis-H. Lafontaine. V. 1- April 20, 1978-. 0228-2755. Periodical. CN. French. bw. Free. Hopital Louis-H Lafontaine, 7401 rue Hochelaga, Montreal Quebec H1N 3M5 Canada. **DD** 362.2109714281.

INFORMATION PAMPHLET - DEPARTMENT OF EMPLOYMENT AND SOCIAL SERVICES. (INFORMATION PAMPHLET). **Main/Corp** Maryland. Dept. of Employment and Social Services. 0092-9476. US. English. Maryland Department of Employment and Social Services, 1315 St Paul Street, Baltimore MD 21202. **LC** KFM1549.A73. **DD** 344.75203.

INFORMATION SHARING INDEX. See Indexes/Abstracts.

INFORMATIONAL LETTER. Main/Corp New York (State). Dept. of Social Services. Periodical. US. English. New York State Department of Social Services, 40 North Pearl Street, Albany NY 12243.

INFORMATSIONEN BIULETIN - SONS, UPRAVLENIE NARODNO ZDRAVE I SOTSIALNI GRIZHI. See Public Health and Safety.

INFORME GENERAL - DIRECCION GENERAL DE INSTITUCIONES PENITENCIARIAS. Main/Corp Spain. Direccion General de Instituciones Penitenciarias. Spanish. ir. **LC** HV7361.

INMATE AND PAROLE POPULATIONS. Main/Corp New York (State). Dept. of Correctional Services. Office of Program Planning, Evaluation, and Research. 0098-3969. US. English. an. Department of Correctional Services,

Sociology: General Works, Theory—Social Pathology, Welfare, Criminology

State Office Building Campus, Albany NY 12226. LC HV7282. **DD** 365.9747.

INNOVATIVE PROGRAMS FOR CHILD CARE, EVALUATION REPORT. (INNOVATIVE PROGRAMS FOR CHILD CARE : EVALUATION REPORT). **Main/Corp** California. State Dept. of Education. Office of Program Evaluation and Research. 0362-7063. US. English. California State Department of Education, 721 Capital Mall, Sacramento CA 95814. LC HV742.C2. **DD** 362.709794.

INSIGHT. 1977. 0145-1588. Periodical. US. English. qt. $30.00. North Carolina Insight, PO Box 430, Raleigh NC 27002. **Tel** (919)832-2839. **Ed** Bill Finger. LC HV1796.N8. **DD** 362.4109756. bk rev. adv acc. **Circ** 2,500. Public policy research on state government operations in North Carolina. A non-government organization which acts as a watchdog on state government.

INSTITUTE OF CRIMINOLOGY & FORENSIC SCIENCES BULLETIN. VFOAT Institute of Criminology Forensic Sciences Bulletin. Began in 1984. 0739-8514. Periodical. US. English. mo. $12.00. Institute of Criminology and Forensic Sciences, Box 28421, San Jose CA 95159. **Tel** (408)448-6210. **Ed** Michael M Zanoni. **DD** 364. **Circ** 200. (ctrl). Addressing issues of interest to those in areas of criminology, criminalistics, and forensic science.

INTERACTION (CALGARY, ALTA.). (INTERACTION). 0712-1725. Periodical. CN. English. qt. Free. Youth Department, Canadian Red Cross Society, Alberta/NWT Division, 737-13th Avenue South West, Calgary Alberta T2R 1J1 Canada. **DD** 361.763.

INTERCOM. V. 1- Fall 1969-. 0092-1106. Periodical. US. English. ir. Riverside City College Library, 4800 Magnolia Avenue, Riverside CA 92506. **Ind/Abst** Curr. Index J. Educ. LC HV8145.C2. **DD** 363.20979493.

INTERCOM (ST. BONIFACE GENERAL HOSPITAL). (INTERCOM). 0226-8795. Periodical. CN. English (includes some text in French). bm. Free. Department of Public Relations, St Boniface General Hospital, 409 Tache Avenue, Winnipeg Manitoba R2H 2A6 Canada. **DD** 362.110971274. (ctrl).

INTERESTED? AND IT'S YOURS. No. 1- Sept. 1976-. 0704-0709. Periodical. CN. English. ty. Free to Boys' and Girls' Club Workers Across Canada. Boys' and Girls' Clubs of Canada, 35 York Street, Montreal Quebec H3Z 1N Canada. **DD** 369.40971.

INTERNATIONAL; BULLETIN. VFOAT International. No. 1- Feb. 1976-. 0700-3625. Periodical. CN. English (French). International Social Service, 55 Parkdale Avenue, Ottawa Ontario K1Y 4G1 Canada. **DD** 361.006171.

INTERNATIONAL CARGO CRIME PREVENTION. Vol. 1, No. 9 (Jan. 1984)-. 0264-9306. Periodical. UK. English. mo. BNA International Inc, 17 Dartmouth Street, London SW1H 9BL England. LC HV6652. **DD** 380.5068. *Business and Crime, Cargoes.*

INTERNATIONAL CHILD WELFARE REVIEW. Began publication with Vol. 1 in 1947. 0020-6342. Periodical. SZ. English. qt. International Union for Child Welfare, PO Box 41, 1211 Geneva 20 Switzerland. **Tel** (022)34 12 20. **Ed** Ceri Hammond. **Ind/Abst** Soc. Work Res. Abstr., GeoRef, Abstr. Soc. Work. NLM W1 IN729. bk rev. adv acc. **Circ** 4,000. (ctrl). A communication medium for people concerned with the child, the youth, the family, social action and community development.

INTERNATIONAL EXCHANGE OF INFORMATION ON CURRENT CRIMINOLOGICAL RESEARCH PROJECTS IN MEMBER STATES. ECHANGE INTERNATIONAL D'INFORMATIONS SUR LES PROJETS DE RECHERCHES CRIMINOLOGIQUES EN COURS DANS LES ETATS MEMBRES. VFOAT Echange International D'Informations sur les Projets de Recherches Criminologiques en Cours Dans les Etats Membres. 1- 1966-. US. English (French). ir. Manhattan Publishing Company, 80 Brook Street, Croton-on-Hudson NY 10520. **Tel** (914)271-5194.

INTERNATIONAL JOURNAL OF BEHAVIOURAL SOCIAL WORK AND ABSTRACTS. *See* Indexes/Abstracts.

INTERNATIONAL JOURNAL OF COMPARATIVE AND APPLIED CRIMINAL JUSTICE. V. 1, No. 1/2- Spring/ Fall 1977-. 0192-4036. Periodical. US. English. sa. $42.00. Wichita State University, Box 95, Administration Department of Justice, Witchita KS 67208. **Tel** (316)689-3710. **Ed** Dae H Chang. **Ind/Abst** Leg. Resour. Index, Sociol. Abstr., Soc. Welf. Soc. Plan./Policy Soc. Dev. LC HV6001. bk rev. **Circ** 800. The journal is designed to provide a publishing opportunity for scholars and scientists who are interested in comparative theory and empirical research in criminal justice.

INTERNATIONAL JOURNAL OF OFFENDER THERAPY AND COMPARATIVE CRIMINOLOGY. V. 16- 1972-. 0306-624X. Periodical. US. English (summaries in French, German and Spanish). *International Journal of Offender Therapy, 0020-7497.*

INTERNATIONAL MEALS ON WHEELS DIRECTORY. *See* Yearbooks, Almanacs, Directories.

INTERNATIONAL REVIEW OF THE RED CROSS. No. 1- Apr. 1961-. 0020-8604. Periodical. English. bm. 30.00. International Committee of Red Cross, 17 Avenue de la Prix, 1211 Geneva Switzerland. **Tel** 346001. **Ed** Michel Testuz. bk rev. **Circ** 2,500. (ctrl). Articles on international humanitarian law, summary of Red Cross activities and happenings in the Red Cross world. *Revue Internationale de la Croix-Rouge. English Supplement.*

INTERNATIONAL SECURITY REVIEW. VFOAT Revue Internationale de la Surete et de la Securite. No. 1- Apr. 1978-. Periodical. UK. English (French and German). bm. Unisaf Publications Ltd, Queensway House, 2 Queensway, Redhill Surrey RH1 1QS England. LC HV8290. **DD** 658.47305.

INTERNATIONAL SOCIAL SECURITY REVIEW. Vol. 20, No. 1-. 0020-871X. Periodical. SZ. English (French, German and Spanish). qt. 40. International Social Security Association, Casle Postale 1, CH-1211 Geneva Switzerland. **Tel** (022) 99 61 11. **Ind/Abst** Int. Labour Doc., CIS Abstr., Excerpta Med., Public Aff. Inf. Serv. Bull., Soc. Work Res. Abstr., Abstr. Soc. Work. NLM W1 IN841W. bk rev. **Circ** 1,600. Analyses of technical and administrative aspects of social security, descriptive studies of schemes, recent developments around the world. *Bulletin of the International Social Security Association.*

INTERNATIONAL SOCIAL WORK. V. 1- Jan. 1958-. 0020-8728. Periodical. II. English (with some contributions in French). qt. $15.00. Sage Publications Ltd, 28 Banner Street, London EC1Y 8QE England. **Ed** Chandra Dave. **Ind/Abst** Soc. Work Res. Abstr., Abstr. Soc. Work. bk rev. adv acc. (ctrl). *Social Welfare in South-East Asia.*

INTERVENANT. (L'INTERVENANT). VFOAT Revue l'Intervenant. Vol. 1, No. 1-. 0823-213X. Periodical. CN. French. bm. $10.00. Association des Intervenants en Toxicomanie du Quebec, Bureau 25/ 1650 rue Berri, Montreal Quebec H2L 4E6 Canada. **DD** 362.2909714.

INTERVENTION. 1969. 0047-1321. Periodical. CN. English (text in French). ir. $23.21. Professional Corporation of Social Workers of Quebec, 5757 Decelles Avenue/Suite 335, Montreal Quebec H3S 2C3 Canada. **Tel** (514)731-2749. **Ind/Abst** Point Repere. bk rev. **Circ** 2,500. (ctrl). The publication publishes articles of interest to social workers, psychologists, etc. that are in the fields of health and social services.

INVEST YOURSELF. 0148-6802. US. English. an. $5.00. Invest Yourself, PO Box 117, New York NY 10009. **Tel** (212)581-5082. **Ed** Susan Angus. LC HV89. **DD** 361.70973. bk rev. adv acc. **Circ** 15,000. Definitive reference book to full-time non-government voluntary service opportunities in North America and throughout the world. 94 pages of up-to-date descriptive listings, 190 agencies, 40,000 opportunities.

IOWA CRIMINAL JUSTICE PLAN ANNUAL ACTION. **Main/Corp** Iowa. Crime Commission. US. English. an. Plans Section, Iowa Crime Commission, 3125 Douglas, Des Moines IA 50310. LC HV7265. **DD** 364.9777.

JAARVERSLAG BETREFFENDE HET EXPERIMENT VERTROUWENSARTSEN INZAKE KINDERMISHANDELING. **Main/Corp** Netherlands (Kingdom, 1815-). Interdepartementale Commissie Kindermishandeling. Dutch. ir.

Interdepartmentale Commissie Kindermishandeling, Staatsuitgeverij, S-Gravenhage Netherlands. LC HV776.

JAARVERSLAG - HARMONISATIERAAD WELZIJNSBELEID. **Main/Corp** Netherlands (Kingdom, 1815-). Harmonisatieraad Welzijnsbeleid. NE. Dutch. ir. Harmonisatieraad Welzijnsbeleid, 2500 EE S-Gravenhage Casuariestraat 32 Postbus 20201, S'Gravenhage Netherlands. LC HV306.

JAHRBUCH - DEUTSCHES ROTES KREUZ. **Main/Corp** Red Cross. Germany (Federal Republic). Deutsches Rotes Kreuz. GW. German. mo. West Kohlhammer Verlag GMBH, Hessbruhlstrasse 69, PF 800430, 7000 Stuttgart 80 West Germany. LC HV580.G3.

JAHRESBERICHT - SCHWEIZERISCHES ROTES KREUZ. **Main/Corp** Schweizerisches Rotes Kreuz. SZ. German. an. Schweizerisches Rotes Kreuz, Rainmattstrasse 10, Bern Switzerland.

JAIL COMMITMENTS AND CONFINEMENTS. **Main/Corp** Virginia. Dept. of Corrections. Research and Reporting Unit. VFOAT Commitments to Jails. US. English. an. Virginia Department of Corrections, Research and Reporting Unit/Reporting Section, PO Box 26963, Richmond VA 23261-6963. LC HV7296. **DD** 365.97550212. *Commitments to Jails.*

JIDO FUKUSHI ROPPO. **Main/Corp** Japan. Japanese. ir. 2800. Law and Statues, 27-4 Yoyogi 2, Shibuya-ku (151) Japan.

JOINT. (LE JOINT). V. 1- Jan. 1976-. 0383-8056. Periodical. CN. French. ir. Free. Centre de Services Sociaux, 201 Charles Lemoyne, Longueuil Quebec J4K 2T5 Canada. **DD** 361.971427.

JOURNAL - AMERICAN CIVIL LIBERTIES UNION FOUNDATION. NATIONAL PRISON PROJECT. (JOURNAL : A PROJECT OF THE AMERICAN CIVIL LIBERTIES UNION FOUNDATION, INC). No. 1 (Fall 1984)-. 0748-2655. Periodical. US. English. qt. $15.00. National Prison Project of the ACLU Foundation, 1346 Connecticut Avenue, Washington DC 20036. **DD** 364.

JOURNAL - CANADIAN RED CROSS SOCIETY. BLOOD PROGRAMME. (JOURNAL : NEWS OF THE BLOOD PROGRAMME IN CANADA : NOUVELLES DU PROGRAMME DE SANG AU CANADA). Feb. 1983-. 0715-8602. Periodical. CN. English (text in French). qt. Free. Canadian Red Cross Society Blood Programme, 95 Wellesley Street East, Toronto Ontario M4Y 1H6 Canada. **DD** 362.1784. (ctrl).

JOURNAL - CONSEIL REGIONAL DE LA SANTE ET DES SERVICES SOCIAUX, REGION 01. **Main/Corp** Centre Regional de la Sante et des Services Sociaux. Region 01. No. 10- Jan./Feb. 1980-. 0228-3425. Periodical. CN. French. bm. Free. Centre Regional de la Sante et des Services Sociaux, 274 rue Potvin, Rimouski Quebec G5L 7P5 Canada. **DD** 361.971477. (ctrl). *CRSSS -01, 0228-3417.*

JOURNAL DE L'AGE D'OR. (LE JOURNAL DE L'AGE D'OR). V. 1, No. 1- Dec. 1974-. 0704-7029. Periodical. CN. French. qt. $5.00. R D Publication Ltee, CP 327 Succursale K, Montreal Quebec H1N 3L3 Canada. **DD** 362.609714.

JOURNAL DU SOMMET POPULAIRE DE TROIS-RIVIERES. (LE JOURNAL DU SOMMET POPULAIRE DE TROIS-RIVIERES). V. 1, No 1 (Feb. 1983)-. 0823-7964. Periodical. CN. French. ir. Free. Journal du Sommet Populaire de Trois-Rivieres, a/s Denis Leclerc, 942 rue Ste-Genevieve, Trois-Rivieres Quebec G9A 3X6 Canada. **DD** 361.80971445.

THE JOURNAL FOR THE OFFICE OF MENTAL RETARDATION & DEVELOPMENTAL DISABILITIES. VFOAT Journal. Vol. 1, No. 1 (July/Aug. 1984)-. 8750-3328. Periodical. US. English. bm. Office of Mental Retardation and Developmental Disabilities, 44 Holland Avenue, Albany NY 12229. **DD** 362. *Giant Steps, 0199-1868.*

JOURNAL HANDICO. (LE JOURNAL HANDICO). **Main/Corp** Handico Inc. No longer published after 197-. 0317-3593. CN. French. **DD** 362.409714.

JOURNAL OF CHILD CARE. Vol. 1, No. 1 (Apr. 1982)-. 0715-5883. Periodical. CN. English. ty. $45.00. Journal of Child Care, 117 Woodpark Boulevard, Calgary Alberta T2W 2Z8 Canada. **Tel**

Sociology: General Works, Theory—Social Pathology, Welfare, Criminology

(403)251-0676. Ed Gerry Fewster and Chris Bagley. **Ind/Abst** Psychol. Abstr. **DD** 362.70971. bk rev. adv acc. **Circ** 700. Child care: research and applications for practitioners.

JOURNAL OF COMMUNITY ACTION. Vol. 1, No. 1 (Sept./Oct. 1981)-. 0277-1705. Periodical. US. English. bm. $24.00. Journal of Community Action, PO Box 42120/Northwest Station, Washington DC 20015. **Ind/Abst** Public Aff. Inf. Serv. Bull. **LC** HN49.C6. **DD** 361.8.

JOURNAL OF CONTINUING SOCIAL WORK EDUCATION. See Education (General).

JOURNAL OF CRIME & JUSTICE. VFOAT Crime & Justice. 0735-648X. Periodical. US. English. an. $22.00. Pilgrimage Press, 646 Main Street, Cincinnati OH 45201. **Tel** (606)421-4142. **LC** HV6201. **DD** 364.05.

JOURNAL OF CRIMINAL LAW & CRIMINOLOGY. See Law.

JOURNAL OF EDUCATION FOR SOCIAL WORK CEASED. 1-V. 20. 0022-0612. Periodical. US. English. ty. **Ind/Abst** Sociol. Abstr., Soc. Welf. Soc. Plan./Policy Soc. Dev., Educ. Index, Ref. Source, Soc. Work Res. Abstr., Curr. Index J. Educ. **LC** HV11. **DD** 361.0071. Available on microfilm from University Microfilms.

JOURNAL OF INDEPENDENT SOCIAL WORK. 0883-7562. Periodical. US. English. qt. The Haworth Press, 75 Griswold Street, Binghamton NY 13904.

JOURNAL OF MENTAL HEALTH ADMINISTRATION. V. 1- Spring 1972-. 0092-8623. Periodical. US. English. sa. $15.00. Association Mental Health Administration, 425 13th Street NW/Suite 1230, Washington DC 20004. **Tel** (202)638-6662. Ed Guy A Rogers. **Ind/Abst** Hospit. Lit. Index. **NLM** W1 JO76KE. adv acc. **Circ** 3,000.

JOURNAL OF OFFENDER COUNSELING. Vol. 1, No. 1 (Nov. 1980)-. 0275-8598. Periodical. US. English. sa. $16.50. American Association Counseling Development, 5999 Stevenson Avenue, Alexandria VA 22304. **Tel** (703)823-9800. **LC** HV9275. **DD** 365.66.

JOURNAL OF PRISON & JAIL HEALTH. VFOAT Journal of Prison and Jail Health. Vol. 2, No. 1 (Spring/Summer 1982)-. 0731-8332. Periodical. US. English. sa. Human Sciences Press, 72 5th Avenue, New York NY 10011. **Tel** (212)243-6000. **Ind/Abst** Excerpta Med., Psychol. Abstr. **LC** HV8833. **DD** 365.66. **NLM** W1 JO844. **CODEN** JPJHD3. Journal of Prison Health, 0192-7051.

JOURNAL OF PROBATION AND PAROLE. (JOURNAL OF PROBATION AND PAROLE : THE JOURNAL OF THE NEW YORK STATE PROBATION OFFICERS ASSOCIATION). VFOAT Probation and Parole Journal. Began with Fall 1978 issues. 0278-1042. US. English. an. $5.00. New York State Probation Officers Association, PO Box 114, New York City NY 10013. Ed Rober A Nunz. **LC** HV9305.N7. **DD** 364.6309747. adv acc. **Circ** 1,000. (ctrl). Current community corrections. Probation and Parole.

JOURNAL OF REHABILITATION. Began with V. 11, 1945. 0022-4154. Periodical. US. English. qt. $35.00. National Rehabilitation Association, 633 South Washington Street, Alexandria VA 22314. **Tel** (703)836-0850. Ed Dick Dietl. **Ind/Abst** Cumul. Index Nurs. Allied Health Lit., CIS Abstr., Hospit. Lit. Index, Curr. Index J. Educ., Soc. Sci. Index, Energy Res. Abstr., Index Med., Soc. Sci. Citation Index, Lang. Lang. Behav. Abstr., Sociol. Abstr., Soc. Work Res. Abstr., Abstr. Soc. Work. **DD** 362. **NLM** W1 JO866R. bk rev. adv acc. **Circ** 15,000. (ctrl). Contains articles of interest to both professionals and consumers in the field of rehabilitation. National Rehabilitation News, 0093-1756.

JOURNAL OF REHABILITATION. V. 1- Jan. 1935-. 0022-4154. US. English. qt. $5.00 Domestic, $5.50 Canada. National Rehabilitation Association, 1522 K Street Northwest, Washington DC 20005. **LC** HD7255.A2. **DD** 362. **CODEN** JOREA.

JOURNAL OF RESEARCH IN CRIME AND DELINQUENCY. (THE JOURNAL OF RESEARCH IN CRIME AND DELINQUENCY). V. 1- Jan. 1964-. 0022-4278. Periodical. US. English. qt. Sage Publications, 275 South Beverly Drive, Beverly Hills CA 90212. **Tel** (213)274-8003. **Ind/Abst** Sociol. Abstr., Soc. Welf. Soc. Plan./Policy Soc. Dev., Excerpta Med., Soc. Work Res. Abstr., Psychol. Abstr., Soc. Sci. Index, Lang. Lang. Behav. Abstr., Soc. Sci. Index, Soc. Sci. Citation Index, Abstr. Soc. Work. **LC** HV6001. **NLM** W1 JO869.

JOURNAL OF SOCIAL SERVICE RESEARCH. V. 1- Fall 1977-. 0148-8376. Periodical. US. English. qt. Haworth Press, 28 East 22nd Street, New York NY 10010. **Tel** (212)228-2800. Ed S K Khinduka. **Ind/Abst** Soc. Work Res. Abstr., Psychol. Abstr. **LC** HV1. **DD** 361.005. **NLM** W1 JO888U. **CODEN** JSSRDV. bk rev. adv acc. **Circ** 523. The journal is a resource for researchers, administrators, planners, and evaluators whose responsibilities include the effective delivery of social services and accountability for those services.

THE JOURNAL OF SOCIAL WELFARE LAW. See Law.

JOURNAL OF SOCIAL WORK & HUMAN SEXUALITY. VFOAT Journal of Social Work and Human Sexuality. Vol. 1, No. 1/2 (Fall/Winter 1982)-. 0276-3850. Periodical. US. English. ir. $87.00. Haworth Press, 28 East 22nd Street, New York NY 10010. **Tel** (212)228-2800. Ed David A Shore. **Ind/Abst** Psychol. Abstr. **LC** HV1. **DD** 361.3. **NLM** W1 JO889D. adv acc. **Circ** 353. A text devoted to human sexuality and medical social work.

JOURNAL OF SOCIAL WORK EDUCATION. See Education (General).

JOURNAL OF SOCIOLOGY AND SOCIAL WELFARE. Began with fall 1973 issue. 0191-5096. Periodical. US. English. ir. University of Connecticut, School of Social Work, West Hartford CT 06117. **Tel** (203)241-4717. Ed Robert Leighncuger. **Ind/Abst** Soc. Welf. Soc. Plan./ Policy Soc. Dev., Soc. Work Res. Abstr., Psychol. Abstr., Sociol. Abstr., Lang. Lang. Behav. Abstr., Abstr. Soc. Work. **LC** HN1. **DD** 301.05. bk rev. Sociological approach to social welfare issues and policies, special thematic issues.

JOURNAL OF TEACHING IN SOCIAL WORK. 0884-1233. Periodical. US. English. qt. The Haworth Press Inc, 28 East 22nd Street, New York NY 10010.

JOURNAL OF THE NATIONAL ASSOCIATION OF DENMARK. 8755-1020. Periodical. US. English. qt. $30.00. National Association of Document Examinors Inc, 22 Morgan Place, Princeton NJ 08540. **DD** 363.

JOURNAL OF THE NATIONAL ORGANIZATION HUMAN SERVICE EDUCATORS. Main/Corp National Organization Human Service Educators. 1979-. 0195-3826. Periodical. US. English. sa. National Organization of Human Service Educators, 2101 Coliseum Boulevard East, Fort Wayne IN 46805. **LC** HV88. **DD** 361.005.

THE JOURNAL OF VOLUNTEER ADMINISTRATION. 1:1 (Fall 1982)-. 0733-6535. Periodical. US. English. qt. $20.00. Volunteer Administration, PO Box 4584, Boulder CO 80306. **Tel** (303)497-0238. Ed Susan Ellis. **Ind/Abst** Hospit. Lit. Index. **LC** HV91. **DD** 361.370973. **Circ** 1,900. Model volunteer programs; research in volunteer studies; issues of national impact on volunteers; all types of programs and settings. Volunteer Administration, 0362-773X.

THE JOURNAL ON POLITICAL REPRESSION. V. 1- June 1975-. 0362-8809. Periodical. US. English. sa. $10.00. Journal of Political Repression Inc, 297 Park Avenue South/ Room 23, New York NY 10010. **LC** HV8143.

JOURNAL - ONTARIO ASSOCIATION OF CHILDREN'S AID SOCIETIES. Main/Corp Ontario Association of Children's Aid Societies. V. 9, No. 7- Sept. 1966-. 0030-283X. Periodical. CN. English. mo. $3.86. Ontario Childrens Aid Society, 2323 Yonge Street/Suite 801, Toronto Ontario M4P 2C9 Canada. **Tel** (416)481-5223. Ed Diane Cresswell. **DD** 362.709713. bk rev. adv acc. **Circ** 9,500. A compilation of articles dealing with the care and protection of children. Journal of the Ontario Children's Aid Societies, 0381-985X.

JOURNAL ST-LOUIS. VAT St Louis Journal (1977), Ephemeria Saint-Loui. Vol. 4, No. 2 (July 1977)-. 0710-2186. Newspaper. CN. English (French, Greek, Portuguese, and Oct./Nov. 1977 - Tagalog). mo. Free. University Settlement, 3553 Saint Urbain, Montreal Quebec H2X 2N6 Canada. **DD** 362.84009714281. (ctrl). St-Louis Journal, 0710-2178.

JOURNAL - WORLD RESOURCES INSTITUTE. (JOURNAL). Began in 1984?. 0883-8100. Periodical. US. English. an. WRI Publications, PO Box 260, Holmes PA 19043. **DD** 363.

JUBILEE. (JUBILEE : NEWS OF THE PRISON FELLOWSHIP OF CANADA). Fall Issue 1983-. 0824-5347. Periodical. CN. English. ir. Free. Prison Fellowship of Canada, 2171 Dunwin Drive/Suite #3, Mississauga Ontario L5L 1X2 Canada. **DD** 365.66. Canadian Jubilee, 0821-5820.

JUGENDHILFE. Periodical. WB. German. mo. Kunst & Wissen Erich Bieber, Dufourstrasse 51, Ch-2008 Zurich Switzerland. **LC** HV763.

JUGOSLOVENSKA REVIJA ZA KRIMINOLOGIJU I KRIVICNO PRAVO. Periodical. YU. Serbo-Croatian -R (text in Croatian some articles have summaries in Russian and English, with some table of contents in French and Russian). qt. $27.00. Jugoslovensko Udruzenje Za Kri, Grananicka 18, Yu 1100 Belgrad Yugoslavia.

JULGADOS DO TRIBUNAL DE ALCADA CRIMINAL DE SAO PAULO. See Law.

JURISPRUDENCIA BRASILEIRA CRIMINAL. See Law.

JUSTICE. 1980-. 0225-4115. CN. text in English and French. an. Societe Canadienne pour la Prevention du Crime, 55 Av Parkdale, Ottawa Ontario K1Y 1E5 Canada. **DD** 365.02571. Directory of Correctional Services in Canada, 0070-5381.

JUSTICE QUARTERLY. See Law Enforcement.

JUSTICE STATISTICS ONTARIO . . . . See Statistics.

JUSTICE SYSTEM IMPROVEMENT : ANNUAL REPORT OF THE PENNSYLVANIA COMMISSION ON CRIME AND DELINQUENCY. Main/Corp Pennsylvania Commission on Crime and Delinquency. US. English. an. Pennsylvania Commission on Crime and Delinquency, Harrisburg PA 17120. **LC** HV7288. **DD** 353.9748008806.

JUSTICIELE KINDERBESCHERMING. See Statistics.

JUVENILE AND ADULT CORRECTIONAL DEPARTMENTS, INSTITUTIONS, AGENCIES AND PAROLING AUTHORITIES, UNITED STATES AND CANADA. (JUVENILE AND ADULT CORRECTIONAL DEPARTMENTS, INSTITUTIONS, AGENCIES, AND PAROLING AUTHORITIES, UNITED STATES AND CANADA). VFOAT Directory, Juvenile and Adult Correctional Departments, Institutions, Agencies, and Paroling Authorities, United States and Canada. 1979 Ed.-. 0190-2555. US. English. an. American Correctional Association, 4321 Hartwick Road/Suite L-208, College Park MD 20740. **LC** HV9463. **DD** 365.02573. Directory: Juvenile and Adult Correctional Departments, Institutions, Agencies, and Paroling Authorities, United States and Canada, 0362-9287.

JUVENILE COURT REPORT. Main/Corp Nebraska Commission on Law Enforcement and Criminal Justice. 1977-. 0362-918X. US. English. Nebraska Commission on Law Enforcement and Criminal Justice, 301 Centennial Mall South/PO Box 94946, Lincoln NE 68508. **LC** HV7277. **DD** 364.3609782. Juvenile Court Report, 0362-918X.

JUVENILE COURT STATISTICS. See Statistics.

JUVENILE COURT STATISTICS. See Statistics.

JUVENILE COURT STATISTICS AND ADOPTION PETITIONS IN KANSAS. See Statistics.

JUVENILE DELINQUENTS. VFOAT Jeunes Delinquants. 0822-2770. Periodical. CN. English (French). an. Statistics Canada, Judicial Division, Publication Distribution, Ottawa Ontario K1A 0T6 Canada. **LC** HV9107. **DD** 365.420971. Annual Report of Juvenile Delinquents for the Year September 30 . . ., 0825-3080.

JUVENILE JUSTICE AND DELINQUENCY PREVENTION PLAN. Main/Corp Mississippi. Criminal Justice Planning Commission. US. English. an. **LC** HV9105.M7. **DD** 364.3609762.

Sociology: General Works, Theory—Social Pathology, Welfare, Criminology

JUVENILE JUSTICE INFORMATION SYSTEM : (JJIS)/ KANSAS BUREAU OF INVESTIGATION, STATISTICAL ANALYSIS CENTER. See Statistics.

JUVENILE JUSTICE PLAN FOR NEW JERSEY, APPLICANTS GUIDE. See Law Enforcement.

JUVENILE JUSTICE PLAN SUMMARY. Main/Corp Wisconsin Council on Criminal Justice. 1981-. US. English. an. LC HV9105.W6. DD 364.3609775. *Criminal Justice Improvement Plan Summary.*

JUVENILE PROBATION ADMISSIONS. Main/Corp Wisconsin. Division of Corrections. Office of Systems and Evaluation. Series/Titl Statistical Bulletin C. 1976-. US. English. an. Office of Systems and Evaluation, Wisconsin Division of Corrections, PO Box 669, Madison WI 53701. LC HV9105.W6. DD 364.6309775. *Juvenile Probation Admissions, 0095-4306.*

KANSAS FINAL COMPREHENSIVE SOCIAL SERVICE PLAN, TITLE XX SOCIAL SECURITY ACT. Main/Corp Kansas. Dept. of Social and Rehabilitation Services. VFOAT Final Comprehensive Social Services Plan, Title XX Social Security Act. Periodical. US. English. an. Kansas Department of Social and Rehabilitation Service, Topeka KS 66612. LC HV86. DD 361.609781.

KANSAS JUVENILE JUSTICE INFORMATION SYSTEM ANNUAL REPORT. 1981-. Periodical. US. English. an. Governors Committee on Criminal Administration, Statistical Analysis Center, 503 Kansas Avenue, Topeka KS 66603. *Kansas Juvenile Case Report.*

KASVATUSNEUVOLATOIMINTA. VERKSAMHETEN VID RADGIVNINGSBYRAER FOR UPPFOSTRINGSFRAGOR. Main/Corp Finland. Sosiaalihallitus Sunnnittelu- Ja Tilastotoimisto. VFOAT Verksamheten Vid Radgivningsbyraer for Uppfostringsfragor. Fl. Finnish (Swedish). ir. Sosiaalihallitus, Suunnittelu-Ja Tilastotoimisto, Valtion Painatuskesus, Pl 516, 00101 Helsinki 10 Finland. LC HV799.F5.

KEBIJAKSANAAN TEKNIS PELAKSANAAN PROYEK-P2S/ KEGIATAN BIDANG REHABILITASI DAN PELAYANAN SOSIAL. Main/Corp Indonesia. Direktorat Jenderal Rehabilitasi Dan Pelayanan Sosial. VAT Kebijaksanaan Teknis Pelaksanaan Proyek-Proyek Kegiatan Bidang Rehabilitasi Dan Pelayanan Sosial. Indonesian. ir. Jl Ir H Juanda No 36, Jakarta Indonesia. LC HV401.

KEEPER'S VOICE. 0274-4872. Periodical. US. English. ir. $10.00. American Association Correctional Office, 2309 State North Office, Saginaw MI 48602. Tel (517)799-8208.

KEISATSU HAKUSHO. Main/Corp Japan. Keisatsucho. Japanese. ir. LC HV7826.

KENKO TO FUKUSHI. Japanese. ir. 470. Kosei Mondai Yenkyukai, 18 Nihonbashi Kayabacho 1 Chuo-ku, Tokyo Japan. LC HV413.A2.

KENKYU HOKOKU SHU - TOKYO-TO SHINSHIN SHOGAISHA FUKUSHI SENTA. Main/Corp Tokyo-To Shinshin Shogaisha Fukushi Senta. Japanese. ir. Tokyo-to Shinshin Shogaisha Fukushi Senta, 43 Toyamamachi, Shinjuku-ku Tokyo Japan. LC HV3024.J3.

KENKYU KIYO - SHINTAI SHOGAISHA FUKUSHI KENKYUKAI. Main/Corp Shintai Shogaisha Fukushi Kenkyukai. Japanese. ir. c/o Kokuritsu Shintai Shogai, Senta 1 Toyamamachi Shinjuku-ku, Tokyo Japan. LC HV3024.A2.

KEY TO NORTH YORK. See Yearbooks, Almanacs, Directories.

KEYWORD INDEX TO TRAINING AND EDUCATIONAL RESOURCES IN AGING. See Indexes/Abstracts.

KIDS. Periodical. UK. English. 2.00. Children's Rights Publications, PO Box 70/5 Stewarts Grove, London SW3 England. LC HV751. DD 362.70942. *Children's Rights.*

KIKAN SHAKAI HOSHO KENKYU. See Economics - Labor.

KINDERCENTRA. Main/Corp Netherlands. Centraal Bureau Voor de Statistiek. VFOAT Public Nurseries. 1977-. Periodical. Dutch. ir. 10.25. Centraal Bureau voor de Statistiek, Staatsuitgeverij, S-Gravenhage Netherlands. LC HV861.N4.

KINSHIP. 0023-1703. Periodical. US. English. qt. Kinship of Ohio, Morning Star, PO Box 39188, Cincinnati OH 45239.

KIYO (KOKURITSU KOBE SHIRYOKU SHOGAI SENTA). (KIYO). Dec. 1981-. Japanese. ir. LC HV2114.H9.

KODINHOITOAPU. Main/Corp Finland. Sosiaalihallitus Sunnnittelu- Ja Tilastotoimisto. Series/Titl Suomen Virallinen Tilasto. VFOAT Hemvardshjalp, Home Help. Began with Vol. for 1971. Fl. Finnish and Swedish, with summaries in English. ir. Valtion Painatuskeskus, Annankatu 44, 00100 Helsinki 10 Finland. LC HA1448, HV315.5.

KOTO SAIBANSHO KEIJI SAIBAN SOKUHO SHU. 1986-. JA. Japanese. ir. 2500. Hosokai 1-1 Kasumigaseki 1 Chiyoda-ku, Tokyo-to 100 Japan.

KRIMINALFORSORGEN. Main/Corp Denmark. Direktoratet for Kriminalforsorgen. VFOAT Prison and Probation. Danish (summaries in English). ir. Justitsministeriet Direktoratet for Kriminalforsorgern, Klareboderne 1 1115 K, Kbenhavn Denmark. LC HV8437.

DER KRIMINALIST. Periodical. German. ir. 1.50 Per issue. Verlag Deutsche Kriminalpolizei, Muth Verlag 4 Dusseldorf II, Kaiser-Friedrich-Ring 9, Dusseldorf West Germany. LC HV6003.

KRIMINALISTIK. Began publication with May 1947 issue under title: Kriminalistische. 0023-4699. Periodical. GW. German. mo $39.77. Kriminalistik-Verlag, Im Weiher 10/PO Box 102640, D-6900 Heidelberg West Germany. Tel 6221/48 92 83. Ind/Abst Foreign Lang. Index, Energy Res. Abstr., Foreign Lang. Index.

KRIMINALISTIK UND FORENSISCHE WISSENSCHAFT. VFOAT Kriminalistik. 1-1970-. Periodical. GE. German. qt. 44,-. Deutscher Buch Export-Import, Leninstrasse 16, DDR-701 Leipzig East Germany. Tel 22900. Ed E Stelzer, O Prokop and W Durwald. Ind/Abst Chem. Abstr. LC HV6939.E3. Treats problems of general criminological theory and methodology as well as the scientific elements of criminology and, inter alia, forensic methods.

KRIMINALSTATISTIKK. REAKSJONER, FENGSLINGER. See Statistics.

KRIMINOLOGISCHE SCHRIFTENREIHE. V. 1- 1961-. Periodical. GW. German. ir. Kriminalistik Verlag, Adademiestrasse 6/PF 102640, 6900 Heidelberg 1 Germany.

KRIMINOLOGISCHES BULLETIN. VFOAT Bulletin de Criminologie. SZ. French (German). sa. Schweizerisches Nationalkomite fur Geistige Gesendheit/Lueget 29, CH-8053 Zurich Switzerland. LC HV7052. DD 364.9494.

KRIMINOLOGISCHES JOURNAL. Periodical. SZ. German. qt. 22.00. Arbeitskreis Junger Kriminolgen, Hanomagstrasse 8, 3 Hannover West Germany. LC HV6003.

KUMPULAN DATA-DATA PEMBINAAN P P.K3.A., PEMBINAAN KEGIATAN KESEJAHTERAAN KELUARGA DAN ANAK, DAN KARANG TARUNA TINGKAT KELURAHAN DI DKI JAKARTA. Main/Corp Jakarta Raya, Indonesia Dinas Sosial. IO. Indonesian. ir. Jalan Gunung Sahari II/6, Jakarta Indonesia. LC HV405.J27.

KYUKYU SHOROPPO. Main/Corp Japan. JA. Japanese. ir. 2300. Zenkoku Kajo Horei Shuppan, c/o Zenkoku Building/17 Sanei-cho, Shinjuku-ku 160, Tokyo-to-Japan.

L.A.E. JOURNAL. Main/Corp Lambda Alpha Epsilon American Criminal Justice Association. VAT Lambda Alpha Epsilon Journal. Periodical. US. English. qt. $10.00. Lambda Alpha Epsilon, American Criminal Justice Association, 4048 Marlow Court, Carmichael CA 95608. LC HV7231. DD 364.05.

LAMBTON COUNTY'S COMMUNITY SERVICE DIRECTORY. See Yearbooks, Almanacs, Directories.

LANARK, LEEDS AND GRENVILLE COMMUNITY INFORMATION DIRECTORY. See Yearbooks, Almanacs, Directories.

LANDESJUGENDPLAN : DURCHFUHRUNGSPLAN. Main/Corp Rhineland-Palatinate. Ministerium fur Soziales, Gesundheit und Sport. German. ir. Ministerium fur Soziales Gesundheit und Sport, Bauhofstrasse 4, Mainz West Germany. LC HV771.R47.

LANDSTINGENS PLANER. Main/Corp Svenska Landstingsforbundet. 1914. SW. Swedish. sm. $16.17. Landstingens Tidskrift, Box 6606, 11384 Stockholm Sweden. Tel 08 2365 60. Ed Ake Ingelmo. LC HV338. DD 361.609485. bk rev. adv acc. Concerns the county councils and their functions (health and medical care, dental service, culture, finances, administration, public transportation etc.).

LAPORAN BALAI PENDIDIKAN DAN LATIHAN TENEGA SOSIAL. Main/Corp Balai Pendidikan dan Latihan Tenega Sosial. Indonesian. ir. Balai Pendidikan dan Latihan Tenega Sosial, Jalan Laksamana Laut R E, Martadinata No 112, Badung Indonesia. LC HV11.

LAPORAN KEGIATAN KANTOR WILAYAH DEP. SOSIAL & DINAS SOSIAL PROPINSI DAERAH TINGKAT I LAMPUNG. Main/Corp Indonesia. Departemen Sosial. Kantor Wilayah Propinsi Lampung. VAT Laporan Kegiatan Kantor Wilayah Departemen Sosial Dan Dinas Sosial Propinsi Daerah Tingkat Satu Lampung. Indonesian. ir. Jln Golak Galik, Teluketung Indonesia. LC HV404.L35.

LAPORAN KERJA - KANTOR WILAYAH DEPARTEMEN SOSIAL PROPINSI KALIMANTAN BARAT. Main/Corp Indonesia. Departemen Sosial. Kantor Wilayah Daerah Tingkat I Kalimantan Barat. Indonesian. ir. LC HV404.K3.

LAPORAN KERJA - PERWAKILAN DEPARTEMEN SOSIAL DAERAH TINGKAT I SUMATERA SELATAN. Main/Corp Indonesia. Departemen Sosial. Perwakilan Daerah Tingkat I Sumatera Selatan. VAT Laporan Kerja - Perwakilan Departemen Sosial Daerah Tingkat Satu Sumatera Selatan. Indonesian. ir. Perwakilan Daerah Tingkat I Sumatera Selatan, Jalan Kapien Anwar Sastro, Palembang Indonesia. LC HV404.S96.

LAPORAN PELAKSANAAN TUGAS-TUGAS & I.E. DAN PEDOMAN PELAKSANAAN TUGAS-TUGAS. Main/Corp Indonesia. Direktorat Jenderal Bantuan Sosial. 1976/77-. Indonesian. ir. LC HV401. *Evaluasi Pelaksanaan Tugas Direktorat Jenderal Bantuan Sosial.*

LAPORAN TAHUNAN - DIREKTORAT JENDERAL URUSAN BENCANA ALAM & DANA BANTUAN SOSIAL. Main/Corp Indonesia. Direktorat Jenderal Urusan Bencana Alam Dan Dana Bantuan Sosial. IO. Indonesian. ir. Jakarta Departemen Sosial, JL IR H Juanda 36, Jakarta Indonesia. LC HV555.I55.

LAPORAN TAHUNAN KEGIATAN OPERASIONIL KANTOR WILAYAH DEPARTEMEN SOSIAL PROPINSI JAWA TENGAH. Main/Corp Indonesia. Departemen Sosial. Kantor Wilayah Propinsi Jaws Tengah. Indonesian. ir. Jalan Pahlawan No 10, Semarang Indonesia. LC HV404.J36.

LAW RELATED TO THE DEPARTMENT OF SOCIAL SERVICES PASSED DURING THE LEGISLATIVE SESSION. See Law.

LAWS RELATING TO JUVENILES IN ONTARIO. See Law.

LEADER. (THE LEADER). VFOAT Canadian Leader. VAT Canadian Leader (1976). Vol. 7, No. 1 (Aug./Sept. 1976). 0711-5377. Periodical. CN. English. mo. $4.00 Per Year, Registered Members, Boy Scouts of Canada, $7.00 Others, $9.00 Other Countries. Canyouth Publications, PO Box 5112 Station F, Ottawa Ontario K2C 3H4 Canada. DD 369.43.0971. *Canadian Leader, 0036-9462.*

LEADING CONSTITUTIONAL CASES ON CRIMINAL JUSTICE. 1973- Ed. 0272-2151. US. English. an. LC KF9618. DD 345.7305.

LEGISLATIVE HISTORY OF TITLES I-XX OF THE SOCIAL SECURITY ACT. See Law.

LEGISLATIVE REPORT ON JUVENILE PROBATION SUBSIDY. Main/Corp Nevada. Division of Juvenile Community Services. 0364-5649. US. English. Department of Human

Sociology: General Works, Theory—Social Pathology, Welfare, Criminology

Resources, 308 North Curry Street, Carson City NV 89701. LC HV7278. DD 364.6.

LEGISLATIVE REVIEW ACTIVITY, REPORT OF THE COMMITTEE ON LABOR AND PUBLIC WELFARE, UNITED STATES SENATE. See Law.

LIBEREZ LES VACANCES. (LIBEREZ LES VACANCES : PUBLICATION DU MOUVEMENT QUEBECOIS DES CAMPS FAMILIAUX). No. 1-. 0712-9599. Periodical. CN. French. ty. Free. Liberez les Vacances, c/o Mouvement Quebecois des Camps Familiaux, 49 East rue Sainte-Catherine, Montreal Quebec H2X 1K7 Canada. DD 362.5809714. (ctrl).

LIBRARY NOTES. Main/Corp United States. Social Security Administration. Periodical. US. English. mo. Library Services and Information Branch, Social Security Administration, Room 570/Altmeyer, 6401 Security Boulevard, Baltimore MD 21235.

LIFECARE INDUSTRY. 1981 Ed.-. 0738-5048. US. English. an. Laventhol & Horwath, 1845 Walnut Street, Philadelphia PA 19103. LC HV1454.2.U6. DD 362.61.

LIFELINE CREDIT PROGRAM ANNUAL REPORT. Fiscal Year 1981-. 0732-1058. US. English. an. State of New Jersey Department of Human Services, Division of Medical Assistance and Health Services CN 714, Trenton NJ 08625. LC HV1468.N5. DD 353.974900844045.

LIFELINE PROGRAM ANNUAL REPORT. Main/Corp New Jersey. Division of Medical Assistance and Health Services. VFOAT Lifeling Annual Report. US. English. an. State of New Jersey Department of Human Services, Division of Medical Assistance and Health Services CN714, Trenton NJ 08625. LC HV4045.5.N5. DD 353.974900845045.

LIGHT. Began publication with V. 3 (Nov. 1931). Periodical. US. English. qt. LC HV1571.

LINKS. 0163-2205. Periodical. US. English. mo. $45.00. Links-NAPRFMR, PO Box 160274, Sacramento CA 95816. Tel (916)451-7265. Ed Charles W Skoien Jr. bk rev. adv acc. Circ 3,000. (ctrl). National and state educational information that pertains to services for the mentally disabled.

LOCAL UNITED WAY ALLOCATIONS. ALLOCATIONS TO AGENCIES AND PROGRAM SERVICES, METROS I-VIII. VFOAT Allocations to Agencies & Program Services, Metros I-VIII. 1980-. US. English. an. United Way of America Research Development & Program Evaluation Division, 801 North Fairfax Street, Alexandria VA 22314. LC HV89. DD 361.8. *Local United Way Allocations. Allocations to Agencies and Services.*

MAANDSTATISTIEK POLITIE, JUSTITIE EN BRANDWEER. Main/Corp Netherlands (Kingdom, 1815-). Centraal Bureau voor de Statistiek. VFOAT Monthly Bulletin of Judicial Statistics. NE. Dutch. ir. 153.75. Centraal Bureau voor de Statistiek, Staatsuitgeverij, S-Gravenhage Netherlands. LC HV7354. *Maandstatistiek Politie en Justitie.*

MADRES DE PLAZA DE MAYO : BOLETIN. VFOAT Madres. No. 2 (Sept. 1980)-. Periodical. AG. Spanish. mo. Casa De Las Madres, Hipolito Yrigoyen 1442, 1089 Buenos Aires Argentina. LC HV6433.A7. DD 323.490982. *Madres de Plaza de Mayo de La Plata.*

MAGAZINES (LIBRARY OF CONGRESS. NATIONAL LIBRARY SERVICE FOR THE BLIND AND PHYSICALLY HANDICAPPED). (MAGAZINES). Began with 1978. 0161-2689. US. English. be. National Library Service for the Blind and Physically Handicapped, Library of Congress, 1291 Taylor Street NW, Washington DC 20542. LC Z5346.A2, HV1571. DD 016.3624105. Issued also in braille and flexible disk.

MAILLON. (LE MAILLON). June 1975-. 0383-7297. Periodical. CN. French. mo. Conseil de l'Age d'Or Region de Laval, 765 Roland Forget Duvernay, Laval Quebec H7E 4C1 Canada. DD 362.63.

MAINE MENTAL HEALTH PLAN. See Public Health and Safety.

MAINE'S STATE PLAN ON DEVELOPMENTAL DISABILITIES. Main/Corp Maine. Council on Developmental Disabilities. VFOAT State Plan of the Developmental Disabilities Planning Council. 0161-3979. US. English. an. 411 State Office Building, Augusta ME 04333. LC HV3006.M2. DD 362.309741.

MANITOBA SOCIAL WORKER. 0715-3481. Periodical. CN. English. mo. $10.00. Manitoba Association of Social Workers, 83 Rutgers Bay, Winnipeg Manitoba R3T 3C9 Canada. DD 361.97127.

MANUAL OF SOCIAL SERVICES IN MANITOBA. Began with 1972/73 issue. 0318-5427. CN. English. Social Planning Council of Winnipeg, 501-177 Lombard Avenue, Winnipeg Manitoba R3B 0W5 Canada. LC HV109.M4. DD 361.00257127.

MATCH NEWSLETTER. (MATCH NEWSLETTER). VFOAT Bulletin Match. VAT Bulletin Match, Match Newsletter (English Edition). Vol. 1, No. 1 (July 1977)-. 0229-5814. Periodical. CN. English. ir. Free. Match International Centre, 401-171 Nepean, Ottawa Ontario K2P 0B5 Canada. DD 362.83091724. (ctrl).

MATERNAL HEALTH NEWS. 0820-6465. Periodical. CN. English. qt. $10.00. Maternal Health Society, PO Box 46563 Station G, Vancouver British Columbia V6R 4G8 Canada. DD 362.1982009711.

MEDICAID UTILIZATION BY PUBLIC ASSISTANCE RECIPIENTS, NEW YORK CITY. 0736-9344. US. English. Human Resources Administration Office of Policy and Economic Research, 71 Worth Street/4th Floor, New York NY 10013. LC HD7102.U5. DD 362.104252097471.

MEDICAL ASSISTANCE, MEDICAID (LANSING). (MEDICAL ASSISTANCE (MEDICAID)). Series/Titl DSS Publication. 0193-9483. US. English. an. Michigan Department of Social Services, 300 South Capitol Avenue, Lansing MI 48926. LC HV86, HD7102.U5. DD 361.9774 S 362.10425.

THE MEDICARE AND MEDICAID DATA BOOK. Series/Titl Health Care Financing Program Statistics. HHS Publication. 1981-. 0743-5959. US. English. an. Free to Libraries. ORD Publications, Room 1A9, Oak Meadows Building, 6325 Security Boulevard, Baltimore MD 21207. Tel (301)594-7772. Ed Alice Young. LC HD7102.U4. DD 362.1042520973. Circ 3,000. (ctrl). Vol. for 1981 distributed to depository libraries in microfiche. Provides statistics on medicare and medicaid programs including eligibility, benefits, service coverage and limitations, utilization, expenditures, financing and administration. *Data on the Medicaid Program.*

MEDICARE, HEALTH INSURANCE FOR THE AGED AND DISABLED. SELECTED STATE DATA. Series/Titl Health Care Financing Program Statistics. HHS Publication. 1973-1977-. 0731-180X. US. English. Ords Publications, Oak Meadows Building/Room 1E9, 6340 Security Boulevard, Baltimore MD 21235. NLM W2 A H24M. *Medicare. Selected State Data, 0090-979X.*

MEDICARE, HEALTH INSURANCE FOR THE AGED AND DISABLED. SUMMARY-UTILIZATION AND REIMBURSEMENT BY PERSON. Series/Titl Health Care Financing Program Statistics. HCFA Pub. VFOAT Summary-Utilization and Reimbursement by Person. 1975-. 0730-143X. US. English. NLM W2 A S63ME. *Medicare, Health Insurance for the Aged and Disabled. Section 1.2, Summary Utilization-and Reimbursement by Person.*

MEDICARE, HEALTH INSURANCE FOR THE AGED. LENGTH OF STAY FOR SELECTED DIAGNOSES, SURGICAL PROCEDURES AND DISCHARGE CHARACTERISTICS. Series/Titl DHEW Publication, No. (SSA). VFOAT Length of Stay for Selected Diagnoses, Surgical Procedures and Discharge Characteristics. 1971-. 0363-5007. Periodical. US. English. an. LC RA981.A2. DD 362.110973. NLM W2 A S63MB. *Medicare, Health Insurance for the Aged. Length of Stay by Diagnosis, 0093-772X.*

MEDICARE MEDICAID INFORMATION. V. 1- July 1976-. 0193-2152. Periodical. US. English. ir. $150.00. Healthcare Publications, 1341 G Street NW, Washington DC 20005. Tel (202)347-5500. NLM W1 ME5509D.

MEDICARE: PARTICIPATING PROVIDERS AND SUPPLIERS OF HEALTH SERVICES. (MEDICARE, PARTICIPATING PROVIDERS AND SUPPLIERS OF HEALTH SERVICES). Series/Titl Health Care Financing Notes. HHS Publication. VFOAT Participating Providers and Suppliers of Health Services. 1979-. 0731-3055. US. English. an. Free to Libraries. Ords Publications, Oak Meadows Building/Room 1A9, 6325 Security Boulevard, Baltimore MD 21235. Tel (301)594-9346. Ed Linda Cantale. NLM W2 A H24MB. Circ 3,000. (ctrl). Presents 83 data on the number of providers and suppliers of services certified to participate in the medicare program.

MEDICARE: USE OF HOSPITAL OUTPATIENT SERVICES. (MEDICARE, USE OF HOSPITAL OUTPATIENT SERVICES). Series/Titl Health Care Financing Notes. 1974-1977-. 0275-4827. US. English. an. Free to Libraries. Ords Publications, Oak Meadows Building, Room 1-A-9, 6325 Security Boulevard, Baltimore MD 21235. Tel (301)594-9346. Ed Linda Cantale. NLM W2 A H63MB. Circ 2,000. (ctrl). Presents data on use of hospital, outpatient services by aged and disabled medicare beneficiaries in 1980.

MEMBERSHIP - CAHRO. (MEMBERSHIP). Main/Corp Canadain Association of Housing and Renewal Officials. VAT Membership - Canadian Association of Housing and Renewal Officials. 0713-7028. CN. English (includes some test in French). Cahro, PO Box 1395, Kingston Ontario K7L 5C6 Canada. DD 363.506071.

MEMBERSHIP DIRECTORY - AMERICAN ASSOCIATION OF HOMES FOR THE AGING. See Yearbooks, Almanacs, Directories.

MEMBERSHIP DIRECTORY - NATIONAL SOCIETY OF FUND RAISING EXECUTIVES. See Yearbooks, Almanacs, Directories.

MENTAL HANDICAP : JOURNAL OF THE BRITISH INSTITUTE OF MENTAL HANDICAP. Vol. 10, No. 1 (Mar. 1982)-. 0261-9997. Periodical. UK. English. qt $16.09. BIMH Publications, Wolverhampton Road, Kidderminster, Worcs DY 10 PP England. Tel (0562)851428. Ed S J Newbould and G B Simon. NLM W1 ME9229P. bk rev. adv acc. Circ 3,500. Original articles on mental and multiple handicap. Of practical application by professionals and families providing services to people with mental handicaps. Book reviews and letters. Apex (Kidderminster, Hereford and Worcester).

MENTAL HEALTH. (MENTAL HEALTH : NATIONAL NEWSLETTER OF THE CANADIAN MENTAL HEALTH ASSOCIATION). VFOAT Sante Mentale. VAT Sante Mentale (Toronto). Vol. 3, No. 1 (Sept. 1979)-. 0821-3305. Periodical. CN. English (with French text on inverted pages). qt. DD 362.206071. *Mental Health News (Toronto, Ont. : 1977), 0705-811X.*

MENTAL HEALTH AND MENTAL RETARDATION SERVICES ANNUAL STATISTICAL REPORT. See Statistics.

MENTAL HEALTH, RETARDATION AND HOSPITALS. Main/Corp Rhode Island. Dept. of Mental Health, Retardation and Hospitals. 1970/71-. 0094-291X. US. English. an. A J Forand Buildings 600 New London Avenue, Cranston RI 02920. LC RA790.65.R4. DD 362.209745.

MENTAL HEALTH STATE PLAN. Main/Corp South Dakota. Dept. of Social Services. 0146-7905. US. English. LC RA790.65.S8. DD 362.209783.

THE MENTAL HEALTH YEARBOOK/DIRECTORY. See Yearbooks, Almanacs, Directories.

MICHIGAN FOUNDATION DIRECTORY. See Yearbooks, Almanacs, Directories.

MICHIGAN STATE PLAN FOR COMPREHENSIVE MENTAL HEALTH SERVICES. Main/Corp Michigan. Dept. of Mental Health. 0148-8945. US. English. an. LC RA790.65.M5. DD 362.209774.

MIGRANT SERVICES STATISTICAL REPORT. See Statistics.

MINNESOTA AID TO FAMILIES WITH DEPENDENT CHILDREN FOR FISCAL YEAR . . . . US. English. an. LC HV699. DD 362.71309776. *Aid to Families with Dependent Children.*

MINNESOTA ALCOHOL PROGRAMS FOR HIGHWAY SAFETY. See Public Health and Safety.

Sociology: General Works, Theory—Social Pathology, Welfare, Criminology

MINNESOTA CHILDREN UNDER STATE GUARDIANSHIP AS DEPENDENT/NEGLECTED, YEAR ENDING JUNE 30 ... ANNUAL REPORT. 1980-. US. English. an. LC HV990.M6. DD 362.7309776. *Minnesota Children Under State Guardianship as Dependent and/or Neglected, 0148-2262.*

MINNESOTA COMPREHENSIVE ANNUAL SERVICES PROGRAM PLAN. Main/Corp Minnesota. Dept. of Public Welfare. 1975/76-. 0363-0935. US. English. an. Department of Public Welfare, Centennial Office Building, St Paul MN 55155. LC HV86. DD 361.9776.

MINNESOTA GENERAL ASSISTANCE ANNUAL REPORT. Main/Corp Minnesota. Dept. of Public Welfare. Operations Review Division. Reports and Statistics. 1977-8-. US. English. an. LC HV98.M65. DD 361.609776. *Minnesota General Assistance Annual Report.*

MINNESOTA INCOME MAINTENANCE, RECIPIENT RATES PER 1000 POPULATION. Main/Corp Minnesota. Dept. of Public Welfare. Research and Statistics Division. US. English. LC HV86. DD 362.58209776.

MINNESOTA MEDICAL ASSISTANCE BIENNIAL REPORT DATA. Main/Corp Minnesota. Dept. of Public Welfare. Research and Statistics Division. Income Maintenance Section. 0085-347X. Periodical. US. English. be. LC HD7102.U5. DD 362.10425209776.

MINNESOTA WOMAN'S YEARBOOK. See Yearbooks, Almanacs, Directories.

MINSEI IIN JIDO IIN NO TEBIKI. Main/Corp Tokyo. Minseikyoku. JA. Japanese. ir. Tokyo-to Minseikyoku, 8-1 Marunouchi, Chiyoda-ku, Tokyo Japan. LC HV415.T6.

MINUTES OF PROCEEDINGS AND EVIDENCE OF THE SPECIAL COMMITTEE ON THE DISABLED AND THE HANDICAPPED. Main/Corp Canada. Parliament. House of Commons. Special Committee on the Disabled and the Handicapped. VFOAT Proces-Verbaux et Temoignages du Comite Special Concernant les Invalides et les Handicapes. Issue No. 1 (June 11/July 9, 1980)-. 0826-3183. CN. English (text in French in parallel columns). Canadian Government Printing Centre, Supply and Services Canada, Hull Quebec K1A 0S9 Canada. LC HV1559.C2. DD 362.40971.

MINUTES OF PROCEEDINGS AND EVIDENCE OF THE SUB-COMMITTEE ON THE PENITENTIARY SYSTEM IN CANADA. Main/Corp Canada. Parliament. House of Commons. Sub-Committee on the Penitentiary System in Canada. VFOAT Proces-Verbaux et Temoignages du Sous-Comite sur le Regime d'Institutions Penitentiaires au Canada. Oct. 26, 1976-. Periodical. CN. English (French in parallel columns). Printing and Publishing, Supply and Services Canada, Ottawa Ontario K1A 0S9 Canada. LC HV7315. DD 365.971.

MISSION IMPOSSIBLE. (MISSION IMPOSSIBLE : JOURNAL INTERNE DU CENTRE DE SERVICES SOCIAUX DU CENTRE DU QUEBEC). Main/Corp Centre de Services Sociaux du Centre du Quebec. Vol. 1, No 1 (Oct. 1983)-. 0822-9619. Periodical. CN. French. ir. Free. CSSCQ, C P 1330, Trois-Rivieres, Quebec G9A 5L2 Canada. DD 361.971445.

MISSOURI TITLE XX PROPOSED COMPREHENSIVE SERVICE PLAN. Main/Corp Missouri. Dept. of Social Services. VFOAT Title 20 Proposed Comprehensive Service Plan. 1982-. US. English. an. Department of Social Services, Broadway State Office Building, Attn: Division of Planning and Budget, Jefferson City MO 65102. LC HV98.M8. DD 353.9778008406. *Proposed Comprehensive Annual Social Services Program Plan.*

MIT PRESS SERIES IN HEALTH AND PUBLIC POLICY. VFOAT M.I.T. Press Series in Health and Public Policy. VAT Massachusetts Institute of Technology Press Series in Health and Public Policy. 1-. 0277-8637. Monographic Series. US. English. MIT Press, Massachusetts Institute of Technology, Cambridge MA 02142. Ed Jeffrey E Harris. DD 362.1. NLM W1 MI938.

THE MITCHELL GUIDE. NEW YORK CITY. VFOAT Mitchell New York City. 0748-8556. US. English. be. $145.00. Mitchell Guide, 195 Nassau Street, PO Box 413, Princeton NJ 08542. LC HV99.N59. DD 361.76320257471.

MITTEILUNGEN - ARBEITSGEMEINSCHAFT FUR JUGENDHILFE. Main/Corp Arbeitsgemeinschaft fur Jugendhilfe. Periodical. GW. German. ir. 5300 Bonn 1 Haager Weg 44, Bonn W Germany. LC HV763.

MITTEILUNGEN AUS STATISTIK UND VERWALTUNG DER STADT WIEN. AU. German. qt. Stadt Wien Geschaftsgruppe, Rathaus, 5 Stiege, 1082 Wien Austria. LC HD7337.V3. DD 363.50943613.

MITTEILUNGEN FUR VERTRIEBENE, FLUCHTLINGE, AUSSIEDLER, HEIMKEHRER, POLITISCHE HAFTLINGE. Periodical. German. qt. Der Hessische Sozialminister, Adolfsallee 53, 62 Wiesbaden West Germany. LC HV640.4.G3. DD 362.87094341. *Mitteilungen fur Vertriebene, Fluchtlinge, Diregssachgeschadigte, Heimkehrer, Politische Haftlinge.*

MONOGRAPH SERIES - CRIMINAL LAW EDUCATION AND RESEARCH CENTER. See Law.

MONOGRAPH SERIES - WISCONSIN UNIVERSITY INSTITUTE FOR RESEARCH ON POVERTY. Main/Corp University of Wisconsin. Institute for Research on Poverty. US. English. ir. Academic Press, 4805 Sand Lake Road, Orlando FL 32887. Tel (305)345-4100.

MONOGRAPH - UNIVERSITY OF WASHINGTON. CENTER FOR SOCIAL WORK RESEARCH. (MONOGRAPH). No. 1-. 0883-7643. Monographic Series. US. English. Center for Social Welfare Research, University of Washington, School of Social Work JH-30, Seattle WA 98195. DD 361.

MONTANA AGING SERVICES PROGRAM BOOK. VFOAT Aging Services Bureau Resource Book. 0270-3823. US. English. an. Aging Services Bureau, PO Box 4210, 111 Sanders, Helena MT 59601. LC HV1468.M9. DD 362.6025786. *Montana State Aging Services Bureau Resource Book, 0097-7551.*

MONTANA COMPREHENSIVE PLAN FOR CRIMINAL JUSTICE IMPROVEMENT. Main/Corp Montana. Board of Crime Control. VFOAT Comprehensive Plan for Criminal Justice Improvement. US. English. an. Montana Board of Crime Control, 1336 Helena Avenue, Helena MT 59601. LC HV7276. DD 364.9786. *Montana Plan for Criminal Justice Improvement.*

MONTANA HUMAN SERVICES DIRECTORY. See Yearbooks, Almanacs, Directories.

MONTHLY STATISTICAL REPORT. See Statistics.

MONTHLY STATISTICAL REPORT. See Statistics.

MONTHLY STATISTICAL REPORT - STATE OF NEW MEXICO, INCOME SUPPORT DIVISION. See Statistics.

MONTHLY STATISTICAL SUMMARY REPORT - STATE OF OHIO, DEPARTMENT OF MENTAL HEALTH AND MENTAL RETARDATION, DIVISION OF BUSINESS ADMINISTRATION, BUREAU OF STATISTICS. See Statistics.

MOVING FORWARD. Vol. 1, No. 1 (Nov., Dec. 1984 1984)-. 0748-9277. Periodical. US. English. bm. $6.00. Moving Forward, PO Box 1304, la Canada CA 91011. DD 362 #2 11.

MUZZLE POINT. Apr. 1969-. 0226-4498. CN. English. ir. Free. Hunter and Firearm Safety, PO Box 24 1495 Saint James Street, Winnipeg Manitoba R3H 0W9 Canada. DD 363.1097127.

NACHRICHTENDIENST. Main/Corp Deutscher Verein fur Offentliche and Private Fursorge. Began publication in 1920. 0012-1185. Periodical. GW. German. mo. Deutscher Verein F Oeffentlich & Private Fuersorge, 6 Frankfurt Main 50 West Germany. LC HV24.

THE NASW PROFESSIONAL SOCIAL WORKERS' DIRECTORY. See Yearbooks, Almanacs, Directories.

NASW REGISTER OF CLINICAL SOCIAL WORKERS. Main/Corp National Association of Social Workers. 1st- Ed. 0277-0695. US. English. be. National Association of Social Workers, 7981 Eastern Avenue, Silver Spring MD 20910. Tel (301)565-0333. LC HV89. DD 361.002573. NLM HV 89 N1112.

NATIONAL CRIMINAL JUSTICE THESAURUS. 0198-6546. US. English. an. National Criminal Justice, Reference Service Box 6000, Rockville MD 20850. LC Z695.1.C84. DD 025.49364.

NATIONAL DIRECTORY OF CHILD ABUSE SERVICES AND INFORMATION. See Yearbooks, Almanacs, Directories.

NATIONAL DIRECTORY OF CHILDREN & YOUTH SERVICES. See Yearbooks, Almanacs, Directories.

NATIONAL JAIL AND ADULT DETENTION DIRECTORY. See Yearbooks, Almanacs, Directories.

THE NATIONAL JOURNAL OF CRIMINAL DEFENSE CEASED. V. 1-7. 0098-9533. US. English. sa. Ind/Abst Public Aff. Inf. Serv. Bull. LC K14. DD 345.730505.

NATIONAL LIFELINER. (THE NATIONAL LIFELINER). V. 12, No. 2- July 1979-. 0709-8677. Periodical. CN. English. qt. Royal Life Saving Society, Canada National Office, 550 Church Street, Toronto Ontario M4Y 2E1 Canada. DD 363.10971. *Lifeliner, 0706-7925.*

NATIONAL NEWS LETTER - FEDERATION OF MILITARY AND UNITED SERVICES INSTITUTES OF CANADA. See Military Science.

NATIONAL NEWSLETTER - CANADIAN ASSOCIATION OF SEXUAL ASSAULT CENTRES. (THE NATIONAL NEWSLETTER). VFOAT Les Nouvelles Nationales. 0824-5045. Periodical. CN. English. bm. Canadian Association of Sexual Assualt Centres, 4-45 Kingsway, Vancouver British Columbia V5T 3H7 Canada. DD 362.8830971.

THE NATIONAL PRISON DIRECTORY : ORGANIZATIONAL PROFILES OF PRISON REFORM GROUPS IN THE UNITED STATES. See Yearbooks, Almanacs, Directories.

NATIONAL SERVICE NEWSLETTER. No. 1- Aug. 1966-. US. English. $10.00. 5140 Sherier Pl NW, Washington DC 20016. Tel (202)244-5828. Ed Donald J Eberly. bk rev. Circ 1,000. Describes latest developments in youth services and conservation corps.

NATIVE SISTERHOOD. Began publication in 1969?. 0703-9190. Periodical. CN. English. ir. $2.50. Native Sisterhood, Box 515, Kingston Ontario K7L 4WT Canada. DD 365.971372.

NCPI HOTLINE. Main/Corp University of Louisville. National Crime Prevention Institute. VAT National Crime Prevention Institute Hotline. Periodical. US. English. mo. National Crime Prevention, Institute School of Police Administration, University of Louisville, Shelby Campus, Louisville KY 40222. *NCPI Associates Newsletter.*

NCSA NEWSLETTER. 0824-4820. Periodical. CN. English. bm. Free. Native Counselling Services of Alberta, 9912-106 Street, Edmonton Alberta T5K 1C5 Canada. DD 362.58. *Native Counselling Services of Alberta News, 0824-4820.*

NEBRASKA COMPREHENSIVE CRIMINAL JUSTICE PLAN. Main/Corp Nebraska Commission on Law Enforcement and Criminal Justice. VFOAT Nebraska Criminal Justice Plan. US. English. an. Nebraska Commission on Law Enforcement and Criminal Justice, 301 Centinnial Mall S, Lincoln NE 68509. LC HV7277. DD 364.978205.

NEBRASKA STATE PLAN FOR REHABILITATION FACILITIES AND SHELTERED WORKSHOPS. Main/Corp Nebraska. Division of Rehabilitation Services. 0090-533X. US. English. an. Nebraska Department of Education, Division of Rehabilitation Services, State Office in Lincoln, 301 Centennial Mall 5, Lincoln NE 68509. LC HD7256.U6. DD 353.97820084.

NEBRASKA STATE PLAN REHABILITATION SERVICES. Main/Corp Nebraska. Division of Rehabilitation Services. US. English. an. LC HD7256.U6. DD 353.9782008484.

NETWORK. (NETWORK : NIAGARA'S HUMAN SERVICES NEWSLETTER). VFOAT Niagara's Human Services Newsletter. Vol. 1, No. 1 (Summer 1984)-.

Sociology: General Works, Theory—Social Pathology, Welfare, Criminology

0827-2417. Periodical. CN. English. qt. Free. Information Niagara, 5017 Victoria Avenue, Niagara Falls Ontario L2E 4C9 Canada. DD 362.971338.

NEVADA COMPREHENSIVE CRIMINAL JUSTICE PLAN. Main/Corp Nevada. Commission on Crime, Delinquency, and Corrections. US. English. Nevada Commission of Crime, Delinquency and Corrections, Carson City NV 89710. LC HV7278. DD 364.979305. *State of Nevada Comprehensive Criminal Justice Plan.*

NEW DIRECTIONS (WINNIPEG, MAN.). (NEW DIRECTIONS). Vol. 1, No. 1 (Oct. 1980)-. 0712-2101. Periodical. CN. English. bm. Free with Membership. New Directions CAMR, 46-825 Sherbrooke Street, Winnipeg Manitoba R3A 1M5 Canada. DD 362.30971274.

NEW ENGLAND JOURNAL OF HUMAN SERVICES. VFOAT Human Services. Vol. 1, issue 1 (Winter 1981)-. 0277-996X. Periodical. US. English. qt. $35.00. Osiris Press Inc, PO Box 529, Canton MA 02021. Tel (617)828-8450. Ind/Abst Hospit. Lit. Index, Sociol. Abstr., Public Aff. Inf. Serv. Bull. LC HV1. DD 362.974. NLM W1 NE387T.

NEW ENGLAND JOURNAL ON PRISON LAW CEASED. V. 1-8. 0095-7364. Periodical. US. English. sa. $10.00. 126 Newbury Street 02116. LC K14. DD 344.7303505.

NEW HAMPSHIRE CRIMINAL CODE : R.S.A. TITLE LXII, AS AMENDED THROUGH JULY 1975. Main/Corp New Hampshire. US. English. ir. Equity Publishing Company, Orford NH 03777. Tel (603)353-4351. (cum index).

NEW HORIZONS IN CORRECTIONS; ANNUAL REPORT. Main/Corp Missouri. Division of Corrections. 0147-5290. US. English. an. Division of Corrections, 911 Missouri Boulevard, Jefferson City MO 65101. LC HV7275. DD 353.977800849.

THE NEW JERSEY MITCHELL GUIDE. (THE NEW JERSEY MITCHELL GUIDE : FOUNDATIONS, CORPORATIONS, AND THEIR MANAGERS). VFOAT Mitchell Guide. 0743-9601. US. English. be. $35.00. Mitchell Guide, 195 Nassau Street, PO Box 412, Princeton NJ 08540. LC HV98.N5. DD 361.7632025749. *Directory of New Jersey Foundations, 0743-9598.*

THE NEW MEXICO PROGRESS. V. 1- Mar. 1909-. Periodical. US. English. mo. School For The Deaf, 1060 Cerrillos Raod, Santa FE NM 87501. Tel (505)982-9756. LC HV2561.

NEW RESEARCH IN MENTAL HEALTH. 1975-. 8756-260X. Periodical. US. English. Ohio Department of Mental Health, House of Program Evaluation and Research, State Office Tower Room 1340J, 30 East Broad Street, Columbus OH 43215. DD 362.

NEW SPIRIT. Feb. 1979-. 0190-1168. Periodical. US. English. mo. $10.00. National Center for Community Action, 1328 New York Avenue Northwest, Washington DC 20005. LC HV95. DD 361.60973.

NEW YORK STATE CRIMINAL LAW REVIEW. See Law.

NEWS AND ROUND TABLE. V. 1- 19 -. Periodical. US. English. bm. $25.00. United Neighboorhood Centers of America, 232 Madison Avenue, New York NY 10016. Tel (212)679-6110. Ed Walter L Smart. bk rev. Circ 1,200. (ctrl). Articles related to the national organization and its local affiliates and other social welfare news.

NEWS - ASSISTANCE LEAGUE OF SOUTHERN CALIFORNIA. (NEWS). Main/Corp Assistance League of Southern California. Vol. 1, No. 1 (Mar. 1982)-. 0736-1459. Periodical. US. English. qt. Assistance League of Southern California, 1370 North Street/Andrews Place, Los Angeles CA 90028. *Assistance League News.*

NEWS BULLETIN OF THE TASK FORCE ON TEENAGE PREGNANCY AND PARENTHOOD. 0821-5545. Periodical. CN. English. ir. 10.00. Vancouver YWCA, 580 Burrard Street, Vancouver British Columbia V6C 2K9 Canada. Tel (604)683-2531. Ed Mary Douglas-Crampton. DD 362.8392088055. bk rev. Circ 1,700. (ctrl). Social service, educational and medical programs information relating to teenage pregnancy and parenthood.

NEWS FROM THE CENTRE - INSTITUTE FOR NONPROFIT ORGANIZATIONS. Main/Corp Institute for Nonprofit Organizations. Began publication in 1979 (V. 1, No. 4). 0225-0446. Periodical. CN. English. ir. Free to Members. Institute for Nonprofit Organizations, 3rd Floor/287 MacPherson Avenue, Toronto Ontario M4V 1A4 Canada. DD 361.7630971. *News from the Centre, 0225-0470.*

NEWS - INTERNATIONAL CHRISTIAN AID. (NEWS). VFOAT ICA News. VAT ICA News (1983), International Christian Aid News (1983). 0824-684X. Periodical. CN. English. bm. Free to Donors. ICA, PO Box 5090, Burlington Ontario L7R 4G5 Canada. DD 361.75. *ICA News (Burlington, Ont.), 0824-6831.*

THE NEWS LETTER. Main/Corp India (Republic). Dept. of Social Welfare. Periodical. English. ir. Room No. 633, 'A' Wing8 Shastri Bhavan 110001 India. LC HV391. DD 362.954.

NEWS LETTER - ONTARIO ASSOCIATION OF FAMILY SERVICE AGENCIES. (NEWS LETTER). Jan. 9th, 1976-. 0227-6771. Periodical. CN. English. mo. Free. Ontario Association of Family Service Agencies, 17 Dundonald Street, Toronto Ontario M4Y 1K5 Canada. DD 362.8209713.

NEWSLETTER - INTERNATIONAL PRISONERS AID ASSOCIATION. Main/Corp International Prisoners Aid Association. 0195-7252. Periodical. US. English. ty. $5.00. International Prisoners Aid Association, IPAA Treasurer, 436 West Wisconsin Avenue, Milwaukee WI 53203.

NEWSLETTER (MISSOURI. STATE EMERGENCY MANAGEMENT AGENCY). (NEWLETTER). Vol. 29, No. 1 (July/ Aug. 1982)-. Periodical. US. English. bm. LC HV555.U62. DD 363.34809778. *Disaster Planning and Operations Newsletter, 0197-6672.*

NEWSLETTER - MONTREAL JOINT HOSPITAL INSTITUTE. (NEWSLETTER). Main/Corp Montreal Joint Hospital Institute. Vol. 1, No. 1 (May 1977)-. 0229-8759. Periodical. CN. English. mo. Free. Montreal Joint Hospital Institute, 1110 Pine Street West, Montreal Quebec H3A 1A3 Canada. DD 362.1109714281.

NEWSLETTER - NANAIMO REFUGEE CO-ORDINATION SOCIETY. (NEWSLETTER). June 15/81-. 0824-5185. Periodical. CN. English. bm. $0.50 per issue. Community Services Facility, 285 Prideaux Street/Suite 225-228, Nanaimo British Columbia V9R 2N2 Canada. DD 362.870971. *Nanaimo Refugee Co-Ordination Society Newsletter.*

NEWSLETTER - NATIONAL ASSOCIATION OF FRIENDSHIP CENTRES. (NAFC NEWSLETTER). Main/Corp National Association of Friendship Centres. VAT National Association of Friendship Centres Newsletter. 0821-6509. Periodical. CN. English. ir. National Association of Friendship Centres, Suite 3/ 200 Cooper Street, Ottawa Ontario K2P 0G1 Canada. DD 362.849707106071.

NEWSLETTER - NATIONAL ASSOCIATION OF SOCIAL WORKERS. CALIFORNIA CHAPTER. (NASW NEWSLETTER). VAT National Association of Social Workers Newsletter. Oct./Nov. 1974-. 0745-5186. Periodical. US. English. mo $15.00. California Chapter of National Association of Social Workers, 11th and L/Suite 210, Sacramento CA 95814. Tel (916)442-0485. Ed Tom Clancy. adv acc. Circ 9,000. (ctrl). News and information related to professional social work in California. *NASW Record.*

NEWSLETTER - NATIONAL LEGAL AID RESEARCH CENTRE. (NEWSLETTER). No. 1 (1981)-. 0715-4186. Periodical. CN. English (French). qt. National Legal Aid Research Centre/Tabaret Hall, University of Ottawa, Ottawa Ontario K1N 6N5 Canada. DD 362.580971.

NEWSLETTER - NIAGARA CHILDREN'S SERVICES COMMITTEE. (NEWSLETTER). Main/Corp Niagara Children's Services Committee. Vol. 1, 1 (Oct. 1979)-. 0229-2742. Periodical. CN. English. qt. Free. Niagara Children's Services Committee, 206 King Street, Saint Catharines Ontario L2R 3J5 Canada. DD 362.706071338.

NEWSLETTER - OPEN DOOR SOCIETY OF OTTAWA. (NEWSLETTER). 0712-3132. Periodical. CN. English. Open Door Society, Ottawa Branch, 1370 Bank Street, Ottawa Ontario K1H 7Y3 Canada. DD 362.734.

NEWSLETTER-SOCIAL WELFARE HISTORY GROUP. Main/Corp Social Welfare History Group. No. 1- 1956-. 0560-3870. Periodical. US. English. ir. $5.00. Social Work Program, 6090 Haley Center Auburn University, Auburn AL 36849. Each issue contains an index to its own contents - no vol index - loose.

NEWSLETTER - S.U.C.C.E.S.S. (NEWSLETTER). VFOAT S.U.C.C.E.S.S. Newsletter. No. 1-. 0823-7999. Periodical. CN. English (Chinese). qt. Free. S U C C E S S, 449 East Hastings Street, Vancouver British Columbia V6A 1P5 Canada. DD 362.8495107110006071133.

NEWSLETTER - TEXAS ADULT PROBATION COMMISSION. Main/Corp Texas Adult Probation Commission. V. 1- Oct. 1978-. Periodical. US. English. Texas Adult Probation Commission, 8100 Cameron Road/Suite 600, Building B, Austin TX 78753. Tel (512)834-8188.

NEWSLETTER - TEXAS UNITED COMMUNITY SERVICES. Main/Corp Texas United Community Services, Inc. Periodical. US. English. ir. Texas United Community Services, PO Box 1487, Austin TX 78767.

NEWSLETTER - U.N.B. TEMPERANCE UNION. (NEWSLETTER). Main/Corp U.N.B. Temperance Union. VAT U.N.B. Temperance Union Newsletter, University of New Brunswick Temperance Union Newsletter, Newsletter - University of New Brunswick Temperance Union. 0708-3599. Periodical. CN. English. ir. $1.00 to Members. U.N.B. Temperance Union, c/o Department of History, University of New Brunswick, Fredericton New Brunswick Canada. DD 362.2920671551.

NEXUS. 0197-8519. Periodical. US. English. qt. Delaware Council on Crime and Justice Inc, 701 Shipley Street, Wilmington DE 19801. LC HV8145.D3. DD 364.9751.

NIEDEROSTERREICHISCHE SOZIALHILFE UND JUGENDWOHLFAHRTSPFLEGE. Main/Corp Lower Austria (Austria). 1974-. German. ir. Amt der Niederosterreichischen Landesregierung, Herrengasse 11-13, Wien Austria. LC HV259.A9. *Niederosterreichische Fursorgestatistik.*

NIHON FUKUSHI NENKAN. 1977-. JA. Japanese. ir. 5500. Rippu Shobo, 6-18 Higashi Gotanda 3, Shinagawa-ku 141 Tokyo Japan. LC HV413.A2.

NIJ REPORTS : A SELECTIVE NOTIFICATION OF INFORMATION PROGRAM OF THE NATIONAL INSTITUTE OF JUSTICE. VFOAT N.I.J. Reports/S.N.I. Reports, NIJ Reports/SNI Reports, N.I.J. Reports. Nov. 1983-. Periodical. US. English. bm. NCJRS User Services, PO Box 6000, Rockville MD 20850. LC Z5703.4.C73 HV7245. DD 016.3640973. *SNI.*

NOIN POKCHI SONGU. VFOAT Journal of the Aged Welfare. V. 1- Series (1978)-. Periodical. Korean (summaries in English). ir. LC HQ1060.

NONPROFIT WORLD REPORT. See Business - General Management.

NORDISK SOSIALT ARBEID. V. 1, No. 1-. 0333-1342. Periodical. Danish (text in Norwegian and Swedish). qt. 140.00. Universitetsforlaget Tidsskriftavdelingen Abonnementsseksjonen, Boks 2959 Toyen, Oslo 6 Norway. LC HV333.

NORTH CAROLINA FIVE YEAR PLAN FOR COMPREHENSIVE MENTAL HEALTH SERVICES : ANNUAL REPORT AND UPDATE. See Public Health and Safety.

NORTH DAKOTA COMPREHENSIVE CRIMINAL JUSTICE PLAN. Main/Corp North Dakota. Combined Law Enforcement Council. VFOAT Crime and Delinquency in North Dakota. 0098-0498. US. English. Combined Law Enforcement Council, Box B, Bismark ND 58501. LC HV7284. DD 364. *North Dakota Comprehensive Law Enforcement Plan.*

NORTH DAKOTA STATE PLAN FOR DEVELOPMENTAL DISABILITIES SERVICES AND FACILITIES CONSTRUCTION. Main/Corp North Dakota. State Dept. of Health. 0091-1070. US. English. North Dakota State Department of Health, 1200 Missouri

Sociology: General Works, Theory—Social Pathology, Welfare, Criminology

Avenue, Bismarck ND 58505. **LC** HV3006.N9. **DD** 362.309784.

NORTH WIND. (THE NORTH WIND). V. 1- Jan. 1975-. 0316-6953. **CN.** English. The North Wind, PO Box 65583, Vancouver British Columbia V5N 5K5 Canada. **DD** 367.971133.

NOUS TOUTES. (NOUS TOUTES : BULLETIN DE L'ASSOCIATION DE GARDIENNAGE DE MONTREAL-NORD). 0821-0381. Periodical. **CN.** French. bm. Free. Association de Gardiennage de Montreal-Nord, 6338 rue Fiset, Montreal Nord Quebec H1G 2B2 Canada. **DD** 362.71206071428.

NOUVELLES DES PETITS FRERES. First issue in 1972. 0382-7992. Periodical. **CN.** French (text in English). sa. Les Petits Freres des Pauvres, 4624 rue Garnier, Montreal Quebec H2J 3S7 Canada. **DD** 362.6309714281.

NSFRE JOURNAL. **Main/Corp** National Society of Fund Raising Executives. **VAT** National Society of Fund Raising Executives Journal. 0196-3295. Periodical. US. English. $5.00. National Society of Fund Raising Executives Inc, Suite 831/1511 K Street, Washington DC 20005. **LC** HG177. **DD** 658.15224.

OAPSW NEWSMAGAZINE. (O A P S W NEWSMAGAZINE). **Main/Corp** Ontario Association of Professional Social Workers. **VAT** Ontario Association of Professional Social Workers Newsmagazine. V. 4, No. 1- Summer 1977-. 0704-3244. Periodical. CN. English. bm. $11.61. Ontario Association of Professional Social Workers, 185 Bloor Street East/Suite 701, Toronto Ontario M4W 3J3 Canada. **Tel** (416)924-1478. **DD** 361.0062713. *O A P S W, 0319-6119.*

LES OBJECTIFS DANS LE DOMAINE DES AFFAIRES SOCIALES ET DE LA FAMILLE. **Main/Corp** Family and Social Affairs Council. 1973/74-. CN. French. Family and Social Affairs Council, 2700 Boul Laurier Ste-Foy, Quebec Province of Quebec 10 Canada. **LC** HV700.C3. **DD** 362.971.

ODYSSEE. (L'ODYSSEE : JOURNAL DES USAGERS DE LA MAISON ST-JACQUES). 0229-8023. Periodical. CN. French. ir. Free. Usagers de la Maison, St-Jacques 1629 rue St-Hubert, Montreal Quebec H2L 3Z1 Canada. **DD** 362.2042509714281.

OEIL DE FEU. V. 1- Jan. 1976-. 0702-8024. Periodical. CN. French. ir. $1.00 Each Number. Comite Provincial des Malades, CP 458 Complexe Desjardins, Montreal Quebec H5B 1B5 Canada. **DD** 362.11062714.

OEIL OUVERT. (L'OEIL OUVERT). 0821-7033. Periodical. CN. French. mo. Free. Association d'Entraide pour le Bien-Etre Emotionnel du Quebec, 12358 rue Lachapelle, Montreal Quebec H4J 2M8 Canada. **DD** 362.2060714. (ctrl).

OF COMPOUND INTEREST. Vol. 1, No. 2 Sept. 30, 1979. 0710-5975. Periodical. CN. English. ir. Free. Co-Ordinator of Children's Services, Vancouver Public Library, 750 Burrard Street, Vancouver British Columbia V6Z 1X5 Canada. **DD** 018.162. *Co-Ordinator of Juvenile Services : Publication, 0710-5967.*

OFAQ'TUALITE. **Main/Corp** Organismes Familiaux Associes du Quebec. V. 1- Dec. 1974-. 0318-5524. CN. French. Free. Organismes Familiaux Associes du Quebec, 1207 rue Saint-Andre, Montreal Quebec H2L 3S8 Canada. **DD** 362.82062714.

OFFENDER EMPLOYMENT REVIEW. 0094-6699. US. English. 1705 Desales Street NW, Washington DC 20590. **LC** KF3468.A73. **DD** 344.7301133.

OFFENDERS ADMITTED TO ADULT CORRECTIONAL INSTITUTIONS. Series/Titl Statistical Bulletin, C. 0093-321X. US. English. an. Division of Corrections, Office of Systems and Evaluation, PO Box 669, Madison WI 53701. **LC** HV7299. **DD** 365.609775.

OFFENDERS IN NEW JERSEY CORRECTIONAL INSTITUTIONS, ANNUAL REPORT. 1982-. US. English. an. **LC** HV9475.N5. **DD** 364.309749.

OFFENDERS ON PAROLE IN NEW JERSEY : ANNUAL REPORT. 1982-. US. English. an. **LC** HV9278. **DD** 364.309749.

OFFENDERS RELEASED FROM ADULT CORRECTIONAL INSTITUTIONS. Series/Titl Statistical Bulletin C. 0092-9956. US. English. an. Department of Health and Social Services, Division of Corrections and Office of Information Management, Madison WI 53707. **LC** HV9305.W6. **DD** 365.647.09775. *Offenders Released from Division of Corrections Adult Institutions in . . . .*

OFFENDERS RELEASED FROM ADULT CORRECTIONAL INSTITUTIONS THROUGH THE MUTUAL AGREEMENT PROGRAM. **Main/Corp** Wisconsin. Division of Corrections. Office of Systems and Evaluation. 1976-. US. English. an. Wisconsin Division of Corrections, Box 669, Madison WI 53701. **LC** HV9305.W6. **DD** 364.3709775.

OFFENSES KNOWN TO POLICE : UNIFORM CRIME REPORT. **Main/Corp** Nebraska Commission on Law Enforcement and Criminal Justice. 1975-. US. English. an. Commission on Law Enforcement and Criminal Justice, 301 Centennial Mall South, PO Box 94946, Lincoln NB 68509. **LC** HV7277. **DD** 364.9782. *Crime in Nebraska, 0360-103X.*

OFFENTLICHE FURSORGE, SOZIALHILFE. See Statistics.

OFFICIAL ANNUAL AUTO THEFT REPORT. See Transportation - Automobiles.

OLD AGE SECURITY, GUARANTEED INCOME SUPPLEMENT, SPOUSE'S ALLOWANCE. See Insurance.

ON RECORD (TORONTO, ONT.). (ON RECORD). 0821-7882. Periodical. CN. English. ty. Free. Family Service Association of Metropolitan Toronto, 22 Wellesley Street East, Toronto Ontario M4Y 1G3 Canada. **DD** 362.8209713541. (ctrl). *N W A on Record.*

ON THE LINE (COLLEGE PARK, MD.). (ON THE LINE). Began with: Vol. 1 in Nov. 1977. 0190-2571. Periodical. US. English. bm.

ON THE SAFE SIDE. V. 1- 1977-. 0226-8094. Periodical. CN. English. mo. Saskatchewan Government Insurance Office, C M Fines Building 2260 11th Avenue, Regina Saskatchewan S4P 0J9 Canada. **DD** 363.1.

ONTARIO GUARANTEED ANNUAL INCOME SYSTEM. GAINS RATE TABLES FOR OLD AGE SECURITY AND GUARANTEED INCOME SUPPLEMENT RECIPIENTS. (ONTARIO GUARANTEED ANNUAL INCOME SYSTEM). **VFOAT** Le Regime de Revenu Annuel Garanti de L'Ontario. July 1974-. 0228-3034. Periodical. CN. English (French). qt. Free. Ministry of Revenue, Queens Park, Toronto Ontario M7A 1X8 Canada. **DD** 362.63.

ONTARIO GUARANTEED ANNUAL INCOME SYSTEM. GAINS RATE TABLES FOR PERSONS NOT ELIGIBLE FOR OLD AGE SECURITY. (ONTARIO GUARANTEED ANNUAL INCOME SYSTEM). **VFOAT** Regime de Revenu Annuel Garanti de l'Ontario. July 1974-. 0228-3026. Periodical. CN. English (French). qt. Free. Ministry of Revenue, Queens Park, Toronto Ontario M7A 1X8 Canada. **DD** 362.63.

ONTARIO WELFARE REPORTER CEASED. (THE ONTARIO WELFARE REPORTER). V. 1-26, No. 6. 0048-1874. Periodical. CN. English. qt. 1240 Bay Street/Suite 404, Ontario M5R 2A7 Canada.

OPTIQUE. (L'OPTIQUE). Vol. 1, No. 1 (Nov. 1982)-. 0823-6232. Periodical. CN. French (text in English). mo. $6.00 for six numbers. Institution Laval, 160 Montee St-Francois, Ville de Laval Quebec H7C 1S5 Canada. **DD** 365.9714271.

ORGANISATION POPULAIRE. V. 1- Feb. 1975-. 0381-1522. Periodical. CN. French. mo. Association pour la Defense des Droits Sociaux, 1750 rue Saint-Denis, Montreal Quebec H2X 3K6 Canada. **DD** 362.509714281. *Droit Populaire.*

THE ORISSA POLICE MAGAZINE. Began in 1964. Periodical. English (Oriya). ir. **LC** HV7809.O7. **DD** 363.2095413.

ORZECNICTWO SADU NAJWYZSZEGO IZBA CYWILNA ORAZ IZBA PRACY I UBEZPIECZEN SPOLECZNYCH. **Main/Corp** Poland. Sad Najwyzszy. PL. Polish. mo. Ars Polona, Krakowskie Przedmiescie 7, 00-068 Warsaw Poland.

OTTAWA NEWSLETTER. **Main/Corp** Canadian Loyalists' Association. No. 1- 197—. 0700-995X. Periodical. CN. English. C.L.A. Newsletter, PO Box 3084 Station C, Ottawa Ontario K1Y 3B5 Canada. **DD** 369.271.

OUTLINE OF ACTIVITIES FOR HOME DEPARTMENT. **Main/Corp** Maharashtra, India (State). Home Dept. **VFOAT** Karyaci Ruparesha, Grha Vibhaga. English (Marathi). ir. **LC** HV7371.M34. **DD** 363.20954792.

OUTLINE OF ACTIVITIES FOR PUBLIC WORKS AND HOUSING DEPARTMENT. **Main/Corp** Maharashtra, India (State). Public Works and Housing Dept. **VFOAT** Karyakramaci Ruparesha, Sarvajanika Bankhakama va Grhanirmana Vibhaga. English (Marathi). ir. **LC** HD4295.Z8. **DD** 363.0954792.

OUTLOOK. Feb. 1, 1970-. 0382-4780. Periodical. CN. English. ir. Lethbridge Correctional Institution, PO Box 490, Lethbridge Alberta T1J 3Z3 Canada. **DD** 365.971234.

PAEDOVITA. Vol. 1, No. 1 (Jan. 1984)-. 0737-5131. Periodical. US. English. qt. $15.00 Individuals, $25.00 Multiple-Reader Institutions, $10.00 Full-Time Students. Paedovita, PO Box 1344, Oak Brook IL 60521. **Ind/Abst** Int. Nurs. Index. **DD** 362. **NLM** W1.

PALESTINE REFUGEES TODAY. 1960. 0031-0336. US. English. qt. Free. UNRWA Headquarters, Vienna International Centre, PO Box 700, 1400 Vienna Austria. **Tel** 26-31. Ed Ron Wilkinson. **LC** HV640.5.A6. **Circ** 11,000. Describes living conditions of Palestine refugees in Jordan, Lebanon, Syria, West Bank and Gaza and world of UNRWA in providing education, health, and welfare services to refugees in these areas.

PAMPHLET - DEPARTMENT OF EMPLOYMENT AND SOCIAL SERVICES. (PAMPHLET). **Main/Corp** Maryland. Dept. of Employment and Social Services. 0092-8720. US. English. Maryland Department of Employment and Social Services, 1315 St Paul Street, Baltimore MD 21202. **LC** KFM1549.A73. **DD** 344.75203.

PANOPTICON. Vol. 1, No. 1 (Nov./Dec. 1980)-. Periodical. Dutch (with summaries in English and French). ir. 1.200. Uitgeverij Kluwer Rechtswetenschappen, Santvoortbeeklaan 21-23, 2100 Deurne, Antwerpen Belgium. **LC** HV7003.

PAPER - PACIFIC GROUP FOR POLICY ALTERNATIVES. (PAPER). No. P-84-1-. 0824-1341. Monographic Series. CN. English. ir. Pacific Group for Policy Alternatives, 22 East 8th Avenue, Vancouver British Columbia V5T 1R4 Canada. **DD** 361.6109711.

PARAQUAD. June 1976-. 0227-7123. Periodical. CN. French. qt. $25.00 Membership. Association des Paraplegiques du Quebec, 4545 Chemin Queen Mary, Montreal Quebec H3W 9Z9 Canada. **DD** 362.4309714. *Caliper.*

PARENTS SECOURS. **VFOAT** Block Parents. Vol. 1, No. 1 (Sept. 1979)-. 0823-3128. Periodical. CN. French (text also in English). ty. Free. Parents-Secours du Quebec, Bureau 2320/890 Est Boulevard Dorchester, Montreal Quebec H2L 2L4 Canada. **DD** 362.71060714.

PAROLE IN THE UNITED STATES. **Main/Corp** National Council on Crime and Delinquency. Research Center. **Series/Titl** Uniform Parole Reports. 1976/77-. US. English. an. US Department of Justice, Law Enforcement Assistance Administration, National Criminal Justice Informantion and Statistics Service, Washington DC 20402. **LC** HV9304. **DD** 364.620973.

PARTNERSHIP (OTTAWA, ONT.). (PARTNERSHIP). **VFOAT** Partenaires. 1 (Oct. 1980)-. 0228-4391. Periodical. CN. English (French). ir. Free. Partnership, c/o Children's Aid Society of Ottawa-Carleton, 1370 Bank Street, Ottawa Ontario K1H 7Y3 Canada. **DD** 362.7330971383.

PATTERNS OF JUVENILE OFFENDING IN NEW ZEALAND. No. 1 (1978-1981)-. English. an. **LC** HV9230.4. **DD** 364.3609931.

PEACE CORPS DIRECTORY, FORMER VOLUNTEERS AND STAFF. See Yearbooks, Almanacs, Directories.

PEDIATRIC SOCIAL WORK. See Medicine - Pediatrics.

PELITA BPKS. **Main/Corp** Balai Penelitian Kesejahteraan Sosial. **VAT** Pelita Balai Penelitian Kesejahteraan Sosial. Periodical. English and Indonesian. ir. Free. Balai Penelitian Kesejahteraan Sosial, Tromolpos 65, Yogyakarta Indonesia. **Tel** (274)3265. Ed Y B Suparlan. **LC** HV11. bk rev. **Circ** 6,000. (ctrl). Social science, social work, family, marriage, women, children and youth humanities.

Sociology: General Works, Theory—Social Pathology, Welfare, Criminology

PEN-VISTA. BILINGUAL EDITION. (PEN-VISTA). V. 1- May 1977-. 0705-3908. Periodical. CN. English (French in parallel columns). mo. Distributed free to inmates of Archambault Maximum Security Institution, $5. Others. Pen-Vista, PO Box 1210, Ste Anne Des Plaines Quebec J0N 1H0 Canada. DD 365.971424.

PENDULUM. Mar. 1979-. 0704-481X. Periodical. CN. English. mo. $7.00. Inmate Committee, Joyceville Institution, PO Box 880, Kingston Ontario K7L 4X9 Canada. DD 365.971372. *Advance, 0709-1710.*

PENELITIAN MASALAH KESEJAHTERAAN SOSIAL ANAK PROPINSI JAWA BARAT. 1982-. Indonesian. ir. LC HV800.I56.

LOS PENITENTES. Periodical. Spanish. ir. Editores Mexicanos Asociados, Lago Chalco No 156, Mexico 17 D F Mexico. Ed Francisco Ochoa Gonzalez.

PENYULUH SOSIAL. VFOAT Majalah Penyuluh Sosial. No. 18- Oct./Nov. 1972-. Indonesian. ir. Direktorat Jenderal Bira Sosial, Jl Ir H Juanda 36, Jakarta Indonesia. LC HV403. *Penjuluh Sosial.*

PEOPLE. V. 25, No. 3/4- Winter 1973/74-. 0094-8462. Periodical. US. English. qt. Centennial Office Building, St Paul MN 55155. LC HV86. DD 361.6209776. *Minnesota Mental Health Mental Retardation Newsletter, 0092-2730; Rap; Minnesota Welfare, 0026-5705.*

PEOPLE. 0145-2932. Periodical. US. English. qt. 325 North Salisbury Street, Raleigh NC 27611. LC HV86. DD 362.9756.

PEOPLE'S YELLOW PAGES OF AMERICA. Began Publication With 1974 Issue. 0097-255X. US. English. $5.00. Heller, 90 Daisy Farms Drive, New Rochelle NY 10804. LC HV89. DD 362.02573.

PERCEPTION. V. 1- Sept./Oct. 1977-. 0704-5263. Periodical. CN. English (text also in French). bm. Canadian Council on Social Development, 55 Avenue Parkdale, CP 3505 Station C, Ottawa Ontario K1Y 4G1 Canada. Tel (613)728-1865. Ed Robert Bisson. Ind/Abst Can. Period. Index, Foreign Lang. Index, Public Aff. Inf. Serv. Bull. LC HV1. DD 361.005, 309.171064. bk review. adv acc. Circ 4,000. A national bilingual magazine devoted to social policy issues in the fields of income security, health care, social services, employment, justice, human rights, native and women's issues, etc. *C W, Canadian Welfare, 0008-5332; Digeste Social, 0382-6287.*

PERFORMANCE BUDGET - DEPARTMENT OF WOMAN AND CHILD WELFARE. Main/Corp Andhra Pradesh (India). Dept. of Woman and Child Welfare. English. an. LC HJ65.A65. DD 354.548400722253.

PERMANENCY REPORT. Vol. 1, No. 1 (Summer 1983)-. Periodical. US. English. qt $10.00. Permanent Fam For Children, 67 Irving Place, New York NY 10003. *Adoption Report.*

PERMANENT DAY CARE COMMISSION. ANNUAL REPORT. Main/Corp Rhode Island. Permanent Day Care Commission. US. English. an. Room 326/State House, Providence RI 22903. LC HV857.R4. DD 353.9745008471.

PERSONAL SOCIAL SERVICES STATISTICS, ESTIMATES. See Statistics.

PERSPECTIVE. Main/Corp South Plains Association of Governments. 0197-2545. US. English. an. South Plains Association of Governments, 1709 26th Street, Lubbock TX 79411. LC HT393.T48. DD 361.60976484.

PERSPECTIVE (MINNESOTA. DEPT. OF CORRECTIONS). (PERSPECTIVE). Vol. 5, Issue 2 (Mar./Apr. 1979)-. Periodical. US. English. Minnesota Department of Corrections, 450 North Syndicate, St Paul MN 55104. *Corrections Perspective.*

PHYSICIANS DRG NEWSLETTER. VFOAT Physicians D.R.G. Newsletter. Began with: V. 1, No. 1 (Apr. 1984). 0748-8211. Periodical. US. English. mo. $159.00. Current Health Concepts, 2049 Centruy Park East/Suite 5117, Los Angeles CA 90067. DD 362.

PLAN CANADA NEWS. Began with Spring 1974 Issue. 0700-9011. Periodical. CN. English. sa. Limited Free Distribution. Foster Parents Plan of Canada, 153 St Clair Avenue West, Toronto Ont M4V 1P8 Canada. DD 362.7106271.

PLANNING FOR THE DEVELOPMENTALLY DISABLED. Main/Corp West Virginia. State Commission on Mental Retardation. US. English. Charleston Commission on Mental Retardation, State Capitol, Charleston WV 25305. LC HV3006.W4. DD 362.309754.

PLANO DE ACAO E ORCAMENTO PROGRAMA. Main/Corp Fundacao Estadual do Bem-Estar do Menor (Rio Grando do Sul, Brazil). Portuguese. an. LC HV747.B94. DD 362.7042.

POINT. (LE POINT). V. 1, No 1 (Feb. 1981)-. 0226-9740. Periodical. CN. French. bm. Association des Eclaireurs Baden-Powell, 70 rue Lahaie, Lavan Quebec H7G 3A8 Canada. DD 369.43060714.

POLIISIN JA TULLIN TIETON TULLEET RIKOKSET, PAIHTYNEENA SAILOON OTETUT JA PYSAKOINTIVIRHEET. Main/Corp Finland. Tilastokeskus. VFOAT Brott som Kommit till Pulisens och Tulens Kanedom, Berudade som Tagits I Forvar och Parkeringsfel. Fl. Finnish (Swedish). ir. Tilastokeskus, Pl 516 00101 10, Helsinki Finland. LC HV7015.5.

POLIZEILICHE KRIMINALSTATISTIK NIEDERSACHSEN MIT INFORMATIONEN AUS DEM LANDESKRIMINALAMT. 0171-2721. German. an. LC HV7349.S38. DD 364.042094359. *Polizeiliche Kriminalstatistik Niedersachsen Mit Informationen aus dem Landeskriminalpolizeiamt.*

POLYGRAPH. V. 1- Mar. 1972-. 0197-7024. Periodical. US. English. qt. $25.00. American Polygraph Association, PO Box 74, Linthicum Heights MD 21090. Ind/Abst Print. Abstr. LC HV8078.A1. DD 364.128. *Journal of the American Polygraph Association.*

POPULATION ANALYSIS OF THE ILLINOIS ADULT PRISON SYSTEM. Main/Corp Illinois. Dept. of Corrections. Division of Research and Long Range Planning. 0093-5603. US. English. Illinois Department of Corrections, PO Box 736, Joliet IL 60434. LC HV7262. DD 365.609773.

POPULATION MOVEMENT. Main/Corp Kentucky State Penitentiary. US. English. Kentucky State Penitentiary, PO Box 128, Eddyville KY 42038-0128. LC HV8482.K4. DD 365.609769.

PORTE-VOIX. (LE PORTE-VOIX). VFOAT Journal Communautaire Joli-Mont. V. 1, No. 6- Dec. 1979-. 0225-3593. Periodical. CN. French. bm. Free. Comite Promoteur du Journal Communautaire Joli-Mont, CP 270, Saint-Theodore de Chertsey Quebec J0K 3K0 Canada. DD 361.97141. (ctrl) *CLSC Joli-Mont, 0708-3122.*

PORTLAND PHYSICIAN SCRIBE. VFOAT Scribe. Vol. 1, No. 1 (Jan. 1983)-. 8756-646X. Periodical. US. English. bw. $3.00 Members, $10.00 Nonmembers. Multnomah County Medical Society, 2188 SW Park Place, Portland OR 97205. DD 362. *Portland Scribe, 0032-4930.*

PPG INDUSTRIES FOUNDATION. (PPG INDUSTRIES FOUNDATION : REPORT). VFOAT P.P.G. Industries Foundation. VAT Pittsburgh Plate Glass Industries Foundation. 0278-9108. US. English. PPG Industries Foundation, 1 Gateway Center, Pittsburgh PA 15222. LC HV97.P67. DD 361.7650973.

PRAIRIE WEEK. (THE PRAIRIE WEED). Vol. 1, No. 1 (Dec. 1, 1978)-. 0229-6632. Periodical. CN. English. qt. $0.25 Each Number, $5.00 for 12 Issues. Prairie Society for Marijuana Research and Individual Liberty, c/o Box 115, Students' Union Building, University of Alberta, Edmonton Alberta T6G 2J7 Canada. DD 363.45.

THE PRESIDIO. Periodical. US. English. Iowa State Penitentiary, Box 316, Fort Madison IA 52629. LC HV8301. DD 365.9777.

THE PRETRIAL REPORTER. V. 1- June 1977-. 0193-4015. Periodical. US. English. bm. $36.00. Pretrial Servs Resource, 918 F Center Street NW/Suite 500, Washington DC 20004-1482. Tel (202)638-3080. Ed (James) Andy Hall. LC KF9632.A15. DD 345.7307205. Research and tech assistance in area of jail overcrowing-particularly P.T. detention and alternatives to incarceration.

PREVENTION UPDATE NEWSLETTER. VFOAT Prevention Update. Vol. 1, No. 1-. 0882-5513. Periodical. US. English. bm. $25.00. Health Promotion Publications, 2952 Mesquite Drive, Riverside CA 92503. DD 362.

PREVIDENCIA SOCIAL, URBANA E RURAL. Periodical. Portuguese. ir. Caixa Postal 326, Cep 13 100 Campinas Brazil.

PRISM. V. 1- Mar. 1975-. 0317-2341. CN. English. School of Social Work, Carleton University, Ottawa Ontario K1S 5B6 Canada. DD 361.0071171384.

THE PRISON JOURNAL. V. 1- Jan. 1921-. 0032-8855. Periodical. US. English. sa. $10.00. Pennsylvania Prison Society, 311 South Juniper Street, Philadelphia PA 19107. Tel (215)732-5990. LC HV7231. DD 365.05. (cum index). *Journal of Prison Discipline and Philanthropy.*

PRISON LAW & ADVOCACY. See Law.

PRISON LAW MONITOR. See Law.

PRISON SERVICE JOURNAL. 1960. 0300-3558. Periodical. UK. English. qt. $4.72. Prison Service Journal, H M Prison Leyhill, Wotton Under Edge Glos GL 12 8HL England. Tel (0)454 260681. Ed Richard Tilt. LC HV7231. bk rev. Circ 2,500. Forum of discussion for penal policy and practice in UK and worldwide articles on all aspects of prison work and life.

PRISON STATISTICS : ENGLAND AND WALES. See Statistics.

PRISON STATISTICS, TASMANIA. See Statistics.

PRISONERS IN STATE AND FEDERAL INSTITUTIONS. (PRISONERS IN STATE AND FEDERAL INSTITUTIONS ON . . .). Series/Titl National Prisoner Statistics Bulletin. Dec. 31, 1971, 1972, and 1973-. 0148-5288. US. English. an. National Criminal Justice Reference Service, Box 6000, Rockville MD 20850. LC HV7245. DD 365.60973. *National Prisoner Statistics. Prisoners in State and Federal Institutions for Adult Felons.*

PRISONS IN SCOTLAND; REPORT. Main/Corp Scotland. Scottish Home and Health Department. UK. English. an. LC HV9649.S6.

PRIVATE FUNDING ADVISOR. Vol. 1, No. 1 (Apr. 1986)-. 0887-2201. Periodical. US. English. mo. $117.00. The Taft Group, 5130 Macarthur Boulevard, Washington DC 20016. DD 361.

PROBATION ADMINISTRATIVE MANAGEMENT SYSTEM. Main/Corp New Jersey. Juvenile Probation Management Information System. US. English. an. Administrative Office of the Courts, State House Annex, Trenton NJ 08625. LC HV9305.N48. DD 364.360974991.

PROBATION AND PAROLE DIRECTORY. See Yearbooks, Almanacs, Directories.

PROBATION & PAROLE STATISTICS. See Statistics.

PROBATION AND PAROLE TERMINATIONS. Main/Corp Wisconsin. Division of Corrections. Office of Systems and Evaluation. Series/Titl Statistical Bulletin, C. 1976-. US. English. an. Division of Corrections, Office of Systems and Evaluation, PO Box 669, Madison WI 53701. LC HV9305.W6. DD 364.6309775. *Probation and Parole Terminations.*

PROBATION JOURNAL. V. 21-. Periodical. UK. English. qt. $7.66. Probation Journal, 3-4 Chivlry Road, London SW11 1HT England. Tel (01)223-4887. Ed Nigel Stone. bk rev. adv acc. Circ 7,000. Social work with offenders in the criminal justice system and divorce court welfare. *Probation.*

PROBATION SERVICE STATISTICS . . . ESTIMATES. See Statistics.

PROCEEDINGS - FLORIDA CORRECTIONAL EDUCATION ASSOCIATION. Main/Corp Florida Correctional Education Association. 0430-7615. US. English. ir. Florida State Prison, PO Box 747, Starke FL 32091.

PROCEEDINGS; INTERAGENCY WORKSHOP - SAM HOUSTON STATE UNIVERSITY. INSTITUTE OF CONTEMPORARY CORRECTIONS AND THE BEHAVIORAL SCIENCES. Main/Corp Sam Houston State University. Institute of Contemporary Corrections and the Behavioral Sciences. 1st- 1965-. US. English. an. Sam Houston State University, Huntsville TX 77340. LC HV9303. DD 364.60973.

Sociology: General Works, Theory—Social Pathology, Welfare, Criminology

PROCEEDINGS OF THE ANNUAL CONGRESS OF CORRECTION OF THE AMERICAN CORRECTIONAL ASSOCIATION. Main/Corp American Correctional Association. 85th- 1955-. 0065-7948. US. English. an. American Correctional Association, 4321 Hartwick Road/Suite 1208, College Park MD 20740. Ed Particia L Millard. Circ 1,200. A compendium of papers presented at ACA'S annual congress of correction. Deals with the most vital issues in corrections today. *Proceedings of the Annual Congress of Correction of The American Prison Association.*

PROCEEDINGS OF THE ANNUAL MEETING - FLORIDA GROUP CHILD CARE ASSOCIATION. Main/Corp Florida Group Child Care Association. US. English. ir. State Department of Public Health, Jacksonville FL 32221. LC HV741.

PROCEEDINGS OF THE INTERNATIONAL CONFERENCE ON SOCIAL WELFARE. Main/Conf International Conference on Social Welfare. 14th- 1968-. 0074-3305. US. English. ir. International Conference on Social Welfare, Koestlergasse 1/29, A-1060 Vienna Austria. *Proceedings of the International Conference of Social Work.*

PROCEEDINGS OF THE NATIONAL CONFERENCE ON PUBLIC GAMING. (PROCEEDINGS). Main/Conf National Conference on Public Gaming. 1973-. 0093-7878. US. English. PO Box 1544, 253 East Palmetto Park Road, Boca Raton FL 33432. LC HV6715. DD 364.1720973.

PROCEEDINGS OF THE RESIDENTIAL CONFERENCE OF THE AUSTRALIAN INSTITUTE OF CRIMINOLOGY. Main/Corp Australian Institute of Criminology. 1st- 1973-. AT. English. ir. Australian Institute of Criminology, 10-16 Colbee Court Phillip, Canberra Australian Capital Territory 2606 Australia. LC HV6024.5. DD 364.994.

PROCEEDINGS OF THE STANDING COMMITTEE ON SOCIAL SERVICES. Main/Corp Newfoundland. House of Assembly. Standing Committee on Social Services. 0712-5216. CN. English. an. LC HV109.N4. DD 354.7180084.

PROCEEDINGS OF THE SUBCOMMITTEE ON CHILDHOOD EXPERIENCES AS CAUSES OF CRIMINAL BEHAVIOUR. Main/Corp Canada. Parliament. Senate. Sub-Committee on Childhood Experiences as Causes of Criminal Behaviour. VFOAT Deliberations du Sous-Comite sur la Delinquance Inputable aux Experiences de l'Enfance. VAT Childhood Experiences as Causes of Criminal Behaviour., Delinquance Imputable aux Experiences de l'Enfance. No. 1- June 30, 1977-. 0707-9044. CN. English (text in French in parallel columns). Printing and Publishing, Supply and Services Canada, Ottawa Ontario K1A OS9 Canada. LC HV6115. DD 364.25.

PRODUCTIVE AGING NEWS. No. 1 (Mar. 1986)-. 0887-3798. Periodical. US. English. mo. $57.00. Mount Sinai Medical Center, 13-30 Annenberg Building/1 Gastav Levy Pl, New York NY 10029. DD 362.

PROGRAM ADMINISTRATION REVIEW OF THE SOCIAL SECURITY DISABILITY INSURANCE AND THE SUPPLEMENTAL SECURITY INCOME VOCATIONAL REHABILITATION PROGRAMS. Main/Corp United States. Rehabilitation Services Administration. VFOAT Program Administrative Review: Special Programs, VR, SSDI, SSI. 0194-3871. US. English. an. US Department of Health Education and Welfare, 200 Independence Avenue SW, Washington DC 20201. LC HD7256.U5. DD 362404820973.

PROGRAM INFORMATION SERIES REPORT. 0091-0511. US. English. Department of Social Welfare Management Information Service, Health & Welfare Agency, 714 P Street, Sacramento CA 95814. LC HV98.C3. DD 361.409794.

PROGRAM PLAN - NATIONAL INSTITUTE OF JUSTICE (U.S.). (PROGRAM PLAN). Main/Corp National Institute of Justice (U.S.). 0735-2808. US. English. an. US Department of Justice, National Institute of Justice, Washington DC 20531. LC HV9471. DD 364.973. *Program Plan.*

PROGRAM PROGRESS SUMMARY. Main/Corp Mississippi. Governor's Office of Volunteer Services. US. English. an. Governor's Office of Volunteer Services, Walter Sillers Building, 500 High Street, Jackson MS 39201. LC HV86. DD 361.3709762.

PROGRAM STATISTICS - MICHIGAN DEPARTMENT OF SOCIAL SERVICES. See Statistics.

PROGRAMS AND PROGRESS. Main/Corp New York (State). Office for the Aging. 0363-0625. US. English. an. Office for the Aging, 855 Central Avenue, Albany NY 12206. LC HV1468.N7. DD 362.609747.

PROGRAMS PROVIDING SERVICES TO BATTERED WOMEN. Series/Titl Domestic Violence Information Series. 0272-4448. US. English. National Clearinghouse on Domestic Violence, Box 2309, Rockville MD 20852. LC HV699. DD 362.83. NLM HV 6626 P964.

PROGRESS REPORT DINAS SOSIAL PROPINSI SUMATERA UTARA. Main/Corp Sumatera Utara, Indonesia. Dinas Sosial. Indonesian. an. Jalan Jenderal A Yani VII/29, Medan Indonesia. LC HV405.S85.

PROGRESS REPORT - MICHIGAN DEPARTMENT OF SOCIAL SERVICES. OFFICE OF YOUTH SERVICES. (PROGRESS REPORT). Main/Corp Michigan. Office of Youth Services. Series/Titl DSS Publication. 1971/72-. 0091-2883. US. English. an. Missouri Department of Social Services, Office of Youth Services, 300 South Capitol Avenue, Lansing MI 48026. LC HV86, HV1435.M5. DD 362.709774.

PROGRESS REPORT PELITA P.K3A. Main/Corp Jakarta Raya, Indonesia. Dinas Sosial. VAT Progres Report Pembangunan Lima Tahun Pembinaan Kegiatan Kesejahteraan Keluarga dan Anak. IO. Indonesian. ir. Dinas Sosial, J1 Gunung Sahari II/6, Jakarta Indonesia. LC HV800.I56.

PROGRESS REPORT - WASHINGTON CRIMINAL JUSTICE EDUCATION AND TRAINING CENTER. Main/Corp Washington Criminal Justice Education and Training Center. US. English. Criminal Justice Education and Training Center, Issaquah WA 98027. LC HV8145.W2. DD 364.

PROJECT INFORMATION EXCHANGE. VFOAT Echange-Renseignements. 1st- Ed. 0704-6693. CN. English (French). an. Canadian Council on Social Development, 55 Parkdale Avenue, Ottawa Ontario K1Y 1E5 Canada. DD 016.362.

PROJECT INFORMATION EXCHANGE. VFOAT Echange-Renseignements. 1976-. 0708-5710. Periodical. CN. English (some text in French). DD 360.

PROJECT STATEMENT DAN PEDOMAN PELAKSANAAN D.I.K. & D.I.P. Main/Corp Indonesia. Direktorat Jenderal Bina Karya. VAT Project Statement dan Pedoman Pelaksanaan Daftar Isian Kegiatan dan Daftar Isian Proyek. Indonesian. ir. Direktorat Jenderal Bira Karya, Jln Ir H Juanda 36, Jakarta Indonesia. LC HV401.

PROMOCAO SOCIAL. Year 1- (No. 1-). Periodical. Portuguese. ir. Secretaria da Promocao Social, rua do Ouvidor 63 - 80 Andar, Sao Paulo Brazil. LC HV194.S3.

PROPOSED COMPREHENSIVE ANNUAL SERVICE PLAN FOR THE COMMONWEALTH OF MASSACHUSETTS UNDER TITLE XX OF THE SOCIAL SECURITY ACT. Main/Corp Massachusetts. Dept. of Social Services. VFOAT Title 20 Proposed Comprehensive Annual Service Plan. July 1, 1980-June 30, 1981-. US. English. an. Massachusetts Department of Social Services, 150 Causeway Street, Boston MA 02114. LC J87, HV98. M39. DD 300.9744 S, 353.9744008406.

PROPOSED COMPREHENSIVE ANNUAL SERVICE PROGRAM PLAN FOR THE STATE OF HAWAII. Main/Corp Hawaii. Dept. of Social Services and Housing. 0148-317X. US. English. an. Services Program Development Administrator, 1390 Miller Street, Honolulu HI 96813. LC HV86. DD 353.99690084.

PROPOSED COMPREHENSIVE ANNUAL SERVICES PLAN. Main/Corp Indiana Office of Social Services. VFOAT State of Indiana Proposed Comprehensive Annual Services Plan. Began with vol. for 1979/80. 0147-6157. US. English. an. Indiana Office of Social Services, 964 North Pennsylvania, Indianapolis IN 46204. LC HV86. DD 353.97720084. *Proposed Comprehensive Annual Services Plan, 0147-6157.*

PROPOSED COMPREHENSIVE ANNUAL SERVICES PROGRAM PLAN. Main/Corp Minnesota. Dept. of Public Welfare. 1978/79-. US. English. an. Gary Haselluhn/Division of Social Services, Department of Public Welfare/Centennial Office Building, St Paul MN 55155. LC HV86. DD 353.9776008405. *Comprehensive Annual Services Program Plan. Proposed Plan, Title XX.*

PROPOSED COMPREHENSIVE ANNUAL SERVICES PROGRAM PLAN. Main/Corp Arkansas. Office of Title XX Services. VFOAT Title XX Proposed Comprehensive Annual Services Program Plan. 1978/79-. US. English. an. Office of Title XX Services, Department of Human Resources, PO Box 1427, Little Rock AR 72203. LC HV98.A65. DD 361.609767. *Proposed Comprehensive Annual Services Program Plan.*

PROPOSED COMPREHENSIVE ANNUAL SERVICES PROGRAM PLAN. Main/Corp Louisiana. Dept. of Health and Human Resources. VFOAT Proposed Title XX Comprehensive Annual Services Program Plan for the State of Louisiana. US. English. an. Department of Health & Human Resources, PO Box 3318, Baton Rouge LA 70821. LC HV86. DD 353.97630084.

PROPOSED COMPREHENSIVE ANNUAL SOCIAL SERVICES PLAN. Main/Corp Alaska. Dept. of Health and Social Services. US. English. an. Alaska Department of Health and Social Services, Juneau AK 99801. LC HV86. DD 361.6209798.

PROPOSED COMPREHENSIVE ANNUAL SOCIAL SERVICES PROGRAM PLAN FOR NEW YORK STATE. Main/Corp New York (State). Dept. of Social Services. 1975/76-. US. English. an. $17.25. New York State Department of Social Services, 40 North Pearl Street, Albany NY 12243. LC HV98.N7. DD 361.9747.

PROPOSED COMPREHENSIVE ANNUAL SOCIAL SERVICES PROGRAM PLAN FOR THE STATE OF WASHINGTON. Main/Corp Washington (State). Dept. of Social and Health Services. US. English. an. David J Holloman/Department of Social and Health Services, Administration and Management Mail Stop OB-41K, Olympia WA 98504. LC HV86. DD 361.609797.

PROPOSED CONNECTICUT STATE PLAN ON AGING. Main/Corp Connecticut. Dept. of Aging. 0160-2101. US. English. Department of Aging, 90 Washington Street, Hartford CT 06115. LC HV1468.C8. DD 362.609746.

PROPOSED MICHIGAN ANNUAL SOCIAL SERVICES PLAN. Main/Corp Michigan. Dept. of Social Services. 1975/76-. 0362-7446. US. English. an. Michigan Department of Social Services, 300 South Capitol Avenue, Lansing MI 48933. LC HV86. DD 362.9774.

PROPOSED MICHIGAN ANNUAL TITLE XX SERVICES PLAN. Main/Corp Michigan. Dept. of Social Services. Title XX Administration Division. Series/Titl DSS Publication. 1980/81-. US. English. an. Title XX Administration, Office of Planning Budget and Evaluation, Michigan Department of Social Services, 300 South Capitol Avenue, PO Box 30037, Lansing MI 48909. LC HV86. DD 361.609774. *Proposed Michigan Annual Title XX Services Plan.*

PROPOSED SERVICES & BUDGETS OF STATE AGENCIES SERVING VIRGINIA'S ELDERLY. (PROPOSED SERVICES & BUDGETS OF STATE AGENCIES SERVING VIRGINIA'S ELDERLY). VFOAT Proposed Services and Budgets of State Agencies Serving Virginia's Elderly. 0737-058X. US. English. be. Virginia Department for the Aging, 830 East Main Street/Suite 950, Richmond VA 23219. LC HV1468.V8. DD 362.609755.

PROPOSED STATE OF CALIFORNIA ANNUAL STATEWIDE SOCIAL SERVICES PLAN. (PROPOSED, STATE OF CALIFORNIA, ANNUAL STATEWIDE SOCIAL SERVICES PLAN). Main/Corp California. Dept. of Health. Social Services Division. 0149-5097. US.

Sociology: General Works, Theory—Social Pathology, Welfare, Criminology

English. an. Sacramento Social Services Division/Department of Health and Welfare, 744 P Street Room 576, Sacramento CA 95814. LC HV86. DD 361.6209794. *Proposed, State of California, Comprehensive Annual Services Program Plan.*

PROPOSED STATE OF ILLINOIS COMPREHENSIVE ANNUAL SERVICES PLAN FOR PROGRAM YEAR. Main/Corp Illinois. Dept. of Public Aid. US. English. an. Illinois Department of Public Aid, 316 South Second Street, Springfield IL 62762. LC HV86. DD 362.9773.

PROPOSED TITLE XX COMPREHENSIVE SERVICES PROGRAM PLAN. Main/Corp Arkansas. Office of Title XX Services. US. English. Department of Human Services, Office of Title XX Services, Donaghey Building/Suite 626, Little Rock AK 72201. LC HV98.A65. DD 361.609767. *Proposed Comprehensive Annual Services Program Plan.*

PROPOSED TITLE XX SOCIAL SERVICES : COMPREHENSIVE ANNUAL SERVICES PROGRAM PLAN FOR THE STATE OF TEXAS. 1976/77-. US. English. an. State Department of Human Resources, John H Reagan Building, Austin TX 78701. LC HV98.T5. *Proposed Title XX Comprehensive Annual Services Program Plan for Texas.*

PROSECUTORS' NOTES. See Law.

PROSPECTIVE PAYMENT GUIDE. Vol. 1, No. 1 (Sept 1983)-. 8756-3274. Periodical. US. English. mo. $249.00. Key Communications Group, 1022 Triangle Towers, 4853 Cordell Avenue, Bethesda MD 20814. DD 362.

PROVIDER (WASHINGTON, D.C.). (PROVIDER). Vol. 12, No. 3 (Mar. 1986)-. 0888-0352. Periodical. US. English. mo. $36.00 Domestic, $49.00 Foreign, Free to Association Members. American Health Care Association, 1200 15th Street NW, Washington DC 20005. LC PAR. DD 362. NLM W1. Issued also in microform by University Microfilms International. *Journal - American Health Care Association, 0360-4969.*

PROVINCE OF ONTARIO. ITS SOCIAL SERVICES. (THE PROVINCE OF ONTARIO, ITS SOCIAL SERVICES). 6th- Ed. 0317-705X. Periodical. CN. English. te. Ontario Welfare Council, 1240 Bay Street, Toronto Ontario M5R 2A7 Canada. DD 361.9713. *Province of Ontario, Its Welfare Services, 0317-7068.*

PROVINCIAL NEWSJOURNAL - INFANT DEVELOPMENT PROGRAMMES OF B.C. (PROVINCIAL NEWSJOURNAL). VAT IDP Newsjournal, Infant Development Programme of B.C. Newsjournal. Vol. 2, No. 1 (May 1983)-. 0824-9946. Periodical. CN. English. ty. $1.00 Per No. Provincial Advisor Infant Development Programme, 2979 West 41st Avenue, Vancouver British Columbia V6N 3C8 Canada. DD 362.4088054. *Newsletter (Infant Development Programme of B.C.), 0823-9924.*

PRZSTEPCZOSC NA SWIECIE. See Law Enforcement.

PSLG. PUBLIC SERVICE & LOCAL GOVERNMENT. (PUBLIC SERVICE & LOCAL GOVERNMENT : PSLG). VFOAT Public Service and Local Government. 0144-4212. Periodical. UK. English. mo. $13.02. BWS Publishing, 4 Addison Bridge Place, London W14 9BR England. Ind/Abst Coal Abstr. LC HD4645. DD 363.0941.

P'TIT ROBERT. (LE P'TIT ROBERT). No. 1-. 0823-6135. Periodical. CN. French. bw. Centre Hospitalier Robert-Giffard Service d'Audio-Visuel, 2601 de la Canardiere, Beauport Quebec G1J 2G3 Canada. DD 362.20971447.

PUBLIC ASSISTANCE FOR MINNESOTA INDIANS. See Ethnic.

PUBLIC ASSISTANCE RECIPIENT AND EXPENDITURE STUDY. Main/Corp Alaska. Dept. of Health and Social Services. Office of Information Systems. US. English. sa. Office of Information Systems, Pouch H81, Juneau AK 99811. LC HV86. DD 353.9798007231.

PUBLIC ASSISTANCE RECIPIENTS IN STANDARD METROPOLITAN STATISTICAL AREAS. See Statistics.

PUBLIC CONTRIBUTIONS ACT. ANNUAL REPORT. (THE PUBLIC CONTRIBUTIONS ACT . . . ANNUAL REPORT . . .). Main/Corp Alberta. Alberta Consumer and Corporate Affairs. 0381-4327. CN. English. an. Alberta Consumer and Corporate Affairs, Office of the Minister, 224 Legislative Building, Edmonton Alberta T5K 2B6 Canada. LC HV109.A5. DD 354.71230084, 361. 763097123. *Public Contributions Act Annual Report, 0381-4327.*

PUBLIC JUSTICE. See Law.

PUBLIC WELFARE. V. 1- Jan. 1943-. 0033-3816. Periodical. US. English. qt. American Public Welfare Association, 1125 15th Street NW/Suite 300, Washington DC 20005. Tel (202)293-7550. Ed Bill Detweiler. Ind/Abst Hospit. Lit. Index, Ref. Source, Soc. Work Res. Abstr., Soc. Sci. Index, Women Stud. Abstr., Am. Hist. Life, Hist. Abstr., Abstr. Soc. Work., Hist. Abstr., Part A, Mod. Hist. Abstr., Hist. Abst., Part B, Twent. Century Abstr. LC HV1. DD 360.5. NLM W1 PU64. bk rev. adv acc. Circ 8,600. (ctrl). Available on microfilm from University Microfilms. Articles range from commentary by national leaders to practical features by human service administrators. Research reports and opinion columns. *Public Welfare News.*

PUBLIC WELFARE ACTIVITIES IN ARIZONA. Main/Corp Arizona. State Dept. of Public Welfare. 0360-6600. US. English. mo. Department of Public Welfare, State Office Building, Phoenix AZ 85009. *Public Welfare Statistics.*

PUBLIC WELFARE DIRECTORY. See Yearbooks, Almanacs, Directories.

PUBLIC WELFARE IN CALIFORNIA. 0362-742X. US. English. an. California Health & Welfare Agency/Department of Social Service, 1500 Fifth Street, Sacramento CA 95814. LC HV98.C3. DD 362.9794.

PUBLIC WELFARE IN OREGON. Main/Corp Oregon. Public Welfare Division. 0090-6522. Periodical. US. English. Public Welfare Division, 312 Public Service Building, Salem OR 97310. LC HV86. DD 362.9795. *Public Welfare in Oregon.*

PUBLIC WELFARE STATISTICS. See Statistics.

PUBLICATION CATALOG OF THE U.S. DEPARTMENT OF HEALTH AND HUMAN SERVICES. Main/Corp United States. Dept. of Health and Human Services. VFOAT Publications Catalog. VAT Publication Catalog of the United States Department of Health and Human Services. Jan. 1979-Dec. 1979-. 0278-0143. US. English. an. US Department of Health and Human Services, 200 Independence Avenue Southwest, Washington DC 20201. LC Z7164.C4, HV97.U5. DD 016.361. NLM ZWA 100 U525C. *Publication Catalog of the U.S. Department of Health, Education, and Welfare, 0275-8210.*

PUBLICATION SERIES. MONOGRAPH SERIES - FACULTY OF SOCIAL WORK. UNIVERSITY OF TORONTO. (PUBLICATION SERIES. MONOGRAPH SERIES). VAT Monograph Series - Faculty of Social Work. University of Toronto. 1-. 0710-0329. Monographic Series. CN. English. Faculty of Social Work, University of Toronto, 246 Bloor Street West, Toronto Ontario M5S 1A1 Canada. DD 361.005. *Occasional Papers in Social Work, 0317-8382.*

PUBLICATION SERIES. WORKING PAPERS ON SOCIAL WELFARE IN CANADA. (PUBLICATION SERIES. WORKING PAPERS ON SOCIAL WELFARE IN CANADA). VFOAT Working Papers on Social Welfare in Canada. VAT Publication Series. Working Papers on Social Work in Canada. 1-. 0710-0299. Monographic Series. CN. English. Faculty of Social Work, University of Toronto, 246 Bloor Street West, Toronto Ontario M5S 1A1 Canada. DD 361.971. *Occasional Papers in Social Work, 0317-8382.*

PUBLICATIONS SERIES. BIBLIOGRAPHIC SERIES - FACULTY OF SOCIAL WORK. UNIVERSITY OF TORONTO. See Bibliographies.

PULSATION (OTTAWA, ONT.). (PULSATION). V. 1, No. 2, (April 1982)-. 0712-6131. Periodical. CN. French (text in English). qt. Free. Pulsation, Hopital Monrfort, 713 Chemin de Montreal, Ottawa Ontario K1K 0T2 Canada. DD 362.110971384. (ctrl). *Hopital Montfort, 0712-6123.*

QRC ADVISOR. VFOAT Q.R.C. Advisor. VAT Quality, Risk, Cost Advisor. Vol. 1, No. 1 (May 1984)-. 0747-7384. Periodical. US. English. mo. $80.00 Domestic, $95.00 Foreign. Aspen Distribution Center, 16792 Oakmont Avenue, Gaithersburg MD 20877. DD 362.

QUAKER COMMITTEE ON JAILS & JUSTICE. (A QUAKER COMMITTEE ON JAILS & JUSTICE : NEWSLETTER). Vol. 6, No. 3 (Fall 1981)-. 0824-6521. Periodical. CN. English. ir. Quaker Committee on Jails & Justice, 60 Lowther Avenue, Toronto Ontario M5R 1C7 Canada. DD 365.9713541. *QCJJ, 0824-331X.*

QUALITY CONTROL IN AFDC, NATIONAL FINDINGS. (QUALITY CONTROL IN AFDC : NATIONAL FINDINGS). Main/Corp United States. Social and Rehabilitation Service. Division of Quality Control Management. 0360-0033. US. English. US Department of Health, Education and Welfare, Social and Rehabilitation Service, Office of Special Initiatives, Division of Quality Control Management, Washington DC 20204. LC HV741. DD 362.70973.

QUALITY CONTROL, STATES' CORRECTIVE ACTION ACTIVITIES. (QUALITY CONTROL : STATES' CORRECTIVE ACTION ACTIVITIES). Main/Corp United States. Social and Rehabilitation Service. Office of Management. 0361-2643. US. English. US Department of Health Education & Welfare, Social & Rehabiation Service, Washington DC 20202. LC HV85. DD 362.973.

QUART MONDE. Main/Corp Association des Amis d'Atad Quart-Monde. 0823-938X. CN. French. an. $1.00 Each Number. Association des Amis d'Atd Quart-Monde, #2 5250 Av du Parc, Montreal Quebec H2V 4G7 Canada. DD 362.50601.

QUARTERLY JOURNAL OF CORRECTIONS. V. 1- Winter 1977-. 0147-9040. Periodical. US. English. qt. $12.00. Quarterly Journal of Corrections, 5983 Macon Cove at Interstate 40, Memphis TN 38134. Ind/Abst Sociol. Abstr., Soc. Welf. Soc. Plan./Policy Soc. Dev. LC HV9261. DD 364.609768.

THE QUARTERLY NEWSLETTER OF THE ONTARIO ASSOCIATION. (DIRECTIONS : THE QUARTERLY NEWSLETTER OF THE ONTARIO ASSOCIATION FOR THE MENTALLY RETARDED). Main/Corp Ontario Association for the Mentally Retarded. Vol. 1, No. 1 (1983)-. 0823-2512. Periodical. CN. English. qt. Free to Members. Ontario Association for the Mentally Retarded, 1376 Bayview Avenue, Toronto Ontario M4G 3A3 Canada. DD 362.309713. *Ontario Reporter, 0708-1103.*

QUARTERLY - PENNSYLVANIA ASSOCIATION ON PROBATION, PAROLE AND CORRECTION CEASED. Main/Corp Pennsylvania Association of Probation, Parole and Correction. Ceased With V. 36, No. 4, Winter 1979-1980?. Periodical. US. English. qt. *Pennsylvania Probation and Parole Quarterly.*

THE QUARTERLY PUBLIC ASSISTANCE REPORT. (THE QUARTERLY PUBLIC ASSISTANCE REPORT FOR . . .). 0731-0838. US. English. qt. Human Resources Administration, Division of Policy and Economic Research, 71 Worth Street/4th Floor, New York NY 10013. *Quarterly Data Report, 0364-880X.*

QUARTERLY PUBLIC ASSISTANCE STATISTICS. See Statistics.

QUARTERLY REPORT FOR THE QUARTER ENDED . . . . Main/Corp Nevada. State Gaming Control Board. Periodical. US. English. qt. LC HV6721.N45. DD 363.4209793. *Quarterly & Fiscal Year Report for . . . of . . . and Year-to-Date Comparisons . . . Comparative Fiscal Year Report . . . .*

QUARTERLY REPORT - NEBRASKA DEPARTMENT OF PUBLIC WELFARE. Main/Corp Nebraska. Dept. of Public Welfare. Division of Research and Statistics. Periodical. US. English. qt. Nebraska State Department of Public Welfare, 301 Centennial Mall South, Lincoln NE 68509. LC HV86. DD 361.6209782. *Monthly Report - Nebraska Department of Public Welfare.*

QUARTERLY STATISTICAL BULLETIN - SPECIAL SERVICES DIVISION. SOCIAL SERVICES BRANCH. DEPARTMENT OF HEALTH AND SOCIAL SERVICES. See Statistics.

Sociology: General Works, Theory—Social Pathology, Welfare, Criminology

QUESTION-MARK. V. 1- 1974?-. Periodical. US. English. mo. $8.50. Mass Correctional Institution, Box 43, Inmate Resident Council, Norfolk MA 02056.

LA QUESTIONE CRIMINALE. Year 1- Jan./Apr. 1975-. Periodical. Italian. ir. 8.000. Societa Editrice Il Mulino, Conto Corrente Postale 8/12926, Bologna Italy. **LC** HV6004. **DD** 364.05.

QUOI DE 9. **VAT** Quoi de Neuf. 0228-6238. Periodical. CN. French. mo. Productions Claude Savoie, 327 Boul. St-Joseph, Hull Quebec J8Y 3Z2 Canada. **DD** 362.1109741221.

R E O. Mar. 1976-June 1981. 0380-2485. Periodical. CN. English (text in French and English text on inverted pages). mo. Quebec Association for the Mentally Retarded, Suite 407/5890 Monkland Avenue, Montreal Quebec H4A 1G2 Canada. **DD** 362.309714.

RAPATRIES : BILAN ANNUEL DU SECRETARIAT D'ETAT AUPRES DU PREMIER MINISTRE CHARGE DES RAPATRIES. FR. French. an. 14 Bd de la Madeleine, 75008 Paris France. **LC** HV640.4.F7. **DD** 362.870944.

R.A.P.H.A.T. REGROUPEMENT DES ASSOCIATIONS DE PERSONNES HANDICAPEES DE L'ABITIBI-TEMISCAMINGUE. (R.A.P.H.A.T. : BULLETIN D'INFORMATION DU REGROUPEMENT DES ASSOCIATIONS DE PERSONNES HANDICAPEES DE L'ABITIBI-TEMISCAMINGUE). **VAT** Regroupement des Associations de Personnes Handicapees de l'Abitibi-Temiscamingue. VOL. 1, NO 1-. 0822-9279. Periodical. CN. French. qt. Free. R.A.P.H.A.T., 330 Est rue Perrault, Rouyn Quebec J9X 3J7 Canada. **DD** 362.40971413.

RAPPORT ANNUEL - COMMISSION QUEBECOISE DES LIBERATIONS CONDITIONNELLES. **Main/Corp** Quebec (Province). Commission Quebecoise des Liberations Conditionnelles. 1978/79-. 0228-8435. CN. French. an. Editeur Officiel du Quebec, 1283 Boul Charest Quest, Quebec Quebec G1N 2C9 Canada. **LC** HV9278. **DD** 354.714008493.

RAPPORT ANNUEL - CONSEIL DES AFFAIRES SOCIALES ET DE LA FAMILLE. **Main/Corp** Quebec (Province). Conseil des Affaires Sociales et de la Famille. 0226-4323. CN. French. an. Editeur Officiel du Quebec, 1283 Boul Charest Quest, Quebec Quebec G1N 2C9 Canada. **LC** HV109.Q4. **DD** 354.714008406. *Rapport d'Activities, 0226-4331.*

RAPPORT ANNUEL - CONSEIL REGIONAL DE LA SANTE ET DES SERVICES SOCIAUX DE QUEBEC. **Main/Corp** CRSS de Quebec (Quebec). **VAT** Rapport Annuel - CRSS de Quebec, Rapport Annuel - Region 03. Conseil de la Sante et des Services Sociaux de la Region de Quebec. 1972-. 0710-2305. CN. French. an. Conseil Regional de la Sante et des Services Sociaux de Quebec, Quebec Canada. **LC** HV110.Q4. **DD** 354.7140084.

RAPPORT ANNUEL - DIRECTION GENERALE DE LA PROBATION ET DES ETABLISSEMENTS DE DETENTION CEASED. (RAPPORT ANNUEL). **Main/Corp** Quebec (Province). Direction Generale de la Probation et Detention. 0317-736X. CN. French. an. **LC** HV9309.Q8. **DD** 354.71400849.

RAPPORT ANNUEL. REGIME DES ALLOCATIONS FAMILIALES DU QUEBEC. (RAPPORT ANNUEL, REGIME DES ALLOCATIONS FAMILIALES DU QUEBEC). **Main/Corp** Regie des Rentes du Quebec. 1976/77-. 0380-5387. CN. French. an. Service des Communications de la Regie des Rentes du Quebec, Case Postale 5200, Quebec PQ G1K Canada. **LC** HV700.C3. **DD** 354.714008482.

RAPPORT D'ACTIVITE - SURETE DU QUEBEC. (RAPPORT D'ACTIVITE). **Main/Corp** Surete du Quebec. Began with V. for 1979. 0227-8367. CN. French. an. Surete du Quebec, Service des Communications, 1701 rue Parthenais/Bureau 730, Montreal Quebec Canada. **LC** HV7642.O4. **DD** 354.714007406. *Rapport des Activites, 0225-3267.*

RAPPORT (TORONTO, ONT.). (RAPPORT). Vol. 1, No. 1 (Apr. 1, 1978)-. 0229-6381. Periodical. CN. English. mo. **DD** 361.8060713541.

RASSEGNA PENITENZIARIA E CRIMINOLOGICA. Yearly V. 1, 1-2 (Jan./June 1979)-. Periodical. IT. Italian (summaries in English, French, German, and Spanish). qt. 20.600. Direzione Generale Per Gli Istituti di Prevenzione E di Pena, Via Arenula 71, Roma Italy. **LC** HV6004. **DD** 364.05. **NLM** W1 RA905. *Quaderni di Criminologia Clinica.*

RAUMPLANUNG, INFORMATIONSHEFTE. VFOAT Amenagement du Territoire, Bulletin d'Information. Periodical. French (German). ir. 20.00. Bundesamt Fur Raumplanung, Bundesrain 20, 3003 Bern Switzerland. **LC** HT395.S9. **DD** 361.609494.

READINGS - AMERICAN ORTHOPSYCHIATRIC ASSOCIATION. (READINGS). Vol. 1, No. 1 (Mar. 1986)-. 0886-3784. Periodical. US. English. qt. $35.00. American Orthopsychiatric Association, 19 West 44th Street, New York NY 10036. **DD** 362.

THE RECORD - TENNESSEE DEPARTMENT OF HUMAN SERVICES. **Main/Corp** Tennessee. Dept. of Human Services. 0360-4608. Periodical. US. English. ir. Department of Human Service, 111 Seventh Avenue North, Nashville TN 37203. **Ind/Abst** Am. Hist. Life, Hist. Abstr. **LC** HV86. **DD** 361.09768. *Tennessee Public Welfare Record.*

RED CROSS TODAY. Nov. 1980-. 0711-4044. Periodical. CN. English. qt. British Columbia-Yukon Division, Canadian Red Cross Society, 4750 Oak Street, Vancouver British Columbia V6H 2N9 Canada. **DD** 361.763. *Across (Vancouver, B.C.), 0711-4036.*

REFERENCE TABLES. DRUG ARRESTS AND DISPOSITIONS. *See* Drug Abuse and Alcoholism.

REFLECTIONS. (REFLECTIONS : CANADIAN JOURNAL OF VISUAL IMPAIRMENT). VFOAT Canadian Journal of Visual Impairment. No. 1 (Spring 1982)-. 0710-1449. CN. English. an. $6.00 Each Volume. Reflections c/o Canadian National Institute For The Blind, 1931 Bayview Avenue, Toronto Ontario M4G 4C8 Canada. **DD** 362.4105.

REFUGE. (REFUGE : CANADA'S NATIONAL NEWSLETTER ON REFUGEES). No. 1 (May 1981)-. 0229-5113. Periodical. CN. English. ir. Refuge, 2nd Floor/8 York Street, Toronto Ontario M5J 1R2 Canada. **DD** 362.870971.

REFUGE. (REFUGE : LE BULLETIN D'ACTUALITES CANADIEN SUR LES REFUGIES). No. 1 (May 1981)-. 0229-5121. Periodical. CN. French. ir. $10.00 Per Issue. Refuge, 2E Etage, 8 rue York, Toronto Ontario M5J 1R2 Canada. **DD** 362.870971.

REFUGEE RESETTLEMENT PROGRAM. **Main/Corp** United States. Office of Refugee Resettlement. 0735-8334. US. English. an. US Department of Health and Human Services, Social Security Administration Office of Refuge Resettlement/1332 Switzer Building, 330 C Street Southwest, Washington DC 20201. **LC** HV640.4.U54. **DD** 362.870973. Vols. for fiscal years 1980 and 1982 distributed to depository libraries in microfiche.

REGINA FRIENDSHIP CENTRE NEWSLETTER. 1- May 6, 1974-. 0317-5782. CN. English. mo. Regina Friendship Centre, 1689 Toronto Street, Regina Saskatchewan S4P 1M3 Canada. **DD** 362.84.

REGIONAL PROFILES OF FELONS CONFINED . . . . June 30, 1982-. US. English. an. Department of Corrections, Research and Reporting Unit, PO Box 26963, Richmond VA 23261. *Regional Profiles of Inmates Confined . . . .*

REGISTRY OF CHARITABLE ORGANIZATIONS. 1977-. US. English. an. Department of Licensing, PO Box 9649, Olympia WA 98504. **LC** HV98.W3. **DD** 361.763025797.

REHABILITATION GAZETTE. V. 13- 1970-. 0361-4166. US. English. an. **Ind/Abst** Excerpta Med. **LC** HV1553. **DD** 362.4048305. **NLM** W1 RE174R. **CODEN** RHGZA. *Toomey J. Gazette.*

RELATORIO ANNUAL - SERVICO SOCIAL DO COMERCIO, ADMINISTRACAO REGIONAL NO ESTADO DO PARA. **Main/Corp** Servico Social do Comercio. Administracao Regional no Estado do Para. BL. Portuguese. an. Servico Social do Comercio Administracao Regional No Estado do Para, Rua Senador Mandel Barata 1873, Balem Brazil. **LC** HV194.P33.

RELATORIO ANUAL AR/SESC/GO. **Main/Corp** Servico Social do Comercio. Administracao Regional no Estado de Goias. Portuguese. an. **LC** HV194.G6. **DD** 354.8173008406. *Relatorio de Atividades.*

RELATORIO ANUAL DE ATIVIDADES REFERENTE AO EXERCICIO DE . . . . **Main/Corp** Servico Social da Industria. Departamento Regional do Rio Grande do sul. Portuguese. an. **LC** HD6957.B82. **DD** 354.816500848506. *Relatorio Anual de Atividades.*

RELATORIO ANUAL - FUNDACAO NACIONAL DO BEM-ESTAR DO MENOR. **Main/Corp** Fundacao Nacional do Bem-Estar do Menor. Portuguese. an. **LC** HV747.B8. **DD** 362.7042. *Relatorio de Atividades.*

RELATORIO ANUAL - SERVICO SOCIAL DO COMERCIO. ADMINISTRACACO REGIONAL DE SAO PAULO. **Main/Corp** Servico Social do Comercio. Administracao Regional no Estado de Sao Paulo. BL. Portuguese. ir. Ria Dr Vola Nova 228 70 Andar, Sao Paulo Brazil. **LC** HV194.S34.

RELATORIO ANUAL - SERVICO SOCIAL DO COMERCIO. ADMINISTRACAO DO MARANHAO. **Main/Corp** Servico Social do Comercio. Administracao Regional do Maranhao. Portuguese. an. **LC** HV194.M36. **DD** 354.8121008406.

RELATORIO ANUAL - SERVICO SOCIAL DO COMERCIO. ADMINISTRACAO REGIONAL EM MINAS GER. **Main/Corp** Servico Social do Comercio. Administracao Regional em Minas Gerais. BL. Portuguese. an. Administracao Regional Em Minas Gerais, rua Tupinambas, 956 Belo Horizonte Brazil. **LC** HV194.M5. **DD** 361.6098151.

RELATORIO DE ATIVIDADES - FUNDACAO PARA O LIVRO DO CEGO NO BRASIL. **Main/Corp** Fundacao Para o Livro do Cego no Brasil. BL. Portuguese. ir. Fundacao Para O Livro do Cego No Brasil, rua Dr Diogo de Faria 558, 04037 Sao Paulo Brazil. **LC** HV1892. **DD** 362.4183. *Relatorio - Fundacao Para o Livro do Cego no Brasil.*

RELATORIO DE ATIVIDADES - SECRETARIA DA SEGURANCA PUBLICA. **Main/Corp** Bahia, Brazil (State). Secretaria de Seguranca Publica. Periodical. Portuguese. ir. **LC** HV7696.B2.

RELATORIO DE ATIVIDADES - SERVICO SOCIAL DO COMERCIO, ADMINISTRACAO REGIONAL NO ESTADO DE GOIAS. **Main/Corp** Servico Social do Comercio. Administracao Regional no Estado de Goias. Portuguese. ir. Servico Social do Comercio Administracao Regional No Estado de Goias, Av Universitaria 1749 Cx Postal, Goiania 309 Brazil. **LC** HV194.G6.

RELATORIO ESTATISTICO (SALVADOR, BRAZIL). (RELATORIO ESTATISTICO). Portuguese. ir. **LC** HV8184.B33. **DD** 3545.8142007406.

RELATORIO ESTATISTICO - SERVICO DE ESTATISTICA POLICIAL E CRIMINAL. *See* Statistics.

RELATORIO - FEBEM/RS. **Main/Corp** Fundacao Estadual do Bem-Estar do Menor. Rio Grande do sul, Brazil. Portuguese. ir. **LC** HV747.B8.

RELATORIO GERAL - FUNDACAO LEGIAO BRASILEIRA DE ASSISTENCIA. **Main/Corp** Legiao Brasileira de Assistencia. BL. Portuguese. ir. Fundacao Legiso Brasileira de Assistencia, Av General Justo 275, Rio de Janeiro Brazil. **LC** HV192. **DD** 362.981.

RELATORIO - POLICIA CIVIL DA BAHIA. **Main/Corp** Policia Civil da Bahia. Portuguese. ir. **LC** HV8184.B33. **DD** 354.8142007406.

RELATORIO QUALITATIVO - SERVICO SOCIAL DO COMERCIO, ADMINISTRACAO REGIONAL EM MINAS GERAIS. **Main/Corp** Servico Social do Comercio. Administracao Regional em Minas Gerais. BL. Portuguese. ir. Administracao Regional em Minas Gerais, rua Tupinambas 956, Belo Horizonte Brazil. **LC** HV194.M54.

RELATORIO SETORIAL, GOVERNO DO ESTADO DE SAO PAULO. **Main/Corp** Sao Paulo, Brazil (State). Secretaria da Promocao Social. BL. Portuguese. ir. Secretaria da Promocao Social, Avenida Casper Libero 464, Sao Paulo Brazil. **LC** HV194.S3. **DD** 354.8161008406.

Sociology: General Works, Theory—Social Pathology, Welfare, Criminology

RELEASES FROM JUVENILE INSTITUTIONS (WISCONSIN. DIVISION OF CORRECTIONS. OFFICE OF INFORMATION MANAGEMENT). (RELEASES FROM JUVENILE INSTITUTIONS). **Series/Titl** Statistical Bulletin, C. Calendar Year 1979-. 0277-7282. US. English. an. Wisconsin Division of Corrections, PO Box 7925, Madison WI 53707. **LC** HV7299. **DD** 364.3609775. *Offenders Released from Juvenile Correctional Institutions, 0362-7470.*

RENDEZVOUS (BRANTFORD, ONT.). (RENDEZVOUS). 0712-7588. Periodical. CN. English (French). ir. Free. Rendezvous, Prison Arts Foundation, 80 Chatham Street, Brantford Ontario N3T 2P1 Canada. **DD** 365.660971. (ctrl).

REPERTOIRE DES CENTRES RESIDENTIELS COMMUNAUTAIRES AU CANADA. 1975-. 0226-0492. CN. French. be. Ministere du Solliciteur General du Canada, Ottawa Ontario K1A 0T6 Canada. **DD** 362.802571.

REPERTOIRE DES ORGANISATIONS MEDICO-SANITAIRES ET SOCIALES PHILANTHROPIQUES PRIVEES ET D'ORIGINE RELIGIEUSE EN HAITI. HT. French. ir. Commission Medicale Chretienne d'Haiti, 68 rue Capois, Port-au-Prince Haiti. **DD** 362.10425097294.

REPERTOIRE DES RESSOURCES COMMUNAUTAIRES DE LA REGION DE LEVIS. 0712-1199. CN. French. ir. $1.00 Each Number. Service d'Entraide, Regroupement et Solidarite, Centre de Benevolat, 106 rue Jean XXIII, Levis Quebec G6V 2K1 Canada. **DD** 361.002571459.

REPERTOIRE DES SERVICES COMMUNAUTAIRES. 1983/84-. 0823-891X. CN. English (text in French). an. $6.00 Per Vol. Information and Reference, Sudbury Public Library, 200 Brady Street, Sudbury Ontario P3E 5K3 Canada. **DD** 361.0025713133. *Directory of Community Services, 0709-0749.*

REPERTOIRE DES SERVICES COMMUNAUTAIRES DE GRANBY ET DES ENVIRONS. First issue in 1971?. 0315-8357. Periodical. CN. French. Centre de Reference et d'Information de Granby, C.P. 332, Granby Quebec Canada. **DD** 361.002571463.

REPERTOIRE DES SERVICES COMMUNAUTAIRES DE LA REGION ST-HYACINTHE-BELOEIL-MONT ST-HILAIRE. 1981-. 0712-1237. CN. French. an. $7,00 LE V $10,00 Le V Avec Classeur A Anneaux. Centre de Reference et d'Information Familiale, CP 190, 1900 Ouest rue Girouard, St-Hyacinthe Quebec J2S 7B4 Canada. **DD** 361.0025714523. *Repertoire des Services Communautaires de la Region St-Hyacinthe-Beloeil, 0712-1229.*

REPERTOIRE DES SERVICES COMMUNAUTAIRES DU GRAND MONTREAL. BIEN-ETRE. SANTE. LOISIRS. *See* Yearbooks, Almanacs, Directories.

REPORT & ACCOUNTS - BRITISH AGENCIES FOR ADOPTION AND FOSTERING. **Main/Corp** British Agencies for Adoption and Fostering. **VFOAT** Report of the Management Committee and Accounts. 1980/81-. UK. English. an. British Agency for Adoption and Fostering, 11 Southwark Street, London SE1 1RQ England. **LC** HV887.G7. **DD** 354.410072305.

REPORT AND EVALUATION. MAINE CRIMINAL JUSTICE INTERNSHIP PROGRAM. (MAINE CRIMINAL JUSTICE INTERNSHIP PROGRAM; REPORT AND EVALUATION). **Main/Corp** Maine. Law Enforcement Planning & Assistance Agency. 0090-9386. US. English. an. Maine Law Enforcement Planning & Assistance Agency, 295 Water Street, Augusta ME 04330. **LC** HV7269. **DD** 363.2209741.

REPORT AND STATEMENT OF ACCOUNTS - LIQUOR CONTROL COMMISSION. **Main/Corp** Victoria, Australia. Liquor Control Commission. 1968/69-. AT. English. ir. $1.50. F D Atkinson, Government Printer, PO Box 203, North Melbourne Victoria 3051 Australia. **LC** HV5675.A3. **DD** 354.9450076106.

REPORT - BRITISH COLUMBIA. FIRST CITIZENS' FUND ADVISORY COMMITTEE. **Main/Corp** British Columbia. First Citizens' Fund Advisory Committee. CN. English. K M McDonald/Queen Printer, Parliament Buildings, Victoria British Columbia V8V 4R6 Canada. **LC** E78.B9. **DD** 362.84.

REPORT. CHILD ABUSE. (REPORT : CHILD ABUSE). **Main/Corp** Washington (State). Dept. of Social and Health Services. 0160-175X. US. English. **LC** HV742.W3. **DD** 362.71.

REPORT - FEDERAL SURPLUS RELIEF CORPORATION. **Main/Corp** Federal Surplus Relief Corporation. Periodical. English. ir.

REPORT - KARNATAKA LEGISLATURE, COMMITTEE ON THE WELFARE OF SCHEDULED CASTES & SCHEDULED TRIBES. **Main/Corp** Karnataka, India. Legislature. Committee on the Welfare of Scheduled Castes and Scheduled Tribes. English. ir. Karnataka Legislature Secretariat, Vidhana Soundha, Bangalore India 560001. **LC** HN690.M9. **DD** 362.8. *Report - Committee on the Welfare of Scheduled Castes and Scheduled Tribes.*

REPORT - KENTUCKY. DEPT. OF CORRECTIONS. **Main/Corp** Kentucky. Dept. of Corrections. 1st- 1962/63-. 0451-6702. US. English. an. **LC** HV8337.

REPORT - KENTUCKY. DEPT. OF ECONOMIC SECURITY. **Main/Corp** Kentucky. Dept. of Economic Security. 1948/49-. US. English. an. State of Kentucky, Department of Economic Security, Frankfort KY 40601. **LC** HV86. **DD** 360.61769.

REPORT - MALAYA (FEDERATION) DEPT. OF SOCIAL WELFARE. **Main/Corp** Malaya (Federation). Dept. of Social Welfare. English. ir. **LC** HV394.M3. **DD** 360.61595.

REPORT - MARYLAND DIVISION OF CORRECTION. **Main/Corp** Maryland. Division of Correction. 0362-9198. US. English. an. Division of Correction, 920 Greenmount Avenue, Baltimore MD 21202. **LC** HV7270. **DD** 353.975200849.

REPORT - MEGHALAYA LEGISLATIVE ASSEMBLY, COMMITTEE ON PETITIONS. **Main/Corp** Meghalaya, India. Legislative Assembly. Committee on Petitions. 1st-1973-. II. English. ir. Meghalaya Legislative Assembly Secretariat, Meghalaya Shillong India. **LC** HV395.M4. **DD** 362.95416.

REPORT - NATIONAL ADVISORY COUNCIL FOR THE HANDICAPPED (AUSTRALIA). *See* Physically Impaired.

REPORT - NEW JERSEY. BUREAU OF STATE USE INDUSTRIES. **Main/Corp** New Jersey. Bureau of State Use Industries. 1954/55-. US. English. an. **LC** HV8929.N5.

REPORT OF ACHIEVEMENTS OF PROGRAMS FOR THE AGING. **Main/Corp** Hawaii. Commission on Aging. 1970/71-. 0090-2233. US. English. an. Commission on Aging, 250 South King Street, Honolulu HI 96813. **LC** HV1468.H3. **DD** 362.6099693.

REPORT OF ACTIVITIES - MAX BELL FOUNDATION. (REPORT OF ACTIVITIES. MAX BELL FOUNDATION). **Main/Corp** Max Bell Foundation. 0828-6507. CN. English. be. Max Bell Foundation, PO Box 122 Toronto-Dominion Centre, Toronto Ontario M5K 1H1. **DD** 361.760971.

REPORT OF ESCAPES - VIRGINIA. DEPT. OF CORRECTIONS. BUREAU OF MANAGEMENT INFORMATION. **VFOAT** Report of Felon Escapes. 0098-5686. US. English. an. Department of Corrections, PO Box 26963, Richmond VA 23261. **LC** HV9475.V8. **DD** 365.641.

REPORT OF OPERATIONS & DEVELOPMENT. **Main/Corp** New York (State). Dept. of Correctional Services. **VFOAT** Report of Operations and Development. Began with 1976 vol. 0276-7759. US. English. an. New York State Department of Correctional Services, Building 2, State Office Building, Campus Albany NY 12226. **LC** HV7282. **DD** 353.97470084906. *Annual Report, 0095-7666.*

REPORT OF PERSONS DISCHARGED FROM PAROLE AND PERSONS VIOLATING PAROLE. **Main/Corp** Virginia. Dept. of Corrections. 0364-6580. US. English. **LC** HV7296. **DD** 364.6209755.

REPORT OF PROBATION SUPERVISION WORKLOAD. **Main/Corp** Virginia. Dept. of Corrections. Bureau of Management Information. 0362-7489. US. English. an. Commonwealth of Virginia, Department of Corrections, Bureau of Management Information, 22 East Cary, Richmond VA 23219. **LC** HV7296. **DD** 364.6309755. *Report of Probation Supervision Workload, 0362-7489.*

REPORT OF RECIDIVISTS COMMITTED TO THE VIRGINIA STATE PENAL SYSTEM. **Main/Corp** Virginia. Dept. of Corrections. Bureau of Management Information. 0363-0633. US. English. an. Commonwealth of Virginia, Department of Corrections, PO Box 26963, Richmond VA 23261. **LC** HV7296. **DD** 365.609755.

REPORT OF THE CRIME VICTIMS COMPENSATION BOARD. (ANNUAL REPORT - CRIME VICTIMS COMPENSATION BOARD). **Main/Corp** New York (State). Crime Victims Compensation Board. 1st- 1967-. 0077-9148. US. English. an. Crime Victims Compensation Board, 855 Central Avenue, Albany NY 12206. **LC** HV8688. **DD** 362.8809747.

REPORT OF THE CRIMINAL INJURIES COMPENSATION BOARD - ONTARIO. **Main/Corp** Ontario. Criminal Injuries Compensation Board. 3D- 1971-. CN. English. Criminal Injuries Compensation Board, Room 201 454/University Avenue, 2 Toronto Ontario Canada. **LC** HV8688. **DD** 362.8809713. *Report of the Law Enforcement Compensation Board.*

REPORT OF THE DEPARTMENT OF COMMUNITY WELFARE SERVICES FOR THE YEAR ENDED 30 JUNE . . . . **Main/Corp** Victoria. Dept. of Community Welfare Services. **VFOAT** Annual Report. AU. English. an. $2.30. Department of Community Welfare Services, 55 Swanston Street, Melbourne 3000 Australia.

REPORT OF THE DEPARTMENT OF SOCIAL WELFARE. **Main/Corp** New Zealand. Dept. of Social Welfare. 1972/73-. NZ. English. an. Government Printing Office NZ, Private Bag, Wellington New Zealand. **LC** HV515.5. **DD** 354.9310084.

REPORT OF THE DIRECTOR - DEPARTMENT OF CHILDREN'S SERVICES. **Main/Corp** Queensland. Dept. of Children's Services. **VFOAT** Annual Report - Department of Children's Services. 1967-. English. ir. **LC** HV802.Q4. **DD** 362.709943. **NLM** W2 KA8 Q3D3R. *Report - State Children Department.*

REPORT OF THE GENERAL DIRECTOR - INTERAMERICAN CHILDREN'S INSTITUTE. **Main/Corp** Interamerican Children's Institute. English. an. Interamerican Children's Institute, Avda 8 de Octubre 2904, Montevideo 2904 Uruguay. **LC** HV703. **DD** 362.7098.

REPORT OF THE GOVERNOR'S EARTHQUAKE COUNCIL. **Main/Corp** California. Governor's Earthquake Council. 0098-2717. US. English. Governor's Earthquake Council, Resources Building/Room 1115, 1416 9th Street, Sacramento CA 98517. **Ind/Abst** GeoRef. **LC** TA654.6. **DD** 363.34.

REPORT OF THE HARRY FRANK GUGGENHEIM FOUNDATION. **Main/Corp** Harry Frank Guggenheim Foundation. 1929/74-. US. English. Harry Frank Guggenheim Foundation, 120 Broadway, New York NY 10005. **LC** HV97.H36. **DD** 361.76.

REPORT OF THE MASTERTON LICENSING TRUST. **Main/Corp** Masterton Licensing Trust. 1st- 1947/48-. English. ir. **LC** HV5685.M3. **DD** 352.9361093127.

REPORT OF THE OHIO DEPARTMENT OF REHABILITATION AND CORRECTION. **Main/Corp** Ohio. Dept. of Rehabilitation and Correction. 0095-7720. US. English. 1944 Morse Road, Columbus OH 43229. **LC** HV7285. **DD** 353.977100849.

REPORT OF THE TASK FORCE ON ALCOHOLISM. **Main/Corp** Massachusetts. Task Force on Alcoholism. US. English. Task Force on Alcoholism, 296 Boylston Street, Boston MA 02116. **LC** HV5297.M39. **DD** 362.29209744.

Sociology: General Works, Theory—Social Pathology, Welfare, Criminology

REPORT - OHIO. DIVISION OF STATE HIGHWAY PATROL. Main/Corp Ohio. Division of State Highway Patrol. 1934-. US. English. LC HV7571.O3.

REPORT ON DEPARTMENT OF HEALTH, OFFICE OF MENTAL RETARDATION, NORTH CENTRAL REGIONAL CENTER. Main/Corp Connecticut. Auditors PF Public Accounts. 0362-8248. US. English. be. Auditors of Public Accounts, 165 Capital Avenue, Hartford CO 06115. LC HV3006.C72. DD 353.974600843.

REPORT ON DEPARTMENT OF SOCIAL SERVICES. Main/Corp Connecticut. Auditors of Public Accounts. 1974/77-. US. English. an. State of Connecticut, Auditors of Public Accounts, State Capitol, Hartford CT 06106. LC HV86. DD 353.97460084. *Report on State Welfare Department.*

REPORT ON SERVICES AND FINANCING OF FAMILY SERVICE AGENCIES IN ONTARIO. (REPORT ON SERVICES AND FINANCING OF FAMILY SERVICE AGENCIES IN ONTARIO IN . . .). Main/Corp Ontario Association of Family Service Agencies. 0825-5237. CN. English. an. Ontario Association of Family Service Agencies, Suite 114/175 Bloor Street East, Toronto Ontario M4W 1E1 Canada. DD 362.828060713. *Services and Financing of Family Service Agencies in Ontario in . . ., 0709-1648.*

REPORT ON SOCIAL DEVELOPMENTS. See Economics - Labor.

REPORT ON THE PROBATION AND WELFARE SERVICE WITH STATISTICS FOR THE YEAR . . . . Main/Corp Ireland. Probation and Welfare Service. English. an. 1.80. Government Publications Sales Office, Government Printing Office Arcade, Dublin 1 Ireland. LC HV9278. DD 354.4170084906.

REPORT ON THE WORK OF THE PRISON DEPARTMENT. Main/Corp Great Britain. Home Office. 1964-. UK. English. an. Her Majestys Stationery Office, PO Box 276, London SW8 5DT England. Tel (01)622-3316. LC HV9646. DD 365.942. *Prisons and Borstals: Report on the Work of the Prison Department, 0346-4289.*

REPORT - OREGON. DEPT OF STATE POLICE. Main/Corp Oregon. Dept. of State Police. US. English. an. LC HV7571.O7. DD 351.74, 364.4.

REPORT OT THE GOVERNOR OF MISSISSIPPI AND TO MEMBERS OF THE MISSISSIPPI LEGISLATURE CONCERNING AID TO DEPENDENT CHILDREN CASES INVOLVING A DISERTING PARENT OR PARENTS. Main/Corp Mississippi. State Dept. of Public Welfare. US. English. LC HV742.M75. DD 362.71309762.

REPORT - PENNSYLVANIA CRIME COMMISSION. (REPORT). Main/Corp Pennsylvania. Crime Commission. 0091-4118. US. English. Crime Commission, 523 East Lancaster Avenue, Saint Davids PA 19087. LC HV7288. DD 364.9748.

REPORT (PERMANENT CHARITY FUND OF BOSTON). (REPORT). Vol. 1, No. 1 (Winter 1980)-. Periodical. US. English. qt. Permanent Charity Fund of Boston, One Boston Place, Boston MA 02106.

REPORT PRESENTED TO THE HOUSE OF REPRESENTATIVES. Main/Corp Oamaru Licensing Trust. 1962/63-. English. ir. LC HV5682.

REPORT - SOCIAL SERVICE BOARD OF NORTH DAKOTA. Main/Corp North Dakota. Social Service Board. 0095-6325. US. English. Social Service Board, State Capitol, Bismarck ND 58505. LC HV1555.N9. DD 361.9784.

REPORT - TEXAS. DEPT OF CORRECTIONS. Main/Corp Texas. Dept. of Corrections. US. English. an. LC HV8363.

REPORT TO COUNCIL ON PROGRAM - NATIONAL INSTITUTE ON AGING. Main/Corp National Institute on Aging. 0277-660X. US. English. an. National Institute on Aging, National Institutes of Health, Bethesda MD 20205. LC HQ1060. DD 362.6071173.

REPORT TO GOVERNOR AND THE LEGISLATURE - STATE OF NEW YORK. COMMISSION ON GAMBLING. (REPORT). Main/Corp New York (State). Commission on Gambling. 0092-0746. US. English. an. Commission on Gambling, 162 Washington Avenue, Albany NY 12210. LC HV6721.N52. DD 353.974700762.

A REPORT TO THE . . . GENERAL ASSEMBLY ON THE STATUS OF THE COMMUNITY BASED JUVENILE VICTIM RESTITUTION PROGRAM AUTHORIZED BY THE 1979 SESSION OF THE SIXTY-EIGHTH GENERAL ASSEMBLY. Main/Corp Iowa State Youth Coordinator's Office. 1st. Ed.-. US. English. an. Iowa State Youth Coordinator's Office, Iowa Office for Planning and Programming, 523 East 12th Street, Des Moines IA 50319. Tel (515)281-3927. Ed JoAnn Callison. LC HV9105.I8. DD 364.68. Circ 100. (ctrl).

REPORT TO THE PRESIDENT - UNITED STATES. PRESIDENT'S COMMITTEE ON MENTAL RETARDATION. (REPORT TO THE PRESIDENT). Main/Corp United States. President's Committee on Mental Retardation. Series/Titl DHHS Publication. 12th-. 0739-5493. US. English. an. US Department of Health and Human Services, Washington DC 20201. LC HV3006.A1. DD 362.30973. 0565-9809 MR.

REPORT - WEST VIRGINIA BOARD OF PROBATION AND PAROLE. Main/Corp West Virginia Board of Probation and Parole. VFOAT Report of the Dept. of Probation and Parole. US. English. an. LC HV9305.W4. DD 364.6209754. *Report of the Director of Probation and Parole.*

REPORT - WORKSHOP FOR CHILD CARE STAFF OF FLORIDA'S CHILD CARING FACILITIES. (REPORT). Main/Conf Workshop for Child Care Staff of Florida's Child Caring Facilities. 0091-8482. US. English. an. $1.00 Per Copy. Florida Group Child Care Association, PO Box 2050, Jacksonville FL 32203. LC HV742.F6. DD 362.73209759.

REPORTED OFFENSES AND ARRESTS. NEW YORK STATE. See Law Enforcement.

REPORTER CANADIEN. (LE REPORTER CANADIEN). 0820-6252. CN. French. qt. Free to Members. Association Canadienne pour les d'Eficients Mentaux, 4700 rue Keele, Downsview Ontario M3J 1P3 Canada. DD 362.30971. *Reporter de Quebec, 0381-1395.*

REPORTS. TO. (REPORTS : TO). Main/Conf Inter-African Conference. Treatment of Offenders. VFOAT Rapports: TO. Periodical. UK. English and French. ir. Europa Publications, 18 Bedford Square, London WC1B 3JN England. DD 338.9.

THE REPORTS - VIRGINIA. DEPT. OF CORRECTIONS. Main/Corp Virginia. Dept. of Corrections. US. English. an. Virginia Department of Corrections, 3117 West Clay Street, Richmond VA 23261. LC HV7296. DD 353.97550084906.

RESEARCH AND DEVELOPMENT PROJECTS IN AGING. Main/Corp United States. Administration on Aging. VAT Research & Development Projects in Aging. 0271-2784. US. English. US Department of Health Education & Welfare, Administration on Aging, 330 Independence Avenue SW, Washington DC 20201. LC HV1457. DD 362.6072073. NLM WT 22 AA1 R4.

RESEARCH AND STATISTICS ANNUAL REPORT. See Statistics.

RESEARCH BULLETIN (GREAT BRITAIN. HOME OFFICE. RESEARCH AND PLANNING UNIT). (RESEARCH BULLETIN). No. 13-. 0305-9871. Periodical. UK. English. sa. Home Office Research and Planning Unit, 50 Queen Anne's Gate, London SW1H 9AT England. LC HV6941. DD 364.941. *Research Bulletin (Great Britain. Home Office. Research Unit).*

RESEARCH, DEMONSTRATION AND EVALUATION STUDIES ON CHILD ABUSE AND NEGLECT. Main/Corp United States. Dept. of Health, Education, and Welfare. Intradepartmental Committee on Child Abuse and Neglect. 1973/74-. 0362-8221. US. English. an. $0.80. LC HV741. DD 362.781971.

RESEARCH-IN-PROGRESS (WASHINGTON, D.C. : 1983). (RESEARCH-IN-PROGRESS). VFOAT Research in Progress. 1982-83-. 0882-6692. Periodical. US. English. $10.00. Independent Sector, 1828 L Street Northwest, Washington DC 20036. DD 361.

RESEARCH REPORT A.F.D.C. (RESEARCH REPORT AFDC). Main/Corp Colorado. Dept. of Social Services. Research and Statistics Section. 0091-5823. US. English. LC HV742.C6.

RESEAU. (LE RESEAU). V. 1, No. 1 (Feb. 1976)-. 0712-2144. Periodical. CN. French. ir. Free. Le Reseau, c/o Centre Hospitalier, Robert-Giffard, 2601 Chemin de la Canardiere, Beauport Quebec GIJ 2G3 Canada. DD 362.110971447. (ctrl).

RESIDENTIAL ACCOMODATION FOR THE ELDERLY AND CERTAIN OTHER ADULTS, SCOTLAND. Began in 1978. UK. English. an. Social Work Services Group, Statistics Branch, 43 Jeffrey Street/Room 424, Edinburgh EHI IDN Scotland. LC HD7287.92.G72. DD 362.6109411.

RESIDENTIAL GROUP CARE & TREATMENT. VFOAT Residential Group Care and Treatment. Vol. 1, No. 1 (Fall 1982)-. 0731-7123. Periodical. US. English. qt. $102.00. Haworth Press, 28 East 22nd Street, New York NY 10010. Tel (212)228-2800. Ed Ord Matek. Ind/Abst Electron. Commun. Abstr. J., ISMEC Bull., Pollut. Abstr. Indexes, Saf. Sci. Abstr. J., Excerpta Med., Sociol. Abstr., Psychol. Abstr. LC HV59. DD 362.73205. bk rev. adv acc. Circ 1,044. Provides an active and contemporary forum for those engaged in the interdisciplinary task of the residential group care of children and youth. *Residential and Community Child Care Administration, 0162-1408.*

RESIDENTS IN WISCONSIN ADULT CORRECTIONAL FACILITIES ON . . . WITH FIVE-YEAR TRENDS FOR . . . . Series/Titl Statistical Bulletin C. June 30, 1982-. US. English. sa. Division of Corrections, Office of Information Management and Operations, Madison WI 53707. LC HV7299. DD 364.309775. *Residents in Wisconsin Adult Correctional Institutions and Community Correctional Residental Centers on . . . with Five-Year Trends for . . ., 0732-1066.*

RESIDENTS IN WISCONSIN ADULT CORRECTIONAL INSTITUTIONS. Main/Corp Wisconsin. Division of Corrections. Office of Systems and Evaluation. Series/Titl Statistical Bulletin C. Periodical. US. English. Department of Health & Social Services, Box 669, Madison WI 53701. LC HV7299. DD 364.309775. *Residents in Wisconsin Adult Correctional Institutions, 0363-0641.*

RESIDENTS IN WISCONSIN ADULT CORRECTIONAL INSTITUTIONS AND COMMUNITY CORRECTIONAL RESIDENTIAL CENTERS. Main/Corp Wisconsin. Division of Corrections. Office of Systems and Evaluation. June 30, 1978-. US. English. sa. Wisconsin Division of Corrections, PO Box 669, Madison WI 53701. *Residents in Wisconsin Adult and Youthful Offender Correctional Institutions and Residential Community Centers.*

RESIDENTS IN WISCONSIN JUVENILE CORRECTIONAL INSTITUTIONS. (RESIDENTS IN WISCONSIN JUVENILE CORRECTIONAL INSTITUTIONS ON . . . WITH FIVE-YEAR TRENDS FOR . . .). 0732-0787. US. English. sa. Division of Corrections Office of Systems and Evaluation, Madison WI 53707. LC HV7299. DD 364.3609775. *Offenders Resident in Wisconsin Juvenile Correctional Institutions on .. with Five-Year Trends for . . . (Madison, Wis. : 1979), 0732-0795.*

RESILOG. VFOAT Resilog. No. 1- Dec. 1978-. 0225-5804. Periodical. CN. English (French). bm. Environment Canada, Waste Management Branch, Inquiry Center, Ottawa Ontario K1A 0H3 Canada. DD 363.7280971. Collator.

RESOLUTION OF CORRECTIONAL PROBLEMS AND ISSUES. VFOAT Resolution. V. 1- Fall 1974-. 0095-3180. Periodical. US. English. qt. $10.00. South Carolina Department of Corrections, PO Box 766, Columbia SC 29202. LC HV9261. DD 364.60973.

RESOURCE DIRECTORY - COMMUNITY SWITCHBOARD OF REGINA CEASED. Main/Corp Community Switchboard of Regina. 1975-1982. 0703-9247. Periodical. CN. English. Community Switchboard of

Sociology: General Works, Theory—Social Pathology, Welfare, Criminology

Regina, 2641 Garnet Street, Regina Saskatchewan S4T 3A8 Canada. **DD** 361.002571244.

RESOURCE MATERIAL SERIES. English. ir. Unafei, 1-26 Harumicho, Fuchu Japan. **LC** HV7431. **DD** 364.4.

RESSOURCES ET VOUS. (RESSOURCES ET VOUS : PERIODIQUE DE LA SOCIETE DE CRIMINOLOGIE DU QUEBEC). No 1 (July. 1981)-. 0714-4288. Periodical. CN. French. bm. 6.00. Societe de Criminologie Quebec, 1 East Notre-Dame Palais de Justice, Montreal Quebec H2Y 1B6 Canada. **Tel** (514)873-6167. **Ed** Samir Rizkalla. **Circ** 500. (ctrl). General description of a resource active in crime prevention, law enforcement or social and community help to Ex-convicts.

REVIEW - LEAGUE OF RED CROSS SOCIETIES. **Main/Corp** League of Red Cross Societies. **VFOAT** Review . . . of the Activities of the League of Red Cross Societies. English. ir. **LC** HV560. **DD** 361.763405. **NLM** W1.

REVIEW OF CURRENT RESEARCH. **Main/Corp** Massachusetts. Dept. of Correction. 0160-1091. US. English. Leverett Saltonstall Building Government Center, 100 Cambridge Street, Boston MA 02202. **LC** HV9274. **DD** 364.609744.

REVIEW REPORT. UNITED WAY NATIONAL ATTITUDE SURVEY. (REVIEW REPORT : UNITED WAY NATIONAL ATTITUDE SURVEY). **Main/Corp** United Way of America. 1976-. 0146-7484. US. English. United Way of America, 301 North Fairfax Street, Alexandria VA 22314. **LC** HV88. **DD** 301.1543361973.

REVISTA BOLIVIANA DE CIENCIAS PENALES. Yearly V. 1, No. 1, (May/June/July 1978)-. Periodical. BO. Spanish. qt. Sociedad Boloviana de Ciencias Penales Secretaria General, Jenaro Sanjines 423 6To. Piso Of 610 Casillas 4171, 4854 La Paz Bolivia. **LC** HV6886. **DD** 364.98405.

REVISTA DE CIENCIAS PENALES. V. 1- March/April 1935-. Periodical. CL. Spanish. ir. $2.50. Editorial Andres Bello Avenida Ricardo, Lyon 946, Providencia Santiago Chile.

REVISTA DE ESTUDIOS PENITENCIARIOS (1961). (REVISTA DE ESTUDIOS PENITENCIARIOS). Yearly V. 17, No. 154 (Sept./Oct. 1961)-. 0210-6035. Periodical. SP. Spanish. ir. Revista Estudios Ministerio de Justioia, Madrid 8 Spain. **Ind/Abst** Foreign Lang. Index. Revista de la Escuela de Estudios Penitenciarios.

REVISTA DE PREVIDENCIA SOCIAL. BL. Portuguese. bm. 2350. Editora Previdenciarai Ltda, Caixa Postal 9117, CEP 01047 Sao Paulo SP Brazil. **LC** HV193. **DD** 361.981.

REVISTA PROMOCAO SOCIAL SAO PAULO. Year 1- (No. 1-). Portuguese. ir. Secretaria do Promocao Social, Rua do Ouvidor 63, Sao Paulo Brazil. **LC** HV194.S3.

REVUE BELGE DE SECURITE SOCIALE. Yearly V. 1- Jan./Feb. 1954-. 0771-1530. Periodical. BE. French. mo. 530. Ministere de la Prevoyance Sociale, rue de la Vierge Niore 3C, 1000 Bruxelles Belgium. **Ind/Abst** Int. Labour Doc., Foreign Lang. Index. **LC** HD7186. **DD** 368.4009493. Revue Belge de Securite Sociale, Revue des Allocations Familiales.

REVUE D'ACTION SOCIALE : AS. **VFOAT** AS. Periodical. French. bm. 950. 15 rue des Croisiers, 4000 Liege Belgium. **LC** HV303. **DD** 362.9493.

REVUE DE DROIT PENAL ET DE CRIMINOLOGIE. Periodical. BE. French. ir. Assn Revue Droit Penal Crimino, Palais de Justice, B-1000 Bruxelles Belgium. **Tel** (02)5111455. adv acc. Journal of criminal law and criminology.

LA REVUE FRANCAISE DE SERVICE SOCIAL. No. 1- 19 -. Periodical. FR. French. qt. 140.-. Association Nationale des Assistants de Service Social, 15 rue de Bruxelles, 75009 Paris France. **Tel** 526.33.79. adv acc. **Circ** 4,000. (ctrl). Journal of studies concerning thought and communication on French social service.

REVUE INTERNATIONALE DE CRIMINOLOGIE ET DE POLICE TECHNIQUE. V. 7- 1953-. 0035-3329. Periodical. French. qt. $34.64. Editions Marcel Meichtry, 22 Chemin de la Caroline, CH1213 Petit Lancy Switzerland. **Tel** 022/92 10 27. **Ind/Abst** Psychol. Abstr. **NLM** W1 RE876H.

RICERCA E AZIONE SOCIALE IN ITALIA. 1- 1967-. Italian. ir. **LC** HN480.

RIFF-RAFF ROCKETTE REVIEW. 0227-1702. Periodical. CN. English. ir. Free. Toc Alpha, 15 Gervais Drive, Don Mills Ontario M3C 1Y8 Canada. **DD** 362.2906071. (ctrl). Toc Alphacate, 0381-6125.

ROKYOIKU KAGAKU. **VFOAT** Soundless World. JA. Japanese. ir. 600 Individual Membership. Ro-Kyoiku Kagaku-kai, c/o Kyoto Daigaku Bungakubu Sonohara Kenkyushitsu, Yoshida, Sakyo-ku, Kyoto Japan. **LC** HV2350.

THE ROLE OF BEHAVIORAL SCIENCE IN PHYSICAL SECURITY. See Law Enforcement.

ROLL OF THE ORDER - PRIORY OF CANADA. (ROLL OF THE ORDER - THE PRIORY OF CANADA). **Main/Corp** Order of St. John. Priory of Canada. **VFOAT** Repertoire des Membres - Le Prieure du Canada. 1974-. 0315-9701. CN. English (text in French, 1979-). an. Priory Secretary, Order of St John, PO Box 388 Station A, Ottawa Ontario K1N 8V4 Canada. **DD** 361.77. Roll of the Order in Canada, 0315-9728.

ROLNIK SPOLDZIELCA. Periodical. PL. Polish. wk. ARS Polona, Krakowskie Przedmiescie 7, 00-068 Warsaw Poland.

ROND-POINT. (ROND-POINT : JOURNAL INTERNE DU CHUS). Vol. 1, No. 1 (May 1980)-. 0227-4531. Periodical. CN. French. mo. Free. Service de l'Information Centre Hospitalier, Universitaire de Sherbrooke, Sherbrooke Quebec J1H 5N4 Canada. **DD** 362.110971466. (ctrl).

RULINGS. CUMULATIVE EDITION : SOCIAL SECURITY RULINGS ON FEDERAL OLD-AGE, SURVIVORS, DISABILITY, SUPPLEMENTAL SECURITY INCOME, AND BLACK LUNG BENEFITS. See Economics - Labor.

RUNAWAY AND OTHERWISE HOMELESS YOUTH, ANNUAL REPORT ON THE RUNAWAY YOUTH ACT. (RUNAWAY AND OTHERWISE HOMELESS YOUTH : ANNUAL REPORT ON THE RUNAWAY YOUTH ACT). **Series/Titl** DHHS Publication. Fiscal year 1978-. 0272-541X. US. English. an. Department of Health and Human Services, 200 Independence Avenue SW, Washington DC 20201. **LC** HV1431. **DD** 362.74. **NLM** W2 A Y8R. Runaway Youth, 0193-1946.

S. O. S. GARDERIES. (S O S GARDERIES). **Main/Corp** S O S Garderies (Organisme). May 1975-. 0700-9666. Periodical. CN. French. ir. SOS Garderies 4258, Av de Lorimer, Montreal Quebec H2H 2B1 Canada. **DD** 372.21609714.

SAAD. IS. English. ir. Ministry of Social Welfare, Jerusalem Israel. **LC** HV4. **DD** 361.0095694.

SAFETY INFORMATION BULLETIN. V. 1- Feb. 1980-. 0226-7128. Periodical. CN. English. Rural Gas Safety Committee, PO Box 1517, Edmonton Alberta T5J 3J9 Canada. **DD** 363.1775.

SAGE ANNUAL REVIEWS OF STUDIES IN DEVIANCE. V. 1-. 0197-9272. Monographic Series. US. English. an. $28.00. Sage Publications Inc, PO Box 776, Beverly Hills CA 90213. **Ed** E Sagarin and C Winick. **NLM** W1 SA125U.

SAGE HUMAN SERVICES GUIDES. V. 1-. Monographic Series. US. English. ir. Sage Publications Inc, 275 South Beverly Drive, Beverly Hills CA 90212.

SAGE RESEARCH PROGRESS SERIES IN CRIMINOLOGY. V. 1-. Monographic Series. US. English. ir. Sage Publications Inc, 275 South Beverly Drive, Beverly Hills CA 90212.

SAHOE POKCHI. **VFOAT** Social Welfare. Periodical. KO. Korean. qt. Hanguk Sahoe Pokchi Hyobuihoe, 427-5 Kongduk-dong Mapo-ku, Seoul Korea. **LC** HV415.5.A44.

ST. JOHN NEWS. **VFOAT** Journal St-Jean. Began with Apr. 1952 issue. 0380-8181. Periodical. CN. English (includes some text in French, Apr. 1952-Mar. 1977). ir. St John Ambulance, PO Box 388 Station A, Ottawa Ontario K1N 8V4 Canada. **DD** 362.1'8.

SALVATION ARMY YOUTH. (SALVATION ARMY YOUTH : SAY). **VFOAT** SAY. 0744-5083. Periodical. US. English. mo. $3.00. Salvation Army, National Headquarters, 799 Bloomfield Avenue, Veronaf NJ 07044.

SANTE, SECURITE SOCIALE. Began with Jan./Feb. 1975 issue. 0338-3423. FR. French. bm. Ministere de la Sante et de la Securite Sociale, La Documentation Francaise, 29 Quai Voltaire, 75340 Paris Cedex 07 France. **Ind/Abst** Foreign Lang. Index, Excerpta Med. **LC** RA407.5.F7. **DD** 362.10944. **NLM** W2 GF7 M45B. Bulletin de Statistiques de Sante et de Securite Sociale.

SAR STATISTICS. See Statistics.

SARC NEWSLETTER. **Main/Corp** Saskatchewan Association of Rehabilitation Centres. **VAT** Saskatchewan Association of Rehabilitation Centres Newsletter. Dec. 1981-. 0821-2716. Periodical. CN. English. ir. Free. SARC Newsletter, 5000 Idlewyld Drive North, Saskatoon Sasketchewan S7L 5Y7 Canada. **DD** 362.40607124. Newsletter (Saskatchewan Association of Rehabilitation Centres), 0821-2414.

SATERN. (SATERN : SATELLITE ASSISTED EMERGENCY RESCUE NEWS). **VFOAT** Satellite-Assisted Emergency Rescue News. No. 1 (Summer 1984)-. 8756-1476. Periodical. US. English. qt. $20.00. Satern, 427 Haverhill Road, Joppa MD 21085. **DD** 363.

SAUF-CONDUIT (DRUMMONDVILLE, QUEBEC). (SAUF-CONDUIT). Vol. 1, No. 1 (July/Aug. 1982)-. 0821-3011. Periodical. CN. French. bm. Free. Organisation Sauf-Conduit, C P 442, Drummondville Quebec J2B 6W3 Canada. **DD** 362.704409714.

SAUVEGARDE DE L'ENFANCE. Began with May 1946 issue. Periodical. FR. French. ir. 260.00. French Association for the Safeguard of Childhood and Adolescence, 28 Place St-Georges, 75442 Paris 02 France. **Tel** 878 1373. **LC** HV761. **DD** 362.70944. **NLM** W1 SA979. bk rev. Includes normal and pathological psychology, sociology, education and assistance of the maladjusted child.

SCANDINAVIAN STUDIES IN CRIMINOLOGY. V. 1-. English. Universitetsforlaget, PO Box 2959-Toyen, Oslo 6 Norway. **Ed** K O Christiansen.

SCHOOL OF SOCIAL WORK. UNIVERSITY OF WINDSOR (CALENDAR) CEASED. (SCHOOL OF SOCIAL WORK; CALENDAR). **Main/Corp** University of Windsor. School of Social Work. 1973/74-1980/81. 0316-8697. Periodical. CN. English. an. University of Windsor, Windsor Ontario N9B 3P4 Canada. **DD** 361.0071171332.

SCHRIFTEN ZUR SOZIALARBEIT DES OSTERREICHISCHEN KOMITEES FUR SOZIALARBEIT. German. ir. **NLM** W1.

SCHWEIZERISCHE ZEITSCHRIFT FUR STRAFRECHT. **VFOAT** Revue Penale Suisse. Vol. 1. 0036-7893. Periodical. SZ. Multilingual (German and French). qt. $44.04. Staempfli & Cie SA, Hallerstrasse 7-9 Postfach 2728, CH-3001 Berne Switzerland. Index in last issue of volume - loose - separately paged. (cum index).

SCHWEIZERISCHES ROTES KREUZ JAHRESBERICHT. **VFOAT** Jahresbericht. Began with 1980?. German. ir. **NLM** W1 SC642R. Rapport Annuel de la Croix-Rouge Suisse.

THE SCOTTISH CIVIC TRUST YEAR BOOK. V. 1- 1973-. UK. English. an. Scottish Civic Trust, 24 George Square, Glasgow G2 18F Scotland. **LC** HV249.S4. **DD** 361.809411. Environment Scotland.

SCOTTISH SOCIAL WORK STATISTICS. See Statistics.

THE SEARCH IS ON FOR PERMANENT HOMES. V. 1, No. 1- Nov. 1978-. Periodical. US. English. qt.

SECURITY REGISTER. Nov. 1973-. 0092-7740. Periodical. US. English. bm. $12.00. Nickerson & Collins Company, 2720 Des Plains Avenue, Des Plains IL 60018. **LC** HV8290. **DD** 658.4705.

SEIRBHIS PHOIBLI : JOURNAL OF THE DEPARTMENT OF THE PUBLIC SERVICE. V. 1, No. 1 (Bealtaine 1980)-. 0332-2688. Periodical. chiefly English. ir. 1.50 Single Issue. Government Publications Sales Office, Sun Alliance House, Molesworth Street, Dublin 2 Ireland.

Sociology: General Works, Theory—Social Pathology, Welfare, Criminology

SELECTED CHARACTERISTICS OF PUBLIC ASSISTANCE RECIPIENTS IN NEW YORK CITY BY COMMUNITY DISTRICT. Main/Corp New York, N.Y. Human Resources Administration. Division of Policy and Economic Research. US. English. City of New York, Human Resources Administration, New York NY 10017. LC HV87.N5. DD 362.52097471.

SELECTED FINANCIAL STATISTICS OF CHARITABLE ORGANIZATIONS. See Statistics.

SEMI-ANNUAL REPORT - UNITED STATES. DEPT. OF HEALTH AND HUMAN SERVICES. OFFICE OF THE INSPECTOR GENERAL. (SEMI-ANNUAL REPORT). Main/Corp United States. Dept. of Health and Human Services. Office of Inspector General. VFOAT Semiannual Report. 1981/82-. 8756-7148. US. English. sa. LC HV85. DD 353.84206. *Annual Report, 0735-181X.*

SEMIANNUAL REPORT. Main/Corp United States. CSA/Office of Community Services. Office of Inspector General. Oct. 1, 1981-Mar. 31, 1982-. US. English. sa. Department of Health and Human Services, Office of Inspector General CSA/OCS, Washington DC 20506. *Semiannual Report to the Congress, 0271-9010.*

SEMINAR ON METHODS AND PROGRAMMES FOR THE PROMOTION OF RURAL YOUTH WORK. Main/Corp International Seminar on Methods and Programmes for the Promotion of Rural Youth Work. Periodical. English. ir. *Seminar on Methods and Programmes for the Promotion of Rural Youth Work.*

SENTENCING STATISTICS, HIGHER CRIMINAL COURTS, VICTORIA. See Statistics.

SERIES - PACIFIC GROUP FOR POLICY ALTERNATIVES. (SERIES). 1-84-1 (Feb. 1984)-. 0824-135X. Monographic Series. CN. English. ir. Pacific Group for Policy Alternatives, 22 East 8th Avenue, Vancouver British Columbia V5T 1R4 Canada. DD 361.6109711.

SERVICE CLUBS IN HAMILTON-WENTWORTH. Oct. 1979-. 0712-7642. CN. English. an. $2.00 Per Vol. Service Clubs in Hamilton-Wentworth, Community Information Service, Hamilton-Wentworth/Suite 601, 155 James Street South, Hamilton Ontario L8P 3A4 Canada. DD 361.002571352. *Service Club Directory of Hamilton and District, 0384-1529.*

SERVICE SOCIAL. V. 1- April 1951-. Periodical. CN. French. ir. $9.28. Universite Laval, Faculte des Sciences Sociales, Quebec G1K 7P4 Canada. Tel (418)656-2438. Ind/Abst Point Repere. LC HV2. (ctrl). Deals with social science, social problems with housing, and deviations and delinquency in Canada.

SERVICE : THIS IS THE RED CROSS. Vol. 38, No. 1 (Spring 1977)-. 0227-034X. Periodical. CN. English. qt. Canadian Red Cross Society, 95 Wellesley Street East, Toronto Ontario M4Y 1H6 Canada. DD 361.77.

SERVICE (TORONTO, ONT.). (SERVICE). Vol. 38, No. 3 (1977)-. 0227-034X. CN. English (French). ir. Canadian Red Cross Society, 95 Wellesley Street East, Toronto Ontario M4Y 1H6 Canada. DD 361.77. *Service (Toronto, Ont.). English, 0227-034X; Service (Toronto, Ont.). French, 0227-0358.*

SERVICES FOR PHYSICALLY DISABLED PEOPLE. 1981/82-. 0712-3736. CN. English. an. Free. Services for Physically Disabled People, c/o Community Information Centre, 18 Queen Street North, Kitchener Ontario N2H 2G8 Canada. DD 362.402571344.

SERVICES FOR SENIORS. 1982/83-. 0820-8530. CN. English. an. $0.50. Community Information Centre, 18 Queen Street North, Kitchener Ontario N2H 2G8 Canada. DD 362.60971344.

SERVICES FOR TEXAS CHILDREN. US. English. an. TDCA, Children and Youth Services Division, Box 13166, Capitol Station, Austin TX 78711. LC HV742.T4. DD 362.795025764.

SERVICO SOCIAL E SOCIEDADE. Yearly V. 1 - No. 1, (Sept. 1979)-. 0101-6628. Periodical. BL. Portuguese. ty. Cortez e Editora, 387 rue Bartira 05009, Sao Paulo SP Brazil. Ind/Abst Foreign Lang. Index. LC HV193. DD 361.981.

THE SEX PROBLEMS COURT DIGEST. See Law.

SHAKAI FUKUSHI NO DOKO. Main/Corp Zenkoku Shakai Fukushi Kyogikai. JA. Japanese. ir. 320. Zenkoku Shakai Fukushi Kyogikai, 3-3-4 Kasumigaseki Chiyoda-ku, Tokyo Japan. LC HV413.A2.

SHAKAI FUKUSHI ROPPO. Main/Corp Japan. JA. Japanese. ir. 3400. Shin Nihon Hoki Shuppan Kabushiki Kaisha, 6 Ichigaya Sadohara-cho 2-chome, Shinjuku-ku 162, Tokyo-to-Japan.

SHAKAI FUKUSHI SHISETSU CHOSA KOKOKU. Main/Corp Tokyo. Minseikyoku. Somubu. Kikakuka. JA. Japanese. ir. Minseikyoku, Somubu Kikakuka, Tokyo-to 81 Marunouchi, Chiyoda-ku 100, Tokyo Japan. LC HV413.

SHAKAI MONDAI KENKYU. VFOAT Journal of Social Problems. Began with July 1951 issue. Periodical. Japanese. ir. Osaka Shakai Jigyo Tanki Daigaku, Yuhigaoka Tennoji-ku (543), Osaka Japan. LC HV4.

SHARING (ROCKVILLE, MD.). (SHARING). Began with V. 1, No. 1, Winter 1976/77. 0162-6876. Periodical. US. English. ir. Project Share, PO Box 2309, Rockville MD 20852. Ind/Abst Index U.S. Gov. Period. NLM W1 SH182.

SHE HUI FU LI CHIH PIAO. VFOAT Social Welfare Indicators Republic of China. CH. Chinese and English. ir. LC HV426.

SICHERHEITSTECHNIK. Periodical. GW. German. bm. $50.32. Forum Verlag Liesenhoff Dappe, KG/Kruppstrasse 26, 4 Duesseldorf 1 West Germany. Tel 0211-721055 156. LC HV7431. DD 362.88.

SICUREZZA SOCIALE OGGI. See Insurance.

SIFKU-INFORMATIONEN. 0170-8694. Periodical. English (German). qt. 7.00 Each Issue. Verien fur Sozialwissenschaftliche Katastrophen- und Unfallforschung, 2300 Kiel 1, Holtenauer Strasse 82, Kiel West Germany. LC HV553. DD 363.3405.

SITREP. AT. English. qt. New South Wales St Emergency, Box 42, Queen Victoria Building, Sydney New South Wales 2000 Australia. LC HV555.A8. DD 361.509944. *Bulletin.*

SLACHTOFFERS VAN MISDRIJVEN. VFOAT Victims of Crime. NE. Dutch (summaries in English). ir. 15.00. Centraal Bureau voor de Statistiek, Prinses Beatrixlaan 428 Postbus 959, 2270 AZ Voorburg Netherland. LC HV6250.3.N4.

SLAMMER. V. 1- Oct. 1974-. 0381-6699. Periodical. CN. English. ir. $5.00. Slammer, Box 3000, Drumheller Alberta T0J 0Y0 Canada. DD 365.971233. *Inside News, 0381-6680.*

SOCIAL ALLOWANCE POLICIES & PROCEDURES MANUAL. Apr. 1978-. 0707-3283. CN. English. sa. LC HV109.A5. DD 361.6097123.

SOCIAL AND REHABILITATIVE SERVICES. Main/Corp Rhode Island. Dept. of Social and Rehabilitative Services. 1970/71-. 0092-5128. US. English. an. Aime, J Forand Building 600 New London Avenue, Cranston RI 02920. LC HV86. DD 362.9745.

SOCIAL CASEWORK. V. 1- Mar. 1920-. 0037-7678. Periodical. US. English. $40.00. Family Service America, 44 East 23rd Street, New York NY 10010. Tel (212)674-6100. Ed Robert A Elfers. LC HV1. NLM W1 S0104L. CODEN SOCAA2. bk rev. adv acc. Circ 10,000. Directed primarily to the interests of social work practitioners and educators. Covers social work theory and practice, professional, experimentation, and research.

SOCIAL DEFENCE. V. 1- July 1965-. 0037-7716. Periodical. II. English. qt $16.00. Controller Government of India Publications, Publications Branch, Old Secretariat, Civil Lines Delhi 6 India. Ind/Abst Psychol. Abstr. LC HV9397. CODEN SDEFDL.

SOCIAL DYNAMICS. V. 1- June 1975-. 0253-3952. Periodical. SA. English. ir. $9.00. Social Dynamics, Department of Sociology University of Cape Town, Rondebosch 7700 Republic of South Africa. Ind/Abst Sociol. Abstr., Soc. Welf. Soc. Plan./Policy Soc. Dev. LC HM1. DD 301.05.

SOCIAL INDICATORS. Main/Corp Australian Bureau of Statistics. No. 1- 1976-. AT. English. ir. 25.50. Australian Bureau of Statistics, PO Box 84, Canberra Australian Capital Territory 2600 Australia. Tel (062)52 6778. LC HN844. DD 309.194. A selection of social indicators and other statistics providing a broad background to social issues in Australia. Presents information on population, families, health, education, working life, crime and justice, housing and welfare.

SOCIAL ISSUES RESOURCES SERIES. VFOAT SIRS. 1977-. 0740-3127. Monographic Series. US. English. ir. Social Issues Resources Series Inc, PO Box 2507, Boca Raton FL 33432. Ed Eleanor Goldstein.

SOCIAL PERSPECTIVES CEASED. 0361-1620. US. English. sa. Post Office Box 1935, University of Alabama 35486. LC HV1. DD 361.005.

SOCIAL PRAXIS CEASED. Began with V. 1/1-. Ceased with V. 8, 1981. 0304-2405. Periodical. NE. English. qt. Ind/Abst Sociol. Abstr., Soc. Welf. Soc. Plan./Policy Soc. Dev., Am. Hist. Life, Hist. Abstr., Part A, Mod. Hist. Abstr.

SOCIAL SECURITY EXPLAINED. See Insurance.

SOCIAL SECURITY FORUM. See Insurance.

SOCIAL SECURITY JOURNAL. See Insurance.

SOCIAL SECURITY MANUAL. See Insurance.

SOCIAL SECURITY PROGRAMS THROUGHOUT THE WORLD. See Insurance.

SOCIAL SECURITY RULINGS ON FEDERAL OLD-AGE, SURVIVORS, DISABILITY, SUPPLEMENTAL SECURITY INCOME, AND BLACK LUNG BENEFITS. CUMULATIVE BULLETIN. See Insurance.

SOCIAL SERVICE ABSTRACTS (LONDON, ENGLAND). See Indexes/Abstracts.

SOCIAL SERVICE REVIEW. V. 1- Mar. 1927-. 0037-7961. Periodical. US. English. qt. $38.00. University of Chicago Press, PO Box 37005, Chicago IL 60637. Tel (312)753-3347. Ind/Abst Abstr. Soc. Work., Public Aff. Inf. Serv. Bull., Soc. Sci. Citation Index, Soc. Sci. Index, Am. Hist. Life, Hist. Abstr., Women Stud. Abstr., Hospit. Lit. Index, Lang. Lang. Behav. Abstr., Sociol. Abstr. Index in last issue of volume - attached. (cum index).

SOCIAL SERVICES BLOCK GRANT APPLICATION, WASHINGTON STATE. US. English. an. State of Washington, Department of Social and Health Services, Olympia WA 98504. LC HV98.W3. DD 353.97970084.

SOCIAL SERVICES IN NOVA SCOTIA. 1973-. 0317-4336. CN. English. an. LC HV109.N9. DD 361.6209716. *Welfare Services in Nova Scotia, 0550-8665; Annual Report.*

SOCIAL SERVICES PERSONNEL IN NORTH CAROLINA COUNTIES. Main/Corp North Carolina. Division of Social Services. 1972/73-. 0099-2070. US. English. an. State Department of Human Resources, 325 North Salisbury Street, Raleigh NC 27611. LC HV86. DD 331.7613629756. *Social Services Personnel in North Carolina, 0092-3613.*

SOCIAL WELFARE. Began publication in 1954. 0037-8038. Periodical. II. English. mo. $8.00. Central Social Welfare Board, Jeevan Deep Building, Parliament Street, New Delhi 1 India. Ed Freda Bedi. LC HV1. bk rev. adv acc. Circ 5,000. Concerns the welfare of women, children and the disabled, Depicts social problems and after affects of urbanisation and problems of villages.

THE SOCIAL WELFARE FORUM; OFFICIAL PROCEEDINGS, ANNUAL FORUM. Main/Corp National Conference on Social Welfare. Began publication with 1957. 0734-2004. US. English. an. National Conference on Social Welfare, 1730 M Street NW/Suite 911, Washington DC 20036. DD 360. NLM W3 NA485. *Official Proceedings -National Council of Social Work.*

SOCIAL WELFARE IN APPALACHIA. V. 1- 1969-. Periodical. US. English. an. LC HV98.W4. DD 361.974.

2633

Sociology: General Works, Theory—Social Pathology, Welfare, Criminology

SOCIAL WELFARE, SOCIAL PLANNING/POLICY & SOCIAL DEVELOPMENT. VFOAT Social Welfare, Social Planning Policy and Social Development. Vol. 1, No. 1 (June 1979)-V. 5, No. 2 (Dec. 1983). 0195-7988. Periodical. US. English. sa. $35.00. Sociological Abstracts Inc, PO Box 22206, San Diego CA 92122. **Tel** (619)565-6603. Ed Leo P Chall and Miriam Chall. **CODEN** SOPODA. adv acc. Covers the applied aspects of sociology: welfare, social planning, policy development and community development.

SOCIAL WORK. V. 1- Jan. 1956-. 0037-8046. Periodical. US. English. bm. $58.00. National Association of Social Workers, 7981 Eastern Avenue, Silver Springs MD 20910. **Tel** (301)565-0333. Ed Carol Meyer. **Ind/Abst** Book Rev. Index, Cumul. Index Nurs. Allied Health Lit., Curr. Index J. Educ., Except. Child Educ. Resour., Hospit. Lit. Index, Psychol. Abstr., Public Aff. Inf. Serv. Bull., Ref. Source, Soc. Work Res. Abstr., Sociol. Abstr., Soc. Sci. Index, Soc. Sci. Citation Index, Lang. Lang. Behav. Abstr., Am. Hist. Life, Soc. Work Res. Abstr., Hist. Abstr., Women Stud. Abstr., Abstr. Soc. Work., Hist. Abstr., Part A, Mod. Hist. Abstr., Hist. Abst., Part B, Twent. Century Abstr. **LC** HV1. **DD** 361.305. **NLM** W1 SO135. **CODEN** SOWOA. bk rev. adv acc. **Circ** 106,000. The premier journal in social welfare. Covers social issues, new techniques, research, and education for social work. *Social Work Journal.*

SOCIAL WORK. V. 1- 1971-. Sl. English. ir. Department of Social Work & Social Administration, University of Singapore, Bukit Timah Road, Singapore 10 Singapore. **LC** HV1. **DD** 361.95952.

SOCIAL WORK AND CHRISTIANITY. (SOCIAL WORK AND CHRISTIANITY : JOURNAL OF THE NATIONAL ASSOCIATION OF CHRISTIANS IN SOCIAL WORK). Vol. 6, No. 1 (Spring 1979)-. 0737-5778. Periodical. US. English. sa. $10.00. North American Association of Christians in Social Work, Box 90, St Davids PA 19087. **Tel** (215)687-5777. Ed David Sherwood. **Ind/Abst** Christ. Period. Index, Guide Soc. Sci. Relig. Period. Lit. bk rev. adv acc. **Circ** 1,000. Integration of Christian faith and social work practice. *Paraclete.*

SOCIAL WORK EDUCATION REPORTER. V. 13- Mar. 1965-. Periodical. US. English. ty. Publication Office, 111 Eighth Avenue, New York NY 10011. *Social Work Education.*

SOCIAL WORK IN EDUCATION. See Education (General).

SOCIAL WORK IN HEALTH CARE. V. 1- Fall 1975-. 0098-1389. Periodical. US. English. qt. Haworth Press, 28 East 22nd Street, New York NY 10010. **Tel** (212)228-2800. Ed Sylvia S Clarke. **Ind/Abst** Sociol. Abstr., Soc. Welf. Soc. Plan./Policy Soc. Dev., Index Med., Cumul. Index Nurs. Allied Health Lit., Biol. Abstr., Energy Res. Abstr., Soc. Work Res. Abstr., Abstr. Soc. Work., Abstr. Hospit. Manage. Stud., Chicago Psychoanal. Lit. Index, Curr. Lit. Aging, Excerpta Med., Hospit. Abstr., Hospit. Lit. Index, Med. Care Rev., Nurs. Dig., Psychol. Abstr., Soc. Work Res. Abstr., Soc. Sci. Citation Index, Abstr. Soc. Work. **LC** HV687.A2. **DD** 362.105. **NLM** W1 SO135P. **CODEN** SWHCDO. bk rev. adv acc. **Circ** 3,152. This journal is devoted to social work theory, practice, and administration in a wide variety of health care settings.

SOCIAL WORK (MANILA, PHILIPPINES). (SOCIAL WORK). Began in 1956. 0583-7057. Periodical. PH. English. qt. Pssc Central Subscription Service, PO Box 655 Greehills, Metro Manila 3113 Philippines. **Tel** 922-9621. Ed Thelma Lee Mendoza. **Ind/Abst** Soc. Sci. Citation Index. **LC** HV1. **DD** 361.305. **NLM** W1 SO135M. bk rev. adv acc. **Circ** 1,000. Prints articles and papers on social development and welfare.

SOCIAL WORK PAPERS OF THE SCHOOL OF SOCIAL WORK, UNIVERSITY OF SOUTHERN CALIFORNIA. Main/Corp Los Angeles. University of Southern California. School of Social Work. V. 12- 0272-9016. Monographic Series. US. English. $3.25 Each Copy. School of Social Work, University of Southern California, University Park, Los Angeles CA 90007. **Ind/Abst** Soc. Work Res. Abstr. *Social Work Papers of the Faculty, Alumni and Students.*

SOCIAL WORK RESEARCH & ABSTRACTS. See Indexes/Abstracts.

SOCIAL WORK TODAY. (SWT. SOCIAL WORK TODAY). V. 8- Oct. 5, 1976-. 0037-8070. Periodical. UK. English. ir. British Association of Social Workers, 16 Kent Street, Birmingham B5 6RD England. **Tel** 622 3911. Ed Nathan Goldberg. **Ind/Abst** Soc. Work Res. Abstr., Abstr. Soc. Work. **NLM** W1 S71. bk rev. adv acc. **Circ** 2,500. *Social Work Today.*

SOCIAL WORK WITH GROUPS (HAWORTH PRESS). (SOCIAL WORK WITH GROUPS). Vol. 1, No. 1 (Spring 1978)-. 0160-9513. Periodical. US. English. qt. $102.00. Haworth Press, 28 East 22nd Street, New York NY 10010. **Tel** (212)228-2800. Ed Catherine P Papell and Beulah Rothman. **Ind/Abst** Sociol. Abstr., Soc. Welf. Soc. Plan./Policy Soc. Dev., Soc. Work Res. Abstr., Psychol. Abstr. **LC** HV45. **DD** 361.405. **NLM** W1 SO137MB. **CODEN** SWGRDU. bk rev. adv acc. **Circ** 1,025. It covers the areas of group work in psychiatric, rehabilitative, and multipurpose social work and social service agencies, crisis theory and groupwork.

SOCIAL WORKER. VFOAT Travailleur Social. V. 1- 1932-. 0037-8089. Periodical. CN. English and French. qt. $27.50. Canadian Association of Social Workers, 55 Parkdale Avenue, Suite 313, Ottawa Ontario K1Y 1E5 Canada. **Tel** (613)728-1865. Ed Gweneth Gowanlock. bk rev. adv acc. **Circ** 9,500. (ctrl). Contains information on: the sharing of social work information, knowledge, skills and research with social workers and with the general public; the examination of social issues; the discussion of regional, national, and international issues in social work and social welfare.

SOCIALE VERSEKERING, PENSIOENVERSEKERING, LEVENSVERZEKERING. See Insurance.

SOLEIL DE TRIEST. 0229-3889. Periodical. CN. French. Free. Centre d'Accueil Pierre-Joseph Triest, 8050 Est rue Notre-Dame, Montreal Quebec H1L 3K5 Canada. **DD** 362.609714281.

SOSIAALIMENOT VUONNA . . . SEKA ENNAKKOTIEDOT VUODELLE . . . = SOCIALUTGIFTERNA AR . . . SAMT FORHANDSUPPGIFTER OM . . . ARS SOCIALUTGIFTER. See Insurance.

SOURCE BOOK (NEW YORK, N.Y.). (THE SOURCE BOOK). VFOAT Sourcebook. 1984-85-. 0740-4549. US. English. an. Unipub, 205 East 42nd Street, New York NY 10017. **LC** HV99.N59. **DD** 361.00257471.

SOURCEBOOK OF CRIMINAL JUSTICE STATISTICS. See Statistics.

SOURCES OF VOLUNTARY AGENCY INCOME. US. English. Child Welfare League of America Inc, Research Center 67 Irving Place, New York NY 10003. **LC** HV741. **DD** 362.795.

SOURD QUEBECOIS. (LE SOURD QUEBECOIS). V. 5, No. 2- Oct. 1975-. 0384-8779. Periodical. CN. French. ir. 50. Per No. Centre des Loisirs des Sourds de Montreal Inc, CP 328 Succursale R, Montreal Quebec H2S 3K9 Canada. **DD** 362.42097114. *Penseur du Sourd, 0384-8760.*

SOUTH DAKOTA COUNTY POOR RELIEF. Main/Corp South Dakota. Dept. of Social Services. 0360-9022. US. English. SD Department of Social Services, Capitol Lake Plaza, Pierre SD 57501. **LC** HV86. **DD** 362.509783.

SOUTH DAKOTA INDIAN RECIPIENTS OF SOCIAL WELFARE. Main/Corp South Dakota. Dept. of Social Services. 0094-372X. US. English. South Dakota Department of Social Services, Capitol Lake Plaza, Pierre SD 57501. **LC** E78.S63. **DD** 362.84.

SOUTHERN COALITION REPORT ON JAILS & PRISONS. V. 1- June 1974-. Periodical. US. English. qt. $5.00. Southern Prison Ministry, PO Box 12044, Nashville TN 37212.

SOZIALE ARBEIT. Vol. 1-. 0490-1606. Periodical. GW. German. mo. Deutsches Zentralinst Soziale, Miquel Strasse 83, 1 Berlin 34 Germany. **Ind/Abst** Excerpta Med., Foreign Lang. Index, PAIS Foreign Lang. Index. **LC** HV3.

SOZIALE SICHERHEIT. See Insurance.

SOZIALE SICHERHEIT. See Insurance.

SOZIALLEISTUNGEN. REIHE 1. VERSICHERTE IN DER KRANKEN- UND RENTENVERSICHERUNG. See Insurance.

SPAN NEWSLETTER. Issue No. 1 (Dec. 1979)-. 0822-6407. Periodical. CN. English. ir. Social Policy and Administration Network, Faculty of Social Work, University of Regina, Regina Saskatchewan S4S 0A2 Canada. **DD** 361.610971.

SPAR BULLETIN. 0715-3376. Periodical. CN. English. ir. Free. United Way Social Planning and Research, 1625 West 8th Avenue, Vancouver British Columbia V6J 1T9 Canada. **DD** 362.5820971133.

SPARKS (MONTREAL, QUEBEC). (SPARKS). Vol. 4, No. 1/2 (Mar./June)-. 0715-3767. Periodical. CN. English. qt. Provincial Committee of Patients, PO Desjardins, PO 458, Montreal Quebec H5B 1B5 Canada. **DD** 362.105. *Sparks from Oeil de Feu, 0715-3406.*

A SPECIAL REPORT - DIVISION OF CORRECTION. Main/Corp Maryland. Division of Correction. 0098-3845. US. English. an. Division of Correction, 920 Greenmount Avenue, Baltimore MD 21202. **LC** HV7270. **DD** 365.9752.

A SPECIAL REVIEW OF THE DEPARTMENT OF HEALTH AND SOCIAL SERVICES, DIVISION OF PUBLIC ASSISTANCE, MEDICAL ASSISTANCE PAYMENTS FOR ABORTIONS. US. English. G L Wilkerson CPA Legislative Auditor, Division of Legislative Audit Pouch W, Juneau AK 90811. **LC** HD7102.U5. **DD** 353.9798008256.

SPECIAL STUDY - TEXAS DEPARTMENT OF CORRECTIONS, RESEARCH, PLANNING, AND DEVELOPMENT DIVISION. Main/Corp Texas. Dept. of Corrections. Research, Planning, and Development Division. No. 42- Jan. 1978-. Monographic Series. US. English. Texas Department of Corrections, Research Planning & Development Division, Huntsville TX 77340. **LC** HV7293. **DD** 364.609764. *Special Study - Texas Department of Corrections, Research and Development Division.*

SPECTRUM (TORONTO, ONT. : 1981). (SPECTRUM). Vol. 1, No. 1 (June/July 1981)-. 0226-9228. Periodical. CN. English. bm. $10.00 for 6 Issues. Spectrum, c/o Pedowie Publishers, 632 Queen Street West, Toronto Ontario M6J 1E Canada. **DD** 362.40971.

SPRINGER SERIES ON SOCIAL WORK. Vol. 1-. Monographic Series. US. English. Ed Albert R Roberts. **NLM** W1.

STAFF OF SCOTTISH SOCIAL WORK DEPARTMENTS. 1978-. 0144-5081. UK. English. an. Social Work Services Group, Statistics Branch, 43 Jeffrey Street/Room 424, Edinburgh EH1 1DN Scotland. **LC** HV249.S5. **DD** 331.1251361609411.

STATE AND REGIONAL DATA, FEDERALLY FUNDED COMMUNITY MENTAL HEALTH CENTERS. Main/Corp United States. National Institute of Mental Health. Division of Biometry. Survey and Reports Branch. 0095-3660. US. English. National Institute of Mental Health, Survey and Reports Branch, Division of Biometry, 5600 Fishers Lane, Rockville MD 20852. **LC** RH790.6. **DD** 362.220973.

STATE ANNUAL EVALUATION REPORT P.L. 89-750, PROJECTS IN STATE INSTITUTIONS FOR DELINQUENT CHILDREN. Main/Corp New Mexico. Dept. of Education. 0091-1089. US. English. New Mexico Department of Education, Education Building, Santa Fe NM 87501. **LC** HV9105.N6. **DD** 362.74309789.

STATE DEVELOPMENT PLAN FOR REHABILITATION FACILITIES. See Economics - Labor.

STATE FACILITIES PLAN. Main/Corp Washington (State). Vocational Rehabilitation Services Division. 0092-5543. US. English. Vocational Rehabilitation Services Division, PO Box 1788, Olympia WA 98504. **LC** HD7256.U6. **DD** 362.85.

STATE MENTAL RETARDATION FACILITY DATA. (STATE MENTAL RETARDATION FACILITY DATA FOR THE FISCAL YEAR . . .). 0743-7676. US. English. an. MIS and Data Services Division, Department of Mental Health and Mental Health Retardation, PO Box 1797, Richmond VA 23214.

STATE OF FLORIDA PROPROSED COMPREHENSIVE ANNUAL SERVICES PROGRAM PLAN FOR SOCIAL SECURITY ACT TITLE XX. Main/Corp Florida. Dept. of Health and Rehabilitative Services. VFOAT Proposed Comprehensive Annual Services Program Plan for Title XX—Social Security

Sociology: General Works, Theory—Social Pathology, Welfare, Criminology

Act. US. English. $5.65. Department of Health and Rehabilitative Services, Tallahassee FL 32304. LC HV86. DD 361.6209759.

STATE OF INDIANA FINAL COMPREHENSIVE ANNUAL SERVICES PLAN. Main/Corp Indiana. Office of Social Services. 1978/79-. US. English. an. Indiana Office of Social Services, 964 North Pennsylvania, Indianapolis IN 46204. LC HV86. DD 361.609772. State of Indiana Final Comprehensive Annual Services Plan.

STATE OF NEVADA, DEPARTMENT OF PAROLE AND PROBATION, AUDIT REPORT. Main/Corp Nevada. Legislative Auditor. 0149-2012. US. English. Legislative Auditor, Legislative Building Capitol Complex, Carson City NV 89710. LC HV9305.N3. DD 353.979300849.

STATE OF NEVADA, DEPARTMENT OF PAROLE AND PROBATION, PAROLEES' REVOLVING LOAN FUND, PRISONER'S WORK RELEASE REVOLVING LOAN FUND, AUDIT REPORT. (AUDIT REPORT, STATE OF NEVADA DEPARTMENT OF PAROLE AND PROBATION, PAROLEES' REVOLVING LOAN FUND). Main/Corp Nevada. Legislative Auditor. 0149-225X. US. English. Legislative Building Capitol Complex, Carson City NV 89710. LC HV9305.N3. DD 353.979300849.

STATE OF NEVADA, DEPARTMENT OF PAROLE AND PROBATION, RESTITUTION TRUST FUND, AUDIT REPORT. (AUDIT REPORT, STATE OF NEVADA DEPARTMENT OF PAROLE AND PROBATION, RESTITUTION TRUST FUND). Main/Corp Nevada. Legislative Auditor. 0149-2144. US. English. Legislative Building Capitol Complex, Carson City NV 79710. LC HV9305.N3. DD 353.979300849.

STATE OF NEVADA UNIFORM CRIME REPORTS . . . ANNUAL REPORT. Main/Corp Nevada. Dept. of Law Enforcement Assistance. VFOAT Nevada Uniform Crime Reports . . . Annual Report. US. English. an. LC HV7278. DD 364.109793.

STATE OF NEW MEXICO UNIFORM CRIME REPORT. Main/Corp New Mexico. State Police. Uniform Crime Reporting Unit. VFOAT Crime in New Mexico. US. English. an. LC HV7281. DD 364.9789.

STATE OF NORTH CAROLINA UNIFORM CRIME REPORT. Main/Corp North Carolina. Police Information Network. VFOAT Crime in North Carolina. 1973-. 0096-3208. US. English. an. Police Information Network, 111 East North Street, Raleigh NC 27601. LC HV7283. DD 364.9756.

STATE OF OREGON ANALYSIS OF CRIMINAL OFFENSES AND ARRESTS. Main/Corp Oregon. Law Enforcement Council. VFOAT Oregon Criminal Offenses and Arrests. 0145-6903. US. English. an. Oregon Law Enforcement Council, 2001 Front Street NE, Salem OR 97310. LC HV7287. DD 364.9795. State of Oregon Analysis of Criminal Offenses and Arrests, 0145-6903.

STATE OF THE STATES ON CRIME AND JUSTICE. Main/Conf National Conference of State Criminal Justice Planning Administrator. 0147-0434. US. English. National Conference of State Criminal Justice Planning Administration, 444 North Capitol Street NW/Suite 305, Washington DC 20001. LC HV8183. DD 364.973.

THE STATE OF THE WORLD'S CHILDREN. Began publication in 1980. Periodical. US. English. an. LC HQ792.2. DD 362.71091724.

STATE PLAN ANNUAL REVISION, DEVELOPMENTAL DISABILITIES SERVICES AND FACILITIES CONSTRUCTION ACT OF 1970. Main/Corp California. Developmental Disabilities Planning and Advisory Counci. US. English. an. State Planning and Advisory Council for Developmental Disabilities, 926 J Street/Room 522, Sacramento CA 95814. LC HV3006.C2. DD 362.309794.

STATE PLAN FOR CHILD WELFARE SERVICES. Main/Corp South Dakota. Dept. of Social Services. 0146-5740. US. English. an. Department of Social Services, State Capital Building Pierre SD 57501. LC HV742.S8. DD 362.709783.

STATE PLAN FOR COMPREHENSIVE MENTAL HEALTH SERVICES : ANNUAL REVIEW AND PROGRESS REPORTS FOR THE STATE OF OKLAHOMA. Main/Corp Oklahoma. Dept. of Mental Health. 0193-4260. US. English. an. Oklahoma State Dept of Mental Health, PO Box 53277 Capitol Station, Oklahoma City OK 73152. LC RA790.65.O5. DD 362.209766.

STATE PLAN FOR PROGRAMS ON AGING UNDER TITLE III AND TITLE VII OF THE OLDER AMERICANS ACT OF 1965 AS AMENDED FOR THE STATE OF NEW HAMPSHIRE. Main/Corp New Hampshire State Council on Aging. VAT State Plan for Programs on Aging Under Title Three and Title Seven on the Older Americans Act of Nineteen Hundred and Sixty-Five as Amended for the State of New Hampshire. 0148-9240. US. English. an. LC HV1468.N4. DD 353.974200846.

STATE PLAN ON AGING FOR THE STATE OF NEBRASKA. Main/Corp Nebraska. Commission on Aging. US. English. Nebraska Commission on Aging, 301 Centennial Mall South, Lincoln NB 68509. LC HV1468.N6. DD 362.6309782.

STATE PLAN ON AGING (ILLINOIS). Main/Corp Illinois. Dept. on Aging. US. English. an. 2401 West Jefferson Street, Springfield IL 62706. LC HV1468.I3. DD 362.609773.

STATE PLAN ON AGING UNDER TITLE III OF THE OLDER AMERICANS ACT FOR SOUTH CAROLINA. Fiscal Years 1981-83-. US. English. an. South Carolina Commission on Aging, 915 Main Street, Columbia SC 29201. LC HV1468.S6. DD 362.609757. State Plan on Aging for the State of South Carolina for Fiscal Year . . . .

STATE PLAN ON AGING UNDER TITLE III OF THE OLDER AMERICANS ACT FOR STATE OF SOUTH DAKOTA. Main/Corp South Dakota. Office of Adult Services and Aging. US. English. State of South Dakota, Department of Social Services, Pierre SD 57501. LC HV1468.S8. DD 362.609783. State Plan on Aging.

STATE VOCATIONAL REHABILITATION AGENCY. PROGRAM DATA. (STATE VOCATIONAL REHABILITATION AGENCY PROGRAM DATA). Main/Corp United States. Rehabilitation Services Administration. 0147-0914. Periodical. US. English. an. Rehabilitation Services Administration, 330 Independence Avenue Southwest, Washington DC 20201. LC HD7256.U5. DD 362.85. NLM W2 A R3SE.

STATE WELFARE AIDS AND COUNTY SHARE OF WELFARE EXPENDITURES. Main/Corp Wisconsin. Division of Family Services. 0508-8984. US. English. Division of Family Services, 1 West Wilson Street, Madison WI 53702. LC HV86. DD 361.6209775. State Welfare Aids and County Share of Welfare Expenditures, 0508-8984.

STATISTICAL ANALYSIS AND CORRECTIONAL POPULATION DATA. See Statistics.

STATISTICAL BULLETIN (OKLAHOMA. DEPT. OF HUMAN SERVICES). See Statistics.

STATISTICAL DATA ON PERSONS RELEASED FROM PAROLE BY DISCHARGE AND VIOLATION. See Statistics.

STATISTICAL INFORMATION ON SCHOOLS OF SOCIAL WORK IN CANADA. See Statistics.

STATISTICAL INFORMATION SERVICE : PERSONAL SOCIAL SERVICES STATISTICS ACTUALS. See Statistics.

STATISTICAL NOTES - REHABILITATION SERVICES ADMINISTRATION. See Statistics.

STATISTICAL PRESENTATION (ILLINOIS. DEPT. OF CORRECTIONS. POLICY DEVELOPMENT DIVISION. RESEARCH AND EVALUATION). See Statistics.

STATISTICAL REPORT - CITY OF LOS ANGELES. SOCIAL SERVICE DEPARTMENT. See Statistics.

STATISTICAL REPORT ON MEDICAL CARE. See Statistics.

STATISTICAL REPORT - SOUTH CAROLINA DEPARTMENT OF SOCIAL SERVICES. See Statistics.

STATISTICAL REPORT (VIRGINIA. DEPT. OF SOCIAL SERVICES. BUREAU OF RESEARCH AND REPORTING). See Statistics.

STATISTICAL REVIEW OF CRIME. See Statistics.

STATISTICAL SUPPLEMENT TO ANNUAL REPORT. See Statistics.

STATISTICS. CALENDAR YEAR REVIEW. See Statistics.

STATISTICS - OFFICE OF FAMILY SERVICES. See Statistics.

STATISTICS - STATE OF TENNESSEE, DEPARTMENT OF HUMAN SERVICES. See Statistics.

STATISTIEK VAN DE KINDEREN DIE RECHT GEVEN OP KINDERBIJSLAG. STATISTIQUE DES ENFANTS BENEFICIAIRES D'ALLOCATIONS FAMILIALES. See Statistics.

STATISTIK IN DER RENTENVERSICHERUNG. See Statistics.

STATISTIK KRIMINALITAS DKI JAKARTA. VFOAT Statistik Kriminalitas D.K.I. Jakarta. IO. Indonesian. ir. Kantor Statistik Propinsi, D K I Jakarta JL Merdeka Selatan 8-9, Jakarta Indonesia. LC HV7104.J34.

STATISTIK KRIMINIL. See Statistics.

STATISTIK LEMBAGA PEMASYARAKATAN DAN KEJAKSAAN. See Statistics.

STATISTIK OVER PENSIONSTAGARNA I FINLAND. See Statistics.

STATISTIKS I.E. STATISTISK INFORMATIONSMATERIALE OM INDVANDRERBRN OG -UNGE. See Statistics.

STATISTIQUES DE SECURITE SOCIALE, ASSOCIATIONS SYNDICALES ET PATRONALES : CONTINENT, ACORES ET MADERE. ESTATISTICAS DE SEGURANCA SOCIAL, ASSOCIACOES SINDICAIS E PATRONAIS : CONTINENTE, ACORES E MADEIRA. See Statistics.

THE STATUS OF CHILDREN, YOUTH, AND FAMILIES. Series/Titl DHHS Publication. 1979-. US. English. be. US Department of Health and Human Services. Status of Children, 0161-4150.

STREET. (THE STREET). V. 1- May/June 1979-. 0227-1869. Periodical. CN. English. bm. Free. Law Enforcement Division, 7th Floor, 10310 Japser Avenue, Edmonton Alberta T5J 2W4 Canada. DD 363.23097123.

STUDIES IN SOCIAL POLICY AND WELFARE. Began in 1976. Monographic Series. UK. English. Heinemann Educational Books Ltd, 22 Bedford Square, London WC1B 3HH England. LC UNC.

STUDIES IN THE CAUSES OF DELINQUENCY AND THE TREATMENT OF OFFENDERS. Main/Corp Great Britain. Home Dept. Vol. 1 1955-. UK. English. ir. H M Stationery Office, PO Box 276, London SW8 5DT England.

STUDIES IN WELFARE POLICY. Series/Titl DSS Publication. No. 1-. 0149-2586. Monographic Series. US. English. ir. Michigan Department of Social Services, 300 South Capitol Avenue, Landing MI 48926. LC UNC. NLM W2 AM5 D6S.

SUCCESS WITH YOUTH REPORT. 1967. 0160-9696. Periodical. US. English. mo. Pace Publications, PO Box 2972, New York NY 10163. Tel (212)685-5450. Ed Samuel Graftin. Helping those who deal with youth; to help youth in health careers, education and all aspects of their lives and endeavors. Youth Report.

SUID-AFRIKAANSE TYDSKRIF VIR STRAFREG EN KRIMINOLOGIE. VFOAT South African Journal of Criminal Law and Criminology. Began with issue for Apr. 1977.

Sociology: General Works, Theory—Social Pathology, Welfare, Criminology

Periodical. Afrikaans (English). bm. D & S Publishers, PO Box 5105, Clearwater FL 33518. **Tel** (800)237-9707. **Ind/Abst** Excerpta Med. LC HV6005. Index in first issue of next volume - loose - unpaged. *Misdaad, Straf en Hervorming.*

SUMMARY INFORMATION ON MASTER OF SOCIAL WORK PROGRAMS. Main/Corp Council on Social Work Education. 0145-7314. US. English. an. Council on Social Work Education, 345 East 46th Street, New York NY 10017. LC HV11. DD 361.0071173.

SUMMARY OF GENERAL STATISTICS. See Statistics.

SUMMARY OF HEALTH AND PERSONAL SOCIAL SERVICES ACCOUNTS. See Public Health and Safety.

SUMMARY OF RESEARCH WITHIN THE UNIT AND OF RESEARCH SUPPORTED BY GRANT. Main/Corp Great Britain. Home Office., Research Unit. UK. English. Research Unit, Horseferry House Dean Ryle Street, London SW1 P2AW England. LC HV6024.5. DD 364.

A SUMMARY OF THE SOUTH DAKOTA CRIMINAL JUSTICE PLAN FOR ACTION. Main/Corp South Dakota. Criminal Justice Commission. **VFOAT** South Dakota Criminal Justice Plan for Action. 0148-4273. US. English. Criminal Justice Commission, 200 West Pleasant Drive, Pierre SD 57501. LC HV7291. DD 364.9783.

SUMMARY OF THE WHITE PAPER ON CRIME. Main/Corp Homu Sogo Kenkyujo. 1963-. English. ir. LC HV7113.

SUOMEN POLIISILEHTI. Periodical. Finnish. sm. LC HV7551.

SUOMEN VIRALLINEN TILASTO. XXI B, SOSIAALIHUOLTO. See Statistics.

THE SUPPLEMENTAL SECURITY INCOME PROGRAM FOR THE AGED, BLIND, AND DISABLED. Began with 1975. 0272-7412. US. English. be. Superintendent of Documents, US Government Printing Office, Washington DC 20402. LC HC110.I5. DD 362.582.

SUPPLEMENTAL SECURITY INCOME : STATE AND COUNTY DATA. US. English. sa.

A SURVEY OF CRIME IN NEBRASKA. Main/Corp Nebraska. Commission on Law Enforcement and Criminal Justice. Statistical Analysis Center. US. English. an. 301 Centennial Mall South, PO Box 92946, Lincoln NE 68509. LC HV7277. DD 364.109782.

SYNERGIST CEASED. Publication began with V. 1, No. 1 (Fall 1971). Ceased with V. 11, No. 1, Spring 1982. 0049-2752. Periodical. US. English. ty. Superintendent of Documents, US Government Printing Office, Washington DC 20402. **Ind/Abst** Index U.S. Gov. Period. LC HQ799.7. DD 361.02.

TABLEAUX, SANTE ET SECURITE SOCIALE. Periodical. French. ir. NLM W2 GF7 M47T.

TAFT CORPORATE GIVING DIRECTORY. See Yearbooks, Almanacs, Directories.

TAFT FOUNDATION REPORTER. 1980-. 0730-6237. US. English. an. $267.00. Taft Corporation, 5130 MacArthur Boulevard NW, Washington DC 20016. Ed Yvette Henry. LC HV97.A3. DD 361.763202573. NLM HV 97.A3 T124. bk rev. Information on Foundation grant giving, including listing of foundations, who to contact, etc. *Taft Foundation Reporter. National Edition, 0197-0240; Taft Foundation Reporter. Regional Edition. Region 1: New England, 0273-3897; Taft Foundation Reporter. Regional Edition. Region 2, New York; Taft Foundation Reporter. Regional Edition. Region 3, New Jersey/Pennsylvania.*

TALK OF THE THAMES. Spring 1981-. 0822-8043. Periodical. CN. English. sa. Upper Thames River Conservation Authority, P O Box 6278 Station D, London Ontario N5W 5S1 Canada. DD 363.739460971325.

TAR PAPER CEASED. **VFOAT** Tarpaper. V. 1-10, No. 3. 0384-0638. Periodical. CN. English. $5.00. Tar Paper, PO Box 2500, Abbotsford British Columbia V2S 4P3 Canada. DD 365.971133.

TECHNICAL NOTES - UNITED STATES. DEPT. OF HEALTH AND HUMAN SERVICES. DIVISION OF CHILDREN, YOUTH, AND FAMILY POLICY. (TECHNICAL NOTES). Fiscal Year 1980-. 0735-7966. US. English. an. Division of Children Youth and Family Policy, Office of Social Services, Policy Office of the Assistant Secretary for Planning and Evaluation, US Department of Health and Human Services, Room 416E/Hubert Humphrey Building, 200 Independent Avenue SW, Washington DC 20201. LC HV85. DD 361.60973. NLM W2 A D3816T. *Technical Notes (United States. Dept of Health, Education, and Welfare. Office of the Assistant Secretary for Planning and Evaluation).*

TECHNICAL REPORT - NATIONAL INSTITUTE OF HEALTH AND FAMILY WELFARE, NEW DELHI. See Public Health and Safety.

TEMAS DE DERECHO PENAL. Periodical. Spanish. ir. LC KHQ5402.Z9. DD 345.85.

TEN YEAR CAPITAL IMPROVEMENTS PROGRAM. Main/Corp South Carolina. Dept. of Corrections. **VFOAT** Capital Improvements Program. Fiscal Years 1979-80/1988-89-. US. English. an. S C Department of Corrections, Division of Resource and Information Management, 4444 Broad River Road, Box 21787, Columbia SC 29210. LC HV7290. DD 353.9757008495.

TENNESSEE DIRECTORY OF SERVICES FOR THE DEVELOPMENTALLY DISABLED. See Yearbooks, Almanacs, Directories.

TEORIA Y PRACTICA. Periodical. Spanish. ir. 1,500. Santa Teresa 6, Madrid Spain. LC HN1.

TERATAI. Periodical. Indonesian. ir. Dinas Bina Karya Jawatan Sosial Prop Sulawesi Selatan, Kantor Jasos Prop Sulsel, Jin Meogisiidi No 3, Ujung Pandang. LC HV404.S94.

TEXAS CRIME POLL. Main/Corp Sam Houston State University. Criminal Justice Center. Survey Research Program. US. English. sa. Sam Houston State University, Texas Criminal Justice Center, Huntsville TX 77340. LC HV6793.T4. DD 364.9764.

TEXAS CRIMINAL JUSTICE HIGHLIGHTS. V. 11- Mar. 1980-. Periodical. US. English. mo. Criminal Justice Division, Office of Governor William P Clements Jf, 411 West 13th Street, Austin TX 78701. *Criminal Justice Highlights, 0884-0164.*

THE TEXAS FRONT IN THE NATION'S STRUGGLE AGAINST POVERTY : ANNUAL REPORT OF THE TEXAS DEPARTMENT OF COMMUNITY AFFAIRS' ECONOMIC OPPORTUNITY DIVISION. Main/Corp Texas. Economic Opportunity Division. US. English. an. Texas Department of Community Affairs, Economic Opportunity Division, Box 13166, Capitol Station, Austin TX 78711. LC HV86. DD 361.6209764. *Texas Front in the Nation's Struggle Against Poverty: Annual Report of Texas Department of Community Affairs' Texas Office of Economic Opportunity.*

TEXAS JUVENILE PROBATION STATISTICAL REPORT : STATISTICAL AND OTHER DATA ON THE JUVENILE JUSTICE SYSTEM IN TEXAS FOR CALENDAR YEARS . . . ABBREVIATED. See Statistics.

THREE-YEAR REPORT - FUND FOR THE CITY OF NEW YORK. (THREE-YEAR REPORT). **Main/Corp** Fund for the City of New York. 0741-8213. US. English. te. LC HV99.N6. DD 361.7632097471.

TIGHTWIRE PUBLICATIONS. VFOAT Tightwire. **VAT** Tightwire (1978). Vol. 3, No. 2 (Mar./Apr. 1978)-. 0702-9004. Periodical. CN. English. bm. $3.00. Tightwire Publications, PO Box 515, Kingston Ontario K7L 4W7 Canada. DD C810.80920692. *Tightwire, 0822-9945.*

TIJDSCHRIFT VOOR CRIMINOLOGIE. Vol. 19. 0165-182X. Periodical. NE. Dutch (summaries in English). bm. $25.43. Uitgevery Boom, Postbus 58, 7940 AB Meppel The Netherlands. **Ind/Abst** Excerpta Med. LC HV6005. bk rev. adv acc. Circ 550. Information for criminologists and law students. *Nederlands Tijdschrift Voor Criminologie.*

T.I.M.E. TIME INSIDE MADE EASIER. (T.I.M.E. : TIME INSIDE MADE EASIER). **VFOAT** Time Inside Made Easier. 0226-9910. Periodical. CN. English. qt. Free. T I M E, c/o John Howard Society, 319 Lisgar Street, Ottawa Ontario K2P 0 Canada. DD 365.971383.

TITLE XX COMPREHENSIVE ANNUAL SERVICES PLAN. Main/Corp New Mexico. Social Services Division. 1979/80-. US. English. LC HV86. DD 361.609789. *Final Comprehensive Annual Services Plan.*

TITLE XX COMPREHENSIVE ANNUAL SERVICES PROGRAM PLAN. Main/Corp Maine. Dept. of Human Services. US. English. Capitol Shopping Center, Western Avenue, Augusta ME 04240. LC HV98.M2. DD 361.6209741.

TITLE XX COMPREHENSIVE ANNUAL SERVICES PROGRAM PLAN. Main/Corp California. Health and Welfare Agency. **VFOAT** Title 20 Comprehensive Annual Services Program Plan. Began in 1976. US. English. an. State of California Health and Welfare Agency, Department of Social Services, 744 P Street, Sacramento CA 95814. *Comprehensive Annual Services Program Plan.*

TITLE XX FINAL COMPREHENSIVE I.E. COMPREHENSIVE ANNUAL SERVICES PLAN. Main/Corp South Dakota. Dept. of Social Services. US. English. an. Department of Social Services, State Office Building, Illinois Street, Pierre SD 57501. LC HV86. DD 361.609783.

TITLE XX NEEDS ASSESSMENT, FISCAL YEAR . . . . 1st (1978/79)-. US. English. an. Free. Iowa Department of Social Services, Division of Planning Services, Bureau of Planning Analysis, Hoover State Office Building, Des Moines IA 50319. LC HV98.I8. DD 362.9777.

TITLE XX, SOCIAL SERVICES. Main/Corp Texas. Dept. of Human Resources. US. English. an. Texas Department of Human Resources, John H Reagan Building, Austin TX 78701.

TITLE XX SOCIAL SERVICES BLOCK GRANT REPORT. VFOAT Title 20 Social Services Block Grant Report. US. English. Missouri Department of Social Services, Broadway State Office Building, Box 1527, Jefferson City MO 65102. LC HV98.M8. DD 353.9778008405.

TOCSIN (KINGSTON, ONT.). (TOCSIN). Vol. 1, Issue 1 (Sept./Oct. 1980)-. 0710-6408. Periodical. CN. English. bm. $5.00. Tocsin, c/o John Howard Society, 771 1/2 Montreal Street, Kingston Ontario K7K 3J4 Canada. DD 365.971352.

TODAY'S DELINQUENT. Vol. 1 (1982)-. 0733-6551. US. English. an. $10.00. National Center for Juvenile Justice, 701 Forbes Avenue, Pittsburgh PA 15219. Tel (412)227-6950. Ed Hunter Hurst. LC HV9104. DD 364.360973. Circ 10,000. Contains articles on current issues in juvenile delinquency.

TOKUSHIMA-KEN CHIIKI BOSAI KEIKAKU. Japanese. ir. LC HV555.J3.

TOKYO NO HIKO SHONEN. JA. Japanese. ir. Tokyo Hatei Saibansho, 2-3 Kasumigaseki 1-chome Chiyoda-ku, Tokyo 110 Japan. LC HV9207.T6.

TOURNESOL. (LE TOURNESOL). V. 1- Jan. 1978-. 0705-2898. Periodical. CN. French. ir. Free. Conseil de la Sante et des Services Sociaux de l Outaousis, 4 rue Georges, Bilodeau Hull Quebec J8Z 1V2 Canada. DD 361.97142. (ctrl).

TOWARZYSTWO D/S UCHOCZCOW W NANAIMO. (TOWARZYSTWO D/S UCHODZCOW W NANAIMO : NEWSLETTER). **VAT** Wiadomosci Towarzystwa d/s Uchodozchow W Nanaimo. Vol. 8, No. 4 (Listop./Grudz. 1982)-. 0824-5177. Periodical. CN. English. bm. $0.50 Each Number. Nanaimo Refugee Co-Ordination Society/Suite 225-228 Community Services Facility 285 Prideaux Street, Nanaimo British Columbia V9R 2N2 Canada. DD 362.870971.

TRABAJO SOCIAL. Spanish. ir. $15.00. Campus Oriente, Diagonal Oriente 3300. LC HV4. *RTS.*

TRAINING AND MANPOWER DEVELOPMENT ACTIVITIES. (TRAINING AND MANPOWER DEVELOPMENT ACTIVITIES SUPPORTED BY THE ADMINISTRATION ON AGING UNDER TITLE IV-A OF THE OLDER AMERICANS ACT OF 1965, AS AMENDED). **Main/Corp** United States. Administration on Aging. Division of Manpower Resources. 0161-8288. US. English. LC HQ1060. DD 362.6071173.

Sociology: General Works, Theory—Social Pathology, Welfare, Criminology

TRAINING FOR SOCIAL WORK; INTERNATIONAL SURVEY. Main/Corp United Nations. Department of Economic and Social Affairs. **Series Corp** United Nations. Document. 1st- 1950-. 0497-834X. English. ir. United Nations Department of Economic and Social Affairs, Sales Section/Room A 3315, New York NY 10017. **LC** JX1977. **DD** 360.7.

TRAINING SCHOOL BULLETIN. (THE TRAINING SCHOOL BULLETIN). 0041-0918. Periodical. US. English. qt. Ed E R Johnstone and Others. **Ind/Abst** Educ. Index. **LC** HV897.N5. **CODEN** TSCBA.

TRAINING SCHOOLS. Main/Corp Canada. Statistics Canada. Judicial Division. **VFOAT** Etablissements de Protection de la Jeunesse. 1971-. 0575-996X. CN. text in English and French. an. $1.05. Statistics Canada, Publications Distribution, Ottawa Ontario K1A 0T6 Canada. **LC** HV9108. **DD** 365.42. *Training Schools, 0575-996X.*

TWO THIRDS (OTTAWA, ONT.). (TWO THIRDS). Fall 1982-. 0715-6650. Periodical. CN. English. qt. Free. Canadian Hunger Foundation, 323 Chapel Street, Ottawa Ontario K1N 7Z2 Canada. **DD** 363.805.

UFFI NEWS. **VFOAT** Info-Miuf. Issue 1 (July 1982)-. 0823-6224. Periodical. CN. English (with French text on inverted pages). ir. Free to Members. Huffi Ottawa, PO Box 112 Station B, Ottawa Ontario K1P 6C3 Canada. **DD** 363.179.

U.I.C. NEWSLETTER. **VAT** Unemployment Insurance Commission Newsletter. Vol. 1, No. 1 (Mar. 1979)-. 0821-2945. Periodical. CN. English. ir. $5.00 6 Numbers. Labour Studies Program, Capilano College, 2055 Purcell Way, North Vancouver British Columbia V7J 3H5 Canada. **DD** 344.71024.

UNAFEI NEWSLETTER. **VFOAT** U.N.A.F.E.I. Newsletter. Periodical. English. ir. **LC** HV7431. **DD** 364.405.

UNDUPLICATED COUNT OF MENTALLY RETARDED PATIENTS SERVED CHILDREN'S HEALTH SERVICES DIVISION. Main/Corp Hawaii. Mental Health Register. US. English. PO Box 3378, Honolulu HI 96801. **LC** HV3006.H3. **DD** 362.78309969.

UNIDAD DE PROMOCION VOLUNTARIA DEL IMSS : REVISTA. **VFOAT** Volunteer Advancement Unit of the Mexican Institute of Social Security, The Voluntary Promotion Unit of the Mexican Institute of Social Security : Review. Yearly V. 1, No. 4, (May/June/July 1979)-. Periodical. MX. English (Spanish). qt. Reforma No 476 80 Piso, Mexico 6 DF Mexico. **LC** HD7131. **DD** 368.400972. *Grupo de Promotoras Sociales Voluntarias del IMSS.*

UNIDADES OPERACIONAIS : ENDERECOS. Main/Corp Servico Social do Comercio. Portuguese. ir. Servico Social Do Comercio, Av General Justo 307, rio de Janeiro Brazil. **LC** HV193.A2.

UNIFORM CRIME REPORT ARREST INFORMATION RELATING TO SUBSTANCE ABUSE IN SOUTH CAROLINA. US. English. Division of Planning Evaluation and Grant Management, 3700 Forest Drive/Suite 300, Columbia SC 29204. **LC** HV4999.3.S6. **DD** 364.1770973021.

UNIFORM CRIME REPORTING. Main/Corp New Mexico State Police. **VFOAT** New Mexico Crime Reports. Began with 1976. US. English. an. New Mexico State Police, PO Box 1628, Santa Fe NM 87501. **LC** HV7281. **DD** 364.9789. *State of New Mexico Uniform Crime Report.*

UNIFORM CRIME REPORTS. Periodical. US. English. qt. US Department of Justice, Federal Bureau of Investigation, 9th Street and Pennsylvania Avenue NW, Washington DC 20535.

UNIFORM CRIME REPORTS, COMMONWEALTH OF PENNSYLVANIA. Main/Corp Pennsylvania. State Police. Bureau of Research and Development. **VFOAT** Crime in Pennsylvania. 1973-. 0095-5752. US. English. an. Bureau of Research and Development/ Pennsylvania State Police, Harrisburg Pa 17101. **LC** HV7288. **DD** 364.9748.

UNIFORM CRIME REPORTS FOR THE UNITED STATES. **VFOAT** Crime in the United States. Vol. 1 (Jan.-July 1930)-. 0082-7592. US. English. an. Superintendent of Documents, US Government Printing Office, Washington DC 20402. **LC** HV6787.

UNIFORM CRIME REPORTS, STATE OF WEST VIRGINIA. (UNIFORM CRIME REPORTS; ANNUAL REPORT). Main/Corp West Virginia. Uniform Crime Reporting Section. **VFOAT** Crime in West Virginia. 0095-1641. US. English. an. West Virginia Uniform Crime Reporting Section, 1800 Washington Street, Charleston WV 25305. **LC** HV7293. **DD** 364.9754.

U.S. IDENTIFICATION MANUAL. (U.S. IDENTIFICATION MANUAL : USIM). **VFOAT** US Identification Manual. **VAT** United States Identification Manual. 0732-6688. Periodical. US. English. qt. $100.00 First Year, $35.00 Each Additional Year. US Identification Manual, 1492 Oddstad Drive, Redwood City CA 94063. **LC** HV8074. **DD** 363.258.

U.S. REGULATORY REPORTER. **VFOAT** United States Regulatory Reporter. Began in 1984. 0749-5005. Periodical. US. English. mo. $325.00. Parexel International Corporation, 55 Wheeler Street, Cambridge MA 02138. **Tel** (617)491-7330. **Ed** Mark Mathieu. **DD** 363. **Circ** 1,000. (ctrl). Regulatory information for the pharmaceutical, chemical, medical device, food, and allied industries. Focuses on regulation and regulatory processes of the FDA and EPA.

UNMARRIED MOTHERS IN WISCONSIN. 1962-. US. English. an. **LC** HV86, HV700.5. **DD** 362.8309775. *Unwed Mothers in Wisconsin and Milwaukee County.*

UNRWA : RESUME DU RAPPORT. Main/Corp United Nations Relief and Works Agency for Palestine Refugees in the Near East. French. ir. Boite Postale No 700, A-1400 Veinne Autriche. **LC** HV640.5.A6. **DD** 362.87.

UP TO THE NECK. 0315-2944. Periodical. CN. English. mo. Up to the Neck, 3553 St Urbain Street, Montreal Quebec H2X 2N6 Canada. **DD** 362.509714281.

UP TO THE NECK. ACTION. (UP TO THE NECK, ACTION). **VFOAT** Action. V. 1- May 1974-. 0315-8624. Periodical. CN. English. mo. 0.25 Each Number. Up to the Neck Action, 3553 St Urbain Street, Montreal Quebec H2X 2N6 Canada. **DD** 362.509714281. *Up to the Neck, 0315-2944.*

URAIAN PENGARAHAN PELAKSANAAN PROGRAM UNIT SEKRETARIAT JENDERAL. Main/Corp Indonesia. Departemen Sosial. Sekretariat Jenderal. Indonesian. ir. Departemen Sosial, Jln Ir H Juanda No 36, Jakarta Indonesia. **LC** HV401.

UTAH DEVELOPMENTAL DISABILITIES STATE PLAN. Main/Corp Utah Council for Handicapped and Developmentally Disabled Persons. US. English. PO Box 11356, Salt Lake City UT 84147. **LC** HV3006.U8. **DD** 362.309792.

UTAH REPORT OF ASSISTANCE, MEDICAL & FOOD STAMP PAYMENTS. Main/Corp Utah. Dept. of Social Services. US. English. qt. Bureau of Statistical Services, Office of Administrative Services, 231 East 4th South, Salt Lake City Utah 84111. **LC** HV86. **DD** 362.109792. *Welfare in Utah.*

UTAH REPORT OF MEDICAID STATISTICS. *See* Statistics.

VALFARDS BULLETINEN. **VFOAT** Valfardsbulletinen. 0280-1418. Periodical. SW. Swedish. ir. 25.00. Valfardsbulletinen, Statistiska Centralbyran Utredningsinstitutet, 115 81 Stockholm Sweden. **LC** HV338.

VANKEINHOIDON HISTORIAPROJEKTIN JULKAISU. No. 1-. 0357-2889. Monographic Series. Finnish (summaries in English). ir. **LC** UNC. **DD** 365.94897.

VANKITILASTO. Main/Corp Finland. Tilastokeskus. **VFOAT** Fangstatistik. Finnish and Swedish. ir. Tilastokeskus, Annankatu 44 00100 10, Helsinki Finland. **LC** HV8435.3.

VEILLEUR. (LE VEILLEUR). V. 1, No 2 (Feb. 1982)-. 0712-6824. Periodical. CN. French. ir. Free to Members, $7.00 Others. Veilleur, 930 rue St Jacques, Longueuil Quebec J4H 3E2 Canada. **DD** 362.60971437. *Journal des Retraites de Longueuil, 0712-6824.*

VERMONT COMPREHENSIVE PLAN FOR CRIMINAL JUSTICE. Main/Corp Vermont. Governor's Commission on the Administration of Justice. US. English. 149 State Street, Montpelier VT 05602. **LC** HV7295. **DD** 364.9743.

VICTIMOLOGY. V. 1- Spring 1976-. 0361-5170. Periodical. US. English. qt. $25.00. Visage Press, 3409 Wisconsin Avenue Northwest, Washington DC 20016. **Ind/Abst** Leg. Resour. Index, Psychol. Abstr., Public Aff. Inf. Serv. Bull. **LC** HV6250. **DD** 364. **NLM** W1 VI17S.

VICTIMS OF CRIME IN TEXAS. TEXAS CRIME TREND SURVEY. (VICTIMS OF CRIME IN TEXAS : TEXAS CRIME TREND SURVEY). Main/Corp Texas. Dept. of Public Safety. Statistical Analysis Center. **VFOAT** Texas Crime Trend Survey. 0149-3647. US. English. Statistical Analysis Center, Box 4087, Austin TX 78773. **LC** HV6250.3.U5. **DD** 362.8809764.

VIGILANTE. **VFOAT** Ching Wei Pao. Began with Mar. 1972 issue. Periodical. Chinese, English or Malay. ir. Vigilante Corps Cultural Sports and Welfare Association, Vigilante Corps Headquarters, 1500 Bendemeer Road 12, Singapore Singapore. **LC** HV7551. **DD** 363.2095952.

VIRGIN ISLANDS DIRECTORY OF SERVICES FOR THE AGING. *See* Yearbooks, Almanacs, Directories.

VOCATIONAL REHABILITATION INDEX. *See* Indexes/Abstracts.

VOICE. (THE VOICE). 0713-0333. Periodical. CN. English. ir. Free to Members. Voice, c/o Elizabeth Fry Society, 195A Bank Street, Ottawa Ontario K2P 1W7 Canada. **DD** 365.706071384. *Newsletter (Elizabeth Fry Society of Ottawa).*

VOIR DIRE (MONTREAL, QUEBEC). (VOIR DIRE). Vol. 1, No 1 (Sept/Oct. 1983)-. 0826-4503. Periodical. CN. French. bm. 9.00. Association des Sourds du Montreal Metropolitain, Bureau 409-A 360 rue Berri, Montreal Quebec H2L 4G9 Canada. **DD** 362.4209714.

VOLUNTARY ACTION LEADERSHIP. 0149-6492. Periodical. US. English. qt. $38.00. Voluntary Action Leadership, 1214 16th Street NW, Washington DC 20036. **Tel** (703)276-0542. **Ind/Abst** Hospit. Lit. Index. **LC** HV91. **DD** 361.7. *Voluntary Action News, 0300-6638.*

VOLUNTARY SECTOR PROGRAM NEWSLETTER. Vol. 1, No. 1 (1981)-. 0715-3295. Periodical. CN. English. sa. Free. Voluntary Sector Program, Room 302-A/ Administrative Studies Building, 4700 Keele Street, North York Ontario M3J 1P3 Canada. **Tel** (416)667-6373. **Ed** Signy L Carson. **DD** 361.70711713541. bk rev. **Circ** 2,000. (ctrl). About management and leadership in the non-profit sector.

VOLUNTEER ADMINISTRATION *CEASED.* V. 1-14. 0362-773X. Periodical. US. English. qt.

VOLUNTEER OPPORTUNITIES. 1982-. 0828-6566. CN. English. be. Community Information Centre, 18 Queen Street North, Kitchener Ontario N2H 2G8 Canada. **DD** 361.3702571344.

VOLUNTEER VIRGINIA. V. 1- Mar. 1975-. Periodical. US. English. qt. State & Office of Volunteerism, 205 North Fourth Street, Richmond VA 23219.

VOLUNTEERING. 1979-1980-. 0275-3030. US. English. an. $3.00 Single Issue. Volunteer: The National Center For Citizen Involvement, 1214 16th Street NW, Washington DC 20036. **LC** HV1. **DD** 361.370973.

VOLUNTEERS IN ACTION. Vol. 1, No. 1 (Jan. 1983)-. 0824-1848. Periodical. CN. English. ir. Free. Canadian Red Cross Society, Prince Edward Island Division, 62 Prince Street, Charlottetown Prince Edward Island C1A 4R2 Canada. **DD** 361.763409717.

V.R.A. BULLETIN BOARD. *See* Public Administration.

VVA VETERAN. **VFOAT** V.V.A. Veteran. **VAT** Vietnam Veterans of America Veteran. 8750-359X. Periodical. US. English. mo. VVA Veteran, 2001 S Street Northwest/Suite 700, Washington DC 20009. **DD** 362.

W-MEMO. *See* Public Administration.

WANTED MISSING PERSONS. **VFOAT** Missing Persons Magazine. Sept. 1984-. 8756-0399. Periodical. US. English. mo. $2.50 Each Issue. Missing Person Publishing Company, PO Box 1006, Port Jervis NY 12771. **DD** 363.

Sound Recordings and Systems

WARERA NINGEN. Periodical. Japanese. ir. LC HV1559.J3.

WASHINGTON JAILS : A REPORT TO THE LEGISLATURE. Main/Corp Washington (State). Adult Corrections Division. US. English. Department of Social and Health Services, Adult Corrections Division, Olympia WA 98504. LC HV7297. DD 365.9797. *Jail Inspection Report.*

WELFARE REFORM POLICY ANALYSIS SERIES. No. 1-. Monographic Series. US. English. ir. Urban Institute, 2100 M Street Northwest, Washington DC 20037.

WESTCHESTER HUMAN SERVICES DIRECTORY. *See* Yearbooks, Almanacs, Directories.

WHO'S MINDING THE CHILDREN?. (WHO'S MINDING THE CHILDREN? : AN ESSENTIAL GUIDE TO DAYCARE IN VANCOUVER, VICTORIA AND THE LOWER MAINLAND BY ERICA HILL). Summer 1981-. 0711-4621. CN. English. an. $3.50 Each Volume. E Hill, 485 West 14th Avenue, Vancouver British Columbia V5Y 1X6 Canada. DD 362.71202571133.

WIRTSCHAFTSSCHUTZ + SICHERHEITSTECHNIK. VFOAT Wirtschaftsschutz und Sicherheitstechnik. 0173-3303. Periodical. GW. German. ir. Kriminalistik Verlag GMBH, Postfach 102640, D-6900 Heidelberg West Germany. Ind/Abst Predicasts. LC HV8290. DD 658.47305.

WISCONSIN CRIMINAL JUSTICE INFORMATION, CRIME AND ARRESTS. Main/Corp Wisconsin. Crime Information Bureau. 1969-. US. English. an. LC HV7299. DD 3641.9775.

THE WORK INCENTIVE PROGRAM - UNITED STATES. DEPT. OF LABOR. (THE WORK INCENTIVE PROGRAM). Main/Corp United STates. Dept. of Labor. 1st- 1969/70-. 0271-8634. US. English. an. US Department of Labor, 200 Constitution Avenue, Washington DC 20213. LC HV85. DD 362.5840973.

WORK RELEASE FOR MISDEMEANANTS IN MINNESOTA. Main/Corp Minnesota. Dept. of Corrections. Division of Research and Planning. 0160-5240. US. English. an. Minnesota Department of Corrections, 430 Metro Square Building/7th and Roberts Streets, St Paul MN 55101. LC HV7273. DD 365.65.

WORLD STATISTICAL DIRECTORY OF VOLUNTEER AND DEVELOPMENT SERVICE ORGANISATIONS. *See* Yearbooks, Almanacs, Directories.

YEAR BOOK OF SOCIAL POLICY IN BRITAIN. *See* Yearbooks, Almanacs, Directories.

YEAR OF ACHIEVEMENT. Main/Corp United States. Office of Human Development. 0148-8570. US. English. an. US Department of Health Education and Welfare, Office of Human Development, Washington DC 20201. LC HV85. DD 353.0084.

YEARLY STATISTICAL REPORT OF THE COMMUNITY REHABILITATION SYSTEM. *See* Statistics.

YEARLY STATISTICAL REPORT OF THE FURLOUGH PROGRAM. *See* Statistics.

YOUR CANADA PENSION PLAN. 1965-. 0317-8951. CN. English (Issued also in French). an. CCH Canadian Limited, Garamond Court, Don Mills Ontario M3C 1Z5 Canada. DD 368.4300971.

YOUR QUEBEC PENSION PLAN. 1965-. 0317-3429. Periodical. CN. English. an. 8.00. CCH Canadian, 6 Garamond Court, Don Mills Ontario M3C 1Z5 Canada. Tel (416)441-2992. DD 368.43009714. Pocket-size booklet explaining Quebec Pension Plan, revisions to Old Age Security Pension, Guaranteed Income Supplement, Spouse's Allowance.

YOUTH IN SOCIETY. Sept./Oct. 1973-. 0307-1790. Periodical. UK. English. mo. 12.00. National Youth Bureau, 17-23 Albion Street, Leicester LE1 6GD England. Tel 0533.554775. Ed R J Rogers. LC HV1441.G7. DD 362.70941. bk rev. adv acc. Circ 3,500. Interprofessional journal for everyone concerned with young people, social and political education and youth affairs.

YOUTH POLICY. Vol. 2, No. 10 (Dec. 1980)-. 8756-0909. Periodical. US. English. ir. $75.00. Youth Policy Institute, Cardinal Station, Washington DC 20064. Tel (301)320-4800. Ed Heather Ford. DD 362. bk rev. Circ 500. Monitors federal policy affecting families. Includes legislation, people and organizations, book reviews, bibliography, and meetings. The publication is non-partisan. *Youth Link (Washington, D.C.).*

YOUTH REPORTER. Oct. 1973-. 0092-5438. Periodical. US. English. mo. US Department of Health Education and Welfare, Office of Youth Development, Washington DC 20201. LC HV9104. DD 364.360973. NLM W1 YO993. *Delinquency Prevention Reporter, 0045-9887.*

YOUTH-SERVING ORGANIZATIONS DIRECTORY. *See* Yearbooks, Almanacs, Directories.

ZENTRALBLATT FUR SOZIALVERSICHERUNG, SOZIALHILFE UND VERSORGUNG. 0044-4278. Periodical. GW. German. mo. Asgard Verlag, Einsteinstrasse 10 Postfach 3080, 5205 Saint Augustin West Germany. Ind/Abst CIS Abstr. NLM W1 ZE794.

SOUND RECORDINGS AND SYSTEMS

1/1. *See* Music.

4-CHANNEL. VAT Four-Channel. 0097-4781. US. English. an. $1.25. Davis Publications, 229 Park Avenue South, New York NY 10003. LC TK7881.8. DD 621.38933.

ABSOLUTE SOUND. (THE ABSOLUTE SOUND). 1973. 0097-1138. Periodical. US. English. qt. $30.00. Absolute Sound, PO Box L, Sea Cliff NY 11579. Tel (516)671-6342. LC TK7881.4. DD 621.389305. adv acc. Circ 19,000. The high end journal for the discriminating listener. We review components and records which attempt to capture naturally, the sound of music for home reproduction.

AMERICAN PHONOGRAPH JOURNAL. V. 1- Mar. 1978-. 0162-0312. Periodical. US. English. qt. $7.00. Mr Tim Christen, PO Box 265, Belmont CA 94002. LC TS2301.P3. DD 621.38933.

AMERICAN RECORD GUIDE. VFOAT ARG. V. 11, No. 2- Oct. 1944-. 0003-0716. Periodical. US. English. bm. $35.00. Salem Research, Route 2 Box 59A South Road, Milbrook NY 12545. Tel (914)677-8177. Ed G Wolf. Ind/Abst Mag. Index, Pop. Mag. Rev., Music Artic. Guide, Music Index, Read. Guide Period. Lit. LC ML1. DD 780.5. bk rev. adv acc. Circ 5,000. Covers classical recordings detailed , informed and forthright reviews and comparisons with other recordings will help you make the best choices. *Listener's Record Guide.*

THE AMERICAN RECORDER. *See* Music.

ANNUAIRE INTERNATIONAL : AUDIOVISUEL. *See* Yearbooks, Almanacs, Directories.

ANNUAL REPORT - TENNESSEE. FILM, TAPE, AND MUSIC COMMISSION. Main/Corp Tennessee. Film, Tape, and Music Commission. Sept. 1980-Dec. 1981-. US. English. an. Tennessee Film Tape and Music Commission, James K Polk Building/16th Floor, Nashville TN 37219.

ANTIQUE RECORDS. Nov. 1972-. Periodical. UK. English. J Hall, KT7 OLH Ditton England. LC ML5. DD 789.912075.

AUDIO. V. 38, No. 3- Mar. 1954-. 0004-752X. Periodical. US. English. mo. CBS Publications, 1515 Broadway, New York NY 10036, (subscription address: Neodata PO Box 2606 Boulder CO 80322). Tel (800)525-9504. Ind/Abst Appl. Sci. Technol. Index, Consum. Index Prod. Eval. Inf. Source, Pop. Mag. Rev., Mag. Index, Music Index, Consum. Index Prod. Eval. Inf. Source. *Audio Engineering, 0275-3804.*

AUDIO AMATEUR. V. 1- Winter 1970-. 0004-7546. Periodical. US. English. qt. Audio Amateur, PO Box 576, Peterborough NH 03458. LC TK7881.7. DD 621.389305.

AUDIO & CAR STEREO TRADE NEWS. VFOAT Audio and Car Stereo Trade News. 0744-8236. Periodical. US. English. mo. $18.00. Audio Trade News, 60 East 42nd Street, New York NY 10017. *Audio Trade News, 0164-9590.*

AUDIO & ELECTRONICS DIGEST. VAT Audio and Electronics Digest. 0164-8985. Periodical. US. English. mo $20.00 Domestic, $30.00 Foreign. Society of Audio Consultants, PO Box 552, Beverly Hills CA 90213.

AUDIO-CASSETTE NEWSLETTER. VFOAT CIS Audio-Cassette Newsletter. 1972. 0270-8663. Periodical. US. English. qt. $15.00. Cassette Information Services, Box 9559, Glendale CA 91206. Tel (818)956-5404. Ed Jerry McKee. Circ 800. Descriptions of new spoken-word audio-cassette programs in education, motivation, entertainment, and "How-to-do-it" categories.

THE AUDIO CRITIC. V. 1- Jan./Feb. 1977-. 0146-4701. Periodical. US. English. ir. Audio Critic, Box 392, Bronxville NY 10708. LC TK7881.4.

AUDIO MARKETNEWS. *See* Business - Marketing.

AUDIO RETAILER. (THE AUDIO RETAILER). V. 1-5, No. 9. 0318-0085. Periodical. CN. English. mo. MacLean Hunter, PO Box 100, Station A, Toronto Ontario M5W 1A7 Canada. DD 381.456213893.

AUDIO (SAN LUIS OBISPO, CALIF.). (AUDIO). VFOAT Audio Blue Book. 1984-. 0883-8437. US. English. an. $125.00. Orion Research Corporation, 1315 Main Avenue/Suite 230, Durango CO 81301. Tel (305)247-8855. Ed Roger Rohrs. Blue books giving used prices on computers, audio stereo, musical instruments, cameras and video. *Audio Reference Guide, 0277-3562.*

AUDIO VISUAL DIRECTORY. *See* Yearbooks, Almanacs, Directories.

THE AUDIO-VISUAL EQUIPMENT DIRECTORY. *See* Yearbooks, Almanacs, Directories.

AUDIO-VISUAL PRESENTATION - CANADIAN JEWISH CONGRESS. AUDIO-VISUAL DEPARTMENT. (AUDIO-VISUAL PRESENTATIONS). Main/Corp Canadian Jewish Congress. Audio-Visual Dept. 0821-5529. CN. English. an. Free. Audio-Visual Department, Canadian Jewish Congress, 1590 Dr Penfield Avenue, Montreal Quebec H3G 1C5 Canada. DD 016.90904924. (ctrl).

AUDIO/VIDEO INTEGRATED CIRCUITS. Series/Titl D.A.T.A. Book Electronic Information Series. VFOAT Audio Video Integrated Circuits. Ed. 1 (1984)-. Periodical. US. English. an. $89.00. D A T A Inc, PO Box 26875, San Diego CA 92126. Tel (619)578-7600. *Consumer Integrated Circuits, 0276-5101.*

AUDIOVIDEO INTERNATIONAL. 0362-1162. Periodical. US. English. mo. $20.00. Dempa Publications, 380 Madison Avenue, New York NY 10017. LC TK7800. DD 621.3805. *Audiovideo.*

AUDIOVISIONE. Year 1- Feb. 1973-. 0303-7622. Periodical. Italian. ir. 4000. Viale Degli Ammiragli 71, Roma 00136 Italy. LC TK7881.7.

AUTOSOUND & COMMUNICATIONS. VAT Autosound and Communications. V. 1- June 1979-. 0194-8679. Periodical. US. English. ir. $50.00. CES Publishing Company, 345 Park Avenue South/ Bernard Rock, New York NY 10010. Tel (212)686-7744. *Communications Retailing.*

AV BULLETIN CEASED. (THE AV BULLETIN). VAT Audio-Visual Bulletin. April 1982-No. 9 (Sept. 1983). 0821-6940. Periodical. CN. English. Free. AV Bulletin, University of Saskatchewan, Ellis Hall/Room 408, Saskatoon Saskatchewan S7N 0W0 Canada. DD 016.61. (ctrl).

AVIDEO. (AV VIDEO). VFOAT A.V. Video. VAT Audiovideo Video. Vol. 6, No. 2 (Feb. 1984)-. 0747-1335. Periodical. US. English. mo. $36.00. Montage Publishing Inc, 25550 Hawthorne Boulevard/Suite 314, Torrance CA 90505. Tel (213)373-9993. Ind/Abst Electron. Commun. Abstr. J., ISMEC Bull., Pollut. Abstr. Indexes, Saf. Sci. Abstr. J. *Audio Visual Directions, 0746-8989.*

Sound Recordings and Systems

THE B.A.S. SPEAKER. Main/Corp Boston Audio Society. VAT Boston Audio Society Speaker. 0195-0908. Periodical. US. English. bm. $20.00. Boston Audio Society, Box 7 Kenmore Square Station, Boston MA 02215.

BILLBOARD INTERNATIONAL AUDIO VIDEO TAPE DIRECTORY. See Yearbooks, Almanacs, Directories.

BILLBOARD INTERNATIONAL DIRECTORY OF RECORDING STUDIOS. See Yearbooks, Almanacs, Directories.

BILLBOARD INTERNATIONAL RECORDING EQUIPMENT & STUDIO DIRECTORY. See Yearbooks, Almanacs, Directories.

BUYER'S GUIDE TO THE WORLD OF TAPE. VFOAT World of Tape. 0090-9033. US. English. $1.50 Single Issue. Billboard Publications Inc, State Road, Great Barrington MA 01230. LC TK7881.6. DD 621.38932.

BUYING GUIDE TO CAR STEREO SYSTEMS. 0272-2291. US. English. $2.95. ABC Leisure Magazines Inc, 825 7th Avenue, New York NY 10019. LC TK7881.85. DD 629.277.

CANADIAN L P & TAPE CATALOGUE. (THE CANADIAN L P & TAPE CATALOGUE). VAT The Canadian Long Play and Tape Catalogue. V. 1- Summer 1975-. 0381-9507. CN. English. M J MacArthur Wrightman, 33 Seguin Street, Ottawa Ontario K1J 6P2 Canada. LC ML156.2. DD 016.789912.

CASH BOX. (THE CASH BOX). 0008-7289. Periodical. US. English. wk. $125.00. Cash Box Publishing Company Inc, 330 West 58th Street, New York NY 10019. Tel (212)586-2640. Ed Mark Albert. LC ML1. DD 789.9105. adv acc. Circ 18,000. An international trade publication concerned with news coverage information and reviews and various national charts regarding today's music, video and home entertainment industries.

CATALOG OF COPYRIGHT ENTRIES. FOURTH SERIES. PART 7. SOUND RECORDINGS. See Copyright, Intellectual Property.

CATALOG OF TELEVISION AND AUDIOVISUAL MATERIALS. See Communication - Broadcasting.

CATALOGUE DISQUES. See Music.

CHI E - DOV' E. IT. Italian. ir. 600. via Carducci 8, 20123 Milano Italy. LC ML21. DD 380.1457802545.

CHICOREL INDEX TO VIDEO TAPES AND CASSETTES. See Indexes/Abstracts.

THE COMPLETE BUYER'S GUIDE TO STEREO/HI-FI EQUIPMENT. VFOAT Speakers. VAT Complete Buyer's Guide to Stereo HiFi Equipment. 0270-627X. Periodical. US. English. bm. $2.50. Service Communications Ltd, 50 Rockefeller Plaza, New York NY 10020. LC TK7881.8. DD 621.389334.

CONSUMER GUIDE. STEREO & TAPE EQUIPMENT TEST REPORTS. (CONSUMER GUIDE : STEREO & TAPE EQUIPMENT TEST REPORTS). 0097-8957. Periodical. US. English. qt $1.50. Consumer Guide, 332 West Main Street, Skokie IL 60076. LC TK7881.8. DD 621.3893.

CULTURE STATISTICS. RECORDING INDUSTRY. See Statistics.

CVQ. CANADIAN VIDEO QUARTERLY. (CVQ : CANADIAN VIDEO QUARTERLY). VFOAT Canadian Video Quarterly. Vol. 1, No. 1-. 0828-5772. Periodical. CN. English. qt. Free. 3M Canada, P O Box 5757, London Ontario N6A 4T1 Canada. DD 778.599. (ctrl).

DB (PLAINVIEW, N. Y.). (DB). Began publication in 1967 with V. 1. 0011-7145. Periodical. US. English. mo. $15.00. Sagamore Publishing Company, 1120 Old Country Road, Plainview NY 11803. Tel (516)433-6530. Ed Larry Zide. Ind/Abst Comput. Control Abstr., Electr. Electron. Abstr., Sci. Abstr. Sect. A. Phys. Abstr., Appl. Sci. Technol. Index, Humanit. Index, Phys. Abstr. CODEN DBSEDB. bk rev. adv acc. Circ 16,000. (ctrl). A central source for previews of new products and new techniques. A forum in which audio pros exchange ideas on how to solve working problems.

DELTIO KRITIKES DISKOGRAPHIAS. See Music.

DIGITAL & AUDIO/VIDEO DISCONTINUED DEVICES. Series/Titl D.A.T.A. Book Electronic Information Series. VFOAT Digital and Audio/Video Discontinued Devices. 8755-738X. US. English. an. D.A.T.A. Inc, PO Box 26875, San Diego CA 92126. LC TK7874.5. DD 621.381730216.

DIRECTORY OF SPOKEN-VOICE AUDIO-CASSETTES. See Yearbooks, Almanacs, Directories.

DISCO 45. See Music.

DISCOTECA ALTA FEDELTA'. Began with No. 12, 1971. Periodical. IT. Italian. ir. $11.00. Casa Editrice l'Esperto, Via Martignoni 1, Milano 20124 Italy. Ind/Abst RILM Abstr. LC ML5. DD 384. Discoteca.

DISCOTECA HI-FI. Periodical. IT. Italian. mo. $14.85. Ed Portoria Spa, Corso Venezia 8, 20121 Milano Italy. LC ML5. DD 789.91205. Discoteca Alto Fedelta.

L'EDITION PHONOGRAPHIQUE D'APRES LE DEPOT LEGAL. Main/Corp France. Bibliotheque Nationale. Departement de la Phonotheque Nationale et de l'Audiovisuel. Service du Depot Legal. 1979-. FR. French. an. 58 rue Richelieu, 75084 Paris Cedex 02 France. LC ML111.5. DD 026.0015540944. Edition Phonographique d'Apres le Depot Legal.

ELECTRONIC SOUND + RTE. VFOAT Electronic Sound und Rte. Periodical. SZ. German. mo. $25.73. At Fachschriftenverlag, Bahnhofstrasse 39-43, CH-5001 Aarau Switzerland. Ind/Abst Comput. Control Abstr., Electr. Electron. Abstr., Sci. Abstr. Sect. A. Phys. Abstr. LC TK7881.7. DD 621.38933205. CODEN ESRTDB. Electronic Sound, Rte.

FIND CATALOG. See Music.

FONOWEEK 40. Periodical. Dutch. ir. 94.85. Koning Wilhelminalaan 12, Amersfoort Netherlands. LC TK7881.7.

THE GRAMOPHONE NEWS. See Music.

GRAMOPHONE RECORD CATALOGUE. Main/Corp Wellington, N.Z. National Film Library. English. ir. A R Shearer, Government Printer, A M P Chambers/187 Featherston Street, Wellington New Zealand. LC ML156.2. DD 011.

GRAMOPHONE. SPOKEN WORD AND MISCELLANEOUS CATALOGUE. 1969-). UK. English. ir. General Gramophone Publ Ltd, 177-179 Kenton Road Harrow, Middlesex HA3 OHA England. Tel 01-907 4476. adv acc. Circ 9,000. Detailed listing of recorded works, on records and cassettes, which fall outside musical categories.

GREEN COMPACT DISC CATALOG. 8756-3851. Periodical. US. English. qt. $10.95. Wayne Green Publishers, WGE Center, Petersborough NH 03458. Tel (603)924-9261. Ed Larry Canale. adv acc. Circ 55,000. Updates compact disc listing on quarterly basis. Also provides disc reviews and CD player reviews. Published by digital audio magazine staff.

HI-FI. French. ir. 10.00. Societe des Editions Radio, 17 rue Bucci, Paris France 75006. LC TK7881.7. DD 621.3893305. Haute-Fidelite.

HI-FI ANSWERS. Periodical. UK. English. mo. $30.65. Haymarket Publishing Service Ltd, 1214 Annsdell Street, Kensingston London W85TR. Tel 01 937 7288. LC TK7881.7. DD 621.38933.

HI-FI NEWS & RECORD REVIEW. VFOAT Hi-Fi News and Record Review. Began with: Vol. 16, No. 1, published in 1971. 0018-1226. Periodical. UK. English. mo. Link House Magazines Ltd, Central House/ 27 Park Street, Croydon CRO 1YD England. Tel 01 760 0054. Hi-Fi News Incorporating Record Review.

HI-FI/STEREO BUYERS' GUIDE. CEASED. Ceased with Jan./Feb. 1981 issue. 0018-1218. Periodical. US. English. bm. $5.95 US, $6.45 US Possessions, Canada. Davis Publications, PO Box 1855, Government Printing, New York NY 10001.

HIFI STEREO. New Series, No.1- Jan. 1975-. Periodical. FR. French. mo. $24.61. Hifi Stero, 2 A 12 rue de Bellevue, Paris XIXE France. Ed Ventllard. LC ML5. DD 789.7. bk rev. adv acc. Circ 35,000. (ctrl). Haut-Parleur.

HIGH FIDELITY. V. 1- Summer 1951-. 0018-1455. Periodical. US. English. mo. Editor/High Fidelity, Great Barrington MA 01230. Ind/Abst Read. Guide Period. Lit. LC ML1. DD 621.38413615, 621.345. Available on microfilm from University Microfilms. Audiocraft for the Hi-Fi Hobbyist, Hi-Fi Music at Home.

HIGH FIDELITY'S BUYING GUIDE TO STEREO COMPONENTS. VFOAT Buying Guide to Stereo Components. 0198-7224. US. English. an. ABC Leisure Magazines Inc, 130 East 59th Street/15th Floor, New York NY 10022. LC TK7881.8. DD 621.389334029473.

HIGH FIDELITY'S BUYING GUIDE TO TAPE SYSTEMS. VFOAT Buying Guide to Tape Systems. 0161-4371. US. English. $1.95 Single Copy. ABC Leisure Magazines Inc, Great Barrington MA 01230. LC TK7881.6. DD 621.38932.

HIGH FIDELITY'S TEST REPORTS. 1973-. 0090-3981. Periodical. US. English. $1.95 Single Issue. Billboard Publications Inc, State Road, Great Barrington MA 01230. LC TK7881.7. DD 621.38933.

HIGH PERFORMANCE REVIEW. Vol. 1, No. 1 (Spring 1981)-. 0277-1357. Periodical. US. English. qt. $29.00. High Performance Review Circulation Manager, POB 2989, Stanford CA 94305. Tel (408)446-3131. Ed David H Tarumoto. LC TK7881.7. DD 621.38933205. bk rev. adv acc. Circ 8,000. Definitive magazine for audiophiles and music lovers. Reviews of stereo components and recordings 100+ CD, LP and cassette reviews in each issue.

THE HOME VIDEO REPORT. 0161-9055. Periodical. US. English. sm. $95.00. Knowledge Industry Publications, 2 Corporate Park Drive, White Plains NY 10604. Video Publisher, 0300-7057.

IAR HOTLINE. VFOAT I.A.R. Hotline. VAT International Audio Review Hotline. #1. 0273-9518. Periodical. US. English. mo. $29.00. International Audio Review, 2449 Dwight Way, Berkeley CA 94704. LC TK7881.7. DD 621.38933205.

THE ILLUSTRATED AUDIO BUYERS GUIDE. VFOAT Audio Buyers Guide. 1984-. 0749-355X. US. English. an. Bill Daniels Company Inc, PO Box 2056, Shawnee Mission KS 66201. LC TS2301.A7. DD 621.3893029473. Illustrated Audio Equipment Encyclopedia, 0739-8948.

THE ILLUSTRATED AUDIO/VISUAL EQUIPMENT REFERENCE CATALOG. VFOAT Audio-Visual. 1984-. 0747-5640. US. English. an. Bill Daniels Company, PO Box 2056, Shawnee Mission KS 66201. LC TS2301.A7. DD 621.38044029473. Illustrated Audio/Visual Equipment Encyclopedia, 0738-0607.

INDEX TO AUDIO EQUIPMENT REVIEWS. See Indexes/Abstracts.

INTERFACE. 0700-9682. Periodical. CN. English. Interface, PO Box 1542, Victoria British Columbia V8W 2X7 Canada. DD 791.405.

JOURNAL - ASSOCIATION FOR RECORDED SOUND COLLECTIONS. Main/Corp Association for Recorded Sound Collections. V. 1- Winter 1967/68-. 0004-5438. Periodical. US. English. ty. $15.00. Phillip Rochlin, ARSC Executive Director, PO Box 75082, Washington DC 20013. Tel (718)834-9603. Ed John W N Francis. Ind/Abst MLA Int. Bibliogr. Books Artic. Mod. Lang. Lit., Music Index, RILM Abstr. LC ML1. DD 789.9105. bk rev. adv acc. Circ 1,100. Features results of major research, technical developments, unusual discoveries, discographies, record and book reviews, general articles, and comprehensive index of such articles in other publications.

JOURNAL OF THE AUDIO ENGINEERING SOCIETY. Main/Corp Audio Engineering Society. V. 1- Jan. 1953-. 0004-7554. Periodical. US. English. ir. Audio Engineering Society Inc, 60 East 42nd Street/Room 449, New York NY 10017. Tel (212)661-8528. Ind/Abst Eng. Index Mon., Eng. Index Bioeng. Abstr., Eng. Index Energy Abstr., Comput. Control Abstr., Electr. Electron. Abstr., Sci. Abstr. Sect. A. Phys. Abstr., Ref. Source, Eng. Index Annu., Eng. Index, Nucl. Sci. Abstr., Appl. Sci. Technol. Index, Sci. Cit. Index, Abr. Ed., Sociol. Abstr., Phys. Abstr., Lang. Lang. Behav. Abstr. LC TK5981. DD 681.84305. CODEN IDIOA3.

Sound Recordings and Systems

LISTENING POST. See Music.

MARKETNEWS. VFOAT Audio Marketnews. Vol. 8, Issue 4 (Apr. 1982)-. 0714-7422. Periodical. CN. English. mo. Marketnews, Hunter-Nichols, 2282 Queen Street East, Toronto Ontario M4E 1G6 Canada. DD 338.47621389305. *Audio Marketnews, 0382-6120.*

MEDIA PROFILES. THE AUDIOVISUAL MARKETING NEWSLETTER. VFOAT Audiovisual Marketing Newsletter. Vol. 1, Issue 1 (Spring 1983)-. 0740-1884. US. English. qt. $48.00. Olympic Media Information, 70 Hudson Street, Hoboken NJ 07030. LC HD9697.A843. DD 384.

THE MIX. 1977. 0164-9957. Periodical. US. English. mo. Mix Publications, PO Box 6395, Albany CA 94706. Tel (415)843-7901. Ed David M Schwartz. bk rev. adv acc. Circ 32,000. (ctrl). Audio, video and music information for the professional and serious amateur. Product information, interviews, industry and directories.

MODERN RECORDING & MUSIC. See Music.

MONDE DU ROCK. See Music.

MUSIC AND RECORDINGS. See Music.

THE MUSIC & SOUND ELECTRONICS RETAILER. See Music.

MUSIC, BOOKS ON MUSIC, AND SOUND RECORDINGS. See Music.

MUSIK REPORT. See Music.

NARAS INSTITUTE JOURNAL. Main/Corp National Academy of Recording Arts and Sciences Institute. VAT National Academy of Recording Arts and Sciences Institute Journal. V. 1- 1977-. 0196-3422. Periodical. US. English. sa. $5.00. College of General Studies Georgia State University, University Plaza, Atlanta GA 30303. Ind/Abst Music Index. LC HD9697.P563. DD 338.477899910973.

THE NEW AMBEROLA GRAPHIC. 0028-4181. Periodical. US. English. qt. $4.00. The New Amberola Phonograph Company, 37 Caledonia Street, Saint Johnsbury VT 05819. Ed Martin F Bryan. LC ML156.9. DD 789.91205. bk rev. adv acc. Circ 700. (ctrl). Publication devoted to the history of sound recordings covering the four decades between 1895 and 1935. Articles, discographies, biographies, book reviews, advertisements, etc.

NEW HI-FI SOUND. VFOAT HI-FI Sound. Periodical. UK. English. 16.00. Haymarket Publishing Ltd, 38-42 Hampton Road, Teddington Middlesex TW11 0JE England. LC TK7881.7. DD 621.38933205. *Popular HI-FI (Teddington, Middlesex).*

NEW ON THE CHARTS. Vol. 1, No. L (Jan. 1976)-. 0276-7031. US. English. mo. $99.00. Music Business Reference Inc, 1501 Broadway, New York NY 10036. Tel (212)921-0165. Ed Leonard Kalikow. LC ML18. DD 338.477802573. adv acc. Circ 4,000. (ctrl). Addresses and phone numbers for companies involved with current hit pop records and music videos. Includes a cumulative index of every hit single and album.

THE NEW SCHWANN. VFOAT New Schwann Record and Tape Guide. Vol. 35, No. 12 (Dec. 1983)-. 0742-7239. Periodical. US. English. mo. $30.00. Schwann Record & Tape Catalogs, 535 Boylston Street, Boston MA 02116. LC REVPAR. *Schwann-1, Record & Tape Guide (Boston, Mass. : 1977), Schwann-2, Record & Tape Guide, 0271-5783.*

NEWSLETTER - CANADIAN INDEPENDENT RECORD PRODUCERS ASSOCIATION. Main/Corp Canadian Independent Record Producers Association. VAT CIRPA Newsletter, Canadian Independent Record Producers Association Newsletter. 1- Aug. 1976-. 0703-1858. Periodical. CN. English. ir. Canadian Independent Record Producers Association, 14 Overlea Boulevard, Toronto Ontario M4H 1A4 Canada. DD 338.477899106271.

NEWSLETTER : CONCERT RECORDINGS. See Music.

LA NOUVELLE REVUE DU SON, DES IDEES, DES NOUVEAUTES, TOUS LES PRIX. Periodical. FR. French. mo. Editions Frequences, 13 Boulevard Ney, 75018 Paris France. LC TK7888.4. DD 621.38939305.

NUMERICAL LISTING OF SUPRAPHON LP RECORDS. See Music.

ORKESTER JOURNALEN. See Music.

PAUL'S RECORD MAGAZINE. See Music.

PERCUSSIONER INTERNATIONAL AUDIO MAGAZINE. 0743-8621. Periodical. US. English. bm. Sal Sofia Industries Inc, # 6 Avenue J, Brooklyn NY 11230.

PHONO. See Music.

PHONOGRAPHIC BULLETIN. No. 1- Summer 1971-. 0253-004X. Periodical. NE. Multilingual (English, German, or French). ir. Hengevelstraat 29, Utrecht Netherlands. Ind/Abst Libr. Inf. Sci. Abstr., Ref. Source. LC ML5. DD 789.912.

PHYSICAL ACOUSTICS : PRINCIPLES AND METHODS. 1982-. Periodical. US. English. ir.

PRO SOUND NEWS. No. 1- Nov. 1978-. 0164-6338. Periodical. US. English. mo. $25.00. Pro Sound News, 220 Westbury Avenue, Subscription Department, Carle Place NY 11514. Tel (516)334-7880. Ed Randy Savicky. adv acc. Circ 15,000. (ctrl). Trade newsmagazine for the professional sound production industry.

PROFESSIONAL AUDIO BUYERS REFERENCE GUIDE. 0747-752X. Periodical. US. English. an. $14.95. SIE Publishing, 976 Fernhill Avenue, Newbury Park CA 91320.

PROFESSIONAL SOUND. VFOAT Professional Sound Blue Book. 1984-. 0883-8445. US. English. an. Orion Research Corporation, 1315 Main Avenue/Suite 230, Durango CO 81301. *Professional Sound Reference Guide, 0276-5578.*

RADIO & RECORDS. See Music.

RECORD & TAPE BUYER'S GUIDE. VAT Record and Tape Buyer's Guide. July 1983-. 0822-9767. CN. English. an. $15.00 Each Volume. The Record, PO Box 201 Station M, Toronto Ontario M6S 4T3 Canada. DD 338.4778991202571.

THE RECORD COLLECTORS JOURNAL. V. 1- July 1975-. 0099-0817. Periodical. US. English. mo. $10.00. Markell Publishing Company, PO Box 1200, Covina CA 91722. LC ML1. DD 789.91205.

RECORD COLLECTORS' SOURCE BOOK. See Hobbies.

RECORD REVIEW (LOS ANGELES, CALIF.). (RECORD REVIEW). V. 1- Jan./Feb. 1977-. 0198-8573. Periodical. US. English. bm. Record Review, PO Box 91878, Los Angeles CA 90009. Tel (213)886-4432. Ind/Abst Music Index. LC ML156.9. DD 789.913105.

RECORDED SOUND. Began with No. 1- May 1961-. Ceased with No. 86, 1984. 0034-1630. Periodical. UK. English. sa. Ind/Abst Libr. Inf. Sci. Abstr., Music Index, RILM Abstr. LC ML5. DD 001.55405. (cum index).

RECORDER REVIEW. 0361-5855. US. English. A Nitka, 166 West 48 Street, New York NY 10036. LC ML1. DD 788.5305.

RECORDING ENGINEER/PRODUCER. Jan./Feb. 1971-. 0034-1673. Periodical. US. English. bm. Recording & Broadcasting Publications, PO Box 2449, Hollywood CA 90078. Tel (213)467-1111. Ed Mel Lambert. LC TK7881.6. DD 621.3893205. bk rev. adv acc. Circ 20,000. (ctrl).

RECORDING INDUSTRY INDEX. See Indexes/Abstracts.

RECORDING WORLD. Spring 1984-. 0743-5827. Periodical. US. English. qt. Innovations International, GPO Box 2367, New York NY 10001. DD 621.

RECORDS IN REVIEW CEASED. VFOAT High Fidelity Annual. Began publication with 1957? Ceased with 1981 issue. 0073-2095. US. English. an. LC ML156.9. DD 789.913. *High Fidelity Record Annual.*

REVISTA DE ACUSTICA. Yearly V. 1- July/Sept/ 1970-. Periodical. SP. English (text and summaries in Spanish). ir. $10.00. Revista de Acustica, Serrano 144, Madrid 6 Spain. Tel 261 88 06.

SAMS TAPE RECORDER SERVICE DATA. Main/Corp Sams (Howard W.) and Company, Inc., Indianapolis. 0162-2447. US. English. 4300 West 62nd Street, Indianapolis In 46268. LC TK7881.6. DD 621.38932. *Sams Photofact Tape Recorder Series.*

SAMS VIDEOCASSETTE RECORDER SERVICE DATA. VFOAT Sams V.C.R. Service Data. VCR45 (Apr. 1981)-. US. English. H W Sams & Company, 4300 West 62nd Street, PO Box 7092, Indianapolis IN 46268. LC TK6655.V5. DD 621.3883320288. *Videocassette Recorder Service Data.*

DAS SCHALLARCHIV. Periodical. AU. German. ir. Arbeits Gem Oesterreicher, Schallarchive Rotenhausgasse 6, A-1090 Wien Austria. LC ML111.5.

SCHWANN-2, RECORD & TAPE GUIDE CEASED. VFOAT Schwann-2, Records & Tapes. VAT Schwann Two, Record and Tape Guide. Began in 1971?. 0271-5783. Periodical. US. English. sa. Schwann Record Catalogs, 137 Newbury Street, Boston MA 02116.

THE SENSIBLE SOUND. 1977. 0199-4654. Periodical. US. English. qt. $18.00. Sensible Sound, 403 Darwin Drive, Snyder NY 14226. Tel (716)839-5049. Ed John A Horan. bk rev. Circ 4,500. A totally candid audio equipment review journal. Unique because advertising from the manufacturers whose equipment we test is not accepted. Sonic purity at an affordable price is our goal.

SON HI-FI MAGAZINE. No.1- Autumn/Winter 1978-. 0708-1588. Periodical. CN. French. bm. $11.61. Les Editions Alcyon, 4351 Esplanade, Montreal Quebec H2W 1T2 Canada. Tel (514)845-7159. Ed Michel Prin. Ind/Abst Point Repere. DD 621.3893305. adv acc. Circ 23,500. (ctrl). To help consumers to listen and to buy well.

SON, VIDEO MAGAZINE. Periodical. FR. French. mo. 140.00. Editions Frequences, 1 Bld Ney, 75018 Paris France. Tel 46 07 01 97. bk rev. adv acc. Circ 30,000. Sound (general), video, music, (jazz, rock, classic), audio and video synthetizers, laboratory tests on sound (hi-fi) and video (VTR-camcorders). *Son Magazine.*

SONO. V. 1-5. 0702-1062. CN. French. mo. $17.56 Foreign. Sono, 2 A 12 rue de Bellevue, 75019 Paris France. Tel (1) 200 33 05. Ed Jean-Paul Poincignon and Charles Pannel. bk rev. adv acc. Circ 28,500. (ctrl). Technical tests on sound reinforcement and electronic music instruments/reports on audio engineering and music shows/technical reports on discotheques, sound recording studios and concerts.

SOUND & VIDEO CONTRACTOR. (SOUND & VIDEO CONTRACTOR : S&VC). VFOAT Sound and Video Contractor. Vol. 1, No. 1 (Sept. 1983)-. 0741-1715. Periodical. US. English. mo. Free to Qualified Persons, $25.00 Others US, $27.00 Others Canada. Sound & Video Contractor, 9221 Quiviria Road, PO Box 12901, Overland Park KS 66212.

SOUND CANADA. V. 4, No. 7- Nov. 1973-. 0383-6908. Periodical. CN. English. mo. $6.00. Sound Magazine, 62 Shaftsbury Avenue, Toronto Ontario M4T 1A4 Canada. Ind/Abst Comput. Control Abstr., Electr. Electron. Abstr., Sci. Abstr. Sect. A. Phys. Abstr. CODEN SOCAD5. *Sound, 0703-6930; Audio Video Canada, 0710-4413.*

SPEAKER BUILDER. Began with Feb. 1980. 0199-7920. Periodical. US. English. qt. $12.00. Audio Amateur Publications, PO Box 576, Peterborough NH 03458. Tel (603)924-9464. Ed Edward T Dell Jr. LC TK5983. DD 621.389332. bk rev. adv acc. Circ 6,000. To help build audio speakers.

SPEAKERS. VFOAT High Fidelity's Buying Guide to Speaker Systems. 0278-1387. US. English. an. $1.95. LC TK5983. DD 621.380282. *High Fidelity's Buying Guide to Speaker Systems, 0147-7676.*

SPECIALISTE. (LE SPECIALISTE). Vol. 1, No 1 (Summer 1982)-. 0712-5151. Periodical. CN. French. qt. Free. Specialiste a/s Camera RL, 368 rue Main, Gatineau Quebec J8P 5K Canada. DD 770.60714221.

STEREO. See Music.

STEREO DIRECTORY & BUYING GUIDE. See Yearbooks, Almanacs, Directories.

STEREO REVIEW. V. 21, No. 5- Nov. 1968-. 0039-1220. Periodical. US. English. mo. CBS Publications, 1515 Broadway, New York NY 10036, (subscription address): Neodata PO Box 2606 Boulder CO 80322). Ind/Abst Mag. Index, Book Rev. Index, Music Artic. Guide, Music Index, Consum. Index Prod. Eval. Inf. Source, Read. Guide Period. Lit., RILM Abstr., Mag. Index, Pop. Mag. Rev. *Hi Fi/Stereo Review.*

STEREO REVIEW'S BUYERS GUIDE. (STEREO REVIEW'S STEREO . . . BUYERS GUIDE). **VFOAT** Stereo Buyer's Guide. 0736-6515. US. English. an. $4.95. CBS Magazines, One Park Avenue, New York NY 10016. **Tel** (212)503-5064. **Ed** William Burton. **LC** TK7881.8. **DD** 621.389334029473. adv acc. Descriptions, features, specifications, and prices on stereo receivers, amplifiers, tuners, turntables, cartridge, tonearms, cassette decks, open-reel decks, blank tape, accessories, speakers, headphones, pocket stereo, signal processors, and compact disc players.

STEREO REVIEW'S TAPE RECORDING & BUYING GUIDE. **VFOAT** Tape Recording & Buying Guide. Began in 1973. 0093-996X. US. English. an. $4.50. Ziff-Davis Publishing Company, PO Box 278, Pratt Station, Brooklyn NY 11205. **Tel** (212)725-3928. **LC** TK 7881.6. **DD** 621.38932. Stereo Review's Tape Recorder Guide.

STEREO TEST REPORTS. 1979-. 0194-1844. Periodical. US. English. $2.95 Each. 1330 Avenue of the Americas, New York NY 10019. **LC** TK7881.8. **DD** 621.389305.

STEREO/HI-FI DIRECTORY. See Yearbooks, Almanacs, Directories.

STEREO/HI-FI EQUIPMENT ANNUAL REVIEW. **VFOAT** Annual Review. **VAT** Stereo Hi-Fi Equipment Annual Review. 0277-6898. US. English. an. $12.00 Domestic, $16.00 Canada, $24.00 Others. Complete Buyer's Guide to Stereo/Hi-Fi Equipment, Box 172, Mt Morris IL 61054. **LC** TK7881.8. **DD** 621.38933.

STEREOPHILE; FOR THE HIGH FIDELITY STEREO PERFECTIONIST. 0585-2544. Periodical. US. English. ir. $32.00. Stereophile, PO Box 1948, Santa Fe NM 87501. **Tel** (505)982-2366. **Ed** Gordon Holt. adv acc. **Circ** 20,000. Reviews high-end audio, stereo equipment.

STEREOPLAY. No. 1 (Jan. 1984)-. Periodical. GW. German. mo. 84.00. Vereinigte Motor-Verlage GMBH & Co KG, Leuschnerstr 1 Postfach 10 42, 7000 Stuttgart West Germany. Hifi Stereophonie, 0018-1382.

THE TALKING MACHINE REVIEW. 0039-9191. Periodical. UK. English. ir. $10.73. Ernie Bayly, 19 Glendale Road, Bournemouth BH6-4JA England. **Ed** Ernie Bayly. bk rev. adv acc. **Circ** 8,000. History of phonographs, disc and cylinder, artistes who recorded and their records etalia.

TAPE. Periodical. UK. English. mo. 3/5/-. Seymour Press Ltd, 334 Brixton Road, SW9 London England. **LC** TK7881.6. **DD** 621.3893205. Sound & Picture Tape Recording Magazine.

TAPE DECK. V. 1- Jan./Feb. 1979-. 0164-4602. Periodical. US. English. an. $4.95. Hampton Internations Comm Inc, 60 East 42nd Street/Suite 3415, New York NY 10017. **Tel** (212)682-7320.

TON REPORT. Periodical. German. ir. Ring der Tonbandfreunde, Postfach 11 01, 3388 Bad Harzburg 1 West Germany. **LC** TK7881.6.

UP DATE - CANADIAN RECORDING INDUSTRY ASSOCIATION. (UP DATE). July 1983-. 0824-6203. Periodical. CN. English. ir. Free. Canadian Recording Industry Association, 89 Bloor Street East, Toronto Ontario M4W 1A9 Canada. **DD** 338.477899120971.

THE VIDEO RETAILER. Vol. 3, Issue 2 (Feb. 1982)-. 0730-3505. Periodical. US. English. mo. National Video Clearinghouse, 100 Lafayette Drive, Syosset NY 11791. **LC** HD9697.V543. **DD** 381.4562138833. Video Programs Retailer, 0199-9745.

VIDEODISC UPDATE CEASED. Vol. 1, No. 1 (July 1982)-. 0733-0421. Periodical. US. English. mo. Vededisc Update, Meckler Publishing, 520 Riverside Avenue, Westport CT 06880.

VIDEOGLOBE. Published since Oct./Nov. 1983. 0824-1449. CN. French. qt. $2.00 Each Number. Videlglobe, 136 rue Merizzi, Ville St-Laurent Quebec H4T 1S4 Canada. **DD** 011.37.

THE VIDEOLOG : PROGRAMS FOR GENERAL INTEREST AND ENTERTAINMENT. See Communication - Broadcasting.

VIDEONEWS. **VAT** Video News. 0145-9023. Periodical. US. English. bw. Phillips Publishing Company, 7315 Wisconsin Avenue/Suite 1200 N, Washington DC 20014. **Tel** (301)986-0666. **Ind/Abst** Predicasts, Infobank, Funk Scott Index Corp. Ind. Vidnews, 0093-5395; Broadband Communications Report; Videocassette & CATV Newsletter.

VIDEOPLAY MAGAZINE (DANBURY, CONN.). (VIDEOPLAY MAGAZINE). **VFOAT** Videoplay. Began with issue for Apr. 1980. 0273-9828. Periodical. US. English. bm. $9.80. Videoplay Magazine, 51 Sugar Hollow Road, Danbury CT 06810. **LC** TK9960. **DD** 621.38833205.

VIDEOPLAYER. 0090-3922. Periodical. US. English. bm. $10.00. 13273 Ventura Boulevard/Suite 213, Studio City CA 91604. **LC** TK6655.V5. **DD** 778.59.

YIN HSIANG CHIH NAN. **VFOAT** Audio Guide Book. CH. Chinese. an. $15.00. Tai-Pei Shih Tien Chi Shang Yeh Tung Yeh Kung Hui, 131 Sung-Chiang Road, Taipei Taiwan. **LC** TK7881.8.

STATISTICS

4TH QUARTER STATISTICAL REPORT & ANNUAL REPORT. **Main/Corp** Alaska. Division of Social Services. US. English. an. Division of Social Services, Pouch H-05, Juneau AK 99811. **LC** HV98.A4. **DD** 361.609798.

A.A.P.-A.U.P.S. UNIVERSITY PRESS STATISTICS. (AAP-AUPS UNIVERSITY PRESS STATISTICS). **VFOAT** University Press Statistics. 0094-7970. US. English. J P Dessauer Inc, One Park Avenue, New York NY 10016. **LC** Z231.5.U6. **DD** 338.470705730973.

ABORTION STATISTICS. ENGLAND & WALES. (ABORTION STATISTICS). **Series/Titl** Series AB. 1974-. 0140-5314. UK. English. an. **LC** HQ767.5.G7. **DD** 301. **NLM** W2 FA1 O3A. The Registrar General's Statistical Review of England and Wales. Supplement on Abortion.

ABRIDGED TRADE STATISTICS FOR TANZANIA, UGANDA, AND KENYA. **Main/Corp** East African Community. East African Customs and Excise Dept. 0304-5919. KE. English. ir. East African Community, Box 30022, Nairobi Kenya. **LC** HF266.E3. **DD** 382.09676.

ABS NEWSTATS. (A B S NEWSTATS). **Main/Corp** Alberta. Bureau of Statistics. **VAT** Alberta Bureau of Statistics Newstats. V. 1- 6 Jan. 1978-. 0709-9541. Periodical. CN. English. Alberta Bureau of Statistics, 480 Terrace Building, 9515-107 Street, Edmonton Alta T5K 2C3 Canada. **DD** 310.5.

ABSTRACT OF BUILDING AND CONSTRUCTION STATISTICS - JAMAICA. See Indexes/Abstracts.

ABSTRACT OF STATISTICS - BARBADOS. STATISTICAL SERVICE. See Indexes/Abstracts.

ABSTRACT OF STATISTICS (PAPUA NEW GUINEA. NATIONAL STATISTICAL OFFICE). See Indexes/Abstracts.

ACADEMIC SCIENCE, SCIENTISTS AND ENGINEERS. DETAILED STATISTICAL TABLES. Periodical. US. English. an. National Science Foundation, Washington DC 20550.

ACCOUNTS . . . AND STUDENT STATISTICS. **Series/Titl** Accounts Series. English. an. 1.50. Government Publications Sales Office, G P O Arcade, Dublin 1 Ireland. **LC** LC148. **DD** 378.1059417.

ACP BASIC STATISTICS. **VFOAT** ACP Statistiques de Base. **VAT** A C P Basic Statistics. English (French). ir. European Community Info Inc, 2100 M Street NW Suite 707, Washington DC 20037. **Tel** (202)862-9500.

ACTIVITE DES COURS ET TRIBUNAUX. STATISTIQUES DIVERSES. **Series/Titl** Statistiques Judiciaires. BE. French. an. 85 Domestic, 135 Foreign. Institut National de Statistique, rue de Louvain, 44 - 1000 Bruxelles Belgium. **Tel** (02)513.96.50. **Circ** 350. (ctrl). Court statistics.

ADDRESS LIST - NATIONAL CLEARINGHOUSE FOR CENSUS DATA SERVICES. See Population Studies.

Statistics

ADMINISTRATION OF JUSTICE STATISTICS . . . ESTIMATES. 1983-84-. 0264-6552. UK. English. an. 9.00. Chartered Institute of Public Finance And Accountancy, 1 Buckingham Pl, Londong SW1E 6HS England. **LC** KD7122.5.A13. **DD** 347.41013, 344.10713.

ADMISSIONS DECISIONS STUDY - FLORIDA. UNIVERSITY. GAINESVILLE. GRADUATE SCHOOL. See Education (General) - Higher Education.

ADVANCE DATA. (ADVANCE DATA FROM VITAL & HEALTH STATISTICS OF THE NATIONAL CENTER FOR HEALTH STATISTICS). Began with No. 1, Oct. 18, 1976. 0147-3956. Monographic Series. US. English. ir. US National Center for Health Statistics, 3700 East-West Highway, Hyattsville MD 20782. **Ind/Abst** Hospit. Lit. Index, Energy Inf. Abstr., Environ. Abstr., Excerpta Med., Popul. Index, Am. Stat. Index. **LC** RA407.3. **DD** 362.160973. **NLM** W2 A N148A.

ADVANCE STATISTICS OF EDUCATION. **VFOAT** Statistique de l'Enseignement-Estimations. 1973/74-. 0575-786X. Periodical. CN. English (French). an. Receiver General for Canada, Statistics Canada Publications, Ottawa Ontario K1A 0T6 Canada. **DD** 370.971.

AEDC JOURNAL. See Economics.

AFFIRMATIVE ACTION INFORMATION. OLYMPIA MSA, METROPOLITAN STATISTICAL AREA (THURSTON COUNTY). **VFOAT** Olympia MSA, Metropolitan Statistical Area (Thurston County). 1984-. US. English. an. Research and Analysis Branch, Washington State Employment Security Department, Olympia WA 98504. **LC** HD5726.O49. **DD** 331.1143. Affirmative Action Information, Olympia Standard Metropolitan Statistical Area.

AFFIRMATIVE ACTION STATISTICS - CALIFORNIA YOUTH AUTHORITY. **Main/Corp** California Youth Authority. Report No. 1- Sept. 1974-. 0362-4110. US. English. sa. California Youth Authority, 4241 Williamsbourgh Drive, Sacramento CA 95823. **LC** HD6274.C3. **DD** 331.133.

AFFIRMATIVE EMPLOYMENT STATISTICS. **Series/Titl** Federal Civilian Workforce Statistics. Sept. 30, 1982-. US. English. be. U S Office of Personnel Management, Compliance and Investigations Group/Office of Workforce Information, 1900 E Street NW, Washington DC 20415. Vols. for Sept. 30, 1982- distributed to depository libraries in microfiche. Equal Employment Opportunity Statistics.

AFRICAN DIRECTORY OF STATISTICIANS. See Yearbooks, Almanacs, Directories.

AFRICAN STATISTICAL YEARBOOK. See Yearbooks, Almanacs, Directories.

AFTERMARKET STATISTICAL YEARBOOK. See Yearbooks, Almanacs, Directories.

AG. ECONOMICS STATISTICAL SERIES. **VFOAT** Ag. Economics Statistics Series. **VAT** Agricultural Economics Statistical Series. 0148-2920. Monographic Series. US. English. North Dakota State University, Department of Agricultural Economics, Commonwealth Morril Hall, Fargo ND 58105. **LC** HD1407. **DD** 338.10212. Agricultural Economics Statistical Series.

AGRARBERICHTERSTATTUNG. HEFT 4, VIEHHALTUNG. **Series/Titl** Statistik Niedersachsen. **VFOAT** Viehhaltung. German. be. Niedersachsisches Landesverwaltungsamt Statistik Schriftenvertrieb, Postfach 107, 3000 Hanover 1 West Germany. **LC** HD9423.7.L69. **DD** 338.1760094359. bk rev. **Circ** 300.

AGRARSTATISTIK CEASED. **VFOAT** Statistique Agricole, Agricultural Statistics. -No. 8 (1972). 0081-4946. Periodical. BE. German and French. ir. 700 Domestic, 1200 Foreign. Institute National Statistique, Rue de Louvain 44, 1000 Bruxelles Belgium. **Tel** (02)513 96 50. **Circ** 500. (ctrl). Agricultural statistics. Agrarstatistische Mitteilungen.

AGRARSTATISTISCHE UBERSICHTEN. **Main/Corp** Landwirtschaftskammer Rheinland. German. ir.

AGRI-VIEW. See Agriculture.

AGRICULTURAL CENSUS - GUJARAT. See Agriculture.

Statistics

AGRICULTURAL FINANCE STATISTICS. Main/Corp United States. Dept. of Agriculture. Economic Research Service. V. 1- 1973-. 0091-3502. US. English. Superintendent of Documents, US Government Printing Office, Washington DC 20402. LC HG2051.U5. DD 332.710973. *Agricultural Finance Review.*

AGRICULTURAL INDUSTRIES FINANCIAL STATISTICS, AUSTRALIA. English. ir. Information Service ABS, PO Box 10, Belconnen Australian Capital Territory 2616 Australia. LC HD9018.A6. DD 338.130994.

AGRICULTURAL LAND RESERVE STATISTICS. 0713-1631. CN. English. an. Provincial Agricultural Land Commission, 4333 Ledger Avenue, Burnaby BC Canada. LC HD319.B8. DD 333.761609711.

AGRICULTURAL OUTLOOK (WASHINGTON, D.C. : 1978-). See Agriculture.

AGRICULTURAL SECTOR. PART IV : FINANCIAL STATISTICS - AUSTRALIAN BUREAU OF STATISTICS. Main/Corp Australian Bureau of Statistics. VFOAT Financial Statistics. Began with 1974/75 issue. 0314-2965. English. ir. Australian Bureau of Statistics, Information Services, PO Box 10, Belconnen ACT 2616, Canberra Australia. LC HD2151. DD 338.13.

AGRICULTURAL STATISTICS. VFOAT Statistique Agricole. Periodical. LU. text in French, German, English and Italian, introductory material in English, Italian, Dutch and Danish. European Community Information Service, 2100 M Street NW/ Suite 707, Washington DC 20037. Tel (202)862-9547. Ind/Abst Foreign Lang. Index, PAIS Foreign Lang. Index. World market prices and official support prices for products under the EC common agricultural policy and current statistics on plant products: land use, areas and products harvested, selection of yield, and agro-meteorological conditions.

AGRICULTURAL STATISTICS. 1936-. Periodical. US. English. an. US Department of Agriculture, Washington DC 20402. *Report, Yearbook of Agriculture.*

AGRICULTURAL STATISTICS AND REVIEW OF AGRICULTURE. VFOAT Agricultural Statistics. Vol. 9 (1973)-. 0715-1438. CN. English. an. PEI Department of Agriculture/Forestry, PO Box 2000, Marketing Branch, Charlottetown Prince Edward Island C1A 7N8 Canada. Tel (902)892-4101. LC HD1790.P74. *Agricultural Statistics (Charlottetown, P.E.I.), 0715-142X.*

AGRICULTURAL STATISTICS FOR ARKANSAS. US. English. an. USDA-SRS Crop Reporting Service Room 5829 Building, Washington DC 20250. Tel (501)378-5145.

AGRICULTURAL STATISTICS FOR ONTARIO. Main/Corp Ontario. Ministry of Agriculture and Food Statistics Section. 1971-. 0568-2894. Periodical. CN. English. an. Receiver General for Canada, Statistics Canada Publications, Ottawa Ontario K1A 0T6 Canada. Tel (613)992-3151. LC HD1790.06. DD 338.109713021.

AGRICULTURAL STATISTICS OF SABAH. Main/Corp Sabah. Dept. of Agriculture. English. ir. Agricultural Information Division, Department of Agriculture, Sabah Malaysia. LC S296.S3. DD 338.1095953.

AGRICULTURAL STATISTICS OF THE AUSTRALIAN CAPITAL TERRITORY. English. ir. Information Services, Canberra 526627 Australia. LC S382.

AGRICULTURAL STATISTICS, UNITED KINGDOM. Main/Corp Great Britain. Ministry of Agriculture, Fisheries and Food. 1954/55-. 0065-4590. UK. English. an. Her Majesty's Stationery Office, PO Box 276, London SW8 5DT England. LC HD1921. DD 338.10941. *Agricultural Statistics, United Kingdom, 0065-4590; Agricultural Statistics, England.*

AGRICULTURAL STATISTICS (WASHINGTON, D.C.). (AGRICULTURAL STATISTICS). Began with 1936. 0082-9714. US. English. an. Superintendent of Documents, US Government Printing Office, Washington DC 20402. LC HD1751. DD 338.10973. *Yearbook of Agriculture (Washington, D.C. : 1926), 0084-3628.*

A.I.D. ECONOMIC DATA BOOK, NEAR EAST AND SOUTH ASIA. Main/Corp United States. Agency for International Development. Statistics and Reports Division. No. 243- Apr. 1967-. 0503-4922. Periodical. US. English. ir. National Technical Information Service, 5285 Port Royal Road, Springfield VA 22161. Tel (905)559-5211. Circ 18,500. (ctrl). Bulletin listing a sampling of reports contained in the NTIS database in five catagories: manufacturing processing industry, agriculture and food, construction, and management and economic development.

AIR CARRIER FINANCIAL STATISTICS. Began with March 31, 1962. 0002-2225. Periodical. US. English. qt. Superintendent of Documents, US Government Printing Office, Washington DC 20402. LC HE9803.A1. DD 387.710973. *Quarterly Report of Air Carrier Financial Statistics.*

AIR QUALITY DATA - STATISTICS. Main/Corp United States. Environmental Protection Agency. National Air Data Branch. Periodical. US. English. qt. National Technical Information Service, 5285 Port Royal Road, Springfield VA 22151. LC TD883.2. DD 363.6. *Air Quality Data from the National Air Surveillance Networks and Contributing State and Local Networks.*

AIR TRANSPORT STATISTICS. FLIGHT CREW LICENCES. 1980-. 0727-2774. AT. English. ir. OIC Aviation Statistics, Air Transport Policy Division, PO Box 3567, Canberra City ACT 2601 Australia.

AIRCRAFT STATISTICS, FIJI. FJ. English. ir. LC HE9898.5.A1. DD 387.7099611021. *Aircraft Statistics.*

AIRPORT STATISTICS, STATEWIDE AIRPORT SYSTEM. Calendar Year 1981 Ed.-. US. English. an. Airports Division/Department of Transportation, Honololu International Airport, Honolulu HI 96819. *State of Hawaii Airport Statistics.*

AJIA SHOKOKU YORAN. Japanese. ir. 2-1 Kasumigaseki 2-Chome Chiyoda-Ku, Tokyo Japan. LC HA1665.

AKHILA BHARATIYA AYAKARA ANKARE. Main/Corp India. Directorate of Inspection (Research, Statistics & Publication). VFOAT All India Income-Tax Statistics. 1967/68-. II. English (Hindi). an. LC HJ4766. DD 336.240954.

AKTIVNOST MESNIH ZAJEDNICA. See Public Administration.

AL-ARD AL-IQTISADI WA-AL-MALI. Main/Corp Bank Al-Sudan. Maslahat Al-Ihsa. Arabic. ir. Bank Al-Sudan, Maslahat Al-Ihsa, PO Box 313, Al-Kartum Sudan. LC HA2275.S8.

AL-IQTISADI AL-KUWAYTI. VFOAT Kuwaiti Economist. Periodical. Arabic or English. ir. Ali Salem Street, PO Box 775, Al-Kuwayt Kuwait. LC HC497.K8.

AL-NASHRAH AL-SHAHRIYAH LIL-IHSA - IDARAT AL-IHSAAT WA-AL-DIRASAT AL-IQTISADIYAH. Main/Corp Mauritania. Direction de la Statistique et des Etudes Economiques. VFOAT Bulletin Mensuel Statistique - Direction de la Statistique et des Etudes Economiques. French. ir. 20.00. B P 240, Nouakchott Mauritania. LC HA2096.5. DD 316.61.

AL-TAQRIR AL-IHSAI AL-TARBAWI AL-SANAWI AN AL-TALIM FI JAMI MADARIS AL-URDUN. See Yearbooks, Almanacs, Directories.

ALABAMA AGRICULTURAL STATISTICS. (ALABAMA AGRICULTURAL STATISTICS. BULLETIN). Began in 1948. 0270-2436. US. English. an. USDA-Crop Reporting Service, P O Box 1071, Montgomery AL 36192. Tel (205)832-7263. LC S31. DD 338.109761.

ALABAMA'S VITAL EVENTS. 1972-. 0095-3431. US. English. an. Special Services Administration, Department of Public Health, Montgomery AL 36104. LC HA221. DD 312.09761. NLM W2 AA4 D6A.

ALASKA AGRICULTURAL STATISTICS. VFOAT Alaska Farm Production. 1963-. US. English. an. $5.00. Alaska Crop & Livestock Reporting Service, PO Box 799, Palmer AK 99645. Tel (907)745-4272. LC S33. DD 338.109798. *Alaska Farm Production, 0516-4850.*

ALASKA PERSONAL LINES STATISTICAL ANALYSIS, PRIVATE PASSENGER AUTOMOBILE INSURANCE, HOMEOWNERS INSURANCE. VFOAT Alaska . . . Private Passenger Auto Insurance and Homeowners Insurance. US. English. an. State of Alaska, Department of Commerce & Economic Development, Division of Insurance Pouch D, Juneau AK 99811. Tel (907)465-2517. Ed Bob Sims. LC HG9970.35.A4. DD 368.09609798. Circ 3,000. Analysis and comparison of homeowners and auto rates in Alaska.

ALASKA STATISTICAL QUARTERLY. Main/Corp Alaska. Dept. of Labor. Research and Analysis Section. VFOAT Statistical Quarterly. 0401-1961. Periodical. US. English. Research & Analysis Section, Box 1149, Juneau AK 99802. LC HD5725.A4. DD 331.12509798. *Alaska Statistical Quarterly, 0401-1961.*

ALBERTA ELECTRIC INDUSTRY. ANNUAL STATISTICS. Series/Titl ERCB 28. Began in 1977. 0706-1420. CN. English. an. $15.00. Energy Resources Conservation Board, 640 Fifth Avenue South West, Calgary Alberta T2P 3G4 Canada. LC TN873.C22, HD9685. C3. DD 333.79160971231 S, 363. 62097123. *Cumulative Annual Statistics: Alberta Electric Industry, 0704-4356.*

ALBERTA ENERGY RESOURCE INDUSTRIES : MONTHLY STATISTICS. Main/Corp Alberta. Energy Resources Conservation Board. Periodical. CN. English. mo. Energy Resources Conservation, 640 5th Avenue SW, Calgary Alberta T2P 3G4 Canada. Tel (403)297-8311.

ALBERTA ENERGY RESOURCE INDUSTRIES, MONTHLY STATISTICS. 0710-6874. Periodical. CN. English. mo. Energy Resources Conservation Board, 640-5th Avenue SW, Calgary Alberta T2P 3G4 Canada. DD 333.79097123. *Monthly Statistics.*

ALBERTA OIL AND GAS INDUSTRY : ANNUAL STATISTICS. 1974-. CN. English. an. $10.00. Alberta Energy Resources Conservation Board, 603 Sixth Avenue SW, Calgary Alberta T2P 0T4 Canada. LC TN873.C22, HD9574. C23. DD 333.7 S, 381.4228097123.

ALBERTA PETROLEUM STATISTICS. Main/Corp Alberta. Bureau of Statistics. 1970/74-. 0382-1943. CN. English. an. Alberta Bureau of Statistics, 480 Terrace Building, Edmonton Alberta Canada. LC HD9574.C23. DD 338.27282097123.

ALBERTA PROVINCIAL PARKS USER STATISTICS. VFOAT User Statistics, Alberta Provincial Parks. 0821-0683. CN. English. an. Limited Free Distribution. Alberta Recreation and Parks, 10405 Jasper Avenue, Edmonton Alberta T5J 3N4 Canada. LC GV191.46.A43. DD 333.783097123.

ALBERTA PUBLIC LIBRARY STATISTICS. Began in 1960?. CN. English. an. LC Z735.A45. DD 027.47123.

ALBERTA STATISTICAL REVIEW. Apr. 1973-. 0317-3925. Periodical. CN. English. an. Alberta Treasury/Bureau of Statistics, Legislative Building, Edmonton Alberta T5K 2B6 Canada. LC HA747.A79. DD 317.123. *Business Trends, 0317-3933.*

ALBUQUERQUE SMSA ANNUAL PLANNING REPORT. Main/Corp New Mexico. Employment Security Commission. Research and Statistics Section. US. English. an. Employment Security Commission Research and Statistics Section, PO Box 1928, Albuquerque NM 87103.

ALCOHOL, TOBACCO AND FIREARMS SUMMARY STATISTICS CEASED. (ALCOHOL, TOBACCO, AND FIREARMS SUMMARY STATISTICS). Series/Titl ATF P. Began with 1972/73. Ceased 1981-1982. 0095-1803. US. English. an. Department of the Treasury, Bureau of Alcohol Tobacco and Firearms, 1200 Pennsylvania Avenue NW, Washington DC 20226. LC HD9354. DD 338.4766310973. *Alcohol and Tobacco Summary Statistics.*

ALGEMENE MILIEUSTATISTIEK. VFOAT General Environmental Statistics. NE. Dutch (summaries in English). ir. Centraal Bureau Voor de Statistiek, Staatsuitgeverij, S-Gravenhage Netherlands. LC TD186.5.N47.

ALL ELECTRIC HOMES IN THE UNITED STATES : ANNUAL BILLS, CITIES OF 50,000 AND MORE. See

Statistics

Engineering - Electricity, Electrical Engineering, Electronics.

ALLGEMEINES STATISTICHES ARCHIV. Vol. 1-. 0002-6018. Periodical. GW. German. ir. $50.44. Vandenhoeck & Ruprecht, Postfach 3753, Theaterstr 13, D-3400 Goettingen West Germany. **Tel** 0551/65061. **Ind/Abst** Math. Rev., Coal Abstr., Foreign Lang. Index, PAIS Foreign Lang. Index. **LC** HA1. **NLM** W1 AL824C. **CODEN** ALSAAX. (cum index).

ALLMAN MANADSSTATISTIK. Main/Corp Sweden. Statistiska Centralbyran. **VFOAT** Monthly Digest of Swedish Statistics. Vol. 1- 1963-. 0039-7253. Periodical. SW. Swedish (English). mo. 39.92. Scb-Distributionen, S-70189 Oerebro Sweden. **Tel** 46 8 7834262. **Ed** Nils Welander. **LC** HA1523. **Circ** 3,000. (ctrl). Statistical data and index series for the last two years and annual data for the last five years. *Kommersiella Meddelanden.*

ALUMINUM STATISTICAL REVIEW. 0065-6666. US. English. an. $25.00. Aluminum Association, 818 Connecticut Avenue NW, Washington DC 20006. **Tel** (202)862-5100. **LC** HD9539.A6. **DD** 338.27492. **Circ** 10,000. (ctrl). Statistical data on aluminum industry, including shipments, markets, supply, foreign trade and per capita consumption in many countries of the world.

AMAMI GUNTO NO GAIKYO. JA. Japanese. ir. Kagoshima-Ken Oshima Shicho, 16-11 Horiecho, Naze Japan. **LC** HA1848.A5.

THE AMERICAN STATISTICIAN. V. 1- Aug. 1947-. 0003-1305. Periodical. US. English. qt. $22.00. American Statistician, 806 15th Street NW/Suite 640, Washington DC 20005. **Tel** (202)393-3253. **Ind/Abst** Math. Rev., Electron. Commun. Abstr. J., ISMEC Bull., Pollut. Abstr. Indexes, Saf. Sci. Abstr. J., Int. Aerosp. Abstr., Public Aff. Inf. Serv. Bull., Soc. Sci. Index, Comput. Control Abstr., Electr. Electron. Abstr., Sci. Abstr. Sect. A. Phys. Abstr., Sci. Cit. Index, Abr. Ed., Sociol. Abstr., Lang. Lang. Behav. Abstr., Phys. Abstr. **LC** HA1. **DD** 310.6273. **NLM** HA 1 A517. **CODEN** ASTAAJ. (cum index). *Bulletin of the American Statistical Association.*

AMERICAN STATISTICS INDEX. *See* Indexes/Abstracts.

AMSTAT NEWS. Main/Corp American Statistical Association. **VAT** American Statistical Association News. Began with No. 1, Jan. 1974. 0163-9617. Periodical. US. English. ir. $13.00. American Statistical Association, 806 15th Street SW, Washington DC 20005. **Tel** (202)393-3253.

AMTLICHE NACHRICHTEN DER BUNDESANSTALT FUR ARBEIT. ARBEITSSTATISTIK... JAHRESZAHLEN. VFOAT Arbeitsstatistik... Jahreszahlen. 0170-2696. German. ir. 15.00. Bundesanstalt fur Arbeit, Regensburger Strasse 104, 8500 Nurnberg West Germany. *Jahreszahlen, Arbeitsstatistik.*

AMTLICHES GEMEINDEVERZEICHNIS FUR RHEINLAND-PFALZ. Series/Titl Statistik Von Rheinland-Pfalz. German. an. Statistisches Landesamt Rheinland-Pfalz, Mainzer Str 15/16, 5427 Bad Ems West Germany. **LC** HA1320, JS5471. R47. **DD** 314.343 S, 352.04343.

ANALYSES OF HOSPITAL RUNNING COSTS, RELATED INCOME AND STATISTICS. Main/Corp Northern Ireland Hospitals Authority. UK. English. an. Her Majestys Stationery Office, 80 Chichester Lane, Belfast BT1 4JY Northern Ireland. **LC** RA987.I6. **DD** 338.433621109416.

ANALYSES OF NEW JERSEY PUBLIC LIBRARY STATISTICS FOR.... **VFOAT** New Jersey Public Library Statistics. 1981-. US. English. an. New Jersey State Department of Education/Division of the State Library, 185 West State Street, Trenton NJ 08625-0520. **Ed** O P Gillock. **LC** Z732.N6. **DD** 027.4749.

ANALYSES OF THE ILLINOIS PUBLIC LIBRARY STATISTICS. (ANALYSES OF THE... ILLINOIS PUBLIC LIBRARY STATISTICS). **VFOAT** Illinois Public Library Statistics. 1974-75-. 0736-5616. US. English. an. Illinois State Library, Centennial Building, Springfield IL 62756. **Ed** Susan Bonzi. **LC** Z732.I2. **DD** 027.4773.

ANALYSIS OF CLASS 1 RAILROADS. *See* Transportation - Railroads.

ANIMALSK PRODUKTION. *See* Agriculture - Livestock and Poultry.

ANKETA O OSTVARIVANJU PRAVA RADNIKA IZ RADNOG ODNOSA. *See* Economics - Labor.

ANKETA O PORODICNIM BUDZETIMA RADNICKIH DOMACINSTAVA. Main/Corp Savezni Zavod za Statistiku (Yugoslavia). **Series Corp** Its Statisticki Bilten. 0300-2543. YU. Serbo-Croatian(R). ir. 4.00 Per Issue. Savezni Zavod za Statistiku, Kneza Milosa 20, Beograd Yugoslavia. **LC** HA1631, HD7045.5.

ANKETA O PRIHODIMA, RASHEDIMA I POTRESNJI DOMACINSTAVA. Main/Corp Savezni Zavod Za Statistiku (Yugoslavia). Began with Vol. for 1963. Serbo-Croatian(R). ir. 10.00. Savezni Zavod za Statistiku, Kneza Milosa 20, Beograd Yugoslavia. **LC** HA1631, HC407.Z9.

ANKETA O SEOSKIM DOMACINSTVIMA. Main/Corp Savezni Zavod za Statistiku (Yugoslavia). **Series Corp** Its Statisticki Bilten. YU. Serbo-Croatian(R). ir. 5.00. Savezui Zavod za Statistiku, Kenza Milosa 20, Beograd Yugoslavia. **LC** HA1631, HN631.

ANNALES DE L'INSTITUT HENRI POINCARE. SECTION B, CALCUL DES PROBABILITES ET STATISTIQUE CEASED. **Main/Corp** Institut Henri Poincare. **VFOAT** Calcul des Probabilites et Statistique. New Series, V. 1-18, No. 1. 0020-2347. Periodical. FR. French. qt. 640. Centrale des Revues-Gauther Villars, 11 rue Gossin, 92543 Montrouge Cedex France. **Tel** 1 43 20 15 50. **Ed** Jacques Neveu. **Ind/Abst** Energy Res. Abstr., Comput. Control Abstr., Electr. Electron. Abstr., Sci. Abstr. Sect. A. Phys. Abstr. **LC** QA273.A1. **DD** 519.205. **CODEN** AHPBAR. bk rev. adv acc. **Circ** 750. This journal, recently reorganized, welcomes high standard manuscripts from all areas of the theory of probabilities. *Annales de l'Institut Henri Poincare.*

ANNALS OF PROBABILITY. (THE ANNALS OF PROBABILITY). V. 1- Feb. 1973-. 0091-1798. Periodical. US. English. qt $80.00. Institute Mathematical Statistics, 3401 Investment Boulevard #6, Hayward CA 94545. **Tel** (415)783-8141. **Ed** Thomas Liggett. **Ind/Abst** Math. Rev., Sci. Cit. Index, Abr. Ed. **LC** HA1. **DD** 519.205. **CODEN** APBYAE. bk rev. adv acc. **Circ** 3,300. Publishes contributions to the theory of probability and statistics and to their applications. *Annals of Mathematical Statistics, 0003-4851.*

ANNALS OF STATISTICS. (THE ANNALS OF STATISTICS). V. 1- Jan. 1973-. 0090-5364. Periodical. US. English. qt. $85.00. Institute Mathematical Statistics, 3401 Investment Boulevard #6, Hayward CA 94545. **Tel** (415)783-8141. **Ed** Willem R van Zwet. **Ind/Abst** Math. Rev., Sci. Cit. Index, Abr. Ed. **LC** HA1. **DD** 519.505. **CODEN** ASTSC7. bk rev. adv acc. **Circ** 4,700. Publishes contributions to the theory of probability and statistics and to their applications. *Annals of Mathematical Statistics, 0003-4851.*

ANNALS OF THE INSTITUTE OF STATISTICAL MATHEMATICS. Main/Corp Tokei Suri Kenkyujo (Tokyo, Japan). Vol. 1, No. 1 (Aug. 1949)-. 0020-3157. Periodical. JA. English. ir. Japan Publishers Trading Co Ltd, PO Box 5030 Tokyo International, Tokyo 100-31 Japan. **Ind/Abst** Math. Rev., Int. Aerosp. Abstr., Sci. Cit. Index, Abr. Ed. **LC** QA276. **DD** 519.905. **CODEN** AISXAD. (cum index).

ANNOTATED BIBLIOGRAPHY OF STATISTICAL METHODOLOGY. 0278-9221. US. English. an. US Department of Health and Human Services/Public Health Service Office of Health Research Statistics and Technology/National Center For Health Statistics, 3700 East-West Highway, Hyattsville MD 20782. **LC** Z7553.M43, RA409. **DD** 362.10723. **NLM** ZWA 950 A615.

ANNUAIRE ABREGE DE STATISTIQUES AGRICOLES, REGION RHONE-ALPES. *See* Yearbooks, Almanacs, Directories.

ANNUAIRE DE STATISTIQUE AGRICOLE (FRANCE. SERVICE REGIONAL DE STATISTIQUE AGRICOLE, POITOU-CHARENTES). *See* Yearbooks, Almanacs, Directories.

ANNUAIRE DE STATISTIQUE AGRICOLE. GUADELOUPE. *See* Yearbooks, Almanacs, Directories.

ANNUAIRE DE STATISTIQUES AGRICOLES. *See* Yearbooks, Almanacs, Directories.

ANNUAIRE DE STATISTIQUES REGIONALES. *See* Yearbooks, Almanacs, Directories.

ANNUAIRE DES STATISTIQUES DU COMMERCE EXTERIEUR. *See* Yearbooks, Almanacs, Directories.

ANNUAIRE DES STATISTIQUES DU COMMERCE EXTERIEUR DU TOGO. *See* Yearbooks, Almanacs, Directories.

ANNUAIRE DU CANADA. *See* Yearbooks, Almanacs, Directories.

ANNUAIRE REGIONAL DE STATISTIQUE AGRICOLE. *See* Yearbooks, Almanacs, Directories.

ANNUAIRE RHONE-ALPES. *See* Yearbooks, Almanacs, Directories.

ANNUAIRE STATISTIQUE DE LA BELGIQUE. *See* Yearbooks, Almanacs, Directories.

ANNUAIRE STATISTIQUE DE LA FRANCE (INSTITUT NATIONAL DE LA STATISTIQUE ET DES ETUDES ECONOMIQUES (FRANCE)). *See* Yearbooks, Almanacs, Directories.

ANNUAIRE STATISTIQUE DE LA SECURITE SOCIALE. *See* Yearbooks, Almanacs, Directories.

ANNUAIRE STATISTIQUE DE LA TUNISIE. *See* Yearbooks, Almanacs, Directories.

ANNUAIRE STATISTIQUE DE L'ALGERIE. *See* Yearbooks, Almanacs, Directories.

ANNUAIRE STATISTIQUE DE L'ENSEIGNMENT. *See* Yearbooks, Almanacs, Directories.

ANNUAIRE STATISTIQUE DE L'INDUSTRIE FRANCAISE DU JUTE ET DES POLIOLEFINES TEXTILES. *See* Yearbooks, Almanacs, Directories.

ANNUAIRE STATISTIQUE DE POCHE - INSTITUT NATIONAL DE STATISTIQUE. *See* Yearbooks, Almanacs, Directories.

ANNUAIRE STATISTIQUE DU LUXEMBOURG. *See* Yearbooks, Almanacs, Directories.

ANNUAIRE STATISTIQUE DU MAROC (RABAT, MOROCCO : 1982). *See* Yearbooks, Almanacs, Directories.

ANNUAIRE STATISTIQUE DU TOGO. *See* Yearbooks, Almanacs, Directories.

ANNUAIRE STATISTIQUE (HAITI.) DEPARTEMENT DE L'EDUCATION NATIONALE. SECTION DE STATISTIQUES). *See* Yearbooks, Almanacs, Directories.

ANNUAIRE STATISTIQUE (INSTITUT NATIONAL DE LA STATISTIQUE ET DE L'ANALYSE ECONOMIQUE). *See* Yearbooks, Almanacs, Directories.

ANNUAIRE STATISTIQUE (LUXEMBURG). *See* Yearbooks, Almanacs, Directories.

ANNUAIRE STATISTIQUE - NOUVELLE-CALEDONIE ET DEPENDANCES. SERVICE DE LA STATISTIQUE. *See* Yearbooks, Almanacs, Directories.

ANNUAIRE STATISTIQUES. *See* Yearbooks, Almanacs, Directories.

ANNUAL ABSTRACT OF GREATER LONDON STATISTICS. *See* Indexes/Abstracts.

ANNUAL ABSTRACT OF STATISTICS - GREAT BRITAIN. CENTRAL STATISTICAL OFFICE. *See* Indexes/Abstracts.

ANNUAL ABSTRACT OF STATISTICS - MALTA. OFFICE OF STATISTICS. *See* Indexes/Abstracts.

ANNUAL ABSTRACT OF STATISTICS - NIGERIA. FEDERAL OFFICE OF STATISTICS. *See* Indexes/Abstracts.

Statistics

ANNUAL - ASSOCIATION OF TRACK AND FIELD STATISTICIANS. Main/Corp Association of Track and Field Statisticians. 0361-8048. US. English. an. Tafnews Press, Box 296, Los Altos CA 94022. LC GV1060.67. DD 796.420212.

ANNUAL BULLETIN OF COAL STATISTICS FOR EUROPE. (ANNUAL BULLETIN OF COAL STATISTICS FOR EUROPE). Main/Corp United Nations. Economic Commission for Europe. VFOAT Bulletin Annuel de Statistiques du Charbon pour l'Europe, Ezhegodnyi Biulleten Evropeiskoi Statistiki Uglia. V. 1- 1962/66-. 0066-3808. US. English (French and Russian). an. $11.00. United Nations Publications, Standing Order Service, New York NY 10017. Tel (212)754-8302. LC WMLC L 82/188. Provides basic data on developments and trends in the field of solid fuels, giving statistics for Europe, Canada and the United States.

ANNUAL BULLETIN OF ELECTRIC ENERGY STATISTICS FOR EUROPE. Main/Corp United Nations. Economic Commission for Europe. VFOAT Bulletin Semestriel de Statistiques pour l'Europe, Ezhegodnyi Bulletin Evropeiskoi Statistiki Elektroenergii. V. 1- 1956-. 0066-3816. US. English (French and Russian). an. Tel (212)754-8302. LC HD9685.A1. DD 621.3.

ANNUAL BULLETIN OF GAS STATISTICS FOR EUROPE. VFOAT Bulletin Annuel de Statistiques du Gaz pour l'Europe, Ezhegodnyi Biulleten Evropeiskoi Statistiki Gaza. V. 1- 1957-. 0066-3824. US. English (text in French and Russian). an. $11.00. United Nations Publications, Sales Section/Room A-3315, New York NY 10017. Tel (212)754-8302. LC HD9581.E8. DD 338.27285094. Provides basic data on development and trends, consumption and production of gas in Europe, Canada, and the United States.

ANNUAL BULLETIN OF GENERAL ENERGY STATISTICS FOR EUROPE. Main/Corp United Nations. Economic Commission for Europe. VFOAT Bulletin Annuel de Statistiques Generales de l'Energie pour l'Fur. V. 1- 1968-. US. English (French and Russian). an. $15.00. United Nations Publications, Sales Section/Room A-3315, New York NY 10017. Tel (212)754-8302. LC HD9555.A1. DD 333.8094. Provides basic data on the energy situation as a whole as well as details on the production of energy for the European countries, Canada and the United States.

ANNUAL BULLETIN OF HOUSING AND BUILDING STATISTICS FOR EUROPE. Main/Corp United Nations. Economic Commission for Europe. VFOAT Bulletin Annuel de Statistiques du Logement et de la Construction pour l'Europe, Ezhegodnyi Biulleten Evropeiskoi Zhilishchoi I Stroitelioi Statistiki. 1st- 1957-. 0066-3840. US. English (French and Russian). an. $12.50. United Nations Publications, Sales Section/Room A 3315, New York NY 10017. Tel (212)754-8302. LC HD9715.A1. DD 338.4769. Information on dwelling construction, materials used and employment in the construction industry. Also includes wholesale price indices of building materials in Europe, Canada and the United States.

ANNUAL BULLETIN OF STATISTICS - INTERNATIONAL TEA COMMITTEE. Main/Corp International Tea Committee. May 1946-. 0305-2370. UK. English. an. $107.28. International Tea Committee, 5 High Timber Street, Sir John Lyon House, London EC4V 3NH England. Tel 01-248 4672. LC HD9198.A1. adv acc. Circ 500. Statistics relating to all aspects of tea trade e.g. production, consumption, exports, imports, acreage, supply, absorption. *Monthly Bulletin of Statistics.*

ANNUAL BULLETIN OF STATISTICS ON COCOA, COFFEE & TEA. VFOAT Nigerian Cocoa Board Statistical Bulletin. 1979-. English. an. Nigerian Cocoa Board Statistics Section, P M B 5032, Ibadan Nigeria. LC HD9017.N53. DD 338.1737409669.

ANNUAL BULLETIN OF STATISTICS, SABAH. Main/Corp Malaysia. Dept. of Statistics. 1964-. MY. English. an. 72.00. Department of Statistics, Publ Section/Jalan Cenderasari, Kuala Lumpur 10-01 Malaysia. Tel 2922133. LC HA1797.S2. DD 315.953. Circ 100. (ctrl).

ANNUAL CROP AND LIVESTOCK SUMMARY. Series/Titl Indiana Crop and Livestock Statistics. 1951. 0148-1932. US. English. an. $4.00. Indiana Crop & Livestock Report, Agricultural Administration Building, West Lafayette IN 47907. Tel (317)494-8371. LC S59. DD 338.109772. Statistical summary of agricultural production during the past year with comparisons. *Annual Crop Summary, Annual Livestock Summary.*

ANNUAL ECONOMIC REPORT. PORTLAND SMSA. VFOAT Portland SMSA. US. English. an. Employment Division/Labor Economist, 1407 SW 4th Avenue, Portland OR 97201. LC HC108.P87. DD 330.97954005.

ANNUAL ELECTRIC POWER SURVEY. See Engineering - Electricity, Electrical Engineering, Electronics.

ANNUAL ELECTRIC POWER SURVEY OF CAPABILITY AND LOAD (CANADA). See Engineering - Electricity, Electrical Engineering, Electronics.

ANNUAL FINANCIAL AND STATISTICAL REPORT - OHIO. DEPT. OF MENTAL RETARDATION AND DEVELOPMENTAL DISABILITIES. (ANNUAL FINANCIAL AND STATISTICAL REPORT). Main/Corp Ohio. Dept. of Mental Retardation and Developmental Disabilities. Fiscal Year 1981-. 0733-4761. US. English. an. Department of Mental Retardation and Developmental Disabilities/Office of Planning, 30 East Broad Street, Columbus OH 43215. LC HV3006.O3. DD 353.97710084306.

ANNUAL GRAZING STATISTICAL REPORT. (ANNUAL GRAZING STATISTICAL REPORT. USE SUMMARY). 0091-438X. US. English. an. US Department of Agriculture, Forest Service, Range Management Staff, Washington DC 20013. LC SD427.G8.

ANNUAL JUDICIAL CONFERENCE STATISTICAL REPORT - MISSOURI. Main/Corp Missouri. Judicial Conference. 0099-0558. US. English. an. Office of State Courts Administrator, Supreme Court Building, Jefferson City MO 65102. LC KFM7871. DD 347.778013.

ANNUAL JUVENILE STATISTICAL REPORT - SUPERIOR COURT OF THE DISTRICT OF COLUMBIA. WASHINGTON, D.C. (ANNUAL JUVENILE STATISTICAL REPORT). Main/Corp District of Columbia. Superior Court. 1970/71-. 0091-1151. US. English. an. LC HV9106.D55. DD 364.3609753. *Statistical Report.*

ANNUAL MANAGEMENT/ ADMINISTRATIVE STATISTICS REPORT ON THE CRIMINAL JUSTICE SYSTEM. Main/Corp Nebraska. Commission on Law Enforcement and Criminal Justice. Statistical Analysis Center. 1977-. US. English. an. PO Box 94946/301 Centinnial Mall South, Lincoln NE 68509. LC HV7277. DD 353.97820084.

ANNUAL MEDICARE PROGRAM STATISTICS. VFOAT Medicare Program Statistics. 1981-. 0741-0190. Periodical. US. English. an. LC HD7102.U4. DD 368.42600973. *Medicare, Health Insurance for the Aged and Disabled. Section 1.2. Summary Utilization-and Reimbursement by Person, 0198-0394.*

ANNUAL OIL AND GAS STATISTICS. VFOAT Statistiques Annuelles des Hydrocarbures et du Gaz Naturel. 1978/1979-. US. English (French). an. $40.00. OECD Publications, 1750 Pennsylvania Avenue Northwest, Washington DC 20006. Tel (202)724-1857. LC HD9575.A12. DD 338.27280212. Presents data on oil and gas balances; sources of imports; production supply, and disposal of crude, finished products, and natural gas; and exports of OECD/IEA countries. *Oil Statistics.*

ANNUAL PLANNING INFORMATION. CHICO STANDARD METROPOLITAN STATISTICAL AREA (BUTTE COUNTY). 1983-84-. US. English. an. Northern Area Labor Market Information Group, 800 Capitol Mall MIC 57, Sacramento CA 95814. LC HD5725.C2. DD 331.10979432021. *Annual Planning Information. Butte County.*

ANNUAL PLANNING INFORMATION, FISCAL YEAR . . . . See Economics - Labor.

ANNUAL PLANNING INFORMATION FISCAL YEAR . . . FOR MONTANA, BILLINGS SMSA, GREAT FALLS SMSA. VFOAT Montana Annual Planning Information. US. English. an. Research and Analysis Bureau Department of Labor & Industry, Box 1728, Helena MT 59624. LC HD5725.M9. DD 331.1109786.

ANNUAL PLANNING INFORMATION FOR COLUMBIA SMSA. Main/Corp Missouri. Division of Employment Security. US. English. an. Division of Employment Security, 2101 Whitegate Drive, PO Box 898, Columbia MO 65205. LC HD5726.C68. DD 331.120977829.

ANNUAL PLANNING INFORMATION FOR MANPOWER PLANNERS. NEW YORK CITY SMSA. Series/Titl BLMI Report. VFOAT New York City SMSA. Fiscal Year 1982-. US. English. an. Bureau of Labor Market Information, Two World Trade Center, New York NY 10047. LC HD5726.N5. DD 331.109471.

ANNUAL PLANNING INFORMATION FOR MANPOWER PLANNERS. SYRACUSE SMSA IN NEW YORK STATE. Series/Titl BLMI Report. VFOAT Syracuse SMSA in New York State. US. English. an. R Evans, 601 James Street, Syracuse NY 13203. LC HD5726.S97. DD 331.10974766.

ANNUAL PLANNING INFORMATION. HUNTINGTON-ASHLAND-IRONTON STANDARD METROPOLITAN STATISTICAL AREA. See Economics - Labor.

ANNUAL PLANNING INFORMATION. LABOR AREA, WATERLOO-CEDAR FALLS SMSA, CETA PRIME SPONSOR JURISDICTION, BLACK HAWK COUNTY. VFOAT Annual Planning Information, Waterloo. US. English. an. Job Service of Iowa, 527 East 5th Street, Waterloo IA 50704. LC HD5725.I8. DD 331.10977737.

ANNUAL PLANNING INFORMATION, MACON, GEORGIA SMSA MIDDLE GEORGIA APDC. US. English. an. Georgia Department of Labor, Employment Security Agency Labor Information Systems, 254 Washington Street SW, Atlanta GA 30334. LC HD5726.M29. DD 331.10975851.

ANNUAL PLANNING INFORMATION. OXNARD-SIMI VALLEY-VENTURA SMSA. VFOAT Annual Planning Information. 0731-4256. US. English. an. State of California/ Employment Development Department, Southern California Employment Data and Research, 1525 South Broadway, Los Angeles CA 90015.

ANNUAL PLANNING INFORMATION REPORT : BEAUMONT-PORT ARTHUR-ORANGE SMSA. Main/Corp Texas. Employment Commission. VFOAT Beaumont-Port Arthur-Orange SMSA. US. English. an. Texas Employment Commission, PO Box 2831, Beaumont TX 77704. LC HD5726.B42. DD 331.1209764145.

ANNUAL PLANNING INFORMATION REPORT. BRYAN-COLLEGE STATION SMSA. VFOAT Bryan-College Station SMSA. US. English. an. LC HD5726.B79. DD 331.1209764242. *Annual Planning Report. Bryan-College Station SMSA.*

ANNUAL PLANNING INFORMATION REPORT : DALLAS-FORT WORTH SMSA. Main/Corp Texas. Employment Commission. US. English. an. LC HD5726.D25. DD 331.12097642812.

ANNUAL PLANNING INFORMATION REPORT. DAYTONA BEACH SMSA. VFOAT Daytona Beach S.M.S.A. Annual Planning Information. US. English. an. Labor Market Analyst, Florida State Employment Service, PO Box 870, Daytona Beach FL 32015. LC HD5726.D32. DD 331.120975921.

ANNUAL PLANNING INFORMATION REPORT FOR FISCAL YEAR . . . SAVANNAH SMSA SAVANNAH/ CHATHAM CONSORTIUM. VFOAT Annual Planning Information for Fiscal Year . . . Savannah. US. English. an. Georgia Department of Labor, Employment Security Agency, PO Box 9089, Savannah GA 31412. LC HD5726.S48. DD 331.109758724.

ANNUAL PLANNING INFORMATION REPORT FOR LANCASTER COUNTY SMSA, LANCASTER COUNTY SDA. US. English. an. Labor Market Information Unit, Office of Employment Security, PO Box 1418, Lancaster PA 17603. LC HD5726.L322. DD 331.120974815.

ANNUAL PLANNING INFORMATION REPORT FOR SOUTHERN ALLEGHENIES SERVICE DELIVERY AREA : INCLUDES ALTOONA SMSA AND JOHNSTOWN SMSA. Main/Corp Pennsylvania. Office of Employment Security. US. English. an. Labor Market Information Unit, Office of

Statistics

Employment Security, 1101 Green Avenue, Altoona PA 16603. **LC** HD5726.J64. **DD** 331.12097487.

ANNUAL PLANNING INFORMATION REPORT : LONGVIEW SMSA. Main/Corp Texas. Employment Commission. US. English. an. **LC** HD5726.L66. **DD** 331.1209764189.

ANNUAL PLANNING INFORMATION REPORT. ORLANDO SMSA AND ORANGE COUNTY, ORLANDO CITY, SEMINOLE COUNTY CETA PRIME SPONSOR AREAS. Main/Corp Florida. Division of Employment Security. **VFOAT** Orlando S.M.S.A. Annual Planning Information. 1981-. US. English. an. Florida State Employment Service, State Office Building, 941 Morse Boulevard, Winter Park FL 32789. **LC** HD5726.O7. **DD** 331.120975924. *Annual Planning Information Report . . . Orlando SMSA, and Orange, and Seminole Counties CETA Prime Sponsor Areas.*

ANNUAL PLANNING INFORMATION REPORT . . . PENSACOLA SMSA AND OKALOOSA COUNTY. Main/Corp Florida State Employment Service. **VFOAT** Pensacola S.M.S.A. Annual Planning Information. US. English. an. Florida State Employment Service, PO Box 1393, 236 West Garden Street, Pensacola FL 32596. **LC** HD5726.P44. **DD** 331.1209759982.

ANNUAL PLANNING INFORMATION, SIOUX CITY SMSA. Began with 1978/79 issue. US. English. an. Free. Job Service of Iowa, 2508 4th Street, Sioux City IA 51101. **LC** HD5726.S56. **DD** 331.10977741. *Annual Planning Report, Sioux City SMSA and Woodbury County.*

ANNUAL PLANNING REPORT, DECATUR SMSA. US. English. an. Illinois Bureau of Employment Security, Research and Analysis, 910 South Michigan Avenue, Chicago IL 60605. **LC** HD5726.D38. **DD** 331.109773582.

ANNUAL PLANNING REPORT. DETROIT SMSA. Main/Corp Michigan. Employment Security Commission. Detroit Labor Market Analysis Unit. US. English. an. Detroit Labor Market Analysis Unit, 7310 Woodward Avenue, Detroit MI 48202. **LC** HD5726.D4. **DD** 331.10977434.

ANNUAL PLANNING REPORT, FISCAL YEAR . . . CHAMPAIGN SMSA. Main/Corp Illinois. Bureau of Employment Security. Research and Analysis Division. US. English. an. Bureau of Employment Security, Research and Analysis, 402 North Randolph, Champaign IL 61820. **LC** HD5726.C36. **DD** 331.1097736.

ANNUAL PLANNING REPORT. OLYMPIA SMSA. **VFOAT** Olympia SMSA. 1982-. US. English. ir. Washington State Employment Security Department, Research and Statistics Branch, Olympia WA 98504. **LC** HD5725.W2. **DD** 331.10979779. *Annual Planning Report, Thurston County.*

ANNUAL PLANNING REPORT : TOPEKA, KANSAS SMSA AND SURROUNDING COUNTIES AREA NO. 8440. **VFOAT** Annual Planning Report: Topeka SMSA. US. English. an. Department of Human Services, Topeka Avenue, Topeka KS 66603. **LC** HD5715.4.T66. **DD** 331.10978163.

ANNUAL PRICE STATISTICS & MARKET TRENDS - IMO STATE, NIGERIA. TRADE DIVISION. Main/Corp Imo State, Nigeria. Trade Division. **VAT** Annual Price Statistics and Market Trends. 1976/77-. English. ir. Ministry of Trade & Co-Operatives, 47 Douglas Road, Owerrie Nigeria. **LC** HB235.N53. **DD** 338.52096694.

ANNUAL REPORT AND CARGO STATISTICS - MACKAY HARBOUR ROAD. Main/Corp MacKay Harbour Board. English. an. MacKay Harbour Board, P O Box 96, MacKay Qld 4740 Australia. **LC** HE560.M24. **DD** 387.1099436.

ANNUAL REPORT AND STATISTICAL DATA - DIVISION OF INSURANCE (MISSOURI). Main/Corp Missouri. Division of Insurance. US. English. an. 11th Floor/Jefferson Building, Jefferson City Mo 65101. **LC** HG8511.M8. **DD** 368.9778.

ANNUAL REPORT FOR THE YEAR ENDED - ZAMBIA. DEPT. OF CENSUS AND STATISTICS. Main/Corp Zambia. Dept. of Census and Statistics. **VFOAT** Report on the Work of the Department of Census and Statistics for the Year Ended . . . . Dec. 1968-. English. an. **LC** HA37. **DD** 354.689400819. *Report for the Eighteen Months Ended 31st December . . . .*

ANNUAL REPORT - JORDAN STATISTICAL TRAINING CENTRE. Main/Corp Jordan Statistical Training Centre. English. ir. **LC** HA35. **DD** 519.50715.

ANNUAL REPORT - NATIONAL CENSUS AND STATISTICS OFFICE (PHILIPPINES). Main/Corp Philippines. National Census and Statistics Office. 1974/75-. PH. English. ir. National Census and Statistics Office, PO Box 779, Manila Philippines. **LC** HA37. **DD** 354.5990081.

ANNUAL REPORT OF MUNICIPAL STATISTICS. Main/Corp Nova Scotia. Dept. of Municipal Affairs. 1st- 1936-. CN. English. an. Department of Municipal Affairs, PO Box 216 Provincial Building, Halifax NS B3J 2M4 Canada. **Tel** (902)424-5634. **Ed** Thomas F LeBlanc. **LC** TS4.N6. **DD** 352.0716. **Circ** 800. (ctrl). Summaries of audited financial statements for Nova Scotia's local governments as well as census information, list of officials with mailing addresses, area and road mileage figures.

THE . . . ANNUAL REPORT OF THE CHAIRMAN OF THE DEVELOPMENT COORDINATION COMMITTEE. STATISTICAL ANNEX 3. US. English. an. Development Coordination Committee, Room 3491A/320 21st Street NW, Washington DC 20523.

ANNUAL REPORT OF THE DIRECTOR OF ECONOMICS AND STATISTICS (SASKATCHEWAN). Main/Corp Saskatchewan. Dept. of Agriculture. Economics and Statistics Branch. 1st- 1964/65-. CN. English. an. Queens Printer, 2045 Broad Street/3rd Floor, Regina Saskatchewan S4P 3V7 Canada. **LC** S161. **DD** 354.712400823305. *Annual Report of the Supervisor of Statistics.*

ANNUAL REPORT OF VITAL STATISTICS, COLORADO. Main/Corp Colorado. Health Statistics Section. **VFOAT** Colorado Vital Statistics. US. English. an. Colorado Department of Health, Health Statistics and Vital Records Division/Public Health Statistics Section, 4210 East 11th Avenue, Denver CO 80220. **LC** HA271. **DD** 312.09788.

ANNUAL REPORT OF VITAL STATISTICS OF MASSACHUSETTS. Main/Corp Massachusetts. Dept. of Public Health. Office of Health Planning & Statistics. **VFOAT** Annual Report of Vital Statistics. Began in 1964. 0542-8998. Periodical. US. English. an. **LC** J87 H2433. **DD** 312.09744.

ANNUAL REPORT OF VITAL STATISTICS OF VERMONT. Main/Corp Vermont. Division of Public Health Statistics. 0147-5843. US. English. an. Vermont Department of Health Statistics Division, 115 Collchester, Burlington VT 05401. **Tel** (802)862-5701. **LC** HA671. **DD** 312. **NLM** W2 AV5 D5A. *Annual Bulletin of Vital Statistics.*

ANNUAL REPORT ON TOBACCO STATISTICS (UNITED STATES). AGRICULTURAL MARKETING SERVICE). (ANNUAL REPORT ON TOBACCO STATISTICS). 1980-. 0747-5314. US. English. an. USDA, Agricultural Marketing Service, Washington DC 20250. **LC** HD9134. **DD** 338.173710973. *Annual Report on Tobacco Statistics, 0747-5314.*

ANNUAL REPORT - STATE OF NEBRASKA. DEPARTMENT OF HEALTH. (STATE OF ILLINOIS STATISTICAL REPORT). Main/Corp Illinois. Office of Planning and Analysis. 1972-. 0090-3787. US. English. State of Illinois, Office of Planning & Analysis, Springfield IL 62706. **LC** HA341. **DD** 317.73.

ANNUAL REPORT STATISTICAL AND FINANCIAL DATA OF THE STATE BOARD OF EDUCATION (NEBRASKA). Main/Corp Nebraska. State Dept. of Education. US. English. an. Nebraska Department of Education, 233 South 10th Street, Lincoln NE 68508. **LC** L172. **DD** 370.9782.

ANNUAL REPORT. STATISTICAL SUPPLEMENT OF THE DEPARTMENT OF INDUSTRIAL RELATIONS. DIVISION OF SAFETY AND INSPECTION. (ANNUAL REPORT : STATISTICAL SUPPLEMENT OF THE DEPARTMENT OF INDUSTRIAL RELATIONS, DIVISION OF SAFETY AND INSPECTION (ALABAMA). Main/Corp Alabama. Department of Industrial Relations. Division of Safety and Inspection. **VFOAT** Annual Statistical Report - Alabama Department of Industrial Relations, Division of Safety and Inspection. 1959/60-. Periodical. US. English. an. Alabama Department of Industrial Relations, Division of Safety and Inspection, Montgomery AL 36130. *Annual Statistical Report - Division of Safety and Inspection.*

ANNUAL REPORT - STATISTICS CANADA. Main/Corp Statistics Canada. **VFOAT** Rapport Annuel de Statistique Canada. 1971/72-. CN. English and French. an. Information Canada, Receiver General for Canada, Statistics Publication Canada, Ottawa Ontario K1A 0T6 Canada. **LC** HA742. **DD** 354.710081. *Annual Report.*

ANNUAL REPORT WITH STATISTICS AND RELATED DATA - JUDICIAL COUNCIL OF THE SUPREME COURT OF LOUISIANA. (ANNUAL REPORT WITH STATISTICS AND RELATED DATA). Main/Corp Louisiana. Judicial Council. 0090-6301. US. English. an. Louisiana Judicial Council, New Orleans LA 70112. **LC** KFL508.A73. **DD** 347.763013.

ANNUAL REPORT - WYOMING DEPARTMENT OF LABOR AND STATISTICS. Main/Corp Wyoming. Dept. of Labor and Statistics. US. English. an. Free. Department of Labor & Statistics, Herschler Building, Cheyenne WY 82002. **Tel** (307)777-7340. **Ed** Albert J Wolff. **LC** HD8053.W8. **DD** 353.97870081. **Circ** 700. (ctrl). Summary of Wyoming DOL activities by division. *Biennial Report.*

ANNUAL REVIEW AND ENERGY STATISTICS. English. an. Secretariat of Queensland Department of Mines, Mineral House 41-59 George Street, Brisbane 4000 Australia. **LC** TJ163.25.A8. **DD** 333.7909943021.

ANNUAL STATE AID ENTITLEMENT STATISTICS . . . , ILLINOIS PUBLIC SCHOOLS. 1982-1983-. US. English. an. Illinois State Board of Education, Department of Finance & Reimbursement, 100 North 1st Street, Springfield IL 62777. **LC** LB2826.I3. **DD** 379.11309773. *Annual State Aid Claim Statistics. Illinois Public Schools.*

ANNUAL STATISTICAL BULLETIN - LESOTHO. Main/Corp Lesotho. Bureau of Statistics. 1963/64-. 0459-1135. English. ir. Lesotho Bureau of Statistics, Maseru Lesotho Africa. **LC** HA1977.B35.

ANNUAL STATISTICAL BULLETIN (NATIONAL COUNCIL ON COMPENSATION INSURANCE). (ANNUAL STATISTICAL BULLETIN). **VFOAT** Statistical Bulletin. 1st Ed. (1981)-. US. English. an. **LC** HD7103.65.U6. **DD** 368.4100973.

ANNUAL STATISTICAL BULLETIN - SWAZILAND. CENTRAL STATISTICAL OFFICE. (ANNUAL STATISTICAL BULLETIN). Main/Corp Swaziland. Central Statistical Office. 0300-2098. English. an. Central Statistical Office, PO Box 456, Mbabane Swaziland. **LC** HA1977.S9. **DD** 316.83.

ANNUAL STATISTICAL BULLETIN - WASHINGTON STATE LIBRARY. Main/Corp Washington (State). State Library, Olympia. US. English. an. Washington State Library, Olympia WA 98504. **LC** Z732.W28. **DD** 027.0025797. *Library News Bulletin. Annual Statistical Issue, 0097-9945.*

ANNUAL STATISTICAL DIGEST - BOARD OF GOVERNORS OF THE FEDERAL RESERVE SYSTEM. (ANNUAL STATISTICAL DIGEST). Main/Corp Board of Governors of the Federal Reserve System (U.S.). 1971/75-. 0148-4338. US. English. an. Federal Reserve System, Board of Governors, Washington DC 20551. **LC** HG181.A1. **DD** 332.0973.

ANNUAL STATISTICAL DIGEST - CENTRAL STATISTICAL OFFICE (PORT-OF-SPAIN). (ANNUAL STATISTICAL DIGEST). Began with No. 1 for 1935/51. 0564-2604. TR. English. an. Government of Trinidad & Tobago, Central Statistical Office, 2 Edward Street, Trinidad West Indies. **LC** HA867. **DD** 317.2983. **NLM** W2 DT7 C3A.

ANNUAL STATISTICAL REPORT - AMERICAN ASSOCIATION OF COLLEGES OF OSTEOPATHIC MEDICINE. (ANNUAL STATISTICAL REPORT). 1981-. 0738-6230. US. English. an. American Association of of Colleges/Osteopathic Medicine, 4720 Montgomery Lane Suite 609, Bethesda MD 20814. **NLM** W 18 A615A.

Statistics

ANNUAL STATISTICAL REPORT : AMERICAN IRON AND STEEL INSTITUTE. Main/Corp American Iron and Steel Institute, New York. Periodical. US. English. an. American Iron & Steel Institute, 1000 16th Street NW, Washington DC 20036.

ANNUAL STATISTICAL REPORT - BOARD OF PARDONS AND PAROLES. Main/Corp Texas. Board of Pardons and Paroles. 19th- 1965/66-. US. English. an. Board of Pardons & Paroles, Stephen F Austin Building/Room 722, Austin TX 78711. LC HV7293. DD 353.976400849.

ANNUAL STATISTICAL REPORT - CEYLON TOURIST BOARD. Main/Corp Ceylon Tourist Board. English. ir. Ceylon Tourist Board. LC G155.C44.

ANNUAL STATISTICAL REPORT (COLORADO. DEPT. OF CORRECTIONS). (ANNUAL STATISTICAL REPORT). US. English. an. 6385 North Academy Boulevard, Colorado Springs CO 80907. LC HV6793.C6. DD 364.309788.

ANNUAL STATISTICAL REPORT - DEPARTMENT OF CORRECTIONS. Main/Corp Louisiana. State Dept. of Corrections. 0098-3144. US. English. an. Department of Corrections, Box 44304 Capitol Station, Baton Rouge LA 70804. LC HV7268. DD 353.976300849.

ANNUAL STATISTICAL REPORT - DEPARTMENT OF PUBLIC INSTITUTIONS, DIVISION ON ALCOHOLISM. Main/Corp Nebraska. Division of Alcoholism. Periodical. US. English. an. Department of Public Instition, PO Box 94728, Lincoln NE 68509. LC HV5280.N2. DD 362.292809782.

ANNUAL STATISTICAL REPORT - DIVISION OF FAMILY SERVICES. (ANNUAL STATISTICAL REPORT). **Main/Corp** Florida. Division of Family Services. 0093-6715. US. English. an. PO Box 2050, Jacksonville FL 32203. LC HV86. DD 362.9759.

ANNUAL STATISTICAL REPORT - DIVISION OF INFORMATION ANALYSIS, TEXAS EDUCATION AGENCY CEASED. **Main/Corp** Texas. Education Agency. Division of Information Analysis. US. English. an. Texas Education Agency Division of Information Analysis, 201 East 11th Street, Austin TX 78701. Tel (512)463-9734. LC L204. DD 370.0764.

ANNUAL STATISTICAL REPORT - EMILY P. BISSELL HOSPITAL (DELAWARE). Main/Corp Emily P. Bissell Hospital. VFOAT Annual Report. US. English. an. Emily P Bissell Hospital, 3000 Newport Gap Pike, Wilmington DE 19808. LC RA982.W582. DD 362.11.097512.

ANNUAL STATISTICAL REPORT FOR INDIANA MENTAL HEALTH CLINICS. Main/Corp Indiana. Dept. of Mental Health. Statistics Office. 0145-6954. US. English. an. Department of Mental Health, 5 Indiana Square, Indianapolis IN 46204. LC RA790.65.I5. DD 362.2209772.

ANNUAL STATISTICAL REPORT, IOWA JUDICIARY. Main/Corp Iowa. Court Administrator of the Judicial Dept. US. English. an. Court Administrator of the Judicial Department, Statehouse, Des Moines IA 50319. LC KFI4271. DD 347.7770130212.

ANNUAL STATISTICAL REPORT, KANSAS. STATE DEPT. OF EDUCATION. Main/Corp Kansas. State Dept. of Education. US. English. an. Kansas State Department of Education, Kansas State Education Building, 120 East 10th Street, Topeka KS 66612. LC L150. DD 370.9781.

ANNUAL STATISTICAL REPORT - KANSAS STATE DEPARTMENT OF EDUCATION. ADMINISTRATION AND FINANCE DIVISION. (ANNUAL STATISTICAL REPORT). **Main/Corp** Kansas. State Dept. of Education. Administration and Finance Division. 0091-9802. US. English. an. State Department of Education, 120 East 10th Street, Topeka KS 66612. LC L150. DD 379.153509781.

ANNUAL STATISTICAL REPORT - MARYLAND. JUVENILE SERVICES ADMINISTRATION. Main/Corp Maryland. Juvenile Services Administration. VFOAT Annual Report - Dept. of Juvenile Services. 1974/75-. US. English. an. Juvenile Services Administration, 201 West Preston Street, Baltimore MD 21201. LC HV742.M3. DD 364.3609752. *Annual Statistical Report.*

ANNUAL STATISTICAL REPORT. MENTAL HEALTH SERVICES. MENTAL RETARDATION SERVICES. VETERANS' HOMES SERVICE (NEBRASKA). Main/Corp Nebraska. Dept. of Public Institutions. Research and Statistics Section. 0146-2148. US. English. an. Department of Public Institutions, Research & Statistics Section, Lincoln NE 68509. LC RA790.65.N2. DD 362.209782.

ANNUAL STATISTICAL REPORT - MISSOURI, STATE FIRE MARSHAL, DEPARTMENT OF PUBLIC SAFETY. (ANNUAL STATISTICAL REPORT - MISSOURI, STATE FIRE MARSHAL). **Main/Corp** Missouri. State Fire Marshal. 0360-2826. US. English. an. Missouri State Fire Marshall, 505 Missouri Boulevard, Jefferson City MO 65101. LC TH9504.M8. DD 353.97780078205.

THE ANNUAL STATISTICAL REPORT OF EXPENDITURES MADE IN CONNECTION WITH ELECTIONS (MISSOURI). Main/Corp Missouri. Office of the Secretary of State. 0149-1962. US. English. an. Secretary of State, PO Box 1370, Jefferson City MO 65101. LC JK1991.5.M8. DD 329.02509778.

ANNUAL STATISTICAL REPORT OF FELONS AND MISDEMEANANTS COMMITTED TO THE VIRGINIA STATE CORRECTIONAL SYSTEM AND FELONS CONFINED IN THE CORRECTIONAL SYSTEM INCLUDING FELON RECIDIVISTS COMMITTED AND CONFINED. Main/Corp Virginia. Dept. of Corrections. Bureau of Research, Reporting and Evaluation. VFOAT Felons, Misdemeanants, Recidivists. 1975/76-. US. English. an. Department of Corrections, Bureau of Research, Reporting and Evaluation, 22 East Cary Street, Richmond VA 23219. LC HV7296. DD 364.309755.

ANNUAL STATISTICAL REPORT OF PENNSYLVANIA COUNTY PRISONS AND JAILS. US. English. an. Pennsylvania Bureau of Corrections, PO Box 598, Camp Hill PA 17011. LC HV8358. DD 365.9748.

ANNUAL STATISTICAL REPORT OF THE DEPARTMENT OF EDUCATION (TENNESSEE). Main/Corp Tennessee. Dept. of Education. 1940/41-. US. English. an. Tennessee Department of Education, Nashville TN 37202. LC L202. DD 379.768. *Annual Report of the Dept. of Education.*

ANNUAL STATISTICAL REPORT OF THE MEMBER INSTITUTIONS - UNITED NEGRO COLLEGE FUND CEASED. **Main/Corp** United Negro College Fund. VFOAT Statistical Report of the Member Institutions. VAT United Negro College Fund Statistical Report of the Member Institutions. Began with issue for 1973/74. Ceased 1980. 0364-4723. US. English. an.

ANNUAL STATISTICAL REPORT OF THE PROCEEDINGS OF THE LOCAL AUTHORITIES PENSION BOARD PURSUANT TO THE LOCAL AUTHORITIES PENSION ACT (ALBERTA) CEASED. **Main/Corp** Alberta. Local Authorities Pension Board. 11th-19th. 0381-4807. Periodical. CN. English. an. 500 10050-112 Street, Alberta T5K 2J1 Canada. LC JS4.A5. DD 352.0055097123. *Annual Statistical Report of the Proceedings of the Public Service Pension Board Pursuant to the Local Authorities Pension Act, 0381-4793.*

ANNUAL STATISTICAL REPORT OF THE PROCEEDINGS OF THE PUBLIC SERVICE MANAGEMENT PENSION BOARD PURSUANT TO THE PUBLIC SERVICE MANAGEMENT PENSION ACT (ALBERTA). Main/Corp Alberta. Public Service Management Pension Board. VAT Annual Report - Public Service Management Pension Board. Annual Report. The Public Service Management Pension Act. 1973-. 0383-3674. CN. English. an. Alberta Pension Administration, 300 Petroleum Plaza, 9945 108th Street, Edmonton Canada. LC JL332.Z2. DD 354.7123005.

ANNUAL STATISTICAL REPORT OF THE PROCEEDINGS OF THE PUBLIC SERVICE PENSION BOARD PURSUANT TO THE PUBLIC SERVICE PENSION ACT (ALBERTA). Main/Corp Alberta. Public Service Pension Board. VFOAT Annual Report. VAT Annual Report - Public Service Pension Board (Edmonton), Annual Report - The Public Service Pension Act, Annual Report of the Public Service Pension Board Pursuant to the Public Service Pension Act. 0383-3666. Periodical. CN. English. an. LC JL332.Z2. DD 354.7123005.

ANNUAL STATISTICAL REPORT OF THE PUBLIC SCHOOLS OF ARKANSAS. Main/Corp Arkansas. Dept. of Education. 0149-3140. US. English. an. LC LB2826.A8. DD 379.12209767.

ANNUAL STATISTICAL REPORT OF THE RETAIL SALES TAX DIVISION INCLUDING ADMISSIONS TAX UNIT FOR THE FISCAL YEAR ENDED . . . - MARYLAND. Main/Corp Maryland. Comptroller's Office. Retail Sales Tax Division. US. English. an. State of Maryland Comptroller of the Treasury, Retail Sales Tax Division, 301 West Preston Street, Baltimore MD 21201.

ANNUAL STATISTICAL REPORT ON TOURISM IN THAILAND. English. an. LC G155.T4. DD 380.145915930444.

ANNUAL STATISTICAL REPORT ON VISITOR ARRIVALS (SINGAPORE). Main/Corp Singapore. Tourist Promotion Board. 0583-4007. English. ir. LC G155.S5. DD 338.47915952.

ANNUAL STATISTICAL REPORT - PENNSYLVANIA DEPT. OF JUSTICE. VFOAT Pennsylvania Bureau of Correction's . . . Annual Statistical Report. US. English. an. LC HV7288. DD 364.309748.

ANNUAL STATISTICAL REPORT - SOUTH DAKOTA DEPARTMENT OF SOCIAL SERVICES. (ANNUAL STATISTICAL REPORT). **Main/Corp** South Dakota. Dept. of Social Services. 0147-6467. US. English. an. Department of Social Services, State Office Building, Illinois Street, Pierre SD 57501. LC HV86. DD 353.97830084. NLM W2 AS8 D4A.

ANNUAL STATISTICAL REPORT - STATE OF MICHIGAN, INSURANCE BUREAU. Main/Corp Michigan. Insurance Bureau. US. English. an. 611 West Ottawa, PO Box 30220, Lansing MI 48909. Tel (517)373-0220. LC HG8538.M5. DD 338.473689774. Lists all the insurance companies that are licensed to do business in Michigan with their addresses. Includes some financial information and miscellaneous topics.

ANNUAL STATISTICAL REPORT - STATE OF NEW MEXICO, HEALTH AND SOCIAL SERVICES DEPARTMENT, STATE WELFARE AGENCY. (ANNUAL STATISTICAL REPORT - STATE OF NEW MEXICO, HEALTH AND SOCIAL SERVICES DEPARTMENT). **Main/Corp** New Mexico. Health and Social Services Dept. 0149-3892. US. English. an. PO Box 2348, Santa Fe NM 87503. LC HV86. DD 361.6209789. NLM W2 AN5 S8S. *Statistical Report - New Mexico State Welfare Agency, 0197-6141.*

ANNUAL STATISTICAL REVIEW (CHARLOTTETOWN, P.E.I.). (ANNUAL STATISTICAL REVIEW). CN. English. an. LC HA747.P73. DD 331.28136130973.

ANNUAL STATISTICAL REVIEW - HONGKONG. TRADE INDUSTRY AND CUSTOMS DEPT. Main/Corp Hong Kong. Trade Industry and Customs Dept. 1977-. English. an. *Annual Statistical Review.*

ANNUAL STATISTICAL REVIEW OF COTTON AND ALLIED TEXTILE INDUSTRY IN JAPAN. No. 1- June 1965-. 0570-2607. English. ir.

ANNUAL STATISTICAL SUMMARY - AMERICAN PAPER INSTITUTE. Main/Corp American Paper Institute. Printing-Writing Paper Division. US. English. an. American Paper Institute, 260 Madison Avenue, New York NY 10016. Tel (212)340-0630. Ed Benjamin Slatin. LC HD9822. DD 338.4767620973. Circ 1,200. Paper industry statistics-long term.

ANNUAL STATISTICAL SUMMARY OF THE STATE OF MARYLAND FAMILY PLANNING PROGRAM. Main/Corp Maryland. Dept. of Health and Mental Hygiene. 0098-390X. US. English. an. Department of Health and Mental Hygiene, 301 West Preston Street, Baltimore MD 21201. LC HQ766.5.U5. DD 362.82.

ANNUAL STATISTICAL SUMMARY : UNFILLED JOB OPENINGS (MASSACHUSETTS). Main/Corp Massachusetts. Occupation/Industry Research Dept. 0146-0293. US. English. an. Occupation/Industry

Statistics

Research Department, Employment Security Building, Government Center, Boston MA 02114. **LC** HD5725.M4. **DD** 331.126.

ANNUAL STATISTICAL SURVEY OF THE ELECTRONICS INDUSTRY. **Main/Corp** Economic Development Committee for the Electronics Industry. UK. English. an. Her Majesty's Stationery Office, PO Box 276, London SW8 5DT England. **LC** HD9696.A3. **DD** 338.4762130942.

ANNUAL STATISTICS AND REPORT - IOWA. DEPT. OF JUSTICE. **Main/Corp** Iowa. Dept. of Justice. Consumer Protection Division. US. English. an. Consumer Protection Division, Hoover Building 2nd Floor/1300 East Walnut, Des Moines IA 50319. **LC** KFI4430. **DD** 353.97770082042.

ANNUAL STATISTICS - DEPARTMENT OF MENTAL HEALTH, STATISTICS BRANCH (INDIANA). **Main/Corp** Indiana. Dept. of Mental Health. Statistics Branch. 0191-2070. US. English. an. **LC** RC445.I62. **DD** 362.2109772.

ANNUAL STATISTICS - MANITOBA HEALTH SERVICES COMMISSION. (ANNUAL STATISTICS). Began in 1976. 0708-7233. CN. English. an. Manitoba Health Services Commission, Box 925 599 Empress Street, Winnipeg Manitoba R3C 2T6 Canada.

ANNUAL STATISTICS OF MEDICAL SCHOOL LIBRARIES IN THE UNITED STATES AND CANADA. 1977-1978-. 0196-6448. US. English. an. $15.00. Houston Academy of Medicine and Texas Medical Center Library, 1133 M D Anderson Boulevard, Houston TX 77030. **LC** Z675.M4. **DD** 026.610973. **NLM** Z 675.M4 M49034. *Medical Library Statistics.*

ANNUAL SUMMARY OF BRITISH COLUMBIA CATCH STATISTICS *CEASED.* **Main/Corp** Canada. Fisheries and Marine Service. Pacific Region. 1972-1975?. CN. English. an. Department of the Environment, Fisheries and Marine Service, 1090 West Pender Street, Vancouver 1 British Columbia Canada V6E 2P1. **LC** HD9464.C22. **DD** 388.3727092071. *Annual Summary of British Columbia Catch Statistics.*

ANNUAL SUMMARY OF VITAL STATISTICS (IDAHO). **Main/Corp** Idaho. Dept. of Health and Welfare. VFOAT Vital Statistics, Idaho. 0362-9279. US. English. an. Department of Health & Welfare, 3105 1 2 State Street, Boise ID 83703. **LC** HA331. **DD** 312.09796. **NLM** W2 AI2 D4A.

ANNUAL SUMMARY OF VITAL STATISTICS, KANSAS (1969). (ANNUAL SUMMARY OF VITAL STATISTICS, KANSAS). 1969-. 0364-2372. US. English. an. Free. Kansas Department of Health, Forbes Field, Topeka KS 66620. **Tel** (913)862-9360. Ed Janet Marquis. **LC** HA381. **DD** 304.609781021. **NLM** W2 AK3 D85AC. Circ 750. (ctrl). Compilation of data collected on births, deaths, marriages, divorces, abortions and stillbirths reported through the vital statistics registration system of Kansas. *Annual Summary of Vital Statistics, State of Kansas.*

ANNUAL SUPPLEMENT TO HONG KONG TRADE STATISTICS, COUNTRY BY COMMODITY IMPORTS. (HONG KONG TRADE STATISTICS. ANNUAL SUPPLEMENT : COUNTRY BY COMMODITY). **Main/Corp** Hongkong. Census and Statistics Dept. 0304-8489. HK. English. ir. Census & Statistics Department, Beaconsfield House/6th Floor, Queens Road, Central Victoria Hong Kong. **LC** HF259.H6. **DD** 382.095125. *Hong Kong Trade Statistics. Supplement.*

ANNUAL SURVEY OF COLLEGES. (ANNUAL SURVEY OF COLLEGES : SUMMARY STATISTICS). VFOAT Summary Statistics. 8755-8696. US. English. an. College Board Publications, Box 886, New York NY 10101. **Tel** 713-6116. Ed Brooke Brestowe. **LC** LA227.3. **DD** 378.73.

ANNUAL SURVEY OF MANUFACTURES. STATISTICS FOR STATES, STANDARD METROPOLITAN STATISTICAL AREAS, LARGE INDUSTRIAL COUNTIES, AND SELECTED CITIES. VFOAT Statistics for States, Standard Metropolitan Statistical Areas, Large Industrial Counties, and Selected Cities. US. English. an. US Department of Commerce, Bureau of the Census, Washington DC 20233.

ANNUAL VITAL STATISTICS REPORT (FRANKFORT, KY.). (ANNUAL VITAL STATISTICS REPORT). 1980-. US. English. an. State Center for Health Statistics, 275 East Main Street, Frankfort KY 40621. **NLM** W2. *Selected Vital Statistics and Planning Data, 0145-5990.*

ANNUARIO DE STATISTICHE INDUSTRIALI. See Yearbooks, Almanacs, Directories.

ANNUARIO DI STATISTICA AGRARIA (ITALY). See Yearbooks, Almanacs, Directories.

ANNUARIO DI STATISTICHE DEL LAVORO. See Yearbooks, Almanacs, Directories.

ANNUARIO DI STATISTICHE GIUDIZIARIE (ITALY). See Yearbooks, Almanacs, Directories.

ANNUARIO DI STATISTICHE METEOROLOGICHE. See Yearbooks, Almanacs, Directories.

ANNUARIO ESTATISTICO (PARAIBA , BRAZIL). See Yearbooks, Almanacs, Directories.

ANNUARIO STATISTICO DEL COMMERCIO INTERNO E DEL TURISMO. See Yearbooks, Almanacs, Directories.

ANNUARIO STATISTICO DELLA ZOOTECNICA, PESCA E CACCIA. V. 16- 1975-. Italian. ir. 5.000. Istituto Central di Statistica, Via Cesare Balbo 16, Roma 00100 Italy. **LC** SF55.I8. **DD** 338.10945. *Annuario di Statistiche Zootecniche, Annuario Statistico della Pesca e della Caccia.*

ANNUARIO STATISTICO DELL'ISTRUZIONE. See Yearbooks, Almanacs, Directories.

ANNUARIO STATISTICO ITALIANO. See Yearbooks, Almanacs, Directories.

ANUARIO DE DADOS ESTATISTICOS DA EDUCACAO E CULTURA. See Yearbooks, Almanacs, Directories.

ANUARIO DE ESTADISTICA. See Yearbooks, Almanacs, Directories.

ANUARIO DE ESTADISTICA AGRARIA. See Yearbooks, Almanacs, Directories.

ANUARIO DE ESTADISTICAS DE TRANSPORTE. See Yearbooks, Almanacs, Directories.

ANUARIO ESTADISTICO - ASOCIACION NACIONAL DE UNIVERSIDADES E INSTITUTOS DE ENSENANZA SUPERIOR. See Yearbooks, Almanacs, Directories.

ANUARIO ESTADISTICO (AUTORIDAD PORTUARIA DE GUAYAQUIL). See Yearbooks, Almanacs, Directories.

ANUARIO ESTADISTICO DE ESPANA. See Yearbooks, Almanacs, Directories.

ANUARIO ESTADISTICO DE LA MINERIA MEXICANA. See Yearbooks, Almanacs, Directories.

ANUARIO ESTADISTICO DE LA SIDERURGIA Y MINERIA DEL HIERRO DE AMERICA LATINA. See Yearbooks, Almanacs, Directories.

ANUARIO ESTADISTICO DE TRANSPORTE. See Yearbooks, Almanacs, Directories.

ANUARIO ESTADISTICO. ENERGIA ELECTRICA. **Main/Corp** Argentine Republic. Oficina Sectorial de Desarrollo de Energia. VFOAT Energia Electrica. Spanish. ir.

ANUARIO ESTADISTICO (INSTITUTO NACIONAL DE ESTADISTICA Y CENSOS (ARGENTINA)). See Yearbooks, Almanacs, Directories.

ANUARIO ESTATISTICO. See Yearbooks, Almanacs, Directories.

ANUARIO ESTATISTICO. See Yearbooks, Almanacs, Directories.

ANUARIO ESTATISTICO - COMISSAO DE FINANCIAMENTO DA PRODUCAO, DEPARTAMENTO DE PESQUISAS ECONOMICAS. See Yearbooks, Almanacs, Directories.

ANUARIO ESTATISTICO (COMPANHIA DE FINANCIAMENTO DA PRODUCAO (BRAZIL)). (ANUARIO ESTATISTICO). Yearly V. 10 (1982)-. Portuguese. an. **LC** HD9014.B8. **DD** 338.130981.

ANUARIO ESTATISTICO - CORREIOS E TELECOMUNICACOES DE PORTUGAL. See Yearbooks, Almanacs, Directories.

ANUARIO ESTATISTICO DA UNIDADE CENTRAL DO SISTEMA DE INFORMACAO DE MERCADO AGRICOLA. See Yearbooks, Almanacs, Directories.

ANUARIO ESTATISTICO DE ENERGIA ELECTRICA. See Yearbooks, Almanacs, Directories.

ANUARIO ESTATISTICO DE TRANSITO NO ESTADO DO PARANA. See Yearbooks, Almanacs, Directories.

ANUARIO ESTATISTICO DO AMAPA. See Yearbooks, Almanacs, Directories.

ANUARIO ESTATISTICO DO ARROZ. See Yearbooks, Almanacs, Directories.

ANUARIO ESTATISTICO DO ESTADO DE SAO PAULO. See Yearbooks, Almanacs, Directories.

ANUARIO ESTATISTICO DO ESTADO DO RIO DE JANEIRO. See Yearbooks, Almanacs, Directories.

ANUARIO ESTATISTICO DOS TRANSPORTES. See Yearbooks, Almanacs, Directories.

ANUARIO ESTATISTICO PARANA. See Yearbooks, Almanacs, Directories.

ANUARIO ESTATISTICO - SERVICO SOCIAL DO COMERCIO, ADMINISTRACAO REGIONAL EM MINAS GERAIS. Portuguese. ir. Servico Social do Comercio, Administracao Regional em Minas Gerais, Rua Tupinambas 956, Belo Horizonte Brazil. **LC** HV194.M54. **DD** 361.6098151.

ANUARIO ESTATSITCO DAS FERROVIAS DO BRASIL. See Yearbooks, Almanacs, Directories.

ANUARIO SIMA : ESTADISTICAS REGIONALES BASICAS DEL MERCADO ARGENTINO. See Yearbooks, Almanacs, Directories.

ANUARUL STATISTIC AL REPUBLICII SOCIALISTE ROMANIA. 1966-. Periodical. RM. Romanian. an. $52.00. Rompresfilatelia, PO Box 1362137, Bucharest Romania. *Anuarul Statistic Al R.P.R., 0304-1387.*

API INDEXES. INDEX TERM USE STATISTICS. See Indexes/Abstracts.

APPARENT PER CAPITA FOOD CONSUMPTION IN CANADA. See Food & Drink.

APPLICATION STATISTICS. 1973-. 0382-912X. Periodical. CN. English. an. Council of Ontario Universities, 130 St George Street/Suite 8039, Toronto Ontario M5S 2T4 Canada. **LC** LA418.O6. **DD** 378.105609713.

APPLIED PSYCHOLOGICAL MEASUREMENT. See Psychology.

APPLIED STATISTICS. VFOAT Journal of the Royal Statistical Society. V. 1- Mar. 1952-. 0570-4936. Periodical. UK. English. ir. $27.58. Royal Statistical Society, 25-26 Enford Street, London WIH 2BH England. **Tel** 01-723-5882. **Ind/Abst** Math. Rev., Life Sci. Collect., GeoRef, Comput. Control Abstr., Electr. Electron. Abstr., Sci. Abstr. Sect. A. Phys. Abstr., Phys. Abstr. **LC** HA1. **NLM** W1 AP53. **CODEN** APSTAG.

ARBEITEN ZUR ANGEWANDTEN STATISTIK. No. 16- 1973-. 0066-5673. Monographic Series. GW. German. ir. Physics-Verlag, Tiergartenstrabe 17, D-6900 Heidelberg 1 West Germany. **Tel** (06221)487492. Ed K A Schaffer, P Schonfeld and W Wetzel. **Ind/Abst** Math. Rev. Monograph series on applied statistics. *Berichte aus dem Institut fur Statistik und Versicherungsmathematik und aus dem Institut fur Angewandte Statistik der Freien Universitat Berlin, 0067-5865.*

ARBEITER IM ANGESTELLTENVERHALTNIS IN DER INDUSTRIE OSTERREICHS. See Economics - Labor.

ARBEITS- UND SOZIALSTATISTIKEN. **Main/Corp** Germany (West). Bundesministerium fur Arbeit und Sozialordnung. German. ir.

Statistics

Bundesministerium Fur Arbeit Und Sozialordnung, 53 Bonn, Bonn West Germany. **LC** HA1233.

DER ARBEITSMARKT IN HESSEN. STATISTISCHE UBERSICHTEN. **VFOAT** Statistische Urersichten. Mar. 1978-. German. mo. Landesarbeitsamt Hessen, Saonestrasse 2-4-6, Frankfurt A M 71 West Germany. **LC** HD5780.H4. **DD** 331.11094341. *Arbeitsmarktlage in Hessen. Statistische Ubersichten.*

DIE ARBEITSSTATTEN DES GROSSHANDELS UND DER HANDELSVERMITTLUNG IN RHEINLAND-PFALZ. Series/Titl Statistik von Rheinland-Pflaz. German. ir. 9.20. Statistisches Landesamt Rheinland-Pfalz, Postfach Mainzer Strasse 15/16, 5427 Bad Ems West Germany.

ARBETSKRAFTSUNDERSOKNINGEN. ARSMEDELTAL. *See* Economics - Labor.

ARBETSMARKNADSSTATISTISK ARSBOK. *See* Yearbooks, Almanacs, Directories.

AREA MANPOWER REVIEW. BALANCE OF CONTRA COSTA COUNTY, CONTRA COSTA COUNTY EXCEPT CITY OF RICHMOND. *See* Economics - Labor.

AREA MANPOWER REVIEW. VALLEJO-FAIRFIELD-NAPA SMSA. NAPA COUNTY SUPPLEMENT. (AREA MANPOWER REVIEW : VALLEJO-FAIRFIELD-NAPA SMSA. NAPA COUNTY SUPPLEMENT). **Main/Corp** California. Employment Development Dept. Northern California Employment Data Research Section. **VAT** Area Manpower Review: Vallejo-Fairfield-Napa Standard Metropolitan Statistical Area. Napa County Supplement. 0145-708X. US. English. Health and Welfare Agency, Employment of Napa County Supplement, PO Box 7774, San Francisco CA 94120. **LC** HD5725.C2. **DD** 331.110979419.

AREA WAGE SURVEY. ALASKA. *See* Economics - Labor.

AREA WAGE SURVEY. COLUMBUS, MISS. *See* Economics - Labor.

AREA WAGE SURVEY. GREENVILLE-SPARTANBURG, SOUTH CAROLINA, METROPOLITAN AREA. *See* Economics - Labor.

AREA WAGE SURVEY. JACKSONVILLE, FLORIDA, METROPOLITAN AREA. *See* Economics - Labor.

AREA WAGE SURVEY. MELBOURNE-TITUSVILLE-COCOA, FLORIDA, METROPOLITAN AREA. *See* Economics - Labor.

AREA WAGE SURVEY. WICHITA FALLS-LAWTON-ALTUS, TEX. - OKLA. *See* Economics - Labor.

ARIZONA STATISTICAL REVIEW. 0518-6242. US. English. an. Valley National Bank, 241 North Central Avenue, Economic Research, Phoenix AZ 85001. **Tel** (602)261-2900. **LC** HA245. **DD** 317.91. *Statistical Review of Arizona.*

ARIZONA SUICIDE STATISTICS. **Main/Corp** Arizona. Dept. of Health Services. Planning and Analysis Management Information Systems. **Series/Titl** Health Information Special Report. US. English. Planning & Analysis Management Information Systems, Arizona Department of Health Services, 1740 West Adams Street, Phoenix AZ 85007. **LC** HB1323.S8. **DD** 312.276.

ARIZONA VITAL HEALTH STATISTICS. **VFOAT** Vital Health Statistics. 1979-. US. English. an. 1740 West Adams Street, Phoenix AZ 85007. **NLM** W2. *Arizona Vital and Health Statistics.*

ARIZONA WAGE STATISTICS AND COPPER OUTPUT. **VFOAT** Wage Statistics and Copper Output. Arizona and United States Copper Mines. Periodical. US. English. ir. Arizona Department of Mineral Resources, Mineral Building Fairgrounds, Phoenix AZ 85007. **LC** HD4976.A8.

ARKANSAS HEALTH MANPOWER STATISTICS. CHIROPRACTORS. (ARKANSAS HEALTH MANPOWER STATISTICS, CHIROPRACTORS). **VFOAT** Chiropractors. Began with 1978. 0198-7062. US. English. an. Division of Health Statistics, Department of Health, 4815 West Markham Street, Little Rock AR 72201. **LC** RZ225.U6. **DD** 331.12916155340.9767. **NLM** W2 AA8 D63AI. *Arkansas Health Manpower Statistics,* 0197-6478.

ARKANSAS HEALTH MANPOWER STATISTICS. DENTISTS. (ARKANSAS HEALTH MANPOWER STATISTICS, DENTISTS). **VFOAT** Dentists. Began with 1978. 0196-7959. US. English. an. Division of Health Statistics, Department of Health, 4815 West Markham Street, Little Rock AR 72201. **LC** RK58.6.A8. **DD** 331.1291617609767. **NLM** W2 AA8 D63AC. *Arkansas Health Manpower Statistics,* 0197-6478.

ARKANSAS HEALTH MANPOWER STATISTICS. LICENSED PRACTICAL NURSES. (ARKANSAS HEALTH MANPOWER STATISTICS : LICENSED PRACTICAL NURSES). **VFOAT** Licensed Practical Nurses. 1978-. 0272-586X. US. English. **NLM** W2 AA8 D63AL. *Arkansas Health Manpower Statistics,* 0197-6478.

ARKANSAS HEALTH MANPOWER STATISTICS. NURSING HOME ADMINISTRATORS. (ARKANSAS HEALTH MANPOWER STATISTICS, NURSING HOME ADMINISTRATORS). **VFOAT** Nursing Home Administrators. Began with 1978. 0196-7894. US. English. an. **LC** RA997.5.A8. **DD** 331.29136216068. **NLM** W2 AA8 D63AD. *Arkansas Health Manpower Statistics,* 0197-6478.

ARKANSAS HEALTH MANPOWER STATISTICS. OPTOMETRISTS. (ARKANSAS HEALTH MANPOWER STATISTICS, OPTOMETRISTS). **VFOAT** Optometrists. Began with 1978. 0196-7916. US. English. an. Division of Health Statistics, Arkansas Department of Health, 4815 West Markham Street, Little Rock AR 72201. **LC** RE959.3. **DD** 331.11916177509767. **NLM** W2 AA8 D63AE. *Arkansas Health Manpower Statistics,* 0197-6478.

ARKANSAS HEALTH MANPOWER STATISTICS. OSTEOPATHS. (ARKANSAS HEALTH MANPOWER STATISTICS, OSTEOPATHS). **VFOAT** Osteopaths. Began with 1978. 0196-7908. US. English. an. Division of Health Statistics, Department of Health, 4815 West Markham Street, Little Rock AR 72201. **LC** RZ325.U6. **DD** 331.129161553309767. **NLM** W2 AA8 D63AF. *Arkansas Health Manpower Statistics,* 0197-6478.

ARKANSAS HEALTH MANPOWER STATISTICS. PHARMACISTS. (ARKANSAS HEALTH MANPOWER STATISTICS, PHARMACISTS). **VFOAT** Pharmacists. Began with 1978. 0196-7940. US. English. an. Division of Health Statistics, Department of Health, 4815 West Markham Street, Little Rock AR 72201. **LC** RS67.U7. **DD** 331.1291615109767. **NLM** W2 AA8 D63AG. *Arkansas Health Manpower Statistics,* 0197-6478.

ARKANSAS HEALTH MANPOWER STATISTICS: PHYSICAL THERAPISTS. (ARKANSAS HEALTH MANPOWER STATISTICS, PHYSICAL THERAPISTS). **VFOAT** Physical Therapists. Began with 1978. 0198-7054. US. English. an. Division of Health Statistics, Department of Health, 4815 West Markham Street, Little Rock AR 72201. **LC** RM699.3.U6. **NLM** W2 AA8 D63AJ. *Arkansas Health Manpower Statistics,* 0197-6478.

ARKANSAS HEALTH MANPOWER STATISTICS. PHYSICIANS. (ARKANSAS HEALTH MANPOWER STATISTICS, PHYSICIANS). **VFOAT** Physicians. Began with 1978. 0272-5843. US. English. an. Division of Health Statistics, Department of Health, 4815 West Markham Street, Little Rock AR 72201. **LC** RA410.8.A8. **DD** 331.12916109767. **NLM** W2 AA8 D63AM. *Arkansas Health Manpower Statistics,* 0197-6478.

ARKANSAS HEALTH MANPOWER STATISTICS. PODIATRISTS. (ARKANSAS HEALTH MANPOWER STATISTICS, PODIATRISTS). **VFOAT** Podiatrists. Began with 1978. 0272-5851. US. English. an. Division of Health Statistics, Department of Health, 4815 West Markham Street, Little Rock AR 72201. **LC** RD563. **DD** 331.129161758509767. **NLM** W2 AA8 D63AN. *0197-6478.*

ARKANSAS HEALTH MANPOWER STATISTICS. REGISTERED NURSES. (ARKANSAS HEALTH MANPOWER STATISTICS : REGISTERED NURSES). **VFOAT** Registered Nurses. 1978-. 0272-5878. US. English. **NLM** W2 AA8 D63AP. *0197-6478.*

ARKANSAS HEALTH MANPOWER STATISTICS, SUMMARIES OF LICENSED HEALTH MANPOWER PROFESSIONALS BY COUNTY. **VFOAT** Summaries of Licensed Health Manpower Professionals by County. Began with 1978. 0277-7231. US. English. an. Division of Health Statistics, Department of Health, 4815 West Markham Street, Little Rock AR 72201. **LC** RA410.8.A8. **DD** 331.12916109676. **NLM** W2 AA8 D63AQ. *Arkansas Health Manpower Statistics. Summaries of Licensed and Allied Health Manpower Professionals by County,* 0730-790X.

ARKANSAS HEALTH MANPOWER STATISTICS. VETERINARIANS. *See* Veterinary Medicine, Animal Culture.

ARKANSAS OIL AND GAS STATISTICAL BULLETIN. **Main/Corp** Arkansas. Oil and Gas Commission. Periodical. US. English. mo. Free. Arkansas Oil & Gas Commission, 314 East Oak, El Dorado AR 71730. **Tel** (501)862-4965. **LC** HD9567.A8. **DD** 338.2728. **Circ** 450. Production of north and south Arkansas.

ARKANSAS VITAL STATISTICS. **Main/Corp** Arkansas. Division of Health Statistics. 0364-0728. US. English. be. Division of Health Statistics, 4815 West Markham Street, Little Rock AR 72201. **LC** HA251. **DD** 312.09767. **NLM** W2 AA8 B9AB. *Arkansas Vital Statistics,* 0364-0728.

ARL STATISTICS. **Main/Corp** Association of Research Libraries. **VAT** Association of Research Libraries Statistics. 1974/75-. 0147-2135. US. English. an. $10.00. Association of Research Libraries, 1527 New Hampshire Avenue NW, Washington DC 20036. **Tel** (202)232-2466. **Ed** Nicola Daval. **LC** Z675.U5. **DD** 027.773. **Circ** 1,200. Describes the collections, staffing levels, expenditures, and interlibrary loan volume of all Association of Research Libraries member libraries in the US and Canada. *Academic Library Statistics,* 0571-6519.

ARSBOK FOR SVERIGES KOMMUNER. *See* Yearbooks, Almanacs, Directories.

ASPECTS STATISTIQUES DE LA REGION PARISIENNE CEASED. **Main/Corp** Institut National de la Statistique et des Etudes Economiques (France). July 1971-June 1976. Periodical. French. mo. INSEE-CNGP, BP 2718, 80027 Amiens Cedex France. **LC** HA1228.S4. *Bulletin de Statistique: Region Parisienne.*

ASPECTS STATISTIQUES DE L'ILE DE FRANCE. **Main/Corp** Institut National de la Statistique et des Etudes Economiques (France). **VFOAT** Aspects Statistiques de la Region Parisienne. July 1976-. 0395-7179. Periodical. FR. French. mo. INSEE-CNGP, BP 2718, 80027 Amiens Cedex France. *Aspects Statistiques de la Region Parisienne.*

ASSISTANCE PAYMENTS STATISTICS. Series/Titl DSS Publication. **VFOAT** Monthly Assistance Payments Statistics. Periodical. US. English. mo. State of Michigan, Data Reporting Section, Department of Social Services, Lansing MI 48909. *Social Services Statistics.*

AN AUDITOR'S APPROACH TO STATISTICAL SAMPLING. US. English. ir. American Institute of CPA, 1211 Avenue of the Americas, New York NY 10036.

AUSLANDER. **Main/Corp** Saxony, Lower. Landesverwaltungsamt. German. ir. 3.60. Niedersachsisches Landesverwaltungsamt, Postfach 107, 3000 Hannover West Germany. **LC** HA1248.S28.

DER AUSSENHANDEL. **Main/Corp** Statistisches Landesamt Baden-Wurttemberg. **Series/Titl** Statistik Von Baden-Wurttemberg. German. ir. 8.00. Statistisches Landesamt Baden-Wurttemberg, Postfach 898, 7000 Stuttgart 1 West Germany. **LC** HA1320.B2, HF196. B28. **DD** 314.346 S, 382.094346.

DER AUSSENHANDEL NORDRHEIN-WESTFALENS. **Main/Corp** North Rhine-Westphalia. Landesamt fur Datenverarbeitung und Statistik. German. ir. 20.00. Landesamt fur Datehverarbeitung und Statistik Nordrhein-Westfalen, Ludwig Beck Strasse 23, 4 Dusseldorf West Germany. **LC** HF3569.N6.

AUSTRALIAN CAPITAL TERRITORY STATISTICAL SUMMARY. 0067-1754. AT. English. ir. Australian Bureau of Statistics, Ground Floor Wing 5 Cameron Offices, Belconnen Australian Capital Territory 2617 Australia. **Tel** (062)52 6627. **LC** HA3008.A9. **DD** 319.47. Information on the population

Statistics

and its characteristics; social statistics and demography, primary production; labour, wages and prices; retail trade; building and transport. *Australian Capital Territory Statistical Summary, 0067-1754.*

AUSTRALIAN ENERGY STATISTICS. 1981-. 0727-2596. AT. English. an. LC HD9502.A87. DD 333.790994.

AUSTRALIAN FIRE, MARINE AND GENERAL INSURANCE STATISTICS. AT. English. ir. Australian Bureau of Statistics, GPO Box 796, Sydney NSW 2001 Australia. LC HG8732. DD 368.994.

AUSTRALIAN JOURNAL OF STATISTICS. V. 1- Apr. 1959-. 0004-9581. AT. English. ir. $40.00. Australian Statistical Publishing Association Inc, c/o Dr D J Daily, Government Printing Office, Box 4 Canberra Australian Capital Territory 2601 Australia. **Tel** 49 4551. **Ed** J S Maritz. **Ind/Abst** Math. Rev., Public Aff. Inf. Serv. Bull. LC HA1. DD 310.994. NLM HA 1 A938. CODEN AUJSA3. (cum index). bk rev. **Circ** 1,600. (ctrl). Papers on statistics.

AUSTRALIAN PETROLEUM STATISTICS. VFOAT Petroleum Statistics. 0300-2101. English. ir. Department of National Development, Processing and Distribution Branch, PO Box 5, Canberra Australian Capitol Territory 2601 Australia. **Tel** (062)458211. **Ind/Abst** GeoRef. LC HD9578.A8. DD 338.4766550994. CODEN APSTDJ. **Circ** 1,100. (ctrl). Provides a summary of Australian production, refining, domestic marketing and international trade in petroleum, coal, uranium and electricity.

AUSTRALIAN SHIPPING AND SHIPBULDING STATISTICS. English. an. LC HE565.A8. DD 387.240994.

AVIATION DAILY'S AIRLINE STATISTICAL ANNUAL. VFOAT Airline Statistical Annual. 0092-2862. US. English. an. $12.00. Ziff-Davis Publishing Co, 1156 15th Street Northwest, Washington DC 20005. LC HE9803.A2. DD 387.740973.

B P STATISTICAL REVIEW OF THE WORLD OIL INDUSTRY. 0081-5039. UK. English. an. Free. British Petroleum Corporation Ltd, 620 Fifth Avenue, New York NY 10020. **Tel** (212)887-9467. (ctrl). Statistical review of world-wide energy trends.

BAHAMAS TOURISM STATISTICS. VFOAT Bahamas Tourism Statistical Review. 1983-. BF. English. an. Ministry of Tourism, Research and Statistics, PO Box N-3701, Nassau Bahamas. *Tourism Statistical Review.*

BALANCE OF PAYMENTS STATISTICS. Main/Corp Zambia. Central Statistical Office. 0304-8985. ZA. English. mo. $38.00. Central Statistics Office, PO Box 1908, Lusaka Zambia. **Tel** (202)477-7000. LC HG3883.Z35. DD 382.17096894.

BALANCE OF PAYMENTS STATISTICS YEARBOOK - INTERNATIONAL MONETARY FUND. See Yearbooks, Almanacs, Directories.

BANGLADESH EXPORT STATISTICS. Main/Corp Bangladesh. Raptani Unnayana Byuro. 1976/78-. English. ir. Export Promotion Bureau Bangladesh, 122-124 Montijheel Commercial Area, Dacca Bangladesh. LC HF3790.6.A45. DD 382.09549200212.

BANK OF ENGLAND STATISTICAL ABSTRACT. See Indexes/Abstracts.

BANK OPERATING STATISTICS. Began with 1967. 0430-1684. US. English. Federal Deposit Insurance Corporation, 559 17th Street NW, Washington DC 20006. LC HG2416. DD 332.120973.

BANKING STATISTICS OF PAKISTAN. Main/Corp State Bank of Pakistan. Dept. of Statistics. 1948-57-. 0067-3811. PK. English. an. $5.00. State Bank of Pakistan, POB 4456 Central Directorate, Katachi Pakistan. LC HG3290.5.S8. **Circ** 485. Covers banking and finance.

BASIC ROAD STATISTICS. UK. English. an. LC HE363.G7. DD 388.10941.

BASIC STATISTICAL DATA OF NEW JERSEY SCHOOL DISTRICTS. Main/Corp New Jersey Education Association. US. English. ir. $3.50. New Jersey Education Association, 180 West Adams Street, Trenton NJ 08608. **Tel** (609)599-4561. LC LB5. DD 370.780749 S, 379.153509749.

BASIC STATISTICS OF THE COMMUNITY. (BASIC STATISTICS OF THE COMMUNITY). 0081-4873. English (also issued in German, French, Italian and Dutch). an. European Community Information Inc, 2100 M Street NW, Suite 707, Washington DC 20037. DD 314. *Basic Statistics for Fifteen European Countries.*

BAUSTATISTIK. GERATEBESTAND IM HOCH- U. TIEFBAU AM . . . . Series/Titl Beitrage zur Osterreichischen Statistik. VFOAT Geratebestand im Hoch- U Tiefbau Am . . . . German. an. LC HA1173, HD9715. A9. DD 314.36 S, 338.4762409436021.

BAUWIRTSCHAFT UND BAUTATIGKEIT IN NORDRHEIN-WESTFALEN. Main/Corp North Rhine-Westphalia (Germany). Landesamt fur Datenverarbeitung und Statistik. Series/Titl Beitrage zur Statistik des Landes Nordrhein-Westfalen. 1973-. German. ir. Landesamt fur Datenverarbeitung und Statistik, Ludwig-Beck-Strasse 23, Dusseldorf 4 West Germany. LC HA1320.N6, HD9715. G33. DD 314.355 S, 338.47690094355. *Bauwirtschaft und Bautatigkeit in Nordrhein-Westfalen.*

BAYERN IN ZAHLEN. V. 1- Jan. 1947-. 0005-7215. Periodical. German. mo. Carl Gerber Verlag, D-8000 Munchen 45 Muthmannstr 4 Germany. **Ind/Abst** Bibliogr. Agric.

B.C. PUBLIC SCHOOL STATISTICS. Main/Corp British Columbia. Educational Data Services. US. English. British Columbia Research, 3650 Wesbrook Mall, Vancouver BC V6S 2L2 Canada. LC LB2833.4.C2. DD 331.12. *B.C. Public School Enrolment Statistics.*

BED USE STATISTICS. Main/Corp Great Britain. Welsh Office. UK. English. an. LC RA987.W2. DD 362.1109429.

BEE FARMING STATISTICS, TASMANIA. Main/Corp Australian Bureau of Statistics. Tasmanian Office. Series/Titl Tasmanian Statistics. AT. English. an. Australian Bureau of Statistics, 188 Collins Street, Hobart Australia. LC SF531. DD 638.109946. *Bee Farming Statistics, Tasmania.*

BEER STATISTICS NEWS. V. 3, No. 6- July 1977-. 0164-4831. Periodical. US. English. mo. $40.00 Domestic, $125.00 Foreign. Beer Marketers Insights, 51 Virginia Avenue, West Nyack NY 10994. **Tel** (914)358-7751. **Ed** Eric Shepard. Computerized data service, with reports highlighting data, showing trends for major brewers in 38 states in US. States grouped by region, and regional analyses also made. *Beer Statistics Monthly, 0164-4467.*

BEFOLKNINGEN I DE ENKELTE KOMMUNER PR. . . . FORDELT EFTER KN, ALDER OG GTESKABÉLIG STILLING. Began with 1. Jan. 1971. 0107-1041. DK. Danish. an. 36.00. Danmarks Statistik, Sejrgade 11, 2100 Kbenhavn Denmark. LC HA1471.

BEFOLKNINGENS BEVGELSER. VFOAT Vital Statistics. 0070-3478. DK. Danish. an. 31.00. Danmarks Statistik, Sejrgade 11, 2100 Kbenhavn Denmark. LC HA1473.

BENELUX : STATISTIEKEN. Main/Corp Benelux Economic Union. VFOAT Benelux Statistiques. Began in 1973. Periodical. BE. Dutch (French). ir. Benelux Economic Union, Regentschapsstraat 39 1000, Brussels Belgium. LC HC310.5.A1. DD 330.949207.

BETALINGSBALANCER. SAMLEDE ANGIVELSER. VFOAT Zahlungsbilanzen. Gesamtangaben., Payments. Global Data. Began with Vol. for 1961/74. Danish (Dutch, English, French, German, and Italian). qt. European Community Information Service, 2100 M Street NW Suite 707, Washington DC 20037. LC HG3883.E83. Gives data on global balance of payments for the EC and its members states, Spain, Portugal, the US and Japan. Also contains comparitive tables for the main balances of payments of industrialized countries. *Zahlungsbiliazen.*

DIE BEVOLKERUNG IN NORDRHEIN-WESTFALEN. Main/Corp North Rhine-Westphalia (Germany). Landesamt fur Datenverarbeitung und Statistik. Series/Titl Beitrage zue Statistik des Landes Nordrhein-Westfalen. German. ir. 6-. Landesamt fur Datenverarbeitung und Statistik Nordrhein-Westfalen, Mauerstr 51, Dusseldorf West Germany. **Tel** (0211)44971. LC HB2056.N6. adv acc. **Circ** 1,100. Statistical returns about population.

BEVOLKERUNGSSTAND UND BEVOLKERUNGSBEWEGUNG. Main/Corp Bremen. Statistisches Landesamt. German. ir. 28 Bremen an der Weide 14/16 Postfach 909, Bremen West Germany. LC HA1271.

BEVOLKINGSSTATISTIEKEN - NATIONAAL INSTITUUT VOOR DE STATISTIEK. Main/Corp Institut National de Statistique (Belgium). 1969. 0304-8888. BE. Dutch. qt. 250 Domestic, 400 Foreign. Nationaal Instituut voor de Statistiek, Leuvenseweg 44, 1000 Brussels Belgium. **Tel** (02)513.96.50. LC HA1391. **Circ** 525. (ctrl). Population studies.

A BIBLIOGRAPHY OF ECONOMIC AND STATISTICAL PUBLICATIONS ON TANZANIA. 1967-. Periodical. English. ir. Bureau of Statistics, PO Box 796, Dars-es-Salaam Tanzania. LC Z7165.T3, HC557.T3. DD 016.3309678.

BICYCLE ACCIDENT STATISTICS. Main/Corp Iowa. Dept. of Public Safety. Research and Statistics Section. 1973-. US. English. Department of Public Safety, Administration Division, Des Moines IA 50319. LC HE5614.3.I8. DD 312.4409777. *Fatal Bicycle Accident Statistics, Iowa, 0147-3220.*

BIENNIAL AND STATISTICAL REPORT - NEBRASKA. DEPT. OF ROADS. Main/Corp Nebraska. Dept. of Roads. US. English. be. PO Box 94759, Lincoln NE 68509. LC HE356.N36. DD 353.97820086406.

BILAN ANNUEL BRETAGNE. FR. French. an. 36 Place du Colombier, Rennes France. LC HA1228.B7. DD 314.41.

BILANS ALIMENTAIRES ET AUTRES BILANS. Main/Corp France. Service Central des Enquetes et Etudes Statistiques. 1956/67-. FR. French. ir. Service Central des Enquetes et Etudes Statistiques, Ministere de l'Agriculture, 4 Avenue de Saint-Mande, 75570 Paris Cedex 12 France. LC HD9012.4. DD 338.10944.

BILANZ DER WOHNBEVOELKERUNG IN DEN GEMEINDEN DER SCHWEIZ. Series/Titl Statistische Quellenwerke der Schweiz. VFOAT Bilan Demographique des Communes Suisses. 1981-. French (German). an. 26.-. Bundesamt fuer Statistik, Hallwylstrasse 15, CH 3003 Bern Switzerland. **Tel** 031/61 8836. LC HA1593. DD 312.09494. adv acc. **Circ** 900. Resident population, live births, deaths, marriages, internal migration, emigration, immigration, population change, regionalized data on population change.

BIOMETRICS. See Biology.

BIRTHS AND DEATHS BY JURISDICTION OF RESIDENCE. MARRIAGES AND DIVORCES BY COUNTY. Main/Corp Ohio. Division of Vital Statistics. 0363-1281. US. English. an. Ohio Department of Health/ Division of Vital Statistics, 65 South Front Street/PO Box 118, Columbus OH 43213. LC HA571. DD 312.09771.

BIRTHS, SOUTH AUSTRALIA. Main/Corp Australian Bureau of Statistics. South Australian Office. 0067-088X. AT. English. an. Australian Bureau of Statistics, Ground Floor Annexe City Mutual Centre, 10-20 Pulteney Street, Adelaide South Australia 5000 Australia. **Tel** (08)228 9439. LC HB1095. DD 312.19423. Registrations by nuptiality, multiple births, age of mother, previous issue, relative ages of parents, age-specific birth rates, fertility and duration of marriage. *Births. South Australia, 0067-088X.*

BIULETYN STATYSTYCZNY. Main/Corp Poland. Glowny Urzad Statystyczny. Jan. 1957-. 0006-4025. PL. Polish (table of contents also in English and Russian). mo. ARS Polona, Krakowskie Przedmiescie 7, 00-068 Warsaw Poland. LC HA1451. DD 314.38.

BOATING INDUSTRY STATISTICAL YEARBOOK. See Yearbooks, Almanacs, Directories.

BOATING REGISTRATION STATISTICS. 0163-7207. US. English. an. $5.00. National Association of Engine and Boat Manufacturers, PO Box 5555, Grand Central Station, New York NY 10017. LC GV776.A2. DD 353.9387723.

Statistics

BOATING STATISTICS. Series/Titl Comdtinst. Began with 1966. US. English. an. Commandant, United States Coast Guard, Washington DC 20593. *Recreational Boating Statistics.*

BOLETIM ANUAL DE ESTATISTICA. Began with 1981 Vol. Portuguese. an. **LC** HD9410.9.B6. **DD** 338.476649070981.

BOLETIM ESTATISTICO. Main/Corp Administracao do Porto de Sao Francisco do Sul. VFOAT Estatistica. Portuguese. mo. Administracao do Porto de Sao Francisco do Sul Assessoria de Planejamento Servico de Estatistica, rua Babitonga 99 CP 7, Sao Francisco do Sul Santa Catarina. **LC** HE563.B8. **DD** 387.1098164.

BOLETIM ESTATISTICO - ADMINISTRACAO DO PORTO DO RECIFE. Main/Corp Administracao do Porto do Recife. BL. Portuguese. mo. Administracao do Porto do Recife, Av Alfredo Listoa Ed A.P.R., Recife Brazil. **LC** HE556.R4. **DD** 387.109813.

BOLETIM ESTATISTICO ANUAL. Main/Corp Administracao do Porto do Recife. BL. Portuguese. an. Assessoria Tecnica de Estatistica, Av Alfredo Lisboa S/N, Recife Brazil. **LC** HE563.B8.

BOLETIM ESTATISTICO ANUAL - COMPANHIA DE ELETRICIDADE DE CEARA. Main/Corp Companhia de Eletricidade de Cera. Portuguese. ir. Diretoria da Area Economico-Financeira, Av Barao de Studart 2917, Aldeota, Fortaleza Brazil. **LC** HD9685.B83.

BOLETIM ESTATISTICO - COMPANHIA PAULISTA DE FORCA E LUZ. Main/Corp Companhia Paulista de Forca e Luz. Periodical. Portuguese. ir. Companhia Paulista de Forca e Luz, Avenida Angelica 2565, Sao Paulo Brazil. **LC** HD9685.B83.

BOLETIM ESTATISTICO. CONSUMO E CONSUMIDORES POR CLASSE E MUNICIPIO ESTADO DE SAO PAULO. (BOLETIM ESTATISTICO : CONSUMO E CONSUMIDORES POR CLASSE E MUNICIPIO, ESTADO DE SAO PAULO). **Main/Corp** Centrais Eletricas de Sao Paulo. Setor de Estudos de Mercado. 0303-7614. Portuguese. ir. **LC** HD9685.B82.

BOLETIM ESTATISTICO DE ENERGIA ELETRICA. BL. Portuguese. qt. Coordenacao de Energia da Secretaria das Minas e Energia do Estado da Bahia, Centro Administrativo da Bahis, Av Luiz Viana Filho S/No 40.000, Bahia Salvador. *Boletim Estatistico Mensal de Energia Eletrica.*

BOLETIM ESTATISTICO - FUNDAFAO INSTITUTO BRASILEIRO DE GEOGRAFIA E ESTATISTICA, DEPARTAMENTO DE DIVULGACAO ESTATISTICA. Main/Corp Fundacao Ibge. Departamento de Divulgacao Estatistica. V. 30- (No. 120-). Portuguese. ir. $18.00. Av Franklin Roosevelt 166, Rio de Janeiro Brazil. **LC** HA973. *Boletim Estatistico.*

BOLETIM MENSAL DAS ESTATISTICAS DO COMERCIO EXTERNO. CONTINENTE, ACORES E MADEIRA. VFOAT Bulletin Mensuel des Exterieur. Continent, Acores et Madere. Vol. 4 (1978)-. Periodical. PO. Portuguese (French). mo. Instituto Nacional Estatisticas, Avenida Antonio Jose de Almedid, 1078 Lisboa Codex Portugal.

BOLETIM MENSAL DAS ESTATISTICAS INDUSTRIAIS. (BOLETIM MENSAL DAS ESTATISTICAS INDUSTRIAIS : CONTINENTE E ILHAS ADJACENTES). **Main/Corp** Instituto Nacional de Estatistica (Portugal). Servicos Centrais. VFOAT Bulletin Mensuel des Statistiques Industrielles : Continent et Iles Adjacentes. Vol. 1- 1976-. 0377-2179. BL. French and Portuguese. ir. Instituto Nacional de Estatistica, Avenida Antonio Jose de Almeida, Lisboa 1 Portugal. **LC** HC391. **DD** 338.09469.

BOLETIM MENSAL DE ESTATISTICA. Main/Corp Angola. Direcao Provincial dos Servicos de Estatistica. Vol. 25- 1969-. AO. Portuguese. mo. Caixa Postal 1215, Luanda Angola. **Ind/Abst** Foreign Lang. Index. **LC** HA2211. *Boletim Mensal de Estatistica.*

BOLETIM MENSUAL DE ESTATISTICA. Main/Corp Macao. Reparticao dos Servicos de Estatistica. VFOAT Monthly Bulletin of Statistics. Jan. 1976-. Periodical. English (Portuguese). mo. Reparticao dos Servicos de Estatistica, PO Box 471, Macao. **LC** HA1950.M3. **DD** 315.126.

BOLETIM TRIMESTRAL (BANCO DE PORTUGAL. DEPARTAMENTO DE ESTATISTICA E ESTUDOS ECONOMICOS). (BOLETIM TRIMESTRAL). Vol. 3, No. 1 (March 1981)-. Portuguese. qt. Banco de Portugal Departamento de Estatistica e Estudos Economicos, Av Da Republica 57, 1094 Lisboa Portugal. **Ind/Abst** Foreign Lang. Index. **LC** HG186.P8. **DD** 330.9469005.

BOLETIM TRIMESTRAL DAS ESTATISTICAS DA AGRICULTURA E DA PESCA : CONTINENTE E ILHAS ADJACENTES. Main/Corp Portugal. Instituto Nacional de Estatistica. Servicos Centrais. VFOAT Bulletin Trimestriel des Statistiques de l'Agriculture et de la Peche : Continent et Iles Adjacentes. French and Portuguese. ir. 60.00. Instituto Nacional de Estatistica, Av Jose De Almeida 1, Lisboa Portugal. **LC** HD2026. **DD** 338.09469.

BOLETIM TRIMESTRAL DE ESTATISTICA (FUNCHAL, MADEIRA ISLANDS). (BOLETIM TRIMESTRAL DE ESTATISTICA). Vol. 1- 1st Quarter 1972-. 0303-1705. PO. Portuguese. qt. 900.00. Edificio da Junta-Geral, Av Arriaga, Funchal Portugal. **Tel** 27454. **LC** HA1577.M3. **DD** 314.698. adv acc. **Circ** 500. (ctrl). Autonomous region of Madeira.

BOLETIM TRIMESTRAL DE ESTATISTICA - INSTITUTO NACIONAL DE ESTATISTICA. DELEGACAO DE S. TOME E PRINCIPE. (BOLETIM TRIMESTRAL DE ESTATISTICA). **Main/Corp** Sao Tome e Principe. Reparticao Provincial dos Servicos de Estatistica. Yearly V. 1- 1st Quarter 1971-. 0303-1675. Portuguese. ir. 120.00. Reparticao Provincial dos Servicos de Estatistica, Caixa Postal No 256, Sao Tome E Principe. **LC** HA2204.S27.

BOLETIN ANUARIO - BANCO CENTRAL DEL ECUADOR. *See* Yearbooks, Almanacs, Directories.

BOLETIN DE ESTADISTICA MINERA. Main/Corp Chile. Direccion de Estadistica y Censos. 0577-7933. Periodical. CL. Spanish. ir. Av Bulnes 418, Santiago Chile 31133384.

BOLETIN ESTADISTICO (BANCO CENTRAL DEL URUGUAY. DEPARTAMENTO DE INVESTIGACIONES ECONOMICAS : 1982). (BOLETIN ESTADISTICO). Spanish. mo. **LC** HG185.U8. **DD** 330.9895005. *Boletin Estadistico Mensuel (Banco Central del Uruguay. Division Asesoria Economica y Estudios),* 0005-4747.

BOLETIN ESTADISTICO (BANCO NACIONAL DE AHORRO Y PRESTAMO. SISTEMAS DE INFORMACION). (BOLETIN ESTADISTICO). VE. Spanish. mo. Banco Nacional de Desarrollo y Prestamo, Calle de Sabana Grande Cruce Con Av los Jabillos Edit Continental, Caracas Venezuela. **LC** HG2156.V42. **DD** 332.320987.

BOLETIN ESTADISTICO DE FAENA Y EXPORTACION. VFOAT Estadisticas. June 1978-. Periodical. Spanish. mo. Unidad de Estudios Economicos, Rincon 549, Montevideo Uruguay.

BOLETIN ESTADISTICO - DIRECCION GENERAL DE ESTADISTICA Y CENSOS. Main/Corp Salvador. Direccion General de Estadistica y Censos. Periodical. ES. Spanish. ir. Direccion General De Estadistica y Censos, Rasale Contreras 145, San Salvador El Salvador. **LC** HA841. **DD** 317.284. *Boletin Estadistico.*

BOLETIN ESTADISTICO (DOMINICAN REPUBLIC. SECRETARIA DE ESTADO DE FINANZAS, DEPARTAMENTO DE ESTUDIOS ECONOMICOS). (BOLETIN ESTADISTICO). Yearly V. 1, No. 2 (April/June 1980)-. Spanish. qt. **Ind/Abst** Foreign Lang. Index. **LC** HJ26. **DD** 336.7293.

BOLETIN ESTADISTICO - EMPRESA PORTUARIA DE CHILE. Main/Corp Empresa Portuaria de Chile. Spanish. ir. Empresa Portuaria de Chile, Depto Explotacion, Sub-Depto Estadistica, Casilla 133, Valparaiso Chile. **LC** HE563.C5.

BOLETIN ESTADISTICO MENSUAL. Main/Corp Banco Central del Paraguay. No. 1- June 1958-. 0522-1161. Periodical. Spanish. mo. **LC** HA1045.

BOLETIN ESTADISTICO, SISTEMA MUTUAL. VFOAT Boletin Estadistico del Sistema Mutual. Periodical. Spanish. mo. *Boletin Estadistico (Banco de la Vivienda del Peru).*

BOLETIN ESTADISTICO TRIMESTRAL (INSTITUTO NACIONAL DE ESTADISTICA (BOLIVIA). (BOLETIN ESTADISTICO TRIMESTRAL). Yearly V. 1, No. 1 (Sept. 1981)-. Spanish. qt. Plaza Mario Guzman Aspiazu, No 1 Casilla 6129, La Paz Bolivia. **Ind/Abst** Foreign Lang. Index. **LC** HC181. **DD** 330.984005.

BOLETIN ESTADISTICO TRIMESTRAL - INSTITUTO NACIONAL DE ESTADISTICA Y CENSOS. (BOLETIN ESTADISTICO TRIMESTRAL). **Main/Corp** Argentine Republic. Instituto Nacional de Estadistica y Censos. Jan./March 1973-. 0325-1969. Periodical. AG. Spanish. ir. Hipolito Yrigoyen 250, Buenos Aires Argentina. **Ind/Abst** Foreign Lang. Index. *Boletin de Estadistica,* 0004-1017.

BOLETIN INFORMATIVO - SUPERINTENDENCIA DE SOCIEDADES, SECCION DE ESTADISTICA. Main/Corp Colombia. Superintendencia de Sociedades. Seccion de Estadistica. Spanish. ir. **LC** HD2837.

BOLETIN MENSUAL DE ESTADISTICA AGRARIA. Main/Corp Spain. Ministerio de Agricultura. July 1973-. 0211-9889. Periodical. SP. Spanish. mo. $10.79. Secretaria General Technica Ser Publ Agrar/Pseo Infanta, Isabel 1, Madrid 7 Spain. **Ind/Abst** Foreign Lang. Index, PAIS Foreign Lang. Index. **LC** S253. **DD** 338.10946.

BOLETIN MENSUAL DE ESTADISTICA (SPAIN. MINISTERIO DE AGRICULTURA, PESCA Y ALIMENTACION). (BOLETIN MENSUAL DE ESTADISTICA). Series/Titl Publicaciones Agrarias. Spanish. mo. **LC** S253. **DD** 338.10946. *Boletin Mensual de Estadistica Agraria.*

BOLETIN MENSUAL ESTADISTICAS AGRICOLAS *CEASED.* **Main/Corp** Puerto Rico. Oficina de Estadisticas Agricolas y Estudios Economicos. PR. Spanish. mo. Departamento de Agricultura, Apartado 10163, Santurce Puerto Rico. **Ind/Abst** Foreign Lang. Index. **LC** S181. *Boletin Mensual de Estadisticas Agricolas.*

BOLLETTINO DELLA DOXA. Main/Corp Doxa, Istituto per le Ricerche Statistiche e l'Analisi dell'Opinione Pubblica, Milan. V. 1- 1946?-. Periodical. IT. Italian. mo. $45.00. Doxa, 6 Galleria S Carlo, 29122 Milano Italy. **Tel** 02 790871. **Circ** 2,000. Results of public opinion surveys in Italy and other countries.

BOLLETTINO MENSILE DI STATISTICA. Year 1 (Nov. 1926)-. 0021-3136. Periodical. IT. Italian. mo. $38.61. Istituto Centrale di Statistic, Via Censare Balbo 16, 00100 Roma Italy. **Ind/Abst** Predicasts, Foreign Lang. Index. **LC** HA1360.

BOLLETTINO STATISTICO QUADRIMESTRALE (ISTITUTO NAZIONALE DELLA PREVIDENZA SOCIALE (ITALY)). (BOLLETTINO STATISTICO QUADRIMESTRALE). Italian. ty. **LC** HD7184. **DD** 368.400945. *Bollettino Statistico Quadrimestrale (Istituto Nazionale della Previdenza Sociale (Italy). Servizio Statistico Attuariale).*

BOTSWANA AGRICULTURAL STATISTICS. GABORONE REGION. 1980-. English. ir. **LC** S338.B6. **DD** 338.1096811.

BOTSWANA AGRICULTURAL STATISTICS. WESTERN REGION. English. ir. **LC** SF55.B54. **DD** 338.1760096811.

BP STATISTICAL REVIEW OF THE WORLD OIL INDUSTRY *CEASED.* VFOAT B.P. Statistical Review of the World Oil Industry. **VAT** British Petroleum Statistical Review of the World Oil Industry. 1969-80. UK. English. an. Britannic House, Moor Lane, London EC2Y 9BU England. **LC** HD9560.4. **DD** 338.82305. *Statistical Review of the World Oil Industry.*

BP STATISTICAL REVIEW OF WORLD ENERGY. VFOAT B.P. Statistical Review of World Energy. 1981-. UK. English. an. British Petroleum Company, Britannic House, Moor Lane, London EC2Y

Statistics

9BU England. **LC** HD9560.4. **DD** 333.7905. *BP Statistical Review of the World Oil Industry.*

BRITISH COLUMBIA CATCH STATISTICS BY AREA AND TYPE OF GEAR (AS REPORTED ON SALES SLIPS RECEIVED BY THE DEPARTMENT). Main/Corp Canada. Fisheries Service. Pacific Region. **CN.** English. an. Department of Fisheries and Forestry, 115 Robson Street, Vancouver 5 British Columbia. **LC** SH224.B7. **DD** 639.209711. *British Columbia Catch Statistics by Area and Type of Gear (as Reported on Sales Slips Received by the Department).*

BRITISH COLUMBIA LABOUR FORCE STATISTICS. VAT Special Report - Research and Planning. Province of British Columbia. Ministry of Labour. May 1977-. 0706-2753. Periodical. **CN.** English. mo. Free. **LC** HD5730.B75. **DD** 331.12509711021. (ctrl).

BRITISH ECONOMY SURVEY. *See* Economics.

BROADCAST STATS. No. 1 (Aug. 17, 1984)-. 0749-2936. Periodical. **US.** English. sm. $350.00. Paul Kagan Associates, 126 Clock Tower Place, Carmel CA 92923. **Tel** (408)624-1536. Ed Sharon Armbrust. Newsletter containing new data on radio and TV market billings, revenue, cash flow, market. By-market history of station sales; digest of financial data.

BUDAPEST STATISZTIKAI ZSEBKONYVE. 1956-. 0438-2242. HU. Hungarian. an. 45.—. Statisztikai Kiado Vallalat, III Kaszasdulo U 2, Budapest Hungary. **Tel** 803-311. **LC** HA1208. **DD** 314.39. **NLM** W2 GH8 K7B. **Circ** 1,500. A statistical pocket-book of Budapest; reviews yearly the development of economic and social life of the Hungarian capital.

BUDAPESTI STATISZTIKAI TAJEKOZTATO. HU. Hungarian. qt. Kozponti Statisztikai Hivatal Fovarosi Igazgatosaga, Statisztikai Kiado Vallalat II, Keleti Karoly U 18/B, Budapest Hungary. **LC** HA1208.B8.

BUDGET IN BRIEF - BUREAU OF STATISTICS AND EVALUATION. Main/Corp Pondicherry (India). Bureau of Statistics and Evaluation. English. ir. **LC** HJ66.P5.

BUDGET : STATISTICAL SURVEY. Main/Corp South Africa. **VFOAT** Begroting. SA. English and Afrikaans. ir. Government Printer, Private Bag X85, Pretoria 0001 South Africa. **LC** HC517.S7. **DD** 354.6800722.

BUILDING STATISTICS. Main/Corp Australian Bureau of Statistics. 0312-3324. **AT.** English. ir. Australian Bureau of Statistics, GPO 796, Sydney New South Wales 2001 Australia. **LC** HD9715.A8. **DD** 338.476900994. *Building Statistics, 0312-3324.*

BUILDING STATISTICS. Main/Corp Papua New Guinea. Bureau of Statistics. PP. English. ir. Bureau of Statistics, PO Wards Strip, Donedobu Papua New Guinea. **LC** HD9715.P23. **DD** 338.4769009953. *Bulletin of Building Statistics.*

BUILDING STATISTICS. Main/Corp New Zealand. Dept. of Statistics. 1976/77-. 0100-3490. NZ. English. ir. Government Bookshop, Mulgrave Street c/o Private Bag, Cubacade Wellington New Zealand. **LC** HD9715.N4. **DD** 338.47669009931. *Building and Construction Statistics.*

BUILDING STATISTICS : BUILDING APPROVALS. Main/Corp Australian Bureau of Statistics. South Australian Office. English. ir. Australian Bureau of Statistics South Australia, Prudential Building/6th Floor, 195 North TCE, Adelaide Australia. **LC** HD9715.A8. **DD** 338.47690099423. *Building Approvals, South Australia.*

BUILDING STATISTICS. NORTHERN TERRITORY. (BUILDING STATISTICS : NORTHERN TERRITORY). **Main/Corp** Australian Bureau of Statistics. 0587-5730. **AT.** English. ir. Australian Bureau of Statistics, GPO 796, Sydney New South Wales 2001 Australia. **LC** HD7382.A3. **DD** 338.476900994. *Building Statistics: Northern Territory, 0587-5730.*

BUILDING STATISTICS QUARTERLY. Main/Corp Singapore. Ministry of National Development. Research-Statistics Unit. Periodical. English. ir. $14.00. 21st Floor National Development Building, Maxwell Road, Singapore 2 Singapore. **LC** HD9715.S5. **DD** 338.47690095952.

BUILDINGS STATISTICS IN KARNATAKA STATE. Main/Corp Karnataka, India. Public Works Dept. Chief Engineer, Communications and Buildings. English. ir. Chief Engineer Communications and Buildings, Public Works Department, Central Office, 50001 Bangalori India. **LC** HD4295.M9. **DD** 338.47690095487. *Building Statistics in Karnataka State.*

BUKU MAKLUMAT PERANGKAAN GETAH BAGI MALAYSIA. Main/Corp Malaysia. Jabatan Perangkaan. **VFOAT** Rubber Statistics Handbook of Malaysia. 1967-. MY. English and Malay. an. 60.00. Department of Statistics, Publishing Section, Jalan Cenderasari, Kuala Lumpur 10-01 Malaysia. **Tel** 2922133. **LC** HD9161.M32. **DD** 338.47678209595. **Circ** 180. (ctrl). *Rubber Statistics Handbook of Malaysia.*

BUKU SAKU STATISTIK INDONESIA. VFOAT Statistical Pocketbook of Indonesia. IO. English and Indonesian. ir. 4.500.-. Biro Pusat Statistik, Jalan Dr Sumoto No 8, Jakarta Indonesia. **Tel** 372808. **LC** HA1811. **DD** 315.98. bk rev. adv acc. (ctrl). *Statistik Indonesia.*

BUKU STATISTIK PADJAK. Main/Corp Indonesia. Direktorat Perentjanaan Penerimaan Dan Penagihan. Indonesian. ir. **LC** HJ4764.

BULITIN PERANGKAAN SOSIAL MALAYSIA. VFOAT Social Statistics Bulletin, Malaysia. 1980-. English (Malay). an. $6.00. **LC** HN700.6. **DD** 306.09595. *Bulitin Perangkaan Sosial Semenanjung Malaysia.*

BULLETIN BIBLIOGRAPHIQUE - INSTITUT NATIONAL DE LA STATISTIQUE ET DES ETUDES ECONOMIQUES, DEPARTEMENT DE LA COOPERATION. Main/Corp Institut National de la Statistique et des Etudes Economiques (France). Departement de la Cooperation. No. 153- Mar./April 1973-. FR. French. ir. 29 Quai Branly, Paris 7 Eme France. **LC** Z7165.F8, HC279. **DD** 016.33096. *Bulletin Bibliographique - Institut National de la Statistique et des Etudes Economiques.*

BULLETIN - CALCUTTA STATISTICAL ASSOCIATION. (CALCUTTA STATISTICAL ASSOCIATION BULLETIN). **Main/Corp** Calcutta Statistical Association. V. 1, No. 1- Aug. 1947-. 0008-0683. Periodical. II. English. qt. $20.00. Calcutta Statistical Association, 35 Ballygunge Circle Road New Sci, Calcutta 700019 India. Ed S K Chatterjee. **Ind/Abst** Math. Rev. **LC** HA1. **NLM** HA 1 C144. **CODEN** CSTBAA. bk rev. **Circ** 345. (ctrl). Publishes articles dealing with advances and critical appraisals relating to various branches of theoretical and applied statistics and allied fields.

BULLETIN DE LA CHAMBRE SYNDICALE DE LA SIDERURGIE FRANCAISE. SERIE BLEUE. VFOAT Bulletin Statistique de la Chambre Syndicale de la Siderurgie Francaise. FR. French. ir. 5 Bis rue de Madrid, 75008 Paris France. **LC** HD9506.A1. **DD** 380.1456720212. *Bulletin de la Chambre Syndicale de la Siderurgie. Serie Bleue, Statistiques Annuelles, Commerce Exterieur.*

BULLETIN DE LA CHAMBRE SYNDICALE DE LA SIDERURGIE FRANCAISE. SERIE ROUGE. VFOAT Bulletin Statistique de la Chambre Syndicale de la Siderurgie Francaise. Serie Rouge. No. 367 (April 1961)-No. 800. FR. French. ir. le Chambre, 5 Bis rue de Madrid, Paris 8 France. **LC** HD9506.A1. **DD** 338.476720212. *Bulletin de la Chambre Syndicale de la Siderurgie. Serie Rose, Statistiques Annuelles, Production.*

BULLETIN DE LA CHAMBRE SYNDICALE DE LA SIDERURGIE FRANCAISE. SERIE VERTE, STATISTIQUES MENSUELLES. VFOAT Bulletin Statistique de la Chambre Syndicale de la Siderurgie Francaise. FR. French. ir. Societe d'Editions Siderurgie, Boite Postale 707-08, 75367 Paris Cedex 08 France. **LC** HD9510.4. **DD** 338.476720212. *Bulletin de la Chambre Syndicale de la Siderurgie Francaise. Serie Verte, Statistiques Mensuelles.*

BULLETIN DE LA CHAMBRE SYNDICALE DE LA SIDERURGIE. SERIE BLEUE, STATISTIQUES ANNUELLES, COMMERCE EXTERIEUR. FR. French. ir. Societe d'Editions Siderurgie, Boite Postale 707-08, 75367 Paris Cedex 08 France. **LC** HD9506.A1. **DD** 382.456710212.

BULLETIN DE STATISTIQUE AGRICOLE (FRANCE). Main/Corp France. Service Central des Enquetes et Etudes Statistiques. Yearly V. 14, No. 7/8- July/August 1974-. FR. French. bm. 100.00. Service Central des Enquetes et Etudes Statistiques, 5 rue Casimir Peruer, 57007 Paris France. **Ind/Abst** Foreign Lang. Index, Predicasts. **LC** S229. *Statistique Agricole.*

BULLETIN DE STATISTIQUE (BELGIUM). Main/Corp Belgium. Institut National de Statistique. **VFOAT** Statistisch Bulletin. V. 1- 1913-. 0045-1703. Periodical. BE. French and Flemish. mo. 900 Domestic, 1200 Foreign. Institut National Statistique, rue de Louvain 44, 1000 Bruxelles Belgium. **Tel** (02)513.96.50. **Ind/Abst** Foreign Lang. Index, Funk Scott Index Corp. Ind., PAIS Foreign Lang. Index. **Circ** 1,075. (ctrl). General statistics about Belgium.

BULLETIN DE STATISTIQUE (CHAD). Main/Corp Chad. Sous-Direction de la Statistique. No. 208- 1st Quarter, 1973-. CD. French. qt. Bulletin de Statistique, BP 453, Ndjamena Chad. **LC** HA2086. **DD** 330.9674304. *Bulletin de Statistique.*

BULLETIN DE STATISTIQUE - DIRECTION DE LA STATISTIQUE ET DE LA DOCUMENTATION (RWANDA). Main/Corp Rwanda. Direction de la Statistique et de la Documentation. 0304-9426. Periodical. French. ir. $7.00 Single Issue. BP 46, Kigala Rwanda. **LC** HA4695. **DD** 316.7571. *Bulletin des Statistique - Direction de l'Office General des Statistiques. Rwanda, 0557-5583.*

BULLETIN DE STATISTIQUE - DIRECTION DE LA STATISTIQUE ET DE LA DOCUMENTATION. SUPPLEMENT ANNUEL (RWANDA). Main/Corp Rwanda. Direction de la Statistique et de la Documentation. No. 1- 1974-. RW. French. an. $7.00. Direction de la Statistique et de la Documentation, BP 46, Kigali Rwanda. **LC** HA2124.R8. **DD** 316.7571.

BULLETIN DE STATISTIQUE - FEDERATION NATIONALE DU BATIMENT. Main/Corp Federation Nationale du Batiment. French. ir. 33 Avenue Kleber, Paris France 75784. **LC** HD9715.F7. **DD** 338.476240944.

BULLETIN DE STATISTIQUE - REPUBLIQUE DU NIGER, MINISTERE DU DEVELOPPEMENT ET DE LA COOPERATION, DIRECTION DE LA STATISTIQUE. Main/Corp Niger. Ministere du Developpement et de la Cooperation. Direction de la Statistique. **VFOAT** Bulletin Trimestriel de Statistique - Republique du Niger, Ministere du Developpement et de la Cooperation, Direction de la Statistique. Periodical. French. ir. 800. Compte Bceao No 1-16-13, Monsieur le Tresorier General de la Republique du Niger, Niamey Nigeria. **LC** HA2097. **DD** 316.626. *Bulletin Trimestriel de Statistique.*

BULLETIN DU STATEC (LUXEMBURG). Main/Corp Luxembourg. Service Central de la Statistique et des Etudes Economiques. V. 9, No. 7/8- July/Aug. 1963-. 0076-1583. Periodical. LU. French. ir. 680. Statistique et Etudes Economiques Statec, 19-21 Bd Royal/PO Box 304, L-2013 Luxembourg Luxembourg. **Tel** 4794-292. **Ind/Abst** Foreign Lang. Index. bk rev. (ctrl). Economic studies of statistical series and inquiries.

BULLETIN - INSTITUTE OF MATHEMATICAL STATISTICS. Main/Corp Institute of Mathematical Statistics. V. 1- Jan. 1972-. 0146-3942. Periodical. **US.** English. bm. $20.00. Institute of Mathematical Statistics, 3401 Investment Boulevard #6, Hayward CA 94545. **Tel** (415)783-8141. Ed William Guenther. **Ind/Abst** Math. Rev. **LC** QA276.A1. **DD** 519.505. **CODEN** ISMBC. adv acc. **Circ** 3,400. Carries the abstracts of all contributed papers presented at the meetings of the Institute and publishes news items of interest to mathematical statisticians and probabilists.

BULLETIN MENSUEL DE STATISTIQUE (CENTRAL AFRICAN REPUBLIC) CEASED. **Main/Corp** Central African Republic. Direction de la Statistique Generale et des Etudes Economiques. CX. French. ir. 2,000. BP 954, Bangui Central African Republic. **LC** HA2084. **DD** 316.741.

BULLETIN MENSUEL DE STATISTIQUE - DIRECTION DE LA STATISTIQUE ET DES ETUDES ECONOMIQUES (GABON). Main/Corp Gabon. Direction de la Statistique et des Etudes Economiques. Began with V. 12, No. 138, Sept. 1970. 0304-9485. French. ir. 12.00. Direction de la Statistique et des Etudes Economiques, BP 2081, Libreville Gabon. **Ind/Abst** Foreign Lang. Index. **LC** HA2090. **DD** 316.721. *Bulletin Mensuel de Statistique.*

Statistics

BULLETIN MENSUEL DE STATISTIQUE (FRANCE). Main/Corp Institut National de la Statistique et des Etudes Economiques (France). V. 1-37, Oct. 1911-Nov./Dec. 1949. Periodical. FR. French. mo. 290. INSEE-CNGP, BP 2718, 80027 Amiens Cedex France. Tel 22 92 73 22. Ind/Abst Foreign Lang. Index, Funk Scott Index Corp. Ind., PAIS Foreign Lang. Index. LC HA1213. adv acc. Indices.

BULLETIN MENSUEL DE STATISTIQUE INDUSTRIELLE (FRANCE). No. 62- April 1978-. 0429-4092. FR. French. ir. 300.00 Domestic, 360.00 Foreign. SESSI, 85 Bd du Montparnasse, 75270 Paris Cedex 06 France. Tel 556 41 08. Ind/Abst Predicasts, Funk Scott Index Corp. Ind. LC HC271. DD 338.0944. Analysis of 700 products and groups of products covering the totality of French industrial activity.

BULLETIN MENSUEL DE STATISTIQUE - INSTITUT NATIONAL DE LA STATISTIQUE (AL-MAHAD). Main/Corp Al-Mahad Al Qqwmi Lil-Ihsa. French. ir. 0.200. Ministere du Plan, Institut National de la Statistique, 31 Avenue de Paris, BP 65, Tunis Tunisia. LC HA2076. DD 316.11. Bulletin Mensuel de Statistique.

BULLETIN MENSUEL DE STATISTIQUE - MINISTERE DU PLAN, DIRECTION DE LA STATISTIQUE (TOGO). Main/Corp Togo. Ministere du Plan. Direction de la Statistique. TG. French. mo. 2000.00. Ministere du Plan, BP 118, Lome Togo. LC HA2126. DD 316.681. Bulletin Mensuel de Statistique.

BULLETIN MENSUEL DE STATISTIQUE : STATISTIQUE ET ECONOMIE (MALI (REPUBLIC)). Main/Corp Mali (Republic). Service de la Statistique Generale et de la Comptabilite Economique Nationale. Jan. 1964-. French. ir. Service de la Statistique, General et de la Comptabilite Economique National, CCP No 3746, Bamako Mali. LC HA2096. DD 316.623. Bulletin Statistique Mensuel.

BULLETIN MENSUEL DE STATISTIQUE (TOGO). Main/Corp Togo. Secretariat d'Etat a la Presidence Charge du Commerce, de l'Industrie et du Plan. Direction de la Statistique. TG. French. mo. 2,000. BP No 118, Lome Togo. LC HA2126. DD 316.681.

BULLETIN MENSUEL DES STATISTIQUES - DIRECTION DE LA STATISTIQUE ET DE LA COMPTABILITE ECONOMIQUE (CONGO (BRAZZAVILLE)). Main/Corp Congo (Brazzaville). Direction de la Statistique et de la Comptabilite Economique. Periodical. CG. French. mo. $18.10. Brazzaville Republique Populaire du Congo, Vice-Presidente du Conseil d'Etat, Commissariat General au Plan, Direction de la Statistique et de la Compatabilite Economique, Boite Postal 2031, Braze Congo. Ind/Abst Foreign Lang. Index, PAIS Foreign Lang. Index. LC HA2088. DD 316.724. Bulletin Mensuel de Statistique.

BULLETIN MENSUEL DES STATISTIQUES DU TRAVAIL. SUPPLEMENT (PARIS, FRANCE : 1982). See Economics - Labor.

BULLETIN MENSUEL D'INFORMATION STATISTIQUE ET ECONOMIQUE. Main/Corp Institut National de la Statistique et de la Demographie. UV. French. ir. 6.000. Institut National de la Statistique et de la Demographie, BP 374, Ouagandougou Upper Volta. LC HA2100. DD 330.9662505. Bulletin Mensuel d'Information Statistique et Economique.

BULLETIN MENSUEL DU COMMERCE EXTERIEUR DE L'UNION ECONOMIQUE BELGO-LUXEMBOURGEOISE. Main/Corp Institut National de Statistique (Belgium). VFOAT Maandelijks Bulletin Over de Buitenlandse Handel van de Belgisch-Luxemburgse Economische Unie. 1948. Periodical. BE. Dutch and French. mo. 2.249 Domestic, 2.600 Foreign. Institut National de Statistique, rue de Louvain 44, 1000 Bruxelles Belgium. Tel 02/513 96 50. Ind/Abst Foreign Lang. Index. LC HF203. DD 382.09493. Circ 400. (ctrl). Import and exports. Bulletin Mensuel du Commerce avec les Pays Etrangers.

BULLETIN OF CROP AND LIVESTOCK STATISTICS. 1976-. English. ir. Statistics Section, Planning Division, Ministry of Agriculture, PO Box 9192, Dar es Salaam Tanzania. LC HD9017.T3. DD 338.109678. Bulletin of Crop Statistics.

BULLETIN OF LABOUR STATISTICS. VFOAT Bulletin des Statistiques du Travail. 1st Quarter, 1965-. 0007-4950. Periodical. US. English (issued also in French and Spanish, 1965-). qt. $39.90. ILO Publications, International Labour Office, CH-1211 Geneva 22 Switzerland. Tel (202)376-2315. Ind/Abst Int. Labour Doc. LC HD4826. DD 331.0212. Articles on methodology and special topics. Includes results of a detailed annual inquiry into wages, hours of work and consumer prices. International Labour Review.

BULLETIN OF STATISTICS - OFFICE OF PLANNING AND STATISTICS, OFFICE OF THE HIGH COMMISSIONER. Main/Corp Pacific Islands (Trust Territory). Office of the High Commissioner. Office of Planning and Statistics. VFOAT Quarterly Bulletin of Statistics. V. 1- Dec. 1977-. English. qt. $1.50 Single Issue. Office of Planning and Statistics Office of the High Commissioner, Saipan Mariana Islands TT 96950. LC HA4010.5. DD 319.65.

BULLETIN OF STATISTICS RELATING TO THE MINING INDUSTRY OF MALAYSIA. Main/Corp Malaysia. Kementerian Pertanian dan Tanah. MY. English. qt. $2.54. Jalan Gurney, Kuala Lumpur Mines Department, Selangor Malaysia. Tel 929797. LC HD9506.M36. DD 338.209595. Circ 150. (ctrl). Includes statistics relating to the mining industry, number of mines, production, employment and power. Does not include petroleum.

BULLETIN OF STATISTICS - THAILAND. CENTRAL STATISTICAL OFFICE. Main/Corp Thailand. Samnakngan Sathiti Klang. V. 1-11, No. 2. Periodical. TH. English (Siamese). qt. National Statistical Office, Larn Luang Road, Bangkok 10100 Thailand 1407-244. Tel 2818618. Circ 1,200. (ctrl). Covers climate, population and vital statistics, production transport and communication, and external price list.

BULLETIN OF THE INTERNATIONAL STATISTICAL INSTITUTE. (BULLETIN DE L'INSTITUT INTERNATIONAL DE STATISTIQUE). VFOAT Bulletin of the International Statistical Institute. Vol. 1, No. 1, 2nd Ed. (1886). 0074-8609. US. English (French, German, and Italian). be. 150. International Statistical Institute, 428 Prinses Beatrixlaan, Voorburg The Netherlands. Tel 70-694341. Ind/Abst Math. Rev. LC HA11. NLM W1 BU539T. CODEN BIISAR. Circ 4,000. Proceedings of the biennial session, all papers presented.

BULLETIN ON MOTOR VEHICLE STATISTICS. 1978-. English. sa. Department of Census and Statistics, PO Box 563, Colombo 7 Sri Lanka. LC HE5689.8. DD 354.54930087834.

BULLETIN - REPUBLIQUE DU BURUNDI, SECRETARIAT GENERAL A LA PRESIDENCE CHARGE DU BUREAU TECHNIQUE D'ETUDES, DEPARTEMENT DES ETUDES ET STATISTIQUES. Main/Corp Burundi. Secretariat General a la Presidence Charge du Bureau Technique d'Etudes. Departement des Etudes et Statistiques. French. qt. Republique du Burundi, B P 1 156, Bujumbura Burundi. LC HA4696. DD 316.7572. Bulletin de Statistique.

BULLETIN STATISTIQUE DE LA DGAC. VFOAT Bulletin Statistique de la D.G.A.C. 0181-1517. FR. French. an. Service des Transports Aeriens SDEEP, Bureau Statistiques, 246 rue Lecourbe, 75732 Paris Cedex 15 France. Bulletin Statistique de la Direction Generale a l'Aviation Civile.

BULLETIN STATISTIQUE - DIRECTION GENERALE DE L'ENSEIGNEMENT COLLEGIAL. (BULLETIN STATISTIQUE : RECHERCHE ET DEVELOPPEMENT). 0229-0766. Periodical. CN. French. Gouvernement du Quebec, 600 St Amable 4E Etage, Quebec G1R 4Z1 Canada. DD 378.1059714.

BULLETIN STATISTIQUE DU SECRETARIAT GENERAL A L'AVIATION CIVILE (FRANCE). Main/Corp France. Secretariat General a l'Aviation Civile. 0302-8607. French. ir. Secretariat General a l'Aviation Civile, 246 rue Lecourbe, Paris France. LC HE9848.A1. DD 387.70944.

BULLETIN TRIMESTRIEL DE STATISTIQUE (DJIBOUTI. DIRECTION NATIONALE DE LA STATISTIQUE). (BULLETIN TRIMESTRIEL DE STATISTIQUE). No. 32 (4th Quarter 1981)-. French. qt. 500 Single Issue. Direction Nationale de la Statistique, BP 1846, Republique de Djibouti. LC HA2108. DD 330.96771005. Bulletin de Statistique et de Documentation (Djibouti. Ministere du Commerce, des Transports et du Tourisme).

BULLETIN TRIMESTRIEL DE STATISTIQUES - DIRECTION DES STATISTIQUES ET DE LA COMPTABILITE NATIONALE. Main/Corp Algeria. Mudiriyat Al-Ihsaat Wa-Al-Muhasabah Al-Wataniya. VFOAT Nashrah Al-Fasliyah Lil-Ihsaat. New Series, Jan./Mar. 1975-. AE. French. qt. Direction des Statistiques et de la Comptabilite Nationale, Chemin IBN-Badis Al-Mou IZ El-Biar, Alger Algeria. LC HA2071. DD 316.5. Bulletin Trimestriel de Statistiques - Direction des Statistiques.

BULLETIN - UNITED STATES. BUREAU OF JUSTICE STATISTICS. See Sociology: General Works, Theory - Social Pathology, Welfare, Criminology.

BULLETIN - UNITED STATES. BUREAU OF LABOR STATISTICS. (BULLETIN). VFOAT Bulletin of the Bureau of Labor Statistics. No. 612 (July 1935)-. 0082-9021. Monographic Series. US. English. US Department of Labor, Bureau of Labor Statistics, Washington DC 20212. LC HD8051. DD 331.0973. (cum index). Bulletin of the United States Bureau of Labor Statistics.

BUSINESS STATISTICS, NEW YORK STATE. Jan./Mar. 1977-. US. English. ir. Quarterly Summary of Business Statistics, New York State.

BUSINESS STATISTICS, NEW YORK STATE. ANNUAL SUMMARY (ALBANY, N.Y. : 1977). (BUSINESS STATISTICS, NEW YORK STATE. ANNUAL SUMMARY). Began with 1977. 0197-3193. US. English. an. New York State Department of Commerce, 99 Washington Avenue, Albany NY 12210. LC HC107.N7. DD 330.9747005. Annual Summary of Business Statistics, New York State.

BUSINESS STATISTICS, NEW YORK STATE. QUARTERLY SUMMARY. Jan./Mar. 1977-. 0197-3185. Periodical. US. English. qt. New York State Department of Commerce, 99 Washington Avenue, Albany NY 12245. LC HA544. DD 330.9747005. Quarterly Summary of Business Statistics, New York.

BUSINESS STATISTICS (UNITED STATES. BUREAU OF ECONOMIC ANALYSIS). (BUSINESS STATISTICS). Began with 1951. 0083-2545. US. English. be. US Government Printing Office, Superintendent of Documents, Washington DC 20402. Statistical Supplement to the Survey of Current Business.

CAA ANNUAL STATISTICS CEASED. Main/Corp Great Britain. Civil Aviation Authority. VAT Civil Aviation Authority Annual Statistics. UK. English. an. LC HE9843.A1. DD 387.70941.

CAB AIR CARRIER TRAFFIC STATISTICS. VFOAT C.A.B. Air Carrier Traffic Statistics. VAT Civil Aeronautics Board Air Carrier Traffic Statistics. Nov. 1980-. 0731-3411. Periodical. US. English. mo. US Government Printing Office, Superintendent of Documents, Washington DC 20402. Ind/Abst Am. Stat. Index. LC HE9803.A1. DD 387.740973. Air Carrier Traffic Statistics (United States. Civil Aeronautics Board. Data Systems Management Division. Financial Section), 0098-0404.

LES CAHIERS DE L'ANALYSE DES DONNEES. VFOAT Analyse des Donnees. 1. Yearly- 1976-. 0339-3097. Periodical. FR. French (summaries in English). qt. $57.20. Centrale des Revues-Dunod, 11 rue Gossin, 92543 Montrouge Cedex France. Tel (1)43 20 15 50. Ed J Benzecri. Ind/Abst GeoRef, Energy Res. Abstr. Index in last issue of volume - attached. bk rev. adv acc. Circ 900. This journal publishes results of specific studies, statistics and programmes designed for data analysis.

CAHIERS ECONOMIQUES. See Economics.

CALIFORNIA ALMANAC. See Yearbooks, Almanacs, Directories.

CALIFORNIA CHILDREN SERVICES INFORMATION AND STATISTICS FOR FISCAL YEARS . . . . US. English. State of California, Department of Health Services, B A Myers Director, 714/744 P Street, Sacramento CA 95814. LC RJ102.5.C2. DD 362.198920009794.

CALIFORNIA CRIPPLED CHILDREN SERVICES STATISTICAL REPORT. VFOAT Statistical Report - Crippled Children Services. 1971/75-. 0190-1591. Periodical. US.

Statistics

English. an. California Children Services Program, 714 P Street/Room 323, Sacramento CA 95827. **Tel** (916)322-2090. **Ed** James N Creeger. **NLM** W2 AC2 B905C. **Circ** 2,000. Program description and statistics for two fiscal years. Statistics are by diagnosis (summary) and by county and state for California. *California Public Health Statistical Report.*

CALIFORNIA LIBRARY STATISTICS. 1983-. 0741-031X. US. English. an. California State Library, PO Box 2037, Sacramento CA 95809. **LC** Z732.C2. **DD** 027.0794. *California Library Statistics and Directory, 0148-4583.*

CALIFORNIA LIBRARY STATISTICS AND DIRECTORY CEASED. 1976-1982. 0148-4583. US. English. an. **LC** Z732.C2. **DD** 0210025794.

CALIFORNIA LIVESTOCK STATISTICS. Main/Corp California Crop and Livestock Reporting Service. 1973-. 0361-9095. US. English. California Crop and Livestock Reporting Service, PO Box 1258, Sacramento CA 95806. **LC** SF13.C3. **DD** 338.176009794. *California Livestock and Poultry Report.*

CALIFORNIA STATISTICAL ABSTRACT. See Indexes/Abstracts.

CANADIAN BANKS STATISTICAL REVIEW. 1983-. 0824-0949. CN. English. an. $45.00 Per Vol. Canadian Bond Rating Service, 1600 Dorchester Boulevard West Suite 610, Montreal Quebec H3H 1P9 Canada. **DD** 332.10971.

CANADIAN CITIZENSHIP STATISTICS. VFOAT Statistique de la Cititennete Canadienne, Statistiques de la Citoyennete Canadienne, Statistique Concernant la Citoyennete Canadienne. 1952-. 0575-8033. CN. English (French). an. 70.00. **LC** JL187. **DD** 323.60971.

CANADIAN FISHERIES. ANNUAL STATISTICAL REVIEW. VFOAT Peches Canadiennes. Vol. 12 (1979)-. CN. English (French). Fisheries & Oceans Department, Communication Director, 200 Kent Street, Ottawa Ontario K1A 0E6 Canada. **Tel** (613)993-0600. **Circ** 1,000. (ctrl). Statistical information on the commercial activities of Canadian fisheries, giving breakdown of quantity and value of catch statistics, exports, imports, and employment. *Annual Statistical Review of Canadian Fisheries.*

CANADIAN FISHERIES ANNUAL STATISTICAL REVIEW. (ANNUAL STATISTICAL REVIEW, CANADIAN FISHERIES). VAT Peches Canadiennes. Revue Statistique Annuelle. Vol. 12 (1979)-. 0713-2158. CN. English (French). an. **LC** SH223. **DD** 338.3727092071. *Annual Statistical Review of Canadian Fisheries, 0382-2249.*

CANADIAN FORESTRY STATISTICS. Main/Corp Canada. Statistics Canada. Forestry Section. VFOAT Statistiques Forestieres du Canada. 1970-. 0575-805X. CN. English (text also in French). an. Receiver General for Canada, Statistics Canada, Ottawa Ontario K1A 0T6 Canada. *Canadian Forestry Statistics, 0575-805X.*

CANADIAN JOURNAL OF STATISTICS. (THE CANADIAN JOURNAL OF STATISTICS). VFOAT Revue Canadienne de Statistique. V. 1- Dec.? 1973-. 0319-5724. Periodical. CN. English (includes some text in French). sa. $46.43. Canadian Journal of Statistics, 675 Denbury Avenue, c/o D F Bray, Ottawa Ontario K2A 2P2 Canada. **Tel** (613)993-7570. **Ed** Donald L McLeish. **Ind/Abst** Math. Rev., Public Aff. Inf. Serv. Bull. bk rev. adv acc. **Circ** 1,250. (ctrl). Publishes original work in the theory and application of statistics in the social physical, biological and engineering sciences.

CANADIAN MEDICAL EDUCATION STATISTICS. VFOAT Statistiques Relatives a l'Enseignement Medical au Canada. 1977/78-. 0225-9451. CN. English (French). an. 18.00. Association of Canadian Medical Colleges, 151 Slater Street, Ottawa Ontario K1P 5H3 Canada. **Tel** (613)237-0070. **Ed** E Ryten. **DD** 610.71171. **NLM** W 18 C213. **Circ** 300. Statistics on enrollment, graduation, admissions, fees, post-MD. residency training, of Canadian Medical Schools.

CANADIAN PLASTICS STATISTICAL YEAR BOOK. See Yearbooks, Almanacs, Directories.

CANADIAN STATISTICAL REVIEW. V. 23- Jan. 1948-. 0008-509X. CN. English. mo. $7.00. Statistics Canada, Publications Distribution, Ottawa Ontario K1A 0T6 Canada. **Ind/Abst** Can. Bus. Index, Public Aff. Inf. Serv. Bull. **LC** HA741. **DD** 330.9710644. *Monthly Review of Business Statistics.*

CANADIAN STATISTICAL REVIEW. ANNUAL SUPPLEMENT TO SECTION 1. (CANADIAN STATISTICAL REVIEW. ANNUAL SUPPLEMENT TO SECTION 1 : SELECTED ECONOMIC INDICATORS). **Main/Corp** Statistics Canada. Current Economic Analysis Division. VFOAT Revue Statistique du Canada. Supplement Annuel de la Section 1 : Certains Indicateurs Economiques. V. 16- 1976-. 0705-5765. CN. English (French). an. $1.05. Canadian Statistical Review, 23 MR H Coats Building, Statistics Canada, Ottawa Ontario K1A 0T6 Canada. **LC** HA741. **DD** 330.97106.

CANADIAN STATISTICAL REVIEW. WEEKLY SUPPLEMENT. VFOAT Revue Statistique du Canada. Supplement Hebdomadaire. Mar. 10, 1948-. 0300-0273. CN. English. wk. **Tel** (800)268-1151. **LC** HA745. **DD** 317.1. Summarizes Canadian economic indicators and statistics showing monthly and quarterly figures for most recent two years. Data is entirely derived from CANSIM.

CANADIAN UNDERWRITER. ANNUAL STATISTICAL REVIEW. Began publication in 1934. 0317-1264. CN. English. an. $13.93. Wadham Publications Ltd, 109 Vanderhoof au Suite 101, Toronto Ontario M4G 2J2 Canada. **DD** 368.971.

CANCER MORTALITY STATISTICS. 0748-7762. US. English. **LC** RC277.T4. **DD** 614.5999. *Cancer Mortality Statistics by County, 0196-2973.*

CANNED FOOD PACK STATISTICS. 0069-018X. US. English. an. $20.00. Tech S Corporation, 1133-20th Street NW, Washington DC 20036. **LC** HD9321.4. **DD** 338.476640280973.

CAPITAL EXPENDITURE AND DEBT FINANCING STATISTICS. 1981-82-. 0263-2985. UK. English. an. 15.00. The Director CIPFA/Statistical Information Service, 1 Buckingham Place, London SW1E 6HS England. **LC** HA741. **DD** 336.343141. *Return of Outstanding Debt as at 31st March . . . .*

CAPITAL INTERNATIONAL PERSPECTIVE (MONTHLY). See Business - Banking & Finance.

CAPITAL PUNISHMENT. See Sociology: General Works, Theory - Social Pathology, Welfare, Criminology.

CARDAMOM STATISTICS (INDIA). Main/Corp India. Cardamon Board. English. ir. Government of India Cardamon Board, Chittoor Road, Cochin India 682018. **LC** HD9210.I5. **DD** 338.17383.

CARIBBEAN TOURISM STATISTICAL REPORT. English. an. Caribbean Tourism Research and Development Centre, Mer Vue Marine Gardens, Christ Church Barbados. **LC** G155.C35. **DD** 380.1459172904520212. *Caribbean Tourism Statistics.*

CARLOAD WAYBILL STATISTICS. 1969-. 0360-4586. US. English. an. Also available on microform.

CASELOAD STATISTICAL REPORT ... FOR SUPREME COURT OF ALABAMA, COURT OF CRIMINAL APPEALS, COURT OF CIVIL APPEALS, CIRCUIT COURTS, DISTRICT COURTS. US. English. an. Administrative Office of Courts, 917 South Court Street, Montgomery AL 36104. **LC** KFA510. **DD** 347.76101, 347.61071.

CASELOAD STATISTICS. STATE VOCATIONAL REHABILITATION AGENCIES. (CASELOAD STATISTICS : STATE VOCATIONAL REHABILITATION AGENCIES). **Main/Corp** United States. Rehabilitation Services Administration. Division of Program Data and Analysis. Office of Administrative Support. 1977/78-. 0566-0009. US. English. an. Department of Health Education and Welfare, Office of Human Development Services, Rehabilitation Services Administration, 330 C Street Southwest, Washington DC 20201. **LC** HD7256.U5. **DD** 362.85. *Caseload Statistics: State Vocational Rehabilitation Agencies, 0566-0009.*

CASH DISPENSERS AND AUTOMATED TELLERS. (CASH DISPENSERS AND AUTOMATED TELLERS : STATISTICAL DATA AND ANALYSIS WITH SELECTED CASE HISTORIES). Began with Vol. for 1972. 0148-5423. US. English. an. Linda Fenner Zimmer, Payment Services Correspondent, 80 Lawn Street, Park Ridge NJ 07656. **LC** HG1616.E7. **DD** 658.89332120973.

CATALOG OF PUBLICATIONS OF THE NATIONAL CENTER FOR HEALTH STATISTICS. Main/Corp National Center for Health Statistics (U.S.). **Series/Titl** DHHS Publication. 1980-. 0278-4912. US. English. an. National Center for Health Statistics, Scientific and Technical Information Branch, 3700 East-West Highway, Hyattsville MD 20782. *Current Listing and Topical Index to the Vital and Health Statistics Series, 0092-7287.*

CATALOGO DE INFORMACOES. Main/Corp Sao Paulo (Brazil : State). Fundacao Sistema Estuadual de Analise de Dados. 1981-. Portuguese. ir. Fundacao Sistema Estadual de Analise de Dados, Caixa Postal 8223, 01033 Sao Paulo SP Brazil. **LC** HA37.B88. **DD** 016.318161.

CATALOGO DE SERIES ESTADISTICAS - INE. Main/Corp Instituto Nacional de Estadisticas (Chile). Spanish. ir. **LC** HA993.

CATALOGUE OF STATISTICAL DATA IN THE PROGRAM REFERENCE CENTRE. (CATALOGUE OF STATISTICAL DATA IN THE PROGRAM REFERENCE CENTER). **Main/Corp** Indian and Inuit Affairs Program (Canada). Program Reference Centre. VFOAT Catalogue de Donnees Statistiques du Centre de Reference du Programme. 11 (Mar. 1978)-. 0707-106X. CN. English (text in French, each with special t.p. and separate paging. French text on inverted pages). an. Free. Program Reference Centre, North Tower/15th Floor, Les Terrasses de la Chaudiere, 10 Wellington Street, Hull Quebec Canada. **LC** Z1209.2.C2, E78.C2. **DD** 018. *Catalogue of Data in the Statistical Information Centre, 0317-8226.*

CATALOGUE OF STATISTICAL INFORMATION ON PAPUA NEW GUINEA. Main/Corp Papua New Guinea. Bureau of Statistics. English. ir. Bureau of Statistics, PO Box 2032, Konedobu Papua New Guinea. **LC** HA37. **DD** 016.3195.

CAUSES OF DEATH. AUSTRALIAN BUREAU OF STATISTICS. TASMANIAN OFFICE. Main/Corp Australian Bureau of Statistics. Tasmanian Office. AT. English. ir. Bureau of Statistics, Tasmanian Office, 188 Collins Street, Hobart Australia. **LC** RA407.5.A8. **DD** 312.209946. **NLM** W2 KA8.1 T2B9C.

CAUSES OF DEATH (BRISBANE, QUEENSLAND). (CAUSES OF DEATH). English. an. 2.10. Australian Bureau of Statistics, Ground Floor Statistics House, 345 Ann Street, Brisbane Queensland 4000 Australia. **Tel** (07)222 6351. **NLM** W2 KA8 B9C. All deaths by cause of death, age group, and sex; deaths of infants under one year by cause, age at death, and sex; death of males and females showing age-specific rates, proportions, and crude death rates for selected causes. *Statistics of the State of Queensland for the Year . . . Part A, Population and Vital.*

CAUSES OF DEATH. BULLETIN. AUSTRALIAN BUREAU OF STATISTICS. (CAUSES OF DEATH). **Main/Corp** Australian Bureau of Statistics. No. 9- 1972-. 0067-0766. AT. English. an. Australian Government Publishing Co, PO Box 84, Canberra Australian Capital Territory 2600 Australia. **Tel** (062) 95 4411. **LC** RA407.5.A8. **DD** 312.20994. **NLM** W2 KA8 B9C. *Causes of Death.*

CBS BIJDRAGEN TOT DE STATISTIEKEN BETREFFENDE DE KAPITAALGOEDERENVOORRAAD ORRAAD. VFOAT C.B.S. Bijdragen tot de Statistieken Betreffende de Kapitaalgoederenvoorraad. 1981-. Dutch (summaries in English). an. 28.65. Staatsuitgeverij, The Hague Netherlands.

CBS JAARSTATISTIEK VAN DE BEVOLKING. VFOAT C.B.S. Jaarstatistiek van de Bevolking. 1981-. NE. Dutch (summaries in English). an. 26.70. Staatsuitgeverij, The Hague Netherlands. **LC** HA1381. *Jaaroverzicht Bevolking en Volksgezondheid.*

CE.D.R.E.S. DOCUMENTI. See Economics - Economics: Land.

CEGB STATISTICAL YEARBOOK. Main/Corp Central Electricity Generating Board. 1964-. 0577-0777. UK. English. an. The Board, Courtney House 18 Warwick Lane, London EC4P England. **LC** WMLC L 83/441.

CEMETERIES AND CREMATORIA STATISTICS ... ACTUALS. 1981-82-. 0263-2969. UK. English. an. Chartered Institute of Public Finance and Accountancy, 1 Buckingham Place, London SW1E 6HS England. **LC** RA630.G73. **DD** 363.75. *Crematoria Statistics, Cemeteries Statistics . . . Actuals.*

Statistics

CENSO AGROPECUARIO; VIII RECENSEAMENTO GERAL. See Agriculture.

CENSUS OF DISTRIBUTION (NEW ZEALAND). Main/Corp New Zealand. Dept of Statistics. 0110-4632. NZ. English. ir. Department of Statistics, Private Bag, Wellington New Zealand. **Tel** 729 119. Statistics show purchases, stocks, sales and other information helpful in evaluating developments in retail trade, wholesale trade and services. *Census of Distribution*.

CENSUS OF MANUFACTURING ESTABLISHMENTS. DETAILS OF OPERATIONS AND SMALL AREA STATISTICS, TASMANIA. 0157-2156. AT. English. an. 2.80. Australian Bureau of Statistics, Commonwealth Government Centre/3rd Floor, 188 Collins Street, Hobart Tasmania 7000 Australia. **Tel** (002)20 9439. **LC** HD9738.A83. **DD** 338.476709946. Details of operations by industry class and subdivision, statistical division and local government area - number of establishments, type of employment, average employment, wages and salaries paid, etc. *Economic Censuses Manufacturing Establishments, Details of Operations and Small Area Statistics*.

CENSUS OF MANUFACTURING SERIES B. CANTERBURY, OTAGO, SOUTHLAND STATISTICAL AREAS. VFOAT Canterbury, Otago, Southland Statistical Areas. US. English. Department of Statistics, Private Bag, Wellington New Zealand. **LC** HD9738.N46. **DD** 338.47000993155.

CENSUS OF MINING ESTABLISHMENTS: INDUSTRY CONCENTRATION STATISTICS, AUSTRALIA. Main/Corp Australian Bureau of Statistics. AT. English. ir. Australian Bureau of Statistics, PO Box 84, Canberra Australian Capital Territory 2600 Australia. **Tel** (062)52 6778. **LC** HD9506.A7. **DD** 338.826220994. Statistics relating to industry concentration concerned with providing measures of the extent to which a few firms are dominant in individual industries.

CENTRAL EXCISE STATISTICS; QUARTERLY BULLETIN. Main/Corp India (Republic). Statistics and Intelligence Branch (Central Excise). II. English. qt. Government of India, Ministry of Works and Housing, Department of Publ Civil Lines, New Delhi 111054 India.

CHA STATISTICAL REPORT. Main/Corp Chicago Housing Authority. 1974-. US. English. an. Chicago Housing Authority, 22 West Madison Street, Chicago IL 60602. **LC** HD7304.C4. **DD** 363.50977311. *Annual Statistical Report - Chicago Housing Authority*.

CHARACTERISTICS OF DOCTORAL SCIENTISTS AND ENGINEERS IN THE UNITED STATES. DETAILED STATISTICAL TABLES. Series/Titl Surveys of Science Resources Series. 1979-. 0734-6468. US. English. be. National Science Foundation, Washington DC 20550. **LC** Q149.U5. **DD** 331.129150973. **NLM** W2 A N37C. Vols. for (1981-) distributed to depository libraries in microfiche. *Characteristics of Doctoral Scientists and Engineers in the United States. Technical Notes and Detailed Statistical Tables*.

CHARITY STATISTICS. UK. English. an. Charities Aid Foundation, 48 Pembury Road, Tonbridge Kent TN9 2JD England.

CHESA TONGGYE YONBO. See Yearbooks, Almanacs, Directories.

CHIFFRES POUR L'ALSACE. 1-. 0395-8191. Periodical. FR. French. qt. INSEE-CNGP, BP 2718, 80027 Amiens Cedex France. *Bulletin Regional de Statistique : ALSAE (Bas-Rhin, Haut-Rhin)*.

CHIIKI TOKEI TEIYO. 1975-. JA. Japanese. ir. Kokuritsu Kokkai Toshokan Chosa Oyobi Rippo Kosakyoku, 10-1 Nagatacho 1, Chiyoda-Ku 100 Tokyo Japan. **LC** HA1844.

CHILD ABUSE AND NEGLECT STATISTICS. Fiscal Year 1981-. US. English. an. Department of Children and Family Services, One North Old State Capitol Plaza, Springfield IL 62706. **LC** HV742.I3. **DD** 362.7044.

CHINA : INTERNATIONAL TRADE. ANNUAL STATISTICAL SUPPLEMENT. (CHINA, INTERNATIONAL TRADE. ANNUAL STATISTICAL SUPPLEMENT). 0739-3512. US. English. an. Documents Expediting Project, Exchange and Gift Division, Library of Congress, Washington DC 20540. **LC** HF3831.5. **DD** 382.095100212. Vols. for (1983-) distributed to depository libraries in microfiche.

CHINA'S CUSTOMS STATISTICS QUARTERLY. VFOAT Chung-Kuo Hai Kuan Tung Chi. 1983.1 (June 1983)-. Periodical. English (Chinese). qt. 80.00. Economic Information and Agency Hong Kong, 342 Hennessy Road, Hong Kong Hong Kong. **Tel** 5-738217. **Circ** 2,000. Provides statistical information on import and export commodities of China. Import and export value by commodities, and country.

CHOLGANG TONGGYE. VFOAT Monthly Steel Statistics. KO. Korean (English). mo. Hanguk Cholgang Hyophoe, 51-8 Susong-Dong, Chongno-Ku Seoul Korea. **LC** HD9526.K6.

CHOLTO TONGGYE YONBO. See Yearbooks, Almanacs, Directories.

CHONGI KONGSAOP TONGGYE CHARYO. See Yearbooks, Almanacs, Directories.

CHUNG-HUA MIN KUO TAI-WAN TI CHU, CHIN JUNG TUNG CHI YUEH PAO. VFOAT Financial Statistics Monthly, Taiwan District, The Republic of China. July 1978-. Periodical. Chinese (English). mo. **LC** HG187.T28. *Republic of China, Taiwan Financial Statistics Monthly*.

CHUNG-KUO TUNG CHI NIEN CHIEN. Chinese. an. $80.00. Hsiang-Kang Ching Chi Tao Pao, She 342 Hsuan Ni Shih Tao, Hsing-Kan China. **LC** HA4631. **DD** 315.1.

CHUYO KYONGJE CHIPYO. VFOAT Major Statistics of Korean Economy. English (Korean). ir. **LC** HC466. *Chuyo Kyongje Chipyo*.

CISLA PRO KAZDEHO. 0578-3208. Periodical. CS. Czech. an. Technicke Literatury, VA Smeckach 30, Praha 1 Czechoslovakia. **LC** HA1191.

CITRUS FRUIT INDUSTRY STATISTICAL BULLETIN. Main/Corp Sunkist Growers, Inc. Information Systems Dept. 0362-014X. US. English. ir. Sunkist Growers Inc, 14130 Riverside Drive, Sherman Oak CA 91423. **LC** HD9259.C54. **DD** 338.17430973.

CIVIL AVIATION STATISTICS OF THE WORLD. 1st- Ed. CN. English. an. International Civil Aviation Organization, c/o Distribution Officer, PO Box 400/Succursal Place de l'Aviation Internatinal, 1000 Sherbrooke Street West, Montreal Quebec H3A 2R2 Canada. **LC** HE9762.5. **DD** 387.70212.

CIVIL JUDICIAL STATISTICS. Main/Corp Great Britain. Lord Chancellor's Departments. UK. English. an. Her Majestys Stationery Office, PO Box 276, London SW8 5DT England. **LC** KD327. **DD** 347.41013.

CIVILIAN MANPOWER STATISTICS. Began with Aug. 1980. 0882-8857. Periodical. US. English. qt. Superintendent of Documents, US Government Printing Office, Washington DC 20402. **Ind/Abst** Am. Stat. Index. *Department of Defense Civilian and Military Personnel, OSD-JCS and Other Defense Activities*.

CNC STATISTIQUES. VFOAT C.N.C. Statistiques. V. 21 (1974)-. FR. French. an. Centre National de la Cinematographie, 12 rue de Lubeck, 75784 Paris France. **LC** PN1993.5.F7. **DD** 384.80944. *Statistiques du Cinema Francais*.

COAL AND COKE STATISTICS. VFOAT Statistique du Charbon et du Coke. V. 51- Jan. 1972-. 0380-6847. Periodical. CN. English and French. mo. Receiver General for Canada, Statistics Canada Publications, Ottawa Ontario K1A 0T6 Canada. *Coal and Coke Statistics for Canada, 0829-9781*.

COASTWISE SHIPPING STATISTICS (ANNUAL). (COASTWISE SHIPPING STATISTICS). VFOAT Statistiques du Cabotage. VAT Statistiques du Cabotage (Edition Annuelle). 1978-. 0225-1507. CN. English (French). an. Receiver General of Canada, Statistics Canada Publications, Ottawa Ontario K1A 0T6 Canada. **Tel** (613)996-9159. **LC** HE769. **DD** 387.5440971. *Shipping Report, Part III, Shipping Report*.

COASTWISE SHIPPING STATISTICS (QUARTERLY). (COASTWISE SHIPPING STATISTICS). Vol. 1, No. 1 (1st Quarter 1981)-. 0228-4405. CN. English (French). qt. $24.00 Domestic, $28.80 Foreign. Publication Sales and Services, Statistics Canada, Ottawa Ontario K1A 0V7 Canada. **LC** HE769. **DD** 387.5440971021. *Shipping Statistics, 0527-6160*.

COCONUT STATISTICS. English. an. $60.00. United Coconut Philippines Inc, 941 Josefa Llanes Escoda Street, Ermita Manila Phillipines. **Tel** 50-54-54. Ed Leonardo F Ignacio Jr. bk rev. adv acc. **Circ** 1,000. (ctrl). Statistics pertinent to the coconut industry in the Philippines and elsewhere. World oils/fats production, imports, exports, prices, Philippine coco trade directory, current policies related to industry.

COFFEE STATISTICS - (INDIA). Main/Corp India (Republic). Coffee Board. VFOAT Coffee in India. 1954/55-. 0536-7093. Periodical. English. ir. **LC** HD9199.I4.

COLLECTIONS DE L'INSEE. (LES COLLECTIONS DE L'INSEE). Main/Corp Institut National de la Statistique et des Etudes Economiques (France). No.1- May 1969-. 0533-0777. FR. French (summaries in English and Spanish). ir. 2280. Institut National de la Statistique et des Etudes Economiques, 18 Boulevard Adlophe Pinard, 75675 Paris Cedex 14 France. **Tel** 22 92 73 22. **LC** HC271. adv acc. Deomographic accounts and planning and employment, enterprises, households, and regions.

LES COLLECTIONS DE L'INSEE. SERIE C : COMPTES ET PLANIFICATION. Main/Corp Institut National de la Statistique et des Etudes Economiques (France). VFOAT Comptes et Planification. Monographic Series. FR. French. ir. Dawson France, BP 40, 91 Palaiseau France. **Ind/Abst** Foreign Lang. Index.

COLLECTIONS DE L'INSEE. SERIE E : ENTREPRISES. Main/Corp Institut National de la Statistique et des Etudes Economiques (France). VFOAT Collections E. No. 1-. Monographic Series. French (summaries in English and Spanish). ir. **Ind/Abst** Foreign Lang. Index.

COLLECTIVE BARGAINING. STATISTICS IN EDUCATION. (COLLECTIVE BARGAINING : STATISTICS IN EDUCATION). V. 1, No. 29- Sept. 1974-. 0700-5121. Periodical. CN. English. wk. $45. H L Willis & Associates, 33 Bloor Street East, Toronto Ontario M4W 3H1 Canada. **DD** 331.890413711009713. *Collective Bargaining in Education, 0700-5113*.

COLORADO COUNTY AND CITY RETAIL SALES BY STANDARD INDUSTRIAL CLASSIFICATION. See Business - Commerce.

COLORADO INSURANCE INDUSTRY STATISTICAL REPORT. 0277-9595. US. English. an. $5.00. Department of Regulatory Agencies Division of Insurance, 303 West Colfax, Suite 500, Denver CO 80204. **Tel** (303)573-3410. **LC** HG8101.C6. **Circ** 250. (ctrl). Insurance operations in Colorado for calendar year and division operations for fiscal year. *Insurance Industry in Colorado, Statistical Report, 0361-6568*.

COLORADO SKI AND WINTER RECREATION STATISTICS. Began with Vol. for 1966. 0147-5746. US. English. University of Colorado, Business Research Division, Campus Box 450, Boulder CO 80309. **LC** GV854.5.C6. **DD** 796.909788.

THE COMMERCIAL AND FINANCIAL CHRONICLE. 0163-2876. Periodical. US. English. wk. $237.00. National News Service Inc, 4 Water Street, Arlington MA 02174. **Tel** (617)643-7900. Ed John Dunne. **Ind/Abst** Manage. Contents, Predicasts. **LC** HG1. **DD** 332.63205. adv acc. **Circ** 910. A compendium of stocks and bond activity compiled from leading stock exchanges around the country. *Commercial and Financial Chronicle. Statistical Section, 0163-058X*.

COMMERCIAL AND INDUSTRIAL FLOORSPACE STATISTICS, ENGLAND. Began with: No. 9 (1977-1980). UK. English. an. Her Majesty's Stationery Office, 49 High Holborn, London WC1V 6HB England. **LC** HD1393.5. **DD** 658.230941. *Commercial and Industrial Floorspace Statistics, England and Wales*.

COMMERCIAL AND INDUSTRIAL FLOORSPACE STATISTICS, WALES. 0262-5334. English. an. 5. Economic And Statistical Services, 1B Welsh Office New, Crown Building, Cathays Park Cardiff CF1 3NQ Wales England. **Tel** (0222)825087. Ed E Swires-Hennessy. **LC** HD1393.5. **DD** 333.38. **Circ** 300. Contains detailed information, including gross and percentage changes for the latest year and since 1974, presented by counties, statistical sub-divisions and districts for seven non-domestic, use classes.

Statistics

COMMITMENTS AND RELEASES : ANNUAL STATISTICAL REPORT. **VFOAT** Annual Statistical Report. US. English. an. **LC** HV9475.M8. **DD** 365.609778.

COMMODITY TRADE STATISTICS. Series **Corp** United Nations.*Statistical Office.*Statistical Papers. 1951-. 0010-3233. Periodical. US. English. ir. United Nations Publications, Sales Section/Room A-3315 New York NY 10017. **Tel** (212)754-8302. **LC** HA13.

COMMONWEALTH RAILWAYS FINANCIAL AND STATISTICAL BULLETIN. **Main/Corp** Australia. Railways Commissioner. AT. English. ir. Australian Government Publishing Service, PO Box 84, Canberra 2600 Australia. **LC** HE3461. **DD** 385.10994.

COMMUNICABLE DISEASE STATISTICS. Series/Titl Series MB2. 1979-. UK. English. an. Her Majesty's Stationery Office, 49 High Holborn, London XC1V 6HB England. **LC** RA643.7.G7. **DD** 312.390942. *Statistics of Infectious Diseases.*

COMMUNICATIONS IN STATISTICS. SIMULATION AND COMPUTATION. (COMMUNICATIONS IN STATISTICS : SIMULATION AND COMPUTATION). **VFOAT** Simulation and Computation. V. B5- 1976-. 0361-0918. Periodical. US. English. bm. $185.00. Marcel Dekker Inc, PO Box 11305 Church Street Station, New York NY 10016. **Ed** D B Owen. **Ind/Abst** Electron. Commun. Abstr. J., ISMEC Bull., Int. Aerosp. Abstr., Bull. Signal., Comput. Control Abstr., Curr. Contents, Phys. Chem. Earth Sci., Curr. Index Stat., Curr. Pap. Phys., Electr. Electron. Abstr., Sci. Abstr. Sect. A. Phys. Abstr., Phys. Briefs, Sci. Cit. Index, Abr. Ed., Stat. Theory Method Abstr., Math. Rev. **LC** QA276.A1. **DD** 591.505. **CODEN** CSSCDB. bk rev. adv acc. *Communications in Statistics, 0090-3272.*

COMMUNICATIONS IN STATISTICS. STOCHASTIC MODELS. Vol. 1, No. 1-. 0882-0287. Periodical. US. English. ty. $90.00. Marcel Dekker Inc, PO Box 11305, Church Street Station, New York NY 10249. **Ed** Marcel F Neuts. **DD** 519. bk rev. adv acc.

COMMUNICATIONS IN STATISTICS. THEORY AND METHODS. (COMMUNICATIONS IN STATISTICS : THEORY AND METHODS). V. A5-. 0361-0926. US. English. $655.10. Marcel Dekker Inc, PO Box 11305 Church Street Station, New York NY 10249. **Ed** D B Owens. **Ind/Abst** Electron. Commun. Abstr. J., ISMEC Bull., Pollut. Abstr. Indexes, Saf. Sci. Abstr. J., GeoRef, Comput. Control Abstr., Electr. Electron. Abstr., Sci. Abstr. Sect. A. Phys. Abstr., Sci. Cit. Index, Abr. Ed., Math. Rev. **LC** QA276.A1. **DD** 519.505. **CODEN** CSTMDC. bk rev. adv acc. *Communications in Statistics, 0090-3272.*

COMMUNIQUE HEBDOMADAIRE (INSTITUT NATIONAL DE STATISTIQUE (BELGIUM) : 1982). (COMMUNIQUE HEBDOMADAIRE). 0771-0410. Periodical. BE. Dutch (French). wk. 650 Domestic, 870 Foreign. rue de Louvain 44, 1000 Bruxelles Belgium. **Tel** (02)513.96.50. **LC** HA1393. **Circ** 500. (ctrl). General statistics about Belgium. *Communique Hebdomadaire (Institut National de Statistique (Belgium) : 1963).*

COMMUNIQUE HEBDOMADAIRE. WEEKBERICHT CEASED. **Main/Corp** Belgium. Institut National de Statistique. **VFOAT** Weekbericht. Periodical. BE. Flemish and French. wk. 650 Domestic, 870 Foreign. Institut National de Statistiques, rue de Louvaine 44, 1000 Bruxelles Belgium. **Tel** (02)513.96.50. **Circ** 650. (ctrl). General statistics about Belgium.

COMMUTER AIR CARRIER TRAFFIC STATISTICS. 0270-448X. US. English. sa. Civil Aeronautics Board, Distribution Section B-22B, Washington DC 20428. **LC** HE9803.A1. **DD** 387.710973.

COMPARABLE COMMODITY STATISTICS OF PRODUCTION, IMPORTS AND EXPORTS, AUSTRALIA. **Main/Corp** Australian Bureau of Statistics. AT. English. an. $2.07. Australian Bureau of Statistics, Government Office Box 796, Sydney New South Wales 2001 Australia. **Tel** 268-4111. **LC** HD9738.A8. **DD** 338.0994.

COMPARATIVE FINANCIAL & STATISTICAL DATA, PUPIL TRANSPORTATION, NEW JERSEY PUBLIC AND PRIVATE SCHOOLS. **Main/Corp** New Jersey. State Dept. of Education. Division of Finance and Regulatory Services. US. English. an. **LC** LB2864. **DD** 371.87209749. *Comparative Financial and Financial Data on Pupil Transportation, New Jersey Public and Private Schools.*

COMPARATIVE MOTOR VEHICLE TRAFFIC ACCIDENT STATISTICS IN CITIES OF 5,000 POPULATION AND OVER. Periodical. US. English. sa. Department of Public Works & Buildings, Bureau of Traffic, Springfield IL 62706. **LC** HE5614.3.I4. **DD** 312.4409773.

COMPARATIVE SAFETY STATISTICS IN OPERATIONS OF U.S. SCHEDULED AIRLINES. **Main/Corp** United States. Civil Aeronautics Board. US. English. an. **LC** TL553.5. **DD** 629.13255.

COMPARATIVE STATEMENT OF ESTIMATES AND STATISTICS ON NARCOTIC DRUGS FOR . . . . Series **Corp** United Nations. Document. **VFOAT** Estado Comparativo de las Previsiones y las Estadisticas de Estupefacientes Facilitadas Para . . . por los Gobiernos en Cumplimiento de los Tratados Internacionales, Etat Comparatif des Evaluations et des Statistiques sur les Stupefiants Fournies pour . . . . US. English, French and Spanish. an. $6.00. United Nations Publications, Sales Section Room A3315, New York NY 10017. **Tel** (212)754-8302. **LC** JX1977, HV5800. **DD** 300.8 S, 362.293. Contains information on movement of narcotic drugs and their production from raw materials to the consumption of the finished products.

COMPENDIO DE ESTADISTICAS SOCIALES. **VFOAT** Compendio Estadisticas Sociales. 1979-. PR. Spanish. ir. $2.00. Junta de Planificacion, Division de Finanzas, Centro Gubernamental Minillas, Edificio Norte, Santurce Puerto Rico 00940. **LC** HA901. **DD** 317.295. *Compendio Estadisticas Sociales.*

COMPENDIO ESTADISTICO. **Main/Corp** Instituto Nacional de Estadisticas (Chile). 1971-. CL. Spanish. an. $10.00. Republica de Chile, Ministerio de Economia, Fomento Resconstruccion, Instituto Nacional Estadistic, Santiago Chile 31133384. **LC** HA991.

COMPENDIO STATISTICO ITALIANO. 1927-. 0301-8628. Italian. ir. 1500. Istituto Central di Statistica, Via Cesare Balbo 16, Roma 00100 Italy. **LC** HA1362. **NLM** W2 GI8 I5C.

COMPENDIUM OF HOUSING STATISTICS - (UNITED NATIONS). **Main/Corp** United Nations. Statistical Office. **VFOAT** Recueil des Statistiques de l'Habitation. 1st- Ed. US. English (French). $31.00. United Nations Publications, Sales Section/Room A 3315, New York NY 10017. **Tel** (212)754-8302. **LC** JX1977, HD7287. **DD** 300.8 S, 301.540212. Includes data on population, dwelling construction, costs of housing and building, land use and environmental pollution.

COMPENDIUM OF LOCAL GOVERNMENT AREA STATISTICS. 0157-2067. English. ir. Australian Bureau of Statistics, Tasmanian Office, 188 Collins Street, Hobart Tasmania. **LC** HA3113. **DD** 319.46. *Compemdium of Municipal Statistics.*

COMPENDIUM OF STATISTICS FOR PAPUA NEW GUINEA. **Main/Corp** Australia. Dept. of External Territories. Statistics Section. 1971-. 0084-9111. AT. English. ir. Australia Department of External Territories, Statistics Section, Canberra Australian Capital Territory 2600 Australia. **LC** HA4007.R3. **DD** 319.5.

COMPENDIUM OF UNIVERSITY STATISTICS. **VFOAT** Compendium de Statistique Concernant les Universites. 1983-. 0826-2292. CN. English (French). an. Free. Association of Universities and Colleges of Canada, 151 Slater Street, Ottawa Ontario K1P 5N1 Canada. **LC** LA417.5. **DD** 378.71. (ctrl).

COMPUTATIONAL STATISTICS & DATA ANALYSIS. **VFOAT** Computational Statistics and Data Analysis. Vol. 1, No. 1 (March 1983)-. 0167-9473. Periodical. English. qt. Elsevier Science Publishers, PO Box 211, 1000 AE Amsterdam Netherlands. **Tel** (020)5803.911. **Ind/Abst** Math. Rev., Electron. Commun. Abstr. J., ISMEC Bull., Pollut. Abstr. Indexes, Saf. Sci. Abstr. J., Comput. Control Abstr., Electr. Electron. Abstr., Sci. Abstr. Sect. A. Phys. Abstr. **LC** QA276.A1. **DD** 519.505. **CODEN** CSDADW.

CONCISE STATISTICAL YEARBOOK OF POLAND. See Yearbooks, Almanacs, Directories.

CONCRETE PIPE INDUSTRY STATISTICS. **Main/Corp** American Concrete Pipe Association. 1974-. 0360-2877. US. English. an. $3.50. American Concrete Pipe Association, 1501 Wilson Boulevard, Arlington VA 22209. **LC** TP885.P5. **DD** 621.8672.

CONFERENCE BOARD STATISTICAL BULLETIN. (STATISTICAL BULLETIN). V. 3, No. 10- Oct. 1970-. 0010-5554. US. English. mo. Conference Board, 845 Third Avenue, New York NY 10022. **Ind/Abst** Predicasts. **LC** HC101. **DD** 339.0973. *Conference Board Statistical Bulletin, 0010-5554.*

CONNECTICARD ANNUAL STATISTICAL REPORT. Mar. 1982 through Feb. 1983-. US. English. an. Interlibrary Loan Center, Connecticut State Library, Hartford CT 06106. **LC** Z713.5.U6. **DD** 025.62. *Connecticard Semi-Annual Statistical Report.*

CONNECTICUT STATE DEPARTMENT OF MENTAL HEALTH FACILITIES. INPATIENT STATISTICS. (CONNECTICUT STATE DEPARTMENT OF MENTAL HEALTH FACILITIES : INPATIENT STATISTICS). **Main/Corp** Connecticut. Dept. of Mental Health. Statistics Section. 0147-0523. US. English. an. Connecticut State Department of Mental Health, 90 Washington Street, Hartford CT 06115. **LC** RC445. **DD** 362.209746.

CONNECTICUT'S PRIVATE MENTAL HOSPITALS : INPATIENT STATISTICS FOR YEAR ENDING . . . . **VFOAT** Private Mental Hospitals, Inpatient Statistics. US. English. an. Statistics Section, Connecticut State Department of Mental Health, 90 Washington Street, Hartford CT 06115. **LC** RC445.C78. **DD** 362.2109746.

CONSTRUCTION PRICE STATISTICS. MONTHLY BULLETIN. (CONSTRUCTION PRICE STATISTICS). **Main/Corp** Statistics Canada. Prices Division. **VFOAT** Statistiques des Prix de la Construction. V. 1- Nov. 1974-. 0319-8243. Periodical. CN. English (French). mo. Receiver General for Canada, Statistics Canada Publications, Ottawa Ontario K1A 0T6 Canada. *Construction Price Statistics.*

CONSTRUCTION STATISTICS YEARBOOK. See Yearbooks, Almanacs, Directories.

CONTAINERIZED CARGO STATISTICS. Began with 1972. 0099-2429. US. English. an. US Department of Transportation Maritime Administration, 400 7th Street SW, Washington DC 20590. **LC** HE597.U6. **DD** 387.544. Vols. for 1980-1982 distributed to depository libraries in microfiche.

CONTINUING EDUCATION FOR THE HEALTH PROFESSIONS, STATISTICAL REPORT. **VFOAT** Statistical Report: Continuing Education for the Health Professions. 1974/75-. 0162-2366. Periodical. US. English. **NLM** W1 CO775QE.

CORPORATION FINANCIAL STATISTICS. **VFOAT** Statistique Financiere des Societes. 1965-. 0575-8262. CN. English (French). an. Receiver General for Canada, Statistics Canada Publications, Ottawa Ontario K1A 0T6 Canada. **LC** HG4090. **DD** 338.740971.

CORPORATION TAXATION STATISTICS. **Main/Corp** Canada. Statistics Canada. Business Finance Division. **VFOAT** Statistique Fiscale des Societes. 1971-. 0576-0119. CN. English (French). an. Receiver General for Canada, Statistics Canada Publications, Ottawa Ontario K1A 0T6 Canada. **LC** HJ4662.A7. **DD** 336.2430971. *Corporation Taxation Statistics, 0576-0119.*

LA COTE D'IVOIRE EN CHIFFRES. **VFOAT** Annuaire Statistique de la Cote d'Ivoire. 1975-. French. ir. Societe Africaine d'Edition, Passage Leblanc, B P 1877, Dakar 6 Ivory Coast. **LC** HC547.I8. **DD** 316.668.

COTTON PRICE STATISTICS. Publication began with Vol. 53, No. 8, Mar. 1972. 0010-9827. Periodical. US. English. mo. US Department of Agriculture, Agricultural Marketing Service, Cotton Division, 4841 Summer Avenue, Memphis TN 38122. **Ind/Abst** Am. Stat. Index. **LC** HD9093.U4. **DD** 338.13. *Cotton Price Statistics, 0010-9827.*

THE COTTON STATISTICS MONTHLY. No. 1 (Jan. 1964)-. 0574-2374. Periodical. English. mo. *Cotton Statistical Journal.*

COTTON : WORLD STATISTICS. **VFOAT** Coton : Statistiques Mondiales, Algodon : Estadisticas Mundiales. Periodical. US. English. qt. **Tel**

Statistics

(202)463-6660. **Ind/Abst** World Text Abstr., Predicasts. *Cotton : Quarterly Statistical Bulletin.*

COUNTDOWN; CANADIAN NURSING STATISTICS CEASED. 1967-1974. 0070-1238. CN. English. an. Canadian Nurses Association, 50 The Driveway, Ottawa Ontario K2P 1E2 Canada. **DD** 331.761610730971. **NLM** W1 CO965.

COUNTY AND CITY DATA BOOK. 1st Ed. (1949)-. 0082-9455. US. English. ir. Superintendent of Documents, US Government Printing Office, Washington DC 20402. **LC** HA202. **DD** 317.3. **NLM** W2 A B9CO. *Statistical Abstract of the United States. Cities Supplement. County Data Book.*

COURT STATISTICS, TASMANIA. 1980-. English. an. Australian Bureau of Statistics, Tasmanian Office, 10th Floor, Commonwealth Government Centre, 188 Collins Street, Box 66-A, Hobart 7001 Australia. **DD** 345.94600212, 349.460500212. *PUBLIC JUSTICE, TASMANIA.*

CRIMINAL STATISTICS, ENGLAND AND WALES. SUPPLEMENTARY TABLES. VOL. 1, PROCEEDINGS IN MAGISTRATES' COURTS. VFOAT Proceedings in Magistrates' Courts. 1980-. UK. English. an. '18.75. Home Office, Horseferry House Dean Rule Street, London SW1 P2AW England. **LC** HA1131. **DD** 312.460942.

CRIMINAL STATISTICS, ENGLAND AND WALES. SUPPLEMENTARY TABLES. VOL. 3, TABLES BY POLICE FORCE AREAS AND SOME COURT AREAS. VFOAT Tables by Police Force Areas and Some Court Areas. 1980-. UK. English. an. 18.75. Home Office, Horseferry House/Dean Rule Street, London SW1 P2AW England. **LC** HA1131. **DD** 312.460942.

CRIMINAL STATISTICS. SCOTLAND. (CRIMINAL STATISTICS, SCOTLAND). **Main/Corp** Scotland. Scottish Home and Health Dept. 0307-6717. UK. English. an. 65. Her Majestys Stationery Office, Scottish Home and Health Department, 13 A Castle Street, Edinburgh EH2 Scotland. **LC** HA1154. **DD** 364.9411. *Statistics Relating to Police Apprehensions and Criminal Proceedings.*

LA CRIMINALITE EN FRANCE EN . EN. . . D'APRES LES STATISTIQUES DE POLICE JUDICIAIRE. Began in 1972. French. ir. **LC** HV6966. **DD** 364.944.

CULTURE STATISTICS : CENTRALIZED SCHOOL LIBRARIES IN CANADA CEASED. **Main/Corp** Canada. Statistics Canada. Cultural Institutions Section. VFOAT Statistiques de la Culture: Bibliotheques Scolaires Centralisees au Canada. 1st- Issue. CN. English (French). Statistics Canada, Publications Distribution, Ottawa Ontario K1A 0T6 Canada. **LC** Z735.A1. **DD** 027.80971.

CULTURE STATISTICS. FILM INDUSTRY. 1st issue (1978)-. 0227-4000. CN. English (French). an. $6.00 Domestic, $7.20 Foreign. Publication Sales & Services, Statistics Canada, Ottawa Ontario K1A OV7 Canada. **LC** PN1993.5.C2. **DD** 384.80971.

CULTURE STATISTICS. GOVERNMENT EXPENDITURES ON CULTURE IN CANADA. (CULTURE STATISTICS, GOVERNMENT EXPENDITURES ON CULTURE IN CANADA). VFOAT Government Expenditures on Culture in Canada, Titre de la Culture au Canada, Statistiques de la Culture, Depenses Publiques au Titre de la Culture au Canada. 1976-77-. 0709-406X. CN. English (French in parallel columns). an. Receiver General for Canada, Statistics Canada Publications, Ottawa Ontario K1A 0T6 Canada. **Tel** (800)268-1151.

CULTURE STATISTICS, NEWSPAPERS AND PERIODICALS. VFOAT Newspapers and Periodicals, Journaux et Periodiques, Statistiques de la Culture, Journaux et Periodiques. 1976-1977-. 0706-7518. Periodical. CN. English (French in parallel columns). an. Receiver General for Canada, Statistics Canada Publications, Ottawa Ontario K1A 0T6 Canada. Presents information on Canada's newspapers and periodicals. Also presents some information on the workings of these media: their revenues, their expenses and the pattern of ownership and control.

CULTURE STATISTICS. PERFORMING ARTS. (CULTURE STATISTICS, PERFORMING ARTS). VFOAT Statistiques de la Culture, les Arts d'Interpretation. 1976-. 0706-2621. CN. English (French). an. Receiver General for Canada, Statistics Canada Publications, Ottawa Ontario K1A 0T6 Canada. Statistics on performing companies: theatre, music, opera and dance. Also data on attendances.

CULTURE STATISTICS. PUBLIC LIBRARIES IN CANADA. (CULTURE STATISTICS, PUBLIC LIBRARIES IN CANADA). VFOAT Public Libraries in Canada, Statistiques de la Culture, Bibliotheques Publiques au Canada. 1st Issue (1975)-. 0704-884X. CN. English (French). ir. $6.35 Domestic, $7.60 Foreign. Publication Sales and Services, Statistics Canada, Ottawa Ontario K1A 0T6 Canada. **LC** Z735.A1. **DD** 027.471. *Public Libraries in Canada, 0317-4921.*

CULTURE STATISTICS. RADIO AND TELEVISION CEASED. (CULTURE STATISTICS, RADIO AND TELEVISION). VFOAT Statistiques de la Culture, Radio et Television. 1978-. 0225-915X. CN. English (French in parallel columns). an. Receiver General for Canada, Statistics Canada Publications, Ottawa Ontario K1A 0T6 Canada. **Tel** (800)268-1151. **LC** PN1992.3.C3. **DD** 384.540971.

CULTURE STATISTICS. RECORDING INDUSTRY CEASED. (CULTURE STATISTICS, RECORDING INDUSTRY). VFOAT Statistiques de la Culture, l'Industrie de l'Enregistrement. 1st issue (1978)-. 0228-3077. CN. English (French). an. Receiver General for Canada, Statistics Canada Publications, Ottawa Ontario K1A 0T6 Canada. **Tel** (800)268-1151. **DD** 338.477899120971.

CURRENT ECONOMIC STATISTICS. Main/Corp Fiji. Bureau of Statistics. FJ. English. qt. $8.00. Fiji Government Printing & Statistics Department, PO Box 98, Suva Fiji. **LC** HC687.F5. **DD** 330.99611.

CURRENT HOUSING REPORTS. SERIES H-111, HOUSING VACANCIES. VACANCY RATES AND CHARACTERISTICS OF HOUSING IN THE UNITED STATES, ANNUAL STATISTICS. VFOAT Housing Vacancies. US. English. an. Superintendent of Documents, US Government Printing Office, Washington DC 20402.

CURRENT INDEX TO STATISTICS. See Indexes/Abstracts.

CURRENT TREND REVIEW. 0362-4269. US. English. 1500 SE 3rd Court/Suite 101, 23441. **LC** HA214. **DD** 309.173092.

DADES BALEARS. 1980-. Spanish. an. Conselleria d'Economia I Hisenda, Service d'Estadistica I Informatica, C Palau Reial 1, Palma de Mallorca-1 Spain. **LC** HA1558.B3. **DD** 314.675.

DADOS ESTATISTICOS DA MOVIMENTACAO DE CARGA E PASSAGEIROS. VFOAT Dados Estatisticos da Navegacao. Portuguese. ir. Av P Vargas 41 CX Postal 1068, Belem Brazil. **LC** HE563.B8.

DADOS ESTATISTICOS : PRODUTOS AGRO PECUARIOS SAIDOS DE MATO GROSSO. Main/Corp Acordo de Classificacao no Estado de Mato Grosso. Periodical. Portuguese. ir. Presidente Marques, Departamento de Estatistica, 559 Brazil. **LC** HD9014.B83.

DAFTAR PENERBITAN PENERBITAN BIRO PUSAT STATISTIK. See Bibliographies.

DAIRY MARKET STATISTICS, ANNUAL SUMMARY. 1974-. 0098-6690. US. English. an. US Department of Agriculture, Agricultural Marketing Service, Washington DC 20250. **LC** HD9275.U3. **DD** 338.1770973. *Dairy Market Statistics, 0091-2123.*

DALGETY FARMERS' ANNUAL WOOL DIGEST. See Textiles.

DATA ON VIETNAM ERA VETERANS. See Military Science.

DATA STATISTIK TEH. Main/Corp Pusat Penelitian Dan Pengembangan Perdagangan. Indonesian. ir. **LC** HD9198.I52.

DATA USER EDUCATION & TRAINING ACTIVITIES. Main/Corp United States. Bureau of the Census. Data User Services Division. VAT Data User Education and Training Activities. 0147-7064. US. English. Commerce Department, Bureau of the Census, Washington DC 20233. **LC** HA35. **DD** 001.433.

DATA USER NEWS. Began with V. 10, No. 1 (Jan. 1975). 0096-9877. Periodical. US. English. mo. Superintendent of Documents, Government Printing Office, Washington DC 20402. **Tel** (202)783-3238. **Ind/Abst** Predicasts, Am. Stat. Index, Index U.S. Gov. Period., Funk Scott Index Corp. Ind. **LC** HA203. **DD** 001.422. *Small-Area Data Notes, 0565-1239.*

DATAMAP. VFOAT Data Map. 1983-. 0264-7745. US. English. Longman Inc, 1560 Broadway, New York NY 10036. **LC** Z7552, HA1. **DD** 016.31.

DATEN ZUR SOZIALSTRUKTUR : DIE MATERIELLE LEBENSSICHERUNG. Main/Corp Statistisches Landesamt Baden-Wurttemberg. **Series/Titl** Statistik Von Baden-Wurttemberg. German. ir. 9.00. Statistisches Landesamt Baden-Wurttemberg, 7000 Stuttgart 1 Postfach 898, Stuttgart West Germany. **LC** HA1320.B2, HC287. B2.

DATEN ZUR UMWELT. Main/Corp Statistisches Landesamt Baden-Wurttemberg. **Series/Titl** Statistik von Baden-Wurttemberg. 1977-. Periodical. German. ir. 10.00. Statistisches Landesamt Baden-Wurttemberg, 7000 Stuttgart 1 Postfach 898, Stuttgart West Germany. **LC** HA1320.B2, TD789. G72B3.

DATOS ESTADISTICOS - EMPRESA NACIONAL DE ENERGIA ELECTRICA. Main/Corp Empresa Nacional de Energia Electrica. Departamento de Planificacion Economica. Spanish. ir. **LC** HD9685.H83.

DDARSAKER.HOVEDTABELLER. Main/Corp Norway. Statistisk Sentralbyra. **Series/Titl** Norges Offisielle Statistikk. VFOAT Causes of Death.Main Tables. 1964-. 0550-032X. NO. Norwegian (English). ir. Statistisk Sentrabyra, PO Box 8131 Dep, Oslo 1 Norawy. **LC** HA1501, RA407.5.N. **DD** 314.81 S, 312.209481. **NLM** W2 GN6 S6D. *HelestatistikkK. Health Statistics.*

DEATHS. Main/Corp Australian Bureau of Statistics. AT. English. ir. Australian Bureau of Statistics, PO Box 84, Collector of Publications, Canberra Australian Capital Territory 2600 Australia. **LC** HB1505. **DD** 312.20994. *Deaths.*

DELAVCI V ZDRUZENEM DELU. Series/Titl Rezultati Raziskovanj. Slovenian. ir. Zavod Sr Slovenije Za Statistiko, Vozarski Pot 12, Ljubljana Yugoslavia.

DELEGACIJE OSNOVNIH SAMOUPRAVNIH ORGANIZACIJA I ZAJEDNICA I SKUPSTINE DRUSTVENO-POLITICKIH ZAJEDNICA. Main/Corp Savezni Zavod za Statistiku (Yugoslavia). VFOAT Delegations of Basic Self-Managing Organizations and of Communities and Assemblies of Socio-Political Communities. YU. Serbo-Croatian. ir. $30.00. Savezni Zavod za Statistiku, Kneza Milosa 20, Beograd Yugoslavia. **LC** HA1631, JN9670.

DELTION STATISTIKE DEMASION OIKONOMIKON. VFOAT Statistical Bulletin of Public Finance. V. 16, 1st Quarter of 1974. 0256-3592. Periodical. GR. Greek, Modern (English). qt. 16.00. National Statistical Service of Greece, 14-16 Lycourgou Street, Athens Greece. **Tel** 3244-746. **Circ** 1,000. Includes data on public finance, i.e. state revenue on expenditures, investments, etc. *Meniaien Deltion Statistikes Demosion Oikonomikon. Monthly Statistical Bulletin of Public Finance.*

DEMOGRAFISCHE GEGEVENS. Main/Corp Rotterdam. Gemeentelijk Bureau Voor Onderzoek en Statistiek. NE. Dutch. an. Gemeentelijk Bur Voor Onder- Zoek En Stat, Postbus 70018, 3000 KX Rotterdam Netherlands. **LC** HA1388.R6.

DEMOGRAPHIC STATISTICS. Main/Corp Jamaica. Dept. of Statistics. JM. English. an. $3.32. Department of Statistics, 9 Shallowfield Road, Kingston 5 Jamaica. **LC** HA891. **DD** 312.097292.

DEMOGRAPHIC YEARBOOK. See Yearbooks, Almanacs, Directories.

DESCRIPTIVE LIST OF PUBLICATIONS AS AT 30 SEPTEMBER . . . . Main/Corp New Zealand. Dept. of Statistics. 1980-. English. an. Free. Enquiries Section, Information Services Division, Department of Statistics, Wellington New Zealand. **Tel** 729-119. **LC** Z7554.N5, HA3173. **DD** 016.31931. A list of official publications that are issued by the department of statistics.

DETAILED MORTALITY STATISTICS, SOUTH CAROLINA. Series/Titl Annual Vital Statistics Series; V. 2. VFOAT Detailed Mortality Statistics, S.C. 1979-. 8755-2744. US. English. an. Office of Vital Records and Public Health Statistics/

Statistics

South Carolina Department of Health and Environmental Control, 2600 Bull Street, Columbia S C 29201. **Tel** (803)758-5511. **LC** RA407.4.S57. **DD** 614.42757021. **Circ** 200. Vital statistics for S.C. (mortality data).

DETAILED STATISTICAL DATA FOR OHIO PUBLIC LIBRARIES. 0160-2705. US. English. an. 65 Front Street, Columbus OH 43215. **LC** Z732.O5. **DD** 027.4771.

DETAILPRISER. Main/Corp Denmark. Danmarks Statistik. 0417-0164. Periodical. Dutch. qt. 50. Danmarks Statistik, Sejrogade 11 Postbox 2550, DK-2100 Copenhagen Denmark. **Tel** (01)29 82 22. **Circ** 775. Average prices for 41 local municipalities collected for 81 items of the Danish consumer price indices. *Detailpriser.*

DEVELOPMENT STATISTICS OF THE PUNJAB. Began in 1972. English. ir. 2 Begum Road, Lahore Pakistan. **LC** HA1730.5.Z9. **DD** 309.15491405. *Development Statistics of Punjab, Sind, N.W.F.P. and Baluchistan.*

DEVELOPMENTS IN STATISTICS. V. 1-. 0163-3384. Periodical. US. English. ir. Academic Press, 4805 Sand Lake Road, Orlando FL 32887. **Tel** (305)345-4100. Ed Paruchuri R Krishnaiah. **Ind/Abst** Math. Rev. **LC** QA276.A1. **DD** 519.505.

DIGEST OF ANNUAL STATISTICS. Main/Corp Hong Kong Tourist Association. Research Dept. English. ir. Hong Kong Tourist Association, Realty Building/Connaught Road PO Box 2597, Hong Kong. **LC** G155.H63. **DD** 338.4791512504.

DIGEST OF CURRENT ECONOMIC STATISTICS, AUSTRALIA. AT. English. mo. Australian Bureau of Statistics, PO Box 84, Canberra Australian Capital Territory 2600 Australia. **Tel** (062)52 6778. **LC** HC601. **DD** 330.994005. A selection of latest available information on the following: production, stocks, foreign trade, retail sales and instalment credit, new capital expenditure by enterprises, etc. *Digest of Current Economic Statistics (Canberra, A.C.T.).*

DIGEST OF EDUCATION STATISTICS. 1962-. Periodical. US. English. an. US Department of Health, Education and Welfare, Education Division, National Center for Education Statistics, Washington DC 20402. *Digest of Educational Statistics.*

DIGEST OF ENVIRONMENTAL POLLUTION AND WATER STATISTICS. No. 3 (1980)-. UK. English. 9.80. Her Majestys' Stationery Office Government Bookshops, 49 High Holborn, London WC1V England. **LC** TD186.5.G7. **DD** 363.7320941. *Water Data, Digest of Environmental Pollution Statistics.*

DIGEST OF PRICE STATISTICS. Began with Vol. for 1976. NR. English. ir. Government Printer, Ministry of Local Government and Information, Printing and Stationery Division, Ibadan Oyo State Nigeria. **LC** HB235.N53. **DD** 338.52096692.

DIGEST OF STATISTICS (INTERNATIONAL CIVIL AVIATION ORGANIZATION). (DIGEST OF STATISTICS - INTERNATIONAL CIVIL AVIATION ORGANIZATION). **VFOAT** Recueil de Statistiques - Organisation de l'Aviation Civile Internationale. Monographic Series. CN. English (French, Russian and Spanish). ir. International Civil Aviation Organization, PO Box 400/1000 Sherbrook Street West, Montreal Quebec H3A 2R2 Canada. **Tel** (514)285-8162. **LC** TL720.A1. **DD** 387.740212. *Digest of Statistics.*

DIGEST OF STATISTICS, NORTHERN IRELAND. Main/Corp Northern Ireland. Dept. of Finance. Statistics and Economics Unit. UK. English. sa. 1.50 Single Issue. H M Stationery Office, 80 Chichester Street, Belfast BT1 4OY Northern Ireland. **LC** HA1138.N6. **DD** 314.16.

DIGEST OF TOURISM STATISTICS. 1980-. BB. English. an. $1.00. Barbados Statistical Service, National Insurance Building, Fairchild Street, Bridgetown Barbados. **LC** G155.B27. **DD** 380.1459172981040212. *Digest of Tourist Statistics.*

DIGEST OF TOURIST STATISTICS. Main/Corp British Tourist Authority. UK. English. 4.00. British Tourist Authority, 64 Sainte James's Street, London SW1A 1NF England. **LC** G155.G7. **DD** 338.47914100212.

DIGEST OF UNITED KINGDOM ENERGY STATISTICS. Main/Corp Great Britain. Dept. of Energy. 1974-. 0307-0603. UK. English. an. Her Majestys Stationery Office, PO Box 276, London SW8 5DT England. **Tel** 01-622 3316. **LC** HD9551.4. **DD** 333.80941. *Digest of Energy Statistics, 0533-8921.*

DIMENSIONS ECONOMIQUES DE LA BOURGOGNE. May 1971-. Periodical. FR. French. mo. 80. INSEE-Cite Administrative Delaborde, BP 1509, 21035 Dijon Cedex France. **Tel** (80)433145. **LC** HA1228.B8. bk rev. **Circ** 1,500. (ctrl). Statistic, economic, and social studies of Burgundy. *Bulletin de Statistique: Bourgogne (Cote-Dor, Nievre, Saone-et-Loire, Yonne), Franche-Comte (Doubs, Jura, Haute-Saone, Territoire de Belfort).*

DIMENSIONS ON DELAWARE; A STATISTICAL ABSTRACT. See Indexes/Abstracts.

DIRECT LABOUR ORGANISATIONS STATISTICS . . . ACTUALS. 1981-82-. UK. English. an. 15.00. CIPFA, 1 Buckingham Place, London SW1E 6HS England.

DIRECTION OF TRADE STATISTICS - INTERNATIONAL MONETARY FUND. (DIRECTION OF TRADE STATISTICS). Jan. 1981-. 0252-306X. Periodical. US. English. mo. $12.00. International Monetary Fund, 700 19th Street NW, Washington DC 20431. **Tel** (202)477-7000. **LC** HF1016. **DD** 382.0212. *Direction of Trade (Monthly), 0012-3226.*

DIRECTION OF TRADE STATISTICS. YEARBOOK - INTERNATIONAL MONETARY FUND. See Yearbooks, Almanacs, Directories.

DIRECTORY OF FEDERAL STATISTICAL DATA FILES. See Yearbooks, Almanacs, Directories.

DIRECTORY OF FEDERAL STATISTICS FOR LOCAL AREAS. A GUIDE TO SOURCES. URBAN UPDATE. See Yearbooks, Almanacs, Directories.

DIRECTORY OF MEMBERS - INTERNATIONAL ASSOCIATION OF SURVEY STATISTICIANS. See Yearbooks, Almanacs, Directories.

DIRECTORY OF PROGRAMS IN STATISTICS AND RELATED AREAS IN CANADIAN UNIVERSITIES. See Yearbooks, Almanacs, Directories.

DIRECTORY OF THE BUSINESS RESEARCH ADVISORY COUNCIL TO THE BUREAU OF LABOR STATISTICS. See Yearbooks, Almanacs, Directories.

DISTRICT STATISTICAL HANDBOOK - (INDIA). Main/Corp Bihar, India (State). District Statistical Office, Monghyr. 0523-3456. II. English. ir. District Statistical Office, Patna India.

DOD STATISTICAL REPORT ON THE MILITARY RETIREMENT SYSTEM / OFFICE OF ACTUARY, DEFENSE MANPOWER DATA CENTER. VFOAT D.O.D. Statistical Report on the Military Retirement System. **VAT** Department of Defense Statistical Report on the Military Retirement System. US. English. an. Office of the Actuary, Defense Manpower Data Center, 1600 North Wilson Boulevard 4th Floor, Arlington VA 22209. **LC** UB443. **DD** 355.1140973.

THE DOLLARS & CENTS OF SHOPPING CENTERS. See Business.

DOMANVERKET : ARSBERATTELSE. Main/Corp Sweden. Domanverket. **Series/Titl** Sveriges Officiella Statistik. Began in 1922. Swedish. an. **LC** HA1521. **DD** 338.1749809485. *Kungl. Domanstyrelsens Forvaltning.*

DOMESTIC AND INTERNATIONAL COMMERCIAL LOAN CHARGE-OFFS. See Business - Banking & Finance.

DOMESTIC TOURISM STATISTICS. VFOAT Statistiques de Tourisme National. English (French and Spanish). ir. World Tourism Organization, Calle Capitan Haya 42 E-Madrid-20 Spain.

DONNEES STATISTIQUES DU LIMOUSIN. July 1971-. Periodical. FR. French. qt. INSEE-CNGP, BO 2718, 80027 Amiens Cedex France. **Tel** 55792625. **LC** HA1228.L5. bk rev. Analyses of subjects of an economic and social nature based on the review of a great number of writings. *Bulletin de Statistique: Limousin (Correze, Creuse, Haute-Vienne).*

DRI-FACS. FINANCIAL AND CREDIT STATISTICS INFORMATION SERVICE. APPLIED REPORTS AND GRAPHICS LIBRARY. (DRI-FACS, FINANCIAL AND CREDIT STATISTICS INFORMATION SERVICE : APPLIED REPORTS AND GRAPHICS LIBRARY). **Main/Corp** Data Resources, Inc. 0271-1931. US. English. 29 Hartwell Avenue, Lexington MA 02173. **LC** HG181. **DD** 332.0973.

DRI-FACS, REFERENCE GUIDE TO U.S. WEEKLY BANKING STATISTICS. (DRI-FACS : REFERENCE GUIDE TO U.S. WEEKLY BANKING STATISTICS). **Main/Corp** Data Resources, Inc. **VFOAT** Reference Guide to U.S. Weekly Banking Statistics. 0271-3470. US. English. Data Resources Inc, 29 Hartwell Avenue, Lexington MA 02173. **LC** HG2493. **DD** 332.10973.

DROPOUT RATE BY SCHOOL DISTRICT. See Education (General).

DUN'S CENSUS OF AMERICAN BUSINESS. See Business.

EAST EUROPEAN STATISTICS SERVICE. Main/Corp East-West S.P.R.L. BE. English. ir. 15 rue Hobbena, 1040 Brussels Belgium. **LC** HC244/A1. **DD** 330.9470005.

ECONOMETRIC REVIEWS. See Mathematics.

ECONOMIC AND FINANCIAL STATISTICS. Main/Corp Central Bank of Barbados. Research Dept. **VFOAT** Economic and Financial Statements. 0378-178X. BB. English. ir. Central Bank of Barbados, PO Box 1016, Bridgetown Barbados. **LC** HC157.B35. **DD** 330.972981.

ECONOMIC AND FINANCIAL STATISTICS REVIEW. Main/Corp Bank Al-Sudan. Maslahat Al-Ihsa. V. 17, No. 2- April/June 1976-. Periodical. English. ir. Bank of Sudan, Statistics Department, PO Box 313, Khartoum Sudan. **LC** HC591.S8. **DD** 330.9624005. *Economic and Financial Bulletin.*

ECONOMIC & STATISTICAL BULLETIN. Main/Corp Andhra Pradesh (India). Bureau of Economics and Statistics. **VAT** Economic and Statistical Bulletin. V. 1- Jan./Feb. 1957-. 0570-0388. Periodical. II. English. qt. Government of Andhra Prades, Bureau of Economics and Statistics, Hyderabad India. **LC** HC437.A73. **DD** 330.95484005. *Hyderabad Government Bulletin on Economic Affairs.*

ECONOMIC AND STATISTICAL BULLETIN - NATIONAL BANK OF GREECE. (ECONOMIC AND STATISTICAL BULLETIN). **Main/Corp** Ethnike Trapeza Tes Hellados. Jan./Feb. 1975-. 0376-9224. Periodical. GR. English. bm. National Bank of Greece, Economic Research Department, Pub 8-4, Athens Greece. **Ind/Abst** Predicasts. **LC** HC291. **DD** 330.949507. *Greece To-Day.*

ECONOMIC INDICATORS OF THE FARM SECTOR. INCOME AND BALANCE SHEET STATISTICS. VFOAT Income and Balance Sheet Statistics. 1979-. 0747-8585. US. English. an. Superintendent of Documents, US Government Printing Office, Washington DC 20402. **LC** HD1769. **DD** 338.10973. *Farm Income Statistics, Balance Sheet of the Farming Sector, 0362-5362.*

ECONOMIC INDICATORS OF THE FARM SECTOR. PRODUCTION AND EFFICIENCY STATISTICS. (ECONOMIC INDICATORS OF THE FARM SECTOR. PRODUCTION AND EFFICIENCY STATISTICS). **VFOAT** Production and Efficiency Statistics. 1979-. 0747-9492. US. English. an. Superintendent of Documents, US Government Printing Office, Washington DC 20402. **LC** HD1751. **DD** 338.160973. *Changes in Farm Production and Efficiency, 0731-3217.*

ECONOMIC INDICATORS OF THE FARM SECTOR. STATE INCOME AND BALANCE SHEET STATISTICS. (ECONOMIC INDICATORS OF THE FARM SECTOR. STATE INCOME AND BALANCE SHEET STATISTICS . . .). **VFOAT** State Income and Balance Sheet Statistics. 1979-. 0747-8569. US. English. an. Superintendent of Documents, US Government Printing Office, Washington DC 20402. *State Farm Income Statistics, 0883-5446; Balance Sheet of the Farming Sector, 0362-5362.*

ECONOMIC STATISTICS QUARTERLY. No. 1 (Feb. 1980)-. Periodical. English. qt. Free. Central Bank of Iceland, PO Box 160, 121 Reykjavik Iceland. **Tel** 01-20500. **LC** HC360.5.A1. **DD** 330.94912005. **Circ** 1,200. News items and brief reports, money and credit financial institutions, balance of payments, exchange rates, treasury, finances, national accounts, production, employment, prices, and incomes.

ECONOMICS, STATISTICS, COOPERATIVES; PROGRAM RESULTS AND PLANS. See Economics.

Statistics

ECONOMIE ET STATISTIQUE. (E & S. ECONOMIE ET STATISTIQUE). No. 97- Feb. 1978-. 0336-1454. Periodical. FR. French (summaries in English and Spanish). mo. 365. INSEE-CNGP, BP 2718, 80027 Amiens Cedex France. Tel 22927322. **Ind/Abst** Int. Labour Doc., Predicasts, Foreign Lang. Index, PAIS Foreign Lang. Index. bk rev. adv acc. Covers production, population, society, daily life, international commerce, fiscal statistics, perspectives, long-term analyses, methods, sampling, models, and conferences. *Economie et Statistique.*

EDUCATION IN CANADA. (EDUCATION IN CANADA, A STATISTICAL REVIEW). Main/Corp Canada. Statistics Canada. Education, Science and Culture Division. Projections Section. VFOAT Education au Canada, Revue Statistique. 1973-. 0706-3679. Periodical. CN. English (French). an. DD 370.971. *Preliminary Statistics of Education, 0575-9374.*

EDUCATION STATISTICS AND GRAPHS. Main/Corp East-Central State, Nigeria. Ministry of Education. 0304-1492. English. ir. LC L675.N52. DD 370.9669.

EDUCATION STATISTICS BULLETIN. VFOAT Bulletin des Statistiques de l'Education. Vol. 6, No. 1-. 0826-8258. Periodical. English (text in French). Tel (800)268-1151. LC L221.H5. DD 370.971. *Education Statistics (Statistics Canada), 0709-7883.*

EDUCATION STATISTICS . . . ESTIMATES. 0307-0514. UK. English. an. 10.00. Chartered Institute of Public Finance and Accountancy, 1 Buckingham Place, London SW1E 6HS England. LC LA630. DD 370.941.

EDUCATION STATISTICS FOR THE UNITED KINGDOM. Main/Corp Great Britain. Dept. of Education and Science. 1967-. UK. English. an.

EDUCATION STATISTICS - (NORTHERN IRELAND). Main/Corp Northern Ireland. Dept. of Education. No. 18- Jan. 1975-. UK. English. 1.50 Single Issue. H M Stationery Office, Northern Ireland Department of Education, 80 Chichester Street, Belfast BT1 4JY Northern Ireland. LC L347. DD 370.9416. *Education Statistics.*

EDUCATION STATISTICS. ONTARIO. (EDUCATION STATISTICS, ONTARIO). Main/Corp Ontario. Ministry of Education. VFOAT Statistiques sur l'Education en Ontario. 1973-. 0317-6428. CN. English (text in French with parallel columns). an. Ministry of Education, Mowat Block, Queen's Park, Toronto Ontario M7A 1L2 Canada. LC L222.O6. DD 370.9713.

EDUCATION STATISTICS (STATISTICS CANADA). (EDUCATION STATISTICS). VFOAT Staristiques de l'Education. Vol. 1, No. 1-V. 5, No. 6. 0709-7883. Periodical. CN. English (text in French). ir. LC L221.H5. DD 370.971. Provides advance and timely information on education in Canada and the provinces. Includes data on enrollment, instructional staffs and finance, for all levels of education. *Service Bulletin (Statistics Canada. Education, Science and Culture Division), 0317-5383.*

EDUCATION STATISTICS - (SWAZILAND). Main/Corp Swaziland. Central Statistical Office. English. ir. Central Statistical Office, PO Box 456, Mbabane Swaziland. LC LA1544.S9. DD 370.9683. *Education Report.*

EDUCATIONAL STATISTICS AT A GLANCE. Main/Corp India (Republic). Ministry of Education and Social Welfare. Statistics and Information Division. II. English. ir. Government of India, Ministry of Education & Social Welfare, Statistics & Information Division, Minto Road, New Delhi India. LC LA1151. DD 390.954.

EDUCATIONAL STATISTICS, DISTRICT-WISE. GUJARAT. VFOAT Gujarat. English. ni. LC LA1154.G8. DD 379.5475.

EDUCATIONAL STATISTICS, DISTRICT-WISE. JAMMU & KASHMIR. VFOAT Jammu & Kashmir. English. ni. LC LA1154.J35. DD 379.5475.

EDUCATIONAL STATISTICS, DISTRICT-WISE. KARNATAKA. VFOAT Karnataka. English. ni. LC LA1154.K29. DD 379.5475.

EDUCATIONAL STATISTICS, DISTRICT-WISE. PUNJAB. VFOAT Punjab. English. ni. LC LA1154.P8. DD 370.95455205.

EDUCATIONAL STATISTICS, DISTRICT WISE. SIKKIM. 1976-77-. English. ni. LC LA1154.S48. DD 370.954167.

EDUCATIONAL STATISTICS OF MALAYSIA MICROFORM. Began with 1938/67 issue. English. ir.

EDUCATIONAL STATISTICS YEARBOOK. See Yearbooks, Almanacs, Directories.

DIE EINFUHR NACH HESSEN. German. ir. 6.50. Hessisches Statistisches Landesamt, Postfach 3205, 6200 Wiesbaden 1 West Germany. LC HA1320, H3569.H4.

ELECTION RESULTS AND STATISTICS (OKLAHOMA). See Public Administration.

ELECTORAL STATISTICS (GREAT BRITAIN). Main/Corp Great Britain. Office of Population Censuses and Surveys. Series/Titl Series El. 1974-. UK. English. an. H M Stationery Office, PO Box 276, London SW8 5DT England. LC JN956. DD 329.02341085.

ELECTRIC POWER STATISTICS. VFOAT Statistique de l'Energie Electrique. 1956-. 0575-8351. CN. English and French. mo. 80.00 Domestic, 90.00 Foreign. Receiver General for Canada, Statistics Canada Publications, Ottawa Ontario K1A 0T6 Canada. Tel (800)268-1151. LC HD9685. DD 338.4. Generation by utilities and industrial establishments, imports and exports, energy made available for use in Canada, cumulative monthly totals for year to date, by province. *Central Electric Stations.*

ELECTRIC POWER STATISTICS. VOLUME 2. ANNUAL STATISTICS. (ELECTRIC POWER STATISTICS. VOLUME II, ANNUAL STATISTICS). VAT Statistique de l'Energie Electrique. Volume 2. Statistiques Annuelles. 1965-. 0380-9765. CN. English. an. $1.40. Publication Sales and Services, Statistics Canada, Ottawa Ontario K1A 0V7 Canada. LC TK26. DD 338.47621310971. *Electric Power Statistics.*

ELECTRIC POWER STATISTICS. VOLUME 3. INVENTORY OF PRIME MOVER AND ELECTRIC GENERATING EQUIPMENT. (ELECTRIC POWER STATISTICS. VOLUME III, INVENTORY OF PRIME MOVER AND ELECTRIC GENERATING AS AT . . .). VFOAT Inventory of Prime Mover and Electric Generating Equipment as at . . , Statistique de l'Energie Electrique Volume III, Inventaire des Moteurs Primaires et des Generateurs Electrigues i.e. Electriques au . . . . 0702-6609. CN. English (French). an. $2.10. Publication Sales and Services, Statistics Canada, Ottawa Ontario K1A 0V7 Canada. LC TK26. DD 621.31210971. *Electric Power Statistics.*

ELECTRIC POWER STATISTICS. VOLUME I, ANNUAL ELECTRIC POWER SURVEY OF CAPABILITY AND LOAD. L'ENERGIE ET DES MINERAUX. VFOAT Annual Electric Power Survey of Capability and Load, Statistique de l'Energie Electrique. Volume I, Enquete Annuelle sur la Puissance Maximate et sur la Charge des Reseaux. 0380-951X. CN. English (French). an. $1.05. Statistics Canada, Publication Distribution, Ottawa Ontario K1A 0T6 Canada. LC TK26. DD 363.620971. *Electric Power Statistics.*

ELECTRIC UTILITY STATISTICAL REFERENCE. 0190-1729. US. English. Donaldson Lufkin & Jenrette Inc, 140 Broadway, New York NY 10005. LC HD9685.U4. DD 338.43.

ELECTRICITY SALES STATISTICS. (ELECTRICITY SALES STATISTICS). 0364-0124. Periodical. US. English. mo. Tennessee Valley Authority, Division of Power Utilization, 721 Power Building, Chattanooga TN 37401. **Ind/Abst** Am. Stat. Index.

ELEMENTARY-SECONDARY SCHOOL ENROLMENT (CANADA). See Education (General).

ELEMENTS DE PREVISIONS. SERIE A. Main/Corp Quebec (Province). Bureau de la Statistique. Service des Etudes Previsionnelles. V. 1- Sept. 1977-. CN. French. Bureau de la Statistique du Quebec, 117 rue Saint Andre, Quebec Quebec G1K 3Y3 Canada. LC HA747.Q4. DD 317.14. *Bulletin Previsionnel. Serie A.*

EMPLOYMENT SECURITY STATISTICAL BULLETIN. VFOAT Statistical Bulletin. Aug. 1979-. 0735-3286. Periodical. US. English. mo. State of Alabama, Department of Industrial Relations, Montgomery AL 36130. LC HD7096.U6. DD 368.44009761. *Statistical Bulletin (Alabama. Division of Employment Security), 0731-3977.*

EMPLOYMENT STATISTICS. Main/Corp New York (State). Dept. of Labor. Division of Research and Statistics. V. 9- 1972-. 0091-0767. US. English. New York State Department of Labor, Division of Research & Statistics, State Office Building Campus, Albany NY 12226. LC HD5725.N7. DD 331.109747. *Employment Statistics.*

EMPLOYMENT STATISTICS (HONG KONG. CENSUS AND STATISTICS DEPT. EMPLOYMENT STATISTICS SECTION). (EMPLOYMENT STATISTICS). English. qt. LC HD5833. DD 331.12095125.

ENERGISTATISTIK. VFOAT Energiestatistik, Energy Statistics. 1969/73-. US. Danish (Dutch, English, French, German, or Italian). mo. European Community Information Service, 2100 M Street NW/ Suite 707, Washington DC 20037. Tel (202)862-9547. LC HD9502.E79. DD 333.79094. Monthly statistics on coal, hydrocarbon, and electrical energy trade and consumption in the European community. *Statistiques de l'Energie. Energy Statistics. Energiestatistik.*

ENERGISTATISTISK ARBOG. See Yearbooks, Almanacs, Directories.

ENERGY STATISTICS. Main/Corp Organization for Economic Cooperation and Development. VFOAT Statistiques de l'Energie. 1973/75-. Periodical. English (French). ir. OECD Publications Center, 1750 Pennsylvania Avenue NW, Washington DC 20006. *Statistics of Energy.*

ENERGY STATISTICS AND MAIN HISTORICAL SERIES. VFOAT Statistiques de l'Energie et Series Historiques Principales. 1981/1982-. US. English (French). an. $20.00. OECD Publications and Information Center, 1750 Pennsylvania Avenue NW/Suite 1207, Washington DC 20006. Tel (202)724-1857. LC HD9502.A1. DD 333.790212. Available on microfiche. Provides detailed statistics on production, trade, and consumption for each source of energy in all OECD countries. *Energy Statistics (Paris, France).*

ENERGY STATISTICS (CHICAGO, ILL.). (ENERGY STATISTICS). Began in 1978. 0739-3075. US. English. qt. Institute of Gas Technology, 3424 South State Street, Chicago IL 60616. LC HD9502.A1. DD 333.790212.

ENERGY STATISTICS YEARBOOK (UNITED NATIONS. STATISTICAL OFFICE). See Yearbooks, Almanacs, Directories.

ENERUGI TOKEI NEMPO. VFOAT Yearbook of Coal, Petroleum and Coke Statistics. 1975-. JA. Japanese. ir. Tsusho Sangyo Chosakai, 15-2 Ginza 6, Chuo-ku 104, Tokyo Japan. LC HD9556.J29. *Sekitan Kokusu Nempo, Sekiyu Tokei Nempo.*

THE ENGINEERING INDUSTRIES IN OECD MEMBER COUNTRIES : NEW BASIC STATISTICS. Main/Corp Organisation for Economic Co-Operation and Development. VFOAT Industries Mecaniques et Electriques dans les pays Membres de l'OCDE: Nouvelles Statistiques de Base. English and French. ir. Director of Information OECD, 2 rue Andre-Pascal, 75775 Paris Cedex 16 France. LC HD9735.A2. DD 338.4094. *Engineering Industries.*

ENQUETE SOCIO-ECONOMIQUE. Main/Corp Institut National de Statistique (Belgium). Periodical. BE. French. ir. 550 Domestic, 660 Foreign. Institut National de Statistique, rue de Louvain 44, 1000 Bruxelles Belgium. Tel (02)513.96.50. LC HA1393 .I57B. DD 314.93. Circ 700. (ctrl). Statistics about population, employment, families, housing, strangers, and instruction.

ENSKILDA FORSAKRINGSANSTALTER. Main/Corp Sweden. Forsakringsinspektionen. 1912-. Swedish. an. Box 5053, Stockholm S10242 5 Sweden. LC HA1521 HG8670. DD 368.9485.

ENVIRONMENTAL ACCIDENT STATISTICS. CN. English. an. Manitoba Environmental Management Division, Environmental Control Services Waste Management, Box 7 Building 2, 139 Tuxedo Avenue, Winnipeg Manitoba R3N 0H6 Canada. *Environmental Accident Report, 0706-5221.*

EPITOIPARI STATISZTIKAI EVKONYV. Hungarian. an. 221.—. Statisztikai Kiado Vallalat, III Kaszasdulo U 2, 1033 Budapest Hungary. Tel 803-311. LC HD9715.H8. Circ 1,000.

Statistics

Reviews the structure and activities of the Hungarian building industry. It gives account of the producing conditions, allocations, costs, results and prices.

EQUAL EMPLOYMENT OPPORTUNITY STATISTICS. Main/Corp United States. Civil Service Commission. Bureau of Personnel Management Information Systems. VFOAT Federal Civilian Workforce Statistics. Nov. 1976-. 0161-245X. US. English. sa. Superintendent of Documents, US Government Printing Office, Washington DC 20402. LC JK723.M54. DD 353.00104. *Minority Group Employment in the Federal Government, 0090-3531; Study of Employment of Women in the Federal Government, 0097-7764.*

ERHEBUNG DER LAND- UND FORSTWIRTSCHAFTLICHEN ARBEITSKRAFTE. Main/Corp Osterreichisches Statistisches Zentralamt. Series/Titl Beitrage zur Osterreichischen Statistik. German. ir. Kommissionsverlag, Osterreichische Staatsdruckerei Renweg 12 A, 1037 Wien Austria. LC HA1173, HD1536. A93. DD 314.36, 331.76309436.

ERLANGER REIHE DER MEDIZINISCHEN STATISTIK UND INFORMATIONSVERARBEITUNG : SCHRIFTENREIHE DES INSTITUTS FUR MEDIZINISCHE STATISTIK UND DOKUMENTATION DER UNIVERSITAT ERLANGEN-NURNBERG. Vol. 1-. German. ir. Ed Lothar Horbach. NLM W1.

ESPOON KAUPUNGIN TILASTOLLINEN VUOSIKIRJA. See Yearbooks, Almanacs, Directories.

ESTADISTICA AGROPECUARIAS. 1-. Periodical. Spanish. ir. Comcorde, Secretaria Tecnica, Avda Rondeau 1908, Montevideo Uruguay.

ESTADISTICA DE CRIMINALIDAD. VFOAT Criminalidad. Spanish. ir. Policia Nacional de Colombia, Carrera 25 No 10-41, Bogota Colombia. LC HV7335.

ESTADISTICA DE ESTABLECIMIENTOS SANITARIOS CON REGIMEN DE INTERNADO. 1973-. 0210-4598. Spanish. ir. NLM W2 GS6 I46EC. *Estadistica de Establecimientos Sanitarios Con Regimen Interno.*

ESTADISTICA DE LA ENSENANZA EN ESPANA. Main/Corp Spain. Instituto Nacional de Estadistica. SP. Spanish. an. Instituto Nacional de Estadistica, Avda Generalisimo 91, Madrid 91 Spain. LC L511. DD 371.2.

ESTADISTICA DE VENTAS A PLAZOS. Spanish. ir. LC HG3756.S7. DD 332.743.

ESTADISTICA DEL COMERCIO EXTERIOR DE ESPANA. Main/Corp Spain. Direccion General de Aduanas. Spanish. ir.

ESTADISTICA DEL SUICIDIO EN ESPANA. Main/Corp Spain. Instituto Nacional de Estadistica. Spanish. ni. LC HB1323.S8. *Estadistica del Suicidio en Espana.*

ESTADISTICA EDUCATIVA. PY. Spanish. ir. Paraguay 1657/Planta Baja, Buenos Aires Argentina. LC LA545.

ESTADISTICA ESPANOLA. No. 1- Oct./Dec. 1958-. 0014-1151. Periodical. SP. Spanish. qt. Insitute Nacioinal de Estadistica, Avda Generalisimo 91, Madrid 16 Spain. Ind/Abst Math. Rev. LC HA1. NLM W2 GS6 I46EA. CODEN ESTEA7.

ESTADISTICA FORESTAL. VFOAT Estadisticas Forestales de Venezuela. Spanish. an. LC SD175. DD 333.750987.

ESTADISTICA LABORAL (BOLIVIA). Main/Corp Bolivia. Subsecretaria de Desarrollo Laboral. Oficina Sectorial de Estadistica. Spanish. ir. LC HD5751.

ESTADISTICA MENSUAL DE EXPORTACION DE FRUTOS DEL PAIS. Periodical. Spanish. mo.

ESTADISTICA MENSUAL : PRECIOS AL POR MAYOR (ARGENTINA). No. 1- Jan. 1973-. Periodical. AG. Spanish. mo. LC HB235.A7.

ESTADISTICA - MINISTERIO DE ALIMENTACION DIRECCION GENERAL DE INFORMATICA Y ESTADISTICA. Main/Corp Peru. Ministerio de Alimentacion. Direccion General de Informatica y Estadistica. VFOAT Estadistica Agropeuaria. Spanish. ir. Cahuide 852 - Jesus Maria. LC HD1901.

ESTADISTICA - OSE. Main/Corp Uruguay. Administracion de Las Obras Sanitarias del Estado. Spanish. ir. LC TD53.

ESTADISTICA PANAMENA; BOLETIN SEMANAL. Main/Corp Panama. Direccion de Estadistica y Censo. Periodical. PN. Spanish. ir. Contraloria Gen Republica, Direccion Estadistica y Censo, Panama 5 Panama.

ESTADISTICA PANAMENA. SERIE H.2 : INFORMACION AGROPECUARIA, PRECIOS PAGADOS POR EL PRODUCTOR AGROPECUARIO. Main/Corp Panama. Direccion de Estadistica y Censo. VFOAT Informacion Agropecuaria, Precios Pagados por el Productor Agropecu. Spanish. ir. LC S562.P33.

ESTADISTICA PANAMENA. SERIE K : ANUARIO DE COMERCIO EXTERIOR. See Yearbooks, Almanacs, Directories.

ESTADISTICA PANAMENA. SITUACION ECONOMICA : HACIENDA PUBLICA Y FINANZAS. Main/Corp Panama. Direccion de Estadistica y Censo. VFOAT Hacienda Publica y Finanzas. 1976-. Spanish. ir. LC HJ21. *Estadistica Panamena. Situacion Economica: Finanzas Publicas y Banca.*

ESTADISTICA PANAMENA. SITUACION POLITICA, ADMINISTRATIVA Y JUSTICIA, SECCION 631 : JUSTICIA. Main/Corp Panama. Direccion de Estadistica y Censo. VFOAT Situacion Politica, Administrativa y Justicia: Justicia. 0378-259X. Spanish. ir. LC HV7322.

ESTADISTICA PANAMENA. SITUACION SOCIAL, SECCION 441- TRABAJO Y SALARIOS : ESTADISTICAS DEL TRABAJO. Main/Corp Panama. Direccion de Estadistica y Censo. VFOAT Estadisticas del Trabajo, Situacion Social: Estadisticas del Trabajo. VAT Estadistica Panamena. Situacion Social, Seccion Cuatrocientos Cuarenta y Uno-Trabajo y Salarios: Estadisticas del Trabajo. 1975-. PN. Spanish. ir. LC HD5738. *Estadistica Panamena. Serio O: Estadisticas del Trabajo.*

ESTADISTICA. SERIE B, PRESTAMOS. VFOAT Prestamos. Spanish. ir. LC LB2340.4.P3. DD 378.362097287. *Estadisticas. Serie B, Prestamos.*

ESTADISTICA Y ACTUARIADO. Periodical. Spanish. ir. Edificio Stolmar, Mezzanina 1 - Altagracia a Salas, Caracas Venezuela. LC HA1.

ESTADISTICAS AGRICOLAS CONTINUAS. Spanish. an. LC HD1806. DD 338.1097281.

ESTADISTICAS AGROPECUARIAS DE LAS ENTIDADES FEDERALES : ANZOATEGUI, MONAGAS, NVA. ESPARTA, SUCRE Y T.F. DELTA AMACURO (VENEZUELA). Main/Corp Venezuela. Ministerio de Agricultura y Cria. Division de Estadistica. Spanish. ir. LC HD1911.

ESTADISTICAS AGROPECUARIAS DE LAS ENTIDADES FEDERALES : APURE, BOLVAR Y T.F. AMAZONAS (VENEZUELA). Main/Corp Venezuela. Ministerio de Agricultura y Cria. Division de Estadistica. VAT Estadisticas Agropecuarias de las Entidades Federales: Apure, Bolvar y Territorio Federal Amazonas. Spanish. ir. LC HD1911.

ESTADISTICAS AGROPECUARIAS DE LAS ENTIDADES FEDERALES : BARINAS, COJEDES, GUARICO Y PORTUGESA (VENEZUELA). Main/Corp Venezuela. Ministerio de Agricultura y Cria. Division de Estadistica. Spanish. ir. LC HD1911.

ESTADISTICAS (CHILE. SERVICIO DE SEGURO SOCIAL). Main/Corp Chile. Servicio de Seguro Social. 1952/56?-. 0577-8174. Periodical. CL. Spanish. ir. Servico de Seguro Social, Av Bulnes 418, Santiago Chile 31133384. *Anuario Estadistico.*

ESTADISTICAS DE LA EDUCACION. 1974-. AG. Spanish. an. Ministerio de Cultura y Educacion, Avda e Madero 235 1 Piso, Buenos Aires Argentina. LC LA545. DD 370.982. *Estadistica Educativa.*

ESTADISTICAS DE PRODUCCION INDUSTRIAL. ANALISIS Y RESULTADOS. SP. Spanish. ir. Servico Sindical de Estadisticas, Madrid Spain. LC HC381. DD 338.0946.

ESTADISTICAS DEL COMERCIO EXTERIOR DE VENEZUELA. Main/Corp Venezuela. Direccion General de Estadistica y Censos Nacionales. VE. Spanish. Instituto Comercio Exterior, Bibl Ctr Comerical Cedros, AV Libertador Carcas Venezuela.

ESTADISTICAS FINANCIERAS INTERNACIONALES - FONDO MONETARIO INTERNACIONAL. (ESTADISTICAS FINANCIERAS INTERNACIONALES). Began in 1981. 0252-3078. US. Spanish. mo. Publications Unit, International Monetary Fund, Washington DC 20431. *International Financial Statistics. Ed. Espanol, 0250-734X.*

ESTADISTICAS INDUSTRIALES (BOLIVIA). Main/Corp Instituto Nacional de Estadistica (Bolivia). Began with 1966/68. BO. Spanish. ir. Instituto Nacional de Estadistica, Ave 6 de Agosto NR 2507, La Paz Bolivia.

ESTADISTICAS JUDICIALES DE ESPANA. Main/Corp Spain. Instituto Nacional de Estadistica. 1959-. 0561-4473. Spanish. be. *Estadistica de los Tribunales Tutelares de Menores, Estadistica Penal de Espana; Estadistica Penitenciaria; Estadistica Judicial Civil y de lo Contencioso-Administrativo.*

ESTADISTICAS PORTUARIAS. Main/Corp Comision Ejecutiva Portuaria Autonoma. Spanish. ir. LC HE563.S1.

ESTADISTICAS SOCIOECONOMICAS, PUERTO RICO. DELETE. VFOAT Socioeconomic Statistics, Puerto Rico. PR. English (Spanish). an. $1.00. Junta de Planificacion, Division de Finanzas, Centro Gubernamental Minillas Edificio Norte, Santurce Puerto Rico 00940. LC HC154.5.A1. DD 317.295.

ESTADISTICS. V. 1- March 1943-. 0014-1135. Periodical. US. chiefly in English or Spanish. qt. Organization of American States, Inter-American Statistical Institute, 17th Street and Constitution Avenue, Washington DC 20006. Ind/Abst Math. Rev., Popul. Index, Public Aff. Inf. Serv. Bull., Foreign Lang. Index. LC HA1. DD 310.627. NLM HA 1 E79. CODEN ESTDA4. (cum index).

ESTADO DA PARAIBA, ANUARIO ESTATISTICO. See Yearbooks, Almanacs, Directories.

ESTATISTICA. Main/Corp Administracao do Porto do Recife. Sub-Setor de Controle e Estatistica. Portuguese. ir. Administracao do Porto do Recife Setor Comerical, Sub-Setor de Controle e Estatistica, Praca Artur Oscar, S/No Recife Pe Brazil. LC HE563.B8. DD 387.1098134.

ESTATISTICA DA ACTIVIDADE MINEIRA NO ESTADO DE ANGOLA. (ESTATISTICA DA ACTIVIDADE MINEIRA). Main/Corp Angola. Direccao Provincial dos Servicos de Geologia e Minas. 0301-6552. Portuguese. ir. Ind/Abst GeoRef. LC HD9506.A58. DD 338.209673. CODEN EMAGDF.

ESTATISTICA DA EDUCACAO NO RIO GRANDE DO SUL. Main/Corp Rio Grande do Sul, Brazil (State). Superintendencia de Estatistica e Informatica. 1972-. Portuguese. ir. LC LA556.

ESTATISTICA DA EDUCACAO. STATISTIQUE DE L'EDUCATION. Main/Corp Portugal. Instituto Nacional de Estatistica. VFOAT Statistique de l'Education. Began with 1940/41 issue. Portuguese. ir. LC L521. DD 370.9469.

ESTATISTICA DAS INSTALACOES ELECTRICAS EM PORTUGAL. Portuguese. ir. LC HD9685.P8.

ESTATISTICA INDUSTRIAL (LISBOA). (ESTATISTICA INDUSTRIAL). VFOAT Statistique Industrielle. Began Publication in 1943?. 0079-418X. Periodical. PO. Portuguese and French. ir. Instituto Nacional de Estatistica, Av Antonio Jose de Almeida, Lisboa L Portugal. LC HC391. DD 338.

ESTATISTICAS DA EDUCACAO NACIONAL. Main/Corp Brazil. Servico de Estatistica da Educacao e Cultura. Began with Vol. for 1960/71. Portuguese. ir. Ministerio da Educaco E Cultura, rua da Imprensa 16 - 3 Andar, Rio de Janeiro Brazil. LC LA555.

ESTATISTICAS DE MORTALIDADE, BRASIL. 1979-. Portuguese. ir. Centro de Documenta Cao do Ministerio da Saude, Esplanada dos Ministerios Bloco G Terreo, 70058 Brasilia DF Brazil. LC HB1393. DD 312.20981.

Statistics

ESTATISTICAS DE SAUDE. ASSISTENCIA MEDICO-SANITARIA. VFOAT Assistencial Medico-Sanitaria. Vol. 1 (1976)-. 0101-3033. Portuguese. an. LC RA984.B8. DD 362.10981021.

ESTATISTICAS DO COMERCIO EXTERNO. VFOAT Statistiques du Commerce Exterieur. Portuguese. ir. Direccao Provincial dos Servicos de Estatistica, Caixa Postal 1215, Luanda Angola. LC HF272.A6. *Comercio Externo.*

ESTIMATES OF REVENUE AND EXPENDITURE. Main/Corp East African Railways Corporation. English. ir. LC HE3419.E3. DD 385.1.

ESTIMATES OF SCHOOL STATISTICS. Began with Vol. for 1958/59. 0077-4278. US. English. an. National Education Association, 1201 Sixteenth Street NW, Washington DC 20036. *Advance Estimates of Public Elementary and Secondary Schools.*

ESTUDIOS FRANCISCANOS. Periodical. SP. Spanish. ty. $9.81. Convento de Capuchinos Admin, Diagonal 450, Barcelona 6 Spain. Tel 319.00.87. Ind/Abst New Testam. Abstr. bk rev. *Revista de Estudios Franciscanos.*

ETUDES ET STATISTIQUES; BULLETIN MENSUEL. Main/Corp Banque des Etats de l'Afrique Centrale. No. 1- April 1973-. FR. French. mo. 17.500. Banque Etats l'Afrique Central, Services Centraux, BP 1917, Yaoundi Cameroun. Tel 222505. Ind/Abst Foreign Lang. Index, PAIS Foreign Lang. Index. LC HG3409.E65. DD 330.967. Circ 1,500. *Etudes et Statistiques.*

ETUDES STATISTIQUES (BRUSSELS, BELGIUM). (ETUDES STATISTIQUES). No. 15-. 0522-7585. BE. French. ir. 150 Domestic, 200 Foreign. Institute National Statistique, rue de Louvain 44, 1000 Bruxelles Belgium. Tel (02)513.96.50. Ind/Abst Foreign Lang. Index. Circ 1,000. (ctrl). General statistical studies. *Etudes Statistiques et Econometriques.*

THE EUROPEAN COMMUNITY : FACTS AND FIGURES. UK. English. Commission of the European Communities, 20 Kensington Palace Gardens, London W8 4QQ England. LC HA1107.5. DD 309.14055.

EUROPEAN ECONOMY. SUPPLEMENT B, ECONOMIC PROSPECTS—BUSINESS SURVEY RESULTS. See Business.

EUROPEAN MARKETING DATA AND STATISTICS. VFOAT EMDAS. Began with: Vol. 1 in 1962. 0071-2930. UK. English. an. $160.00. Gale Research Co, Book Tower, Detroit MI 48226. Tel (313)961-2242. LC HA1107. DD 338.094. Some 300 tables furnish at-a-glance comparisons between the countries covered. Fifteen major sections cover such broad areas as population, employment, production, trade, economy, standard of living, consumer expenditures, consumption, etc.

EUROPEAN SUPPLIES BULLETIN. See Fish Culture and Fisheries.

EUROSTAT, ACP: ANNUAIRE DES STATISTIQUES DU COMMERCE EXTERIEUR. See Yearbooks, Almanacs, Directories.

EUROSTAT, BULLETIN TRIMESTRIEL DES STATISTIQUES SIDERURGIQUES. (STATISTISK KVARTALSBULLETIN FOR JERN OG STAL). Main/Corp Statistical Office of the European Communities. VFOAT Vierteljahrliches Statistisches Bulletin Eisen und Stahl, Quarterly Iron and Steel Statistical Bulletin, Bulletin Trimestriel des Statistiques Siderurgiques. 1976-77. 0378-3510. titles and text also in Danish, French, German, Dutch, and Italian. ir. LC HD9525.A2. DD 338.47672094. *Iron and Steel.*

EUROSTAT, GENERAL GOVERNMENT ACCOUNTS AND STATISTICS. (GENERAL GOVERNMENT ACCOUNTS AND STATISTICS). VFOAT Comptes et Statistiques des Administrations Publiques. Began with Vol. for 1970/77. 0255-3953. LU. Dutch (English and French). an. Statistical Office of the European Communities, PO Box 1907, L-2920 Luxemburg-Kirchberg Luxembourg. LC HC240.9.I5. DD 339.34. *Nationalregnskaber, Ens Arbog.*

EUROSTAT NEWS. Main/Corp Statistical Office of the European Communities. 1976-. Periodical. LU. English. qt. European Communities Information Service, 2100 M Street NW/Suite 707, Washington DC 20037. Ind/Abst Int. Labour Doc. LC HA1107.5. DD 314.

EUROSTAT REVIEW. VFOAT Revue Eurostat. 1970-1979-. US. Dutch (text in English and French). an. $12.80. E C I S, 2100 M Street Northwest/Suite 707, Washington DC 20037. Tel (202)862-9500. LC HA1107.5. DD 314. Ten year review of general macroeconomic data for the members of the European communities with comparative data for the US and Japan.

EUROSTAT, SKOVSTATISTIK. (SKOVSTATISTIK). VFOAT Forststatistik, Forest Statistics. 0255-3988. Danish (Dutch, English, French, German and Italian). ir. European Community Information Service, 2100 M Street NW/Suite 707, Washington DC 20037. LC SD177.

EUROSTAT, STATISTIQUES MENSUELLES DE LA VIANDE. (MANEDLIG STATISTIK FOR KD). Main/Corp Statistical Office of the European Communities. VFOAT Statistiques Mensuelles de la Viande, Monatliche Statistik von Fleisch, Monthly Statistics of Meat. Began in 1967. 0378-3553. Periodical. LU. Danish (Dutch, English, French, German, and Italian). mo. European Community Information Service, 2100 M Street NW/Suite 707, Washington DC 20037. Tel (202)862-9500. LC HD9425.E83. DD 338.4766490094.

EUROSTAT, STATISTIQUES MENSUELLES DES OEUFS. (MANEDLIG STATISTIK FOR G). Main/Corp Statistical Office of the European Communities. VFOAT Monatliche Statistik von Eiern, Monthly Statistics of Eggs. 1976-. 0378-3537. Periodical. Danish (Dutch, English, French, German, and Italian). mo. European Community Information Inc, 2100 M Street NW/Suite 707, Washington DC 20037. Tel (202)862-9500. LC HD9284.E97. DD 338.17754094. *Landbrug: Maneds Statistik: G.*

EUROSTAT, STATISTIQUES MENSUELLES DU LAIT. (MANEDLIG STATISTIK FOR MLK). Main/Corp Statistical Office of the European Communities. VFOAT Statistiques Mensuelles du Lait, Monatliche Statistik von Milch, Monthly Statistics of Milk. Began in 1974. 0378-3545. US. Danish, Dutch, English, French, German, and Italian. ir. $34.15. European Community Information Service, 2100 M Street NW, Suite 707, Washington DC 20037. LC HD9282.E9. DD 338.1771094.

EUROSTATISTIK, DATEN ZUR KONJUNKTURANALYSE / EUROSTATISTICS, DATA FOR SHORT-TERM ECONOMIC ANALYSIS / STATISTICAL OFFICE OF THE EUROPEAN COMMUNITIES. VFOAT Eurostatistics, Data for Short-Term Economic Analysis. 1982, 1-. 0252-8266. Periodical. German (English and French). mo. European Community Information Service, 2100 M Street Northwest/Suite 707, Washington DC 20037. Tel (202)862-9547. Includes statistics on unemployment, consumer price index, industrial production, steel, energy, extra community trade, intra-community trade, exchange rates, and public finance. *Eurostatistik, Data til Konjunkturanalyse Eurostatistiken, Daten zur Konjunkturanalyse.*

EXPERIMENTS ON LIVING ANIMALS : STATISTICS. UK. English. an. 1.25. Her Majesty's Stationery Office, PO Box 276, London SW8 5DT England. LC QP45. DD 619.0212. *Experiments on Living Animals . . . Return Showing the Number of Experiments on Living Animals . . . .*

EXPLANATORY MEMORANDUM AND STATISTICAL SUPPLEMENT, PAKISTAN RAILWAY BUDGET. Main/Corp Pakistan. Railway Board. VFOAT Railway Budget. English. ir. Government of Pakistan, Karachi 15 B Pakistan. LC HE3300.5. DD 353.9549100875.

EXTERNAL TRADE STATISTICS. 1955-. 0555-6546. NZ. English. an. Government Printing Office of New Zealand, Private Bag, New Zealand. LC HF155. DD 382. *Statistical Yearbook. Trade Statistics Supplement.*

EXTERNAL TRADE STATISTICS, SRI LANKA. English. sa. Sri Lanka Government Publ Bureau, The Superintendent, Colombo Sri Lanka. LC HF3770.8. DD 382.09549300212.

FACT BOOK ON DIRECT MARKETING. STATISTICAL UPDATE. 1983-. 0739-9464. US. English. be. $81.95. Direct Marketing Association Inc, 6 East 43rd Street, New York NY 10017. Tel (212)689-4977. Ed Virginia Starke. LC HF5410. DD 658.84. Circ 1,000. Data and background compiled and written by top industry people to help plan direct marketing compaigns. *Fact Book on Direct Response Marketing. Statistical Update, 0735-5130.*

FACT BOOK : TABLES AND CHARTS ON THE NEW YORK METROPOLITAN REGION. Main/Corp New York City Council on Economic Education. 1970-. US. English. be. $12.00. New York City Council on Economic Education, 150 Nassau Street/Room 1603, New York NY 10038. Tel (312)374-1244. Ed Albert Alexander. A concise one-volume collection of selecting economic and related statistics about New York City and the surrounding region.

FACT SHEET - SASKATCHEWAN. BUREAU OF STATISTICS. (FACT SHEET). 1980-. 0713-7281. CN. English. an. Bureau of Statistics, 3475 Albert Street, T C Douglas Building, Regina Saskatchewan S4S 6X6 Canada. DD 317.124. *Saskatchewan Annual Fact Sheet, 0713-729X.*

FACTS. See Metals & Metallurgy.

FACTS & FEATURES - ONTARIO RESEARCH FOUNDATION. (FACTS & FEATURES). VAT Facts and Features - Ontario Research Foundation. Vol. 1, No. 1 (Mar. 1980)-. 0710-6092. Periodical. CN. English. bm. Ontario Research Foundation, Sheridan Park Research Committee, Mississauga Ontario L5K 1B3 Canada. DD 001.409713541.

FACTS AND FIGURES OF THE AUTOMOBILE INDUSTRY. See Transportation - Automobiles.

FACTS AND FIGURES OF THE AUTOMOTIVE INDUSTRY. See Transportation - Automobiles.

FAITS & CHIFFRES. VFOAT Faits et Chiffres. French. ir. Le Nouvel Observateur, 9 rue d'Aboukir, 75002 Paris France.

FALL PUPIL ENROLLMENT AND TEACHER STATISTICS, ILLINOIS PUBLIC SCHOOLS. 1964/65-. US. English. an. Illinois State Board of Education, 100 North First Street, Springfield IL 62777. LC LC144.I3. DD 373.1219773.

FAO MONTHLY BULLETIN OF STATISTICS. VFOAT Bulletin Mensuel FAO de Statistiques, Boletin Mensual FAO de Estadisticas. Vol. 1, No. 1 (Jan. 1978)-. 0379-0010. Periodical. English (text in French and Spanish). mo. UNIPUB, PO Box 1222, Ann Arbor MI 46106. Tel (800)521-8110. Ind/Abst Biol. Agric. Index, Predicasts, Public Aff. Inf. Serv. Bull. A source of current facts and data on world food and agricultural conditions, with an analysis of the factors influencing them. *Monthly Bulletin of Agricultural Economics and Statistics.*

FARM CREDIT STATISTICS. VFOAT Statistiques du Credit Agricole. 1983-. 0825-7019. CN. English (French in parallel columns). an. Farm Credit Corporation Canada Research Division, PO Box 2314, Station D, Ottawa Ontario K1P 6J9 Canada. DD 332.710971. *Federal Farm Credit Statistics (1981), 0823-4264.*

FARMER COOPERATIVE STATISTICS. 1976-77-. 0742-9495. US. English. an. Agricultural Cooperative Service, USDA, 500 12th Street South West/Room 550, Washington DC 20250. LC HD1491.U5. DD 334.6830973 S, 334.6830973. *Statistics of Farmer Cooperatives.*

FEDERAL AND INDIAN LANDS COAL, PHOSPHATE, POTASH, SODIUM, AND OTHER MINERAL PRODUCTION, ROYALTY INCOME, AND RELATED STATISTICS CEASED. Main/Corp Geological Survey (U.S.). Conservation Division. 1971-1980. US. English. an. *Mineral Production, Royalty Income, and Related Statistics on Oil, Gas, and other Leasable Minerals, Federal and Indian Lands.*

FEDERAL AND INDIAN LANDS OIL AND GAS PRODUCTION, ROYALTY INCOME, AND RELATED STATISTICS CEASED. Main/Corp Geological Survey (U.S.). Conservation Division. Began with 1970 issue. Ceased in 1980. US. English. an. *Mineral Production, Royalty Income, and Related Statistics on Oil, Gas, and other Leasable Minerals, Federal and Indian Lands.*

FEDERAL COURT MANAGEMENT STATISTICS. 1983-. 0741-692X. US. English. an. Administrative Office of the United States Courts, Washington DC 20544. LC KF180. DD 347.73200212,

Statistics

347.30720212. V. for 1983- distributed to depository libraries in Microfiche. *Management Statistics for United States Courts, 0099-0434.*

FEDERAL FUNDS FOR RESEARCH, DEVELOPMENT, AND OTHER SCIENTIFIC ACTIVITIES. DETAILED STATISTICAL TABLES. APPENDICES C AND D. (FEDERAL FUNDS FOR RESEARCH, DEVELOPMENT, AND OTHER SCIENTIFIC ACTIVITIES). 1973-. Periodical. US. English. an. US National Science Foundation, Division of Science Resources Studies, 1800 G Street NW, Washington DC 20550.

FEDERAL JUDICIAL WORKLOAD STATISTICS. (FEDERAL JUDICIAL WORKLOAD STATISTICS DURING THE TWELVE MONTH PERIOD ENDED . . .). VFOAT Federal Judicial Workload Statistics for the Twelve-Month Period Ended . . . . 0192-625X. Periodical. US. English. qt. Administrative Office of the United States Courts, Statistical Analysis and Reports Division, Washington DC 20544. LC KF180. DD 347.7313.

FEDERAL MILK ORDER MARKET STATISTICS. (FEDERAL MILK ORDER MARKET STATISTICS. ANNUAL SUMMARY). Began with 1962. 0501-4670. US. English. an. US Department of Agriculture, Agricultural Marketing Service, Washington DC 20250. Tel (202)447-4115. Ed John P Rourke. LC HD1751, HD9282. U3A28. DD 338.10973 S, 381.41710973. Circ 1,500. Vols. for 1982- distributed to depository libraries in microfiche. Data on the amount of milk marketed by dairy farmers, prices paid for milk, and production and consumption of milk and dairy products. *Federal Milk Order Market Statistics. Supplement.*

FEDERAL RESERVE CHART BOOK ON FINANCIAL AND BUSINESS STATISTICS. HISTORICAL SUPPLEMENT. Main/Corp Board of Governors of the Federal Reserve System (U.S.). 1957-58. US. English. qt. Board of Governors, Federal Reserve System, Mailstop 138, Washington DC 20551. Tel (202)452-3244. Ind/Abst Am. Stat. Index. *Federal Reserve Charts on Bank Credit, Money Rates, and Business. Historical Supplement.*

FEDERAL STATISTICS. Main/Corp United States. Office of Management and Budget. Statistical Policy Division. 1st- Ed. 0146-7395. US. English. $1.55. Executive Office of the President, Office of Management and Budget, Statistical Policy Division, Washington DC 20402. LC HA37. DD 001.433.

FEED EGG RATIO AND STATISTICAL SUMMARY. Main/Corp New York (State). Dept. of Agriculture and Markets. Division of Marketing. Apr. 5, 1957-. Periodical. US. English. wk.

FELLMONGERING, WOOLSCOURING AND CARBONISING. Main/Corp Australian Bureau of Statistics. Series Corp Australian Bureau of Statistics. Production Summary. Apr. 1974-. Periodical. English. ir. *Fellmongering, Woolscouring and Carbonising.*

FERTILISER & ALLIED AGRICULTURAL STATISTICS, NORTHERN REGION. VFOAT Fertiliser and Allied Agricultural Statistics, Northern Region. II. English. an. 15.00. Fertiliser Association of India, Northern Region Near Jawaharlal Nehru University, New Delhi 110 067 India. LC HD9483.I4. DD 338.476686209541.

FERTILISER STATISTICS. Main/Corp Fertiliser Association of India. Began publication with volume for 1955. 0430-327X. II. English. an. Fertiliser Association of India, Near Jawaharlal/Nehru University, New Delhi 110067 India. Tel 66 7144.

FEUILLE D'INFORMATION . . . HOJA DE INFORMACION . . . SURVEY. See Food & Drink.

FIBV STATISTICAL DATA. Main/Corp International Federation of Stock Exchanges. 1975/76-. English. ir. Federation International des Bourses de Valeurs, 22 Boulevard de Courcelles, 75017 Paris France. LC HG4551. DD 332.642.

FIBV STATISTICS. VFOAT F.I.B.V. Statistics. English. ir. Federation Internationale des Bourses de Valeurs, 22 Blvd de Courcelles, 75017 Paris France. LC HG4551. DD 332.642. *FIBU Statistical Data.*

FIELD CROPS STATISTICS, CALIFORNIA. Series/Titl Field Crops Statistics Bulletin. Began in 1967/76. 0734-4333. US. English. LC SB187.U6. DD 338.173009794. *California Field Crops Statistics.*

FILMFORDERUNG . . . STATISTIK, FILMEINFUHR, STATISTIK. VFOAT Encouragement du Cinema . . ., Statistique, Importation de Films . . ., Statistique. French (German). an. Bundesamt fur Kulturpflege, Sektion Film, 3000 Bern 6 Switzerland. LC PN1993.5.S9. DD 384.809494. *Filmforderung, Statistik.*

FINAL STATISTICAL REPORT - CALIFORNIA. PRUNE MARKETING COMMITTEE. (FINAL STATISTICAL REPORT). 0737-4852. US. English. 103 World Trade Center, San Francisco CA 94111-4293. LC HD9259.P73. DD 380.14566480421.

FINANCES OF PUBLIC SCHOOL SYSTEMS. (FINANCES OF PUBLIC SCHOOL SYSTEMS IN . . .). 0270-8868. US. English. an. $3.00. Customer Services Section, Data User Services Division, Bureau of the Census, Washington DC 20233. Tel (301)763-5847. Ed Vance Kane. LC LB2825. DD 379.1210973. Data on finances of both independent and dependent public school systems by states. Presents statistics for individual systems with more than 20,000 enrollment.

FINANCIAL AND OPERATING STATISTICS CLASS I MOTOR CARRIERS OF PASSENGERS. Main/Corp United States. Interstate Commerce Commission. Bureau of Accounts. VAT Financial and Operating Statistics Class One Motor Carriers of Passengers. Jan./June 1975-. 0362-9317. US. English. sa. LC HE5623. DD 388.322. *Revenues, Expenses, other Income, and Statistics of Class I Motor Carriers of Passengers.*

FINANCIAL AND OTHER STATISTICS - CITY OF OTTAWA. (FINANCIAL AND OTHER STATISTICS). Main/Corp Ottawa (Ont.). Dept. of Finance. VFOAT Statistiques Financieres et Autres. 0823-5104. CN. English (French, with text on inverted pages). sa. Department of Finance, City of Ottawa, 111 Sussex Drive, Ottawa Ontario K1N 5A1 Canada. LC HJ9014.O6. DD 336.71384. *Financial and Other Statistics.*

FINANCIAL AND STATISTICAL REPORT - LOUISIANA. Main/Corp Louisiana. Dept. of Transportation and Development. 1976/77-. US. English. an. State of Louisiana, Department of Transportation and Development, PO Box 94245, Baton Rouge LA 70804-9245. LC HE356.L8. DD 388.109763. *Financial and Statistical Report.*

FINANCIAL AND STATISTICAL REPORT - MICHIGAN. Main/Corp Michigan. Public School Employees' Retirement System. US. English. an. Michigan Public School Employees, Retirement System 2nd Floor South Wing, S T Mason Building, Lansing MI 48913. LC LB2842.2. DD 331.252.

FINANCIAL AND STATISTICAL REPORT: SPECIAL EDUCATION (ILLINOIS). Main/Corp Illinois. Office of the Superintendent of Public Instruction. Handicapped Children Section. VFOAT Special Education Financial and Statistical Report for Handicapped Children. US. English. an. Illinois Department of Public Instruction/ Handicapped Children Section, 325 South 5th Street, Sprinfield IL 62706. LC LC4032.I6. DD 371.909773.

FINANCIAL AND STATISTICAL SUPPLEMENT (AUSTRALIA). Main/Corp Australia. Postmaster-General's Dept. English. ir. $0.65. Postmaster-General's Department, 199 William Street, Melbourne 3000 Australia. LC J905, HE7391.A33. DD 328.9401 S, 354.9400873.

FINANCIAL STATISTICS. CANADA'S PROVINCES AND REPRESENTATIVE MUNICIPALITIES CEASED. (FINANCIAL STATISTICS : CANADA'S PROVINCES AND REPRESENTATIVE MUNICIPALITIES). 1968-1980 Ed. 0071-5123. CN. English. an. Wood Gundy Ltd, Royal Trust Tower, PO Box 274 Toronto Dominion Centre, Toronto Ontario M5K 1J5 Canada. DD 336.71. *Canadian Government and Municipal Financial Statistics, 0576-5293.*

FINANCIAL STATISTICS. CANADIAN PROVINCES AND SELECTED MUNICIPALITIES. (FINANCIAL STATISTICS, CANADIAN PROVINCES AND SELECTED MUNICIPALITIES). 0820-7267. CN. English. an. Wood Gundy Ltd, Royal Trust Tower, PO Box 274, Toronto-Dominion Centre, Toronto Ontario M5R 1J5 Canada. DD 336.71. *Financial Statistics: Canada's Provinces and Representative Municipalities, 0071-5123.*

FINANCIAL STATISTICS. EXPLANATORY HANDBOOK. Began in 1977. UK. English. an. 4.10. Her Majesty's Stationery Office, PO Box 569, London SE1 9NH England. LC HG186.G7. DD 332.0941. *Financial Statistics. Notes and Definitions.*

FINANCIAL STATISTICS OF EDUCATION IN CYPRUS. Main/Corp Cyprus. Statistics and Research Dept. English. ir. Statistics and Research Department/Printing Office, Nicosia Cyprus. LC LB2965.C9. DD 379.152095645.

FINANCIAL STATISTICS OF INSTITUTIONS OF HIGHER EDUCATION. CURRENT FUNDS, REVENUES AND EXPENDITURES SUMMARY DATA. (FINANCIAL STATISTICS OF INSTITUTIONS OF HIGHER EDUCATION : CURRENT FUNDS, REVENUES AND EXPENDITURES SUMMARY DATA). Main/Corp National Center for Education Statistics. 0565-7458. US. English. National Center for Education Statistics, Washington DC 20202. LC LB2342. DD 379.12140973.

FINANCIAL STATISTICS OF INSTITUTIONS OF HIGHER EDUCATION. STATE DATA. Began with 1975/76. 0161-3073. US. English. an. Statistical Information Office, National Center for Education Statistics, 400 Maryland Avenue SW, Washington DC 20202. LC LB2342. DD 378.020973. *Financial Statistics of Institutions of Higher Education. Current Funds Revenues and Expenditures. State Data, 0148-9305.*

FINANCIAL STATISTICS OF JAPAN. Fiscal Year 1983-. 0289-1522. English. an. Research and Planning Division, Minister's Secretariat, Ministry of Finance, 1-1 Kasumigaseki 3-Chome Chiyoda-Ku, Tokyo 100 Japan. LC HG41. DD 332.0952. *Quarterly Bulletin of Financial Statistics.*

FINANCIAL STATISTICS OF JOINT STOCK COMPANIES IN INDIA. 1950-51-1962-63-. English. ir. LC HG4240. DD 338.740954.

FINANCIAL STATISTICS OF PUBLIC UTILITIES. ELECTRIC AND GAS COMPANIES. Periodical. US. English. an. $67.00. CA Turner & Association Inc, PO Box F, Bloomingdale IL 60108. Tel (312)893-7233. Ed Robert Webb. Circ 500. Financial and statistical data on electric and gas public utilities.

FINANCIAL STATISTICS OF SELECTED ELECTRIC UTILITIES. 1982-. 0747-7635. US. English. an. LC HD9685.U4. DD 338.43363620973. *Statistics of Privately Owned Electric Utilities in the United States, . . . Classes A and B Companies, 0161-9004; Statistics of Publicly Owned Electric Utilities in the United States.*

FINANCIAL STATISTICS OF TELEPHONE AND WATER COMPANIES. Began publication in 1964?. 0430-4853. US. English. an. $43.00. C A Turner & Association Inc, PO Box F, Bloomingdale IL 60108. Tel (312)893-7233. Ed Robert Webb. Circ 500. Financial and statistical data on telephone and water public utilities.

FINANCIAL STATISTICS OF THE MAJOR PRIVATELY OWNED UTILITIES IN NEW YORK STATE. Main/Corp New York (State). Dept. of Public Service. 0363-2113. US. English. an. Department of Public Service, Empire State Plaza Agency Building 3, Albany NY 12223. LC HD2767.N. DD 338.761363609747.

FINANCIAL STATISTICS, TAIWAN DISTRICT, THE REPUBLIC OF CHINA. CH. English. mo. Economic Research Department Central Bank of China, 2 Roosevelt Road Section 1, Taipei Taiwan 107 China. LC HG187.T28. DD 332.0951249. *Taiwan Financial Statistics Monthly.*

FINANCIAL STATISTICS, VERMONT SCHOOL SYSTEMS. (FINANCIAL STATISTICS : VERMONT SCHOOL SYSTEMS). Main/Corp Vermont. Dept. of Education. 0363-3012. US. English. Vermont State Department of Education, PO Box 567, Montpelier VT 05602. LC L208. DD 379.12209743.

FINANCING THE OREGON UNEMPLOYMENT INSURANCE PROGRAM. (FINANCING THE OREGON UNEMPLOYMENT INSURANCE PROGRAM : ACTUARIAL REPORT AND STATISTICAL

Statistics

HANDBOOK). **Main/Corp** Oregon. Employment Division. Research and Statistics Section. 0149-0109. US. English. Employment Division, Department of Human Resources, 875 Union Street NE, Salem OR 97311. LC HD7096.U6. DD 353.97950083.

FIRE LOSSES IN BRITISH COLUMBIA. See Fire Prevention.

FISHERIES STATISTICS. (FISHERIES STATISTICS. QUEBEC). **Main/Corp** Canada. Statistique Canada. Division des Industries Manufacturieres et Primaires. **VFOAT** Statistique des Peches. Quebec. 1970-. 0527-5253. CN. French (English). an. Receiver General for Canada, Statistics Canada Publications, Ottawa Ontario K1A 0T6 Canada. *Fisheries Statistics. Quebec, 0527-5253.*

FISHERIES STATISTICS. BRITISH COLUMBIA AND YUKON CEASED. **Main/Corp** Canada. Dominion Bureau of Statistics. Industry Division. **VFOAT** Statistique des Peches. Colombie-Britannique et Yukon, La Statistique des Peches. Colombie-Britannique et Yukon. 1964-1969. 0380-0253. CN. text in English and French. ir. Receiver General for Canada, Statistics Canada Publications, Ottawa Ontario K1A 0T6 Canada. **Tel** (800)268-1151. *Fisheries Statistics. British Columbia, 0527-5199.*

FISHERIES STATISTICS OF BRITISH COLUMBIA CEASED. 0524-5346. Periodical. CN. English. an. Bureau of Statistics, Publications Distribution, Ottawa Ontario K1A 0T6 Canada. **DD** 338.372709711.

FISHERIES STATISTICS OF JAPAN. JA. English. an. Government Publishing Service Center, 2-1 1 Chome Kasumigaseki, Chiyoda-Ku Tokyo 100 Japan. **Tel** (03)504-3885. LC SH301. DD 338.3727092052. (ctrl).

FISHERIES STATISTICS : ONTARIO CEASED. **Main/Corp** Statistics Canada. **VFOAT** La Statistique des Peches : Ontario. Periodical. CN. Multilingual (English and French). ir. Receiver General for Canada, Statistics Canada Publications, Ottawa Ontario K1A 0T6 Canada.

FISHERIES STATISTICS. PRINCE EDWARD ISLAND. **Main/Corp** Canada. Statistique Canada. Division des Industries Manufacturieres et Primaires. **VFOAT** Statistique des Peches. Ile-du-Prince-Edouard. 1970-. 0575-8556. CN. text in English and French. an. Receiver General for Canada, Statistics Canada Publications, Ottawa Ontario K1A 0T6 Canada. *Fisheries Statistics.*

FISHERY STATISTICS OF THE UNITED STATES. **VFOAT** Fishery Statistics of the U.S. Began in 1939. 0095-7682. US. English. an. US Department of Commerce, National Oceanic and Atmospheric Administration, National Marine Fisheries Service, Washington DC 20402. LC SH11. DD 338.3727092073. *Fishery Industries of the United States.*

FISKERISTATISTIKK. Series/Titl Norges Offisielle Statistikk. **VFOAT** Fishery Statistics. Began in 1962. Norwegian (English). an. 13.00. LC HA1501 SH279. DD 314.81 338.372709481. *Norges Fiskerier.*

FISKERISTATISTISK ARBOG. See Yearbooks, Almanacs, Directories.

FLORIDA ACCIDENTAL DEATH STATISTICS. **Main/Corp** Florida. Dept. of Health and Rehabilitative Services. US. English. $2.64. State of Florida, Department of Health and Rehabilitative Services, Jacksonville FL 32231. LC HB1355.F6. DD 312.2709759.

FLORIDA AGRICULTURAL STATISTICS. **Main/Corp** Florida Crop and Livestock Reporting Service. **VFOAT** Commercial Citrus Inventory. 1966?. US. English. ir. Florida Crop & Livestock Reporting Service, 1222 Woodward Street, Orlando FL 32803. LC HD9259.C54. DD 338.174309759.

FLORIDA AGRICULTURAL STATISTICS. CITRUS SUMMARY. (FLORIDA AGRICULTURAL STATISTICS : CITRUS SUMMARY). **Main/Corp** Florida Crop and Livestock Reporting Service. 0428-6414. US. English. an. 1222 Woodward Street, Orlando FL 32803. LC HD9259.C54. DD 338.174309759. *Florida Agricultural Statistics : Citrus Summary.*

FLORIDA AGRICULTURAL STATISTICS. COMMERCIAL CITRUS INVENTORY. (FLORIDA AGRICULTURAL STATISTICS : INVENTORY OF COMMERCIAL CITRUS ACREAGE). **Main/Corp** Florida Crop and Livestock Reporting Service. **VFOAT** Inventory of Commercial Citrus Acreage. 1965-. 0092-3656. US. English. 1222 Woodward Street, Orlando FL 32803. LC SB369.2.F6. DD 338.1743.

FLORIDA AGRICULTURAL STATISTICS. DAIRY SUMMARY. (FLORIDA AGRICULTURAL STATISTICS : DAIRY SUMMARY). **Main/Corp** Florida Crop and Livestock Reporting Service. **VFOAT** Dairy Summary. 0428-6421. US. English. an. $2.50. Florida Crop and Livestock Reporting Service, 1222 Woodward Street, Orlando FL 32803. **Tel** (305)648-6013. LC HD9282.U5. DD 338.17709759. (ctrl). *Florida Agricultural Statistics: Dairy Summary.*

FLORIDA AGRICULTURAL STATISTICS : POULTRY SUMMARY. US. English. an. 1222 Woodward Street, Orlando FL 32803. LC HD9437.U63. DD 338.1765009759. *Florida Agricultural Statistics: Poultry and Egg Summary.*

FLORIDA AGRICULTURAL STATISTICS. VEGETABLES PRELIMINARY SUMMARY PLANTED ACREAGE. (FLORIDA AGRICULTURAL STATISTICS : VEGETABLES PRELIMINARY SUMMARY, PLANTED ACREAGE). **Main/Corp** Florida Crop and Livestock Reporting Service. 0094-5854. US. English. 1222 Woodward Street, Orlando FL 32803. LC HD9220.U53. DD 338.17509759.

FLORIDA AIR QUALITY STATISTICAL REPORT. (FLORIDA ... AIR QUALITY STATISTICAL REPORT). 0738-1050. US. English. LC TD224.F6. DD 363.7392209759.

FLORIDA EMPLOYMENT STATISTICS. **Main/Corp** Florida. Division of Employment Security. Periodical. US. English. mo. Florida Department of Labor & Employment Security, Tallahassee FL 32301. LC HD5725.F6. DD 331.1109759. *Florida Employment Statistics, 0364-8311.*

THE FLORIDA OUTLOOK. See Economics.

FLORIDA STATISTICAL ABSTRACT. See Indexes/Abstracts.

FLORIDA VITAL STATISTICS. HRS DISTRICT SUPPLEMENT. US. English. Office of Vital Statistics, Public Health Statistics Section, PO Box 210 Jacksonville FL 32231. **Tel** (904)359-6960. LC HA311. DD 312.09759. Circ 800. Vital statistics data for births, deaths, fetal deaths, marriages and dissolutions for state of Florida, counties and districts.

FLOW OF FUNDS SUMMARY STATISTICS. Series/Titl Federal Reserve Statistical Release. Periodical. US. English. qt. Board of Governors of the Federal Reserve System, Washington DC 20551.

F.O. LICHT'S INTERNATIONAL SWEETENER REPORT. See Agriculture.

FOLKMANGD. **Main/Corp** Sweden. Statistiska Centralbyran. Series Corp ITS Sveriges Officiella Statistik. **VFOAT** Population. SW. Swedish (summaries in English). ir. PO Box 23116, 10435 Stockholm 23 Sweden. LC HA1523. DD 312.09485. *Folkmangden Inom Administrativa Omraden.*

FOOD CONSUMPTION STATISTICS. **VFOAT** Basis Statistics OECD/OCDE Statistiques de Base Alimentaires, Statistiques de la Consommation des Denrees Alimentaires. 1954-1966-. English (French). ir. $56.00. OECD Publishing Center, 1750 Pennsylvania Avenue NW, Washington DC 20006. **Tel** (202)724-1857. LC HD9000.1. DD 339.48641300212. Microfiche.

FOOD OUTLOOK. STATISTICAL SUPPLEMENT. **VFOAT** Food Outlook Statistical Supplement. 1981-. English. an. LC HD9000.1. DD 338.19.

FOOD STAMP PROGRAM. STATISTICAL SUMMARY OF OPERATIONS. (FOOD STAMP PROGRAM : STATISTICAL SUMMARY OF OPERATIONS). **Main/Corp** United States. Food and Nutrition Service. May 1973-. 0276-0320. US. English. mo. US Department of Agriculture, Food and Nutrition Service, Washington DC 20250.

FOOTBALL STATISTICIANS' MANUAL. **VFOAT** NCAA Football Statisticians' Manual. Periodical. US. English. an. $2.75. National Collegiate Athletic Association, PO Box 1906, Shawnee Mission KS 66222. **Tel** (913)384-3220. Official statistics rules, including special interpretations and approved rulings.

FOOTWEAR STATISTICS. **VFOAT** Statistique de la Chaussure. V. 47- Jan. 1972-. 0380-707X. Periodical. CN. text in English and French. mo. 40.00 Domestic, 50.00 Foreign. Receiver General for Canada, Statistics Canada Publications, Ottawa Ontario K1A 0T6 Canada. **Tel** (800)268-1151. Production of footwear in Canada, by type of footwear. *Production of Leather Footwear, 0380-7088.*

FOREIGN AGRICULTURAL TRAINING ACTIVITIES : ANNUAL STATISTICAL SUMMARY. **Main/Corp** United States. Dept. of Agriculture. Economic Research Service. International Training Office. 1973-. Periodical. US. English. an.

FOREIGN COMMERCE STATISTICAL REPORT. PORT OF BALTIMORE AND OTHER MARYLAND PORTS. (FOREIGN COMMERCE STATISTICAL REPORT : PORT OF BALTIMORE AND OTHER MARYLAND PORTS). **Main/Corp** Maryland. Port Administration. 0191-0434. US. English. an. Maryland Port Administration, World Trade Center, Baltimore MD 21202. LC HF3163.B2. DD 382.097526.

FOREIGN TRADE STATISTICAL DIGEST. **Main/Corp** Bank Al-Sudan. Idarat Al-Buhuth Al-Iqtisadiyah. V. 1- 1968-. 0522-246X. SJ. English. ir. Bank of Sudan, Research Dept, Khartoum Sudan. LC HF273.S8. DD 382.09624.

FOREIGN TRADE STATISTICS. **Main/Corp** Israel. Lishkah Ha-Merkazit Li-Statistikah. Jan./Mar.-Jan./June 1969. 0021-1990. IS. English. an. $30.00. Central Bureau of Statistics, PO Box 13015, Jerusalem Israel. **Tel** (72)211400. LC HF259.P3. DD 382.095694. Detailed classified (BTN) statistics on the imports and exports of Israel, by commodity value and country of origin/destination.

FOREIGN TRADE STATISTICS FOR AFRICA. SERIES A : DIRECTION OF TRADE. **Main/Corp** United Nations. Economic Commission for Africa. **VFOAT** Statistiques Africaines du Commerce Exterieur. Series A : Echanges par Pays. No. 11-. US. English (French). ir. $8.50. United Nations Publications, Sales Section/Room A-3315, New York NY 10017. **Tel** (212)754-8302. Focuses on trade issues by country. *Foreign Trade Statistics of Africa. Series A: Direction of Trade, 0071-7398.*

FOREIGN TRADE STATISTICS FOR AFRICA. SERIES B : TRADE BY COMMODITY. **VFOAT** Statistiques Africaines du Commerce Exterieur. Serie B. Echanges par Produits. No. 14-. US. English (French). ir. $9.00. United Nations Publications, Sales Section/Room A-3315, New York NY 10017. **Tel** (212)754-8302. Focuses on African trade issues, by commodity. *Foreign Trade Statistics of Africa. Series B: Trade by Commodity.*

FOREIGN TRADE STATISTICS MONTHLY. **Main/Corp** Israel. Central Bureau of Statistics. V.26, No. 1- Jan. 1975-. Periodical. IS. English. mo. *Monthly Foreign Trade Statistics.*

FOREIGN TRADE STATISTICS OF ASIA AND THE PACIFIC. SERIES A. V. 8, No. 2- 1969-. Periodical. US. English. ir. $12.50. United Nations Publications, Sales Section/Room A-3315, New York NY 10017. **Tel** (212)754-8302. LC JX1977, HF3751. DD 300 S, 382.095. Statistics on import/export trade in the Asian/Oceanic region. Tables give data for overall trade, trade between countries, intraregional trade and major specific products. *Foreign Trade Statistics of Asia and The Far East Series A.*

FOREIGN TRADE STATISTICS OF ASIA AND THE PACIFIC. SERIES B. V. 7, No. 1-. Periodical. US. English. ir. $17.50. United Nations Publications, Sales Section/Room A-3315, New York NY 10017. **Tel** (212)754-8302. LC JX1977. DD 300 S, 382.09500212. Statistical data on trade by commodity in the Asia/Oceanic region. *Foreign Trade Statistics of Asia and the Far East. Series B.*

FOREIGN TRADE STATISTICS OF THE PHILIPPINES. Periodical. PH. English. an. National Census and Statistics Office, PO Box 779, Manila Philippines.

FOREST SERVICE ANNUAL REPORT. STATISTICS. (FOREST SERVICE ANNUAL REPORT). **Main/Corp** British Columbia. Forest Service. 1976-. 0706-2982. CN. English. an. 3.00. Queen's Printer, Victoria British Columbia V8V 4R6 Canada. **Tel** 387-1901.

FOREST STATISTICS FOR IOWA. **Main/Corp** North Central Forest Experiment Station (St. Paul, Minn.). 0146-4159. US. English. Free. St Paul North Forest Experiment Station, Folwell Avenue, St Paul MN 55018. **Tel** (612)642-5233. Ed Robert D

Statistics

Wray. **LC** SD11, SD144.I8. **DD** 333.750977 S, 333.7509777. **Circ** 4,000. (ctrl). One of a series (Resource Bulletins) reporting on periodic statewide inventories of forest resources.

FORTHCOMING EVENTS - STATISTICAL SOCIETY OF CANADA *CEASED.* (FORTHCOMING EVENTS : FROM THE OFFICE OF THE CANADIAN JOURNAL OF STATISTICS, STATISTICAL SOCIETY OF CANADA). Vol. 1, No. 1 (1980)-. 0711-1061. Periodical. CN. English (includes some text in French). sa. Free. Canadian Journal of Statistics, 675 Denbury Avenue, Ottawa Ontario K2A 2P2 Canada. **DD** 519.5.

FORUM STATISTICUM. Periodical. French (text in German and Italian). ir. Eidgenossisches Statistisches AMT, 3003 Bern Switzerland. **LC** HA37. **DD** 314.94.

LA FRANCHE-COMTE EN QUELQUES CHIFFRES. FR. French. ir. Institut National de la Statistique et des Etudes Economiques, Service Regional de Besancon, 2 rue de l'Industrie, Besan France. **LC** HA1228.F7. **DD** 314.445.

FREIGHT COMMODITY STATISTICS. MOTOR CARRIERS OF PROPERTY. VFOAT Freight Commodity Statistics of Class 1 Motor Carriers of Property Operating in Intercity Service— Common and Contract, in the United States. 0194-0562. Periodical. US. English. an. US Government Printing Office, Superintendent of Documents, Washington DC 20402. **LC** HE5623. **DD** 388.3240973. *Freight Commodity Statistics.*

FREIGHT COMMODITY STATISTICS OF CLASS I RAILROADS IN THE UNITED STATES. VFOAT Freight Commodity Statistics: Class I Railroads. 33rd-. US. English. an. Interstate Commerce Commission, Bureau of Accounts, Washington DC 20423. *Freight Commodity Statistics of Class I Steam Railways in the United States.*

FROZEN FOOD PACK STATISTICS. Main/Corp American Frozen Food Institute. Began in 1946. 0469-7405. US. English. an. $50.00. American Frozen Food Institute, 1838 El Camino Real/Suite 202, Burlingame CA 94010. **Tel** (415)697-6835. (ctrl). Frozen food production statistics by style and container size.

FRUIT (AUSTRALIAN BUREAU OF STATISTICS). (FRUIT). 1980-81-. English. an. Australian Bureau of Statistics, 10-20 Pulteney Street, Adelaide 5000 Australia. **LC** HD9258.A8. **DD** 338.1740994.

FYLKESTINGSVALGET. Main/Corp Norway. Statistisk Sentralbyra. **Series/Titl** Norges Offiselle Statistikk. VFOAT County Council Elections. 1975-. Norwegian (English). ir. **LC** HA1501, JS6218.S7.

GABUN : WIRTSCHAFTLICHE ENTWICKLUNG. Main/Corp Bundesstelle fur Aussenhandelsinformation (Germany). 1968/73-. German. ir. Bundesstelle fur Aussenhandelsinformation, Blaubach 13 5 1, Koln West Germany. **LC** HA2090.

THE GAMBIA EDUCATION STATISTICS. VFOAT Education Statistics. English. an. 10.00. **LC** LA1620. **DD** 370.96651.

GARTENBAU- UND FELDGEMUSE-ANBAUERHEBUNG. *See* Horticulture and Plant Culture.

GAS FACTS. *See* Petroleum and Natural Gas.

GASSTATISTIK FUR DIE BUNDESREPUBLIK DEUTSCHLAND. VFOAT Gasstatistik. German. ir. ZFGW Verlag, Postfach 901080, D-6000 Frankfurt West Germany. Zusammenstellung der Statistischen Angaben der Gasversorgungsunternehmen in der Bundesrepublik Deutschland und in West-Berlin.

GEHALTS- UND LOHNSTRUKTURERHEBUNG. Series/Titl Statistik von Baden-Wurttemberg. GW. German. ir. Statistisches Landesamt Baden-Wurttemberg, Postfach 898, 7000 Stuttgart 1 West Germany. **LC** HA1320.B2, HD5030. B3. **DD** 314.346 S, 331.294346.

GEMEINDEDATEN. Main/Corp Bayerisches Statistisches Landesamt. German. ir. Bayerisches Statistisches Landesamt, Neuhauser Str 51, 8 Munchen 2 West Germany. **LC** HA1261. **DD** 314.33.

DIE GEMEINDEN NORDRHEIN-WESTFALEN. Main/Corp North Rhine-Westphalia. Landesamt fur Datenverarbeitung und Statistik. German. ir. 13.-. Landesamt fur Datenverarbeitung und Statistik, 4000 Dusseldorf Mauerstr 51, Dusseldorf West Germany. **Tel** (0211)44971. **LC** HA1320.N6. adv acc. **Circ** 1,200. Selected statistical returns about the 396 communities of Nordrhein-Westfalen.

GENERAL AVIATION STATISTICAL DATABOOK. 1982 Ed.-. US. English. an. General Aviation Manufacturers Association, 1025 Connecticut Avenue NW/Suite 517, Washington DC 20036. *General Aviation Statistical Data.*

GEORGIA DESCRIPTIONS IN DATA. 1982-. 0741-0182. US. English. an. $7.50. Office of Planning and Budget, 608 Trinity-Washington Street SW, Atlanta GA 30334. **Tel** (404)656-0911. Ed Robin Kirkpatrick and Thomas Wagner. **LC** HA321. **DD** 317.58. **Circ** 1,000. (ctrl). Contains statistics for Georgia on education, income, population, employment, health, taxes, business, industry, government, agriculture, public safety and natural resources.

GEORGIA OFFICIAL AND STATISTICAL REGISTER. 1971/72-. US. English. ir. $15.00. Department of Archives and History, 330 Capitol Avenue SE, Atlanta GA 30334. **Tel** (404)656-2370. Ed Marian B Holmes. **Circ** 1,800. (ctrl). Reference source of Georgia state government. Includes biographical sketches of Georgia officials in federal and state levels of government, duties of state agencies, last election results, etc. *Georgia's Official and Statistical Register.*

GEORGIA STATISTICAL ABSTRACT. *See* Indexes/Abstracts.

GEORGIA VITAL AND MORBIDITY STATISTICS. Main/Corp Georgia. Dept. of Human Resources. US. English. an. 47 Trinity Avenue SW, Atlanta GA 30334. **LC** HA321. **DD** 312.0975. *Georgia Vital and Morbidity Statistics.*

DAS GESUNDHEITSWESEN IN NORDRHEIN-WESTFALEN. Main/Corp North Rhine-Westphalia (Germany). Landesamt fur Datenverarbeitung und Statistik. **Series/Titl** Beitrage zur Statistik des Landes Nordrhein-Westfalen. German. ir. 23.50. Landesamt fur Datenverarbeitung und Statistik, Mauerstr 51, 4000 Dusseldorf West Germany. **Tel** (0211)44971. **LC** HA1320.N6, RA407.5. G4. adv acc. **Circ** 300.

GOHAN TOKEI. Series/Titl Norin Suisan Tokei Hokoku. VFOAT Statistics of Plywood. JA. Japanese. ir. Nihon Gohan Kogyo Kumiai Rengokai, c/o Meisan Building, 18-17 Nishi Shinbashi 1-chome, Minato-ku, Tokyo-to Japan. **LC** HD9769.P63.

GOLD STATISTICS AND ANALYSIS. 0736-1777. US. English. J Aron & Co, 160 Water Street, New York NY 10038. **LC** HG293. **DD** 338.274105.

GOVERNMENT FINANCE STATISTICS YEARBOOK. INTERNATIONAL MONETARY FUND. *See* Yearbooks, Almanacs, Directories.

GRAIN STATISTICS WEEKLY. Main/Corp Canadian Grain Commission. Economics and Statistics Division. Aug. 11, 1971-. 0381-3010. Periodical. CN. English. wk. *Canadian Grain Position,* 0410-5125.

GUIDE STATISTIQUE DE LA FISCALITE DIRECTE LOCALE. FR. French. ir. 29-31 Quai Voltaire, 75340 Paris Cedex 07 France.

GUIDE TO FEDERAL GOVERNMENT LABOUR STATISTICS. VFOAT Guide de la Statistique du Travail du Gouvernement Federal. CN. English and French. $1.00. Information Canada/Receiver General Canada, Statistics Publication Canada, Ottawa Ontario K1A 0T6 Canada. **LC** HD8103. **DD** 331.1077.

GUIDE TO FOREIGN TRADE STATISTICS. 0565-0933. US. English. $4.75. US Department of Commerce, Bureau of the Census, Washington DC 20233. **LC** HF105. **DD** 382.0973. The Foreign Trade Statistics program involves the compilation and dissemination of thousands of facts relating to imports and exports of the United States.

GUIDE TO OFFICIAL STATISTICS. Main/Corp Great Britain. Central Statistical Office. 1976-. UK. English. 7.50. Her Majestys Stationery Office, PO Box 276, London SW8 5DT England. **LC** HA37. **DD** 016.3141.

GUIDE TO PETROLEUM STATISTICAL INFORMATION. 1983-. 0742-8464. US. English. an. American Petroleum Institute, 156 William Street, New York NY 10038. **LC** Z6972, HD9560.1. **DD** 016.33827282.

GUJARAT STATISTICAL REVIEW. 0379-3419. Periodical. II. English. ir. $5.00. R T Ratani, Department of Statistics, Gujarat University, Ahmedabad 380004 India. **Ind/Abst** Math. Rev. **LC** QA276.A1. **DD** 519.505. **CODEN** GSTRD3.

GYPSUM PRODUCTS. Main/Corp Canada. Statistique Canada. Division des Industries Manufacturieres et Primaires. VFOAT Produits de Gypse. V. 23- Jan. 1972-. 0380-7223. Periodical. CN. English and French. mo. Receiver General for Canada, Statistics Canada Publications, Ottawa Ontario K1A 0T6 Canada. *Gypsum Products.*

HA-YARHON HA-STATISTI LE-YISRAEL. Main/Corp Israel. Lishkah Ha-Merkazit Li-Statistikah. VFOAT Statistical Bulletin of Israel. V. 18- Jan. 1967-. 0021-1982. IS. English and Hebrew. ir. $26.60. Government Publishing House, Street B No 29 Hakirya, Tel-Aviv Yerushalayim Israel. **Tel** (00-972)2-211400. **LC** HA1931. Periodic offical statistics on various branches of Israel's society, demography and economy. *Yarhon Ha-Statisti Le-Yisrael, Helek A: Hevrah.*

HA-YARHON HA-STATISTI LE-YISRAEL. MUSAF. Main/Corp Israel. Lishkah Ha-Merkazit Li-Statistikah. VFOAT Statistical Bulletin of Israel. V. 18- Jan. 1967-. IS. English or Hebrew. ir. Government Printing House, Street B No 29 Hakirya, Yerushalayim Israel. **LC** HA1931.

HAGSKYRSLUR ISLANDS *CEASED.* VFOAT Statistique de l'Islande, Statistics of Iceland. No. 1-132. IC. Icelandic. ir. Statistical Bureau of Iceland, Central Bank of Iceland, Reykjauik Iceland. **LC** HA1491. **DD** 314.912.

HALF-YEARLY BULLETIN OF ELECTRIC ENERGY STATISTICS FOR EUROPE. Main/Corp United Nations. Economic Commission for Europe. VFOAT Bulletin Semestriel de Statistiques de l'Energie Electrique pour l'Europe, Polugodovoi Biulleten Evropeiskoi Statistiki Electroenergii. V. 10- 1965-. 0503-3772. Periodical. US. English (in French and Russian). ir. United Nations Publications, Sales Section/Room A-3315, New York NY 10017. *Quarterly Bulletin of Electric Energy Statistics for Europe.*

HALSO- OCH SJUKVARD VID FORSVARET. Main/Corp Sweden. Forsvarets Sjukvardsstyrelse. Centralplaneringen. 1970/72-. Swedish. ir. Forsvarets Sjukvardsstyrelse Centralplaneringen, Fack 104 40 14, Stockholm Sweden. **LC** HA1521. *Halso - Och Sjukvard Vid Forsvaret.*

HAMBURG IN ZAHLEN. June 21 1947-. Periodical. German. ir. **Tel** 040-3681-719. bk rev. (ctrl). Report on statistics of the city of Hamburg, West Germany. Includes selected texts and large section of statistical figures.

HAMBURGER KREBSDOKUMENTATION. Series/Titl Statistik des Hamburgischen Staates. 0170-3064. GW. German. ir. Statistisches Landesamt, Steckelhorn 12, 2000 Hamburg 11 West Germany.

THE HANDBOOK OF BASIC ECONOMIC STATISTICS. Began in 1947. 0017-7199. Periodical. US. English. mo. $132.00. Economic Statistics Bureau, PO Box 10163, Washington DC 20018. **Tel** (202)393-5070. Ed Charles L Franklin. **LC** HC101. **DD** 330.97300212. Contains government statistics. Each supplement includes end-of-month business summary and economic highlights.

HANDBOOK OF BASIC STATISTICS OF MAHARASHTRA STATE. Main/Corp Maharashtra, India (State). Directorate of Economics and Statistics. 1974-. II. English. ir. 0.80. Govenment of Maharashtra, Yervada Prison Press, Poona 6 Maharashtra India. **LC** HA1728.M3. **DD** 315.4792. *Handbook of Basic Statistics.*

HANDBOOK OF ECONOMIC STATISTICS. 0195-9018. US. English. an. US Government Printing Office, Superintendent of Documents, Washington DC 20402. **LC** HA155. **DD** 330.904. Vols. for 1980- distributed to depository libraries in microfiche.

HANDBOOK OF ECONOMIC STATISTICS. US. English. an. Superintendent of Documents, US Government Printing Office, Washington DC 20402.

HANDBOOK OF EMPLOYMENT SECURITY PROGRAM STATISTICS. Main/Corp Oklahoma. State Employment Service. 0361-2902. US. English. ir. Oklahoma Employment Security Commission, Will Rogers Memorial Office

Statistics

Building, Oklahoma City OK 73105. **LC** HD7096.U6. **DD** 368.44009766. *Handbook of Employment Security Program Statistics.*

HANDBOOK OF HOUSING STATISTICS. VFOAT Avasiya Sankhyiki Pustika. Began in 1979. English. an. **LC** HD7361.A3. **DD** 363.50954.

HANDBOOK OF INTERNATIONAL TRADE AND DEVELOPMENT STATISTICS. Main/Corp United Nations Conference on Trade and Development. VFOAT Manuel de Statistiques du Commerce International et du Developpement. 1969-. US. English (French). an. $50.00. United Nations Publications, Sales Section/Room A-3315, New York NY 10017. Tel (212)754-8302. Complete basic collection of statistical data relevant to the analysis of world trade and development.

HANDBOOK OF INTERNATIONAL TRADE AND DEVELOPMENT STATISTICS. SUPPLEMENT. Main/Corp United Nations Conference on Trade and Development. VFOAT Supplement, Manuel de Statistiques du Commerce International et du Developpement. Began with V. for 1970?. US. English (French). an. **LC** HF1016. **DD** 382.021.

HANDBOOK OF LABOR STATISTICS. Began with 1924-26. 0082-9056. US. English. Superintendent of Documents, Government Printing Office, Washington DC 20402. **LC** HD8051. **DD** 331.0973, 331.0973. Vols. for 1983- Distributed to depository libraries in microfiche.

HANDBOOK OF SELECTED AGRICULTURAL STATISTICS. VFOAT Guide de Donnees Statistiques Agricoles. 1984-. CN. English. an. **LC** S133. **DD** 338.10971021. *Selected Agricultural Statistics for Canada and the Provinces, 0832-4795.*

HANDBOOK OF STATISTICS - INDIAN ENGINEERING ASSOCIATION. Main/Corp Indian Engineering Association. Began publication July 1963. 0073-6333. II. English. ir. Indian Exchange 7th Floor, Calcutta India. **LC** HA1725.

HANDBOOK OF STATISTICS. JAMMU AND KASHMIR. (HANDBOOK OF STATISTICS, JAMMU AND KASHMIR). 0377-7219. II. English. ir. Directorate of Economics and Statistics, Spinagar India. **LC** HA1728.K35. **DD** 315.46.

HANDBOOK OF STATISTICS (NORTH-HOLLAND PUBLISHING COMPANY). (HANDBOOK OF STATISTICS). Vol. 1-. Monographic Series. US. English. ir. Elsevier North-Holland Inc, 52 Vanderbilt Avenue, New York NY 10017. **Ind/Abst** Math. Rev., Comput. Control Abstr., Electr. Electron. Abstr., Sci. Abstr. Sect. A. Phys. Abstr.

HANDBOOK OF STATISTICS ON COTTON TEXTILE INDUSTRY. Began in 1968. English. an. Textile Center, P d'Mello Road, Bombay 400009 India. **LC** HD9886.I4. **DD** 338.47677210954.

HANDBOOK ON AGRICULTURAL STATISTICS FOR ASIA AND THE PACIFIC. Began with Vol. for 1978. English. an. **LC** S270. **DD** 338.1095. *Handbook on Cereal and Fertilizer Statistics for Asia and the Pacific.*

HAN'GUK CHONJA KONGOP TONGGYE YON'GAM. *See* Yearbooks, Almanacs, Directories.

HAWAII FACTS AND FIGURES. Began with: 1946/47. US. English. an. $2.71. Chamber of Commerce of Hawaii, 735 Bishop Street, Honolulu HI 96813. Ed C L Hodge. *General Information about Honolulu, Hawaii, U.S.A. and the Territory, Combined with Business Statistics.*

HAYATI ISTATISTIKLER : IL VE ILCE MERKEZLERINDE OLUMER. Main/Corp Devlet Istatistik Enstitusu (Turkey). Series Corp Its Yayn. Publication. VFOAT Vital Statistics. English and Turkish. ir. Devlet Istatistik Enstitusu, Ankara Turkey. **LC** HA1911, HB1455.

HEALTH AND PERSONAL SOCIAL SERVICES STATISTICS FOR ENGLAND WITH SUMMARY TABLES FOR GREAT BRITAIN. (HEALTH AND PERSONAL SOCIAL SERVICES STATISTICS FOR ENGLAND). Main/Corp Great Britain. Dept. of Health and Social Security. 1973-. 0307-0824. UK. English. an. 3.00. Her Majestys Stationery Office, 49 High Holborn, Longon WC1V 6HB England. **LC** RA407.5.G7. **DD** 362.10942. **NLM** W2 FA1 D425H. *Health and Personal Social Services Statistics for England and Wales with Summary Tables for Great Britain, 0300-988X.*

HEALTH AND PERSONAL SOCIAL SERVICES STATISTICS FOR WALES. Main/Corp Great Britain. Welsh Office. VFOAT Ystadegau Iechyd a Gwasanaethau Cymdeithasol Personol. No. 1- 1974-. 0307-0840. UK. English. an. 2.15. **LC** HV249. **DD** 362.1109429. **NLM** W2 FA1 W27K.

HEALTH CARE EXPENDITURES IN KANSAS. *See* Public Health and Safety.

HEALTH CARE FINANCING REVIEW. *See* Public Health and Safety.

HEALTH MANPOWER STATISTICS. Began with Vol. for 1981. 0740-1701. US. English. an. Department of Defense, Washington Headquarters Services, Directorate for Information Operations and Reports, The Pentagon, Washington DC 20310. **LC** UH223. **DD** 355.3450973.

HEALTH RESOURCES STATISTICS. Main/Corp United States. National Center for Health Statistics. Series/Titl Public Health Service Publication. 1965-. 0083-1956. US. English. an. National Center for Health Statistics, Rockville MD 20852. **LC** RA407.3. **DD** 362.10973. **NLM** W2 A N148H.

HEALTH STATISTICS IN THE NORDIC COUNTRIES. VFOAT Helsestatistikk I de Nordiske Land. English (Norwegian). ir. Nordic Medical Statistical Commission (Nomesko). **LC** RA407.5.S34. **DD** 362.10948.

HEALTH STATISTICS PLAN. Main/Corp United States. Dept. of Health, Education, and Welfare. 0147-0949. US. English. an. US Department of Health Education & Welfare, Washington DC 20202. **LC** RA407.3. **DD** 353.00841. **NLM** W2 A H3H.

HEALTH STATISTICS REPORT. CANCER DATA. VFOAT Cancer Data. Began with 1972 issue. 0548-9415. NZ. English. an. 15.00. National Health Statistics Centre, Department of Health, Wellington New Zealand. Tel 844 167. **LC** RC279.N47. **DD** 312.3994009931. **NLM** W2 KN4 N24C. **Circ** 450. (ctrl). New Zealand cancer data. *Cancer Data.*

HEALTH STATISTICS REPORT : HOSPITAL AND SELECTED MORBIDITY DATA. Main/Corp National Health Statistics Centre (N.Z.). VFOAT Hospital and Selected Morbidity Data. 1971-. NZ. English. ir. 17.00. National Health Statistics, PO Box 5013, Wellington NZ. Tel 844-167. **LC** RA407.5.N4. **DD** 312.309931. **NLM** W2 KN4 D4HB. **Circ** 450. (ctrl). Statistics of causes of admission (morbidity) into New Zealand hospitals. Includes length of stay and number of operations. *Medical Statistics Report.*

HELSINGIN VAESTO. VFOAT Helsingfors Befolkning. 0357-3370. FI. Finnish. an. Toolontorinkatu 2 B, 00260 Helsinki 26 Finland. **LC** HA1450.5.Z9.

HENKIKIRJOITETTU VAESTO KUNNITTAIN. Main/Corp Finland. Tilastokeskus. VFOAT Mantalskriven Befolkning Kommunvis. Finnish and Swedish. ir. Tilastokeskus, Annankatu 44 00100 10, Helsinki Finland. **LC** HA1448.

DIE HESSISCHE AUSFUHR. German. ir. 6.50. Hessisches Statistisches Landesamt, Postfach 3205, 6200 Wiesbaden 1 West Germany. **LC** HA1320, HF3569. H4.

HIGHER EDUCATION FINANCIAL STATISTICS. US. English. an. Pennsylvania Department of Education, Division of Data Services, 333 Market Street/PO Box 911, Harrisburg PA 17108. **LC** LB2342. **DD** 378.12209748.

HIGHER EDUCATION STATISTICAL ABSTRACT. *See* Indexes/Abstracts.

HIGHWAY TRAFFIC STATISTICS. Main/Corp North Carolina. Division of Highways. Planning and Research Branch. 0364-0825. US. English. **LC** HE371.N75. **DD** 388.31409756.

HIGHWAYS AND TRANSPORTATION STATISTICS . . . ESTIMATES. 1981-82-. 0260-9894. UK. English. an. 9.00. Chartered Institute of Public Finance and Accountancy, 1 Buckingham Palace, London SW1E 6HS England. **LC** HE243.A15. **DD** 388.049.

HISTORICAL ENERGY STATISTICS. V. 3- 1979-. US. English. Department of Natural Resources and Conservation, Energy Division, Helena MT 59601. Ed R Itami. **LC** HD9502.U53. **DD** 333.7909786. *Montana Historical Energy Statistics.*

HISTORICAL STATISTICAL BULLETIN. VFOAT Bulletin Statistique Historique. Vol. 1 (1950-1959)-. English (French and Spanish). an. ICCAT Secretariat, Principe de Vergara 17, Madrid 1 Spain. **LC** SH351.T8. **DD** 338.37278.

HISTORICAL STATISTICS OF FOREIGN TRADE. VFOAT Statistiques Retrospectives du Commerce Exterieur. US. English (French). an. $11.00. OECD Publications and Information Center, Suite 1207/1750 Pennsylvania Avenue NW, Washington DC 20006. Tel (202)724-1857. **LC** HF1016. **DD** 382.0212.

HOMICIDE IN CANADA, A STATISTICAL PERSPECTIVE. VFOAT L'Homicide au Canada, Perspective Statistique. 1982-. 0825-432X. CN. English (French). an. $11.10 Domestic, $13.30 Foreign. Publication Sales and Services, Statistics Canada, Ottawa Ontario K1A 0T6 Canada. **DD** 364.1520971. *Homicide Statistics (Statistics Canada), 0706-2788.*

HOMICIDE STATISTICS (STATISTICS CANADA) CEASED. (HOMICIDE STATISTICS). VFOAT Statistique de l'Homicide. 1976-1981. 0706-2788. CN. English (French). an. Receiver General for Canada, Statistics Canada Publications, Ottawa Ontario K1A 0T6 Canada. **LC** HV6535.C3. **DD** 312.2760971. Also available in microfiche. *Murder Statistics, 0575-917X.*

HONG KONG ANNUAL DIGEST OF STATISTICS. 1978-. English. an. 90.00 Domestic, $12.00. Government Information Services, Beaconsfield House/Queens Road, Central Victoria Hong Kong. Tel 5 233191. **LC** HA1950.H6. **DD** 315.125. **Circ** 1,000. The most comprehensive collection of data series from government departments and data from major census and surveys.

HONG KONG MONTHLY DIGEST OF STATISTICS. Main/Corp Hong Kong. Census and Statistics Dept. 0300-418X. HK. English. mo. 336 Domestic, 456 Foreign, $44.80 US. Hong Kong Government Information Systems, Beaconsfield House/6th Floor, Queens Road Center, Victoria Hong Kong. **LC** HA1950.H6. **DD** 315.125. **Circ** 2,000. Contains main data series from all government departments and up-to-date statistical information on the social and economic characteristics of Hong Kong.

HONG KONG REVIEW OF OVERSEAS TRADE. *See* Business - Commerce.

HONG KONG SOCIAL & ECONOMIC TRENDS. *See* Economics.

HONG KONG TRADE STATISTICS. Main/Corp Hong Kong. Census and Statistics Dept. HK. English. mo. $190.00. Census and Statistics Department, Beaconsfield House/6th Floor, Queens Road, Central Victoria Hong Kong. **LC** HF259.H6. **DD** 382.095125. *Hong Kong Trade Statistic.*

HOSPITAL ANNUAL STATISTICS. VFOAT La Statistique Annuelle des Hopitaux. 1976-. 0228-5142. CN. English. an. 100.00 Domestic, 113.00 Foreign. Receiver General for Canada, Statistics Canada Publications, Ottawa Ontario K1A 0T6 Canada. Tel (800)268-1151. Public, private and federal general and allied special hospitals: number of facilities and approved bed complement, by province, type of hospital, service and size, etc. *Hospital Statistics (Statistics Canada. Hospitals Section).*

HOSPITAL IN-PATIENT STATISTICS, WESTERN AUSTRALIA CEASED. English. ir. Australian Bureau of Statistics, 1 3 St Georges Terrace, Perth Western Australia 6000 Australia. Tel 3235323. **LC** RA992.W47. **DD** 362.1109941.

HOSPITAL INDICATORS. *See* Medicine - Medical Centers, Hospitals.

HOSPITAL MORBIDITY STATISTICS. (HOSPITAL MORBIDITY STATISTICS : BASED ON THE EXPERIENCE OF PROVINCIAL HOSPITAL INSURANCE PLANS IN CANADA, JANUARY 1- DECEMBER 31 . . .). 0712-2306. CN. English. an. Receiver General for Canada, Statistics Canada, Ottawa Ontario K1A 0T6 Canada. **DD** 362.110971.

Statistics

HOSPITAL STATISTICS. Main/Corp American Hospital Association. 0090-6662. US. English. an. $49.50. American Hospital Association, PO Box 99376, Chicago IL 60693. Tel (312)280-6029. LC RA981.A2. DD 362.110973. NLM W1 HO885D.

HOSPITAL STATISTICS : PRELIMINARY ANNUAL REPORT. Main/Corp Canada. Statistics Canada. Health Division. Institutional Statistics Section. VFOAT La Statistique Hospitaliere: Rapport Annuel Preliminaire. 1977/78-. 0381-8802. CN. English (French). an. $3.60. Statistics Canada, Health Division, Institutional Statistics Section, Ottawa Ontario K1A 0T6 Canada. DD 362.110971. *Hospital Statistics.*

HOSPITAL STATISTICS. PUBLIC AND PRIVATE HOSPITALS. MENTAL HEALTH SERVICES. (HOSPITAL STATISTICS : PUBLIC AND PRIVATE HOSPITALS, MENTAL HEALTH SERVICES). Main/Corp Ontario. Ministry of Health. Ministry Information System Division. 1974-. 0703-0525. CN. English. an. Publications Centre, Ministry of Government Services, MacDonald Block/Room 3B7, Queen's Park Toronto Ontario M7A 1R5 Canada. LC RA983.A4. DD 362.109713. NLM W2 DC2.1 O5M6HA. *Mental Health Services, 0704-3236; Hospital Statistics: Public and Private Hospitals, 0317-395X.*

HOSPITAL STATISTICS. VOLUME 1. BEDS, SERVICES, PERSONNEL. (HOSPITAL STATISTICS, V. I). Main/Corp Canada. Statistics Canada. Hospitals Section. VFOAT Statistique Hospitaliere, V. I. 1973-. 0383-574X. CN. English (French). an. $3.50. Information Canada, Statistics Canada, Ottawa Ontario Canada. *Hospital Statistics, V. I, Hospital Statistics, V. II.*

HOURLY PRECIPITATION DATA. HAWAII AND PACIFIC. See Earth Sciences - Meteorology.

HOUSING AND CONSTRUCTION STATISTICS. No. 1 (1st Quarter 1972)-No. 32 (4th Quarter 1979). UK. English. ir. $42.14. Her Majestys Stationery Office, PO Box 276, London SW8 5DT England. Tel (01)622 3316. LC HD7333.A3. DD 338.476240944. *Housing Statistics, Great Britain, Monthly Bulletin of Construction Statistics.*

HOUSING AND CONSTRUCTION STATISTICS (ANNUAL). (HOUSING AND CONSTRUCTION STATISTICS). 0308-9819. UK. English. an. 21.00. Directorate of Statistics, STCG3 Division/Department of the Environment, 2 Marsham Street, London SW1P 3EB England. LC HD7333.A3. DD 338.476240941.

HOW NORTH CAROLINA RANKS EDUCATIONALLY AMONG FIFTY STATES. See Education (General).

HUNGARY, STATISTICAL DATA. English. ir. 18.-. Statistical Publications House, PO Box 99, Budapest H-1300 Hungary. Tel 803-311. LC HA1201. DD 314.39. Circ 35,000. This popular small-format book gives a comprehensive picture of Hungary's economic and social development by way of thousands of statistical data; in Hungarian, English, German and Russian.

HUNTER CASUALTY REPORT. See Recreation, Leisure - Outdoor Life.

IDAHO AGRICULTURAL STATISTICS. Main/Corp Idaho Crop and Livestock Reporting Service. 1972-. 0094-1271. Periodical. US. English. an. Idaho Statistical Reporting Service, Box 1699, Boise ID 83701. LC S53. DD 338.109796.

IDAHO HIGHWAY STATISTICS. US. English. LC HE356.I2. DD 388.109796.

IFO SPIEGEL DER WIRTSCHAFT. See Economics - International Economics.

IHSAAT AL-IQTISADIYAH WA-AL-MALIYAH LIL-BUNUK WA-AL-TA-MIN. Arabic. ir. Jihaz Al-Markazi, Lil-Tabiah Al-Ammah, Wa-Al-Ihsa Tariq Salah Salim Madinat Nasr Al-Qahirah Egypt. LC HG3386.

IHSAAT AL-TALIM FI AL-MAMLAKAH AL-ARABIYAH AL-SAUDIYAH. VFOAT Educational Statistics in the Kingdom of Saudi Arabia. Began with Vol. for 1974/75. Arabic (English). an. LC L564.S33. *Educational Statistics in the Kingdom of Saudi Arabia.*

ILLINOIS AGRICULTURAL STATISTICS. Began in 1951. 0422-2562. US. English. an. $5.00. US Department of Agriculture, Crop Reporting Board, South Building/Room 5829, Washington DC 20250. LC 555. DD 338.1.

IMPORTACION-EXPORTACION, URUGUAY. See Business - Commerce.

INCHON KYOYUK TONGGYE YONBO. See Yearbooks, Almanacs, Directories.

INDAGINE SPECIALE SULLE VACANZE DEGLI ITALIANI. See Economics - Labor.

INDEKS; MESECHI PREGLED PRIVREDNE STATISTIKE FNRJ. See Indexes/Abstracts.

INDEX OF ONTARIO GOVERNMENT STATISTICS FOR MUNICIPALITIES. See Indexes/Abstracts.

INDEX OF STATISTICS PUBLISHED BY THE DEPARTMENT OF HEALTH. See Indexes/Abstracts.

INDEX TO INTERNATIONAL STATISTICS. See Indexes/Abstracts.

INDEX TO STATISTICS CANADA QUESTIONNAIRES. See Indexes/Abstracts.

INDICADORES DE COYUNTURA (BUENOS AIRES, ARGENTINA). See Economics - Economic History, Conditions.

INDICADORES DE PRODUCCION Y VENTAS DEL SECTOR INDUSTRIAL. See Economics.

INDICADORES ECONOMICOS (BANCOO DE MEXICO (1925-). SUBDIRECCION DE INVESTIGACION ECONOMICA). See Economics.

INDICATOR. See Real Estate.

INDICATORI MENSILI. Main/Corp Istitito Centrale di Statistica (Italy). IT. Italian. mo. $14.85. Istituto Centrale di Statistic, Via Censare Balbo 16, 00100 Roma Italy. LC HA1363. *Sintesi Grafica della Vita Economica Italiana.*

INDICATORS OF INDUSTRIAL ACTIVITY. See Economics - Labor.

INDICE DE VENTAS NOMINALES DE COMERCIO INTERIOR. See Indexes/Abstracts.

INDICES DE PRECIOS. See Economics.

INDIVIDUAL INCOME TAX ANNUAL STATISTICAL REPORT. 1972-. US. English. an. State of Iowa, Department of Revenue, Research and Statistics Division/Hoover State Office Building, Des Moines IA 50319. LC HJ4655.I77. DD 336.2409777. *Income Tax Annual Statistical Report.*

INDONESIA STATISTICS. Main/Corp First National City Bank (New York, N.Y.). 0376-9984. English. ir. First National City Bank, PO Box 2463, Jakarta Indonesia. LC HA1815. DD 315.98. *Indonesia: Economic Statistics.*

INDONESIA TOURIST STATISTICS. 1975-. English. ir. Directorate General of Tourism, Jln Kramat Raya, PO Box 409 Jkt, Jakarta Indonesia. LC G155.I5. DD 338.4791598043. *Tourist Statistics.*

INDUSTRIAL ACCIDENT STATISTICS, TASMANIA. 0314-1721. English. an. Australian Bureau of Statistics, Commonwealth Government Centre/3rd Floor, 188 Collins Street, Hobart Tasmania 7000 Australia. Tel (002)20 9409. LC HD7262.5.A8. DD 312.4309946. Fatal and non-fatal accidents, time lost, cost of claims, type of accident, accident factor, nature of injury, site of injury, month of occurrence, industry group, occupational group, age group and duration of time lost. *Industrial Accident Statistics (Hobart, Tasmania).*

INDUSTRIAL CORPORATIONS : FINANCIAL STATISTICS, PRELIMINARY DATA. Main/Corp Canada. Statistics Canada. VFOAT Societes Industrielle : Statistique Financiere Donnees Provisoires. Periodical. CN. English and French. qt. LC HG4090. DD 338.740971.

INDUSTRIAL PRODUCTION : HISTORICAL STATISTICS. SUPPLEMENT. Main/Corp Organisation for Economic Co-Operation and Development. VFOAT Production Industrielle: Statistiques Retrospectives. Supplement. No. 1- Jan. 1978-. English (French). ir. $5.00. OECD Publications Center, Suite 1207/1750 Pennsylvania Avenue, Washington DC 20006. Tel (202)724-1857. LC HC10. DD 338.005.

INDUSTRIAL PRODUCTION : HISTORICAL STATISTICS. SUPPLEMENT = PRODUCTION INDUSTRIELLE : STATISTIQUES RETROSPECTIVES. SUPPLEMENT. Main/Corp Organization for Economic Cooperation and Development. VFOAT Production Industrielle: Statistiques Retrospectives. No. 1- Jan. 1978-. Periodical. English (French). ir. OECD Publishing Center, 1750 Pennsylvania Avenue NW, Washington DC 20006.

INDUSTRIAL RESEARCH AND DEVELOPMENT STATISTICS . . . (WITH . . . FORCASTS). VFOAT Statistiques sur la Recherche et le Developpement Industriels (Avec des Previsions pour . . . . 1st issue (1982)-. 0824-8133. CN. English (French). an. $8.85 Domestic, $10.60 Foreign. Publication Sales and Services, Statistics Canada, Ottawa Ontario K1A 0V7 Canada. DD 338.4750971.

INDUSTRIAL STATISTICS YEARBOOK. VFOAT Industrial Statistics Year Book. 1982-. US. English (French). an. United Nations, Publishing Division, New York NY 10017. Tel (212)754-8302. LC HC59. DD 338.0021. Provides statistics on industrial establishments, employers/employees, wages, output in various sectors, investments, commodity production data of individual products and other areas. *Yearbook of Industrial Statistics.*

INDUSTRIAL STRUCTURE STATISTICS. VFOAT Statistiques des Structures Industrielles. US. English (French). an. $17.00. OECD Publications and Information Center, Suite 1207/1750 Pennsylvania Avenue Northwest, Washington DC 20006. Tel (202)724-1857. LC HC10. DD 338.0021. Provides detailed statistics on production, value added, employment, exports, imports, investments, wages and salaries, and supplements to wages and salaries for over 60 industries in 20 OECD countries.

INDUSTRIAS MANUFACTURERAS. See Economics - Economics: Industry & Production.

DIE INDUSTRIE IN NORDRHEIN-WESTFALEN. Main/Corp North Rhine-Westphalia (Germany). Landesamt fur Datenverarbeitung und Statistik. Series/Titl Beitrage zur Statistik des Landes Nordrhein-Westfalen. German. ir. 9.50. Landesamt fur Datenverarbeitung, 4000 Dusseldorf West Germany. LC HA1320.N6, HC287. N6.

INDUSTRIE- UND GEWERBESTATISTIK. Series/Titl Beitrage zur Osterreichischen Statistik. 1982-. German. ir. LC HA1173, HC261. DD 314.36 S, 338.09436021.

INDUSTRIELLE PRODUKTION. See Economics - Economics: Industry & Production.

INDUSTRIENS KONJUNKTURINDIKATORER. See Economics - Economics: Industry & Production.

INDUSTRIESTATISTIK. Main/Corp Osterreichisches Statistisches Zentralamt. Series/Titl Beitrage zur Osterreichischen Statistik. 1- 1969-. German. ir. LC HA1173. *Osterreichs Industrie.*

INDUSTRIJSKA PREDUZECA. Main/Corp Savezni Zavod za Statistiku (Yugoslavia). Serbo-Croatian(R). ir. 5.00. Savezni Zavod za Statistiku, Kneza Milosa 20, Beograd Yugoslavia. LC HA1631, HC407.Y6.

INDUSTRISTATISTIK. VFOAT Industrial Statistics. Began with 1966/67. 0070-3532. DK. Danish. an. 22.13. Danmarks Statistik, Sejrgade 11, 2100 Kbenhavn Denmark. Tel (01)298222. LC HC351. Circ 1,300. Employment and wage and salary statistics, price and quantity indexes, accounts and investment statistics. *Industriel Produktionsstatistik.*

INDUSTRISTATISTIKK (1961). (INDUSTRISTATISTIKK). Series/Titl Norges Offisielle Statistikk. VFOAT Industrial Statistics. 1961-. 0078-1886. NO. Norwegian (English). ir. Statistisk Sentralbyra, PO Box 8131 DEP, Oslo 1 Norway. LC HA1501. DD 338. *Norges Industri: Produksjonsstatistikk.*

INDUSTRY CONCENTRATION STATISTICS : MANUFACTURING CENSUS, AUSTRALIA. Main/Corp Australian Bureau of Statistics. AT. English. ir. Australian Bureau of Statistics, PO Box 84, Canberra Australian Capital Territory 2600 Australia. LC HD9738.A8. DD 338.0994.

INDUSTRY REVIEW. US. English. an. $3.00. Carpet and Rug Institute, Box 2048, Dalton GA 30720. Tel (404)278-3176. Ed Betty Hickman. LC HD9937.U5. DD 338.477367973. bk rev. Circ 600. Statistical report presenting seven year summary of carpet industry shipments in square yards and dollars; import, export data; and information on fiber consumption, backing,

Statistics

and artificial turf. *Review: State of the Industry,* 0092-0495.

INFORMACION ESTADISTICA MENSUAL. Main/Corp Banco Central de Costa Rica. Spanish. ir. LC HG185.C7.

INFORMACION ESTADISTICA MENSUAL. COMERCIO EXTERIOR DE COSTA RICA. BALANZA COMERCIAL. VFOAT 5103 Rica. Spanish. mo. LC HF3251. DD 382.17097286021.

INFORMACION SOBRE INFORMACION. Vol. 1, No. 1-. MX. Spanish. mo. Balderas No 71 Mezzanine, Mexico 1 DF. LC HA37. DD 310.6072.

INFORMACIONES ESTADISTICAS. 0379-7015. Periodical. Spanish. ir. NLM W2 DC8 M63I.

INFORMACIONES ESTADISTICAS DOMINICANAS. Main/Corp Dominican Republic. Direccion General de Estadistica y Censos. Periodical. MX. Spanish. ir. Iztapalapa Av Michoacan Puris, 09340 Mexico DF Mexico. *Informaciones Estadisticas Dominicanas.*

INFORMAT. (INFOMAT, WEEKLY BULLETIN). Began with July 13, 1973 issue. 0380-0547. Periodical. CN. English. wk. Receiver General for Canada, Statistics Canada Publications, Ottawa Ontario K1A 0T6 Canada. LC HA741. DD 354.7100819. *Statistics Canada Weekly,* 0380-0555.

INFORMATIONS STATISTIQUES RAPIDES (INSTITUT NATIONAL DE LA STATISTIQUE ET DES ETUDES ECONOMIQUES (FRANCE)). (INFORMATIONS STATISTIQUES RAPIDES). 0336-3791. French. mo. 2 Single Issue. I.N.S.E.E., BP 2718, 80027 Amens Cedex France. LC HA2307. DD 316.981.

INFORMATIONS STATISTIQUES RAPIDES - SERVICE DE LA STATISTIQUE CEASED. Main/Corp New Caledonia. Service de la Statistique. NL. French. ir. 1972. Institut Territorial de la Statistique et des Etudes Economiques, BP 823, Noumea New Caledonia. Tel 27.54.81. LC HA4007.N4. DD 330.9932. bk rev. Data of detail for the following topics: finance, prices, production, trade, building. mining, employment, transport, touring.

INFORMATIVO DO SEITE. Main/Corp Rio Grande do Sul, Brazil (State). Sistema Estadual de Informacao Tecnica e Estatistica. Portuguese. ir. Rua Buque de Caixas 1691, 90 000 Porto Alegre Brazil. LC HA37.B88.

INFORMATIVO ESTADISTICO. Main/Corp Chile. Universidad, Santiago. Instituto de Investigaciones Estadisticas. No. 1- 19 -. 0577-8514. Periodical. CL. Spanish. ir. Santiago Univ de Chile, Casilla 10220, Santiago Chile.

INFORMATIVO ESTADISTICO (CHILE. DIVISION TECNICA DE ESTUDIO Y FOMENTO HABITACIONAL. SECCION ESTADISTICAS). (INFORMATIVO ESTADISTICO). Spanish. ir. LC HD7324.A3. DD 338.47690830983.

INFORME AL CONGRESO NACIONAL. Main/Corp Colombia. Departamento Administrativo Nacional de Estadistica. 1959-. 0588-3555. CK. Spanish. ir. Administra Nacional Estadistic, Bogota Columbia. LC HA37. DD 318.61. *Informe del Jeff Al Congreso Nacional.*

INFORME ANUAL DE ESTADISTICAS VITALES. VFOAT Annual Report on Vital Statistics. English (Spanish). an. LC HA901. DD 312.097295.

INFORME ESTADISTICO (INSTITUTO NACIONAL DE SEGUROS (SAN JOSE, COSTA RICA)). (INFORME ESTADISTICO). CR. Spanish. ir. Apartado Postal 10061, San Jose Costa Rica.

INFORME ESTADISTICO ANUAL, SETOR METALURGICO. BL. Portuguese. an. Conselho de Nao-Ferrosos e de Siderurgia Consider, Secretaria Executiva Esplanada dos Ministerios, Bloco 6 50 Andar, Cep 70 053 Brasilia DF Brazil. LC HD9506.B7. DD 338.2740981. *Informe Estatistico, Produtos Metalurgicos (Annual).*

INFORME ESTADISTICO, SETOR METALURGICO. BL. Portuguese. mo. Conselho de Nao-Ferrosos e de Siderurgia, Secretaria Executiva Esplanada dos Ministerios, Bloco 6 50 Andar, Cep 70 053 Brasilia DF Brasil. LC HD9506.B7. DD 338.2740981. *Informe Estatistico, Produtos Metalurgicos (Monthly).*

INFORME FINANCIERO Y ESTADISTICO, INSTITUTO NACIONAL DE ELECTRIFICACION, Y ESTADISTICAS DEL SECTOR ELECTRICO NACIONAL. Main/Corp Instituto Nacional de Electrificacion. Unidad Economica y Financiera. Spanish. ir. Unidad Economica y Financiera, Departamento de Planificacion, 6A Avenida 2-73, Zona 4, Guatemala CA.

INFORME SOBRE CHILE. CL. Spanish. ir. Editorial Gestion, Avda Los Leones 2279, Santiago Chile. LC HA993. DD 318.3.

INLAND WATERBORNE COMMERCE STATISTICS. Main/Corp American Waterways Operators. 0517-581X. US. English. an. Free. American Waterways Operators Inc, 1600 Wilson Boulevard/Suite 1000, c/o N Schuster, Arlington VA 22307. Tel (703)841-9300. Ed Wendy Allen. LC HE617.5. DD 386.0973. (ctrl). Annual compilation of statistics relating to freight movements of various commodities by barge on the waterways network.

INNER LONDON EDUCATION STATISTICS. Main/Corp London. Inner London Education Authority. 1964/65-. Periodical. UK. English. an. Inner London Education Authority, 14 King Street, London WC2 8HN England. LC L343. DD 370.9421.

INPATIENT HEALTH FACILITIES STATISTICS, UNITED STATES. 1978-. 0733-981X. US. English. ir. NLM W2 A N148VN No. 24, etc. *Inpatient Health Facilities as Reported from the MFI Survey,* 0091-9454.

THE INSTITUTE OF MATHEMATICAL STATISTICS DIRECTORY. See Yearbooks, Almanacs, Directories.

INSTRUCTIONAL MANUAL. DATA PREPARATION. VITAL STATISTICS. (VITAL STATISTICS : INSTRUCTION MANUAL, DATA PREPARATION). Main/Corp United States. National Center for Health Statistics. Data Preparation Branch. 1962-. 0190-5538. US. English. an. Data Preparation Branch, PO Box 12214, Research Triangle Park NC 27709. NLM W2 A N1481V.

INSURANCE BUSINESS STATISTICS. Series/Titl Business Monitor. 1976-. UK. English. an. LC HG8594. DD 338.47368941.

INSURANCE REPORT AND STATISTICS OF FIJI. Main/Corp Fiji. Bureau of Statistics. 1977-. FJ. English. ir. Fiji Bureau of Statistics, PO Box 2221, Suva Fiji. LC J961, HG8738. DD 300 S, 368.99611. *Insurance Statistics of Fiji.*

INSURANCE STATISTICS. 1969/70- 1971-. Periodical. English. 5.00. Government Printing Office Publications, Private Bag, Wellington New Zealand. Tel 729-119. The New Zealand Insurance Industry.

INTER-INDUSTRY STUDY OF THE NEW ZEALAND ECONOMY. See Economics.

THE INTERCONNECT SURVEY. See Communication.

INTERNATIONAL AIR CHARTER STATISTICS. Main/Corp Canada. Statistics Canada Aviation Statistics Centre. VFOAT Statistique des Affretements Aeriens Internationaux. VAT Statistique Internationale des Affretements Aeriens. V. 2- Jan./March 1971-. 0705-4297. CN. English (French). qt. Receiver General for Canada, Statistics Canada Publications, Ottawa Ontario K1A 0T6 Canada. LC HE9815.A1. DD 387.74. *International Air Charter Statistics,* 0705-4297.

INTERNATIONAL COTTON INDUSTRY STATISTICS. V. 1- 1958-. 0538-6829. Periodical. English. an. $34.64. International Textile Manufacturers Federation, Postfach 289, CH-8039 Zuerich Switzerland. Tel 01/201 70 80 or 201 77 47. LC HD9870.4. *International Cotton Loom Statistics.*

INTERNATIONAL ENERGY STATISTICAL REVIEW. Publication Began with Apr. 1978. 0163-3724. Periodical. US. English. mo. $50.00. National Technical Information Service, 5285 Port Royal Road, Springfield VA 22161. Tel (703)487-4630. LC HD9560.4. DD 333.7. *International Energy Biweekly Statistical Review,* 0160-1512.

INTERNATIONAL FINANCIAL STATISTICS. Main/Corp International Monetary Fund. V. 1- Jan. 1948-. 0020-6725. Periodical. US. English. mo. $100.00. International Monetary Fund, 19th and H Street, Washington DC 20431. Tel (202)477-7000. Ind/Abst Funk Scott Index Corp. Ind., Public Aff. Inf. Serv. Bull., Predicasts. LC HG3881. DD 332.05.

INTERNATIONAL FINANCIAL STATISTICS ANUARIO. See Yearbooks, Almanacs, Directories.

INTERNATIONAL FINANCIAL STATISTICS YEARBOOK - INTERNATIONAL MONETARY FUND. See Yearbooks, Almanacs, Directories.

INTERNATIONAL MARKETING DATA AND STATISTICS. 1st- Ed. UK. English. an. $160.00. Gale Research Company, Book Tower, Detroit MI 48226. Tel (313)961-2242. LC HA42. DD 382.09. Provides comparative statistical data on 132 countries located in Asia, Africa, Australasia, and the Americas. Sections cover population, employment, production, trade, economy, standard of living, consumption, communications, and more.

INTERNATIONAL OIL AND GAS DEVELOPMENT. See Petroleum and Natural Gas.

INTERNATIONAL RESEARCH DOCUMENT. No. 1- 1975-. 0098-5643. US. English. US Department of Commerce, Bureau of the Census, Washington DC 20230. Ind/Abst Popul. Index. LC HA42. DD 310.8.

INTERNATIONAL STATISTICAL REVIEW. VFOAT Revue Internationale de Statistique. Vol. 40, No. 1 (April 1972)-. 0306-7734. Periodical. UK. English (French, summaries in the same languages). ty. $24.74. International Statistical Institute, POB 950 428, Prinses Beatrixlaan, 2270 AZ Voorgurg Netherlands. Tel 70-694341. Ed O E Barndorff Nielsen. Ind/Abst Math. Rev., GeoRef, Comput. Control Abstr., Electr. Electron. Abstr., Sci. Abstr. Sect. A. Phys. Abstr., Bibliogr. Index Geol., Bibliogr. Index, Sci. Cit. Index, Abr. Ed., Phys. Abstr. LC HA11. DD 519.505. NLM HA 1 I61R. CODEN ISTRDP. Index published separately - free - automatically sent. Articles on statistical theory, probability and applications. *Revue de l'Institut Internationale de Statistique.*

INTERNATIONAL STATISTICAL TRAINING PROGRAMS. Main/Corp United States. Bureau of the Census. International Statistical Programs Center. US. English. Training Branch, International Statistical Program Center, Bureau of the Census, Washington DC 20233. LC HA35. DD 001.42207.

INTERNATIONAL STEEL STATISTICS : SUMMARY TABLES. 1977-. UK. English. an. Tel 01-686-9050. Publication setting out summary tables for all the countries covered in the series. The tables cover iron ore, pig iron, scrap, crude steel, finished steel products and finished steel trade.

INTERNATIONAL STEEL STATISTICS, UNITED KINGDOM. Main/Corp British Steel Corporation Statistical Services. 0307-7608. UK. English. LC HD9521.4. DD 338.476691.

INTERNATIONAL TEXTILE MACHINERY SHIPMENT STATISTICS. V. 1- 1978-. SZ. English. an. $34.64. International Textile Manufacturers Federation, Postfach 289, CH-8039 Zurich Switzerland. LC HD9850.1. DD 382.4568176770212. *International Cotton Industry Statistics Supplement.*

INTERNATIONAL WHALING STATISTICS. 1- 1930-. 0020-9090. English. ir. International Whaling, 3201 Sandefjord Norway. Tel (022 023) 3971. Ind/Abst Life Sci. Collect. LC HD9469.W5. DD 639.28. Circ 350. (ctrl). Whale catches by country, species, size, sex and whaling grounds. Production of meat, oil and by-product; number and size of foetuses.

INVENTORY OF FINANCIAL AND STATISTICAL INFORMATION FOR CALIFORNIA LONG-TERM CARE FACILITIES. Main/Corp California Health Facilities Commission. 1977/78-. US. English. an. California Health Facilities Commission, 717 K Street, Sacramento CA 95814. Tel (916)322-2810. LC RA997.5.C3. DD 362.1609794. bk rev. Health facility financial utilization and patient data for California; for use by purchasers, providers, planners, insurers, media schools and consumers.

INVESTICIJE SR SRBIJE. Began with Vol. for 1966-1970. YU. Serbo-Croatian -R. ir. 100.00. Republicki Zavod za Statistiku Sr Srbije, M Rakica 5, Beograd Yugoslavia. LC HA1651, HC407 Z7S46.

Statistics

INVESTMENT STATISTICS CEASED. Main/Corp Statistics Canada Construction Division. VFOAT Statistique des Investissements. V. 1-5, No. 2. 0380-7053. Periodical. CN. English (text in French). $2.80.

INVESTMENT STATISTICS. MANUFACTURING SUB-INDUSTRIES AND SELECTED ENERGY RELATED INDUSTRIES. OUTLOOK. (INVESTMENT STATISTICS, MANUFACTURING SUB-INDUSTRIES AND SELECTED ENERGY RELATED INDUSTRIES). VFOAT Statistiques des Investissements, Sour-Industries Manufacturieres et Certaines Industries Energetiques. Outlook 1981-. 0229-7361. CN. English (French in parallel columns). an. $4.50 Domestic, $5.40 Foreign. Statistics Canada, Publications Distribution, Ottawa Ontario K1A 0T6 Canada. LC HC120.C3. DD 338.43670971. *Investment Statistics, Capital and Repair Expenditures, Manufacturing Sub-Industries, Canada, 0708-4196.*

IOWA AGRICULTURAL STATISTICS. 0364-9040. US. English. an. 201 Walnut Street, Des Moines IA 50309. LC S61. DD 630.9777.

IOWA PUBLIC LIBRARY STATISTICS. US. English. an. Free. State Library of Iowa, Office of Library Development, Historical Building, Des Moines IA 50319. LC Z732.I6. DD 024.4777.

IOWA REGIONAL LIBRARY SYSTEM STATISTICS. US. English. an. State Library of Iowa, Office of Library Development, Historical Building, Des Moines IA 50319. LC Z675.R35. DD 020.6232777.

IRISH STATISTICAL BULLETIN. VFOAT Feasachan Staidrimh na Heireann. Vol. 39, No. 1 (Mar. 1964)-. Periodical. English. qt. 4.95. Government Publications Sales Office, Molesworth Street, Dublin 2 Ireland. Tel 710309. Ind/Abst Predicasts, Public Aff. Inf. Serv. Bull. Circ 1,200. *Irish Trade Journal and Statistical Bulletin.*

IRON AND STEEL INDUSTRY. ANNUAL STATISTICS FOR THE UNITED KINGDOM. Main/Corp British Steel Corporation. 1969-. 0572-709X. UK. English. an. $61.30. UK Iron and Steel Statistics Bureau, NLA Tower 12, Addiscombe Road, Croydon CR9 3JH England. Tel 01-686-9050. Circ 1,000. (ctrl). Fifty detailed statistical tables relating to the UK iron and steel industry with historical comparisons and detailed trade information. *Iron and Steel. Annual Statistics of the United Kingdom.*

ISLE OF MAN DIGEST OF ECONOMIC AND SOCIAL STATISTICS. Main/Corp Man, Isle of. Treasury. Economics Section. UK. English. Central Government Offices, Bucks Road, Douglas Isle of Man. Tel (0624)26262. Ed J H Wesster. LC HA1138.M3. DD 314.279. Circ 750. (ctrl). *Digest of economic and social statistics of the Isle of Man.*

L'ITALIA SCACCHISTICA. Yearly V. 1, No. 1-. 0021-2849. Periodical. IT. Italian. mo. $22.00. Italia Scacchistica, Via Passeroni 6, 20135 Milano Italy.

IZBORI NA DELEGACII I DELEGATI ZA SOBORITE NA SOBRANIJATA. Main/Corp Macedonia (Republic). Republicki Zavod za Statistika. Series/Titl Statisticki Pregled. Macedonian. ir. 50.00. Republicki Zavod za Statistika, Maksim Gorki 26, Skopje Yugoslavia. LC HA1, JS6949.M3.

JAARBOEK (AMSTERDAM (NETHERLANDS). BESTUURSINFORMATIE. AFDELING STATISTIEK). See Yearbooks, Almanacs, Directories.

JAARSTATISTIEK OVER DE INTERNATIONALE TRAFIEK DER HAVENS. Main/Corp Institut National de Statistique (Belgium). BE. Dutch. an. Koninkrijk Belgie, Ministerie van Economische Zaken, Nationaal Instituut voor de Statistiek, Leuvenseweg 44, 1000 Brussels Belgium. LC HE563.B3. *Statistique Annuelle de Trafic International des Ports.*

DAS JAHR IN ZAHLEN. Main/Corp Industrie- und Handelskammer zu Lubeck. German. ir. Industrie- und Handelskammer fur Lubeck, 24 Lubeck 1 Breite Strasse 6-8, Lubeck West Germany. LC HA1330.L8.

JAHRBUCH ZUR MEDIENSTATISTIK UND KOMMUNIKATIONSPOLITIK. See Yearbooks, Almanacs, Directories.

JAHRBUCHER FUR STATISTIK UND LANDESKUNDE VON BADEN-WURTTEMBERG. See Yearbooks, Almanacs, Directories.

JAHRESSTATISTIK . . . DER AMBULANTEN BERATUNGS- UND BEHANDLUNGSSTELLEN FUR SUCHTKRANKE IN DER BUNDESREPUBLIK DEUTSCHLAND. VFOAT Annual Statistical Report . . . of the Out-Patient Advisory and Treatment Facilities for Addicts in the Federal Republic of Germany. Began With: 1/1/1980 Bis 31/12/80. German. an. NLM W1.

JAHRESSTATISTIK DES AUSSENHANDELS DER SCHWEIZ. STATISTIQUE ANNUELLE DU COMMERCE EXTERIEUR DE LA SUISSE. Main/Corp Switzerland Edigenossische Oberzolldirektion. 1885-. SZ. Multilingual (French and German). mo. $91.53. Eidg Oberzolldirektion Abt Han, Direction General des Douanes, Monijoustrasse 40, CH3003 Bern Switzerland. Tel 01 61 66 06. bk rev. Foreign trade statistics: imports and exports by quantity and value.

JAKARTA PUSAT DALAM ANGKA STATISTIK. Main/Corp Jakarta Pusat, Indonesia. Walikota. Indonesian. ir. Walikota Jakarta Pusat, Jl Pegangsaan Barat, Jakarta Indonesia. LC HA1818.J34.

THE JAPAN COTTON STATISTICS AND RELATED DATA. 0447-5321. JA. English. an. $20.00. Japan Cotton Traders Association, PO Box Osaka Central 951 8-2 1 Chome, Nishiku Osaka Japan. LC HD9086.J3.

JAPAN (JAPAN. SORIFU. TOKEIKYOKU). (JAPAN). 1979-. JA. English. ir. Statistics Bureau, Prime Minister's Office, Wakamatsu- cho Shinjuku-ku Tokyo 162 Japan. LC HA4621. DD 952.005. *Statistical Handbook of Japan.*

JAPAN PETROLEUM & ENERGY WEEKLY. MONTHLY STATISTICAL SUPPLEMENT. VFOAT Japan Petroleum and Energy Weekly. Periodical. JA. English. mo. $650.00 US, Airmail which Includes Subscription to Japan Petroleum and Energy Weekly. Japan Petroleum Consultants Ltd, CPO Box 1185, Tokyo 100-91 Japan. LC HD9576.J3. DD 338.4766550952.

JAWA TENGAH DALAM ANGKA. Began with 1971 Vol. English (Indonesian). an. Kantor Statistik Propinsi Jateng, UL Pahlawan No 6, Semarang Indonesia. LC HA4607.J385. *Djawa Tengah Dalam Angka.*

JOURNAL DE LA SOCIETE DE STATISTIQUE DE PARIS. Main/Corp Societe de Statistuque de Paris. Vol. 1. 0037-914X. Periodical. FR. French. qt. $39.91. Berger Levrault, 18 rue des Glacis 11X, 54017 Nancy Cedex France. Ind/Abst Popul. Index, Foreign Lang. Index. LC HA1. NLM W1 JQ317Q. (cum index).

JOURNAL OF BUSINESS & ECONOMIC STATISTICS. (JOURNAL OF BUSINESS & ECONOMIC STATISTICS : A PUBLICATION OF THE AMERICAN STATISTICAL ASSOCIATION). VFOAT Journal of Business and Economic Statistics. Vol. 1, No. 1 (Jan. 1983)-. 0735-0015. Periodical. US. English. qt. American Statistical Association, 806 15th Street NW, Washington DC 20005. Tel (202)393-3253. LC HB137. DD 330.072.

JOURNAL OF ECONOMIC COOPERATION AMONG ISLAMIC COUNTRIES. See Economics.

JOURNAL OF EDUCATIONAL STATISTICS. V. 1- Spring 1976-. 0362-9791. Periodical. US. English. qt. $20.00. American Education Research Association, 1230 17th Street NW, Washington DC 20036. Tel (202)223-9485. Ed Lawrence J Hubert. Ind/Abst Curr. Index J. Educ., Psychol. Abstr. LC LB2846. DD 370.212. bk rev adv acc. Circ 2,300. Demonstrates, primarily through concrete example, how the educational statistician can contribute to sound productive, and creative educational decision making and practice.

JOURNAL OF PHILIPPINE STATISTICS. V. 1- July 1941-. 0022-3603. Periodical. PH. English. qt $33.60. National Census and Statistics Office, PO Box 779, Manila Philippines. Ind/Abst Public Aff. Inf. Serv. Bull. LC HA1821. DD 319.14.

JOURNAL OF STATISTICAL PHYSICS PHYSICS. V. 1- 1969-. 0022-4715. Periodical. US. English. sm. $900.00 Domestic, $1,002.00 Foreign. Plenum Press, 233 Spring Street, New York NY 10013. Tel (212)620-8000. Ed Joel L Lebowitz. Ind/Abst Math. Rev., Int. Aerosp. Abstr., Comput. Control Abstr., Electr. Electron. Abstr., Sci. Abstr. Sect. A. Phys. Abstr., Appl. Mech. Rev., Eng. Index Mon., Eng. Index, Curr. Contents, Ref. Z., Nucl. Sci. Abstr., Solid State Abstr. J., Sci. Res. Abstr. J., Spin, Energy Res. Abstr., Phys. Abstr., Sci. Cit. Index, Abr. Ed. LC QC175. DD 530.13205. CODEN JSTPSB. bk rev. adv acc. This journal accepts original and review papers in the fields of statistical mechanics and thermodynamics of equilibrium and non-equilibrium processes; also plasma physics and non-linear dynamics.

JOURNAL OF STATISTICAL PLANNING AND INFERENCE. V. 1- Feb. 1977-. 0378-3758. Periodical. English. bm. Elsevier Science Publishers, PO Box 211, 1000 AE Amsterdam The Netherlands. Tel (020)5803.911. Ind/Abst Math. Rev., Manage. Contents, Comput. Control Abstr., Electr. Electron. Abstr., Sci. Abstr. Sect. A. Phys. Abstr. LC QA276.A1. DD 001.422. CODEN JSPIDN.

JOURNAL OF STATISTICAL RESEARCH. V. 4, No. 1- Jan. 1970-. Periodical. BG. English. $5.00. University of Dhaka, Director Institute of Statistical Research and Training, Dhaka 2 Bangladesh. Tel 501298. Ed Q M Rahman. Ind/Abst Math. Rev. bk rev. Circ 200. (ctrl). This is a core journal on statistical theory and methods. Abstracts of articles appear in the Curriculum Index to Statistics-Application, Methods and Theory; Statistical Theory and Method Abstracts; Bowker Serial Directories, etc. *Bulletin of the Institute of Statistical Research and Training.*

JOURNAL OF THE AMERICAN STATISTICAL ASSOCIATION. VFOAT J.A.S.A. Began with Vol. 18, 1922. 0162-1459. Periodical. US. English. qt. $70.00. Journal of American Statistical Association, 806 15th Street NW/ Suite 640, Washington DC 20005. Tel (202)393-3253. Ind/Abst Math. Rev., Trade Ind. Index, Electron. Commun. Abstr. J., ISMEC Bull., Pollut. Abstr. Indexes, Saf. Sci. Abstr. J., Excerpta Med., Energy Inf. Abstr., Environ. Abstr., Popul. Index, Index Econ. Artic. J. Collect. Vol., Int. Aerosp. Abstr., Comput. Control Abstr., Electr. Electron. Abstr., Sci. Abstr. Sect. A. Phys. Abstr., Ref. Source, Comput. Rev., Sci. Cit. Index, Abr. Ed. LC HA1. NLM HA1 A512. CODEN JSTNAL. (cum index). Available on microfilm. *Quarterly Publication of the American Statistical Association.*

JOURNAL OF THE AUSTRALIAN MATHEMATICAL SOCIETY. SERIES A, PURE MATHEMATICS AND STATISTICS. See Mathematics.

JOURNAL OF THE INDIAN SOCIETY OF AGRICULTURAL STATISTICS. Main/Corp Indian Society of Agricultural Statistics. Began publication with Mar. 1948 issue. 0019-6363. Periodical. II. English (title given also in Hindi). sa. 120 Domestic, $30.00 Foreign. Institute of Agricultural Research Statistics, Post Box 310, New Delhi 12 India. Tel 581861. Ed Prem Narain. Ind/Abst Bibliogr. Agric. bk rev. Circ 600. (ctrl). The journal publishes original articles in statistics and its application to agriculture and allied fields; also reviews books and periodicals recently brought out.

JOURNAL OF THE INDIAN STATISTICAL ASSOCIATION. Main/Corp Indian Statistical Association. Began publication in 1963. 0537-2585. Periodical. II. English. an. $20.00. Indian Statistical Association, University of Poona, Poona 411007 India. Ind/Abst Math. Rev. LC HA1. CODEN ISAJB6.

JOURNAL OF THE ROYAL STATISTICAL SOCIETY. SERIES A. GENERAL. (JOURNAL OF THE ROYAL STATISTICAL SOCIETY. SERIES A (GENERAL)). Main/Corp Royal Statistical Society, London. V. 1- 1838/39-. 0035-9238. Periodical. UK. English. ir. $36.78. Royal Statistical Society, 25/26 Enford Street, London WIH 2BH England. Tel 01-723-5882. Ind/Abst Math. Rev., Sci. Cit. Index, Abr. Ed., Bibliogr. Index Geol. (cum index).

JOURNAL OF THE ROYAL STATISTICAL SOCIETY. SERIES B. (METHODOLOGICAL). (JOURNAL OF THE ROYAL STATISTICAL SOCIETY. SERIES B (METHODOLOGICAL)). Main/Corp Royal Statistical Society, London. V. 1- 1934-. 0035-9246. Periodical. UK. English. ir. $29.12. Royal Statistical Society, 25/26 Enford Street, London WIH 2BH England. Tel 01-723-5882. Ind/Abst Math. Rev., Sci. Cit. Index, Abr. Ed.

Statistics

JOURNAL OF THE STATISTICAL AND SOCIAL INQUIRY SOCIETY OF IRELAND. Began publication in 1861?. 0081-4776. Periodical. English. an. Statistical and Social Inquiry Society, Central Statistics Office, Dublin 2 Ireland. Ind/Abst Public Aff. Inf. Serv. Bull. *Journal of the Dublin Statistical Society.*

JUDICIAL STATISTICS, ENGLAND AND WALES, FOR THE YEAR/CHANCELLOR'S DEPARTMENT. Series/Titl CMND. VFOAT Judicial Statistics. UK. English. an. 9.10. Her Majesty's Stationery Office, 49 High Holborn, London WC1V 6HB England. LC KD327. DD 347.42013.

JUMIN KIHON DAICHO NI YORU TOKYO-TO NO SETAI TO JINKO. Main/Corp Tokyo. Somukyoky. Tokeibu Jinko Tokeika. JA. Japanese. ir. LC HA1849.T6.

JUSTICE STATISTICS ONTARIO . . . . CN. English. Provincial Secretary for Justice, Whitney Block Queen's Park, Toronto Ontario M7A 1A2 Canada. LC HV8157. DD 364.9713.

JUSTICIELE KINDERBESCHERMING. Main/Corp Netherlands (Kingdom, 1815-). Central Bureau voor de Statistiek. Hoofdafdeling Statistieken Van Criminaliet en Rechtspleging. VFOAT Statistics of Judicial Child Protection. Dutch. ir. 8.95. Centraal Bureau Voor de Statistiek, Staatsuitgeverij, S-Gravenhage Netherlands.

JUSTITIELE STATISTIEK. 1951-. Dutch. an. Staatsuit Afd Verkoop, Fluwelengurgwal 18, Den Haag The Netherlands. *Justitieele Statistiek en Failinssementsstatistiek.*

JUVENILE COURT STATISTICS. Main/Corp United States. Office of Youth Development. US. English. US Department of Health Education and Welfare, Office of Youth Development, Washington DC 20201. LC HV9091. DD 345.7308.

JUVENILE COURT STATISTICS. Main/Corp National Center for Juvenile Justice. 1974-. 0091-3278. US. English. an. National Center for Juvenile Justice, 701 Forbes Avenue, Pittsburgh PA 152193. Tel (412)227-6950. Summary data from states, jurisdictions and possessions on the general nature and extent of problems brought before juvenile courts. *Juvenile Court Statistics, 0091-3278.*

JUVENILE COURT STATISTICS AND ADOPTION PETITIONS IN KANSAS. Main/Corp Kansas. State Dept. of Social Welfare. US. English. an. Kansas State Department of Social Welfare, Topeka KS 66620. LC HV9093.K2. DD 364.3609781.

JUVENILE JUSTICE INFORMATION SYSTEM : (JJIS)/ KANSAS BUREAU OF INVESTIGATION, STATISTICAL ANALYSIS CENTER. VFOAT JJIS. 1982-. US. English. an. Kansas Bureau of Investigation, Statistical Analysis Center, 3420 Van Buren, Topeka KS 66611. *Kansas Juvenile Justice Information System.*

KABUPATEN GRESIK DALAM ANGKA. VFOAT Kabupaten Gresik Dalam Tahun . . . . V. 1981-. Indonesian. an. Kantor Statistik Kabupaten Gresik, JL Kyai Haji Wakhid Hasyim No 9A, Gresik Indonesia. LC HA4607.S87. *Statistik Kabupaten Daerah Tingkat II Gresik.*

KACHIKU EISEI TOKEI. Main/Corp Japan. Norin Suisansho Chikusankyoky. VFOAT Statistics on Animal Hygiene. JA. Japanese (English). an. Norin Kosaikai, 2-1 Kasumigaseki 1, Chiyoda-ku 100, Tokyo Japan. LC SF705. *Kachiku Eisei Tokei.*

KANSAS HIGHWAY & TRAFFIC STATISTICS. VFOAT Kansas Highway and Traffic Statistics. 1978-. US. English. an. Kansas Bureau of Investigation, Statistical Analysis Center, 3420 Van Buren, Topeka KS 66611.

KANSAS HIGHWAY AND TRAFFIC STATISTICS. VFOAT Highway and Traffic Statistics. 1982-. Periodical. US. English. be. *Kansas Highway and Traffic Statistics.*

KANSAS MORBIDITY INCIDENCE. Main/Corp Kansas. Bureau of Registration and Health Statistics. V. 1- Jan. 1979-. 0453-2252. US. English. mo. Kansas Department of Health and Evaluation, Building 740 Forbes Air Force Base, Topeka KS 66620. *Kansas Morbidity Incidence, 0453-2252.*

KANSAS STATISTICAL ABSTRACT. See Indexes/Abstracts.

KATALOG. Main/Corp Malaysia. Jabatan Perangkaan. MY. English (Malay). ir. Kentua Perangkawan, Jabatan Perangkaan, Jl Cenderasari Kuala Lumpur Malaysia. Tel 2922133. LC Z7554.M24, HA4600.6. DD 016.31595. Circ 500. *Katalok.*

KEIZAI TOKEI GEPPO. Main/Corp Nihon Ginko. Tokeikyoku. VFOAT Economic Statistics Monthly. No. 70-. English (Japanese). ir. 600. Nihon Ginko Tokeikyoku 2-1, Nihonbashi Honhokucho 2-chome, Chuo-ku 103, Tokyo Japan. LC HG41. *Kinyu Tokei Geppo.*

KENTUCKY DESKBOOK OF ECONOMIC STATISTICS. Main/Corp Kentucky. Dept. of Commerce Division of Research and Planning. 0361-591X. US. English. Kentucky Department of Commerce, Box 817/Versailles Road, Frankfort KY 40601. LC HC107.K4. DD 330.976904. *Deskbook of Kentucky Economic Statistics, 0363-7301.*

KENYA STATISTICAL DIGEST. Main/Corp Kenya. Central Bureau of Statistics. V. 10, No. 2- June 1972-. Periodical. English. ir. 11. Kenya Bureau of Statistics, PO Box 30266, Nairobi Kenya. LC HA1977.K4. DD 316.762. *Kenya Statistical Digest.*

KENYA STATISTICAL DIGEST. V. 1- Sept. 1963-. Periodical. English. qt. $4.06. Government Printer of Kenya, PO Box 30128, Nairobi Kenya East Africa. *Kenya Trade and Supplies Bulletin.*

KEY BUSINESS RATIOS. See Business.

KEY EDUCATION STATISTICS. 1981-. 0217-0582. English. an. LC LA1239.6. DD 370.95957.

KLATEN DALAM ANGKA. Indonesian. an. Biro Pusat Statistik, Kantor Statistik Kabupaten Klaten, Komplek Pem Da Tk II, Klaten Indonesia. LC HA1817.K57. *Kabupaten Klaten Dalam Angka.*

KNIGOIZDAVANE I PECHAT V NARODNA REPUBLIKA BULGARIIA : STATISTICHESKI SBORNIK. Main/Corp Bulgaria. Tsentralno Statistichesko Upravlenie. 1962/63-. 0525-0528. Periodical. BU. Bulgarian. ir. Hemus, 6 Boulevard Rusky, Sofia Bulgaria. *Knigi I Periodichni Izdaniia V N.R. Bulgariia.*

KOKUSEI CHIIKI TOKEI HANDOBUKKU. VFOAT Regional Statistics of Japan. 1984-. 0289-4912. JA. Japanese. an. Kokuritsu Kokkai Toshokan Chosa Rippo Kosakyoku 10-1, Nagata-Cho 1 Chiyoda-Ku, Tokyo-to 100 Japan. *Kokkai Chiiki Tokei Teiyo.*

KOMMUNEVALGET. Main/Corp Norway. Statistisk Sentralbyra. Series Corp Its Norges Offisielle Statistikk. VFOAT Municipal Elections. English and Norwegian. ir. 8.00. LC HA1501 JS6218.S7.

KOMUNALNI FONDOVI U GRADSKIM NASELJIMA. Main/Corp Savenzi Zavod za Statistiku (Yugoslavia). Serbo-Croatian(R). ir. 4.00. Savezni Zavod za Statistiku, Kneza Milosa 20, Beograd Yugoslavia. LC HA1631, HD2768.

KONOMISK UTSYN. Series/Titl Norges Offisielle Statistikk. VFOAT Economic Survey. 0078-1924. Periodical. NO. Norwegian (with English summaries). ir. 80.-. Statistisk Sentralbyra, PO Box 8131 DEP, N-0033 Oslo 1 Norway. Tel 41.38.20. Ed Olav Bjerkholt. LC HC365. DD 330. Circ 3,000. Reviews on Norwegian national economy. Quarterly and annual national accounts. Results from the research activity on (macro-) economics in the Central Bureau of Statistics. *Statistisk Konomisk Oversikt.*

KONSOROP SUJU TONGHYANG. Main/Corp Korea (Republic). Kyongje Kikowgwom. Chosa Tonggyeguk. VFOAT Monthly Statistics of Value of Construction Order Received. Periodical. Korean. ir. LC HD9715.K8.

KOREA STATISTICAL HANDBOOK. 1977-. KO. English. ir. National Bureau of Statistics, Economic Planning Board, 90 Gyeongwun-Gong Jongro-Gu, Seoul South Korea. LC HA4630.5. DD 315.195. *Statistical Handbook of Korea.*

KORNYEZETSTATISZTIKAI ADATGYUJTEMENY. Main/Corp Hungary. Kozponti Statisztikai Hivatal Kommunalis es Igazgatasi Szolgaltatasok Statiszitkai Osztalaya. HU. Hungarian (English and Russian). ir. 250.-. Statisztikai Kiado Vallalat, 1033 Budapest III, Kaszasdulo U 2, Budapest Hungary. Tel 801-311. LC TD171.5.H9. Circ 5,000. Covers the quality of the earth, soil, waters, forests, biosphere and air in Hungary, the protection of the environment.

KORTBEGRIP VAN LANDBOUSTATISTIEK. See Indexes/Abstracts.

KREISDATEN. Main/Corp Bayerisches Statistisches Landesamt. German. ir. Munchen Bayerisches Statistisches Landesmat, 8 Munchen 2 Neuhauser Str 51, Munchen West Germany. LC HA1261. *Daten Zur Gebietsreform.*

KREISFREIE STADTE UND LANDKREISE IN ZAHLEN. Series/Titl Statistische Berichte Niedersachsen. 1981-. GW. German. an. 7.50. Niedersachsisches Landesverwaltungsamt Statistik, Postfach 107, 3000 Hannover 1 West Germany. LC HA1248.L68. DD 314.359. bk rev. Circ 400.

KREISSTANDARDZAHLEN. Main/Corp North Rhine-Westphalia. Landesamt fur Datenverarbeitung und Statistik. VFOAT Statistisches Angaben fur Kreisfriei Stadte und Kreise des Landes Nordrhein-Westfalen. German. ir. 9.-. Landesamt fur Datenverarbeitung und Statistik, 4000 Dusseldorf 1, Postfach 1105 Mauerstrasse 51, Dusseldorf West Germany. Tel (0211)44971. LC HA1320.N6. adv acc. Circ 1,200. Statistical returns about different areas subdivided into the 54 districts of Nordrhein-Westfalen. *Kreisstandardzahlen des Landes Nordrhein-Westfalen.*

KRIMINALSTATISTIKK. REAKSJONER, FENGSLINGER. Series/Titl Norges Offisielle Statistikk. VFOAT Criminal Statistics. Sanctions, Imprisonments. 1978-. NO. English (Norwegian). ir. 15.00. Statistisk Sentralbyra, Dronningensgt 16 Postbok 8131, Oslo 1 Norway. LC HA1501, HV7033. DD 314.81, 312.4609481. *Kriminalstatistikk. Fanger, Kriminalstatistikk Reaksjoner.*

HAI KUAN TUNG CHI. VFOAT Customs Statistics. Periodical. CC. Chinese. qt. 1.00. Hai Kuan Tung Chi Fa Hsing Tsu, Pei-Ching China. LC HJ7071. DD 354.5100724605.

KULKERESKEDELMI STATISZTIKAI EVKONYV. Main/Corp Hungary. Kozponti Statisztikai Hivatal. Kulkereskedelmi Osztaly. Hungarian. ir. 260.-. Kozponti Statisztikai Hivatal, Statisztikai Kiado Vallalat, II Keleti Karoly U 18/B, Budapest Hungary. Tel 803-311. LC HF192.5. Circ 1,500. A statistical data collection which yearly reviews the volume and structure of the export-import trade of Hungary, detailed by article groups and in relations by countries and kinds of foreign exchange.

KULTURNO-UMETNISKA IN PROSVETNA DEJAVNOST. Main/Corp Zavod Sr Slovenije za Statistiku. Slovenian. an. Zavod Sr Slovenije za Statistiko, Vozarski Pot 12, Ljubljana Yugoslavia. LC HA1634.S58.

KUNSTHARSEN E.D. INDUSTRIE PRODUKTIESTATISTIEKEN. VFOAT Kunstharsen en Dergelijke Industrie Produktiestatistieken. Dutch (summaries in English). an. 8.10. Centraal Bureau Voor de Statistik, Prinses Beatrixlaan 428 Postbus 959, 2270 AZ Voorburg Netherlands.

KYONGBUK KYOYUK TONGGYE YONBO. See Yearbooks, Almanacs, Directories.

KYONGGI KYOYUK TONGGYE YONBO. See Yearbooks, Almanacs, Directories.

KYONGNAM KYOYUK TONGGYE YONBO. See Yearbooks, Almanacs, Directories.

LABOR FORCE STATISTICS. (STATE OF HAWAII LABOR FORCE STATISTICS. Main/Corp Hawaii. Dept. of Labor and Industrial Relations. Research and Statistics Office. 0147-4758. US. English. an. Honolulu Department of Labor, PO Box 2359, Honolulu HI 96804. LC HD5725.H3. DD 331.1109969.

LABOR MARKET TRENDS. NORFOLK SMSA. VFOAT Norfolk SMSA, Norfolk S.M.S.A., Labor Market Trends. US. English. LC HD5726.N58. DD 331.120975552. *Labor Market Trends. Norfolk-Virginia Beach-Portsmouth, Virginia-North Carolina Metropolitan Area.*

LABOUR STATISTICS. Main/Corp Australian Bureau of Statistics. 1975-. AT. English. an. 5.39. Australian Bureau of Statistics, PO Box 10, Belconnen Australian Capital Territory 2600 Australia. Tel (062)52 5979. LC HD8841. DD 331.0994. Gives a wide coverage of labor statistics concerning earnings,

Statistics

trade unions, job satisfaction, industrial disputes, unemployment. *Labour Report.*

**LABOUR STATISTICS REPORT FOR
. . . .** No. 1 (1982)-. English. an. 2.00. LC HD5811.95. DD 331.125095645021.

LABOUR STATISTICS : WAGE RATES, EARNINGS AND AVERAGE HOURS WORKED IN THE PRINTING AND NEWSPAPER INDUSTRY, ENGINEERING INDUSTRY, BUILDING INDUSTRY AND COMMERCE. Main/Corp South Africa. Dept. of Statistics. VFOAT Arbeidstatistieke. SA. Afrikaans and English. ir. 3.75. Government Printer, Private Bag X85, Pretoria 0001 South Africa. LC HD5091.Z9. DD 331.2968.

DIE LAND- UND FORSTWIRTSCHAFT. Main/Corp Statistisches Landesamt Baden-Wurttemberg. Series/Titl Statistik von Baden-Wurttemberg. German. ir. LC HA1320.B2, HD1960., B27. DD 314.346 S, 338.1094346.

LAND- UND FORSTWIRTSCHAFT, FISCHERI. REIHE 2.1.7, AUSSERBETRIEBLICHE EINKOMMEN UND ARBEITSVERHALTNISSE FUR AUSGEWAHLTE BETRIEBSGRUPPEN. See Agriculture.

LANDBOUWCIJFERS. See Agriculture.

LANDBOUWSTATISTIEKEN. Main/Corp Institut National de Statistique (Belgium). 1967. Periodical. BE. Dutch. mo. 700 Domestic, 1200 Foreign. National Instituut de Statistieke, Leuvenseweg 44, 1000 Brussel Belgium. Tel (02)513.96.50. LC HD1981. Circ 400. (ctrl). Agricultural statistics.

LANDBRUGSMARKEDER. PRISER. See Agriculture.

LANDBRUGSSTATISTIK. VFOAT Agrarstatistik, Agricultural Statistics. No. 1 (1974)-. Periodical. German (title also in French, Italian and Dutch). bm. European Community Information Center, 2100 M Street NW/Suite 707, Washington DC 20037. *Statistique Agricole.*

LANDBRUGSSTATISTIK. VFOAT Agricultural Statistics. DK. Danish (English). an. Danmarks Statistik, Sejrgade 11, 2100 Kbenhavn 0 Denmark. LC S245. DD 338.109489.
Landbrugsstatistik Herunder Gartneri Og Skovbrug.

LANDERBERICHT : GABUN. Main/Corp Germany (West). Statistisches Bundesamt. Series/Titl Statistik des Auslandes. German. ir. 10.40. W Kohlhammer GMBH, Stuttgart West Germany. LC HA2090.

LANDERBERICHT : NIGERIA. Main/Corp Germany (West). Statistisches Bundesamt. Series/Titl Statistik des Auslandes. GW. German. ir. 10.70. W Kohlhammer, Hessbruhlstrasse 69, PF 800430, 7000 Stuttgart 80 West Germany. LC HA1977.N5. DD 316.69.

LANDERBERICHT : SAMBIA. Main/Corp Germany (West). Statistisches Bundesamt. Statistik des Auslandes. German. ir. 12.80. W Kohlhammer GMBH, Stuttgart West Germany. LC HA1977.Z35.

LANDERBERICHT : UNGARN. Main/Corp Germany (West). Statistisches Bundesamt. Statistik des Auslandes. VFOAT Ungarn. German. ir. 13.00. Verlag W Kohlhammer GMBH, Statistisches Bundesamt, Stuttgart West Germany. LC HA1205.

LANDERBERICHT : ZAIRE. Main/Corp Germany (West). Statistisches Bundesamt. VFOAT Zaire. GW. German. ir. 12.40. W Kohlhammer, Hessbruhlstrasse 69, PF 800430, 7000 Stuttgart 80 West Germany. LC HA4711. DD 316.751.

LANDERBERICHTE : DEMOKRATISCHE VOLKSREPUBLIK KOREA. Main/Corp Germany (West). Statistisches Bundesamt. Series/Titl Statistik des Auslandes. GW. German. ir. 8.60. W Kohlhammer, Hessbruhlstrasse 69, PF 800430, 7000 Stuttgart 80 West Germany. LC HA1857.A2. DD 315.193.

LANDERKURZBERICHT : NAMIBIA (SUDWESTAFRIKA). Main/Corp Germany (West). Statistisches Bundesamt. Series/Titl Statistik des Auslandes. VFOAT Namibia (Sudwestafrika). German. ir. W Kohlhammer GMBH, Stuttgart West Germany. LC HA1977.N3.

LANDERKURZBERICHTE : BAHAMAS. Main/Corp Germany (West). Statistisches Bundesamt. GW. German. ir. Kohlhammer, Hessbruhlstrasse 69, PF 800430, 7000 Stuttgart 80 West Germany. LC HA861. DD 317.296.

LANDERKURZBERICHTE : BAHRAIN, KATAR. Main/Corp Germany (West). Statistisches Bundesamt. GW. German. ir. 2.00 Single Issue. Verlag W Kohlhammer, Hessbruhlstrasse 69, PF 800430, 7000 Stuttgart 80 West Germany. LC HA1950.B3. DD 315.365.

LANDERKURZBERICHTE : BIRMA. Main/Corp Germany (West). Statistisches Bundesamt. VFOAT Birma. 0072-2227. GW. German. ir. W Kohlhammer, Hessbruhlstrasse 69, PF 800430, 7000 Stuttgart 80 West Germany. LC HA1693. DD 315.91.

LANDERKURZBERICHTE : BOLIVIEN. Main/Corp Germany (West). Statistisches Bundesamt. GW. German. ir. W Kohlhammer, Hessbruhlstrasse 69, PF 800430, 7 Stuttgart West Germany. LC HA965. DD 318.4.

LANDERKURZBERICHTE : BRASILIEN. Main/Corp Germany (West). Statistisches Bundesamt. 0435-785X. GW. German. ir. W Kohlhammer, Hessbruhlstrasse 69, PF 800430, 7 Stuttgart West Germany. LC HA984. DD 318.1.

LANDERKURZBERICHTE : BURUNDI. Main/Corp Germany (West). Statistisches Bundesamt. VFOAT Burundi. GW. German. ir. W Kohlhammer, Hessbruhlstrasse 69, PF 800430, 7000 Stuttgart 80 West Germany. LC HA2124.B86. DD 316.7572.

LANDERKURZBERICHTE : CHILE. Main/Corp Germany (West). Statistisches Bundesamt. VFOAT Chile. GW. German. ir. W Kohlhammer, Hessbruhlstrasse 69, PF 800430, 7 Stuttgart West Germany. LC HA1004. DD 318.3.

LANDERKURZBERICHTE : FRANZ. - GUAYANA. Main/Corp Germany (West). Statistisches Bundesamt. Series/Titl Statistik des Auslandes. GW. German. ir. 3.40. W Kohlhammer, Hessbruhlstrasse 69, PF 800430, 7000 Stuttgart 80 West Germany. LC HA1037.F7. DD 318.82.

LANDERKURZBERICHTE : INDONESIEN. Main/Corp Germany (West). Statistisches Bundesamt. GW. German. ir. W Kohlhammer, Hessbruhlstrasse 69, PF 800430, 7 Stuttgart 80 West Germany. LC HA1815. DD 315.98.

LANDERKURZBERICHTE : JORDANIEN. Main/Corp Germany (West). Statistisches Bundesamt. GW. German. ir. W Kohlhammer, Hessbruhlstrasse 69, PF 800430, 7000 Stuttgart 80 West Germany. LC HA1950.J6. DD 315.695.

LANDERKURZBERICHTE : KHMER, REP. (KAMBODSCHA). Main/Corp Germany (West). Statistisches Bundesamt. GW. German. ir. Verlag GMBH, Hessbruhlstrasse 69, PF 800430, 7000 Stuttgart 80 West Germany. LC HA1755. DD 315.96. *Landerkurzberichte: Kambodscha.*

LANDERKURZBERICHTE : KONGO. Main/Corp Germany (West). Statistisches Bundesamt. German. ir. W Kohlhammer, Philipp-Reis-Strasse 3, 6500 Stuttgart 42 West Germany. LC HA2088. *Landerkurzberichte: Kongo (Brazzaville).*

LANDERKURZBERICHTE : KUBA. Main/Corp Germany (West). Statistisches Bundesamt. VFOAT Kuba. 0072-2871. GW. German. ir. W Kohlhammer, Hessbruehlstrasse 69, PF 800430, 7 Stuttgart West Germany. LC HA875. DD 317.291.

LANDERKURZBERICHTE : MEXIKO. Main/Corp Germany (West). Statistisches Bundesamt. GW. German. ir. W Kohlhammer, Hessbruehlstrasse 69, PF 800430, 7 Stuttgart 80 West Germany. LC HA765. DD 317.2.

LANDERKURZBERICHTE : NEPAL. Main/Corp Germany (West). Statistisches Bundesamt. VFOAT Nepal. GW. German. ir. W Kohlhammer, Hessbruhlstrasse 69, PF 800430, 7000 Stuttgart 80 West Germany. LC HA1950 .N5. DD 315.496.

LANDERKURZBERICHTE : NICARAGUA. Main/Corp Germany (West). Statistisches Bundesamt. 0072-3150. GW. German. ir. W Kohlhammer, Hessbruhlstrasse 69, PF 800430, 7 Stuttgart West Germany. LC HA835. DD 317.285.

LANDERKURZBERICHTE : PANAMA. Main/Corp Germany (West). Statistisches Bundesamt. VFOAT Panama. GW. German. ir. W Kohlhammer, Hessbruehlstrasse 69, PF 800430, 7 Stuttgart West Germany. LC HA853. DD 317.287.

LANDERKURZBERICHTE : PERU. Main/Corp Germany (West). Statistisches Bundesamt. VFOAT Peru. 0072-3274. GW. German. ir. W Kohlhammer, Hessbruehlstrasse 69, PF 800430, 7 Stuttgart 80 West Germany. LC HA1064. DD 318.5.

LANDERKURZBERICHTE : PHILIPPINEN. Main/Corp Germany (West). Statistisches Bundesamt. GW. German. ir. W Kohlhammer, Hessbruehlstrasse 69, PF 800430, 7 Stuttgart 80 West Germany. LC HA1825. DD 315.99.

LANDERKURZBERICHTE : REPUBLIK KOREA. Main/Corp Germany (West). Statistisches Bundesamt. Series/Titl Statistik des Auslandes. VFOAT Republik Korea. GW. German. ir. 3.40. W Kohlhammer, Hessbruhlstrasse 69, PF 800430, 7000 Stuttgart 80 West Germany. LC HA1855. DD 315.19.

LANDERKURZBERICHTE : VENEZUELA. Main/Corp Germany (West). Statistisches Bundesamt. 0072-369X. GW. German. ir. W Kohlhammer, Hessbruehlstrasse 69, PF 800430, 7 Stuttgart 80 West Germany. LC HA1095. DD 318.7.

LANDERKURZBERICHTE : ZYPERN. Main/Corp Germany (West). Statistisches Bundesamt. VFOAT Zypern. GW. German. ir. W Kohlhammer, Hessbruehlstrasse 69, PF 800430, 7000 Stuttgart 80 West Germany. LC HA1950.C9. DD 315.645.

DIE LANDWIRTSCHAFT IN RHEINLAND-PFALZ. See Agriculture.

LANGUAGE CENSUS REPORT. See Linguistics.

LAPORAN KEPALA KANTOR SENSUS DAN STATISTIK DKI JAKARTA. Main/Corp Jakarta Raya (Indonesia). Kantor Sensus dan Statistik. 1977/78-. IO. Indonesian. ir. Kantor Sensus dan Statistik DKI Jakarta, Jl Merdeka Selatan 8-9, Jakarta Indonesia. LC HA1818.J34. *Laporan Kantor Sensus & I.E. dan Statistik D.K.I. Jakarta.*

LAPORAN STATISTIK BRI. Main/Corp Bank Rakyat Indonesia. VFOAT Statistical Report, BRI. Periodical. IO. English (Indonesian). ir. Bank Rakyat Indonesia, JL MH Thamrin 2, Jakarta Indonesia. LC HG3308.R33. DD 332.109598.

LAPORAN STATISTIK BULANAN - BAGIAN PENGUMPULAN DAN PENGOLAHAN DATA, BIRO PERENCANAAN, DEPARTEMEN TENAGA KERJA, TRANSMIGRASI DAN KOPERASI. Main/Corp Indonesia. Departmen Tenaga Kerja, Transmigrasi dan Koperasi. Biro Perencanaan. Bagian Pengumpulan dan Pengolahan Data. June 1975-. Indonesian. ir. Bagian Pengumpulan dan Pengolahan Data, Biro Perencanaan, Jl Let Jen Haryono Mt, Jakarta Indonesia. LC HD5824. *Laporan Statistik Bulanan - Bagian Penelitian dan Statistik, Departemen Tenaga Kerja, Transmigrasi dan Koperas.*

LAPORAN TAHUNAN - KANTOR WILAYAH DEPARTEMEN PERINDUSTRIAN PROPINSI SULAWESI TENGAH. Main/Corp Indonesia. Departemen Perindustrian. Kantor Wilayah Propinsi Sulawesi Tengah. Indonesian. ir. Jl Let Jen S Parman, Palu Indonesia. LC HC448.S782.

LEAD AND ZINC STATISTICS. Main/Corp International Lead and Zinc Study Group. VFOAT Statistiques du Plomb et du Zinc. 0023-9577. Periodical. UK. Multilingual (English and French). mo. International Lead & Zinc Study, Metro House, 58 St James Street, London SW1A 1LD England. Tel (212)754/234. Ind/Abst Funk Scott Index Corp. Ind.

LECTURE NOTES IN STATISTICS (SPRINGER-VERLAG). (LECTURE NOTES IN STATISTICS). 1-. Monographic Series. US. English. Springer Verlag-New York Inc, 175 5th Avenue, New York NY 10010. Tel (212)460-1584. Ind/Abst Comput. Control Abstr., Electr. Electron. Abstr., Sci. Abstr. Sect. A. Phys. Abstr. Contains notes on statistics.

LECTURE NOTES - INSTITUTE OF MATHEMATICAL STATISTICS, UNIVERSITY OF COPENHAGEN. Began publication with first issue in 1972. Periodical. English. ir. Copenhagen Universitet, Institute for Matematisk Statistisk, Copenhagen Denmark.

Statistics

LEISURE AND RECREATION STATISTICS ESTIMATES. UK. English. an. 7.50. Chartered Institute of Public Finance and Accountancy, 1 Buckingham Place, London SW1E 6HS England. **LC** GV76.E5. **DD** 990.01350942.

LES COLLECTIONS DE L'ENSEE. SERIE R: REGIONS. (LES COLLECTIONS DE L'INSEE. SERIE R : REGIONS). **Main/Corp** Institut National de la Statistique et des Etudes Economiques (France). **VFOAT** Regions. 1- 1969-. Monographic Series. French (summaries in English and Spanish). ir. **Ind/Abst** Foreign Lang. Index.

LIBRARY AND INFORMATION SCIENCE EDUCATION STATISTICAL REPORT. 1983-. 0739-506X. US. English. an. $25.00. ALISE, 471 Park Lane, State College PA 16803-3208. **Tel** (814)238-0254. Ed Timothy W Sineath. **LC** Z668. **DD** 020.710973. **Circ** 300. In-depth statistical reports from ALISE member graduate library schools on faculty, students, curriculum, finance, and continuing education. *Library Education Statistical Report, 0743-6602.*

LIBRARY NEWS BULLETIN. ANNUAL STATISTICAL ISSUE. (LIBRARY NEWS BULLETIN : ANNUAL STATISTICAL ISSUE). **Main/Corp** Washington (State). State Library, Olympia. 0097-9945. US. English. an. Washington State Library, Olympia WA 98504. **LC** Z732.W28. **DD** 021.009797.

LIBRARY STATISTICS OF COLLEGES AND UNIVERSITIES IN THE PACIFIC NORTHWEST. See Library and Information Science.

LIBRARY STATISTICS OF COLLEGES AND UNIVERSITIES. INSTITUTIONAL DATA. Began with issue for 1971. US. English. bm. US Department of Health Education and Welfare, Education Division, National Center for Education Statistics, Washington DC 20201. **LC** Z675.U5. **DD** 027.70973. Vols. for 1979- distributed to depository libraries in microfiche. *Library Statistics of Colleges and Universities. Data for Individual Institutions, 0083-274X.*

LIBRARY STATISTICS OF ILLINOIS COLLEGES AND UNIVERSITIES. (LIBRARY STATISTICS OF ILLINOIS COLLEGES AND UNIVERSITIES : INSTITUTIONAL DATA). **Main/Corp** Illinois. State Library, Springfield. 0094-2626. US. English. an. Illinois State Library, Springfield IL 62706. **LC** Z732.I2. **DD** 027.709773.

LICNI DOHOCI. Main/Corp Savezni Zavod za Statistiku (Yugoslavia). **Series Corp** Its Statisticki Bilten. 0300-2535. YU. Serbo-Croatian -R. an. 5.00 Single Issue. Savezni Zavod za Statistku, Kneza Milosa 20, Beograd Yugloslavia. **LC** HA1631, HC407.Y6.

LIST OF MEMBERS OF THE INTERNATIONAL STATISTICAL INSTITUTE. Main/Corp International Statistical Institute. **VFOAT** Liste des Membres de l'Institut International de Statistique. English and French. ir. Institut International de Statistique, 428 Prinses Beatrixlaan, Voorburg Netherlands. **LC** HA11. **DD** 310.621.

LIST OF PUBLICATIONS - AUSTRALIAN BUREAU OF STATISTICS, QUEENSLAND OFFICE. Main/Corp Australian Bureau of Statistics. Queensland Office. 1974-. 0312-7397. AT. English. an. Australian Bureau of Statistics, Statistics House 345 Ann Street, Brisbane Queensland 4000 Australia. **LC** Z4019. **DD** 015.943. *List of Publications.*

LIST OF SCHOOLS, ADDRESSES AND STATISTICS. Main/Corp South Africa. Dept. of Bantu Education. **VFOAT** Lys Van Skole, Adresse en Statistiek. SA. Afrikaans or English. ir. South Africa Department of Bantu Education, Private Bag X212, Pretoria South Africa. **LC** L971.S6. **DD** 370.2568.

LISTING OF SUPPLEMENTARY DOCUMENTS - STATISTICS CANADA. LIBRARY. See Bibliographies.

LIVESTOCK AND ANIMAL PRODUCTS STATISTICS. Main/Corp Canada. Statistics Canada. Livestock and Animal Products Section. **VFOAT** Statistique du Betail et des Produits Animaux. 1970-. 0068-7154. CN. English (French). an. Receiver General for Canada, Statistics Canada Publications, Ottawa Ontario K1A 0T6 Canada. *Canadian Livestock and Animal Products Statistics, 0068-7154.*

LIVESTOCK AND MEAT STATISTICS. SUPPLEMENT. Began with 1973. 0190-5678. US. English. an. Superintendent of Documents, US Government Printing Office, Washington DC 20402. **LC** HD1851, HD9414. **DD** 338.10973 S, 338.17600973. *Livestock and Meat Statistics.*

LIVESTOCK AND WOOL PRODUCTION IN LOCAL GOVERNMENT AREAS, STATISTICAL AGRICULTURAL AREAS, AND STATISTICAL DIVISIONS. Began with 1971 Vol. AT. English. an. Australian Bureau of Statistics, St Andrews House, Box 796 GPO, Sydney New South Wales 2001 Australia. **LC** SF55.A8. **DD** 338.1762009944. *Livestock and Wool Production in Local Government Areas and Statistical Divisions.*

LIVESTOCK STATISTICS. Main/Corp Australian Bureau of Statistics. 1974-. AT. English. an. Australian Bureau of Statistics, PO Box 796, Sydney New South Wales 2001 Australia. **LC** SF15.A8. **DD** 636.00994. *Livestock Statistics.*

LIVESTOCK STATISTICS OF LESOTHO. English. ir. Bureau of Statistics, PO Box 455, Maseru 100 Lesotho. **LC** SF55.L45. **DD** 338.1760096816.

LIVESTOCK STATISTICS, TASMANIA. English. an.

LMI TRENDS. CHICAGO SMSA *CEASED.* **VFOAT** Chicago SMSA, L.M.I. Trends, Chicago S.M.S.A. **VAT** Labor Market Informaiton Trends. Chicago Standard Metropolitan Statistical Area. May 1981-. 0733-4788. US. English. Illinois Bureau of Employment Security, 910 South Michigan Avenue, Chicago IL 60605. **LC** HD5726.C4. **DD** 331.120977311. *Labor Force Trends. Chicago Standard Metropolitan Statistical Area.*

LMI TRENDS. DECATUR SMSA (MACON COUNTY). VFOAT Decatur SMSA (Macon County). US. English. State of Illinois Department of Labor, Bureau of Employment Security, Research & Analysis Division, 910 South Michigan Avenue, Chicago IL 60605. *LMI Trends. Decatur Standard Metropolitan Statistical Area.*

LMI TRENDS. ROCKFORD SMSA. VFOAT Rockford SMSA. **VAT** Labor Market Information Trends. Rockford Standard Metropolitan Statistical Area. May 1981-. Periodical. US. English. mo. Illinois Bureau of Employment Security, Research & Analysis Division, 910 South Michigan Avenue, Chicago IL 60605. *Labor Area Trends. Rockford SMSA.*

LNNINGER OG INNTEKTER. Series/Titl Norges Offisielle Statistikk. **VFOAT** Wages, Salaries, and Income. 1980-. English (text in Norwegian). ir. 15.00. **LC** HA1501 Subser., HD5050.

LNNS- OG SYSSELSETTINGSSTATISTIKK FOR ANSATTE I SKOLEVERKET. Main/Corp Norway. Statistisk Sentralbyra. **Series/Titl** Norges Offisielle Statistikk. **VFOAT** Wage and Employment Statistics for Employees in Publicly Maintained Schools. 1977-. NO. Norwegian (English). ir. I Kommisjon Hos H Aschehoug Og Universitetsforlaget, Sehesteds Plass, Oslo 1 Norway. **LC** HA1501 SUBSER, LB2844.N8. **DD** 314.81 S, 331.28137009481. *Lnnsstatistikk for Ansatte I Skoleverket.*

LNNSSTATISTIKK FOR ANSATTE I FORRETNINGSMESSIG TJENESTEYTING OG I INTERESSEORGANISASJONER. DELETYEES IN BUSINESS. Series/Titl Norges Offisielle Statistikk. **VFOAT** Wage Statistics for Employees in Business Services and in Business, Professional and Labour Associations. NO. English (Norwegian). ir. 10.00. Statistisk Sentralbyra, Dronningensgt 16 Postbok 8131, Oslo 1 Norway. **LC** HA1501, HD8039.M4N77. **DD** 314.81 S, 331.29481.

LNNSSTATISTIKK FOR ANSATTE I VAREHANDEL = WAGE STATISTICS FOR EMPLOYEES IN WHOLESALE AND RETAIL TRADE. Main/Corp Norway. Statistisk Sentralbyra. **Series/Titl** Norges Offisielle Statistikk. 1960-. English (Norwegian). ir. **LC** HA1501. **DD** 381.09481.

LOCAL AUTHORITY AIRPORTS, ACCOUNTS AND STATISTICS. Main/Corp Chartered Institute of Public Finance and Accountancy. Statistical Information Service. 1978/79-. UK. English. 5.00. Chartered Institute of Public Finance and Accountancy, 1 Buckingham Place, London SW1E 6HS England. **LC** HE9797.5.G7. **DD** 387.71. *Financial Costs, Statistics of Local Authority Airports.*

LOCAL AUTHORITY ELECTION STATISTICS. 1977-. English. ir. **LC** JS8348.5. *Local Authority Elections.*

LOCAL AUTHORITY STATISTICS. 1960/61-. Periodical. English. 9.00. Government Printing Office Publications, Private Bag, Wellington New Zealand. **Tel** 729-119. Transactions of individual local authorities in such areas as transport, water supply, airports, libraries, real estate, and refuse, drainage and sewerage. *Local Authorities Handbook of New Zealand.*

LOCAL HOUSING STATISTICS : ENGLAND AND WALES. Main/Corp Great Britain. Dept. of the Environment. UK. English. qt. 0.96. HMSO, Department of the Environment, 49 High Holborn, WC1V6HB London England. **LC** HD7334.A3. **DD** 301.540942. Provides quarterly statistics on a cumulative basis, with the full year's figures normally being published in August. *Local Housing Statistics: England and Wales.*

LOCKHEED AIRCRAFT CORPORATION. Main/Corp United States. Bureau of Labor Statistics. 1937/51-. 0273-432X. US. English. US Department of Labor, Bureau of Labor Statistics, Washington DC 20212. **LC** HD4973, HD4966. A452U5. **DD** 331.2973, 331.2829109794.

LONDON STATISTICS *CEASED.* Ceased with: 1938/1939. UK. English. an. London County Council, Local Government and Statistical Department, London England. **Ind/Abst** Contents Curr. Leg. Period., Index Leg. Period., Curr. Law Index, Leg. Resour. Index, Soc. Sci. Citation Index.

LOONSTRUCTUURONDERZOEK. See Economics - Labor.

LUFTFARTSSTATISTIKK. VFOAT Civil Aviation Statistics Norway. 0800-4072. NO. English (Norwegian). an. Luftfartsverket, Storgt 10, 0155 Oslo 1 Norway. **LC** HE9859.A1. **DD** 387.709481021.

MAANDSTATISTIEK BOUWNIJVERHEID. Main/Corp Netherlands (Kingdom, 1815-). Centraal Bureau Voor de Statistiek. **VFOAT** Monthly Bulletin on Construction Statistics. Vol. 15- Jan. 1973-. Dutch. ir. Centraal Bureau Voor de Statistiek, Prinses Beatrixlaan 428 Voorburg S-Gravenhage Netherlands. **LC** HD9715.N2. *Maandstatistiek van de Bouwnijverheid.*

MAANDSTATISTIEK FINANCIEWEZEN. Main/Corp Netherlands (Kingdom, 1815-). Centraal Bureau Voor de Statistiek. **VFOAT** Monthly Bulletin of Financial Statistics. Vol. 21- Jan. 1973-. NE. Dutch. mo. 108.25. Staatsuitgeverij, Postbus 20014 Christoffel Plantijnst 2, 2500 EA'S Gravenhage Netherlands. **Tel** 070/78-95-70. **LC** HG23. *Maandstatistiek van het Financiewezen.*

MAANDSTATISTIEK POLITIE EN JUSTITIE. Main/Corp Netherlands. Centraal Bureau Voor de Statistiek. **VFOAT** Monthly Bulletin of Judicial Statistics. Vol. 1- Jan. 1957-. 0548-1937. NE. Dutch. mo. $77.77. Staatsuitgeverij, Christoffel Plantijnstraat 1, 2515 TZ'S-Gravenhage Netherlands. *Criminele Politieke Statistiek.*

MAANDSTATISTIEK VAN DE BUITENLANDSE HANDEL PER GOEDERENSOORT. Main/Corp Netherlands. Centraal Bureau Voor de Statistiek. **VFOAT** Monthly Statistical Bulletin of Foreign Trade, by Commodities. Vol. 17- 1966-. 0024-8738. NE. Dutch. mo 165.35. Staatsuitgeverij, Christoffel Plantijnstraat 1, 2515 TZ'S-Gravenhage Netherlands. **LC** HF205. *Maandstatistiek van de In-, Uit- en Doovoer per Goederensoort.*

MAANDSTATISTIEK VAN DE BUITENLANDSE HANDEL PER LAND. Main/Corp Netherlands. Centraal Bureau voor de Statistiek. **VFOAT** Monthly Statistical Bulletin of Foreign Trade, by Countries. Vol. 1- Jan. 1950-. 0024-8746. NE. Dutch. mo. 96.30. Staatsuitgeverij, Christoffel Plantijnstraat 1, 2515 TZ'S-Gravenhage Netherlands. *Maandstatistiek van de In-, Uit- en Doorvoer van Nederland.*

MAANDSTATISTIEK VAN VERKEER EN VERVOER. VFOAT Monthly Bulletin of Transport Statistics. Vol. 47, No. 8 (Aug. 1984)-. Periodical. NE. Dutch. mo. 9.00. Centraal Bureau Voor de Statistiek, Prinses Beatrixlaan 428, Postbus

Statistics

959, 2270 AZ Voorburg Netherlands. LC HE69. *CBS Maandstatistiek Van Verkeer en Vervoer.*

MAATALOUSTILASTOLLINEN KUUKAUSIKATSAUAS. Main/Corp Finland. Maatilahallitus. Tilastotoimisto. VFOAT Monthly Review of Agricultural Statistics. Fl. Multilingual (English and French). ir. Maatilahallitus Tlastotoimisto, Mariankatu 23, 00170 Helsinki 17 Finland. LC S242.F5. *Maataloustilastollinen Kuukausikatsaus.*

MAIN ECONOMIC INDICATORS. See Economics - International Economics.

MAINE REGISTER, STATE YEARBOOK AND LEGISLATIVE MANUAL. See Yearbooks, Almanacs, Directories.

MAINE SCHOOL STATISTICS. 0542-1098. US. English. an. Division of Management Information, State Dept of Educational and Cultural Services, State House Station #23, Augusta Maine 04333. LC L156. DD 379.12209741.

MAJOR PROGRAMS, BUREAU OF LABOR STATISTICS. Main/Corp United States. Bureau of Labor Statistics. 1969-. 0160-2985. US. English. an. Bureau of Labor Statistics, 411 9th Street NW, Washington DC 20212. LC HD8051. DD 331.072073. *Major BLS Programs.*

MALAWI MONTHLY STATISTICAL BULLETIN. Periodical. English. mo. National Statistical Office, PO Box 333, Zomba Malawi. LC HA1977.M3. DD 316.897.

MALAWI STATISTICAL YEARBOOK. See Yearbooks, Almanacs, Directories.

MALUKU DALAM ANGKA. Indonesian. ir. JI Pattimura, Ambon Indonesia. LC HA1817.M34.

MANADSSTATISTIK OVER UTRIKESHANDELN. Series/Titl Sveriges Officiella Statistik. VFOAT Monthly Bulletin of Foreign Trade. Ceased with: Dec. 1967. Periodical. SW. Swedish. mo. $28.21. Almqvist & Wiksell, PO Box 45150/108 Drottninggatan, S-104 Stockholm Sweden. Tel 08/23 79 90.

MANEDLIGE BULLETIN OVER UDENRIGSHANDELEN. MONATSBULLETIN DER AUSSENHANDELSSTATISTIK. See Business - Commerce.

MANEDSSTATISTIKK OVER UTENRIKSHANDELEN. Main/Corp Norway. Statistisk Sentralbyra. VFOAT Monthly Bulletin of External Trade. Vol. 48-. Periodical. NO. Norwegian. mo. 120.00. Central Bureau of Statistics, Skippergt 15, PO Box 8131, N-0033 Oslo 1 Norway. Tel (02)413820. LC HF215. bk rev. Circ 1,300. Contains detailed data on imports and exports. *Manedsoppgaver Over Vareomsetningen Med Utlandet.*

MANITOBA AGRICULTURE STATISTICS. July 1979-. 0713-3359. Periodical. CN. English. Free. Manitoba Department of Agriculture, Statistics Section 903-401, York Avenue, Winnipeg Manitoba R3C 0P8 Canada. Tel (204)945-4533. DD 338.1097127. bk rev. (ctrl) Major responsibility is to acquire and provide selected data on Manitoba agriculture for use by government, farm organizations and farmers, researchers and the general public.

MANITOBA STATISTICAL REVIEW. Main/Corp Manitoba. Bureau of Statistics. V. 1, No. 3- 1976-. 0700-2971. Periodical. CN. English. qt. $50. Manitoba Bureau of Statistics, 615-155 Carlton Street, Winnipeg Manitoba R3C 3HB Canada. Tel (204)945-2985. Circ 200. (ctrl) Compendium of socio-economic statistics on Manitoba with comparisons with other provinces. Quarterly (57 tables), 4th quarter (95 tables). *Manitoba Digest of Statistics, 0700-298X; Manitoba Price Statistics, 0317-7475.*

MANUAL DE ESTADISTICA AGRARIA. SP. Spanish. an. $1.31. Secretaria General Technica, ser Publ Agrar, Pseo Infanta Isabel 1, Madrid 7 Spain. LC HD2022.

MANUFACTURING INVESTMENT STATISTICS. CAPITAL APPROPRIATIONS AND CAPITAL INVESTMENT AND SUPPLY CONDITIONS. (MANUFACTURING INVESTMENT STATISTICS : CAPITAL APPROPRIATIONS AND CAPITAL INVESTMENT AND SUPPLY CONDITIONS). Main/Corp Conference Board. July 1978-. 0195-8313. US. English. Conference Board Inc, 845 Third Avenue, New York NY 10022. Ind/Abst Predicasts. LC HG4050. DD 338.43. *Manufacturing Investment Statistics. Capital Appropriations, 0361-4239; Manufacturing Investment Statistics. Capital Investment and Supply Conditions, 0362-9708.*

MANUFACTURING SERIES A. NO. 1, GENERAL STATISTICS. VFOAT Census of Manufacturing Series A. Began with Vol. for 1974/76. English. an. Department of Statistics, Private Bag, Wellington New Zealand. LC HD9738.N46. DD 338.470009931. *Statistics of Industrial Production.*

MARINE RECREATIONAL FISHERY STATISTICS SURVEY. PACIFIC COAST. 1979-1980-. US. English. be. US Department of Commerce, National Oceanic and Atmospheric Administration, National Marine Fisheries Service and National Fishery Statistics Program, Washington DC 20230.

MARKET RESEARCH EUROPE. See Business - Marketing.

MARKET RESEARCH IN GREAT BRITAIN. See Business - Marketing.

MARKET STATISTICS. Main/Corp Chicago Board Options Exchange. 0146-731X. US. English. Chicago Board Options Exchange, LaSalle at Jackson, Chicago IL 60604. LC HG5131.C4. DD 332.67.

MARYLAND STATISTICAL ABSTRACT. See Indexes/Abstracts.

MASIKA ANKARA SARA. See Indexes/Abstracts.

MASSACHUSETTS AGRICULTURAL STATISTICS. Main/Corp New England Crop and Livestock Reporting Service. VFOAT Agricultural Statistics, Massachusetts. Began with Vol. for 1972. 0092-9794. US. English. an. Massachusetts Department of Agriculture, 100 Cambridge Street, Boston MA 02202. LC S73. DD 338.109774.

MASSACHUSETTS LOBSTER FISHERY STATISTICS. 14th(1980)-. US. English. an. LC SH11, SH380.2.U6. DD 639.2 S, 338.3725384109744. *Massachusetts Coastal Lobster Fishery Statistics.*

MATERNAL AND CHILD HEALTH STATISTICS : NORTH CAROLINA. 1972-. US. English. an. Department of Health Resources, Division of Health Services, Raleigh NC 27611. LC RG530.3.U52. DD 312.23756.

MATHEMATICS AND STATISTICS RESEARCH DEPARTMENT PROGESS REPORT. Main/Corp Oak Ridge National Laboratory. Mathematics and Statistics Research Dept. VFOAT Progress Report - Mathematics and Statistics Research Department. US. English. US Department of Energy, Office of Energy Technology, Oak Ridge National Laboratory, 5285 Port Royal Road, Springfield VA 22161.

MAY ROCZNIK STATYSTYKI MIEDZYNARODOWEJ. Series Corp Poland. Gowny Urzad Statystyczny. Seria Statystyka Miedzynarod. 1972-. Polish. ir. 25.00. Gowny Urzad Statstyczny Department Wydawnictw, Warszawa Poland. LC HA173.P6.

MEAT STATISTICS. Main/Corp Australian Bureau of Statistics. AT. English. ir. Australian Bureau of Statistics, GPO Box 796, Sydney New South Wales 2001 Australia. LC HD9428.A8. DD 338.476490094. *Meat Industry.*

MEDICAL MANPOWER IN NEW ZEALAND. STATISTICS. 1978-. Periodical. NZ. English. ir. Medical Council of New Zealand, PO Box 5135, Wellington New Zealand. LC RA410.9.N42. DD 331.12516106952. NLM W1 ME3813.

MEDICARE—— USE OF HOME HEALTH SERVICES (HEALTH CARE FINANCING PROGRAM STATISTICS). See Public Health and Safety.

MEMBERSHIP AND STATISTICAL DIRECTORY - NEW ENGLAND GAS ASSOCIATION. See Yearbooks, Almanacs, Directories.

MEMBERSHIP DIRECTORY - AMERICAN STATISTICAL ASSOCIATION. MONTREAL CHAPTER. See Yearbooks, Almanacs, Directories.

MEMBERSHIP DIRECTORY OF THE FEDERAL STATISTICS USERS' CONFERENCE. See Yearbooks, Almanacs, Directories.

MEMBERSHIP DIRECTORY - STATISTICAL SOCIETY OF CANADA. See Yearbooks, Almanacs, Directories.

MEMENTO DE STATISTIQUE AGRICOLE : DORDOGNE. French. ir. Ministere de l'Agriculture, Direction Departementale de l'Agriculture Service Statistique, 7 Place Francheville, 24016 Perigueux France. LC S230.D67.

MEMORIA ESTADISTICA : SEGUROS PRIVADOS. Main/Corp Spain. Direccion General de Seguros. Spanish. ir. LC HG8677.

MENIAION STATISTIKON DELTION (TRAPEZA TES HELLADOS. DIEUTHYNSIS OIKONOIKON MELETON). (MENIAION STATISTIKON DELTION). VFOAT Meniaio Statistiko Deltio, Monthly Statistical Bulletin. GR. Greek, Modern (English). mo. $45. Bank of Greece, Economic Research, PO Box 105, Athens Greece. Tel 3202392. Circ 3,000. Statistical data on money and banking, public finance, balance of payments, production and prices. *Meniaion Deltion.*

MENTAL HEALTH AND MENTAL RETARDATION SERVICES ANNUAL STATISTICAL REPORT. Main/Corp Nebraska. Dept. of Public Institutions. US. English. an. Department of Public Institutions, PO Box 94728, Lincoln NE 68509. LC HV3006.N2. DD 362.209782.

MENTAL HEALTH SERVICE SYSTEM REPORTS. SERIES CN, MENTAL HEALTH NATIONAL STATISTICS. VFOAT Mental Health National Statistics. No. 1-. 0278-6877. Monographic Series. US. English. NLM W1 ME928EN.

MENTAL HEALTH STATISTICS. Main/Corp Illinois. Dept. of Mental Health and Developmental Disabilities. 1974/75-. US. English. an. Department of Mental Health & Developmental Disabilities, 401 State Office Building, Springfield IL 62706. LC RA790.65.I4. DD 362.209773. *Mental Health Statistics in Illinois.*

MENTAL HEALTH STATISTICS. Main/Corp Missouri. Dept. of Mental Health. 1975/76-. 0196-562X. US. English. an. LC RA790.65.M8. DD 362.209778. NLM W2 AM8 D35M.

MENTAL HEALTH STATISTICS. VOLUME 3. INSTITUTIONAL FACILITIES, SERVICES AND FINANCES. (MENTAL HEALTH STATISTICS. VOLUME III : INSTITUTIONAL FACILITIES, SERVICES AND FINANCES). Main/Corp Statistics Canada. Health Division. Institutional Statistics Section. VFOAT La Statistique de l'Hygiene Mentale. Volume III : Installations, Services et Finances des Etablissements. 1976-. 0380-6545. CN. English (French). an. $10.00. Statistique Canada, Publications Division, Ottawa Ontario K1A 0T6 Canada. Tel 991-1641. LC RA790.7.C2. DD 362.20971. Circ 1,200. Information on the medical and clinographic characteristics of patients discharged from general hospitals and mental hospitals, with psychiatric diagnoses. *Mental Health Statistics. Volume III: Institutional Facilities, Services and Finances, 0380-6545.*

MERCHANDISING. . .STATISTICAL AND MARKETING REPORT. VFOAT Merchandising Statistical Issue and Marketing Report. 56th (1978)-. US. English. an. Billboard Publications, 1515 Broadway, New York NY 10036. Forecast.

METAL BULLETIN HANDBOOK. See Metals & Metallurgy.

METAL STATISTICS. 54th- Ed. 0170-9933. GW. English. an. Metallgesellschaft AG, Volkswirtschaft, Postfach 3274, D-6000 Frankfurt AM 1 West Germany. LC HD9539.A1. *Statistical Tables on Aluminium, Lead, Copper, Zinc, Tin, Cadmium, Nickel, Mercury, and Silver.*

METAL STATISTICS; THE PURCHASING GUIDE OF THE METAL INDUSTRIES. Began Publication in 1908. US. English. an. $62.00. American Metal Markets, 7 East 12th Street, New York NY 10003. Tel (212)741-4429. DD 671, 669.

I METALLI NON FERROSI IN ITALIA; STATISTICHE. IT. Italian. ir. Associazione Nazionale Industrie Metalli Non Ferrosi, Via Lepoardi 18, Milano Italy. LC HD9539.A3.

Statistics

METHODOLOGY REPORTS. (MENTAL HEALTH STATISTICS SERIES). 0098-4949. US. English. National Institute of Mental Health, 5600 Fishers Lane, Rockville MD 20852. LC RA790.6. DD 362.20973.

METRON. See Mathematics.

MEZOGAZDASAGI ERO- ES MUNKAGEPEK. HU. Hungarian. ir. 67.—. Statisztikai Kiado Vallalat III, Kaszasdulo U. 2, 1033 Budapest Hungary. Tel 803-311. Circ 800. Gives a survey on all power engines and machineries used in agriculture in Hungary. It reports the stock on the 31st of December every year, detailed by categories and territories.

MICHIGAN AGRICULTURAL STATISTICS. 0277-5824. US. English. an. Michigan Department of Agriculture, Lewis Cass Building, PO Box 30017, Lansing MI 48909. LC S75. DD 338.109774.

MICHIGAN HEALTH STATISTICS. Main/Corp Center for Health Statistics (Michigan). 1970-. 0539-7413. US. English. an. 3500 North Logan Street, Lansing MI 98914. LC RA407.4.M5. DD 312.09774. Michigan Public Health Statistics.

MICHIGAN LIBRARY STATISTICS (MICHIGAN. STATE BOARD OF EDUCATION). (MICHIGAN LIBRARY STATISTICS). 1981-1982. US. English. an. LC Z732.M6. DD 027.4774. Michigan Library Statistics (Michigan. Dept. of Education : 1978).

MICHIGAN STATE EMPLOYEES' RETIREMENT SYSTEM. (MICHIGAN STATE EMPLOYEES' RETIREMENT SYSTEM FINANCIAL AND STATISTICAL REPORT). Main/Corp Michigan. Dept. of Administration. 0092-9212. US. English. an. Department of Administration, Stevens T Mason Building, 2nd Floor West Wing, Lansing MI 48913. LC JK5860.P4. DD 353.9774005.

MICHIGAN STATISTICAL ABSTRACT. See Indexes/Abstracts.

MID-YEAR STATISTICS OF THE NATIONAL CREDIT UNION ADMINISTRATION. (MID-YEAR ... STATISTICS OF THE NATIONAL CREDIT UNION ADMINISTRATION). Main/Corp United States. National Credit Union Administration. 1980-. 0277-0881. US. English. National Credit Union Administration, 1775 G Street NW, Washington DC 20456. LC HG2037. DD 334.220973.

MIGRANT SERVICES STATISTICAL REPORT. Main/Corp Michigan. Dept. of Social Services. Series/Titl DSS Publication. US. English. Department of Social Services, Lansing MI 48926. LC HV86. DD 361.9774 S, 362.85. Migrant Services Report, 0360-9359.

MIGRATION AND TOURISM STATISTICS. Main/Corp Kenya. Central Bureau of Statistics. 1968/71-. 0377-1385. English. ir. 10.00. Central Bureau of Statistics, Ministry of Finance & Planning, Box 30266, Nairobi Kenya. LC G155.K4. DD 338.47916762044.

MIGRATION AND TOURISM STATISTICS. English. an. LC JV8975.S48. DD 325.696.

MILITARY MANPOWER STATISTICS. Began with issue for Apr. 1979. 0741-1340. Periodical. US. English. mo. Director for Information Operations and Reports, WHS the Pentagon, Washington DC 20301. Ind/Abst Am. Stat. Index. LC UB23. DD 355.220973.

MILITARY PERSONNEL AND DEPENDENTS IN HAWAII. Main/Corp Hawaii. Dept. of Planning and Economic Development. 0363-8359. US. English. State of Hawaii/Department of Planning and Economic Dev, PO Box 2359, Honolulu HI 96804. LC HA329.1, UA26.H38. DD 319.69 S, 355.33809969.

MILJSTATISTIKK. Main/Corp Norway. Statistisk Sentralbyra. Series/Titl Statistiske Analyser. VFOAT Environmental Statistics. 1976-. Norwegian (summaries in English). ir. LC HC365.

MINERAL COMMODITY SUMMARIES. See Earth Sciences - Mineralogy.

MINERAL STATISTICS YEARBOOK. 1977-. 0707-2570. CN. English. an. LC HD9506.C23. DD 338.2097124. Mineral Statistical Yearbook, 0080-651X.

MINI TOKEI HANDO BUKKU. JA. Japanese. ir. Sorifu Tokeikyoku, 95 Wakamatsu-Cho Shinjuku-Ku, Tokyo-To 162 Japan. LC HA4621.

MINING STATISTICS : NORTH OF 60. Main/Corp Canada. Northern Economic Development Branch. Mining Section. VFOAT Statistiques Minieres:. CN. Multilingual (English and French). National Economic Development Branch Mining Section, Information Canada Receiver General Canada, Statistics Publications Canada, Ottawa Ontario K1A 0T6 Canada. LC HD9506.C2. DD 338.209712.

MINNESOTA AGRICULTURAL STATISTICS. 1944/45-. US. English. an. $5.50. Minnesota State Documents Center, 117 University Avenue, St Paul MN 55155. Tel (612)296-2230. Minnesota Annual Crop and Livestock Statistics.

MINNESOTA HEALTH STATISTICS. 1972-. 0094-5641. US. English. an. Minnesota Health Statistics, 717 Delaware Street SE, Minneapolis MN 55440. LC RA407.4.M6. DD 312.09776. NLM W2 AM6 S6MI. Issued also in microfiche by: Minnesota State Document Depository System. Minnesota Vital Statistics.

MINNESOTA POCKET DATA BOOK. VFOAT Minnesota Data Book. 1973-. 0094-3983. US. English. be. $24.95. Minnesota State Planning Agency, Development Planning Division, St Paul MN 55166. LC HA454. DD 317.76.

MINNESOTA POPULATION ESTIMATES. US. English. an. State Demography Unit, Minnesota Department of Energy Planning and Development, 101 Capitol Square Building, 550 Cedar Street, St Paul MN 55101. LC HA451. DD 312.809776.

MINNESOTA STATISTICAL ABSTRACT. See Indexes/Abstracts.

MINNESOTA STATISTICAL PROFILE. Main/Corp Minnesota. Dept. of Economic Development. Research Division. 1976-. US. English. 480 Cedar Street, St Paul MN 55101. LC HA451. DD 317.76. Minnesota Profile.

MISSIONNAIRES CATHOLIQUES CANADIENS. STATISTIQUES. (MISSIONNAIRES CATHOLIQUES CANADIENS, STATISTIQUES). VFOAT Canadian Catholic Missionaries, Statistics. Began publication in 197-. 0225-3801. CN. English (French). be. Canadian Religious Conference, Missions Department, 324 Laurier Avenue East, Ottawa Ontario K1N 6P6 Canada. DD 266.20212.

MISSISSIPPI FINANCIAL STATISTICS FOR HIGHWAY PLANNING ON STATE HIGHWAYS, COUNTY ROADS, CITY STREETS. (MISSISSIPPI FINANCIAL STATISTICS FOR HIGHWAY PLANNING ON STATE HIGHWAYS COUNTY ROADS CITY STREETS). 0096-333X. US. English. an. LC HE356.M7. DD 388.1109762. Mississippi Statistics for Highway Planning on State Highways, County Roads, City Streets.

MISSISSIPPI MORBIDITY REPORT. 0745-2535. Periodical. US. English. mo. Mississippi State Department of Health, Bureau of Technical Services, Office of Epidemiology, PO Box 1700, Jackson MS 39205.

MISSISSIPPI OFFICIAL AND STATISTICAL REGISTER. VFOAT Official and Statistical Register. 0196-4755. US. English. ir. Mississippi Secretary of State, PO Box 136, Jackson MS 39205. LC J87. DD 353.9762002. Mississippi Blue Book.

MISSISSIPPI STATISTICAL ABSTRACT. See Indexes/Abstracts.

MISSOURI JUVENILE COURT STATISTICS. 1978-. Periodical. US. English. an. Missouri Juvenile Court Statistics.

MISSOURI VITAL STATISTICS. Main/Corp Missouri Center for Health Statistics. 1973-. 0098-1974. US. English. an. Missouri Vital Statistics, Box 570, Jefferson City MO 65102-0570. Tel (314)751-8074. Ed Wayne Schramm. LC HA471. DD 312.09778. NLM W2 AM8 B9V. Circ 700. (ctrl). Missouri vital statistic data in the state containing a short two or three page analytical article relating to public health data of interest. Missouri Vital Statistics.

MITTEILUNGEN DES DIREKTORIUMS DER OSTERREICHISCHEN NATIONALBANK. See Business - Banking & Finance.

MONTANA AGRICULTURAL STATISTICS. V. 1-. US. English. be. LC HD1775.M9. DD 338.1.

MONTANA HISTORICAL ENERGY STATISTICS. 1976-. US. English. an. Montana Energy Office, Capitol Station, Helena MT 59601. LC HD9502.U53. DD 333.7909786.

MONTANA LIBRARY DIRECTORY, WITH STATISTICS OF MONTANA PUBLIC LIBRARIES. VFOAT Statistics of Montana Public Libraries. 0094-873X. US. English. LC Z732.M9. DD 021.0025786. Statistics of Montana Public Libraries, 0735-7818.

MONTANA VITAL STATISTICS. Main/Corp Montana. Dept. of Health and Environmental Sciences. Bureau of Records & Statistics. 1970-. 0077-1198. US. English. an. Montana Department of Health and Environmental Sciences, Bureau of Records and Statistics, Cogswell Building, Helena MT 59601. LC HA481. DD 312.09786. NLM W2 AM9 S7A. Annual Statistical Supplement.

MONTHLY ABSTRACT OF STATISTICS. See Indexes/Abstracts.

MONTHLY BENEFIT STATISTICS (UNITED STATES. RAILROAD RETIREMENT BOARD. BUREAU OF RESEARCH). (MONTHLY BENEFIT STATISTICS). 0364-7129. Periodical. US. English. mo. Bureau of Research, US Railroad Retirement Board, Chicago IL 60611. Ind/Abst Am. Stat. Index, Index U.S. Gov. Period. LC HD7116.R118.

MONTHLY BULLETIN OF STATISTICS, THE REPUBLIC OF CHINA. Main/Corp China (Republic : 1949-). Hsing Cheng Yuan. V. 1- July 1975-. CH. English. mo. $35.00. Li Ming Cultural Enterprise Company, 1 Chung Hsiao East Road, Section 1, Taipei Taiwan. Tel 3814910. Ind/Abst Public Aff. Inf. Serv. Bull. LC HA1710.5. DD 315.1249.

MONTHLY BULLETIN OF STATISTICS - UNITED NATIONS. (MONTHLY BULLETIN OF STATISTICS). VFOAT Bulletin Mensuel de Statistique. Vol. 1, No. 1 (Jan. 1947)-. 0041-7432. US. English (French). mo. $150.00. United Nations Publications, Sales Section/Room A-315, New York NY 10017. Tel (212)754-8324. Ind/Abst Ship Abstr., Funk Scott Index Corp. Ind. LC HC57. DD 330.90021. Contains worldwide statistical data on all areas of economic activity. Monthly Bulletin of Statistics (United Nations. Statistical Office : 1946).

MONTHLY BULLETIN - STATISTICS OF FOREIGN TRADE. ORGANIZATION FOR ECONOMIC COOPERATION AND DEVELOPMENT. SERIE A CEASED. (STATISTICS OF FOREIGN TRADE : MONTHLY BULLETIN. SERIES A). VFOAT Statistiques du Commerce Exterieur. June 1974-1982. 0377-1547. FR. English (French). mo. LC HF91. DD 382.0212. Statistics of Foreign Trade. Series A: Overall Trade by Countries.

MONTHLY COFFEE STATISTICS. V. 1- (No. 1-). 0730-3254. Periodical. US. English. mo. $85.00. 114 Liberty Street, New York NY 10016.

MONTHLY DIGEST OF STATISTICS - BARBADOS. Main/Corp Barbados Statistical Service. Apr. 1974-. 0378-8873. Periodical. BB. English. ir. Barbados Statistical Service, National Insurance Building, Bridgetown Barbados. LC HA865. DD 317.2981. Quarterly Digest of Statistics.

MONTHLY DIGEST OF STATISTICS (GREAT BRITAIN. CENTRAL STATISTICAL OFFICE). (MONTHLY DIGEST OF STATISTICS). Began with: No. 1 (Jan. 1946). Periodical. UK. English. mo. $107.28. Her Majestys Stationery Office, PO Box 276, London SW8 5DT England. Tel (01)622-3316. LC HC251. DD 330.942. Contains 20 broadly ranging subjects, including population, employment, social services, retailing and manufacturing.

MONTHLY DIGEST OF STATISTICS - SINGAPORE. Main/Corp Singapore. Dept. of Statistics. V. 1- Jan. 1962-. SI. English. mo. $27.66. Government of Singapore Chief Statistician, Maxwell Road, PO Box 3010, Singapore 9050. Tel 20826. LC HA1797.S5. DD 315.957. Singapore. Circ 900. It gives the latest available data on the demographic and economic characteristics of. Malayan Statistics.

MONTHLY DIGEST OF STATISTICS - ZAMBIA. Main/Corp Zambia. Central Statistical Office. V. 1- Apr. 1964-. 0027-0377. Periodical. ZA. English. mo. 40.00. Central Statistical Office, Box

31908, Lusaka Zambia. **Tel** 211231. **Circ** 1,000. (ctrl). Time series of data on population and migration, agriculture, employment, production, external trade transport, government accounts, money and banking, prices, national accounts education, and health. *Monthly Digest of Statistics.*

MONTHLY DIGEST OF STATISTICS (ZIMBABWE. CENTRAL STATISTICAL OFFICE). (MONTHLY DIGEST OF STATISTICS (ZIMBABWE. CENTRAL STATISTICAL OFFICE)). Began in Mar. 1980. Periodical. English. ir. Central Statistical Office, PO Box 8063, Causeway Salisbury Rhodesia. *Monthly Digest of Statistics (Zimbabwe, Rhodesia. Central Statistical Office).*

MONTHLY GAS UTILITY STATISTICAL REPORT. **Main/Corp** American Gas Association. Periodical. US. English. mo. American Gas Association, 1515 Wilson Boulevard, Arlington VA 22209. **Tel** (703)841-8400.

MONTHLY MIGRATION AND TOURIST STATISTICS FOR . . . . Began in 1980. Periodical. English. mo. *Monthly Migration and Tourist Statistics.*

MONTHLY NEWSPRINT STATISTICS. CANADIAN PULP AND PAPER ASSOCIATION. (MONTHLY NEWSPRINT STATISTICS). **VFOAT** Statistiques Mensuelles de Papier Journal. Jan. 1977-. 0709-602X. Periodical. CN. English (French). mo. American Paper Institute, 260 Madison Avenue, New York NY 10016. **Tel** (202)797-5800. **Ind/Abst** Abstr. Bull. Inst. Paper Chem., Funk Scott Index Corp. Ind. **DD** 338.47676286. *Monthly Newsprint Report, 0316-4268.*

MONTHLY PETROLEUM STATISTICS REPORT *CEASED.* Began Apr. 1975. 0364-0205. Periodical. US. English. mo. Superintendent of Documents, US Government Printing Office, Washington DC 20402. **Ind/Abst** Energy Inf. Abstr., Environ. Abstr., Am. Stat. Index. *Weekly Petroleum Statistics Report, Petroleum Situation Report.*

MONTHLY PRODUCTION OF SELECTED INDUSTRIES OF INDIA. **Main/Corp** India (Republic). Central Statistical Organisation. Periodical. II. English. mo. $23.40. Deputy Director, Government of India, Ministry of Planning, Department of Statistics, Central Statistical Organisation, Industrial Statistics Wing 1, Council House Street, Calcutta-700001 India. **Tel** 23-6534. **LC** HC431. **DD** 338.0954. **Circ** 185. (ctrl). Provisional monthly production data and indices of industrial production (base 1970=100) at various levels of industrial classification for the country for a few months. *Monthly Statistics of the Production of Selected Industries of India.*

MONTHLY REPORT OF THE IRON & STEEL STATISTICS. **VFOAT** Tekko Gekkan Tokei. Began in Jan. 1958. 0497-1140. Periodical. JA. English. mo. $11.75. Japan Iron & Steel Federation, Keidanren Kaiden 9-4 1-chome, Tokyo 100 Japan.

MONTHLY REVIEW OF CANADIAN FISHERIES STATISTICS. **Main/Corp** Statistics Canada. Manufacturing and Primary Industries Division. **VFOAT** la Statistique Mensuelle des Peches du Canada. V. 26- Jan. 1972-. Periodical. CN. English (French). mo. Receiver General for Canada, Supply & Services, Ottawa Ontario K1A 0S9 Canada. *Monthly Review of Canadian Fisheries Statistics.*

MONTHLY STATISTICAL BULLETIN (INTERNATIONAL TIN COUNCIL) *CEASED.* (MONTHLY STATISTICAL BULLETIN). Vol. 18 (1974)-V. 27 (1983). UK. English. mo. 36.00. International Tin Council, Haymarket House, 1 Oxendon Street, London SW1Y 4EQ England. **LC** HD9539.T5. **DD** 338.274530212. *Statistical Bulletin (International Tin Council).*

MONTHLY STATISTICAL BULLETIN (MAJLIS PENGELUAR-PENGELUAR GETAH MALAYSIA). (MONTHLY STATISTICAL BULLETIN). Began with issue for September 1973. 0126-5865. Periodical. MY. English. mo. $19.06. Malaysian Rubber Production Council, PO Box 2688, Kuala Lumpus West Malaysia. **Tel** 482677. **LC** HD9161.M32. **DD** 338.173895209795. *Monthly Statistical Bulletin (Majlis Pengeluar P2 S Getah Tanah Melayu), 0303-1640.*

MONTHLY STATISTICAL BULLETIN OF BANGLADESH. **Main/Corp** Bangladesh. Bureau of Statistics. V. 1- Mar. 1972-. 0377-1555. English. mo. $60.00. Bandladesh Bureau of Statistics, Bangladesh Secretariat, Dacca Bangladesh. **LC** HA1730.8. **DD** 315.492. *Monthly Bulletin of Statistics.*

MONTHLY STATISTICAL BULLETIN OF WEST MALAYSIA. **Main/Corp** Malaysia. Dept. of Statistics. Periodical. English. mo. 60.00. Department of Statistics, Jalan Cenderasari, Kuala Lumpur 10-01 Malaysia. **Tel** 2922/33. **LC** HA1791. **DD** 315.95. bk rev. **Circ** 500. (ctrl).

MONTHLY STATISTICAL DIGEST WEST BENGAL. (MONTHLY STATISTICAL DIGEST, WEST BENGAL). **Main/Corp** West Bengal. Bureau of Applied Economics and Statistics. 0043-308X. II. English. ir. 17.28. Bureau of Applied Economics and Statistics, Calcutta India. **LC** HA1728.B42. **DD** 315.414. *Monthly Statistical Digest West Bengal, 0043-308X.*

MONTHLY STATISTICAL REPORT. **Main/Corp** District of Columbia. Department of Public Welfare. V. 1- Jan. 1946-. Periodical. US. English. Department of Public Welfare, Superintendent of Documents, US Government Printing Office, Washington DC 20402. **LC** HV87.W3. **DD** 360.9753.

MONTHLY STATISTICAL REPORT. **Main/Corp** American Petroleum Institute. Statistics Dept. V. 1- 1977-. Periodical. US. English. mo. $10.00. American Petroleum Institute, 1220 L Street NW, Washington DC 20005. **Tel** (202)682-8378. This report will analyze and comment on the significance of trends reflected in the weekly data.

MONTHLY STATISTICAL REPORT. **Main/Corp** New York (City). Human Resources Administration. Periodical. US. English. mo. The City of New York, Department of Social Services, New York NY 10013. **LC** HV87.N5. **DD** 361.63097471. *Monthly Statistical Report.*

MONTHLY STATISTICAL REPORT - STATE OF NEW MEXICO, INCOME SUPPORT DIVISION. **Main/Corp** New Mexico. Income Support Division. **VFOAT** Monthly Report. April 1978-. Periodical. US. English. mo. **LC** HV86. **DD** 361.609789. *Quarterly Statistical Report.*

MONTHLY STATISTICAL REVIEW - GOVERNMENT OF SASKATCHEWAN, BUREAU OF STATISTICS. **Main/Corp** Saskatchewan. Bureau of Statistics. V. 4- Jan. 1978-. CN. English. mo. Bureau of Statistics, 3475 Albert Street, TC Douglas Building, Regina Saskatchewan S4S 6X6 Canada. **Tel** 787-6327. **LC** HA747.S3. **DD** 317.124. **Circ** 600. Economic and social statistics for the province of Saskatchewan. *Saskatchewan Monthly Statistical Review.*

MONTHLY STATISTICAL SUMMARY REPORT - STATE OF OHIO, DEPARTMENT OF MENTAL HEALTH AND MENTAL RETARDATION, DIVISION OF BUSINESS ADMINISTRATION, BUREAU OF STATISTICS. (MONTHLY STATISTICAL SUMMARY REPORT - STATE OF OHIO, DEPARTMENT OF MENTAL HEALTH AND MENTAL RETARDATION). **Main/Corp** Ohio. Dept. of Mental Health and Mental Retardation. Bureau of Statistics. May 1972-. 0090-7456. US. English. mo. Ohio Mental Health & Mental Retardation Department, Statistics Bureau, Columbus OH 43215. **Tel** (614)466-2596. **NLM** W2 AO3 D48M. *Monthly Statistical Summary Report - State of Ohio, Department of Mental Hygiene and Correction, Division of Business, Bureau of Statistics, 0090-7464.*

MONTHLY STATISTICS. ALBERTA COAL INDUSTRY. **Main/Corp** Alberta. Energy Resources Conservation Board. 0382-2168. Periodical. CN. English. mo. $11.61. Energy Resources Conservation Board, 640 5th Avenue Southwest, Calgary Alberta T2P 3G4 Canada. **Tel** (403)297-8311.

MONTHLY STATISTICS. ALBERTA ELECTRIC ENERGY INDUSTRY. **Main/Corp** Alberta. Energy Resources Conservation Board. 0319-3705. Periodical. CN. English. mo. $7.74. Energy Resources Conservation, 640 5th Avenue Southwest, Calgary Alberta T2P 3G4 Canada. **Tel** (403)297-8311.

MONTHLY STATISTICS OF EMPLOYMENT. **Main/Corp** New Zealand. Dept. of Labour (1954-). Research and Planning Division. Periodical. NZ. English. ir. Department of Labour, Private Bag, Wellington New Zealand. **LC** HD5850.4. **DD** 331.1209931. *Monthly Statistics of Employment.*

MONTHLY STATISTICS OF FOREIGN TRADE. **VFOAT** Statistiques Mensuelles du Commerce Exterieur. Jan. 1983-. 0474-5388. Periodical. US. English (French). mo. $68.00. OECD Publications Center, 1750 Pennsylvania Avenue Northwest, Washington DC 20006. **Tel** (202)724-1857. **LC** HF91. **DD** 382.0212. Available on microfiche. A detailed regional analysis of trade of the main country groupings in the OECD area. *Statistics of Foreign Trade. Monthly Bulletin. Series A, 0377-1547.*

MONTHLY STATISTICSL SUMMARY - AMERICAN PAPER INSTITUTE *CEASED.* (MONTHLY STATISTICAL SUMMARY). **Main/Corp** American Paper Institute. V. 59, No. 8 Aug. 1981. 0003-0341. US. English. mo. American Paper Institute, 260 Madison Avenue, New York NY 10016. **Tel** (212)340-0630. **Ed** Benjamin Slatin. **Ind/Abst** Abstr. Bull. Inst. Paper Chem. **LC** HD9824. **DD** 338.4767620973. **Circ** 1,000. Paper industry statistics, current.

MONTHLY SUMMARY OF JUTE GOODS STATISTICS. **Main/Corp** Bangladesh Jute Mills Association. English. ir. 6.00. Bangladesh Jute Mills Association, 62/63 Motijheel, Dacca Bangladesh. **LC** HD9156.J8. **DD** 338.4767713095492. *Monthly Summary of Jute Goods Statistics.*

MONTHLY SUMMARY OF STATISTICS. **Main/Corp** Australian Bureau of Statistics. Queensland Office. English. mo. Australian Bureau of Statistics, Ground Floor Statistics House, 345 Ann Street, Brisbane Queensland 4000 Australia. **Tel** (07)222 6351. **LC** HA3071. **DD** 319.43. Latest statistics on: building approvals and activity, building materials, wholesale price indexes, building societies (permanent) and coal production. *Queensland Statistics.*

MONTHLY SUMMARY OF STATISTICS, AUSTRALIA. **Main/Corp** Australian Bureau of Statistics. July 1979-. AT. English. mo. 49.20. Australian Bureau of Statistics, PO Box 84, Canberra Australian Capital Territory 2600 Australia. **Tel** (062)52 6778. **LC** HC601. **DD** 330.994005. Data on a wide range of items classified in varying degree of details for population and vital statistics, employment and unemployment, internal and overseas trade, etc. *Monthly Review of Business Statistics, 0311-9025.*

MONTHLY SUMMARY OF STATISTICS, NEW SOUTH WALES. **Main/Corp** Australian Bureau of Statistics. New South Wales Office. No. 551- Sept. 1979-. AT. English. mo. 22.30. Australian Bureau of Statistics, 3rd Floor St Andrews House, Sydney Square, Sydney New South Wales 2000 Australia. **Tel** (02)268 4611. **LC** HA3011. **DD** 330.994400212. Covers population and vital statistics, employment and unemployment, wages and prices, production, building, finance, trade, transport and welfare. *New South Wales Monthly Summary of Business Statistics, 0028-680X.*

MONTHLY SUMMARY OF STATISTICS, TASMANIA. No. 396 (June 1978)-. 0314-2094. English. mo. 22.30. Australian Bureau of Statistics, Commonwealth Government Centre/3rd Floor, 188 Collins Street, Hobart Tasmania 7000 Australia. **Tel** (002)20 9409. **LC** HA3007.T37. **DD** 319.46. Contains tables dealing with: population and vital statistics, employment and unemployment, wages and prices, production statistics, building, finance and trade. *Monthly Summary of Statistics (Australian Bureau of Statistics. Tasmania Office).*

MONTHLY SUMMARY OF STATISTICS : WESTERN AUSTRALIA. AT. English. mo. Australian Bureau of Statistics, 1 3 St Georges Terrace, Perth WA 6000 Australia. **LC** HA3159. **DD** 319.41. *Monthly Statistical Summary, Western Australia.*

MONTHLY SUMMARY OF VITAL STATISTICS. **Main/Corp** Kansas. Bureau of Registration and Health Statistics. V. 1- Jan. 1979-. 0449-7732. US. English. mo. Kansas Department of Health & Environment, Building 740 Forbes Air Force Base, Topeka KS 66620. *Monthly Summary of Vital Statistics, 0449-7732.*

MONTHLY TRADE BULLETIN - MINISTRY OF FINANCE, PLANNING AND ECONOMIC DEVELOPMENT, STATISTICS DIVISION. **Main/Corp** Uganda. Ministry of Finance, Planning and Economic Development. Statistics Division. English. ir. 22/-. PO Box 13, Entebbe Uganda. **LC** HF266.U4. **DD** 382.096761. *Monthly Trade Bulletin.*

MONTHLY VITAL STATISTICS REPORT. (MONTHLY VITAL STATISTICS REPORT : PROVISIONAL STATISTICS FROM THE NATIONAL CENTER FOR HEALTH STATISTICS).

Statistics

Began with: Vol. 1, No. 1 (Jan. 1952). 0364-0396. Periodical. US. English. mo. Department of Health and Human Services, Public Health Service, Office of Health Research Statistics and Technology, National Center for Health Statistics, 3700 East-West Highway, Hyattsville MD 20782. Ind/Abst Popul. Index, Predicasts, Am. Stat. Index. LC HA203. DD 312.0973. NLM W2 A N148M. *Current Mortality Analysis, Monthly Marriage Report, Monthly Vital Statistics Bulletin.*

MORTALITY STATISTICS. (MORTALITY STATISTICS. CHILDHOOD). Series/Titl Series DH3. 1980-. UK. English. an. Her Majesty's Stationery Office, Government Bookshops, 49 High Holborn, London WC1V 6HB England. LC HB1323.I4. DD 312.2088054. *Mortality Staticics. Childhood and Maternity.*

MORTALITY STATISTICS. PERINATAL AND INFANT : SOCIAL AND BIOLOGICAL FACTORS. Series/Titl Series DH3. 1978,1979-. Periodical. UK. English.

MOSKVA V TSIFRAKH. Main/Corp Statisticheskoe Upravlenie Goroda Moskvy. UR. Russian. an. 0.65. Izdatelstvo Statistika, Ul Kirova 39, Moskva Russian SFSR. LC HA1449.M8.

MOTOR CARRIER STATISTICAL SUMMARY. Main/Corp American Trucking Associations. Division of Research and Economics. 1977-. 0196-5352. Periodical. US. English. qt. Division of Research and Economics, American Trucking Associations Inc, 1616 P Street NW, Washington DC 20036. *Truck Beat, Intercity Truck Tonnage, 0569-8839.*

MOTOR VEHICLE STATISTICS. (MOTOR VEHICLE STATISTICS : STATISTICAL DATA). Main/Corp New York (State). Dept. of Motor Vehicles. 1975-. 0147-9210. US. English. an. New York State Department of Motor Vehicles, Albany NY 12228. LC HE5614.3.N5. DD 388.314. *Accident Facts.*

MOTOR VEHICLE STATISTICS (BENUE STATE (NIGERIA). (MOTOR VEHICLE STATISTICS). English. an. LC HE5707.7.B46. DD 354.6695.

MOTORCYCLE STATISTICAL ANNUAL. 1977-. 0149-3027. US. English. an. Motorcycle Industry Council, 4100 Birch Street/Suite 101, Newport Beach CA 92660. LC HD9710.5.U5. DD 380.14562922750973.

MULKA CHONGNAM (HANGUK UNHAENG). (MULKA CHONGNAM). VFOAT Price Statistics Summary. Periodical. English (Korean). ir. 3,930. Hanguk Unhaeng, 110 3-Ka Namdaemunno, Chung-Ku Seoul Korea. LC HB235.K6.

LA MUTUALITE SOCIALE AGRICOLE, STATISTIQUES. Main/Corp Union des Caisses Centrales de la Mutualite Agricole. FR. French. ir. 8-10 rue d'Astorg, Paris 8 Eme France. LC HD7116.A3. DD 368.4.

NAGALAND BUDGET. SOME FACTS AND CHARTS. See Business - Public Finance.

NAN-KA-KAN SHIRYO SENTA HOKOKU. VFOAT Reports of the Reference Center of the Scientific Research for Southwest Pacific Area, Kagoshima University. Periodical. JA. Japanese (English). ir.

NARODNOE KHOZIAISTVO LENINGRADA I LENINGRADSKOI OBLASTI. Main/Corp Leningrad, Russian S. F. S. R. Statisticheskoe Upravlenie. UR. Russian. 1.05. Fontanka 59, Leningrad Russian SFSR. LC HA1448.L4.

NARODNOE KHOZIAISTVO SSSR: STATISTICHESKII EZHEGODNIK. See Yearbooks, Almanacs, Directories.

NARODNOE KHOZIAISTVO UKRAINSKOI SSR. UR. Russian. Tekhnika, Pushkinskaia 28, Kiev USSR. LC HA1448.U6.

NATIONAL ACCIDENT SAMPLING SYSTEM. See Transportation - Roads and Traffic.

NATIONAL ACCOUNTS STATISTICS. ANALYSIS OF MAIN AGGREGATES. VFOAT Analysis of Main Aggregates. 1982-. US. English. *Yearbook of National Accounts Statistics.*

NATIONAL ACCOUNTS STATISTICS. MAIN AGGREGATES AND DETAILED TABLES. VFOAT Main Aggregates and Detailed Tables. 1982-. US. English. Publishing Division, United Nations, New York NY 10017. *Yearbook of National Accounts Statistics, 0084-3881.*

NATIONAL ACCOUNTS STATISTICS (ORGANISATION FOR ECONOMIC CO-OPERATION AND DEVELOPMENT) CEASED. (NATIONAL ACCOUNTS STATISTICS). VFOAT Statistique des Comptes Nationaux, National Accounts of OECD Countries. -1963-1980. FR. Multilingual (English and French). an. $4.50. 1750 Pennsylvania Avenue Northwest, Washington DC 20006. LC HC79.I5. DD 339.3. *Statistics of National Accounts.*

NATIONAL ACCOUNTS STATISTICS (PORT MORESBY, PAPUA NEW GUINEA). (NATIONAL ACCOUNTS STATISTICS). Bull. No. 1 (1974/75)-. PP. English. ir. National Statistical Office Bureau of Statistics, PO Wards Strip, Port Moresby Papua New Guinea. LC HC687.P33. DD 339.209953.

NATIONAL ANNUAL MEDICAID STATISTICS. Series/Titl Health Care Financing Program Statistics. HHS Publication. 0737-4917. US. English. an. $18.00. ORD Publications, Room 1A9 Oak Meadows Building 6325 Security Boulevard, Baltimore MD 21207. Tel (301)597-2420. Ed Gerri Michael. LC HD7102.U4. DD 362.1042520973. bk rev. Circ 4,000. Health care financing issues and innovative delivery systems as related to the Medicaid and Medicare programs.

NATIONAL COAL BOARD STATISTICAL TABLES. Main/Corp Great Britain. National Coal Board. 0307-7691. UK. English. National Coal Board, Hobart House Grosvenor Place, London SW1X 7AE England. LC HD9551.4. DD 338.2720941.

THE NATIONAL COMMITTEE ON VITAL AND HEALTH STATISTICS. Main/Corp United States. National Committee on Vital and Health Statistics. Series/Titl DHHS Publication. Fiscal Years 1979 and 1980-. US. English. Office of Health Research Statistics and Technology, National Center for Health Statistics, 3700 East-West Highway, Hyattsville MD 20782. *Annual Report of the United States National Committee on Vital and Health Statistics.*

NATIONAL ECONOMIC PROJECTIONS SERIES. See Economics - Economics: Industry & Production.

NATIONAL FOOD REVIEW. ECONOMICS, STATISTICS, AND COOPERATIVES SERVICE, US DEPARTMENT OF AGRICULTURE. See Agriculture.

NATIONAL HMO CENSUS. See Public Health and Safety.

NATIONAL INCOME AND EXPENDITURE. See Business - Public Finance.

NATIONAL INCOME AND PRODUCT. See Economics.

NATIONAL INSTITUTE ON DRUG ABUSE STATISTICAL SERIES, QUARTERLY REPORT. SERIES D. VFOAT Data from the Client Oriented Data Acquisition Process (CODAP). No. 1- Oct./Dec. 1976-. Periodical. US. English. qt. National Institute of Drug Abuse, Room 11-A 56/5600 Fishers Lane, Rockville MD 20857. Tel (202)443-6637. *National Institute on Drug Abuse Statistical Series, Quarterly Report, 0145-1065.*

NATIONAL INSTITUTE ON DRUG ABUSE STATISTICAL SERIES. SERIES C. VFOAT C.O.D.A.P. Topical Reports. 0731-2458. Monographic Series. US. English. National Institute on Drug Abuse, Division of Scientific and Program Information, 5600 Fishers Lane, Rockville MD 20857. DD 362.29. NLM W2 A N223S.

NATIONAL INSTITUTE ON DRUG ABUSE STATISTICAL SERIES. SERIES H. VFOAT Statistical Series. No. 1-. Monographic Series. US. English.

NATIONAL MONTHLY MEDICAID STATISTICS CEASED. Series/Titl Health Care Financing Program Statistics. HHS Publication. Sept. 1978-. 0277-5611. Periodical. US. English. $18.00. HCFA ORDS Publications, 6325 Security Boulevard, 1A9 Oak Meadows Building, Baltimore MD 21207. Tel (301)597-2420. Ed Gerri Michael. Ind/Abst Am. Stat. Index. LC HD7102.U4. DD 362.1042520973. NLM W2. bk rev. Circ 4,000. Health care financing issues and innovative delivery systems as related to the Medicine and Medicaid programs. *Medicaid Statistics (United States. Health Care Financing Administration. Office of Research), 0163-7584.*

NATIONAL PARK STATISTICAL ABSTRACT. See Indexes/Abstracts.

NATIONAL SAMPLE SURVEY OF HOUSEHOLDS BULLETIN. Main/Corp Philippines. National Census and Statistics Office. PH. English. qt. National Census & Statistics, PO Box 779, Manila Philippines. LC HD5825. DD 331.109599. *BCS Survey of Households Bulletin.*

NATIONAL TRANSPORTATION STATISTICS. Began with 1977. 0161-8628. US. English. an. Superintendent of Documents, US Government Printing Office, Washington DC 20402. LC HE203. DD 380.50973. Vols. for 1981- distributed to depository libraries in microfiche. *Summary of National Transportation Statistics, 0145-2541; Energy Statistics, 0360-8980.*

NATIONAL URBAN MASS TRANSPORTATION STATISTICS. (NATIONAL URBAN MASS TRANSPORTATION STATISTICS : ANNUAL REPORT, SECTION 15 REPORTING SYSTEM). VFOAT Section 15 Reporting System. 1st (fiscal years ending between July 1, 1978 and June 30, 1979)-. 0737-2981. US. English. an. National Technical Information Service, 5285 Port Royal Road, Springfield VA 22161. LC HE4401. DD 338.40973. Vols. for (1978/79) distributed to depository libraries in microfiche.

NAUCHNI TRUDOVE (VISSHE TEKHNICHESKO UCHILISHTE ANGEL KUNCHEV—RUSE). (NAUCHNI TRUDOVE). VFOAT Nauchnye Trudy. V. 23, Ser. 1-. Monographic Series. Bulgarian (summaries in English and Russian). ir. *Nauchni Trudove.*

NEBRASKA AGRICULTURAL STATISTICS. US. English. an. $5.00. USDA-Statistics Reporting Service, PO Box 81069, Lincoln NE 68501. Tel (402)471-5541.

NEBRASKA HIGHWAY STATISTICS : STATE AND LOCAL ROAD AND STREET DATA. Main/Corp Nebraska. Dept. of Roads. Highway Statistical Unit. US. English. LC HE356.N36. DD 388.109782.

NEBRASKA STATISTICAL HANDBOOK. Main/Corp Nebraska. Dept. of Economic Development. Division of Research. 0097-9325. US. English. an. Department of Economic Development, POB 94666, Lincoln NE 68509. Tel (402)471-3111. Ed Shirley Kling. LC HA491. DD 371.82. Circ 1,200. Facts on Nebraska's population, labor force, income, industry and business, agriculture, resources, education, government, energy and other subjects; county level data on many subjects.

NEBRASKA STATISTICAL REPORT OF ABORTIONS. Main/Corp Nebraska. Division of Health Data and Statistical Research. 1974-. 0095-3105. US. English. LC HQ767.5.U5. DD 301. *Nebraska Statistical Report of Abortions, 0095-3105.*

NEKI POKAZATELJI TEHNICKOG RAZVOJA PRIVREDE JUGOSLAVIJE. Main/Corp Savezni Zavod za Statistiku (Yugoslavia). Series Corp Its Statisticki Bilten. YU. Serbo-Croatian -R. ir. 5.- Single Issue. Savezni Zavod za Statistku, Kneza Milosa 20, Beograd Yugoslavia. LC HA1631, HD6331. *Statistika Nove Tehniki.*

NEMZETKOZI STATISZTIKAI EVKONYV CEASED. Main/Corp Hungary. Kozponti Statisztikai Hivatal. Hungarian. ir. Statisztikai Kiado Vallalat, Kaszasdulo u 2, H-1033 Budapest Hungary. LC HA162.

NEVADA AGRICULTURAL STATISTICS. Main/Corp Nevada Crop and Livestock Reporting Service. 0196-0636. US. English. an. Free. Agricultural Statistician, PO Box 8888, Reno NV 89507.

NEVADA ANNUAL PLANNING STATISTICS FOR STATE, LAS VEGAS SMSA, RENO SMSA, BALANCE-OF-STATE. US. English. an. Nevada Employment Security Department, Employment Security Research Section, 500 East

Statistics

Third Street, Carson City NV 89713. **LC** HD5725.N3. **DD** 331.1209793. *Nevada Annual Planning Report for State, Las Vegas SMSA, Reno SMSA, Balance of State.*

NEVADA LIBRARY DIRECTORY AND STATISTICS. US. English. Nevada State Library, Library Development Division Capitol Complex, Carson City NV 89710. **LC** Z732.N38. **DD** 027.0025793. *Statistics with Directory of Nevada Libraries and Library Personnel.*

NEVADA STATISTICAL ABSTRACT. See Indexes/Abstracts.

NEW DIRECTIONS FOR PROGRAM EVALUATION. See Social Sciences (General).

NEW ENGLAND ECONOMIC INDICATORS. See Economics - Economic History, Conditions.

NEW ENGLAND MILK MARKET STATISTICS. Series/Titl Federal Order. **VFOAT** New England Market Statistics. US. English. **LC** HD9282.U5. **DD** 338.17710974.

NEW HAMPSHIRE AFFIRMATIVE ACTION DATA. Main/Corp New Hampshire. Dept. of Employment Security. 0149-9211. US. English. 32 South Main Street, Concord NH 03301. **Tel** (603)224-3311. Ed Wesley S Noyes Jr. **LC** HD5725.N4. **DD** 331.133. **Circ** 1,000. An average data on population, labor force, applicants and employment by occupation and industry by sex and minority status.

NEW HAMPSHIRE LIBRARY STATISTICS. 1965-. 0749-0313. US. English. an. **LC** Z733. **DD** 027.0742. *Library Statistics.*

NEW HAMPSHIRE REGISTER, STATE YEAR-BOOK AND LEGISLATIVE MANUAL. See Yearbooks, Almanacs, Directories.

NEW JERSEY ECONOMIC INDICATORS. See Economics - Economic History, Conditions.

NEW JERSEY PUBLIC LIBRARIES. (NEW JERSEY PUBLIC LIBRARIES STATISTICS). **Main/Corp** New Jersey. Library Development Bureau. **VFOAT** Public Libraries in New Jersey Statistics. 0093-1098. US. English. Library Development Bureau, 185 West State Street Box 1598, Trenton NJ 08625. **LC** Z732.N6. **DD** 027.4749. *New Jersey Public Library Statistics . . . Directory.*

NEW MEXICO AGRICULTURAL STATISTICS. V. 1- 1962-. US. English. an. USDA, PO Box 1809, Las Cruces NM 88004. **Tel** (505)523-8168. Ed Don Gerhardt. **LC** HD1775.N6. **Circ** 1,500. (ctrl). New Mexico agricultural statistics.

NEW MEXICO HIGHWAY STATISTICS AND RELATED INFORMATION. (NEW MEXICO . . . HIGHWAY STATISTICS AND RELATED INFORMATION). **VFOAT** Highway Statistics and Related Information. 0731-017X. US. English. an. New Mexico State Highway Department, Planning Research Section, PO Box 1149, Sante Fe NM 87503. **LC** HE356.N6. *Highway Statistics and Related Information, 0363-3993.*

NEW MEXICO LIBRARY STATISTICS. 0278-9329. US. English. an. New Mexico State Library, PO Box 1629, Santa Fe NM 87503. **LC** Z675.S7. **DD** 027.5789.

NEW MEXICO MONTHLY VITAL STATISTICS REPORT. US. English. mo. Department of Health & Environment, Health Services Division, PO Box 968 Plaza San Mateo, Sante Fe NM 87503. **LC** HA531. **DD** 312.09789.

NEW MEXICO SELECTED HEALTH STATISTICS. Main/Corp New Mexico. Health and Environment Dept. 1976-. 0161-5416. US. English. an. State of New Mexico, Health & Environment Department, Sante Fe NM 87501. **LC** RA407.4.N6. **DD** 312.09789. **NLM** W2 AN5 H5SN. *New Mexico Selected Health Statistics, 0161-5416.*

NEW MEXICO STATISTICAL ABSTRACT. See Indexes/Abstracts.

NEW SOUTH WALES YEARBOOK. See Yearbooks, Almanacs, Directories.

NEW YORK STATE ANNUAL ENERGY REVIEW, ENERGY CONSUMPTION, SUPPLY, AND PRICE STATISTICS. VFOAT Energy Consumption, Supply, and Price Statistics. 1960-1979-. US. English. an. **LC** HD9502.U53. **DD** 333.791309747. *New York State Energy Consumption and Supply Statistics, 0272-8346.*

NEW YORK STATE STATISTICAL YEARBOOK. See Yearbooks, Almanacs, Directories.

NEW YORK STATE'S . . . HIGHWAY SUFFICIENCY RATINGS. See Transportation - Roads and Traffic.

NEW ZEALAND CIVIL AVIATION STATISTICS (WELLINGTON, N.Z. : 1976-80). (NEW ZEALAND CIVIL AVIATION STATISTICS). 1976-80-. 0467-8966. English. ir. **LC** TL529. **DD** 387.7409931. *New Zealand Civil Aviation Statistical Statement.*

NEW ZEALAND ECONOMIC STATISTICS CEASED. English. ir. Bank of New Zealand, PO Box 2392, Wellington New Zealand. **LC** HG188.N45. **DD** 330.993103.

NEW ZEALAND HOTEL/MOTEL INVENTORY AND ROOM OCCUPANCY RATES (LICENSED). See Hotels/Motels.

NEW ZEALAND HOUSEHOLD SURVEY REPORT. See Home Economics.

NEW ZEALAND MEDICAL MANPOWER STATISTICS. 0111-7793. English. ir. Management Services and Research Unit, Department of Health, PO Box 5013, Wellington New Zealand. **LC** RA410.9.N42. **DD** 331.1251610695209931. *Medical Manpower in New Zealand. Statistics.*

NEW ZEALAND OPERATIONAL RESEARCH. See Business.

NEWBORN. (THE NEWBORN). Series/Titl Special Report - Division of Vital Statistics. 1961/64-. 0226-9481. Periodical. CN. English. ir. **NLM** W2 DC2.1 B8D415S NO.89 ETC. *Physicians' Notice of Birth Statistics, British Columbia.*

NEWS BULLETIN. See Public Administration.

NEWS - BUREAU OF LABOR STATISTICS. Main/Corp United States. Bureau of Labor Statistics. US. English. US Department of Labor, Labor Statistics, 441 G Street NW, Washington DC 20212.

NEWS OF THE COOPERATIVE HEALTH STATISTICS SYSTEM CEASED. Began with Jan./Feb. 1974. 0094-3045. Periodical. US. English. bm. US Department of Health and Human Services, Public Health Service, Office of Health Research Statistics and Technology, National Center for Health Statistics, 3700 East-West Highway, Hyattsville MD 20782. **Ind/Abst** Am. Stat. Index. **LC** RA407.3. **DD** 362.10973. **NLM** W2 A N148N. *Registrar and Statistician, 0093-478X.*

NEWSLETTER - FEDERAL STATISTICS USERS' CONFERENCE. Main/Corp Federal Statistics Users' Conference. 0014-9225. US. English. mo. $30.00. Federal Statistics Users' Conference, 1030 Fifteenth Street Northwest, Washington DC 20005. **Ind/Abst** Predicasts. **DD** 317.

NEWSLETTER - STATISTICAL SOCIETY OF CANADA. (NEWSLETTER). **VFOAT** Bulletin. Vol. 6, No. 1 (Apr. 1978)-. 0228-1104. Periodical. CN. English (French with text on inverted pages, Apr. 1978-). ir. Free. A Plante, PO Box 8888 Station A, Montreal Quebec H3C 3P8 Canada. **DD** 519.506071. (ctrl). *Newsletter (Statistical Science Association of Canada), 0229-3536; Joint Bulletin (Statistical Science Association of Canada), 0229-3544.*

NEYAGAWA-SHI TOKEISHO. Japanese. ir. Neyagawa Shiyakusho, 1-1 Honmachi, Neyagawa 582 Japan. **LC** HA1849.N47.

NIEDERSACHSEN IN ZAHLEN. German. ir. 1.80. Niedersachsisches Landesverwaltungsamt, Schriftenvertrieb Postfach 107 3000 Hannover 1, Giebelstrasse 65, Hannover West Germany. **LC** HA1301.

NIHON ARUMANAKKU. 1984-. JA. Japanese. ir. 5000. Kyoikusha Shuppan Sabisu Kabushiki Kaisha c/o Maruju Building 11-10, Fujimi 2 Chiyoda-ku, Tokyo-to 102 Japan. **LC** HA4621.

NIHON HYOJUN SANGYO BUNRUI. GOJUON SAKUIN HYO. (NIHON HYOJUN SANGYO BUNRUI; GOJUON SAKUIN HYO). Began in 1949. 0303-6065. JA. Japanese. ir. 1600. Zenkoku Tokei Kyokai Rengokai, 3-1-1 Kasumigaseki Chiyoda-ku, Tokyo Japan. **LC** HA40.I6.

NIHON TOKEI GAKKAISHI. (NIHON TOKEI GAKKAI SHI). **VFOAT** Journal of the Japan Statistical Society. Vol. 1, No. 1-. 0389-5602. JA. English (Japanese). ir. Nihon Tokei Gakkai, c/o Tokei Suri Kenkyujo, 6-7 Minami Azabu, Minato-ku, Tokyo-to Japan. **Ind/Abst** Math. Rev. **LC** HA1.

NIHON TOKEI NENKAN. See Yearbooks, Almanacs, Directories.

NIVELES MINIMOS DE PRODUCTIVIDAD. See Agriculture.

NONGCHON MULKA CHONGNAM. VFOAT Statistics on Prices in Rural Areas. English (Korean). ir. Nongop Hyoptong Chohap Chunganghoe, 75 Chungjongno 1-ka Chung-ku, Seoul Korea. **LC** HD9016.K6.

NONGOP KIBAN CHOSONG SAOP TONGGYE YONBO. See Yearbooks, Almanacs, Directories.

NORDESTE EM NUMEROS. Main/Corp Brazil. Superintendencia do Desenvolvimento do Nordeste. Divisao de Comercio. Portuguese. ir. Av Prof Moraes Rego, S/N Cidade Universitaria, Recife Brazil. **LC** HA973.

NORIN SUISANSHO TOKEIHYO. See Yearbooks, Almanacs, Directories.

NORTH CAROLINA BOATING ACCIDENT STATISTICS. 0148-8090. US. English. an. State of North Carolina Wildlife Resources Commission, Raleigh NC 27611. **LC** GV776.N74. **DD** 614.81.

NORTH CAROLINA STATE GOVERNMENT STATISTICAL ABSTRACT. See Indexes/Abstracts.

NORTH DAKOTA ACADEMIC LIBRARY STATISTICS. Main/Corp North Dakota. State Library Commission. Series/Titl North Dakota Library Notes. 0094-5455. US. English. an. **LC** Z732.N9. **DD** 021.009784 S, 027.709784.

NORTH DAKOTA AGRICULTURAL STATISTICS (FARGO, N.D.). (NORTH DAKOTA AGRICULTURAL STATISTICS). Series/Titl Ag. Statistics. **VFOAT** Agricultural Statistics. 0737-1624. US. English. an. $4.00. Agriculture Communications, Morrill Hall, North Dakota State University, Fargo ND 58105. **Tel** (701)237-5771. **LC** S99. **DD** 338.109784. *North Dakota Crop & Livestock Statistics.*

NORTH-HOLLAND SERIES IN STATISTICS AND PROBABILITY. VAT North Holland Series in Statistics and Probability. Vol. 1-. 0168-1974. Monographic Series. US. English. ir. Elsevier Science Publishing Co Inc, 52 Vanderbilt Avenue, New York NY 10017. **Ind/Abst** Math. Rev., Comput. Control Abstr., Electr. Electron. Abstr., Sci. Abstr. Sect. A. Phys. Abstr. **LC** UNC. **DD** 519.5. **CODEN** NHSPDQ.

NORTHERN TERRITORY STATISTICAL SUMMARY. Main/Corp Australian Bureau of Statistics. 1974-. 0067-0855. AT. English. an. 5.30. Australian Bureau of Statistics, 5th Floor MLC Building, 81 Smith Street, Darwin Northern Territory 5790 Australia. **Tel** (089)81 5222. **LC** HA3052. **DD** 319.429. Information on the population and its characteristics: social statistics and demography, primary production, labour, wages, and prices, retail trade, building and transport and finance. *Northern Territory Statistical Summary, 0067-0855.*

NORTHWEST TERRITORIES STATISTICAL ABSTRACT. See Indexes/Abstracts.

NOTE ANNUELLE DE STATISTIQUE - DIRECTION DE LA STATISTIQUE ET DE LA COMPTABILITE NATIONALE. Main/Corp Cameroon. Dept. of Statistics and National Accounts. Yearly V. 1973/74-. French. ir. 75.00. Department of Statistics and National Accounts, Boite Postale No 660, Yaounde Cameroon. **LC** HA2141. **DD** 316.711.

NOTE D'INFORMATIONS STATISTIQUES (CAMEROON. SERVICE PROVINCIAL DES STATISTIQUES DU LITTORAL : ANNUAL). (NOTE D'INFORMATIONS STATISTIQUES). CM. French. an. Ministere de l'Economie et du Plan Secretariat General Service, Provincial des Statistiques du Littoral, BP 794 Douala, Republique Unie du Cameroun. **LC** HA4719.Z9. **DD** 316.7113.

NOTE TRIMESTRIELLE DE CONJONCTURE. See Economics.

NOTES D'INFORMATION ET STATISTIQUES. Main/Corp Banque Centrale des Etats de l'Afrique de l'Ouest. No. 1- 1956-. 0005-559X. Periodical. SG. French. ir. $14.00. Banque

Statistics

Centrale des Etats, Siega Avenue du Barachois/Boite, Postale 3108, Dakar Senegal. Ind/Abst Foreign Lang. Index.

NOTES ON LABOUR STATISTICS. Main/Corp Canada. Statistics Canada. Manpower Research and Development Section. VAT Etudes des Statistiques du Travail. 1971-. 0318-2983. CN. English (text in French, 1972). an. $0.75. Manpower Research and Development Section, Coates Building Pasture, Ottawa Ontario K1A 0T6 Canada. LC HD8103. DD 331.10971.

NOTIZIARIO STATISTICO - ANFIA. See Transportation - Automobiles.

NOTIZIE STATISTICHE. IT. Italian. ir. Instituto Nazionale della Previdenza Sociale, Servizio Statistico Attuariale, Roma TI Italy. LC HD7182. DD 368.400945021.

NOTIZIE STATISTICHE. Main/Corp Istituto Nazionale della Previdenza Sociale. Servizio Statistico Attuariale. IT. Italian. ir. Inst Nazionale Previdenza Soc, Servizio Statistico Attuariale, Rome TI Italy.

NUNG KUNG SHANG PU TUNG CHI PIAO. Main/Corp China. Nung Kung Shang Pu. US. Chinese. Center for Chinese Research Material, Association of Research Libaries, 1527 New Hampshire Avenue, Washington DC 20036. LC HA1701. DD 315.1.

NZ FERTILISER STATISTICS. Main/Corp New Zealand. Ministry of Agriculture and Fisheries. Economics Division. VFOAT New Zealand Fertiliser Statistics. 1975-. NZ. English. ir. Ministry of Agriculture and Fisheries, Economics Division, PO Box 2298, Wellington New Zealand. LC HD9483.N47. DD 338.476686209931. *Statistical Review of Fertilisers in New Zealand.*

OCCASIONAL PAPER (COOK ISLANDS. STATISTICS OFFICE). (OCCASIONAL PAPER). No. 1-. Monographic Series. English. ir. $0.59. Statistics Office, PO Box 125, Rarotonga Cook Islands. Tel #392.

OCCASIONAL PAPER - RESERVE BANK OF AUSTRALIA. See Business - Banking & Finance.

OCCUPATIONAL SAFETY AND HEALTH STATISTICS OF THE FEDERAL GOVERNMENT. Began with 1972. 0092-8712. US. English. an. Occupational Safety and Health Administration, 200 Constitution Avenue, Washington DC 20210. LC JK850.A3. DD 614.8. NLM W2 A O14O.

OCCUPATIONAL WAGE INFORMATION IN MICHIGAN AND FLINT SMSA. VFOAT Occupational Wage Information, Michigan. US. English. an. Occupational Employment Statistics Unit, 7310 Woodward Avenue, Detroit MI 48202. LC HD4976.M46. DD 331.2209774. *Occupational Wage Information in Michigan.*

OECD FINANCIAL STATISTICS. METHODOLOGICAL SUPPLEMENT. VFOAT Statistiques Financieres de l'O.C.D.E. Supplement Methodologique. 1981-. 0304-3371. FR. English (French in parallel columns). an. Publications de l'OCDE, 2 rue Andre-Pascal, 75775 Paris Cedex 16 France. LC HG176.5. DD 332.05. Purpose is to facilitate the interpretation of the statistics published in three parts by explaining their methods of calculation and their institutional context. *OECD Financial Statistics, 0048-2188.*

OECD FINANCIAL STATISTICS. MONTHLY SUPPLEMENT : INTEREST RATES. Main/Corp Organization for Economic Cooperation and Development. VFOAT Statistiques Financieres de l'OCDE. Supplement Mensuel : Taux d'Interet. VAT Organization for Economic Cooperation and Development Financial Statistics. Monthly Supplement: Interest Rates. Periodical. FR. English (French). mo. Organization for Economic Cooperation and Development, 2 rue Andre-Pascal, 75775 Paris Cedex 16 France. LC HB549.O6. DD 332.80212.

OECD FINANCIAL STATISTICS. PART 1, FINANCIAL STATISTICS MONTHLY. VFOAT Statistiques Financieres de l'OCDE. 1re Partie, Statistiques Financieres Mensuelles. Oct. 1980-. 0304-3371. FR. English (French). mo. Director of Information OECD, 2 rue Andre-Pascal, 75775 Paris France. LC HG176. DD 332.0212. *OECD Financial Statistics. Monthly Supplement.*

OECD FINANCIAL STATISTICS. PART 2, FINANCIAL ACCOUNTS OF OECD COUNTRIES. VFOAT Statistiques Financieres de l'OCDE. 2E Partie, Comptes Financiers des Pays de l'OCDE. 1981, 1-. US. English (French). sa. OECD Publications and Information Center/Suite 1207 1750 Pennsylvania Avenue Northwest, Washington DC 20006. Tel (202)724-1857. LC HG176. DD 332..05. Provides flow-of-funds and balance-sheet accounts detailed by sectors and by financial instruments. *OECD Financial Statistics.*

OECD FINANCIAL STATISTICS. PART 3, NON-FINANCIAL ENTERPRISES FINANCIAL STATEMENTS. VFOAT Non-Financial Enterprises Financial Statements, Statistiques Financieres de l'OCDE. 3E Partie, Comptes des Enterprises Non Financieres. 1981-. US. English (French). an. OECD Publications and Information Center, Suite 1207 /1750 Pennsylvania Avenue Northwest, Washington DC 20006. Tel (202)724-1857. LC HG4001. DD 338.7405. Gives balance-sheets, statements of income and sources and uses of funds for a representative sample of companies in 12 countries. *OECD Financial Statistics.*

OFFENTLICHE FURSORGE, SOZIALHILFE. Main/Corp Osterreichisches Statistisches Zentralamt. Series/Titl Beitrage zur Osterreichischen Statistik. German. an. Kommissionsverlag Osterreichische Staatsdruckerei, Renweg 12 A, Wien Austria. LC HA1173, HD7169. *Offentliche Fursorce.*

OFFICE MONITOR, STATISTICS. (OFFICE MONITOR. STATISTICS). Main/Corp Toronto (Ont.). Planning and Development Dept. 83-. 0823-9967. Periodical. CN. English. 3.00. City of Toronto Planning and Development Department, Toronto City Hall, Toronto Ontario M5H 2N2 Canada. Tel (416)362-7185. Ed Steve Dyns. DD 690.523. Circ 1,000. (ctrl). A review of office growth and office market conditions in Toronto. *City Monitor, 0714-4334.*

OFFICIAL BASEBALL REGISTER. See Recreation, Leisure - Sports.

OFFICIAL HERD RECORDING STATISTICS. Main/Corp New South Wales. Dept. of Agriculture. Division of Dairying. (1975/76-1976-). Periodical. English. ir.

THE OFFICIAL NATIONAL COLLEGIATE ATHLETIC ASSOCIATION BASKETBALL STATISTICIANS' MANUAL. VFOAT Basketball Statisticians' Manual. US. English. an. National Collegiate Athletic Association, PO Box 1906, Shawnee Mission KS 66222.

OFFICIAL YEAR BOOK OF THE COMMONWEALTH OF AUSTRALIA. See Yearbooks, Almanacs, Directories.

OHIO AGRICULTURAL STATISTICS. US. English. an. $5.00. USDA, 200 North High Street, Columbus OH 43215. Tel (614)469-5590. LC S101. DD 338.109771.

OHIO JUVENILE COURT STATISTICS. 0094-2677. US. English. an. LC KFO71.55. DD 345.771081.

OIL AND GAS PRODUCTION STATISTICS. Main/Corp North Dakota. Geological Survey. 0363-2512. US. English. $3.50. North Dakota Geological Survey, Grand Forks ND 58202. LC TN872.N9. DD 338.272809782. *Production Statistics and Engineering Data: Oil in North Dakota.*

OIL AND GAS STATISTICS. Main/Corp Colorado. Oil and Gas Conservation Commission. 0360-0238. US. English. $3.00. Oil and Gas Conservation Commission, Columbine Building/Room 237, 1845 Sherman Street, Denver CO 80203. LC HD9567.C6. DD 338.272809788. *Colorado Oil and Gas Statistics.*

OIL WORLD STATISTICS. 0306-770X. UK. English. an. -/10. Institute of Petroleum, Information Services Department, 61 Cavendish Street, London W1 England. LC HD9560.4. DD 338.272805.

OIL/ENERGY STATISTICS BULLETIN AND CANADIAN OIL REPORTS. VFOAT Oil/Energy Statistics Bulletin. VAT Oil, Energy Statistics Bulletin and Canadian Oil Reports. 0276-5977. Periodical. US. English. bw. Oil Statistics Company Inc, Babson Park MA 02157. Tel (617)237-6620.

OKINAWA-KEN TOKEI NENKAN. No. 16-Issue. JA. Japanese. ir. Okinawa-Ken, 2-32 Senzaki 1-Chome, Naha Japan. LC HA1848.R9. *Ryukyu Tokei Nenkan.*

OKLAHOMA AGRICULTURAL STATISTICS. 1976-. US. English. an. $5.00. Oklahoma State Department of Agriculture, 2800 Lincoln Boulevard, Oklahoma City OK 73105. Tel (405)525-9226. Ed Burt Bartlett. LC S103. DD 338.109766. Circ 2,000. (ctrl). Publication usually issued in August, contains all major crop and livestock statistics for Oklahoma and each county. Length averages 108 pages. *Oklahoma Agriculture.*

OKLAHOMA FARM STATISTICS. Vol. 1, No. 1 (Jan. 20, 1981)-. 0279-7712. Periodical. US. English. sm. $10.00. USDA-SRS, Crop Reporting Service, Oklahoma Farm Statistics, Room 5829/S Building, Washington DC 20250.

OKLAHOMA HEALTH STATISTICS. Main/Corp Oklahoma. Public Health Statistics Division. 0098-5651. US. English. an. Oklahoma State Department of Health, Public Health Statistics Division, NE Tenth and Stonewall, PO Box 53551, Oklahoma City OK 73117. LC RA4074.O6. DD 312.09766.

OKLAHOMA OCCUPATIONAL EMPLOYMENT STATISTICS; BULLETIN. VFOAT OOES. Oklahoma Occupational Employment Statistics. No.1- Sept. 1975-. 0147-8052. US. English. Will Rogers Memorial Office Building/Room 310, Oklahoma City OK 73105. LC HD5725.O35. DD 331.125109766.

ONDERZOEK HUISHOUDENS MET EENMALIGE UITKERING. VFOAT Survey of Households Receiving Non-Recurrent Benefit. Periodical. NE. Dutch. an. 8.40. Centraal Bureau voor de Statistiek, Prinses Beatrixlaan 428 Postbus 959, 2270 AZ Voorburg Netherlands.

ONTARIO HYDRO STATISTICAL YEARBOOK. See Yearbooks, Almanacs, Directories.

ONTARIO POPULATION STATISTICS. Main/Corp Ontario. Ministry of Treasury, Economics and Intergovernmental Affairs. Municipal Planning & Development Branch. CN. English. an. $2.00. Ministry of Treasury Municipal Planning & Development Branch, Parliament Buildings, Toronto Ontario Canada. LC HB3530.O5. DD 312.09713.

ONTARIO STATISTICS. 1975-. 0319-7751. CN. English. an. $11.61. Treasurer of Ontario, Ministry of Government Service, 880 Bay Street/5th Floor, Toronto Ontario M7A 1N8 Canada. Tel (416)965-6015. LC HA748.O55. DD 317.13. *Ontario Statistical Review, 0078-5113.*

OPEN DOORS. See Education (General) - Higher Education.

OPERATING REVENUE AND EXPENSE STATISTICS CLASS A AND B PRIVATE GAS UTILITIES IN WISCONSIN. Main/Corp Public Service Commission of Wisconsin. Accounts and Finance Division. 0098-3225. US. English. LC HD2767.W6, HD9581. U52. DD 363.609775 S, 338.43.

OPSTINE U SR SRBIJI. Main/Corp Serbia (Federated Republic, 1945-). Zavod Za Statistiku. YU. Serbo-Croatian -C. ir. 80.00. Republicki Zavod Za Statistiku, Milana Rakica 5, Beograd Yugoslavia. LC HA1651. *Statisticki Pokazatelji O Opstinama.*

OREGON AGRICULTURAL STATISTICS. VFOAT Oregon Agricultural Statistics. 0748-2647. US. English. an. Oregon Crop and Livestock Reporting Service, 1735 Federal Building, 1220 SW Third Avenue, Portland OR 97204. LC HD1775.O7. DD 338.109795.

OREGON PROPERTY TAX STATISTICS. Main/Corp Oregon. Dept. of Revenue. Research and Special Services Division. 1975-. 0145-4269. US. English. an. Department of Revenue, Research and Special Services Division, 402 State Office Building, Salem OR 97310. LC HJ4121.O7. DD 336.2209795. *Summary of Assessment and Tax Rolls.*

OREGON PUBLIC HEALTH STATISTICS REPORT. Main/Corp Oregon. Vital Statistics Section. VFOAT Oregon State Health Division, Vital Statistics Annual Report. US. English. an. Oregon State Health Division, Vital Statistics Section, Portland OR 97201. LC RA407.4.O7. DD 312.09795. NLM W2 AO7 S8BA.

Statistics

OREGON SALMON AND STEELHEAD SPORT CATCH STATISTICS. VFOAT Steelhead Sport Catch Statistics. 1970-79-. 0731-3306. US. English. an. Oregon Department of Fish and Wildlife, PO Box 3503, Portland OR 97208. LC SH686. DD 333.956.

ORIGIN OF KENTUCKY COLLEGE AND UNIVERSITY ENROLLMENTS. See Education (General) - Higher Education.

ORIGINAL STATISTICS, ENGLAND AND WALES. SUPPLEMENTARY TABLES. VOL. 2, PROCEEDINGS IN THE CROWN COURT. VFOAT Proceedings in the Crown Court. 1980-. UK. English. an. 12.75. Home Office, Horseferry House Dean Rule St, London SW1 P2AW England. LC HA1131.A3. DD 312.460942.

OSNOVNI UCILISTA VO SRM SPORED GRADSKO-SELSKO PODRACJE. Main/Corp Macedonia (Republic). Republicki Zavod Za Statistika. Macedonian. ir. 50.00. Republicki Zavod Za Statistika, Dame Gruev 1, Skopje Yugoslavia. LC HA1, LB3219.Y8.

OTHER MISCELLANEOUS MANUFACTURING INDUSTRIES = AUTRES INDUSTRIES MANUFACTURIERES DIVERSES. See Manufacturing.

OUTER CONTINENTAL SHELF STATISTICS : OIL, GAS, SULFUR, SALT, LEASING, DRILLING, PRODUCTION, INCOME CEASED. Main/Corp Geological Survey (U.S.). Conservation Division. 1971-1980. US. English. an. *Outer Continental Shelf Oil, Gas, Sulfur and Salt, Leasing, Drilling, Production, Income and Related Statistics.*

OVERSEAS TRADE STATISTICS OF THE UNITED KINGDOM. Jan. 1970-. 0436-3574. Periodical. UK. English. mo. $308.02. Her Majestys Stationery Office, PO Box 276, London SW8 5DT England. Tel 01-622 3316. Provides details of trade by country in terms of broad groups of commodities, and analyses trade by commodity in terms of both value and quantity, firstly down to the level of individual SITC items and secondly to the level of individual UK tariff headings. *Overseas Trade Accounts of the United Kingdom.*

OWNER OCCUPIED HOUSING STATISTICS FROM HOMESTEAD REBATE AND INCOME TAX DATA MATCH. Feb. 1979-. US. English. LC HJ4121.N5. DD 363.5097749021.

PAKISTAN STATISTICAL YEARBOOK. See Yearbooks, Almanacs, Directories.

PALESTINIAN STATISTICAL ABSTRACT. See Indexes/Abstracts.

PALMOIL STATISTICAL HANDBOOK. 1980-. English. ni. $5.00. Porla, PO Box 2184, Kuala Lumpur 01-02 Malaysia. LC HD9490.5.P343. DD 338.17385109595.

PANORAMA DE L'ECONOMIE DE LA REUNION. See Economics.

PAST AND LIKELY FUTURE OF 58 RESEARCH LIBRARIES, 1951-1980. See Library and Information Science.

PENDUDUK JAWA-BARAT, HASIL REGISTRASI PENDUDUK. Main/Corp Jawa Barat, Indonesia. Kantor Sensus dan Statistik. 1972-. IO. Indonesian. ir. Kantor Sensus & Statistik Java-Barat, Jalan Jendral Gatotsubroto 77, Bandung Indonesia. LC HA1817.J35.

PENDUDUK JAWA TENGAH, HASIL REGISTRASI PENDUDUK. VFOAT Penduduk Jawa Tengah. Indonesian. ir. (024)311195. Biro Pusat Statistik, Kantor Statistik Propinsi Jawa Tengah, JL Pahlawan No 6, Semarang Indonesia. LC HA1817.J38. *Penduduk Jawa Tengah, Hasil Registrasi.*

PENDUDUK SUMATERA UTARA. Main/Corp Sumatera Utara, Indonesia. Kantor Sensus dan Statistik. 1973-. Indonesian. ir. Kantor Sensus dan Statistik, Jln Sukamulia 13 Atas, Medan Indonesia. LC HA1817.S9.

PENNSYLVANIA COUNTY DATA BOOK. 1979-. English. an. Tel (717)787-7532. Circ 600. Overall statistical view of Pennsylvania counties. Individual report published for each of Pennsylvania's 67 counties. *Pennsylvania County Industry Report.*

PENNSYLVANIA MASS TRANSIT STATISTICAL REPORT. VFOAT Mass Transit Statistical Report. US. English. an. Pennsylvania Department of Transportation, Room 1215 Transportation & Safety Building, Harrisburg PA 17120. LC HE4487.P4. DD 338.409748.

PENNSYLVANIA STATISTICAL ABSTRACT. See Indexes/Abstracts.

PENNSYLVANIA VITAL STATISTICS, ANNUAL REPORT. VFOAT Pennsylvania Vital Statistics. 1979-. US. English. an. Director, Bureau of Health Data Systems, Health Data Center, Pennsylvania Department of Health, PO Box 90, Harrisburg PA 17120. LC HA604. DD 312.09748. *Natality and Mortality Statistics Annual Report.*

PERANGKAAN PERTANIAN SARAWAK. Began with 1976 vol. in English. an. LC HD2080.6.Z9. DD 338.1095954. *Agricultural Statistics of Sarawak.*

PERFIL MUNICIPAL. Main/Corp Sao Paulo (Brazil : State). Fundacao Sistema Estadual de Analise de Dados. V. 1- 1979-. BL. Portuguese. an. $300. Fundacao Sistema Estadual de Analise de Dados, Caixa Postal 8223, 01033 Sao Paulo Brazil. LC HA988.S2.

PERIODIC REPORT - FOOD AND AGRICULTURE ORGANIZATION OF THE UNITED NATIONS, ASIA AND FAR EAST COMMISSION ON AGRICULTURAL STATISTICS. Main/Corp Food and Agriculture Organization of the United Nations. Asia and Far East Commission on Agricultural Statistics. English. ir. LC HD2056. DD 338.1095.

PERKEMBANGAN HARGA DAN PENDUDUK DI KAB. DATI II SIDOARJO. Series/Titl Statistik Harga dan Penduduk. Indonesian. ir. LC HA4607.S52.

PERKEMBANGAN STATISTIK HARGA-HARGA PROPINSI RIAU. Indonesian. sa. LC HB235.I5.

PERSONAL IM OFFENTLICHEN DIENST. See Public Administration.

PERSONAL SOCIAL SERVICES STATISTICS, ESTIMATES. 1974/75-. Periodical. UK. English. an. 5.00. LC HV245. DD 361.60941. NLM W1 PE846. *Social Services Statistics Estimates, 0307-045X.*

PERSONS NOT IN THE LABOUR FORCE. See Economics - Labor.

PERSPECTIVES STATISTIQUES. (PERSPECTIVES STATISTIQUES : REVUE STATISTIQUE ANNUELLE DE LA REGIE DES RENTES DU QUEBEC). Vol. 1 (1981)-. 0712-8223. CN. French. an. Case Postale 5200, Quebec G1K 7S9 Canada. LC HD7130.Q4. DD 368.4009714. *Bulletin Statistique (Regie des Rentes du Quebec).*

PETIT GUIDE STATISTIUQE DE LA LORRAINE. Main/Corp Institut National de la Statistique et des Etudes Economiques. Observatoire Economique de l'Est. French. ir. 34 Quai Claude Lorrain, Nanncy France. LC HA1228.L65.

PETROLE. ELEMENTS STATISTIQUES (1968). (PETROLE). 1968-. FR. French. ir. Comite Professionnel du Petrole, 51 Boulevard de Courcelles, 75008-Paris France. Ind/Abst Energy Res. Abstr. LC HD9572.2. DD 338.27280944. *Activite de l'Industrie Petroliere, 0515-3468.*

PETROLEO Y OTROS DATOS ESTADISTICOS. Began with 1958. 0083-5390. VE. Spanish. ir. Ministerio de Minias, Hidrocarburos, Division de Economica Petrolera, Caracas Venezuela. LC HD9574.V4.

PETROLEUM STATISTICS. VFOAT Statistiques du Petrole. 1977-. English (French). ir. European Community Information Service, 2100 M Street NW/Suite 707, Washington DC 20037. LC HD9575.E97. DD 338.27282094. *Oliestatistik.*

PETUNJUK KELURAHAN WILAYAH JAKARTA BARAT. Main/Corp Jakarta Raya, Indonesia. Kantor Sensus dan Statistik. 1977-. IO. Indonesian. ir. Kantor Sensus dan Statistik Dki Jakarta, Jl Medan Merdeka Selatan, No 89 Lantai XX, Jakarta Indonesia. LC HA1818.J34. *Buku Petunjuk Kelurahan Wilayah Jakarta Barat.*

PETUNJUK KELURAHAN WILAYAH JAKARTA PUSAT. Main/Corp Jakarta Raya, Indonesia. Kantor Sensus dan Statistik. 1977-. IO. Indonesian. ir. Kantor Sensus dan Statistik Dki Jakarta, Jl Medan Merdeka Selatan No, 8 9 Lantai XX, Jakarta Indonesia. LC HA1818.J34. *Buki Petunjuk Kelurahan Wilayah Jakarta Pusat.*

PETUNJUK KELURAHAN WILAYAH JAKARTA SELATAN. Main/Corp Jakarta Raya, Indonesia. Kantor Sensus dan Statistik. 1977-. Periodical. IO. Indonesian. ir. Kantor Sensus dan Statistik Dki Jakarta, Jl Medan Merdeka Selatan No 8 9., Lantai XX, Jakarta Indonesia. LC HA1818.J34. *Buku Petunjuk Kelurahan Wilayah Jakarta Selatan.*

PETUNJUK KELURAHAN WILAYAH JAKARTA TIMUR. Main/Corp Jakarta Raya, Indonesia. Kantor Sensus dan Statistik. 1977-. IO. Indonesian. ir. Kantor Sensus dan Statistik Dki Jakarta, Jl Medan Merdeka Selatan No 89, Lantai XX, Jakarta Indonesia. LC HA1818.J34. *Buku Petunjuk Kelurahan Wilayah Jakarta Timur.*

PETUNJUK KELURAHAN WILAYAH JAKARTA UTARA. Main/Corp Jakarta Raya, Indonesia. Kantor Sensus dan Statistik. 1977-. IO. Indonesian. ir. Kantor Sensus dan Statistik Dki Jakarta, Jl Medan Merdeka Selatan No 89, Lantai XX, Jakarta Indonesia. LC HA1818.D5. *Buku Petunjuk Kelurahan Wilayah Jakarta Utara.*

PEULOT U-FIRSUMIM STATISTIYIM HADASHIM BE-YISRAEL. VFOAT New Statistical Projects and Publications in Israel. Periodical. English and Hebrew. ir. 20.00. Government Publishing House, Street B No 29 Hakirya, Tel-Aviv Israel. LC HA37. *Peulot Statistiyot Hadashot.*

PHILIPPINE FORESTRY STATISTICS. PH. English. an. Bureau of Forest Development, Diliman, Quezon City Philippines. Tel 96-21-41. LC SD229. DD 333.7509599. Circ 700. (ctrl). Forestry activities, forest resources, forest land uses, products utilization, trade and revenues derived from the utilization of forest resources.

PHILIPPINE STATISTICAL YEARBOOK. See Yearbooks, Almanacs, Directories.

THE PHILIPPINE STATISTICIAN. V. 1- June 1952-. 0031-7829. Periodical. PH. English. sa. $5.00. PSSC/Central Subscription Service, PO Box 655-Greenhills, Metro Manila 3113 Philippines. Tel 922-9621. Ed Burton T Onate. bk rev. adv acc. Circ 1,000. Presents papers and articles on theoretical and applied statistics.

PHSB STUDIES. Main/Corp North Carolina. Dept. of Human Resources. Public Health Statistics Branch. VAT Public Health Statistics Branch Studies. No. 1- Jan. 1977-. 0164-2782. Periodical. US. English. Public Health Statistics Branch, Division of Health Services, Department of Human Resources, PO Box 2091, Raleigh NC 27602. LC HQ407.4.N8. DD 301.4209756. NLM W2 AN8 P9P.

PLANNING AND DEVELOPMENT STATISTICS . . . ACTUALS. 0260-8642. UK. English. an. 10.00. Chartered Institute of Public Finance and Accountancy, 1 Buckingham Place, London SW1E 6HS England. LC HD601.A1. DD 352.94180942.

PLANNING AND DEVELOPMENT STATISTICS. ESTIMTES. Main/Corp Chartered Institute of Public Finance and Accountancy. Statistical Information Service. UK. English. an. CIPFA Secretary, 1 Buckingham Place, London SW1E 6HS England. LC HT169.G72. DD 309.2120941.

POCKET BOOK OF HEALTH STATISTICS. Main/Corp India (Republic). Central Bureau of Health Intelligence. English. ir. Central Bureau of Health Intelligence, New Delhi India. LC RA407.5.I4. DD 312.0954.

POCKET BOOK OF LABOUR STATISTICS (NEW DELHI, INDIA). (POCKET BOOK OF LABOUR STATISTICS). English. an. 20.00. All India Organization of Employers, Federation House, New Delhi India. LC HD5817. DD 331.0954.

POCKET BOOK OF PUNJAB LABOUR STATISTICS. Main/Corp Punjab (India). Labour Dept. 1972-. II. English. ir. Office of the Labour Commissioner, Department of Labour, Chanigarh Punjab India. LC HD8689.P8. DD 331.10954552.

Statistics

POCKET DATA BOOK. USA. (POCKET DATA BOOK, USA). VAT Pocket Data Book, United States of America. Began with 1967. 0079-2403. US. English. te. Superintendent of Documents, US Government Printing Office, Washington DC 20402. LC HA195. DD 317.3.

POCKET YEAR BOOK, AUSTRALIA. See Yearbooks, Almanacs, Directories.

THE POCKET YEAR BOOK OF TASMANIA. See Yearbooks, Almanacs, Directories.

POCKETBOOK OF PHILIPPINE STATISTICS. PH. English. ir. National Economic and Development Authority, PO Box 1116, Manila Phillipines. LC HA4611. DD 315.99.

POCKETBOOK OF STATISTICS: JAMAICA. JM. English. an. Department of Statistics, 9 Swallowfield Road, Kingston 5 Jamaica. Tel (809)92-28371. Ed Booth. LC HA891. DD 317.292. Circ 1,500. (ctrl). The publication deals with population, migration, health, education, housing, labor and employment transport and communication, external trade consumer price indices among other economic topics.

POHOM TONGGYE YONBO. See Yearbooks, Almanacs, Directories.

POHOM TONGGYE YON'GAM. See Yearbooks, Almanacs, Directories.

LE POINT ECONOMIQUE DE L'AUVERGNE. Main/Corp Institut National de la Statistique et des Etudes Economiques (France). May 1971-. Periodical. FR. French. bm. INSEE-CNGP, BP 2718, 80027 Amiens Cedex France. LC HA1228.A9. Bulletin de Statistique: Auvergne (Allier, Cantal, Haute-Loire, Puy-de-Dome).

POLICE FORCE STATISTICS. Main/Corp Chartered Institute of Public Finance and Accountancy. UK. English. 1/-/-. Chartered Institute of Public Finance and Accountancy, 1 Buckingham Place, SW1E 6HS London England. LC HV8195. DD 363.20942.

POLICE STATISTICS ACTUALS. UK. English. an. '2.50. Statistical Information Service, Chartered Institute of Public Finance and Accountancy, 1 Buckingham Place, London SW1E 6HS England. LC HV8196.A2. DD 363.20942.

POLICE STATISTICS (CHARTERED INSTITUTE OF PUBLIC FINANCE AND ACCOUNTANCY. STATISTICAL INFORMATION SERVICE). (POLICE STATISTICS). UK. English. an. LC HV8195.A2. DD 363.20941.

POLICE STATISTICS, TASMANIA. 1978-79-. 0705-8187. English. ir. Tasmanian Office, Australian Bureau of Statistics, 188 Collins Street, Hobart Australia. LC HV8280.A5. DD 363.20996.

POLICY STATISTICS SERVICE. 0163-8920. US. English. ir. The National Underwriter, 420 East 4th Street, Cincinnati OH 45202. Tel (201)963-2300.

POPULATION AND DWELLINGS, STATISTICAL DIVISIONS, SUB-DIVISIONS, AND LOCAL GOVERNMENT AREAS, WESTERN AUSTRALIA. AT. English. ir. Australian Bureau of Statistics, 1-3 St George's Terrace, Perth Western Australia 6000 Australia. LC HA3007.W47. DD 319.41. Population, Dwellings, and Vital Statistics, Statistical Divisions, Subdivisions and Local Government Areas, Western Australia.

POPULATION AND VITAL STATISTICS REPORT. See Population Studies.

PORT STATISTICS. 1 (1980)-. 0263-9149. UK. English. an. 20.00. British Ports Association, Commonwealth House 1-19/New Oxford Street, London WC1A 1DZ England. LC HE557.G7. DD 387.10941021. Annual Digest of Port Statistics.

PORT STATISTICS . . . AND SUPPLEMENTARY INFORMATION. 0550-6522. English. an. Maritime Service Board of N S W, Box 32 GPO, Sydney 2001 Australia. LC HE559.A8. DD 387.109944. Port Statistics.

PORT STATISTICS FOR THE FOREIGN TRADE OF THE UNITED KINGDOM. 1961/62-. UK. English. an. LC HF3501. DD 382.0941.

POST-SECONDARY STATISTICS ENROLMENT DATA. Main/Corp British Columbia. Educational Data Services. VFOAT B.C. Post-Secondary Statistics. CN. English. British Columbia Research, 3650 Wesbrook Mall, Vancouver British Columbia V6S 212 Canada. LC LC148. DD 378.1059711.

POSTCENSAL ANNUAL ESTIMATES OF POPULATION FOR CENSUS DIVISIONS AND CENSUS METROPOLITAN AREAS . . . COMPONENT METHOD. (POSTCENSAL ANNUAL ESTIMATES OF POPULATION FOR CENSUS DIVISIONS AND CENSUS METROPOLITAN AREAS, JUNE 1 . . . COMPONENT METHOD)). Vol. 1 (1982)-. 0825-1320. CN. English (text in French). an. $5.00 Domestic, $6.00 Other Countries. Statistics Canada, Publication Sales and Services, Ottawa Ontario K1A 0T6 Canada. LC HA741. DD 304.620971021.

POTATO STATISTICAL YEARBOOK. See Yearbooks, Almanacs, Directories.

POULTRY MARKET STATISTICS. Main/Corp United States. Agricultural Marketing Service. 1972-. 0565-1980. US. English. an. US Department of Agriculture, Agricultural Marketing Service, Washington DC 20250. LC HD1751, HD9437.U6. DD 338.10973 S, 338.176500973. Poultry Market Statistics, 0565-1980.

PREISE UND LOHNE. Main/Corp Statistisches Landesamt Baden-Wurttemberg. Series/Titl Statistik van Baden-Wurttemberg. 1975/76-. German. an. Postfach 898, 7000 Stuttgart 1 West Germany. LC HA1320.B2, HD7029.

PRELIMINARY NATIONAL ACCOUNTS STATISTICS. SUPPLEMENT. English. ir. LC HC155.5.Z7. DD 339.72975.

PRELIMINARY NATIONAL MEDICAID STATISTICS. Series/Titl Health Care Financing Program Statistics. 1978-. 0730-7934. US. English. an. $18.00. ORD Publications, Room 2F1 Oak Meadows Building 6325 Security Boulevard, Baltimore MD 21207. Tel (301)597-2420. Ed Gerri Michael. NLM W2 A H24P. bk rev. Circ 4,000. Health care financing issues and innovative delivery systems as related to the Medicare and Medicaid programs.

PRELIMINARY NATIONAL MONTHLY MEDICAID STATISTICS. Series/Titl Health Care Financing Program Statistics. Oct.-Dec. 1978-. 0730-7977. Periodical. US. English. qt. $18.00. ORD Publications, Room 2F1 Oak Meadows Building 6325 Security Boulevard, Baltimore MD 21207. Tel (301)597-2420. Ed Gerri Michael. NLM W2 A H24P. bk rev. Circ 4,000. Health care financing issues and innovative delivery systems as related to the Medicaid and Medicare programs.

PRIKLADNAIA INFORMATIKA. Vol. 1-. UR. Russian. Izdatelstvo Finansy I Statistika, Moskva Ul. Chernyshvskogo 7, Moskva Russian SFSR.

PRINCIPAL MANUFACTURING STATISTICS, ALBERTA. Main/Corp Alberta. Bureau of Statistics. 1971/73-. 0382-1951. CN. English. an. Alberta Bureau of Statistics, 480 Terrace Building, Edmonton Alberta Canada. LC HD9734.C3. DD 338.097123.

PRISON STATISTICS : ENGLAND AND WALES. UK. English. an. 2.50. H M Stationery Office, 49 High Holborn, London WC1V 6HB England. Tel (0603)622211. LC HV9649.E5. DD 365.60942. Statistics of receptions and population of prison department establishments in England and Wales.

PRISON STATISTICS, TASMANIA. 1978-79-. 0705-8179. English. an. Australian Bureau of Statistics, Tasmanian Office, 10th Floor, Commonwealth Government Centre, 188 Collins Street, GPO Box 66-A, Hobart 7001 Australia. LC HV9430.A6. DD 364.309946. Public Justice, Tasmania.

PROBABILITY AND MATHEMATICAL STATISTICS. 1-. 0079-5607. Monographic Series. US. English. ir. Academic Press, 4805 Sand Lake Road, Orlando FL 32887. Tel (305)345-4100. Ed M M Rao. Ind/Abst Math. Rev.

PROBATION & PAROLE STATISTICS. Main/Corp Saskatchewan. Dept. of Social Services. Planning and Evaluation Division. 1973/74-. 0317-3828. Periodical. CN. English. an. Department of Social Services, 2210 Albert Street, Regina Saskatchewan S4P 2Y3 Canada. LC HV9309.S3. DD 364.63097124. Probation & Parole Statistics, 0317-3828.

PROBATION SERVICE STATISTICS . . . ACTUALS. 1982-83-. 0140-8291. UK. English. an. 9.00. Chartered Institute of Public Finance and Accountancy, 1 Buckingham Palace, London SW1E 6HS England.

PROBATION SERVICE STATISTICS . . . ESTIMATES. 1983-84-. 0264-6544. UK. English. an. 9.00. CIPFA Statistical Information Service, 1 Buckingham Pl, London SW1E 6HS England. LC HV9346.A5. DD 364.630942.

PROCEEDINGS OF THE BUSINESS AND ECONOMIC STATISTICS SECTION. (PROCEEDINGS OF THE BUSINESS AND ECONOMIC STATISTICS SECTION). Main/Corp American Statistical Association. Business and Economic Statistics Section. 114th-. 0066-0736. US. English. ir. American Statistical Association, 806 15th Street NW, Suite 640, Washington DC 20005. Tel (202)393-3253. LC HA1. DD 310.6273.

PROCEEDINGS OF THE SECTION ON STATISTICAL EDUCATION. Main/Corp American Statistical Association. Section on Statistical Education. US. English. an. 806 15th Street NW, Washington DC 20005.

PROCEEDINGS OF THE SOCIAL STATISTICS SECTION. Main/Corp American Statistical Association. Social Statistics Section. 1st- 1958-. 0066-0752. US. English. an. American Statistical Association, 806 15th Street NW/Suite 640, Washington DC 10005. Tel (202)393-3253. LC HA1. DD 310.6073. NLM W1 PR5863.

PROCEEDINGS OF THE STANDING SENATE COMMITTEE ON NATIONAL FINANCE. (PROCEEDINGS OF THE STANDING COMMITTEE ON NATIONAL FINANCE). Main/Corp Canada. Parliament. Senate. Standing Committee on National Finance. VFOAT Deliberations du Comite Senatorial Permanent des Finances Nationales. VAT Deliberations du Comite Senatorial Permanent des Finances Nationales (Edition Anglaise et Francaise), National Finance (Ottawa), Finances Nationales (Ottawa). Feb. 27th, 1969-. 0576-3851. Periodical. CN. text in English and French in parallel columns, Nov. 9, 1976-. Statistics Canada, Ottawa Ontario K1A 0T6 Canada. Proceedings of the Standing Senate Committee on Finance, Deliberations du Comite Senatorial Permanent des Finances Nationales, Nov. 9, 1976, 0576-3843.

PROCEEDINGS OF THE STATISTICAL COMPUTING SECTION. Main/Corp American Statistical Association. Statistical Computing Section. 1975-. 0149-9963. US. English. an. $10.00. American Statistical Association, 806 15th Street Northwest, Washington DC 20005. LC QA276.4. DD 519.50183.

PRODUCTION CREDIT ASSOCIATIONS OPERATING STATISTICS. (PRODUCTION CREDIT ASSOCIATIONS, OPERATING STATISTICS). 0272-9768. US. English. an. Farm Credit Association, Office of Supervision, Washington DC 20578. LC HG2051.U5. DD 332.710973.

PRODUCTION STATISTICS AND ACTIVITY REPORT. Main/Corp Manitoba. Petroleum Branch. Mar. 1979-. 0704-3864. Periodical. CN. English. mo. Production Statistics and Schedule of Wells, 0319-7255.

PRODUCTION STATISTICS AND SCHEDULE OF WELLS. Main/Corp Manitoba. Mines Branch. Periodical. CN. English. mo. Minister of Finance Manitoba, 103 Legislative Building, Winnipeg Manitoba Canada.

PRODUKTIESTATISTIEKEN : VEEVOEDERINDUSTRIE CEASED. Main/Corp Netherlands. Centraal Bureau voor de Statistiek. NE. Dutch. ir. 4.00. Central Bureau Voor de Statistiek, Prinses Beatrixlaan 428, Voorburg Netherlands. LC HD9056.N4.

PROGRAM STATISTICS - MICHIGAN DEPARTMENT OF SOCIAL SERVICES. (PROGRAM STATISTICS). Main/Corp Michigan. Dept. of Social Services. Series/Titl DSS Publication. 0093-7835. US. English. LC HV86. DD 361.9774 S, 362.9774.

PROJECTIONS OF EDUCATION STATISTICS TO . . . . 1984/85-. US. English. be. Superintendent of Documents, US Government Printing Office, Washington DC 20402. NLM W2 A N1478P. Eric Version for 1990/91, Vols. 1

Statistics

and 2, distributed to depository libraries in microfiche. *Projections of Educational Statistics.*

PROJECTIONS. SELECTED EDUCATION STATISTICS FOR PENNSYLVANIA. (PROJECTIONS : SELECTED EDUCATION STATISTICS FOR PENNSYLVANIA). Main/Corp Pennsylvania. Division of Education Statistics. 0160-4155. US. English. LC LA355. DD 371.219748.

PROJECTS, PRODUCTS, AND SERVICES OF THE NATIONAL CENTER FOR EDUCATIONAL STATISTICS. Main/Corp National Center for Education Statistics. 0092-6620. US. English. an. US Department of Health, Education and Welfare, Education Division, National Center for Education Statistics, Washington DC 20402. LC L112. DD 371.00973.

PROPERTY TAX STATISTICAL REPORT FORM THE OFFICE OF STATE TAX COMMISSIONER . . . ON . . . PROPERTY TAXES LEVIED AND PROPERTY VALUATION. US. English. North Dakota Tax Department, State Capitol, Bismarck ND 58505. LC HJ4121.N9. DD 336.2209784. *Statistical Report (North Dakota. Tax Dept.).*

PRVI STATISTICNI PODATKI ZA LETO . . . (Z OCENO). Slovenian. an. Zavod Sr Slovenije Za Statistiko, Vozarski Pot 12, Ljubljana Yugoslavia.

PRZEGLAD STATYSTYCZNY. Vol. 1-. 0033-2372. Periodical. PL. Polish (tables of contents also in Russian and English). qt. ARS Polona, Krakowskie Przedmiescie 7, 00-068 Warsaw Poland. Ind/Abst Math. Rev. LC HA1. DD 310.5. CODEN PZSTAD.

PUBLIC ASSISTANCE RECIPIENTS IN STANDARD METROPOLITAN STATISTICAL AREAS. Feb. 1981-. 0736-9301. US. English. an. Superintendent of Documents, US Government Printing Office, Washington DC 20402. LC HV90. DD 362.580973. *Public Assistance Recipients and Cash Payments by State and County, 0272-3697.*

PUBLIC COMMON SCHOOL ENROLLMENT FORECASTS FOR . . . THE BIENNIUM BUDGET, STATE OF WASHINGTON. See Education (General).

PUBLIC FINANCE STATISTICS. Main/Corp Pakistan. Finance Division. PK. English. ir. Government of Pakistan, Finance Division, Karachi 15B Pakistan. LC HJ67.5. DD 336.5491.

PUBLIC HEALTH STATISTICS. Main/Corp Louisiana. Office of Public Health Statistics. 0148-5555. Periodical. US. English. qt. E H Atkins Statistical Officer, PO Box 60630, New Orleans LA 70160. LC RA74. DD 312.09763. NLM W2 AL6 D41L. *Public Health Statistics, 0148-5555.*

PUBLIC HEALTH STATISTICS (MADISON, WIS. : 1977). (PUBLIC HEALTH STATISTICS). VFOAT Public Health Statistics, Wisconsin. 1977-. US. English. an. NLM W2. *Public Health Statistics, Wisconsin.*

PUBLIC LAND STATISTICS. Began with 1962. 0082-9110. US. English. an. Superintendent of Documents, US Government Printing Office, Washington DC 20402. LC HD183. DD 333.10973. *Statistical Appendix to the Annual Report of the Director, Bureau of Land Management, to the Secretary of the Interior.*

PUBLIC LIBRARIES IN QUEENSLAND, STATISTICAL BULLETIN. Began with issue for 1968/72. AT. English. an. $2.95. Library Board of Queensland, William Street, Brisbane 4000 Australia. LC Z870.Q44. DD 027.4943.

PUBLIC LIBRARY STATISTICS. Main/Corp Chartered Institute of Public Finance and Accountancy. 0537-9466. UK. English. an. $1.50. Chartered Institute of Public Finance & Accountancy, 1 Buckingham Place, London England. LC Z791.A1. DD 027.442.

PUBLIC LIBRARY STATISTICS . . . ESTIMATES. 0307-0522. UK. English. an. 6.00 for Nonsubscribers. Chartered Institute of Public Finance and Accountancy, 1 Buckingham Place, London SW1E 6HS England. LC Z791.A1. DD 027.441.

PUBLIC WELFARE STATISTICS. Main/Corp Virginia. Dept. of Welfare. V. 1- Jan. 1939-. Periodical. US. English. qt. Bureau of Research & Reporting, 8007 Discovery Drive, Richmond VA 23288. Tel (804)281-9204. LC HV86.

PUBLICATIONS DE L'INSTITUT DE STATISTIQUE DE L'UNIVERSITE DE PARIS. Main/Corp Universite de Paris. Institut de Statistique. V. 1- 1952-. 0041-9184. Periodical. FR. French. sa. $26.61. Institut de Statistique, Tour 45-55 E3-4 Place Jussieu, 75230 Paris Cedex 05 France. Tel 329-12021. Ind/Abst Math. Rev. LC HA1. CODEN PBSPA3.

PUBLICATIONS OF THE AUSTRALIAN BUREAU OF STATISTICS. Main/Corp Australian Bureau of Statistics. 0312-4819. English. ir. The Commonwealth Statistician, Treasury Building, Box 17 GPO, 2600 Canberra Australia. LC Z7554.A77, HA37.A8. DD 016.3194. *Publications of the Commonwealth Bureau of Census and Statistics.*

PUBLICATIONS OF THE UNIVERSITY OF KUOPIO. COMMUNITY HEALTH. SERIES STATISTICS AND REVIEWS. VFOAT Community Health. 0358-3058. Monographic Series. English. ir. NLM W1 PU736UF.

PUBLICATIONS STATISTIQUES DES ADMINISTRATIONS. Main/Corp Institut National de la Statistique et des Etudes Economiques (France). French. ir. 8.00. INSEE, 195 rue de Bercy, Paris France 75012. LC Z7554.F7, HA1213. DD 016.3144.

PULP & PAPER STATISTICS. Main/Corp Nihon Seishi Rengokai. JA. English. an. $17.00. Japan Publications Trading Company, Ltd, PO Box 5030 Tokyo International, Tokyo 100-31 Japan. LC HD9836.J3. DD 338.476760952. *Pulp & Paper Statistics.*

PULPWOOD AND WOOD RESIDUE STATISTICS. Main/Corp Statistics Canada. Manufacturing and Primary Industries Division. VFOAT Statistiques de Bois a Pate et Dechets de Bois. V. 15- Jan. 1972-. 0575-9536. CN. English (French). mo. 50.00 Domestic, 60.00 Foreign. Receiver General for Canada, Statistics Canada Publications, Ottawa Ontario K1A 0T6 Canada. Tel (800)268-1151. LC HD9769.W53. DD 338.47676120971. Cumulative data on production, consumption, and inventories of pulpwood, and wood residue for Canada and the provinces. *Pulpwood and Wood Residue Statistics, 0575-9536.*

PUPIL TRANSPORTATION SYSTEM. ILLINOIS PUBLIC SCHOOLS. (PUPIL TRANSPORTATION STATISTICS, ILLINOIS PUBLIC SCHOOLS). Series/Titl Circular Series A. 0092-4644. US. English. 216 East Monroe, Springfield IL 62706. LC L142, LB2864. DD 371.8709773.

PURPOSE AND METHODS IN FISHERIES STATISTICS. DOCUMENT. (PURPOSE AND METHODS IN FISHERIES STATISTICS : DOCUMENT). VFOAT Buts et Methodes en Matiere de Statistiques des Peshes. No. 1- 1952-. 0426-7680. Monographic Series. English and French. ir. FAO of United Nations, Via delle Terme di Caracalla, 00100 Rome Italy. DD 338.3.

PUSAN KYOYUK TONGGYE YONBO. VFOAT Statistic Year Book, Busan Education. Korean. an. LC L614.P87.

QUALITY CONTROL AND APPLIED STATISTICS. V. 1- 1956-. 0033-5207. Periodical. US. English. mo. Executive of Sciences Institute Inc, PO Drawer No M, Whippany NY 07981. Tel (201)887-1233. Ed Arnold J Rosenthal. Index in last issue of volume - attached. Quality control applied statistic, experimental design, data analysis and abstracts.

QUARTERLY ABSTRACT OF STATISTICS. See Indexes/Abstracts.

QUARTERLY AGRICULTURAL STATISTICAL BULLETIN. Main/Corp Zambia. Ministry of Rural Development. Statistics Section. ZA. English. ir. 50. Ministry of Rural Development, Statistics Section, Lusaka Zambia. LC HD2130.Z15. DD 338.1096894. *Statistical Bulletin.*

QUARTERLY BANKING STATISTICS. Main/Corp Bangladesh Bank. Statistics Dept. BG. English. ir. Bangladesh Bank, PO Box 325, Dacca 2 Bangladesh. LC HG3290.6.A5. DD 332.1095492.

QUARTERLY BULLETIN OF COCOA STATISTICS. VFOAT Bulletin Trimestriel de Statistiques du Cacao. Began with Dec. 1974 issue. 0308-4469. UK. English (French, Russian, and Spanish). qt. 25. International Cocoa Organization, 22 Berners Street, London W1P 3DB United Kingdom. Tel (01)637-3211. LC HD9200.A1. DD 382.413740212. Statistics on world cocoa economy, prediction, consumption, exports, imports, prices.

QUARTERLY BULLETIN OF CONSTRUCTION STATISTICS. Main/Corp Bahamas. Dept. of Statistics. English. ir. $1.00. Department of Statistics, Cabinet Office, PO Box N 3904, Nassau Barnabas. LC HD9715.B3. DD 338.47690097296.

QUARTERLY BULLETIN OF ELECTRIC ENERGY STATISTICS FOR EUROPE CEASED. Main/Corp United Nations. Economic Commission for Europe. VFOAT Bulletin Trimestriel de Statistiques de l'Energie Electrique pour l'Europe, Trekhmesiachnyi Evropeiskii Biulleten' Statistiki Electroenergii. V. 1-9. Periodical. English (French and Russian). ir. United Nations Publications, Sales Section/Room A-3315, New York NY 10017.

QUARTERLY BULLETIN OF FINANCIAL STATISTICS CEASED. Main/Corp Japan. Okurasho. Daijin Kanbo. Chosa Kikakuka. 1968-82. JA. English. ir. Research and Planning Division, Minister's Secretariat, Ministry of Finance, 3-1 Kasumigaseki, Chiyoda-ku Tokyo 100 Japan. LC HG41. DD 332.0952. *Quarterly Bulletin of Financial Statistics.*

QUARTERLY BULLETIN OF STATISTICS FOR ASIA AND THE PACIFIC. Main/Corp United Nations. Economic and Social Commission for Asia and the Pacific. V. 3, No. 3- Sept. 1973-. 0125-0019. US. English. qt. $9.50. United Nations Publications, Sales Section/Room A-3315, New York NY 10017. Tel (212)754-8302. Ind/Abst Predicasts, Funk Scott Index Corp. Ind. LC JX1977, HA1665. DD 300.8 S, 315. Regional statistics on a cross-section of economic and social topics. *Quarterly Bulletin of Statistics for Asia and The Far East.*

QUARTERLY BULLETIN OF STEEL STATISTICS FOR EUROPE. VFOAT Bulletin Trimestriel de Statistiques de l'Acier pour l'Europe. No. 1 (Dec. 1950)-. 0041-7378. Periodical. SW. English (French). qt. $8.50. United Nations Publications, Sales Section/Room A-3315, New York NY 10017. Tel (212)754-8302. Ind/Abst Funk Scott Index Corp. Ind. LC HD9525.A2.

QUARTERLY COMMODITY STATISTICS. Main/Corp Lembaga Pemasaran Pertanian Persekutuan. English. ir. 4th & 5th Floors Bangkok Bank Building, Kuala Lumpur Malaysia. LC HD9016.M3. DD 338.17.

QUARTERLY DIGEST OF STATISTICS. Main/Corp Malta. Office of Statistics. No. 1- Mar. 1960-. English. qt. Central Office of Statistics, O Auberge de Castille, Valletta Malta. LC HA1117.M3. DD 314.585.

QUARTERLY ECONOMIC AND STATISTICAL REVIEW. See Economics.

QUARTERLY ECONOMIC SUMMARY. STATISTICAL SUPPLEMENT. VFOAT Statistical Supplement. Vol. 1, No. 1 (Apr. 1985)-. 0828-0878. Periodical. CN. English. qt.

QUARTERLY FINANCIAL STATISTICS OF CREDIT UNIONS ET CAISSES POPULAIRES. Main/Corp Manitoba. Bureau of Statistics. VFOAT Financial Statistics of Credit Unions. Statistiques Financieres des Caisses Populaires. V. 1- Dec. 1973-. Periodical. CN. English (includes some text in French). qt. LC HG2039.C2. DD 334.2.

QUARTERLY LABOUR FORCE STATISTICS. VFOAT Statistiques Trimestrielles de la Population Active. 1983, No. 1-. 0255-3627. Periodical. English (French in parallel columns). qt. $24.00. OECD Publications Center, 1750 Pennsylvania Avenue NW, Washington DC 20006. Tel (202)724-1857. Ind/Abst Predicasts. This quarterly bulletin provides data for the short-term evolution of the major labour force components and employment by sector. *Labour Force Statistics. Quarterly Supplement to the Yearbook.*

QUARTERLY NATIONAL ACCOUNTS BULLETIN. See Economics - International Economics.

Statistics

QUARTERLY OIL AND GAS STATISTICS. VFOAT Statistiques Trimestrielles du Petrole et du Gaz Naturel. 1st Quarter 1984-. Periodical. US. English (French). qt. $95.00. OECD Publications and Information Center, 1750 Pennsylvania Avenue/Suite 1207, Washington DC 20006. Tel (202)724-1857. **Ind/Abst** Predicasts. LC HD9560.1. DD 338.2728021. Statistics on oil and gas supply and demand in the OECD area including trade, production, refinery, intake and output, final consumption and stock levels. *Quarterly Oil Statistics.*

QUARTERLY OIL STATISTICS CEASED. **Main/Corp** Organisation for Economic Co-operation and Development. VFOAT Statistiques Trimestrielles du Petrole. 1976, 4th Quarter-1983, 4th Quarter. 0378-6536. Periodical. FR. English (French). qt. $95.00. OECD Publication Center, 1750 Pennsylvania Avenue NW, Washington DC 20006. **Ind/Abst** Predicasts, Energy Inf. Abstr., Environ. Abstr., Ship Abstr., GeoRef, Energy Res. Abstr. LC HD9560.1. DD 338.27282021. *Statistiques Petrolieres Trimestrielles.*

QUARTERLY PUBLIC ASSISTANCE STATISTICS. Jan./Mar. 1981-. 0735-0856. US. English. qt. $12.00 Domestic, $15.00 Foreign. Superintendent of Documents, US Government Printing Office, Washington DC 20402. LC HV85. DD 362.973021. *Public Assistance Statistics (United States. Social Security Administration. Office of Research and Statistics), 0145-952X; Applications and Case Discontinuances of AFDC; Disposition of Public Assistance Cases Involving Questions of Fraud.*

QUARTERLY REPORT, PROVISIONAL DATA, DATA FROM THE CLIENT ORIENTED DATA ACQUISITION PROCESS. (NATIONAL INSTITUTE ON DRUG ABUSE STATISTICAL SERIES. SERIES D, QUARTERLY REPORT, PROVISIONAL DATA. DATA FROM THE CLIENT ORIENTED DATA ACQUISITION PROCESS). VFOAT Quarterly Report, Provisional Data. Data from the Client Oriented Data Acquisition Process. Began with No. 2, Jan./Mar. 1979. 0161-603X. Periodical. US. English. qt. Division of Scientific and Program Information, National Institute on Drug Abuse, 5600 Fishers Lane, Rockville MD 20857. **Ind/Abst** Am. Stat. Index. LC HV5825. DD 362.290973. *Data from the Client Oriented Data Acquisition Process, 0145-1065.*

QUARTERLY REVIEW OF DRILLING STATISTICS FOR THE UNITED STATES. 0033-5789. Periodical. US. English. qt. American Petroleum Institute, Statistical Publications, 1801 K Street NW, Washington DC 20006. **Ind/Abst** GeoRef, Energy Inf. Abstr., Environ. Abstr. CODEN QRDSB.

QUARTERLY STATISTICAL ABSTRACT. See Indexes/Abstracts.

QUARTERLY STATISTICAL BULLETIN. Main/Corp Tanzania. Bureau of Statistics. VFOAT Taarifa ya Tarakumu. (V.23, No.3-Sept. 1973-). Periodical. Swahili. ir. *Monthly Statistical Bulletin.*

QUARTERLY STATISTICAL BULLETIN (INTERNATIONAL TIN COUNCIL). (QUARTERLY STATISTICAL BULLETIN). Vol. 28, No. 1 (Mar. 1984)-. Periodical. UK. English. qt. International Tin Council, Haymarket House 1 Oxendon Street, London SW1Y 4EQ England. Tel 01 930 0451. Circ 600. Mine and shelter production of tin, tin consumption, stocks and trade. Production, apparent consumption and trade in tinplate, tin prices and turnover. *Monthly Statistical Summary (International Tin Council).*

QUARTERLY STATISTICAL BULLETIN ON COFFEE. Vol. 1, No. 1 (Jan.-Mar. 1977)-. 0140-5225. UK. English (French, Portuguese, or Spanish). qt. $36.00. International Coffee Organization, 22 Berners Street, London W1 England. LC HD9199.A1. DD 380.1413730212.

QUARTERLY STATISTICAL BULLETIN - SPECIAL SERVICES DIVISION. SOCIAL SERVICES BRANCH. DEPARTMENT OF HEALTH AND SOCIAL SERVICES. (QUARTERLY STATISTICAL BULLETIN). Apr. 1980/Mar. 1981-. 0824-930X. Periodical. CN. English. qt. DD 361.9717. *Quarterly Statistical Bulletin, 0225-2139.*

QUARTERLY STATISTICAL REPORT - EDISON ELECTRIC INSTITUTE. STATISTICAL DEPT. (QUARTERLY STATISTICAL REPORT). 1982, 2nd Quarter-. 0749-9183. Periodical. US. English. qt. Edison Electric Institute, 1111 19th Street Northwest, Washington DC 20036. DD 333. *Total Electric Utility Industry in the United States, including Alaska and Hawaii.*

QUARTERLY STATISTICS - DE NEDERLANDSCHE BANK N.V. Main/Corp Nederlandsche Bank (Amsterdam, Netherlands). Periodical. English. qt. $28.00. Kluwer Academic Publishers, Box 322, 3300 AH Dordrecht Nederlands. LC HC321. DD 330.9692005.

QUARTERLY STATISTICS OF MANUFACTURERS' SALES. INDEX OF COMMODITIES. See Indexes/Abstracts.

QUARTERLY VITAL STATISTICS REVIEW CEASED. Jan./Mar. 1971-Oct./Dec. 1982. 0095-7887. Periodical. US. English. qt. New York State Department of Health, Office of Biostatistics, Albany NY 12208. LC RA407.4.N7. DD 312.09747. **NLM** W2 AN6 D3Q. *Monthly Vital Statistics Review, 0095-7879.*

QUATERLY STATISTICS ON THE WORKING OF CAPITAL ISSUES CONTROL. Main/Corp India (Republic). Dept. of Economic Affairs. 0536-8014. Periodical. English. ir. LC HG5735.

THE QUEENSLAND POCKET YEAR BOOK. See Yearbooks, Almanacs, Directories.

QUEENSLAND YEAR BOOK. See Yearbooks, Almanacs, Directories.

R & S REPORT. No. 1- Jan. 1973-. 0093-3481. US. English. ir. Research and Statistics Office, State Department of Health, PO Box 3378, Honolulu HI 96801. LC HB3525.H3. DD 312.09969. **NLM** W2 AH3 D45R.

RAC NEWSLETTER. See Engineering.

RACE RELATIONS SURVEY. See Sociology: General Works, Theory.

RADNE ORGANIZACIJE VANPRIVREDNIH DELATNOSTI. Main/Corp Savezni Zavod za Statistiku (Yugoslavia). Serbo-Croatian(R). ir. 4.00. Savezni Zavod Za Statistiku, Kneza Milosa 20, Beograd Yugoslavia. LC HA1631, HA1632.

RADNICI I CIST LICNI DOHODAK PO OPSTINAMA U SRBIH. Series/Titl Statisticki Pregled za Opstine Socijalisticke Republike Bosne I Hercegovine. Serbo-Croatian -R. sa. LC HA1188.B6, HC407. Z7.

RAIL PASSENGER STATISTICS IN THE NORTHEAST CORRIDOR. Main/Corp United States. Federal Railroad Administration. US. English. National Technical Information Service, 5285 Port Royal Road, Springfield VA 22161.

RAILROAD ACCIDENTS IN OREGON. (RAILROAD ACCIDENTS IN OREGON, STATISTICS SUMMARY AND ANALYSIS). Main/Corp Oregon. Public Utility Commissioner. 0093-2140. US. English. an. Public Utility Commissioner, Labor and Industries Building, Salem OR 97310. Tel (503)378-6351. Ed David J Astle. LC HE1780.5.O7. DD 312.44. Circ 600. (ctrl). Statistics and analysis of accidents at rail crossings in Oregon. Also includes section on railroad employee accidents. *Statistical Report, Railroad Accidents.*

RAILWAY TRANSPORT IN CANADA, COMMODITY STATISTICS. VFOAT Transport Ferroviaire du Canada, Statistiques sur les Merchandises. 1982-. 0823-3969. CN. English (French). an. $8.85 Domestic, $10.60 Foreign. Publication Sales and Services, Statistics Canada, Ottawa Ontario K1A 0T6 Canada. LC HE2801. DD 385.240971. *Railway Transport. Part 5, Freight Carried by Principal Commodity Classes, 0706-2087.*

RAILWAY TRANSPORT. PART 1, COMPARATIVE SUMMARY STATISTICS. VFOAT Transport Ferroviaire. 1958-. 0706-2028. CN. text in English and French, English only, 1958-1970. an. $1.05. Statistics Canada, Publications Distribution, Ottawa Ontario K1A 0T6 Canada. DD 385.0971. *Railway Transport.*

RAILWAY TRANSPORT. PART 2, FINANCIAL STATISTICS. VFOAT Transport Ferroviaire. 1958-. 0706-2044. CN. French (text in English only, 1958-1970). an. 70.00. Statistics Canada, Publications Distribution, Ottawa Ontario K1A 0T6 Canada. DD 385.1. *Railway Transport.*

RAILWAY TRANSPORT. PART III, EQUIPMENT, TRACK AND FUEL STATISTICS. VFOAT Transport Ferroviaire. 1958-. 0706-2060. CN. English (French; in English only, 1958-1970). an. $5.40. LC HE2801. DD 385.370971. *Railway Transport.*

RAILWAY TRANSPORT. PART IV, OPERATING AND TRAFFIC STATISTICS. VFOAT Transport Ferroviaire. 1958-. 0706-2079. CN. English (French; English only, 1958-1970). an. Receiver General for Canada, Statistics Canada Publications, Ottawa Ontario K1A 0T6 Canada. LC HE2801. DD 385.0971. *Railway Transport.*

RAILWAY TRANSPORT: RAILWAY COMMODITY ORIGIN AND DESTINATION STATISTICS. (RAILWAY TRANSPORT, RAILWAY COMMODITY ORIGIN AND DESTINATION STATISTICS). VFOAT Railway Commodity Origin and Destination Statistics, Transport Ferroviaire, Statistiques sur l'Origine et la Destination des Merchandises Transportees par Chemin de Fer. 1st Issue (1976/1979)-. 0229-883X. CN. English (text in French in parallel columns). an. 22.00 Domestic, 23.00 Foreign. Receiver General for Canada, Statistics Canada Publications, Ottawa Ontario K1A 0T6 Canada. LC HE2379. DD 385.240971. Provides a four-year summary of tonnages and related revenues of CN and CP Rail for principal commodities and commodity groups by provinces of original and destination.

RAPPORT D'ACTIVITE - SERVICE PROVINCIAL DE STATISTIQUE DU CENTRE-SUD. Main/Corp Cameroon. Service Provincial de Statistique du Centre-Sud. French. ir. Service Provincial de Statistique du Centre-Sud, BP 1.501, Yaounde Cameroon. LC HA2141. DD 316.671105.

RAPPORT D'ACTIVITES - REPUBLIQUE UNIE DU CAMEROUN, SERVICE PROVINCIAL STATISTIQUE DU NORD CAMEROUN. Main/Corp Cameroon. Service Provincial Statistique du Nord Cameroun. CX. French. ir. Service Provincial Statistique du Nord Cameroun, B.P. 251, Garoua, Cameroun Africa. LC HA2141. DD 316.7112.

RAPPORT - SVERIGES LANTBRUKSUNIVERSITET, INSTITUTIONEN FOR EKONOMI OCH STATISTIK. Main/Corp Sveriges Lantbrukuniversitet. Institutionen for Ekonomi Och Statistik. VFOAT Report - Department of Economics and Statistics. 112-. 0347-982X. Monographic Series. SW. Swedish (English with summaries in Swedish and English). ir. Sveriges Lantbruksuniversitet, Institutionen for Ekonomi och Statistik, S-750 07 Uppsala Sweden. *Rapport Fran Institutionen for Ekonomi Och Statistik.*

RASSEGNA DI STATISTICHE DEL LAVORO. Year 1- Jan./Feb. 1949-. 0033-961X. Periodical. Italian. bm. 48,000.00 Domestic, 60,000.00 Foreign. Servizio Italiano Pubblicazion, Viale dell'Astronomia 30, 00144 Rome Italy. Tel (06)5920509. **Ind/Abst** Foreign Lang. Index, PAIS Foreign Lang. Index. LC HD4826. (cum index). Offers articles by specialists as well as statistics on Italian labor topics, such as employment and unemployment, salaries, social security, cost of living and international comparisons.

RASSEGNA STATISTICA DELL'ECONOMIA LIGURE. Began with issue for July/Aug. 1967. IT. Italian. bm. Ufficio Studi e Statistica della Cassa di Risparmio di Genova e Imperia, Via Cassa di Risparmio 15, 16123 Genova Italy. LC HC307.L5.

RATE SUPPORT GRANT STATISTICS. 1979-80-. 0142-5137. UK. English. 2.50. K Hyde Honorary Treasurer, County Hall, Truro TR1 3AY England. LC HJ1023. DD 336.185.

RECREATION STATISTICS. 0362-7837. US. English. Department of the Army, Office of the Chief of Engineers, the Pentagon, Washington DC 20310. LC GV191.4. DD 333.780973.

RECUEIL STATISTIQUE DU POITOU-CHARENTES. French. ir. Direction Regionale de l'I.N.S.E.E., 5 rue Sainte-Catherine, Poitiers France. LC HA1228.P6. DD 944.65.

REGIONAL BREAKDOWN OF WORLD TOURISM STATISTICS. VFOAT Repartition Regionale des Statistiques du Tourisme Mondial. Began in 1979 with vol. for 1973-1977. SP. English

Statistics

(French and Spanish). ir. World Tourism Organization, Calle Capitan Haya 42, E-Madrid-20 Spain. *Regional Breakdown of World Travel Statistics*.

REGIONAL STATISTICS CEASED. No. 11-15. UK. English. an. 5.00. Her Majesty's Stationery Office, 49 High Holborn, London WC1V 6HB England. LC HA1123. DD 314.1. *Abstract of Regional Statistics*.

REGIONAL STATISTICS : COMMUNITY'S FINANCIAL PARTICIPATION IN INVESTMENTS = STATISTIQUES REGIONALES : CONCOURS FINANCIERS DE LA COMMUNAUTE AUX INVESTISSEMENTS. Main/Corp Statistical Office of the European Communities. English (French). ir. Eurostat, 2100 M Street NW/Suite 707, Washington DC 20037. LC HG5430.5.A2. DD 332.6094.

REGIONALISIERTE SCHULERPROGNOSEN. Main/Corp North Rhine-Westphalia (Germany). Landesamt fur Datenverarbeitung und Statistik. Series/Titl Beitrage zur Statistik des Landes Nordrhein-Westfalen. German. ir. 7.50. Landesamt fur Datenverarbeitung und Statistik Nordrhein-Westfalen, Postfach 1105, 4000 Dusseldorf 1 West Germany. LC HA1320.N6, L401.

REGIONALSTRUKTUR BADEN-WURTTEMBERG : GEMEINDEN. Main/Corp Statistisches Landesamt Baden-Wurttemberg. Series/Titl Statistik von Baden-Wurttemberg. GW. German. ir. Statistisches Landesamt Baden-Wurttemberg, Postfach 898, 7000 Stuttgart 1 West Germany. LC HA1320.B2, HA1248. B32.

LE REGIONI IN CIFRE. Main/Corp Italy. Istituto Centrale di Statistica. Italian. ir. Istituto Centrale di Statistica, Via Cesare Balbo 16, Roma 00100 Italy. LC HA1362.

RELATORIO DE ATIVIDADES - COMPANHIA AGRICOLA DE MINAS GERAIS. Main/Corp Companhia Agricola de Minas Gerais. 1983-. Portuguese. ir. LC HD9014.B84. DD 354.815100823305. *Relatorio*.

RELATORIO ESTATISTICO DE INFORMACOES ECONOMICO-TRIBUTARIAS. Portuguese. an. LC HJ5715.B8. DD 336.2713098151.

RELATORIO ESTATISTICO - SERVICO DE ESTATISTICA POLICIAL E CRIMINAL. Main/Corp Bahia, Brazil (State). Servico de Estatistica Policial e Criminal. Portuguese. an. LC HV7333.B33. DD 364.981420212.

REPERES; ECONOMIE DU LANGUEDOC-ROUSILLON. April 1972-. 0395-9031. Periodical. FR. French. qt. INSEE-CNGP, BP 2718, 80027 Amiens Cedex France. *SUD*.

REPERES ET REFERENCES STATISTIQUES SUR LES ENSEIGNEMENTS ET LA FORMATION. VFOAT Reperes et References Statistiques. 1st Ed. (Ed. 1984)-. 0761-3423. FR. French. an. 50. 58 Boulevard du Lycee, 92170 Vanves Cedex France.

REPORT FROM THE DEPARTMENT OF MATHEMATICS AND STATISTICS. VFOAT Rapport du Department of Mathematics and Statistics. 0824-4944. Monographic Series. CN. English. McGill University, Department of Mathematics and Statistics, Burnside Hall, 805 Sherbrooke Street West, Montreal Quebec H3A 2K6 Canada. DD 510.

REPORT OF EDUCATIONAL STATISTICS. Main/Corp Delaware. State Board of Education. 1970/71-. 0362-8787. US. English. an. Department of Public Instruction, Townsend Building, Dover DE 19901. LC LA252. DD 370.9751. *Annual Report - State Department of Public Instruction, Part I. Statistical Section*.

REPORT OF MEDICAL ASSISTANCE & COUNTY INDIGENT STATISTICS. VFOAT Report of Medical Assistance and County Indigent Statistics. FY 1979-80-. US. English. an. Free. Bureau of Cost Management, Division of Health Care Financing and Standards, PO Box 2500, Salt Lake City UT 84110. Tel (801)533-7329. LC HD7102.U5. DD 362.10425209792. Circ 500. Expenditure and program analysis of public medical assistance programs in Utah. *Utah Report of Medicaid Statistics, 0193-4252*.

REPORT OF STATISTICAL INFORMATION FOR INDIANA SCHOOL CORPORATIONS. Main/Corp Indiana. Dept. of Public Instruction. US. English. an. LC L146.

REPORT OF THE REGISTRAR-GENERAL OF CEYLON ON VITAL STATISTICS FOR . . . . 1950-. 0254-0924. English. an. NLM W2 JC4 R3V. *Report on Vital Statistics for the Year, 0254-0916*.

REPORT OF THE STATISTICAL COMMISSION. Main/Corp United Nations. Economic and Social Council. Statistical Commission. VFOAT Report to the Economic and Social Council on the . . . Session of the Commission. 1st Session (Jan. 27/Feb. 7, 1947)-. US. English. ir. United Nations, Sales Section Room A 3315, New York NY 10017. Tel (212)754-8302. LC JX1977. DD 310.611.

REPORT OF VITAL STATISTICS FOR OHIO. Main/Corp Ohio. Division of Vital Statistics. VFOAT Vital Statistics. 0147-5614. US. English. an. Ohio Department of Health, 65 South Front Street/PO Box 118, Columbus OH 43213. LC HA571. DD 312.09771. *Report of Vital Statistics*.

REPORT ON MATERNAL DEATHS IN AUSTRALIA. Began with: 1964-66. 0728-604X. AT. English. te. NLM W2 KA8 N2RR. *Maternal Deaths in the Commonwealth of Australia*.

REPORT ON THE . . . AGRICULTURE SURVEY. See Agriculture.

REPORT ON THE DISTILLED LIQUOR INDUSTRY. Main/Corp Canada. Bureau of Statistics. 1919/20-. Periodical. CN. English. an. Statistics Canada Publications Distributions, Ottawa Ontario K1A 0T6 Canada. LC HD9364.C3. DD 338.476635.

REPORT ON THE GENERAL HOUSEHOLD SURVEY FIRST ROUND. Vol. 1 (June 1976-July 1977)-. English. ir. 2.00. LC HA4733. DD 312.09664.

REPORT ON THE INTERNATIONAL TECHNICAL CONFERENCE ON EXPERIMENTAL SAFETY VEHICLES. See Indexes/Abstracts.

REPORT ON THE PROBATION AND WELFARE SERVICE WITH STATISTICS FOR THE YEAR . . . . See Sociology: General Works, Theory - Social Pathology, Welfare, Criminology.

REPORT ON VITAL STATISTICS & REGISTRATIONS. Main/Corp Barbados. Registration Office. BB. English. ir. Barbados Government Print Office, Bridgetown Barbados West Indies. LC HA865. DD 312.0972981.

REPORT SERIES ON MENTAL HEALTH STATISTICS. SERIES B. ANALYTICAL AND SPECIAL STUDY REPORTS. VFOAT Analytical and Special Study Reports. No. 6- 1974-. 0363-9800. Monographic Series. US. English. ir. NLM W2 A N204MD. *Mental Health Statistics. Series B*.

REPORTS OF STATISTICAL APPLICATION RESEARCH, UNION OF JAPANESE SCIENTISTS AND ENGINEERS. (REPORTS OF STATISTICAL APPLICATION RESEARCH). V. 1- March 1951-. 0034-4842. Periodical. JA. English. qt. Japan Publishers Trading Company Ltd, PO Box 5030, Tokyo International, Tokyo 100-31 Japan. Ind/Abst Math. Rev., Int. Aerosp. Abstr., Comput. Control Abstr., Electr. Electron. Abstr., Sci. Abstr. Sect. A. Phys. Abstr., Phys. Abstr. LC HA1. CODEN RARJAT.

REPORTS. ST. (REPORTS : ST). Main/Conf Inter-African Conference on Statistics. VFOAT Reports: Statistics. 1- 1955-. 0414-0532. Periodical. UK. English. ir. Europa Publications, 18 Bedford Square, London WC1B 3JN England. DD 316.

RESEARCH AND STATISTICS ANNUAL REPORT. Main/Corp South Dakota. State Dept. of Public Welfare. Division of Research and Statistics. 0099-2305. US. English. an. SD Department of Public Welfare, Division of Research and Statistics, Office Building, Number One, Pierre SD 57501. LC HV86. DD 353.97830084.

RESEARCH BULLETIN - COMMONWEALTH OF MASSACHUSETTS, DEPARTMENT OF EDUCATION, DIVISION OF RESEARCH AND STATISTICS. See Education (General).

RESEARCH - TRAFFIC INJURY RESEARCH FOUNDATION OF CANADA. See Transportation - Roads and Traffic.

RESENHA ESTATISTICA DO RIO GRANDE DO SUL. 0102-0226. BL. Portuguese. ir. Fundacao de Economia e Estistica, Caixa Postal 2355, 90.000 Porot Alegre Brazil. LC HC188.R4. DD 318.165.

RESIDENT & RECORDED LIVE BIRTHS, INFANT DEATHS, AND DEATHS FOR ILLINOIS LARGER CITIES. VFOAT Resident and Recorded Live Births, Infant Deaths, and Deaths for Illinois Larger Cities. 1979-. US. English. an. Illinois Department of Public Health, 535 West Jefferson, Springfield IL 62706. LC HA341. DD 312.09773. *Resident and Recorded Live Births, Infant Deaths, and Deaths for the Larger Cities in Illinois*.

RESOURCE-DATA BOOK. 0091-3758. US. English. an. State Capital Area Planning Council, Capital Station, Austin TX 78711. LC HA651. DD 317.64.

RESTAURANT, CATERER AND TAVERN STATISTICS. VFOAT Statistiques des Restaurants, Traiteurs et Tavernes. 0226-2320. CN. English (French). mo. $18.00. LC TX910.C2. DD 338.476479571. *Restaurant Statistics, 0008-2627*.

RETENCION Y DESGRANAMIENTO : EDUCACION PRIMARIA, EDAD ESCOLAR. Main/Corp Argentine Republic. Ministerio de Cultura y Educacion. Departamento de Estadistica. VFOAT Estadisticas de la Educacion. Periodical. Spanish. ir. Ministerio de Cultura y Educacion, Departamento de Estadistica, Av E Madero 235-1Er Piso, Buenos Aires Argentina.

THE REVIEW OF ECONOMICS AND STATISTICS. See Economics.

REVISTA DE ESTADISTICA Y GEOGRAFIA. Vol. 1, No. 1 (Jan.-March 1980)-. Periodical. MX. Spanish. qt. Subdireccion de Integracion de Informacion, Insurgentes Sur 795, Piso 9 Mexico 18 DF. LC HA37. DD 317.2.

REVISTA DE STATISTICA. 0556-6398. Periodical. RM. Romanian (some issues have summaries and tables of contents in English, French, and Russian). mo. Ilexim Press, PO Box 1-136-1-137, Bucharest Romania. Ind/Abst Coal Abstr. LC HA1.

REVUE DE STATISTIQUE APPLIQUEE. V. 1- 1953-. 0035-175X. Periodical. FR. French. qt. 415. Science Statistique (Ceresta), 10 rue Bertin Poiree, 75001 Paris France. Tel 42 33 97 14. Ind/Abst Math. Rev., Energy Res. Abstr. NLM W1 RE805G. CODEN RVSTA7. Circ 800. Publishes papers on applied statistics.

REVUE ECONOMIQUE - CHAMBRE DE COMMERCE DE LAVAL. See Business.

REVUE STATISTIQUE DU CANADA. SUPPLEMENT. No. 1- 1953-. 0823-311X. Periodical. CN. French. be. Canadian Bureau of Statistics, Publications Distribution, Ottawa Ontario K1A 0T6 Canada. LC HA745. DD 317.1.

REVUE STATISTIQUE DU QUEBEC. Main/Corp Quebec Bureau of Statistics. VFOAT Quebec Statistical Review. CN. English and French. $2.00. Quebec Bureau of Statistics, Quebec Official Publisher, Parliament Buildings, Quebec Canada. LC HA747. DD 317.14. *Statistique*.

REVUE STATISTIQUE DU QUEBEC CEASED. VFOAT Quebec Statistical Review. VAT Quebec Statistical Review (1973). Began with V. 12, No. 1. Ceased with V. 19, No. 1/2/3/4. 0383-4603. Periodical. CN. English (text also in French Sept. 1973-Mar. 1975). qt. Ind/Abst Foreign Lang. Index. *Statistiques (Quebec Bureau of Statistics. Statistical Information Centre), 0039-0550*.

RHODE ISLAND BASIC ECONOMIC STATISTICS. Main/Corp Rhode Island. Economic Research Division. 0361-0632. US. English. Rhode Island Department of Economic Development, One Weybosset Hill, Providence RI 02903. LC HA614. DD 317.45. *Rhode Island Basic Economic Statistics, 0361-0632*.

RICE STATISTICS YEARBOOK. VFOAT Annuaire Statistique du Riz. 1st- Ed. LB. English and French. an. LC HD9066.A46. DD 338.173180966.

RIKSREVISIONSVERKETS TAXERINGSSTATISTISKA UNDERSOKNING TAXERINGSARET . . . . Series/Titl Sveriges Officiella Statistik. Statistiska Meddelanden. SW. Swedish. an. Liber Distribution, Prenumerationsorder, 162 89 Stockholm Sweden.

Statistics

RINDERRASSENERHEBUNG. Main/Corp Osterreichisches Statistisches Zentralamt. Series/Titl Beitrage zur Osterreichischen Statistik. German. ir. Kommissionsverlag Osterreichische Staatsdruckerei, Rennweg 12A, 1037 Wien Austria. LC HA1173, SF196.A8.

RIVISTA ITALIANA DI ECONOMIA, DEMOGRAFIA E STATISTICA. 0035-6832. Periodical. IT. Italian. qt. 40.000. Rivista Italiana di Economia Demografia e Statistica, Via Filippo Nicola 1 49, 00136 Rome Italy. Tel 06-3451503. Ind/Abst Foreign Lang. Index. LC HB3599. bk rev. Circ 850. (ctrl). Problems on economics, demography, statistics, sociology, book reviews and other scientific information. *Rivista Italiana di Demografia e Statistica.*

RIVON LI-STATISTIKAH SHEL TAHBURAH. Main/Corp Israel. Lishkah Ha-Merkazit Li-Statistikah. VFOAT Quarterly Transport Statistics. Kereck 1- Yanuar 1974-. English and Hebrew. ir. $8.00. Ha-Lishkah Ha-Merkazit Li-Statistikah, Street B No 29 Hakirya, Yerushalayim Israel. Tel (00-972)2-211400. LC HE96.I8. Periodic official statistics on all divisions of Israel's land, air and sea transportation and various special surveys.

ROAD STATISTICS IN KARNATAKA STATE. Main/Corp Karnataka, India. Public Works Dept. Statistical Unit. English. ir. Public Works Department, Statistical Unit, Communications and Buildings Central Office 1, Bangalore India. LC HE365.I44. DD 388.1095487. *Road Statistics in Mysore State.*

ROCZNIK STATYSTYCZNY. *See* Yearbooks, Almanacs, Directories.

ROCZNIK STATYSTYCZNY MIAST. Series/Titl Statystyka Polski. 1980-. PL. Polish. an. 90.00. 00-068 Warszawa, Ksiegarnia Naukowa Im. Bolesawa Prusa, UL. Krakowskie Przemdiescie 7, Warszawa Poland. LC HA1451.

ROCZNIK STATYSTYCZNY MIASTA KOSZALINA CEASED. V. 1- 1971-. PL. Polish. ir. 20.00 Single Issue. Gowna Ksiegarnia Naukowa Im B Prusa, Warszawa Ul Krakowski Przedmiescie 7, Koszalin Poland. LC HA1458.K66.

ROCZNIK STATYSTYCZNY MIASTA NYSY CEASED. V. 1- 1971-. PL. Polish. ir. 20.00 Single Issue. Gowna Ksiegarnia Naukowa Im B Prusa, Warszawa ul Krakowskie Przedmiescie 7, Nysa Poland. LC HA1458.N9.

ROCZNIK STATYSTYCZNY MIASTA PIOTRKOWA TRYBUNALSKIEGO. V. 1- 1971-. Polish. ir. 20. Gowna Ksiegarnia Naukowa Im B Prusa, Ul Krakowskie Przedmiescie 7, Warszawa Poland. LC HA1458.P5.

ROCZNIK STATYSTYCZNY MIASTA WOCAWKA CEASED. V. 1- 1971-. PL. Polish. ir. 20.00. Warsawa Gowna Ksiegarna Naukowa, IM B Prusa UL Krakowskie Przedmiescie 7, Warszawa Poland. LC HA1458.W55.

ROCZNIK STATYSTYCZNY MIASTA ZDUNSKIEJ WOLI. V. 1- 1971-. PL. Polish. ir. 20.00. Warszawa Gowna Ksiegarnia Naukowa Im B Prusa, Ul Krakowskie Przedmiescie 7, Warszawa Poland. LC HA1458.Z47.

ROCZNIK STATYSTYCZNY POWIATU BARTOSZYCE CEASED. V. 1- 1971-. PL. Polish. ir. 20 Single Issue. Gowna Ksiegarnia Naukowa Im B Prusa, Warszawa Ul Krakowskie Przedmiescie 7, Bartoszyce Poland. LC HA1457.B36.

ROCZNIK STATYSTYCZNY POWIATU CHRZANOW I MIASTA JAWORZNO CEASED. V. 1- 1971-. Polish. ir. 20.00. Gowna Ksiegarnia Naukowa Im B Prusa, Warszawa Ul Krakowskie Przedmiescie 7, Chrzanow Poland. LC HA1457.C47.

ROCZNIK STATYSTYCZNY POWIATU IAWA CEASED. V. 1- 1971-. PL. Polish. ir. 20 Single Issue. Gowna Ksiegarnia Naukowa Im B Prusa, Warszawa Ul Krakowskie Przedmiescie 7, Iawa Poland. LC HA1457.I4.

ROCZNIK STATYSTYCZNY POWIATU KROSNO. V. 1- 1971-. Polish. ir. 20.00. Powiatowy Inspektorat Statystyczwy, Warszawa Cowna Ksiegarnia Naukowa Im B Prusa UL Krakowskie, Przedmiescie 7, Krosno Poland. LC HA1457.K75.

ROCZNIK STATYSTYCZNY POWIATU MRAGOWO CEASED. V. 1- 1971-. PL. Polish. ir. 20 Single Issue. Gowna Ksiegarnia Naukowa Im B Prusa, Warszawa Ul Krakowskie Przedmiescie 7, Mragowa Poland. LC HA1457.M7.

ROCZNIK STATYSTYCZNY POWIATU OSTRODA. V. 1- 1971-. PL. Polish. ir. 20. Powiatowy Inspektorat Statystyezay, UL Krakowskie Przedmiescie 7, Ostroda Poland. LC HA1457.O8.

ROCZNIK STATYSTYCZNY POWIATU TARNOW CEASED. V. 1- 1971-. PL. Polish. ir. 20.00 Single Issue. Gowna Ksiegarnia Naukowa Im B Prusa, Warszawa ul Krakowskie Przedmiescie 7, Tarnow Poland. LC HA1457.T3.

ROCZNIK STATYSTYCZNY POWIATU ZOTOW CEASED. V. 1- 1971-. PL. Polish. ir. 20. Gowna Ksiegarnia Naukowa IM B Prusa, Warszawa UL Krakowskie Przedmiescie 7, Zotow Poland. LC HA1457.Z6.

ROCZNIK STATYSTYCZNY WOJEWODZTW. Series/Titl Statystyka Polski. 1976-. Polish. ir. 42.00. Gowna Ksiegarnia Naukowa Im Bolesawa Prusa, Ul Krakowskie Przedmiescie 7, Warszawa Poland. LC HA1451. *Statystyka Wojewodztw.*

ROCZNIK STATYSTYCZNY WOJEWODZTWA WROCAWSKIEGO I MIASTA WROCAWIA. Began with vol. for 1976. Polish. an. 40.00. Ksiegarnia Im Marchlewskiego, Rynek 60, 50-116 Wrocaw Poland. LC HA1457.W76. *Rocznik Statystyczny Wojewodztwa Wrocawskiego, Rocznik Statystyczny Miasta Wrocawia.*

ROENI U SR SRBIJI. Began with vol. for 1970-1976. YU. Serbo-Croatian(R). ir. 80.00. Republicki Zavod za Statistiku Sr Srbije, M Rakica 5, Beograd Yugoslavia. LC HA1651, HA1634. S47.

ROSTOCKER MATHEMATISCHES KOLLOQUIUM. *See* Mathematics.

DE ROTTERDAMSE HAVEN IN CIJFERS. VFOAT Le Port de Rotterdam en Chiffres, The Port of Rotterdam in Figures. 1982-. NE. Dutch (English, French, and German). an. Kamer van Koophandel en Fabrieken voor Rotterdam en de Beneden-Maas, Coolsingel 58, 3011 AE Rotterdam The Netherlands. *Rotterdam: Statistiek van Handel, Nijverheid en Verkeer.*

ROUND-UP OF ECONOMIC STATISTICS. Main/Corp Australia. Treasury. AT. English. mo. $36.90. Australian Government Publishing Service, PO Box 84, Canberra Australian Capital Territory 2600 Australia. Tel (062) 95 4411. LC HC601. DD 330.99406.

THE RUBBER INDUSTRY STATISTICAL REPORT, AND, CHANGING MARKETS AND MANUFACTURING PATTERNS IN THE SYNTHETIC RUBBER INDUSTRY. VFOAT Changing Markets and Manufacturing Patterns in the Synthetic Rubber Industry. US. English. an.

RUBBER, PRODUCTION, SHIPMENTS, AND STOCKS. *See* Rubber.

RUBBER STATISTICAL BULLETIN. V. 1- July 1946-. 0035-9548. Periodical. UK. English. mo. $57.00 Domestic, $67.00 Foreign. International Rubber Study Group, Brettenham House 5-6 Lancaster Place, London WC2E 7ET England. Tel 01-836 6811. *Statistical Bulletin.*

RURAL COMMUNICATION STATISTICS IN KARNATAKA STATE. Main/Corp Karnataka, India. Public Works Dept. 1973-. English. ir. LC HE365.I44. DD 388.1095487. *Rural Communication Statistics in Mysore State.*

RURAL STATISTICS OF THE AUSTRALIAN CAPITAL TERRITORY. Main/Corp Australian Bureau of Statistics. AT. English. ir. Australian Bureau of Statistics, PO Box 84, Canberra Australian Capital Territory 2600 Australia. LC HD2155.A8. DD 338.109947. *Rural Statistics of the Australian Capital Territory.*

SAARLAND HEUTE. German. ir. Statistisches Amt des Saarlendes, Hardenbergstrasse 3, 6000 Saarbrucken. LC HA1320.S24. DD 314.342.

SAARLANDISCHE KREISZAHLEN. August 1981-. 0486-7890. German. ir. 4.00. Statistisches Amt Des Saarlandes, Postfach 409, Hardenbergstr 3 6600 Saarbrucken West Germany. LC HA1248.S23. DD 314.342.

SAENGMYONG POHOM TONGGYE YONBO. *See* Yearbooks, Almanacs, Directories.

SAIKIN NO JINKO DOTAI. Main/Corp Japan. Koseisho. Tokei Johobu. No. 10-. Japanese. ir. LC HA1831. *Tokei Chosabu.*

ST. CLOUD SMSA LABOR MARKET INFORMATION SUMMARY FOR . . . . VFOAT St. Cloud S.M.S.A. Labor Market Information Summary for . . . . US. English. an. Minnesota Department of Economic Security, Central Minnesota Labor Market Information Center, 2700 North 1st Street/Room 2700, St Cloud MN 56301. LC HD5726.S27. DD 331.120977647. *St. Cloud SMSA Annual Planning Information Report.*

SAISEKI TOKEI NENPO. *See* Yearbooks, Almanacs, Directories.

SALARIES, WAGES AND FRINGE BENEFITS OF OKLAHOMA CITIES AND TOWNS. *See* Economics - Labor.

SALARY STATISTICS FOR LARGE PUBLIC LIBRARIES. Main/Corp Enoch Pratt Free Library. 0423-1937. US. English. ir. Enoch Pratt Free Library, 400 Cathedral Street, Baltimore MD 21201. LC Z682.3. DD 023.8.

SAMOUPRAVLJANJE U BANKAMA I ZAJEDNICAMA OSIGURANJA. VFOAT Self-Management in Banks and Communities of Insurance. 1979-. Serbo-Croatian. ir. 5.00. Savezni Zavod za Statistiku, Kneza Milosa BR 20, Beograd Yugoslavia. LC HA1631, HG3232.

SAMOUPRAVLJANJE U USTANOVAMA DRUSTVENIH SLUZBI. Main/Corp Savezni Zavod Za Statistiku (Yugoslavia). Serbo-Croatian(R). ir. 10.00. Savezni Zavod Za Statistiku, Kneza Milosa 20, Beograd Yugoslavia. LC HA1631, HD5660.Y8.

SAMOUPRAVNE INTERESNE ZAJEDNICE. Main/Corp Savezni Zavod Za Statistiku (Yugoslavia). 1973-. Serbo-Croatian(R). ir. 10.00. Savezni Zavod Zu Statistiku, Kneza Milosa 20, Beograd Yugoslavia. LC HA1631, HS71.Y8.

SAMPLE SURVEYS OF CURRENT INTEREST. Began with: 1st (Feb. 28, 1949). US. English. ir. United Nations Statistical Office, Publications Sales Section/Room A 3315, New York NY 10017. LC HA13. DD 311.22. (cum index).

SAN FRANCISCO STATISTICAL ABSTRACT. *See* Indexes/Abstracts.

SANFORD EVANS GOLD BOOK OF MOTORCYCLE DATA AND USED PRICES. *See* Motorcycles.

SANFORD EVANS GOLD BOOK OF SNOWMOBILE DATA AND USED PRICES. *See* Transportation.

SANKHYIKIYA DAYARI. Main/Corp Uttar Pradesh (India) Directorate of Economics and Statistics. VFOAT Statistical Diary. Hindi and English. ir. India Department of Economics and Statistics, Lucknow India. LC HA1728.U7.

SANKHYIKIYA PUSTIKA. Main/Corp Delhi (Union Ter.). Bureau of Economics and Statistics. VFOAT Statistical Hand Book. Began publication in 1970. Periodical. II. Hindi (English). ir. Bureau of Economics & Statistics, New Delhi India.

SAOBRACAJ I VEZE. Main/Corp Savezni Zavod za Statistiku (Yugoslavia). Series Corp Its Statisticki Bilten. Serbo-Croatian(R). ir. 30.-. Kneza Milosa 20, Beograd Yugoslavia. LC HA1631.

SAOBRACAJNE NEZGODE NA PUTEVIMA. Main/Corp Yugoslavia. Savezni Zavod za Statistiku. VFOAT Transport Accidents on Roads. YU. Serbo-Croatian. ir. 15.00. Savezni Zavod za Statistiku, Kneza Milosa Br 20, Beograd Yugoslavia. LC HA1631, HE5614.5. Y8.

SAR STATISTICS. VFOAT S.A.R. Statistics. VAT Search and Rescue Statistics. 0163-2833. US. English. an. United States Coast Guard, 400 Seventh Street SW, Washington DC 20591. LC TL553.8. DD 361.58.

SARVEKSHANA. V. 1- July 1977-. Periodical. II. English (with summaries in Hindi). ir. $10.00. Chief Executive Officer, National Sample Survey Organisation, Sardar Patel Bhavan Parliament Street, New Delhi 110001 India. LC HA1724. DD 315.4. Index in last issue of volume - attached.

SASKATCHEWAN PROVINCIAL HIGHWAYS ACCIDENT STATISTICS. VFOAT Accident Statistics. VAT Accidents Statistics (Regina). Began publication 1973?. 0318-2819. CN. English. Saskatchewan Highways & Transportation, 1855 Victoria Avenue, Regina Saskatchewan S4P 3V5 Canada. DD 388.314.

SCANDINAVIAN JOURNAL OF STATISTICS. (SCANDINAVIAN JOURNAL OF STATISTICS, THEORY AND APPLICATIONS). V. 1- 1974-. 0303-6898. Periodical. SW. English. ty. $68.00.

Statistics

Almqvist & Wiksell, 108 Drottninggatan, PO Box 45150, S-104 30 Stockholm Sweden. **Tel** (08)783-4490. **Ed** Benat Rosen. **Ind/Abst** Math. Rev., Comput. Control Abstr., Electr. Electron. Abstr., Sci. Abstr. Sect. A. Phys. Abstr., Phys. Abstr. **LC** QA276.A1. **DD** 519.505. **NLM** W1 SC154BN. **CODEN** SJSADG. **adv acc. Circ** 1,000. Publishes research papers on statistical theory and its applications including relevant aspects of probability.

SCBS BILKALENDER. VFOAT S.C.B.S Bilkalender. V. 1 (1983)-. Swedish. an. Statistiska Centralbyran, Aarsbok Foer Snerige, 115 81 Stockholm Sweden.

SCHEDULE B, STATISTICAL CLASSIFICATION OF DOMESTIC AND FOREIGN COMMODITIES EXPORTED FROM THE UNITED STATES. Main/Corp United States. Bureau of the Census. VFOAT Statistical Classification of Domestic and Foreign Commodities Exported from the United States. Began with: Nov. 1941. US. English. ir. $40.00. US Department of Commerce, Bureau of the Census, Washington DC 20233. **Tel** (202)783-3238. *Schedule B, Statistical Classification of Domestic and Foreign Commodities Exported from the United States.*

SCHEDULE C-I. CLASSIFICATION OF COUNTRY AND TERRITORY DESIGNATIONS FOR U.S. IMPORT STATISTICS. (SCHEDULE C-I, CLASSIFICATION OF COUNTRY AND TERRITORY DESIGNATIONS FOR U.S. IMPORT STATISTICS). VFOAT Classification of Country and Territory Designations for U.S. Import Statistics. Began with Jan. 1, 1976. 0191-4057. US. English. US Department of Commerce, Bureau of the Census, Washington DC 20233. **LC** HF3005. **DD** 382.50973. *U.S. Foreign Trade. Schedule C, Classification of Country Designations.*

SCHOOL MEDIA STATISTICS. Main/Corp New Jersey. Library Development Bureau. VFOAT Statistics, New Jersey School Media Programs. 0098-3179. US. English. Library Development Bureau, 116 West State Street, Trenton NJ 08608. **LC** Z675.S3. **DD** 027.809749. *School Media Statistics.*

DIE SCHULDEN DES LANDES, DER GEMEINDEN, GEMEINDEVERBANDE UND ZWECKVERBANDE AM . . . . See Business - Public Finance.

DIE SCHWEIZ IN KURVEN = LA SUISSE EN DIAGRAMMES. VFOAT Suisse en Diagrammes. Periodical. SZ. French (German). ir. 85.00. Economica Verlag AG, Dorneckstr 105, 4143 Dornach Switzerland. **LC** HA1604. **DD** 314.94.

SCHWEIZERISCHE BIBLIOGRAPHIE FUR STATISTIK UND VOLKSWIRTSCHAFT. VFOAT Bibliographie Suisse de Statistique et d'Economie Politique,. Yearly V. 1-. introductory matter in German and French. ir. $17.32. Federal Office of Statistics, Hallwylstr 15, CH-3003 Berne Switzerland. **LC** Z7552. **DD** 016.3.

SCHWEIZERISCHE BIBLIOTHEKEN. BIBLIOTHEQUES SUISSES. Main/Corp Switzerland. Bundesamt fur Statistik. Series/Titl Beitrage zur Schweizerischen Statistik. VFOAT Bibliotheques Suisses. SZ. French (German). ir. 4.00. Bundesamt fur Statistik, Hallwylstrasse 15, CH 3003 Bern Austria. **LC** HA1593, Z837.A1.

SCHWEIZERISCHE VERKEHRSSTATISTIK. Main/Corp Switzerland. Eidgenossisches Statistisches Amt. VFOAT Statistique Suisse des Transports. 1976-. French (German). ir. **LC** HE263.

SCHWEIZERISCHE ZEITSCHRIFT FUR VOLKSWIRTSCHAFT UND STATISTIK. See Economics - Economic Theory.

SCIENCE STATISTICS. See Science (General).

SCOTTISH ABSTRACT OF STATISTICS. See Indexes/Abstracts.

SCOTTISH HEALTH STATISTICS. 1957/58-. UK. English. an. 10.00. Her Majestys Stationery Office, 13 A Castle Street, Edinburgh EH2 3AR Scotland. **LC** RA243. **DD** 312.09411. **NLM** W2 FS2 D4SC.

SCOTTISH HOUSING STATISTICS. No. 1, 1st Quarter 1978-. UK. English. an. **LC** HD7335.A3. **DD** 338.476908309411. *Housing Return for Scotland.*

SCOTTISH LOCAL GOVERNMENT FINANCIAL STATISTICS. 1975-76 to 1977-78-. UK. English. an. 10.00. Her Majesty's Stationery Office, 13A Castle Street, EH2 3AR Scotland. **LC** HJ9043. **DD** 352.109411. *Local Financial Returns, Scotland.*

SCOTTISH SEA FISHERIES STATISTICAL TABLES. 1939/48-. 0080-8202. UK. English. an. *Sea Fisheries: Statistical Tables.*

SCOTTISH SOCIAL WORK STATISTICS. Main/Corp Great Britain. Scottish Education Dept. Social Work Services Group. 1971-. UK. English. an. 0.82. Her Majestys Stationery Office, 13 A Castle Street, Edinburgh EH2 Scotland. **LC** HV241. **DD** 362.941.

SEA FISHERIES STATISTICAL TABLES. 1919/20-. 0072-6702. UK. English. an. Her Majesty's Stationery Office, PO Box 276, London SW8 5DT England. **LC** SH225. **DD** 338.3727.

SEAMIC HEALTH STATISTICS. Main/Corp Nihon Kokusai Iryodan. Tonan Ajia Iryo Joho Senta. Committee on Health Statistics. Series/Titl SEAMIC Publication. VAT Southeast Asian Medical Information Center Health Statistics. 1979-. JA. English. ir. Southeast Asian Medical Information Center, International Medical Foundation of Japan, No 6 Toyo-Kaiji Building 7-2 Shinbashi 4-chome, Minato-ku 105, Tokyo Japan. **LC** RA407.5.A7842. **DD** 362.10959.

SEC MONTHLY STATISTICAL REVIEW. VAT Securities and Exchange Commission Monthly Statistical Review. Vol. 39, No. 8 (Aug. 1980)-. 0272-7846. US. English. mo. Superintendent of Documents, United States Government Printing Office, Washington DC 20402. **Tel** (202)783-3238. **Ind/Abst** Predicasts, Am. Stat. Index. **LC** HG4501. **DD** 332.60973. *Statistical Bulletin (United States. Securities and Exchange Commission), 0039-0410.*

SEDAROT STATISTIYOT. Main/Corp Ha-Merkaz Le-Tikhnun U-Fituah Haklai Ve-Hityashvuti. VFOAT Statistical Series. Hebrew (with summary in English). ir. Hakiria P O B 7011, Tel Aviv Israel. **LC** HD2111.P32.

SEHAR HUTS SHEL YISRAEL. Series Corp Israel. Ha-Lishkan Ha-Merkazit Le-Statistikah. Sidrat Pirsumin Meyuadim - Ha Lishkah Ha-Merkazit Le-Statistikah. VFOAT Israel's Foreign Trade. 1951-. 0075-1421. Periodical. IS. English, Hebrew. ir. Central Bureau of Statistics, PO Box 13015, 91 130 Jerusalem Israel. **LC** HA1931. **DD** 382.

SEKAI DAITOSHI HIKAKU TOKEI NEMPYO. VFOAT Comparative Statistical Table of World Large Cities. 1961-. Japanese and English. ir.

SELECTED AGRICULTURAL STATISTICS FOR CANADA CEASED. VFOAT Donnees Statistiques Agricoles Canadiennes. VAT Donnees Statistiques Agricoles Canadiennes (1975). 1972-1980. 0317-512X. CN. English (French). an. Sir John Carling Building, Carling Avenue, Ottawa Ontario K1A 0C5 Canada. **LC** S133. **DD** 338.10971. *Agricultural Statistics for Canada, 0380-5484; Donnees Statistiques Agricoles Canadiennes, 1975, 0380-5492.*

SELECTED AGRICULTURAL STATISTICS FOR CANADA. Main/Corp Canada. Dept. of Agriculture. Economics Branch. Communications Unit. VFOAT Donnees Statistiques Agricoles Canadiennes. CN. English and French. an. Sir John Carling Building, Carling Avenue, Ottawa Ontario K1A 0C5 Canada. **LC** S133. **DD** 338.10971.

SELECTED FINANCIAL STATISTICS OF ASSOCIATIONS. Main/Corp Statistics Canada. Merchandising and Services Division. VFOAT Certaines Statistiques Financieres d'Associations. CN. English and French. $0.70. Information Canada, 171 Slater Street, Ottawa Ontario K1A 0S9 Canada. **LC** HD2429.C3. **DD** 338.43.

SELECTED FINANCIAL STATISTICS OF CHARITABLE ORGANIZATIONS. Main/Corp Statistics Canada. VFOAT Certaines Statistiques Financieres des Oeuvres de Charite. 1972/73-. 0318-8787. CN. English (text in French in parallel columns). an. **LC** HV101. **DD** 361.7. *Selected Financial.*

SELECTED MANPOWER STATISTICS. 0501-9427. US. English. an. Department of Defense, Washington Headquarters Services, Washington DC 20301. **LC** UA17.5.U5. **DD** 355.220973. Vols. for (1980-) distributed to depository libraries in microfiche.

SELECTED MEDICAL CARE STATISTICS. 0884-1152. Periodical. US. English. qt. US Government Printing Office, Superintendent of Documents, Washington DC 20402.

Ind/Abst Am. Stat. Index. **LC** UH223. **DD** 355.3450973.

SELECTED STATISTICAL DATA - MARYLAND STATE BOARD FOR COMMUNITY COLLEGES. Main/Corp Maryland. State Board for Community Colleges. 0099-2089. US. English. State Board for Community Colleges, State Treasury Building, Annapolis MD 21404. **LC** LB2328. **DD** 378.154309752.

SELECTED STATISTICS ON STUDENTS AND STAFF IN NEW YORK CITY SCHOOL DISTRICTS. Main/Corp University of the State of New York. Information Center on Education. 0099-0485. US. English. an. University of the State of New York, Information Center on Education, Albany NY 12224. **LC** L183.N5. **DD** 371.10097471.

SELECTED STATISTICS ON TECHNOLOGICAL INNOVATION IN INDUSTRY. Main/Corp Canada. Statistics Canada. Science Statistics Section. VFOAT Certaines Statistiques sur l'Innovation Technologique dans l'Industrie. CN. English and French. Information Canada, 171 Slater Street, Ottawa Ontario K1A 0S9 Canada. **LC** HC120.T4. **DD** 338.

SELECTED STATISTICS ON THE OFFICE OF ATTORNEY GENERAL. Main/Corp National Association of Attorneys General. Committee on the Office of Attorney General. 0145-2436. US. English. 3901 Barrett Drive, Raleigh NC 27609. **LC** KF5107.Z9. **DD** 353.9.

SENTENCING STATISTICS, HIGHER CRIMINAL COURTS, VICTORIA. 0725-654X. English. an. Research Section Law Department, 271 William Street, Melbourne 3000 Victoria Australia. **LC** HV8708. **DD** 364.6509945.

SERI STATISTIK PENGANGKUTAN KERETA API. RAILWAYS STATISTICS. Series/Titl Statistik Perhubungan. VFOAT Statistik Pengangkutan Kereta Api. 0445-9474. Indonesian (English). ir. Biro Pusat Statistik, Jalan Dr Sutomo No 8, Jakarta Indonesia. **Tel** 372808. **LC** HE3331. bk rev. adv acc.

SERIE ESTADISTICA (MENDOZA) (ARGENTINA : PROVINCE). DIRECCION AGROPECUARIA). (SERIE ESTADISTICA). No. 1 (1979)-. Spanish. ir.

SERIES STATISTIQUES DE BRUXELLES. Main/Corp Universite Libre de Bruxelles. Departement d'Economie Appliquee. VFOAT Statistische Reeksen van Brussel. Flemish and French. ir. 900.00. Editions du Dulbea, 50 Avenue F D Roosevelt, 1050 Bruxelles Belgium. **LC** HA1404. **DD** 339.09493.

SERVICE BULLETIN : ENERGY STATISTICS. Main/Corp Statistics Canada. VFOAT Bulletin de Service : La Statistique de l'Energie. 0008-266X. CN. Multilingual. **LC** HD9554.C292. **DD** 333.80971. *Service Bulletin: Energy Statistics.*

SEXUALLY TRANSMITTED DISEASE (STD) STATISTICAL LETTER. VFOAT Sexually Transmitted Disease Statistical Letter. 0190-5759. US. English. US Department of Health and Human Services, Public Health Service Centers for Disease Control, Center for Prevention Services, Division of Veneral Disease Control, Atlanta GA 30333. **LC** RC200.1. **DD** 312.395100973. **NLM** W2 A C75VE. *VD Statistical Letter, 0363-2032.*

SEZNAM PREJETIH STATISTICNIH PUBLIKACIJ, KNJIG IN REVIJ V . . . . Periodical. Slovenian. mo. **LC** Z7555, HA154. *Seznam Prejetih Knjig, Revij in Statisticnih Pulikacij V . . . .*

SHIGEN TOKEI NEMPO. VFOAT Yearbooks of Mining, Non-Ferrous Metals, and Products Statistics. JA. Japanese. ir. 4900. Tsusan Tokei Kyokai, 15-18 Ginza 5, Chuo-ku 104, Tokyo Japan. **LC** HD9506.J3. *Hitetsu Kindoku Seihin Tokei Nempo, Hitetsu Kinzoku To Jukyu Tokei Nempo; Hompo Kogyo No Susei.*

SHIPPING STATISTICS. Main/Corp Institut fur Serverkehrswirtschaft Bermen. VFOAT Statistik der Schiffahrt. English (German). mo. $80.02. Instutute of Shipping Economic Boersenhof A/AM Dom 5A, D2800 Bremen 1 West Germany. **Tel** (04 21)32 10 40. **Ind/Abst** Public Aff. Inf. Serv. Bull. **LC** HE561. **DD** 387.50212.

SHIPPING STATISTICS AND ECONOMICS. VFOAT SSE. Shipping Statistics and Economics. No. 1- Nov. 1970-. 0306-1817. Periodical. UK. English. mo. $375.00. Drewey

Statistics

Shipping Consultants, 34 Brook Street Mayfair, London W1Y 2LL England. **Tel** 629 5362. **Ind/Abst** Public Aff. Inf. Serv. Bull. bk rev. adv acc. (ctrl). Monthly updated record of the whole tanker and dry cargo charter markets, extensive data on shipping demand, fleet developments, freight rates with tables/charts.

SHIPPING STATISTICS OF FIJI. English. ir. Bureau of Statistics, PO Box 2221, Government Buildings, Suva Fiji. **LC** HE933.5. **DD** 387.5099611021. *Shipping Statistics (Suva, Fiji).*

SHUTOKEN TOKEI YORAN. 1974-. JA. Japanese. ir. Kokudocho Daitoshiken Seibikyoku, 6-19 Azabudai 1-chome Minato-ku, Tokyo Japan. **LC** HA1849.T6.

SIAM JOURNAL ON SCIENTIFIC AND STATISTICAL COMPUTING. Main/Corp Society for Industrial and Applied Mathematics. V. 1- Mar. 1980-. 0196-5204. Periodical. US. English. qt. $78.00. Business Manager SIAM Publications, 1405 Architects Building, 117 South 17th Street, Philadelphia PA 19103. **Tel** (215)564-2929. **Ed** Charles William Gear. **Ind/Abst** Math. Rev., Electron. Commun. Abstr. J., ISMEC Bull., Pollut. Abstr. Indexes, Saf. Sci. Abstr. J., Int. Aerosp. Abstr., Comput. Control Abstr., Electr. Electron. Abstr., Sci. Abstr. Sect. A. Phys. Abstr., Sci. Cit. Index, Abr. Ed., Phys. Abstr., Comput. Rev. **LC** QA297. **DD** 519.405. **CODEN** SIJCD4. **Circ** 1,500. Contains articles on numerical statistical and nonnumerical techniques, for solving scientific and statistical problems on computers. Emphasis is on the implementation of such techniques with computer languages.

SINGAPORE EXTERNAL TRADE STATISTICS. Main/Corp Singapore. Dept. of Statistics. 1956-74. 0583-3647. Sl. English. qt. Singapore National Printers Presss, PO Box 485, Singapore.

SINGAPORE STATISTICAL BULLETIN. Main/Corp Singapore. National Statistical Commission. V. 1- June 1972-. Sl. English. ir. $1.00 Each Issue. 31-B Goldhill Plaza Newton Road, 11 Singapore Singapore. **Ind/Abst** Math. Rev., Public Aff. Inf. Serv. Bull. **LC** HA37.S5. **DD** 315.952.

SINGAPORE STATISTICAL CHARTS. 0129-7015. Sl. English. an. $10.00. Singapore National Printers, Publications Sales Division Ground Floor Fullerton Building, Singapore. **LC** HA4600.67. **DD** 315.957.

SINGAPORE STATISTICAL NEWS : SSN. Vol. 6, No. 1-. 0217-4316. Periodical. English. qt. The Editor/Singapore Statistical News, Maxwell Road P O Box 3010, Singapore 9050 Singapore. *NSC Statistical News.*

SINO-US TRADE STATISTICS. **VAT** Sino-United States Trade Statistics. 0196-4607. US. English. an. $25.00. National Council for US-China Trade, 1050 17th Street Northwest/Suite 350, Washington DC 20036. **Tel** (202)429-0340. **Ed** Marianna Graham. **LC** HF3128. **DD** 382.0951073. **Circ** 5,000. (ctrl). Publication of US-China trade statistics, including information on thousands of imports and exports in both value and volume terms for the past five years.

SINOPSE ESTATISTICA ACRE. Main/Corp Fundacao Ibge. Departamento de Divulgacao Estatistica. Portuguese. ir. Fundacao Ibge, Depatamento de Divulgacao Estatistica, Av Franklin Roosevelt 166, Rio de Janeiro Brazil. **LC** HA988.A2.

SINOPSE ESTATISTICA AMAPA. Main/Corp Fundacao Ibge. Departamento de Divulgacao Estatistica. Portuguese. ir. Departamento de Divulgacao Estatistica, Av Franklin Roosevelt 166, Rio de Janeiro Brazil. **LC** HA988.A45. **DD** 318.11.

SINOPSE ESTATISTICA DA REGIAO NORTE. 1981-. Portuguese. ir. Fundacao Instituto Brasileiro de Geografia e Estatistica, Av Brasil 15.671, Lucas 21.241, Rio de Janeiro RJ Brazil. **LC** HA973. **DD** 318.1.

SINOPSE ESTATISTICA DA REGIAO SUL. 1982-. Portuguese. an. Fundacao Instituto Brasileiro de Geografia e Estatistica Ibge, Av Franklin Roosevelt 166, Centro 20.021, Rio de Janeiro RJ Brazil. **LC** HA988.S68. **DD** 318.16.

SINOPSE ESTATISTICA DO BRASIL. Main/Corp Fundacao Instituto Brasileiro de Geografia e Estatistica. V. 5- 1977-. BL. Portuguese. be. $25.00. Inst Brasileiro De Geog E Estat, Av Brasil 15-671 P De Lucas, 21241 Rio de Janeiro Brasil. **Tel** 2304747. **LC** HA984. **DD** 318.1. adv acc. **Circ** 5,000.

Presents analytical comments and statistical data on social, cultural, economic, geophysical, demographic and political-administrative situation of Brazil. *Sinopse Estatistica Do Brasil.*

SINOPSE ESTATISTICA RORAIMA. Main/Corp Fundacao Ibge. Departamento de Divulgacao Estatistica. Series/Titl Sinopses Estaduais. Portuguese. ir. Av Franklin Roosevelt 166, Rio de Janeiro Brazil. **LC** HA988.R87.

SINTESIS ESTADISTICA - MINISTERIO DI ECONOMIA, JUNTA NACIONAL DE CARNES DE LA REPUBLICA ARGENTINA. Main/Corp Argentine Republic. Junta Nacional de Carnes. AG. Spanish. ir.

SINTESIS ESTADISTICA REGIONAL. No. 1 (1980-1981/Sept. 1982)-. Spanish. ir. **LC** HC191. **DD** 330.983005.

SITUATION ECONOMIQUE DE LA REPUBLIQUE RWANDAISE. Main/Corp Rwanda. Direction Generale de la Documentation et de la Statistique Generale. French. ir. B P 46, Kigali Rwanda. **LC** HC557.R8. **DD** 330.96757104.

SJULYKKESSTATISTIKK. Main/Corp Norway. Statistisk Sentralbyra. Series/Titl Norges Offisielle Statistikk. **VFOAT** Marine Casualties. Norwegian (English). ir. **LC** HA1501.

SKATTESTATISTIK. **VFOAT** Steuerstatistik, Steuerstatistik, Tax Statistics. 1968/73-. English (French, German, and Italian). ir. Centre Europeen, Boite Postale 1907, Luxembourg Luxembourg. **LC** HJ2599.5. **DD** 336.20094.

SMSA STATISTICS, DATA FROM THE CLIENT ORIENTED DATA ACQUISITION PROCESS. Series/Titl National Institute on Drug Abuse Statistical Series. Series E DHHS Publication. **VFOAT** S.M.S.A. Statistics, Data from the Client Oriented Data Acquisition Process. **VAT** Standard Metropolitan Statistical Area Statistics, Data from the Client Oriented Data Acquisition Process. 0161-5033. US. English. an. National Institute on Drug Abuse Division of Data and Information Development, 5600 Fishers Lane, Rockville MD 20857. **LC** HV5825. **DD** 362.29.

SOCIAL SECURITY STATISTICS. Main/Corp Great Britain. Dept. of Health and Social Security. 1972-. UK. English. an. 2.25. HMSO Department of Health and Social Security, 49 High Holborn, WCLV 6HB London England. **LC** HD7165. **DD** 368.400942.

SOCIAL TRENDS. (SOCIAL TRENDS : A PUBLICATION OF THE GOVERNMENT STATISTICAL SERVICE). No. 1-. 0306-7742. UK. English. an. Her Majestys Stationery Office, PO Box 276, London SW8 5DT England. **Tel** (01)622-3316. **Ind/Abst** Sociol. Abstr., Soc. Welf. Soc. Plan./Policy Soc. Dev., Lang. Lang. Behav. Abstr. **LC** HA1134. **DD** 314.2.

SOLIDARITE, SANTE. ETUDES STATISTIQUES. Nos. 1-2 (Jan./Feb. Mar./April 1984)-. Periodical. FR. French. bm. 190.00 Domestic, 220.00 Foreign. La Documentation Francaise, 29-31 Quai Voltaire, 75340 Paris Cedex France. *Sante, Securite Sociale.*

SOME STATISTICS ON BACCALAUREATE AND HIGHER DEGREE PROGRAMS IN NURSING. Main/Corp National League for Nursing. Division of Research. 0081-203X. US. English. an. National League for Nursing, 10 Columbus Circle, New York NY 10019. **LC** RT79. **DD** 610.73071173. *Some Statistics on Baccalaureate and Higher Degree Programs in Nursing, 0081-203X.*

SOURCEBOOK OF CRIMINAL JUSTICE STATISTICS. Began with 1973. 0360-3431. US. English. an. NIJ/NCJRS, Box 6000, Rockville MD 20850. **LC** HV7245. **DD** 364.973.

SOURCES OF MORBIDITY DATA FROM THE CLEARINGHOUSE ON CURRENT MORBIDITY STATISTICS PROGRAMS. Main/Corp United States. Division of Public Health Methods. **VFOAT** Sources of Morbidity Data. 1- 1953-. 0500-3210. Periodical. US. English. Superintendent of Documents US Government Printing Office, Washington DC 20402.

SOUTH AFRICAN STATISTICAL JOURNAL. **VFOAT** Suid-Afrikaanse Statistiese Tydskrif. V. 1-. 0038-271X. Periodical. SA. English. sa. 20.00. PO Box 27321 Sunnyside, 0132 Pretoria South Africa. **Ed** T de Wet. **Ind/Abst** Math. Rev. **LC** QA276.A1. **NLM** HA 1 S719. **CODEN** SASSB5. **Circ** 550. Research and applications of statistics and the usage of data.

SOUTH AUSTRALIAN YEAR BOOK. See Yearbooks, Almanacs, Directories.

SOUTH CAROLINA CROP STATISTICS. **VFOAT** South Carolina Crop Statistics, State and County Data. Began with Vol. for 1961. US. English. an. $5.00. USDA SRS, Crop Reporting Board, Room 5829/S Building, Washington DC 20250. **Tel** (803)758-2426. **LC** HD1775.S6, S111. **DD** 338.1 S, 338.109757.

SOUTH CAROLINA PUBLIC LIBRARY ANNUAL STATISTICAL SUMMARY. **VFOAT** Public Library Annual Statistical Summary. FY 1980-. US. English. an. SC State Library, 1500 Senate Street, Columbia SC 29201. **LC** Z732.S72. **DD** 027.0757.

SOUTH CAROLINA VITAL AND MORBIDITY STATISTICS. Main/Corp South Carolina. Division of Biostatistics. 1974-. 0094-6338. US. English. an. 2600 Bull Street, Columbia SC 29201. **Tel** (803)758-5511. **LC** HA621. **DD** 312.09757. **NLM** W2 AS6 D65S. **Circ** 500. Vital statistics for S.C. *South Carolina Vital and Morbidity Statistics, 0094-6338.*

SOUTH DAKOTA EDUCATIONAL STATISTICS DIGEST. Main/Corp South Dakota. Division of Elementary and Secondary Education. 0360-4772. US. English. Department of Education and Cultural Affairs, 411 East Capitol, Pierre SD 57501. **LC** LA364. **DD** 370.9783.

SOUTH DAKOTA VITAL STATISTICS. 1979-. 0732-0442. US. English. an. Vital Records Program, State Department of Health, Joe Foss Building, Pierre SD 57501. **LC** HA631. **DD** 312.09783. *South Dakota Vital Statistics Annual Report, 0095-4802.*

SOUTHWEST EMPLOYMENT & EARNINGS. See Economics - Labor.

SPECIAL STUDIES PAPER - DIVISION OF RESEARCH AND STATISTICS, FEDERAL RESERVE BOARD. Main/Corp United States. Board of Governors of the Federal Reserve System. US. English. Federal Reserve Board, Division of Research and Statistics, Washington DC 20551. **LC** HG538. **DD** 332.4973.

SREDNJE USMERENO OBRAZOVANJE (PO REGIONIMA I OPSTINAMA). Pocetak Skolske 1980/81 G.-. Serbo-Croatian -R. ir. 80.00. Republicki Zavod za Statistiku Sr Srbije, M Rakica 5, Beograd Yugoslavia.

STAFF PAPER IN ECONOMICS AND STATISTICS. 0091-2190. US. English. Superintendent of Documents, US Government Printing Office, Washington DC 20402. **LC** HC101. **DD** 330.973092.

STANDARD METROPOLITAN STATISTICAL AREAS. Main/Corp United States. Office of Management and Budget. Statistical Policy Division. 0362-5397. US. English. Office of Management and Budget, Robert Brown 726 Jackson Place NW, Washington DC 20503. **LC** HT334.U5. **DD** 317.3.

STANDARD METROPOLITAN STATISTICAL AREAS STATISTICS, DATA FROM THE CLIENT ORIENTED DATA ACQUISITION PROCESS. (SMSA STATISTICS, DATA FROM THE CLIENT ORIENTED DATA ACQUISITION PROCESS). Main/Corp United States. National Institute on Drug Abuse. Division of Scientific and Program Information. Periodical. US. English. an. National Institute on Drug Abuse, Division of Scientific and Program Information, 5600 Fishers Lane, Rockville MD 20857.

STATE AND METROPOLITAN AREA DATA BOOK. 1979-. 0276-6566. US. English. an. Superintendant of Documents, US Government Printing Office, Washington DC 20402. **LC** HA202. **DD** 317.3. **NLM** W2 A B9S.

STATE AND REGIONAL ECONOMIC ILLINOIS DATA BOOK. See Economics.

STATE COURT CASELOAD STATISTICS, ADVANCE REPORT. 1975-. US. English. an. US Department of Justice, Law Enforcement Assistance Administration, National Criminal Justice Information and Statistics Service, Washington DC 20531.

Statistics

STATE COURT CASELOAD STATISTICS, ANNUAL REPORT. 1975-. US. English. an. Superintendent of Documents, US Government Printing Office, Washington DC 20402. LC KF180. DD 347.7313.

STATE DATA CENTER DATA DEVELOPMENTS BULLETIN. No. 1 (Jan. 1983)-. Periodical. US. English. mo. Free. Department of Commerce, 99 Washington Avenue, Albany NY 12245. Tel (518)474-6005. Ed Leonard M Gaines. LC HA37.U7. DD 310.60747. Circ 1,200. Newsletter containing news about the release of data and reports from the US Census Bureau or other sources regarding New York state.

STATE OF HAWAII DATA BOOK. (THE STATE OF HAWAII DATA BOOK). Main/Corp Hawaii. Dept. of Planning And Economic Development. 1967-. 0073-1080. US. English. an. $15.00. State of Hawaii, PO Box 2359, Department of Planning & Economic Development, Honolulu HI 96804. Tel (808)548-4620. Ed Robert C Schmitt. LC HA329.1. DD 319.69. Circ 3,000. More than 700 pages of data about the state of Hawaii with detailed index and 24 subject sections. *Statistical Abstract of Hawaii.*

STATE OF NORTH CAROLINA UNIFORM CRIME REPORT. See Sociology: General Works, Theory - Social Pathology, Welfare, Criminology.

STATE STATISTICS, DATA FROM THE CLIENT ORIENTED DATA ACQUISITION PROCESS. Series/Titl National Institute on Drug Abuse Statistical Series. Series E. DHHS Publication. VFOAT Data from the Client Oriented Data Acquisition Process. 0161-4967. US. English. an. National Institute on Drug Abuse, Division of Data and Information Development, 5600 Fishers Lane, Rockville MD 20857. LC HV5825. DD 362.29.

STATEMENT OF ACCOUNTS AND STATISTICS. Main/Corp Electricity Council. UK. English. an. 1.50. Electricity Council, 30 Millbank, London SW1P 4RD England. LC HD9685.G73. DD 363.620942.

STATISTICA. Year 1- (No. 1-) Jan./Mar. 1941-. 0390-590X. Periodical. Italian. ir. Ind/Abst Math. Rev., Foreign Lang. Index, Popul. Index, Index Econ. Artic. J. Collect. Vol. NLM HA 1 S797. CODEN STATDJ. (cum index). *Nuovi Problemi di Politica, Storia ed Economia. Supplemento Statistico.*

STATISTICA ANNUALE DEL COMMERCIO CON L'ESTERO. Main/Corp Istituto Centrale di Statistica (Italy). 0075-1871. IT. Italian. an. $13.06. Istituto Centrale di Statist, Via Cesare Balbo 16, Roma Italy. LC HF199.

STATISTICA NEERLANDICA. Year 9, No. 1/2-. 0039-0402. Periodical. NE. Dutch (English). qt. 125.- Domestic, $37.50 US, 32.50 UK. Vereniging voor Statistiek, Kruislaan 413, 1098 SJ Amsterdam Netherlands. Tel (20)592-4048. Ind/Abst Math. Rev. LC HA1. bk rev. Scientific statistical research journal including review papers on subfields of probability and statistics. *Statistics (Vereniging voor Statistiek).*

STATISTICAL ABSTRACT. See Indexes/Abstracts.

STATISTICAL ABSTRACT. See Indexes/Abstracts.

STATISTICAL ABSTRACT - CENTRAL STATISTICAL OFFICE. See Indexes/Abstracts.

STATISTICAL ABSTRACT - EMPLOYEES' STATE INSURANCE CORPORATION. See Indexes/Abstracts.

STATISTICAL ABSTRACT, INDIA. See Indexes/Abstracts.

STATISTICAL ABSTRACT - NEW YORK STATE DEPARTMENT OF STATE. See Indexes/Abstracts.

STATISTICAL ABSTRACT OF COLORADO. See Indexes/Abstracts.

STATISTICAL ABSTRACT OF IRELAND. See Indexes/Abstracts.

STATISTICAL ABSTRACT OF ISRAEL. See Indexes/Abstracts.

STATISTICAL ABSTRACT OF LATIN AMERICA. See Indexes/Abstracts.

STATISTICAL ABSTRACT OF MAHARASHTRA STATE. See Indexes/Abstracts.

STATISTICAL ABSTRACT OF OHIO. See Indexes/Abstracts.

STATISTICAL ABSTRACT OF OKLAHOMA (1972). See Indexes/Abstracts.

STATISTICAL ABSTRACT OF PUBLIC FINANCE IN PUNJAB. See Indexes/Abstracts.

STATISTICAL ABSTRACT OF PUBLIC FINANCE OF HARYANA STATE. See Indexes/Abstracts.

STATISTICAL ABSTRACT OF THE DEMOCRATIC SOCIALIST REPUBLIC OF SRI LANKA. See Indexes/Abstracts.

STATISTICAL ABSTRACT OF THE UNITED STATES. See Indexes/Abstracts.

STATISTICAL ABSTRACT - PRESIDENT'S OFFICE, CENTRAL STATISTICAL BUREAU, DIRECTORATE OF DEVELOPMENT AND PLANNING (DAR ES SALAAM). See Indexes/Abstracts.

STATISTICAL ABSTRACT. REPUBLIC OF KENYA. See Indexes/Abstracts.

STATISTICAL ABSTRACT - STATISTICS AND RESEARCH DEPARTMENT. See Indexes/Abstracts.

STATISTICAL ANALYSIS AND CORRECTIONAL POPULATION DATA. Main/Corp Pennsylvania. Bureau of Correction. US. English. Pennsylvania Bureau of Correction, PO Box 598, Camp Hill PA 17011. LC HV8358. DD 365.97480212.

STATISTICAL ANALYSIS OF DAIRY PROCESSOR MARKET GUIDE. Main/Corp Dairy & Food Industries Supply Association. 0092-8992. US. English. an. Dairy & Food Industries Supply Association, Washington DC 20015. LC HD9275.U3. DD 338.1770973.

A STATISTICAL ANALYSIS OF THE WORLD'S MERCHANT FLEETS SHOWING AGE, SIZE, SPEED, AND DRAFT BY FREQUENCY GROUPINGS. (A STATISTICAL ANALYSIS OF THE WORLD'S MERCHANT FLEETS). 1956-. 0081-4768. US. English. an. US Maritime Administration, Washington DC 20590. LC HE731. DD 387.24.

STATISTICAL ANALYSIS OF WOOL PRODUCTION IN SOUTHERN AFRICA, PRODUCTION AREAS. VFOAT Statistiese Ontleding van wol Geproduseer in Suidelike Afrika Produksiegebiede. Afrikaans (English). an. LC HD9907.S6. *Statistical Analysis of Wool Produced in Southern Africa.*

STATISTICAL AND ACCOUNTING REPORT. Main/Corp Marlyand. Dept. of Health and Mental Hygiene. Laboratories Administration. VFOAT Report of Statistical and Cost Accounting of Laboratory Examinations for the Laboratories Administration. 1973-. 0147-6807. US. English. an. Maryland Department of Health & Mental Hygiene, 111 North Calvert Room A 200, Baltimore MD 20212. LC RA4283.M37. DD 353.9752007231. *Statistical and Cost Accounting Report, 0161-2255.*

STATISTICAL AND COST SUPPLEMENT TO A REPORT ON SCHOOL BUILDINGS IN UTAH. SEPTEMBER, 1975. US. English. an. Office of the State, Superintendent of Public Instruction, 260 East 5th South, Salt Lake City UT 84111. LC LB3218. DD 371.0109792.

STATISTICAL AND FISCAL DIGEST. Main/Corp Rhode Island. Dept. of Employment Security. 29th- 1964-. US. English. an. LC HD8053.R4. *Annual Report -Rhode Island Department of Employment Security.*

STATISTICAL AND NARRATIVE SUMMARY OF THE EXECUTIVE BUDGET. US. English. an. LC HJ11. DD 353.9747007225605.

STATISTICAL ANNUAL - CHICAGO BOARD OF TRADE. (STATISTICAL ANNUAL). -1978. 0163-5409. US. English. an. $9.45. Chicago Board of Trade Statistical Annual, LaSalle & Jackson, 141 West Jackson, Room 336A, Chicago IL 60604. Tel (312)435-3632. Ed Leslie Villarosa. LC HF296. DD 332.6440977311. Circ 3,000. Statistical data on grains, forest products, energy, options on soybeans, interest rates, options on T-bonds, futures, metals. Includes historical weather data, consumer prices and related topics. *Annual Report.*

STATISTICAL ANNUAL - COFFEE, SUGAR & COCOA EXCHANGE, INC. (STATISTICAL ANNUAL). 1980-. 0731-9576. US. English. an. Coffee/Sugar & Cocoa Exchange Inc, Four World Trade Center, New York NY 10048. LC HG6047.C57. DD 332.644.

STATISTICAL ANNUUAL (WINNIPEG COMMODITY EXCHANGE). (STATISTICAL ANNUAL). CN. English. an. Winnipeg Commodity Exchange, 678-167 Lombard Avenue, Winnipeg Manitoba R3B 0V7 Canada.

STATISTICAL BASEBOOK SERIES - ECONOMICS SERVICE, DEPARTMENT OF FISHERIES OF CANADA. Main/Corp Canada. Department of Fisheries. Economics Service. No. 3- 1958-. 0527-6942. Monographic Series. CN. English. ir. Department of Fisheries of Canada, Economics Service, Ottawa Ontario Canada. DD 639. *Basebook on Fishery Statistics.*

STATISTICAL BULLETIN CEASED. Main/Corp Trinidad and Tobago. Central Statistical Office. V. 1-12. English. ir. No 2 Edward Street, Port-of-Spain Trinidad. LC HA867. DD 317.2983.

STATISTICAL BULLETIN (BOTSWANA). (STATISTICAL BULLETIN). Vol. 1, No. 1 (June 1976)-. English. qt. 2.00. Government Printer, PO Box 87, Gaborone Botswana. LC HA4706. DD 316.811.

STATISTICAL BULLETIN (CENTRAL BANK OF THE PHILIPPINES). (STATISTICAL BULLETIN). Vol. 3, No. 1 (Mar. 1951)-. English. an. LC HC451. DD 330.9599005.

STATISTICAL BULLETIN - CIPEC DOCUMENTATION CENTRE. (CIPEC STATISTICAL BULLETIN). Main/Corp Intergovernmental Council of Copper Exporting Countries. Documentation Centre. VAT Consejo Intergubernamental de Paises Exportadores de Cobre Statistical Bulletin. 0254-2552. FR. English (French and Spanish). ir. Intergovernmental Council of Copper Exporting Countries, 177 Avenue du Roule, 92200 Neuilly sur Seine France. LC HD9539.C5. DD 338.27430212.

STATISTICAL BULLETIN (INTERNATIONAL TIN COUNCIL) CEASED. (STATISTICAL BULLETIN). Vol. 1 (Apr. 1957)-. 0020-8949. Periodical. UK. English. *Statistical Bulletin.*

STATISTICAL BULLETIN (LEMBAGA LETRIK NEGARA TANAH MELAYU. BAHAGIAN PERNIAGAAN). (STATISTICAL BULLETIN). English. ir. LC HD9685.M25. DD 363.62.

STATISTICAL BULLETIN - METROPOLITAN LIFE INSURANCE COMPANY CEASED. (STATISTICAL BULLETIN - METROPOLITAN LIFE). Main/Corp Metropolitan Life Insurance Company. V. 1-62. 0026-1513. Periodical. US. English. qt. $20.00. Metropolitan Life Insurance, One Madison Avenue, New York NY 10010. Tel (212)578-6731. Ed Charles B Arnold and Joan W Parks. Ind/Abst Popul. Index, Bus. Period. Index, Biol. Abstr., Index Med., Hospit. Lit. Index. LC HG8963.M5. DD 368.3. NLM W1 ST316E. CODEN SBMLAS. (cum index). Circ 10,000. Statistical analysis and information on longevity, mortality, morbidity, population trends, health promotion, cost-effective use of health resources.

STATISTICAL BULLETIN - METROPOLITAN LIFE INSURANCE COMPANY. (STATISTICAL BULLETIN : SB). VFOAT SB. Vol. 65, No. 1 (Jan.-Mar. 1984)-. 0741-9767. Periodical. US. English. qt. $20.00. Statistical Bulletin, Metropolitan Life Insurance Company, One Madison Avenue, New York NY 10010. Ed Charles B Arnold and Joan W Parks. Ind/Abst Energy Res. Abstr., Bus. Period. Index, Index Med., Hospit. Lit. Index, Popul. Index. LC HG8963.M5. DD 304.60973. NLM W1. Circ 6,000. Offers specialized information on longevity, mortality, population, accidents, disability, cost effective use of health care resources, health promotion and related subjects. *Statistical Bulletin (Metropolitan Life Foundation), 0736-4822.*

Statistics

STATISTICAL BULLETIN - NORTHWEST ATLANTIC FISHERIES ORGANIZATION. (STATISTICAL BULLETIN). VFOAT N.A.F.O. Statistical Bulletin. Vol. 29 (1979)-. 0250-6394. CN. English. an. 22.00. Northwest Atlantic Fisheries, PO Box 638, Dartmouth Nova Scotia B2Y 3Y9 Canada. Tel (902)469-9105. Ed V M Hodder. LC SH1. DD 338.372709211. Circ 600. Publication of detailed catch and effort statistics by type and size of fishing vessel, fishing gear, statistical area and country for all fishing activity in the Northwest Atlantic. Statistical Bulletin (International Commission for the Northwest Atlantic Fisheries), 0074-266X.

STATISTICAL BULLETIN OF THE OAS. Main/Corp Organization of American States. VAT Statistical Bulletin of the Organization of American States. V. 1- Jan./Mar. 1979-. 0250-6289. US. English. sa. $12.00. OAS General Secretariat, 1889 F Street NW, Washington DC 20006. Tel (202)789-3000. Ind/Abst Public Aff. Inf. Serv. Bull. LC HA755. DD 318. Synthesis of Economic Performance in Latin America.

STATISTICAL BULLETIN (OKLAHOMA. DEPT. OF HUMAN SERVICES). (STATISTICAL BULLETIN). Jan. 1980-. Periodical. US. English. qt. NLM W2 AO5 D25S. Statistical Bulletin (Oklahoma. Dept. of Institutions, Social and Rehabilitative Services).

STATISTICAL BULLETIN : PRODUCTION STATISTICS. Main/Corp Jamaica. Dept. of Statistics. JM. English. an. Department of Statistics, 9 Swallowfield Road, Kingston 5 Jamaica.

STATISTICAL BULLETIN (VICTORIA, SEYCHELLES). (STATISTICAL BULLETIN). Vol. 1, No. 1 (2nd Quarter 1980)-. English. qt. 25.00 Each Issue. Government Printer, PO Box 205, Union Vale Seychelles. LC HA2301. DD 316.96. Seychelles Statistical Bulletin.

STATISTICAL COMPILATION - ADMINISTRATIVE OFFICE OF THE COURTS. (STATISTICAL COMPILATION). Main/Corp Maryland. Administrative Office of the Courts. 0093-4186. Periodical. US. English. mo. Administrative Office of the Courts, Courts of Appeal Building, Baltimore MD 21401. LC KFM1271. DD 347.752013.

STATISTICAL DATA. Main/Corp North Carolina. Drug Commission. 0145-8531. US. English. an. North Carolina Drug Commission, 3800 Barrett Drive, Raleigh NC 27609. LC HV5831.N8. DD 364.17.

STATISTICAL DATA OF THE AMSTERDAM PORT AND OTHER NORTH SEA CANAL PORT AREAS. VFOAT Statistisch Overzicht van de Amsterdamse Haven en Andere Havens in Het Noorzeekanaalgebied. Dutch (English). ir. Port Management of Amsterdam, Havengebouw de Ruijterkade 7, 1013 AA Amsterdam Netherlands. Tel (20) 221201. Statistics issued by the Port Management of Amsterdam in co-operation with the other north sea canal port areas.

STATISTICAL DATA ON PERSONS RELEASED FROM PAROLE BY DISCHARGE AND VIOLATION. Main/Corp Virginia. Dept. of Corrections. 0097-7667. US. English. Department of Corrections, PO Box 26963, Richmond VA 23261. LC HV7296. DD 364.6209755. Statistical Data on Persons Released from Parole by Discharge and Violation.

STATISTICAL DATA. STATEWIDE STATISTICS, CURRENT EXPENDITURES BY DISTRICT, RANKING OF STATISTICS BY DISTRICT. (STATISTICAL DATA). Main/Corp Mississippi. Dept. of Education. Division of Administration and Finance. 0148-3617. US. English. an. Mississippi Department of Education, 1328 Lynch Street, Jackson MS 39203. LC LB2826.M7. DD 379.12209762.

STATISTICAL DIGEST (BANK OF JAMAICA. RESEARCH DEPT.). (STATISTICAL DIGEST). Periodical. English. mo. LC HG2824. DD 330.97292005. Bank of Jamaica Statistical Digest.

STATISTICAL DIGEST - LEGISLATIVE BUDGET AND FINANCE COMMITTEE. Main/Corp Pennsylvania. General Assembly. Legislative Budget and Finance Committee. 1978/79-. US. English. an. Legislative Budget and Finance Committee Senate, PO Box 80, Main Capitol Building, Harrisburg PA 17120. LC HJ11. DD 353.974800722305. Selected Financial and Related Statistical Facts of the Commonwealth of Pennsylvania.

STATISTICAL ECOLOGY SERIES. VFOAT Statistical Ecology. Vol. 4-. Monographic Series. US. English. ir. International Co-Operative Publishing House, PO Box 245, Burtonsville MD 20730. Tel (301)384-2627. Ind/Abst Math. Rev. LC UNC.

STATISTICAL HANDBOOK. Main/Corp West Bengal. Bureau of Applied Economics and Statistics. II. English. ir. 5.88. Government of West Bengal, Bureau of Applied Economics & Statistics, Calcutta West Bengal India. LC HA1728.B42. DD 315.414. Statistical Hand Book.

STATISTICAL HANDBOOK (NEW ZEALAND WOOL BOARD). (STATISTICAL HANDBOOK). 1977/78 Season-. 0110-1242. NZ. English. an. New Zealand Wool Board, 139-141 Featherston Street, Wellington New Zealand. LC HD9908.N45. DD 338.1763145. Statistical Handbook (New Zealand Wool Marketing Corporation).

STATISTICAL HANDBOOK OF THE UNITED ARAB REPUBLIC. 19 -1952/67. English. ir. Presidency of UAR-Central Agency, 140 Tahrir Street, Dokki Cairo Egypt. LC HA4686. DD 316.2. Statistical Pocket-Book of the United Arab Republic.

STATISTICAL HANDBOOK - WEST VIRGINIA LEAGUE, INC. (STATISTICAL HANDBOOK). Main/Corp West Virginia Research League. 0091-6102. US. English. an. $5.63. West Virginia Research League, 1107 Charleston National Plaza, Charleston WV 25301. Tel (304)346-9451. Ed Sarah F Roach. LC HJ760. Circ 2,100. A concise, convenient and usable source of selected statistical facts and figures relating to state and local government in West Virginia.

STATISTICAL INDICATORS FOR ASIA AND THE PACIFIC. Vol. 7, No. 2 (June 1977)-. 0252-4457. Periodical. English. qt. $9.50. United Nations, Room DC2-853, New York NY 10017. LC HC411. DD 330.950021. Statistical Indicators in Escap Countries.

STATISTICAL INDICATORS OF SHORT TERM ECONOMIC CHANGES IN ECE COUNTRIES. Periodical. English. mo. $45.00. United Nations Publications, Sales Section/Room A-3315, New York NY 10017. Tel (212)754-8324. Provides current statistical and economic indicators on Europe and USA.

STATISTICAL INFORMATION ON SCHOOLS OF SOCIAL WORK IN CANADA CEASED. Main/Corp Statistics Canada. Post-Secondary Education Section. VFOAT Information Statistique sur les Ecoles de Service Sociale au Canada. 1972-. 0318-7160. Periodical. CN. English (text in French). an. 0.70. Statistics Canada, Publication Distribution, Ottawa Ontario K1A 0T6 Canada. LC HV11. DD 362.071171. Statistical Information on Schools of Social Work in Canada, 0318-7160.

STATISTICAL INFORMATION ON WESTERN STATE OF NIGERIA CONTROLLED PRODUCE. Main/Corp Western Nigeria Marketing Board. Statistics Section. No. 9- 1973-. English. ir. LC HD9017.N53. DD 338.1096692.

STATISTICAL INFORMATION RELEVANT TO THE HEALTH SERVICES. Main/Corp Ireland (EIRE). Dept. of Health. Planning Unit. English. ir. 40. Government Publications Sale Office, Government Printing Office Arcade, Dublin 1 Ireland. LC RA407.5.I73. DD 362.109417.

STATISTICAL INFORMATION RESPECTING THE MUNICIPALITIES OF THE PROVINCE OF MANITOBA. 1973-. 0580-5333. Periodical. CN. English. an. Minister of Municipal Affairs, 1 Manitoba Canada. LC HJ9014.M3. DD 352.12097127. Statistical Information Respecting the Municipalities of the Province of Manitoba (Manitoba. Dept. of Urban Development and Municipal Affairs), 0580-5333.

STATISTICAL INFORMATION SERVICE : PERSONAL SOCIAL SERVICES STATISTICS ACTUALS. Main/Corp Chartered Institute of Public Finance and Accountancy. UK. English. 3.00 Each. Institute of Finance and Accountancy, 1 Buckingham Palace, London SW 1E 6HS England. LC HV249.E86. DD 362.620942.

STATISTICAL INFORMATION SERVICE : POLICE FORCE AND REGIONAL CRIME SQUAD STATISTICS, ACTUALS. Main/Corp Chartered Institute of Public Finance and Accountancy. UK. English. 1.20 Each. 1 Buckingham Place, London SW1E 6HS England. LC HV8195.A2.

STATISTICAL JOURNAL OF THE UNITED NATIONS ECONOMIC COMMISSION FOR EUROPE. Vol. 1, No. 1 (June 1982)-. 0167-8000. Periodical. NE. English. qt. Elsevier Science Publishers, PO Box 211, 1000 AE Amsterdam Netherlands. Tel (020)5803.911. Ind/Abst Index Econ. Artic. J. Collect. Vol. LC HA1. DD 310.601.

STATISTICAL LEAFLET - DEPARTMENT OF FISH AND GAME. Main/Corp Alaska. Department of Fish and Game. 0516-4311. Periodical. US. English. ir.

STATISTICAL MECHANICS. V. 1- 1973-. 0305-9960. UK. English. be. 28.00 Vols. 1 and 2. Royal Society of Chemistry, Blackhorse Road, Letchworth Herts SG6 1HN England. LC QC174.7. DD 530.132.

STATISTICAL NEWS FROM THE HEALTH DATA CENTER. Main/Corp Pennsylvania. Health Data Center. Began publication in 1980. Periodical. US. English. bm. Free. Health Data Center, Pennsylvania Department of Health, PO Box 90, Harrisburg PA 17108. Tel (717)783-2548. Ed Jerry Orris. Circ 500. Various articles on the Pennsylvania health statistics especially natality, mortality, marriage, divorce, hospital and nursing home data.

STATISTICAL NEWS LETTERS - INTERNATIONAL COUNCIL FOR THE EXPLORATION OF THE SEA. Main/Corp International Council for the Exploration of the Sea. No. 1- Aug. 1957-. 0074-4352. Monographic Series. DK. English. ir. International Council for the Exploration of the Sea, DK1261 Copenhagen K Denmark. LC SH1. DD 639, 551.4.

STATISTICAL NOTES FOR HEALTH PLANNERS. Main/Corp National Center for Health Statistics (U.S.). 0147-278X. US. English. National Center for Health Statistics, 5600 Fishers Lane, Rockville MD 20857. Ind/Abst Popul. Index. LC RA790.6. DD 362.20973. NLM W2 A N148S.

STATISTICAL NOTES - REHABILITATION SERVICES ADMINISTRATION. (STATISTICAL NOTES). Main/Corp United States. Rehabilitation Services Administration. 0093-9463. US. English. Rehabilitation Services Administration, 330 Independence Avenue Southwest, Washington DC 20201. LC HD7256.U5. DD 362.85.

STATISTICAL OUTLINE OF INDIA. Main/Corp Tata Services Limited. Dept. of Economics and Statistics. II. English. ir. 20 Domestic, $4.00 Foreign. Tata Services Ltd, Department of Economics and Statistics, Bombay House, Bombay 400023 India. Tel 204-5928. LC HC431. DD 330.95405. Circ 18,000. Covers latest statistics on various aspects of Indian economy and also tables showing international comparisons. Statitsical Outline of India.

STATISTICAL PAPERS. SERIES F. Main/Corp United Nations. Statistical Office. 049X-014X. Periodical. UK. English. ir. Her Majestys Stationery Office, PO Box 276, London SW8 5DT England. Tel 01-622 3316.

STATISTICAL PAPERS - UNITED NATIONS. STATISTICAL OFFICE. Main/Corp United Nations. Statistical Office. Series Corp United Nations. Document. Ser. A- 1949-. English. ir. United Nations Statistical Office, PO Box 5850, New York NY 10163. LC JX1977. DD 310.82.

STATISTICAL POCKET BOOK, NEPAL. Main/Corp Nepal. Central Bureau of Statistics. 1974-. NP. English. ir. 10.31. Central Bureau of Statistics, Kathmandu Nepal. Tel 2-12606. LC HA1950.N5. DD 315.496. (ctrl). Covers area and population, forest, mineral production, water, power and irrigation, education, health, tourism, transport and communication, climate, food and agriculture, industry, government, finance, and prices.

Statistics

STATISTICAL POCKET-BOOK OF AFGHANISTAN. 1350 1971 or 2-. English. ir. LC HA1675. DD 315.81.

STATISTICAL POCKET BOOK OF BANGLADESH. VFOAT Bamladesa Parisamkhyana Paketa Bai. 1978-. BG. Bengali (English; material also in Urdu) an. $10.00. Bangladesh Bureau of Statistic, Bangladesh Secretariat, Dacca Bangladesh. LC HA4590.6. DD 315.492.

STATISTICAL POCKET BOOK OF HUNGARY. Main/Corp Hungary, Kozponti Statisztikai Hivatal. 1961-. Periodical. HU. English. an. Akademiai Kiado, POB 24, 1363 Budapest Hungary. LC HA1201.

STATISTICAL POCKET BOOK OF THE DEMOCRATIC SOCIALIST REPUBLIC OF SRI LANKA. 11th- 1978-. CE. English. ir. 5.45. PO Box 563, Colombo 7 Sri Lanka. Tel 595291. LC HA1697. DD 315.493. Circ 3,932. Contains statistical data on population and vital statistics, agriculture, social conditions, education, health, national accounts, public finance, geography, etc. *Statistical Pocket Book of the Republic of Sri Lanka (Ceylon).*

STATISTICAL POCKET-BOOK OF YUGOSLAVIA. VFOAT Statistical Pocket Book of Yugoslavia. 1955-. 0585-1815. YU. English. an. Federal Institute for Statistics, Kneza Milosa 20, Beograd Republic of Yugoslavia. LC HA1631. DD 314.

STATISTICAL POCKETBOOK OF HUNGARY. VFOAT Magyar Statisztikai Zsebkonyv. 0441-473X. HU. English and Hungarian (some volumes include separately paged section in Hungarian with separate title page). an. Akademiai Kiado, POB 24, 1363 Budapest Hungary.

STATISTICAL PRESENTATION (ILLINOIS. DEPT. OF CORRECTIONS. POLICY DEVELOPMENT DIVISION. RESEARCH AND EVALUATION). (STATISTICAL PRESENTATION). 1979-. US. English. an. Illinois Department of Corrections, Research and Evaluation Unit, 160 North La Salle, Chicago IL 60601. LC HV9475.I3. DD 364.609773.

STATISTICAL PROFILE - IOWA DEPARTMENT OF TRANSPORTATION. (STATISTICAL PROFILE - DEPARTMENT OF TRANSPORTATION). Main/Corp Iowa. Dept. of Transportation. 0160-1970. US. English. an. Iowa Department of Transportation, 800 Lincoln Way, Ames IA 50010. LC HE28.I8. DD 380.509777.

STATISTICAL PROFILE. NORTH CAROLINA PUBLIC SCHOOLS. (STATISTICAL PROFILE, NORTH CAROLINA PUBLIC SCHOOLS). 0148-2742. US. English. an. North Carolina Department of Public Education, Raleigh NC 27602. LC LA340. DD 370.9756.

STATISTICAL PROFILE OF ILLINOIS SCHOOL ADMINISTRATORS. 1980/81-. US. English. an. Illinois State Board of Education, Department of Planning Research and Evaluation, 100 North First Street, Springfield IL 62777. LC LB2831.624.I4. DD 371.20109773.

STATISTICAL PROFILE OF IOWA. Main/Corp Iowa Development Commission. US. English. an. Iowa Development Commission, 250 Jewett Building/Research & Supplies Division, Des Moines IA 50309. Tel (515)281-3036. LC HA371. DD 317.77. Factual information about the economic environment within the state of Iowa.

STATISTICAL PROFILE OF ZAMBIAN EDUCATION. Main/Corp Zambia. Ministry of Education. Began with Vol. for 1975. English. ir. Ministry of Education, PO Box R W 93, Lusaka Zambia. LC LA1595. DD 370.96894.

STATISTICAL PROFILE. THE SOFT DRINK INDUSTRY IN THE UNITED STATES. (STATISTICAL PROFILE : THE SOFT DRINK INDUSTRY IN THE UNITED STATES). Main/Corp National Soft Drink Association. VFOAT Soft Drink Industry in the United States. 1974-. 0360-2427. US. English. an. $17.00. National Soft Drink Association, 1101 16th Street Northwest, Washington DC 20036. Tel (202)463-6706. LC HD9348.U5. DD 338.47663620973. A collection of data pertaining to all aspects of the soft drink industry.

THE STATISTICAL RECORD. (V.4- 1974-). Periodical. UK. English. qt. Weatherbys, 59 High Street, Ascot Berkshire SL57HP England. Tel (099)21476.

STATISTICAL REFERENCE BOOK OF INTERNATIONAL ACTIVITIES. Main/Corp John E Fogarty International Center for Advanced Study in the Health Sciences. International Cooperation and Geographic Studies Branch. VFOAT National Institutes of Health Statistical Reference Book of International Activities. Began with fiscal year 1972. 0361-0764. US. English. an. John E Fogarty International Center for Advanced Study in the Health Sciences, International Coordination and Geographic Studies Branch, 9000 Rockville Pike, Bethesda MD 20205. NLM W2 A J6S. *Statistical Reference Book of International Activities.*

STATISTICAL REFERENCE INDEX ANNUAL. See Indexes/Abstracts.

STATISTICAL REGISTER OF SOUTH AUSTRALIA CEASED. -1975/76. AT. English. ir. Australian Bureau of Statistics, PO Box 10, Belconnen Australian Capital Territory 2616 Australia. Tel (062)52-5979. LC HA3093. DD 319.423.

STATISTICAL REPORT. Main/Corp Lahore Chamber of Commerce & Industry. Research and Statistical Dept. English. ir. Lahore Chamber of Commerce & Industry, 11 Race Course Road, Lahore Pakistan. LC HA1730.5. DD 330.9549105.

STATISTICAL REPORT: ANNUAL LINE OF BUSINESS REPORT. (STATISTICAL REPORT, ANNUAL LINE OF BUSINESS REPORT : REPORT OF THE BUREAU OF ECONOMICS, FEDERAL TRADE COMMISSION). VFOAT FTC, Annual Line of Business Report. 0192-8260. US. English. an. Federal Trade Commission, 6th Street & Pennsylvania Avenues NW, Washington DC 20580. LC HG4051. DD 338.740973.

STATISTICAL REPORT - CANADIAN ASSOCIATION OF GRADUATE SCHOOLS. Main/Corp Canadian Association of Graduate Schools. Began with 1967 issue. 0318-1510. Periodical. CN. English. an. $19.35. COU Holdings Ltd, 130 St George Street/Suite 8039, Toronto Ontario M5S 2T4 Canada. DD 378.15530971.

STATISTICAL REPORT - CITY OF LOS ANGELES. SOCIAL SERVICE DEPARTMENT. (STATISTICAL REPORT). Main/Corp Los Angeles. Dept. of Social Service. 0090-6565. US. English. Los Angeles Department of Social Service, 313 North Figueroa Street, Los Angeles CA 90012. LC HV87.L7. DD 360.979493.

STATISTICAL REPORT - DEPT. OF LABOR AND INDUSTRIES. Main/Corp Washington (State). Dept. of Labor and Industries. 1950/51-. Periodical. US. English. sa. LC HD8083.W2. DD 331.061797. *Report.*

STATISTICAL REPORT - DIV. OF THE WOMEN'S HOSPITAL. VAT Statistical Report - Division of the Women's Hospital. 1965-. 0125-4839. English. ir. NLM WX 2 JT3 B2W8S. *Statistical Report - the Women's and Children's Hospital, Bangkok.*

STATISTICAL REPORT - EXECUTIVE OFFICE FOR U.S. ATTORNEYS. (STATISTICAL REPORT). Main/Corp Executive Office for U.S. Attorneys. 1978/79-. 0740-8277. US. English. an. US Department of Justice, Executive Office for US Attorneys, Washington DC 20530. LC KF180. DD 347.7313, 347.30713. Vols. for Fiscal Year 1982- distributed to depository libraries in microfiche. *United States Attorney's Offices Statistical Report, 0162-668X.*

STATISTICAL REPORT - GEORGIA DEPARTMENT OF EDUCATION. (STATISTICAL REPORT). Main/Corp Georgia. Dept. of Education. 0094-1557. US. English. State Office Building, Department of Education, Atlanta GA 30334. LC L138. DD 370.9758.

STATISTICAL REPORT - LOUISIANA, HEALTH AND SOCIAL AND REHABILITATION SERVICES ADMINISTRATION. (STATISTICAL REPORT). Main/Corp Louisiana. Health and Social and Rehabilitation Services Administration. 0098-8057. US. English. an. Health & Social & Rehabilitation Services Administration, PO Box 60630, Public Health Station, New Orleans LA 70160. LC RA981.L6. DD 362.1109763. *Annual Statistical Report.*

STATISTICAL REPORT - MENTAL HEALTH PROGRAMS. DEPARTMENT OF HEALTH. (STATISTICAL REPORT - MENTAL HEALTH PROGRAMS). Main/Corp British Columbia. Mental Health Programs. 1973-. 0383-3518. CN. English. an. Department of Health, Mental Health Programs, Parliament Building, Victoria British Columbia Canada. LC RC448. DD 362.2109711. *Statistical Report, 0706-4004.*

STATISTICAL REPORT - NORTH DAKOTA TAX DEPARTMENT. Main/Corp North Dakota. Tax Dept. US. English. North Dakota Tax Department, State Capitol, Bismark ND 58505.

STATISTICAL REPORT OF ACCIDENTS. Main/Corp West Virginia. Safety Responsibility Division. 0093-2418. US. English. 1800 Washington Street East, Charleston WV 25305. LC HE5614.3.W4. DD 312.44.

STATISTICAL REPORT OF INFORMATION REGARDING THE ENROLLMENT, FINANCES, COURSEWORK, CREDIT HOURS, AND DEGREES AT THE PUBLIC SENIOR COLLEGES AND UNIVERSITIES OF MISSISSIPPI. Main/Corp Mississippi. Board of Trustees of State Institutions of Higher Learning. 0094-4122. US. English. LC LA313.5. DD 378.762.

STATISTICAL REPORT OF PROPERTY ASSESSMENT AND TAXATION. Main/Corp Kansas. Division of Property Valuation. 0098-0056. US. English. an. Division of Property Valuation, State Capitol Building, Topeka KS 66606. LC HJ4217. DD 333.33209781. *Statistical Report of General Property Assessment and Taxation.*

STATISTICAL REPORT OF SASKATCHEWAN PUBLIC HOSPITALS. Main/Corp Saskatchewan Hospital Services Plan. 1973-. 0701-7049. CN. English. an. LC RA983.A4. DD 362.11097124. *Report of Public General Hospitals, 0701-7057.*

STATISTICAL REPORT OF THE FIRE COMMISSIONER. Main/Corp Alberta. Office of the Fire Commissioner. 1978-. 0715-2256. CN. English. an. LC TH9506.A8. DD 363.372097123. *Annual Report, 0568-899X.*

STATISTICAL REPORT OF THE JAMAICA LIBRARY SERVICE. English. an. LC Z753.J2. DD 027.07292.

STATISTICAL REPORT ON GAMBLING. Main/Corp Iowa. Dept. of Revenue. Research & Statistics Division. US. English. an. LC HJ5339. DD 353.97770076.

STATISTICAL REPORT ON LEGALLY INDUCED ABORTIONS. UTAH. (STATISTICAL REPORT ON LEGALLY INDUCED ABORTIONS, UTAH). VFOAT Abortions in Utah. 1974/75-. 0164-2715. US. English. an. NLM W2 AU8 B7S.

STATISTICAL REPORT ON MEDICAL CARE. Main/Corp South Dakota. Division of Social Welfare. 0098-9800. US. English. an. SD Division of Social Welfare, Capitol Lake Plaza, Pierre SD 57501. LC HD7102.U5. DD 368.42009783.

STATISTICAL REPORT ON MERGERS AND ACQUISITIONS. 0731-0692. US. English. an. F T C Bureau of Economics, Washington DC 20850. LC HD2775. DD 338.830973. *F.T.C. Statistical Report on Mergers and Acquisitions, 0094-1662.*

STATISTICAL REPORT ON THE NATIONAL AGRICULTURAL EXHIBITION. SP. English. ir. Central Statistical Office, 2 Victoria Avenue, Port of Spain Trinidad West Indies. LC S557.T752. DD 630.740972983.

STATISTICAL REPORT ON THE OPERATION OF THE UNEMPLOYMENT INSURANCE ACT. VFOAT Rapport Statistique sur l'Application de la Loi sur l'Assurance-Chomage. V. 31- Jan. 1972-. 0382-4098. Periodical. CN. English (French). qt. Receiver General for Canada, Statistics Canada, Ottawa Ontario K1A 0T6 Canada.

STATISTICAL REPORT. RURAL ELECTRIC BORROWERS. VFOAT Rural Electric Borrowers. 1980-. US. English. an. Superintendent of Documents, US Government

Statistics

Printing Office, Washington DC 20402. LC HD9688.U5. DD 338.76213930973. Vols. for (1983-) distributed to depository libraries in microfiche. *Annual Statistical Report. Rural Electric Borrowers (Washington, D.C. : 1971).*

STATISTICAL REPORT. RURAL TELEPHONE BORROWERS. Series/Titl REA Bulletin. VFOAT Rural Telephone Borrowers. 1980-. 0731-8251. US. English. an. Superintendent of Documents, Government Printing Office, Washington DC 20402. LC HE8801. DD 384.63. Vols. for (1981-) distributed to depository libraries in microfiche. *Annual Statistical Report. Rural Telephone Borrowers.*

STATISTICAL REPORT SERIES - DIVISION OF EDUCATIONAL STATISTICS. Main/Corp Pennsylvania. Division of Education Statistics. No. 19- 1971/72-. US. English. an. Department of Education, Box 911, Harrisburg PA 17126. LC L194. DD 370.9748. *Statistical Report Series - Bureau of Educational Statistics.*

STATISTICAL REPORT SERIES (WYOMING. STATE DEPT. OF EDUCATION. PLANNING & VOCATIONAL SERVICES DIVISION). (STATISTICAL REPORT SERIES). Monographic Series. US. English. Planning & Vocational Services Division, State Department of Education, Cheyenne WY 82002. *Statistical Report Series (Wyoming. State Dept. of Education. Division of Administrative Services).*

STATISTICAL REPORT - SOUTH CAROLINA DEPARTMENT OF SOCIAL SERVICES. VFOAT Statistics - South Carolina Department of Social Services. V. 35, No. 11- May 1972-. 0163-6898. Periodical. US. English. NLM W2 AS6 S72P. *Public Welfare Statistics - South Carolina Department of Public Welfare.*

STATISTICAL REPORT - STATE OF ALASKA, ALASKA OIL AND GAS CONSERVATION COMMISSION. (STATISTICAL REPORT). 1978-. 0273-1916. US. English. an. Alaska Oil and Gas Conservation Commission, 30001 Porcupine Drive, Anchorage AK 99501. LC TN872.A7. DD 333.8231609798. *Statistical Report (Alaska. Division of Oil and Gas Conservation).*

STATISTICAL REPORT - STATE OF NEW YORK, OFFICE OF COURT ADMINISTRATION. (STATISTICAL REPORT - STATE OF NEW YORK OFFICE OF COURT ADMINISTRATION). Main/Corp New York (State). Office of Court Administration. 0098-2016. US. English. Office of Court Administration, 270 Broadway, New York NY 10007. LC KFN5070. DD 347.747013.

STATISTICAL REPORT (VIRGINIA. DEPT. OF SOCIAL SERVICES. BUREAU OF RESEARCH AND REPORTING). (STATISTICAL REPORT). VFOAT Public Welfare Statistics. Vol. 44, No. 1 (Sept. 1982)-. US. English. qt. Commonwealth of Virginia, Department of Social Services, Bureau of Research and Reporting, 8007 Discovery Drive, Richmond VA 23288. LC HV86. DD 362.9755021. *Statistical Report (Virginia. Dept. of Welfare. Bureau of Research and Reporting).*

STATISTICAL REPORT (WEST VIRGINIA. OFFICE OF OIL AND GAS). (STATISTICAL REPORT). VFOAT Oil and Gas Statistical Report. US. English. an. State of West Virginia, Department of Mines, Charleston WV 25305. LC HD9567.W4. DD 338.762233809753021.

STATISTICAL REPORTS AND TABLES. 1975/76-. 0711-9518. CN. English. an. Ministry of Human Resources, Parliament Buildings, Victoria British Columbia V8V 1X4 Canada. *Statistical Reports and Tables.*

STATISTICAL RESEARCH MONOGRAPHS. Vol. 1-. 0081-5020. Monographic Series. US. English. ir. University of Chicago Press, PO Box 37005, Chicago IL 60637.

STATISTICAL REVIEW. (STATISTICAL REVIEW, GROCERS BAGS, GROCERS SACKS AND MERCHANDISE BAGS). Main/Corp Paper Bag Institute, New York. 1974-. 0162-8097. US. English. an. Paper Bag Institute, 41 East 42nd Street, New York NY 10017. LC HD9839.P28. DD 338.47676330212. *Grocers Bags and Grocers Sacks, 0091-617X; Merchandise Bags.*

STATISTICAL REVIEW - AUSTRALIAN TOURIST COMMISSION. Main/Corp Australian Tourist Commission. English. ir. GPO Box 73B, 3001 Melbourne Australia. LC G155.A75. DD 338.479194046.

STATISTICAL REVIEW (JAMAICA. DEPT. OF STATISTICS). (STATISTICAL REVIEW). Aug. 1981-. Periodical. English. mo. Department of Statistics, 9 Swallowfield Road, Kingston 5 Jamaica. LC HA891. DD 317.292.

STATISTICAL REVIEW OF COAL IN CANADA. 1977-. 0707-2767. CN. English. an. LC TN806.C2. DD 333.7. *Coal in Canada.*

STATISTICAL REVIEW OF CRIME. AT. English. ir. Victorian Police, Government Printer, PO Box 203, North Melbourne Victoria Australia. LC HV7396. DD 364.9945.

STATISTICAL REVIEW OF NORTHERN IRELAND AGRICULTURE. Began in 1974/75. UK. English. an. Her Majesty's Stationery Office, Chichester House, Chichester Street, Belfast BT1 4JY Northern Ireland. LC HD1930.N65. DD 338.109416.

STATISTICAL REVIEW OF THE FUR SEASON IN NORTHERN FUR CONSERVATION AREAS. Main/Corp Saskatchewan. Fisheries and Wildlife Branch. Statistical Division. CN. English. LC SK283.6.C2. DD 338.3729323097124.

A STATISTICAL REVIEW OF TOURISM IN HONG KONG. Main/Corp Hong Kong Tourist Association. Research Dept. English. ir. HKTA Research Department, 35th Floor Connaught Centre Connaught Road C, Hong Kong Hong Kong. LC G155.H63. DD 338.4791512504.

STATISTICAL REVIEW - ONTARIO. MINISTRY OF CONSUMER AND COMMERCIAL RELATIONS. (STATISTICAL REVIEW - MINISTRY OF CONSUMER AND COMMERCIAL RELATIONS). Main/Corp Ontario. Ministry of Consumer and Commercial Relations. 1972/73-. 0317-8161. CN. English. an. 555 Yonge Street, Toronto Ontario M4Y 1Y7 Canada. LC HC117.O6. DD 381.3.

STATISTICAL SERVICES DIRECTORY. *See* Yearbooks, Almanacs, Directories.

STATISTICAL SERVICES IN JAPAN. 1978-. JA. English. ir. Director, International Statistical Affairs Division, Office of Statistical Standards, Administrative Management, Agency 3-1-1 Kasumigaseki, Chiyoda-ku 100, Tokyo Japan. LC HA37. DD 310.6052.

STATISTICAL SERVICES OF THE UNITED STATES GOVERNMENT. Main/Corp United States. Office of Management and Budget. Statistical Policy Division. 0362-4315. US. English. $3.40. Superintendent of Documents, US Government Printing Office, Washington DC 20402. LC HA37. DD 001.4220973. *Statistical Services of the United States Government, 0362-4315.*

STATISTICAL SOFTWARE NEWSLETTER. 0173-5896. Periodical. English (German). ir. LC QA276.4. DD 519.505.

STATISTICAL SOURCE DIRECTORY FOR NEW JERSEY STATE GOVERNMENT. *See* Yearbooks, Almanacs, Directories.

STATISTICAL STANDARDS AND STUDIES. Main/Conf Conference of European Statisticians. Series Corp United Nations. Document ST/CES. Began publication with first issue in 1963. 0069-8458. US. English. $8.50. United Nations Publications, Sales Section/Room A3315, New York NY 10017. Tel (212)754-8302. LC JX1977. *Statistics of air quality including some methods.*

STATISTICAL STATEMENT - SALES AND USE TAX DIVISION, ARIZONA DEPT. OF REVENUE. (STATISTICAL STATEMENT). Main/Corp Arizona. Sales and Use Tax Division. 0147-3409. US. English. an. LC HJ5715.U6. DD 336.271. *Statistical Statement.*

STATISTICAL STATEMENTS RELATING TO THE CO-OPERATIVE MOVEMENT IN INDIA, FOR THE YEAR . . . . English (Vols. for 1978-9- also have preliminary information in Hindi). an. LC HD3537. DD 334.0954. *Statements Showing Progress of the Co-Operative Movement in India.*

STATISTICAL STATEMENTS RELATING TO THE COOPERATIVE MOVEMENT IN INDIA. Main/Corp Reserve Bank of India. II. English. ir. Reserve Bank of India, Economic Department, PO Box 1036, Bombay India 400 001. LC HD3537. DD 334.058.

STATISTICAL SUMMARY. Main/Corp Onondaga County Public Library. 0883-3494. US. English. an. Onondaga County Public Library, 335 Montgomery Street, Syracuse NY 13202.

STATISTICAL SUMMARY : AIR CARRIER ENFORCEMENT CASES. Main/Corp United States. Federal Aviation Administration. Office of the General Counsel. VFOAT Air Carrier Enforcement Cases. US. English. an. US Department of Transportation, US Federal Aviation Administration, Office of the General Counsel, Washington DC 20402. LC KF2422.5. DD 343.730978.

STATISTICAL SUMMARY - CANADIAN GAS ASSOCIATION. Main/Corp Canadian Gas Association. 1960-. 0068-8800. CN. English. an. Free. Canadian Gas Association, 55 Scarsdale Road, Don Mills Ontario M3B 2R3 Canada. DD 338.22850971. (ctrl).

STATISTICAL SUMMARY - COMMONWEALTH OF VIRGINIA, STATE MILK COMMISSION. Main/Corp Virginia. Milk Commission. 0363-0072. US. English. State Milk Commission, Ninth Street Office Building, Richmond VA 23219. LC HD9282.U5. DD 338.177109755.

STATISTICAL SUMMARY, FEDERAL MEAT AND POULTRY INSPECTION FOR FISCAL YEAR. (STATISTICAL SUMMARY, FEDERAL MEAT AND POULTRY INSPECTION FOR FISCAL YEAR . . .). 1980-. 0277-3724. US. English. an. USDA, Food Safety and Inspection Service, Washington DC 20250. LC HD9410.9.U5. DD 353.0082336043. *Federal Meat and Poultry Inspection Statistical Summary for . . . .*

STATISTICAL SUMMARY - FLORIDA CANNERS ASSOCIATION. Main/Corp Florida Canners Association. 0430-7585. US. English. an. PO Box 780, Winter Haven FL 33880. LC HD9259.C54. DD 338.476648.

STATISTICAL SUMMARY - FLORIDA CITRUS PROCESSORS ASSOCIATION. Main/Corp Florida Citrus Processors Association. 0270-7691. US. English. an. $6.00. Florida Citrus Processors Association, PO Box 780, Winter Haven FL 33882. Tel (813)293-4171. LC HD9259.C54. DD 338.476648043509759.

STATISTICAL SUMMARY FOR THE PUBLIC SCHOOLS OF ARKANSAS. 1938/40-. US. English. Arkansas Department of Education, Education Building, State Capitol Grounds/Room 404A, Little Rock AR 72201.

STATISTICAL SUMMARY - LOUISIANA STATE DEPARTMENT OF HOSPITALS CEASED. Main/Corp Louisiana. State Dept. of Hospitals. US. English. bm. $175.00. Louisiana State Department of Hospitals, Baton Rouge LA 70804. Tel (813)974-3161. Ind/Abst Chem. Abstr., Sci. Cit. Index, Abr. Ed., Int. Aerosp. Abstr., Index Med. LC HV3006.L8. DD 362.1109763. NLM W2 AL6 S6SB.

STATISTICAL SUMMARY OF DEPARTMENTAL ACTIONS. Main/Corp Los Angeles, Calif. Dept. of City Planning. VFOAT Annual Report Summary of the Department of City Planning. Periodical. US. English. an. Department of City Planning, 561 City Hall, Los Angeles CA 90012. LC HT168.L6. DD 352.960979494.

STATISTICAL SUMMARY OF PROGRAMS. Main/Corp New York (State). Division of Housing and Community Renewal. US. English. an. New York State Division of Housing and Community Renewal, 2 World Trade Center, New York NY 10047. *Statistical Summary of Programs.*

STATISTICAL SUMMARY OF THE COLORADO JUDICIARY. July, 1978 to June 30, 1979-. 0731-6992. US. English. an. Office of the State Court Administrator, Two East Fourteenth Avenue, Denver CO 80203. LC KFC1871. DD 347.788013, 347.880713.

STATISTICAL SUMMARY OF THE OFFICE OF REGISTRATION AND RECORDS. Main/Corp Wyoming. University. Office of Registration and Records. 0096-1264. US. English. University of Wyoming, PO Box 3008,

Statistics

University Street, Laramie WY 82070. LC LD6252.7. DD 378.78795.

STATISTICAL SUPPLEMENT TO ANNUAL REPORT. (ANNUAL REPORT OF THE NEW YORK STATE DEPARTMENT OF SOCIAL SERVICES. STATISTICAL SUPPLEMENT). **Main/Corp** New York (State). Dept. of Social Services. 1974-. 0364-4715. US. English. an. LC HV86. DD 361.9747 S, 361.6209747. *New York State Social Statistics.*

STATISTICAL SUPPLEMENT TO THE ANNUAL REPORT OF THE ADMINISTRATIVE DIRECTOR OF THE COURTS. Main/Corp New Jersey. Administrative Office of the Courts. 1977/78-. US. English. an. State House Annex CN-037, Trenton NJ 08625.

STATISTICAL SUPPLEMENT TO THE TOP MANAGEMENT REPORT. (TOP MANAGEMENT REPORT. STATISTICAL SUPPLEMENT). **Main/Corp** American Management Association. Executive Compensation Service. 0098-2504. US. English. Amacom, 135 West 50th Street, New York NY 10020. LC HD4965.5.U6. DD 658.40720973.

STATISTICAL SURVEY OF CZECHOSLOVAKIA. English. ir. 15. Orbis Publishing House, Praque Czechoslovakia. LC HA1195. DD 314.37. *Czechoslovakia Statistical Abstract, 0591-0587.*

STATISTICAL SURVEY OF JAPAN'S ECONOMY. Began in 1969. JA. English. an. $15.00. Keizai Gaiko Kenkyukai, Seno Building, 14-9 3-Chome Roppongi, Minato-Ku Tokyo 106 Japan. LC HC461. DD 330.952005. *Statistical Survey of Economy of Japan.*

STATISTICAL SURVEY OF THE EAST AFRICAN COMMUNITY INSTITUTIONS. Main/Corp East African Community. East African Statistical Dept. 1972-. English. ir. LC HD4350.E25. DD 341.249.

STATISTICAL TABLES - DEPARTMENT OF EMPLOYMENT SECURITY. (STATISTICAL TABLES - STATE OF VERMONT, DEPARTMENT OF EMPLOYMENT SECURITY). **Main/Corp** Vermont. Dept. of Employment Security. 0095-1382. US. English. LC HD7096.U6. DD 331.109743.

STATISTICAL TABLES FOR ANNUAL REPORT. SUPPLEMENT. Main/Corp New Hampshire. Dept. of Employment Security. Economic Analysis and Reporting Section. US. English. an. State of New Hampshire, Department of Employment Security, 32 South Main Street, Concord NH 03301. **Tel** (603)224-3311. Ed Wesley S Noyes Jr. LC HD5725.N4. DD 331.1209742. **Circ** 250. Detailed statistical data on claimants, employers and services provided to job applicants. *Statistical Supplement for .. Annual Report, New Hampshire.*

STATISTICAL TABLES FROM ANNUAL STATEMENTS. Main/Corp New York (State). Insurance Dept. **VFOAT** NY Statistical Tables. US. English. an. $6.50. Superintendent of Insurance Agency B-1, Empire State Plaza, Suozzo, Albany NY 12223. **Tel** (518)474-4557. Includes statistical tables from annual statements and an annual report of the superintendent of insurance to the legislature.

STATISTICAL THEORY AND METHOD ABSTRACTS. See Indexes/Abstracts.

STATISTICAL TRAINING PROGRAMS BY THE U.S. BUREAU OF THE CENSUS. Main/Corp United States. Bureau of the Census. International Statistical Programs Center. **VAT** Statistical Training Programs by the United States Bureau of the Census. Periodical. US. English. an.

STATISTICAL YEAR BOOK - CENTRAL BUREAU OF STATISTICS. See Yearbooks, Almanacs, Directories.

STATISTICAL YEAR BOOK OF THE ELECTRIC UTILITY INDUSTRY. (STATISTICAL YEAR BOOK OF THE ELECTRIC UTILITY INDUSTRY FOR . . .). **VFOAT** EEI Statistical Year Book. Began with Vol. for 1960. 0361-3607. US. English. an. $30.00. Edison Electric Institute, 1111 19th Street NW, Washington DC 20036. LC HD9685.U4. DD 338.4736362. *Electric Utility Industry in the United States.*

STATISTICAL YEAR BOOK, THAILAND. See Yearbooks, Almanacs, Directories.

STATISTICAL YEAR BOOK - THE AUSTRALIAN GAS INDUSTRY. See Yearbooks, Almanacs, Directories.

STATISTICAL YEAR BOOK. TIN, TINPLATE, CANNING. See Yearbooks, Almanacs, Directories.

STATISTICAL YEARBOOK. See Yearbooks, Almanacs, Directories.

STATISTICAL YEARBOOK (ARAB MEMBER STATES). See Yearbooks, Almanacs, Directories.

STATISTICAL YEARBOOK - CENTRAL STATISTICAL OFFICE. See Yearbooks, Almanacs, Directories.

STATISTICAL YEARBOOK FOR ASIA AND THE PACIFIC. See Yearbooks, Almanacs, Directories.

STATISTICAL YEARBOOK FOR LATIN AMERICA. See Yearbooks, Almanacs, Directories.

STATISTICAL YEARBOOK. GOLD OPTIONS DATA. See Yearbooks, Almanacs, Directories.

STATISTICAL YEARBOOK - INTERNATIONAL NORTH PACIFIC FISHERIES COMMISSION. See Yearbooks, Almanacs, Directories.

STATISTICAL YEARBOOK. METALS FUTURES DATA. See Yearbooks, Almanacs, Directories.

STATISTICAL YEARBOOK - NEW YORK MERCANTILE EXCHANGE. See Yearbooks, Almanacs, Directories.

STATISTICAL YEARBOOK OF BANGLADESH. See Yearbooks, Almanacs, Directories.

STATISTICAL YEARBOOK OF CHINA. See Yearbooks, Almanacs, Directories.

STATISTICAL YEARBOOK OF MEMBER STATES OF THE COUNCIL FOR MUTUAL ECONOMIC ASSISTANCE. See Yearbooks, Almanacs, Directories.

STATISTICAL YEARBOOK OF MUNICIPAL FINANCE. See Yearbooks, Almanacs, Directories.

STATISTICAL YEARBOOK OF THE NETHERLANDS. See Yearbooks, Almanacs, Directories.

STATISTICAL YEARBOOK OF THE SOCIALIST FEDERAL REPUBLIC OF YUGOSLAVIA. See Yearbooks, Almanacs, Directories.

STATISTICAL YEARBOOK OF THE SOCIALIST REPUBLIC OF ROMANIA. See Yearbooks, Almanacs, Directories.

STATISTICAR : ORGAN STATISTICKOG DRUSTVA SRBIJE ZA TEORIJSKU I PRIMENJENU STATISTIKU. Periodical. Serbo-Croatian -C. ir. 60.00 Each Issue. LC HA1.

STATISTICHE SOCIALI. Vol. 1 (Ed. 1975)-. Italian. ir. 7.000. LC HN476. DD 306.0945.

STATISTICHESKI IZVESTIIA. 1970?-. Periodical. BU. Bulgarian. mo. Hemus, 6 Boulevard Rusky, Sofia Bulgaria.

THE STATISTICIAN. V. 1- July 1950-. 0039-0526. Periodical. UK. English. ir. $94.00. Carfax Publishing Company, PO Box 25 Abingdon, Oxfordshire OX14 3UE England. **Ed** R R Harris. **Ind/Abst** Electr. Electron. Abstr., Phys. Abstr., Comput. Control Abstr., Public Aff. Inf. Serv. Bull. bk rev. adv acc. Publishes articles encouraging the application of statistical principles to administrative and research problems.

STATISTICIANS AND OTHERS IN ALLIED PROFESSIONS. VFOAT Statistical Membership Directory—ASA, ENAR, WNAR, IMS. 1961-73. 0081-508X. US. English. $15.00 Each Issue. American Statistical Association, 806 15th Street Northwest, Washington DC 20005.

STATISTICKA REVIJA. V. 1- March 1951-. 0039-0534. Periodical. Slovak (summaries in French and English). qt. Jugoslovenska Knjica, PO Box 36, Beograd Yugoslavia. **Ind/Abst** MLA Int. Bibliogr. Books Artic. Mod. Lang. Lit., Lang. Lang. Behav. Abstr., Sociol. Abstr. LC HA37.Y83.

STATISTICKI GODISNJAK. Main/Corp Stara Pazova, Serbia (District). Narodni Odbor. Year. 1952-. YU. Serbo-Croatian(R). an. $32.00. Jugoslovenska Knjica, PO Box 36, Beograd Yuguslavia. LC HA1657.S7.

STATISTICKI GODISNJAK SR SRBIJE. 1974-. Serbo-Croatian -C. ir. 100.00. Republicki Zavod za Statistiku, Milana Rakica 5, Beograd Yugoslavia. LC HA1651. *Statisticki Godisnjak N. R. Srbije.*

STATISTICS. Main/Corp Great Britain. Board of Inland Revenue. **VFOAT** Inland Revenue Statistics. 1971-. UK. English. H M Stationery Office, PO Box 276, London SW8 5DT England. LC HJ40. DD 336.0242. *Report of the Commissioners of Her Majesty's Inland Revenue.*

STATISTICS. Main/Corp States of Malaya Chamber of Mines. English. ir. State of Malaya Chamber of Mines, No 1 Post Office Road Perak, Ipoh Malaysia. LC HD9506.M36. DD 338.209595.

STATISTICS. V. 8-. Periodical. English (summaries in German and Russian). ir. 120.00. 108 Berlin, Leipziger Strasse 3-4, Akademie-Verlag DDR, Berlin East Germany. **Ind/Abst** Math. Rev., Energy Res. Abstr., Comput. Control Abstr., Electr. Electron. Abstr., Sci. Abstr. Sect. A. Phys. Abstr. LC QA276.A1. DD 519.505. CODEN MOSSD5. *Mathematische Operationsforschung und Statistik.*

STATISTICS & DECISIONS. VFOAT Statistics and Decisions. Vol. 1, No. 1-. Periodical. English. qt. R Oldenbourg Verlag, Postfach 801360, D-8000 Munchen 80 West Germany. **Tel** 089/4112. **Ind/Abst** Math. Rev.

STATISTICS & PROBABILITY LETTERS. VFOAT Statistics and Probability Letters. Vol. 1, No. 1 (July 1982)-. 0167-7152. Periodical. English. bm. Elsevier Science Publishers, PO Box 211, 1000 AE Amsterdam Netherlands. **Tel** (020)5803.911. **Ind/Abst** Electron. Commun. Abstr. J., ISMEC Bull., Pollut. Abstr. Indexes, Saf. Sci. Abstr. J.

STATISTICS ANNUAL - B.C. TRACK & FIELD ASSOCIATION. (STATISTICS ANNUAL - B. C. TRACK & FIELD ASSOCIATION). **Main/Corp** British Columbia Track & Field Association. **VAT** Statistics Annual - British Columbia Track and Field Association. 1973-. 0705-2421. CN. English. an. B C Track and Field Association, 2447 Sugarpine Street, Abbotsford British Columbia V2T 3M7 Canada. DD 796.4209711. *British Columbia Annual Statistics, 0709-5503.*

STATISTICS (BRITISH TELECOM). (STATISTICS). **VFOAT** Telecommunications Statistics. UK. English. British Telecom Headquarters Service and Performance Department, THQ/SP1.2, 2-12 Gresham Street, London EC2V 7AG England. LC HE8091. DD 384.0941.

STATISTICS. CALENDAR YEAR REVIEW. (STATISTICS : CALENDAR YEAR REVIEW). **Main/Corp** North Dakota. Social Service Board. 0362-0360. US. English. an. Social Service Board of North Dakota, c/o Bureau of Governmental Affairs, Grand Forks ND 58201. LC HV86. DD 362.9784. *North Dakota Welfare Statistics, Calendar Year Review, 0549-8449.*

STATISTICS CANADA CATALOGUE. Main/Corp Statistics Canada. User Advisory Services Division. CN. English (French). be. Free. Publications Distribution, Statistics Canada, Ottawa Ontarion K1A 0T6 Canada. LC Z1373, J103. DD 015.71.

STATISTICS CONCERNING INDIAN EDUCATION. 1952-. 0498-7136. US. English. an. US Department of the Interior, Bureau of Indian Affairs Office of Indian Education Programs, Washington DC 20240. LC E97.

STATISTICS FOR MUNICIPAL AUTHORITIES IN PENNSYLVANIA. 0147-4626. US. English. an. PA Department of Community Affairs, Forum Building, Room 321A, Harrisburg PA 17120. LC HD4606.P4. DD 336.748.

STATISTICS FOR SELECTED S.M.S.A.'S. (STATISTICS FOR SELECTED SMSA'S). **Main/Corp** Pennsylvania. Dept. of Commerce., Bureau of Statistics, Research and

Statistics

Planning. Series/Titl Pennsylvania Industrial Census Series. 0556-4689. US. English. Bureau of Statistics, Research and Planning, Department of Commerce, Harrisburg PA 17120. LC HC107.P4. DD 338.09748. *Statistics for Selected SMSA'S.*

STATISTICS FROM RELIGIOUS ORGANIZATIONS. Main/Corp Papua New Guinea. Bureau of Statistics. English. ir. Bureau of Statistics, PO Box 2032, Papua New Guinea. LC BV3680.N5. DD 266.009953.

STATISTICS IN MEDICINE. Vol. 1, No. 1 (Jan.-Mar. 1982)-. 0277-6715. Periodical. UK. English. qt. John Wiley and Sons, Baffins Lane, Chichester Sussex P019 1UD England. Ind/Abst Excerpta Med., Index Med. LC RA409. DD 610.72. NLM W1 ST319N. CODEN SMEDDA.

STATISTICS NOVA SCOTIA. 0226-5095. Periodical. CN. English. mo. Statistical Services Branch, Department of Development, PO Box 519, Halifax Nova Scotia B3J 2R7 Canada. DD 317.1605. *Nova Scotia Statistics, 0226-5087.*

STATISTICS OF CIVIL COURTS IN THE STATE OF TAMIL NADU FOR THE YEAR . . . . 1971-. English. an. DD 347.5482013, 345.4820713. *Administration Report of the Civil Courts Statistics.*

STATISTICS OF DECISIONS ON PLANNING APPLICATIONS : ENGLAND AND WALES. Main/Corp Great Britain. Dept. of the Environment. Series/Titl Statistics for Town and Country Planning. Series I: Planning Decisions. UK. English. an. -/50. Her Majesty's Stationery Office, PO Box 276, London SW8 5DT England. LC HT169.G7. DD 309.2120942. *Statistics of Decisions on Planning Applications.*

STATISTICS OF EDUCATION. Main/Corp Great Britain. Dept. of Education and Science. No. 1- 1965/66-. UK. English. ir.

STATISTICS OF EDUCATION IN CYPRUS. Main/Corp Cyprus. Tmeme Statistikes Kai Ereunon. English. an. 300. LC LA1480. DD 370.95645.

STATISTICS OF EDUCATION IN LAGOS STATE. Main/Corp Lagos State, Nigeria. Ministry of Education and Community Development. V. 1- 1968-. 0331-0477. NR. English. ir. Lagos State Ministry of Education & Community Development, 216 Yakubu Gowon Street, Lagos Nigeria. LC LA1634.L3. DD 370.96691.

STATISTICS OF EDUCATION IN THE UNITED STATES. Main/Corp United States. Office of Education. 1958/59-. US. English. an. LC L111. DD 373.73. *Biennial Survey of Education in the United States.*

STATISTICS OF ELECTRIC COMPANIES. 0093-5042. US. English. an. LC HD9685.U6. DD 363.62.

STATISTICS OF ELECTRIC, GAS, STEAM HEAT, TELEPHONE, TELEGRAPH AND WATER COMPANIES. Main/Corp Oregon. Public Utility Commissioner. VFOAT Oregon Utility Statistics, Electric, Gas, Steamheat, Telephone, Telegraph, Water. 0091-0546. US. English. an. Oregon Public Utility Commissioner, Public Service Building, Salem OR 97310. LC HD2767.O7. DD 363.609795.

STATISTICS OF EMPLOYMENT IN LOCAL BODIES IN WEST BENGAL. Main/Corp West Bengal. Bureau of Applied Economics and Statistics. 0511-5507. II. English. ir. West Bengal Government Press, Duplicating Section, Alipore India. LC JS7025.W4. DD 331.761331795095414. *Statistics of Employment in Local Bodies in West Bengal.*

STATISTICS OF EMPLOYMENT UNDER THE PUBLIC SERVICE ACT. Main/Corp Australia. Public Service Board. Project Services Branch. Statistical Section. AT. English. ir. Australia Public Service Board Project Services Branch, Statistical Section, PO Box 84, Canberra ACT 2600 Australia. LC JQ4045. DD 331.76135494.

STATISTICS OF FOREIGN TRADE. SERIES B, ANNUAL, TABLES BY REPORTING COUNTRIES CEASED. VFOAT Statistiques du Commerce Exterieur. Serie B, Annuaire, Tableaux par Pays Declarants. 1978-1980. 0474-5396. English (French). bm. $36.00. OECD Publications Center, 1750 Pennsylvania Avenue NW, Washington DC 20006. LC HF1016. DD 382.0212.

Statistics of Foreign Trade. Series B, Trade by Commodities : Country Summaries.

STATISTICS OF FOREIGN TRADE. SERIES B. TRADE BY COMMODITIES : COUNTRY SUMMARIES. Main/Corp Organization for Economic Cooperation and Development. VFOAT Statistiques du Commerce Exterieur. Echanges par Produits : Resume par Pays. Periodical. English (French). ir. OECD Publications Center, 2 rue Andre Pascal, 75775 Paris Cedex 16 France. LC HF91. DD 382. *Statistics of Foreign Trade. Series B. Trade by Commodities: Analytical Abstracts, Statistiques du Commerce Exterier. Exchanges par Produits: Tableaux Analytiques.*

STATISTICS OF FRATERNAL BENEFIT SOCIETIES. 1966-. 0532-6109. US. English. an. $8.00. National Fraternal Congress of America, 230 West Monroe Street/Suite 726, Chicago IL 60606. Tel (312)782-3446. LC HG9226. DD 368.36300973. *Combined Statistics and Consolidated Chart of Fraternal Societies.*

STATISTICS OF GAS COMPANIES. Main/Corp Washington (State). Utilities and Transportation Commission. Accounting Section. 0090-9068. US. English. an. Utilities & Transportation Commission, Accounting Section, Highways-Licenses Building, Olympia WA 98501. LC HD9581.U52. DD 363.6309797. *Statistics of Gas Companies.*

STATISTICS OF HIGHER EDUCATION. Main/Corp National Council for Higher Education. General Secretariat. English. ir. LC LA1813. DD 378.624.

STATISTICS OF HOSPITAL CASES DISCHARGED. BRITISH COLUMBIA. (STATISTICS OF HOSPITAL CASES DISCHARGED). Main/Corp British Columbia. Hospital Programs. Research Division. No. 14- 1974-. 0524-5354. CN. English. an. Hospital Programs, Parliament Buildings, Victoria British Columbia Canada. LC RA983.A4. DD 362.1109711. *Statistics of Hospital Cases Discharged, 0524-5354.*

STATISTICS OF INCOME. CORPORATION INCOME TAX RETURNS. VFOAT Corporation Income Tax Returns. Began with 1954/55. 0160-9920. US. English. an. Superintendent of Documents, US Government Printing Office, Washington DC 20402. DD 336.243. (cum index). *Statistics of Income.*

STATISTICS OF INCOME. FIDUCIARY INCOME TAX RETURNS. (STATISTICS OF INCOME : FIDUCIARY INCOME TAX RETURNS). Main/Corp United States. Internal Revenue Service. 0161-6803. US. English. US Department of Treasury, Internal Revenue Service, Washington DC 20402. LC HJ5805. DD 336.2760973. *Statistics of Income: Fiduciary, Gift, and Estate Tax Returns.*

STATISTICS OF INCOME : INCOME TAX RETURNS. Main/Corp New Jersey. Division of Taxation. Research and Statistics Section. 1976-. US. English. an. Department of Treasury, Division of Taxation, Trenton NJ 08625. LC HJ11. DD 336.24209749.

STATISTICS OF INCOME. INDIVIDUAL INCOME TAX RETURNS. VFOAT Individual Income Tax Returns. Begin with 1954. US. English. an. Superintendent of Documents, US Government Printing Office, Washington DC 20402. LC HJ4652. DD 336.2420973.

STATISTICS OF INCOME. INTERNATIONAL INCOME AND TAXES. DOMESTIC INTERNATIONAL INCOME AND TAXES. SUPPLEMENTAL REPORT. Main/Corp United States. Internal Revenue Service. VFOAT International Income and Taxes. Domestic International Income and Taxes. Supplemental Report, International Income and Taxes. US. English. US Treasury Department, Washington DC 20402.

STATISTICS OF INCOME. PARTNERSHIP RETURNS (1977). (STATISTICS OF INCOME. PARTNERSHIP RETURNS). VFOAT Partnership Returns. 1977-. 0734-1709. US. English. ir. US Government Printing Office, Superintendent of Documents, Washington DC 20402. LC HJ4653.C7. DD 336.207. *Statistics of Income. Business Income Tax Returns, Sole Proprietorships, Partnerships.*

STATISTICS OF INCOME. SOI BULLETIN. VFOAT SOI Bulletin, Statistics of Income, S.O.I. Bulletin. Vol. 1, No. 1 (Summer 1981)-. 0730-0743. Periodical. US. English. qt. $25.00. US Government Printing Office, Superintendent of Documents, Washington DC 20402. Tel (202)783-3238. LC HJ4653.S7. DD 336.200973. *Preliminary Statistics of Income. Individual Income Tax Returns, Statistics of Income, Preliminary. Business Income Tax Returns, Sole Proprietorships, Partnerships; Statistics of Income, Preliminary. Corporation.*

STATISTICS OF INCOME. SOLE PROPRIETORSHIP RETURNS. VFOAT Sole Proprietorship Returns. 0744-0030. US. English. an. US Government Printing Office, Superintendent of Documents, Washington DC 20402. LC HJ4653.C7. DD 336.207. *Statistics of Income. Business Income Tax Returns, Sole Proprietorships, Partnerships.*

STATISTICS OF INCOME, SUPPLEMENTAL REPORT. INTERNATIONAL INCOME AND TAXES, FOREIGN INCOME AND TAXES REPORTED ON U.S. INCOME TAX RETURNS. VFOAT International Income and Taxes. 1976-1979-. 0882-1216. US. English. Superintendent of Documents, US Government Printing Office, Washington DC 20402. LC HJ4653.C7. DD 336.243. *Statistics of Income. Supplemental Report. International Income and Taxes. Foreign Tax Credit Claimed on Corporation Income Tax Returns, 0882-1755.*

STATISTICS OF INCOME, SUPPLEMENTAL REPORT. INTERNATIONAL INCOME AND TAXES, U.S. CORPORATIONS AND THEIR CONTROLLED FOREIGN CORPORATIONS. VFOAT International Income and Taxes, U.S. Corporations and Their Controlled Foreign Corporations. 1974-1978-. US. English. Superintendent of Documents, US Government Printing Office, Washington DC 20402. *Supplemental Statistics of Income. International Income and Taxes, U.S. Corporations and Their Controlled Foreign Corporations.*

STATISTICS OF INCOME, SUPPLEMENTAL REPORT. SALES OF CAPITAL ASSETS REPORTED ON INDIVIDUAL INCOME TAX RETURNS. VFOAT Sales of Capital Assets Reported on Individual Income Tax Returns. US. English. Superintendent of Documents, US Government Printing Office, Washington DC 20402.

STATISTICS OF INTERSTATE NATURAL GAS PIPELINE COMPANIES. Main/Corp United States. Energy Information Administration. 0162-9670. US. English. an. US Department of Energy, Energy Information Administration, Washington DC 20426. LC TN880. DD 338.4766570973. *Statistics of Interstate Natural Gas Pipeline Companies, 0162-9670.*

STATISTICS OF LOCAL PUBLIC SCHOOL SYSTEMS; STAFF. Main/Corp National Center for Education Statistics. VFOAT Elementary and Secondary Education. Fall 1970-. US. English. Superintendent of Documents, US Government Printing Office, Washington DC 20402. LC LA217. DD 371.010973.

STATISTICS OF MARINE PRODUCTS EXPORTS. English. ir. Marine Products Exports Development Authority Etc, M G Road, Cochin India. LC HD9466.I5. DD 382.437092054.

STATISTICS OF MISSOURI NONPUBLIC ELEMENTARY AND SECONDARY SCHOOLS. Main/Corp Missouri. Dept. of Education. 0090-7154. US. English. Missouri Department of Education, PO Box 480, 100 East Capital Avenue, Jefferson City MO 65101. LC LC50.M8. DD 371.0209778.

STATISTICS OF MOTOR CARRIERS CLASS I, II, III, & IV. Main/Corp Oregon. Public Utility Commissioner. VFOAT Statistics: Motor Carriers Operating in Oregon. US. English. LC HE5633.O7. DD 388.32409795. *Statistics of Motor Carriers Class 1, 2, & 3, 0094-6273.*

STATISTICS OF NAVY MEDICINE. Vol. 1, No. 1 (Sept. 1945)-. 0146-3020. Periodical. US. English. qt. Bureau of Medicine and Surgery, 23rd and E Street, Washington DC 20390. ind/Abst Am. Stat. Index. LC VG100. DD 359.3450973. NLM W2 A5 B9S.

STATISTICS OF OHIO LIBRARIES FOR . . . . Periodical. US. English. an.

STATISTICS OF PAPER AND PAPERBOARD CEASED. 0097-4730. US. English. an. $25.00. American Paper Institute, 260 Madison Avenue, New York NY 10016. LC

Statistics

HD9839.P33. **DD** 338.4767620973. *Paperboard Industry Statistics, Statistics of Paper.*

STATISTICS OF PAPER, PAPERBOARD AND WOOD PULP. 19th Ed. (1981)-. 0731-8863. US. English. an. $235.00 Domestic, $260.00 Foreign. American Paper Institute Inc, 260 Madison Avenue, New York NY 10016. **Tel** (212)340-0630. Ed Benjamin Slatin. **LC** HD9839.P33. **DD** 338.4767620973021. **Circ** 1,000. Long term annual statistical data on paper and paperboard industry. *Statistics of Paper and Paperboard.*

STATISTICS OF PROMOTIONS AND APPEALS. **Main/Corp** Australia. Public Service Board. Project Services Branch. Statistical Section. AT. English. ir. Australia Public Service Board Project Service Branch, Statistical Section, PO Box 84, Canberra ACT 2600 Australia. **LC** JQ4045. **DD** 331.76135494.

STATISTICS OF PUBLIC ELEMENTARY AND SECONDARY SCHOOL SYSTEMS. Fall 1979-. US. English. an. Statistical Information Office National Center for Education Statistics, 400 Maryland Avenue Southwest, Washington DC 20202. **LC** LA210. **DD** 371.010973. Eric Version for 1979-1980 distributed to depository libraries in microfiche. *Statistics of Public Elementary and Secondary Day Schools, 0095-8182.*

STATISTICS OF PUBLIC LIBRARIES. Began with 1955/56. US. English. ir. Superintendent of Documents, US Government Printing Office, Washington DC 20402. Eric Version for 1977/1978 distributed to depository libraries in microfiche.

STATISTICS OF PUBLIC SCHOOL LIBRARIES/MEDIA CENTERS. Began with Fall 1974. 0733-2041. US. English. ir. **LC** Z675.S3. **DD** 027.80973.

STATISTICS OF PUBLIC SCHOOL SYSTEMS IN THE TWENTY LARGEST U.S. CITIES. Fall 1980-. 0742-3888. US. English. an. **LC** LA216. **DD** 373.73.

STATISTICS OF RAILROADS OF CLASS I IN THE UNITED STATES *CEASED.* (STATISTICS OF RAILROADS OF CLASS I IN THE UNITED STATES : STATISTICAL SUMMARY). **Main/Corp** Association of American Railroads. Economics and Finance Dept. 1957/67-1972/82. 0091-4894. US. English. **LC** HE2713. **DD** 385.0973. *Statistics of Railroads of Class I, United States.*

STATISTICS OF ROAD ACCIDENTS IN KARNATAKA STATE. **Main/Corp** Karnataka, India. Public Works Dept. Statistical Unit. English. ir. **LC** HE5614.5.I38. **DD** 388.314.

STATISTICS OF ROAD TRAFFIC ACCIDENTS IN JAPAN. JA. English. ir. International Association of Traffic and Safety Sciences, 6-20 2-Chome, Yaesu Chou-Ku 10 4, Tokyo Japan. **LC** HE5614.5.J3. **DD** 312.440952.

STATISTICS OF SOUTH DAKOTA PUBLIC LIBRARIES. **Main/Corp** South Dakota State Library Commission. 0099-0655. US. English. South Dakota State Library, 322 South 4th Street, Pierre SD 57501. **LC** Z732.S9. **DD** 027.4783.

STATISTICS OF THE AIR BORNE FOREIGN TRADE OF INDIA. II. English. ir. Government of India, 214 Acharya Jagadish Bose Road, Calcutta 700017 India. **LC** HE9788.5.I4. **DD** 382.0954005.

STATISTICS OF THE INDEPENDENT TELEPHONE INDUSTRY *CEASED.* VFOAT Annual Statistical Volume of the United States Independent Telephone Association, Independent Telephone Statistics, Telephone Statistics for the Year . . . . -1984. 0083-1298. US. English. an. US Independent Telephone Association, 1801 K Street NW, Washington DC 20004.

STATISTICS OF THE MISUSE OF DRUGS UNITED KINGDOM, SUPPLEMENTARY TABLES. 0143-1463. UK. English. 2.00. Home Office Statistical Department, Room 1706 Tolworth Tower, Surbiton Surrey KT6 7DS England. **LC** HV5840.G7. **DD** 364.1770941.

STATISTICS OF TIMBER EXPORTS FROM SINGAPORE IN . . . . SI. English. an. Timber Industry Board, 4th Floor Realty Centre, 15-16th/J Enggor Street, Singapore 0207 Singapore. **LC** HD9766.S55. **DD** 382.41498095957021.

STATISTICS OF VIRGINIA PUBLIC LIBRARIES AND INSTITUTIONAL LIBRARIES. 1975/76-. 0731-8464. US. English. an. Virginia State Library, 11th and Capital Streets, Richmond VA 23219. **LC** Z732.V8. **DD** 027.4755. *Statistics of Virginia Public Libraries, 0095-3490.*

STATISTICS OF WAGES, EARNINGS AND HOURS OF WORK . . . AND PREVIOUS YEARS. Periodical. English. ir. Government Publications Sale Office, Government Printing Office Arcade, Dublin 1 Ireland.

STATISTICS OF WESTERN AUSTRALIA : FINANCE. **Main/Corp** Australian Bureau of Statistics. Western Australian Office. AT. English. ir. Australian Bureau of Statistics, Western Australian Office, 1-3 St Georges Terrace, Perth Western Australia 6000 Australia. **LC** HJ96. **DD** 332.09941. *Statistics of Western Australia: Finance.*

STATISTICS OF WESTERN AUSTRALIA : MINING. 1974/75-. AT. English. ir. Australian Bureau of Statistics, GPO Box 796, Sydney New South Wales 2001 Australia. **LC** HD9506.A7. **DD** 338.209941. *Western Australia Mineral Exploration, Economic Census: Mining Establishments, Details of Operation, Western Australia.*

STATISTICS OF WESTERN AUSTRALIA : RURAL INDUSTRIES. **Main/Corp** Australia. Bureau of Statistics. Western Australian Office. 1972/73-. Periodical. AT. English. ir. *Statistics of Western Australia, Rural Industries.*

STATISTICS OF WESTERN AUSTRALIA : TRADE, INTERSTATE AND OVERSEAS. 1972/73-. AT. English. ir. Australian Bureau of Statistics Western Australian Office, 1 3 Street Geroges Terrace, Perth WA 6000 Australia. **LC** HF291. **DD** 382.09941. *Statistics of Western Australia: Trade.*

STATISTICS OF WESTERN AUSTRALIA : TRADE, OVERSEAS. 1972/73-. AT. English. ir. Australian Bureau of Statistics, Western Australian Office, 1-3 St Georges Terrace, Perth Western Australia 6000 Australia. **LC** HF291. **DD** 382.09941. *Statistics of Western Australia: Trade.*

STATISTICS OF WORLD TRADE IN STEEL (NEW YORK, N.Y. : 1976). (STATISTICS OF WORLD TRADE IN STEEL). VFOAT Statistiques du Commerce Mondial de l'Acier. 1976-. US. English (preface in French and Russian). an. $8.50. United Nations Publications, Sales Section/Room A-3315, New York NY 10017. **Tel** (212)754-8302. **LC** HD9510.4. **DD** 382.456720212. Provides basic data on exports of semi-finished and finished steel products from Europe and other steel exporting countries in the world. *Annual Bulletin of Statistics of World Trade in Steel for Europe.*

STATISTICS - OFFICE OF FAMILY SERVICES. **Main/Corp** Louisiana. Office of Family Services. Oct./Dec. 1976-. US. English. **LC** HV86. **DD** 362.9763. *Statistics.*

STATISTICS ON ALASKA'S DRUG ABUSE TREATMENT PROGRAMS AND HEROIN COST STUDY. 1975/76-. 0164-1638. Periodical. US. English. an. **NLM** W2 AA5 O34S. *Statistics on Alaska's Drug Abuse Treatment Programs, 0164-1646.*

STATISTICS ON ALCOHOL AND DRUG USE IN CANADA AND OTHER COUNTRIES. Aug. 1982-. 0715-7657. CN. English. an. Marketing Services Addiction Research Foundation, 33 Russell Street, Toronto Ontario M5S 2S1 Canada. **LC** HV5306. **DD** 362.29220971021. *Statistical Supplement to the Annual Report, 0225-333X.*

. . . STATISTICS ON BANKING. **Main/Corp** Federal Deposit Insurance Corporation. 1981-. Periodical. US. English. an.

STATISTICS ON JUDICIAL ADMINISTRATION. **Main/Corp** Great Britain. Lord Chancellor's Departments. 1973-. UK. English. an. 1.50. HMSO Stationery Office, Lord Chancellor's Departments 49 High Holborn, WC1V 6HB London England. **LC** KD327. **DD** 347.420130212.

STATISTICS ON MARRIAGES. Periodical. English. an. **LC** HB1265.A3. **DD** 306.81095957021.

STATISTICS ON NARCOTIC DRUGS FOR . . . FURNISHED BY GOVERNMENTS IN ACCORDANCE WITH THE INTERNATIONAL TREATIES AND MAXIMUM LEVELS OF OPIUM STOCKS. -1979. US. English. an. $12.50. United Nations, Room A-3315, New York NY 10017. **Tel** (212)754-8302. **NLM** W2 MU5. Contains information on drug manufacture, consumption stocks, and seizure of illicit narcotics.

STATISTICS ON OPERATIONS. **Main/Corp** New York (State). Dept. of Labor. US. English. an. Department of Labor, State Office Building Campus, Albany NY 12226. **LC** HD8053.N7. **DD** 331.109747. *Statistics on Operations.*

STATISTICS ON SALES OF SPORT FISHING LICENCES IN CANADA. VFOAT Fishing Licences. V. 1- 1966/71-. 0711-821X. CN. English (French). Fisheries & Oceans Department of Canada, 240 Sparks Street, Ottawa Ontario K1A 0E6 Canada. **Tel** (613)995-2041. **LC** SH571. **DD** 354.7100858.

STATISTICS ON SCHEDULED BANKS IN PAKISTAN. **Main/Corp** State Bank of Pakistan. Dept. of Statistics. Began publication Dec. 1961. 0039-0577. Periodical. English. qt. State Bank of Pakistan, PO Box 4456, Central Directorate, Karachi Pakistan. **LC** HG3290.5.S8.

STATISTICS ON SOCIAL WORK EDUCATION IN THE UNITED STATES. 1974-. 0163-1403. US. English. an. Council on Social Work Education, 111th Avenue/Suite 501, New York NY 10011. **LC** HV11. **DD** 361.0071173. *Statistics on Graduate Social Work Education in the United States, 0091-7192.*

STATISTICS - ONTARIO MINISTRY OF NATURAL RESOURCES. (STATISTICS - MINISTRY OF NATURAL RESOURCES). **Main/Corp** Ontario. Ministry of Natural Resources. 1973-. 0383-5898. CN. English. an. Ministry of Natural Resources, Information Service, Toronto Ontario Canada. **LC** QH77.C2. **DD** 354.713008232.

STATISTICS, PUBLIC SCHOOL FINANCE DIVISION. US. English. Department of Finance & Administration, Public School Finance Division, Santa Fe NM 87501. **LC** LB2826.N6. **DD** 379.12209789. *Statistics (New Mexico.) Public School Finance Division.*

STATISTICS QUARTERLY - BUREAU OF STATISTICS. (STATISTICS QUARTERLY). VAT Statistics Quarterly - Northwest Territories. Began with Dec. 1979 issue. 0225-9907. Periodical. CN. English. qt. 15.00. Government of the Northwest Territories, Department of Information, Yellowknife North West Territories X1A 2L9 Canada. **Tel** (403)873-7147. **LC** HA747.N6. **DD** 317.19205. **Circ** 900. Provides statistical data on the Northwest Territories.

STATISTICS RELATING TO DGTD UNITS. **Main/Corp** India (Republic). Directorate General of Technical Development. VAT Statistics Relating to Directorate General of Technical Development Units. 1977-. II. English. ir. 15.00 Domestic, 45.40. Govt of India, Directorate of Public Relations & Publications Directorate General of Technical Develop Udyog Bhevan Maulana Ozad Road, New Delhi 110011 India. **LC** HC431. **DD** 338.0954. *Annual Report - Directorate General of Technical Development.*

STATISTICS RELATING TO REGIONAL AND MUNICIPAL GOVERNMENTS IN BRITISH COLUMBIA. 0702-0988. CN. English. an. Department of Municipal Affairs, Parliament Buildings, Victoria British Columbia V8V 1X4 Canada. **LC** HJ9014.B7. **DD** 317.11.

STATISTICS SOURCES. 1st Ed-. 0585-198X. US. English. ir. $250.00. Gale Research Company, Book Tower, Detroit MI 48226. **Tel** (313)961-2242. Ed Paul Wasserman. **LC** Z7551, HA1. **DD** 016.31. **NLM** Z 7551. This reference work is designed basically to identify primary sources of statistical data, especially in American publications, of national rather than regional scope.

STATISTICS - STATE OF TENNESSEE, DEPARTMENT OF HUMAN SERVICES. (STATISTICS - DEPARTMENT OF HUMAN SERVICES). **Main/Corp** Tennessee. Dept. of Human Services. April 1975-. 0361-896X. US. English. mo. State Office Building, Nashville TN 37219. **LC** HV86. **DD** 362.0768. *Statistics.*

STATISTIEK DER BRANDEN. VFOAT Fire Statistics. NE. Dutch. an. 11.00. Centraal Bureau Voor de Statistiek, Staatsuitgeverij, S-Gravenhage Netherlands. **LC** TH9557.

STATISTIEK DER GEMEENTEBEGROTINGEN. VFOAT Statistics of the Municipal Budgets. 1983-. Dutch. an. 12.10. Staatsuitgeverij, The Hague Netherlands. **LC** HJ9054. *Statistiek der Gemeentefinancien Begrotingen.*

STATISTIEK DER PROVINCIALE FINANCIEN. VFOAT Statistics of the Provincial Finances of the Netherlands. 0168-3837. NE. Dutch. ir. 15.00. Centraal Bureau Voor de Statistiek, Prinses

Statistics

Beatrixlaan 428 Postbus 959, 2270 AZ Voorburg Netherlands. LC HJ1204.

STATISTIEK FINANCIEN VAN ONDERNEMINGEN, HANDEL. VFOAT Statistics of Finances of Enterprises, Trade. 0168-8405. NE. Dutch (summaries in English). ir. 14.40. Centraal Bureau Voor de Statistiek, Prinses Beatrixlaan 428, Postbus 959, 2270 AZ Voorburg Netherlands.

STATISTIEK VAN DE ANN-, AF- EN DOORVOER. GOEDERENVERVOER PER GOEDERENSOORT VAN EN NAAR DE ZEEHAVENS VAN ROTTERDAM EN AMSTERDAM. VFOAT Goederenvervoer per Goederensoort van en Naar de Zeehavens van Rotterdam en Amsterdam. NE. Dutch. ir. 24.50. Centraal Bureau Voor de Statistiek, Prinses Beatrixlaan 428 Postbus 949, 2270 Az Voorburg Netherlands.

STATISTIEK VAN DE ANN-, AF- EN DOORVOER. GOEDERENVERVOER PER LAND VAN EN NAAR DE ZEEHAVENS VAN ROTTERDAM EN AMSTERDAM. VFOAT Goederenvervoer per Land van en Naar de Zeehavens van Rotterdam en Amsterdam. 0168-3241. NE. Dutch. ir. 35.00. Centraal Bureau Voor de Statistiek, Prinses Beatrixlaan 428 Postbus 959, 2270 AZ Voorburg Netherlands.

STATISTIEK VAN DE ELEKTRICITEITS—VOORZIENING IN NEDERLAND. Dutch. ir. LC HD9685.N2.

STATISTIEK VAN DE KINDEREN DIE RECHT GEVEN OP KINDERBIJSLAG. STATISTIQUE DES ENFANTS BENEFICIAIRES D'ALLOCATIONS FAMILIALES. Dutch (French). ir. Jan Jacobsplein 6, 1000 Brussels Belgium. LC HD4925.5.B4. *Statistique des Enfants Beneficiaires. D'Allocations Familiales.*

STATISTIEK VAN DE LAND- EN TUINBOUW. VFOAT Statistics on Agriculture. NE. Dutch (summaries in English). an. Centraal Bureau Voor de Statistiek, Staatsuitgeverij, Christoffel Plantijnstraat 1, 2515 Tz's Gravenhage Netherlands. LC S239. DD 338.109492.

STATISTIEK VAN DE SCHEEPVAARTBEWEGING. VFOAT Census of Inland Shipping at Docks and Bridges. Dutch. an. Staatsuitgeverij, S-Gravenhage The Hague Netherlands. LC HE674. *Statistiek van de Scheepvaartbeweging in Nederland.*

STATISTIEK VAN DE VERKEERSONGEVALLEN OP DE OPENBARE WEG. 1950-. Dutch. ir. LC HE5614.

STATISTIEK VAN HET AUTOPARK. Main/Corp Netherlands (Kingdom, 1815-). Centraal Bureau voor de Statistiek. Dutch. ir. Centraal Bureau voor de Statistiek, Staatsuitgeverij, S-Gravenhage Netherlands. LC HE5674.

STATISTIEK VAN HET BEROEPSONDERWIJS. BEROEPSBEGELEIDEND ONDERWIJS LEERLINGWEZEN. VFOAT Beroepsbegeleidend Onderwijs Leerlingwezen, Statistics on Vocational Training. Part-Time Training Apprenticeship Scheme, Part-Time Apprenticeship Scheme. NE. Dutch. an. 5.00. Centraal Bureau voor de Statistiek, Staatsuitgeverij, S-Gravenhage Netherlands. LC HD5715.5.N45.

STATISTIEK VAN HET BEROEPSONDERWIJS : ECONOMISCH EN ADMINISTRATIEF ONDERWIJS, LAGER ALGEMEEN VOORTGEZET ONDERWIJS, MIDDENSTANDSONDERWIJS CEASED. Main/Corp Netherlands. Centraal Bureau Voor de Statistiek. NE. Dutch. ir. 7.00. Centraal Bureau Voor de statistiek, Staatsuitgeverij, S-Gravenhage Netherlands. LC HF1155.

STATISTIEK VAN HET BEROEPSONDERWIJS. KUNSTONDERWIJS. VFOAT Statistics on Vocational Training. 0168-5503. NE. Dutch. an. 9.50. Centraal Bureau voor de Statistiek, Prinses Beatrixlaan 428, Postbus 959, 2270 Az Voorburg, S-Gravenhage Netherlands. LC NX354.A1.

STATISTIEK VAN HET BEROEPSONDERWIJS : LERAREN BIJ HET KUNSTONDERWIJS. Main/Corp Netherlands (Kingdom, 1815-). Centraal Bureau voor de Statistiek. Hoofdafdeling Statistieken van Onderwijs en Wetenschappen. VFOAT Statistics on Vocational Training: Teachers on Art Colleges. Dutch. ir. 6.50. LC N88.5.N4.

STATISTIEK VAN HET BEROEPSONDERWIJS. LERAREN EN BEVOEGDHEIDSSITUATIE BIJ HET HUISHOUD- EN NIJVERHEIDSONDERWIJS. VFOAT Statistics on Vocational Training. NE. Dutch. an. 10.55. Centraal Bureau voor de Statistiek, Prinses Beatrixlaan 428, Postbus 959 2270 AZ, Voorburg Netherlands. LC LC1047.85.

STATISTIEK VAN HET BEROEPSONDERWIJS : LERAREN EN BEVOEGDHEIDSSITUATIE BIJ HET SOCIAAL-PEDAGOGISCH ONDERWIJS. Main/Corp Netherlands (Kingdom, 1815-). Centraal Bureau voor de Statistiek. Hoofdafdeling Statistieken van Onderwijs en Wetenschappen. VFOAT Statistics on Vocational Training. Dutch. ir. LC LB1725.N4.

STATISTIEK VAN HET BEROEPSONDERWIJS : NIEUWE LERARENOPLEIDINGEN WAARIN OPGENOMEN MIDDELBARE AKTENOPLEIDINGEN. VFOAT Nieuwe Lerarenopleidingen Waarin Opgenomen Middelbare Aktenopleidingen. Dutch. ir. 6.75. Centraal Bureau Voor de Statistiek, Staatsuitgeverij, S-Gravenhage Netherlands. LC LB1737.N4.

STATISTIEK VAN HET BEROEPSONDERWIJS : OPLEIDINGSSCHOLEN VOOR KLEUTERLEIDSTERS, PEDAGOGISCHE ACADEMIES. Main/Corp Netherlands. Centraal Bureau Voor de Statistiek. Dutch. ir. 5.50. Centraal Bureau Voor de Statistiek, Staatsuitgeverij, S-Gravenhage Netherlands. LC LB1732.5.

STATISTIEK VAN HET BEROEPSONDERWIJS. TECHNISCH ONDERWIJS, NAUTISCH ONDERWIJS. VFOAT Statistics on Vocational Training. Technical Training, Nautical Training, Technisch Onderwijs, Nautisch Onderwijs, Technical Training, Nautical Training. NE. Dutch (summaries in English). ir. 10.50. Central Bureau voor de Statiskiek, Staatsuitgeverij, S-Gravenhage Netherlands. LC T127.

STATISTIEK VAN HET BUITENGEWOON ONDERWIJS. VFOAT Statistics on Special Education. NE. Dutch. an. 12.10. Centraal Bureau Voor de Statistiek, Prinses Beatrixlaan 428, Postbus 959, 2270 Az Voorburg Netherlands. LC LC4036.N4.

STATISTIEK VAN HET CONSUMPTIEF KREDIET. VFOAT Statistics of Consumptive Credit. NE. Dutch. an. Centraal Bureau Voor de Statistiek, Prinses Beatrixlaan 428 Postbus 959, 2270 Az Voorburg Netherlands.

STATISTIEK VAN HET GEWOON LAGER ONDERWIJS. Dutch. ir. 6.50. Centraal Bureau Voor de Statistiek, Staatsuitgeverij, S-Gravenhage Netherlands. LC LA803.A2. *Statistiek van het Gewoon- en Voortgezet Gewoon Lager Onderwijs.*

STATISTIEK VAN HET GEWOON LAGER ONDERWIJS EN HET BUITENGEWOON ONDERWIJS. INSTROOM, DOORSTROOM EN UITSTROOM VAN HOOFDEN EN ONDERWIJZERS CEASED. VFOAT Statistics on Primary and Special Education: In, Through- and Outflow of Teachers, Instroom, Doorstroom en Uitstroom van Hoofden en Onderwijzers, In-, Through- and Outflow of Teachers. NE. Dutch (summaries in English). an. 6.50. Centraal Bureau Voor de Statistiek, Staatsuitgeverij, S-Gravenhage Netherlands. LC LB2831.646.N4.

STATISTIEK VAN HET INTERNATIONAAL GOEDERENVERVOER. VFOAT Statistics of the International Goods Traffic. NE. Dutch. an. Centraal Bureau voor de Statistiek, Prinses Beatrixlaan 428, Postbus 959, 2270 AZ Voorburg Netherlands. LC HE199.N4. DD 380.52409492021.

STATISTIEK VAN HET WETENSCHAPPELIJK ONDERWIJS. VFOAT Statistics on University Education. 0168-5058. NE. Dutch (summaries in English). an. Central Bureau voor de Statistiek, Princess Beatrixlaan 428, Postbus 959, 2270 AZ Voorburg Netherlands. NLM W2 GN4 C3SA.

STATISTIEK VREEMDELINGENVERKEER. VFOAT Tourism Statistics. NE. Dutch. an. 19.25. Centraal Bureau voor de Statistiek, Prinses Beatrixlaan 428, Postbus 2270, AZ Voorburg Netherlands. LC G155.N2. *Statistiek van het Vreemdelingenverkeer.*

STATISTIEKE VAN ADMINISTRASIERADE. VFOAT Statistics of Administration Boards. SA. Afrikaans (English). ir. The Government Printer, Department of Statistics, Bosman Street, Private Bag X85, Pretoria 0001 South Africa. LC HJ9587.7.

STATISTIEKE VAN MOTOR- EN ANDER VOERTUIE SOOS OP . . . . VFOAT Statistics of Motor and Other Vehicles as at . . . . June 30 1981-. Afrikaans (English). an. 2.50. Government Printer, Bosman Street Private Bag X85, Pretoria 0001 South Africa. *Statistieke van Motor- en Ander Voertuie, Alle Voertuie.*

STATISTIEKE VAN NUWE VOERTUIE GELISENSIEER. Main/Corp South Africa. Dept. of Statistics. VFOAT Statistics of New Vehicles Licensed. Afrikaans and English. ir. The Government Printer, Private Bag X85, Pretoria 0001 South Africa. LC HE5704.4.

STATISTIEKE VAN PLAASLIKE OWERHEDE, ORANJE-VRYSTAAT, TRANSVAAL. Main/Corp South Africa. Dept. of Statistics. VFOAT Local Government Statistics, Orange Free State, Transvaal. Multilingual (Afrikaans, English). ir. 3.75. Department of Statistics, The Government Printer, Private Bag X85 0001, Pretoria South Africa. LC HA2221.

STATISTIESE OORSIG VAN SWART ONTWIKKELING CEASED. Main/Corp Bureau for Economic Research, Co-Operation and Development (South Africa). VFOAT Statistical Survey of Black Development. Afrikaans (English). ir. Bureau for Economic Research Co-Operation and Development, PO Box 2312, Pretoria 0001 South Africa. LC DT763.6. DD 305.8968.

STATISTIK. Main/Corp Perhutani, P. N. Indonesian. ir. LC SD97.I6.

STATISTIK AIR MINUM. VFOAT Water Supply Statistics. English (Indonesian). ir. Biro Pusat Statistik, Jl Dr Sutomo No 8, Jakarta Indonesia. Tel 372808. LC HD4465.I55. DD 333.91009598. bk rev. adv acc. (ctrl)

STATISTIK ARSBOK FOR SVERIGE. See Yearbooks, Almanacs, Directories.

STATISTIK BIOSKOP & REKREASI. VFOAT Statistik Bioskop dan Rekreasi. 1981-. IO. Indonesian. an. Kantor Statistik Propinsi, D K I Jakarta, Jl Merkdeka, Selatan 8-9, Jakarta Indonesia.

STATISTIK COKLAT. Main/Corp Balai Penelitian Perkebunan Bogor. 1970/72. English and Indonesian. ir. LC HD9200.I5.

STATISTIK DER ALLGEMEINBILDENDEN SCHULEN IN NIEDERSACHSEN. German. ir. Niedersachsischen Kultusminister, Schiffgraben 12, 3000 Hannover West Germany. LC LA770.S3. DD 371.0094359.

STATISTIK DES AUSLANDES. LANDERBERICHT. BAHREIN. VFOAT Landerbericht. GW. German. ir. Verlag W Kohlhammer GMBH, Hessbruhlstrasse 69, Postfach 800430, 7000 Stuttgart 80 West Germany. LC HC415.38.A1. DD 330.95365005.

STATISTIK DES AUSLANDES. LANDERBERICHT. BANGLADESCH. VFOAT Landerbericht. GW. German. ir. 11.00. Verlag W Kohlhammer GMBH, Hessbruhlstrasse 69, Postfach 800430, 7000 Stuttgart 80 West Germany. LC HA4590.6. DD 315.492.

STATISTIK DES AUSLANDES. LANDERBERICHT. BOLIVIEN. VFOAT Landerbericht. GW. German. ir. 7.70. Verlag W Kohlhammer GMBH, Hessbruhlstrasse 69, Postfach 800430, 7000 Stuttgart 80 West Germany.

STATISTIK DES AUSLANDES. LANDERBERICHT. DEMOKRATISCHE VOLKSREPUBLIK KOREA. VFOAT Landerbericht. KO. German. ir. 7.70. Verlag W Kohlhammer GMBH, Hessbruhlstrasse 69, Postfach 800430, 7000 Stuttgart 80 West Germany.

STATISTIK DES AUSLANDES. LANDERBERICHT. ECUADOR. VFOAT Landerbericht. GW. German. ir. 7.70. Verlag W Kohlhammer GMBH, Hessbruhlstrasse 69, Postfach

Statistics

800430, 7000 Stuttgart 80 West Germany. **LC** HA1025. **DD** 318.66. *Landerberichte. Ecuador.*

STATISTIK DES AUSLANDES. LANDERBERICHT. EG-STAATEN. **VFOAT** Landerbericht. **GW.** German. ir. 7.70. Verlag W Kohlhammer GMBH, Hessbruhlstrasse 69, Postfach 800430, 7000 Stuttgart 80 West Germany.

STATISTIK DES AUSLANDES. LANDERBERICHT. ELFENBEINKUSTE. **VFOAT** Landerbericht. **GW.** German. ir. 7.70. Verlag W Kohlhammer GMBH, Hessbruhlstrasse 69, Postfach 800430, 7000 Stuttgart 80 West Germany. **LC** HA2096. **DD** 316.662. *Landerberichte: Elfenbeinkuste.*

STATISTIK DES AUSLANDES. LANDERBERICHT. GRIECHENLAND. **VFOAT** Landerbericht. **GW.** German. ir. 7.70. Verlag W Kohlhammer GMBH, Hessbruhlstrasse 69, Postfach 800430, 7000 Stuttgart 80 West Germany. **LC** HA1351. **DD** 314.95.

STATISTIK DES AUSLANDES. LANDERBERICHT. GUATEMALA. **VFOAT** Landerbericht. Guatemala. **GW.** German. ir. 7.70. Verlag W Kohlhammer GMBH, Hessbruhlstrasse 69, Postfach 800430, 7000 Stuttgart 80 West Germany. **LC** HA811. **DD** 317.281.

STATISTIK DES AUSLANDES. LANDERBERICHT. GUYANA. **VFOAT** Landerbericht. Guyana. **GW.** German. ir. 7.90. Verlag W Kohlhammer GMBH, Hessbruhlstrasse 60, Postfach 800430, 7000 Stuttgart 80 West Germany. **LC** HA1033. **DD** 318.81.

STATISTIK DES AUSLANDES. LANDERBERICHT. HAITI. **VFOAT** Landerbericht. Haiti. **GW.** German. ir. 7.70. Verlag W Kohlhammer GMBH, Hessbruhlstrasse 69, Postfach 800430, 7000 Stuttgart 80 West Germany. **LC** HA881. **DD** 317.294.

STATISTIK DES AUSLANDES. LANDERBERICHT. INDONESIEN. **VFOAT** Indonesien, Landerbericht. **GW.** German. ir. 7.70. Verlag W Kohlhammer GMBH, Hessbruhlstrasse 69, Postfach 800430, 7000 Stuttgart 80 West Germany. **LC** HA4601. **DD** 315.98.

STATISTIK DES AUSLANDES. LANDERBERICHT. IRAN. **VFOAT** Landerbericht. **GW.** German. ir. 7.70. Verlag W Kohlhammer GMBH, Hessbruhlstrasse 69, Postfach 800430, 7000 Stuttgart 80 West Germany. *Landerberichte: Iran.*

STATISTIK DES AUSLANDES. LANDERBERICHT. JAMAIKA. **VFOAT** Landerbericht. Jamaika, Jamaika. **GW.** German. ir. 7.70. Verlag W Kohlhammer GMBH, Hessbruhlstrasse 69, Postfach 800430, 7000 Stuttgart 80 West Germany. **DD** 317.292. Each issue contains an index to its own contents - no vol index - loose.

STATISTIK DES AUSLANDES. LANDERBERICHT. JAPAN. **VFOAT** Landerbericht. **GW.** German. ir. 7.70. Verlag W Kohlhammer GMBH, Hessbruhlstrasse 69, Postfach 800430, 7000 Stuttgart 80 West Germany. **LC** HA4621. **DD** 315.2.

STATISTIK DES AUSLANDES. LANDERBERICHT. JORDANIEN. **VFOAT** Landerbericht. **GW.** German. ir. 7.70. Verlag W Kohlhammer GMBH, Hessbruhlstrasse 69, Postfach 800430, 7000 Stuttgart 80 West Germany. *Landerberichte: Jordanien.*

STATISTIK DES AUSLANDES. LANDERBERICHT. KAMERUN. **VFOAT** Landerbericht. **GW.** German. ir. 14.20. Verlag W Kohlhammer GMBH, Hessbruhlstrasse 69, Postfach 800430, 7000 Stuttgart 80 West Germany. **LC** HA4719. **DD** 316.711.

STATISTIK DES AUSLANDES. LANDERBERICHT. KATAR. **VFOAT** Landerbericht. **GW.** German. ir. 7.70. Verlag W Kohlhammer GMBH, Hessbruhlstrasse 69, Postfach 800430, 7000 Stuttgart 80 West Germany. **LC** HC415.37.A1. **DD** 330.95363005.

STATISTIK DES AUSLANDES. LANDERBERICHT. KENIA. **VFOAT** Landerbericht. **GW.** German. ir. 16.80. Verlag W Kohlhammer GMBH, Hessbruhlstrasse 69, Postfach 800430, 7000 Stuttgart 80 West Germany. **LC** HA4693. **DD** 316.762.

STATISTIK DES AUSLANDES. LANDERBERICHT. KOLUMBIEN. **VFOAT** Landerbericht. **GW.** German. ir. 7.70. Verlag W Kohlhammer GMBH, Hessbruhlstrasse 69, Postfach 800430, 7000 Stuttgart 80 West Germany. *Landerberichte: Kolumbien.*

STATISTIK DES AUSLANDES. LANDERBERICHT. LIBYEN. **VFOAT** Landerbericht. **GW.** German. ir. 7.70. Verlag W Kohlhammer GMBH, Hessbruhlstrasse 69, Postfach 800430, 7000 Stuttgart 80 West Germany.

STATISTIK DES AUSLANDES. LANDERBERICHT. MADAGASKAR. **VFOAT** Landerbericht. **GW.** German. ir. 7.70. Verlag W Kohlhammer GMBH, Hessbruhlstrasse 69, Postfach 800430, 7000 Stuttgart 80 West Germany.

STATISTIK DES AUSLANDES. LANDERBERICHT. MALAWI. **VFOAT** Landerbericht. **GW.** German. ir. 7.70. Verlag W Kohlhammer GMBH, Hessbruhlstrasse 69, Postfach 800430, 7000 Stuttgart 80 West Germany.

STATISTIK DES AUSLANDES. LANDERBERICHT. MALI. **VFOAT** Landerbericht. **GW.** German. ir. 7.70. Verlag W Kohlhammer GMBH, Hessbruhlstrasse 69, Postfach 800430, 7000 Stuttgart 80 West Germany.

STATISTIK DES AUSLANDES. LANDERBERICHT. OMAN. **VFOAT** Landerbericht. **GW.** German. ir. 7.70. Verlag W Kohlhammer GMBH, Hessbruhlstrasse 69, Postfach 800430, 7000 Stuttgart 80 West Germany.

STATISTIK DES AUSLANDES. LANDERBERICHT. SAMBIA. **VFOAT** Landerbericht. **GW.** German. ir. 9.70. Verlag W Kohlhammer GMBH, Hessbruhlstrasse 69, Postfach 800430, 7000 Stuttgart 80 West Germany.

STATISTIK DES AUSLANDES. LANDERBERICHT. SESCHELLEN. **VFOAT** Landerbericht. Seschellen. **GW.** German. ir. 7.70. Verlag W Kohlhammer GMBH, Hessbruhlstrasse 69, Postfach 800430, 7000 Stuttgart 80 West Germany. **LC** HA4739.9. **DD** 316.96.

STATISTIK DES AUSLANDES. LANDERBERICHT. SOMALIA. **VFOAT** Landerbericht. **GW.** German. ir. 7.70. Verlag W Kohlhammer GMBH, Hessbruhlstrasse 69, Postfach 800430, 7000 Stuttgart 80 West Germany. **LC** HA4690. **DD** 316.773.

STATISTIK DES AUSLANDES. LANDERBERICHT. TSCHAD. **VFOAT** Landerbericht. **GW.** German. ir. 7.70. Verlag W Kohlhammer GMBH, Hessbruhlstrasse 69, Postfach 800430, 7000 Stuttgart 80 West Germany.

STATISTIK DES AUSLANDES. LANDERBERICHT. TUNESIEN. **VFOAT** Landerbericht. **GW.** German. ir. 7.70. Verlag W Kohlhammer GMBH, Hessbruhlstrasse 69, Postfach 800430, 7000 Stuttgart 80 West Germany. *Landerberichte: Tunesien.*

STATISTIK DES AUSLANDES. LANDERBERICHT. TURKEI. **VFOAT** Turkei. **GW.** German. ir. 7.70. Verlag W Kohlhammer GMBH, Hessbruhlstrasse 69, Postfach 800430, 7000 Stuttgart 80 West Germany. **LC** HA4556.5. **DD** 315.61.

STATISTIK DES AUSLANDES. LANDERBERICHT. ZYPERN. **VFOAT** Landerbericht. **GW.** German. ir. 7.70. Verlag W Kohlhammer GMBH, Hessbruhlstrasse 69, Postfach 800430, 7000 Stuttgart 80 West Germany.

STATISTIK DES AUSLANDES. LANDERKURZBERICHT. BOTSUANA, LESOTHO, SWASILAND. **VFOAT** Landerkurzbericht. **GW.** German. ir. 5.40. Verlag W Kohlhammer GMBH, Hessbruhlstrasse 69, Postfach 800430, 7000 Stuttgart 80 West Germany. **LC** HA4706. **DD** 316.81. *Statistik des Auslandes. Landerkurzbericht. Botsuana.*

STATISTIK DES AUSLANDES. LANDERKURZBERICHT. CHINA (TAIWAN). **GW.** German. ir. 4.80. Verlag W Kohlhammer GMBH, Hessbruhlstrasse 69, Postfach 800430, 7000 Stuttgart 80 West Germany. **LC** HA4646. **DD** 315.1249.

STATISTIK DES AUSLANDES. LANDERKURZBERICHT. DOMINIKANISCHE REPUBLIK. **VFOAT** Landerkurzbericht. **GW.** German. ir. 5.10. Verlag W Kohlhammer GMBH, Hessbruhlstrasse 69, Postfach 800430, 7000 Stuttgart 80 West Germany. **LC** HA886. **DD** 317.293.

STATISTIK DES AUSLANDES. LANDERKURZBERICHT. KARIBISCHE STAATEN. **VFOAT** Landerkurzbericht. Karibische Staaten. **GW.** German. ir. 5.10. Verlag W Kohlhammer GMBH, Hessbruhlstrasse 69, Postfach 800430, 7000 Stuttgart 80 West Germany. **LC** HA855.5. **DD** 317.29.

STATISTIK DES AUSLANDES. LANDERKURZBERICHT. PAZIFISCHE STAATEN. **VFOAT** Landerkurzbericht. **GW.** German. ir. 5.40. Verlag W Kohlhammer GMBH, Hessbruhlstrasse 69, Postfach 800430, 7000 Stuttgart 80 West Germany. **LC** HA4001. **DD** 319.

STATISTIK DES AUSLANDES. LANDERKURZBERICHT. VEREINIGTE ARABISCHE EMIRATE. **VFOAT** Landerkurzbericht. **GW.** German. ir. 4.80. Verlag W Kohlhammer GMBH, Hessbruhlstrasse 69, Postfach 800430, 7000 Stuttgart 80 West Germany. **LC** HA4566. **DD** 315.357.

STATISTIK EKSPOR HASIL HUTAN BUKAN KAYU. **Main/Corp** Indonesia. Direktorat Bina Sarana Usaha Kehutanan. Indonesian. ir. Direktorat Bina Sarana Usaha Kehutanan, Jl Kalemba Raya 16, Jakarta Indonesia. **LC** HD9766.I7. *Statistik Ekspor Hasil Hutan Non Kayu.*

STATISTIK ENERGI. **VFOAT** Energy Statistics. English (Indonesian). an. Biro Pusat Statistik, Jl Dr Sutomo No 8, Jakarta Indonesia. Tel 372808. **LC** HD9502.I5. **DD** 333.7909598. bk rev. adv acc. (ctrl).

STATISTIK FRAN ENSKILDA LANDER. **Main/Corp** Statistiska Centralbyrans Bibliotek (Sweden). 0280-7610. SW. Swedish. an. Statistiska Centralbyrans Bibliotek, 115 81 Stockholm Sweden. **LC** Z7552, HA154.

STATISTIK HARGA HARGA PROPINSI KALIMANTAN TIMUR. **Series/Titl** Bulletin Statistik Tahunan. Indonesian. an. Kantor Sensus & Statistik Propinsi Kalimantan Timur, Jl Kemakmuran Temindung PO Box 127, Samarinda Indonesia. **LC** HB235.I5.

STATISTIK HARGA . . . SULAWESI SELATAN. **VFOAT** Price Statistics . . . Sulawesi Selatan. 1980-. English (Indonesian). an. Kantor Statistik Propinsi Sulawesi Selatan, Jl Haji Bau No 6, Ujung Pandang Indonesia. **LC** HB235.I5. **DD** 338.528095984.

STATISTIK IN DER RENTENVERSICHERUNG. **Series/Titl** Schriften zur Rortbildung. Seminar 1-. Periodical. **GW.** German. ir. Verband Deutscher Rentenversicherungstrager, Eysseneckstr 55, Frankfurt Am Main West Germany. **LC** HD7177. **DD** 368.400943.

STATISTIK INDONESIA. See Yearbooks, Almanacs, Directories.

STATISTIK INDONESIA. STATISTICAL POCKETBOOK, INDONESIA. **VFOAT** Statistical Pocketbook, Indonesia. 1964/67-1976. English (Indonesian). ir. $10.85. Biro Pusat Statistik, Jalan Dr Sutomo No 8, PO Box 3, Jakarta Indonesia. **LC** HA1811. **DD** 315.98. *Statistical Pocketbook of Indonesia.*

STATISTIK INDUSTRI BALI. 1975-1981-. Indonesian. ir. Kantor Statistik Propinsi Bali, JL Raya Puputan, Denpasar Indonesia. **LC** HC448.B3.

STATISTIK INDUSTRI KARET REMAH (CRUMB RUBBER). 1980 and 1981-. IO. English (Indonesian). ir. Biro Pusat Statistik, Jl Dr Sutomo No 8, Jakarta Indonesia.

STATISTIK INDUSTRI KECIL. **VFOAT** Small Scale Industrial Statistics. English (Indonesian). ir. Biro Pusat Statistik, Jl Dr Sutomo No 8, Jakarta Indonesia. Tel 372808. **LC** HD2346.I6. **DD** 338.64209598. bk rev. adv acc. (ctrl).

STATISTIK JAWA BARAT. **Main/Corp** Jawa Barat, Indonesia. Kantor Sensus dan Statistik. 1971-. Indonesian. ir. Kanor Sensus Dan Statistik, IL Jend Gatotsubroto 77, Bandung Indonesia. **LC** HA1817.J35.

STATISTIK - KAMMER DE GEWERBLICHEN WIRTSCHAFT FUR WIEN. **Main/Corp** Vienna. Kammer de Gewerblichen Wirtschaft fur Wien. German. ir. Stubenring 8-10, Wien I Austria. **LC** HA1189.V6.

STATISTIK KEAGAMAAN. Indonesian. ir. **LC** BP63.I5.

STATISTIK KENDARAAN BERMOTOR DAN PANJANG JALAN. **Main/Corp** Indonesia. Biro Pusat Statistik. **Series/Titl** Statistik Perhubungan. Indonesian. ir. Biro Pusat Statistik, Jln Dr Sutomo No 8, Jarkarta Indonesia. **LC** HE5695.

STATISTIK KEUANGAN DESA. **VFOAT** Village Government Financial Statistics. English (Indonesian). an. $4.80. Bagian Statistik Tahunan dan

Statistics

Penerbitan, Biro Pusat Statistik, Jl Dr Sutomo No 8, PO Box 3, Jakarta Indonesia. Tel 372808. LC HJ9555. DD 336.014598. bk rev. adv acc. (ctrl). *Statistik Keuangan Pemerintahan Desa.*

STATISTIK KEUANGAN DESA JAWA DAN MADURA. VFOAT Village Government Financial Statistics, Java and Madura. 1977/1978-. 0126-4397. IO. English (Indonesian). an. $4.80. Bagian Statistik Tahunan dan Penerbitan, Biro Pusat Statistik, Jl Dr Sutomo No 8, PO Box 3, Jakarta Indonesia. Tel 372808. LC HJ9575. DD 336.014598. bk rev. adv acc. (ctrl). *Statistik Keuangan Pemerintahan Desa.*

STATISTIK KOTAMADYA PASURUAN. 1980-. IO. Indonesian. an. Kantor Statistik Kotamadya Pasuruan, Jl Panglima Sudirman No 84, Pasuruan Indonesia. LC HA4608.P37. *Statistik Kotamadya Daerah Tingkat II Pasuruan.*

STATISTIK KRIMINIL CEASED. Main/Corp Indonesia. Biro Pusat Statistik. Series/Titl Statistik Sosial. VFOAT Crime Statistics. IO. Indonesian. ir. Biro Pusat Statistik, Jl Dr Sutomo No 8, Jakarta Indonesia. LC HV7101.

STATISTIK KUNJUNGAN WISATAWAN ASING KE INDONESIA. VFOAT Statistics on International Tourist Arrivals to Indonesia. English (Indonesian). ir. LC G155.I5. DD 382.4591598040212.

STATISTIK LEMBAGA PEMASYARAKATAN DAN KEJAKSAAN. 1981-. Indonesian. an. LC HV9804.J39.

STATISTIK LINGKUNGAN HIDUP INDONESIA. 1982-. Indonesian. ir. Biro Pusat Statistik, Jl Dr Sutomo No 8, Jakarta Indonesia. Tel 372808. LC HC447. bk rev. adv acc. (ctrl).

STATISTIK OVER LUFTFARTSAKTIVITETER. DK. Danish. qt. Statens Luftfartsvsen Luftfartsdirektoratet, Gammel Kongevej 60, 1850 Kbenhavn V Denmark.

STATISTIK OVER PENSIONSTAGARNA I FINLAND. VFOAT Statistical Yearbook of Pensioners in Finland. 0780-7554. Swedish (with English summaries). an. LC HD7197.3.

STATISTIK PENDIDIKAN DILUAR LINGKUNGAN DEPARTEMEN P & K. Feb. 1978-. IO. Indonesian. ir. $1.35. Bagian Statistik Tahunan dan Penerbitan, Biro Pusat Statistik, Jl Dr Sutomo No 8, PO Box 3, Jakarta Indonesia. Tel 372808. LC LA1271. bk rev. adv acc. (ctrl). *Statistik Pendidikan Diluar Lingkungan Departemen P & K Daerah Jawa, Bali dan Sumatera Utara.*

STATISTIK PENDIDIKAN DILUAR LINGKUNGAN DEPARTEMEN P & K DI-SUMATERA UTARA. Main/Corp Sumatera Utara, Indonesia. Kantor Sensus dan Statistik. Indonesian. ir. LC LA1272.

STATISTIK PENDIDIKAN (SEKOLAH, MURID DAN GURU). Main/Corp Indonesia. Badan Pengembangan Pendidikan. VAT Statistik Pendidikan (Sekolah, Murid dan Guru) Departemen/Lembaga Pemerintah Diluar Departemen Pendidikan dan Kebudayaan. Indonesian. ir. Badan Pengembangan Pendidikan, Departemen Pendidikan Dau Kebudayaan, Jln Jenderal Sudirman, Jakarta Indonesia. LC LA1270.

STATISTIK PENDIDIKAN SMA SELURUH INDONESIA. Main/Corp Proyek Pengembangan Informasi Pendidikan. VAT Statistik Pendidikan Sekolah Menengah Atas Seluruh Indonesia. English and Indonesian. ir. Selatan Departemen Pendidikan Dan Kebudayaan, Jln Jend Sudirman Senayan, Jakarta Indonesia. LC LA1272.

STATISTIK PENDIDIKAN ST SELURUH INDONESIA. Main/Corp Proyek Pengembangan Informasi Pendidikan. VAT Statistik Pendidikan Sekolah Tehnik Seluruh Indonesia. IO. English and Indonesian. ir. Departemen Pendidkian dan Kebudayaan, Jl Jenderal Sudirman, Jakarta Indonesia. LC T163.I6.

STATISTIK PERHUTANI JAWA TENGAH. Main/Corp Perhutani Jawa Tengah. Indonesian. ir. LC SD97.I6.

STATISTIK PERJALANAN WISATAWAN DOMESTIK JAWA TENGAH. Indonesian. ir. Biro Pusat Statistik, Kantor Statistik Propinsi Jateng, JL Pahlawan No 6, Semarang Indonesia. LC G155.I5.

STATISTIK PERUMAHAN DAN LINGKUNGANNYA. 1981-. IO. Indonesian. ir. Biro Pusat Statistik, Jl Dr Sutomo No 8, Jakarta Indonesia. LC HD7365.A3.

STATISTIK RESTORAN : HASIL PELAKSANAAN SURVEI KHUSUS RESTORAN DI 12 PROPINSI. IO. Indonesian. ir. Biro Pusat Statistik, Jl Dr Sutomo No 8, Jakarta Indonesia. Tel 372808. LC TX945. bk rev. adv acc. (ctrl).

STATISTIK TANAMAN BAHAN MAKANAN. Indonesian. ir. Kantor Statistik Propinsi Bali, JL Raya Puputan, Denpasar Indonesia. LC SB176.I5.

STATISTIK UBER NS-PROZESSE. Periodical. German. ir. Prasidium der VVN-Bund der Antifaschisten, 6 Frankfurt/Main, Rossestrasse 4, Frankfurt West Germany. DD 341.69.

STATISTIKA. Main/Corp Bulgaria. Glavna Direktsiia Na Statistikata. Periodical. BU. Bulgarian. bm. Hernus, 6 Boulevard Rusky, Sofia Bulgaria. LC HA1621.

STATISTIKA : CASOPIS PRO TEORII A PRAXI SOUSTAVY SOCIALNE EKONOMICKYCH INFORMACI. Periodical. Czech. mo.

STATISTIKAH SHENATIT SHEL HA-MOSADOT HA-BANKAIYIM. VFOAT Annual Statistics of the Banking System. 1974-1978-. English (Hebrew). an. LC HG3260.A6. DD 332.1095694.

STATISTIKE EPETERIS DEMOSION OIKONOMIKON. See Yearbooks, Almanacs, Directories.

STATISTIKE EPETERIS TES HELLADOS / STATISTICAL YEARBOOK OF GREECE / HELLENIC REPUBLIC, NATIONAL STATISTICAL SERVICE OF GREECE. See Yearbooks, Almanacs, Directories.

STATISTIKE TOU DELOTHENTOS EISODEMATOS PHYSIKON PROSOPON KAI TES PHOROLOGIAS AUTOU. Main/Corp Ethnike Statistike Hyperesia Tes Hellados. Greek, Modern. ir. $1.00. Ethnike Statistike Hyperesia Hellados, Athenai Greece. LC HC291.

STATISTIKEN UBER DEN AUSSENHANDEL. ANALYTISCHE UBERSICHTEN : AUSFUHR. VFOAT Foreign Trade Statistics. 1958-. 0585-1661. Periodical. German, French Italian, Dutch, and English. qt. Statistical Office of the European Communities, Brussels Belgium. LC HF181. DD 383. *Jahrbuch des Aussenhandels Nach Ursprungs-Und Bestimmungslandern, 0561-9270.*

STATISTIKS I.E. STATISTISK INFORMATIONSMATERIALE OM INDVANDRERBRN OG -UNGE. VFOAT Statistisk Informationsmateriale om Indvandrerbrn Og -unge. Jan. 1982-. Danish. ir. LC HV786.

STATISTIQUE AGRICOLE. PRINCIPAUX RENSEIGNEMENTS, REGIONS NORD-PAS DE CALAIS ET PICARDIE. VFOAT Principaux Renseignements, Regions Nord-Pas de Calais et Picardie. 0243-7155. FR. French. an. 25 rue Evrard de Fouilloy, 80041 Amiens Cedex France. LC S230.N673. DD 338.1094427. *Statistique Agricole. Regions Nord-Picardie.*

STATISTIQUE AGRICOLE : REGION PARISIENNE. French. ir. Ministere de l'Agriculture, 33 rue Chanzy, Paris France 75011. LC HD1950.P35.

STATISTIQUE ANNUELLE (CHARBONNAGES DE FRANCE. DIRECTION DE L'INFORMATIQUE ET DE L'ETUDE DES MARCHES). (STATISTIQUE ANNUELLE). French. an. LC HD9552.1. DD 333.8220944. *Statistique Annuelle (Charbonnages de France. Service d'Informatique et d'Etudes des Marches).*

STATISTIQUE ANNUELLE DES VEHICULES NEUFS IMMATRICULES EN BELGIQUE. JAARLIJKSE STATISTIEK DER NIEUWE VOERTUIGEN IN BELGIE INGESCHREVEN. VFOAT Jaarlijkse Statistiek der Nieuwe Voertuigen in Belgie Ingeschreven. Dutch (French). ir. Febiac, Boulevard de la Woluwe 46 Bie 6, B-1200 Bruxelles Belgium. LC HE5673.A45.

STATISTIQUE - BUREAU DE LA STATISTIQUE DU QUEBEC. (STATISTIQUES). Vol. 1, No. 1 (Mar. 1981)-. 0227-0668. CN. French. qt. $15.00. Editeur Officiel du Quebec, 1283 Boul Charets Ouest, Quebec Quebec G1N 2C9 Canada. Ind/Abst Foreign Lang. Index. LC HA747. DD 317.14. *Revue Statistique du Quebec.*

STATISTIQUE CRIMINELLE DE LA BELGIQUE. Series/Titl Statistiques Judiciaires. Began with 1944. BE. French. an. 125 Domestic, 175 Foreign. Institut National de Statistique, rue de Louvain 44, 1000 Bruxelles Belgium. Tel (02)513.96.50. LC HV7353. DD 364.94930212. Circ 350. (ctrl). Statistics about criminality.

STATISTIQUE DE L'INDUSTRIE MINERALE CEASED. VFOAT Annales des Mines. FR. French. an. Service du Traitement, 85 Boulevard du Monntparnasse, 75006 Paris France. Tel 556.41.08. LC TN71. DD 338.20944. *Statistique de l'Industrie Minerale.*

STATISTIQUE DU TRAFIC INTERNATIONAL (U.E.B.L.). Began with Vol. For 1977. BE. French. qt. 600 Domestic, 800 Foreign. Institut National de Statistique, Rue de Louvain 44, 1000 Bruxelles Belgium. Tel (02)513 96 50. LC HF3601.5. DD 380.109493. Circ 295. (ctrl). Statistics about the international traffic in the Belgian seaports. *Statistique du Trafic International des Ports. Chiffres Provisoires.*

STATISTIQUE MEDICALE DANS LES ARMEES. VFOAT Statistique Medicale des Armees. 0291-851X. FR. French. an. Centre de Traitement de l'Information Medicale des Armees, 69 Avenue de Paris, 94160-Saint-Mande France. LC UH271. DD 355.3450944.

STATISTIQUE MENSUELLE DE L'ENERGIE (FRANCE. SERVICE D'ETUDE DES STRATEGIES ET DES STATISTIQUES INDUSTRIELLES). (STATISTIQUE MENSUELLE DE L'ENERGIE). FR. French. mo. 83 Bd du Montparnasse, 75270 Paris Cedex 06 France. LC HD9502.F7. DD 333.790944. *Statistique Mensuelle de l'Energie (France. Delegation Generale a l'Energie).*

STATISTIQUES AGRICOLES, ANNUAIRE. See Yearbooks, Almanacs, Directories.

STATISTIQUES & ETUDES FINANCIERES. SERIE ORANGE CEASED. VFOAT Statistiques et Etudes Financieres. No. 1 (1971)-. Periodical. French. qt. *Statistiques & Etudes Financieres.*

STATISTIQUES & ETUDES : MIDI-PYRENEES. June 1971-. Periodical. FR. French. qt. INSEE-CNGP, BP 2718, 80027 Amiens Cedex France. LC HA1228.A78. *Bulletin de Statistique: Midi-Pyrenees (Ariege, Aveyron, Haute-Garonne, Gers, Lot, Hautes-Pyrenees, Tarn, Tarn-et-Garonne).*

STATISTIQUES AVICOLES. VFOAT Poultry Statistics. 0300-5690. Periodical. CN. English (French, 1972-73). mo. 117 rue Saint Andre, Quebec Quebec G1K 3Y3 Canada. LC HD9437.C23. DD 338.1765009714. *Couvirs: Mise en Elevage.*

STATISTIQUES : BATIMENTS, TRANSPORTS. Main/Corp France. Direction de l'Equipement et des Transports. Bureau A 2. French. ir. LC HE6981. DD 383.420944.

STATISTIQUES (CAISSE NATIONALE DE L'ASSURANCE MALADIE DES TRAVAILLEURS SALARIES, (FRANCE). DEPARTEMENT STATISTIQUE). (STATISTIQUES). 1981-. FR. French. an. 66 Avenue du Maine, 75682 Paris Cedex 14 France. *Statistiques de l'Annee.*

STATISTIQUES (CAISSES CENTRALES DE MUTUALITE SOCIALE AGRICOLE (FRANCE). (STATISTIQUES). FR. French. ir. 8-10 rue d'Astorg, Paris 8E France.

STATISTIQUES DE LA CONSTRUCTION. Main/Corp France. Bureau des Systemes d'Information sur la Construction et l'Urbanisation. Series/Titl Etudes sur la Construction et l'Equipement. FR. French. an. Documentation Francaise, 29-31 Quai Voltaire, 75340 Paris Cedex 07 France. LC HD9715.F7. DD 338.476240944.

STATISTIQUES DE LA CONSTRUCTION ET DU LOGEMENT. Main/Corp Belgium. Institut National de Statistique. 1971-. 0772-7712. BE. French (Dutch). an. 375

Statistics

Domestic, 425 Foreign. Institut National de Statistique, Rue de Louvain 44, 1000 Bruxelles Belgium. **Tel** (02)513 96 50. **LC** HD9715.B4. **DD** 338.4769009493. **Circ** 825. (ctrl). Statistics about building, construction and housing.

STATISTIQUES DE LA JUSTICE. CONTINENT ET ILES ADJACENTES. (STATISTIQUES DE LA JUSTICE : CONTINENT ET ILES ADJACENTES). **Main/Corp** Portugal. Instituto Nacional de Estatistica. Servicos Centrais. **VFOAT** Estatisticas da Justica : Continente e Ilhas Adjacentes. 0253-0600. Portuguese (French). be. **DD** 347.4690130212.

STATISTIQUES DE L'AGRICULTURE, DES PECHES ET DE L'ALIMENTATION. 0828-2501. CN. French. **LC** HD9014.C4. **DD** 338.109713021.

STATISTIQUES DE L'ENSEIGNEMENT. French. ir. Ministere de l'Education Nationale, Direction de la Planification Statistique et Information, Kigali Rwanda. **LC** LA2090.R95. **DD** 370.967571.

STATISTIQUES DE L'ENSEIGNEMENT AU GABON. French. ir. Ministere de Education Nationale, BP 334, Libreville Gabon Africa. **LC** LA1821.G3. **DD** 370.96721.

STATISTIQUES DE L'ENSEIGNEMENT SECONDAIRE. Main/Corp Luxemburg. Ministere de l'Education Nationale. Service des Statistiques. French. ir. Ministere de l'Education Nationale, Service des Statistiques, 12 rue du St Esprit, Luxembourg Luxembourg. **LC** LA1040.L8. **DD** 373.4934.

STATISTIQUES DE L'INDUSTRIE FRANCAISE DES PATES, PAPIERS ET CARTONS. Main/Corp Centre d'Etudes et de Productivite des Industries des Papiers, Cartons et Celluloses. French. ir. 154 Boulevard Haussmann, Paris France 75008. **LC** HD9832.4. *Quelques Donnees Statistiques sur l'Industrie Francaise des Pates, Papiers, Cartons.*

STATISTIQUES DE L'INDUSTRIE GAZIERE EN FRANCE. Main/Corp France. Direction du Gaz, de l'Electricite et du Charbon. French. ir. Ministere de l'Industrie et de la Recherche, 24 rue de l'Universite, Paris France 75700. **LC** TP733.F8. **DD** 338.4766570944. *Statistiques Officielles de l'Industrie Gaziere en France.*

STATISTIQUES DE PERSONNEL. Main/Corp France. Ministere des P.T.T., Direction du Personnel et des Affaires Sociales. French. an. **LC** HE6981. **DD** 331.76138030944.

STATISTIQUES DE PLANNING FAMILIAL. Main/Corp Tunisia. Division de la Population. French. sa. **LC** HQ766.5.T83. **DD** 362.82.

STATISTIQUES DE RECETTES PUBLIQUES DES PAYS MEMBRES DE L'OCDE: UNE CLASSIFICATION NORMALISEE. Main/Corp Organisation for Economic Co-Operation and Development. **VFOAT** Revenue Statistics of OECD Member Countries : A Standardized Classification. Began with 1965/70?. French (English). ir. $8.25. OECD Publications Center, Suite 1207/1750 Pennsylvania Avenue, Washington DC 20006. **Tel** (202)724-1857. **LC** HJ2279. **DD** 336.20091713.

STATISTIQUES DE SECURITE SOCIALE, ASSOCIATIONS SYNDICALES ET PATRONALES : CONTINENT, ACORES ET MADERE. ESTATISTICAS DE SEGURANCA SOCIAL, ASSOCIACOES SINDICAIS E PATRONAIS : CONTINENTE, ACORES E MADEIRA. Main/Corp Instituto Nacional de Estatistica (Portugal). Servicos Centrais. **VFOAT** Estatisticas de Seguranca Social, Associacoes Sindicais e Patronais. 0377-211X. French (Portuguese). ir. **LC** HD6490.W38. *Statistiques des Associations Patronales, Syndicales et Prevoyance Sociale: Continent, Acores et Madeira.*

STATISTIQUES DE TRAFIC. Main/Corp Western European Airport Association. English and French. ir. Aeroport de Paris, 94396 Orly Aerogare, Paris France. **LC** HE9778. **DD** 387.740212.

STATISTIQUES DE TRAFIC : BULLETIN MENSUEL. Main/Corp Aeroport de Paris. Section Etudes Statistiques. French. ir. Aeroport de Paris, 94396 Orly Aerogare, Paris France. **LC** HE9797.5.F72. **DD** 387.740944. *Statistiques de Trafic.*

STATISTIQUES DE TRAFIC : GRANDS AEROPORTS DE L'OUEST DE L'EUROPE. Main/Corp Aeroport de Paris. Service Statistique. 1951-. 0078-947X. French. ir. Western European Airport Association, 291 B D Raspazl, 75014 Paris France. **LC** HE9842.A4. **DD** 387.7.

STATISTIQUES DE TRAFIC. RESULTATS GENERAUX. French (English). ir. **LC** HE9778. **DD** 387.740212.

STATISTIQUES DEMOGRAPHIQUES. Main/Corp Belgium. Institut National de Statistique. 1969-. 0067-5490. Periodical. BE. French. ir. 200 Domestic, 320 Foreign. Institute National de Statistique, rue de Louvain 44, 1000 Bruxelles Belgium. **Tel** (02)513.96.50. **Ind/Abst** Foreign Lang. Index, PAIS Foreign Lang. Index. **NLM** W2 GB4 I5SF. **Circ** 650. (ctrl). Population studies.

STATISTIQUES DES BENEFICIAIRES DE PRESTATIONS DE RETRAITE ET DE SURVIE. VFOAT Statistiek van de Personen die een Rust- en Overlevingsprestatie Genieten. 1970-. Flemish and French. ir. Place Jean Jacobs 6, 1000 Bruxelles Belgium. **LC** HD7106.B3.

STATISTIQUES DES COMPTES POUR L'EXERCICE . . . DES COMMUNES, DES DEPARTEMENTS, DES REGIONS ET DES ETABLISSEMENTS PUBLICS LOCAUX. Series/Titl Finances du Secteur Public Local. **VFOAT** Communes, les Departements, les Regions, les Etablissements Publics Locaux. FR. French. an. 93 rue de Rivoli, Paris 1Er France. **LC** HJ9779.F7. **DD** 336.01444. *Statistiques des Comptes des Communes, des Departements et de Leurs Etablissements Publics.*

STATISTIQUES DES PERSONNES ASSUJETTIES AU STATUT SOCIAL DES TRAVAILLEURS INDEPENDANTS. VFOAT Statistiek der Personen die Onder de Toepassing Vallen van het Sociaal Statuut der Zelfstandigen. Flemish and French. ir. Place Jean Jacobs 6, 1000 Bruxelles Belgium. **LC** HD7186.

STATISTIQUES DES REGIMES D'ASSURANCE MALADIE. FR. French. ir. 66 Avenue de Maine, 75682 Paris France.

STATISTIQUES DES SOCIETES. Main/Corp Portugal. Instituto Nacional de Estatistica. Servicos Centrais. **VFOAT** Estatisticas das Sociedades. 1970-. French (Portuguese). ir. Imprensa Nacional, Av Antonie Jose de al Eida, 1078 Lisboa Codex Portugal. **LC** HD2889. *Estatisticas das Sociedades.*

STATISTIQUES DES TRANSPORTS CEASED. **Main/Corp** Institut National de Statistique (Belgium). BE. French. mo. 360.00. rue de Louvain 44, Bruxelles Belgium. **Ind/Abst** Foreign Lang. Index. **LC** HF203. **DD** 380.509493. *Statistiques du Commerce et des Transports.*

STATISTIQUES DES TRANSPORTS ET COMMUNICATIONS : CONTINENT, AZORES ET MADERE. Main/Corp Instituto Nacional de Estatistica (Portugal). Servicos Centrais. **VFOAT** Estatisticas dos Transportes e Comunicacoes : Continente, Acores e Madeira. 1976-. 0377-2292. French (Portuguese). ir. Instituto Nacional de Estatistica, Servicos Centrais, Avenida Antonio Jose de Almeida 1, Lisboa Portugal. **LC** HE77. **DD** 380.305. *Statistiques des Transports: Continente et Iles Adjacentes.*

STATISTIQUES DIVERSES. Series/Titl Statistiques Judiciaires. French. an. 85 Domestic, 135 Foreign. Institut National de Statistique, rue de Louvain 44, Brussels 1000 Belgium. **Tel** (02)513.96.50. **DD** 347.493013, 344.930713. **Circ** 350. (ctrl). Law and court statistics.

STATISTIQUES DU BATIMENT ET DE L'HABITATION : CONTINENT, AZORES ET MADERE = ESTATISTICAS DA CONSTRUCAO E DA HABITACAO : CONTINENTE, ACORES E MADEIRA. Main/Corp Portugal. Instituto Nacional de Estatistica. Servicos Centrais. **VFOAT** Estatisticas da Construcao e da Habitacao :. Periodical. French and Portuguese. ir. 140.00. Av Antonio Jose de Almeida 1, Lisboa Portugal. **LC** HD7352.A3.

STATISTIQUES DU COMMERCE. Main/Corp Institut National de Statistique (Belgium). 1972-. French. ir. 360. Institut National de Statistique, rue de Louvain 44, Bruxelles Belgium. **Ind/Abst** Foreign Lang. Index. **LC** HF203. **DD** 380.09493. *Statistiques du Commerce et des Transports.*

STATISTIQUES DU COMMERCE EXTERIEUR DE L'UNION ECONOMIQUE BELGO-LUXEMBOURGEOISE. VFOAT Statistiques du Commerce Exterieur. French. mo. 3250. Institut National de Statistique, Rue de Louvain, 44 Centre Albert/8th Etage, 1000 Bruxelles Belgium. **Tel** 02/513.96.50. **LC** HF3601. **DD** 382.094920021. **Circ** 500. (ctrl). Statistics: import, export and foreign trade.

STATISTIQUES DU COMMERCE INTERIEUR ET DES TRANSPORTS. No. 1-2 (Jan.-Feb. 1985)-. Periodical. French. mo. Institut National de Statistique, rue de Louvain, 44 1000 Bruxelles Belgium. **Tel** 02/513.96.50. **LC** HF3601. **DD** 380.09493021. **Circ** 500. (ctrl). Statistics about inland trade and transportation. *Statistiques des Transports.*

STATISTIQUES DU TOURISME. Main/Corp France. Ministere de la Jeunesse, des Sports et des Loisirs. FR. French. ir. 100. Editions de la Documentation Francaise, 29-31 Quai Voltaire, 75340 Paris Cedex 07 France. **LC** G155.F8. **DD** 338.479144048305. *Statistiques du Tourisme.*

STATISTIQUES DU TOURISME. VFOAT Estatisticas do Turismo. 1969-. 0377-2306. French (Portuguese). qt. Documentation Francaise, 124 rue Henri Barbusse, 93308 Aubervilliers Cedex France. **Tel** 834-9275. **LC** G155.P75.

STATISTIQUES DU TRAVAIL; BULLETIN MENSUEL. SUPPLEMENT. Main/Corp France. Ministere du Travail et de la Participation. 53-. French. ir. *Statistiques du Travail.*

STATISTIQUES ET COMMENTAIRES DU COMMERCE EXTERIEUR. Main/Corp Chad. Sous-Direction de la Statistique. French. ir. **LC** HF3918. **DD** 382.096743.

STATISTIQUES ET INDICATEURS DES REGIONS FRANCAISES. Main/Corp Institut National de la Statistique et des Etudes Economiques (France). **Series/Titl** Collections de l'Insee. French (summaries in English and Spanish). ir. 40.00. La Documentation Francaise, 29-31 Quai Voltaire, Paris 7E France. **LC** HC271, HC280.Z6. **DD** 330.08 S, 309.250944. *Statistiques et Indicateurs des Regions Francaises.*

STATISTIQUES ET RESULTATS COMPLEMENTAIRES. Main/Corp Caisse Nationale des Allocations Familiales. French. ir. CNAF Caisse Nationale des Allocations Familiales, 63 Bd Haussmann 8, Paris France. **LC** HV700.F8. **DD** 362.82.

STATISTIQUES F. O. A. : DISTRIBUTION DES FUELS-OILS. Main/Corp Comite Professionnel du Petrole, Paris. VAT Statistiques Fuel-Oils A(?): Distribution des Fuel-Oils. Periodical. French. ir. Comite Professional du Patrole, 51 Boulevard de Courcelles, Paris France 75508. **LC** HD9572.4. **DD** 381.42282. *Statistique Mensuelles de la Distribution des Fuel-Oils.*

STATISTIQUES FINANCIERES. Main/Corp Al-Bank Al-Markazi-Al-Tunisi. No. 1- Sept. 1972-. French. ir. **LC** HG188.T77. **DD** 332.09611.

STATISTIQUES FINANCIERES. Main/Corp Belgium. Institut National de Statistique. No 1- 1972-. BE. French. ir. 375 Domestic, 525 Foreign. Institute National Statistique, rue de Louvain 44, 1000 Bruxelles Belgium. **Tel** (02)513 96 50. **LC** HG21. **Circ** 600. (ctrl). Covers income statistics; and sales of real estate.

STATISTIQUES FINANCIERES DU GOUVERNEMENT DU QUEBEC. Main/Corp Bureau de la Statistique du Quebec. Service des Finances, des Gouvernements et des Institutions a But Non Lucratif. Began with V. for 1976/77. 0705-579X. CN. French. an. **LC** HJ13. **DD** 354.7140072. *Statistiques Financieres du Gouvernement du Quebec, 0705-579X.*

LES STATISTIQUES FINANCIERES EN . . . . Series/Titl Les Regimes de Retraite au Quebec. 1974-. CN. French. Direction des Communications Regie des Rentes du Quebec, Case Postal 5200, Quebec G1K 7S9 Canada. **LC** HD7105.35.C2. **DD** 331.25209714.

STATISTIQUES FINANCIERES INTERNATIONALES - FONDS MONETAIRE INTERNATIONAL. (STATISTIQUES FINANCIERES INTERNATIONALES). Began in 1981. 0252-2977. Periodical. US. French.

Statistics

mo. $52.00. Attention Publications Unit, International Monetary Fund, Washington DC 20431. *International Financial Statistics. Ed. Francais,* 0250-7331.

STATISTIQUES FISCALES DES PARTICULIERS DU QUEBEC. Main/Corp Quebec (Province) Ministere du Revenu. 1973-. 0382-358X. CN. French. an. Ministere du Revenu, Quebec Canada.

STATISTIQUES : HOUILLE, COKES, AGGLOMERES, METALLURGIE, CARRIERES. Main/Corp Belgium. Administration des Mines. VFOAT Statistieken : Steenkolen, Cokes, Agglomeraten, Metaalnijverheid, Groven. Dutch and French. ir. Ministere des Affaires Economiques, rue Monteyer 3, Bruxelles 1040 Belgium. LC HD9555.B4.

STATISTIQUES INDUSTRIELLES. Main/Corp Institut National de Statistique (Belgium). Jan./Feb. 1967-. Periodical. BE. French. mo. 700 Domestic, 1200 Foreign. Institute National de Statistiques, rue de Louvain 44, 1000 Bruxelles Belgium. **Tel** (02)513.96.50. **Ind/Abst** Predicasts, Foreign Lang. Index, Funk Scott Index Corp. Ind. LC HC311. DD 338.09493. **Circ** 600. (ctrl). Statistics about industrial production; statistics about building and housing. *Bulletin de Statistique.*

STATISTIQUES JUDICIAIRES. Main/Corp Belgium. Institut National de Statistique. 1969-. Monographic Series. BE. French. ir. 250 Domestic, 540 Foreign. Institute National Statistique, 44 rue de Louvain, Brussels 1000 Belgium. **Tel** (02)513.96.50. **Ind/Abst** Foreign Lang. Index. **Circ** 350. (ctrl). Statistics about the courts' activities, law and criminality.

STATISTIQUES (MADAGASCAR. DIVISION DE CONTROLE DES QUALITES ET DU CONDITIONNEMENT DES PRODUITS AGRICOLES). (STATISTIQUES). French. ir. LC HD9017.M25. DD 338.109691.

STATISTIQUES (MOROCCO. KITABAT AL-DAWLAH LIL-TAKHTIT WA-AL-TANMIYAH AL-JIHAWIYAH. IDARAT AL-IHSA). (STATISTIQUES). VFOAT Ihsaat. Arabic (French). mo. Direction de la Statistique, BP 178, Rabat Morocco. LC HJ2181.Z9. *Bulletin Mensuel de Statistique (Morocco. Maslahah Al-Markaziyah Lil-Ihsaiyat).*

STATISTIQUES POUR L'ECONOMIE NORMANDE. June 1971-. 0395-8973. Periodical. FR. French. bm. INSEE-CNGP, BP 2718, 80027 Amiens Cedex France. *Bulletin de Statistique: Basse-Normandie (Calvados, Manche, Orne), Haute-Normandie (Eure, Seine-Maritime).*

STATISTIQUES, PRESTATIONS DE LOGEMENT. Main/Corp Caisse Nationale des Allocations Familiales. Periodical. FR. French. ir. CNAF, 47 rue da la Chaussee D Antin, Paris Cedex 09 France. LC HD7338.A3. DD 362.5.

STATISTIQUES - REGIE NATIONALE DES CHEMINS DE FER DU CAMEROUN. Main/Corp Regie Nationale des Chemins de fer du Cameroun. French. ir. LC HE3442. *Statistique - Regie des Chemins de fer du Cameroun.*

STATISTIQUES SCOLAIRES. Main/Corp Togo. Ministere de l'Education Nationale. Direction de la Planification, des Statistiques et de la Conjoncture. French. ir. Ministere de l'Education Nationale, BP 339, Lome Togo. LC L708.T6. DD 370.96681.

STATISTIQUES SOCIALES. 1970-. 0067-5563. Periodical. BE. French. ir. 250 Domestic, 400 Foreign. Institut National de Statistiques, rue de Louvain 44, 1000 Bruxelles Belgium. **Tel** (02)513.96.50. **Ind/Abst** Foreign Lang. Index. NLM W2 GB4 I5SK. **Circ** 700. (ctrl). Social statistics: employment, unemployment, earnings, working accidents, and prices. *Bulletin de Statistique.*

STATISTIQUES TRIMESTRIELLES DEFINITIVES. (STATISTIQUES TRIMESTRIELLES - CONSEIL NATIONAL DU CREDIT). Main/Corp France. Conseil National du Credit. FR. French. ir. Secretariat General du Conseil National du Credit, BP 230-01, 75024 Paris Cedex 01 France. LC HG3729.F78. DD 332.0944.

STATISTIQUES - UNIVERSITE LAVAL. Main/Corp Universite Laval. No 1- 1963/64-. 0708-1545. CN. French. an. Bureau de Registraire, Pavillon de la Bibliotheque, Universite Laval, Quebec Quebec G1K 7P4 Canada. DD 378.71447.

STATISTISCH BULLETIN - CENTRAAL BUREAU VOOR DE STATISTIEK. Main/Corp Netherlands (Kingdom, 1815-). Centraal Bureau voor de Statistiek. Dutch. ir. 42.25. Centraal Bureau voor de Statistiek, Prinses Beatrixlaan 428, Postbus 959, 2270 Az Voorburg Netherlands. LC HA1381.

DIE STATISTISCH ERFASSTEN ARBEITSERGEBNISSE DER STAATLICHEN ALLGEMEINBIBLIOTHEKEN UND GEWERKSCHAFTSBIBLIOTHEKEN DER HAUPTSTADT DER DDR BERLIN. German. an. LC Z803.A1. DD 027.0431.

STATISTISCH-PROGNOSTISCHER BERICHT. VFOAT Statistisch Prognostischer Bericht. 1981/82-. German. an. LC HA1248.B32. DD 303.494346. *Statistischer und Prognostischer Jahresbericht.*

STATISTISCH ZAKBOEK. Main/Corp Netherlands. Centraal Bureau voor de Statistiek. VFOAT Pocket Yearbook. 1926-. NE. Dutch. an. C B S, Postbus 959, 2270 AW Voorburg Netherlands. LC HA1381.

STATISTISCHE BEIHEFTE ZU DEN MONATSBERICHTEN DER DEUTSCHEN BUNDESBANK. REIHE 1 : BANKENSTATISTIK NACH BANKENGRUPPEN. Main/Corp Deutsche Bundesbank. 0419-9014. Periodical. GW. German. ir. Deutsche Bundesbank, Wilhelm Epsteinstrasse 14, 6000 Frankfurt West Germany.

STATISTISCHE BEIHEFTE ZU DEN MONATSBERICHTEN DER DEUTSCHEN BUNDESBANK. REIHE 2 : WERTPAPIERSTATISTIK. Main/Corp Deutsche Bundesbank. 0418-8314. Periodical. GW. German. ir. Deutsche Bundesbank Wilhelm Epsteinstrasse 14, 6000 Frankfurt West Germany.

STATISTISCHE BEIHEFTE ZU DEN MONATSBERICHTEN DER DEUTSCHEN BUNDESBANK. REIHE 3 : ZAHLUNGSBILANZSTATISTIK. Main/Corp Deutsche Bundesbank. 0418-8322. Periodical. GW. German (summaries in English). ir. Deutsche Bundesbank, Wilhelm Epsteinstrasse 14, 6000 Frankfurt West Germany.

STATISTISCHE BEIHEFTE ZU DEN MONATSBERICHTEN DER DEUTSCHEN BUNDESBANK. REIHE 4 : SAISONBEREINIGTE WIRTSCHAFTSZAHLEN. Main/Corp Deutsche Bundesbank. 0418-8330. Periodical. GW. German (summaries in English). ir. Deutsche Bundesbank, Wilhelm Epsteinstrasse 14, 6000 Frankfurt West Germany.

STATISTISCHE BERICHTE DES STATISTISCHEN AMTES DES SAARLANDES. Main/Corp Saarland. Statistisches Amt. German. ir. Hardenbergstrasse 3, Saarbruchen W Germany. LC HA1320.S24.

STATISTISCHE HEFTE. VFOAT Cahiers Statistiques, Statistical Papers. Vol. 1-. 0039-0631. Periodical. GW. German (some articles in English with summaries in English, French and Russian). qt. $52.00. Springer Verlag New York Inc, 175 5th Avenue, New York NY 10010. **Tel** (212)460-1500. Ed G Bamberg, W Janko, H Schneewiss and H J Skala. **Ind/Abst** Math. Rev., Public Aff. Inf. Serv. Bull. LC HA15. NLM HA 1 S85. bk rev. Covers statistics (especially in the social sciences), operations, research, economics and decision theory.

STATISTISCHE MEDEDELINGEN, NEDERLANDSE ANTILLEN. Began in 1953. Periodical. NE. Dutch (text in English and Spanish). mo. Department Sociale en Economisch Zak, Bureau voor Statistiek Curaco, Nederlandse Antillen.

STATISTISCHE MITTEILUNGEN. 0175-7350. German. ir. Statistisches Landesamt Bremen, Postfach 10 13 09, An Weide 14/16, 2800 Bremen 1 West Germany. *Statistische Mitteilungen Freier Hansestadt Bremen.*

STATISTISCHE NACHRICHTEN. Main/Corp Osterreichisches Statistisches Zentralamt. Began publication in Apr. 1923. 0029-9960. Periodical. AU. German. mo. $60.41. Carl Ueberreuter Druck Verlag, Postfach 60, A-1095 Wien Austria. **Ind/Abst** Foreign Lang. Index, PAIS Foreign Lang. Index. LC HA1173. *Mitteilungen des Bundesamtes fur Statistik.*

STATISTISCHE NACHRICHTEN (SAARLAND, GERMANY). (STATISTISCHE NACHRICHTEN). Edition 1 and 2, 1981-. German. qt. 10.00. Statistisches Amt des Saarlandes, Postfach 409 Hardenbergstr 3, 6600 Saarbrucken West Germany. LC HA1248.S23. DD 314.342.

STATISTISCHE RUNDSCHAU FUR DAS LAND NORDRHEIN-WESTFALEN. Main/Corp North Rhine-Westphalia. Landesamt fur Datenverarbeitung und Statistik. German. ir. 6.00 Quarterly. Landesamt fur Datneverarbeitung und Statistik, Ludwig-Beck-Strasse 23, Dusseldorf 4 West Germany. LC HA1320.N6. DD 314.355. *Statistische Rundschau fur das Land Nordrhein-Westfalen.*

STATISTISCHE RUNDSCHAU FUR DAS RUHRGEBIET CEASED. Main/Corp Landesamt fur Datenverarbeitung und Statistik Nordrhein-Westfalen. GW. German. ir. 10.00. Landesamt fur Datenverarbeitung und Statistik Nordrhein-Westfalen, Maverst 51, 4000 Dusseldorf West Germany. **Tel** (0211)44971. LC HA1320.R8. adv acc. **Circ** 1,100. *Statistische Rundschau fur das Ruhrgebiet: Siedlungsverband Ruhrkohlenbezirk.*

STATISTISCHE UBERSICHTEN : BESTAND UND BEDARF AN CHEMIKERN IN DER CHEMISCHEN INDUSTRIE DER BUNDESREPUBLIK DEUTSCHLAND. Main/Corp Fonds der Chemischen Industrie zur Forderung von Forschung, Wissenschaft und Lehre. German. ir. Fonds der Chemischen Industrie, 6000 Frankfurt Am Main, Karlstrasse 21, Frankfurt West Germany. LC TP186.

STATISTISCHE UBERSICHTEN : CHEMIE AN DER HOCHSCHULEN DER BUNDESREPUBLIK DEUTSCHLAND. Main/Corp Fonds der Chemischen Industrie zur Forderung von Forschung, Wissenschaft und Lehre. German. ir. Fonds der Chemischen Industrie, 6000 Frankfurt Am Main, Karlstrasse 21, Frankfurt West Germany. LC QD49.G3. DD 540.71143.

STATISTISCHE UBERSICHTEN FUR DAS JAHR (UNIVERSITAT KIEL. INSTITUTS FUR WELTWIRTSCHAFT. BIBLIOTHEK). (STATISTISCHE UBERSICHTEN FUR DAS JAHR). German. an. Bibliothek des Instituts fur Weltwirtschaft an der Universitat Kiel, Dusternbrokker WEG 120, Postfach 4309, D-2300 Kiel 1 West Germany. LC Z802.K54. DD 027.7433. *Statistische Ubersichten und Bericht (Universitat Kiel. Institut fur Weltwirtschaft. Bibliothek).*

STATISTISCHES HANDBUCH FUR DIE REPUBLIK OSTERREICH. Main/Corp Osterreichisches Statistisches Zentralamt. Vol. 1-17, 1920-37. AU. German. ir. $37.79. Verlag der Osterreichischen St Rennweg 12A, 1037 Wien Austria. LC HA1171.

STATISTISCHES JAHRBUCH BERLIN. See Yearbooks, Almanacs, Directories.

STATISTISCHES JAHRBUCH DER NORDRHEIN-WESTFALISCHEN INDUSTRIE- UND HANDELSKAMMERN. See Yearbooks, Almanacs, Directories.

STATISTISCHES JAHRBUCH DER SCHWEIZ. See Yearbooks, Almanacs, Directories.

STATISTISCHES JAHRBUCH . . . FUR DIE BUNDESREPUBLIK DEUTSCHLAND. See Yearbooks, Almanacs, Directories.

STATISTISCHES JAHRBUCH NORDRHEIN-WESTFALEN. See Yearbooks, Almanacs, Directories.

STATISTISCHES TASCHENBUCH. Main/Corp Hamburg., Statistisches Landesamt. 1967-. Periodical. GW. German. an. 10.00. Statistisches Landesamt Hanbg, Steckelhoern 12, 2000 Hamburg 11 West Germany. **Tel** 040-3681-719. (ctrl). Most important results from all areas of official statistics concerning population, education, culture, public health, commerce, harbor traffic and the finances of the city of Hamburg West Germany.

STATISTISCHES TASCHENBUCH DER DEUTSCHEN DEMOKRATISCHEN REPUBLIK. (STATISTICAL POCKET BOOK OF THE GERMAN DEMOCRATIC REPUBLIC). VFOAT Statistical Pocket Book. Began in 1959. 0585-1785. German. an. LC HA1248.A2.

Statistics

STATISTISK ARBOG. See Yearbooks, Almanacs, Directories.

STATISTISK ARBOG. See Yearbooks, Almanacs, Directories.

STATISTISK ARBOG FOR NORGE. See Yearbooks, Almanacs, Directories.

STATISTISK ARBOK. See Yearbooks, Almanacs, Directories.

STATISTISK ARSBOK FOR FINLAND. See Yearbooks, Almanacs, Directories.

STATISTISK MANEDSHEFTE. Main/Corp Norway. Statistisk Sentralbyra. Vol. 1-. 0029-3636. NO. Norwegian. mo. 150.-. Central Bureau of Statistics, POB 8131 Dep, 0033 Oslo 1 Norway. Tel (02)413820. Ind/Abst Funk Scott Index Corp. Ind. LC HA1503. (cum index). bk rev. Circ 4,400. Economic statistics (indexes finance trade).

STATISTISK MANEDSOVERSIGT. VFOAT Monthly Review of Statistics. 1983:1-. 0108-5603. DK. Danish (text in English). mo. 150.00. Danmarks Statistik, Sejrgade 11, DK-2100 Copenhagen Denmark. LC HC351. DD 330.9489. *Konjunkturoversigt, 0106-2417.*

STATISTISK TIDSKRIFT CEASED. Main/Corp Sweden. Statistiska Centralbyran. VFOAT Statistical Review. Vol. 1-165, 1860-1919. 0039-7261. Periodical. SW. Swedish (summaries in English). bm. Energy Economics Research Ltd, 7-9 Queen Victoria Street, Reading Berks RG1 1SY England. Ind/Abst Am. Hist. Life, Hist. Abstr., Part A, Mod. Hist. Abstr., Hist. Abst., Part B, Twent. Century Abstr., Popul. Index, Energy Res. Abstr. LC HA1523. DD 314.85. (cum index).

STATISTISK VAREFORTEGNELSE FOR UTENRIKSHANDELEN. Series/Titl Statistisk Sentralbyras Handbker. Norwegian. ir. LC HA1503, HF215.

STATISTISKA MEDDELANDEN. Main/Corp Gothenburg, Sweden. Stadskontoret. VFOAT Statistical Review. Swedish. ir. Fredsgatan 1, Fack 1510 401 10 1, Goteborg Sweden. LC HA1539.G6. *Meddelanden.*

STATISTISKA MEDDELANDEN. Main/Corp Televerket. SW. Swedish. mo. AB Nordiska Bokhandeln, Subscription Department, Stockholm 1 Sweden. LC HE9311.

STATISTISKA MEDDELANDEN. P. Series/Titl Sveriges Officiella Statistik. VFOAT Statistiska Meddelanden. English (Swedish). ir. LC HB235.S8. DD 338.52809485.

STATISTISKA MEDDELANDEN. SERIE T, TRANSPORT OCH KOMMUNIKATIONER. Series/Titl Sveriges Officiella Statistik. VFOAT Transport Och Kommunikationer. 0082-0334. Monographic Series. Swedish. ir. Liber Distribution, 162 89 Vallingby, Stockholm Sweden. LC HE260.A15. *Statistiska Meddelanden. T.*

STATISTISKA MEDDELANDEN. T. Series/Titl Sveriges Officiella Statistik. VFOAT Statistiska Meddelanden. Monographic Series. Swedish. ir. LC HE260.A15.

STATISTISKE EFTERRETNINGER. VFOAT Frerne og Grnland. 1983:1-. 0108-5557. Monographic Series. DK. Danish. ir. 15.00. Danmarks Statistik, PB 2550 Sejrgade 11, 2100 Kbenhavn Denmark. *Statistiske Efterretninger.*

STATISTISKE EFTERRETNINGER. VFOAT Uddannelse og Kultur. 1983:1-. 0108-5492. Monographic Series. DK. Danish. ir. 28.00. Danmarks Statistik, PB 2550 Sejrgade 11, 2100 Kbenhavn Denmark. *Statistiske Efterretninger.*

STATISTISKE EFTERRETNINGER. ARBEJDSMARKED. VFOAT Arbejdsmarket. 1983:1-. 0108-5514. Monographic Series. DK. Danish. ir. 34.00. Danmarks Statistik, PB 2550 Sejrgade 11, 2100 Kbenhavn Denmark. *Statistiske Efterretninger.*

STATISTISKE EFTERRETNINGER. BEFOLKNING OG VALG. VFOAT Befolkning og Valg. 1983:1-. 0108-5530. Monographic Series. DK. Danish. ir. 29.00. Danmarks Statistik, PB 2550, Sejrgade 11, 2100 Kbenhavn Denmark. *Statistiske Efterretninger.*

STATISTISKE EFTERRETNINGER. BYGGE- OG ANLGSVIRKSOMHED. VFOAT Bygee- og Anlgsvirksomhed. 1983:1-. 0108-5549. Monographic Series. DK. Danish. ir. 50.00. Danmarks Statistik, PB 2550 Sejrgade 11, 2100 Kbenhavn Denmark. *Statistiske Efterretninger.*

STATISTISKE EFTERRETNINGER. GENEREL ERHVERVSSTATISTIK OG HANDEL. VFOAT Generel Erhvervsstatistik og Handel. 1983:1-. 0108-5573. Monographic Series. DK. Danish. ir. 19.00. Danmarks Statistik, PB 2550 Sejrgade 11, 2100 Kbenhavn Denmark. *Statistiske Efterretninger.*

STATISTISKE EFTERRETNINGER. INDKOMST, FORBRUG OG PRISER. VFOAT Indkomst, Forbrug og Priser. V. 1, 1983:1 (Feb. 7 1983)-. 0108-5565. Periodical. DK. Danish. ir. 44.00. Danmarks Statistik, Sejrgade 11, 2100 Kbenhavn Denmark. LC HC360.I5. *Statistiske Efterretninger.*

STATISTISKE EFTERRETNINGER. INDUSTRI OG ENERGI. VFOAT Industri og Energi. 0108-5468. Monographic Series. DK. Danish. ir. 42.00. Danmarks Statistik, Sejrgade 11, 2100 Kbenhavn Denmark. LC HC351. *Statistiske Efterretninger.*

STATISTISKE EFTERRETNINGER. LANDBRUG. VFOAT Landbrug. 1983:1-. 0108-5522. Monographic Series. DK. Danish. ir. 48.00. Danmarks Statistik, PB 2550 Sejrgade 11, 2100 Kbenhavn Denmark. *Statistiske Efterretninger.*

STATISTISKE EFTERRETNINGER. NATIONALREGNSKAB, OFFENTLIGE FINANSER, BETALINGSBALANCE. VFOAT Nationalregnskab, Offentlige Finanser, Betalingsbalancer. 1983:1-. 0108-545X. Monographic Series. DK. Danish. ir. 32.00. Danmarks Statistik, PB 2550 Sejrgade 11, 2100 Kbenhavn Denmark. *Statistiske Efterretninger.*

STATISTISKE EFTERRETNINGER. PENGE- OG KAPITALMARKED. VFOAT Penge- og Kapitalmarked. 1983:1-. 0108-5476. Monographic Series. DK. Danish. ir. 65.00. Danmarks Statistik, PB 2250 Sejrgade 11, 2100 Kbenhavn Denmark. *Statistiske Efterretninger.*

STATISTISKE EFTERRETNINGER. UDENRIGSHANDEL. VFOAT Udenrigshandel. 1983:1-. 0108-5506. Monographic Series. DK. Danish. ir. 200.00. Danmarks Statistik, PB 2550 Sejrgade 11, 2100 Kbenhavn Denmark. *Statistiske Efterretninger, Manedsstatistik Over Udenrigshandelen.*

STATISTISKE OVERSIKTER - STATISTISK SENTRALBYRA CEASED. Main/Corp Norway. Statistisk Sentralbyra. Series/Titl Norges Officielle Statistik. Norges Offisielle Statistikk. VFOAT Statistical Survey - Statistisk Sentralbyra. Began publication in 1914. 0468-8171. Periodical. NO. Norwegian and English. ir. Statistisk Sentralbyra, PO Box 8131 DEP, Oslo 1 Norway. LC HA1505. DD 314.

STATISZTIKAI EVKONYV. See Yearbooks, Almanacs, Directories.

STATISZTIKAI EVKONYV - KOZPONTI STATISZTIKAI HIVATAL (BUDAPEST). (STATISZTIKAI EVKONYV). VFOAT Statistical Yearbook. 0073-4039. HU. Hungarian (Multilingual). an. Kozponti Statisztikai Hivatal II, Keleti Karoly U, Budapest 181B Hungry. LC HA1201. DD 314.39. NLM W2 GH8 K7SV. *Magyar Statisztika Evkonyv.*

STATISZTIKAI HAVI KOZLEMENYEK. Main/Corp Hungary. Kozponti Statisztikai Hivatal. 0018-781X. Periodical. HU. Hungarian. mo. 480. Statistical Publishing House, H-1300 Budapest PO Box 99. Tel 688-635. Ed Gy Holka. LC HA1201. DD 314. Reports the results of the monthly quarterly data-collections. Gives information on Hungarian demographical population changes, employment, national economy, branches of money, social and cultural situation.

STATISZTIKAI SZEMLE. Main/Corp Hungary. Kozponti Statisztikai Hivatal. VFOAT Statisticheskoe Obozrenie, Statistical Review. Began in 1949. 0039-0690. Periodical. Hungarian (summaries in Hungarian, English, and Russian). mo. 396. Statistical Publishing House, H-1300 Budapest, PO Box 99. Tel 688-635. Ed F Gyulaj. Ind/Abst Popul. Index. bk rev. Covers all fields of social and economic life, giving comprehensive information to statisticians and economists. Reviews regularly the newest examination methods, the news of statistical organizations and of special literature. *Magyar Statisztikai Szmele.*

STATISZTIKAI TAJEKOZTATO. SZAKKONYVTARAK. VFOAT Szakkonyvtarak. 0139-0236. Periodical. Hungarian. an. LC Z675.A2.

STATS. V. 1- May 30, 1964-. SA. English. mo. $28.91. George Warman Publications Pty Ltd, PO Box 3847, 77 Hout Street, Cape Town 8000 South Africa. Tel (021) 24 5320. Ed W S Pretorius. Circ 500. Supplies up-dated economic trend indicators, also statistics from a wide range of sources on a variety of subjects.

STATSTILSKUD TIL ENERGIBESPARENDE FORANSTALTINGER I FORBINDELSE MED INDUSTRIELLE PROCESSER M.V. Main/Corp Denmark. Teknologiradet., Sekretariatet. 1977/78-. DK. Danish. ir. Sekretariatet for Teknologiradet, Bredgade 31, 1260 Kbenhavn K Denmark. LC HD3646.D4.

STATSTILSKUD TIL PRODUKTUDVIKLING. Main/Corp Denmark. Teknologiradet. Sekretariatet. 1977/78-. DK. Danish. ir. Sekretariatet for Teknologiradet, Bredgade 31, 1260 Kbenhavn K Denmark. LC HD69.N4.

STATUS. July 1976-. 0147-0477. Periodical. US. English. mo. $3.60. Bureau of the Census, Subscriber Services Section, Washington DC 20233. Tel (301)763-4100. LC HC101. DD 317.3. NLM W1 ST37.

STATUS, PROGRESS, AND PROBLEMS IN FEDERAL AGENCY ACCOUNTING. 0730-3440. US. English. an. US General Accounting Office, Document Handling and Information Service Facility, PO Box 6015, Gaithersburg MD 20760. LC HJ9801. DD 353.007231.

STATYSTYKA GMIN. Series/Titl Statystyka Polski. 1983-. PL. Polish. ir. 300.00. Ksiegarnia Noukowa lm Bolesawa Prusa Ul, Krakowskie Przedmiescie 7, 00-068 Warszawa Poland.

STEAM-ELECTRIC PLANT FACTORS. See Energy.

STEIRISCHE STATISTIKEN. 0039-1093. German. qt. Amt der Steiermarkischen Landesregierung, Landesamtdirektion, Referat Statistik Neue Burg 8010, Graz Austria. LC HA1188.S8. DD 314.365.

STRASSEN, BRUCKEN UND PARKEINRICHTUNGEN. Main/Corp North Rhine-Westphalia (Germany). Landesamt fur Datenverarbeitung und Statistik. Series/Titl Beitrage zur Statistik des Landes Nordrhein-Westfalen. German. ir. 9.50. Landesamt fur Datenverarbeitung und Statistik Nordrhein-Westfalen, 4000 Dusseldorf 1 Postfach 1105, Dusseldorf West Germany. LC HA1320.N6.

STRUCNI ISPITI RADNIKA. Main/Corp Savenzi Zavod za Statistiku (Yugoslavia). Series Corp Its Statisticki Bilten. YU. Serbo-Croatian(R). ir. 10.00. Savezui Zavod za Statistiku, Kneza Milosa 20, Beograd Yugoslavia. LC HA1631, HF5549.5. R3.

STRUKTURTALL FOR KOMMUNENES KONOMI. See Business - Public Finance.

STUDENTIM BA-UNIVERSITAOT. VFOAT Students in Universities. English (Hebrew). ir. LC HA1931, L A1443. DD 378.198095694.

STUDI DI STATISTICA. Main/Corp Naples. Universita. Istituto di Statistica e Demografia. Book 1- 1973-. Italian. ir. 4.500. LC HB848.

STUDIES IN OFFICIAL STATISTICS. No. 1-. Monographic Series. UK. English. ir. Her Majestys Stationery Office, PO Box 276, London SW8 5DT England. Tel (01)622-3316. LC HA37.

SUDAN GUIDE. VFOAT Murshid Al-Sudan. Began with Vol. for 1980. Arabic (English). an. Planning & Management Consultancy, PO Box 60, Kh North Industrial Area, Khartoum Sudan. LC HA4687. DD 316.24.

SUGAR MARKET STATISTICS. July 1980-. Periodical. US. English. qt. $5.00. USDA/SRS, Room 5829, South Building, Washington DC 20250. *Sugar and Sweetener Report, 0362-9511.*

SUID-AFRIKAANSE STATISTIEKE. VFOAT South African Statistics. 0081-2544. SA. Afrikaans and English. ir. Pretoria Government Printer, Private Bag X85, Pretoria 0001 South Africa. LC HA1991. DD 316.8. *Suid-Afrikaanse Statistieke.*

SUMMARY OF AGRICULTURAL STATISTICS FOR ONTARIO. VFOAT Agricultural Statistics for Ontario. 0227-8685. Periodical. CN. English. Ontario Ministry of Agriculture & Food, 801 Bay Street, Toronto Ontario M7A 1B3 Canada. DD 338.109713.

SUMMARY OF CURRENT EDUCATION STATISTICS (AKURE, NIGERIA). (A SUMMARY OF CURRENT EDUCATION STATISTICS). English. an. LC LA1630. DD 370.9669.

Statistics

SUMMARY OF CURRENT INCOME TAX STATISTICS. (A SUMMARY OF CURRENT INCOME TAX STATISTICS). **Main/Corp** Western State, Nigeria. Ministry of Economic Planning and Reconstruction. Statistics Division. 0331-0434. English. ir. Ministry of Economic Planning and Reconstruction, Statistics Division, Ibadan Nigeria. **LC** HJ4794.N5. **DD** 336.24209669.

SUMMARY OF GENERAL STATISTICS. Main/Corp Virginia. Dept. of Mental Health and Mental Retardation. 0098-2725. US. English. Department of Mental Health & Mental Retardation, Richmond VA 23220. **LC** RC445. **DD** 362.2.

SUMMARY OF KENTUCKY EDUCATION. (SUMMARY OF KENTUCKY EDUCATION STATISTICS). **Main/Corp** Kentucky. Dept. of Education. Bureau of Administration and Finance. 0362-6679. US. English. Kentucky Department of Education, 1923 Capital Praza Tr, Frankfort KY 40601. **LC** LA292. **DD** 320.9769.

SUMMARY OF MONTHLY STATISTICS. ALBERTA ENERGY RESOURCE INDUSTRIES. (ALBERTA ENERGY RESOURCE INDUSTRIES; SUMMARY OF MONTHLY STATISTICS). **Main/Corp** Alberta. Energy Resources Conservation Board. Feb. 1972-. 0382-2176. Periodical. CN. English. Energy Resources Conservation Board, 603 Sixth Avenue South West, Calgary Alberta T2P 0T4 Canada. *Alberta Resource Industries.*

SUMMARY OF NATIONAL TRANSPORTATION STATISTICS. VFOAT National Transportation Statistics. 1st- 1971-. Periodical. US. English. an. US Department of Transportation, Washington DC 20402.

SUMMARY OF NATURAL GAS STATISTICS. US. English. an. Ohio Division of Energy, State Office Tower, 30 East Broad Street, Columbus OH 43215. **LC** HD9581.U52. **DD** 338.2728509771.

SUMMARY OF PASSPORT STATISTICS. 0565-9566. Periodical. US. English. qt. State Department Passport Service, 1425 K Street NW/Room 338, Washington DC 20524. **Tel** (202)523-4232. Ind/Abst Am. Stat. Index. **LC** JX4253.U6. **DD** 353.0089806.

SUMMARY OF STATISTICS. BUREAU OF STATISTICS, KONEDOBU. (SUMMARY OF STATISTICS). 0377-5844. English. an. The Statistician-National Statistical Office, PO Wards Strip, Papua New Guinea. **LC** HA4007.P3. **DD** 319.53.

SUMMARY STATISTICS OF CPB-QUALIFIED PUBLIC RADIO STATIONS. Main/Corp National Center for Education Statistics. 0092-900X. US. English. Superintendent of Documents, US Government Printing Office, Washington DC 20402. **LC** HE8698. **DD** 384.540973.

SUMMARY STATISTICS OF PUBLIC TV LICENSEES. 0095-1919. US. English. **LC** HE8700.8. **DD** 384.54520973.

SUOMEN TILASTOLLINEN VUOSIKIRJA. See Yearbooks, Almanacs, Directories.

SUOMEN VIRALLINEN TILASTO. XXI B, SOSIAALIHUOLTO. VFOAT Sosiaalihuolto, Finlands Officiella Statistik. XXI B, Socialvard, Official Statistics of Finland. XXI B, Social Welfare. Began with: 14 (1970). English (text in Finnish and Swedish). ir. NLM W2 GF5 S86S. *Suomen Virallinen Tilasto. XXI B, Sosiaalihuoltotilaston Vuosikirja.*

SUPPLEMENT BIJ DE SOCIAAL-ECONOMISCHE MAANDSTATISTIEK. VFOAT Sociaal-Economische Maandstatistiek. Vol. 1984, No. 1-. Periodical. Dutch. ir. Centraal Bureau voor de Statistiek, Prinses Beatrixlaan 428, Postbus 958, 2270 AZ Voorburg Netherlands.

SUPPLEMENT TO THE STATISTICAL YEARBOOK AND THE MONTHLY BULLETIN OF STATISTICS. See Yearbooks, Almanacs, Directories.

SURVEY OF CONTRACTING STATISTICS. Began with Dec. 1978. 0193-9327. US. English. an. Department of the Navy, 800 North Quincy Street, Arlington VA 22217. **LC** VC267.U6. **DD** 355.6211.0973. *Survey of Procurement Statistics,* 0565-8497.

A SURVEY OF PAY AND RELATED PERSONNEL PRACTICES OF MUNICIPAL FIRE DEPARTMENTS. See Fire Prevention.

SURVEY STATISTICIAN. No. 1- Feb. 1979-. Periodical. English. ir. IASS, c/o INSEE, 18 Boulevard Adolphe Pinard, 75675 Paris Cedex 14 France. **LC** HA1. **DD** 310.6. *Newsletter - International Association of Survey Statisticians.*

SUSANMUL KYETONG PANMAEGO TONGGYE YONBO. VFOAT Statistics on Cooperative Sale of Fishery Products. 1981-. English (Korean). an. Susanop Hyoptong Chohap Chunganghoe, 88 Kyongun-Dong, Chongno-ku Seoul Korea. **LC** HD9466.K58. *Susanmul Kyetong Panmaego Tonggye.*

SYSTEMATISCHE VERZEICHNISSE. ALPHABETISCHES WARENVERZEICHNIS FUR DIE BINNENHANDELSSTATISTIK. See Indexes/Abstracts.

TAARIFA YA TARAKIMU. Main/Corp Tanzania. Bureau of Statistics. VFOAT Quarterly Statistical Bulletin. Swahili and English. ir. 1/30. Tanzania Bureau of Statistics, PO Box 1801, Dar es Salaam Tanzania. **LC** HA2131. *Monthly Statistical Bulletin.*

TABEL AKHIR STATISTIK PENDIDIKAN SLTP/SLTA SMP SELURUH INDONESIA. Main/Corp Proyek Pengembangan Informasi Pendidikan. IO. English and Indonesian. ir. Departemen Pendidikan Dan Kebudayaan, Jln Jeneral Sudirman, Jakarta Indonesia. **LC** LA1272.

TABLEAUX DE L'ECONOMIE CHAMPENOISE. VFOAT T.E.C. French. ir. 32. Direction Regionale de Reims, 1 rue de l'Arbalete, 51079 Reims Ce France. **Tel** 26882412. **LC** HA1228.C5. **DD** 314.43. **Circ** 1,000. Our main subjects are local studies about population, industry education, housing and urban development in Champagne Ardenne.

TABLEAUX ECONOMIQUES DE L'ILE-DE-FRANCE. VFOAT Tableaux Economiques de l'Ile de France. Began with 1978 vol. FR. French. ir. Observatoire Economique de Paris Tour Gamma, A 195 rue de Bercy, 75582 Paris Cedex 12 France. **LC** HA1228.I47. **DD** 314.434.

TABLEAUX ECONOMIQUES DE MIDI-PYRENEES. 1981-. French. an. Observatoire Economique Regional Midi-Pyrenees, 36 rue des 36 Ponts, 31054 Toulouse Cedex France. **LC** HA1228.M53. **DD** 330.9448600212.

TAIWAN FINANCIAL STATISTICS MONTHLY. Main/Corp China (Republic). Economic Research Department. VFOAT Republic of China Taiwan Financial Statistics Monthly. 1951?-. 0496-7046. CH. English (Chinese). ir. Central Bank of China, 2 Roosevelt Road, Economic Research Department, Taipei Taiwan 107 Republic of China.

TAIWAN STATISTICAL DATA BOOK. CH. English. an. $7.10. CMC Taipei Laison Office, PO Box 22048, Taipei Taiwan 100 Republic of China. **Tel** (886)752-9244. **LC** HA1710.5. **DD** 315.1249. **Circ** 1,000. Annual statistics for area, population, national income, agriculture, industry, transportation, communication, banking, prices, external trade, etc.

TASMANIAN YEAR BOOK. See Yearbooks, Almanacs, Directories.

TAXATION STATISTICS. Main/Corp Canada. Taxation. VFOAT Statistique Fiscale. 1946-. 0700-1665. Periodical. CN. English (title only, 1946-1959, 1967-1970, text in English only, 1946-1959, 1967-1970). an. Department of National Revenue Taxation, 875 Heron Road, Ottawa Ontario K1A 0L8 Canada. **LC** HJ4661. **DD** 336.200971. *Statistique Fiscale.*

TAXATION STATISTICS. Main/Corp Australia. Dept. of the Treasury. Taxation Branch. AT. English. ir. Commonwealth Government Printer Office, PO Box 84, Canberra ACT 2600 Australia. **LC** HJ90. **DD** 336.200994.

TEA STATISTICS. Main/Corp India. Tea Board. 0536-7026. English. ir. **LC** HD9198.I4. *Indian Tea Statistics.*

TEA STATISTICS (CALCUTTA, INDIA : 1982). (TEA STATISTICS). English. an. J Thomas & Company, Private Limited Nilhat House 11 R N Mukherjee Road, Calcutta 700001 India. **LC** HD9198.I4. **DD** 338.173720954.

TEACHING STATISTICS. Vol. 1, No. 1 (Jan. 1979)-. 0141-982X. Periodical. UK. English. ty. 5.50 Domestic, $10.00 US, 7.00 Others. Teaching Statistics/University of Sheffield, Department of Probability & Statistics, Sheffield S3 7RH England. **Tel** 0742-78555. Ed Peter Holmes. bk rev. adv acc. **Circ** 1,400. Informative and entertaining articles showing teachers of statistics, mathematics and other science subjects how to use statistical ideas in teaching.

TECHNICAL NOTES - U.S. DEPARTMENT OF COMMERCE, BUREAU OF THE CENSUS. (TECHNICAL NOTES - BUREAU OF THE CENSUS). **Main/Corp** United States. Bureau of the Census. VAT Technical Notes - United States Department of Commerce, Bureau of the Census. 0082-9536. US. English. US Dept of Commerce/Bureau of Census, Washington DC 20230. **LC** HA37. **DD** 519.508.

TECHNICAL PAPER - U.S. DEPARTMENT OF COMMERCE, SOCIAL AND ECONOMICS STATISTICS ADMINISTRATION, BUREAU OF THE CENSUS. (TECHNICAL PAPER (UNITED STATES. BUREAU OF THE CENSUS)). VAT Technical Paper - United States Department of Commerce, Social and Economics Statistics Administration, Bureau of the Census. No. 1-. 0082-9544. Monographic Series. US. English. Superintendent of Documents, US Government Printing Office, Washington DC 20402. **LC** UNC.

TECHNICAL REPORT SERIES OF THE LABORATORY FOR RESEARCH IN STATISTICS AND PROBABILITY. VFOAT Serie de Monographies du Laboratoire de Recherche en Statistique et Probabilites. 0823-1664. Monographic Series. CN. English. ir. Mrs Gill Murray Technical Editor and Coordinator for the Laboratory for Research in Statistics and Probability, Room 611/ Arts Tower, Carleton University, Colonel by Drive, Ottawa Ontario K1S 5B6 Canada. **DD** 519.05.

TELECOMMUNICATIONS EQUIPMENT INDUSTRY STATISTICAL REVIEW. US. English. an. North American Telephone Association, 511 2nd Street NE, Washington DC 20002. **LC** HD9696.T443. **DD** 380.145621380973.

TELECOMMUNICATIONS STATISTICS. Main/Corp Statistics Canada. Communications Section. VFOAT Statistique des Telecommunications. 1972-. 0703-7252. Periodical. CN. English (French). an. Receiver General for Canada, Statistics Canada Publications, Ottawa Ontario K1A 0T6 Canada. **Tel** (613)992-2959. **LC** HE7811. **DD** 384.0971. *Telegraph and Cable Statistics.*

TELEPHONE STATISTICS. Main/Corp Canada. Statistics Canada. Communications Section. VFOAT Statistique du Telephone. 1972-. 0380-7843. Periodical. CN. English (French). an. Receiver General for Canada, Statistics Canada Publications, Ottawa Ontario K1A 0T6 Canada. **LC** HE8861. **DD** 384.60971. *Telephone Statistics, 0380-7843.*

TELEPHONE STATISTICS : SELECTED FINANCIAL DATA FOR WISCONSIN TELEPHONE COMPANIES. Main/Corp Public Service Commission of Wisconsin. Accounts and Finance Division. 0097-9198. US. English. Public Service Commission of Wisconsin, Accounts & Finance Division, Madison WI 53703. **LC** HE8805.W6. **DD** 385.6309775. *Telephone Statistics: Selected Financial Data for Wisconsin Telephone Companies, 0097-9198.*

TENDANCES DE LA CONJONCTURE. April 1969-. 0497-2007. Periodical. FR. French. ir. 570. INSEE-CNGP, BP 2718, 80027 Amiens Cedex France. **Tel** 22927322. adv acc. Conjunctural data.

TENNESSEE AGRICULTURAL STATISTICS. 1963-. 0497-2317. US. English. an. USDA-SRS Crop Reporting Board, Room 5829- South Building, Washington DC 20250. **LC** S115. **DD** 338.109768.

TENNESSEE DAIRY STATISTICS. VFOAT Tennessee Dairy Statistics and Summary. Began with 1978 issue. 0748-4119. US. English. an. **LC** HD9275.U7. **DD** 338.17709768.

Statistics

TENNESSEE DATA FOR AFFIRMATIVE ACTION PLANS. STATE, SMSA'S. COUNTIES, ANNUAL AVERAGE. (TENNESSEE DATA FOR AFFIRMATIVE ACTION PLANS : STATE, SMSA'S, COUNTIES, ANNUAL AVERAGE). **Main/Corp** Tennessee. Dept. of Employment Security. **VFOAT** Data for Affirmative Action Plans. 0360-5345. US. English. an. 519 Cordell Hull Building, Nashville TN 37219. LC HD5725.T4. DD 331.1109768.

TENNESSEE STATISTICAL ABSTRACT. See Indexes/Abstracts.

TEOLLISUUSTILASTO. Series/Titl Suomen Virallinen Tilasto. **VFOAT** Industrial Statistics. 1884-. Finnish (English and Swedish). an. Valtion Painatuskeskus, Annankatu 44, 00100 Helsinki Finland. LC HA1448, HC337.F5.

TEXAS COMMERCIAL HARVEST STATISTICS. Series/Titl Management Data Series. 0734-7278. US. English. an. Texas Parks & Wildlife Department, 4200 Smith School Road, Austin TX 78744. LC SH222.T4. DD 333.37209764.

TEXAS FIELD CROP STATISTICS. Main/Corp Texas Crop and Livestock Reporting Service. 0092-153X. US. English. an. Texas Department of Agriculture, PO Box 12847, Austin TX 78711. LC S117. DD 633.009764.

TEXAS FRUIT AND PECAN STATISTICS. Main/Corp Texas Crop and Livestock Reporting Service. 0092-2005. US. English. PO Box 70, Austin TX 78767. LC HD9247.T4. DD 338.17409764.

TEXAS JUDICIAL SYSTEM ANNUAL REPORT OF STATISTICAL AND OTHER DATA. (TEXAS JUDICIAL SYSTEM ANNUAL REPORT OF STATISTICAL AND OTHER DATA FOR CALENDAR YEAR . . .). **VFOAT** Texas Judicial System Annual Report. 53rd (1981)-. 8756-6869. US. English. an. 1414 Colorado Street/Suite 600, PO Box 12066, Austin TX 78711. LC KFT1271. DD 347.764013, 347.640713. Annual Report of Statistical and Other Data of the Texas Judicial System for Calendar Year . . . , 8756-6850.

TEXAS JUVENILE PROBATION STATISTICAL REPORT : STATISTICAL AND OTHER DATA ON THE JUVENILE JUSTICE SYSTEM IN TEXAS FOR CALENDAR YEARS . . . ABBREVIATED. 1980-81-. US. English. an. LC HV9105.T44. DD 364.6309764.

TEXAS LIVESTOCK, DAIRY, AND POULTRY STATISTICS. 1980-. US. English. an. USDA Economics and Statistics Service, Agricultural Statistician, Box 70, Austin TX 78767. LC HD9417.T4. DD 338.176009764. Texas Livestock Statistics, 0091-1550; Texas Dairy Statistics; Texas Poultry Statistics.

TEXAS LIVESTOCK STATISTICS. Main/Corp Texas Crop and Livestock Reporting Service. 0091-1550. US. English. Charles E Candill Agricultural Statistician, PO Box 70, Austin TX 78767. LC HD9417.T4. DD 338.176009764.

TEXAS PUBLIC LIBRARY STATISTICS FOR . . . . 1968-. 0082-3120. US. English. an. LC Z732.T25. DD 027.4764. Texas Public Library Statistics, 0082-3120.

TEXAS VITAL STATISTICS (AUSTIN, TEX. : 1960) CEASED. (TEXAS VITAL STATISTICS). 1960-1961. 0495-257X. US. English. an. Department of Health Resources, 1100 West 49th Street, Austin TX 78756. LC HA651. DD 312.09764. NLM W2 AT4 S7TI. Vital Statistics in Texas.

THAMES WATER STATISTICS. UK. English. an. Thames Water Authority, Reading Bridge House, Reading England. LC TC464.T4. DD 363.6109422.

THEORY OF PROBABILITY AND ITS APPLICATIONS. See Mathematics.

THOMAS GROCERY REGISTER. FOOD MARKETERS' HANDBOOK, KEY INDUSTRY STATISTICS AND TRADE CALENDAR. **VFOAT** Food Marketers' Handbook. 1983-. 0739-3423. US. English. an. Thomas Publishing Company, One Penn Plaza, New York NY 10119. LC HD9321.1. DD 381.45641300973.

THE THOROUGHBRED RECORD. FOREIGN STATISTICAL REVIEW. **VFOAT** Foreign Statistical Review. 1984-. US. English. wk. $78.00. The Thoroughbred Record, PO Box 4240, Lexington KY 40544. Tel (606)276-5311. Ed Timothy T Capps. bk rev. adv acc. Circ 14,000. A thoroughbred breeding and racing publication over 111 years old. Thoroughbred Record Breeders Book.

TIDS NOG. See Sociology: General Works, Theory.

TILASTOKATSAUKSIA. Main/Corp Finland. Tilastokeskus. **VFOAT** Statistiska Oversikter, Bulletin of Statistics. 46, No. 3-. Fl. English (Finnish, and Swedish). ir. $36.63. Statistikcentralen, PB 504, SF-00101 Helsinki 10 Finland. Tel 358017341. LC HA1450.5. DD 314.897. Circ 2,000. Statistical data in population, production, commerce, banking, transport, communication, national accounts, prices, wages, labour, state finances, etc., seasonally adjusted series included. Tilastokatsauksia.

TILASTOTIEDOTUS. RT. **VFOAT** Statistisk Rapport. RT. 0355-2322. Monographic Series. Fl. Finnish (Swedish). ir. Government Printing Centre, POB 516, SF00100 Helsinki 10 Finland.

TILK : NELJANNESVUOSIKATSAUS. Main/Corp Helsinki. Tilastokeskus. **VFOAT** Tilk : Kvartalsoversikt, Tilk : Quarterly Review. 1979-. Fl. Finnish (Swedish, with summaries in English). ir. Helsingin Kaupunki, Tilstokeskus, Toolontorinkatu 2 B, 00260 Helsinki 26 Finland. LC HA1450.5.Z9. Tilastollisia Kuukausitietoja Helsingista.

TIMELNNINGER, ARBEJDSTID. STUNDENVERDIENSTE, ARBEITSZEIT. See Economics - Labor.

TIN STATISTICS. 1963/73-. UK. index in English, French, Spanish and Russian. an. International Tin Council, Haymarket House, 1 Oxendon Street, London SW1Y 4EQ England. Tel 01 930 0451. LC HD9539.T5. DD 338.476736. Circ 600. Mine and shelter production of tin, tin consumption, stocks and trade. Production, apparent consumption and trade in tinplate, tin prices and turnover. Statistical Year Book. Tin, Tinplate, Canning, 0074-9117.

TJENESTEYTING, FORRETNINGSMESSIG TJENESTEYTING, UTLEIE AV MASKINER OG UTSTYR, RENOVASJON OG REINGJRING, VASKERI- OG RENSERIVIRKSOMHET. AND SIMILAR SERVICES, LAUNDRIES, LAUNDRY SERVICES AND CLEANING AND DYEING PLANTS /. Series/Titl Norges Offisielle Statistikk. **VFOAT** Services, Business Services, Machinery and Equipment Rental and Leasing, Sanitary and Similar Services, Laundries, Laundry Services and Cleaning and Dyeing Plants. English (Norwegian). an. 18.00. LC HA1501, HD9986.N8. DD 314.81, 338.470009481.

TOBACCO AND TOBACCO PRODUCTS STATISTICS. Main/Corp Statistics Canada. Manufacturing and Primary Industries Division. **VFOAT** Statistiques du Tabac et des Produits du Tabac. **VAT** Statistiques du Tabac et des Produits du Tabac (1975). V. 42- Jan./March 1975-. 0380-2183. Periodical. CN. English (French). qt. $2.80. Statistics Canada, Publications Distribution, Ottawa Ontario K1A 0T6 Canada. Tobacco and Tobacco Products Statistics Quarterly, 0380-2175.

TOKEI CHOSA SORAN. Japanese. ir. Gyosei Kanricho Kanrikyoku Tokei Shukan, c/o Chuo Godo Chosa, 4-Gokan 1-1 Kasumigaseki 3 Chuo-ku (100), Tokyo Japan. LC Z7554.J3, HA1844.

TOKEI DE MIRU KEN NO SUGATA. Japanese. an. LC HA4621.

TOKYO-TO TOKEI CHOSA ICHIRAN. See Bibliographies.

TOLDTARIFSTATISTIK. Main/Corp Statistical Office of the European Communities. **VFOAT** Zolltarifstatistik, Tariff Statistics. Periodical. Danish, Dutch, English, French, German, and Italian. ir. $60.75. European Community Information Service, 2100 M Street NW/Suite 707, Washington DC 20037. LC HF1044.E8. DD 382.7094. Statistiques Tarifaires. Zolltarifstatistiken.

TONG KYE WEOL BO. (TONGGYE WOLBO). **VFOAT** Monthly Economic Statistics. V. 35, No. 12, (Dec. 1981)-. 0300-0850. KO. English (Korean). mo. 555 Single Issue. Hanguk Unhaeng, 110 3-ka Namdaemun-no, Chung-ku Seoul. LC HC466.A1. Tonggye Wolbo (Hanguk Unhaeng. Chosabu).

TONGGYE YONBO (SUNCHON-SI, KOREA). See Yearbooks, Almanacs, Directories.

TORONTO STATISTICS. Apr. 1981-. 0822-7411. CN. English. an. City of Toronto, Clerk's Office, Toronto Ontario M5H 2N2 Canada. DD 317.13541.

TORONTO STOCK EXCHANGE REVIEW. See Business - Investments.

TORTENETI STATISZTIKAI TANULMANYOK. 1- 1975-. HU. Hungarian (summaries in English and Russian). ir. Statisztikai Kiado Vallalat, Il Keleti Karoly U 18/B, Budapest Hungary. Ind/Abst Am. Hist. Life, Hist. Abstr., Part A, Mod. Hist. Abstr., Hist. Abst., Part B, Twent. Century Abstr. LC HA1205. Torteneti Statisztikai Evkonyv.

TOURISM AND HOTEL SERVICES STATISTICS QUARTERLY. Main/Corp Israel. Lishkah Ha-Merkazit Li-Statistikah. **VFOAT** Rivon Statistile-Tayarut Ule-Sherute Haarahah. IS. English (Hebrew). ir. 65.00. Government Publishing House, B Street, No 29 Hakirya, Tel-Aviv Isreal. LC TX910.I75. DD 338.47647945694. Yarhon Statisti Le-Tayarut Ule-Serute Harahah, 0302-8224.

TRABAJOS DE ESTADISTICA Y DE INVESTIGACION OPERATIVA. 0041-0241. SP. English or Spanish. ty. 30.00. Sociedade de Estadistica e Investigacion Operativa, Serrano 123, 28006 Madrid Spain. Tel (91)2619800. Ind/Abst Math. Rev., Foreign Lang. Index. LC HA1. DD 519.505. bk rev. Circ 1,800. Trabajos de Estadistica.

TRACK NEWSLETTER. See Recreation, Leisure - Sports.

TRADE AND SHIPPING STATISTICS. 1930-. Periodical. IE. English. ir. Dublin Stationery Office, Street Martin House Waterloo Road, Dublin 4 Ireland. LC HF189.

TRADE UNION STATISTICS : AUSTRALIA. Main/Corp Australian Bureau of Statistics. English. an. Australian Bureau of Statistics, PO Box 84, Canberra Australian Capital Territory 2600 Australia. Tel (062)52 6778. LC HD6891. DD 331.880994. Number of separate trade unions; financial and total members classified by state, territory and sex; proportion of employed wage and salary earners who were members of unions. Trade Union Statistics: Australia.

TRANSPORT STATISTICS. Main/Corp Botswana. Ministry of Works and Communications. Statistics Unit. 1976/78-. English. ir. Botswana Government Information Service, PO Box 51, Gaberone Botswana Africa. LC HE99.9.A3. DD 380.5096811.

TRANSPORT STATISTICS IN THE UNITED STATES. 68th (1954)-. US. English. an. Government Printers Office, Washington DC 20402. LC HE2708. DD 380.50973. Annual Report on the Statistics of Railways in the United States.

TRANSPORT STATISTICS (NEW ZEALAND. DEPT. OF STATISTICS). (TRANSPORT STATISTICS). NZ. English. Department of Statistics, Private Bag, Wellington New Zealand. LC HE297.5. DD 380.509931.

TRANSPORT STATISTICS OF JAPAN. Mar. 1982-. English. ir. Ministry of Transport, 2-1-3 Kasumigaseki, Chiyoda-ku Tokyo 100 Japan. LC HE277.A15. DD 380.50952.

TRANSPORT STATISTICS REPORT. **VFOAT** Transport Statistics. 1980-1981-. 0110-3458. English. ir. $4.00. Department of Statistics, Private Bag, Wellington New Zealand. LC HE297.5. DD 380.509931. Transport Statistics (New Zealand. Dept. of Statistics).

TRANSPORT THEORY AND STATISTICAL PHYSICS. V. 1- Jan. 1971-. 0041-1450. Periodical. US. English. qt. $195.00. Marcel Dekker Inc, PO Box 11305, Church Street Station, New York NY 10249. Tel (212)696-9000. Ed Paul Nelson. Ind/Abst Math. Rev., Eng. Index Annu., Eng. Index Mon., Eng. Index Bioeng. Abstr., Eng. Index Energy Abstr., Comput. Control Abstr., Electr. Electron. Abstr., Sci. Abstr. Sect. A. Phys. Abstr., Chem. Abstr., Spin, Nuci. Sci. Abstr., Int. Aerosp. Abstr., Energy Res. Abstr., Appl. Mech. Rev., Phys. Abstr. LC QC175.2. DD 531.113705. CODEN TTSPB4. bk rev. adv acc. (ctrl). The international vehicle for work on both numerical and analytical methods in neutron transport theory. Devoted entirely to advancing our understanding of basic transport phenomena.

TRANSPORTATION IN AMERICA. See Transportation.

TRAVEL STATISTICS. Main/Corp Jordan. Wizarat Al-Siyahah Wa-Al-Athar. JO. English. ir. Ministry of Tourism & Antiques, Hasemite Kingdom of Jordan PO Box 88, Amman Jordan. LC G155.J6. DD 338.47915695044.

Statistics

TRAVEL STATISTICS, JAMAICA.
English. an. 85 Knutsford Boulevard, Kingston 5 Jamaica. LC G155.J25. DD 380.14591729046.

TRAVELLER ACCOMMODATION STATISTICS. Main/Corp Statistics Canada. Merchandising and Services Division. VFOAT de Voyageurs. 1969-. 0380-5956. CN. English (French). an. 15.00 Domestic, 16.00 Foreign. Receiver General for Canada, Statistics Canada Publications, Ottawa Ontario K1A 0T6 Canada. Tel (800)268-1151. Statistics on hotels, motels, tourist camping grounds and other types of traveller accommodations (e.g. receipts, employment, expenses, occupancy). *Hotels, 0410-5419.*

TRENDS - BUREAU OF RESEARCH AND STATISTICS. Main/Corp North Carolina. Employment Security Commission. Bureau of Research and Statistics. VFOAT Employment Security Commission of North Carolina Trends. V. -Sept. 1961. Periodical. US. English. mo. LC HD5725.N8. DD 331.1209756. *Trends - Employment Security Commission of North Carolina.*

TRENDS IN BHPR PROGRAM STATISTICS. GRANTS, AWARDS, LOANS. Series/Titl Health Professions Reference DHHS Publication. VFOAT Trends in B.H.P.R. Program Statistics. VAT Trends in Bureau of Health Professions Program Statistics. Grants, Awards, Loans. FY 1957-79-. US. English. an. US Department of Health and Human Services, Health Resources Administration, Bureau of Health Professions Program, Management Information Systems Branch, 3700 East-West Highway, Hyattsville MD 20782. *Trends in BHM Program Statistics. Grants, Awards, Loans, 0147-3425.*

TRIBUNAUX CORRECTIONNELS, COURS D'APPEL, CONSEILS DE GUERRE ET COUR MILITAIRE. French. an. 85 Domestic, 135 Foreign. Institut National de Statistique, rue de Louvain 44, Bruxelles 1000 Belgium. Tel (02)513.96.50. DD 347.493013, 344.930713. Circ 350. (ctrl). Court statistics.

TROMESECNI PREGLED MEUNARODNE STATISTIKE. Main/Corp Savezni Zavod za Statistiku (Yugoslavia). Vol. 6- Jan./March 1973-. Serbo-Croatian -R. ir. 120.00. Savezni Zavod za Statistiku, Kneza Milosa 20, Beograd Yugoslavia. LC HA173.Y8. *Mesecni Pregled Meunarodne Statistike.*

TRUCK DATA BOOK. See Transportation - Automobiles.

TRUSTEED PENSION PLANS FINANCIAL STATISTICS. Main/Corp Canada. Statistics Canada. Pensions Section. VFOAT Regimes de Pensions en Fiducie Statistique Financiere. 1970-. 0575-9978. CN. text in English and French. an. $1.05. Receiver General for Canada Statistics Canada Publications, Ottawa Ontario K1A 0T6 Canada. *Trusteed Pension Plans Financial Statistics, 0575-9978.*

TUBERCULOSIS STATISTICS. Main/Corp Statistics Canada. Health and Welfare Division. VFOAT Statistique de la Tuberculose. 34 V. 2- 1970-. CN. English and French. an. Information Canada, Receiver General Canada, Statistics Publishing Canada, Ottawa Ontario K1A 0T6 Canada. LC RC314. DD 312.2699500971. *Tuberculosis Statistics.*

TUBERCULOSIS STATISTICS. MORBIDITY AND MORTALITY. (TUBERCULOSIS STATISTICS, MORBIDITY AND MORTALITY). VFOAT La Statistique de la Tuberculose, Morbidite et Mortalite. 1975-. 0708-4277. CN. French (English). an. 8.00 Domestic, 9.00 Foreign. Receiver General for Canada, Statistics Canada Publications, Ottawa Ontario K1A 0T6 Canada. NLM W2 DC2 S8TA. Admissions, discharges and deaths of patients during the year and patients in institutions at the end of the year classified by medical, social and personal characteristics; and historical tables. *Tuberculosis Statistics, Morbidity and Mortality, Facilities and Services, 0706-4365.*

TUBERCULOSIS STATISTICS. STATES AND CITIES. (TUBERCULOSIS STATISTICS, STATES & CITIES). VFOAT Tuberculosis Statistics. VAT Tuberculosis Statistics. States & Cities. Began with 1970. 0146-7298. US. English. Center for Disease Control, Bureau of State Services, Technical Information Services, Atlanta GA 30333. Tel (404)329-2580. LC RC313. DD 312.399500973. NLM W2 A C242T.

TUINBOUWCIJFERS. See Horticulture and Plant Culture.

TUOMIOISTUIMISSA KASITELLYT RIKOS-, SIVIILI- JA HALLINTOOIKEUDELLISET ASIAT. Main/Corp Finland. Tilastokeskus. VFOAT Vid Domstolarna Handlagda Kriminalcivil- Och Forvaltningsrattsliga Mal Och Arenden, Criminal, Civil and Administrative Cases Concluded in Courts. Finnish (Swedish, with summaries in English). ir. LC HA1448. DD 314.897 S 347.4897013, 314.897 344.8970713.

TURKIYE ISTATISTIK YLLG. See Yearbooks, Almanacs, Directories.

TWENTIETH CENTURY PETROLEUM STATISTICS. 1945. US. English. an. $35.00. Degolyer & MacNaughton, One Energy Square, Dallas TX 75206. Circ 2,000. Information regarding world wide oil and gas production.

TYOELAKEJARJESTELMAN TILASTOLLINEN VUOSIKIRJA. OSA I, TILASTOTIETOJA TYOELAKKEEN SAAJISTA. VFOAT Tilastotietoja Tyoelakkeen Saajista. Began with issue for 1980. 0358-9625. English summaries. an. 90.-. Elaketurvakeskus Tutkimusosasto Opastinsilta 7, 00520 Helsinki 52 Finland. Tel 90-1511. LC HV315.5. DD 331.252094897. Circ 1,100. (ctrl). Statistical information on employment, pension recipients in Finland. *Tilastotietoja Tyoelakkeen Saajista.*

U. K. PETROLEUM INDUSTRY STATISTICS RELATING TO CONSUMPTION AND REFINERY PRODUCTION. VFOAT United Kingdom Petroleum Industry Statistics Relating to Consumption and Refinery Production. 0476-4536. Periodical. UK. English. ir. Institute of Petroleum, 61 New Cavendish Street, London W1M 8AR England. LC HD9571.4.

UAE OIL STATISTICAL REVIEW. English. ir. Ministry of Petroleum and Mineral Resources Statistics Department, PO Box 59, Abu Dhabi Truical States. LC HD9578.U47. DD 338.2728209535.

UCENYE ZAPISKI PO STATISTIKE. (UCHENYE ZAPISKI PO STATISTIKE). V. 1-. 0503-0021. UR. Russian. ir. Ind/Abst Math. Rev. LC HA1.A38.

U.K. PETROLEUM INDUSTRY STATISTICS. CONSUMPTION AND REFINERY PRODUCTION. VFOAT UK Petroleum Industry Statistics. 0141-4305. UK. English. Institute of Petroleum, 61 New Cavendish Street, London W1M 8AR England. LC HD9571.1. DD 338.476655380941.

U.K. SUPPLIES BULLETIN. See Fish Culture and Fisheries.

UKAZATELE HOSPODARSKEHO VYVOJE V ZAHRANICI. Began with Vol. for 1951. Czech. be. 200.00. Ustredi Vedeckych Technickych a Ekonomickych Informaci, 113 57 Praha 1, Konviktska 5, Praha Czechoslovakia. LC HA154.

ULASTIRMA ISTATISTIKLERI. Main/Corp Devlet Istatistik Enstitusu (Turkey). VFOAT Transportation Statistics. 1966-. Turkish (English). ir. LC HA1911. *Kara ve Deniz Tastlar, Kabotaj ve Milletlerarasi Deniz Trafigi ve Nakliyati.*

UNDERVISNINGSSTATISTIKK : AVSLUTTET UTDANNING. Main/Corp Norway. Statistisk Sentralbyra. Series Corp Its Norges Offisielle Statistikk. VFOAT Educational Statistics. 1971-. English and Norwegian. ir. 9.00. LC HA1501 LA892.

UNDUPLICATED COUNT OF MENTALLY RETARDED PATIENTS SERVED CHILDREN'S HEALTH SERVICES DIVISION. See Sociology: General Works, Theory - Social Pathology, Welfare, Criminology.

UNEMPLOYMENT, UNDEREMPLOYMENT, AND RELATED STATISTICS, AUSTRALIA. AT. English. ir. Information Services of the Australian Bureau of Statistics, PO Box 84, Canberra Australian Capital Territory 2600 Australia. LC HD5850. DD 331.137994.

UNIFORM CRIME REPORT FOR THE STATE OF MICHIGAN. See Law Enforcement.

UNIFORM CRIME REPORTS, STATE OF FLORIDA. See Law Enforcement.

UNIFORM CRIME REPORTS, STATE OF NEW JERSEY. See Law Enforcement.

UNITED KINGDOM BALANCE OF PAYMENTS. Main/Corp Great Britain. Central Statistical Office. 1963-. UK. English. ir. Her Majestys Stationery Office, PO Box 276, London SW8 5DT England. Tel 01-622-3316. *United Kingdom Balance of Payments.*

UNITED KINGDOM ENERGY STATISTICS. Main/Corp Great Britain. Dept. of Trade and Industry. UK. English. 3.50. HMSO, Department of Trade and Industry, 49 High Holborn, WC1V 6HB London England. LC HD9502.G7. DD 333.7.

UNITED KINGDOM MINERAL STATISTICS. 1973-. UK. English. an. Her Majestys Stationery Office, PO Box 276, London SW8 5DT England. LC HD9506.G7. DD 338.20942.

U.S. AID STATISTICS. Series/Titl International Policy Report. Fiscal Year 1977-. US. English. an. Center for International Policy, 120 Maryland Avenue Northeast, Washington DC 20002.

U.S. CENSUS REPORT. See Business - Marketing.

U.S. CIVIL AIRMEN STATISTICS. VAT United States Civil Airmen Statistics. 0364-927X. US. English. an. US Department of Transportation, Federal Aviation Administration Office of Management Systems, 800 Independence Avenue SW, Washington DC 20591. LC TL521. DD 331.11. Vols. for (1983-) distributed to depository libraries in microfiche.

U.S. DECENNIAL LIFE TABLES. ACTUARIAL TABLES BASED ON UNITED STATES LIFE TABLES. VFOAT Actuarial Tables Based on United States Life Tables. US. English. ir. Department of Health Education and Welfare, Health Service, Health Resources Administration, National Center for Health Statistics, Washington DC 20402.

U.S. DECENNIAL LIFE TABLES. UNITED STATES LIFE TABLES. (U.S. DECENNIAL LIFE TABLES; UNITED STATES LIFE TABLES). VFOAT United States Life Tables. 1975-. Periodical. US. English. US Department of Health, Education and Welfare, National Center for Health Statistics, Rockville MD 20402.

U.S. DECENNIAL LIFE TABLES. UNITED STATES LIFE TABLES BY CAUSES OF DEATH. VFOAT United States Life Tables by Causes of Death. 1959/61-. US. English. ir. US Department of Health Education and Welfare, Public Health Service, Health Resources Administration, Washington DC 20402.

U.S. FATS AND OILS STATISTICS. Main/Corp United States. Dept. of Agriculture. Economic Research Service. VAT United States Fats and Oils Statistics. 0146-8782. US. English. an. US Department of Agriculture, Economic Research Service, Washington DC 20520. LC HD1751, HD9490.U5. DD 338.10973 S, 338.4766430973.

U.S. FOREIGN AGRICULTURAL TRADE STATISTICAL REPORT, CALENDAR YEAR. (U.S. FOREIGN AGRICULTURAL TRADE STATISTICAL REPORT). VFOAT US Foreign Agricultural Trade Statistical Report. VAT United States Foreign Agricultural Trade Statistical Report. Began with FY 1970. 0362-0530. US. English. an. Superintendent of Document, US Government Printing Office, Washington DC 20402. LC HD9002. DD 382.410973. *U.S. Foreign Agricultural Trade by Commodities, 0565-2545; U.S. Foreign Agricultural Trade by Countries, 0565-2553.*

U.S. FOREIGN TRADE. CONCORDANCE OF STATISTICAL CLASSIFICATIONS OF DOMESTIC AND FOREIGN COMMODITIES EXPORTED FROM THE UNITED STATES. (U.S. FOREIGN TRADE : CONCORDANCE OF STATISTICAL CLASSIFICATIONS OF DOMESTIC AND FOREIGN COMMODITIES EXPORTED FROM THE UNITED STATES). Main/Corp United States. Bureau of the Census. VFOAT Concordance of Statistical Classifications of Domestic and Foreign Commodities Exported from the United States. VAT United States Foreign Trade. Concordance of Statistical Classifications of Domestic and Foreign Commodities Exported from the United States. 1978-. 0193-1687.

Statistics

US. English. Superintendent of Documents, US Government Printing Office, Washington DC 20402. LC HF1042. DD 382.0973.

U.S. INTERNATIONAL AIR TRAVEL STATISTICS (CALENDAR YEAR). (U.S. INTERNATIONAL AIR TRAVEL STATISTICS). VFOAT US International Air Travel Statistics. VAT United States International Air Travel Statistics. Began with 1979. US. English. ir. $200.00. DOT/ Transportation Systems Center, Collection Officer Kendall Square, Cambridge MA 02142. Tel (617)494-2450. Number of U.S. citizens and aliens arriving and departing U.S. gateways on all international flights by world area and country.

U.S. LONG-TERM REVIEW. See Economics.

U.S. MEDICAL LICENSURE STATISTICS AND LICENSURE REQUIREMENTS. (U.S. MEDICAL LICENSURE STATISTICS . . . AND LICENSURE REQUIREMENTS . . .). VFOAT US Medical Licensure Statistics . . . and Licensure Requirements . . . . 1980-81-. 0741-6326. US. English. Department of Data Planning and Evaluation (2-SE), American Medical Association, 535 North Dearborn Street, Chicago IL 60610.

U.S. REGIONAL. VFOAT US Regional. VAT United States Regional. 8755-7398. US. English. Data Resources Inc, 24 Harwell Avenue, Lexington MA 02173. LC HA37. DD 016.3173.

UNITED STATES UNDERWATER FATALITY STATISTICS. 0161-2557. US. English. an. US Department of Commerce, National Oceanic & Atmospheric Administration, Washington DC 20230. LC RC1220.D5. DD 614.81.

UNIVERSITY AND COLLEGE LIBRARIES; STATISTICS OF NORTH CAROLINA. 0098-7816. US. English. an. NC Department of Cultural Resources, Box 5125, Raleigh NC 27607. LC Z732.N8. DD 027.709756.

UNIVERSITY STATISTICS. Main/Corp Australian Bureau of Statistics. 1972, Pt. 3-. AT. English. ir. Australian Bureau of Statistics, PO Box 84 Collectors Publ, Canberra Australian Capital Territory, 2600 Australia. LC L750. DD 378.94. *University Statistics.*

UNUTRASNJA TRGOVINA. Main/Corp Yugoslavia. Savezni Zavod za Statistiku. Series Corp Its Statisticki Bilten. 0300-2462. YU. Serbo-Croatian(R). ir. 10.00 Each Issue. Savezni Zavod za Statistku, Kneza Milosa 20, Beograd Yugloslavia. LC HA1631, HF3732.3.

US-CHINA TRADE STATISTICS. VFOAT US China Trade Statistics. VAT United States-China Trade Statistics. 1981-. 0732-8478. US. English. an. $25.00. National Council for US-China Trade, 1050 17th Street Northwest/Suite 350, Washington DC 20036. Tel (202)429-0340. Ed Marianna Graham. LC HF3128. DD 382.09510730212. Circ 5,000. (ctrl). Publication of US-China trade statistics, including imports and exports in both value and volume terms for the past five years. *US-Sino Trade Statistics.*

USA STATISTICS IN BRIEF. VFOAT U.S.A. Statistics in Brief. Began with 1972. US. English. an. Superintendent of Documents, US Government Printing Office, Washington DC 20402.

USSR FACTS & FIGURES ANNUAL. VFOAT U.S.S.R. Facts and Figures Annual. VAT Union of Soviet Socialist Republics Facts and Figures Annual. V. 1- 1977-. 0148-7760. US. English. an. Box 555, Gulf Breeze FL 32561. LC HA1446. DD 314.7. NLM DK 1 U11.

UTAH EMPLOYMENT, WAGES, AND REPORTING UNITS BY FIRM SIZE. See Economics - Economics: Industry & Production.

UTAH ENERGY STATISTICAL ABSTRACT. See Indexes/Abstracts.

UTAH REPORT OF MEDICAID STATISTICS. V. 1- 1977/78-. 0193-4252. US. English. an. Department of Social Services, 44 Medical Drive, Salt Lake City UT 84111. LC HD7102.U5. DD 362.10425209792.

UTAH STATISTICAL ABSTRACT. See Indexes/Abstracts.

UTAH VITAL STATISTICS, ANNUAL REPORT (UTAH. BUREAU OF HEALTH STATISTICS). (UTAH VITAL STATISTICS, ANNUAL REPORT). 1977-. 0736-4601. US. English. an. Bureau of Health Statistics, 150 West North Temple, Salt Lake City UT 84103. LC HA664. DD 312.09792. *Annual Report of Utah Vital Statistics, 0500-7720.*

UTBILDNINGSSTATISTISK ARSBOK. See Yearbooks, Almanacs, Directories.

UTDANNINGSSTATISTIKK : GRUNNSKOLER. Main/Corp Norway. Statistisk Sentralbyra. Series/Titl Norges Offisielle Statistikk. VFOAT Educational Statistics. Norwegian (English). ir. 8.00. LC HA1501, LA894.

UTDANNINGSSTATISTIKK : OVERSIKT. Main/Corp Norway. Statistisk Sentralbyra. Series/Titl Norges Offisielle Statistikk. VFOAT Educational Statistics : Survey. 1974-. Norwegian (English). ir. LC HA1501, LA892.7.

UTDANNINGSSTATISTIKK : VAKSENOPPLRING. Main/Corp Norway. Statistisk Sentralbyra. Series/Titl Norges Offisielle Statistikk. VFOAT Educational Statistics : Adult Education. 1975/76-. Periodical. English (Norwegian). ir. LC HA1501, LC5256.N7. DD 314.81 S.

UTILITY INVESTMENT STATISTICS, UTILITY APPROPRIATIONS CEASED. (UTILITY INVESTMENT STATISTICS : UTILITY APPROPRIATIONS). Main/Corp Conference Board. 0360-523X. Periodical. US. English. qt. Conference Board, 845 Third Avenue, New York NY 10022. Ind/Abst Predicasts. LC HD2766. DD 338.43. *Investment Statistics. Utility Appropriations, 0090-9726.*

VALTIOLLISET VAALIT : KANSANEDESTAJAIN VAALIT. Main/Corp Finland. Tilastokeskus. Series/Titl Suomen Virallinen Tilasto. VFOAT Statliga Val : Riksdagsmannavalen, National Elections : Parliamentary Elections. English (Finnish and Swedish). ir. Tilastokeskus, Valtion Painatuskeskus, Markkionointiosasto, Pl 516, 001 01 Helsinki Finland. LC HA1448, JN6719.A15. DD 314.897 S, 324.94897033.

VALTIOLLISET VAALIT : TASAVALLAN PRESIDENTIN VALITSIJAMIESTEN VAALIT = STATLIGA VAL : VAL AV ELEKTORER FOR VALET AV REPUBLIKENS PRESIDENT. Main/Corp Finland. Tilastokeskus. Series/Titl Suomen Virallinen Tilasto. VFOAT Statliga Val: Val av Elektorer for Valet av Republikens President, National Elections : Elections of Presidential Electors. English (Finnish and Swedish). ir. Tilastokeskus, Valtion Painatuskeskus, Markkinointiosasto, Pl 516, 001 01 Helsinki Finland. LC HA1448, JN6711. DD 314.897 S, 324.94897033.

VALTION TILASTOJULKAISUT. STATENS STATISTISKA PUBLIKATIONER. GOVERNMENT STATISTICS. Main/Corp Finland. Tilastokeskus. VFOAT Statens Statistiska Publikationer. Fl. English (Finnish and Swedish). mo. Free. Tilastokeskus, Pl 504, 00101 Helsinki 10 Finland. LC Z7554.F5, HA1448.F4. DD 016.314897.

VEJVISER I DANMARKS STATISTIKS PUBLIKATIONER. See Bibliographies.

VEJVISER I STATISTIKKEN. 0109-8314. Danish. ir. 37.00. Danmarks Statistik, Sejrgade 11, 2100 Kbenhavn Denmark. Tel 01 29 82 22. LC Z7554.D3, HA1471. Circ 3,500. Description of contents and collection methods in the various fields of statistics such as surveys, censuses, analyses, compilations, etc. *Vejviser I Danmarks Statistiske Publikationer, 0107-1009.*

VERARBEITENDES GEWERBE. Series/Titl Statistik von Baden-Wurttemberg. GW. German. ir. Statistisches Landesamt Baden-Wurttemberg, Postfach 898, 7000 Stuttgart 1 West Germany. LC HA1320.B2, HC287. B23. DD 314.346, 338.094346.

DIE VERKEHRSWIRTSCHAFT. Main/Corp Statistisches Landesamt Baden-Wurttemberg. Series/Titl Statistik von Baden-Wurttemberg. German. ir. Statistisches Landesamt Baden-Wurttemberg, Postfach 898, 7000 Stuttgart 1 West Germany. LC HA1320.B2, HE249. Z7B25.

VERMONT ENERGY STATISTICS. VFOAT Energy Statistics. US. English. an. State Energy Office, Fuel Management Division, State Office Building, Montpelier VT 05602. LC TJ163.25.U6. DD 333.7909743.

VERMONT FACTS AND FIGURES. 0092-5144. US. English. Vermont Department of Budget and Management, Pavilion Office Building, Montpelier VT 05602. LC HA671. DD 317.43.

VEROFFENTLICHUNGEN DES HESSISCHEN STATISTISCHEN LANDESAMTES. Main/Corp Hesse. Statistisches Landesamt. German. ir. Statistischen Landesamtes, Rheinstrasse 35/37, 6200 Wiesbaden 1 West Germany. LC HA1320.H6. DD 314.341.

VEROFFENTLICHUNGEN DES LANDESAMTES FUR DATENVERARBEITUNG UND STATISTIK NORDRHEIN-WESTFALEN. See Indexes/Abstracts.

VERSLAG VAN DIE OUDITEUR-GENERAAL OOR DIE REKENINGS VAN DIE BANTOESAKE-ADMINISTRASIERAAD, SUID-ORANJE-VRYSTAATGEBIED. Main/Corp South Africa. Controller and Auditor-General. VFOAT Report of the Auditor-General on the Accounts of the Southern Orange Free State Area Bantu Affairs Administration Board. 1973/75-. SA. Afrikaans (English). ir. 2.15. The Government Printer, Pretoria South Africa. LC HJ9080A. DD 354.685008.

VERZEICHNIS DER ALLGEMEINBILDENDEN SCHULEN. Main/Corp Saxony, Lower. Landesverwaltungsamt. Series/Titl Verzeichnisse von Niedersachsen. GW. German. ir. Niedersachsisches Landesverwaltungsamt, Postfach 107, 3000 Hannover West Germany. Tel (0511)108-9466. LC L930.L68. Computer prints of addresses of all state schools in the state of Lower Saxony/West Germany.

VESTNIK STATISTIKI. Series 1 V. 1- 1919-. 0042-4692. Periodical. UR. Russian. mo. $47.50. Victor Kamkin Inc (70127), 12224 Parklawn Drive, Rockville MD 20852. Tel (301)881-5973. Ind/Abst Popul. Index, Sociol. Abstr., Lang. Lang. Behav. Abstr. LC HA1431. (cum index).

VIDEO MARKETING SURVEYS AND FORECASTS. See Communication - Broadcasting.

VIRGINIA AGRICULTURAL STATISTICS. Main/Corp Virginia Cooperative Crop Reporting Service. 0360-3830. US. English. an. Virginia Department of Agriculture & Commerce, Richmond VA 23219. LC HD1775.V5, S123. DD 338.109755 S, 338.109755.

VISITATION AND OUTDOOR RECREATION STATISTICAL REPORT. CN. English. an. LC GV191.46.S2. DD 333.783097124.

VITAL AND HEALTH STATISTICS. SER. 14. DATA ON NATIONAL HEALTH RESOURCES. VFOAT Data on National Health Resources. No. 1- Nov. 1968-. US. English. ir. Ind/Abst Index Med. NLM W2 A N148VN.

VITAL & HEALTH STATISTICS. SERIES 3, ANALYTICAL AND EPIDEMIOLOGICAL STUDIES. Series/Titl DHHS Publication. VFOAT Vital and Health Statistics. No. 21-. Monographic Series. US. English. Ind/Abst Index Med. NLM W2. *Vital and Health Statistics. Series 3, Analytical Studies, 0083-2065.*

VITAL AND HEALTH STATISTICS. SERIES 3, ANALYTICAL STUDIES CEASED. VFOAT Analytical Studies. No. 1-No. 20. 0083-2065. Monographic Series. US. English. ir. Ind/Abst Energy Res. Abstr. NLM W2.

VITAL AND HEALTH STATISTICS. SERIES 4, DOCUMENTS AND COMMITTEE REPORTS. No. 1-. 0083-2073. US. English. Superintendent of Documents, US Government Printing Office, Washington DC 20402. Ind/Abst Index Med. LC HA37. DD 312.0973. NLM W2 A N148VD.

VITAL & HEALTH STATISTICS. SERIES 5, COMPARATIVE INTERNATIONAL VITAL AND HEALTH STATISTICS REPORTS. Series/Titl DHHS Publication. VFOAT Comparative International Vital and Health Statistics Reports. No. 1-. Monographic Series. US. English. NLM W2.

VITAL AND HEALTH STATISTICS. SERIES 13 : DATA FROM THE NATIONAL HEALTH SURVEY. DATA ON HEALTH RESOURCES UTILIZATION. Main/Corp United States. National Center for Health Statistics. No. 22-. US. English. $1.35. US Department of Health Education & Welfare, National Center for Health Statistics, Hyattsville MD 20202. LC RA407.3. DD 362.110973. *Vital and Health Statistics. Series 13: Data from the*

Statistics

National Health Survey. Data from the Hospital Discharge Survey.

VITAL AND HEALTH STATISTICS. SERIES 23. DATA FROM THE NATIONAL SURVEY OF FAMILY GROWTH. (VITAL AND HEALTH STATISTICS. SERIES 23, DATA FROM THE NATIONAL SURVEY OF FAMILY GROWTH). **VFOAT** Data from the National Survey of Family Growth. Began with: No. 1 (Nov. 1977). 0278-5234. Monographic Series. US. English. 3700 East West Highway, Hyattsville MD 20782. **Ind/Abst** Index Med., Popul. Index. **LC** UNC. **DD** 363.990973. **NLM** W2 A N148VW.

VITAL STATISTICS. 1- Fall 1978-. 0164-0151. Periodical. US. English. qt. $12.00. Wolf Run Books, PO Box 10671, Eugene OR 97440. **Tel** (503)343-9391.

VITAL STATISTICS ANNUAL REVIEW. Main/Corp Alberta. Vital Statistics Division. 1975/76-. 0707-7548. CN. English. an. Vital Statistics Division, Department of Public Health, Edmonton Alberta Canada. **LC** RA185.A5. **DD** 312.097123. *Annual Report of the Department of Health Including Vital Statistics Division, 0702-9500.*

VITAL STATISTICS (NEW HAMPSHIRE. BUREAU OF VITAL RECORDS & HEALTH STATISTICS). (VITAL STATISTICS). **VFOAT** Vital Statistics Report for the State of New Hampshire. 1980-. 0737-1896. US. English. an. Bureau of Vital Resources and Health Statistics, Division of Public Health Services, Health and Welfare Building, Haxen Drive, Concord NH 03301. **LC** HA5111. **DD** 312.09742. **NLM** W2 AN3 S4P. *Vital Statistics Report for the State of New Hampshire, 0270-3378.*

VITAL STATISTICS OF NEW YORK STATE. 1972-. 0097-9449. Periodical. US. English. an. New York Vital Statistics Review, New York State Department of Health, Empire State Plaza, Albany NY 12237. **LC** HA544. **DD** 312.09747. **NLM** W2 AN6 D3S. *Vital Statistics for New York State, 0097-9449.*

VITAL STATISTICS OF THE UNITED STATES. Series/Titl DHHS Publication. 1937-. 0083-6710. US. English. an. US Government Printing Office, Superintendent of Documents, Washington DC 20402. **LC** HA203. **DD** 312.0973. **NLM** W2. *Birth, Stillbirth, and Infant Mortality Statistics for the Continental United States, the Territory of Hawaii, the Virgin Islands, Mortality Statistics . . . Annual Report.*

VITAL STATISTICS. PART 2D, NCHS PROCEDURES FOR MORTALITY MEDICAL DATA SYSTEM FILE PREPARATION AND MAINTENANCE. VFOAT NCHS Procedures for Mortality Medical Data System File Preparation and Maintenance. US. English. US Department of Health and Human Services, Public Health Service, Office of Health Research Statistics and Technology, National Center for Health Statistics, Hyattsville MD 20782.

VITAL STATISTICS. PRELIMINARY ANNUAL REPORT. (VITAL STATISTICS; PRELIMINARY ANNUAL REPORT). **Main/Corp** Canada. Statistics Canada. Vital Statistics Section. **VFOAT** Statistique de l'Etat Civil. 1970-. 0317-3143. Periodical. text in English and French. ir. **NLM** W2 DC2 S83V. *Vital Statistics.*

VITAL STATISTICS. PRELIMINARY ANNUAL REPORT. (VITAL STATISTICS). **VFOAT** Statistique de l'Etat Civil. 1950-. 0317-3143. CN. English (French). an. $1.40. Statistics Canada, Publications Distribution, Ottawa Ontario K1A 0T6 Canada. **NLM** W2 DC2 S83V. *Quarterly Report of Births, Marriages and Deaths, Preliminary Annual Report of Vital Statistics of Canada.*

VITAL STATISTICS (QUARTERLY) *CEASED.* (VITAL STATISTICS). **VFOAT** Statistique de l'Etat Civil. V. 20- Jan. 1972-. 0317-3135. Periodical. CN. English (French). qt. Receiver General for Canada, Statistics Canada Publications, Ottawa Ontario K1A 0T6 Canada. **Tel** (613)991-1775. **Ed** Anita Rappaport. **LC** HA741. **DD** 312.0971. **NLM** W2 DC2 B9V. adv acc. **Circ** 3,000. Statistical study of chronic renal failure in Canada covering some of the following treatments: peritoneal dialysis, haemodialysis and transplantation. *Monthly Report of Vital Statistics, 0829-6553.*

VITAL STATISTICS REPORT. Main/Corp Georgia. Dept. of Human Resources. Program and Management Analysis Unit. 1972-. 0094-0690. US. English. an. 47 Trinity Avenue, Atlanta GA 30334. **LC** HA321. **DD** 312.09758. *Georgia Vital and Morbidity Statistics.*

VITAL STATISTICS REPORT. Main/Corp Philippines (Republic). National Census and Statistics Office. PH. English. an. $14.40. National Census & Statistics Office, PO Box 779, Manila Philippines. **LC** HA1821. **DD** 315.99.

VITAL STATISTICS. SPECIAL REPORTS. US. English. ir. US National Office of Vital Statistics, Washington DC 20241. **LC** HA203. **DD** 614.10973.

VITAL STATISTICS. VOLUME 2. MARRIAGES AND DIVORCES. (VITAL STATISTICS. VOLUME II. MARRIAGES AND DIVORCES). **Main/Corp** Statistics Canada. Vital Statistics and Disease Registries Section. **VFOAT** La Statistique de l'Etat Civil. Volume II. Mariages et Divorces. 1976-. 0700-1460. CN. English (French). an. Receiver General for Canada, Statistics Canada Publications, Ottawa Ontario K1A 0T6 Canada. **LC** HB1149. **DD** 312.50971. **NLM** W2 DC2 S83VB. *Vital Statistics. Volume II. Marriages and Divorces, 0700-1460; Vital Statistics.*

VITAL STATISTICS. VOLUME 3, MORTALITY, SUMMARY LIST OF CAUSES *CEASED.* (VITAL STATISTICS. VOLUME III, MORTALITY, SUMMARY LIST OF CAUSES). **VFOAT** Statistique de l'Etat Civil Volume III, Mortalite, Liste Sommaire des Causes. 1978-1981. 0225-7394. CN. English (French). an. 7.00 Domestic, 8.00 Foreign. Publications Distribution, Statistics Canada, Ottawa Ontario K1A 0T6 Canada. **LC** HB1359. **DD** 312.20971. **NLM** W2 DC2 S83VA. *Vital Statistics. Vol. III, Deaths, 0700-1479.*

VITAL STATISTICS. VOLUME I, BIRTHS *CEASED.* **VFOAT** Statistique de l'Etat Civil, L'Etat Civil. Volume I. Naissances. 1975/76-. 0700-1452. CN. French (English). an. $1.40. Distribution des Publications Statistique Canada, Ottawa Ontario K1A 0T6 Canada. **NLM** W2 DC2 S83VC. *Vital Statistics (Statistique Canada), 0527-6438.*

VOCATIONAL AND TECHNICAL EDUCATION SELECTED STATISTICAL TABLES. Main/Corp United States. Office of Education. Division of Vocational and Technical Education. **Series/Titl** Vocational Education Information. US. English. US Department of Health Education & Welfare, Division of Vocational and Technical Education, Washington DC 20202. **LC** LC1045. **DD** 379.155.

VUES SUR L'ECONOMIE D'AQUITAINE. May 1971-. Periodical. FR. French. bm. INSEE-CNGP, BP 2718, 80027 Amiens Cedex France. **LC** HA1228.A75. *Bulletin de Statistique: Aquitaine (Dordogne, Gironde, Landes, Lot-et-Garonne, Pyrnees-Atlantiques).*

VUOSIKIRJA (ALKO OY). (VUOSIKIRJA). **VFOAT** Arsbok, Alcohol Statistics. 0356-6730. Finnish (Swedish). an. **LC** HD9365.F5. **DD** 380.145663109489702I.

WAGE DIFFERENCES AMONG LARGE CITY GOVERNMENTS AND COMPARISONS WITH INDUSTRY AND FEDERAL PAY. *See* Economics - Labor.

WAHL ZUM NIEDERSACHSISCHEN LANDTAG DER . . . . *See* Political Science.

WASHINGTON AGRICULTURAL STATISTICS. Main/Corp Washington Crop and Livestock Reporting Service. 0095-4330. US. English. 3136 Federal Office Building, Seattle WA 98174. **LC** S125. **DD** 338.109797. *Annual Crop Report.*

WASTE DISPOSAL STATISTICS BASED ON ESTIMATES. Main/Corp Society of County Treasurers. UK. English. Society of County Treasurers, County Hall TR1 3BD, Truro England. **LC** TD793.7. **DD** 363.6.

WASTE DISPOSAL STATISTICS . . . ESTIMATES. VFOAT Waste Disposal Statistics Based on Estimates. UK. English. 5.00. Chartered Institute of Public Finance and Accountancy, 1 Buckingham Place, London SW1E 6HS England. **LC** TD793.7. **DD** 363.7280942. *Waste Disposal Statistics Based on Estimates.*

A WATER INDUSTRY STATISTICAL PROFILE. Main/Corp Missouri Public Service Commission. Office of Economic Research. 0149-029X. US. English. an. $4.50. Public Service Commission c/o Economic Research, PO Box 360, Jefferson City MO 65101. **LC** HD4464.M8. **DD** 338.43.

WATER TRANSPORT STATISTICS OF INDIA. 1972/73-. II. English. ir. Government of India, Transportation Research Division, New Delhi 110054 India. **LC** E563.I5. **DD** 387.00954. *Statistics of Water Transport Industries.*

WEEKLY INSIDERS DAIRY & EGG LETTER. *See* Agriculture - Dairy & Related Technologies.

WEEKLY INSIDERS POULTRY REPORT. *See* Agriculture - Livestock and Poultry.

WEEKLY INSIDERS TURKEY LETTER. *See* Agriculture - Livestock and Poultry.

WEEKLY PETROLEUM STATUS REPORT. *See* Petroleum and Natural Gas.

WEEKLY PRODUCTION AND DRILLING STATISTICS, ALBERTA OIL AND GAS INDUSTRY *CEASED.* **Main/Corp** Alberta. Energy Resources Conservation Board. June 7th, 1971-Dec. 24-31, 1979?. 0032-9827. Periodical. CN. English. wk. Energy Resources Conservation, 640 5th Avenue Southwest, Calgary Alberta T2P 3G4 Canada. *Weekly Production and Drilling Statistics, Alberta Oil and Gas Industry, 0032-9827.*

WEEKLY STATISTICAL BULLETIN - AMERICAN PETROLEUM INSTITUTE, STATISTICS DEPARTMENT. Main/Corp American Petroleum Institute. Dept. of Statistics. V. 56, No. 47- Nov. 21, 1975-. US. English. wk. American Petroleum Institute, 2101 L Street NW, Washington DC 20037. *Weekly Statistical Bulletin.*

WEEKLY STATISTICAL SUGAR TRADE JOURNAL. VFOAT Willet & Gray's Weekly Statistical Sugar Trade Journal. **VAT** Willet and Gray's Weekly Statistical Sugar Trade Journal. 0043-1923. Periodical. US. English. wk. $65.00. Willett & Gray Inc, PO Box N, Brightwaters NY 11718. **LC** HD9100.1. **DD** 380.141360973.

WEST VIRGINIA AGRICULTURAL STATISTICS. Series/Titl C.R. Bulletin. US. English. an. West Virginia Crop Reporting Service, c/o State Department of Agriculture, Charleston WV 25305. **LC** S127, HD1775.W4. **DD** 630.9754, 338.109754.

WEST VIRGINIA LABOR FORCE ANNUAL AVERAGES HOURS & EARNINGS. WEST VIRGINIA STANDARD METROPOLITAN STATISTICAL AREAS. (WEST VIRGINIA LABOR FORCE ANNUAL AVERAGES HOURS & EARNINGS : WEST VIRGINIA STANDARD METROPOLITAN STATISTICAL AREAS). **Main/Corp** West Virginia. Dept. of Employment Security. Research and Statistics Division. 0097-7837. US. English. an. West Virginia Department of Employment Security, Research and Statistics Division, 112 California Avenue, Charleston WV 25305. **LC** HD5725.W4. **DD** 331.1109754.

WESTERN AUSTRALIA LOCAL GOVERNMENT FINANCE STATISTICS. Main/Corp Australian Bureau of Statistics. Western Australian Office. AT. English. ir. Australian Bureau of Statistics Western Australian Office, 1-3 Street Georges Terrace, Perth Western Australia 6000 Australia. **LC** HJ9096. **DD** 336.01409941. *Western Australia Local Government Finance Statistics.*

WESTERN AUSTRALIA, WAGE AND SALARY EARNERS IN CIVILIAN EMPLOYMENT. *See* Economics - Labor.

WESTERN AUSTRALIAN WINE STATISTICS. Main/Corp Australian Bureau of Statistics. Western Australian Office. 1975/77-. AT. English. ir. Australian Bureau of Statistics, 1-3 St Georges Terrace, Perth Western Australia 6000 Australia. **LC** HD9388.A83. **DD** 338.476632009941.

WIADOMOSCI STATYSTYCZNE *CEASED.* **Main/Corp** Poland. Gowny Urzad Statystyczny. **VFOAT** Nouvelles Statistiques de l'Office Centrale de Statistique. Vol. I I II- 1923-. 0043-518X. PL. Polish (French; Polish only, Oct. 18, 1923-Jan. 3, 1925). mo. ARS Polona, Krakowskie Przedmiescie 7, 00-068 Warsaw Poland. **Ind/Abst** Popul. Index. **LC** HA1451.

WILDFIRE STATISTICS. Began with 1968. 0360-8034. US. English. an. USDA Forest Service, State and Private Forestry Cooperative Fire Protection

Statistics

Staff, Washington DC 20250. **Ind/Abst** Bibliogr. Agric. **LC** SD421. **DD** 634.96180973. Vols. for (1979-) distributed to depository libraries in microfiche. *Forest Fire Statistics.*

WISCONSIN CRIMINAL JUSTICE INFORMATION, CRIME AND ARRESTS. *See* Sociology: General Works, Theory - Social Pathology, Welfare, Criminology.

WISCONSIN STATISTICAL ABSTRACT. *See* Indexes/Abstracts.

WOHNGELD IN NORDRHEIN-WESTFALEN. Main/Corp North Rhine-Westphalia (Germany). Landesamt fur Datenverarbeitung und Statistik. **Series/Titl** Beitrage zur Statistik des Landes Nordrhein-Westfalen. 1974/76-. German. ir. 4.-. Landesamt fur Datenverarbeitung, 4000 Dusseldorf 1, Postfach 1105, Dusseldorf West Germany. **Tel** (0211)44971. **LC** HA1320.N6, HD7339. N6. adv acc. **Circ** 200. Statistical returns about public housing allowance.

WOLFMAN REPORT ON THE PHOTOGRAPHIC INDUSTRY IN THE UNITED STATES. *See* Photography & Photographs.

WOMEN AND MINORITY MANPOWER STATISTICS. Main/Corp Maine. Manpower Research Division. 0149-8959. US. English. an. Manpower Research Division, Employment Security Commission Maine Department of Manpower Affairs, 20 Union Street, Augusta ME 04330. **LC** HD5725.M3. **DD** 331.409741.

WOOD PULP AND FIBER STATISTICS. Main/Corp American Paper Institute. Pulp, Fiber and Raw Materials Group. V.38-1974-. Periodical. US. English. an. $75.00. American Paper Institute Publishing Department, 260 Madison Avenue, New York NY 10016. **Tel** (212)340-0630. *Wood Pulp Statistics.*

WOOL QUARTERLY. *See* Textiles.

WOOL STATISTICS. 1948-. UK. English. an. $18.38. Commonwealth Secretariat Publishers, Marlborough House, Pall Mall, London SW1Y 5HX England. **Tel** (01)839-3411. Ed M J Godfrey. Reviews world wool and wool textile situations and outlook. Contains comprehensive up-to-date statistics on sheep numbers, raw wool production, consumption, trade and prices.

WOOL STATISTICS, AUSTRALIA. Main/Corp Australian Bureau of Statistics. AT. English. ir. **LC** HD9908.A8. **DD** 338.47677310994.

WORKER'S COMPENSATION CLAIMS. *See* Economics - Labor.

WORKERS' COMPENSATION STATISTICS. Main/Corp Papua New Guinea. Bureau of Statistics. 0377-6522. English. ir. Bureau of Statistics, PO Box 2032, Konedobu Papua New Guinea. **LC** HD7262.5.P34. **DD** 368.41009953.

WORKING PAPERS. *See* Economics.

THE WORLD ALMANAC & BOOK OF FACTS. *See* Yearbooks, Almanacs, Directories.

WORLD DEBT TABLES. *See* Economics - International Economics.

WORLD GRAIN TRADE STATISTICS. 1954/56-. 0084-182X. title and text in English 1954/56. ir. Unipub, 345 Park Avenue South, New York NY 10010. **LC** HD9030.4. **DD** 382.

WORLD HEALTH STATISTICS ANNUAL. VFOAT Annuaire de Statistiques Sanitaires Mondiales. 1962-. 0250-3794. SZ. English (French). an. World Health Organization, 27 Av Appia CH-1211, Geneva 27 Switzerland. **LC** RA651. **DD** 312.205. **NLM** W2 MW6 W9S. *Statistiques Epidemiologiques et Demographiques Annuelles.*

WORLD HEALTH STATISTICS QUARTERLY. Main/Corp World Health Organization. VFOAT Rapport Trimestriel de Statistiques Sanitaires Mondiales. V. 31-. 0379-8070. English (French). ir. $40.00. World Health Organization, PO Box 5284, Church Street Station, New York NY 10249. **Tel** (202)861-3200. **Ind/Abst** Excerpta Med., Index Med., Popul. Index. **LC** RA651. **DD** 312.305. **NLM** W2 MW6 W9RA. Focus has shifted in recent years away from mere presentation of statistical data to the interpretation of data as a means to improve the use of quantitative information for administrative and research purposes. *World Health Statistics Report.*

WORLD METAL STATISTICS. V. 20, No. 6- June 1967-. 0043-8758. Periodical. UK. English. mo. 570.00 Domestic, $1,200.00 Foreign. World Bureau of Metal Statistics, 41 Doughty Street, London WC1N 2LF England. **Tel** (01)405 2771. **Ind/Abst** Public Aff. Inf. Serv. Bull. *World Non-Ferrous Metal Statistics.*

WORLD MINERAL STATISTICS. 1970/74-. UK. English. ir. Her Majestys Stationery Office, PO Box 276, London SW8 5DT England. **Tel** (01)622 3316. **LC** HD9506.A1. **DD** 338.20212. *Statistical Summary of the Mineral Industry.*

WORLD SHIPPING STATISTICS. 1975-. UK. English. an. H P Drewry/Shipping Consultants, 1-4 Argyll Street, London England. **LC** HE563.A3. **DD** 387.5440212.

WORLD SOLID FUELS, ELECTRICITY, GAS, IRON AND STEEL AND PETROLEUM STATISTICS. 1957-. Periodical. UK. English. ir. Ministry of Power, Statistics Branch, London WC1 England. **DD** 338.2, 338.39. *World Solid Fuels, Electricity, Gas, and Petroleum Abstracts, 0432-4676.*

WORLD STAINLESS STEEL STATISTICS. UK. English. an. 150.00 Domestic, $350.00 Foreign. World Bureau of Metal Statistics, 41 Doughty Street, London WC1N 2LF England. **Tel** (01)834-3888. **LC** HD9529.S62. **DD** 338.47762. bk rev. **Circ** 300. World stainless steel production and consumption statistics.

WORLD STATISTICS IN BRIEF. VFOAT United Nations Statistical Pocketbook. 1st- Ed. US. English. an. $5.00. United Nations Publications, Room A-3315, New York NY 10017. **Tel** (212)754-8302. **LC** JX1977. **DD** 310.5 S, 310.5. Pocketsize reference book giving statistical data from 156 countries on demography, labor force, national accounts, agriculture, industry, trade, finance, tourism, transport, communication, education, health and nutrition.

WORLDCASTS. PRODUCT. *See* Economics - Economics: Industry & Production.

WORLDWIDE MANPOWER DISTRIBUTION BY GEOGRAPHICAL AREA. *See* Economics - Labor.

WYOMING AGRICULTURAL STATISTICS. 1973-. 0363-9339. US. English. an. Free. Wyoming Crop and Livestock Reporting Service, PO Box 1148, Cheyenne WY 82001. **Tel** (307)772-2181. Ed Samuel J Hundley. **LC** S131. **DD** 630.9787. Statistics about agriculture in Wyoming at the state and county level on crops, livestock and prices.

WYOMING COVERED EMPLOYMENT AND WAGE DATA BY INDUSTRY AND COUNTY. *See* Economics - Labor.

WYOMING LABOR FORCE TRENDS. *See* Economics - Labor.

WYOMING OIL AND GAS STATISTICS. 0360-2923. US. English. an. $6.00. Wyoming Oil & Gas Statistics, PO Box 2640, Casper WY 82602. **Tel** (307)234-7147. **LC** TJ163.4.U6. **DD** 338.272809787.

WYOMING POPULATION AND EMPLOYMENT FORECAST REPORT. *See* Economics - Labor.

WYOMING STATISTICAL REVIEW. VFOAT Employment Security Statistical Review, Wyoming. US. English. an. Wyoming Statistical Review, PO Box 2760, Casper WY 82602. **Tel** (307)235-3296. Ed Deana Hauf. **LC** HD7096.U6. **DD** 368.44009787. **Circ** 75. Contains historical data for Wyoming concerning job openings, work applications, job placements, claims for unemployment insurance benefits, and payments of unemployment insurance benefits act.

YARHON LI-STATISTIKAH SHEL MEHIRIM. Main/Corp Isreal. Lishkah Ha-Merkazit Li-Statistikah. VFOAT Monthly Price Statistics. V. 18- February 1967-. Hebrew (summaries in English). ir. 25.00. Government Publishing House, Street B No 29, Hakirya Tel-Aviv Israel. **LC** HB235.P3. *Yarhon Ha-Statisti Le-Yisrael. Helek D: Mehirim.*

YEAR BOOK, AUSTRALIA. *See* Yearbooks, Almanacs, Directories.

YEAR BOOK - INSURANCE ACCOUNTING AND STATISTICAL ASSOCIATION. *See* Yearbooks, Almanacs, Directories.

YEAR BOOK OF LABOUR STATISTICS. *See* Yearbooks, Almanacs, Directories.

YEAR BOOK OF TRANSPORT STATISTICS. *See* Yearbooks, Almanacs, Directories.

YEARBOOK OF FISHERY STATISTICS. *See* Yearbooks, Almanacs, Directories.

YEARBOOK OF FOREIGN TRADE STATISTICS, THIRD COUNTRIES. *See* Yearbooks, Almanacs, Directories.

YEARBOOK OF INDUSTRIAL STATISTICS CEASED. 1974-1981. US. English. an. United Nations Publications, Sales Section/Room A-3315, New York NY 10017. **LC** HC59. **DD** 338.0021. *Growth of World Industry.*

YEARBOOK OF INTERNATIONAL TRADE STATISTICS. *See* Yearbooks, Almanacs, Directories.

YEARBOOK OF INVESTMENT STATISTICS. *See* Yearbooks, Almanacs, Directories.

YEARBOOK OF LABOR STATISTICS. *See* Yearbooks, Almanacs, Directories.

YEARBOOK OF NATIONAL ACCOUNTS STATISTICS. *See* Yearbooks, Almanacs, Directories.

YEARBOOK OF NORDIC STATISTICS. *See* Yearbooks, Almanacs, Directories.

YEARBOOK OF STATISTICS: SINGAPORE. *See* Yearbooks, Almanacs, Directories.

YEARBOOK OF WORLD ENERGY STATISTICS. *See* Yearbooks, Almanacs, Directories.

YEARLY BULLETIN OF PRICE STATISTICS, RETAIL, WHOLESALE. Main/Corp Kuwait. Al-Idarah Al-Markaziyah Lil-Ihsa. English. ir. Kuwait Central Statistics Office, Box 26188, Kuwait Kuwait. **LC** HB235.K9. **DD** 339.42.

YEARLY STATISTICAL REPORT OF THE COMMUNITY REHABILITATION SYSTEM. Main/Corp Massachusetts. Dept. of Correction. Division of Research. VFOAT Statistical Report of the Community Rehabilitation System. 0146-2717. US. English. an. **LC** HV9305.M4. **DD** 364.6309744.

YEARLY STATISTICAL REPORT OF THE FURLOUGH PROGRAM. Main/Corp Massachusetts. Dept. of Correction. US. English. an. **LC** HV9305.M4. **DD** 365.643.

YIELD AND PRICE STATISTICS FOR TEXAS AGRICULTURAL PRODUCTS. 1974/78-. US. English. an. **LC** S117. **DD** 338.109764.

YLEISISSA ALIOIKEUKSISSA SYYTETYT JA TUOMITUT. VFOAT Vid de Allmanna Underratterna Atalade Och Domda. FI. Finnish (Swedish). an. Government Printing Centre, PO Box 516, SF-00101 Helsinki 10 Finland.

YUNYU TOKEI HIMMOKU HYO. Main/Corp Nihon Kanzei Kyokai. VFOAT Import Statistical Schedule, Japan. English or Japanese. an. $48.50. OCS America Inc, 14th & F Street NW, c/o Mr Shoji, Washington DC 20045. **Tel** (202)347-4233. **LC** HF1044.J3.

YUSHUTSU TOKEI HIMMOKU HYO. Main/Corp Nihon Kanzei Kyokai. VFOAT Export Statistical Schedule: Japan. JA. Japanese and English. $32.06. Japan Tariff Association Ed, 4-7-8 Kojimachi Chiyada ku, Tokyo Japan. **LC** HF1044.J3.

ZAHLEN ZUR KOHLENWIRTSCHAFT. Main/Corp Statistik der Kohlenwirtschaft. 0723-0036. GW. German. ir. Verlag Glueckauf GMBH, Postfach 1794, 43 Essen West Germany. **Ind/Abst** Coal Abstr. **LC** HD9553.4.

ZAHLENSPIEGEL. Main/Corp Germany (West). Bundesministerium fur Innerdeutsche Beziehungen. German. ir. Bundesministerium fur Innerdeutsche Beziehungen, Distributor: Gesamtdeutsches Institut, Postfach 1640, 5300 Bonn 1 West Germany. **LC** HA1233.

ZAMBIA IN FIGURES. Main/Corp Zambia. Central Statistical Office. English. ir. Central Statistical Office, PO Box 1908, Lusaka Zambia. **LC** HA4703. **DD** 316.894.

Technology (General)

ZAPOSLENOST I LICNI DOHOCI PO KVALIFIKACIJAMA. Serbo-Croatian -R. ir. LC HA1634.B67.

ZEITREIHENANALYSE IM RAHMEN DER AUSSENHANDELS- UND SEEGUTERSVERKEHRSSTATISTIK. Main/Corp Bremen. Statistisches Landesamt. Periodical. German. ir. Statistisches Landesamt, An der Weide 14-16 Postfach 10 13 09, 2800 Bermen 1 West Germany. LC HF3570.B8.

ZEITSCHRIFT DES BAYERISCHEN STATISTISCHEN LANDESAMTS. Main/Corp Bayerisches Statistisches Landesamt. GW. German. an. Bayerisches Statistisches Neuhauserstr 511, 8000 Munchen 2 West Germany. LC HA1261. NLM W2 GG4.1 B3S7Z. *Zeitschrift des Koniglich Bayerischen Statistischen Bureau.*

ZIVILLUFTFAHRT IN OSTERREICH. Main/Corp Osterreichisches Statistisches Zentralamt. Series Corp Its Beitrage zur Osterreichischen Statistik. 1955/59-. Monographic Series. German. ir. LC HA1173.

ZUSETSU EPOKA TOKEI SHIRYO. VFOAT Epoka Tokei Shiryo. Japanese. ir. Obunsha, Yokoderacho Shinjuku-ku (162), Tokyo Japan. LC HA1844.

TECHNOLOGY (GENERAL)

AAMI TECHNOLOGY ASSESSMENT REPORT. See Medicine.

ABSTRACTS IN BIOCOMMERCE. See Indexes/Abstracts.

ABSTRACTS OF ROMANIAN SCIENTIFIC AND TECHNICAL LITERATURE. See Indexes/Abstracts.

ABSTRACTS OF THESES ACCEPTED IN PARTIAL FULFILLMENT OF THE REQUIREMENTS FOR THE DOCTOR'S DEGREE - MASSACHUSETTS INSTITUTE OF TECHNOLOGY. See Indexes/Abstracts.

ACHIEVEMENTS OF CZECHOSLOVAK SCIENCE AND TECHNOLOGY WHICH WERE AWARDED STATE PRIZES. See Science (General).

ACTA POLYMERICA. See Textiles.

ACTA POLYTECHNICAE WRATISLAVIENSIS. Main/Corp Breslau. Politechnika. No. 1- 1972-. PL. in English. qt. ARS Polona, Krakowskie Przedmiescie 7, 00-068 Warsaw Poland. LC T1. DD 608.

ACTA TECHNICA. VFOAT Conference on Dimensioning and Strength Calculation. V. 1, Issue No. 1-. 0001-7035. Periodical. HU. English (text in French, German or Russian). mo. $44.00. Akademiai Kiado, POB 24, 1363 Budapest Hungary. Tel 111-010. Ed M Major. Ind/Abst Int. Aerosp. Abstr., GeoRef, Met. Abstr., World Alum. Abstr., Bibliogr. Agric., Comput. Control Abstr., Electr. Electron. Abstr., Sci. Abstr. Sect. A. Phys. Abstr., Appl. Mech. Rev., Comput. Abstr., Eng. Index, Math. Rev., Eng. Index Annu., Eng. Index Mon., Eng. Index Bioeng. Abstr., Eng. Index Energy Abstr. LC T4. CODEN ATSHA8. (cum index). bk rev. adv acc. Circ 700.

ACTA TECHNICA CSAV. Vol. 7-. 0001-7043. Periodical. Czech. bm. $141.63. Kubon and Sagner, Postfach 34 01 08, D8 Muenchen 34 West Germany. Tel (089)52 20 27. Ind/Abst Math. Rev., Fluidex, Eng. Index Annu., Eng. Index Mon., Eng. Index Bioeng. Abstr., Eng. Index Energy Abstr., Int. Aerosp. Abstr., Met. Abstr., World Alum. Abstr., Chem. Abstr., Comput. Control Abstr., Electr. Electron. Abstr., Sci. Abstr. CODEN ATCVA4. Subjects covered by this journal are electrotechniques, engineering and building industries, hydrodynamics, theory of material and mechanics. *Acta Technica.*

ACTIVITIES OF THE FEDERAL COUNCIL FOR SCIENCE AND TECHNOLOGY AND THE FEDERAL COORDINATING COUNCIL FOR SCIENCE, ENGINEERING AND TECHNOLOGY. See Science (General).

ADATE. ASSOCIATION POUR LE DEVELOPPEMENT DE L'AUDIO-VISUEL ET DA LA TECHNOLOGIE EN EDUCATION. See Education (General) - Theory, Practice of Education.

ADVANCED MANUFACTURING TECHNOLOGY. See Manufacturing.

ADVANCED SOLAR ENERGY TECHNOLOGY NEWSLETTER. See Energy.

ADVANCED TECHNOLOGY IN THE PACIFIC NORTHWEST. VFOAT Directory and Guide to Advanced Technology in the Pacific Northwest. Vol. 1 (Winter 84-85)-. 8755-7258. US. English. sa. $72.00. Quanix Data Services Inc, 2545 Southwest Spring Garden Street, Portland OR 97219. Tel (503)245-7665. Ed D E Smith. DD 338. adv acc. Circ 2,000. Directory of advanced technology in Pacific Northwest. Covers over 1,000 firms detailed in Oregon, Washington and Idaho in five categories.

ADVANCED TECHNOLOGY IN WASHINGTON STATE. See Yearbooks, Almanacs, Directories.

ADVANCES IN CEREAL SCIENCE AND TECHNOLOGY. See Food & Drink.

ADVANCES IN URETHANE SCIENCE AND TECHNOLOGY. See Plastics.

AEROJET TECHNOLOGY. See Aeronautics, Astronautics.

AEROSPACE/DEFENSE MARKETS & TECHNOLOGY. See Military Science.

AFRICAN TECHNICAL REVIEW. VFOAT Technical Review. Mar. 1983-. Periodical. UK. English. mo. $60.00. Expediters of the Printed Word Ltd, 527 Madison Avenue, New York NY 10022. Tel 01 828 6107. Ed Jonquil Phelan. LC T1. DD 609.6. bk rev. adv acc. Circ 17,383. (ctrl). New developments/ contracts in Black Africa, including oil, commodities, banking, finance, insurance, airlines, power generation, commerical vehicles, freight handling, construction, miningand telecoms. *West African Technical Review.*

AGENCY OF INDUSTRIAL SCIENCE AND TECHNOLOGY : AIST. Main/Corp Kogyo Gijutsuin (Japan). VFOAT AIST. JA. English. ir. Agency of Industrial Science and Technology, Technology Research and Information Division, 1-3-1 Kasumigaseki, Chiyoda-ku, Tokyo Japan. LC T177.J3. DD 607.252.

AHA HOSPITAL TECHNOLOGY ALERTS. VFOAT A.H.A. Hospital Technology Alerts. VAT American Hospital Association Technology Alerts. Began with issue for June 1982?. 0735-4479. Periodical. US. English. American Hospital Association, PO Box 99376, Chicago IL 60693. Tel (312)289-6029. *Alerts.*

AHA HOSPITAL TECHNOLOGY SERIES. VFOAT A.H.A. Hospital Technology Series. VAT American Hospital Association Hospital Technology Series. Began in 1982?. 0735-4681. US. English. $150.00. American Hospital Association, PO Box 99376, Chicago IL 60693. Tel (312)280-6029. Ind/Abst Hospit. Lit. Index.

A.I.D. EVALUATION SPECIAL STUDY. See Science (General).

AIIE TRANSACTIONS CEASED. Main/Corp American Institute of Industrial Engineers. VAT American Institute of Industrial Engineers Transactions. V. 1-13. 0569-5554. US. English. qt. Ind/Abst Math. Rev., Electron. Commun. Abstr. J., ISMEC Bull., Pollut. Abstr. Indexes, Saf. Sci. Abstr. J., Eng. Index Mon., Eng. Index Bioeng. Abstr., Eng. Index Energy Abstr., Ship Abstr., Coal Abstr., Int. Aerosp. Abstr., Eng. Index Annu., ABI/Inform, Comput. Control Abstr., Electr. Electron. Abstr., Sci. Abstr. Sect. A. Phys. Abstr. LC T55.4. DD 658.5005. CODEN AIITAJ. *Journal of Industrial Engineering.*

AIPE FACILITIES MANAGEMENT, OPERATIONS & ENGINEERING. See Engineering.

AL-ILM. See Science (General).

AMERICA LATINA 2001 I.E. DOS MIL UNO. VFOAT America Latina 2001. VAT America Latina dos Mil Uno. No. 1- Jan./Feb. 1976-. Periodical. Spanish. ir. $33.00. Bogota anif etc, Asociacion Nacionel de Instituciones Financireras, Cale 35 No 4-8A Apartado Aero 29765, Bogota Columbia. LC T24.A1.

AMERICAN JOURNAL OF E.E.G. TECHNOLOGY. See Medicine - Neurology.

AMTS- UND MITTEILUNGSBLATT DER BUNDESANSTALT FUR MATERIALPRUFUNG. See Engineering.

ANAIS - SEMINARIO SOBRE ENERGIA DE BIOMASSAS NO NORDESTE. Main/Conf Seminario Sobre Energia de Biomassas No Nordeste (Brazil). 1.- 1979-. BL. Portuguese. ir. LC TP360.

ANNUAIRE DES COMITES - ASTED. See Yearbooks, Almanacs, Directories.

L'ANNUAIRE INTERNATIONAL DES FOIRES-EXPOSITIONS & I.E. ET SALONS SPECIALISES. See Yearbooks, Almanacs, Directories.

ANNUAL INTERNATIONAL INDUSTRIAL ENGINEERING CONFERENCE. See Engineering.

ANNUAL PROCEEDINGS - ASSOCIATED SCIENTIFIC AND TECHNICAL SOCIETIES OF SOUTH AFRICA. See Science (General).

ANNUAL PROGRESS REPORT, TRACT C-A. (ANNUAL PROGRESS REPORT : TRACT C-A). 1977/1978-. 8756-0518. US. English. an. Gulf Oil Corporation/Standard Oil Company, 9725 East Hampden Avenue, Denver CO 80231. Ind/Abst GeoRef. DD 665.

ANNUAL REPORT - BNF METALS TECHNOLOGY CENTRE. Main/Corp BNF Metals Technology Centre. 1974-. UK. English, French, or German. an. BNF Metals Technology Centre, Grove Laboratories Denchworth Road, Wantage OX12 9BJ England. LC TA459. DD 669.006242576. *Annual Report.*

ANNUAL REPORT - INTERNATIONAL INSTITUTE FOR APPLIED SYSTEMS ANALYSIS. Main/Corp International Institute for Applied Systems Analysis. VFOAT IIASA Annual Report. 1973-. 0304-7121. AT. English. ir. International Institute for Applied Systems Analysis, 2361 Lexenburg Australia. LC T57.6.A1. DD 003.0621.

ANNUAL REPORT - MASSACHUSETTS TECHNOLOGY DEVELOPMENT CORPORATION. (ANNUAL REPORT). Main/Corp Massachusetts Technology Development Corporation. Fiscal year 1979-. 0275-1917. US. English. an. Massachusetts Technology Development Corporation, 131 State Street, Suite 620, Boston MA 02109. LC HG3729.U49. DD 332.742.

ANNUAL REPORT OF THE FEDERAL INSTITUTE OF INDUSTRIAL RESEARCH. Main/Corp Federal Institute of Industrial Research, Oshodi. English. ir. LC T177.N5.

ANNUAL REPORT OF THE POLICY COORDINATION GROUP FOR TECHNOLOGY DEVELOPMENT, CONGRESS OF THE UNITED STATES. (ANNUAL REPORT OF THE POLICY COORDINATION GROUP FOR TECHNOLOGY DEVELOPMENT). Main/Corp United States. Congress. Policy Coordination Group for Technology Development. 1st- 1978-. 0271-0250. US. English. an. Superintendent of Documents, US Government Printing Office, Washington DC 20402. LC T10.63.A1. DD 353.0085605.

ANNUAL REPORT OF THE PUBLIC TECHNOLOGY, NATIONAL AERONAUTICS AND SPACE ADMINISTRATION TECHNOLOGY APPLICATION PROGRAM. Main/Corp Public Technology, Inc. 0095-7674. US. English. an. Public Technology Inc, 1301 Pennsylvania Avenue NW, Washington DC 20004. LC TD159.A1. DD 338.7616.

ANNUAL REPORT ON HIGH-TECH MATERIALS. VFOAT Annual Report on High Tech Materials. 1984. . .1985-. 8755-9978. US. English. an. $285.00. Technical Insights Inc, PO Box 1304, Fort Lee NJ 07024.

ANNUAL REPORT ON RESEARCH & DEVELOPMENT - TECHNICAL INSIGHTS, INC. (ANNUAL REPORT ON RESEARCH & DEVELOPMENT). Main/Corp Technical Insights, Inc. VFOAT Annual Report on Research and Development. 1982/1983-. 0739-6325.

Technology (General)

US. English. an. $315.00. Technical Insights Inc, PO Box 1304, Fort Lee NJ 07024. LC T175. DD 607.205.

ANNUAL REPORT - SOUTH CAROLINA, STATE BOARD FOR TECHNICAL AND COMPREHENSIVE EDUCATION. Main/Corp South Carolina. State Board for Technical and Comprehensive Education. US. English. an. State Board for Technical and Comprehensive Education, 1429 Senate Street, Colombia SC 29201. LC T74.S6. DD 607.11757.

ANNUAL REPORT - SOUTHERN RESEARCH INSTITUTE. Main/Corp Southern Research Institute, Birmingham, Ala. 1st- 1945-. 0361-6452. US. English. an. Southern Research Institute, 2000 Ninth Avenue South, Birmingham AL 35205. LC T176. DD 607.

ANNUAL REPORT TO CONGRESS ON THE USE OF ALCOHOL IN MOTOR FUELS. Main/Corp United States. Office of the Assistant Secretary for Conservation and Solar Energy. Office of Alcohol Fuels. 1st- 1979-. 0271-5341. US. English. an. $5.25. National Technical Information Service, 5285 Port Royal Road, Springfield VA 22161. LC TP358. DD 629.2538.

ANNUAL REPORT TO THE CONGRESS BY THE OFFICE OF TECHNOLOGY ASSESSMENT. (ANNUAL REPORT TO THE CONGRESS FOR . . .). Main/Corp United States. Congress. Office of Technology Assessment. Began with 1974. 0095-2109. US. English. an. Superintendent of Documents, US Government Printing Office, Washington DC 20402. LC T174.5. DD 328.73076. NLM W2 A C83A.

ANNUAL REPORT TO THE CONGRESS BY THE OFFICE OF TECHNOLOGY ASSESSMENT. Main/Corp United States. Congress. Office of Technology Assessment. Series/Titl OTA. 1973-. 0095-2109. Periodical. US. English. an. Congress of the United States, Office of Technology Assessment, Washington DC 20510.

ANNUAL TECHNICAL CONFERENCE TRANSACTIONS - AMERICAN SOCIETY FOR QUALITY CONTROL CEASED. (ANNUAL TECHNICAL CONFERENCE TRANSACTIONS). Main/Corp American Society for Quality Control. 19th-34th. 0360-6929. US. English. an. $13.00. 161 West Wisconsin Avenue, Milwaukee WI 53203. Ind/Abst Eng. Index Annu., Eng. Index Energy Abstr. LC TP149. CODEN AQATAZ. Annual Convention Transactions.

ANNUAL TECHNICAL CONFERENCE TRANSACTIONS - AMERICAN SOCIETY FOR QUALITY CONTROL. Main/Corp American Society for Quality Control. US. English. an. $30.00. American Society for Quality Control, 230 West Wells Street/Suite 7000, Milwaukee WI 53203.

ANNUAL TECHNICAL REPORT. US. English. an. Bismarck Plant Materials Center, Bismarck ND 58505.

ANNUARIO SEAT. VOL. B, ELETTROTECNICA, TERMOTECNICA E ATTREZZATURE INDUSTRIALI. See Yearbooks, Almanacs, Directories.

ANUARIO - ABDIB. See Yearbooks, Almanacs, Directories.

ANUDANOM KI MANGEM (INDIA. DEPT. OF SCIENCE AND TECHNOLOGY). See Science (General).

APPLICATIONS OF CRYOGENIC TECHNOLOGY. V. 1- 1968-. 0093-8815. US. English. an. Scholium International, 265 Great Neck Road, Great Neck NY 11021. Tel (212)445-8700. Ind/Abst Chem. Abstr. LC TP480. DD 621.5905. CODEN ACGTAZ.

APPLIED MICROBIOLOGY AND BIOTECHNOLOGY. See Biology - Microbiology.

APPLIED RESEARCH SUMMARY OF AWARDS. Began with fiscal year 1979. 0275-939X. US. English. an. National Science Foundation, 1800 G Street NW, Washington DC 20550. LC T176. DD 338.973.

APPROPRIATE TECHNOLOGY. V. 1- 1974-. 0305-0920. Periodical. UK. English. qt $16.85. Intermediate Technology Publ Ltd, 120-126 Lavender Avenue, Mitcham Surrey CR4 3HP England. Ind/Abst Excerpta Med., Bibliogr. Agric., Energy Inf. Abstr., Environ. Abstr., Fluidex. LC T1. DD 609.1724.

APPROPRIATE TECHNOLOGY DOCUMENTATION BULLETIN. Began in 1973. Periodical. II. English. ir. $10.00. Siet Institute, Yousufguda, Hyderabad 500045 India. LC T27.I4. DD 338.470954.

APPROTECH : JOURNAL OF THE INTERNATIONAL ASSOCIATION FOR THE ADVANCEMENT OF APPROPRIATE TECHNOLOGY FOR DEVELOPING COUNTRIES. Began in Nov. 1978. Periodical. US. English. qt. $15.00. University of Michigan, 603 East Madison Street/IAATCD, Ann Arbor MI 48109. Tel (313)665-7166. Ed M C W Smith. bk rev. adv acc. Circ 350. (ctrl). Includes agriculture, health, education, economics, technical innovation, rural development and marketing.

ARBEITSSCHUTZ, ARBEITSHYGIENE. 16. Yearly (1/80)-. 0138-1555. Periodical. GE. German. qt. 13,-. Deutscher Buch Export-Import, Leninstrasse 16, DDR-701 Leipzig East Germany. Tel 4656446. NLM W1 AR128P. bk rev adv acc. Circ 8,000. (ctrl). Occupational safety research, accidents, diseases, noise and vibration control, analysis, statistics, management and planning, training and education, safety techniques, safetylaw, publications, etc. Informationen Arbeitsschutz, Arbeitshygiene, 0138-1458.

ARIES' BIOTECHNOLOGY CHEMONOMIES REPORT. See Economics.

ARSBERATTELSE - NORDFORSK. Main/Corp Scandinavian Council for Applied Research. Danish, Norwegian or Swedish. ir. Nordforsk, Huvudsekretariatet, Box 5103 S-102 43 5, Stockholm Sweden. LC T177.S33.

ARSBERETNING - DENMARK. KEMIKALIEKONTROLLEN. Main/Corp Denmark. Kemikaliekontrollen. VFOAT Bekmpelsesmidler Gifte Og Sundhedsfarlige Stoffer. Danish. ir. Skovbrynet 12, 2800 Lyngby Denmark. LC TP201.

ARSBERETNING - HERMETIKKINDUSTRIENS LABORATORIUM. Main/Corp Hermetikkindustriens Laboratorium. Norwegian. ir. Postboks 68-4011, Stavanger Norway. LC TP370.8.

ARTS & METIERS. See Engineering.

ASIA 2000. VFOAT Asia Two Thousand. Periodical. HK. English. bm. $18.00 (Introductory Rate), $24.00 (Regular Rate). Asia 2000, 10th Floor, 146 Prince Edward Road W, Kowloon Hong Kong. LC T27.A1. DD 609.5.

ASK. See Business.

ASSESSMENT ACTIVITIES. Main/Corp United States. Congress. Office of Technology Assessment. US. English. Congress of the United States, Office of Technology Assessment, Washington DC 20510.

ATAC, ASOCIACION DE TECNICOS AZUCAREROS DE CUBA. (ATAC). Main/Corp Asociacion de Tecnicos Azucareros de Cuba. VAT Associacion de Tecnicos Azucareros de Cuba. 0366-242X. CU. Spanish. bm. Empresa Ediciones Cubanas, Obispo 461 Apartado 605, Ciudad de la Habana Cuba. LC TP375.

ATCP. See Paper & Pulp Industry.

ATINDEX. See Indexes/Abstracts.

ATIVIDADES DESENVOLVIDAS. Main/Corp Instituto de Pesquisas Technologicas. Portuguese. ir. Cidade Universitaria Armando de Salles Oliveria, Caixa Postal 7141, Sao Paulo Brazil. LC T173.S255. DD 607.11816.

ATV-H. Main/Corp Akademiet for de Tekniske Videnskaber, Copenhagen. VAT Akademiet for de Tekniske Videnskaber-Handbog. Danish. ir. 40.00. Akademiet for de Tekniske Videnskaber, Luntoftevej 266 2800, Lyngby Denmark. LC T173.C75.

ATZ. AUTOMOBILTECHNISCHE ZEITSCHRIFT. See Transportation - Automobiles.

AUSLANDISCHE MESSEN, AUSSTELLUNGEN, KONGRESSE. AU. German. ir. Wirtschaftforderungsinstitut, Hoher Markt 3, 1011 Wien Austria. LC T391.

AVTOMATIZIROVANNYE SISTEMY UPRAVLENIIA. V. 1- 1974-. UR. Russian. 1.10 Single Issue. Izd-vo Leningradskogo Universiteta, 199164 Universitetskaia Nab 7/9, Leningrad USSR. LC T58.6.

BANGLADESH SCIENCE AND TECHNOLOGY INDEX. See Indexes/Abstracts.

BATTELLE TODAY. No. 1- Aug. 1976-. 0145-8477. Periodical. US. English. qt. Battelle Office of Corporate Communications, 505 King Avenue, Columbus OH 43201. Ind/Abst Electron. Commun. Abstr. J., ISMEC Bull., Pollut. Abstr. Indexes, Saf. Sci. Abstr. J., Predicasts, Energy Inf. Abstr., Environ. Abstr., Int. Packag. Abstr., Met. Abstr., World Alum. Abstr., Pap. Board Abstr., Print. Abstr. Research Outlook (Columbus), 0092-1122.

BC R+D. BRITISH COLUMBIA RESEARCH AND DEVELOPMENT. (BC R+D). VFOAT British Columbia Research and Development. Vol. 1, No. 1 (Oct. 1982)-. 0825-7469. Periodical. CN. English. bm. DD 607.2711.

BEDRIJF EN TECHNIEK. See Manufacturing.

BERETNING. Main/Corp Akademiet for de Tekniske Videnskaber (Denmark). Began in 1939. Danish. ir. LC T4.

BERICHT - FORSCHUNGSFORDERUNGSFONDS FUR DIE GEWERBLICHE WIRTSCHAFT. Main/Corp Forschungsforderungsfonds fur die Gewerbliche Wirtschaft. GW. German. an. Forschungsforderungsfonds der Gewerbliche Wirtschaft, Karntner Strasse 21-23, 1015 Wien Austria. LC T177.A9. DD 330.06043613.

BERICHT - HOHERE TECHNISCHE BUNDES-LEHR- UND VERSUCHSANSTALT WIEN I. Main/Corp Hohere Technische Bundes-Lehr-und Versuchsanstalt Wien I. AU. German. ir. 1010 Wien L Schellingrasse 13, Wien Austria. LC T173.V65.

BERKALA ITB. Main/Corp Institut Teknologi Bandung. Periodical. IO. Indonesian. ir. Institut Teknologi Bandung, Jl Tamansari 64, Bandung Indonesia. LC T173.B127. ITB.

BETON-TECHNIK. 1. Yearly issue 1 (Feb. 1980)-. 0138-2101. Periodical. GE. German (summaries in English, German and Russian). bm. 28.50. Deutscher Buch Export-Import, Leninstrasse 16, DDR-701 Leipzig East Germany. Tel 2041316. bk rev. (ctrl). Informs about various themes as technology, constructions, directions, preproduction, monolithbeton and transport of industrial branch of beton, also practical experiences and scientific results. Baustoffindustrie. Ausgabe B: Bauelemente.

BIBLIOGRAPHIC GUIDE TO TECHNOLOGY. See Bibliographies.

BIOCYCLE. See Sanitation, Environmental Technology.

BIOPROCESSING TECHNOLOGY. Vol. 7, No. 1 (Jan. 1985)-. 0885-5625. Periodical. US. English. mo. $244.00 Domestic, $280.00 Foreign. Technical Insights Inc, PO Box 1304, Fort Lee NJ 07024. Ind/Abst Abstr. Bull. Inst. Paper Chem. DD 660. Biomass Digest, 0163-6766.

B.I.O.S. MISCELLANEOUS REPORT. Main/Corp Great Britain. British Intelligence Objectives Sub-Committee. No. 1- 1945-. UK. English. ir. Her Majestys Stationery Office, PO Box 286, London SW8 5DT England. LC T7. DD 608.2.

BIOSENSORS. See Biology - Biochemistry.

BIOTECHNIQUES. See Biology.

BIOTECHNOLOGY ADVANCES. Vol. 1, No. 1 (1983)-. 0734-9750. Periodical. UK. English. sa. $110.00. Pergamon Press, 395 Sawmill River Road, Elmsford NY 10523. Ind/Abst Chem. Abstr. LC TP248.2. DD 660.605. NLM W1. CODEN BIADDD. Issued also in Microform.

BIOTECHNOLOGY AND BIOENGINEERING SYMPOSIUM. See Engineering.

BIOTECHNOLOGY MONTHLY UPDATE. VFOAT Biotechnology. 0738-4076. US. English. mo. $150.00 Domestic, $175.00 Foreign. G V Olsen Associates, 170 Broadway, New York NY 10038.

BIO/TECHNOLOGY - NATURE PUBLISHING COMPANY. See Biology.

Technology (General)

BIULETYN - POLAND. URZAD PATENTOWY. Main/Corp Poland. Urzad Patentowy. V. 1- Feb. 26, 1973-. PL. Polish. bw. ARS Polona, Krakowskie Przedmiescie 7, 00-068 Warsaw Poland. LC T201.

BLATTER FUR TECHNIKGESCHICHTE. Main/Corp Vienna. Forschungsinstitut fur Technikgeschichte. 0067-9127. US. German. ir. Springer Verlag-New York Inc, 175 5th Avenue, New York NY 10010. Tel (212)460-1584. LC T15.A1.

BOLETIM - INSTITUTO DO AZEITE E PRODUTOS OLEAGINOSOS. Main/Corp Instituto do Azeite e Produtos Oleaginoso. Yearly V. 1- Jan./June 1973-. 0304-5196. Portuguese. ir. Instituto do Azeite e Produtos Oleaginosos, Av de Sidonio Pais 10 10., 1, Lisboa Portugal. Ind/Abst Bibliogr. Agric. LC TP670.

BOLETIM TECNICO CEPED. (BOLETIM TECNICO). Began in 1974. 0100-1949. Periodical. Portuguese. sa. Centro de Pesquisas e Desenvolvimento Ceped Gerencia de Desenvolvimento, Caixa Postal 09, Camacari Bahia Brazil. Ind/Abst Chem. Abstr. LC T4. CODEN BTCPDY.

BOLETIN INFORMATIVO - SISTEMA NACIONAL DE INFORMACION CIENTIFICA Y TECNOLOGICA. See Science (General).

BOLETIN - OFICINA REGIONAL DE CIENCIA Y TECNOLOGIA DE LA UNESCO PARA AMERICA LATINA Y EL CARIBE. See Science (General).

BORSODI MUSZAKI ES IPARGAZDASAGI ELET CEASED. Periodical. HU. Hungarian. qt. 3530 Miskolc Szemere U 4, Miskolc Hungary. LC T4.

BOSTID DEVELOPMENTS. See Science (General).

BRITISH JOURNAL OF NON-DESTRUCTIVE TESTING. See Engineering.

BRITISH TECHNOLOGY INDEX. See Indexes/Abstracts.

BROADCAST TECHNOLOGY. See Communication - Broadcasting.

BRYGMESTEREN. See Food & Drink.

BUILDING INDUSTRY TECHNOLOGY. See Building and Construction.

BUILDING TECHNOLOGY PROJECT SUMMARIES. Main/Corp National Engineering Laboratory (U.S.). Center for Building Technology. 1977-78-. 0149-1679. US. English. US Department of Commerce, National Bureau of Standards, National Engineering Laboratory, Center for Building Technology, Washington DC 20402. CODEN XNBSAV. *Building Technology Project Summaries, 1049-1679.*

BULETIN INSTITUSI JURUTERA MALAYSIA. VFOAT Bulletin I.E.M. 0126-9909. Periodical. English (Malay). mo. $10.00. Editor, PO Box 223, P J Petaling Jaya Selangor Malaysia. LC TA1. DD 620.005. *Bulletin (Institusi Jurutera Malaysia).*

BULETINUL STIINTIFIC SI TEHNIC AL INSTITUTULUI POLITEHNIC TRAIAN VUIA TIMISOARA. SERIA CHIMIE. VFOAT Buletinul Stiintific Si Techic Al Institutului Politehnic Traian Vuia Timisoara. Periodical. RM. English (French, German, and Romanian). ir. Ilexim Service Export-Import Presa, Press Department, Str 30 Decembrie Nr 3-5 POB 136-137, Bucharest Romania.

BULETINUL STIINTIFIC SI TEHNIC AL INSTITUTULUI POLITEHNIC TRAIAN VUIA TIMISOARA. SERIA CONSTRUCTII. VFOAT Buletinul Stiintific Si Tehnic Al Institutului Politehnic Traian Vuia Timisoara. Periodical. RM. English (French, German, and Romanian). ir. Ilexim Services, Export-Import Presa/Press Department Str 30 Decembrie Nr 3-5/POB 136-137, Bucharest Romania.

BULETINUL STIINTIFIC SI TEHNIC AL INSTITUTULUI POLITEHNIC TRAIAN VUIA TIMISOARA. SERIA ELECROTEHNICA. VFOAT Buletinul Stiintific Si Tehnic Al Institutului Politehnic Traian Vuia Timisoara. Periodical. RM. English (French and German). ir. Ilexim Services, Export-Import Presa/Press Department, Str 30 Decembrie Nr 3-5 POB 136-137, Bucharest Romania.

BULETINUL STIINTIFIC SI TEHNIC AL INSTITUTULUI POLITEHNIC TRAIAN VUIA TIMISOARA. SERIA MECANICA. VFOAT Buletinul Stiintific Si Tehnic Al Institutului Politehnic Traian Vuia Timisoara. Periodical. RM. English (French, German, and Romanian). ir. Ilexim Services, Export-Import Presa/Press Department, Str 30 Decembrie Nr 3-5 POB 136-137, Bucharest Romania.

BULETINUL UNIVERSITATII DIN GALATI. FASCICULA VI, TEHNOLOGIA SI CHIMIA PRODUSELOR ALIMENTARE. See Food & Drink.

BULLETIN - CANADIAN SOCIETY OF LABORATORY TECHNOLOGISTS. Main/Corp Canadian Society of Laboratory Technologists. V. 4, No. 1- Jan./Feb. 1976-. 0381-5838. Periodical. CN. English (includes some text in French). bm. Canadian Society of Laboratory Technologists, PO Box 830, Hamilton Ontario L8N 3N8 Canada. Tel (416)528-8642. Ed Kurt Davis. DD 610.695305. adv acc. Circ 21,100. (ctrl). Professional organization newsletter - applicable to Canadian Society of Laboratory Technologist members only. *News Bulletin,* 0381-5846.

BULLETIN OF SCIENCE, TECHNOLOGY & SOCIETY. See Science (General).

BULLETIN OF THE UNESCO REGIONAL OFFICE OF SCIENCE AND TECHNOLOGY FOR AFRICA. See Science (General).

BUSINESS, INDUSTRY, TECHNOLOGY SERVICES. See Business.

CADERNOS DE TECNOLOGIA E CIENCIA. V. 1, No. 1, (June 1978)-. 0101-2991. Periodical. BL. Portuguese. mo. Editora Tama Ltda, Rua Voluntarios da Patria 34 Casa 1 Caixa Postal 44.140, CEP 22.180 Rio de Janeiro RJ Brazil. Ind/Abst Foreign Lang. Index. LC T4. DD 605.

CAHIERS DU CENTRE SCIENTIFIQUE ET TECHNIQUE DU BATIMENT. See Science (General).

CALENDAR OF EVENTS. TRADE FAIRS AND EXHIBITIONS. Main/Corp Deutsche Lufthansa (1953-). VFOAT Trade Fairs and Exhibitions. English. ir. Deutsche Lufthansa AG, Special Business-Travel 75 Airport, 6000 Frankfurt-Main West Germany. LC T394. DD 380.14567074.

CALTECH. Main/Corp California Institute of Technology. VAT California Institute of Technology. 0160-502X. Periodical. US. English. bm. Caltech, 1201 East California Boulevard, Pasadena CA 91109. CODEN CALTD3.

CANADIAN INSTITUTE OF FOOD SCIENCE AND TECHNOLOGY JOURNAL. See Food & Drink.

CARIRI. Main/Corp Caribbean Industrial Research Institute. English. ir. Carribean Industrial Research Institute, University Post Office, St Augustine Trinidad. LC T177.T7. DD 607.272983.

CATALOG OF PROFESSIONAL DEVELOPMENT SEMINARS. Main/Corp Control Data Corporation. Institute for Advanced Technology. US. English. Institute of Advanced Technology, 6003 Executive Boulevard, Rockville MD 20852. Tel (800)638-6590. Circ 500,000. (ctrl). A collection of technical and management seminars designed for the professional community. All seminars are real world skill oriented. Seminars are regularly scheduled in major cities.

CATJ. See Communication - Telecommunications.

CBI EDUCATION & TRAINING BULLETIN. Main/Corp Confederation of British Industry. Periodical. UK. English. qt. $21.45. Confederation of British Industry, 103 New Oxford Street, London WC1A 1DU England. LC T107. DD 331.2592.

CELLULOSE CHEMISTRY AND TECHNOLOGY. See Chemistry.

CERAMURGIA. 0045-6152. Periodical. IT. Italian (summaries in English, French and German). bm. $70.00. Ceramurgia, Casella Postalla, 48018 Faenza Italy. Ind/Abst Eng. Index Annu., Eng. Index Mon., Eng. Index Bioeng. Abstr., Eng. Index Energy Abstr., GeoRef, Chem. Abstr., Bibliogr. Index Geol., Eng. Index. LC TP785. CODEN CRGIAR.

CEREAL FOODS WORLD. See Food & Drink.

CESKOSLOVENSKA INFORMATIKA. 0322-8509. Periodical. CS. Czech (some summaries in English, French, German, and Russian). mo. Artia, PO Box 790, Ve Smeckach 30, Praha 1 Czechoslovakia. Ind/Abst Libr. Inf. Sci. Abstr., Comput. Control Abstr., Electr. Electron. Abstr., Sci. Abstr. Sect. A. Phys. Abstr. LC T10.6.

CESKOSLOVENSKE VYZKUMNE ZPRAVY A DISERTACE. See Science (General).

CHALMERS TEKNISKA HOGSKOLAS HANDLINGAR. VFOAT Handlingar, Transactions of the Chalmers University of Technology. No. 1-. 0069-2417. Monographic Series. SW. Swedish (German and English). ir. Chalmers Tekniska Hogskola, 404 20 Goteberg S, Gothenburg Sweden. Ind/Abst Int. Aerosp. Abstr. LC T7. DD 608.2.

CHEMICAL INDUSTRY. V. 1- March 1950-. Periodical. JA. English. mo. 90.00. Maruzen Company Ltd, PO Box 5050, 100-31 Tokyo Japan. Tel 03-405-9767. adv acc. Circ 32,000. (ctrl). Mainly about ultramodern techniques of petroleum, electronics, chemical technology. It reports wide divisions of special articles, from iron and steel to atomic energy.

CHEMICAL TECHNOLOGY REVIEW. No. 1-. 0198-6880. Monographic Series. US. English. ir. Noyes Data Corporation, Mill Road at Grand Avenue, Park Ridge NJ 07656. Tel (201)391-8484. Ind/Abst Eng. Index Mon., Eng. Index Bioeng. Abstr., Eng. Index Energy Abstr., GeoRef, Eng. Index Annu., Bibliogr. Index Geol. LC UNC. CODEN CTYRBN. *Chemical Process Review.*

CHEMIEINGENIEURTECHNIK. (CHEMIE-INGENIEUR-TECHNIK). VFOAT CIT. V. 21- 1949-. 0009-286X. Periodical. German. mo. VCH Publishers Inc, 303 12th Avenue NW, Deerfield Beach FL 33442. Tel (305)428-5566. Ind/Abst CIS Abstr., Coal Abstr., Comput. Control Abstr., Electr. Electron. Abstr., Funk Scott Index Corp. Ind., Phys. Abstr., Eng. Index Energy Abstr., Energy Inf. Abstr., Fluidex, Excerpta Med., Environ. Abstr., Int. Aerosp. Abstr., Sci. Abstr. Sect. A. Phys. Abstr., Met. Abstr., World Alum. Abstr., Bibliogr. Agric., Chem. Abstr., Nuci. Sci. Abstr., Eng. Index Annu., Phys. Abstr., Eng. Index Mon., Energy Res. Abstr., Predicasts, Sel. Water Resour. Abstr., Sci. Cit. Index, Abr. Ed., Pet. Abstr. CODEN CITEAH. *Angewandte Chemie. B, Technisch-Wirtschaftlicher Teil,* 0170-9054; *Beihefte Verfahenstechnik.*

CHEMTECH. (CHEM TECH). V. 1- Jan. 1971-. 0009-2703. Periodical. US. English. mo. $50.00 Domestic, $54.00 Canada. Controller of American Chemical Society, 1155 16th Street NE, Washington DC 20036. Ind/Abst Appl. Sci. Technol. Index, Abstr. Bull. Inst. Paper Chem., Art Archaeol. Tech. Abstr., Chem. Abstr., Coal Abstr., Energy Inf. Abstr., Energy Res. Abstr., Eng. Index Annu., Eng. Index Mon., Eng. Index Bioeng. Abstr., Eng. Index Energy Abstr., Environ. Abstr., Excerpta Med., Fluidex, Int. Aerosp. Abstr., Predicasts, World Surf. Coat. Abstr., Gen. Sci. Index. LC TP1. DD 660.05. CODEN CHTEDD. Available on microfiche from Special Issues Sales, American Chemical Society, Washington, D.C. *Industrial & Engineering Chemistry,* 0019-7866.

CHENGDU KEJI DAXUE XUEBAO. (CHENG-TU KO CHI TA HSUEH HSUEH PAO). VFOAT Journal of Chengdu University of Science and Technology. Began in 1979?. 0253-2263. Periodical. Chinese (English). qt. 0.80. Chung-Kuo Kuo Chi Shu Tien, PO Box 2820, Pei-Ching China Mainland. Ind/Abst Math. Rev., Chem. Abstr. LC Q4. DD 505. CODEN CKDXDB.

CHET, CHEMIE EXPERIMENT + TECHNOLOGIE. See Chemistry.

CHIHO KOKYO DANTAI SHIKEN KENKYU KIKAN SORAN. 1976-. Japanese. ir. Tokyo-to Doboku Gijutsu Kenkyujo, 1-18 Konan 1-chome Minato-ku, Tokyo Japan. LC T177.J3.

CHINESE SCIENCE AND TECHNOLOGY. See Science (General).

CHUGOKU KOGYO GIJUTSU. Edition- (Oct. 1973)-. JA. Japanese. ir. Chugoku Kogyo Gijutsu Kyokai, Kotsubo Danchi Hiromachi, Kure 737-01 Japan. LC T178.C48.

Technology (General)

CHUGOKU KOGYO GIJUTSU SHIKENJO NEMPO. Japanese. ir. 15000 Hiromachi, 737-01 Kure Japan. LC T178.C48.

CHUNG-KUO KO CHI SHIH LIAO. See Science (General).

CHUNGSO KIOP CHONGBO MONGNOK. Series/Titl Chongbo Charyo. KO. Korean. ir. Chungso Kiop Chinhung Kongdan, 1-1040 Youido-Dong Yongdungpo-ku, Seoul Korea. LC Z7913, T45.

CHUSHO KIGYO GIJUTSU JITTAI CHOSA. VFOAT Gijutsu Kaihatsu Kadai Hokokusho. Began with report for 1972. Japanese. ir. c/o Sankaido Building, 9-13 Akasaka 1, Minato-ku (107), Tokyo Japan. LC T4.

CIECIA Y DESARROLLO. See Science (General).

CIENCIA DA INFORMACAO. See Library and Information Science.

CIENCIA Y TECNOLOGIA DE VENEZUELA. See Science (General).

CIRP ANNALS . . . MANUFACTURING TECHNOLOGY. See Engineering.

CLINICAL INSTRUMENT SYSTEMS. See Medicine - Pathology.

COAL PROCESSING TECHNOLOGY. Series/Titl CEP Technical Manual. V.1- 1974-. 0147-1708. US. English. ir. American Institute of Chemical Engineers, 345 East 47th Street, New York NY 10017. Ind/Abst Eng. Index Annu., Eng. Index Mon., Eng. Index Bioeng. Abstr., Eng. Index Energy Abstr., Coal Abstr., Chem. Abstr. CODEN CPRTD2.

COAL TECHNOLOGY REPORT. VFOAT Coal. V. 1, No. 1 (July 11, 1983)-. 0738-9876. Periodical. US. English. bw. $180.00. Coal Technology Report, 1401 Wilson Boulevard/Suite 1000, Arlington VA 22209. *ERD, Energy Research Digest, 0195-4474.*

COLOMBIA, CIENCIA Y TECNOLOGIA. See Science (General).

COLORADO HIGH TECHNOLOGY DIRECTORY. See Yearbooks, Almanacs, Directories.

COMMENT CA MARCHE. V. 1-. Periodical. CN. French. wk. $1. Per No. Comment Ca Marche, CP 305 Succursale Bourassa, Montreal Quebec H2C 3G2 Canada. DD 603.

COMMUNICATION TECHNOLOGY IMPACT : CTI. Vol. 1, No. 1 (April 1979)-. 0142-5854. Periodical. UK. English. mo. $190.00. Elsevier Science Publishers, PO Box 211, 1000 AE Amsterdam Netherlands. Tel (212)867-9040. Ed I H Marshall. Ind/Abst Predicasts, Libr. Inf. Sci. Abstr. Print. Abstr., Electron. Pub. Abstr. The journal publishes papers which contribute to knowledge in the use of composite materials in engineering structures.

COMMUNICATOR OF SCIENTIFIC AND TECHNICAL INFORMATION. (THE COMMUNICATOR OF SCIENTIFIC AND TECHNICAL INFORMATION). Began publication with No. 29 in 1976?. 0308-6925. Periodical. UK. English. qt. Institute Scientific Technical Communicators, 17 Bluebridge Avenue, Brookman's Park, Hatfield Herts AL9 7RY England. Tel (0707) 55392. Ed Penny Morgan. Ind/Abst Libr. Inf. Sci. Abstr. adv acc. Circ 1,700. Caters to interests of technical authors, editors and illustrators plus teachers of communication skills. *Communicator (Institute of Scientific and Technical Communicators).*

COMPILATION OF ABSTRACTS OF THESES SUBMITTED BY CANDIDATES FOR DEGREES. See Indexes/Abstracts.

COMPOSITE INDEX FOR CRC HANDBOOKS. See Indexes/Abstracts.

COMPTES RENDUS DE RECHERCHES. Main/Corp Institut pour l'Encouragement de la Recherche Scientifique dans l'Industrie et l'Agriculture. VFOAT Verslagen Over Navorsingen. No. 1- Nov. 1949-. Periodical. Dutch (English, French or German). ir. LC T2.

COMPUT-A-CAL. See Computers and Computer Science.

CONDIZIONAMENTO DELL'ARIA, RISCALDAMENTO, REFRIGERAZIONE. See Heating, Plumbing, & Refrigeration.

CONFERENCE BRIEFS. Main/Corp United States. National Bureau of Standards. Periodical. US. English. qt. Department of Commerce, National Bureau of Standards, Office of Information Activities, Washington DC 20234.

CONFERENCES & EXHIBITIONS INTERNATIONAL. VFOAT Conferences and Exhibitions International. 0260-8316. Periodical. UK. English. mo. Conferences & Exhibitions Publications Ltd, Wardrobe Chambers, 146A Queen Victoria Street, London EC4V 4DQ England. LC T391. DD 382.1. *Conferences + Exhibitions, 0306-9397.*

CONNECTION TECHNOLOGY. See Engineering - Electricity, Electrical Engineering, Electronics.

COPY TECHNOLOGY REVIEW. VFOAT CTR. Periodical. US. English. mo. Copy Technology Consulting Company, 3871 Narcissus Way, Denver CO 80237.

CORPORATE TECHNOLOGY DIRECTORY. See Yearbooks, Almanacs, Directories.

CPST: COMPUTER PROGRAMS IN SCIENCE AND TECHNOLOGY. See Science (General).

CSIR ANNUAL REPORT. See Science (General).

CTI : CURRENT TECHNOLOGY INDEX. See Indexes/Abstracts.

CURRENT AWARENESS IN BIOTECHNOLOGY. See Biology.

CURRENT AWARENESS IN PARTICLE TECHNOLOGY : (CONTINUATION OF PARTICULATE INFORMATION). See Engineering - Chemical Engineering.

CURRENT CONTENTS. ENGINEERING & TECHNOLOGY. See Engineering.

CURRENT RESEARCH IN THE NETHERLANDS : TECHNOLOGICAL SCIENCES. 1979/1980-. NE. English. ir. Netherlands Organization for the Advancement of Pure Research, Juliana Van Stolberglaan 148, Rglaan 148 PO Box 2509, The Hague The Netherlands.

CURRENT TECHNOLOGY INDEX (ANNUAL). See Indexes/Abstracts.

CURRENT TECHNOLOGY INDEX : CTI. See Indexes/Abstracts.

CYBERNETICA. See Computers and Computer Science.

CZECHOSLOVAK HEAVY INDUSTRY. 1955-. 0011-4618. Periodical. English (French, German, Russian, and Spanish). mo. $33.00. Artia, PO Box 790 VE Smeckach 30, Praha 1 Czechoslovakia. Ind/Abst Fluidex, Comput. Control Abstr., Electr. Electron. Abstr., Sci. Abstr. Sect. A. Phys. Abstr., Met. Abstr., World Alum. Abstr., Phys. Abstr. LC T4. DD 609.437. CODEN CZHIAK.

DALIL AL-MAARID WA-AL-ASWAQ AL-DAWLIYAH. Arabic. ir. Al-Ghurfah Al-Tijariyah Al-Sinaiyah Al-Riyad Al-Mamlakah Al-Arabiyah Al-Saudiyah, Shari Abd Al-Aziz IBN Abd Allah IBN Turki, Al-Riyad Saudi Arabia. LC T391.

DATA ON RESEARCH UTILISATION. English. ir. LC T177.I4. DD 607.254.

DEJINY VED A TECHNIKY. See Science (General).

DENKI KAGAKU. V. 38- Jan. 1970-. Periodical. JA. Japanese (English). mo. 100.00. Maruzen Company Ltd, PO Box 5050, 100-31 Tokyo Japan. Tel 03-214-6001. Ind/Abst Comput. Control Abstr., Electr. Electron. Abstr., Sci. Abstr. Sect. A. Phys. Abstr., Phys. Abstr., Sci. Cit. Index, Abr. Ed. CODEN DNKKA2. Circ 4,000. (ctrl) A journal of academic studies about electrical chemistry and industrial, physical chemistry. *Journal of the Electrochemical Society of Japan, Denki Kagaku Oyobi Kogyo Butsuri Kagaku; DK Newsletter.*

DERWENT BIOTECHNOLOGY ABSTRACTS. See Indexes/Abstracts.

DESIGN NEWS. V. 1- Nov. 1946-. 0011-9407. Periodical. US. English. sm. Cahners Publishing Company, 221 Columbus Avenue, Boston MA 02116. Tel (303)388-4511. Ind/Abst Eng. Index Annu., Eng. Index Mon., Eng. Index Bioeng. Abstr., Eng. Index Energy Abstr., Pop. Mag. Rev., Met. Abstr., World Alum. Abstr., Appl. Sci. Technol. Index, Predicasts, Energy Inf. Abstr., Environ. Abstr., Mag. Index, Funk Scott Index Corp. Ind. CODEN DIGNAO.

DEUTSCHER FACHHOCHSCHULFUHRER. 17 Edition. GW. German. ir. VDE Verlag GMBH, Bismarckstrasse 33, D1000 Berlin 12 West Germany. Tel 0 30/ 3 341 30 41. LC T123. *Deutscher Ingenieurschulfuhrer.*

DIRECTIONS. See Computers and Computer Science.

DIRECTORY - AMERICAN COUNCIL OF INDEPENDENT LABORATORIES. See Yearbooks, Almanacs, Directories.

DIRECTORY OF AMERICAN RESEARCH AND TECHNOLOGY. See Yearbooks, Almanacs, Directories.

DIRECTORY OF EXPERT WITNESSES IN TECHNOLOGY. See Yearbooks, Almanacs, Directories.

DIRECTORY OF FEDERAL TECHNOLOGY RESOURCES. See Yearbooks, Almanacs, Directories.

DIRECTORY OF PUBLIC HIGH TECHNOLOGY CORPORATIONS. See Yearbooks, Almanacs, Directories.

DIRECTORY OF RESEARCH INSTITUTES & INDUSTRIAL LABORATORIES IN ISRAEL. See Yearbooks, Almanacs, Directories.

DIRECTORY OF SCIENTIFIC & TECHNICAL RESEARCH CENTRES IN MALAYSIA. See Yearbooks, Almanacs, Directories.

DIRECTORY OF SCIENTIFIC RESOURCES IN GEORGIA. See Yearbooks, Almanacs, Directories.

DISCUSSION PAPER. See Science (General).

DISPLAYS. See Engineering - Electricity, Electrical Engineering, Electronics.

DNIAS ANNUAL REPORT + 1. Main/Corp Kankyo to Kogyo O Musubu Kai. VAT DNIAS Annual Report Plus One. 0303-5514. JA. Japanese. ir. Kankyo to Kogyo O Musubu Kai, 7-22-1 Roppongi Minato-ku, Tokyo Japan. LC T4.

DOCUMENTATION BULLETIN (VAIKUNTHBHAI MEHTA SMARAK TRUST, DOCUMENTATION CENTRE-CUM-REFERENCE LIBRARY). (DOCUMENTATION BULLETIN). II. English. qt. NKM International House, 5th Floor, 178 Backbay Reclamation Madam Cama Road, Bombay 400 020 India.

DOE/ET. See Energy.

DOKUMENTATION TRIBOLOGIE. See Engineering - Mechanical Engineering & Machinery.

DONGBEI GONGXUEYUAN XUEBAO. (TUNG-PEI KUNG HSUEH YUAN HSUEH PAO). 0253-4258. Periodical. CH. Chinese (abstracts in English). qt. Chung-Kuo Kuo Chi Shu Tien, PO Box 2820, Pei-Ching China. Ind/Abst Math. Rev., Chem. Abstr. LC T4. DD 605. CODEN THYPDK.

DOSTIZHENIIA I PERSPEKTIVY. Began in 1978. 0204-2495. Periodical. UR. Russian (summaries in English). 1.85. Mezhdunarodnyi Tsentr Nauchnoi I Tekhicheskoi Informatsii, Ul Kuusinena 21B, 125252 Moskva USSR. LC T4.

DREXEL TECHNICAL JOURNAL. V. 1- 1938-. 0012-6179. Periodical. US. English. qt. $2.00. Circulation Manager, The Drexel Technical Journal, Drexel University, 32nd and Chestnut Streets, Philadelphia PA 19104. Ind/Abst Chem. Abstr. LC T1. CODEN DTJODK.

DRYING TECHNOLOGY. Vol. 1, No. 1-. 0737-3937. Periodical. US. English. $95.00 US, $108.80 Canada. M Dekker Journals, Box 11305 Church Street Station, New York NY 10249. Ind/Abst Abstr. Bull. Inst. Paper Chem. LC TP363. DD 660.28426. CODEN DRTEDQ.

DSIR BULLETIN. See Science (General).

Technology (General)

E&TR, ENERGY AND TECHNOLOGY REVIEW. See Energy.

EAST-WEST TECHNOLOGY DIGEST. (EAST/WEST TECHNOLOGY DIGEST). 0145-1421. Periodical. US. English. mo. $44.88. Welt Publishing Company, 1413 K Street NW, Washington DC 20005. Tel (202)371-0555. Ed Brian Benninghoff. **Ind/Abst** Chem. Abstr. **CODEN** EWTDDZ. Newsletter reporting recently developed products and processes from USSR and East Bloc countries that are available for licensing and purchase in the West. *Soviet Technology Digest.*

EDUCATIONAL GUIDE : TECHNICAL INSTITUTES, COMMUNITY COLLEGES. See Education (General).

EDUCATIONAL MEDIA AND TECHNOLOGY YEARBOOK. See Yearbooks, Almanacs, Directories.

EDUCATIONAL RESOURCES & TECHNIQUES. See Education (General).

EFOC, FIBER OPTICS & COMMUNICATIONS PROCEEDINGS. See Communication - Telecommunications.

ELECTROCHEMICAL INDUSTRIES AND TECHNOLOGY. See Chemistry.

ELECTRONIC SERVICING & TECHNOLOGY. VFOAT Electronic Servicing and Technology. Vol. 1, No. 1 (Nov. 1981)-. 0278-9922. Periodical. US. English. mo. $18.00. Intertec Publishing Corporation PO Box 12901, Overland Park KS 66212. Ed Nils Conrad Persson. **LC** TK7870. **DD** 621.3810288. bk rev. adv acc. **Circ** 55,799. (ctrl). This editorial format is tailored for the professional whose livelihood is centered in the commercial electronics servicing industry. *Electronic Servicing, 0013-497X; Electronic Technician/Dealer.*

ELECTRONICS TODAY INTERNATIONAL. See Engineering - Electricity, Electrical Engineering, Electronics.

ELEMENTS OF TECHNOLOGY CEASED. VFOAT Elements of Technology for Educators. Began with Vol. 1, Fall 1969. Ceased with Vol. 7, No. 4. 0046-1806. Periodical. CN. English. qt. $4.00. Elements of Technology, 542 Mount Pleasant Road/ Suite 103, Toronto Ontario M4S 2M7 Canada.

ELETTRONICA E TELECOMUNICAZIONI. See Communication - Telecommunications.

EMERGENCY RESPONCE GUIDEBOOK. (EMERGENCY RESPONSE GUIDEBOOK : GUIDEBOOK FOR HAZARDOUS MATERIALS INCIDENTS). 1984-. 0747-816X. US. English. an. US Department of Transportation, Materials Transportation Bureau Atten: DMT-11, Washington DC 20590. **LC** T55.3.H3. **DD** 604.70289. *Hazardous Materials . . . Emergency Response Guidebook.*

EMERGING TECHNOLOGY. Periodical. US. English. Donaldson Lufkin & Jenrette Securities Corporation, 140 Bradway, New York NY 10005.

ENERGIE ALTERNATIVE HTE. See Energy.

ENERGY DIGEST. See Energy.

ENERGY MANAGEMENT TECHNOLOGY. See Energy.

ENERGY MANAGER. See Energy.

ENERGY TECHNOLOGY REVIEW. See Energy.

ENGENHARIA NA INDUSTRIA. 0100-0608. Portuguese. ir. $100. Engetec, Caixa Postal 9336, Sao Paulo CEP 01000 Brazil. **Ind/Abst** Chem. Abstr. **LC** T4. **CODEN** ENINDF. *Engenharia.*

ENGINEERING AND TECHNOLOGY GRADUATES. See Engineering.

ENGINEERING. CORNELL QUARTERLY. See Engineering.

ENGINEERING DIGEST (TORONTO, ONT.). See Engineering.

ENGINEERS' SALARIES, SPECIAL INDUSTRY REPORT. See Engineering.

ENVOL. See Business.

EQUIPMENT & TECHNOLOGY INTERNATIONAL. VAT Equipment and Technology International. V. 1- 1975-. 0098-5376. US. English. Intercontinental Publications Inc, 1010 Washington Boulevard, Stamford CT 06904. **LC** T1. **DD** 605.

EREKUTORONIKUSU. See Engineering - Electricity, Electrical Engineering, Electronics.

ERGONOMIIA. Bulgarian. ir. 4.101 Single Issue. **LC** T59.7.

EURO ABSTRACTS : SCIENTIFIC AND TECHNICAL PUBLICATIONS AND PATENTS. See Indexes/Abstracts.

EUROPEAN JOURNAL OF OPERATIONAL RESEARCH. V. 1- 1977-. 105. Periodical. English. bm. $386.21. Elsevier Science Publishers, PO Box 211, 1000 AE Amsterdam Netherlands. Tel (020)5803.911. **Ind/Abst** Math. Rev., Electron. Commun. Abstr. J., ISMEC Bull., Pollut. Abstr. Indexes, Saf. Sci. Abstr. J., Manage. Contents, Eng. Index Annu., Eng. Index Mon., Eng. Index Bioeng. Abstr., Eng. Index Energy Abstr., Coal Abstr., Excerpta Med., Ship Abstr., ABI/Inform, Comput. Control Abstr., Electr. Electron. Abstr., Sci. Abstr. Sect. A. Phys. Abstr., Energy Res. Abstr. **LC** T57.6. **DD** 001.424. **CODEN** EJORDT.

EXHAUST NEWS. 0192-7469. Periodical. US. English. mo. Exhaust News, 113 McCullar, Burleson TX 76028. **Tel** (817)292-1900.

THE EXHIBITOR'S HANDBOOK. Began with Vol. for 1980. 0260-1508. UK. English. 12.95. Kogan Page Ltd, 120 Pentonville Road, London N1 England. **LC** T396. **DD** 659.152025.

EXPO INTER. VFOAT Catalogue Foires. FR. French. an. 490. BIEF, 21 Avenue Secretan, 75019 Paris France. **LC** T391. **DD** 380.1.

FA MING TIEN TI. VFOAT World of Invention. Began with Feb. 1974 issue. Periodical. Chinese. ir. $8.50. Room 304 Cathay Chang An Building No 108 Chang An East Road Sec 2-104, Taipei China. **LC** T4.

THE FADUM REPORT. 0748-3236. Periodical. US. English. Fadum Report, 218 Briar Lane, Westwood MA 02090. **DD** 676.

FARM COMPUTER NEWS (DES MOINES , IOWA : 1985). See Agriculture.

FEDERAL SCIENTIFIC AND TECHNICAL COMMUNICATION ACTIVITIES, PROGRESS REPORT. See Science (General).

FEDERAL TECHNOLOGY TRANSFER. Vol. 5, No. 6 (Nov./Dec. 1985)-. Periodical. US. English. bm. National Technology Transfer Institute, 7206 Ben Franklin Building/1200 Pennsylvania Avenue, Washington DC 20044. *Technology Utilization.*

FEN. FINITE ELEMENT NEWS. (FINITE ELEMENT NEWS : FEN). VFOAT FEN. Jan. 1976-. 0309-6688. Periodical. UK. English. bm. $52.00. Finite Element News, 260 Lesmill Road, Don Mills Ontario M3B 2T5 Canada. **Tel** (416)447-5353. Ed John Robinson. **Ind/Abst** Fluidex. bk rev. adv acc. **Circ** 1,500. (ctrl). Finite element methods.

FISICA E TECNOLOGIA. See Physics.

FLUSSIGES OBST. See Food & Drink.

FONDERIE, FONDEUR D'AUJOURD'HUI. See Metals & Metallurgy.

FOOD TECHNOLOGY. See Food & Drink.

FOOD TECHNOLOGY IN AUSTRALIA. See Food & Drink.

FOOD TECHNOLOGY IN NEW ZEALAND. See Food & Drink.

FOOD TECHNOLOGY REVIEW. See Food & Drink.

FOR INDUSTRIAL ARCHEOLOGY. (IA). VFOAT Industrial Archeology. V. 1, No. 1-. 0160-1040. Periodical. US. English. an. $5.00. Treasurer SIA, National Museum of History and Technology/Room 5020, Washington DC 20560. **Ind/Abst** Avery Index Archit. Period. **LC** T37. **DD** 609.

FORSCHUNG AN DER TECHNISCHEN UNIVERSITAT BERLIN. Main/Corp Berlin. Technische Universitat. Kommission fur Forschung und Wissenschaftlichen Nachwuchs. German. ir. Strasse des 17 Juni 135, 1 Berlin 12 West Germany. **LC** T173.

FORSCHUNG IM INGENIEURWESEN. See Engineering.

FORSCHUNGSBERICHTE AUS TECHNIK UND NATURWISSENSCHAFTEN. See Science (General).

FORTSCHRITTE DER VERFAHRENSTECHNIK. See Engineering.

FORTSCHRITTE DER VERFAHRENSTECHNIK. ABTEILUNG B, MECHANISCHE VERFAHRENSTECHNIK. See Engineering - Chemical Engineering.

FREDDO. Began in 1951. 0016-0296. Periodical. IT. Italian. ir. 40,000. Propaganda Editoriale Grafica, Via F LLI Brassan 2, Milano Italy 20126. **Tel** 25.79.841. Ed Paolo Sonino. **Ind/Abst** Chem. Abstr. **CODEN** FREDAZ. bk rev. adv acc. **Circ** 1,750. High-level technical articles on refrigeration, existing plants, machinery and components, research, laws and regulations.

FRENCH TECHNICAL BULLETIN. Began with: 1961, No. 2?. Periodical. US. English. **LC** HC276.2. **DD** 330.944005. *French Economic and Technical Bulletin.*

FT ABSTRACTS IN SCIENCE AND TECHNOLOGY. See Indexes/Abstracts.

FUJITSU SCIENTIFIC & TECHNICAL JOURNAL. VAT Fujitsu Scientific and Technical Journal. Vol. 1 (Apr. 1965)-. 0016-2523. Periodical. JA. English. qt. $30.00. Kinokuniya Book-Store Co Ltd, 17-7 Shinjuky 3-chome, Shinjuku-ku Tokyo 160-91 Japan. **Tel** (415)439-0161. Ed Hiroshi Yamada. **Ind/Abst** Eng. Index Annu., Eng. Index Mon., Eng. Index Bioeng. Abstr., Eng. Index Energy Abstr., Int. Aerosp. Abstr., Comput. Control Abstr., Electr. Electron. Abstr., Sci. Abstr. Sect. A. Phys. Abstr., Met. Abstr., World Alum. Abstr., Chem. Abstr., Phys. Abstr., Eng. Index. **CODEN** FUSTA4. Specific studies and reports on ultra high technological fields such as electrical engineering.

FUKUOKA DAIGAKU KOGAKU SHUHO. VFOAT Fukuoka University Review of Technological Sciences. JA. Japanese (summaries in English). ir. 11 Nanakuma, Nishi-ku, Fuokuoka Japan. **Ind/Abst** Chem. Abstr. **LC** T4. **CODEN** FDKSDF.

FUTURES RESEARCH QUARTERLY. Vol. 1, No. 1 (Spring 1985)-. 8755-3317. Periodical. US. English. qt. $50.00 Members, $60.00 Non-Members. World Future Society, 4916 Saint Elmo Avenue, Bethesda MD 20814-5089. **Tel** (301)656-8274. **Ind/Abst** Curr. Index J. Educ. **DD** 303. bk rev. adv acc. **Circ** 1,500. A professional journal on strategic planning, policy analysis, technical forecasting, issues on management, and other futures-related areas. *World Future Society Bulletin, 0049-8092.*

FUTURIBLERNE. Periodical. Danish. ir. 125.00. Landssekretaer B Olsen, S L 22, 5683 Haarby Denmark. **LC** T174.

GEC JOURNAL OF SCIENCE & TECHNOLOGY. See Science (General).

GEKKAN NIRA. Main/Corp Sogo Kenkyu Kaihatsu Kiko. VFOAT Nira. Began with Aug. 1979. Periodical. JA. Japanese. ir. Sogo Kenkyu Kaihatsu Kiko, c/o Mitsui Building, 37-Kai 1-1 Nishi Shinjuku, 2-chome Shinjuku-ku, Tokyo 160 Japan. **LC** T175 /B .S54A.

GENERAL CATALOG OF INFORMATION SERVICES. Main/Corp United States. National Technical Information Service. US. English. an. National Technical Information Service, 5285 Port Royal Road, Springfield VA 22161. *NTIS Information Services General Catalog for North America.*

GENETIC TECHNOLOGY NEWS. Vol. 1, No. 1 (Feb. 1981)-. 0272-9032. Periodical. US. English. mo. $248.00 Domestic, $284.00 Foreign. Technical Insights Inc, PO Box 1304, Fort Lee NJ 07024. **Tel** (201)568-4744. Ed Albert S Hester. Interpretive news on opportunities to apply genetic engineering in medicine, agriculture and industry.

GEOTHERMAL ENERGY TECHNOLOGY. VFOAT G.E.T. Jan. 15, 1983-. 0736-6620. Periodical. US. English. sm. $40.00 Domestic, $80.00 Others. National Technical Information Service, 5285 Port Royal Road, Springfield VA 22161. **LC** Z5853.G4, TJ280.7. **DD** Q16.6214405. *Geothermal Energy Update, 0146-194X.*

Technology (General)

GIJUTSU JOHO. Japanese. ir. 60 Ogura 649-62, Wakayama Japan. **LC** T4 .G573.

GIJUTSU KAIHATSU KANKEI INDEKKUSU. See Bibliographies.

GIJUTSU KENKYU HONBU GIHO. VFOAT Technical Report. JA. Japanese (with summaries in English). ir. Boeicho Gijutsu Kenkyu Honbu Gijutsubu Chosaka, 2-24 Ikejiri 1, Setagaya-ku Tokyo-to 154 Japan.

GIJUTSU TO NINGEN. No. 1- (Sukan No. 1-)-. Japanese. mo. 6500. Agune, 52 Suidocho Shinuku-ku 162, Tokyo Japan. **LC** T4.

GOVERNMENT EQUIPMENT NEWS. VFOAT GEN. Began in 1980. 0111-1590. English. bm. $28.16. Cranwell Publishing Company Ltd, PO Box 3397, Auckland New Zealand. **Tel** (09)418 0346. **Ed** David Reddaway. **adv acc. Circ** 2,600. (ctrl). Designed to keep government and local bodies abreast of the availability of new and improved products. It is divided into four main trade indexes-environment, construction, administration, parks and reserves. *Australasian Environment.*

GUIA INDUSTRIAL ABRIL. 1973-. Portuguese. ir. 100.00. Editora Abril Ltda Grupo Tecnica, Caixa Postal 30 777, Sao Paulo Brazil. **LC** T12.5.B7.

GUIDE TO EEC TECHNICAL DIRECTIVES. No. 1- Dec. 1972-. English. ir. -/-/50 Single Issue. Institute for Industrial Research and Standards, Ballymun Road 9, Dublin Ireland. **LC** T59.2.E75.

GUIDE TO THE HIGH TECHNOLOGY INDUSTRIES. 1st Ed.-. 0738-2324. US. English. an. Ballinger Publishing Company, 54 Church Street, Cambridge MA 02138.

GYOMU NEMPO - OSAKA FURITSU KOGYO GIJUTSU KENKYUJO. **Main/Corp** Osaka Furitsu Kogyo Gijutsu Kenkyujo. VFOAT Osaka Furitsu Kogyo Gijutsu Kenjyujo Gyomu Nempo. JA. Japanese. ir. Osaka Furitsu Kogyo Gijutsu Kenkyujo, 1-53 Enokojima 2-chome, Nishi-ku, Osaka Japan. **LC** T178.O73.

HAKODATE KOGYO KOTO SEMMON GAKKO KIYO. VFOAT Research Reports, Hakodate Technical College. No. 1-. JA. Japanese (with some summaries in English). ir. No 226 Tokuracho Hakodate, Hokkaido Japan. **Ind/Abst** Chem. Abstr. **CODEN** HKSKDY.

HANDBOOK AND ANNUAL REVIEW. See Economics - Economics: Industry & Production.

HANDBOOK OF POLYTECHNIC COURSES. 1972/73-. 0305-6376. UK. English. International Publications Service, 114 East 32nd Street, New York NY 10016. **LC** T107. **DD** 607.1042.

HANDBUCH - ARBEITSGEMEINSCHAFT INDUSTRIELLER FORSCHUNGSVEREINIGUNGEN. **Main/Corp** Arbeitsgemeinschaft Industrieller Forschungsvereinigungen. Periodical. German. ir. Arbeitsgemeinschaft Industrieller Forschungsvereinigungen, 5000 Koln 51, Bayenthalgurtel 23, Koln West Germany. **LC** T177.G4.

HANGUK KISUL. Periodical. English (French, Korean, and Spanish). ir. Hanguk Kisul Yongyok Hyophoe, San 76-561 Yoksam-dong, Kangnam-ku Seoul Korea. **LC** T174.3.

HAN'GUK SIKPUM KWAHAKHOE CHI. See Food & Drink.

HARVARD STUDIES IN TECHNOLOGY AND SOCIETY. Periodical. US. English. ir. Harvard University Press, 79 Garden Street, Cambridge MA 02138. **Tel** (617)661-3761.

HASIL RAPAT KERJA - LEMBAGA PENELITIAN DAN PENDIDIKAN INDUSTRI. **Main/Corp** Lembaga Penelitian dan Pendidikan Industri. Indonesian. ir. Lembaga Penelitian dan Pendidikan Industri, Kotak Pos 2802, Jakarta Indonesia. **LC** T163.I6.

HEI-LUNG-CHIANG FA HSIAO. Periodical. CC. Chinese. qt. 0.50. Hei-Lung-Chiang Sheng Ching Kung Yeh Yen Chiu So Harbin China. **LC** TP500. **DD** 663.1305.

HI-HAKAI KENSA. (HIHAKAI KENSA). VFOAT Journal of N.D.I. VAT Journal of Non-Destructive Inspection. Began in 1952. 0367-5866. Periodical. JA. Japanese. mo. 65.00. Maruzen Company Ltd, PO Box 5050, 100-31 Tokyo Japan. **Tel** 03-863-6521. **Ind/Abst** Chem. Abstr. **CODEN** HIHKAU. **Circ** 5,000. (ctrl). Report of technical studies about nondestructive inspection, data, and explanations.

HIGH TECHNOLOGY. V. 1- Feb. 1980-. 0195-4091. Periodical. US. English. mo. $35.00. United Technical Publications Inc, 645 Stewart Avenue, Garden City NY 11530. **LC** TK7800. **DD** 621.38105.

HIGH TECHNOLOGY (BOSTON, MA). (HIGH TECHNOLOGY). Vol. 1, No. 1 (Sept./Oct. 1981)-. 0277-2981. US. English. mo. $18.00. High Technology, PO Box 2606, Boulder CO 80322. **Tel** (617)227-4700. **Ed** Robert C Haavind. **Ind/Abst** Abstr. Bull. Inst. Paper Chem., Int. Aerosp. Abstr., Nexis, Predicasts, Energy Inf. Abstr., Environ. Abstr., Energy Res. Abstr., Gen. Sci. Index. **LC** T1. **DD** 605. **adv acc. Circ** 300,000. The only magazine covering the business of emerging technologies, written for Wall Street to Silicon valley.

HIGH TEMPERATURE SCIENCE. See Chemistry - Physical and Theoretical Chemistry.

HISTORY AND TECHNOLOGY. See History (General).

HISTORY OF TECHNOLOGY. 1st-. 0307-5451. UK. English. an. $22.50. Mansell, 6 All Saints Street, London N1 9RL England. **Tel** 01-837 6676. **Ed** Norman Smith. **Ind/Abst** Am. Hist. Life, Hist. Abstr., Part A, Mod. Hist. Abstr., Hist. Abst., Part B, Twent. Century Abstr. **LC** T14.7. **DD** 609. **Circ** 750. A collection of essays on the technical problems of different periods and societies and the measures taken to solve them.

HISTORY, TECHNOLOGY, AND ART MONOGRAPH. See History (General).

HITACHI REVIEW. V. 1- Jan. 1952-. 0018-277X. Periodical. JA. English. bm. Japan Publishers Trading Company Ltd, PO Box 5030, Tokyo International Tokyo 100-31 Japan. **Ind/Abst** Eng. Index Mon., Eng. Index Bioeng. Abstr., Eng. Index Energy Abstr., Fluidex, Excerpta Med., Comput. Control Abstr., Electr. Electron. Abstr., Sci. Abstr. Sect. A. Phys. Abstr., Met. Abstr., World Alum. Abstr., Chem. Abstr., Nuci. Sci. Abstr., Sel. Water Resour. Abstr., Eng. Index, Eng. Index Annu., Electron. Pub. Abstr., Phys. Abstr. **LC** T1. **CODEN** HITAAQ.

HITACHI TECHNOLOGY. 0018-277X. JA. English. an. Ohm-sha Company Ltd, 1 Kanda Nishiki-cho 3-chome Chiyoda-ku, Tokyo 10 Japan. **LC** T1. **DD** 605.

HOJA INFORMATIVA DE LA SECCION DE HISTORIA DE LA CIENCIA Y LA TECNOLOGIA DEL INSTITUTO DE INVESTIGACIONES HISTORICAS, UNIVERSIDAD NACIONAL AUTONOMA DE MEXICO. See Science (General).

HOKKAI GAKUEN DAIGAKU KOGAKUBU KENKYU HOKOKU. No. 1-. Japanese. ir. Minami 26-Jo Chuo-ku (062), Nishi 11-chome, Sapporo Japan. **Ind/Abst** Coal Abstr. **LC** T4.

HOKKAIDO KOGYO DAIGAKU KENKYU KIYO. (KENKYU KIYO). VFOAT Memoirs of the Hokkaido Institute of Technology. Began in 1970. 0385-0862. Japanese (some in English). an. Hokkaido Kogyo Daigaku, 419-2 Teine Maeda Nishi-ku, Sapporo-shi 061-24 Japan. **Ind/Abst** Comput. Control Abstr., Electr. Electron. Abstr., Sci. Abstr. Sect. A. Phys. Abstr., Chem. Abstr. **LC** T4. **CODEN** HODKDL.

HOKKAIDO KOGYO KAIHATSU SHIKENJO NEMPO. JA. Japanese. ir. Hokkaido Kogyo Kaihatsu Shikenjo, 41-2 Higashi-Tsukisamu Toyohira-ku, Sapporo 061-01 Japan. **LC** T178.H64.

HOLZTECHNOLOGIE. Began publication in July 1960. 0018-3881. Periodical. GE. German (summaries in English, French, and Russian). qt. $23.95. Kunst & Wissen Erich Bieber, Dufourstrasse 51, CH-8008 Zurich Switzerland. **Tel** 011-41-1-69 44 20. **Ind/Abst** Excerpta Med., Abstr. Bull. Inst. Paper Chem., CIS Abstr., Pap. Board Abstr., Chem. Abstr. Bibliogr. Agric. **LC** TA419.A1. **CODEN** HLZTAW.

HOME MECHANIX. Jan. 1985-. 8755-0423. Periodical. US. English. mo. $12.00 US, $17.00 Foreign. Home Mechanix, Subscription Department, PO Box 2830, Boulder CO 80322. **DD** 605. *Mechanix Illustrated,* 0025-6587.

HSTC BULLETIN. See Science (General).

HSUEH PAO (WU-HAN KUNG HSUEH YUAN). (HSUEH PAO). VFOAT Wuhan Gongxueyuan Xuebao. Periodical. CH. Chinese. qt. 24.00. Wu-Han Kung Hsueh Yuan, Hsueh Pao Ma Fang Shan, Wu-Chang China. **Tel** 71939. **Ed** Gao Shixiu. **LC** T4. **DD** 605. **Circ** 1,500. (ctrl). A comprehensive publication. Each issue covers mainly the research achievements related to the design and manufacture of machine, forging, casting, material protection, enterprise management, automobiles, tribology, etc.

HUA TUNG FANG CHIH KUNG HSUEH YUAN HSUEH PAO. VFOAT Huadong Fangzhi Gongxueyuan Xuebao. Vol. 7, Vol. 1 – Vol. 21. 0253-2433. Periodical. CC. Chinese. qt. $16.00. Post Office, Shanghai China. **Tel** 522430. **Ed** Yan Haojing. **Ind/Abst** World Text Abstr., Chem. Abstr. **LC** TS1300. **DD** 677.005. **CODEN** HFGXDC. **adv acc. Circ** 1,450. Textile science and technology, fiber sciences, man-made fibers, mechanical engineering, automation, chemical engineering, apparel, textile machinery, computer applications, applied physics: applied chemistry, mathematics, and management. *Shang-Hai Fang Chih Kung Hsueh Yuan Hsueh Pao,* 0253-309X.

HUA ZHONG GONG XUEYUAN XUEBAO. (JOURNAL OF HUAZHONG INSTITUTE OF TECHNOLOGY). VFOAT Hua Chung Kung Hsueh Yuan Hsueh Pao. Vol. 1, No. 1 (Sept. 1979)- 1982. 0253-4274. Periodical. CC. English. bm. $16.40. China Publication Centre, PO Box 2820, Beijing China. **Ind/Abst** Math. Rev., Comput. Control Abstr., Electr. Electron. Abstr., Sci. Abstr. Sect. A. Phys. Abstr. **LC** T1. **DD** 605. **CODEN** JJHTDL.

HUMAN SYSTEMS MANAGEMENT. See Business - General Management.

HYBRID CIRCUIT TECHNOLOGY. See Engineering - Electricity, Electrical Engineering, Electronics.

T A I C H NEWS. VAT Technical Assistance Information Clearing House News. No. 1- , 1964-. 0039-8209. Periodical. US. English. ir. Technical Assistance Information Clearing House, 200 Park Avenue South, New York NY 10003. **Tel** (212)777-8210.

IDEAS EN ARTE Y TECNOLOGIA. See The Arts (General) - Art.

IDSA PAPERS. (IDSA PAPERS). VFOAT I.D.S.A. Papers. VAT Industrial Designers Society of America Papers. Vol. 1 (1981)-. 0277-173X. Periodical. US. English. an. Free to Members, $20.00 Nonmembers. Industrial Designers Society of America, 6803 Poplar Place, McLean VA 22101. **LC** TS171.A1. **DD** 745.205.

IMAGE. See Medicine.

IMBALLAGGIO. 0019-2708. Periodical. IT. Italian. mo. $45.74. Etas Kompass Periodici Tecnici, Via Mantegna 6, 20154 Milano Italy.

IMPACT ASSESSMENT BULLETIN. Vol. 1, No. 2 (Winter 1982)-. 0734-9165. Periodical. US. English. qt. $36.00. International Association of Impact Assessment, Georgia Institute of Technology, Atlanta GA 30322. **Tel** (404)894-3195. **Ed** Larry Canter. **LC** T174.5. **DD** 333.7105. bk rev. **Circ** 550. Publication of short articles, professional experience, reviews, and news, and professional opportunities. *IAIA Bulletin.*

IMPACT : OFFICE AUTOMATION : TRENDS AND GUIDELINES IN MANAGING AUTOMATED OFFICE SYSTEMS. Jan. 1978-. 0194-9845. Periodical. US. English. mo. $45.00. Impact Information Technology, Maryland Road, Willow Grove PA 19090. **Tel** (215)659-4300. **Ed** Lou Pilla. **Circ** 1,000. (ctrl). Trends and guidelines in managing automated office systems. *Impact: Information Technology Technology,* 0194-9845.

INDEX OF TECHNICAL PUBLICATIONS. See Indexes/Abstracts.

INDEX TO SCIENTIFIC & TECHNICAL PROCEEDINGS. See Indexes/Abstracts.

AN INDEX TO STANDARD INTEREST PROFILES IN SCIENCE AND TECHNOLOGY. See Indexes/Abstracts.

THE INDIAN JOURNAL OF TECHNICAL EDUCATION. See Education (General).

Technology (General)

INDIAN JOURNAL OF TECHNOLOGY. Began with: Vol. 1, No. 1 (Jan. 1, 1963). 0019-5669. Periodical. II. English. mo. 40.00. Publishing and Information Directorate, Hillside Road, New Delhi 110054 India. Ed Subbiah Arunachalam. Ind/Abst Eng. Index Mon., Eng. Index Annu., Eng. Index Energy Abstr., Eng. Index Bioeng. Abstr., Fluidex, Life Sci. Collect., World Text Abstr., Excerpta Med., Coal Abstr., Old Testam. Abstr., Energy Inf. Abstr., Environ. Abstr., Minproc, GeoRef, Int. Aerosp. Abstr., Comput. Control Abstr., Electr. Electron. Abstr., Sci. Abstr. Sect. A. Phys. Abstr., Met. Abstr., World Alum. Abstr., Biol. Abstr., Chem. Abstr., Nucl. Sci. Abstr., Bibliogr. Agric., Eng. Index, Sci. Cit. Index, Abr. Ed., Phys. Abstr. LC T1. DD 605. CODEN IJOTA8. bk rev. adv acc. Circ 1,000. Original research papers and occasional review articles in mechanical, chemical engineering, metallurgy, applied chemistry, applied mathematics, etc. *Journal of Scientific and Industrial Research. Section D: Technology*, 0368-4237.

INDUSTRIA USOARA. SERIA B. Romanian (abstracts in English, French, German and Russian). ir. 140.00. Centrul de Documentare Si Publicatii Tehnice M I U, 30/07 02 00 Bucurest Romania. Ind/Abst Coal Abstr. LC T4.

INDUSTRIAL ARCHAEOLOGY. V. 1- May 1964-. 0019-7971. Periodical. UK. English. qt. Graphmitre Ltd, 1 West Street, Tavistock Devon England. LC T37. DD 609.

INDUSTRIAL ARCHAEOLOGY REVIEW. V. 1- Autumn 1976-. 0309-0728. Periodical. UK. English. ty. $50.00. Association for Industrial Archaeology, Wharfage Ironbridge Telford, Shropshire TF8 7AW England. Tel 0952-45-3522. Ed Marilyn Palmer. Ind/Abst Am. Hist. Life, Hist. Abstr., Art Archaeol. Tech. Abstr., Repert. Int. Litt. Art. LC T37. DD 609.41. bk rev. adv acc. Circ 1,000. (ctrl). Articles on conservation and industrial archaeology, photographs and book reviews.

INDUSTRIAL ARTS INITIATIVE. VFOAT Initiative. VAT Initiative (Fredericton). 0710-1945. Periodical. CN. English. ty. Free. New Brunswick Teachers' Association, PO Box 752, Fredericton New Brunswick E3B 5R6 Canada. Ind/Abst Can. Educ. Index. DD 607.12715. (ctrl).

INDUSTRIAL DIAMOND REVIEW. VFOAT IDR. Began in 1940. 0019-8145. Periodical. UK. English. bm. $53.00. Kenion Advertising, Marish Wharf, St Marys Road, Slough Berks SL3 6DA England. Tel 23456. Ed P A Daniel. Ind/Abst Electron. Commun. Abstr. J., ISMEC Bull., Pollut. Abstr. Indexes, Saf. Sci. Abstr. J., Eng. Index Annu., Eng. Index Mon., Eng. Index Bioeng. Abstr., Eng. Index Energy Abstr., Excerpta Med., Ref. Source, Eng. Index. LC TJ1193. DD 621.92. CODEN INDRA9. (cum index). bk rev. adv acc. Circ 12,000. Diamond and CBN tools are used in metalworking, civil engineering, mining and in the glass, ceramics, electronics, etc., industries. IDR looks at new applications in all these industries. *Bibliography of Industrial Diamond Applications.*

INDUSTRIAL EDUCATION. See Education (General).

INDUSTRIAL ENGINEERING (INSTITUTE OF INDUSTRIAL ENGINEERS). (INDUSTRIAL ENGINEERING). VFOAT IE. Vol. 13, No. 10 (Oct. 1981)-. 0019-8234. Periodical. US. English. mo. $37.50. Institute of Industrial Engineers, 25 Technology Park, Atlanta Norcross GA 30092. Tel (404)449-0460. Ind/Abst ABI/Inform, Math. Rev., CIS Abstr., Eng. Index Annu., Eng. Index Mon., Eng. Index Bioeng. Abstr., Eng. Index Energy Abstr., Excerpta Med., Ship Abstr., Comput. Control Abstr., Electr. Electron. Abstr., Sci. Abstr. Sect. A. Phys. Abstr., Ref. Source, Energy Inf. Abstr., Environ. Abstr. LC T55.4. DD 670.5. CODEN IDLEB9. Also issued in microfilm. *Industrial Engineering (American Institute of Industrial Engineers)*, 0019-8234.

INDUSTRIAL HANDLING REVUE. Periodical. SZ. German. ir. AGIFA Verlag, Universitatstrasse 120, Postfach 257, 8033 Zurich Switzerland. LC T59.5.

INDUSTRIAL HEATING. See Metals & Metallurgy.

INDUSTRIAL NEWS AND RESEARCH. Periodical. English. ir. Singapore Institute of Standards and Industrial Research, PO Box 2611, Singapore Singapore. LC T1. DD 605.

INDUSTRIAL RESEARCH IN BRITAIN. 1st- Ed. 0073-7615. UK. English. ir. $195.00. Gale Research Company, Book Tower, Detroit MI 48226. LC T177.G7. DD 607. Detailed entries furnish valuable information about a wide range of organizations, firms, and agencies engaged in industrial research in the United Kingdom.

INDUSTRIAL RESEARCH LABORATORIES OF THE UNITED STATES. 1st- Ed. 0073-7623. US. English. ir R R Bowker Company, 205 East 42nd Street, New York NY 10017. LC T176. DD 607. NLM T 176 I142.

INDUSTRIAL RESEARCH LABORATORIES OF THE UNITED STATES. (INDUSTRIAL RESEARCH LABORATORIES OF THE UNITED STATES, INCLUDING CONSULTING RESEARCH LABORATORIES). 3rd Ed.-. 0073-7623. US. English. ir. $149.00. RR Bowker Company, PO Box 1807, Ann Arbor MI 48106. Tel (212)916-1600. NLM T 176 I42. (ctrl). Descriptive information on 12,500 industrial organizations in the U.S. up-to-date, alphabetical listings, laboratory addresses, officers, administrators, research personnel. *Research Laboratories in Industrial Establishments of the United States of America.*

INDUSTRIAL ROBOT. (THE INDUSTRIAL ROBOT). V. 1- Sept 1973-. 0143-991X. Periodical. UK. English. qt. $99.00. Air Science Company, PO Box 143, Corning NY 14830. Tel (607)962-5591. Ed Brian Rooks. Ind/Abst Electron. Commun. Abstr. J., ISMEC Bull., Pollut. Abstr. Indexes, Saf. Sci. Abstr. J., Eng. Index, Bioeng. Abstr., Eng. Index Energy Abstr., Fluidex, Comput. Control Abstr., Electr. Electron. Abstr., Sci. Abstr., Appl. Sci. Technol. Index. CODEN IDRBAT. bk rev. adv acc. (ctrl). Unique international coverage of design, development and application of robots in industry for engineers and managers.

INDUSTRIAL WORLD. Began 1946. 0019-8889. Periodical. US. English. mo. $80.00. Johnston International Publishing Company, 386 Park Avenue South, New York NY 10016. Tel (212)689-0120. Ind/Abst Excerpta Med.

INDUSTRIE ET ARTISANAT. Main/Corp Paris. Ecole Pratique des Hautes Etudes. Section des Sciences Economiques et Sociales. 1- 1965-). 0073-7739. Monographic Series. US. French. ir. Walter de Gruyter Inc, 200 Saw Mill River Road, Hawthorne NY 10532. Tel (914)747-0110.

INDUSTRY AND SCIENTIFIC RESEARCH MEMORANDA. See Science (General).

INFO-TECH (MONTREAL, QUEBEC). (INFO-TECH). Vol. 1, No. 5 May 1979 Vol. 3 No. 2 Jan./Feb. 1981. 0710-9725. Periodical. CN. French. bm. DD 606.0714. *Informatech (Montreal, Quebec)*, 0710-9717.

INFORMACION CIENTIFICA Y TECNOLOGICA. See Science (General).

INFORMATION AND DOCUMENTS - BCEOM. Main/Corp Bureau Central d'Etudes pour les Equipements d'Outre-Mer. 1- Nov. 1973-. English. ir. BCEOM, 15 Square Max-Hymans, Paris 15E France. LC T1. DD 309.213091724.

INFORMATION TECHNOLOGY. Vol. 3, No. 1 (Jan. 1984)-. Periodical. UK. English. qt. Butterworth Scientific Limited, PO Box 63, Westbury House/Bury Street, Guildford GU2 5BH England. *Information Technology, Research and Development.*

INFORMATIONS ET DOCUMENTS - BCEOM. Main/Corp France. Bureau Central d'Etude pour les Equipements d'Outre-Mer. Periodical. FR. French (summaries in English and Spanish). ir. Bureau Central d'Etudes Pour les Equipments d'Outre-Mer, 15 Square Max-Hymans, Paris 15E France. LC T2.

INFORMATIONSTAG FUR SPRENGTECHNIK INTERNATIONAL : PROCEEDINGS. English (German). an. Wirtschaftsforderungsinstitut der Kammer der Gewerblichen Wirtschaft fur Oberosterreich, Wiener Strasse 150, 4024 Linz Austria.

INFORMATIQUE ET BUREAUTIQUE. See Computers and Computer Science.

INGENIEUR-ARCHIV. See Engineering - Mechanical Engineering & Machinery.

INNOVATION. Began with Dec. 1975 issue. 0334-3847. Periodical. English. mo. $30.00. A G Publications Ltd, PO Box 7422, 31 070 Haifa Israel. Tel 04-255104. Ed A Greenfield. Ind/Abst Predicasts. Circ 4,000. A report on industrial R & D and science based industry in Israel. *Technical Progress in Israel*.

INSIDE R & D. (INSIDE R & D : THE WEEKLY REPORT ON TECHNICAL INNOVATION). VFOAT Inside R and D. 0300-757X. Periodical. US. English. wk. $382.00 Domestic, $437.00 Foreign. Technical Insights Inc, PO Box 1304, Fort Lee NJ 07024. Tel (201)568-4744. Ed Richard Consolas. Ind/Abst Predicasts, Funk Scott Index Corp. Ind. R&D breakthroughs in industry, government and academic labs, with emphasis on technology transfer.

INSTRUMENTATION IN THE FOOD AND BEVERAGE INDUSTRY; PROCEEDINGS. See Food & Drink.

INTEC. Main/Corp Comite de Investigaciones Tecnologicas de Chile. Spanish. ir. Avda Santa Maria 6500 Casilla 667, Santiago Chile. LC T4.

INTERNATIONAL ANNUAL JOURNAL OF ARTS, SCIENCES, ENGINEERING, AGRICULTURE, AND TECHNOLOGY. See Science (General).

INTERNATIONAL GAS TECHNOLOGY HIGHLIGHTS. See Petroleum and Natural Gas.

INTERNATIONAL HIGH TECHNOLOGY REPORT. VFOAT IHTR. 0882-3553. Periodical. US. English. mo. $197.00. Amersham Associates, Woodward Building, 733 15th Street NW/Suite 1036, Washington DC 20005. Tel (202)328-8709. Ed David S Harvey. DD 621. Circ 150. A report on key trends in overseas high technology development from a business viewpoint.

INTERNATIONAL JOURNAL FOR DEVELOPMENT TECHNOLOGY. English. qt. $25.00. International Center Technical Research, 11/12 Pall Mall, London SW1Y 5LU England. Tel 930-682516. Ed B Nath. bk rev. Circ 1,400. Provides a forum for the discussion of technologies relevant to the less developed countries and the way they can be identified, developed, and applied.

INTERNATIONAL JOURNAL OF COSMETIC SCIENCE. Began with Feb. 1979 issue. 0142-5463. Periodical. UK. English (text in French). bm. $135.00. Blackwell Scientific Publishers, PO Box 88, Oxford OX2 0EL England. Tel 240201. Ed J M Blakeway. Ind/Abst Pestdoc, Ringdoc, Vetdoc, Excerpta Med., Biol. Abstr., Chem. Abstr., Sci. Cit. Index, Abr. Ed. LC TP983. DD 668.5505. NLM W1 IN766F. CODEN IJCMDW. bk rev. adv acc. Circ 2,400. Publishes original and review articles aimed at cosmetic scientists, dermatologists, and those microbiologists, pharmacists and chemists working on products which come in contact with the human body. *Journal of the Society of Cosmetic Chemists*, 0037-9832.

INTERNATIONAL JOURNAL OF MODELLING & SIMULATION. See Science (General).

INVATAMINTUL LICEAL SI TEHNIC PROFESIONAL. VFOAT Revista Invatamintul Liceal Si Tehnic Profesional. Periodical. RM. Romanian. mo. Ilexim Press Department, PO Box 1-136-1-137, Bucharest Romania. LC T61. *Invatamintul Profesional Si Tehnic.*

INVENTORS' VOICE. Vol. 1, No. 1 (May-June 1983)-. 0748-7851. Periodical. US. English. qt. $15.00. Affiliated Inventors Foundation Inc, 501 Iowa Avenue, Colorado Springs CO 80909.

IRCS MEDICAL SCIENCE. BIOMEDICAL TECHNOLOGY. See Biology.

IRON AND STEEL ENGINEER. V. 1- 1924-. 0021-1559. Periodical. US. English. mo. Association of Iron and Steel Engineers, Suite 2350/Three Gateway Center, Pittsburgh PA 15222. Tel (412)281-6323. Ed Charles J Labee. Ind/Abst Eng. Index Mon., Eng. Index Bioeng. Abstr., Eng. Index Energy Abstr., Excerpta Med., Coal Abstr., Comput. Control Abstr., Electr. Electron. Abstr., Sci. Abstr. Sect. A. Phys. Abstr., Met. Abstr., World Alum. Abstr., Chem. Abstr., Eng. Index Annu., Eng. Index Mon., Sel. Water Resour. Abstr., Appl. Sci. Technol. Index, ISMEC Bull., Phys. Abstr., Eng. Index. LC TS300. DD 672.05. CODEN IRSEA5. bk rev. adv acc. Circ 10,000. (ctrl). Information relating to the design, construction, operation and maintenance of iron and steel producing facilities and related equipment.

Technology (General)

ISA TRANSACTIONS. Main/Corp Instrument Society of America. V. 1- Jan. 1962-. 0019-0578. Periodical. US. English. qt. $75.00. Instrument Society of America, 67 Alexander Drive/PO Box 12277, Triangle Park NC 27709. **Tel** (919)549-8411. **Ed** G E Dreifke and W S Bloor. **Ind/Abst** Eng. Index Mon., Eng. Index Bioeng. Abstr., Eng. Index Energy Abstr., Fluidex, Sel. Water Resour. Abstr., Excerpta Med., Coal Abstr., Energy Inf. Abstr., Environ. Abstr., Comput. Control Abstr., Electr. Electron. Abstr., Sci. Abstr. Sect. A. Phys. Abstr., Met. Abstr., World Alum. Abstr., Biol. Abstr., Chem. Abstr., Eng. Index Annu., Eng. Index Mon., Nucl. Sci. Abstr., Int. Aerosp. Abstr., Appl. Sci. Technol. Index, Index Med., Energy Res. Abstr., Phys. Abstr., Hospit. Lit. Index. **NLM** W1 I27. **CODEN** Isataz. **Circ** 1,000. (ctrl). Forty most significant papers from thousands given at symposia and conferences yearly; subjects: technology for instrumentation and process control. Ten papers in each issue.

ISR, INTERDISCIPLINARY SCIENCE REVIEWS. See Science (General).

ISSUES IN SCIENCE AND TECHNOLOGY. See Science (General).

ITOGI NAUKI I TEKHNIKI. SERIIA EKONOMIKA, ORGANIZATSIIA, TEKHNOLOGIIA I OBORUDOVANIE POLIGRAFICHESKOGO PROIZVODSTVA. See Economics.

IZOBRETENIIA I RATSIONALIZATORSKIE PREDLOZHENIIA V OBLASTI MEDITSINY. See Medicine.

IZVESTIJA AKADEMII NAUK BELORUSSKOJ SOVETSKOJ SOCIALISTICESKOJ RESPUBLIKI. See Science (General).

IZVESTIJA SIBIRSKOGO OTDELENIJA AKADEMII NAUK SSSR. SERIJA TEHNICESKIH NAUK. (IZVESTIIA SIBIRSKOGO OTDELENIIA AKADEMII NAUK SSSR. SERIIA TEKHNICHESKIKH NAUK). **Main/Corp** Akademiia Nauk SSSR. Sibirskoe Otdelenie. 0002-3434. Periodical. UR. Russian. ty. Victor Kamkin Inc, 12224 Parklawn Drive, Rockville MD 20852. **Tel** (301)881-5973. **Ind/Abst** Math. Rev., Eng. Index Annu., Eng. Index Mon., Eng. Index Bioeng. Abstr., Eng. Index Energy Abstr., Int. Aerosp. Abstr., Met. Abstr., World Alum. Abstr., Chem. Abstr., Energy Res. Abstr. **CODEN** IZSTA4. *Izvestiia Sibirskogo Otdeleniia Akademii Nauk SSSR.*

JAPAN HIGH TECH REVIEW. Began with Vol. 1, No. 1 (Jan. 1984)-. 0743-4871. Periodical. US. English. mo. $295.00. The Mead Group, PO Box 44952, Phoenix AZ 85064.

JAPAN INDUSTRIAL & TECHNOLOGICAL BULLETIN. (THE JAPAN INDUSTRIAL & TECHNOLOGICAL BULLETIN). **VFOAT** Japan Industrial and Technological Bulletin. 0385-6542. Periodical. JA. English. mo. Japan External Trade Organization, Machinery and Technology Department, 2-5 Toranomon 2-chome Minato-ku Tokyo 105 Japan. **Ind/Abst** Met. Abstr., World Alum. Abstr. **LC** T1. **DD** 605.

JAPAN SEMICONDUCTOR TECHNOLOGY NEWS. **VFOAT** JST News. Began with Vol. 1, No. 1 (Feb. 1982). 0286-8210. Periodical. US. English. bm. $97.50. Jack K Burgess Inc, 2175 Lemoine Avenue, Fort Lee NJ 07024.

JETI. See Energy.

JOHNS HOPKINS STUDIES IN THE HISTORY OF TECHNOLOGY. New Ser., No. 1-. Monographic Series. US. English. ir. Johns Hopkins University Press, 701 West 40th Street/Suite 275, Baltimore MD 21211. **Tel** (301)339-6987.

JOURNAL OF APPLIED MEASUREMENTS. V. 1- July/Aug. 1977-. 0092-2447. Periodical. US. English. bm. 745 North Hollywood Way, Burbank CA 91505. **LC** T50. **DD** 620.0044.

JOURNAL OF CARDIOVASCULAR ULTRASONOGRAPHY. See Medicine - Cardiovascular Diseases.

JOURNAL OF CHEMICAL TECHNOLOGY AND BIOTECHNOLOGY. V. 29-32. 0142-0356. Periodical. UK. English. mo. $157.00. Blackwell Scientific Publisher, PO Box 88, Oxford OX2 OEL England. **Ind/Abst** Sel. Water Resour. Abstr., Pestdoc, Ringdoc, Vetdoc, Excerpta Med., Coal Abstr., Energy Inf. Abstr., Environ. Abstr., World Surf. Coat. Abstr., Minproc. Met. Abstr., World Alum. Abstr., Chem. Abstr., Energy Inf. Abstr., Environ. Abstr., Abr. Ed., Comput. Control Abstr., Phys. Abstr., Sci. Abstr. Sect. A. Phys. Abstr., Electr. Electron. Abstr., Eng. Index. **LC** TP1. **DD** 660.05. **NLM** W1 JO581U. **CODEN** JCTBDC. *Journal of Applied Chemistry and Biotechnology, 0375-9210.*

JOURNAL OF CHEMICAL TECHNOLOGY AND BIOTECHNOLOGY. BIOTECHNOLOGY. See Science (General).

JOURNAL OF CHEMICAL TECHNOLOGY AND BIOTECHNOLOGY. CHEMICAL TECHNOLOGY. **VFOAT** Chemical Technology. Vol. 33A, No. 1 (Jan. 1983)-. 0264-3413. Periodical. UK. English. 70 Domestic, $157.00 US/Canada and 84 Others. Society of Chemical Industry, 14 Belgrave Square, London SW1X 8PS England. **Tel** (0865)240201. **Ed** J Melling. **Ind/Abst** Excerpta Med., Life Sci. Collect., Pestdoc, Ringdoc, Vetdoc, Sel. Water Resour. Abstr., Minproc, Coal Abstr., Chem. Abstr. **LC** TP1. **DD** 660.05. **NLM** W1. **CODEN** JCTTDW. adv acc. **Circ** 1,400. (ctrl). Papers and review articles on original investigations or technological achievements: industrial chemical processes, microbes, tissue cells, enzymes in industry, biotechnology and chemical technology. *Journal of Chemical Technology and Biotechnology, 0142-0356.*

JOURNAL OF EDUCATIONAL TECHNOLOGY SYSTEMS. Began with Summer 1972 issue. 0047-2395. Periodical. US. English. qt. $66.00. Baywood Publishing Company, Inc, 120 Marine Street/PO Box Box D, Farmingdale NY 11735. **Tel** (516)249-2464. **Ed** Thomas T Liao and David C Miller. **Ind/Abst** Comput. Control Abstr., Electr. Electron. Abstr., Sci. Abstr. Sect. A. Phys. Abstr., Educ. Index, Curr. Index J. Educ., Phys. Abstr. **LC** LB1028.3. **DD** 371.305. **CODEN** JETSB7. Investigates and reports on actual classroom experience in the use of all technology: video disks, closed circuit TV, computers, and all audio-visual materials.

JOURNAL OF FOOD TECHNOLOGY. See Food & Drink.

JOURNAL OF GEOTECHNICAL ENGINEERING. See Engineering.

JOURNAL OF IMAGING TECHNOLOGY. **VFOAT** Imaging Technology. Vol 10, No. 1 (Feb. 1984)-. 0747-3583. Periodical. US. English. bm. $70.00 Domestic. Society of Photographic Scientists and Engineers, 7003 Kilworth Lane, Springfield VA 22151. **Ind/Abst** Comput. Control Abstr., Electr. Electron. Abstr., Eng. Index Annu., Eng. Index Mon., Eng. Index Bioeng. Abstr., Eng. Index Energy Abstr., Sci. Abstr. Sect. A. Phys. Abstr. *Journal of Applied Photographic Engineering, 0098-7298.*

JOURNAL OF INDUSTRIAL TECHNOLOGY. **VFOAT** Industrial Technology. Began in 1984. 0882-6404. Periodical. US. English. qt. $20.00. National Association of Industrial Technology, College of Eastern Michigan University, Upsilanti MI 48197. **Tel** (313)487-0358. **Ed** David K Gore. **DD** 607. adv acc. **Circ** 3,000. A national technical journal featuring reviewed and non-reviewed articles and items of interest to persons involved in industrial technology and industrial technology education.

JOURNAL OF MEDICAL ENGINEERING & TECHNOLOGY. See Medicine.

JOURNAL OF NUCLEAR MEDICINE TECHNOLOGY. See Medicine.

JOURNAL OF PROTECTIVE COATINGS & LININGS. **VFOAT** Journal of Protective Coatings and Linings. Began in June 1984. 8755-1985. Periodical. US. English. mo. $24.00. Technology Publishing Company, PO Box 89, Pittsburgh PA 15230. **DD** 667.

JOURNAL OF QUALITY TECHNOLOGY. See Manufacturing.

JOURNAL OF SCIENCE AND TECHNOLOGY. See Science (General).

JOURNAL OF TECHNOLOGY. V. 1- June 1956-. 0047-2824. II. English. sa. $6.00. Bengal Engineering College, Howrah 711103, West Bengal India. **Ind/Abst** Math. Rev., Int. Aerosp. Abstr., Comput. Control Abstr., Electr. Electron. Abstr., Sci. Abstr. Sect. A. Phys. Abstr., Appl. Mech. Rev., Phys. Abstr. **CODEN** JTBEAD.

THE JOURNAL OF TECHNOLOGY TRANSFER. Began in 1976. Periodical. US. English. sa. $33.00 Domestic, $42.00 Foreign. Technology Transfer Society, 279 South Beverly Drive, Box 1078, Beverly Hills CA 90212. **Tel** (213)274-3815. **Ed** James Jolly. bk rev. **Circ** 650. Original papers on technology transfer, assessment, forecasting and utilization, theory and practice in business, universities and medical laboratories.

JOURNAL OF THE NATIONAL TECHNICAL ASSOCIATION. Main/Corp National Technical Association. **VFOAT** NTA Journal. 0271-776X. Periodical. US. English. qt. $30.00. National Technical Association, 1425 H Street NW/Suite 715 South B, Washington DC 20005. **Ind/Abst** Coal Abstr., Chem. Abstr., Energy Res. Abstr. **CODEN** JNTADI.

KAGAKU SOCHI. **VFOAT** Plant and Process. Began in 1959. 0368-4849. Periodical. JA. Japanese. mo. 70.00. Maruzen Company Ltd, PO Box 5050, 100-31 Tokyo Japan. **Ind/Abst** Coal Abstr., Chem. Abstr. **CODEN** KASOB7. (ctrl). Technical subscription about chemical industry.

KAIHO - KANTO GAKUIN DAIGAKU KOGAKUBU KOGAKKAI. Main/Corp Kanto Gakuin Daigaku Kogakubu Kogakkai. JA. Japanese. ir. 4834 Mutsuura Kanazawa-ku (236), Yokohama Japan. **LC** T4.

KANTO GAKUIN DAIGAKU KOGAKU SOGO KENKYUJO HO. **VFOAT** Bulletin of Institute of Technology. Ed.- March 1978-. English (Japanese). ir. Kanto Gakuin Daigaku, 4834 Rokuuracho Kanazawa-ku, Yokohama 236 Japan. **LC** T4.

KEIRYO KENKYUJO NEMPO. JA. Japanese. ir. 10-4 Kaga 1-chome Itabashi-ku (173), Tokyo Japan. **LC** T50.

KENKYU HOKOKU (KOGYO GIJUTSUIN (JAPAN)). (KENKYU HOKOKU). **VFOAT** Kogyo Gijutsuin Kyodo Hokoku, Bulletin of Agency of Industrial Science and Technology. No. 1-. Periodical. JA. Japanese (summaries in English). ir. **Ind/Abst** Chem. Abstr. **LC** T177.J3. **CODEN** KHKGDS.

KENKYU KIYO - AKASHI KOGYO KOTO SEMMON GAKKO. See Education (General) - Higher Education.

KHIMICHESKAIA TEKHNOLOGIIA I KHIMIIA. Began in 1973. Periodical. UR. Russian. 1.24. **LC** TP1.

KIBERNETIKA, AUTOMATIZACIJA POSLOVANJA : MESECNI CASOPIS ZAVODA ZA EKONOMSKI EKSPERTIZE. **VFOAT** Automatizacija Poslovanja,. V. 21, No. 10 (Oct. 1980)-. Periodical. Serbo-Croatian -R. mo. Zavod za Ekonomske Ekspertize, 11071 Novi Beograd Palmira, Toljatija 3, Postanski Fah 104, Beograd Yugoslavia. **LC** T57.5. *Automatizacija Poslovanja.*

KIKAI GIJUTSU KENKYUJO SHOHO. See Engineering - Mechanical Engineering & Machinery.

KISUL ILLYOK. V. 1-. Periodical. KO. Korean. ir. Hanguk Kisul Komjong Kongdon, 286 Yang-dong Ghung-ku, Seoul South Korea. **LC** T163.K6.

KISUL SIDAE. V. 1-. Periodical. KO. Korean. bm. Hanguk Chigop Hullyon Kwalli Kongdan, 370-4 Kongdok-dong, Mapo-ku Seoul Korea. **LC** T163.K6.

KLASSIFIKATSIIA I KODIROVANIE. Began in 1971. Periodical. UR. Russian. mo. 0.20 Single Issue. Vniiki, 103001 K-1 Ul Shuseva 4, Moskva Russian SFSR. **LC** T14.

KOGIKEN NYUSU. Main/Corp Kansai Daigaku, Osaka Kogyo Gijutsu Kenkyujo. V. 4, No. 4- (First issue No. 16-). Japanese. ir. Kansai Daigaku Kogyo Gijutsu Kenkyujo, 3-35 Yamatecho 3/Suita 564, Japan. **LC** T178.K28.

KOGYO GIJUTSU. V. 1-. Periodical. JA. Japanese. ir. 4488. Gijutsu Kaihatsu Shinkokai Shuppanbu, 20-8 Nishi Shinbashi 2-chome Minato-ku 105, Tokyo Japan. **LC** T4.

Technology (General)

KOGYO GIJUTSUIN SHIKEN KENKYUJO KENKYU KEIKAKU. JA. Japanese. ir. 3000. Nihon Sangyo Gijutsu Shinko Kyokai, c/o Dai Nijumori Building, 7-3 Nishi Shinbashi, 2 Minato-ku (105) Tokyo Japan. **LC** T177.J3.

KOGYO GIJUTSUIN SHOKAI. Main/Corp Japan. Kogyo Gijutsuin. Japanese. ir. 3-1 Kasumigaseki 1, Chiyoda-ku (100 Japan) Tokyo. **LC** T177.J3.

KONFERENTSII, SOVESHCHANIIA, SIMPOZIUMY I VYSTAVKI, PROVODIMYE V STRANAKH- CHLENAKH TSENTRA. Main/Corp Mezhdunarodnyi Tsentr Nauchnoi I Tekhnicheskoi Infromatsil. UR. Multilingual (Russian, undetermined). 0.42 Single Issue. Liubertsy, Oktiabrskii Prospekt 403, Moskva Russia. **LC** T6.

KONGOP KISUL KYOYUK. VFOAT Journal of Vocational and Technical Education. Periodical. English (Korean). mo. Kongop Kyoyuk Yonguso, 172 Kongnung-dong, Tobong-ku Seoul Korea. **LC** T61.

KONGOP KISUL YONGU. VFOAT Journal of Industrial Technology. V. 1- No. 1- 1981-. Periodical. English (Korean). ir. Hansa Taehak Kongop Kisul, Yonguso 2881 Taemyong, 3-dong- Nam-ku Taegu Korea. **Ind/Abst** Energy Res. Abstr. **LC** T4.

KOSETSU SHIKENJO GIJUTSU SHIDO JIREI RISUTO. JA. Japanese. an. Chusho Kigyo Joho Senta, c/o Sankaido Building/9-13 Akasaka 1-chome Minato-ku, Tokyo 107 Japan. **LC** Z7914.R5, T177.J3.

KOSETSU SHIKENJO KENKYU BUNKEN SHOROKUSHU. JA. Japanese. an. Chusho Kigyo Joho Senta, c/o Sankaido Building 9-13 Akasaka 1-chome Minato-ku, Tokyo 107 Japan. **LC** Z7914.R5, T177.J3.

KOSETSU SHIKENJO KENKYU SEIKA SHOROKUSHU. See Bibliographies.

KS CHONGNAM. VFOAT K.S. Chongnam. Korean. an. 12.000. Hanguk Kongop Pyojun Hyophoe, 105-153 Kongduk-dong, Mapo-ku Seoul Korea. **LC** T59.2.K6.

KUMAMOTO KOGYO DAIGAKU KENKYU HOKOKU. (KENKYU HOKOKU). VFOAT Bulletin of the Kumanoto Institute of Technology. Began in 1976. 0385-132X. Periodical. Japanese. sa. Kumamoto Kogyo Daigaku, 22-ban 1-go Ikeda 4-chome, Kumamoto-shi 860 Japan. **Ind/ Abst** Chem. Abstr. **LC** T4. **CODEN** KHKDDJ.

KUNG YEH YUEH KAN. First published in Aug. 1975-. Chinese. ir. $3.00 Single Issue. Industry Magazine, Rooms 302/Tak Cheong Commercial Building, 215 Portland Street, Mongkok Kowloon, Chiu-Lung Hong Kong. **LC** T4.

KUSTE. (DIE KUSTE). 1.- Yearly Vol. 0452-7739. Periodical. GW. German. ir. Westholsteinische Verlag & Co, Postfach 1880, D-2240 Heide West Germany. **Tel** 0481/691-1. **Ind/Abst** Fluidex, Ship Abstr., GeoRef. **LC** TC203. **CODEN** KUSTAP. **Circ** 700. All new knowledge about technical news in order to secure the German coast.

KWAGIWON SOSIK. Periodical. KO. Korean. qt. Hanguk Hwahak Kisurwon, 207-43 Chongnyangni-dong Tong Daemun-ku, Seoul Korea. **LC** T178.H344.

KWAGIYON SOSIK. Main/Corp Han'Guk Kwahak Kisul Yon'Guso. Periodical. KO. Korean. ir. Hanguk Kwahak Kisui Yonguso, 39-1 Hawolgok-dong, Songbuk-ku, Seoul South Korea. **LC** T178.H34.

KYOKAN KENKYU GYOSEKI ICHIRAN. VFOAT Tokyo Kogyo Daigaku Kyokan Kenkyu Gyoseki Ichiran. 1973/75-. JA. English or Japanese. ir. 12-1 Ookayama 1, Meguro-ku 1952 Tokyo Japan. **LC** Z7913, T45.

KYOKAN KENKYU YOROKU. Main/Corp Boei Daigakko (Japan). VFOAT Digest of Researches by Faculty Members, National Defense Academy. Began with 1956 issue. JA. Japanese. an. Boli Daigakko, 10-20 Hashirimizu, 1-Chome, Yokosuka 239 Japan. **LC** T4.

KYUSHU KOGYO GIJUTSU SHIKENJO HOKOKU. TOKUSHUGO. VFOAT Reports of the Government Industrial Research Institute, Kyushu. March 1980-. 0286-2018. Periodical. JA. English (Japanese). ir. Kyushu Kogyo Gijutsu Shikenjo Shukumachi, Tosu-shi, Saga-ken 841 Japan. **Ind/Abst** Coal Abstr.

KYUSHU KOGYO GIJUTSU SHIKENJO NEMPO. JA. Japanese. ir. Kyushu Kogyo Gijutsu Shikenjo, 807-A Shukumachi, Tosu 841 Japan. **LC** T178.K9.

LASERS & APPLICATIONS. VFOAT Lasers and Applications. Vol. 1, No. 1 (Sept. 1982)-. 0733-303X. Periodical. US. English. mo. $45.00. High Tech Publications Inc, 23717 Hawthorne Boulevard/Suite 306, Torrance CA 90505. **Tel** (213)378-0261. **Ed** Thomas R Farre. **LC** TA1671. **DD** 621.36605. bk rev. adv acc. **Circ** 32,000. (ctrl). Published for engineers, designers and scientists in indepth news, practical design techniques and up-to-date new product information from the most experienced editorial team in the business.

LAW/TECHNOLOGY. See Law.

LEADER (RESEARCH TRIANGLE PARK (N.C.)). See Business.

LEADING CONSULTANTS IN TECHNOLOGY. 1983-. 0749-9000. US. English. ir. $225.00. J Dick Publishing, Division of Research Publications, 801 Greenbay Road/Suite 200, Lake Bluff IL 60044. **Tel** (203)397-2600. **DD** 609. 17,000 profiles of prominent consultants in science and engineering. Endexed by 1,500 areas of expertise and city/state. Source: Who's Who in Technology Today.

LIBRARY TECHNOLOGY REPORTS. See Library and Information Science.

LINDE REPORTS ON SCIENCE AND TECHNOLOGY. See Science (General).

LISTE DESCRIPTIVE DES ETABLISSEMENTS PUBLICS D'ENSEIGNEMENT DE SECOND DEGRE DISPENSANT UN ENSEIGNEMENT PROFESSIONNEL DE CYCLE COURT OU DE CYCLE LONG: TERRITOIRES D'OUTRE-MER. See Education (General) - Special Aspects of Education.

LISTY CUKROVARNICKI CASOPIS PRO PRUMSYL CUKROVARNICKY V CECHACH. Periodical. CS. CZECH. mo. Artia, PO Box 790, Praha 1 Czechoslovakia. **LC** TP375.

LITHIC TECHNOLOGY. See Archaeology.

THE LOCALNETTER DESIGNER'S HANDBOOK. 0740-6932. US. English. an. $65.00 US, $90.00 Foreign. Architecture Technology Corporation, PO Box 24322, Minneapolis MN 55424. **LC** TK5105.5. **DD** 384.

LOGISTICS SPECTRUM. V. 1- Sept. 1967-. 0024-5852. Periodical. US. English. qt. $30.00 Domestic, $35.00 Foreign. Dir of Publications SLE, Suite 922/Park Plaza 303 Williams Avenue, Huntsville AL 35801. **Tel** (205)539-3800. **Ed** Elizabeth P Crowe. **Ind/Abst** Predicasts, Int. Aerosp. Abstr. **LC** U168. **DD** 355.4105. bk rev. adv acc. **Circ** 9,500. (ctrl). Journal for individuals working, studying, or interested in the career fields of logistics technology, management, engineering, education, products support, and physical distribution.

LOGOS (ARGONNE, ILL.). See Science (General).

M. I. T. EAST ASIAN SCIENCE SERIES. Main/Corp Massachusetts Institute of Technology. Monographic Series. US. English. ir. Mass Institute of Technology, 28 Carlton Street, Cambridge MA 02142.

MCCUTCHEON'S FUNCTIONAL MATERIALS. NORTH AMERICAN EDITION. (MCCUTCHEON'S FUNCTIONAL MATERIALS). VFOAT Functional Materials. 0734-0559. US. English. an. $45.00. McCutcheons Publ, 175 Rock Road, Glen Rock NJ 07452. **Tel** (201)652 2655. **LC** TP202. **DD** 660.

MCGRAW-HILL'S BIOTECHNOLOGY NEWSWATCH. VFOAT Newswatch. Vol. 1, No. 1 (Sept. 7, 1981)-. 0275-3685. Periodical. US. English. sm. $457.00. McGraw Hill Publications, 1221 Avenue of the Americas, New York NY 10020. **Tel** (212)997-6090. **Ind/Abst** Nexis.

MAJALLAT AL-INMA AL-ARABI LIL-ULUM WA-AL-TAQNIYAH. See Science (General).

MAN, SOCIETY, TECHNOLOGY CEASED. (MAN/SOCIETY/TECHNOLOGY). V. 30-42. 0022-1813. Periodical. US. English. ir. $20.00. American Industrial Arts Association, 1914 Association Drive, Reston VA 22091. **Ind/Abst** Educ. Index, Curr. Index J. Educ., Ref. Source, Media Rev. Dig. **LC** T61. **DD** 607.1. Journal of Industrial Arts Education.

MANAGEMENT JOURNAL. Periodical. US. English. mo. free. Pacific Telephone and Nevada Bell, Room 628 140 New Montgomery Street, San Francisco CA 94105. **Tel** (415)452-3833. **Ed** Christine M Infante. **Circ** 30,000. (ctrl). Outlooks on technology, government regulation, and international issues affecting telecommunications industry and general management topics.

MANAGEMENT TECHNOLOGY (NEW YORK, N.Y. : 1983). (MANAGEMENT TECHNOLOGY). Vol. 1, No. 1 (May 1983)-. 0736-5225. Periodical. US. English. mo. $36.00 US, $48.00 Canada. International Thomson, Technology Information Inc, 11 Commerce Street, Norwalk CT 06850. **LC** T58.6. **DD** 658.403805.

MANUFACTURING TECHNOLOGY. Began with June 28, 1983. Periodical. US. English. wk. $130.00. National Technical Information Service, 5285 Port Royal Road, Springfield VA 22161.

MANUFACTURING TECHNOLOGY HORIZONS. Vol. 1, No. 1 (Jan./Feb. 1982)-. 0278-4424. Periodical. US. English. bm. $60.00. Tech Tran Consultants Inc, PO Box 206, Lake Geneva WI 53147. **Tel** (414)248-2200. **Ed** John D Meyer. **Ind/Abst** Predicasts, Met. Abstr., World Alum. Abstr. bk rev. Digest of major developments in manufacturing processes and equipment.

MARKETS YEAR BOOK. See Yearbooks, Almanacs, Directories.

MASS HIGH TECH. VAT Massachusetts High Technology. Vol. 1, No. 1 (Oct. 25, 1982)-. 8750-2100. Periodical. US. English. bw. $25.00. Mass High Tech, 113 Terrace Hall Avenue, Burlington MA 01803. **Tel** (617)229-2768. **Ed** Joeth Barias. **DD** 621. bk rev. adv acc. **Circ** 30,000. (ctrl). News of a general nature for technical professionals in the high technology industry in New England. Includes electronics, communications, computers and defence.

MEASUREMENTS & CONTROL. (M & C, MEASUREMENTS & CONTROL). VAT Measurements and Control. V. 11- Jan./Feb. 1977-. 0148-0057. Periodical. US. English. bm. $22.00. Measurements & Data Corp, 2994 West Library Avenue, Pittsburgh PA 15216. **Tel** (412)343-9666. **Ind/Abst** Ref. Source. **LC** T50. **DD** 389.105. M & D, Measurements & Data, 0025-6323.

MECHANIX ILLUSTRATED CEASED. V. 20, No. 2-V. 80, No. 680. 0025-6587. Periodical. US. English. mo. $11.94 Domestic, $16.94 Foreign. Subscription Department, PO Box 2830, Boulder CO 80322. **Ind/Abst** Energy Inf. Abstr., Environ. Abstr., Pop. Mag. Rev., Energy Res. Abstr., Read. Guide Period. Lit., Consum. Index Prod. Eval. Inf. Source. **LC** T1. **DD** 605. Modern Mechanix, Electronics Illustrated.

MECHANO BUYERS DIRECTORY. NORTHERN CALIFORNIA. See Yearbooks, Almanacs, Directories.

MECHELECIV. V. 1- July 1942-. 0047-6382. Periodical. US. English. bm. $2.00. Mecheleciv, Davis-Hodgkins House The George Washington University 2142 G Street Northwest, Washington DC 20052. **Tel** (202)676-3998. **Ed** Daniel L Briller. adv acc. **Circ** 10,000. A student published, student written, student operated technical magazine. Cooperatively published with the Engineer Alumni Association at George Washington University, Washington DC.

MEDIA AND METHODS. See Education (General).

MEDICAL PROGRESS THROUGH TECHNOLOGY. See Medicine.

MEDIZINTECHNIK. VFOAT Engineering in Medicine. 98- Yearly volume. 0344-9416. Periodical. German. qt. 6.63. A W Genter Verlag, Postfach 688, Forststr 131, 7000 Stuttgart 1 West Germany. **Tel** 0711/63-83-56. **Ed** R D Bockman. **Ind/Abst** Excerpta Med., Chem. Abstr. **NLM** W1 ME858A. **CODEN** MDZNDG. bk rev. adv acc. **Circ** 6,500. General field of medical technology, diagnosis, therapeutic rehabilitation. Medizinische Technik, 0025-8504.

MEMORIA ANUAL - SOCIEDAD DE FOMENTO FABRIL. Main/Corp Sociedad de Fomento Fabril, Santiago de Chile. Spanish. ir. Sociedad de Fomento Fabril, Agustinas 1357 Pisos 11-120, Casilla 44-D, Santiago Chile. **LC** T93.

Technology (General)

Memoria que Presenta el Consejo Directivo de la Sociedad de Fomento Fabril.

MEZHVUZOVSKII SBORNIK NAUCHNYKH TRUDOV - PERMSKII POLITEKHNICHESKII INSTITUT. Main/Corp Perm, Russia (City). Politekhnicheskii Institut. Monographic Series. UR. Russian. LC T4. *Sbornik Nauchnykh Trudov (Permskii Politekhnicheskii Institut).*

MIDIST BULLETIN D'INFORMATION. See Science (General).

MILES ANALECTA. Main/Corp Miles Laboratories, Inc., Elkhart Ind. V.1-. 0146-6011. US. English. LC TP248.3. DD 660.6305.

MIND, THE MEETINGS INDEX. SERIES SEMT, SCIENCE, ENGINEERING, MEDICINE, TECHNOLOGY. See Indexes/Abstracts.

MITSUBISHI JUKO GIHO. Began in 1964. 0387-2432. Periodical. English (Japanese). bm. $43.00. Japan Publishers Trading Company Ltd, PO Box 5030, Tokyo International, Tokyo 100-31 Japan. Ind/Abst Coal Abstr., Int. Aerosp. Abstr., Chem. Abstr. CODEN MIJGAF.

MITTEILUNGEN DES AMTES FUR STANDARDISIERUNG, MESSWESEN UND WARENPRUFUNG. Main/Corp Germany (East). Amt fur Standardisierung, Messwesen und Warenprufung. Periodical. German. sa. Amt fur Standardisierung, Messwesen und Warenprufung, Wallstrasse 16 102, Berlin West Germany. LC T59.2.G32.

MODELTEC. See Hobbies.

MOLY CORROSION INHIBITORS. (MOLY CORROSION INHIBITORS : AN AMAX NEWSLETTER). Vol. 1, No. 1 (Oct. 1981)-. 0730-9155. Periodical. US. English. ir. Free. Climax Molybdenum Company, One Greenwich Plaza, Greenwich CT 06830. Tel (203)629-6474. Circ 10,000. (ctrl). This publication describes use of molybdenum chemicals as corrosion inhibitors, among applications such as water treatment, engine coolants, synthetic metalworking, fluids and oilfield fluids.

MONOGRAFIAS (INSTITUTO DE PESQUISAS TECNOLOGICAS). (MONOGRAFIAS). Series/Titl Publicacao IPT. 1-. 0102-1958. Monographic Series. Portuguese. ir. Ind/Abst GeoRef.

MONTHLY TECHNICAL REVIEW. V. 1- Mar. 1957-. 0027-061X. Periodical. SZ. English. mo. Kunst & Wissen Erich Bieber, Dufourstrasse 51, CH-8008 Zurich Switzerland. Ind/Abst Fluidex, Excerpta Med., Met. Abstr., World Alum. Abstr. LC TA1. CODEN MTCRAM.

MULTI-INDUSTRY R&D VOLUME. See Science (General).

NAGAOKA GIJUTSU KAGAKU DAIGAKU KENKYU HOKOKU. VFOAT Technical Report of the Technological University of Nagaoka. 0388-5631. JA. Japanese (English). ir. Nagaoka Gijutsu Kagaku Daigaku, 1603-1 Aza Nagamine Kami-tomiokamachi, Nagaoka-shi 949-54 Japan. Ind/Abst Chem. Abstr. LC T4. CODEN NKHUD7.

NAGOYA KOGYO GIJUTSU SHIKENJO NEMPO. Japanese. ir. Kohyo Gijutsuin Nagoya, Kogyo Gijutsu Shienjo Hiratecho 1-chome Kita-ku, Nagoya 462 Japan. LC T178.N3.

NANJING GONGXUEYUAN XUEBAO. (HSUEH PAO). VFOAT Nan-Ching Kung Hsueh Yuan Hsueh Pao. Began in 1979. 0253-4282. Periodical. Chinese (abstracts in English). ir. 0.70. Kai Hsueh Yan, Post Office, Nanking China Mainland. Ind/Abst Comput. Control Abstr., Electr. Electron. Abstr., Sci. Abstr. Sect. A. Phys. Abstr., Chem. Abstr. LC T4. DD 605. CODEN NKHPDQ.

NASA TECH BRIEFS. See Aeronautics, Astronautics.

NATIONAL AEROSPACE STANDARDS. See Aeronautics, Astronautics.

NATIONAL INSTITUTES OF HEALTH INTERNATIONAL AWARDS FOR BIOMEDICAL RESEARCH AND RESEARCH TRAINING. See Medicine.

NATUUR EN TECHNIEK. See Biology.

NATUURKUNDE RAPPORT. Main/Corp Netherlands (Kingdom, 1815-). Commissie Modernisering Leerplan Natuurkunde. Dutch. ir. Commissie Modernisering Leerplan Natuurkunde, Staatsuitgeverij, S-Gravenhage Netherlands. LC T127.

NAUKA I TEKHNIKA. VFOAT Zinatne Un Tehnika. Began with Aug. 1960 issue. Periodical. UR. Russian. mo. $29.00. Victor Kamkin Inc, 12224 Parklawn Drive, Rockville MD 20852. Tel (301)881-5973. Ind/Abst Int. Aerosp. Abstr. LC T4.

NAUKA I TEKHNIKA ZA MLADEZHA. Periodical. Bulgarian. ir. LC T4.

NAVY TECHNICAL DISCLOSURE BULLETIN. See Naval Science, Navigation.

NDERTUESI. Periodical. AA. Albanian. bm. $3.56. Book Distribution Enterprise, rue Konferenca e Pezes, Tirana Albania. Ind/Abst Excerpta Med. LC T4.

NEC GIHO. VFOAT NEC Technical Journal. 0285-4139. JA. Japanese (with summaries in English). ir. Nippon Denki Bunka Senta, c/o Nippon Denki Bekkan, 31-ban 25-go Shiba 2-chome, Minato-ku 105 Tokyo-to Japan. Ind/Abst Math. Rev. LC TK7800.

NEMPO. Main/Corp Kagoshima-Ken Kogyo Shikenjo. JA. Japanese. an. Kagoshima-ken Kogyo Shikenjo, 7-6 Take 1-chome, Kagoshima-shi 890 Japan. Ind/Abst Chem. Abstr. LC T178.K24. CODEN KKPODU.

NEMPO. Main/Corp Fukui-ken Kogyo Shikenjo. JA. Japanese. an. Fukui-ken Kogyo Shikenjo, 920 Wakaecho, Fukui-shi 910 Japan. Ind/Abst Chem. Abstr. LC T178.F84. CODEN FKSNDL.

NETWORKS. V. 1- 1971-. 0028-3045. Periodical. US. English. qt. John Wiley & Sons Inc, 605 Third Avenue, New York NY 10158. Tel (800)526-5368. Ind/Abst Math. Rev., Comput. Control Abstr., Electr. Electron. Abstr., Sci. Abstr. Sect. A. Phys. Abstr., Comput. Rev., Phys. Abstr. LC T57.85. DD 003.05. CODEN NTWKAA.

NEUE TECHNIK. VFOAT Nouvelles Techniques, New Techniques. Began in 1959. 0028-3398. Periodical. SZ. German (French or English). mo. $50.46. Diagonal Verlags AG, Zuercherstrasse 63, 5400 Baden Switzerland. Ed O Boldinger. Ind/Abst CIS Abstr., Comput. Control Abstr., Electr. Electron. Abstr., Sci. Abstr. Sect. A. Phys. Abstr., Energy Res. Abstr., Appl. Mech. Rev. LC TJ212. CODEN NETEA8. bk rev. adv acc. Industrial electronics.

NEW & EMERGING TECHNOLOGY. VFOAT New and Emerging Technology. 0882-6382. Periodical. US. English. mo. $89.50. Midwest Technology Information Center, S-211 Della College, University Center MI 48710. Tel (517)686-9155. Ed Tom E Fallon. bk rev. Circ 1,340. Broad report on wide-ranging developments in technology, accenting research and development, entrepreneurs, venture capital, and government.

NEW ISSUES IN HIGH TECHNOLOGY. Jan./Apr. 1983-. 0738-7334. US. English. qt. American Investor Information Services, 1627 Spruce Street, Philadelphia PA 19103. LC HD9696.A3. DD 338.762138170973.

NEW SILVER TECHNOLOGY. See Metals & Metallurgy.

NEW TECHNOLOGY INDEX. See Indexes/Abstracts.

NEW USES FOR SULPHUR TECHNOLOGY SERIES. No. 1-. 0225-2643. Periodical. CN. English. ir. Free. Sulphur Development Institute of Canada, Suite 830, 202 6th Avenue South West, Calgary Alberta T2P 2W6 Canada. DD 661.63. (ctrl).

NEW ZEALAND JOURNAL OF MEDICAL LABORATORY TECHNOLOGY. See Medicine.

THE NEWCOMEN BULLETIN. See Engineering.

NEWS DIGEST - ITA. See Business - Marketing.

NEWS REVIEW ON SCIENCE AND TECHNOLOGY. See Science (General).

A NEWSLETTER FOR INVENTORS. 0270-2401. Periodical. US. English. $21.00. United Inventors and Scientists, 9017 Reseda Boulevard, Northridge CA 91324.

NEWSLETTER - NATIONAL TECHNICAL ASSOCIATION. Main/Corp National Technical Association. 0276-2471. Periodical. US. English. mo. National Technical Association Inc, 1425 H Street NW, Suite 715, Washington DC 20005. Tel (202)638-6370.

NEWSLETTER - WATERLOO RESEARCH INSTITUTE, UNIVERSITY OF WATERLOO. Main/Corp University of Waterloo. Research Institute. Mar. 1973-. 0700-3412. Periodical. CN. English. sa. Free. Waterloo Research Institute, University of Waterloo, Waterloo Ontario N2L 3G1 Canada. DD 605. (ctrl).

NEWSLINE (SPRINGFIELD, VA.). (NEWSLINE). VFOAT NTIS Newsline. No. 1 (Spring 1980)-. Periodical. US. English. National Technical Information Service, 5285 Port Royal Road, Springfield VA 22161.

NIHON GAKUJUTSU KAIGI DAI 5-BU SHUHO. Main/Corp Japan. Nihon Gakujutsu Kaigi. Dai 5-BU. JA. Japanese. ir. Nihon Gakijutsu Kaigi, 2-34 Roppongi 7 Minato-ku, Tokyo 106 Japan. LC T4.

NIHON KYOIKU KOGAKU ZASSHI. VFOAT Japan Journal of Educational Technology. Periodical. Japanese (with summaries in English). qt. Nihon Gakkai Jimu Senta Jigyobu 20-6 Mukogaoka 1, Bunkyo-ku Tokyo-to 113 Japan. LC LB1028.35.

NONTOXIC & NATURAL NEWSLETTER. VFOAT Nontoxic and Natural Newsletter. Vol. 1, No. 1 (Jan./Feb. 1985)-. 0882-2867. Periodical. US. English. $10.00. Nontoxic Lifestyles Inc, PO Box 210019, San Francisco CA 94121. DD 602.

NOTRE DAME TECHNICAL REVIEW. (THE NOTRE DAME TECHNICAL REVIEW). V. 1- Nov. 1949-. 0029-4543. Periodical. US. English. qt.

NOVATEUR. (LE NOVATEUR). Vol. 1, No 1-. 0825-0596. Periodical. CN. French. qt. Centre de Recherche Industrielle du Quebec, 333 rue Franquet, C P 9038, Ste-Foy Quebec G1V 4C7 Canada. Tel (418)659-1550. DD 331.09714. Circ 7,000. Content is designed to incite manufacturing firms to seek and use available industrial and technological information to their benefit.

NOVYE KNIGI ZA RUBEZHOM : SERIIA B. TEKHNIKA. 1957-. Periodical. UR. Russian. mo. $63.00. Victor Kamkin Inc, 12224 Parklawn Drive, Rockville MD 20852. Tel (301)881-5973. LC Z7911. *Novye Knigi za Rubezhom.*

NR TECHNOLOGY. 0307-9007. Periodical. UK. English. qt. Malaysian Rubber Bureau, 1925 K Street NW, Washington DC 20006. Tel (202)452-0544. Ind/Abst Fluidex, World Text Abstr., World Surf. Coat. Abstr., Int. Packag. Abstr., Chem. Abstr. CODEN NRRDAI.

NSDB TECHNOLOGY JOURNAL CEASED. VAT National Science Development Board Technology Journal. V. 1- Jan./Mar. 1976-. 0115-2777. Periodical. PH. English. ir. $15.00. College, Laguna 3720 Philippines. Ind/Abst Excerpta Med., Art Archaeol. Tech. Abstr., Chem. Abstr. LC T1. DD 609.599. CODEN NSTJDM.

NSIAA NEWS. VFOAT NSIAA Newsletter. VAT Nova Scotia Industrial Arts Association News. Vol. L, No. 1 (June 1982)-. 0712-6298. Periodical. CN. English. ir. $10.00. NSIAA News, c/o Nova Scotia Teachers Union, PO Box 1060, Armdale Nova Scotia B3L 4L7 Canada. DD 607.716.

NSTA TECHNOLOGY JOURNAL. VFOAT N.S.T.A. Technology Journal. Vol. 7, No. 1 (Jan./Mar. 1982)-. Periodical. English. qt. 40.00 Domestic, 24.00 Foreign. NSTA Bicutan, Taguig Metro Manila, Manila Philippines. Tel 8450961. Ed Darhl S Andaya. Ind/Abst Chem. Abstr., Bibliogr. Agric., Excerpta Med. LC T1. DD 609.599. CODEN NTJODS. bk rev. adv acc. Circ 2,000. A publication devoted to a range of interdisciplinary fields, particularly those exemplifying various relevant technologies. Serves as major medium for applied and technology researches of NSTA (Philippine's National Science and Technology Authority). *NSDB Technology Journal, 0115-2777.*

NTIS ANNUAL REPORT. Main/Corp United States. National Technical Information Service. VAT National Technical Information Service Annual Report. 0192-7094. US. English. an. National Technical Information Service, 5285 Port Royal Road, Springfield VA 22161. LC T10.63.A1. DD 353.00824.

Technology (General)

NTIS TITLE INDEX ON MICROFICHE. See Indexes/Abstracts.

NTISEARCH : CURRENT PUBLISHED SEARCHES FROM THE NTIS BIBLIOGRAPHIC DATA FILE. See Bibliographies.

NY TEKNIK. Began in 1967. Periodical. US. Swedish. LC T4.

NYENGU BOGO - NYENNAM DAIHAGGYO GONNEB GISUR NYENGUSO. (YONGU POGO). VFOAT Report. Began in 1973. 0250-3395. Periodical. English (Korean). an. Yongnam Taehakkyo Chulpanbu, 214-1 Tae-Dong Kyongsan-Up, Kyongbuk Korea. Ind/Abst Chem. Abstr. LC T4. CODEN YNTPDO.

OBZOR POLSKOI TEKHNICHESKOI LITERATURY. See Indexes/Abstracts.

OCEAN TECHNOLOGY & ENGINEERING. VAT Ocean Technology and Engineering. 0364-6424. US. English. wk. $84.00. National Technical Information Service, 5285 Port Royal Road, Springfield VA 22161. Tel (703)487-4650.

ODBORNA SKOLA. Periodical. CS. Czech. ir. Artia, PO Box 790, Praha 1 Czechoslovakia. LC T61.

ODBORNA VYCHOVA. Began in 1951. Periodical. CS. Czech. ir. Artia, PO Box 790, Praha 1 Czechoslovakia. LC T61.

OFFICE OF INSTRUCTIONAL TECHNOLOGY NEWSLETTER. (OFFICE OF INSTRUCTIONAL TECHNOLOGY NEWSLETTER : AN INFORMAL PUBLICATION OF THE STATE DEPARTMENT OF EDUCATION'S OFFICE OF INSTRUCTIONAL TECHNOLOGY). Vol. 1, No. 1 (Feb. 1984)-. 0747-0649. Periodical. US. English. qt. Office of Instructional Technology Newsletter, Drawer L, Columbia SC 29250. South Carolina Scene/ITV-Radio Newsletter, 0745-2861.

OFFICE: TECHNOLOGY AND PEOPLE. VFOAT Office: Technology & People. Vol. 1, No. 1 (Mar. 1982)-. 0167-5710. Periodical. English. qt. Elsevier Science Publishers, PO Box 211, 1000 AE Amsterdam Netherlands. Tel (020)5803 911. Ed P G W Keen. Ind/Abst Manage. Contents, Comput. Control Abstr., Electr. Electron. Abstr., Sci. Abstr. Sect. A. Phys. Abstr. bk rev. adv acc. Focuses on impacts of computer technology on people involved in office work: staff, managers, clerical workers and administrators.

OHIO RESEARCH AND DEVELOPMENT FACILITIES. 0092-9964. US. English. Ohio Research & Development Facilities, Bureau of Economic Research, 65 South Front Street, Columbus OH 43215. LC T176. DD 607.2771.

ONTARIO INDUSTRIAL ARTS BULLETIN. (THE ONTARIO INDUSTRIAL ARTS BULLETIN). Vol. 37, No. 1 (Spring 1978)-. 0227-3764. Periodical. CN. English. sa. Ontario Industrial Arts Teachers, 3726 Saint Clair Avenue East, Scarborough Ontario M1M 1T6 Canada. Ind/Abst Can. Educ. Index. DD 607.1. Bulletin, 0381-8004.

ONTARIO TECHNOLOGIST. See Engineering.

OPERATIONS RESEARCH LETTERS. (OPERATIONS RESEARCH LETTERS : A JOURNAL OF THE OPERATIONS RESEARCH SOCIETY OF AMERICA . . .). Vol. 1, No. 1 (Oct. 1981)-. 0167-6377. Periodical. English. bm. Elsevier Science Publishers, PO Box 211, 1000 AE Amsterdam Netherlands. Tel (020)5803.911. Ind/Abst Math. Rev., Eng. Index Annu., Eng. Index Mon., Eng. Index Bioeng. Abstr., Eng. Index Energy Abstr., Comput. Control Abstr., Electr. Electron. Abstr., Sci. Abstr. Sect. A. Phys. Abstr. LC T57.6.A1. DD 658.4034. CODEN ORLED5.

OSAKA KOGYO GIJUTSU SHIKENJO, KIHO. See Engineering.

OSIAGNIECIA NAUKOWO-BADAWCZE POLITECHNIKI GDANSKIEJ W . . . ROKU. Periodical. Polish. ir. 40.00. LC T173.G37. DD 670.28.

OTA PRIORITIES. Main/Corp United States. Congress. Office of Technology Assessment. VAT Office of Technology Assessment Priorities. 1979-. 0273-4818. US. English. an. Office of Technology Assessment, Congress of the United States, Washington DC 20510. NLM W1 O68.

OTOMATSYAH TAASIYATIT BE-HASHKAAH KETANAH CEASED. Vol. 3- December 1972-. Periodical. Hebrew. qt 12.00. Shevil Ha-Merets 4, Tel-Aviv Israel. LC T59.5. Otomatsyah Taasiyatit, 0303-1411; Otomatsyah Be-Haskkaah Ketanah, 0303-1403.

PAKISTAN JOURNAL OF SCIENTIFIC AND INDUSTRIAL RESEARCH. See Science (General).

PAPERS AND DISCUSSIONS - ASSOCIATION OF MINE MANAGERS OF SOUTH AFRICA. See Engineering - Mining Engineering.

PERIODICAL HOLDINGS LIST - TECHNICAL INFORMATION CENTRE. BELL-NORTHERN RESEARCH. (PERIODICAL HOLDINGS LIST - TECHNICAL INFORMATION CENTRE, BELL-NORTHERN RESEARCH). Main/Corp Bell-Northern Research. Technical Information Centre. 1975-. 0383-8633. Periodical. CN. English. Technical Information Centre, Bell-Northern Research, PO Box 3511 Station C, Ottawa Ontario K1Y 4H7 Canada. DD 016.605. Periodical Holdings, 0383-8625.

PHILIPS TECHNICAL REVIEW. V. 1- Jan. 1936-. 0031-7926. Periodical. NE. English. ir. 80.00 Domestic, 35.00 US. Philips Research Laboratories, PO Box 80000, 5600 JA Eindhoven The Netherlands. Ind/Abst Electron. Commun. Abstr. J., Eng. Index Mon., Eng. Index Bioeng. Abstr., Eng. Index Energy Abstr., Excerpta Med., Ship Abstr., GeoRef, CIS Abstr., Comput. Control Abstr., Electr. Electron. Abstr., Sci. Abstr. Sect. A. Phys. Abstr., Met. Abstr., World Alum. Abstr., Int. Aerosp. Abstr., Eng. Index Mon., Eng. Index Annu., Chem. Abstr., Nuci. Sci. Abstr., Sociol. Abstr., Lang. Lang. Behav. Abstr., Appl. Mech. Rev., Bibliogr. Index Geol. LC TK1. DD 621.305. CODEN PTREAN. (cum index). Circ 3,500. General technical and scientific journal.

PHILIPS TECHNISCH TIJDSCHRIFT. Periodical. NE. Dutch. mo. 20.00 Foreign. Philips Research Laboratories, PO Box 80000, 5600 JA Eindhoven The Netherlands. LC T4. Circ 1,900. General, technical and scientific journal; Dutch edition of Philips Technical Review.

PIANO TECHNICIAN'S JOURNAL. VFOAT Piano Technicians Journal. V. 1- Jan. 1958-. 0031-9562. Periodical. US. English. mo. $85.00. The Piano Technicians Guild, 9140 Ward Parkway, Kansas City MO 64114. Tel (816)444-3500. Ed Larry Goldsmith. Ind/Abst Music Index. LC ML1. bk rev. adv acc. Circ 4,000. A technical journal for those interested in the tuning, maintenance, repair or rebuilding of fine pianos. Tuner's Journal Piano Technician.

PILS. See Library and Information Science.

PLI KNOW HOW. See Manufacturing.

P/M TECHNOLOGY NEWSLETTER. VAT Powder Metallurgy Technology Newsletter. Vol. 11, No. 1 (Jan. 1982)-. 0734-4805. Periodical. US. English. mo. American Powder Metallurgy Institute, 105 College Road, Princeton NJ 08540. Tel (609)452-7700. P/M Technology, 0146-972X.

POLISH TECHNICAL REVIEW. 0032-3012. Periodical. English. bm. $48.00. Ruch, Wronia 33, Warsaw Poland. Ind/Abst Excerpta Med., Coal Abstr., Comput. Control Abstr., Electr. Electron. Abstr., Sci. Abstr. Sect. A. Phys. Abstr., Met. Abstr., World Alum. Abstr., Chem. Abstr. LC T26.P5. CODEN PTRWA9.

POLYTECHNISCHE BILDUNG UND ERZIEHUNG. Periodical. SZ. German. mo. Kunst & Wissen Erich Bieber, Dufourstrasse 51, CH-8008 Zurich Switzerland. Tel 011-41-1-69 44 20. LC T123. DD 607.43105. Index in last issue of volume - attached.

POPULAR MECHANICS (CHICAGO, ILL. : 1959). (POPULAR MECHANICS). Vol. 112, No. 2 (Aug. 1959)-. 0032-4558. Periodical. US. English. mo. Hearst Corporation, 224 West 57th Street, New York NY 10019, (subscription address: Communication Data Services 110 Tenth Street Des Moines IA 50309). Tel (800)247-5470. Ind/Abst Coal Abstr., Energy Inf. Abstr., Environ. Abstr., Pop. Mag. Rev., Energy Res. Abstr., Consum. Index Prod. Eval. Inf. Source, Abr. Read. Guide, Read. Guide Period. Lit. LC T1. DD 605. Popular Mechanics Magazine, 0736-993X.

POPYURA SAIENSU. See Science (General).

PORRIMER. See Chemistry.

POWTECH. Main/Conf International Powder Technology and Bulk Solids Conference. Series/Titl Powder Technology Publication Series, No. 1 etc. 1st- 1971-. UK. English. ir. Heyden & Son Ltd, 247 South 41st Street, Philadelphia PA 19104.

PRACE OSRODKA BADAWCZO-ROZWOJOWEGO PRZETWORNIKOW OBRAZU. No. 1-. 0208-9092. PL. Polish. ir. Osrodek Badawczo-Rozwojowy Przetwornikow Obrazu Ul Duga 44/50, 00-241 Warszawa Poland. Ind/Abst Comput. Control Abstr., Electr. Electron. Abstr., Sci. Abstr. Sect. A. Phys. Abstr., Chem. Abstr. CODEN PBRODW.

PRACE. RADA VI : VSEOBECNA. Main/Corp Prague. Ceske Vysoke Uceni Technicke. V. 1-. Czech (summaries in Russian, German, and English). ir. LC T4.

PRIBORY I TEHNIKA EKSPERIMENTA. (PTE. PRIBORY I TEKHNIKA EKSPERIMENTA). Jul 1956-. 0032-8162. Periodical. UR. Russian. bm. $82.50. Victor Kamkin Inc (70705), 12224 Parklawn Drive, Rockville MD 20852. Tel (301)881-5973. Ind/Abst Int. Aerosp. Abstr., Comput. Control Abstr., Electr. Electron. Abstr., Sci. Abstr. Sect. A. Phys. Abstr., Chem. Abstr., Phys. Abstr. LC QC53. CODEN PRTEAJ.

PROBABLE LEVELS OF R&D EXPENDITURES IN . . . . US. English. an. Battelle Memorial Institute, 505 King Avenue, Columbus OH 43201. Tel (614)424-7728.

PROCEEDINGS - AMERICAN INDUSTRIAL ARTS ASSOCIATION. Main/Corp American Industrial Arts Association. 19 -. US. English. an. American Association of Industrial Arts, 1914 Association Drive, Reston VA 22091. Tel (202)833-4211.

PROCEEDINGS - ELECTRIC FURNACE CONFERENCE. (PROCEEDINGS). Main/Conf Electric Furnace Conference. VFOAT Electric Furnace Proceedings. Vol. 16 (1958)-. 0096-0128. US. English. an. $60.00. Iron & Steel Society of American Institute of Mining Metallurgical and Petroleum Engineers, 410 Commonwealth Drive, PO Box 411, Warrendale PA 15086. Tel (412)776-1585. Ed Lawrence Kuhn. Ind/Abst Eng. Index, Chem. Abstr., Energy Res. Abstr., Eng. Index Mon., Eng. Index Annu., Eng. Index Energy Abstr., Eng. Index Bioeng. Abstr. CODEN EFCPAY. Circ 600. Proceedings, 0096-0136.

PROCEEDINGS - INDUSTRIAL WASTE CONFERENCE. Main/Corp Industrial Waste Conference, Purdue University, Lafayette, Ind. 1st- 1944-. US. English. an. Industrial Waste Conference, Purdue University, Ann Arbor Science Publishers, PO Box 1425, Ann Arbor MI 48106. Ind/Abst Abstr. Bull. Inst. Paper Chem. LC TP995.A1. DD 620.288.

PROCEEDINGS - INSTITUTE OF FOOD SCIENCE AND TECHNOLOGY (U.K.). See Food & Drink.

PROCEEDINGS - INTERNATIONAL CEMENT SEMINAR. (PROCEEDINGS). Main/Conf International Cement Seminar. VFOAT I.C.S. Proceedings. 0277-8211. US. English. an. $40.00. 300 West Adams Street, Chicago IL 60606. Ind/Abst Chem. Abstr. LC TP881. DD 666.9405. CODEN PCESDK.

PROCEEDINGS - IRONMAKING CONFERENCE. Main/Conf Ironmaking Conference. VFOAT Ironmaking Proceedings. 0099-6874. Periodical. US. English. an. $60.00. Iron and Steel Society of AIME, 410 Commonwealth Drive, PO Box 411, Warrendale PA 15086. Tel (412)776-1585. Ed Lawrence Kuhn. Ind/Abst Eng. Index Mon., Eng. Index Bioeng. Abstr., Eng. Index Energy Abstr., Chem. Abstr., Eng. Index Annu., Eng. Index Mon. CODEN PIRCB9. Circ 600. Proceedings - Blast Furnace, Coke Oven, and Raw Materials Committee of the Iron and Steel Division, the Metallurgical Society of the American Institute of Mining, Metallurgical and Petroleum Engineers, 0096-5138.

PROCEEDINGS - JAPAN CONGRESS ON MATERIALS RESEARCH. Main/Corp Japan Congress on Materials Research. JA. English. an. Nihon Zairyo Gakkai, 1-101 Yoshido Qzumidono-cho, Sakyo-ku Kyoto-shi Japan.

PROCEEDINGS OF ANNUAL MEETING AND TECHNICAL CONFERENCE, NUMERICAL CONTROL SOCIETY. (PROCEEDINGS OF . . . ANNUAL MEETING AND TECHNICAL CONFERENCE, NUMERICAL CONTROL

Technology (General)

SOCIETY). **Main/Corp** Numerical Control Society. Meeting and Technical Conference. **VFOAT** Annual Meeting and Technical Conference Proceedings. 19th (Apr. 18-21, 1982)-. 0078-2688. US. English. an. AIM Technical, 111 East Wacker Drive/Suite 600, Chicago IL 60601. **Ind/Abst** Eng. Index Annu., Eng. Index Mon., Eng. Index Bioeng. Abstr., Eng. Index Energy Abstr. **LC** TJ1189. **DD** 621.90230285. **CODEN** NCSPAM. *Proceedings of . . . International Technical Conference.*

PROCEEDINGS OF INNOVATION CANADA INC. 1979-. 0711-0235. CN. English. an. $65.00. Innovation Canada Inc, 533 Arbor Road, Mississauga Ontario L5G 2J6 Canada. **DD** 658.57. *Proceedings of the Innovation Canada Seminar, 0708-3416.*

PROCEEDINGS OF THE . . . PROCESS TECHNOLOGY CONFERENCE. **Main/Conf** Process Technology Conference. 1980-. Periodical. US. English. an. **Ind/Abst** Eng. Index Annu., Eng. Index Mon., Eng. Index Bioeng. Abstr., Eng. Index Energy Abstr. **CODEN** PPTCE3.

PROCEEDINGS - SYMPOSIUM ON INSTRUMENTATION FOR THE PROCESS INDUSTRIES (TEXAS A & M UNIVERSITY). (PROCEEDINGS). **Main/Conf** Annual Symposium on Instrumentation for the Process Industries. **VFOAT** Texas A & M Symposium Proceedings . . . Instrumentation for the Process Industries. 25th (1970)-. 0738-3231. US. English. an. Instrument Society of America, 67 Alexander Drive, PO Box 12277, Research Triangle Park NC 27709. **Tel** (919)549-8411. **LC** TP157. **DD** 660.281. *Proceedings.*

PRODUCTIVITY AND TECHNOLOGY. *See* Economics - Economics: Industry & Production.

PRODUTTIVITA. Yearly V. 1- Oct. 1950-. Periodical. Italian. ir. **Ind/Abst** CIS Abstr. **LC** T4.

LE PROGRES TECHNIQUE. 0397-8060. Periodical. French. ir. 120.00. Association Nationale de la Recherche Technique, 101 Avenue Raymond-Poincare, Paris 75116 France. **Ind/Abst** Energy Res. Abstr., Met. Abstr., World Alum. Abstr., Chem. Abstr. **LC** T175. **DD** 338.9. **CODEN** PRTCDG.

PROGRESS IN FILTRATION AND SEPARATION. Began with 1979. 0167-6938. English. Elsevier Science Publishing Company Inc, PO Box 1663, Grand Central Station, New York NY 10163. **Tel** (212)370-5520. **Ind/Abst** Chem. Abstr. **LC** TP156.F5. **DD** 660.28424505. **CODEN** PFSEDZ.

PROGRESS IN TECHNOLOGY. **Main/Corp** Society of Automotive Engineers. **VFOAT** Technical Progress Series. 0583-936X. Monographic Series. US. English. ir. Society of Automotive Engineer, 400 Commonwealth Drive, Warrendale PA 15096. **Tel** (412)776-4970.

PROGRESS REPORT - COAST INSTITUTE OF TECHNOLOGY. **Main/Corp** Coast Institute of Technology. English. ir. Mombosa Kenya 90424. **LC** T173.M645. **DD** 607.1167623.

PROMYSHLENNOST' ARMENII. Aug. 1958-. 0033-1163. Periodical. UR. Russian. mo. $21.50. Victor Kamkin Inc (77807), 12224 Parklawn Drive, Rockville MD 20852. **Tel** (301)881-5973. **LC** T4.

PROTECTIA MUNCII. RM. Romanian. qt. Ilexim Press Department, PO Box 1-136-1-137, Bucharest Romania. **Ind/Abst** Coal Abstr., CIS Abstr. **LC** T55.A1.

PT, PROCESTECHNIEK. (PT. PROCESTECHNIEK). **VFOAT** Procestechniek. **VAT** Polytechnisch Tijdschrift. Volume 37, No. 1 (Jan. 1982)-. 0032-4094. Periodical. NE. Dutch. mo. Stam Tijdschriften BV Postbus 235, 2280 AE Rijswijk The Netherlands. **Tel** 070 99 24 44. **Ind/Abst** Chem. Abstr., Coal Abstr., Comput. Control Abstr., Electr. Electron. Abstr., Excerpta Med., Sci. Abstr. Sect. A. Phys. Abstr. **CODEN** PTPTBP. *Polytechnisch Tijdschrift. Procestechniek.*

PUBLIC TECHNOLOGY NEWS. *See* Public Administration.

PUBLICATION OF TECHNICAL PAPERS AND PROCEEDINGS OF THE ANNUAL MEETING OF SUGAR INDUSTRY TECHNOLOGISTS, INC. **Main/Corp** Sugar Industry Technologists, Inc. 24th-1965-. 0099-9032. US. English. an. Sugar Industry Technologists, 288 Lancaster Pike, Malvera PA 19355. **Ind/Abst** Chem. Abstr., Bibliogr. Agric. **LC** TP375. **DD** 664.1205. **CODEN** PTPPAC. *Publication of Technical Papers and Proceedings of the Annual Meeting.*

PUBLICATIONS - TECHNICAL RESEARCH CENTRE OF FINLAND. (PUBLICATIONS). Began in 1981?. 0358-5069. Monographic Series. English. ir. Technical Research Centre of Finland, Vuorimiehentie 5, SF-02150 Espoo 15 Finland. **Ind/Abst** Life Sci. Collect., Chem. Abstr. **CODEN** PTRFDT. *Publication - Technical Research Centre of Finland. Materials and Processing Technology, 0355-3388; Publication - Technical Research Centre of Finland, Building and Technology and Community Development.*

PUBLIKATIONEN ZU WISSENSCHAFTLICHEN FILMEN, SEKTION TECHNISCHE WISSENSCHAFTEN, NATURWISSENSCHAFTEN. 0073-8433. German (summaries in English and French). ir. 7.00 Single Issue. Naturwissenschaften, Nonnenstieg 72 34, Wissenschaften West Germany. **Ind/Abst** Energy Res. Abstr. **LC** T65.5.M6.

PYROTECHNICA. Began with Oct. 1977. 0272-6521. Periodical. US. English. $15.00. Pyrotechnica Publications, 2302 Tower Drive, Austin TX 78703. **LC** TP300. **DD** 662.105.

QUALITY TECHNOLOGY HANDBOOK. 2d- Ed. UK. English. ir. Business Press International Ltd, Perrymount Road, Haywards Heath, West Sussex RH163BR England. *Quality Technology.*

QUALITY TODAY. Began with Feb. 1983 issue. 0264-2344. Periodical. UK. English. mo. Business Press International Ltd, Perrymount Road/Haywards Heath, West Sussex England. **Ind/Abst** Fluidex, Comput. Control Abstr., Electr. Electron. Abstr., Sci. Abstr. Sect. A. Phys. Abstr., Energy Res. Abstr., Met. Abstr., World Alum. Abstr. **CODEN** QUTODG. *Measurement and Inspection Technology.*

QUARTERLY LITERATURE REVIEW OF THE REMOTE SENSING OF NATURAL RESOURCES. 1974-. 0160-8754. Periodical. US. English. qt. $150.00. Technology Application Center, University of New Mexico, Albuquerque NM 87131. **Tel** (505)277-3622. Ed Raul Campos-Marquetti. **Ind/Abst** GeoRef. **LC** G70.4. **DD** 621.3678. **CODEN** QLRRDK. **Circ** 150. (ctrl) Documented data obtained from space, aircraft or ground-based stations relating to remote sensing sensors or remote sensing of natural resources.

QUEBEC TECHNOLOGIE. Dec./Jan. 1980-. 0711-5288. Periodical. CN. French. bm. Free. Quebec Technologie, c/o La Corporation Professionnelle des Technologues des Sciences Appliquees du Quebec, 4152 rue St-Denis, Montreal Quebec H2W 2M5 Canada. **DD** 606.0714. (ctrl). *Technicien (Corporation des Techniciens Professionnels du Quebec).*

QUEST. **VFOAT** TRW/DSSG/Quest. V. 1- Winter 1976/77-. 0149-6670. Periodical. US. English. TRN Defense and Space Systems Group, One Space Park, Redondo Beach CA 90278. **Ind/Abst** Int. Aerosp. Abstr. **LC** T1. **DD** 620.005.

R & D MANAGEMENT. V. 1- Oct. 1970-. 0033-6807. Periodical. UK. English. ty. 60.00. Basil Blackwell and Mott Ltd Journals Department, 108 Cowley Road, Oxford OX1 1JF England. **Tel** 0865 722146. Ed Sidney Eaton and Alan Pearson. **Ind/Abst** Manage. Contents, World Text Abstr., Ship Abstr., ABI/Inform, Int. Aerosp. Abstr., Comput. Control Abstr., Electr. Electron. Abstr., Sci. Abstr. Sect. A. Phys. Abstr., Manage. Market. Abstr., Electron. Pub. Abstr., Public Aff. Inf. Serv. Bull. **LC** T175.5. **DD** 658.5705. **CODEN** RDMAAW. bk rev. adv acc. **Circ** 1,000. Promotes a better understanding of the problems of managing research and development wherever they occur throughout the world.

R & D REVIEW. 0361-4689. US. English. General Electric Company, PO Box 8, Schenectady NY 12301. **Ind/Abst** Energy Inf. Abstr., Environ. Abstr. **LC** T1. **DD** 621.305.

R.A.I.R.O. RECHERCHE OPERATIONNELLE. (RAIRO : RECHERCHE OPERATIONNELLE). **VFOAT** Recherche Operationnelle, RAIRO : Operations Research. V. 11-Feb. 1977-. 0399-0559. Periodical. FR. English (French). qt. 180.00. Centrale des Revues, Dunod-Gauthier-Villars, BP 119, 93104 Montreuil Cedex France. **Ind/Abst** Math. Rev., Comput. Control Abstr., Electr. Electron. Abstr., Sci. Abstr. Sect. A. Phys. Abstr., Energy Res. Abstr. **LC** T57.6. **DD** 658.4034. **CODEN** RSROD3. *Revue Francaise d'Automatique, Informatique, Recherche Operationnelle: Recherche Operationnelle.*

R&D CONTRACTS MONTHLY. (R & D CONTRACTS MONTHLY). **VAT** Research and Development Contracts Monthly. 0033-6793.
Periodical. US. English. mo. $72.00. Government Data Publications, 1120 Connecticut Avenue Northeast, Washington DC 20036. **Tel** (718)627-0819. Ed Siegfried Lobel. **Ind/Abst** Predicasts, Funk Scott Index Corp. Ind. Each issue lists research and development, design, research engineering and prototype production contracts and is divided into three pre-sorted sections of immediately usable 100% current data.

RAPPORT D'ACTIVITE - CENTRE NATIONAL DE DOCUMENTATION SCIENTIFIQUE ET TECHNIQUE. **Main/Corp** Belgium. Centre National de Documentation Scientifique et Technique. 0069-1968. BE. French. ir. Bibliotheque Royal Albert ler, Boulevard de l'Empereur 4, 1000 Bruxelles Belgium. **Ind/Abst** GeoRef. **LC** T10.65.B4. **DD** 607.24933. **NLM** Z 699.A1 C397R. **CODEN** CDORBV.

RAPPORT D'ACTIVITE DE LA MIDIST. *See* Science (General).

RAPPORT D'ACTIVITE - INSTITUT DE RECHERCHES TECHNOLOGIQUES. **Main/Corp** Institut de Recherches Technologiques (Libreville, Gabon). 1976/77-. French. ir. Centre National de la Recherche Scientifique et Technologique Institut de Recherches Technologiques, B P 14 070 Akebe, Libreville Republique Gabonaise. **LC** T177.G23. **DD** 607.26721.

RAPPORT D'ACTIVITES SUR LES RECHERCHES A L'ENSTA. **Main/Corp** Ecole Nationale Superieure de Techniques Avancees. **VFOAT** Activites Recherche - Ecole Nationale Superieure de Techniques Avancees. French. ir. Ecole Nationale Superieure de Techniques Avancees, 32 Blvd Victor, Paris France 75015. **LC** T178.E32. **DD** 620.0072044361. *Activities Recherche - Ecole Nationale Superieure de Techniques Avancees, 0376-6268.*

RAPPORT TECHNIQUE (UNIVERSITE LAVAL. DEPARTEMENT D'INFORMATIQUE). (RAPPORT TECHNIQUE). RT/7501-. Monographic Series. CN. English (French). ir. Dep d'Informatique Faculte des Sciences et de Genie Universite Laval, Quebec Quebec G1K 7P4 Canada.

RD, RESEARCH DEVELOPMENT *CEASED.* **VFOAT** Research Development. V. 11-29, No. 2. 0034-5199. Periodical. US. English. mo. $72.00. Technical Publishing Company, 875 3rd Avenue, New York NY 10022. **Tel** (212)605-9400. **Ind/Abst** Energy Inf. Abstr., Environ. Abstr., Int. Aerosp. Abstr., Chem. Abstr., Meteorol. Geoastrophys. Abstr., Sel. Water Resour. Abstr., Electr. Electron. Abstr., Phys. Abstr., Comput. Control Abstr., Sci. Cit. Index, Abr. Ed., Bus. Period. Index, Funk Scott Index Corp. Ind., Sci. Abstr. Sect. A. Phys. Abstr. **LC** T175. **DD** 607.2. **CODEN** REDEA8. *Industrial Laboratories, 0096-1671.*

RECOGNITION TECHNOLOGIES TODAY. *See* Computers and Computer Science.

REFERATIVNYI ZHURNAL : KHIMICHESKOE, NEFTEPERERABATYVAIUSHCHEE I POLIMERNOE MASHINOSTROENIE. Began in 1970. Periodical. UR. Russian. mo. 1.04 Single Issue. Liubertsy, 10 Moskovskoi Obl, Oktiabrskii Prospekt 403, Moskva Russian SFSR. **LC** TP155.5.

REGULATORY FOCUS. V. 1, No. 1 (1981)-. Periodical. US. English. bm. $85.00. HLW Technical Regulatory Services, 287 Childs Road, Bashing Redge NJ 07920. **Tel** (201)953-2000.

RELATORIO DE ATIVIDADES - CENTRO FEDERAL DE EDUCACAO TECNOLOGICA DO PARANA. **Main/Corp** Centro Federal de Educacao Tecnologica do Parana. Portuguese. ir. **LC** T92.P35. **DD** 607.118162.

RELATORIO DE ATIVIDADES - SECRETARIA DE TECNOLOGIA INDUSTRIAL. **Main/Corp** Brazil. Secretaria de Tecnologia Industrial. BL. Portuguese. an. Superintendencia da Borracha, Av Almirante Baroso 81, 4 Andar Rio de Janeiro Brazil. **LC** T25.B8.

REPERTORIO DEL FILM INDUSTRIALE. Italian. ir. 3,000. F Angeli, Casella Postalle 4294, Milano Italy. **LC** T65.5.M6.

REPORT - INDIA (REPUBLIC). DEPT. OF SCIENCE AND TECHNOLOGY. *See* Science (General).

REPORT OF THE DEPARTMENT OF SCIENTIFIC AND INDUSTRIAL RESEARCH. *See* Science (General).

Technology (General)

REPORT ON RESEARCH AND DEVELOPMENT - GREAT BRITAIN. DEPT. OF INDUSTRY. Main/Corp Great Britain. Dept. of Industry. UK. English. 1.25 Each Copy. H M Stationery Office, Great Britain Department of Industry, PO Box 276, London SW8 5DT England. LC T177.G7. DD 338.4760941. *Report on Research and Development.*

REPORT - THE UNIVERSITY OF MAURITIUS. Main/Corp Mauritius. University. English. ir. Mauritius Printing CY, Place D Armes/ Government Printers Office, Port Louis Mauritius. LC T173.P64. DD 607.116982.

RESEARCH & DEVELOPMENT (BARRINGTON, ILL.). (RESEARCH & DEVELOPMENT). VFOAT Research and Development. Vol. 26, No. 1 (Jan. 1984)-. 0746-9179. Periodical. US. English. Free to qualified subscribers, $36.00 Others. Research & Development, Circulation Department, Box 5365, New York NY 10101. Ind/Abst Predicasts, Bus. Period. Index, Eng. Index Annu., Eng. Index Mon., Eng. Index Bioeng. Abstr., Eng. Index Energy Abstr., Fluidex, Coal Abstr., Chem. Abstr. LC T175. DD 607.2. CODEN REDEEA. (ctrl) *Industrial Research & Development, 0160-4074.*

RESEARCH AND DEVELOPMENT BULLETIN. See Science (General).

RESEARCH & DEVELOPMENT. TELEPHONE DIRECTORY. See Yearbooks, Almanacs, Directories.

RESEARCH AND INDUSTRY. V. 1- Jan. 1956-. 0034-513X. Periodical. II. English. qt. $23.00. Publishers and Information Directorate, Hillside Road, New Delhi 110012 India. Ind/Abst Eng. Index Annu., Eng. Index Mon., Eng. Index Bioeng. Abstr., Eng. Index Energy Abstr., Energy Inf. Abstr., Environ. Abstr., Energy Res. Abstr., Chem. Abstr., Bibliogr. Agric., Sci. Cit. Index, Abr. Ed., ISMEC Bull., Eng. Index. LC T1. DD 607.254. CODEN RSIDAO.

RESEARCH BULLETIN - INDIAN INSTITUTE OF TECHNOLOGY, BOMBAY. Main/Corp Indian Institute of Technology, Bombay. V. 1- 1976-. English. ir. Indian Institute of Technology, Powai 400076 India. LC T1. DD 605.

RESEARCH IN PHILOSOPHY & TECHNOLOGY. VAT Research in Philosophy and Technology. V. 1- 1978-. 0161-7249. US. English. an. $52.50. Jai Press, PO Box 1678, Greenwich CT 06836. Tel (203)661-7602. LC T14. DD 601.

RESEARCH IN PHILOSOPHY & TECHNOLOGY. SUPPLEMENT. VFOAT Research in Philosophy and Technology. 1 (1984)-. 8756-9299. US. English. $49.50. Jai Press Inc, 36 Sherwood Place/PO Box 1678, Greenwich CT 06836. Tel (203)661-7602. Ed Paul Durbin. LC T14. DD 601.

RESEARCH ON TECHNOLOGICAL INNOVATION, MANAGEMENT AND POLICY. Vol. 1 (1983)-. 0737-1071. US. English. an. $49.50. Jai Press Inc, 36 Sherwood Place PO Box 1678, Greenwich CT 06836. Tel (203)661-7602. Ed Richard Rosenbloom. LC HD45. DD 658.406305.

RESEARCH REVIEW (HARVARD UNIVERSITY. PROGRAM ON TECHNOLOGY AND SOCIETY). (RESEARCH REVIEW). No. 1-8. 0073-0823. Monographic Series. US. English. ir. Harvard University Press, 79 Garden Street, Cambridge MA 02138. Tel (617)661-3761. LC UNC. DD 600.

REUSE RECYCLE. See Conservation & Natural Resources.

REVIEW OF NEW ENERGY TECHNOLOGY. VFOAT New Energy Technology. Vol. 1, No. 1 (Apr. 1984)-. 0748-4011. Periodical. US. English. mo. $250.00 Domestic, $275.00 Foreign. Review of New Energy Technology, PO Box 609, Littleton CO 80160.

REVISTA BRASILEIRA DE TECNOLOGIA. 1- 1970-. Periodical. BL. English or Portuguese, with summaries in other languages. bm. $1.29. CNPQ/Coordenacao Editorial, Avenue West, 3N Quadra 511 Bloca A 1A, 70750 Brasilia DF Brazil. Ind/Abst Eng. Index, Appl. Mech. Rev.

RISK ANALYSIS. (RISK ANALYSIS : AN OFFICIAL PUBLICATION OF THE SOCIETY FOR RISK ANALYSIS). Vol. 1, No. 1 (March 1981)-. 0272-4332. Periodical. US. English. qt. $110.00 Domestic, $123.00 Foreign. Plenum Publishing Company, 233 Spring Street, New York NY 10013. Tel (212)620-8000. Ed Curtis Travis. Ind/Abst Eng. Index Annu., Eng. Index Mon., Eng. Index Bioeng. Abstr., Eng. Index Energy Abstr., Excerpta Med., Energy Inf. Abstr., Environ. Abstr., Comput. Control Abstr., Electr. Electron. Abstr., Sci. Abstr. Sect. A. Phys. Abstr., Energy Res. Abstr. LC T174.5. DD 658.403. NLM W1 RI285D. CODEN RIANDF. bk rev. adv acc. This journal provides a focal point for new developments in risk analysis for scientists from a wide range of disciplines. Covers topics of interest to researchers, deals with health risk engineering, math and theoretical aspects of risks.

RIVISTA DELLA STAZIONE SPERIMENTALE DEL VETRO. Vol. 1, No. 1 Jan./Feb. 1971. Periodical. IT. Italian. bm. 35.64. Stazione Sperimentale del Vetro, Via Briati 10, 30121 Mirano Venice Italy. Tel 041/739422. bk rev. adv acc Circ 2,000. (ctrl). Science and technology of silicates, properties, measurement and control, raw materials, glass furnaces and refractories, manufacturing processes, pollution, history and art, literature, abstracts, book reviews.

ROCKY MOUNTAIN HIGH TECHNOLOGY DIRECTORY. See Yearbooks, Almanacs, Directories.

RUTGERS COMPUTER & TECHNOLOGY LAW JOURNAL. See Law.

SAENGSAN KISUL YONGU. VFOAT Production Technology Research. Periodical. KO. Korean (with summaries in English). ir. Choson Taehakkyo SAengsan Kisul Yonguso 17 Pullo-dong, Tong-ku Kwangju-si Korea. LC T4.

SALT RESEARCH AND INDUSTRY. 0581-3999. Periodical. II. English. qt. 70.00 Domestic, 13.00 England, $23.00 US. Publishing & Information Directorate, Hillside Road, New Delhi 110012 India. Ed S P Ambasta and S S Nathan. Ind/Abst Chem. Abstr. CODEN SRSIBQ. bk rev. adv acc. Circ 700. Addressed specially to industrial executives. Provides information on new products, processes instruments and analytical techniques which are of direct industrial interest.

SAMS TRANSISTOR RADIO. See Engineering - Electricity, Electrical Engineering, Electronics.

SANDIA TECHNOLOGY. Main/Corp Sandia Laboratories. 0734-5879. Periodical. US. English. National Technical Information Service, US Department of Commerce, 5285 Port Royal Road, Springfield VA 22161. Ind/Abst GeoRef.

SANOP KISUL. Main/Corp Han'Guk Sanop Unhaeng. VFOAT Industry & Technology. Periodical. Korean. ir. 120 Single Issue. LC T4.

SANOP, KISUL TONGHYANG. VFOAT Survey of Industrial & Technological Development. Periodical. KO. Korean. mo. 48,000. Hanguk Sanop Kyongje Kisul Yonguwon, 206-9 Chongnyangni-dong Tongdaemun-ku, Seoul Korea. LC T4.

LE SAVOIR & I.E. ET L'ACTION. Periodical. French. ir. $14.00. Periodica, 7045 Av du Parc, Montreal 303-Quebec Canada. LC T2. DD 605.

SCHRIFTENREIHE. Main/Corp Badische Anilin- und Soda-Fabrik. Unternehmensarchiv. German. ir. LC TP7. *Schriftenreihe.*

SCHRIFTENREIHE DER TECHNISCHEN HOCHSCHULE IN WIEN. V. -4. 0344-8770. Monographic Series. German. ir. Springer Verlag, Postfach 367, Moelkerbastei 5, A-1011 Vienna Austria. Ind/Abst Chem. Abstr. CODEN STHWDT.

SCHWEISSTECHNIK. (SCHWEISSTECHNIK : ZEITSCHRIFT FUR SCHWEISSTECHNIK). VFOAT Soudure : Journal de la Soudure. No. 51, No. 1-. 0376-2181. Periodical. SZ. German (text in French or Italian). mo. Assn Suisse pour Tech Soudage, Zwingliplatz 3, 8022 Zurich Switzerland. Ind/Abst CIS Abstr., Eng. Index Annu., Eng. Index Mon., Eng. Index Bioeng. Abstr., Eng. Index Energy Abstr., Excerpta Med., Chem. Abstr. CODEN SCHWA9. *Zeitschrift fur Schweisstechnik.*

SCHWEIZERISCHE TECHNISCHE ZEITSCHRIFT. VFOAT Revue Technique Suisse, Rivista Tecnica Svizzera. 1926-. 522. Periodical. SZ. German. sm. $54.42. Schweiz Technische Zeitschrift, Weinbergstrasse 41, 8023 Zurich Switzerland. Ind/Abst Excerpta Med., Int. Aerosp. Abstr., CIS Abstr., Comput. Control Abstr., Electr. Electron. Abstr., Sci. Abstr. Sect. A. Phys. Abstr., Met. Abstr., World Alum. Abstr. LC T3. DD 605. CODEN STZTA5. *Schweizerische Techniker-Zeitung, Technik und Betrieb.*

SCIENCE & TECHNOLOGIE. See Science (General).

SCIENCE AND TECHNOLOGY. See Science (General).

SCIENCE AND TECHNOLOGY : A PURCHASE GUIDE FOR BRANCH AND PUBLIC LIBRARY. See Library and Information Science.

SCIENCE AND TECHNOLOGY : ANNUAL REPORT TO THE CONGRESS. See Science (General).

SCIENCE & TECHNOLOGY IN JAPAN. See Science (General).

SCIENCE & TECHNOLOGY QUARTERLY. See Science (General).

SCIENCE AND TECHNOLOGY RESEARCH IN PROGRESS. See Science (General).

SCIENCE, MEDICINE, AND TECHNOLOGY IN EAST ASIA. See Medicine.

SCIENCES ET TECHNIQUES. See Science (General).

SCIENCES, TECHNIQUES, INFORMATIONS CRIAC. See Science (General).

SCIENCETECH BULLETIN. Periodical. English. mo. Technology Bhawan, New Mehrauli Road, New Delhi 110029 India. LC T27.I4. DD 609.54.

SCIENTIAE. See Science (General).

SCIENTIFIC ACTIVITIES OF THE POLISH ACADEMY OF SCIENCES, INSTITUTE OF FUNDAMENTAL TECHNOLOGICAL RESEARCH. See Science (General).

SCIENTIFIC AMERICAN. See Science (General).

SCIENTIFIC AND TECHNICAL BOOKS AND SERIALS IN PRINT. See Science (General).

SCIENTIFIC AND TECHNICAL INFORMATION PROCESSING. See Science (General).

SCIENTIFIC AND TECHNICAL SOCIETIES OF CANADA. See Science (General).

SCIENTIFIC HONEYWELLER. See Science (General).

SEARCH. See Science (General).

SEKIYU GIJUTSU KYOKAISHI. VFOAT Journal of the Japanese Association of Petroleum Technologists. V. 1- Oct. 1933-. 0370-9868. Periodical. JA. abstracts in English or Japanese. bm. 68.00. Maruzen Company Ltd, PO Box 505, 100-31 Tokyo Japan. Tel 03-279-5841. Ind/Abst Coal Abstr., GeoRef, Chem. Abstr. CODEN SGKYAO. Circ 2,500. (ctrl). Report of research and monographs about petroleum technology.

SEKKO TO SEKKAI. See Chemistry.

SENSOR REVIEW. Vol. 1, No. 1 (Jan. 1981)-. 0260-2288. Periodical. UK. English. qt. $99.00. Air Science Company, PO Box 143, Corning NY 14830. Tel (607)962-5591. Ed Jack Hollingum. Ind/Abst Electron. Commun. Abstr. J., ISMEC Bull., Pollut. Abstr. Indexes, Saf. Sci. Abstr. J., Eng. Index Annu., Eng. Index Mon., Eng. Index Bioeng. Abstr., Eng. Index Energy Abstr., Comput. Control Abstr., Electr. Electron. Abstr., Sci. Abstr. Sect. A. Phys. Abstr., Chem. Abstr. CODEN SNRVDY. bk rev. adv acc. Circ 3,000. (ctrl). Coverage of international technical development and radio growth in new types of sensors and new areas of application as well as business development.

SERIE DE INVESTIGACIONES TECNICAS. Main/Corp Escuela Nacional de Agricultura. Colegio de Postgraduados. (No.12- 1969-). Periodical. Spanish. ir. *Serie de Investigaciones.*

Technology (General)

SERIE INFORMACION Y DOCUMENTACION. Main/Corp Comision Nacional de Investigacion Cientifica y Tecnologica. CL. Spanish. ir. Comisson Nacional Investment Cient, Casilla 297 V, Santiago Chile.

SEZNAM CESKOSLOVENSKYCH STATNICH A OBOROVYCH NOREM A NOREM RVHP. VFOAT Seznam Csn a on a Norem Rvhp. Czech. an. 63.00. LC T59.2.C95. *Seznam Platnych Ceskoslovenskych Statnich a Oborovych Norem.*

SEZNAM PLATNYCH CESKOSLOVENSKYCH STATNICH A OBOROVYCH NOREM. Main/Corp Czechoslovakia. Urad Pro Normalizaci a Mereni. Czech. ir. Urad Pro Normalizaci A Meveni, Vinohradska Trida 32, Praha Czechoslovakia. LC T59.2.C95. *Seznam Platnych Ceskoslovenskych Statnich Norem.*

SHINKU TANKU NEMPO. JA. Japanese. an. Zenkoku Kampo Hambai Kyoko Kumiai, c/o Okurasho Insatsukyoku, 2-4 Toranomon 2, Minato-ku 107, Tokyo Japan. LC AZ188.J3.

SILICON VALLEY. VFOAT Silicon Valley Magazine. 8756-7830. Periodical. US. English. bm. $10.00. Technoglyph Inc, PO Box 60145, Sunnyvale CA 94088. Tel (408)249-8020. Ed Norbert J Stein. DD 338. adv acc. Circ 15,000. Covers the people and products of Silicon Valley.

SILIKATTECHNIK. See Chemistry.

SIMENTU. VFOAT Cement. Periodical. Korean. qt. Hanguk Yanghoe Kongop Hyophoe, 25-5 Chungmu-ro 1-ka, Chung-ku Japan. LC TP880.K6.

SIMENTU KAGONGOP. VFOAT Cement Processing Industry. Periodical. Korean. qt. Hanguk Simentu Kagongop Hyoptong Chohap Yonhaphoe, 204-6 Nonhyon-dong Kangnam-ku, Seoul Korea. LC TP880.K6.

SIN CHEPUM, SIN KISUL. VFOAT Industrial Technology. Periodical. KO. Korean. ir. 3,000. Hanguk Kwahak Kisul Chongho Sento, 206-9 Chongyangni-dong Tongdaemun-ku, Seoul Korea. LC T4.

SKAD OSOBOWY W ROKU AKADEMICKIM . . . . Main/Corp Politechnika Odzka. PL. Polish. an. Redakcja Wydawnictw Naukowych Politechniki Odzkiej, 93-005 Odz Ul, Wolczanska 219 Poland. LC T173.L8.

SNIPS (FREDERICTON, N.B.). (SNIPS). 0710-2216. Periodical. CN. English. ty. Free. New Brunswick Teachers' Association, PO Box 752, Fredericton New Brunswick E3B 5R6 Canada. Ind/Abst Can. Educ. Index. DD 607.12715. (ctrl). *Industrial Teacher, 0710-2208.*

SOBRE LOS DERIVADOS DE LA CANA DE AZUCAR (HAVANA, CUBA : 1983). (SOBRE LOS DERIVADOS DE LA CANA DE AZUCAR). VFOAT Revista I.C.I.D.C.A. Periodical. CU. Spanish (summaries in English). ty. ICIDCA, Apartado 4026, Habina 10 Cuba. LC TP375. DD 664.11805. *Revista Sobre los Derivados de la Cana de Azucar.*

SOLID FUEL. No. 1- Apr. 5, 1966-. Periodical. UK. English. bw. LC TP315. DD 6626205.

SOVIET PROGRESS IN POLYURETHANES SERIES. US. English. ir. Technomic Publishing Company, 851 New Holland Avenue, Lancaster PA 17604. Tel (717)291-5609.

SPECULATIONS IN SCIENCE AND TECHNOLOGY. See Science (General).

SPEEDNEWS. See Aeronautics, Astronautics.

SPINOFF. 1976-. 0148-2203. US. English. an. Superintendent of Documents, US Government Printing Office, Washington DC 20402. LC T1. DD 605. *Technology Utilization Program Report, 0098-0749.*

STAHL UND EISEN. See Metals & Metallurgy.

STATE OF THE ART REPORT. Ser. 10, No. 1-. 0276-8267. Monographic Series. UK. English. ir. Pergamon Press, 395 Sawmill River Road, Elmsford NY 10523. *Infotech State of the Art Report, 0734-8487.*

STATISTIEK VAN HET BEROEPSONDERWIJS. TECHNISCH ONDERWIJS, NAUTISCH ONDERWIJS. See Statistics.

STATISTIK PENDIDIKAN ST SELURUH INDONESIA. See Statistics.

STROJNISKI VESTNIK. See Engineering - Mechanical Engineering & Machinery.

STUDIEHANDBOK. Main/Corp Stockholm. Tekniska Hogskolan. Swedish. ir. Tekniska Hogskolan, 100 44, Stockholm 70 Sweden. LC T173.S889.

SUGAR TECHNOLOGY REVIEWS. See Food & Drink.

SURVEY OF RESEARCH IN FLORIDA. Main/Corp Florida State Improvement Commission. US. English. ir. Florida State Improvement Committee, Tallahassee FL 32304. LC AZ513.F6.

SYSTEM DYNAMICS NEWSLETTER. US. English. an. $7.25. Systems Dynamic Group-MIT, Building E40-294, Cambridge MA 02139. Tel (617)253-1550.

SZABVANYOSITAS : A MAGYAR SZABVANYUGYI HIVATAL MUSZAKI TUDOMANYOS LAPJA. Periodical. Hungarian (summaries in English and Russian). mo. Magyar Szabvanyugyi Hivatal, Budapest VIII, Ulloi Ut 24 Budapest Hungary. LC T59. *Szabvanyugyu Kozlemenyek.*

SZILIKATTECHNIKA. See Chemistry.

TA-LIEN KUNG HSUEH YUAN HSUEH PAO. 0253-0031. Periodical. Chinese (abstracts in English). qt. Chung-Kuo Kuo Chi Shu Tien, PO Box 2820, Pei-Ching China. Ind/Abst Math. Rev., Comput. Control Abstr., Electr. Electron. Abstr., Sci. Abstr. Sect. A. Phys. Abstr., Chem. Abstr. LC T4. DD 605. CODEN TKHPDO.

TABLE PAR DENOMINATIONS DE MARQUES DE FABRIQUE, DE COMMERCE OU DE SERVICE. FR. French. an. 26 Bis rue de Leningrad, 75800 Paris Cedex 08 France. LC T271.V1. DD 602.75. *Bulletin Officiel de la Propriete Industrielle. Table par Denominations de Marques de Fabrique, de Commerce ou de Service.*

TAEHAN SANOP KONGHAKHOE CHI. See Engineering.

TAIKABUTSU OVERSEAS. Vol. 1, No. 1 (Apr. 1981)-. 0285-0028. Periodical. English. qt. 40,000. Technical Association of Refractories, 1-11-7 Toranomon, Minato-ku 105, Tokyo Japan. Tel 03-508-0051. Ed Ichiro Isshibashi. Ind/Abst Coal Abstr., Chem. Abstr., Met. Abstr., World Alum. Abstr. CODEN TAOVD7. adv acc. Circ 300. Discusses Japan's refractory and growth of technology.

TAIYUAN GONGXUEYUAN XUEBAO. (TAI-YUAN KUNG HSUEH YUAN HSUEH PAO). VFOAT Journal of Taiyuan Institute of Technology. 0253-2387. Periodical. Chinese (with abstracts in English, 1982). qt. 0.50. Post Office Tai-Yuan China. Ind/Abst Chem. Abstr. LC T4. DD 650. CODEN TGXUDN.

TAP CHI KHOA HOC KY THUAT. Periodical. Vietnamese. ir. Vien Khoa Hoc Vietnam, 70 Tran Hung Dao, Ha-Noi Vietnam. LC T4. *Khoa Hoc Ky Thuat.*

TECH NOTES. TESTING & INSTRUMENTATION. VFOAT Testing & Instrumentation. Periodical. US. English. mo. National Technical Information Service, Springfield VA 22161.

TECH TALK (CAMBRIDGE, MASS.). (TECH TALK). Periodical. US. English. ir. $15.00. Tech Talk, c/o Business Manager, Massachusetts Institute of Technology/Room 5-113, Cambridge MA 02139.

TECHNICA. Began in 1952. Periodical. German. bw. Ind/Abst Excerpta Med., Ship Abstr., Comput. Control Abstr., Electr. Electron. Abstr., Sci. Abstr. Sect. A. Phys. Abstr., CIS Abstr., Energy Res. Abstr., Met. Abstr., World Alum. Abstr. LC T4. CODEN TCHNAR.

TECHNICAL AND SPECIALISED PERIODICALS PUBLISHED IN BRITAIN. See Bibliographies.

TECHNICAL BOOKS & MONOGRAPHS. See Bibliographies.

TECHNICAL BULLETIN (EGGS AUTHORITY). (TECHNICAL BULLETIN). Began in 1977. 0263-5178. UK. English.

TECHNICAL COMMUNICATION. 0049-3155. Periodical. US. English. qt. Technical Communication, PO Box 64025, Baltimore MD 21264. Tel (301)528-4105. Ind/Abst Eng. Index Mon., Eng. Index Bioeng. Abstr., Eng. Index Energy Abstr., Int. Aerosp. Abstr., Libr. Inf. Sci. Abstr., Bus. Period. Index, Ref. Source, Eng. Index Annu., Print. Abstr. LC T11. DD 808.066602105. CODEN TLCMBT. *Technical Communications, 0049-3155.*

TECHNICAL EDUCATION NEWS. V. 1- Aug. 1941-. 0146-0137. Periodical. US. English. ir. Free to Educators. Gregg/McGraw-Hill, Princeton Road, Hightstown NJ 08520. Ind/Abst Curr. Index J. Educ. LC T61. DD 607.

TECHNICAL EDUCATION REPORTER. V. 1- May/June 1974-. 0095-6317. Periodical. US. English. bm. $70.00. Technical Education Research Centers, 44 Battle Street, Cambridge MA 02138. LC T61. DD 607.

TECHNICAL INSIGHTS ANNUAL REPORT ON GENETIC TECHNOLOGY. VFOAT Annual Report on Genetic Technology. 1983. . .1984-. 0741-3661. US. English. an. $230.00. Technical Insights Inc, POB 1304, Fort Lee NJ 07024. LC TP248.6. DD 660.6.

TECHNICAL NEWS - PERKIN-ELMER CORPORATION. (TECHNICAL NEWS). 0736-6965. Periodical. US. English. qt. Editorial Office Optical Group, 100 Wooster Heights, Danbury CT 06810. Ind/Abst Comput. Control Abstr., Electr. Electron. Abstr., Sci. Abstr. Sect. A. Phys. Abstr., Chem. Abstr., Met. Abstr., World Alum. Abstr. CODEN TNPEDI.

TECHNICAL PUBLICATIONS (NEW ZEALAND. WAIKATO VALLEY AUTHORITY). (TECHNICAL PUBLICATIONS). 1 (Feb. 1979)-. Monographic Series. English. ir.

TECHNICAL SERIES (INTERGOVERNMENTAL OCEANOGRAPHIC COMMISSION). (TECHNICAL SERIES). 1-. 0074-1175. Monographic Series. US. English. UNIPUB, PO Box 1222, Ann Arbor MI 48106. Tel (212)764-2791.

TECHNICAL SERVICES QUARTERLY. Vol. 1, Nos. 1/2 (Fall/Winter 1983)-. 0731-7131. Periodical. US. English. qt. $60.00. Haworth Press, 28 East 22nd Street, New York NY 10010. Tel (212)228-2800. Ed Gary Pitkin. LC Z688.5. DD 025.0202854. adv acc. Circ 544. A journal devoted to helping the technical services professional and paraprofessional be informed of current developments and future trends.

TECHNICAL TRANSLATION BULLETIN. V. 7- 1960 or 1961-. Periodical. UK. English. ty $39.00. Learned Information Inc, 143 Old Marlton Pike, Medford NJ 08055. Tel (609)654-6266. Ind/Abst Lang. Teach. *Engineering Translator's Bulletin.*

TECHNICIAN EDUCATION YEARBOOK. See Yearbooks, Almanacs, Directories.

TECHNIK. (DIE TECHNIK). Vol. 1-. 0040-1099. Periodical. GW. German. mo. Kunst & Wissen Erich Bieber, Dufourstrasse 51, CH-8008 Zurich Switzerland. Ind/Abst CIS Abstr., Energy Res. Abstr., Excerpta Med. LC T3. DD 605.

TECHNIK REPORT. Sept. 1974-. Periodical. AU. German. ir. Verlag Technik-Report, Gudrunstrasse 121, 1100 Wien Austria. LC T3. DD 605.

TECHNIK UND GESELLSCHAFT (FRANKFURT AM MAIN, GERMANY). (TECHNIK UND GESELLSCHAFT). Year Book 1-. 0723-0664. GW. German. an. Campus Verlag, Myliusstrasse 15, 6000 Frankfurt I West Germany.

TECHNIKA CHRONIKA. Year 1- (No. 1-). Periodical. GR. Greek, Modern. mo. $30.00. Technical Chamber of Greece, Rue Karageorgi Servias 4, Athens 125 Greece. Ind/Abst Comput. Control Abstr., Electr. Electron. Abstr., Sci. Abstr. Sect. A. Phys. Abstr., Energy Res. Abstr., Phys. Abstr. LC T4. CODEN TECHAW.

TECHNIQUE MODERNE. (LA TECHNIQUE MODERNE). 1.- Year. 0040-1250. Periodical. FR. French. bm. $87.81. Sirpe Editeur, 76 rue de Rivoli, 75004 Paris France. Tel 278 72 20. Ind/Abst Excerpta Med., Coal Abstr., Int. Aerosp. Abstr., Comput. Control Abstr., Electr. Electron. Abstr., Sci. Abstr. Sect. A. Phys. Abstr., Energy Res. Abstr., Chem.

Technology (General)

Abstr., Met. Abstr., World Alum. Abstr., Phys. Abstr. LC T2. CODEN TEMDA2. bk rev. adv acc. Circ 3,000. (ctrl). Technical progresses for industry.

TECHNISCH-WISSENSCHAFTLICHE ABHANDLUNGEN DER OSRAM-GESELLSCHAFT. See Science (General).

TECHNISCHE FORTSCHRITTSBERICHTE. GE. German. ir. Deutscher Buch Export-Import, Leninstrasse 16, DDR-701 Leipzig East Germany.

TECHNISCHE GEMEINSCHAFT. Began with Oct. 1953 issue. Periodical. German. mo. Ind/Abst Coal Abstr. LC T3.

TECHNISCHE MITTEILUNGEN. Main/Corp Switzerland. Generaldirektion der Post-, Telegraphen und Telephon-Verwaltung. **VFOAT** Bulletin Technique, Bollettino Tecnico. Vol. 1- Feb. 1923-. GW. German. mo. Vulkan-Verlag, Dr W Classen Pstfch 103962 Hollestrasse 1G, D-4300 Essen 1 West Germany. Tel 0201/22 18 15. Ed Ing E Steinmetz. Ind/Abst Comput. Control Abstr., Electr. Electron. Abstr., Sci. Abstr. Sect. A. Phys. Abstr., Met. Abstr., World Alum. Abstr. LC TK4. CODEN TMPTAJ. bk rev. adv acc. Circ 2,800. Actual information from industry, economy and science.

TECHNISCHER JAHRESBERICHT. Main/Corp Berufsgenossenschaft der Feinmechanik und Elektrotechnik. GW. German. ir. 5 Koln 51 Oberlander Ufer 130, Koln W Germany. LC T55.A1.

TECHNOCRAT. See Engineering.

TECHNOLOGICAL FORECASTING AND SOCIAL CHANGE. V. 2- 1970-. 0040-1625. Periodical. US. English. ir. $164.00. Elsevier Science Publishing Company Inc, PO Box 1663, Grand Central Station, New York NY 10163. Tel (212)370-5520. Ind/Abst Eng. Index, Eng. Index Mon., Int. Aerosp. Abstr. CODEN TFSCB3. *Technological Forecasting.*

TECHNOLOGUE. (LE TECHNOLOGUE). V. 4, No. 1, (April 1984)-. 0825-5172. Periodical. CN. French. mo. Corporation Professionnelle des Technologues des Sciences Appliquees du Quebec, 4152 rue St-Denis, Montreal Quebec H2W 2M5 Canada. DD 606.0714. *Bulletin d'Information (Corporation Professionnelle des Technologues des Sciences Appliquees du Quebec), 0711-530X.*

TECHNOLOGY AND CULTURE. V. 1- Winter 1959-. 0040-165X. Periodical. US. English. qt. $48.00. University of Chicago Press, PO Box 37005, Chicago IL 60637. Tel (312)753-3347. Ind/Abst Am. Hist. Life, Hist. Abstr., Part A, Mod. Hist. Abstr., Hist. Abst., Part B, Twent. Century Abstr., Excerpta Med., Sociol. Abstr., Soc. Welf. Soc. Plan./Policy Soc. Dev., Int. Aerosp. Abstr., Art Archaeol. Tech. Abstr., Writ. Am. Hist., Soc. Sci. Index, Energy Inf. Abstr., Environ. Abstr., Lang. Lang. Behav. Abstr., Soc. Sci. Citation Index. LC T1. NLM W1 TE211. Available on microfilm from University Microfilms.

TECHNOLOGY ASSESSMENT. V. 1- 1972-. 0092-2234. Periodical. US. English. Gordon & Breach, 440 Park Avenue South, New York NY 10016. LC T174.5. DD 301.243.

TECHNOLOGY ASSESSMENT & FORECAST. VAT Technology Assessment and Forecast. Began with 5th, Aug. 1975. 0364-9105. US. English. Superintendent of Documents, US Government Printing Office, Washington DC 20402. LC T223.J4. DD 608.773. *Technology Assessment and Forecast, 0364-9105.*

TECHNOLOGY (BOCA RATON, FLA.). (TECHNOLOGY). Series/Titl Social Issues Resources Series. V. 1, Article 1-. 0273-2580. US. English. an. Social Issues Resources Series Inc, PO Box 2507, Boca Raton FL 33432. Ed E C Goldstein. LC T14.5. DD 303.483.

TECHNOLOGY BOOK GUIDE. Series/Titl Computext Book Guide Series. 1974-. 0091-7885. US. English. an. G K Hall, 70 Lincoln Street, Boston MA 02111. LC Z7913, T45. DD 016.6.

TECHNOLOGY (BOULDER, COLO.). (TECHNOLOGY). Vol. 1, No. 1 (Nov./Dec. 1981)-. 0276-8259. Periodical. US. English. bm. $24.00 Domestic, $28.00 Foreign. Technology, PO Box 2528, Boulder CO 80321. Ind/Abst Abstr. Bull. Inst. Paper Chem., Energy Inf. Abstr., Environ. Abstr., Int. Aerosp. Abstr., Predicasts. LC T1. DD 605.

TECHNOLOGY EXCHANGE BULLETIN. V. 1- Oct. 1978-. 0163-2698. Periodical. US. English. mo. $24.00 Domestic, $30.00 Foreign. Institute for Invention and Innovation, PO Box 436, Arlington MA 02174.

TECHNOLOGY FOR LARGE SPACE SYSTEMS. SUPPLEMENT. Series/Titl NASA SP. 1 (July 1979)-. 0278-5765. US. English. National Technical Information Service, Springfield VA 22161. LC Z5064.S8, T L875. DD 016.62944.

TECHNOLOGY FORECASTS AND TECHNOLOGY SURVEYS. Began publication in 1968?. 0886-0890. Periodical. US. English. mo. PWG Publications, 205 South Beverly Drive, Beverly Hills CA 90212. Ind/Abst Predicasts. DD 600.

TECHNOLOGY IN SOCIETY. V. 1- Spring 1979-. 0160-791X. Periodical. US. English. qt. $73.00. Pergamon Press, Maxwell House Fairview Park, Elmsford NY 10523. Ind/Abst Excerpta Med., Sociol. Abstr., Soc. Welf. Soc. Plan./Policy Soc. Dev., Energy Inf. Abstr., Environ. Abstr., Int. Aerosp. Abstr., Energy Res. Abstr. LC T14.5. DD 303.48305. Available in microfilm and microfiche.

TECHNOLOGY IRELAND. V. 1- Apr. 1969-. 0040-1676. Periodical. IE. English. mo. Inst for Industrial Research & Standards, Ballymun Road Glasnevin, Dublin 9 Ireland. Ind/Abst Excerpta Med., Coal Abstr., Int. Packag. Abstr., Electron. Pub. Abstr. LC T1. DD 605.

TECHNOLOGY NETWORK (DENVER, COLO.). (TECHNOLOGY NETWORK). Vol. 1, No. 1 (Sept. 1983)-. 0740-252X. Periodical. US. English. wk. Technology Network, PO Box 5400 TA, Denver CO 80217-5400.

TECHNOLOGY NOTEBOOK (TECHNICAL UNIVERSITY OF NOVA SCOTIA). (TECHNOLOGY NOTEBOOK). Vol. 1, No. 1 (Oct. 1, 1982)-. 0824-0353. Periodical. CN. English. wk. $50.00. Technical University of Nova Scotia, PO Box 1000, Halifax Nova Scotia B3J 2X4 Canada. DD 609.71.

TECHNOLOGY NY NEWSLETTER. VFOAT Technology N.Y. Newsletter. Vol. 1, No. 1 (May 1983)-. 0732-7382. Periodical. US. English. mo. $100.00. Technology New York, Rensselaer Technology Park, 250 Jordan Road. Tel (518)283-8444. Ed Joseph Phillips. Covers high technology developments in business, the public sector and academia, focusing principally on New York state in its coverage.

TECHNOLOGY REIMBURSEMENT REPORTS. (TECHNOLOGY REIMBURSEMENT REPORTS : TRR). VFOAT TRR. Vol. 1, No. 1 (Feb. 1, 1985)-. 0882-2611. Periodical. US. English. wk. $250.00. F-D-C Reports, 5550 Friendship Boulevard Suite 1, Chevy Chase MD 20815. Ind/Abst Pharm. News Index. DD 338.

TECHNOLOGY REPORTS OF THE OSAKA UNIVERSITY. Main/Corp Osaka Daigaku. Kogakubu. V. 1- 1951-. 0030-6177. Periodical. English. ir. Ind/Abst Math. Rev., Electron. Commun. Abstr. J., ISMEC Bull., Pollut. Abstr. Indexes, Saf. Sci. Abstr. J., Eng. Index Annu., Eng. Index Mon., Eng. Index Bioeng. Abstr., Eng. Index Energy Abstr., Fluidex, Coal Abstr., Int. Aerosp. Abstr., Comput. Control Abstr., Electr. Electron. Abstr., Sci. Abstr. Sect. A. Phys. Abstr., Chem. Abstr., Met. Abstr., World Alum. Abstr. CODEN TROUAI.

THE TECHNOLOGY REPORTS OF THE TOHOKU UNIVERSITY. LIST OF OTHER PUBLICATIONS. See Bibliographies.

TECHNOLOGY REVIEW. V. 1- Jan. 1899-. 0040-1692. Periodical. US. English. ir. $27.00. PO Box 978, Farmingdale NY 11737. Tel (617)253-8292. Ed John I Mattill. Ind/Abst Comput. Rev., Guide Soc. Sci. Relig. Period. Lit., Mag. Index, Eng. Index, Bibliogr. Index Geol., Excerpta Med., Coal Abstr., ABI/Inform, Appl. Sci. Technol. Index, Book Rev. Index, Energy Inf. Abstr., Environ. Abstr., Energy Res. Abstr., Chem. Abstr., Hospit. Lit. Index, Int. Aerosp. Abstr., Nuci. Sci. Abstr., Predicasts, Read. Guide Period. Lit., Sel. Water Resour. Abstr., GeoRef, Public Aff. Inf. Serv. Bull., Pollut. Abstr. Indexes, Funk Scott Index Corp. Ind., Sci. Cit. Index, Abr. Ed., Eng. Index Annu. LC T171. NLM W1 TE211M. CODEN TEREAU. bk rev. adv acc. Circ 75,000. The national magazine of technology edited at the Massachusetts Institute of Technology. It looks at the potential and problems of today's rapid technological advancements.

TECHNOLOGY TODAY. V. 1- Sept./Oct. 1976 -. 0148-3595. Periodical. US. English. bm. $6.00. Enland Publications, PO Box 341, Canyon TX 79015. LC T73. DD 607.1173.

TECHNOLOGY TODAY (ONTARIO RESEARCH FOUNDATION). (TECHNOLOGY TODAY). 0712-9467. Periodical. CN. English. qt. Ontario Research Foundation, Sheridan Park Research Community, Mississauga Ontario L5K 1B3 Canada. DD 609.713. *Ontario Research Newsletter.*

TECHNOLOGY UPDATE. Vol. 38, No. 21 (May 29, 1982). 0732-5533. Periodical. US. English. wk. $190.00 US, $215.00 Foreign. Predicasts Inc, 11001 Cedar Avenue, Cleveland OH 44106. Tel (216)795-3000. Ed David R Burwasser. NLM ZQ 1 T24. Selected journal abstracts regarding new technology, new processes and applications, impacts on society, research management, technical education, technology transfer, embargo and regulation. *Technical Survey (Newark, N.J.), 0040-1005.*

TECHNOLOGY UTILIZATION PROGRAM REPORT. Series/Titl NASA SP. 1981. 0098-0749. US. English. bm. $110.00. Technology Utilization, 7206 Ben Franklin Building, 1200 Pennsylvania Avenue, Washington DC 20044. Tel (703)276-9426. Ed Charles Rechnagel. LC T1. DD 605. Circ 3,500. (ctrl). The magazine makes availabe inventions and abstracts from government and university research laboratories for transfer to US industry.

TECNOLOGIA Y GESTION. VFOAT Iram, Tecnologia y Gestion. Periodical. AG. Spanish. qt. Instituto Argentino de Racionalizacion de Materiales Chile, 1192 Buenos Aires Argentina. LC TA401. *Iram, Tecnologia y Gestion.*

TEHNIKA. Began 1946. 0040-2176. Periodical. Serbo-Croatian -R (summaries in English, French, German and Russian). mo. Jugoslovenska Knjica, PO Box 36, Beograd Yuguslavia. Ind/Abst Coal Abstr., Comput. Control Abstr., Electr. Electron. Abstr., Sci. Abstr. Sect. A. Phys. Abstr., Energy Res. Abstr., Met. Abstr., World Alum. Abstr. CODEN TEHBA5.

TEHNIKA I NAUKA. (TEKHNIKA I NAUKA). Began in 1973. 0321-3269. Periodical. UR. Russian. mo. $30.50. Victor Kamkin Inc (70983), 12224 Parklawn Drive, Rockville MD 20852. Tel (301)881-5973. Ind/Abst Int. Aerosp. Abstr. LC T4. *Nauchno-Tekhnicheskie Obshchestva.*

TEKNISK TIDSKRIFT-NY TEKNIK. VFOAT NY Teknik-Teknisk Tidskrift. Began with issue for Feb. 22, 1979. Periodical. SW. Swedish. ir. 200.00. Ingenjors Forlaget, Box 27315, 102 54 Stockholm Sweden. Ind/Abst Energy Res. Abstr., Int. Packag. Abstr. LC T4. *NY Teknik, Teknisk Tidskrift.*

TEKNOLOGI. V. 1- Apr. 1977-. Periodical. English (Malay). ir. Universiti Teknologi Malaysia, Jl Gurney, Kuala Lumpur Malaysia. LC T1.

TEMAT. Periodical. PL. Polish. ir. RSW Prasa-Ksiazka-Ruch Centrala Kolporta Zu Prasy I Wydawnictw, Ulica Towarowa 28, 00-958 Warszawa Poland. LC T212. *Wynalazczosci Racjonalizacja.*

TEORETICHESKIE VOPROSY AVTOMATIZIROVANNYKH SISTEM UPRAVLENIIA. Main/Corp Riga. Universitate. Ekonomiskas Kibernetikas Katedra. Vol. 1- 1973-. UR. Russian. 0.70 Each Issue. Redktsionno-Izdatelskii Otdel LGU, 50 Bulv Rainisa 19 50, Riga Latvian USSR. LC T58.6.

TI, TECHNICAL INFORMATION FOR INDUSTRY. Main/Corp South African Council for Scientific and Industrial Research. V. 1- Jan. 1963-. Periodical. SA. English. mo. CSIR-Publishing Division, PO Box 395, Pretoria 0001 South Africa. Tel 86-9211. Ind/Abst Energy Res. Abstr.

TIEN HSIN CHI SHU. VFOAT Telecoms Technical Quarterly. V. 1, (August 1981)-. Periodical. CH. Chinese (with summary in English). qt. Directorate General of Telecommunications, 31 Aikuo East Road, Taipei Taiwan 106 Republic of China. LC TK5101.A1. DD 621.3805.

TOHOKU KOGYO GIJUTSU SHIKENJO HOKOKU. VFOAT Reports of the Government Industrial Research Institute, Tohoku. No. 1-. Japanese (with summaries in English). ir. Tohoku Kogyo Gijutsu Shikenjo, Nigatake Haranomachi (983), Sendai Japan. Ind/Abst Chem. Abstr. LC T177.J3. CODEN TGSHDR.

TOKAI DAIGAKU KIYO : KOGAKUBU. VFOAT Proceedings of the Faculty of Engineering of Tokai University. 1958-. Periodical. JA. Japanese or English, with abstracts in English. ir. c/o Tokai Building, 27-4 Shinjuku 3, Shinjuku-Ku 160 Tokyo Japan. LC T4.

Technology (General)

TOKYO TORITSU KOGYO GIJUTSU SENTA KENKYU HOKOKU. VFOAT Report of the Tokyo Metropolitan Industrial Technic Institute. Periodical. JA. Japanese (abstracts in English). ir. Tokyo Toritsu Kogyo Gijutsu Senta, 13-10 Nishigaoka 3, Kita-Ku, Tokyo-To Japan. **Ind/Abst** Chem. Abstr. **CODEN** TKGHDT.

TOLEDO TECHNICAL TOPICS. (TOLEDO TECHNICAL TOPICS : OFFICIAL PUBLICATION OF TOLEDO TECHNICAL COUNCIL). Vol. 20, No. 8 (July-August 1966)-. 0745-9297. Periodical. US. English. qt. Toledo Technical Topics, 2801 West Bancroft, Toledo OH 43606. *Toledo Technical Journal.*

TOLUENE XYLENES ANNUAL. See Chemistry.

TOPICS IN ENZYME AND FERMENTATION BIOTECHNOLOGY. V. 1- 1977-. 0140-0835. UK. English. an. John Wiley and Sons Ltd, 605 Third Avenue, New York NY 10158. **Ind/Abst** Life Sci. Collect., Chem. Abstr., Bibliogr. Agric. **LC** TP248.3. **DD** 660.63. **NLM** W1 TO539LP. **CODEN** TEFBDW.

TOTTORI-KEN KOGYO SHIKENJO KENKYU HOKOKU. No. 1 (1979)-. JA. Japanese. ir. Tottori-Ken Kogyo Shikenjo 390, Akisato Tottori 680 Japan. **LC** T178.T67.

TRADE SHOW CONVENTION GUIDE. VFOAT Tradeshow Convention Guide. US. English. an. $55.00. 1515 Broadway, New York NY 10036.

TRADESHOW. (TRADESHOW 150). VFOAT Annual Edition of the Tradeshow .... 0145-5559. US. English. an. $15.00. 1605 Cahuenga Boulevard, Los Angeles CA 90028. **LC** T391. **DD** 659.152.

TRANET : TRANSNATIONAL NETWORK FOR APPROPRIATE/ ALTERNATIVE TECHNOLOGIES. Began in 1976. Periodical. US. English. qt. $25.00. Tranet, PO Box 567, Rangeley ME 049707. **Tel** (217)864-2252. Ed Dan Behrman. bk rev. **Circ** 2,500. (ctrl). A network of appropriate technology and local self-reliance. Exchange with one another thru this newsletter. Directory going to grass-roots organizations in 124 countries.

TRANSACTIONS - NEWCOMEN SOCIETY FOR THE STUDY OF THE HISTORY OF ENGINEERING AND TECHNOLOGY. See Engineering.

TRANSACTIONS OF SHASE JAPAN. **Main/Corp** Kuki Chowa Eisei Kogakkai. Began in 1963. 0081-1610. JA. English. qt. 120.00. Maruzen Company Ltd, PO Box 5050, 100-31 Tokyo Japan. **Tel** (03)363-8261. Ed Ikuo Sato. **Ind/Abst** Appl. Mech. Rev., Eng. Index. **LC** TH7201. adv acc. **Circ** 20,000. (ctrl). The journal about air conditioning systems, water supply and drainage, hygienic engineering.

TRANSACTIONS OF THE INSTITUTE OF METAL FINISHING. See Metals & Metallurgy.

TREATISE ON ADHESION AND ADHESIVES. V. 1- 1967-. 0082-6235. US. English. ir. Marcel Dekker, 270 Madison Avenue, New York NY 10016. **Tel** (212)696-9000. Ed R L Patrick. **LC** TP968. **DD** 668.3. This is an ongoing series. Each title in the series has a different subject.

TREND. Began in 1969. Periodical. Czech (Some summaries in English and Russian). ir. 120.00. Ustredi Vedeckych Technickych A Ekonomickych, Konviktska 5, Praha Czechoslovakia. **LC** T174.

TRENDS IN TECHNOLOGY. Periodical. English. ir. Economic Development Foundation, 6764 Ayala Avenue Makati Rizal/PO Box 1896, Manila Philippines. **LC** TR1. **DD** 605.

TRUDY TSNIITMASH. **Main/Corp** Tsentralnyi Nauchno-Issledovatelskii Institut Tekhnologii I Mashinostroeniia. **VAT** Trudy Tsentralnogo Nauchno-Issledovatelskogo Institut Tekhnologii Mashinostroeniia. UR. Russian. 1.80 Each Issue. **LC** T4. *Trudy.*

TSUSHO SANGYOSHO KOGYO GIJUTSUIN SHIKOKU KOGYO GIJUTSU SHIKENJO YORAN. **Main/ Corp** Sikoku Kogyo Gizyutu Sikensyo. JA. Japanese. ir. Shikoku Kogyo Gijutsu Shikenjo, 3-3 Hananomiyacho 2-chome (760), Takamatsu Japan. **LC** T178.S55.

TUBS IN ZAHLEN. **Main/Corp** Technische Universitat Carolo-Wilhelmina. Planungs- und Informationszentrum. **VAT** Technische Universitat Braunschweig in Zahlen. German. ir. Technische Universitat Braunschweig in Zahlen, Abt - Jerusalem Str 6, Braunschweig West Germany. **LC** T173.B7997.

TUTKIMUKSIA - VALTION TEKNILLINEN TUTKIMUSKESKUS. (TUTKIMUKSIA). VFOAT Forskningsrapporter, Research Reports, Forskningrapporter - Statens Tekniska Forskningscentral. 1/1981-. 0358-5077. Monographic Series. English. ir. Valtion Teknillinen Tutkimuskeskus, Elintarvikelaboratorio, Biologinkuja 1, 02150 Espoo 15 Finland. **Ind/Abst** Biol. Abstr., Comput. Control Abstr., Electr. Electron. Abstr., Sci. Abstr. Sect. A. Phys. Abstr., Chem. Abstr. **LC** UNC. **CODEN** TUTUDX.

UNITED STATES CONVENTIONS AND TRADE SHOWS. US. English. US Department of Commerce, Washington DC 20402. **LC** T391. **DD** 607.3473.

U.S. / R&D. VFOAT GDP'S U.S. / R&D. June 1975-. Periodical. US. English. mo. $72.00. Government Data Publications, 1120 Connecticut Avenue NW, Washington DC 20036. **Tel** (718)627-0819. Ed Siegfried Lobel. bk rev. Contains articles on studies, contracts, trends, developments, special events, depth reports, analyses, political currents, new products and techniques, meetings and exclusives.

UNITED TECHNOLOGIES MAGAZINE. V. 1- Winter 1980-. Periodical. US. English. United Technologies Corporation, United Technologies Building, Hartford CT 06101. *United Technologies Bee Hive.*

UPDATE (ELIZABETHTOWN, PA.). See Aeronautics, Astronautics.

UPRAVLENIE BOLSHIMI SISTEMAMI : BIBLIOGRAFICHESKII UKAZATEL LITERATURY : OTECHESTVENNAIA LITERATURA. See Indexes/Abstracts.

URETHANE PLASTICS AND PRODUCTS. See Plastics.

UURIMUSI. **Main/Corp** Tallinna Polutehniline Instituut. Poliitilise Okonoomia Kateeder. UR. Estonian. **LC** T4.

VENTURE PRODUCT NEWS. VFOAT Venture/Product News. 0738-7199. Periodical. US. English. mo. $250.00. Genium Publishing Company, 1145 Catalyn Street, Schenectady NY 12303. **Tel** (518)377-8854. Ed Robert A Roy. bk rev. Newsletter lists approximately 80 products and processes available to others via licensing from US and foreign industry, universities, research and development labs, government agencies, individuals and other sources.

VIDEOTEX WORLD. See Computers and Computer Science.

VITA NEWS. **VAT** Volunteers in Technical Assistance News. 1977. Periodical. US. English. qt. $15.00. Volunteers in Technical Assistance, 1815 Lynn Street/Suite 200, Arlington VA 22209. **Tel** (703)276-1800. Ed Margaret Crouch. bk rev. adv acc. **Circ** 10,000. (ctrl). Offers information and assistance aimed at helping people and groups select and implement technologies appropriate to their situations.

VOLUND. 1953-. 0048-2277. Norwegian. an. **LC** T183.

VORTRAGE - RHEINISCH-WESTFALISCHE AKADEMIE DER WISSENSCHAFTEN, N, NATUR-, INGENIEUR- UND WIRTSCHAFTSWISSENSCHAFTEN. See Science (General).

VYNALEZY A ZLEPSOVACI NAVRHY. Periodical. CS. Czech. mo. 72.00. Postovni Novinova Sluzba, Ustredni Expedice Tisku, Odd Vyvoz Tisku, Jindrisska 14, Praha 1 Czechoslovakia. **LC** T26.C9.

WASHINGTON REMOTE SENSING LETTER. See Science (General).

WATERLINES. **VAT** Water Lines. 0262-8104. Periodical. UK. English. qt. Intermediate Technology Publications Ltd, 9 King Street, London WC2E 8HN England.

WEHRTECHNIK. See Military Science.

WEST EUROPE REPORT. SCIENCE AND TECHNOLOGY. See Science (General).

WIRE ROPE NEWS & SLING TECHNOLOGY. VFOAT Wire Rope News and Sling Technology. 0740-1809. Periodical. US. English. bm. $15.00 Domestic, $25.00 Foreign. Edward J Bluvias T/A VS Enterprises, PO Box 871, Clark NJ 07066. *Wire Rope News.*

WISSENSCHAFT AKTUELL. See Science (General).

WISSENSCHAFT UND FORTSCHRITT. See Science (General).

WISSENSCHAFTLICHE ZEITSCHRIFT DER TECHNISCHEN UNIVERSITAT DRESDEN. **Main/Corp** Technische Universitat Dresden. V. 10, No. 5-. 0043-6925. Periodical. GE. English. ir. Deutscher Buch Export-Import, Leninstrasse 16, DDR-701 Leipzig East Germany. **Ind/Abst** Fluidex, Excerpta Med., Coal Abstr., Comput. Control Abstr., Electr. Electron. Abstr., Sci. Abstr. Sect. A. Phys. Abstr., Chem. Abstr., Eng. Index Mon., Nuci. Sci. Abstr., Math. Rev., Int. Aerosp. Abstr., Energy Res. Abstr., Phys. Abstr., Comput. Rev. **CODEN** WZTUAU. *Wissenschaftliche Zeitschrift.*

WOCHENBLATT FUR PAPIERFABRIKATION. See Paper & Pulp Industry.

WORLD MEETINGS, UNITED STATES AND CANADA. See Science (General).

WORLD'S FAIR (CORTE MADERA, CALIF.). (WORLD'S FAIR). Vol. 1, No. 1 (Feb. 1981)-. 0273-480X. Periodical. US. English. qt. $24.00. World's Fair, PO Box 339 Department ABE, Corte Madera CA 94925. **Tel** (415)924-6035. Ed Alfred E Heller. bk rev. adv acc. **Circ** 5,000. The people, pagentry and politics of fairs and exhibitions of the past and the present. Accurate, lively accounts of great international events of all kinds.

WPI JOURNAL. **Main/Corp** Worcester Polytechnic Institute, Worcester, Mass. **VAT** Worcester Polytechnic Institute Journal. 1869. 0148-6128. Periodical. US. English. qt. Worcester Polytechnic Institute, Alumni Association, Worcester MA 01609. **Tel** (617)793-5609. Ed Kenneth L McDonnell. **LC** TA1. **DD** 607.117443. **Circ** 22,000. (ctrl). Alumni magazine, stories on issues in education, engineering, science. People and technology oriented. *Journal of the Worcester Polytechnic Institute.*

XIANDAI HUAGONG. (HSIEN TAI HUA KUNG). VFOAT M.C.I., Modern Chemical Industry. Began in 1980. 0253-4320. Periodical. CH. Chinese (added contents in English). bm. 0.45. The Scientific and Technical Information Research Institute of the Ministry of Chemical Industry, PO Box 1410, Beijing China. **Ind/Abst** Chem. Abstr. **LC** TP155. **DD** 660.205. **CODEN** HTKUDJ.

YONBO. **Main/Corp** Soul Taehakkyo. Kongkwa Taehak. VFOAT Soul Taehakkyo Kongkwa Taehak Yonbo. V. 1- (1981-82)-. KO. Korean. an. Soul Taehakkyo Kongkwa Taehak, San 56-1 Sillim-dong Kwanak-ku, Seoul Korea. **LC** T173.S4588.

YONGU NONMUNJIP (HANGUK ENOJI YONGUSO). (YONGU NONMUNJIP). Periodical. English (Korean). ir. Hanguk Enoji Yonguso, 170-2 Kongnung-dong, Tobong-ku Seoul Korea. **LC** T9001. *Yongu Nonmunjip (Hanguk Wonjaryok Yonguso).*

YONGU NONMUNJIP (ULSAN KONGKWA TAEHAK. PYONGSOL KONGOP CHONMUN TAEHAK). (YONGU NONMUNJIP). VFOAT U.J.C.T. Report. Periodical. English (Korean). ir. **Ind/Abst** Energy Res. Abstr. **LC** T4.

YORAN - HOKKAIDO KOGYO KAIHATSU SHIKENJO. **Main/Corp** Hokkaido Kogyo Kaihatsu Shikenjo. JA. Japanese. ir. Hokkaido Kogyo Kaihatsu Shikenjo, 41-2 Higashi Tsukisappu, Toyohira-Ku 061-01 Tokyo Japan. **LC** T178.H64.

YORAN - KYUSHU KOGYO GIJUTSU SHIKENJO. **Main/Corp** Kyushu Kogyo Gijutsu Shikenjo. Japanese. ir. Shukumachi (841), Tokyo Japan. **LC** T178.K9.

YORAN- TOHOKU KOGYO GIJUTSU SHIKENJO. **Main/Corp** Tohoku Kogyo Gijutsu Shikenjo. JA. Japanese. ir. Tohoku Kogyo Gijutsu Shikenjo, Haramachi-Nigatake Miyagi-Ken, Sendai 983 Japan. **LC** T178.T63.

ZAHLENSPIEGEL. 1976-. German. ir. Technische Universitat Hannover, 3000 Hannover 1, Welfengarten 1B, Hannover West Germany. **LC** T173.

ZBORNIK VEDECKYCH PRAC VYSOKEJ SKOLY TECHNICKEJ V KOSICIACH. 1968-. 0371-4616. Periodical. English (German, Russian, and Slovak, with summaries in the other languages). ir. ALFA,

Textiles

Vydavatelstvo Technickej a Ekonomickej Literatury, Hurbanovo Nam 3, Bratislava Czechoslovakia. **Ind/Abst** Chem. Abstr., Met. Abstr., World Alum. Abstr. **LC** TA4. **DD** 605. **CODEN** SVVSAU. *Sbornik Vedecych Prac Vysokej Skoly Technickej v Kosiciach.*

ZEITSCHRIFT FUR LEBENSMITTEL-UNTERSUCHUNG UND -FORSCHUNG. See Food & Drink.

ZEITSCHRIFT FUR WIRTSCHAFTLICHE FERTIGUNG. See Manufacturing.

ZHONGGUO KEXUE JISHU DAXUE XUEBAO. See Science (General).

ZPRAVODAJ - FEDERALNI MINISTERSTVO PRO TECHNICKY A INVESTICNI ROZVOJ, MINISTERSTVO VYSTAVBY A TECHNIKY CSR, MINISTERSTVO VYSTAVBY A TECHNIKY SSR. **Main/Corp** Czechoslovakia. Federalni Ministerstvo Pro Technicky a Investicni Rozvoj. Vol. 3- Un. 1971-. CS. Czech. ir. 8.00. Federalni Ministerstvo Pro Technicky A Investicni, Rozvoj Slezska 9, Praha 2 Czechoslovakia. **LC** T26.C9. *Zpravodaj - Federalni Vybor pro Technicky a Investicni Rozvoj, Ministerstvo Vystavby a Techniky CSR a SSR.*

TEXTILES

AATCC TECHNICAL MANUAL. VFOAT Technical Manual of the American Association of Textile Chemists and Colorists. **VAT** American Association of Textile Chemists and Colorists Technical Manual. Vol. 39 (Sept. 1963)-. 0734-8894. US. English. an. American Association of Textile Chemists and Colorists, PO Box 12215, Research Triangle Park NC 27709. **Ind/Abst** Art Archaeol. Tech. Abstr. *Technical Manual of the American Association of Textile Chemists and Colorists, 0883-4539.*

ACTA POLYMERICA. V. 30- Jan. 1979-. Periodical. SZ. German (English or Russian). mo. Kunst & Wissen Erich Bieber, Dufourstrasse 51, CH-8008 Zurich Switzerland. **Tel** 01/69 44 20. **Ind/Abst** World Text Abstr., Abstr. Bull. Inst. Paper Chem., Art Archaeol. Tech. Abstr., Chem. Abstr., Energy Res. Abstr., Sci. Cit. Index, Abr. Ed. **LC** TS1300. **DD** 668.905. **CODEN** ACPODY. *Faserforschung und Textiltechnik.*

THE AGENT. Periodical. US. English. sa. Halper Publishing Company, 300 West Adams Street, Chicago IL 60606. **LC** TS1312. **DD** 677.058.

EL ALGODON HACE SUS CUENTAS. **Main/Corp** Servicio Comercial de la Industria Textil Algodonera. Seccion Estudios de Mercado. **Series Corp** Its Estudio. Began with Vol. for 1956. Spanish. ir. 750. Av Jose Antonio 670, (10) Barcelona Spain. **LC** HD9885.S69.

AMERICAN COIN-OP. Vol. 14, No. 2 Feb. 1973-. 0092-2811. Periodical. US. English. mo. American Trade Magazines Inc, 500 North Dearborn Street, Chicago IL 60610. **Tel** (312)337-7700. **LC** HD9999.L38. **DD** 338.4766713. *Coin-Op.*

AMERICAN DRYCLEANER. VFOAT American Dry Cleaner. Began with Vol 1934 issue. 0002-8258. Periodical. US. English. mo. $20.00. American Trade Magazines, 500 North Dearborn Street, Chicago IL 60610. **Tel** (312)337-7700. **LC** HD9999.C48. **DD** 338.47667120973. *Cleaners and Dyers Advertiser.*

AMERICAN DYESTUFF REPORTER. V. 1- Oct. 8, 1917-. 0002-8266. Periodical. US. English. mo. S A F International Inc, Suite 2/Promenade A Harmon, Cove Towers, Secaucus NJ 07094. **Tel** (201)867-9230. **Ind/Abst** Eng. Index Annu., Eng. Index Mon., Eng. Index Bioeng. Abstr., Eng. Index Energy Abstr., World Text Abstr., Predicasts, Excerpta Med., Energy Inf. Abstr., Environ. Abstr., Abstr. Bull. Inst. Paper Chem., Chem. Abstr., Appl. Sci. Technol. Index, Biogr. Index, Sci. Cit. Index, Abr. Ed., Funk Scott Index Corp. Ind., Eng. Index. **LC** TP890. **DD** 667.205. **CODEN** ADREAI. *Textile Colorist and Converter, 0096-591X.*

AMERICAN LAUNDRY DIGEST. 0002-9718. Periodical. US. English. mo. $22.00. American Trade Magazines Inc, 500 North Dearborn Street, Chicago IL 60610. **Tel** (312)337-7700. **Ind/Abst** Hospit. Lit. Index. **DD** 338.

AMERICA'S TEXTILES (GREENVILLE, S.C. : 1983). (AMERICA'S TEXTILES). Vol. 12, No. 1 (Jan. 1983)-. 0737-0040. Periodical. US. English. mo. $43.00. Billian Publishing Company, PO Box 88, Greenville SC 29602. **Ind/Abst** World Text Abstr., Chem. Abstr. **LC** TS1300. **DD** 677.005. **CODEN** AMTXDF. *America's Textiles. Reporter/Bulletin, 0095-8921; America's Textiles, 0194-4428.*

AMERICA'S TEXTILES. KNITTER/APPAREL EDITION CEASED. (AMERICA'S TEXTILES). **VAT** America's Textiles. Knitter Apparel Edition. 0194-4428. Periodical. US. English. mo. $97.00. Billian Publishing Company, 2100 Powers Ferry Road Suite 125, Atlanta GA 30339. **Tel** (404)955-5656.

AMERICA'S TEXTILES. REPORTER/BULLETIN EDITION CEASED. (AMERICA'S TEXTILES REPORTER/BULLETIN). Vol. 35, No. 9 (Sept. 1971)-. 0095-8921. Periodical. US. English. mo. $43.00. Billiam Publishing Company, 2100 Powers Ferry Road, Atlanta GA 30339. **Tel** (404)955-5656. Ed Bud Newcome. **Ind/Abst** Chem. Abstr. **LC** TS1300. **DD** 677.005. bk rev. adv acc. **Circ** 36,500. (ctrl). Serves the textile industry from raw fiber through end product. The knitting/apparel supplement serves manufacturers and processers of knitted garments and fabrics. *Textile Bulletin, America's Textile Reporter, 0003-1607.*

ANITAF DIRECTORY. See Yearbooks, Almanacs, Directories.

ANNOTATED DIRECTORY OF SELF-PUBLISHED TEXTILE BOOKS. See Yearbooks, Almanacs, Directories.

ANNUAIRE STATISTIQUE DE L'INDUSTRIE FRANCAISE DU JUTE ET DES POLIOLEFINES TEXTILES. See Yearbooks, Almanacs, Directories.

ANNUAL REPORT - AHMEDABAD TEXTILE MILLS' ASSOCIATION. **Main/Corp** Ahmedabad Textile Mills' Association. English. an. Ahmedabad Textile Mills' Association Ranchhodlal, Marg Ashram Road, Ahmedabad India 380009. **LC** HD9866.I64. **DD** 338.4767700605475.

ANNUAL REPORT AND ACCOUNTS FOR . . . - TEXTILE INSTITUTE. **Main/Corp** Textile Institute (Manchester, Greater Manchester). UK. English. an. 10 Black Friars Street, Manchester United Kingdom. **LC** TS1300. **DD** 677.00601. *Report, Balance Sheet and Accounts.*

ANNUAL REPORT AND STATEMENT OF ACCOUNTS - NATIONAL TEXTILE CORPORATION LIMITED. **Main/Corp** National Textile Corporation Limited. 0376-5504. English. ir. National Textile Corp Ltd, 8th Floor Surya Kiran Building 19 Kasturba Gandhi Marg, New Delhi India. **LC** HD9866.I64. **DD** 338.767700954.

ANNUAL REPORT OF THE U.S. CONSUMER PRODUCT SAFETY COMMISSION ON FLAMMABLE FABRICS DATA. **Main/Corp** United States. Consumer Product Safety Commission. **VAT** Annual Report of the United States Product Safety Commission on Flammable Fabrics Data. 0192-1029. US. English. an. Consumer Product Safety Commission, 1111 18th Street NW, Washington DC 20207. **LC** TS1449. **DD** 677. *Flammable Fabrics Report.*

ANNUAL REPORT - TEXTILE MACHINERY MANUFACTURERS' ASSOCIATION. **Main/Corp** Textile Machinery Manufacturers' Association. English. an. **LC** TS1525.

ANNUAL REPORT - WOOL RESEARCH ORGANISATION OF NEW ZEALAND. **Main/Corp** Wool Research Organisation of New Zealand. 1961/62-. English. an.

ANNUAL STATISTICAL REVIEW OF COTTON AND ALLIED TEXTILE INDUSTRY IN JAPAN. See Statistics.

ANNUAL TEXTILE INDUSTRY TECHNICAL CONFERENCE. **Main/Conf** Textile Industry Technical Conference. 0094-9884. US. English. an. $5.00. IEEE, 345 East 47th Street, New York NY 10017. **Ind/Abst** Index IEEE Publ., Eng. Index Annu., Eng. Index Mon., Eng. Index Bioeng. Abstr., Eng. Index Energy Abstr. **LC** TK4035.T4. **DD** 677.028. **CODEN** IATTD7.

APTMA DIRECTORY OF MEMBERS. See Yearbooks, Almanacs, Directories.

ARENA TEKSTIL. V. 1- 1969-. 0518-4010. English or Indonesian. ir. Institut Teknologi Tekstil, Jl Jenderal A Yani 318, Bandung Indonesia. **Ind/Abst** Chem. Abstr. **LC** TS1300. **CODEN** ARTKDB.

ARS TEXTRINA. VFOAT Art of Weaving. Vol. 1 (Dec. 1983)-. 0824-9091. Periodical. CN. English. sa. $70.00. Charles Babbage Research Centre, PO Box 272 St Norbert Postal Station, Winnipeg Manitoba R3V 1L6 Canada. **Tel** (204)474-8313. Ed R G Stanton. **DD** 677.02824205. **Circ** 250. Investigation of mathematical patterns associated with weaving, interest in the history, theory, practice, and development of textile knowledge in general.

BANDINDUSTRIE EN OVERIGE TEXTIELINDUSTRIE PRODUKTIESTATISTIEKEN. VFOAT Manufacture of Narrow Fabrics and of Other Textiles Production Statistics. NE. Dutch (summaries in English). ir. 10.15. Centraal Bureau Voor de Statistiek, Prinses Beatrixlaan 428 Postbus 959, 2270 Az Voorburg Netherlands.

BANGLADESH JOURNAL OF JUTE & FIBRE RESEARCH. **VAT** Bangladesh Journal of Jute and Fibre Research. V. 1- July 1976-. 0253-5424. Periodical. BG. English. be. Secretary Bangladesh Jute Res, Tejgaon, Dacca 15 Bangladesh. **Ind/Abst** Chem. Abstr. **CODEN** BJJRD5.

BOLETIN DEL INSTITUTO DE INVESTIGACION TEXTIL Y DE COOPERACION INDUSTRIAL. **Main/Corp** Instituto de Investigacion Textil y de Cooperacion Industrial. 0210-251X. Periodical. SP. Spanish. sa. Universidad Politecnica Barcelona, Auda Gregorio Maranon S/N, Barcelona Spain. **Ind/Abst** Chem. Abstr. **LC** TS1300. **CODEN** BIIBDD.

BOOK OF PAPERS FOR THE CANADIAN TEXTILE SEMINAR. INTERNATIONAL. (BOOK OF PAPERS FOR THE CANADIAN TEXTILE SEMINAR (INTERNATIONAL)). **Main/Corp** Canadian Textile Seminar (International). 9th- 1964-. 0384-112X. Periodical. CN. English. ir. Textile Technical Fed Canada, 4920 de Maisonneuve Boulevard West, Montreal Quebec H3Z 1NL Canada. **Ind/Abst** Chem. Abstr. **DD** 677. **CODEN** CTBPA3. *Book of Papers for the Canadian Textile Seminar, 0384-1111.*

BOOK OF PAPERS, NATIONAL TECHNICAL CONFERENCE. (BOOK OF PAPERS). **Main/Conf** National Technical Confernece. Began in 1974. 0192-4699. US. English. an. AATCC, Box 12215, Research Triangle Park NC 27709. **Tel** (919)549-8141. **Ind/Abst** Eng. Index Annu., Eng. Index Mon., Eng. Index Bioeng. Abstr., Eng. Index Energy Abstr., Chem. Abstr., Eng. Index. **LC** TP890.5. **DD** 677.0283505. **CODEN** BPNADG. **Circ** 2,000. Published in conjunction with AATCC's International Conference and Exhibition. Each contains the full texts of all available papers. Soft covers.

BROADWOVEN FABRICS, GRAY. (CURRENT INDUSTRIAL REPORTS. MQ-22T, BROADWOVEN FABRICS (GRAY)). VFOAT Broadwoven Fabrics (Gray). Publication began with July 1976. 0145-8957. US. English. qt. $8.00. US Government Printing Office, Superintendent of Documents, Washington DC 20402. **Ind/Abst** Predicasts, Am. Stat. Index. Presents timely data on the production, inventories, and orders of approximately 5,000 products, which presents 40 percent of all US manufacturing. *Current Industrial Reports. MQ-22T. 1, Cotton Broadwoven Gray Goods, 0364-1759; Current Industrial Reports. MQ-22T. 2, Manmade Fiber Broadwoven Gray Goods, 0145-4919; Current Industrial Reports. MQ-22T. 3, Wool Broadwoven Goods, 0145-501X.*

BROADWOVEN GRAY FABRIC PRODUCTION. SEASONAL ADJUSTMENT SUPPLEMENT. (CURRENT INDUSTRIAL REPORTS. MQ-22T, BROADWOVEN GRAY FABRIC PRODUCTION, SEASONAL ADJUSTMENT SUPPLEMENT). VFOAT Broadwoven Gray Fabric Production, Seasonal Adjustment Supplement. 0730-0905. US. English. Customer Services, Bureau of the Census, Washington DC 20233.

BULLETIN - ASSOCIATION DES TISSERANDS DU QUEBEC. (BULLETIN). **VAT** Bulletin - Association of Quebec Weavers. Vol. 1, No. 1 (Oct. 81)-. 0714-8119. Periodical. CN. English (French). ir. Free to Members. Bulletin Association of

Textiles

Quebec Weavers, PO Box 47/Rural Route 1, Hudson Quebec J0P 1H0 Canada. **DD** 746.1409714.

BULLETIN DE LIAISON DU CENTRE INTERNATIONAL D'ETUDE DES TEXTILES ANCIENS. **Main/Corp** Centre International d'Etude des Textiles Anciens. No. 1- 1955-. Periodical. FR. French. sa. Bulletin de Liason Centre, 34 rue de la Charite, 69002 Lyon France. **Ind/Abst** World Text Abstr.

CARPET & RUG INDUSTRY. **VAT** Carpet and Rug Industry. 0192-4486. Periodical. US. English. mo. $38.00. Rodman Publications Inc, 26 Lake Street, PO Box 555, Ramsey NJ 07446. **Ind/Abst** World Text Abstr.

CARPET AND RUGS. See Manufacturing.

CARPET, MAT AND RUG INDUSTRY (FINAL). (CARPET, MAT AND RUG INDUSTRY). **VFOAT** Industrie des Tapis et Carpettes, Industrie des Tapis, des Carpettes et de la Moquette. 1960-. 0527-4893. CN. English (French). an. Receiver General for Canada, Statistics Canada Publications, Ottawa Ontario K1A 0T6 Canada. **DD** 338.47677643. *Miscellaneous Textiles Industries, 0527-5733.*

CARPET REVIEW EXPORT. See Business - Commerce.

CARPET SPECIFIER'S HANDBOOK. (THE CARPET SPECIFIER'S HANDBOOK). **Main/Corp** Carpet and Rug Institute. 1974- Ed. 0095-6457. US. English. an. Carpet and Rug Institute, Box 2048, Dalton GA 30720. **LC** TS1772. **DD** 677.64305.

CATALOG OF ARTICLES AND PAPERS ON NONWOVEN FABRICS. **VFOAT** Nonwoven Articles/Papers and Patents. US. English. an. Rando Machine Corp, 1700 Broadway, New York NY 10019. **LC** TS1828. **DD** 016.6776.

CHEMICKE VLANKNA. (CHEMICHE VLAKNA). Began publication in 1951. 0528-9432. Periodical. Czech. bm. **Ind/Abst** Chem. Abstr., World Text Abstr., Abstr. Bull. Inst. Paper Chem. **CODEN** CMVLA8.

CHEMIEFASERN, TEXTIL-INDUSTRIE. 0340-3343. Periodical. GW. German. mo. $73.41. Deutscher Fachverlag GMBH, Postfach 100606, Schumannstr 27, 6000 Frankfurt 1 West Germany. **Tel** 069/74331. **Ind/Abst** Predicasts, Abstr. Bull. Inst. Paper Chem., CIS Abstr., Chem. Abstr., Funk Scott Index Corp. Ind. **LC** TS1300. *Chemiefasern + I.E. und Textil-Anwendungstschnik. Textil-Industrie.*

CLARK'S DIRECTORY OF SOUTHERN TEXTILE MILLS. See Yearbooks, Almanacs, Directories.

COIR. V. 1- Aug. 1956-. 0530-0495. Periodical. II. English. qt. $10.00. Coir Board, PO Box 1752, Ernakulam South Cochen 16 India. **LC** TS1544.C6.

COLOURAGE. Began in 1954. 0010-1826. II. English. bw. 75.00. Colour Publications Pvt Ltd, 126A Dhuruwadi Off Dr Nariman, Bombay 400025 India. **Tel** 430 9610/9318/6319. Ed R V Raghavan. **Ind/Abst** Predicasts, Chem. Abstr., Energy Inf. Abstr., Environ. Abstr., World Text Abstr. **LC** TP890. **DD** 667.305. **CODEN** COLOBG. bk rev. adv acc. **Circ** 6,400. Technical articles, special columns and news reports pertaining to the textile wet processing and dyestuffs industries.

COMITEXTIL. BULLETIN. **VFOAT** Comitextil. 75/1-. Periodical. BE. English (French). bm. $59.28. Comitextil, 24 rue Montoyer, B-1040 Bruxelles Belgium. **Tel** 02 230 95 80. **Ind/Abst** World Text Abstr. **Circ** 400. Bulletin on European textile industry giving information on economics, politics, external trade, monographies on textile and clothing at international levels. *Comitextil. Documents, Comitextil. Information; Comitextil. Presse.*

CONSUMER PURCHASES AND PRICE TRENDS OF TEXTILES. **Main/Corp** India (Republic). Textiles Committee. No. 88-. Periodical. II. English. mo. **LC** HD9866.I6. **DD** 381.4567700954. *Consumer Purchases of Textiles.*

CORRELATION, TEXTILE AND APPAREL CATEGORIES WITH TARIFF SCHEDULES OF THE UNITED STATES ANNOTATED. **VFOAT** Textile and Apparel Categories with Staff Schedules of the United States Annotated. US. English. an. US Department of Commerce, International Trade Administration, Office of Textiles and Apparel, Washington DC 20230.

COTON ET FIBRES TROPICALES. See Horticulture and Plant Culture.

COTTON AND WOOL. OUTLOOK & SITUATION CEASED. (OUTLOOK & SITUATION. COTTON AND WOOL). **VAT** Cotton and Wool. Outlook and Situation. No. 26 (Feb. 1981)-No. 39, (May 1984). 0744-2890. Periodical. US. English. qt. $18.00. Superintendent of Documents, US Government Printing Office, Washington DC 20402. **Tel** (202)783-3238. **Ind/Abst** World Text Abstr., Predicasts, Am. Stat. Index. **LC** HD9074. **DD** 338.173510973. *Cotton and Wool Situation, 0360-2184.*

THE COTTON DIGEST INTERNATIONAL. See Agriculture.

COTTON FIBER AND PROCESSING TEST RESULTS. See Manufacturing.

THE COTTON GIN AND OIL MILL PRESS. See Agriculture.

COTTON INTERNATIONAL. 1970-. 0070-0673. US. English. an. $12.00. Meister Publishing Co, 37841 Euclid Avenue, Willoughby OH 44094. **Tel** (216)942-2000. **Ind/Abst** Bibliogr. Agric. **LC** TS1550. **DD** 677205. *Cotton.*

COTTON : MONTHLY REVIEW OF THE WORLD SITUATION. See Agriculture - Crop Production and Soil.

THE COTTON STATISTICS MONTHLY. See Statistics.

COTTON : WORLD STATISTICS. See Statistics.

COTTON YARN AND CLOTH MILLS (FINAL). (COTTON YARN AND CLOTH MILLS). **Series/Titl** Annual Census of Manufactures. **VFOAT** Fabriques de Files et de Tissus de Coton, Filature et Tissage du Coton. 1960-1980. 0527-5016. CN. text in English and French, English only, 1960-1965. an. 70.00. Canada Dominion Bureau of Statistics, Industry and Merchandising Division, Ottawa Ontario Canada. **DD** 338.47677210971. *Cotton Textile Industries, 0384-2878.*

CURRENT INDUSTRIAL REPORTS. M22D, CONSUMPTION ON THE WOOLEN SYSTEM AND WORSTED COMBING. See Manufacturing.

DALGETY FARMERS' ANNUAL WOOL DIGEST. **VFOAT** Annual Wool Digest. 1983-84 season-. AT. English. an. Free. Public Relations Department of Dalgety Farmers Limited, Government Printing Office, Box 261, Sydney New South Wales 2001 Australia. **Tel** (02)238-2000. Ed Terence C Anderson. **Circ** 10,000. A digest of the Australian wool market statistics and information and summary of New Zealand and South African wool markets. *Dalgety-N.Z.L. Annual Wool Digest.*

DAVISON'S KNIT GOODS TRADE; THE STANDARD. 1st- 1906-. 0070-2943. US. English. an. Davison Publishing Co, Box 477, Ridgewood NJ 07451. **LC** TT695. Each issue contains an index to its own contents - no vol index - loose.

DAVISON'S SALESMAN'S BOOK. 63rd- Ed. 0363-5252. US. English. an. Davisons Pub Co, Box 477, Ridgewood NJ 07451. **Tel** (201)445-3135. Ed Bruce W Nealy. **LC** TS1312. **DD** 338.47677002573. adv acc. (ctrl). Textile Directory listing mills, dyers, finishers in US and Canada. Listings include personnel, and products produced. *Davison's Textile directory for Executives and Salesmen.*

DAVISON'S TEXTILE BLUE BOOK. **VFOAT** Textile Blue Book. US. English. an. PO Box 477, Ridgewood NJ 07451. *Davison's Textile Blue Book United States and Canada.*

DAVISON'S TEXTILE BUYERS GUIDE (1980). (DAVISON'S TEXTILE BUYERS GUIDE). **VFOAT** Davison Textile Buyers Guide. Began with 1980. 0734-4708. US. English. an. Davison Publishing Co, PO Box 477, Ridgewood NJ 07451. **LC** HD9850.3. **DD** 681.7677029473. *Davison's Textile Buyers Guide and Buyer's Guide, 0730-5990.*

DEUTSCHE SEILER-ZEITUNG. 0012-0758. Periodical. German. mo.

THE DIRECTORY OF TEXTILE PLANT PROCESSES. See Yearbooks, Almanacs, Directories.

DIRECTORY OF WOOL, HOSIERY & FABRICS. See Yearbooks, Almanacs, Directories.

DRYCLEANER NEWS. 1951. 0012-6802. Periodical. US. English. mo. Zachin Publications Inc, 70 Edwin Avenue/PO Box 2180, Waterbury CT 06722. **Tel** (203)755-0158. Ed Jack Goldberg. adv acc. **Circ** 9,000. (ctrl). Business, industry and technical advice for drycleaners in the Northeast.

EN BREF. (EN BREF : JOURNAL DE L'ASSOCIATION DES TISSERANDS D'ICI). V. 1, No. 1 (Winter 1979/80)-. 0228-8710. Periodical. CN. French. ir. $2.00 Per Number. Association des Tisserands d'Ici, 402 Est rue St-Paul, Montreal Quebec H2Y 1H4 Canada. **DD** 746.1409714.

ESTIMATED POUNDAGE EQUIVALENTS. **Main/Corp** Canadian Textiles Institute. **VFOAT** Study of Canadian Imports of Manufactured Textiles. 1975/76-. CN. English. an. Canadian Textiles Institute, 1002 Commerce House, 1808 Beaver Hall Hill, Montreal Quebec H2Z 1T6 Canada. *Pounds and Square Yards Study, 0318-3408.*

FABRIC FACTS. **Main/Corp** IFI Research Center. No. C-139- Feb. 1973-. 0470-1348. Periodical. US. English. bm. International Fabricare Institute, 12251 Tech Road, Silver Spring MD 20904. **LC** TP932.3. **DD** 667.1205. *Fabric Facts.*

FABRIC STORES. **VFOAT** List of Fabric Stores. 0147-2143. US. English. $75.00. Leads-Prospects Inc, 1182 Broadway, New York NY 10001. **LC** HD9869.F33. **DD** 381.45677002573.

FABRICS-FASHIONS. **Main/Corp** IFI Research Center. No. FF-219- 1973-. 0097-2495. US. English. International Fabricare Institute/IFI Research Center, 12251 Tech Road, Silver Spring MD 20904. **LC** TP932.3. **DD** 667.1205. *Fabrics-Fashions.*

FANG CHIH HSUEH PAO. Began in 1980. 0253-9721. Periodical. CH. Chinese. mo. 0.40. Chung-Kuo Kuo Chi Shu Tien, PO Box 2820, Peking China. **Ind/Abst** World Text Abstr., Chem. Abstr. **LC** TS1300. **DD** 677.005. **CODEN** FCHPDI.

FARBE. (DIE FARBE). Began publication with July 1952 issue. 0014-7680. Periodical. GW. German. ir. 198.00. Verlag Muster Schmidt, Postfach 421 Turnstrasse 7, D-3400 Goettingen West Germany. **Tel** 551/71741. Ed Manfred Richter. **Ind/Abst** Art Archaeol. Tech. Abstr., World Surf. Coat. Abstr. **LC** TP890. Scientific journal that deals with all questions concerning color in an optical sense. Problems concerning the visibility of color, testing of color, comparison, color reflection of light sources, and color spectrum.

FASHION TEXTILES MODE. **VFOAT** Textiles Mode. V. 1- Summer 1973-. 0318-8701. Periodical. CN. text in English and French. qt. $10. Fashion Textiles Mode Publishing Ltd, Bureau 311, 1396 St Catherine Street West, Montreal Quebec H3G 1P9 Canada. **DD** 677.02860971.

FEM EGO. V. 1- Summer 1975-. 0318-871X. Periodical. CN. English and French. qt. $10.00. Fashion Textiles Mode Publishing, Suite 311/1396 St Catherine Street West, Montreal Quebec H3G 1P9 Canada. **DD** 746.9205. *Fashion Textiles Mode, 0318-8701.*

FIBERARTS. V. 3- Jan./Feb. 1976-. 0164-324X. Periodical. US. English. bm. $22.00. Lark Communications, 50 College Street, Asheville NC 28801. **Tel** (704)253-0468. **Ind/Abst** Art Archaeol. Tech. Abstr., Art Index. **LC** TT697. **DD** 746.05. The magazine of textiles. Articles on weaving, wearables, dyeing, needlework, sewing. Artists, techniques and design. *Fibercraft Newsletter.*

FIBERSCOPE. V. 1-. 0198-8387. Periodical. US. English. an. $18.00. Interweave Press, 306 North Washington, Loveland CO 80537. Ed L Jane Patrick. **LC** N6494.F47. **DD** 746.0904. bk rev. adv acc. **Circ** 35,000. Handwoven designs, full color photography, complete project instructions to encourage the beginner and challenge the experienced weaver. In-depth features, outstanding craftsmen.

FIBRE E COLORI. Yearly V. 1-20. No. 6-. 0015-055X. Periodical. IT. Italian. mo. Periodici Aracne Nuova Srl, Via Padova 41, 20127 Milano Italy. **LC** TS1688.A1. **CODEN** FICLAK.

FIBRE MARKET NEWS. 0046-3728. Periodical. US. English. ir. $85.00. Market News Publishing Corporation, 156 5th Avenue, New York NY 10010. **Tel** (212)255-2277. Ed Anthony J Abitante. adv acc. **Circ** 2,700. Covers all aspects of recycling secondary fibres. Offers market reviews and prices.

FIBRE, YARN, AND CLOTH MILLS. **VFOAT** Fabrication de Fibres, Files et Tissus. 1981-. 0319-8901. CN. English (French). an. $6.35 Domestic,

Textiles

$7.60 Foreign. **LC** HD9864.C2. **DD** 338.4767700971. *Cotton Yarn and Cloth Mills (Final), 0527-5016; Man-Made Fibre, Yarn, and Cloth Mills, 0300-3795; Wool Yarn and Cloth Mills (Final), 0300-1202; Knitting Mills, 0384-3343.*

FINISHED BROADWOVEN FABRIC PRODUCTION. See Manufacturing.

FINISHED FABRICS. PRODUCTION, INVENTORIES, AND UNFILLED ORDERS. See Manufacturing.

FLAME RETARDANCY OF POLYMERIC MATERIALS. V. 1- 1973-. 0361-6320. US. English. ir. Plenum Press, c/o H Feldman, 233 Spring Street, New York NY 10013. **Tel** (212)620-8000. Ed W C Kuryla and others. **Ind/Abst** Chem. Abstr. **CODEN** FRPMBG.

GEOTECHNICAL FABRICS REPORT. Vol. 1, No. 1 (Summer 1983)-. 0882-4983. Periodical. US. English. bm. $30.00. Geotechnical Fabrics Report, 345 Cedar Building/Suite 450, St Paul MN 55101. **Tel** (612)222-2508. Ed Joan R Haglund. **Ind/Abst** World Text Abstr. **DD** 677. adv acc. **Circ** 3,500. (ctrl) Gives detailed reports and case histories on latest geosynthetic product developments, techniques and applications. Written for the civil engineer, installer, manufacturer and specifier.

GOUE VAG = GOLDEN FLEECE. See Agriculture - Livestock and Poultry.

HALI; THE INTERNATIONAL JOURNAL OF ORIENTAL CARPETS AND TEXTILES. VFOAT Hali. V. 1- Spring 1978-. 0142-0798. Periodical. UK. English (German). qt. Hali, 20 East 53rd Street, New York NY 10022. **Tel** (212)319-6825. Ed Alan Marcuson. **LC** NK2808. **DD** 746.7505. Index in last issue of volume - attached. bk rev. adv acc. **Circ** 15,000. Devoted to the history, provenance, market for antique oriental rugs and textiles.

HANDBOOK OF STATISTICS ON COTTON TEXTILE INDUSTRY. See Statistics.

HANDWOVEN. 1979. 0198-8212. Periodical. US. English. ir. $18.00. Interweave Press, 306 North Washington Avenue, Loveland CO 80537. **Tel** (303)669-7672. Ed Jane Patrick. **LC** TT848. **DD** 746.1405. bk rev. adv acc. **Circ** 29,000. Handwoven designs to encourage the beginner and challenge the experienced weaver, full-color photography, complete instructions, yarn recommendations, history, plus more in every issue. *Interweave, 0198-8220.*

HANGUG SEMNYU GONHAGHOIJI. (HAN'GUK SOMYU KONGHAKHOE CHI). VFOAT Journal of the Korean Society of Textile Engineers and Chemists. 0253-6420. Periodical. Korean (added contents page and abstracts in English). ir. **Ind/Abst** Chem. Abstr. **LC** TS1300. **CODEN** HSKCDQ. *Somyu Konghakhoe Chi.*

HAN'GUK UIRYU HAKHOE CHI. See Clothing and Fashion.

HOME FASHIONS TEXTILES. See Interior Design - Home Furnishings.

HOME TEXTILES TODAY. V. 1- Sept. 1979-. 0195-3184. Periodical. US. English. sm. $54.00. Home Textiles Today, PO Box 2754, High Point NC 27261. **Tel** (919)889-0113. Ed Marge Axelrod. adv acc. **Circ** 11,000. The business and fashion newspaper of the home textiles industry.

HOSIERY NEWS. Vol. 61, No. 6 (Apr. 1982)-. 0742-8065. Periodical. US. English. mo. National Association of Hosiery Manufacturers, PO Box 35098, Charlotte NC 28235. **Ind/Abst** World Text Abstr. **LC** HD9969.H6. **DD** 338.4768730973. *Hosiery Newsletter, 0018-540X.*

HUA TUNG FANG CHIH KUNG HSUEH YUAN HSUEH PAO. See Technology (General).

IEEE ANNUAL TEXTILE INDUSTRY TECHNICAL CONFERENCE. Main/Corp Institute of Electrical and Electronics Engineers. VFOAT Textile Industry Technical Conference. 1972-. Periodical. US. English. ir. Institute of Electrical and Electronic Engineers, 445 Hoes Lane, Publishing Sales, Piscataway NJ 08854.

I.F.I. NEWS REPORTER. (IFI NEWS REPORTER). **Main/Corp** International Fabricare Institute. Drycleaning Division. **VAT** International Fabricare Institute News Reporter. No. 369- April 1972-. 0095-7569. Periodical. US. English. mo. International Fabricare Institute, Drycleaning Division/ 909 Burlington Avenue, Silver Spring MD 20910. **LC** HD9999.C48. **DD** 338.4766710973. *Bulletin Service. Reporter.*

INDIAN JOURNAL OF TEXTILE RESEARCH. V. 1- Mar. 1976-. 0377-8436. Periodical. II. English. qt. $17.00. Asia Books and Periodicals Company, 11 Darya Ganj, New Delhi 110002 India. Ed R N Shaima. **Ind/Abst** World Text Abstr., Abstr. Bull. Inst. Paper Chem., Art Archaeol. Tech. Abstr., Chem. Abstr. **CODEN** IJTRDU. bk rev. adv acc. Papers reporting results of fundamental and applied research in the field of textile technology.

INDIAN SILK. V. 1- May 1962-. 0019-6355. Periodical. II. English. mo. $24.00. Central Silk Board, Government of India, 94B Marine Drive, Bombay 2 India. **LC** HD9910.1.

INDIAN TEXTILE INDUSTRY ANNUAL. in publication since 1936. English. ir. Ed M P Gandhi. **LC** HD9866.I6.

INDIAN TEXTILE JOURNAL. (THE INDIAN TEXTILE JOURNAL). Began publication in 1890. 0019-6436. Periodical. II. English. mo. $38.00. Indian Textile Journal Pvt Ltd, 5 Burjurji Bharucha Marg Fort, Bombay 400 023 India. **Ind/Abst** World Text Abstr., Art Archaeol. Tech. Abstr., Chem. Abstr. **LC** TS1300. **CODEN** INTJAV.

INDUSTRIA USOARA. (INDUSTRIA USOARA. TEXTILE, TRICOTAJE, CONFECTII TEXTILE). VFOAT Textile, Tricotaje, Confectii Textile. Vol. 25, No. 7 (July 1974)-. 0019-7785. Periodical. RM. Romanian. mo. $57.00. Rompresfilatelia, PO Box 1362137, Bucharest Romania. **Ind/Abst** World Text Abstr., Art Archaeol. Tech. Abstr., Chem. Abstr. **CODEN** IUSAAE. *Industria Usoara. Seria A.*

INDUSTRIAL FABRIC PRODUCTS REVIEW. V. 42, No. 10- Feb. 1966-. 0019-8307. Periodical. US. English. $24.00 Domestic, $25.00 Foreign. Industrial Fabrics Association International, 350 Endicott Building, St Paul MN 55101. **Ind/Abst** World Text Abstr. *Canvas Products Review.*

INDUSTRIAL LAUNDERER. 0046-9211. Periodical. US. English. mo. $20.00. Institute Industrial Launderer, 1730 M Street NW, Washington DC 20036. **Tel** (202)296-6744. Ed David Ritchey. adv acc. **Circ** 2,700. Wide range of general management and specific how-to articles tailored to the industrial laundry industry.

INDUSTRIE TEXTILE. (L'INDUSTRIE TEXTILE). 0019-9176. Periodical. FR. French. ir. $79.82. L'Industrie Textile, 36 rue Ballu, 75009 Paris France. **Tel** (1)974.15.96. **Ind/Abst** CIS Abstr., Excerpta Med., Chem. Abstr., Bibliogr. Agric., Predicasts. **CODEN** INTPAF. Subscription includes "L'Industrie Textile" (11 issues) and its knitwear supplement "Filiere Maille" (5 times a year).

L'INDUSTRIE TEXTILE DANS LES PAYS DE L'O.C.D.E. TEXTILE INDUSTRY IN O.E.C.D. COUNTRIES. Main/Corp Organisation for Economic Co-Operation and Development. VFOAT Textile Industry in O.E.C.D. Countries. 1962/63-. English (French). ir. OECD Publishing Center, 1750 Pennsylvania Avenue NW, Washington DC 20006. **LC** HD9850.1. **DD** 338.47677. *Industrie Textile: Etude Statistique.*

INDUSTRY REVIEW. See Statistics.

INDUSTRY WAGE SURVEY. TEXTILE MILLS AND TEXTILE DYEING AND FINISHING PLANTS. See Economics - Labor.

INFORMATION SUR LES TEXTILES SYNTHETIQUES ET CELLULOSIQUES. VFOAT Information on Man-Made Fibres. 1972-. FR. English (French and German). an. 29 rue de Courcelles, 75008 Paris France. **LC** HD9929.2.A1. **DD** 338.476774021. *Information sur les Textiles Cellulosiques et Synthetiques.*

INSIDE TEXTILES. 1980. 0733-8244. Periodical. US. English. bw. $187.00. Inside Textiles, PO Box 1309, Point Pleasant NJ 08742. **Tel** (201)295-8258. Ed Noreen Heimbold. Covers manufacturing and marketing of textiles and apparel.

INSTRUMENTATION IN THE TEXTILE INDUSTRY. 0276-2951. Periodical. US. English. Instrument Society of America, PO Box 12277, Research Triangle Park NC 27709.

INTERIOR TEXTILES. See Interior Design - Home Furnishings.

INTERNATIONAL COTTON INDUSTRY STATISTICS. See Statistics.

INTERNATIONAL DIRECTORY OF THE NONWOVEN FABRICS INDUSTRY. See Yearbooks, Almanacs, Directories.

INTERNATIONAL DYER. (THE INTERNATIONAL DYER, TEXTILE PRINTER, BLEACHER AND FINISHER). 0020-658X. Periodical. UK. English. mo. Business Press International Ltd, Perrymount Road/Haywards Heath, West Sussex RH16 3BR England. **Ind/Abst** World Text Abstr., Art Archaeol. Tech. Abstr., Chem. Abstr., Sel. Water Resour. Abstr. **CODEN** IDBFAT. *Dyer, Texile Printer, Bleacher and Finisher.*

INTERNATIONAL TEXTILE BULLETIN. DYEING/PRINTING/ FINISHING/ITS. VFOAT Dyeing/Printing/ Finishing. VAT International Textile Service Bulletin. Dyeing/Printing/Finishing. Periodical. English. qt. $23.25. Internationaler Textil Service, Kesslerstrasse 9, PO Box, CH-8952 Schlieren Switzerland. **Tel** 01/ 730 58 53. **Ind/Abst** Eng. Index Annu., Eng. Index Mon., Eng. Index Bioeng. Abstr., Eng. Index Energy Abstr., World Text Abstr. **CODEN** ITBFD8.

INTERNATIONAL TEXTILE MACHINERY SHIPMENT STATISTICS. See Statistics.

INTERNATIONAL TEXTILE MANUFACTURING. See Manufacturing.

INTERNATIONAL TEXTILE REVIEW. 1979-. US. English. an. $97.00 US, $118.50 Foreign. McGraw-Hill Publications, 457 National Press Building, Washington DC 20045. **LC** HD9850.1. **DD** 338.47677005.

INTERNATIONAL TEXTILES. V. 1- 1933-. 0020-8914. Periodical. UK. Dutch (English, French, German and Spanish). mo. $180.00. International Textiles, Benjamin Dent Lt, 33 Bedford Place, London WC1B 5JX England.

INTERNATIONAL TEXTILES INTERIOR. VFOAT Interior. 1960-. 0020-8922. Periodical. GW. English (French and German). mo. W E Saarbach GMBH, Postfach 101610, D-5000 Koeln 1 West Germany. **Tel** 02 21-23 46 31.

INVESTIGACION E INFORMACION TEXTIL Y DE TENSIOACTIVOS. 0302-5268. Periodical. SP. Spanish (summaries in English, French, and German). qt. $15.00. Investigacion e Informacion, Jorge Girona Salgado S/N, Barcelona 34 Spain. **Ind/Abst** World Text Abstr., Chem. Abstr., Bibliogr. Agric. **LC** TS1300. **CODEN** IITTCS. *Investigacion e Informacion Textil.*

ISHIKAWA-KEN KOGYO SHIKENJO SHIKENJO HOKOKU. (SHIKENJO HOKOKU). VAT Shikenjo Hokoku - Ishikawa-Ken Kogyo Shikenjo. 0285-869X. JA. Japanese. ir. Ishikawa-Ken Kogyo Shikenjo, 4-133 Yonaizumimichi, Kanazawa 921 Japan. **Ind/Abst** Chem. Abstr. **LC** TS1300. **CODEN** IKSHD2.

IZVESTIIA VYSSHIKH UCHEBNYKH ZAVEDENII. TEKHNOLOGIIA TEKSTILNOI PROMYSHLENNOSTI. 0021-3497. Periodical. UR. Russian. bm. Victor Kamkin Inc, 12224 Parklawn Drive, Rockville MD 20852. **Tel** (301)881-5973. **Ind/Abst** Abstr. Bull. Inst. Paper Chem., Art Archaeol. Tech. Abstr., Chem. Abstr., Bibliogr. Agric. **CODEN** IVTTAF.

JAPAN TEXTILE NEWS. 0021-4752. Periodical. JA. English. mo. Osaka Senken Ltd, 4-4 Bingomachi Higashi-Ku, Osaka 541 Japan. **Ind/Abst** Chem. Abstr. **CODEN** JTENAL.

JOURNAL - INDIAN COTTON MILLS' FEDERATION. Main/Corp Indian Cotton Mills' Federation. Began with May 1964 issue. Periodical. II. English. ir. 100.00. Indian Cotton Mills' Federation, Elphinstone Building, 10 Ver Nariman Road, Bombay India. **Tel** 86 20 43. Ed C V Radhakrishnan. **LC** HD9086.I4. **DD** 338.47677210954. bk rev. adv acc. **Circ** 2,000. Deals with matters of textiles. Contains special articles, reports and statistical tables connected with textiles, etc.

JOURNAL OF COATED FABRICS. V. 3- July 1973-. 0093-4658. Periodical. US. English. qt. $115.00. Technomic Publishing Company Inc, 851 New Holland Avenue/Box 3535, Lancaster PA 17604. **Tel** (717)291-5609. Ed Peter Larcombe. **Ind/Abst** Eng. Index Mon., Eng. Index Bioeng. Abstr., Eng. Index Energy Abstr., World Text Abstr., Excerpta Med., Chem. Abstr., Eng. Index Annu., Eng. Index. **LC**

Textiles

TS1512. **DD** 677.02864. **CODEN** JCTFAL. bk rev. **Circ** 350. Technical studies on coated fabrics. Information on materials, processes, product applications, properties and performance, patents, fire safety, and government regulations. *Journal of Coated Fibrous Materials.*

JOURNAL OF INDUSTRIAL FABRICS. Vol. 1, No. 1 (Summer 1982)-. 0276-7953. Periodical. US. English. qt. $40.00. Industrial Fabrics Association International, 345 Cedar Building/Suite 450, St Paul MN 55101. **Tel** (612)222-2508. Ed Joan Haglund. **Ind/Abst** World Text Abstr., Chem. Abstr. **Circ** 500. (ctrl). Technical journal for the industrial fabric industry devoted to the dissemination of information about all aspects of current fiber and fabric technology.

JOURNAL OF TEXTILE INDUSTRY. Began in 1967. Periodical. English. qt. $8.00. Journal of Textile Industry, V E 1516 Nazimbad, Karachi Pakistan. **LC** HD9866.P3. **DD** 338.476770095491.

JOURNAL OF THE SOCIETY OF DYERS AND COLOURISTS. **Main/Corp** Society of Dyers and Colourists. V. 1- Nov. 1884-. 0037-9859. Periodical. UK. English. ir. 60. Society of Dyers and Colourists, PO Box 244/82 Gratton Road, Bradford Yorks BD1 2JB England. **Tel** 725138. Ed P M Dinsdale. **Ind/Abst** World Text Abstr., Sel. Water Resour. Abstr., Energy Inf. Abstr., Environ. Abstr., Excerpta Med., World Surf. Coat. Abstr., Art Archaeol. Tech. Abstr., Chem. Abstr., Biogr. Index, Sci. Cit. Index, Abr. Ed. **LC** TP890. **DD** 667.305. **CODEN** JSDCAA. Index in last issue of volume - attached. bk rev. adv acc. **Circ** 4,000. (ctrl). An internationally recognised vehicle for the publication of academic, theoretical and technological articles on subjects allied to all aspects of coloration.

JOURNAL OF THE TEXTILE ASSOCIATION. (JOURNAL). **Main/Corp** Textile Association (India). V. 33- March 1972-. 0368-4636. Periodical. English. ir. **Ind/Abst** World Text Abstr., Chem. Abstr. **LC** TS1300. **DD** 677.005. **CODEN** JTXAA9. *Textile Digest.*

JTN. No. 276- Nov. 1977-. Periodical. English. ir. $44.00 Seamail, $67.10 Airmail. 14 Kawaramachi, 3-Chome Higaski-Ku Osaka 541, Odaka Japan. **Ind/Abst** World Text Abstr., Chem. Abstr. **LC** HD9866.J3. **DD** 338.4767700952. **CODEN** JTNNDZ. *Japan Textile News*, 0021-4752.

JUTE AND JUTE FABRICS, BANGLADESH. Newsletter 1 (Jan. 1975)-. Periodical. BG. English. mo. Sec Bangladesh Jute Research Institute, Sher-E-Banlanagar, Dacca 15 Bangladesh. **Ind/Abst** Art Archaeol. Tech. Abstr., Bibliogr. Agric. **LC** HD9156.J8. **DD** 338.17354095492.

KASEN GEPPO. VFOAT Japan Synthetic Textile Monthly. V. 1- Nov. 1948-. 0368-475X. Periodical. Japanese. mo. **Ind/Abst** Chem. Abstr. **CODEN** KAGEAI.

KIITO KENSAJO JIGYO SEISEKI HOKOKU. **Main/Corp** Yokohama Kiito Kensajo. VFOAT Norinsho Kiito Kensajo Jigyo Hokoku. Japanese. ir. **LC** TS1669.

KJI CEASED. VFOAT Knitwear Jersey International. Periodical. UK. English. bm. 5.00. Knitwear Jersey International, Eastern Boulevard, Leicester LE2 7BN England. **LC** TT679. **DD** 338.4767766105. *Jersey Fabrics International*, 0144-9028.

KNIT FABRIC PRODUCTION. (CURRENT INDUSTRIAL REPORTS. MA-22K, KNIT FABRIC PRODUCTION). 0744-2300. US. English. an. $1.00. Data User Services Division Customer Services Publication, Bureau of the Census, Washington DC 20233. **Tel** (301)763-4100. Presents timely data on the production, inventories, and orders of approximately 5,000 products, which represents 40 percent of all US manufacturing.

KNITOVATIONS. 0160-6336. Periodical. US. English. Woolknit Associates Inc, 501 Madison Avenue, New York NY 10022. **LC** TT679. **DD** 338.47687.

KNITTING MILLS. VFOAT Bonneterie. 1970-1980. 0384-3343. CN. English (French). an. $1.05. Statistics Canada, Manufacturing and Primary Industries Division, Ottawa Ontario K1A 0T6 Canada. **DD** 338.476776610971. *Hosiery and Knitting Mills*, 0575-8734.

KYOTO DAIGAKU NIHON KAGAKU SENI KENKYUJO KOENSHU. VFOAT Annual Report of the Research Institute for Chemical Fibers, Japan. 0368-6280. JA. Japanese. ir. Japan Publications Trading Company Ltd, PO Box 5030 Tokyo International, Tokyo 100-31 Japan. **Ind/Abst** Chem. Abstr. **CODEN** KNKKAB.

LAMB CROP & WOOL. *See* Agriculture - Livestock and Poultry.

THE LATIN AMERICAN TEXTILE INDUSTRY DIRECTORY. *See* Yearbooks, Almanacs, Directories.

LENZINGER BERICHTE. No. 1- 1953-. 0024-0907. Periodical. AU. German (English summaries). ir. 180.-. Chemiefaser Lenzing, Aktiengesellschaft, 4860 Lenzing Austria. **Tel** (07672)2511-2232. Ed E Falilhansl. **Ind/Abst** World Text Abstr., Abstr. Bull. Inst. Paper Chem., Art Archaeol. Tech. Abstr., Chem. Abstr. **LC** TS1300. **CODEN** LEBEAW. adv acc. **Circ** 2,000. (ctrl). Covers man-made fiber production. End-uses, raw materials, viseosefiber, testing, environmental-protection, and processing.

LITERATURSCHAU POLYMERE UND CHEMIEFASERSTOFFE CEASED. V. 20-. Periodical. GE. German. mo. Deutscher Buch Export-Import, Leninstrasse 16, DDR-701 Leipzig East Germany. **LC** Z7914.T3 TS1548.5. *Literaturschau Faserstoffe und Textiltechnik.*

LLOYD'S CANADIAN TEXTILE DIRECTORY. *See* Yearbooks, Almanacs, Directories.

MAN-MADE FIBERS OF JAPAN. 0303-7215. English. ir. Japan Chemical Fibers Association, No 3 Nihonbashi Muromachi 3-Chome Chuo-Ku, Tokyo Japan. **LC** HD9866.J3. **DD** 338.4767740952.

MAN-MADE FIBRE, YARN AND CLOTH MILLS CEASED. VFOAT Fabrication de Fibres, Files et Tissus Artificiels et Synthetiques. 1970-1980. 0300-3795. CN. English (French). an. 70. **DD** 338.47677. *Synthetic Textile Mills*, 0527-6306.

MAN-MADE TEXTILES IN INDIA. V. 16, No. 8- Aug. 1973-. 0377-7537. Periodical. II. English. mo. 120.-. Silk & Art Silk Mills Research Association, Dr Annie Beasant Road, Worli Bombay 400 025 India. **Tel** 4935351. Ed A Kaplash. **Ind/Abst** Chem. Abstr., World Text Abstr. **LC** TS1640. **DD** 677.40954. **CODEN** MMTIBW. bk rev. adv acc. **Circ** 1,500. Deals with all aspects of the man-made fibre and textile industry. It also deals with the latest machinery developments in the industry and new technology. *Silk and Rayon Industries of India.*

MAN-MADE TEXTILES IN INDIA. II. English. ir. Colour Publications, 126 A Dhuruwadi Off Dr Nariman, Bombay 400025 India. **LC** TS1548.5. **DD** 677.405.

MARINE TEXTILES. 0885-9949. Periodical. US. English. bm. $18.00. Industrial Fabrics Association International, 345 Cedar Street/Suite 450, St Paul MN 55101.

MELLIAND-TEXTILBERICHTE. (MELLIAND TEXTILBERICHTE : INTERNATIONAL TEXTILE REPORTS : TEXTILTECHNIK, TEXTILMASCHINEN, TEXTILVEREDLUNG, TEXTILCHEMIE, TEXTILINDUSTRIE). VFOAT Textiltechnik, Textilmaschinen, Textilveredlung, Textilchemie, Textilindustrie. No. 57, Issue 1 (Jan. 1976)-. 0341-0781. Periodical. German. mo. **Ind/Abst** Abstr. Bull. Inst. Paper Chem., World Text Abstr., Excerpta Med., Predicasts, Art Archaeol. Tech. Abstr., Energy Res. Abstr., Chem. Abstr. **LC** TS1300. **DD** 677.005. **CODEN** MTIRDL. *Melliand Textilberichte International* (Heidelberg, Germany).

MELLIAND TEXTILBERICHTE-INTERNATIONAL. ENGLISH EDITION. (MELLIAND TEXTILBERICHTE INTERNATIONAL). VFOAT Melliand Textile Reports. V. 1- 1972-. 0198-7275. Periodical. US. English. mo. $365.00. Ralph McElroy Company Inc, Box 5776, Austin TX 78763. **Tel** (512)451-3461. Ed Werner Szyleyko. **Ind/Abst** Funk Scott Index Corp. Ind., Chem. Abstr. **LC** TS1300. **DD** 677.02805. **Circ** 350. Publishes articles marking current developments in virtually every field of textile science: textile technology, textile finishing, machinery, etc.

MERIYASU KONGOP YONBO. VFOAT Annual on Korean Knitting Industry. Korean. ir. **LC** HD9969.K7.

MODERN FIBRES. 0377-1490. English. ir. 20.00. Association of Man-Made Fibre Industry, 78 Beer Nariman Road, Bombay India. **LC** HD9929.2.I5. **DD** 338.4767740954.

MODERN TEXTILES CEASED. V. 50, No. 7-V. 62, No. 9. 0096-4980. Periodical. US. English. mo. $20.00 Domestic, $25.00 Foreign. Rayon Publishing Corporation, 303 5th Avenue, New York NY 10016. **Ind/Abst** Chem. Abstr. **CODEN** MNTXAF. *Technical Review and Register, Modern Textiles Magazine*, 0026-8488.

MOHAIR AUSTRALIA. (V. 7, No. 3- Sept. 1977-). Periodical. English. ir.

MONTHLY COTTON LINTERS REVIEW. 0027-0318. US. English. mo. US Department of Agriculture, Agricultural Marketing Service, Cotton Division, 4841 Summer Avenue, Memphis TN 38122. **LC** HD9093.U4. **DD** 338.173510973. *Monthly Cotton Linters Review*, 0027-0318.

MONTHLY FIBRE REPORT. **Main/Corp** Wigglesworth and Company. Jan. 1961-. Periodical. UK. English. mo. $20.00. Wigglesworth and Company Ltd, 69 Southwark Bridge Road, London SE1 0NG England.

NAN'S KNIT-KNACKS. VFOAT Knit-Knacks. VAT Knit-Knacks (Montebello). V. 1- Apr. 1977-. 0705-3681. Periodical. CN. English (includes some text in French). qt. Nans Knit-Knacks, 2180 Yonge Street, PO Box 43, Toronto Ontario M4S 2B9 Canada. **Tel** (416)487-5914. **DD** 746.432.

NARROW FABRICS. *See* Manufacturing.

NATIONAL CLOTHESLINE (MIDWEST EDITION). (THE NATIONAL CLOTHESLINE). 0744-6306. Periodical. US. English. mo. $10.00. The National Clothesline, 717 E Chelten Avenue, Philadelphia PA 19144. **Tel** (215)843-9795.

NORTH CAROLINA WORK INJURIES IN THE TEXTILE MILL PRODUCTS INDUSTRY. *See* Industrial Health & Safety.

OSTERREICHISCHE TEXTILE-ZEITUNG. Periodical. AU. German. wk. Osterreichische Textil Zeitung, Industriestrabe 2, A-2380 Perchtoldsdorf. **Tel** 86-49-21.

OUTLOOK AND SITUATION REPORT. COTTON AND WOOL. *See* Agriculture - Crop Production and Soil.

PAPERMAKERS' AND OTHER FELTS CEASED. VFOAT Feutres de Papetier et Autres. -V. 12, No. 2 (June 1983). 0706-2567. Periodical. CN. English (French). qt. **DD** 677.62.

PATENTSCHAU FASERSTOFFE UND TEXTILTECHNIK. AUSGABE A, CHEMIEFASERSTOFFE EINSCHL. POLYMERE UND ORG. AUSGANGSSTOFFE. VFOAT Chemiefaserstoffe Einschl. Polymere und Org. Ausgangsstoffe. Periodical. German. ir. 27.00 Quarterly. Institut fur Polymerenchemie der ADW der DDR, Kantstr 55, Teltow-Seehof 153 East Germany. **LC** TS1300. **DD** 677.02830272. *Patentschau Faserstoffe und Textiltechnik. Ausgabe A, Faserstoffe Einschl. Grundsubstanzen.*

PROCEEDINGS OF THE TECHNOLOGICAL CONFERENCE. **Main/Corp** Ahmedabad Textile Industry's Research Association. 1st- 1959-. II. English. an. 10.00. Ahmedabad Textile Indian Research Association, PO Polytechnic, Ahmedabad 380 015 India. **Tel** 442671. **Circ** 2,000. Papers in the field of textiles and allied subjects.

PRODUKTIESTATISTIEKEN : TRICOT-EN KOUSEINDUSTRIE CEASED. **Main/Corp** Netherlands. Centraal Bureau voor de Statistiek. Dutch. ir. **LC** HD9969.K7.

PROTEXTILE : LE CENTRE QUEBECOIS DE PRODUCTIVITE DU TEXTILE. Bulletin 1 (June/July 1984)-. 0825-8031. Periodical. CN. English. bm. Free. Protestile, 3000 rue Boule, St-Hyacinthe Quebec J2S 1H9 Canada. **DD** 338.47677009714.

REINIGER + WASCHER. (REINIGER + I.E. UND WASCHER). VAT Reiniger und Wascher. V. 23, No. 4, April 1970-. 0034-3625. Periodical. GW. German. mo. $36.52. Verlag Neuer Merkur GMBH, Postfach 460805, Ingolstadterstr 63A, 8000 Munchen 46 West Germany. **Ind/Abst** Excerpta Med., CIS Abstr. **LC** TP932. *Wascher + I.E. und Reiniger.*

REPORT - LINEN FLAX CORPORATION OF NEW ZEALAND. **Main/Corp** Linen Flax Corporation of New Zealand. 1st- 1946-. NZ. English. ir. Linen Flax Corporaton of

Textiles

New Zealand, Wellington New Zealand. LC HD9155.N44. **DD** 338.47677LL.

REVIEW OF PROGRESS IN COLORATION AND RELATED TOPICS. V. 1- June 1967/Sept. 1969-. 0557-9325. UK. English. an. $19.16. Society of Dyers and Coulourists, Box 244/82 Grattan, Bradford West Yorkshire BD1 2JB England. **Tel** 725138. **Ed** Anita Hallan. **Ind/Abst** World Text Abstr., Abstr. Bull. Inst. Paper Chem., Chem. Abstr. LC TP890. **DD** 667.305. **Circ** 4,000. (ctrl). A review to critically assess various fields under consideration. Topics include: dyes, pigments, coloration of textile and non-textile substrates.

RUG NEWS. See Interior Design.

SALARIE SYNDIQUE. See Clothing and Fashion.

SAWTRI SPECIAL PUBLICATION. VFOAT S.A.W.T.R.I. Special Publication. Monographic Series. English. ir. South African Wool Textile Research Institute, Box 1124, Port Elizabeth 6000 South Africa. **Tel** (041)53-2131. **Ed** P Horn. **Ind/Abst** Chem. Abstr. **CODEN** SASPDW. **Circ** 230. (ctrl). Textile related topics such as the physical and chemical properties of natural fibers or blends of wool, cotton and mohair with synthetics of one another.

SENI GAKKAI SHI. VFOAT Seni Gakkaishi, Journal of the Society of Fiber and Technology, Japan. Began in 1944. 0037-9875. Periodical. JA. Japanese. mo. $134.00. Japan Publishers Trading Company Ltd, PO Box 5030, Tokyo International, Tokyo 100-31 Japan. **Ind/Abst** Abstr. Bull. Inst. Paper Chem., Excerpta Med., World Text Abstr., Chem. Abstr. **CODEN** SENGA5. Seni Kogyo Gakkai Shi Seni to Kogyo.

SERIE DE INGENIERIA DE LA CALIDAD. Series **Corp** Asociacion de Investigacion Textil Algodonera. Coleccion de Manuales Tecnicos. Spanish. ir. Asociacion de Investigacion Textil Algodonera, Avda Jose Antonio 670, Barcelona Spain. LC HD9885.S69.

SHEETS, PILLOWCASES, AND TOWELS. (CURRENT INDUSTRIAL REPORTS. MQ-23X, SHEETS, PILLOWCASES, AND TOWELS). 0145-496X. US. English. qt. $8.00. Data User Services Division, Customer Services Publication, Bureau of the Census, Washington DC 20233. **Tel** (301)763-7536. **Ind/Abst** Predicasts, Am. Stat. Index. LC HD9969.H833. **DD** 338.4768. Detailed statistics on textiles, apparel, and footwear.

SKINNER'S BRITISH TEXTILE REGISTER. VFOAT British Textile Register. 1st-Ed. UK. English, French, German and Spanish. 10.50. RAC House, Lansdowne Road, Croydon CR9 2HH England. LC TS1312. **DD** 338.47677002542. British Textile Industry, Lancashire Textile Industry; Skinner's Cotton and Man-Made Fibres Directory of the World; Skinner's Hosiery and Knit Goods Directory; Skinner's Wool Trade Directory of the World; Yorkshire Textile Industry.

SOMYU YONGAM. VFOAT Textile Year Book. 1980-. KO. Korean. an. Hanguk Somyu Snaop, Yonhaphoe 10-1, 2 Ka Hoehyon-Dong, Chung-Ku Seoul Korea. LC HD9866.K65.

SOUTHERN AFRICA TEXTILES. VFOAT SA Textiles. Began with issue for Aug. 1952. Periodical. SA. English. mo. $12.39. The Phoneix Group, PO Box 69264, Bryanston 2021 Republic South Africa. **Ind/Abst** Chem. Abstr. LC TS1300. **CODEN** TISADK.

SOUTHERN TEXTILE NEWS. Began in 1945. 0038-4607. Periodical. US. English. wk. $15.00. Southern Textile News, PO Box 668926, Charlotte NC 28266. **Tel** (704)394-5111. **Ed** Marjorie T Richardson. adv acc. **Circ** 6,000. (ctrl). Textile news paper containing industry editorial comment; industry machinery, facility and personnel news and textile machinery and ancillary equipment, advertising (both new and used).

SOUTHWEST CLEANING. Vol. 1, No. (May 1982)-. 0744-7124. Periodical. US. English. mo. Southwest Cleaning, PO Box 340195, Dallas TX 75234.

SPIN-OFF. (SPIN OFF). V. 1- 1977-. 0198-8239. US. English. qt. $10.00. Interweave Press, 306 N Washington Avenue, Loveland CO 80537. **Tel** (303)669-7672. **Ed** Lee Raven. LC TT847. **DD** 746.1205. bk rev. adv acc. **Circ** 10,000. 60 or more pages of how-to's, history, fiber use and properties, news and technical information on handspun designs, plus in-depth articles and photography.

SPUN YARN PRODUCTION. See Manufacturing.

STATISTICAL HANDBOOK (NEW ZEALAND WOOL BOARD). See Statistics.

STOCKS OF WOOL AND RELATED FIBERS. (CURRENT INDUSTRIAL REPORTS. MA-22M, STOCKS OF WOOL AND RELATED FIBERS). 0149-0583. US. English. be. $1.00. Data User Services Division, Customer Services Publication, Bureau of the Census, Washington DC 20233. **Tel** (301)763-4100. LC HD9891. Information on raw wool, tops, noils, and related fibers, including synthetic staple, owned or held on consignment for growers or US agents of foreign exporters. Current Industrial Reports. M22M, Stocks of Wool and Related Fibers.

SUMMARY OF COTTON FIBER AND PROCESSING TEST RESULTS. 0565-2030. US. English. Standards Section, Cotton Division AMS, USDA, 4841 Summer Avenue, Memphis TN 38122. LC TS1542. **DD** 677.2130973.

SURFACE DESIGN JOURNAL. VFOAT SDJ. Vol. 2, No. 3 (Summer 1978)-. 0197-4483. Periodical. US. English. qt. $45.00. Surface Design Association, 311 East Washington Street, Fayetteville TN 37334. **Tel** (615)433-6804. **Ed** Stephen Blumrich. bk rev. adv acc. **Circ** 1,500. For those interested in the coloring and patterning of fabric and fiber with dyes, pigments, or manipulation. Surface Design.

SZOVETKEZETI IPAR. Periodical. HU. Hungarian. ir. Ikisz, Budapest V Pesti Barnabas UTCA 6, Budapest Hungary. LC HD9865.H9.

TECHNICAL BULLETIN - I.F.I. RESEARCH CENTER. (TECHNICAL BULLETIN - IFI RESEARCH CENTER). **Main/Corp** IFI Research Center. No. T-486- March 1973-. 0095-666X. US. English. IFI Research Center, 12251 Tech Road, Silver Spring MD 20904. LC TP932. **DD** 667.1205. Technical Bulletin - International Fabricare Institute, Drycleaning Division.

TECHNICAL MANUAL AND YEAR BOOK OF THE AMERICAN ASSOCIATION OF TEXTILE CHEMISTS AND COLORISTS. See Yearbooks, Almanacs, Directories.

TECHNICAL REVIEW & REGISTER. **Main/Corp** American Association for Textile Technology. VFOAT AATT Technical Review and Register. 1968-. 0065-7069. US. English. an. Rayon Publishing Company, 5th Avenue, New York NY 10016. LC TS1300.A16. **DD** 677.005. Annual Conference, Annual Conference; Full Text of Annual Conference.

TEINTURE ET APPRETS. Began in 1948. 0040-2206. Periodical. FR. French. bm. Siege Social et Bureaux, 97 rue du Bas-Saut, 60230 Chambly France. **Ind/Abst** Chem. Abstr. **CODEN** TNAPA7.

TEKSTIILITEOLLISUUDEN VUOSIKIRJA. TEXTILINDUSTRINS ARSBOK. See Yearbooks, Almanacs, Directories.

DE TEX. Began in 1942?. Periodical. Dutch. mo. LC TS1300. **DD** 677.05.

DE TEX - TEXTILIS. No. 6 (June 1973)-. Periodical. Multilingual (Dutch and French). bm. $14.83. De Tex Textiles, 92 Savaanstraat, Ghent Belgium. **Ind/Abst** Art Archaeol. Tech. Abstr. De Tex Textilis.

TEXSCOPE; USA TEXTILE INDUSTRY OVERVIEW. VFOAT USA Textile Industry Overview. 0092-3540. US. English. Werner Management Consultants Inc, 1450 Broadway, New York NY 10018. LC HD9853. **DD** 338.4767700973.

TEXTIELVERZORGING : VAKBLAD VAN DE NVW EN DE VCW. Jan. 1984-. Periodical. Dutch. mo. **Ind/Abst** Excerpta Med. LC TP932. **DD** 667.1205. Vakblad voor Textielreiniging.

TEXTIL OCH KONFEKTION CEASED. Vol. 1- Feb. 1944-. 0040-4845. Periodical. SW. Swedish. ir. 225.-. Sveriges Textilindustriforbund, Box 16124, S103 23 Stockholm Sweden. **Tel** (08)24 40 40. **Ed** Olof Myr. **Ind/Abst** World Text Abstr. LC TS1300. **DD** 677.05. adv acc. **Circ** 8,900. (ctrl). Fashion and marketing news for managers and employees in the textile and garment trade, technical news for technicians in the textile, clothing, footwear and leather industries. Skandinavisk Tidskrift For Textilindustri.

TEXTIL-PRAXIS INTERNATIONAL. (TEXTIL PRAXIS INTERNATIONAL). 0040-4853. Periodical. GW. German (supplement in English). mo. 229.20. Konradin-Verlag, Postfach 100252, Ernst Mey Str 8, 7022 Leinfelden West Germany. **Tel** (0711)75940. **Ed** Horst Meyrahn. **Ind/Abst** Chem. Abstr., Excerpta Med., Predicasts, CIS Abstr., Art Archaeol. Tech. Abstr. LC TS1300. **DD** 677.005. bk rev. adv acc. **Circ** 7,170. Magazine for spinning, fabric manufacturing, dyeing, finishing industries. Textil-Praxis.

TEXTILBETRIEB. Vol. 89, No. 10-. 0340-4188. Periodical. German. ir. **Ind/Abst** Excerpta Med., World Text Abstr., CIS Abstr., Art Archaeol. Tech. Abstr., Chem. Abstr. LC TS1300. **CODEN** TXTBAS. Spinner, Weber, Textilveredlung.

TEXTILBRANSCHEN. 0040-4888. Periodical. Swedish. ir. 225.-. Textilbranschen, Textil och Konfektion, Textilbranschens Forlags AB, S-10561 Stockholm Sweden. **Tel** (08)24 40 40. **Ed** Olof Myr. adv acc. **Circ** 8,900. (ctrl). Fashion and marketing news for managers and employees in the textile and garment trade, technical news for technicians in the textile, clothing, footwear and leather industries. Textil Och Konfektion.

TEXTILE ASIA. V. 1- Oct. 1970-. 0049-3554. Periodical. English. mo. $36.00. Business Press Ltd, Tak Yan Com Block/GPO Box 185, Hong Kong China. **Tel** 5-233744. **Ed** Kayser Sung. **Ind/Abst** World Text Abstr., Chem. Abstr. LC TS1399. **DD** 338.4'7'677095. **CODEN** TASIDM. bk rev. adv acc. **Circ** 15,000. (ctrl). Textile and clothing technology, reports on and analyses of international textile trade, management features, new equipment reports, fashion trends, news about textile companies and people.

THE TEXTILE BOOKLIST. 0149-5682. Periodical. US. English. qt. $14.00. Textile Booklist, c/o Kaaren Buffington, PO Box 4392, Arcata CA 95521. **Tel** (707)822-7716. **Ed** Kaaren Buffington. **Ind/Abst** Index Book Rev. Humanit. bk rev. **Circ** 2,000. (ctrl). Digest of book news and reviews: textiles, fiber arts, needle arts, costumes, plus listing of new books and textile shows and happenings around the world.

TEXTILE CHALLENGER. See Economics - Labor.

TEXTILE CHEMIST AND COLORIST. V. 1- Jan. 1969-. 0040-490X. Periodical. US. English. mo. $30.00 US/Canada, $40.00 Foreign. American Association of Textile Chemists and Colorists, PO Box 12215, Research Triangle Park NC 27709. **Tel** (919)549-8141. **Ed** Jack Kissiah. **Ind/Abst** Eng. Index Annu., Eng. Index Mon., Eng. Index Bioeng. Abstr., Eng. Index Energy Abstr., Excerpta Med., World Text Abstr., Energy Inf. Abstr., Environ. Abstr., Abstr. Bull. Inst. Paper Chem., Art Archaeol. Tech. Abstr., Chem. Abstr., Bibliogr. Agric., Eng. Index. LC TP890. **DD** 677.0282505. **CODEN** TCCOB6. bk rev. adv acc. **Circ** 10,200. Contains current news and features on all phases of textile wet processing plus reporting in-depth on AATCC activities. July issue is the Annual Buyer's Guide.

TEXTILE CLEANING TECHNOLOGY. **Main/Corp** International Fabricare Institute. 0094-5781. Periodical. US. English. mo. $40.00. International Fabricare Institute, PO Box 940, Joliet IL 60434. LC TP932.3. **DD** 667.1205.

TEXTILE DIRECTIONS. V. 9- 1st Quarter 1974-. Periodical. US. English. qt. $7.00. Geer Publishing Company, 1440 Broadway, New York NY 10018. LC TT679. **DD** 677.005. Textile-Knit Directions, 0147-0132.

TEXTILE DYER & PRINTER. V. 1- 1967-. 0040-4926. Periodical. II. English. bw. 35.00. Sevak Publications, PO Box 7110, Wadala Bombay 400 031 India. **Tel** 412 34 36. **Ed** K S S Raghavan. **Ind/Abst** World Text Abstr., Art Archaeol. Tech. Abstr., Chem. Abstr. LC TP890. **CODEN** TDYPAN. bk rev. adv acc. **Circ** 5,000. (ctrl). Devoted to wet processing industry.

TEXTILE DYER & PRINTER : ANNUAL NUMBER. English. ir. Sevak Publications, Unit No B-26 Royal Optical Industrial Estate Wadala -31, Bombay India. LC TP890. **DD** 667.305.

TEXTILE EXPORTS OF JAPAN : COUNTRY BY COMMODITY. **Main/Corp** Yushutsu Seni Tokei Kyokai (Japan). VFOAT Seni Yushutsu Tokei Geppyo: Kunibetsu Shohinbetsu. JA. English and Japanese (English only, 19(66)-68). ir. Yushutsu Seni Tokei Kyokai, c/o Textile Exporters' House 4, Bingomachi 4-chome Higashi-ku, Osaka 540 Japan. LC HD9866.J3. **DD** 382.4567700952.

TEXTILE FLAMMABILITY DIGEST. V. 1-1973-. 0738-9620. Periodical. US. English. mo. $60.00. LeBlanc Research Corporation, PO Box 295, North Kingstown RI 02852. **Tel** (401)884-5785. **Ed** R Bruce LeBlanc. bk rev. **Circ** 200. Abstracts of all literature, patents, meetings, and other information on textile flammability and flame resistance.

TEXTILE HISTORY. Began with: Vol. 1, No. 1 (Dec. 1968). 0040-4969. Periodical. UK. English. qt. 20.00. Magazine Subscription Ltd, Oakfield House/Perrymount Road, Haywards Heath RH16 3DH England. **Tel** (01)405 7686. **Ind/Abst** Repert. Int. Litt. Art, Avery Index Archit. Period. **LC** HD9850.1. **DD** 338.47677005. Textile history.

TEXTILE HORIZONS. Vol. 1, No. 1 (Sept. 1981)-. 0260-6518. Periodical. UK. English. mo. Textile Institute, 10 Blackfriars Street, Manchester M3 5DR United Kingdom. **Ind/Abst** Eng. Index Annu., Eng. Index Mon., Eng. Index Bioeng. Abstr., Eng. Index Energy Abstr., Excerpta Med., World Text Abstr., Abstr. Bull. Inst. Paper Chem., Predicasts. **LC** HD9850.1. **DD** 338.47677005. *Textile Institute and Industry, 0039-8357.*

TEXTILE INDUSTRY & TRADE JOURNAL. Began in Jan. 1963. 0040-4993. Periodical. II. English. bm. $25.00. Indian Export Trade Journal, Savajuganj, Baroda 5 India. **Ind/Abst** Art Archaeol. Tech. Abstr. **LC** TS1300. **DD** 677.005.

THE TEXTILE INSTITUTE AND INDUSTRY *CEASED.* V. 1-19, No. 8. 0039-8357. Periodical. UK. English. mo. **Ind/Abst** Excerpta Med., Predicasts, Art Archaeol. Tech. Abstr., Ref. Source, Chem. Abstr. **CODEN** TIINA6. *Journal of the Textile Institute, 0040-5000.*

TEXTILE JAPAN. Began publication in 1953. 0082-366X. English. an. Japan Publications Trading Company Ltd, PO Box 5030, Tokyo International, Tokyo 100-31 Japan. **LC** TS1405. **DD** 677.058.

TEXTILE MANUAL. **VFOAT** Manual of the Textile Industry of Canada. 41st- Ed. 0381-551X. CN. English. an. $7.50. 4999 St Catherine Street West/Suite 446, Montreal Quebec H3Z 1T3 Canada. **LC** TS1326. **DD** 338.4767700971. *Manual of the Textile Industry of Canada, 0076-4183.*

TEXTILE MANUFACTURER & KNITTING WORLD. **VFOAT** Knitting World & Textile Manufacturer. V. 102, No. 1202- May 1975-. Periodical. UK. English. mo. 10.00. 33 King Street, London M2 6AA England. **LC** TS1300. **DD** 338.4767700941. *Textile Manufacturer, British Knitting Industry.*

TEXTILE MONTH. Jan. 1968-. 0040-5116. Periodical. UK. English. mo. $117.00. Business Press International Limited, Perrymont Road, Haywards Health West Sussex RH163BR England. **Ind/Abst** Eng. Index Annu., Eng. Index Mon., Eng. Index Bioeng. Abstr., Eng. Index Energy Abstr., Excerpta Med., World Text Abstr., Predicasts, Funk Scott Index Corp. Ind., Eng. Index. **LC** TS1300. **DD** 677.005. **CODEN** TXMOAW. *Man-Made Textiles and Skinner's Record, Textile Recorder.*

TEXTILE MUSEUM JOURNAL. *See* Museums.

TEXTILE ORGANON (1952). (TEXTILE ORGANON). Began with: Vol. 23, in 1952. 0040-5132. Periodical. US. English. mo. $25.00. Textile Economics Bureau Inc, 101 Eisenhower Parkway, Roseland NJ 07068. **Tel** (202)228-1107. **Ind/Abst** World Text Abstr., Predicasts, Public Aff. Inf. Serv. Bull. **LC** HD9929.5.U6. **DD** 338.4767746. *Rayon Organon.*

TEXTILE PRODUCTS AND PROCESSES. V. 1- Oct. 1978-. 0162-9468. Periodical. US. English. mo. $45.00. McGraw Hill Publications, 4170 Asford Dunwoody Road/Suite 420, Atlanta GA 30319. **Tel** (404)252-0626. **LC** TS1300. **DD** 677.005. adv acc. (ctrl).

THE TEXTILE RECORDER BOOK OF THE YEAR. 1947/48-. UK. English. an. **LC** TS1301. **DD** 677.05. *Textile Recorder Year Book.*

TEXTILE RESEARCH JOURNAL. V. 15, No. 2- Feb. 1945-. 0040-5175. Periodical. US. English. mo. $115.00. Textile Research Institution, PO Box 625, Princeton NJ 08542. **Tel** (609)924-3150. **Ed** R K Tower. **Ind/Abst** Eng. Index Mon., Eng. Index Bioeng. Abstr., Eng. Index Energy Abstr., Life Sci. Collect., Excerpta Med., World Text Abstr., Predicasts, Abstr. Bull. Inst. Paper Chem., Int. Aerosp. Abstr., Art Archaeol. Tech. Abstr., Chem. Abstr., Eng. Index Annu., Eng. Index Mon., Bibliogr. Agric., Appl. Sci. Technol. Index, Eng. Index, Sel. Water Resour. Abstr. **LC** TS1300. **DD** 677.05. **CODEN** TRJOA9. bk rev. **Circ** 2,000. Contains fundamental and applied scientific information in the physical, chemical, and engineering sciences related to the textile and allied industries. *Textile Research, 0096-5928.*

TEXTILE TECHNOLOGY DIGEST. V. 1-June 1944-. 0040-5191. Periodical. US. English. mo. Institute of Textile Technology, PO Box 391, Charlottesville VA 22902. **Tel** (804)296-5511. **Ed** Linda Cahill. **Ind/Abst** World Text Abstr., Abstr. Bull. Inst. Paper Chem. **LC** TS1300. **DD** 016.677. bk rev. Textiles, fibers, textile equipment and processes, apparel, dyeing and finishing, industrial fabrics, yarn and fabric manufacturing, drycleaning.

TEXTILE TRENDS. 1958. 0040-5205. Periodical. II. English. mo. $100.00. Eastland Publications Pr Ltd, 44 Chittaranjan Avenue, Calcutta 700 012 India. **Tel** 27-3096. **Ed** Mukul Guha. **LC** TS1300. bk rev. adv acc. **Circ** 4,000. Various articles, news, write-ups on textile and allied industries for the textile and allied industries exclusively served by us.

TEXTILE WEEK. V. 1- May 22, 1978-. 0161-9713. Periodical. US. English. wk. $156.00. McGraw-Hill Publications, 1175 Peachtree Street NE, Atlanta GA 30361. **LC** HD9851. **DD** 338.4767700973.

TEXTILE WORLD. 0040-5213. Periodical. US. English. mo. $72.00. Textile World, McGraw Hill Publishing, PO Box 416, Hightstown NJ 08520. **Tel** (609)426-5000. **Ind/Abst** Eng. Index Annu., Eng. Index Mon., Eng. Index Bioeng. Abstr., Eng. Index Energy Abstr., Excerpta Med., World Text Abstr., Predicasts, CIS Abstr., Art Archaeol. Tech. Abstr., Bus. Period. Index, Chem. Abstr., Appl. Sci. Technol. Index, Funk Scott Index Corp. Ind., Bus. Period. Index, Eng. Index. **CODEN** TEWOAH. adv acc. (ctrl). *Textile World Journal, 0096-5936; Posselt's Textile Journal, 0096-8358; Textiles; Textile Advance News.*

TEXTILES. V. 1- Feb. 1972-. 0306-0748. Periodical. UK. English. ir. 12.00. Shirley Institute, Didsbury, Manchester M20 8RX England. **Tel** (061)445 8141. **Ed** Maureen Sawbridge. **Ind/Abst** Abstr. Bull. Inst. Paper Chem., Art Archaeol. Tech. Abstr., Predicasts, World Text Abstr., Funk Scott Index Corp. Ind. bk rev. Descriptions in non-technical language of science and technology of fibres, textile materials, clothing, industrial and other fibre-containing products. *Shirley Link.*

TEXTILES PANAMERICANOS. V. 1- May 1941-. 0049-3570. Periodical. US. Spanish. qt. $20.00. Billian Publishing, 2100 Powers Ferry Road/Suite 125, Atlanta GA 30339. **Tel** (404)955-5656. **Ed** Jim Woodroffe. **LC** TS1300. adv acc. **Circ** 14,400.

TEXTILES SUISSES. **VFOAT** Swiss Textiles. SZ. Multilingual (French, English, German). qt. $33.64. Office Suisse d'Expansion Comm, Avenue de l'Avant Poste 4, CH-1001 Lausanne Switzerland. **Tel** (021)23.18.24. **Ed** Peter Pfister. adv acc. **Circ** 12,500. (ctrl). Devoted to Swiss clothing fabrics and their use in int. haute couture and ready-to-wear, and accessories/company-profiles. Only Swiss products are being published.

TEXTILIA. V. 46- July 1970-. Periodical. IT. Italian. bm. $45.14. Periodici Aracne Nuova SRL, Via Padova 41, 20127 Milano Italy. **Tel** 28-40-130. **Ind/Abst** World Text Abstr., Chem. Abstr. **CODEN** TXTLAO. *Revista Tessile, Raion e Fibre; Fibre e Colori.*

A TEXTILIPARI KUTATO INTEZET KOZLEMENYEI. (TEXTILIPARI KUTATO INTEZET KOZLEMENYEI). Began in 1976. 0133-2082. Monographic Series. Hungarian. bm. **Ind/Abst** World Text Abstr., Chem. Abstr. **CODEN** TKIKDE.

TEXTILTECHNIK. Vol. 23. 0323-3804. Periodical. SZ. German. mo. $45.12. Kunst & Wissen Erich Bieber, Dufourstrasse 51, CH-8008 Zurich Switzerland. **Tel** (011)41169 44 20. **Ind/Abst** Excerpta Med., World Text Abstr., CIS Abstr., Art Archaeol. Tech. Abstr., Chem. Abstr. **LC** TS1300. **CODEN** TEXTC5. *Deutsche Textiltechnik.*

TEXTILVEREDLUNG. Yearly Vol. 1 Jan. 1966-. 0040-5310. Periodical. SZ. German. mo. 52.50. Geschaftsstelle Basel, Postfach 146, CH-4013 Basel Switzerland. **Tel** (061)243265. **Ed** A Barthold. **Ind/Abst** Excerpta Med., World Text Abstr., Abstr. Bull. Inst. Paper Chem., CIS Abstr., Art Archaeol. Tech. Abstr., Chem. Abstr. **LC** TS1510. **DD** 677.005. **CODEN** TXLVAE. bk rev. adv acc. **Circ** 3,000. Magazine for people working in the textile industry, the chemical industry, (dyestuffs, finishes) and the machine industry (machines for the texture finishing industry). Also for schools for textile engineering and universities (chemistry of dyestuffs).

TEXTRACTS. No. 1- July 1953-. 0495-3789. Periodical. US. English. mo. $75.00. Varley Textile Associates, 32 West 40th Street, New York NY 10018. **Tel** (212)840-7022. **Ed** Gerald M Varley. bk rev. A summary of domestic and international textile, apparel, industrial news, and technology.

TEXTURED YARN PRODUCTION. *See* Manufacturing.

TJENESTEYTING, FORRETNINGSMESSIG TJENESTEYTING, UTLEIE AV MASKINER OG UTSTYR, RENOVASJON OG REINGJRING, VASKERI- OG RENSERIVIRKSOMHET. AND SIMILAR SERVICES, LAUNDRIES, LAUNDRY SERVICES AND CLEANING AND DYEING PLANTS /. *See* Statistics.

TRI NEWS AND RESEARCH BRIEFS. VAT Textile Research Institute News and Research Briefs. Periodical. US. English. Textile Research Institute, PO Box 625, Princeton NJ 08540. **Ind/Abst** World Text Abstr.

TRSA ORGANIZATION. **Main/Corp** Textile Rental Services Association of America. **VAT** Textile Rental Services Association of America Organization. 0748-7142. US. English. TRSA, 1250 East Hallandale Beach Boulevard, Hallandale FL 33009.

UNITED STATES COTTON QUALITY REPORT FOR GINNINGS. 0093-4429. US. English. USDA Cotton Division, 4841 Summer Avenue, Memphis TN 38122. **Tel** (901)521-2934. **Ind/Abst** Am. Stat. Index.

UPHOLSTERY MANUFACTURING MANAGEMENT. *See* Manufacturing.

WAGA KUNI NO KOKOGYO : SENI KOGYO HEN; SENI RYUTSU HEN. **Main/Corp** Japan. Tsusho Sangyosho. Daijin Kambo. Chosa Tokeibu. JA. Japanese. ir. Daijin Kambo, 3-Ban 1-Go Kasumigaseki 1-Chome Chiyoda-Ku, Tokyo 100 Japan. **LC** HD9866.J3.

WARP AND WEFT. Began with issue for Nov. 1947. 0732-6890. Periodical. US. English. mo. $12.00. Warp & Weft, 533 North Adams Street, McMinnville OR 97128. **Tel** (503)472-5760. **Ed** Russell E Groff. bk rev. adv acc. **Circ** 450. (ctrl). For handweavers with 4-harness looms. A sample with directions on how-to-weave each month plus book reviews and other articles concerning handweaving.

THE WEAVERS JOURNAL *CEASED.* No. 97, Spring 1976. Ceased with No. 130. Periodical. UK. English. qt. Association of the Guilds of Weavers Spinners and Dyers, BCM 963, London WC1N 3XX England. *Quarterly Journal of the Association of the Guilds of Weavers, Spinners, and Dyers.*

THE WEAVER'S JOURNAL. V. 1- (Issue 1-). 0160-3817. Periodical. US. English. qt. $42.00. The Weavers Journal, PO Box 14238, St Paul MN 55114. **Tel** (612)646-7445. **Ed** Karen Searle. **LC** TT848. **DD** 746.1405. bk rev. adv acc. **Circ** 10,000. Technical and educational information on weaving, spinning, and dyeing. Historical information, project ideas, instructions, and inspiration. Themes: clothing, rugs, fibers and ethnic textiles.

WOLGAN SOMYU. **VFOAT** Somyu. Periodical. KO. Korean. mo. 2,000. Wolgan Somyusa 73-1, 2-Ka Inhyon-Dong Chung-Ku, Seoul Korea. **LC** HD9866.K6.

WOOL. V. 1- 1948-. English. an. $1.12. Massey Wool Association Inc, PO Box 421, Palmerston North New Zealand. **Ind/Abst** Bibliogr. Agric.

WOOL & CARPET REVIEW. **VFOAT** Wool and Carpet Review. Vol. 1, No. 1 (1981)-. Periodical. English. qt. 260.00. Naeem Tahir, 23 Carvan Building Link McLeod Road, PO Box 1834, Lahore Pakistan. **LC** HD9937.P18. **DD** 338.47677643095491.

WOOL AND MOHAIR. Began with 1964. US. English. ir. $1.25. USDA, c/o John Lawler ESS-NED Crop Branch, 500 12th Street NW, Washington DC 20250. *Wool Production and Value.*

WOOL AND WOOLENS OF INDIA. (WOOL & WOOLLENS OF INDIA). Began in 1964. 0043-7808. Periodical. II. English. qt. $20.00. Indian Woollen Mills Federation, Churchgate Cham 7th Floor, 5 New Marine Line, Bombay 400020 India. **Ind/**

Theater

Abst World Text Abstr., Chem. Abstr. CODEN WWIDA5.

WOOL, AUSTRALIA. AT. English. ir. Information Services, Australian Bureau of Statistics, Belconnen Australian Capital Territory 2616 Canberra Australia. LC HD9908.A8. DD 338.47677310994.

WOOL OUTLOOK CEASED. (THE WOOL OUTLOOK). Main/Corp Australia. Bureau of Agricultural Economics. No. 1-43. Periodical. AT. English. sa. Australian Government Publishing Service, PO Box 84, Canberra Australian Capital Territory 2600 Australia. Tel 062/95 4411. LC HD9890.1. DD 338.176314.

WOOL PRODUCTION AND DISPOSAL—TASMANIA. 0156-7829. English. ir. Tasmanian Office, Australian Bureau of Statistics, 10th Floor, Commonwealth Government Centre, 188 Collins Street, GPO Box 66-A, Hobart 7001 Australia. LC HD9908.A83. DD 338.1763145. *Wool Production Statistics, Tasmania.*

WOOL QUARTERLY. V. 1- Jan.1979-. 0142-1921. Periodical. UK. English. qt. $119.17. Commonwealth Secretariat, Marlbourogh House/Pall Mall, London SW1Y 5HX England. Tel (01)839-3411. Ed M Godfrey. Ind/Abst World Text Abstr. Deals with world wool, wool textile situation outlook and summaries developments affecting wool supplies and markets. Also comprises detailed analytical statistical tables on all countries with an interest in sector.

WOOL RECORD WEEKLY MARKET REPORT. Periodical. UK. English. wk. $139.00. Wool Record Ltd, 91 Kirkgate, Bradford BD1 1TB England. Tel (0274)731907. Ed Martin Black. Ind/Abst World Text Abstr. bk rev. adv acc. Commentary of wool and yarn prices and wool futures markets around the world. *Weekly Wool Chart and Private Business Report (45.8 W855).*

WOOL STATISTICS. See Statistics.

WOOL STATISTICS, AUSTRALIA. See Statistics.

WOOL TECHNOLOGY AND SHEEP BREEDING. See Agriculture - Livestock and Poultry.

WOOL YARN AND CLOTH MILLS (FINAL) CEASED. (WOOL YARN AND CLOTH MILLS). VFOAT Filature et Tissage de la Laine. 1970-1980. 0300-1202. CN. English (French). an. 70. DD 338.476773. *Wool Mills (Canada. Dominion Bureau of Statistics), 0576-0089.*

WORLD FIBRE NEWS. Periodical. UK. English. wk. $18.00. 222 Strand, London WC2R 1BA England. LC HD9850.1. DD 338.47677. *Jute Markets & Prices, Textile Production.*

WORLD TEXTILE ABSTRACTS. See Indexes/Abstracts.

WYOMING WOOL GROWER. See Agriculture - Livestock and Poultry.

YORAN - SENI KOBUNSHI ZAIRYO KENKYUJO. Main/Corp Seni Kobunshi Zairyo Kenkyujo. VFOAT Outline of the Research Institute for Polymers and Textiles. JA. Japanese and English. ir. Kogyo Gijutsuin Sani Kobunshi Zairyo Kenkyujo, 4-Banchi Sawatari, Kanagawa-Ku (221), Yokohama Japan. LC TA417.S36.

THEATER

ABRACADABRA. V. 1- Dec. 1978-. 0708-9600. Periodical. CN. English. Free to members, $15.00 Others. Association of British Columbia Drama Educators, c/o British Columbia Teachers Federation, 2235 Burrard Street, Vancouver BC V6J 3H9 Canada. Ind/Abst Can. Educ. Index. DD 792.0710711.

ACADEMY PLAYERS DIRECTORY. See Yearbooks, Almanacs, Directories.

ACQUISITIONS - METROPOLITAN TORONTO LIBRARY. THEATRE DEPARTMENT. See Bibliographies.

AL-SINIMA WA-AL-MASRAH. See Motion Picture.

AMERICAN THEATRE. Vol. 1, No. 1 (Apr. 1984)-. 8750-3255. Periodical. US. English. mo. $24.00. Theatre Communications Group, American Theatre, 355 Lexington Avenue, New York NY 10017. Tel (212)697-5230. Ed Jim O'Quinn. DD 792. bk rev. adv acc. Circ 14,000. Feature articles highlight developments in all aspects of theater; regular monthly columns update nationwide performance activity, international events, book reviews, and awards. *Theatre Communications, 0275-5971.*

ANNUAL REPORT - THEATRE ARTS DEPARTMENT. Main/Corp Dar es Salaam. University. Theatre Arts Dept. TZ. English. ir. University of Dar es Salaam, Theatre Arts Department, Dar es Salaam Tanzania. LC PN2078.T342. DD 792.0711678.

L'ANNUEL DU THEATRE. FR. French. an. 120.00. L'Annuel du Theatre, 30 rue de la Belique, 92190 Meudon France. LC PN2003. DD 792.05.

ANUARIO DO TEATRO BRASILEIRO. See Yearbooks, Almanacs, Directories.

ARCHIVIO DEL TEATRO ITALIANO. See Genealogy and Heraldry - Archives.

ASIAN THEATRE JOURNAL. (ASIAN THEATRE JOURNAL : ARJ). VFOAT ATJ. Vol. 1, No. 1 (Spring 1984)-. 0742-5457. Periodical. US. English. sa. $20.00. University of Hawaii Press, 2840 Kolowalu Street, Honolulu HI 96822. Tel (808)948-8255. This illustrated journal is dedicated to the performing arts of Asia, focusing upon both traditional and modern theatrical forms.

ASIAN THEATRE REPORTS. 1977-. 0161-4908. Periodical. US. English. an. Asian Theatre Organization of the University of Hawaii, 1770 East-West Road, Honolulu HI 96822. LC PN2860. DD 792.095.

ASTR, AMERICAN SOCIETY FOR THEATRE RESEARCH NEWSLETTER. Main/Corp American Society for Theatre Research. VFOAT ASTR Newsletter. VAT American Society for Theatre Research Newsletter. No. 1- , 1957-71. 0044-7927. Periodical. US. English. sa. P T Dircks, C W Post Center Greenvale, Long Island NY 11548.

AUSTRALASIAN DRAMA STUDIES. Vol. 1, No. 1 (Oct. 1982)-. 0810-4123. Periodical. AT. English. sa. $11.07. University of Queensland, Department of English, St Lucia Qld 4067 Australia. Tel (07)3772135. Ed Veronica Kelly and Richard Foheringham. bk rev. adv acc. Circ 500. Theatre documentation and criticism with an emphasis on Australian and New Zealand drama.

THE BEST PLAYS. VFOAT Burns Mantle Yearbook. 1894/99-. US. English. an. Dood Mead & Company, Box 14100, Nelson Place East Hill Pike, Nashville TN 37214. LC PN6112. DD 812.5082. (cum index).

BIBLIOGRAPHIC GUIDE TO THEATRE ARTS. See Bibliographies.

BILLBOARD INDEX. See Indexes/Abstracts.

BOLETIM INFORMATIVO DO INSTITUTO NACIONAL DE ARTES CENICAS. Periodical. BL. Portuguese. ir. Av Rio Branco 257, 130 Andar CEP 20040 Rio de Janeiro Brazil.

BRITISH ALTERNATIVE THEATRE DIRECTORY. See Yearbooks, Almanacs, Directories.

BRITISH THEATRE DIRECTORY. See Yearbooks, Almanacs, Directories.

BRITISH THEATRE REVIEW. 1974-. UK. English. an. Vance-Offord Publications Ltd, Twelve Trinity Trees, Eastbourne Sussex BN21 3LE England. LC PN2580. DD 792.0941.

BROADSIDE. (BROADSIDE : NEWSLETTER OF THE THEATRE LIBRARY ASSOCIATION). Vol. 1, No. 1 (1940)-. 0068-2748. Periodical. US. English. qt. Free to Members. Theatre Library Association, 111 Amsterdam Avenue, New York NY 10025. DD 026.792.

BUHNENTECHNISCHE RUNDSCHAU. Vol. 1, No. 1-. 0007-3091. Periodical. GW. German. bm. WE Saarbach GMBH, Postfach 101610, D5000 Koeln 1 West Germany. Ed W Unruh. Ind/Abst Archit. Period. Index. LC WMLC L 83/1180. Available on microfilm from University of Pittsburgh.

BULLETIN OF THE COMEDIANTES. See Literature.

BULLETIN PROVINCIAL - ASSOCIATION CANADIENNE DU THEATRE POUR LA JEUNESSE DU NOUVEAU-BRUNSWICK. (BULLETIN PROVINCIAL). VFOAT Provincial Newsletter. Fall 1979-. 0228-8079. Periodical. CN. English. qt. Free. New Brunswick Canadian Child and Youth Drama Association Newsletter, c/o R Hallum, 248 Wellington Street, Fredericton New Brunswick E3B 3A5 Canada. DD 792.022609715. (ctrl).

CAHIERS JEAN GIRAUDOUX. See Literature.

CALIFORNIA THEATRE ANNUAL. 1980-81-. 0733-5806. Periodical. US. English. an. $35.00. California Theatre Annual, 9025 Wilshire Boulevard Suite 210, Beverly Hills CA 90211. Tel (213)273-8161.

CALLBOARD. VAT Call Board. Periodical. US. English. qt. $11.61. Nova Scotia Drama League, 5516 Spring Garden Road/Suite 305, Halifax Nova Scotia B3J 1G6 Canada. Tel (902)425-3876. Ed Astrid Bruner. bk rev. adv acc. Circ 500. A publication of news and reviews of theatre activity local and national.

CANADA ON STAGE. VFOAT Canadian Theatre Review Yearbook. 1975-. 0380-9455. CN. English. an. University of Toronto Press, 5201 Dufferin Street, Downsview Ontario M3H 5T8 Canada. Tel (416)667-7782. DD 792.0971. *Canadian Theatre Review Yearbook, 0316-1323.*

CANADIAN DRAMA. VFOAT L'Art Dramatique Canadien. V. 1- Spring 1975-. 0317-9044. Periodical. CN. English (includes some text in French). sa. $11.61. University of Waterloo, Department of English, Waterloo Ontario N21 3G1 Canada. Tel (519)885-1211. Ed Ugene Benson. DD C812.009. bk rev. adv acc. Circ 300. To advance awareness of Canadian dramatists and their work among scholars, teachers, students, theatre professionals and amateurs and the theatre going public.

CANADIAN NEWSLETTER CEASED. (THE CANADIAN NEWSLETTER). VAT Canadian Newsletter. ITI, Canadian Newsletter. International Theatre Institute. Fall 1979-. 0711-3234. Periodical. CN. English. qt. $0.50 Per No., Free to Subscribers of Canadian Theatre Review. CTR Publications, York University, 4700 Keele Street, Downsview Ont M3J 1P3 Canada. DD 792.05.

CANADIAN THEATRE CHECKLIST. 1979/80-. 0226-5125. CN. English. ir. University of Toronto Press, 63A St George Street, Toronto Ontario M5S 1A6 Canada. Tel (416)667-3768. DD 792.0971. *Checklist of Canadian Theatres, 0705-5064.*

CANADIAN THEATRE REVIEW. Vol. 1- Winter 1974-. 0315-0836. Periodical. CN. English. qt. 35.00. University of Toronto Press, Journals Department, 5201 Dufferin Street, Downsview Ontario M3H 5T8 Canada. Tel (416)667-7781. Ed Robert Wallace. Ind/Abst MLA Int. Bibliogr. Books Artic. Mod. Lang. Lit., Can. Period. Index, Index Book Rev. Humanit., Years Work Eng. Stud. LC PN2009. DD 792.05. bk rev. adv acc. Circ 1,500. (ctrl). Covers the Canadian theatre.

CATALOG OF THE THEATRE AND DRAMA COLLECTIONS. Main/Corp New York Public Library. Research Libraries. 1967-. Periodical. US. English. ir. G K Hall, 70 Lincoln Street, Boston MA 02111. Tel (617)423-3990.

CENTRE STAGE MAGAZINE. V. 1- Sept. 1975-. 0380-4720. Periodical. CN. English. c/o Royal Alexandra Theatre, 260 King Street West, Toronto Ontario M5V 1H9 Canada. DD 792.0299.

CESKE DIVADLO. Periodical. CS. Czech. ir. Divadelni Ustav, Celetna 17, Praha 1 Czechoslovakia. LC PN2859.C9.

CHILDREN'S THEATRE REVIEW. (CHILDREN'S THEATRE REVIEW : THE JOURNAL OF THE CHILDREN'S THEATRE ASSOCIATION OF AMERICA). 0009-4196. Periodical. US. English. qt. American Theatre Association, 1029 Vermont Avenue NW, Washington DC 20005. Ind/Abst Curr. Index J. Educ. LC PN3157. DD 792.022605.

CHU I. VFOAT Drama Arts. First published in Oct. 1973-. Periodical. Chinese (issue for Oct. 1973 has title only in characters). ir. $38.00. LC PN2009.

CHU I I SHU LUN TSUNG. See The Arts (General) - Performing Arts.

Theater

CHU TAN. VFOAT Jutan. First published in 1982. Periodical. CH. Chinese. bm. 0.35. Post Office Tien-Chin, Tien-Chin China. LC PN2870. DD 792.0951.

CHUNG-KUO HSI CHU NIEN CHIEN. 1981-. CH. Chinese. an. 4.30. Hsin Hua Shu Tien, Pei-Ching Fa Hsing So, Peking China. LC PN2870. DD 792.0976.

CINE EN LA CULTURA ARGENTINA Y LATINOAMERICANA. VFOAT Cine. Periodical. Spanish. mo. Integral Producciones SRL, Paraguay 542, 30 E 1057 Buenos Aires Argentina.

CITADEL SCENE. (THE CITADEL SCENE). V. 1- Jan./Feb. 1975-. 0317-364X. CN. English. Citadel Theatre, 10018 102nd Street, Edmonton Alberta T5J 0V7 Canada. DD 792.0971233.

CIVILITA VENEZIANA. FONTI E TESTI. SERIE TERZA : LETTERE, MUSICA E TEATRO. See Music.

COLECCION TEATRO. No. 1- 1951-. 0587-9957. Periodical. SP. Spanish. ir. Ediciones Alfil, Comandante Azcarraga, Madrid 16 Spain.

COLECCION TEATRO ECUATORIANO CONTEMPORANEO. VFOAT Teatro Ecuatoriano Contemporaneo. No. 1-. EC. Spanish. ir. General Pintag 309 y Juala, Quito Ecudor. LC PQ8216.D7.

CONTRIBUTIONS IN DRAMA AND THEATRE STUDIES. No. 1-. 0163-3821. Monographic Series. US. English. ir. Greenwood Press, 88 Post Road West, Box 5007, Westport CT 06881. Tel (203)226-3571. Ed Joseph Donohue.

CRITICAL DIGEST. V. 1- Sept. 7, 1947-. 0045-9070. Periodical. US. English. sm. \$15. Critical Digest, 225 West 34th Street/Room 918, New York NY 10001. Tel (212)361-4400. Ed Ted M Kraus. bk rev. Available on microfilm from Xerox University Microfilms. Digest of news, reviews, comments on NYC and London theatre.

CRITIQUE (CLANDEBOYE, MAN.). (CRITIQUE). Autumn 1982-. 0821-5561. Periodical. CN. English. qt. \$10.00. Critique, 300 Summergrome Street, Clandeboye Manitoba R0C 0P0 Canada. DD 791.437505.

CU DIRECTORY. See Yearbooks, Almanacs, Directories.

CUADERNOS DE POSTGRADO : PUBLICACIONES DE LA UNIVERSIDAD AUTONOMA DE SANTO DOMINGO. No. 1-. Periodical. DR. Spanish. ir. Editora de la UASD, Apartado Postal No 1355, Santo Domingo Republica Dominicana.

THE CUE. 0197-7962. Periodical. US. English. \$2.50. Steffen Publishing, Holland Patent NY 13354. *Cue of Theta Alpha Phi.*

CUE (FARINGDON, OXFORDSHIRE). (CUE). 1 (Sept.-Oct. 1979)-. 0144-6088. Periodical. UK. English. bm. \$19.92. Twynam Publishing Ltd, Kitemore Faringdon, Oxfordshire SN78HR England. Tel 0367 21141. Ed James R Twunam. Ind/Abst Archit. Period. Index. bk rev. adv acc. Circ 2,000. Concerns technical aspects of the theatre including lighting, sound, scenography and costume. Also, theatre architecture, actor/audience involvement. Includes informed opinions by producers, directors, and designers.

DEPOIMENTOS. Series/Titl Colecao Depoimentos. 1-. Periodical. Portuguese. ir. LC PN2473. DD 792.0981.

DIE DEUTSCHE BUHNE. Began with Vol. for 1929. Periodical. German. mo. 72.-. Quatermarkt 5, 5000 Koln 1, Koln West Germany. Tel (0221)210762. Ed Wolfgang Ruf. LC PN2004. DD 792.0943. bk rev. adv acc. Circ 3,000. (ctrl) Informs and discusses on all aspects of German (and international) theater including opera, dance and general questions of management and culture politics.

DIDASCALIES : CAHIERS OCCASIONNELS DE L'ENSEMBLE THEATRAL MOBILE. VFOAT Textes pour Didascalies. Periodical. BE. French. ir. 400. Ensemble Theatral Mobile, 86 rue de la Caserne, 1000 Bruxelles Belgium. Tel 32.2.513.73.00. Ed Marc Liebens. All subjects in connection with theater: contemporary, theater's texts, analysis, critique, photography, etc.

DIONISO. V. 3, No. 1, (Year 1931)-. Periodical. IT. Italian (occasional articles in English). ir. Instituto Nazionale Drama Antico, Siracusa Italy. *Bollettino.*

DIRECTORY OF AMERICAN COLLEGE THEATRE. See Yearbooks, Almanacs, Directories.

DIRECTORY OF CANADIAN THEATRE SCHOOLS. See Yearbooks, Almanacs, Directories.

DIRECTORY OF NIGHTCLUBS, HOTELS, THEATRES, LOUNGES & DISCOTHEQUES. See Yearbooks, Almanacs, Directories.

DIRECTORY OF THE AMERICAN THEATRE ASSOCIATION, INC. See Yearbooks, Almanacs, Directories.

DISCUSSIONS IN DEVELOPMENTAL DRAMA. See Literature.

DIVADLO. Periodical. CS. Czech. ir. Artia, Ve Smeckach 30/PO Box 790, Praha 1 Czechoslovakia. LC PN2859.C9.

DIXIT.01. VAT Dixit.Zero Un. Vol. 1, No 1 (Winter 1984)-. 0825-0340. Periodical. CN. French. ir. 25.00. Editions Cooperatives de la Melee, CP 67 Succursale C, Montreal Quebec H2L 4J6 Canada. Tel (514)524-9422. DD C841.5408. bk rev. adv acc. Circ 1,000. (ctrl). Children's theater, adult theater (engaged), poetry and novels, re-editions of Gueseguers novels and stories.

DRAMA. No. 1- Summer 1946-. Periodical. UK. English. qt. Ind/Abst Abstr. Engl. Stud., Subj. Index Period., Int. Index Period., Book Rev. Index, Index Book Rev. Humanit., Humanit. Index. LC PN2001. DD 792.0941. Index published separately - free - automatically sent. (cum index). Available on microfilm. *Interim Drama.*

DRAMA-LOGUE. VFOAT Hollywood Drama-Lodge. 0272-2720. Periodical. US. English. wk. \$36.00. Drama-Logue Casting News, PO Box 38771, Hollywood CA 90038. Tel (213)464-5079.

THE DRAMA REVIEW. See The Arts (General) - Performing Arts.

DRAMA, THE QUARTERLY THEATRE REVIEW. V. 1, July 1919-July 1920. 0012-5946. Periodical. UK. English. qt. \$22.98. British Theatre Association, 9 Fitzroy Square, London WIP 6AE England. Tel 01387 2666. Ed Christopher Edwards. Ind/Abst Humanit. Index, Mag. Index, Book Rev. Index. LC PN2001. DD 792.0942. (cum index). bk rev. adv acc. Circ 7,000. Includes reviews, articles and features on subsidised, commercial, experimental, fringe and young people's theatre and theatre personalities in the UK and abroad.

DRAMATICS. V. 1- Jan. 1929-. 0012-5989. US. English. ir. Dramatics Magazine, 3368 Central Parkway, Cincinnati OH 45225. LC PN3175.A1. DD 371.89505.

THE DRAMATISTS GUILD QUARTERLY. V. 1- Spring 1964-. 0012-6004. Periodical. US. English. qt. Free to Members. Dramatists Guild Inc, 234 West 44th Street, New York NY 10036. LC PN2000. DD 792.0973. *Dramatists Bulletin.*

DRAMATISTS SOURCEBOOK. VFOAT T.C.G.'s Dramatists Sourcebook, TCG's Dramatists Sourcebook. 1981-82-. 0733-1606. US. English. an. \$7.95. Theatre Communications Group, 355 Lexington Avenue, New York NY 10017. Tel (212)697-5230. Ed M Elizabeth Osborn. LC PN2289. DD 792.02573. Revised guide to professional theatre opportunities for the playwright and dramaturist. Lists publishing outlets, workshops, conferences, services, etc. *Information for Playwrights.*

DRAMATURGIES NOUVELLES. V. 3, No. 2, (Dec. 1981)-. 0715-9145. Periodical. CN. French. ir. Centre d'Essai des Auteurs Dramatiques, Bureau 300/426 Est rue Sherbrooke, Montreal Quebec H2L 1J6 Canada. DD C842.54060714281. *Dramaturgies Nouvelles, en Bref, 0715-9137.*

IL DRAMMA. V. 1- (No. 1-446) Dec. 1925- April 1945-. 0012-6012. Periodical. IT. Italian. ir. Licosa Libreria Comm Sansani, Via Lamarmora 45, 50121 Firenze Italy. Ind/Abst MLA Int. Bibliogr. Books Artic. Mod. Lang. Lit. LC PN1605. DD 808.82. (cum index).

EDUCATIONAL THEATRE NEWS. V. 1- Feb. 1954-. 0013-1997. Periodical. US. English. bm.

ELIZABETHAN THEATRE. (THE ELIZABETHAN THEATRE). Main/Conf International Conference on Elizabethan Theatre. V. 1- 1969-. 0317-4964. CN. English. MacMillan of Canada, 70 Bond Street, Toronto Ontario M5B 1X3 Canada. Ed D Galloway. Ind/Abst MLA Int. Bibliogr. Books Artic. Mod. Lang. Lit. LC PN2589. DD 792.0942.

EMPIRICAL RESEARCH IN THEATRE. V. 1- Summer 1971-. 0361-2767. US. English. an. \$11.50. Center Communication Research, Bowling Green University, c/o B H Lee, Bowling Green OH 43403. Tel (419)372-2531. Ind/Abst Sociol. Abstr., Lang. Lang. Behav. Abstr. LC PN2075. DD 792.072.

ENACT. No. 1- 1967-. Periodical. II. English. ir. \$15.00. Enact, c/o Pauls Peers, E44-11 Okhla Industrial Area, New Delhi 110020 India.

ENCORE. 0071-0164. Periodical. US. English. an. \$2.00. National Association of Dramatic Speech Arts, North Carolina A & T State University, Greensboro NC 27411. Tel (919)379-7852. Ed H D Flowers, II. bk rev. adv acc. Circ 1,000. A magazine designed by theatricians in historically black institutions. New plays, research and innovative theatre programs and projects featured.

ENGEKI NEMPO. VFOAT Japanese Theatre Annual. Began with 1966 Edition. JA. Japanese. ir. LC PN2920.

ENGEKIGAKU. VFOAT Studies on Theatre Arts. JA. Japanese. an. Waseda Daigaku Bungakubu, Engeki Kenkyushitsu 42-Banchi Toyama-Machi, Shinjuku-Ku Tokyo-To-Japan. LC PN2009.

ESSAYS IN THEATRE. Vol. 1, No. 1 (Nov. 1982)-. 0821-4425. Periodical. CN. English. sa. \$12.00. Essays in Theatre, Department of Drama University of Guelph, Guelph Ontario N1G 2W1 Canada. DD 792.05.

ESTUDIS ESCENICS. (ESTUDIS ESCENICS : QUADERNS DE L'INSTITUT DEL TEATRE DE LA DIPUTACIO DE BARCELONA). 22 (March 1983)-. 0212-3819. Periodical. SP. Catalan (summaries in English, French and Spanish). ir. Ind/Abst MLA Int. Bibliogr. Books Artic. Mod. Lang. Lit. LC PQ6098.7. DD 792.05. *Estudios Escenicos.*

EXIL. V. 1-2. 0315-4165. Periodical. CN. French. mo. G.P.D.U. C.P. 1443 Succursale B, Hull Quebec J8X 3Y3 Canada. DD 792'.05.

EXPRESS - ASSOCIATION QUEBECOISE DE JEUNE THEATRE. (L'EXPRESS). V. 1, No 1 (Feb. 1983)-. 0823-7506. Periodical. CN. French. ir. Free. Association Quebecoise du Jeune Theatre, 426 Est rue Sherbrooke, Montreal Quebec H2L 1J6 Canada. DD 792.060714. (ctrl).

EXPRESSION (MONTREAL, QUEBEC). (EXPRESSION). Dec. 2/3 78-. 0714-8054. Periodical. CN. French. ty. \$2.00 Per No. Expression, c/o APEDQ, #4/229 rue St-Vincent Ouest, Montreal Quebec H2T 2L6 Canada. DD 792.028070714. *Communic-Action.*

GEORGE SPELVIN'S THEATRE BOOK. VFOAT Theatre Book. Vol. 1, No. 1 (Spring, 1978)-. 0730-6431. Periodical. US. English. ty. \$16.00. Proscenium Press, PO Box 361, Newark DE 19711. Tel (215)255-4083. Ed G Spelvin.

GODISNJAK JUGOSLOVENSKIH POZORISTA. VFOAT Godisnjak Jugoslovenskih Kazalista. Began with issue for 1978/79. 0351-9120. Serbo-Croatian. an. Sterijno Pozorje, Zmaj-Jovina 22/I, 2100 Novi Sad Yugoslavia. LC PN2850.

GRYPHON THEATRE NEWS. Vol. 1, No. 1 (Fall 1979)-. 0710-2747. Periodical. CN. English. qt. Free. Gryphon Theatre News, 124 Brock Street, Barrie Ontario L4N 2M2 Canada. DD 792.0971317.

THE GUIDE TO SELECTING PLAYS. Main/Corp French, Samuel, Firm, Publishers. UK. English. ir. 2.00. Samuel French Ltd, 52 Fitzroy Street, London W1P 6JR England. Tel 01-387-9373. Ed Amanda Smith. LC PN6112.5. DD 016.80882. Circ 20,000. Synopses of story, cast and characters of over 2,000 modern plays.

GUTHRIE NEW THEATER. V. 1- 1976-. 0145-3750. US. English. an. \$4.95 Single Issue. Grove Press, 196 West Houston, New York NY 10014. LC PS634. DD 812.5408.

HANDBOOK - NATIONAL ASSOCIATION OF SCHOOLS OF THEATRE (U.S.). (HANDBOOK). Main/Corp National Association of Schools of Theatre (U.S.). 1984-1985-. 0739-9839. US. English. be. \$5.00. National Association of Schools of Theatre, 11250 Roger Bacon Drive/Suite 5, Reston VA 22090. Tel (703)437-0700. LC PN2078.U6. DD 792.07073. Circ

Theater

500. Standards for accreditation for educational programs in theatre.

HSI CHU HSUEH HSI. See Literature.

HSI CHU I SHU (SHANG-HAI HSI CHU HSUEH YUAN). (HSI CHU I SHU). VFOAT Theatre Arts. Began with Mar. 1978 issue. Periodical. Chinese. ir. 0.70. Chung-Kuo Kuo Chi Shu Tien, PO Box 2820, Pei-Ching China Mainland. LC PN2009. DD 792.05.

HSI CHU LUN TSUNG. VFOAT Xijuluncong. 1957-. Periodical. CC. Chinese. qt. 0.65. Hsin Hua Shu Tien, Peking China. LC PN2870. DD 792.0951.

HUA HSUEH SHIH CHI. VFOAT Huaxue Shiji. Began in 1979. Periodical. CH. Chinese. bm. $4.73. China Publication Centre, PO Box 2820, Beijing China. Ind/Abst Chem. Abstr. CODEN HUSHDR.

INFORMATION FOR PLAYWRIGHTS. -1980/81. US. English. an. Theatre Communications Group, 255 Lexington Avenue, New York NY 10017. Tel (212)697-5230.

INTERNATIONAL BIBLIOGRAPHY OF THEATRE. See Bibliographies.

INTERSCNA; ACTA SCNOGRAPHICA. V. 1- 1971-. Periodical. CS. Czech (with summaries in English, French, German, and Russian). bm. $17.50. Artia, VE Smehach 30, Praha 1 Czechoslovakia. Ind/Abst CIS Abstr. *Interscena, 0539-1989; Acta Scnographica, 0567-8110.*

THE IRISH THEATRE SERIES. 1- 1970-. Periodical. US. English. ir. Humanities Press, Atlantic Highlands NJ 07716. Ed Hogan, Kilroy, Burnham and Miller. A continuing series of monographs which provide a fresh and comprehensive survey of Irish theater. Each title is complete in itself.

JAHRBUCH DER WIENER GESELLSCHAFT FUR THEATERFORSCHUNG. See Yearbooks, Almanacs, Directories.

JAVISKO. Periodical. Slovak. ir. 48.00. PNS - Ustredna Expedicia Tlace, Gottwaldovo Namestie 48, V Bratislave Czechoslovakia. LC PN2859.C93.

JEN MIN HSI CHU (PEKING, CHINA) CEASED. (JEN MIN HSI CHU). VFOAT Renmin Xiju. Vol. 1- July. Periodical. CC. Chinese. mo. $0.34 Single Issue. LC PN2870. *Jen Min Hsi Chu (Chung-Kuo Hsi Chu Chia Hsieh Hui).*

JEU (MONTREAL, QUEBEC). (JEU). VFOAT Cahiers de Theatre Jeu. 1 (Winter 1976)-. 0382-0335. Periodical. CN. French. qt. 40.00 Domestic, 48.00 Foreign. Cahiers de Theatre Jeu Inc, PO Box 1600/Station E, Montreal Quebec H2T 3B1 Canada. Tel (514)288-2808. LC PN2305.Q4. DD 792.09714. bk rev. adv acc. Circ 1,500. Informs about various tendencies of contemporary theatre in Quebec and other countries. Editorial promotes circulation of theatrical testamonies by practitioners and, through socio-political questioning, the historicization of the theatrical practice.

JEUNE THEATRE (ASSOCIATION QUEBECOISE DU JEUNE THEATRE). (JEUNE THEATRE). Vol. 7, No. 1-. 0315-0402. Periodical. CN. French. mo. Free. Jeune Theatre, 952 rue Cherrier, Montreal Quebec H2L 1H7 Canada. DD 792.060714. (ctrl).

JOHN WILLIS' THEATRE WORLD CEASED. VFOAT Theatre World. Vol. 28 (1971/1972)-V. 36 (1979/1980). US. English. an. *Theatre World (New York, N.Y. : 1966).*

KOKURITSU GEKIJO ENGEIJO. Began with No. 1, (Mar./Apr. 1979)-. Periodical. JA. Japanese. ir. Kokuritsu Gekijo 4-Ban, 1-Go Hayabusa-Cho Chiyoda-Ku, Tokyo-To 102 Japan. LC PN2920.

LATIN AMERICAN THEATRE REVIEW. 1- Fall 1967-. 0023-8813. Periodical. US. English (Spanish or Portuguese). sa. $36.00. Center of Latin American Studies, The University of Kansas, Lawrence KS 66045. Tel (913)864-4213. Ed George Woodyard. Ind/Abst MLA Int. Bibliogr. Books Artic. Mod. Lang. Lit. LC PN2309. bk rev. Circ 1,500. Analytic discussion of Latin American drama in Spanish, Portuguese and English; reviews of books, performances, etc.

LETTURE. Began in 1964. 0024-144X. IT. Italian. ir. 20. Scurani Alessandro, Piazza San Fedele 4, Milan Italy. Tel 00.02.804441. Ind/Abst MLA Int. Bibliogr. Books Artic. Mod. Lang. Lit. LC AS221. Circ 6,200. Books and performances, theater and movies.

LIAISON. No. 1- Summer 1978-. 0227-227X. Periodical. CN. French. ir. 0.50 Per No. Liaison, Bureau 202/45 rue Rideau, Ottawa Ontario K1N 6A0 Canada. DD 792.09713.

LITTERATUR, TEATER, FILM. See Literature.

THE LONDON STAGE, 1660-1800. US. English. LC PN2592. DD 792.09421.

LONDON THEATRE RECORD. Vol. 1, Issues 1/2 (1-28 Jan. 1981)-. 0261-5282. UK. English. bw. 60 Domestic, $95.00 US. London Theatre Rocord, 4 Cross Deep Gardens, Twickenham TW1 4QU Middlesex England. Tel (01)892-6087. Ed Ian Herbert. LC PN2596.L6. bk rev. adv acc. Complete reviews and technical credits for all new theatre in London and much outside. Simply, the most imformative UK theater journal.

MARQUEE. (MARQUEE : THE JOURNAL OF THE THEATRE HISTORICAL SOCIETY). Began publication with Vol. 1 (Feb. 1969). 0025-3928. Periodical. US. English. ir. $15.00. Theatre Historical Society, PO Box 767, San Francisco CA 94101. Tel (415)983-8688. Ed Robert Headley Jr. Ind/Abst Avery Index Archit. Period. bk rev. Circ 1,000. History and photographs of theatre buildings.

MEDIEVAL ENGLISH THEATRE. V. 1- Oct. 1979-. 0143-3784. Periodical. UK. English. sa. 4.00 Domestic, 5.00 Foreign. University of Leeds, Peter Meredith, Department of English, Leeds LS2 9JT England. Tel (0532)431751. Ed Meg Twycross and Peter Meredith. Circ 400. Practices of theatre in England in Middle Ages; Anglo-Saxon period to late sixteenth-century; mysteries, moralities, mummings, interlodes, etc.

MICKERY MOUTH & TONEEL TEATRAAL. Dutch. ir. 20.00. Rozengracht 117, Amsterdam Netherlands. LC PN2002. *Toneel, Mickery Mouth.*

MIME JOURNAL. No. 1- 1974-. 0145-787X. Periodical. US. English. sa. $32.00. Performing Arts Center, Grand Valley State Colleges, Allendale MI 49401. Tel (714)621-8186. Ed Thomas Leabhart. Circ 500. A profusely illustrated monograph published on mime and movement theater subjects. Recent topics include Decroux, Copeau, Noh masks, essays on modern and post-modern mime.

MINNESOTA DRAMA EDITIONS. 0076-9142. Monographic Series. US. English. ir. University of Minnesota Press, 2037 University Avenue SE, Minneapolis MN 55455. Tel (612)373-3266. Ed Michael Langham. Only one volume, No. 8, Oedipus the King, remains in print.

MODERN DRAMA. Began with May 1958 issue. 0026-7694. Periodical. CN. English. qt. $27.09. University of Toronto Press, Journals Department, 5201 Dufferine Street, Downsview Ontario M3H 5T8 Canada. Ind/Abst MLA Int. Bibliogr. Books Artic. Mod. Lang. Lit., Annu. Bibliogr. Engl. Lang. Lit., Film Lit. Index, Ref. Source, Humanit. Index, Index Book Rev. Humanit., Soc. Sci. Index. DD 809.2005.

MODERN INTERNATIONAL DRAMA. Began with Sept. 1967 Issue. 0026-7856. Periodical. US. English. sa. $10.00. Modern International Drama, SUNY at Binghamton, Binghamton NY 13901. Tel (607)777-2704. Ed G E Wellwarth. LC PN6111. DD 808.8204. adv acc. Circ 550. (ctrl). Publication of previously untranslated plays.

MODERN IRISH PLAYS. 1-. Monographic Series. English. ir. Co-Op Books Publishing Ltd, 16 Lower Liffey Street, Dublin 1 Ireland. LC UNC.

MUSIK & I.E. OG TEATER. See Music.

MUSIK & THEATER (SAINT GALL, SWITZERLAND). See Music.

NASHI DEBIUTANTY. Series/Titl Samodeiatelnyi Teatr. Periodical. UR. Russian. 0.20. Izdatelstvo Iskusstvo, Sobinobskii Per 3, 103009 Moskva USSR.

NATIONAL THEATRE SCHOOL OF CANADA. VFOAT Ecole National de Theatre du Canada. Began with 1961 issue. 0383-1256. CN. English (French). an. Free. National Theatre School of Canada, 5030 St Denis Street, Montreal Quebec H2J 2L8 Canada. DD 792.0710714281.

NATO NEWS & VIEWS. VAT National Association of Theatre Owners News and Views. 0279-120X. Periodical. US. English. ir. $30.00. National Association of Theater Owners, 1560 Broadway, New York NY 10036. Tel (212)730-7420.

Ed Wayne R Green. Circ 2,400. (ctrl). News and information of interest to motion picture theatre owners and executives. *NATO Flash Bulletin.*

NEW FREEDOM QUARTERLY. 8755-0598. Periodical. US. English. qt. $15.00. New Freedom Theater Inc, 1346 N Broad Street, Philadelphia PA 19121.

NEW PLAYS USA. VFOAT TCG New Plays USA. Vol. 1 (1982)-. 0731-4523. US. English. be. Theatre Communications Group, 335 Lexington Avenue, New York NY 10017. Tel (212)697-5230. Ed James Leverett and M Elizabeth Osborn. Presents complete texts of plays by outstanding contemporary playwrights, both American and international.

NEW YORK THEATRE CRITICS' REVIEWS. VFOAT Theatre Critics' Reviews. 0028-7784. Periodical. US. English. ir. Proscenium Publications, 4 Park Avenue Towers Suite 21D, New York NY 10016. Tel (212)532-2570. (cum index). *Critics' Theatre Reviews.*

THE NEW YORK TIMES THEATER REVIEWS. 1870-85-. 0160-0583. US. English. be. Times Books, 130 Fifth Avenue, New York NY 10011. Tel (212)620-5900. LC PN2266. DD 792.0973.

NEWS LETTER - CANADIAN ACTORS' EQUITY ASSOCIATION. Main/Corp Canadian Actors' Equity Association. June 1976-. 0384-0476. Periodical. CN. English. Canadian Actors' Equity Association, 64 Shuter Street, Toronto Ontario M5B 2G7 Canada. DD 792.06271. *News Letter, 0384-0484.*

NEWS - THEATRE ONTARIO. (NEWS). VFOAT Theatre Ontario News. No. 1-. 0821-4476. Periodical. CN. English. bm. 12.00. Theatre Ontario, 344 Bloor Street West, Toronto Ontario M5S 1W9 Canada. Tel (416)366-2938. Ed Angie Bahr Fostaty. DD 792.09713. bk rev. Circ 2,500. (ctrl). Features profiles, articles, and on stage listings on professional, community and educational theatre in Ontario.

NEWSLETTER - ASSOCIATION OF BRITISH COLUMBIA DRAMA EDUCATORS. Sept./Oct. 1978-. 0708-9597. Periodical. CN. English. Free to Members. Association of British Columbia Drama Educators, c/o British Columbia Teachers Federation, 2235 Burrard Street, Vancouver British Columbia V6J 3H9 Canada. DD 792.0710711. *W A D E, 0708-9589.*

NEWSLETTER - PLAYWRIGHTS UNION OF CANADA. (NEWSLETTER). Summer 1984-. 0827-3073. Periodical. CN. English. qt. 15. Playwrights Union of Canada, 6th Floor 8 York Street, Toronto Ontario M5J 1R2 Canada. Tel (416)947-0201. Ed Dave Carley. DD C812.5406071. adv acc. Circ 1,000. (ctrl). A newsletter published as a service to our membership which focuses on current news and developments in the Canadian theatre industry. *Newsletter (Guild of Canadian Playwrights), 0824-5460; Newsletter (Playwrights Canada).*

NEWSLETTER - SASKATCHEWAN DRAMA ASSOCIATION. (NEWSLETTER). Vol. 1, No. 2 (Fall 1980)-. 0824-2038. Periodical. CN. English. qt. Saskatchewan Drama Association, 1031 King Crescent, Saskatoon Saskatchewan S7K 0N9 Canada. DD 792.097124. *SDA Newsletter, 0229-0758.*

NEWSLETTER - THEATRE CANADA. Main/Corp Theatre Canada. VFOAT Bulletin de Nouvelles - Theatre Canada. Oct. 1971-Mar. 1978. 0703-5659. Periodical. CN. English (French, Oct. 1971-Jan. 1977). qt. Theatre Canada, 45 Rideau Street, Ottawa Ontario K1N 5W8 Canada. DD 792.0971. *Nouvelles.*

NIHON NO JIDO ENGEKI. VFOAT Children's Theatre in Japan. 1982-. JA. Japanese. an. Nihon Jido Engeki Kyokai, 19-3 Jingumae 6 Shibuya-ku, Tokyo-to 150 Japan.

NINETEENTH CENTURY THEATRE RESEARCH. V. 1- Spring 1973-. 0316-5329. Periodical. US. English. sa. $5.00. University of Arizona, Department of English, Tucson AZ 85721. Ind/Abst Abstr. Engl. Stud., MLA Int. Bibliogr. Books Artic. Mod. Lang. Lit., Recent Publ. Artic. LC PN1851. DD 792.0942. *NCTR Newsletter, 0710-5576.*

NORSK TEATERARBOK. 1975-. Norwegian. ir. Aschehoug, Sehesteds Gate 3, Oslo Norway. LC PN2760.

NUMMO. Summer 1977-. 0149-3663. Periodical. US. English. an. $1.00. Carl Morrison Jr, Department of Theatre, Illinois University, Normal IL 61761.

ON-STAGE STUDIES. VFOAT On Stage Studies. Began with No. 3 (1979). 0749-1549. US. English. an. $3.50. University of Colorado, Campus Box 261, Boulder CO 80309. **Tel** (303)492-7355. **Ed** Martin Cobin. **LC** PR2885. **DD** 822.33. **Circ** 500. (ctrl). Insights into Shakespeare texts and production methods by those engaged in the production of Shakespeare's plays. *Colorado Shakespeare Festival Annual, 0198-831X.*

OOBA GUIDEBOOK OF THEATRES. **Main/Corp** Off Off Broadway Alliance. **VAT** Off Off Broadway Alliance Guidebook of Theatres. V. 1- 1975-. 0361-6606. US. English. Off Off Broadway Alliance, 162 West 56 Street, New York NY 10019. **LC** PN2277.N5. **DD** 792.097471.

OPAL. (THE OPAL). 0030-3062. Periodical. CN. English. bm. $11.61. Ontario Puppetry Association, 171 Avondale, Willowdale Ontario M2N 2V4 Canada.

OPERA-MUSICAL THEATER. VFOAT Orera, Musical Theater. Began with 1979/80. 8756-856X. US. English. an. National Endowment for the Arts, 2401 E Street NW, Washington DC 20506. **DD** 782. *Opera Orchestra.*

PASSING SHOW (NEW YORK, N.Y.). *See* Genealogy and Heraldry - Archives.

PAYS THEATRAL. (LE PAYS THEATRAL). Vol. 1, No. 1 (Saison 77/78)- . -. 0705-4750. Periodical. CN. French. ir. Free. Theatre d'Aujourd'ui, 1297 Papineau, Montreal Quebec H2K 4H3 Canada. **DD** 792.09714. (ctrl).

PESTI MUSOR. VFOAT PM. Periodical. HU. Hungarian. wk. Akademiai Kiado, POB 24, 1363 Budapest Hungary. **LC** PN2616.B8.

PIECE PAR PIECE. V. 1, No. 1, (April 1980)-. 0226-2355. Periodical. CN. French. mo. Free. Theatre de L'Atelier, Piece par Piece, CP 221, Succursale Jacques-Cartier, Sherbrooke Quebec J1J 3Y2 Canada. **DD** 792.0971466.

PLATFORM (LONDON, ENGLAND : 1979). (PLATFORM). 1 (Winter 1979)-. Periodical. UK. English. ir. 3.00 for issues 4-6 Institutions 5, Abroad 6. Platform 18/Vauxhall Grove, London SW8 England.

PLAYS AND PLAYERS. VFOAT Plays & Players. Began with V. 1, 1953. 0032-1559. Periodical. UK. English. mo. 0.90 Single Issue. Hansom Books, Brevet Publishing Ltd, PO Box 252, 2 Old Pye Street, London SW1P 2LD England. **Ind/Abst** Humanit. Index. **LC** PN2001. **DD** 792.0941. *Theatre World, Encore (London, Eng.).*

PLAYS IN PROCESS. 1979. 0736-0711. US. English. ir. $60.00. Theatre Communications Group, 355 Lexington Avenue, New York NY 10017. **Tel** (212)697-5230. **Ed** James Leverett. **Circ** 370. A national script circulation service that offers a first-hand look at some of America's most important new dramatic writing.

PLAYS : THE DRAMA MAGAZINE FOR YOUNG PEOPLE. 1964-. Periodical. US. English. ir. $19.00. Plays Inc, 120 Boylston Street, Boston MA 02116. **Tel** (617)423-3157. **Ed** Sylvia K Burack. **Ind/Abst** Read. Guide Period. Lit., Child. Mag. Guide. Index in last issue of volume - attached. (cum index). bk rev. adv acc. **Circ** 21,300. A complete source of one-act plays and programs for young people: holiday plays, skits, dramas, mysteries, folk tales, dramatized classics, parodies, plays for reading improvement and to improve communication skills.

PRATIQUES THEATRALES. No. 13 (Fall 1981)-. 0714-8178. Periodical. CN. French. ir. $14.70. University of Quebec-Montreal, 200 rue Sherbrooke Ouest, Montreal Quebec H2X 3P2 Canada. **Ind/Abst** Point Repere. **DD** 792.09714. *Grande Replique, 0704-7576.*

PROGRAMA. No. 1- July 1978-. Portuguese. ir. 50.00 Each Issue. Teatro do Grupo de Campolide, Av D Carlos I N 61-1, Lisboa Portugal. **LC** PN2796.L52.

PROLOG. No. 1- May 1973-. 0271-7743. Periodical. US. English. qt. $6.00. Theater Sources Inc, 104 North St Mary, Dallas TX 75214.

PROMPTS. *See* Genealogy and Heraldry - Archives.

QUADERNI DI TEATRO. Yearly V. 1- August 1978-. 0391-4038. Periodical. IT. Italian. qt. Nuova Vallecchi, Via Gino Capponi 26 Conto Corrente Postale N 5/20373, 50121 Firenze Italy. **LC** PN2005. **DD** 792.09455.

QUELLEN ZUR THEATERGESCHICHTE. Vol. 1-. AU. German. ir. Verband Wissen Gesellschaften Osterreichs, Lindengasse 37, A 1070 Wien Austria. **Tel** 93 47 56. **Ed** Otto Schindler. **LC** PN2616.V5. **Circ** 400. Monographs of edited sources and documents concerning different periods in the history of the theatre.

REACH TH' PEOPLE. Vol. 1, No. 1 (April 1984)-. 0825-7507. Periodical. CN. English. ir. Free to Members. Black Theatre Canada, 109 Vaughan Road, Toronto Ontario M6C 2L9 Canada. **DD** 792.08996.

RECORDS OF EARLY ENGLISH DRAMA. (RECORDS OF EARLY ENGLISH DRAMA : NEWSLETTER). **VFOAT** Reed Newsletter. Began with June 1976. 0700-9283. Periodical. CN. English. sa. $3.86. University of Toronto, Erindale College, English Department, Mississauga L5L 1C6 Canada. **Tel** (416)978-3916. **Ed** Joanna Dutka. **Ind/Abst** MLA Int. Bibliogr. Books Artic. Mod. Lang. Lit. **LC** PR641. **DD** 822.009. **Circ** 600. Documents dealing with Medieval and Renaissance English drama.

REEL PEOPLE. 0196-2647. US. English. Peter Glenn Publications Ltd, 17 East 48th Street, New York NY 10017. **Tel** (212)688-7940. **Ed** Ronn Robinson. **LC** PN1998.A2. **DD** 791.430280257471. adv acc. **Circ** 2,000. (ctrl). A pictorial directory of New York SAG and AFTRA performers.

RENAISSANCE DRAMA. 7-9, 1964-66. 0486-3739. US. English. ir. Northwestern University Press, Box 1093, Evanston IL 60201. **Tel** (312)491-5313. **Ed** Leonard Barkan. **Ind/Abst** Abstr. Engl. Stud., MLA Int. Bibliogr. Books Artic. Mod. Lang. Lit., Annu. Bibliogr. Engl. Lang. Lit., Years Work Eng. Stud. **LC** PN1785. **DD** 809.20902. adv acc. Drama of all nations in the 15th, 16th, and 17th Century. *Renaissance Drama: A Report on Research Opportunities.*

REPERTOIRE THEATRAL DU QUEBEC. 1979/80-. 0226-1804. CN. French. an. 10. Jeu Inc, CP 1600 Succe E, Montreal Quebec H2T 3B1 Canada. **Tel** (514)288-2808. **DD** 792.09714. adv acc. **Circ** 1,500. Aims and activities of more than 800 theatrical companies and organs of Quebec and French theatre in North America. Many helpful addresses in Europe.

REPORT - THEATRES BRANCH *CEASED.* (ANNUAL REPORT - MINISTRY OF CONSUMER AND COMMERCIAL RELATIONS, THEATRES BRANCH). **Main/Corp** Ontario. Theatres Branch. Ceased with 1981/1982 issue. 0826-6514. CN. English. an.

RESEARCH OPPORTUNITIES IN RENAISSANCE DRAMA. *See* Literature.

REVISTA DE TEATRO. No. 1- Nov./Dec. 1960-. 0484-7369. Periodical. BL. Spanish. qt. $30.00. Soc Brasileira Autor Teatrais, Av Almirante Barroso 97-30 Andar, Rio de Janeiro Brazil. **Tel** (021)2-40-7231. **Ed** Helcio Pereira da Silva. **LC** PN2008. adv acc. **Circ** 4,500. (ctrl). Copyright, theater news in general, national theater play published in each issue, articles on theater and performing arts in general.

REVUE D'HISTOIRE DU THEATRE. **VFOAT** Revue de la Societe d'Histoire du Theatre. Vol. 1-. 0035-2373. Periodical. FR. French. qt. $39.00. Societe D Histoire du Theatre, 98 Boulevard Kellermann, 75013 Paris France. **Tel** (1)45 88 46 55. **Ind/Abst** Am. Hist. Life, Hist. Abstr., Part A, Mod. Hist. Abstr., Hist. Abst., Part B, Twent. Century Abstr., MLA Int. Bibliogr. Books Artic. Mod. Lang. Lit., Annu. Bibliogr. Engl. Lang. Lit., Years Work Eng. Stud. **LC** PN2003. **DD** 792. bk rev. Each issue contains unpublished studies and documents about theater in France and abroad. Also, international bibliography of performance arts, summaries of books and exhibitions.

REVUE ROUMAINE D'HISTOIRE DE L'ART. SERIE THEATRE, MUSIQUE, CINEMA. V. 7- 1970-. Periodical. RM. Romanian (contributions in Russian, English, French, German or Spanish). an. Rompresfilatelia, PO Box 1362137, Bucharest Romania. *Revue Roumaine d'Histoire de l'Art.*

ROYAL SHAKESPEARE COMPANY; A COMPLETE RECORD OF THE YEAR'S WORK. 0142-9434. Periodical. UK. English. an. $5.75. Royal Shakespeare Company BKSP, 47 Aldwych, London WC2 England.

SAN FRANCISCO THEATRE. 0146-9576. Periodical. US. English. qt. $8.00. San Francisco Theatre Magazine, 408 Columbus Avenue, San Francisco CA 94133.

SCEN OCH SALONG. Periodical. Swedish. ir. **LC** PN2006.

SCENA. Periodical. Polish. ir. **LC** PN2859.P6. *Teatr Ludowy.*

EN SCENE. Vol. 1, No 1 (Jan. 1983)-. 0822-5095. Periodical. CN. French. ir. Nouvelle Compagnie Theatrale, 4353 Est rue Ste-Catherine, Montreal Quebec H1V 1Y2 Canada. **DD** 792.05. *N C T, 0705-3630; Acte 1 du Texte— a la Representation, 0711-7213.*

SCENE CHANGES. V. 1- Feb. 1973-. 0381-8098. Periodical. CN. English. mo. Theatre Ontario, 8 York Street, Toronto Ontario M5J 1R2 Canada. **DD** 792.09713. *Dialog (Theatre Ontario), 0708-7667.*

SEGISMUNDO. 1, 1-. 0582-396X. SP. Spanish. sa. Consejo Superior de Investigaciones Cientificas, Vitruvio 8, Apartado 14 458, 28006 Madrid Spain.

SHAKESPEARE QUARTO FACSIMILES. **Main/Corp** Shakespeare Association (Great Britain). **VFOAT** Shakespeare Quartos in Collotype Facsimile. Monographic Series. UK. English. ir. Oxford University Press, 16-00 Pollitt Drive, Fair Lawn NJ 07414. **Ed** W W Greg.

SHAN-HSI HSI CHU. VFOAT Shanxixiju. Periodical. CH. Chinese. mo. 0.30. Post Office, Hsi-An Shih China. **LC** PN2875.S54. **DD** 792.095143.

SHANG-HAI HSI CHU. VFOAT Shanghai Xiju. Began with Oct. 1959 issue. Periodical. CC. Chinese. bm. China Publication Centre, PO Box 2820, Beijing China. **LC** PN2009. **DD** 792.0951.

THE SHORT PLAY SERIES. No. 1- 1966-. 0083-9403. Monographic Series. US. English. ir. Proscenium Press, PO Box 361, Newark DE 19711.

SIMON'S DIRECTORY OF THEATRICAL MATERIALS, SERVICES & INFORMATION. *See* Yearbooks, Almanacs, Directories.

SIPARIO. Vol. 1- (N. 1-) 1946-. Periodical. IT. Italian. qt. $53.46. C A M A SAS, Viale Montello N 12, 20125 Milano Italy. **Ind/Abst** MLA Int. Bibliogr. Books Artic. Mod. Lang. Lit.

SLOVENSKE DIVADLO. V. 1- 1953-. 0037-699X. Periodical. Czech. ir. Kubon & Sagner, Postfach 38 01 08, Hess-Strasse 39/41, D-8 Munchen 34 West Germany. **Tel** (089)52 20 27. Focusses on all questions of the Slovak theatre, carries articles dealing with aesthetical and theoretical subjects as well as problems of contemporary stage art in drama, opera, operetta and ballet.

SOUTHERN THEATRE. Began with: Vol 7 In Fall 1963. 0584-4738. Periodical. US. English. qt. $8.00. Fisher Harrison Publications, 338 North Elm Street, Greensboro NC 27401. **Tel** (919)272-3645. **Ed** Mary Ann Blazek. adv acc. Popular Magazine of timely articles for theatre people in the southeastern region of the country. *Southern Theatre News.*

SOVETSKIE KHUDOZHNIKI TEATRA I KINO. Periodical. UR. Russian. 2.37. UL Cherniakhovskoga 4A 125319, Moskva USSR. **LC** PN2091.S8.

SOVIET THEATRE. Periodical. UR. English. qt. $13.80. Soviet Theatre. **LC** PN2724. **DD** 792.0947.

SPECIAL BULLETIN - THEATRE CANADA. **Main/Corp** Theatre Canada. **VFOAT** Bulletin Special - Theatre Canada. Began publication in 1973?. 0703-5640. Periodical. CN. English (French). Theatre Canada, 45 Rideau Street, Ottawa Ontario K1N 5E8 Canada. **DD** 792.0971.

SPEECH AND DRAMA. Began in 1951. UK. English. sa. $5.75. Speech and Drama, 14 Florence Road, Brighton Sussex BN16DJ England. **Ed** Kenneth Pickering. **LC** PN4071. **DD** 001.54. bk rev. adv acc. **Circ** 1,200. Teaching and performing of speech, educational drama, theatre arts, poetry, prose, articles, book reviews, advertisements, forthcoming events.

THE STAGE AND TELEVISION TODAY. No. 4062- Feb. 19, 1959-. 0038-9099. Periodical. UK. English. wk. 34.00. Carson & Comerford Ltd, Stage House 47 Bermondsey Street, London Bridge London SE13XT England. **Tel** 01-403 1818. **Ed** Peter Happle. bk rev. adv acc. **Circ** 39,800. All matters relating to theatre and television of interest to professionals and serious students. *Stage.*

STRATFORD FESTIVAL STORY. (THE STRATFORD FESTIVAL STORY). 1953/61-. 0085-6789. Periodical. CN. English. an. Stratford Festival, PO Box 520, Stratford Ontario N5A 6V2 Canada. **DD** 792.0971323. *Story of the Stratford Festival, Canada, 0318-2975.*

STRATFORD FOR STUDENTS. 1978-. 0822-9066. Periodical. CN. English. sa. Stratford Festival, PO Box 520, Stratford Ontario N5A 6V2

Theater

Canada. **DD** 822.33. *Stratford School Newsletter, 0317-2082.*

STRATFORD-UPON-AVON STUDIES. 0081-5969. UK. English. ir. Holmes & Meir Publishing, 30 Irving Place, New York NY 10003. **Tel** (212)254-4100. **Ind/Abst** Years Work Eng. Stud.

STUBS. Began publication in 1942. 0081-6051. US. English. ir. Meyer Schattner, 246 West 44th Street, New York NY 10036. **LC** PN2277.N5. **DD** 792.02957472.

SUMMER THEATRES. VFOAT Leo Shull's Summer Theatres. US. English. an. Leo Shull Publications, 1501 Broadway/29th Floor, New York NY 10036. **Tel** (212)354-7600. **LC** PN2269. **DD** 792.

SZENE SCHWEIZ. VFOAT Scene Suisse. Periodical. SZ. French (German and Italian). an. Richard Wagner-Str 19, 8002 Zurich Switzerland. **LC** PN2800. **DD** 792.09494.

SZINHAZ. Vol. 1-. 0039-8136. Periodical. HU. Hungarian. mo. Akademiai Kiado, POB 24, 1363 Budapest Hungary. **Ind/Abst** MLA Int. Bibliogr. Books Artic. Mod. Lang. Lit.

TEATER I DANMARK. VFOAT Theatre in Denmark. 0106-7672. Danish (English). ir. **LC** PN2740. **DD** 790.209489. *Theatre in Denmark.*

TEATERRADETS INDSTILLING. Main/Corp Denmark. Teaterradet. DK. Danish. ir. Teaterradet, Frederiksborggade 20, 3 1360 Kbenhavn K Denmark. **LC** PN2044.D4.

TEATR. V. 13, No. 9- 1/15 May 1958-. Periodical. PO. Polish. mo. ARS Polona, Krakowskie Przedmiescie 7, 00-068 Warsaw Poland. *Teatr I Film.*

TEATR. UR. Russian (Multilingual). mo. $45.00. Victor Kamkin Inc (70962), 12224 Parklawn Drive, Rockville MD 20852. **Tel** (301)881-5973. **LC** Z2504.D7, PN2724. *Novosti Nauchnoi Literatury: Teatr.*

TEATRO (BUENOS AIRES, ARGENTINA). (TEATRO). **VFOAT** Revista Teatro San Martin. Yearly V. 1, No. 1, (Temporada 1980/81)-. Periodical. AG. Spanish. qt. Av Corrientes 1530/50 Piso, 1042-Buenos Aires Argentina.

TEATRO CONTEMPORANEO. Periodical. IT. Italian. ty. 54.000. Roma, Viale Mazzini, 146-00195 Roma Italy.

TEATTERI. US. Finnish. **LC** PN2006.

TEL QUE NOUS LE PENSONS ET AVONS ENVIE DE LE DIRE. V. 1-. 0317-5243. CN. French. Edition Jeunesse Quebec, 801 12E Rue, Quebec Quebec G1J 2N1 Canada.

THEATER. German. ir. 19.20. Friedrich Verlag Velber, 3016 Seelze 6 West Germany. **LC** PN2004.

THEATER. V. 9- Fall 1977-. 0161-0775. Periodical. US. English. ir. $18.00. Theatre Magazine, 222 York Street, New Haven CT 06520. **Tel** (203)436-1417. Ed Joel Schecter. **Ind/Abst** Humanit. Index, MLA Int. Bibliogr. Books Artic. Mod. Lang. Lit., Film Lit. Index, Index Book Rev. Humanit. **LC** PN2000. **DD** 792.05. adv acc. **Circ** 1,000. Publishes new plays, reviews, interviews with writers and directors. It focuses on the best new plays in America and abroad. *Yale/Theatre, 0044-0167.*

THEATER DER ZEIT. Vol. 1-. 0040-5418. Periodical. SZ. German. mo. $37.71. Kunst and Wissen Erich Bieber, Dufourstrasse 51, CH-8008 Zurich Switzerland. **Tel** 011-41-1-69 44 20. **Ind/Abst** RILM Abstr. **LC** PN2004. **DD** 792.05.

THEATER HEUTE. Vol. 1-, Sept. 1960-. 0040-5507. Periodical. GW. German. ir. W E Saarbach GMBH, Postfach 101610, D-5000 Koeln 1 West Germany. **LC** PN2004. **DD** 792.05.

THEATER IN OSTERREICH. Series/Titl Jahrbuch der Wiener Gesellschaft fur Theaterforschung. 1980/81-. German. ir. Verband der Wissenschaftlichen Gesellschaften Osterreichs, Lindengasse 37, A1070 Wien Austria. **Tel** 93 47 56. Ed Oto G Schindler. **LC** PN2616.V5, PN2614. **DD** 792.9436 S, 792.0295436. **Circ** 400. Lists up a season's performances on Austrian stages.

THEATER-RUNDSCHAU. Publication began 1955. 0040-5442. Periodical. GW. German. mo. 29.40. Theater Rundschau Verlag, Bonner Talweg 10, D-5300 Bonn West Germany. **Tel** 21-87-56. bk rev. adv acc. **Circ** 50,000. Articles on the intellectual situation of theatre, music, literature; reports on German first performances; portraits of dramatists and composers, speaking countries.

THEATER (WASHINGTON, D.C.). (THEATER). Fiscal Year L980-. 8756-4335. US. English. an. National Endowment for the Arts, 1100 Pennsylvania Avenue NW, Washington DC 20506. **LC** PN2044.U6. **DD** 792.079. *Theatre (Washington, D.C.), 8756-4335.*

THEATERGESCHISCHTE OSTERREICHS. V. 1, No. 1- 1964-. Periodical. German. ir. **LC** PN2610.

THE THEATERGOER. VFOAT Theater Goer. Vol. 1, No. 1 (May 1981)-. 0734-3736. Periodical. US. English. mo. $36.00. The Theatergoer, PO Box 889 Midtown Station, New York NY 10018. **Tel** (212)921-8012. Ed Peter Bailey. bk rev. **Circ** 500. Newsletter gives news of broadway, off-broadway, London and regional theater.

THEATERWORK MAGAZINE. VFOAT Theater Work Magazine. Vol. 2, No. 5 (July/Aug. 1982)-. 0735-1895. Periodical. US. English. bm. $9.00 Domestic, $15.00 Foreign. Cherry Creek Inc, 406 South 3rd Street, Saint Peter MN 56082. **LC** PN2000. **DD** 792.05. *Theaterwork, 0736-1130.*

THEATERZEITSCHRIFT. VFOAT Theater Zeitschrift. No. 1 (Sept. 1982)-. 0723-1172. Periodical. GW. German. qt. 34.-. Theater Zeit Schrift Redaktion, Grobbeerenstrabe 13A, D-1000 Berlin 61 West Germany. **Tel** (030)2161079. **LC** PN2004. **DD** 792.0943. bk rev. adv acc. **Circ** 1,650. The only existing scholarly journal in West Germany on matters of performing arts, media and cultural politics.

THEATRE. 1954/55-. UK. English. an. Ed I Brown. **LC** PN2580. **DD** 792.0942. Each issue contains an index to its own contents - no vol index - loose.

THEATRE. VFOAT Trident. V. 1, No 2- Oct./Nov. 1976-. 0705-0453. Periodical. CN. French. bm. Free. Theatre du Trident, Edifice Palais Montcalm, 975 Place d'Youville, Quebec Quebec G1R 3P1 Canada. **DD** 792.09714471. *Theatru du Trident, 0705-0445.*

LE THEATRE. 1- 1968-. 0563-3966. Periodical. FR. French. ir. Christian Bourgeois, 8 rue Garanciere, Paris 6EME France. Ed Fernando Arrabal.

THE THEATRE ANNUAL. 1942-. 0082-3821. US. English. ir. $10.00. University of Akron, Department of Theatre & Dance, Akron OH 44303. **Tel** (216)375-6846. Ed Wallace Sterling. **Ind/Abst** Abstr. Engl. Stud., MLA Int. Bibliogr. Books Artic. Mod. Lang. Lit. **LC** PN2012. **DD** 792.058. **Circ** 400. Information and research in the history and arts of the theatre.

THEATRE B. C. Began publication in 1968?. 0382-7623. Periodical. CN. English. ir. Theatre B C, c/o Community Arts Council of Greater Vancouver 315 West Cordova Street, Vancouver BC V6B 1E5 Canada. **DD** 792.09711.

THEATRE CANADA. 1971-. 0316-1056. Periodical. CN. text in English and French. an. Theatre Canada, 8th Floor 170 Metcalfe Street, Ottawa Ontario K2P 1P3 Canada. **DD** 792.0971. *Dominion Drama Festival.*

THEATRE CHECKLIST. No. 13-. Monographic Series. UK. English. qt. $35.00. TQ Subscriptions, Division of Drama, University of Southern California, University Park, Los Angeles CA 90007.

THEATRE CRAFTS. VFOAT TC. V. 1- Mar./Apr.1967-. 0040-5469. Periodical. US. English. mo. $55.00. Theatre Crafts Association, PO Box 630, Holmes PA 19043. **Tel** (212)677-5997. **Ind/Abst** Mag. Index, Book Rev. Index, Read. Guide Period. Lit. **LC** PN2275.C3. **DD** 790.2097946. (cum index). *Theatre Directory of the Bay Area, 0730-9260.*

THEATRE CRAFTS DIRECTORY. See Yearbooks, Almanacs, Directories.

THEATRE DESIGN AND TECHNOLOGY CEASED. (THEATRE DESIGN AND TECHNOLOGY : JOURNAL OF THE U.S. INSTITUTE FOR THEATRE TECHNOLOGY). No. 13 (May 1968)-No. 43 (Winter 1976). 0040-5477. Periodical. US. English. qt. $24.00. US Institute for Theatre Technology, 330 West 42nd Street, Suite 1702, New York NY 10036. **Tel** (212)563-5551. Ed Tina Margolis. **Ind/Abst** Avery Index Archit. Period. **LC** NA1. bk rev. adv acc. **Circ** 3,000. (ctrl). Available on microfilm from University Microfilms. *Theatre Design & Technology (Pittsburgh, Pa.), 0040-5477.*

THEATRE DIRECTORY. See Yearbooks, Almanacs, Directories.

THEATRE DIRECTORY OF THE SAN FRANCISCO BAY AREA. See Yearbooks, Almanacs, Directories.

THEATRE-DRAMA & SPEECH INDEX. See Indexes/Abstracts.

LE THEATRE EN POLOGNE. VFOAT The Theatre in Poland. Yearly V. 1- (No. 1/2-). 0363-4008. Periodical. PL. English (French). mo. ARS Polona, Krakowskie Przedmiescie 7, 00-068 Warsaw Poland. **LC** PN2859.P6. (cum index).

THEATRE FACTS. VFOAT T.C.G. Survey. 80-. US. English. an. $5.00. Theatre Communications Group Inc, 355 Lexington Avenue, New York NY 10017. **LC** PN2293.E35. **DD** 338.437920973. *TCG Survey, 0271-4124.*

THEATRE HISTORY STUDIES. Vol. 1 (1981)-. 0733-2033. Periodical. US. English. an. $6.00. University of North Dakota, PO Box 8182 Theatre Arts Department, Grand Forks ND 58202. **Tel** (701)777-3446. Ed Ron Engle. **LC** PN2000. **DD** 792.09. bk rev. adv acc. **Circ** 600. Illustrated theatre history journal devoted to research in all areas and fields of interest in national and international theatre history.

THEATRE IN THE AMERICAS. VFOAT Teatro en las Americas, Theatre des Ameriques, Teatro nas Americas. Vol. 1, No. 1 (Spring 1981)-. 0278-8446. Periodical. US. English (Spanish, French and Portuguese). qt. $8.00 Domestic, $10.00 Foreign. Theatre of Latin America Inc, 1860 Broadway/Room 1715, New York NY 10023.

THEATRE INFORMATION BULLETIN. 1944. 0040-5515. Periodical. US. English. wk. $90.00. Proscenium Publications, 4 Park Avenue, New York NY 10016. **Tel** (212)532-2570. Ed Joan Marlowe and Betty Blake.

THEATRE IRELAND. 1-. 0263-6344. Periodical. US. English. qt. $15.00. Robert Lowery, 114 Paula Boulevard, Selden NY 11784. **Tel** (516)698-8243.

THEATRE JOURNAL. VFOAT TJ. V. 31- Mar. 1979-. 0192-2882. Periodical. US. English. qt. $34.00. Johns Hopkins University Press, 701 West 40th Street/Suite 275, Baltimore MD 21211. **Tel** (301)338-6987. Ed Timothy Murray. **Ind/Abst** Abstr. Engl. Stud., MLA Int. Bibliogr. Books Artic. Mod. Lang. Lit., Book Rev. Index, Curr. Contents, Soc. Behav. Sci., Curr. Index J. Educ., Educ. Index, Humanit. Index, Index Book Rev. Humanit., Years Work Eng. Stud. **LC** PN3171. **DD** 792.05. bk rev. adv acc. **Circ** 1,500. Examines all aspects of theatre studies. Publishes contributions from practitioners as well as scholars. *Educational Theatre Journal, 0013-1989.*

THE THEATRE LIBRARY ASSOCIATION. See Library and Information Science.

THEATRE NEWS. V. 1- Oct. 1968-. 0563-4040. Periodical. US. English. ir. $24.00. American Theatre Association, 1010 Wisconsin Avenue NW/Suite 620, Washington DC 20007. **Tel** (202)342-7530. Ed Malcolm Bessom. bk rev. adv acc. **Circ** 8,000. News of interest to theatre educators and professionals.

THEATRE NOTEBOOK. Vol. 1 (Oct. 1945)-. 0040-5523. Periodical. UK. English. ty. $18.75. The Society for Theater Research, 77 Kinnerton Street, London SW1X 8ED England. Ed George Speiaght. **Ind/Abst** Abstr. Engl. Stud., MLA Int. Bibliogr. Books Artic. Mod. Lang. Lit., Annu. Bibliogr. Engl. Lang. Lit., Index Book Rev. Humanit., Humanit. Index, Archit. Period. Index, Years Work Eng. Stud. adv acc. **Circ** 1,500. History and technique of British theatre.

THEATRE ORGAN. V. 12- Feb. 1970-. 0040-5531. Periodical. US. English. bm. $20.00. American Theatre Organ Society, PO Box 420490, Sacramento CA 95842. **Tel** (916)481-7084. *Theatre Organ/Bombarde.*

THEATRE PROFILES. V. 1- 1973-. 0361-7947. US. English. be. Theatre Communications Group, 355 Lexington Avenue, New York NY 10017. **Tel** (212)697-5230. Ed Laura Ross. **LC** PN2266. **DD** 792.0973. Illustrated; artistic profiles plus financial and production information on over 175 theatres across the US.

THEATRE QUEBEC. Vol. 1, No. 1-. 0825-4494. Periodical. CN. English. ir. Free. Centre d'Essai des Auteurs Dramatiques, 426 Sherbrook Street East, Montreal Quebec H2L 1J6 Canada. **DD** 792.09714281. (ctrl).

THEATRE RESEARCH INTERNATIONAL. V. 1- Oct. 1975-. 0307-8833. Periodical. UK. summaries in French. ty. $50.00. Drama Department, Glasgow University, Glasgow G12 8QE Scotland. **Tel** (041)339-8855. Ed Claude Schumacher. **Ind/Abst** Am. Hist. Life, Hist. Abstr., Part A, Mod. Hist. Abstr., Hist. Abst., Part B, Twent. Century Abstr., MLA Int. Bibliogr. Books Artic. Mod. Lang. Lit., Ref. Source, Index Book Rev. Humanit., Humanit. Index, Years Work Eng. Stud., Hist. Abstr. **LC** PN2001. **DD** 790.205. bk rev. adv acc. **Circ** 1,000. Performance acting, production techniques, theater, history architecture, criticism, theory, actor's social conditions, finances, sponsorship, aesthetics. *Theatre Research, New Theatre Magazine.*

THEATRE REVIEW. 1972/73-. UK. English. an. 4.00. W H Allen Company, 44 Hill Street, WIX 8LB London England. **LC** PN2580. **DD** 792.9.

THEATRE SOUTHWEST. V. 1- Feb. 1975-. 0743-5452. Periodical. US. English. ty. $8.00. Theatre Southwest, 102 Seretean OSU, Stillwater OK 74078. **Tel** (405)624-6094. Ed Kenneth D Cox. bk rev. adv acc. **Circ** 1,200. (ctrl) Scholarship and features of southwestern American and world theatre. Approximately 40-8 1/2 x 11 pages.

THEATRE STUDIES. No. 18- 1971/72-. 0362-0964. US. English. an. $6.00. Theater Studies, 1089 Drake Union, Columbus OH 43210. **Tel** (614)422-6614. Ed Alan Woods. **Ind/Abst** Abstr. Engl. Stud., MLA Int. Bibliogr. Books Artic. Mod. Lang. Lit., Theatre Drama Speech Index, Annu. Bibliogr. Mod. Humanit. Res. Assoc., Guide Perform. Arts, Avery Index Archit. Period. **LC** PN1620.O45. **DD** 792.05. bk rev. **Circ** 500. (ctrl). A journal of traditional theatre history, largely American and European. Journal also features book reviews of important research in the discipline. *Ohio State University Theater Collection Bulletin.*

THEATRE SURVEY. V. 1- 1960-. 0040-5574. Periodical. US. English. sa. $10.00. Professor Roger W Herzel, Department of Theatre, State University of New York at Albany, Albany NY 12222. **Tel** (513)442-4205. Ed Roger W Herzel. **Ind/Abst** Am. Hist. Life, Hist. Abstr., Part A, Mod. Hist. Abstr., Hist. Abst., Part B, Twent. Century Abstr., Abstr. Engl. Stud., MLA Int. Bibliogr. Books Artic. Mod. Lang. Lit., Writ. Am. Hist., Years Work Eng. Stud., Index Book Rev. Humanit., Humanit. Index, Recent Publ. Artic. **LC** PN2000. **DD** 792.05. bk rev. adv acc. **Circ** 1,200. (ctrl). All aspects of theatre history, all periods and nations.

THEATRE TIMES. (THEATRE TIMES : A PUBLICATION OF THE ALLIANCE OF RESIDENT THEATRES/NEW YORK). Vol. 1, No. 1-. 0732-300X. Periodical. US. English. bm. $15.00. Alliance of Resident Theatres, 325 Spring Street/Room 315, New York NY 10013. **Tel** (212)898-5257. Ed Mindy N Levine. bk rev. **Circ** 3,000. (ctrl). The trade newspaper of New York City's nonprofit theatre, reports on artistic and management issues important to off and on-broadway theatre.

THEATRE YEAR : A SELECTION OF PHOTOGRAPHS. Oct. 1979 - Nov. 1980-. 0261-2348. UK. English. an. 5.95. In Parenthesis Ltd, 21 Wellington Street, London WC2 England. **LC** PN2595. **DD** 792.9509421.

THEATREPHILE. Vol. 1, No. 1 (Dec. 1983)-. 0265-2609. Periodical. UK. English. qt. $26.05. Theatrephile, 5 Dryden Street, London WC2E 9NW England. **Tel** 01 240 2430. Ed D F Chesmire and Sean McCarthy. **LC** PN2001. **DD** 792.09. adv acc. **Circ** 1,000. History of theatre, popular theatre and leisure entertainments of all periods to present day.

THEATRIKA. Periodical. Greek, Modern. mo. Ekdoseis Choros, Aiginitou 9, Athenai Greece. **LC** PN2009.

TONEEL TEATRAAL. Vol. 95- Jan. 1974-. Periodical. Dutch. ir. 55.00 Domestic, 79.00 Foreign. Nederlands Theater Institute, Herengracht 106, 1016 BP Amsterdam Netherlands. **Tel** (020)235104. **LC** PN2002. Reviews, interviews, and essays on drama, dance, and opera; text fragments of new Dutch foreign plays. *Mickery Mouth & Toneel Teatraal.*

TORONTO THEATRE REVIEW. V. 1- Feb. 1977-. 0225-638X. Periodical. CN. English. ir. $6.00 Canada and US, $10.00 Others. Toronto Theatre Review, Box 41 Station P, Toronto Ontario M5S 2S6 Canada. **DD** 792.09713541.

TQ. THEATRE QUARTERLY CEASED. (THEATRE QUARTERLY). V. 1-10 (No. 1-40). 0049-3600. Periodical. UK. English. **Ind/Abst** Abstr. Engl. Stud., Humanit. Index. **LC** PN2001. **DD** 792.05.

UBU REPERTORY THEATER PUBLICATIONS. VFOAT UBU. Vol. 1-. 0738-4009. Monographic Series. US. English (French). qt. $6.25. UBU Repertory Theater, 149 Mercer Street, New York NY 10012. **Tel** (212)925-0999. Ed Catherine Temerson. **LC** UNC. Contemporary French-language plays in English translation.

UKRAINSKYI TEATR. Rik Zasnuvanuia 1936. Periodical. UR. Ukrainian. bm. **LC** PN2725.U4.

V SOVETSKOM TEATRE. 0201-9272. Periodical. UR. Russian. qt. VAAP-Inform, 103104 Moskva, B Bronnaia 6A, Moskva Russian SFSR. **LC** PN2724.

WAGNER NEWS (LONDON, ENGLAND). *See* Music.

WER SPIELTE WAS?. Began with 1977 issue. German. an. 5.00. Direktion fur das Buhnenrepertoire, Griechische Allee, Berlin East Germany. **LC** PN2640. **DD** 792.0943. *Dramatiker und Komponisten auf den Buhnen der Deutschen Demokratischen Republik.*

WEST COAST PLAYS. 1-. 0147-4502. Periodical. US. English. qt. $25.00. California Theatre Council, East Columbia Building/Suite 621, 849 South Broadway, Los Angeles CA 90014. **Tel** (213)622-6727. Ed Robert Hurwitt. **LC** PS569. **DD** 812.5405. bk rev. adv acc. **Circ** 2,000. A collection of the best new plays from trend-setting theatres along the west coast. Selected and edited by California magazine theatre critic Robert Hurwitt.

WORD PLAYS. (WORD PLAYS : AN ANTHOLOGY OF NEW AMERICAN DRAMA). Series/ Titl PAJ Playscripts. VFOAT Wordplays. 1st Ed-. 0749-7768. US. English. ir. **DD** 812.

WU TAI MEI SHU YU CHI SHU = STAGE ART AND TECHNOLOGY. VFOAT Stage Art and Technology. 1981, 1-. Periodical. CH. Chinese. ir. 1.20. Hsin Hua Shu Tien, Pei-Ching Fa Hsing So, Peking China. **LC** PN2009. **DD** 792.02.

YOUNG CINEMA & THEATRE. VFOAT Jeune Cinema & Theatre. 0513-5958. Periodical. English (French). qt. $3.00. International Union of Student, Parizska 1, 110 01 Praha 1 Czechoslovakia. **Tel** 23 12 812. **DD** 791. **Circ** 20,000. Devoted to the presentation of students and young cinema and theater phenomenas and streams with the emphasis on the third world countries. *Young Cinema.*

TOBACCO

ABSTRACTS OF PAPERS PRESENTED AT THE . . . TOBACCO ROOT GEOLOGICAL SOCIETY CONFERENCE. *See* Indexes/Abstracts.

ANNALES DU TABAC. SECTION 1, RECHERCHE ET DEVELOPPEMENT. 0399-0206. Periodical. French (summaries in English and German). ir. 53 Quai d'Orsay, 75340 Paris Cedex 07 France. *Annales du Tabac. Section 1, Recherche et Ingegnierie.*

ANNUAL REPORT AND ACCOUNTS - TOBACCO EXPORT PROMOTION COUNCIL. Main/Corp Tobacco Export Promotion Council. 0304-6648. English. ir. World Trade Centre, 123-C Mount Road, 600006 Madras India. **LC** HD9146.I4. **DD** 354.54008233.

ANNUAL REPORT OF THE TOBACCO BOARD (PORT LOUIS, MAURITIUS). Main/Corp Port Louis, Mauritius. Tobacco Board. English. ir. Tobacco Board Mauritius, 37 Sir William Newton Street, Port Louis Mauritius. **LC** HD9147.M3.

ANNUAL REPORT ON TOBACCO STATISTICS (UNITED STATES). AGRICULTURAL MARKETING SERVICE. *See* Statistics.

ANNUAL REPORT - R. J. REYNOLDS INDUSTRIES. Main/Corp R. J. Reynolds Industries, Inc. 1970-. US. English. an. Free upon request. Reynolds Boulevard, Winston-Salem NC 27102.

ANNUAL REPORT - TOBACCO WORKING GROUP, NATIONAL INSTITUTES OF HEALTH. Main/Corp National Cancer Institute. Tobacco Working Group. Periodical. US. English. an. National Cancer Institute, National Institutes of Health, 9000 Rockville Pike, Bethesda MD 20014.

ARSREDOVISNING - SVENSKA TOBAKS AB. Main/Corp Svenska Tobaks Aktiebolaget. 1969-. Periodical. Swedish. ir. *Verksamhetsaet . . . Arsredovisning Och Revisionsberattelse.*

AUSTRALIAN TOBACCO GROWERS' BULLETIN. No. 1-. Periodical. English. ir.

BEITRAGE ZUR TABAKFORSCHUNG INTERNATIONAL. V. 9, No. 4 (July 1978)-. 0173-783X. Periodical. German (articles also in English with summaries in English, French, and German). ir. Verband der Cigarettenindustrie, Harvestehuder Weg 88, D-2000 Hamburg West Germany. **Ind/Abst** Excerpta Med., Biol. Abstr., Chem. Abstr., Life Sci. Collect., Bibliogr. Agric. **LC** TS2220. **DD** 679.705. **CODEN** BTAID3. *Beitrage zur Tabakforschung.*

BHARATIYA TAMBAKU. V. 1- April/June 1971-. II. in Hindi. ir. 4.00. Tambaku Vikasa Nidesalaya, 3-A Eldams Road, Teynampet Madrasa 600018 India. **LC** SB278.I58.

BOLETIM INFORMATIVO : COMERCIO EXTERIOR - EXPORTACAO DE FUMO EM FOLHAS. Main/Corp Instituto Bahiano do Fumo. BL. Portuguese. ir. Rua da Belgica, 2-Ed Roosevelt Lo Andar, Salvador Brazil. **LC** HD9144.B73.

CANADIAN TOBACCO GROWER. (THE CANADIAN TOBACCO GROWER). Began publication in 1953. 0008-5189. Periodical. CN. English. mo. Cash Crop Farming Publishing Ltd, 222 Argyle Avenue, Delhi Ontario N48 2Y2 Canada. **Tel** (519)582-2510. Ed David MacLaren. adv acc. **Circ** 4,500. (ctrl). Serving growers of flue-cured tobacco in Canada.

CUBA TABACO. Periodical. CU. Spanish. ir. Amargura No. 103, Esq A San Ignacio, Zona 1 Ciudad Habana. **LC** HD9144.C9.

DOHANYIPAR. Began 1954. 0012-4931. Periodical. HU. Hungarian. bm. Akademiai Kiado, POB 24, 1363 Budapest Hungary. **Ind/Abst** Chem. Abstr., Bibliogr. Agric. **CODEN** DOHAAW.

FINANZEN UND STEUERN. REIHE 9. 1.2 : TABAKGEWERBE. Main/Corp Germany (West). Statistisches Bundesamt. **VAT** Finanzen Und Steuern. Reihe Neun.Eins.Zei: Tabakgewerbe. German. ir. 3.20. **LC** HD9143.4. *Finanzen und Steuren. Reihe 8: Tabakgewerbe Enschl. Tabakhandel.*

THE FLUE CURED TOBACCO FARMER. 0015-4512. Periodical. US. English. ir. $8.00. Specialized Agriculture Publishers, 3000 Highwoods Boulevard, Box 95075, Raleigh NC 27625. **Tel** (919)872-5040. **Ind/Abst** Bibliogr. Agric.

FOREIGN AGRICULTURE CIRCULAR. TOBACCO. 0145-0867. US. English. mo. $25.00 Domestic, $40.00 Foreign. US Department of Agriculture, Foreign Agriculture Service, Washington DC 20250. **Tel** (202)382-9516. **Ind/Abst** Am. Stat. Index. **Circ** 800. Report highlights latest information on imports and exports of tobacco, world prices, world developments affecting tobacco demand and supply, and US tobacco industry and trade developments.

GYOTEI HOKOKU - NIHON SEMBAI KOSHA UTSUNOMIYA TABAKO SHIKENJO. Main/Corp Utsunomiya Tabako Shikenjo. VFOAT Tabako Shikenjo Gyotei Hokoku. JA. Japanese. ir. Utsunomiya Tabako Shikenjo, 1900 Oaza Izui, Koyama 323 Japan. **LC** SB278.J3.

HANGUK YONCHO HAKHOE CHI. VFOAT Journal of the Korean Society of Tobacco Science. Periodical. KO. Korean (summaries in English). ir. Hanguk Yoncho Hakhoe, 112 Inui-Dong, Chongno-Ku, Seoul South Korea. **LC** TS2249.

HATABAKO KENKYU. Japanese. ir. Semba: Jigyo Kyokai, 11 Nishikubo Sakuragawacho, Minato-Ku, Tokyo Japan. **LC** SB278.J3.

INDIAN TOBACCO. 0445-7951. English. ir. World Trade Centre, 123 C Mount Road, 600006 Madras India. **LC** HD9146.I4. **DD** 338.173710954.

Tobacco

INDIAN TOBACCO (GUNTUR, INDIA). (INDIAN TOBACCO). 1981-. English. ir. Post Bag No 451, Lakshmipuram, Guntur 522007 India. LC HD9146.I4. DD 633.71029454.

INFORME ANUAL - PROGRAMA NACIONAL DE TABACO (PARAGUAY). COMISION DE EJECUCION. Main/Corp Programa Nacional de Tabaco (Paraguay). Comision de Ejecucion. Spanish. an. LC SB278.P37. DD 633.7109892.

KENKYU HOKOKU.—NIHON SEMBAI KOSHA CHUO KENKYUJO. Main/Corp Nihon Sembai Kosha. Chuo Kenkyujo. VFOAT Scientific Papers of the Central Research Institute, Japan Tobacco & Salt Public Corporation. 0369-4372. Multilingual (Japanese and English). ir. Nihon Sembai Kosha, Umegaoka Midori-Ku, Yokohama Japan. Ind/Abst Chem. Abstr., Bibliogr. Agric. LC TS2220. CODEN NISHA6.

KOKUNAISAN HATABAKO KAISETSUSHO. Main/Corp Nihon Semabi Kosha. Genryo Hombu. 1975-. Japanese. ir. Nihon Sembai Kosha, 11 Nishikubo Sakuragawacho, Shipa-Ku Tokyo Japan. LC SB278.J3. *Kokunaisan Hatabako Kaisetsusho.*

LIGHTER. (THE LIGHTER). VFOAT Le Briquet. 1931. 0024-340X. Periodical. CN. French (text in English). qt. Free. Secretary Editorial Board, Communications Branch, Agriculture Canada, Ottawa Ontario K1A 0C7 Canada. Tel (613)995-8963. Ind/Abst Bibliogr. Agric. Circ 1,600. (ctrl). A journal devoted to tobacco research and the tobacco industry in Canada.

NEWS LETTER (FLUE-CURED TOBACCO COOPERATIVE STABILIZATION CORPORATION). (NEWS LETTER). VFOAT Newsletter. Jan. 4, 1954-. Periodical. US. English. mo.

NORTH CAROLINA INTEGRATED TOBACCO PEST MANAGEMENT . . . ANNUAL REPORT. 1974-. US. English. an. *North Carolina Tobacco Pest Management Annual Report.*

NORTH CAROLINA TOBACCO REPORT. Main/Corp North Carolina. Dept. of Agriculture. US. English. an. LC HD9137.N8.

OUTLOOK AND SITUATION REPORT. TOBACCO. VFOAT Tobacco. TS-187 (March 1984)-. Periodical. US. English. qt. Superintendent of Documents, US Government Printing Office, Washington DC 20402. Ind/Abst Am. Stat. Index, Predicasts. *Tobacco Outlook & Situation, 0277-1829.*

REPORT OF THE COUNCIL FOR TOBACCO RESEARCH-U.S.A., INC. (REPORT OF THE COUNCIL FOR TOBACCO RESEARCH—U.S.A., INC). Main/Corp Council for Tobacco Research—U.S.A. 0361-1612. US. English. an. Council for Tobacco Research USA, 110 East 59th Street, New York NY 10022. LC R850.A1. DD 615.952379. NLM W1 CO955B.

REPORT ON THE TOBACCO INDUSTRIES. Main/Corp Canada. Bureau of Statistics. Periodical. CN. English (French). an. LC HD9144.C2. DD 338.476791371.

RESEARCH PAPER - TOBACCO RESEARCH COUNCIL. No. 1- 1966-. 0082-4607. Monographic Series. UK. English. ir. Tobacco Research Council, Glen House Stag Place, London SW1E 5AG England. NLM W1 RE2322. *Tobacco Manufacturers' Standing Committee. Research Papers.*

REVIEW OF THE CANADIAN TOBACCO INDUSTRY. 0712-7863. CN. English. an. Free. Public Relations Department, Imperial Tobacco Ltd, PO Box 6500, Montreal Quebec H3C 3L6 Canada. DD 338.173710971. *Annual Industry Review (1968), 0712-7855.*

SHISHA CHIHOKYOKU TABAKO KOSAKU SHIKEH SEISEKI. Main/Corp Nihon Sembai Kosha. Seisan Hombu. Japanese. ir. Nihon Sembai Kosha Seisan Hombu, 2 Akasaka Aoicho, Minato-Ku 107 Tokyo Japan. LC SB278.J3. *Chihokyoku Tabako Kosaku Shiken Seiseki.*

SMOKESHOP. See Business.

SMOKING AND HEALTH BULLETIN. See Public Health and Safety.

SNUFF BOTTLE REVIEW. No. 1- Jan. 1975-. Periodical. English. ir.

SOUTHERN TOBACCO JOURNAL. 0300-6239. Periodical. US. English. mo. Southern Trade Publications Company, PO Box 9377, Greensboro NC 27408.

TABAC AU CANADA. (LE TABAC AU CANADA . . . : UN RAPPORT). 1981-. 0713-5467. CN. French. an. Conseil Canadien des Fabricants des Produits du Tabac, 1808 Ouest rue Sherbrooke, Montreal Quebec H3H 1E5 Canada. DD 338.4767970971.

TABAK. 1934, No. 1-. Periodical. UR. Russian. qt. $16.00. Victor Kamkin Inc (70960), 12224 Parklawn Drive, Rockville MD 20852. Tel (301)881-5973. Ind/Abst Bibliogr. Agric.

TABAKO BYOGAICHU SOGO BOJO TENJI NOJO SEISEKI. 1942- 1967-. JA. Japanese. ir. LC SB608.T7.

TAIWAN SHENGYANJIU GONGMAIJU YONGYE SHIYAN-SUO YANJIU HUIBAO. (TAI-WAN SHENG YEN CHIU KUNG MAI CHU YEN YEH SHIH YEN SO YEN CHIU HUI PAO). Main/Corp Tai-Wan Sheng Yen Chiu Kung Mai Chu. Yen Yeh Shih Yen So. VFOAT Bulletin of the Tobacco Research Institute, Taiwan Tobacco & Wine Monopoly Bureau. No. 3- Aug. 1975-. 0379-4199. Periodical. Chinese (summaries in English). sa. Ind/Abst Excerpta Med., Chem. Abstr., Bibliogr. Agric. CODEN BTRBDX.

TAMBAE (HANGUK YONCHO HAKHOE). (TAMBAE). VFOAT Tobacco Korea. Periodical. KO. Korean. ir. Hanguk Yoncho Hakhoe, 21-4 Cho-dong, Chung-ku, Seoul South Korea. LC SB273.

TAMBAE YONGU NONMUNJIP. VFOAT Research Papers of Tobacco Science. Periodical. English (Korean). ir. Hanguk Insam Yoncho, Yonguso 112 In Ui-dong, Chongno-Ku Seoul Korea. LC SB278.K6.

THE TAX BURDEN ON TOBACCO. V. 1- 1966-. 0563-6191. US. English. an. Tobacco Tax Council, 5407 Patterson Avenue, Richmond VA 23226. LC HD9130.1. DD 336.27867970973.

TECHNICAL BULLETIN (CENTRAL TOBACCO RESEARCH INSTITUTE (INDIA)). (TECHNICAL BULLETIN). Monographic Series. English. ir.

TJI : TOBACCO JOURNAL INTERNATIONAL. VFOAT Tobacco Journal International. 0039-8748. Periodical. English (Dutch, French, German, Italian and Spanish). bm. $50.00. Mainzer Verlagsanstalt und Druckerie Will und Rothe GMBH, Co, KG Pressehaus Gro E Bleiche 44-50 P O B 3120, D-6500 Mainz West Germany. LC HD9130.1. DD 338.1737105.

TO-DO-FU-KENBETSU SEIZO TABAKO URIWATASHI JISSEKI. Main/Corp Nihon Sembai Kosha. Eigyo Hombu. Japanese. ir. LC HD9146.J19.

TOBACCO. Founded 1881. 0040-8271. Periodical. UK. English. mo. Industrial Newspapers Ltd, Queensway House 2 Queensway, Redhill Surrey RHI 105 England. LC HD9130.1. DD 338.476791371.

TOBACCO ABSTRACTS. See Indexes/Abstracts.

TOBACCO ALLOTTED, BY COUNTIES AND KINDS. US. English. an. Department of Agriculture, Agricultural Stabilization & Conservation Service, Washington DC 20250.

TOBACCO AND TOBACCO PRODUCTS STATISTICS. See Statistics.

THE TOBACCO FARMER. Periodical. US. English. qt. Georgia Agricultural Commodity Commission, PO Box 396, Lifton GA 31794.

THE TOBACCO GROWER. (THE TOBACCO GROWER : THE OFFICIAL PUBLICATION OF THE TOBACCO GROWERS ASSOCIATION OF NORTH CAROLINA, INC). Began With V. 1, No. 1 in July 1984. 8756-4750. Periodical. US. English. mo. $15.00. TGANC, 1315 Brooks Avenue, Raleigh NC 27607. Tel (919)781-2307. Ed Chris Bickers. DD 633. bk rev. adv acc. Circ 3,000. Latest information on political developments especially Washington, management practices, agronomy and economics affecting tobacco growers.

TOBACCO IN CANADA. (TOBACCO IN CANADA . . . : A REPORT). 1981-. 0713-5459. CN. English. an. Canadian Tobacco Manufacturers' Council, 1808 Sherbrooke Street West, Montreal Quebec H3H 1E5 Canada. DD 338.4767970971.

TOBACCO INTERNATIONAL. V. 172- Jan. 8, 1971-. 0049-3945. Periodical. US. English. bw. Tobacco International, 551 Fifth Avenue, New York NY 10017. Tel (212)661-5980. Ind/Abst Excerpta Med., Int. Packag. Abstr., Chem. Abstr., Bibliogr. Agric. LC HD9130.1. DD 338.47679705. CODEN TBCIAE. *Tobacco.*

TOBACCO MARKET REVIEW. BURLEY. VFOAT Burley. TOB-LA-26 (1981 Crop)-. 0742-1869. US. English. an. U S D A, Agricultural Marketing Service, Washington DC 20250. LC HD9134. DD 381.413717. Vols. for 1982- distributed to depository libraries in microfiche. *Tobacco Market Review. Light Air-Cured. Burley, Type 31, 0196-8688.*

TOBACCO MARKET REVIEW. FIRE-CURED AND DARK AIR-CURED. Began with TOB-FDA-19, 1975 Crop, 1976-76 season. 0272-2771. US. English. an. US Department of Agriculture, Agricultural Marketing Service, Washington DC 20250. LC HD9134. DD 338.17371. Vols. for (1981-) distributed to depository libraries in microfiche. *Fire-Cured and Dark Air-Cured Tobacco Market Review, 0498-2150.*

TOBACCO MARKET REVIEW: FLUE-CURED. (TOBACCO MARKET REVIEW. FLUE-CURED). 0193-6514. US. English. an. US Department of Agriculture, Agricultural Marketing Service, Washington DC 20250. LC HD9134. DD 338.17371. *Flue-Cured Tobacco Market Review, 0498-1782.*

TOBACCO MARKET REVIEW. SOUTHERN MARYLAND. 0364-7420. US. English. US Department of Agriculture, Agricultural Marketing Service, Washington DC 20250. LC HD9137.M3. DD 381.41371097524.

TOBACCO PRODUCTS INDUSTRIES. Series/Titl Annual Census of Manufactures. VFOAT Industrie du Tabac. 1970-. 0300-0249. CN. English (French). an. Receiver General for Canada, Statistics Canada Publications, Ottawa Ontario K1A 0T6 Canada. *Tobacco and Tobacco Products.*

TOBACCO QUARTERLY. Vol. 1, No. 1 (Jan. 1979). 0142-1913. Periodical. UK. English. qt. $119.17. Commonwealth Secretariat, Marlborough House/Pall Mall, London SW1Y 5HX England. Tel 01-839-3411. Circ 500. Providing detailed information on tobacco leaf production, exports, imports, stocks, prices and consumption. Also gives data on production, consumption, exports and imports of cigarettes, cigars/cigarillos, and other tobacco manufacturers' products.

TOBACCO REPRINT SERIES. 0743-4707. Periodical. US. English. ir. Free to Qualified Subscribers. Tobacco Literature Service, Box 711 2314 D H Hill Library North Carolina State University, Raleigh NC 27695-7111. Tel (919)737-2836. DD 633. Circ 400. (ctrl). Reprints of published NCSU tobacco related research.

TOBACCO STOCKS. See Business - Investments.

TOBACCO TAX GUIDE. Main/Corp United States. Internal Revenue Service. VFOAT Tobacco Tax Guide. Periodical. US. English. ir. US Treasury Department, Internal Revenue Service, Washington DC 20402.

TR, TOBACCO REPORTER. VFOAT Tobacco Reporter. 0361-5693. US. English. mo. Harcourt Brace Jovanovich Publications, 1 East First Street, Duluth MN 55802. LC HD9130.1. DD 338.1737105. *Tobacco Reporter, 0040-8328.*

TUPAKKATUOTTEIDEN KULUTUS. VFOAT Tobakskonsumtion. 1960-1978-. English (Finnish and Swedish, 1960-1978-1979-1981-). an. Government Printing Centre, PO 516, SF-00101 Helsinki 10 Finland.

UNITED STATES TOBACCO AND CANDY JOURNAL. Vol. 211, No. 14 (July 22-Aug. 7, 1983)-. 0741-2258. Periodical. US. English. bw. $24.00 Domestic, $30.00 Canada, $65.00 Other Countries. BMT Publications, 254 West 31st Street, New York NY 10001. Ind/Abst Trade Ind. Index, Infobank. LC HD9130.1. DD 381.456641530973. *United States Tobacco Journal, 0041-8137.*

WIADOMOSCI TYTONIOWE. Periodical. PL. Polish. mo. ARS Polona, Krakowskie Przedmiescie 7, 00-068 Warsaw Poland.

WORLD SMOKING & HEALTH. (WORLD SMOKING & HEALTH : AN AMERICAN CANCER SOCIETY JOURNAL). VAT World Smoking and Health. Began with Fall/Winter 1976 issue. 0161-7672. Periodical. US. English. Free. American Cancer Society, 4 West 35th Street, New York NY 10001. Ed Adele Paroni. LC RA1242.T6. DD 613.8505. NLM W1 WO899. Circ 10,000. (ctrl). Articles discussing the world smoking epidemic and the harmful effects of smoking. Includes epidemiologic studies and cessation suggestions.

WORLD TOBACCO. No. 1- June 1963-. 0043-9126. Periodical. UK. English (summaries in French and German, also Spanish from June 1964). qt. 55.00. Industrial Newspapers Ltd, Queensway House, 2 Queensway, Redhill Surrey RH1 1QS England. Tel (0737)68611. Ed George Gaye. Ind/Abst Predicasts. LC SB273. bk rev. adv acc. Circ 4,389. A journal for managers and key decision makers involved in the international tobacco and allied industries.

YEN YEH SHIH YEN SO NIEN PAO. VFOAT Annual Report of Tobacco Research Institute, Taiwan Tobacco & Wine Monopoly Bureau. Thai. an.

YON YONCHO. Periodical. KO. Korean. ir. Yop Yoncho Saengsan Chohap Yonhaphee, 86 Chunghak-Dong Chongno-Ku, Seoul South Korea. LC SB278.K6.

ZIMBABWE TOBACCO TODAY. V. 3, No. 3- Mar. 1980-. Periodical. English. mo. $50.00. Thomsom Publications Zimbabwe Pty Ltd, Box 1683, Salisbury Rhodesia. LC SB278.R45. DD 633.71096891. *Rhodesian Tobacco Today*.

TRANSPORTATION

AASHTO QUARTERLY. Main/Corp American Association of State Highway and Transportation Officials. VAT American Association of State Highway and Transportation Officials Quarterly. V. 55, No. 2-Apr. 1976-. 0147-4847. Periodical. US. English. qt. $6.00. AASHTO Quartely, 444 North Capitol Street NW/Suite 225, Washington DC 20001. Tel (202)624-5800. Ed Mariann Humphreys. LC TE1. DD 388.0973. Articles cover topics of wide variety relating to planning, building and maintaining the nation's transportation systems. *American Highway & Transportation Magazine*, 0147-4820.

ACCELERATION AND PASSING ABILITY. Main/Corp United States. National Highway Traffic Safety Administration. Series/Titl Consumer Aid Series. 0360-6090. US. English. US Department of Transportation, National Highway Safety Administration, Washington DC 20590. LC TL1, TL154. DD 629.2832.

ACCIDENTS OF MOTOR CARRIERS OF PASSENGERS. See Public Health and Safety.

ACCIDENTS OF MOTOR CARRIERS OF PROPERTY. See Public Health and Safety.

ACTIVITES DE L'INSTITUT DE RECHERCHE DES TRANSPORTS. Main/Corp Institut de Recherche des Transports. French. ir. I R T, 2 Avenue du General Malleret-Joinville B P 28, Archeil 94110 France. LC TA1071.

ADMINISTRATION REPORT - KARNATAKA STATE ROAD TRANSPORT CORPORATION. Main/Corp Karnataka State Road Transport Corporation. 12th- 1972/73-. English. ir. Transport House, Shanthinagar, 27, Bangalore India. LC HE5691.M9. DD 388.1.1. *Administration Report*.

ADVANCE BULLETIN OF INTERSTATE COMMERCE ACTS ANNOTATED. See Business - Commerce.

ADVANCED VEHICLE NEWS. VFOAT Advanced Vehicle News and Electric Vehicle News. Vol. 12, No. 1 (Feb. 1983)-. 0739-5388. Periodical. US. English. qt $15.00. Advanced Vehicle News, PO Box 5200, Westport CT 06881. Ind/Abst Predicasts, Energy Res. Abstr. LC TL220. *Electric Vehicle News*, 0095-7526.

ADVISORY BULLETIN - OFFICE OF PIPELINE SAFETY OPERATIONS. Main/Corp United States. Office of Pipeline Safety Operations. Periodical. US. English. mo. US Department of Transportation, Materials Transportation Bureau, Office of Pipeline Safety Operations, 400 7th Street SW, Washington DC 20590.

AFFIRMATIVE ACTION PLAN - ALASKA. DEPT. OF TRANSPORTATION AND PUBLIC FACILITIES. (AFFIRMATIVE ACTION PLAN). Main/Corp Alaska. Dept. of Transportation and Public Facilities. 0742-6097. US. English. an. Department of Transportation and Public Facilities, Pouch Z, Juneau AK 99811. LC HE213.A4. DD 353.97980087500683.

AIR FREIGHT DIRECTORY. See Yearbooks, Almanacs, Directories.

AIRLINE & TRAVEL FOOD SERVICE. See Food & Drink.

ALASKA PASSENGER TRAFFIC SURVEY. 1950-. 0401-1813. Periodical. US. English. ir. Alaska Department of Economic Development & Planning, Division ECP Enterprise/Porich EE, Juneau AK 99811. LC HE213.A4. DD 387.7.

ALBERTA CHECK STOP PROGRAM. ANNUAL REPORT CEASED. (ALBERTA CHECK STOP PROGRAM : ANNUAL REPORT). Main/Corp Alberta. Dept. of the Solicitor General. VAT Alberta Check Stop. Annual Report. 1st- 1973/74?. 0703-041X. Periodical. CN. English. an. Department of the Solicitor General, 10310 Jasper Avenue, Edmonton Alberta T5J 1Y8 Canada. LC HE5620.D7. DD 363.41.

ALBERTA MOTOR TRANSPORT DIRECTORY. See Yearbooks, Almanacs, Directories.

ALBERTA MOTORIST CEASED. -V. 22, No. 2 (Mar./Apr. 1980). 0002-4856. Periodical. CN. English. bm. $7.74. Kingsway Publishing Western Ltd, 304 10010-105 Street, Edmonton Alberta T5G 2X8 Canada. Tel (403)428-9578. *Voice of Motordom*.

ALBERTA TRANSPORTATION. VAT Alberta Transportation Magazine, Transportation (Edmonton). V. 1- Feb./Mar. 1978-. 0705-4629. Periodical. CN. English. bm. Alberta Transportation, 4999-98 Ave Twin Atria, Edmonton Alberta T6B 2X3 Canada.

ALBERTA TRANSPORTATION (CALGARY, ALTA.). (ALBERTA TRANSPORTATION). VAT Western Canada Oil & Gas Directory. Alberta Transportation. No. 1-. 0821-7718. CN. English. an. Alberta Transportation, 4135 Edmonton Trail NE, Calgary Alta T2E 3 Canada. DD 380.5240257123.

ALCOHOL, DRUGS, AND TRAFFIC SAFETY : CURRENT RESEARCH LITERATURE. See Drug Abuse and Alcoholism.

ALMANAK PERHUBUNGAN DAN PARIWISATA INDONESIA. See Yearbooks, Almanacs, Directories.

AMERICAN MCD. NATIONAL EDITION. See Yearbooks, Almanacs, Directories.

AMERICAN MCD. NEW ENGLAND EDITION. See Yearbooks, Almanacs, Directories.

AMERICAN MCD. PACIFIC STATES EDITION. See Yearbooks, Almanacs, Directories.

AMERICAN MOTOR CARRIER. 0003-0066. Periodical. US. English. bm. $1.50. American Motor Carrier, 473 Hemlock Dr, Marietta GA 30064. Tel (404)427-6362. Ed W H Hooker. adv acc. Circ 28,000. (ctrl). Activities of trucking companies and individual truckers and official information from state public service commissions and from the Interstate Commerce Commission.

THE AMERICAN TRANSPORTATION BUILDER. V. 54, No. 5- May 1977-. 0149-4511. Periodical. US. English. qt $15.00. ARTBA, 525 School Street SW, Washington DC 20024. Tel (202)488-2722. LC TE1. DD 388.10973. *American Road Builder*, 0003-0856.

AMERICAN TRUCKER. 0199-3305. Periodical. US. English. mo. $12.00. MTN Publications, PO Box 6391, San Bernardino CA 92412. Tel (714)889-1167. Ed Steve Sturgess. adv acc. Circ 47,000. The magazine for trucking professionals who own and operate their own trucks.

ANALYSIS AND FORECASTS. VFOAT Europa Transport. 1st-. English. an. Directorate-General for Transport, Commission of the European Communities, 200 rue de la Loi, 1049 Brussels Belgium. LC HE199.E87. DD 380.524094.

ANALYSIS OF MOTOR CARRIER ACCIDENTS INVOLVING VEHICLE DEFECTS OR MECHANICAL FAILURE. US. English. an. Department of Transportation, Federal Highway Administration, Washington DC 20590.

T & DM, TRANSPORTATION & DISTRIBUTION MANAGEMENT. VFOAT Transportation & Distribution Management. VAT T and DM, Transportation and Distribution Management, Transportation and Distribution Management. V. 14- Jan./Feb. 1974-. 0039-8276. Periodical. US. English. bm. $15.00 Domestic, $25.00 Foreign. Traffic Service Corporation, 815 Washington Building, Washington DC 20005. *Transportation & Distrubution Management*, 0049-4496.

ANNUAIRE - ASSOCIATION DES ROUTES ET TRANSPORTS DU CANADA. See Yearbooks, Almanacs, Directories.

ANNUAL CONFERENCE PROCEEDINGS - INSTITUTE OF TRANSPORTATION ENGINEERS, CANADA. Main/Corp Institute of Transportation Engineers. District 7, Canada. 1976-. 0705-677X. CN. English. an. Institute of Transportation Engineers District 7 Canada, PO Box 96 Station K, Toronto Ontario M4P 2G1 Canada. DD 388.31.

ANNUAL FINANCIAL REPORT FOR THE FISCAL YEAR ENDING AUGUST 31 . . . - TEXAS. STATE DEPT. OF HIGHWAYS AND PUBLIC TRANSPORTATION. Main/Corp Texas. State Dept. of Highways and Public Transportation. US. English. an. State Department of Highways and Public Transportation, Austin TX 78701. LC HE28.T4. DD 353.9764007232.

ANNUAL FINANCIAL REPORT, STATE OWNED TOLL BRIDGES. Main/Corp California. Dept. of Transportation. US. English. an. Department of Transportation, 1425 River Park Drive, Sacramento CA 95815. LC HE376.A2. DD 388.114.

ANNUAL MEETING. PROCEEDINGS. CANADIAN URBAN TRANSIT ASSOCIATION. (PROCEEDINGS - CANADIAN URBAN TRANSIT ASSOCIATION, MEETING). Main/Corp Canadian Urban Transit Association. Meeting. 68th- 1972/73-. 0316-7933. CN. English. an. Canadian Urban Transit Association, 140 Bay Street/Suite 220, Union Station, Toronto Ontario MJ5 2L5 Canada. Tel (416)481-3309. LC HE4501. DD 388.406271.

ANNUAL PROGRESS REPORT - MICHIGAN DEPARTMENT OF TRANSPORTATION. Main/Corp Michigan. Dept. of Transportation. Series/Titl MDOT Report. 27th- 1977-. US. English. an. Department of Transportation, Transportation Building, 425 West Ottawa, Box 30050, Lansing MI 48909. LC HE356.M5. DD 388.109774. *Annual Progress Report - Michigan Department of State Highways and Transportation*.

ANNUAL REPORT. Main/Corp Australia. Dept. of Transport. 1982-83-. 0812-5384. English. an. GPO Box 84, Canberra Australian Capital Territory 2601 Australia. LC HE289.A15. DD 354.9400875006. *Annual Report*.

ANNUAL REPORT - ALBERTA TRANSPORTATION. (ANNUAL REPORT). Main/Corp Alberta. Alberta Transportation. 1975/76-. 0702-7702. CN. English. an. LC HE357.Z6. DD 354.712300875006. *Annual Report*, 0318-4757.

ANNUAL REPORT AND CARGO STATISTICS - MACKAY HARBOUR ROAD. See Statistics.

ANNUAL REPORT - ARIZONA DEPARTMENT OF TRANSPORTATION. Main/Corp Arizona. Dept. of Transportation. 1974-. 0149-7405. US. English. an. Public Information Office, 206 17th Avenue South, Phoenix AZ 85007. LC HE28.A6. DD 353.97910087505.

ANNUAL REPORT - ARIZONA DEPARTMENT OF TRANSPORTATION, ADMINISTRATIVE SERVICES DIVISION. Main/Corp Arizona. Dept. of Transportation. Administrative Services Division. US. English. an. Arizona Department of Transportation,

Transportation

206 17th Avenue South, Phoenix AZ 85007. LC HE356.A7. DD 353.9791008781.

ANNUAL REPORT - ARKANSAS. STATE HIGHWAY & TRANSPORTATION DEPT. Main/Corp Arkansas. State Highway & Transportation Dept. US. English. an. LC HE213.A7. DD 353.976700875006.

ANNUAL REPORT : BALTIMORE REGION. Main/Corp Metropolitan Transit Authority (Baltimore County, MD.). US. English. an. Metropolitan Transit Authority, 1515 Washington Boulevard, Baltimore MD 21230. LC HE4491.B3. DD 388.41322097526.

ANNUAL REPORT - CANADA. TRANSPORT CANADA. Main/Corp Canada. Transport Canada. VFOAT Rapport Annuel. 1972-. CN. English (French). an. LC HE30.A3. DD 354.710087506. Annual Report.

ANNUAL REPORT - CANADIAN NATIONAL. Main/Corp Canadian National. 1979-. 0824-8265. CN. English. an. Free. Corporate Communications Canadian National, PO Box 8100, Montreal Quebec H3C 3N4 Canada. Tel (514)877-4758. LC HE2801. DD 385.06571. Circ 40,000. (ctrl). Covers financial reviews and outlook for this integrated transport and communications company, operating throughout Canada and with international links. 0225-1868.

ANNUAL REPORT, DELAWARE TURNPIKE. Main/Corp Delaware. Dept. of Transportation. 1976/77-. US. English. an. Deleware Department of Transportation, Dover DE 19901. LC HE356.D4. DD 353.9751008642. Annual Report, Delaware Turnpike.

ANNUAL REPORT - DEPARTMENT OF HIGHWAYS AND TRANSPORTATION. Main/Corp Delaware. Dept. of Highways and Transportation. 1970/71-. 0095-7593. US. English. an. Department of Highways and Transportation, Dover DE 19901. LC HE356.D4. DD 353.975100864.

ANNUAL REPORT - DEPT. OF TRANSPORTATION AND PUBLIC FACILITIES (ALASKA). Main/Corp Alaska. Dept. of Transportation and Public Facilities. 1977-. US. English. an. LC HE28.A4. DD 353.9798087505. Annual Report, Annual Report.

ANNUAL REPORT, INDIANA PUBLIC TRANSPORTATION. VFOAT Indiana Public Transportation. US. English. an. Division of Public Transportation, 143 West Market Street Suite 300, Indianapolis IN 46204. LC HE309.I6. DD 353.977200878406.

ANNUAL REPORT - MAINE DEPARTMENT OF TRANSPORTATION. Main/Corp Maine. Dept. of Transportation. 1st- 1972/73-. 0094-5048. US. English. an. Maine Department of Transportation, Augusta ME 04330. LC HE28.M2. DD 353.97410087.

ANNUAL REPORT - MASS TRANSIT DIVISION. DEPARTMENT OF TRANSPORTATION. STATE OF OREGON. (ANNUAL REPORT). Main/Corp Oregon. Mass Transit Division. 0090-3906. US. English. an. Oregon Mass Transit Division, Highway Building, Salem OR 97310. LC HE4411.O7. DD 353.97950087832.

ANNUAL REPORT - METROPOLITAN TRANSIT COMMISSION. Main/Corp Metropolitan Transit Commission. 1975-. 0082-710X. US. English. an. 330 Metro Square, St Paul MN 55101. LC HE310.T85. DD 352.918409776579.

ANNUAL REPORT, MICHIGAN TRANSPORTATION FUND. Main/Corp Michigan. State Transportation Commission. Series/Titl MDOT Report. Fiscal year ending Sept. 30, 1979-. US. English. an. Transportation Commission/Michigan Department of Transportation, Transportation Building.425 West Ottawa PO Box 30050, Lansing MI 48909. LC HE356.M5. DD 353.977400864206.

ANNUAL REPORT - MILWAUKEE COUNTY TRANSIT BOARD. Main/Corp Milwaukee County Transit Board. No. 1- 1975-76-. Periodical. US. English. an. Milwaukee County Transit Board, 901 9th Street North, Milwaukee WI 53233.

ANNUAL REPORT - MISSOURI HIGHWAY AND TRANSPORTATION COMMISSION. Main/Corp Missouri Highway and Transportation Commission. 1981-. US. English. an. Update.

ANNUAL REPORT - NATIONAL MOTOR VEHICLE SAFETY ADVISORY COUNCIL. Main/Corp United States. National Motor Vehicle Safety Advisory Council. 0360-3040. US. English. an. US Department of Transportation, Federal Highway Administration, Washington DC 20590. LC TL242. DD 353.00783.

ANNUAL REPORT - NATIONAL PORT AUTHORITY. Main/Corp National Port Authority. English. ir. National Port Authority, PO Box 1849, Monrovia Liberia. LC HE559.L5. DD 354.6662008771.

ANNUAL REPORT - NEW JERSEY. DEPT. OF TRANSPORTATION. (ANNUAL REPORT). Main/Corp New Jersey. Dept. of Transportation. 1979-. 0085-395X. US. English. an. Office of Public Affairs, Bureau of Publications, New Jersey Department of Transportation, 1035 Parkway Avenue, Trenton NJ 08625. LC HE28.N5. DD 353.974900875006. Annual Report of the New Jersey Department of Transportation, 0085-395X.

ANNUAL REPORT - NEW YORK (STATE). METROPOLITAN TRANSPORTATION AUTHORITY. Main/Corp New York (State). Metropolitan Transportation Authority. 1967/1968-. 0543-6494. US. English. an. Metropolitan Transportation Authority, 1700 Broadway, New York NY 10019. LC HE4491.N69. Annual Report.

ANNUAL REPORT - NORTH CAROLINA, PUBLIC TRANSPORTATION DIVISION. Main/Corp North Carolina. Public Transportation Division. US. English. an. Office of the Assistant Secretary for Planning, Public Transportation Division, Raleigh NC 27611. LC HE309.N8. DD 353.975600878406.

ANNUAL REPORT - NOVA SCOTIA DEPARTMENT OF TRANSPORTATION. (ANNUAL REPORT FOR THE FISCAL YEAR ENDED MARCH 31 . . .). Main/Corp Nova Scotia. Dept. of Transportation. VFOAT Department of Transportation Report. 1980-. 0823-9169. CN. English. an. LC TE27.N7. DD 354.71600864. Annual Report, 0701-7693.

ANNUAL REPORT OF THE CANADIAN TRANSPORT COMMISSION. Main/Corp Canadian Transport Commission. VFOAT Rapport Annuel. CN. English (text in French). an. LC WMLC L 83/1204. Annual Report of the Canadian Transport Commission.

ANNUAL REPORT OF THE COMMISSIONER OF TRANSPORTATION TO THE GOVERNOR - TENNESSEE. Main/Corp Tennessee. Dept. of Transportation. VFOAT Annual Report to the Governor by the Commissioner. 0363-3330. US. English. an. Department of Transportation, Andrew Jackson State Office Building, Nashville TN 37219. LC HE28.T2. DD 353.97680087505.

THE ANNUAL REPORT OF THE DIRECTOR GENERAL OF TRANSPORT (WESTERN AUSTRALIA). Main/Corp Western Australia. Office of the Director General of Transport. 15th (June 30th, 1981)-. English. an. Exchange House, 68 St George's Terrace, Perth West Australia. LC HE104.W47. DD 354.94100875006.

ANNUAL REPORT OF THE IDAHO TRANSPORTATION DEPARTMENT. Main/Corp Idaho. Transportation Dept. 1st- 1974/75-. 0145-7039. US. English. an. Idaho Transportation Department, Boise ID 83720. LC HE28.I28. DD 353.979600875.

ANNUAL REPORT OF THE ONTARIO HIGHWAY TRANSPORT BOARD. Main/Corp Ontario. Highway Transport Board. 1971-. CN. English. an. LC HE5635.O5. DD 354.71300878305. Annual Report.

ANNUAL REPORT OF THE PUBLIC SERVICE COMMISSION OF SOUTH CAROLINA. Main/Corp South Carolina. Public Service Commission. 1st- 1879-. 0361-7807. US. English. an. Owen Building/8th Floor, PO Drawer 11649, Columbia SC 29211. DD 385.09757.

ANNUAL REPORT - OFFICE OF DIRECTOR. OREGON DEPARTMENT OF TRANSPORTATION. (ANNUAL REPORT). Main/Corp Oregon. Dept. of Transportation. Office of Director. 0090-6247. US. English. an. Oregon Department of Transportation, Office of Director, State Highway Building, Salem OR 97310. LC HE28.O7. DD 353.97950087.

ANNUAL REPORT ON HAZARDOUS MATERIALS TRANSPORTATION : HAZARDOUS MATERIALS TRANSPORTATION ACT (TITLE I, PUBLIC LAW 93-633). See Law.

ANNUAL REPORT - PHYSICAL RESEARCH UNIT (MINNESOTA). Main/Corp Minnesota. Dept. of Transportation. Physical Research Unit. US. English. an. Minnesota Department of Transportation, John Ireland Boulevard/Room 810, St Paul MN 55155. LC TE192. DD 625.70720776.

ANNUAL REPORT - SOUTH AFRICAN TRANSPORT SERVICES. Main/Corp South African Transport Services. 1980-81-. SA. English. an. Office of the General Manager, South African Transport Services, Johannesburg South Africa. LC HE3459.S7. DD 354.6800875006. Annual Report.

ANNUAL REPORT - THE URBAN TRANSIT AUTHORITY OF BRITISH COLUMBIA CEASED. Main/Corp British Columbia. Urban Transit Authority. 1978/79-. CN. English. an. Urban Transit Authority, 844 Courtney Street, PO Box 610, Victoria British Columbia V8W 2P3 Canada. LC HE4508.B7. DD 354.71100878406.

ANNUAL REPORT TO CALIFORNIA LEGISLATURE. Main/Corp California Transportation Commission. 1st (1984)-. US. English. an. California Transportation Commission, 1120 N Street, PO Box 1139, Sacramento CA 95805. Tel (916)445-1690. Ed Robert Remen. Circ 900. Summary of policies of California transportation commission, major upcoming issues for consideration by California legislature, and monitoring of highway program's implementation.

ANNUAL REPORT TO CONGRESS - NATIONAL TRANSPORTATION SAFETY BOARD. (ANNUAL REPORT TO CONGRESS). Main/Corp United States. National Transportation Safety Board. VFOAT National Transportation Safety Board Annual Report to Congress. Began with 1967. 0565-8365. US. English. an. National Transportation Safety Board, 800 Independence Avenue SW, Washington DC 20594.

ANNUAL REPORT TO DIRECTOR - ALASKA. DEPT. OF TRANSPORTATION AND PUBLIC FACILITIES. RESEARCH SECTION. Main/Corp Alaska. Dept. of Transportation and Public Facilities. Research Section. US. English. an. LC TA1024.A4. DD 629.040720798.

ANNUAL REPORT - TRANSPORT COMMISSION. (ANNUAL REPORT OF THE COMMISSIONER OF TRANSPORT). Main/Corp Western Australia. Transport Commission. 0312-4797. English. ir. Western Australian Transport Commission, 136-138 Stirling Highway, 6009 Perth Australia. LC HE112. DD 354.94100875.

ANNUAL REPORT - TRANSPORTATION RESEARCH CENTER OF OHIO. Main/Corp Transportation Research Center Of Ohio. 0149-4341. US. English. an. Ohio Department of Transportation, 25 South Front Street, PO Box 899, Columbus OH 43216. LC HE192.5. DD 388.072077146.

ANNUAL REPORT - UNITED STATES. DEPT. OF TRANSPORTATION. Main/Corp United States. Dept. of Transportation. Began with 1966/67. US. English. an. Superintendent of Documents, US Government Printing Office, Washington DC 20402. LC HE206.3. DD 353.00875.

ANNUAL REPORT - UNITED STATES. MATERIALS TRANSPORTATION BUREAU. OFFICE OF OPERATIONS AND ENFORCEMENT. (ANNUAL REPORT). Main/Corp United States. Materials Transportation Bureau. Office of Operations and Enforcement. 0277-3120. US. English. an. Office of Operations and Enforcement, US Department of Transportation, Research and Special Programs Administration, Materials Transportation Bureau, Washington DC 20590. LC HE199.5.D3. DD 353.00783.

ANNUAL REPORT - UTAH VALLEY AREA TRANSPORTATION STUDY. Main/Corp Utah Valley Area Transportation Study. 0364-2542. US. English. an. Mountainland Association of Governments, 160 East Center Street, Provo UT 84601. LC HE28.U8. DD 380.509792.

Transportation

ANNUAL ROAD FINANCE REPORT OF THE 65 INCORPORATED PLACES IN ARIZONA. Main/Corp Arizona. Dept. of Transportation. Planning Survey Group. VAT Annual Road Finance Report of the Sixty-Five Incorporated Places in Arizona. 1973/74-. 0148-4028. US. English. an. Arizona Department of Transportation, 206 South 17th Avenue 222 East, Phoenix AZ 85007. LC HE356.A7. DD 388.11.

ANNUAL SUMMARY OF SPEED LIMIT 55 MONITORING PROGRAM (MINNESOTA). Main/Corp Minnesota. Dept. of Transportation. US. English. an. Minnesota Department of Transportation, Transportation Building, St Paul MN 55155. LC HE5620.S6. DD 388.314409766.

ANNUAL TITLE VI PROGRAM REVIEW AND UPDATE. See Public Administration.

EL ANO DEL TRANSPORTE. No. 1- 1975/76-. Spanish. ir. 1000. Edisport, Isaac Peral, Madrid 12 Spain. LC HE8.

ANUARIO BRASILEIRO DE TRANSPORTES. See Yearbooks, Almanacs, Directories.

ANUARIO DE ESTADISTICAS DE TRANSPORTE. See Yearbooks, Almanacs, Directories.

ANUARIO DE TRANSPORTES Y COMUNICACIONES. See Yearbooks, Almanacs, Directories.

ANUARIO ESTADISTICO DE TRANSPORTE. See Yearbooks, Almanacs, Directories.

ANUARIO ESTATISTICO DOS TRANSPORTES. See Yearbooks, Almanacs, Directories.

APPLICATION AND INSTRUCTIONS FOR INTERNATIONAL REGISTRATION PLAN. See Law.

APPLICATION AND INSTRUCTIONS FOR VEHICLE PRORATION. Main/Corp Illinois. Office of Secretary of State. Commercial and Farm Truck Division. US. English. an. Office of the Secretary of State, Commercial and Farm Truck Division, Centennial Building, Room 300, Springfield IL 62756. Published in an attempt to answer all questions concerning the requirements of the trucking industry in the state of Illinois. Basically a reference manual for prorate applications.

APPROVED EXPENDITURE AND REVENUE BUDGETS AND CAPITAL WORKS PROGRAMME. Main/Corp East African Harbours Corporation. VFOAT Approved Revenue and Expenditure Budgets and Capital Works Programme, Original. 0304-8535. English. ir. LC HE559.A362. DD 387.106567.

ARABIAN TRANSPORT. UK. English. an. Beacon Publishing, Weston Favell, Northampton NN3 4NW England. LC HE268.6.A15. DD 380.502553. *Arabian Transport Directory.*

ATLANTIC TRUCK TRANSPORT REVIEW. V. 18, No. 12- Dec. 1969-. 0004-6868. Periodical. CN. English. qt. $5.81. Atlantic Provinces Trucking Association, 567 Coverdale Road/Suite 7A, Riverview New Brunswick E1B 3K7 Canada. Tel (506)386-4413. Ed Dale Elliott. adv acc. Circ 1,200. Up-to-date industry development, information on new products, people and appointments, human interest angles- people or company profiles, major scheduled events. *Maritime Truck Transport Review, 0542-7193.*

AUSTRALIAN TRANSPORT. 1975. 0005-0385. Periodical. AT. English. mo. 44. Magazine Art Pty Ltd, 35 Willis Street, Hampton Vic 3188 Australia. Tel 03 5989555. Ed J Spiers. Ind/Abst APAIS, Aust. Public Aff. Inf. Serv. bk rev. adv acc. Circ 3,000. (ctrl). Circulated to senior executives in the Australian transport industry and covers all information on shipping, airlines and highway transportation.

AUTOMOTIVE AGE. 0005-1470. Periodical. US. English. mo. $24.00. Automotive Age, Kelley Blue, PO Box 1290/2950 A7 Airway, Costa Mesa CA 92626. Tel (714)957-2600. Ind/Abst Predicasts.

AUXILIAIRES DES TRANSPORTS TERRESTRES. Main/Corp France. Departement des Statistiques des Transports. FR. French. ir. Department des Statistiques des Transport, 21 rue Mathurin Regnier, 75732 Paris Cedex 15 France. LC HE199.F8. DD 380.5240944.

AUXILIARY, BIBLIOGRAPHY OF PUBLICATIONS. See Bibliographies.

BACKGROUND ON TRANSPORTATION. COAL AND THE RAILROADS. VFOAT Coal and the Railroads. US. English. an. Association of American Railroads, 1920 L Street NW, Washington DC 20036.

BALANCE PREVENTIVO - SOCIEDAD PRIVADA MUNICIPAL TRANSPORTES DE BARCELONA. (BALANCE PREVENTIVO - SOCIEDAD PRIVADA MUNICIPAL TRANSPORTES DE BARCELONA). Main/Corp Sociedad Privada Municipal Transportes de Barcelona. 0304-8993. SP. Spanish. ir. Sociedad Privada Municipal Transportes de Barcelona, Luchana 99, Barcelona 5 Spain. LC HE4899.B4.

BARRETT TRANSPORTATION NEWSLETTER. 0883-1777. Periodical. US. English. mo. $120.00. Traffic Service Corporation, 1325 G Street/Suite 900, Washington DC 20005. DD 380.

BERETNING OG REGNSKAB - KBENHAVNS SPORVEJE. Main/Corp Kbenhavns Sporveje. DK. Danish (summaries in English). ir. Gothersgade 53, Kbenhavn Denmark. LC HE4859.C7. *Arsberetning.*

BIBLIOGRAPHIE D'ECONOMIE DES TRANSPORTS. See Bibliographies.

BIENNIAL REPORT - DEPARTMENT OF TRANSPORTATION, STATE OF WISCONSIN. Main/Corp Wisconsin. Dept. of Transportation. 0364-1422. US. English. be. Department of Transportation, Hill Farms State Office Building, 4802 Shelboyan Avenue, Madison WI 53702. LC HE28.W6. DD 353.97750087.

BIENNIAL REPORT - ILLINOIS. GENERAL ASSEMBLY. LEGISLATIVE ADVISORY COMMITTEE TO THE REGIONAL TRANSPORTATION AUTHORITY. Main/Corp Illinois. General Assembly. Legislative Advisory Committee to the Regional Transportation Authority. June 1984-. US. English. be. Illinois Legislative Advisory Committee to the Regional Transportation Authority, 2049 Stratton Building, Springfield IL 62706.

BIENNIAL REPORT - MISSOURI HIGHWAY AND TRANSPORTATION COMMISSION. Main/Corp Missouri Highway and Transportation Commission. 32nd (July 1,1978-June 30, 1980)-. US. English. be. Missouri Highway and Transportation Commission, PO Box 270, Jefferson City MO 65102. Tel (314)751-2840. LC TE24.M8. DD 353.977887806. Circ 500. (ctrl). Finances and operations of Missouri Highway and Transportation Department for fiscal 2-year period. *Biennial Report.*

BIENNIAL REPORT - NORTH CAROLINA DEPARTMENT OF TRANSPORTATION. Main/Corp North Carolina. Dept. of Transportation. US. English. be. North Carolina Department of Transportation, PO Box 25201, Raleigh NC 27611. LC HE213.N8. DD 353.975600875005.

BIENNIAL REPORT - STATE DEPARTMENT OF HIGHWAYS AND PUBLIC TRANSPORTATION. (BIENNIAL REPORT - STATE DEPARTMENT OF HIGHWAYS AND PUBLIC TRANSPORTATION, FINANCE DIVISION). Main/Corp Texas. State Dept. of Highways and Public Transportation. Finance Division. 30th- 1974/76-. 0147-8362. Periodical. US. English. be. Texas State Department of Highway/Public Transportation, Austin TX 78701. LC HE356.T4. DD 353.9764008781. *Biennial Report - State Highway Department of Texas, 0147-8370.*

BIENNIAL REPORT - STATE OF MINNESOTA DEPARTMENT OF PUBLIC SERVICE. See Public Administration.

BIENNIAL STATEWIDE TRANSPORTATION NEEDS REPORT TO THE ARIZONA LEGISLATURE. Main/Corp Arizona. Dept. of Transportation. 1st- 1976-. US. English. be. Arizona Department of Transportation, 206 South 17th Avenue, Phoenix AZ 85007. LC HE356.A7. DD 388.109791. *Inventory of Highway Needs (Excluding Interstate Systems), Status of Road Systems Mileages.*

BOTTIN DE L'AUTO, DU CYCLE ET DE LA MOTO INDUSTRIES CONNEXES. French. ir. LC TL12. DD 338.47629202544. *Bottin de l'Auto du Cycle: Motocycle, Motoculture, Nautisme, Industries Connexes.*

BOTTIN DU TRANSPORT. 1975-. French. ir. Societe Didot-Bottin, 28 rue du Docteur-Finlay, 75738 Cedex 15 Paris France. LC HE199.F8.

BREAKDOWN OF REGISTRATION BY TYPE VEHICLE BY COUNTY. VFOAT Report of Registrations. US. English. an. LC HE5633.P4. DD 353.97480087834.

BREATH TESTS IN NEW ZEALAND. See Law Enforcement.

BUDAPESTI KOZLEKEDESI VALLALAT HIVATALOS KOZLONYE. Hungarian. ir. Kozlekedesi Vallalat, VII Akacfa U 15, Budapest Hungary. LC HE311.H82.

BUDGET - NATIONAL TRANSPORTATION SAFETY BOARD. See Business - Banking & Finance.

BULLETIN DU C.R.T. (BULLETIN DU C R T). Main/Corp Universite de Montrsal. Centre de Recherche sur les Transports. VAT Bulletin de Centre de Recherche sur les Transports. V. 1- July 1976-. 0703-2935. Periodical. CN. French. ir. Free. Centre de Recherche sur les Transports, Universite de Montreal, CP 6128 Succursale A, Montreal Quebec H3C 3J7 Canada. DD 380.505. (ctrl).

BULLETIN - NATIONAL HIGHWAY INSTITUTE. Main/Corp United States. National Highway Institute. Periodical. US. English. US Department of Transportation, Federal Highway Administration, National Highway Institute, Washington DC 20590.

BULLETIN - NEW JERSEY MOTOR TRUCK ASSOCIATION. Main/Corp New Jersey Motor Truck Association. VFOAT NJMTA Bulletin. 1914. 0028-5838. Periodical. US. English. mo. $6.00. New Jersey Motor Truck Association, c/o Robert Behre, 160 Tices Lane, East Brunswick NJ 08816. Tel (201)254-5000. Ed Robert J Behre. adv acc. Circ 2,800. (ctrl). Publishes news and feature stories that relate to the trucking industry, particularly in New Jersey.

BULLETIN - TRANSPORTATION SAFETY ASSOCIATION OF ONTARIO. See Industrial Health & Safety.

BUNGA RAMPAI PERHUBUNGAN. See Communication.

BUS & TRUCK TRANSPORT. VFOAT Bus and Truck Transport in Canada. V. 1- 1925-. 0007-635X. Periodical. CN. English. mo. $30.18. MacLean Hunter, Circulation Accounting Department, PO Box 100/Station A, Toronto Ontario M5W 1A7 Canada. Ind/Abst Can. Bus. Index.

BUS FACTS (AMERICAN BUS ASSOCIATION). (BUS FACTS). 1981 Ed.-. 0734-5917. US. English. an. American Bus Association, 1025 Connecticut Avenue NW, Washington DC 20036. *Report from the American Bus Association, 0278-1565.*

BUS RIDE. 0192-8902. Periodical. US. English. bm. $17.50. Friendship Publications Inc, PO Box 1472, Spokane WA 99210. Tel (509)328-9181. Ed William A Luke. bk rev. adv acc. Circ 12,500. (ctrl). Trade journal for the bus industry.

BUS RIDE. BUS INDUSTRY DIRECTORY. See Yearbooks, Almanacs, Directories.

BUS VERKEHR. VFOAT Busverkehr. Periodical. German. mo. 60.00. Kirschbaum Verlag, Siegfriedstrasse 28, 5300 Bonn 2 West Germany.

BUS WORLD. V. 1-. 0162-9689. Periodical. US. English. qt. $7.00. Sunrise Enterprises, PO Box 39, Woodland Hills CA 91365. Tel (818)710-0208. Ed Ed Stauss. LC TL232. DD 388.3423305. bk rev. adv acc. Circ 7,000. Enthusiast journal of buses and bus systems. Reports on new and oil buses; intercity, transit and school buses.

BUSES ANNUAL. 0068-4376. UK. English. an. Terminal House, Shepperton Middlesex TW17 8AS England. Ed R A Smith. LC HE5601.

CAB FARE. 0732-1236. Periodical. US. English. bm. Heanue System, 115 Broad Street, Boston MA 02110.

Transportation

CANADIAN DRIVER OWNER. (CANADIAN DRIVER/OWNER). V. 1- Winter 1972/73-. 0315-6826. Periodical. CN. English. bm. $8.51. MacLean Hunter, PO Box 100 Station A, Toronto Ontario M5W 1A7 Canada. Ind/Abst Can. Bus. Index.

CANADIAN HIGHWAY CARRIERS GUIDE. VFOAT Guide des Transporteurs Routiers Canadiens. 1976-. 0702-8733. CN. English (and French). an. $21.63. Southam Communications Ltd, 1450 Don Mills Road, Don Mills Ontario M3B 2X7 Canada. Tel (416)445-6641. Ed Michelle Ramsay. DD 388.32402571. adv acc. *Highway Carriers Guide, 0315-7520.*

CANADIAN RECREATIONAL VEHICLE GUIDE. VFOAT Guide Canadien du Vehicule Recreatif. 1981-. 0710-4405. CN. English (text also in French). $35.00. Canadian Recreational Vehicle Guide, 1208 Beaupre Avenue, Ste-Foy Quebec G1W 4C1 Canada. DD 381.45629226029471.

CANADIAN SPECIAL TRUCK EQUIPMENT MANUAL. See Economics - Economics: Industry & Production.

CANADIAN TRANSPORTATION & DISTRIBUTION MANAGEMENT. V. 71, No. 11- Nov. 1968-. 0008-5200. Periodical. CN. English. mo. Southam Communications Ltd, 1450 Don Mills Road, Don Mills Ontario M3B 1X2 Canada. Tel (416)445-6641. Ind/Abst Manage. Contents, Can. Bus. Index. *Canadian Transportation, 0319-4388.*

CANADIAN TRUCKERS' GUIDE. 0824-5509. CN. English. an. $3.00 Per Vol. Canadian Truckers' Guide, 270-10691 Shellbridge Way, Richmond British Columbia V6X 2W8 Canada. DD 388.34.

CANALS CANADA. (CANALS CANADA : NEWSLETTER OF THE CANADIAN CANAL SOCIETY). Issue No. 1 (Jan. 1983)-. 0826-1954. Periodical. CN. English. ir. Free to Members. Canadian Canal Society, PO Box 1652, St Catharines Ontario L2R 7K1 Canada. DD 386.406071.

CAR RENTAL/LEASING INSIDER. 0008-6053. Periodical. US. English. ir. $88.00. Atlantic Commercial Enterprise, 2315 Broadway, New York NY 10024. Tel (212)873-5900. Ed Michael Ehrhardt. Circ 2,439. (ctrl). A newsletter for professionals in the automobile rental and leasing business.

CARGO HANDLING ABSTRACTS : AN ICHCA INFORMATION ACCESS PUBLICATION. See Indexes/Abstracts.

CARGO SYSTEMS INTERNATIONAL. V. 1- Nov. 1973-. 0306-0985. Periodical. UK. English. mo. $41.61. C S Publications Ltd, 54 Cheam Common Road, Worcester Park, Surrey KT4 8RJ England. Tel (01)330-3911. Ed Clive Woodbridge. Ind/Abst Eng. Index Annu., Eng. Index Mon., Eng. Index Bioeng. Abstr., Eng. Index Energy Abstr., Fluidex, Ship Abstr., Coal Abstr., Excerpta Med., Eng. Index. LC TA1215. DD 380.52. CODEN CSYIBN. bk rev. adv acc. Circ 8,000. Ports and terminal operations, container industry; ships and shipping, intermodalism, and cargo handling. *ICHCA Monthly Journal.*

CATALOG OF PUBLICATIONS - NATIONAL RESEARCH COUNCIL (U.S.) TRANSPORTATION RESEARCH BOARD. See Bibliographies.

CBS WEGVERVOERVERWANTE BEDRIJVEN. Series/Titl Produktiestatistieken Transport, Opslat en Communicatie. VFOAT C.B.S. Wegvervoerverwante Bedrijven. NE. Dutch (summaries in English). an. 7.50. Centraal Bureau voor de Statistiek Voorburg, Prinses Beatrixlaan 428, Postbus 959, 2270 AZ Voorburg Netherlands.

CDE STOCK OWNERSHIP DIRECTORY : TRANSPORTATION INDUSTRY. See Yearbooks, Almanacs, Directories.

CENSUS OF TRANSPORTATION. Main/Corp United States. Bureau of the Census. VFOAT Commodity Transportation Survey. 1963-. US. English. ir. Department of Commerce, Social and Economic Statistics Administration, Bureau of the Census, Washington DC 20402.

CHARTERED INSTITUTE OF TRANSPORT JOURNAL CEASED. (JOURNAL). VFOAT Journal of the Chartered Institute of Transport, Transport. Began with V. 34, No. 4. Ceased V. 38, No. 14. 0020-3181. Periodical. UK. English. bm. Ind/Abst Int. Aerosp. Abstr., Public Aff. Inf. Serv. Bull. DD 380.505. *Journal.*

CHIAO TUNG CHIEN SHE. Periodical. CH. Chinese. mo. $30.00. Chung Kuo Chiao Tung Chien She Hsueh Hui, 4 Lane 77 Chin Shan St, Tai Pei Taiwan. LC HE7. DD 380.505.

CHILTON'S COMMERCIAL CARRIER JOURNAL. VFOAT Commercial Carrier Journal. Vol. 139, No. 9 (Sept. 1982)-. 0734-1423. Periodical. US. English. mo. $35.00. Chilton Company, Chilton Way, Radnor PA 19089. Tel (215)964-4000. *Chilton's CCJ.*

CHILTON'S DISTRIBUTION FOR TRAFFIC & TRANSPORTATION DECISION MAKERS. VFOAT Chilton's Distribution for Traffic and Transportation Decision Makers. Vol. 79, No. 9 (Sept. 1980)-. 0273-6721. Periodical. US. English. mo. Free to Qualified Personnel, $40.00 Others. Chilton Company, Chilton Way, Radnor PA 19089. Tel (215)964-4386. Ed Joseph Barks. Ind/Abst ABI/Inform, Predicasts, Bus. Period. Index. DD 388. bk rev. adv acc. Circ 70,000. (ctrl). Available on microfilm. The magazine for freight transportation, business, logistics, physical distribution, traffic management, warehousing, international trade, shipping, materials management. *Chilton's Distribution, 0195-7244.*

CHILTON'S TRUCK & OFF-HIGHWAY INDUSTRIES. VFOAT Chilton's Truck and Off-Highway Industries. V. 1, No. 4 (July/Aug. 1979)-. 0194-1410. Periodical. US. English. bm. Chilton Company, Chilton Way, Radnor PA 19089. Tel (215)964-4000. Ind/Abst Eng. Index Annu., Eng. Index Bioeng. Abstr., Eng. Index Energy Abstr., Eng. Index Mon., ISMEC Bull. DD 338. CODEN TOINDH. *Truck & Off-Highway Industries, 0164-3436.*

CHRISTIAN AIRMAN CEASED. No. 1-85. 0381-0275. Periodical. CN. English. qt. Air Division of Christian Transportation, 512 Yonge Street Rear, Toronto Ontario M4Y 1X9 Canada.

CHRISTIAN BUS DRIVER CEASED. (THE CHRISTIAN BUS DRIVER). No. 1-, No. 83. 0382-8727. Periodical. CN. English.

CITT NEWS. VAT Canadian Institute of Traffic and Transportation News. 0227-5708. Periodical. CN. English. mo. Canadian Institute of Traffic and Transportation, Suite 515, 515/44 Victoria Street, Toronto Ontario M5C 1Y2 Canada. DD 380.506071.

COAL PRODUCTION & TRANSPORTATION. ANNUAL CONFERENCE. See Economics - Economics: Industry & Production.

COAL TRAFFIC. 1980-81-. 0738-1794. US. English. an. $75.00. National Coal Association, 1130 17th Street Northwest, Washington DC 20036. Tel (202)463-2631. LC HE199.5.C6. DD 380.524, 338.2. *Coal Traffic Annual, 0069-4916.*

COAL TRANSPORTATION REPORT. 1980. 0732-8397. Periodical. US. English. bw. $377.00. Suite 1000/1133 15th Street NW, Washington DC 20005. Tel (202)775-0240. Ed James N Heller. bk rev. Only newsletter in US on coal transportation. Covers technical, legislative, regulatory, legal, and marketing aspects of coal transport by rail, barge, truck, and slurry.

COAST MARINE & TRANSPORTATION DIRECTORY. See Yearbooks, Almanacs, Directories.

CODIFICACION DE NORMAS DE TRANSITO Y TRANSPORTES - (COLOMBIA). Spanish. ir. $60.00. Apartado Aereo 9188, Bogota Colombia.

COMMERCE YEARBOOK OF ROAD TRANSPORT. See Yearbooks, Almanacs, Directories.

COMMERCIAL TRANSPORT. Periodical. SA. English. $27.67. Thomson Publications South Africa Pty Ltd, PO Box 8308, Johannesburg 2000 South Africa. Tel 789 2144. LC HE5601. DD 388.32405. *Commercial Transport and Freight, 0376-5849.*

COMMUTED RATE SCHEDULE FOR TRANSPORTATION OF HOUSEHOLD GOODS. US. English. US Government Printing Office, Superintendent of Documents, Washington DC 20402.

THE COMMUTER. (THE COMMUTER : A PUBLICATION OF THE NATIONAL CLEARINGHOUSE FOR COMMUTER PROGRAMS). 0734-3817. Periodical. US. English. $20.00 Membership. National Clearinghouse for Commuter Programs, University of Maryland, 1195 Student Union, College Park MD 20742.

CONNECTICUT MASTER TRANSPORTATION PLAN. Main/Corp Connecticut. Dept. of Transportation. 1st- 1971-. 0090-8460. US. English. an. State of Connecticut, Department of Transportation, Wethersfield CT 06109. LC HE28.C8. DD 380.509746.

CONSOLIDATED TRANSPORTATION PROGRAM - (MARYLAND). Main/Corp Maryland. Dept. of Transportation. 1972-. 0090-6530. US. English. Maryland Department of Transportation, PO Box 717, Baltimore MD 21203. LC HE356.M3. DD 388.109752.

CONSULTOR. Periodical. Spanish (summaries in English). ir. $50.00. Republica Argentina Centro de Informaciones del Transporte Internacional, Cerrito 40 - 1 B, Buenos Aires Argentina. LC HE7. DD 380.505. (cum index).

CORPORATE REPORT - ONTARIO TRANSPORTATION DEVELOPMENT CORPORATION. Main/Corp Ontario Transportation Development Corporation. 1973-. 0702-9365. CN. English. Ontario Transportation Development Corporation, 20 Eglinton Avenue West, 14th Floor, Toronto Ontario M4R 1K8 Canada. LC HE311.C32. DD 388.409713.

COST OF TRANSPORTING FREIGHT BY CLASS I AND CLASS II MOTOR COMMON CARRIERS OF GENERAL COMMODITIES, BY REGIONS OR TERRITORIES. Main/Corp United States. Interstate Commerce Commission. Bureau of Accounts. Series Corp Its Statement. US. English. Superintendent of Documents, US Government Printing Office, Washington DC 20402.

COUNTY STATE AID HIGHWAY APPORTIONMENT DATA. Main/Corp Minnesota. Dept. of Transportation. US. English. an. Minnesota Department of Transportation, Room 810, John Ireland Boulevard, St Paul MN 55155. LC HE356.M6. DD 353.97760072236864205.

CRUISING AROUND THE WORLD. See Travel.

CTA QUARTERLY. Main/Corp Chicago Transit Authority. VAT Chicago Transit Authority Quarterly. V. 1- Autumn 1974-. 0361-2791. Periodical. US. English. qt. Public Affairs Department, Chicago Transit Authority, Merchandise Mart Plaza, PO Box 3555, Chicago IL 60654. LC HE310.C45. DD 388.40977311.

CUADROS ESTADISTICOS SOBRE EL SECTOR TRANSPORTE. Main/Corp Costa Rica. Ministerio de Obras Publicas Y Transportes. Departamento de Estudios Economicos. 1974-. Spanish. ir. LC HE33. DD 380.5097286.

CURRENT OPERATING EXPENSES AND SCHEDULE OF FIXED CHARGES. Main/Corp Massachusetts Bay Transportation Authority. VFOAT Massachusetts Bay Transportation Authority Budget. US. English. an. Massachusetts Bay Transportation Authority, 50 High Street, Boston MA 02110. LC HE310.B6. DD 352.9184042.

N A D A RECREATIONAL VEHICLE APPRAISAL GUIDE. Main/Corp National Automobile Dealers Association. Periodical. US. English. ir. National Automobile Dealer Used Car Guide, PO Box 7800, Costa Mesa CA 92628. Tel (213)967-3981. Ed Don Christy Jr. Lists values from 1977 to 1983. All types of recreation vehicles and optional equipment.

T D C PROJECT DIRECTORY. See Yearbooks, Almanacs, Directories.

DANGEROUS GOODS : NEWSLETTER. 0710-0914. Periodical. CN. English. qt. Transport Dangerous Goods Dir, Tower B Place de Ville, Ottawa Ontario K1A 0N5 Canada. Tel (613)992-4624. DD 363.17560971.

DATOS - SOCIEDAD PRIVADA MUNICIPAL. TRANSPORTES DE BARCELONA, S.A. (DATOS - SOCIEDAD PRIVADA MUNICIPAL TRANSPORTES DE BARCELONA). Main/Corp Sociedad Privada Municipal Transportes de Barcelona. 0376-8112. SP. Spanish. ir. Sociedad Privada Municipal Transportes de Barcelona, Luchana 99, Barcelona 5 Spain. LC HE4899.B4.

Transportation

DDR VERKEHR. Began publication with 1, Jan. 1968. 0011-4820. Periodical. SZ. German (table of contents in Russian, English and French). mo. Kunst & Wissen Erich Bieber, Dufourstrasse 51, CH-8008 Zurich Switzerland. LC HE5. DD 380.509431.

DEFENSE TRANSPORTATION JOURNAL. V. 23, No. 5- Sept./Oct. 1967-. 0011-7625. Periodical. US. English. bm. $25.00. National Defense Transportation Association, 727 North Washington Street/Suite 200, Alexandria VA 22314-1976. Tel (703)836-3303. Ed Joseph Mattingly. Ind/Abst Predicasts. bk rev. adv acc. Circ 7,500. (ctrl). To advance knowledge and science in defense transportation (defense transportation is the partnership between the commercial transportation industry and the government transporter.). *National Defense Transportation Journal, 0193-8851.*

DELAWARE VALLEY GUIDE TO TRANSPORTATION. 0277-1136. US. English. $2.00 Members of the Chamber of Commerce, $5.00 for Non-members. Penjerdel Corporation, 1528 Walnut Street, Philadelphia PA 19102. *DELAWARE VALLEY TRANSPORTATION FACTS & FACILITIES.*

DELTA NU ALPHIAN; A JOURNAL OF TRANSPORTATION AND LOGISTICS CEASED. Main/Corp Delta Nu Alpha Transportation Fraternity. VFOAT Alphian. 0161-2395. Periodical. US. English. ir. Delta Nu Alpha Transportation Fraternity, 1040 Woodcock Road, Orlando FL 32803. Tel (305)894-0384.

DEPARTMENT OF TRANSPORTATION. STATE OF RHODE ISLAND. (DEPARTMENT OF TRANSPORTATION, STATE OF RHODE ISLAND). Main/Corp Rhode Island. Dept. of Transportation. 1974/75-. 0148-298X. US. English. Room 210/State Office Building, Providence RI 02903. LC HE28.R4. DD 353.97450087505. *Transportation.*

DESIGN, ART & ARCHITECTURE IN TRANSPORTATION CEASED. VFOAT Annual Report on Design, Art, and Architecture in Transportation. VAT Design, Art, and Architecture in Transportation. 1st issue 1978. Ceased with 3rd Annual Report, Jan. 1981. 0193-0346. US. English. an. US Department of Transportation, Office of the Secretary of Transportation, 400-7th Street SW, Washington DC 20590.

DESTINATION PHILADELPHIA. (DESTINATION : PHILADELPHIA). V. 1- Nov. 1972-. 0090-3833. Periodical. US. English. bm. Philadelphia Port Corporation, 940 Public Ledger Building, Independence Square, Philadelphia PA 19106. LC HE554.P5. DD 387.10974811.

DIRECTION. Vol. 55, No. 3 (March 1973)-. 0092-7449. US. English. mo. $42.00. National Moving & Storage Association, 124 South Royal Street, Alexandria VA 22314. Tel (703)549-6003. LC HF5487. DD 658.785.

DIRECTORY - BRITISH COLUMBIA MOTOR TRANSPORT ASSOCIATION. See Yearbooks, Almanacs, Directories.

DIRECTORY OF METROPOLITAN PLANNING ORGANIZATIONS AND STATE TRANSPORTATION AGENCIES. See Yearbooks, Almanacs, Directories.

A DIRECTORY OF REGULARLY SCHEDULED, FIXED ROUTE, LOCAL PUBLIC TRANSPORTATION SERVICE IN URBANIZED AREAS OVER 50,000 POPULATION. See Yearbooks, Almanacs, Directories.

DIRECTORY OF THE TRANSPORTATION RESEARCH BOARD. See Yearbooks, Almanacs, Directories.

DIREKTORI PERUSAHAAN TRUK (ANTAR PROPINSI) DI JAWA. See Yearbooks, Almanacs, Directories.

DOMESTIC LIGHT TRUCKS & VANS TUNE-UP MECHANICAL SERVICE & REPAIR. VFOAT Domestic Light Trucks and Vans Tune-Up Mechanical Service & Repair. US. English. an. Mitchell Manuals Inc, PO Box 26260, San Diego CA 92126. Tel (619)578-8770. Ed Dan Kelley. LC TL230.2. DD 629.287305. adv acc. (ctrl). Complete service and repair information for 1985 domestic light trucks. Includes tune-up, computerized engine controls, all electrical and mechanical components and systems. *Domestic Light Trucks Tune-Up-Mechanical Transmission Service & Repair.*

DOT AWARDS TO ACADEMIC INSTITUTIONS. (FY . . . DOT AWARDS TO ACADEMIC INSTITUTIONS). VFOAT D.O.T. Awards to Academic Institutions. VAT Fiscal Year . . . Department of Transportation Awards to Academic Institutions. 0731-6852. US. English. an. Free. US Department of Transportation, Office of the Secretary, Program of University Research, Washington DC 20590. Tel (617)494-2718. Ed George K Megerian. LC HE192.5. DD 350.5072073. Circ 6,000. Vols. for 1980- distributed to depository libraries in microfiche. Listing of all university research and training sponsored by the US Department of Transportation in February 1985. *Awards to Academic Institutions by the Department of Transportation, 0099-2267.*

DOT EMPLOYMENT FACTS. See Public Administration.

DRIVERS LICENSES. Main/Corp United States. Federal Highway Administration. 0097-8655. US. English. US Department of Transportation, Federal Highway Administration, Washington DC 20590. LC HE5623. DD 388.3.

DUN & BRADSTREET REFERENCE BOOK OF TRANSPORTATION. VFOAT Reference Book of Transportation. 0093-9528. US. English. Trinc Transportation Consultants, Suite 4200/485 l'Enfant Plaza SW, Washington DC 20024. LC HE5623.A45. DD 380.5202573. *Dun's Reference Book of Transportation.*

DVZ DEUTSCHE VERKEHRS-ZEITUNG. (DEUTSCHE VERKEHRS-ZEITUNG : DVZ). VFOAT DVZ. 0342-166X. GW. German. ir. 282,- Domestic, 282,- Foreign. Deutscher Verkehrs Verlag GMBH, D-2000 Nordkanal Strasse 36, PF 101609 Hamburg West Germany. Tel 040/23714-01. Ed Wolfhart Schlichting and Herbert Zernikow. Ind/Abst Energy Res. Abstr. bk rev. adv acc. Circ 13,000. (ctrl). Forwarding, warehousing, transhipment, traffic by surface, air or sea, in land navigation, container and trailer exchange, foreign country sections, and register of forwarding agents.

ECHO DU TRANSPORT. (L'ECHO DU TRANSPORT). V. 1- May 1977-. 0705-7040. Periodical. CN. French. mo $12.00. Lecho du Transport, 435 rue Norman, Ville St-Pierre Quebec H8R 1A4 Canada. DD 388.32409714.

EER ENERGY PRICE FORECASTS. V. 1-. 0273-155X. Periodical. US. English. bm. $95.00. Fairmont Press, PO Box 14227, Atlanta GA 30324. Tel (404)447-5314. Ed Yanuck & Brown. Circ 200. Detailed long range price data for commercial, industrial, transportation and residential fuels covering 15 fuel types. Separate forecasts for each of 10 regions of the US.

ELECTRIC VEHICLE PROGRESS. V. 1- April 1, 1979-. 0190-4175. Periodical. US. English. sm. $267.00. Alexander Research & Communications, 1133 Broadway/Suite 1407, NewYork NY 10010. Tel (212)206-7979. Ed Laurence A Alexander. bk rev. News about the research and development of electric and hybrid vehicles.

ELECTRICAL COMPONENT LOCATOR : DOMESTIC CARS, LIGHT TRUCKS & VANS. 1983-. US. English. an.

ELECTRICAL COMPONENT LOCATOR. DOMESTIC CARS, LIGHT TRUCKS & VANS, IMPORTED CARS & TRUCKS. Series/Titl Manuals for the Automotive Professional. 0743-6076. US. English. Mitchell Manuals Inc, PO Box 26260, San Diego CA 92126. Tel (619)578-8770. Ed Dan Kelley. LC TL272. DD 629.25405. adv acc. (ctrl). Locator charts and illustrations guide you to electrical components on 1978-85 domestic cars and light trucks, or 1977-84 imported cars and light trucks.

ENQUETE PERMANENTE SUR L'UTILISATION DES VEHICULES DE TRANSPORT EN COMMUN DE PERSONNES EN . . . . FR. French. an. Le Department 55, rue Brillat-Savarin, 75658 Paris Cedex 13 France. LC HE5668. DD 388.3220944.

EPITHEORESIS SYNKOINONIAKOU DIKAIOU. 0376-8767. Greek, Modern. mo. 500.00. Mr O Onouphriades, Metamorphoseos 3, Athenai Greece. LC K5.

ESTIMATES. PART III, CANADIAN TRANSPORT COMMISSION. CN. English (French). $9.00 Domestic, $10.80 Foreign. Canadian Government Publishing Centre, Supply and Services Canada, Ottawa Ontario K1A 0S9 Canada. LC HE215.A15. DD 354.7100875.

ESTIMATES. PART III, TRANSPORT CANADA. VFOAT Budget des Depenses. CN. English (French). $12.00 Domestic, $14.40 Foreign. Canadian Government Publishing Centre, Supply and Services Canada, Ottawa Ontario K1A 0S9 Canada. LC HE215.A15. DD 354.7100875.

ESTIMATES. PART III, TRANSPORT CANADA, DEPARTMENTAL ADMINISTRATIVE PROGRAM, MARINE TRANSPORTATION PROGRAM, SURFACE TRANSPORTATION PROGRAM. VFOAT Budget des Depenses. CN. English (French). $12.00 Domestic, $14.40 Foreign. Canadian Government Publishing Centre, Supply and Services Canada, Ottawa Ontario K1A 0S9 Canada. LC HE215.A15. DD 354.7100875.

LES ETUDES DE TRANSPORT EN . . . . FR. French. ir. 244 Boulevard Saint-Germain VIIE, 75775 Paris Cedex 16 France. LC HE192.55.F8. DD 380.5072044.

EUROPEAN TRANSPORT LAW. See Law.

EZVESTIJA AKADEMII NAUK SSSR. ENERGETIKA I TRANSPORT. See Energy.

FAHRPLANE. Main/Corp Austria. Generaldirektion der Osterreichischen Bundesbahnen. Periodical. German. ir. 40.00. LC HE9.A8. *Amtliches Osterreichisches Kursbuch.*

FEDERAL MOTOR VEHICLE FLEET REPORT. (FEDERAL MOTOR VEHICLE FLEET REPORT FOR THE FISCAL YEAR ENDING . . .). June 30, 1972-. 0093-0180. US. English. an. Transportation and Public Utilities Service, General Services Administration, Washington DC 20406. LC JK1677.M7. DD 353.007134. *Annual Motor Vehicle Report.*

FEDERAL MOTOR VEHICLE SAFETY STANDARDS AND REGULATIONS. (FEDERAL MOTOR VEHICLE SAFETY STANDARDS AND REGULATIONS, WITH AMENDMENTS AND INTERPRETATIONS). Main/Corp United States. National Highway Traffic Safety Administration. 0364-6858. Periodical. US. English. $35.00 Domestic, $43.75 Foreign. US Department of Transportation, National Highway Traffic Safety Administration, Washington DC 20402.

FERRIES, BRIDGES, BOAT TOURS. 1967-. 0711-0332. CN. English. an. Canadian Government Travel Bureau, 235 Queen Street/4th Floor East, Ottawa Ontario K1A 0H6 Canada. DD 386.24202571. *Cruises and Boat Tours, Canada, 0711-0324.*

FERRIES, BRIDGES, CRUISES. VAT Ferries, Bridges & Cruises, Ferries, Bridges and Cruises. 0708-3300. CN. English. an. Canadian Government Travel Bureau, 235 Queen Street/4th Floor East, Ottawa Ontario K1A 0H6 Canada. DD 386.24202571. *Ferries, Bridges, Boat Tours, 0711-0332.*

FIELD & STREAM GUIDE TO CAMPING ON WHEELS. See Recreation, Leisure - Outdoor Life.

A FINANCIAL ANALYSIS OF THE FOR-HIRE TANK TRUCK INDUSTRY FOR THE YEAR . . . . Began in 1973. US. English. an. National Tank Truck Carriers Inc, 1616 P Street NW, Washington DC 20036. Tel (202)797-5425.

FINANCIAL AND OPERATING STATISTICS CLASS I MOTOR CARRIERS OF PASSENGERS. See Statistics.

FINANCIAL STATEMENT AFTER ALLOCATION - FLORIDA. DEPT. OF TRANSPORTATION. Main/Corp Florida. Dept. of Transportation. 0145-2924. US. English. an. State of Florida Department of Transportation, The Capitol, Tallahassee FL 32304. LC HE28.F6. DD 353.97590087.

FISCAL YEAR BUDGET ESTIMATES - DEPT. OF TRANSPORTATION, OFFICE OF THE SECRETARY. Main/Corp United States. Dept. of Transportation. Office of the Secretary. 0278-2987. US. English. an. Department of Transportation, Office of the Secretary, 400 Seventh Street SW, Washington DC 20590.

Transportation

FLEET EQUIPMENT. Vol. 10, No. 4 (Apr. 1984)-. 0747-2544. Periodical. US. English. mo. $20.00 (U.S.), $30.00 (Canada). Fleet Equipment, Circulation Manager, 7300 North Cicero Avenue, Lincolnwood IL 60646. LC TL230.2. DD 629.287405. *Fleet Maintenance and Specifying, 0095-3245.*

FLEET OWNER. BIG FLEET EDITION. (FLEET OWNER). Vol. 77, No. 2 (Feb. 1982)-. 0731-9622. Periodical. US. English. mo. $25.00. Fleet Owner, McGraw Hill Publishing Company Attn Cheryl Ross, PO Box 416, Hightstown NJ 08520. Tel (609)426-5000. Ind/Abst Trade Ind. Index. adv acc. (ctrl). *Fleet Owner, 0015-3567.*

FLEET SUPERVISOR. See Business - General Management.

FLORIDA TRUCK NEWS. V. 1- Sept. 1947-. 0015-4334. Periodical. US. English. mo. Florida Trucking Association Inc, 704 Gilmore Street, Jacksonville FL 32204.

FLYING MODELS. See Hobbies.

FOUR WHEELER. 0015-9123. Periodical. US. English. mo. Twentieth Century Publications, PO Box 7116, Canoga Park CA 91303.

FREIGHT COMMODITY STATISTICS. MOTOR CARRIERS OF PROPERTY. See Statistics.

FREIGHT DATA MICROFORM. VFOAT Freight Classification Data File, Basic. US. English. qt. Commander, Defense Logistics Services Center, Attn: DLSC-AP, Federal Center, Battle Creek MI 49016.

FREIGHT FORWARDERS AND AIR ROUTING GUIDE. 1st- Ed. US. English. an. $15.00. G R Leonard & Company, 2121 Shermer Road, Northbrook IL 60062. Tel (312)498-2121.

FREIGHT NEWS (1983). (FREIGHT NEWS). Periodical. UK. English. $26.05. Link House Magazines Ltd, Link House Dingwall Avenue, Croydon CR9 2TA England. Tel 01-686 2599. *Freight News International Weekly.*

FREIGHT NEWS EXPRESS. Periodical. UK. English. Tel 01-994 6477. adv acc. Circ 15,000. (ctrl). News/features, of freight transport worldwide by road, rail, air, and sea. *Freight News (1983).*

FREIGHT SERVICE DIRECTORY. CHICAGO EDITION. See Yearbooks, Almanacs, Directories.

FREIGHTER TRAVEL NEWS. See Travel.

FROM THE STATE CAPITALS. TRANSPORTATION POLICIES. VFOAT Transportation Policies. 0749-2774. Periodical. US. English. mo. $125.00. Wakeman/Walworth Inc, PO Box 1939, New Haven CT 06509. *From the State Capitals. Parking Regulations, 0741-3513; From the State Capitals. Urban Transit, 0741-3564.*

GEFAHRLICHE LADUNG. VFOAT Dangerous Cargo. 0016-5808. GW. English or German. mo. $62.77. K O Storck & Company, Verlag und Druckerel GMBH, Stahltwiete 7, 2000 Hamburg 50 West Germany. Tel 040/8500071. Ed H Meder and U Heins. Ind/Abst Ship Abstr., Energy Res. Abstr. LC T55.3.H3. bk rev. adv acc. Circ 4,000. Transport, storage and handling of hazardous cargoes, fire and disaster prevention, oil spill prevention and combat, regulation.

GO SYSTEM TIMETABLE. 0225-9842. Periodical. CN. English. Toronto Area Transit Operating Authority, Toronto Ontario Canada. DD 380.52209713541.

GO WEST (BURLINGAME, CALIF. : 1982). See Business - General Management.

GO WEST MAGAZINE. VFOAT Go. Ceased Sept. 1982?. 0745-2675. Periodical. US. English. mo. Go West Magazine, 1240 Bayshore Highway, Burlingame CA 94010. Tel (415)579-3510. Ed Buck Luetscher. adv acc. Circ 50,000. (ctrl). Serves the managerial needs of operators of medium and heavy trucks in the pacific, mountain, and southwestern states. *Go West (Burlingame, Calif. : 1980), 0884-7258.*

GRANT AWARDS - U.S. DEPARTMENT OF TRANSPORTATION. (GRANT AWARDS). 0090-6492. US. English. an. US Department of Transportation, Assistant Secretary for Administration, Office of Installations and Logistics, Washington DC 20590. LC HE17. DD 380.5.

GREEN GUIDE FOR ELECTRIC LIFT TRUCKS. 0731-9819. US. English. an. $175.00. Nielsen/Dataquest Inc, 2800 West Bayshore Road, Palo Alto CA 94303.

GREEN GUIDE FOR LIFT TRUCKS. 0731-9827. US. English. an. $175.00. Nielsen/Dataquest Inc, 2800 West Bayshore Road, Palo Alto CA 94303.

GREEN GUIDE FOR OFF-HIGHWAY TRUCKS & TRAILERS. VAT Green Guide for Off Highway Trucks and Trailers. 0731-9835. Periodical. US. English. ir. $195.00. Dataquest Inc, 1290 Ridder Park Drive, San Jose CA 95131. Tel (408)971-9001.

GUIA COLOMBIANA DEL TRANSPORTE. 1977-. Spanish. ir. Apartado Aereo 8010, Bogota Columbia. LC HE235.

GUIA NACIONAL DO TRANSPORTE RODOVIARIO DE CARGA. Portuguese. ir. Associacao Nacional das Empresas de Transportes, Rua Araujo 216 - 10 Andar, Sao Paulo Brazil. LC HE5653.A1.

GUIDE DU TRANSPORT PAR CAMION INC. VFOAT Truck Transport Guide Inc. 0706-9995. CN. English (French). an. $30.00. Guide du Transport par Camion, 3675 Boulevard des Sources Bureau 110, Dollard Ormeaux H9B 2TG Canada. Tel (514)683-1461. DD 388.32402571. adv acc. Circ 6,000. (ctrl). Publicity on transportation means for Canada and USA, transportation guide.

HANDBOOK - CHARTERED INSTITUTE OF TRANSPORT. Main/Corp Chartered Institute of Transport. Began in 1971. 0306-9559. UK. English. an. Free. Chartered Institute of Transport, 80 Portland Place, London W1N 4DP England. Tel (01)636-9952. Ed L Aldridge. LC HE243.A1. DD 380.506241. Circ 8,000. Describes the aims, activities and qualifications of the Chartered Institute of Transport, the international professional body for managers in transportation.

HAZARDOUS CARGO BULLETIN. Jan. 1980-. 0143-6864. Periodical. UK. English. mo. 43. Intapress Publishing Limited, 38 Tavistock Street, London WC2E 7PB England. Tel (01)240-0837. Ed Michael Corkhill. Ind/Abst Fluidex, Coal Abstr., Int. Packag. Abstr., Energy Res. Abstr. bk rev. adv acc. Circ 5,000. News and regulations covering the transport and handling of oils, gases and chemicals.

HAZARDOUS MATERIALS TRANSPORTATION. 0197-3177. Periodical. US. English. sm. $237.00. Cahners Publishing Co, PO Box 716, Back Bay Annex, Boston MA 02117. Tel (617)536-7780.

HEAVY-DUTY DISTRIBUTION. 0191-6777. Periodical. US. English. mo. $25.00. Kona Cal Inc, 707 Lake Cook Road, Deerfield IL 60015. Tel (312)498-3180.

HEAVY TRUCK SALESMAN. Vol. 1, No. 1 (July/Aug 1983)-. 0740-3941. Periodical. US. English. bm. $30.00. Newport Publications Division HIC Corporation, 4001 Westerly Place, PO Box 2, Newport Beach CA 92658-0617. Tel (714)833-0512. Ed David Kolman. LC HD9710.35.U6. DD 629.2240688. adv acc. Circ 20,000. (ctrl). Serves new truck and trailer dealerships, factory branches, rental and leasing companies, equipment dealers, manufacturers, engine distributors and other facilities.

HELICOPTERS. VFOAT Helicopters in Canada. VAT Helicopters in Canada (1983). V. 3, No. 3 (Winter 1983)-. 0227-3160. Periodical. CN. English. qt. $10.00. Helicopters, Suite 158/1224-53 Avenue Northeast, Calgary Alberta T2E 7E2 Canada. DD 387.733520971. *Helicopters Canada, 0826-1237.*

HIGHWAY & URBAN MASS TRANSPORTATION. VAT Highway and Urban Mass Transportation. 0364-3468. Periodical. US. English. Superintendent of Documents, US Government Printing Office, Washington DC 20402. LC HE308. DD 388.40973. *Highway Transportation.*

HIGHWAY SAFETY LITERATURE. No. 1-72-1. 0300-6905. US. English. qt. Transportation Research Board, 2101 Constitution Avenue Northwest, Washington DC 20418. Tel (202)334-3250. Ed Nancy Ackerman. Ind/Abst Am. Stat. Index. LC HE5614. Circ 3,500. (ctrl). An abstract journal on safety aspects of drivers, vehicles, pedestrians, roadways, alcohol and drug use, traffic management, hazardous materials, environmental effects, insurance and legislation.

HIGHWAY TRANSPORT BOARD BULLETIN. No. 57/26 (July 2, 1957)-. 0701-8568. Periodical. CN. English. wk. Free. Ontario Trucking Association, 555 Dixon Road, Rexdale Ontario M9W 1H8 Canada. DD 388.32409713. (ctrl). *Members' Bulletin (Automotive Transport Association of Ontario), 0229-9755.*

HIGHWAYS AND TRANSPORTATION STATISTICS . . . ESTIMATES. See Statistics.

HOME & AWAY. See Travel.

HOME SERVICES AND TRANSPORTATION. See Sociology: General Works, Theory - Social Pathology, Welfare, Criminology.

HONG KONG DEPARTMENTAL REPORT BY THE COMMISSIONER FOR TRANSPORT. Main/Corp Hong Kong. Transport Dept. English. ir. $8.00. J R Lee, Government Printer, Java Road, Hong Kong. LC HE96.H6. DD 354.51250087.

HOOSIER MOTORIST HOME & AWAY. See Travel.

HOW TO RECOVER FOR LOSS OR DAMAGE TO GOODS IN TRANSIT. 1976-. US. English. ir. Matthew Bender & Company Inc, 1275 Broadway, Albany NY 12201. Tel (800)833-9844. Index published separately - free - upon request.

IFW. INTERNATIONAL FREIGHTING WEEKLY. (INTERNATIONAL FREIGHTING WEEKLY : IFW). VFOAT IFW. Began publication in 1962. 0032-5007. Periodical. UK. English. wk. $68.96. MacLean Hunter Ltd, 76 Oxford Street, London W1N 9FD England. Tel 01-434 2233. Ed Derek North. Ind/Abst Predicasts, Ship Abstr. adv acc. Circ 20,679. (ctrl). Read by personnel responsible for the movement and handling of international cargo. The UK's only weekly freight newspaper. *Ports and Terminals/International Freighting.*

IMPLEMENTATION DIVISION ACTIVITIES REPORT. VFOAT Implementation Division Activities. US. English. an. US Department of Transportation, Federal Highway Administration, Office of Research and Development, Implementation Division, Washington DC 20590. *Implementation Division Activities, 0161-2239.*

IMPORTED CARS & TRUCKS TUNE-UP MECHANICAL SERVICE & REPAIR. VFOAT Imported Cars and Trucks Tune-Up Mechanical Service and Repair. 0737-3341. US. English. an. Mitchell Manuals Inc, Box 26260, San Diego CA 92126. Tel (619)578-8770. Ed Dan Kelley. LC TL152. DD 629.28722. adv acc. (ctrl). Complete service and repair information for 1984 imported cars and light trucks. Includes tune-up, computerized engine controls, all electrical and mechanical components and systems. *Tune-Up Mechanical Service and Repair. Imported Cars & Trucks, 0193-7995.*

IN TRANSIT. Vol. 65, No. 2 (Feb. 1957)-. 0019-3291. Periodical. US. English. mo. $5.00. Amalgamated Transit Union, 5025 Wisconsin Avenue, Washington DC 20016.

INBOUND TRAFFIC GUIDE. See Business - Purchasing.

INFO PREVENTION. Vol. 1, No. 1 (Nov./Dec. 1983)-. 0822-6776. Periodical. CN. French. bw. Free. Association Paritaire pour la Sante et la Securite du Travail du Secteur Transport et Entreposage, 1550 East Boulevard St-Joseph, Montreal Quebec H2J 1M7 Canada. DD 363.119380509714. (ctrl).

INFORMATION - ASSOCIATION QUEBECOISE DU TRANSPORT ET DES ROUTES INC. (INFORMATION - L'ASSOCIATION QUEBECOISE DU TRANSPORT ET DES ROUTES). Main/Corp Association Quebecoise du Transport et des Routes. V. 1- May 1975-. 0319-1818. Periodical. CN. French. bm. l'association Quebecoise du Transport et des Routes Inc, c/o Ecole Polytechnique, CP 6079/Succursale A, Montreal Quebec H3C 3A7 Canada. DD 380.5062714.

INFORMATION SERIES. GROUP 2. DESIGN AND CONSTRUCTION OF TRANSPORTATION FACILITIES. (INFORMATION SERIES. GROUP 2 : DESIGN AND CONSTRUCTION OF TRANSPORTATION FACILITIES). 0148-8473. Periodical. US. English. ir.

Transportation

Transportation Research Board, 2101 Constitution Avenue NW, Washington DC 20418.

INFORME AL CONGRESO NACIONAL. Main/Corp Colombia. Ministerio de Obras Publicas y Transporte. Spanish. ir. LC HE50.A3. DD 380.509861.

INFORME ANUAL - PUERTO RICO PORTS AUTHORITY. Main/Corp Puerto Rico Ports Authority. English (Spanish). an. LC HE9797.5.P9. DD 354.729500877106.

INTER-REGIONAL DRY CARGO MOVEMENTS. Main/Corp Organisation for Economic Co-Operation and Development. VFOAT Mouvements Interregionaux de Cargaisons Seches. FR. English and French. ir. 2 rue Andre-Pascall, 75777 Cedex 16 France. LC HE563.A3. DD 387.5440212.

INTERNATIONAL BULK JOURNAL. (INTERNATIONAL BULK JOURNAL : IBJ). VFOAT IBJ. 0260-1087. Periodical. UK. English. mo. $153.24. IBJ Associates, Ranmore House/Ranmore Road, Darking Surrey RH4 1HE England. Tel (0306)887433. Ed Richard G Peckham. Ind/Abst Coal Abstr., Fluidex. bk rev. adv acc. Circ 7,500. (ctrl). All aspects of seaborne dry bulk trade, transport and handling.

INTERNATIONAL CONGRESS PROCEEDINGS. Main/Corp International Union of Public Transport. English. ir. International Union of Public Transport, Avenue de l Uruguay 19, B-1050 Brussels Belgium. LC TF701. DD 388.04205. *Proceedings*.

INTERNATIONAL MOTOR BUSINESS. No. 122 (Apr. 1985)-. 0267-8225. Periodical. UK. English. qt. $355.00. Economist Publications Ltd, The Economist Intelligence Unit, PO Box 1DW, 40 Duke Street, London W1A 1DW England. Tel 01-493-6711. Issued also on microfilm by World Microfilms Publications Ltd. Examines recent developments, current trends and short term prospects for the passenger car and commercial vehicle sectors of the world's principal producing countries. *Motor Business*.

INTERNATIONAL REGISTER OF FORWARDING AGENTS. VFOAT Internationales Spediteur-Verzeichnis, Repertoire International de Transitaires. Periodical. English. ty. LC HE5999.A3. DD 380.524025.

INTERNATIONAL TRANSPORT POLICY. Periodical. US. English. Tel (212)354-4480. Reports on international air and sea transport policy developments in intergovernmental organizations, in labor, business, and trade groups, and in the US government.

INTERNATIONALES VERKEHRSWESEN. 0020-9511. Periodical. German. bm. 103.80. Tetzlaff Verlag GMBH, Postfach 4006, D-6100 Darmstadt 1 West Germany. Tel (6151)3801. Ind/Abst Excerpta Med. LC HE5. DD 380.505. bk rev. adv acc. Circ 4,100. Technical, economic, legal, and political aspects of international transportation. *IV*.

INTERSTATE INFORMATION REPORT. US. English. mo. $30.00. American Trucking Association, 2200 Mill Road, Alexandria VA 22314. Tel (703)838-1788. Ed Jan Balkin. Circ 1,800. Digest of state legislation, regulatory activities and court cases which affect motor carriers in the trucking industry today.

I.R.T. DIGEST. (IRT DIGEST). Main/Corp Institute for Rapid Transit. 0094-2707. US. English. Institute for Rapid Transit, 1612 K Street Northwest, Washington DC 20006. LC HE4201. DD 388.40973.

ISR, INTERNATIONLE BERG- UND SEILBAHNRUNDSCHAU. VFOAT Internationle Berg- und Seilbahnrundschau, International Aerial Tramway Review. Periodical. German (English and French). ir. 900.-. Bohmann Verlag AG, Leberstrasse 122, A-1011 Wien Austria. Tel (0222)74 15 95. Ed Gerda Stockhammer. LC TJ1385. DD 621.86805. adv acc. Circ 3,000. (ctrl). Concerns cable car technique, slope grooming and artificial snowmaking. *Internationale Berg- Und Seilbahn-Rundschau*.

ITE JOURNAL. Main/Corp Institute of Transportation Engineers. VAT Institute of Transportation Engineers Journal. V. 48, No. 6- June 1978-. 0162-8178. Periodical. US. English. mo. $13.00. Institute of Transportation Engineers, 1815 North Fort Meyer Drive/Suite 905, Arlington VA 22209. Ind/Abst Eng. Index Annu., Eng. Index Mon., Eng. Index Bioeng., Eng. Index Energy Abstr., Excerpta Med., Energy Inf. Abstr., Environ. Abstr., Ref. Source, Appl. Sci. Technol. Index, Energy Res. Abstr. LC HE331. DD 380.505. CODEN ITEJDZ. Microfilm Copies. *Transportation Engineering, 0148-0170*.

ITOGI NAUKI I TEKHNIKI : SERIIA ORGANIZATSIIA UPRAVLENIIA TRANSPORTOM. VFOAT Seriia Organizatsiia Upravleniia Transportom. Began in 1978. Periodical. UR. Russian. 0.75. LC HE255.

JAARVERSLAG - NEDERLANDSCHE SCHEEPVAART UNIE. Main/Corp Nederlandsche Scheepvaart Unie. Dutch. ir. Dr H Colinjnlaan, 204 Rijsuijk Netherlands. LC HE945.N63.

JAHRESBERICHT DES VERBANDES SCHWEIZERISCHER TRANSPORTUNTERNEHMUNGEN DES OFFENTLICHEN VERKEHRS. Main/Corp Verband Schweizerischer Transportunterenhumngen des Offentlichen Verkehrs. VFOAT V.S.T. Jahresbericht, Rapport Annuel de l'Union des Entreprises Suisses de Transports Publics. French (German). an. LC HE263.A15. DD 380.509494.

JANE'S FREIGHT CONTAINERS. 1st- Ed. 0075-3033. US. English. an. $125.00. Janes Publishing Inc, 135 West 50 Street/12th Floor, New York NY 10020. Tel (212)586-7745. Ed Patrick Finlay. LC TA1215. DD 380.53. adv acc. Reference book on container industry listing port facilities, freight movement, airfreight and road transport, and manufacturers of containers and companies with related services.

JANE'S URBAN TRANSPORT SYSTEMS. VFOAT Urban Transport Systems. 1st Ed. (1982)-. UK. English. an. $110.00. Janes Publishing Inc, 135 West 50th Street/12th Floor, New York NY 10020. Tel (212)586-7745. Ed Chris Bushell and Peter Stonham. LC HE4201. DD 388.4. adv acc. Reference book covering world's major urban transport systems, including metro, light rail, tram, bus and trolleybus. Also lists manufacturers, products, consultants and their projects.

JIDOSHA CHOSA NEMPO. Japanese. ir. Nihon Jiodosha Kaigisho, c/o Kokusai Kanko Kaikan, 8-3 Marunouchi 1 Chiyoda-ku (100), Tokyo Japan. LC HE5697.A1.

JOURNAL OF ADVANCED TRANSPORTATION. V. 13- Spring 1979-. 0197-6729. Periodical. US. English. ir. $60.00. Institute for Transportation, 1410 Duke University Road, Durham NC 27705. Tel (919)489-2356. Ed C M Harman. Ind/Abst Electron. Commun. Abstr. J., ISMEC Bull., Pollut. Abstr. Indexes, Saf. Sci. Abstr. J., Eng. Index Mon., Eng. Index Bioeng. Abstr., Eng. Index Energy Abstr., Int. Aerosp. Abstr., Fluidex, Eng. Index Annu., Energy Res. Abstr., Appl. Mech. Rev., Eng. Index. LC TF1300. DD 388.05. CODEN JATRDC. Circ 500. Urban mass transportation is emphasized. Engineering aspects include structures, vehicles and control. Economics, planning and socio-political aspects of transportation included. *High Speed Ground Transportation Journal, 0018-1501*.

JOURNAL OF BUSINESS LOGISTICS. VFOAT Business Logistics. V. 1- Spring 1978-. 0735-3766. Periodical. US. English. sa. $25.00. 1775 College Road, Columbus OH 43210. Tel (614)422-0331. Ed Bernard J La Londe. Ind/Abst Manage. Contents. bk rev. Circ 5,000. Provides information, new theory or techniques, and researched generalizations about thought and practice in transportation and distribution. Presents views and syntheses which impact the future.

JOURNAL OF TRANSPORT ECONOMICS AND POLICY. V. 1- Jan 1967-. 0022-5258. Periodical. UK. English. ir. $68.00. University of Bath, Claverton Down, Bath BA2 7AY England. Tel 0225-61244. Ed M E Beesley. Ind/Abst Manage. Contents, Ship Abstr., Energy Inf. Abstr., Environ. Abstr., Index Econ. Artic. J. Collect. Vol., ABI/Inform, Public Aff. Inf. Serv. Bull., Soc. Sci. Citation Index. LC HE1. bk rev. adv acc. Circ 1,350. Covers all forms of transport and is essential reading for professionals concerned with transport-administrators, planners, engineers and economists.

JOURNAL OF TRANSPORT HISTORY. (THE JOURNAL OF TRANSPORT HISTORY). Vol. 1, No. 1 (May 1953)-V. 7, No. 4 (Nov. 1966). 0022-5266. Periodical. UK. English. sa. $60.00. Manchester University Press, Journals Department, Oxford Road, Manchester M13 9PL England. Tel 061-273-5539. Ed C L Turnbull and T R Gourvish. Ind/Abst Am. Hist. Life, Hist. Abstr., Part A, Mod. Hist. Abstr., Hist. Abst., Part B, Twent. Century Abstr., Hist. Abstr., Recent Publ. Artic. LC HE1. DD 380.509. bk rev. adv acc. Circ 472. Covers all aspects of the social and economic history of transportation.

JOURNAL OF TRANSPORTATION ENGINEERING. See Engineering - Civil Engineering.

KOKUSAI UNYU TOKEI. Japanese. ir. LC HE7.

KOTSU SHOROPPO. Main/Corp Japan. Began in 1961. JA. Japanese. ir. 950. Taisei Shuppansha, 1-7-11 Hanegi Setagaya-Ku, Tokyo Japan.

KOTSUGAKU KENKYU: KENKYU NEMPO. Began with the issue for 1957. JA. Japanese. ir. Nikon Kotsu Kuokai, 5-6 Izumicho 2 Kokubunji (185), Kokubunji Japan. LC HE7.

KOZLEKEDESI ES HIRKOZLESI EVKONYV. See Communication.

KOZLEKEDESTUDOMANYI SZEMLE. VFOAT Scientific Review of Communication. V. 1-. 0023-4362. Periodical. HU. Multilingual (English and Hungarian). mo. Akademiai Kiado, POB 24, 1363 Budapest Hungary. Ind/Abst Comput. Control Abstr., Electr. Electron. Abstr., Sci. Abstr. Sect. A. Phys. Abstr. LC TA1001. CODEN KOSZAZ. *Magyar Kozlekedes, Mely- es Vizepites*.

KRAKS FRAGTLISTE. 0105-0346. Danish. an. Nytorv 17, 1450 Kbenhavn Denmark. LC HE199.D4. *Kraks Fragtsmandsliste*.

LAMY TRANSPORT (SOCIETE LAMY). See Law.

LARGE CLASS I HOUSEHOLD GOODS CARRIERS SELECTED EARNINGS DATA. Main/Corp United States. Interstate Commerce Commission. Bureau of Accounts. Periodical. US. English. qt. Free. Interstate Commerce Commission, Bureau of Accounts, Washington DC 20433. Tel (202)275-7833. Circ 550. Report showing latest earnings and traffic volume data of certain large class I household goods carriers.

LARGE CLASS I MOTOR CARRIERS OF PROPERTY SELECTED EARNINGS DATA. Main/Corp United States. Interstate Commerce Commission. Bureau of Accounts. US. English. Interstate Commerce Commission, Bureau of Accounts, Washington DC 20433.

LEISURE WHEELS. V. 10 - May 1979-. 0709-7093. Periodical. CN. English. mo. $10.00. Murray Publications Ltd, PO Box 7302 Station E, Calgary Alberta T3C 3M2 Canada. Tel (403)263-2707. Ed M Gimbel. DD 796.7905. bk rev acc. Circ 25,000. (ctrl). *Taylor's Leisure Wheels, 0318-3467*.

LETNI PREGLED PROMETA IN ZVEZ. Main/Corp Zavod Sr Slovenije Za Statistiko. 1978-. YU. Slovenian. an. Zavod Sr Slovenije za Statistiko, Vozarski Pot 12, Ljubljana Poland. LC HE80.5. *Letni Pregled Prometa*.

THE LEXINGTON NEWSLETTER. 1942. Periodical. US. English. qt. $10.00. Lexington Group Transportation, 1010 Zephyr, Plainview TX 79072. Tel (806)296-6576. Ed Don L Hofsommer. bk rev. Circ 450. (ctrl). Bibliographic and membership information; transportation history.

LIGHT, MEDIUM, HEAVY TRUCK SHOP MANUAL. US. English. Ford Parts & Service Division, 20000 Rotunda Drive, Dearborn MI 48121. LC TL230.5.F57. DD 629.287405.

LIGHT TRUCK EQUIPMENT NEWS CEASED. V. 2, Issue 7- Aug. 1979-. 0225-9737. Periodical. CN. English. mo. Warren Publishers, 1730 Amico Boulevard, Mississauga Ontario L4W 1Y3 Canada. DD 629.22305. *4 X 4 Pickup & Van Equipment News, 0709-5104*.

LIMOUSIN LEADER. (THE LIMOUSIN LEADER). V. 1- April 1974-. 0381-5552. Periodical. CN. English. $19.35. Limousin Leader, Bay 5A 3101, 19th Street Northeast, Calgary Alberta T2E 6X8 Canada. DD 636.242.

LIMOUSIN WORLD. Vol. 1, No. 1 (Oct. 1983)-. 8750-2127. Periodical. US. English. mo. $15.00. Limousin World Inc, 6408 South College Avenue, Fort Collins CO 80524. DD 636.

Transportation

LIMOUSINE & CHAUFFEUR. VFOAT Limousine and Chauffeur. 8750-7374. Periodical. US. English. bm. $20.00 US, $35.00 Canada. Limousine & Chauffeur, 2500 Artesia Boulevard, Redondo Beach CA 90278.

LIVE ANIMALS REGULATIONS. Main/Corp International Air Transport Association. VFOAT IATA Live Animals Regulations. VAT International Air Transport Association Live Animals Regulations. 0256-4742. CN. English. an. $15.00. Traffic Services Administrator International Air Transport Association, 2000 Peel Street, Montreal Quebec H3A 2R4 Canada. DD 387.744.

THE LOGISTICS AND TRANSPORTATION REVIEW. Began in 1972. 0047-4991. Periodical. CN. English. qt. 28.00. University of British Columbia, Faculty Commerce Business Administration, Vancouver British Columbia V6T 1W5 Canada. Tel (604)228-6767. Ed W G Waters II. Ind/Abst Electr. Electron. Abstr., Phys. Abstr., Comput. Control Abstr., Manage. Contents. LC U168. DD 355.41105. bk rev. adv acc. Circ 1,000. An international refereed journal publishing informative articles from across the spectrum of logistics and transportation research.

MAANDSTATISTIEK VAN VERKEER EN VERVOER. See Statistics.

MCD. MIDDLE ATLANTIC EDITION. See Yearbooks, Almanacs, Directories.

MAGAZINE TOUT TERRAIN. (LE MAGAZINE TOUT TERRAIN : GUIDE DE L'ACHETEUR). VFOAT Tout Terrain. Vol. 1, No. 1-. 0829-4445. Periodical. CN. French. sa. Free. Publications CRV, Bureau 221 3414 Ave du Parc, Montreal Quebec H2X 2H5 Canada. DD 629.2204205. (ctrl).

MASS TRANSIT. VFOAT MT. V. 1- June 1974-. 0364-3484. Periodical. US. English. mo. $25.00. Mass Transit, 555 National Press Building, Washington DC 20045. Tel (202)638-0330. Ind/Abst Trade Ind. Index, Appl. Sci. Technol. Index, Avery Index Archit. Period., Bus. Period. Index. LC HE4201. DD 388.405.

MASTER PLAN FOR TRANSPORTATION. (A MASTER PLAN FOR TRANSPORTATION). Main/Corp New Jersey. Dept. of Transportation. 1968-. 0092-1254. US. English. Department of Transportation, 1035 Parkway Avenue, Trenton NJ 08625. LC HE28.N5. DD 711.7309749.

MBTA BUDGET, REPORT OF ADVISORY BOARD BUDGET COMMITTEE. Main/Corp Massachusetts Bay Transportation Authority. Budget Committee. 1978-. US. English. Massachusetts Bay Transportation Authority, 50 High Street, Boston MA 02110. LC HE310 .B6. DD 352.1252. MBTA Itemized Budget and Report of Advisory Budget Committee, 0363-1346.

MECHANICAL PARTS/LABOR ESTIMATING GUIDE. (MECHANICAL PARTS/LABOR ESTIMATING GUIDE. IMPORTED CARS & TRUCKS). VFOAT Mechanical Parts Labor Estimating Guide. Vol. 23, No. 5 (1982)-. 8755-6057. US. English. an. Mitchell Manuals Inc, PO Box 26260, San Diego CA 92126. Tel (619)578-8770. Ed Bill Jillard. LC TL152. DD 629.287. Mechanical part numbers and prices, estimated labor times for 1974-86 domestic cars. Separate times for combined operations. Skill level codes and model identification illustrations. Imported Cars & Trucks Mechanical Parts/Labor Estimating Guide, 0277-156X.

MECHANICAL PARTS/LABOR ESTIMATING GUIDE. DOMESTIC TRUCKS (SAN DIEGO, CALIF. : 1982). (MECHANICAL PARTS/LABOR ESTIMATING GUIDE. DOMESTIC TRUCKS). VFOAT Mechanical Parts Labor Estimating Guide. Vol. 23, No. 3 (1982)-. 8755-1764. US. English. an. Mitchell Manuals Inc, Box 26260, San Diego CA 92126. Tel (619)578-8770. Ed Bill Jillard. DD 629. adv acc. (ctrl). Mechanical parts numbers and prices, estimated labor times for 1973-85 domestic light trucks and vans. Includes skill level codes and model identification illustrations. Domestic Trucks Mechanical Parts/Labor Estimating Guide, 0732-4316.

MEMBERSHIP DIRECTORY - CANADIAN URBAN TRANSIT ASSOCIATION. See Yearbooks, Almanacs, Directories.

MEMBERSHIP DIRECTORY - INSTITUTE OF TRANSPORTATION ENGINEERS. See Yearbooks, Almanacs, Directories.

MEMORIA - TRANSPORTS DE BARCELONS. Main/Corp Transports de Barcelona. Spanish. an. S P M Transports de Barcelona S A, Ronda de Sant Pau 43, Barcelona 15 Spain. LC HE4899.B4. DD 388.4094672. Memoria y Balance.

MET, MIDDLE EAST TRANSPORTATION. VFOAT Middle East Transportation. Periodical. UK. English. mo. Free to Qualified, $62.00 Others. Middle East Transportation, Marketing Department, Room 1402/14th Floor Crown House, London Road, Morden Surrey SM4 50X England. LC HE268.2.A1. DD 380.50956.

METRO GUIDE (MONTREAL, QUEBEC). (METRO GUIDE). 1981/82-. 0714-4776. CN. French. an. Free. Publications Metro Guide, Bureau 1405, 3637 East Boulevard Cremazie, Montreal Quebec H1Z 2J9 Canada. DD 388.42809714281.

METRO (REDONDO BEACH, CALIF.) CEASED. (METRO). VFOAT Metropolitan. Began with issue for Sept./Oct. 1975 Ceased with Vol. 81, No. 2 (Mar./Apr. 1985). 0162-6221. Periodical. US. English. bm. Free to qualified subscribers. $9.00 Domestic, $12.00 Canada. Bobit Publishing Company, 2500 Artesia Boulevard, Redondo Beach CA 90278. Tel (213)376-8788. LC HE5601. DD 388.4132205. Also available on microfilm from University Microfilms International. Metropolitan.

METROSTROI. Periodical. UR. Russian. ir. $16.00. Victor Kamkin Inc (70572), 12224 Parklawn Drive, Rockville MD 20852. Tel (301)881-5973. LC TF845.

MICHIGAN SCHOOL BUS ACCIDENTS. Main/Corp Michigan. Dept. of State Police. 0097-8744. US. English. an. Michigan Department of State Police, 714 South Harrison Road, East Lansing MI 48823. LC HE5614.3.M4. DD 388.314.

MICHIGAN SNOWMOBILER. 0746-2098. Periodical. US. English. bm. $4.00 Domestic, $5.00 Foreign. Michigan Snowmobiler, 207 Main Street, East Jordan MI 49727.

MIDDLE EAST INDUSTRY & TRANSPORT. VFOAT Middle East Industry and Transport. VAT Middle East Industry and Transport. Issue No. 34 (Jan./Feb. 1981)-. 0261-1473. Periodical. UK. English. bm. $60.00. International Communications, 122 East 42nd Street/Room 1121, New York NY 10017. Tel (212)867-5159. Ed Norma Di Marco. LC HE268.2 .A15. DD 380.50956. bk rev adv acc. Circ 6,500. (ctrl). Middle East Transport.

MILK AND LIQUID FOOD TRANSPORTER. V. 18, No. 5- Apr. 1978-. 0199-2317. Periodical. US. English. mo. Milk & Liquid Food Transporter, N80 W12878 Fond du Lac Avenue, PO Box 878, Menomonee Falls WI 53051. Milk Hauler and Liquid Food Transporter.

MINERALS TRANSPORTATION; PROCEEDINGS. Main/Conf International Symposium on Transport and Handling of Minerals. V. 1- 1971-. 0094-7466. US. English. be. $27.50. 500 Howard Street, San Francisco CA 94105. LC HE199.5.O7. DD 380.142.

MINNESOTA MOTOR VEHICLE LAW. See Law.

MINUTES OF PROCEEDINGS AND EVIDENCE OF THE STANDING COMMITTEE ON NORTHERN PIPELINES. See Petroleum and Natural Gas.

MINUTES OF PROCEEDINGS AND EVIDENCE OF THE STANDING COMMITTEE ON TRANSPORT. Main/Corp Canada. Parliament. House of Commons. Standing Committee on Transport. VFOAT Proces-Verbaux et Temoignages du Comite Permanent des Transports. CN. English (French). Canadian Government Publishing Centre, Supply and Services Canada, Hull Quebec K1A 0S9 Canada. LC HE215. DD 380.50971. Minutes of Proceedings and Evidence of the Standing Committee on Transport and Communications.

MOBILE HOME & RV TRAILER GUIDE, NEW & USED VALUES. Main/Corp Kelley Blue Book Co. VAT Mobile Home and Recreational Vehicle Trailer Guide, New & Used Value. 0364-7374. US. English. $20.00. Kelley Blue Book Company, 4005 Long Beach Boulevard, Long Beach CA 90807. LC HD9710.A1. DD 381.456292260973.

MOBILE LIVING IN CANADA. See Housing and Urban Development.

MOBILITY TRENDS. Periodical. English. qt. Allied Van Lines Inc, PO Box 4403, Chicago IL 60680.

MODERN TRAMWAY AND LIGHT RAIL TRANSIT. VFOAT Modern Tramway. No. 508 (Apr. 1980)-. 0144-1655. Periodical. UK. English. mo. 8.00. Light Rail Transit Association, 6 Hermitage Woods Crescent, Surrey GU21 1UE England. Ed W J Wyse. LC TF701. DD 388.4605. bk rev. adv acc. Circ 3,000. (ctrl). General transport in light rail and trams. Modern Tramway and Light Rapid Transit.

MONDE A BICYCLETTE. See Bicycles and Bicycling.

MOODY'S TRANSPORTATION MANUAL. VFOAT Transportation Manual. 1983-. Periodical. US. English. ir. Moody's Investors Service, 99 Church Street, New York NY 10007. Moody's Manual of Investments: American and Foreign. Railroad Securities.

MOTEUR QUEBEC. V. 4, No. 1- Jan./Feb. 1978-. 0707-6215. Periodical. CN. French. mo. $15.00 Domestic, $22.00 US, $30.00 Other Countries. Les Editions J D L, Bureau 910/1253 Av du College McGill, Montreal Quebec H3B 2Y5 Canada. DD 629.222205. Derriere le Volant, 0383-9176.

MOTONEIGISTE CANADIEN. First edition in 1975. 0381-694X. Periodical. CN. French. an. $13.00. CRV Publishing Company Ltd, 3414 Park Avenue/Suite 221, Montreal Quebec H2X 2H5 Canada. Tel (514)282-0191. Ed J G Langlois. DD 796.9. bk rev. adv acc. Circ 100,000.

MOTOR ACCIDENTS IN NEW ZEALAND. 0550-5089. Periodical. NZ. English. ir. Ministry of Transport, Private Bag, Wellington New Zealand. LC HE5614.5.N45. DD 388.314.

MOTOR CARRIER ANNUAL REPORTS. Main/Corp American Trucking Associations. 0160-4570. US. English. an. 1616 P Street NW, Washington DC 20036. LC HE5623.A1. DD 388.3240973.

MOTOR CARRIER STATISTICAL SUMMARY. See Statistics.

MOTOR CARRIERS. FREIGHT AND HOUSEHOLD GOODS MOVERS. (MOTOR CARRIERS—FREIGHT AND HOUSEHOLD GOODS MOVERS). 1975-. 0705-5978. CN. English (French in parallel columns). an. $2.10. DSS, Ottawa Ontario Canada. LC HE5635. DD 388.3240971. Motor Carriers, Moving and Storage Household Goods, 0575-9137.

MOTOR CARRIERS FREIGHT QUARTERLY. Main/Corp Statistics Canada. Transportation Section. VFOAT Entrepreneurs en Camionnage. CN. English and French. qt. Statistics Canada, Transportation Section, Publication Distribution, Ottawa Ontario K1A 0T6 Canada. LC HE5635. DD 388.3240971. Motor Carriers.

MOTOR COACH AGE. 0739-117X. Periodical. US. English. bm. $20.00. Motor Bus Society Inc, PO Box 7058, West Trenton NJ 08628. LC HE5601.

MOTOR HOMES, CAMPERS, VAN CONVERSIONS, SURFER VANS. VFOAT Kelley Blue Book RV Guide. 0094-8446. US. English. ir. $33.00. Kelley Blue Book, PO Box 1290, 2950 A7 Airway, Costa Mesa CA 92626. Tel (714)957-2600. LC HD9710.U5. DD 380.1456908790973.

THE MOTOR INDUSTRY OF GREAT BRITAIN. 1930. UK. English. an. $55.17. Society of Motor Manufacturers & Traders, Forbes House Halkin Street, London SW1X 7DS England. Tel 01-550-3231. Ed M Murphy. Circ 900. Vehicles in use, production, new registrations, imports and exports, UK production by model, UK exports by manufacturer, plus miscellaneous information akin to the motor industry.

MOTOR SPECIFICATIONS AND PRICES. VFOAT Stone & Cox Motor Specifications & Prices. Began in 1922. Periodical. UK. English. an. 15.00. Stone & Cox Publications Ltd, 44 Fleet Street, London EC4Y 1BS England. Tel 01-353-1622. Ed Ernest Holland. LC HD9710.G7. adv acc. Circ. 1,500. Specifications, prices, recommended insurance group ratings for all models of UK manufactured and non-UK private cars and motorcycles for the past 14 years.

MOTOR TRUCK. V. 33, No. 6- June 1964-. 0027-2108. Periodical. CN. English. mo. Wadham Publishing Ltd, 109 Vanderhoff Avenue/Suite 101, Toronto Ontario M4G 2J2 Canada. Tel (416)445-6641. Ind/Abst Can. Bus. Index. DD 388.3240971. Motor Truck & Coach, 0380-0849.

Transportation

THE MOTORCYCLIST'S POST. 1967. 0164-9256. Periodical. US. English. mo. $8.00. Motorcyclist Post, PO Box 154, Rochdale MA 01542. **Tel** (617)885-5221. **Ed** Robert F Frink. bk rev. adv acc. **Circ** 9,800. Motorcycle activity and sport riding in New England area.

MOVING HOUSE AND HOME. 0279-0971. Periodical. US. English. qt. $15.00. Moving Market Inc, 420 Lexington Avenue/Suite 2616, New York NY 10170. **Tel** (212)661-6630.

MUYOK UNSONG. VFOAT Monthly Trade & Transport. V. 1- (Oct. 1984)-. Periodical. KO. Korean. mo. Chusik Hoesa Kago Puresu, 4 Naesu-dong Chongno-ku, Seoul Korea. **LC** HE199.A2.

NATION ON THE MOVE. VFOAT Nation en Mouvement. 1972-. 0317-2643. Periodical. CN. English (French). an. Road & Transportation Association of Canada, 1765 St Laurent Boulevard, Ottawa Ontario K1G 3V4 Canada. **DD** 354.71008781. Highway Finance, 0073-215X.

NATIONAL BUS TRADER. Began in Dec. 1977. 0194-939X. Periodical. US. English. mo. $15.00. National Bus Trader, 6322 Marshall Drive, Woodridge IL 60517. **LC** TL232. **DD** 629.222330973.

NATIONAL HIGHWAY AND AIRWAY CARRIERS AND ROUTES. 0275-3286. US. English. sa. $94.00. National Highways Carriers Directory, 936 South Betty Drive-PO Box U, Buffalo Grove IL 60090. **Tel** (312)541-6565. adv acc. **Circ** 10,500. Guide for routing freight between all points in U.S. and Canada; includes terminal locations and phone numbers, company officials, type of service and states served. National Highway Carriers Directory and Routes, including Air Cargo Transports.

NATIONAL LEGAL BIBLIOGRAPHY. SUBJECT AREA LIST. TRANSPORTATION AND MARITIME LAW. See Bibliographies.

NATIONAL MOTORIST. 0279-3083. Periodical. US. English. bm. National Motorist, 1 Market Plaza, San Francisco CO 94105. **Tel** (415)777-4000.

NATIONAL MOVING & STORAGE TIMES. VFOAT National Moving and Storage Times. Vol. 1, No. 1 (Apr. 13, 1984)-. 0747-3877. Periodical. US. English. wk. NMSA, 124 South Royal Street, Alexandria VA 22314.

NATIONAL SCHOOL BUS REPORT. V. 1- June/July 1971-. Periodical. US. English. qt. $50.00. National School Transportation Association, PO Box 324, Farifax VA 22030. **Tel** (703)644-0700. **LC** LB2864. **DD** 371.870973.

NATIONAL TANK TRUCK CARRIER DIRECTORY. See Yearbooks, Almanacs, Directories.

NATIONAL TRANSPORTATION SAFETY BOARD DECISIONS. **Main/Corp** United States. National Transportation Safety Board. Began with V. 1, Apr. 1967- Dec. 1972. 0094-761X. US. English. Superintendent of Documents, Government Printing Office, Washington DC 20402. **LC** KF2172.A2. **DD** 344.73047.

NATIONAL TRANSPORTATION STATISTICS. See Statistics.

NATIONAL URBAN MASS TRANSPORTATION STATISTICS. See Statistics.

NDOT NEWS. **Main/Corp** Nevada. Dept. of Transportation. V. 19, No. 9- Nov./Dec. 1979-. Periodical. US. English. **LC** HE356.N37. **DD** 388.109293. Nevada Highway News.

NEBRASKA PUBLIC TRANSPORTATION. **Main/Corp** Nebraska. Dept. of Roads. Office of Engineering Services. Planning Division. US. English. **LC** HE4487.N2. **DD** 353.97820087805.

NEW CONCEPTS IN URBAN TRANSPORTATION. V. 2- July 15, 1972-. 0148-8457. Periodical. US. English. ir. Transportation Research Board, 2101 Constitution Avenue, Washington DC 20418. Personal Rapid Transit.

NEWSLETTER - UNIVERSITY OF TORONTO. YORK UNIVERSITY. JOINT PROGRAM IN TRANSPORTATION. (NEWSLETTER - UNIVERSITY OF TORONTO/YORK UNIVERSITY JOINT PROGRAM IN TRANSPORTATION). **Main/Corp** Joint Program in Transportation. V. 1- July 1971-. 0318-1235. Periodical. CN. English. bm. Joint Program in Transportation, c/o Centre for Urban and Community Studies, 150 St George Street, Toronto Ontario M5S 1A1 Canada.

NIHON NO KANCHO, SONO HITO TO SOSHIKI. UNYUSHO. VFOAT UNYUSHO. JA. Japanese. ir. 30000. Seisaku Jiho Shinsha, 19-4 Akasaka 6 Minato-Ku, Tokyo-To 107 Japan. **LC** HE277.A15.

NOTES FROM UNDERGROUND. No. 1- 1964-. 0550-0974. US. English. mo. $20.00. Committee Better Transit Inc, PO Box 3106, Long Island City NY 11103. **Tel** (718)728-0091. **Ed** Stephen B Dobron. **LC** AP2. bk rev. **Circ** 2,400. News and views on urban transportation, with special emphasis on the New York-New Jersey metropolitan area. Renaissance.

NOUVELLE VOIX DE L'ANCAI. (LA NOUVELLE VOIX DE L'ANCAI). **Main/Corp** Association Nationale des Camionneurs-Artisans. Vol. 1, No. 1 (Sept. 1983)-. 0822-5435. Periodical. CN. French. mo. Association Nationale des Camionneurs-Artisans, Bureau 373/2030 Boulevard Pere Lalievre, Duberger Quebec G1P 2X1 Canada. **DD** 388.324060714. Voix (Drummondville, Quebec), 0823-4655.

DAS NUTZFAHRZEUG. 1.- Yearly Vol. Periodical. GW. German. mo. $30.44. Vogel Fachzeitschriften GMBH, Postfach 80 20 20, D-8000 Munchen 80 West Germany. **Tel** 089-4 32 80 217. **Ed** Theo Delfried Dolmina. **LC** TL3. bk rev. adv acc. **Circ** 5,000. (ctrl). Fleet operating, vehicle specificiations, test reports on trucks and trailers, and transport business information.

OAG AIR CARGO GUIDE. VFOAT Air Cargo Guide. 0191-152X. US. English. mo. $57.00. OAG Cargo Guide, 2000 Clearwater Drive, Oak Brook IL 60521. **Tel** (312)654-6000. **Ed** Red Howe. adv acc. **Circ** 9,000. Reference publication for worldwide commercial airfreight schedules and related information.

OCCASIONAL PAPER - CENTRE FOR TRANSPORTATION STUDIES. UNIVERSITY OF BRITISH COLUMBIA. (AN OCCASIONAL PAPER). 0712-1067. Monographic Series. CN. English. Centre for Transportation Studies, University of British Columbia, Vancouver British Columbia V6T 1W5 Canada. **DD** 380.5072.

OCCASIONAL STUDENT PAPER - CENTRE FOR TRANSPORTATION STUDIES. UNIVERSITY OF BRITISH COLUMBIA. (AN OCCASIONAL STUDENT PAPER). VFOAT Student Paper. 0229-9704. CN. English. ir. Centre for Transportation Studies, University of British Columbia, Vancouver British Columbia B6T 1W5 Canada. **DD** 380.50971.

OFFICIAL FINANCIAL STATEMENT. **Main/Corp** Florida. Dept. of Transportation. June 1980-. US. English. an. State of Florida, Department of Transportation, Fiscal Mail Station 42, Tallahassee FL 32301. **LC** HE28.F6. **DD** 353.9759007231. Official Financial Statements.

THE OFFICIAL INTERMODAL EQUIPMENT REGISTER. 1969. 0190-6690. Periodical. US. English. qt. $32.00. Intermodal Publishers Company, 424 West 33rd Street, New York NY 10001. **Tel** (212)563-7210. adv acc. Dimensions and capacities tariff for containers, trailers and chassis in intermodal use by listed companies. Reporting marks, type codes series.

OFFICIAL MOTOR CARRIER DIRECTORY. See Yearbooks, Almanacs, Directories.

OFFICIAL STEAMSHIP GUIDE INTERNATIONAL. See Travel.

ON THE MOVE (BUFFALO, N.Y.). (ON THE MOVE). Vol. 1, No. 1 (Jan. 1981)-. Periodical. US. English. mo. Niagare Frontier, Transportation Authority, 181 Ellicott Street, Buffalo NY 14205.

ONTARIO TRUCKING TODAY. VFOAT OTT. VAT OTT. Ontario Trucking Today. July 1983-. 0824-0248. Periodical. CN. English. ir. 24.95. c/o Naylor Communications Ltd, 419-720 Spadina Avenue, Toronto Ontario M5S 2T9 Canada. **Tel** (416)961-1028. **Ed** Janice Kray. **DD** 388.32409713. adv acc. **Circ** 2,200. (ctrl). Trucking association magazine.

OPEN WHEEL. 0279-0254. Periodical. US. English. bm. $14.95. Lopez Automotive Group, 602 Montgomery Street, Alexandria VA 22314. **Tel** (703)836-5881. **Ed** Dick Berggren. bk rev. adv acc. **Circ** 55,000. Dedicated to behind the scenes coverage of events and personalities along with in-depth technical articles and brillant color photography.

OPERATING COSTS OF TRUCKS IN CANADA. CN. English. $22.75. Canadian Government Publication Centre, Supply and Services Canada, Ottawa Ontario K1A 059 Canada. **LC** HE5635. **DD** 388.324.

ORCAMENTO DA DESPESA PARA . . . 1, CLASSIFICACAO ORGANICA, FUNCIONAL E ECONOMICA. **Main/Corp** Portugal. Departamento dos Transportes. VFOAT Orcamento da Despesa para . . . . Portuguese. ir. **LC** HE262.A15. **DD** 354.46900875.

OREGON DRIVERS. 1981-. US. English. an. **LC** HE5633.O7. **DD** 338.31409795. Oregon's Driving Population.

OREGON TRANSPORTATION COMMISSION POLICIES. 0148-9704. US. English. an. Department of Transportation, State Highway Building, Salem OR 97310. **LC** HE28.O7.

OTA VIEWPOINT. VAT Ontario Trucking Association Viewpoint. 0824-2224. Periodical. CN. English. ir. Free to Members. Ontario Trucking Association, 555 Dixon Road, Rexdale Ontario M9W 1H8 Canada. **DD** 388.32409713.

OVERSEAS ARRIVALS AND DEPARTURES. **Main/Corp** Australian Bureau of Statistics. AT. English. mo. Australian Bureau of Statistics, PO Box 84, Canberra Australian Capital Territory 2600 Australia. **Tel** (062)52 6778. **LC** HE104. **DD** 387. Short summary of data; category of movement. For short-term visitors arriving and residents departing, intended length of stay, purpose of journey, and principal destination or country of usual residence. Overseas Arrivals and Departures.

OVERWEIGHT VEHICLES-PENALTIES & PERMITS : REPORT TO CONGRESS FROM THE SECRETARY OF TRANSPORTATION. VAT Overweight Vehicles- Penalties and Permits. Nov. 1981-. US. English. an. U S Department of Transportation, Federal Highway Administration, Superintendent of Documents, US Government Printing Office, Washington DC 20402. Vols. for 1981- distributed to depository libraries in microfiche. Overweight Vehicle Penalties and Permits.

OWEN'S COMMERCE & TRAVEL AND INTERNATIONAL REGISTER CEASED. VFOAT Owen's Commerce & Travel, Owen's Commerce and Travel and International Register. 1964-81. 0078-7167. UK. English. an. **LC** HF3872. **DD** 380.1025. Owen's African and Middle East Commerce & Travel and International Register.

OWNER OPERATOR. Began in 1969. 0475-2112. Periodical. US. English. bm. $10.00. Chilton Company, Chilton Way, Radnor PA 19089. **Tel** (215)964-4261. **Ed** Leon Witconis. **LC** HE5601. **DD** 388. adv acc. **Circ** 90,515. (ctrl). Publication for owners and operators of one-to-ten heavy duty, over-the-road trucks. Contents: new products, business management, taxes, how-to-do-it, technical, legislation and news.

PACIFIC SHIPPER. 0030-8900. Periodical. US. English. wk. $40.00. Pacific Shipper Inc, 1139 Howard, San Francisco CA 94103-3970. **Tel** (415)981-7171. **Ed** Robert Bowman. adv acc. **Circ** 7,500. Schedules for worldwide shipping and cargo moving. Editorial ads include maritime, air, and intermodal transportation for importers, exporters, traffic managers, FRT forwarder, CHB.

PACKUNG & TRANSPORT. VFOAT Packung und Transport. 0724-8490. Periodical. GW. German. mo. 72.00. Handelsblatt GMBH, Kasernenstrasse 67 Postfach 11, 4000 Dusseldorf West Germany. **Ind/Abst** Predicasts, Int. Packag. Abstr. Packung & Transport in Chemie, Kosmetik, Pharmazie.

PAPERS AND PROCEEDINGS - WESTERN TRANSPORTATION LAW SEMINAR. (PAPERS AND PROCEEDINGS). **Main/Conf** Western Transportation Law Seminar. 1978-. 0271-4396. US. English. an. Association of ICC Practitioners, 1112 ICC Building, Washington DC 20423. **LC** KF2179.A2. **DD** 343.73093, 347.30393. Transportation Law Seminar. Papers and Proceedings, 0164-1689.

PARKING PROGRESS. V. 1-14, No. 4/5 (Bulletin No. 1-154/155). 0553-3104. Periodical. US. English. mo. Applied Parking Techniques, PO Box 707, Reston VA 22070.

Transportation

PASSENGER TRANSPORT. V. 1- Apr. 30, 1943-. 0364-345X. Periodical. US. English. bm. $52.00. American Public Transit Association, 1225 Connecticut Avenue Northwest/Suite 200, Washington DC 20036. Tel (202)828-2846. Ed Belinda Reilly. LC HE4441. DD 388.305. adv acc. Circ 4,600. (ctrl). Newspaper of transit industry- keeps you in touch with capitol hill actions, ridership increases, people in industry, UMTA grants, updates on individual systems.

PENNSYLVANIA MASS TRANSIT STATISTICAL REPORT. See Statistics.

PERIODICA POLYTECHNICA. TRANSPORTATION ENGINEERING. TRANSPORT. (PERIODICA POLYTECHNICA : TRANSPORTATION ENGINEERING. TRANSPORT). VFOAT Transportation Engineering, Transport. V. 1- 1973-. 0303-7800. Periodical. HU. chiefly in English or German, some articles in Russian. qt. $11.00. Akademiai Kiado, POB 24, 1363 Budapest Hungary. Ind/Abst Fluidex, Int. Aerosp. Abstr. LC TA1001.

PHYSICAL CONDITION REPORT OF COMMERCIAL DRIVERS INVOLVED IN ACCIDENTS. Main/Corp United States. Bureau of Motor Carrier Safety. 0090-2896. US. English. Department of Transportation, Federal Highway Administration, Bureau of Motor Carrier Safety, 400 7th Street SW, Washington DC 20590. LC HE5614.2. DD 614.862. NLM W2 A U8702P.

PILOTE. Periodical. FR. French. mo. $36.36. Dargaud Editeur, 12 rue Blaise Pascal, 92200 Neuilly/Seine France.

PIPELINE SAFETY ADVISORY BULLETIN. Main/Corp United States. Materials Transportation Bureau. No. 78-4- July 1978-. US. English. mo. US Department of Transportation, Research and Special Programs Administration, Materials Transportation Bureau, 400 7th Street SW, Washington DC 20590. Advisory Bulletin - Office of Pipeline Safety Operations.

PLANNING AND RESEARCH PROGRAM. Main/Corp Iowa. Dept. of Transportation. US. English. an. Department of Transportation, 800 Lincoln Way, Ames IA 50010. LC HE213.I8. DD 353.977700875006.

PLEINS FEUX SUR LE TAXI. First issue in 1973?. 0701-1725. Periodical. CN. French (text in English). .25 Per Number. Pleins Feux sur le Taxi, 5310 Boulevard Couture, Montreal Quebec H1R Canada. DD 388.41321.

POCKET-BOOK ON TRANSPORT IN INDIA. II. English. ir. $7.20. LC HE271. DD 380.50954.

PRIVATE CARRIER. (THE PRIVATE CARRIER). V. 1- Jan. 1964-. 0032-8871. Periodical. US. English. mo. $25.00. American Trucking Association, 2200 Mill Road, Alexandria VA 22314. Tel (704)838-1995. Ed Thomas L Moore. LC HE5623.A1. DD 388.3243. adv acc. Circ 35,000. (ctrl). Information regarding legal, legislative, regulatory, technical, safety and operational developments in the field of private carriage.

PROBLEMS OF TRANSPORTATION IN JAPAN. 1- 1975-. English. ir. LC HE277. DD 380.50952.

PROBLEMY PRAWA PRZEWOZOWEGO. See Law.

PROCEEDINGS. ANNUAL MEETING - TRANSPORTATION RESEARCH FORUM. (PROCEEDINGS : ANNUAL MEETING). Main/Corp Transportation Research Forum. 0091-2468. US. English. $12.00. Grant C Vietsch, 181 East Lake Shore Drive, Chicago IL 60611. LC HE11. DD 380.505. Papers: Annual Meeting - Transportation Research Forum.

PROCEEDINGS OF THE ... INTERNATIONAL TECHNICAL CONFERENCE ON SLURRY TRANSPORTATION. Main/Conf International Technical Conference on Slurry Transportation. 1st (1976) -. Periodical. US. English. ir.

PROCEEDINGS OF THE SEMINAR SERIES ON TRANSPORTATION. Main/Corp University of Manitoba. Center for Transportation Studies. V. 4- 1970/71-. 0076-3993. CN. English. an. University of Manitoba, Center for Transportation Studies, Winnipeg Manitoba R3T 2N2 Canada. DD 380.50971. Proceedings of the Colloquium Series on Transportation, 0069-584X.

PROCEEDINGS OF THE SPECIAL COMMITTEE OF THE SENATE ON A NORTHERN GAS PIPELINE. See Petroleum and Natural Gas.

PROCEEDINGS OF THE STANDING SENATE COMMITTEE ON TRANSPORT AND COMMUNICATIONS. See Communication.

PROCEEDINGS - SEMINAR SERIES ON TRANSPORTATION. Main/Conf Seminar Series on Transportation. CN. English. an. LC HE1. DD 380.505. Proceedings.

PROCEEDINGS - SOUTHEASTERN ASSOCIATION OF STATE HIGHWAY AND TRANSPORTATION OFFICIALS. Main/Corp Southeastern Association of State Highway and Transportation Officials (U.S.). Meeting. US. English. an. Department of Highways and Transportation, 1221 East Broad Street, Richmond VA 23219.

PROCEEDINGS - SOUTHEASTERN ASSOCIATION OF STATE HIGHWAY AND TRANSPORTATION OFFICIALS (U.S.). MEETING. (PROCEEDINGS). Main/Corp Southeastern Association of State Highway and Transportation Officials (U.S.). Meeting. 0735-0805. US. English. an. Department of Highways and Transportation, 121 East Broad Street, Richmond VA 23219. LC HE208. DD 380.50975.

PROGRAMME DE RECHERCHE - INSTITUT DE RECHERCHE DES TRANSPORTS. Main/Corp Institut de Recherche des Transports. French. ir. 2 Avenue du General, Malleret-Joinville B P 28, Arcrieil 94114 France. LC HE192.5. DD 380.5072044.

PROGRESS REPORT ON TRIP ENDS GENERATION RESEARCH COUNTS. Main/Corp California. Dept. of Transportation. 0092-6159. US. English. California Department of Transportation, PO Box 3366 Rincon Annex, San Francisco CA 94119. LC HE373.U53. DD 388.31409794.

PROGRESS REPORT TO THE GOVERNOR'S HIGHWAY SAFETY OFFICE. Main/Corp University of North Carolina (System) Highway Safety Research Center. 0149-6328. Periodical. US. English. qt. University of North Carolina Press, Chapel Hill NC 27515. LC HE5614.3.N6. DD 614.86209756.

PROLONGEMENT DU METRO. (METRO EXTENSION; COMMUNIQUE). Main/Corp Montreal Urban Community. Metropolitan Transit Bureau. No. 1- June 1972-. 0315-1603. Periodical. CN. English (French with special T P and separate paging). Montreal Urban Community Metropolitan Transit Bureau, 1701 du Havre, Montreal Quebec Canada.

PROMET I VEZE. Serbo-Croatian -R. an. 130.00. Republicki Zavod Za Statistiku Sr, Hrvatske Zagreb Ilica 3 Yugoslavia. LC HE265.5.Z7.

PRZEGLAD KOMUNIKACYJNY. Vol. 1- 1962-. Periodical. PL. Polish (table of contents also in Russian, English, and French). mo. ARS Polona, Krakowskie Przedmiescie 7, 00-068 Warsaw Poland. LC HE7.

PUBLIC TRANSIT REPORT. 0148-4087. Periodical. US. English. bw. Business Publishers Inc, 951 Pershing Drive, Silver Spring MD 20910. Tel (301)587-6300. Ed Dede Ryan. A report on public transit systems throughout the US, with information from Washington (Capital Hill and the Department of Transportation) as well as local transit companies.

PUBLIC UTILITIES AND TRANSPORTATION NEWSLETTER. See Public Administration.

PUBLICATION - CENTRE DE RECHERCHE SUR LES TRANSPORTS. UNIVERSITE DE MONTREAL. (PUBLICATION). 0709-9851. Monographic Series. CN. French (English). ir. Universite de Montreal Centre de Recherche sur les Transport, Case Postale 6128 Succursale A, Montreal Quebec H3C 3J7 Canada. DD 380.50724. Dan Geofisika.

PUBLICATION INDEX - TRANSPORTATION RESEARCH BOARD. See Indexes/Abstracts.

PUBLICATION SERIES - TRANSPORT GROUP. DEPARTMENT OF CIVIL ENGINEERING. UNIVERSITY OF WATERLOO. (PUBLICATION SERIES - UNIVERSITY OF WATERLOO, DEPARTMENT OF CIVIL ENGINEERING, TRANSPORT GROUP). Main/Corp University of Waterloo. Transport Group. 0316-5922. Newspaper. CN. English. Transport Group, University of Waterloo, Waterloo Ontario N26 3G1 Canada. DD 380.5.

PUPIL TRANSPORTATION SYSTEM. ILLINOIS PUBLIC SCHOOLS. See Statistics.

PURCHASING PREFERENCE SURVEY. TRAFFIC TRANSPORTATION. See Business - Purchasing.

PYRAMID. Mar. 1978-. 0709-4272. Periodical. CN. English. 25.00. Alberta Trucking Association, PO Box 5520 Station A, Calgary Alberta T2H 1X9 Canada. Tel (403)253-8401. Ed Jim Bradbury. DD 388.324097123. adv acc. Circ 1,500. (ctrl). Index to trucking companies and the points they serve in Alberta and across Canada. Reference text for provincial regulations carries information relating to carriage of hazardous materials. Trucking Bulletin, 0704-6502.

QUARTERLY BULLETIN. Main/Corp Co-Ord. Transport Industries Research Council of Australia. Periodical. English. ir. $0.80. Transport Industries Research Council of Australia, 14 Kennington Road, Camp Hill Australia. LC HE192.5. DD 380.5072.

QUEENSLAND TRANSPORT. Main/Corp Australian Bureau of Statistics. Queensland Office. 1974/75-. English. an. Australian Bureau of Statistics, Ground Floor Statistics House, 345 Ann Street, Brisbane Queensland 4000 Australia. Tel (07)222 6351. LC HE104. DD 380.509943. Shipping: cargo loaded and discharged at each port, destinations and origins of cargo loaded and discharged; land transport: government railway operations, motor vehicles registed and revenue collected, etc.

RAIL, BUS AND AIR TRANSPORT. See Business - Commerce.

RAPPORT ANNUEL - CANADIAN NATIONAL. Main/Corp Canadian National. CN. French. an. Free. Corporate Communications Canadian National, PO Box 8100, Montreal Quebec H3C 3N4 Canada. Tel (514)877-4758. LC HE2801. DD 385.06571. Circ 10,000. (ctrl). Covers financial review and outlook for this integrated transport and communications company, operating throughout Canada and with international links. Canadian National Railways, Annual Report.

RAPPORT ANNUEL - COMMISSION DES TRANSPORTS DU QUEBEC. Main/Corp Quebec (Province). Commission des Transports. 1977/78-. 0702-0996. CN. French. an. Editeur Officiel du Quebec, 1283 Boul Charest Quest, Quebec Province of Quebec G1N 2C9 Canada. LC HE30.Q4. DD 354.71400875006. Rapports des Activites de la Commission des Transports du Quebec, 0318-5303.

RASPISANIE DVIZHENIIA RECHNYKH PASSAZHIRSKIKH SUDOV OSNOVNYKH TRANSPORTNYKH LINII NA NAVIGATSIIU. UR. Russian. 0.25. Transport, Basmannyi Tup 6A, Moskva Russia. LC HE675.

RECENT TRANSPORTATION LITERATURE FOR PLANNING AND ENGINEERING LIBRARIANS. See Bibliographies.

RECHERCHE EN MATIERE D'ECONOMIE DES TRANSPORTS. See Economics.

RECREATIONAL VEHICLE BLUE BOOK. 0733-4745. US. English. sa. National Market Reports Inc, 300 West Adams Street, Chicago IL 60606. Tel (312)726-2802. LC TL298. DD 629.226029473.

REFERATIVNYI ZHURNAL : ORGANIZATSIIA I BEZOPASNOST DOROZHNOGO DVIZHENIIA. VFOAT Organizatsiia i Bezopasnost Dorozhnogo Divzheniia. Began in 1974. UR. Russian. mo. 0.26. Liuberttsy-10 Moskovskoi Obl Oktiabrskii Prospekt D 403, Moskva 140010 Russia 403. LC HE5601.

Transportation

REFERATIVNYI ZHURNAL : PROMYSHLENNYI TRANSPORT. VFOAT Promyshlennyi Transport. Jan. 1962-. Periodical. UR. Russian (tables of contents also in English). mo. Victor Kamkin Inc (01520), 12224 Parklawn Drive, Rockville MD 20852. **Tel** (301)881-5973. *Referativnyi Zhurnal: Transport.*

REFLET. (REFLET : BULLETIN DE LA COMMISSION DE TRANSPORT DE LA RIVE SUD DE MONTREAL). **Main/Corp** Commission de Transport de la Rive sud de Montreal. V. 1, No. 1 (June 1978)-. 0227-4558. Periodical. CN. French. bm. Free to Employees. Reflet CTRSM, Bureau 100 1000 rue de Serigny, Longueuil Quebec J4K 5B1 Canada. **DD** 388.406571437.

REFRIGERATED TRANSPORTER. 0034-3129. Periodical. US. English. mo. $25.00. Tunnell Publications, 1602 Harold Street, Houston TX 77006. **Tel** (713)523-8124. Ed Gary Macklin. bk rev. adv acc. **Circ** 15,000. (ctrl). Equipment specifications, maintenance of equipment, operating refrigerated truck fleets.

REGULATORY REPORTER (OTTAWA, ONT.). *See* Communication.

RELATORIO DAS ATIVIDADES - EMPRESA BRASILEIRA DE PLANEJAMENTO DE TRANSPORTES. **Main/Corp** Empresa Brasileira de Planejamento de Transportes. Portuguese. ir. Setor de Autarquias Sul Quadra, 2 Bloco G 70.000, Brasilia Brazil. **LC** HE233. **DD** 354.8100875.

RELATORIO DE ATIVIDADES - PARAIBA (BRAZIL : STATE)-SERCRETARIA DOS TRANSPORTES E OBRAS. **Main/Corp** Paraiba (Brazil : State). Secretaria dos Transportes e Obras. Portuguese. ir. **LC** HE233.Z7. **DD** 354.8133087506.

RELATORIO SETORIAL, GOVERNO DO ESTADO DE SAO PAULO. **Main/Corp** Sao Paulo, Brazil (State). Secretaria dos Transportes. BL. Portuguese. ir. **LC** HE233.Z7.

REPORT AND STATEMENT OF ACCOUNTS FOR THE YEAR ENDED 30TH JUNE - METROPOLITAN (PERTH) PASSENGER TRANSPORT TRUST. **Main/Corp** Metropolitan (Perty) Passenger Transport Trust. **VFOAT** Annual Report. English. an. Perth Metropolitan Passenger Transport Trust, 10 Adelaide Terrace, Perth Western Australia. **LC** HE311.A852. **DD** 352.9184099411.

REPORT - MINISTER OF TRANSPORTATION AND HIGHWAYS. (REPORT FOR THE FISCAL YEAR . . .). **Main/Corp** British Columbia. Ministry of Transportation and Highways. **VFOAT** Annual Report. **VAT** Annual Report - Ministry of Transportation, Communications and Highways (Victoria. 1980). 1979/80-. 0706-1897. CN. English. an. Province of British Columbia, 1450 Government Street, Information Services, Victoria British Columbia V8W 3E7 Canada. **LC** HE215.Z7. **DD** 354.71106875006. *Report for the Fiscal Year . . .*, 0708-7691.

REPORT NO. D.O.T.-T.S.T. (REPORT NO. DOT-TST). **Main/Corp** United States. Office of Noise Abatement. 0092-9646. US. English. US Department of Transportation, Office of Noise Abatement, Washington DC 20590. **LC** TD891. **DD** 363.6.

REPORT NO. T.E.S. *See* Sanitation, Environmental Technology.

REPORT OF OPERATIONS : HIGHWAYS, BUSES, AERONAUTICS, RAILROADS. **Main/Corp** New Jersey. Dept. of Transportation. US. English. Department of Transportation, 1035 Parkway Avenue, Trenton NJ 08625. **LC** HE28.N5. **DD** 380.509749.

REPORT OF THE MINISTRY OF TRANSPORT (NEW ZEALAND). **Main/Corp** New Zealand. Ministry of Transport. English. ir. **LC** HE297.5.A1. **DD** 354.9310087.

REPORT OF THE ROAD TRANSPORT DEPARTMENT. **Main/Corp** Sierra Leone. Road Transport Dept. 1947-. SL. English. ir. Government Printing Department, Road Transport Department, Freetown Sierre Leone Africa. **LC** HE5704.S5. **DD** 388.3.

A REPORT ON TRANSPORTATION IN VERMONT. **Main/Corp** Vermont. Agency of Transportation. **VFOAT** Biennial Report of the Vermont Agency of Transportation. 2nd- 1976/78-. US. English. be. Vermont Agency of Transportation, Montpelier VT 05602. **LC** HE28.V5. **DD** 353.974300875005. *Report on Transportation in Vermont.*

REPORT TO CONGRESS CONCERNING THE DEMONSTRATION OF FARE-FREE MASS TRANSPORTATION. **Main/Corp** United States. Urban Mass Transportation Administration. 1975-. 0360-750X. US. English. an. US Department of Transportaton, Federal Highway Administration, Washington DC 20590. **LC** HE17. **DD** 388.4.

REPORT TO THE CONGRESS OF THE UNITED STATES ON URBAN TRANSPORTATION POLICIES & ACTIVITIES. **Main/Corp** United States. Dept. of Transportation. **VFOAT** Urban Transportation Policies & Activities. 0098-0617. US. English. US Department of Transportation, Federal Highway Administration, Washington DC 20590. **LC** HE308. **DD** 388.40973.

A REPORT TO THE PRESIDENT ON THE NATIONAL CARGO SECURITY PROGRAM CEASED. **Main/Corp** United States. Dept. of Transportation. Began with 1975/76. Ceased with 1980. 0145-174X. US. English. an. US Department of Transportation, 400 7th Street SW, Washington DC 20590. **LC** HV8290. **DD** 363.233. Vol. for 1978 distributed to depository libraries in microfiche.

A REPORT TO THE PRESIDENT ON THE NATIONAL CARGO SECURITY PROGRAM. **Main/Corp** United States. Dept. of Transportation. 1- 1976-. Periodical. US. English. an.

REPORT, WASHINGTON STATE TRANSPORTATION PLAN UPDATE. **VFOAT** Washington State Transportation Plan Update. 1983-1995-. US. English. be. State of Washington, Department of Transportation, Highway Administration Building, Olympia WA 98504. **LC** HE213.W2. **DD** 380.5068.

RESEARCH IN TRANSPORTATION ECONOMICS. *See* Economics.

RESEARCH REPORT - AUSTRALIAN ROAD RESEARCH BOARD. **Main/Corp** Australian Road Research Board. No. 1-. AT. English. ir. 10.00 Domestic. Australian Road Research Board, PO Box 156 Bag 4, Nunawading Vermont South Victoria 313 Australia. **Tel** (03)235-1555. **Circ** 500. Results of research work performed or sponsored by the Australian Road Research Board.

RESEARCH REPORT - CENTER FOR TRANSPORTATION STUDIES. UNIVERSITY OF MANITOBA. (RESEARCH REPORT - UNIVERSITY OF MANITOBA, CENTRE FOR TRANSPORTATION STUDIES). **Main/Corp** University of Manitoba. Centre for Transportation Studies. 0316-7984. Monographic Series. CN. English. ir. University of Manitoba, Center for Transportation Studies, Winnipeg Manitoba R3T 2N2 Canada. **DD** 380.5. *Research Progress Report*, 0316-7976.

RESEARCH REPORT - UNIVERSITY OF TORONTO, YORK UNIVERSITY. JOINT PROGRAM IN TRANSPORTATION. (RESEARCH REPORT - UNIVERSITY OF TORONTO - YORK UNIVERSITY JOINT PROGRAM IN TRANSPORTATION). **Main/Corp** Joint Program in Transportation. No. 1- 1972-. 0316-9456. Monographic Series. CN. English. Centre for Urban & Communite Studies, 150 St George Street, University of Toronto, Toronto Ontario M5R 2E9 Canada. **DD** 380.5.

REVISTA BRASILEIRA DE TRANSPORTES. No. 1- July/Sept. 1966-. Periodical. BL. Portuguese. ir. Grupo Executivo de Integracao da Politica de Transportes, R Alcindo Guanabara, 24 S/814 GB ZC-06, Rio de Janeiro Brazil. **LC** HE7. **DD** 380.50981.

REVISTA TRANSPORTURILOR SI TELECOMUNICATIILOR. Year 1-. Periodical. RM. Romanian (abstracts in English, French, German, and Russian). mo. Ilexim Press Department, PO Box 1-136-1-137, Bucharest Romania. **Ind/Abst** Coal Abstr., Int. Aerosp. Abstr. **LC** TA1001.

REVUE. **Main/Corp** International Union of Public Transport. 9091- Mar. 1952-. Periodical. French (English, German). ir. **LC** HE4201.

REVUE DE L'UITP. **VFOAT** UITP Revie. Periodical. French (English, German). qt. 2000. International Union of Public Transport, Avenur de Uruguay 19, B-1050 Brussels Belgium. **Tel** (02)673 33 25. bk rev. adv acc. **Circ** 2,000. General information about urban and regional public transportation in the world. *Revue*, 0539-1121.

RIVISTA INTERNAZIONALE DI ECONOMIA DEI TRASPORTI. *See* Economics.

RIVON LI-STATISTIKAH SHEL TAHBURAH. *See* Statistics.

ROAD MOTOR VEHICLES. FUEL SALES. (ROAD MOTOR VEHICLES—FUEL SALES). **VFOAT** Vehicules Automobiles-Ventes de Carburants. 1975-. 0703-654X. CN. English (French in parallel columns). an. Receiver General for Canada, Statistics Canada Publications, Ottawa Ontario K1A 0T6 Canada. **Tel** (613)992-3151. **LC** HD9574.C2. **DD** 381.45665538270971021. *Motor Vehicle.*

ROADSIDE VEHICLE INSPECTION REPORT. *See* Public Administration.

ROCZNIK STATYSTYCZNY TRANSPORTU. 1945/66-. PL. Polish. ir. 77.00. Gowny Urzad Statystyczny, 00068 Warsaw Poland. **LC** HE255.T. **DD** 380.509438.

ROUTES ET TRANSPORTS. No.14- May 1975-. 0319-3780. CN. French. qt. $11.61. Association Quebecoise du Tran Routes, 6290 Perinault/#103, Montreal Quebec H4K 1K5 Canada. **Tel** (514)331-5810. Ed Guy Pare. **Ind/Abst** Point Repere. **DD** 625.709714. bk rev. adv acc. **Circ** 2,000. (ctrl). All matters related to the technology of transportation. *Routes du Quebec*, 0318-6245.

ROUTIER. (LE ROUTIER). V. 1- Nov. 1979-. 0225-4638. Periodical. CN. French. mo. $3.00 Domestic, $23.00 Foreign. Publications Expresses M F Inc, 465 rue Deslauriers, Ville Sainte-Laurent Quebec H1W 1B2 Canada. **DD** 388.32409714.

RTAC FORUM. **VFOAT** Tribune de l'ARTC. Vol. 1, No. 1 (April 1977)-. Periodical. CN. English (French). qt. $55.71. Roads & Transportation Association of Canada, 1765 St Laurent Boulevard, Ottawa Ontario K1G 3V4 Canada. **Tel** (613)521-4052. Ed D A Woods. **Circ** 900. Refereed quarterly journal carrying technical and policy papers on all aspects of the transport sector.

RUNZHEIMER REPORTS ON TRANSPORTATION. 0730-8655. Periodical. US. English. mo. $195.00. Runzheimer International, 555 Skokie Boulevard/Suite 245, Northbrook IL 60062. **Tel** (312)291-9011. Ed Adlore Chaudier. Covers all aspects of corporate fleet management.

RUSSELL'S OFFICIAL NATIONAL MOTOR COACH GUIDE. (RUSSELL'S OFFICIAL NATIONAL MOTOR COACH GUIDE FOR UNITED STATES, CANADA, MEXICO, CENTRAL AMERICA). Began with V. 9 (Oct. 1936) issue. 0036-0171. Periodical. US. English. mo. $63.20 Domestic, $82.40 Foreign. Russells Guides Inc, 834 3rd Avenue SE, PO Box 278, Cedar Rapids IA 52406. **Tel** (319)364-6138. Ed Tom Whitters. **LC** HE5623.A1. **DD** 388.3221097. adv acc. **Circ** 9,000. Bus schedules throughout the US and Canada. *Russell's National Motor Coach Guide.*

RV TRADE DIGEST. **VAT** Recreational Vehicle Trade Digest. Began in 1981?. 0745-0389. Periodical. US. English. mo. $24.00. Continental Publishing Company, PO Box 25583, Chicago IL 60625. **Tel** (312)539-1936.

RV WORLD. *See* Recreation, Leisure.

RVBUSINESS. **VFOAT** R.V. Business, RV Business. **VAT** Recreational Vehicle Business. Vol. 33, No. 5 (Aug. 1982)-. 0744-9569. Periodical. US. English. mo. $12.00. T L Enterprises Inc, 29901 Agoura Road, Agoura CA 91301. **Ind/Abst** Trade Ind. Index. **LC** TL298. **DD** 338.47629226. *Recreational Vehicle Dealer*, 0886-0041.

R.V.R. RECREATIONAL VEHICLE RETAILER CEASED. (RECREATIONAL VEHICLE RETAILER). **VFOAT** RVR. 0090-3841. Periodical. US. English. mo. $8.00. 23945 Craftsman Road, Calabasas CA 91302. **LC** HD9710.A1. **DD** 381.456292260973.

RVS, THE FAMILY CAMPING VEHICLES. **VFOAT** R.V.S, The Family Camping Vehicles. -1981. 0734-7715. US. English. an. Recreational Vehicle Industry Association, PO Box 2999, Reston VA 22090-0999. **Tel** (703)620-6003. **LC** HD9710.38.U6. **DD** 381.456292260973. Historical review and update of production and shipment statistics of RV manufacturing. Provides data on market percentages by size and type of vehicles. Wholesale and retail volume from 1976. *Facts and Trends (Chantilly, Va.).*

Transportation

SAILING DIRECTIONS (ENROUTE) FOR NEWFOUNDLAND, LABRADOR AND HUDSON BAY. Main/Corp Defense Mapping Agency Hydrographic Center. US. English. ir. Receiver General for Canada, Supply & Services Canada, Ottawa Ontario K1A 0S9 Canada.

SAILING DIRECTIONS (ENROUTE) FOR NOVA SCOTIA, AND THE ST. LAWRENCE. Main/Corp Defense Mapping Agency. Hydrographic Center. US. English. ir. Receiver General for Canada, Supply & Services Canada, Ottawa Ontario K1A 0S9 Canada. Tel (819)997-256.

SAMFERDSEL TRANSPORT. V. 1-. 0036-3774. Periodical. Norwegian. ir. LC HE363.N6. *Samferdsel Norsk Vegtidsskrift.*

SANFORD EVANS GOLD BOOK OF SNOWMOBILE DATA AND USED PRICES. VFOAT Gold Book Official Snowmobile Guide. 1972/73-. 0318-9422. Periodical. CN. English. an. 7.95. Sanford Evans Communications Ltd, Box 6900, 1077 St James Street, Winnipeg Manitoba R3C 3B1 Canada. Tel (204)775-0201. Ed G B Henry. DD 338.4362922. An annual publication with registration data and realistic retail values for new and used snowmobiles.

SANGYO SHARYO. See Engineering.

SASKATCHEWAN TRUCKING. VFOAT Trucking. Vol. 1, No. 1 (Winter 1980/81)-. 0229-9666. Periodical. CN. English. qt. 15.00. Naylor Communications Ltd, 100 Sutherland Avenue, Winnipeg Manitoba R2W 3C7 Canada. Tel (204)947-0222. Ed Will Oliver. DD 388.324097124. adv acc. Circ 3,000. (ctrl). A trucking periodical, produced for the Saskatchewan Trucking Association. General stories on trucking, company profiles, new products, etc. *Saskatchewan Shippers Directory (1980)*, 0227-5902.

SBTD. SHIP-BY-TRUCK DIRECTORY. See Yearbooks, Almanacs, Directories.

SCHEDULES FOR THE FINANCIAL REPORT, FISCAL YEAR ENDED JUNE 30 . . . . Main/Corp Connecticut. Dept. of Transportation. 1982-. US. English. an. LC HE213.C6. DD 354.74600875. *Financial Report*, 0197-3568.

SCHOOL BUS FLEET. 0036-6501. Periodical. US. English. bm. $12.00. Bobit Publishing Company, 2500 Artesia Boulevard, Redondo Beach CA 90278. Tel (312)724-8440. *School Bus Transportation.*

SCHOOL BUS PURCHASES. See Education (General) - School Organization and Administration.

SCHOOL TRANSPORTATION. Vol. 1, No. 1 (Dec. 11, 1980)-. 0273-0936. Periodical. US. English. ir. $86.00. School Transportation Director, 421 National Press Building NW, Washington DC 20045. Tel (202)829-7244. Ed Roseann Schwaderes. News of federal, state and local developments which can affect local school transportation safety, funding, or management practices.

SCHWEIZERISCHE VERKEHRSSTATISTIK. See Statistics.

SCHWEIZERISCHE ZEITSCHRIFT FUR VERKEHRSWIRTSCHAFT. VFOAT Revue Suisse d'Economie des Transports. V. 32-. 0251-0987. Periodical. SZ. French or German. qt. Orell Fuessli Zeitschriften, Dietzingerstrasse 3, 8036 Zurich Switzerland. Ind/Abst Foreign Lang. Index, Public Aff. Inf. Serv. Bull. LC HE5. DD 380.509494. *Schweizerisches Archiv fur Verkehrswissenschaft und Verkehrspolitik.*

SELECTED LIST OF RECENT ACQUISITIONS OF THE TRANSPORTATION LIBRARY. See Bibliographies.

SELECTED PAPERS FROM THE TRANSPORTATION SEMINAR SERIES. VFOAT Transportation Seminar Series. 0229-8627. Periodical. CN. English. ir. Free. Department of Civil Engineering, University of New Brunswick, Fredericton New Brunswick E3B 5A3 Canada. DD 380.50971. (ctrl).

SEMIANNUAL REPORT TO THE CONGRESS - UNITED STATES. DEPT. OF TRANSPORTATION. OFFICE OF INSPECTOR GENERAL. (SEMIANNUAL REPORT TO THE CONGRESS). Main/Corp United States. Dept. of Transportation. Office of Inspector General. VFOAT Semi-Annual Report to the Congress. Apr. 1, 1981-Sept. 30, 1981-. 8755-4836. US. English. sa. US Department of Transportation, Office of Inspector General, Washington DC 20590. LC HE206.3. DD 353.8606. *Semiannual Report*, 8755-4488.

SERVICE AND METHODS DEMONSTRATION PROGRAM. ANNUAL REPORT, EXECUTIVE SUMMARY. (SERVICE AND METHODS DEMONSTRATION PROGRAM ANNUAL REPORT. EXECUTIVE SUMMARY). 0196-6405. US. English. an. National Technical Information Service, 5285 Port Royal Road, Springfield VA 22161. LC HE308. DD 388.40973.

SERVICE BULLETIN. VFOAT Chek-Chart Service Bulletin. Vol. 1 (1929)-. 0731-471X. Periodical. US. English. mo. $14.95. Gousha Chek-Chart, 2001 The Alameda, San Jose CA 95150. Tel (408)296-1060. Ed Jo Phelps. Circ 20,000. (ctrl). Automotive repair and maintenance procedures and news. Car manufacturers latest tips and bulletins. Tricks and secrets of the auto repair trade.

THE SHOCK AND VIBRATION BULLETIN. See Engineering - Mechanical Engineering & Machinery.

SHOCK AND VIBRATION MONOGRAPH SERIES. See Engineering - Mechanical Engineering & Machinery.

SIGNAL. (THE SIGNAL). Signal No. 1 (Feb. 1977)-. 0228-3824. Periodical. CN. English. ir. Department of Education, 693 Taylor Avenue, Winnipeg Manitoba Canada. DD 371.872097127. *Transportation Bulletin* (Manitoba. Dept. of Education).

S.I.T.R.A.M. RESULTATS GENERAUX, TRAFIC INTERIEUR ET INTERNATIONAL. VFOAT Sitram. FR. French. ir. 20.00. 55 rue Brillat-Savarin, 75658 Paris Cedex 13 France. LC HE199.F8. DD 380.5240944.

S.I.T.R.A.M. : RESULTATS GENERAUX, TRAFIC INTERNATIONAL. Main/Corp France. Departement des Statistiques des Transports. VFOAT Systeme d'Information sur les Transports de Marchandises: Resultats Generaux, Trafic International. French. ir. 21 rue Mathurin-Reginer, Paris France 75732. LC HE199.F8. DD 380.5240944.

SNOW-GOER. (SNOW-GOER : THE MAGAZINE OF CANADIAN SNOWMOBILING). Vol. 1, No. 1 (Winter 1981)-. 0711-6454. Periodical. CN. English. ir. $1.50 Each Number. Snow-Goer, c/o 2nd Floor, 100 Steelcase Road East, Markham Ontario L3R 1E Canada. DD 796.940971.

SNOWMOBILE CANADA. VFOAT Recreational Vehicle Life. VAT Recreational Vehicle Life. Snowmobile Canada. V. 8, No. 1- Sept./Oct. 1976-. 0705-3789. Periodical. CN. English. ir. $6.97. CRV Publishing Company Ltd, 3414 Park Avenue, Montreal Quebec H2X 2H5 Canada. Tel (514)282-0191. Ed Reg Fife. DD 796.9. bk rev. adv acc. Circ 100,000. *0319-101X.*

SNOWMOBILE SPORTS. See Recreation, Leisure - Sports.

SNOWMOBILE WEST. 1974. 0164-6540. Periodical. US. English. ir. $19.00. Harris Publishing Inc, PO Box 981, Idaho Falls ID 83401. Tel (208)522-5187. Ed Steve Jones. adv acc. Circ 125,000. (ctrl). Articles are written on studies made with all makes and models of snowmobiles and snowmobile equipment plus anything of interest to snowmobilers.

SOUTH DAKOTA MOTOR CARRIER. 0038-3333. Periodical. US. English. mo. South Dakota Motor Carriers Association, 310 First Avenue, Rock Rapids IA 51246.

SPECIAL REPORT - TRANSPORTATION RESEARCH BOARD, NATIONAL RESEARCH COUNCIL. Main/Corp National Research Council (U.S.). Transportation Research Board. 144-. 0360-859X. Monographic Series. US. English. ir. Transportation Research Board, 2101 Constitution Avenue NW, Washington DC 20418. Ind/Abst Eng. Index Annu., Eng. Index Mon., Eng. Index Bioeng. Abstr., Eng. Index Energy Abstr., Chem. Abstr., GeoRef, Bibliogr. Index Geol., Eng. Index. LC UNC. CODEN SRTBDC. *Special Report.*

SPECIALIZED TRANSPORTATION PLANNING AND PRACTICE. Vol. 1, No. 1 (Mar. 1982)-. 0276-8631. Periodical. US. English. ir. $146.00. Gordon & Breach, PO Box 197, London WC2e 9PX England. Ed William G Bell. LC HV1553. DD 362.40483. CODEN STPPDE. bk rev. adv acc. Also issued in microfilm and microfiche.

DER STADTVERKEHR. Began with Mar. 1956 issue. Periodical. GW. German. mo. 56.00. Verlag Werner Stock, Postfach 14 09 45/Koessener Strasse 11, 4800 Bielefeld 14 West Germany. Tel 521-441644. LC TA1001. Public transportation in the city.

STATISTICAL PROFILE - IOWA DEPARTMENT OF TRANSPORTATION. See Statistics.

STATISTICS OF MOTOR CARRIERS CLASS I, II, III, & IV. See Statistics.

STATISTIEK VAN HET INTERNATIONAAL GOEDERENVERVOER. See Statistics.

STATISTIQUES DES TRANSPORTS. See Statistics.

STATISTISKA MEDDELANDEN. SERIE T, TRANSPORT OCH KOMMUNIKATIONER. See Statistics.

STATISTISKA MEDDELANDEN. T. See Statistics.

STATISTISKE EFTERRETNINGER. SAMFRDSEL OG TURISME. VFOAT Samfrdsel Og Turisme. 0108-5484. Monographic Series. German. ir. 67.00. Danmarks Statistik, Sejrgade 11, 2100 Kbenhavn Denmark. LC HE257. *Statistiske Efterretninger.*

THE STATUS OF OHIO'S CAPITAL AND OPERATING NEEDS FOR PUBLIC TRANSPORTATION. Main/Corp Ohio. Dept. of Transportation. US. English. an. Ohio Department of Transportation, 25 South Front Street, PO Box 899, Columbus OH 43216. LC HE309.O36. DD 388.4042.

STEERING WHEEL. 0039-1298. Periodical. US. English. mo. $10.50. Texas Motor Transportation Association, PO Box 1669, Austin TX 78767. Tel (512)478-2541. Ed Deborah A Swift. adv acc. Circ 3,500. (ctrl). News on truck and bus equipment, safety, public relations, related economic and government issues, personnel management and news about association activities.

SUBURBAN TRANSPORTATION SERVICE GUIDE. V. 1- 1975-. 0360-5353. US. English. $10.00. Russell's Guides Inc, 817 2nd Avenue SE, Cedar Rapids IA 52406. LC HE9.U5. DD 388.402573.

SUMMARY OF ACTIVITIES, OFFICE OF RESEARCH. Main/Corp Connecticut. Dept. of Transportation. Office of Research. VFOAT Summary of Activities. Began with 1976/77 issue. US. English. an. Connecticut Department of Transportation, Wolcott Hill Road, PO Drawer A, Wethersfield CT 06109. LC HE213.C6. DD 380.50720746.

SUMMARY OF ACTIVITIES - UNITED STATES. CONGRESS. HOUSE. COMMITTEE ON PUBLIC WORKS AND TRANSPORTATION. (SUMMARY OF ACTIVITIES). Main/Corp United States. Congress. House. Committee on Public works and Transportation. 0740-9435. US. English. be. LC KF31.8. DD 344.7306, 347.3046.

SUMMARY OF AWARDS, ... PROGRAM OF UNIVERSITY RESEARCH. VFOAT University Research Summary of Awards. Began with 1976/77. US. English. an. US Department of Transportation, Research and Special Programs Administration, Transportation Programs Bureau, Office of University Research, Washington DC 20590. LC HE192.5. DD 380.5072073. *Summary of Awards & Published Reports*, 0147-4340.

SUMMARY OF NATIONAL TRANSPORTATION STATISTICS. See Statistics.

SUMMARY OF UMTA'S TRANSIT ASSISTANCE PROGRAM. Main/Corp United States. Urban Mass Transportation Administration., Office of Transit Assistance. VFOAT Summary of U.M.T.A.'S Transit Assistance Program. VAT Summary of Urban Mass Transportation Administration's Transit Assistance Program. 0277-5859. US. English. US Department of Transportation, Urban Mass Transportation, Administration Office of Tranist Assistance, Washington DC 20590. LC HE308. DD 338.4042.

SURVEY OF STATE INVOLVEMENT IN PUBLIC TRANSPORTATON. (SURVEY OF STATE INVOLVEMENT IN PUBLIC TRANSPORTATION : A REPORT OF THE STANDING COMMITTEE ON PUBLIC TRANSPORTATION). Began with 1980 issue. 0743-4499. US. English. an. American Association of State Highway and Transportation, Officials 444 North Capitol Street NW/Suite 225, Washington DC 20001. **LC** HE4401. **DD** 388.4042.

SYNTHESIS OF HIGHWAY PRACTICE. **Main/Corp** National Cooperative Highway Research Program. 0547-5570. US. English. ir. Transportation Research Board, 2101 Constitution Avenue NW, Washington DC 20418. **Ind/Abst** Eng. Index Annu., Eng. Index Mon., Eng. Index Bioeng. Abstr., Eng. Index Energy Abstr., Eng. Index, GeoRef. **CODEN** NCHSBB.

TAMPA PORT HANDBOOK. 0163-6790. US. English. an. $5.00. Howard Publication Inc, PO Box 4728, Jacksonville FL 32201. **Tel** (904)355-2601. **Ed** Hayes H Howard. **LC** HE554.T3. **DD** 387.10975965. adv acc. **Circ** 6,000. Directory of marine, air, rail and motor transportation and related industries.

TARHEEL WHEELS. 0039-968X. Periodical. US. English. bm. Tarheel Wheels, PO Box 2977, Raleigh NC 27602.

THIS BUSINESS OF TRUCKING. 0229-0065. Periodical. CN. English. bm. Free. Saskatchewan Trucking Association, 1335 Wallace Street, Regina Saskatchewan S4N 3Z5 Canada. **DD** 388.324097124. (ctrl).

THIS IS SAR & H : ROAD TRANSPORT HANDBOOK. **Main/Corp** South African Railways and Harbours. SA. English. ir. Thomson Publications, PO Box 8308, Johannesburg 2000 South Africa. **LC** HE5704.4. **DD** 388.320968.

THOMAS COOK CONTINENTAL TIMETABLE. *See* Travel.

THOMAS COOK OVERSEAS TIMETABLE. *See* Travel.

TIJDSCHRIFT VOOR VERVOERSWETENSCHAP. Began in 1965. 0040-7623. Periodical. NE. Dutch. qt. 110.-. Ned Vervoerwetenschappelijk Institute, Polakweg 13, 2288 GG Rijswijk Netherlands. **Tel** 70-993341. **Ind/Abst** Excerpta Med., Ship Abstr. **LC** HE7. bk rev. adv acc. **Circ** 500. A multidisciplinary and multimodel journal covering all facets of transport. Provides a forum for the practising researcher and the decisionmaker at political and business levels.

TIME-SENSITIVE DELIVERY GUIDE. **VFOAT** TSDG. Issue No. 1 (Fall 1981)-. 0731-0722. US. English. ir. $119.00. Time Sensitive Delivery Guide Inc, PO Box 720455, Atlanta GA 30328. **Tel** (404)955-3000. **LC** HE5895. **DD** 380.52.

TODAY'S TRANSPORT INTERNATIONAL. 0040-859X. Periodical. US. English. bm. $30.00. Lineal Publishing Company, 23 Leroy Avenue, Darien CT 06820. **Tel** (203)655-7676. **Ed** George Loinaz. **LC** HF5415.6. **DD** 658.7805. bk rev. adv acc. **Circ** 16,000. (ctrl). Publication for fleet owners and management including trucking, materials handling bus and taxi fleets in Mexico, Centraland South America.

TOXIC MATERIALS TRANSPORT. V. 1- 1980-. 0275-3766. Periodical. US. English. bw. Business Publishers Inc, 951 Pershing Drive, Silver Spring MD 20910. **Tel** (301)587-6300. **Ed** Andrew Stephens. Coverage of both federal and local issues and legislation regulation of carriers. Focus also on accident response, routing, requirements technological developments, compliance efforts and costs.

TR NEWS. **VFOAT** T.R. News. No. 104 (Jan.-Feb. 1983)-. 0738-6826. Periodical. US. English. bm. $25.00. Transportation Research Board, 2101 Constitution Avenue, Washington DC 20418. **Tel** (202)334-3218. **LC** TE1. **DD** 380.5072073. **Circ** 8,000. Discussions of the activities and programs of the Board, government, and industry. Features articles on timely subjects, abstracts of current transportation literature, and announcements of TRB publications and meetings. *Transportation Research News, 0095-2656.*

TRACTION YEARBOOK. *See* Yearbooks, Almanacs, Directories.

TRAFFIC ENGINEERING & CONTROL. V. 2- 1960-. 0041-0683. Periodical. UK. English. ir. Printerhall Publishing Ltd, 25 Crown Street Kettering, Northants NN16 8QU England. **Tel** Kettering 517320. **Ed** Keith Lumley. **Ind/Abst** Eng. Index Mon., Eng. Index Bioeng. Abstr., Eng. Index Energy Abstr., Excerpta Med., Energy Inf. Abstr., Environ. Abstr., Comput. Control Abstr., Electr. Electron. Abstr., Sci. Abstr. Sect. A. Phys. Abstr., Eng. Index Mon., Eng. Index Annu., Phys. Abstr., Comput. Abstr., Eng. Index. **LC** HE331. **DD** 388.3105. **CODEN** TENCA4. bk rev. adv acc. **Circ** 2,500. (ctrl). Road Safety.

TRAFFIC MANAGEMENT. V. 1- Jan. 1962-. 0041-0691. Periodical. US. English. mo. $45.00. Cahners Publishing, 270 St Paul Street, Denver CO 80206. **Tel** (617)964-3030. **Ed** Francis J Quinn. **Ind/Abst** Manage. Contents, ABI/Inform, Comput. Control Abstr., Electr. Electron. Abstr., Sci. Abstr. Sect. A. Phys. Abstr., Bus. Period. Index. **LC** HE1. **CODEN** TRMADJ. adv acc. **Circ** 70,000. (ctrl). News and features on transportation, physical distribution systems and management.

TRAFFIC TOPICS. (TRAFFIC TOPICS : CURRENT NEWS ON TRANSPORTATION). **VFOAT** Current News on Transportation. Vol. 1, No. 1-. 0735-7613. Periodical. US. English. qt. $30.00. National Retail Merchants Association, 100 West 31st Street, New York NY 10001. **Tel** (212)244-8780. **Ed** Beatrice Cohen. **DD** 380. bk rev. (ctrl). Covers regulatory matters pertaining to transportation and responsibilities of traffic managers such as transportation, cost routing, modes of transportation, loss and damage claims.

THE TRAFFIC WORLD. Vol. 11, No. 1 (Jan. 4, 1913)-. 0041-073X. Periodical. US. English. wk. $76.00. Traffic Service Corporation, 1435 G Street/Suite 815 Washington DC 20005. **Tel** (202)626-4500. **Ed** Carlo Salzano. bk rev. adv acc. **Circ** 15,000. News magazine of transportation and distribution management. *Traffic World and Traffic Bulletin, Federal Trade Reporter.*

TRAFIC ROUTIER (MONTREAL, QUEBEC). (TRAFIC ROUTIER). V. 1, No. 1, (April 1981)-. 0229-6497. Periodical. CN. French. ir. $2,50 Each Number. Publications Amylitho Inc, 4270 rue Papineau, Montreal Quebec H2H 1S9 Canada. **DD** 388.32409714.

TRAILER/BODY BUILDERS. **VFOAT** Trailer Body Builders. 1953. 0041-0772. Periodical. US. English. mo. Trailer Body Builders, 1602 Harold Street, Houston TX 77006. **Tel** (713)523-8124. **Ed** Paul Shenck. bk rev. adv acc. **Circ** 12,000. (ctrl). For manufacturers and distrubutors of truck trailers, truck bodies and related equipment and components.

TRAM- EN AUTOBUSBEDRIJVEN. **Series/Titl** Produktiestatistieken Transport, Opslag en Commuunicatie. **VFOAT** Tram and Buscompanies. 1981-. 0168-5775. NE. Dutch (summaries in English). an. 7.50. Centraal Bureau Voor de Statistiek, Prinses Beatrixlaan 428, Postbus 955, 2270 AZ Voorburg Netherlands. *Produktiestatistieken Transport, Opslag en Communicatie: Tram- en Autobusbedrijven.*

TRANSACTION. No. 437 (Jan./Feb. 1982)-. 0714-8100. Periodical. CN. English. bm. Free. Transaction, c/o Christian Publications, Unit 5 Building 2/2222 South Sheridan Way, Mississauga Ontario L5J 2M4 Canada. **DD** 248.88. *Postal Christian Witness, 0700-7787; Christian Airman, 0381-0275; Christian Bus Driver, 0382-8727; Automotive Christian, 0382-5299; Christian Sailor, 0714-8089; Christian Railroader, 0714-8097.*

TRANSIT CANADA MAGAZINE. V. 11- Jan./Feb. 1975-. 0380-3295. Periodical. CN. English. bm. $10.00 Canada and US, $12.00 Other Countries. Transit Canada, PO Box 6103 Station A, Toronto Ontario M5W 1P5 Canada. **DD** 388.413220971. *Canadian Coach Magazine, 0045-4559.*

TRANSIT JOURNAL *CEASED.* V. 1-7, No. 2. 0097-8299. Periodical. US. English. qt. $18.00. American Public Transit Association, 1100 17th Street NW, Washington DC 20036. **LC** HE305. **DD** 388.405.

TRANSIT NEWS CANADA. No. 1 (Jan. 82)-. 0712-8355. Periodical. CN. English (includes some text in French). bm. $8.00. Transit News Canada, TNC Publishers, 651 Wavell Avenue, Ottawa Ontario K1A 3A9 Canada. **DD** 388.40971.

TRANSIT OPERATING REPORT. **Main/Corp** American Public Transit Association. Statistical Dept. 0361-6371. US. English. an. American Public Transit Association, 1100 17th Street Northwest/Suite 1200, Washington DC 20036. **LC** HE308. **DD** 388.40973.

TRANSITIONS (CINCINNATI, OHIO). (TRANSITIONS). Spring 1980-. 0278-2804. Periodical. US. English. qt. $18.00. ATE Management and Service Company, 617 Vine Street/Suite 800, Cincinnati OH 45202. **Tel** (513)3481-7424. **Ed** Doreen Gurbacka. bk rev. **Circ** 1,500. Articles in journal format on topics of interest to public transit professionals. Such topics include operations, funding, marketing, maintenance, and service alternatives.

TRANSLOG. Publication began with Feb. 1970. 0041-1639. Periodical. US. English. mo. Superintendent of Documents, US Government Printing Office, Washington DC 20402. **Tel** (202)783-3238. **Ind/Abst** Index U.S. Gov. Period. **LC** UC270. **DD** 358.250973. *Transportation Proceedings.*

TRANSPO. V. 1- Summer 1978-. 0706-3954. Periodical. CN. English (text in summer 1978). an. Free. Transport Canada, Public Affairs Branch, Ottawa Ontario K1A 0N5 Canada. **Tel** (613)996-4006. **Ed** Peter Twidale. **Circ** 6,000. (ctrl). Canadian transportation, mainly involving Transport Canada, the Federal Government Department. *Transport Canada.*

TRANSPO TOPICS. (TRANSPO TOPICS : NEWSLETTER OF THE OFFICE OF GOVERNMENTAL AFFAIRS). Aug. 1982-. 0748-7274. Periodical. US. English. US Department of Transportation, Division of Consumer Affairs, 400 7th Street NW, Washington DC 20590. **Tel** (202)426-4518. *Dialog (United States. Dept. of Transportation. Office of Governmental Affairs), Transportation Consumer.*

TRANSPORT 2000. **VAT** Transport Two Thousand. Jan./Feb. 1976-. 0362-3815. Periodical. US. English. bm. $15.00. Transport 2000, 870 Market Street/Suite 954, San Francisco CA 94102-2904. **Tel** (415)982-6592. **Ed** Lawrence V Cott. **Ind/Abst** Predicasts, Funk Scott Index Corp. Ind. **LC** TA1001. **DD** 380.505. adv acc. **Circ** 12,000. An international distributed magazine focusing on cargo and transportation activities worldwide with special emphasis on intermodalism. We cover air surface and marine related issues and news. *Intermodal World.*

TRANSPORT-ACTION. No. 6 (Fall/Autumn 1980)-. 0227-3020. Periodical. CN. English (French). qt. Tranport 2000, Box/CP 858 Station B, Ottawa Ontario K1P 5P9 Canada.

TRANSPORT-ACTION. No. 5 (Summer 1980)-. 0227-3020. Periodical. CN. English (French). bm. $11.61. Transport Action, Box CP 858 Station B, Ottawa Ontario K1P 5P9 Canada. **Tel** 594-3290. **DD** 380.50971. A newsletter on all facets of public transportation policy, technology and operation. *Trans-Action, 0226-5966.*

TRANSPORT AND COMMUNICATIONS: SOUTH AUSTRALIA. **Main/Corp** Australian Bureau of Statistics. South Australian Office. AT. English. ir. Information Service, Australian Bureau of Statistics, GPO Box 2272, Adelaide 5001 Australia. **LC** HE104.S68. **DD** 380.3099423.

TRANSPORT & TOURISM JOURNAL. Periodical. II. English. ir. 8.00. 1969 Ganj Mir Khan, Daryaganj Delhi-6, New Delhi India. **LC** HE7. **DD** 338.47915404505.

TRANSPORT (CHARTERED INSTITUTE OF TRANSPORT). (TRANSPORT). Vol. 1, No. 1 (Mar./Apr. 1980)-. 0144-3453. Periodical. UK. English. bm. $38.00. City Press, Fairfax House, Colchester CO1 1RJ UK England. **Tel** (206)451213. **Ed** David Robinson. **Ind/Abst** Public Aff. Inf. Serv. Bull., Energy Res. Abstr. bk rev. adv acc. **Circ** 20,000. Content includes features, book reviews, letters, case studies, technology, personal profiles, news digest and special reports. *Journal, 0020-3181.*

TRANSPORT (DE)REGULATION REPORT. **VFOAT** Transport Deregulation Report. 0733-0197. Periodical. US. English. mo. $167.00. Cahners Newsletter Center, PO Box 716, Back Bay Annex, Boston MA 02117. **Tel** (657)536-7780.

TRANSPORT DEVELOPMENT NEWS. July 1971-. 0381-3444. Periodical. CN. English. bm. Transportation Development Agency, 2085 Union, Montreal Quebec K3A 2C3 Canada.

TRANSPORT-DIENST. 0721-6955. Periodical. GW. German. wk. 134,50. Transport-Dienst & Wirtschafts Correspondent, Stubbenhuk 10/ POB 11 03 29, 2000 Hamburg 10 West Germany. **Tel** 040/36 49 81. **Ed** Wolfgang H G Friske. **LC** HE5. bk rev. adv acc. **Circ** 3,500. Reports and informations on: shipping, ports, air transport, rail and road transport, forwarding, international transport news, transport-engineering.

Transportation

TRANSPORT-DIENST + WIRTSCHAFTS-CORRESPONDENT. VFOAT Transport-Dienst und Wirtschafts-Correspondent. Periodical. German. wk. Schiffahrts-Verlag Hansa C. Schroedter & Co, Stubbenhuk 10, Postfach 11 03 39, 2000 Hamburg 11 West Germany. LC HE5. DD 380.52405. *Transport-Dienst.*

TRANSPORT ECONOMICS. Aug. 1941-. 0041-1434. Periodical. US. English. mo. US Interstate Commerce Commission, Bureau of Economics, 1112 ICC Building, Washington DC 20423. LC HE17. DD 385. (cum index).

THE TRANSPORT ENGINEER. See Engineering.

TRANSPORT HISTORY. V. 1- Mar. 1968-. 0041-1469. Periodical. UK. English. ty. $25.29. Graphmitre Ltd, 1 West Street, Tavistock Devon PL19 8DS England. Ind/Abst Ref. Source, Am. Hist. Life, Avery Index Archit. Period., Hist. Abstr.

THE TRANSPORT MANAGER'S HANDBOOK. UK. English. an. $16.95. Kogan Page, 16 Grays Inn Road, London England. Ed David Lowe. LC KD2579.A1. DD 343.420948. Includes new material on changes to the EEC driving hours law, and regulations concerning the fitting of anti-spray equipment and the classification, packaging and labelling of dangerous substances.

TRANSPORT MONTREAL. (TRANSPORT MONTREAL : REPERTOIRE DU TRANSPORT). VFOAT The Transportation Register. 1980-. 0229-2408. CN. English (French). an. Anchor Press, Division of Shipping Register Publications, Suite 204/1434 Saint Catherine Street West, Montreal Quebec H3G 1R4 Canada. DD 380.5025714281. *Montreal, Repertoire du Transport. Montreal, the Transportation Register, 0225-4603; Guide du Port de Montreal, 1980, 0225-4727.*

TRANSPORT OF DANGEROUS GOODS. Main/Corp United Nations. Committee of Experts on the Transport of Dangerous Goods. (1953-1956). Series Corp United Nations. Document. 1964-. English. ir. $40.00. United Nations Publications, Sales Section, New York NY 10017. Tel (212)754-8302. LC JX1977. Contains significant recommendation on transporting dangerous goods, definitions, instructions and technical information of relevance to international shippers and inspection authorities.

TRANSPORT OF THUNDER BAY. VFOAT Port of Thunder Bay. Vol. 1, No. 1 (Spring 1983)-. 0822-580X. Periodical. CN. English. qt. Lakehead Harbour Commission, PO Box 2266, Thunder Bay Ontario P7C 5E Canada. DD 387.10971312.

TRANSPORT REVIEW. No. 5084- Mar. 12, 1976-. Periodical. UK. English. wk. 10.00. 205 Euston Road, London NW1 England. Tel (01)387-4771. Ed J Finney. LC HD6668.R3. DD 380.50941. bk rev. adv acc. *Railway Review.*

TRANSPORT REVIEWS. Vol. 1, No. 1 (Jan/Mar 1981)-. 0144-1647. Periodical. UK. English (summaries in French, German and Spanish). qt. $96.00. Taylor & Francis Inc, 242 Cherry Street, Philadelphia PA 19106.

TRANSPORT ROUTIER DU QUEBEC. VFOAT Quebec Road Transport. 1st Edition in 1942?. 0049-447X. Periodical. CN. French (text in English). mo. $15.48. Transport Routier du Quebec, 4855 rue Boyer Bureau 100, Montreal Quebec H2J 3E6 Canada. Tel (514)527-1359. Ed M Jacques Alary. adv acc. Circ 7,400. (ctrl). New rules in transportation, new products available for trucks and cars.

TRANSPORT STATISTICS. See Statistics.

TRANSPORT STATISTICS (NEW ZEALAND. DEPT. OF STATISTICS). See Statistics.

TRANSPORT STATISTICS OF JAPAN. See Statistics.

TRANSPORT STATISTICS REPORT. See Statistics.

TRANSPORT TOPICS. 1935. 0041-1558. Periodical. US. English. wk. American Trucking Association, 2200 Mill Road, Alexandria VA 22314. Tel (703)838-1770. Ed William Smith. LC HE5601. DD 388.3. adv acc. Circ 34,000. National business newspaper of the trucking industry— national, state and local news concerning managment of operations and maintenance of for-hire and private truck fleets. *A.T.A. News Bulletin.*

TRANSPORTATION. V. 1- May 1972-. 0049-4488. Periodical. English. qt. $81.00. Elsevier Science Publishers, PO Box 211, 1000 AE Amsterdam Netherlands. Tel (020)5803.911. Ind/Abst Avery Index Archit. Period., Eng. Index, Eng. Index Annu., Eng. Index Mon., Eng. Index Bioeng. Abstr., Eng. Index Energy Abstr., Int. Aerosp. Abstr., Appl. Sci. Technol. Index, Energy Res. Abstr. LC HE7. DD 380.505. CODEN TRPOB6.

TRANSPORTATION AND TRAVEL. OFFICIAL TABLE OF DISTANCES, FOREIGN TRAVEL. See Travel.

TRANSPORTATION (BOCA RATON, FLA.). (TRANSPORTATION). Series/Titl Social Issues Resources Series. V. 1, Article 1-. 0273-2602. US. English. an. Social Issues Resources Series Inc, PO Box 2507, Boca Raton FL 33432. Ed Eleanor C Goldstein. LC HE202.5. DD 380.50973.

TRANSPORTATION BUSINESS. Vol. 2, No. 3 (Oct. 1982)-. 0821-5634. Periodical. CN. English. mo. $15.00 Canada, $25.00 US and England. Transportation Business, 277 Lakeshore Road/Suite 209, Oakville Ontario L6J 6J3 Canada. DD 380.50971. *Quarterly Report on Transportation, 0711-0049.*

TRANSPORTATION. CURRENT LITERATURE. (TRANSPORTATION; CURRENT LITERATURE). V. 51, No. 1- Jan. 5, 1972-. 0091-1410. US. English. wk. US Department of Transportation, Library Services Division, 400 Sixth Street, Washington DC 20590. LC Z7295. DD 016.3805. *Highways. Current Literature.*

TRANSPORTATION ENERGY ACTIVITIES OF THE U.S. DEPARTMENT OF TRANSPORTATION. Main/Corp United States. Dept. of Transportation. Office of the Secretary. VFOAT Transportation Energy Technical Assistance, Research, and Planning Activities of the U.S. Department of Transportation. Began with Dec. 1979. US. English. Technology Sharing Program Office of the Secretary, Department of Transportation, Room 9402 I-40, 400 7th Street SW, Washington DC 20590.

TRANSPORTATION ENERGY BULLETIN. Periodical. US. English. Transportation Association of America, Suite 1107/1100 17th Street NW, Washington DC 20036.

TRANSPORTATION ENERGY RESEARCH. See Energy.

TRANSPORTATION ENGINEER. V. 1- Sept. 1953-. 0041-1604. Periodical. US. English. bm. $24.00. Newport Publications, 4001 Westerly Place, PO Box W, Newport Beach CA 92658. Tel (714)833-0512. Ed Ken Kelley. adv acc. Circ 12,500. The only US based magazine written expressly for heavy/ specialized carriers and crane rigging operators. *American Cartagemen and Heavy Haulers.*

TRANSPORTATION FACTS AND TRENDS. VFOAT Transportation Facts & Trends. 1st- Ed. US. English. an. Transportation Association of America, Suite 1107/1100 17th Street NW, Washington DC 20036.

TRANSPORTATION FOCUS. 0098-0129. US. English. Department of Transportation, Room 4113/1120 N Street, Sacramento CA 95814. LC HE1. DD 380.505.

TRANSPORTATION FORUM. VFOAT Tribune des Transports. Vol. 1/1 (June 1984)-. 0826-8193. Periodical. CN. English (French). qt. $30.00. Roads and Transportation Association of Canada, 1765 St Laurent Boulevard, Ottawa Ontario K1G 3V4 Canada. DD 380.50971. *R T A C Forum, 0703-7090.*

TRANSPORTATION GUIDE. CN. English. an. $36.95. Southam Communications Ltd, 1450 Don Mills Road, Don Mills, Ontario M3B 2X7 Canada. Tel (416)445-6641. Ed Michelle Ramsay. DD 380.502571. adv acc. Circ 14,500. (ctrl). Serves transportation and distribution managers offering information on air, highway, marine, rail and freight forwarding services.

TRANSPORTATION IN AMERICA. 1st Ed. (Mar. 1983)-. US. English. an. $25.00. Transportation Policy Association, PO Box 33633 Farragut Station, Washington DC 20033. Tel (202)638-5244. Circ 600. (ctrl). Statistical analysis of freight/passenger transport by modes and including current/historical data. Includes outlays, traffic distribution, employment/wage- fringe levels, capital outlays number of units, etc. *Transportation Facts & Trends, 0564-1292.*

TRANSPORTATION JOURNAL. V. 1- Fall 1961-. 0041-1612. Periodical. US. English. qt. $30.00. American Society of Transportation and Logistics, PO Box 33095, Louisville KY 40232. Tel (502)451-8150. Ed John C Spychalski. Ind/Abst Coal Abstr., Energy Inf. Abstr., Energy Res. Abstr., Environ. Abstr., Public Aff. Inf. Serv. Bull., Ship Abstr., Bus. Period. Index, Soc. Sci. Citation Index. LC HE1. DD 380.505. CODEN TRNJA. bk rev. Circ 3,500. (ctrl). Available in microform from University Microfilms International. Publication of articles designed to advance the traffic, transportation and physical distribution management profession. Review of new books in transportation.

TRANSPORTATION LAW JOURNAL. See Law.

TRANSPORTATION MONITORING REPORT. Main/Corp Data Resources, Inc. Transportation Service. V. 1- May 1978-. 0162-699X. US. English. mo. Data Resources Inc, Transportation Service, 29 Hartwell Avenue, Lexington MA. LC HE203. DD 380.52.

TRANSPORTATION NOISE BULLETIN. V. 1- Oct. 1971-. 0094-0682. US. English. National Academy of Sciences Highway Research Council, 2101 Constitution Avenue NW, Washington DC 20418. LC TD893.6.T7. DD 363.6.

TRANSPORTATION PAPER. Main/Corp Joint Program in Transportation. No. 1- 1972-. Monographic Series. CN. English. Centre for Urban & Community Studies, 150 St George Street University of Toronto, Toronto Ontario M5S 2E9 Canada. DD 380.5.

TRANSPORTATION PLANNING AND TECHNOLOGY. V. 1- Apr. 1972-. 0308-1060. Periodical. US. English. ir. $264.00. Gordon & Breach, PO Box 197, London WC2E 9PX England. Ed N J Ashford. Ind/Abst Math. Rev., Eng. Index Annu., Eng. Index Mon., Eng. Index Bioeng. Abstr., Eng. Index Energy Abstr., Excerpta Med., Comput. Control Abstr., Electr. Electron. Abstr., Sci. Abstr. Sect. A. Phys. Abstr., Eng. Index, Phys. Abstr. CODEN TPLTAK. bk rev. adv acc.

TRANSPORTATION PRACTITIONERS JOURNAL. Vol. 52, No. 1 (FAll 1984)-. 8756-9302. Periodical. US. English. qt. $20.00 Active and Retired Members, $50.00 Nonmembers. Transportation Practitioners Journal, 1211 Connecticut Avenue, NW/Suite 310, Washington DC 20036. Ind/Abst Index Leg. Period. *ICC Practitioners' Journal, 0018-8859.*

TRANSPORTATION QUARTERLY. Vol. 36, No. 1 (Jan. 1982)-. 0278-9434. Periodical. US. English. qt. Free. Eno Foundation for Transportation, PO Box 55 Saugatuck Station, Westport CN 06880. Tel (203)227-4852. Ed Wilbur S Smith. Ind/Abst Electron. Commun. Abstr. J., ISMEC Bull., Pollut. Abstr. Indexes, Saf. Sci. Abstr. J., Eng. Index, Energy Inf. Abstr., Environ. Abstr., Avery Index Archit. Period., Public Aff. Inf. Serv. Bull., Energy Res. Abstr., Appl. Sci. Technol. Index, Public Aff. Inf. Serv. Bull. LC HE331. DD 380.505. CODEN TRQUDV. Circ 5,000. (ctrl). Broad range of transportation topics from authors in academic, government, and industrial fields. *Traffic Quarterly, 0041-0713.*

TRANSPORTATION REPRINT. Main/Corp Joint Program in Transportation. No. 1- 1971-. Monographic Series. CN. English. Centre for Urban & Community Studies, 150 St George Street University of Toronto, Toronto Ontario M5S 2E9 Canada. DD 380.5.

TRANSPORTATION RESEARCH CEASED. V. 1-12. 0041-1647. Periodical. UK. English. bm. Pergamon Press, 395 Sawmill River Road, Elmsford NY 10523. Tel (914)592-7700. Ind/Abst Math. Rev., Excerpta Med., Energy Inf. Abstr., Environ. Abstr., Ship Abstr., Eng. Index Annu., Int. Aerosp. Abstr., Soc. Sci. Citation Index, Sci. Cit. Index, Abr. Ed., Phys. Abstr., Comput. Control Abstr., Manage. Contents, Appl. Sci. Technol. Index, Electr. Electron. Abstr., Eng. Index Mon., Energy Res. Abstr., Sci. Abstr. Sect. A. Phys. Abstr. LC HE192.5. CODEN TRREBK. Available on microfilm from Microform International Marketing Corp.

TRANSPORTATION RESEARCH ABSTRACTS. See Indexes/Abstracts.

TRANSPORTATION RESEARCH NEWS CEASED. No. 55-103. 0095-2656. Periodical. US. English. bm. $6.00. Transportation Research Board, National Research Council, 2101 Constitution Avenue NW, Washington DC 20418. Ind/Abst Eng. Index Annu., Eng. Index Mon., Eng. Index

Transportation

Bioeng. Abstr., Eng. Index Energy Abstr. **LC** TE1. **DD** 380.505. **CODEN** TRENDI. *Highway Research News, 0018-1749.*

TRANSPORTATION RESEARCH. PART A : GENERAL. V. 13A- Feb. 1979-. 0191-2607. Periodical. UK. English. bm. $96.00. Pergamon Press Inc, Maxwell House, Fairview Park, Elmsford NY 10523. **Ind/Abst** Eng. Index Annu., Eng. Index Mon., Eng. Index Bioeng. Abstr., Eng. Index Energy Abstr., Excerpta Med., Int. Aerosp. Abstr., Comput. Control Abstr., Electr. Electron. Abstr., Sci. Abstr. Sect. A. Phys. Abstr., Energy Res. Abstr., Appl. Sci. Technol. Index. **LC** HE192.5. **DD** 380.505. **CODEN** TRAGDB. *Transportation Research, 0041-1647.*

TRANSPORTATION RESEARCH. PART B : METHODOLOGICAL. VFOAT Transportation Research-B. V. 13B- Mar. 1979-. 0191-2615. Periodical. UK. English. bm. $110.00 Institution, $45.00 Individuals whose institution has a library subscription. Subscription Fulfillment, Manager Pergamon Press Ltd, Headington Hill Mall, Oxford OX3 OBW England. **Ind/Abst** Math. Rev., Eng. Index Annu., Eng. Index Mon., Eng. Index Bioeng. Abstr., Eng. Index Energy Abstr., Excerpta Med., Coal Abstr., Int. Aerosp. Abstr., Comput. Control Abstr., Electr. Electron. Abstr., Sci. Abstr. Sect. A. Phys. Abstr., Energy Res. Abstr., Appl. Sci. Technol. Index. **LC** HE192.5. **DD** 380.5072. **CODEN** TRBMDY. Available on microfilm and microfiche. *Transportation Research, 0041-1647.*

TRANSPORTATION RESEARCH RECORD. No. 480-. 0361-1981. Monographic Series. US. English. ir. Transportation Research Board, 2101 Constitution Avenue, Washington DC 20418. **Tel** (202)334-3218. **Ind/Abst** Eng. Index Annu., Eng. Index Mon., Eng. Index Bioeng. Abstr., Eng. Index Energy Abstr., Coal Abstr., GeoRef, Chem. Abstr., Sel. Water Resour. Abstr., Bibliogr. Index Geol., Eng. Index. **LC** TE7. **DD** 380.508. **CODEN** TRREDM. **Circ** 3,000. Contains several technical papers on a given subject. The papers are usually prepared for an annual meeting and accepted for publication through a technical review process. *Highway Research Record, 0073-2206.*

TRANSPORTATION REVIEW. VFOAT Data Resources Transportation Review. 0197-419X. Periodical. US. English. Data Resources Inc, 29 Hartwell Avenue, Lexington MA 02173. **LC** HE1. **DD** 380.505.

TRANSPORTATION SCIENCE. V. 1- Feb. 1967-. 0041-1655. Periodical. US. English. qt. Operations Research Society of America, PO Box 64237, Baltimore MD 21264. **Tel** (301)528-4146. **Ind/Abst** Electron. Commun. Abstr. J., ISMEC Bull., Pollut. Abstr. Indexes, Saf. Sci. Abstr. J., Eng. Index Mon., Eng. Index Bioeng. Abstr., Eng. Index Energy Abstr., Ship Abstr., Int. Aerosp. Abstr., Comput. Control Abstr., Electr. Electron. Abstr., Sci. Abstr. Sect. A. Phys. Abstr., Eng. Index Annu., Eng. Index, Math. Rev., Appl. Sci. Technol. Index, Phys. Abstr., Sci. Cit. Index, Abr. Ed. **LC** TA1001. **DD** 380.505. **CODEN** TRSCBJ. Available on microfilm from the Microfilm Dept., Waverly Press.

TRANSPORTATION (SPRINGFIELD, VA.). (TRANSPORTATION). 0163-1527. Periodical. US. English. wk. $94.00. National Technical Information Service, 5285 Port Royal Road, Springfield VA 22161. **Tel** (703)487-4650. **Ind/Abst** Eng. Index, Soc. Sci. Citation Index, Humanit. Index.

THE TRANSPORTATION SYSTEM MANAGEMENT REPORT FOR NORTHEASTERN ILLINOIS. (THE ... TRANSPORTATION SYSTEM MANAGEMENT REPORT FOR NORTHEASTERN ILLINOIS). **Main/Corp** Chicago Area Transportation Study. 1982-. 0741-2266. US. English. an. Chicago Area Transportation Study, 300 West Adams Street, Chicago IL 60606. **LC** HE310.C45. **DD** 388.068. *Transportation System Management Plan for Northeastern Illinois, 0743-6092.*

TRANSPORTATION TELEPHONE TICKLER. Periodical. US. English. an. Journal of Commerce, 445 Marshall Street, Phillipsburg NJ 08865. **Tel** (201)859-1300. **LC** HE9.U5. **DD** 385.1. *The Journal of Commerce Transportation Telephone Tickler, 0447-9181.*

TRANSPORTATION U.S.A CEASED. (TRANSPORTATION USA). Began with summer 1974. Ceased with V. 7, No. 1, (Fall 1980). 0094-9922. Periodical. US. English. qt. Superintendent of Documents, US Government Printing Office, Washington DC 20402. **Ind/Abst** Energy Inf. Abstr., Environ. Abstr., Index U.S. Gov. Period., Public Aff. Inf. Serv. Bull. **LC** HE17. **DD** 380.50973.

TRANSPORTE MODERNO. 0041-1698. Periodical. US. Spanish. bm. Lineal Publishing Company, 23 Leroy Avenue, Darien CT 06820. **Tel** (203)226-7463. **LC** HE7.

TRANSPORTING PERSONAL FIREARMS. 0883-0932. US. English. Sparrow Publishing House, PO Box 817, Boulder City NV 89005.

TRANSPORTRECHT. *See* Law.

TRANSPORTS. 1.- Yearly V. (No. 1-). Periodical. FR. French. ir. 455,24. Editions Techniques Economique, 3 rue Soufflot, 75005 Paris France. **Tel** (1)634 10 30. Ed E Epstein. **Ind/Abst** Predicasts. **LC** HE3.

TRANSPORTS ROUTIERS DE MARCHANDISES. **Main/Corp** France. Departement des Statistiques des Transports. VFOAT Enquete Annuelle d'Entreprise. FR. French. ir. Ministere de Lequipement, 21 rue Mathuring-Regnier, 75732 Paris Cedex 15 France. **LC** HE5668. **DD** 388.3240944.

TRANSPOTECH. V. 1- Mar. 1979-. 0709-5368. Periodical. CN. English (French). bm. $8.00 Members, $12.00 Nonmembers. Roads and Transportation Association of Canada, 1765 Sainte Laurent Boulevard, Ottawa Ontario K1G 3V4 Canada. **DD** 016.3805.

TRANSPR. *See* Law.

TRAVEL SCOOP. Jan. 15, 1983-. 0822-9228. Periodical. CN. English. ir. $28.00. Travel Scoop, 1000 Dundas Street E/Suite 7, Toronto Ontario M4M 1R7 Canada. **Tel** (416)465-6871. Ed Robin Cardozo. **DD** 910.5. bk rev. **Circ** 1,000. Newsletter devoted to money-saving values in travel, with special interest items for senior citizens, the disabled and single travelers. Also includes consumer rights about travel.

TRAVEL TO WORK. VFOAT Deplacements Entre le Domicile et de le Lieu de Travail. 1976-1980-. CN. English (French). $7.20. Publication Sales And Services, Statistics Canada, Ottawa Ontario K1A 0V7 Canada. **LC** HD5717.5.C2. **DD** 388.413140971021.

TRAVELAGE WEST. *See* Travel.

TRINC'S BLUE BOOK OF THE TRUCKING INDUSTRY. VFOAT Blue Book of the Trucking Industry. Began publication with vol. for 1944. 0082-6499. US. English. an. Trinc's Transportation Consultants, Suite 303/8200 Greensboro Drive, McLean VA 22101. **Tel** (703)448-1146. **LC** HE5623.A1.

TROLLEY COACH NEWS. Periodical. US. English. qt. $12.00 Domestic, $15.00 Canada. North American Trackless Trolley Association, 2125 Bashford Manor Lane, Louisville KY 40218. **LC** TL232. **DD** 388.41322305.

TRUCK & EQUIPMENT SALESMAN. VFOAT Truck and Equipment Salesman. Vol. 1, No. 1 (Jyly/Aug. 1981)-. 0279-2176. Periodical. US. English. bm. $12.00 Domestic, $30.00 Foreign. Chilton Company, Chilton Way, Radnor PA 19089. **LC** HD9710.35.U6. **DD** 629.2240688.

TRUCK & TRAILER BUYER'S GUIDE. VFOAT Truck and Trailer Buyer's Guide. 8756-5129. Periodical. US. English. mo. $15.00. PO Box 153873, Irving TX 75015. **LC** TL230.A1. **DD** 629.224029473.

THE TRUCK BLUE BOOK LEASE GUIDE, RESIDUAL PROJECTIONS. (THE TRUCK BLUE BOOK LEASE GUIDE, RESIDENTIAL PROJECTIONS). VFOAT Truck Blue Book Lease Guide. Vol. 1, No. 1 (Jan. 1-Mar. 31, 1985)-. 8756-4041. US. English. qt. $50.00 Domestic, $60.00 Canada. National Market Reports Inc, PO Box 6500, Chicago IL 60680. **DD** 629.

TRUCK BROKER DIRECTORY. *See* Yearbooks, Almanacs, Directories.

TRUCK CAMPER TRADE-IN GUIDE. 0749-4548. US. English. an. $8.95. **LC** HD9710.U52. **DD** 629.226. *Official Truck Camper Trade-in Guide, 0094-1131.*

TRUCK CANADA. V. 21, No. 5- May 1973-. 0315-5501. Periodical. CN. English. mo. $27.09. Sentinel Business Publication, 6420 Victoria Street/Suite 8, Montreal Quebec H3W 2S7 Canada. **Tel** (514)731-3523. Ed Carole Clifford. bk rev. adv acc. **Circ** 21,500. (ctrl). Technical data maintenance, fleet operations, and product information on heavy-duty trucks. *Truck Transportation Canada, 0315-551X.*

TRUCK INSIDER. 0041-3399. Periodical. US. English. ir. $88.00. Atcom Inc, 2315 Broadway, New York NY 10024. **Tel** (212)873-5900. Ed Michael Ehrhardt. **Circ** 800. (ctrl). A newsletter for truck dealers and professionals in the truck sales, rental and leasing business.

TRUCK LUBRICATION GUIDE. 0162-3435. US. English. an. $31.80. Gousha Chek-Chart, 2001 The Alameda PO Box 6227, San Jose CA 95159. **Tel** (408)296-1060. **Circ** 2,600. Covers periodic maintenance and lubrication of all sizes of on-highway trucks, in tabular data form.

TRUCK TAXES BY STATES. **Main/Corp** American Trucking Associations. Dept. of Research and Transport Economics. US. English. an. American Trucking Association, 1616 P Street Northwest, Washington DC 20036.

TRUCK WEIGHT STUDY. **Main/Corp** Mississippi. Transportation Planning Division. 0364-703X. US. English. an. **LC** TL230.A1. **DD** 629.224.

TRUCK WEIGHT SURVEY. **Main/Corp** Tennessee. Dept. of Transportation. Bureau of Planning and Programming. 0360-7399. US. English. an. **LC** TL230.A1. **DD** 388.324.

TRUCKER'S ALMANAC. *See* Yearbooks, Almanacs, Directories.

TRUCKIN'. 0277-5743. Periodical. US. English. mo. $17.98. McMullen Publishing Company, 2145 West La Palma, Anaheim CA 92801. **Tel** (714)635-9040.

TRUCKS (NEW YORK, N.Y. : 1985). (TRUCKS). VFOAT Trucks Magazine. Vol. 1, No. 1 (Jan. 1986)-. 0884-8947. Periodical. US. English. bm. $17.00 Non-drivers, $12.00 Class 7 & 8 Truckers. Trucks Magazine Inc, 20 Waterside Plaza, New York NY 10010.

TSC ANNUAL REPORT. VFOAT T.S.C. Annual Report. 1978-. US. English. an. US Department of Transportation Systems, Research and Special Programs Transportation Systems Center, Kendall Square, Cambridge MA 02142.

U T U NEWS CANADA. *See* Economics - Labor.

UKRAINSKA RSR. UKRAINSKAIA SSR. UKRAINIAN SSR. *See* Engineering.

ULASTIRMA ISTATISTIKLERI. *See* Statistics.

UNFALLVERHUTUNGSBERICHT STRASSENVERKEHR : BERICHT DES BUNDESMINISTERS FUR VERKEHR UBER MASSNAHMEN AUF DEM GEBIET DER UNFALLVERHUTUNG IM STRASSENVERKEHR. VFOAT Bericht des Bundesministers fur Verkehr Uber Massnahmen auf dem Gebiet der Unfallverhutung im Strassenverkehr. 0722-8333. German. ir. **LC** HE5614.5.G3.

UNIFIED WORK PROGRAM. **Main/Corp** Illinois. Dept. of Transportation. Office of Planning, Programming, and Environmental Science. 0361-9079. US. English. an. Illinois Department of Transportation, 2300 South Dirkse, Springfield IL 62764. **LC** HE28.I3. **DD** 309.2509773.

U.S. DEPARTMENT OF TRANSPORTATION ANNUAL REPORT. **Main/Corp** United States. Dept. of Transportation. VFOAT Annual Report - U.S. Department of Transportation. 1st- 1967-. Periodical. US. English. an. US Department of Transportation, Washington DC 20590.

UNITED STATES DEPARTMENT OF TRANSPORTATION YEAR-END REPORT. (YEAR-END REPORT). 0093-9897. US. English. US Department of Transportation, Office of Public Affairs, Washington DC 20590. **LC** HE17. **DD** 353.0087.

U.S. GREAT LAKES PORTS. VAT United States Great Lakes Ports. 0145-1308. Periodical. US. English. qt. US Department of Transportation, St Lawrence Seaway Development Corporation, 800 Independence Avenue SW/Room 832-FOB 10A, Washington DC 20591.

U.S. MOPED, 3 & 4 WHEELER, MOTOR SCOOTERS, ETC. IMPORTS. VFOAT US Moped, Three and Four Wheeler, Motor Scooters, etc., Imports. 0742-4523. US. English. mo.

Transportation—Automobiles

$15.00. W C Single, 6040 Boulevard East, West New York NY 07093.

UNTERNEHMEN UND ARBEITSSTATTEN. REIHE 1 : DIE KOSTENSTRUKTUR IN DER WIRTSCHAFT. III. VERKEHRSGEWERBE. Main/Corp Germany (West). Statistisches Bundesamt. VFOAT Kostenstruktur in der Wirtschaft. 0072-3975. German. ni.

URBAN INNOVATION ABROAD. See Public Administration.

URBAN TRANSIT FACTS IN CANADA. 1983-. 0821-2996. CN. English. an. $10.00 Each Number. Canadian Urban Transit Association, Suite 220/Union Station 140 Bay Street, Toronto Ontraio M5J 2L5 Canada. DD 388.40971. *Transit Fact Book and Membership Directory, 0706-7658.*

URBAN TRANSPORT NEWS. 0195-4695. Periodical. US. English. bw. $180.00. Urban Transport News, Suite 407, 733 15th Street NW, Washington DC 20005. Tel (202)628-7986. Ed Robert M Loebelson. Coverage of developments in public transportation. This includes buses, subways, light rail, commuter rail and the manufacturers and the operators of mass transit equipment.

URBAN TRANSPORTATION ABROAD. Vol. 3, No. 1 (Spring 1980)-. Periodical. US. English. qt. $40.00. International Center/Academy for State & Local Government, 444 N Capitol Street/Suite 349, Washington DC 20001. Tel (212)638-1445. Ed George G Wynne. bk rev. Circ 5,000. Newsletter on public transportation technology, innovation and trends from around the world relevant to US concerns. *Urban Transit Abroad.*

URBAN TRANSPORTATION ABSTRACTS. See Indexes/Abstracts.

URBAN TRANSPORTATION OFFICIALS. Mar. 1981 -. 0278-7253. US. English. an. Free to Members. US Conference of Mayors, 1620 Eye Street NW, Washington DC 20006. LC HE308. DD 352.918402573.

VACUUM CIRCUITS. (VACUUM CIRCUITS : DOMESTIC CARS, LIGHT TRUCKS & VANS, IMPORTED CARS & TRUCKS). Series/Titl Manuals for the Automotive Professional. VFOAT Mitchell Vacuum Circuits. 1969/78-. 0747-5063. US. English. Mitchell Manuals Inc, PO Box 26260, San Diego CA 92126. Tel (619)578-8770. Ed Dan Kelley. adv acc. (ctrl). Our vaccum circuit diagrams make tune-ups, emission and air conditioning servicing easier. Covers 1979-85 domestic and 1979-84 imported cars and light trucks.

VARSHIKA KARYA-VIVARANA. Main/Corp Uttara Pradesa Rajya Saraka Parivahana Nigama. Hindi. an. Free. LC HE365.I44.

VEHICLE WEIGHT AND USE DATA COLLECTED ON MINNESOTA ROADS. Main/Corp Minnesota. Dept. of Transportation. US. English. be. Department of Transportation, St Paul MN 55101. LC TL230.A1. DD 388.34409776.

VERKEHR. Main/Corp Brabant, North, (Province). Provinciale Waterstaat. Dutch. ir. LC HE69.

VERKEHR. REIHE 5 : STRASSENVERKEHR. II. PERSONENVERKEHR. Main/Corp Germany (West). Statistisches Bundesamt. German. ir. 7.00. LC HE249.

VERKEHRSANNALEN. VFOAT Verkehrs Annalen. 0379-0223. Periodical. AU. German. ir. Alle, 1010 Wien Gauermanngasse 4 Austria. Ind/Abst Ship Abstr.

DIE VERKEHRSWIRTSCHAFT. See Statistics.

VERKEHRSWIRTSCHAFTLICHE ZAHLEN. GW. German. ir. Free. Breitenbachstr 1, 6 Frankfurt Main 93 West Germany. Tel 0697919365. Ed Georg Dierschke. LC HE249. adv acc. Circ 4,500. (ctrl). Statistics of goods transport in, from, and to West Germany.

VERSLAG VAN DIE RAAD VAN SUID-AFRIKAANSE VERVOERDIENSTE VIR DIE JAAR GEEINDIG . . . . Main/Corp South African Transport Services Board. 1981-. Afrikaans (English). an. LC HE284.4.A15. DD 354.680087.5006.

VESTNIK DOPRAVY. Main/Corp Czechoslovakia. Federalni Ministerstvo Dopravy. CS. Czech. ir. Dopravy a Spoju, Zasobovaci Sklad Zeleznic, Zelivskeho 2, 130.00 Praha 3 Czechoslovakia. LC HE7.

VESTNIK VSESOIUZNOGO NAUCHNO-ISSLEDOVATELSKOGO INSTITUTA ZELEZNODOROZNOGO TRANSPORTA. (VESTNIK VSESOIUZNOGO NAUCHNO-ISSLEDOVATELSKOGO INSTITUTA ZHELEZNODOROZHNOGO TRANSPORTA). VFOAT Vestnik Vniizht. Began in Aug. 1956. 0042-4749. Periodical. UR. Russian. ir. $41.50. Victor Kamkin Inc, 12224 Parklawn Drive, Rockville MD 20852. Tel (301)881-5973. Ind/Abst Chem. Abstr. CODEN VVNZAA. Index in last issue of volume - attached. *Tekhnika Zheleznykh Dorog.*

VIE E TRASPORTI. Periodical. IT. Italian. mo. $32.08 Foreign. La Fiaccola, Via C Ravizza 62, 20149 Milano Italy. Tel 02/481.4939 - 481.4355. Ed Ing Ernesto Stagni. LC TE4. adv acc. Circ 7,500. Technical magazine on transport problems (road, rail, air, sea and waterway). Construction and use of equipment and organisation of transport systems of people and goods. *Rivista Della Strada.*

VIRGINIA HIGHWAY AND TRANSPORTATION COMMISSION ANNUAL REPORT. Began with vol. for 1974/75. US. English. an. Virginia Highway and Transportation Department, 1221 East Broad Street, Richmond VA 23219. LC TE24.V. DD 353.97550087805. *Report.*

EN VRAC (NORANDA, QUEBEC). (EN VRAC). V. 1, No 1 (Feb. 1983)-. 0715-7525. Periodical. CN. French. bm. Free. Poste Transport de Vrac, Region 08, Bureau 109/138 Avenue Murdoch, Noranda Quebec J9X 1E1 Canada. DD 388.32406071413. (ctrl). *Revue du Camionneur.*

VST REVUE. VFOAT V.S.T. Revue. Periodical. German. mo. 25.00. VST, Dalholzliweg 12, 3000 Bern 6 Switzerland. LC HE5. DD 380.509494. *Offentliche Verkehr.*

WASHINGTON TRANSPORTATION NEWSLETTER. 0091-5734. Periodical. US. English. wk. Washington Transportation Association, Suite 532 1629 K Street Northwest, Washington DC 20006. LC HE1.

WESTERN MOTOR FLEET. V. 36 Dec. 1970/Jan. 1971-. 0043-3950. Periodical. CN. English. bm. $20.12. Mercury Publications Ltd, 945 King Edward Street, Winnipeg Manitoba R3H OP8 Canada. *Western Motor Fleet and Highway News, 0380-4836.*

WESTERN TRUCK NEWS. Vol. 1, No. 5 (June 1980)-. 0229-6268. Periodical. CN. English. mo. $6.00. Western Truck News, PO Box 4653, Edmonton Alberta T6E 5G5 Canada. DD 388.324097123. *Western Truck, 0229-625X.*

WHEELS OF TIME. Vol. 1, No. 1 (Oct. 1980)-. 0738-565X. Periodical. US. English. bm. $15.00. American Truck Historical Society, 201 Office Park Drive, Birmingham AL 35223. Tel (205)879-2131. Ed Charles B Rawson. LC TL230.A1. DD 629.2240973. bk rev. adv acc. Circ 7,500. (ctrl). Historical information about trucks, the trucking industry and its pioneers. Many photos.

WHITE PAPER ON TRANSPORTATION SAFETY IN JAPAN. '83-. English. an. IATSS 6-20, 2-chome Yaesu, Chuo-ku Tokyo 104 Japan. LC HE5614.5.J3. DD 363.120952. *Japanese Government White Paper on Transportation Safety.*

WOODALL'S RV BUYER'S CATALOG. Main/Corp Woodall Publishing Company. VFOAT RV Buyer's Catalog. 0162-7015. US. English. $5.95. Woodall Publishing Company, 500 Hyacinth Place, Highland Park IL 60035.

WOODALL'S RV BUYER'S GUIDE. Main/Corp Woodall Publishing Company. VAT Woodall's Recreational Vehicle Buyer's Guide. 0162-7368. US. English. $2.95. Woodall Publishing Company, 500 Hyacinth Place, Highland Park IL 60035.

WOODALL'S RV OWNER'S HANDBOOK. VFOAT RV Owner's Handbook. VAT Woodall's Recreational Vehicle Owner's Handbook. V. 1-. 0192-4532. US. English. an. Woodall Publication Company, 11 North Skokie Highway, Lake Bluff IL 60044.

WYOMING URBAN AREAS . . . ANNUAL REPORT. 1982-. US. English. Urban Transportation Planning Unit Wyoming Highway Department, PO Box 1708, Cheyenne WY 82002-9019. LC HE309.W8. DD 338.409787.

YEAR BOOK OF TRANSPORT STATISTICS. See Yearbooks, Almanacs, Directories.

ZAGADNIENIA TRANSPORTU. Polish (Summaries in English). ir. 42.00 Each Issue. Panstwowe Wydawn Naukowe, Instytut Transportu Samochodowego, Ul Stalingradzka 40, Pok 322, Warszawa Poland. LC HE7.

ZEITSCHRIFT FUR VERKEHRSRECHT. Vol. 1-. Periodical. AU. German. mo. $36.77. Manzxche Verlagsbuchhandlung Kohlmark 16, 1014 Wien Austria. (cum index).

ZEITSCHRIFT FUR VERKEHRSWISSENSCHAFT. 1. Volume, No. 1-. 0044-3670. Periodical. GW. German. bm. Verkehrs Verlag J Fischer, Postfach 140140, 4 Dusseldorf 14 West Germany. Ind/Abst Excerpta Med., Foreign Lang. Index, PAIS Foreign Lang. Index. LC HE5. DD 380.505.

AUTOMOBILES

3WHEELING. See Recreation, Leisure - Sports.

4 X 4. REGLEMENTS GENERAUX, FONDS DE POINTS. See Recreation, Leisure - Sports.

1001 CUSTOM AND ROD IDEAS. VFOAT Custom & Rod Ideas. VAT One Thousand and One Custom and Rod Ideas. 0030-2546. Periodical. US. English. mo. $13.50 Domestic, $15.50 Foreign. 1001 Custom and Rod Ideas, P O Box 49659, Los Angeles CA 90049.

AA HANDBOOK (ZAMBIA). Main/Corp Automobile Association of Zambia. English. ir. Associated Reviews, PO Box 717, Ndola Zambia. LC TL119.Z34. DD 916.894044.

THE AAA TRAVELER. MUSKINGUM AAA EDITION. (THE AAA TRAVELER). VFOAT A.A.A. Traveler. VAT American Automobile Association Traveler. Muskingum AAA Edition. 0744-6535. Periodical. US. English. bm. $1.00. Ohio Automobile Club, 1120 Maple Avenue, Zanesville OH 43701. *Motor Travel, 0279-5779.*

AAA WORLD. HAWAII. (AAA WORLD). 0731-8723. Periodical. US. English. bm. $4.00. The Automobile Club of Hawaii, Outrigger East Hotel, 150 Kaiulani Avenue, Honolulu, HI 96815. *Motoring in Hawaii.*

AAA WORLD (MISSISSIPPI EDITION). (AAA WORLD). VFOAT A.A.A. World. VAT American Automobile Association World. Vol. 4, No. 3 (May/June 1984)-. 0743-0663. Periodical. US. English. bm. $4.00. AAA World, Mississippi Edition, P.O. Box 16529, Jackson, MS 39236. *AAA World, 0277-1047.*

AAA WORLD. NEW MEXICO. (AAA WORLD). VAT American Automobile Association World. New Mexico. Vol. 1, No. 1 (May/June 1981)-. 0277-1020. Periodical. US. English. bm. $4.00. American Automobile Association, New Mexico Division, 2201 San Pedro Boulevard NE, Building 3, Albuquerque, NM 87110. *American Motorist, 0199-0268.*

AAA WORLD. POTOMAC. (AAA WORLD). VAT American Automobile Association World. Potomac. Vol. 1, No. 1 (May/June 1981)-. 0279-0270. Periodical. US. English. bm. $4.00. American Automobile Association, Potomac Division, 8111 Gatehouse Road, Falls Church, VA 22047. *American Motorist, 0199-0268.*

AAA WORLD. WISCONSIN. (AAA WORLD). VAT American Automobile Association World. Wisconsin. Vol. 1, No. 1 (May/June 1981)-. 0277-1411. Periodical. US. English. bm. $4.00. American Automobile Association, Wisconsin Division, 433 W Washington Avenue, Madison WI 53703. *Traveler.*

ACCELERATORS AND STORAGE RINGS. V. 1-. 0272-5088. Monographic Series. English. ir. Harwood Publications, PO Box 786 Cooper Station, New York NY 10276. Ind/Abst Chem. Abstr. CODEN ASRGDU.

AE. AUTOMOTIVE EXECUTIVE. (AUTOMOTIVE EXECUTIVE : AE). VFOAT AE. Vol. 1, No. 1 (Sept. 1979)-. 0195-1564. Periodical. US. English. mo. $12.00 Domestic, $15.00 Canada. Automotive Executive, 8400 Westpark Drive, McLean VA 22102. LC HD9710.U5. DD 629.2068. *Cars & Trucks, 0027-5778.*

AFTERMARKET EXECUTIVE. V. 1- Oct. 1978-. 0162-6604. Periodical. US. English. bm. $25.00. Automotive Parts and Accessories Association, 1025

Transportation—Automobiles

Connecticut Avenue NW, Washington DC 20036. LC HD9710.3.A1. DD 658.8962920973.

AFTERMARKET STATISTICAL YEARBOOK. See Yearbooks, Almanacs, Directories.

AIR COOLED NEWS. Began in 1953. Periodical. US. English. ty. LC TL215.F85.

AIRSTREAM SERVICE MANUAL. Main/Corp Airstream, Inc. 0160-3019. US. English. Airstream Inc, Jackson Center OH 45334. LC TL297. DD 629.2876.

A.L.A. SIGHTS TO SEE BOOK. See Travel.

ALBERTA MOTORIST (EDMONTON, ALTA.). (ALBERTA MOTORIST). V. 1, No. 1 (Jan/Feb 1984)-. 0826-4937. CN. English. bm. $10.00. Alberta Motorist, 11648-142 Street, Edmonton Alberta T5M 1V4 Canada. DD 629.283097123. *Alberta Magazine, 0228-1082.*

ALFA OWNER. 0364-930X. Periodical. US. English. mo. Alfa Romeo Owners Club Inc, 2304 San Pasqual Valley Road, Escondido CA 92027. LC TL215.A35. DD 629.2222.

ALGEMENE VERKEERSWAARNEMINGEN. Main/Corp Limburg, Netherlands (Province). Provinciale Waterstaat. Onderafdeling Verkeerszaken. 0300-1830. Dutch. ir. Provinciale Waterstaat Limburg, Stadhuisstraat 4, Limburg The Netherlands. LC HE5674.L5.

ALMANACH DE L'AUTO (MONTREAL, QUEBEC). See Yearbooks, Almanacs, Directories.

AMERICAN CLEAN CAR. See Business.

ANALYSIS OF BICYCLE/MOTOR VEHICLE COLLISIONS REPORTED IN MANITOBA. (AN ANALYSIS OF BICYCLE/MOTOR VEHICLE COLLISIONS REPORTED IN MANITOBA, JANUARY 1,-DECEMBER 31 . . .). 0711-9453. CN. English. Free. Department of Highways, Division of Driver and Vehicle Licensing, 1075 Portage Avenue, Winnipeg Manitoba R3G 0S1 Canada. Tel (204)945-5751. LC HE5614.5.C2. DD 388.314. Circ 300. Statistical breakdown of reported accidents in Manitoba involving collsions between bicycles and motor vehicles.

ANNUAIRE DE L'AUTOMOBILE. See Yearbooks, Almanacs, Directories.

ANNUAL COST OF DOING BUSINESS REPORT FOR ASIA WAREHOUSE DISTRIBUTORS. See Business.

ANNUAL NATIONAL VEHICLE POPULATION PROFILE. IMPORT CARS. (ANNUAL NATIONAL VEHICLE POPULATION PROFILE : IMPORT CARS). Main/Corp Polk (R. L.) and Company, Inc. 0148-6861. US. English. an. LC HE5623.A1. DD 388.340973.

ANNUAL NATIONAL VEHICLE POPULATION PROFILE. LIGHT TRUCKS. (ANNUAL NATIONAL VEHICLE POPULATION PROFILE : LIGHT TRUCKS). Main/Corp Polk (R. L.) and Company, Inc. 0148-6276. US. English. an. LC HE5623.A1. DD 629.22.

ANNUAL REPORT - AMERICAN BUS ASSOCIATION. (ANNUAL REPORT). Main/Corp American Bus Association. 1982-. 0738-2685. US. English. an. American Bus Association, 1025 Connecticut Avenue NW, Washington DC 20036. LC HE5623. DD 388.3220973. *Report from the American Bus Association, 0278-1565.*

ANNUAL REPORT - DEPARTMENT OF MOTOR VEHICLES (WESTERN AUSTRALIA). Main/Corp Western Australia. Dept. of Motor Vehicles. 1973/74-. English. ir. LC HE5717. DD 354.94100878305.

ANNUAL REPORT - STATE OF NEW YORK, DEPARTMENT OF MOTOR VEHICLES. Main/Corp New York (State). Dept. of Motor Vehicles. 1st- 1961-. 0196-6723. US. English. an. LC HE5633.N7. DD 388.309747.

ANNUAL REPORT - STATE OF OHIO, THE STATE UNDERGROUND PARKING COMMISSION. Main/Corp State Underground Parking Commission. 0145-7764. US. English. an. 60 East State Street, Columbus OH 43215. LC HE5633.O3. DD 353.977100878312.

ANNUAL REPORT TO CONGRESS ON THE AUTOMOTIVE TECHNOLOGY DEVELOPMENT PROGRAM. VFOAT Automotive Technology Development Program. 1st (1979)-. 0270-756X. US. English. an. US Department of Energy, Washington DC 20585. LC TL1. DD 629.2305.

ANNUAL REPORT TO CONGRESS ON THE IMPLEMENTATION OF PUBLIC LAW 94-413, THE ELECTRIC & HYBRID VEHICLE RESEARCH, DEVELOPMENT & DEMONSTRATION ACT OF 1976. Main/Corp United States. Office of Electric and Hybrid Vehicle Systems. 1st-1977-. 0161-0759. US. English. an. LC TL220. DD 629.229305.

ANNUAL REPORT - VOLVO. Main/Corp Volvo, Aktiebolaget. English. ir. AB Volvo, S-405 08, Gotenburg Sweden. LC HD9710.S84. DD 338.7629209485. *Annual Report For . . . .*

ANNUARIO SEAT. VOL. I, TRASPORTI, CARTOTECNICA ED EDITORIA. See Yearbooks, Almanacs, Directories.

ANTIQUE & CLASSIC CARS, TRUCKS, MOTORCYCLES. Series/Titl The Official Collector's Price Report. VFOAT Antique and Classic Cars, Trucks, Motorcycles. 1st Ed.-. 0747-9786. US. English. an. $3.50. The House of Collectibles Inc, Orlando Central Park/1900 Premier Row, Orlando FL 32809. LC TL7.A1. DD 629.22075.

ANTIQUE AUTOMOBILE. (THE ANTIQUE AUTOMOBILE). 1937. 0003-5831. Periodical. US. English. bm. $12.00. Antique Automobile, 501 West Governor Road, Hershey PA 10733. Tel (717)534-1910. Ed William E Bomgardner. LC TL1. DD 629.2222075. bk rev. adv acc. Circ 40,000. (ctrl). Contains many fine historical articles, tour accounts, technical articles on restorations, and other material. Brief items on Antique Automobile Club of American news and meets. *Bulletin of the Antique Automobile Club of America.*

ANUARIO DA INDUSTRIA BRASILEIRA DE AUTOPECAS. See Yearbooks, Almanacs, Directories.

APA BULLETIN (1980). (APA BULLETIN). VFOAT Bulletin APA. Vol. 6, No. 2 (Winter 1980)-. 0229-7027. Periodical. CN. French. Association pour la Protection des Automobilistes, 292 Boul St Joseph Ouest, Montreal Quebec H2V 2N7 Canada. DD 338.47629222205. *Bulletin aux Consommateurs, 0229-9011; Consumer Bulletin (Montreal, Quebec : 1979), 0229-9003.*

ATA INGEGNERIA AUTOMOTORISTICA. VFOAT ATA. Periodical. IT. Italian. mo. $50.00. Via Carlo Alberta 61, 10 123 Torino Italy. LC TL4. DD 629.205. *ATA.*

ATZ. AUTOMOBILTECHNISCHE ZEITSCHRIFT. (AUTOMOBILTECHNISCHE ZEITSCHRIFT). VFOAT ATZ. 0001-2785. GW. German. mo. $80.48. Franckh Verlags W Keller and Company, PO Box 640, D-7000 Stuttgart 1 West Germany. Tel (0711)21910. Ed Claus Keller. Ind/Abst CIS Abstr., Energy Res. Abstr., Eng. Index Annu., Eng. Index Mon., Eng. Index Bioeng. Abstr., Eng. Index Energy Abstr., Excerpta Med., Fluidex, Eng. Index. CODEN AUTZA6. bk rev. adv acc. Circ 3,700. (ctrl). A technical journal for engineers, constructors and the management of the automobile industry. *Motorwagen, 0369-1330; Auto-Technik, 0365-8090.*

AUTO COLLECTOR NEWS. MIDWEST ED. (AUTO COLLECTOR NEWS). Vol. 2, No. 1 (Aug. 1984)-. 8750-1511. Periodical. US. English. mo. $15.00 Domestic, $20.00 Foreign. Midwest Car Collector, PO Box 1806, Cedar Rapid IA 52406. *Midwest Car Collector, 0746-2174.*

AUTO EXKLUSIV. Periodical. German. mo. 68.00. Tobinium-Verlag, Henzmannstr 27, 4800 Zofingen Switzerland.

AUTO GUIDE. Main/Corp Duval, Jacques, 1934-. 1974-. CN. English (French). LC TL1.D87. DD 629.222205.

THE AUTO INDEX. See Indexes/Abstracts.

AUTO-INDUSTRIE EN ASSEMBLAGEBEDRIJVEN, AUTO-ONDERDELENINDUSTRIE, VLIEGTUIGBOUW- EN VLIEGTUIGREPARATIEBEDRIJVEN. Series/Titl Produktiestatistieken Industrie. VFOAT Manufacture and Assembly of Motor Vehicles, Manufacture of Parts and Accessories For Motor Vehicles, Manufacture and Repair or Aircraft. 1981-. Dutch (summaries in English). an. 10.55. Central Bureau voor de Statistiek, Prinses Beatrixlaan 428 Postbus 959, 2270 AZ Voorburg Netherlands. LC HD9710.N4.

AUTO INDUSTRY MAGAZINE. Vol. 1, No. 1 (July 1983)-. 0746-3774. Periodical. US. English. mo. $12.00. Target Publishing Inc, Rt 1 Box 470, Newton NJ 07860.

L'AUTO-JOURNAL. Began with Jan. 15, 1950 issue. FR. French. sm. Soc Presse Auto Journal, 43 Boulevard Barbes, 75018 Paris Cedex France. Tel 257 11 88. LC TL2. DD 629.222205.

AUTO LAUNDRY NEWS. 0005-0776. Periodical. US. English. ir. $15.00. Columbia Communications, 370 Lexington Avenue, New York NY 10024. Tel (212)532-9290.

AUTO MERCHANDISING NEWS. See Business.

AUTO MODIFIEE. See Recreation, Leisure - Sports.

AUTO-MOTOR. Periodical. HU. Hungarian. sm. Akademiai Kiado, POB 24, 1363 Budapest Hungary. LC TL4.

AUTO PLUS. Vol. A, No. 4-. 0711-2912. Periodical. CN. French. ir. $12.50 Canada, $18.00 US, $25.00 Others. EPH Inc, Bureau 11/1459 rue Belanger, Montreal Quebec H2G 1A5 Canada. DD 629.222205. *Grand Tourisme Magazine, 0227-4515.*

AUTO PREVENTION. (AUTO PREVENTION : BULLETIN D'INFORMATION DE L'ASSOCIATION SECTORIELLE, SERVICES AUTOMOBILES). VFOAT Bulletin D'Information de L'Association Sectorielle, Services Automobiles. V. 1, No. 1 (Mar/April 1984)-. 0825-4990. Periodical. CN. French. bm. Free. Association Sectorielle Services Automobiles, Bureau 340 1425 Rue de la Montagne, Montreal Quebec H3G 1Z3 Canada. DD 363.11933847629222209714.

AUTO-QUEBEC. (AUTO-QUEBEC : REVUE OFFICIELLE DE LA FEDERATION AUTO-QUEBEC). 0821-7343. Periodical. CN. French. bm. Federation Auto-Quebec, 1415 Est rue Jarray, Montreal Quebec H2E 2Z7 Canada. DD 796.7209714.

AUTO RACING DIGEST. See Recreation, Leisure - Sports.

AUTO RACING USA. See Recreation, Leisure - Sports.

AUTO RACING/USA. See Recreation, Leisure - Sports.

AUTO REPORTS. 0148-9410. Periodical. US. English. bm. $5.00. Hi-Torque Publications, 16200 Ventura Boulevard, Encino CA 91436. LC TL1. DD 629.222205. *U.S. Auto Reports, 0095-5299.*

AUTO SPORT. See Recreation, Leisure - Sports.

AUTO SPORT CANADA. See Recreation, Leisure - Sports.

AUTO TRIM NEWS. Began in 1952. 0005-0865. Periodical. US. English. mo. $12.00. Auto Trim News, PO Box 86, North Bladwin NY 11510. Tel (516)223-4334. Ed Nat Danas. LC TL1. DD 629.26. bk rev. adv acc. Circ 8,000. (ctrl). Upholsters to the nation's autos, boats and trucks. Restylers who do cosmetic changes for above. Restorers of classic cars.

AUTOBODY AND THE RECONDITIONED CAR. Began with Issue for Aug. 1938. 0005-0911. Periodical. US. English. mo. Spokesman Publishing Company, 431 Ohio Pike, Cincinnati OH 45230. Tel (513)528-5530. LC TL1. *Automobile Trimmer and Painter.*

THE AUTOCAR. V. 1- Nov. 1895-. Periodical. UK. English. wk. $81.21. Haymarket Publishing Ltd, 38-42 Hampton Road, Teddington Middlesex TW11 0JE England. Tel 01-977 8787. Ed Matthew Carter. LC TL1. bk rev. adv acc. Circ 50,000. Road tests; new car descriptions; driving impressions, everything to do with cars. *Motor Car & Motorcycle, Horseless Carriage and Journal of Automobility.*

AUTOCLUB. VFOAT Auto Club. No. 1-. Periodical. Spanish. bm. Auto Club, Avda Del Libertado 1850, Buenos Aires Argentina.

AUTOFACTS NEW CAR GUIDE. VFOAT New Car Guide. 0149-5763. US. English. an. $1.50. Davis Publications, 229 Park Avenue South, New York NY 10003. LC TL1. DD 629.222205.

AUTOKOZLEKEDES. 0587-2243. Periodical. Hungarian. ir. 60.00. Lapkiado Vallalat, Hagyar Posta Kozponti Hirlapiroda Budapest V Jozsef Nador T, Budapest Hungary. LC HE5601.

AUTOMOBIL. V. 55, No. 4- Apr. 1975-. 0304-8721. Periodical. English and/or Afrikaans. ir. Mead and McGrouther, PO Box 741, Johannesburg South

Transportation—Automobiles

Africa. LC HD9710.S7. DD 338.476292220968. *Automobile In Southern Africa.*

AUTOMOBIL-INDUSTRIE. Vol. 1-. 0005-1306. Periodical. GW. German. qt. $27.60. Vogel Verlag, Postfach 67-40, D-8700 Wurzburg 1 West Germany.

AUTOMOBILE. (L'AUTOMOBILE). 0005-1330. Periodical. CN. French. bm. $6.19. Wadham Publishing Ltd, 109 Vanderhoof Avenue/Suite 101, Toronto Ontario M4G 2J2 Canada. Ind/Abst Point Repere.

L'AUTOMOBILE. No. 1- Sept. 1946-. Periodical. FR. French. mo. $34.00. Zone Indust de la Gaudre, BP 38, 91410 Dourdan France. Tel 459 68 68. Ed Dargound P Laureys. LC TL2. bk rev.

AUTOMOBILE ABSTRACTS. See Indexes/Abstracts.

AUTOMOBILE ALMANAC. See Yearbooks, Almanacs, Directories.

AUTOMOBILE BUYERS' GUIDE. 1968-. English. ir. LC TL12. DD 338.47629202554.

AUTOMOBILE IN CIFRE. Italian. an. LC TL4. DD 629.222205.

AUTOMOBILE INDUSTRY TRENDS. 0198-781X. Periodical. US. English. qt. Sanford C Bernstein & Company, 717 Fifth Avenue, New York NY 10022.

AUTOMOBILE INSURANCE EXPERIENCE. See Insurance.

AUTOMOBILE INSURANCE LOSSES COLLISION COVERAGES INITIAL RESULTS. See Insurance.

AUTOMOBILE INSURANCE LOSSES COLLISION COVERAGES VARIATIONS BY MAKE AND SERIES. See Insurance.

AUTOMOBILE INSURANCE THEFT LOSSES BY MAKE AND SERIES, MODELS. See Insurance.

AUTOMOBILE INTERNATIONAL. 0099-2615. Periodical. US. English. ir. Johnston International Publ., 386 Park Avenue South, New York, NY 10016. Tel (212)689-0120. Ed Bernard Zinober. adv acc. Circ 28,029. (ctrl). Serves the vehicle aftermarket outside of North America with service-oriented articles addressed to repair shops, vehicle distributors, fleets and parts dealers.

AUTOMOBILE MANUFACTURERS' MEASUREMENTS. US. English. an. Federal Maritime Commission, 1100 L Street NW, Washington DC 20573. LC TL1. DD 629.22220212.

AUTOMOBILE QUARTERLY. V. 1- Spring 1962-. 0005-1438. Periodical. US. English. qt. $39.95. Automobile Quarterly, PO Box 348, Route 22 Sharadin Road, Kutztown PA 19530. Tel (215)683-8352. Ind/Abst Appl. Sci. Technol. Index. LC TL1. DD 629.205. (cum index). Circ 25,000. (ctrl). A quarterly hardbound magazine whichs covers the cars of yesterday, today and tomorrow.

AUTOMOBILE RED BOOK. VFOAT Red Book. 0736-7953. US. English. bm. $32.00. National Market Reports Inc, 300 West Adams Street, Chicago IL 60606. LC HD9710.U5. DD 629.222029473. *Red Book (Chicago, Ill. : 1979), 0484-1697.*

AUTOMOBILE YEAR. SZ. English (French, German and Italian). an. 69. Editions 24 Heures, Ar de la Gare 39, CH-1001 Lausanne Switzerland. Tel 021 20 31 11. Ed J R Piccard. adv acc. Circ 14,000. International annual on production cars, automobile industry and car racing. *Annual Automobile Review.*

AUTOMOBILES CITROEN. RAPPORT. FR. French. ir. Mundoprint-France, 117 A 167 Quai Andre Citroen, Paris 15E France. LC HD9710.F74. DD 338.762920944.

AUTOMOBILISM : THE JOURNAL OF THE FEDERATION INTERNATIONALE DE L'AUTOMOBILE. Periodical. English (summaries in French, German, Italian, and Spanish). qt. 110. Fia Secretariat, 8 Place De La Concorde, 75008 Paris France. LC TL4. DD 629.222205. *Automobilismo E Automobilismo Industriale.*

AUTOMOTIVE AIR CONDITIONING AND HEATING SERVICE MANUAL. BOOK SUPPLEMENT. (AUTOMOTIVE AIR CONDITIONING AND HEATING SERVICE MANUAL : BOOK SUPPLEMENT). Main/Corp Mitchell Manuals, Inc. VFOAT Automotive Air Conditioning and Heating Service Manual. 0194-0023. US. English. Mitchell Manuals Inc, PO Box 80527, San Diego CA 92138. LC TL271. DD 629.277.

AUTOMOTIVE BODY REPAIR NEWS. 0192-0995. Periodical. US. English. mo. $35.00. 300 West Kaje Street, Chicago IL 60606. LC TL255. DD 629.260288. *Automotive Service and Body News.*

AUTOMOTIVE CHAIN STORE (NEW YORK, N.Y.). (AUTOMOTIVE CHAIN STORE). Began in 1983. 0746-2077. Periodical. US. English. mo. $25.00. Automotive Chain Store, 77 North Miller Road, Akron OH 44313. LC HD9710.A1. DD 381.456292068. *ACS Magazine, 0738-663X.*

AUTOMOTIVE ENGINEER. V. 1- Oct. 1975-. 0307-6490. Periodical. UK. English. bm. $75.00. Mechanical Engineering Publishing, PO Box 361, Birmingham AL 35201. Tel (205)991-6925. Ed John Fenton. Ind/Abst Electron. Commun. Abstr. J., ISMEC Bull., Pollut. Abstr. Indexes, Saf. Sci. Abstr. J., Eng. Index Mon., Eng. Index Bioeng. Abstr., Eng. Index Energy Abstr., Fluidex, Ship Abstr., Coal Abstr., Excerpta Med., Met. Abstr., World Alum. Abstr., Ref. Source, Eng. Index Mon., Eng. Index Annu., Energy Res. Abstr., Eng. Index. LC TL1. DD 629.205. adv acc. Coverage includes research design, development and production in the automotive industry. Topics encompass the manufacture of various vehicles based on automotive engineering principles and technology. *JAE, Journal of Automotive Engineering, 0307-1820; Automotive Design Engineering.*

AUTOMOTIVE ENGINEERING. 0098-2571. Periodical. English. ir. $8.00 Members, $16.00 Nonmembers. Society of Automotive Engineers, 400 Commonwealth Drive, Warrendale PA 15096. Tel (412)776-4841. bk rev adv acc. Circ 67,000. (ctrl). Serves the automotive design and production industries and contains state-of-the-art information for application in the design of new and improved vehicle systems. *SAE Journal of Automotive Engineering, 0097-711X.*

AUTOMOTIVE EXECUTIVE (1974). (AUTOMOTIVE EXECUTIVE). VFOAT AE. Spring 1974-. Periodical. US. English. mo. $12.00. Automotive Executive, 8400 Westpark Drive, McLean VA 22102. Tel (703)821-7150. LC HD9710.U5. DD 658.9292220973.

AUTOMOTIVE FLEET. 1961-. 0005-1519. Periodical. US. English. mo. $18.00. Bobit Publishing Company, 2500 Artesia Boulevard, Redondo Beach CA 90278. Tel (213)376-8788.

AUTOMOTIVE INDEPENDENT. Vol. 28, No. 1 (Jan. 1980)-. 0199-6908. Periodical. US. English. mo. $12.00. Independent Automotive Service Association, PO Box 929, Bedford TX 76021. Tel (817)283-6205. Ed Charles Seitz. bk rev. adv acc. Circ 5,300. Business news regarding auto and truck repairs, management, technical news, equipment and tool information, association news, and repair tips. *Independent Garageman, 0445-5266.*

AUTOMOTIVE LITERATURE INDEX. See Indexes/Abstracts.

AUTOMOTIVE MARKET REPORT. See Business - Marketing.

AUTOMOTIVE MARKETER. Issue No. 18- Fall 1976-. 0702-8318. Periodical. CN. English. an. Wadham Publications Ltd, 109 Vanderhoof Avenue/Suite 101, Toronto Ontario M4G 2J2 Canada. Ind/Abst Can. Bus. Index. DD 338.4762920971. *Automotive Mass Marketer, 0067-2572.*

AUTOMOTIVE NEWS. 0005-1551. Periodical. US. English. wk. $25.00. Automotive News, 965 East Jefferson, Detroit MI 48207. Ind/Abst Trade Ind. Index, Predicasts, Infobank, Bus. Period. Index. LC TL1. DD 338.4762920205. *Automotive Service, Automotive Daily News.*

AUTOMOTIVE NEWS. MARKET DATA BOOK. VFOAT Automotive News. 1976-. US. English. an. $45.00. Crain Communications Inc, 1400 Woodbridge Avenue, Detroit MI 48207. Tel (313)446-6000. Ed Andrew R McGill. adv acc. Circ 64,000. Comprehensive data on 1985 automotive calendar year and 1986 model cars and trucks. Includes statistics and analysis of motor vehicle production, sales and registrations, products and spccs, prices, options, equipment and much more. *Automotive News. Almanac Issue.*

AUTOMOTIVE Q & A. Main/Corp Williams, Doug. VFOAT Q & A. VAT Automotive Questions and Answers, Automotive Q&A. 0196-0156. Periodical. US. English. sm. Automotive Q & A, 20420 Briarcliff, Detroit MI 48221. Tel (313)341-0654.

AUTOMOTIVE REBUILDER. V. 1- Oct. 1964-. 0567-2317. Periodical. US. English. mo. Babcox Business Publications, Babcox Building 11 South Forge Street, Akron OH 44304. Tel (216)535-6117. LC TL1. DD 658.929287.

AUTOMOTIVE RETAILER. 0005-1578. Periodical. CN. English. mo. Automotive Retailer Publ, 1687 West Broadway, Vancouver British Columbia V6J 1X5 Canada. Ind/Abst Can. Bus. Index.

AUTOMOTIVE REVIEW. V. 1- Jan. 1978-. 0706-506X. Periodical. CN. English. bm. Free to members. Ontario Retail Gasoline and Automotive Service Association, Suite 210/312 Dolomite Drive, Downsview Ontario M3J 2N2 Canada. DD 629.28609713.

AUTOMOTIVE SERVICE DATA BOOK. VAT Data Book (Toronto). 1978-. 0705-6281. CN. English. an. $6.50 Canada, $8.50 US & UK, $9.50 Others. MacLean-Hunter Ltd, 481 University Avenue, Toronto Ontario M5W 1A7 Canada. DD 629.2872. *Canadian Service Data Book, 0068-9629.*

AUTOMOVIL INTERNACIONAL. 0193-0907. Periodical. US. English. ir. $80.00. Johnston International Publ., 386 Park Avenue South, New York, NY 10016. Tel (212)689-0120. Ed Bernard Zinober. adv acc. Circ 20,115. (ctrl). Serves the vehicle aftermarket in Latin America with service-oriented articles addressed to repair shops, vehicle distributors and parts dealers.

AUTOPARTS DISTRIBUTOR. VAT APD. Vol. 1, No. 1 (Jan. 1984)-. 0827-2808. Periodical. CN. English. bm. $3.00 Per No. APD Publications, 41 Mutual Street, Toronto Ontario M5B 2A7 Canada. DD 338.4762920971.

AUTOSCOPE. (L'AUTOSCOPE). Vol. 1, No. 1 (Jan./Feb. 1983)-. 0823-7018. Periodical. CN. French (text in English). bm. Free. Autoscope, 10525 rue Clark, Montreal Quebec H3L 2S5 Canada. DD 381.45629209714. (ctrl).

AUTOWEEK. 0192-9674. Periodical. US. English. wk. $23.00. Crain Communications, 740 North Rush Street, Chicago IL 60611. Tel (312)649-5456. Ed Leon Mandell. adv acc. Circ 160,000. Serving the interest of automotive enthusiasts. *Autoweek and Competition Press.*

AVANTI NEWSLETTER. VFOAT Newsletter. 0741-9252. Periodical. US. English. qt. $10.00. 13150 el Capitan Way, Delhi CA 95315. LC TL215.A94. *Avanti Owners Association International Newsletter.*

AVION OWNER'S MANUAL. Main/Corp Avion Coach Corporation. US. English. PO Box 7300, Riverside CA 92516. LC TL297. DD 643.

AVTOEXPORT ROUND-UP. Periodical. UR. English. qt. V/O Avtoexport, 14 Ui Volkhonda, 119902 Moscow Russian SFSR. LC HD9710.R9. DD 338.4762920947.

AVTOMOBILNAIA PROMYSHLENNOST. 1958-. 0005-2337. Periodical. UR. Russian. mo. $33.50. Victor Kamkin Inc (70003), 12224 Parklawn Drive, Rockville MD 20852. Tel (301)881-5973. Ind/Abst Met. Abstr., World Alum. Abstr. *Avtomobilnaia I Traktornaia Promyshlennost.*

AVTOMOBILNYI TRANSPORT KAZAKHSTANA. Periodical. UR. Russian. mo. 1.80. 83 GSP-1 Pr Seifullina 460, Alma-Ata Kazakh SSR. LC HE5699.K3.

BAGNALL'S VPO INDUSTRY NEWS. VFOAT VPO Industry News. VAT Van Pickup and Off Road Industry News. 0195-9727. Periodical. US. English. mo. $10.00 Domestic, $15.00. Bagnall Brothers Publishing Company, 4262 Campus Drive/Suite A, Newport Beach CA 92660.

BATTERY MAN. 1921-. 0005-6359. Periodical. US. English. mo. Independent Battery Manufacturers Association Inc, 100 Larchwood Drive, Largo FL 33540. Tel (813)586-1408. Ind/Abst Predicasts, Energy Res. Abstr., Funk Scott Index Corp. Ind.

BIENNIAL REPORT - VIRGINIA DIVISION OF MOTOR VEHICLES. Main/Corp Virginia. Division of Motor Vehicles. US. English. be. Virginia Division of Motor Vehicles, 2220 West Broad Street, Richmond VA 23220. LC HE5633.V8. DD 353.9755008783.

BILEN, MOTOR OG SPORT. Periodical. Danish. ir. Palle Fogtdal, Nrre Farimagsgade 49, 1364 Kvenhaven Denmark. LC TL4. *Bilen Og Baden.*

Transportation—Automobiles

BITS ABOUT WHEELS CEASED. Began with Sept. 1969 issue. 0383-9923. Periodical. CN. English. ir. Ontario Safety League, 409 King Street West, Toronto Ontario M5V 1K1 Canada. DD 629.283205.

BLACK BOOK. IMPORT CAR FACT BOOK. (IMPORT CAR FACT BOOK). 0742-0854. US. English. National Auto Research, PO Box 758, Gainesville GA 30503. LC TL1. DD 629.2222.

BLACK BOOK. OLD CAR MARKET GUIDE. (BLACK BOOK. OLD CAR ... MARKET GUIDE). VFOAT Old Car ... Market Guide. 0747-4393. Periodical. US. English. bm. $36.00. Black Book, PO Box 758, Gainesville GA 30503. DD 629.

BLACK BOOK USED SPECIALTY VEHICLE AND TRUCK GUIDE. Jan./Feb. 1975-. 0318-9368. CN. English (includes some text in French). bm. $30. National Auto Research Canada, 67 Ellesmere Road, Scarborough Ontario M1R 4B8 Canada. DD 338.436292230971. *Black Book Used Truck Guide, 0318-935X.*

BMW NEWS. 0164-8659. Periodical. US. English. mo. $10.50. BMWMOA, PO Box 74, Newark CA 94560. LC TL448.B18. DD 629.227506073.

BODYSHOP. V. 1- Jan./Feb. 1970-. 0045-2319. Periodical. CN. English. bm. $10.83. Wadham Publications Ltd, 109 Vanderhoof Avenue, Toronto Ontario M4G 2J2 Canada. Tel (416)425-9021.

BRAKE & FRONT END. VFOAT Brake and Front End. 0193-726X. Periodical. US. English. mo. $23.00. Babcox Publications Inc, 11 South Forge Street, Akron OH 44304. Tel (216)535-6117. Ed Jeffrey S Davis. LC TL275.A1. DD 629.2460288. adv acc. Circ 29,000. (ctrl). For auto repair shops engaged in brake, steering and suspension service. Semi-technical descriptions of mechanical systems and repair techniques, plus management articles, product reviews and industry news. *Brake and Front End Service.*

BRAKES. See Public Health and Safety.

BRANHAM AUTOMOBILE REFERENCE BOOK, SHOWING IN ILLUSTRATED FORM THE LOCATION OF MOTOR AND SERIAL NUMBERS ON ALL PASSENGER CARS AND TRUCKS. US. English. an. $10.25. Branham Publishing Company, PO Box 1948, Santa Monica CA 90406. Tel (213)394-8585. LC TL151. DD 629.2085.

BROKEN SPOKE. (THE BROKEN SPOKE). VFOAT Rayon Casse. Began with Jan. 1959 issue. 0045-3226. Periodical. CN. English. mo. $3.00. Calgary Sports Car Club, Box 844, Calgary Alberta T2P 2J8 Canada. DD 796.7705.

BUDGET GUIDE TO CAR REPAIR. VFOAT Car Repair. 0360-1110. US. English. an. $1.25. Davis Publications, 229 Park Avenue South, New York NY 10003. LC TL152. DD 629.2872205.

BULLETIN ON MOTOR VEHICLE STATISTICS. See Statistics.

BUYER'S GUIDE REPORTS. 10 YEARS OF USED CAR PRICES. VFOAT 10 Years of Used Car Prices. 0748-1632. US. English. mo. Pace Publications Inc, 1845 North Farwell Avenue, Milwaukee WI 53202. LC HD9710.U5. DD 629.2222029473.

BUYER'S GUIDE REPORTS. USED CAR PRICES. VFOAT Used Car Prices. 0740-1302. Periodical. US. English. mo. $22.00. Pace Publications Inc, 1410 East Capitol Drive, Milwaukee WI 53211.

BUYER'S GUIDE REPORTS/CARFACTS. NEW & USED FOREIGN CAR PRICES. (BUYER'S GUIDE REPORTS : NEW & USED FOREIGN CAR PRICES). VFOAT New and Used Foreign Car Prices. 0740-1280. Periodical. US. English. Pace Publications, 1410 East Capitol Drive, Milwaukee WI 53211.

BUYER'S GUIDE REPORTS/CARFACTS. NEW & USED FOREIGN CAR PRICES. (BUYER'S GUIDE REPORTS : NEW & USED FOREIGN CAR PRICES). VFOAT New and Used Foreign Car Prices. 0740-1280. US. English. qt. $9.00. Pace Publications Inc, 1410 East Capitol Drive, Milwaukee WI 53211. LC HD9710.U5. DD 629.2222029473. *Buyer's Guide Reports. New Car Prices.*

BUYER'S GUIDE REPORTS/CARFACTS. NEW AND USED TRUCK AND VAN PRICES. VFOAT New and Used Truck and Van Prices. 0740-1310. Periodical. US. English. ty. $5.00. Pace Publications Inc, 1410 East Capitol Drive, Milwaukee WI 53211. LC TL230.A1.

BUYER'S GUIDE REPORTS/CARFACTS. NEW CAR PRICES. (BUYER'S GUIDE REPORTS. NEW CAR PRICES). VFOAT New Car Prices. 0740-1299. Periodical. US. English. $11.00. Pace Publications Inc, 1020 North Broadway/Suite 111, Milwaukee WI 53211. Tel (414)272-9977. Ed Emily Maid. adv acc. Automotive pricing cost and list including options.

C. A. S. C. RACE REGULATIONS. (RACE REGULATIONS). Main/Corp Canadian Automobile Sport Clubs. 1975-. 0381-9906. CN. English. Canadian Automobile Sport Clubs, PO Box 97 Station A, Willowdale Ontario M2N 5S7 Canada. DD 796.720971. *Race & Solo Regulations, 0381-9892.*

CALIFORNIA WHOZ WHO. VFOAT Who's Who Behind Personalized California License Plates. 1979-. 0195-6949. US. English. $6.95. Mike Farley, 9701 Wilshire Boulevard/Suite 800, Beverly Hills CA 90212. LC HE5620.L5. DD 388.3422.

CANADIAN AFTERMATH. (THE CANADIAN AFTERMARKET). V. 1, No. 1 (April/May 1982)-. 0821-2651. Periodical. CN. English. bm. $10.00. Wheelspin News Inc, 3045 Universe Drive, Mississauga Ontario L4X 2E2 Canada. DD 338.4762920971.

CANADIAN BLACK BOOK. 1978/1971-. 0705-6966. CN. English. ir. William Ward Publications Ltd, 85 Ellesmere Road/Suite 201, Scarborough Ontario M1R 4B8 Canada. Tel (416)447-8545. DD 629.2220212. *Black Book Vehicle Identification Guide, 0316-4896.*

CANADIAN BLACK BOOK. ONTARIO. (CANADIAN BLACK BOOK; OFFICIAL USED CAR MARKET GUIDE). Sept. 20, 1976-. 0384-8434. Periodical. CN. English (includes some text in French). bm. National Auto Research Canada, 67 Ellesmere Road, Scarborough Ontario M1R 4B8 Canada. DD 338.4762920971. *Black Book.*

CANADIAN BLACK BOOK USED SPECIALTY VEHICLE AND TRUCK GUIDE. Sept./Oct. 1976-Nov./Dec. 1978. 0384-6962. Periodical. CN. English (includes some text in French). bm. William Ward Publishing Ltd, 85 Ellesmere Road/Suite 201, Scarborough Ontario M1R 4B8 Canada. Tel (416)447-8545. DD 338.47629202571. *Black Book Used Specialty Vehicle and Truck Guide, 0318-9368.*

CANADIAN BLACK BOOK USED SPECIALTY VEHICLE AND TRUCK VALUATIONS. Jan./Feb. 1979-. 0822-5176. Periodical. CN. English (includes some text in French). bm. $30.00. Canadian Black Book Used Specialty Vehicle and Truck Valuations, 67 Ellesmere Road, Scarborough Ontario M1R 4B8 Canada. DD 338.436292240216. *Canadian Black Book Used Specialty Vehicle and Truck Guide, 0384-6962.*

CANADIAN CAMPING AND RV DEALER. VAT Canadian Camping and Recreational Vehicle Dealer. Vol. 1, No. 1 (Oct./Nov. 1975)-. 0710-9326. Periodical. CN. English. ir. 11.00. CRV Publishing Company, 3414 Park Avenue/Suite 221, Montreal Quebec H2X 2H5 Canada. Tel (514)282-0191. Ed W E Taylor. DD 381.456292260971. adv acc. Circ 6,000. Covers advertising, editorial, listing of shows, and accessories. *Vehicules de Recreation, Trade (1975).*

CANADIAN MOTORIST CEASED. Began publication in 1914?. 0008-4530. Periodical. CN. English. Ontario Motor League, 2 Carlton Street, Toronto Ontario M5B 1K4 Canada.

CANADIAN MOTORSPORT ANNUAL. (THE CANADIAN MOTORSPORT ANNUAL ...). 1980/81-. 0711-3064. CN. English. an. $3.00. Wheelspin News Inc, 3045 Universal Drive, Mississauga Ontario L4X 2E2 Canada. DD 796.705.

CANADIAN RED BOOK. V. 1- June/Aug. 1958-. 0045-527X. Periodical. CN. English (includes some text in French). mo. $37.92. MacLean Hunter, Circulation/Accounting Department, PO Box 100 Station A, Toronto Ontario M5W 1A7 Canada. Tel (416)596-5082.

CAR AND DRIVER. V. 1- July 1955-. 0008-6002. Periodical. US. English. mo. $9.98 Domestic, $12.98 Canada. CBS Publications, 1515 Broadway, New York NY 10036; (subscription address: Neodata PO Box 2606 Boulder CO 80322). Ind/Abst Pop. Mag. Rev., Consum. Index Prod. Eval. Inf. Source, Read. Guide Period. Lit., Mag. Index. LC TL236. Available on microfilm. *Sports Cars Illustrated.*

CAR AND DRIVER ROAD TEST ANNUAL. VFOAT Road Test Annual. 8755-626X. US. English. an. $3.95. Ziff-Davis Publishing Company, 1 Park Avenue, New York NY 10016. DD 629.

CAR AND TRUCK APPRAISALS. Main/Corp American Auto Appraisal. Began in 1923. Periodical. US. English. qt. American Auto Appraisal, PO Box 930, Royal Oak MI 48068. LC HD9710.U5. DD 338.43.

CAR CARE. VFOAT Money Saving Car Care. 0275-391X. Periodical. US. English. an. $2.25. Performance Publications Inc, Box 99, Amawalk NY 10501. LC TL152. DD 629.2872205.

CAR CARE GUIDE. 1973-. 0162-3443. US. English. an. $39.75. Gousha Chek-Chart, 2001 The Alameda/PO Box 6227, San Jose CA 95126. Tel (408)296-1060. Ed Robert Colver. Circ 30,000. Ten years of automotive maintenance services, comprehensive lubrication recomendations and popular automotive systems specifications including a monthly service bulletin highlighting current technology, service, manufacturers updates.

CAR CARE HANDBOOK. 0147-7684. US. English. $1.50. Times Mirror Magazines Inc, 380 Madison Avenue, New York NY 10017. LC TL152. DD 629.28822.

CAR. CLUB AUTOMOBILE ROUTIER. (CAR : CLUB AUTOMOBILE ROUTIER). VFOAT Club Automobile Routier. Autumn 1981-. 0712-8614. Periodical. CN. French. ir. Free to Members. CAR, c/o Corporation des Routiers du Quebec, Bureau 208/3019, East Sherbrooke Montreal Quebec H1W 1B2 Canada. DD 629.2222060714.

CAR COLLECTOR AND CAR CLASSICS. VFOAT Car Collector. V. 2- Feb. 1979-. 0164-5552. Periodical. US. English. mo. $24.00. Car Collector, 8601 Dunwoody Place/Suite 144, Atlanta GA 30338. Tel (404)998-4603. Ed Don Peterson. LC TL1. DD 629.2222075. bk rev. adv acc. Circ 40,000. (ctrl). Covers the antique, classic, special interest and sports car fields. Generous use of color. Top writers in this field display and in classified ads. *Car Collector, 0734-5046; Car Classics, 0095-0556.*

CAR COSTS. Began with 1972 issue. 0705-1298. CN. English. an. Canadian Automobile Association, 1775 Courtwood Crescent, Ottawa Ontario K2C 3J2 Canada. Tel (613)224-5173. Ed Michael S McNeil. DD 629.2222. Circ 8,000. (ctrl). Booklet describing how to calculate costs of owning and operating an automobile in Canada.

CAR CRAFT ANNUAL. 0743-3182. Periodical. US. English. an. $4.95 Domestic, $5.95 Canada. Petersen Publishing Company, 6725 Sunset Boulevard, Los Angeles CA 90028. LC TL210. DD 629.22805.

CAR CRAFT HOW TO BUILD A STREET MACHINE. VFOAT How to Build a Street Machine. No. 1-. 0731-4825. US. English. $2.50. Petersen Publishing Company, Department CC7/PO Box 3299, Los Angeles CA 90028. LC TL236. DD 629.228.

CAR DEALER INSIDER. 0148-6721. Periodical. US. English. ir. $88.00. Atcom Inc, 2315 Broadway, New York NY 10024. Tel (212)873-5900. Ed Al Burns. Circ 3,400. (ctrl). A newsletter for automobile dealers in the new car retailing business.

CAR MECHANICS. Began publication in 1958. 0008-6037. Periodical. UK. English. mo. Business Publications Ltd, Canada House/Kildare Close, Ruislip HA4 9XB England. Tel 01-928-3388.

CAR PRICES. VFOAT Car Prices Magazine. 1966. 0739-1722. US. English. an. $3.25. Peoples Publishing Company, 901 West Victoria Street/Suite B, Compton CA 90224. Tel (213)537-0896. Ed Rosemary Anderson. adv acc. Circ 100,000. Car price catalogue.

CAR-PUTER'S AUTOFACTS. (CAR-PUTER'S AUTOFACTS : USED CAR PRICES). VFOAT Autofacts: Used Car Prices. 0094-8527. US. English. $1.50. 229 Park Avenue South, New York NY 10003. LC HD9710.U5. DD 381.456292220973.

CAR-PUTER'S NEW CAR YEARBOOK. See Yearbooks, Almanacs, Directories.

CAR SERVICE MANUAL. VFOAT Mobil Car Service Manual. 0743-6084. US. English. an. Mobil Oil Corporation/ Technical Publications, 3225 Gallows Road, Fairfax VA 22037. LC TL152. DD 629.28722.

CAR STEREO. See Engineering - Electricity, Electrical Engineering, Electronics.

Transportation—Automobiles

CAR STYLING QUARTERLY. V. 1- Winter 1973-. Periodical. US. English (Japanese). qt. Kaneko Enterprises Inc, 15641 Product Ln Suite A-10, Huntington Beach CA 92649. Tel (714)891-1929. LC TL240.

CARAVAN. 1973/74-. 0303-7576. Italian. ir. 5000. l'Editrice dell'Automobile, Viale Regina Margherita 279, Roma 00198 Italy. LC TL297.

CARGUIDE. VFOAT Carguide Preview. 0384-9309. CN. English. an. $2. Formula Publications Ltd, 1255 Yonge Street/Suite 105, Toronto Ontario M4T 1W6 Canada. DD 629.222205.

CARMAG. (CARMAG : CANADIAN AUTOMOBILE REPAIR & MAINTENANCE). VAT Canadian Automobile Repair & Maintenance Magazine. Vol. 2, No. 1 (Spring 1981)-. 0710-7277. Periodical. CN. English. bm. $7.50. CARM Publishing, 287 Pacpherson Avenue, Toronto Ontario M4V 1A4 Canada. Tel (416)928-1096. Ed Ed Belitsky. DD 629.2872205. bk rev. adv acc. Circ 55,000. Includes car care, car evaluations, new automotive products vintage and classic cars, how to repair and service vehicles. *Canadian Automobile Repair & Maintenance, 0710-7285.*

CARS. Periodical. US. English. $10.00. Popular Publications, 420 Lexington Avenue, New York NY 10170. LC TL236. DD 629.228. *Hi-Performance Cars.*

CARS & PARTS. VFOAT Cars and Parts. 1957. 0008-6975. Periodical. US. English. mo. $20.00. Amos Press Inc, PO Box 482, 911 Vandemark Road, Sidney OH 45365. Tel (513)498-2111. Ed Robert J Stevens. adv acc. Circ 87,000. (ctrl). Readers collect cars from all eras. Editorial focus: authenticity, restoration, history. How-to's, swap meets, questions answered, classified marketplace for cars, parts, accessories and services.

CARS & PARTS ANNUAL. VFOAT Cars and Parts Annual. Periodical. US. English. an. $3.95. Amos Press, 911 Vandemark Road, Sidney OH 45365. LC TL7. DD 629.2222075.

CARS IN PROFILE. Collection 1- 1973-. UK. English. 4. Profile Publications Ltd, Coburg House Sheet Street, Windsor England. LC TL236. DD 629.22220904.

CART NEWS MEDIA GUIDE. VFOAT C.A.R.T. News Media Guide. VAT Championship Auto Racing Teams News Media Guide. 8755-7703. US. English. $6.00. Championship Auto Racing Teams Inc, 2655 Woodward Avenue/Suite 275, Bloomfield Hills MI 48013. LC GV1033. DD 796.720973.

CAT. CANADIAN AUTOMOTIVE TRADE. (C A T, CANADIAN AUTOMOTIVE TRADE). VFOAT CAT, Canadian Automotive Trade. V. 51, No. 9- Sept. 1969-. 0319-1990. Periodical. CN. English. bm. 52.00. MacLean Hunter, PO Box 100 Station A, Toronto Ontario M5W 1A7 Canada. Tel (416)596-5930. Ed Richard Jacobi and David Booth. adv acc. Circ 31,000. (ctrl). Tabloid publication servicing the Canadian garbage owner and mechanic with management and technical articles, troubleshooting, etc. *Canadian Automotive Trade, 0008-2945.*

CBS CARROSSERIE-AANHANGWAGEN- EN OPLEGGERINDUSTRIE. Series/Titl Produktiestatistieken Industrie. VFOAT C.B.S. Carrosserie, Aanhangwagen- en Opleggerindustrie. 1980-. NE. Dutch (summaries in English). an. 10.55. Staatsuitgeverij, The Hague Netherlands. LC HD9710.3.N4. *Carrosserie-, Aanhangwagen- en Opleggerindustrie Produktiestatistieken.*

CENTRE LINE. Began publication in 1969?. 0702-8369. Periodical. CN. English. ir. Ontario Motor League, 160 Bloor Street East, Toronto Ontario M4W 1C6 Canada. DD 388.309713.

CHABOTAP. See Insurance.

CHADONGCHA SAENGHWAL. VFOAT Car Life. V. 1- (1984, 9)-. Periodical. KO. Korean. mo. 30,800. Chadongcha Saenghwal, 58-1 1-ka Sinmunno Chongno-ku, Seoul Korea. LC TL4.

CHAGONGBO. Periodical. Korean. mo. LC HD9710.K6.

CHANGING CHALLENGE : GENERAL MOTORS QUARTERLY. Began with: V. 1, Winter 1974. Periodical. US. English. qt. General Motors, 3044 West Grand Boulevard, Detroit MI 48202.

CHECKPOINT. (CHECKPOINT : THE OFFICIAL PUBLICATION OF THE UNITED STATES AUTO CLUB, MOTORING DIVISION, INC). VFOAT Check Point. 0747-2080. Periodical. US. English. qt. United States Auto Club, Motoring Division, 250 East Carpenter Freeway, Irving TX 75062.

CHEVROLET CAMARO SHOP MANUAL. VFOAT Camaro Shop Manual. 0735-0066. US. English. an. Chevrolet Motor Division, General Motors Corporation, Detroit MI 48202. LC TL215.C33. DD 629.28722.

CHEVROLET CORVETTE SHOP MANUAL. VFOAT Corvette Shop Manual. 0735-3251. US. English. Chevrolet Motor Division, General Motors Corporation, Detroit MI 48203. LC TL215.C6. DD 629.28722.

CHI CHE KUNG CHENG. VFOAT Qiche Gongcheng. Periodical. Chinese (abstracts in English). qt. .40. Chung-Kuo Kuo Chi Shu Tien, PO Box 2820, Peking China. LC TL4. DD 629.205.

CHI E NELL'AUTOMOBILISMO ITALIANO. IT. English, French, German and Italian. ir. 2,550. Editrice Dell Automobile, V le Regina Margherita 279, 00198 Rome Italy. LC TL12. DD 338.47629222202545.

CHILTON'S AUTO REPAIR MANUAL. VFOAT Auto Repair Manual. 1968-. 0069-3634. Periodical. US. English. an. Chilton Book Company, Chilton Way, Radnor PA 19089-0230. LC TL152. Each issue contains an index to its own contents - no vol index - loose. *Glenn's Auto Repair Manual.*

CHILTON'S AUTOMOTIVE INDUSTRIES. V. 154- Jan. 1976-. 0273-656X. Periodical. US. English. mo. Chilton Company, Chilton Way, Radnor Way 19089. Tel (215)964-4245. Ed John McElroy. Ind/Abst Appl. Sci. Technol. Index, Bus. Period. Index, Trade Ind. Index, Energy Inf. Abstr., Energy Res. Abstr., Environ. Abstr., Excerpta Med. LC TL1. DD 629.205. adv acc. Circ 75,000. (ctrl). News, features, new products, and technology literature in regard to design, manufacturing and purchasing within the motor vehicle original equipment market. *Automotive Industries, 0005-1527.*

CHILTON'S AUTOMOTIVE MARKETING. VFOAT Automotive Marketing. V. 7- Jan. 1978-. 0193-3264. Periodical. US. English. mo. $36.00 Domestic, $70.00 Foreign. Chilton Company, Chilton Way, Radnor PA 19089. Tel 964-4000. Ed Charles Haberstroh. Ind/Abst Trade Ind. Index. DD 381. adv acc. Circ 24,500. (ctrl). Retailing parts, accessories, and chemicals to do-it-yourself customers. *Chilton's AM.*

CHILTON'S AUTOMOTIVE SERVICE MANUAL. (CHILTON'S . . . AUTOMOTIVE SERVICE MANUAL). VFOAT Chilton's . . . Motor/Age Professional Automotive Service Manual. 1980-. 0736-1793. US. English. an. Chilton Book Company, Chilton Way, Radnor PA 19089. LC TL152. DD 629.2872205. *Chilton's Motor/Age Professional Automotive Service Manual, 0363-2393.*

CHILTON'S IMPORT AUTOMOTIVE SERVICE MANUAL. VFOAT Import Automotive Service Manual. 0742-0307. Periodical. US. English. ir. Chilton Book Company, Chilton Way, Radnor PA 19089.

CHILTON'S IMPORT CAR REPAIR MANUAL. VFOAT Import Car Repair Manual. 5th- 1979-. 0271-3608. US. English. ir. Chilton Company, PO Box 1412, Riverton NJ 08077. Tel (215)964-4000. Each issue contains an index to its own contents - no vol index - loose. *Chilton's Import Automotive Repair Manual.*

CHILTON'S IMPORT LABOR GUIDE AND PARTS MANUAL. VFOAT Import Labor Guide and Parts Manual. 1981-. 0742-0323. Periodical. US. English. Chilton Book Company, Chilton Way, Radnor PA 19089.

CHILTON'S LABOR GUIDE AND PARTS MANUAL. (CHILTON'S . . . LABOR GUIDE AND PARTS MANUAL). 1980-. 0749-5579. US. English. an. Chilton Book Company, Chilton Way, Radnor Pa 19089-0230. DD 338. *Chilton's Motor/Age Professional Labor Guide and Parts Manual, 0361-9397.*

CHILTON'S MOTOR-AGE SERVICE HANDBOOK. (CHILTON'S MOTOR/AGE SERVICE HANDBOOK). 0097-4773. US. English. an. $2.50 Per Copy. Chilton Book Company, Chilton Way, Radnor PA 19089. LC TL152. DD 629.2872205.

CHILTON'S MOTOR/AGE. VFOAT Chilton's Motor Age. V. 89- Jan. 1970-. 0193-7022. Periodical. US. English. mo. $12.00. Chilton Company, Chilton Way, Radnor PA 19089. Tel (215)964-4000. Ed Stanley Stephenson. DD 388. adv acc. Circ 136,000. (ctrl). Available on microfilm.

CHILTON'S MOTOR/AGE PROFESSIONAL LABOR GUIDE AND PARTS MANUAL. 1977-. Periodical. English. ir.

CHILTON'S MOTOR/AGE PROFESSIONAL MECHANIC'S REFERENCE GUIDE. (CHILTON'S MOTOR/AGE . . . PROFESSIONAL MECHANIC'S REFERENCE GUIDE). VFOAT Professional Mechanic's Reference Guide. VAT Chilton's Motor Age Professional Mechanic's Reference Guide. 0737-2663. US. English. LC TL152. DD 629.287220212.

CHILTON'S TRUCK AND VAN SERVICE MANUAL. (CHILTON'S TRUCK AND VAN SERVICE MANUAL : GASOLINE AND DIESEL ENGINES). VFOAT Chilton Motor/Age Professional Truck and Van Service Manual. 0742-0331. US. English. Chilton Book Company, Chilton Way, Radnor PA 19089. LC TL230.2. DD 629.2873.

THE CLASSIC CAR. (CLASSIC CAR). V. 1- Jan. 1953-. 0009-8310. Periodical. US. English. qt. $18.00. Classic Car Club of America, PO Box 443, Madison NJ 07940. Tel (201)377-1925. LC TL7. Circ 4,800. Hobby magazine for classic car collectors.

CLASSIC CAR BIMONTHLY. VFOAT Classic Car Series. 0740-4794. Periodical. US. English. bm. $3.50 Single Issue. Consumer Guide, 3841 West Oakton Street, Skokie IL 60076.

THE CLASSIC MG YEARBOOK. See Yearbooks, Almanacs, Directories.

COAST CAR COLLECTOR. See Hobbies.

COLLECTOR'S CAR. See Hobbies.

COLLECTORS MOTOR NEWS. (COLLECTORS MOTOR NEWS : CMN). VFOAT CMN. Vol. 23, No. 1 (Jan. 1984)-. 0746-8687. Periodical. US. English. mo. $13.75 Domestic, $17.70 Canada. Collectors Motor News, 919 South Street, Long Beach CA 90805. LC TL7.A1. DD 629.2222075. *Antique Motor News, 0570-3476 ; Cars for Sale.*

COLLISION ESTIMATING GUIDE. (MITCHELL COLLISION ESTIMATING GUIDE). VFOAT Mitchell Domestic Collision Estimating Guide. 0731-2431. US. English. ir. $131.50. Mitchell Manuals Inc, PO Box 26260, San Diego CA 92126. Tel (800)854-7030. LC TL152. DD 629.28722029473. *Collision Estimating Guide with Parts Numbers, 0364-3328.*

COLLISION ESTIMATING GUIDE DOMESTIC. (MITCHELL COLLISION ESTIMATING GUIDE DOMESTIC). Began in 1981. 0735-9039. US. English. ir. Mitchell Manuals Inc, PO Box 26260, San Diego CA 92126. LC TL152. DD 629.28722029473. *Mitchell Collision Estimating Guide, 0731-2431.*

COLLISION ESTIMATING GUIDE, DOMESTIC OLDER MODELS. VFOAT Mitchell Collision Estimating Guide, Domestic Older Models. Vol. 23, No. 4 (Oct. 1981)-. 0883-3117. Periodical. US. English. qt. $65.00. Mitchell Manuals Inc, PO Box 26260, San Diego CA 92126. *Collision Estimating Guide. Older Models. Domestic Edition, 0735-1224.*

COLLISION ESTIMATING GUIDE IMPORTED. (MITCHELL COLLISION ESTIMATING GUIDE IMPORTED). Vol. 22, No. 10 (Oct. 1981)-. 0735-858X. US. English. mo. $90.00. Mitchell Manuals Inc, PO Box 26260, San Diego CA 92126. LC TL152. DD 629.28722. *Imported Collision Estimating Guide, 0730-2398.*

COLLISION ESTIMATING GUIDE, IMPORTED OLDER MODELS. (MITCHELL COLLISION ESTIMATING GUIDE, IMPORTED OLDER MODELS). 0735-7826. US. English. qt. $61.50. Mitchell Mannuals Inc, PO Box 26260, San Diego CA 92126. Tel (800)854-7030. LC TL152. DD 629.28722. *Mitchell Collision Estimating Guide. Older Models. Imported Edition, 0277-3147.*

COLLISION ESTIMATING GUIDE WITH PARTS NUMBERS CEASED. VFOAT Collision Estimating Guide. Began with V. -17, No. 10. 0364-3328. US. English. mo. 4926 Savannah Street,

Transportation—Automobiles

PO Box 80427, San Diego CA 92138. LC TL152. DD 338.43629287220973.

COMMERCIAL MOTOR. (THE COMMERCIAL MOTOR). **VFOAT** CM. Began with Vol. 1, March 1, 1905. 0010-3063. Periodical. UK. English. wk. Business Press International Ltd, Perrymount Road, Haywards Heath West Sussex RH163BR England. **Ind/Abst** CIS Abstr. Available on microfilm from University Microfilms.

COMMUNIQUE - CANADIAN AUTOMOBILE ASSOCIATION. **Main/Corp** Canadian Automobile Association. V. 1- Nov. 1970-. 0380-6987. Periodical. CN. English. ir. Canadian Automobile Association, 150 Gloucester Street, Ottawa Ontario K2P 0A6 Canada. DD 388.30971.

THE COMPLETE BOOK OF ENGINES. No. 1- 1965-. 0069-7974. US. English. an. LC TL210.

THE COMPLETE CHEVROLET BOOK. 1st- Ed. 0069-7982. US. English. Petersen Publishing Co, 6725 Sunset Boulevard, Los Angeles CA 90028. LC TL215.C5. DD 629.2222.

THE COMPLETE FORD BOOK. **VFOAT** Petersen's Complete Ford Book. US. English. $2.00. Petersen Publishing Company, 6725 Sunset Boulevard, Los Angeles CA 90028. LC TL215.F7. DD 629.2222.

COMPUTERIZED ENGINE CONTROLS. (COMPUTERIZED ENGINE CONTROLS : DIAGNOSIS & TESTING). **Series/Titl** Manuals for the Automotive Professional. US. English. an. Mitchell Manuals Inc, PO Box 26260, San Diego CA 92126. **Tel** (619)578-8770. Ed Dan Kelley. Diagnosis, testing and trouble shooting computer-controlled systems in 1981-85 domestic and 1981-84 imported vehicles. Wiring diagrams, flow charts, procedures and illustrations.

CONDUCTEUR AVERTI. Vol. 1, No. 1-. 0228-9083. Periodical. CN. French. mo. Ligue de Securite du Quebec, 6785 Ouest rue St-Jacques, Montreal Quebec H4B 1V3 Canada. DD 629.28305.

CONFERENCE RECORD OF PAPERS PRESENTED AT THE ANNUAL CONFERENCE - IEEE VEHICULAR TECHNOLOGY CONFERENCE. See Engineering - Electricity, Electrical Engineering, Electronics.

CONSUMER GUIDE. AUTO. (CONSUMER GUIDE : AUTO). 0097-8337. US. English. an. $1.95 Per Copy. Consumer Guide, 3323 West Main Street, Skokie IL 60076. LC TL5. DD 629.222205.

CONSUMER GUIDE. CARS. See Consumer Interests.

CONSUMER REPORTS GUIDE TO USED CARS. 1978/79-. 0162-4091. US. English. Consumers Union of the USA, 256 Washington Street, Mount Vernon NY 10550. LC TL154. DD 629.2222.

CONTINENTAL HANDBOOK & GUIDE TO WESTERN EUROPE. **VFOAT** Continental Handbook and Guide to Western Europe. 1932-. 0589-5413. UK. English. an. RAC Motoring Services Ltd, Lansdowne Road, Croydon CR9 2IA England. LC GV1025.A2. DD 914.0455.

THE CORMORANT NEWS BULLETIN. **VFOAT** Cormorant News-Bulletin. 0045-8554. Periodical. US. English. mo. $20.00. The Packard Club, PO Box 1347, Orinda CA 94563. Ed Alan Adams. DD 629. bk rev. adv acc. Circ 3,000. (ctrl). Ads and contents aimed toward preservation of the Packard automobile 1899-1958.

CORVETTE. (CORVETTE; SPORTS CAR OF AMERICA). 1980-. 0271-0889. US. English. an. $34.50, $44.50 with hard case and framing prints. Michael Bruce Associates Inc, Post Office Box 396, Powell OH 43065. LC TL215.C6. DD 629.2222.

CORVETTE, THE SENSUOUS AMERICAN. V. 1- 1976-. 0362-3777. Periodical. US. English. ty. $29.95. PO Box 396, Powell OH 43065. LC TL215.C63. DD 629.2222.

COURRIER DES FAMILLES. (LE COURRIER DES FAMILLES). V. 1- Fall 1978-. 0702-0376. Periodical. CN. French. qt. $1.00 Per No. Le Courrier des Familles, C P 3 Succursale F, Montreal Quebec H3J 2K8 Canada. DD 338.479171404.

CPI : CARS OF PARTICULTAR INTEREST. **VAT** Cars of Particular Interest. Periodical. US. English. qt. $16.00. CPI, P O Box 11409, Baltimore MD 21239. **Tel** (301)252-5759. **Ind/Abst** Bibliogr. Index Geol. Value guide to cars of particular interest.

CROSSROADS. V. 7, No. 3- May/June 1980-. 0199-9230. Periodical. US. English. ir. $7.97. Signature Publications, 2020 Dempster Street, Evanston IL 60202. Montgomery Ward Auto Club News News, 0199-3321.

CUMULATIVE INDEX OF SAE TECHNICAL PAPERS. See Indexes/Abstracts.

DEPENSES D'AUTOMOBILE. (LES DEPENSES D'AUTOMOBILE). 1976-. 0714-5586. CN. French. an. Free. Association Canadienne des Automobilistes, 1775 Croissant Courtwood, Ottawa Ontario K2C 3J2 Canada. DD 629.222205. Fraid d'Utilisation d'Une Auto, 0714-5593.

DETAILLANT. (LE DETAILLANT). **VFOAT** Nouvelles Gulf Canada. No. 1- 1976-. 0383-6762. Periodical. CN. French. Gulf Oil Canada, 800 Bay Street, Toronto Ontario M5S 1Y8 Canada. DD 338.766550971. Nouvelles Gulf Canada, 0380-3465.

DETROIT AUTOMOTIVE SERVICES. NEW CAR INVOICE GUIDE. **VFOAT** New Car Invoice Guide. 8755-6936. US. English. National Auto Research Division, PO Box 758, Gainesville GA 30503. LC HD9710.U5. DD 629.222029473.

DIEMEX-WHARTON. PROYECTO AUTOMOTRIZ. PROYECCIONES PREVIAS A LA JUNTA. **VFOAT** Proyecto Automotriz. 8755-0881. US. English ((June 1982-)). LC HD9710.M4. DD 338.4762920972.

DIESEL CAR DIGEST. 0160-7065. Periodical. US. English. qt. $13.00. Diesel Car Digest, PO Box 160253, Sacramento CA 95816. LC TL229.D5. DD 629.22.

DIESEL MAGAZINE. **VAT** Diesel (Guelph). July-Aug. 1981-. 0711-3374. Periodical. CN. English. bm. $7.74. McBain Publications Inc, 70 Ontonabee Drive/Kitchener, Ontario N2C 1L6 Canada. **Tel** (519)894-4000. Ed John McBain. DD 629.250605. bk rev. adv acc. Circ 15,000. (ctrl). Tests diesel-powered cars, trucks and machinery; announces new products; explains service procedures; responds to consumer enquiries; and editorializes on all research and development in the field.

DIGEST OF MOTOR LAWS. **Main/Corp** American Automobile Association. 0093-4062. US. English. an. $6.00. American Automobile Association, 1712 G Street NW, Washington DC 20006. **Tel** (703)222-6343. LC KF2210.Z95. DD 343.730944.

DIRECTORY AND REGISTER - ROLLS ROYCE OWNERS' CLUB. See Yearbooks, Almanacs, Directories.

DIRECTORY OF AUTO AFTERMARKET SUPPLIERS. See Yearbooks, Almanacs, Directories.

DIRECTORY OF AUTOMOTIVE CONSULTANTS. See Yearbooks, Almanacs, Directories.

DIRECTORY OF MEMBERS - VEHICLE BUILDERS & REPAIRERS ASSOCIATION. See Yearbooks, Almanacs, Directories.

DISCOVERY; THE ALLSTATE MOTOR CLUB MAGAZINE. See Travel.

DISMANTLERS DIGEST. See Business.

DISTRIBUTION OF MOTOR VEHICLE REGISTRATION FEES AND FUEL TAXES TO OHIO CITIES. **Main/Corp** Ohio. Dept. of Taxation. 0145-1782. US. English. Research and Statistics Section, PO Box 530, Columbus OH 43216. LC HJ5359. DD 336.185.

DOMESTIC AND IMPORTED VEHICLES TOWING MANUAL. 0735-0333. US. English. an. $8.95. AAA, 8111 Gatehouse Road, Falls Church VA 20047. LC TL154. DD 629.286. Domestic Vehicles Towing Manual, 0272-8125.

DOMESTIC CARS MECHANICAL PARTS/LABOR ESTIMATING GUIDE. **VFOAT** Mechanical Parts/Labor Estimating Guide. **VAT** Domestic Cars Mechanical Parts Labor Estimating Guide. Vol. 22, No. 1 (1981)-. 0273-5385. Periodical. US. English. an. **Tel** (619)578-8770. LC TL152. DD 629.28722. adv acc. (ctrl). Mechanical part numbers and prices, estimated labor times for 1974-86 domestic cars. Separate times for combined operations. Skill level codes and model identification illustrations. Mechanical Parts/Labor Estimating Guide. Domestic Cars, 0276-878X.

DOMESTIC CARS. TUNE-UP, MECHANICAL TRANSMISSION SERVICE & REPAIR. (DOMESTIC CARS : TUNE-UP MECHANICAL TRANSMISSION SERVICE & REPAIR). **Main/Corp** Mitchell Manuals, Inc. **VFOAT** Tune-Up, Mechanical Transmission Service & Repair. 1978-. 0272-8745. US. English. Mitchell Manuals Inc, Box 80427, San Diego CA 92138. LC TL152. DD 629.28722.

DORDOGNE, PERIGORD, LIMOUSIN. **Main/Corp** Michelin Tyre Company. 2d- Ed. UK. English. Michelin Tyre Company Ltd, 81 Fulham Road, London SW36 RD England. LC GV1025.F7. DD 914.4720483. Dordogne, Perigord, Limousin, Quercy.

DRIVE (WINNIPEG, MAN.). (DRIVE). Vol. 1, No. 1 (Nov./Dec. 1981)-. 0712-5755. Periodical. CN. English. bm. Free to Members. Drive, c/o Manitoba Motor League, PO Box 1400, Winnipeg Manitoba R3C 2Z3 Canada. DD 796.78097127. Manitoba Motorist, 0380-0172.

DRIVER. **VFOAT** Air Force Driver. Vol. 1, No. 1 (June 1967)-. 0002-2373. Periodical. US. English. mo. Superintendent of Documents, Government Printing Office, Washington DC 20402. **Tel** (202)783-3238. **Ind/Abst** Index U.S. Gov. Period. LC TL1.

DRIVER EDUCATION BULLETIN. See Education (General).

DRIVERS AND RIDERS LICENCES. English. ir. National Statistical Office, PO Wards Strip, Konedobu Papua New Guinea. LC HE5717.8. DD 354.95300878321. Drivers and Riders Licenses Issued.

DUNE BUGGIES AND HOT VWS. **VFOAT** Hot VWs. **VAT** Dune Buggies and Hot Volkswagens. 1970-. 0012-7132. Periodical. US. English. mo. $29.50. Dune Buggies and Hot VWs, 2949 Century Plaza Cosa Mesa CA 92627. **Tel** (714)979-2560. Ed Lane Evans. LC TL236.7. DD 629.2222. bk rev. adv acc. Circ 107,688. Edited for Volkswagen owners, off-road enthusiasts, racers and general automotive enthusiasts. Features include technical articles, how-to-do-it's, and competition coverage. Dune Buggies.

DUQUETTE'S SHOW CAR QUARTERLY. **VFOAT** Show Car Quarterly. No. 1 (July 1984)-. 0748-3341. Periodical. US. English. qt. $12.00. Duquett's Show Car Quarterly Magazine, 7901 Northeast 10th Suite 204, Midwest City OK 73110. DD 629.

EDMUND'S AUTO-PEDIA. **Main/Corp** Edmund Publications Corporation (West Hempstead, N.Y.). **VFOAT** Glove Compartment Necessity. 0270-5354. US. English. ir. $2.50. Special Marketing Division of Dell Distributing Inc, One Dag Hammarskjold Plaza 245 East 47th Street, New York NY 10017. LC TL151. DD 629.2.

EDMUND'S ECONOMY CAR BUYING GUIDE. (EDMUND'S . . . ECONOMY CAR BUYING GUIDE). **VFOAT** Economy Car Buying Guide. Summer 1982-. 0732-5835. US. English. $2.50. Edmund Publications Corporation, 515 Hempstead Turnpike, West Hempstead NY 11552. LC TL162. DD 629.2222029473.

EDMUND'S FOREIGN CAR PRICES. **VFOAT** Foreign Car Prices. Began in 1969. 0531-7886. Periodical. US. English. sa. Edmund Publications Corporation, 515 Hempstead Turnpike, West Hempstead NY 11552. LC TL162. DD 338.43.

EDMUND'S NEW CAR PRICES. Periodical. US. English. ir. Edmunds Publications Corporation, 515 Hempstead Turnpike, West Hempstead NY 11552. **Tel** (516)292-0044.

EDMUND'S USED CAR PRICES. **VFOAT** Used Car Prices. Began in 1967. 0424-5059. Periodical. US. English. qt. Edmunds Publications Corporation, 515 Hempstead Turnpike, West Hempstead NY 11552. **Tel** (516)292-0044.

EINGEFUHRTE MOTORFAHRZEUGE. VEHICULES A MOTEUR IMPORTES. **Main/Corp** Switzerland. Eidgenossisches Statistisches AMT. **Series Corp** Its Statistische Quellenwerke der Schweiz. **VFOAT** Vehicules a Moteur Importes. French and German. ir.

Transportation—Automobiles

Publikationsdienst, Hallurylstrasse 15, CH 3003 Bern Switzerland. LC HD9710.S9. DD 314.94 S, 382.45629209494. *Eingefuhrte Motorfahrzeuge.*

ELECTRIC AND HYBRID VEHICLES PROGRAM. US. English. an. National Technical Information Service, US Department of Commerce, Springfield VA 22161. LC TL220. DD 629.229305. *Annual Report to Congress for FY ... Electric and Hybrid Vehicle Program.*

ELECTRIC UTILITY FLEET MANAGEMENT. Vol. 1, No. 1 (Feb. 15, 1982)-. 0744-3501. Periodical. US. English. bm. $10.00. Pritchard Publishing, PO Box 960/4 Dennison Road, Durham NH 03824. Tel (603)868-7131. Ed Parm F Pritchard. bk rev. adv acc. Circ 3,400. (ctrl). The magazine for specifying, purchasing, operating and maintaining cars, trucks, construction/maintenance equipment and tools used by the Electric Utility Industry.

ELECTRIC VEHICLE DEVELOPMENTS. (ELECTRIC VEHICLE DEVELOPMENTS : EVD). VFOAT EVD. Began with Mar. 1979 issue. 0141-9811. Periodical. UK. English. qt. $36.78. Research Applications Ltd, City University/Northhampton Square, London EC1V OHB England. Ind/Abst Coal Abstr., Energy Inf. Abstr., Environ. Abstr., Comput. Control Abstr., Electr. Electron. Abstr., Sci. Abstr. Sect. A. Phys. Abstr., Energy Res. Abstr., Phys. Abstr. CODEN EVDEDJ.

ELECTRIC VEHICLE NEWS CEASED. V. 1-11. 0095-7526. Periodical. US. English. qt. $10.00. PO Box 533, Westport CT 06880. Ind/Abst Energy Inf. Abstr., Environ. Abstr. LC TL220. DD 629.229305.

ELECTRONIC FUEL INJECTION, DIAGNOSIS & TESTING. Series/Titl Manuals for the Automotive Professional. VFOAT Electronic Fuel Injection. 0741-6334. US. English. an. Mitchell Manuals Inc, PO Box 26260, San Diego CA 92126. Tel (619)578-8770. Ed Dan Kelley. LC TL214.F78. DD 629.253. adv acc. (ctrl). Diagnose, test, adjust, and repair 1975-86 domestic and 1968-85 imported car and light truck electronic fuel injection systems with this guide.

EMISSION CONTROL SERVICE & REPAIR, IMPORTED CARS & TRUCKS. SUPPLEMENT. Series/Titl Manuals for the Automotive Professional. VFOAT Emission Control Service and Repair, Imported Cars & Trucks. 0741-6342. US. English. an. Mitchell Manuals Inc, PO Box 26260, San Diego CA 92126. LC TL214.P6. DD 629.25280288. *Emission Control Service and Repair, Imported Cars and Trucks. Supplement, 0741-6342.*

ENGINEERING KNOW-HOW IN ENGINE DESIGN. See Engineering - Mechanical Engineering & Machinery.

ENONCES DE PRINCIPE - ASSOCIATION CANADIENNE DES AUTOMOBILISTES. Main/Corp Association Canadienne des Automobilistes. Publication began with 1974/75?. 0225-9222. CN. French. an. Association Canadienne des Automobilistes, 150 rue Gloucester, Ottawa Ontario K2P 0A6 Canada. DD 388.0971.

EVAC NEWS. VAT Electric Vehicle Association of Canada News. 82/12 (Dec. '82)-. 0822-3432. Periodical. CN. English. bm. Free. Electric Vehicle Association of Canada, Suite 500/275 Slater Street, Ottawa Ontario K1P 5HP Canada. DD 629.229305. *EV Circuit (Electric Vehicle Association of Canada), 0825-5547.*

EXERCICE - CHAMBRE SYNDICALE DES CONSTRUCTEURS D'AUTOMOBILES ET DE MOTOCYCLES DE BELGIQUE ET FEDERATION BELGE DES INDUSTRIES DE L'AUTOMOBILE ET DU CYCLE REUNIES. Main/Corp Chambre Sydnicale des Constructeurs d'Automobiles et de Motocycles de Belgique et Federation Belge des Industries de l'Automobile et du Cycle Reunies. VFOAT Boekjaar - Syndikale Kamer der Auto- en Motorrijwielen-Constructeurs Van Belgie en Belgische Federatie der Auto- en Rijwielnijverheden Verenigd. Flemish and French. ir. Boulevard de la Woluwe 46, Bruxelles Belgium. LC HD9710.B3.

FACTS AND FIGURES OF THE AUTOMOBILE INDUSTRY. CN. English. ir. Canadian Automobile Chamber of Commerce, Toronto Ontario Canada. LC HD9710.C2.

FACTS AND FIGURES OF THE AUTOMOTIVE INDUSTRY. 1958-. 0316-3504. Periodical. CN. English. an. Motor Vehicle Manufacturers, 300 New Center Building, Detroit MI 48124. Tel (313)872-4311. DD 338.476292. *Facts and Figures of the Automobile Industry, 0316-3555.*

FAMILY MOTOR COACHING. 0360-3024. Periodical. US. English. mo. $15.00. Family Motor Coaching Association, PO Box 44144, Cincinnati Ohio 45244. LC TL298. DD 796.7.

FERNVERKEHR DEUTSCHER LASTKRAFTFAHRZEUGE ... IN SEINER BEWEGUNG NACH VERKEHRSGEBIETEN, GUTERHAUPTGRUPPEN UND WICHTIGEREN GUTERGRUPPEN : GEMEINSAMER BERICHT DER BUNDESANSTALT FUR DEN GUTERFERNVERKEHR UND DES KRAFTFAHRT-BUNDESAMTES. Series/Titl GD. VFOAT BAG/KBA Fermverlejr Deutscher. German. an. LC HE5669. DD 388.3240943.

FICHIER CENTRAL DES AUTOMOBILES, PARC ET IMMATRICULATIONS. FR. French. an. 55-57 Rue Brillat-Savarin, 75013 Paris France. LC HE5668. DD 388.320944021. *Parc des Vehicules Utilitaires Immatricules, Immatriculations des Vehicules Utilitaires.*

THE FIFTH WHEEL. CEASED with Jan. 1984?. 0015-0819. Periodical. US. English. mo. Indiana Motor Truck Association Inc, PO Box 41193, Indianapolis IN 46241. Tel (317)244-7851.

FINANCIAL ANALYSIS OF THE MOTOR CARRIER INDUSTRY. 0099-2445. US. English. American Trucking Associates, Public Relations Department, 1616 P Street North West, Washington DC 20036. Tel (703)838-1772. LC HE5623. DD 388.324.

FISCAL YEAR ... ALABAMA TRANSIT DATA REPORT. US. English. an. LC HE5633.A2. DD 388.32209761.

FISHER BODY SERVICE MANUAL. Main/Corp General Motors Corporation. Fisher Body Division. 0164-0437. US. English. LC TL255. DD 629.26028.

FIX YOUR VOLKSWAGEN. 0071-5697. US. English. an. Ed Larry Johnson.

FLEET OWNER. SMALL FLEET EDITION. (FLEET OWNER). V. 73, No. 13- Dec. 1978-. 0162-1025. Periodical. US. English. mo. $25.00 US, $30.00 Canada. Fulfillment Manager, Fleet Owner, PO Box 430, Highstown NJ 08520. LC TL165. DD 388.3240973.

FOLIO. See Insurance.

FORESIGNT (TORONTO, ONT.). See Public Health and Safety.

FRENCH RIVIERA. COTE D'AZUR. 1st- Ed. UK. English. LC GV1025.F7.

FROM THE STATE CAPITALS. MOTOR VEHICLE REGULATION. VFOAT Motor Vehicle Regulation. 0016-1810. Periodical. US. English. wk. $175.00. Wakeman/Walworth Inc, PO Box 1939, New Haven CT 06509. Tel (203)562-8518. Examines state motor vehicle safety regulations, inspections, emission standards, drunken driving laws, motorist licensing, insurance and education.

FUEL CONSUMPTION GUIDE. VFOAT Guide sur la Consommation de Carburant. 1st- Ed. 0225-9214. CN. English (French). an. Transport Canada, Road Safety, Ottawa Ontario K1A 0N5 Canada. DD 629.253.

GENERAL COMPETITION RULES. See Recreation, Leisure - Sports.

THE GOLD BOOK (EL PASO, TEX.). (THE GOLD BOOK). Periodical. US. English. qt. Gold Book, 910 Tony Lama Street, El Paso TX 79915. Ed Q Craft.

GOOD SAM CLUB'S RECREATIONAL VEHICLE OWNERS DIRECTORY. See Yearbooks, Almanacs, Directories.

GRAND PRIX DU CANADA. (GRAND PRIX LABATT DU CANADA : PROGRAM). VFOAT Grand Prix Labatt. 0710-3778. CN. English (French). an. $3.00 Each Number. Grand Prix Labatt du Canada, c/o Promaction Inc, 363 rue St-Francois-Xavier/Suite 300, Montreal Quebec H2Y 3P9 Canada. DD 796.7209714281. *Album Souvenir Grand Prix du Canada Montreal.*

GRAND PRIX LABATT DU CANADA. REGLEMENTS. (REGLEMENTS). Main/Corp Grand Prix du Canada. VFOAT Regulations. VAT Grand Prix Labatt du Canada. Regulations. 0822-5222. CN. English (French with translation on opposite pages). an. Grand Prix du/Canada Bassin Olympiquell Ile Notre-Dame, Montreal Quebec H3C 1A0 Canada. DD 796.7209714.

GUIDE D'ACHAT DE LA VOITURE USAGEE. 0820-8964. CN. French. an. $3.00. Association Canadienne des Automobilistes, 1775 Croissant Courtwood, Ottawa Ontario K1C 3J2 Canada. Tel (613)226-7631. DD 629.2222. Circ 75,450.

GUIDE DE L'AUTO. (LE GUIDE DE L'AUTO). 1967-. 0315-9205. Periodical. CN. French. an. $3.00. Messageries Internationales du Livew, 4550 rue Hochelaga, Montreal Quebec H1V 1C6 Canada. LC TL2. DD 629.22205.

GUIDE DE L'AUTOMOBILE AMERICAINE. (LE GUIDE DE L'AUTOMOBILE AMERICAINE). 1981-. 0228-9776. CN. French. an. $2.95 Per No. Editions & Publications Heraud, Bureau 11/1459 Belanger, Montreal Quebec H2G 1A5 Canada. Ed Daniel Heraud. DD 629.22205. *Guide de l'Automobile Nord-Americaine, 0226-1960.*

GUIDE MOTOR CLUB'S ANNUAL EMERGENCY ROAD SERVICE GUIDE. VFOAT Emergency Road Service Guide. No. 1- 1977-. 0160-1318. US. English. an. Guide Motor Club, 450 West 33rd Street, New York NY 10001. LC TL153. DD 629.2860257471.

GUIDE ROUTIER ET TOURISTIQUE : MADAGASCAR, REUNION, MAURICE, COMORES ET SEYCHELLES. See Travel.

GUIDE TO THE MOTOR INDUSTRY OF JAPAN. VFOAT Motor Industry of Japan. JA. English. an. 4,000. Japan Motor Industrial Federation Inc, Otemachi Building Otemachi, Chiyoda ku Tokyo 100 Japan. Tel 211-8731. Ed Kohki Fujimori. adv acc. Circ 20,000. Covers Tokyo Motor Show, the automobile manufacturers, general catalogues, specifications, motor vehicle statistics, directory of organizations and manufacturers.

HANDBOOK AND DIRECTORY - CLASSIC CAR CLUB OF AMERICA. See Yearbooks, Almanacs, Directories.

HEAD LIGHTS. 8081/1-. 0228-4715. Periodical. CN. English. Ontario Safety League, 409 King Street West, Toronto Ontario M5V 1K1 Canada. DD 629.283205. *Bits About Wheels, 0383-9923.*

HEADLAMP (ARMDALE, N.S.). (HEADLAMP). Vol. 1, No. 1 (Feb. '79)-. 0229-6667. Periodical. CN. English. qt. Free to Members. Headlamp c/o Deta Nova Scotia Teachers' Union, PO Box 1060, Armdale Nova Scotia B3L 4L7 Canada. DD 629.283207.

THE HEADLIGHT. Periodical. US. English. mo. National Car Rental System, Public Relations Department, 5501 Green Valley Drive, Minneapolis MN 55437.

HEAVY TRUCK COLLISION ESTIMATING GUIDE : CHEVROLET, DIAMOND REO, DODGE, FORD, FREIGHTLINER, GMC, INTERNATIONAL, KENWORTH, MACK, PETERBILT, WHITE. Main/Corp Mitchell Manuals, Inc. 0272-8591. US. English. Mitchell Manuals Inc, PO Box 80427, San Diego CA 92138. LC TL230.2. DD 629.2874.

HEAVY TRUCK EQUIPMENT NEWS CEASED. VFOAT HTEN. V. 1-10, Issue 2. 0318-1367. CN. English. ir. $7.95. PO Box 2159, Bramalea Ontario L6T 3S4 Canada. DD 629.22405.

HEMMINGS MOTOR NEWS. Periodical. US. English. mo. Tel (802)442-3101. adv acc. Advertisements for antique auto flea markets, car shows, etc.

HIGH SPEED DIESEL REPORT. Vol. 1, No. 1 (Jan.-Feb. 1982)-. 0730-5303. Periodical. US. English. bm. $30.00. Diesel & Gas Turbine Publishing, 13555 Bishops Court, Brookfield WI 53005. Tel (414)784-9177. Ed Rob Wilson. LC TJ795.A1. DD 621.43605. adv acc. Circ 16,500. (ctrl). Provides in-depth coverage of major technical developments

Transportation—Automobiles

specifically related to the vehicular, industrial and marine markets for volume produced high speed diesel engines.

HIGHWAY USER REVENUES AND DISTRIBUTION FOR THE CALENDAR YEAR ENDING .... US. English. LC HE5633.A8. DD 388.114.

HOME & AUTO. VAT Home and Auto. 0162-8801. Periodical. US. English. ir. $25.00. Home & Auto Buyers Guide, 1 East First Street, Duluth MN 55802. Tel (218)723-9517. Ed Dick Weinberg. Ind/Abst Trade Ind. Index, Predicasts. adv acc. Circ 22,000. (ctrl). Retail automotive aftermarket industry, reporting, analyzing, merchandising trends, techniques, advertising, promotion, display and packaging. A number of annual studies on automotives for the do-it-yourself consumer.

HOME & AUTO. See Business - Purchasing.

HOME & AWAY MINNESOTA. VFOAT Home & Away. VAT Home and Away Minnesota. V. 1- Jan./Feb. 1980-. 0199-5383. Periodical. US. English. bm. $3.00. 7 Travelers Trail, Burnsville MN 55337. Tel (612)890-2500. Ed Judie Gibbish. adv acc. Circ 210,000. Articles cover popular vacation destinations, foreign and domestic travel tips, cruises, tours, car care information, consumer issues. *Minnesota Motorist, 0026-5381.*

HORSELESS CARRIAGE GAZETTE. V. 17, No. 4- 19 -. 0018-5213. Periodical. US. English. bm. $8.00. Horseless Carriage Club of America, 9031 East Florence Avenue/Arlington Square, Downey GA 90240. LC TL1. DD 388.32109. *Horseless Carriage Club Gazette.*

HOT ROD. V. 6, No. 5- May 1953-. 0018-6031. Periodical. US. English. mo. $15.94. Petersen Publishing Company, 6725 Sunset Boulevard, Los Angeles CA 90028. Tel (213)657-5100. Ed Leonard Emanuelson. Ind/Abst Mag. Ind., Pop. Mag. Rev. adv acc. Circ 509,000. The hottest technology and trends for street machines, from how-to's to performance specs on foreign and domestic cars. *Hot Rod Magazine.*

HOT ROD ANNUAL. (HOT ROD . . . ANNUAL). VFOAT Petersen's Hot Rod Annual. 1982-. 0735-083X. US. English. an. $6.95 US, $8.50 Canada. Petersen Publishing Company, 6725 Sunset Boulevard, Los Angeles CA 90028. LC TL236. DD 629.228. adv acc. Circ 200,000.

HOT ROD MAGAZINE CHEVROLET. VFOAT Hot Rod Chevrolet. 0271-0919. Periodical. US. English. $2.50 US, $3.25 Canada. Petersen Publishing Company, 6725 Sunset Boulevard, Los Angeles CA 90028. LC TL215.C5. DD 629.2222. adv acc. Circ 200,000.

HOT ROD MAGAZINE CORVETTE. VFOAT Corvette. 0273-0383. Periodical. US. English. $2.50 US, $3.50 Canada. Petersen Publishing Company, 6725 Sunset Boulevard, Los Angeles CA 90028. LC TL215.C6. DD 629.2222.

HOT ROD MAGAZINE ENGINES. VFOAT Engines. 0730-4811. US. English. $2.95 US, $3.50 Canada. Petersen Publishing Company, 6725 Sunset Boulevard, Los Angeles CA 90028. Circ 200,000.

HOT ROD MAGAZINE KIT CAR. VFOAT H.R. Kit Car Annual. 0731-3314. Periodical. US. English. an. Petersen Publishing Company, 6725 Sunset Boulevard, Los Angeles CA 90028. Ed Dave Fults. adv acc. Circ 150,000. *Hot Rod Magazine Kit Car Annual.*

HOT ROD MAGAZINE PICKUPS & MINI-TRUCKS. VFOAT Pickups & Mini-Trucks. VAT Hot Rod Magazine Pickups and Mini-Trucks. 0730-5044. US. English. $2.50 US, $3.25 Canada. Petersen Publishing Company, 6725 Sunset Boulevard, Los Angeles CA 90028. LC TL230. DD 629.8273.

HOT ROD PERFORMANCE AND CUSTOM DIRECTORY. See Yearbooks, Almanacs, Directories.

I.B.C.A.M. (IBCAM). Main/Corp Institute of British Carriage and Automobile Manufacturers. VFOAT Institute Journal. V. 1- Jan. 1974-. 0306-2910. Periodical. UK. English. mo. Institute of British Carriage and Automobile Manufacturing, Thames Meadow, 59 Henley Road, Shillingford OX9 8EZ England. LC TL1. *Institute Bulletin.*

ILLINOIS TRUCK NEWS. 0019-2309. Periodical. US. English. mo. Illinois Trucking Associations, Mannheim Road at Madison, Hillside IL 60162.

IMPORTCAR (AKRON, OHIO : 1982). (IMPORTCAR). VFOAT Import Car. Vol. 4, No. 1 (Jan. 1982)-. 0735-7877. Periodical. US. English. mo. Babcox Business Publishers, Babcox Building, 11 Forge Street, Akron OH 44304. Tel (216)535-6117. LC TL159. DD 629.222205. *Babcox's Importcar (Akron, Ohio : 1980), 0278-6532.*

IMPORTED CARS & TRUCKS, ELECTRICAL SERVICE & REPAIR. VFOAT Mitchell Manuals for Automotive Professionals. Electrical Service & Repair, Imported Cars & Trucks. VAT Imported Cars and Trucks, Electrical Service and Repair. US. English. an. Mitchell Manuals Inc, 9889 Willow Creek Road/PO Box 26260, San Diego CA 92126. Tel (619)578-8770. Ed Dan Kelley. adv acc. (ctrl). Testing, servicing, and repair of alternators, starters, regulators, ignition systems and others electrical components on 1975-84 imported cars and light trucks. Wiring diagrams included.

IMPORTED CARS & TRUCKS, TRANSMISSION SERVICE & REPAIR. VFOAT Imported Cars and Trucks, Transmission Service & Repair. 0741-0158. US. English. an. Mitchell Manuals Inc, PO Box 26260, San Diego CA 92126. Tel (619)578-8770. Ed Dan Kelley. LC TL262. DD 629.24405. adv acc. (ctrl). This manual explains servicing, trouble shooting and overhaul of manual and automatic transaxles and transmissions for 1975-84 imported cars and light trucks. *Transmission Service & Repair, Imported Cars & Trucks.*

IMPORTED INTERCHANGE. IMPORTED CARS & LIGHT TRUCKS. VFOAT Imported Interchange. 0742-2628. US. English. an. $75.00. Mitchell Manuals Inc, Box 26260, San Diego CA 92126. Tel (619)578-8770. Ed Ken Young. LC TL159. DD 629.20216. Parts interchange listings for 16 imported manufacturers. Coverage back to early 60's on some models. Covers major mechanical parts and collision parts.

IN THE DRIVER'S SEAT. 0702-5785. Periodical. CN. English. mo. Free. Ontario Safety League, 409 King Street West, Toronto Ontario M5V 1K1 Canada. DD 629.204205. (ctrl).

IN VERKEHR GESETZTE NEUE MOTORFAHRZEUGE. Main/Corp Liechtenstein. Amt Fur Volkswirtschaft. German. ir. Amt fur Volkswirtschaft des Furstentums Liechtenstein, FI 9490 Liechtenstein, Vaduz Liechtenstein. LC HE5667.9. DD 388.320943648.

IN VERKEHR GESETZTE NEUE MOTORFAHRZEUGE. VEHICULES A MOTEUR NEUFS MIS EN CIRCULATION. Main/Corp Switzerland. Statistisches Amt. Series Corp Its Statistische Quellenwerke der Schweiz. VFOAT Vehicules a Moteur Neufs Mis En Circulation. French and German. ir. Publikationsdienst, Hallurylstrasse 15, CH 3003 Bern Switzerland. LC HA9710 .S9. *Eingefuhrte Motorfahrzeuge.*

INDEPENDENT MERCEDES BENZ BUSINESS DIRECTORY. See Yearbooks, Almanacs, Directories.

THE INDIANAPOLIS 500 YEARBOOK. See Yearbooks, Almanacs, Directories.

INDUSTRIA AUTOMOBILISTICA BRASILEIRA. BL. Portuguese. ir. Anfavea, Avenida Paulista 2073 - 15 Andar Conj 1503 A 1510 Sao Paulo Brazil. LC HD9710.B8. DD 338.476292220981.

INFOLETTER - ONTARIO RETAIL GASOLINE AND AUTOMOTIVE SERVICE ASSOCIATION. Main/Corp Ontario Retail Gasoline and Automotive Service Association. VAT Orga Infoletter, Ontario Retail Gasoline and Automotive Service Association Infoletter. Vol. 1- Dec. 1979-. 0228-0477. Periodical. CN. English. mo. Ontario Retail Gasoline and Automotive Service Association, Suite 102/101 Queensway West, Mississauga Ontario L5B 2P7 Canada. DD 629.28609713. *Automotive Review, 0706-506X.*

INSURANCE THEFT LOSSES. VANS, PICKUPS AND UTILITY VEHICLES MODELS. See Insurance.

INTERNATIONAL AUTOMOTIVE REVIEW. 0261-2267. Periodical. UK. English. qt. Automotive Research and Management Consultants Ltd, 1045 Eastlawn Drive, Highland Heights OH 44143.

INTERNATIONAL JOURNAL OF VEHICLE DESIGN. (INTERNATIONAL JOURNAL OF VEHICLE DESIGN : THE JOURNAL OF THE INTERNATIONAL ASSOCIATION FOR VEHICLE DESIGN). V. 1- Oct. 1979-. 0143-3369. Periodical. UK. English. bm. $155.00. Inderscience Enterprises Ltd, POB 301/Queens House, Don Road, Jersey Channel Islands UK. Tel 9080 653945. Ed M A Dorgham. Ind/Abst Electron. Commun. Abstr. J., ISMEC Bull., Pollut. Abstr. Indexes, Saf. Sci. Abstr. J., Eng. Index Annu., Eng. Index Mon., Eng. Index, Eng. Index Bioeng. Abstr., Eng. Index Energy Abstr., Excerpta Med., Int. Aerosp. Abstr., Comput. Control Abstr., Electr. Electron. Abstr., Sci. Abstr. Sect. A. Phys. Abstr., Met. Abstr., World Alum. Abstr., Sci. Cit. Index, Abr. Ed., Phys. Abstr., Appl. Mech. Rev. LC TL1. DD 629.23105. CODEN IJVDDW. bk rev. adv acc. Circ 75,000. Topics include vehicle engineering and components, transport, design, energy, materials, electronics, manufacturing, product planning, aerodynamics, environment, safety, thermo and fluid mechanics, vibration.

IOWA ACCIDENT FACTS. See Public Health and Safety.

JAGUAR JOURNAL. 0743-3913. Periodical. US. English. qt. $5.00 Members, $7.50 Non-Members. The Editor Jaguar Journal, 600 Willow Tree Road, Leonia NJ 07605. LC TL215.J3. DD 629.2222.

THE JAMA FORUM. VFOAT J.A.M.A. Forum. Vol. 1, No. 1 (Apr. 1982)-. Periodical. JP. English. ir. Automobiles. Japan Automobile Manufacturers Association Inc, Ohte-Machi Building, 6-1 Ohte-Machi 1-chome Chiyoda-ku, Tokyo Japan. LC HD9710.J3. DD 338.4762920952.

JANE'S MILITARY VEHICLES AND GROUND SUPPORT EQUIPMENT. VFOAT Military Vehicles and Ground Support Equipment. 0263-2594. UK. English. an. $125.00. Janes Publishing Inc, 135 West 50th Street/12th Floor, New York NY 10020. Tel (212)586-7745. Ed Christopher F Foss and Terry J Gander. LC UG615. DD 358.18. adv acc. Reference book on non-combat military vehicles and support equipment worldwide. Includes mine equipment, armored engineer vehicles, bridging systems, demolition and NBC equipment. *Jane's Combat Support Equipment, 0143-1420.*

JOBBER AND WAREHOUSE EXECUTIVE. 0021-7042. Periodical. US. English. mo. $30.00. Hunter Publishing Company, 950 Lee Street, Des PLaines IL 60016. Tel (312)296-0770. Ed James Halloran. LC HD9710 A1. bk rev. adv acc. Circ 40,000. (ctrl). The audience are executives at automotive parts replacement warehouses and jobber stores. *Jobber Executive.*

JOBBER NEWS. Began publication in 1932. 0021-7050. Periodical. CN. English. ir. 24.00. Wadham Publications Ltd, 109 Vanderhoof Avenue, Toronto Ontario M4G 2J2 Canada. Tel (416)425-9021. Ed Bob Blans. adv acc. Circ 11,500. (ctrl). Canada's leading aftermarket publication serving the key buying and selling personnel of WD's jobbers and now mass merchandisers, hardware chains and national accounts.

JOBBER-RETAILER. (JOBBER RETAILER). V. 1- Apr. 1977-. 0148-5792. Periodical. US. English. ir. $24.00. Bill Automotive Group, 110 North Miller Road, Akron OH 44313. Tel (216)867-4401. LC HD9710.A1. DD 338.47629205.

JOBBER RETAILER MARKET MANUAL. 1983-. US. English. $20.00. Jobber Retailer, 110 North Miller Road, Akron OH 44313. Tel (216)867-4401. Ed Greg Smith. LC HD9710.3.U5. DD 629.20688. adv acc. Circ 35,000. (ctrl). Complete information to allow the automotive parts jobber to run their businesses more profitably. How-to educational approach is used.

JOBBER TOPICS. Began in 1934. 0021-7069. Periodical. US. English. mo. $20.00. Irving Cloud Publishing Company, 7300 North Cicero Avenue-Lincolnwood, Chicago IL 60646. Tel (312)588-7300. Ed Jack Creighton. Ind/Abst Trade Ind. Index. bk rev. adv acc. Circ 71,645. (ctrl). Edited for automotive jobbers, redistributing jobbers, and automotive warehouse distributors.

JOURNAL OF THE SOCIETY OF AUTOMOTIVE ENGINEERS OF JAPAN. 0385-7298. Periodical. JA. Japanese. mo. 145.00 Domestic. Maruzen Company Ltd, PO Box 5050, 100-31, Tokyo Japan. Tel 03-262-8211. Ed

Transportation—Automobiles

Katsumi Kageyama. **Circ** 20,000. (ctrl). Report of technical study about car-industry, introduction of these and explanation, announcement of complete car or excellent parts, and introduction of documents.

JOURNAL PISTES CIRCUITS. VFOAT Pistes et Circuits. First issue in 1972. 0702-8555. Periodical. CN. French (text in English). mo. .50 Per Number. Promotions P C, CP 71 Ste-Rose, Laval Quebec H7L 1K8 Canada. **DD** 796.7205.

JSAE REVIEW. No. 1- 1978-. 0389-4304. Periodical. US. English. ty. $30.00. Society of Automotive Engineers Inc, 400 Commonwealth Drive, Warrendale PA 15096. **Tel** (412)776-4841. **Ind/Abst** Fluidex, Predicasts, Met. Abstr., World Alum. Abstr., Chem. Abstr. **CODEN** JREVDY. Published three times a year by JSAE. This technical magazine covers developments in the Japanese automotive industry, contains abstracts of JSAE papers and reports of the Ministry of Transport.

KART SPORT. Vol. 1, No. 1 (May 1982)-. 0744-5962. Periodical. US. English. mo. Kart Sport/Subscription Order, Kart Sport Magazine, 5510 Ashborn Road, Baltimore MD 21227.

KARTING DIGEST. See Travel.

KEEPIN' TRACK OF CORVETTES. 1976. 0191-474X. Periodical. US. English. mo. $19.00. Keepin' Track of Vettes, PO Box 48, Spring Valley NY 10977. **Tel** (914)425-2649. Ed Shelli Finkel. bk rev. adv acc. **Circ** 30,000. Published for the Corvette enthusiast: includes restoration, technical and mechanical how-to information, covers Corvette racing, club activities and more.

KEIJIDOSHA YUSO TOKEI CHOSA HOKOKUSHO. 1986 No. 10 Oct. 10, 1981-. JA. Japanese. ir. Unyusho Daijin Kambo Joho Kanribu Tokeika, c/o Godo Chosha, 3-Gokan 1-3 Kasumigaseki 2, Chiyoda-ku Tokyo Japan. **LC** HE5697.

KELLEY BLUE BOOK, OFFICIAL GUIDE FOR OLDER CARS. VFOAT Kelley Blue Book Auto Market Report, Official Guide for Older Cars. Periodical. US. English. qt. $40.00. Kelley Blue Book, PO Box 1290, Costa Mesa CA 92625.

KELLEY BLUE BOOK RV TRAILER GUIDE. VFOAT Kelley Blue Book. US. English. sa. $33.00. Kelley Blue Book, PO Box 1290, Costa Mesa CA 92626. **Tel** (714)957-2600. **LC** TL297. **DD** 629.226029473. *Travel Trailers, 5th Wheel Trailers, Camping Trailers RV Guide, New & Used Values 0145-3785.*

KFZ I.E. KRAFTFAHRZEUG-BETRIEB UND AUTOMARKT. VFOAT KFZ-BETRIEB UND AUTOMARKT. Yearly V. 62-. 0047-3049. Periodical. GW. German. sm. Vogel Verlag, Postfach 67 40, D-8700 Wurzburg 1 West Germany. **LC** TL3. **DD** 629.22205. *KFZ-BETRIEB, AUTOMARKT.*

KRAFTFAHRZEUGTECHNIK. Began publication with Sept. 1950 issue. 0023-4419. Periodical. SZ. German. mo $24.84. Kunst & Wissen Erich Bieber, Dufourstrasse 51, CH-8008 Zurich Switzerland. **Tel** 011-41-1-69 44 20. **Ind/Abst** Excerpta Med. **LC** TL3.

KUORMA-AUTO LINJALIIKENNE. **Main/Corp** Finland. Tilastokeskus. VFOAT Linjetrafik Med Lastbilar. Finnish and Swedish. ir. Tilastokeskus, Annankatu 44 00100 10, Helsinki Finland. **LC** HE5675.3.

LEMON-AID CEASED. 1976-1981. 0383-7084. CN. English. an. Editions Edmonston, Montreal Quebec Canada. **DD** 629.2222205.

LEMON-AID NEW CAR GUIDE. (LEMON-AID NEW CAR GUIDE . . .). 1982-. 0714-5861. CN. English. an. $7.95 Per Vol. Lemon-Aid New Car Guide, c/o Musson Book Company, 30 Lesmill Road, Toronto Ontario M3B 2T6 Canada. **DD** 629.222205. *Lemon-Aid, 0383-7084.*

LEMON-AID USED CAR GUIDE. (LEMON-AID USED CAR GUIDE . . .). 1982-. 0714-587X. CN. English. an. $7.95 Per Vol. Lemon-Aid Used Car Guide, Musson Book Company, 30 Lesmill Road, Toronto Ontario M3B 2T6 Canada. **DD** 629.222205. *Lemon-Aid, 0383-7084.*

LICENCES ISSUED TO DRIVERS AND RIDERS OF MOTOR VEHICLES. Series/Titl Territory of Papua and New Guinea Statistical Bulletin. English. an. **LC** HE5717.8. **DD** 354.9530087834.

LIGHT TRUCK EQUIPMENT NEWS. V. 1- July 10, 1978-. 0707-7939. Newspaper. CN. English. ir. $5.00. Warren Publishing, 1730 Amico Boulevard, Mississauga Ontario L4W 1Y3 Canada. **DD** 629.22305.

MAANDCIJFERS VAN DE INVOER, UITVOER EN ASSEMBLAGE VAN MOTORVOERTUIGEN. **Main/Corp** Netherlands (Kingdom, 1815-). Centraal Bureau Voor de Statistiek. NE. Dutch. Centraal Bureau Statistiek, Klooster weg 1, Heerlen Netherlands. **Tel** 045-736666. **LC** HD9710.N4. *Maandcijfers Van de Invoer, Uitvoer en Assemblage van Motorrijtuigen.*

MAGAZINE CONTRE-JOUR. See Recreation, Leisure - Sports.

MANUAL PARA LA REPARACION DE AUTOMOVILES Y CAMIONES, GUIA DEL COMERCIO Y LA INDUSTRIA AUTOMOTOR. VFOAT Guia Del Comercio Y la Industria Automotor. Spanish. ir. **LC** TL152. **DD** 338.47629.28702582.

MECANO (FLEURIMONT, QUEBEC : 1982). (MECANO). 0820-893X. Periodical. CN. French. ir. Centre d'Inspection et de Prevention Automobile de l'Estrie, 1573 Est rue King, Fleurimont Quebec J1G 1E3 Canada. **DD** 629.2872205. *Journal des Membres de C.I.P.A.E., 0823-5627.*

MECHANICAL PARTS/LABOR ESTIMATING GUIDE. DOMESTIC GLASS. Series/Titl Manuals for the Automotive Professional. VFOAT Mitchell Mechanical Parts/Labor Estimating Guide. US. English. qt. Mitchell Manuals Inc, PO Box 26260, San Diego CA 92126. **Tel** (619)578-8770. Ed Bill Jillard. adv acc. (ctrl). Mechanical part numbers and prices, estimated labor times for 1974-86 domestic cars. Separate times for combined operations. Skill level codes and model identification illustrations.

MEMBERS & CARS. **Main/Corp** Antique Automobile Club of Ottawa. 1982-. 0714-8569. CN. English. an. Free to Members. Antique Automobile Club of Ottawa, PO Box 2525 Station D, Ottawa Ontario K1P 5W6 Canada. **DD** 629.2222. *AACO Membership Roster, 0714-8569.*

MEMBERS' HANDBOOK - AUTOMOBILE ASSOCIATION OF KENYA. **Main/Corp** Automobile Association of Kenya. 1979-. English. ir. Free to Members. Media Services, PO Box 50095, Nairobi Kenya. **LC** GV1025.K4. **DD** 916.762044. *AA Guide to Motoring in Kenya.*

MEMBERSHIP ROSTER - PRIVATE TRUCK COUNCIL OF AMERICA. (MEMBERSHIP ROSTER). **Main/Corp** Private Truck Council of America. 0742-0773. US. English. Private Truck Council of America, 1101 17th Street Northwest, Washington DC 20036. **LC** HE5623. **DD** 388.32406073.

MICHIGAN CAR RECYCLING PROJECT ANNUAL REPORT. Periodical. US. English. an.

MICHIGAN LIVING. See Travel.

MID AMERICAN AUTO RACING NEWS. See Recreation, Leisure - Sports.

MIDWEST RACING NEWS. See Recreation, Leisure - Sports.

THE MILESTONE CAR. V. 1- Summer 1972-. Periodical. US. English. qt. $2.00 Each Issue. Milestone Car Society, 13150 El Capitan Way, Delhi CA 95315. **LC** TL1. **DD** 629.222205.

MINNESOTA . . . MOTOR VEHICLE CRASH FACTS (MINNESOTA. DEPT. OF PUBLIC SAFETY. OFFICE OF TRAFFIC SAFETY : 1982). (MINNESOTA . . . MOTOR VEHICLE CRASH FACTS). VFOAT Motor Vehicle Crash Facts. 1982-. US. English. an. Office of Traffic Safety, Department of Public Safety, 207 Transportation Building, St Paul MN 55155. **LC** HE5614.3.M5. **DD** 312.4409776. *Minnesota . . . Motor Vehicle Crash Data, 0737-0121.*

MISCELLANEOUS VEHICLE MANUFACTURERS. See Manufacturing.

MITCHELL TECH SERVICE BULLETIN. VFOAT Mitchell Tech Service Bulletins. Vol. 1-. 8755-4453. Periodical. US. English. Mitchell Manuals Inc, PO Box 26260, San Diego CA 92126. **Tel** (619)578-8770. Ed Dan Kelley. **LC** TL152. **DD** 629.287. adv acc. (ctrl). Complete source for latest factory changes in domestic and imported vehichle repairs.

MITCHELL TECHNICAL SERVICE BULLETIN, COLLISION. VFOAT Technical Service Bulletin, Collision. Vol. 1, Issue No. 1 (Mar. 1, 1980)-. 0276-2382. Periodical. US. English. mo. $56.50. Mitchell Manuals Inc, PO Box PO Box 26260, San Diego CA 92126. **Tel** (619)578-8770.

MODEL AUTO REVIEW. 0267-2715. Periodical. English. ir. 14.70. R & V Ward, 120 Gledhow Valley Road, Leeds LS27 6LX Great Britain. **Tel** (0532)686685. Ed Roderick C Ward. bk rev. adv acc. **Circ** 6,000. Leading publication worldwide for collectors of model and toy road vehicles. All scales, materials, kits and handbuilt. Mostly male adult readership.

MODERN TRUCKIN. VFOAT Trucking. Issue 1-. 0735-4800. Periodical. US. English. $2.00 Single Issue. Arden Communications, PO Box 99, Amawalk NY 10501. **LC** TL230.A1. **DD** 629.22405.

MONTHLY GASOLINE REPORTED BY STATES. Jan. 1983-. US. English. mo. Federal Highway Administration, Highway Statistics Division, 400 7th Street SW/Room 3300, Washington DC 20590. *Monthly Motor Gasoline Reported by States.*

MOOTTORIAJONEUVO- JA KUMIKORJAAMOT. **Main/Corp** Finland. Tilastokeskus. VFOAT Reparation av Motorfordon, Dack och Slangar. Finnish and Swedish. ir. Tilastokeskus, Annankatu 44 00100 10, Helsinki Finland. **LC** HD9710.F5.

MOT AUTO-JOURNAL. Periodical. German. ir. 1.80 Single Issue. Vereinigte Motor-Verlage, 7 1 Leuschnerstrasse 1, Postfach 1042, Stuttgart West Germany. **LC** TL3. **DD** 629.205. *MOT, Motor Rundschau.*

MOTEUR ET EQUIPEMENT. VFOAT Incorporant Transport Commercial et Revue-Moteur. Vol. 62, No. 9 (Sept. 1981)-. 0712-7898. Periodical. CN. French. ir. $16.00 Per Year. Moteur et Equipement, MacLean-Hunter, 625 Avenue du President Kennedy, Montreal Quebec H3A 1K5 Canada. **DD** 388.3240971.

MOTOR AGE MECHANICS NEWSLETTER. VFOAT Mechanics Newsletter. 1, 81-. 0278-9418. Periodical. US. English. ir. $25.00. Chilton Company, PO Box 1412, Riverton NJ 08077. **Tel** (215)964-4150.

MOTOR AUTO REPAIR MANUAL. 0098-1745. US. English. an. Hearst Corporation, c/o Donald Powell, 317 Round Hill Road, Pelham AL 35124. **Tel** (205)663-0353. **LC** TL152. **DD** 629.28722. *Motor's Auto Repair Manual.*

MOTOR CRASH ESTIMATING GUIDE. VFOAT Crash Estimating Guide. 0194-9411. US. English. ir. $133.00. Hearst Corporation, c/o Ronald Powell, 317 Round Hill Road, Pelham AL 35124. **Tel** (205)663-0353.

MOTOR EARLY MODEL CRASH ESTIMATING GUIDE. VFOAT Motor's Crash Estimating Guide. V. 1- Winter 1977-. 0160-1644. US. English. qt. Hearst Corporation, Joan Harris, Customer Service, Box 10116, Des Moines IA 50530. **LC** TL152. **DD** 338.4362928705.

MOTOR EMISSION CONTROL MANUAL. VFOAT Emission Control Manual. 2 (1975)-. 0743-1031. US. English. Motor, 555 West 57th Street, New York NY 10019. Ed Joe Oldham and Lou Forier. **LC** TL214.P6. **DD** 629.252805. *Motor's Emission Control Manual, 0743-1031.*

MOTOR HANDBOOK. 0094-1514. Periodical. US. English. an. Motor Handbook, 250 West 55th Street, New York NY 10019. **LC** TL152. **DD** 629.28705. *Motor's Handbook.*

MOTOR IMPORTED CAR CRASH ESTIMATING GUIDE. VFOAT Imported Car Crash Estimating Guide. 0164-6346. US. English. mo. $140.00. Hearst Corporation, c/o Ronald Powell, 317 Round Hill Road, Pelham AL 35124. **Tel** (205)663-0353. **LC** TL152. **DD** 338.43629287220973.

MOTOR IMPORTED CAR REPAIR MANUAL. PROFESSIONAL SERVICE TRADE EDITION. (MOTOR IMPORTED CAR REPAIR MANUAL). **Main/Corp** Motor. 0163-9110. US. English. Motor, 1790 Broadway, New York NY 10019. **LC** TL152. **DD** 629.2872205.

Transportation—Automobiles

MOTOR IN CANADA. April 1917-. 0027-190X. Periodical. CN. English. mo. 18.00 Domestic, 30.00 US, 36.00 Foreign. Sanford Evans Communications Ltd, Box 6900/1077 St James St, Winnipeg Manitoba R3C 3B1 Canada. Tel (204)775-0201. Ed James Buchok. adv acc. Circ 13,500. (ctrl). Articles of interest to those involved in the automotive aftermarket mainly in western Canada. Articles include features , service advice, new products and literature. *Motor and Sport.*

MOTOR INDUSTRY YEAR BOOK. See Yearbooks, Almanacs, Directories.

MOTOR ITALIA. 1926. Periodical. IT. Italian. qt. $14.85. Stamperia Artistica Nazionale, Corso Siracusa 37, 10136 Torino Italy. Ed Gianni Rogliatti. LC TL4. bk rev. adv acc. Circ 20,000. Motoring, new car descriptions (both technical and historical). Occasional truck, boat and component descriptions.

MOTOR LIGHT TRUCK & VAN REPAIR MANUAL. VFOAT Motor Light Truck and Van Repair Manual. 1984-. US. English. an. Motor, 250 West 55th Street, New York NY 10019. *Motor Truck Repair Manual, 0098-3624; Motor Truck & Diesel Repair Manual, 0362-6938.*

MOTOR MATERIAL : M.M. VFOAT M.M. Periodical. JA. Japanese. mo. 6500. Mota Matereriarusha, 64 Kanda Jinbo-cho 1 Chiyoda-ku, Tokyo-to Japan. LC TL159.

MOTOR MINIATURES. Vol. 1, No. 1 (Nov. 1980)-. 0229-6128. Periodical. CN. English. qt $5.95 Domestic for 4 Numbers, $6.95 US for 4 Numbers. Motor Miniatures Wheelspin News, 3045 Universal Drive, Mississauga Ontario L4X 2E2 Canada. DD 629.22105.

MOTOR NEWS ANALYSIS. 1945. 0027-1942. Periodical. US. English. wk. $99.00. News Analysis Inc, 32068 Olde Franklin Drive, Farmington Hills MI 48018. Tel (313)851-1377. Ed Maynard M Gordon. bk rev. adv acc. Circ 2,100. Newsletter concentrating on marketing and future product development trends in the US and foreign automotive industries.

MOTOR NORTH. Began publication in 1972. 0300-6301. Periodical. US. English. mo. $29.00. R-6-S, 6420 Zane Avenue North/Suite 201, Minneapolis MN 55429. Tel (612)535-8383.

MOTOR PARTS AND TIME GUIDE. 0098-1656. US. English. mo. Hearst Corporation, c/o Ronald Powell, 317 Round Hill Road, Pelham AL 35124. Tel (205)663-0353. LC TL152. DD 658.816. *Motor's Parts and Time Guide.*

MOTOR RACING YEAR. See Recreation, Leisure - Sports.

MOTOR REISE REVUE. Began with Dec. 1957 issue. Periodical. GW. German. ir. 15.00. Niederrad Lyoner Strasse 16, Postfach 71 0166, 6 Frankfurt AM Main West Germany. LC TL3.

MOTOR SERVICE (CHICAGO, ILL. : 1951). (MOTOR SERVICE). Sept. 15, 1951-. 0027-1977. Periodical. US. English. mo. $30.00. Hunter Publishing Company, 950 Lee Street, Des Plaines IL 60016. Tel (312)296-0770. LC TL1. DD 629.2872205. *Motor Service Magazine (Chicago, Ill. : 1950).*

MOTOR SPORT YEARBOOK. See Yearbooks, Almanacs, Directories.

MOTOR; THE AUTOMOTIVE BUSINESS MAGAZINE. 0027-1748. Periodical. US. English. mo. $12.00. Hearst Corporation, c/o Ronald Powell, 317 Round Hill Road, Pelham AL 35124. Tel (205)663-0353.

MOTOR TREND. V. 1- Sept. 1949-. 0027-2094. Periodical. US. English. mo. $15.94. Petersen Publishing Company, 6725 Sunset Boulevard, Los Angeles CA 900298. Tel (213)657-5100. Ed Tony Swan. Ind/Abst Pop. Mag. Rev., Read. Guide Period. Lit., Consum. Index Prod. Eval. Inf. Source, Abr. Read. Guide, Mag. Index. LC TL1. DD 629.205. adv acc. Circ 778,000. America's automotive authority filled with road tests, service features, forecasts, and racing news. *Car Life, Sports Car Graphic; Wheels Afield.*

MOTOR TREND NEW CAR BUYER'S GUIDE. 0160-8886. US. English. an. $1.95. Petersen Publishing Company, 6725 Sunset Boulevard, Los Angeles CA 90028. LC TL5. DD 629.22205.

MOTOR TRUCK & DIESEL REPAIR MANUAL. VAT Motor Truck and Diesel Repair Manual. 0362-6938. US. English. an. Motor, 1790 Broadway, New York NY 10019. LC TL230.A1. DD 629.2874. *Motor's Truck & Diesel Repair Manual.*

MOTOR TRUCK REPAIR MANUAL. 0098-3624. Periodical. US. English. an. Motor, 250 West 55th Street, New York NY 10019. LC TL230.A1. DD 629.287405.

MOTOR VACUUM & WIRING DIAGRAM DIAGNOSTIC MANUAL. PROFESSIONAL SERVICE TRADE EDITION. (MOTOR VACUUM & WIRING DIAGRAM DIAGNOSTIC MANUAL). Main/Corp Motor (New York). VFOAT Vacuum & Wiring Diagram Diagnostic Manual. VAT Motor Vacuum and Wiring Diagram Diagnostic Manual. Professional Service Trade Edition. 0273-1029. US. English. Motor, 224 West 57th Street, New York NY 10019. LC TL272. DD 629.2540288.

MOTOR VEHICLE. (THE MOTOR VEHICLE). Main/Corp Statistics Canada. Transportation Section. VFOAT Vehicules a Moteur. 1971-. 0410-5575. Periodical. CN. English (French). an. $0.50. Statistics Canada, Transportation Section, Ottawa Ontario K1A 0T6 Canada. LC HE5635. DD 388.34220971. *Motor Vehicle.*

MOTOR VEHICLE CARRIERS. Main/Corp Virginia. State Corporation Commission. 1951-. US. English. an. LC HE5633.V8.

MOTOR VEHICLE CENSUS, TASMANIA. Main/Corp Australian Bureau of Statistics. AT. English. ir. Free. Australian Bureau of Statistics, Commonwealth Government Centre 3rd Floor, 188 Collins Street, Hobart Tasmania 7000 Australia. Tel (002)20 9409. LC HE5709.T37. DD 388.3409946. Number of motor cars and station wagons, utilities, panel vans, rigid and articulated trucks, other truck type vehicles, buses and motor cycles on register in each State and Territory and Australia at 30 September 1985.

MOTOR VEHICLE CENSUS, WESTERN AUSTRALIA. AT. English. ir. Australian Bureau of Statistics, Level 1 Merlin Centre, 30 Terrace Road, Perth Western Australia 6000 Australia. Tel (09)323 5140. LC HE5709.W47. DD 388.3409941. Number of motor cars and station wagons, utilities, panel vans, rigid and articulated trucks, other truck type vehicles, buses and motor cycles on register in each State and Territory and Australia at 30 September 1985.

MOTOR VEHICLE DATA BOOK. Began publication in 1947/48?. 0316-6198. Periodical. CN. English. an. 21.75. Sanford Evans Communications Ltd, Box 6900/1077 St James Street, Winnipeg Manitoba R3C 3B1 Canada. Tel (204)775-0201. Ed G B Henry. DD 629.2220212. Passenger car statistics for vehicle identification and registration. Includes vehicle weight, wheelbase, serial numbers, engine stats and manufacturers retail prices.

MOTOR VEHICLE IDENTIFICATION. 0736-8437. US. English. an. Motor Vehicle Manufacturers Association of the United States, 300 New Center Building, Detroit MI 48202.

MOTOR VEHICLE INDUSTRIES. VFOAT Fabrication de Vehicules Automobiles. 1981-. 0319-9088. CN. English (French). an. $4.75 Domestic, $5.70 Foreign. Statistics Canada, Publication Sales and Services, Ottawa Ontario K1A 0V7 Canada. *Motor Vehicle Manufacturers, 0575-9129; Miscellaneous Vehicle Manufacturers, 0527-5741.*

THE MOTOR VEHICLE. PART II : MOTIVE FUEL SALES. VFOAT Vehicules a Moteur. Partie : II Ventes de Carburants. CN. English and French. an. $0.70. Minister of Industry, Trade and Commerce, Publishing Centre, Supply and Services Canada, Ottawa K1A 0S9 Canada. LC HD9574.C2. DD 381.45665538270971.

MOTOR VEHICLE STATISTICS. See Statistics.

MOTOR VEHICLE STATISTICS (BENUE STATE (NIGERIA). See Statistics.

MOTOR VEHICLE THEFTS IN CANADA CEASED. VFOAT Vols de Vehicules Automobiles au Canada. May 1963-Sept./Oct. 1974. 0828-3532. CN. English (English). $1.05. Information Canada, 171 Slater Street, Ottawa Ontario K1A 0S9 Canada. LC HV6665.C2. DD 364.162. Also available in microfiche.

MOTOR VEHICLES ASSESSED VALUATIONS. VOLUME B. See Business - Public Finance.

MOTOR VEHICLES (PORT-VILA, VANUATU). (MOTOR VEHICLES). VFOAT Vehicules Automobiles. 1970-1981-. English (French). an. LC HE5718.4. DD 388.309934021. *New Registrations of Motor Vehicles and Motor Vehicles on the Register.*

MOTORFAHRZEUGBESTAND IN DER SCHWEIZ NACH KANTONEN UND ORTSCHAFTEN. Main/Corp Switzerland. Statistisches Amt. VFOAT Effectif des Vehicules a Moteur en Suisse par Cantons et Localites. French and German. ir. 24.00. Eidgenossisches Statistisches Amt, Hallwylstrasse 15, Bern Switzerland. LC HE5683.

MOTORIST (WINSTON-SALEM, N.C.). (THE MOTORIST). 8750-3107. Periodical. US. English. qt. $1.00. Winston Salem Automobile Club, 611 Coliseum Drive, Winston Salem NC 27106. *Winston-Salem Travelife.*

MOTOR'S IMPORTED CAR REPAIR MANUAL. (MOTOR IMPORTED CAR REPAIR MANUAL). 0090-1563. US. English. Motor, 555 West 57th Street, New York NY 10019. LC TL152. DD 629.2872205. *Motor's Imported Car Repair Manual, 0090-1563.*

MOTORTECH. Vol. 1, No. 1 (Spring 1981)-. 0027-1748. Periodical. US. English. Motortech, PO Box 1714, Sandusky OH 44870. LC TL152. DD 629.2872205.

MUFFLER DIGEST. 0164-6044. Periodical. US. English. mo. $34.00. MD Publication Inc, 1036 South Glenstone, Springfield MO 65804. Tel (417)866-3917.

MY LITTLE SALESMAN TRUCK CATALOG. 0192-7027. Periodical. US. English. mo. $60.00. My Little Salesman Inc, PO Box 2328, Eugene OR 97402. Tel (503)689-2711.

N.A.D.A. MOBILE HOME APPRAISAL GUIDE. Main/Corp National Automobile Dealers Association. 0095-6538. US. English. ty. National Automobile Dealers Association, PO Box 7800, Costa Mesa CA 92628. Tel (703)821-7192. Ed Don Christy Jr. LC HD9715.7.U62. DD 381.456908790973. Used values 1956-1983. Optional equipment section.

NADA NEWSLETTER. Main/Corp National Automobile Dealers Association. VAT National Automobile Dealers Association Newsletter. 0164-3592. Periodical. US. English. mo. $50.00. National Automobile Dealers Association, 8400 West Park Drive, McLean VA 22101. Tel (703)821-7108.

N.A.D.A. OFFICIAL USED CAR GUIDE. Main/Corp National Automobile Dealers Association. VAT National Automobile Dealers Association Official Used Car Guide. 0027-5794. Periodical. US. English. mo. $32.00. National Automobile Dealers Association, 8400 West Park Drive, McLean VA 22102. Tel (800)252-6232. Ed Lynn A Weaver. (ctrl). Prices on used cars: domestic, imports and light trucks.

N.A.D.A. OLDER CAR, R.V., MOTORCYCLE : AN OFFICIAL N. A.D.A. VALUE GUIDE. VFOAT N.A.D.A. Older R.V., Car, Motorcycle. VAT National Automobile Dealers Association Older Car, RV, Motorcycle. 1980-. Periodical. US. English. ty. $40.00. National Automobile Dealers Association, PO Box 7800, Costa Mesa CA 92628. Tel (703)821-7192. Ed Don Christy Jr. Used values from 1967 to 1976.

N.A.D.A. RECREATION VEHICLE APPRAISAL GUIDE. Main/Corp National Automobile Dealers Association. 0092-4601. US. English. ty. $26.00. PO Box 1407, Covina CA 91722. LC HD9715.7.U6. DD 381.456292260973.

N.A.D.A. TITLE AND REGISTRATION BOOK. See Law.

NASCAR NEWSLETTER. See Recreation, Leisure - Sports.

NATIONAL ADLETTER. (THE NATIONAL ADLETTER : MONTHLY NEWSLETTER OF THE NATIONAL ASSOCIATION OF ANTIQUE AUTOMOBILE CLUBS OF CANADA CORPORATION). Vol. 1, Issue No. 1 (Jan./Feb./Mar. 1980)-. 0228-6874. Periodical. CN. English. mo. Free to Members. N A A A C C C, Suite 302/19 Richmond Street West, Toronto Ontario M5H 1Y9 Canada. DD 629.22220750971.

Transportation—Automobiles

NATIONAL NEW CAR PRICE GUIDE. VFOAT National Appraisal Guides New Car Price Guide. US. English. an. National Automobile Dealers Association, 8400 West Park Drive, Mclean VA 22101.

NATIONAL SERVICE DATA. VFOAT National Service Data. US. English. Mitchell Manuals Inc, PO Box 80427, San Diego CA 92138. LC TL152. DD 629.28722.

NATIONAL SERVICE DATA, TRANSMISSION MANUAL. Main/Corp Mitchell Manuals, Inc. VFOAT Transmission Service & Repair, Domestic Cars. Periodical. US. English. an. Mitchell Manuals Inc, PO Box 80427, San Diego CA 92138.

NATIONAL TRUCK CHARACTERISTIC REPORT. Main/Corp United States. Office of Highway Planning. Planning Services Branch. 0148-222X. US. English. an. US Department of Transportation, Federal Highway Administration, Washington DC 20590. LC TL230.A1. DD 629.224.

NEW CAR COST GUIDE. VFOAT AIS New Car Cost Guide. 1956. 0731-4787. US. English. ir. $73.00. Automobile Invoice Service, PO Box 6227, San Jose CA 95150. Tel (408)296-2211. Ed Christine Boldt. bk rev. Circ 8,000. An invaluable consumer reference book, lists dealer invoice and suggested retail prices for domestic cars, light trucks and popular imports.

NEW CAR PRICES : BUYER'S GUIDE. 1980-. Periodical. US. English. ty.

NEW DRIVER. 0279-6384. Periodical. US. English. qt. $3.90. Curriculum Innovations Inc, 3500 Western Avenue, Highland Park IL 60035. Tel (312)432-2700. Ed Margaret Mucklo. Circ 150,000. A periodical for driver education students stressing behind-the-wheel safety and skill, energy conservation, maintenance, consumer and legal issues. Teacher's guide included with each issue. *Scholastic Wheels, 0161-2727.*

NEW MODEL PRODUCT INFORMATION MANUAL, PONTIAC. Main/Corp General Motors Corporation. Pontiac Motor Division. VFOAT Pontiac New Product Information Manual. US. English. Pontiac Motor Division, General Motors Corporation, Pontiac MI 48053. LC TL215.P68. DD 629.222205.

NEW MOTOR VEHICLE SALES (ANNUAL). (NEW MOTOR VEHICLE SALES). VFOAT Ventes de Vehicules, Automobiles Neufs. 1961-1978. 0575-920X. Periodical. CN. English. an. Receiver General for Canada, Statistics Canada Publications, Ottawa Ontario K1A 0T6 Canada. DD 381.4562920971. *New Motor Vehicle Sales and Motor Vehicle Financing (Annual), 0703-0150.*

NEW YORK AUTO REPAIR NEWS. VFOAT Auto Repair News. 0191-4979. Periodical. US. English. mo. $3.00. Van Allen Publishing Company, Box 354, Hicksville NY 11502.

NEW YORK MOTORIST. 0028-7385. Periodical. US. English. mo. New York Motorist, 28 East 78th Street, New York NY 10021.

NEWS FROM THE CLUB - CLUB AUTOMOBILE DU QUEBEC. (NEWS FROM THE CLUB). Vol. 1, No. 1 (May 1976)-. 0228-4847. Periodical. CN. English. ir. Free to English-Speaking Members. Quebec Automobile Club, PO Box 9600, 2600 Laurier Boulevard, Ste-Foy Quebec G1V 4K8 Canada. DD 796.7060714.

NOMAD NEWS. 0149-6301. Periodical. US. English. mo. $20.00. National Nomad Club, 4691 South Mariposa Drive, Englewood CO. LC TL215.N57. DD 629.2222.

NORD DE LA FRANCE : CHAMPAGNE, ARDENNES. FR. French. ir. Pneu Michelin, 46 Av de Breteuil, 75 Paris France. LC DC611.C451. DD 914.430483.

NORMANDIE. See Recreation, Leisure - Sports.

NORTHWESTERN TOUR BOOK. See Travel.

NOTIZIARIO STATISTICO - ANFIA. Main/Corp Associazione Nazionale Fre Industrie Automobilistiche. VAT Notiziario Statistico - Associazione Nazionale Fre Industrie Automobilistiche. V. 19- Jan. 1977-. Periodical. Italian. ir. ANFIA, Corso Galileo Ferraris 61, Torino 10128 Italy. LC HD9710.I8. *Bollettino Statistico.*

NUWE VOERTUIE GEREGISTREER. VFOAT New Vehicles Registered. SA. Afrikaans (English). an. 2.50. Government Printer, Bosman Street, Private Bag X85, Pretoria 0001 South Africa. LC HE5704.4.

OFF-ROAD. 0363-1745. Periodical. US. English. mo. $13.50 Domestic, $15.50 Foreign. Off-Road, PO Box 49659, Los Angeles CA 90049. Ind/Abst Consum. Index Prod. Eval. Inf. Source. LC TL235.6. DD 629.22. *Off-Road Vehicles and Adventure.*

OFFICIAL ANNUAL AUTO THEFT REPORT. Main/Corp Massachusetts. Registrar of Motor Vehicles. VFOAT Annual Auto Theft Report. US. English. an. Commonwealth of Massachusetts Registry of Motor Vehicles, 100 Nashua Street, Boston MA 02114. LC HV6661.M4. DD 364.162.

THE OFFICIAL PRICE GUIDE TO COLLECTOR CARS. See Hobbies.

OFFICIAL WISCONSIN AUTOMOBILE VALUATION GUIDE. (OFFICIAL WISCONSIN AUTOMOBILE VALUATION GUIDE : FOR USE IN STATE OF WISCONSIN). Main/Corp Wisconsin Automobile and Truck Dealers Association. 0736-7988. US. English. bm. $32.00 Single Subscription. National Market Reports Inc, 300 West Adams Street, Chicago IL 60606-5.

OFICINA. Periodical. Portuguese. ir. 1.00 single issue. Departamento de Circulacao Consultas, Caixa Postal 5095, Sao Paulo Brazil. LC TL152.

OHIO MOTORIST. 0030-0985. Periodical. US. English. mo. *Motorist.*

OLD CAR VALUE GUIDE. 0475-1876. US. English. an. Crafts Publications, 1462 Vandervilt, El Paso TX 79935. Tel (915)592-5713. Ed Quentin Craft. LC TL7. DD 629.2222075. adv acc. Circ 25,000. (ctrl). Collector car values, photos, original factory specifications on all cars 1897 to 1980 plus automobile history on 500 makes, classic color section plus over 200 black and white photos.

OLD CARS. 0048-1637. Periodical. US. English. wk. $21.50. Krause Publications Inc, 700 East State Street, Iola WI 54990. Tel (715)445-2214. Ed John Gunnell. bk rev. adv acc. Circ 80,000. The newspaper for the old car enthusiast. Contains the information you need to make the hobby more fun and profitable for you.

OLD CARS PRICE GUIDE. 0194-6404. US. English. qt. $21.00. Krause Publications Inc, 700 East State Street, Iola WI 54990. Tel (715)445-2214. Ed Dennis Schrimpf. adv acc. Circ 85,000. (ctrl). Price guide of old cars with grading qualities.

ON & OFF ROAD MAINTENANCE AND FUEL COST INDEX. VFOAT On-Road and Off-Road Cost Index. 1984-. 0749-5692. US. English. an. Cost Research Institute Inc, PO Box 5227, 912 Highland Avenue, Albany GA 31706. LC TL151.5. DD 629.287042.

ONTARIO TRUCKING UPDATE. Vol. 1, No. 1 (Mar. 1, 1982)-. 0713-8482. Periodical. CN. English. bw. Free. Member Services and Administration Division, Ontario Trucking Association, 555 Dixon Road, Rexdale Ontario M9W 1H8 Canada. DD 388.32409713. (ctrl). *News Round-Up, 0882-5966.*

OPERATING AUTHORITY BULLETIN. Main/Corp Alberta Trucking Association. VFOAT Trucking Bulletin. June 30, 1975-. 0383-8994. Periodical. CN. English. Alberta Trucking Association, 5112 3rd Street SE, PO Box 5520 Station A, Calgary Alberta T2H 1J6 Canada. DD 388.324097123. *Operating Authority Bulletin, 0319-390X.*

OREGON MOTOR VEHICLE ACCIDENTS. US. English. an. Motor Vehicles Division, Department of Transportation, Salem OR 97314. LC HE5614.3.O7. DD 312.4409795.

ORGA NEWSLINE. (O R G A NEWSLINE). Main/Corp Ontario Retail Gasoline and Automotive Service Association. VAT Ontario Retail Gasoline and Automotive Service Association Newsline. V. 1- Dec. 1979-. 0228-0469. Periodical. CN. English. Ontario Retail Gasoline and Automotive Service Association, Suite 102/101 Queensway West, Mississauga Ontario L5B 2P7 Canada. DD 629.28609713. *Automotive Review, 0706-506X.*

ORGANIZATION CHART MANUAL. Main/Corp California. Dept. of Motor Vehicles. US. English. an. Department of Motor Vehicles, Staff Services Section, Division of Administration, PO Box 11828, Sacramento CA 95953. LC HE5633.C2. DD 353.97940087834.

THE PACKARD CORMORANT. V. 22, No. 4- Winter 1976-. 0362-9368. Periodical. US. English. qt. $20.00. The Packard Club, Box 2808, Oakland CA 94618. Ed Alan Adams. LC TL215.P25. DD 629.2222. bk rev. adv acc. Circ 3,999. (ctrl). Our publication is dedicated to information regarding the Packard automobile of 1899-1958. *Cormorant.*

PACKARDS INTERNATIONAL MOTOR CAR CLUB. 0364-9261. Periodical. US. English. qt. $3.00 Single Issue. 302 French Street, Santa Ana CA 92701. LC TL215 .P25. DD 388.3422.

PADVERVOERTARIEFBOEK EN LYS VAN STOPPLEKKE. See Indexes/Abstracts.

PARAIBA, PERNAMBUCO, ALAGOAS : ESTATISTICA DE TRAFEGO NO NORDESTE. Main/Corp Brazil. Superintendencia do Desenvolvimento do Nordeste. Departamento de Desenvolvimento Local. Portuguese. ir. LC HE5653.

PARC AUTOMOBILE DU BURUNDI. French. an. Service National des Etudes et Statistiques, BP 1156, Bujumbura Republique du Burundi. LC HE5703.8. DD 388.340967572. *Parc Automobile Prive du Burundi.*

PARC ET IMMATRICULATIONS DES VEHICULES UTILITAIRES. FR. French. an. 55-57 rue Brillat Savarin, 75013 Paris France. LC HE5668. DD 388.320944.

PARKING. 0031-2193. Periodical. US. English. bm. $35.00. National Parking Association Inc, 2000 K Street Northwest, Washington DC 20006. LC HE371.A2. DD 388.4740973.

PERFORMANCE DATA, NEW PASSENGER CARS AND MOTORCYCLES. Main/Corp United States. National Highway Traffic Safety Administration. Series/Titl Consumer Information Series, V. 4. Periodical. US. English. ir. *Performance Data for New Passenger Cars and Motorcycles.*

PETERSEN'S 4 WHEEL & OFF-ROAD. VFOAT 4 Wheel & Off-Road. VAT Petersen's Four Wheel and Off Road. 0162-3214. Periodical. US. English. mo. $9.76. Petersen Publishing Company, 6725 Sunset Boulevard, Los Angeles CA 90028. Tel (213)657-5100. Ed Michael Coates. LC TL235.6. DD 629.22. adv acc. Circ 300,900. The nation's #1 off-road magazine, with tips on technology and techniques, travel tours, pictorial guides, and racing.

PETERSEN'S BIG BOOK OF AUTO REPAIR. VFOAT Big Book of Auto Repair. 1977- Ed. 0730-3580. US. English. an. $14.95 (U.S.), $18.50 (Canada). Petersen Publishing Company, 6725 Sunset Boulevard, Los Angeles CA 90028. LC TL152. DD 629.28722.

PETERSEN'S CIRCLE TRACK. VFOAT Circle Track. Vol. 1, No. 1 (Oct. 1982)-. 0734-5437. Periodical. US. English. mo. $49.95. Petersen Publishing Company, 6725 Sunset Boulevard, Los Angeles CA 90028. Tel (213)657-5100. Ed C J Baker. adv acc. Circ 86,600. The latest on Indy cars stocks, sprints and the teams and technology behind them- plus track reviews and race reports.

PETERSEN'S COMPLETE BOOK OF PLYMOUTH, DODGE, CHRYSLER. VFOAT Complete Book of Plymouth, Dodge, Chrysler. 1973-. 0092-4512. US. English. $2.00. Petersen Publishing Company, 6725 Sunset Boulevard, Los Angeles CA 90028. LC TL215.C55. DD 629.2222.

PETERSEN'S HOW TO TUNE YOUR CAR. 6Th-. 0271-3527. Periodical. US. English. $5.95 A Copy. Petersen Publishing Company, 6725 Sunset Boulevard, Los Angeles CA 90028. LC TL210. DD 629.25040288. *How to Tune Your Car.*

PETERSEN'S WHEELS AFIELD. VFOAT Wheels Afield. V. 1- Feb. 1967-. Periodical. US. English. mo. Petersen's Publishing Company, 6725 Sunset Boulevard, Los Angeles CA 90028. LC TL298. DD 629.22605.

PICKUP, VAN & 4WD ROAD TEST ANNUAL AND BUYERS' GUIDE. See Business - Purchasing.

PONTIAC CHASSIS SHOP MANUAL. (PONTIAC; CHASSIS SHOP MANUAL). Main/Corp General Motors Corporation., Pontiac Motor Division. 1960-. 0149-9637. US. English. Pontiac Motor Division, General Motors Corporation, 660 East South Boulevard, Truck Division, Pontiac MI 48053. LC TL215.P68. DD 629.24028.

Transportation—Automobiles

PONTIAC SHOP MANUAL SUPPLEMENT. Main/Corp General Motors of Canada. VFOAT Pontiac Chassis Shop Manual. 1973-. 0700-3447. CN. English. an. General Motors of Canada Ltd, 36 Overlea Boulevard, Toronto Ontario M4H 1B7 Canada. DD 629.2872. *Pontiac Service Manual. Supplement, 0700-3439.*

POPULAR & PERFORMANCE CAR REVIEW. VFOAT Popular and Performance Car Review. May 1984-. 0747-1483. Periodical. US. English. mo. $7.50. Car Review, PO Drawer 7157, Lakeland FL 33807. *Car Exchange, 0164-0836.*

POPULAR HOT RODDING. V. 1- June 1962-. 0032-4523. Periodical. US. English. mo. Argus Publishers Corporation, 12301 Wilshire Boulevard, Los Angeles CA 90025. Tel (213)820-3601. LC TL236. DD 629.22805.

PORSCHE PANORAMA. 0147-3565. Periodical. US. English. mo. $8.00. Porsche Club of America, 5616 Clermont Drive, Alexandria VA 22310. LC TL215.P75. DD 629.22805.

PRESS. (PRESS). VAT Press (Weston). Jan. 1979-. 0820-0076. Periodical. CN. English. bm. Driving School Association of Ontario, 1778 Weston Road, Weston Ontario M9N 1V8 Canada. DD 629.2830710713. *Newsletter (Driving School Association of Ontario), 0823-1850.*

PREVOYANCE. See Public Health and Safety.

PRIVATE PASSENGER AUTOMOBILE INSURANCE. See Insurance.

PROCEEDINGS OF STAPP CAR CRASH CONFERENCE. Main/Conf Stapp Car Crash Conference. First conference held in 1955. 0585-086X. US. English. an. Society of Automotive Engineering, 400 Commonwealth Drive, Warrendale PA 15096. Tel (412)776-4970. Ind/Abst Eng. Index.

PROCEEDINGS OF STAPP CAR CRASH CONFERENCE. (STAPP CAR CRASH CONFERENCE PROCEEDINGS). 27th (Oct. 17-19, 1983)-. 0585-086X. US. English. an. Society of Automotive Engineers, 400 Commonwealth Drive, Warrendale PA 15096. LC TL6. DD 629.231. *Proceedings of ... Stapp Car Crash Conference, 0585-086X.*

PROCEEDINGS ... OF THE ANNUAL CONVENTION. Main/Corp Automotive Engine Rebuilders Association (U.S.). US. English. an. LC TL1. DD 629.250627.

PROFESSIONAL DRIVER EDUCATION. Vol. 1, No. 1 (Oct. 1977)-. 0228-9237. Periodical. CN. English. bm. $12.00. Professional Driver Education, 22 Oakmount Road/No 1008, Toronto Ontario M6P 2M7 Canada. DD 629.283207.

THE PROFESSIONAL'S TIRE HANDBOOK. VFOAT Modern Tire Dealer's Professional Tire Handbook. 0161-7214. US. English. $4.00 Each Issue. Hartman Communications, 633 Third Avenue, New York NY 10017. LC TL270. DD 629.48.

QUARTERLY/JOURNAL. See Medicine.

QUATTRORUOTE. Began in 1956. Periodical. IT. Italian. mo. $39.00. Editoriale Domus, Via A Grandi 5/7, 20089 Rozzano Milan Italy. Tel 02/824721. Ed Raffaele Mastrostefano. LC TL4. adv acc. Circ 610,000. World famous motortrade magazine which anticipates Italian and foreign novelties, strict technical tests pointing out merits and faults, up-to-date pricelist for new and second-hand cars.

THE QUINLAN PRIVATE TRUCK LAW REPORT. See Law.

O R G A NEWS. See Petroleum and Natural Gas.

RACECAR. See Recreation, Leisure - Sports.

THE RADIATOR. Periodical. English. ir. LC HD9710.N5. DD 338.476292.

RADIATOR REPORTER & PRICING GUIDE. VFOAT Radiator Reporter and Pricing Guide. 0739-2060. Periodical. US. English. mo. $69.00 Domestic, $83.00 Canada. Radiator Reporter, PO Box 38, Grosse Ile MI 48138.

RALLY ONTARIO. COMPETITION NEWS. See Recreation, Leisure - Sports.

READING-BERKS AUTO CLUB MAGAZINE. 0744-7043. Periodical. US. English. bm. Reading-Berks Auto Club, POB 1696, Reading PA 19603.

RECREATION VEHICLE FINANCING. See Business - Public Finance.

REGISTERED MOTOR VEHICLES. Main/Corp Papua New Guinea. Bureau of Statistics. English. ir. Bureau of Statistics, PO Box 2032, Konedobu Papua New Guinea. LC HE5718.P3.

REGISTRERADE FORDON EFTER FABRIKAT DEN .... Series/Titl Sveriges Officiella Statistik. Statistiska Meddelanden. VFOAT Registered Vehicles by Make on .... English (Swedish). ir. Liber Distribution, 162 89 Vallingby, Stockholm Sweden. LC HE260.A15, HE5680.

REGISTRY OF VEHICLES SINGAPORE ANNUAL REPORT. See Public Administration.

REKISTERIIN MERKITYT UUDET MOOTTORIAJONEUVOT. Main/Corp Finland. Tilastokeskus. VFOAT Inregistrerade Nya Motorfordon. English, Finnish and Swedish. ir. Tilastokeskus, Annankatu 44 00100 10, Helsinki Finland. LC HE5675.3.

THE REPAIR CAR/NEW CAR DIRECTORY. See Yearbooks, Almanacs, Directories.

REPORT - INTERNATIONAL TECHNICAL CONFERENCE OF EXPERIMENTAL SAFETY VEHICLES. Main/Conf International Technical Conference on Experimental Safety Vehicles. 1st- 1971-. 0093-1411. US. English. $3.00. Superintendent of Documents, US Government Printing Office, Washington DC 20402. LC TL242. DD 629.276.

REPORT OF THE MOTOR VEHICLE LICENSE DIVISION OF THE OKLAHOMA TAX COMMISSION. Main/Corp Oklahoma Tax Commission. US. English. ir. LC HE5633.O5. DD 629.21342.

REPORT ON OPERATION OF THE STATE MOTOR VEHICLE POOL. See Public Administration.

REPORT: PRIVATE PASSENGER AUTOMOBILE INSURANCE. See Insurance.

RESEARCH REPORT - DEPARTMENT OF MOTOR VEHICLES. RESEARCH AND TECHNOLOGY DIVISION. (RESEARCH REPORT). Main/Corp Washington (State). Dept. of Motor Vehicles. Research and Technology. 0092-3583. US. English. State of Washington, Department of Motor Vehicles & Research Technology, Olympia WA 98504. LC TL24.W2. DD 629.205.

RESEARCH REPORT - U. S. LAND LOCOMOTION RESEARCH LABORATORY, CENTER LINE, MICHIGAN. See Engineering.

REVUE JURIDIQUE DU CONSOMMATEUR. (LA REVUE JURIDIQUE DU CONSOMMATEUR). V. 1- Aug./Sept. 1975-. 0318-8574. Periodical. CN. French. bm. $10. Per No. Association pour la Protection des Automobilistes, 292 Ouest Boulevard St-Joseph, Montreal Quebec H2V 2N7 Canada. DD 343.7107.

RIKUUN YORAN. Main/Corp Japan. Fukuoka Rikuunkyoku. Japanese. ir. 1300. Kyushu Rikuun Kyoryokukai, 6-2 Akasaka 2-chome Chuo-ku, Fukuoka Japan. LC HE5697.K93.

ROAD & TRACK. See Recreation, Leisure - Sports.

ROAD & TRACK'S BUYER'S GUIDE. 0094-5692. US. English. $2.00. Bond/Parkhurst Publications, 1499 Monrovia Avenue, Newport Beach CA 92663. LC TL5. DD 629.2222.

ROAD & TRACK'S ROAD TEST ANNUAL & BUYER'S GUIDE. Series/Titl CBS Leisure Transportation Series. VFOAT Road Test Annual & Buyer's Guide. VAT Road and Track's Road Test Annual and Buyer's Guide. Began with 1978. 0278-2669. US. English. an. $2.95. CBS Publications, 1515 Broadway, New York NY 10036, (subscription address: Neodata PO Box 2606 Boulder CO 80322). LC TL1. DD 629.222205.

ROAD MOTOR VEHICLES. (ROAD MOTOR VEHICLES. REGISTRATIONS). VFOAT Vehicles Automobiles. 0706-067X. CN. English (French). an. $5.40. LC HE5635. DD 354.710087834. *Road Motor Vehicles. Registrations (Statistics Canada. Surface Transport Section).*

ROAD TEST. V. 1- Dec. 1964-. 0557-1537. Periodical. US. English. mo. $14.00 Domestic, $17.00 Foreign. Road Test Subscriptions, Mount Morris IL 61504. LC TL1. DD 629.282405.

THE ROAD WAY. Began in 1935. Periodical. UK. English. mo. Road Haulage Association, 104 New Kings Road, London SW6 4LN England. LC HE5601. DD 388.3.

ROD ACTION. See Recreation, Leisure - Sports.

ROSTER - MCLAUGHLIN BUICK CLUB OF CANADA. Main/Corp McLaughlin Buick Club of Canada. 1973-. 0317-610X. Periodical. CN. English. an. McLaughlin Buick Club of Canada, 99 Simcoe Street South, Oshawa Ontario L1H 4G7 Canada. DD 629.2222. *Membership Roster and Car List, 0317-6118.*

ROTARY ROCKET. 0194-6439. Periodical. US. English. qt. $16.00. RX-7 Club of America Inc, 4020 Palos Verdes Drive N/Suite 108, Rolling Hills Estate CA 90274.

ROULEZ SANS VOUS FAIRE ROULER CEASED. VFOAT Arret, Roulez Sans Vous Faire Rouler. 1975-1981 Ed. 0383-7092. CN. French. an. Editions Edmonston, Montreal Quebec Canada. DD 629.222205.

RUNNING BOARD. (THE RUNNING BOARD). V. 8- Jan. 1969-. 0048-8771. Periodical. CN. English. mo. Edmonton Antique Car Club, Box 102, Edmonton Alberta T5J 2G9 Canada. *Edmonton Antique Car Club Bulletin, 0380-8106.*

RV BUSINESS. VFOAT R.V. Business. Vol. 34, No. 7 (Oct. 1983)-. Periodical. US. English. mo. $12.00. T L Enterprises, 29901 Agoura Road, Agoura CA 91301. Tel (213)991-4980. Ind/Abst Trade Ind. Index. *RVBusiness.*

RV BUYERS GUIDE. VFOAT R.V. Buyers Guide. 0742-6208. US. English. $2.95. 29901 Agoura Road, Agoura CA 91301. LC TL298. DD 629.226029.

RVBUSINESS. ANNUAL DIRECTORY AND BUYER'S GUIDE. See Yearbooks, Almanacs, Directories.

RVS, AMERICA'S FAMILY CAMPING VEHICLES. VFOAT R.V.S, America's Family Camping Vehicles. 1982-. 8756-4246. US. English. an. Recreation Vehicle Industry Association, 14650 Lee Road, Chantilly VA 22021. LC HD9710.38.U6. DD 381.456292260973. *RVS, The Family Camping Vehicles, 0734-7715.*

S S G M. SERVICE & GARAGE MANAGEMENT. (S S G M, SERVICE STATION & GARAGE MANAGEMENT). V. 5, No. 8- Aug. 1975-. 0381-548X. Periodical. CN. English. mo. $27.86. Wadham Publications Ltd, 109 Vanderhoof Avenue/Suite 101, Toronto Ontario M4G 2J2 Canada. Tel (416)445-6641. Ind/Abst Can. Bus. Index. DD 658.9162928605. *Service Station and Garage Management, 0037-2668.*

S.A.E. AUSTRALASIA. (THE SAE—AUSTRALASIA : JOURNAL OF THE SOCIETY OF AUTOMOTIVE ENGINEERS - AUSTRALASIA). VFOAT SAE Australasia. Vol. 27 (Jan./Feb. 1967)-. 0036-0651. Periodical. AU. English. bm. $26.57. Society of Automotive Engineers, 191 Royal Parade, Parkville Victoria 3052 Australia. Tel 347-2220. Ind/Abst Met. Abstr., World Alum. Abstr. *IAAE Journal.*

SAE HANDBOOK. (S.A.E. HANDBOOK). 0362-8205. US. English. an. Society of Automotive Engineering, 400 Commonwealth Drive, Warrendale PA 15096. Tel (412)776-4970. Ind/Abst Eng. Index. LC TL151.

SAE TRANSACTIONS. See Engineering.

SAFETY RELATED RECALL CAMPAIGNS FOR MOTOR VEHICLES AND MOTOR VEHICLE EQUIPMENT, INCLUDING TIRES. DETAILED REPORTS. (SAFETY RELATED RECALL CAMPAIGNS FOR MOTOR VEHICLES AND MOTOR VEHICLE EQUIPMENT, INCLUDING TIRES : DETAILED REPORTS). Main/Corp United States. National Highway Traffic Safety Administration. 0146-7026. Periodical. US. English. qt. National Technical Information Service, 5285 Port Royal Road, Springfield VA 22161. LC TL242. DD 629.234.

SANFORD EVANS GOLD BOOK OF USED CAR PRICES. July 1969-. 0381-8179. Periodical. CN. English. mo. 55.00. Sanford Evans Communications Ltd, Box 6900/1077 St James Street, Winnipeg Manitoba R3C 3B1 Canada. Tel

Transportation—Automobiles

(204)775-0201. Ed G B Henry. Reporting service of retail and wholesale prices for used cars and light duty trucks. Nine model years are covered and prices are supplied for three major markets. *Sanford Evans Used Car Market Report.*

SCALE AUTO ENTHUSIAST. See Hobbies.

SCOUT FOUR WHEEL DRIVE ANNUAL. 0147-3506. US. English. an. $1.95 Single Issue. Popular Publications, 420 Lexington Avenue, New York NY 10170. LC TL215.S36. DD 629.2222.

THE SERVICE JOB ANALYSIS. See Economics - Economics: Industry & Production.

SERVICE STATION MANAGEMENT. (SERVICE STATION MANAGEMENT SSM). VFOAT SSM. Mar. 1958-. 0488-3896. Periodical. US. English. mo. $30.00. Hunter Publishing Company, 950 Lee Street, Des Plaines IL 60016. Tel (312)296-0770. Ed Frank Victoria. LC TL153.A1. adv acc. Circ 110,000. (ctrl). Automotive repair and service data, management and marketing tips for small shops, industry and government news and events.

SEVICE MANUAL DODGE TRUCKS AND UTILITY VEHICLES. Main/Corp Chrysler Corporation. VFOAT Trucks 150-400, Dodge Ramcharger, Plymouth Trailduster Service Manual. US. English. an. Chrysler Corporation, Service Department, PO Box 40, Detroit MI 48288.

SHIP-BY-TRUCK OFFICIAL ONTARIO DIRECTORY AND BUYER'S GUIDE. See Yearbooks, Almanacs, Directories.

SKINNED KNUCKLES. 0164-3509. Periodical. US. English. mo. $33.00. Skinned Knuckles, 175 May Avenue, Monrovia CA 91016. Tel (818)358-6255. bk rev. adv acc. Circ 7,500. Devoted exclusively to the restoration, operation, and maintenance of all authentic collector vehicles.

SOLO. REGLEMENTS. See Recreation, Leisure - Sports.

SOUTH CAROLINA DRIVER'S HANDBOOK. VFOAT Driver's Handbook. 1977-. US. English. ir. *South Carolina Driver's Handbook.*

SOUTHERN MOTOR CARGO. Began in 1945. 0038-4372. Periodical. US. English. mo. $25.00. Southern Motor Cargo Magazine, Box 4169, Memphis TN 38104. Tel (901)276-5424. LC TL230.A1.

SPECIAL-INTEREST AUTOS. 1970. 0049-1845. Periodical. US. English. bm. $14.00 Domestic, $16.00 Foreign. Special Interest Publications, PO Box 196, Bennington VT 05201. Tel (802)442-3101. Ed David Brownell. adv acc. Circ 38,000. Covers collectable cars 1925-1975.

SPECIALTY & CUSTOM DEALER. VAT Specialty and Custom Dealer. 0193-7278. Periodical. US. English. mo. Babcox Publications, 11 South Forge Street, Akron OH 44304. Tel (216)535-6117. Ed Jim MacQueen. LC HD9710.3.U5. DD 380.145629205. adv acc. Circ 23,000. (ctrl). The business management magazine for speed and custom equipment retailers. *Speed & Custom Dealer.*

SPORT AUTO. See Recreation, Leisure - Sports.

SPORTS CAR. 0300-6387. Periodical. US. English. mo. Paul Oxman Publishing Inc, 17165 New Hope Street, Unit M, Fountain Valley CA 92708. Tel (714)979-8855.

SPORTS CARS IN REVIEW. 0096-3313. US. English. an. Henry Ford Museum, Dearborn MI 48121. LC TL236. DD 629.2222.

STAPP CAR CRASH AND FIELD DEMONSTRATION CONFERENCE. Main/Conf Demonstration Conference. First conference held in 1955. English. ir. LC TL6.

STATE GUIDE FOR RV MANUFACTURERS. See Manufacturing.

STATE OF OKLAHOMA ANNUAL VEHICLE REGISTRATION REPORT. Main/Corp Oklahoma Tax Commission. 0364-4820. US. English. an. Oklahoma Tax Commission, 2501 Lincoln Boulevard, Oklahoma City OK 73194. LC HE5633.O5. DD 353.97660087834.

STATE OF WISCONSIN MOTOR VEHICLE REGISTRATIONS FISCAL YEAR END REPORT. US. English. an. LC HE5633.W6. DD 388.3309775.

STATEMENT OF POLICY - CANADIAN AUTOMOBILE ASSOCIATION. Main/Corp Canadian Automobile Association. Began with 1974/75 issue. 0702-2441. Periodical. CN. English. an. Canadian Automobile Association, 150 Gloucester Street, Ottawa Ontario K2P 0A7 Canada. DD 388.0971. *Policies and Resolutions, 0702-2476.*

STATISTIEK VAN HET AUTOPARK. See Statistics.

STATISTIEKE VAN MOTOR- EN ANDER VOERTUIE SOOS OP . . . . See Statistics.

STATISTIEKE VAN MOTORVOERTUIE : NUWE VOERTUIE GELISENSIEER. Main/Corp South Africa. Dept. of Statistics. VFOAT Motor Vehicle Statistics. SA. Afrikaans and English. ir. 60. Government Printer, Private Bag X85, Pretoria 0001 South Africa. LC HE5704.S6. DD 354.680087834.

STATISTIEKE VAN NUWE VOERTUIE GELISENSIEER. See Statistics.

STATISTIK KENDARAAN BERMOTOR DAN PANJANG JALAN. See Statistics.

STATISTIQUE ANNUELLE DES VEHICULES NEUFS IMMATRICULES EN BELGIQUE. JAARLIJKSE STATISTIEK DER NIEUWE VOERTUIGEN IN BELGIE INGESCHREVEN. See Statistics.

STOCK CAR CLASSIFICATION GUIDE. 0731-2008. US. English. National Hot Rod Association, PO Box 150, North Hollywood CA 91603. LC TL236. DD 629.2280212.

STOP. 0139-6501. Periodical. Slovak. ir. 6.00 Each Issue. Ustredna Expecicia Tlace Gottwaldovo Nam 48/VII, V Bratislave Czechoslovakia. LC TL4.

DER STRASSENGUTERVERKEHR. Periodical. German. ir. LC HE5667.A1.

STRASSENVERKEHRSZAHLUNGEN. GW. German. LC HE5601. DD 388.30943.

STREET MACHINES & BRACKET RACING. VAT Street Machines and Bracket Racing. 0192-1967. Periodical. US. English. $1.95 Each Copy. Petersen Publishing Company, 6725 Sunset Boulevard, Los Angeles CA 90028. LC TL236. DD 629.228.

STREET RODDING ILLUSTRATED. 8750-3298. Periodical. US. English. bm. $11.25. McMullein Publishing, 2145 West La Palma Avenue, Anaheim CA 92801-178. Tel (714)635-9040. Ed Philippe Danh. DD 629. adv acc. Circ 80,000. Covers the building and rebuilding of 1948 and earlier cars using late model engines and suspension. Also covers both outdoor and indoor shows featuring this type of vehicle. Lots of technical information and how-to articles for the home street rod builder.

STRUKTUR BIAYA BUS DAN TRUK UMUM. 0126-494X. IO. Indonesian. ir. Biro Pusat Statistik, Jl Dr Sutomo No 8, Jakarta Indonesia. Tel 372808. LC HE5695. bk rev. adv acc. (ctrl).

SUMMARY OF . . . MOTOR VEHICLE LICENSE ISSUE AS COMPARED TO . . . . VFOAT Summary of Motor Vehicle License and Title Issue. US. English. an. LC HE5633.V8. DD 388.3209755021.

SUMMARY OF NEW MOTOR VEHICLES REGISTERED. Main/Corp Papua New Guinea. Bureau of Statistics. English. ir. Bureau of Statistics, PO Box 2032, Konedobu Papua New Guinea. LC HE5718.P3. DD 388.3409953.

SUMP. See Recreation, Leisure - Sports.

SUPER CHEVY. 0146-2628. Periodical. US. English. mo. $15.00. Super Chevy, 12301 Wilshire Boulevard, Los Angeles CA 90025. Tel (213)820-3601.

SUPER SERVICE STATION. Began with issue for June 1929. 0039-5676. Periodical. US. English. mo. $30.00. Irving Cloud Publishing Company, 7300 North Cicero Avenue Lincolnwood, Chicago IL 60646. Tel (312)588-7300. Ed Bob Weber. Ind/Abst Trade Ind. Index. LC TL153.A1. DD 629.28605. adv acc. Circ 120,000. (ctrl). Topics include features on automotive service and repair, operations, management for service stations, tire dealers, mass merchandisers with auto service facilities, and independent repair shops (garages).

SUPER STOCK & DRAG ILLUSTRATED. See Recreation, Leisure - Sports.

SUPER STOCK & DRAG ILLUSTRATED'S PULLING POWER. See Recreation, Leisure - Sports.

SURVEY AND ANALYSIS OF BUSINESS CAR POLICIES & COSTS. See Business.

SURVEY OF MOTOR VEHICLE USAGE, ACCIDENT EXPOSURE DATA. AT. English. an. Australian Bureau of Statistics, PO Box 84, Canberra Australian Capital Territory 2600 Australia. LC HE5709. DD 388.3210994.

TAXIDIA STEN EUROPE. Greek, Modern. ir. 200.00. EKD Hellenews, Platia Karitsy 6, T T 124 Athenai Greece. LC D923.

TAXIDIA STEN HELLADA KAI TEN KYPRO. Greek, Modern. ir. 60.00. Ekd Hellenews, Platia Karitsy 6, T T 124 Athenai Greece. LC DF727.

TAYLOR'S LEISURE WHEELS. VFOAT Leisurewheels. V. 4, No. 6- June 1972-. 0318-3467. Periodical. CN. English. mo. DD 796.7905. *Travel Leisure, 0049-4550.*

TECHNICAL DIGEST - I.E.E.E. VEHICULAR TECHNOLOGY ANNUAL CONFERENCE. (TECHNICAL DIGEST). Main/Conf IEEE Vehicular Technology Conference. VAT Technical Digest - Institute of Electrical and Electronics Engineers Vehicular Technology Annual Conference. 0092-3680. US. English. an. $5.00. Institute of Electrical and Electronics Engineers, 345 East 47th Street, New York NY 10017. LC TL272.5. DD 388.3028.

TEMPEST CHASSIS SHOP MANUAL. Main/Corp General Motors Corporation. Pontiac Motor Division. 1961-. 0149-5089. US. English. Pontiac Motor Division, General Motors Corporation, 660 East South Boulevard, Truck Division, Pontiac MI 48053. LC TL215.T4. DD 629.28722.

THOROUGHBRED & CLASSIC CARS. VAT Thoroughbred and Classic Cars. Periodical. UK. English. mo. Business Press International, Perrymount Road Haywards Heath, West Sussex RH163BR England. LC TL1. DD 629.222209.

THUNDERBIRD ILLUSTRATED. V. 1- Fall 1974-. 0145-4110. Periodical. US. English. qt. $15.00. Thunderbird Publications, PO Box 6446, Orange CA 92667. LC TL215.T46. DD 338.3422.

TIRE SCIENCE & TECHNOLOGY. VAT Tire Science and Technology. V. 1- Feb. 1973-. 0090-8657. Periodical. US. English. qt. $18.00. Tire Society Inc, D A Benko, 68 Spring Garden Drive, Munroe Falls OH 44262. Tel (216)644-5405. Ind/Abst Eng. Index Mon., Eng. Index Bioeng. Abstr., Eng. Index Energy Abstr., Int. Aerosp. Abstr., Eng. Index Annu., Eng. Index, ISMEC Bull., Appl. Mech. Rev. LC TL270. DD 629.248. CODEN TSTCAU.

TIRES. See Public Health and Safety.

T'NT. TRUCK 'N TRAILER. (T 'N T, TRUCK 'N TRAILER). VFOAT Truck 'n Trailer. No. 6- May 10, 1976-. 0703-6906. Periodical. CN. English. ir. $5.50. Pace Publications Ltd, 3049 Jarrow Avenue, Mississauga Ontario L4X 2C6 Canada. DD 388.3240971. *Truck & Trailer, 0319-7492.*

TRANSMISSION DIGEST. (TRANSMISSION DIGEST : TD). VFOAT TD. Vol. 1, No. 1 (Sept. 1981)-. 0277-8300. Periodical. US. English. mo. $18.00. M D Publications, PO Box 1067-sss, Springfield MO 65805. Tel (417)866-3917. Ed Lola Miller. adv acc. Circ 17,000. (ctrl). Information for and about the automotive transmission field: manufacturing, distribution, and repair.

TRANSMISSION MECHANICAL PARTS/LABOR ESTIMATING GUIDE. Series/Titl Manuals for the Automotive Professional. VFOAT Mitchell Transmission Mechanical Parts/Labor Estimating Guide. US. English. qt. $155.00. Mitchell Information Services, PO Box 26260, San Diego CA 92126.

TRAVEL TRAILERS, 5TH WHEEL TRAILERS, CAMPING TRAILERS RV GUIDE, NEW & USED VALUES. Main/Corp Kelley Blue Book Co. VAT Travel Trailers, Fifth Wheel Trailers, Camping Trailers Recreational Vehicle Guide, New and Used Values. 0145-3785. US. English. $20.00. Kelley Blue Book Company, 4005

Transportation—Automobiles

Long Beach Boulevard, Long Beach CA 90807. **LC** TL297. **DD** 629.226029473.

TRUCK. Periodical. UK. English. mo. $22.68. F F Publishing Ltd, 97 Earls Court Road, London W8 6QH England. **Tel** (01)370-0333. **LC** TL230.A1. **DD** 388.32405.

TRUCK & VAN BUYER'S GUIDE. **VFOAT** Petersen's Truck & Van Buyer's Guide. **VAT** Truck and Van Buyer's Guide. 0190-3101. US. English. an. $1.95. Petersen Publishing Company, 6725 Sunset Boulevard, Los Angeles CA 90028. **LC** TL230.A1. **DD** 629.223.

TRUCK BODY AND TRAILER MANUFACTURERS. **Main/Corp** Statistics Canada. Manufacturing and Primary Industries Division. **Series/Titl** Annual Census of Manufacturers. **VFOAT** Fabricants de Carrosseries de Camions et Remorques. 1970-. 0527-6365. Periodical. CN. English (text in French). an. 20.00 Domestic, 21.00 Foreign. Receiver General for Canada, Statistics Canada Publications, Ottawa Ontario K1A 0T6 Canada. **Tel** (800)268-1151. *Truck Body and Trailer Manufacturers, 0527-6365.*

TRUCK DATA BOOK. Began with 1949/50 issue. 0564-3392. Periodical. CN. English. an. 21.75. Sanford Evans Communications Ltd, Box 6900/1077 St James Street, Winnipeg Manitoba R3C 3B1 Canada. **Tel** (204)775-0201. **Ed** G B Henry. **DD** 629.2240212. Truck statistics for truck identification and registration. Includes vehicle weight, wheelbase serial numbers and engine stats.

TRUCK NEWS (TORONTO, ONT.). (TRUCK NEWS). Vol. 1, Issue 1 (May 1981)-. 0712-2683. Periodical. CN. English. ir. Free. Truck News, 120 Heward Avenue, Toronto Ontario M4M 2T7 Canada. **DD** 388.3240971.

TRUCK OPERATING COSTS. **Main/Corp** New Zealand. Ministry of Transport. Economics Division. 1975-. English. ir. 5.00. Ministry of Transport, Private Bag, Wellington 1 New Zealand. **Tel** 721253. **LC** HE5717.5. **DD** 388.324. **Circ** 1,000. A breakdown of the private economic costs of operating different sized trucks in New Zealand. Two broad components: running and standing costs. *Car and Truck Operating Costs.*

TRUCK TRAILERS. See Manufacturing.

TRUCKING BULLETIN. **VFOAT** A T A News Bulletin. **VAT** Alberta Trucking Association News Bulletin (Oct. 1975). No. 64- Oct. 1975-. 0704-6502. Periodical. CN. English. ir. Free to Members. Alberta Trucking Association, PO Box 5520 Station A, Calgary Alberta T2H 1X9 Canada. **DD** 388.324097123. *A T A News Bulletin, 0380-8920.*

TRUCKS 26,000 PLUS. **VAT** Trucks Twenty-Six Thousand Plus. V. 5- Feb. 1977-. 0146-9622. Periodical. US. English. bm. $15.00. McGraw Hill, 1221 Avenue of the Americas, New York NY 10020. **LC** HE5623.A1. **DD** 388.3240973. *26 Plus, 0091-410X.*

TURBO. Periodical. Hebrew. mo. **LC** TL4.

TUV AUTO-REPORT. **Main/Corp** Vereinigung der Technischen Uberwachungs-Vereine. **VAT** Technischer Uberwachungs-Vereine Auto-Report. German. ir. Verlag Tuv Rheinlan Gmbh, Am Grauen Stein Postfach, 5 Koln 1 West Germany. **LC** TL3.

THE U.S. AUTO INDUSTRY, U.S. FACTORY SALES, RETAIL SALES, IMPORTS, EXPORTS, APPARENT CONSUMPTION, SUGGESTED RETAIL PRICES, AND TRADE BALANCES WITH SELECTED COUNTRIES FOR MOTOR VEHICLES. **Series/Titl** USITC Publication. **VFOAT** US Auto Industry, US Factory Sales, Retail Sales, Imports, Exports, Apparent Consumption, Suggested Retail Prices, and Trade Balances with Selected Countries for Motor Vehicles. **VAT** United States Auto Industry: United States Factory Sales, Retail Sales, Imports, Exports, Apparent Consumption, Suggested Retail Prices, and Trade Balances with Selected Countries for Motor Vehicles. 1964-81-. 8755-4607. US. English. an. Office of the Secretary, United States International Trade Commission, Washington DC 20436. **LC** HD9710.U5. **DD** 380.24562920973. *Automotive Trade Statistics. Series A, Motor Vehicles, 0147 8400; Automotive Trade Statistics. Series B: Passenger Automobiles, 0164-0097.*

U.S. AUTOMOBILE INDUSTRY (TRANSPORTATION SYSTEMS CENTER). (THE U.S. AUTOMOBILE INDUSTRY : REPORT TO THE CONGRESS FROM THE SECRETARY OF TRANSPORTATION). **VFOAT** US Automobile Industry. **VAT** United States Automobile Industry. Began with 1980. US. English. an. Superintendent of Documents, US Government Printing Office, Washington DC 20402. **LC** HD9710.U5. **DD** 338.4762920973.

U.S. AUTOMOTIVE SERVICES BULLETIN. **VFOAT** US Automotive Services Bulletin. **VAT** United States Automotive Services Bulletin. 0734-6573. Periodical. US. English. qt. Data Resources Inc, 29 Hartwell Avenue, Lexongton MA 02173. **LC** HD9710.U5. **DD** 338.4762920973.

USED CAR BUYER'S GUIDE. 1981 Ed.-. 0820-8956. CN. English. an. $3.00. Canadian Automobile Association, 1775 Courtwood Crescent, Ottawa Ontario K2C 3J2 Canada. **Tel** (613)226-7631. **DD** 629.2222. **Circ** 75,450.

UTAH MOTORIST. (UTAH MOTORIST : OFFICIAL PUBLICATION OF THE AUTOMOBILE CLUB OF UTAH). Vol. 1, No. 1 (Winter 1983)-. 0745-4562. Periodical. US. English. bm. $1.00. Automobile Club of Utah, 560 East 5th South, Salt Lake City UT 84404.

VEHICLE CODE. **Main/Corp** California. **VFOAT** California Vehicle Code. US. English. an. $3.00. Department of Motor Vehicles Attn S Wiseman, 2415 First Avenue, Sacramento CA 95818. Each issue contains an index to its own contents - no vol index - loose.

VEHICLE IDENTIFICATION. 8756-940X. US. English. $15.00. Lee Books, PO Box 906, Novato CA 94948. **Tel** (415)897-3550. **Ed** Lee S Cole. **LC** TL154. **DD** 629.2222027. Books on vehicle theft, fire fraud and identification procedures and methods.

VEHICLE IDENTIFICATION GUIDE. 0364-9563. US. English. Motor, 250 West 55th Street, New York NY 10019. **LC** TL154. **DD** 629.222207.

VEHICULES A MOTEUR NEUFS MIS EN CIRCULATION. **Main/Corp** Institut National de Statistique (Belgium). French. ir. 250 Domestic, 300 Foreign. Institut National de Statistique, rue de Louvain 44, 1000 Bruxelles Belgium. **Tel** (02)513.96.50. **LC** HE5673. **Circ** 165. (ctrl). Statistics about the new cars in traffic.

VEICULOS LICENCIADOS. **Main/Corp** Espirito Santo, Brazil (State). Departamento Estadual de Estatistica. Portuguese. ir. **LC** HE5653.E76.

VETTE. 0199-7890. Periodical. US. English. bm. $16.66. CSK Publishing Company Inc, 29 Grove Street, South Hackensack NJ 07606. **Tel** (201)440-2770.

VETTE VUES MAGAZINE. 0279-8476. Periodical. US. English. mo. $28.00. Vette Vues, Drawer A, Sandy Springs GA 30328. **Tel** (404)252-2575. **Ed** James B Prather. bk rev. adv acc. **Circ** 25,000. For Chevrolet Corvette owners only. Cars and parts for sale. Articles and events.

VINTAGE AUTO ALMANAC. See Yearbooks, Almanacs, Directories.

THE VINTAGE FORD. V. 1- Mar./Apr. 1966-. 0042-6350. Periodical. US. English. bm. $15.00. Model T Ford Club of America, Box 7400, Burbank CA 91510. **Tel** (818)842-2010. **Ed** Bruce W McCalley. **LC** TL215.F7. bk rev. adv acc. **Circ** 6,000. General coverage of the model T Ford, its history and current activities.

VINTAGE LORRY ANNUAL. No. 1- 1979-. Periodical. UK. English. an. International Publications Service Collings Inc, 114 East 32nd Street, New York NY 10016. **LC** TL230.A1. **DD** 629.2240941.

THE VINTAGE TRIUMPH. 0147-9695. Periodical. US. English. bm. $20.00. Vintage Triumph Register, Box 36477, Grosse Point MI 48236. **Tel** (203)481-0533. **Ed** Steven Rossi. **LC** TL215.T7. **DD** 629.2222. bk rev. **Circ** 3,000. Articles and information to assist and encourage the ownership, operation and enjoyment of Triumph sports cars and motor cars.

VOIX DE L'ANCAI. (LA VOIX DE L'ANCAI). **Main/Corp** Association Nationale des Camionneurs-Artisans. V. 1-10, No.7. 0317-2937. CN. French. mo. Les Publications Plus Inc, 225 rue Lindsay, Drummondville Quebec J2C 1P2 Canada. **Tel** (819)477-6811. **DD** 388.32409714.

VOLKSWAGEN GREATS. **VFOAT** VW Greats. 0049-6723. Periodical. US. English. bm. $7.00 Domestic, $9.00 Foreign. Volkswagen Greats, PO Box 49659, Los Angeles CA 90049.

VOZAC I SAOBRACAJ. Periodical. Serbo-Croatian -R. ir. 33.00. Savez Udrunzenja Vozaca I Automehanicara SRH, Draskoviceva 27/1, Zagreb Yogoslavia. **Tel** (041)417-009. **LC** TL4. adv acc. *Vozac.*

VW & PORSCHE. **VAT** Volkswagen and Porsche. 0273-6748. Periodical. US. English. bm. $11.00. Argus Publishers Corporation, 12301 Wilshire Boulevard, Los Angeles CA 90025. **Tel** (213)820-3601.

VW TRENDS. **VFOAT** V.W. Trends. **VAT** Volkswagen Trends. 8750-3301. Periodical. US. English. mo. $12.00. McMullen Publishing Inc, 2145 West La Palma Avenue, Anaheim CA 92801-178. **DD** 629.

THE VW/AUDI FRONTDRIVER. **VAT** Volkswagen/Audi Frontdriver. 0162-167X. Periodical. US. English. bm. $6.00. Dasher Owners of America, 153 North Mechanic Street, Cumberland MD 21502. **LC** TL215.D34. **DD** 629.222. *VW Frontdriver, 0148-6853.*

WARD'S AUTO WORLD. V. 5- Feb. 1969-. 0043-0315. Periodical. US. English. mo. Ward's Communications Inc, 28 West Adams Street/Suite 1805, Detroit MI 48226. **Tel** (313)962-4433. **Ind/Abst** Predicasts, Infobank, Bus. Period. Index, Funk Scott Index Corp. Ind. **LC** HD9710.U5. **DD** 338.476292220973. *Ward's Quarterly.*

WARD'S AUTOMOTIVE REPORTS. Periodical. US. English. wk. **Ind/Abst** Predicasts. **LC** HD9710.U5.

WARD'S AUTOMOTIVE YEARBOOK. See Yearbooks, Almanacs, Directories.

THE WAY OF THE ZEPHYR. 0748-1683. Periodical. US. English. bm. $18.00 Membership US, Canada, and Mexico. Lincoln Zephry Owner's Club, 2107 Steinruck Road, Elizabethtown PA 17022. **LC** TL215.Z46. **DD** 629.222.

WESTERN AUSTRALIA MOTOR VEHICLE REGISTRATION. **Main/Corp** Australian Bureau of Statistics. Western Australian Office. AT. English. ir. Australian Bureau of Statistics, 1 3 St Georges Terrace, Perth WA 6000 Australia. **LC** HE5717. **DD** 354.9410087834.

WESTEUROPA QUELLEN ZUM KRAFTFAHRZEUGMARKT. **Main/Corp** Bundesstelle fur Aussenhandelsinformation (Germany). **Series/Titl** Marktinformation. German. ir. 10.00. Bundesstelle fur Aussenhandelsinformation, Postfach 10 8, 5 Koln 1 West Germany. **LC** HD9710.A1.

WHAT CAR?. Periodical. UK. English. mo. $30.65. Haymarket Publishing Ltd, 1214 Annsdell Street, Kensington London W85TR England. **Tel** (01)937-7288. **LC** TL1. **DD** 629.222205.

THE WHEEL EXTENDED. V. 1- Spring 1971-. Periodical. JA. English. qt. Toyota Motor Sales Company Ltd, 3-18 2-chome Kudan Minami, Chiyoda-ku Tokyo 102 Japan. **LC** HE277.A1. **DD** 380.50952.

WHEEL-O-RAMA. (WHEEL-O-RAMA : OFFICIAL SHOWTIME MAGAZINE OF THE NCSA). **VFOAT** NCSA Wheel-O-Rama. Vol. 1, No. 1 (Mar. 1985). 0882-6676. Periodical. US. English. qt. $18.00. National Custom Show Association, 836 South Wayne Avenue, Columbus OH 43204. **Tel** (614)279-2172. **Ed** Margaret Frum. **DD** 629. adv acc. **Circ** 2,00. (ctrl). Consists of car pictures and stories about the cars and owners. Also automotive clubs and their members and sponsored events, for sale and wanted car items, and advertisements.

WNY MOTORIST. **VAT** Western New York Motorist. V. 70, No. 6 (June 1977)-. 0149-3175. Periodical. US. English. mo. Automobile Club Western NY, 976 Delaware Avenue, Buffalo NY 14240. **LC** TL1. **DD** 338.321097479. *Western New York Motorist, 0043-3977.*

WOLGAN UNJON SEGYE. **VFOAT** Unjon Segye. 1st Vol. (1984/2)-. Periodical. KO. Korean. mo. 16,000. Wolgan Unjon Segye, 48-24 Mia 4-Dong Tobong-ku, Seoul Korea. **LC** TL4.

WORKING PAPER - ROLE OF THE AUTOMOBILE STUDY. TRANSPORT CANADA. (WORKING PAPER - ROLE OF THE AUTOMOBILE STUDY, TRANSPORT CANADA). **Main/Corp** Canada. Ministry of Transport. Role of the Automobile Study. **VAT** Role of the Automobile Study. Working Paper. No. 1- 0228-2011. Monographic Series. CN. English (includes summary in French). Transport Canada, Strategic Planning Group, Ottawa Ontario K1A 0N5 Canada. **DD** 388.

THE WORLD AUTOMOTIVE MARKET. 1969-. US. English. an. $22.00 Domestic, $24.00 Foreign. Auto International-Johnston International

Transportation—Railroads

Publishers, 386 Park Avenue South, New York NY 10016. **Tel** (212)689-0120. Ed Bernard Zinober. **Circ** 3,000. Statistical analysis of worldwide vehicle production, registration, trade as well as reports on U.S. exports of automotive products. *World Automotive Market Survey.*

WORLD CARS. US. English. an. $48.85. Herald Books, Box 17, Pelham NY 10803. **Tel** (914)576-1121.

WORLD OF WHEELS. Vol. 1, No. 1 (Fall 1983)-. 0824-5487. Periodical. CN. English. qt. $1.50. World of Wheels, Suite 100/ 4035 Wilson Avenue, Montreal Quebec H4A 2V1 Canada. **DD** 629.222205.

RAILROADS

ACCIDENT/INCIDENT BULLETIN. *See* Public Health and Safety.

ADDISIONELE KAPITAALBEGROTING. **Main/Corp** South African Railways and Harbours. **VFOAT** Additional Capital Budget. Afrikaans (English). ir. .80. **LC** HE3426.

AMERICAN RAILS. Began in 1985. 8750-5762. Periodical. US. English. bm. $8.50 Domestic, $9.50 Foreign. White Publishing, PO Box 286, 208 North Stewart Street, Geneseo IL 61254. **DD** 385. *Midwestern Rails, 8750-5819.*

AMTLICHES KURSBUCH. **Main/Corp** Schweizerische Bundesbahnen. Generaldirektion. **VFOAT** Indicateur Officiel, Orario Ufficiale. Periodical. German. qt. **LC** HE3214. **DD** 656.

AMTRAK MATRIX SYSTEM ANNUAL ORIGIN/DESTINATION PASSENGER COUNT. 1977-. US. English. an. US Federal Railroad Administration, Office of Rail Systems Analysis and Information, Washington DC 20590.

AMTRAK'S INVENTORY AND PROPERTY CONTROLS NEED STRENGTHENING. 0275-9829. US. English. an. US Government Accounting Office, Distribution Section, 441 G Street NW, Washington DC 20548. **LC** HE2791. **DD** 353.0087500687.

ANALYSIS OF CLASS 1 RAILROADS. US. English. an. $75.00. Association of American Railroads, 1920 L Street NW/Room 663, Washington DC 20036. **Tel** (202)835-9361. adv acc. Financial and operating statistics for Class 1 Railroads within the following categories: fuel consumption, net worth, investment base, revenue expenses, income, employment, etc. *Operating & Traffic Statistics, 0738-0003.*

ANNUAL BUDGET STATEMENT OF PAKISTAN RAILWAYS. **Main/Corp** Pakistan. Ministry of Railways. English. ir. Government of Pakistan, Ministry of Railways, Karachi 15 B Pakistan. **LC** HE3300.5. **DD** 354.54910072252.

ANNUAL MEETING - ASSOCIATION OF AMERICAN RAILROADS. COMMUNICATION AND SIGNAL DIVISION. MEETING. (ANNUAL MEETING). **Main/Corp** Association of American Railroads. Communication and Signal Division. Meeting. **VFOAT** Proceedings . . . Annual Meeting. 0744-2920. US. English. an. Communication and Signal Division AAR, 1920 L Street NW, Washington DC 20036. **LC** TF615. **DD** 625.165. *Proceedings, Annual Meeting.*

ANNUAL PROCEEDINGS, PRE-CONVENTION REPORT - LOCOMOTIVE MAINTENANCE OFFICERS ASSOCIATION (U.S.). (ANNUAL PROCEEDINGS . . . PRE-CONVENTION REPORT). **Main/Corp** Locomotive Maintenance Officers Association (U.S.). **VFOAT** LMOA. 0883-6035. US. English. an. Locomotive Maintenance Officers Association, 3144 Brereton Court, Huntington WV 25705. *Pre-Convention Report, Annual Proceedings of the Annual Meeting.*

ANNUAL REPORT - AUSTRALIAN NATIONAL RAILWAYS COMMISSION. **Main/Corp** Australian National Railways Commission. 1975-76-. English. an. Free. Australian National Railways Commission, Norwich Centre, 55 King William Road, North Adelaide South Australia 6005 Australia. **Tel** (08)217-4775. **LC** HE3461. **DD** 385.0994. **Circ** 3,000. (ctrl). *Report on the Operations of the Commonwealth Railways.*

ANNUAL REPORT - EAST AFRICAN RAILWAYS CORPORATION. **Main/Corp** East African Railways Corporation. 1970-. English. ir. 30. Kenya Railways Corporation, PO Box 30121, Nairobi Kenya. **Tel** 21211. **LC** HE3419.E3. **DD** 385.096. **Circ** 2,500. (ctrl). Statement of revenue and expenditure for each year covering the activities of the corporation.

ANNUAL REPORT FOR YEAR ENDED 30 JUNE - QUEENSLAND RAILWAYS. **Main/Corp** Queensland Railways. English. an. **LC** HE3501. **DD** 385.065943.

ANNUAL REPORT - IOWA STATE COMMERCE COMMISSION. *See* Business - Commerce.

ANNUAL REPORT - NATIONAL RAILWAYS OF ZIMBABWE. **Main/Corp** National Railways of Zimbabwe. English. an. Office of the Board, PO Box 782, Bulawayo Zimbabwe. **Tel** 363111. **LC** HE3427. **Circ** 1,100. (ctrl).

ANNUAL REPORT - NORFOLK SOUTHERN CORPORATION. **Main/Corp** Norfolk Southern Corporation. 1982-. 0748-8750. US. English. an. Norfolk Southern Corporation, PO Box 3609, Norfolk VA 23514-3609. *Annual Report - Southern Railway Company, Annual Report.*

ANNUAL REPORT OF KENTUCKY & INDIANA TERMINAL RAILROAD COMPANY. **Main/Corp** Kentucky & Indiana Terminal Railroad Company. **VAT** Annual Report of Kentucky and Indiana Terminal Railroad Company. 1900/01-. 0363-7557. US. English. an. 2910 North Western Parkway, Louisville KY 40212.

ANNUAL REPORT OF RAILROAD ACCIDENTS OCCURRING IN CALIFORNIA AND REPORTED UNDER GENERAL ORDER 22-B AND . . . . US. English. an. California Public Utilities Commission, State Building, San Francisco CA 94102. **LC** HE1780.5.C2. **DD** 312.4409794. *Annual Report of Railroad Accidents Reported under General Order No. 22-B for Year . . . .*

ANNUAL REPORT OF THE NORTH COMMISSION (ALASKA). **Main/Corp** Alaska. Northern Operations of Rail Transportation and Highways Commission. 1968-. Periodical. US. English. ir. Alaska Northern Operations of Rail Transportation and Highways Commission, Juneau AK 99801. **LC** HE2709.

ANNUAL REPORT OF THE RAILROAD COMMISSION OF TEXAS, GAS UTILITIES DIVISION. *See* Petroleum and Natural Gas.

ANNUAL REPORT - ROCHESTER-GENESEE REGIONAL TRANSPORTATION AUTHORITY. **Main/Corp** Rochester-Genesee Regional Transportation Authority. **VFOAT** Annual Report of the Rochester-Genesee Regional Transportation Authority. Began with 1974/75. US. English. an. Rochester-Genesee Regional Transportation Authority, 1372 East Main Street, PO Box 90629 Beechwood Station, Rochester NY 14609. **LC** HE4491.R68. **DD** 352.91840974788.

ANNUAL REPORT - TRANSPORT USERS CONSULTATIVE COMMITTEE FOR WALES. **Main/Corp** Transport Users Consultative Committee for Wales. 1974-. UK. English. an. Government Bookshops, 49 High Holborn, London WC1V 6HB England. **LC** HE59. **DD** 354.4290087506. *Report.*

ANNUAL REPORT - UNITED STATES RAILWAY ASSOCIATION. **Main/Corp** United States Railway Association. 1973/74-. 0363-3187. US. English. an. $1.05. Superintendent of Documents, US Government Printing Office, Washington DC 20402. **LC** HE2715. **DD** 353.0087505.

ANNUAL REPORT - VIA RAIL CANADA INC. (ANNUAL REPORT). **Main/Corp** Via Rail Canada. **VFOAT** Rapport Annuel. **VAT** Rapport Annuel - Via Rail Canada Inc. 1977-. 0706-5698. CN. English (French). an. Via Rail Canada Inc, Box 8116, Montreal Quebec H3C 3N3 Canada.

ANUARIO ESTATSITCO DAS FERROVIAS DO BRASIL. *See* Yearbooks, Almanacs, Directories.

A.R.P.S. YEAR BOOK & STEAM PRESERVATION GUIDE. **Main/Corp** Association of Railway Preservation Societies. **VFOAT** Railway Forum. UK. English. -/65. 31 Old Croft Road, Walton on the Hill, Stafford England. **LC** TF1. **DD** 625.1007402.

ARSREDOVISNING. **Main/Corp** Statens Jarnvagar (Sweden). **VFOAT** SJ Arsredovisning. 1980/81-. SW. Swedish. an. SJ Centralforvaltning, 105 50 Stockholm Sweden. **LC** HE3181. *Verksamhetsberattelse.*

AUTO-TRAIN MAGAZINE. V. 1- Nov. 1973-. 0092-6515. Periodical. US. English. qt. $3.00. 1801 K Street Northwest, Washington DC 20006. **LC** F206. **DD** 917.504405.

AVTOMATIKA, TELEMEHANIKA I SVJAZ. (AVTOMATIKA, TELEMEKHANIKA I SVIAZ). V. 1- Jan. 1957-. 0005-2329. Periodical. UR. Russian. mo. $25.50. Victor Kamkin Inc (70002), 12224 Parklawn Drive, Rockville MD 20852. **Tel** (301)881-5973. **Ind/Abst** Electron. Commun. Abstr. J., ISMEC Bull., Pollut. Abstr. Indexes, Saf. Sci. Abstr. J., Comput. Control Abstr., Electr. Electron. Abstr., Sci. Abstr. Sect. A. Phys. Abstr., Phys. Abstr. **LC** TF615. **CODEN** ATSVAG.

AWARDS . . . FIRST DIVISION, NATIONAL RAILROAD ADJUSTMENT BOARD. **Main/Corp** United States. National Railroad Adjustment Board. V. 1- 1936-. Periodical. US. English. **LC** HD5503. **DD** 331.1550973.

B & M BULLETIN. **VAT** Boston and Maine Bulletin. 0362-2711. Periodical. US. English. qt. $2.00 Single Issue. PO Box 223/Harwood Station, Littleton MA 01460. **LC** TF25.B8. **DD** 385.0974.

BAXTER'S EURAILPASS TRAVEL GUIDE. *See* Travel.

BEDRYFSBEGROTINGS. **Main/Corp** South African Railways and Harbours. **VFOAT** Working Estimates. SA. Afrikaans (English). ir. 1.70. South African Railways and Harbours, Cape Town South Africa. **LC** HE3426. **DD** 354.680072225.

BEGROTING VAN DIE ADDISIONELE BEDRYFSUITGAWE. **Main/Corp** South African Railways and Harbours. **VFOAT** Estimates of the Additional Working Expenditure. Afrikaans (English). ir. 0.90. **LC** HE3426. **DD** 354.6800722253.

BIENNIAL REPORT OF THE ALABAMA PUBLIC SERVICE COMMISSION. **Main/Corp** Alabama Public Service Commission. 1916/18-. US. English. be. **LC** HE2702.

LE BILAN. **Main/Corp** Octra (Gabon). FR. French. ir. Cabinet Daniel Verpeaux, 35 Quai d'Anjou, 75004 Paris France. **LC** HE3438. **DD** 354.67210087506.

BRANCHLINE (OTTAWA, ONT.). (BRANCHLINE). 0824-233X. Periodical. CN. English. mo. Free to members. Branchline, P O Box 141 Station A, Ottawa Ontario K1N 8V1 Canada. **DD** 385.0971.

BRMNA JOURNAL. (THE BRMNA JOURNAL). **VAT** British Railway Modellers of North America Journal. 0229-0553. Periodical. CN. English. mo. Free. British Railway Modellers of North America, 666 Island Park Drive, Ottawa Ontario K1Y 0B7 Canada. **DD** 625.1905. (ctrl). *British Railway Modellers' Association Journal.*

B.R.M.N.A. MEMBERSHIP DIRECTORY. *See* Yearbooks, Almanacs, Directories.

BULLETIN - AMERICAN RAILWAY ENGINEERING ASSOCIATION. **Main/Corp** American Railway Engineering Association. **VFOAT** Area Bulletin. 0003-0694. Periodical. US. English. ir $52.00. American Railway Engineer Association, 50 F Street NW, Washington DC 20001. **Tel** (202)639-2190. Ed W A Grotz Jr. **Ind/Abst** GeoRef, Bibliogr. Index Geol. **DD** 625. adv acc. **Circ** 4,200. Contains reports of associations, technical committees, papers on railway engineering, consturction, maintenance and research results. *Bulletin.*

BULLETIN DE DOCUMENTATION ET D'INFORMATION - DIRECTION DES ETUDES GENERALES. **Main/Corp** Regie Autonome des Transports Parosiens. Direction des Etudes Generales. **VFOAT** Documentation, Information - RATP. Periodical. FR. French. ir. Direction des Etudes Generales, 53 Ter Quai des Grands Augustins, 75271 Paris Cedex 06 France. **LC** HE4769.P33. **DD** 388.4. *Bulletin d'Information et de Documentation Generale.*

BULLETIN DES TRANSPORTS INTERNATIONAUX PAR CHEMINS DE FER. *See* Law.

2762

Transportation—Railroads

BULLETIN - RAILWAY AND LOCOMOTIVE HISTORICAL SOCIETY CEASED. Main/Corp Railway and Locomotive Historical Society. No. 1-126, 1921-Apr. 1972. Periodical. US. English. sa. $15.00. Railway and Locomotive Historical Society, PO Box 1418, Westford MA 01886-4818. Tel (617)692-6649. Ed Robert C Post. Ind/Abst Am. Hist. Life, Hist. Abstr. bk rev. adv acc. Circ 3,000. (ctrl). Covers formation, consolidation and present history, and locomotives and equipment of rail lines in the United States, Canada and Mexico.

BULLETIN (TOY TRAIN OPERATING SOCIETY : 1973). See Hobbies.

DIE BUNDESBAHN. Vol. 23 No. 18- Sept. 1949-. 0007-5876. Periodical. GW. German. mo. $72.72. Hestra Verlag Hernincel & Dr, Postfach 4244, Holzhofallee 33, 6100 Darmstadt 1 West Germany. **Ind/Abst** Excerpta Med. Reichsbahn.

CANADIAN NATIONAL RAILWAYS AND CANADIAN PACIFIC LIMITED. VFOAT Les Chemins de fer Nationaux du Canada et Canadien Pacifique Limitee. 1968/1972-. 0317-6711. CN. English (French). an. $0.70. Statistics Canada, Surface Transport Section, Publication Distribution, Ottawa Ontario K1A 0T6 Canada. LC HE2801. DD 385.0971.

CANADIAN RAIL. No. 135- July/Aug. 1962-. 0008-4875. Periodical. CN. English. bm. Canadian Railroad Historical Association, PO Box 282, St Eustache Quebec J7R 4K6 Canada. Tel (514)473-7766. Ed Fred Angus. Circ 1,300. Canada's only railway magazine that covers the latest in technological developments, historical articles and essays, and photo stories of Canada's railways. CRHA News Report.

CANADIAN RAILWAY CLUB NEWS. VFOAT Nouvelles Club du Rail Canadien. V. 1- Jan. 1979-. 0226-157X. Periodical. CN. English (French). Free. Canadian Railway Club, PO Box 162 Station A, Montreal Quebec H3C 1C5 Canada. DD 385.06071. (ctrl).

CANADIAN RAILWAYMAN. VFOAT Cheminot. V. 1- April 1966-. 0045-5261. Periodical. CN. English (French, each with special title page and separate paging. French text on inverted pages). ir. $3.98. c/o Labor Room 106, 400 First Street NW, Washington DC 20001. Tel (202)628-9260. Ed Collin Gribbons. Circ 33,000. Railway labor.

CANADIAN TRANSPORT. VFOAT Transport Canadien. Began publication in 1954. 0045-5466. Periodical. CN. English (includes some text in French, 1954-1963). mo. $4.65. Canadian Brotherhood of Railroad Employees, 2300 Carling Avenue, Ottawa K2B 2G1 Ontario Canada. Also available on microfilm from University Microfilms International, Ann Arbor MI. Canadian Railway Employees' Monthly, 0319-6933.

CAR AND LOCOMOTIVE CYCLOPEDIA OF AMERICAN PRACTICE. See Encyclopedias & General Reference Books.

CARLOAD WAYBILL STATISTICS. See Statistics.

CENTRAL RAILWAY CHRONICLE. 0008-9532. Periodical. US. English. qt. $3.00. Central Railway Chronicle, 39 Paul Place, Buffalo NY 14210. Tel (615)825-0248. Ed Clarence M Voll. bk rev. adv acc. Circ 300. (ctrl). Reports of meetings, concentrated reports of railroad operation and railroad history.

CHEMINS DE FER : BULLETIN OFFICIEL. 0009-2924. Periodical. FR. French. bm. 180. Assn Amis ded Chemins de Fer, Gare de l'Est, Paris 10E France. Tel (1) 42 03 96 31. adv acc. Circ 4,000. (ctrl). Technical and historic studies of France and foreigner railways-national, city lines, subways.

CHI CHE TIEN CHUAN TUNG. VFOAT Jichedianchuandong. Periodical. CC. Chinese. qt. 0.25. Guoji Shudian, PO Box 2820, Beijing China. LC TF975. DD 625.26305.

CHOLTO CHARYANG KISUL. VFOAT Rolling Stock Engineering. Periodical. Korean. qt. Cholto Charyang Kisul Kongsa, 17-2 Piltong 2-ka Chung-ku, Seoul Korea. LC TF371.

CHOLTO TONGGYE YONBO. See Yearbooks, Almanacs, Directories.

CIGGT REPORT. VFOAT C I G G T Report. VAT Canadian Institute of Guided Ground Transport Report. No. 1972-. 0383-2449. Monographic Series. CN. English. Canadian Institute of Guided Ground Transport, Queen's University, Kingston Ontario K7L 3N6 Canada. DD 625.1. Working Paper Series (Canadian Institute of Guided Ground Transport), 0702-8709.

CIRCULAR - ASSOCIATION OF AMERICAN RAILROADS, OPERATIONS AND MAINTENANCE DEPARTMENT, MECHANICAL DIVISION. (CIRCULAR - ASSOCIATION OF AMERICAN RAILROADS, MECHANICAL DIVISION). Main/Corp Association of American Railroads. Mechanical Division. 0148-723X. US. English. ir. $72.00. Association of American Railroads, Mechanical Division, 59 East Van Buren Street, Chicago IL 60605. Tel (312)939-0770. LC TF340.

CLASS I FREIGHT LINE-HAUL RAILROADS SELECTED EARNINGS DATA. VFOAT Class One Freight Line-Haul Railroads Selected Earnings Data. March 31, 1983-. 0749-548X. Periodical. US. English. qt. Free. Interstate Commerce Commission, Washington DC 20423. Tel (202)275-7833. DD 385. Circ 500. (ctrl). Report showing latest earnings and traffic volume data of Class One Freight Railroads. Class I Line-Haul Railroads Selected Earnings Data, 0361-3402.

CLEAR TRACK. 0193-3477. Periodical. US. English. mo. $54.00. National Railroad Construction & Maintenance, 9331 Waymond Avenue, Highland IN 46332. Tel (219)924-1709.

COMMODITY FLOW ANALYSIS : CANADIAN CARLOAD ALL-RAIL TRAFFIC. Main/Corp Canada. Transport Commission. Traffic and Tariffs Branch. VFOAT Analyse de Volume de Denrees. CN. English and French. an. Information Canada, 171 Slater Street, Ottawa Ontario K1A 0S9 Canada. LC HE2801. DD 385.240971.

COMMONWEALTH RAILWAYS FINANCIAL AND STATISTICAL BULLETIN. See Statistics.

CONRAIL PERFORMANCE REVIEW. Main/Corp United States Railway Association. 1981-. 0735-1593. US. English. an. United States Railway Association, 955 l'Enfant Plaza SW, Washington DC 20595. LC HE2791. DD 385.06573. Report to Congress on Conrail Performance.

DB; DEINE BAHN. VFOAT Deine Bahn. Periodical. GW. German. ir. 1.75 Single Issue. Eisenbahn-Fachverlag, Bonifazius Platz 3, 65 Mainz West Germany. LC TF3. DD 625.100943. Eisenbahnfachmann, Eisenbahner.

DET, DIE EISENBAHNTECHNIK CEASED. VFOAT Eisenbahntechnik. Year. 21-31, No.6. Periodical. German (summaries in English, French and Russian). ir. Oranienburger Strasse 13/14, 102 Berlin West Germany. Ind/Abst Excerpta Med. LC TF3. DD 625.1005. CODEN DETEBZ. Deutsche Eisenbahntechnik.

DEUTSCHES BUNDESBAHN-ADRESSBUCH. TEIL 2 : GLEISANSCHLUSSBESITZER UND-MITBENUTZER. VAT Deutsches Bundesbahn-Adressbuch. Teil Zwei: Gleisanschlussbesitzer und-Mitbenutzer. German. ir. Hestra-Verlag, Holzhofallee 33, Darmstadt West Germany.

DEVELOPING RAILWAYS. 1974-. UK. English. an. Business Press International Ltd, Perrymount Road, Haywards Heath West Sussex RH16 3BR England. LC HE1009. DD 385.091724. International Railway Progress.

DOCUMENTATION - SNCB, DIRECTION DU PERSONNEL ET DES SERVICES SOCIAUX. DOCUMENTATIE - NMBS, DIRECTIE VAN HET PERSONNEEL EN DE SOCIALE DIENSTEN. Main/Corp Societe Nationale des Chemins de fer Belges. Direction du Personnel et des Services Sociaux. VFOAT Documentatie - NMBS, Directie van het Personnel en de Sociale Diensten. BE. Dutch. ir. 750. Direction du Personnel et des Services Sociaux, 51-13 rue de France, 1070 Bruxelles Belgium. Tel (02)5238080. LC Z7231. DD 016.38509493. Railway transportation articles. Bulletin Mensuel de Documentation.

THE DSI-RAIL ROUTING SUPPLEMENT. VFOAT DSI Rail Routing Supplement. VAT Distribution Sciences Inc. Rail Routing Supplement. 0883-1831. US. English. bm. $15.00. National Railway Publishing Co, 424 West 33rd Street, New York NY 10001.

DZIENNIK TARYF I ZARZADEN KOLEJOWYCH. WYDAWNICTWO MINISTERSTWA KOMUNIKACJI. Main/Corp Poland. Ministerstwo Komunikacji. Yr. 1- 1. July 1928-. Polish. ir. LC HE3139.7. DD 385.09438.

EISENBAHNINGENIEUR. (DER EISENBAHNINGENIEUR). 0013-2810. Periodical. GW. German. mo. $41.63. Tetzlaff Verlag GMBH, Havelstrasse 9, D-6100 Darmstadt West Germany. Tel 06151/380-1. Ed Tetzlaff Verlag GMBH. Ind/Abst Comput. Control Abstr., Electr. Electron. Abstr., Sci. Abstr. Sect. A. Phys. Abstr., Energy Res. Abstr. CODEN ESBGAP. bk rev. adv acc. Circ 11,300. All questions of engineering in the field of railroad technology are covered. Zeitschrift, Eisenbahnbau; Eisenbahntechnik.

ELEKTRISCHE BAHNEN. Began publication in 1925. 0013-5437. Periodical. GW. English. mo. 182.-. R Oldenbourg Verlag, Postfach 801360, D-8000 Munchen 80 West Germany. Tel 089/41 12. Ind/Abst Eng. Index Annu., Eng. Index Mon., Eng. Index Bioeng. Abstr., Eng. Index Energy Abstr., Coal Abstr., Int. Aerosp. Abstr., Energy Res. Abstr., Comput. Control Abstr., Electr. Electron. Abstr., Sci. Abstr. Sect. A. Phys. Abstr., Phys. Abstr., Eng. Index. LC TF701. CODEN ELBAAQ. Zentralblatt fur den Elektrischen Zugbetrieb.

ELSNERS TASCHENBUCH DER EISENBAHNTECHNIK. 1970-. GW. German. an. $12.88. Tetzlaff Verlag GMBH, Postfach 4006, Havelstrasse 9, D6100 Darmstadt 1 West Germany. Tel 06151/380-1. LC TF151. adv acc. Railroad engineering, construction, telecommunication, signaling, machinery, and electro-engineering. Elsners Taschenbuch fur den Bautechnischen Eisenbahndienst, Elsners Taschenbuch fur den Fernmelde- und Signaltechnischen Eisenbahndienst; Elsners Taschenbuch fur den Maschinen- und Elektrotechnischen.

ESTIMATES OF REVENUE AND EXPENDITURE. See Statistics.

ETR; EISENBAHNTECHNISCHE RUNDSHAU. VFOAT Eisenbahntechnische Rundshau. 0013-2845. Periodical. GW. German. mo. 194. Hestra Verlag, Postfach Holzhofallee 33, D-61 Darmstadt West Germany. Tel 6151-33481. Ed Teng Hafner and Prof Schuclk. Ind/Abst Energy Res. Abstr. bk rev. adv acc. Circ 6,050. Leading German publication for the whole field of railroading.

EURAIL GUIDE. 1971-. 0085-0330. US. English. an. Eurail Guide Annual, 27540 Pacific Coast Highway, Malibu CA 90265. Tel (213)457-7286. LC HE3004. DD 914.0455. Complete information concerning tourist train rides. Covers 115 countries.

EXAMINATION OF UNITED STATES RAILWAY ASSOCIATION'S FINANCIAL STATEMENTS. 0272-7021. US. English. US General Accounting Office, Document Handling and Information Services Facility, PO Box 6015, Gaithersburg MD 20760. LC HE2714. DD 353.0087506.

EXPLANATORY MEMORANDUM AND STATISTICAL SUPPLEMENT, PAKISTAN RAILWAY BUDGET. See Statistics.

FACTS & FIGURES (NIHON KOKUYU TETSUDO). Main/Corp Nihon Kokuyu Tetsudo. English. ir. LC HE3351.

FAHRT FREI. Began publication in 1949. US. German. bw. Kunst & Wissen Erich Bieber, Dufourstrasse 51, CH-8008 Zurich Switzerland. LC Microfilm 05509 HE, HE3080.5. Verkehr: Ausgabe Eisenbahn.

FEDERAL RAILROAD ADMINISTRATION SPRING PREVIEW. Main/Corp United States. Federal Railroad Administration. US. English. an. US Department of Transportation, Federal Railroad Administration, 400 7th Street SW, Washington DC 20590.

FERROVIAS DO BRASIL. 1946-. BL. Portuguese. ir. Serviceo Grafico do Instituto Brasileiro de Geografia Estatistica, AV Brasil 15 671 P de Lucas, 20000 Rio de Janeiro Brasil. LC HE2921. DD 385.

THE FINANCIAL CONDITION OF PENN CENTRAL TRANSPORTATION COMPANY. (THE FINANCIAL CONDITION OF PENN CENTRAL TRANSPORTATION COMPANY : ANNUAL REPORT TO THE PRESIDENT AND THE CONGRESS). Main/Corp United States. Dept. of

Transportation—Railroads

Transportation. 0098-3128. US. English. an. Department of Transportation, Federal Highway Administration, Washington DC 20590. LC HE2791. DD 385.106574.

THE FINANCIAL CONDITION OF THE CENTRAL RAILROAD COMPANY OF NEW JERSEY. (THE FINANCIAL CONDITION OF THE CENTRAL RAILROAD COMPANY OF NEW JERSEY : ANNUAL REPORT TO THE PRESIDENT AND THE CONGRESS). Main/Corp United States. Dept. of Transportation. 0098-2288. US. English. an. Department of Transportation, Federal Highway Administration, Washington DC 20590. LC HE2791. DD 385.065749.

FLAGS, DIAMONDS, AND STATUES. 0271-7638. Periodical. US. English. qt. $12.00. Anthracite Railroads Historical Society, PO Box 119, Bridgeport PA 19405. Ed Richard W Jahn. LC TF23.1. DD 385.09748. Circ 1,500. (ctrl). Historical articles dealing with the motive power, right-of-way and corporate aspects of the Anthracite railroads of Pennsylvania (LV, RDG, CNJ, DL&W, and LNE).

FREIGHT COMMODITY STATISTICS OF CLASS I RAILROADS IN THE UNITED STATES. See Statistics.

FUTURAIL : REVUE BIMESTRIELLE DE L'OCTRA - OFFICE DU CHEMIN DE FER TRANSGABONAIS. Periodical. FR. French. bm. 200.00. Cabinet Daniel Verpeaux, 35 Quai d'Anjou, 75004 Paris France. LC HE3438. DD 385.096721.

GESCHAFTSBERICHT UND RECHNUNGSABSCHLUSS - STEIERMARKISCHE LANDESBAHNEN. Main/Corp Steiermarkische Landesbahnen. German. ir. Radetzky Strasse 31, Graz Austria. LC HE3060.S74.

GUDOK. Began publication in Dec. 1917. UR. Russian. da. $32.50. Victor Kamkin Inc (50019), 12224 Parklawn Drive, Rockville MD 20852. Tel (301)881-5973. LC MICROFILM S-521TF, TF4.

HEADLIGHTS. V. 23, No. 1- Jan. 1961-. 0091-8059. Periodical. US. English. $8.00. Electric Railroaders Association, 145 Greenwich Street, New York NY 10006. LC TF701. DD 388.42. ERA Headlights.

ILLINOIS CENTRAL GULF NEWS. Periodical. US. English. ir.

ILLINOIS RAIL PLAN . . . UPDATE. Began in 1978. US. English. an. Illinois Department of Transportation Auditorium, 2300 South Dirksen Parkway, Springfield IL 62764. LC HE2709. DD 385.068. Illinois Rail System Plan, Annual Update.

ILLINOIS RAIL SYSTEM PLAN. ANNUAL UPDATE. Main/Corp Illinois. Dept. of Transportation. VFOAT Illinois Rail Plan, Annual Update. US. English. an. Illinois Department of Transportation Auditorium, 2300 South Dirksen Parkway, Springfield IL 62764. LC HE2709. DD 385.068.

INDIAN RAILWAYS. V. 1- Apr. 1956-. 0019-6274. Periodical. II. English. mo. $3.50. The Ministry of Railways, Government of India, New Delhi India. LC TF4.

INDIANA . . . STATE RAIL PLAN UPDATE. Began with 1979. US. English. an. Public Service Commission of Indiana, 901 State Office Building/100 North Senate Avenue, Indianapolis MD 46204. LC HE2771.I6. DD 385.068.

INFORMATION BOOKLET - STATE RAILWAY OF THAILAND. Main/Corp State Railway of Thailand. 0585-1300. English. ir. LC HE3309.S5. DD 354.59300826.

INTERNATIONAL RAILWAY JOURNAL AND RAPID TRANSIT REVIEW. (INTERNATIONAL RAILWAY JOURNAL AND RAPID TRANSIT REVIEW : IRJ). VFOAT IRJ. Vol. 19, No. 1 (Jan. 1979)-. 0744-5326. Periodical. US. English (summaries in French, German, and Spanish). mo. $23.00. International Railway Journal, PO Box 8, Falmouth Cornwall 11 4RJ England. Tel (203)582-9546. Ed Mike Knutton. Ind/Abst Excerpta Med. LC TF1. DD 385.05. adv acc. Circ 10,000. (ctrl). Worldwide railway developments analysed in business and economic terms for principal officers of railways, and railway equipment manufacturers and suppliers. International Railway Journal, 0020-8450.

INTERSTATE COMMERCE COMMISSION'S REPORT TO THE PRESIDENT AND THE CONGRESS. EFFECTIVENESS OF THE ACT. AMTRAK. (AMTRAK : EFFECTIVENESS OF THE ACT). Main/Corp United States. Interstate Commerce Commission. VFOAT Report on the Effectiveness of the Rail Passenger Service Act of 1970 (Public Law 91-518). 0147-2178. US. English. an. $1.50 Per Issue. Interstate Commerce Commission, 1222 ICC Bld, Washington DC 20423. LC HE2708. DD 385.0973.

JAHRBUCH DES EISENBAHNFREUNDES. See Yearbooks, Almanacs, Directories.

JAHRBUCH DES EISENBAHNWESENS. See Yearbooks, Almanacs, Directories.

JANE'S WORLD RAILWAYS. 1st- Ed. 0075-3084. UK. English. an. $125.00. Jane's Publishing Inc, 135 West 50th Street/12th Floor, New York NY 10070. Tel (212)586-7745. Ed Geoffrey Freeman Allen. LC TF1. DD 385.05. adv acc. Reference guide to all rail transport. Divided into two main sections- manufacturers and systems. Details cover all types of equipment and rail networks by country.

JAPANESE RAILWAY ENGINEERING. V. 1- July, 1959-. 0448-8938. Periodical. JA. English (beginning in 1960. Includes summaries in French). qt. 30.00 Domestic. Maruzen Company Ltd, PO Box 5050, 100-31 Tokyo Japan. Tel 03-237-0871. Ind/Abst Eng. Index Annu., Eng. Index Mon., Eng. Index, Eng. Index Bioeng. Abstr., Eng. Index Energy Abstr., Comput. Control Abstr., Electr. Electron. Abstr., Sci. Abstr. Sect. A. Phys. Abstr., Phys. Abstr. CODEN JAREBT. (ctrl). The journal which introduces the techniques of Japanese railways to the world.

JARNVAGSHOBBY. 1-. Periodical. Swedish. ir. Forlag J Jango, Riksradsvagen 78, S-121 60 Johanneshov Sweden. LC TF197.

JOURNAL - INSTITUTE OF RAIL TRANSPORT. Main/Corp Institute of Rail Transport. V. 1- Apr. 1965-. 0020-3114. Periodical. English. ir. LC HE3291.

JOURNAL OF THE INSTITUTION OF ENGINEERS (INDIA. See Engineering - Mechanical Engineering & Machinery.

JREA. 0447-2322. Periodical. JA. Japanese. mo. 450 Single Issue. Nihon Tetsudo Gijutsu Kyokai Suidobashi Nishiguchi Kaikan Nai, 20-8 Misaki-cho 2-chome Chiyoda-ku, Tokyo-to 101 Japan. LC TF4.

THE KEYSTONE - PENNSYLVANIA RAILROAD TECHNICAL AND HISTORICAL SOCIETY. (THE KEYSTONE). Vol. 1, No. 1 (Apr. 1968)-. 0744-4036. Periodical. US. English. qt. Business Office of Pennsylvania Railroad, Technical and Historical Society, PO Box 389, Upper Darby PA 19082.

KOKUTETSU SHUTOKEN NYUSU. VFOAT Shutoken Nyusu. Began with June 1971 issue. JA. Japanese. ir. Nihon Kokuyu Tetsudo Shutoken Hombu Kohoka, 6-5 Marunouchi 1, Chiyoda-ku (100), Tokyo Japan. LC HE3359.T55.

KREPLAN. Main/Corp Denmark. Generaldirektratet for Statsbanerne. Danish. ir. 5. Generaldirektratet for Statsbanerne, Slvgade 40, 1349 Kbenhavn Denmark. LC HE3151.

KURSBUCH - DEUTSCHE BUNDESBAHN. Main/Corp Deutsche Bundesbahn. German. ir. 7.00 Single Issue. Zentrale Transportleitung, Kursbuchstelle der Deutschen Bundesbahn, Kaiserstrasse 3 65 1, Mainz West Germany. LC HE3074. Amtliches Kursbuch.

KURSBUCH: INTERNATIONALER + I.E. UND BINNENVERKEHR. Main/Corp Deutsche Reichbahn (East Germany). VFOAT Kursbuch der Dr Internationaler + I.E. und Binnenverkehr. English, French, German or Russian. ir. 3.50 Single Issue. Wilhelm-Pick-Str 49, 1054 Berlin West Germany. LC HE3080.5. DD 385.209431.

LIVE STEAM. 0364-5177. Periodical. US. English. mo. Live Steam, PO Box 629, Traverse City MI 49684. Tel (616)941-7160. LC TJ630. DD 621.105. Live Steam Magazine, 0300-7804.

LOCOMOTIVE ENGINEER. See Engineering.

LOCOMOTIVE QUARTERLY. Began with Fall 1976 issue. 0276-6736. Periodical. US. English. qt. $32.00. Locomotive Quarterly, PO Box 383, Mount Vernon NY 10552. LC TJ605. DD 625.2605.

LOCOMOTIVE ROSTERS OF NORTH AMERICA. VFOAT Locomotive Fleet Statistics. Began with 1972 issue?. 0380-3856. CN. English. an. $7. per copy. Northam Directory Associates, PO Box 560 Station A, Montreal Quebec H3C 2T6 Canada. DD 625.26097.

THE LOG TRAIN. (THE LOG TRAIN : JOURNAL OF THE MOUNTAIN STATE RAILROAD & LOGGING HISTORICAL ASSOC). Vol. 1, No. 1-2 (July/Oct. 1982)-. 0743-281X. US. English. qt. $15.00. PO Box 89, Cass WV 24927. Tel (304)456-4362. Ed Max S Robin. LC TF678. DD 385.5405. bk rev. adv acc. Circ 300. (ctrl). A journal devoted to the history of railroading in West Virginia with emphasis on logging railroads.

LOK-MAGAZIN. 1.- 1962. Periodical. GW. German. bm. 68.40. Franckhsche Vghndl W Keller & Co Kosmos VG, PO 640, D7000 Stuttgart 1 West Germany. Tel 0711/21910. Ed Horst J Obermayer. LC TJ605. bk rev. adv acc. Circ 9,000. Technics and history of railroads, especially in Germany and middle Europe.

LONDON PASSENGER TRANSPORT. No. 1- 0309-5428. Periodical. UK. English. ir. London Passenger Transport Research Group, 24 Cranbourn Street, London WC2H 7AA England. LC HE4719.L82. DD 388.4109421.

MAINLINE MODELER. V. 1, No. 1 (Jan./Feb. 1980)-. 0199-5421. Periodical. US. English. mo. $28.00. Hundman Publishing, 5115 Monticello Drive, Edmond WA 98020. Tel (206)743-2607. LC TF1975. DD 625.1905.

MANAGEMENT COMPENSATION, RAILROADS. 0273-0332. US. English. an. Charles M Rice, 408 Olive Street, Suite 823, Jefferson Memorial Station, St Louis MO 63102. LC HD4965.5.U6. DD 331.281385. Management Compensation in the Railroad Industry, 0160-8657.

MANTETSUKAI HO. JA. Japanese. ir. 2000. Mantetsukai, c/o Matsuo Building 2-4, Ginza 7, Chuo-ku 104 Tokyo Japan. LC HE3290.M5.

MANUAL OF THE AMERICAN RAILWAY ENGINEERING ASSOCIATION. Main/Corp American Railway Engineering Association. 0065-9940. US. English. ir. American Railway Association, 2000 L Street NW, Washington DC 20036. Tel (202)835-9336.

MEMORIA - URUGUAY. ADMINISTRACION DE FERROCARRILES DEL ESTADO. Main/Corp Uruguay. Administracion de Ferrocarriles del Estado. VFOAT AFE. Spanish. an. LC HE2981. DD 385.09895. Memoria y Balance.

METRO. 1967/69-. Multilingual (French). ir. Union Internationale des Transports Publics, Avenue de l'Uruguay 19 B-1050, Bruxelles Belgium. LC Z7234.S9, HE4211. DD 016.38842.

MILEPOST. Began publication in Aug. 1975?. 0227-2458. Periodical. CN. English. mo. Free to Members. Midwestern Rail Association, PO Box 1855, Winnipeg Manitoba R3C 3R1 Canada. DD 385.09712.

MINTETSU TOKEI NEMPO. 1975-. JA. Japanese. ir. 2500. Seifu Shiryoto Fukyo Chosakai, c/o Hasegawa Building 7-1 Akasaka 1, Minato-ku 107 Tokyo Japan. LC HE3951. Shitetsu Tokai Nempo.

MINTETSU YORAN. JA. Japanese. ir. Denkisha Kenkyukai Tetsudo Kankokai, 4-1 Marunouchi 3, Chiyoda-ku Tokyo Japan. LC HE3354.

MODEL RAILROAD BUYERS GUIDE. 1st- Ed. US. English. $6.00. Boynton and Associates, 8001 Forbes Place/Suite 210D, Springfield VA 22151. LC TF197. DD 338.4762519.

MODEL RAILROADER. V. 1- Jan. 1934-. 0026-7341. Periodical. US. English. mo. $22.50. Kalmbach Publishing Company, 1027 7th Street, Milwaukee WI 53233. Tel (414)272-2060. Ed Russ Larson. Ind/Abst Mag. Index, Consum. Index Prod. Eval. Inf. Source. LC TF197. bk rev. adv acc. Circ 185,000. Presents information on building and operating model railroads. Each issue contains material designed to instruct and inspire model railroad hobbyists.

DER MODELLEISENBAHNER. Periodical. SZ. German. mo. Kunst & Wissen Erich Bieber, Dufourstrasse 51, CH-8008 Zurich Switzerland. Tel 011-41-1-69 44 20. LC TF197.

MODERN RAILROADS (CAHNERS PUB. CO. : 1982). (MODERN RAILROADS). Vol. 37, No. 9 (Sept. 1982)-. 0736-2064. Periodical. US. English. mo. $35.00 Domestic, $40.00 Canada.

Transportation—Railroads

Modern Railroads, 270 St Paul Street, Denver CO 80206. **Ind/Abst** Predicasts, Energy Inf. Abstr., Environ. Abstr. **LC** TF1. **DD** 625.1005. *MR. Modern Railroads Rail Transit, 0193-3272.*

MODERN RAILWAYS. Began with No. 160 (Jan. 1962). 0026-8356. Periodical. UK. English. mo. 30.50. Ian Allan Ltd, Coombelands House, Addlestone Weybridge KT15 1HY England. **Tel** 0932 58511. Ed J Abbott. **Ind/Abst** Coal Abstr., Ref. Source. bk rev. adv acc. **Circ** 33,000. News and feature articles on engineering, economics and operation of British and overseas railroads. *Trains Illustrated.*

MONTHLY REVIEW OF TECHNICAL LITERATURE. **Main/Corp** British Railways. Research and Development Division. V. 23, No. 3- Mar. 1973-. 0007-1714. Periodical. UK. English. mo. Research and Development Division, London Road, Derby DE2 8UP England. **LC** T1. **DD** 625.1005. *Monthly Review of Technical Literature, 0007-1714.*

MORIKO NENJI HOKOKU. **Main/Corp** Nihon Kokuyu Tetsudo. Morioka Kojikyoku. **VAT** Nihon Kokuyu Tetsudo Morioka Kojikyoku Nenji Hokoku. Began with the Report for 1954-. Japanese. ir. Nihon Kokyuo Tesudo, 1-43 Ekimaedori, Morioka 020 Japan. **LC** TF106.I93.

MOTIVE POWER INTERNATIONAL. 1- Fall 1973-. 0381-9868. Periodical. CN. English. qt. $1.25 Each Number. Motive Power International, PO Box 39, Port Moody British Columbia V3H 3E1 Canada. **DD** 625.2605.

MUTUAL MAGAZINE (PHILADELPHIA, PA. : 1983). (THE MUTUAL MAGAZINE). **VFOAT** Mutual. Began in 1980. 0740-672X. Periodical. US. English. mo. $.60 Members. Room 359 Amtrak Station 30th Street, Philadelphia PA 19104. **LC** HE2791. **DD** 331.7613850974. *Mutual, 0162-2676.*

NACHRICHTEN - DEUTSCHE GESELLSCHAFT FUR EISENBAHNGESCHICHTE. **Main/Corp** Deutsche Gesellschaft fur Eisenbahngeschichte. GW. Germany. qt. Deutsche Gesellschaft Eisenbah, Elbinger Str 12C Postfach 2063, 7500 Karlsruhe 1 West Germany. **LC** HE3071. *DGEG-Nachrichten.*

NARROW GAUGE AND SHORT LINE GAZETTE. 0148-2122. Periodical. US. English. bm. $18.00. Gazette Publications, One First Street/Suite C, PO Box 26, Los Altos CA 94022. **Tel** (415)941-3823. Ed Bob Brown. **LC** TF197. **DD** 625.1905. bk rev. adv acc. **Circ** 15,500. History and modeling of Narrow Gauge and Short Line Railroads.

NATIONAL RAILWAY BULLETIN. V. 41- 1976-. 0885-5099. Periodical. US. English. National Railway Historical Society, 734 St John Street, Allentown PA 18103. **Ind/Abst** Writ. Am. Hist. **LC** HE2715. **DD** 385.0973. *Bulletin.*

NATIONAL RAILWAYS OF ZIMBABWE. **VFOAT** National Railways of Zimbabwe Magazine. Periodical. English. mo. 3.50. Publicity Office, National Railways of Zimbabwe, Box 596, Bulawayo Zimbabwe Africa. **Tel** 3635. Ed J J Mpofu. **LC** HE3419.R4. **DD** 385.096891. bk rev. adv acc. **Circ** 19,500. (ctrl). House magazine of the National Railways of Zimbabwe. *Rhodesia Railways Magazine.*

NEMZETKOZI VASUTI OSSEZEKOTTETESEK KIVONATOS MENETRENDJE. **Main/Corp** Hungary. Kozlekedes- es Postaugyi Miniszterium. Vasuti Foosztaly. 0300-2330. Hungarian. ir. Vi Nepkoztarsas ag Utja 73-75, Budapest Hungary. **LC** HE3059.5.

NETWORK (MELBOURNE (VIC.)). (NETWORK : RAILWAYS OF AUSTRALIA QUARTERLY). **VFOAT** Railways of Australia Network. 0159-7302. Periodical. EN. English. qt. $16.00. Railways of Australia Committee, 325 Collins Street, Melbourne 3000 Australia. **LC** TF121. **DD** 385.0994. *Railways of Australia Network.*

THE NEW ENGLAND STATES LIMITED. 0162-1599. Periodical. US. English. qt. $8.00. PO Box 701, Keene NH 03431. **LC** HE2714. **DD** 385.0974.

NEWS BULLETIN - SASKATCHEWAN RAIL COMMITTEE. **Main/Corp** Saskatchewan Rail Committee. 1- Mar. 1977-. 0708-028X. Periodical. CN. English. ir. Free. Saskatchewan Rail Committee, PO Box 3594, Regina Saskatchewan S4P 3L7 Canada. **DD** 385.0627124. (ctrl).

NORDENS JARNVAGAR. English and Swedish. ir. F Stenvall, Kopenhamnsvagen 47A, S-217 71 Malmo Sweden. **LC** TF88.5.

NORDISK JARNBANETIDSKRIFT. **VFOAT** Jarnbanetidskrift. Periodical. Swedish. ir. **LC** TF4.

OBB JOURNAL. **Main/Corp** Austria. Generaldirektion der Osterreichischen Bundesbahnen. **VAT** Osterreichische Bundesbahnen Journal. 1976-. Periodical. German. ir. 315.00. Generaldirektion der Osterreichischen Bundesbahnen, Elisabethstrasse 9, Wien 1010 Austria. **LC** HE3051. *Obb in Wort und Bild.*

THE OFFICIAL RAILWAY EQUIPMENT REGISTER. 0030-0373. Periodical. US. English. qt. National Railway Publication Company, 424 West 33rd Street, New York NY 10001. **Tel** (212)563-7210.

THE OFFICIAL RAILWAY GUIDE. NORTH AMERICAN FREIGHT SERVICE EDITION. (THE OFFICIAL RAILWAY GUIDE). V. 106, No. 8- Jan./Feb. 1974-. 0190-6704. Periodical. US. English. bm. $42.00. National Railway Publishers Inc, 424 West 33rd Street Maria, Faradans New York NY 10001. **Tel** (212)563-7210. *Official Guide of the Railways and Steam Navigation Lines of the United States, Puerto Rico, Canada, Mexico and Cuba.*

THE OFFICIAL RAILWAY GUIDE. NORTH AMERICAN TRAVEL EDITION. UNITED STATES, CANADA AND MEXICO. (THE OFFICIAL RAILWAY GUIDE). 0273-9658. Periodical. US. English. mo. $64.00. The Official Railway Guide, 424 West 33rd Street, New York NY 10001. **LC** HE2727. **DD** 385.2042. *Official Railway Guide. North American Passenger Travel Edition, 0094-5218.*

PACIFIC NEWS. 0030-879X. Periodical. US. English. mo. Interurbans Publications, PO Box 6128, Glendale CA 91205. **Tel** (818)240-4777. **DD** 385.

PACIFIC RAIL NEWS. **VFOAT** Pacific News. No. 252 (Oct. 1984)-. 8750-8486. Periodical. US. English. mo. $25.00. Interurbans Publications, PO Box 6128, Glendale CA 91205. **Tel** (818)240-4777. Ed James W Walker Jr. **DD** 385. bk rev. adv acc. **Circ** 86,400. A magazine covering the railway scene and urban transit west of the Mississippi in news stories, features and photographs. *Pacific News, 0030-879X.*

PASSENGER TIMETABLE : GREAT BRITAIN INTER-CITY, LOCAL AND SUBURBAN SERVICES, IRISH, CHANNEL ISLAND, COASTAL SERVICES. **Main/Corp** British Railways Board. UK. English. 1.80. British Railways Board, Charges Publications, Room 4A Melbury House, Melbury Terrace, London NW1 6JU England. **LC** HE3014. **DD** 385.220941.

PASSENGER TIMETABLE : INTERNATIONAL, INTER-CITY, SEALINK, SEASPEED SERVICES, GREAT BRITAIN-CONTINENT OF EUROPE. **Main/Corp** British Railways Board. **VFOAT** International, Inter-City, Sealink, Seaspeed Services, Great Britain-Continent of Europe. UK. English. an. 14. British Railways Board, 222 Marylebone Road, London NW1 6JU England. **Tel** (01)262-3232. **LC** HE3014. **DD** 385.22. **Circ** 180,000. British rail passenger timetable issued in May and September giving comprehensive details of all train services run in Great Britain.

PASSENGER TRAIN JOURNAL. 0160-6913. Periodical. US. English. mo. $24.00 Domestic, $27.00 Canada. Passenger Train Journal, PO Box 860, Homewood IL 60430. **LC** HE2583. **DD** 385.220973. *PTJ. Passenger Train Journal, 0160-6352.*

PERMANENT WAY. V. 1- (No. 1-). 0031-5516. Periodical. JA. English. qt. Japan Publishers Trading Co Inc, PO Box 5030 Tokyo International, Tokyo 100-31 Japan. **Tel** (914)592-2077. **Ind/Abst** Eng. Index Annu., Eng. Index Mon., Eng. Index Bioeng. Abstr., Eng. Index Energy Abstr., Eng. Index. **LC** TF240. **CODEN** PRMWA4.

PINE TREE FLYER. (PINE TREE FLYER : PUBLICATION OF THE RAILROAD HISTORICAL SOCIETY OF MAINE). Vol. 1, No. 1 (Fall 1981)-. 0743-4448. Periodical. US. English. qt. Free to members, included in dues. Railroad Historical Society of Maine, Box 8057, Portland ME 04104. **DD** 385.

THE POCKET LIST OF RAILROAD OFFICIALS. **VFOAT** Pocket List. V. 1- (Serial No. 1-). 0032-1826. US. English. qt. National Railway Publishing Company, 424 West 33rd Street, New York NY 10001. **Tel** (212)563-7210. **LC** HE2723.

PRESUPUESTO PRO PROGRAMA - INSTITUTO AUTONOMO ADMINISTRACION DE FERROCARRILES DEL ESTADO, DIVISION DE PRESUPUESTO. **Main/Corp** Instituto Autonomo Administracion de Ferrocarriles del Estado (Venezuela). Division de Presupuesto. VE. Spanish. ir. Instituto Autonomo Administracion de Ferrocarriles del Estado, Oficina de Planificacion y Presupuesto, Caracas Venezuela. **LC** HE2991. **DD** 354.8700875.

PROCEEDINGS ... ANNUAL CONVENTION. **Main/Corp** American Railway Engineering Association. 68th-. US. English. an. $52.00. American Railway Association, 2000 L Street NW, Washington DC 20036. **Tel** (202)835 9336. *Proceedings of the ... Annual Convention of the American Railway Engineering Association.*

PROCEEDINGS OF THE ANNUAL MEETING AND REGIONAL MEETING - AMERICAN ASSOCIATION OF RAILROAD SUPERINTENDENTS. (PROCEEDINGS OF THE ANNUAL MEETING AND REGIONAL MEETING). **Main/Corp** American Association of Railroad Superintendents. 0276-7724. US. English. an. American Association of Railroad Superintendents, 18154 Harwood Avenue, Homewood IL 60430. *Proceedings of the Annual Meeting.*

PROCEEDINGS OF THE NEW ENGLAND RAILROAD CLUB. **Main/Corp** New England Railroad Club, Boston. US. English. qt. New England Rail Road Club, Box 445, Pembroke MA 02359. **LC** TF1.

PROCEEDINGS - SOUTHERN AND SOUTHWESTERN RAILWAY ASSOCIATION. **Main/Corp** Southern and Southwestern Railway Association. Periodical. US. English. qt. $3.00. Southern Southwest Railway Association, Box 1744, Roanoke VA 24008. *Proceedings.*

PROCEEDINGS, TECHNICAL CONFERENCE - AMERICAN RAILWAY ENGINEERING ASSOCIATION. **Main/Corp** American Railway Engineering Association. V. 75- 1974-. 0271-4450. US. English. an. American Railway Engineering Association, 2000 L Street Northwest, Washington DC 20036. **Ind/Abst** Eng. Index. **CODEN** ARWPA4. *Proceedings of the Annual Convention of the American Railway Engineering Association.*

PROGRESSIVE RAILROADING. (PROGRESSIVE RAILROADING : THE EXECUTIVE VIEWPOINT). V. 1- 1958-. 0033-0817. Periodical. US. English. mo. $50.00. Murphy-Richter Publ Company, 2 North Riverside Plaza/Suite 2115, Chicago IL 60606. **Tel** (312)454-9155. Ed Phil Murphy. adv acc. (ctrl). Railroad technology.

PRZEGLAD KOLEJOWY ELEKTROTECHNICZNY. Began in 1953. Periodical. PL. Polish. mo. Ars Polona, Krakowskie Przedmiescie 7, 00-068 Warsaw Poland. **LC** TF4. *Przeglad Kolejowy.*

PRZEGLAD KOLEJOWY MECHANICZNY. Began with Sept. 1953 issue. 0033-2224. Periodical. PL. Polish. mo. ARS Polona, Krakowskie Przedmiescie 7, 00-068 Warsaw Poland. **Ind/Abst** CIS Abstr. **LC** TF340. *Przeglad Kolejowy.*

PRZEGLAD KOLEJOWY PRZEWOZOWY. Began in 1953. Periodical. PL. Polish. mo. Ars Polona, Krakowskie Przedmiescie 7, 00-068 Warsaw Poland. **LC** TF504. *Przeglad Kolejowy.*

QUARTERLY FREIGHT LOSS AND DAMAGE CLAIMS. CLASS 1, LINE-HAUL RAILROADS. Periodical. US. English. qt. Interstate Commerce Commission, Bureau of Accounts, Washington DC 20423.

QUARTERLY REPORTS OF THE RAILWAY TECHNICAL RESEARCH INSTITUTE. (QUARTERLY REPORTS - RAILWAY TECHNICAL RESEARCH INSTITUTE). **Main/Corp** Tetsudo Gijutsu Kenkyujo, Tokyo. V. 1- March 1960-. 0033-9008. Periodical. JA. English. qt. $137.00. Kenyusha Inc, 1-45-6 Hikariecho Kokubunji, Tokyo Japan. **Tel** 0425 (72) 7157. **Ind/Abst** Eng. Index Annu., Eng. Index Mon., Eng. Index Bioeng. Abstr., Eng. Index Energy Abstr., Comput. Control Abstr., Electr. Electron. Abstr., Sci. Abstr. Sect. A. Phys. Abstr. **CODEN** QRTIA8. (cum index). **Circ** 600. Covers the activities of the Railway Technical Research Institute of the Japanese National Railways.

RAIL AND TRANSIT. Nov./Dec. 1975-. 0382-9057. Periodical. CN. English. bm. Upper Canada Railway Society, PO Box 122 Postal Station

A, Toronto Ontario M5W 1A2 Canada. **DD** 385.0971. *Newsletter, 0382-9049.*

RAIL CLASSICS. 0194-9187. Periodical. US. English. bm. $13.50. Challenge Publications Inc, 7950 Deering Avenue, Canoga Park CA 91304. **Tel** (213)887-0550. **LC** TF1. **DD** 385.0973.

RAIL CLASSICS & RAILWAY QUARTERLY. **VFOAT** Rail Classics and Railway Quarterly. Vol. 13, No. 3 (May 1984)-. 0743-9075. Periodical. US. English. bm. $13.50. Rail Classics, 10968 via Frontera, San Diego CA 92127. **LC** TF1. **DD** 385.05. *Rail Classics, 0194-9187; Railway Quarterly, 0191-1805.*

RAIL ENGINEERING INTERNATIONAL (1981). (RAIL ENGINEERING INTERNATIONAL). Vol. 10, No. 4 (Oct./Dec. 1981)-. 0141-4615. Periodical. UK. English. qt. $7.00 Domestic $8.00 Foreign. Little Leighs, Chelmsford CM3 1PF Essex England. **Ind/Abst** Electron. Commun. Abstr. J., ISMEC Bull., Pollut. Abstr. Indexes, Saf. Sci. Abstr. J., Eng. Index Annu., Eng. Index Mon., Eng. Index Bioeng. Abstr., Eng. Index Energy Abstr., Fluidex, Excerpta Med. **LC** TF1. **DD** 625.1005. **CODEN** REGIAX. *Railway Engineer International.*

RAIL-HIGHWAY CROSSING ACCIDENT/INCIDENT AND INVENTORY BULLETIN. **VAT** Rail Highway Crossing Accident Incident and Inventory Bulletin. Began with No. 1, 1978. 0197-5315. US. English. an. US Department of Transportation, Federal Railroad Administration, 400 7th Street SW, Washington DC 20590. **LC** HE1780. **DD** 312.440973. *Rail-Highway Grade-Crossing Accidents/Incidents Bulletin for the Year Ended December 31, ...*

RAIL HOBBYIST. September 1984-. 0738-1778. Periodical. US. English. mo. $18.00 Domestic, $26.00 Foreign. PO Box 789, Hurst TX 76053. **DD** 385.

RAIL INTERNATIONAL. 1st- Year. 0020-8442. Periodical. BE. English (French, German and Russian). mo. 3200. International Railway Congress Association, rue de France 85, B-1070 Bruxelles Belgium. **Ind/Abst** Eng. Index Annu., Eng. Index Mon., Eng. Index Bioeng. Abstr., Eng. Index Energy Abstr., Comput. Control Abstr., Electr. Electron. Abstr., Sci. Abstr. Sect. A. Phys. Abstr., Phys. Abstr., Eng. Index. **LC** TF1. **DD** 625.1005. **CODEN** RAIIAF. bk rev. adv acc. (ctrl). Publishes articles, original technical papers, dealing with all branches of railway science and management, including economic, financial and social questions. *Monthly Bulletin - International Railway Congress Association, Bulletin - International Railway Union, Bulletin - International Railway Union, Office for Research and Experiments.*

RAIL PASSENGER STATISTICS IN THE NORTHEAST CORRIDOR. *See* Statistics.

LE RAIL SYNDICALISTE. 0150-1313. Periodical. FR. French. mo. Le Rail Syndicaliste, 60 rue Vergniaud, 75640 Paris Cedex 13 France. **LC** HD6681.A1.

RAIL TRANSIT DIRECTORY. *See* Yearbooks, Almanacs, Directories.

RAIL TRANSPORT, AUSTRALIA. 1979-80-. English. an. Australian Bureau of Statistics, PO Box 84, Canberra Australian Capital Territory 2600 Australia. **Tel** (062)52 6778. **LC** HE289. **DD** 385.0994. Shows details of Government railway statistics relating to the traffic and financial operations of the State and Commonwealth Government railway systems. *Rail, Bus and Air Transport.*

RAILFAN & RAILROAD. **VAT** Railfan and Railroad. V. 2, No. 10- May 1979-. 0163-7266. Periodical. US. English. bm. $11.00. Carstens Publications, Box 700, Newton NJ 07860. **Tel** (201)383-3355. **Ed** James A Boyd. **Ind/Abst** Ref. Source. **LC** TF1. **DD** 385.0973. bk rev. adv acc. **Circ** 53,000. Railroad news magazine of contemporary railroading: rail history, books, video, collecting, traction, narrow gauge, rail museums, posters, movies, fantrips, railroadiana, events. *Railroad Magazine, 0033-8761; Railfan.*

RAILPACE NEWSMAGAZINE. **VFOAT** Railpace Magazine. 0745-5267. Periodical. US. English. mo. $27.00. Railpace Company Inc, PO Box 927, Piscataway NJ 08854. **LC** TF1. **DD** 385.0973.

RAILPLAN SOUTH DAKOTA. **Main/Corp** South Dakota. Division of Railroads. Began in 1978. US. English. an. Department of Transportation, Division of Railroads, Pierre SD 57501. **LC** HE2771.S8. **DD** 385.068.

RAILROAD ACCIDENT INVESTIGATION REPORTS. **Main/Corp** United States. Federal Railroad Administration. Office of Safety. 0160-1261. US. English. US Department of Transportation, Federal Railroad Administration, Office of Safety, 400 7th Street SW, Washington DC 20590. **LC** HE1780. **DD** 614.8630973.

RAILROAD ACCIDENT REPORT. BRIEF FORMAT. (RAILROAD ACCIDENT REPORTS, BRIEF FORMAT). Began with 1976. 0148-0200. US. English. ir. National Technical Information Service, 5285 Port Royal Road, Springfield VA 22161. **Tel** (703)487-4630. **LC** HE17, HE1780. **DD** 629.04208 S 385.

RAILROAD ACCIDENTS IN OREGON. *See* Statistics.

RAILROAD CAR JOURNAL. No. 1- Aug. 1971-. 0091-5572. Periodical. US. English. $3.50 Single Issue. Kratville Publications, 516 Furnam Building, Omaha NE 68101. **LC** TF371. **DD** 625.2405.

RAILROAD EMPLOYEE FATALITIES INVESTIGATED BY THE FEDERAL RAILROAD ADMINISTRATION. (RAILROAD EMPLOYEE FATALITIES INVESTIGATED BY THE FEDERAL RAILROAD ADMINISTRATION IN . . .). Began with vol. for 1976. 0730-5230. US. English. an. US Department of Transportation, Federal Railroad Administration, 400 7th Street SW, Washington DC 20590. **LC** HE1780. **DD** 363.1220973. Vols. for (1982-) distributed to depository libraries in microfiche. *Railroad Employee Fatalities Investigated in . . ., 0160-886X.*

RAILROAD FACTS (WASHINGTON, D.C.). (RAILROAD FACTS). 1983 Ed.-. 0742-1850. US. English. an. Association of American Railroads, Office of Information and Public Affairs, 1920 L Street Northwest, Washington DC 20036. **LC** HE2713. **DD** 385.0973. *Yearbook of Railroad Facts, 0084-3997.*

RAILROAD HISTORY. No. 127- Oct. 1972-. 0090-7847. Periodical. US. English. sa. $6.00. Harvard Business School, Boston MA 02163. **Ind/Abst** Am. Hist. Life, Hist. Abstr., Part A, Mod. Hist. Abstr., Hist. Abst., Part B, Twent. Century Abstr., Writ. Am. Hist. **LC** TF1. **DD** 385.09. *Bulletin.*

RAILROAD MODEL CRAFTSMAN. *See* Hobbies.

RAILROAD NOTES (NEW YORK, N.Y. : 1976). (RAILROAD NOTES). Vol. 1, No. 1 (Feb. 1976)-. 0741-8124. Periodical. US. English. ir. $5.00. Lavor Research Association, 80 East 11th Street, New York NY 10003. **Tel** (212)473-1042. **Ed** Franz J Lehman. **Circ** 1,200. Critic of the rail industry as it affects the public, the economy and rail workers. *Railroad Notes (New York, N.Y. : 1943).*

RAILROAD RESEARCH BULLETIN *CEASED.* Began with V. 1, Spring 1984-. Ceased with V. 8, No. 2, Autumn 1981. 0097-0042. US. English. sa. Railroad Research Information Service, 2101 Constitution Avenue NW, Washington DC 20418. **LC** HE2704. **DD** 385.0973 S, 385.0973.

RAILROAD REVENUES, EXPENSES, AND INCOME : CLASS I RAILROADS IN THE UNITED STATES. **Main/Corp** Association of American Railroads. Economics and Finance Dept. 3rd Qtr. 1967-. Periodical. US. English. qt. $20.00. Association of American Railroads, 1920 L Street NW/Room 663, Washington DC 20036. **Tel** (202)835-9361. adv acc. Detailed financial data of most recent quarter and cumulative period of year compared with the same periods of previous year. *Railroad Revenues, Expenses and Income.*

THE RAILROADIANA EXPRESS. 0199-3445. Periodical. US. English. qt. Railroadiana Collectors Association Inc, PO Box 1107, Wheaton IL 60187.

RAILS SOUTH. 0194-8881. Periodical. US. English. bm. $6.00. White Publishing, Box 286, Geneseo IL 61254. **Tel** (309)944-3227.

RAILWAY AGE. V. 1- April 1, 1870-. 0033-8826. Periodical. US. English. mo. Simmons Boardman Publishing Corporation, 508 Birch Street, Bristol CT 06010. **Tel** (203)582-9546. **Ind/Abst** Bus. Period. Index, Eng. Index, Mag. Index, Electr. Electron. Abstr., Phys. Abstr., Comput. Control Abstr., Funk Scott Index Corp. Ind., Public Aff. Inf. Serv. Bull. **LC** TF1. **DD** 385.05. **CODEN** RAAGA3. *Railway Age, Railway Review.*

THE RAILWAY BUDGET : ANNUAL DEVELOPMENT PROGRAMME. **Main/Corp** Pakistan. Railway Board. English. ir. Government of Pakistan, Ministry of Railways, Karachi 15 B Pakistan. **LC** HE3300.5. **DD** 354.549100875.

THE RAILWAY BUDGET : ANNUAL DEVELOPMENT PROGRAMME OF THE PAISTAN WESTERN RAILWAY. **Main/Corp** Pakistan. Railway Board. English. ir. Government of Pakistan, Ministry of Railways, Karachi 15 B Pakistan. **LC** HE3300.5.Z8. **DD** 354.9549100875.

THE RAILWAY BUDGET : DEMANDS FOR GRANTS FOR THE PAKISTAN RAILWAYS. **Main/Corp** Pakistan. Railway Board. English. ir. Government of Pakistan, Ministry of Railways, Karachi 15 3 Pakistan. **LC** HE3300.5. **DD** 353.9549100875.

THE RAILWAY BUDGET : IMPROVEMENT FUND WORKS PROGRAMME. **Main/Corp** Pakistan. Railway Board. English. ir. Government of Pakistan, Karachi 15 B Pakistan. **LC** HE3300.5. **DD** 353.9549100875.

THE RAILWAY BUDGET IN BRIEF. **Main/Corp** Pakistan. Railway Board. English. ir. Government of Pakistan, Ministry of Railways, Karachi 15 B Pakistan. **LC** HE3300.5. **DD** 354.9549100875.

RAILWAY CARLOADINGS. **Main/Corp** Canada. Statistique Canada. Section des Transports de Surface. **VFOAT** Chargements Ferroviaires. V. 51- June 1974-. 0380-6308. Periodical. CN. English and French. mo. Receiver General for Canada, Statistics Canada Publications, Ottawa Ontario K1A 0T6 Canada. *Railway Carloadings, 0380-6308.*

RAILWAY CARMEN'S JOURNAL. V. 1- 1895-. 0033-8850. Periodical. US. English. mo. Brotherhood Railway Carmen of the United States and Canada, 4929 Main Street, Kansas City MO 64112. **LC** HD6350.R25.

RAILWAY CLERK INTERCHANGE *CEASED.* **VFOAT** Interchange. Vol. 69, No. 1 (Jan. 1970)-V. 84, No. 5 (June/July 1985). 0033-8869. Periodical. US. English. mo. $2.50. Railway Clerk Interchange, 3 Research Place, Rockville MD 20850. **Tel** (301)948-4910. *Railway Clerk, 0270-0778.*

RAILWAY FREIGHT TRAFFIC. **Main/Corp** Statistics Canada. Surface Transport Section. **VFOAT** Trafic Marchandises Ferroviaire. V. 52- 1st Quarter 1974-. 0317-3437. CN. English (French). qt. $4.20. Statistics Canada, Publication Distribution IC, Ottawa Ontario K1A 0T6 Canada. **LC** HE2801. **DD** 385.2640971. *Railway Freight Traffic, 0317-3437.*

RAILWAY FREIGHT TRAFFIC. **Main/Corp** Statistics Canada. Surface Transport Section. **VFOAT** Trafic Marchandises Ferroviaire. 1974-. 0317-3445. CN. Multilingual (text in French). an. Receiver General for Canada, Statistics Canada Publications, Ottawa Ontario K1A 0T6 Canada. **Tel** (800)268-1151. **LC** HE2379. **DD** 385.240971. Provincial and national data on revenue freight carried by Class I and II railways by Canada. Shows origination, terminations, receipts from and deliveries to US rail connections, by 320 SCC-based commodity classes. *Railway Freight Traffic, 0317-3445.*

RAILWAY GAZETTE INTERNATIONAL. V. 126, No. 19- Oct. 1970-. 0373-5346. Periodical. UK. English. mo. $39.00. Business Press International Ltd, Perrymount Road/ Haywards Heath, West Sussex Rh16 3BR England. **Ind/Abst** CIS Abstr., Coal Abstr., Comput. Control Abstr., Electr. Electron. Abstr., Sci. Abstr. Sect. A. Phys. Abstr., Met. Abstr., World Alum. Abstr., Ref. Source, Eng. Index, Phys. Abstr., Eng. Index Annu., Eng. Index Mon. **LC** TF1. **DD** 385.105. **CODEN** RWGIAN. *Railway Gazette, 0033-8907.*

RAILWAY HISTORY MONOGRAPH. (THE RAILWAY HISTORY MONOGRAPH). V. 1- Jan. 1972-. 0093-8505. Periodical. US. English. qt. $10.00. J B Publishing Company, 430 Ivy Avenue, Crete NE 68333. **Tel** (402)826-3356. **Ed** William F Rapp. **LC** TF15. **DD** 385.09. bk rev. **Circ** 100. Articles dealing with railway history-all phases.

RAILWAY LINE CLEARANCES. 0190-6763. US. English. an. National Railway Publishing Inc, 424 West 33rd Street, New York NY 10007. **Tel** (212)563-7210. **LC** TF22. **DD** 385.3120973.

RAILWAY MAGAZINE. (THE RAILWAY MAGAZINE). 0033-8923. Periodical. UK. English. mo. $40.30. Business Press International Ltd, Perrymount Road, Haywards Heath, West Sussex RH163BR England. **Ind/Abst** Ref. Source. **LC** TF1.

Transportation—Railroads

RAILWAY PASSENGER CAR ANNUAL. V. 1- 1973/74-. 0094-2278. US. English. an. RPC Publication, PO Box 211, Park Forest IL 60466. LC TF455. DD 385.330973.

RAILWAY QUARTERLY. 0191-1805. Periodical. US. English. qt. $9.00. Challenge Publishing, 7950 Deering Avenue, Canoga Park CA 91304. Tel (213)887-0550. LC TF1. DD 385.0973.

RAILWAY TRANSPORT. Main/Corp Canada. Statistics Canada. Surface Transport Section. VFOAT Transport Ferroviaire. CN. English and French. an. Information Canada, Receiver General for Canada, Statistics Publications Canada, Ottawa Ontario K1A 0T6 Canada. LC HE2801. DD 385.0971. *Railway Transport.*

RAILWAY TRANSPORT IN CANADA , COMMODITY STATISTICS. See Statistics.

RAILWAY TRANSPORT. PART 1, COMPARATIVE SUMMARY STATISTICS. See Statistics.

RAILWAY TRANSPORT. PART 2, FINANCIAL STATISTICS. See Statistics.

RAILWAY TRANSPORT. PART 5, FREIGHT CARRIED BY PRINCIPAL COMMODITY CLASSES CEASED. VFOAT Transport Ferroviaire. 1958-1981. 0706-2087. CN. French (text in English only, 1958-1969). an. $2.10. Dominion Bureau of Statistics, Public Finance and Transportation Division, Transportation and Public Utilities Section, Ottawa Ontario Canada. DD 385.240971. *Railway Transport.*

RAILWAY TRANSPORT. PART III, EQUIPMENT, TRACK AND FUEL STATISTICS. See Statistics.

RAILWAY TRANSPORT. PART IV, OPERATING AND TRAFFIC STATISTICS. See Statistics.

RAILWAY TRANSPORT: RAILWAY COMMODITY ORIGIN AND DESTINATION STATISTICS. See Statistics.

RAILWAY WORLD ANNUAL. 0082-5891. UK. English. an. $8.25. Ian Allen Ltd, Coombelands House, Addlestone Weybridge KT15 1HY England. Tel 58511. adv acc. Circ 10,000. Annual for rail enthusiasts. Varied content, old and new in the style of parent monthly magazine. *Trains.*

RAILWAYS. VFOAT Railways Southern Africa. Mar. 1977-. Periodical. SA. English. bm. 36.00. Target Communications, PO Box 404, 2153 Jukskei Park South Africa. Tel (011)704-1539. Ed R E Bull. Ind/Abst Comput. Control Abstr., Electr. Electron. Abstr., Sci. Abstr. Sect. A. Phys. Abstr., Phys. Abstr. LC TF1. DD 625.1005. bk rev. adv acc. Circ 2,000. (ctrl). Aimed at engineers in national railways, mines and industry. It conveys developments in railway technology in general. It covers systems, products, people, internationally and locally and other items. *Railway Engineering.*

RAPPORT ANNUEL - COMPAGNIE DES CHEMINS DE FER KINSHASA-DILOLO-LUBUMBASHI. Main/Corp Compagnie des Chemins de fer Kinshasa-Dilolo-Lubumbashi. French. ir. Compaguie des Chemins de fer Kinshasa-Dilolo-Lubumbashi, Place de la Gare, Lubumbashi Zaire. LC HE3460.K5. DD 385.096751.

RAPPORT ANNUEL - SOCIETE NATIONALE DES CHEMINS DE FER LUXEMBOURGEOIS. Main/Corp Societe Nationale des Chemins de fer Luxembourgeois. VFOAT C.F.L. EN . . . . 1962-. French. an. LC HE3130.5. DD 385.0604935.

RELATORIO ANUAL - REDE FERROVIARIA FEDERAL, S. A., SUPERINTENDENCIA REGIONAL, PORTO ALEGRE. Main/Corp Rede Ferroviaria Federal, S.A. Superintendencia Regional, Porto Alegre. BL. Portuguese. ir. LC HE2909.R42. DD 385.09816.

REPORT OF THE COMPTROLLER AND AUDITOR GENERAL OF INDIA, UNION GOVERNMENT (RAILWAYS). Main/Corp India (Republic). Comptroller and Auditor-General. 1970/71-. English. ir. $1.19. Controller of Publications, 6 New Delhi India. LC HE3291. DD 354.5400875. *Central Government Audit Report, Railways.*

REPORT OF THE SELECT COMMITTEE ON RAILWAY ACCOUNTS. Main/Corp South Africa. Parliament. House of Assembly. Select Committee on Railway Accounts. VFOAT Verslag van die Gekose Komitee oor Spoorwegrekenings. SA. Afrikaans (English). ir. 8.70. House of Assembly, Select Committee on Railway Accounts, Government Printer, Pretoria 0001 South Africa. LC HE3419.S8. DD 385.1.

REPORT ON THE USE OF THE GRADE CROSSING PROTECTION FUND. 1978-. US. English. an. LC HE1618.A3. DD 385.312. *Report on use of Grade Crossing Protection Fund.*

REVENUE FREIGHT LOADED AND RECEIVED FROM CONNECTIONS BY COMMODITIES. Began in 1979. Periodical. US. English. wk. $40.00. Association of American Railroads, 1920 L Street NW, Washington DC 20036. Tel (202)835-9100. *Revenue Freight Loaded by Commodities and Total Received from Connections.*

REVISTA AIT. Main/Corp Asociacion de Investigacion del Transporte (Spain). VAT Revista Asociacion de Investigacion del Transporte. Periodical. Spanish (summaries in English, French, and German). ir. Asociacion de Investigacion del Transporte, Alberto Alcocer 38, Madrid-16 Spain. LC TF4. DD 625.105.

REVUE GENERALE DES CHEMINS DE FER. 0035-3183. Periodical. FR. French. ir. $56.93. Centrale des Revues, 11 rue Gossin, 92543 Montrouge Cedex France. Tel 656 52 66. Ind/Abst Eng. Index, Excerpta Med., Comput. Control Abstr., Electr. Electron. Abstr., Sci. Abstr., Phys. Abstr., Sci. Abstr. Sect. A. Phys. Abstr., Eng. Index Annu., Eng. Index Mon., Eng. Index Energy Abstr., Eng. Index Bioeng. Abstr. CODEN RGCFAl. *Revue Generale des Chemins de Fer et des Tramways.*

REVUE GENERALE DES CHEMINS DE FER CEASED. V. 1-20. Periodical. FR. French. mo. $15.96. Centrale des Revues-Dunod, 11 rue Gossin, 92543 Montrouge Cedex France. Tel (1)43 20 15 50. Ed Jean Philippe Bernard. bk rev. adv acc. Circ 4,200. Technical aspects of railway transportation in its widest dense-trains-underground networks and new technologies.

REVUE GENERALE DES CHEMINS DE FER. (FRENCH RAILWAY REVIEW). Vol. 1, No. 1 (Apr. 1983)-. Periodical. UK. English (French). bm. $96.00. Berkshire Ltd. NH Oxford Academic Publishing Company, 242 Banbury Road, Oxford OX2 7DW England. Ind/Abst Comput. Control Abstr., Electr. Electron. Abstr., Sci. Abstr. Sect. A. Phys. Abstr. LC TF1. DD 625.1005.

RT&S. RAILWAY TRACK & STRUCTURES. VFOAT Railway Track & Structures. V. 75- Jan. 1979-. Periodical. US. English. mo. Simmons Boardman Publishing, 508 Birch Street, Bristol CT 06010. Tel (203)582-9546. Ind/Abst Eng. Index. *Railway Track & Structures.*

S & L MUSEUM NEWSLETTER. See Museums.

SERI STATISTIK PENGANGKUTAN KERETA API. RAILWAYS STATISTICS. See Statistics.

SHORELINER. 0162-0282. Periodical. US. English. qt. $8.50. Ronald Hall, 290 North Elm Street, Wallingford CT 06492. LC TF25.N726. DD 625.100974.

SHORELINER SUPPLEMENT. 0162-0746. US. English. Ronald Hall, 280 North Elm Street, Wallingford CT 06492. LC TF25.N726. DD 385.09746.

THE SHORT LINE. 0199-4050. Periodical. US. English. bm. $10.00. The Short Line, PO Box 607, Pleasant Garden NC 27313. Tel (919)674-2168. Ed Garreth M McDonald. bk rev. Circ 1,600. Description of all new shortline-industrial railroad operations. Periodic listings of all rail operations in a given state or area. Disposition/acquisition rail equipment.

SIGNAL UND DRAHT. VFOAT Signal + Draht. 0037-4997. Periodical. GW. German. mo. 136.80. Tetzlaff Verlag Gmbh, Havelstrasse 9, D-6100 Darmstadt West Germany. Tel 06151/380-1. Ed Tetzlaff Verlag Gmbh. Ind/Abst Comput. Control Abstr., Electr. Electron. Abstr., Sci. Abstr. Sect. A. Phys. Abstr. CODEN SIGDAN. bk rev. adv acc. Circ 3,000. Signaling, data processing, process control, measuring and regulating, telecommunications, automation and office machines for the railway sector.

SIGNAL UND SCHIENE. Vol. 1-. 0037-5004. Periodical. SZ. German. mo. $8.21. Kunst & Wissen Erich Bieber, Dufourstrasse 51, CH-8008 Zurich Switzerland. Tel (011)411694420. Ind/Abst Excerpta Med., Comput. Control Abstr., Electr. Electron. Abstr., Sci. Abstr. Sect. A. Phys. Abstr. LC TF3. CODEN SIGSAY.

THE SIGNALMAN'S JOURNAL. V. 1- Jan. 1920-. 0037-5020. Periodical. US. English (French). mo. $10.00. Signalmans Journal, 601 Golf Road/PO Box U, Mt Prospect IL 60056. Ed R T Bates. LC HD6350.R39. adv acc. Circ 15,000. Edited for the men and women who install, test, inspect and maintain signal equipment and systems on railroads and transit systems.

SINTESE FERROVIARIA BRASILEIRA. Began with 1980 V. Portuguese. an. LC HE2921. DD 385.0981.

SISTEMA FERROVIARIO DO BRASIL. Began with V. for 1964. Portuguese. ir. Rede Ferroviaria Federal SA, Diretoria de Planejamento, Departamento Geral de Estatistica, Centro ZC-14 Caixa Postal 1693, 20.000 Rio de Janeiro Brazil. LC HE2921. DD 385.0981.

SISTEMA FERROVIARIO RFFSA. Main/Corp Rede Ferroviaria Federal, S.A. Departamento Geral de Estatistica. VAT Sistema Ferroviario Rede Ferroviaria Federal Sociedade Anonima. Portuguese. ir. LC HE2930.R5. DD 385.314.

THE SOO. (THE SOO : THE MAGAZINE OF THE SOO LINE HISTORICAL AND TECHNICAL SOCIETY). No. 1 (Sept. 1977)-. 0733-5296. Periodical. US. English. qt. $11.00 Membership, $3.00 Each Issue. J Fishbein Secretary, PO Box 1126, Manitowoc WI 54220. LC TF25.S65. DD 385.0977.

SOUNDER NEWSLETTER (SNOQUALMIE, WASH. : 1980). See History (General) - History of North, South, and Central America.

SOUTHERN PACIFIC LOCOMOTIVE DIRECTORY. See Yearbooks, Almanacs, Directories.

SOUTHERN PACIFIC MOTIVE POWER ANNUAL. Began with Vol. for 1966-1967. 0584-4568. US. English. ir. Chatham Publishing Company, PO Box 283, Burlingame CA 94010. LC TJ603.3.S6. DD 625.2660978.

SPRECHSTELLENVERZEICHNIS. Main/Corp Austria. Generaldirektion der Osterreichischen Bundesbahnen. German. an. LC HE3054. DD 385.025436.

STANDARD TRANSPORTATION COMMODITY CODE. Main/Corp Association of American Railroads. Began with 1963 issue. 0160-6875. US. English. Association of American Railroads, American Railroads Building, 50 F Street NW, Washington DC 20001. LC HF1052. DD 338.0012.

STATE RAIL PLAN, ANNUAL UPDATE. Main/Corp West Virginia Railroad Maintenance Authority. US. English. an. West Virginia Railroad, Maintenance Authority, 922 Quarrier Street, Charleston WV 25301. LC TF24.W4. DD 385.09754.

STATE RAIL PLAN . . . UPDATE. US. English. an. Commonwealth of Massachusetts, Executive Office of Transportation & Construction, 1 Ashburton Place, Boston MA 02108. LC HE2771.M4. DD 385.068.

STATISTICS OF RAILROADS OF CLASS I IN THE UNITED STATES. See Statistics.

STATISTIQUES - REGIE NATIONALE DES CHEMINS DE FER DU CAMEROUN. See Statistics.

STEAM PASSENGER SERVICE DIRECTORY. See Yearbooks, Almanacs, Directories.

SUJI DE MIRU MINTETSU. Japanese. ir. 200. Unyu Keizai Kenkyu Senta, 1 Shiba Kotohiracho Minato-ku, Tokyo 105 Japan. LC HE3351.

SUMMARY AND ANALYSIS, RAILROAD-HIGHWAY GRADE CROSSING ACCIDENTS. Main/Corp Washington Utilities and Transportation Commission. 0360-0734. US. English. Washington Utilities and Transportation Commission, Highways-Licenses Building, Olympia WA 98501. LC HE1618.A3. DD 388.314.

Transportation—Roads and Traffic

SUMMARY AND ANALYSIS. RAILROAD OPERATIONAL ACCIDENTS. (SUMMARY AND ANALYSIS RAILROAD OPERATIONAL ACCIDENTS). **Main/Corp** Washington Utilities and Transportation Commission. 0147-9717. US. English. an. LC HE1780.5.W2. DD 385.

SUMMARY OF ACCIDENTS INVESTIGATED BY THE FEDERAL RAILROAD ADMINISTRATION. (SUMMARY OF ACCIDENTS INVESTIGATED BY THE FEDERAL RAILROAD ADMINISTRATION IN THE . . .). 0092-2781. US. English. an. Federal Railroad Administration, Office of Safety, 400 Seventh Street SW, Washington DC 20590.

SUMMARY OF ACCIDENTS/INCIDENTS REPORTED BY ALL LINE-HAUL AND SWITCHING AND TERMINAL RAILROAD COMPANIES. Periodical. US. English. mo. US Department of Transportation, Federal Aviation Administration, 400 7th Street SW, Washington DC 20590. *Summary of Accidents Reported by all Line-Haul Switching and Terminal Railroad Companies, 0565-5307.*

SUMMARY OF O-D TRIPS (ALL TRAINS). Main/Corp Amtrak. VFOAT Ranking Summary of O/D Trips. 1977-. US. English. ir. Federal Railroad Administration, Office of Rail Systems Analysis and Information, 400 7th Street SW, Washington DC 20590.

SUPPLEMENTARY BUDGET STATEMENT OF PAKISTAN RAILWAYS. Main/Corp Pakistan. Railway Board. English. ir. Government of Pakistan, Karachi 15 B Pakistan. LC HE3300.5. DD 354.54910072254.

SVENSK JARNVAGSTARIFFTAXA OCH SVERIGES JARNVAGSSTATIONER OCH POSTANSTALTER. Swedish. an. LC HE3184.

TECHNICAL PAPERS PRESENTED AT GENERAL SESSIONS AND COMMITTEE WORKSHOPS. ANNUAL MEETING. (TECHNICAL PAPERS PRESENTED AT GENERAL SESSIONS AND COMMITTEE WORKSHOPS . . . ANNUAL MEETING). Main/Corp Association of American Railroads. Communication and Signal Division. Meeting. VFOAT Technical Papers and Committee Reports . . . Annual Meeting. 19th (1979)-. 0730-935X. US. English. an. Communication and Signal Section AAR, 1920 L Street NW, Washington DC 20036. LC TF615. DD 625.16505. *Technical Papers Presented at General Sessions and Committee Workshops . . . Annual Meeting, 0730-935X.*

TEXAS RAILROAD COMMISSION SECONDARY RECOVERY APPLICATION SUMMARY. Main/Corp Railroad Commission of Texas. VFOAT Secondary Recovery Railroad Commission Application Summaries. US. English. an. PO Box 12156, Capitol Station, Austin TX 78711. LC TN872.T4. DD 338.2728209764.

THIS IS SAR & H : RAILWAYS HANDBOOK. Main/Corp South African Railways and Harbours. VFOAT This is South African Railways. SA. English. ir. Thomson Publications, PO Box 8308, Johannesburg 2000 South Africa. LC HE3419.S8. DD 3850968.

THOMAS COOK INTERNATIONAL TIMETABLE. Jan. 1977-. 0141-2701. Periodical. UK. English (French, and German). mo. Thomas Cook Ltd, Thorpe Wood, Peterborough PE3 6SB England. LC HE3004. DD 385.2042094. *Thomas Cook Continental Timetable.*

TRACTION AND TRANSMISSION. A MONTHLY SUPPLEMENT TO ENGINEERING. *See* Engineering - Electricity, Electrical Engineering, Electronics.

TRAFFIC WORLD. *See* Transportation - Roads and Traffic.

TRAINS (MILWAUKEE, WIS. : 1954). (TRAINS). Vol. 14, No. 5 (Mar. 1954)-. 0041-0934. Periodical. US. English. mo. $59.00. Kalmbach Publishing Company, 1027 North 7th Street, Milwaukee WI 53233. Tel (414)272-2060. LC TF1. DD 385.0973. *Trains & Travel.*

TRAKCJA I WAGONY. V. 1- Jan. 1978-. Periodical. PL. Polish. ir. Centrala Kolpotazu Prasy I Wydawnictw RSW Prasa-Ksiazka-Ruch, UI Towarowa 28, 00-958 Warszawa Poland. LC TF4.

TRANSIT FACT BOOK. Main/Corp American Public Transit Association. 1974/75-. 0149-3132. US. English. an. $1.00. American Public Transit Association, 1225 Connecticut Avenue NW/Suite 200, Washington DC 20036. LC HE4441. DD 388.40973. *Transit Fact Book.*

TRANSPORT STATISTICS IN THE UNITED STATES. *See* Statistics.

IL TRENO. Main/Corp Azienda Autonoma Delle Ferrovie Dello Stato (Italy). IT. Italian. ir. 5000 Single Issue. Conto Corrente Postale Intestato A: Banca Nacionale Delle Comunicazione, Ufficio Ragineria Dei Servizi Centrale FS, Roma Italy. LC HE3094.

TROLLEY TALK. Began with Sept. 1954 issue. 0148-8406. Periodical. US. English. bm. 59 Euclid Avenue, Cincinnati OH 45215. LC TF701. DD 388.460973.

TRUDY. Main/Corp Vsesoiuznyi Nauchno-Issledovatelskii Institut Vagonstroeniia. UR. Russian. 1.10 Each Issue. LC TF371.

TRUDY INSTITUTOV INZHENEROV ZHELEZNODOROZHNOGO TRANSPORTA. Monographic Series. UR. Russian. Ind/Abst Math. Rev., Chem. Abstr. LC TF4. CODEN TIITDR. *Trudy.*

TURNOUT. (THE TURNOUT). No. 1- Sept. 1972-. 0227-244X. Periodical. CN. English. mo. $12.00. Canadian Railroad Historical Association, Toronto & York Division, PO Box 5849 Terminal A, Toronto Ontario M5W 1P3 Canada. Tel (416)244-3718. Ed John P Picur. DD 385.0971. bk rev. adv acc. Circ 165. (ctrl). Club newsletter containing regional railroad and historical news and short features. Uses black and white photographs only.

U.S. RAIL NEWS. VAT United States Rail News. 0275-3758. Periodical. US. English. bw. US Rail News, PO Box 7005, Huntington Woods MI 48070. Tel (301)587-6300. Ed Andrew Stephens. Report on all aspects of the US rail industry- legislation, regulation, funding, business news on mergers and acquisitions, labor relations, marketing techniques and successes.

UPDATE, NEW JERSEY STATE RAIL PLAN. VFOAT New Jersey State Rail Plan. US. English. an. New Jersey Department of Transportation, 1035 Parkway Avenue, Trenton NJ 08625. Tel (609)292-1530. LC HE2771.N5. DD 385.068. Circ 400. (ctrl). Evaluation of New Jersey rail line segments for inclusion in the state rail assistance program.

VERKEHR. REIHE 2 : EISENBAHNVERKEHR. Main/Corp Germany (West). Statistisches Bundesamt. Series/Titl Fachserie 8. 1976-. German. ir. 16.10. LC HE3071. DD 385.20943. *Verkehr. Reihe 4: Eisenbahverkehr.*

VERKEHR UND TECHNIK. 0042-4005. Periodical. GW. German. mo. 146.40. Erich Schmidt Verlag GMBH, PO Box 7330-40, Viktoriastr 44-A, D4800 Bielefeld 1 West Germany. Tel 0521/66061. Ind/Abst Excerpta Med. LC TF3. bk rev. adv acc. Circ 3,236. (ctrl). Traffic and technical science magazine.

VERKSAMHETSBERATTELSE CEASED. Main/Corp Statens Jarnvagar. 1970/71-. Swedish (summaries in English, French, and German). ir. LC HE3181. *Budgetarsredovisning.*

VIRGINIA STATE RAIL PLAN . . . UPDATE. US. English. an. Rail Transportation Division, Virginia Department of Highways and Transportation, 1221 East Broad Street, Richmond VA 23219. LC HE2771.V8. DD 385.068.

WESTERN CANADIAN STEAM LOCOMOTIVE DIRECTORY. *See* Yearbooks, Almanacs, Directories.

WESTERN RAILROADER AND WESTERN RAILFAN. 0149-4996. Periodical. US. English. mo. $3.00. PO Box 688, San Mateo CA 94401. LC TF23.6. DD 385.0978.

WHEEL CLICKS. 0043-4744. Periodical. US. English. mo. Pacific Railroad Society, PO Box 8726, San Marino CA 91108.

THE WISCONSIN STATE RAIL PLAN. VFOAT Wisconsin Railroad Plan. 1977-. US. English. an. Wisconsin Department of Transportation, Madison WI 53701. LC TF24.W6. DD 385.09775.

WORKING PAPER SERIES - CANADIAN INSTITUTE OF GUIDED GROUND TRANSPORT. (WORKING PAPER SERIES). 0702-8709. CN. English. ir. Canadian Institute of Guided Ground Transport, Queen's University, Kingston Ontario Canada. DD 625.1.

YEARBOOK OF RAILROAD FACTS. *See* Yearbooks, Almanacs, Directories.

ZEITSCHRIFT FUR EISENBAHNWESEN UND VERKEHRSTECHNIK. (ZEITSCHRIFT FUR EISENBAHNWESEN UND VERKEHRSTECHNIK : ZEV). VFOAT ZEV. Vol. 96, Issue 1 (Jan. 1972)-. 0373-322X. Periodical. German. mo. 236.-. Georg Siemens Verlagsbuchhandlung, Lutzowstrasse 105/106 Postfach 3148, D-1000 Berlin 30 West Germany. Tel (030)2613415. Ed Manfred Benzenberg. Ind/Abst Eng. Index Annu., Eng. Index Mon., Eng. Index Bioeng. Abstr., Eng. Index Energy Abstr., Excerpta Med., Int. Aerosp. Abstr., Comput. Control Abstr., Electr. Electron. Abstr., Sci. Abstr. Sect. A. Phys. Abstr., Chem. Abstr., Eng. Index Mon. Author Index, Energy Res. Abstr. LC T3. CODEN ZEVGAK. bk rev. adv acc. Circ 4,000. The oldest technical scientific journal for railways and transport of Germany. *Glasers Annalen.*

ZELEZNICNI OBZOR. Periodical. CS. Czech. mo. Artia, PO Box 790, Praha 1 Czechoslovakia. LC HD8039.R12.

ZHELEZNODOROZHNYI TRANSPORT. Periodical. UR. Russian. mo. $41.50. Victor Kamkin Inc (70280), 12224 Parklawn Drive, Rockville MD 20852. Tel (301)881-5973. LC HE7.

ROADS AND TRAFFIC

200TH HIGHEST HOUR TRAFFIC VOLUMES, TENNESSEE. VFOAT Two Hundredth Highest Hour Traffic Volumes, Tennessee. US. English. LC HE371.T2. DD 388.314209768.

AAMVA BULLETIN. *See* Law Enforcement.

ACCIDENT AND VIOLATION ANALYSIS FOR LICENSED OREGON DRIVERS. Main/Corp Oregon. Motor Vehicles Division. 0360-9847. US. English. Department of Transportation Motor Vehicle Division, Salem OR 97314. LC HE5614.3.O7. DD 363.125209795021.

ACCIDENTS DE LA CIRCULATION SUR LA VOIE PUBLIQUE. *See* Public Health and Safety.

ACQUISITIONS TRIMESTRIELLES - FONDS D'ETUDES POUR LA SECURITE ROUTIERE. SERVICE DOCUMENTATION. Main/Corp Fonds d'Etudes pour la Securite Routiere. Service Documentation. VFOAT Driemaandelijkse Aanwinsten. No. 1 (April/June 1981)-. 0304-0690. Periodical. BE. French (Dutch, English, and German). ir. Fonds d'Etudes pour la Securite Routiere, Chassee de Haecht 1405, 1130 Bruxelles Belgium.

ACTIVITIES - COMMITTEE ON RIGHT-OF-WAY, AMERICAN ASSOCIATION OF STATE HIGHWAY AND TRANSPORTATION OFFICIALS. (ACTIVITIES, ANNUAL REPORT OF PROGRESS AND PAPERS ON HIGHWAY RIGHT-OF-WAY PROBLEMS). Main/Corp American Association of State Highway and Transportation Officials. Right-of-Way Committee. 0363-2059. US. English. an. American Association of State Highway & Transportation, 400 17th Street SW, Washington DC 20590. LC KF5525.Z95. DD 388.106273. *Activities, Annual Report of Progress and Papers on Highway Right-of-Way Problems Presented at Annual Convention.*

ALASKA AND THE ALASKA HIGHWAY. Main/Corp American Automobile Association. 1946-. US. English. an. LC F909. DD 917.98.

ALASKA HIGHWAYS ANNUAL TRAFFIC VOLUME REPORT. Main/Corp Alaska. Dept. of Transportation and Public Facilities. Transportation Planning Division. VFOAT Annual Traffic Volume Report. US. English. an. $5.00. LC HE371.A5. DD 388.31409798.

ALBERTA TRAFFIC COLLISION FACTS. 1982-. 0825-5709. CN. English. an. Alberta Transportation Safety Branch, Twin Atria Building, 4999-98 Avenue, Edmonton Alberta T6B 2X3 Canada. LC HE5614.5.C2. DD 363.1252097123. *Alberta Collision Facts, 0825-5695.*

ANNUAL CONFERENCE PROCEEDINGS. THEME SESSIONS - ROADS AND TRANSPORTATION ASSOCIATION OF CANADA. (ANNUAL CONFERENCE PROCEEDINGS, THEME SESSIONS - ROADS AND TRANSPORTATION ASSOCIATION OF

Transportation—Roads and Traffic

CANADA). **Main/Corp** Roads and Transportation Association of Canada. 1975-. 0380-657X. CN. English. an. $7.50. Roads and Transportation Association of Canada, Ottawa Ontario Canada. **DD** 380.50971. *Proceedings of the Annual Conference, 0080-3324.*

ANNUAL NEVADA STREET AND HIGHWAY CONFERENCE. (NEVADA STREET AND HIGHWAY CONFERENCE). **Main/Conf** Nevada Street and Highway Conference. **Series/Titl** Engineering Report 49. 0550-7898. US. English. an. University of Nevada, Civil Engineering Department, Reno NV 89507. **LC** TA1. **DD** 625.709793.

ANNUAL REPORT - ARIZONA STATE HIGHWAY COMMISSION. (ANNUAL REPORT). **Main/Corp** Arizona. State Highway Commission. 0092-2854. US. English. an. Arizona Department of Transportation, State Highway Commission, 20 South 17th Avenue 222 E, Phoenix AZ 85026. **LC** TE24.A6. **DD** 353.9791008781.

ANNUAL REPORT, HIGHWAY SAFETY IMPROVEMENT PROGRAMS IN VIRGINIA. *See* Public Health and Safety.

ANNUAL REPORT - INDIANA. TOLL ROAD DIVISION. **Main/Corp** Indiana. Toll Road Division. 28th (1981)-. US. English. an. Toll Road Division, 52551 Ash Road, PO Box 1, Granger IN 46530. **LC** HE356.I6. **DD** 353.77200864204406. *Annual Report.*

ANNUAL REPORT - MISSISSIPPI STATE HIGHWAY DEPARTMENT. **Main/Corp** Mississippi. Highway Dept. 0363-5295. US. English. an. PO Box 1850, Jackson MS 39205. **LC** HE356.M7. **DD** 353.976200878105.

ANNUAL REPORT - MISSOURI HIGHWAY AND TRANSPORTATION COMMISSION. **Main/Corp** Missouri Highway and Transportation Commission. 1983-. US. English. an. **LC** HE356.M8. **DD** 353.977800875006. *Review.*

ANNUAL REPORT - MOTOR VEHICLE BRANCH. (ANNUAL REPORT - MANITOBA. MOTOR VEHICLE BRANCH). **Main/Corp** Manitoba. Motor Vehicle Branch. **VAT** Annual Report - Manitoba. Department of Highways and Transportation. Motor Vehicle Branch. 0225-1728. CN. English. an. Free. Department of Highways and Transportation, Motor Vehicle Branch, 1075 Portage Avenue, Winnipeg Manitoba R3G 0S1 Canada. **LC** HE5614.5.C2. **DD** 363.1252097127021. (ctrl).

ANNUAL REPORT - NATIONAL SWEDISH ROAD AND TRAFFIC RESEARCH INSTITUTE CEASED. **Main/Corp** Statens Vag- Och Trafikinstitut. -1981/82. 0346-752X. SW. English. ir. National Road and Traffic Research Institute, Fack 581 01 Linkoping, Stockholm Sweden. **LC** HE363.S8. **DD** 354.485008781.

ANNUAL REPORT - NEW JERSEY HIGHWAY AUTHORITY, GARDEN STATE PARKWAY, GARDEN STATE ARTS CENTER. **Main/Corp** New Jersey Highway Authority. 0149-1261. US. English. an. **LC** HE356.N5. **DD** 388.1209749.

ANNUAL REPORT - NEW MEXICO TRAFFIC SAFETY COMMISSION. **Main/Corp** New Mexico. Traffic Safety Commission. 0363-3977. US. English. an. 339 P E R A Building, Santa Fe NM 87503. **LC** HE5614.3.N47. **DD** 353.978900783.

ANNUAL REPORT OF FATAL & INJURY MOTOR VEHICLE TRAFFIC ACCIDENTS. (ANNUAL REPORT OF FATAL AND INJURY MOTOR VEHICLE TRAFFIC ACCIDENTS). 1973-. 0276-7678. US. English. an. $3.40. Staff Services Section/ California Highway Patrol, PO Box 898, Sacramento CA 95804. **LC** HE5614.3.C3. **DD** 363.125209794021.

ANNUAL REPORT OF THE BOARD OF EXAMINERS FOR COUNTY HIGHWAY AND CITY STREET SUPERINTENDENTS (NEBRASKA). (ANNUAL REPORT). **Main/Corp** Nebraska. Board of Examiners for County Highway and City Street Superintendents. 0098-6364. US. English. an. State of Nebraska, Board of Examiners for County & City Street Superintendents, Lincoln NE 68509. **LC** HE356.N36. **DD** 353.9782008781.

ANNUAL REPORT OF THE MOTOR ACCIDENTS BOARD FOR THE YEAR ENDED 30 JUNE . . . (VICTORIA). **Main/Corp** Victoria. Motor Accidents Board. English. an. **LC** HE5614.5.A8. **DD** 354.9450087831.

ANNUAL REPORT OF THE SOUTH CAROLINA DEPARTMENT OF HIGHWAYS AND PUBLIC TRANSPORTATION TO THE GENERAL ASSEMBLY. **Main/Corp** South Carolina. Dept. of Highways and Public Transportation. 1976/77-. US. English. an. 1100 Senate Street, Box 191, Columbia SC 29202. **LC** HE356.S5. **DD** 353.975700878105.

ANNUAL REPORT OF THE STATE OF ALABAMA HIGHWAY DEPARTMENT. **Main/Corp** Alabama. State Highway Dept. 1st- 1911/12-. 0160-9246. US. English. an. State of Alabama, State Highway Department, Montgomery AL 36104. **LC** TE24.A2. **DD** 625.7061761.

ANNUAL REPORT OF THE TRAFFIC BOARD FOR THE YEAR ENDING JUNE 30 . . . (WESTERN AUSTRALIA). **Main/Corp** Western Australia. Traffic Board. 1982-. English. an. **LC** HE368.Z6. **DD** 354.94100878106. *Annual Report.*

ANNUAL REPORT ON HIGHWAY SAFETY IMPROVEMENT PROGRAMS. **Main/Corp** United States. Dept. of Transportation. 1st- 1973/74-. 0098-3209. US. English. an. Superintendent of Documents, US Government Printing Office, Washington DC 20402. **LC** HE5614.2. **DD** 388.3140973.

ANNUAL REPORT ON RURAL TRAFFIC MOVEMENT IN ETHIOPIA. English. an. **LC** HE373.E85. **DD** 388.3140963.

ANNUAL REPORT ON THE PUBLIC INFORMATION AND EDUCATION COUNTERMEASURE OF ALCOHOL SAFETY ACTION PROJECTS. **Main/Corp** United States. National Highway Traffic Safety Administration. Office of Driver and Pedestrian Traffic Safety Programs. 0099-2380. US. English. an. US Department of Transportation, Federal Highway Administration, Washington DC 20590. **LC** HE5620.D7. **DD** 614.862.

ANNUAL REPORT - OPERATION C.A.R.E. (U.S.). **Main/Corp** Operation C.A.R.E. (U.S.). US. English. an. Combined Accident Reduction Effort, 301 State Office Building, 100 North Senate Avenue, Indianapolis IN 46204. **LC** HE5614.2. **DD** 363.1250973.

ANNUAL REPORT, SAFETY. US. English. an. **LC** HE5614.3.I5. **DD** 312.44.

ANNUAL REPORT, SOUTH DAKOTA GOVERNOR'S TRAFFIC SAFETY PROGRAM. **Main/Corp** South Dakota. Division of Highway Safety. State & Community Programs. US. English. an. Department of Public Safety, Division of Highway Safety, Pierre SD 57501. **LC** HE5614.3.S8. **DD** 614.86209783.

ANNUAL REPORT - SOUTH DAKOTA. STATE HIGHWAY COMMISSION. **Main/Corp** South Dakota. State Highway Commission. 1913-1916, 1918/1919-. US. English.

ANNUAL REPORT, STATUS OF THE STATE SYSTEM OF EXPRESS HIGHWAYS AND FREEWAYS (KANSAS). **Main/Corp** Kansas. Dept. of Transportation. Planning and Development Dept. 4th-1976-. US. English. an. Kansas Department of Transportation, Planning & Development, Topeka KS 66612. **LC** HE356.K2. **DD** 388.12. *Annual Report, Status of the State System of Express Highways and Freeways.*

ANNUAL REPORT - TEXAS HIGHWAY DEPARTMENT. **Main/Corp** Texas. State Highway Dept. 0147-6017. US. English. an. Texas Highway Department, Finance Department, Austin TX 78701. **LC** HE356.T4. **DD** 353.97640087805.

ANNUAL REPORT TO THE OKLAHOMA TURNPIKE AUTHORITY. *See* Public Administration.

ANNUAL REPORTS - INDIANA STATE HIGHWAY COMMISSION, DIVISION OF ACCOUNTING & CONTROL. **Main/Corp** Indiana. State Highway Commission (1961-1981). Division of Accounting and Control. **VAT** Annual Reports - Indiana State Highway Commission, Division of Accounting and Control. 0363-9312. US. English. an. **LC** HE356.I6. **DD** 353.9772008781.

ANNUAL SPEED STUDY, WASHINGTON . . . AND CERTIFICATION OF 55 MPH ENFORCEMENT. US. English. an. Department of Transportation, Highway Administration Building, Olympia WA 98504. **LC** HE371.W2. **DD** 338.214409797. *Annual Speed Study (Olympia, Wash.).*

ANNUAL TRAFFIC REPORT (CARSON CITY, NEVADA). (ANNUAL TRAFFIC REPORT). US. English. an. $7.50. **LC** HE371.N3. **DD** 388.314209793. *Annual Traffic Report, Nevada Highways.*

ANNUAL TRAFFIC REPORT (WASHINGTON STATE). **Main/Corp** Washington (State). Public Transportation and Planning Division. US. English. an. Washington State Transportation Commission, Highway Administration Building, Olympia WA 98504. **LC** HE371.W2. **DD** 388.314209797.

ANNUAL WORK PROGRAM - WASHINGTON TRAFFIC SAFETY COMMISSION. *See* Public Health and Safety.

ANUARIO ESTATISTICO DE TRANSITO NO ESTADO DO PARANA. *See* Yearbooks, Almanacs, Directories.

ARIZONA TRAFFIC. **Main/Corp** Arizona. Dept. of Transportation. Planning Survey Group. 0360-7720. US. English. an. Arizona Department of Transportation, 206 South 17th Avenue, Phoenix AZ 85007. **LC** HE356.A7. **DD** 388.31409791. *Arizona Traffic.*

ARIZONA'S TRAFFIC ACCIDENT SUMMARY. (ARIZONA TRAFFIC ACCIDENT SUMMARY). **Main/Corp** Arizona. Office of Highway Safety. 1974-. 0096-9796. US. English. an. Arizona Department of Transportation, 20 South 17th Avenue 222 East, Phoenix AZ 85007. **Tel** (602)255-7724. **LC** HE5614.3.A6. **DD** 388.314. *Arizona's Traffic Accident Summary, 0096-9796.*

ARKANSAS HIGHWAY COMMISSION ANNUAL REPORT TO THE GOVERNOR OF ARKANSAS. **Main/Corp** Arkansas. State Highway Commission. US. English. an. State Highway Commission, POB 2261, Little Rock AR 72203. **LC** HE28.A8. **DD** 353.97670086406.

ASPECTS TECHNIQUES DE LA SECURITE ROUTIERE. VFOAT Technical Aspects of Road Safety. Began with Mar. 1960 Issue. Periodical. French (English, Flemish, and/or German). qt. **LC** HE5601. **DD** 363.12505. (cum index).

AUSTRALIAN ROAD INDEX. *See* Indexes/Abstracts.

AUSTRALIAN ROAD RESEARCH. V. 1- Mar. 1962-. 0005-0164. Periodical. AT. English. qt. 30.00. Australian Road Research Board, PO Box 156 Bag 4, Nunawading Vermont Victoria 3131 Australia. **Tel** (03)235-1555. Ed Keiran Sharp. **Ind/Abst** Eng. Index Mon., Eng. Index Bioeng. Abstr., Eng. Index Energy Abstr., Chem. Abstr., Nuci. Sci. Abstr., Eng. Index Annu., Eng. Index. **LC** TE121. **CODEN** ARDRAH. bk rev. **Circ** 2,000. Road research; discussion, enquiry and solutions to road, traffic, and road transport problems and description of the Australian road research board's activities.

AUSTRALIAN ROADS. AT. English. an. NAASRA Secretariat, 5th Level Legal & General Abuse, PO Box 489, Milsons Point NSW 2061. **Tel** (02)957-6188. **LC** TE121. **DD** 625.70994. **Circ** 4,000. (ctrl).

AUTOMATIC TRAFFIC RECORDER REPORT. 1979-. US. English. an. **LC** HE371.W8. **DD** 388.314209787. *Automatic Counter Report.*

AUTOSTRADE. Yearly V. 1- Jan. 1959-. Periodical. IT. Italian. mo. Concessioni e Costruzioni Autostrade SPA, Trade Spa Via A Nibby 20, Rome Italy. **LC** TE4. **DD** 338.12205. (cum index).

AVERAGE DAILY TRAFFIC FLOWS : PERTH METROPOLITAN REGION. **Main/Corp** Western Australia. Main Roads Dept. English. ir. **LC** HE373.A983. **DD** 388.4131409941.

AVERAGE DAILY TRAFFIC VOLUMES ON INTERSTATE, ARTERIAL AND PRIMARY ROUTES. 0094-7415. US. English. Division of Traffic and Safety, Richmond VA 23219. **LC** HE371.V8. **DD** 388.31409755. *Average Daily Traffic Volumes on Interstate and Primary Routes.*

AVTOMOBILNYE DOROGI. Began in July 1954. 0005-2353. Periodical. UR. Russian. mo. $40.50. Victor Kamkin Inc (70004), 12224 Parklawn Drive, Rockville MD 20852. **Tel** (301)881-5973. **Ind/Abst** Energy Res. Abstr. Index in last issue of volume - attached. *Stroitelstvo Dorog.*

BASIC ROAD STATISTICS. *See* Statistics.

Transportation—Roads and Traffic

BERICHT UBER DIE FORDERUNG VON FORSCHUNGS- UND ENTWICKLUNGSVORHABEN UND UBER DIE ERTEILUNG VON FORSCHUNGS- UND ENTWICKLUNGSAUFTRAGEN. Main/Corp Austria. Bundesministerium fur Bauten und Technik. Bundesstrassenverwaltung. VFOAT Jahresbericht - Bundesministerium fur Bauten und Technik, Bundesstrassenverwaltung. German. ir. Bundesministerium fur Bauten und Technik, Stubenring 1, A-1010 Wien Austria. LC TE192.

DER BERLIN-VERKEHR. Main/Corp Berlin (West Berlin). Der Senator fur Verkehr und Betriebe. German. ir. Senator fur Verkear und Betriebe, Nurnberger Strasse 53-55, 1 Berlin 30 West Germany. LC HE363.G34.

BETTER ROADS. VFOAT Better Roads Magazine. V. 1- 1931-. 0006-0208. Periodical. US. English. mo. Better Roads, PO Box 558, Park Ridge IL 60068. Tel (312)693-7710. Ed William Dannhausen. Ind/Abst Eng. Index Annu., Eng. Index Mon., Eng. Index Bioeng. Abstr., Eng. Index Energy Abstr., Energy Inf. Abstr., Environ. Abstr., Eng. Index. CODEN BEROAW. bk rev. adv acc. Circ 39,000. (ctrl). Governmental road, street, bridge construction, maintenance, traffic control safety, funding at federal, state, county, town/township road and city street levels.

BID OPENING REPORT. Main/Corp United States. Federal Highway Administration. 0146-9037. US. English. US Department of Transportation, Federal Highway Administration, Washington DC 20590. LC HE355.A3. DD 388.11.

BIENNIAL AND STATISTICAL REPORT - NEBRASKA. DEPT. OF ROADS. See Statistics.

BIENNIAL HIGHWAY IMPROVEMENT PROGRAM. Main/Corp Indiana. Dept. of Highways. Division of Planning. July 1, 1982 to June 30, 1984-. US. English. an. Indiana Department of Highways/Division of Planning, Room 1205/State Office Building, 100 North Senate Avenue, Indianapolis IN 46204. LC TE24.I6. DD 388.1.

BIENNIAL REPORT - NORTH DAKOTA STATE HIGHWAY DEPARTMENT. Main/Corp North Dakota. State Highway Dept. US. English. be. North Dakota State Highway Department, Capitol Grounds, Bismarck ND 58505. LC TE24.N9. DD 353.97840086405. Report.

BIENNIAL REPORT OF ALTERATIONS TO THE STATE HIGHWAY SYSTEM. Main/Corp Connecticut. Bureau of Highways. Division of Engineering Services. Engineering Data and Inventory Section. VFOAT Alterations to the State Highway System. 1977-. 0098-9754. US. English. be. LC HE356.C7. Biennial Report of Alterations to the State Highway System, 0098-9754.

BOLETIN DE INFORMACION DEL LABORATORIO DE CARRETERAS Y GEOTECNIA. Main/Corp Laboratorio de Carreteras y Geotecnia (Spain). Began with Jan./Feb. 1980 issue. 0210-9085. Periodical. SP. Spanish. bm. Laboratorio de Carreteras y Geotecnia Jose Luis Escario, Alfonso XII 3, Madrid-7 Spain. Ind/Abst GeoRef. LC TE4.M3.

BOSTON EXTENSION : ANNUAL AUDIT REPORT OF THE MASSACHUSETTS TURNPIKE AUTHORITY TO THE FIRST NATIONAL BANK OF BOSTON AS TRUSTEE. Main/Corp Massachusetts Turnpike Authority. US. English. an. Massachusetts Turnpike Authority, Suite 3000/Prudential Center, Boston MA 02199. LC HE356.M4. DD 353.97440087812.

BULLETIN - VIRGINIA DEPARTMENT OF HIGHWAYS AND TRANSPORTATION. Main/Corp Virginia. Dept. of Highways and Transportation. 0360-9413. Periodical. US. English. bm. Virginia Department of Highways and Transportation, 1221 East Broad Street, Richmond VA 23219. Ind/Abst Sociol. Abstr., MLA Int. Bibliogr. Books Artic. Mod. Lang. Lit., Lang. Lang. Behav. Abstr. LC TE24.V8. DD 625.709755. Virginai Highway Bulletin.

CA. VAT Carreteras Autopistas. No. 1- May 1975-. Periodical. Spanish. ir. 1,400. Asociacion Espanola de la Carretera, Serrano 57, Madrid Spain. LC TE4.

CAROLINA HIGHWAYS. Began in 1949. 0008-6789. Periodical. US. English. bm. Carolina Highways, Box 191, Columbia SC 29202. LC HE356.S5. DD 388.109757.

CAUSEWAYS & THEATRE PROJECTS. ANNUAL REPORT. (CAUSEWAYS & THEATRE PROJECTS; ANNUAL REPORT). Main/Corp Jones Beach State Parkway Authority. VAT Causeways and Theatre Projects: Annual Report. 0277-6286. US. English. an. Jones Beach State Parkway Authority, Babylon NY 11702.

CENTERLINE. VFOAT Nebraska Centerline. US. English. Accident Record Bureau, Lincoln NE 68508. LC HE5614.3.N35. DD 388.314.

LA CIRCULATION ROUTIERE : FAITS ET CHIFFRES. Main/Corp Union Routiere de France. French. ir. Union Routiere de France, 54 Avenue Marceau, Paris France 75008. LC HE373.F7.

CITY STREET FINANCIAL REPORT (OREGON. DEPT. OF TRANSPORTATION.). Main/Corp Oregon. Dept. of Transportation. Finance Branch. US. English. an. LC HE356.O7. DD 388.41109795.

CODE OF FEDERAL REGULATIONS. 23, HIGHWAYS. See Law.

COMPARATIVE MOTOR VEHICLE TRAFFIC ACCIDENT STATISTICS IN CITIES OF 5,000 POPULATION AND OVER. See Statistics.

CONCEPTS FOR TRAFFIC SAFETY. 1- Spring 1968-. 0588-9715. Periodical. US. English. 151 Farmington Avenue, Hartford CT 06156. Drivotrainer Digest.

CONTAGENS DE TRAFEGO : TEMPORADA DE VERAO. Main/Corp Rio Grande do Sul, Brazil (State). Departamento Autonomo de Estradas de Rodagem. 1977-. BL. Portuguese. ir. Secretaria dos Transportes, Departamento Autonomo de Estradas de Rodagem, Porto Alegre Brazil. LC HE373.B72. DD 388.31409816. Contagens de Trafego: Temporada de Verao.

CONTINUOUS COUNT TRAFFIC DATA. Main/Corp Georgia. Traffic Survey Branch. 1972-. 0094-9965. US. English. an. LC HE371.G4. DD 388.31409758. Continuous Count Traffic Data.

CONTINUOUS COUNT TRAFFIC DATA. Main/Corp Georgia. Dept. of Transportation. Periodical. US. English. an. Continuous Count Traffic Data.

CONTINUOUS TRAFFIC COUNT DATA AND TRAFFIC CHARACTERISTICS ON NEBRASKA STREETS AND HIGHWAYS. Main/Corp Nebraska. Dept. of Roads. Traffic Analysis Unit. 0091-844X. US. English. LC HE371.N25. DD 388.31409782.

COUNTY ROAD AND BRIDGE EXPENDITURE REPORT. Main/Corp Mississippi. Legislature. Audit Committee. US. English. Mississippi Legislature, Legislative Audit Committee, PO Box 1204, Jackson MS 39205. LC HE356.M7. DD 353.97620087811.

COUNTY ROAD FINANCIAL REPORT. Main/Corp Oregon. Dept. of Transportation. Finance Branch. 0364-4758. US. English. an. LC HE356.O7. DD 388.1109795. County Road Financial Report, 0364-4758.

CURRENT LITERATURE IN TRAFFIC AND TRANSPORTATION. V. 1- Jan./Feb. 1960-. 0011-3654. Periodical. US. English. mo. Transportation Center Library, Northwestern University, Deering Library, Evanston IL 60201. Tel (312)492-5273. LC Z7164.T8, HE151. DD 016.3805. Current Literature in Transportation.

DAILY TRAFFIC WORLD. 0195-4490. Periodical. US. English. da. $375.00. Traffic Service Corporation, 1325 G Street NW/Suite 900, Washington DC 20005.

DELAWARE TURNPIKE ANNUAL REPORT. VFOAT Annual Report. US. English. an. LC HE356.D4. DD 353.9751008642.

DER-PE RELATORIO. Main/Corp Pernambuco (Brazil). Departamento de Estradas de Rodagem. VFOAT D.E.R.-P.E. Relatorio. 1981-. Portuguese. ir. LC HE359.B9. DD 354.813400864206. Relatorio Anual.

DETAILS OF WORKS FOR DEMANDS 39, ROADS AND BRIDGES AND 52, CAPITAL OUTLAY ON ROADS AND BRIDGES FOR THE YEAR . . . . Main/Corp Tamil Nadu (India). VFOAT Detailed Roads and Bridges Budget. 1980-81-. English. an. 4.35. LC HE365.I44. DD 354.548200864. Detailed Roads and Bridges Budget.

DISTANCES ROUTIERES. 0714-2153. CN. French. ir. Gouvernement du Quebec, 600 St Amable 4E Etage, Quebec G1R 4Z1 Canada. DD 388.1209714.

ERFAHRUNGSAUSTAUSCH UBER ERDARBEITEN IM STRASSENBAU. German. ir. Bundesanstalt fur Strassenwesen, Bruler Strasse 1, 5 Koln 51 West Germany. LC TE210.

EXPENDITURE REPORT - STATE OF COLORADO, DEPARTMENT OF HIGHWAYS. (EXPENDITURE REPORT - DEPARTMENT OF HIGHWAYS). Main/Corp Colorado. Dept. of Highways. VFOAT Annual Report - State of Colorado Department of Highways. 0146-7506. US. English. an. State of Colorado, Department of Highways, 1375 Sherman Street, Denver CO 80203. LC HE356.C6. DD 353.9788008781.

FATAL ACCIDENT REPORTING SYSTEM (WASHINGTON, D.C. : 1979). (FATAL ACCIDENT REPORTING SYSTEM). 1979-. 0732-9792. US. English. an. US Department of Transportation, National Highway Traffic Safety Administration, 400 Seventh Street SW, Washington DC 20590. LC HE5614.2. DD 312.2790973. FARS, Fatal Accident Reporting System. Annual Report, 0195-6930.

FATAL MOTOR VEHICLE ACCIDENT COMPARATIVE DATA REPORT. 0737-6332. US. English. an. New Jersey State Police, Fatal Accident Unit, Traffic Bureau, Box 7068, West Trenton NJ 08625. LC HE5614.3.N44. DD 312.4409749. New Jersey Fatal Motor Vehicle Accidents and Fatalities Review, Comparative Data Report, 0097-9457.

FEDERAL HIGHWAY ADMINISTRATION NEWSLETTER. OFFICE OF HIGHWAY PLANNING. Issue No. 1 (Nov. 1977)-. Periodical. US. English. ir. Publications and Visual Aids Branch, Office of Management Systems, Room 6415 Nassif Building, Washington DC 20590.

FEDERAL HIGHWAY ADMINISTRATION NEWSLETTER. REGION 15 DEMONTRATION PROJECTS. Issue No. 1 (Jan. 1975)-. Periodical. US. English. ir. Publications and Visual Aids Branch, Office of Management Systems, Room 4422 Nassif Building, Washington DC 20590.

FEDERALLY COORDINATED PROGRAM OF HIGHWAY RESEARCH AND DEVELOPMENT. Began with 1974/75. 0361-4204. US. English. an. US Department of Transportation, Federal Highway Administration, Offices of Research Development and Technology, Washington DC 20590. LC TE192. DD 625.7072073. Research and Development Program, 0098-0234.

FINANCIAL AND STATISTICAL REPORT - LOUISIANA. See Statistics.

FINANCIAL REPORT TO MANAGEMENT. Main/Corp Kentucky. Bureau of Highways. Division of Accounts. US. English. sa. Commonwealth of Kentucky Department of Transportation, Frankfort KY 406. LC HE28.K4. DD 353.9769007231.

FLORIDA SUMMARY OF ACCIDENT DATA. Main/Corp Florida. Dept. of Transportation. Division of Safety. 0092-007X. US. English. Florida Department of Transportation, Division of Safety, Tallahassee FL 32304. LC HE5614.3.F6. DD 388.314.

FOCUS ON NEBRASKA HIGHWAYS. Main/Corp Nebraska. Dept. of Roads. US. English. LC HE356.N36. DD 388.109782.

FORSCHUNGSGESELLSCHAFT FUR STRASSEN- UND VERKEHRSWESEN (GERMANY). (TATIGKEITSBERICHT). German. ir. Alfred-Schutte-Allee 10, 5000 Koln 21 West Germany. Tatigkeitsbericht der Forschungsgesellschaft fur das Strassenwesen.

FORSCHUNGSPROGRAMM - BUNDESANSTALT FUR STRASSENWESEN, BEREICH UNFALLFORSCHUNG. Main/Corp Bundesanstalt fur Strassenwesen (Germany). Bereich Unfallforschung. 0170-5431. GW. German. ir. Bundesstelle fur Aussenhandelsinformation, 5000 Koln 1, Postfach 510530, Bruhler Strasse 1, Koln West Germany. Tel (02204)43421. LC HE5614.5.G3. Circ 2,000. Program of accident research (road

Transportation—Roads and Traffic

safety) of the ministry of transport of the Federal Republic of Germany.

THE FREEWAY EVOLUTION. Main/Corp California. Division of Highways. District 7. US. English. Department of Transportation, Division of Highways, District 7, Los Angeles CA 90053. LC HE356.C2. DD 388.122097949.

FREEWAY/L.A. (FREEWAY/L.A. : NEWSLETTER OF DIGNITY/LOS ANGELES). VFOAT Freeway LA. VAT Freeway Los angeles. 0740-3003. Periodical. US. English. mo. Dignity/LA, PO Box 27516, Los Angeles CA 90026. *Caterpillar.*

FROM THE STATE CAPITALS. HIGHWAY FINANCING AND CONSTRUCTION. VFOAT Highway Financing and Construction. 0016-1705. Periodical. US. English. wk. $175.00. Wakeman/Walworth Inc, PO Box 1939, New Haven CT 06509. Tel (203)/562-8518. *Highway financing and construction: furnishes updates on the allocation of funds for highway, street and bridge construction, extension, repair, renovation, replacement, and truck weight limits and fees.*

GLC ROAD SAFETY SECTION ANNUAL REPORT. Main/Corp Greater London Council. Road Safety Section. VFOAT G.L.C. Road Safety Section Annual Report. UK. English. an. Greater London Council, The County Hall, London SE1 7PB England. LC HE5614.5.G7. DD 363.12509421.

HANSHIN KOSOKU DORO KODAN NEMPO. Main/Corp Hanshin Kosoku Doro Kodan. 1962/66-. Japanese. ir. c/o Osaka Senta Building, 68 Kita Kutarocho 4-Chome, Higashi-Ku (541), Osaka Japan. LC HE365.J34.

HIGHWAY ACCIDENT REPORTS. SUMMARY FORMAT. 1980, Issue No. 1-. 8755-9196. Periodical. US. English. $55.00. National Technical Information Service, 5285 Port Royal Road, Springfield VA 22161. Tel (703)487-4630. DD 363.

HIGHWAY & VEHICLE SAFETY REPORT. VAT Highway and Vehicle Safety Report. 1974. 0161-0325. Periodical. US. English. bw. $117.00. Highway & Vehicle Safety Report, POB 3367/SC Station 297 Main, Branford CT 06405. Tel (203)488-9808. Ed S Paul Stamler. (ctrl). *News and analysis of all areas of vehicle and highway safety: legislation, regulation, litigation, reports, recalls, defect investigations, research statistics, etc.*

HIGHWAY MILEAGE REPORT FOR NEW YORK STATE. US. English. an. LC HE356.N7. DD 388.109747.

HIGHWAY RESEARCH ABSTRACTS. *See* Indexes/Abstracts.

HIGHWAY SAFETY IMPROVEMENT PROGRAM, ANNUAL REPORT. Main/Corp North Dakota. State Highway Dept. US. English. an. LC HE5614.3.N63. DD 614.86209784.

HIGHWAY SAFETY LITERATURE (NATIONAL RESEARCH COUNCIL (U.S.). TRANSPORTATION RESEARCH BOARD). (HIGHWAY SAFETY LITERATURE). Fall 1982-. 0738-5277. Periodical. US. English. qt. Transportation Research Board, National Academy of Sciences, 2101 Constitution Avenue NW, Washington DC 20418. Ind/Abst Am. Stat. Index. LC HE5614. DD 363.12505. *Highway Safety Literature (United States. National Highway Traffic Safety Administration : 1973), 0738-5277.*

HIGHWAY SAFETY PERFORMANCE. FATAL AND INJURY ACCIDENT RATES ON PUBLIC ROADS IN THE UNITED STATES. (HIGHWAY SAFETY PERFORMANCE . . . FATAL AND INJURY ACCIDENT RATES ON PUBLIC ROADS IN THE UNITED STATES). VFOAT Fatal and Injury Accident Rates on Public Roads in the United States. 8755-8688. US. English. an. US Department of Transportation, Federal Highway Administration, Washington DC 20590. LC HE5614.2. DD 363.12520973021. Vols. for (1983-) distributed to depository libraries in microfiche. *Fatal and Injury Accident Rates on Federal-Aid and Other Highway Systems, 0565-0437.*

HIGHWAY SAFETY PLAN. Main/Corp Florida. Governor's Highway Safety Commission. US. English. an. LC HE5614.3.F6. DD 363.125609759.

HIGHWAY SAFETY PLAN. Main/Corp Washington (State). Traffic Safety Commission. US. English. Washington Traffic Safety Commission, Olympia WA 98504. LC HE5614.3.W2. DD 363.125609797.

HIGHWAY SAFETY PLAN. Main/Corp Oregon Traffic Safety Commission. Began with Vol. for 1978. US. English. an. Oregon Traffic Safety Commission, 325 13th Street, Salem OR 97310. LC HE5614.3.O7. DD 363.1255609795.

HIGHWAY SAFETY PLAN. Main/Corp Wisconsin. Office of the Governor. VFOAT State of Wisconsin Highway Safety Plan. US. English. an. Wisconsin Department of Transportation, Office for Highway Safety, 4802 Sheboygan Avenue/Room 936, Madison WI 53702. LC HE5614.3.W5. DD 363.1255609775.

HIGHWAY SAFETY PLAN FOR MISSOURI. Fiscal Year 1983-. US. English. an. LC HE5614.3.M8. DD 363.12509778. *Missouri's Highway Safety Plan.*

HIGHWAY SAFETY PROGRAM, ANNUAL REPORT OF ACTIVITIES. (HIGHWAY SAFETY PROGRAM : ANNUAL REPORT OF ACTIVITIES). Main/Corp Nevada Office of Highway Safety. 0097-9465. US. English. an. Office of Highway Safety, 555 Wright Way, Carson City NV 89701. LC HE5614.3.N42. DD 353.979300878314.

THE HIGHWAY SAFETY STEWARDSHIP REPORT. (THE . . . HIGHWAY SAFETY STEWARDSHIP REPORT : REPORT OF THE SECRETARY OF TRANSPORTATION TO THE UNITED STATES CONGRESS). 6th(1980)-. 0277-2310. US. English. an. Office of Highway Safety, Washington DC 20590. LC HE5614.2. DD 363.12560973. *Highway Safety Improvement Programs.*

HIGHWAY SUFFICIENCY REPORT. Main/Corp Maine. Dept. of Transportation. Bureau of Planning. 0147-9539. US. English. Maine Department of Transportation, Augusta ME 04333. LC TE24.M2. DD 388.109741.

HIGHWAY TAXES AND FEES. 0732-8230. US. English. Federal Highway Administration, Washington DC 20590. LC HE355.A3. DD 353.9372.

HIGHWAY TRAFFIC ACCIDENT REPORT. VFOAT Washington State Highway System, Traffic Accident Report. 1977-. US. English. an. Department of Transportation, Highway Administration Building, Olympia WA 98504. LC HE5614.3.W2. DD 312.4409797. *Washington State Annual Traffic Accident Report, 0093-2167.*

HIGHWAY TRAFFIC STATISTICS. *See* Statistics.

HIGHWAY TRANSPORTATION RESEARCH AND DEVELOPMENT STUDIES. Main/Corp United States. Federal Highway Administration. 0092-3389. US. English. $4.20. Superintendents of Documents, US Government Printing Office, Washington DC 20402. LC TE1. DD 625.7072073. *R & D Highway & Safety Transportation Systems Studies.*

HIGHWAY TRUST FUND ANNUAL REPORT CEASED. (HIGHWAY TRUST FUND . . . ANNUAL REPORT : COMMUNICATION FROM THE FISCAL ASSISTANT SECRETARY OF THE TREASURY . . .). Main/Corp United States. Dept. of the Treasury. -25th. 0742-177X. US. English. an. LC HE355.A3. DD 353.00864204506.

HIGHWAY USER QUARTERLY. Winter 1974-. 0094-7393. US. English. qt. $3.00. Highway Users Federation for Safety and Mobility, 1776 Massachusetts Avenue, Washington DC 20036. Ind/Abst Public Aff. Inf. Serv. Bull. LC HE331. DD 388.10973. *Highway User, 0018-1765.*

HIGHWAYS AND TRANSPORTATION. (HIGHWAYS AND TRANSPORTATION : JOURNAL OF THE INSTITUTION OF HIGHWAYS AND TRANSPORTATION & HTTA). Vol. 30, No. 8/9 (Aug./Sept. 1983)-. 0265-6868. Periodical. UK. English. mo. 22.00. East Midland Allied Press, 41 Broadway, Peterborough Bretton Court Bretton PE3 8DZ England. Ind/Abst Excerpta Med. LC TE1. DD 625.705. *Highway Engineer, 0306-6452.*

THE HSRI RESEARCH REVIEW CEASED. Main/Corp Michigan. University Highway Safety Research Institute. VAT Highway Safety Research Institute Research Review. V. 7, No. 5-L2, No. 6. 0146-8545. Periodical. US. English. bm. Free. Highway Safety Research Institute, University of Michigan, Huron Parkway and Baxter Road, Ann Arbor MI 48109. Ind/Abst Eng. Index Annu., Eng. Index Mon., Eng. Index Energy Abstr., Public Aff. Inf. Serv. Bull. NLM W1 H148. CODEN HSRRD4. *HSRI Research, 0364-3476.*

IDAHO HIGHWAY STATISTICS. *See* Statistics.

IOWA ACCIDENT FACTS. *See* Public Health and Safety.

IOWA MOTOR VEHICLE TRAFFIC ACCIDENT FACTS. US. English. Research and Statistics Section, Motor Vehicle Division, Iowa Department of Transportation, Grimes State Office Building, Des Moines IA 50319. LC HE5614.3.I8. DD 388.314.

JOURNAL OF TRAFFIC MEDICINE. (JOURNAL OF TRAFFIC MEDICINE/IAATM NEWSLETTER). VFOAT IAATM Newsletter. V. 1- May 1973-. 0345-5564. Periodical. US. English. qt. $5.99. Health and Association Inc, IAATM Association for Accident and Traffic Medicine, Box 22, Morton Grove IL 60053. Ind/Abst Excerpta Med. NLM W1 JO966KH.

JOURNAL OF TRAFFIC SAFETY EDUCATION. V. 18- Oct. 1970-. 0164-1344. Periodical. US. English. qt. $8.00. California Driver Education Association, c/o Larry Collins, 4348 Lomina Avenue, Lakewood CA 90713. Tel (213)429-0469. Ed Larry Collins. Ind/Abst Educ. Index. LC HE5614.3.C3. DD 614.86207120794. bk rev. adv acc. Circ 2,500. (ctrl). *Mostly deals with driver and passenger safety, drivers education and training. Also deals with research, engineering and law enforcement. California Journal of Traffic Safety Education.*

KANSAS HIGHWAY & TRAFFIC STATISTICS. *See* Statistics.

KANSAS HIGHWAY AND TRAFFIC STATISTICS. *See* Statistics.

KOTSU ANZEN KOGAI KENKYUJO NEMPO. 1970/71-. JA. Japanese. ir. 38-1 Shinkawa 6-chome, Tokyo Japan. LC HE5614.5.J3.

LARGE CLASS I HOUSEHOLD GOODS CARRIERS SELECTED EARNINGS DATA. *See* Transportation.

LOCAL HIGHWAY INVENTORY. US. English. an. NY State Department of Transportation, Data Services Bureau, Albany NY 12230. LC HE356.N7. DD 388.109747. *Local Highway Systems Inventory: City and Village Street Mileage, Local Highway Systems Inventory: Town and Country Road Mileage.*

T M B EXPRESS. Main/Corp Halifax, N.S. Traffic Management Board. VFOAT Express. V. 1- June 1976-. 0703-4679. Periodical. CN. English. ir. Free. Traffic Management Board, 3rd Floor/City Hall, Halifax Nova Scotia Canada. DD 388.41310971622.

MAIN ROADS CEASED. Began in 1929. 0025-0597. Periodical. AT. English. qt. Department of Main Roads, 309 Castlereagh Street, Sydney New South Wales Australia. Ind/Abst Public Aff. Inf. Serv. Bull. LC TE1. DD 625.705.

THE MAINE TRAIL. *See* Engineering - Civil Engineering.

MANITOBA HIGHWAY NEWS. V. 1- Mar./Apr. 1971-. 0380-4852. Periodical. CN. English. bm. $12.00. Manitoba Trucking Association, 25 Bunting Street, Winnipeg Manitoba R2X 2P5 Canada. Tel (304)632-6600. Ed Al Harris. adv acc. Circ 3,500. (ctrl). *Serves the field of highway motor transport in Canada with special emphasis on the industry in the four western provinces. Western Motor Fleet and Highway News, 0380-4836.*

MANUAL ON UNIFORM TRAFFIC CONTROL DEVICES FOR STREETS AND HIGHWAYS. Main/Corp United States. National Advisory Committee on Uniform Traffic Control Devices. VFOAT Manual on Uniform Traffic Control Devices. 1978-. US. English. ir. Superintendent of Documents, US Government Printing Office, Washington DC 20402. Tel (202)783-3238.

MEMBERSHIP ROSTER - NATIONAL INDUSTRIAL TRAFFIC LEAGUE. Main/Corp National Industrial Traffic League. 0198-7127. US. English. National Industrial Traffic League, 1909 K Street NW/Suite 410, Washington DC 20006. LC HF5780.U6. DD 381.06073.

MERGE. Main/Corp Kansas. Highway Safety Coordinating Office. Issue 1- Nov./Dec. 1972-. 0364-2518. US. English. Kansas Highway Safety Cordinating Office, 535 Kansas Avenue, Topeka KS 66603. LC HE5614.3.K3. DD 388.314.

MINNESOTA AUTOMATIC TRAFFIC RECORDER DATA SUMMARY. US. English. LC HE371.M6. DD 388.314209776.

MISSISSIPPI FINANCIAL STATISTICS FOR HIGHWAY PLANNING ON STATE HIGHWAYS, COUNTY ROADS, CITY STREETS. *See* Statistics.

Transportation—Roads and Traffic

MISSISSIPPI HIGHWAY TRAFFIC REPORT. VFOAT Mississippi . . . Highway Traffic. US. English. LC HE371.M7. DD 388.314209762.

MISSISSIPPI PUBLIC ROAD MILEAGE AS OF DEC 31. VFOAT Mississippi State Highway Department Public Road Mileage as of December 31. US. English. an. LC HE356.M7. DD 388.109762.

MISSOURI ANNUAL HIGHWAY SAFETY WORK PROGRAM. Main/Corp Missouri. Division of Highway Safety. 0091-1097. US. English. an. Missouri State Highway Department, Division Highway Safety, Main Office Building, Jefferson MO 65101. LC HE5614.3.M8. DD 388.314.

MISSOURI HIGHWAY NEWS CEASED. Mar. 1943-Jan. 1980. Periodical. US. English. mo.

MONTANA AUTOMATIC COUNTERS. VFOAT Montana Automatic Traffic Counters. US. English. an. LC HE371.M9. DD 388.31409786.

MOTOR VEHICLE TRAFFIC ACCIDENTS. Main/Corp Statistics Canada. Transportation Section. VFOAT Accidents de la Circulation Routiere. CN. English and French. an. $1.00. Information Canada, Receiver General for Canada, Statistics Canada Publications, Ottawa Ontario K1A 0T6 Canada. LC HE5614.5.C2. DD 312.44. Motor Vehicle Traffic Accidents.

MUNICIPAL STATE AID STREET APPORTIONMENT DATA (MINNESOTA. DEPT. OF TRANSPORTATION). (MUNICIPAL STATE AID STREET APPORTIONMENT DATA). US. English. an. Minnesota Department of Transportation, State Transportation Building, St Paul MN 55155. LC HE356.M6. DD 388.11409776. Municipal State Aid Street Apportionment Data (Minnesota. Dept. of Highways), 0096-994X.

NATIONAL ACCIDENT SAMPLING SYSTEM. 0741-1723. US. English. an. National Highway Traffic Safety Administration, US Government Printing Office, Washington DC 20402. LC HE5614.2. DD 312.4450973.

NATIONAL COOPERATIVE HIGHWAY RESEARCH PROGRAM REPORT. (REPORT - NATIONAL COOPERATIVE HIGHWAY RESEARCH PROGRAM). 1-. 0077-5614. Monographic Series. US. English. ir. Transportation Research Board, 2101 Constitution Avenue NW, Washington DC 20418. Ind/Abst Eng. Index Annu., Eng. Index Mon., Eng. Index Bioeng. Abstr., Eng. Index Energy Abstr., Chem. Abstr., Eng. Index. LC TE7. CODEN NCHRDA.

THE NATIONAL TRAFFIC LAW NEWS. See Law.

NEBRASKA HIGHWAY STATISTICS : STATE AND LOCAL ROAD AND STREET DATA. See Statistics.

NEW HAMPSHIRE'S FATAL TRAFFIC ACCIDENT FACTS. US. English. an. New Hampshire Department of Public Works and Highways, John O Morton Building, Concord NH 03301. LC HE5614.3.N43. DD 363.125209742. Fatal Traffic Accident Statistics for the State of New Hampshire.

NEW MEXICO HIGHWAY STATISTICS AND RELATED INFORMATION. See Statistics.

NEW MEXICO TRAFFIC ACCIDENT DATA. 1980-. US. English. an. Traffic Safety Bureau, Motor Vehicle Division, State of New Mexico P E R A Building, PO Box 1028, Santa Fe NM 87503. LC HE5614.3.N47. DD 312.4409789. New Mexico . . . Vehicular Accident Summary.

NEW YORK STATE'S . . . HIGHWAY SUFFICIENCY RATINGS. VFOAT Highway Sufficiency Ratings. US. English. New York State Department of Transportation State Campus, Building 4/Room 108, Albany NY 12232. LC TE24.N7. DD 625.709747021.

NORTH CAROLINA MUNICIPAL EXPENDITURES FROM STATE STREET-AID ALLOCATIONS. Main/Corp North Carolina. Division of Highways. Planning and Research Branch. 0361-9532. US. English. an. North Carolina Department of Transportation & Highway Safety, PO Box 25201, Raleigh NC 27611. LC HE356.N8. DD 338.43.

NORTH CAROLINA TRAFFIC ACCIDENT SUMMARY. US. English. an.

NORTH DAKOTA ACCIDENT FACTS. Main/Corp North Dakota. Traffic Engineering Division. 1973-. 0095-7712. US. English. LC HE5614.3.N63. DD 388.314. Traffic Accident Facts and Statistical Report.

NORTH DAKOTA HIGHWAY SAFETY IMPROVEMENT PROGRAM, ANNUAL REPORT. Main/Corp North Dakota. Traffic Engineering Division. VFOAT Highway Safety Improvement. 0361-8099. US. English. an. LC HE5614.3.N63. DD 388.312.

NORTH DAKOTA HIGHWAY SAFETY PLAN. VFOAT Highway Safety Plan. US. English. an. North Dakota State Highway Department, Capitol Grounds, Bismarck ND 58505. LC HE5614.3.N63. DD 363.125609784.

NORTH DAKOTA TRAFFIC REPORT. Main/Corp North Dakota. Transportation Services Division. 1974-. 0549-852X. US. English. an. LC HE371.N8. DD 388.31409784. North Dakota Traffic Report.

NORTH DAKOTA VEHICULAR ACCIDENT FACTS. 0362-9171. US. English. an. Planning Division, North Dakota State Highway Department, 600 East Boulevard Avenue, Bismark ND 58505-01781. LC HE5614.3.N63. DD 363.125209784021.

OHIO TURNPIKE COMMISSION ANNUAL REPORT. (ANNUAL REPORT - OHIO TURNPIKE COMMISSION). Main/Corp Ohio. Turnpike Commission. 0271-8413. US. English. an. Ohio Turnpike Commission, 682 Prospect Street, Berea OH 44017. LC HE356.O3. DD 388.1.

OKLAHOMA TRAFFIC ACCIDENT FACTS. Main/Corp Oklahoma. Dept. of Public Safety. Services & Records Division. US. English. an. Services and Records Division, Department of Public Safety, Box 11415, Oklahoma City OK 73136. LC HE5614.3.O5. DD 312.4409766.

ONTARIO TRAFFIC SAFETY. V. 1- Apr. 1958-. 0702-8040. CN. English. bm. Ministry of Transportation, 1201 Wilson Avenue/1st Floor West Tower, Downsview Ontario M3M 1J8 Canada. Tel (416)248-3501.

OREGON TRAFFIC ACCIDENTS. FOCUS ON MOTORCYCLES. Main/Corp Oregon. Motor Vehicles Division. 1976-. US. English. an. Oregon Motor Vehicles Division, 1905 Lana Avenue NE, Salem OR 97314. LC HE5614.3.O7. DD 363.1259. Oregon Motorcycle Accidents, 0092-9913.

OREGON TRAFFIC ACCIDENTS, TRUCK. 1981-. US. English. an. LC HE5614.3.O7. DD 363.1259. Oregon Truck Accidents.

PACIFIC TRAFFIC. VFOAT Pacific Traffic Magazine. 1953. 0030-8943. Periodical. US. English. mo. $24.00 Domestic, $150.00 Foreign. Pacific Traffic, PO Box 11477, Marina Del Rey CA 90292. Tel (213)822-3132. Ed Nicole Knowlton. adv acc. Circ 13,500. (ctrl). Serves the field of traffic and distribution management which ship and/or store goods and merchandise via air, rail, truck, or ship throughout the world.

THE PAN AMERICAN HIGHWAY SYSTEM. 1947-. US. English. LC GV1025.S75.

PLANNING AND RESEARCH PROGRAM. Main/Corp District of Columbia. Office of Transportation Policies and Plans. 1979/80-. US. English. be. Office of Transportation Policies and Plans, Department of Transportation, Washington DC 20036. LC HE356.5.W3. DD 388.4068.

PLANO RODOVIARIO ESTADUAL. Main/Corp Maranhao, Brazil (State). Departamento de Estradas de Rodagem. Portuguese. ir. LC HE359.B9. DD 388.109812.

POLICY FOR ROADS: ENGLAND. Main/Corp Great Britain. Dept. of Transport. 1978-. UK. English. ir. Her Majesty's Stationery Office, PO Box 569, London SE1 England. Tel (01)211-5656. LC HE363.G7. DD 388.10942. Roads in England.

LA PREVENTION ROUTIERE INTERNATIONALE : PUBLICATION TRIMESTRIELLE DE LA PRI. VFOAT International Road Safety. Periodical. English (text in French and German). qt. $15.00. Banque de Neuflize, 3 Avenue Aoche, 75008 Paris France.

PROCEEDINGS - COMMITTEE ON COMPUTER TECHNOLOGY. (PROCEEDINGS : NATIONAL CONFERENCE). Main/Corp American Association of State Highway Officials Committee on Computer Technology. 1970-. 0091-5122. US. English. an. American Association of State Highway Officials, 444 Capital Street NW/Suite 225, Washington DC 20001. Tel (202)624-5800. LC TE5. DD 625.702854. National Conference - A.A.S.H.O Committee on Electronics, 0091-5130.

PROCEEDINGS - HIGHWAY ENVIRONMENT CONFERENCE. Main/Conf Highway Environment Conference. 10th- 1973-. 0317-0373. Periodical. CN. English. Publications Department of Centre for Continuing Education, University of British Columbia, Vancouver British Columbia V6T 1W5 Canada. DD 625.77. Proceedings, 0317-0381.

PROCEEDINGS OF THE AMERICAN ASSOCIATION FOR AUTOMOTIVE MEDICINE CONFERENCE. See Medicine.

PUERTO RICO HIGHWAY IMPROVEMENT PROGRAM. Main/Corp Wilbur Smith and Associates. 0092-8941. US. English. an. 4500 Jackson Boulevard, Columbia SC 29202. LC HE359. DD 388.1097295.

RAPPORT ANNUEL DE LA CAISSE NATIONALE DES AUTOROUTES. Main/Corp Caisse Nationale des Autoroutes. FR. French. ir. Caisse Nationale des Autoroutes, 56 rue de Lille, 75007 Paris France. LC HE363.F7. DD 354.4400864205.

RAPPORT ANNUEL DU CONSEIL D'ADMINISTRATION SUR L'ACTIVITE DE LA CAISSE NATIONALE DES AUTOROUTES EN . . . . Main/Corp Caisse Nationale des Autoroutes. Conseil d'Administration. FR. French. an. 56 rue de Lille, 75007 Paris France. LC HE363.F7. DD 354.440864205. Rapport Annuel de la Caisse Nationale des Autoroutes.

RAPPORT (CONSEIL SUPERIEUR DE LA SECURITE ROUTIERE (BELGIUM)). (RAPPORT). BE. French. ir. Conseil Superieur de la Securite Routiere Rond-Point Robert Schuman 9, Bte 7, 1040 Bruxelles Belgium.

RAPPORT D'ACTIVITE - CENTRE DE RECHERCHES ROUTIERES. Main/Corp Centre de Recherches Routieres. BE. French. ir. Centre de Recherches, Routieres, Boulevard de la Woluwe 42, 1200 Bruxelles Belgium. Ind/Abst Eng. Index Annu., Eng. Index Mon., Eng. Index Bioeng. Abstr., Eng. Index Energy Abstr. CODEN CRRCDX.

RELATORIO ANUAL DO DNER. Main/Corp Brazil. Departamento Nacional de Estradas de Rodagem. VFOAT Relatorio Anual. Portuguese. an. LC HE359.B6. DD 354.8100864206.

RELATORIO DE ATIVIDADES - PARA (BRAZIL : STATE). DEPARTAMENTO DE ESTRADAS DE RODAGEM. DIRETORIA DE PLANEJAMENTO. Main/Corp Para (Brazil : State). Departamento de Estradas de Rodagem. Diretoria de Planejamento. Portuguese. ir. LC HE359.B9. DD 354.811500864206.

RELATORIO DE TRABALHOS RODOVIARIO SIC. Main/Corp Bahia (Brazil : State). Departamento de Estradas de Rodagem. VFOAT Relatorio de Trabalhos Rodoviarios. Portuguese. an. LC HE359.B9. DD 388.122098142.

RELATORIO - DEPARTAMENTO DE ESTRADAS DE RODAGEM. Main/Corp Sao Paulo, Brazil (State). Departamento de Estradas de Rodagem. Portuguese. ir. LC HE359.B9.

REPORT - KENTUCKY. DEPT OF HIGHWAYS. Main/Corp Kentucky. Dept. of Highways. US. English. an. Commonwealth of Kentucky, Department of Transportation, Frankfort KY 40601. LC HE356.K4. DD 625.7.

REPORT OF THE MISSISSIPPI RIVER PARKWAY COMMISSION TO THE . . . GENERAL ASSEMBLY OF ILLINOIS. Main/Corp Mississippi River Parkway Commission (Ill.). 1st (1981)-. US. English. an. State of Illinois, Mississippi River Parkway Commission, Room 121/Capitol Building, Springfield IL 62706. LC HE356.I3. DD 353.977300864206.

REPORT OF THE SASKATCHEWAN SAFETY COUNCIL PUBLIC OPINION POLL. See Public Health and Safety.

A REPORT ON ACTIVITIES UNDER THE HIGHWAY SAFETY ACT OF 1966 AS AMENDED. VFOAT Traffic Safety. Began with 1974. US. English. an. National Highway Traffic Safety Administration, 400 Seventh Street SW,

Transportation—Roads and Traffic

Washington DC 20590. LC HE5614.2. DD 614.86. *Report on Activities of the National Highway Traffic Safety Administration and the Federal Highway Administration Under the Highway Safety Act of 1966.*

REPORT ON TRAFFIC ACCIDENTS AND INJURIES. (REPORT ON TRAFFIC ACCIDENTS AND INJURIES FOR . . .). 1979-. 0735-8539. US. English. an. US Government Printing Office, Superintendent of Documents, Washington DC 20402. LC HE5614.2. DD 363.12520973. Vols. for 1979/1980- distributed to depository libraries in microfiche.

A REPORT ON TRAVEL ON SASKATCHEWAN HIGHWAYS. Main/Corp Saskatchewan. Dept. of Highways and Transportation. Planning Branch. VFOAT Travel on Saskatchewan Highways. 1971. CN. English. an. Saskatchewan Highways & Transportation, 1855 Victoria Avenue, Regina Saskatchewan S4P 3V5 Canada. LC HE373.C4. *Travel on Saskatchewan Highways.*

REPORT TO THE PEOPLE. Main/Corp Oklahoma. Highway Safety Office. US. English. an. Oklahoma Highway Safety Office, G-80 Jim Thorpe Building, Oklahoma City OK 73105. LC HE5614.3.O5. DD 614.86209766.

REPRINT. Main/Corp Virginia Council of Highway Investigation and Research. No.1- Oct. 1949-. English. ir.

RESEARCH REPORT - AUSTRALIAN ROAD RESEARCH BOARD. See Transportation.

RESEARCH RESULTS DIGEST - NATIONAL COOPERATIVE HIGHWAY RESEARCH PROGRAM. Main/Corp National Cooperative Highway Research Program. Began with Dec. 1968 issue. 0547-5554. Periodical. US. English. ir. Transportation Research Board, 2101 Constitution Avenue NW, Washington DC 20418. LC UNC.

RESEARCH - TRAFFIC INJURY RESEARCH FOUNDATION OF CANADA. (RESEARCH). Sept. 1978-. 0821-7807. Periodical. CN. English. ir. Free. Traffic Injury Research Foundation of Canada, 171 Nepean Street, Ottawa Ontario K2P 0B4 Canada. Tel (613)238-5238. DD 363.125. Reports which deal with the statistical, legal, behavioral, psychological, pharmacological, medical and engineering aspects of traffic accidents.

RESULTATER AF MANUELLE TRAFIKTLLINGER I . . . I FASTE PUNKTER PA VEJNETTET. 1982-. Danish. an. LC HE373.D4.

REVISTA DO DER PERNAMBUCO. Main/Corp Pernambuco, Brazil (State). Departamento de Estradas de Rodagem. VAT Revista do Departamento de Estradas de Rodagem Pernambuco. Periodical. Portuguese. ir. Caixa Postal 412, Recife Brazil. LC HE359.B9. *Noticias.*

REVISTA RODOVIARIA. Yearly V. 1- August 1972-. Periodical. Portuguese. ir. Divisao de Servicos Especiais do Daer, Av Borges de Medeiros No 1555, 120 Porto Alegre Brazil. LC TE4.

ROAD ACCIDENTS GREAT BRITAIN. Main/Corp Great Britain. Dept. of Transport. UK. English. 2.25. Directorate of Statistics, 2 Marsham Street, London SW1P 3EB England. LC HE5614.5.G7. DD 388.314.

ROAD ACCIDENTS (IN GREAT BRITAIN). Main/Corp Great Britain. Dept. of the Environment. 1969-. UK. English. an. 0.70. Her Majestys Stationery Office, PO Box 276, London SW8 5DT England. LC HE5614.5.G7. DD 614.862. *Road Accidents.*

ROAD ACCIDENTS, WALES. VFOAT Damweiniau Ffyrdd, Cymru. 0263-9653. UK. English (Welsh). an. LC HE5614.5. DD 312.44.

ROAD RESEARCH. VFOAT Annual Report of the Road Research Laboratory. English. ir.

ROAD STATISTICS IN KARNATAKA STATE. See Statistics.

ROAD TRAFFIC ACCIDENTS. Main/Corp South Africa. Dept. of Statistics. Series Corp ITS Report. VFOAT Padverkeerongelukke. Afrikaans (English). ir. 0.60. South Africa Department of Statistics, Government Printer, Bosman Street, Private Bag X85, Pretoria South Africa. LC HE5614.5.S6. DD 312.44. *Road Traffic Accidents.*

ROAD TRAFFIC ACCIDENTS INVOLVING CASUALTIES. Main/Corp Australian Bureau of Statistics. Western Australian Office. AT. English. qt. Australian Bureau of Statistics, Level 1 Merlin Centre, 30 Terrace Road, Perth Western Australia 6000. Tel (09)323 5140. LC HE5614.5.A8. DD 312.274. Provides detailed national data on road traffic accidents which resulted in deaths or admissions to hospitals. *Western Australia Road Traffic Accidents Involving Casualties.*

ROAD TRAFFIC ACCIDENTS INVOLVING CASUALTIES, TASMANIA. Main/Corp Australian Bureau of Statistics. Tasmanian Office. AT. English. an. Australian Bureau of Statistics, Commonwealth Government Centre 3rd Floor, 188 Collins Street, Hobart Tasmania 7000 Australia. Tel (002)20 9409. LC HE5614.5.A8. DD 312.4409946. Persons killed in road traffic accidents.

ROAD TRAFFIC REPORTS. 1970-. 0306-5286. UK. English. mo. 25.00. Kenneth Mason Publishing Ltd, 8 North Street Emsworth, Hampshire PO10 7DD England.

ROAD TRAFFIC SAFETY RESEARCH COUNCIL REPORT. Main/Corp New Zealand. Road Traffic Safety Research Council. English. ir. .20 Single Issue. Road Traffic Safety Research Council, PO Box 4140, Wellington New Zealand. LC HE5614.5.N45. DD 614.8620720931.

ROADS. Periodical. US. English. New York Good Roads Association, 116 Washington Avenue, Albany NY 12210. *Roads Bulletin.*

ROADS & BRIDGES. VFOAT Roads and Bridges. Vol. 23, No. 1 (Jan. 1985)-. 8750-9229. Periodical. US. English. mo. $15.00 Domestic, $22.50 Foreign. Scranton Gillette Communications, 380 Northwest Highway, Des Plaines IL 60016. DD 625. Issued also in microform by University Microfilms International. *Roads (Des Plaines, ILL.) 0746-3111.*

ROADS IN SCOTLAND. Main/Corp Great Britain. Scottish Development Dept. UK. English. 25/-. Scottish Development Department, Her Majesty's Stationery Office, 13A Castle Street, Edinburgh EH2 3AR Scotland. LC HE363.G74. DD 388.109411.

ROADWAYS OF MISSISSIPPI. Periodical. US. English. mo. PO Box 1850, Jackson MS 39205. LC HE356.M7. DD 388.109762.

ROBOT. Periodical. SA. Afrikaans (English). bm. Free. National Road Safety Council, Private Bag X147, 0001 Pretoria South Africa. Tel 285929. LC HE5614.5.S6. DD 614.86205. adv acc. Circ 20,000. (ctrl). Journal of South African safety procedures; educational lifestyle for children and adults.

RODOVIARISMO. V. 1- Oct. 1973-. BL. Portuguese. ir. Associacao Radoviaria do Brasil, rua Cristiano Viano 397 Cerqueira Cesar, CEP 05411 Sao Paulo Brazil. LC HE359.B9. DD 388.109816.

RODOVIAS INAUGURADAS. Main/Corp Pernambuco (Brazil). Departamento de Estradas de Rodagem. Portuguese. ir. LC HE359.B9. DD 388.1098134.

LES ROUTES QUEBECOISES. Main/Corp Quebec (Province). Roads Dept. CN. French. an. 1283 Boul Charest Ouest, Quebec Province of Quebec 61N 2CP Canada. LC HE357.Z6. DD 388.109714.

RTAC NEWS. Main/Corp Roads and Transportation Association of Canada. VFOAT Association des Routes et Transports du Canada. Nouvelles de l'Artc. V. 1- Jan. 1975-. 0317-1280. CN. English (also issued in French under title: Nouvelles de l'Artc). bm. $15.48. Road & Transport Association Canada, 1765 St Laurent Boulevard, Ottawa Ontario K1G 3V4 Canada. Tel (613)521-4052. Ed Gilbert Morier. DD 380.506271. adv acc. Circ 1,800. (ctrl). Bimonthly on the Association's numerous technical activities and transportation in general. *Road and Wheel, 0035-7197; Inside RTAC, 0317-1299.*

RURAL COMMUNICATION STATISTICS IN KARNATAKA STATE. See Statistics.

RURAL SPEEDS ON PRIMARY HIGHWAYS AND SECONDARY ROADS. US. English. an. LC HE5620.S6. DD 388.314409756.

SAFETY IMPROVEMENT WORK PROGRAM. US. English. an. LC HE5614.3.D3. DD 363.125609751.

SAFETY I.S.H.C. Main/Corp Indiana. State Highway Commission (1961-1981). 0097-9295. US. English. an. LC HE5614.3.I5. DD 353.977200878314.

SAFETY SADISTICS. See Public Health and Safety.

SAOBRACAJNE NEZGODE NA PUTEVIMA. See Statistics.

SASKATCHEWAN PROVINCIAL HIGHWAYS ACCIDENT STATISTICS. See Statistics.

SASKATCHEWAN TRAFFIC ACCIDENT FACTS. 1979-. 0711-9178. CN. English. Traffic Safety Engineering Branch, Saskatchewan Highways and Transportation, 1855 Victoria Avenue, Regina Saskatchewan S4P 3V5 Canada. LC HE5614.5.C2. DD 312.445097124. *Saskatchewan Provincial Highways Accident Statistics, 0318-2819.*

SEATTLE TRAFFIC ACCIDENT SUMMARY. 1980 & 1981-. US. English. Free. Seattle Engineering Department, Seattle Municipal Building, 600 Fourth Avenue/Room 910, Seattle WA 98104. Tel (206)625-2347. Ed Elizabeth Whitney. Circ 400. (ctrl). Overview of major vehicle accidents in Seattle; highlighting pedestrian, pedacycle, motorcycle, and DWI accidents. *Seattle Traffic Collision Summary.*

SERVICE AND METHODS DEMONSTRATION PROGRAM. ANNUAL REPORT. (SERVICE AND METHODS DEMONSTRATION PROGRAM ANNUAL REPORT). Main/Corp United States. Office of Transportation Management, and Demonstration. 0147-9954. US. English. an. US Department of Tranaportation, Federal Highway Administration, Washington DC 20590. LC HE308. DD 388.40973.

SIKKERHEDSMSSIG VURDERING OG PRIORITERING AF MINDRE ANLGSARBEJDER PA HOVEDLANDEVEJE. Danish. ir. LC HE5614.5.D4.

SISTEMA RODOVIARIO DO ESTADO DO PARANA. Portuguese. an. LC HE359.B9. DD 388.1098162021.

S.I.T.R.A.M., TRAFIC INTERNATIONAL. VFOAT Resultats Trimestriels. 0181-5334. FR. French. qt. 55 rue Brillat-Savarin, 75658 Paris Cedex 13 France.

SIX-YEAR HIGHWAY PROGRAM. Main/Corp Arkansas. State Highway Commission. 0093-6197. US. English. an. State Highway Commission, PO Box 2261, Little Rock AR 72203. LC HE356.A8. DD 388.109767.

SOUTH CAROLINA HIGHWAY SAFETY PLAN. VFOAT Highway Safety Plan. Fiscal Year 1979-. US. English. an. 1205 Pendleton Street, Columbia SC 29201. LC HE5614.3.S6. DD 363.125609757.

SOUTH DAKOTA HIGHWAY FINANCE. US. English. be. LC HE356.S6. DD 388.1109783.

SOUTH DAKOTA HIGHWAY SAFETY MANAGEMENT SYSTEM PLAN. Main/Corp South Dakota. Division of Highway Safety. US. English. Department of Public Safety, Division of Highway Safety, Pierre SD 57501. LC HE5614.3.S8. DD 614.86209783.

SOUTH DAKOTA HIGHWAY SAFETY WORK PROGRAM. Main/Corp South Dakota. Division of Highway Safety. 0361-3461. US. English. Pierre Department of Public Safety, Pierre SD 57501. LC HE5614.3.S8. DD 614.8620710783. *South Dakota Highway Safety Work Program, 0361-3461.*

SOUTH DAKOTA MOTOR VEHICLE TRAFFIC ACCIDENT SUMMARY. VFOAT Motor Vehicle Traffic Accident Summary. US. English. Department of Commerce and Regulation, Accident Records Program, 118 West Capitol Avenue, Pierre SD 57501-2080. LC HE5614.3.S8. DD 363.125209783021.

SOUTH DAKOTA TRAFFIC ACCIDENT FACTS. Main/Corp South Dakota. Dept. of Public Safety. 0147-0760. US. English. LC HE5614.3.S8. DD 388.314.

A SPECIAL REPORT ON PUERTO RICO HIGHWAY AUTHORITY. Main/Corp Government Development Bank for Puerto Rico. English. ir. Government Development Bank for Puerto Rico, PO Box 4200, San Juan Puerto Rico 00940. LC HE359.P92. DD 388.1097295.

SPEED MONITORING REPORT. VFOAT New Jersey Speed Monitoring Report. 1st Quarter (1976/77)-. Periodical. US. English. qt. LC HE5620.S6. DD 388.314409749.

STATE AID TO MUNICIPALITIES FOR HIGHWAYS AND STREETS. Main/Corp Massachusetts. Dept. of Public Works. 0091-6064. US. English. Mr George M Joseph, Principal Federal

Transportation—Roads and Traffic

Aid Engineer, 100 Nashua Street, Boston MA 02145. LC HE5633.M4.

STATE OF COLORADO ANNUAL HIGHWAY SAFETY WORK PROGRAM. Main/Corp Colorado. Division of Highway Safety. 0097-000X. US. English. an. 4201 East Arkansas Avenue, Denver CO 80222. LC HE5614.3.C6. DD 388.314. *State of Colorado Annual Highway Safety Work Program, 0097-000X.*

STATE OF IDAHO ANNUAL WORK PROGRAM. Main/Corp Idaho. Traffic Safety Commission. 0094-5706. US. English. an. 2419 West State Street, Boise ID 83702. LC HE5614.3.I2. DD 614.86209796.

STATE OF MICHIGAN'S ANNUAL HIGHWAY SAFETY PLAN. (STATE OF MICHIGAN'S ANNUAL HIGHWAY SAFETY PLAN FOR . . .). Main/Corp Michigan. Office of Highway Safety Planning. VFOAT Annual Highway Safety Plan. 0731-1966. US. English. an. Office of Highway Safety Planning, Michigan Department of State Police, General Office Building, 7150 Harris Drive, Lansing MI 48913. LC HE5614.3.M4. DD 363.125609774. *Annual Highway Safety Work Plan, 0094-1069.*

STATE OF NORTH CAROLINA HIGHWAY DETOUR BULLETIN. Main/Corp North Carolina. Dept. of Transportation. 0362-7225. US. English. PO Box 25201, Raleigh NC 27611. LC TE220. DD 388.314.

STATE OF WISCONSIN HIGHWAY SAFETY PLAN. VFOAT Wisconsin Highway Safety Plan. 1978/79-. US. English. an. Wisconsin Department of Transportation, Office of Highway Safety Coordination, James Wilson Plaza, Suite 803, 131 West Wilson Street, Madison WI 53702. LC HE5614.3.W5. DD 363.125609775.

STATE OF WISCONSIN STATE SUMMARY. TYPE AND AMOUNT OF AIDS PAID TO ALL GOVERNMENTAL UNITS AND COUNTRIES. (STATE SUMMARY : TYPE AND AMOUNT OF AIDS PAID TO ALL LOCAL GOVERNMENTAL UNITS AND COUNTIES). Main/Corp Wisconsin. Dept. of Transportation. Division of Planning. 0090-1067. US. English. an. State of Wisconsin, Department of Transportation, 4802 Sheboygan Avenue, Madison WI 53702. LC HE356.W5. DD 388.11.

STATE ROAD ANNUAL REPORT. Main/Corp Utah. Dept. of Finance. 0146-8359. US. English. an. Utah Department of Finance, Salt Lake City UT 84114. LC HE365.U8. DD 388.11.

STATISTICAL REPORT OF ACCIDENTS. See Statistics.

STATISTICS OF ROAD ACCIDENTS IN KARNATAKA STATE. See Statistics.

STATISTICS OF ROAD TRAFFIC ACCIDENTS IN JAPAN. See Statistics.

STATISTIEK VAN DE VERKEERSONGEVALLEN OP DE OPENBARE WEG. See Statistics.

STATISTIQUES DES TRANSPORTS ET COMMUNICATIONS : CONTINENT, AZORES ET MADERE. See Statistics.

STATUS REPORT - INSURANCE INSTITUTE FOR HIGHWAY SAFETY. (STATUS REPORT). Main/Corp Insurance Institute for Highway Safety. 0018-988X. Periodical. US. English. sm. Insurance Institute for Highway Safety, Watergate Six Hundred, Washington DC 20037. Tel (202)333-0770. Ed James H Mooney. LC HE5614. DD 614.862. Circ 14,500. (ctrl). A newsletter by the Institute, an independent, nonprofit scientific and educational organization on highway safety.

STATUS REPORT - PENNSYLVANIA TRANSPORTATION INSTITUTE. Main/Corp Pennsylvania Transportation Institute. 0360-1188. US. English. Pennsylvania State University, 226 Fenske Laboratory, University Park PA 16802. LC HE192.5. DD 380.50720748.

STRASSEN, BRUCKEN UND PARKEINRICHTUNGEN. See Statistics.

STRASSEN- VERKEHRSTECHNIK. (STRASSENVERKEHRSTECHNIK). 0039-2219. Periodical. GW. German. bm. Kirschbaum Verlag, Siegfriedstrasse 28, Postfach 9109, D-53 Godesberg Germany. Ind/Abst Excerpta Med., Comput. Control Abstr., Electr. Electron. Abstr., Sci. Abstr. Sect. A. Phys. Abstr. LC HE363.G29. CODEN SVKTAC.

STRASSENVERKEHRSSICHERHEIT IM JAHRE . . . . Series/Titl Beitrage zur Osterreichischen Statistik. 1979-. German. an. Kommissionsverlag Carl Ueberreuter, Alser Strasse 24, 1095 Wien Austria. LC HA1173, HE5614.5. A9.

STRASSENVERKEHRSUNFALLE. Main/Corp Saxony, Lower. Landesverwaltungsamt. German. ir. Niedersachsisches Landesverwaltungsamt, Auerstrasse 14, Hannover West Germany. LC HE5614.5.G3.

STRASSENVERKEHRSUNFALLE IN DER SCHWEIZ. VFOAT Accidents de la Circulation Routiere en Suisse. French (German). ir. 24.00. Bundesamt fur Statistik, Hallwylstrasse 15, CH 3003 Bern Switzerland. Tel (031)618853. Accidents and road traffic in Switzerland.

STREET FINANCE REPORT FOR IOWA CITIES. VFOAT Report of Municipal Street Finance. US. English. an. Iowa Department of Transportation, 800 Lincoln Way, Ames IA 50010. LC HE356.I8. DD 388.4042. *Annual Street Finance Report for the Incorporated Cities and Towns of Iowa.*

SUJI DE MIRU JIDOSHA. Japanese. ir. Nihon Jidosha Kaigisho, c/o Kokusai Kanko Kaikan 8-3 Marunouchi Chiyoda-ku, Tokyo 100 Japan. LC HE5697.A6.

SUMMARY AND ANALYSIS, RAILROAD-HIGHWAY GRADE CROSSING ACCIDENTS. See Transportation - Railroads.

SUMMARY OF ACCIDENT DATA. Main/Corp Virginia. Division of Traffic & Safety. 0146-7468. US. English. Virginia Department of Highway Highways Transporation, 1221 East Broad Street, Richmond VA 23219. LC HE5614.3.V8. DD 388.314.

SUMMARY OF ACCIDENTS INVOLVING THE DRINKING DRIVER. Main/Corp Washington State Patrol. 0146-1192. US. English. LC HE5614.3.W2. DD 614.862. *Drinking Driver Accident Summary, 0095-3350.*

SUMMARY OF ACTIVITIES - GOVERNOR'S HIGHWAY SAFETY PROGRAM. Main/Corp North Carolina. Governor's Highway Safety Program. 0361-2295. US. English. NC Department of Transportation and Highway Safety, PO Box 25201, Raleigh NC 27611. LC HE5614.3.N6. DD 338.314.

SUMMARY OF ALL REPORTED MOTOR VEHICLE TRAFFIC ACCIDENTS AND ACTIVITIES OF ALL FIELD PERSONNEL AND DRIVER SERVICES DIVISION IN THE STATE OF MISSISSIPPI. Main/Corp Mississippi. Driver Services Division. Statistical Bureau. VFOAT Annual Summary. US. English. an. Mississippi Highway Safety Patrol, Driver Services Division, Jackson MS 39205. LC HE5614.3.M55. DD 312.4409762.

SUMMARY OF IOWA COUNTY ENGINEERS ANNUAL HIGHWAY REPORTS. US. English. an. Department of Transportation, State Capitol, Des Moines IA 50319. LC HE356.I8. DD 388.11409777.

SUMMARY OF MOTOR VEHICLE TRAFFIC ACCIDENTS. ALEXANDRIA. Jan.-Dec. 1981-. 0741-448X. US. English. mo. Free. Louisiana Department of Public Safety Traffic Records Unit, PO Box 66614, Baton Rouge LA 70896. LC HE5614.4.A44. DD 312.440976369.

SUMMARY OF MOTOR VEHICLE TRAFFIC ACCIDENTS. BATON ROUGE. Jan.-Dec. 1981-. 0741-4471. US. English. mo. Free. Louisiana Department of Public Safety Traffic Records Unit, PO Box 66614, Baton Rouge LA 70896.

SUMMARY OF MOTOR VEHICLE TRAFFIC ACCIDENTS. GRETNA. Jan.-Dec. 1981-. 0741-4455. US. English. mo. Free. Louisiana Department of Public Safety Traffic Records Unit, PO Box 66614, Baton Rouge LA 70896. LC HE5614.4.G73. DD 312.440976338.

SUMMARY OF MOTOR VEHICLE TRAFFIC ACCIDENTS INVESTIGATED/REPORTED BY STATE POLICE. (SUMMARY OF MOTOR VEHICLE TRAFFIC ACCIDENTS. INVESTIGATED/REPORTED BY STATE POLICE). Jan.-Dec. 1981-. 0741-4366. US. English. mo. Free. Louisiana Department of Public Safety Traffic Records Unit, PO Box 66614, Baton Rouge LA 70896. LC HE5614.3.L8. DD 312.4409763.

SUMMARY OF MOTOR VEHICLE TRAFFIC ACCIDENTS. KENNER. Jan.-Dec. 1981-. 0741-4439. US. English. mo. Free. Louisiana Department of Public Safety Traffic Records Unit, PO Box 66614, Baton Rouge LA 70896.

SUMMARY OF MOTOR VEHICLE TRAFFIC ACCIDENTS. MONROE. Jan./Dec. 1981-. 0741-4404. US. English. mo. Free. Louisiana Department of Public Safety Traffic Records Unit, PO Box 66614, Baton Rouge LA 70896. LC HE5614.4.M66. DD 312.440976387.

SUMMARY OF MOTOR VEHICLE TRAFFIC ACCIDENTS. NEW IBERIA. Jan.-Dec. 1981-. 0741-4390. US. English. mo. Free. Louisiana Department of Public Safety/Traffic Records Unit, PO Box 66614 Baton Rouge LA 70896. LC HE5614.4.N48. DD 312.440976349.

SUMMARY OF MOTOR VEHICLE TRAFFIC ACCIDENTS. NEW ORLEANS. Jan.-Dec. 1981-. 0741-4374. US. English. mo. Free. Louisiana Department of Public Safety Traffic Records Unit, PO Box 66614, Baton Rouge LA 70896. LC HE5614.4.N49. DD 312.440976335.

SUMMARY OF MOTOR VEHICLE TRAFFIC ACCIDENTS. URBAN. Jan./Dec. 1981-. 0741-4331. US. English. mo. Free. Louisiana Department of Public Safety Traffic Records Unit, PO Box 66614, Baton Rouge LA 70896. LC HE5614.3.L8. DD 312.4409763.

SUMMARY OF PROGRESS - NATIONAL COOPERATIVE HIGHWAY RESEARCH PROGRAM. Main/Corp National Cooperative Highway Research Program. 1962/66-. 0547-5562. US. English. National Academy of Sciences, 2102 Constitution Avenue, Washington DC 20418. LC TE153. DD 388.1072073.

A SURVEY OF OUT-OF-STATE PASSENGER CARS AND OUT-OF-STATE CAMPER VEHICLES ON INTERSTATE, ARTERIAL AND PRIMARY HIGHWAYS IN VIRGINIA. Main/Corp Virginia. Division of Traffic & Safety. VFOAT Virginia Visitor Travel Survey. 0363-4027. US. English. Virginia Department of Highways & Transportation, 1221 East Broad Street, Richmond VA 23219. LC HE5614.3.V8. DD 388.314.

SYLLABUS - CITT. (SYLLABUS). Main/Corp Canadian Institute of Traffic and Transportation. VAT Syllabus - Canadian Institute of Traffic and Transportation. 0710-1376. CN. English. an. Canadian Institute of Traffic and Transportation, Suite 515/44 Victoria Street, Toronto Ontario M5C 1Y2 Canada. DD 380.5071171.

TABULATION SHOWING ANNUAL AVERAGE DAILY TRAFFIC VOLUME AT RECORDER LOCATIONS AND PERCENT OF CHANGE IN VOLUME OVER PREVIOUS YEARS. Main/Corp Florida. State Road Department. Division of Traffic and Planning. US. English. ir. State of Florida, Road Department, Tallahassee FL 32304. LC HE371.F6.

TECHNICAL REPORTS OF THE NATIONAL HIGHWAY TRAFFIC SAFETY ADMINISTRATION. Main/Corp United States. National Highway Traffic Safety Administration. US. English. US Department of Transportation, National Highway Traffic Safety Administration, Technical Services Administration, 400 7th Street SW, Washington DC 20402.

TEEN-AGE DRIVERS. Main/Corp Washington State Patrol. 0093-917X. US. English. LC HE5614.3.W2. DD 388.314.

TENNESSEE MOTOR VEHICLE TRAFFIC ACCIDENT FACTS. Main/Corp Tennessee. Dept. of Safety. Planning and Research Section. 0360-5396. US. English. an. Andrew Jackson State Office Building, Nashville TN 37219. LC HE5614.3.T2. DD 388.314.

TEXAS HIGHWAYS. Began publication in 1954. 0040-4349. Periodical. US. English. mo. $10.00 Domestic, $15.00 Foreign. Texas Highways Circulation, State Department of Highway and Public Transportation, Austin TX 78701. Tel (512)465-7408. Ed Frank Lively. LC TE24.T4. DD 917.64046305. Circ 330,000. (ctrl). Interprets scenic, recreational, historical, cultural, and ethnic treasures of the state of Texas. *Construction & Maintenance Bulletin.*

Transportation—Ships & Shipping

TEXAS TRAFFIC SAFETY REPORT. Began in 1974?. Periodical. US. English. ir. State Department of Highways & Public Transportation, 11th & Brazos, Austin TX 78701.

TIELIIKENNEONNETTOMUUDET. VAGTRAFIKOLYCKOR. Main/Corp Finland. Tilastokeskus. VFOAT Road Traffic Accidents. 1978-. Fl. Finnish (Swedish). ir. Tilastokeskus, Valtion Painatuskeskus, Markkinointiosasto, PI 516, 00101 Helsinki 10 Finland. LC HE5614.5.F5. *Tieliikennevahingot.*

TOLLWAYS. May 1964-. Periodical. US. English. ir. International Bridge Tunnel & Turnpike, 1225 Connecticut Avenue NW, Washington DC 20036. *Tolls.*

TORO KYOTONG. Periodical. KO. Korean. mo. Toro Kyotong Anjon Hyophoe, 198-16 Kwanhun-dong Chongno-ku, Seoul Korea. LC HE5614.K6.

TRAFFIC ACCIDENT FACTS. Main/Corp Florida. Division of Highway Patrol. Traffic Homicide and Records Section. 1978-. 0095-6104. US. English. an. Department of Highway Safety & Motor Vehicles, Bureau of Records & Training, Tallahassee FL 32301. LC HE5614.3.F6. DD 363.125209759. *Traffic Accident Facts, 0095-6104.*

TRAFFIC ACCIDENT FACTS (DOVER, DEL.). (TRAFFIC ACCIDENT FACTS). 0738-3657. US. English. an. Department of Public Safety, Division of State Police, PO Box 430, Dover DE 19901. LC HE5614.3.D3. DD 312.4409751.

TRAFFIC ADMINISTRATIVE SUMMARY. Main/Corp Kentucky. State Police. US. English. an. LC HE5614.3.K4. DD 312.4409769.

TRAFFIC CHARACTERISTICS ON ILLINOIS HIGHWAYS. Main/Corp Illinois. Dept. of Transportation. Office of Policy and Planning. 1975-. 0082-5832. US. English. Illinois Department of Transportation, 2300 South Dirksen Parkway, Springfield IL 62764. LC HE371.I3. DD 388.31409773. *Traffic Characteristics on Illinois Highways, 0082-5832.*

TRAFFIC DATA FROM AUTOMATIC TRAFFIC RECORDER STATIONS. Main/Corp Virginia. Division of Traffic & Safety. VFOAT Automatic Traffic Recorder Data. US. English. an. Virginia Department of Highways, Division of Traffic & Safety, Richmond VA 23216. LC HE371.V8. DD 388.31409755.

TRAFFIC QUARTERLY CEASED. V. 1-35. 0041-0713. Periodical. US. English. qt. ENO Foundation for Transportation, Box 55 Saugatuck Station, Westport CT 06880. Ind/Abst Electron. Commun. Abstr. J., ISMEC Bull., Pollut. Abstr. Indexes, Saf. Sci. Abstr. J., Eng. Index Annu., Eng. Index Mon., Eng. Index Bioeng. Abstr., Eng. Index Energy Abstr., Energy Inf. Abstr., Environ. Abstr., Avery Index Archit. Period. Second Ed. Revis. Enlarged Suppl., Int. Aerosp. Abstr., Appl. Sci. Technol. Index, Eng. Index Mon., Public Aff. Inf. Serv. Bull. LC HE331. DD 388.3. CODEN TRAQA4. (cum index).

TRAFFIC SAFETY ANNUAL REPORT. Main/Corp Canada. Road and Motor Vehicle Traffic Safety Branch. VFOAT Rapport Annual, Securite Automobile. 1st- 1970/71-. CN. English and French. an. Transport Canada, Public Affairs Branch, Ottawa Ontario Canada K1A 0N5. LC HE5614.5.C2. DD 354.7100783.

TRAFFIC SAFETY EVALUATION RESEARCH REVIEW. Vol. 2, No. 1 (Spring 1983)-. 0741-5133. Periodical. US. English. bm. National Highway Traffic Safety Administration, Superintendent of Documents, Government Printing Office, Washington DC 20402. LC HE5614.2. DD 363.12560973.

TRAFFIC VOLUMES AND SUPPLEMENTARY DATA, CENTRAL MOUNTAINS DIVISION, CITY OF GOSFORD AND SHIRE OF COLO. English. an. Department of Main Roads, 309 Castlereagh Street, Sydney New South Wales Australia. LC HE373.A982. DD 388.314209944. *Traffic Volumes and Supplementary Data, Central Mountains Division and Colo-Gosford Shires.*

TRAFFIC VOLUMES ON THE CALIFORNIA STATE HIGHWAY SYSTEM. Main/Corp California. Office of Traffic Engineering. VFOAT Traffic Volumes on California State Highways. 1978-. 0145-9813. US. English. an. $5.00. Department of Transportation, Division of Operations, Sacramento CA 95802. LC HE371.C2. DD 388.314209794. *Traffic Volumes on the California State Highway System, 0145-9813.*

TRAFFIC WORLD. Began publication in 1907. 0041-073X. Periodical. US. English. wk. $60.00. Traffic Service Corporation, 1325 G Street NW/Suite 900, Washington DC 20005. LC HE2714. Available on microfilm from University Microfilms. *Federal Trade Reporter.*

TRAFIKBLINKEN CEASED. Swedish. ir. Trafikskyddet, Stora Robertsgatan 20 00120 12, Helsingfors Finland. **Tel** (90)56671. Ed Matti Jarvinen. LC HE5614.5.F5. bk rev.

TRANSPORTATION RESEARCH IN CANADA. 1973-. 0381-8284. CN. English. an. Roads and Transportation Association of Canada, 875 Carling Avenue, Ottawa Ontario K1S 5A4 Canada. DD 388.1072071. *Road Research in Canada, 0381-8292.*

TRIO. TRAFFIC RULINGS, INTERPRETATIONS, OPINIONS. Main/Corp New York (State). Dept. of Motor Vehicles. VFOAT Traffic Bulings, Interpretations, Opinions. V. 1- 1961/62-. US. English. State of New York, Department of Motor Vehicles, Albany NY 12224. DD 343.7470946, 347.4703946.

TWENTY YEAR HIGHWAY NEEDS STUDY. Main/Corp Maryland. Dept. of Transportation. 0090-5879. US. English. Maryland Department of Transportation, State Highway Administration, PO Box 717, Baltimore MD 21203. LC HE356.M3. DD 388.109752. *Twenty Year Highway Needs Study.*

VAGTRAFIKOLYCKOR MED PERSONSKADA. Main/Corp Sweden. Statistiska Centralbryan. Series Corp ITS Sveriges Officiella Statistik. VFOAT Road Traffic Accidents with Personal Injury. English or Swedish. ir. Statistiska Centralbryan, S 102 50 Stockholm Sweden. LC HE5614.5.S8. *Vagtrafikolyckor.*

VEHICLE MILES AND MONTHLY VARIATIONS OF TRAVEL ON MISSOURI HIGHWAYS. VFOAT Vehicle Miles of Travel and Monthly Variations of Traffic. 1979-. US. English. an. LC HE371.M8. DD 388.31409778. *Traffic Trends on Missouri Highways.*

THE VOICE OF THE PEDESTRIAN. See Public Health and Safety.

VOLUME OF TRAFFIC ON THE PRIMARY ROAD SYSTEM OF IOWA. VFOAT Volume of Traffic on the Primary Road System. US. English. be. $12.50. State of Iowa Department of Transportaion, Ames IA 50010. LC HE356.I8. DD 388.314209777.

WEGENVERSLAG. Main/Corp Utrecht (Province). Commissie Wegen, Verkeer en Vervoer. Dutch. ir. LC HE363.N24.

WESTERN ROADS : OFFICIAL JOURNAL OF THE MAIN ROADS DEPARTMENT, WESTERN AUSTRALIA. Vol. 1, No. 1 (Jan. 1976)-. Periodical. AT. English. qt. Western Main Roads Department, GPO Box S 1400, Perty 6001 W Australia. LC TE122.W47. DD 388.109941.

WISCONSIN ANNUAL HIGHWAY SAFETY WORK PROGRAM. Main/Corp Wisconsin. Division of Highway Safety Coordination. 0148-7728. US. English. an. Division of Safety Coordination, James Wilson Plaza, Suite 803/131 West Wilson Street, Madison WI 53702. LC HE5614.3.W5. DD 614.86209775.

WISCONSIN HIGHWAY IMPROVEMENT & MAINTENANCE PROGRAM. Main/Corp Wisconsin. Dept. of Transportation. 1978/79-. US. English. an. *Wisconsin Highway Improvement Program.*

WORK IN PROGRESS. Main/Corp University of Michigan. Highway Safety Research Institute. 1975-. 0731-1834. US. English. an. Highway Safety Research Institute, The University of Michigan, Huron Parkway and Baxter Road, Ann Arbor MI 48109. NLM W1 UN944MA. *Highway Safety Research Institute, 0278-5331.*

WORKING PAPER PUB. - SNOW AND ICE CONTROL WORKING GROUP. (WORKING PAPER PUB). VAT Working Paper - Snow and Ice Control Working Group. 0712-9106. Periodical. CN. English. Institute for Environmental Studies, Front Campus, Toronto Ontario M5S 1A6 Canada. DD 625.763.

WORLD HIGHWAYS. 1949. 0043-8529. Periodical. US. English. ir. $6.25. International Road Federation, 525 School Street SW/Suite 302, Washington DC 20024. **Tel** (202)554-2106. Ed Hugh M Gillespie. bk rev. Circ 4,800. Information on road and transportation projects worldwide; notices of IRF meetings and activities.

WORLD SURVEY OF CURRENT RESEARCH AND DEVELOPMENT ON ROADS AND ROAD TRANSPORT. VFOAT IRF Research and Development. 0277-3805. US. English. an. National Technical Information Service, 5285 Port Royal Road, Springfield VA 22161. **Tel** (703)487-4650. LC TE1. DD 625.705. *Highway Research in Progress, 0440-8004.*

WYOMING'S COMPREHENSIVE REPORT ON TRAFFIC ACCIDENTS. VFOAT Comprehensive Report on Traffic Accidents. 1982-. 0747-8771. US. English. an. Wyoming Highway Department, Highway Safety Branch, Safety Analysis Section, PO Box 1708, Cheyenne WY 82002-9019. LC HE5614.3.W9. DD 312.4409787. *Wyoming's Fatal Accident Facts.*

THE YEAR'S WORK - INSURANCE INSTITUTE FOR HIGHWAY SAFETY. (THE YEAR'S WORK). Main/Corp Insurance Institute for Highway Safety. 1980-1981-. 0276-7325. US. English. an. Free. Insurance Institute for Highway Safety, Watergate 600 New Hampshire Avenue/Suite 300, Washington DC 20037. LC HE5614.2. DD 363.1250973.

YHTEENVETO TIELIIKENNEVAHINGOISTA. VFOAT Sammandrag AV Vagtrafikolyckorna. Finnish and Swedish. ir. Tilastokeskus, Annankatu 44 00100 10, Helsinki Finland. LC HE5614.5.F5.

YOUR HIGHWAY DEPARTMENT, ARKANSAS. (YOUR HIGHWAY DEPARTMENT). Main/Corp Arkansas. State Highway Dept. 0094-9914. US. English. State Highway Department, PO Box 1067, Little Rock AR 72201. LC HE356.A8. DD 353.9767008781.

ZEITSCHRIFT FUR VERKEHRSSICHERHET. Vol. 1-. 0044-3654. Periodical. GW. German (English or French). qt. $51.13. Verlag Tuv Rheinland GMBH, Postfach 101750, D-5000 Koln 1 West Germany. **Tel** (0221)8393-2850. Ind/Abst Foreign Lang. Index. LC HE331.

SHIPS & SHIPPING

THE ABC SHIPPING GUIDE. UK. English. mo. $101.50 US. ABC Travel Guides Ltd, World Timetable Centre Church Street, Dunstable LU5 4HB England. **Tel** (0582)600111. Ed A Bates. LC HE568. adv acc. Circ 7,000. Comprehensive worldwide guide to passenger shipping services, cruises, transocean lines, car ferries and cargo passenger lines plus schedules and fares and included.

ACTIVITES - PORT AUTONOME DE MARSEILLE. See Business - Commerce.

AISA GUIDE TO SHIPPING COOPERATIVES. See Economics - Cooperatives.

AL-NASHRAH AL-SANAWIYAH LIL-MILAHAH WA-AL-NAQL AL-BAHRI. VFOAT Annual Bulletin of Sea-Borne Traffic. Began in 1880. UA. Arabic (and English). an. Jihaz Al-Markazi Lil-Tabiah Al-Ammah Wa-Al-Ihsa, Tariq Salahsalim, Madinat Nasr Cairo Egypt. LC HE702.7. DD 387.5440962.

ALASKA SHIPPERS GUIDE. 1981-. 0271-8987. US. English. an. $19.95. Alaska Northwest Publishing Company, Box 4-EEE, Anchorage AK 99509. LC HE9.U5. DD 380.524025798.

ALASKA VESSEL REGISTER. US. English. an. LC SH222.A4. DD 353.97980082.

ALMANAK INSA. See Yearbooks, Almanacs, Directories.

AMERICAN DROP-SHIPPERS DIRECTORY. See Yearbooks, Almanacs, Directories.

AMERICAN MARINE REGISTER. 0091-5491. US. English. ir. $100.00. American Marine Register, PO Box 5468, North Little Rock AR 72119. LC HE553. DD 387.102573.

AMERICAN SHIPPER. Began with Vol. 18, No. 5 (May 1976) issue. 0160-225X. Periodical. US. English. mo. $15.00 Domestic, 50.00 Foreign. Howard Publications Inc, 33 South Hogan Street, PO Box 4728, Jacksonville FL 32201. Ind/Abst Trade Ind.

Transportation—Ships & Shipping

Index, Bus. Period. Index. **LC** HF1. **DD** 387.00973. *Florida Journal of Commerce, American Shipper,* 0097-6237.

ANNALES (INSTITUT MEDITERRANEEN DES TRANSPORTS MARITIMES (FRANCE)). (ANNALES). 1984-. Periodical. French (summaries in English). an. La Calade, 13080 Aix-En-Provence France.

ANNUAIRE MARITIME NATIONAL. *See* Yearbooks, Almanacs, Directories.

ANNUAL CARGO REPORT. US. English. an. Department of Transportation, Bureau of Waterways, New London CT 06320. **LC** HE767.N38. **DD** 387.164097465.

ANNUAL CONVENTION OF THE HUDSON BAY ROUTE ASSOCIATION. **Main/Corp** Hudson Bay Route Association. CN. English. an. Hudson Bay Route Association, Box 10 Hudson Bay, Saskatchewan Canada. **LC** HE564.B4. **DD** 389.544062712.

ANNUAL DEPARTMENTAL REPORT - DIRECTOR OF MARINE, SARAWAK. **Main/Corp** Sarawak. Marine Dept. 0581-7803. English. ir. **LC** HE880.S3.

ANNUAL REPORT - AMERICAN BUREAU OF SHIPPING. **Main/Corp** American Bureau of Shipping. 0569-3578. Periodical. US. English. an. American Bureau of Shipping, 45 Broad Street Northwest, New York NY 10004. **LC** VK1. **DD** 387.505.

ANNUAL REPORT AND ACCOUNTS - BRITISH WATERWAYS BOARD. **Main/Corp** Great Britain. British Waterways Board. 0436-3639. UK. English. an. Her Majesty's Stationery Office, PO Box 276, London SW8 5DT England. **Ind/Abst** Life Sci. Collect. **LC** HE663. **DD** 387.00942.

ANNUAL REPORT AND REVIEW OF OPERATIONS - PORT OF MELBOURNE AUTHORITY. **Main/Corp** Port of Melbourne Authority. 1981-82-. English. an. Port of Authority Building, World Trade Center, Melbourne 3005 Australia. **LC** HE560.M4. **DD** 387.1. *Annual Report.*

ANNUAL REPORT AND STATEMENT OF ACCOUNTS - SRI LANKA MADHYAMA NAV GASTU KARYAMSAYA. **Main/Corp** Sri Lanka Madhyama Nav Gastu Karyamsaya. VFOAT Annual Report. English. an. **LC** HE876.8. **DD** 354.549300877506.

ANNUAL REPORT - AUSTRALIAN CHAMBER OF SHIPPING. **Main/Corp** Australian Chamber of Shipping. AT. English. an. Australian Chamber of Shipping, 60 Pitt Street, Sydney Australia.

ANNUAL REPORT - BRITISH COLUMBIA FERRY CORPORATION. **Main/Corp** British Columbia Ferry Corporation. 1979-. 0226-2754. CN. English. an. British Columbia Ferry Corporation, 818 Broughton Street, Victoria British Columbia V8W 1E4 Canada. **DD** 386.609711.

ANNUAL REPORT - CYPRUS PORTS AUTHORITY. **Main/Corp** Cyprus Ports Authority. 1st- 1977-. CY. English. ir. Cyprus Ports Authority, 23 Crete Str, Nicosia Cyprus. **LC** HE559.C9. **DD** 354.564500877105.

ANNUAL REPORT - NATIONAL MARITIME BOARD (SINGAPORE). **Main/Corp** Singapore. National Maritime Board. English. ir. National Maritime Board, 20 South Quay, Singapore Singapore. **LC** HE885. **DD** 354.5952008775.

ANNUAL REPORT - PORT AUTHORITY OF NY & NJ. (ANNUAL REPORT - THE PORT AUTHORITY OF NY & NJ). **Main/Corp** Port Authority of New York and New Jersey. VAT Annual Report - Port Authority of New York and New Jersey. 0362-9449. US. English. an. New York Public Affairs Department, PO Box 544 Lenox Hill Station, New York NY 10021. **LC** HE554.N7. **DD** 353.9747008771. *Report.*

ANNUAL REPORT - SAINT LAWRENCE SEAWAY DEVELOPMENT CORPORATION. (ANNUAL REPORT). **Main/Corp** St. Lawrence Seaway Development Corporation. Began with 1954/55. 0558-194X. US. English. an. Saint Lawrence Seaway Development Corporation, 800 Independence Avenue SW, Washington DC 20591. **LC** HD1694. **DD** 386.509714. Vol. for 1978 distributed to depository libraries in microfiche.

ANNUAL REPORT - SOUTH AUSTRALIA. DEPT. OF MARINE AND HARBORS. **Main/Corp** South Australia. Dept. of Marine and Harbors. English. ir. **LC** HE559.A8. **DD** 354.9423008771.

ANNUAL REPORT - WESTERN AUSTRALIAN COASTAL SHIPPING COMMISSION. **Main/Corp** Western Australian Coastal Shipping Commission. AT. English. ir. Western Australian Coastal Shipping Commission PO Box 394, Fremantal WA 6160 Australia. **LC** HE945.W42. **DD** 387.509941.

ANUARIO DE PORTOS E NAVIOS. *See* Yearbooks, Almanacs, Directories.

ANUARIO DEL PUERTO AUTONOMO DE BARCELONA. *See* Yearbooks, Almanacs, Directories.

ANUARIO ESTADISTICO (AUTORIDAD PORTUARIA DE GUAYAQUIL). *See* Yearbooks, Almanacs, Directories.

APPENDIX (LLOYD'S REGISTER OF SHIPPING). (APPENDIX). UK. English. an. Lloyds Register of Shipping, 17 Battery Place, New York NY 10004.

ARAB SHIPPING. VFOAT Arab Shipping Guide, Al-Dalil Al-Bahri Lil-Alam Al-Arabi. Began with 1978 Vol. 0141-4151. UK. Arabic (English, 1978-). an. Free to seatrade subscribers. Seatrade Publications Ltd, Whitehall Building 17 Battery Place, New York NY 10004.

ARBOK OVER SKANDINAVISKE SKIPSREDERIER. *See* Yearbooks, Almanacs, Directories.

ARGO. Periodical. English or Greek. ir. $35.00. E Batis, 145 Kountourioutou and King, George Strs, 7, Peiraieus Greece. **LC** HE561.

ASIAN FISHING AND SHIPPING MAGAZINE. *See* Fish Culture and Fisheries.

ASIAN SHIPPING. No. 1 (Jan. 1978)-. Periodical. HK. English. mo. $16.25. Asian Shipping, PO Box 20014 Hennessy Road, Hong Kong Hong Kong. **Tel** 5-278399. Ed A G Barnett. **LC** HE873. **DD** 387.5095. bk rev. adv acc. **Circ** 5,300. (ctrl). The shipping industry in East and South East Asia with associated developments in shipbuilding and marine engineering.

ATLANTIC CANADA SHIPPING PROJECT NEWSLETTER. **Main/Corp** Memorial University of Newfoundland. Maritime History Group. VFOAT Maritime History Group Newsletter. VAT Newsletter - Maritime History Group (1980). Dec. 1980-. 0710-247X. CN. English. an. Maritime History Group, Memorial University of Newfoundland, St John's Newfoundland A1C 5S7 Canada. **DD** 387.509715. *Canadian Shipping Project Newsletter,* 0708-0727.

AUSTRALASIAN SHIPPING RECORD. V. 1- 1970-. Periodical. AT. English. bm. Australasian Maritime Historical Society, PO Box 33, Magill SA 5072 Australia.

AUSTRALIAN SHIPPING. 1983-. 0812-0730. English. an. **LC** HE565.A8. **DD** 387.2450994. *Australian Shipping and Shipbuilding.*

AUSTRALIAN SHIPPING AND SHIPBULDING STATISTICS. *See* Statistics.

BANGLADESH SHIPPING DIRECTORY. *See* Yearbooks, Almanacs, Directories.

BAY & DELTA YACHTSMAN. VAT Bay and Delta Yachtsman. 0191-4731. Periodical. US. English. mo. $12.00. Bay & Delta Yachtsman, 2019 Clement Avenue, Alameda CA 94501. **Tel** (415)865-7500.

BI-LINGUAL MAGAZINE. **Main/Corp** Nigerian Ports Authority. Management Services Division. VFOAT Revue Bilingue. 1981-. 0189-2029. English (French). an. Management Services Division, Nigerian Ports Authority, 26-28 Marina Lagos Nigeria. **LC** HE559. **DD** 354.66900877106.

BIENNIAL REPORT - INTERNATIONAL CARGO HANDLING CO-ORDINATION ASSOCIATION. **Main/Corp** International Cargo Handling Co-Ordination Association. UK. English. be. International Cargo Handling Co-Ordination Association, Abford House, 15 Wilton Road, London SW1V 1LX England. **LC** HE561. **DD** 380.52.

BIENNIAL REPORT - ARKANSAS WATERWAYS COMMISSION. (REPORT). **Main/Corp** Arkansas. Waterways Commission. 0093-6200. US. English. be. Waterways Commission, 138 National Old Line Building, Little Rock AR 72201. **LC** HE624.A8. **DD** 353.976700876.

BINNENVAARTBEDRIJVEN. **Series/Titl** Produktiestatistieken Transport, Opslag en Communicatie. VFOAT Inland Shipping. 0168-5627. NE. Dutch (summaries in English). an. 7.50. Centraal Bureau Voor de Statistiek, Prinses Beatrixlaan 428 Postbus 959, 2270 AZ Voorburg Netherlands. *Binnenvaartbedrijven: Produktiestatistieken Transport, Opslag en Communicatie.*

BOLETIM ESTATISTICO. *See* Statistics.

BOLETIM ESTATISTICO - ADMINISTRACAO DO PORTO DO RECIFE. *See* Statistics.

BOLETIM ESTATISTICO ANUAL. *See* Statistics.

BOLETIN ESTADISTICO - EMPRESA PORTUARIA DE CHILE. *See* Statistics.

BRANDON'S SHIPPER & FORWARDER. VAT Brandon's Shipper and Forwarder. 0006-9086. Periodical. US. English. wk. $38.00. Brandons Shipper & Forwarder, 424 W 33rd Street, New York NY 10001. **Tel** (212)714-3100. Ed Jon Jacobs. adv acc. **Circ** 5,500. Shipping news and schedules covering activities of liner shipping companies and US import and export trade.

BULK CARRIERS IN THE WORLD FLEET. (BULK CARRIERS IN THE WORLD FLEET AS OF . . .). 0565-680X. US. English. an. US Department of Transportation, Maritime Administration Office of Trade Studies and Subsidy Contracts, 400 Seventh Street SW, Washington DC 20590. **LC** HE565.A3. **DD** 387.245. Vols. for 1982- distributed to depository libraries in microfiche.

BULLETIN ANNUEL DES STATISTIQUES - REPUBLIQUE TUNISIENNE, OFFICE DES PORTS NATIONAUX. **Main/Corp** Diwan Al-Mawani Al-Qawmiyah. TI. French. ir. Office des Ports Nationaux, 23 rue Despagne, Tunis Tunisia. **LC** HE559.T8. **DD** 387.109611.

CAMEROON INTER-PORTS : ORGANE DE LIAISON ET D'INFORMATION DE L'OFFICE NATIONAL DES PORTS DU CAMEROUN. Periodical. English (and French). ir. Office National des Ports du Cameroun, 5 Boulevard Leclerc, BP 4020, Douala Cameroon Africa. **LC** HE559.C35. **DD** 387.10967113.

CANADIAN FORWARDER CEASED. (THE CANADIAN FORWARDER). No. 1-661. 0045-4877. Periodical. CN. English. bw.

CANADIAN PORTS AND SEAWAY DIRECTORY. *See* Yearbooks, Almanacs, Directories.

CANADIAN SAILINGS. (CANADIAN SAILING). July 5, 1982-. 0821-5944. Periodical. CN. English. wk. $25.00. Canadian Sailings, 4606 St Catherine Street West, Montreal Quebec H3Z 1S3 Canada. **DD** 387.5440971.

CANADIAN SAILOR. 0008-4972. Periodical. CN. English (text also in French). mo. Seafarers International Union of Canada, 634 St James Street West, Montreal Quebec Canada. **Tel** (514)842-8161. Ed Andrew C Boyle. **Circ** 1,000. (ctrl). A review of activities which have occurred in each port, president's editorial letters to the editor seafarers' training institute graduates.

CANADIAN SHIPBUILDING AND ALLIED INDUSTRIES. April 1980-. 0714-8364. CN. English. ir. $10.00. Canadian Shipbuilding and Ship Repairing Association, Suite 801/100 Sparks Street, Ottawa Ontario K1P 5B7 Canada. **DD** 338.476238302571. *Canadian Shipbuilding,* 0227-2164.

CANADIAN SHIPPING AND MARINE ENGINEERING. V. 41, No. 8- May 1970-. 0008-4980. Periodical. CN. English. mo. 25.00 Domestic, $40.00 US, 50.00 Others. Arthurs Publications Ltd, 5200 Dixie Suite 204, Mississauga Ontario L4W 1E4 Canada. **Tel** (416)625-5277. Ed Patrick Brophy. **Ind/Abst** ASTIS Bibliogr., ASTIS Curr.

Transportation—Ships & Shipping

Aware. Bull., Can. Bus. Index, Electron. Commun. Abstr. J., Excerpta Med., ISMEC Bull., Pollut. Abstr. Indexes, Ship Abstr., Ocean. Abstr. bk rev. adv acc. Circ 3,300. (ctrl) Technical articles on shipbuilding, marine engineering, naval architecture, offshore structures and allied subjects. *Canadian Shipping and Marine Engineering News*, 0318-3025.

CARIBBEAN PORTS HANDBOOK. English. be. 26.00. Creative Communications Inc Ltd, PO Box 105, Kingston 10 Jamica West Indies. Tel (805)926-2217. Ed Anthony Gambrill. LC HE555.A3. DD 387.1091821. adv acc. Circ 1,000. (ctrl). A comprehensive guide to port entry for over 130 ports in the Caribbean, Gulf of Mexico and adjacent areas.

CARIBBEAN SHIPPING : THE JOURNAL OF THE CARIBBEAN SHIPPING ASSOCIATION. Periodical. JM. English. ty. $12.00. Creative Communications Inc Ltd, PO Box 105, Kingston 10 Jamaica. LC HE785. DD 387.164091821.

CASUALTY RETURN. MERCHANT SHIPS TOTALLY LOST, BROKEN UP, ETC. (CASUALTY RETURN; MERCHANT SHIPS TOTALLY LOST, BROKEN UP, ETC). 0261-2151. Periodical. UK. English. qt. Ind/Abst Ship Abstr.

THE CENTRAL LIVESTOCK CO-OPERATIVE SHIPPER CEASED. VFOAT Co-Operative Shipper. V. 31- 1951-. 0193-2373. Periodical. US. English. bm. $2.00. Central Livestock, Room 104/Livestock Exchange Building South, St Paul MN 55075. Tel (612)451-1844. *Central Co-Operative Shipper.*

THE CHADBURN. Began publication Summer 1976?. Periodical. US. English. Great Lakes Historical Society, 480 Main Street, Vermillion OH 44089. DD 977.006277122.

HAI CHIAO SHIH YEN CHIU. Periodical. CH. Chinese. an. 0.50. Fu-Chien Sheng Chuan-Chou, Shih Yu Tien Chu, Fu-Chien China. LC HE894. DD 387.50951.

CHUNG-KUO HAI YUN. VFOAT Maritime China. Periodical. CH. Chinese (English). qt. $55.00. Maritime China, 4306 China Resources Building, 26 Harbour Road, Hong Kong. Tel (5)736211. Ed Christa Tam. LC HE894. DD 387.50951. bk rev. adv acc. Circ 6,000. (ctrl). A bi-lingual joint venture in its 4th year, Maritime China keeps China up-to-date with international shipping and informs the rest of the world about the Chinese industry.

COAST MARINE & TRANSPORTATION DIRECTORY. See Yearbooks, Almanacs, Directories.

COASTWISE SHIPPING STATISTICS (ANNUAL). See Statistics.

COASTWISE SHIPPING STATISTICS (QUARTERLY). See Statistics.

CODE OF FEDERAL REGULATIONS. 46, SHIPPING. VFOAT Shipping, CRF. 46, Shipping. US. English. an. US Government Printing Office, Superintendent of Documents, Washington DC 20402. Vols. for 1984 distributed to some depository libraries in microfiche.

COMMERCE YEARBOOK OF PORTS, SHIPPING AND SHIPBUILDING. See Yearbooks, Almanacs, Directories.

CONTAINERIZED CARGO STATISTICS. See Statistics.

CURRENT ISSUES IN INTERNATIONAL SHIP FINANCE. Series/Titl Commercial Law and Practice Course Handbook Series. 1984-. 0883-0517. US. English. Practising Law Institute, 810 Seventh Avenue, New York NY 10019. *Current Issues in Ship Financing*, 0883-0592.

DADOS ESTATISTICOS DA MOVIMENTACAO DE CARGA E PASSAGEIROS. See Statistics.

DAILY DEPOSITORY SHIPPING LIST. 0145-0646. Periodical. US. English. Superintendent of Documents, US Government Printing Office, Washington DC 20402.

DANSK ILLUSTRERET SKIBSLISTE. Main/Corp Arhus Havn (Firm). VFOAT Danish Illustrated List of Ships. Danish (English). ir. Arhus Havn, Europaplads 2, 8000 Arhus C Denmark. LC HE565.D4.

DECISIONS. See Law.

DESENVOLVIMENTO DO ORCAMENTO DA RECEITA E DESPESA -ADMINISTRACAO DOS PORTOS DO DOURO E LEIXOES. Main/Corp Administracoa dos Portos do Douro E Leixoes. Portuguese. ir. LC HE558.O6.

DIARKES KODIX NAUTERGATIKES & NAUTILIAKES NOMOTHESIAS. See Law.

DIRECTORY. FLORIDA PORTS AND WATERWAYS. See Yearbooks, Almanacs, Directories.

DIRECTORY OF SERVICES. PORT OF SAINT JOHN, NEW BRUNSWICK. See Yearbooks, Almanacs, Directories.

DIRECTORY OF SHIPOWNERS, SHIPBUILDERS, & MARINE ENGINEERS. See Yearbooks, Almanacs, Directories.

DIRKZWAGER'S GUIDE TO THE NEW WATERWAY, ROTTERDAM, DORDRECHT, EUROPOORT, AND BOTLEK. NE. English. an. LC HE558.R75. DD 387.109492. *Dirkzwager's Guide to the New Waterway, Rotterdam and Dordrecht.*

DOCK AND HARBOUR AUTHORITY. (THE DOCK AND HARBOUR AUTHORITY). V. 1- Nov. 1920-. 0012-4419. Periodical. UK. English. mo. 36.00. Foxlow Publishing Company, 20 Harcourt Street, London W1H 2AX England. Tel (01)723-1486. Ed Anthony Burt. Ind/Abst Electron. Commun. Abstr. J., ISMEC Bull., Pollut. Abstr. Indexes, Saf. Sci. Abstr. J., Eng. Index Mon., Eng. Index Bioeng. Abstr., Eng. Index Energy Abstr., Fluidex, Life Sci. Collect., Ship Abstr., Excerpta Med., Eng. Index Annu., Eng. Index Mon., Nuci. Sci. Abstr., Public Aff. Inf. Serv. Bull., Ocean. Abstr., Eng. Index. LC TC1. CODEN DHBAAL. bk rev. adv acc. Circ 2,800. The worlds leading port journal for over sixty year. An up to the moment guide to essential for senior personnel of ports and relative industries.

DUNIA MARITIM. IO. Indonesian. ir. 1100. JL. Merdeka Timur 5, Jakarta Indonesia. LC HE887.

ECONOMIC & SHIPPING REVIEW. V. 1- Jan. 1979-. Periodical. IO. English. ir. 7.500. Insa Jalan Bungar Besar 54, Jakarta Indonesia. LC HE561. DD 387.509598.

EEC SHIPPING. VAT European Economic Community Shipping. 1978-. 0141-4585. UK. English. an. Whitehall Building, 17 Battery Place, New York NY 10004.

ESCAP REVIEW : SHIPPING AND PORTS. Main/Corp United Nations. Economic and Social Commission for Asia and the Pacific. VFOAT Shipping and Ports. No. 1- 1976-. Periodical. English. ir.

ESTADISTICAS PORTUARIAS. See Statistics.

ESTATISTICA. See Statistics.

EXAMINATION OF THE PANAMA CANAL COMMISSION'S FINANCIAL STATEMENTS. (EXAMINATION OF THE PANAMA CANAL COMMISSION'S FINANCIAL STATEMENTS FOR THE YEARS ENDED . . .). Sept. 30, 1982 and 1981-. 0743-7404. US. English. an. US General Accounting Office, Document Handling and Information Services Facility, PO Box 6015, Gaithersburg MD 20760. LC HE538. DD 353.00876444. Vols. for 1982/81- distributed to depository libraries in microfiche. *Examination of Financial Statements of the Panama Canal Commission for the Years Ended . . . .*

FAIRPLAY INTERNATIONAL SHIPPING WEEKLY. V. 250- (No. 4723-). 0307-0220. UK. English. wk. $99.00. Fairplay International Publishers, 52-54 Southwark Street, Longon SE1 1UJ England. Tel 01-403-3164. Ind/Abst Fluidex, Ship Abstr. LC HE561. DD 387.54405. *Fairplay.*

FAIRPLAY WORLD SHIPPING YEAR BOOK. See Yearbooks, Almanacs, Directories.

FAR EAST SHIPPING. 1st Ed. (1980/81)-. 0144-8781. Periodical. UK. English. Seatrade Publications, Whitehall Building, 17 Battery Place, New York NY 10004. LC HE890.5. DD 387.544095.

FINLANDS SJOFART. VFOAT Suomen Merenkulu. Began with issue for Oct. 1917. 0356-5718. Periodical. Swedish (Finnish). mo. Ind/Abst Ship Abstr. LC HE730.

FORD'S INTERNATIONAL CRUISE GUIDE. 1st- ed. 0015-7066. Periodical. US. English. qt. $30.00. Fords Travel Guides, Box 505, Woodland Hills CA 91365. Tel (818)347-1677. Ed Merrian E Clark. LC HE568. DD 910.202. adv acc. Circ 12,000. Worldwide coverage of cruises. Lists sailing dates. fares, ships, ports of call, length of cruise, pictures and history of the world's cruise ships.

FOREIGN FLAG MERCHANT SHIPS OWNED BY U.S. PARENT COMPANIES. (FOREIGN FLAG MERCHANT SHIPS OWNED BY U.S. PARENT COMPANIES AS OF . . .). VAT Foreign Flag Merchant Ships Owned by United States Parent Companies. Began with Dec. 31, 1972. 0736-2471. US. English. an. US Department of Transportation, Maritime Administration, Washington DC 20590. LC HE565.U5. DD 387.2450973. Vols. for 1978, 1982- distributed to depository libraries in microfiche. *Foreign Flag Ships Owned by United States Parent Companies, Oceangoing Merchant Type Ships of 1,000 Gross Tons and Over as of . . . .*

GATEWAYS OF EASTERN AFRICA. No. 1- June 1971-. 0302-8089. Periodical. English. ir. Wissenschaftliche Verlagsges, Postfach 40, D-7000 Stuttgart 1 West Germany. LC HE550. DD 387.10967.

GEORGIA ANCHORAGE. VFOAT Anchorage. Began Publication with Vol. 1 1960?. 0016-8149. Periodical. US. English. bm. Free. Georgia Ports Authority, PO Box 2406, Savannah GA 31402. Tel (912)964-3882. Ed Sharon Sweetser. LC HE554.A3. DD 387.109758. adv acc. Circ 10,000. Vessel operations, cargo information, people in the business, noteworthy local events, and transportation industry events and trends.

GESCHAFTSBERICHT (SCHWEIZERISCHE REEDEREI UND NEPTUN AG). Main/Corp Schweizerische Reederei und Neptun Ag. 1975-. German. ir. Schweizerische Reederei und Neptun Ag, Wiesandamm 4, Basel 4019 Switzerland. LC HE683.Z9. *Geschaftsbericht.*

GOSPODARKA MORSKA. 1982-. Polish. ir. 500.00. Instytut Morski, 80-830 Gdansk, Skrytka Pckzt 82 Poland. LC HE848.7.

GREAT LAKES NAVIGATION. 1973-. 0824-8583. CN. English. an. $15.48. Canadian Marine Publications, 1434 St Catherine Street West/ Suite 512, Montreal Quebec Canada. LC HE554.A5. DD 386.50977.

GREENWOOD'S GUIDE TO GREAT LAKES SHIPPING. VFOAT Guide to Great Lakes Shipping. 2nd- Ed. 0072-7490. US. English. an. Fresh Water Press Inc, 334 the Arcade, Cleveland 14 Ohio 44114. Tel (216)241-0373. Ed Micheal J Dills. LC HE630.G7. adv acc. Circ 1,700. (ctrl). Comprehensive overview of great lakes shipping-includes all aspects of waterborne commerce. *Guide to Great Lakes Freighters.*

GUIA - ADMINISTRACAO-GERAL DO PORTO DE LISBOA. Main/Corp Portugal. Administracao Geral do Porto de Lisboa. 1970-. PO. Portuguese. ir. Ministerio dos Transportes e Comunicacoes, Cais do Sodre 2, Lisboa Portugal. LC HE558.L45. DD 387.10946942. *Guia do Porto de Lisboa.*

GUIDE TO AMERICAN OFFSHORE FLEETS. OFFSHORE SERVICE VESSELS. VFOAT American Offshore Fleets. 1979-. 0197-1131. US. English. an. $150.00. Fleet Data Service, PO Box 2576, Nacogdoches TX 75963-2576. Tel (409)569-0375. Ed James O Covington. Circ 250. Reference to American-owned petroleum support vessels including capacities and capabilities on over 2,500 crew, utility and supply vessels. *FDS Guide to American Offshore Vessels.*

GUIDE TO AMERICAN OFFSHORE FLEETS. TUGS. VFOAT Guide to American Offshore Tug Fleets. 1979-. 0197-1123. Periodical. US. English. an. $95.00. Fleet Data Service, PO Box 2576, Nacogdoches TX 75963. Tel (409)569-0375. Ed James O Covington. Circ 250. Reference to American-owned coastal, harbor and offshore tugs including capabilities and specifications on over 1,300 tugs. *FDS Guide to Major American Tug Fleets.*

Transportation—Ships & Shipping

GYOMU GAIYO - HOKKAI KAIUNKYOKU. Main/Corp Japan. Hokkai Kaiunkyoku. Japanese. ir. Nishi 11-Chome, Minami 26-JO Chuo-Ku 062. LC HE891.

HAESA YONGAM. 1982-. English (Korean). an. 25,000. Koria Swiping Kajetu Sa, 43-1 Tongui-Dong, Chongno-Ku Seoul Korea. LC HE892.5.

HAEUN HANGMAN. Periodical. KO. Korean. ir. Haeun Hangmanchong, 263 Yonji-Dong Chongno-Ku, Seoul Korea. LC HE561.

HAEUN PYOLLAM. See Yearbooks, Almanacs, Directories.

THE HAMPTON ROADS SHIPPING NEWS. 0744-1061. Periodical. US. English. wk. $12.00. Hampton Roads Shipping News, 740 Duke Street, Duke Grace, Building 310, Norfolk VA 23510. Tel (804)625-4776. *Shipping News, 0744-3498.*

HANG YUN CHOU KAN. Periodical. Chinese. wk. LC HE561. DD 387.505.

HARBOUR & SHIPPING. Began publication in 1918. 0017-7636. Periodical. CN. English. mo. $25.00 Domestic, $30.00 US. Progress Publishing Company, 335 Burrard Street/C310 Marine Building, Vancouver British Columbia Canada. Tel (604)685-4385. Ed Liz Bennett. Ind/Abst Fluidex, Ship Abstr. bk rev. adv acc. Circ 2,000. (ctrl). A marine journal covering local and worldwide port and shipping news including new construction of ships, marine law and insurance columns, new products, nautical nostalgia, etc.

HARBOUR & SHIPPING. ANNUAL PORT ISSUE. 1974-. CN. English. an. Progress Publishing Company, 355 Burrard Street, 310 Marine Boulevard, Vancouver British Columbia. DD 387.10971133.

HARBOUR & SHIPPING. ANNUAL SHIPBUILDING EDITION. VFOAT Annual Shipbuilding Edition. 1973-. CN. English. an. Progress Publishing Company, Marine Building, 355 Burrard Street, Vancouver British Columbia Canada. DD 338.4762382009711.

HARBOUR & SHIPPING. ANNUAL SHIPPING DIRECTORY. See Yearbooks, Almanacs, Directories.

IMO NEWS. 1982, No. 2. Periodical. UK. English. qt. International Maritime Organ 101-104 Piccadilly, London W1V OAE England. LC HE561.5. DD 387.505. *IMCO News.*

INDIAN MARINE DIRECTORY. See Yearbooks, Almanacs, Directories.

INDIAN SHIPPING. V. 1- 1949-. Periodical. II. English. mo. $20.00. Indian National Shipowners Association, 22 Maker Tower F Cuffe Parade, Bombay 400005 India. Tel (211268)215718. Ed B V Nilkund. bk rev. adv acc. Circ 1,000.

INFORMATIVO. Main/Corp Brazil. Departamento Nacional de Portos e Vias Navegaveis. 1- 1966?-. 0524-2932. Periodical. BL. Portuguese. mo. Fun Dacao Getulio Verga, Caxia Postfach 9052, 188 ZC02 Rio de Janeiro Brazil.

INLAND RIVER GUIDE. 1st- Ed. 0198-859X. US. English. an. $35.00. Waterways Journal, 319 North 4th Street/Suite 666, St Louis MO 63102. Tel (314)241-7354. Ed Dan Owen. LC HE627. DD 386.02573. adv acc. Circ 3,500. Quick reference directory covering the inland waterways and Gulf coast; lists barge and towing companies, shipyards, public and private terminals, professional firms, contractors, divers, service firms, etc.

INLAND TOWBOAT NEWSLETTER. V. 1- Jan. 1980-. 0197-1115. Periodical. US. English. mo. $48.00. Fleet Data Service, 6362 Windswept/Suite 220, Houston TX 77057.

INLAND WATERBORNE COMMERCE STATISTICS. See Statistics.

INTERSTATE PORT HANDBOOK. VFOAT Interstate Port Handbook of Illinois and Indiana. 0074-9982. US. English. $25.00. Vance Pub Corporation, 300 West Adams Street, Chicago IL 60606. LC HE554.A5. DD 368.2.

INVENTORY OF AMERICAN INTERMODAL EQUIPMENT. Main/Corp United States. Maritime Administration. 0097-9341. US. English. Superintendent of Documents, US Government Printing Office, Washington DC 20402. LC HE17. DD 387.544.

IRELAND, PORTS & SHIPPING HANDBOOK. VFOAT Ireland, Ports and Shipping Handbook. 0260-924X. UK. English. an. 10. Charter Publications, 11 London Road/Downham Market, Norfolk PE38 9B Ireland. Tel 0366 387344. Ed J Moriarty. LC HE557.I75. DD 387.109415. Circ 6,000. (ctrl). Guide to the ports and shipping services of Ireland.

JAARBOEK VAN DE HAVEN VAN ANTWERPEN. See Yearbooks, Almanacs, Directories.

JAARSTATISTIEK OVER DE INTERNATIONALE TRAFIEK DER HAVENS. See Statistics.

JACKSONVILLE PORT HANDBOOK. 0160-2241. US. English. an. $5.00. Howard Publications Inc, 1314 Seaboard Coast Line Building/PO Box 4728, Jacksonville FL 32201. LC HE554.J3. DD 387.109759121.

JACKSONVILLE SEAFARER. V. 1- Jan. 1952-. 0447-2462. Periodical. US. English. mo. $5.00. Howard Publications, PO Box 4728, Jacksonville FL 32201. Tel (904)355-2601. LC HE554.J3. DD 387.129759121.

JANE'S MERCHANT SHIPS. VFOAT Merchant Ships. 1982-. UK. English. an. Janes Publishing Inc, 135 West 50 Street/12th Floor, New York NY 10020. Tel (212)586-7745. Ed David Greenman. LC VM391. DD 623.82405. adv acc. Guide to merchant ship identification with 10,000 common scale line drawings. Vessels are classified by Talbot-Booth recognition system. Covers 1,400 ships; updated information.

JOURNAL OF ABSTRACTS OF THE BRITISH SHIP RESEARCH ASSOCIATION. See Indexes/Abstracts.

JURISPRUDENCE DU PORT D'ANVERS. VFOAT Recjtspraak der Haven Van Antwerpen. Dutch (summaries in French). ir. 1375. Lloyd Anversois SA, Compte Cheques Postaux No 273.75, Antwerpen Belgium. *Jurisprudence du Port d'Anvers et des Autres Villes Commerciales et Industrielles de la Belgique.*

KAIJO HOAN TOKEI NEMPO. Main/Corp Japan. Kaijo Hoancho. Began with the report for 1950. JA. Japanese. ir. Kaijo Hoancho, 1-3 Kasumigaseki 2-chome, Chiyoda-ku 100 Tokyo Japan. LC HE891.

KAINAN SHIMPANCHO SAIKETSU REI SHU. Main/Corp Japan. Koto Kainan Shimpancho. V. 1-. JA. Japanese. ir. 2000. Koto Kainan Shimpancho, 1-17-2 Nishi-Shinbashi Minato-ku, Tokyo Japan.

KAUPPAMERENKULUN SEKA HUOLINTA- JA AHTAUSTOIMINNAN TASETILASTO. Main/Corp Finland. Tilastokeskus. VFOAT Balansstatistiken Over Handelssjoarten Samt Speditions- OCH Stuveriverksamheten. English, Finnish, and Swedish. ir. Tilastokeskus, Valtion Painatuskeskus Ann Ankatu 44 00100 10, Helsinki Finland. LC HE563.F5.

KEHRWIEDER. Periodical. German. ir. 1.60 Single Issue. Verband Deutscher Reeder, Postfach 325, 2 Hamburg 36 West Germany. LC HE730.

KIBERNETIKA NA MORSKOM TRANSPORTE. Periodical. UR. Russian. Vyshcha Shkola, Gogolevskaia 7, Kiev Russian SFSR.

KISARAZU-KO TOKEI NEMPO. Main/Corp Chiba, Japan (Prefecture). Dobokubu. Kowan Kanrika. 1971-. Japanese. ir. LC HE563.J3. *Kisarazu-Ko Tokei Nempo.*

KOREA SHIPPING GAZETTE. Periodical. KO. English (Korean). ir. 17.000. Korea Shipping Gazette Company, CPO Box 3198, Seoul South Korea. LC HE892.5.

KORIA SWIPOJU CHONOL. VFOAT Korea Shippers' Journal. English (Korean). wk. 900 Single Issue. Koria Swipoju Chonol, 23-1 Cho-dong 1-ka Chung-ku, Seoul Korea. LC HE561.

LA MARINE MARCHANDE EN . . . . (LA MARINE MARCHANDE). Main/Corp Comite Central des Armateurs de France, Paris. FR. French. an. Journal de la Marine Marchande, 190 B Haussmann, 75008 Paris France. Ind/Abst Ship Abstr. LC HE833. DD 387.50944.

LAKE LOG CHIPS. V. 1, No. 7- May 2, 1972-. 0270-5680. Periodical. US. English. bw. $9.00. c/o Jerome Library, Bowling State University, Bowling Green OH 43403. Tel (419)372-0012. Ed David T Glick. bk rev. Circ 1,600. A newsletter of Great Lakes commerce with emphasis upon ships and people written from an historical perspective. *Great Lakes Calender.*

LALU LINTAS ANGKUTAN ANTAR PULAU MENURUT GOLONGAN BARANG, DAERAH ASAL, DAN TUJUAN. VFOAT Inter Island Cargo Traffic by Commodity Group, Region of Origin, and Region of Destination. IO. English (Indonesian). an. $3.60. Bagian Statistik Tahunan Dan Penerbitan, Biro Pusat Statistik, Jl Dr Sutomo, No 8, PO Box 3, Jakarta Indonesia. LC HE887.

LAPORAN PERUSAHAAN - BIRO KLASIFIKASI INDONESIA. Main/Corp Indonesia. Biro Klasifikasi. IO. Indonesian. ir. Jalan Yos Sudarso, No 38-39 Tanjung Priok, Jakarta Indonesia. LC HE887.

LAPORAN-TAHUNAN - BADAN PENGUSAHAAN PELABUHAN PASAR IKAN. Main/Corp Badan Pengusahaan Pelabuhan Pasar Ikan. IO. Indonesian. an. LC HE560.J33.

LAPORAN TAHUNAN - DEPALINDO. Main/Corp Dewan Pemakai Jasa Angkutan Laut Indonesia. 1976-. English or Indonesian. ir. Depalindo, Jl Museum No 2, Jakarta Indonesia. LC HE730.

LAPORAN TAHUNAN DIREKTORAT NAVIGASI. Main/Corp Indonesia. Direktorat Navigasi. Indonesian. ir. Direktorat Nanigasi, JL Merdeka Timur No 5, Jakarta Indonesia. LC HE563.I6.

LIST OF INSPECTED TANK BARGES & TANKSHIPS. Main/Corp United States. Coast Guard. VAT List of Inspected Tank Barges and Tankships. 0145-7705. US. English. sa. $9.25. National Technical Information Service, 5285 Port Royal Road, Springfield VA 22151. LC HE589.U5. DD 387.245.

LIST OF MEMBERS - BALTIC AND INTERNATIONAL MARITIME CONFERENCE. Main/Corp Baltic and International Maritime Conference. 1979-. DK. English. ir. Bimco 19 Kristianiagade, DK-2100 Copenhagen Denmark. LC HE564.A2. DD 387.5025.

LIST OF SHIPOWNERS, INDEX TO FORMER NAMES OF SHIPS, COMPOUND NAMES OF SHIPS. See Indexes/Abstracts.

LISTE OFFICIELLE DES NAVIRES DE MER BELGES ET DE LA FLOTTE DE LA FORCE NAVALE. Main/Corp Belgium. Administration de la Marine et de la Navigation Interieur. French. ir. Administration de la Marine et de la Navigation Interieur, 30 rue Belliard, 1040 Bruxelles Belgium. LC HE565.B4. DD 387.209493.

LLOYD'S CONFIDENTIAL INDEX OF STEAM AND MOTOR VESSELS. See Indexes/Abstracts.

LLOYD'S LOADING LIST. UK. English. ir. LLP Maritime & Business Publication, 87 Terminal Drive, Plainview New York 11803. LC HE568. DD 387.51656. *General Weekly Shipping List.*

LLOYD'S MARITIME AND COMMERCIAL LAW QUARTERLY. See Law - International Law.

LLOYD'S MARITIME ATLAS. VFOAT Maritime Atlas. 1st- Ed. 0076-020X. UK. English. ir. $41.50. LLP Maritime & Business Publ, 87 Terminal Drive, Plainview NY 11803. Tel (212)867-2080. LC G1060.

LLOYD'S MARITIME DIRECTORY. See Yearbooks, Almanacs, Directories.

LLOYD'S PORTS OF THE WORLD. VFOAT Ports of the World. 1982-. UK. English. an. $148.50. LLP Maritime and Business Publ Inc, 87 Terminal Drive, Plainview NY 11803. Tel (516)349-1010. *Ports of the World (London), 0079-4066.*

LLOYD'S REGISTER SHIPBUILDING RETURNS : MERCHANT SHIPS OF 100 TONS GROSS AND UPWARDS. Periodical. UK. English. qt. Lloyds Register of Shipping, 17 Battery Place, New York NY 10004.

LLOYD'S SHIP MANAGER. VFOAT Ship Manager. Began publication with V. 1, No. 1 (Apr. 1980). 0309-6254. Periodical. UK. English. mo.

Transportation—Ships & Shipping

$115.00. Lloyd's of London Press, 3/4 Lime Street, London EC3M 7HA England. **Tel** (01)247 9461. **Ed** David Tinsley. **Ind/Abst** Fluidex, Ship Abstr. bk rev. adv acc. **Circ** 6,000. Technical monthly for ship operations and management. *Nautical Review.*

LLOYD'S SINGAPORE PORT SERVICES INDEX. *See* Indexes/Abstracts.

LOGISTICS OUTLOOK FOR SHIPPERS. VFOAT Data Resources Logistics Outlook for Shippers. Vol. 1, No. 1 (Winter 1982-1983)-. 0737-917X. Periodical. US. English. Data Resources Inc, 24 Hartwell Avenue, Lexington MA 02173. LC HF5761. DD 658.78805.

THE LOOKOUT. 0024-6425. Periodical. US. English. qt. $5.00. Seamans Church Institute, 15 State Street, New York NY 10004.

MARAD. (MARAD : THE ANNUAL REPORT OF THE MARITIME ADMINISTRATION FOR FISCAL YEAR . . .). **Main/Corp** United States. Maritime Administration. VFOAT Annual Report of the Maritime Administration for Fiscal Year . . . . Began with 1968/69. 0882-9004. US. English. an. US Department of Transportation, Maritime Administration, Washington DC 20590. LC HE745. DD 353.00877506. *Annual Report of the Maritime Administration, 0083-1670.*

LA MARINA MERCANTE IBEROAMERICANA. Spanish. ir. LC HE798. *Marina Mercante Argentina.*

MARINE BUYERS' DIRECTORY. *See* Yearbooks, Almanacs, Directories.

MARINE DIGEST. V. 1- Sept. 9, 1922-. 0025-3197. Periodical. US. English. wk. $18.00. Marine Digest, PO Box 3954, Seattle WA 98124. **Tel** (206)682-2484. **Ed** T J Dwyer. LC HE561. DD 387.5. bk rev. adv acc. **Circ** 3,500. (ctrl). To promote all facets of maritime and transportation industry and allied fields.

MARINE DIRECTORY. *See* Yearbooks, Almanacs, Directories.

MARINE ENGINEERING/LOG (BRISTOL, CONN. : 1979). *See* Naval Science, Navigation.

MARINE STORES INTERNATIONAL. *See* Engineering.

MARITIME HISTORY. Began with: Vol. 1 (Apr. 1971). Periodical. UK. English. sa. Graphmitre Ltd, 1 West Street, Tavistock Devon England. LC HE561. DD 387.50941.

MARITIME POLICY AND MANAGEMENT. V. 4- July 1976-. 0308-8839. Periodical. UK. English. qt. 17.00. Taylor & Francis Ltd, Ranking Road, Basingstore Hank RG24 0PR England. **Tel** (0222)42588. **Ed** J J Evans. **Ind/Abst** Electron. Commun. Abstr. J., ISMEC Bull., Pollut. Abstr. Indexes, Saf. Sci. Abstr. J., Fluidex, Life Sci. Collect., Ship Abstr., CIS Abstr., Ocean. Abstr. LC HC92. DD 333.91005. bk rev. **Circ** 400. *Maritime Studies and Management.*

MARITIME STUDIES AND MANAGEMENT. V. 1- July 1973-. UK. English. an. 8.00. Scientechnica Ltd, 823-825 Bath Road, Bristol BS4 5NU England. LC HC92. DD 333.91005.

MARITIME TRANSPORT. **Main/Corp** Organization for Economic Cooperation and Development. Maritime Transport Committee. 1953/54-. 0474-5884. Periodical. English. an. $15.00. OECD Publications Center, 1750 Pennsylvania Avenue Northwest, Washington DC 20006. **Tel** (202)724-1857. Information on international shipping developments and detailed data on world seaborne trade, world merchant fleets and the freight market.

MARITIMES SHIPPING HERALD AND MARINE ENGINEERING JOURNAL. (THE MARITIMES SHIPPING HERALD AND MARINE ENGINEERING JOURNAL). VFOAT Journal de la Marine Marchande des Maritimes. V. 1- April 1974-. 0315-4289. Periodical. CN. English and French. mo. $9.28. Maritimes Shipping Herald, PO Box 1137, 115 Prince William Street, St John New Brunswick E2L 2B4 Canada. **Tel** (506)652-6817.

MAY DAY PICTORIAL NEWS. 1961. 0025-6129. Periodical. US. English. mo. $24.00. Wion Publications, Pier 38-40, San Francisco CA 94107. **Tel** (415)495-6353. **Ed** William Wion. adv acc. **Circ** 5,298. (ctrl). General information on merchant marine ship building, repair ship service, and ship supply manufacturers.

MEDLEMSFORTEGNELSE. **Main/Corp** Norsk Skibsmglerforbund. VFOAT List of Members and Scale of Agency Charges. Norwegian. ir. LC HE610.N6.

MEMORIAS DE LOS PUERTOS. **Main/Corp** Spain. Direccion General de Puertos y Senales Maritimas. Spanish. ir. LC HE557. . .S6.

MERCHANT FLEETS OF THE WORLD. Began with Dec. 31, 1955. 0499-8847. US. English. an. Office of Public Affairs, Maritime Administration, 400 7th Street SW/Room 7215, Washington DC 20590. Vol. for 1981 distributed to depository libraries in microfiche.

MERENKULKU. KAUPPALAIVASTO. VFOAT Kauppalaivasto, Sjofart. Handelsflottan, Navigation. Merchant Fleet. 0430-5574. Fl. English (Finnish and Swedish). an. Government Printing Centre, PO Box 516, SF-00101 Helsinki 10 Finland. LC HA1448, HE563.F5.

MERENKULKU. MERILIIKENNE SUOMEN JA ULKOMAIDEN VALILLA. VFOAT Meriliikenne Suomen Ja Ulkomaiden Valilla, Sjofart. Sjofarten Mellan Finland och Utlandet, Navigation. Shipping Between Finland and Foreign Countries. 0430-5582. Fl. Finnish (Swedish). an. Government Printing Centre PO Box 516, SF-00101 Helsinki 10 Finland. LC HA1448, HE563.F5.

MINUTES OF PROCEEDINGS AND EVIDENCE OF THE SUB-COMMITTEE ON HARBOUR AND WHARF FACILITIES (ATLANTIC REGIONS) OF THE STANDING COMMITTEE ON NATIONAL RESOURCES AND PUBLIC WORKS. **Main/Corp** Canada. Parliament. House of Commons. Sub-Committee on Harbour and Wharf Facilities (Atlantic Regions). VFOAT Proces-Verbaux et Temoignages du Sous-Comite sur les Installations Portuaires et les Quais (Regions de l'Atlantique) du Comite Permanent des Ressources Nationales et des Travaux Publics. May 11, 1973-. CN. English (French in parallel columns). Queen's Printer, Publications Branch, Ottawa Ontario Canada. LC HE554.A3. DD 387.10971.

MODEL SHIP BUILDER. *See* Hobbies.

MONTHLY BULLETIN, PORT OF CHITTAGONG. **Main/Corp** Chittagong Port Authority. VFOAT Port of Chittagong Monthly Bulletin. English. ir. Chittagong Port Authority, PO Box 2013, Chittagong Bangladesh. LC HE560.C5. DD 387.10954923. *Monthly Bulletin, Port of Chittagong.*

MOTOR SHIP. (THE MOTOR SHIP). Began with: No. 449 (Oct. 1957). 0027-2000. Periodical. UK. English. mo. $130.00. Business Press International Ltd, Perrymount Road, Haywards Heath, West Sussex RH163BR England. **Ind/Abst** Trade Ind. Index, Life Sci. Collect., Eng. Index Annu., Eng. Index Mon., Eng. Index Bioeng. Abstr., Eng. Index Energy Abstr., Excerpta Med., Coal Abstr., Ship Abstr., Comput. Control Abstr., Electr. Electron. Abstr., Sci. Abstr. Sect. A. Phys. Abstr. LC VM1. DD 623.8231. CODEN MOSHA3. *British Motor Ship.*

NATIONAL PORTS COUNCIL BULLETIN. VFOAT Bulletin / National Ports Council. No. 1 (Spring 1972)-. 0305-5701. Periodical. UK. English. ir. National Ports Council, Commonwealth House, 1-19 New Oxford Street, London WC1A 1DZ England. **Ind/Abst** Ship Abstr. *Research and Technical Bulletin.*

NAUTILIAKE. Year 21, No. 912/3- I July/Aug. 1977-. Periodical. English (Greek). ir. 145.00. Nautiliake Ekdoseis Epe, Perikleous 62, Eleusina Greece. **Tel** (6)4125005. **Ed** David C Glass. LC HE561. DD 387.509495. bk rev. adv acc. **Circ** 3,265. All aspects of shipping with particular emphasis on the Greek shipping section including information on involvement in the chartering sale and purchase markets. *Nautiliake, Nautergatike.*

NAUVAHANA AURA PARIVAHANA MANTRALAYA KI ANUDANOM KI MANGEM = DEMANDS FOR GRANTS OF MINISTRY OF SHIPPING AND TRANSPORT. **Main/Corp** India (Republic). Ministry of Shipping and Transport. Hindi (English). ir. Government Press, General Manager, Ring Road, New Delhi India. LC HE879.

NEW JERSEY AND NEW YORK PORT HANDBOOK. VFOAT N.J. and N.Y. Port Handbook. 0742-2695. US. English. $25.00. WWS/World Ports, 77 Moehring Drive, Blauvelt NY 10913-2093. LC HE767.N5. DD 387.16402947471.

NIHON NO KAIUN SANGYO. (JAPANESE SHIPPING IN . . .). JA. English. an. Japanese Shipowners' Association, 6-4 Hirakawacho 2-chome, Chiyoda-ku Tokyo Japan. LC HE563.J3. DD 387.50952. *Review of Japanese Shipping.*

NORD-OSTSEE-KANAL JAHRESBERICHT. English (German). an. Wasser und Schiffahrtsdirektion Nord, Hindenburgufer 247, 2300 Kiel West Germany. LC HE449.K3. DD 386.470943512.

OAG WORLDWIDE CRUISE & SHIPLINE GUIDE. VFOAT Worldwide Cruise & Shipline Guide. VAT Official Airline Guide Worldwide Cruise and Shipline Guide. V. 1- Jan./Feb. 1975-. 0097-8779. Periodical. US. English. bm. Official Airline Guide, 2000 Clearwater Drive, Oak Brook IL 60521. **Tel** (800)323-3537/Outside IL.

OCEANOGRAPHIC SHIP OPERATING SCHEDULES. 1961/62-. US. English. an. Office of the Oceanographer, 200 Stovall Street, Alexandria VA 22332. LC WMLC L 82/276.

OFFICIAL MANITOBA SHIP-BY-TRUCK DIRECTORY. *See* Yearbooks, Almanacs, Directories.

OFFICIAL SOUTHERN CALIFORNIA PORTS MARITIME DIRECTORY AND GUIDE. *See* Yearbooks, Almanacs, Directories.

THE OFFICIAL STEAMSHIP SERVICE DIRECTORY. *See* Yearbooks, Almanacs, Directories.

OFFICIEL FORTEGNELSE OVER DANSKE SKIBE MED KENDINGSSIGNALER. VFOAT Danmarks Skibsliste. DK. Danish. an. Farvandsdirektoratet, Nautisk Afdeling, Esplanaden 19, 1263 Kbenhavn K Denmark. LC HE565.D4.

OUTWARD OVERSEAS CARGO, AUSTRALIA . . . AND . . . . *See* Business - Commerce.

OUTWARD OVERSEAS SHIPPING CARGO. **Main/Corp** Australian Bureau of Statistics. 0312-6382. AT. English. an. Australian Bureau of Statistics, Government Printing Office 796, Sydney New South Wales 20001 Australia. LC HE563.A8. DD 387.5440994.

OVERSEAS AND COASTAL SHIPPING. **Main/Corp** Australian Bureau of Statistics. 1974/75-. AT. English. ir. Australian Bureau of Statistics, Government Printing Office Box 796, Sydney New South Wales 2001 Australia. LC HE563.A8. DD 387.5440994. *Overseas Shipping Cargo.*

OWNERS OF VESSELS APPEARING IN THE RECORD. **Main/Corp** American Bureau of Shipping. 0097-6113. US. English. American Bureau of Shipping, 45 Broad Street Northwest, New York NY 10004. LC HE565.U5. DD 387.20973.

PACIFIC MARINER MICROFORM. Periodical. US. English. qt. $8.75. Pacific Mariner, 314 West Hastings Street/Suite 303, Vancouver British Columbia V6B 1K8 Canada. **Tel** (604)688-2271. **Ed** Gilbert Handsbee. bk rev. adv acc. **Circ** 25,000. (ctrl). Canadian commercial marine journal disseminating news of the shipbuilding, fishing, industries, marine products, technology, ports, harbours news and offshore oil and gas. *Norwester (Seattle, Wash.).*

PACIFIC MARITIME MAGAZINE. Began in 1984. 0741-7586. Periodical. US. English. mo. $12.00. Fremont Office Building, Suite 309, 3429 Fremont Place North, Settle WA 98103. **Tel** (206)547-1166. **Ed** B Glenn Ledbetter. adv acc. **Circ** 6,000. Covers marine transportation, construction and ports on the West Coast of North America. Our readers are operators of tugs, barges, cargo and passenger vessels, dredges, crew and supply boats. *Port Reporter, 0738-4165.*

THE PANAMA CANAL REVIEW. V. 1- May 1950-. 0031-0646. Periodical. English. ir. $1.50. Panama Canal Review, Box M, Balboa Heights Canal Zone. LC HE2830.P2. DD 386.445.

THE PANAMA CANAL SPILLWAY. VFOAT Spillway del Canal de Panama. 0364-8044. Periodical. US. English (Spanish). bw. Panama Canal Information Office, APO Miami FL 34011. LC HE538. DD 386.44405. *Spillway.*

PAPERS PRESENTED TO THE . . . ANNUAL TECHNICAL CONFERENCE - CANADIAN SHIPBUILDING AND SHIP REPAIRING ASSOCIATION. (PAPERS PRESENTED TO THE . . . ANNUAL TECHNICAL CONFERENCE). **Main/Corp** Canadian

Transportation—Ships & Shipping

Shipbuilding and Ship Repairing Association. Technical Section. Conference. VFOAT Exposes Presentes a la ... Conference Technique. Mar. 2, 1982-. 0820-0556. CN. English. an. $15.00 Per Number. Conference Papers, c/o Canadian Shipbuilding and Ship Repairing Association, Suite 801/100 Sparks Street, Ottawa Ontario K1P 5B7 Canada. DD 623.8200971. *Papers Presented to the Technical Section Annual Meeting, 0227-2172.*

PERFORMANCE BUDGET OF PORTS AND FISHERIES DEPARTMENT (PORTS ORGANISATION). Main/Corp Gujarat (India). Ports and Fisheries Dept. 1982-83-. English. an. 2.30. LC HE559.I4. DD 354.5475008771.

THE PLATOU REPORT. Main/Corp Platou (R.S.) A/S. English. ir. PO Box 1357 Vika, 1 Oslo Norway. LC HE561. DD 387.54405.

POMORSTVO. V. 1- Sept. 1946-. Periodical. Serbo-Croatian -R. ir. LC HE730.

PORT BUSTAMANTE ... HANDBOOK. English. ir. Port Bustamante Handbook, c/o the Shipping Association of Jamaica, 5-7 King Street, Kingston Jamaica West Indies. LC HE556.K55. DD 387.1097292.

PORT DE MONTREAL. VFOAT Port of Montreal. V. 1- Winter 1975/76-. 0706-5396. Periodical. CN. English (French). qt. Conseil des Ports Nationaux Edifice du Port de Montreal, Aile No 1 Cite du Havre, Montreal Quebec H8P 1J9 Canada. DD 386.809714281.

PORT FOLIO, PORT OF CHITTAGONG. Main/Corp Chittagong Port Authority. VFOAT Port of Chittagong Monthly Bulletin. Periodical. English. ir. Chittagong Port Authority, PO Box 2013, Chittagong Bangladesh. LC HE560.C5. DD 387.10954923. *Monthly Bulletin, Port of Chittagong.*

PORT GALVESTON. 0360-0505. US. English. R Nesbitt, PO Box 328, Galveston TX 77550. LC HF3163.G2. DD 380.109764139. *Galveston.*

PORT OF BALTIMORE HANDBOOK. (HANDBOOK). 0465-1146. US. English. be. Maryland Port Administration, Port Promotion Department, The World Trade Center, Baltimore MD 21202. LC HE554.B3. DD 387.1097526.

PORT OF BOSTON HANDBOOK. Main/Corp Boston Shipping Association. V. 1- 1975/76-. 0149-208X. US. English. $2.50. Port of Boston Handbook, 223 Lewis Wharf, Boston MA 02110. LC HE554.B6. DD 387.10974461.

PORT OF DETROIT WORLD HANDBOOK. 0160-5526. US. English. an. Fourth Seacoast Publishing Company Inc, 24145 Little Mack, St Clair Shores MI 48080. LC HE554.D4. DD 386.80977434.

PORT OF HALIFAX BULLETIN. June 1975-. 0380-1497. Periodical. CN. English. mo. Free. Halifax-Dartmouth Commission, 900 Cogswell Tower, Scotia Square, Halifax Nova Scotia B3J 3K1 Canada. Tel (902)429-1400. Ed Vangie Sadler. DD 387.10971622. adv acc. Circ 6,700. (ctrl). This magazine gives shipping schedules, news of services, routings and cargo related to port. Highlights events, companies, and people of interest to users of port's many facilities, including shippers and receivers. *Halifax, Gateway to North America, 0380-1500.*

PORT OF HELSINKI HANDBOOK. 0359-7431. English. an. Port of Helsinki Authority, Etelaranta 10 P O Box 26, 00131 Helsinki 13 Finland. Tel 358-0-1691. Ed Liisa Melin. LC HE558.H45. DD 387.10948971. Circ 1,000. (ctrl). Description of harbour facilities. Detailed information about Stevedoring, warehousing, and transportation services in the Port of Helsinki.

PORT OF HOUSTON MAGAZINE. V. 1- Jan. 1959-. 0032-4825. Periodical. US. English. mo. Port of Houston, PO Box 2562, Houston TX 77001. LC HE554.H65. *Port of Houston Bulletin, Houston Port Book.*

PORT OF KINGSTON HANDBOOK. JM. English. ir. Shipping Association of Jamaica, PO Box 40, Kingston 15 Jamaica. LC HE556.K55. DD 387.1097292.

PORT OF LONDON. V. 45- (No. 537-). UK. English. qt. 5.00. Port of London Authority, Leslie Ford House, Tilbury Dock, Essex England. Tel 03752 75477. Ed Terry Hatton. Ind/Abst Fluidex. LC HE558.L8. DD 387.109421. bk rev. adv acc. Circ 8,000. Articles which have a London connection, general, technical, historical and commercial. *PLA Monthly.*

PORT OF NEW ORLEANS ANNUAL DIRECTORY. See Yearbooks, Almanacs, Directories.

PORT OF TOKYO. English. ir. Bureau of Port and Harbour, Tokyo Metropolitan Government, 8 Marunouchi 3, Chiyoda-ku, Tokyo Japan. LC HE560.T6. DD 387.10952135.

PORT STATISTICS. See Statistics.

PORT STATISTICS ... AND SUPPLEMENTARY INFORMATION. See Statistics.

PORT STATISTICS FOR THE FOREIGN TRADE OF THE UNITED KINGDOM. See Statistics.

PORTS. '83-. 0262-1630. UK. English. 5.00. Charter Publications Ltd, Bank Chambers Downham Market, Norfolk PE38 9BU England. LC HE557.G7. DD 387.10941. *BTDB Ports.*

PORTS ANNUAL. CANADIAN PORTS EDITION. (PORTS ANNUAL). VFOAT Shipping Register. 1978-. 0225-5456. CN. English. an. Shipping Register Publications, 175 5th Avenue, New York NY 10010. DD 386.80971. *Ports Annual. North American Ports Ed., 0823-5678.*

PORTS DESIGNATED IN APPLICATION OF THE INTERNATIONAL HEALTH REGULATIONS. Main/Corp World Health Organization. VFOAT Ports Notifies en Application du Reglement Sanitaire International. English and French. ir. 4.00. World Health Organization, 1211 Geneve 27, Geneva Switzerland. LC HE951. DD 387.1. NLM W2 MW6 W9PC.

PORTS OF NEW SOUTH WALES. Vol. 2, No. 1 (June 1978)-. 0313-4075. Periodical. English. qt. Maritime Services Board of New South Wales, Box 32 GPO, Sydney New South Wales 2000 Australia. Ed T Williams. *Ports of New South Wales Journal.*

PROCEEDINGS - AMERICAN MERCHANT MARINE CONFERENCE. Main/Conf American Merchant Marine Conference. V. 1- 1935-. 0364-7374. US. English. an. Propeller Club of the United States, 1730 M Street NW/Suite 413, Washington DC 20036. Tel (202)223-1401. LC HE745. DD 387.506373.

PUERTOS ESPANOLES. Periodical. SP. Spanish. ir. 750. (Edificio Astygi) Planta 7A, Madrid Spain. LC HE557.S6. DD 387.10946.

QUEBRA-MAR. Periodical. Portuguese. sa. Administracao do Porto do Recife, Praca Artur Oscar S/N, Recife Brazil. LC HE556.R4. DD 387.1098134.

RAPPORT ANNUEL - OFFICE NATIONAL DES PORTS DU CAMEROUN. Main/Corp Cameroon National Ports Authority. VFOAT Annual Report. English (French, 1983-). ir. National Ports Authority, Bureau de Douala, BP 513, Lome Cameroon. LC HE559.C35. DD 387.16096711.

RAPPORT D'ACTIVITE - NATIONAL SHIPPERS COUNCIL OF CAMEROON. Main/Corp National Shippers Council of Cameroon. CM. French. ir. C N C C, B P 1588, Douala Cameroun.

RECHNOI TRANSPORT. 1941-1953, 1955-. Periodical. UR. Russian. mo $25.50. Victor Kamkin Inc (70787), 12224 Parklawn Drive, Rockville MD 20852. Tel (301)881-5973. LC TC601. *Vodnyi Transport, Morksoi Flot.*

RECORD OF THE AMERICAN BUREAU OF SHIPPING. Main/Corp American Bureau of Shipping. Began with: 1933. US. English. an. $435.00. American Bureau of Shipping, 65 Broadway Street, New York NY 10006. Tel (212)440-0535. Items include propulsion engine design and number, licensees name, compliance with the Marine Pollution Convention, information on offshore installations classed by ABS. *Record of American and Foreign Shipping.*

REED'S TUG WORLD NEWSLETTER. VFOAT Tug World Newsletter. No. 1 (Oct. 1983)-. Periodical. UK. English. ir. Ind/Abst Ship Abstr. *Reed's Special Ships, 0140-8046.*

REGISTER OF OFFSHORE UNITS, SUBMERSIBLES & DIVING SYSTEMS. Main/Corp Lloyd's Register of Shipping. VAT Register of Offshore Units, Submersibles, and Diving Systems. 1977/78-. UK. English. an. 42. Lloyd's Register of Shipping, 71 Fenchurch Street, London EC3M 4BS England. LC VM466.O35. DD 622.29028. Lists mobile drilling rigs, submersibles, diving systems, work units, etc. Also owners with their addresses, telex and telephone number.

REGISTER OF SHIPS (BUREAU VERITAS). (REGISTER OF SHIPS). VFOAT Registre Maritime. English (French). ir. 290 062 Bveritas, Paris France. LC HE565.A3. DD 623.820216. *Registre Maritime.*

REGISTER OF SHIPS (LLOYD'S REGISTER OF SHIPPING). (REGISTER OF SHIPS). UK. English. an. Lloyds Register of Shipping, 17 Battery Place, New York NY 10004. Tel (212)425-8050. LC HE565.A3. DD 623.82405. *Lloyd's Register of Shipping.*

REGISTER OF SHIPS : SUBSIDIARY SECTIONS. Main/Corp Lloyd's Register of Shipping. UK. English. an. Lloyds Register of Shipping, 17 Battery Place, New York NY 10004. LC HE565.A3. DD 387.20212.

REGISTROVAIA KNIGA MORSKIKH SUDOV SSSR. VFOAT Register Book of Sea-Going Ships of the USSR. UR. English (Russian). Registr SSSR, Glavnoe Upravlenie, 192041 Leningrad, Dvortsovaia Naberezhnaia 8, Leningrad Russia SFSR. LC HE565.S65.

RELATORIO ANUAL - COMPANHIA DOCAS DO CEARA. Main/Corp Companhia Docas do Ceara. Portuguese. ir. LC HE556.C4.

RELATORIO ANUAL - EMPRESA DE PORTOS DO BRASIL. Main/Corp Empresa de Portos do Brasil. Portuguese. an. LC HE563.B8. DD 387.10981. *Relatorio.*

REPORT AND ACCOUNTS - BRITISH TRANSPORT DOCKS BOARD. Main/Corp British Transport Docks Board. UK. English. an. LC HE557.G7.

REPORT AND ACCOUNTS FOR THE YEAR ENDED 30TH JUNE - PAKISTAN NATIONAL SHIPPING CORPORATION. Main/Corp Pakistan National Shipping Corporation. PK. English. an. PNSC Building, Moulvi Tamizuddin Khan Road, Karachi Pakistan. LC HE880.5. DD 387.50655491. *Report and Accounts-National Shipping Corporation.*

REPORT AND ACCOUNTS - SINGAPORE SHIPPING ASSOCIATION. Main/Corp Singapore Shipping Association. English. ir. Singapore Shipping Association, Units 2305/6, 23rd Floor, Tong Eng Building, 101 Cecil Street, Singapore. LC HE885. DD 387.50605957.

REPORT & ACCOUNTS TO BE SUBMITTED AT THE ANNUAL GENERAL MEETING OF SHAREHOLDERS. Main/Corp Compagnie Financiere de Suez. English. ir. Paris Financiere de Suez, 1 rue d'Astorg, Paris France 75008. LC HE543. DD 386.43065. *Report & Accounts to be Submitted at the General Meeting of Shareholders.*

REPORT ON SURVEY OF U.S. SHIPBUILDING AND REPAIR FACILITIES. See Economics - Economics: Industry & Production.

REPORT - SINGAPORE. MARINE DEPT. Main/Corp Singapore. Marine Dept. English. ir. LC HE880.S5. DD 387.5.

RESULTATS DE L'EXPLOITATION DES PORTS MARITIMES. FR. French. ir. Ministere des Transports, Direction Generale de la Marine Marchande, Paris France. LC HE557.F8. DD 387.10944.

RIVISTA DI INFORMAZIONI MARITTIME. Yearly V. 1- 1974-. 0390-3842. Italian. ir. 15.000. Societa Editrice Mariana in Acc Sempl Flore E C, C/C Postale, Rome Italy. Ind/Abst Ship Abstr. LC HE839. DD 387.0945. *Bollettino di Informazioni Marittime.*

DE ROTTERDAMSE HAVEN IN CIJFERS. See Statistics.

RULES & REGULATIONS FOR THE CONSTRUCTION AND CLASSIFICATION OF STEEL VESSELS. VAT Rules and Regulations for the Construction and Classification of Steel Vessels. UK. English. an. $110.00. Lloyds Register, 17 Battery Place, New York NY 10004. Tel (212)425-8050. LC HE565.A31.

Transportation—Ships & Shipping

SCALE SHIP MODELER. 0194-780X. Periodical. US. English. bm. $13.50. Challenge Publications Inc, 7950 Deering Avenue, Canoga Park CA 91304. Tel (213)887-0550. LC VM298. DD 623.820105.

SCANDINAVIAN SHIPPING GAZETTE. V. 1- 1916-. Periodical. English. mo. $20.00. Scandinavian Shipping Gazette, 20 Bernhard Bangs Alle, DK-2000 Copenhagen F Denmark. LC HE561.

SCHIFFSTECHNIK. 0036-6064. Periodical. GW. German (English). qt. 110,00. Schiffahrtsverlag Hansa C Schroedtr und Co, Stubbenhuk 10, 2000 Hamburg 11 West Germany. Tel (040)373964. Ed Ing Kurt Wendel. Ind/Abst Eng. Index Mon., Eng. Index Bioeng. Abstr., Eng. Index Energy Abstr., Ship Abstr., Eng. Index Annu., Eng. Index Mon. CODEN SCFTAO. adv acc. Academic contributions of shipping (hydrodynamic, statics, resistance, etc.). *Forschungshefte fur Schiffstechnik, Schiffbau, Schiffsmaschinenbau.*

SEA BREESE (BOSTON, MASS.). (THE SEA BREEZE). 1827. Periodical. US. English. sa. $1.50. Boston Seamans Friend Society, 45 Church Street, Boston MA 02116. Tel (617)426-1665. adv acc. Circ 2,600. Information of activities going on at Seaman's House, programs, meetings, news of various seaman. Also events and happenings on the waterfront.

SEA BREEZES. 0036-9977. Periodical. UK. English. mo. $35.00. Jocast Ltd, 202 Cotton Exchange/Old Hall Street, Liverpool LE 9LA England. Ed C J M Carter. Ind/Abst Ship Abstr. LC HE753.P32.

SEAFARER (JACKSONVILLE, FLA.). (SEAFARER). Vol. 34, No. 1 (Jan. 1985)-. 0882-7788. Periodical. US. English. mo. $5.00. Seafarer Magazine, Box 4728, Jacksonville FL 32201. LC HE554.J3. DD 387.109759121. *Jacksonville Seafarer, 0447-2462.*

SEAPORTS AND THE SHIPPING WORLD. Aug. 1968-. 0037-0150. Periodical. CN. English. mo. Gallery Publishers Ltd, 4634 St Catherine Street West, Montreal Quebec H3Z 2W6 Canada. Tel (514)934-0373. Ed Brian O'N Gallery. Ind/Abst Can. Bus. Index. LC HE561. DD 387.05. adv acc. (ctrl) Covers the marine shipping industry in Canada. *Seaports and the Transport World, 0559-2429.*

SEAPORTS AND THE SHIPPING WORLD. SPRING ISSUE. 1969-. CN. English. an. Gallery Publications Ltd, 1165 Greene Avenue, Montreal Quebec H3Z 2A2 Canada. DD 387.00971. *Seaports and the Transport World. Spring Issue.*

SEATRADE. V. 1- Nov. 1970-. 0037-0428. Periodical. UK. English. mo. Seatrade Publications Ltd, Whitehall Building, 17 Battery Place, New York NY 10004. Ed Paul Bartlett. Ind/Abst Life Sci. Collect., Excerpta Med., Predicasts, Ship Abstr., Public Aff. Inf. Serv. Bull., Funk Scott Index Corp. Ind. LC HE561. bk rev. adv acc. In-depth coverage of current events giving insight into the politics, economics and policies affecting the international shipping business.

SEATRADE US YEARBOOK. See Yearbooks, Almanacs, Directories.

SEAWAY MARITIME DIRECTORY. See Yearbooks, Almanacs, Directories.

SEAWAY REVIEW. V. 1- Spring 1970-. 0037-0487. Periodical. US. English. qt. $20.00. Seaway Review, 221 Water Street, Boyne City MI 49712. Tel (616)582-2814. Ed Michelle Cortright. Ind/Abst Coal Abstr., Ship Abstr. LC HE381.A2. DD 386.4709713. bk rev. adv acc. Circ 16,000. For the people who design, build, own, operate and buy for the giant US and Canadian Great Lakes and inland waterways fleets.

SEMPAKU SETSUBI KANKEI HOREI. 1965-. JA. Japanese. ir. 1500. 4-51 Minami Motocho, Shinjuku-ku Tokyo 160 Japan.

SENKYO KAIUN NEMPO. Main/Corp Nihon Senshu Kyokai. 1956/57-. JA. Japanese. ir. Nihon Senshu Kyokai, c/o Osaka Building 2 Gokan 2-2 Uchisaiwaicho 2-chome Chiyoda-ku, Tokyo Japan. LC HE891.

SFART. Vol. 1-. Periodical. Danish. bm. LC HE730.

SHIP & BOAT INTERNATIONAL. VAT Ship and Boat International. 0037-3834. Periodical. UK. English. mo. $87.60. Metal Bulletin Plc, Park House, 3 Park Terrace, Worcester Park Surrey England. Tel (01)330-4311. Ed R G White. Ind/Abst Fluidex, Life Sci. Collect., Excerpta Med., Ocean. Abstr. LC VM320. DD 623.82005. bk rev. adv acc. Circ 5,000. Specialist coverage of vessels less than 100m in length and below 5000 grt from new orders to datasheets and from equipment news to freight reports. *Ship & Boat Builder International, International Tug and Workboat.*

SHIPBROKER. (THE SHIPBROKER). Began in 1931. 0142-6680. Periodical. UK. English. $91.95. Ryston Publications, Bank Chambers/Downham Market, Norfolk PE38 9BU England. Tel (44)366 387344. Ed John Ison. Ind/Abst Ship Abstr. LC HE610.G7. bk rev. adv acc. Circ 6,000. Shippings international business monthly.

THE SHIPBROKERS' REGISTER. English. ir. S Monseu Company Inc Shipbrokers, New York NY 11361. LC HE610.E9. DD 387.1640254.

SHIPBUILDING AND REPAIR (FINAL) CEASED. (SHIPBUILDING AND REPAIR). Series/Titl Annual Census of Manufactures. VFOAT Construction et Reparation de Navires. 1960-1980. 0527-6144. CN. English. an. 70. DD 338.47623830971. *Shipbuilding Industry (Canada. Dominion Bureau of Statistics), 0700-0014.*

SHIPBUILDING IN KOREA. English. ir. LC VM113.K6. DD 623.83095195.

SHIPCARE & MARITIME MANAGEMENT. VAT Shipcare and Maritime Management. Began publication with Vol. 11, No. 9 in Sept. 1979. 0263-7944. Periodical. UK. English. mo. $74.00. Industrial and Marine Publications Ltd, Queensway House, 2 Queensway, Redhill Surrey RH1 1QS England. Tel (0737)68611. Ed Michael Hood. Ind/Abst Electron. Commun. Abstr. J., ISMEC Bull., Pollut. Abstr. Indexes, Saf. Sci. Abstr. J., Life Sci. Collect., Excerpta Med., Ship Abstr. bk rev. adv acc. Circ 5,000. The only journal in the world covering the areas of ship repair, conversions and maintenance, offering shipowners information on the most cost effective way of ship operation. *Tanker & Bulker Maritime Management, Shipcare International, 0140-8461.*

SHIPPERS' TIMES. 0217-1139. Periodical. English (Chinese). mo. Free to All SNSC Members. Singapore National Shippers, Council 47 Hill Street, Singapore Chinese Chamber of Commerce & Industry Building, Singapore 0617 Singapore. LC HE561. DD 387.505.

SHIPPING AND CARGO MOVEMENTS. 1980-. English. an. Department of Statistics, Private Bag, Wellington New Zealand. LC HE563.N55. DD 387.109931.

SHIPPING & MARINE INDUSTRIES JOURNAL. V. 1- Oct. 1972-. Periodical. II. English. mo. 72.00. Shipping & Marine Inc, 3 Radhe Nivas, 36th Road Bandra, Bombay 400050 India. Tel 6427281/273187. Ed V J Joseph. Ind/Abst Ship Abstr. LC HE561. DD 387.505. bk rev. adv acc. Circ 12,500. A journal devoted to shipping and shipbuilding, offshore and under water activities. Fisheries ports, oceanography, shipping and marine industries journal.

SHIPPING AND PORT REVIEW. V. 1-9, Aug. 1958-Nov./Dec. 1966. 0037-3885. Periodical. II. English. bm. Wachel Molla Mansion, Calcutta 13 India. LC HE561.

SHIPPING, COMMERCE AND INDUSTRY. See Business - Commerce.

SHIPPING DIGEST. Began with issue for Mar. 12, 1923. 0037-3893. Periodical. US. English. wk. Geyer McAllister Publications, PO Box 1129, Dover NJ 07801. LC HE561. DD 656.

SHIPPING REPORT. PART 3. COASTWISE SHIPPING. (SHIPPING REPORT, III). Main/Corp Canada. Statistics Canada. Water Transport Section. VFOAT Transport Maritime, Partie III. 1973-. 0318-8930. CN. English (French). an. $1.40. Information Canada, Statistics Canada, Water Transport Section, Ottawa Ontario K1A 0T6 Canada. *Shipping Report, Part III.*

SHIPPING REPORT. PART 4. ORIGIN AND DESTINATION FOR SELECTED PORTS. (SHIPPING REPORT, PART IV). Main/Corp Statistics Canada. Transportation Section. VFOAT Transport Maritime, Partie IV. 1970-. 0575-9757. CN. text in English and French. an. $2.80. Statistics Canada, Publications Distribution, Ottawa Ontario K1A 0T6 Canada. *Shipping Report, Part IV.*

SHIPPING STATISTICS. See Statistics.

SHIPPING STATISTICS AND ECONOMICS. See Statistics.

SHIPPING STATISTICS OF FIJI. See Statistics.

SHIPPING WORLD AND SHIPBUILDER. (SHIPPING WORLD & SHIPBUILDER). 0037-3931. Periodical. UK. English. mo. Benn Publications, 25 New Street Square, London EC4A 3JA England. Ed A Thorpe. Ind/Abst Eng. Index Annu., Eng. Index Mon., Eng. Index Bioeng. Abstr., Eng. Index Energy Abstr., Fluidex, Life Sci. Collect., Coal Abstr., Ship Abstr., CIS Abstr. CODEN SWSBA5. *Shipbuilder and Marine Engine Builder, Shipping World and World Shipbuilding.*

SHIPS AND THE SEA (MENOMONEE FALLS, WIS.). (SHIPS AND THE SEA). No. 1 (Winter 1983)-. 0745-3183. Periodical. US. English. qt. Phoenix Publications, N89 West 16342 Main Street, Menomonee Falls WI 53051.

SHIPS MONTHLY. V. 1- Jan. 1966-. 0037-394X. Periodical. UK. English. mo. Waterway Prod Ltd, Kottingham HS, Dale Street, Burton-on-Treat Staffs, DE14 3rd England. Tel 0283 64290. Ed Robert Shopland. Ind/Abst Ship Abstr. LC VM1. DD 623.82005. bk rev. adv acc. Circ 25,000. Photographs and illustrated articles on all kinds of ships-/mercantile and naval, sail and steam, past and present.

SHOWBOATS INTERNATIONAL. 0749-2952. Periodical. US. English. bi. $12.00 Domestic, $22.00 Canada. Showboats International, 3886 State Street, Santa Barbara CA 93105. DD 387. *Showboats.*

SINGAPORE MARINE ENGINEERS REVIEW. See Engineering.

SINGAPORE SHIPBUILDING & REPAIRING DIRECTORY. See Yearbooks, Almanacs, Directories.

SINGAPORE SHIPPING & AIR TRANSPORTATION INDUSTRIES DIRECTORY. See Yearbooks, Almanacs, Directories.

SINGAPORE SHIPPING 'N' SHIPBUILDER. Periodical. Sl. English. mo. $24.00. Cosmic Media, PO Box 3163, Singapore Singapore. LC HE561. DD 387.505.

SJULYKKESSTATISTIKK. See Statistics.

SKANDINAVISK SMASKIPSFART. Norwegian. mo. 65.00. Selvigs Forlag, Postboks 162 Sentrum 1, Oslo Norway. LC HE730. *Smaskipsfart.*

SOUTH AFRICAN SHIPPING NEWS AND FISHING INDUSTRY REVIEW. (THE SOUTH AFRICAN SHIPPING NEWS AND FISHING INDUSTRY REVIEW). Began with Jan. 1946 issue. 0038-2671. SA. English. bm. $12.39. Marine Information Services, PO Box 487, Stellenbosch 7600 South Africa. Tel (02231)4040. Ed Michael Stuttaford. Ind/Abst Ship Abstr. LC HE561. adv acc. Circ 1,240. Industrial shipping, fishing, marine mineral exploitation, harbours in Southern Africa.

SOUTH CAROLINA STATE PORTS AUTHORITY, CHARLESTON, SOUTH CAROLINA. REPORT OF STATE AUDITOR AND FINANCIAL STATEMENTS. Main/Corp South Carolina. State Auditor. US. English. State of South Carolina Office of the State Auditor, PO Box 11333, Columbia SC 29211. LC HE554.A3. DD 353.9757008771.

SOUTH FLORIDA PORTS HANDBOOK. 0160-2233. US. English. an. $5.00. Howard Publications, 1314 Seaboard Coast Line Building, PO Box 4728, Jacksonville FL 32201. LC HE554.A3. DD 387.109759.

STATE HARBORS & BOATING FACILITIES. VFOAT State Harbors and Boating Facilities. US. English. an. LC HE553. DD 387.109798.

A STATISTICAL ANALYSIS OF THE WORLD'S MERCHANT FLEETS SHOWING AGE, SIZE, SPEED, AND DRAFT BY FREQUENCY GROUPINGS. See Statistics.

STATISTICAL DATA OF THE AMSTERDAM PORT AND OTHER NORTH SEA CANAL PORT AREAS. See Statistics.

STATISTIEK VAN DE BINNENVLOOT. Main/Corp Netherlands (Kingdom, 1815-). Centraal Bureau voor de Statistiek. Hoofdafdeling Statistieken van Verkeer en Vervoer. VFOAT Statistics of the Inland Fleet. 1979-. NE. Dutch. be. 10.25. Centraal Bureau voor de Statistiek, Staatsuitgeverij, S-

Transportation—Ships & Shipping

Gravenhage Netherlands. **LC** HE674. *Statistiek van de Binnenvloot*.

STATISTIEK VAN DE SCHEEPVAARTBEWEGING. *See* Statistics.

STATISTIK BONGKAR MUAT BARANG DI PELABUHAN INDONESIA. Main/Corp Indonesia. Biro Pusat Statistik. **Series/Titl** Statistik Perhubungan. **VFOAT** Cargo Loading and Unloading at Ports in Indonesia. English and Indoensian. ir. Biro Pusat Statistik, Jln Dr Sutomo No 8, Jakarta Indonesia. **Tel** 372808. **LC** HF247. bk rev. adv acc. (ctrl).

STATISTIK PERHUBUNGAN - BIRO PUSAT STATISTIK (LALU LINTAS ANGKUTAN BARANG ANTAR PULAU MENURUT JENIS PELAYARAN). (LALU LINTAS ANGKUTAN BARANG ANTAR PULAU MENURUT JENIS PELAYARAN). **Series/Titl** Statistik Perhubungan. **VFOAT** Inter Island Cargo Traffics by Shipping Sector. 0216-6909. IO. English (Indonesian). ir. $2.80. Bagian Statistik Tahunan dan Penerbitan, Biro Pusat Statistik, Jl Dr Sutomo No 8, PO Box 3, Jakarta Indonesia. **Tel** 372808. **LC** HE887. bk rev. adv acc. (ctrl).

STATISTIQUE DE LA NAVIGATION MARITIME. **VFOAT** Statistiek van de Zeevaart. BE. Dutch (French (1955-71)). an. 5.00, $10.00. Secretariat General Benelux, rue de la Regence 39, 1000 Bruxelles Belgium. **Tel** (32)025193811. **Ed** P Vandu Meiven. **LC** HE843. **Circ** 3,000. Statistics of maritime transportation originating in or destined to religion and Dutch seaports.

STATISTIQUE DU TRAFIC INTERNATIONAL DES PORTS. Main/Corp Institut National de Statistique (Belgium). French. ir. Royaume de Belgique, Ministere des Affaires Economiques Institut National de Statistique, rue de Louvain 44, 1000 Bruxelles Belgium. **LC** HE563.A3. **DD** 387.10122.

STATISTIQUE DU TRAFIC INTERNATIONAL (U.E.B.L.). *See* Statistics.

SUDOSTROENIE. No. 22- 1974-. UR. Russian. mo. $56.00. Victor Kamkin Inc (70890), 12224 Parklawn Drive, Rockville MD 20852. **Tel** (301)881-5973. **Ind/Abst** Ship Abstr., CIS Abstr., Chem. Abstr., Energy Res. Abstr. **LC** VM7. **CODEN** SUDODQ. *Sudostroenie I Morskie Sooruzheniia*.

SUOMEN KAUPPALAIVASTO. FINLANDS HANDELSFLOTTA. **VFOAT** Finlands Handelsflotta, The Finnish Merchant Marine. 1.- 1918-. Finnish (English, Swedish). an. **LC** HE565.F5.

SYSTEME D'INFORMATION SUR LES TRANSPORTS DE MARCHANDISES. APPLICATION, COMMENT EVALUER LA PART DU TRAFIC MARITIME NE DE NOTRE COMMERCE EXTERIEUR QUI ECHAPPE AUX PORTS FRANCAIS. **VFOAT** Application, Comment Evaluer la Part du Trafic Maritime ne de Notre Commerce Exterieur qui Echappe aux Ports Francais. 0181-5334. FR. French. ir. 55 rue Brillat-Savarin, 75658 Paris Cedex 13 France. **LC** HE597.F8. **DD** 382.094400212.

THE TANKER REGISTER. 1960-. UK. English. an. $282.00. Taylor & Francis Inc, 242 Cherry Street, Philadelphia PA 19106. **Tel** (215)238-0939. **LC** HE566.T3. **DD** 387.245. *Register of Tank Vessels of the World*.

TANKERS IN THE WORLD FLEET. (TANKERS IN THE WORLD FLEET AS OF JAN. 1 . . .). 0741-062X. US. English. an. US Department of Transportation, Maritime Administration, Washington DC 20590. **LC** HE566.T3. **DD** 387.245. Vols. for 1982- distributed to depository libraries in microfiche.

TECHNIKA I GOSPODARKA MORSKA. Periodical. PL. Polish (table of contents and summary in English). mo. *Technika Morza I Wybrzeza*.

THIS IS SAR & H : HARBOURS & PIPELINES HANDBOOK. Main/Corp South African Railways and Harbours. SA. English. ir. Thomson Publication, PO Box 8308, Johannesburg 2000 South Africa. **LC** HE559.S6. **DD** 387.10968.

TRADE AND SHIPPING STATISTICS. *See* Statistics.

TRADE AND SHIPPING, TASMANIA. 1976-77-. AT. English. an. Government Printing Tasmania, GPO Box 66A, Hobart Tasmania 7001 Australia. **LC** HF287. **DD** 382.0994600212. *Trade and Shipping (Hobart, Tasmania : 1973)*.

TRAFIC. Main/Corp Port Autonome de Paris. French. ir. Port Autonomi de Paris, 2 Quai de Grenelle, Paris France 75015. **LC** HE558.P2. **DD** 387.1094436.

TRANSACTIONS (TM). *See* Engineering - Mechanical Engineering & Machinery.

TRANSPORTATION LINES ON THE ATLANTIC, GULF, AND PACIFIC COASTS. Main/Corp United States. Army. Corps of Engineers. **Series/Titl** Transportation Series, 5. 0361-9125. US. English. Waterborne Commerce Statistics Center, PO Box 60267, New Orleans LA 70160. **LC** HE565.U68. **DD** 387.5240973.

TRANSPORTATION LINES ON THE GREAT LAKES SYSTEM. 0361-8978. US. English. an. District Engineer, US Army Engineer District New Orleans, New Orleans LA 70160. **LC** HE565.U71. **DD** 386.540977.

TRANSPORTATION LINES ON THE MISSISSIPPI RIVER SYSTEM AND THE GULF INTRACOASTAL WATERWAY. Main/Corp United States. Army. Corps of Engineers. **Series/Titl** Transportation Series, 4. 0361-8986. US. English. Waterborne Commerce Statistics Center, PO Box 60267, New Orleans LA 70160. **LC** HE565.U74. **DD** 386.350977. *Transportation Lines on the Mississippi River System and the Gulf Intracoastal Waterway*.

TRANSPORTATION SERIES. No. 1- 1926-. Monographic Series. English. ir. **LC** HE623.

TRANSPORTS MARITIMES (NATIONAL SHIPPERS COUNCIL OF CAMEROON). (TRANSPORTS MARITIMES : REVUE TRIMESTRIELLE PUBLIEE PAR LE CONSEIL NATIONAL DES CHARGEURS DU CAMEROUN). Dec. 1980-. Periodical. English (French). qt. C N C C , B P 1588, Douala Cameroun. **LC** HE905.4. **DD** 387.544096711.

TRAVERSIERS, PONTS ET CROISIERES. *See* Travel.

TSUKO SEMPAKU JITTAI CHOSA HOKOKUSHO. Main/Corp Japan. Kaijo Hoancho. Keibi Kyunanbu. Koko Anzenka. Kaijo Kostu Kikakushitsu. JA. Japanese. ir. 1-3 Kasumigaseki 2 Chiyoda-ku, Tokyo Japan. **LC** HE497.A1.

TURKISH SHIPPING. 1984 - 0266-7193. Periodical. UK. English. Free to Seatrade Subscribers. Seatrade, 11/12 Bury Street, London EC3 5AT United Kingdom. **LC** HE873.4. **DD** 387.509561.

UNITED STATES OCEANBORNE FOREIGN TRADE ROUTES. Began with 1975/76. 0161-8830. US. English. an. Maritime Administration, Washington DC 20590. **LC** HE745. **DD** 387.51. *Essential United States Foreign Trade Routes*.

VESSEL INVENTORY REPORT. June 30, 1976-. 0735-2220. Periodical. US. English. sa. US Department of Transportation, Maritime Administration, Office of Trade Studies and Statistics, Division of Statistics, Washington DC 20590. Vols for June 1981, June '83, Jan. '83 distributed to depository libraries in microfiche. *Vessel Inventory Report : United States Flag, Dry Cargo and Tanker Fleets, 1,000 Gross Tons and Over*.

VIA PENSACOLA. V. 1- May 1957-. 0505-4176. Periodical. US. English. ir. Pensacola Port Authority, Pensacola FL 32504.

WATER TRANSPORT STATISTICS OF INDIA. *See* Statistics.

WATER TRANSPORTATION (STATISTICS CANADA. SURFACE AND MARINE TRANSPORT SECTION). (WATER TRANSPORTATION). **VFOAT** Transport Par Eau. 0380-0342. CN. English (French). an. 32.00 Domestic, 33.00 Foreign. Receiver General of Canada, Statistics Canada Publications, Ottawa Ontario K1A 0T6 Canada. **Tel** (613)996-9159. **LC** HE769. **DD** 387.00971. Presents principal statistics on private, government and for-hire water carriers. Includes number, kind, operating status and registry of vessels; gives property value, additions and retirements. Contains an explanation of methodology, a glossary, questionnaires and a list of related publications. *Water Transportation (Statistics Canada. Water Transport Section)*, 0380-0342.

THE WATERWAYS JOURNAL. Began in Apr. 1887. 0043-1524. Periodical. US. English. wk. $18.00. Waterways Journal, 666 Security Building/319 North 4th Street, St Louis MO 63102. **Tel** (314)241-7354. **Ed** Jack Simpson. **LC** HE623. **DD** 386.20973. bk rev. adv acc. **Circ** 8,000. (ctrl). Weekly marine newspaper relating to the inland waterways of the U.S.

WEEKLY BULLETIN. PORT OF NEW ORLEANS. 0192-382X. Periodical. US. English. wk. $26.00. Port Publishing Company, 1004 International Building, New Orleans LA 70130. **Tel** (504)568-1851.

WORLD PORT INDEX. *See* Indexes/Abstracts.

WORLD PORTS. V. 1- Sept./Oct. 1978-. 0194-4681. Periodical. US. English. bm. $9.00 US, Canada, Mexico, Central and South America; $20.00 Others. World Ports, PO Box 1067, Blair Station, Silver Spring MD 20910. **LC** HE550. **DD** 387.105. *World Ports/American Seaport*.

WORLD PORTS & HARBOURS ABSTRACTS (INCORPORATING INTERNATIONAL DREDGING ABSTRACTS). *See* Indexes/Abstracts.

WORLD SHIPPING STATISTICS. *See* Statistics.

WORLDWIDE TANKER NOMINAL FREIGHT SCALE. **VFOAT** Worldscale. Began in 1969. UK. English. sa. Worldscale Association (NYC). **LC** HE594. **DD** 387.51.

WWS. WORLD WIDE SHIPPING GUIDE. (WWS, WORLD WIDE SHIPPING GUIDE). **VFOAT** World Wide Shipping Guide. 0162-0088. US. English. an. $41.25. World Wide Shipping Guide, 77 Moehring Drive, Blauvelt NY 10913. **Tel** (914)359-1934. **LC** HE561. **DD** 387.544025.

WWS/WORLD PORTS. **VFOAT** World Ports. VAT WWS World Ports, World Wide Shipping World Ports. Vol. 44, No. 1 (Mar. 1981)-. 0278-6664. Periodical. US. English. bm. WWS World Ports, 77 Moehring Drive, Blauvelt NY 10913. **Tel** (914)359-1934. **Ind/Abst** Life Sci. Collect., Coal Abstr., Ship Abstr. **LC** HE561. **DD** 387.1091812. *American Seaport*, 0161-6323.

YEARBOOK, SHIPYARDS, BOATBUILDERS, AND MARINE ENGINEERS. *See* Yearbooks, Almanacs, Directories.

YEDION - HA-MAKHON HA-YISREELI LE-HEKER HA-SAPANUT. Main/Corp Makhon Ha-Yisreeli Le-Heker Ha-Sapanut. **VFOAT** Information Paper - Israel Shipping Research Institute. Periodical. IS. English (Hebrew). ir. Israel Shipping and Aviation Research Institute, 65 Haatzmauth Road, POB 1860 Haifa, Hefan Israel. **Tel** (04)520756. **Ed** Miriam Ofek. **Ind/Abst** Ship Abstr. **LC** HE730. **DD** 387.5095694. (ctrl). Summaries of important news and developments worldwide in shipping, aviation, and ports.

ZEEVAARTVERWANTE BEDRIJVEN. **Series/Titl** Produktiestatistieken Transport, Opslag en Communicatie. **VFOAT** Supporting Services to Maritime Transport. 0168-3187. NE. Dutch (summaries in English). an. 7.50. Centraal Bureau voor de Statistiek, Prinses Beatrixlaan 428, Postbus 959, 2270 AZ Voorburg Netherlands.

ZEITSCHRIFT FUR BINNENSCHIFFAHRT. 15. Oct. 1894-. Periodical. German. ir. **Ind/Abst** Ship Abstr. **LC** HE669.

ZESZYTY NAUKOWE WYDZIAU EKONOMIKI TRANSPORTU. EKONOMIKA TRANSPORTU MORSKIEGO. Main/Corp Danzig. Uniwersytet. Wydzia Ekonomiki Transportu. **VFOAT** Ekonomika Transportu Morskiego. Polish (summaries in English and Russian). ir. 12.00 Each Issue. **LC** HE730.

ZOSEN GIJUTSU. **VFOAT** Shipbuilding & Engineering. 0387-2203. Periodical. JA. Japanese. mo. 15000. Japan Indasutoriaru Paburisshingu, c/o Suzuki Building 10-1, Azabu Juaban 3, Minato-ku 106, Tokyo-to Japan. **Ind/Abst** Coal Abstr. **LC** VM4.

ZOSEN YEAR BOOK. See Yearbooks, Almanacs, Directories.

ZOSEN ZOKI TOKEI GEPPO. JA. Japanese. mo. Unyusho Daijin Kambo Joho Kanribu, c/o Godo Chosha Dai 3-go Kan Unyusho, 9-kai 925-Goshitsu 1-3 Kasumigaseki 2, Chiyoda-ku, Tokyo-to Japan. LC VM299.7.J3.

ZOSHU RENRAKU. Main/Corp Japan. Kaijo Hoancho. Sempaku Gijutsubu. Japanese. ir. LC VM4.

TRAVEL

1HE CVR HOTEL GUIDE TO SOUTHERN AFRICA. See Hotels/Motels.

AA GUIDE TO CAMPING AND CARAVANNING. Main/Corp Automobile Association (Great Britain). VFOAT Guide to Camping and Caravanning. 1973-. UK. English. an. Automobile Association, PO Box 51 Fanum House, Basingstoke RG21 2BR England.

THE AAA TRAVELER. MUSKINGUM AAA EDITION. See Transportation - Automobiles.

AAA WORLD. HAWAII. See Transportation - Automobiles.

AAA WORLD (MISSISSIPPI EDITION). See Transportation - Automobiles.

AAA WORLD. WISCONSIN. See Transportation - Automobiles.

ABC AIR TRAVEL ATLAS. Main/Corp ABC Travel Guides Ltd. VFOAT Air Travel Atlas. Periodical. UK. English. sa. 16.60. ABC International, World Timetable Centre Church Street, Dunstable Bedfordshire LU5 4HB England. Tel (0592)600111. Ed V Freeman. LC G1046.P6. DD 912.138772. adv acc. Circ 14,000. This guide gives an overall view of all major domestic and international scheduled air routes, plus 150 country codes, average journey times and time zone map.

THE ABC SHIPPING GUIDE. See Transportation - Ships & Shipping.

ACCOMODATION AND TRAVEL FACTS : NORWAY. See Hotels/Motels.

ADIRONDACK ALMANACK. See Yearbooks, Almanacs, Directories.

ADVENTURE (CANADIAN HOSTELLING ASSOCIATION). (ADVENTURE). VFOAT Aventure. VAT Aventure (Vanier. 1977), Programme de Vacances Aventure. '77-. 0710-2771. CN. English (French). an. Free. Canadian Hostelling Association, 333 River Road, Vanier Ontario K1L 8B9 Canada. DD 917.10464. Aventure, 0383-8935.

AFRICA CALLS FROM ZIMBABWE RHODESIA. No. 116-120. Periodical. RH. English. bm. Africa Calls Ltd, Box 8045 Causeway, Salisbury Rhodesia. Tel 705911. Ed C Wilson. LC DT962.A2. DD 968.91005. adv acc. Circ 13,000. Tourist articles pictures information on Zimbabwe. Rhodesia Calls.

AFRICA UPDATE. 0194-4584. Periodical. US. English. qt. Africa Update Inc, 300 Madison Avenue, New York NY 10017. Tel (914)235-7620.

AGENCY LIST, GEOGRAPHIC - AIR TRAFFIC CONFERENCE OF AMERICA. DATA SERVICES DIVISION. Main/Corp Air Traffic Conference of America. Data Services Division. VFOAT ATC Agency List. 0270-2797. US. English. qt. $100.00. Air Traffic Conference of America, 1709 New York Avenue Northwest, Washington DC 20006. LC G154. DD 338.47910402573.

AGENCY LIST NUMERIC SEQUENCE - AIR TRAFFIC CONFERENCE OF AMERICA. PUBLICATIONS SERVICES DIVISION. Main/Corp Air Traffic Conference of America. Publications Services Division. VFOAT Agency List Numeric. Periodical. US. English. Air Traffic Conference of America, 1709 New York Avenue Northwest, Washington DC 20006. LC G154. DD 338.4791730025.

AGENT WEST. VAT Agent West Traveletter Weekly (1979). V. 2, No. 25-34 (Issue 49-58). 0225-4565. Periodical. CN. English. wk. $74.10. Bizletter Publishers, 1425 West Pender Street, Vancouver British Columbia V6G 2S3 Canada. Tel (604)688-0481. DD 338.479105. Agent West Traveletter Weekly, 0827-3510.

AGENT WEST (1984). (AGENT WEST). V. 7, No. 31 (Sept. 4, 1984)-. 0827-3537. Periodical. CN. English. wk. Free. Agent West, 1425 West Pender Street, Vancouver British Columbia V6C 2S3 Canada. DD 338.479105. (ctrl). Agent West Weekly, 0827-3529.

AIR TRAVEL BARGAINS. 1965-. 0065-4868. US. English. an. Pocket Books Inc, PO Box 408 Coconut Grove, Miami FL 33133. Tel (305)445-0916.

AIRLINE HANDBOOK. (THE AIRLINE HANDBOOK). 0095-4683. US. English. an. $15.00. Aero Travel Research-A, PO Box 3694, Cranston RI 02910. Tel (401)941-6140. Ed Paul K Martin. LC HE9768. DD 387.7025. adv acc. Circ 10,000. Guide to the operations of 2,000 world airlines scheduled charter, commuter and cargo. Covers routes, destinations lists, aircraft, histories, addresses, news developments, and statistics.

AL-MUSAFIR AL-ARABI. VFOAT The Arab Traveller. No. 1, (March/April 1985)-. 0267-0194. Periodical. UK. Arabic. bm. $33.00. The Arab Traveller, Regent Arcade House, 19/25 Argyll Street, London W1V 1AA United Kingdom. Tel 01-734 1655. Ed Terence Mirabelli. bk rev adv acc. Circ 23,000. (ctrl).

A.L.A. SIGHTS TO SEE BOOK. (ALA SIGHTS TO SEE BOOK). Main/Corp Automobile Legal Association. 1973-. 0090-8614. US. English. an. Automobile Legal Association, 1047 Commonwealth Avenue, Boston MA 02215. LC E158. DD 917.3049205. A.L.A. Green Book.

ALABAMA GUEST GUIDE; A TOUR THROUGH THE HEART OF DIXIE. US. English. an. PO Box 6191, Birmingham AL 35209. Ed B E Jones and G Butts.

ALASKA (BLAKE PUBLISHING COMPANY). See Geography.

ALASKA, MARINE HIGHWAY. NORTHWEST TRAVEL GUIDE. (ALASKA MARINE HIGHWAY : NORTHWEST TRAVEL GUIDE). VFOAT Northwest Travel Guide. 1983/Spring 84-. 0824-5967. CN. English. an. $1.95 Per No. Northwest Travel Guides, 211 Wood Street, Whitehorse Yukon Territory Y1A 2E4 Canada. DD 917.9804505. B.C.-Yukon-Alaska Plus the Alaska Marine Highway.

ALBERTA, NORTHWEST TERRITORIES. NORTHWEST TRAVEL GUIDE. (ALBERTA, NORTHWEST TERRITORIES : NORTHWEST TRAVEL GUIDE). VFOAT Northwest Travel Guide. 3rd Annual Ed. (1983/Spring 1984)-. 0826-0301. CN. English. an. $1.95 Per No. Northwest Travel Guides, 211 Wood Street, Whitehorse Yukon Y1A 2E4 Canada. DD 917.12304305. Northwest Travel Guide to the Northwest Territories, 0710-3360.

ALDEN'S CONCISE TORONTO GUIDE. 1983/84 Ed.-. 0827-3162. CN. English. be. $6.95 Per Vol. Alden's Concise Toronto Guide, 1737 Pharmacy Avenue, Scarborough Ontario M1T 1H1 Canada. DD 917.13541044.

ALL ABOUT ARIZONA : THE HEALTHFUL STATE. 1957-. US. English. be. Harian Publications, 1 Vernon Avenue, Floral Park NY 11001. LC F809.3. DD 917.91.

ALL OF MEXICO AT LOW COST. 1st- Ed. US. English. $2.50. Harian Publications, 1 Vernon Avenue, Floral Park NY 11001. LC F1209. DD 917.20482.

ALOHA. V. 1- Jan./Mar. 1978-. 0147-5436. Periodical. US. English. bm. $14.95. Aloha, PO Box 28816, San Diego CA 92128. Tel (808)523-9871. Ed Rita Ariyoshi. LC DU620. DD 996.9005. bk rev adv acc. Circ 60,000. (ctrl). Travel and history to Hawaii and the Pacific.

LES ALPES. See Geography.

AMENAGEMENT DE L'ESPACE ET DU TEMPS ET DEVELOPPEMENT DU TOURISME : ACTES DU CONSEIL SUPERIEUR DU TOURISME. VFOAT Actes du Conseil Superieur du Tourisme. Session 1979-1980-. FR. French. ir. 29-31 Quai Voltaire, 75340 Paris Cedex 07 France. LC G155.F8. DD 380.145914404838.

AMERICAN EXECUTIVE TRAVEL COMPANION. Main/Corp Guides to Multinational Business, Inc. VFOAT Guide to Traveling on Business In 50 States. 0363-535X. US. English. an. Guides to Multinational Business Inc, Box 92, Boston MA 02138. LC E158. DD 917.30492.

AMERICAN TRAVELER (ATLANTA, GA). (AMERICAN TRAVELER : OFFICIAL PUBLICATION OF THE SEPTEMBER DAYS CLUB). V. 7, No. 4 (Spring 1984)-. 0747-0843. Periodical. US. English. qt. American Traveler, 2751 Buford Highway NE, Atlanta GA 30324. September Days, 0746-5009.

AMERICAN URBAN GUIDENOTES : THE NEWSLETTER OF GUIDEBOOKS. VFOAT Guidenotes : The Newsletter of Guidebooks. Vol. 1, No. 1 (Summer 1979)-. US. English. qt. $10.00. American Urban Guide, PO Box 186, Washington DC 20044. Ed John Fondersmith. Ind/Abst Avery Public Period. Circ 200. Deals primarily with current guidebooks, mostly for the US. Also includes some guidebook history.

AMERICAS. PORTUGUESE EDITION. See Geography.

AMOCO TRAVELER. V. 1, Issue 1 (Spring 1981)-. 0275-5564. Periodical. US. English. qt. Amoco Traveler, PO Box 9018, Des Moines IA 50306. DD 910.

ANNALS OF TOURISM RESEARCH. VFOAT ATR, Annals of Tourism Research. 0160-7383. Periodical. US. English. qt. $65.00. Pergamon Press, 395 Sawmill River Road, Elmsford NY 10523. Tel (715)232-2339. Ind/Abst Public Aff. Inf. Serv. Bull., Soc. Sci. Citation Index, Abstr. Anthropol. LC G155.A1. DD 338.479105.

ANNUAIRE TOURISTIQUE ET DIPLOMATIQUE DU CAMEROUN. See Yearbooks, Almanacs, Directories.

ANNUAL CONFERENCE PROCEEDINGS - TRAVEL RESEARCH ASSOCIATION CEASED. (ANNUAL CONFERENCE PROCEEDINGS). Main/Corp Travel Research Association. 0276-8968. US. English. an. Travel & Tourism Research Association, PO Box 8066 Foothill Station, Salt Lake City UT 84108. Tel (801)581-3351. Ed Mari Lou Wood. LC G149.5. DD 910.4072. Circ 1,200. (ctrl). Speeches, panels, workshops presented at 16th annual conference theme: the battle for market share, strategies in research and marketing (as complete as possible).

ANNUAL REPORT - AUSTRALIAN TOURIST COMMISSION. Main/Corp Australian Tourist Commission. AT. English. ir. Commonwealth Government Printing Office, PO Box 84, Canberra Australian Capital Territory 2600 Australia. LC J905, G155.A75. DD 328.9401 S, 338.47919404605.

ANNUAL REPORT - BARBADOS BOARD OF TOURISM. See Public Administration.

ANNUAL REPORT - ENGLISH TOURIST BOARD. Main/Corp English Tourist Board. UK. English. an. 60. English Tourist Board, 4 Grosvenor Gardens, London SW1W 0DU England. LC G155.G7. DD 354.41008243.

ANNUAL REPORT OF THE BRITISH TOURIST AUTHORITY. See Geography.

ANNUAL REPORT OF THE QUEENSLAND TOURIST & TRAVEL CORPORATION. Main/Corp Queensland Tourist & Travel Corporation. 1980-. AT. English. an. Queensland Tourist & Travel Corporation, 307 Queen Street, Brisband 4001 Australia. LC G155.A75. DD 382.45919430463.

ANNUAL REPORT - OKLAHOMA TOURISM AND RECREATION DEPARTMENT. Main/Corp Oklahoma. Tourism and Recreation Dept. 1949-8770. US. English. an. 500 Will Rogers Building, Oklahoma City OK 73105. LC G155.U6. DD 353.976600826.

ANNUAL REPORT ON BARBADOS. See Geography.

ANNUAL REPORT ON DOMINICA, B.W.I. See Geography.

ANNUAL REPORT ON JAMAICA. See Geography.

Travel

ANNUAL REPORT ON ST. LUCIA, B.W.I. See Geography.

ANNUAL REPORT - TAMILNADU TOURISM DEVELOPMENT CORPORATION. Main/Corp Tamilnadu Tourism Development Corporation. English. ir. Tamilnadu Tourism Development Corporation, V S T Motors Buildings 34 Mount Road, Madras 2 India. LC G155.I4. DD 338.761915482045.

ANNUAL REVIEW - TRAVEL ALBERTA. Main/Corp Alberta. Travel Alberta. 1st - 1972/73-. 0319-8723. CN. English. an. Travel Alberta, Capital Square, 10065 Jasper Avenue/12th Floor, Edmonton Alberta T5J 0H4 Canada. LC G155.C3. DD 917.123043.

ANNUAL STATISTICAL REPORT - CEYLON TOURIST BOARD. See Statistics.

ANNUAL STATISTICAL REPORT ON TOURISM IN THAILAND. See Statistics.

ANNUAL STATISTICAL REPORT ON VISITOR ARRIVALS (SINGAPORE). See Statistics.

THE ANNUAL WORLD TOURISM OVERVIEW. (THE . . . ANNUAL WORLD TOURISM OVERVIEW). VFOAT World Tourism Overview. Began in 1976. 0744-1940. US. English. an. American Express Publishing Corporation, 1350 Avenue of the Americas, New York NY 10019. LC G155.A1. DD 380.1459104.

ANNUARIO SEAT. VOL. G, TURISMO E TEMPO LIBERO. See Yearbooks, Almanacs, Directories.

ANUARIO TURISTICO DE PERNAMBUCO. See Yearbooks, Almanacs, Directories.

ARKANSAS TRAVEL AND TOURISM REPORT. US. English. an. LC G155.U6. DD 381.459176045.

ARRIVAL. July 1981-. 0711-544X. Periodical. CN. English. mo. $29.40. bk rev. adv acc. Arrival Publishing Company, 1425 West Pender Street 2nd Floor, Vancouver British Columbia V6G 2S3 Canada. Tel (604)688-0481. DD 910.5.

ARTHUR FROMMER'S DOLLARWISE GUIDE TO NEW ENGLAND. See Geography.

ASIA-PACIFIC TRAVEL INDEX. See Indexes/Abstracts.

ASIA TRAVEL TRADE. Periodical. English. mo. Tel 5-749317. bk rev. adv acc. Circ 20,000. (ctrl). Travel industry magazine for management. Concentrates on operational rather than travel product information. Has gained authoritative reputation.

ASIA TRAVEL TRADE DIRECTORY. See Yearbooks, Almanacs, Directories.

ASPEN VACATION GUIDE. See Recreation, Leisure.

ASTA TRAVEL NEWS. Main/Corp American Society of Travel Agents. VAT American Society of Travel Agents Travel News. Began in 1949. 0001-2637. Periodical. US. English. mo. $10.00. Communications International, 488 Madison Avenue/11th Floor/Suite 1120, New York NY 10022. LC G149. DD 910.5. ASTA News.

ATLANTIC CITY MAGAZINE. 1977. 0194-9993. Periodical. US. English. mo. $9.95. Menus International Inc, 1637 Atlantic Avenue, Atlantic City NJ 08401. Tel (609)348-6886. adv acc. Circ 18,000.

AUSTRIA. See Geography.

BADEN-WURTTEMBERG. V.1- Aug. 1951-. Periodical. GW. German. ir. G Braun Verlag, Karl Friedrichstrasse 14-18, D7500 Karlsruhe West Germany.

BAHAMAS TOURISM STATISTICS. See Statistics.

BARRY BERNDES' ANNUAL EDITION OF SAN DIEGO GUIDE. VFOAT San Diego Guide. 1st- 1969-. 0145-8345. US. English. $1.95. San Diego Guide, PO Box 81544, San Diego CA 92138. LC F869.S22. DD 917.9498.

BAXTER'S EURAILPASS TRAVEL GUIDE. VFOAT Eurailpass Travel Guide. 1972/73-. 0146-8707. US. English. an. Rail Europe, PO Box 3255, Alexandria VA 22302. LC HE3004. DD 385.2042094. Eurail, 0146-8723.

BAZAK GUIDE TO ISRAEL. See Geography.

BAZAK GUIDE TO SPAIN. 0302-6221. US. English. ir. $4.95. Bazak Israel Guidebook Publishers, 60 East 42nd Street Suite 411, New York NY 10017. LC DP14. DD 914.60482.

BELIZE BUSINESS AND TRAVEL DIRECTORY. See Yearbooks, Almanacs, Directories.

THE BELTWAY NATURALIST. No. 1 (Mar. 1984)-. 0749-436X. Periodical. US. English. bm. $9.00. Dominion House, 4616 Briar Parch Court, Fairfax VA 22032. DD 508.

BERKSHIRE TRAVELLER ALMANACK. See Yearbooks, Almanacs, Directories.

BETTER HOMES AND GARDENS CLOSE TO HOME VACATION IDEAS. VFOAT Vacation Ideas. Periodical. US. English. 1716 Locust Street, Des Moines IA 50336. LC E169.02. DD 917.304924.

BIRNBAUM'S EUROPE. Series/Titl A Stephen Birnbaum Travel Guide. VFOAT Europe. 1985-. 0883-2498. US. English. an. $14.95. Houghton Mifflin, 2 Park Street, Boston MA 02108. Europe, 0193-7936.

BIRNBAUM'S EUROPE FOR BUSINESS TRAVELERS. Series/Titl A Stephen Birnbaum Travel Guide. VFOAT Europe for Business Travelers. 1985-. 0749-4815. US. English. an. $7.95 Per Issue. Houghton Mifflin Co, 2 Park Street, Boston MA 02108. LC D909. DD 914.04558.

BIRNBAUM'S FRANCE. Series/Titl A Stephen Birnbaum Travel Guide. VFOAT France. 1985-. 0749-2553. US. English. an. $11.95. Houghton Mifflin Co, 2 Park Street, Boston MA 02108. DD 914.

BIRNBAUM'S GREAT BRITAIN AND IRELAND. Series/Titl A Stephen Birnbaum Travel Guide. VFOAT Great Britain and Ireland. 1985-. 0884-1195. US. English. an. $11.95. Houghton Mifflin Company, Travel Guide Department/GG, 2 Park Street, Boston MA 02108. LC DA650. DD 914.104. Great Britain and Ireland, 0278-0860.

BIRNBAUM'S HAWAII. Series/Titl A Stephen Birnbaum Travel Guide. VFOAT Hawaii. 1985-. 0883-2471. US. English. an. $12.95. Houghton Mifflin Co, 2 Park Street, Boston MA 02108. Ed S Birnbaum. Hawaii (Boston, Mass.), 0732-9024.

BIRNBAUM'S SOUTH AMERICA. Series/Titl A Stephen Birnbaum Travel Guide. VFOAT South America. 1985-. 0883-2463. US. English. an. $12.95. Travel Guides Department GG, Houghton Mifflin Company, 2 Park Street, Boston MA 02108. South America, 0193-7944.

BIRNBAUM'S THE CARIBBEAN, BERMUDA, AND THE BAHAMAS. Series/Titl A Stephen Birnbaum Travel Guide. VFOAT Caribbean, Bermuda, and the Bahamas. 1985-. 0883-248X. US. English. an. $11.95. Houghton Mifflin Company, 2 Park Street, Boston MA 02108. Ed S Birnbaum.

BIRNBAUM'S UNITED STATES. Series/Titl A Stephen Birnbaum Travel Guide. VFOAT United States. 1985-. 0883-2501. US. English. an. $11.95. Travel Guides Department GG, Houghton Mifflin Co/2 Park Street, Boston MA 02108. United States, 0162-2420.

BIRNBAUM'S USA FOR BUSINESS TRAVELERS. Series/Titl A Stephen Birnbaum Travel Guide. VFOAT USA for Business Travelers. 1985-. 0883-251X. US. English. an. $7.95. Houghton Mifflin Co, 2 Park Street, Boston MA 02108. USA for Business Travelers, 0739-6384.

BLUEWATER CIRCLE DRIVES CEASED. Began publication in 1948?. 0318-269X. Periodical. CN. English. an. Free. J D Thomson Tourist Promotions Ltd, Dresden Ontario N0P 1M0 Canada. DD 917.132044.

BLUEWATER ONTARIO VACATION GUIDE. 33rd Ed. (1981/82)-. 0715-3058. CN. English. an. Free. Bluewater Ontario Vacation Guide, Thomson Tourist Promotions, 5 Municipal Street, Guelph Ontario N1G 1G8 Canada. DD 917.13204405. Bluewater Vacation Guide, 0318-2681; Bluewater Circle Driver, 0318-269X.

BLUEWATER VACATION GUIDE CEASED. VFOAT Bluewater Ontario Vacation Guide. 1969/70-1980. 0318-2681. Periodical. CN. English. an. Free. J D Thomson/Tourist Promotions, Dresden Ontario N0P 1M0 Canada. DD 917.132044.

BOLETIN DE INVESTIGACIONES E INFORMACION TURISTICA. Main/Corp Corporacion Nacional de Turismo de Colombia. Spanish. ir. Apartado Aereo 8400, Bogota Columbia. LC G155.C6.

BONJOUR QUEBEC. Vol. 1, No. 1 (July 1980)-. 0229-0898. Periodical. CN. English (text also in French). qt. Free. Association Touristique de la Region de Quebec, 975 Place d'Youville, Palais Montcalm, Suite 300, Quebec Quebec G1R 3P1 Canada. DD 917.1447005.

BOTTIN MONDAIN; TOUT PARIS, TOUTE LA FRANCE. FR. French. ir. $88.00. Didot Bottin, 28 rue de Docteur Finlay, 75738 Paris Cedex 15 France. LC DC704. DD 914.43610025.

BRASIL, MEETING FACILITIES. See Hotels/Motels.

BRASIL : TOURIST CALENDAR. VFOAT Brasil: Calendrier Touristique. BL. Portuguese. ir. Embratur, Cebitur, Rua Barata Ribeiro 272 CEP, 22.040 Rio de Janeiro Brazil.

BRITISH COLUMBIA, VANCOUVER ISLAND. NORTHWEST TRAVEL GUIDE. (BRITISH COLUMBIA, VANCOUVER ISLAND : NORTHWEST TRAVEL GUIDE). VFOAT Northwest Travel Guide B.C. 39th Ed. (1983/Spring 84)-. 0826-0230. CN. English. an. Northwest Travel Guides, 211 Wood Street, Whitehorse Yukon Territory Y1A 2E4 Canada. DD 917.1104. Northwest Travelguide: British Columbia, 0705-3363.

BRITISH HONDURAS. See Geography.

BRITISH ISLES AND IRELAND TRAVEL GUIDE. VFOAT AAA Travel Guide, British Isles and Ireland. 0095-1579. US. English. an. 2.00. 8111 Gatchouse Road, Falls Church VA 22042. LC GV1025.G7. DD 914.104857.

BUDGET TRAVEL IN CANADA (UNITED STATES EDITION). See Business - Public Finance.

BUDGETS OF NATIONAL TOURISM ADMINISTRATIONS. 1979-1981-. English. be. LC G155.A1. DD 351.827. Budgets of National Tourist Administrations.

BUDGETS OF NATIONAL TOURIST ADMINISTRATIONS. 1967/68-. English (Part 1 in French and Spanish, Part 2 in English). an. $50.00. World Tourism Organization, Calle Capitan Haya 42, E-Madrid 20 Spain. Tel 279-2804.

BULLETIN - TOURING OFFICE OF THE CANADA COUNCIL. Main/Corp Canada Council. Touring Office. VFOAT Bulletin - Office des Tournees du Conseil des Arts. VAT Touring Office Bulletin of the Canada Council. V. 1- Apr. 1975-. 0703-6078. Periodical. CN. English (French). ty. Touring Office of the Canada Council, 151 Sparks Street, Ottawa Ontario K1P 5V8 Canada.

BULLETIN VOYAGES. Published since 1978?. 0706-215X. Periodical. CN. French. wk. 0.25 Per Number. DD 338.479105.

BUS TOURS MAGAZINE. 0199-6096. Periodical. US. English. bm. Bus Tours Magazine, 6322 Marshall Drive, Woodridge IL 60517.

BUSINESS TRAVEL REVIEW. 0746-9497. Periodical. US. English. mo. Maxco Publishing, 339 Main Road, Montville NJ 07405.

BUSINESS TRAVELER'S REPORT. VFOAT BTR. 0270-7969. Periodical. US. English. mo. $72.00. Business Travel Newsletter Associates, 210 E 52nd Street, New York NY 10022. Tel (305)483-2600.

THE BUSINESS TRAVELER'S SURVIVAL GUIDE, ATLANTA. 1981-. US. English. an. Business Travelers Inc, 730 Fifth Avenue, New York NY 10019.

BUSINESS TRAVELLER. Vol. 1, No. 1 (June 1984)-. 0827-2948. Periodical. CN. English. mo. Free to Travel Industry, $26.00 Others. Business Traveller, c/o Druid Publishing Corporation, 24 Bellair Street, Toronto Ontario M5R 2C7 Canada. DD 380.1459104.

CALENDARIO TURISTICO. See Economics.

Travel

CALGARY MAGAZINE. V. 1- Sept. 1978-. 0707-4409. Periodical. CN. English. mo. $9.00 Per Year. Pacific West Publications, 139—17th Avenue Southwest, Calgary Alberta Canada. DD 917.1233.

CALIFORNIA EXPLORER. V. 1- Aug. 1978-. 0164-8748. Periodical. US. English. ir. $20.00. California Explorer, 238 Francisco Street, San Francisco CA 94133-2013. Tel (415)362-6636. Ed Stuart Weiss. Circ 10,000. History and travel to little known outdoor places in California and the West.

CAMINHOS DO TURISMO. Yearly V. 1- April 1974-. Portuguese. ir. Assesoria de Imprensa da Secretaria de Turismo, Porto Alegre Brazil. LC G155.B7.

CAMPING TRAILER & TRAVEL TRAILER TRADE-IN-GUIDE. VFOAT Camping Trailer and Travel Trailer Trade-In Guide. 0736-1939. US. English. $7.95. Technical Publications, Division Intertec Publishing Corporation, PO Box 12901, Overland Park KS 66212. LC HD9710.38.A2. DD 629.226029473.

CANADA. Series/Titl The Get'em and Go Travel Guides. 0193-7952. US. English. an. $15.00. Houghton Mifflin Company, 2 Park Street, Boston MA 02107. LC F1009. DD 917.104646.

CANADA (NEW YORK, N.Y. 1983). (CANADA). Series/Titl Fisher Annotated Travel Guides. 1983-. 0883-2641. US. English. an. Fisher Travel Guides Inc, 401 Broadway Suite 2300, New York NY 10013. Tel (212)334-9245. Ed Robert C Fisher. Circ 15,000. First American annotated guidebook to award stars to Canadian tourist sights. Also, first guidebook planned for the experienced traveler.

CANADIAN MOSAIC. See Geography.

CANADIAN STUDENT TRAVELLER. (THE CANADIAN STUDENT TRAVELLER). V. 1- Spring 1978-. 0706-9758. Periodical. CN. English. sa. Free. Association of Student Councils, 44 George Street, Toronto Ontario Canada. DD 910.202.

CANADIAN TOURIST ASSOCIATION MEMBERSHIP DIRECTORY. See Yearbooks, Almanacs, Directories.

CANADIAN TOURIST GUIDE. VFOAT Canadian Tourist. VAT Canadian Tourist (Western Canada Ed.). No. 1-. 0824-3530. CN. English. an. $2.50 Per Vol., Free to Qualified Subscribers. Canadian Tourist Guide, 1212-31 Avenue NE, Calgary Alberta T2E 7S8 Canada. DD 917.1204305. (ctrl).

CANADIAN TRAVEL COURIER. V. 1- June 30, 1965-. 0008-5219. Periodical. CN. English. bw. MacLean Hunter, PO Box 100, Station A, Toronto Ontario M5W 1A7 Canada. Ind/Abst Can. Bus. Index. Also available in microfiche format.

CANADIAN TRAVEL NEWS. V. 13, No. 15- May 2, 1974-. 0319-7107. Periodical. CN. English. bw. Southam Communications Ltd, 1450 Don Mills Road, Don Mills Ontario M3B 1X2 Canada. Tel (416)445-6641. Ind/Abst Can. Bus. Index. Canadian Travel News Weekly, 0319-7093.

CANADIAN TRAVEL PRESS. V. 1- Sept. 5, 1968-. 0045-5490. Periodical. CN. English. ir. 20.00 Domestic, 25.00 USA. Baxter Publishing Company, 310 DuPont Street, Toronto Ontario M5R 1VP Canada. Tel (416)968-7252. Ed Timothy Baxter. adv acc. Circ 18,000. (ctrl). Travel magazine dealing with everything that involves the traveler and industry.

CANADIAN TRAVEL SURVEY : CANADIANS TRAVELLING IN CANADA. VFOAT Enquete sur les Voyages Canadiens : Canadiens Voyageant au Canada. V. 1, No. 1 (July-Sept. 1978)- V. 1 No. 2 (Oct./Dec 1978). 0709-4418. CN. English (French). an. $16.00. Publication Sales and Services Statistics Canada, Ottawa Ontario K1A 0V7 Canada. LC G155.C3. DD 381.4591710400212.

CANADIAN TRAVEL SURVEY. DOMESTIC TRAVEL. (CANADIAN TRAVEL SURVEY). VFOAT Enquete sur les Voyages des Canadiens. 4th Quarter 1978-. 0229-821X. Periodical. CN. English (text also in French). Canadian Government Office of Tourism, 235 Queen Street 4th Floor East, Ottawa K1A 0H6 Ontario Canada. DD 338.4791710405.

CAREERS GUIDE TO THE TOURISM, HOSPITALITY, RECREATION INDUSTRY. VFOAT Career Guide to the Tourism, Hospitality, Recreation Industry. 1979/81-. 0225-2678. Periodical. CN. English. be. Canadian Government Office of Tourism, 235 Queen Street 4th Floor, Ottawa Ontario K1A 0H6 Canada. DD 331.7616479471.

CARIBBEAN FLITE GUIDE. See Aeronautics, Astronautics.

CARIBBEAN FOCUS. See Geography.

CARIBBEAN TOURISM STATISTICAL REPORT. See Statistics.

CARTE-CALENDRIER DES FETES POPULAIRES DU QUEBEC. See Recreation, Leisure.

THE CAYMAN ISLANDS HOLIDAY GUIDE. English. ir. $1.00 Single Issue. Northwester Company, PO Box 243, Grand Caymen Island Caymen Islands. LC F1891.C5. DD 917.2921046.

CENTRAL EUROPE AND SCANDINAVIA TRAVEL GUIDE. VFOAT AAA Travel Guide: Central Europe and Scandinavia. 0094-3657. US. English. American Automobile Association (AAA), 8111 Gatehouse Road, Falls Church VA 22042. LC GV1025.A2. DD 914.

CENTRAL FLORIDA SCENE (ORLANDO, FLA. : 1981). (CENTRAL FLORIDA SCENE). VFOAT Orlando Florida Scene. Vol. 8, No. 7 (April 1981)-. 0734-8290. Periodical. US. English. mo $15.00. Central Scene Publications, PO Box 7624, Orlando FL 32854. Orlando Florida Scene, 0273-6675.

CHATEAUX DE LA LOIRE. French. ir. Pneu Michelin, 46 Avenue de Bretzuil, Paris France 75341. LC GV1025.F7. Chateaux de la Loire.

CHEVRON USA. VAT Chevron United States of America. 0199-5707. Periodical. US. English. qt. H M Gousha Company, PO Box 6227, San Jose CA 95150. LC E158. DD 917.304927.

CHILTON'S GOING PLACES. VFOAT Going Places. V. 1- Nov./Dec. 1976-. 0192-8023. Periodical. US. English. bm. $7.50 Domestic, $9.00 Foreign. Chilton Co, Chilton Way, Radnor PA 19089. LC G149. DD 910.5.

THE CHINA GUIDEBOOK. 1st Ed. (1979/80)-. 0734-6549. US. English. an. Eurasia Press, 302 5th Avenue, New York NY 10001. LC DS712. DD 915.10458.

CHINA TOURISM. No. 43-. Periodical. HK. English. ir. $28.00 US, $105.00 Foreign. H K China Tourism Press, 1C Tsing Building 334-336 King's Road, Hong Kong. LC DS712. DD 951.0505. China Tourism Pictorial.

CHINA TOURISM PICTORIAL. Periodical. English. mo. $12.87. Hong Kong China Tourism Press, IC 334-336 Kings Road, Hong Kong. LC DS712. DD 915.1045805.

CHUNG-KUO TAO YU. See Geography.

CHUNG-KUO YU WEN (JEN MIN CHIAO YU CHU PAN SHE). (CHUNG KUO YU WEN). VFOAT Zhongguo Yuwen. Began with July, 1952 issue. 0578-1949. Periodical. CH. Chinese. bm. $5.40. China Publication Centre, PO Box 2820, Beijing China. Ind/Abst Am. Hist. Life, Hist. Abstr., Hist. Abstr., Part A, Mod. Hist. Abstr., Hist. Abst., Part B, Twent. Century Abstr.

CICERONE. 0193-4244. Periodical. US. Spanish. bm. 2759 SW 27th Avenue, Miami FL 33133. LC G149. DD 910.5.

CITY AND SUBURBAN TRAVEL. V. 1- 1957-. 0045-6985. Periodical. US. English. mo. Transit Research Foundation, Box 3542, Terminal Annex, Los Angeles CA 90054.

COLCHESTER COUNTY, NOVA SCOTIA, TRAVEL GUIDE. (COLCHESTER COUNTY TRAVEL GUIDE). Vol. 1, No. 1 (Summer 1984)-. 0828-7651. CN. English. an. Colchester County Travel Guide, PO Box 697, Truto Novia Scotia B2N 5E7 Canada. DD 917.1612.

COMMONWEALTH (RICHMOND, VA.). (COMMONWEALTH). V. 1- May 1934-. 0010-3365. Periodical. US. English. mo. Cygnet Communications, 121 College Place, Norfolk VA 23510. Tel (804)625-4800. Ind/Abst Public Aff. Inf. Serv. Bull. LC HF1. DD 917.55. Metro, Richmond Lifestyle, 0199-0152.

CONNAISSONS NOS VOISINS. See Geography.

CORPORATE MEETINGS & INCENTIVES. VFOAT Corporate Meetings and Incentives. Vol. 1, No. 1 (Sept./Oct. 1982)-. 0745-1636. Periodical. US. English. ir. $25.00. 1 East First Street, Duluth MN 55802. Tel (218)723-9517. Ed Connie Goldstein. LC HD5260. DD 910.202. adv acc. Circ 40,000. (ctrl). It provides focus on domestic worldwide meeting and incentive destinations. Reviews facilities and locations. Worldwide Meetings & Incentives, 0273-8805.

CORPORATE TRAVEL. Began in 1985. 0882-8709. Periodical. US. English. mo. Corporate Travel, 1051 Broadway/Room 930, New York NY 10036.

CORSE. Main/Corp Pneu Michelin (Firm). Series/Titl Guides Verts Michelin. 1-. Ed. FR. French. ir. Manufacture Francaise des Pneumatiques Michelin, 46 Av de Breteuil, 75431 Paris Cedex 07 France. LC DC611.C812. DD 914.49450483.

COUNTRY MAGAZINE. VFOAT Country. Vol. 1, No. 1 (Oct. 1980)-. 0271-759X. Periodical. US. English. mo $18.00. Country Magazine, PO Box 246, Alexandria VA 22313. Tel (703)548-6177. Ed Walter Nicklin. LC E169.02. DD 975. bk rev. adv acc. Circ 100,000. Regional publication covering travel, leisure and history in Virginia, Maryland, Pennsylvania, North Carolina, Delaware, West Virginia, the District of Columbia and southern New Jersey.

COUNTRY VACATIONS IN ALBERTA. See Recreation, Leisure.

CRUISE TRAVEL MAGAZINE. 0199-5111. Periodical. US. English. bm. $22.00. World Publishing Company, PO Box 10139, Des Moines IA 50340, (subscription address: Communication Data Services PO Box 4966 Des Moines IA 50340). Tel (312)491-6440.

CRUISING AROUND THE WORLD. VFOAT Cruising. Vol. 1, No. 1 (Apr. 1982)-. 0744-6004. Periodical. US. English (French and Spanish). mo. $17.00. Cruising Around The World, PO Box 738, Miami Beach FL 33139. Tel (305)361-7305. Ed Frank A Estrada. adv acc. Circ 23,000. (ctrl). Travel trade magazine that contains information in general of the travel industry, cruise lines schedules, new hotels, destinations, tourist shopping, vacation planning, attractions and tours.

DALIL AL-SIYAHAH FI AMRIKA. VFOAT Arab Traveler-U.S.A., Arab Traveler-USA. Summer 1983-. Periodical. US. Arabic. qt. Free. Decor International Inc, 4545 42nd Street NW/Suite 303, Washington DC 20016.

DATAMEX. WESTERN HEMISPHERE. (DATAMEX). 0091-9160. US. English. $150.00. American Express Company, PO Box 65, Wall Street Station, New York NY 10005. LC G153. DD 910.202. American Express International Index.

DEPARTURES (DON MILLS, ONT.). (DEPARTURES). Began with V. 1, No. 1 (Apr. 1981). 0828-783X. Periodical. CN. English. qt. $6.00 Per Year. Departures Publishing, Suite 909/75 The Donway West, Don Mills Ontario M3C 2E9 Canada. DD 910.5.

DESTINATION SOUTH CAROLINA. 0749-4211. Periodical. US. English. qt. America on the Move South Inc, 2350 Arlington Ridge Road, Arlington VA 22202.

DESTINATION (TORONTO, ONT.). (DESTINATION). 0229-2130. Periodical. CN. English. qt. Free. Destination, 2625 Yonge Street, Toronto Ontario M4P 2J6 Canada. DD 910.5. (ctrl).

DESTINATIONS. Vol. 1, No. 1 (Fall 1980)-. 0275-8024. Periodical. US. English. ty. $9.00. Circulation Department, 13-30 Corporation, 505 Market Street, Knoxville TX 37902. LC G149. DD 910.405.

DIAKOPES. Greek, Modern. ir. 60.00. Praktoreion Hellenikou Typou, Kolokotroni 23, Diakopes Greece. LC G155.G73.

DIGEST OF ANNUAL STATISTICS. See Statistics.

DIGEST OF TOURISM STATISTICS. See Statistics.

DIGEST OF TOURIST STATISTICS. See Statistics.

DIRECTORIO DE LA INDUSTRIA TURISTICA DE EL SALVADOR. See Yearbooks, Almanacs, Directories.

Travel

DIRECTORY AKOMODASI JAWA, BALI DAN SUMATERA UTARA. See Yearbooks, Almanacs, Directories.

DIRECTORY HOTEL PARIWISATA & TRAVEL BUREAU. See Yearbooks, Almanacs, Directories.

DIRECTORY OF INCENTIVE TRAVEL INTERNATIONAL. See Yearbooks, Almanacs, Directories.

DIRECTORY PERUSAHAAN BIS (ANTAR PROPINSI). See Yearbooks, Almanacs, Directories.

DISCOVER AMERICA SALES GUIDE. VFOAT Travel Trade, Discover America Sales Guide. V. 1- 1966/67-. 0419-4071. US. English. ir. Travel Trade, 605 Fifth Avenue, New York NY 10017.

DISCOVER OUR WORLD (TORONTO, ONT.). (DISCOVER OUR WORLD). 0714-9131. CN. English. an. Free. Discover Our World, c/o Convention & Tourist Bureau of Metropolitan Toronto, Toronto Eaton Centre, 220 Yonge Street/Suite 110, Box 510, Toronto Ontario M5B 1H9 Canada. **DD** 917.1354104405. *You've Got Friends in Toronto, 0714-9123.*

DISCOVER WILLIAMSBURG. 1980-. US. English. an. Virginia Gazette Inc, PO Box 419, Williamsburg VA 23185.

DISCOVERING ETHIOPIA. See History (General) - History of Africa.

DISCOVERY GUIDE (TORONTO, ONT.). (DISCOVERY GUIDE). 1982-. 0821-7920. CN. English. an. Free. Convention & Tourist Bureau of Metropolitan Toronto, Toronto Eaton Centre, 220 Yonge Street, Box 510, Toronto Ontario M5B 2H1 Canada. **Tel** (416)979-3133. Ed Cathy Stewart. **DD** 917.1354104405. adv acc. **Circ** 450,000. (ctrl). The only guide a visitor can use to plan a comprehensive visit to the Metropolitan Toronto area. It is a complete ongoing source of information about Toronto. *Discover our World (Toronto, Ont.), 0714-9131.*

DISCOVERY; THE ALLSTATE MOTOR CLUB MAGAZINE. V. 1- Summer 1961-. 0012-3641. Periodical. US. English. qt. $4.00. Allstate Enterprises, 3701 West Lake Street, Glenview IL 60025-8205. **Tel** (312)291-5642. Ed Mary Kaye Stray. **Ind/Abst** Pop. Mag. Rev. adv acc. **Circ** 1,500,000. The magazine of American travel. Each issue focuses on people and places that make America what it is today. Vacation plans and geographic areas of interest are featured.

DIVER TRAVEL ANNUAL. 1983-. 0820-9952. CN. English. an. $2.00. Diver Travel Annual, c/o Seagraphic Publications, 3732 West Broadway, Vancouver British Columbia V6R 2C1 Canada. **DD** 797.2305.

DIVERSION. See Geography.

DIVRE SAR HAT-TAYYARUTIM HAGASAT HASAAT HAT-TAQSIV LA-KENESET. See Geography.

DOCUMENTATION TOURISTIQUE. No. 1 (May 1969)-. Periodical. FR. French. qt. 400. Centre Hautes Tourishques, 18 rue de l'Opera, 13100 Aix-En-Provence France. **Tel** 42 38 17 65. adv acc. **Circ** 256. International and pluridisciplinary approach of tourism, leisure and outdoor recreation. Analytical bibliography.

DOMESTIC TOURISM STATISTICS. See Statistics.

DOMESTIC TRAVEL IN VICTORIA. English. ir. Victorian Government Travel Authority, 500 Bourke Street, Melbourne Victoria 3000 Australia. **LC** G155.A75. **DD** 381.45919450463.

EASTERN EUROPE TRAVEL GUIDE. VFOAT AAA Travel Guide, Eastern Europe: Bulgaria, Czechoslovakia, Hungary, Poland, Romania, U.S.S.R. 0094-8632. US. English. $2.00. American Automobile Association, 8111 Gatehouse Road, Church Falls VA 22042. **LC** DR16. **DD** 914.70485.

EASTERN TRAVEL SALES GUIDE. Vol. 1, No. 1 (Spring/Summer 1983 Ed.)-. 0739-4780. US. English. sa. $60.00. Cabell Travel Publications, 11411 Cumpston Street, North Hollywood CA 91601. **Tel** (818)980-6260. Ed Gregory T Frisbee. **LC** G154. **DD** 380.145917304927025. adv acc. **Circ** 2,000. (ctrl). Geographical listings of retail travel agencies, wholesale tour operators, airlines, cruise lines, car/motorhome rentals, state tourist offices and government tourist offices.

ECHO DES VOYAGES. (L'ECHO DES VOYAGES). No. 060 i.e. No. 1 (Feb. 4, 1980)-. 0228-667X. Periodical. CN. French. wk. $10.00. l'Echo des Voyages, CP 97 Snowdon, Montreal Quebec H3X 3T3 Canada. **DD** 910.5.

THE ECONOMIC REVIEW OF TRAVEL IN AMERICA. (THE ... ECONOMIC REVIEW OF TRAVEL IN AMERICA). 0733-642X. US. English. an. $50.00. US Travel Data Center, Suite 610/1899 L Street Northwest, Washington DC 20036. **Tel** (202)293-1040. **LC** G155.U6. **DD** 380.14591730492. **Circ** 300. Details the economic contribution of the travel industry to the US. Includes foreign arrivals and departures, employments, energy consumption.

ECONOMIC REVIEW OF WORLD TOURISM. Began in 1966. English. ir. $24.00. World Tourism Organization, Calle Capitan Haya 42, E-Madrid-20 Spain. **Tel** 279-2804. **LC** G155.A1. **DD** 338.4791.

THE ENDLESS VACATION - RESORT CONDOMINIUMS INTERNATIONAL. (THE ENDLESS VACATION). 0279-4853. Periodical. US. English. mo. $52.00. Endless Vacation Publications Inc, Robert Ancell/PO Box 80260, Indianapolis IN 46280-0260. **Tel** (317)848-0500. Ed Helen A Wernle. **LC** TX907. **DD** 910.202. adv acc. **Circ** 500,000. An upscale magazine for international travelers. Articles feature destinations around the globe. Columns offer sound, practical advice to vacationers. *Annual Directory Edition, 0276-9085; Endless Vacation (Vacation Horizons International), 0883-8852.*

ENDLESS VACATION - VACATION HORIZONS INTERNATIONAL. (ENDLESS VACATION). 0883-8852. US. English. an. $43.00. Endless Vacation Publications Inc, PO Box 80260, Indianapolis IN 46280. *Vacation Horizons International Annual Directory Edition, 0749-4939.*

ENGLAND AND SCOTLAND ON $ ... A DAY. VAT England and Scotland on ... Dollars a Day. 1980/81-. 0271-3977. US. English. an. $5.95. 380 Madison Avenue, New York NY 10017. Ed S Haggart and D Porter. **LC** DA650. **DD** 914.204858. *England on $15 a Day.*

ESCAPE (SALT LAKE CITY, UTAH). (ESCAPE). Vol. 2, No. 1 (Spring 1983)-. 0745-6182. Periodical. US. English. qt. $8.00. Sunsets Unlimited Travel Club, PO Box 15100, Salt Lake City UT 84115.

ESPANA, PORTUGAL. Main/Corp Pneu Michelin (Firm). 1973-. English (French, German, Italian, Portuguese, and Spanish). ir. Pneu Michelin, 46 Avenue de Breteuil, Paris France 75341. **LC** DP14. **DD** 914.60483.

ETUDES ET MEMOIRES. Main/Corp Paris. Ecole Pratique des Hautes-etudes. Centre d'Etudes Economiques. Began publication in 1952. 0078-9585. Monographic Series. FR. French. ir. Centre des Hautes Etudes Tour, 18 rue de l'Opera, 13100 Aix En Provence France. **Tel** (42)381765. Ed R Baretse. bk rev. **Circ** 300. Tourism and outdoor recreation, multidisciplinary approach.

EURAIL GUIDE. See Transportation - Railroads.

EUROPE FOR TRAVELERS. Vol. 1, No. 1 (Spring 1985). 0883-0231. Periodical. US. English. qt. $8.00. Europe for Travelers, Europe Inc, 408 Main Street, Nashua NH 03060. **Tel** (603)888-0633. Ed Carol Grasso. **DD** 910. bk rev. adv acc. **Circ** 5,000. (ctrl). A leisure publication for the frequent European traveler. Travel with zest, fun and spirit. Also provides practicalities, calendar of events, access to travel literature/maps.

EUROPE ON $ ... A DAY. See Geography.

EUROPEAN TRAVEL & LIFE. VFOAT European Travel and Life. Vol. 1, No. 1 (May/June 1985)-. 0882-7737. Periodical. US. English. bm. $24.00 Domestic, $36.00 Foreign. European Travel & Life, PO Box 860, Farmingdale NY 11737. **DD** 051.

EXPLORATION. 0097-806X. US. English. **Ind/Abst** Abstr. Engl. Stud. **LC** PN56.T7. **DD** 910.4.

EXXON TRAVEL CLUB CANADA VACATION TRAVEL GUIDE. Main/Corp Travelvision. VFOAT Canada Vacation Travel Guide. 1977-. 0272-8311. US. English. an. Simon & Schuster, 1230 Avenue of the Americas, New York NY 10020. **LC** F1009. **DD** 917.104646. *Exxon Travel Club Illustrated Canada Vacation Travel Guide, 0272-8303.*

EXXON TRAVEL CLUB MEXICO VACATION TRAVEL GUIDE. Main/Corp Travelvision. VFOAT Mexico Vacation Travel Guide. 1977- Ed. 0270-8434. US. English. an. $3.95. Simon & Schuster, 1230 Avenue of the Americas, New York NY 10020. **LC** F1209. **DD** 917.204833. *Exxon Travel Club Mexico Illustrated Vacation Travel Guide, 0270-8442.*

EXXON TRAVEL CLUB TRAVEL GUIDE. CANADA. VFOAT Canada. US. English. an. $5.95. Simon & Schuster, 1230 Avenue of the Americas, New York NY 10020. *Exxon Travel Club Canada Vacation Travel Guide, 0272-8311.*

EXXON TRAVEL CLUB TRAVEL GUIDE. CENTRAL USA. VFOAT Central USA. 17th Ed. (1983)-. 0743-6467. US. English. an. **LC** F787. **DD** 917.7. *Exxon Travel Club Central U.S.A. Vacation Travel Guide.*

EXXON TRAVEL CLUB VACATION TRAVEL GUIDE. NORTHEAST U.S.A. Main/Corp Travelvision. VFOAT Vacation Travel Guide. VAT EXXON Travel Club Vacation Travel Guide. Northeast United States of America. 1977-. 0194-4037. US. English. an. $3.95. Simon & Schuster, 1230 Avenue of the Americas, New York NY 10020. **LC** F2.3. **DD** 917.4044. *Illustrated Vacation Travel Guide. Northeast Recreation Region, 0194-3804.*

EXXON TRAVEL CLUB VACATION TRAVEL GUIDE. SOUTHEASTERN U.S. VFOAT Vacation Travel Guide. 1981 Ed.-. 0735-6749. Periodical. US. English. an. **LC** F207.3. **DD** 917.50443. *Exxon Travel Club Vacation Travel Guide. Southeast U.S.A.*

EXXON TRAVEL CLUB ... VACATION TRAVEL GUIDE. WESTERN U.S. VFOAT Vacation Travel Guide. Began in 1981. US. English. an. $4.95. Simon & Schuster, 1230 Avenue of the Americas, New York NY 10020. **LC** F595.2. **DD** 917.90433. *Exxon Travel Club West U.S.A. Vacation Travel Guide, 0198-9642.*

FABULOUS MEXICO - WHERE EVERYTHING COSTS LESS. 1960-. 0429-9639. US. English. an. Harian Publications, 1 Vernon Avenue, Flora Park NY 11001.

THE FAR EAST AND SOUTHWEST PACIFIC CEASED. 1968-1982. 0084-229X. US. English. an. $4.50. Stryker-Post Publications Incorporated, 888 17th Street Northwest, Washington DC 20006. **LC** DS502. **DD** 915.

FARFADET. (LE FARFADET). V. 1- Dec. 1979-. 0225-8269. Periodical. CN. French. qt. Free. Bureau de Tourisme et des Congres de Granby, CP 261, Granby Quebec J1G 8E5 Canada. **DD** 338.479171463. *Tour de Ville, 0316-6553.*

FARM, RANCH & COUNTRY VACATIONS. VAT Farm, Ranch and Country Vacations. 30th- 1979-. 0195-8437. US. English. be. $6.50. Farm & Ranch Vacations Incorporated, 36 East 57th Street, New York NY 10022. **LC** TX907. **DD** 647.9473. *Country Vacations U.S.A., 0147-3867.*

FEDERAL TRAVEL DIRECTORY (WASHINGTON, D.C. : 1981). See Yearbooks, Almanacs, Directories.

FENG KUANG HUA PAO. SCENERY PICTORIAL. VFOAT Scenery Pictorial. First published in Nov. 1975-. Periodical. Chinese (legends and some summaries also in English). ir. $3.00 Single issue. Scenery Publishers, Room 408, 10 Queen's Rd C, Hong Kong Hong Kong. **LC** G149.

FIELDING'S BERMUDA AND THE BAHAMAS. See Geography.

FIELDING'S CARIBBEAN. See Geography.

FIELDING'S ECONOMY EUROPE. See Geography.

FIELDING'S EUROPE. 32nd Ed. (1979)-. 0192-5326. US. English. an. Fielding Travel Books, c/o W Morrow & Company, 105 Madison Avenue, New York NY 10016. Ed Temple Fielding. **LC** D909. **DD** 914.0455. *Fielding's Travel Guide to Europe, 0071-4801.*

FIELDING'S FAR EAST. See Geography.

FIELDING'S LOW-COST EUROPE CEASED. VFOAT Low-Cost Europe. VAT Fielding's Low Cost Europe. 1974- Ed. 0095-6406. US. English. an. $3.50. 105 Madison Avenue, New York NY 10016. **LC** D909. **DD** 914.0455. *Fielding's Super-Economy Europe.*

FIELDING'S MEXICO. See Geography.

FIESTA (MCALLEN, TEX.). See Restaurants.

FINLAND HANDBOOK. See Geography.

Travel

FIRSTCLASS. VAT First Class. 0192-2289. Periodical. US. English. bm. $7.50. Airline Passengers Association, 800 West Airport Freeway, Irving TX 75062. LC G149. DD 910.405.

FITNESS VACATIONS. Vol. 1, No. 1 (Spring/Summer 1985)-. 0749-4076. Periodical. US. English. qt. $8.00. Rodale Press Inc, 33 East Minor Street, Emmaus PA 18049. DD 910.

FLASHMAPS INSTANT GUIDE TO BOSTON. See Geography.

FLIGHT REPORTS. See Aeronautics, Astronautics.

FLORIDA TOUR BOOK. VFOAT Tour Book, Florida. Fall 1965-. 0516-9674. US. English. American Automobile Association, 1712 G Street NW, Washington DC 98111. LC GV1024. DD 917.59046.

FLORIDA TOURISM HOTLINE. 0743-0744. Periodical. US. English. mo. $65.00 Domestic, $80.00 Foreign. Florida Business Reports, PO Box 030009, Fort Lauderdale FL 33303. *Florida Letter on Tourism.*

FOCUS ON JAMAICA. 0015-5160. Periodical. English. sa. Publishing & Distributing Company Ltd, Mitre House/177 Regent Street, London W1 England. Ed Kenneth Jones.

FOCUS ON PAKISTAN. V. 1- Feb 1971-. 0046-4325. Periodical. PK. English. qt. Pakistan Tourism Development Corporation, Hotel Metropole Club Road, Karachi 4 Pakistan. DD 915.49005.

FODOR'S ALASKA. See Geography.

FODOR'S AMSTERDAM. 1984-. 0883-6043. US. English. an. Fodor's Travel Guides, 2 Park Avenue, New York NY 10016. DD 914.923.

FODOR'S BERMUDA. See Geography.

FODOR'S BOSTON. 1984-. 0882-0074. US. English. an. Fodor's Travel Guides, 2 Park Avenue, New York NY 10016. LC F73.18. DD 917.44610443.

FODOR'S BUDGET BRITAIN. See Geography.

FODOR'S BUDGET CANADA. VFOAT Budget Canada. 0736-8992. US. English. an. $6.95. Fodor's Modern Guides, 2 Park Avenue, New York NY 10016. LC F1009. DD 917.104646.

FODOR'S BUDGET CARIBBEAN. VFOAT Budget Caribbean. 0193-9122. US. English. an. $5.95. Fodor's Modern Guides, 2 Park Avenue, New York NY 10016. Ed E Fodor. LC F2171.2. DD 917.29045.

FODOR'S BUDGET EUROPE. VFOAT Budget Europe. 1980-. 0197-4998. US. English. an. $10.95 Single Issue. Fodor's Modern Guides, 2 Park Avenue, New York NY 10016. LC D909. DD 914.04558. *Fodor's Europe on a Budget, 0276-0738.*

FODOR'S BUDGET FRANCE. VFOAT Budget France. 0194-4150. US. English. an. $8.95 Cloth. Fodor's Modern Guides, 2 Park Avenue, New York NY 10016. Ed R Moore and E Fodor. LC DC16. DD 914.40483.

FODOR'S BUDGET GERMANY. VFOAT Budget Germany. 0193-9033. US. English. an. $4.95. Fodor's Modern Guides, 2 Park Avenue, New York NY 10016. Ed E Fodor. LC DD16. DD 914.30487.

FODOR'S BUDGET HAWAII. See Geography.

FODOR'S BUDGET ITALY. See Geography.

FODOR'S BUDGET JAPAN. See Geography.

FODOR'S BUDGET MEXICO. VFOAT Budget Mexico. 0196-1829. US. English. $9.95 Cloth, $5.95 Traveltex. Fodor's Modern Guides, 2 Park Avenue, New York NY 10016. LC F1209. DD 917.204833.

FODOR'S BUDGET SCANDINAVIA. VFOAT Budget Scandinavia. 0748-2620. US. English. an. Fodor's Travel Guides, 2 Park Avenue, New York NY 10016. LC DL4. DD 914.80488.

FODOR'S BUDGET SPAIN. See Geography.

FODOR'S BUDGET TRAVEL IN AMERICA. VFOAT Budget Travel in America. 1979-. 0192-8287. US. English. an. $10.95. Fodor's Modern Guides, 2 Park Avenue, New York NY 10016. Ed E Fodor. LC E158. DD 917.304926.

FODOR'S CALIFORNIA. VFOAT California. 0192-9925. US. English. an. $9.95. Fodor's Modern Guides, 2 Park Avenue, New York NY 10016. LC F859.3. DD 917.94045.

FODOR'S CARIBBEAN AND THE BAHAMAS. VFOAT Caribbean and the Bahamas, Fodor's Caribbean. 1980-. 0271-4760. Periodical. English. $10.95. Fodor's Modern Guides, 2 Park Avenue, New York NY 10016. LC F1612. DD 917.290452. *Fodor's Caribbean, Bahamas and Bermuda, 0098-2547.*

FODOR'S CENTRAL AMERICA. See Geography.

FODOR'S CHICAGO. VFOAT Chicago. 1984-. 0743-9326. US. English. an. Fodor's Travel Guides, 2 Park Avenue, New York NY 10016. LC F548.18. DD 917.73110443. *Fodor's Chicago and the Great Lakes Recreation Areas.*

FODOR'S COLORADO. See Geography.

FODOR'S CRUISES EVERYWHERE. VFOAT Cruises Everywhere. 1977-. 0160-3914. US. English. an. $12.95. Ed E Fodor and R C Fisher. LC G550. DD 910.202.

FODOR'S EGYPT. 0147-8176. US. English. $9.95. D McKay Co, 2 Park Avenue, New York NY 10016. LC DT45. DD 916.2045.

FODOR'S FLORIDA. VFOAT Florida. 0193-9556. US. English. an. $5.95. Fodor's Modern Guides, 2 Park Avenue, New York NY 10016. Ed E Fodor. LC F309.3. DD 917.59046.

FODOR'S GERMANY : WEST AND EAST. VFOAT Fodor's Germany. 1974-. 0192-0952. US. English. $12.95. Fodor's Modern Guides, 750 Third Avenue, New York NY 10017. LC DD16. DD 914.30487. *Fodor's Germany, 0071-6391.*

FODOR'S HONG KONG AND MACAU. VFOAT Hong Kong and Macau. 1984-. 0882-0066. US. English. $9.95. Fodor's Travel Guides, 2 Park Avenue, New York NY 10016. LC DS796.H74. DD 915.125045.

FODOR'S INDIA. See Geography.

FODOR'S ISLAMIC ASIA: IRAN, AFGHANISTAN, PAKISTAN. VFOAT Islamic Asia: Iran, Afghanistan, Pakistan. 1973-. UK. English. '3.25. Hooder & Stoughton, Mill Rd PO Box 700 Dunton Green, Sevenoaks Kent 450111, London England. Ed E Fodor and W Curtis. LC DS254. DD 915.

FODOR'S JAPAN. VFOAT Japan. 1983-. 0736-9956. US. English. an. $15.95. Fodor's Modern Guides, 2 Park Avenue, New York NY 10016. Ed Eugene Fodor. LC DS811. DD 915.20448. *Fodor's Japan and Korea, 0098-1613.*

FODOR'S JORDAN AND THE HOLY LAND. VFOAT Jordan and the Holy land. 1979-. 0193-9114. US. English. $10.95. Fodor Modern Guides, 2 Park Avenue, New York NY 10016. LC DS153.2. DD 915.695044.

FODOR'S MEXICO. VFOAT Mexico. 1972-. 0196-5999. US. English. an. David McKay Company, 2 Park Avenue, New York NY 10016. Ed E Fodor and M Lockett. LC F1216. DD 917.20482.

FODOR'S MID-ATLANTIC. See Geography.

FODOR'S MIDWEST. See Geography.

FODOR'S NEW ENGLAND. VFOAT New England. 0192-3412. US. English. an. $10.95 Cloth, $7.95 Paperbound. Fodor's Modern Guides, 2 Park Avenue, New York NY 10016. LC F2.3. DD 917.4044.

FODOR'S NEW ORLEANS. See Geography.

FODOR'S NEW YORK CITY WITH ATLANTIC CITY. VFOAT New York City with Atlantic City. 1985-. 0882-7338. US. English. an. Special Marketing at Fodor's Travel Guides, 2 Park Avenue, New York NY 10016. LC F128.18. DD 917.4710443. *Fodor's New York City and Nearby Attractions, 0736-9395.*

FODOR'S NORTH AFRICA. VFOAT North Africa. 1980-. 0197-1271. US. English. $13.95. Fodor's Modern Guides, 2 Park Avenue, New York NY 10016. Ed E Fodor. LC DT184. DD 916.10448.

FODOR'S PARIS. VFOAT Paris. Began with Vol. for 1974. 0149-1288. US. English. David McKay Company, 2 Park Avenue, New York NY 10016. LC DC708. DD 914.4360483.

FODOR'S PEOPLE'S REPUBLIC OF CHINA. VFOAT People's Republic of China. 1979-. 0192-2378. US. English. an. $14.95. Fodor's Modern Guides, 2 Park Avenue, New York NY 10016. Ed R C Fisher and L Brown. LC DS712. DD 915.1045. *Each issue contains an index to its own contents - no vol index - loose.*

FODOR'S ROCKIES AND PLAINS. VFOAT Rockies and Plains. 0191-0515. US. English. an. $10.95. Fodor's Modern Guides, 750 3rd Avenue, New York NY 10017. LC F721. DD 917.8043.

FODOR'S ROME. See Geography.

FODOR'S SAN FRANCISCO AND NEARBY ATTRACTIONS. VFOAT San Francisco and Nearby Attractions. 0743-9334. US. English. an. Fodor's Modern Guides Inc, 2 Park Avenue, New York NY 10016. LC F869.S33. DD 917.9460453.

FODOR'S SCANDINAVIA. See Geography.

FODOR'S SCOTLAND. See Geography.

FODOR'S SOUTH-EAST ASIA. VFOAT South-East Asia. 1975-. 0160-8991. US. English. an. D McKay Company, 2 Park Avenue, New York NY 10016. LC DS504. DD 915.904. *Fodor's Japan and East Asia.*

FODOR'S SOUTHWEST. (FODOR'S SOUTHWEST). 0147-8656. US. English. an. $10.95. D McKay Company, 730 Third Avenue, New York NY 10017. Ed E Fodor, S Birnhaum and R Fisher. LC F787. DD 917.6044.

FODOR'S SUNBELT LEISURE GUIDE. VFOAT Sunbelt Leisure Guide. 0196-1055. US. English. an. $12.95. Fodor's Modern Guides, 2 Park Avenue, New York NY 10016. LC F207.3. DD 917.3.

FODOR'S THE SOUTH. See Geography.

FODOR'S TUNISIA. See Geography.

FODOR'S USA. VFOAT USA. VAT Fodor's United States of America. 0147-8745. US. English. an. $14.95. D McKay Company, 750 Third Avenue, New York NY 10017. LC E158. DD 917.30492.

FODOR'S WASHINGTON, D.C. VFOAT Washington, D.C. 1984-. 0743-9741. US. English. an. Fodor's Travel Guides, 2 Park Avenue, New York NY 10016. Ed E Fodor. LC F192.3. DD 917.53044. *Fodor's Washington, D.C. and Vicinity, 0739-9383.*

THE FOOTLOOSE LIBRARIAN. Began in Sept. 1981. 0733-3196. Periodical. US. English. bm. $25.00. The Footloose Librarian, Box 972, Minneapolis MN 55401. Tel (612)333-8076. Ed William J Cutts. bk rev. adv acc. Circ 600. A travel newsletter and network for librarians in the US and overseas. Members may swap services, e.g. Bed n' Breakfast, Housing Exchange.

FORD'S DECK PLAN GUIDE. Main/Corp Ford's Travel Guides. VFOAT Deck Plan Guide. 1st Ed.-. 0096-1353. US. English. $50.00. Fords Travel Guide, Box 505, Woodland Hills CA 91364. Tel (818)347-1677. Ed Merrian E Clark. LC VM381. DD 387.243. adv acc. Circ 5,000. Deck plans of over 130 cruise ships, all fold out pages, hard bound cover, post type construction permits, up-dating, updates are offered annually.

FORD'S FREIGHTER TRAVEL GUIDE. 30th Ed. (Winter 1967-68)-. 0015-7058. Periodical. US. English. sa. $14.00. Fords Travel Guides, Box 505, Woodland Hills CA 91365. Tel (818)347-1677. Ed Merrian E Clark. LC HE566.F7. DD 387.54205. adv acc. Circ 12,000. Covers information on passenger carrying freighters, barge cruises on the inland waterways of Europe, yacht charters, etc. All the more casual types of water travel. *Ford's Freighter Travel Guidebook.*

FOREFRONT : NEWS FROM NEW ZEALAND CEASED. VFOAT Forefront. V. 21- Feb. 1973-. UK. English. mo. Public Relations Officer, New Zealand House Haymarket, London SW1 England. LC DU400. DD 919.3103305. *Forefront of New Zealand Affairs.*

FOREIGN LODGING LIST. See Hotels/Motels.

FOREIGN TOURIST ARRIVALS BY SELECTED STATES- AND PORTS-OF-ENTRY. 1978-. 0270-7985. US. English. an. US Department of Commerce, US Travel Service, Washington DC 20230. LC G155.U6. DD 338.479173040212. *Foreign Visitor Arrivals by Selected Ports, 0192-6144.*

FOREIGN TRAVEL IMMUNIZATION GUIDE. See Public Health and Safety.

FRAM. See Geography.

FRANCE (FISHER TRAVEL GUIDES (FIRM)). (FRANCE). Series/Titt Fisher Annotated Travel Guides. 1983-. 0883-2617. US. English. an. Fisher Travel Guides, 200 Park Avenue South, New York NY 10003. Ed Georgia I Hesse.

FREE CHINA WEEKLY CEASED. VFOAT Tzu Yu Chung-Kuo Chou Pao. V. 1-24, No. 51. English. wk. $2.50. PO Box 337, Taipei China. LC DS895.F68. DD 915.124903505.

Travel

FREIGHTER TRAVEL NEWS. Began publication in 1957. 0016-089X. Periodical. US. English. mo. $14.00. Freighter Travel Club, PO Box 12693, Salem OR 97309. Ed Leland J Pledger. bk rev. adv acc. **Circ** 3,000. (ctrl). First-hand reports of freighter and other unique water travel. Includes comments and answers to specific questions and advertising relevant to freighter travel.

DER FREMDENVERKEHR + I.E. UND DAS REISEBURO. *See* Economics - Economics: Industry & Production.

FROM THE STATE CAPITALS. TOURIST BUSINESS PROMOTION. VFOAT Tourist Business Promotion. 0734-1199. Periodical. US. English. mo. $75.00. Wakeman/Walworth Inc, PO Box 1939, New Haven CT 06509. **Tel** (203)562-8518. New plans and projects to lure vacationers, travellers and convention-goers. Developments on construction and renovation of convention centers and stadiums. Redevelopment of downtown and tourist attractions are also discussed. *From the State Capitals. Tourist Business Promotion Report.*

FROMMER'S AUSTRALIA ON $ . . . A DAY. VFOAT Australia on $ . . . a Day. 8755-5425. US. English. be. $9.95. Frommer/Pasmantier Publishers, 1230 Avenue of the Americas, New York NY 10020. Ed J Godwin. LC DU95. DD 919.40463. *Australia on $ . . . a Day.*

FROMMER'S DOLLARWISE GUIDE TO EGYPT. VFOAT Dollarwise Guide to Egypt. 1982-1983 Ed.-. 0731-4566. US. English. an. $6.95. Frommer/Pasmantier Publishers, 1230 Avenue of the Americas, New York NY 10020. LC DT45. DD 916.20454. *Arthur Frommer's Dollarwise Guide to Egypt.*

FROMMER'S DOLLARWISE GUIDE TO ENGLAND & SCOTLAND. VFOAT Dollarwise Guide to England and Scotland. VAT Frommer's Dollarwise Guide to England and Scotland. 0276-8674. US. English. $6.95. Frommer/Pasmantier Publishers, 380 Madison Avenue, New York NY 10017. LC DA650. DD 914.204858.

FROMMER'S DOLLARWISE GUIDE TO FLORIDA. VFOAT Dollarwise Guide to Florida. 0732-0728. US. English. $6.25. Frommer/Pasmantier Publishers, 1230 Avenue of the Americas, New York NY 10020. LC F309.3. DD 917.590463.

FROMMER'S DOLLARWISE GUIDE TO FRANCE. VFOAT Dollarwise Guide to France. 0276-976X. US. English. an. Frommer/Pasmantier Publishers, 1230 Avenue of the Americas, New York NY 10020. LC DC29.3. DD 914.404838.

FROMMER'S DOLLARWISE GUIDE TO GERMANY. VFOAT Dollarwise Guide to Germany. 0731-4442. US. English. an. Frommer/Pasmantier Publishers, 1230 Avenue of the Americas, New York NY 10020. LC DD16. DD 914.304878. *Arthur Frommer's Dollarwise Guide to Germany, 0272-0035.*

FROMMER'S DOLLARWISE GUIDE TO ITALY. *See* Geography.

FROMMER'S DOLLARWISE GUIDE TO NEW ENGLAND. VFOAT Dollarwise Guide to New England. 0732-4871. US. English. an. Frommer/Pasmantier Publishers, 1230 Avenue of the Americas, New York NY 10020. LC F2.3. DD 917.40443.

FROMMER'S DOLLARWISE GUIDE TO PORTUGAL, MADEIRA & THE AZORES. VFOAT Dollarwise Guide to Potugual, Madeira & the Azores. 1982-1983 Ed.-. 0732-0477. US. English. Frommer/Pasmantier Publishers, 1230 Avenue of the Americas, New York NY 10020. LC DP516. DD 914.690444. *Arthur Frommer's Dollarwise Guide to Portugal, Madeira and the Azores.*

FROMMER'S DOLLARWISE GUIDE TO THE CARIBBEAN INCLUDING BERMUDA & THE BAHAMAS. VFOAT Frommer's Dollarwise Guide to the Caribbean Including Bermuda and the Bahamas. 1982/83 Ed.-. 0882-6919. US. English. be. $10.95. Frommer/Pasmantier Publishers, 1230 Avenue of the Americas, New York NY 10020. Ed D Porter. LC F2171.2. *Arthur Frommer's Dollarwise Guide to the Caribbean, including Bermuda & the Bahamas, 0198-7178.*

FROMMER'S DOLLARWISE GUIDE TO THE SOUTHEAST AND NEW ORLEANS. VFOAT Dollarwise Guide to the Southeast and New Orleans. 0731-8588. US. English. $6.95. Frommer/Pasmantier Publishers, 1230 Avenue of the Americas, New York NY 10020. LC F207.3. DD 917.50443. *Arthur Frommer's Dollarwise Guide to the Southeast and New Orleans, 0731-857X.*

FROMMER'S ENGLAND & SCOTLAND ON $ . . . A DAY. VFOAT England & Scotland on $ . . . a Day. 1982-1983 Ed.-. 8755-5395. US. English. an. $9.95. Frommer/Pasmantier Publishers, 1230 Avenue of the Americas, New York NY 10020. LC DA650. DD 914.204858. *England and Scotland on $ . . . a Day, 0271-3977.*

FROMMER'S EUROPE ON $ . . . A DAY. VFOAT Europe on $ . . . a Day. VAT Frommer's Europe on . . . Dollars a Day. 1981-1982 Ed.-. 0730-1510. US. English. an. $10.95. Frommer/Pasmantier Publishers, 1230 Avenue of the Americas, New York NY 10020. LC D909. DD 914.04558. *Europe on $ . . . a Day, 0271-8596.*

FROMMER'S GREECE ON $ . . . A DAY. VFOAT Greece on $ . . . a Day. VAT Frommer's Greece on Twenty Dollars a Day. 8755-7835. US. English. an. $7.25. Fromme/Pasmantier Publishers, 1230 Avenue of the Americas, New York NY 10020. Ed J Wilcock. DD 914.

FROMMER'S GUIDE TO AMSTERDAM & HOLLAND. VFOAT Guide to Amsterdam & Holland. VAT Frommer's Guide to Amsterdam and Holland. 1981-1982 Ed.-. 0277-3546. US. English. an. $2.95. Frommer/Pasmantier Publishers, 380 Madison Avenue, New York NY 10017. LC DJ16. DD 914.920473.

FROMMER'S GUIDE TO ATHENS. VFOAT Guide to Athens. 1981-1982 Ed.-. 0277-4534. US. English. $2.95. Frommer/Pasmantier Publishers, 380 Madison Avenue, New York NY 10017. LC DF916.5. DD 914.95120476. *Arthur Frommer's Guide to Athens.*

FROMMER'S GUIDE TO BOSTON. VFOAT Guide to Boston. 1981-1982 Ed.-. 0277-4399. US. English. $2.95. Frommer/Pasmantier Publishers, 380 Madison Avenue, New York NY 10017. LC F73.18. DD 917.44610443. *Arthur Frommer's Guide to Boston.*

FROMMER'S GUIDE TO DUBLIN & IRELAND. VFOAT Guide to Dublin & Ireland. 1981-1982 Ed.-. 0277-4437. US. English. $2.95. Frommer/Pasmantier Publishers, 380 Madison Avenue, New York NY 10017. LC DA995.D8. DD 914.183504824.

FROMMER'S GUIDE TO HAWAII. VFOAT Guide to Hawaii. 1981-1982 Ed.-. 0277-4801. US. English. $2.95. Frommer/Pasmantier Publishers, 380 Madison Avenue, New York NY 10017. LC DU622. DD 919.69044.

FROMMER'S GUIDE TO LAS VEGAS. VFOAT Arthur Frommer's Las Vegas. 1981-1982 Ed.-. 0277-1241. US. English. $2.95. Frommer/Pasmantier, 380 Madison Avenue, New York NY 10017. LC F849.L35. DD 917.9313. *Arthur Frommer's Guide to Las Vegas.*

FROMMER'S GUIDE TO LISBON, MADRID & THE COSTA DEL SOL. VFOAT Guide to Lisbon, Madrid & the Costa del Sol. 1981-1982 Ed. 0277-6960. US. English. be. $4.95. Frommer/Pasmantier Publishers, 1230 Avenue of the Americas, New York NY 10020. **Tel** (212)245-6400. LC DP757. DD 914.6.

FROMMER'S GUIDE TO LONDON. VFOAT Arthur Frommer's London. 1981-1982 Ed.-. 0277-3228. US. English. be. $4.95. Frommer/Pasmantier Publishers, 1230 Avenue of the Americas, New York NY 10020. **Tel** (212)245-6400. LC DA679. DD 914.21204858. *Arthur Frommer's Guide to London.*

FROMMER'S GUIDE TO LOS ANGELES. VFOAT Guide to Los Angeles. 1981-1982 Ed.-. 0277-6952. US. English. $2.95. Frommer/Pasmantier Publishers, 380 Madison Avenue, New York NY 10017. LC F869.L83. DD 917.94940453. *Arthur Frommer's Guide to Los Angeles.*

FROMMER'S GUIDE TO MEXICO CITY & ACAPULCO. VFOAT Guide to Mexico City & Acapulco. VAT Frommer's Guide to Mexico City and Acapulco. 1981-1982 Ed.-. 0277-4798. US. English. $2.95. Frommer/Pasmantier Publishers, 380 Madison Avenue, New York NY 10017. LC F1386.A4. DD 917.253.

FROMMER'S GUIDE TO MONTREAL & QUEBEC CITY. (FROMMER'S . . . GUIDE TO MONTREAL & QUEBEC CITY). VFOAT Frommer's . . . Guide to Montreal and Quebec City. 0737-4283. US. English. $3.95. Frommer/Pasmantier Publishers, 1230 Avenue of the Americas, New York NY 10020. Ed Tom Brosnahan. LC F1054.5.M83. DD 917.14281044.

FROMMER'S GUIDE TO NEW ORLEANS. VFOAT Guide to New Orleans. 1981-1982 Ed.-. 0277-4410. US. English. $2.95. Frommer/Pasmantier Publishers, 380 Madison Avenue, New York NY 10017. LC F379.N53. DD 917.63350463.

FROMMER'S GUIDE TO NEW YORK. VFOAT Guide to New York. 1981-1982 Ed.-. 0277-4380. US. English. be. $2.50. Frommer/Pasmantier Publishers, 1230 Avenue of the Americas, New York NY 10020. **Tel** (212)245-6400. Ed F Hammel. LC F128.18. DD 917.4710443. *Arthur Frommer's Guide to New York.*

FROMMER'S GUIDE TO PARIS. VFOAT Guide to Paris. 1981-1982 Ed.-. 0277-4402. US. English. be. $2.50. Frommer/Pasmantier Publishers, 1230 Avenue of the Americas, New York NY 10020. **Tel** (212)245-6400. Ed S Haggart and D Porter. LC DC708. DD 914.43604838.

FROMMER'S GUIDE TO PHILADELPHIA. (FROMMER'S . . . GUIDE TO PHILADELPHIA). VFOAT Guide to Philadelphia. 1985/86-. 0883-7759. US. English. $4.95. Frommer/Pasmantier Publishers, 1230 Avenue of the Americas, New York NY 10020. Ed J Golan. LC F158.18. DD 917.48110443. *Frommer's . . . Guide to Philadelphia & Atlantic City, 0739-7143.*

FROMMER'S GUIDE TO ROME. VFOAT Guide to Rome. 1981-1982 Ed.-. 0277-6979. US. English. be. $3.95. Frommer/Pasmantier Publishers, 1230 Avenue of the Americas, New York NY 10020. **Tel** (212)245-6400. LC DG804. DD 914.563204928. *Arthur Frommer's Guide to Rome.*

FROMMER'S GUIDE TO SAN FRANCISCO. VFOAT Guide to San Francisco. 1981-1982 Ed.-. 0277-4429. US. English. Frommer/Pasmantier Publishers, 380 Madison Avenue, New York NY 10017. *Arthur Frommer's Guide to San Francisco.*

FROMMER'S GUIDE TO WASHINGTON, D.C. VFOAT Guide to Washington, D.C. 1983-1984 Ed.-. US. English. be. $2.50. Frommer/Pasmantier Publishers, 1230 Avenue of the Americas, New York NY 10020. **Tel** (212)578-0829. Ed F Hammel. *Arthur Frommer's Guide to Washington, D.C.*

FROMMER'S HAWAII ON $ . . . A DAY. *See* Geography.

FROMMER'S INDIA ON $ . . . & $ . . . A DAY. VFOAT Frommer's India on $. . . and $. . . a Day. 1985-86 Ed.-. 0883-7422. Periodical. US. English. be. Frommer/Pasmantier Publishers, 1230 Avenue of the Americas, New York NY 10020. Ed J Aaron.

FROMMER'S ISRAEL ON $ . . . & $ . . . A DAY. VFOAT Frommer's Israel on $ . . . and $ . . . a Day. VAT Frommer's Israel on . . . Dollars and . . . Dollars a Day. Began with 1982/83 Ed. 8755-8440. US. English. be. $9.95. Frommer/Pasmantier Publishers, 1230 Avenue of the Americas, New York NY 10020. Ed T Brosnahan and S Brilliant. LC DS103. DD 915.6940454. *Israel on $ . . . a Day.*

FROMMER'S MEXICO & GUATEMALA ON $ . . . & $ . . . A DAY. VFOAT Frommer's Mexico and Guatemala on $ . . . & $ . . . a Day. 0275-6854. US. English. an. $6.95. Frommer/Pasmantier Publishers, 1230 Avenue of the Americas, New York NY 10020. **Tel** (212)245-6400. LC F1209. DD 917.204833. *Mexico and Guatemala on $ . . . & $ . . . a Day.*

FROMMER'S MEXICO ON $20 A DAY. (FROMMER'S MEXICO ON $ . . . A DAY). VFOAT Mexico on $ . . . a Day. VAT Frommer's Mexico on Twenty Dollars a Day. US. English. an. $9.95. Frommer/Pasmantier Publishers, 380 Madison Avenue, New York NY 10017. Ed T Brosnahan and J Kretchman. *Frommer's Mexico & Guatemala on $ . . . & $ . . . a Day, 0275-6854.*

FROMMER'S NEW YORK ON $ . . . A DAY. VFOAT New York on $ . . . a Day. Began with 1982-1983 Ed. 8755-5433. US. English. be. $8.95. Frommer/Pasmantier Publishers, 1230 Avenue of the Americas, New York NY 10020. Ed J Hamburg and N Ketay. LC F128.18. DD 917.4710443. *New York on $ . . . a Day, 0278-128X.*

FROMMER'S NEW ZEALAND ON $ . . . & $ . . . A DAY. VFOAT Frommer's New Zealand on $ . . . and $ . . . a Day. 1982-83 Ed.-. 8755-5417. US. English. $6.95. Frommer/Pasmantier

Travel

FROMMER'S SOUTH AMERICA ON $ . . . A DAY. VFOAT South America on $ . . . a Day. VAT Frommer's South America on . . . Dollars a Day. 0277-7827. US. English. $5.95. Frommer/Pasmantier Publishers, 1230 Avenue of the Americas, New York NY 10020. Ed A Greenberg. LC F2224. DD 918.0438.

FROMMER'S SPAIN & MOROCCO ON $20 A DAY. (FROMMER'S SPAIN & MOROCCO ON $ . . . A DAY). VFOAT Frommer's Spain and Morocco on $ . . . a Day, Frommer's Spain and Morocco Plus the Canary Islands on $ . . . a Day, Spain and Morocco on $ . . . A Day, Spain & Morocco on $ . . . a Day. VAT Frommer's Spain and Morocco on Twenty Dollars a Day. 1981-1982 Ed-. 0276-9875. US. English. $5.95. Frommer/Pasmantier Publishers, 1230 Avenue of the Americas, New York NY 10020. Ed S M Haggart and D Porter. LC DP14. DD 914.60483.

FROMMER'S WASHINGTON, D.C. ON $ . . . A DAY. VFOAT Washington, D.C. on $ . . . a Day. Began with 1982-1983 Ed. 8755-5441. US. English. be. $8.95. Frommer/Pasmantier Publishers, 1230 Avenue of the Americas, New York NY 10020. Ed B Bryant. LC F192.3. DD 917.53044. Washington, D.C. on $ . . a Day, 8755-545X.

FROMMER'S WHERE TO STAY, USA. VFOAT Where to Stay, USA. 1982-1983 Ed-. 8756-8748. US. English. Ed M A Cohen. LC TX907. DD 647.9473. Where to Stay, USA.

GEMEINDERVERZEICHNIS DER SCHWEIZ. See Geography.

GEO-KATALOG. See Geography.

GETAWAY. Began publication in 1978 or 1979. 0225-6673. Periodical. CN. English. qt. $4.00 Domestic, $5.50 Foreign. Getaway Publications Ltd, 1181 Homer Street, Vancouver British Columbia V6B 2B1 Canada. DD 910.5. A C T A Getaway, 0705-1425.

GETTING THERE BY TRAIN, TRANSIT, BOAT & BUS. VFOAT Getting There. Vol. 1, No. 1 (Summer 1981)-. 0731-5473. Periodical. US. English. qt. $7.00 Domestic, $8.00 Foreign. Transport Research and Communications, PO Box 3175, Saxonville Station MA 01701. LC WMLC L 83/616.

GLIMPSES OF MICRONESIA. 23/1-. Periodical. English. qt. $12.00. Glimpses of Micronesia, PO Box 8066, Tamuning GU 96911. Tel (671)477-3483. Ed Pedro C Sanchez. LC DU647. DD 996.5005. bk rev. adv acc. Circ 4,000. (ctrl). A regional publication for Micronesia lovers, travel buffs, and readers interested in America's last frontier. Discover our part of the world. Glimpses of Micronesia & the Western Pacific, 0273-6578.

GLOBEHOPPER. (THE GLOBEHOPPER). VFOAT Globe Hopper. Vol. 1, No. 1 (Oct./Nov. 1981)-. 0711-7108. Periodical. CN. English. bm. 9.28. The Globehopper, 619 Huron Street, Toronto Ontario Canada M5R 2R8. Tel (416)960-0944. Ed Joanna Ebbutt. DD 910.5. adv acc. Circ 100,000. A consumer travel magazine written with the active (as opposed to "armchair") traveller in mind, covering all (safe) parts of the globe, and all modes of travel.

GOA TODAY. Began in 1966. 0017-1484. Periodical. English. ir. LC DS498. DD 915.4799.

THE GOLF TRAVELER. See Recreation, Leisure - Sports.

GOMER'S BUDGET TRAVEL DIRECTORY. See Yearbooks, Almanacs, Directories.

GOMER'S GUIDES FROM THE ATLANTIC TO THE MISSISSIPPI. 0147-6602. US. English. $3.95. Hammond Inc, 515 Valley Street, Maplewood NJ 07040. LC F106. DD 917.4044.

GOMER'S GUIDES FROM THE MISSISSIPPI TO THE PACIFIC. See Geography.

GRAND MANAN HISTORIAN. See Geography.

LA GRANDE GUIDA DELLE VACANZE, ITALIA. 1982-. Italian. an. Via Borromei 5, 20123 Milano Italy. LC DG416. DD 914.504928.

GREAT EXPEDITIONS. V. 1- March/April 1978-. 0706-7682. Periodical. CN. English. bm. $12. US, $16. Foreign. Great Expeditions Inc, Box 46499, Vancouver British Columbia V6R 4G7 Canada. DD 910.5.

GREAT LAKES TOUR BOOK. VFOAT Tour Book, Great Lakes. US. English. an. American Automobile Association, 8111 Gatehouse Road, Falls Church VA 22042. LC F539.3. DD 917.7043. Great Lakes States.

GREAT LAKES TRAVEL & LIVING. VFOAT Great Lakes Travel and Living. 0887-6223. Periodical. US. English. bm. $15.00. PO Box 423, Morris IL 61054-0423.

GREATER VANCOUVER VISITORS GUIDE. Began with Sprint 1978 issue?. 0709-2687. Periodical. CN. English. qt. Greater Vancouver Convention and Visitors Bureau, 650 Burrard Street, Vancouver British Columbia V6C 2L2 Canada. DD 917.1133. Vancouver Visitors Guide, 0381-6370.

GREECE AND YUGOSLAVIA ON $15 & $20 A DAY. 0270-4358. US. English. $4.95. Frommer/Pasmantier Publishing Corp, 380 Madison Avenue, New York NY 10017. LC DF716. DD 914.950476.

GROSS- UND EINZELHANDEL, GASTGEWERBE, REISEVERKEHR. REIHE 8 : REISEVERKEHR. IV. GRENZUBERSCHREITENDER REISEVERKEHR. Main/Corp Germany (West). Statistisches Bundesamt. VAT Gross- und Einzelhandel, Gastgewerbe, Reiseverkehr. Reihe Acht: Reiseverkehr. Vier. Grenzuberschreitender Reiseverrkehr. German. ir. 3.20 Single Issue. Verlag W Kohlhammer GMBH, Phillipp-Reis-Str, 36500 Mainz 42 West Germany. LC G155.G3.

THE GROSSE POINTER. 0017-4629. Periodical. US. English. mo. $12.00 Members, $25.00 Nonmembers. Detroit Publication Consultants, 25875 Jefferson Street, Clair Shores MI 48081.

GUELPH MAGAZINE. Vol. 1, No. 1 (April 1980)-. 0710-3425. Periodical. CN. English. mo. $1.00 Per No. Quintus Enterprises, 19 Prospect Avenue, Guelph Ontario N1E 4W7 Canada. DD 917.1343005.

GUELPH THIS WEEK. V. 1- April 11, 1979-. 0226-6326. Newspaper. CN. English. wk. Free. Guelph This Week, 17-219 Silvercreek Parkway, Guelph Ontario N1H 7K4 Canada. DD 790.0971343.

GUIA COMPLETA DE LA CIUDAD DE MEXICO, DISTRITO FEDERAL Y SUS ALREDEDORES. VFOAT Guia Roji, Mexico. Spanish. ir. Republica de Colombia, No 23, Mexico 1 DF Mexico. Guia Roji (Guia Roja) : Informacion y Guia de la Ciudad de Mexico.

GUIA DE PIURA. 1.- Ed. Spanish. ir. M Razuri, Jr Cuzco 602, Piura Peru. LC F3451.P5.

GUIA DE TURISMO : REPUBLICA ARGENTINA. Main/Corp Ediciones Cicerone. VFOAT Guia de Turismo de la Republica Argentina. Yearly V. 1- 1977-. Spanish. ir. Eidciones Cicerone, Peru 327 2 Piso e, Buenos Aires Argentina. LC F2808.5. DD 918.2046.

GUIA DE VALENCIA : TURISTICA, URBANA, COMERCIAL. Spanish. ir. Editones Guisa, Gran via Marques del Turia 64, Velencia Spain. LC DP402.V15.

GUIDE - AMERICAN TOURIST ASSOCIATION. (GUIDE - AMERICAN TOURIST ASSOCIATION. GUIDE A T A). Main/Corp American Tourist Association. VFOAT Guide A T A. 1973-. 0317-3704. Periodical. CN. text in English and French. American Tourist Association Ltd, 300 Arran Street, St Lambert Quebec Canada. DD 917.14044. American Travel Guide, Canada, 0317-3690.

GUIDE DE LA ROUTE, PROVINCES DE L'ATLANTIQUE ET DU QUEBEC. 1978-. 0225-2600. CN. French. an. Free to Members. Association Canadienne des Automobilistes, 1775 Courtwood Crescent, Ottawa Ontario K2C 3J2 Canada. Tel (613)226-7631. Ed Michael S McNeil. DD 917.15044. adv acc. Circ 15,000. (ctrl). A French language tourbook listing accomodations, sites to see, things to do, etc. in the province of Quebec and the maritime provinces.

GUIDE DE L'INDUSTRIE TOURISTIQUE. VAT Nouveau-Brunswick. Guide de l'Industrie Touristique. Published since 1978. 0709-3306. Periodical. CN. French. Ministere du Tourisme, CP 12345, Fredericton New Brunswick E3B 5C3 Canada.

GUIDE DE ROUTE. Main/Corp Club Automobile Quebec. VFOAT Road Book. First issue in 1925?. 0318-9414. CN. French. Club Automobile Quebec, 871 Chemin Satin-Louis, Quebec Quebec G1K 7T2 Canada. DD 917.14044.

GUIDE DES MANIFESTATIONS DE PROMOTION TOURISTIQUE. FR. French. an. 17 rue de l'Ingenieur Keller, 75740 Paris Cedex 15 France. LC G155.F8. DD 380.14591440405.

GUIDE DU CAMPEUR. (GUIDE DU CAMPEUR : GUIDE OFFICIEL DE L'ASSOCIATION DES TERRAINS DE CAMPING DU QUEBEC). '84-. 0828-5896. CN. French. an. $2.00 Per Vol. Association des Terrains de Camping du Quebec, 8775 Boulevard Lacordaire, St-Leonard Quebec H1R 2A9 Canada. DD 647.9471409. Guide Officiel du Campeur, 0822-5184.

GUIDE GRIMALDI DE MONTREAL. See Geography.

GUIDE ROUTIER ET TOURISTIQUE : MADAGASCAR, REUNION, MAURICE, COMORES ET SEYCHELLES. MG. French. ir. Automobile Club de Madagascar, Service du Guide Route, BP 571, Tananarive Malagasy Republic. LC GV1025.M3. DD 916.91045. Guide Routier, 0572-2330.

GUIDE TO ATLANTIC CANADA. See Geography.

GUIDE TO NORTH SUMATRA INDONESIA. See Geography.

GUIDE TO TRAVEL AND RESIDENCE EXPENSES FOR THE MULTINATIONAL EXECUTIVE. 0193-9130. US. English. an. Travel and Living Costs Worldwide Inc, Harvard Square Box 92, Cambridge MA 02138. LC G153.4. DD 910.202.

GUIDE TO U.S. CITIES. 1977/78-. 0705-3711. CN. English. MacLean-Hunter Ltd, 481 University Avenue, Toronto Ontario M5W 1A7 Canada. DD 917.3.

GUIDE TOURISTIQUE EUROPEEN POUR ISRAELITES. VFOAT European Travel Guide for Jews. English and French. ir. $1.20. Pelikaanstraat 106-108, 2000 Antwerp Belgium. LC DS102.9. DD 914.045502403924.

HAMILTON. See Geography.

HAMILTON GUIDEBOOK. 0227-6267. CN. English. an. Free. Hamilton Guidebook, 110 George Street, Hamilton Quebec L8P 1E2 Canada. DD 917.1352. (ctrl).

HANDEL, GASTGEWERBE, REISEVERKEHR. REIHE 7.3 : URLAUBS- UND ERHOLUNGSREISEN. Main/Corp Germany (West). Statistisches Bundesamt. 1975-. German. an. 5.40. LC G155.G3. Gross- und Einzelhandel, Gastgewerbe, Reiseverkehr. Reihe 8: Reiseverkher. III. Urlaubs- und Erholungsreisen.

HAPPENINGS (TORONTO, ONT.). (HAPPENINGS). Sept./Oct. 1982-. 0822-4846. Periodical. CN. English. qt. Free. Metropolitan Toronto Convention & Visitors Association, Suite 110/Toronto Eaton Centre, Box 510, 220 Yonge Street, Toronto Ontario M5B 2H1 Canada. Tel (416)979-3133. Ed Cathy Stewart. DD 917.1354104405. adv acc. Circ 855,000. (ctrl). A colourful, current look at Toronto's attractions, tours, events, and entertainment with features on our dining and shopping experiences. Great Happenings in Metro Toronto, 0227-3373.

THE HAPPY WANDERER. 0195-2080. Periodical. US. English. bm. Happy Wanderer, 7342 North Lincoln Avenue, Skokie IL 60077. Tel (312)676-1900. Ed Mark Greenfield. adv acc. Circ 250,000.

HARYANA REVIEW. See Geography.

HASIL PENGOLAHAN KARTU-KARTU EMBARKASI WISATAWAN DI SUMATRA UTARA. Main/Corp Sumatera Utara, Indonesia. Kantor Sensus dan Statistik. English (Indonesian). ir. LC G155.I5.

HAWAII ISLAND GUIDE. Began in 1982. 0744-5792. Periodical. US. English. mo. Hawaii Island Guide, 1314 South King Street/Suite 863, Honolulu HI 96814. Aloha Hawaii, 0279-4934.

HAWAII ON $ . . . A DAY. VAT Hawaii on . . . Dollars a Day. 0197-8527. US. English. an. $4.95. Frommer/Pasmantier Publishing Corp, 380 Madison Avenue, New York NY 10017. Ed S Levey. LC DU622. DD 919.69044.

HEALTH INFORMATION FOR INTERNATIONAL TRAVEL. 1974-. 0095-3539. US. English. an. US Government Printing Office, Superintendent of Documents, Washington DC

Travel

20402. Tel (202)783-3238. LC RA783.5. DD 614.4202491. NLM W2 A C17H.

THE HIMALAYAN JOURNAL. See Recreation, Leisure - Outdoor Life.

HOLIDAY NIAGARA. Began with May 1972 issue. 0318-9104. CN. English. ir. 25 Per No. Holiday Niagara, PO Box 951, Niagara Falls Ontario L2E 6V8 Canada. DD 917.133904.

HOLIDAY TIME IN THAILAND. V. 1- June 1960-. 0439-3678. Periodical. TH. English. mo. Tourist Organ of Thailand, Ratchadammden Avenue, Bangkok Thailand. LC DS561. DD 915.93.0444.

HOME & AWAY. VAT Home and Away. V. 1- Jan./Feb. 1980-. 0199-7009. Periodical. US. English. bm. $2.50. Home & Away, Box 3985, 5011 Capitol Avenue, Omaha NE 68103. Tel (402)390-1000. Ed Barc Wade. adv acc. Circ 1,750,000. Domestic and foreign travel, outdoor recreation, automotive safety and do-it-yourself auto repair, travel hints and how-to's. *Nebraska Living*.

HOME & AWAY MINNESOTA. See Transportation - Automobiles.

HONEYMOON HIDEAWAYS. 1st Ed (1983)-. 0736-6736. US. English. an. $7.50. KB Associates Inc, PO Box 53200, Atlanta GA 30355.

HOOSIER MOTORIST HOME & AWAY. VFOAT Home & Away. VAT Hoosier Motorist Home and Away. V. 1- Jan./Feb. 1980-. 0199-6975. Periodical. US. English. bm. $2.50. Home and Away, PO Box 88505, Indianapolis IN 46208-0505. Tel (317)923-1500. Ed Hugh Orr. adv acc. Circ 180,000. (ctrl). Articles about different travel destinations for AAA Hoosier Motor Club Members. *Hoosier Motorist*.

HOTEL & MOTEL RED BOOK. VAT Hotel and Motel Red Book. 1963-. 0073-3490. US. English. an. $32.00. Pac Tel Publishing, c/o Valerie Dow, 1600 South Main Street/Suite 290, Walnut Creek CA 94596. Tel (800)874-7717. Ed Valerie A Dow. DD 647. adv acc. Circ 40,000. Desk-top lodging directory designed for business travelers, travel planners and secretaries. It is the official directory of the American Hotel and Motel Association. *Hotel Red Book*.

HOTLINE. See Geography.

HSIEN TAI AO-MEN. VFOAT Macau Travelling Magazine. Chinese. ir. $1.00 Single Issue. H D & Macau Press, PO Box 174 Macau Macao. LC DS796.M2.

HSING-TAO LU YU. See Geography.

ICTA JOURNAL. Main/Corp Institute of Certified Travel Agents. VAT Institute of Certified Travel Agents Journal. V. 1- Spring 1979-. 0194-0007. US. English. sa. Institute of Certified Travel Agents, 148 Linden Street, Wellesley MA 02181. LC G154. DD 658.9191.

I.C.T.A. ROSTER. (ICTA ROSTER). Main/Corp Institute of Certified Travel Agents. 0094-3517. US. English. Institute of Certified Travel Agents, PO Box 9206, Arlington VA 22209. LC G154. DD 338.479106273.

IDEGENFORGALMI EVKONYV. VFOAT Statisticheskii Ezhegodnik Turizma. 1980-. 0230-4414. Hungarian (summaries in English and Russian). an. LC G155.H9. DD 380.14591439. *Idegenforgalmi Statisztika*.

IDEGENFORGALMI KOZLEMENYEK. Periodical. Hungarian. ir. LC G155.A1.

IDEGENFORGALOM. See Geography.

THE ILLINOIS WEEKENDER. See Geography.

IMAGE DE LA MAURICIE. V. 2- Sept. 1977-. 0704-7428. Periodical. CN. French. mo. La Mauricie Touristique, 564 Boulevard de Prairies, Cap-de-la-Madeleine Quebec G8T 1K9 Canada. DD 917.14465005. *La Mauricie Touristique, 0700-3188*.

IMAGE TOURISTIQUE. MAURICIE, BOIS-FRANCS, CENTRE DU QUEBEC. (IMAGE TOURISTIQUE, MAURICIE, BOIS-FRANCS, CENTRE DU QUEBEC). VFOAT Image Touristique du Centre du Quebec, Mauricie, Bois-Francs. Summer 1981-. 0712-273X. Periodical. CN. French. ir. Free. Publicite GM Inc, 564 rue des Prairies, Cap-de-la-Madeleine Quebec G8T 1K9 Canada. DD 917.144650405.

IMT. Mar. 1973-. Periodical. Polish. ir. 80. RSW Prasa-Ksiaku-Ruch, Ruch Poland. LC G155.A1. *Swiatowid*.

IN BRITAIN. Vol 22- Dec. 1966—. Periodical. UK. English. mo. $24.95. British Tourist Authority, 64 St James Street, London SW1A 1NF England. Tel (212)581-4700. *Coming Events in Britain*.

IN JOPLIN METROPOLITAN. See Geography.

INCENTIVE TRAVEL AND BUSINESS MEETINGS. See Economics - Labor.

INCENTIVE TRAVEL MANAGER. Vol. 1- Nov./Dec. 1973-. 0092-1920. Periodical. US. English. mo. $80.00. Brentwood Publishing Corporation, PO Box 49045, Los Angeles CA 90049. Tel (213)826-8388. Ed Esther Gross. LC HD5261. DD 910.5. bk rev. adv acc. Circ 29,682. Interest of sales or marketing executives of corporations and travel advisors who conceive, plan and implement incentive travel programs.

INDIANA. VFOAT Indiana Magazine. 0193-3345. Periodical. US. English. qt. Indiana Department of Commerce, State House/Room 336, Indianapolis IN 46204. LC F530. DD 917.7204405.

INDONESIA (INDONESIA. DIREKTORAT JENDERAL PARIWISATA). (INDONESIA : TRAVEL INFORMATION MANUAL). VFOAT Indonesia Travel Information Manual. English. an. Directorate General of Tourism JL Kramat Raya 81, PO Box 409, Jakarta Indonesia. LC DS614. DD 915.980438.

INDONESIA TOURIST STATISTICS. See Statistics.

INDUSTRIA TURISTICA. 0019-7777. Periodical. US. Spanish. mo. $10.00. Charles Francis Publishing Inc, 7235 NW 19th Street/Suite G, Miami FL 33126.

INLAND SHORES. Issue 7-. 0149-9815. Periodical. US. English. qt $11.00 Domestic, $13.00 Canada. Inland Shores Magazine, Inland Marketing Corporation, J A Heesler President, 222 South Flemming Road, Woodstock IL 60098. LC F551. DD 917.7043. *Inland Shores, 0149-9815*.

INTERNATIONAL ADVENTURE TRAVELGUIDE. VFOAT Adventure Travelguide. VAT International Adventure Travel Guide. 1978-. 0148-2300. US. English. an. $9.95. Timber Press, PO Box 92, Forest Grove OR 97116. LC GV191.35. DD 790.025.

INTERNATIONAL ADVENTURERS NEWSLETTER. (THE INTERNATIONAL ADVENTURERS NEWSLETTER). Vol. 1 (Jan./Feb. 1983)-. 0820-8948. Periodical. CN. English. bm. Free to Members. International Adventurers Society, PO Box 444/Station D, Toronto Ontario M6P 3K1 Canada. DD 910.5.

INTERNATIONAL BAHAMA LIFE. Periodical. English. ir. $16.00. O N Johnson/Johnson Publications, PO Box N-1505 Commonwealth of Bahamas, Nassau Bahamas. LC F1650. DD 917.296005.

INTERNATIONAL BUSINESS TRAVEL AND RELOCATION DIRECTORY. See Yearbooks, Almanacs, Directories.

INTERNATIONAL GUIDE, VICTORIA AND VANCOUVER ISLAND. 1981-. 0229-4419. CN. English. an. Free. 1200 West 73rd/ Suite 512, Avenue, Vancouver British Columbia V6P 6G5 Canada. DD 917.1134. (ctrl). *International Guide, Victoria, 0226-2932*.

INTERNATIONAL LIVING. 0277-2442. Periodical. US. English. mo. $36.00. International Living, 824 East Baltimore Street, Baltimore MD 21203. Tel (301)235-7961.

INTERNATIONAL TOURISM QUARTERLY. June 1971-. Periodical. UK. English. qt. Economist Intelligence Unit Ltd, Spencer House, 27 St James Place, London SW1A 1NT England. LC G155.A1. DD 338.479105. (cum index).

INTERNATIONAL TRAVEL NEWS. 1976. 0191-8761. Periodical. US. English. mo. $12.00. Martin Publications Inc, 2120 28th Street, Sacramento CA 95818. Tel (916)457-3643. Ed David Tykol. bk rev. adv acc. Circ 26,000. (ctrl). For the high-frequency international traveler. Airline cruise train, lodging bargains plus information feature articles and many tips from subscribers on where and how to go.

IRELAND OF THE WELCOMES. Began with V. 1, No. 1 (May/June 1952). 0021-0943. Periodical. US. English. bm. Ireland of the Welcomes, PO Box 2606, Boulder CO 80322.

IRELAND TODAY. See Geography.

ISIZWE. See Geography.

ISR, INTERNATIONLE BERG- UND SEILBAHNRUNDSCHAU. See Transportation.

ITALY (FISHER TRAVEL GUIDES (FIRM)). (ITALY). Series/Titl Fisher Annotated Travel Guides. 83/84-. 0883-2633. US. English. an. Fisher Travel Guides Inc, 401 Broadway, New York NY 10013. Tel (212)334-9248. Ed Robert C Fisher. Circ 20,000. First American guidebook to award stars to Italian hotels, restaurants and sights. First annotated travel guide anywhere. First guidebook planned for the experienced traveler.

ITINERAIRE. See Economics - Economics: Industry & Production.

J+ I.E. UND W TOURING TELEX. Main/ Corp Telex-Verlag Jaeger+Waldmann. VFOAT Touring Telex. Multilingual (German). ir. Telex-Verlag Jaeger and Waldman, Holzhofallee 38, D-6100 Darmstadt West Germany. LC G153. DD 910.202. *Jaeger+ i. e. und Waldmann Touring Telex*.

JAEGER'S INTERTRAVEL. GW. English (French, German, Italian or Spanish). an. Jaeger International Publishing, PO Box 320, D6100 Darmstadt BRD Germany. LC G154. DD 910.25.

JAPAN, THE OFFICIAL GUIDE. Periodical. JA. English. ir. Japan Travel Bureau, PO Box 5030 Tokyo International Tokyo 10031 Japan. LC DS805. DD 915.2. *Official Guide to Japan*.

JAX FAX TRAVEL MARKETING MAGAZINE. VFOAT JAX FAX. VAT Jet Airtransport Exchange Facts Travel Marketing Magazine. 0279-7984. Periodical. US. English. mo. $12.00. Jet Airtransport Exchange, 280 Tokeneke Road, Darien CT 06820. Tel (203)655-8746. Ed Mona Moore. adv acc. Circ 20,000. (ctrl). Tour and airlines listings for travel agents and tour operators. *JAX FAX, 0148-9542*.

THE JEWISH TRAVEL GUIDE. Began publicaiton with 1951 issue. 0075-3750. UK. English. an. $9.25. Sepher Hermon Press Inc, 53 Park Place/ Suite 503, New York NY 10007. Tel (212)349-1860. LC G153. DD 910.2.

JOURNAL DES VOYAGES. (LE JOURNAL DES VOYAGES). V. 1- 2 Oct. 1978-. 0225-0462. Periodical. CN. French. ir. $12.38. Journal des Voyages, 1872 Vercheres, Longueuil Quebec G4K 2Z9 Canada. Tel (514)651-6580. DD 338.479105.

JOURNAL OF TRAVEL RESEARCH. 0047-2875. Periodical. US. English. qt. $65.00. Business Research Division, 307 College of Business, University of Colorado, Boulder CO 80309. Tel (303)492-8227. Ed C R Goeldner. Ind/Abst Int. Labour Doc., ABI/Inform, Ref. Source. LC G155.A1. DD 910.72. adv acc. Circ 1,900. Provides new information about travel research, new techniques, creative views, generalizations about travel; research, thought, practice and synthesis of travel research materials. *Travel Research Bulletin, 0147-2399*.

JOYER TRAVEL REPORT CEASED. 0145-9473. Periodical. US. English. mo. $29.00 General, $19.00 One Year Introductory Rate. Phillips Publishing Inc, 8401 Connecticut Avenue, Washington DC 20001.

KARTING DIGEST. V. 1- Jan. 1975-. 0192-1134. Periodical. US. English. mo. $10.00. K Dee Publisher, PO Box 1659, Opa Locka FL 33055. LC GV1029.5. DD 796.7605.

KAUPERTS DEUTSCHLAND STADTE-HOTEL- UND REISEFUHRER. See Hotels/Motels.

KENT DIRECTORY. See Yearbooks, Almanacs, Directories.

KEY. THIS WEEK IN MIAMI BEACH. VFOAT Key. 0192-3536. Periodical. US. English. wk. $55.00. McCaskill Publishers Company Inc, PO Box 530565, Miami FL 33153. *This Week in Miami Beach*.

KOSOY'S TRAVEL GUIDE TO EUROPE. VFOAT Travel Guide to Europe. VAT Kosoy Travel Guide to Europe, Travel Guide to Europe (Toronto). 0711-4680. CN. English. ir. $5.95 Per Vol. Kosoy Travel Guides, 40 Shallmar Boulevard, Toronto Ontario M6C 2J9 Canada. DD 914.0455.

KOSOY'S TRAVEL GUIDE TO FLORIDA AND THE SOUTH. VFOAT Travel Guide to Florida and the South. VAT Kosoy Travel Guide to Florida and the South. 2nd Ed.-.

Travel

0711-4702. CN. English. ir. $5.95 Per Vol. Kosoy Travel Guides, 40 Shallmar Boulevard, Toronto Ontario M6C 2J9 Canada. DD 917.5. *Kosoy's Budget-Travel Guide to Florida, 0711-4907.*

KUAN KUANG TUNG CHI NIEN PAO.
VFOAT Annual Report on Tourism Statistics, Republic of China. 1972-. Chiefly Chinese. ir. Ministry of Communications, PO Box 1490, Taipei China. LC G155.T25.

KUAN KUANG TZU LIAO.
VFOAT Monthly Report on Tourism, Republic of China. Periodical. chiefly Chinese. ir. Ministry of Communications, PO Box 1490, Taipei China. LC G155.F6. *Kuan Kuang Yueh Pao.*

KULTURBRIEF.
V. 1- Sept. 1971-. Periodical. GW. English. mo. Kennedyallee 91-103, D 53 Bonn 1 Bundesrepublik Deutschland. DD 914.3038705. *Cultural News from Germany, 0011-2879.*

KWANGWANG CHONGBO.
See Geography.

KYOTO-SHI KANKO CHOSA NEMPO.
JA. Japanese. an. Kyoto-shi Bunka Kankokyoku, Okazaki Saishojicho, Sakayo-ku 606, Kyoto-shi Japan. LC G155.J27.

LABRADOR WEST HAS SOMETHING FOR EVERYONE.
See Yearbooks, Almanacs, Directories.

LATIN AMERICAN TRAVEL & PAN AMERICAN HIGHWAY GUIDE.
0075-8159. US. English. an. Compsco Publishing Co, 663 5th Avenue, New York NY 10022. Ed E A Jahn. LC F1409.2. DD 918.043.

THE LEARNING TRAVELER. U.S. COLLEGE-SPONSORED PROGRAMS ABOARD: ACADEMIC YEAR.
See Education (General) - Higher Education.

THE LEARNING TRAVELER. U.S. COLLEGE-SPONSORED PROGRAMS ABROAD, ACADEMIC YEAR.
See Education (General) - Special Aspects of Education.

THE LEARNING TRAVELER. VOL. 2, VACATION STUDY ABROAD.
See Education (General) - Special Aspects of Education.

LEISURE, RECREATION, AND TOURISM ABSTRACTS.
See Indexes/Abstracts.

LEISUREWAYS.
See Recreation, Leisure.

LET'S GO.
See Geography.

LET'S GO. BUDGET GUIDE TO GREECE.
See Geography.

LET'S GO : THE BUDGET GUIDE TO BRITAIN AND IRELAND.
See Geography.

LET'S GO : THE BUDGET GUIDE TO EUROPE.
VFOAT Let's Go. 1st Ed. (1982)-. US. English. an. St Martins Press, 175 5th Avenue, New York NY 10016. Tel (212)674-5151.

LET'S GO : THE BUDGET GUIDE TO FRANCE.
Main/Corp Harvard Student Agencies. VFOAT Let's Go: France. 1978-. US. English. an. St Martins Press, 175 5th Avenue, New York NY 10016. Tel (800)221-7945. Ed Ralph E Hall and James B Witkin. LC DC16. DD 91.404837.

LET'S GO. THE BUDGET GUIDE TO GREECE, ISRAEL, AND EGYPT.
(LET'S GO : THE BUDGET GUIDE TO GREECE, ISRAEL, AND EGYPT). VFOAT Let's Go : Greece, Israel and Egypt. 1982-. US. English. an. St Martins Press, 175 5th Avenue, New York NY 10016. Ed Daniel M Mandil. DD 914.950476.

LET'S GO. THE BUDGET GUIDE TO ISRAEL AND EGYPT.
VFOAT Lets' Go. Budget Guide to Israel and Egypt, Let's Go. Israel & Egypt, Let's Go. Israel and Egypt, Budget Guide to Israel and Egypt, Israel and Egypt, Israel & Egypt, Let's Go. 1984-. 0882-9535. US. English. an. $7.95. St Martin's Press, 175 5th Avenue, New York NY 10010. *Let's Go. Budget Guide to Greece, Israel, and Egypt 0276-6779.*

LET'S GO : THE BUDGET GUIDE TO ITALY.
Main/Corp Harvard Student Agencies. VFOAT Let's Go: Italy. 1980/81-. 0192-2920. US. English. an. $5.50 Domestic, $7.50 Foreign. Harvard Student Agencies, Thayer Hall-B, Harvard University, Cambridge MA 02138. Ed J Metz. LC DG416. DD 914.504928. *Let's Go: The Budget Guide to Italy, 0192-2920.*

LET'S GO. THE BUDGET GUIDE TO SPAIN, PORTUGAL & MOROCCO.
VFOAT Budget Guide to Spain, Portugal & Morocco, Let's Go. Spain, Portugal and Morocco, Spain, Portugal & Morocco, Spain, Portugal and Morocco, Let's Go. Spain, Portugal & Morocco. 1984-. 0885-3541. US. English. an. $7.95. St Martin's Press, 175 5th Avenue, New York NY 10010. LC DP14. DD 914.604.

LET'S GO. THE BUDGET GUIDE TO THE USA.
VFOAT Let's Go. VAT Let's Go. The Budget Guide to the United States of America. 1981-. 0275-9837. US. English. $5.95. Elsevier-Dutton Publishing Co Inc, 2 Park Avenue, New York NY 10016. Ed K W Warren. LC E158. DD 917.304927.

LET'S GO. THE STUDENT GUIDE TO THE UNITED STATES AND CANADA.
(LET'S GO : THE STUDENT GUIDE TO THE UNITED STATES AND CANADA). VFOAT Student Guide to the United States and Canada. 1972/73-. 0090-788X. US. English. be. $3.95. Harvard Student Agencies Inc, E P Dutton & Co, 2 Trowbridge Street, New York NY 02138. LC E169.02. DD 917.045305.

LET'S HALT AWHILE IN GREAT BRITAIN.
See Hotels/Motels.

LIDE A ZEME.
See Geography.

LODGINGS FOR LE$$. WEST EDITION.
Main/Corp Rand McNally and Company. VFOAT Lodgings for Less. 0883-3672. US. English. $4.95. Lodgings for Less, Mobil Travel Guide, PO Box 5483, Denver CO 80217-9990. Ed Helen Clark and Alice Wisel. bk rev. Circ 30,000. Hotel and motel listings for people on a budget. Prices are $39.00 per night or less for two. Listings taken from the Mobil Travel Guide.

LOOK AT LONDON.
See Geography.

LU YU TIEN TI (SHANGHAI, CHINA).
(LU YU TIEN TI). VFOAT Luyou Tiandi. Periodical. CH. Chinese. ir. 0.38. Post Office, Shanghai China. LC DS712. DD 915.10457.

MANITOBA VACATION GUIDE.
0703-6248. CN. English. Department of Tourism Recreation and Cultural Affairs, 200 North Three Lakeview Square, 185 Carlton Street, Winnipeg Manitoba R3C 0P3 Canada. LC F1062. DD 917.127043. *Manitoba Canada Vacation Handbook, 0703-6256.*

MARCHE BYWARD.
See Geography.

MARKETING VOYAGES.
V. 1- Sept. 1977-. 0703-9905. Periodical. CN. French. mo. $23.21. Les Editions Gi-Plan Inc, 674 Place Publique/Suite 215, Laval PQ H7X 1G1 Canada. Tel (514)689-2543. Ed Gerard Giguere. DD 338.479105. adv acc. Circ 7,500. (ctrl). Covers the travel industry, wholesale and retail.

A MARMAC GUIDE TO ATLANTA.
VFOAT Atlanta. 2nd Ed.-. 0735-827X. US. English. an. Marmac Publishing Company, 6303 Barfiled Road/Suite 208, Atlanta GA 30328. LC F294.A83. DD 917.582310443. *How, When, & Where in Atlanta, 0275-2212.*

A MARMAC GUIDE TO HOUSTON AND GALVESTON.
VFOAT Marmack Guide to Houston. 1st-. 0735-8261. US. English. an. $6.95. Marmac Publishing Company, 6303 Barfield Road/Suite 208, Atlanta GA 30328. LC F394.H83. DD 917.6414110463.

MARYLAND TRAVEL SCENE.
Began in 1961. 0300-7502. Periodical. US. English. bm.

THE MAVERICK GUIDE TO AUSTRALIA.
Series/Titl Pelican Guide Series. 1979-. 0730-0018. US. English. an. Pelican Publishing Company, 1101 Monroe Street, Gretna LA 70053. Tel (504)368-1175. LC DU95. DD 919.40463. Offers hundreds of valuable inside tips on what to do and see in Australia as well as what to avoid. "For travelers heading down under.. almost required reading." ALA Booklist.

THE MAVERICK GUIDE TO HAWAII.
Series/Titl Pelican Guide Series. Began with 1977 Vol. 0278-6613. US. English. an. Pelican Publishing Company, 1101 Monroe Street, Gretna LA 70053. Tel (504)368-1175. LC DU622. DD 919.69044. Updated regularly, there is no better guide to Hawaii. A consumer-oriented book that is as fun to read as it is reliable to use. "You can do no better than to take along The Maverick Guide to Hawaii." UPI.

THE MAVERICK GUIDE TO NEW ZEALAND.
Series/Titl Pelican Guide Series. 0278-5501. US. English. an. $10.95. Bob and Sara Bone Maverick Guides, Pelican Publishing Company, 1101 Monroe Street, Gretna LA 70053. Tel (504)368-1175. Ed Bob Bone. LC DU405.5. DD 919.310437. Information on all the islands and the many things to see and do while visiting.

MEETINGS & INCENTIVE TRAVEL.
VAT Meetings and Incentive Travel. V. 9- Jan./Feb. 1980-. 0225-8285. Periodical. CN. English. bm. $33.67. Southam Communications Ltd, 1450 Don Mills Road, Don Mills Ontario M3B 1X2 Canada. Tel (416)445-6641. Ind/Abst Can. Bus. Index. DD 658.8106. *Canadian Sales Meetings & Conventions, 0318-1049.*

MEMBERSHIP ROSTER - AMERICAN SOCIETY OF TRAVEL AGENTS INC.
Main/Corp American Society of Travel Agents. 0360-6597. US. English. an. $35.00. American Society of Travel Agents Inc, 360 Lexington Avenue, New York NY 10017. LC G154. *List of Members.*

MEXICO.
Series/Titl Get'em and Go Travel Guides. 1979-. 0162-5500. US. English. an. $15.00. Houghton Mifflin, 2 Park Street, Boston MA 02107. Ed S Birnbaum. LC F1209. DD 917.204833.

MEXICO (FISHER TRAVEL GUIDES (FIRM).
(MEXICO). Series/Titl Fisher Annotated Travel Guides. 1983-. 0883-2625. US. English. an. Fisher Travel Guides, 200 Park Avenue South, New York NY 10003. Ed F Lemkowitz.

THE MEXICO TRAV'LER.
8756-1395. Periodical. US. English. mo. $25.00. The Mexico Trav'ler, 121 North College/Suite 301, Ft Collins CO 80524. DD 917.

MICHELIN GREAT BRITAIN AND IRELAND.
Main/Corp Michelin Tyre Company, Ltd. UK. English, French, German and Italian. $5.25. Michelin Tyre Public Ltd Company, Coal House, Lyon Road, Harrow Middlesex HA1 2DQ England. Tel (01)861-2121. LC TX910.G7. DD 647.9441. Selection of hotels and restaurants in Great Britain and Ireland.

MICHIGAN LIVING.
VFOAT Michigan Living A.A.A. Motor News. Vol. 63, No. 9 (Mar. 1981)-. 0735-1798. Periodical. US. English. mo. $6.00. Automobile Club of Michigan, Auto Club Drive, Dearborn MI 48126. Tel (313)336-1523. Ed Len Barnes. LC TL1. DD 917.74. bk rev. adv acc. Circ 825,000. Coverage of oneday, weekend or extended vacation travel in Michigan, USA and worldwide. Michigan events, entertainment, dining and the outdoors. Autos and auto industry news. *Michigan Living Motor News, 0161-2859.*

MIDEASTERN TOUR BOOK.
VFOAT Tour Book: Mideastern. 0569-2865. Periodical. US. English. ir. American Automobile Association, 8111 Gatehouse Road, Fall Church VA 22042. LC E106. DD 917.3.

THE MIDWEST MOTORIST.
1971. 0026-3435. Periodical. US. English. bm. $3.00. Auto Club of Missouri, 12901 North Forty Drive, St Louis MO 63141. Tel (314)576-7350. Ed Michael J Right. adv acc. Circ 328,000. Features articles on travel, area history, auto safety, highway and transportation news, automotive news, and consumer issues.

MIGRATION AND TOURISM STATISTICS.
See Statistics.

MINNESOTA CALENDAR OF EVENTS.
1977-. US. English. an. Minnesota Office of Tourism, 240 Bremer Building 419 North Robert Street, St Paul MN 55101.

MOBIL TRAVEL GUIDE. CALIFORNIA AND THE WEST.
(MOBIL TRAVEL GUIDE : CALIFORNIA AND THE WEST). VFOAT California and the West. 1969-. 0076-9827. US. English. an. $4.95. Mobil Travel Bureau, Box 25, Versailles KY 40383. LC F859.3. DD 917.94045. *Mobil Travel Guide: Good Food, Lodging and Sightseeing, California and the West, 0076-9827.*

MOBIL TRAVEL GUIDE. GREAT LAKES AREA.
(MOBIL TRAVEL GUIDE : GREAT LAKES AREA). 0076-9789. US. English. an. Mobil Travel Guide, PO Box 7600, Chicago IL 60680. DD 917.70433. *Mobil Travel Guide: Great Lakes Area.*

MOBIL TRAVEL GUIDE. MAJOR CITIES . . . .
1980-. Periodical. US. English. an. Mobil Travel Bureau, Box 25, Versailles KY 40383. *Mobil City Vacation & Business Guide.*

MOBIL TRAVEL GUIDE. NORTHWEST AND GREAT PLAINS STATES.
VFOAT Northwest and Great Plains States. Began with: 1962/63. 0076-9819. US. English. an. Rand McNally, 23 East Madison, Chicago IL 60602. DD 917.8.

MOBIL TRAVEL GUIDE SOUTHEASTERN STATES.
(MOBIL TRAVEL GUIDE : SOUTHEASTERN STATES). 0076-9835. US. English. an. Rand McNally, 23 East

Travel

Madison, Chicago IL 60602. **LC** F207.3. **DD** 917.6044. *Mobil Travel Guide: Good Food, Lodging, and Sightseeing in Southeastern States.*

MONTHLY MIGRATION AND TOURIST STATISTICS FOR . . . . See Statistics.

MONTREAL . . . , LE GUIDE DES MONTREALAIS. (MONTREAL . . . , LE GUIDE DES MONTREALAIS). 84-. 0823-8723. CN. French. an. $5.95 Each Number. Editions Quebecor, 225 Est rue Roy, Montreal Quebec H2W 2N6 Canada. **DD** 917.142810025.

MOUNTAIN VACATION & TRAVEL GUIDE COVERING WESTERN NORTH CAROLINA. Main/Corp Carolina Life, Inc. **VAT** Mountain Vacation and Travel Guide Covering Western North Carolina. 0162-6523. US. English. an. $3.50. Carolina Life Inc, PO Box 548, Hendersonville NC 28739.

MOVIMIENTO DE VIAJEROS EN ESTABLECIMIENTOS TURISTICOS. Main/Corp Spain. Instituto Nacional de Estadistica. Jan. 1976-. Spanish. ir. **LC** TX910.S7. *Estadistica del Movimiento de Viajeros en Establecimientos Turisticos.*

MOVING TO & AROUND ALBERTA. See Geography.

MOVING TO & AROUND MARITIMES & NEWFOUNDLAND. See Geography.

MOVING TO & AROUND SASKATCHEWAN. See Geography.

MOVING TO & AROUND TORONTO & AREA. VAT Moving To and Around Toronto and Area. Vol. 9, No. 3 (Jan. 15, 1982)-. 0713-8377. CN. English. an. Moving Publications, 1939 Leslie Street, Don Mills Ontario M3B 2M3 Canada. **DD** 917.1354044. *Moving to Toronto & Area,* 0226-7829.

MOVING TO & AROUND VANCOUVER & B.C. See Geography.

MOVING TO & AROUND WINNIPEG & MANITOBA. VAT Moving to and Around Winnipeg and Manitoba. Vol. 10, No. 4 (Feb. 4, 1983/84)-. 0715-7053. CN. English. be. **DD** 917.1274. *Moving to Winnipeg,* 0702-9209.

MOVING TO AUSTIN. Vol. 11, No. 9 (1984/85)-. 0825-2432. CN. English. an. $4.95 Each Number. **DD** 917.6431. *Moving to San Antonio/Austin,* 0715-9641.

MTM. MOTORCOACH TOUR MART. (MTM, MOTORCOACH TOUR MART). 1978-. 0161-9551. US. English. an. $70.00. Grace J Talmage and Associates, 2600 Martin Road, Willow Grove PA 19090. **LC** G153.4. **DD** 917.30492.

MULTINATIONAL EXECUTIVE TRAVEL COMPANION. 1970. 0093-7487. US. English. an. $50.00 Domestic, $70.00 Foreign. Guides Multinational Business, Harvard Square/PO Box 92, Cambridge MA 02138. **Tel** (617)868-2288. **Ed** Chriss Traeff. **LC** G153. **DD** 910.202. adv acc. (ctrl). The only business-travel guide covering over 145 major cities worldwide with hard to find information on travel, hotel/motels, restaurants, and entertainment.

MUSKOKA LIFE. Vol. 1, No. 1 (May/June 1982)-. 0820-876X. Periodical. CN. English. ir. Muskoka Community Newspapers, PO Box 10000, Bracebridge Ontario P0B 1C0 Canada. **DD** 917.13160405.

MYRA WALDO'S TRAVEL GUIDE TO NORTHERN EUROPE. VFOAT Travel Guide to Northern Europe. 1980-. 0195-8763. US. English. $9.95. MacMillan Publishing Company, Front & Brown Streets, Riverside NJ 08370. **Tel** (212)702-2000. **LC** D965. **DD** 914.04558. *Myra Waldo's Travel and Motoring Guide to Europe.*

MYRA WALDO'S TRAVEL GUIDE TO SOUTH AMERICA. VFOAT Travel Guide to South America. 0196-0024. Periodical. US. English. ir. MacMillan Publishing Company, Front & Brown Streets, Riverside NJ 08370. **Tel** (212)702-2000. **LC** F2211. **DD** 918.0438.

MYRA WALDO'S TRAVEL GUIDE TO SOUTHERN EUROPE. VFOAT Travel Guide to Southern Europe. 1980-. 0196-3651. US. English. ir. $9.95. MacMillan Publishing Company, Front & Brown Streets, Riverside NJ 08370. **Tel** (212)702-2000. **LC** D974. **DD** 914.04558. *Myra Waldo's Travel and Motoring Guide to Europe.*

MYRA WALDO'S TRAVEL GUIDE TO THE ORIENT AND ASIA. 0195-7759. US. English. ir. $10.95. MacMillan Publishing Company, Front & Brown Streets, Riverside NJ 08370. **Tel** (212)702-2000. **LC** DS4. **DD** 915.04428. *Myra Waldo's Travel Guide to the Orient and the Pacific.*

MYRA WALDO'S TRAVEL GUIDE TO THE SOUTH PACIFIC. 1980-. 0195-7767. US. English. ir. $10.95. MacMillan Publishing Company, Front & Brown Streets, Riverside NJ 08370. **Tel** (212)702-2000. *Myra Waldo's Travel Guide to the Orient and the Pacific.*

NAGUNE. VFOAT Traveler. V. 1- (4. 1984)-. Periodical. KO. Korean. mo. 27,000. Chusik Hoesa Nara Munhwa, 1-28 Chong-dong Chung-ku, Seoul 100 Korea. **LC** G149.

NATIONAL DIRECTORY OF FREE TOURIST ATTRACTIONS. See Yearbooks, Almanacs, Directories.

NATIONAL GEOGRAPHIC TRAVELER. See Geography.

NATIONAL TRAVEL EXPENDITURE STUDY. Main/Corp United States Travel Data Center. 0362-7829. US. English. an. US Travel Data Center, 1899 L Street NW #610, Washington DC 20036. **Tel** (202)293-1040. **LC** G155.U6. **DD** 338.4791730492. **Circ** 400. (ctrl). Total travel spending and averages for various categories and trip and traveler characteristics.

NATIONAL TRAVEL SURVEY. FULL YEAR REPORT. Began in 1974. 0737-2620. US. English. an. $90.00. US Travel Data Center, 1899 L Street NW #610, Washington DC 20036. **Tel** (202)293-1040. **LC** G155.U6. **DD** 380.14591730492. **Circ** 600. (ctrl). Analysis of American travelers' trip and travel characteristics.

NEW HORIZONS WORLD GUIDE. VFOAT Pan Am's Travel Facts about 138 Countries. 1951-. 0553-0601. US. English. ir. Pan American Airways, Pan Am Building, 48th Floor, New York NY 10017.

NEW YORK ON $ . . . A DAY. VAT New York on . . . Dollars a Day. 1980-81 Ed-. 0278-128X. US. English. ir. $4.95. Simon & Schuster, 1230 Avenue of the Americas, New York NY 10020. **LC** F128.18. **DD** 917.4710443. *New York on $ . . . $ . . . a Day.*

NEWCOMER'S GUIDE TO METROPOLITAN WASHINGTON. VFOAT Washingtonian. 1st- Ed. 0362-3262. US. English. Washingtonian Books, 1828 L Street Northwest, Washington DC 20036. **LC** F192.3. **DD** 917.53044.

NEWSLETTER - TRAVELING EXHIBITION INFORMATION SERVICE. (NEWSLETTER). V. 1, No. 1 (March/April 1981)-. 0733-463X. Periodical. US. English. bm. $28.00. Traveling Exhibition Information Service, PO Box 1608, Largo FL 34294. **Tel** (813)581-7328.

NEWSLINE - TRAVEL INDUSTRY ASSOCIATION OF AMERICA. (NEWSLINE). 0749-985X. Periodical. US. English. mo. Travel Industry Association of America, 1899 L Street Northwest, Washington DC 20036. **DD** 910.

NIAGARA'S SEASONS. 1981-. 0714-4202. CN. English. an. Free. Niagara's Seasons, c/o Region Niagara Tourist Council, PO Box 3025, Saint Catharines Ontario L2R 7E9 Canada. **DD** 917.133804405.

NIGERIA TOURIST GUIDE. VFOAT Guide du Tourisme Nigerien. 1969-. English and French. ir. Nigerian Tourist Association, 47 Marina, PO Box 2944, Lagos Nigeria. **LC** DT515.2. **DD** 916.69.

NOMAD. V. 1- Aug. 1977-. 0705-3940. Periodical. CN. English. bm. $3. per issue. Nomad, 251 Consumer Road/Suite 817, Willowdale Ontario M2J 4R3 Canada. **DD** 910.5.

NORMAN FORD'S FLORIDA. (NORMAN FORD'S FLORIDA : A COMPLETE GUIDE TO FINDING WHAT YOU SEEK IN FLORIDA). **VFOAT** Norman D. Ford's Florida. Began with: 1953. 0546-3432. US. English. ir. $5.80. Harian Publishing, 1 Vernon Avenue, Floral Park NY 11001. **Tel** (516)437-3440. **LC** F306. **DD** 975.9005.

NORTH AMERICA TRAVEL AGENCY DIRECTORY. See Yearbooks, Almanacs, Directories.

NORTHEASTERN TOUR BOOK. VFOAT Tour Book Northeastern, Connecticut, Maine, Massachusetts, New Hampshire, New York, Rhode Island, Vermont. 0468-6853. US. English. an. American Automobile Association, 1712 G Street, Washington DC 20006. **LC** GV1024. **DD** 917.4044. *Northeastern States.*

NORTHERN AFFAIRS. SPECIAL TRAVEL EDITION. (NORTHERN AFFAIRS). Summer/Fall 1979-. 0226-1626. Periodical. CN. English (summaries in French). Ministry of Northern Affairs, 10 Wellesley Street, 9th Floor, Toronto Ontario M4Y 1G2 Canada. **DD** 917.13104405.

NORTHLAND TODAY MAGAZINE. See General Interest - General Interest-North America.

NORTHWEST BOAT TRAVEL. See Boats and Boating.

NORTHWESTERN TOUR BOOK. VFOAT Tour Book, Northwestern: Idaho, Montana, Oregon, Washington, Wyoming. 0094-078X. US. English. an. American Automobile Association, 8111 Gatehouse Road, Falls Church VA 22042. **LC** GV1024. **DD** 917.9. *Northwestern States.*

NOTES DU CENTRE D'ETUDES DU TOURISME. (LES NOTES DU CENTRE D'ETUDES DU TOURISME). Vol. 1, (June, 15, 1977)-. 0229-2718. Periodical. CN. French. ir. Free. Centre d'Etudes du Tourisme, CP 8000 Succursale A, Montreal Quebec H3C 3L4 Canada. **DD** 016.3384791714.

NOVA SCOTIA TOURISM NEWS *CEASED.* **VAT** Tourism News (Halifax). Apr. 1981-March/Apr. 1983. 0821-0829. Periodical. CN. English. bm. Nova Scotia Tourism News, 5871 Spring Garden Road, Halifax Nova Scotia B3J 2R5 Canada. **DD** 338.479171604405. *Traveller & Travel Industry Reporter,* 0710-250X.

NUDIST PARK GUIDE. US. English. $6.00. American Sunbathing Association, 810 North Mills Avenue, Orlando FL 32803. **Tel** (305)933-2064. **Ed** Arne Eriksen. **LC** GV451. **DD** 917.3. adv acc. **Circ** 20,000. (ctrl). Provides information on nudist clubs throughout North America. Individual club pages include directions, facilities, recreation opportunities, accommodations, scheduled events and more.

OAG TRAVEL PLANNER & HOTEL/MOTEL GUIDE. EUROPEAN ED. (OAG TRAVEL PLANNER & HOTEL/MOTEL GUIDE). **Main/Corp** Official Airline Guides, Inc. **VFOAT** Travel Planner & Hotel/Motel Guide. **VAT** Official Airline Guides Travel Planner and Hotel/Motel Guide. European Ed. 0162-735X. Periodical. US. English. qt. $70.00. Official Airline Guide, Inc, 2000 Clearwater Drive, Oak Brook IL 60521. **Tel** (312)654-6000. **Ed** Margaret E Nester. **LC** D909. **DD** 914.0455. adv acc. **Circ** 20,000. Features city, hotel and ground information. Includes airport diagrams and city maps. Detailed directory sections. Provides basic travel information, events, travel documents required and consular locations.

OAG TRAVEL PLANNER & HOTEL/MOTEL GUIDE. NORTH AMERICAN ED. (OAG TRAVEL PLANNER & HOTEL/MOTEL GUIDE). **VFOAT** Travel Planner & Hotel/Motel Guide. **VAT** Official Airline Guides Travel Planner and Hotel/Motel Guide. 0193-3299. Periodical. US. English. qt. $72.32. Official Airline Guides Inc, 2000 Clearwater Drive, Oak Brook IL 60521. **Tel** (800)323-3537. *OAG Travel Planner & Hotel-Motel Guide,* 0090-0869 Laboratory.

OAG TRAVEL PLANNER & HOTEL/MOTEL GUIDE (PACIFIC AREA EDITION). (OAG TRAVEL PLANNER & HOTEL/MOTEL GUIDE). **VFOAT** OAG Travel Planner and Hotel/Motel Guide. **VAT** Official Airline Guides Travel Planner and Hotel/Motel Guide. Vol. 1, No. 1 (Jan.-Mar. 1985)-. 8750-8672. Periodical. US. English. qt. $70.00. Official Airline Guides, 2000 Clearwater Drive, Oak Brook IL 60521. **Tel** (312)654-6000. **Ed** Margaret E Nester. **DD** 919. adv acc. **Circ** 10,000. Features city, hotel and ground information. Includes airport diagrams and city maps. Detailed directory sections. Provides basic travel information, events, travel documents required and consular locations.

OAG WORLDWIDE CRUISE & SHIPLINE GUIDE. See Transportation - Ships & Shipping.

ODYSSEUS (FLUSHING, N.Y.). (ODYSSEUS). 1st Ed-. 0883-3664. US. English. an. Odysseus Enterprises, PO Box 7605, Flushing NY

Travel

11352. **Tel** (718)445-2471. Ed Joseph H Bain. adv acc. **Circ** 20,000. Accommodations and travel guide for the gay community (USA/International).

OFFICIAL ARROW STREET GUIDE OF OTTAWA & DISTRICT. VFOAT Ottawa & District Including Hull. 0316-8077. Periodical. CN. English. an. Might Directories, 220 Bartley Drive, Toronto Ontario M4A 1G2 Canada. **DD** 917.1384.

THE OFFICIAL GUIDE TO TRAVEL AGENT & TRAVEL CAREERS. See Occupations and Careers.

OFFICIAL STEAMSHIP GUIDE INTERNATIONAL. (OFFICIAL STEAMSHIP GUIDE). V. 64, No. 2- Aug. 1963-. 0030-0381. US. English. mo. $56.00. Transportation Guide Inc, 111 Cherry Street, New Canaan CT 06840. **Tel** (203)966-9784. Ed Marlene Dobrin. adv acc. **Circ** 10,000. A magazine listing all cruises in the world. *Official Steamship & Airways Guide International.*

OFFICIAL TOURING GUIDE TO EAST AFRICA. 1967-. English. ir. Africa News Publishers Ltd, Automobile Association of East Africa, A A House Westlands, PO Box 40087, Nairobi Kenya. LC GV1025.K4. **DD** 916.7604.

THE ON-YOUR-OWN GUIDE TO ASIA. 0162-5950. US. English. an. Box 4543, Stanford CA 94305. **Tel** (415)497-3228. Ed Terry George. LC DS504. **DD** 915.0442. A travel guidebook emphasizing economical accommodations, unusual places of interest and local customs and culture.

ONTARIO TOURISM NEWS. Began with Summer 1978 issue. 0707-1442. Periodical. CN. English. qt. Ontario Ministry of Industry & Tourism, Hearst Block 900 Bay Street, Toronto Ontario M7A 2E1 Canada.

ONTARIO VACATION FARMS. 0712-1636. CN. English. an. Free. Ontario Vacation Farm Association, Rural Route #2 Vankleek Hill Ontario K0B 1R0 Canada. **DD** 917.13044.

ONTARIO/CANADA CAMPING. Main/Corp Ontario. Ministry of Industry and Tourism. CN. English. Queen's Park, Toronto Canada M7A 2E5 Canada. LC GV191.46.O6. **DD** 917.13044.

THE ORIGINAL NEW ENGLAND GUIDE. VFOAT New England Guide. 0734-4066. US. English. an. $3.00. Historical Times Inc, 2245 Kohn Road, Box 8200, Harrisburg PA 17105. **Tel** (717)657-9555. Ed Kathie Kull. LC F1.3. **DD** 917.40443. adv acc. **Circ** 175,000. Comprehensive travel information for those vacationing in New England primarily during the spring, summer and fall seasons. Helps with planning and serves as an on-the-road- guide. *New England Guide.*

OTTAWA MAGAZINE. VFOAT Ottawa. Vol. 23, No. 4 (Apr. 1980)-V. 24, No. 2 (Mar. 1981). 0225-557X. Periodical. CN. English (text in French, Apr. 1980-May 1981). mo. $33.27. Ottawa Magazine, 340 MacLaren Street/Suite 2, Ottawa Ontario K2P 0M6 Canada. **Tel** (613)234-7751. Ed Lousi Valenzuela. **DD** 790.0971384. bk rev. adv acc. **Circ** 44,500. (ctrl). Citystyle magazine reflecting life in Ottawa, Nepean, Gloucester and the Valley. Includes profiles of Ottawans, and Consumer Guides. *What's on in Ottawa Magazine, 0043-468X; Ottawa Citylife.*

OTTAWA NEWCOMER. (THE OTTAWA NEWCOMER). No. 1-. 0826-0265. Periodical. CN. English. mo. Free. Capital Guide Publishers, Suite 200/450 Rideau Street, Ottawa Ontario K1N 5Z4 Canada. **DD** 917.138040405. (ctrl). *Moving Magazine, 0715-805X.*

OU. V. 1- May 1976-. 0705-0429. Periodical. CN. English (French). qt. Free. Systemes Ou, PO Box 191, Magog Quebec J1X 3W8 Canada. **DD** 338.479714604. (ctrl).

OUTLOOK FOR SUMMER TRAVEL. Series/Titl Special Studies in Travel Economics and Marketing. Began with issue for 1982. 0748-0830. US. English. an. $60.00. US Travel Data Center, 1899 L Street Northwest/Suite 610, Washington DC 20036. **Tel** (202)293-1040. LC G155.U6. **DD** 380.145917304927. **Circ** 400. Forecasts the level of vacation travel activity for the upcoming summer in various key market segments.

OVERSEAS ASSIGNMENT DIRECTORY SERVICE. See Yearbooks, Almanacs, Directories.

PACIFIC AREA DESTINATION HANDBOOK. 1976/77-. 0363-4817. US. English. an. $75.00. Pacific Area Travel Association, 228 Grant Avenue, San Francisco CA 94108. LC DS4. **DD** 919.04.

PACIFIC HOTEL DIRECTORY AND TRAVEL GUIDE. See Yearbooks, Almanacs, Directories.

PACIFIC TRAVEL NEWS. V. 1- Jan. 1957-. 0030-8951. Periodical. US. English. mo. Free Members, $10.00 Chapter Members. Pacific Travel News, 274 Brannan Street, San Francisco CA 94107. LC G155.P25. **DD** 910.091823.

PAGES. (PAGES : PILOTS' AIRPORT GUIDE TO ENTERTAINMENT AND SERVICES). VFOAT P.A.G.E.S. 0742-4981. US. English. an. $15.95. Osage Aero Co, PO Box 809, Fair Lawn NJ 07410. Ed A Martin. LC TX907. **DD** 917.40443. **Circ** 5,000. Guide to airports in the Northeast. Describes hotels, motels and car rentals near airports that are used by private pilots.

PAKISTAN HOTEL AND TRAVEL REVIEW. See Hotels/Motels.

PAKISTAN HOTELS & TOURISM. See Hotels/Motels.

PAN-AFRICAN JOURNAL CEASED. Began with Vol. 1 in 1968. Ceased with Vol. 10, No. 1 in 1977. 0031-0565. Periodical. US. English. qt. $15.00. 49 Sheridan Avenue, Albany NY 12210. Ind/Abst MLA Int. Bibliogr. Books Artic. Mod. Lang. Lit., Am. Hist. Life, Hist. Abstr., Part A, Mod. Hist. Abstr., Hist. Abst., Part B, Twent. Century Abstr. LC DT1. **DD** 916.005.

THE PAN AMERICAN YEARBOOK. See Yearbooks, Almanacs, Directories.

PANORAMA. Began in 1913. 0031-0867. Periodical. English. wk. $42.04. Medianet BV, PO Box 6298, 2001 HG Haarlem Netherlands. LC AP15.

PAPINEAU'S GUIDE TO ASEAN LANDS OF TROPICAL BEAUTY. 1st- Ed.-. SI. English. ir. Andre Publications, Tanglin PO Box 7, Singapore 10 Singapore. LC DS504. **DD** 915.904.

PAPINEAU'S GUIDE TO BALI. VFOAT Guide to Bali. SI. English (French and German). ir. MPH Magazines, 5 Stadium Walk, 3rd Floor/Room 5, Singapore 1439 Singapore. LC DS647.B2. **DD** 915.986. *Papineau's Guide to Bali, Island Paradise.*

PAPINEAU'S GUIDE TO BANGKOK, CITY OF ENCHANTMENT. VFOAT Guide to Bangkok. English. ir. Andre Publications, Tanglin PO Box 7, Singapore 10. LC DS589.B2. **DD** 915.93.

PAPINEAU'S GUIDE TO JAKARTA. (PAPINEAU'S GUIDE TO JAKARTA, INDONESIA'S CONVENTION CITY). 1973-. 0377-2659. SI. English. ir. Andre Publications, 154A Emerald Hill Road-9, Singapore. LC DS646.29.D5. **DD** 915.982.

PAPINEAU'S GUIDE TO SINGAPORE. VFOAT Guide to Singapore. 31st Ed. (1980)-. 0129-8682. SI. English. an. 5 Stadium Walk, Suite 5/Third Floor, Singapore 1439 Singapore. LC DS598.S7. **DD** 915.957045. *Papineau's Guide to Singapore and Spotlight on Malaysia.*

PAPINEAU'S GUIDE TO SRI LANKA. VFOAT Guide to Sri Lanka. 1st Ed.-. 0129-9743. English. ir. $5.00 U.S. MPH Magazines, National Stadium, Zone 4 Kallang, Singapore 1439. LC DS489. **DD** 915.493043.

PAPINEAU'S GUIDE TO THAILAND. VFOAT Guide to Thailand. 0129-8534. English. ir. MPH Magazines Pte Ltd, Suite 5/3rd Floor Stadium Walk, Singapore 1439 Singapore. LC DS566.2. **DD** 915.930444.

PAPINEAU'S GUIDE TO THE PHILIPPINES. VFOAT Guide to the Philippines. 1st- Ed. SI. English. an. Andre Publications, Tanglin PO Box 7, Singapore 10 Singapore. LC DS654. **DD** 915.99044.

PASSEPORT. V. 1- March 1980-. 0228-2631. Periodical. CN. French. $6. Publications Passeport, 502 1121 Ouest Sainte-Catherine, Montreal Quebec H3B 1J5 Canada. **DD** 910.202.

PASSPORT (CHICAGO, ILL.). (PASSPORT). Began publication in 1966?. 0031-272X. Periodical. US. English. mo. $120.00. Enterprise Publishers, 20 North Wacker Drive/Suite 3417, Chicago IL 60606. **Tel** (312)332-3571.

PELICAN GUIDE TO THE BAHAMAS. 1st Ed.-. 0740-5529. US. English. be. Pelican Publishing Company, 1101 Monroe Street/Box 189, Gretna LA 70053. **Tel** (504)368-1175. LC F1652. **DD** 917.2960452. An in-depth look at the 700 Islands that comprise the Bahamas. Complete first-hand information, from low-cost to luxury. The most comprehensive guidebook available on the subject.

PERLY'S GUIDE TO METROPOLITAN TORONTO CEASED. Ceased with Vol. for 1981/82 or 1983/84 (23rd or 24th edition). 0712-161X. Periodical. CN. English. be. 5.50. Perly's Maps Ltd, 1050 Eglinton West, Toronto Ontario M6C 2C5 Canada. **DD** 917.13541. *Perly's Guide., 0712-1601.*

PLACES. V. 1- Mar. 1974-. 0094-3452. Periodical. US. English. qt. $7.00. Editod Places, 432 Locust Street, Indiana PA 15701. LC G149. **DD** 910.

PLACES OF INTEREST TO WOMEN. See Women.

PLEASURE BOATING. See Boats and Boating.

PLEASURE HUNT MAGAZINE. VFOAT Pleasure Hunt. 0883-2382. Periodical. US. English. bm. $15.75. Pleasure Hunt Magazine, PO Box 1003, Levittown PA 19058. **DD** 917.

POLK'S SAGUENAY DIRECTORY. See Yearbooks, Almanacs, Directories.

THE PRIVILEGED TRAVELER. 0887-4131. Periodical. US. English. bm. $39.00. The Privileged Traveler Inc, 42 Usonia Road, Pleasantville NY 10570.

PROCEEDINGS - TRAVEL OUTLOOK FORUM CEASED. Main/Conf Travel Outlook Forum. VFOAT Travel Outlook Forum Proceedings (197 -). 0160-4651. US. English. an. $70.00. US Travel Data Center, 1899 L Street NW, Washington DC 20036. **Tel** (801)581-3351. LC G155.U6. **DD** 338.4791730492.

PROGRAM REPORT OF THE UNITED STATES TRAVEL SERVICE. Main/Corp United States. Travel Service. VFOAT Meeting Competition for World Tourism Dollar in the '70S. 0502-5397. US. English. an. Secretary of Commerce Washington DC 20230. LC G155.U6. **DD** 338.47917304.

PROMET TURISTA U PRIMORSKIM OPCINAMA. Began with Vol. for 1975. Serbo-Croatian -R. ir. 200.00. Republicki Zavod za Statistiku Sr Hrvatske, Ilica 3, Zagreb Yugoslavia. *Promet Turista u Primorskim Mjestima.*

PROVINCE. 1st Ed.-. UK. English. Michelin, Lyon Road, Harrow HA12DQ M12DX England. **Tel** 01-861 2121. LC DC611.P958. **DD** 914.4904838. Tourist guide to Provence region of France. Sightseeing tours, history of region, description of sights.

PROVIDENCE VISITOR CEASED. Newspaper. US. English.

QUARTERLY TRAVEL REPORT. Jan.-Mar. 1979-. Periodical. English. ir. Ackerman & Palumbo, 1666 Kennedy Causeway, Miami Beach FL 33141.

QUEBEC VOYAGES. VFOAT Marketing Voyages. No. 1- Summer 1979-. 0225-0454. Periodical. CN. English (French and German). sa. $1.50 Each Number. Systemes Marketing Voyages Ltee, Suite 502/1121 Sainte Catherine Street West, Montreal Quebec H3B 1J5 Canada. **DD** 338.479171404.

RANCH & COAST. VFOAT Ranch & Coast Magazine. VAT Ranch and Coast. 0164-8780. Periodical. US. English. mo. $24.00 California. Ranch & Coast Magazine, PO Box 806, Solana Beach CA 92075.

RAPPORT ANNUEL DES ACTIVITES - ASSOCIATION TOURISTIQUE REGIONALE RICHELIEU RIVE-SUD. See Economics - Economics: Industry & Production.

RECOMMEND FLORIDA. VFOAT Recommend. 0034-1452. Periodical. US. English. mo. PO Box 2226, Hollywood CA 33022. **Tel** (305)949-4218.

THE RECORD. See Geography.

RED DEER, ALBERTA, CITY DIRECTORY. See Yearbooks, Almanacs, Directories.

REGINA MAGAZINE. 1- 1977-. 0704-6685. CN. English. an. Regina Chamber of Commerce, 2145 Albert Street, Regina Saskatchewan S4P 2V1 Canada. **DD** 917.1244. *Regina, 0315-212X.*

REGIONAL BREAKDOWN OF WORLD TOURISM STATISTICS. See Statistics.

RELATORIO DE ATIVIDADES - SECRETARIA DE ESTADO DO TURISMO DO RIO GRANDE DO SUL. Main/Corp Rio Grande do Sul, Brazil (State). Secretaria de Turismo. Portuguese. ir. LC G155.B7.

Travel

RELATORIO - EMPRESA DE TURISMO DA BAHIA. Main/Corp Empresa de Turismo da Bahia. Portuguese. ir. Empresa de Turismo du Bahia, rua Marechal Floriano 1-Canela, Salvador Brazil. LC G155.B7.

RELAX (BANNOCKBURN, ILL.). (RELAX). Vol. 1, No. 1 (Mar. 1985)-. 0882-6544. Periodical. US. English. mo. $24.00 Domestic, $30.00 Foreign. P & C Publishing Inc, 2333 Waukegan Road/Suite S-280, Bannockburn IL 60015. DD 910.

REPORT - NEW ZEALAND. DEPT. OF TOURIST AND PUBLICITY. Main/Corp New Zealand. Dept. of Tourist and Publicity. Began with report for 1924/25. English. ir. LC G155.N5. DD 910.

REPORT OF THE DEPARTMENT OF TRAVEL INDUSTRY. See Economics - Industry & Production.

REPORT - QUEENSLAND. GOVERNMENT TOURIST BUREAU. Main/Corp Queensland. Government Tourist Bureau. English. ir. LC G155.Q4.

RESOURCES FOR TOURISM, HOSPITALITY, RECREATION. 1979/81-. 0225-266X. CN. English. be. Canadian Government Office de Tourism, 235 Queen Street/4th Floor, Ottawa Ontario K1A 0H6 Canada. LC G155.C3. DD 910.402371, 331.7616479471.

RETIREMENT PARADISES OF THE WORLD. 17th- Ed. 0193-4341. US. English. $4.95. LC G153. DD 910.4. Bargain Paradises of the World, 0408-568X.

REVUE DE TOURISME. VFOAT Tourist Review, Zeitschrift fur Fremdenverkehr. Jan. 1946-. 0044-2755. Periodical. SZ. Multilingual (English, French, German, and Italian). ir. $23.25. Stamppfli & Cie Ag, Postfach 2728, 3012 Berne Switzerland. Tel 4131/23 23 23. Ed C Kaspar. Ind/Abst Foreign Lang. Index, PAIS Foreign Lang. Index. bk rev. adv acc. Circ 2,000.

REVUE VOYAGEUR. (LA REVUE VOYAGEUR). VFOAT Voyageur Magazine. Vol. 1, No. 1 (July/August 1984)-. 0824-1309. Periodical. CN. English (French). qt. Free. La Revue Voyageur Magazine, c/o Publications de Vacances Quebec, 575 Arago Street West, Quebec Quebec G1N 2M4 Canada. Tel (418)687-3442. Ed Curtis J Sommerville. DD 910.5. adv acc. Circ 150,000. (ctrl). An on-board bus publication distributed through the Voyageur and Voyageur Colonial bus system in the Province of Quebec and the Province of Ontario.

ROAD & TRACK ROAD ATLAS & TRAVEL GUIDE. Series/Titl CBS Leisure Transportation Series. VFOAT Road & Track's Road Atlas & Travel Guide. VAT Road and Track Road Atlas and Travel Guide. 0198-0386. Periodical. US. English. qt. CBS Publications, PO Box 7350, Greenwich CT 06830. LC G1201.P2. DD 912.73.

ROCKY MOUNTAIN MAGAZINE MEETING AND CONVENTION GUIDE TO THE ROCKY MOUNTAIN REGION. (ROCKY MOUNTAIN MAGAZINE ... MEETING AND CONVENTION GUIDE TO THE ROCKY MOUNTAIN REGION). VFOAT Meeting and Convention Guide to the Rocky Mountain Region. Vol. 1 (1982)-. 0731-1737. US. English. an. Rocky Mountain Country Ltd Partnership, 1741 High Street, Denver CO 80218.

ROLLIN' HOMES. V. 1- Apr. 1976-. 0703-8674. Periodical. CN. English. qt. .50 Per No. Rollin Homes Publications, RR #4, Brampton Ontario L67 3S1 Canada. DD 796.7905.

ROME. Main/Corp Pneu Michelin (Firm). 1.- Ed. French. ir. Pneu Michelin, 46 Avenue de Breteuil, 75341 Paris Cedex 07 France. LC DG804. DD 914.56320492.

ROTEIROS DE VIAGEM. No. 1- Jan. 1973-. Periodical. BL. Portuguese. ir. 50.00. Editora de Turismo Ltda, rua Libero Badaro 182 70.80/90 Andares, Sao Paulo Brazil. LC F2516.

RUNZHEIMER REPORTS ON TRAVEL MANAGEMENT. 0730-8663. Periodical. US. English. mo. $245.00. Runzheimer International, 555 Skokie Boulevard/Suite 245, Northbrook IL 60062. Tel (312)291-9011. Ed Judith Godshalk. Covers all aspects of corporate travel management.

RUTAS GUIA TURISTICA DE BARCELONA. VFOAT Rutas de Barcelona. English, French, German, and Spanish. ir. Ger/Publi, Sants 340-344, Entlo. 3, Barcelona Spain. LC DP302.B36.

ST. CATHARINES. (ST. CATHARINES : YOUR OFFICIAL GUIDE TO THE GARDEN CITY). 1983-. 0824-6572. CN. English. an. Free. St Catharines & District Chamber of Commerce, 60 James Street Box 940, St Catharines Ontario L2R 6Z4 Canada. DD 917.1338.

ST. GEORGE MAGAZINE. VFOAT St. George. 0882-8741. Periodical. US. English. qt. $6.00. St George Magazine, 95 East Tabernacle/Suite 201, St George UT 84770. DD 917.

SASKATOON THE BEAUTIFUL. Began publication in 1967. 0827-2956. CN. English. an. Free. Dominion Heritage Publishing, 508-606 Victoria Avenue, Saskatoon Saskatchewan S7N 0Z1 Canada. DD 917.1242.

SAV-ON-HOTELS. See Hotels/Motels.

SCOPE WHEELERS CANADIAN CAMPGROUND GUIDE. See Geography.

SCOTLAND, WHERE TO STAY, HOTELS AND GUEST HOUSES. See Hotels/Motels.

SEE THE TREASURE COAST. 0746-3944. Periodical. US. English. mo. Brownell Associates, 3675 Clark Road, Sarasota FL 33583. See Vero Beach, Ft. Pierce, Stuart Resort Area, 0273-5644.

SEKIRAT SAR HA-TAYARUT BA-KENESET AL PEULOT MISRADO. Main/Corp Israel. Misrad Ha-Tayarut. Hebrew. ir. LC G155.I78.

SELLING TRAVEL. V. 1- Feb. 1973-. 0316-3822. CN. English. mo. J Stephenson, 67 Richmond Street West 401, Toronto Ontario M5H 1Z5 Canada. DD 338.4791. Vacation.

SIDE STREETS OF THE WORLD. VFOAT Side Streets. Jan. 1984-. 0741-7624. Periodical. US. English. mo. $36.50. T McBrian Communications Inc, 80 Varick Street, New York NY 10013. Tel (212)431-1652. Ed Sheila F Buckmaster. A newsletter that concentrates on different destinations.

SIGNATURE. V. 1- 1966-. 0037-5039. Periodical. US. English. ir. Diners Club, 880 3rd Avenue, New York NY 10022, (subscription address: Communications Data Services PO Box 4966 Des Moines IA 50340). Tel (03)3208888. LC AP2. bk rev. adv acc. Circ 210,000. (ctrl). Travel and entertainment overseas information. A general, light reading magazine for Diners Club members in Australia.

SIGNPOST FOR NORTHWEST HIKERS. See Recreation, Leisure - Sports.

SOUL JOURNEY. Feb. 1973-. 0091-6323. Periodical. US. English. mo. Communicators Ltd, 1014 National Press Building, Washington DC 20004. LC G149. DD 910.5.

THE SOURCE II. VAT Source Two. Vol. 1, No. 1 (Aug./Sept. 1981)-. 0278-4386. Periodical. US. English. bm. $60.00. Armin D Lehmann Associates Inc, 309 Santa Monica Boulevard, Suite 304, Santa Monica CA 90401.

SOUTH AMERICA TRAVEL DIGEST. Began publication with 1st Ed. in 1965?. 0584-3103. US. English. an. $9.95. Travel Digests, 30695 Ganado Drive, Rancho Palos Verdes CA 90274. Tel (213)541-6161. LC F2201.

SOUTH AMERICAN EXPLORER. Began with Vol. for 1977. Periodical. US. English. qt. $24.00. South American Explorers Club, 2239 East Colfax Avenue #205, Denver CO 80206. Tel (303)320-0388. Ed Don Montague and Linda Rojas. LC F2224. DD 918.043. bk rev. adv acc. Circ 6,000. Articles on South America related to exotic and unusual travel, ecology, Andes, Amazon mountaineering, hiking, history and field sciences such as botany, anthropology, archaeology, geology and etc.

SOUTH DAKOTA. See Economics.

SOUTH WEST NOVA. V. 2- Summer/Autumn 1978-. 0708-9821. Periodical. CN. English. Free. Lescarbot Print, Box 402, 4 Alma Street, Yarmouth Nova Scotia B5A 4B3 Canada. DD 917.163. In Town, 0702-8156.

THE SOUTHERN AFRICAN AND INDIAN OCEAN ISLANDS TRAVEL INDUSTRY'S YEARBOOK, DIRECTORY AND WHO'S WHO. See Yearbooks, Almanacs, Directories.

SOUTHERN EUROPE TRAVEL GUIDE. VFOAT AAA Travel Guide: Southern Europe. 0094-3614. US. English. American Automobile Association, 8111 Gatehouse Road, Falls Church VA 22042. LC GV1025.A2. DD 914.

SPAIN. Main/Corp Michelin Tyre Company, Ltd. Tourist Service. 1st- Ed. UK. English. Michelin Tyre Company, 81 Fulham Road, London SW3 6RD England. LC DP43. DD 914.60482.

STATISTICAL REVIEW - AUSTRALIAN TOURIST COMMISSION. See Statistics.

A STATISTICAL REVIEW OF TOURISM IN HONG KONG. See Statistics.

STATISTIEK VREEMDELINGENVERKEER. See Statistics.

STATISTIK KUNJUNGAN WISATAWAN ASING KE INDONESIA. See Statistics.

STATISTIK PERJALANAN WISATAWAN DOMESTIK JAWA TENGAH. See Statistics.

STATISTIQUES DU TOURISME. See Statistics.

STATISTIQUES DU TOURISME. See Statistics.

A STEPHEN BIRNBAUM TRAVEL GUIDE. VFOAT Stephen Birnbaum Travel Guides. 0749-2561. Monographic Series. US. English. ir. Houghton Mifflin Company, 2 Park Street, Boston MA 02108. DD 910. Get Em and Go Travel Guide, 0162-5497.

SUMMARY AND ANALYSIS OF INTERNATIONAL TRAVEL TO THE U.S. VAT Summary and Analysis of International Travel to the United States. 0095-3482. Periodical. US. English. qt. Superintendent of Documents, US Government Printing Office, Washington DC 20402. LC G155.U6. DD 338.47917304926. Summary and Analysis of International Travel to the U.S., 0095-3482.

SUMMER GUIDE. (SUMMER GUIDE : ROCKY MOUNTAIN MAGAZINE'S COMPLETE GUIDE TO SUMMER IN THE ROCKIES). VFOAT Rocky Mountain Magazine's Summer Guide. Vol. 1, No. 1 (Summer 1981)-. 0275-8482. Periodical. US. English. an. $2.95. Rocky Mountain Magazine, 1741 High Street, Denver CO 80218. LC F721. DD 917.80433.

SUNSET WESTERN TRAVEL ADVENTURES. 1st- Ed. 0191-3468. US. English. an. Lane Publishing Company, 85 Willow Road, Menlo Park CA 94025. LC F595.2. DD 917.8043.

SUOMEN MATKAILU. See Hotels/Motels.

SURINAME DIRECTORY OF COMMERCE, INDUSTRY AND TOURISM. See Yearbooks, Almanacs, Directories.

SURVEY AND ANALYSIS OF BUSINESS TRAVEL POLICIES & COSTS. Series/Titl Runzheimer Management Report. VAT Survey and Analysis of Business Travel Policies and Costs. 1982-1983-. 0735-0376. US. English. Runzheimer and Company Publications Division, 555 Skokie Boulevard, Northbrook IL 60062. Tel (312)291-9011. Ed Judith Godshalk. LC HD28. DD 658.383. A statistical survey of corporate business travel practices.

SURVEY OF OVERSEAS VISITORS TO SINGAPORE. Main/Corp Singapore. Tourist Promotion Board., Research Dept. 1975-. English. ir. LC G155.S5. DD 338.47915952045.

SURVEY OF STATE TRAVEL OFFICES. Main/Corp United States Travel Data Center. VFOAT State Travel Offices. 0361-8307. US. English. an. United States Travel Data Center, 1899 L Street NW, Washington DC 20036. LC G155.U6. DD 353.9382.

SURVEY OF TRAVEL IN KENTUCKY. 0146-4698. US. English. an. Department of Public Information, Commonwealth of Kentucky, 1923 Capitol Plaza Trail, Frankfort KY 40601. LC G155.U6. DD 338.4791769044.

TABUAS ITINERARIAS DO ESTADO DA BAHIA. V. 1- 1972-. Portuguese. ir. Departamento Geografia e Estatistica, Avenida Luiz Viana Filho S/N - Paralela, Salvador Brazil. LC GV1025.B7. DD 918.14.

LE TEMPS DES VACANCES. Periodical. CN. French. ir. Temps des Vacances, Bureau 10/400 Ouest rue St Antoine, Montreal Quebec H2Y 1J9 Canada. DD 917.104646.

TEMPS LIBRE. (TEMPS LIBRE : LE MAGAZINE DE L'ORGANISATION POUR LE TOURISME ETUDIANT AU QUEBEC (OTEQ)). Vol. 1, No 1

Travel

(Autumn 1983)-. 0823-5708. Periodical. CN. French. qt. 9.00. Temps Libre, Organisation pour le Tourisme Etudiant du Quebec, 4545 Pierre-de-Coubertin, CP 1000, Succursale 1000, Montreal Quebec H1V 3R2 Canada. Tel (514)252-3119. DD 91088375. adv acc. Circ 50,000. (ctrl). Low budget travel, transportation, accomodation, specialized services for youth and student youth exchange programs; description of books and guides. Outdoor activities.

TEOROS. VFOAT Cahiers de Recherche Teoros. Vol. 1, No. 1 (Feb. 1982)-. 0712-8657. Periodical. CN. French. ty. $5.42. Universite Quebec, CP 888, Succursale A, Montreal Quebec H3C 3P8 Canada. Tel (514)282-3650. DD 338.479171404405.

THAILAND TRAVEL TRADE YEARBOOK. See Yearbooks, Almanacs, Directories.

THIS IS ALASKA. 8756-4920. US. English. an. $5.95. Blake Publishing Company, 1021 West 25th Avenue, Anchorage AK 99510. LC F902.3. DD 917.98045.

THIS WEEK ON PEI. VFOAT This Week. VAT This Week on Prince Edward Island. 0710-0256. Periodical. CN. English. wk. Free from May 15th - Oct 15th for tourists. Walt Wheeler Publications Ltd, Box 1131, Charlottetown Prince Edward Island C1A 7M8 Canada. Tel (902)566-4600. Ed Debbie Gamble-Arsenault. DD 790.09717. adv acc. Circ 270,000. (ctrl) Details of events taking place during tourist season on Prince Edward Island. Restaurant reviews, attractions, accommodations and shopping.

THOMAS COOK BUSINESS TRAVELER. VFOAT Business Traveler. Vol. 1, No. 1 (Spring 1982)-. 0731-728X. Periodical. US. English. qt Norback & Company, 352 Nassau Street, Princeton NJ 08540.

THOMAS COOK CONTINENTAL TIMETABLE. VFOAT Indicateur Europeen Cook. 1873. UK. English. bm. $79.95. Forsyth Travel Library, PO Box 2975, Shawnee Mission KS 66201. Tel (800)367-7984. LC HE3004. DD 385.2042. adv acc. Circ 25,000. Comprehensive English language European and British railroad and local shipping schedule. Published over a century, widely used throughout the travel industry recommended for eurailpass. Cooks Continental Timetable.

THOMAS COOK CONTINENTAL TIMETABLE (PETERBOROUGH, CAMBRIDGESHIRE : 1981). (THOMAS COOK CONTINENTAL TIMETABLE). VFOAT Continental Timetable. Jan. 1981-. 0144-7467. Periodical. UK. English (French, German, and Italian). mo. adv acc. Circ 198,000. Railway and local shipping services guide for Europe. Thomas Cook International Timetable.

THOMAS COOK OVERSEAS TIMETABLE. Winter 1980-. 0144-7475. UK. English (French, Italian, German, Spanish, and Portuguese). bm. 59.95. Thomas Cook Ltd, Bluebell Cottage/PO Box 36, Peterborough PE3 6SB England. Tel (800)367-7984. LC HE1805. DD 385.204205. adv acc. Circ 10,000. Detailed surface transportation schedule for worldwide rail ferry and intercity bus services. Covers world except Europe and Britain. Widely used within travel industry as a reference. Thomas Cook International Timetable.

TIAC NEWSLETTER. (INFORMATION AITC). Main/Corp Association de l'Industries Touristique du Canada. VFOAT TIAC Newsletter. V. 23, No. 1, I.E. V. 25, No. 1, (May 1981)-V. 25, No. 3 (Dec. 1981). 0701-1741. Periodical. CN. French (English). bm. Association de l'Industrie Touristique du Canada, Bureau 1016/130 rue Albert, Ottawa Ontario K1P 5G4 Canada. DD 338.4791710405. T I A C Newsletter, 0701-1741.

TIACTION. Vol. 1, No. 1 (June 1982)-. 0715-5638. Periodical. CN. English (with French in parallel columns). bm. Free. Tiaction, c/o Tourist Industry Association of Canada, Suite 1016/130 Albert Street, Ottawa Ontario K1P 5G4 Canada. DD 338.4791710405. Tourism Canada, 0712-1849.

TIROLER VERKEHRSWIRTSCHAFTLICHE ZAHLEN. German. ir. Verein zur Jorderung des Instituts fur Verkehr und Tourismus, Wilhelm-Greil Strasse 4, Innsbruck Austria. LC G155.A8.

TMR. TRAVEL MARKETING REPORT. See Engineering.

TOERISME EN MIGRASIE. Main/Corp South Africa. Dept. of Statistics. VFOAT Tourism and Migration. Afrikaans (English). ir. 6.25. Departement van Statistiek, The Government Printer, Pretoria South Africa. LC G155.S57. DD 338.479168046.

TOLL-FREE TRAVEL/VACATION PHONE DIRECTORY. See Yearbooks, Almanacs, Directories.

TOUR BOOK. ALABAMA, LOUISIANA, MISSISSIPPI. (TOUR BOOK : ALABAMA, LOUISIANA, MISSISSIPPI). VFOAT Alabama, Louisiana, Mississippi Tour Book. 0361-4948. US. English. an. American Automobile Association, 8111 Gatehouse Road, Falls Church VA 22042. LC F324.3. DD 917.6.

TOUR BOOK. ARIZONA, NEW MEXICO. (TOUR BOOK : ARIZONA, NEW MEXICO). VFOAT Arizona, New Mexico Tour Book. 0362-3599. US. English. an. American Automobile Association, 8111 Gatehouse Road, Falls Church VA 22042. LC F809.3. DD 917.8904505.

TOUR BOOK. ARKANSAS, KANSAS, MISSOURI, OKLAHOMA. (TOUR BOOK : ARKANSAS, KANSAS, MISSOURI, OKLAHOMA). Main/Corp American Automobile Association. VFOAT Arkansas, Kansas, Missouri, Oklahoma. 0363-1486. US. English. an. American Automobile Association, 8111 Gatehouse Road, Falls Church VA 22042. LC F409.3. DD 917.6.

TOUR BOOK. ATLANTIC PROVINCES AND QUEBEC. (TOUR BOOK : ATLANTIC PROVINCES AND QUEBEC). Main/Corp American Automobile Association, Canadian Automobile Association. VAT Atlantic Provinces and Quebec, New Brunswick, Newfoundland, Nova Scotia, Prince Edward Island, Quebec. Tour Book. 0363-1788. US. English. an. American Automobile Association, 8111 Gatehouse Road, Falls Church VA 22042. LC F1035.8. DD 917.15'044. Eastern Canada Tour Book, 0569-2857.

TOUR BOOK. COLORADO, UTAH. (TOURBOOK : COLORADO, UTAH). Main/Corp American Automobile Association. VFOAT Colorado, Utah: Tourbook. 0362-9821. US. English. an. American Automobile Association, 8111 Gatehouse Road, Falls Church VA 22042. LC F774.3. DD 917.88043.

TOUR BOOK. CONNECTICUT, MASSACHUSETTS, RHODE ISLAND. (TOUR BOOK : CONNECTICUT, MASSACHUSETTS, RHODE ISLAND). Main/Corp American Automobile Association. VFOAT Connecticut, Massachusetts, Rhode Island Tour Book. 0363-1494. US. English. an. American Automobile Association, 8111 Gatehouse Road, Falls Church VA 22042. LC F92.3. DD 917.4.

TOUR BOOK. GEORGIA, NORTH CAROLINA, SOUTH CAROLINA. (TOUR BOOK : GEORGIA, NORTH CAROLINA, SOUTH CAROLINA). VFOAT Georgia, North Carolina, South Carolina Tour Book. 0361-4956. US. English. an. American Automobile Association, 8111 Gatehouse Road, Falls Church VA 22042. LC F284.3. DD 917.5.

TOUR BOOK. HAWAII. (TOUR BOOK : HAWAII). VFOAT Hawaii, Tour Book. 0160-6921. US. English. an. American Automobile Association, 8111 Gatehouse Road, Falls Church VA 22042. LC DU622. DD 919.69044.

TOUR BOOK. IDAHO, MONTANA, WYOMING. (TOUR BOOK : IDAHO, MONTANA, WYOMING). VFOAT Idaho, Montana, Wyoming Tour Book. 1976/77-. 0363-2695. US. English. an. American Automobile Association, 8111 Gatehouse Road, Falls Church VA 22042. LC F744.3. DD 917.8.

TOUR BOOK. ILLINOIS, INDIANA, OHIO. (TOUR BOOK : ILLINOIS, INDIANA, OHIO). Main/Corp American Automobile Association. VFOAT Illinois, Indiana, Ohio Tour Book. 0363-1508. US. English. an. American Automobile Association, 8111 Gatehouse Road, Falls Church VA 22042. LC F539.3. DD 917.7.

TOUR BOOK. KENTUCKY, TENNESSEE. (TOUR BOOK : KENTUCKY-TENNESSEE). VFOAT Kentucky-Tennessee Tour Book. 0361-4964. US. English. an. American Automobile Association, 8111 Gatehouse Road, Falls Church VA 22402. LC F449.3. DD 351.892.

TOUR BOOK. MAINE, NEW HAMPSHIRE, VERMONT. (TOUR BOOK : MAINE, NEW HAMPSHIRE, VERMONT). Main/Corp American Automobile Association. VFOAT Maine, New Hampshire, Vermont Tour Book. 0363-1516. US. English. an. American Automobile Association, 8111 Gatehouse Road, Falls Church VA 22042. LC F17.3. DD 917.4.

TOUR BOOK. MICHIGAN, WISCONSIN. (TOUR BOOK : MICHIGAN, WISCONSIN). Main/Corp American Automobile Association. VFOAT Michigan, Wisconsin Tour Book. 0363-1524. US. English. an. American Automobile Association, 8111 Gatehouse Road, Falls Church VA 22042. LC F564.3. DD 917.74044.

TOUR BOOK. NEW JERSEY, PENNSYLVANIA. (TOUR BOOK : NEW JERSEY, PENNSYLVANIA). Main/Corp American Automobile Association. VFOAT New Jersey, Pennsylvania Tour Book. 0363-1532. US. English. an. American Automobile Association, 8111 Gatehouse Road, Falls Church VA 22042. LC F132.3. DD 917.48044.

TOUR BOOK. NEW YORK. (TOUR BOOK : NEW YORK). Main/Corp American Automobile Association. VFOAT New York Tour Book. 0363-1540. US. English. an. American Autombile Association, 8111 Gatehouse Road, Falls Church VA 22042. LC F117.3. DD 917.47044.

TOUR BOOK. ONTARIO. (TOUR BOOK : ONTARIO). Main/Corp American Automobile Association. VFOAT Ontario, Tour Book. 0363-1559. US. English. an. American Automobile Association, 8111 Gatehouse Road, Falls Church VA 22042. LC F1057. DD 917.13044.

TOUR BOOK. OREGON, WASHINGTON. (TOUR BOOK : OREGON, WASHINGTON). VFOAT Oregon, Washington Tour Book. 0363-1567. US. English. an. American Automobile Association, 8111 Gatehouse Road, Falls Church VA 22042. LC F874.3. DD 917.95044.

TOUR BOOK. TEXAS. (TOUR BOOK : TEXAS). Main/Corp American Automobile Association. VFOAT Texas Tour Book. 0363-1575. US. English. an. American Automobile Association, 8111 Gatehouse Road, Falls Church VA 22042. LC F384.3. DD 917.64046.

TOUR BOOK. WESTERN CANADA AND ALASKA. (TOUR BOOK : WESTERN CANADA AND ALASKA). VFOAT Western Canada and Alaska, Alberta, British Columbia, Manitoba, Saskatchewan, Northwest Territories, Yukon Territory and Alaska Tour Book. 0362-3602. US. English. an. American Automobile Association, 8111 Gatehouse Road, Falls Church VA 22042. LC F1060.4. DD 917.1204305.

TOUR BRITISH COLUMBIA. VAT Tour B.C. 0226-3513. Monographic Series. CN. English. Free. Public Information Office, Tourism British Columbia, 1117 Wharf Street, Victoria British Columbia V8W 2Z2 Canada. DD 917.11044. Discover British Columbia.

TOURBOOK. MID-ATLANTIC. (TOURBOOK : MID-ATLANTIC). Main/Corp American Automobile Association. VFOAT Mid-Atlantic: Delaware. District of Columbia, Maryland, Virginia West Virginia, Tourbook. 0364-0086. US. English. an. American Automobile Association, 8111 Gatehouse Road, Falls Church VA 22042. LC F106. DD 917.5044.

TOURBOOK. NORTH CENTRAL. VFOAT Tour Book. 0733-8368. US. English. an. American Automobile Association, 8111 Gatehouse Road, Falls Church VA 22042. LC GV1024. DD 917.7. North Central Tour Book, 0733-835X.

TOURING. Periodical. FR. French. ir. 50.00. Touring Club de France, 65 Avenue de la Grande-Armee, 75782 CCP 32-58 Paris France. LC G149. DD 910.5.

TOURING & TRAVEL. V. 17, No. 1- May 1975-. 0318-4390. CN. English. qt. $6.00. Groupmark Canada, 199 Bay Street/4th Floor, Toronto Ontario M5J IL4 Canada. DD 796.705. Driving, 0318-4439.

TOURING (TOURING CLUB MONTREAL). (TOURING). Vol. 60, No. 1 (Apr. 1980)-. 0229-5466. Periodical. CN. English (French). qt. Free. Touring Club Montreal, 1425 de la Montagne Street, Montreal Quebec H3G 2R7 Canada. DD 796.7060714281. (ctrl). Bonne Route, 0229-5474.

TOURISM AND HOTEL SERVICES STATISTICS QUARTERLY. See Statistics.

TOURISM BRITISH COLUMBIA (1981). (TOURISM BRITISH COLUMBIA). Vol. 5, No. 1 (July 1981)-. 0713-1593. Periodical. CN. English. Province of British Columbia, 1450 Government Street, Information Services, Victoria British Columbia V8W 3E7 Canada. DD 338.47917110405. Newsletter, 0225-9680.

TOURISM IN ENGLISH. UK. English. English Tourist Board, 4 Grosvenor Gardens, London SW1W 0DU England. LC G155.G7. DD 338.47914204857.

Travel

TOURISM IN JAPAN. JA. English. ir. Department of Tourism and Ministry of Transport, 1-3 Kasumigaseki 2-chome Chiyoda-ku, Tokyo Japan. LC G155.J27. DD 380.14591520448.

TOURISM MANAGEMENT. See Business - General Management.

TOURISM POLICY AND INTERNATIONAL TOURISM IN OECD MEMBER COUNTRIES. Main/Corp Organization for Economic Cooperation and Development. Tourism Committee. 1974-. English. ir. Organization for Economic Cooperation and Development, 2 rue Andre-Pascal, 75775 Paris Cedex 16 France. LC G155.A1. DD 382.4591. *International Tourism and Tourism Policy in OECD Member Countries.*

TOURISM REPORT. English. an. LC G155.M73. DD 380.14591729750452.

TOURISME+. Yearly V. 1, April 1980-. 0226-6601. Periodical. CN. French. bm $19.35. Tourisme Press Inc, 429 St Vincent/Room 304, Montreal Quebec H2Y 3A6 Canada. Tel (514)397-9535. Ed Nicole LaBonte. DD 338.479105. adv acc. Circ 5,545. (ctrl). Trade publication published in French for the French Canadian travel industry.

TOURISME DANS LE CANTON DU VALAIS. Main/Corp Switzerland. Statistisches Amt. VFOAT Tourismus im Kanton Wallis. SZ. French (German). ir. Bureau Federal de Statistique, Hallwylstr 15, CH 3003 Berne Switzerland. LC G155.S8. DD 338.47914947.

LE TOURISME EN FRANCE. Began with 1976 Vol. FR. French. ir. 19 rue de Calais, 75009 Paris France. LC G155.F8. DD 380.14591440405.

TOURISME OUTAOUAIS. (TOURISME OUTAOUAIS : BULLETIN D'INFORMATION DE L'ASSOCIATION TOURISTIQUE DE L'OUTAOUAIS). Vol. 1, No 1 (Feb. 1982)-. 0712-6832. Periodical. CN. French. qt. Free. Tourisme Outaouais, 768 Boulevard, St Joseph Hull Quebec J8Y 4B8 Canada. DD 338.4791714220406. (ctrl).

TOURISMUS IM KANTON GRAUBUNDEN. Main/Corp Switzerland. Eidgenossisches Statistisches Amt. VFOAT Tourisme dans le Canton des Grisons. French and German. ir. 75.00. Eidgenossisches Statistisches Amt, Publikationsdienst, Hallwylstrasse 15, 3003 Bern Switzerland. LC G155.S8. DD 338.47914947047.

TOURISMUS IN DER SCHWEIZ IN DER HOTELLERIE UND DEN UBRIGEN BEHERBERGUNGSFORMEN. See Hotels/Motels.

TOURISMUS IN FREMDENORTEN UND STADTEN. Main/Corp Switzerland. Statistisches Amt. VFOAT Tourisme dans Quelques Centres Touristiques et Villes. French and German. ir. 85.00. Hallwylstrasse 15, CH-3003 Bern Switzerland. LC G155.S8.

TOURIST & HOTEL GUIDE FOR LEBANON. English. ir. Librairie Orientale, Place de l'Etoile BP 1986, Beirut Lebanon. LC DS80.A5. DD 915.692044.

TOURIST BULGARIA. English. mo. $33.00. Hemus, 6 Boulevard Rusky, Sofia Bulgaria. LC G155.B8. DD 380.14591497704.

TOURIST DEPARTURES AND MAIN DESTINATIONS. English (French and Spanish). ir. WTO Publications Section, Capitan Haya 42, Madrid 20 Spain. LC G155.A1. DD 380.14591040212.

TOURIST GUIDE. VFOAT Guide Touristique. 1975-. 0381-9523. CN. text in English and French. an. $2.50 Each Number. Editiour Ltd, 300 Arran Street, St Lambert Quebec J4R 1K5 Canada. DD 917.14044. *Guide, 0317-3704.*

TOURIST GUIDE BOOK. Main/Corp Nadi Al-Sayyarat Wal-Al-Rihlat Al-Misri. 1973-. English. ir. 10 Kasr E-Nil Street, Cairo UAR Egypt. LC DT45. DD 916.2045.

TOURIST GUIDE BOOK OF ONTARIO. Began publication in 1921. 0319-0439. Periodical. CN. English. an. Free. Tourist Guide Book of Ontario, 1215 Ouellette Avenue, PO Box 580, Windsor Ontario N9A 6N3 Canada. Tel (519)255-1212. Ed M Lancaster. DD 917.13044. adv acc. Circ 150,000. (ctrl). A tourist publication on Ontario and surrounding border areas listing cities, towns, places to stay, dine and shop. Helpful in vacation planning.

TOURIST RECEPTION CENTER STUDY. Main/Corp Manitoba. Dept. of Tourism, Recreation, and Cultural Affairs. Research and Planning Branch. VFOAT Tourist Reception Centre Survey. CN. English. LC G155.C3. DD 338.4791712704.

TOURIST RECEPTION CENTRE SURVEY. CN. English. LC G155.C3. DD 380.145917127043.

TOURIST REPORT. Main/Corp Malawi. National Statistical Office. English. ir. National Statistical Office, PO Box 333, Zomba Malawi. LC G155.M32. DD 338.4791689704405.

TOURIST TRADE OF INDIA. Periodical. II. English. ir. A 3 Delisle Road, Byculla 27 Bombay India. LC G155.I5. DD 338.479154045.

TOURISTIC ANALYSIS REVIEW. No. 1 (1973)-. Periodical. FR. English. qt. $53.21. Centre des Hautes Etudes Tour, 18 rue de I Opera, 13625 Aix-En-Provence France. Tel (42) 381765. Ed R Baredt. bk rev. Circ 250. International approach of tourism and outdoor recreation.

DIE TOURISTISCHE NACHFRAGE DER BUNDESDEUTSCHEN IN DER SCHWEIZ. VFOAT La Demande Touristique des Allemands de l'Ouest en Suisse. French (German). ir. Bundesamt fur Statistik Publikationsdienst, Hallwylstrasse 15, CH-3003 Bern Switzerland.

TOURMALINE. V. 1- 1973-. Periodical. English. ir. 20.00. Ceylon Tourist Board, 25 Galle Face Centre Road 3, Colombo (Sri Lanka). LC DS488. DD 915.493043. *Tourists' Ceylon Quarterly.*

TOURS AND VISITS DIRECTORY. See Yearbooks, Almanacs, Directories.

TRA DIGEST. Main/Corp Travel Research Associates. VAT Travel Research Associates Digest. V. 1- Summer/Fall 1975-. 0360-7534. US. English. sa. $30.00. Travel Research Associates, 203 Middlesex Turnpike, Burlington MA 01803. LC G153. DD 910.202.

TRADEMARK INFORMATION FOR TRAVELERS. Began with Apr. 1, 1977. US. English. Department of the Treasury, US Customs Service, Washington DC 20229. *Trademark Information.*

TRANSITIONS. Began publication in 1977. 0276-4717. Periodical. US. English. qt. Transitions Abroad, Box 344, Amherst MA 01004. Tel (413)256-0373. Ed Clayton A Hubbs. bk rev. adv acc. Circ 10,000. (ctrl). The leading magazine guide to international work, travel, and study for independent people. Double emphasis on budget, travel and interaction with people of host country.

TRANSPORT & TOURISM JOURNAL. See Transportation.

TRANSPORTATION AND TRAVEL. OFFICIAL TABLE OF DISTANCES, FOREIGN TRAVEL. (TRANSPORTATION AND TRAVEL : OFFICIAL TABLE OF DISTANCES, FOREIGN TRAVEL). Main/Corp United States. Dept. of the Army. 0197-3320. US. English. LC UG633, G109. DD 358.4 S, 910.40287.

TRAVEL 800. VAT Travel Eight Hundred. 1972. 0192-155X. Periodical. US. English. qt. $25.00. Cabell Travel Publications, 11411 Cumpston Street, North Hollywood CA 91601. Tel (818)980-6260. Ed Kelli Marshall. adv acc. Circ 8,000. A reservation guide-travel industry publication.

THE TRAVEL AGENT. V. 4, No. 10- Oct. 1933-. 0041-199X. Periodical. US. English. ir. $15.00. Fairchild Publications, Marjorie Leonard, 7 East 12th Street, New York NY 10003. Tel (212)741-6184. *American Travel Agent's Magazine.*

EL TRAVEL AGENT INTERNACIONAL. Apr. 1979-. 0194-620X. Periodical. US. Spanish. mo. Travel Agent y American Traveler Inv, 2 West 46th Street, New York NY 10036.

TRAVEL AGENTS' ANNUAL PRODUCTION, UNITED STATES ONLY. VFOAT A.T.C. Agency List. 8755-7738. US. English. Publication Services, Air Traffic Conference of America, 1709 New York Avenue NW, Washington DC 20006. LC G155.U6. DD 380.14591002573.

TRAVEL AGENTS' HANDBOOK (WASHINGTON, D.C.). (TRAVEL AGENTS' HANDBOOK). 8755-8203. US. English. Publications Services of the Air Traffic Conference of America, 1709 New York Avenue Northwest, Washington DC 20006. LC G154. DD 380.1459104023.

TRAVEL & LEARNING ABROAD. VFOAT Travel and Learning Abroad. Vol. 1, No 1 (July/Aug. 1984)-. 0748-7398. Periodical. US. English. bm. $16.00. Raico Publishing Company, 67 Main Street, Brattleboro VT 05301. DD 370.

TRAVEL & LEISURE. VAT Travel and Leisure. V. 1- Feb./Mar. 1971-. 0041-2007. Periodical. US. English. mo. $25.00. American Express Publishing Corporation, PO Box 777, Great Neck NY 11025, (subscription address: Communication Data Services 112 Tenth Street Des Moines IA 50309). Tel (212)382-5643. Ed Pamela Fiori. Ind/Abst Access. LC G149. DD 910.5. adv acc. Circ 925,000. (ctrl). Available on microfilm from University Microfilms. The how-to book of travel-where to stay, eat, see and do. Regular columns include travel and health, travel and money and traveling photographer. *Travel & Camera.*

TRAVEL & TOURISM EXECUTIVE NEWSLETTER : OFFICIAL PUBLICATION OF THE ASSOCIATION OF TRAVEL MARKETING EXECUTIVES, INC. (ATME). VFOAT Travel and Tourism Executive Newsletter. Periodical. US. English. mo. $85.00. Association of Travel Marketing Executives Inc, 804 D Street NE, Washington DC 20002. Tel (203)535-3866. *Travel Marketing News.*

TRAVEL BETWEEN CANADA AND OTHER COUNTRIES. Main/Corp Canada. Statistique Canada. Division des Flux Financiers et des Entreprises Multinationales. VFOAT Voyages Entre le Canada et les Autres Pays (Edition Mensuelle), Voyages Entre le Canada et les Autres Pays (Edition Trimestrielle), Voyages Entre le Canada and Other Countries. VAT Travel Between Canada and Other Countries (Quarterly Edition). V. 29- Jan. 1973-. 0380-2094. Periodical. CN. English (French). qt. Receiver General for Canada, Statistics Canada Publications, Ottawa Ontario K1A 0T6 Canada. *Travel Between Canada and Other Countries, 0380-2094.*

TRAVEL BUSINESS REPORT. VFOAT Travel Business. 0884-0687. Periodical. US. English. mo. $48.00. Travel Business Report, PO Box 889/Midtown Station, New York NY 10018. DD 338. *Travel Business.*

TRAVEL DESTINATION CANADA. Vol. 1, No. 1 (May 15, 1981)-. 0712-1261. Periodical. CN. English. bm. $12.00. Baxter Publishing Company, 310 Dupont Street, Toronto Ontario M5R 1VP Canada. Tel (416)968-7252. Ed Edith Baxter. DD 338.4791710405. adv acc. Circ 10,000. (ctrl). Canadian meeting, convention and travel information for the international travel trade.

TRAVEL EXPENSE MANAGEMENT. VFOAT Travel Expense Management Digest. 0272-569X. Periodical. US. English. mo. $95.00. Management Alternatives, PO Box 4270, Grand Central Station, New York NY 10163. DD 658.

TRAVEL FOOD & DUTY FREE INTERNATIONAL. VFOAT Travel Food and Duty Free International. 0746-7990. Periodical. US. English. bm. Alexander Morton, 665 Lavilla Drive, Miami Springs FL 33166. *Duty Free International, 0279-1684.*

TRAVEL GUIDE CARIBBEAN, BAHAMAS, BERMUDA, AND OTHER PORTS OF CALL. VFOAT Travel Guide to Caribbean, including the Bahamas and Bermuda. 0730-6873. US. English. an. $2.00. AAA, 8111 Gatehouse Road, Falls Church VA 22047. LC F2171. DD 917.290452. *Caribbean, Bahamas, Bermuda, and other Ports of Call Travel Guide.*

TRAVEL GUIDE FLORIDA. Vol. 1, No. 1-. 0277-4097. US. English. $2.50. Traveler Publications Inc, 1731 NW 6th Street/Suite 24, Box 1284 Gainesville FL 32601. LC G1316.E63. DD 917.590463.

TRAVEL GUIDE, MEXICO. VFOAT Travel Guide to Mexico. 0732-2313. US. English. an. AAA, 8111 Gatehouse Road, Falls Church VA 22047. LC F1209. DD 917.20433.

TRAVEL GUIDE, MEXICO AND CENTRAL AMERICA. VFOAT Travel Guide to Mexico and Central America. 0732-0434. US. English. an. American Automobile Association, 8111

Travel

Gatehouse Road, Falls Church VA 22047. LC F1209. DD 917.204833.

TRAVEL GUIDE TO MEXICO, CENTRAL AMERICA AND SOUTH AMERICA. (A TRAVEL GUIDE TO MEXICO, CENTRAL AMERICA AND SOUTH AMERICA). VFOAT Kosoy Travel Guide to Mexico, Central America and South America. 0711-4710. CN. English. ir. $6.95 Each Volume. Kosoy Travel Guides, 40 Shallmar Boulevard, Toronto Ontario M6C 2J9 Canada. DD 918.043.

TRAVEL HANDBOOK. VFOAT Travel. US. English. ir. US Department of Housing and Urban Development, 451 7th Street SW, Washington DC 20410.

TRAVEL HOLIDAY. V. 151, No. 2- Feb. 1979-. 0199-025X. Periodical. US. English. mo. $11.00. Travel Magazine Inc, Travel Building, Floral Park NY 1101. Tel (516)352-9700. Ind/Abst Read. Guide Period. Lit., Mag. Index, Book Rev. Index. LC G149. DD 910.405. Travel, Incorporating Holiday, 0161-7184.

TRAVEL IDEAS. 1971-. 0085-7351. US. English. an. $1.35. Special Interest Publications, 1716 Locust Street, Des Moines IA 50303. LC GV1024. DD 917.049205. Better Homes and Gardens Travel Ideas.

TRAVEL IN VIRGINIA. Began with 1975 vol. US. English. an. Virginia State Travel Service, 6 Nort 6th Street, Richmond VA 23219. LC G155.U6. DD 380.145917550443. Economic Analysis of Travel in Virginia.

TRAVEL INDUSTRY INDICATORS. 8756-8799. Periodical. US. English. mo. $75.00 Domestic, $85.00 Foreign. Travel Industry Indicators, PO Box 6627, Miami FL 33154. Tel (212)737-7231. Ed James V Cammisa Jr. DD 330.

TRAVEL INDUSTRY PERSONNEL DIRECTORY. See Yearbooks, Almanacs, Directories.

THE TRAVEL INDUSTRY WASHINGTON REPORT. VFOAT Washington Report. 0272-5649. Periodical. US. English. mo. Travel Industry Publications, 804 D Street NE, Washington DC 20002. Tel (202)484-2600.

TRAVEL INDUSTRY WORLD YEARBOOK. See Yearbooks, Almanacs, Directories.

TRAVEL MANITOBA MARKETING SUMMARY. CN. English. LC G155.C3. DD 380.145917127043.

TRAVEL MARKETING AND AGENCY MANAGEMENT GUIDELINES. 0275-3545. Periodical. US. English. bm. $60.00. Travel Marketing, PO Box 2781, Culver City CA 90230. Tel (213)204-0673. Ed Evelyn Reichman. bk rev. Circ 500. Concise, practical, legal management and marketing articles in 8-page bimonthly advice letter for travel agencies.

TRAVEL MASTER. See Hotels/Motels.

TRAVEL NORTH AMERICA. V. 1- Fall 1973-. 0147-1422. Periodical. US. English. qt. $12.00. Subscription Service Department, Box 278, Neptune NJ 07753. LC G155.N58. DD 338.479170453.

TRAVEL PRINTOUT. Began in 1972. 0744-6233. Periodical. US. English. mo. $55.00. US Travel Data Center, 1899 L Street NW #610, Washington DC 20036. Tel (202)293-1040. Ed Ida Simmons. bk rev. Circ 2,000. A newsletter reporting results of research on travel by Americans, the cost of travel, and the level of travel activity in the US.

TRAVEL SMART. Began with vol. for 1976. 0741-5826. Periodical. US. English. mo. $80.00. Communications House, 40 Beechdale Road, Dobbs Ferry NY 10522. Tel (914)693-8300. Ed H J Teison. bk rev. Circ 10,000. How to travel better for less; the ultimate travel 'insider'. Joy of Travel, 0277-7738.

TRAVEL STATISTICS. See Statistics.

TRAVEL STATISTICS, JAMAICA. See Statistics.

TRAVEL TO THE USSR. VAT Travel to the Union of Soviet Socialist Republics. 0320-0167. Periodical. UR. Russian English, German, and French. bm. Travel to the USSR Moscow 70751 Russia. Tel 228-39-01. Ed V Chernov. LC DK29. adv acc. Circ 200,000. (ctrl). Covers tourism in the USSR the country's nature, tourist centres and places of interest, historical and cultural landmarks, the art of the Soviet people. Travel to the Soviet Union.

TRAVEL TRADE DIRECTORY. See Yearbooks, Almanacs, Directories.

TRAVEL TRADE; THE BUSINESS PAPER OF THE TRAVEL INDUSTRY. V. 1- July 1929-. 0041-2066. Periodical. US. English. wk. $8.00. Travel Trade Publications, 6 East 46th Street, New York NY 10017. Tel (212)883-1110.

TRAVEL TRAILERS, 5TH WHEEL TRAILERS, CAMPING TRAILERS RV GUIDE, NEW & USED VALUES. See Transportation - Automobiles.

TRAVEL TRENDS IN THE UNITED STATES AND CANADA. 1969- ed. US. English. $45.00. University of Colorado, Business Research Division, Boulder CO 80302. Tel (303)492-8227. Ed C R Goeldner. Circ 500. (ctrl). Statistics on US and Canada on visits to recreation areas, number of tourists, tourist expenditures, length of stay, economic impact of tourism, mode of transportation, etc.

TRAVEL WEEKLY. 0041-2082. Periodical. US. English. sw. Ziff Davis Publishing Company, PO Box 5830, Cherry Hill NJ 08034. Tel (609)795-7012. Ind/ Abst Trade Ind. Index, Infobank.

TRAVELAGE SOUTHEAST. VFOAT Travel Age Southeast. 0744-1592. Periodical. US. English. bw. $25.00. Official Airline Guide, 880 7th Avenue, New York NY 10106. Tel (800)323-3537/Outside IL.

TRAVELAGE WEST. Began with Vol. for 1969. 0041-1973. Periodical. US. English. wk. $25.00 Domestic, $60.00 Foreign. Travelage West Publishing, 100 Grant Avenue, San Francisco CA 94108. Tel (415)781-8359. Ed Martin Deutsch. bk rev. adv acc. Circ 37,000. (ctrl). Geared to retail travel agents, industry and publication.

TRAVELCADE MAGAZINE. 0363-1796. Periodical. US. English. mo. $9.00. Travelcade Publications Inc, Box 58 Germantown Pike, Lafayette Hill PA 19444. LC G149. DD 910.5.

TRAVELER'S ALMANAC. See Yearbooks, Almanacs, Directories.

TRAVELER'S TOLL-FREE TELEPHONE DIRECTORY. See Yearbooks, Almanacs, Directories.

TRAVELIFE. 0228-5916. Periodical. CN. English. ir. $1.25 Each Number. Travelife Publications Ltd, 12th Floor, 797 Don Mills Road, Don Mills Ontario M3C 1V2 Canada. DD 910.5.

TRAVELLER ACCOMMODATION STATISTICS. See Statistics.

TRAVELLER'S ENCYCLOPAEDIA. VAT Ontario/Canada Traveller's Encyclopaedia. 0711-9119. CN. English. an. Ministry of Tourism and Recreation, Province of Ontario, Queen's Park, Toronto Ontario M7A 2E5 Canada. LC F1057. DD 917.13044. Welcome to the Traveller's Encyclopaedia of Ontario/Canada, 0706-1668.

TRAVELLER'S GUIDE TO CANADIAN BED & BREAKFAST COUNTRY PLACES. (A TRAVELLER'S GUIDE TO CANADIAN BED & BREAKFAST COUNTRY PLACES). VFOAT Canadian Bed & Breakfast Country Places. 1983 Ed.-. 0822-6288. CN. English. an. DD 647.9471. Country Bed and Breakfast Places in Canada, 0822-627X.

TRAVELLER'S GUIDE TO THE MIDDLE EAST. 1st- Ed. UK. English. an. $60.00. International Communications, 122 East 42nd Street/Room 1121, New York NY 10017. Tel (212)867-5159. Ed John Seekings. LC DS43. DD 915.604405. bk rev. adv acc. Circ 6,810. (ctrl).

THE TRAVELLERS REVIEW. 0732-779X. Periodical. US. English. bm. $15.00. The Travellers Review, PO Box 3008, Princeton NJ 08540.

TRAVELWARE. VFOAT Travel Ware. Vol. 174, No. 5 (July 1984)-. 0747-475X. Periodical. US. English. mo. $24.00. Business Journals, 22 South Smith Street, Norwalk CT 06855. DD 338. Luggage & Travelware, 0193-0559.

TRAVELWEEK BULLETIN. VFOAT C T M Travelweek Bulletin. VAT CTM Travelweek Bulletin, Concepts Travel Media Travelweek Bulletin. V. 5, Issue 40- Sept. 29, 1977-. 0225-6207. Periodical. CN. English. ir. 30.00 Travelweek Bulletin, PO Box 575 Station F, Toronto Ontario M4Y 2L8 Canada. Tel (416)924-0963. Ed Jill Wykes. DD 338.479105. adv acc. Circ 7,000. (ctrl). Canada's only travel trade publication. C T M Weekly Bulletin, 0380-2019.

TRAVERSIERS, PONTS ET CROISIERES. 0708-3319. CN. French. an. Office de Tourisme du Quebec, 235 Queen Street/4th Floor East, Ottawa Ontario K1A 0H6 Canada. DD 386.24202571.

TRAVLTIPS. VFOAT Travltips Freighter Bulletin. 0162-9816. Periodical. US. English. bm. $15.00. Travltips Cruise & Freighter Travel Association, 163-09 Depot Road, Flushing NY 11358. Tel (212)939-2400.

TTG ASIA YEARBOOK. See Yearbooks, Almanacs, Directories.

TURISMO EN CIFRAS. DR. Spanish. an. Cesar Nicolas Penson No. 59, Santo Domingo Republica Dominicana. LC G155.D65. DD 380.14591729304540212.

TURISMO, ENCUESTA. Main/Corp Nicaragua. Oficina Ejecutiva de Encuestas y Censos. Spanish. ir. Oficina Ejecutiva de Encuestas y Censas, Apartado 4031, Managua Nicaragua. LC G155.N53.

IL TURISMO NEL CANTONE TICINO. VFOAT Tourismus Im Kanton Tessin. German (Italian). an. 85.00. Ufficio Federale di Statistica, Hallwylstrasse 15, Bern 3003 Switzerland. LC G155.S8.

TURISTA MAGAZIN. Periodical. HU. Hungarian. mo. Akademiai Kiado, POB 24, 1363 Budapest Hungary. LC DB917. Turista.

TURIZAM. Main/Corp Savezni Zavod Za Statistiku (Yugoslavia). Series Corp Its. Statisticki Bilten. Serbo-Croatian. ir. Kneza Milosa 20, Beograd Yugoslavia. LC HA1631, G155.Y8.

UNDERGROUND GUIDE TO KAUAI, HAWAII. Began in 1980. 0733-1649. US. English. an. $5.95. Lenore W Horowitz, 813 Aster Boulevard, Rockville MD 20850. Tel (301)279-2264. Ed Lenore W Horowitz. LC DU628.K3. DD 919.6941044. Circ 6,000. Detailed descriptions of Kauai's best beaches, adventures, hidden beauty, and sports. Reliable recommendations about restaurants, tours, and shopping. Special tips for traveling with children.

UNITED KINGDOM & IRELAND TRAVEL TRADE DIRECTORY. See Yearbooks, Almanacs, Directories.

VACACIONES EN CASAS DE LABRANZAS. Main/Corp Spain. Direccion General de Empresas y Actividades Turisticas. Spanish. ir. Ministerio de Comercio y Secretaria de Estado de Turismo, Alcala Num 44, Madrid-14 Spain. LC TX910.S7.

VACANCES-FAMILLES-INFORMATION. (VANCANCES-FAMILLES-INFORMATION). V. 1- Nov. 1972-. 0700-821X. Periodical. CN. French. qt. $3.00. Societe Vacances-Familles Inc, 1661 Av du Parc, Sainte-Foy Quebec G1W 3Z3 Canada. DD 910.5.

VACATION. Fall/Winter 1974-. 0316-991X. Periodical. CN. English. qt. Free to Travel Agents in Canada and Eastern United States, $2.00 Others. Vacation Magazine Inc, 111 Pears Avenue, Toronto Ontario M5R 1S9 Canada. DD 910.5.

VACATION & TRAVEL GUIDE. Main/Corp Rand McNally and Company. VAT Vacation and Travel Guide. 0193-9831. US. English. an. $7.95. Rand McNally & Company, 23 East Madison, Chicago IL 60602. Tel (312)332-4627. LC E158. DD 917.304926.

VACATION TRAVEL BY CANADIANS IN THE UNITED STATES. VFOAT Canadian Vacation Travel. 0362-6040. US. English. an. UD Travel and Tourism Administration, Department of Commerce, Washington 20230. LC G155.U6. DD 381.45917304926. Vols. for (1977, V.1-) distributed to depository libraries in microfiche.

VACCINATION CERTIFICATE REQUIREMENTS FOR INTERNATIONAL TRAVEL AND HEALTH ADVICE TO TRAVELLERS CEASED. VFOAT Health Advice to Travellers. Jan. 1981-. 0254-296X. SZ. English. an. World Health Organization, PO Box 5284 Church Street Station, New York NY 10249. Tel (202)861-3200. LC RA638. DD 614.405. NLM W1 VA228B. Certificats de Vaccination Exiges dans les Voyages Internationaux, 0512-3011.

VALLEE DES FORTS. (LA VALLEE DES FORTS). VFOAT Valley of the Forts. 1981/82-. 0711-7906. CN. English (French). an. $1.15 Each

Travel

Number. Valley of the Forts, c/o Cartaffiche, 23 rue des Oblats, Lasalle Quebec H8R 3K9 Canada. **DD** 917.143005.

VE VENEZUELA. 1965. 0042-2932. Periodical. VE. text in Spanish and English. ir. $6.00. VE Venezuela, Surface Mail, Apartado del Este 60182, Caracas Venezuela. **Tel** 2835237. **Ed** Lynn Grossberg. adv acc. **Circ** 10,000. (ctrl). Tourist attractions of Venezuela and the Caribbean.

VENTURE ROAD. (VENTURE ROAD : THE OFFICIAL PUBLICATION OF THE VENTURE TOURING SOCIETY). Began in 1985?. 0883-7821. Periodical. US. English. mo. $24.00. The Venture Touring Society, 1615 South Eastern Avenue, Las Vegas NV 89104. **DD** 796.

VERY SPECIAL RESORTS. 1973-. 0093-4003. US. English. Berkshire Traveller Press, Stockbridge MA 01262. **LC** TX907. **DD** 917.0453.

VICTORIA GUIDELINE. Began with May 13, 1977 issue. 0715-6723. Periodical. CN. English. wk. Free. Guideline Publications, 11-415 West Cordova Street, Vancouver British Columbia V6B 1E7 Canada. **DD** 790.0971134. (ctrl). *Vancouver and Victoria Visitors Guideline, 0702-2425.*

VICTORIAN TRAVELER'S COMPANION. **Main/Corp** Victorian Society in America. 1980-. 0198-9626. US. English. an. Victorian Society in America, East Washington Square, Philadelphia PA 19105. **LC** E159. **DD** 917.304926.

VIKING TOURIST GUIDE. **VAT** Viking (Yarmouth. 1978). 0828-4849. Periodical. CN. English. ir. Free. Viking Tourist Guide, PO Box 128, Yarmouth Nova Scotia B5A 4B1 Canada. **DD** 917.15044. *Viking, 0049-6448.*

VISITOR ACCOMMODATIONS, FACILITIES, AND SERVICES FURNISHED BY CONCESSIONERS IN THE NATIONAL PARK SYSTEM. **Main/Corp** United States. National Park Service. 1976-77-. US. English. be. US Department of the Interior, National Park Service, Washington DC 20402.

VISITOR GUIDE TO FRONTIER VISTA TRAVEL REGION. *See* Geography.

VISITOR GUIDE TO PRAIRIE VALLEYS TRAVEL REGION. *See* Geography.

VISITOR GUIDE TO WOODLAND PARK TRAVEL REGION. *See* Geography.

VISITOR TRAVEL TO NOVA SCOTIA. Began with 1973 issue. 0709-6194. CN. English. an. Free. Research Section, Department of Tourism, PO Box 456, Halifax Nova Scotia B3J 2R5 Canada.

VISITORS & CONVENTION SERVICES NEWSLETTER. **VAT** Visitors and Convention Services Newsletter. 0713-7613. Periodical. CN. English. mo. Visitors & Convention Services, City of London, PO Box 5035, London Ontario N6A 4L9 Canada. **DD** 338.4791713260405.

VISTA USA. (VISTA/U.S.A). **VAT** Vista United States of America. 1965. 0507-1577. Periodical. US. English. qt. $3.00. Exxon Travel Club Inc, PO Box 3633, Houston TX 77001. **Tel** (201)538-7600. **Ed** Patrick W Sarver. **LC** G149. **Circ** 900,000. (ctrl). Travel-related and general interest articles.

VOICE OF TOURISM. (THE VOICE OF TOURISM). V. 1- Jan. 1967-. 0380-5476. Periodical. CN. English. qt. Alberta Tourist Association, 105 - 8th Avenue Southeast, Calgary Alberta T2G 0K4 Canada. **DD** 338.479171230405.

VOILA QUEBEC. (VOILA QUEBEC : LE GUIDE TOURISTIQUE DE QUEBEC : THE TOURIST GUIDE TO QUEBEC). V. 1, No. 1 (Summer 1979)-. 0228-698X. Periodical. CN. English (French). qt. $2.00 Each Number. Voila Quebec, 3765 Boulevard Hamel, Quebec Quebec G2E 2H1 Canada. **DD** 917.14471005.

VOYAGE EN GROUPE. **VFOAT** Group Travelling. Vol. 1, No. 1 (Jan./Feb. 1982)-. 0711-6136. Periodical. CN. English (text in French only, Jan./Feb. 1982-July/Aug. 1983). bm. 6.00. Voyage en Groupe, 425 rue Harris, St-Laurent Quebec H4N 2G8 Canada. **Tel** (514)744-3867. **Ed** Andre Quesnel. **DD** 917.140405. adv acc. **Circ** 10,000. (ctrl). Magazine which gives ideas to people in charge of groups on where to go and how to reach the different resources and tourist attractions that can receive groups.

WARDAIR WORLD (1983). (WARDAIR WORLD). Autumn/Winter 1983-. 0822-9678. Periodical. CN. French. qt. Wardair World, Suite 601/211 Yonge Street, Toronto Ontario M5B 1M4 Canada. **DD** 910.5. *Monde de Wardair, 0821-7963.*

WASHINGTON CALENDAR MAGAZINE. 1st-. 0161-0260. Periodical. US. English. mo. $10.00. Washington Calendar Magazine Inc, 7900 Westpark Drive, McLean VA 22101. **LC** F192.3. **DD** 917.53044.

WATERLOO REGION MAGAZINE. **VFOAT** Waterloo Region. Vol. 5, No. 1 (Winter 1983)-. 0826-7529. Periodical. CN. English. qt. 3.00. Fairway Press, 225 Fairway Road, Kitchener Ontario N2G 4E5 Canada. **Tel** (519)894-1630. **Ed** Audrey Wicken. **DD** 917.1344044. adv acc. **Circ** 42,500. (ctrl). A complete tourist guide to Kitchener, Waterloo, Cambridge and surrounding towns and villages; accomodations, attractions, entertainment, shopping and dining, tours and events are also covered. *Waterloo Region, 0710-2828.*

W.D. FARMER'S VACATION & RETIREMENT HOMES FOR PLEASANT LIVING. 0271-2717. US. English. $3.50. W D Farmer, PO Box 49463, Atlanta GA 30359. **LC** TH4835. **DD** 728.720973.

WELCOME BACK MAGAZINE. 0828-6221. CN. English. an. Free. Welcome Back Magazine, PO Box 1352, Kingston Ontario K7L 5C6 Canada. **DD** 917.137204405. (ctrl).

WELCOME TO CZECHOSLOVAKIA. 0043-2210. CS. English. qt. Orbis Press Agency, 120 41 Praha 2, Vinohradska 46 Czechoslovakia. Tourist review.

WELCOME TO GREY/BRUCE. *See* Geography.

WHAT'S ON IN OTTAWA. (WHAT'S ON). **VFOAT** Voici Ottawa-Hull. **VAT** Voici Ottawa-Hull (Ed. Mensuelle). Vol. 23, No. 1 (Feb. 1980)-. 0043-468X. Periodical. CN. English (French). mo. $9.28. Capital Guide Publishers, 450 Rideau Street/#200, Ottawa Ontario K1N 5Z4 Canada. **Tel** (613)238-4736. **DD** 790.0971384. *What's on (Visitor Edition), 0043-468X.*

WHERE TO GO IN LOS ANGELES. 0743-8540. US. English. an. $12.95. Karen Eklund, 5243 Horizon Drive, Malibu CA 90265.

WHERE TO GO IN MINNEAPOLIS & ST. PAUL. **VAT** Where To Go in Minneapolis and Saint Paul. 1st Ed. -. 0739-9693. US. English. be. $14.95. Where To Go Inc, PO Box 204, Excelsior MN 55331. **Tel** (612)546-1318. **Ed** Jeffrey Kaufman. **LC** F614.M6. **DD** 917.765790453. adv acc. **Circ** 20,000. A delectable menu of what's grand, elegant, charming, cosmopolitan, and distinctively Minnesota about the Minneapolis and St. Paul area.

WHERE TO STAY IN SCOTLAND, BED AND BREAKFAST. *See* Hotels/Motels.

WHO GOES WHERE. UK. English. 2.40. Alan Darby Publications, Plymouth Road, Birmingham B4S 8JE England. **LC** G153. **DD** 910.202.

WHOLE WORLD HANDBOOK. (WHOLE WORLD HANDBOOK : A GUIDE TO TRAVEL, STUDY AND WORK ABROAD). 1972-. Periodical. US. English. an. $5.95. EP Dutton & Company Inc, 2 Park Avenue, New York NY 10003.

WISCONSIN ESCAPE. **VFOAT** Escape. 0273-9755. Periodical. US. English. mo. $9.00. Heidel Publishing Inc, PO Box 1009, Green Lake WI 54941. *Wisconsin Holiday News, 0191-8982.*

WOLGAN YOHAENG. **VFOAT** Monthly Travel & Leisure. V. 1- (1984/1)-. Periodical. KO. Korean. mo. 2,500 Each Issue. Wolgan Yohaeng, Chungang Ucheguk Sasoham, 10078 Seoul Korea. **LC** G149.

WOMAN'S GUIDE TO WASHINGTON, D.C. (A WOMAN'S GUIDE TO WASHINGTON, D.C.) 0090-080X. US. English. Montag Associates, 1120 Connecticut Avenue Northwest, Washington DC 20036. **LC** F191. **DD** 917.53044.

WOMEN'S TRAVEL CONNECTIONS. **VFOAT** Connections. Vol. 3, No. 2 (Feb. 1985)-. 0882-8458. Periodical. US. English. an. $24.00. PO Box 6117, New York NY 10150. **Tel** (212)751-6758. **Ed** Jeanine Moss. **DD** 910. bk rev. **Circ** 2,000. A newsletter for the woman traveler, covering lodging, dining, transport, culture, security, shopping and publications. *Connections (New York, N.Y.: 1983).*

WOODALL'S EXPLORING AMERICA, FLORIDA. EDICION ESPANOL. (WOODALL'S EXPLORING AMERICA, FLORIDA). 0198-1102. US. English. an. Woodall Publishing Company, 500 Hyacinth Place, Highland Park IL 60635.

WOODALL'S FLORIDA. 0198-1110. US. German. an. Woodall Publishing Company, 500 Hyacinth Place, Highland Park IL 60035. **Tel** (312)433-4550. adv acc. Contains expanded listings for all campgrounds listed in each state or group of states.

WOODALL'S FLORIDA CAMPGROUND DIRECTORY. *See* Yearbooks, Almanacs, Directories.

WOODALL'S TRAILER & RV TRAVEL CEASED. **VFOAT** Trailer & RV Travel. **VAT** Woodall's Trailer and Recreational Vehicle Travel. V. 42- (Issue No. 493-). 0160-3000. Periodical. US. English. mo. $8.50. Woodall Publishing Company, 10 Caravan Court, Marion OH 43302. **LC** TL1. **DD** 796.7905. *Woodall's Trailer Travel, 0043-7727.*

WOODALL'S TRAILERING PARKS & CAMPGROUNDS. CANADIAN EDITION. (WOODALL'S TRAILERING PARKS & CAMPGROUNDS). **VAT** Trailering Parks & Campgrounds. **VAT** Woodall's Trailering Parks and Campgrounds. Canadian Edition. 0362-3823. US. English. Woodall Publishing Company, 500 Hyacinth Place, Highland Park IL 60035. **LC** TX907. **DD** 647.947.

WOODALL'S TRAILERING PARKS AND CAMPGROUNDS DIRECTORY. *See* Yearbooks, Almanacs, Directories.

WOODALL'S TRAILERING PARKS & CAMPGROUNDS. WESTERN EDITION. *See* Recreation, Leisure - Outdoor Life.

WORKING HOLIDAYS (LONDON, ENGLAND). (WORKING HOLIDAYS). UK. English. $7.00 Each Volume. Working Holidays, c/o Canadian Bureau for International Education, Suite 809/141 Laurier West, Ottawa Ontario K1P 5J3 Canada. **DD** 914.0455.

WORKING HOLIDAYS. SUPPLEMENT FOR NORTH AMERICAN READERS. 0828-8070. CN. English. an. Working Holidays. **DD** 914.0455.

WORLD BOOK & TRAVEL REPORT. **VAT** World Book and Travel. V. 1- Winter 1976-. 0146-4248. US. English. $5.95. 2000-B Governor's Circle, Houston TX 77092. **LC** Z1035.A1. **DD** 028.1.

WORLD STUDY & TRAVEL FOR TEACHERS. *See* Education (General).

WORLD TRAVEL. **VFOAT** Tourisme Mondial. 0043-9169. Periodical. SP. English (French, Spanish). bm. World Tourism Organization, Calle Capitan Haya 42, E Madrid 20 Spain. **Tel** 279-2804. **Ind/Abst** Excerpta Med.

WORLD TRAVEL DIRECTORY. *See* Yearbooks, Almanacs, Directories.

WORLD TRAVEL MANAGERS. V. 1- 1973-. 0090-421X. US. English. an. $22.00. Cabell-Shordon Publishing Company, 11411 Cumpston Street, North Hampton CA 91601. **LC** G154. **DD** 338.4791025.

WORLD TRAVELING. V. 1- Sept. 1978-. 0163-1780. Periodical. US. English. bm. $11.00. World Traveling, 30943 Club House Lane, Farmingdale Hills MI 48018. **Tel** (313)626-6068. **Ed** Terri Mitar. bk rev. adv acc. **Circ** 70,000. The only travel magazine with a travel guide enclosed (International Go Getter's Guide to . . .).

WORLDWIDE ADVENTURE TRAVELGUIDE. **VFOAT** Adventure Travelguide. 1979-. Periodical. US. English. an. $9.95. American Adventurers Association, Suite 301/444 NE Ravenna Boulevard, Seattle WA 98115. *International Adventure Travelguide, 0148-2300.*

YANKEE MAGAZINE'S GUIDE TO NEW ENGLAND CEASED. **VFOAT** Guide to New England. Periodical. US. English. sa. $1.25 Each Issue. 03444. **LC** F2.3. **DD** 917.4044. *Yankee Guide to the New England Countryside.*

YANKEE MAGAZINE'S TRAVEL GUIDE TO NEW ENGLAND. **VFOAT** Travel Guide to New England. Summer/Fall 1981-. 0740-6215. Periodical. US. English. an. $2.50 Each Issue. Yankee Publishers Inc, Main Street, Dublin NH 03444. **LC** F2.3. **DD** 917.40443. *Yankee Magazine's Guide to New England.*

Veterinary Medicine, Animal Culture

YORKTON, SASKATCHEWAN, CITY DIRECTORY. See Yearbooks, Almanacs, Directories.

YOUTH GROUP TRAVEL DIRECTORY. See Yearbooks, Almanacs, Directories.

YUGOSLAV TOURIST NEWS AND COMMERCIAL INFORMATION. V. 1- (No. 1-). Periodical. YU. English. mo. Yugoslav Tourist Association, Mose Pijade 8/11, Belgrade Yugoslavia. **LC** G155.Y8.

YUGOSLAVIA; HOTEL AND TOURIST DIRECTORY. See Yearbooks, Almanacs, Directories.

YUGOSLAVIA. HOTELSKE CENE. See Hotels/Motels.

YUGOSLAVIA TRAVEL AGENTS' MANUAL. VFOAT Yugoslavia. English. ir. Poslovna Zajednica Turistickih Organizacija Udruzenog Rada Jugoslavije, Majke Jevrosime 51/V, 11000 Beograd Yugoslovia. **LC** G154. **DD** 914.970424025.

YUKON, ALASKA HIGHWAY. NORTHWEST TRAVEL GUIDE. (YUKON, ALASKA HIGHWAY : NORTHWEST TRAVEL GUIDE). VFOAT Northwest Travel Guide. 39th Annual Ed. (1983/Spring 84)-. 0826-0389. CN. English. an. $1.95 Per Issue. Northwest Travel Guides, 211 Wood Street, Whitehorse Yukon Territory Y1A 2E4 Canada. **DD** 917.19104305. *Northwest Travel Guide : Alaska, Yukon, Alaska Highway, 0705-3355.*

Z MAGAZINE. No. 1- June 1969-. Periodical. ZA. English. mo. Zambia Information Service, PO Box RW 20, Ridgeway Lusaka Zambia. **Ind/Abst** MLA Int. Bibliogr. Books Artic. Mod. Lang. Lit. **LC** DT963.A2. **DD** 916.894005.

ZENKOKU RYOKO GYOSHA MEIBO. See Yearbooks, Almanacs, Directories.

VETERINARY MEDICINE, ANIMAL CULTURE

A.A.E.P. DIRECTORY. See Yearbooks, Almanacs, Directories.

AAHA DIRECTORY OF MEMBERSHIP. See Yearbooks, Almanacs, Directories.

AAHA MEMBERSHIP. Main/Corp American Animal Hospital Association. VFOAT AAHA Directory of Membership. VAT American Animal Hospital Association Membership. 1965. 0272-0078. US. English. bm. $142.00. American Animal Hospital Association, P O Box 768, Mishawaka IN 46544. **Tel** (219)256-0280. **Ed** Wm Jackson. **LC** SF604.5. **DD** 636.083202573. bk rev. adv acc. **Circ** 11,300. (ctrl). Professional publication for veterinarians who are small animal practitioners.

A.A.V. NEWSLETTER (1984). (A.A.V. NEWSLETTER). Vol. 5, No. 1 (Mar. 1984)-. Periodical. US. English. $35.00. A A V Newsletter Office, 5770 Lake Worth Road, Lake Worth FL 33463. **Tel** (305)439-2421. **Ed** Linda R Harrison. bk rev. adv acc. **Circ** 1,500. A professional association publication addressing exotic bird medicine and surgery. Of interest to veterinarians, aviculturists, pet shops, zoos, wildlife rehabilitators and biologists. *Newsletter (Association of Avian Veterinarians).*

ACCUMULATIVE VETERINARY INDEX. See Indexes/Abstracts.

ACTA MEDICA VETERINARIA. V. 1 Jan./Apr. 1955-. 0001-6136. Periodical. Italian (articles in English, French, German, Portuguese or Spanish). Editoriale Scientifica SRL, Via Chiatamone 60/B, 80121 Napoli Italy. **Ind/Abst** Bibliogr. Agric., Biol. Abstr., Chem. Abstr. **NLM** W1 AC856M. **CODEN** AMVEAX.

ACTA VETERINARIA. (ACTA VETERINARIA (BELGRADE)). VFOAT Acta Veterinaria. V. 1- 1951-. 0567-8315. Periodical. YU. Serbo-Croatian-C (summaries in English, French or German). ir. $36.00. Acta Veterinaria-Belgrade, Veterinarski Fakultet Bul JNA 18, 11000 Beograd Yugoslavia. **Tel** (011)685-261. **Ed** Milovan Tovanovic. **Ind/Abst** Life Sci. Collect., Biol. Abstr., Chem. Abstr., Sci. Cit. Index, Abr. Ed. **NLM** W1 AC9553. **CODEN** ACVTA8. **Circ** 1,000. Animal physiology along with pathology, endocrinology, immunology, animal nutrition, parasitology, radiology, surgery, toxicology, etc.

ACTA VETERINARIA ACADEMIAE SCIENTIARUM HUNGARICAE CEASED. (ACTA VETERINARIA). V. 1-30, No. 4. 0001-7205. Periodical. English (text in English, French, German or Russian with summaries in one or more of the other languages). qt. **Ind/Abst** Life Sci. Collect., Pestdoc, Ringdoc, Vetdoc, Biol. Abstr., Index Med., Chem. Abstr., Nuci. Sci. Abstr., Sel. Water Resour. Abstr. **NLM** W1 AC9555. **CODEN** AVASAX. *Acta Veterinaria Hungarica.*

ACTA VETERINARIA JAPONICA. V. 1- 1956-. 0001-7221. Periodical. JA. English (Japanese). ir. Research Institute of Veterinary Science, Nihon University, Shimo-Umo, Tokyo Japan.

ACTA VETERINARIA SCANDINAVICA. V. 1, Issue 1- 1959-. 0044-605X. Periodical. DK. English (papers in German or French, with summaries in German and a Scandinavian language). qt. $54.68. Den Danske Pyriage Forening, Alhambraues 15, DK 1826 Copenhagen Denmark. **Ind/Abst** Life Sci. Collect., Pestdoc, Ringdoc, Vetdoc, Excerpta Med., Bibliogr. Agric., Biol. Abstr., Chem. Abstr., Index Med., Nuci. Sci. Abstr., Energy Res. Abstr., Sci. Cit. Index, Abr. Ed. **NLM** W1 AC956E. **CODEN** AVSCA7.

L'ACTION VETERINAIRE. Began in 1946. 0001-7523. Periodical. FR. French. ir. $69.18. Compagnie Gen Developpement, 15-17 rue Godefroy Cavaignac, 75541 Paris Cedex 11 France. **Tel** 379-0630.

ADVANCES IN VETERINARY SCIENCE AND COMPARATIVE MEDICINE. V. 13- 1969-. 0065-3519. US. English. ir. Academic Press, 4805 Sand Lake Road, Orlando FL 32887. **Tel** (305)345-4100. **Ed** C E Cornelius. **Ind/Abst** Life Sci. Collect., Pestdoc, Ringdoc, Vetdoc, Excerpta Med., Chem. Abstr., Index Med., Bibliogr. Agric., Sci. Cit. Index, Abr. Ed. **NLM** W1 AD885. **CODEN** AVSCB8. *Advances in Veterinary Science, 0096-7653.*

AFRICAN JOURNAL OF ECOLOGY. V. 17- Mar. 1979-. 0141-6707. Periodical. UK. English. qt. $126.00. Blackwell Scientific Publications, PO Box 88 Osney Mead, Oxford OX2 0EL England. **Tel** 0865 240201. **Ed** S K Eltringham. **Ind/Abst** Life Sci. Collect., Sel. Water Resour. Abstr., Biol. Abstr., Sci. Cit. Index, Abr. Ed. **LC** QL337.E25. **DD** 599.005. **CODEN** AJOEDE. bk rev. adv acc. **Circ** 451. *Ecology of African animals- populations, behaviour, breeding, etc. East African Wildlife Journal.*

AGRICULTURE INTERNATIONAL. See Agriculture.

AMERICAN BEE JOURNAL. V. 1- Jan. 1861-. 0002-7626. Periodical. US. English. mo. $11.40. Dadant and Sons, 51 South 2nd Street, Hamilton IL 62341. **Tel** (217)847-3324. **Ed** Joe M Graham. **Ind/Abst** Life Sci. Collect., Energy Inf. Abstr., Environ. Abstr., Biol. Abstr., Chem. Abstr., Bibliogr. Agric. **LC** SF521. **DD** 638.1405. **CODEN** ABJOAS. bk rev. adv acc. **Circ** 19,000. Available on microfilm from University Microfilms. Edited for hobbyist and commercial beekeepers. Explains all aspects of beekeeping and honey production on special features of honey handling, colony management and the latest in scientific research.

AMERICAN JOURNAL OF VETERINARY RESEARCH. V. 1- (No. 1-). 0002-9645. Periodical. US. English. mo. American Journal Veterinary, 930 North Meacham Road, Schaumburg IL 60196. **Tel** (312)885-8070. **Ind/Abst** Life Sci. Collect., Pestdoc, Ringdoc, Vetdoc, Excerpta Med., Index Med., Chem. Abstr., Bibliogr. Agric., Energy Res. Abstr., Biol. Agric. Index, Sci. Cit. Index, Abr. Ed., Hospit. Lit. Index. **LC** SF601. **DD** 619.05. **NLM** W1 AM53. **CODEN** AJVRAH.

THE AMERICAN KENNEL CLUB SHOW, OBEDIENCE AND FIELD TRIAL AWARDS. See Pets.

AMERICAN KENNEL CLUB STUD BOOK REGISTER. See Pets.

THE AMERICAN RACING PIGEON NEWS. Publication began in 1885. 0003-0686. Periodical. US. English. mo. 34 East Franklin Street, Bellbrook OH 45305. **Tel** (215)275-1729. **LC** SF481. **DD** 636.59605. *Homing Exchange.*

AMI DES BETES. (L'AMI DES BETES). Vol. 1, No. 1 (Jan. 1984)-. 0824-8494. Periodical. CN. French. mo. $1.00. L'Ami des Betes, 6748 rue Saint-Hubert, Montreal Quebec H2S 2M6 Canada. **DD** 636.009714.

ANALES DEL INSTITUTO DE INVESTIGACIONES VETERINARIAS. See Yearbooks, Almanacs, Directories.

ANATOMIA, HISTOLOGIA, EMBRYOLOGIA. (ZENTRALBLATT FUR VETERINARMEDIZIN. REIHE C, ANATOMIA, HISTOLOGIA, EMBRYOLOGIA : JOURNAL DE WELTVEREINIGUNG DER VETERINARANATOMEN). VFOAT Anatomia, Histologia, Embryologia. Began in March 1973. 0340-2096. Periodical. English (French, German, and Spanish; summaries in all languages). qt. $210.20. Paul Parey Scientific Publishing, 35 West 38th Street #3W, New York NY 10018. **Tel** (212)730-0518. **Ed** James Breazile and Bernd Vollmerhaus. **Ind/Abst** Life Sci. Collect., Excerpta Med., Biol. Abstr., Curr. Contents, Sci. Cit. Index, Abr. Ed., Autom. Subj. Citation Alert, Index Med., Ringdoc, Vetdoc, Index Vet., Vet. Bull., Energy Res. Abstr., Pestdoc, Nutr. Abstr. Rev. **NLM** W1 AN192F. **CODEN** AHEMA5. bk rev. adv acc. **Circ** 500. Official journal of the World Association of Veterinary Anatomists. *Zentralblatt fur Veterininmedizin. Reihe C, Anatomie, Histologie, Embryologie, 0300-8649.*

ANIMAL BLOOD GROUPS AND BIOCHEMICAL GENETICS. V. 1- 1970-. 0003-3480. Periodical. English. qt. $68.00. Centre for Agricultural Publishing and Documentation, PO Box 4, 6700 AA Wageningen Netherlands. **Ind/Abst** Life Sci. Collect., Excerpta Med., Index Med., Curr. Contents Agric. Food Vet. Sci., Biol. Abstr., Chem. Abstr., Bibliogr. Agric., Sci. Cit. Index, Abr. Ed. **NLM** W1 AN228F. **CODEN** ABBGBX.

ANIMAL BREEDING ABSTRACTS. See Indexes/Abstracts.

ANIMAL CARE MATTERS. Vol. 80, No. 1 (Sept. 1980)-. Periodical. US. English. qt. US Department of Agriculture/ Animal and Plant Health Inspection Service, Veterinary Services/Animal Care Programs, Hyattsville MD 20782.

ANIMAL DISEASE OCCURRENCE. VFOAT Incidence des Maladies Animales. Vol. 1- July 1980-. 0144-3879. Periodical. UK. English. sa. $309.70. Commonwealth Agricultural Bureau, Farnham House/Farnham Royal, Slough SL2 3BN England. **Tel** (02814) 2662. **Ed** J R Metcalfe. **Ind/Abst** Life Sci. Collect. adv acc. Contains abstracts and also data tables on the occurance of diseases of animals in specified countries.

ANIMAL HEALTH & NUTRITION. VFOAT Animal Health and Nutrition. Vol. 40, No. 8 (Sept. 1985)-. 0888-028X. Periodical. US. English. mo. Sandstone Building, Mt Morris IL 61054. **Ind/Abst** Biol. Agric. Index, Bibliogr. Agric. **DD** 636. *Animal Nutrition & Health, 0003-3553.*

ANIMAL HEALTH MONTHLY NEWSLETTER. Periodical. US. English. mo.

ANIMAL HEALTH YEARBOOK. See Yearbooks, Almanacs, Directories.

ANIMAL HUSBANDRY JOURNAL. Vol. 1, No. 1 (Jan. 1985)-. 8756-4742. Periodical. US. English. mo. $18.00. Animal Husbandry Journal, PO Box 111, Freedom ME 04941. **DD** 636.

ANIMAL MORBIDITY REPORT CEASED. Ceased publication in 1981. 0091-0872. Periodical. US. English. qt. US Department of Agriculture, Animal & Plant Health Inspection Service, Veterinary Services, Hyattsville MD 20782. **Ind/Abst** Am. Stat. Index.

ANIMAL MORBIDITY REPORT (ANNUAL). (ANIMAL MORBIDITY REPORT). US. English. an. Veterinary Services Animal & Plant Health Inspection Service, US Department of Agriculture, Hyattsville MD 20782. **LC** SF623. **DD** 636.08944273.

THE ANIMAL PEOPLE'S DIRECTORY. See Yearbooks, Almanacs, Directories.

ANIMAL PRODUCTION. V. 1- Mar. 1959-. 0003-3561. Periodical. UK. English. bm. $135.00. Scottish Academic Press Limited, 33 Montgomery Street, Edinburgh EH7 5JX Scotland. **Tel** 031/556 2796. **Ind/Abst** Life Sci. Collect., Pestdoc, Ringdoc, Vetdoc, Excerpta Med., Biol. Abstr., Chem. Abstr., Nuci. Sci. Abstr., Bibliogr. Agric., Biol. Agric. Index, Sci. Cit. Index, Abr. Ed. **CODEN** ANIPA8. (cum index).

Veterinary Medicine, Animal Culture

Report of Proceedings-British Society of Animal Production.

ANIMAL PRODUCTION BULLETIN. No. 1-. Monographic Series. English. ir.

ANIMAL PROTECTION NEWS. -V. 1, No. 3 (Winter 1979). 0738-5838. Periodical. US. English. qt. American Humane Association, PO Box 1266, Childrens Division, Denver CO 80201. *American Humane Magazine*, 0149-5224.

ANIMAL REGULATION STUDIES CEASED. V. 1-3. 0378-4282. Periodical. English. qt. $47.75 US, 117.- Others. Elsevier Scientific Publishing Company, PO Box 211, Amsterdam The Netherlands. Ind/Abst Chem. Abstr. LC HV4701. DD 179.305. CODEN ARESDS.

ANIMAL REPRODUCTION SCIENCE. V. 1- May 1978-. 0378-4320. Periodical. English. ir. Journal Information Center, 52 Vanderbilt Avenue, New York NY 10017. Ind/Abst Life Sci. Collect., Excerpta Med., Chem. Abstr. NLM W1 AN228V. CODEN ANRSDV.

ANIMAL SCIENCE RESEARCH REPORT (BLACKSBURG, VA.). (ANIMAL SCIENCE RESEARCH REPORT). No. 1 (July 1981)-. US. English. an.

ANIMAL TECHNOLOGY : JOURNAL OF THE INSTITUTE OF ANIMAL TECHNICIANS. Vol. 34, No. 1 (May 1983)-. 0264-4754. Periodical. UK. English. sa. NLM W1. *Journal - Institute of Animal Technicians.*

ANIMAL WELFARE. Jan./Feb. 1976-. UK. English. 0.10. British Union for the Abolition of Vivisection, 47 Whitehall, London SW1 England. LC HV4905. DD 636.083. *A V Times*.

ANIMAL WELFARE. LIST OF LICENSED DEALERS. VFOAT List of Licensed Dealers. 0882-0457. US. English. an. U.S.D.A. Animal and Plant Health Inspection Services, Veterinary Services, Washington DC 20250.

ANIMAL WELFARE. LIST OF LICENSED EXHIBITORS. VFOAT List of Licensed Exhibitors. 0747-5128. US. English. an. USDA Animal and Plant Health Inspection Service, Veterinary Services, Washington DC 20250.

ANIMAL WELFARE. LIST OF REGISTERED EXHIBITORS. VFOAT List of Registered Exhibitors. US. English. an. USDA Animal and Plant Health Inspection Service, Veterinary Services, Washington DC 20250.

ANIMAL WELFARE. LIST OF REGISTERED RESEARCH FACILITIES. VFOAT List of Registered Research Facilities. 0747-5144. US. English. an. USDA Animal and Plant Health Inspection Service, Veterinary Services, Washington DC 20250.

ANIMALIA. V. 1- Jan./Mar. 1974-. Periodical. English. ir. World Federation for the Protection of Animals, Dreikonigstresse 37, Zurich CH-8002 Switzerland. LC HV4701. DD 636.083. *WFPA News*.

ANIMALS CANADA. See Pets.

ANIMAL'S DEFENDER. V. 7, No. 4- April 1963-. Periodical. UK. English. bm. $4.60. National Anti-Vivisection Society, 51 Harley Street, London W1N 1DD England. NLM W1 AN23A. *Animal's Defender and Anti-Vivisection News*.

ANIMALS FOR RESEARCH. 7th- July 1968-. 0547-8626. Periodical. US. English. $7.75. National Academy of Sciences, 2101 Constitution Avenue NW, Washington DC 20418. Tel (202)389-6692. NLM QY 26 A598. *Laboratory Animals. Part II. Animals for Research*, 0195-9506.

ANIMALS' VOICE. V. 1- Mar. 1960-. 0700-8392. CN. English. Ontario Humane Society, 696 Yonge Street, Toronto M4Y 2A7 Canada.

ANNAIRE OFFICIEL - ACADEMIE DE MEDECINE VETERINAIRE DU QUEBEC. See Yearbooks, Almanacs, Directories.

ANNALES DE RECHERCHE VETERINAIRES. (ANNALES DE RECHERCHES VETERINAIRES). VFOAT Annals of Veterinary Research. V. 1- 1970-. 0003-4193. Periodical. FR. French (English with summaries in the alternate language). qt. $77.16. Serv Publications INRA, Rte de St Cyr, F78000 Versailles France. Tel 30 21 74 22. Ind/Abst Life Sci. Collect., Pestdoc, Ringdoc, Vetdoc, Excerpta Med., Index Med., Biol. Abstr., Chem. Abstr., Bibliogr. Agric., Sci. Cit. Index, Abr. Ed. NLM W1 AN381. CODEN ARCVBP. bk rev. Circ 1,000. Scientific aspects in the field of veterinary and comparative medicine and related subjects. *Recherches Veterinaires*.

ANNOTATED BIBLIOGRAPHY (COMMONWEALTH BUREAU OF ANIMAL HEALTH). See Bibliographies.

ANNUAL FINANCIAL REPORT - TEXAS ANIMAL HEALTH COMMISSION. See Business - Public Finance.

ANNUAL REPORT - INDIAN VETERINARY RESEARCH INSTITUTE. (ANNUAL REPORT). Main/Corp Indian Veterinary Research Institute. 1947/48-. 0304-7067. English. ir. LC SF779.M78. DD 636.08905.

ANNUAL REPORT - INSTITUTE OF ANIMAL AND FOOD SCIENCES (AUSTRALIA). Main/Corp Institute of Animal and Food Sciences (Australia). 1979/80-. 0158-7390. AT. English. an. $2.22. Commonwealth Scientific and Industrial Research Organization, PO Box 89/314, Albert Street, East Melbourne Victoria 3002 Australia.

ANNUAL REPORT - MINNESOTA. BOARD OF ANIMAL HEALTH. Main/Corp Minnesota. Board of Animal Health. US. English. an. Board of Animal Health, LL 70 Metro Square Building, 7th & Roberts Streets, St Paul MN 55101. LC SF624.M6. DD 353.97760082336. *Annual Report*.

ANNUAL REPORT - NATIONAL HYDATIDS COUNCIL. (ANNUAL REPORT YEAR ENDED 31 MARCH . . .). Main/Corp National Hydatids Council (N.Z.). Began with 16th (1975/76). 0110-9901. NZ. English. an. Ministry of Agriculture and Fisheries, Dominion Farmers' Institute Building, PO Box 2298 Featherston Street, Wellington New Zealand. LC SF810.H8. DD 636.70894554. NLM W1 NA485PB.

ANNUAL REPORT - NATIONAL INSTITUTE OF HEALTH (U.S.). DIVISION OF RESEARCH SERVICES. (ANNUAL REPORT). Main/Corp National Institutes of Health (U.S.). Division of Research Services. Fiscal Year 1977-. 0735-1992. US. English. an. National Institutes of Health, Division of Research Services, 9000 Rockville Pike, Bethesda MD 20205. NLM W2 A N212A.

ANNUAL REPORT OF THE ANIMAL HEALTH TRUST. Main/Corp Animal Health Trust. Began with: 1977/78. 0142-6591. UK. English. an. 2.25. Animal Health Trust, Lauwades Hall, Kennett Newmarket CB8 7PN Suffolk England. Tel Newmarket 751030. NLM W1 AN228W. Animal Health Trust Annual Report 1985. *Animal Health*.

ANNUAL REPORT OF THE DEPARTMENT OF ANIMAL HUSBANDRY AND VETERINARY SERVICES IN KARNATAKA, INDO-DANISH PROJECT HESSARGHATTA AND BANGALORE DAIRY, BANGALORE. Main/Corp Karnataka, India. Dept. of Animal Husbandry and Veterinary Services. II. English. ir. Department of Animal Husbandry & Veterinary Services, Krishi Bhavan, New Delhi India. LC SF15.I42. DD 354.5487008233.

ANNUAL REPORT OF THE DEPARTMENT OF VETERINARY SERVICES AND ANIMAL INDUSTRY (MALAWI). Main/Corp Malawi. Dept. of Veterinary Services and Animal Industry. English. ir. LC SF719.M3.

ANNUAL REPORT - UNITED STATES. ANIMAL HEALTH SCIENCE RESEARCH ADVISORY BOARD. Main/Corp United States. Animal Health Science Research Advisory Board. 0275-5009. US. English. an. US Department of Agriculture, Science and Education Administration, Washington DC 20250. LC SF600. DD 636.089072073.

ANNUAL SCIENTIFIC REPORT OF THE I.V.R.I. CAMPUS, BANGALORE, FOR THE YEAR . . . . Main/Corp I.V.R.I. Campus, Bangalore. VAT Annual Scientific Report of the Indian Veterinary Research Institute Campus, Bangalore, for the Year . . . . English. an.

ANNUAL SHOW - VANCOUVER ISLAND CAGE BIRD SOCIETY. Main/Corp Vancouver Island Cage Bird Society. Began with 1952 issue. 0317-0160. Periodical. CN. English. an. Vancouver Island Cage Bird Society, c/o 3631 Cedar Hill Road, Victoria British Columbia V8P 3Z3 Canada. DD 636.68606271134.

ANNUARIO STATISTICO DELLA ZOOTECNICA, PESCA E CACCIA. See Statistics.

ANUARIO BRASILEIRO DE MEDICINA VETERINARIA. See Yearbooks, Almanacs, Directories.

AOMORI-KEN CHIKUSAN SHIKENJO HOKOKU. VFOAT Bulletin of the Aomori Zootechnical Experiment Station. Periodical. JA. Japanese (with summaries in English). ir. Aomori-Ken Chikusan Shikenjo, 51 Oaza Noheji Aza Biwano Noheji-Machi Kamikita-Gun, Aomori-Ken 039-31 Japan. LC SF55.J3.

APHIS 82. Main/Corp United States. Animal and Plant Health Inspection Service. US. English. US Department of Agriculture/ Animal & Plant Health Inspection Service, Hyattsville MD 20782. LC SB981. DD 353.008233.

A.P.H.S. 91. (APHS 91). Main/Corp United States. Animal and Plant Health Service. VAT Animal and Plant Health Service Ninety-One. 0094-2618. US. English. US Department of Agriculture, Animal & Plant Health Inspection Service, Hyattsville MD 20782. LC S21. DD 630. *ARS 91*.

APICULTURAL ABSTRACTS. See Indexes/Abstracts.

AQUARAMA. See Pets.

AQUATIC MAMMALS. See Zoology-Vertebrate and Invertebrate.

ARCHIV FUR EXPERIMENTELLE VETERIARMEDIZIN. See Genealogy and Heraldry - Archives.

ARCHIV FUR TIERARZTLICHE FORTBILDUNG. See Genealogy and Heraldry - Archives.

ARCHIV FUR TIERERNAHRUNG. See Genealogy and Heraldry - Archives.

ARCHIVES DE L'INSTITUTE RAZI. See Genealogy and Heraldry - Archives.

ARCHIVIO VETERINARIO ITALIANO. See Genealogy and Heraldry - Archives.

ARCHIVOS DE MEDICINA VETERINARIA. See Genealogy and Heraldry - Archives.

ARCHIVOS DE ZOOTECNIA. See Genealogy and Heraldry - Archives.

THE ARIZONA VETERINARIAN. Periodical. US. English. bm. Arizona Veterinary Medical Association, 6040 North 7th Street, Phoenix AZ 85012. Tel (602)274-4657.

ARK. No.54- 1978-. Periodical. UK. English. ty. 3. Catholic Study Circle Animal Welfare, 39 Onslow Gardens So, Woodford London E18Ind England. Tel (01)9890478. Ed Kevin Daley. bk rev. adv acc. Circ 2,000. To promote concern and respect for animals by prayer, example and propaganda through the Ark magazine. We embrace the christian condition of care for animals. *Journal From the Royal College of Art*.

ARKANSAS ANIMAL MORBIDITY REPORT. 1956-. 0093-142X. Periodical. US. English. qt. Free. Arkansas Department of Health, 4815 West Markham, Little Rock AR 72205. Tel (501)661-2264. Ed Thomas D McChesney. Ind/Abst Bibliogr. Agric. Circ 500. Statistical information on diseases in animals in Arkansas; updated veterinary medical narratives.

ARKANSAS HEALTH MANPOWER STATISTICS. VETERINARIANS. VFOAT Veterinarians. Began with 1978. 0196-7924. US. English. an. Division of Health Statistics, Department of Health, 4815 West Markham Street, Little Rock AR 72201. LC SF756.475.A8. DD 331.125163608909767. NLM W2 AA8 D63AH. *Arkansas Health Manpower Statistics*, 0197-6478.

ARQUIVOS DO INSTITUTO BIOLOGICO. Vol. 9 (1938)-. 0020-3653. Periodical. BL. Portuguese (summaries and some articles in English). qt. $25.00. Do Instituto Biologico, Caixa Postal 7119, 01000 Sao Paulo Brazil. Tel 011 572-9822. Ed Jose Reis July. Ind/Abst Chem. Abstr. NLM W1 AR921KI. CODEN AIBOA3. (cum index). Circ 2,000. Research on plant and animal parasitology and pathology. *Archivos Do Instituto Biologico*.

Veterinary Medicine, Animal Culture

ARSRAPPORT FRA STATENS HUSDYRBRUGSFORSG. Main/Corp Statens Husdyrbrugsforsg. (1974-). Periodical. Danish. ir.

THE AUBURN VETERINARIAN. V. 1- 1945-. Periodical. US. English. ir. $10.00 Domestic, $20.00 Foreign. Auburn Veterinarian, School of Veterinary Medicine, Auburn AL 36849. Tel (205)826-4546. Ed Susan Holland & Laurel Gardiner. bk rev. adv acc. Circ 900. Articles pertaining to veterinary medical problems of the southeast USA region.

AUDIT REPORT, LIVESTOCK AND HORSE SHOW PREMIUMS AND AWARDS, AND CONSTRUCTION. COUNTY, DISTRICT AND STATE, STATE LIVESTOCK SHOW ASSETS. (AUDIT REPORT, LIVESTOCK AND HORSE SHOW PREMIUMS AND AWARDS, AND CONSTRUCTION - COUNTY, DISTRICT AND STATE, STATE LIVESTOCK SHOW ASSETS). Main/Corp Arkansas. General Assembly. Division of Legislative Audit. 0149-7758. US. English. be. LC SF117.65.A8. DD 338.13.

AUSTRALIAN ADVANCES IN VETERINARY SCIENCE. VFOAT Proceedings of the Annual Conference of the Australian Veterinary Association. 1978-. 0155-5995. AT. English. an. $23.76. Australian Veterinary Association Ltd, 134-136 Hampden Road, Artarmon NSW 2064 Australia. Tel 411 2733. Ind/Abst Chem. Abstr. CODEN AAVSDS.

AUSTRALIAN VETERINARY JOURNAL. V. 3- 1927-. 0005-0423. Periodical. AT. English. mo. 140.00. Australian Veterinary Journal, 272 Brunswick Road, Brunswick Australia 3056. Tel (03)387-2982. Ed K L Hughes. Ind/Abst Life Sci. Collect., Pestdoc, Ringdoc, Vetdoc, Excerpta Med., Biol. Abstr., Chem. Abstr., Nuci. Sci. Abstr., Index Med., Bibliogr. Agric., Sci. Cit. Index, Abr. Ed. NLM W1 AU698. CODEN AUVJA2. bk rev. adv acc. Circ 4,000. (ctrl). Clinical findings and research on health of agricultural and companion animals and wildlife. *Journal of the Australian Veterinary Association.*

AUSTRALIAN VETERINARY PRACTITIONER. 0310-138X. Periodical. AT. English. qt. 40.00 Foreign. PO Box 243, Bondi New South Wales 2026 Australia. Tel (02)309-1990. Ed R Atwell. Ind/Abst Life Sci. Collect., Sci. Cit. Index, Abr. Ed. bk rev acc. Circ 1,000. Applicable to practising small animal veterinarians.

THE AV MAGAZINE. VAT Anti-Vivisection Magazine. V. 85- Jan. 1977-. 0274-7774. Periodical. US. English. mo. $10.00. American Anti-Vivisection Society, 801 Old York Road/ Noble Park, Jenkintown PA 19046. Tel (215)887-0816. Ed William A Cave. NLM W1 A164. bk rev. Circ 11,000. (ctrl). Intended to abolish painful experiments on animals through appropriate legislation: concerns animals' rights and allied subjects.

AVIAN DISEASES. V. 1- May 1957-. 0005-2086. Periodical. US. English. qt. $30.00. American Association of Avian Pathologists, University of Pennsylvania, New Bolton Center, Philadelphia PA 19348-1692. Tel (215)444-5800. Ed D P Anderson. Ind/Abst Life Sci. Collect., Can. Environ., Pestdoc, Ringdoc, Vetdoc, Index Med., Biol. Abstr., Chem. Abstr., Bibliogr. Agric. NLM W1 AV401. CODEN AVDIAI. adv acc. Circ 1,750.

AVIAN PATHOLOGY. (AVIAN PATHOLOGY : JOURNAL OF THE W.V.P.A). Began with: Vol. 1, No. 1 (1972) 0307-9457. Periodical. UK. English (articles in French or German). qt. $40.00. Worlds Veterinary Poultry Association, Houghton Poultry Research Station, Houghton PE 17 2DA England. Tel 0480 64101. Ed P M Biggs. Ind/Abst Life Sci. Collect., Pestdoc, Ringdoc, Vetdoc, Biol. Abstr., Bibliogr. Agric., Sci. Cit. Index, Abr. Ed. NLM W1 AV414. CODEN AVPADN. bk rev. adv acc. Circ 700. Concerned with diseases of domestic poultry and other birds, original papers on all disciplines associated with the study of disease including bacteriology, epizootiology, genetics, immunology, toxicology, and virology.

BEE FARMING STATISTICS, TASMANIA. See Statistics.

BEITRAGE ZUR TROPISCHEN LANDWIRTSCHAFT UND VETERINARMEDIZIN. V. 11- 1973-. 0301-567X. Periodical. SZ. German (added table of contents and summaries in English, French, Russian and Spanish). qt. Kunst & Wissen Erich Bieber, Dufourstrasse 51, CH-8008 Zurich Switzerland. Tel (01)694420. Ind/Abst Life Sci. Collect., Excerpta Med., Index Med., GeoRef, Chem. Abstr., Bibliogr. Agric., Bibliogr. Index Geol. NLM W1 BE461L. CODEN BTLVBR. *Beitrage zur Tropischen und Subtropischen Landwirtschaft und Tropenveterinarmedizin, 0005-8203.*

BENCHMARK PAPERS IN ANIMAL BEHAVIOR. V. 1- 1974-. 0093-4720. Periodical. US. text mostly in English. ir. Academic Press, 4805 Sand Lake Road, Orlando FL 32819. NLM W1 BE514.

BENCHMARK PAPERS IN BEHAVIOR. 13-. 0277-0032. Monographic Series. US. English. ir. Academic Press, 4805 Sand Lake Road, Orlando FL 32819. Ed M W Schein and S W Porges. LC UNC. DD 591.51. NLM W1 BE514B. *Benchmark Papers in Animal Behavior, 0093-4720.*

BERLINER UND MUNCHENER TIERARZTLICHE WOCHENSCHRIFT. Vol. 1- 1885-. 0005-9366. Periodical. German. mo. $133.20. Paul Parey Scientific Publishing, 35 West 38th Street 3 West, New York NY 10018. Tel (212)730-0518. Ed J Boch. bk rev adv acc. Circ 800. The oldest veterinary medical journal for the practitioner. *Munchener Tierarztliche Wochenschrift.*

BIENNIAL REPORT OF EXAMINING AND LICENSING BOARDS - MINNESOTA. VETERINARY MEDICINE BOARD. Main/Corp Minnesota. Veterinary Medicine Board. US. English. be. 717 Delaware Street SE, Minneapolis MN 55414. LC SF624.M6. DD 353.9776008233.

BIENNIAL SYMPOSIUM ON ANIMAL REPRODUCTION; PROCEEDINGS. Main/Conf Symposium on Animal Reproduction. 1st- 1953-. 0570-1244. US. English. ir. $10.00. American Society of Animal Science, 309 West Clark Street, Champaign IL 61820. Tel (217)356-3182.

BILTEN DOKUMENTACIJE. SERIJA A2 : STOCNA PROIZVODNJA I VETERINARSTVO. VFOAT Bulletin of Documentation. Series A2 : Stockbreeding and Veterinary Medicine. V. 28, No. 1- Jan. 1977-. 0006-2707. Periodical. Serbo-Croatian -R. ir. *Bilten Dokumentacije: Biljna Proizvodnja Istocarstvo. Bulletin of Documentation: Plant Production, Stockbreeding.*

BIOLOGIZACE A CHEMIZACE ZIVOCISNE VYROBY-VETERINARIA. (BIOLOGIZACE A CHEMIZACE ZIVOCISNE VYROBY - VETERINARIA). VFOAT Biological and Chemical Factors in Animal Production, Veterinaria. Vol. 14- 1978-. 0139-8571. Periodical. CS. Czech (Slovak). ir. $8.00. Artia, Smecky 30, Prague 1 Czechoslovakia. Ind/Abst Life Sci. Collect., Chem. Abstr., Curr. Contents, Bibliogr. Agric. NLM W1 BI836. CODEN BCZVDE. *Veterinaria Spofa, Biologizace A Chemizace Vyzivy Zvirat.*

BIULLETEN. Vol. 1-. 0366-4899. Monographic Series. UR. Russian. Ind/Abst Chem. Abstr. NLM W1 BI99LR. CODEN BVEVA5.

BOLETIM DE DEFESA SANITARIA ANIMAL. Yearly V. 8, No. 1-41974. Periodical. Portuguese. ir.

BOLETIM DE INDUSTRIA ANIMAL. Began with Nova Ser., V. 4, N. 1 (Jan. 1941). 0067-9615. Periodical. Portuguese (some summaries in English). sa. 155. Instituto de Zootecnia, Caixa Postal 60 Nova Odessa, Sao Paulo Brazil. Tel (0194)661410. Ed Nelson Morato Ferraz Meirelles. Ind/Abst Bibliogr. Agric. NLM W1 BO164P. Circ 2,400. Concerning upon animal science and animal production of ruminants and no ruminants and forage crops. *Revista de Industria Animal.*

THE BOVINE PRACTITIONER. No. 1- Jan. 1967-. 0524-1685. US. English. an. $20.00. Dr Eric I Williams, 1226 North Lincoln, Stillwater OK 74074. Tel (405)624-7472. Ed Eric I Williams. Ind/Abst Life Sci. Collect., Biol. Abstr. CODEN BOVPBO. bk rev adv acc. Circ 8,000. (ctrl). A journal for veterinarians and others interested in cattle diseases and presentation.

BRITISH CATTLE VETERINARY ASSOCIATION PROCEEDINGS FOR. UK. English. an.

BRITISH HOMING WORLD. V. 1- (No.). Periodical. UK. English. wk. 21.84. British Homing World, 26 High Street, Welshpool Powys SY21 7JP Wales United Kingdom. Tel 0938 2360. Ed J R Thomas. Articles dealing with management and conditioning of pigeons for racing. Up-to-date news and race results. particulars of winning birds regularly featured.

BRITISH VETERINARY JOURNAL. (THE BRITISH VETERINARY JOURNAL). V. 105- 1949-. 0007-1935. Periodical. UK. English. bm. 49.00. Williams and Wilkins, 428 Preston Street, Baltimore MD 21202. Tel (01)630-7881. Ed J M Payne. Ind/Abst Life Sci. Collect., Pestdoc, Ringdoc, Vetdoc, Excerpta Med., CIS Abstr., Bibliogr. Agric., Sel. Water Resour. Abstr., Index Med., Biol. Abstr., Chem. Abstr., Nuci. Sci. Abstr. NLM W1 BR771. CODEN BVJOA9. bk rev. adv acc. Circ 1,100. Scientific papers of world wide interest in the field of veterinary surgery and medicine series of reviews and specialties to meet veterinary development needs. *Veterinary Journal.*

BRUCELLOSIS BULLETIN : COOPERATIVE STATE-FEDERAL BRUCELLOSIS ERADICATION PROGRAM. See Agriculture.

BULETINUL INSTITUTULUI AGRONOMIC CLUJ-NAPOCA. SERIA ZOOTEHNIE SI MEDICINA VETERINARA. Main/Corp Institutul Agronomic Dr. Petru Groza. VFOAT Seria Zootehnie Si Medicina Veterinara. V. 32- 1978-. RM. Romanian (English). an. Institutl Agronomic, Str Manastur Nr 3, Cluj-Naspoca Romania. Ind/Abst Chem. Abstr. CODEN BIAVDX. *Buletinul Institutului Agronomic Cluj-Napoca.*

BULLETIN - AMERICAN ANIMAL HOSPITAL ASSOCIATION. Main/Corp American Animal Hospital Association. VFOAT Bulletin of the American Animal Hospital Association. Periodical. US. English. 3612 East Jefferson Boulevard, South Bend IN 46615.

BULLETIN ANALYTIQUE D'ENTOMOLOGIE MEDICALE ET VETERINAIRE. Main/Corp O.R.S.T.O.M. V. 1- 1953/54-. 0007-4098. Periodical. French.

BULLETIN DE LA SOCIETE DES SCIENCES VETERINAIRES ET DE MEDECINE COMPAREE DE LYON CEASED. Began with V. 70, No.1- 1968-. Ceased in 1981?. 0301-1194. FR. French. ir. Ind/Abst Bibliogr. Agric. NLM W1 BU515T. *Bulletin de la Societe des Sciences Veterinaires de Lyon.*

BULLETIN DE L'ACADEMIE VETERINAIRE DE FRANCE. Vol. 81- 1928-. 0001-4192. Periodical. FR. French. qt. Academie Veterinaire de France, 60 Boulevard Latour-Maubourg, 75007 Paris France. Ind/Abst Life Sci. Collect., Pestdoc, Ringdoc, Vetdoc, Chem. Abstr., Bibliogr. Agric., Sci. Cit. Index, Abr. Ed. NLM W1 BU527. CODEN BAVFAV. *Bulletin - Societe Centrale de Medecine Veterinaire.*

BULLETIN DES G.T.V. (BULLETIN DES G.T.V. DOSSIERS TECHNIQUES VETERINAIRES). Main/Corp Groupement Techniques Veterinaires. VFOAT Dossiers Techniques Veterinaires. Began in 1973?. 0399-2519. Periodical. French. bm. Section Nationale des Groupements Veterinaires Practiciens, de Syndicat National des Veterinaires Francais, 10 Place Leon-Blum, 75001 Paris France. Ind/Abst Chem. Abstr., Bibliogr. Agric. CODEN BGTVDC.

BULLETIN - OFFICE INTERNATIONAL DES EPIZOOTIES (PARIS). Main/Corp International Office of Epizottics, Paris. Began with May/June 1931 issue. 0300-9823. Periodical. English (French or Spanish). mo. $66.00. Office International des Epizooties, 12 rue de Prony, Paris 75017 France. Tel (1)227 65 76. Ed E Meissonnier. Ind/Abst Excerpta Med., Biol. Abstr., Bibliogr. Agric. LC SF781. DD 636.08969. NLM W1 BU901D. CODEN OTEBA6. bk rev. adv acc. Circ 1,000. (ctrl). Animal diseases, animal epidemiology, veterinary services, reports, outbreaks, contagious diseases of animals, epizootics, etc. *Bulletin Mensuel - Office International des Epizooties.*

BULLETIN TECHNIQUE - CENTRE DE RECHERCHES ZOOTECHNIQUES ET VETERINAIRES DE THEIX. (BULLETIN TECHNIQUE - CENTRE DE RECHERCHES ZOOTECHNIQUES DE THEIX). Main/Corp Centre de Recherches Zootechniques et Veterinaires de Theix. 0395-7519. Periodical. French. qt. $9.98. Centre Recherche de Theix, 63110 Beaumont France. Ind/Abst Bibliogr. Agric.

BULLETIN - WISCONSIN VETERINARY MEDICAL ASSOCIATION. Main/Corp Wisconsin Veterinary Medical Association. 0512-1345. US. English. mo. Wisconsin Veterinary Medical

Veterinary Medicine, Animal Culture

Association, 540 West Washington Avenue, Madison WI 53703.

CADASTRO DAS INSTITUICOES DE PESQUISA, PESQUISADORES E SUAS ATIVIDADES NO RIO GRANDE DO SUL : I. MEDICINA VETERINARIA. 1975-. Portuguese. ir. Caixa Postal 1646 90.000, Porto Alegre Brazil. LC SF611.

LES CAHIERS BLEUS VETERINAIRES. 1-. 0526-765X. Monographic Series. French. ir. Ind/Abst Bibliogr. Agric.

THE CALIFORNIA VETERINARIAN. Began in Sept. 1947. 0008-1612. Periodical. US. English. bm. $30.00. California Veterinatian Medical Association, 1024 Country Club Drive, Moraga CA 94556. Tel (415)376-2020. Ed Vivian Antonali. Ind/Abst Pestdoc, Ringdoc, Vetdoc, Bibliogr. Agric. NLM W1 CA443F. adv acc. Circ 4,500. Veterinary medicine articles, advertising, classifieds, association news, calendar.

CANADA CHINCHILLA. March 1983-. 0823-2504. Periodical. CN. English (includes some text in French). mo. National Chinchilla Breeders of Canada, PO Box 64, Carleton Place Ontario K7C 3P3 Canada. DD 636.93234. *Monthly Bulletin, 0027-8963.*

CANADIAN JOURNAL OF ANIMAL SCIENCE. V. 37. June 1957-. 0008-3984. Periodical. CN. English (some text and summaries in French). qt. 56.00. Agricultural Institute of Canada, Burnside Building 151/Slater Street 907, Ottawa Ontario K1P 5H4 Canada. Tel (613)232-9459. Ed J Buchanan-Smith. Ind/Abst Life Sci. Collect., Pestdoc, Ringdoc, Vetdoc, Energy Inf. Abstr., Environ. Abstr., Sel. Water Resour. Abstr., Nucl. Sci. Abstr., Biol. Abstr., Chem. Abstr., Bibliogr. Agric., Biol. Agric. Index, Sci. Cit. Index, Abr. Ed., Pollut. Abstr. Indexes. CODEN CNJNAT. Circ 1,600. Contains information on breeding and genetics; meat, physiology, ruminant; non-ruminant. *Canadian Journal of Agricultural Science, 0366-6557.*

CANADIAN JOURNAL OF COMPARATIVE MEDICINE. VFOAT Revue Canadienne de Medecine Comparee. V. 32, No. 2- April 1968-. 0008-4050. Periodical. CN. English (includes some text in French). qt. Canadian Journal of Comparative Medicine, 339 Booth Street, Ottawa Ontario K1R 7K1 Canada. Tel (613)236-1162. Ind/Abst Life Sci. Collect., Can. Environ., Pestdoc, Ringdoc, Vetdoc, Excerpta Med., Energy Inf. Abstr., Environ. Abstr., Biol. Abstr., Chem. Abstr., Nutr. Abstr. Rev., Nucl. Sci. Abstr., Bibliogr. Agric., Index Med., Sci. Cit. Index, Abr. Ed. NLM W1 CA586. CODEN CJCMAV. *Canadian Journal of Comparative Medicine and Veterinary Science.*

CANADIAN SOCIETY OF ANIMAL SCIENCE. PROCEEDINGS OF THE ANNUAL MEETING OF THE GENERAL SOCIETY AND THE WESTERN BRANCH. (PROCEEDINGS OF THE ANNUAL MEETING OF THE GENERAL SOCIETY AND THE . . . BRANCH). 21st- 1971-. 0318-1839. CN. English. an. Canadian Society of Animal Science, Suite 907/151 Slater Street, Ottawa Ontario K1P 5H4 Canada. *Proceedings of the Annual Meeting of the General Society and the . . . Branch, 0068-9696.*

CANADIAN VET SUPPLIES. VFOAT Vet Supplies. Vol. 1, No. 1 (Summer 1984)-. 0825-754X. Periodical. CN. English. qt. Free to Veterinarian and Animal Health Technicians in Canada, $10.00 Others. SELC Publishing Inc, 1 Phillipsburg Street, PO Box 1320, Bedford Quebec J0J 1A0 Canada. Tel (514)248-3356. Ed Anne-Lise Brien. DD 636.089028. (ctrl).

CANADIAN VETERINARY JOURNAL. (THE CANADIAN VETERINARY JOURNAL). VFOAT Revue Veterinaire Canadienne. V. 1- Jan. 1960-. 0008-5286. Periodical. CN. includes some text in French. mo. $35. US. 339 Booth Street, Ottawa Ontario K1R 7K1 Canada. Tel (613)236-1162. Ed W T Nagge. Ind/Abst Life Sci. Collect., Pestdoc, Ringdoc, Vetdoc, Nucl. Sci. Abstr., Biol. Abstr., Chem. Abstr., Index Med., Sci. Cit. Index, Abr. Ed. NLM W1 CA665S. CODEN CNVJA9. bk rev. adv acc. Circ 4,500. (ctrl). Contains case reports, papers, letters to the editors.

CANADIAN WOOL GROWER. V. 44, No. 1- Fall 1973-. 0319-7387. Periodical. CN. English. sa. 2.50. Canadian Co-Op Wool Growers, PO Box 130/Carleton Place Ontario K7C 3P3 Canada. Tel (613)275-2714. Ed E Bjergso. adv acc. Circ 14,000.

Canadian wool, sheep, and sheep supplies. *Canadian Wool Grower and Sheep Breeder, 0045-5598.*

CANINE PRACTICE. V. 1- May/June 1974-. 0094-4904. Periodical. US. English. bm. $30.00. Veterinary Practice Publishing Company, PO Box 4457, Santa Barbara CA 93103. Tel (805)965-1028. Ed John B Carricaburu. Ind/Abst Life Sci. Collect. NLM W1 CA704P. CODEN CPCEAF. bk rev. adv acc. Circ 4,500. A journal of canine medical and surgical problems, procedures, and diagnostic dilemnas in day-to-day practitioner experience.

CARING FOR ANIMALS (OTTAWA, ONT.). (CARING FOR ANIMALS). Vol. 1, No. 1 (Spring 1984)-. 0825-1711. Periodical. CN. English. sa. Free. Canadian Federation of Humane Societies, 101 Champagne Avenue South, Ottawa Ontario K1S 4P3 Canada. Tel (613)728-2516. Ed Stephanie Brown. DD 636.0885. bk rev. Circ 2,500. (ctrl). News, philosophy, editorial, information on alternatives to live animals used in research, teaching, testing. Laboratory animal welfare oriented. Directed to animal care and use committees.

CDC VETERINARY PUBLIC HEALTH NOTES. VAT Center for Disease Control Veterinary Public Health Notes. - 4th Quarter 1981. 0360-7836. Periodical. US. English. ir. Center for Disease Control, 1600 Clifton Road, Clifton GA 30333. Ind/Abst Am. Stat. Index. LC SF601. *CDC Veterinary Public Health Notes, 0360-7836.*

CEYLON VETERINARY JOURNAL. 0009-0891. CE. English. an. $10.00. Ceylon Veterinary Association, University of Sri Lanka, Peradiniya Ceylon. Tel Kandy 88311. Ed S T Fernando. adv acc. Circ 500. Original articles, short communications, and reviews pertaining to research in veterinary medicine and animal husbandry.

CHEIRON. V. 1- Oct. 1972-. 0379-542X. Periodical. II. English. bm. $15.00. Prints India, 11 Darya Ganj, New Delhi 110002 India. Ind/Abst Life Sci. Collect., Chem. Abstr., Bibliogr. Agric. NLM W1 CH154E. CODEN CHRNAR.

CHIBA-KEN SANGYO SHIKENJO TOKUBETSU HOKOKU. No. 1-. JA. Japanese. ir. Chiba-Ken Sangyo Shikenjo, 1055 Aburai, Togane-Shi 283, Togane Japan. LC SF553. J3.

CHIKUSAMBUTSU SEISANHI CHOSA HOKOKU. Main/Corp Japan. Norinsho. Norin Keizaikyoku. Tokei Johobu. 1981-. JA. Japanese. ir. Norin Tokei Kyokai, c/o Otori Building, 11-Ban 14-Go Meguro, 2-chome Meguro-ku, Tokyo 153 Japan. LC SF15.J3. *Chikusambutsu Seisanhi Chosa Hokoku.*

CHIKUSAN NO KENKYU. VFOAT Animal Husbandry. V. 1- Jan. 1947-. Periodical. JA. Japanese. mo. 11 Domestic, 165 Foreign. Yokendo, 5-30-15 Hongo, Bunkyo-ku Tokyo Japan. Tel 814-0911. Ed Akira Suzuki. Ind/Abst Chem. Abstr., Bibliogr. Agric. CODEN CKNKAJ. bk rev. adv acc. Circ 20,000. Articles covering scientific technologies of animal breeding, nutrition, feeds, management, and veterinary concerning dairy, beef, pork, poultry, sheep and laboratory animals.

CHIRURGIA VETERINARIA. REFERATE. ABSTRACTS. REVUES. See Indexes/Abstracts.

CHUNG-KUO HSU MU HSUEH HUI HUI CHIH. VFOAT Journal of the Chinese Society of Animal Science. V.4,No.3-4-. summaries in English. ir.

CHUNG-KUO SHOU I TSA CHIH. VFOAT Chinese Journal of Veterinary Medicine. Periodical. CH. Chinese. mo. 0.30. Chung-Kuo Kuo Chi Shu Tien, PO Box 2820, Pei-Ching China. LC SF604. DD 636.08905.

CIENCIAS VETERINARIAS (HEREDIA, COSTA RICA). (CIENCIAS VETERINARIAS). V. 1, No. 1 (Sept.-Dec. 1979)-. 0250-5649. Periodical. Spanish. ir. Ind/Abst Bibliogr. Agric. NLM W1 CI266F.

CLINICA VETERINARIA; RASSEGNA DI POLIZIA SANITARIA E DI IGIENE. Began publication in 1878. 0009-9082. Periodical. IT. Italian. mo. $11.88. Instituto Sierotera Pico, Milanese S Belfanti, Via Darwin, Milan Italy. Ind/Abst Chem. Abstr., Bibliogr. Agric., Pestdoc, Ringdoc, Vetdoc, Excerpta Med. NLM W1 CL61. CODEN CLVEAE.

CO-OPERATIVE STATE-FEDERAL BRUCELLOSIS ERADICATION PROGRAM. (COOPERATIVE STATE-FEDERAL BRUCELLOSIS ERADICATION PROGRAM). Main/Corp United States. Animal and Plant Health Inspection Service. Veterinary Services. 1971/72-. 0503-5031. US. English. US Department of Agriculture, Animal and Plant Health Inspection Service, Federal Building, Hyattsville MD 20782. LC SF809.B8. DD 636.208945650973. *Cooperative State-Federal Brucellosis Eradication Program.*

COMMUNITY ANIMAL CONTROL. V. 1, No. 1 (March/April 1982). 0278-2863. Periodical. US. English. bm. $15.00. Katherine B Morgan, PO Box 43488, Tucson AZ 85733. Tel (602)881-1220. Ed Katherine B Morgan. LC HV4764. DD 363.78. bk rev. adv acc. Circ 7,500. (ctrl).

COMPARATIVE ANIMAL NUTRITION. V. 1- 1976-. 0304-5374. Monographic Series. SZ. English. ir. S Karger, PO Box, CH-4009 Basel Switzerland. Tel 061-39 08 80. Ed M Rechcigl Jr. Ind/Abst Chem. Abstr., Bibliogr. Agric. NLM W1 CO434N. CODEN CANUDG. Each issue contains an index to its own contents - no vol index - loose. This series represents a unique effort to present the study of nutrition within the context of the entire animal kingdom from a comparative point of view.

THE COMPENDIUM ON CONTINUING EDUCATION FOR THE PRACTICING VETERINARIAN. Began with: V. 1, No. 8 (Aug. 1979). 0193-1903. Periodical. US. English. mo. $41.00. Veterinary Learning Systems, 50 Hightstown Road, Princeton NJ 08550. Tel (609)799-5700. DD 636. Circ 21,000. *Compendium on Continuing Education for the Small Animal Practitioner, 0164-5455.*

COMPENDIUM PHARMACO-THERAPEUTIQUE VETERINAIRE. VFOAT CDMV Compendium. 1st Ed. (1983)-. 0822-868X. CN. French. an. Compendium Pharmaco-Therapeutique Veterinaire, CP 608, Saint-Hyacinthe Quebec J2S 6H5 Canada. DD 636.0895105.

COMPILATION OF LAW RELATING TO THE PRACTICE OF VETERINARY MEDICINE AND SURGERY. (COMPILATION OF LAWS RELATING TO THE PRACTICE OF VETERINARY MEDICINE AND SURGERY, WITH RULES AND REGULATIONS, GENERAL PROVISIONS OF THE BUSINESS AND PROFESSIONS CODE, INCLUDING THE CONSUMER AFFAIRS ACT, AND EXCERPTS FROM THE GOVERNMENT CODE - (CALIFORNIA)). 0362-5532. US. English. Consumer Affairs Building, 1020 N Street, Sacramento CA 95814. LC KFC547.V3. DD 344.794049.

THE COMPREHENSIVE DESK REFERENCE OF VETERINARY PHARMACEUTICALS & BIOLOGICALS. VFOAT Veterinary Pharmaceuticals & Biologicals. VAT Comprehensive Desk Reference of Veterinary Pharmaceuticals and Biologicals. 1976/77. 0145-9708. Periodical. US. English. sa. $37.50. Veterinary Medicine Publishing Company, PO Box 13265, Edwardsville KS 66113. Ed R A Le Clair. NLM SF 917. *Complete Desk Reference of Veterinary Pharmaceuticals & Biologicals.*

CONTEMPORARY ISSUES IN SMALL ANIMAL PRACTICE. Vol. 1-. Monographic Series. US. English. Churchill Livingston, 1560 Broadway, New York NY 10036. NLM W1.

COOPERATIVE STATE-FEDERAL HOG CHOLERA ERADICATION PROGRAM. Main/Corp United States. Animal and Plant Health Inspection Service. 0503-504X. US. English. LC SF973. DD 636.408945140973. *Cooperative State-Federal Hog Cholera Eradication Program.*

COOPERATIVE STATE-FEDERAL TUBERCULOSIS ERADICATION PROGRAM. Main/Corp United States. Animal and Plant Health Inspection Service. Veterinary Services. 0498-2452. US. English. LC SF808. DD 636.08945420973. *Cooperative State-Federal Tuberculosis Eradication Program.*

THE CORNELL VETERINARIAN. V. 1- June 1911-. 0010-8901. Periodical. US. English. qt. 18.00 US and Canada, 22.00 Others. Cornell Veterinarian, New York State Veterinarian College, Ithaca NY 14853. Tel (607)256-5454. Ed Lennart Krook. Ind/Abst Life Sci. Collect., Pestdoc, Ringdoc, Vetdoc, Excerpta Med., Coal Abstr., Index Med., Biol. Abstr., Chem. Abstr., Biol. Agric. Index, Sci. Cit. Index, Abr. Ed. NLM W1 CO881. CODEN COVEAZ. bk rev. adv acc. Circ 1,200. (ctrl). Current veterinary medicine research and reports.

CORNELL VETERINARIAN. SUPPLEMENT. Began publication with No. 1 in 1966. 0589-7432. US. English. be. $18.00 US & Canada, $22.00 other countries. Cornell Veterinarian,

Veterinary Medicine, Animal Culture

New York State Vet College, Ithaca NY 14853. **Tel** (607)256-5454. **Ed** Lennart Krook. bk rev. adv acc. **Circ** 1,100. This journal publishes papers of veterinary medicine research and current diseases of animals.

CSIRO RANGELANDS RESEARCH. **VFOAT** C.S.I.R.O. Rangelands Research, Rangelands Research. AT. English. an. **LC** SF85.4.A8. **DD** 636.010994.

CURRENT CONTENTS. AGRICULTURAL, FOOD & VETERINARY SCIENCES. See Agriculture.

CURRENT TECHNIQUES IN SMALL ANIMAL SURGERY. V.1- 1975-. Monographic Series. US. English.

CURRENT TOPICS IN VETERINARY MEDICINE AND ANIMAL SCIENCE. V. 4-. 0166-2333. Periodical. English. ir. Kluwer Boston Inc, 190 Old Derby Street, Hingham MA 02043. **Ind/Abst** Chem. Abstr., Bibliogr. Agric. **NLM** W1 CU822B. **CODEN** CTVSDD. *Current Topics in Veterinary Medicine, 0165-4586.*

CURRENT VETERINARY THERAPY. 1964/65-. 0070-2218. US. English. W B Saunders Company, West Washington Square, Philadelphia PA 19105. **Ed** R W Kirk. **Ind/Abst** Chem. Abstr. **LC** SF745. **DD** 636.0896. **NLM** W1 CU823. **CODEN** CVTHDI.

CYNOMAG. V. 1, No. 3- May 1973-. 0317-1965. CN. French. mo. Free to Members, .75 Per Number for Nonmembers. Club Canin de Montreal, 12337 Charles Renard, Riviere des Prairies Quebec Canada. **DD** 636.70062714281.

DANSK VETERINAERTIDSSKRIFT. Began with V. 58, Jan. 1975. 0106-6854. Periodical. DK. Danish. ir. Den Dansk Dyrlaegeforening, Alhambravej Isal, 1826 Kobenhavn V Denmark. **Ind/Abst** Bibliogr. Agric. **NLM** W1 DA693. *Medlemsblad for den Dansk Dyrlaegeforening, 0011-6564.*

DEUTSCHER KLEINTIER-ZUCHTER. AUSGABE KANINCHEN. **VFOAT** Ausgabe Kaninchen. Periodical. German. ir.

DEUTSCHES TIERARZTEBLATT. 22.- Yearly Volume. 0340-1898. Periodical. GW. German. mo. 132.-. Schluetersche Verlag Druckerei, Postfach 5440, D-3000 Hannover 1 West Germany. **Tel** 511-12360. **Ind/Abst** Bibliogr. Agric. **NLM** W1 DE997C. bk rev. adv acc. (ctrl) Bulletin of the veterinary committees of the West German states, official publication of the German Veterinary Society. *Deutsches Tierarzteblatt und Mitteilungsblatt der Tierarztekammern der l'Ander, 0301-0465.*

DEVELOPMENTAL STUDIES AND LABORATORY INVESTIGATIONS CONDUCTED BY VETERINARY SERVICES DIAGNOSTIC LABORATORIES. **Main/Corp** United States. Animal and Plant Health Inspection Service. 0361-9745. US. English. US Department of Agriculture, Animal and Plant Inspection Service, Washington DC 20220. **LC** SF771. **DD** 636.0896075.

DEVELOPMENTS IN ANIMAL AND VETERINARY SCIENCES. 0167-5168. Monographic Series. English. ir. **Ind/Abst** Life Sci. Collect., Chem. Abstr. **CODEN** DAVSDR.

DIRECTORY - AMERICAN VETERINARY MEDICAL ASSOCIATION. See Yearbooks, Almanacs, Directories.

DIRECTORY OF ANIMAL DISEASE DIAGNOSTIC LABORATORIES. See Yearbooks, Almanacs, Directories.

DIRECTORY OF LICENSED VETERINARIANS. See Yearbooks, Almanacs, Directories.

DIRECTORY - ONTARIO VETERINARY ASSOCIATION. See Yearbooks, Almanacs, Directories.

DLEETEMAL SCIENCE. See Indexes/Abstracts.

DOBUTSU IYAKUHIN KENSAJO NENPO. (ANNUAL REPORT OF THE NATIONAL VETERINARY ASSAY LABORATORY). **Main/Corp** Norin Suisansho Dobutsu Iyakuhin Kensajo (Japan). **VFOAT** Norin Suisansho Dobutsu Iyakuhin Kensajo Nempo. 0388-7421. JA. Japanese (with summaries in English). an. Norin Suisansho Dobutsu Iyakuhin Kensajo, 15-1 Tokura 1 Kokubunji, Tokyo 185 Japan. **Ind/Abst** Chem. Abstr. **LC** SF917. **CODEN** DIKNAA.

LES DOSSIERS DE L'ELEVAGE. **VFOAT** Dossiers Veterinaires des Elevages Rationnels. 0150-0112. Periodical. FR. French. ir. Point Veterinaire, 25 rue Bourgelat, 94700 Maisons Alfort France.

DTW. DEUTSCHE TIERARZTLICHE WOCHENSCHRIFT. **VFOAT** Deutsche Tierarztliche Wochenschrift. 78.-Yearly volume. 0341-6593. Periodical. GW. German. mo. 175.-. M & H Schaper Verlag, Ptfch 810669, Grazier Strasse 20, D3000 Hannover 81 West Germany. **Tel** (0511)85687301. **Ed** Hapke. **Ind/Abst** Bibliogr. Agric., Chem. Abstr., Energy Inf. Abstr., Energy Res. Abstr., Environ. Abstr., Index Med., Life Sci. Collect., Pestdoc, Ringdoc, Vetdoc. **NLM** W1 D17. **CODEN** DDTWDG. bk rev. adv acc. **Circ** 1,000. Animal production health diagnosis, treatment, prophylaxis vaccination residues in food, laboratory medicine, hygiene environment. *Deutsche Tierarztliche Wochenschrift, 0012-0847.*

DU UND DAS TIER. 1971-. Periodical. GW. German. bm. M & H Schaper Verlag, Ptfch 810669, Grazer Strasse 20, D3000 Hannover 81 West Germany. **Tel** 05 11/ 83 00 18. *Tier-Illustrierte.*

EGYPTIAN JOURNAL OF ANIMAL PRODUCTION. V. 12- 1972-. 0302-4520. Periodical. UA. English (Vols. for 1972- have added title page and summaries in Arabic). sa. $37.00. National Information and Documentation Center, A1-Tahrir St Dokki, Cairo AR Egypt. **Ind/Abst** Chem. Abstr., Bibliogr. Agric. **CODEN** EGAPBW. *Arabic United Arab Republic Journal of Animal Production.*

EGYPTIAN JOURNAL OF VETERINARY SCIENCE. V. 9- 1972-. 0301-8199. Periodical. UA. English (summaries in Arabic). sa. $37.00. National Information & Documentation Center, A1-Tahrir St Dokki, Cario AR Egypt. **Ind/Abst** Excerpta Med., Chem. Abstr. **NLM** W1 EG916. **CODEN** EJVSAU. *United Arab Republic Journal of Veterinary Science.*

L'ELEVEUR DE LAPINS. Periodical. FR. French. qt. $22.08. Editions du Boisbaudry, 35 rue Carnot, 35000 Rennes France.

ELLENIKE KTENIATRIKE. (HELLENIKE KTENIATRIKE). **VFOAT** Medecine Veterinaire Hellenique, Hellenic Veterinary Medicine. Vol. 1- 1958-. 0018-0068. Periodical. GR. Greek, Modern (some summaries in English, French or German). qt. $30.00. Medecine Veterinaire, Mongenthou 1 E Kteniatrike, Thessalonki Greece. **Tel** 30 031 271 229. **Ed** Nicolas Aspiotis Morgentour. **Ind/Abst** Bibliogr. Agric., Biol. Abstr., Chem. Abstr. **NLM** W1 HE788M. **CODEN** EKTEAJ. bk rev. adv acc.

ENCUESTA NACIONAL DE BOVINOS, X REGION, PROV. OSORNO. **VFOAT** Encuesta Nacional de Bovinos, Decima Region, Prov. Osorno. 1979-. Spanish. ir. **LC** SF196.C5. **DD** 338.17620098353.

ENERGIE- UND NAHRSTOFFBEDARF LANDWIRTSCHAFTLICHER NUTZTIERE. No. 1-. Monographic Series. German. ir.

EQUINE VETERINARY AND RESEARCH DIRECTORY. See Yearbooks, Almanacs, Directories.

EQUINE VETERINARY DATA. V. 1- Jan. 1, 1980-. 0739-9065. Periodical. US. English. sm. $120.00. Equine Veterinary Data, Box 1127, Wildomar CA 92395. **Tel** (714)678-1083. **Ed** Wm E Jones. (ctrl). Professional newsletter for equine practitioners. Latest information on veterinary care of horses.

EQUINE VETERINARY JOURNAL. V. 1- July 1968-. 0425-1644. Periodical. UK. English. bm. 38. British Veterinary Association, 7 Mansfield Street, London W1M OAT England. **Tel** 0638 666160. **Ed** Peter Rossdale. **Ind/Abst** Life Sci. Collect., Index Med., Curr. Contents, Biol. Abstr., Index Vet., Bibliogr. Agric., Vet. Bull., Sci. Cit. Index, Abr. Ed. **NLM** W1 EQ967. **CODEN** EQVJAI. bk rev. adv acc. **Circ** 2,400. Original reports of work related to all aspects of equine veterinary medicine.

EXPERIMENTAL HUSBANDRY CEASED. No. 1-38. 0071-3414. Periodical. UK. English. ir. $10.00. Her Majesty's Stationery Office, PO Box 276, London SW8 5DT England. **Tel** 01-622-3316. **Ind/Abst** Bibliogr. Agric., Biol. Abstr., Chem. Abstr. **CODEN** EXHUAU.

EXPERIMENTS ON LIVING ANIMALS : STATISTICS. See Statistics.

FACT SHEET - FOOD ANIMAL CONCERNS TRUST. (FACT SHEET). 0882-3022. Periodical. US. English. Fact Inc, PO Box 14599, Chicago IL 60614. **DD** 636.

FDA VETERINARIAN. APR. 1979-. Periodical. US. English. FDA Veterinarian, Rockville MD 20857. *Animal Drug Memo.*

THE FEDERAL VETERINARIAN. 1922. 0164-6257. Periodical. US. English. mo. $30.00. National Association of Federal Veterinarians, 1522 K Street NW/Suite 828, Washington DC 20005-1202. **Tel** (212)223-3590. **Ed** Edward L Menning. **NLM** W1 FE243. bk rev. adv acc. **Circ** 2,000. Abstracts, articles about meat/poultry inspection, foodborne and zoonotic diseases, animal drug and food residues, regulated animal diseases, plus legislation affecting federal veterinarians. *Bureau Veterinarian.*

FEED & FEEDING DIGEST. **VFOAT** Feed and Feeding Digest. Periodical. US. English. **Ind/Abst** Bibliogr. Agric. *The Feed Trader and Retailer.*

FELINE PRACTICE. V. 1- Sept./Oct. 1971-. 0046-3639. Periodical. US. English. bm. $30.00. Veterinary Practice Publishing Company, PO Box 4457, Santa Barbara CA 93103. **Tel** (805)965-1028. **Ed** John B Carricaburu. **Ind/Abst** Life Sci. Collect., Accumu. Vet. Index, Biol. Abstr., Curr. Contents, Index Vet., Bibliogr. Agric. **NLM** W1 FE459. **CODEN** FELPBG. bk rev. adv acc. **Circ** 5,500. A journal devoted to feline medicine and surgery for the practitioner.

FORTSCHRITTE DER VERHALTENSFORSCHUNG. **VFOAT** Advances in Ethology. No. 8- 1972-. Monographic Series. English. Paul Parey Verlag, PO Box 106304/ Spitalerstr 12 D-2000, Hamburg 1 West Germany. **Tel** 040-33 96 9-134. *Zeitschrift fur Tierpsychologie. Beiheft.*

FORTSCHRITTE DER VETERINARMEDIZIN. **VFOAT** Advances in Veterinary Medicine. 15- 1971-. 0301-2794. Monographic Series. GW. German (summaries in English, French, and Spanish). Paul Parey Verlag, PO Box 106304, Spitalerstr 12, D-2000 Hamburg 1 West Germany. **Tel** 040-33 96 9-134. **Ind/Abst** Excerpta Med., Biol. Abstr., Chem. Abstr., Sci. Cit. Index, Abr. Ed. **NLM** W1 FO893. **CODEN** AVYMAX. *Zentralblatt fur Veterinarmedizin. Beiheft, 0514-714X.*

GANADERIA. **Main/Corp** Colombia. Ministerio de Agricultura. 1976/78-. Spanish. ir. Ministerio de Agricultura, Oficina de Comunicaciones, Carrera 10 No 20-30, Bogota de Colombia. **LC** SF15.C7.

DE GEITEHOUDER. See Agriculture - Livestock and Poultry.

GENETIQUE, SELECTION, EVOLUTION. Vol. 15, No 1-. 0754-0264. Periodical. French (text in English with summaries and tables of contents in both languages). qt. 425.00. Institut National de la Recherche Agronomique, Regisseur des Recettes, 78000 Versailles France. **Ind/Abst** Life Sci. Collect. **LC** SF105. **DD** 636.0821. *Annales de Genetique et de Selection Animale.*

THE GEORGIA VETERINARIAN. (GEORGIA VETERINARIAN). V. 1- Sept. 1948-. Periodical. US. English. bm. $15.00. Georgia Veterinarian Medical Association, Box 4185 Campus Station, Athens GA 30601. **Tel** (404)542-3461. **Ed** J T Mercer. **Ind/Abst** Bibliogr. Agric. **NLM** W1 GE451K. bk rev. adv acc. **Circ** 2,000. Association business, case reports and scientific articles.

GOAT VETERINARY SOCIETY JOURNAL. Began in 1979?. Periodical. English. ir. David Chennells, Lucks Hall Annia Cross, Bradfield Berks England.

A GUIDE FOR ACCREDITED VETERINARIANS. **Main/Corp** United States. Animal and Plant Health Inspection Service. Veterinary Services. US. English. US Department of Agriculture, Animal & Plant Health Inspection Service, Hyattsville MD 20782. **LC** SF740. **DD** 636.089440973. *A Guide for Accredited Veterinarians.*

GUIDE FOR THE CARE AND USE OF LABORATORY ANIMALS. 1969-. US. English. Science and Health Reports, National Institution of Health, Bethesda MD 20205. *Guide for Laboratory Animal Facilities and Care.*

GUINEA-PIG NEWS LETTER CEASED. **VAT** Guinea Pig News Letter. Ceased with No. 16. 0309-1821. Periodical. UK. English. Medical Research Council, Laboratory Animals Centre, Woodmansterne Road, Carshalton Surrey SM5 4EF England. **NLM** W1 GU806.

GYOMU HOKOKU. **Main/Corp** Yamaguchi-Ken Chikusan Shikenjo. 0389-0724. Japanese. ir. Yamaguchi-ken Chikusan, Shikenjo Isa-Cho Mine-shi, Yamaguchi-ken 759-22 Japan. **LC** SF83.J32.

HAMSTER INFORMATION SERVICE. 0739-4276. Periodical. US. English. qt. $12.00 Domestic, $15.00 Foreign. The Hamster Society, Bio-Research Institute, 9 Commercial Avenue, Cambridge MA 02141.

HAN'GUK CHUKSAN HAKHOE CHI. VFOAT Korean Journal of Animal Sciences. 0367-5807. Periodical. KO. Korean (summaries in English). ir. c/o Department of Animal Science, College of Agriculture, Seoul National University, Suweon Korea 170. **Ind/Abst** Biol. Abstr., Chem. Abstr. **LC** SF1. **CODEN** HGCHAG. *Chi. The Research Bulletin.*

HANGUK CHUKSAN KWAHAK YONGU POGO. VFOAT Annual Research Reports of the Korea Institute of Animal Sciences. V. 1- Series (1981)-. Periodical. KO. English (Korean). an. Hanguk Chuksan Kwahak Yonguso, 129 Ami-ri Pubal-Myon Ich On-Gun, Kyonggi-do Korea 172-18. **LC** SF1.

HANGUK SUUI KONGJUNG POGON HAKHOE CHI. VFOAT Korean Journal of Veterinary Public Health. Periodical. KO. Korean (English). ir. Hanguk Suui Kongjung Pogon Hakhoe 50, 3-Ka Chungmu-Ro, Chung-ku, Seoul South Korea. **LC** SF740.

HISTORIA MEDICINAE VETERINARIAE. 1-. 0105-1423. Periodical. DK. Dutch (summaries in English, German, and French). qt. $33.00. Historia Medicinae, Sondergade 39, DK-4130 Viby Sjaelland Denmark. **Ed** Josef Parmas. **Ind/Abst** Bibliogr. Agric. **LC** SF615. **DD** 636.08909. **NLM** W1 HI781. bk rev. adv acc. **Circ** 300. A new journal designed to satisfy the curiosity of persons interested in the history of veterinary medicine as a science and as a profession. It is the only international journal devoted to this subject.

HODOWCA GOEBI POCZTOWYCH. *See* Pets.

HOME QUARTER. Vol. 1, No. 1 (Autumn '81)-. 0823-6410. Periodical. CN. English. qt. Stockmen's Memorial Foundation, 2116-27 Avenue NE, Calgary Alberta T2E 7A6 Canada. **DD** 636.2006071233.

HSU MU SHOU I HSUEH PAO. VFOAT Acta Veterinaria et Zootechnica Sinica. Began in 1956?. 0529-5127. Periodical. CC. Chinese (with summaries in English). qt. 0.70. Chung-Kuo Kuo Chi Shu Tien, PO Box 2820, Pei-Ching China. **LC** SF604. **DD** 636.08905.

HUMANE EDUCATION. V. 1- Fall 1977-. 0149-8061. Periodical. US. English. qt. $10.00. National Association for Advisory of Human Education, PO Box 362, East Haddam CT 06423. **Tel** (203)434-8666. **Ed** Willow Ann Soltow. **LC** HV4712. **DD** 636.083. Provieds teaching ideas, worksheets and other support materials for educators interested in teaching about animals and the environment.

ILCA ANNUAL REPORT. **Main/Corp** International Livestock Centre for Africa. VFOAT I.L.C.A. Annual Report. English. an. ILCA, PO BOX 5689, Addis Abara Ethiopia. **LC** SF83.A35. **DD** 636.0096.

ILMOITUS TARTTUVISTA ELAINTAUDEISTA. VFOAT Rapport Om Smittsamma Djursjunkdomar. Periodical. Finnish (text in French and Swedish). mo. *Ilmoitus Tarttuvista Kotielaintaudeista Suomessa.*

ILRAD : ANNUAL REPORT OF THE INTERNATIONAL LABORATORY FOR RESEARCH ON ANIMAL DISEASES. **Main/Corp** International Laboratory for Research on Animal Diseases. VFOAT I.L.R.A.D. 1981-. English. an. *Annual Report (International Laboratory for Research on Animal Diseases).*

ILRAD REPORTS. VFOAT I.L.R.A.D. Reports. VAT International Laboratory for Research on Animal Diseases Reports. Vol. 1, No. 1 (July 1983)-. Periodical. English. qt.

IN PRACTICE. Vol. 1, No. 1 (Jan. 1979)-. 0263-841X. Periodical. UK. English. bm. 18. British Veterinary Association, 7 Mansfield Street, London W1M 0AT England. **Tel** (01)636-6541. **Ed** Edward Boden. **Ind/Abst** Index Med., Biol. Abstr., Bibliogr. Agric., Biol. Agric. Index. **NLM** W1 IN102M. **CODEN** IPRCDH. adv acc. **Circ** 11,000. (ctrl). Postgraduate journal comprising clinical papers on conditions and problems encountered in veterinary practice.

INAUGURAL-DISSERTATION. **Main/Corp** Justus Liebig-Universitat. Fachbereich Veterinarmedizin. No.18- 971-. Periodical. German. ir. *Inaugural-Dissertation.*

INAUGURAL-DISSERTATION. **Main/Corp** Munich. Universitat. Fachbereich Tiermedizin. 1974, No. 71-. Periodical. German. ir. *Inaugural-Dissertation.*

INDEX-CATALOGUE OF MEDICAL AND VETERINARY ZOOLOGY. SUPPLEMENT. *See* Indexes/Abstracts.

INDEX OF VETERINARY SPECIALITIES. *See* Indexes/Abstracts.

INDEX VETERINARIUS. *See* Indexes/Abstracts.

INDIAN JOURNAL OF ANIMAL HEALTH. 1962. 0019-5057. Periodical. II. English. sa. $15.00. 61-4 Belgachia Road, Calcutta India 700037. **Tel** 52 8351. **Ed** A Chatterjee. **Ind/Abst** Life Sci. Collect., Biol. Abstr., Bibliogr. Agric., Chem. Abstr. **NLM** W1 IN206NJ. **CODEN** IJAHA4. bk rev. adv acc. **Circ** 2,500. (ctrl). Dedicated to promote the art of veterinary and animal husbandry services including their relation to public health and agriculture.

THE INDIAN JOURNAL OF ANIMAL REPRODUCTION : JOURNAL OF THE INDIAN SOCIETY FOR THE STUDY OF ANIMAL REPRODUCTION. Periodical. English. sa. $20.00. Prints India, 11 Darya Ganj, New Delhi 110002 India.

INDIAN JOURNAL OF ANIMAL RESEARCH. V. 5- June 1971-. 0367-6722. Periodical. II. English. sa. $20.00. Agricultural Research Commission, Sadar Karnal 132001, Karnal Haryan India. **Ind/Abst** Life Sci. Collect., Biol. Abstr., Chem. Abstr., Bibliogr. Agric. **CODEN** IALRBR. *Indian Journal of Science and Industry. Section B: Animal Sciences, 0019-5618.*

INDIAN JOURNAL OF ANIMAL SCIENCES. (THE INDIAN JOURNAL OF ANIMAL SCIENCES). Began with: V. 39, No. 1 (Feb. 1969). 0367-8318. Periodical. II. English. mo. $40.00. Indian Council of Agricultural Sciences, Krishi Bhavan, New Delhi India. **Ind/Abst** Life Sci. Collect., Pestdoc, Ringdoc, Vetdoc, Excerpta Med., Biol. Abstr., Chem. Abstr., Bibliogr. Agric. **NLM** W1 IN206NR. **CODEN** IJLAA4. *Indian Journal of Veterinary Science and Animal Husbandry.*

INDIAN VETERINARY JOURNAL. (THE INDIAN VETERINARY JOURNAL). Began publication in 1924. 0019-6479. Periodical. II. English. mo. $20.00. Indian Veterinary Journal, No 10 Avenue Road, Madras 34 India. **Ed** R Krishnamurti. **Ind/Abst** Life Sci. Collect., Pestdoc, Ringdoc, Vetdoc, Biol. Abstr., Chem. Abstr., Bibliogr. Agric., Sci. Cit. Index, Abr. Ed. **LC** SF604. **NLM** W1 IN278. **CODEN** IVEJAC. adv acc.

INFORMATIONS TECHNIQUES DE SERVICES VETERINAIRES. Periodical. FR. French. qt. $33.26. Informations Techniques de Services Veterinaires, 44-46 Boulevard de Grenelle, 75732 Paris Cedex 15 France. *Informations Techniques des Directions des Services Veterinaires.*

INTERNATIONAL JOURNAL FOR THE STUDY OF ANIMAL PROBLEMS. V. 1- Jan./Feb. 1980-. 0195-7554. Periodical. US. English. bm. Journal Department, Institute for the Study of Animal Problems, 2100 L Street NW, Washington DC 20037 DELETNGTON, DC 20037. **Ind/Abst** Life Sci. Collect., Biol. Abstr., Psychol. Abstr., Energy Inf. Abstr., Environ. Abstr. **LC** HV4701. **DD** 179.305. **NLM** W1 IN652M. **CODEN** IJSPEK. *Bulletin of the Institute for the Study of Animal Problems.*

THE IOWA STATE UNIVERSITY VETERINARIAN. V. 1- Fall 1938-. 0099-5266. Periodical. US. English. sa. $8.00. Iowa State University Student Chapter of the American Veterinary Association, Ames IA 50010. **Tel** (515)294-3282. **Ed** John H Greve. bk rev. adv acc. **Circ** 2,500. (ctrl). Semiannual student journal features clinical reports and news (student, faculty, and alumni).

IRISH VETERINARY JOURNAL. 0368-0762. Periodical. UK. English. mo. 31.00. Irish Veterinary Association, 53 Lansdowne Road, Ballsbridge Dublin 4 Ireland. **Tel** 01-685263. **Ed** P J Hartigan. **Ind/Abst** Life Sci. Collect., Excerpta Med., Chem. Abstr., Bibliogr. Agric., Sci. Cit. Index, Abr. Ed. **NLM** W1 IR459. **CODEN** IVTJAJ. bk rev. adv acc. **Circ** 2,000. Science articles/papers describing cases encountered during general practice and studies of cases met within the laboratory. General news and items of interest to practicioners also included.

JAARSTATISTIEK VAN DE VEEVOEDERS. **Main/Corp** Netherlands (Kingdom, 1815-). Ministerie Van Landbouw en Visserij. Directie Algemene Zaken. Afdeling Statistiek en Documentatie. Dutch. ir. Ministere Van Landbow en Visserij, 1E Van Den Boschstraat 4, S-Gravenhage Netherlands. **LC** SF95.

JAPANESE JOURNAL OF VETERINARY SCIENCE. (THE JAPANESE JOURNAL OF VETERINARY SCIENCE). V. 1- Feb. 1939-. 0021-5295. Periodical. JA. Japanese (articles and table of contents in English). bm. 80.00. Maruzen Company Ltd, PO Box 5050, 100-31 Tokyo Japan. **Tel** 03-379-0636. **Ind/Abst** Life Sci. Collect., Pestdoc, Ringdoc, Vetdoc, Index Med., Biol. Abstr., Chem. Abstr., Bibliogr. Agric., Sci. Cit. Index, Abr. Ed. **NLM** W1 NI916J. **CODEN** NJUZA9. adv acc. **Circ** 4,700. (ctrl). An organ paper of the Japanese Society of Veterinary Science. *Journal - Japanese Society of Veterinary Science.*

JOURNAL - INSTITUTE OF ANIMAL TECHNICIANS *CEASED.* V. 16, No. 3-V. 33, No. 2. 0020-2711. Periodical. UK. English. qt. **Ind/Abst** Bibliogr. Agric., Biol. Abstr. **NLM** W1 JO478K. **CODEN** IATJA8. *Journal of the Animal Technicians Association, 0307-465X.*

JOURNAL - NORTH AMERICAN WOLF SOCIETY. (JOURNAL OF THE NORTH AMERICAN WOLF SOCIETY). **Main/Corp** North American Wolf Society. 0740-0152. Periodical. US. English. ty. $15.00. North American Wolf Society, Route 2 Troy Pike/Windhover Farm, Versailles KY 40383.

JOURNAL OF ANIMAL SCIENCE. V. 1- Feb. 1942-. Periodical. US. English. mo. American Society of Animal Science, 309 West Clark Street, Champaign IL 61820. **Tel** (217)356-3182. **Ind/Abst** Biol. Abstr., Chem. Abstr., Nuci. Sci. Abstr., Int. Aerosp. Abstr., Index Med., Sel. Water Resour. Abstr., Bibliogr. Agric., Sci. Cit. Index, Abr. Ed. **CODEN** JANSAG. *Record of Proceedings of the Annual Meeting - American Society of Animal Production.*

THE JOURNAL OF EQUINE MEDICINE AND SURGERY. V. 1- Jan. 1977-. 0147-0833. Periodical. US. English. mo. $40.00 Veterinarians, $20.00 Veterinarian Students. Veterinary Publications Inc, Business and Editorial Offices, 44 Nassau Street, Princeton NJ 08540. **Ind/Abst** Life Sci. Collect., Chem. Abstr., Sci. Cit. Index, Abr. Ed., Bibliogr. Agric. **LC** SF951. **DD** 636.0896005. **NLM** W1 JO644C. **CODEN** JESUDA.

THE JOURNAL OF EQUINE MEDICINE AND SURGERY. SUPPLEMENT. No. 1- 1978-. Monographic Series. US. English.

JOURNAL OF EQUINE VETERINARY SCIENCE. Vol. 1, No. 1 (Jan./Feb. 1981)-. 0737-0806. Periodical. US. English. bm. $50.00. Journal of Equine Veterinary Science, Subscription Department, PO Box 1127, Wildomar CA 92395. **NLM** W1 JO644CD.

JOURNAL OF RANGE MANAGEMENT. V. 1- Oct. 1948-. 0022-409X. Periodical. US. English. bm. $56.00. Society for Range Mangaement, 2760 W 5th Avenue, Denver CO 80204. **Tel** (303)571-0174. **Ed** Patricia G Smith. **Ind/Abst** Can. Environ., Life Sci. Collect., Excerpta Med., Pestdoc, Ringdoc, Vetdoc, Coal Abstr., Energy Inf. Abstr., Environ. Abstr., GeoRef, Biol. Abstr., Chem. Abstr., Nuci. Sci. Abstr., Sel. Water Resour. Abstr., Bibliogr. Agric., Biol. Agric. Index, Bibliogr. Index Geol., Sci. Cit. Index, Abr. Ed. **LC** SF85. **DD** 636.08423, 636.081. **CODEN** JRMGAQ. bk rev. adv acc. **Circ** 6,800. (ctrl). Technical articles on range management including range plant physiology, grazing effects, wildlife, watershed and economics.

THE JOURNAL OF SMALL ANIMAL PRACTICE. V. 1- Apr. 1960-. 0022-4510. Periodical. UK. English. mo. $195.00. British Small Animal Veterinarian Association, 5 Street Georges Terrace, Cheltenham Gloucestershire United Kingdom. **Tel** 0242 580324. **Ed** H E Carter. **Ind/Abst** Life Sci. Collect., Excerpta Med., Pestdoc, Ringdoc, Vetdoc, Nuci. Sci. Abstr., Bibliogr. Agric., Index Med., Biol. Abstr., Chem. Abstr., Sci. Cit. Index, Abr. Ed. **NLM** W1 JO877L. **CODEN** JAPRAN. bk rev. adv acc. **Circ** 3,500. Scientific and topical papers on techniques and investigations in small animal medicine and surgery.

THE JOURNAL OF THE AMERICAN ANIMAL HOSPITAL ASSOCIATION. **Main/Corp** American Animal Hospital Association. V. 4- Feb. 1968-. 0587-2871. Periodical. US. English. bm. $25.00 General Free to Members. American Hospital Association, 3612 East Jefferson Boulevard, South Bend IN 46615. **Ind/Abst** Life Sci. Collect., Excerpta Med., Chem. Abstr., Biol. Abstr., Bibliogr. Agric., Biol.

Agric. Index. **LC** SF601. **DD** 636.08905. **NLM** W1 JO908A. **CODEN** JAAHBL. *Animal Hospital, 0570-1198.*

JOURNAL OF THE AMERICAN VETERINARY MEDICAL ASSOCIATION. **Main/Corp** American Veterinary Medical Association. V. 48-. Periodical. US. English. sm. American Veterinary Medical Association, 930 North Meacham Road, Schaumburg IL 60196. **Tel** (312)885-8070. **Ind/Abst** Index Med., Sci. Cit. Index, Abr. Ed., Hospit. Lit. Index, Chem. Abstr., Biol. Agric. Index.

JOURNAL OF THE SOUTH AFRICAN VETERINARY ASSOCIATION. **VFOAT** Tydskrif van die Suid-Afrikaanse Veterinere Vereniging. V. 43- Mar. 1972-. 0301-0732. Periodical. SA. some texts in Afrikaans with English summaries. qt. 86.00. South African Veterinary Association, PO Box 25033, Monument Park, Pretoria 0105 South Africa. **Tel** (012)346 1150. **Ed** N P J Kriek. **Ind/Abst** Life Sci. Collect., Excerpta Med., Pestdoc, Ringdoc, Vetdoc, Index Med., Biol. Abstr., Chem. Abstr., Bibliogr. Agric. **NLM** W1 JO955Q. **CODEN** JAVTAP. bk rev. adv acc. Scientific veterinary medical journal. *Journal of the South African Veterinary Medical Association, 0038-2809.*

JOURNAL OF VETERINARY ORTHOPEDICS. V. 1- July/Sept. 1979-. 0199-0187. Periodical. US. English. qt. Veterinary Practice Publishers Company, PO Box 4457, Santa Barbara CA 93103. **Tel** (805)965-1028. **Ed** J W Alexander. **LC** SF910.5. **DD** 636.08973005. bk rev. adv acc. **Circ** 2,000. A cross-species specialty journal devoted to orthopedic diseases, surgical procedures and orthopedic instrumentation.

JOURNAL OF VETERINARY PHARMACOLOGY AND THERAPEUTICS. V. 1- Mar. 1978-. 0140-7783. Periodical. UK. English. qt. $120.00 $120.00 US and Canada. Blackwell Scientific Publishing Ltd, PO Box 88, Oxford OX2 0EL England. **Tel** 0865-240201. **Ed** Charles Short and Peter Lees. **Ind/Abst** Pestdoc, Ringdoc, Vetdoc, Index Med., Biol. Abstr., Chem. Abstr., Bibliogr. Agric., Sci. Cit. Index, Abr. Ed. **NLM** W1 JO97Q. **CODEN** JVPTD9. bk rev. adv acc. **Circ** 600. Clinical aspects of veterinary pharmacology and pharmacological topics of veterinary relevance.

JOURNAL OF WILDLIFE DISEASES. V. 6- Jan. 1970-. 0090-3558. Periodical. US. English. qt. $40.00. Wildlife Disease Association, PO Box 886, Ames IA 50010. **Tel** (515)233-1931. **Ed** Donald J Forrester. **Ind/Abst** Can. Environ., Life Sci. Collect., Excerpta Med., Energy Inf. Abstr., Environ. Abstr., ASTIS Bibliogr., ASTIS Curr. Aware. Bull., Chem. Abstr., Biol. Abstr., Index Med., Sel. Water Resour. Abstr., Bibliogr. Agric., Energy Res. Abstr., Sci. Cit. Index, Abr. Ed. **NLM** W1 JO972D. **CODEN** JWIDAW. bk rev. (ctrl). *Bulletin of the Wildlife Disease Association, 0098-373x.*

JOURNAL OF ZOO ANIMAL MEDICINE. V. 1- Sept. 1970-. 0093-4526. Periodical. US. English. qt. Free with Membership. Journal of Zoo Animal Medicine, 500 Ringgold Street, Brownsville TX 78520. **Ind/Abst** Life Sci. Collect. **NLM** W1 JO974M. **CODEN** JZAMD9.

KACHIKU EISEI TOKEI. *See* Statistics.

KAJIAN VETERINAR MALAYSIA. V. 6, No. 2- Nov. 1974-. 0126-9437. Periodical. MY. English (summaries in English and Maylay). sa. $15.00. Faculty of Veterinary Medicine and Animal Science, University of Pertanian Malaysia, Serdang Selangor Malaysia. **Tel** 386101-10. **Ed** Sheikh Omar Abdul Rahman. **Ind/Abst** Life Sci. Collect. **NLM** W1 KA41VC. bk rev. adv acc. **Circ** 300. (ctrl). Papers on various aspects of veterinary medicine and animal science. *Kajian Veterinaire, 0047-309X.*

KANAGAWA-KEN SANGYO SENTA SHIKEN KENKYU KOKOKU. No. 1-. JA. Japanese. ir. Kanagawa-Ken Sangyo Senta, 2010 Nakashinden, Ebina Japan. **LC** SF541. *Shiken Chosa Seiseki Gaiyo.*

KANSAS VETERINARIAN. Periodical. US. English. bm. $10.00. Kansas Veterinary Medical Association, 227 South Wind Place, Manhattan KS 66502. **Tel** (913)539-4273.

THE KENNEL DOCTOR. 0886-7917. Periodical. US. English. mo. $42.00. 4833 Spring Lake Road, Rhinelander WI 54501. **DD** 636.

KLEINTIER-PRAXIS. 1st Vol. Apr. 1956-. 0023-2076. Periodical. GW. German (with summaries in English, French, and Italian and an added table of contents in English). ir. M & H Schaper Verlag, Ptfch 810669, Grazer Strasse 20, D3000 Hannover 81 West Germany. **Tel** 05 11/ 83 00 18. **Ind/Abst** Life Sci. Collect., Pestdoc, Ringdoc, Vetdoc, Energy Res. Abstr., Bibliogr. Agric., Sci. Cit. Index, Abr. Ed. **NLM** W1 KL183.

LAB ANIMAL. V. 1- Jan. 1972-. 0093-7355. Periodical. US. English. ir. Media Horizons Inc, 50 West 23rd Street, New York NY 10010. **Tel** (212)645-1000. **Ind/Abst** Bibliogr. Agric. **NLM** W1 LA125.

LABCHOWS DIGEST. **VAT** Lab Chows Digest. V. 1- Nov. 1977-. 0190-2474. Periodical. US. English. Ralston Purina Company, Checkerboard Square, St Louis MO 63188. **NLM** W1 LA139. *Laboratory Animal Digest, 0458-5925.*

LABORATORY ANIMAL HANDBOOKS. *See* Medicine.

LABORATORY ANIMAL SCIENCE. V. 21- Feb. 1971-. 0023-6764. Periodical. US. English. bm. $60.00. American Association for Laboratory Animal Science, 210 North Hammes Avenue/Suite 205, Joliet IL 60435. **Tel** (815)729-1161. **Ind/Abst** Life Sci. Collect., Excerpta Med., Pestdoc, Ringdoc, Vetdoc, Nuci. Sci. Abstr., Bibliogr. Agric., Biol. Abstr., Chem. Abstr., Index Med., Int. Aerosp. Abstr., Energy Res. Abstr. **NLM** W1 LA206J. **CODEN** LBASAE. *Laboratory Animal Care, 0094-5331.*

LABORATORY ANIMALS. V. 1- Apr. 1967-. 0023-6772. Periodical. UK. English. qt. 85. Laboratory Animals Ltd, 1 Thrifts Mead, Theydon Bois, Epping Essex CM16 7NF England. **Ed** Sharrock. **Ind/Abst** Life Sci. Collect., Excerpta Med., Bibliogr. Agric., Biol. Abstr., Chem. Abstr., Nuci. Sci. Abstr., Index Med., Sci. Cit. Index, Abr. Ed. **LC** UNC. **NLM** W1 LA206K. **CODEN** LBANAX. bk rev. adv acc. **Circ** 1,700. All aspects of laboratory animal science.

LABORATORY PRIMATE NEWSLETTER. V. 1- Jan. 1962-. 0023-6861. Periodical. US. English. qt. Allan M Schrier, Psychology Department, Brown University, Providence RI 02912. **LC** SF407.P7. **DD** 636.98. **NLM** W1 LA231H.

LAC MANUAL SERIES. **VFOAT** Manual Series - Laboratory Animals Centre. **VAT** Laboratory Animals Centre Manual Series. No. 1- 1974-. 0144-0314. Monographic Series. UK. English. ir. **NLM** W1 L1M.

LAC NEWS. **Main/Corp** Medical Research Council (Gt. Brit.). Laboratory Animals Centre. No. 51- Jan. 1977-. 0308-9568. Periodical. UK. English. sa. *LAC News Letter.*

LANDWIRTSCHAFTLICHES ZENTRALBLATT. ABTEILUNG IV. VETERINARMEDIZIN. V. 1- Jan. 1956-. 0023-821X. Periodical. SZ. German. mo. Kunst & Wissen Erich Bieber, Dufourstrasse 51, CH-8008 Zurich Switzerland.

LIAO-NING HSU MU SHOU I. **VFOAT** Liao Ning Xu Mu Shou Yi. Periodical. CC. Chinese. bm. 0.32. Post Office, Liao-Yang Shih China. **LC** SF604. **DD** 636.08905.

LISTE - D'ACQUISITIONS - BIBLIOTHEQUE DE MEDECINE VETERINAIRE. (LISTE D'ACQUISITIONS). **Main/Corp** Universite de Montreal. Bibliotheque de Medecine Veterinaire. 0822-952X. Periodical. CN. French. mo. Bibliotheque de Medecine Veterinaire/ Universite de Montreal, C P 5000, St-Hyacinthe Quebec J2S 7C6 Canada. **DD** 016.636089.

LITHIUM AND ANIMAL BEHAVIOR. **Series/Titl** Annual Research Reviews. V. 1- 1977-. 0705-4718. CN. English. ir. Human Sciences Press, 72-5th Avenue, New York NY 10011. **Ed** D F Smith. **Ind/Abst** Life Sci. Collect., Psychol. Abstr. **DD** 615.2381. **NLM** W1 LI821N.

LIVESTOCK HEALTH AND HUSBANDRY REPORT. **Main/Corp** New South Wales. Division of Animal Industry. 0312-8547. AT. English. ir. New South Wales Department of Agriculture, State Office Block, Phillip Street, Sydney Australia. **LC** SF15.A8. **DD** 338.176009944. *Livestock Health and Animal Husbandry Report, 0312-8539.*

LUCRARI STIINTIFICE. SERIA C. ZOOTEHNIE SI MEDICINA VETERINARA. (LUCRARI STIINTIFICE. SERIA C : ZOOTEHNIE SI MEDICINA VETERINARA). **VFOAT** Zootehine si Medicina Veterinara. 4- 1960-. 0524-8108. Periodical. Romanian (tables of contents and summaries in English, French, and Russian). ir. **Ind/Abst** Bibliogr. Agric. **NLM** W1 LU315I. *Annurul Lucrarilor Stiintifice.*

THE MCLEAN GUIDE TO KENNELS OF AMERICA. **VFOAT** Kennels of America. 1st- Ed. 0093-2531. US. English. 19425. **Ed** C D McLean. **LC** SF428. **DD** 636.708202573.

THE MADRAS VETERINARY COLLEGE ANNUAL. *See* Education (General) - Higher Education.

MAGYAR ALLATORVOSOK LAPJA. **VFOAT** Vengerskii Veterinarnyi Zhurnal. V. 1-. 0025-004X. Periodical. HU. Hungarian (Summaries and tables of contents in English, Russian, and German). mo. $34.50. Hirlapkiado, Blaha Lujza 3, 1959, Budapest Hungary. **Tel** (1)413-023. **Ed** Ferenc Hollo. **Ind/Abst** Life Sci. Collect., Pestdoc, Ringdoc, Vetdoc, Chem. Abstr., Curr. Contents. **NLM** W1 MA388. **CODEN** MGALA5. bk rev. adv acc. **Circ** 3,500. (ctrl). Founded in 1878, features scientific and practical papers with broad English abstracts. *Allatorvosi Lapok.*

MAINELINE. V. 1- July 1974-. 0316-8581. Periodical. CN. English. mo. $5., North America, $10., Foreign. Maine-Anjou Canada Ltd, 120 Petroleum Building, 310 9th Avenue SW, Calgary Alberta T2P 1K5 Canada. **DD** 636.242.

MAINSTREAM (ANIMAL PROTECTION INSTITUTE OF AMERICA). *See* Pets.

MAJOR PROBLEMS IN VETERINARY MEDICINE. V. 1-. 0741-5575. Monographic Series. US. English. ir. WB Saunders, West Washington Square, Philadelphia PA 19105. **Tel** (800)523-0713. **NLM** W1 MA492Y.

MALAYSIAN VETERINARY JOURNAL. (THE MALAYSIAN VETERINARY JOURNAL). 0126-5652. Periodical. English. an. University of Malaya, Central Animal Facility, Kuala Lumpur Malaya. **Ind/Abst** Life Sci. Collect., Biol. Abstr. **NLM** W1 MA5247SF. **CODEN** MVEJDP. *Journal of the Malaysian Veterinary Medical Association.*

MANAGEMENT ECONOMICS BULLETIN. (MANAGEMENT/ECONOMICS BULLETIN). Oct. 15, 1981-. 0821-6932. Periodical. CN. English. ir. Society of Ontario Veterinarians, Suite 412 131 Bloor Street West, Toronto Ontario M5S 1R1 Canada. **Tel** (416)968-9130. **Ed** Gida Nason. **DD** 636.089068. adv acc. **Circ** 2,00. (ctrl). Carries both classified and commerical ads. Classified sections include employment wanted/employment available, practices wanted/practices for sale, equipment wanted/equipment for sale.

MARKET REPORT & NEWSLETTER. **VFOAT** Market Report and Newsletter. 0747-4121. Periodical. US. English. wk. $2.50 for Members. Arizona Cattle Growers' Association, 5025 East Washington/Suite 110, Phoenix AZ 85034. **DD** 636.

MEDECIN VETERINAIRE DU QUEBEC. (LE MEDECIN VETERINAIRE DU QUEBEC). V. 10, No. 1- Jan. 1980-. 0225-9591. Periodical. CN. French. qt. Le Medecin Veterinaire du Quebec, 220 Avenue Pratte/Bureau 301, Saint-Hyacinthe Quebec J2S 4B6 Canada. **Ind/Abst** Point Repere, Biol. Abstr. **DD** 636.08905. **CODEN** MVEQDC. *M V-Quebec, 0704-6995.*

MEDYCYNA WETERYNARYJNA. Vol. 1- May/June 1945-. 0025-8628. Periodical. PL. Polish. mo. ARS Polona, Krakowskie Przedmiescie 7, 00-068 Warsaw Poland. **Ind/Abst** Life Sci. Collect., Excerpta Med., Pestdoc, Ringdoc, Vetdoc, Bibliogr. Agric., Biol. Abstr., Chem. Abstr., Nuci. Sci. Abstr. **NLM** W1 ME8718. **CODEN** MDWTAG.

THE MERCK VETERINARY MANUAL. (MERCK VETERINARY MANUAL). 0076-6542. US. English. ir. Merck & Company, PO Box 2000, Rahway NJ 07065. **Tel** (201)574-5403.

METHODS OF ANIMAL EXPERIMENTATION. US. English. ir. Academic Press, 4805 Sand Lake Road, Orlando FL 32819. **Tel** (305)345-4100.

MINK. Began with 1976. 0749-8683. US. English. an. Crop Reporting Board, Statistical Reporting Service, USDA, Washington DC 20250. **LC** SF405.M6. **DD** 338.176974447. *Mink Production.*

MINNESOTA NUTRITION CONFERENCE. 0271-1893. US. English. an. $8.00. University of Minnesota, Office of Special Programs, 405 Coffey Hall, 1429 Eckles, St Paul MN 55108. **Tel** (612)373-0725. **Ed** Gerald Wagner. **Ind/Abst** Chem. Abstr. **CODEN** MNCPDB. **Circ** 500. Scientific papers and research findings on animal nutrition.

Veterinary Medicine, Animal Culture

THE MINNESOTA VETERINARIAN. V. 1- 1961-. Periodical. US. English. sa. *Veterinary Grad.*

MISSOURI VETERINARIAN. Periodical. US. English. ir. Missouri Student Chapter of American Veterinarian Medical Association, University of Missouri, Columbia MO 65201.

MODERN VETERINARY PRACTICE. VFOAT MVP. V. 54- Jan. 1973-. 0362-8140. Periodical. US. English. mo. American Veterinary Publishers, Drawer KK, Santa Barbara CA 93102. **Tel** (800)235-6947. **Ind/Abst** Life Sci. Collect., Pestdoc, Ringdoc, Vetdoc, Energy Res. Abstr., Biol. Abstr., Chem. Abstr., Index Med., Bibliogr. Agric., Sci. Cit. Index, Abr. Ed. **NLM** W1 MO177. **CODEN** MVPRAX. *MVP, Modern Veterinary Practice.*

MONATSHEFTE FUR VETERINARMEDIZIN. Vol. 1- July 1946-. 0026-9263. Periodical. German (Added table of contents and summaries in English and Russian). sm. $64.00. VCH Publishers Inc, 303 North West 12th Avenue, Deerfield Beach FL 33442. **Tel** (305)428-5566. **Ind/Abst** Life Sci. Collect., Excerpta Med., Pestdoc, Ringdoc, Vetdoc, Biol. Abstr., Chem. Abstr., Bibliogr. Agric., Sci. Cit. Index, Abr. Ed. **LC** SF603. **NLM** W1 MO359. **CODEN** MVMZA8.

MONTHLY LETTER (MONTANA. ANIMAL HEALTH DIVISION). (MONTHLY LETTER). Jan. 1972-. Periodical. US. English. mo. *Monthly Letter (Montana. Livestock Sanitary Board).*

MORPHOGENESE DER TIERE. REIHE 1. DESKRIPTIVE MORPHOGENESE. Vol. 1- 1978-. Monographic Series. German. ir.

NATIONAL INSTITUTE OF ANIMAL HEALTH QUARTERLY. Main/Corp Kachiku Eisei Shikenjo, Tokyo. VFOAT Quarterly - National Institute of Animal Health. V. 1- Spring 1961-. 0027-951X. Periodical. English. qt. **Ind/Abst** Life Sci. Collect., Excerpta Med., Index Med., Biol. Abstr., Bibliogr. Agric. **LC** SF601. **NLM** W1 NA486CE. **CODEN** NIAHAI. *Bulletin of the National Institute of Animal Health.*

NATIONAL TICK SURVEILLANCE PROGRAM. 0503-5090. US. English. US Department of Agriculture, Animal & Plant Health Inspection Service, Washington DC 20402. **LC** SF810.T5. **DD** 636.0894433. **NLM** W2 A A5N.

NEBRASKA HEALTH MANPOWER REPORTS. VETERINARIANS. (NEBRASKA HEALTH MANPOWER REPORTS : VETERINARIANS). Main/Corp Nebraska. Division of Health Data and Statistical Research. 0148-3722. US. English. an. Nebraska Department of Health, 1003 O Street, Lincoln NE 68508. **LC** SF624.N2. **DD** 331.11. **NLM** W2 AN1 D34NV.

NEW METHODS (BERKELEY, CALIF.). (NEW METHODS). Vol. 4, No. 1 (May 1981)-. 0277-3015. Periodical. US. English. mo. $18.00 Domestic, $23.00 Canada. New Methods, PO Box 2605, San Francisco CA 94122. **Tel** (415)664-3469. Ed Ronald S Lippert. **DD** 636. bk rev. adv acc. **Circ** 5,600. National network service in the animal and veterinary fields. Resource bank for information. *Methods.*

NEW ZEALAND VETERINARY JOURNAL. V. 1- 1952-. 0048-0169. Periodical. NZ. English. mo. 160. New Zealand Veterinary Association, PO Box 524, Wellington New Zealand. **Tel** 04 720 103. Ed Julie A Lord. **Ind/Abst** Life Sci. Collect., Excerpta Med., Pestdoc, Ringdoc, Vetdoc, Biol. Abstr., Chem. Abstr., Index Med., Bibliogr. Agric., Sci. Cit. Index, Abr. Ed. **NLM** W1 NE986. **CODEN** NEZTAF. bk rev. adv acc. **Circ** 1,800. (ctrl). Refereed scientific articles covering a wide range of veterinary subjects. Also letters to the editor.

'NEWS" FOR THE CANADIAN RABBIT BREEDER. (THE NEWS FOR THE CANADIAN RABBIT BREEDER). VFOAT Nouvelles Nationales Pour le Cuniculteur Canadien. 0545-8269. Periodical. CN. English. bm. E McCallum, RR No 3 Lambeth, Ontario N0L 1S0 Canada.

NEWSLETTER - AMERICAN ASSOCIATION OF EQUINE PRACTIONERS. See Horses and Horsemanship.

NEWSLETTER - B.C.A.I. CENTRE. (NEWSLETTER). Main/Corp B.C. Articicial Insemination Centre. VAT Newsletter - British Columbia Artificial Insemination Centre. 0715-4526. Periodical. CN. English. qt. Newsletter British Columbia Artificial Insemination Centre Milner, British Columbia V0X 1T0 Canada. **DD** 636.08245.

NEWSLETTER - FLOWER VETERINARY LIBRARY. See Library and Information Science.

NEWSLETTER - HUMANE SOCIETY OF OTTAWA-CARLETON. (NEWSLETTER). 0712-2950. Periodical. CN. English. ty. Free to Members. Humane Society of Ottawa-Carleton, 101 Champagne Avenue South, Ottawa Ontario K1S 4P3 Canada. **DD** 179.306071383.

NEWSLETTER - SCIENTISTS' CENTER FOR ANIMAL WELFARE (WASHINGTON, D.C.). (NEWSLETTER). VFOAT Scientists Center Newsletter. (Vol. 1, No. 1 (Dec. 1978-Jan. 1979)-. 0742-5260. Periodical. US. English. ty. $20.00. Scientists Center for Animal Welfare, PO Box 3755, Washington DC 20007. **NLM** W1 NE977TC.

NNALES DE GENETIQUE ET DE SELECTION ANIMALE. V. 1-. 0003-4002. Periodical. FR. French (chiefly in English with some German). qt. Institut National de la Recherche Agronomique, Regisseur des Recettes, 78000 Versailles France. **Ind/Abst** Chem. Abstr., Biol. Abstr., Bibliogr. Agric. **LC** SF105. **DD** 636.082105. **NLM** W1 AN336AD. **CODEN** AGQSA8.

NORDISK VETERINARMEDICIN. 0029-1579. Periodical. DK. Multilingual. mo. $39.21. Den Danske Dyraegeforening, Alhambraues 15, DK 1826 Copenhagen Denmark. **Ind/Abst** Biol. Abstr., Chem. Abstr., Energy Res. Abstr., Excerpta Med., Index Med., Life Sci. Collect., Pestdoc, Ringdoc, Vetdoc, Sci. Cit. Index, Abr. Ed. **NLM** W1 NO228. **CODEN** NOVTAV. *Norsk Veterinrtidsskrift, Skandinavisk Veterinartidsskrift; Suomen Elainlaakarilehti Svensk Veterinartidskrift.*

NORIN SUISANSHO KACHIKU EISEI SHIKENJO NEMPO. 1977-. JA. Japanese. ir. Buneido, 27-18 Hongo 2-chome, Bunkyo-ku 113, Tokyo Japan. **LC** SF705. *Norinsho Kachiku Eisei Shikenjo Nempo.*

NORINSHO KACHIKU EISEI SHIKENJO NEMPO. Began with the Report for 1958. JA. Japanese. ir. 1900. Buneido, 27-18 Hongo 2-chome Bunkyo-ku, Tokyo 113 Japan. **LC** SF705.

NORTH CAROLINA VETERINARIAN. V. 1- 1956-. 0029-263X. Periodical. US. English. qt.

NOS ANIMAUX. See Pets.

NOUVELLES ACQUISITIONS - UNIVERSITE DE MONTREAL, BIBLIOTHEQUE DE MEDECINE VETERINAIRE. See Bibliographies.

NRCHA NEWS. VAT National Reined Cow Horse Association News. 8756-2197. Periodical. US. English. mo. PCQHA, PO Box 254822, Sacramento CA 95865. **DD** 636. *Cutter (Sacramento, Calif.), 0746-7443.*

NUTRIENT REQUIREMENTS OF DOMESTIC ANIMALS. 0160-6948. Monographic Series. US. English. ir. National Research Council, 2101 Constitution Avenue, Washington DC 20520. **Ind/Abst** Chem. Abstr., Bibliogr. Agric. **CODEN** NRDAA7.

OEGUK KWAHAK KISUL TONGBO. SUUI CHUKSAN. VFOAT Zhivotnovodstvo i Veterinariia. Periodical. Korean. ir. **LC** SF1.

OFFICIAL PROCEEDINGS, ANNUAL MEETING - AMERICAN ASSOCIATION OF FEED MICROSCOPISTS. Main/Corp American Association of Feed Microscopists. 0569-2628. US. English. an. University of Maryland, Center of Adult Education, College Park MD 20742. **Ind/Abst** Chem. Abstr. **LC** SF97. **DD** 636.0855. **CODEN** OPFMAG.

THE OKLAHOMA VETERINARIAN. Vol. 1- 1954-. 0474-0785. Periodical. US. English. ir. $12.00. Oklahoma Veterinarian, 1547 South Lewis, Tulsa OK 74104.

OMV-NOUVELLES CEASED. (O M V-NOUVELLES). Main/Corp Ordre des Medecins Veterinaires du Quebec. VAT Ordre des Medecins Veterinaires-Nouvelles. Began 1974? Ceased with Vol. 10, No. 3, 1979. 0705-2111. Periodical. CN. French. bm. 12.50. Ordre des Medecins Veterinaires du Quebec, Bureau 505/250 Ouest East, Boulevard Sainte-Joseph, Montreal Quebec H2T 1H7 Canada. **DD** 636.08905. *C M V-Nouvelles.*

ONDERSTEPOORT JOURNAL OF VETERINARY RESEARCH. (THE ONDERSTEPOORT JOURNAL OF VETERINARY RESEARCH). V. 25- 1951-. 0030-2465. Periodical. English. ir. **Ind/Abst** Life Sci. Collect., Pestdoc, Ringdoc, Vetdoc, Biol. Abstr., Chem. Abstr., Nuci. Sci. Abstr., Index Med., Bibliogr. Agric. **NLM** W1 ON108. **CODEN** OJVRAZ. (cum index). *Onderstepoort Journal of Veterinary Science and Animal Industry.*

ONZE VOGELS. Periodical. NE. Dutch. mo. Bondsbureau N B V V, P B 74, Bergen OP Zoom Netherlands. **LC** SF461.A1.

PAKISTAN VETERINARY JOURNAL. Vol. 1, No. 1 (Jan. 1981)-. 0253-8318. Periodical. English. qt. 25.00. University of Agriculture, Faculty Veterinary Science, Faisalabad Pakistan. **Tel** 25911-20/437. Ed M Infan. **Ind/Abst** Biol. Abstr., Chem. Abstr. **CODEN** PVJODU. bk rev. adv acc. **Circ** 1,000. Contains veterinary parasitology, pathology; pharmacology; microbiology; medicine; surgery and animal reproduction-artificial insemination; obstetrics and gynecology.

PEOPLE, ANIMALS, ENVIRONMENT. VFOAT People-Animals-Environment. Vol. 1, No. 1 (Spring 1983)-. 8755-5875. Periodical. US. English. sa. $10.00. Delta Society, 212 Wells Avenue South, Suite C, Renton WA 98055. **Tel** (206)226-7357. Ed Linda M Hines. **DD** 636. bk rev. **Circ** 2,500. Overviews of programs that use animals in therapy and community programs bringing people and animals together. Conference information, book reviews, resource materials.

PERFORMANCE BUDGET ON ANIMAL HUSBANDRY & VETERINARY. Main/Corp Assam (India). Veterinary Dept. English. an. Veterinary Department, Gauhati Assam India. **LC** SF604. **DD** 354.541620082336.

PERFORMANCE HORSEMAN. See Horses and Horsemanship.

PHILIPPINE JOURNAL OF VETERINARY MEDICINE. V. 1- June 1962-. 0031-7705. Periodical. PH. English. sa. $16.00. University of Philippines, College of Veterinary Medicine, Quezon City D55 Phillippines. **Ind/Abst** Life Sci. Collect., Biol. Abstr., Chem. Abstr., Bibliogr. Agric. **NLM** W1 PH576P. **CODEN** PJVMAV.

PIG VETERINARY SOCIETY PROCEEDINGS. VFOAT Proceedings - Pig Veterinary Society. V. 1- 1976-. 0141-3074. Periodical. UK. English. ir. $13.80. Pig Veterinary Society Proceedings, c/o T W Heard Grove House, Corston Malmesbury Wilts SN16 OHL England. **Tel** (06662)3355. Ed The Pig Veterinary Society. Proceedings of papers given at Pig Veterinary Society meetings.

PLANO NACIONAL DO COMBATE A FEBRE AFTOSA: RELATORIO. Main/Corp Brazil. Coordenacao do Combate a Febre Aftosa. 1972-. Portuguese. ir. Ed Embaixador, 4O Andar (S C S), Brasilia Brazil. **LC** SF793.

PLAYBOAR MAGAZINE. 0710-0361. Periodical. CN. English. qt. $2.50 Per. No. Playboar Magazine, PO Box 353 Station A, Kingston Ontario K7M 6R7 Canada. **DD** 636.400207.

POINT VETERINAIRE. (LE POINT VETERINAIRE). V. 7, No. 32-. 0335-4997. Periodical. FR. French. ir. 450. Le Point Veterinaire, 25 rue Bourgelat, 94700 Maison Alfort France. **Tel** 353.20.01. **Ind/Abst** Bibliogr. Agric. adv acc. **Circ** 6,000. (ctrl). Technical information for veterinary practitioners on pathology, surgery, therapeutics, epidemiology, etc. of large and small animals (dogs, cats, horses, cows, goats, sheep, poultry, etc.).

POLSKIE ARCHIWUM WETERYNARYJNE. See Genealogy and Heraldry - Archives.

PRACTICA BOVINA CEASED. Vol. 1, No. 1 (Mar.-Apr. 1980)-. 0273-740X. Periodical. US. Spanish. bm. $43.00. Veterinary Practice Publishing Company, PO Box 4457, Santa Barbara CA 93103.

PRAKTISCHE TIERARZT. (DER PRAKTISCHE TIERARZT). Vol. 1-. 0032-681X. Periodical. GW. German. mo. $68.98. Schlutersche Verlag Druckerei, Georgswall 4, Postfach 5440, D-3000 Hanover West Germany. **Ind/Abst** Pestdoc, Ringdoc, Vetdoc, Energy Res. Abstr., Life Sci. Collect., Chem. Abstr., Bibliogr. Agric., Sci. Cit. Index, Abr. Ed. **NLM** W1 PR283. **CODEN** PRTIAV. bk rev. adv acc. **Circ** 6,000. (ctrl).

Veterinary Medicine, Animal Culture

PRATIQUE MEDICALE & CHIRURGICALE DE L'ANIMAL DE COMPAGNIE. VFOAT Pratique Medicale et Chirurgicale de L'Animal de Compagnie. Began with: V. 18, No. 1 (Jan./Feb. 1983). 0758-1882. Periodical. French (summaries in English, German, Italian and Spanish). bm. Ind/Abst Bibliogr. Agric., Pestdoc, Ringdoc, Vetdoc. *Animal de Compagnie.*

PRAXIS VETERINARIA. Periodical. In Serbo-Croatian. bm. Free. Pliva, I L Ribara 89, 41000 Zagreb Yugoslavia. Tel 412-070. Ind/Abst Chem. Abstr. CODEN PRVEDW. bk rev. Circ 5,000. (ctrl). We publish scientific and technical works of veterinary medicine as well as genetic engineering related to the development of veterinary medicine and cattle feeding.

PREVENTIVE VETERINARY MEDICINE. Vol. 1, No. 1 (Aug. 1982)-. 0167-5877. Periodical. English. bm. Elsevier Science Publishers, PO Box 211, 1000 AE Amsterdam Netherlands. Tel (020)5803.911. Ind/Abst Life Sci. Collect. NLM W1 PR507Z.

PROCEEDINGS, ANNUAL MEETING OF THE UNITED STATES ANIMAL HEALTH ASSOCIATION. Main/Corp United States Animal Health Association. 1969-. 0082-8750. US. English. an. $20.00. US Animal Health Association, PO Box 28176, Richmond VA 23228. Tel (804)266-3275. Ind/Abst Leg. Contents, Curr. Law Index, Leg. Resour. Index, Index Leg. Period., Index Med. Circ 1,300. Study of animal health science, milk and meat hygiene and information relating to the unification of laws, regulations, policies and methods pertaining to milk and meat hygiene. *Proceedings, Annual Meeting of the United States Livestock Sanitary Association.*

PROCEEDINGS, ANNUAL MEETING - WESTERN SECTION, AMERICAN SOCIETY OF ANIMAL SCIENCE. Main/Corp American Society of Animal Science. Western Section. V. 14- 1963-. 0569-7832. US. English. an. American Society of Animal Science, 309 West Clark Street, Champaign IL 61820. Tel (217)356-3182. Ind/Abst Chem. Abstr., Bibliogr. Agric. CODEN PMWSA7. *Proceedings, Annual Meeting.*

PROCEEDINGS OF ANNUAL MEETING - AMERICAN ASSOCIATION OF VETERINARY LABORATORY DIAGNOSTICIANS. Main/Corp American Association of Veterinary Laboratory Diagnosticians. 18th-. 0098-3534. Periodical. US. English. an. Veterinary Medicine Diagnosticians Laboratory, University of Missouri, Columbus MO 65217. Ind/Abst Chem. Abstr. LC SF771. DD 636.0896076. NLM W1 PR584RV. CODEN PAMDDZ.

PROCEEDINGS OF THE ANNUAL CONFERENCE. Main/Corp Australian Veterinary Association. 53d- 1976-. 0312-8555. Periodical. English. ir.

PROCEEDINGS OF THE ANNUAL CONVENTION - AMERICAN ASSOCIATION OF BOVINE PRACTITIONERS. CONVENTION. (PROCEEDINGS OF THE . . . ANNUAL CONVENTION). Main/Corp American Association of Bovine Practitioners. Convention. VFOAT Boving Proceedings. Began with Vol. for 1971. 0743-0450. US. English. an. $20.00. Heritage Press, 1226 North Lincoln, Stillwater OK 74074. Tel (405)624-7472. Ed Eric I Williams. Ind/Abst Bibliogr. Agric. bk rev. adv acc. Circ 6,000. (ctrl). A journal for veterinarians and others in allied fields that are interested in cattle diseases and prevention. A report of our annual meeting.

PROCEEDINGS OF THE ANNUAL CONVENTION OF THE AMERICAN ASSOCIATION OF EQUINE PRACTITIONERS. Main/Corp American Association of Equine Practitioners. 1956. 0065-7182. US. English. an. $20.00. American Association of Equine Practitioners, Route 5, 22363 Hillcrest Circle, Golden CO 80401. Tel (303)526-0820. Ed Frank J Milne. Ind/Abst Life Sci. Collect. NLM W1 PR584NN. (cum index). Scientific papers given at the annual convention of equine medicine.

PROCEEDINGS OF THE ANNUAL MEETING - AMERICAN SOCIETY OF ANIMAL SCIENCE. WESTERN SECTION. Main/Corp American Society of Animal Science. Western Section. V. 1- 1950-. 0569-7832. US. English. an. University of Nevada, c/o Dr B Bohman, Animal Science Department, Reno NV 89507.

PROCEEDINGS OF THE CANADIAN ASSOCIATION FOR LABORATORY ANIMAL SCIENCE. Main/Corp Canadian Association for Laboratory Animal Science. Convention. 0708-7624. CN. English. an. Canadian Association for Laboratory Animal Science, 2627 Morley Trail North West, Calgary Alberta T2M 4G6 Canada. Ind/Abst Chem. Abstr. DD 636.0885. CODEN PCASDY.

PROCEEDINGS OF THE KAL KAN SYMPOSIUM FOR THE TREATMENT OF SMALL ANIMAL DISEASES. Main/Conf Kal Kan Symposium for the Treatment of Small Animal Diseases. 4th (1980)-. US. English. an. Kal Kan Professional Services, 3386 East 44th Street, Vernon CA 90058. *Proceedings of the Kal Kan Symposium for the Treatment of Dog & Cat Diseases.*

PROCEEDINGS OF THE TECHNICAL CONFERENCE ON ARTIFICIAL INSEMINATION AND REPRODUCTION. Main/Conf Technical Conference on Artificial Insemination and Reproduction. 0190-4531. US. English. be. National Association of Animal Breeders, PO Box 1033, Columbia MO 65201. LC SF105.5. DD 636.08245.

PRODUCTEUR AGRICOLE. *See* Agriculture.

PROGRESS IN CANINE PRACTICE. Series/Titl Modern Veterinary Reference Series. V. 1- 1967-. 0091-0643. US. English. ir. American Veterinary Publishers Inc, Drawer KK, Danta Barbara CA 93102. NLM ZSF 991 P964.

PROGRESS REPORT - FUND FOR THE REPLACEMENT OF ANIMALS IN MEDICAL EXPERIMENTS. Main/Corp Fund for the replacement of Animals in medical experiments. No. 1- Apr. 1970-. Monographic Series. UK. English. sa. Secretary Frame, 34 Stoney Street, Nottingham NG1 1NB England. Tel (0602)584740. Ed DR Gilly Griffin. Circ 2,500. A newsletter published quarterly, giving details on the work of frame and on current happenings within the area of animal experimentation.

PULSE. Began publication in 1959. 0555-6953. Periodical. US. English. $20.00. Southern California Veterinary Medical Association, 8338 Rosemead Boulevard, Pico Riveres CA 90660. Tel (213)723-1746.

QUARTERLY INDEX - VETERINARY INTERFACE (OAKDALE, CALIF.). (QUARTERLY INDEX). Vol. 1, No. 1 (Jan./Mar. 1983)-. 0740-2430. US. English. qt. $55.00 Domestic, $65.00 Foreign. Veterinary Interface, 5679 Claribel Road, Oakdale CA 95361. Tel (209)847-6570. Ed M M Mastin. adv acc. Circ 700. Periodical indes and abstract covering 18 veterinary journals. Each article, case report, letter, abstract, etc., on dogs, cats, laboratory animals, and exotic pets and indexed.

QUEENSLAND JOURNAL OF AGRICULTURAL AND ANIMAL SCIENCES. *See* Agriculture.

RABBIT BRAIN RESEARCH. Periodical. English. ir. Elsevier Science Publishing Company, PO Box 1663, Grand Central Station, New York NY 10163.

RABBITS. Vol. 1, No. 1 (Dec. 1977)-. 0277-3171. Periodical. US. English. mo. $12.00. Countryside Publications Ltd, 312 Portland Road, Waterloo MI 53594. Tel (414)478-2115. Ed Jerome Belanger. LC SF451. DD 636.931. bk rev. adv acc. Circ 6,000. Rabbit raising: commercial meat/fur, hobby, and pets. *Countryside.*

RABBITS IN CANADA. V. 5, No. 7- July 1970-. 0033-7242. Periodical. CN. English. bm. 7.00. Clay Publishing Company Ltd, Bewdley Ontario Canada. Tel (416)797-2281. Ed Charlotte Clay. bk rev. adv acc. Circ 500. (ctrl). Commercial rabbit growing plus fancier breeding. *Thumper.*

THE RANCH MAGAZINE. Began with Oct. 1971 issue. 0145-8515. Periodical. US. English. mo. $18.40. Texas Sheep & Goat Raisers Association, PO Box 2678, San Angelo TX 76901. Tel (915)655-4434. Ed Scott Campbell. Ind/Abst Bibliogr. Agric. LC SF371. DD 636.3005. bk rev. adv acc. Circ 6,200. (ctrl). Sheep, Angora goat and cattle raiser information, market updates, wool and Mohair fashions. *Sheep and Goat Raiser, 0037-3397.*

RAT NEWS LETTER. No. 1- Apr. 1977-. 0309-1848. Periodical. UK. English. ir. University of Pittsburgh, Department of Pathology, School of Medicine, Dr Cramer, Pittsburgh PA 15261. Tel (01)643-8000. NLM W1 RA9475.

RECENT ADVANCES IN ANIMAL NUTRITION. Series/Titl Studies in the Agricultural and Food Sciences. 1977-. Monographic Series. UK. English. an. Ind/Abst Chem. Abstr. CODEN RAANES.

RECUEIL DE MEDECINE VETERINAIRE. 0034-1843. Periodical. French. bm. Ecole Natl Veterinaire Alfort Administration & Redaction, 94704 Maisons-Alfort Cedex France. Tel (1)4375 12 10. Ind/Abst Excerpta Med., Pestdoc, Ringdoc, Vetdoc, Life Sci. Collect., Bibliogr. Agric., Biol. Abstr. NLM W1 RE114. CODEN RMVEAG. bk rev. adv acc. Circ 6,000. Dealing with veterinary medicine each issue is concerned with research, post-graduate education and review.

REGISTERED HOLSTEIN TOTAL PERFORMANCE SIRE SUMMARIES. Main/Corp Holstein-Friesian Association of America. VFOAT Sire Summaries. US. English. an. $10.00. The Association, 1 South Main Street, Box 808, Brattleboro VT 05301.

REPORT - INSTITUTE OF ANIMAL PHYSIOLOGY. Main/Corp Institute of Animal Physiology (Great Britain). 1960/61-. UK. English. be. 1.30. 49 High Holborn, Cambridge WC1V 6HB England. LC SF768. DD 636.0892005.

REPORT TO CONGRESS, ADMINISTRATION OF THE WILD FREE-ROAMING HORSE AND BURRO ACT. VFOAT Administration of the Wild Free-Roaming Horse and Burro Act. 0739-3989. US. English. US Department of the Interior, Bureau of Land Management, 18th and C Street NW, Washington DC 20240. LC SF959.E5. DD 353.0082328. Vols. for (1982-) distributed to depository libraries in microfiche. *Report to Congress by the Secretary of the Interior and the Secretary of Agriculture on Administration of the Wild Free-Roaming Horse and Burro Act, Public Law 92-195, 0739-4071.*

REPORTED ARTHROPOD-BORNE ENCEPHALITIDES IN HORSES AND OTHER EQUIDAE. Main/Corp United States. Animal and Plant Health Inspection Service. US. English. an. $3.00. US Department of Agriculture, Animal and Plant Health Inspection Service, Federal Building, Hyattsville MD 20782. LC SF960.3.U6. DD 636.108945983200973. *Reported Arthropod-Borne Encephalitides in Horses and Other Equidae.*

REPORTS OF THE SCIENTIFIC COMMITTEE FOR ANIMAL NUTRITION. 1st Ser. (1979)-. US. English. ir. $1.85. European Community Information Service, 2100 M Street NW/Suite 707, Washington DC 20037. LC SF95. DD 636.08505.

REPOSITORIO DE TRABALHOS DO L.N.I.V. Main/Corp Laboratorio Nacional de Investigacao Veterinaria. VAT Repositorio de Trabalhos do Laboratorio Nacional de Investigacao Veterinaria. Portuguese (summaries in English and French). ir. Laboratorio Nacional de Investigacao Veterinaria, Estrada de Benfica 701, Lisboa Portugal. Ind/Abst Bibliogr. Agric. LC SF604.

REPRODUCTION, NUTRITION, DEVELOPPEMENT. V. 20, No. 1A-. 0181-1916. Periodical. French (English). ir. 450 Foreign. Ind/Abst Life Sci. Collect., Excerpta Med., Pestdoc, Ringdoc, Vetdoc, Index Med., Biol. Abstr., Energy Res. Abstr., Chem. Abstr. LC SF768. DD 636.0892. NLM W1 RE213LN. CODEN RNDED4. *Annales de Biologie Animale, Biochimie, Biophysique, 0003-388X.*

RESEARCH ANIMALS IN CANADA. July 1980-. 0229-1223. CN. English. an. Canadian Council on Animal Care, 1105-151 Slater Street, Ottawa Ontario K1P 5H3 Canada. DD 636.088502571.

RESEARCH IN VETERINARY SCIENCE. V. 1- Jan. 1960-. 0034-5288. Periodical. UK. English. bm. British Veterinary Association, 7 Mansfield Street, London W1M 0AT England. Tel 01 636 6541. Ed E Boden. Ind/Abst Life Sci. Collect., Excerpta Med., Pestdoc, Ringdoc, Vetdoc, Index Med., Biol. Abstr., Chem. Abstr., Bibliogr. Agric., Sci. Cit. Index, Abr. Ed. LC SF601. DD 636.08905. NLM W1 RE231. CODEN RVTSA9. adv acc. (ctrl). Original research on the health and disease of animals including comparative medicine.

Veterinary Medicine, Animal Culture

RESEARCH REPORT - COMMONWEALTH SCIENTIFIC AND INDUSTRIAL RESEARCH ORGANIZATION. DIVISION OF ANIMAL HEALTH. 1982-83-. 0812-7336. English. ir. *Annual Report, 0069-7273.*

RESOURCE. V. 1- Sept. 1975-. 0700-5237. Periodical. CN. English. be. Free. Canadian Council on Animal Care, 151 Slater Street, Ottawa Ontario K1P 5H3 Canada. DD 636.08850971.

RESSOURCE. V. 1, No. 2, April 1976-. 0700-5245. Periodical. CN. French. be. Free. Conseil Canadien de Protection des Animaux, 151 rue Slater, Ottawa Ontario K1P 5H3 Canada Canada. DD 636.08850971.

RESULTATS DEFINITIFS DE L'ENQETE SUR LE CHEPTEL BOVIN. Main/Corp France. Service Central des Enquetes et Etudes Statistiques. Series/Titl Production Animale. FR. French. ir. Service Central des Enquetes et Etudes Statistiques, 4 Ave. de Saint-Mande, 75570 Paris Cedex 12 France. LC SF196.F7. DD 338.176200944.

RESUMENES. SERIE ZOOTECNIA E INSEMINACION ARTIFICIAL. V. 4, No. 3/4- March/April 1973-. Periodical. Spanish. ir.

REVIEW OF APPLIED ENTOMOLOGY. SERIES B, MEDICAL AND VETERINARY. Began with: Vol. 1 in Jan. 1913. 0305-0084. Periodical. UK. English. mo. $172.00. Commonwealth of Agricultural Bureaux, Farnham House, Farnham Royal, Slough SL2 3BN England. Tel (02814)2662. Ed J R Metcalfe. LC SF601. DD 595.705. NLM Z 5858.E2 R454. CODEN RAEBA8. Index published separately - free - automatically sent. (cum index). adv acc. Deals with insects and other arthropods transmitting disease or otherwise injurious to man and to animals of significance to man.

REVIEW OF MEDICAL AND VETERINARY MYCOLOGY. Began in 1951. 0034-6624. Periodical. UK. English. qt. 231.80. Commonwealth Agricultural Bureau, Farnham House Farnham Royal, Slough SL2 3BN England. Tel (02814) 2662. Ed J R Metcalfe. adv acc. Mycosis of man and farm, domestic and wild animals, allergic disorders of man and animals associated with fungi, poisoning of man and animals by fungi, etc, and general and systematic mycology and fungicides. *Annotated Bibliography of Medical Mycology.*

REVIEW - VETERINARY INSTITUTE FOR TROPICAL AND HIGH ALTITUDE RESEARCH, SAN MARCOS UNIVERSITY INVESTIGATION CENTRE. Main/Corp Universidad Nacional Mayor de San Marcos. Instituto Veterinario de Investigaciones Tropicales y de Altura. Cectro de Investigacion. VFOAT Informe - Instituto Veterinario de Investigacioner Tropicales y de Altura. U.N.M.S.M. Centro de Investigacion. No. 21- July/Dec. 1971. Periodical. Spanish. ir.

REVISTA DA FACULDADE DE MEDICINA VETERINARIA E ZOOTECNIA DA UNIVERSIDADE DE SAO PAULO. Main/Corp Universidade de Sao Paulo. Faculdade de Medicina Veterinaria e Zootecnia. V. 9- 1972-. 0303-7525. Periodical. BL. Portuguese. sa. 60 Single Issue. Cidade Universitaria, CEP 05508 Sao Paulo Brazil. Ind/Abst Bibliogr. Agric., Chem. Abstr. LC SF604. NLM W1 RE369T. CODEN RVZUAB. *Revista da Faculdade de Medicina Veterinaria.*

REVISTA DE CRESTEREA ANIMALELOR. V. 24, No. 7- July 1974-. Periodical. RM. Romanian (added table of contents in English, French, and Russian). mo. Ilexim Press Department, PO Box 1-136-1-137, Bucharest Romania. Ind/Abst Pestdoc, Ringdoc, Vetdoc, Chem. Abstr., Bibliogr. Agric. CODEN RCAND7. *Revista de Zootehnie si Medicina Veterinaria.*

REVISTA DE LA FACULTAD DE CIENCIAS VETERINARIAS : ORGANO DE LA FACULTAD DE CIENCIAS VETERINARIAS. V. 27, No. 1-8 (1977-1978)-. Periodical. Spanish (text in English summaries). ir. *Revista de Medicina Veterinaria y Parasitologia.*

REVISTA DE MEDICINA VETERINARIA. V. 1- Aug. 1915-. 0325-6391. Periodical. AG. English summaries. bm. $100.00. Sociedad de Medicina Veterinar, Chile 1856, Buenos Aires Argentina. Ind/Abst Chem. Abstr., Bibliogr. Agric. NLM W1 RE436V. CODEN RMEVAG. *Revista - Sociedad de Medicina Veterinaria.*

REVISTA MUNDIAL DE ZOOTECNIA. No. 1-. Periodical. Spanish. qt $10.00. UNIPUB, 205 East 42nd Street, New York NY 10017. LC SF1.

REVISTA PORTUGUESA DE CIENCIAS VETERINARIAS. 1- 1902. 0035-0389. Periodical. PO. Portuguese (summaries in English and French). qt. 900. Sociedade Portuguesa Ciencias Veterinarias, rue D Dinis 2-A RC, 1200 Lisbon Portugal. Tel 680188. Ed Manuel Maria Bettencourt de Sa Nogueira. bk rev. adv acc. Circ 1,000. (ctrl). Scientific papers about veterinary medicine and animal production; bibliographic indexes and abstracts; technical book reviews; short news about veterinary life in Portugal and in the world.

REVUE D'ELEVAGE ET DE MEDECINE VETERINAIRE DES PAYS TROPICAUX. Jan./Mar. 1947-. 0035-1865. Periodical. FR. French (summaries in English and Spanish). qt. $43.90. Semaine des Hopitaux, 15 rue Saint Benoit, 75278 Paris Cedex 06 France. Tel (800)645-7512. Ind/Abst Excerpta Med., Pestdoc, Ringdoc, Vetdoc, Index Med., Life Sci. Collect., Curr. Contents, Agric. Biol. Environ. Sci., Bibliogr. Agric. NLM W1 RE8088. *Recueil de Medecine Veterinaire Exotique.*

REVUE LAITIERE FRANCAISE. 0035-3590. Periodical. FR. French. mo. $46.57. Revue Laitiere Francaise, 15 rue Danielle Casanova, 75001 Paris France. Tel 261-52-74. Ind/Abst Excerpta Med., Int. Packag. Abstr., Bibliogr. Agric. LC SF221. DD 338.17705. *Industrie Laitiere.*

REVUE - OFFICE INTERNATIONAL DES EPIZOOTIES. (REVUE SCIENTIFIQUE ET TECHNIQUE). VFOAT Revue Scientifique et Technique de l'OIE. Vol. 1, No. 1 Mar. 1982-. 0253-1933. Periodical. English (French and Spanish). qt. Ind/Abst Pestdoc, Ringdoc, Vetdoc, Biol. Abstr. LC SF781. DD 636.0896905. CODEN RTOEDX.

REVUE TRIMESTRIELLE D'INFORMATION TECHNIQUE ET ECONOMIQUE. Main/Corp Communaute Economique du Betail et de la Viande. Secretariat Executif. Periodical. French. ir. Communaute Economique du Betail et de la Viande Secretariat Executif, BP 638, Ouagadougou Haute-Volta (Upper Volta). LC SF55.A39. DD 338.17608830966.

ROCZNIKI AKADEMII ROLNICZEJ W POZNANIU - WYDZIA ZOOTECHNICZNY. Main/Corp Akademia Rolnicza W Poznaniu. Wydzia Zootechniczny. 19-1973-. Polish (summaries in English and Russian). ir. 12.00. Wydawn Uczelniane Akademii Rolniczej, Ul Armii Czerwonej 77, Poznan Poland. LC SF1. *Roczniki Wyzszej Szkoy Rolniczej W Poznaniu - Wydzia Zootechniczny.*

ROCZNIKI NAUK ROLNICZYCH. SERIA E. WETERYNARII. VFOAT Annaly Selskokhoziaistvennykh Nauk. Seriia E. V. 66- 1953- Ceased in 1960?. Periodical. PL. Polish (summaries in Russian and English). sa. Ind/Abst Sel. Water Resour. Abstr.

R.T.V.A. (REVUE TECHNIQUE VETERINAIRE DE L'ALIMENTATION : RTVA). VFOAT RTVA. 0483-786X. Periodical. FR. French. mo. Editions Meteore, 42 rue de Louvre, 75001 Paris, France. Ind/Abst Chem. Abstr. CODEN RRTADW.

SANSHI SHIKENJO NEMPO. 1960-. Japanese. ir. LC SF553.J3.

SAPPORO HISHIRYO KENSAJO JIGYO HOKOKU : SHIRYO NO BU. Main/Corp Norin Suisansho Sapporo Hishiryo Kensajo. 1977-. Japanese. ir. LC SF15.J3. *Sapporo Hishiryo Kensajo Jigyo Hokoku: Shiryo No Bu.*

SASKATCHEWAN VETERINARY MEDICAL ASSOCIATION NEWSLETTER. (NEWSLETTER). VAT Newsletter - Saskatchewan Veterinary Medical Association. Vol. 1, No. 1 (May 1968)-. 0711-2467. Periodical. CN. English. ir. Free. Saskatchewan Veterinary Medical Association, 15 Hawthorne Crescent, Regina Saskatchewan S4S 4Y1 Canada. DD 636.089097124.

SBORNIK NAUCHNYKH RABOT SIBNIVI. Main/Corp Sibirskii Nauchno-Issledovatel'skii Veterinarnyi Institut. No. 22- 1975-. Periodical. UR. Russian. ir. *Sbornik Nauchnykh Rabot.*

SCHWEIZER ARCHIV FUR TIERHEILKUNDE. See Genealogy and Heraldry - Archives.

SCIENTIFIC PROCEEDINGS - AMERICAN COLLEGE OF VETERINARY INTERNAL MEDICINE. Main/Corp American College of Veterinary Internal Medicine. 1979-. CN. English. ir. University of Guelph, American College of Veterinary Internal Medicine, 805 Horseshoe Lane, Blacksburgh VA 24060. *Proceedings of the Annual Scientific Meeting of the American College of Veterinary Internal Medicine.*

SCIENTIFIC PROCEEDINGS FROM THE ANNUAL MEETING - AMERICAN COLLEGE OF VETERINARY OPHTHALMOLOGISTS. Main/Corp American College of Veterinary Ophthalmologists. 1st-3d. 0147-2666. Periodical. US. English. an. American College of Veterinary Ophthalmologists, 617 Building 229 H, Chapel Hill NC 27177. Tel (919)966-5296. NLM W1 SC862G.

THE SCOTTISH TERRIER QUARTERLY. Vol. 1, No. 1 (Spring 1984)-. 0747-3532. Periodical. US. English. bm. The Scottish Terrier Quarterly, 4401 Zephyr Street, Wheat Ridge CO 80033-3299.

SELEZIONE VETERINARIA. Main/Corp Istituto Zooprofilattico Sperimentale della Lombardia e dell 'Emilia. V. 1- 1960-. 0037-1521. Periodical. IT. Italian. mo. 15.000 Domestic, Free Foreign. Istituto Zooprofilattico Sperimentale della Lombardia e dell 'Emila, Sel Veterinaria/V Bianchi 7, 25125 Brescia Italy. Tel 030-42161. Ind/Abst Chem. Abstr., Bibliogr. Agric. CODEN SVETDJ. Circ 2,800. Large summary foreign publications and original publications on biology, microbiology, fish culture and fisheries, sanitation, and environmental technology.

SHEEP REPORT FROM THE DEPARTMENT OF ANIMAL SCIENCE. Periodical. US. English. bm. $5.00. Agricultural Newsletter Service, University of Illinois, 120 Munford Hall Urbana IL 61801. Tel (217)333-1000.

SHEEP RETURNS. Main/Corp New Zealand. Dept. of Statistics. NZ. English. ir. Department of Statistics, Private Bag, Wellington New Zealand. LC SF375.5.N4. DD 338.1763009931. *Annual Sheep Returns.*

SHEEP TOPICS. July 1982-. 0715-8378. Periodical. CN. English. DD 636.3097124.

SHELTER SENSE. V. 1- April 1978-. 0734-3078. Periodical. US. English. mo. $8.00. The Humane Society of the United States, 2100 L Street NW, Washington DC 20037. Tel (202)452-1100. Ed Deborah L Reed. Circ 3,000. A monthly newsletter for humane and animal control workers to help them increase their professionalism, reduce animal suffering, and solve community animal problems.

SMALL ANIMAL ABSTRACTS. See Indexes/Abstracts.

SOUTH AFRICAN JOURNAL OF ANIMAL SCIENCE. VFOAT Suid-Afrikaanse Tydskrif vir Veekunde. V. 1- 1971-. 0375-1589. Periodical. SA. Multilingual (English and Afrikaans, with summaries in both languages). sa. 20.00. Bureau for Scientific Publishing, PO Box 1758, 0001 Pretoria South Africa. Tel (012)260207. Ed R I Mackie. Ind/Abst Life Sci. Collect., Biol. Abstr., Chem. Abstr., Bibliogr. Agric. CODEN SAJAC9. bk rev. adv acc. Circ 1,000. Original research in animal science. *Proceedings, Agroanimalia.*

THE SOUTHWESTERN VETERINARIAN. V. 1- May 1948-. 0038-495X. Periodical. US. English. ty. $15.00. Texas A & M University, School Veterinary Medicine, College Station TX 77843. Tel (409)845-0806. Ed Constance Dobbs. Ind/Abst Life Sci. Collect., Biol. Abstr., Chem. Abstr., Nuci. Sci. Abstr., Bibliogr. Agric., Sci. Cit. Index, Abr. Ed. NLM W1 SO969R. CODEN SOVEA7. bk rev. adv acc. Circ 11,000. A student run, non-refereed journal covering current research and clinical applications in veterinary medicine.

SOV FOR VETERINARIANS. (THE SOV FOR VETERINARIANS : NEWSLETTER OF THE SOCIETY OF ONTARIO VETERINARIANS). VAT Society of Ontario Veterinarians for Veterinarians. Vol. 1, No. 1 (Jan. 1982)-. 0712-5399. Periodical. CN. English. bm. Sov for Veterinarians, Suite 412/151 Bloor Street, West Toronto Ontario M5S 1R1 Canada. DD 636.089060713.

Veterinary Medicine, Animal Culture

THE SPECULUM. V. 1-2, Winter 1946-Spring 1947. 0739-3806. Periodical. US. English. sa. Ohio State University of Veterinary Medicine, 190 Coffeyn Road, Columbus OH 43210. Tel (513)475-6951.

THE SRI LANKA VETERINARY JOURNAL : THE OFFICIAL JOURNAL OF THE SRI LANKA VETERINARY ASSOCIATION. Vol. 30, No. 1 (Jan./June 1982)-. Periodical. English. sa. Veterinary Research Institute, Gannoruwa, Peradeniya Sri Lanka. Ind/Abst Life Sci. Collect. Ceylon Veterinary Journal, 0009-0891.

STAL. SCIENCES ET TECHNIQUES DE L'ANIMAL DE LABORATOIRE. VFOAT STAL. V. 1- 1976-. 0339-722X. Periodical. FR. French. qt. $25.28. Mons J Maillard, Inra-Centre de Tours B P 1, 37380 Monnaie La France. Ind/Abst Life Sci. Collect., Biol. Abstr. NLM W1 S645. CODEN STALDT.

THE STATE VETERINARY JOURNAL. Periodical. UK. English. Ind/Abst Bibliogr. Agric.

THE STOCK FINDER. VFOAT Stockfinder. Vol. 1-. US. English. $495.00. Veterinary Information Company Inc, Langmuir Lab Suite 108-110 Brown Road, Ithaca NY 14850. Tel (607)257-4303. Ed Lawrence S Rivkin. (ctrl) An online database of products (drugs and supplies) used in the animal health field. World-wide access by computer and electronic ordering are featured.

SUDAN JOURNAL OF VETERINARY SCIENCE AND ANIMAL HUSBANDRY. (THE SUDAN JOURNAL OF VETERINARY SCIENCE AND ANIMAL HUSBANDRY). V. 1- March 1960-. 0562-5084. Periodical. English. ir. 30.00. Sudan Veterinary Association, PO Box 2382, Khartoum Sudan. NLM W1 SU161.

TAEHAN SUUI HAKHOE CHI. VFOAT Korean Journal of Veterinary Research. Periodical. English (Korean). ir. Institute of Veterinary Research, Office of Rural Development, Anyang Korea. LC SF604.

TANZANIAN VETERINARY BULLETIN : THE TROPICAL VETERINARIAN. Vol. 1, No. 1-. Periodical. English. ir. Tanzanian Veterinary Bulletin, PO Box 643, Morogoro Tanzania.

TEXAS VETERINARY MEDICAL JOURNAL. 0040-4756. Periodical. US. English. bm. $30.00. Texas Veterinary Medical Association, 612 Scarbrough, Austin TX 78701. Tel (512)472-4224. Ed David Lancaster. adv acc. Circ 3,000. (ctrl). Contains news of veterinary science, practice, management, organized veterinary medicine and individual veterinarians. Texas Veterinary Bulletin.

THERIOGENOLOGY. V. 1- Jan. 1974-. 0093-691X. Periodical. US. English. mo. $80.00. Geron-X Inc, PO Box 1108, Los Altos CA 94022. Tel (415)493-0871. Ed Victor Shille. Ind/Abst Life Sci. Collect., Biol. Abstr., Energy Res. Abstr., Chem. Abstr., Bibliogr. Agric., Sci. Cit. Index, Abr. Ed. NLM W1 TH677K. CODEN THGNBO. bk rev. adv acc. Circ 850. Current and concise reports about reproduction in domestic and wild animals. Information is published as original research, review, and clinical articles and economic and ecological evaluations.

TIERARZTLICHE PRAXIS. Vol. 1- 1973-. 0303-6286. Periodical. GW. German. qt. $72.64. Hans Marseille Verlag Burkeinstrassee 12 D8000 Munich 22 West Germany. Ind/Abst Pestdoc, Ringdoc, Vetdoc, Index Med. NLM W1 TI349.

TIERARZTLICHE UMSCHAU. Vol. 1-. 0049-3864. Periodical. GW. English summaries. mo. 149.-. Terra Verlag, Neuhauser Strasse 21, Postfach 1222, D-7750 Konstanz West Germany. Tel 07531/54031. Ed Eberhard Heizmann and O Straub. Ind/Abst Life Sci. Collect., Pestdoc, Ringdoc, Vetdoc, Energy Res. Abstr., Bibliogr. Agric., Sci. Cit. Index, Abr. Ed. NLM W1 TI352. bk rev. adv acc. Circ 7,200. All aspects of veterinary medicine. Tierarztliche Rundschau.

TIJDSCHRIFT VOOR DIERGENEESKUNDE. VFOAT Netherlands Journal of Veterinary Science. Vol. 43- 1916-. 0040-7453. Periodical. NE. Dutch (English). sm. 102.41. Koninklijke Nederlandse M Dier Julianalaan, 10 PO Box 14031, 3508 SB Utrecht Netherlands. Ind/Abst Life Sci. Collect., Pestdoc, Ringdoc, Vetdoc, Chem. Abstr., Sci. Cit. Index, Abr. Ed., Biol. Abstr., Index Med., Index Vet., Vet. Bull., Landwirtsch. Zentralbl., Bibliogr. Agric., Curr. Contents Agric. Biol. Environ. Sci. NLM W1 TI652. CODEN TIDIAY. Tijdschrift voor Veeartsenijkunde.

TRENDS : AN AMERICAN ANIMAL HOSPITAL ASSOCIATION PUBLICATION. VFOAT AAHA Trends. Vol. 1, No. 1 (Apr. 1985)-. 0883-1696. Periodical. US. English. bm. Free to Members. American Animal Hospital Association, P O Box 768, Mishawaka IN 46544. DD 362.

TROPICAL ANIMAL HEALTH AND PRODUCTION. V. 1- Aug. 1969-. 0049-4747. Periodical. UK. English (summaries in French and Spanish). qt $64.00. Longman Group Ltd, Fourth Avenue, Harlow Essex CM19 5AA England. Tel (031)556 2796. Ind/Abst Life Sci. Collect., Excerpta Med., Pestdoc, Ringdoc, Vetdoc, Index Med., Biol. Abstr., Chem. Abstr., Bibliogr. Agric., Curr. Contents Agric. Food Vet. Sci., Sci. Cit. Index, Abr. Ed. LC SF601. DD 636.0896988305. NLM W1 TR88. CODEN TAHPAJ.

TROPICAL ANIMAL PRODUCTION. V. 1- 1976-. 0250-5576. Periodical. English. qt. $18.00. Tropicalanimal Production, Apartados Nums 1256 Y 1258, Santo Domingo Dominican Republic. Tel 594-2511. Ind/Abst Chem. Abstr., Bibliogr. Agric. CODEN TANPDI.

TROPICAL VETERINARIAN. 1/1/83 (Aug. 1983)-. 0253-4851. Periodical. English. qt. $79.00. NLM W1. CODEN TRVTDJ.

TROPICAL VETERINARY AND ANIMAL SCIENCE RESEARCH : TVASR. VFOAT TVASR. Vol. 1, No. 1 (Mar. 1983)-. Periodical. English. qt.

TSETSE AND TRYPANOSOMIASIS INFORMATION QUARTERLY. V. 1- 1978-. 0142-193X. Periodical. UK. English. qt. 17.50 Domestic, $25.00. O D A, Tropical Development and Research Institute, College House, Wrights Lane, London W8 5SJ England. Tel (01)937-8191. Ed J M Child. NLM ZWC 705 T879. (ctrl). Abstracts, bibliographic references and news items on all aspects of tsetse flies and human and animal trypanosomiasis in Africa.

TUNG HAI HSU MU. VFOAT Hsu Mu Hsi Hsi Kan. First published in June 1978-. CH. Chinese. ir. Tung Hai Ta Hsueh, Hsu Mu Hsueh Hui, PO Box 884, Taichung Taiwan. LC SF55.T28.

THE U.P. VETERINARY JOURNAL CEASED. Ceased with Vol.4. Periodical. English. ir. United Provinces Veterinary Magazine.

UPDATE - ONTARIO VETERINARY ASSOCIATION. (UPDATE). VAT Ontario Veterinary Association Update. Vol. 1, No. 1 (Mar. 1983)-. 0821-6320. Periodical. CN. English. qt. 75.00. Ontario Veterinary Association, Suite 24-25/340 Woodlawn Road West, Guelph Ontario N1H 2X1 Canada. Tel (519)824-5600. Ed O Osborne. DD 636.089060713. Circ 2,800. (ctrl). Newsletter to the Ontario Veterinary profession published by the provincial licensing and regulatory body, containing matters of interest regarding veterinary medicine and professional ethics. OVA Update, 0821-6320.

VERBESSERUNG DER EIWEISSVERSORGUNG DER LANDWIRTSCHAFTLICHEN NUTZTIERE. Periodical. German (summaries in English and Russian). ir. 22.10. Akademie-Verlag, DDR-108 Berlin, Leipziger, Strasse 3-4, Berlin East Germany. LC SF98.P7.

VERKSAMHETSBERATTELSE : FORSOK. HUSDJURSEEKTIONEN. Main/Corp Sveriges Lantbruksuniversitet. Lantbruksvetenskapliga Fakulteten. 1976/77. Periodical. Swedish. ir. Verksamhetsberattelse: Forsok. Husdjurssektionen.

VETERINAR-MEDIZINISCHE NACHRICHTEN. VFOAT Veterinar Medizinische Nachrichten. 19 -75. 0083-5862. Periodical. GW. German. sa. N G Elwert Verlag, Postfach 1128, Reitgasse 7+9, D3550 Marburg West Germany. Ind/Abst Chem. Abstr. CODEN VMZNA5.

VETERINARIA. (VETERINARIA MEXICO). Vol. 7, No. 1 (Jan./March 1976)-. 8581-5092. Periodical. MX. Spanish (text in English summaries). qt. $10.00. Universidad Nacional Autonoma de Mexico, Revista de la Facultad de Medicine Veterinaria y Zootecnica, Ciudad Universitaria, 04510 Deleg Couaocan, Mexico DF Mexico. Ed Raymuado Martinaz Pena. Ind/Abst Life Sci. Collect. bk rev. Circ 2,000. (ctrl). Contains information on veterinary medicine and zoo techniques. Veterinaria (Universidad Nacional Automona de Mexico. Facultad de Medicina Veterinaria y Zootecnia).

VETERINARIA TROPICAL. V. 1- Jan./Dec. 1976-. 0379-8275. Periodical. VE. Spanish (articles in summaries in English and Spanish). Ceniap, Apartado No 70 las Delicias, Maracay 300 Venezuela. NLM W1 VE899T. Boletin del Instituto de Investigaciones Veterinarias.

VETERINARIANS' PRODUCT & THERAPEUTIC REFERENCE. VFOAT Veterinarians' P & TR. 1972-. US. English. Therapeutic Communications, 435 Bloomfield Avenue, Caldwell NJ 07006. LC SF917. DD 636.08951016.

VETERINARIIA (UKRAINE. MINISTERSTVO SILSKOHO HOSPODARSTVA). (VETERINARIIA). 0321-0502. Periodical. UR. Russian. mo. $33.50. Victor Kamkin Inc (70130), 12224 Parklawn Drive, Rockville MD 20852. Tel (301)881-5973. Ind/Abst Bibliogr. Agric., Chem. Abstr., Pestdoc, Ringdoc, Vetdoc. NLM W1 VE938G. CODEN VMSKAT.

DIE VETERINARMEDIZIN. 1.- Volume. 0049-6057. Periodical. GW. German. bm. 231.-. Terra Verlag, Neuhauser Str 21/Postfach 1222, D-7750 Konstanz West Germany. Tel 07531/54031. Ed Eberhard Heizmann Eissner. LC SF603. NLM ZSF 615 V58. bk rev. adv acc. Circ 2,000. Abstracts of originals as they appear in leading veterinary medicine journals worldwide. Jahresbericht Veterinarmedizin.

VETERINARNA SBIRKA. 0324-1017. Periodical. BU. Russian. mo. $24.00. Hemus, 6 Boulevard Rusky, Sofia Bulgaria. Ind/Abst Bibliogr. Agric. NLM W1 VE916H.

VETERINARNI MEDICINA. Began May 1962. 0375-8427. Periodical. CS. Czech (table of contents and summaries also in Russian, English and German). mo. Artia, PO Box 790, Praha 1 Czechoslovakia. Ind/Abst Index Med., Life Sci. Collect., Excerpta Med., Chem. Abstr., Bibliogr. Agric., Sci. Cit. Index, Abr. Ed. CODEN VTMDAR.

VETERINARNO MEDITSINSKI NAUKI. VFOAT Veterinary Science. Vol. 1- 1964-. 0506-8215. Periodical. BU. Bulgarian (English and Russian summaries and added tables of contents). mo. Hemus, 6 Boulevard Rusky, Sofia Bulgaria. Ind/Abst Life Sci. Collect., Excerpta Med., Index Med., Biol. Abstr., Chem. Abstr. NLM W1 VE916R. CODEN VMDNAV.

VETERINARSKI GLASNIK. V. 1- 1947-. 0350-2457. Periodical. Serbo-Croatian -C (table of contents in Roman). mo. $83.65. Fam Book Service, 69 5th Avenue, New York NY 10003. Ind/Abst Life Sci. Collect., Bibliogr. Agric. NLM W1 VE919.

VETERINARSTVI. 0506-8231. Periodical. CS. Czech (added table of contents in English, German and Russian). mo. Artia, PO Box 790, Praha 1 Czechoslovakia. Ind/Abst Pestdoc, Ringdoc, Vetdoc, Chem. Abstr., Bibliogr. Agric. NLM W1 VE92. CODEN VTERAT.

VETERINARY ANESTHESIA. V. 1- July 1974-. 0149-3949. Periodical. US. English. ty. Ind/Abst Chem. Abstr., Bibliogr. Agric. NLM W1 VE923H. CODEN VEANDV.

VETERINARY BIOLOGICAL PRODUCTS. LICENSEES. Periodical. US. English. Veterinary Services, Animal and Plant Health Inspection Service, US Department of Agriculture, Hyattsville MD 20782. Establishments Holding U.S. Veterinary Licenses to Produce Biological Products.

THE VETERINARY BULLETIN. V. 1- Apr. 1931-. 0042-4854. Periodical. UK. English. mo. $716.30. Commonwealth Agriculture Bureaux, Farnham Royal NR, Slough SL2 3BN England. Tel (02814)2662. Ed J R Metcalfe. Ind/Abst Pestdoc, Ringdoc, Vetdoc, Bibliogr. Agric. LC SF601. DD 636.089, 619.05. NLM ZSF 615 V587. adv acc. Covers the field of animal health. Special emphasis on prevention, control and treatment of diseases; effects of disease on production of food, skins, wool and health aspects of animal husbandry. Tropical Veterinary Bulletin, Veterinary Reviews.

VETERINARY CLINICAL PATHOLOGY. V. 6, No. 3- Nov/Dec. 1977-. 0275-6382. Periodical. US. English. qt. $25.00. Veterinary Practice Publishing Company, PO Box 4457, Santa Barbara CA 93103. Tel (805)965-1028. Ed A H Rebar DVM. Ind/Abst Chem. Abstr., Bibliogr. Agric. CODEN VCPADJ. bk rev. adv acc. **Circ** 1,000. The official publication of the American Association for Veterinary Clinical Pathology. *Bulletin of the American Society of Veterinary Clinical Pathologists, 0147-0701.*

THE VETERINARY CLINICS OF NORTH AMERICA. LARGE ANIMAL PRACTICE. (THE VETERINARY CLINICS OF NORTH AMERICA : LARGE ANIMAL PRACTICE). **VFOAT** Large Animal Practice. V. 1-. 0196-9846. Monographic Series. US. English. sa. $45.00. W B Saunders Company, West Washington Square, Philadelphia PA 19105. **Tel** (215)574-3395. **Ind/Abst** Life Sci. Collect., Excerpta Med., Index Med., Chem. Abstr., Energy Res. Abstr. **LC** UNC. **NLM** W1 VE929L. **CODEN** VCNPDK. **Circ** 2,000. Hardbound. Practical updates for the clinician on the latest advances plus topics of current interest. Illustrated. *Veterinary Clinics of North America, 0091-0279.*

THE VETERINARY CLINICS OF NORTH AMERICA. SMALL ANIMAL PRACTICE. **VFOAT** Small Animal Practice. V. 9, No. 1- Feb. 1979-. 0195-5616. Monographic Series. US. English. bm. $60.00. W B Saunders Company, West Washington Square, Philadelphia PA 19105. **Tel** (215)574-3395. **Ind/Abst** Life Sci. Collect., Excerpta Med., Index Med., Biol. Abstr., Energy Res. Abstr., Sci. Cit. Index, Abr. Ed. **LC** UNC. **NLM** W1 VE929S. **CODEN** VNAPDW. **Circ** 6,000. Hardbound. Practical updates for the clinician on the latest advances plus topics of current interest. Illustrated. *Veterinary Clinics of North America, 0091-0279.*

VETERINARY COMPUTING. Vol. 1, No. 1 (Sept. 1983)-. 8755-0946. Periodical. US. English. mo. American Veterinary Publications, PO Drawer KK, Santa Barbara CA 93102. **DD** 636.

VETERINARY ECONOMICS. V. 1- Oct. 1960-. 0042-4862. Periodical. US. English. mo. $30.00. Veterinary Medicine Publishing Company, PO Box 13265, Edwardsville KS 66113. **Tel** (913)492-4300. **Ed** Michael D Sollars. **Ind/Abst** Account. Index. Suppl., Bibliogr. Agric. **NLM** W1 VE93R. adv acc. **Circ** 38,000. (ctrl). Articles on management, finance, economics targeted to the veterinarian. Can use tax articles.

VETERINARY HISTORY. No. 1-12, Summer 1973-Winter 1978/79. 0301-6943. Periodical. UK. English. sa. 3.50 Domestic, 4.00 Foreign. Veterinary History, Tan-Y-Coed Penlon Bangor, Gwynedd United Kingdom. **Ed** A W Johnson. **NLM** W1 VE931H. (cum index). bk rev. **Circ** 165. All matters connected with history of veterinary art and science, livestock farming and related subjects.

VETERINARY IMMUNOLOGY AND IMMUNOPATHOLOGY. V. 1- Nov. 1979-. 0165-2427. Periodical. English. mo. Elsevier Science Publishers, PO Box 211, 1000 AE Amsterdam Netherlands. **Tel** (020)5803.911. **Ind/Abst** Life Sci. Collect., Index Med., Biol. Abstr., Chem. Abstr., Bibliogr. Agric., Sci. Cit. Index, Abr. Ed. **NLM** W1 VE931HJ. **CODEN** VIIMDS.

VETERINARY MEDICAL REVIEW. NO. 1-116. Periodical. US. English. bm. Free. University of Missouri, College of Veterinary Medicine, Columbia MO 65211. **Tel** (314)882-2461. **Circ** 1,400. (ctrl). Provides news of the college; carries at least one major scientific article per issue; indexed by Index Veterinarius.

VETERINARY MEDICINE (EDWARDSVILLE, KAN.). (VETERINARY MEDICINE). Vol. 80, No. 1 (Jan. 1985)-. 8750-7943. Periodical. US. English. mo. $33.95. Veterinary Medicine Publishing Company, 690 South 4th Street, PO Box 13265, Edwardsville KS 66113. **Tel** (800)255-6864. **Ed** Bruce Novotny. **Ind/Abst** Biol. Agric. Index, Life Sci. Collect., Pestdoc, Ringdoc, Vetdoc. **DD** 636. bk rev. adv acc. **Circ** 22,000. A journal of practical continuing education for veterinarians. Articles help veterinarians solve dignostic and therapeutic problems. *VM/SAC, Veterinary Medicine/Small Clinician, 0042-4889.*

VETERINARY MICROBIOLOGY. V. 1- July 1976-. 0378-1135. Monographic Series. NE. English. bm. **Ind/Abst** Life Sci. Collect., Excerpta Med., Index Med., Biol. Abstr., Chem. Abstr., Bibliogr. Agric. **NLM** W1 VE933F. **CODEN** VMICDQ.

VETERINARY NEWS. V. 1- 1939-. 0360-1730. Periodical. US. English. mo. New York State Veterinary Medical Society, 150 State Street, Albany NY 12207. **NLM** W1 VE933Q.

VETERINARY NEWS (ITHACA, N.Y.). (CORNELL FELINE HEALTH CENTER VETERINARY NEWS). Winter 1983-. Periodical. US. English. qt. Cornell Feline Health Center, New York State College of Veterinary Medicine, Ithaca NY 14853. **Tel** (607)256-5454. **Ed** June E Tuttle. **Circ** 24,000. A newsletter for the veterinary professional which focuses on current feline health topics. *Cornell Feline Health Center News.*

VETERINARY PARASITOLOGY. V. 1- June 1975-. 0304-4017. Periodical. NE. English. Elsevier Science Publishers, PO Box 211, 1000 AE Amsterdam Netherlands. **Tel** (020)5803911. **Ind/Abst** Life Sci. Collect., Excerpta Med., Index Med., Biol. Abstr., Chem. Abstr., Sci. Cit. Index, Abr. Ed. **NLM** W1 VE933U. **CODEN** VPARDI.

VETERINARY PATHOLOGY. V. 8- 1971-. 0300-9858. Periodical. US. English (German). bm. $60.00. Veterinary Pathology, PO Box 64025, Baltimore MD 21264. **Tel** (301)528-4105. **Ind/Abst** Life Sci. Collect., Excerpta Med., Pestdoc, Ringdoc, Vetdoc, Index Med., Chem. Abstr., Bibliogr. Agric., Sci. Cit. Index, Abr. Ed. **LC** SF769. **DD** 636.08960705. **NLM** W1 VE933V. **CODEN** VTPHAK. *PATHOLOGIA VETERINARIA.*

VETERINARY PHARMACEUTICALS & BIOLOGICALS. (VETERINARY PHARMACEUTICALS & BIOLOGICALS : VPB). **VFOAT** Veterinary Pharmaceuticals and Biologicals. 1980/1981-. 0272-4669. US. English. be. Harwal Publishing Company, 326 West State Street, Media PA 19063. **Ed** Carl E Aronson. **NLM** SF 917 C737. *Complete Desk Reference of Veterinary Pharmaceuticals & Biologicals (Media, PA.).*

VETERINARY PRACTICE. **VFOAT** VP, Veterinary Practice. V. 1- Sept. 1969-. 0042-4897. Periodical. UK. English. sm. A E Morgan Publications Ltd, Stanley House, 9 West Street, Epsom Surrey KT187RL England. **Tel** 01-393 0941/5. *Veterinary News, 0506-8282.*

THE VETERINARY QUARTERLY. V. 1- Jan. 1979-. 0165-2176. Periodical. NE. English. qt. $46.00. Martinus Nijhoff Publishers, PO Box 163, 3300 AD Dordrecht Netherlands. **Tel** 078-334233. **Ed** J Goudswaard. **Ind/Abst** Life Sci. Collect., Pestdoc, Ringdoc, Vetdoc, Index Med., Curr. Contents, Chem. Abstr., Biol. Abstr., Bibliogr. Agric., Sci. Cit. Index, Abr. Ed. **NLM** W1 VE9332F. **CODEN** VEQUDU. bk rev. adv acc. **Circ** 1,000. The journal intends to bridge the gap between veterinary practice and specialisms, by publishing the results of applied veterinary research. *Tijdschrift Voor Diergeneeskunde.*

VETERINARY RADIOLOGY. Vol. 20, No. 3-6-. 0196-3627. Periodical. US. English. bm. $62.00. J B Lippincott Company, East Washington Square, Philadelphia PA 19105. **Tel** (215)238-4273. **Ed** Donald E Thrall. **Ind/Abst** Life Sci. Collect., Biol. Abstr., Bibliogr. Agric. **DD** 636. **NLM** W1 VE9332J. **CODEN** VERAD9. adv acc. **Circ** 743. Original reports and case histories by specialists in radiology and all allied fields. *Journal of the American Veterinary Radiology Society, 0066-1155.*

VETERINARY RECORD. (THE VETERINARY RECORD). V. 1- 1888/89-. 0042-4900. Periodical. UK. English. wk. British Veterinary Association, 7 Mansfield Street, London W1M 0AT England. **Tel** (01)636-6541. **Ind/Abst** Life Sci. Collect., Excerpta Med., Pestdoc, Ringdoc, Vetdoc, Index Med., Chem. Abstr., Biol. Agric. Index, Biol. Agric. Index, Hospit. Lit. Index. **NLM** W1 VE934. **CODEN** VETRAX. *Veterinary Record and Transactions of the Veterinary Medical Association.*

VETERINARY REGISTER. 1973-. US. English. be. 700 North High School Road/Suite 200, Indianapolis IN 46224. **LC** SF624.I64. **DD** 636.089025772. *List of Graduate Licensed Veterinarians Registered in Indiana.*

VETERINARY RESEARCH COMMUNICATIONS. Vol. 4, No. 2 (Aug. 1980)-. 0165-7380. Periodical. English. qt. Elsevier Science Publishers, PO Box 211, 1000 AE Amsterdam Netherlands. **Tel** (020)5803.911. **Ind/Abst** Life Sci. Collect., Excerpta Med., Index Med., Biol. Abstr., Chem. Abstr. **NLM** W1 VE934M. **CODEN** VRCODX. *Veterinary Science Communications, 0378-4312.*

VETERINARY SCIENCE COMMUNICATIONS *CEASED.* V. 1-4, No. 1. 0378-4312. Periodical. English. ir. $56.70. **Ind/Abst** Chem. Abstr., Bibliogr. Agric. **NLM** W1 VE936.

VETERINARY SCOPE. V. 1- 1954-. Periodical. US. English. ir. Free. Upjohn Company, 9823-190-45, Kalamazoo MI 49001. **Tel** (616)385-6693. **Ed** Ronald A Miller. **Circ** 35,000. (ctrl). Newsletter concerning practical veterinary medicine topics, veterinary pharmaceutical research and development; issued twice annually; readers include practicing veterinarians, veterinary educators and students.

VETERINARY SERVICES BIOLOGICS NOTICE. No. 24- – Jan. 1977-. Periodical. US. English. United States, Department of Agriculture, Animal and Plant Health Inspection Service, Federal Building, Hyattsville MD 20782.

VETERINARY SURGERY. **VFOAT** VS. V. 7- Jan./Mar. 1978-. 0161-3499. Periodical. US. English. qt. $55.00. J B Lippincott Company, East Washington Square, Philadelphia PA 19105. **Tel** (215)238-4273. **Ed** Colin E Harvey. **Ind/Abst** Biol. Abstr., Bibliogr. Agric. **LC** SF911. **DD** 636.0897005. **NLM** W1 VE938C. **CODEN** VESUD6. adv acc. **Circ** 2,023. Publishes informative, up-to-the-minute reports on clinical and research topics of special interest to veterinary surgeons and anesthesiologists. *Journal of Veterinary Surgery.*

VETERINARY TECHNICIAN. Vol. 5, No. 1 (Jan./Feb. 1984)-. Periodical. US. English. ir. $24.00. Veterinary Learning Systems, 50 Hightstown Road, Princeton Junction NJ 08550. **Tel** (609)882-5600. **Ed** Richard B Ford. adv acc. **Circ** 8,000. Reviewed articles and features covering various aspects of veterinary medicine as it applies to veterinary staff. *Animal Health Technician, 0733-6004.*

VETERINER HEKIMLER DERNEGI DERGISI. **VFOAT** Acta Veterinaria Turcica. 1974-. 0377-6395. Periodical. Turkish. ir. **NLM** W1 VE938F. *Turk Veteriner Hekimleri Dernegi Dergisi, 0376-8104.*

VLAAMS DIERGENEESKUNDIG TIJDSCHRIFT. **VFOAT** Flemish Veterinary Journal. V. 1- July 1931-. 0303-9021. Periodical. BE. English Summaries. bm. $13.83. Vlaams Diergeneeskundig Tijds, Casinoplein 24, B-9000 Gent/Belgium. **Tel** 091/23 37 65. **Ed** M Pensaert. **Ind/Abst** Life Sci. Collect., Pestdoc, Ringdoc, Vetdoc, Chem. Abstr., Bibliogr. Agric., Sci. Cit. Index, Abr. Ed. **NLM** W1 VL21. **CODEN** VDTIAX. bk rev. adv acc. **Circ** 1,450. (ctrl). The journal publishes original and review articles on different aspects of veterinary medicine, meat inspection included. All animal species are treated.

WESTERN AUSTRALIA SHEEP, LAMBING AND WOOL CLIP. **Main/Corp** Australian Bureau of Statistics. Western Australian Office. AT. English. ir. Australian Bureau of Statistics, GPO Box 796, Sydney New South Wales 2001 Australia. **LC** SF375.5.A8. **DD** 636.3009941. *Sheep, Lambing and Wool Clip.*

WIENER TIERARZTLICHE MONATSSCHRIFT. 0043-535X. Periodical. AU. German. ir. 830.-. Verlag Ferdinand Berger & Sohne, Wiener Strasse 21-23, A-3580 Horn Austria. **Tel** (02082)2317-0. **Ind/Abst** Life Sci. Collect., Pestdoc, Ringdoc, Vetdoc, Bibliogr. Agric., Chem. Abstr., Sci. Cit. Index, Abr. Ed. **NLM** W1 WI41. **CODEN** WTMOA3. bk rev. adv acc. *Tierarztliche Zeitschrift, 0371-7569.*

WILDLIFE DISEASE NEWSLETTER. Periodical. US. English.

WISCONSIN REGISTERED LICENSED VETERINARIANS. BULLETIN. US. English. an. Veterinary Examining Board, 110 North Henry Street, Madison WI 53703. **LC** SF611. **DD** 636.089025775. **NLM** SF 25 W811.

WORLD ANIMAL REVIEW. No. 1- 1972-. 0049-8025. Periodical. IT. English. qt. $10.00. Unipub, PO Box 1222, Ann Arbor MI 48106. **Tel** (800)521-8110. **Ind/Abst** Life Sci. Collect., Energy Inf. Abstr., Environ. Abstr., Chem. Abstr., Bibliogr. Agric., Sci. Cit. Index, Abr. Ed. **NLM** W1 WO849E. **CODEN** WARVAI. Covers development in animal production, health and animal products with particular reference to Asia, Africa, and Latin America.

WORLD ANIMAL SCIENCE. B, DISCIPLINARY APPROACH. **VFOAT** Disciplinary Approach. 1-. Monographic Series. English. ir.

WORLD CATALOGUE OF VETERINARY FILMS/VIDEO TAPES AND FILMS/VIDEO TAPES OF VETERINARY INTEREST. 1983-. English. ir. **NLM** SF 775. *World Catalogue of Veterinary Films and Films of Veterinary Interest.*

WORLD DIRECTORY OF SCHOOLS FOR ANIMAL HEALTH ASSISTANTS. *See* Yearbooks, Almanacs, Directories.

WORLD DIRECTORY OF VETERINARY SCHOOLS. See Yearbooks, Almanacs, Directories.

WORLD REVIEW OF ANIMAL PRODUCTION. 0043-8979. Periodical. IT. articles in English. qt. International Publishing Entr, Via di Tor Vergata 85-87, 00133 Roma Italy. Tel 6140653. Ind/Abst Life Sci. Collect., Pestdoc, Ringdoc, Vetdoc, Chem. Abstr., Bibliogr. Agric. CODEN WRAPAY.

WYNIKI OCENY SWIN NA PODSTAWIE BADAN PRZEPROWADZONYCH W STACJACH KONTROLI UZYTKOWOSCI RZEZNEJ TRZODY CHLEWNEJ INSTYTUT ZOOTECHNIKI ZA ROK . . . . VFOAT Results of Evaluation in Pig Testing Stations of the Institute of Animal Production, Results of Evaluation in Pig Testing Stations of the Institute of Animal Production in . . . Instytut Zootechniki W Polsce, Zakad Informacji Zootechnicznej. Polish. an.

YANKEE HORSETRADER. See Horses and Horsemanship.

YELLOWSTONE GRIZZLY BEAR INVESTIGATIONS. (YELLOWSTONE GRIZZLY BEAR INVESTIGATIONS : REPORT OF THE INTERAGENCY STUDY TEAM). Main/Corp Interagency Grizzly Bear Study Team. 0192-8031. US. English. an. US Department of the Interior National Park Service, Washington DC 20240. LC QL737.C27. DD 599.74446.

YEN CHIU SHIH YEN PAO KAO - TAI-WAN TANG YEH KU FEN YU HSIEN KUNG SSU HSU CHAN YEN CHIU SO. Main/Corp Tai-Wan Tang Yeh Ku Fen Yu Hsien Kung Ssu. Hsu Chan Yen Chiu So. VFOAT Annual Research Report - Animal Industry Research Institute, Taiwan Sugar Corporation. CH. Chinese (with English summaries). ir. Animal Industry Research Institute, Taiwan Sugar Corporation Chunan, Miaoli Taiwan Republic of China. LC SF55.T28.

YORKIE TALES. 0883-7686. Periodical. US. English. mo. $24.00. Magestic Publications, Suite 331/2005 Palo Verde, Long Beach CA 90815. DD 636.

ZEITSCHRIFT FUR VERSUCHSTIERKUNDE. VFOAT Journal of Experimental Animal Science. Vol. 1- 1961-. 0044-3697. Periodical. GE. Multilingual (German and English). bm. $75.00. VCH Publishers Inc, 303 Northwest 12th Avenue, Deerfield Beach FL 33442. Tel (305)428-5566. Ind/Abst Life Sci. Collect., Excerpta Med., Pestdoc, Ringdoc, Vetdoc, Index Med., Biol. Abstr., Chem. Abstr., Curr. Contents, Bibliogr. Agric., Sci. Cit. Index, Abr. Ed. NLM W1 ZE66. CODEN ZEVRAJ.

ZENTRALBLATT FUR VETERINARMEDIZIN. BEIHEFT. 1-14. Monographic Series. German (summaries in English, French, and Spanish). ir. Paul Parey Verlag, PO Box 106304, Spitalerstr 12, D-2000 Hamburg 1 West Germany. Tel 040-33 96 9-134.

ZENTRALBLATT FUR VETERINARMEDIZIN. REIHE A. VFOAT Journal of Veterinary Medicine. Series A. V. 10- Jan. 1963-. 0514-7158. Periodical. WB. German (English, French, and Spanish). $415.20. Paul Parey Scientific Publishing, 35 West 38th Street #3W, New York NY 10018. Tel (212)730-0518. Ed M Berchtold, A Mayr, H Spoerri and E G White. Ind/Abst Life Sci. Collect., Excerpta Med., Pestdoc, Ringdoc, Vetdoc, Biol. Abstr., Curr. Contents, Agric. Biol. Environ. Sci., Curr. Contents. Life Sci., Index Med., Chem. Abstr., Index Vet., Bibliogr. Agric., Energy Res. Abstr. NLM W1 ZE799B. CODEN ZVRAAX. bk rev. adv acc. Circ 500. Physiology, endocrinology, biochemistry, pharmacology, internal medicine, surgery, genetics, animal breeding, obstetrics and gynecology, andrology, animal nutrition and feeding, genetics and special pathology. Zentralblatt fur Veterinarmedizin, 0044-4294.

ZENTRALBLATT FUR VETERINARMEDIZIN. REIHE B. VFOAT Journal of Veterinary Medicine. Series B. Volume 10 Feb. 1963-. 0514-7166. Periodical. WB. German (English, French or Spanish). mo. $415.20. Paul Parey Scientific Publishing, 35 West 38th Street West, New York NY 10018. Tel (212)730-0518. Ed M Berchtold, A Mayr, H Spoerri and E G White. Ind/Abst Life Sci. Collect., Excerpta Med., Pestdoc, Ringdoc, Vetdoc, Biol. Abstr., Curr. Contents, Agric. Biol. Environ. Sci., Curr. Contents. Life Sci., Index Med., Chem. Abstr., Nutr. Abstr. Rev., Index Vet., Bibliogr. Agric., Energy Res. Abstr. NLM W1 ZE799C. CODEN ZVRBA2. bk rev. adv acc. Circ 500. Infectious diseases, immonology, food hygiene, veterinary health. Zentralblatt fur Veterinarmedizin, 0044-4294.

ZIMBABWE VETERINARY JOURNAL. Vol. 11, No. 1/2 (June 1980)-. Periodical. English. qt. 8.00. Faculty of Veterinary Science, PO Box MP 167, Mount Pleasant, Harare Zimbabwe. Tel 303211. Ed J A Lawrence. Ind/Abst Bibliogr. Agric. bk rev. adv acc. Circ 300. Original and review papers on diseases of domestic and wild animals in Southern Africa. Rhodesian Veterinary Journal, 0253-3278.

ZOO-SANITARY SITUATION IN MEMBER COUNTRIES IN . . . . VFOAT Zoo Sanitary Situation in Member Countries in . . . 1981-. English. ir. LC SF740. DD 636.08944021.

ZOOMORPHOLOGIE CEASED. V. 82-95, No. 3. 0340-6725. German. ir. 196.00. Springer-Verlag, Heidelberger Platz 3, D-1000 Berlin 33 West Germany. LC QL1. NLM W1 ZO614L. Zeitschrift fur Morphologie der Tiere, 0044-3131.

ZOOTECHNIKA. Main/Corp Akademia Rolnicza W Warszawie. 9- 1973-. Polish (summaries in English and Russian). ir. 14.00. Akademia Rolnicza W Warszawie, Ul Rakowiecka 41, Warszawa Poland. LC SF1. Zootechnika.

ZOOTECNICA INTERNATIONAL. Periodical. text and summaries in Arabic, English, French, or German. ir.

ZPRAVY MUZEA VETERINARNI MEDICINY. Main/Corp Udvvl. Kabinet Dejin A Muzeum Veterinarni Mediciny. Vol. 1- 1975/76-. Czech. ir. NLM W1 U205.

ZWIERZETA LABORATORYJNE. (ZWIERZETA LABORATORYJNE). Vol. 1- 1963-. 0084-5825. Monographic Series. English (Polish). ir. Panstow Wydawn, Zakad Hodowli Zwierzat Doswiadczalnych, Instytut Biologii Doswiadczalnej Im M Nenkiego Pan, Ul Pasteura 3, 02-093 Warszawa Poland. Ind/Abst Life Sci. Collect., Chem. Abstr. LC QL55. NLM W1 ZW201. CODEN ZWLAAA.

WATER RESOURCES

305 (B) TECHNICAL REPORT FOR OKLAHOMA. See Sanitation, Environmental Technology.

ADVANCE PROGRAM - BONNEVILLE POWER ADMINISTRATION. See Engineering - Electricity, Electrical Engineering, Electronics.

ADVANCES IN WATER RESOURCES. VFOAT Adv. Water Resource. Began with Sept. 1977 issue. 0309-1708. Periodical. UK. English. qt. $130.00. Computational Mechanics Centre, 400 West Cummings Park Suite 6200, Woburn MA 01801. Ed G F Pinder and C A Brebbia. Ind/Abst Fluidex, Can. Environ., Life Sci. Collect., Sel. Water Resour. Abstr., Ship Abstr., Coal Abstr., Excerpta Med., Int. Aerosp. Abstr., GeoRef, Bibliogr. Agric., Energy Res. Abstr. LC TC1. DD 627.05. CODEN AWREDI. bk rev. Circ 20,000. Covers both the theoretical and practical aspects of water resources engineering. Promotes the interchange of ideas for engineers and scientists interested in more qualitative aspects of the water sciences.

AGRICULTURAL WATER MANAGEMENT. V. 1- Dec. 1976-. 0378-3774. Periodical. NE. English. qt. Elsevier Science Publishers, PO Box 211, 1000 AE Amsterdam Netherlands. Tel (020)5803.911. Ind/Abst Can. Environ., Life Sci. Collect., Sel. Water Resour. Abstr., Energy Inf. Abstr., Environ. Abstr., GeoRef, Biol. Abstr., Bibliogr. Agric., Biol. Agric. Index. LC S494.5.W3. DD 631.6. CODEN AWMADF.

AL-MAJALLAH AL-ILMIYAH LIL-MAWARID AL-MAIYAH. VFOAT Journal of Water Resources. Journal 1, No. 1-. Periodical. Arabic (and English). sa. S B 26054, Waziriyah Baghdad Iraq.

Water Resources

ANNUAL FINANCIAL REPORT - TEXAS DEPARTMENT OF WATER RESOURCES. Main/Corp Texas. Dept. of Water Resources. Administrative Services Division. Fiscal Services Section. US. English. an. Texas Department of Water Resources, PO Box 13087, Austin TX 78701. LC TC424.T4. DD 353.976400722368232516.

ANNUAL OPERATING PLAN. FRYINGPAN-ARKANSAS PROJECT, COLORADO. (ANNUAL OPERATING PLAN : FRYINGPAN-ARKANSAS PROJECT, COLORADO). Main/Corp United States. Dept. of the Interior. Water and Power Resources Service. Lower Missouri Region. VFOAT Fryingpan-Arkansas Project, Colorado. VAT Annual Operating Plan. Fryingpan Arkansas Project, Colorado. 0270-2037. US. English. an. US Department of the Interior, Water and Power Resources Service, Regional Office, Lower Missouri Region, PO Box 25247, Building 20/Denver Federal Center, Denver CO 80225. LC HD1695.C7. DD 333.9162097881. Annual Operating Plan. Fryingpan-Arkansas Project, Colorado, 0270-2037.

ANNUAL PROGRESS REPORT - WATER MANAGEMENT RESEARCH PROJECT. (ANNUAL PROGRESS REPORT, WATER MANAGEMENT RESEARCH PROJECT SUBMITTED TO THE U. S. AGENCY FOR INTERNATIONAL DEVELOPMENT). Main/Corp Colorado. State University, Fort Collins. Water Management Research Project. VFOAT Water Management Research in Arid and Sub-Humid Lands of Less Developed Countries. 1974/75-. 0198-1994. US. English. an. Colorado State University, Fort Collins CO 80523. LC TC401. DD 333.910091724.

ANNUAL PROJECT HISTORY. MANN CREEK PROJECT. (ANNUAL PROJECT HISTORY : MANN CREEK PROJECT). Main/Corp United States. Bureau of Reclamation. 1966-. Periodical. English. ir.

ANNUAL REPORT AND ACCOUNTS - WATER RESEARCH CENTRE. Main/Corp Water Research Centre. 1978/79-. 0144-9370. Periodical. UK. English. an. NLM W1 WA692AB. Annual Report - Water Research Centre, 0143-2443.

ANNUAL REPORT - ARIZONA. DEPT. OF WATER RESOURCES. (ANNUAL REPORT). Main/Corp Arizona. Dept. of Water Resources. 1980-1981-. 0743-5134. US. English. an. LC HD1694.A7. DD 353.9791008232506. Annual Report, 0091-6366.

ANNUAL REPORT, BASIN AND STATE PRIORITIES, PROPOSED WATER AND RELATED LAND RESOURCES ACTIVITIES. Main/Corp United States. Missouri River Basin Commission. 3rd- 1977/80-. 0160-4171. US. English. an. Missouri River Basin Commission, Suite 403/10050 Regency Circle, Omaha NE 68114. LC TC425.M7. DD 333.91020978. Annual Report, Basin Priority of Proposed Water and Related Land Resources Activities, 0363-2539.

ANNUAL REPORT - CENTRAL WATER PLANNING UNIT. Main/Corp Great Britain. Central Water Planning Unit. UK. English. an. Central Water Planning Unit, Reading Bridge House, Reading RG1 8PS England. Ind/Abst GeoRef. LC TC457. DD 354.41008232.

ANNUAL REPORT - COLORADO RIVER BOARD OF CALIFORNIA. Main/Corp California. Colorado River Board. 0575-2310. US. English. an. Colorado River Board of California, 302 California State Building, 217 West First Street, Los Angeles CA 90012. LC TC423.6. DD 353.9794008232.

ANNUAL REPORT - DELAWARE RIVER BASIN COMMISSION. Main/Corp Delaware River Basin Commission. Began with 1961/63 issue. 0418-5455. US. English. an. Water Resources Association of the Delaware River Basin, Box 867 David Road, Valley Forge PA 19481. Tel (215)783-0634. Ed Bruce E Stewart. Circ 800. (ctrl). Update on association accomplishments and activities, committee reports, financial information, and a look at the future.

ANNUAL REPORT FOR THE FISCAL YEAR JULY 1 . . . TO JUNE 30 - METROPOLITAN WATER DISTRICT OF SOUTHERN CALIFORNIA. Main/Corp Metropolitan Water District of Southern California. VFOAT Annual Report. 1980-1981-. US. English. an. LC TD224.C3. DD 352.610979493. Annual

Water Resources

Report Appendix for the Fiscal Year July 1 . . . to June 30 . . . .

ANNUAL REPORT - GREAT LAKES BASIN COMMISSION. (ANNUAL REPORT). Main/Corp United States. Great Lakes Basin Commission. 0271-7174. US. English. an. Great Lakes Basin Commission, 3475 Plymouth Road, PO Box 999, Ann Arbor MI 48106. Ind/Abst GeoRef.

ANNUAL REPORT - KANSAS-OKLAHOMA ARKANSAS RIVER COMMISSION. Main/Corp Kansas-Oklahoma Arkansas River Commission. 1968-. Periodical. US. English. an. Kansas State Library, 3rd Floor/Statehouse, Topeka KS 66612. LC WMLC L 83/455.

ANNUAL REPORT - KANSAS WATER RESOURCES RESEARCH INSTITUTE. Main/Corp Kansas Water Resources Research Institute. 1963/64-. 0160-2659. US. English. an. Kansas Water Resources, Research Institute, 146 D Waters Hall, Manhattan KS 66502. Ind/Abst GeoRef. LC TC424.K2. DD 333.91009781.

ANNUAL REPORT - MANITOBA WATER SERVICES BOARD. (ANNUAL REPORT OF THE MANITOBA WATER SERVICES BOARD). Main/Corp Manitoba Water Services Board. 1st- 1972/73-. 0318-3912. CN. English. an. Manitoba Water Services Board, 693 Taylor Avenue, Winnipeg Manitoba R3M 2K2 Canada. LC TD227.M3. DD 354.712700871. *Annual Report, 0542-5646.*

ANNUAL REPORT - MARYLAND. STATE WATER QUALITY ADVISORY COMMITTEE. Main/Corp Maryland. State Water Quality Advisory Committee. US. English. an. Maryland Department of Health and Mental Hygiene, Office of Environmental Programs, PO Box 13387, Baltimore MD 21203.

ANNUAL REPORT - MISSOURI RIVER BASIN COMMISSION. (ANNUAL REPORT). Main/Corp Missouri River Basin Commission. Began with 1972/73. 0092-7945. US. English. an. Missouri River Basin Commission, 10050 Regency Circle, Suite 403, Omaha NE 68114. LC HD1695.M45. DD 333.9100978.

ANNUAL REPORT - NEW ENGLAND RIVER BASINS COMMISSION CEASED. Main/Corp New England River Basins Commission. -1981. 0077-8265. US. English. an. 55 Court Street, Boston MA 02108. LC TC423.15. DD 333.9100974.

ANNUAL REPORT - NEW JERSEY WATER SUPPLY AUTHORITY. Main/Corp New Jersey Water Supply Authority. 1982-. US. English. an.

ANNUAL REPORT - NEW MEXICO WATER RESOURCES RESEARCH INSTITUTE. 1965-. US. English. an. New Mexico Water Resources Institute, New Mexico State University, Box 3167, Las Cruces NM 88003.

ANNUAL REPORT - NEW SOUTH WALES. WATER RESOURCES COMMISSION. Main/Corp New South Wales. Water Resources Commission. 1976-1977-. 0155-9834. AT. English. an. Water Resources Commission, Ibis House, 201-211 Miller Street, North Sydney Australia. LC TC922. DD 354.944008232506. *Report of the Water Resources Commission of New South Wales.*

ANNUAL REPORT - NORTH DAKOTA WATER RESOURCES RESEARCH INSTITUTE. Main/Corp North Dakota Water Resources Research Institute. US. English. an. North Dakota State University, North Dakota Water Resources, Research Institute, Fargo ND 58102.

ANNUAL REPORT OF THE DEPARTMENT OF WATER AND NATURAL RESOURCES ON THE WATER RESOURCES MANAGEMENT SYSTEM (SOUTH DAKOTA). Main/Corp South Dakota. Dept. of Water and Natural Resources. US. English. an. LC TC424.S8. DD 353.9783008232506.

ANNUAL REPORT OF THE IDAHO DEPARTMENT OF WATER RESOURCES. Main/Corp Idaho. Dept. of Water Resources. 0362-3289. US. English. an. Idaho Department of Water Resources, Statehouse, Boise ID 83720. LC GB705.I2. DD 353.9796008232.

ANNUAL REPORT OF THE SASKATCHEWAN WATER SUPPLY BOARD OF THE PROVINCE OF SASKATCHEWAN. (ANNUAL REPORT OF THE SASKATCHEWAN WATER SUPPLY BOARD). Main/Corp Saskatchewan Water Supply Board. 1st.- 1966-. 0586-5522. Periodical. CN. English. an. Saskatchewan Water Supply Board, 2345 Broad Street, Regina Saskatchewan S4P Canada. LC TD227.S3. DD 354.712400871.

ANNUAL REPORT OF THE WATER RESOURCES RESEARCH INSTITUTE OF THE UNIVERSITY OF WYOMING. Main/Corp University of Wyoming. Water Resources Research Institute. 1st- 1964/65-. 0084-3202. Periodical. US. English. ir. University of Wyoming, PO Box 3413, Laramie WY 82071. DD 333.9.

ANNUAL REPORT - OHIO RIVER BASIN COMMISSION. Main/Corp Ohio River Basin Commission. 1970/71-. 0149-6875. US. English. an. 36 East 4th Street/Suite 208-20, Cincinnati OH 45202. LC TC425.O4. DD 353.008232.

ANNUAL REPORT - OKLAHOMA WATER RESOURCES BOARD. Main/Corp Oklahoma Water Resources Board. 0099-1635. US. English. an. Oklahoma Water Resources Board, Dialex Building/2241 NW 40th Street, Oklahoma City OK 73112. LC TD224.O5. DD 353.9766008232506.

ANNUAL REPORT ON THE COMPREHENSIVE WATER RESOURCES PLAN (WEST VIRGINIA). Main/Corp West Virginia. Dept. of Natural Resources. 0095-4659. US. English. an. West Virginia Department of Natural Resources, 1800 Washington Street, Charleston WV 25305. LC TC424.W4. DD 333.91009754.

ANNUAL REPORT - PRAIRIE PROVINCES WATER BOARD. Main/Corp Prairie Provinces Water Board. VAT Annual Reports - Prairie Provinces Water Board. 1969/72-. 0704-8726. CN. English. an. Prairie Provinces Water Board, 403 1955 Smith Street, Regina Saskatchewan S4P 2N9 Canada. LC TC427.P7. DD 354.712008232.

ANNUAL REPORT - THE WATER RESOURCES COMMISSION, STATE OF MICHIGAN. Main/Corp Michigan. Water Resources Commission. 1st-. US. English. an. LC HD1694.M5. DD 333.91.

ANNUAL REPORT TO THE FLORIDA LEGISLATURE. Main/Corp Coordinating Council on the Restoration of the Kissimmee River Valley and Taylor Crrk-Nubbin Slough Basin (Fla.). 1st- 1977-. US. English. an. 2562 Executive Center Circle East, Tallahassee FL 32301.

ANNUAL REPORT - UNIVERSITY OF ALASKA, FAIRBANKS. INSTITUTE OF WATER RESOURCES. Main/Corp University of Alaska, Fairbanks. Institute of Water Resources. US. English. an. Institute of Water Resources, University of Alaska, Fairbanks AK 99701. LC TC424.A4. DD 553.709798.

ANNUAL REPORT - UNIVERSITY OF ALASKA, FAIRBANKS. INSTITUTE OF WATER RESOURCES/ENGINEERING EXPERIMENT STATION. (ANNUAL REPORT). Main/Corp University of Alaska, Fairbanks. Institute of Water Resources/Engineering Experiment Station. 1983-. 8755-2965. US. English. an. Free. Institute of Water Resources, Engineering Station, University of Alaska-Fairbanks, Fairbanks AK 99701. Tel (907)474-7775. Ed Alan C Parlson. LC TC424.A4. DD 333.91100720798. Circ 2,000. Contains information on: hydrology, geochemistry, microbiology, fisheries, alternative energy, artic engineering, biotechnology, forestry, nearshore oceanography, environmental impact and solar energy. *Annual Report (1980), 0749-0461.*

ANNUAL REPORT - UNIVERSITY OF DELAWARE, WATER RESOURCES CENTER. Main/Corp University of Delaware. Water Resources Center. 1965-. Periodical. US. English. ir. University of Delaware, Water Resources Center, Newark DE 19711. DD 333.9, 628.

ANNUAL REPORT - UNIVERSITY OF TEXAS AT AUSTIN. CENTER FOR RESEARCH IN WATER RESOURCES. (ANNUAL REPORT - CENTER FOR RESEARCH IN WATER RESOURCES, THE UNIVERSITY OF TEXAS AT AUSTIN). Main/Corp Texas. University at Austin. Center for Research In Water Resources. VFOAT CRWR Annual Report. 1965. 0276-0177. US. English. ir. Center for Research in Water Resources, 10100 Burnet Road, Austin TX 78758. Tel (512)471-3131. bk rev. Reports of water related research.

ANNUAL REPORT - UNIVERSITY OF THE DISTRICT OF COLUMBIA. WATER RESOURCES RESEARCH CENTER. Main/Corp University of the District of Columbia. Water Resources Research Center. US. English. an. University of the District of Columbia, VNC, Washington DC 20008.

ANNUAL REPORT - VERMONT WATER RESOURCES RESEARCH CENTER. Main/Corp Vermont Water Resources Research Center. US. English. an. Water Resources Research Center, The University of Vermont, 601 Main Street, Burlington VT 05401.

ANNUAL REPORT - VIRGINIA WATER RESOURCES RESEARCH CENTER. (ANNUAL REPORT). Main/Corp Virginia Water Resources Research Center. Began in 1973. 0736-3923. US. English. an. Virginia Water Resources Research Center, Virginia Polytechnic Institute and State University, 617 North Main Street, Blacksburg VA 24060. LC TC424.V8. DD 333.9109755. *Water Resources Research in Virginia, Annual Report, 0095-1250.*

ANNUAL REPORT - WATER RESOURCES RESEARCH CENTER. Main/Corp University of Hawaii. Water Resources Research Center. 1965/66-. 0440-5013. US. English. an. Free. University of Hawaii, Honolulu HI 96822. Tel (808)948-7847. Ed Faith N Fujimura. Ind/Abst GeoRef. LC TD224.H3. DD 627. CODEN RHWRDS. Circ 500. (ctrl). Water quality, stream fauna, drip irrigation, groundwater, wastewater irrigation, pesticides, 2-D infiltration, virus monitoring, evaporation, rainfall, and electrical resistivity publications.

ANNUAL REPORT - WESTERN STATES WATER COUNCIL. Main/Corp Western States Water Council. 1st- 1966-. 0511-8182. Monographic Series. US. English. ir. 220 South 2nd East/Suite 200, Salt Lake City UT 84111. LC HD1695.W4. DD 333.9.

ANNUAL WATER-RESOURCES REVIEW, WHITE SANDS MISSILE RANGE, NEW MEXICO. 1977-. US. English. an. Open-File Services Section, Western Distribution Branch, Geological Survey, Box 25425, Federal Building, Denver CO 80225. *Annual Water-Resources Review, White Sands Missile Range, 0731-5120.*

AQUA. (AQUA). Began publication in 1952. 0003-7214. Periodical. UK. English and French. bm. Pergamon Press, 395 Sawmill River Road, Elmsford NY 10523. Ind/Abst Chem. Abstr., Sel. Water Resour. Abstr., Sel. Water Resour. Abstr., Fluidex, GeoRef, Chem. Abstr., Bibliogr. Agric., Bibliogr. Index Geol. LC TD201. DD 3636105. CODEN AQUAAA.

AQUARIUS (LOGAN, UTAH). (AQUARIUS). Special issue No. 1-. 0587-341X. US. English. an. Utah Water Research Laboratory, Utah Water Research Laboratory, Utah State University, Logan Utah 84322-8200. Ind/Abst GeoRef. A newsletter for the Utah Center for Water Resources, Utah State University.

AQUEDUCT. V. 40, No. 5- May 1973-. 0092-0622. Periodical. US. English. qt. Metropolitan Water District Southern California, PO Box 54153, Los Angeles CA 90054. *Aqueduct News.*

ARCHIVES REPORT. *See* Genealogy and Heraldry - Archives.

ARIZONA DEPARTMENT OF WATER RESOURCES BULLETIN. 1 (Jan. 1983)-. 0749-1735. Monographic Series. US. English. ir. Ind/Abst GeoRef.

ATMOSPHERIC WATER RESOURCES SERIES. VFOAT UWRL/A. A1-A2. Monographic Series. US. English. Utah Water Research Laboratory, College of Engineering, Utah State University, Logan UT 84322.

AUDITED ANNUAL FINANCIAL REPORT - TEXAS. DEPT. OF WATER RESOURCES. *See* Business - Public Finance.

AUSTRALIAN WATER RESOURCES COUNCIL HYDROLOGICAL SERIES. *See* Earth Sciences - Hydrology.

AWWA MAINSTREAM. VFOAT Mainstream. VAT American Water Works Association Mainstream. Vol. 25, No. 3 (Mar. 1981)-. 0273-3218. Periodical. US. English. mo. $12.00. American Water Works Association, 6666 West Quincy Avenue, Denver CO

Water Resources

80209. **Tel** (303)794-7711. Ed Mary A Parmelee. bk rev. adv acc. **Circ** 37,000. (ctrl). News and feature items about the drinking water industry, including coverage of governmental actions, water utility experiences, technological advances, and association activities. *Willing Water.*

AWWA/AWWARF MERGED INDEX. See Indexes/Abstracts.

BACKFLOW PREVENTION. Began in July 1984. 8755-3457. Periodical. US. English. mo. $20.00. SFA Enterprises Inc, PO Box 33209, Northglenn CO 80233. **Tel** (303)451-0980. Ed Dee Cooperider. **DD** 696. bk rev. adv acc. **Circ** 3,000. Focus on cross connections between plumbing systems, portable water systems and the prevention of contamination due to backflow.

BASIC DATA REPORT. See Earth Sciences - Hydrology.

BASIC DATA SERIES. GROUND-WATER RELEASE. VFOAT Ground-Water Release. Began with: No. 1, published in 1969. 0160-9548. US. English. ir. Kansas Geological Survey, University of Kansas, Lawrence KS 66044. **Ind/Abst** GeoRef. **LC** UNC. **DD** 553.79097814. **CODEN** GSKSDT.

BASIN BIBLIOGRAPHY. See Bibliographies.

BIBLIOGRAPHY OF WATER QUALITY RESEARCH REPORTS. See Bibliographies.

BIENNIAL REPORT - NORTH DAKOTA. STATE WATER CONSERVATION COMMISSION. **Main/Corp** North Dakota. State Water Conservation Commission. 1st- 1937/38-. US. English. be. **LC** TC824.N9.

BIENNIAL REPORT OF THE DEPARTMENT OF WATER RESOURCES. **Main/Corp** Nebraska. Dept. of Water Resources. 32d- 1957/58-. 0466-6992. US. English. be. Free. State of Nebraska, Department of Water Resources, Lincoln NE 68508. **Tel** (402)471-2363. Ed Susan France. **LC** HD1694.N2. **DD** 333.9109782. **Circ** 350. Current listing of Nebraska's water rights and an overview of events concerning water in Nebraska.

BIENNIAL REPORT UNDER THE GREAT LAKES WATER QUALITY AGREEMENT OF 1978. **Main/Corp** International Joint Commission. 1st (June 1982)-. 0736-8410. US. English. be. **LC** TD223.3. **DD** 354.18710977.

BOLETIM - MINISTERIO DA AGRICULTURA, DEPARTAMENTO NACIONAL DA PRODUCCAO MINERAL, SERVICO DE AGUAS. See Earth Sciences - Hydrology.

BOLETIN INFORMATIVO (ARGENTINA.) DEPARTAMENTO GENERAL DE IRRIGACION. (BOLETIN INFORMATIVO). 0325-8106. Periodical. Spanish. ir.

THE BRITISH WATER SUPPLY YEAR BOOK. See Yearbooks, Almanacs, Directories.

BULLETIN - CALIFORNIA. DEPT. OF WATER RESOURCES. (BULLETIN - STATE OF CALIFORNIA, DEPARTMENT OF WATER RESOURCES). **VFOAT** State Water Resources Board Bulletin. Began in 1956. 0084-8263. Monographic Series. US. English. ir. State of California, Department of Water Resources, Sacramento CA 95802. **Ind/Abst** Eng. Index Annu., Eng. Index Mon., Eng. Index Bioeng. Abstr., Eng. Index Energy Abstr., GeoRef. **LC** GB705.C2. **DD** 333.9. **CODEN** CAWRAF. *Bulletin.*

BULLETIN - CAPITAL AREA GROUND WATER CONSERVATION COMMISSION. **Main/Corp** Capital Area Ground Water Conservation Commission. No. 1-. 0161-9179. Monographic Series. US. English. bm. **LC** GB1025.L8. **DD** 553.790796318.

BULLETIN - DEPARTMENT OF NORTHERN AFFAIRS AND NATIONAL RESOURCES. WATER RESOURCES BRANCH. (BULLETIN - DEPARTMENT OF NORTHERN AFFAIRS AND NATIONAL RESOURCES, WATER RESOURCES BRANCH). **Main/Corp** Canada. Department of Northern Affairs and National Resources. Water Resources Branch. Monographic Series. US. English. ir.

BULLETIN - ILLINOIS STATE WATER SURVEY. **Main/Corp** Illinois State Water Survey. No. 15- 1917-. 0360-9804. Monographic Series. US. English. ir. **Ind/Abst** GeoRef, Chem. Abstr., Bibliogr. Agric. **CODEN** ISWSA6. *Water Survey Series.*

BULLETIN - MISSISSIPPI BOARD OF WATER COMMISSIONERS. (BULLETIN). **Main/Corp** Mississippi Board of Water Commissioners. 0462-8128. Monographic Series. US. English. ir. **Ind/Abst** GeoRef. **DD** 628. **CODEN** MBWBAG.

BULLETIN - OREGON STATE WATER RESOURCES BOARD. **Main/Corp** Oregon. State Water Resources Board. No. 1- 1956-. 0471-900X. Periodical. US. English. ir.

BULLETIN - WATER RESEARCH INSTITUTE (MORGANTOWN). (BULLETIN - WATER RESEARCH INSTITUTE). **Main/Corp** West Virginia University. Water Research Institute. No. 1- 1969-. 0512-4727. Monographic Series. US. English. West Virginia University, Water Research Institute, Morgantown WV 26506.

BULLETIN - WATER RESOURCES RESEARCH CENTER (UNIVERSITY OF NEW HAMPSHIRE). **Main/Corp** University of New Hampshire. Water Resources Research Center. **VFOAT** WRRC Bulletin. Vol. 1 1967-. 0548-4901. Monographic Series. US. English. ir. University of New Hampshire, Water Resource Research Center, Durham NH 03824. **DD** 628.

BUSINESS MONITOR. REPORT ON THE CENSUS OF PRODUCTION : WATER SUPPLY. See Business.

CALIFORNIA STATE AGENCIES' WATER QUALITY RELATED ACTIVITIES. **Main/Corp** California. State Water Resources Control Board. US. English. an. California State Water Resources Control Board, Division of Planning and Research, PO Box 100, Sacramento CA 95801. **LC** TD224.C3. **DD** 353.9794008232506.

CALIFORNIA STATE WATER PROJECT. ANNUAL REPORT. (CALIFORNIA STATE WATER PROJECT : ANNUAL REPORT). **Main/Corp** California. Department of Water Resources. **Series Corp** Its Bulletin. **VFOAT** Annual Report. California State Water Project. 1963-. 0090-5968. Periodical. US. English. ir. California State Water Project, Sacramento CA 95819. **LC** HD1694.C3. **DD** 627.

THE CALIFORNIA STATE WATER PROJECT. APPENDIX A, . . . ANNUAL FINANCIAL REPORT. **Main/Corp** California. Dept. of Water Resources. 0736-4636. US. English. an. State of California Resources Agency, Department of Water Resources, PO Box 388, Sacramento CA 95802. **LC** HD1694.C2. **DD** 353.9794007231.

THE CALIFORNIA STATE WATER PROJECT. APPENDIX E, WATER OPERATIONS IN THE SACRAMENTO-SAN JOAQUIN DELTA CEASED. **VFOAT** Appendix E, Water Operations in the Sacramento San Joaquin Delta, Water Operations in the Sacramento-San Joaquin Delta. 1962-1975-. 0736-2617. US. English. an. State of California, Resources Agency, Department of Water Resources, PO Box 388, Sacramento CA 95802. **LC** TC425.D34. **DD** 333.9115097945.

THE CALIFORNIA STATE WATER PROJECT, CURRENT ACTIVITIES AND FUTURE MANAGEMENT PLANS CEASED. **Main/Corp** California. Dept. of Water Resources. 0741-9198. US. English. an. **LC** HD1694.C3. **DD** 333.91009794. *California State Water Project, Activities and Future Management Plans.*

CALIFORNIA WATER. 1978-. 0195-8658. Periodical. US. English. an. State of California/ Department of Water Resources, PO Box 388, Sacramento CA 95802. **LC** TC424.C2. **DD** 333.91009794.

THE CALIFORNIA WATER PLAN OUTLOOK. **Main/Corp** California. Dept. of Water Resources. 1974-. 0147-9164. US. English. $5.00. State of California/ Department of Water Resources, PO Box 388, Sacramento CA 95802. **Tel** (916)445-3553. Ed William J Helms. **LC** HD1694.C2. **DD** 333.91009794. **Circ** 1,000. (ctrl). Shows current water situation in California including weather, reservoir storage, stream flows, runoff forecasts and snow and tide data. *Water for California-Outlook.*

THE CALIFORNIA WATER PLAN OUTLOOK. SUMMARY REPORT. (THE CALIFORNIA WATER PLAN OUTLOOK, SUMMARY REPORT). **Main/Corp** California. Dept. of Water Resources. 1974-. 0147-9806. US. English. State of California, Department of Water Resources, PO Box 388, Sacramento CA 95802. **LC** TC424.C2. **DD** 333.91009794.

CANADA WATER ACT. ANNUAL REPORT. (THE CANADA WATER ACT : ANNUAL REPORT). **Main/Corp** Canada. Environment Canada. **VFOAT** Loi Sur les Ressources en Fau du Canada: Rapport Annuel. 1978/79-. 0227-4747. CN. English (French). an. Environment Canada, Publications Distribution, Ottawa Ontario K1A 0T6 Canada. **Ind/Abst** GeoRef. **LC** TC426. **DD** 333.9100971. *Canada Water Act: Annual Report, 0227-4787.*

CANADA WATER YEAR BOOK. See Yearbooks, Almanacs, Directories.

CANADIAN WATER RESOURCES JOURNAL. **VFOAT** Revue Canadienne des Ressources en Eau. V. 1- Oct. 1976-. 0701-1784. Periodical. CN. English (includes some text in French). qt. 12.00. Canadian Water Resources Association, 765 Grain Exchange Building/167 Lombard Avenue, Winnipeg Manitoba R3B 0V3 Canada. **Ind/Abst** Can. Environ., Sel. Water Resour. Abstr., ASTIS Bibliogr., ASTIS Curr. Aware. Bull. **DD** 333.9100971. *Reclamation, 0380-7509.*

CENSUS OF MISSOURI PUBLIC WATER SUPPLIES. **Main/Corp** Missouri. Division of Environmental Quality. 1977-. 0190-5015. US. English. be. **LC** TD224.M8. **DD** 363.6109778. *Census of Public Water Supplies in Missouri.*

CHUNG-KUO SHUI TU PAO CHIH. See Agriculture - Crop Production and Soil.

CIVIL WORKS WATER RESOURCES DEVELOPMENT PROGRAM. **Main/Corp** North Carolina. Dept. of Natural and Economic Resources. 0145-9619. US. English. **LC** TC424.N8. **DD** 333.910209756.

CIVIL WORKS WATER RESOURCES DEVELOPMENT PROGRAM. **Main/Corp** North Carolina. Dept. of Natural Resources and Community Development. US. English. Department of Natural Resources & Community Development, Office of Water Resources, Development Section, PO Box 27687, Raleigh NC 27611. **LC** TC424.N8. **DD** 363.6109756. *Civil Works Water Resources Development Program, 0145-9619.*

COLLECTED REPRINTS - WATER RESOURCES RESEARCH CENTER, UNIVERSITY OF HAWAII. **Main/Corp** University of Hawaii. Water Resources Research Center. **VFOAT** WRRC Contribution. V. 1- 1966/68-. US. English. ir. University of Hawaii, 2540 Dole Street, Holmes Hall 283, Honolulu HI 96822. **Tel** (808)948-7848. Ed Faith N Fujimura. **Circ** 300. (ctrl). Hawaii water resources: rainfall, wastewater reuse, solar radiation, water rights, groundwater, storm runoff, seawater indicator bacteria, floods, conservation economics, runoff impoundment.

COLORADO RIVER STORAGE PROJECT AND PARTICIPATING PROJECTS IN FISCAL YEAR . . . . **Main/Corp** United States. Dept. of the Interior. Water and Power Resources Service. Upper Colorado Region. 22nd Annual Report, 1978-. US. English. an. Upper Colorado Region Office, Box 11568, 125 South State, Salt Lake City UT 84147. *Colorado River Storage Project and Participating Projects, Annual Report.*

COLORADO WATER RESOURCES CIRCULAR. No. 15-. 0092-2684. US. English. ir. Colorado Water Conservation, 1845 Sherman Street, Denver CO 80203. **Ind/Abst** GeoRef. **LC** GB1025.C7. **DD** 553.709788. **CODEN** CLWCBE. *Ground Water Series. Circular, 0160-0974.*

CONNECTICUT WATER RESOURCES BULLETIN. No. 1-. 0589-400X. Monographic Series. US. English. Connecticut Department of Environmental Protection, State Office Building/Room 112, Hartford CT 06106. **Ind/Abst** GeoRef. **LC** TD201. **DD** 553.709746. **CODEN** CWCBAL. *Connecticut Water Resources Bulletin.*

CONSERVATION DISTRICT BOARDS OF MANITOBA ANNUAL REPORT. **VFOAT** Conservation Districts of Manitoba Annual Report. Began in 1977. 0708-5648. CN. English. an. **LC** TC427.M3. **DD** 354.71270082326. *Watershed*

Water Resources

Conservation District Boards of Manitoba Annual Report, 0228-1902.

DECISION - STATE OF CALIFORNIA, STATE WATER RESOURCES CONTROL BOARD. Main/Corp California. State Water Resources Control Board. 0098-1958. US. English. LC KFC162. DD 346.7940432. *DECISION.*

DENVER WATER NEWS. Periodical. US. English. mo. $2.40. Department of Natural Resources, 1313 Sherman Street Street/Room 818, Denver CO 80203. Tel (303)839-3581.

DEPARTMENT PUBLICATIONS - STATE OF CALIFORNIA, RESOURCES AGENCY, DEPARTMENT OF WATER RESOURCES. (DEPARTMENT PUBLICATIONS - STATE OF CALIFORNIA, DEPT. OF WATER RESOURCES). Main/Corp California. Dept. of Water Resources. July/Dec. 1972-. 0360-3946. US. English. an. Department of Water Resources, PO Box 388, Sacramento CA 95802. LC GB705.C2. DD 016.5514809794. *Abstracts of DWR Publications.*

DESALINATION. V. 1- Apr. 1966-. 0011-9164. Periodical. English. ir. 1028.00 Domestic, $380.75 US. Elsevier Science Publishers, PO Box 211, 1000 AE Amsterdam Netherlands. Ed Mirian Balaban. Ind/Abst Electron. Commun. Abstr. J., ISMEC Bull., Pollut. Abstr. Indexes, Saf. Sci. Abstr. J., Eng. Index, Phys. Abstr., Sci. Cit. Index, Abr. Ed., Ocean. Abstr., Fluidex, Life Sci. Collect., Can. Environ., Sel. Water Resour. Abstr., Excerpta Med., Energy Inf. Abstr., Environ. Abstr., Comput. Control Abstr., Electr. Electron. Abstr., Sci. Abstr., Chem. Abstr., Bibliogr. Agric., Energy Res. Abstr., Curr. Contents, Appl. Sci. Technol. Index, Eng. Index, Eng. Index Annu., Eng. Index Mon. LC TD478. CODEN DSLNAH. bk rev. adv acc. Dedicated to keeping pace with the water desalting and purification field in all its aspects, theoretical and applied research, technological and industrial development, and the experience of operators and users.

DEUTSCHE GEWAESSERKUNDLICHE MITTEILUNGEN. Began with Vol. 1, April 1957. 0012-0235. Periodical. GW. German. bm. 45.-. Bundesanstalt fuer Gewaesserkunde, Kaiserin Augusta Anlagen 15, Postbox 309, 54 Koblenz West Germany. Tel (0261)12431. Ed H Liebscher. Ind/Abst Life Sci. Collect., Excerpta Med., GeoRef, Chem. Abstr., Energy Res. Abstr., Electron. Commun. Abstr. J., Pollut. Abstr. Indexes, ISMEC Bull., Saf. Sci. Abstr. J. LC GB651. CODEN DGMTAO. bk rev. Circ 1,600. (ctrl). Quantitative and qualitative hydrology, water pollution control, water protection (from basic research to practical use in water resources management). *Mitteilungen.*

DEVELOPMENTS IN WATER TREATMENT. See Chemistry.

DICTIONARY CATALOG OF THE WATER RESOURCES CENTER ARCHIVES. SUPPLEMENT. See Genealogy and Heraldry - Archives.

DIRECTORY OF AMERICAN WATER WORKS ASSOCIATION. ONTARIO SECTION. See Yearbooks, Almanacs, Directories.

DIRECTORY OF FEDERAL AND STATE OFFICIALS ENGAGED IN WATER RESOURCES DEVELOPMENT. See Yearbooks, Almanacs, Directories.

DIRECTORY OF WATER RESOURCES EXPERTISE. See Yearbooks, Almanacs, Directories.

DOKUMENTATION WASSER. See Engineering.

DRIP/TRICKLE IRRIGATION. VFOAT Drip Trickle Irrigation. V. 1- 1976-. 0276-8232. Periodical. US. English. qt. $10.00 Domestic, $20.00 Foreign. Agribusiness Publications, 627 North Fresno Street, Fresno CA 93701.

L'EAU ET L'INDUSTRIE. (EAU ET L'INDUSTRIE). 0337-9329. Periodical. FR. French. mo. $51.88. P Johanet et Fils, 7 Avenue Fd Roosevelt, 75008 Paris France. Ind/Abst GeoRef, Chem. Abstr. CODEN EINUDQ.

ECOLOGICAL ASPECTS OF USED-WATER TREATMENT. V. 1- 1975-. Monographic Series. UK. English. ir. Academic Press, 4805 Sand Lake Road, Orlando FL 32887. Tel (305)345-4100. Ed C R Curds and H A Hankes. Each issue contains an index to its own contents - no vol index - loose.

FEDERAL-STATE-PRIVATE SNOW SURVEYS AND WATER SUPPLY OUTLOOK FOR ALASKA (ANCHORAGE, ALASKA : 1983). See Earth Sciences - Meteorology.

FLUORIDATED DRINKING WATER, PROFICIENCY TESTING. US. English. mo. Center for Disease Control, Atlanta GA 30333.

FROM THE STATE CAPITALS. WATER SUPPLY. VFOAT Water Supply. 0734-1237. Periodical. US. English. mo. $95.00. Wakeman/Wolworth Inc, PO Box 1939, New Haven CT 06509. Tel (203)562-8518. Subjects include construction and financing of reservoirs and treatment plants, pollution controls, water development rights and irrigation projects.

GAUGING STATION RECORDS - SASKATOON SOUTHEAST WATER SUPPLY PROJECT. (GAUGING STATION RECORDS, SASKATOON SOUTHEAST WATER SUPPLY PROJECT). VFOAT Saskatoon Southeast Water Supply Project, Gauging Station Records. Began with 1966/67 issue. 0225-2694. Periodical. CN. English. an. Saskatchewan Water Corporation, Victoria Place 111 Fairford Street East, Moosejaw Saskatchewan S6H 7X5 Canada. Tel (306)694-3980. LC TD227.S33. DD 333.9102110971242. (ctrl). Publication of hydrometric data in Saskatchewan.

GEWASSERSCHUTZ, WASSER, ABWASSER. (GEWASSERSCHUTZ, WASSER, ABWASSER : GWA). VFOAT GWA. Began in 1968. 0342-6068. Monographic Series. German. ir. Ind/Abst Chem. Abstr. CODEN GWABDO.

GIDROTEKHNICHESKOE STROITEL'STVO. 0016-9714. UR. Russian. mo. $47.50. Victor Kamkin Inc (70224), 12224 Parklawn Drive, Rockville MD 20852. Tel (301)881-5973. Ind/Abst Fluidex, Electr. Electron. Abstr., Sci. Abstr. Sect. A. Phys. Abstr., Sci. Abstr. Sect. A. Phys. Abstr., Comput. Control Abstr., Phys. Abstr. CODEN GTSTA8.

GIDROTEKHNIKA I MELIORATSIIA. Began publication in 1949. 0016-9722. UR. Russian. mo. $33.50. Victor Kamkin Inc (70223), 12224 Parklawn Drive, Rockville MD 20852. Tel (301)881-5973. Ind/Abst GeoRef, Chem. Abstr., Bibliogr. Agric. LC TC1. CODEN GIMEAQ.

GOSPODARKA WODNA. 0017-2448. Periodical. PL. Polish (tables of contents also in Russian, French, and English). mo. Ars Polona, Krakowskie Przedmiescie 7, 00-068 Warsaw Poland. Ind/Abst Chem. Abstr., Energy Res. Abstr. CODEN GOWOAC.

GREAT LAKES RESEARCH CHECKLIST. No. 1- Dec. 1959-. 0072-7326. US. English. sa. Great Lakes Commission, 2200 Bonistell Boulevard, Ann Arbor MI 48109. Ed Albert G Ballert. LC UNC. DD 016.977. (ctrl). Bibliography of Great Lakes articles and books.

GREAT LAKES RESEARCH VESSELS SUPPLEMENT; PRELIMINARY SCHEDULES. 1979-. US. English. an. Great Lakes Basin Commission, PO Box 999, Ann Arbor MI 48106. *Great Lakes Research Vessels : Capabilities and Preliminary Schedules.*

GREAT LAKES WATER LEVELS (QUINQUENNIAL). (GREAT LAKES WATER LEVELS). 1860-1970-. US. English. an. Department of Commerce-NOAA, National Ocean Survey Office, Rockville MD 20852. Tel (313)226-3650. Vols. for (1860-1980-) Distributed to depository libraries in microfiche.

GREEN RIVER WATERSHED NEWS. V. 1, No. 1- May 1979-. Periodical. US. English. ir.

GROUND-WATER DATA FOR MICHIGAN. VFOAT Ground Water Data for Michigan. Began in 1973. 0098-3691. US. English. an. Michigan Department of the Interior, Box 30028, R Thomas Segall, Lansing MI 48909. LC GB1025.M5. DD 553.7909774. Vols. for (1980-) distributed to depository libraries in microfiche. *Summary of Ground-Water Hydrologic Data in Michigan, 0085-6924.*

GROUND-WATER LEVELS IN NEW MEXICO. BASIC DATA REPORT. VFOAT Basic Data Report. Began with 1961. 0548-6165. US. English. an. Office of the State Engineer, Sante Fe MN 87503. Tel (505)827-6110. LC GB1025.N6. DD 551.49209789. CODEN NMEBA. Circ 500. Water resource data and investigations agency annual report. *Ground-Water Levels in New Mexico.*

GROUND-WATER LEVELS IN THE UNITED STATES. NORTH-CENTRAL STATES. Main/Corp United States. Geological Survey. 0499-5198. US. English. US Department of the Interior, US Geological Survey, 1200 South Eads Street, Arlington VA 22202. *Water Levels and Artesian Pressure in Observation Wells in the United States.*

GROUND-WATER LEVELS IN THE UNITED STATES. SOUTH-CENTRAL STATES. Main/Corp United States. Geological Survey. 1956-59-. 0502-1464. US. English. US Department of the Interior, US Geological Survey, 1200 South Eads Street, Arlington VA 22202. *Water Levels and Artesian Pressure in Observation Wells in the United States.*

GROUND-WATER LEVELS IN THE UNITED STATES. SOUTHWESTERN STATES. Main/Corp United States. Geological Survey. Series Corp Its Water-Supply Paper. 1956/60-. US. English. US Department of the Interior, US Geological Survey, 1200 South Eads Street, Arlington VA 22202. *Water Levels and Artesian Pressure in Observation Wells in the United States.*

GROUND WATER QUALITY MONITORING PROGRAM. Vol. 3 (1980)-. 0738-1204. US. English. an. LC TD224.M6. DD 363.7394. *Groundwater Quality Monitoring Program, 0738-1204.*

HIMIJA I TEHNOLOGIJA VODY. (KHIMIIA I TEKHNOLOGIII VODY). V. 1- Sept./Oct. 1979-. 0204-3556. Periodical. UR. Russian (summaries in English). bm. $40.50. Victor Kamkin Inc (71043), 1224 Parklawn Drive, Rockville MD 20852. Tel (301)881-5973. Ind/Abst Electron. Commun. Abstr. J., ISMEC Bull., Pollut. Abstr. Indexes, Saf. Sci. Abstr. J., Coal Abstr., Chem. Abstr. LC TD204. CODEN KTVODL.

HYDATA CEASED. VFOAT Hydata Water Resources Index. V. 1-14. 0018-8115. Periodical. US. English. mo. Ind/Abst Fluidex, Sel. Water Resour. Abstr. NLM Z 7935 H992. CODEN HYDTAD.

HYDRO-ABSTRACTS. See Indexes/Abstracts.

HYDROLOGIC REPORT. (HYDROLOGIC REPORT - LOS ANGELES COUNTY FLOOD CONTROL DISTRICT). Main/Corp Los Angeles County Food Control District. 0147-3697. US. English. an. Los Angeles County Department of Public Works, PO Box 2418 Terminal Annex, Los Angeles CA 90051. Tel (213)226-4191. Ind/Abst GeoRef. LC TC425.L65. DD 551.480979493. (ctrl). Hydraulic data for Los Angeles county: precipitation, runoff, evaporation, dam operation, conservation and groundwater.

I.C.I.D. BULLETIN. (ICID BULLETIN). VFOAT Irrigation and Drainage Bulletin. VAT International Commission on Irrigation and Drainage Bulletin. July 1968/Jan. 1969-Jan. 1975. 0300-2810. Periodical. II. English (French). sa. $10.00. International Commision on Irrigation and Drainage, 48 Myaya Marg Chanaky Apuri, New Delhi 21 India. Ind/Abst Eng. Index Annu., Eng. Index Mon., Eng. Index Bioeng. Abstr., Eng. Index Energy Abstr., Can. Environ., Bibliogr. Agric. LC TC801. DD 333.91305. CODEN IIDBAS. *Annual Bulletin.*

ILRI PUBLICATION (INTERNATIONAL INSTITUTE FOR LAND RECLAMATION AND IMPROVEMENT). (ILRI PUBLICATION). VFOAT I.L.R.I. Publication. No. 27-. 0167-4072. Monographic Series. English. ir. 30.-. International Institute for Land Reclamation and Improvement, PO Box 45, 6700 AA Wageningen The Netherlands. Tel 08370-19100. Ed N A de Riddoir. Ind/Abst Eng. Index Annu., Eng. Index Mon., Eng. Index Bioeng. Abstr., Eng. Index Energy Abstr., Chem. Abstr. CODEN ILPUDX. bk rev. (ctrl). Water management, irrigation drainage, and land reclamation in developing countries. *Publication - International Institute for Land Reclamation and Improvement.*

IMPACT OF WATER RESOURCES DEVELOPMENT. Vol. 1- Oct. 1982-. Periodical. US. English. Environment Information Center, 124 East 39th Street, New York NY 10016. LC TC401. DD 333.91005.

INDIAN JOURNAL OF POWER AND RIVER VALLEY DEVELOPMENT. Began publication with December 1950 issue. 0019-5537. Periodical. II. English. mo. $30.00. Books

Water Resources

and Journals Private Ltd, 612 Madan Street, Calcutta 13 India. **Tel** 271711. **Ed** P K Menon. **Ind/Abst** Fluidex, Energy Inf. Abstr., Environ. Abstr., GeoRef, Comput. Control Abstr., Electr. Electron. Abstr., Sci. Abstr. Sect. A. Phys. Abstr., Nucl. Sci. Abstr., Sel. Water Resour. Abstr., Bibliogr. Agric., Eng. Index, Energy Res. Abstr., Phys. Abstr., Bibliogr. Index Geol. **LC** TC1. **CODEN** IJPRA7. bk rev. adv acc. **Circ** 2,000. (ctrl). Devoted to development of power and water resources.

INFORMATION CIRCULAR - MISSOURI. DIVISION OF GEOLOGICAL SURVEY AND WATER RESOURCES. *See* Earth Sciences - Geology.

INFORMATION EAUX. *See* Sanitation, Environmental Technology.

INTERNATIONAL HYDROGRAPHIC BULLETIN. BULLETIN HYDROGRAPHIQUE INTERNATIONAL. **VFOAT** Bulletin Hydrographique International. Began publication in 1928. 0020-6938. Periodical. English (French). mo. $17.96. International Hydrographical Bureau, BP 345-7 Avenue, President JF Kennedy, MC 98000 Monaco. **Tel** 33/93/50 65 87. **LC** VK588.

INTERNATIONAL JOURNAL OF WATER RESOURCES DEVELOPMENT. Vol. 1, No. 1 (Apr. 1983)-. 0790-0627. Periodical. IE. English. qt. $95.00. Tycooly International Publishing Ltd, 6 Charlemont Terrace, Dublin Ireland. **Tel** 353-11. **Ed** Asit K Biswos. bk rev. adv acc. Covers all aspects of water development and management, and reports on the application of the latest research results to solve real world problems.

INTERNATIONAL WATER REPORT. *See* Sanitation, Environmental Technology.

INVESTIGATIONS OF INDIANA LAKES AND STREAMS. V. 1, No. 4/9-7, No. 6. 0075-0239. Monographic Series. US. English. ir. Indiana University and Indiana Department of Natural Resources, Department of Zoology, Bloomington IN 47401. **Ind/Abst** Biol. Abstr. *Investigations of Indiana Lakes.*

IRC BULLETIN. **VFOAT** EPA IRC Bulletin. **VAT** Instructional Resources Center Bulletin. 1977. Periodical. US. English. qt. $4.50. EPA Instructional Resources Center, Ohio State University 1200 Chambers, Columbus OH 43212. **Tel** (614)422-6717. **Ed** Robert W Howe. bk rev. **Circ** 900. Provides information on water quality education and training with an emphasis on publications, audio-visual aids, and training opportunities. Also includes selected information on recent events.

IRRICAB. *See* Agriculture.

IRRIGATION AGE. 0021-1656. Periodical. US. English. mo. $15.00. Webb Publishing Company, 1999 Shephard Road, St Paul MN 55116. **Ind/Abst** Sel. Water Resour. Abstr., Energy Inf. Abstr., Environ. Abstr.

IRRIGATION AND POWER. (IRRIGATION & POWER : THE JOURNAL OF THE CENTRAL BOARD OF IRRIGATION & POWER). **VFOAT** Irrigation and Power. Vol. 8, No. 1 (Jan. 1951)-. 0367-9993. Periodical. II. English. qt. $20.00. Central Board of Irrigation Power, Malcha Marg Chanakyapuri, New Delhi 11 0021 India. **Ind/Abst** Eng. Index Annu., Eng. Index Mon., Eng. Index Bioeng. Abstr., Eng. Index Energy Abstr., Fluidex, Sel. Water Resour. Abstr., GeoRef, Bibliogr. Agric., Energy Res. Abstr., Bibliogr. Index Geol., Eng. Index. **CODEN** IRPWAA.

IRRIGATION EFFICIENCY : A BIBLIOGRAPHY. *See* Bibliographies.

IRRINEWS. **VFOAT** Newsletter of the International Irrigation Information Center. No. 1- Oct. 1975-. 0304-3606. Periodical. CN. English. qt. Free Domestic, $5.00 Foreign. International Irrigation Information Center, Volcani Center, POB 49, Bet Dagan Israel. **Tel** (03)980356. **Ed** J Shalhevet. **Ind/Abst** Fluidex. bk rev. **Circ** 5,000. (ctrl). Articles on all aspects of irrigation technology worldwide including new equipment, environmental effects, country and region focus, plant-water relations. Also book reviews, international courses.

IWSA YEAR BOOK : AN OFFICIAL PUBLICATION OF THE INTERNATIONAL WATER SUPPLY ASSOCIATION. *See* Yearbooks, Almanacs, Directories.

IZVESTIIA. **Main/Corp** Bulgarska Akademiia Na Naukite Naukite, Sofia. Institut Po Vodni Problemi. 1-1963-. 0525-0811. Periodical. BU. Bulgarian (summaries in Russian English or French). ir. Bulgarski Academiia Naukite Institute, PO Vodni Problemi Sofia Bulgaria.

JAPAN'S WATERWORKS YEARBOOK. *See* Yearbooks, Almanacs, Directories.

JOHNSON DRILLERS JOURNAL. (THE JOHNSON DRILLERS JOURNAL). V. 34, No. 2-V. 56, No. 4 1962-. 0021-7271. Periodical. US. English. qt. Johnson Division UOP Inc, Box 43118, St Paul MN 55164. **Ind/Abst** Sel. Water Resour. Abstr., GeoRef, Bibliogr. Index Geol. *Johnson National Drillers Journal.*

JOURNAL - AMERICAN WATER WORKS ASSOCIATION. *See* Sanitation, Environmental Technology.

JOURNAL (AMERICAN WATER WORKS ASSOCIATION). (JOURNAL). Vol. 40, No. 1 (Jan. 1948)-. 0003-150X. Periodical. US. English. mo. $50.00. American Water Works Association, 6666 West Quincy Avenue, Denver CO 80235. **Tel** (303)794-7711. **Ind/Abst** Can. Environ., Sel. Water Resour. Abstr., Abstr. Bull. Inst. Paper Chem., GeoRef, Appl. Sci. Technol. Index, Energy Res. Abstr. **CODEN** JAWWA5. *Journal of the American Water Works Association.*

THE JOURNAL OF FRESHWATER. Began with Winter 1977 issue. 0276-0142. Periodical. US. English. qt. Teh Freshwater Biological Research Foundation/Freshwater Society, 2500 Shadywood Road/Box 90, Navarre MN 55392. **Ind/Abst** Bibliogr. Agric. **LC** QH96.A1. **DD** 333.9105.

JOURNAL OF IRRIGATION AND DRAINAGE ENGINEERING. *See* Engineering - Civil Engineering.

JOURNAL OF THE NEW ENGLAND WATER WORKS ASSOCIATION. **Main/Corp** New England Water Works Association. V. 1- 1886-. 0028-4939. Periodical. US. English. qt. $20.00 Domestic, $25.00 Foreign. New England Water Works Association, 850 R Providence Highway, Dedham MA 02026. **Tel** (617)329-9650. **Ed** James J Matera. **Ind/Abst** Eng. Index Mon., Eng. Index Bioeng. Abstr., Eng. Index Energy Abstr., Fluidex, Excerpta Med., GeoRef, Biol. Abstr., Chem. Abstr., Eng. Index Annu., Eng. Index, Sel. Water Resour. Abstr., Bibliogr. Index Geol. **LC** TD201. **CODEN** JNEWA6. (cum index). bk rev. adv acc. **Circ** 1,700. (ctrl). Journal containing the essentials of professional reporting in the field of water works. *Transactions.*

JOURNAL OF THE WATER RESOURCES PLANNING AND MANAGEMENT DIVISION CEASED. **Main/Corp** American Society of Civil Engineers. Water Resources Planning and Management Division. V. 102-108, No. WR3. 0145-0743. US. English. ir. $4.00. American Society of Civil Engineers, 345 East 47th Street, New York NY 10017. **Ind/Abst** Eng. Index Annu., Eng. Index Mon., Eng. Index Energy Abstr., Sel. Water Resour. Abstr., Energy Inf. Abstr., Environ. Abstr., ASCE Annu. Comb. Index, Int. Aerosp. Abstr., GeoRef, Bibliogr. Agric., Coal Abstr. **LC** TC401. **DD** 333.91005. **CODEN** JWRDDC. Available on microfilm. *Proceedings of the American Society of Civil Engineers,* 0097-417X.

JOURNAL OF WATER RESOURCES PLANNING AND MANAGEMENT. **VFOAT** A.S.C.E. Water Resources Planning and Management. Vol. 109, No. 1 (Jan. 1983)-. 0733-9496. Periodical. US. English. qt. $56.00. American Society of Civil Engineers, 345 East 47th Street, New York NY 10017. **Tel** (212)705-7275. **Ind/Abst** Fluidex, Can. Environ., Coal Abstr., Excerpta Med., ASCE Annu. Comb. Index, ASCE Publ. Inf., Trans. Am. Soc. Civ. Eng., Appl. Sci. Technol. Index, Sel. Water Resour. Abstr. **LC** TC401. **DD** 333.91005. **CODEN** JWRMD5. **Circ** 4,000. Examines social, economic, environmental, and administrative concerns relating to the utilization and conservation of water. *Journal of the Water Resources Planning and Management Division,* 0145-0743.

KANSAS WATER NEWS. V. 1- Nov./Dec. 1957-. 0022-8869. Periodical. US. English. sa. Kansas Water Resources Board (Depository), Topeka KS 66613. **Ind/Abst** GeoRef. **CODEN** KAWNAN.

KANSAS WATER PLAN. US. English. Kansas Water Office, 109 SE Ninth/Suite 200, Topeka KS 66612. **LC** TC424.K2. **DD** 333.911509781.

KUTATASI JEGYZEK, ANNOTACIOK, TANULMANYOK. Series/Titl Vituki Kozlemenyek. English (Hungarian). an. Vizgazdalkodasi Tudomanyos Kutato Kozpont, Kvassay Jeno Ut 1, 1453 Budapest Hungary. **Tel** (361)338160. **Ed** A Szollosi-Nagy. **LC** TC465.5. **DD** 628.05. (ctrl). Full list of research projects and brief summaries of reports completed of the Research Centre for Water Resources Development Vituki.

LIBRARY BULLETIN - TEXAS DEPARTMENT OF WATER RESOURCES. **Main/Corp** Texas. Dept. of Water Resources. V. 9, No. 9- Sept. 1977-. 0148-7876. Periodical. US. English. mo. Department of Water Resources, PO Box 13807 Capitol Station, Austin TX 78701. **Tel** (512)475-3781. *Library Bulletin - Texas Water Development Board,* 0146-1761.

LLANO ESTACADO PLAYA LAKE WATER RESOURCES STUDY. (LLANO ESTACADO PLAYA LAKE WATER RESOURCES STUDY : A SPECIAL INVESTIGATION : STATUS REPORT). Fiscal Year 1978-. US. English. Water and Power Resources Services, Southwest Regional Office, 317 East Third, Amarillo TX 79101. *Llano Estacado Total Water Management Study.*

MEDEDELING - INSTITIT VOOR CULTUURTECHNIEK EN WATERHUISHOUDING. **Main/Corp** Instituut voor Cultuurtechniek en Waterhuishouding. No. 1- 1958-. 0074-0411. Monographic Series. NE. Dutch. ir. Free. Institute for Land & Water Management Research, 6700 A Wageningen Netherlands. **Tel** 08370-19100. **Ed** Ing Bram ten Cate. (ctrl). Covers water management, plant-soil-water relationships, soil technology, groundwater and surface water quality, land layout and farm economics, land development projects and their economic evaluation.

MEMBERSHIP DIRECTORY AND INDUSTRY BUYERS' GUIDE - IRRIGATION ASSOCIATION. *See* Yearbooks, Almanacs, Directories.

MERCURY IN WATER; A BIBLIOGRAPHY. *See* Bibliographies.

MIDDLE EAST WATER & SEWAGE. **VFOAT** Wutar and Suwij Al-Sharq Al-Awsat, Ab va Fazilab-I Khavrmiyanah. V. 1- July/Aug. 1977-. 0140-5098. Periodical. UK. English. bm. $68.00. Industrial & Marine Publications Ltd, Queensway House 2 Queensway, Redhill Surrey RHI 105 England. **Ind/Abst** Electron. Commun. Abstr. J., ISMEC Bull., Pollut. Abstr. Indexes, Saf. Sci. Abstr. J., Fluidex. **LC** TD311.A1. **DD** 628.05.

MINUTES OF THE MEETING - ARKANSAS-WHITE-RED BASINS INTER-AGENCY COMMITTEE. **Main/Corp** Arkansas-White-Red Basins Inter-Agency Committee. 1st-. 0403-1911. Periodical. US. English. ir. Southwestern Division/Corps of Engineers, Dallas TX 75235. **LC** HD1695.A8. **DD** 333.9. (cum index).

MISSOURI RIVER BASIN REGION, WATER RESOURCES RESEARCH INSTITUTES. **VFOAT** Water Resources Budget Projection. English. ir. **LC** HD1695.M45. **DD** 333.91.

MONTANA WATER SUPPLY OUTLOOK. Jan. 1, 1982-. US. English. mo. **LC** TD224.M9. **DD** 553.7809786. *Water Supply Outlook for Montana and Federal-State-Private Cooperative Snow Surveys,* 0566-0416.

MONTHLY WATER LEVEL BULLETIN, GREAT LAKES AND MONTREAL HARBOUR. **Main/Corp** Canadian Hydrographic Service. **VFOAT** Bulletin Mensuel des Niveaux de l'Eau des Grands Lacs et du Port de Montreal. Oct. 1974-. 0381-3371. Periodical. CN. English (French, April 1975-). mo. Free. Environment Canada, Department of the Environment Ocean and Aquatic Sciences, PO Box 5050, Burlington Ontario L7R 4A6 Canada. *Monthly Water Level Bulletin, Great Lakes and Montreal Harbour,* 0381-3371.

NATIONAL WATER CONDITIONS. July 1982-. 0736-2609. Periodical. US. English. mo. Geological Survey, National Center Stop 329, Reston VA 22092. **Ind/Abst** Energy Inf. Abstr., Sel. Water Resour. Abstr., Environ. Abstr., Energy Res. Abstr. **LC** GB701. **DD** 553.70973. *Water Resources Review (1982).*

NATIONAL WATER LINE. 0271-0692. Periodical. US. English. bw. National Water Resources Association, 955 l'enfant Plaza, North Building SW, Washington DC 20024.

NATIONAL WATER QUALITY INVENTORY : REPORT TO CONGRESS. Began with 1974. US. English. be. U S Environmental Protection Agency, Office of Water Regulations and Standards, Washington DC 20460. **LC** TD223. **DD** 363.61.

Water Resources

NATIONAL WATERSHED CONGRESS; PROCEEDINGS. 1st- 1954-. 0470-3480. US. English. an. National Watershed Congress, 1025 Vermont Avenue NW, Washington DC 20005. Ind/Abst GeoRef. LC HD1694. DD 333.91.

NEBRASKA WATER SURVEY PAPER. No. 2- Dec. 1944-. 0090-6727. Monographic Series. US. English. ir. University of Nebraska-Lincoln, 113 Nebraska Hall, 901 North 17th Street, Lincoln NE 68588-0517. Tel (402)472-3471. Ind/Abst GeoRef, Bibliogr. Index Geol. LC GB1025.N2. CODEN NWSPAQ. *Nebraska Water Survey Bulletin.*

NEVADA WATER SUPPLY OUTLOOK AND FEDERAL-STATE-PRIVATE COOPERATIVE SNOW SURVEYS. VFOAT Nevada Water Supply Outlook. Periodical. US. English. mo. US Department of Agriculture, Soil Conservation Service/3rd Floor, Reno NV 89505. Tel (702)784-5869. Ind/Abst Am. Stat. Index. Circ 1,000. (ctrl). Listing of current values for water supply and forecasted streamflow in Nevada and Eastern California. *Water Supply Outlook for Nevada and Federal-State-Private Cooperative Snow Surveys.*

NEWSLETTER - CANADIAN NATIONAL COMMITTEE. INTERNATIONAL WATER RESOURCES ASSOCIATION. (NEWSLETTER). Main/Corp International Water Resources Association. Canadian National Committee. VFOAT Bulletin d'Information. VAT Bulletin d'Information - Comite National Canadien. Association Internationale des Ressources en Eau. No. 1 (Sept. 1974)-. 0821-2309. Periodical. CN. English. ir. Free. CNC-IWRA Newsletter, c/o Environment Canada, Ottawa Ontario K1A 0E7 Canada. DD 333.91005.

NOR'WESTER (SEATTLE, WASH. : 1972). (THE NOR'WESTER). Began in 1972?. 8750-6076. Periodical. US. English. mo. $12.00. 3918- 1st Northeast, Seattle WA 98105.

NOTES ON WATER RESEARCH. No. 1- Dec. 1975-. 0307-6652. Monographic Series. UK. English. Water Research Centre, Stevenage Laboratory, Elder Way, Herts 5PQ 1TH England. Ind/Abst Life Sci. Collect., Pap. Board Abstr. LC TD201. DD 614.772. *Notes on Water Pollution, 0434-4456.*

OKHRANA PRIRODNYKH VOD URALA. UR. Russian. 0.56 Each Issue. Sredne-Uralskoe Knizhnoe Izd-Vo, Malysheva 24, Sverdlovsk Russia. LC TD286.U7.

ONTARIO PIPELINE. Mar. 1971-. 0380-1624. Periodical. CN. English. ty. American Water Works, 6666 West Quincy Avenue, Denver CO 80235. Tel (416)252-7060. Circ 2,000. (ctrl).

OPFLOW. V. 1- Jan. 1975-. 0149-8029. Periodical. US. English. mo. $9.50. American Water Works Association, 6666 West Quincy Avenue, Denver CO 80235. Tel (303)794-7711.

PACIFIC WATERSHED ENHANCEMENT. Vol. 2, No. 1-. 0730-921X. Periodical. US. English. mo. $30.00. Mattole Center for Science and Education, PO Box 96, Honeydew CA 95545. *Enhancement Newsletter, 0278-3657.*

PCB IN WATER : A BIBLIOGRAPHY. See Bibliographies.

PERFORMANCE BUDGET. Main/Corp Orissa, India. Irrigation and Power Dept. T. English. ir. LC TC904.O7. DD 354.5413008242.

PHILIPPINES WATER RESOURCES ABSTRACTS. See Indexes/Abstracts.

POLLUTION AND WATER RESOURCES, COLUMBIA UNIVERSITY SEMINAR SERIES. (POLLUTION AND WATER RESOURCES COLUMBIA UNIVERSITY SEMINAR SERIES). Vol. 13, Pt. 1-. 0278-0925. US. English. ir. Pergamon Press, Maxwell House, Fairview Park, Elmsford NY 10523. Ind/Abst GeoRef. *Proceedings of University Seminar on Pollution and Water Resources, 0278-0917.*

PREAUTHORIZATION PLANNING ACTIVITIES OF THE BUREAU OF RECLAMATION, THE CORPS OF ENGINEERS, AND THE SOIL CONSERVATION SERVICE. (PREAUTHORIZATION OF PLANNING ACTIVITIES OF THE BUREAU OF RECLAMATION, THE CORPS OF ENGINEERS, AND THE SOIL CONSERVATION SERVICE). Main/Corp Arkansas-White-Red Basins Inter-Agency Committee. Standing Committee on Exchange of Program Information. 0565-0631. US. English. LC TC423.6. DD 333.91020976.

PROCEEDINGS - INTERNATIONAL WATER CONFERENCE. (THE INTERNATIONAL WATER CONFERENCE ANNUAL MEETING : PROCEEDINGS). Main/Conf International Water Conference. 1940. 0074-9575. US. English. an. $40.00. Engineers Society of Western Pennsylvania, 530 William Penn Place, Pittsburgh PA 15219. Tel (412)261-0710. Ind/Abst Eng. Index Mon., Eng. Index Bioeng. Abstr., Eng. Index Energy Abstr., Chem. Abstr., Eng. Index Annu. CODEN AMICDX. adv acc. Circ 1,500. (ctrl). Contains papers and discussions of papers presented annually at each conference on the subject of industrial water.

PROCEEDINGS-MISSISSIPPI WATER RESOURCES CONFERENCE. Main/Conf Mississippi Water Resources Conference. 1st- 1966-. 0076-9533. US. English. an. Ind/Abst GeoRef, Chem. Abstr. CODEN MWRPAA.

PROCEEDINGS OF THE ANNUAL CONFERENCE ON WATER FOR TEXAS. Main/Conf Conference on Water for Texas. VFOAT Water for Texas. 2nd- 1956-. 0495-2340. Periodical. US. English. ir. Texas A & M University/Water Resources Institute, College Station TX 77843. LC TD201. DD 333.9.

PROCEEDINGS OF THE ANNUAL MISSOURI RIVER BASIN GOVERNORS' CONFERENCE. Main/Conf Missouri River Basin Governors' Conference on Water. First conference held in 1976. 0160-5518. US. English. Missouri River Basin Commission, Suite 403/ 10050 Regency Circle, Omaha NE 68114. LC HD1695.M45. DD 333.91.

PROCEEDINGS OF THE MEETING. Main/Corp Interstate Commission on the Potomac River Basin. VFOAT Water Resources in the Economic Development of the Shenandoah Valley. 1963?-. US. English. LC HD1695.P65.

PROCEEDINGS OF THE NATIONAL GROUND WATER QUALITY SYMPOSIUM. Main/Conf National Ground Water Quality Symposium. 1st- Aug. 1971-. US. English. ir. $31.25. National Water Well Association, 500 West Wilson Bridge Road, Worthington OH 43085. Tel (614)846-9355. Ind/Abst GeoRef.

PROCEEDINGS - SOUTH CAROLINA GOVERNOR'S CONFERENCE ON WATER RESOURCES. (PROCEEDINGS). Main/Conf South Carolina Governor's Conference on Water Resources. VFOAT Proceedings of the Conference. 0731-9495. US. English. an. South Carolina Water Resources Commission, 3830 Forest Drive, PO Box 4515, Columbia SC 29240. LC TC424.S7. DD 333.91009757.

PROGRESS REPORT - SOCIETE D'ENERGIE DE LA BAIE JAMES. See Business.

PROJECT COMPLETION REPORT - WATER RESOURCES CENTER. Main/Corp Ohio State University. Water Resources Center. VFOAT Termination Report - Water Resources Center. 1969-. Monographic Series. US. English. ir. *Research Project Completion Report - Water Resources Center.*

PROJECT SKYWATER; PROCEEDINGS. Main/Conf Skywater Conference. 1st- 1967-. US. English. US Department of Interior, Bureau of Reclamation Division of Atmospheric Water Resources Management, Denver CO 80220.

PROJECTS RECOMMENDED FOR DEAUTHORIZATION, ANNUAL REPORT. SUPPLEMENT. Main/Corp United States. Dept. of the Army. No. 1- 1976-. 0362-9201. US. English. an. US Gov't Printers Office, Washington DC 20402. LC TC423. DD 333.9100973.

PUBLICATION - ARKANSAS WATER RESOURCES RESEARCH CENTER. Main/Corp Arkansas Water Resources Research Center. Periodical. US. English. Ind/Abst GeoRef. LC GB705.A8. DD 333.9. CODEN PAWCDE. *Publication - Water Resources Research Center, 0571-043X.*

PUBLICATION-CALIFORNIA STATE WATER RESOURCES CONTROL BOARD. Main/Corp California. State Water Resources Control Board. 0096-1728. Monographic Series. US. English. Ind/Abst GeoRef. CODEN CWQPAV. *Publication - State Water Quality Control Board.*

PUBLICATION - CORNELL UNIVERSITY WATER RESOURCES AND MARINE SCIENCES CENTER. Main/Corp Cornell University. Water Resources and Marine Sciences Center. No. 22- 1969-. Monographic Series. US. English. ir. Water Resources & Marine Science Center, Cornell University, 468 Hollister Hall, Ithaca NY 14850. LC TD224.N7. *Publication -Cornell University Water Resources Center.*

PUBLICATION IWR. Main/Corp University of Alaska. Institute of Water Resources. Monographic Series. US. English. ir. University of Alaska, Institute of Water Resources, Fairbanks AK 99701.

PUBLICATIONS OF THE UTAH WATER RESEARCH LABORATORY. Main/Corp Utah Water Research Laboratory. US. English. ir. Utah Water Research Laboratory, Utah State University, Logan UT 84322-8200. Tel (801)750-3186. Ed Donna Falkenborg. Ind/Abst Bibliogr. Index Geol. Hydraulics and hydrology, water quality, water resources planning, atmospheric water resources.

PUBLICATIONS OF THE WEST VIRGINIA GEOLOGICAL SURVEY. See Earth Sciences - Geology.

QUADERNI - ISTITUTO DI RICERCA SULLE ACQUE. Main/Corp Istituto di Ricerca Sulle Acque (Italy). Began in 1970. 0390-6329. Periodical. Italian. ty. Ind/Abst GeoRef, Chem. Abstr. CODEN QIRADG.

RAPPORT MANUSCRIT CANADIEN DES SCIENCES HALIEUTIQUES ET AQUATIQUES. (RAPPORT MANUSCRIT CANADIEN DES SCIENCES HALIETIQUES ET AQUATIQUES). 0706-6589. CN. French (summaries in English). an. Gouvernement du Quebec, Supply and Services, Ottawa Ontario K1A 0S9 Canada. DD 333.9100971.

RAPPORTO DI ATTIVITA. Main/Corp Istituto di Ricerca Sulle Acque (Italy). Italian. ir. Via Reno 1, 00198 Roma Italy. LC TC479. DD 333.9100945.

RECLAMATION RESEARCH. US. English.

REFERENCE HANDBOOK FOR USE WITH THE PRINCIPLES, STANDARDS, AND PROCEDURES FOR WATER RESOURCES PLANNING (LEVEL C). US. English. an. US Water Resources Council, 2120 L Street Northwest, Washington DC 20037.

REPERTOIRE . . . DES PRODUITS ET SERVICES, DOMAINE DE L'EAU. 1982-. 0711-5997. CN. French. Free. Repertoire des Produits et Services Domaine de l'Eau, a/s AQTE, Bureau 2/6290 rue Perinault, Montreal Quebec H4K 1K5 Canada. Tel (514)337-4446. Ed Raymond Larivee. DD 338.761627025714. adv acc. Circ 10,000. Roster of manufacturers and distributors in water and wastewater treatment in Quebec-Province Canada. *Bottin des Fournisseurs AQTE, 0709-8170.*

REPORT - CALIFORNIA WATER RESOURCES CENTER. Main/Corp University of California. Water Resources Center. No. 34-. 0575-4968. Monographic Series. US. English. an. University of California, Davis Water Resources Center, Davis CA 95616. Ind/Abst Eng. Index Annu., Eng. Index Mon., Eng. Index Bioeng. Abstr., Eng. Index Energy Abstr., Chem. Abstr., GeoRef, Bibliogr. Index Geol. CODEN RUCCD8. *Report - University of California, Water Resources Center, Universitywide, 0375-5975.*

REPORT - NORTH CAROLINA. UNIVERSITY. WATER RESOURCES RESEARCH INSTITUTE. No. 1- 1966?-. 0078-1525. Periodical. US. English. ir. $8.00. Water Resources Research Institute, 124 Riddick Building, Raleigh NC 27607.

REPORT - NORTH CAROLINA. UNIVERSITY. WATER RESOURCES RESEARCH INSTITUTE. Main/Corp North Carolina. University. Water Resources Research Institute. No. 1- 1966-. Monographic Series. US. English. ir.

REPORT OF INVESTIGATION - ILLINOIS STATE WATER SURVEY. (REPORT OF INVESTIGATION (ILLINOIS STATE WATER SURVEY)). 1-. 0097-5672. Monographic

Water Resources

Series. US. English. Illinois State Geological Survey, National Resources Building, Urbana IL 61801. **Ind/Abst** Eng. Index Annu., Eng. Index Mon., Eng. Index Bioeng. Abstr., Eng. Index Energy Abstr., GeoRef, Biol. Abstr., Chem. Abstr., Sel. Water Resour. Abstr. **LC** GB705.I3. **DD** 628.1. **CODEN** ILWIAT.

REPORT OF INVESTIGATIONS - WEST VIRGINIA GEOLOGICAL AND ECONOMIC SURVEY. See Earth Sciences - Geology.

REPORT OF THE SECRETARY FOR WATER DEVELOPMENT. Main/Corp Rhodesia. Ministry of Water Development. Periodical. English. ir. Report of the Director.

REPORT ON RESEARCH AND DEVELOPMENT - GREAT BRITAIN. OVERSEAS DEVELOPMENT ADMINISTRATION. Main/Corp Great Britain. Overseas Development Administration. 1979-. UK. English. an. 3.75. Her Majesty's Stationery Office, 49 High Holborn, London WCIV 6HB England. **LC** HD20.3. **DD** 338.914101724. Report on Research and Development.

REPORT - OREGON. WATER RESOURCES DEPT. (REPORT FOR . . .). Main/Corp Oregon. Water Resources Dept. VFOAT Report for the Period . . . . Jan. 1979 to Dec. 1980-. 8756-0240. US. English. be. Oregon Water Resources Department, 555 13th Street Northeast, Salem OR 97310. **Ind/Abst** GeoRef. **LC** TC424.O7. **DD** 353.97950082325. Report for the Period . . . , 8756-0240.

REPORT - RALPH M. PARSONS LABORATORY FOR WATER RESOURCES AND HYDRODYNAMICS, DEPARTMENT OF CIVIL ENGINEERING, MASSACHUSETTS INSTITUTE OF TECHNOLOGY. (REPORT - RALPH M. PARSONS LABORATORY FOR WATER RESOURCES AND HYDRODYNAMICS). Main/Corp Ralph M. Parsons Laboratory for Water Resources and Hydrodynamics. 1950. 0361-6746. Monographic Series. US. English. ir. Ralph M Parsons Laboratory, Department of Civil Engineers, Building 48-309, Cambridge MA 02139. **Tel** (617)253-4111. **Ind/Abst** Life Sci. Collect., GeoRef, Eng. Index. **CODEN** MHYTAK. **Circ** 200. Technical reports on hydrodynamics, coastal engineering, hydrology, water resources, environmental engineering and aquatic sciences. Report - Hydrodynamics Laboratory, Massachusetts Institute of Technology, 0146-7107.

REPORT SERIES (CANADA. INLAND WATERS DIRECTORATE). (REPORT SERIES - INLAND WATERS DIRECTORATE). No. 24- 1973-. 0318-5869. Monographic Series. CN. English (some nos. include abstract in French). Free. Inland Waters Directorate, Place Vincent Massey, Ottawa Ontario K1A 0H3 Canada. **Ind/Abst** Eng. Index Annu., Eng. Index Mon., Eng. Index Bioeng. Abstr., Eng. Index Energy Abstr., GeoRef, ASTIS Bibliogr., ASTIS Curr. Aware. Bull. **DD** 551.4. **CODEN** CIWRA3. Report Series, 0375-6009.

REPORT - STATE ENGINEER'S OFFICE, WYOMING WATER PLANNING PROGRAM. Main/Corp Wyoming. Water Planning Program. 0160-8851. Monographic Series. US. English. US Geological Survey, Water Resources Division, PO Box 1125, Cheyenne WY 82001. **Ind/Abst** GeoRef. **CODEN** WWPPB9.

REPORT - TEXAS DEPARTMENT OF WATER RESOURCES. Main/Corp Texas. Dept. of Water Resources. 214-. 0191-0426. Monographic Series. US. English. Texas Department of Water Resources, Post Office Box 13087, Austin TX 78711. **Ind/Abst** GeoRef, Chem. Abstr. **LC** TD224.T4. **DD** 333.91009764. **CODEN** RTDRDH. Report - Texas Water Development Board, 0082-3562.

REPORT - TEXAS TECH UNIVERSITY, WATER RESOURCES CENTER. Main/Corp Texas Tech University. Water Resources Center. 0163-1160. Monographic Series. US. English. ir. Texas Tech University, Water Resource Center, PO Box 4630, Lubbock TX 79409. **LC** TD224.T4. **DD** 333.91009764S, 333.91009764.

REPORT - UNIVERSITY OF CONNECTICUT. INSTITUTE OF WATER RESOURCES. (REPORT - INSTITUTE OF WATER RESOURCES, UNIVERSITY OF CONNECTICUT). Main/Corp University of Connecticut. Institute of Water Resources. VFOAT Report - Institute of Water Resources of The University of Connecticut. No. 1- 1967-. 0069-9063. Monographic Series. US. English. University of Connecticut, Institute of Water Resources, Storrs CT 06268. **Tel** (203)486-4523. **Ind/Abst** GeoRef. **CODEN** CUWRAJ. Water resources reports based on research supported under the U.S. geological survey.

REPORT - UNIVERSITY OF CONNECTICUT. INSTITUTE OF WATERRESOURCES. Main/Corp University of Connecticut. Institute of Water Resources. No.1- 1967-. Monographic Series. US. English.

REPORT - WATER RESEARCH COMMISSION. Main/Corp Water Research Commission. 1971/73-. English. ir. Water Research Commission, PO Box 824, Van der Stel Building, Pretorius Street, Pretoria South Africa. **LC** HD1699.S58. **DD** 333.9100968.

REPORT - WATER RESOURCES RESEARCH INSTITUTE, CLEMSON UNIVERSITY. (REPORT - WATER RESOURCES RESEARCH INSTITUTE). Main/Corp Clemson University. Water Resources Research Institute. VFOAT Technical Report - Water Resources Research Institute. No 1-. 0069-4657. Monographic Series. US. English. Clemson University, Water Resources Research Institute, Clemson SC 29631. **Ind/Abst** Chem. Abstr., GeoRef. **CODEN** CUWRBK.

REPORT - WATER RESOURCES RESEARCH INSTITUTE OF THE UNIVERSITY OF NORTH CAROLINA. (REPORT - WATER RESOURCES RESEARCH INSTITUTE OF THE UNIVERSITY OF NORTH CAROLINA). No. 1-. 0078-1525. Monographic Series. US. English. ir. University of North Carolina, Water Resources Research Institute, Box 5504, Raleigh NC 27607. **Ind/Abst** Eng. Index Annu., Eng. Index Mon., Eng. Index Bioeng. Abstr., Eng. Index Energy Abstr., Chem. Abstr., GeoRef. **LC** HD1694.N8. **DD** 333.9. **CODEN** RWRCDT.

RESEARCH AND DEVELOPMENT NEWS. Vol. 1- Aug. 1960-. 0486-476X. Periodical. US. English. sm. Water Information Center Inc, 7 High Street, Huntington NY 11743.

RESEARCH NEEDS IN THE SOUTHERN REGION; WATER AND WATERSHEDS. Main/Corp Joint Task Force of the Southern Region Agricultural Experiment Stations. Periodical. US. English.

RESEARCH PUBLICATION - INSTITUTE FOR RESEARCH ON LAND AND WATER RESOURCES. PENNSYLVANIA STATE UNIVERSITY. See Economics - Economics: Land.

RESEARCH REPORT - UNIVERSITY OF KENTUCKY. WATER RESOURCES RESEARCH INSTITUTE. (RESEARCH REPORT UNIVERSITY OF KENTUCKY WATER RESOURCES RESEARCH INSTITUTE). Main/Corp University of Kentucky. Water Resources Research Institute. No. 62-. 0277-884X. Monographic Series. US. English. **Ind/Abst** GeoRef, Chem. Abstr. **CODEN** RRUIDR. Research Report - University of Kentucky. Water Resources Institute, 0453-5669.

RESEARCH REPORT - WATER RESOURCES RESEARCH CENTER. Main/Corp University of New Hampshire. Water Resources Research Center. No. 1- June 1969-. Monographic Series. US. English. ir. University of New Hampshire, Water Resource Research Center, Durham NH 03824. **DD** 628.

RESEARCH REPORT WI. Main/Corp North Dakota State University. Water Resources Research Institute. Monographic Series. US. English. ir. NDSU WRRI, 202 Ceres Hall, Fargo ND 58102. WI. Water Resources Research Institute.

REVIEW OF THE LITERATURE ON FOREST MANAGEMENT PRACTICES, HYDROLOGY, AND WATER QUALITY PROTECTION AND MANAGEMENT. See Forestry.

REVUE FRANCAISE DES SCIENCES DE L'EAU. VFOAT French Journal of Water Science. Vol. 1, No. 1-. 0750-7186. Periodical. FR. French. qt. $50.00. Lavoisier Abonnements, 11 rue Lavoisier, 75384 Paris Cedex 08 France. **Tel** 42.65.71.67. Ed Bontoux. **Ind/Abst** Chem. Abstr. **CODEN** RFSEDN. bk rev. adv acc. **Circ** 1,000. (ctrl). Publishes original papers in water research: microbiology, chemistry, hydrogeology, water supplies, toxicology, pollution, hydraulics, quality.

RIKUSUIGAKU ZASSHI. (RIKUSUI-GAKU ZASSHI). VFOAT Japanese Journal of Limnology. V. 1- Dec. 1931-. 0021-5104. Periodical. JA. Japanese (with English titles and summaries). qt $86.50. Japan Publishing Trading Company, PO Box 5030, International Tokyo 100-31 Japan. **Ind/Abst** Life Sci. Collect., Excerpta Med., Sel. Water Resour. Abstr., GeoRef, Biol. Abstr., Chem. Abstr. **CODEN** RIZAAU.

RIVER BASIN BULLETIN. 1-. 0083-856X. Monographic Series. US. English. ir. West Virginia Geological Survey, PO Box 879, Morgantown WV 26507-0879. **Tel** (304)594-2331. Ed Fred Schroyer. **Ind/Abst** GeoRef, Bibliogr. Index Geol. **LC** UNC. **CODEN** WVBBAP. **Circ** 200. Technical reports on the West Virginia river basin.

RIVER TEMPERATURES AT SELECTED STATIONS IN PACIFIC NORTHWEST, SAMPLED OR REPORTED BY INDICATED AGENCIES. (RIVER TEMPERATURES AT SELECTED STATIONS IN PACIFIC NORTHWEST : WEEKLY REPORT). Main/Corp United States. Geological Survey. Northwest Water Resources Data Center. Sept. 20-Oct. 6, 1975-. 0146-8103. Periodical. US. English. wk. PO Box 3202, Portland OR 97208.

RIVERLANDER. 1- Jan./Feb. 1946-. Periodical. AT. English. qt $4.43. Murray Valley League, Rundle Mall, PO Box 89, Adelaide South Australia 5000 Australia. **Tel** 08 227 3001. bk rev. adv acc. **Circ** 7,000. Concerned with multiple uses of the River Murray and the research and management required.

ROCKY MOUNTAIN MINERAL LAW NEWSLETTER. WATER LAW. See Law.

SCIENCES ET TECHNIQUES DE L'EAU. See Earth Sciences - Hydrology.

A SELECTED ANNOTATED BIBLIOGRAPHY ON THE ANALYSIS OF WATER RESOURCE SYSTEMS. See Bibliographies.

SELECTED WATER RESOURCES ABSTRACTS. See Indexes/Abstracts.

SNOW SURVEY BULLETIN. VFOAT British Columbis Snow Survey Bulletin. 0045-303X. Periodical. CN. English. mo. Ministry of the Environment, Parliament Building, Water Investigation, Victoria British Columbia V8V 1X5 Canada. **Tel** (604)387-1111. Snow Survey Report.

SPECIAL GROUND-WATER REPORT (LITTLE ROCK). (SPECIAL GROUND-WATER REPORT). No. 1- 1960-. 0571-026X. Monographic Series. US. English. ir. Arkansas Geological & Conservation Commission, 3815 West Roosevelt Road, Little Rock AR 72204. **DD** 551.4.

A SPECIAL REPORT - WATER RESOURCES AUTHORITY. Main/Corp Puerto Rico. Water Resources Authority. PR. English. ir. Government Development Bank for Puerto Rico, PO Box 42001, San Juan Puerto Rico 00940. **LC** HD9685.P92. **DD** 354.729500871.

STANDARDS. Main/Corp American Water Works Association. Series/Titl ANSI/AWWA B200-78. ANSI/AWWA B701-78. ANSI A21.1-1967. ANSI A21.4-1974. ANSI A21.5-1972. ANSI A21.6-1975. ANSI A21.8-1975. ANSI A21.10-1971. ANSI/AWWA C110-77. ANSI A21.11-1972. ANSI A21.12-1971. VFOAT AWWA Standards. US. English. ir. $160.00. American Water Works Association, 6666 West Quincy Avenue, Denver CO 80235. **Tel** (303)794-7711.

THE STATE OF TEXAS WATER QUALITY MANAGEMENT, ANNUAL WORK PROGRAM. Main/Corp Texas. Dept. of Water Resources. 0741-3386. US. English. an. Texas Department of Water Resources, PO Box 13087, Austin TX 78711. **LC** TD224.T4. **DD** 353.9764008232506. State of Texas Water Quality Management Program, 0160-6905.

THE STATE OF TEXAS WATER QUALITY MANAGEMENT PROGRAM. (STATE OF TEXAS WATER QUALITY MANAGEMENT PROGRAM). Main/Corp Texas. Dept. of Water Resources. 0160-6905. US. English. an. Texas Department of Water Resources, Post Office Box 13087, Austin TX 78711. **LC** TD224.T4. **DD** 614.77209764. State of Texas Water Quality Management Program, 0160-6905.

Water Resources

STATE WATER PLAN PUBLICATION. Main/Corp Nebraska. Natural Resources Commission. 0092-6442. US. English. Natural Resources Commission, PO Box 94725, Lincoln NE 68509. LC TC424.N2. DD 333.91009782.

STATE WATER PROGRAM. Main/Corp Washington (State). Dept. of Ecology. Planning and Development Division. 1st- 1971/73-. US. English. be. State of Washington, Department of Ecology, Olympia WA 98504. LC HD1694.W2. DD 333.91009797.

STATISTIK AIR MINUM. See Statistics.

STORAGE IN RESERVOIRS, DAILY DISCHARGE RECORDS OF MISCELLANEOUS STREAMS AND CANAL DIVERSIONS. VFOAT Daily Discharge Records of Miscellaneous Streams and Canal Diversions. 1969-1970-. US. English. an. Nebraska Department of Water Resources, PO Box 94676, Lincoln NB 68509. LC TD224.N18. DD 333.91021309782. Canal Diversions and Miscellaneous Stream Discharge Records.

STUDIES AND REPORTS IN HYDROLOGY. VFOAT Etudes de Rapports d'Hydrologie, Etudes et Rapports d'Hydrologie, Estudios e Informes de Hidrologia, Isledovaniia I Doklady po Gidrologii. No. 1- 1969-. 0081-7449. Monographic Series. English (some material in French, Russian, and Spanish). ir. UNIPUB, PO Box 1222, Ann Arbor MI 48106. Tel 4568-3999. Ed John S Gladwell. Ind/Abst GeoRef. DD 551.4. CODEN IHSRB9. (ctrl). Individual reports on aspects of scientific hydrology, water resources planning and management, education and training — available for purchase.

STUDII DE ECONOMIA APELOR. Main/Corp Institutul de Studii, Cercetari Si Proiectari Pentru Gospodarirea Apelor. 2- 1972-. Romanian (summaries in English, French and Russian). ir. Splaiul Indepentei 294 17, Bucuresti Romania. LC TC401. Studii de Economia Apelor.

SUIDO JITSUMU ROPPO. Main/Corp Japan. 1977-. JA. Japanese. ir. 4050. Gyosei, 52 Nishi Goken-Cho Shinjuku-ku, Tokyo-to 162 Japan.

SUIRI KAGAKU. VFOAT Water Science. (No.103- June 1975-). 0039-4858. Periodical. JA. Japanese. bm. 800. Suiri Kagaku Kenkyusho, 1-7-22 Koraku, Bunkyo-ku Tokyo Japan. Tel 03-816-3391. Ed Masao Yosimura. Ind/Abst Life Sci. Collect. Circ 1,900. Deals with water science.

SUMMARY OF GROUND WATER DATA FOR TENNESSEE. Main/Corp Tennessee. Division of Water Resources. Series Corp Its Miscellaneous Publication. 0093-0539. US. English. an. Tennessee Division of Water Resources, 2611 West End Avenue, Nashville TN 37203. LC GB1025.T2. DD 553.7909768.

SURFACE WATER RECORDS OF ALASKA. 1960/61-1963/64. Periodical. US. English. an.

SURFACE WATER RECORDS OF WASHINGTON. 1960/61-1963/64. US. English. an. US Geological Survey/Water Resources Division, 604 South Pickett Street East Distributor, Alexandria VA 22304. LC GB1225.W3. DD 553.7809797.

SURFACE WATER-SUPPLY OF THE UNITED STATES. (SURFACE WATER-SUPPLY OF THE UNITED STATES. PT. 3, V. 1-4. OHIO RIVER BASIN). VFOAT Ohio River Basin. 1907/08-. Periodical. US. English. ir. Ohio River Basin, US Department of the Interior, Geological Survey, Washington DC 20402.

SURFACE WATER-SUPPLY OF THE UNITED STATES. (SURFACE WATER-SUPPLY OF THE UNITED STATES. PT. 1, V. 1-3. NORTH ATLANTIC SLOPE BASINS). VFOAT North Atlantic Slope Basins. 1907/08-. Periodical. US. English. ir.

SURFACE WATER-SUPPLY OF THE UNITED STATES. (SURFACE WATER-SUPPLY OF THE UNITED STATES. PT. 4, V. 1-2. ST. LAWRENCE RIVER BASIN). VFOAT St. Lawrence River Basin. 1907/08-. Periodical. US. English. ir.

SURFACE WATER-SUPPLY OF THE UNITED STATES. (SURFACE WATER-SUPPLY OF THE UNITED STATES. PT. 5, V. 1-3. HUDSON BAY AND UPPER MISSISSIPPI RIVER BASINS). VFOAT Hudson Bay and Upper Mississippi River Basins. 1907/08-. Periodical. US. English. ir. Hudson Bay and Upper Mississippi River Basins, US Department of the Interior, Geological Survey, Washington DC 20402.

SURFACE WATER-SUPPLY OF THE UNITED STATES. (SURFACE WATER-SUPPLY OF THE UNITED STATES. PT. 11, V. 1-4. PACIFIC SLOPE BASINS IN CALIFORNIA). VFOAT Pacific Slope Basins in California. 1907/08-. Periodical. US. English. ir.

SURFACE WATER-SUPPLY OF THE UNITED STATES. (SURFACE WATER-SUPPLY OF THE UNITED STATES. PT. 15. ALASKA). VFOAT Alaska. 1961/65-. Periodical. US. English. ir. US Department of the Interior, 1200 South Eads Street, Arlington VA 22202. Quantity and Quality of Surface Water of Alaska.

SURFACE WATER YEAR-BOOK OF GREAT BRITAIN. See Yearbooks, Almanacs, Directories.

SURFARE WATER DATA. BRITISH COLUMBIA. (SURFACE WATER DATA). Main/Corp Water Survey of Canada. VFOAT Donnees sur les Eaux de Surface. VAT Donnees sur les Eaux de Surface. Colombie-Britannique. 1965-. 0576-2367. CN. English (title only, 1965-1974). an. Ind/Abst GeoRef. LC GB1230.B7. DD 553.7809711.

TECHNICAL MEMORANDUM - AMERICAN SOCIETY OF CIVIL ENGINEERS. URBAN WATER RESOURCES RESEARCH PROGRAM. (TECHNICAL MEMORANDUM - ASCE URBAN WATER RESOURCES RESEARCH PROGRAM). Main/Corp American Society of Civil Engineers. Urban Water Resources Research Program. VFOAT Technical Memorandum - American Society of Civil Engineers Urban Water Resources Research Program. No. 1-. 0066-0612. Monographic Series. US. English. American Society of Civil Engineers, 745 East 47th Street, New York NY 10017. Ind/Abst Eng. Index, GeoRef, Energy Res. Abstr. CODEN AUWTB4.

TECHNICAL MEMORANDUM OF THE DIVISION OF WATER. See Earth Sciences - Hydrology.

TECHNICAL PAPER - DIVISION OF WATERS. Main/Corp Minnesota. Division of Waters. No. 1- Jan. 1958-. 0462-6699. Monographic Series. US. English. ir. Minnesota Department of Natural Resources, 350 Centennial Building, St Paul MN 55155. DD 333.9.

TECHNICAL PAPER - HUDSON RIVER BASIN STUDY GROUP, NEW YORK STATE DEPARTMENT OF ENVIRONMENTAL CONSERVATION. (TECHNICAL PAPER). VFOAT Hudson River Basin Level B Water and Related Land Resources Study. No. 1-. Monographic Series. US. English. Hudson River Basin Study Group, New York State Department of Environmental Conservation, Room 422/50 Wolf Road, Albany NY 12233.

TECHNICAL PROCEEDINGS. ANNUAL CONFERENCE AND INTERNATIONAL TRADE FAIR OF THE NATIONAL WATER SUPPLY IMPROVEMENT ASSOCIATION. (TECHNICAL PROCEEDINGS). Main/Corp National Water Supply Improvement Association. Conference and International Trade Fair. 0278-6206. US. English. an. $100.00. National Water Supply IMP Association, 26 Newbury Road, Ipswich MA 01938. Tel (714)963-5661. Ind/Abst Chem. Abstr. CODEN TPASDX.

TECHNICAL PUBLICATION SERIES - AMERICAN WATER RESOURCES ASSOCIATION. Main/Corp American Water Resources Association. TPS 79/1-. 0731-9789. Monographic Series. US. English. ir. American Water Resources Association, St Anthony Falls Hydraulic Laboratory, Mississippi River at 3rd Avenue SE, Minneapolis MN 55414. Ind/Abst GeoRef. Proceedings Series - American Water Resources Association, 0375-5606.

TECHNICAL REPORT - CORNELL UNIVERSITY WATER RESOURCES AND MARINE SCIENCES CENTER. Main/Corp Cornell University. Water Resources and Marine Sciences Center. 0197-0526. Monographic Series. US. English. ir. National Technical Information Service, 5285 Port Royal Road, Springfield VA 22161. Ind/Abst GeoRef. LC UNC. Technical Report -Cornell University, Water Resources Center.

TECHNICAL REPORT - INSTITUTE OF WATER RESEARCH (EAST LANSING). (TECHNICAL REPORT - INSTITUTE OF WATER RESEARCH, MICHIGAN STATE UNIVERSITY). Main/Corp Michigan State University. Institute of Water Research. No. 1-. 0580-9746. Monographic Series. US. English. ir. Ind/Abst GeoRef. CODEN TRMWDH.

TECHNICAL REPORT - LOUISIANA WATER RESOURCES RESEARCH INSTITUTE. (TECHNICAL REPORT). No. 1-. 0459-8768. Monographic Series. US. English. ir. Ind/Abst GeoRef. LC TC424.L8.

TECHNICAL REPORT - TEXAS WATER RESOURCES INSTITUTE. (TECHNICAL REPORT). Began with: No. 37, published June 1971. 0275-5483. Monographic Series. US. English. Texas A & M University, Texas Water Resources Institute, College Station TX 77843. Ind/Abst GeoRef. LC TD224.T4. DD 553.709764. CODEN TRTIDA. Technical Report - Water Resources Institute, Texas A & M University.

TECHNICAL REPORT (UNIVERSITY OF HAWAII AT MANOA. WATER. (TECHNICAL REPORT - WATER RESOURCES RESEARCH CENTER, UNIVERSITY OF HAWAII). 0272-8729. US. English. LC TC1. DD 553.709969. Technical Report (University of Hawaii (Honolulu). Water Resources Research Center), 0073-1307.

TECHNICAL REPORT (UNIVERSITY OF MARYLAND, COLLEGE PARK. WATER RESOURCES RESEARCH CENTER). (TECHNICAL REPORT). Monographic Series. US. English. ir.

TECHNICAL REPORT - WATER RESOURCES RESEARCH CENTER, UNIVERSITY OF GUAM. Main/Corp University of Guam. Water Resources Research Center. No. 1-. 0272-9555. Monographic Series. GU. English. ir. WRRC University of Guam, PO Box EK, Agana GU 96910. Ind/Abst GeoRef. LC UNC.

LA TECHNIQUE DE L'EAU ET DE L'ASSAINISSEMENT. 1.- Year (No. 1-). 0040-120X. Periodical. BE. French. ir. Technique de l'Eau et de l'Assainissement, rue Tenbosch 43, 1050 Bruxelles Belgium. Tel (02)6470073. Ind/Abst Bibliogr. Index Geol.

TECHNIQUES OF WATER-RESOURCES INVESTIGATIONS OF THE UNITED STATES GEOLOGICAL SURVEY. VFOAT Model for Simulation of Flow in Singular and Interconnected Channels. 0565-596X. Monographic Series. US. English. ir. Branch of Distribution, US Geological Survey, 1200 South Eads Street, Arlington VA 22202. LC TC177. CODEN XTWRA.

TEXAS WATER DEVELOPMENT BOARD PUBLICATIONS CATALOG. VFOAT Publications Catalog - Texas Water Development Board. 0564-7495. US. English. Water Development Board, PO Box 13087, Austin TX 78711.

TEXAS WATER REPORT. 0492-9829. Periodical. US. English. wk. $47.25. Texas Water Report, Box 12368, Austin TX 78711. Tel (512)478-5663.

THAMES WATER STATISTICS. See Statistics.

TRIENNIAL REPORT ON WATER RESOURCES DEVELOPMENT. Main/Corp United Nations. Dept. of Economic and Social Affairs. Series Corp United Nations. Document. 0091-1593. US. English. te. United Nations Publications, Sales Section Room A3315, New York NY 10017. LC JX1977. DD 333.91.

U.S. WATER NEWS. VFOAT U. S. Water News. VAT United States Water News. Began with Vol. 1, No. 1 (July 1984). 0749-1980. Periodical. US. English. mo. $28.00. U S Water News, 230 Main Street, Halstead KS 67056. Tel (316)835-2222. Ed Thomas C Bell. DD 627. adv acc. Circ 50,000. (ctrl). Addresses important water news in the areas of federal, state, and local water policy, water rights; water quality and pollution; law suits, innovative conservation practices; new irrigation techniques.

VIZMINOSEGI ES VIZTECHNOLOGIAI KUTATASI EREDMENYEK. See Sanitation, Environmental Technology.

VODNYE RESURSY. No. 1- 1974-. 0302-5454. Periodical. UR. Russian. bm. $78.00. Victor Kamkin Inc (70134), 12224 Parklawn Drive, Rockville MD

Water Resources

20852. Tel (301)881-5973. Ind/Abst Bibliogr. Agric., Chem. Abstr. CODEN VDRSBK.

WASHINGTON STATE'S WATER. (WASHINGTON STATE'S WATER : A REPORT). Main/Corp State of Washington Water Research Center. 7th- 1971-. 0161-5912. US. English. an. Washington Water Research Center, Washington State University, Pullman WA 99163. LC TD224.W2. DD 333.91009797. *Washington's Water, 0161-5904.*

WASHINGTON'S WATER RESOURCES PROGRAM. FY 1981 and FY 1982-. 0741-1383. US. English. Washington State Department of Ecology, Mail Stop PV-11, Olympia WA 98504. LC TC424.W2. DD 333.91009797. *Washington's Water Resources, Recommendations to the Legislature.*

WASSER UND ABWASSER IN FORSCHUNG UND PRAXIS. 0512-5030. Monographic Series. GW. German. ir. Engineering. Erich Schmidt Verlag GMBH, POB POB 7330/ Viktoriastr 44-A, D4800 Bielefeld 1 West Germany. Tel 0521/66061. Ind/Abst Chem. Abstr. CODEN WAFPDB. Water and waste water studies. research and experience.

WASSERHAUSHALT UND BODENNUTZUNG. See Earth Sciences - Hydrology.

WASSERVERSORGUNG UND ABWASSERBESEITIGUNG IN DER WIRTSCHAFT. Series/Titl Statistik Niedersachsen. GW. German. ir. Niedersachsiches Landesverwaltungsamt Statistik, Postfach 107, 3000 Hannover 1 West Germany. LC TD273.

WASSERWIRTSCHAFT. 0043-0978. Periodical. GW. German. mo. $56.16. Franckh Verlags W Keller & Company, PO Box 640, D7000 Stuttgart 1 West Germany. Ind/Abst Eng. Index Annu., Eng. Index Mon., Eng. Index Bioeng. Abstr., Eng. Index Energy Abstr., Fluidex, Excerpta Med., Coal Abstr., GeoRef, Chem. Abstr., Energy Res. Abstr. CODEN WSWTAR. *Deutsche Wasserwirtschaft.*

WATER CEASED. (WATER . . .). 1968-1980. US. English. an. Ind/Abst Bibliogr. Agric. LC TD365. DD 628.1605.

WATER CEASED. No. 1-43. 0305-3105. Periodical. UK. English. qt. 1 Queen Anne's Gate, London SW1H 9BT England. Ind/Abst Excerpta Med., GeoRef. LC TD257. DD 363.61. *British Water Supply.*

WATER & IRRIGATION REVIEW. See Agriculture - Crop Production and Soil.

WATER AND LAND RESOURCE ACCOMPLISHMENTS. FEDERAL RECLAMATION PROJECTS, SUMMARY REPORT. See Conservation & Natural Resources.

WATER AND SEWER PROGRAMS FOR OHIO. Main/Corp Ohio. Dept. of Economic and Community Development. 1974-. 0148-2785. US. English. an. Department of Economic and Community Development, 30 East Broad Street, Columbus OH 43215. LC TD224.O3. DD 363.61.

WATER BULLETIN. (WATERBULLETIN). No. 1 (April 1, 1982)-. 0262-9909. Periodical. UK. English. wk. 45.-. Water Authorities Association, 1 Queen Anne's Gate, London SW1H 9BT England. Tel (01)222 8111. Ed Les Freeman. Ind/Abst Coal Abstr., Excerpta Med., Fluidex. LC TD257. DD 363.610941. bk rev. adv acc. Circ 5,744. Reports on the water industry in the United Kingdom; news and in-depth features plus information and advisory section. *Water (London, England), 0305-3105; Bulletin (National Water Council (Great Britain)).*

WATER CIRCULAR. VFOAT Utah State Engineer Water Circular. No. 1- 1965-. 0502-8450. Monographic Series. US. English. ir. State of Utah, Department of Natural Resources, Salt Lake City UT 84114. LC WMLC L 82/102. DD 551.4.

WATER DEVELOPMENT, SUPPLY AND MANAGEMENT. See Earth Sciences - Hydrology.

WATER EQUIPMENT NEWS. 1971. 0194-1194. Periodical. US. Enlgish. mo. Free. Mut & Jef Enterprises Inc, PO Box 367, Urbana IL 61801. Tel (217)344-7443. Ed Jeffrey Farlow-Cornell. bk rev. adv acc. Circ 23,400. (ctrl). A digest of new and used equipment for water suppliers and a summary of news in the industry and throughout all of North America.

A WATER INDUSTRY STATISTICAL PROFILE. See Statistics.

WATER INFORMATION BULLETIN. No. 1-. 0511-3598. Monographic Series. US. English. ir. Idaho Department of Water Resources, Statehouse, Boise ID 83720. Ind/Abst Chem. Abstr., GeoRef. LC TD224.I2. DD 333.91009796. CODEN WBIRD5.

WATER INFORMATION NEWS SERVICE. V. 1- 1976-. Periodical. US. English. sm. Water Information News Service, 1730 M Street NW/Suite 1100, Washington DC 20026. Tel (202)857-1435.

WATER INTERNATIONAL. English. qt. $66.75. Elsevier Sequoia SA, PO Box 851, CH-1001 Lausanne 1 Switzerland. Index in last issue of volume - loose - unpaged.

WATER INVENTORY REPORT. VFOAT Ohio Water Inventory Report. No. 24-. US. English. $2.50. Fountain Square, Columbus OH 43224. LC TD224.O3. *Ohio Water Plan Inventory: Report.*

WATER JOURNAL. V. 1- 1916-. Periodical. US. English. ty. Free. Rockwell International Corporation, 400 North Lexington Avenue, Pittsburgh PA 15208. Tel (412)247-3000. Ed Jack F Pektas. Ind/Abst Electron. Commun. Abstr. J., ISMEC Bull., Pollut. Abstr. Indexes, Saf. Sci. Abstr. J. Circ 15,000. (ctrl). Information for water utility directors, meter shop managers, distribution directors and others involved in managing municipal or privately owned water utilities.

WATER LAW NEWSLETTER (BOULDER, COLO. : 1976). See Law.

WATER LINE NEWSLETTER. V. 1- Jan. 1977-. 0196-075X. Periodical. US. English. mo. Water Resources Planning, Department of Natural Resources, 3rd Floor/Centennial Building, St Paul MN 55155.

WATER MANAGEMENT BULLETIN (SOUTH FLORIDA WATER MANAGEMENT DISTRICT). (WATER MANAGEMENT BULLETIN). Vol. 4, No. 1 (Spring 1978)-. 0738-3274. Periodical. US. English. qt. South Florida Water Management Distribution, Box V, 3301 Gun Club Road, West Palm Beach FL 33402. Tel (305)686-8800. *Bulletin from Your Water Managers, 0741-2614.*

WATER MANAGEMENT TECHNICAL REPORT. Main/Corp Colorado State University. No.1- 1969-. Monographic Series. US. English. Ind/Abst GeoRef. CODEN CSWDAV.

WATER NEWS. V. 6, No. 7- Oct. 1975-. Periodical. US. English. mo. $9.00. Virginia Polytechnic Institute & State University, 617 North Main Street, Blacksburg VA 24060. Tel (703)961-5624. Ed Elizabeth Crumbley. Circ 6,000. (ctrl). Devoted to water (and land-related) resource issues, primarily in Virginia. *News - Virginia Water Resources Research Center, 0091-0228.*

WATER NEWS (CAMBRIDGE, ONT.). (WATER NEWS). Vol. 1, No. 1 (Mar. 1982)-. 0821-0233. Periodical. CN. English. qt. Free. Canadian Water Association, c/o J S Bauer, PO Box 729, Cambridge Ontario N1R 5W6 Canada. DD 333.9110971.

WATER NEWSLETTER. Main/Corp University of Minnesota. Water Resources Research Center. VFOAT Water. 0544-3482. US. English. ir. Water Resources Research Center University of Minnesota, 866 Biological Science Center, 1445 Gortner Avenue, St Paul MN 55108.

WATER NEWSLETTER; WATER SUPPLY, WASTE DISPOSAL, CONSERVATION. See Sanitation, Environmental Technology.

WATER OPERATION AND MAINTENANCE BULLETIN. Began with No. 75, Mar. 1971. 0145-2800. Periodical. US. English. qt. Bureau of Reclamation, PO Box 25007, Denver CO 80225. Tel (303)234-3000. LC TC801. DD 627.5205. (cum index). *Irrigation Operation and Maintenance Bulletin.*

WATER QUALITY BULLETIN. V. 1- Jan. 1976-. 0706-8158. Periodical. CN. English. qt. Ind/Abst Can. Environ., Energy Inf. Abstr., Environ. Abstr., Chem. Abstr. CODEN WQBUDG.

WATER QUALITY OF TENNESSEE SURFACE STREAMS. Main/Corp Tennessee. Stream Pollution Control Board. 1960-. US. English. an. LC TD224.T2.

WATER QUALITY SERIES (LOGAN, UTAH). (WATER QUALITY SERIES). VFOAT Report Q. 78-001-. 0270-9503. Monographic Series. US. English. ir. Utah Water Research Laboratory, College of Engineering, Utah State University, Logan UT 84322. Ind/Abst GeoRef.

WATER QUALITY/WATER RIGHTS. Main/Corp California. State Water Resources Control Board. 1978-80-. 0733-2955. US. English. be. LC TD224.C3. DD 363.739409794. *State of California Water Resources Control Board, 0193-0974.*

WATER RESEARCH. V. 1- Jan. 1967-. 0043-1354. Periodical. UK. English. mo. Pergamon Press, 395 Sawmill River Road, Elmsford NY 10523. Tel (914)592-7700. Ind/Abst Eng. Index, Sci. Cit. Index, Abr. Ed., Energy Res. Abstr., Ocean. Abstr., Pestdoc, Ringdoc, Vetdoc, Pet. Abstr., Life Sci. Collect., Excerpta Med., Can. Environ., Coal Abstr., Abstr. Bull. Inst. Paper Chem., GeoRef, Comput. Control Abstr., Electr. Electron. Abstr., Sci. Abstr., Biol. Abstr., Chem. Abstr., Nuci. Sci. Abstr., Sel. Water Resour. Abstr., Bibliogr. Agric., Appl. Sci. Technol. Index, Sci. Abstr. Sect. A. Phys. Abstr., Eng. Index Annu., Eng. Index Mon., Pollut. Abstr. Indexes. LC TD420. DD 628.16805. NLM W1 WA692A. CODEN WATRAG. Available on microform from Micro Mark. *Air and Water Pollution.*

WATER RESEARCH QUARTERLY. (WATER RESEARCH QUARTERLY : AN INFORMATION SERVICE OF THE AWWA RESEARCH FOUNDATION). Vol. 1, No. 1 (Oct. 1982)-. 0734-7227. Periodical. US. English. qt. $30.00 US, Canada, and Mexico $40.00 Others. A W W A Research Foundation, 6666 West Quincy Avenue, Denver CO 80235. Tel (303)794-7711. Ed Sharon Crnkovich. Circ 4,500. Primarily a report on foundation projects and activities; also has articles of special interest to the water supply industry.

WATER RESOURCE DATA FOR INDIANA. (WATER RESOURCES DATA. INDIANA). Series/Titl U.S. Geological Survey Water-Data Report. VFOAT USGS Water Resources Data. Water Year 1981-. 0364-4340. US. English. an. US Department of the Interior, US Geological Survey, National Technical Information Service, 5285 Port Royal Road, Springfield VA 22161. LC GB1225.I3. DD 553.709772. Vols. for (1982-) distributed to depository libraries in microfiche. *Water Resources Data for Indiana, 0364-4340.*

WATER RESOURCES. V. 1- Jan./Feb. 1974-. 0097-8078. Periodical. US. English (Translated from Russian). bm. $395.00 Domestic, $440.00 Foreign. Plenum Publishing Corporation, 227 West 17th Street, New York NY 10011. Tel (212)620-8000. Ed G V Voropaer. Ind/Abst Excerpta Med., Coal Abstr., Sel. Water Resour. Abstr., GeoRef, Chem. Abstr. LC GB746. DD 553.70947. CODEN WARED4. An international survey of water resource problems. This journal evaluates the water resources of specific geographical areas and reviews, regularities of water resources formation and scientific principles for their optical use.

WATER RESOURCES ACTIVITIES IN ILLINOIS. Main/Corp Geological Survey (U.S.). Water Resources Division. 0276-6477. US. English. an. District Chief, US Geological Survey WRD, PO Box 1026, 605 North Neil Street, Champaign IL 61820. LC TC424.I3. DD 353.008232509773.

WATER RESOURCES BASIC RECORDS REPORT. No. 7- 0731-7638. Monographic Series. US. English. U S Geological Survey, PO Box 66492, Baton Rouge LA 70806. Ind/Abst GeoRef. LC TA24.L7. CODEN LDBRAU. *Basic Records Reports.*

WATER RESOURCES BULLETIN. V. 1- 1965-. 0043-1370. Periodical. US. English. bm. $65.00 Domestic, $75.00 Foreign. American Water Resources Association, 5410 Grosvenor Lane/Suite 220, Bethesda MD 20814. Tel (301)493-8600. Ed Milton Potash. Ind/Abst Eng. Index Annu., Eng. Index Mon., Eng. Index Bioeng. Abstr., Eng. Index Energy Abstr., Excerpta Med., Can. Environ., Coal Abstr., GeoRef, Int. Aerosp. Abstr., Chem. Abstr., Bibliogr. Agric., Energy Res. Abstr., Bibliogr. Index Geol., Pollut. Abstr. Indexes, Sci. Cit. Index, Abr. Ed. LC GB651. DD 333.91. NLM W1 WA692AE. CODEN WARBAQ. bk rev. Circ 3,800. The water resources bulletin is an interdisciplinary peer reviewed journal containing original and technical articles dealing with all aspects of water resources studies.

WATER-RESOURCES BULLETIN. 0094-7636. US. English. Utah Geological & Mineral Survey, 606 Black Hawk Way, Salt Lake City UT 84108. LC TD224.U8. DD 553.709792 S. *Water-Resources Bulletin.*

Water Resources

WATER RESOURCES BULLETIN. GROUND WATER SERIES. (WATER RESOURCES BULLETIN : GROUND WATER SERIES). Monographic Series. CN. English. Ind/Abst GeoRef. LC TD227.O5. DD 553.7909713. CODEN OWRBAO.

WATER RESOURCES COORDINATION DIRECTORY. See Yearbooks, Almanacs, Directories.

WATER RESOURCES DATA. ALASKA. Series/Titl U.S. Geological Survey Water-Data Report. VFOAT Alaska. 0741-0689. US. English. an. US Department of the Interior Geological Survey, 1515 East 13th Avenue, Anchorage AK 99501. LC GB1225.A4. DD 553.709798. Vols. for (1982-) distributed to depository libraries in microfiche. *Water Resources Data for Alaska.*

WATER RESOURCES DATA. COLORADO. Series/Titl U.S. Geological Survey Water-Date Report. VFOAT Colorado. 0741-0697. US. English. an. US Department of the Interior, US Geological Survey, National Technical Information Service, 5285 Port Royal Road, Springfield VA 22161. LC GB1225.C6. DD 553.709788. Vols. for 1981- distributed to depository libraries in microfiche. *Water Resources Data for Colorado.*

WATER RESOURCES DATA FOR ARIZONA CEASED. Began in 1964/65-. Ceased with 1980. US. English. ir. LC GB1225.A6. DD 553.7809791. *Surface Water Records of Arizona.*

WATER RESOURCES DATA FOR CALIFORNIA CEASED. Series/Titl U.S. Geological Survey Water-Data Report. Began with 1964/65. 0364-4057. US. English. an. National Technical Information Service, Springfield VA 22161. LC GB1225.C3. DD 553.7809794. *Surface Water Records of California.*

WATER RESOURCES DATA FOR FLORIDA. (WATER RESOURCES DATA. FLORIDA). Series/Titl U.S. Geological Survey Water-Data Report. VFOAT Florida. Began with water year 1981. 0275-2689. US. English. an. US Department of the Interior, US Geological Survey, National Technical Information Service, 5285 Port Royal Road, Springfield VA 22161. LC GB1225.F6. DD 553.709759. Vols. for (1982-) distributed to depository libraries in microfiche. *Water Resources Data for Florida, 0275-2689.*

WATER RESOURCES DATA FOR GEORGIA CEASED. Series/Titl U.S Geological Survey Water-Data Report. Began with 1964/65. 0093-5980. US. English. an. National Technical Information Service, Springfield VA 22161 VA 22161. LC TD224.G4. DD 553.709758. *Surface Water Records of Georgia.*

WATER RESOURCES DATA FOR IDAHO. (WATER RESOURCES DATA. IDAHO). Series/Titl U.S. Geological Survey Water-Data Report. VFOAT Idaho. 0364-4324. US. English. an. US Department of the Interior, Geological Survey, Box 036, Federal Building, 550 West Fort Street, Boise ID 83724. LC GB1225.I2. DD 553.709796. Vols. for 1982- distributed to depository libraries in microfiche. *Water Resources Data for Idaho, 0364-4324.*

WATER RESOURCES DATA FOR ILLINOIS. (WATER RESOURCES DATA. ILLINOIS). Series/Titl U.S. Geological Survey Water-Data Report. VFOAT Illinois. Water Year 1981-. 0364-4332. US. English. an. US Department of the Interior, US Geological Survey, National Technical Information Service, 5285 Port Royal Road, Springfield VA 22161. LC GB1225.I27. DD 553.709773. Vols. for 1981- distributed to depository libraries in microfiche. *Water Resources Data for Illinois, 0364-4332.*

WATER RESOURCES DATA FOR KENTUCKY. (WATER RESOURCES DATA. KENTUCKY). Series/Titl U.S. Geological Survey Water-Data Report. VFOAT USGS Water Resources Data. Water Year 1981-. 0364-4081. US. English. an. US Department of the Interior, US Geological Survey, National Technical Information Service, 5285 Port Royal Road, Springfield VA 22161. LC GB1225.K4. DD 553.709769. Vols. for 1981- distributed to depository libraries in microfiche. *Water Resources Data for Kentucky, 0364-4081.*

WATER RESOURCES DATA FOR MARYLAND AND DELAWARE. (WATER RESOURCES DATA. MARYLAND AND DELAWARE). Series/Titl U.S. Geological Survey Water-Data Report. VFOAT Maryland and Delaware. Water Year 1981-. 0364-4367. US. English. an. US Department of the Interior, US Geological Survey, National Technical Information Service, 5285 Port Royal Road, Springfield VA 22161. LC GB1225.M3. DD 553.709752. *Water Resources Data for Maryland and Delaware, 0364-4367.*

WATER RESOURCES DATA FOR MASSACHUSETTS AND RHODE ISLAND. Series/Titl U.S. Geological Survey Water-Data Report. Water Year 1975-. US. English. an. National Technical Information Service, 5285 Port Royal Road, Springfield VA 22161. *Water Resources Data for Massachusetts, New Hampshire, Rhode Island and Vermont.*

WATER RESOURCES DATA FOR MICHIGAN. (WATER RESOURCES DATA. MICHIGAN). Series/Titl U.S. Geological Survey Water-Data Report. VFOAT USGS Water Resources Data. Michigan, U.S.G.S. Water Resources Data. Michigan. Water Year 1981-. 0364-4375. US. English. an. US Department of the Interior, US Geological Survey, National Technical Information Service, 5285 Port Royal Road, Springfield VA 22161. LC GB1225.M5. DD 553.709744. Vols. for 1981- Distributed to depository libraries in microfiche. *Water Resources Data for Michigan, 0364-4375.*

WATER RESOURCES DATA FOR MINNESOTA. (WATER RESOURCES DATA. MINNESOTA). Series/Titl U.S. Geological Survey Water-Data Report. VFOAT Minnesota. Water Year 1981-. 0364-4383. US. English. an. US Department of the Interior, US Geological Survey, National Technical Information Service, 5285 Port Royal Road, Springfield VA 22161. LC GB1225.M6. DD 553.709776. Vols. for 1981- distributed to depository libraries in microfiche. *Water Resources Data for Minnesota, 0364-4383.*

WATER RESOURCES DATA FOR MINNESOTA : WATER YEAR. 1975-. Monographic Series. US. English. an. *Water Resources Data for Minnesota.*

WATER RESOURCES DATA FOR MISSISSIPPI. Series/Titl U.S. Geological Survey Water-Data Report. VFOAT USGS Water Resources Data for Mississippi. Began with 1964/65. 0364-510X. US. English. an. National Technical Information Service, 5285 Port Royal Road, Springfield VA 22161. *Surface Water Records of Mississippi.*

WATER RESOURCES DATA FOR MONTANA. (WATER RESOURCES DATA. MONTANA). Series/Titl U.S. Geological Survey Water-Data Report. VFOAT USGS Water Resources Data. Water Year 1981-. 0364-4073. US. English. an. US Department of the Interior, US Geological Survey, National Technical Information Service, 5285 Port Royal Road, Springfield VA 22161. LC GB1225.M9. DD 553.709786. *Water Resources Data for Montana, 0364-4073.*

WATER RESOURCES DATA FOR NEBRASKA. (WATER RESOURCES DATA. NEBRASKA). Series/Titl U.S. Geological Survey Water-Data Report. VFOAT USGS Water Resources Data. Water Year 1981-. 0363-1974. US. English. an. US Department of the Interior, US Geological Survey, National Technical Information Service, 5285 Port Royal Road, Springfield VA 22161. LC GB705.N2. DD 553.709782. Vols. for 1981- distributed to depository libraries in microfiche. *Water Resources Data for Nebraska, 0363-1974.*

WATER RESOURCES DATA FOR NEW JERSEY. 1964/65-. 0095-4187. US. English. an. US Geological Survey/Water Resources Division, 604 South Pickett Street East Distributor, Alexandria VA 22304. LC TD224.N5. DD 553.709749. *Surface Water Records of New Jersey.*

WATER RESOURCES DATA FOR NEW MEXICO. (WATER RESOURCES DATA. NEW MEXICO). Series/Titl U.S. Geological Survey Water-Data Report. VFOAT USGS Water Resources Data. Water Year 1981-. 0364-4065. US. English. an. US Department of the Interior, US Geological Survey, National Technical Information Service, 5285 Port Royal Road, Springfield VA 22161. LC GB1225.N6. DD 553.709789. Vols. for (1983-) distributed to depository libraries in microfiche. *Water Resources Data for New Mexico, 0364-4065.*

WATER RESOURCES DATA FOR NEW YORK. Series/Titl U.S. Geological Survey Water-Data Report. VFOAT U.S.G.S. Water Resources Data for New York. Began with 1964/65. 0147-2283. US. English. an. National Technical Information Service, 5285 Port Royal Road, Springfield VA 22151. Ind/Abst Chem. Abstr. LC GB1225.N7. DD 553.709747. CODEN WRDYDB. *Surface Water Records of New York.*

WATER RESOURCES DATA FOR NORTH CAROLINA : WATER YEAR. 1975-. Monographic Series. US. English. an. *Water Resources Data for North Carolina.*

WATER RESOURCES DATA FOR NORTH DAKOTA. Series/Titl U.S. Geological Survey Water-Data Report. VFOAT U.S.G.S. Water Resources Data for North Dakota. Began with 1965/66. 0364-4405. US. English. an. US Geological Survey, Water Resources Division, 604 South Street East Distributor, Alexandria VA 22304. LC GB1225.N9. DD 553.7809784. *Water Resources Data for North Dakota and South Dakota, 0197-0518.*

WATER RESOURCES DATA FOR NORTH DAKOTA : WATER YEAR. 1975-. Monographic Series. US. English. an. *Water Resources Data for North Dakota.*

WATER RESOURCES DATA FOR OHIO : WATER YEAR. 1975-. Monographic Series. US. English. an.

WATER RESOURCES DATA FOR OKLAHOMA CEASED. Series/Titl U.S. Geological Survey Water-Data Report. VFOAT U.S.G.S Water Resources Data for Oklahoma. Began with 1964/65. 0095-5671. US. English. an. National Technical Information Service, Springfield VA 22161. LC GB1225.O5. DD 553.709766. *Surface Water Records of Oklahoma, 0733-0022.*

WATER RESOURCES DATA FOR OREGON (PORTLAND, OR.). (WATER RESOURCES DATA FOR OREGON). Series/Titl U.S. Geological Survey Water-Data Report. VFOAT U.S.G.S. Water Resources DATA for Oregon. Began Publication with 1965 issue. US. English. an. National Technical Information Service, 5285 Port Royal Road, Springfield VA 22151. LC GB705.O7. DD 553.709795. *Surface Water Records of Oregon.*

WATER RESOURCES DATA FOR PENNSYLVANIA. (WATER RESOURCES DATA. PENNSYLVANIA). Series/Titl U.S. Geological Survey Water-Data Report. VFOAT USGS Water Resources Data. Water Year 1981-. 0197-0755. US. English. an. US Department of the Interior, US Geological Survey, National Technical Information Service, 5285 Port Royal Road, Springfield VA 22161. LC GB1225.P4. DD 553.709748. Vols. for 1981- distributed to depository libraries in microfiche. *Water Resources Data for Pennsylvania, 0197-0755.*

WATER RESOURCES DATA FOR SOUTH CAROLINA. (WATER RESOURCES DATA. SOUTH CAROLINA). Series/Titl U.S. Geological Survey Water-Data Report. VFOAT South Carolina. Water Year 1981-. 0732-9997. US. English. an. US Department of the Interior, US Geological Survey, National Technical Information Service, 5285 Port Royal Road, Springfield VA 22161. LC GB1225.S6. DD 553.709757. Vols. for (1983-) distributed to depository libraries in microfiche. *Water Resources Data for South Carolina, 0732-9997.*

WATER RESOURCES DATA FOR TENNESSEE. (WATER RESOURCES DATA. TENNESSEE). Series/Titl U.S. Geological Survey Water-Data Report. VFOAT USGS Water Resources Data. Water Year 1982-. 0163-9447. US. English. an. US Department of the Interior, US Geological Survey, National Technical Information Service, 5285 Port Royal Road, Springfield VA 22161. LC GB1225.T4. DD 553.709768. *Water Resources Data for Tennessee, 0163-9447.*

WATER RESOURCES DATA FOR UTAH. Series/Titl U.S. Geological Survey Water-Data Report. VFOAT U.S.G.S. Water Resources Data for Utah. Began with 1964/65. 0360-1633. US. English. an. National Technical Information Service, 5285 Port Royal Road, Springfield VA 22161. LC GB705.U8. DD 553.70972. *Surface Water Records of Utah.*

WATER RESOURCES DATA FOR VIRGINIA. (WATER RESOURCES DATA. VIRGINIA). Series/Titl U.S. Geological Survey Water-Data Report. VFOAT Water Resources Data, Virginia. 0276-1319. US. English. an. US Department of the Interior, US Geological Survey, National Technical Information Service, 5285 Port Royal Road, Springfield VA 22161. LC GB1225.V8. DD 553.709755. *Water Resources Data for Virginia, 0276-1319.*

Water Resources

WATER RESOURCES DATA FOR WASHINGTON. (WATER RESOURCES DATA. WASHINGTON). Series/Titl U.S. Geological Survey Water-Data Report. VFOAT Washington. Water Year 1981-. 0364-3557. US. English. an. US Department of the Interior, US Geological Survey, National Technical Information Service, 5285 Port Royal Road, Springfield VA 22161. LC GB1225.W3. DD 553.709797. Vols. for 1981- distributed to depository libraries in microfiche. *Water Resources Data for Washington, 0364-3557.*

WATER RESOURCES DATA FOR WEST VIRGINIA. (WATER RESOURCES DATA. WEST VIRGINIA). Series/Titl U.S. Geological Survey Water-Data Report. VFOAT West Virginia. Water Year 1981-. 0364-4421. US. English. an. US Department of the Interior, US Geological Survey, National Technical Information Service, 5285 Port Royal Road, Springfield VA 22161. LC TD224.W4. DD 553.709754. *Water Resources Data for West Virginia, 0364-4421.*

WATER RESOURCES DATA FOR WYOMING. (WATER RESOURCES DATA. WYOMING). Series/Titl U.S. Geological Survey Water-Data Report. VFOAT Wyoming. Water Year 1981-. 0364-3565. US. English. an. US Department of the Interior, US Geological Survey, National Technical Information Service, 5285 Port Royal Road, Springfield VA 22161. LC GB1225.W8. DD 553.709787. *Water Resources Data for Wyoming, 0364-3565.*

WATER RESOURCES DATA. KANSAS. Series/Titl U.S. Geological Survey Water-Data Report. VFOAT USGS Water Resources Data. Water Year 1981-. 0741-4803. US. English. an. US Department of the Interior, Us Geological Survey, National Technical Information Service, 5285 Port Royal Road, Springfield VA 22161. LC GB1225.K2. DD 553.709781. Vols. for 1981- distributed to depository libraries in microfiche. *Water Resources Data for Kansas, 0741-4803.*

WATER RESOURCES DATA. LOUISIANA. Series/Titl U.S. Geological Survey Water-Data Report. VFOAT Water Resources Data, Louisiana. Water Year 1981-. US. English. an. US Department of the Interior, US Geological Survey, National Technical Information Service, 5285 Port Royal Road, Springfield VA 22161. LC GB1225.L6. DD 553.709763. *Water Resources Data for Louisiana, 0276-1297.*

WATER RESOURCES DATA. MISSOURI. Series/Titl U.S. Geological Survey Water-Data Report. VFOAT Missouri. 1981-. 0741-6296. US. English. an. US Department of the Interior, US Geological Survey, National Technical Information Service, 5285 Port Royal Road, Springfield VA 22161. LC GB1225.M65. DD 553.709778. Vols. for 1981- distributed to depository libraries in microfiche. *Water Resources Data for Missouri, 0741-6296.*

WATER RESOURCES DATA. NEVADA. Series/Titl U.S. Geological Survey Water-Data Report. VFOAT Water Resources Data, Nevada. US. English. an. US Department of the Interior, US Geological Survey, National Technical Information Service, 5285 Port Royal Road, Springfield VA 22161. Vols. for (1982-) distributed to depository libraries in microfiche. *Water Resources Data for Nevada, 0364-4391.*

WATER RESOURCES DATA. NEW HAMPSHIRE AND VERMONT. Series/Titl U.S. Geological Survey Water-Data Report. VFOAT Water Resources Data, New Hampshire and Vermont. Water Year 1981-. US. English. an. US Geological Survey, Water Resources Division, 150 Causeway Street, Boston MA 02114. Vols. for 1981- distributed to depository libraries in microfiche. *Water Resources Data. New Hampshire and Vermont, 0735-8903.*

WATER RESOURCES DATA, NORTH CAROLINA. (WATER RESOURCES DATA. NORTH CAROLINA). Series/Titl U.S. Geological Survey Water-Data Report. VFOAT USGS Water Resources Data, North Carolina. 0734-5747. US. English. an. US Department of the Interior, US Geological Survey, National Technical Information Service, 5285 Port Royal Road, Springfield VA 22161. LC GB1225.N8. DD 553.709756. Vols. for 1981- issued to depository libraries in microfiche. *Water Resources Data for North Carolina, 0734-5747.*

WATER RESOURCES DATA. PUERTO RICO AND THE U.S. VIRGIN ISLANDS. Series/Titl U.S. Geological Survey Water-Data Report. VFOAT U.S.G.S. Water Resources Data. Water Year 1983-. 8756-9809. US. English. an. US Department of the Interior, US Geological Survey, National Technical Information Service, 5285 Port Royal Road, Springfield VA 22161. LC GB717. DD 551.48097295. Vols. for Water Year 1983- distributed to depository libraries in microfiche. *Water Resources Data. Puerto Rico, 8756-9795.*

WATER RESOURCES DATA. SOUTH DAKOTA. Series/Titl U.S. Geological Survey Water-Data Report. VFOAT South Dakota. Water Year 1981-. 0741-451X. US. English. an. US Department of the Interior, US Geological Survey, National Technical Information Service, 5285 Port Royal Road, Springfield VA 22161. LC GB1225.S8. DD 553.709783. Vols. for 1981- distributed to depository libraries in microfiche. *Water Resources Data for South Dakota.*

WATER RESOURCES DATA SUMMARY. VFOAT Idaho Water Resources Data Summary. US. English. an. US Department of the Interior, Federal Building Box 042 550 West Fort Street, Boise ID 83724.

WATER RESOURCES DATA. TEXAS. Series/Titl U.S. Geological Survey Water-Data Report. VFOAT Texas. 0742-1575. US. English. an. US Department of the Interior, US Geological Survey, National Technical Information Service, 5285 Port Royal Road, Springfield VA 22161. LC GB1025.T4. DD 553.709764. Vols. for 1981- distributed to depository libraries in microfiche. *Water Resources Data for Texas, 0742-1575.*

WATER RESOURCES DATA. WISCONSIN. Series/Titl U.S. Geological Survey Water-Data Report. VFOAT Wisconsin. Water Year 1981-. 0740-8803. US. English. an. US Department of the Interior, US Geological Survey, National Technical Information Service, 5285 Port Royal Road, Springfield VA 22161. LC GB1225.W6. DD 553.709775. Vols. for 1981- distributed to depository libraries in microfiche. *Water Resources Data for Wisconsin, 0740-8803.*

WATER RESOURCES DEVELOPMENT BY THE U.S. ARMY CORPS OF ENGINEERS IN ARKANSAS (1979). (WATER RESOURCES DEVELOPMENT BY THE U.S. ARMY CORPS OF ENGINEERS IN ARKANSAS). VFOAT Water Resources Development in Arkansas. Began with 1979. US. English. be. Southwestern Division, US Army Corps of Engineers, 1114 Commerce Street, Dallas TX 75242. *Water Resources Development in Arkansas.*

WATER RESOURCES DEVELOPMENT BY THE U.S. ARMY CORPS OF ENGINEERS IN IDAHO (1979). (WATER RESOURCES DEVELOPMENT BY THE U. S. ARMY CORPS OF ENGINEERS IN IDAHO). VFOAT Water Resources Development, Idaho. VAT Water Resources Development by the United States Army Corps of Engineers in Idaho. Jan. 1979-. US. English. be. The Division, PO Box 2870, Portland OR 97208. *Water Resources Development in Idaho by the U.S. Army Corps of Engineers.*

WATER RESOURCES DEVELOPMENT BY THE U.S. ARMY CORPS OF ENGINEERS IN ILLINOIS. VFOAT Water Resources Development in Illinois. US. English. be. Division Engineer, US Army Division North Central, 536 South Clark Street, Chicago IL 60605.

WATER-RESOURCES DEVELOPMENT BY THE U.S. ARMY CORPS OF ENGINEERS IN NEVADA. VFOAT Water Resources Development, Nevada. US. English. qt. Division Engineer, US Army Engineer Division South Pacific, Corps of Engineers, 630 Sansome Street, San Francisco CA 94111.

WATER RESOURCES DEVELOPMENT BY THE U.S. ARMY CORPS OF ENGINEERS IN NORTH CAROLINA. VFOAT Water Resources Development in North Carolina. US. English. US Army Engineer Division, South Atlantic Corps of Engineers, 510 Title Building, 30 Pryor Street SW, Atlanta GA 30303.

WATER RESOURCES DEVELOPMENT BY THE U.S. ARMY CORPS OF ENGINEERS IN TEXAS. VFOAT Water Resources Development in Texas. US. English. US Army Engineer Division Southwestern, 1114 Commerce Street, Dallas TX 75242.

WATER RESOURCES DEVELOPMENT BY THE US ARMY CORPS OF ENGINEERS, CHARLESTON DISTRICT. VFOAT Water Resources Development in South Carolina. US. English. ir. U S Army Engineer Division, Corps of Engineers, 510 Title Building, 30 Pryor Street SW, Atlanta GA 30303. Tel (404)331-6641. LC TC424.S7. DD 333.91021509757. (ctrl). Status report on all existing water resources studies and projects completed or underway by U.S. Army Corps of Engineers in the state of South Carolina.

WATER RESOURCES DEVELOPMENT BY THE US ARMY CORPS OF ENGINEERS IN KANSAS. VFOAT Water Resources Development in Kansas. US. English. Division Engineer, US Army Engineer Division Southwestern, Main Tower Building, 1200 Main Street, Dallas TX 75202. LC TC424.K2. DD 333.911509781.

WATER RESOURCES DEVELOPMENT BY THE US ARMY CORPS OF ENGINEERS IN OKLAHOMA. VFOAT Water Resources Development in Oklahoma. 0744-0480. US. English. be. Division Engineer, US Army Division Southwestern, Main Tower Building, 1200 Main Street, Dallas TX 75202. LC TC424.O5. DD 333.911509766.

WATER RESOURCES DEVELOPMENT IN GEORGIA. 1981-. US. English. ir. US Army Engineer Division, South Atlantic Corps of Engineers, 510 Title Building, 30 Pryor Street SW, Atlanta GA 30303. Tel (404)331-6641. (ctrl). Status report on existing water resources studies and projects completed of underway by U.S. Army Corps of Engineers in the state of Georgia. *Water Resources Development, United States Army Corps of Engineers, In Georgia.*

WATER RESOURCES DEVELOPMENT IN IOWA. (WATER RESOURCES DEVELOPMENT IN IOWA . . . BY THE US ARMY CORPS OF ENGINEERS). 1981-. 0732-6408. US. English. be. US Army Engineer Division North Central, 536 South Clark Street, Chicago IL 60605. LC TC424.I8. DD 353.0082325. *Water Resources Development by the U. S. Army Corps of Engineers in Iowa (Chicago, Ill. : 1979).*

WATER RESOURCES DEVELOPMENT IN LOUISIANA (UNITED STATES. ARMY. CORPS OF ENGINEERS. LOWER MISSISSIPPI VALLEY DIVISION : 1981). (WATER RESOURCES DEVELOPMENT IN LOUISIANA/BY THE US ARMY CORPS OF ENGINEERS). 1981-. US. English. be. Division of Engineer, US Army Engineer Division, Lower Mississippi Valley, PO Box 80, Vicksburg MS 39180. *Water Resources Development by the U.S. Army Corps Engineers in Louisiana (1979).*

WATER RESOURCES DEVELOPMENT IN MICHIGAN (UNITED STATES. ARMY. CORPS OF ENGINEERS. NORTH CENTRAL DIVISION : 1981). (WATER RESOURCES DEVELOPMENT IN MICHIGAN). 1981-. 0278-5781. US. English. US Army Engineer Division North Central, 536 South Clark Street, Chicago IL 60605. LC TC424.M5. DD 333.911509776. *Water Resources Development by the U.S. Army Corps of Engineers in Michigan.*

WATER RESOURCES DEVELOPMENT IN MINNESOTA. 1981-. 0278-5447. US. English. be. U S Army Engineer Division, North Central 536 South Clark Street, Chicago IL 60605. LC TC424.M6. DD 333.911509776. *Water Resources Development by the U.S. Army Corps of Engineers in Minnesota.*

WATER RESOURCES DEVELOPMENT IN MISSISSIPPI BY THE US ARMY CORPS OF ENGINEERS. VFOAT Water Resources Development by the U.S. Army Corps of Engineers. 0503-5481. US. English. ir.

WATER RESOURCES DIVISION TRAINING BULLETIN. Main/Corp Geological Survey (U.S.). Water Resources Division. US. English. an. US Geological Survey, Box 25046 Denver Federal Center, Denver CO 80225.

WATER RESOURCES FOR IOWA. (WATER RESOURCES DATA. IOWA). Series/Titl U.S. Geological Survey Water-Data Report. VFOAT Iowa. 0364-4359. US. English. an. US Department of the Interior, US Geological Survey, National Technical Information Service, 5285 Port Royal Road, Springfield VA 22161. LC GB1225.I8. DD 553.709777. Vols. for 1981- distributed to depository libraries in microfiche. *Water Resources Data for Iowa, 0364-4359.*

WATER RESOURCES-INFORMATION SERIES REPORT. (WATER RESOURCES. INFORMATION SERIES. REPORT). 0548-3557. Monographic Series. US. English. ir. State of Nevada,

Water Resources

Division of Water Resources, Carson City NV 89701. **Ind/Abst** GeoRef, Chem. Abstr. **DD** 333.9. **CODEN** NCGRAZ. *Ground-Water Resources. Information Series. Report.*

WATER-RESOURCES INVESTIGATIONS CEASED. VFOAT U.S.G.S. Water-Resources Investigations. VAT Water Resources Investigations. Began with 1-72, published in 1972. Ceased in 1982. 0092-332X. Monographic Series. US. English. ir. US Geological Survey, National Center, 12201 Sunrise Valley Drive, Reston VA 22092. **Ind/Abst** GeoRef, ASTIS Bibliogr., ASTIS Curr. Aware. Bull., Chem. Abstr., Bibliogr. Agric. **LC** GB701. **DD** 553.70973. **CODEN** WRIND3.

WATER-RESOURCES INVESTIGATIONS IN ARIZONA. US. English. Chief Hydrologist, US Geological Survey, 420 National Center, Reston VA 22092.

WATER RESOURCES INVESTIGATIONS IN FLORIDA. VFOAT Summary Statements of Water Resources Investigations in Florida. 0195-3885. US. English. US Geological Survey, Water Resources Division, District Office, 325 John Knox Road, Suite F-240, Tallahassee FL 32303. **LC** TC424.F6. **DD** 553.709759.

WATER-RESOURCES INVESTIGATIONS IN MISSOURI. US. English. Chief Hydrologist, US Geological Survey, 420 National Center, Reston VA 22092.

WATER-RESOURCES INVESTIGATIONS IN NEVADA. 0277-9293. US. English. Free. District Chief, Water Resources Division, US Geological Survey, Room 227 Federal Building, 705 North Plaza Street, Carson City NV 89710. **LC** TC424.N3. **DD** 333.91009793.

WATER RESOURCES INVESTIGATIONS IN NEW YORK. 0277-3651. US. English. an. Open-File Services Section Branch of Distribution, US Geological Survey, Box 25425 Federal Center, Denver CO 80225.

WATER-RESOURCES INVESTIGATIONS IN NORTH CAROLINA. US. English. Chief Hydrologist, US Geological Survey, 420 National Center, Reston VA 22092. *Water Resources Investigations in North Carolina.*

WATER-RESOURCES INVESTIGATIONS IN NORTH DAKOTA. US. English. Chief Hydrologist, US Geological Survey, 420 National Center, Reston VA 22092.

WATER-RESOURCES INVESTIGATIONS IN OREGON. US. English. Chief Hydrologist, US Geological Survey, 420 National Center, Reston VA 22092.

WATER-RESOURCES INVESTIGATIONS IN SOUTH CAROLINA. US. English. Chief Hydrologist, US Geological Survey, 420 National Center, Reston VA 22092.

WATER-RESOURCES INVESTIGATIONS IN TEXAS. Main/Corp Geological Survey (U.S.). Water Resources Division. Texas District. Began with 1971-72. US. English. an. US Geological Survey, Water Resources Division, Texas District, 300 East 8th Street/Room 649, Austin TX 78701. *Program of the Water Resources Division, Texas District for the Fiscal Year and Summary of District Activities during Fiscal Year,* 0565-6060.

WATER-RESOURCES INVESTIGATIONS OF THE U.S. GEOLOGICAL SURVEY IN MISSOURI. Fiscal Year 1980-. US. English. an. US Geological Survey and Water Resources Division, 1400 Independence Road/Mail Stop 200, Rolla MO 65401 65401. *Programs and Activities of the Missouri District, Water Resources Division, U.S. Geological Survey.*

WATER-RESOURCES INVESTIGATIONS OF THE U.S. GEOLOGICAL SURVEY NEW MEXICO DISTRICT. Main/Corp United States. Geological Survey. Water Resources Division. New Mexico District. VAT Water Resources Investigations of the United States Geological Survey New Mexico District. 1977/78-. 0196-1357. US. English. an. US Geological Survey, Water Resources Division, PO Box 26659, Albuquerque NM 87125. **LC** GB658.7. **DD** 553.709789.

WATER RESOURCES JOURNAL. Dec. 1962-. 0377-8053. Periodical. US. English. qt. United Nations Publications, Sales Section/Room A 3315, New York NY 10017. **Ind/Abst** GeoRef, Bibliogr. Agric. **LC** JX1977, GB773. **DD** 300.8, 553.7095. **NLM** W1 WA692AG. *Flood Control Journal.*

WATER RESOURCES MONOGRAPH. VFOAT Water Resources Monograph Series. Began in 1971. 0270-9600. Monographic Series. US. English. ir. American Geophysical Union, 2000 Florida Avenue NW, Washington DC 20009. **Tel** (202)462-6903. **Ind/Abst** GeoRef, Bibliogr. Index Geol. This book series brings information from the research community to the practitioner. Each book describes a specific technique or approach to water resources planning.

WATER RESOURCES NEWSLETTER CEASED. Began with No. 1- Oct. 1963-. Ceased in 1981. 0311-7987. Periodical. English. bm. **Ind/Abst** GeoRef. **LC** TC521. **DD** 333.9100994. **CODEN** WRNLAJ.

WATER RESOURCES PLANNING SERIES. Report P-78-001-. 0270-9481. Monographic Series. US. English. ir. Utah Water Research Laboratory, College of Engineering, Utah State University, Logan UT 84322. **Ind/Abst** GeoRef.

WATER RESOURCES PROGRAM. Main/Corp Delaware River Basin Commission. 0273-4338. US. English. an. **LC** TC425.D3. **DD** 333.91009749.

WATER RESOURCES REFERENCE SERVICES. Periodical. US. English. mo. Water Resources Center, University of Wisconsin-Madison, 1975 Willow Drive, Madison WI 53706. **LC** TD201.

WATER RESOURCES REPORT. Main/Corp South Dakota Geological Survey. No. 1-. 0584-3685. Monographic Series. US. English. ir. Science Center, University of South Dakota, Vermillion SD 57069. **Ind/Abst** GeoRef. **LC** GB1025.S8. **DD** 333.9. **CODEN** SDWRB9.

WATER RESOURCES REPORT (MISSOURI. DIVISION OF GEOLOGY AND LAND SURVEY.). (WATER RESOURCES REPORT). No. 31 (1976)-. 0076-9614. Monographic Series. US. English. ir. Missouri Department of Natural Research, PO Box 250, Rolla MO 65401. **Ind/Abst** GeoRef, Bibliogr. Index Geol. **CODEN** MGWAAE. *Water Resources Report,* 0076-9614.

WATER RESOURCES RESEARCH. V. 11 Feb. 1965-. Periodical. US. English. mo. $295.00. American Geophysical Union, 2000 Florida Avenue NW, Washington DC 20009. **Tel** (202)462-6903. Ed Ronald Cummings and Donald Nielsen. **Ind/Abst** Eng. Index Annu., Eng. Index Mon., Eng. Index Bioeng. Abstr., Eng. Index Energy Abstr., Fluidex, Excerpta Med., Can. Environ., Coal Abstr., Abstr. Bull. Inst. Paper Chem., Index Econ. Artic. J. Collect. Vol., GeoRef, Energy Inf. Abstr., Environ. Abstr., Int. Aerosp. Abstr., Comput. Control Abstr., Electr. Electron. Abstr., Sci. Abstr. Sect. A. Phys. Abstr., Chem. Abstr., Bibliogr. Agric., Energy Res. Abstr., Sel. Water Resour. Abstr. **LC** GB651. **DD** 553.70973. **NLM** W1 WA692AH. **CODEN** WRERAQ. (ctrl). Available on microfilm. Original contributions on physical, chemical, biological and social aspects of water science and water law.

WATER RESOURCES RESEARCH SERIES (NASHVILLE). (WATER RESOURCES RESEARCH SERIES). No. 1 (1969)-. 0092-3699. Monographic Series. US. English. ir. Tennessee Department of Conservation, Division of Water Resources, 2611 West End, Nashville TN 37203. **Ind/Abst** GeoRef. **CODEN** TWRSAS.

WATER RESOURCES RESEARCH SUPPORT PROGRAM. Main/Corp Canada. Inland Waters Directorate. VFOAT Programme de Subvention a la Recherche sur les Ressources en Eau. 1973/1974-. 0317-6703. Periodical. CN. text in English and French. Free. Inland Waters Directorate, Place Vincent Massey, Ottawa Ontario K1A 0H3 Canada. **LC** GB658. **DD** 551.48072071.

WATER RESOURCES REVIEW. 1940-. 0043-1400. Periodical. US. English. mo. Geological Survey Interior Department, 582 National Center, Reston VA 22092. **Ind/Abst** Am. Stat. Index. **LC** GB701.

WATER RESOURCES SEMINAR SERIES. Main/Corp Hawaii. University, Honolulu. Water Resources Research Center. No. 1- July/Dec. 1971-. 0091-2913. Periodical. US. English. sa. **LC** TC424.H3. **DD** 333.91009969.

WATER RESOURCES SERIES. No. 1- May 1966-. 0084-3210. Monographic Series. US. English. University of Wyoming, Water Resources/Research Institute, PO Box 3008, Laramie WY 82070. **Ind/Abst** GeoRef. **DD** 628. **CODEN** WUWWAG.

WATER RESOURCES SERIES (DUBLIN, DUBLIN). (WATER RESOURCES SERIES). VOL. 1-. Monographic Series. English. ir.

WATER RESOURCES SERIES (NASHVILLE, TENN.). (WATER RESOURCES SERIES). 0495-1026. Monographic Series. US. English. ir. State of Tennessee, Department of Conservation/Division of Water Resources, 2611 West End, Nashville TN 37203. **Ind/Abst** Chem. Abstr. **LC** GB651. **DD** 553.70968. **CODEN** TWWRAG.

WATER RESOURCES SPECIAL REPORT. No. 1-. 0161-2867. Monographic Series. US. English. Louisiana Department of Public Works, Baton Rouge LA. **Ind/Abst** Chem. Abstr., GeoRef. **CODEN** LWSRBB.

WATER RESOURCES SUMMARY (LITTLE ROCK). (WATER RESOURCES SUMMARY). 0518-6374. Monographic Series. US. English. ir. Arkansas Geological Commission, 3815 West Roosevelt Road, Little Rock AR 72204. **LC** TC424.A8. **DD** 551.4.

WATER RESOURCES SYMPOSIUM. No. 1- 1968-. 0083-7709. US. English. ir. Center of Research Water Resource, 10100 Burnet Road, Austin TX 78758. **Tel** (512)471-3131. **Ind/Abst** GeoRef, Chem. Abstr., Energy Res. Abstr., Bibliogr. Index Geol. **NLM** W3 WA34. **CODEN** WARSA9. Conference proceedings related to water use.

WATER REUSE. VFOAT OWRT/RU. 79/1-. Monographic Series. US. English. ir. OWRT, Room 1310, 18th & C Streets NW, Washington DC 20240.

WATER SUPPLY. (WATER SUPPLY : THE REVIEW JOURNAL OF THE INTERNATIONAL WATER SUPPLY ASSOCIATION). Vol. 1, No. 1 (Mar. 1983)-. 0735-1917. Periodical. UK. English (French). qt. Pergamon Press, 395 Sawmill River Road, Elmsford NY 10523. **Ind/Abst** Fluidex, Chem. Abstr. **LC** TD201. **DD** 628.105. **CODEN** WASUDN. Available on microfiche simultaneously with the paper edition, and on microfilm at the end of the subscription year.

WATER SUPPLY & MANAGEMENT. VFOAT Water Supply and Management. V. 1, No. 3-. 0364-7714. Periodical. UK. English. bm. $140.00 North America. Pergamon Press Inc, Maxwell House, Fairview Park, Elmsford NY 10523. **Ind/Abst** Eng. Index Annu., Eng. Index Mon., Eng. Index Bioeng. Abstr., Eng. Index Energy Abstr., Fluidex, Excerpta Med., Can. Environ., Coal Abstr., Energy Inf. Abstr., Environ. Abstr., Sel. Water Resour. Abstr., GeoRef, Chem. Abstr., Bibliogr. Agric. **LC** TD201. **DD** 333.9115. **CODEN** WSMADP. Available on microfilm and microfiche. *Aqua (Oxford, Oxfordshire),* 0147-3298.

WATER SUPPLY OUTLOOK FOR ARIZONA AND FEDERAL-STATE-PRIVATE COOPERATIVE SNOW SURVEYS CEASED. 0364-4987. US. English. US Department of Agriculture, Soil Conservation Service, Federal Building/Room 3008, 230 North First Avenue, Phoenix AZ 85025. **Ind/Abst** Am. Stat. Index. **LC** GB2425.A6. **DD** 551.579791.

WATER SUPPLY OUTLOOK FOR NEVADA AND FEDERAL-STATE-PRIVATE COOPERATIVE SNOW SURVEYS CEASED. 0196-3325. US. English. US Department of Agriculture Soil Conservation Service, PO Box 4850, Reno NV 89505. **Tel** (702)784-5869. Ed John R Capurro. **LC** TD224.N2. **DD** 553.709793. Circ 1,000. (ctrl). Listing of current values for water supply and forecasted streamflow in Nevada and eastern California. *Water Supply Outlook and Federal-State-Private Cooperative Snow Surveys for Nevada.*

WATER SUPPLY OUTLOOK FOR OREGON AND FEDERAL-STATE-PRIVATE COOPERATIVE SNOW SURVEYS CEASED. VFOAT Water Supply Outlook for Oregon. Publication began with Jan. 1967. 0566-0394. Periodical. US. English. ir. US Department of Agriculture, Soil Conservation Service, 1220 SW Third Avenue, Portland OR 97204. **Ind/Abst** Am. Stat. Index. *Water Supply Outlook and Federal-State-Private Cooperative Snow Surveys for Oregon.*

WATER SUPPLY OUTLOOK FOR THE NORTHEASTERN UNITED STATES. *See Earth Sciences - Hydrology.*

WATER SUPPLY OUTLOOK FOR THE WESTERN UNITED STATES. See Earth Sciences - Hydrology.

WATER SUPPLY OUTLOOK FOR UTAH AND FEDERAL-STATE-PRIVATE COOPERATIVE SNOW SURVEYS. 0364-4995. Periodical. US. English. mo. Soil Conservation Service, West Technical Service Center, Room 111 NW Broadway, Portland OR 97209. Ind/Abst GeoRef, Am. Stat. Index. LC GB2425.U8. DD 553.709792.

WATER SUPPLY OUTLOOK FOR WASHINGTON AND FEDERAL-STATE-PRIVATE COOPERATIVE SNOW SURVEYS. VFOAT Water Supply Outlook for Washington. 0364-5347. US. English. ir. US Department of Agriculture, Soil Conservation Service Room 360 US Courthouse, Spokane WA 99201. Tel (509)456-3715. Ind/Abst Am. Stat. Index. LC TD224.W2. DD 553.7809797. Circ 7,000. Snow water content and expected summer stream flow.

WATER SUPPLY OUTLOOK FOR WYOMING AND FEDERAL-STATE-PRIVATE COOPERATIVE SNOW SURVEYS CEASED. VFOAT Water Supply Outlook for Wyoming, Water Supply Summary and Outlook for Wyoming. 0364-5363. Periodical. US. English. ir. Soil Conservation Service, PO Box 2440, Casper WY 82601. Ind/Abst Am. Stat. Index. LC GB2425.W8. DD 551.48309787. *Federal-State-Cooperative Snow Surveys and Water Supply Forecasts for Wyoming.*

WATER SUPPLY PAPERS OF THE INSTITUTE OF GEOLOGICAL SCIENCES. RESEARCH REPORT. No. 4-. Monographic Series. UK. English (some numbers have summaries also in French and German). Her Majesty's Stationery Office, 49 High Holborn, London WC1 England. Ind/Abst GeoRef. CODEN GWRRAI. *Water Supply Papers of the Geological Survey of Great Britain.*

WATER SUPPLY REPORT (EAST LANSING). (WATER SUPPLY REPORT). No. 1- 1957-. 0543-8519. Monographic Series. US. English. ir. Michigan Geological Survey Division, Box 30028, R Thomas Segall, Lansing MI 48909. DD 333.9.

WATER UTILITY OPERATING DATA. 0276-7481. US. English. be. $15.00 Members, $30.00 Others. AWWA, 6666 West Quincy Avenue, Denver CO 80235. LC HD4461. DD 363.610973. *AWWA Operating Data for Water Utilities, 0194-1828.*

WATER WELL JOURNAL. VFOAT WWJ. Summer 1947-. 0043-1443. Periodical. US. English. mo. $11.00. Water Well Journal Publishing Company, 500 West Wilson Bridge Road, Worthington OH 43085. Tel (614)846-4967. Ed Anita Bacco Stanley. Ind/Abst Excerpta Med., Sel. Water Resour. Abstr., GeoRef, Bibliogr. Index Geol. LC TD405. DD 622.37905. CODEN WWJOA9. adv acc. Circ 30,000. (ctrl). The 'voice of the ground water industry' for over 30 years. Each month covers topics of importance to drillers, suppliers, manufacturers and scientists alike. *Illinois Well Driller.*

WATER WELL RECORDS FOR ONTARIO. Main/Corp Ontario. Water Resources Branch. Series/Titl Water Resources Bulletin. Ground Water Series. Began publication in 1975. 0226-4552. Periodical. CN. English. Hydrology and Monitoring Section Water Resources Branch Ministry of the Environment, 135 St Clair Avenue West, Toronto Ontario M4V 1P5 Canada. DD 628.11409713.

WATERMASTER SERVICE IN THE RAYMOND BASIN. US. English. an. LC TD224.C3. DD 333.91170979493. *Watermaster Service in the Raymond Basin, Los Angeles County.*

WATERMASTER SERVICE IN THE WEST COAST BASIN, LOS ANGELES COUNTY. Main/Corp California. Dept. of Water Resources. Southern District. US. English. an. Department of Water Resources, PO Box 388, Sacramento CA 95802. LC TD224.C3. DD 333.9104170979493.

WATERSCHAPSBELANGEN. Periodical. NE. Dutch. 93,50. Unie Van Waterschappen, Postbus 29740, 2502 LS Den Haag Netherlands. Tel 070-469797. Ind/Abst Excerpta Med. LC HD1683.N2. bk rev. adv acc. Water-management, water-resources, press-releases, studies about water-problems, new land-reclamation, dikes, etc. juridical articles.

WESTERN WATER. Sept./Oct. 1975-. 0735-5424. Periodical. US. English. bm. $15.00. Western Water Education Foundation, 1007 Seventh Street #315, Sacramento CA 95814. Tel (916)444-6240. Ed Rita Schmidt Sudman. Ind/Abst Energy Inf. Abstr., Environ. Abstr., GeoRef, Public Aff. Inf. Serv. Bull. Circ 12,000. Educational non-partisan material on California water issues. *Western Water News.*

WORLD BANK STUDIES IN WATER SUPPLY AND SANITATION. VFOAT Studies in Water Supply and Sanitation. Began publication in 1982. Monographic Series. UK. English.

WORLD WATER. V. 1- May 1978-. 0140-9050. Periodical. UK. English. mo. $75.00. Thomas Telford, 26/34 Old Street PO Box 101, London EC1P 1JH England. Tel (51)236-1155. Ed Robin Wiseman. Ind/Abst Fluidex, Excerpta Med., Energy Inf. Abstr., Environ. Abstr., Sel. Water Resour. Abstr., GeoRef. LC TD201. DD 363.6105. bk rev. adv acc. Circ 14,000. (ctrl). International magazine covering water supply, wastewater treatment, irrigation, hydroelectricity and desalination. Owned by Institution of Civil Engineers in the United Kingdom.

WORLDWIDE DIRECTORY OF NATURAL AND HOT SPRINGS. See Yearbooks, Almanacs, Directories.

WRC INFORMATION (WATER RESEARCH CENTRE). (WRC INFORMATION). VAT Water Research Centre Information. V. 5, No. 1 (3rd Jan. 1978)-. Periodical. UK. English. wk. *WRC Information : Publications and Meetings.*

W.R.C. RESEARCH REPORT. (WRC RESEARCH REPORT). Main/Corp Illinois. University at Urbana-Champaign. Water Resources Center. VAT Water Resources Center Research Report. No. 63-. 0073-5442. US. English. 2535 Hydrosystems Laboratory, Urbana IL 61801. Ind/Abst Biol. Abstr., GeoRef, Eng. Index Annu., Eng. Index Mon., Eng. Index Mon., Eng. Index Bioeng. Abstr., Eng. Index Energy Abstr. LC HD1694. DD 333.91008. CODEN IUWRAH. *WRC Research Report, 0073-5442.*

WRRC BULLETIN. (BULLETIN). VFOAT W.R.R.C. Bulletin. VAT Water Resources Research Center Bulletin. 1-. 0544-3466. Monographic Series. US. English. ir. University of Minnesota, 866 Biological Sciences Center, St Paul MN 55108. Ind/Abst Eng. Index Annu., Eng. Index Mon., Eng. Index Bioeng. Abstr., Eng. Index Energy Abstr., GeoRef, Eng. Index. CODEN MWCBAT.

WRRI BULLETIN. Main/Corp Auburn University. Water Resources Research Institute. VAT Water Resources Research Institute Bulletin. 0097-5729. Monographic Series. US. English. Free. Water Resources Research Institute, c/o Auburn University, 205 Samford Hall, Auburn AL 36830. Ind/Abst GeoRef, Biol. Abstr., Chem. Abstr. LC TC1. CODEN WRRBA9.

WRRI REPORT. Main/Corp New Mexico Water Resources Research Institute. VAT Water Resources Research Institute Report. No. 3-. 0731-7557. Monographic Series. US. English. ir. New Mexico Water Resources and Research Institute, New Mexico State University, Box 3167, Las Cruces NM 88003. Ind/Abst GeoRef. CODEN NMWRAG. *W.R.R.I. Publication.*

WSIA JOURNAL. VFOAT Water Supply Improvement Association Journal. Vol. 8, No. 2 (July 1981)-. 0730-9570. Periodical. US. English. sa. National Water Supply Improvement Association, PO Box 387, Topsfield MA 01938. Tel (617)887-8101. Ind/Abst Chem. Abstr., GeoRef, Energy Res. Abstr. CODEN WSIAD5. *NWSIA Journal, 0145-4382.*

YEAR REPORT - TEMPORARY STATE COMMISSION ON THE WATER SUPPLY NEEDS OF SOUTHEASTERN NEW YORK. (YEAR REPORT). Main/Corp New York (State). Temporary State Commission on the Water Supply Needs of Southeastern New York. 1st- 1971/72-. 0092-2676. US. English. an. Department of State, Temporary State Commission on Water Supply, 162 Washington Avenue, Albany NY 12231. LC TD224.N7. DD 333.91009.747.

YUKON WATER MANAGEMENT. (YUKON WATER MANAGEMENT : A BULLETIN OF THE WESTWATER RESEARCH CENTRE). No. 1 (Sept. 1981)-. 0711-1223. Periodical. CN. English. ir. Free. Westwater Research Centre, University of British Columbia, 1933 West Mall, Vancouver British Columbia V6T 1W5 Canada. DD 331.9115097191.

ZEITSCHRIFT FUR KULTURTECHNIK UND FLURBEREINIGUNG. 0044-2984. Periodical. GW. German. bm. 228.-. Paul Parey Verlag, PO Box 106304, Spitalerstr 12, D-2000 Hamburg 1 West Germany. Tel 030/2599040. Ed B Scheffer. Ind/Abst Life Sci. Collect., Excerpta Med., Chem. Abstr., Energy Res. Abstr., Energy Inf. Abstr., Environ. Abstr. CODEN ZKUFAK. bk rev. adv acc. (ctrl). Contains articles on rural engineering and development such as soil technology, land consolidation, water management, hydraulic engineering, regional planning, environment conservation and related problems in developing countries.

ZEITSCHRIFT FUR WASSER- UND ABWASSER FORSCHUNG. See Sanitation, Environmental Technology.

ZEITSCHRIFT FUR WASSERRECHT. VFOAT ZFW. Zeitschrift fur Wasserrecht. Vol. 1-. 0044-3735. Periodical. German. qt. Ind/Abst Energy Res. Abstr.

WOMEN

13TH MOON. See Literature.

LA ABOGADA INTERNACIONAL. THE INTERNATIONAL WOMAN LAWYER. See Law - International Law.

ACTION. Began with May 1973 issue. 0701-1547. Periodical. CN. English. bm. $2. Manitoba Action Committee On the Status of Women, 447 Webb Place, Winnipeg Manitoba R3B 2P2 Canada. DD 301.412097127.

ACTION ADAPTATION. See Emigration and Immigration.

ACTIVITIES OF THE AFRICAN TRAINING AND RESEARCH CENTRE FOR WOMEN. Main/Corp African Training and Research Centre For Women. English. ir. LC HQ1788. DD 305.4096.

A.D.F.C. INFORME. See Economics - Labor.

AEGIS. See Political Science - Civil Rights.

AFRICA WOMAN CEASED. Began with Oct./Nov. 1975 issue. 0308-5821. Periodical. UK. English. bm. $1.25. 54 West 82nd Street, New York NY 10024. LC HQ1101. DD 301.412096.

AGENCY ACCOUNTABILITY SURVEY. See Economics - Labor.

AGORA (TOKYO, JAPAN : 1972). (AGORA). Began in 1972. Periodical. JA. Japanese. sa. 6000 Membership, 1500 Single Issue. Boc Shuppanbu, 9-6 Shinjuku 1, Shinjuku-ku Tokyo-to 160 Japan. LC HQ1761.

A.I.A.W. HANDBOOK OF POLICIES AND OPERATING PROCEDURES. See Recreation, Leisure - Sports.

AL-JAWHARAH. Periodical. Arabic. ir. 15.00. Muassasat Al-Ahd Lil-Sihafah Wa-Al-Tibaah Wa-Al-Nashr, PO Box 2531, Al-Dawhah Qatar. Tel 414575. Ed Abdullah Al-Aussaini. LC AP95.A6. bk rev. adv acc. Circ 16,000. (ctrl). This is the only women magazine here, so we cover all that concerns women and her home, fashions, child care, cosmetics, etc.

AL-JAZAIRIYAH. VFOAT Djazairia, Jazairia. Began in 1970. Periodical. AE. Arabic. mo. LC HQ1791.5.

AL-MARAH AL-JADIDAH. V. 1- March 1975-. Periodical. Arabic. ir. 0.05. PO Box 363, Al-Khartum Sudan. LC HQ1104.

AL-RAIDAH. No. 1- May 1976-. Periodical. Arabic. ir. $5.00. P O Box 11-4080, Bayrut Lebanon. LC HQ1784.

AL-SHARQIYAH. VFOAT Elle. Periodical. Arabic. ir. 185.00. Al-Sharikah Al-Sharqiyah Al-Alamiyah, 6 R Ancelle, 92521 Neuilly Y-Sue-Seine Cedex Paris France. LC AP95.A6.

ALLE KVINNER; MAGAZINE FOR WOMEN. Periodical. NO. Norwegian. wk. Bladcentraalen, Postboks 5162, Majorstuen Oslo 3 Norway.

ALMANACH DE LA FEMME. See Yearbooks, Almanacs, Directories.

AMINA. Periodical. FR. French. mo. 230.00. S A F E P, 11 Rue de Teheran, 75008 Paris France. Tel 562 74 76 . LC HQ1101. Magazine of female information.

ANGELA LUISA. 0279-3385. Periodical. US. Spanish. mo. Angela Luisa, Box 1807, Hato Rey Puerto Rico 00919.

Women

ANNABEL. No. 1- Mar. 1966-. Periodical. UK. English. mo. $19.81. D C Thomson & Company Ltd, 7 Bank Street, Dundee DD1 9HU Scotland. Tel 0382 23131. LC HQ1101.

ANNOTATED GUIDE TO WOMEN'S PERIODICALS IN THE U.S. & CANADA. (THE ANNOTATED GUIDE TO WOMEN'S PERIODICALS IN THE U.S. & CANADA). VFOAT Annotated Guide to Women's Periodicals in the United States and Canada. Vol. 2, No. 1 (Apr. 1983)-. 0741-9899. Periodical. US. English. sa. $20.00. The Women's Programs Office, Earlham College c/o N.S.I.W.S., Box E-94, Earlham College, Richmond IN 47374. Tel (317)962-6561. Ed Terry Mehlman. DD 016. adv acc. Circ 200. (ctrl). Provides up-to-date information on over 250 feminist and alternative women's periodicals. Arranged by subject. Title and geographical indicies. *Annotated Guide to Women's Periodicals in the U.S.*

ANNUAL REPORT - ADVISORY COUNCIL ON THE STATUS OF WOMEN. Main/Corp Canada. Advisory Council on the Status of Women. VFOAT Rapport Annuel - Conseil Consultatif de la Situation de la Femme. 1973/74-. 0705-6028. CN. English (and French. Vols. for 1973/74- have special title page and separate paging, with French text on inverted pages). an. Free. Advisory Council on the Status of Women, 63 Sparks Street, PO Box 1541 Station B, Ottawa Ontario K1P 5R5 Canada. LC HQ1453. DD 354.710084.

ANNUAL REPORT AND REPORT OF . . . TRAINING PROGRAMME - EASTERN AND SOUTHERN AFRICAN MANAGEMENT INSTITUTE. Main/Corp Eastern and Southern African Management Institute. VFOAT Training for Development Planning and Women: An African Perspective. 1st (16 Sept. 1980-15 Sept. 1981)-. English. an. Eastern and Southern African Management Institute, PO Box 3030, Arusha Tanzania. LC HN780.Z9. DD 307.14088042.

ANNUAL REPORT - ARIZONA WOMEN'S COMMISSION. Main/Corp Arizona Women's Commission. VFOAT Women In Arizona. US. English. an. Arizona Women's Commission, 333 East McDowell Road, Phoenix AZ 85004. LC HQ1438.A6. DD 353.979100813. *Women in Arizona.*

ANNUAL REPORT - COMMISSION ON THE STATUS OF WOMEN OF SOUTH DAKOTA. Main/Corp South Dakota. Commission On the Status of Women. 0362-9252. US. English. an. Commission on the Status of Women, Capitol Lake Plaza Building No 300 711 Wells, Pierre SD 57501. LC HQ1438.S6. DD 353.9783008.

ANNUAL REPORT - GOVERNOR'S COMMISSION ON THE STATUS OF WOMEN (MASSACHUSETTS). Main/Corp Massachusetts. Governor's Commission on the Status of Women. US. English. an. Governor's Commission on the Status of Women, Room 1105/100 Cambridge Street, Boston MA 02202. LC HQ1438.M4. DD 353.974400996.

ANNUAL REPORT INCLUDING . . . OBJECTIVES AND ACTION PLANS - EQUAL OPPORTUNITIES FOR WOMEN. (ANNUAL REPORT INCLUDING . . . OBJECTIVES AND ACTION PLANS). Main/Corp Canada. Health and Welfare Canada. Equal Opportunity for Women. 0823-5864. CN. English (French). an. LC RA184. DD 354.710084.

ANNUAL REPORT - MAYOR'S COMMITTEE ON THE STATUS OF WOMEN (HONOLULU). (ANNUAL REPORT). Main/Corp Honolulu. Mayor's Committee on the Status of Women. 1972-. 0091-8121. US. English. an. Mayor's Committee on the Status of Women, Honolulu HI 96813. LC HQ1438.H3. DD 301.41209969.

ANNUAL REPORT - NATIONAL ADVISORY COUNCIL ON WOMEN'S EDUCATIONAL PROGRAMS. (ANNUAL REPORT). Main/Corp United States. National Advisory Council on Women's Educational Programs. VFOAT Women's Education, the Challenge of the 80's. Began with 2nd, 1976. 0162-0541. US. English. an. National Advisory Council on Women's Educational Programs, 1832 M Street Northwest/Suite 821, Washington DC 20036. LC LC1481. DD 376.973. *Annual Report, 0364-3174.*

ANNUAL REPORT - NATIONAL COMMISSION ON THE ROLE OF FILIPINO WOMEN (PHILIPPINES). Main/Corp Philippines. National Commission On the Role of Filipino Women. Began with 1975 vol. English. ir. Commission on the Role of Filipino Women, 1145 J P Laurel Street, San Miguel Metro, Manila Philippines. LC HQ1757. DD 354.59900996.

ANNUAL REPORT - NATIONAL COUNCIL ON WOMEN AND DEVELOPMENT (GHANA). Main/Corp Ghana. National Council on Women and Development. 1975/76-. English. ir. National Council on Women and Development, PO Box M.53, Accra Ghana. LC HQ1816. DD 354.66700996.

ANNUAL REPORT - NEBRASKA COMMISSION ON THE STATUS OF WOMEN. Main/Corp Nebraska. Commission on the Status of Women. 0149-3973. US. English. an. Commission on the Status of Women, PO Box 94985 01 Centinnial Mall South, Lincoln NE 68509. LC KFN91.W6. DD 346.782013.

ANNUAL REPORT OF THE NATIONAL WOMEN'S ADVISORY COUNCIL . . . . Main/Corp National Women's Advisory Council (Australia). 1st (1979)-. English. an. LC HQ1821. DD 354.9400813.

ANNUAL REPORT - PROVINCIAL ADVISORY COUNCIL ON THE STATUS OF WOMEN, NEWFOUNDLAND AND LABRADOR. (ANNUAL REPORT). Main/Corp Provincial Advisory Council on the Status of Women, Newfoundland and Labrador. June 6, 1980-Mar. 31, 1981-. 0715-1152. CN. English. an. Provincial Advisory Council on the Status of Women of Newfoundland and Labrador, 131 Lemarchant Road, Saint John's Newfoundland A1C 2H3 Canada. LC HQ1459.N5. DD 354.71800813.

ANNUAL REPORT - SASKATCHEWAN ADVISORY COUNCIL ON THE STATUS OF WOMEN. Main/Corp Saskatchewan. Advisory Council on the Status of Women. 1st- 1974/75-. 0384-9872. CN. English. an. LC HQ1459.S27. DD 305.42097124.

ANNUAL REPORT - STATE OF HAWAII. STATE COMMISSION ON THE STATUS OF WOMEN. (ANNUAL REPORT). Main/Corp Hawaii. State Commission on the Status of Women. 1st- 1972-. 0092-9190. US. English. an. State Commission on the Status of Women, 250 South King Street, Honolulu HI 96813. LC KFH91.W6. DD 346.969013.

ANNUAL REPORT - STATE OF IOWA, COMMISSION ON THE STATUS OF WOMEN. Main/Corp Iowa. Commission on the Status of Women. 0362-6687. US. English. an. Free. Commission on the Status of Women, 300 Fourth Street, Des Moines IA 50319. Tel (515)281-4461. Ed Rebecca Ann Burke. LC HQ7438.I7. DD 353.977700996. Circ 2,600. Informs women about state and federal public policies which affect them; additionally, it has up-to-date information on women's organizational activities, particularly the Commission's.

ANNUAL REPORT - TENNESSEE COMMISSION ON THE STATUS OF WOMEN. Main/Corp Tennessee. Commission on the Status of Women. 1st- 1974-. 0149-7561. US. English. an. 100 Andrew Jackson Building, Nashville TN 37219. LC KFT91.W6. DD 346.768013.

ANNUAL REPORT. THE STATUS OF WOMEN IN FLORIDA. (THE STATUS OF WOMEN IN FLORIDA). Main/Corp Florida. Governor's Commission on the Status of Women. 1973-. 0093-7118. US. English. an. Governor's Commission on the Status of Women, The Capitol, Tallahassee FL 32304. LC HQ1438.F6. DD 301.41209259.

ANNUAL REPORT TO THE GOVERNOR AND LEGISLATURE - NEW MEXICO. COMMISSION ON THE STATUS OF WOMEN. Main/Corp New Mexico. Commission on the Status of Women. US. English. an. Commission on the Status of Women, Suite 811/Plaza Del Sol/600 2nd Street NW, Albuquerque NM 87102. LC HQ1438.N55. DD 353.9789008.

ANNUAL REPORT - TOKYO JOSHI DAIGAKU. CENTER FOR WOMEN'S STUDIES. Main/Corp Tokyo Joshi Daigaku. Center for Women's Studies. JA. English (Japanese). an. Center for Women's Studies, Tokyo Woman's Christian University, Tokyo Japan. LC HQ1180. DD 305.4071152135.

ANNUAL REPORT - VERMONT GOVERNOR'S COMMISSION ON THE STATUS OF WOMEN. Main/Corp Vermont. Governor's Commission on the Status of Women. US. English. an. Governor's Commission on the Status of Women, 126 State Street, Montpieler VT 05602. LC HQ1438.V47. DD 353.974300813.

ANNUAL REPORT - WEST VIRGINIA WOMEN'S COMMISSION. Main/Corp West Virginia Women's Commission. US. English. an. West Virginia Women's Commission, WB 9 Capitol Complex, Charleston WV 25305. LC HQ1438.W47. DD 353.975400813.

APOSTROPHE (SILLERY, QUEBEC). (APOSTROPHE). 1-. 0715-9900. Periodical. CN. French. qt. $4,95 Per No. Apostrophe, App 1/1337 Av Maguire, Sillery Quebec G1T 1Z2 Canada. DD 305.4205.

ARBOG FOR KVINDESTUDIER VED AUC. See Yearbooks, Almanacs, Directories.

ASIAN WOMAN. Periodical. US. English. qt. $25.00. Asian Women's Institute, 475 Riverside Drive/Room 439, New York NY 10115.

ATLANTIS (WOLFVILLE, N.S.). (ATLANTIS). V. 1- Fall 1975-. 0702-7818. Periodical. CN. English (French). sa. 16.00. Mount Saint Vincent University, 166 Bedford Highway, Halifax Nova Scotia B3M 2J6 Canada. Tel (902)443-4450. Ed Susan M Clark, Deborah C Poff and Margaret Conrad. Ind/Abst Altern. Press Index, MLA Int. Bibliogr. Books Artic. Mod. Lang. Lit., Women Stud. Abstr., Am. Hist. Life, Hist. Abstr. LC HQ1180. DD 305.405. bk rev. adv acc. Circ 500. (ctrl). Available on microfilm from Micromedia Ltd. Interdisciplinary journal devoted to critical research and creative writing on all topics relating to the study of women. Bilingual, refereed; articles must be non-sexist.

AUTRE PAROLE. See Religion, Mythology, Rationalism.

AWA. Periodical. French. ir. 4000. B P 2578, Dakar Senegal. LC HQ1102. DD 301.41209663.

AWC NEWS. See Music.

AWOURA. No. 1- Feb. 1972?-. Periodical. IV. French. ir. BP 2273, Abidjan Ivory Coast. LC AP27. DD 054.1.

B.C.N.W.S. NEWSLETTER. VAT B.C. Native Women's Society Newsletter, British Columbia Native Women's Society Newsletter. 0828-6582. Periodical. CN. English. bm. Free to members. BC Native Women's Society, 116 Seymour Street, Kamloops British Columbia V2C 2E1 Canada. DD 305.488970711.

BERITA KOWANI. Main/Corp Kongres Wanita Indonesia. 1979-. IO. Indonesian. ir. Humas Kowani, J1. HOS Cokroaminoto 67, Jakarta-Pusat Indonesia. LC HQ2004.A1. *Berita Kongres Wanita Indonesia, Kowani.*

BIBI. Began with Apr. 1972 issue. 0376-6624. French or Lingala. ir. Lutayi-Kanza, 33 Av Victoire Com Kasa-Vubu B P 6507 Kin/Mdolo, Kinshasa Congo. LC HQ1810. DD 301.412091751.

BIG MAMA RAG. 1- 1973-. 0277-7533. Periodical. US. English. mo. Big Mama Rag, 1724 Gaylord, Denver CO 80206. Ind/Abst Altern. Press Index.

BLACK MARIA. V. 1- 1971-. 0045-222X. Periodical. US. English. qt. Black Maria, PO Box 25187, Chicago IL 60625. Ed Laurie Fortman. bk rev. adv acc. Circ 1,000. (ctrl). Feminist arts publication that caters especially to women. Literature and artwork.

BODY TALK. Vol. 1, No. 1 (Fall 1984)-. 0749-1018. Periodical. US. English. qt. Women's Center, POB 43222, Cincinnati OH 45243.

BOLETIM (PORTUGAL. COMISSAO DA CONDICAO FEMININA). (BOLETIM). No. 1 (Jan. 1975)-. Periodical. Portuguese. ir. LC HQ1697. DD 305.4209469.

BOLETIN DOCUMENTAL SOBRE LAS MUJERES. Periodical. Spanish. ir. Apt Postal 42 Suc A, Cuernavaca Mexico. LC HQ1104.

BOTTIN DES FEMMES PROFESSIONNELLES ET COMMERCANTES (MONTREAL). (BOTTIN DES FEMMES PROFESSIONNELLES ET COMMERCANTES). VFOAT Career Women on

Women

Record. 1981-. CN. French (text in English). an. Free. Le Bottin des Femmes, 376 Est rue Sherbrooke, Montreal Quebec H2X 1E6 Canada. DD 331.4025714281. *Bottin des Femmes Professionnelles et Commerciales (Montreal District Centre-Ouest), 0712-8452.*

BREAKING THE SILENCE (OTTAWA, ONT.). (BREAKING THE SILENCE). Vol. 1, No 1 (Spring 1982)-. 0713-4266. Periodical. CN. English. qt. 12 Domestic. Breaking the Silence, PO Box 4857/Station E, Ottawa Ontario K1S SJ1 Canada. Tel (613)231-3677. Ed Sherry Galey and Joan Riggs. DD 362.830971384. bk rev. Circ 1,500. Social issues of relevance to women. We are committed to practice a forum for women to voice their concerns, ideas and experiences.

BREAKTHROUGH. V. 1, No. 4- Oct. 1975-. 0384-160X. Periodical. CN. English. ir. Breakthrough, 115B Stong College, York University, Downsview Ontario M3J 1P3 Canada. DD 301.41209713541. *Women's Newsletter, 0384-1596.*

BREAKTHROUGH FOR WOMEN. VAT Breakthrough (Toronto). No. 1 (June 1980)- -. 0228-7293. Periodical. CN. English. qt. PO Box 506 Station A, Toronto Ontario M6W 1E6 Canada. DD 305.420971.

BROADSIDE. V. 1- Oct. 1979-. 0225-6843. Periodical. CN. English. mo. $34.05. Broadside Communications Ltd, PO Box 494 Station P, Toronto Ontario Canada M5S 2T1. Tel (416)598-3512. Ed Philinda Masters. DD 305.420971. bk rev. adv acc. Circ 2,500. Feminist newspaper, local, national and inter-national coverage of women's movement plus analysis of arts, politics, and news from Canadian women perspective.

BROOMSTICK. (BROOMSTICK : A PERIODICAL BY, FOR, & ABOUT WOMEN OVER FORTY). Periodical. US. English. bm. $20.00. Options for Women Over 40, 3543 18th Street, San Francisco CA 94110. Tel (415)552-7460. Ed Mickey Spencer and Polly Taylor. Ind/Abst Altern. Press Index. bk rev. adv acc. Circ 3,000. A feminist magazine by, for, and about women over 40.

BULLETIN - LIGUE DES FEMMES DU QUEBEC. (BULLETIN). Vol. 1, No. 1 (Jan. 1981)-. 0228-5886. Periodical. CN. French. qt. Free. Ligue des Femmes du Quebec, 2000 Av de l'Hotel de Ville, Montreal Quebec H2X 3B2 Canada. DD 362.83060714.

BULLETIN - OTTAWA WOMEN'S NETWORK. (BULLETIN). 0824-6599. Periodical. CN. English. bm. Ottawa Women's Network, PO Box 2053 Station D, Ottawa Ontario K1P 5W3 Canada. DD 305.4306071384. *Newsletter (Ottawa Women's Network), 0824-6580.*

BULLETIN - U.S. DEPT. OF LABOR, EMPLOYMENT STANDARDS ADMINISTRATION, WOMEN'S BUREAU. See Economics - Labor.

BUSINESS. V. 1- June 1979-. 0708-5842. Periodical. CN. English. mo. $8.00 Domestic, $10.00 US/United Kingdom. Women's Conference Institute, 43 Victoria Street/Suite 30, Toronto Ontario M5C 2A2 Canada. DD 331.481658.

BUSINESS & PROFESSIONAL WOMAN. (THE BUSINESS & PROFESSIONAL WOMAN). Began in 1934. 0045-3587. Periodical. CN. English. qt. $2.32. Canadian Federation of Business and Professional Women, 56 Sparks Street/Room 115, Ottawa Ontario K10 5A9 Canada. Tel (613)234-7619.

BUSINESS WOMAN. Vol. 1, No. 1 (Oct. & Nov. 1981)-. 0279-3954. Periodical. US. English. bm. $12.00. Business Woman, PO Box 23276, San Jose CA 95153. Tel (408)226-3311. Ed Carole J Holcomb. bk rev. adv acc. Circ 7,500. Business related articles for the upwardly mobile businesswoman. Articles suitable for management, entrepreneurial career women.

BY APPOINTMENT ONLY. (BY APPOINTMENT ONLY : REGINA WOMEN'S NETWORK ENGAGEMENT CALENDAR). VFOAT Regina Women's Network Engagement Calendar. 1984-. 0824-5355. CN. English. an. $7.95 Per Volume. Regina Women's Network, PO Box 3422, Regina Saskatchewan S4P 3N8 Canada. DD 920.72097124.

CALGARY WOMAN. VFOAT Chandelle. VAT Chandelle (Lethbridge). Summer, 1982. Vol. 1, No. 3 (July 1982)-. 0824-2860. Periodical. CN. English. qt. Calgary Woman, 1416 Ashgrove Road, Lethbridge Alberta T1K 3L7 Canada. DD 051. *Chandelle (Calgary, Alta.), 0824-2879.*

CALGARY WOMEN'S NEWSPAPER. Began with Feb. 1975 issue. 0702-9241. Periodical. CN. English. mo. $4.00. Calgary Women's Newspaper, 223 12th Avenue SW/Room 321, Calgary Alberta T2R 0G9 Canada. DD 301.4120971233.

THE CALIFORNIA WOMAN. 0008-1663. Periodical. US. English. qt. $2.00. California Federation of Business & Professional Women's Club, 833 Market Street/Suite 809, San Francisco CA 94103. Tel (415)776-0625. Ed Ginger Jarvis. adv acc. Circ 8,000. (ctrl). Magazine for working women.

CANADIAN HOME LEAGUER CEASED. (THE CANADIAN HOME LEAGUER). Began in 1953? Ceased V. 30, No. 10, April 1983. 0008-3771. Periodical. CN. English. an. $2.00. The Salvation Army, 20 Albert Street, Toronto Ontario M5G 1A6 Canada. *Home Leaguer, 0315-4904.*

CANADIAN LIVING. V. 1- Dec. 1975-. 0382-4624. Periodical. CN. English. mo. $16.98. Canadian Living, 50 Holly Street, Toronto Ontario M4S 3B3 Canada. Tel (416)482-8600. Ed Judy Brandow. Ind/Abst Can. Period. Index. DD 051. adv acc. Circ 500,000. A home service magazine designed to give Canadian women "a helping hand," whether they are working full or part-time or at home with their families.

CANADIAN WOMAN STUDIES. VFOAT Les Cahiers de la Femme. Vol. 3, No. 3 (Spring 1982)-. 0713-3235. Periodical. CN. English (French). qt. 28.00 Domestic, 31.00 Foreign. Canadian Woman Studies, 212 Founders College, York University, 4700 Keele Street, Downsview Ontario M3J 1P3 Canada. Tel (416)667-3725. Ed Elizabeth Brady. Ind/Abst Can. Period. Index. DD 305.40971. bk rev. adv acc. Circ 3,500. Bilingual (French and English) feminist journal, containing articles, book reviews, poetry, artwork. *Canadian Women's Studies, 0706-8204.*

THE CELIBATE WOMAN. VFOAT Celibate Woman Journal. Vol. 1, No. 1 (July 1982)-. 0735-4398. Periodical. US. English. sa. $8.00. The Celibate Woman, 3306 Ross Place, Martha Allen, Washington DC 20008. Tel (202)966-7783. Ed Martha Leslie Allen. A journal for women who are celibate or considering this liberating way of relating to others. For all women wishing to explore issues relating in any way to celibacy.

CHALLENGE. Periodical. US. English. mo. $15.00. National Federation of Republican Women, 310 First Street SE, Washington DC 20003. Tel (202)863-8770. Ed Kathy Hunter. (ctrl). *Winning Spirit.*

CHATELAINE. V. 1- March 1928-. 0009-1995. Periodical. CN. English. mo. 12.00. MacLean Hunter Agency Sales Division, 777 Bay Street 8th Floor, Toronto Ontario M5W 1A7 Canada. Tel (416)596-5523. Ed Mildred Istona. Ind/Abst Can. Period. Index, Mag. Index. bk rev. adv acc. A magazine for Canadian women featuring solution-oriented articles on subjects of special interest to women and their dynamic roles in today's changing society. *Canadian Home Journal.*

CHRONICLE - CANADIAN FEDERATION OF UNIVERSITY WOMEN. (THE CHRONICLE). VFOAT Chronique. VAT Chronique - Federation Canadienne des Femmes Diplomees des Universites. Began with 1920 issue. 0316-330X. CN. English (includes some text in French, 1920-1976/77). ty. Canadian Federation of University, Women Maliposa College, Wakesiah Campus, 900 5th Street, Nanimo British Columbia V9R 5S5 Canada. DD 301.41206271.

CHRYSALIS CEASED. No. 1-. 0197-1867. Periodical. US. English. qt. $15.00 Domestic, $18.00 Foreign, $22.00 Institutional. Chrysalis Subscriptions, PO Box 28761, San Diego CA 92128. Ind/Abst Women Stud. Abstr. LC HQ1101. DD 301.41205.

THE CHURCH WOMAN. See Religion, Mythology, Rationalism.

CITY WOMAN. V. 1- Sept./Oct. 1978-. 0707-6940. Periodical. CN. English. ir. $7.74. Comac Communications Ltd, 2300 Yonge Street, Suite 401, Toronto Ontario M4P 1E4 Canada. Tel (416)482-8260. Ed Karen Hanley. DD 301.4120971. bk rev. adv acc. Circ 200,000. (ctrl). A publication geared towards the career interests of professional women.

CLASS. CANADIAN LADIES ASSOCIATION OF SHOOTING SPORTS. See Recreation, Leisure - Sports.

CLEARINGHOUSE FOR FEMINIST MEDIA. Began publication with 1971 issue? 0319-6925. Periodical. CN. English. ir. 25 Per No., Free to Members, $1. Membership. Clearinghouse for Feminist Media, PO Box 207, Ancaster Ontario Canada. DD 301.412.

CLP FAWCETT BIBLIOFEM. See Bibliographies.

CNA MEMO. VAT Comite National d'Action sur le Statut de la Femme Memo. 0712-3191. Periodical. CN. French. ir. $6.00. CNA Memo, Suite 306/40 East Avenue St-Clair, Toronto Ontario M4T 1M9 Canada. DD 305.4206071.

COACHING. WOMEN'S ATHLETICS. See Recreation, Leisure - Sports.

COLLECTIONS. See Genealogy and Heraldry - Archives.

THE COLLEGIATE CAREER WOMAN. Vol. 8, No. 2 (Winter 1980/81)-. 8755-9218. Periodical. US. English. ty. $12.75. LC HD6093. DD 331.40973. *Collegiate Woman's Career Magazine, 0095-0653.*

COLLEGIATE WOMAN'S CAREER MAGAZINE CEASED. Vol. 1-8, No. 1. 0095-0653. Periodical. US. English. ty. $15.00. PO Box 202, Centerport NY 11721. LC HD6093. DD 331.40973.

COMMON GROUND (CHARLOTTETOWN, P.E.I.). (COMMON GROUND). V. 1, No. 1 (March/April 1982)-. 0715-478X. Periodical. CN. English. bm. $4.00. Common Ground, 81 Prince Street, Charlottetown Prince Edward Island C1A 4R3 Canada. DD 305.409717.

COMMUNIQUE - INSTITUTE FOR THE STUDY OF WOMEN. (COMMUNIQUE). Main/Corp Institute for the Study of Women. Spring 1982-. 0821-2589. Periodical. CN. English. ty. Free. Institute for the Study of Women, Mount Saint Vincent University, 166 Bedford Highway, Halifax Nova Scotia B3M 2J6 Canada. DD 305.405.

COMMUNIQUELLES. ENGLISH. (COMMUNIQUELLES). Vol. 7, No. 3 (April 1981)-. 0710-5126. Periodical. CN. English. ir. Free to Residents of Quebec, $2.00 Residents Outside of Quebec. Editions Communiquelles, 3585 St-Urbain Street, Montreal Quebec H2X 2N6 Canada. DD 305.409714. *Bulletin, 0709-0080.*

COMMUNIQU'ELLES. FRANCAIS. (COMMUNIQU'ELLES). Vol. 7, No. 3 (April 1981)-. 0710-5118. Periodical. CN. French. ir. Free to Residents of Quebec, $2.00 Residents Outside of Quebec. Editions Communiquelles, 3585 rue St-Urbain, Montreal Quebec H2X 2N6 Canada. DD 305.409714. *Bulletin (Centre d'Information et de Reference pour Femmes : 1978), 0708-7926.*

COMPAGNA. Vol. 1- Jan. 1972-. Periodical. Italian. ir. 4,500. Edizioni Dedalo, Viale Orazio Flacco 15, Bari Italy 70124. LC HQ1104.

COMPLETE WOMAN. Vol. 1, No. 1 (Oct. 1981)-. 0278-0534. Periodical. US. English. bm. $7.50. Associated Publishing Inc, 1165 North Clark Street, Suite 607, Chicago IL 60610. Tel (312)266-8680.

CONDITIONS. See Literature.

CONFESSIONS INTIMES. 0227-0323. Periodical. CN. French. ir. $2.00 Per No. Fax Services, 225 Est rue Roy, Montreal Quebec H2W 2M9 Canada. DD 054.1.

CONNEXIONS. No. 1 (Summer 1981)-. Periodical. US. English. qt. $25.00. Connexions, 4228 Telegraph Avenue, Oakland CA 94609. Tel (415)654-6725. Ind/Abst Altern. Press Index. bk rev. adv acc. Circ 4,000. Translations or reprints from international press by and about the concerns of women in other countries. Issues are thematic.

CONTRIBUTIONS IN WOMEN'S STUDIES. No. 1-. 0147-104X. Monographic Series. US. English. ir. Greenwood Press, 88 Post Road West, Box 5007, Westport CT 06881. Tel (203)226-3571. LC UNC. These texts and monographs are concerned with both the historical aspects of women's studies and the progress and problems of today's woman.

COSMOPOLITAN. V. 132, No. 4- April 1952-. 0010-9541. Periodical. US. English. mo. $28.93. National Magazine Company, PO Box 1000, Haywards Heath Sussex England. Ind/Abst Mag. Index, Pop. Mag. Rev., Media Rev. Dig. LC AP2. *Hearsts International Combined with Cosmopolitan.*

THE COUNTRYWOMAN. Began publication with Mar. 1934 issue. Periodical. UK. English. LC HD6073.A38.

COURAGE. Periodical. German. ir. 3.00 Single Issue. 1 Berlin 62 Postfach 309, Berlin West Germany. LC HQ1103.

Women

CRAFTSWOMAN. See The Arts (General) - Arts & Crafts, Handicrafts, Decorative Arts.

CRITICAL MATRIX. Series/Titl Princeton Working Papers in Women's Studies. Monographic Series. US. English. bm. Princeton University, 218 Palmer Hall, Princeton NJ 08544.

CSW REPORT OF THE COMMISSION ON THE STATUS OF WOMEN. Main/Corp Pennsylvania. Commission on the Status of Women. 1st- 1972/73-. 0097-9481. US. English. an. Commission on the Status of Women, Room 609 Main Capitol Building, Harrisburg PA 17120. LC HQ1438.P4. DD 323.4.

DAUGHTERS OF SARAH. See Religion, Mythology, Rationalism.

DEMOCRATIC WOMEN. (DEMOCRATIC WOMEN : ORGAN OF THE DEMOCRATIC WOMEN'S UNION OF CANADA). 0828-654X. Periodical. CN. English. mo. $0.50 Per Issue. Democratic Women's Union of Canada, PO Box 382 Station U, Toronto Ontario M8Z 5P7 Canada. DD 335.0088042.

DES LUTTES ET DES RIRES DE FEMMES. V. 2, No. 1- Oct./Nov. 1978-. 0709-4841. Periodical. CN. French. bm. $1.50. Des Luttes et des Rires de Femmes, CP 687, Station N, Montreal Quebec H2X 3N4 Canada. DD 301.41205. Pluri-Elles, 0709-485X.

DIRECTORY OF FINANCIAL AIDS FOR WOMEN. See Yearbooks, Almanacs, Directories.

DIRECTORY OF ORGANIZATIONS PROMOTING EQUAL EMPLOYMENT OPPORTUNITIES FOR WOMEN, CALIFORNIA. See Yearbooks, Almanacs, Directories.

DIRECTORY OF RESEARCH FUNDING SOURCES FOR WOMEN. See Yearbooks, Almanacs, Directories.

DIRECTORY OF WOMEN ATTORNEYS IN THE UNITED STATES. See Yearbooks, Almanacs, Directories.

DIRECTORY OF WOMEN HISTORIANS. See Yearbooks, Almanacs, Directories.

DIRECTORY OF WOMEN IN MARQUIS WHO'S WHO PUBLICATIONS. See Yearbooks, Almanacs, Directories.

A DIRECTORY OF WOMEN IN PHILOSOPHY. See Yearbooks, Almanacs, Directories.

DIRECTORY OF WOMEN IN THE MATHEMATICAL SCIENCES. See Yearbooks, Almanacs, Directories.

DIRECTORY OF WOMEN OWNED BUSINESSES AND PROFESSIONAL WOMEN : METRO ST. LOUIS AREA. See Yearbooks, Almanacs, Directories.

DIRECTORY OF WOMEN-OWNED BUSINESSES. WASHINGTON-BALTIMORE METROPOLITAN AREA. See Yearbooks, Almanacs, Directories.

DIRECTORY OF WOMEN PHYSICIANS IN THE U.S. See Yearbooks, Almanacs, Directories.

DIRECTORY OF WORKING WOMEN. See Yearbooks, Almanacs, Directories.

DONNA. Yearly V. 1- July 15, 1979-. 0225-4786. Periodical. CN. Italian (includes some text in English). sm. 50. Per No. Donna, Unit 13, 101 Toro Road, Downsview Ontario M3J 2Z1 Canada. DD 051.

DONNE RURALI.—. Italian. bm.

DOSSIER AFEAS. VAT Dossier - Association Feminine d'Education et d'Action Sociale. 0822-5605. Periodical. CN. French. mo. Association Feminine d'Education et d'Action, Sociale Bureau 200/180 Est Dorchester, Montreal Quebec H2X 1N6 Canada. DD 305.4205.

EARTH'S DAUGHTERS. Vol. 1, No. 1 (Feb. 1971)-. 0163-0989. Periodical. US. English. ir. $18.00. Earth's Daughters, Box 41 Central Park Station, Buffalo NY 14215. Tel (716)837-7778. LC PS508.W7. DD 810.809287. Circ 1,000. We are a feminist arts periodical by and for women and specializing in work supportive of women in all their diversity. We publish mainly poetry and short prose;.

EMMA. Periodical. German. mo. 3.00 Single Issue. Emma-Frauenverlags GMBH, 5000 Koln 1 Kolpingplatz La, Koln West Germany. LC HQ1103. DD 301.4120943.

ENHANCE NEWSLETTER. VAT Enhance. Vol. 1, No. 1-. 0823-8693. Periodical. CN. English. bm. Enhance Newsletter, PO Box 16042 Station F, Ottawa Ontario K2C 3S9 Canada. DD 305.405.

ENTRELLES. (L'ENTRELLES). V. 1, No. 2- Mar. 1979-. 0225-5545. Periodical. CN. French. bm. Free. L'Entrelles, CP 1398 Succursale B, Hull Quebec J8X 3Y1 Canada. DD 305.4097142. Femme d'ICI, 0225-5537.

THE EPISCOPAL WOMEN'S HISTORY PROJECT. See Religion, Mythology, Rationalism - Protestantism.

ESSENCE. V. 1- May 1970-. 0014-0880. Periodical. US. English. mo. Essence, 1500 Broadway, New York NY 10036, (subscription address: Neodata PO Box 2606 Boulder CO 80322). Tel (212)730-4260. Ind/Abst Pop. Mag. Rev., Media Rev. Dig., Read. Guide Period. Lit., Mag. Index, Psychol. Abstr. LC E185.86. DD 051. Available on microfilm from University Microfilms.

ESTIMATES. PART III, CANADIAN ADVISORY COUNCIL ON THE STATUS OF WOMEN. VFOAT Budget des Depenses. CN. English (French). $3.00 Domestic, $3.60 Foreign. Canadian Government Publishing Centre, Supply and Services Canada, Ottawa Ontario K1A 0S9 Canada. LC HQ1457. DD 305.40971.

ESTIMATES. PART III, STATUS OF WOMEN CANADA. VFOAT Budget des Depenses. CN. English (French). $3.00 Domestic, $3.60 Foreign. Canadian Government Publishing Centre, Supply And Services Canada, Ottawa Ontario K1A 0S9 Canada. LC HQ1457. DD 354.7100813.

EVERY WOMAN'S ALMANAC. See Yearbooks, Almanacs, Directories.

THE EXECUTIVE FEMALE. See Business - General Management.

FARM WOMAN NEWS. See Agriculture.

FEDERATION NEWSLETTER (UNITARIAN UNIVERSALIST WOMEN'S FEDERATION). (FEDERATION NEWSLETTER : A JOURNAL OF THE UNITARIAN UNIVERSALIST WOMEN'S FEDERATION). VFOAT UUWF Federation Newsletter. V. 1, No. 1 (Oct. 15, 1976)-. Periodical. US. English. qt. Unitarian Universalist Women's Federation, 25 Beacon Street, Boston MA 02108.

FEM. Began with Oct./Dec. 1976 issue. Periodical. MX. Spanish. qt. $24.00. Nueva Cultura Feminista AC, Ave Mex 76 Loc 8, Col P Tizapan, 01080 Mexico 20 D F Mexico. Tel 550-73-06. LC HQ1104. DD 305.4205. adv acc. Circ 16,000. (ctrl). International Feminist.

FEMINA. No. 1- July 1974-. Periodical. HT. French. ir. $10.00. Comite Haitien de Cooperation Avec la CIM-OEA, 53 Ruelle Roy, Port-au-Prince Haiti. LC HQ1511. DD 305.4097294.

FEMININ PLURIEL. V. 1, No. 1 (Sept. 1981)-. 0707-9036. Periodical. CN. French. mo. $2,00 each no., $16,00 yearly. Parallele 4 Communications, Audio-Scripto-Visuelles, 4936 Coolbrook, Montreal Quebec H3X 2K9 Canada. DD 054.1.

DER FEMINIST. Began in 1976. Periodical. German. sa. Der Feminist, Christrosenweg 5, Munchen 70 West Germany. LC HQ1103. DD 305.4205.

FEMINIST BOOKSTORE NEWS. 0741-6555. Periodical. US. English. bm. $40.00 Domestic, $45.00 Foreign. Feminist Bookstore News, P O Box 882554, San Francisco CA 94188. Tel (415)431-2093. Ed Carol Seajay. bk rev. adv acc. Circ 500. The trade magazine of the Women-in-Print movement. Reviews 60-80 books of feminist interest per issue with complete ordering information for small presses. Feminist Bookstore Newsletter.

FEMINIST FORUM. 5th issue-. 0732-6378. Periodical. UK. English. Free to regular subscribers of Women's Studies International Forum. Pergamon Press, Maxwell House, Fairview Park, Elmsford NY 10523. LC HQ1101. DD 305.405. Women's Studies International Quarterly Forum, 0733-0065.

FEMINIST ISSUES. Vol. 1, No. 1 (Summer 1980)-. 0270-6679. Periodical. US. English. sa. $25.00. Transaction Periodicals Consortium, Rutgers University, Department 2000, New Brunswick NJ 08903. Tel (201)932-2280. Ed Mary Jo Lakeland. Ind/Abst Altern. Press Index. LC HQ1101. DD 305.4205. bk rev. adv acc. Circ 800. Feminist social and political theory, devoted to an international exchange of ideas. Includes articles by English-language feminists as well as texts by women of other countries.

FEMINIST PERIODICALS. (FEMINIST PERIODICALS : A CURRENT LISTING OF CONTENTS). Vol. 1, No. 1-. 0742-7441. Periodical. US. English. qt. Free Wisconsin Residents,, $12.00 Individuals & Women's Programs, includes all Office Publications, $24.00 Institutions, includes all Office Publications. Women's Studies, Librarian-At- Large, University of Wisconsin System, 112A Memorial Library, 728 State Street, Madison WI 53706.

FEMINIST REVIEW. 1-. 0141-7789. Periodical. UK. English. ty. $50.00. Feminist Review, 11 Carleton Gardens, Brecknock Road, London N19 5AQ England. Ind/Abst Sociol. Abstr., Soc. Welf. Soc. Plan./Policy Soc. Dev., Altern. Press Index. LC HQ1154. DD 305.4205. bk rev. adv acc. Circ 3,500. Explores the diverse, theoretical and strategic issues and the differing experiences of women, in the struggle for a socialist feminist future.

FEMINIST STUDIES. VFOAT FS, Feminist Studies. V. 1- Summer 1972-. Periodical. US. English. ty. Ind/Abst Women Stud. Abstr.

FEMME. V. 1- Feb. 1975-. 0318-2452. CN. French. mo. $1.00 each no., $10.00 yearly. Editions Lizon, 385 Boul Lebeau Ville Saint-Laurent, Montreal Quebec H4N 1S3 Canada. DD 054.1.

FEMME DU QUEBEC. March/April 1979-. 0708-6423. Periodical. CN. French. mo. $1.25 each no. Femme du Quebec, 8 rue Cook 3E, Montreal Quebec G1R 5T7 Canada. DD 301.41209714.

FEMMES D'ACTION. V. 10, No. 1 (Printemps/Ete 1980)-. 0226-9902. Periodical. CN. French. qt. Federation des Femmes Canadiennes-Francaises Piece, 525 325 rue Dalhousie, Ottawa Ontario K1N 7G2 Canada. DD 305.406071. Femme d'Action, 0226-9899.

FEMMES D'ICI. V. 12- Sept. 1977-. 0705-3851. Periodical. CN. French. Association Feminine d'Education et d'Action Sociale, Bureau 200/180 East Boulevard Dorchester, Montreal Quebec H2X 1N6 Canada. DD 301.41205. A F E A S, 0381-7598.

FEMMES ET RUSSIE (PARIS, FRANCE : 1981). (FEMMES ET RUSSIE). Series/Titl Des Femmes Du M.L.F. Editent—. 1981-. Periodical. FR. French (in Russian). ir. 2 Rue de la Roquette, 75011 Paris France. LC HQ1663. DD 305.420947. Des Femmes Russes.

FFQ PETITE PRESSE. VAT Federation des Femmes du Quebec Petite Presse, Petite Presse. V. 1, No. 1 (Jan. 1981)-. 0228-8478. Periodical. CN. French. ir. Free to Members, $5.00 Nonmembers. Federation des Femmes du Quebec, Bureau 3115/1600 rue Berri, Montreal Quebec H2L 4E4 Canada. DD 305.409714. Bulletin (Federation des Femmes du Quebec), 0700-4621.

FILLES D'AUJOURD'HUI. V. 1, No. 1-. 0227-0315. Periodical. CN. French. mo. $14.70. Groupe Quebecor Inc, CP 70 Succ N, Montreal Quebec Canada H2X 3M2. Tel (514)282-9600. DD 054.1.

FILMS BY AND/OR ABOUT WOMEN. See Motion Picture.

FINANCIALLY YOURS. See Economics - Labor.

FLARE. V. 1- Sept. 1979-. 0708-4927. Periodical. CN. English. ir. $14.00. MacLean Hunter, Agency Sales Division, 777 Bay Street/8th Floor, Toronto Ontario M5W 1A7 Canada. Tel (416)596-5523. Ed Bonnie Hurowitz. DD 051. bk rev. adv acc. Canada's only national fashion, beauty and lifestyle magazine for young working women. Miss Chatelaine, 0026-5918.

FOCUS ON WOMEN. See Drug Abuse and Alcoholism.

FOCUS WOMEN. (FOCUS WOMEN : STATUS OF WOMEN/UVIC ACTION GROUP . . . ANNUAL CONFERENCE REPORT). Main/Corp Victoria Status of Women Action Group. Conference. 0713-8547. CN. English. Victoria Status of Women Action Group, 1429 Monterey Avenue, Victoria British Columbia V8S 4V9 Canada. DD 305.4206071134.

FOR INSURANCE WOMEN, NORTHEAST UPDATE. See Insurance.

Women

FORWARD (MADISON, WIS.). (FORWARD). 0745-3086. Periodical. US. English. ir. $1.50. Wisconsin League of Women Votes, 625 West Washington Avenue, Madison WI 53703. **Tel** (608)256-0827.

DIE FRAU IN DER OFFENEN GESELLSCHAFT CEASED. Periodical. GW. German. qt. 18. Eichholz-Verlag, Argelanderstrasse 173, 53 Bonn West Germany. **Ind/Abst** Coal Abstr. **LC** HQ1103.

FRAUEN UND FILM. See Motion Picture.

FRAUENJAHRBUCH. 1st Edition. German. ir. Verlag Frauenoffensive, 8 Munchen 80 Kellerstr 39, Munchen West Germany. **LC** HQ1103. **DD** 301.412.

FREE SPACE. 0821-5294. Periodical. CN. English. mo. Free Space, 1 19 St Francis Street, Ottawa Ontario K1Y 1W6 Canada. **DD** 305.40971384.

THE FREEDOM SOCIALIST. 0272-4367. Periodical. US. English. qt. $6.00. Freeway Hall Publications, 5018 Rainier Avenue South, Seattle WA 98118. **Tel** (206)722-2453. Ed Robert Crisman. **Ind/Abst** Altern. Press Index. bk rev. **Circ** 10,000. (ctrl). The intractable voice of revolutionary socialist feminism.

FRIENDLY WOMAN. (THE FRIENDLY WOMAN). 0740-5618. Periodical. US. English. qt. $4.00 Regular, $2.00 Low Income. Friendly Woman, University Friends Meeting, 4001 9th Avenue NE, Seattle WA 98105.

FROM THE STATE CAPITALS. WOMEN AND THE LAW. See Law.

FRONTIERS. V. 1- Fall 1975-. 0160-9009. Periodical. US. English. ty. $28.00. Frontiers, University of Colorado, Women Studies Program, Boulder CO 80309. **Tel** (303)492-5065. Ed Kathi George. **Ind/Abst** Am. Hist. Life, Hist. Abstr., Part A, Mod. Hist. Abstr., Hist. Abst., Part B, Twent. Century Abstr., MLA Int. Bibliogr., Books Artic. Mod. Lang. Lit., Sociol. Abstr., Soc. Welf. Soc. Plan./Policy Soc. Dev., Hist. Abstr., Hum. Resour. Abstr., Women Stud. Abstr., Public Aff. Inf. Serv. Bull. bk rev. adv acc. **Circ** 1,200. Appeals to academic and community feminists by publishing articles and creative work that are substantive and accessible to all readers interested in women's issues.

FU NU SHENG HUO. Periodical. CC. Chinese. mo. 0.25. Post Office, Cheng-Tu Shih China. **LC** HQ1766. **DD** 305.40951.

FWZ REVIEW. See History (General) - History of Asia.

GAZETTE DES FEMMES. (LA GAZETTE DES FEMMES). V. 1- Oct. 1979-. 0704-4550. Periodical. CN. French. bm. Free. Conseil du Statut de la Femme du Quebec, 8 rue Cook, 3E Etage/ Bureau 300, Quebec G1R 5J7 Canada. **Tel** (418)643-4326. **Ind/Abst** Point Repere. **DD** 305.409714. bk rev. **Circ** 48,000. General information on women's movement and feminism issues; new rights, research reports, book reviews. *Le Bulletin du C S F, 0708-3378.*

GENDAI NI IKIRU JOSEI JITEN. VFOAT Josei Jiten. 1981-. JA. Japanese. an. 3800. NIchigai Asoshietsu, c/o Dai 3 Chimokawa Building, 23-8 Omori Kita 1-chome, Ota-ku 143, Tokyo Japan. **LC** HQ1762.

GFWC CLUBWOMAN. VFOAT G.F.W.C. Clubwoman. VAT General Federation of Women's Clubs Clubwoman. 0745-2209. Periodical. US. English. bm. $4.00. General Federation of Women's Club, 1734 North Street NW, Washington DC 20036. **LC** HQ1871. **DD** 367.088042.

GOOD HOUSEKEEPING (NEW YORK, N.Y.). See Home Economics.

GRAPEVINE. (GRAPEVINE : THE NEWSLETTER OF THE LESBIAN MOTHERS' DEFENCE FUND). Summer 1979-. 0229-446X. Periodical. CN. English. ty. $2.00. Lesbian Mothers' Defence Fund, PO Box 38/ Station E, Toronto Ontario M6H 4E1 Canada. **DD** 306.8743.

HANGUK YWCA. VFOAT Korea YWCA. Periodical. KO. Korean. mo. Taehan YWCA Yonghaphoe, 1-3 1-Ka Myong-dong Chung-ku, Seoul Korea. **LC** BV1360.K8.

HARVARD WOMEN'S LAW JOURNAL. See Law.

HASILP2S MAJELIS PERMUSYAWARATAN KOWANI. Main/Corp Kongres Wanita Indonesia. Majelis Permusyawaratan. VAT Hasil-Hasil Majelis Permusyawaratan Kongres Wanita Indonesia. 1-1975-. Indonesian. ir. **LC** HQ1752.

HEALTH CARE FOR WOMEN INTERNATIONAL. See Medicine - Gynecology & Obstetrics.

HECATE. V. 1- Jan. 1975-. 0311-4198. Periodical. AT. English. sa. $7.38. Hecate, PO Box 99, St Lucia Queensland 4067 Australia. **Tel** 3773848. Ed Carole Ferrier. **Ind/Abst** Women Stud. Abstr., Altern. Press Index, Aust. Public Aff. Inf. Serv. bk rev. adv acc. **Circ** 2,000. Interdisciplinary writing from women's liberation socialist perspectives about Australia and elsewhere, plus creative writing.

HELICON NINE. V. 1- Spring/Summer 1979-. 0197-3371. Periodical. US. English. ty. $15.00. Helicon Nine, PO Box 22412, Kansas City MO 64113. **Tel** (913)381-6383. Ed Gloria Bando Hickok. **LC** NX164.W65. **DD** 700.88042. adv acc. **Circ** 3,500. Publishes literature, poetry, historical articles, essays, original art, showing the breadth and richness of women's creative achievements. A cross-general focus is attained by juxtaposing past and contemporary writers and artists.

HERIZONS. (HERIZONS : THE MANITOBA WOMEN'S NEWSPAPER). Vol. 2, No. 1 Sept. 15, 1981. 0711-7485. Periodical. CN. English. ir. $5.00. Manitoba Women's Newspaper, Box 551, Winnipeg Manitoba R3C 2J3 Canada. **DD** 305.420971. *Manitoba Women's Newspaper, 0228-7285.*

HEURES CLAIRES DES FEMMES. New Ser. No. 1- Mar. 1957-. Periodical. FR. French. ir. Union des Femmes Francaises, 15 rue Martel, Paris France 75480. *Heures Claires, Femmes Francaises.*

HOME AND COUNTRY : THE MAGAZINE OF THE NATIONAL FEDERATION OF WOMEN'S INSTITUTES. VFOAT Home and Country. Periodical. FR. English. mo. $6.99. Adprint, 69 Thorpe Road, Norwich NR1 1UA England.

THE HOMEMAKER OF THE NATIONAL EXTENSION HOMEMAKERS COUNCIL. See Home Economics.

HOMEMAKER'S MAGAZINE. V. 8- Jan./ Feb. 1973-. 0318-7802. Periodical. CN. English. ir. $18.58. Comac Communications Ltd, 2300 Yonge Street/Suite 401, Toronto Ontario M4P 1E4 Canada. **Tel** (416)482-8260. Ed Jane Gale. **Ind/Abst** Can. Period. Index. adv acc. **Circ** 1,400,000. (ctrl). Reflection of goals and concerns of today's woman, from traditional areas- food, fashion, decor and beauty-to politics, career aspirations and community responsibilities, with particular emphasis on personal relationships. *Homemaker's Digest, 0318-7810.*

THE HOOSIER BUSINESS WOMAN. 0194-5319. Periodical. US. English. qt. $1.20. IFBPWC, 305 South Harrison Street, Shelbyville IN 46176.

HOT FLASH : A NEWSLETTER FOR MIDLIFE AND OLDER WOMEN. Periodical. US. English. qt. $25.00. Hot Flash, Suny/ Behavior and Social Science, c/o J Porcino, Stony Brook NY 11794. **Tel** (516)246-3305. bk rev. **Circ** 7,000. A newsletter which addresses the myriad of health issues which affect all women in the second half of their lives.

HURRICANE ALICE. Vol. 1, No. 1 (Spring 1983)-. 0882-7907. Periodical. US. English. qt. $9.00. Hurricane Alice, 207 Lind Hall, 207 Church Street SE, Minneapolis MN 55455. **Tel** (612)376-7134. Ed Martha Roth. **DD** 305. bk rev. adv acc. **Circ** 1,000. We are a feminist cultural review, committed to re-viewing all the works of culture with a fresh feminist eye.

HUSMODERN. 0018-8026. Periodical. Swedish. Swedish Torsgaten 21, 10544 Stockholm Sweden.

HYSTERIA (HYSTERIA MAGAZINE COLLECTIVE). (HYSTERIA). Vol. 1, No. 1 (Spring 1980)-. 0229-5385. Periodical. CN. English. qt. $11.61. Hysteria, Box 2481/Station B, Kitchener Ontario N2H 6M3 Canada. **Tel** (519)576-8094. Ed Catherine Edwards. **DD** 305.4205. bk rev. adv acc. **Circ** 1,200. A feminist periodical about social, cultural, and artistic issues of interest to women and a showcase for their fiction, poetry and original art and photography.

IMAGES. 1972. 0384-5990. Periodical. CN. English. ir. 15.00 Domestic, $15.00 US. Images, PO Box 736, Nelson British Columbia V1L 5R4 Canada. **Tel** (604)352-9916. **DD** 301.41205. bk rev. adv acc. **Circ** 750. A rural Canadian feminist paper with articles, news, fiction, poetry and graphics on issues which concern women in rural British Columbia and the world.

INDEX/DIRECTORY OF WOMEN'S MEDIA. See Indexes/Abstracts.

INTER-AMERICAN COMMISSION OF WOMEN : NEWSLETTER. Vol. No. 34 (Sept. 1981)-. Periodical. US. English. General Secretariat of the Organization of American States, 1889 F Street Northwest, Washington DC 20006. **LC** HQ1239. **DD** 305.40601. *News Bulletin of the Inter-American Commission of Women.*

INTER-FEMMES. Main/Corp Equipe Inter-Femmes. V. 1- April 1979-. 0709-0099. Periodical. CN. French. Free. Equipe Inter-Femmes #4, 180 Sanborn, Sherbrooke Quebec J1H 1T3 Canada. **DD** 301.41205. (ctrl).

INTERCAMBIOS FEMENILES. See Education (General) - Higher Education.

THE INTERCONNECTION JOURNAL. 0746-9292. Periodical. US. English. bm. WESA, 363 West Drake, Ft Collins CO 80526. *HER Street Journal, 0745-0303.*

INTERFEM. Vol. 1, No. 1 (Nov. 1983)-. 0742-9436. US. English. mo. $48.00. Interfem Inc, PO Box 17379, Milwaukee WI 53217. **LC** HQ1101. **DD** 305.420973.

THE INTERNATIONAL CONGRESS ON WOMEN IN MUSIC NEWSLETTER. See Music.

INTERNATIONAL JOURNAL OF WOMEN'S STUDIES. Vol. 1, No. 1 (Jan./ Feb 1978)-. 0703-8240. Periodical. CN. English. $45.00. Eden Press, 4626 St Catherine Street West, Montreal Quebec H3Z 1S3 Canada. **Tel** (514)931-3910. **Ind/Abst** Am. Hist. Life, Hist. Abstr., MLA Int. Bibliogr., Books Artic. Mod. Lang. Lit., Women Stud. Abstr., Psychol. Abstr. **LC** HQ1101. **DD** 301.405. **NLM** W1 IN791U.

INTERNATIONAL LEAGUE OF WOMEN COMPOSERS NEWSLETTER. See Music.

INTERNATIONAL WOMEN'S NEWS JOURNAL OF THE INTERNATIONAL ALLIANCE OF WOMEN, INCORPORATING LE DROIT DES FEMMES. VFOAT Journal of the International Alliance of Women. V. 73- Feb. 1978-. 0020-9120. Periodical. UK. English (French). qt. 5.00. International Alliance Women, 7 Ullswater, 53 Putney Hill, London SW15 6RY England. **Tel** (01)788-7427. Ed Jan Marsh. bk rev. **Circ** 1,000. (ctrl). Equal rights and equal responsibilities between men and women; status of women throughout the world.

IOWA WOMAN. Jan./Feb. 1980-. 0271-8227. Periodical. US. English. qt. $15.00. Iowa Woman, PO Box 680, Iowa City IA 52244. Ed Valerie Staats. **LC** HQ1438.I7. **DD** 305.409777. bk rev. **Circ** 600. (ctrl). A quarterly journal of literature information, and art dedicated to publishing the work of midwestern women.

JERSEY WOMAN. V. 1- Feb./Mar. 1979-. 0197-4610. Periodical. US. English. bm. $9.00. Jersey Women Magazine, 85 Portland Avenue, Bergenfield NJ 07261. **Tel** (201)384-0201. Ed Louise Hafesh. bk rev. adv acc. **Circ** 15,000. Only magazine in New Jersey written for and by New Jersey women, promotes the talents and accomplishments of state females. Also provides forum for exchange of ideas, news information, career updates and fashion.

JOURNAL - CANADIAN FEDERATION OF UNIVERSITY WOMEN. Main/Corp Canadian Federation of University Women. V. 21, No. 3- Fall 1977-. 0705-3843. Periodical. CN. English (French in parallel Columns). Free. E Conway, 16111-78A Avenue, Edmonton Alberta T5R 3G2 Canada. **DD** 301.41206271. (ctrl). *Bulletin, 0319-7417.*

JOURNAL OF FEMINIST STUDIES IN RELIGION. See Religion, Mythology, Rationalism.

JOURNAL OF REPRINTS OF DOCUMENTS AFFECTING WOMEN. See Law.

Women

JOURNAL OF THE . . . CONVENTION. Main/Corp National Woman's Relief Corps. US. English. an. National Women's Relief Corps, 2916 Broadway, Toledo OH 43614. Index in last issue of volume - attached. *Journal of the . . . National Convention.*

JOURNAL OF THE NATIONAL ASSOCIATION FOR WOMEN DEANS, ADMINISTRATORS, & COUNSELORS. See Education (General) - School Organization and Administration.

JOURNAL OF WOMEN'S MINISTRIES. See Religion, Mythology, Rationalism.

JUGOSHI NOTO. No. 1-. Periodical. Japanese. ir. 1500. JCA, Shuppan 1-42, Kanda Jinbo-Cho, Chiyoda-ku Japan. LC HQ1761.

JUNIOR LEAGUE REVIEW. 0274-8584. Periodical. US. English. ir. $2.00. Association of Junior League, 825 3rd Avenue, New York NY 10022. Tel (212)355-4380. Ed Betsey B Steeger. LC HQ1903. DD 369.5. bk rev. adv acc. Circ 160,000. Contains articles on issues of general interest to women and trends affecting voluntary sector. Reports on activities of the Association, individual leagues, other community organizations.

KAIHATSU TO KENSHU. See Occupations and Careers.

KALLIOPE. See Humanities.

KENA. Spanish. mo $36.00. Hispanic Books Distribution, 240 East Yvon Drive, Tucson AZ 87504. Tel (602)887-8879. General interest periodical for the young career woman, mother or working wife.

KINESIS. V. 4, No. 29- Jan. 1974-. 0317-9095. Periodical. CN. English. mo. 40.00. Vancouver Status of Women, 400 A West 5th Avenue, Vancouver British Columbia V5Y 1J8 Canada. Tel (604)873-5925. Ed Esther Shannon. bk rev. adv acc. Circ 2,000. Status of women, Kinesis has reported on the victories, defeats activism and commitments of women across Canada and around the world for fourteen years. *Newsletter,* 0317-9109.

KINGSTON WOMEN'S CENTRE NEWSLETTER. Began publication in 197-. 0383-9915. Periodical. CN. English. ir. Kingston Women's Centre, 200 Montreal Street, Kingston Ontario K7K 3G4 Canada. DD 301.41205.

KUANG-TUNG FU NU. VFOAT Guangdongfunu. 1982, 1-. Periodical. CH. Chinese. mo. 0.23. Kuang-Chou Shih Yu Chu Canton China. LC AP95.C4. DD 305.42095127.

LA TRIBUNE - INTERNATIONAL WOMEN'S TRIBUNE CENTRE. (LA TRIBUNE). Began with No. 1 June 1983. 0748-4593. Periodical. US. French. sa. International Women's Tribune Centre, 777 U N Plaza 12th Floor, New York NY 10017.

LADIES' HOME JOURNAL. V. 6, No. 7- June 1889-. 0023-7124. Periodical. US. English. mo. $20.00. Hochman Association, 120 East 56th Street, New York NY 10022. Tel (212)371-4932. Ind/Abst Mag. Index, Read. Guide Period. Lit., Consum. Index Prod. Eval. Inf. Source. LC AP2. DD 640.5. The magazine women believe in. *Ladies Home Journal and Practical Housekeeper.*

LADY GOLFER. See Recreation, Leisure - Sports.

LADY'S CIRCLE. 0023-7191. Periodical. US. English. mo $12.97. Lopez Publications, 23 West 26th Street, New York NY 10010. Tel (212)689-3933. Ed Mary Jane Cahill. bk rev. adv acc. Circ 60,963. Articles on personalities, gallant survivors, compassionate do-gooders, diet, fashion/beauty, needlework, knitting and crochet, medicine, psychology, how to save money, how-to crafts, children.

LEGACY (AMHERST, MASS.). See Literature.

LETRAS FEMENINAS. See Literature.

LILITH (NEW YORK, N.Y.). See Religion, Mythology, Rationalism - Judaism.

LISTING OF WOMEN'S GROUPS, CANADA. See Yearbooks, Almanacs, Directories.

LUNDI. (LE LUNDI). V. 1- Feb. 19, 1977-. 0704-7886. Periodical. CN. French. wk. Le Lundi, CP 216 Succursale Longueil, Longueuil Quebec J4K 4Y3 Canada. Tel (514)285-1241. DD 054.1.

LUTHERAN WOMEN. See Religion, Mythology, Rationalism - Protestantism.

LYSISTRATA. May 1975-. 0318-1480. Periodical. CN. English. Women's Centre, 552 Pandora Avenue, Victoria British Columbia Canada. DD 301.41206271134. *Newsletter,* 0318-1472.

MADAME AU FOYER. V. 1- Oct. 1966-. 0541-6620. Periodical. CN. French. mo. $18.58. Comac Communications Ltd, 2300 Yonge Street/Suite 401, Toronto Ontario M4P 1E4 Canada. Tel (416)482-8260. Ed Pierrette Laberge-Ferth. adv acc. Circ 330,600. (ctrl) Reflection of goals and concerns of today's woman, from traditional areas- food, fashion, decor and beauty-to politics, career aspirations, and community responsibilities, with particular emphasis on personal relationships.

MAENAD. Vol. 1, No. 1 (Fall 1980)-. 0275-5629. Periodical. US. English. qt. $24.00 Institutions, $19.00 International. Paula Estey, PO Box 738, Gloucester MA 01930. LC HQ1101. DD 305.40973.

MANITOBA WOMEN'S NEWSPAPER. (THE MANITOBA WOMEN'S NEWSPAPER). Vol. 1, No. 1 (Mar. 1980)-V. 1, No. 10 (July 1981). 0228-7285. Periodical. CN. English. mo $5.42. Manitoba Women's Newspaper, 447 Webb Place, Winnipeg Manitoba R3B 2P2 Canada. Tel (204)477-1730. Ed D Holmberg-Schwartz. DD 305.420971. bk rev. adv acc. Spunky, attractive, national feminist magazine offering a comprehensive overview of issues critical to Canadian women. Covers women's health issues, childcare, employment, and legal reform.

MANUSHI. Periodical. II. English (and Hindi). bm. 24.00. Manushi, C1/202 Lajpat, Nagar-1 New Delhi 110024 India. Tel 617022. Ed Madhu Kishwar. Ind/Abst Altern. Press Index. LC HQ1104. DD 305.40954. bk rev. Circ 10,000. Life conditions, struggles, achievements of Indian women, past and present; civil rights and other movements for change; women oriented fiction, poetry, and film reviews.

MARIE-PIER. 0823-6356. Periodical. CN. French. wk. $59.00. Marie-Pier, C P 216 Succursale Longueuil, Longueuil Quebec J4K 4 Canada. DD 054.1.

MARIEMOU. VFOAT Maryam. No. 1- Jan. 1968-. 0047-5920. Periodical. French (Arabic). ir. LC HQ1804.M38.

THE MARYLAND CLUBWOMAN. (THE MARYLAND CLUB WOMAN). 0279-3490. Periodical. US. English. qt. $2.00. Mrs J N May, Circulation Manager, 717 Cabin Branch Lane, Linthicum MD 21090. LC HQ1905.M3. DD 396.062752.

ME NAISET. 0025-6277. Fl. Finnish. wk. $116.48. Sanoma Corporation, PO Box 240, SF-00101 Helsinki 10 Finland. LC AP80.

MEDIA REPORT TO WOMEN. See Communication.

MEMBERSHIP DIRECTORY - AMERICAN MEDICAL WOMEN'S ASSOCIATION. See Yearbooks, Almanacs, Directories.

MEMORIA (TURIN, ITALY). See History (General).

M/F. VAT M F. Began with: No. 1, in 1978. 0141-948X. Periodical. UK. English. sa. M/F London, 24 Ellerdale Road, London NW3 6BB England. Ind/Abst Sociol. Abstr., Soc. Welf. Soc. Plan./Policy Soc. Dev. (cum index). bk rev. adv acc. Circ 2,000. Microform. Includes women's studies, psychoanalysis, film, visual and literary arts, law, women's theory, policies of women and sexual difference.

MICHIGAN OCCASIONAL PAPERS IN WOMEN'S STUDIES. No. 1- Fall 1978-. 0731-163X. Monographic Series. US. English. ir. University of Michigan, 368 Lorch Hall, Ann Arbor MI 48109. LC UNC. *University of Michigan Papers in Women's Studies.*

MINERVA (ARLINGTON, VA.). See Military Science.

THE MISSISSIPPI BUSINESS WOMAN. See Business.

MON AMIE (MONTREAL, QUEBEC). (MON AMIE). Vol. 1, No 1 (May 81)-. 0229-9127. Periodical. CN. French. mo. $0.79 Each Number. Groupe Quebecor Inc, 225 Est rue Roy, Montreal Quebec H2W 2N6 Canada. DD 054.1.

THE MONTHLY EXTRACT; AN IRREGULAR PERIODICAL. 1972-. Periodical. US. English. bm. New Moon Publications Inc, 2 Hemlock Drive, Stamford CT 06902.

MONTREAL WOMEN'S YELLOW PAGES. VFOAT Pages Jaunes des Femmes de Montreal. June 1973-. 0705-8934. Periodical. CN. English (with French on inverted pages, 1973). ir. $4.00 Each Number. Montreal Women's Yellow Pages, 3585 St-Urbain, Montreal Quebec H2X 2N6 Canada. DD 362.8302571427.

MOTERIS. No. 1- Spalis/Gr. 1955-. 0463-6309. Periodical. CN. Lithuanian. bm. 15.00. Moteris, 1011 College Street, Toronto Ontario M6H 1A5 Canada. Tel (416)634-0393. Ed Nora Kulpaviciene. LC HQ1104. DD 059.9192. Circ 2,500. Magazine for Lithuanian women.

MOVING OUT. No. 1-Mar. 1971-. Periodical. US. English. sa. $9.00. Moving Out, Box 21249, Detroit MI 48221. Tel (313)478-0529. Ed Margaret Kaminksi. bk rev. adv acc. Circ 500. Also available on microfilm from Bell & Howell. Feminist literary and arts journal publishes quality poetry, fiction, articles, art, photos, interviews, criticism, reviews, parts-of-novels, long-poems, plays concerning women's lives and literature.

MS. V. 1- July 1972-. 0047-8318. Periodical. US. English. mo. MS Foundation for Education and Communication Inc, 370 Lexington Avenue, New York NY 10017, (subscription address: Fulfillment Corporation of America 205 West Center Street Marion OH 43302). Tel (212)719-9800. Ind/Abst Abr. Read. Guide, Read. Guide Period. Lit., Book Rev. Index, Consum. Index Prod. Eval. Inf. Source, Film Lit. Index, Media Rev. Dig., Pop. Mag. Rev., Women Stud. Abstr., Mag. Index. LC HQ1101. DD 301.412097.

MUJERES. Began in 1959?. Periodical. CU. Spanish. ir. $0.30. Apartado 2545, Habana 2 Cuba. LC AP63.

THE MUSICAL WOMAN. See Music.

THE NABW JOURNAL. See Business - Banking & Finance.

NAC MEMO. VAT National Action Committee on the Status of Women Memo. 0712-3183. Periodical. CN. English. ir. $6.00 Per Year. NAC Memo, Suite 306/40 Saint Clair Avenue East, Toronto Ontario M4T 1M9 Canada. DD 305.4206071.

NAGWS GUIDE, BASKETBALL. See Recreation, Leisure - Sports.

NAGWS GUIDE. BASKETBALL, VOLLEYBALL. See Recreation, Leisure - Sports.

NAGWS GUIDE. FIELD HOCKEY. See Recreation, Leisure - Sports.

NAGWS GUIDE. FLAG FOOTBALL, SPEEDBALL, SPEED-A-WAY. See Recreation, Leisure - Sports.

NAGWS GUIDE. GYMNASTICS. See Recreation, Leisure - Sports.

NAGWS GUIDE. LACROSSE. See Recreation, Leisure - Sports.

NAGWS GUIDE. SOCCER. See Recreation, Leisure - Sports.

NAGWS GUIDE. SOFTBALL. See Recreation, Leisure - Sports.

NAGWS GUIDE, SYNCHRONIZED SWIMMING. See Recreation, Leisure - Sports.

NAGWS GUIDE. TEAM HANDBALL, RACQUETBALL, ORIENTEERING. See Recreation, Leisure - Sports.

NAGWS GUIDE. TENNIS. See Recreation, Leisure - Sports.

NAGWS GUIDE. TRACK AND FIELD. See Recreation, Leisure - Sports.

NAGWS GUIDE. VOLLEYBALL. See Recreation, Leisure - Sports.

NAGWS RULES : BASKETBALL. See Recreation, Leisure - Sports.

NAGWS RULES. SKIING. See Recreation, Leisure - Sports.

NAGWS/ABO BASKETBALL CASEBOOK. See Recreation, Leisure - Sports.

Women

NASE ZITTJA. (OUR LIFE). VFOAT Nashe Zhyttia. 0740-0225. Periodical. US. English. mo. UNWLA Inc, 203 Second Avenue, New York NY 10003. **Tel** (212)674-5508. Ed Olga Liskiwskyi. LC HQ1104. bk rev. **Circ** 4,000. (ctrl). The official publication of Ukrainian National Women's League of America. Printed monthly in Ukranian with approximately seven pages in English.

NATIONAL BUSINESS WOMAN.
0027-8831. Periodical. US. English. bm. National Federation of Business & Professional Women, 2012 Massachusetts Avenue Northwest, Washington DC 20036. **Tel** (202)293-1100. adv acc. **Circ** 144,000. (ctrl). Articles on women's issues. *Independent Woman.*

NATIONAL DIRECTORY OF WOMEN ELECTED OFFICIALS. *See* Yearbooks, Almanacs, Directories.

NATIONAL DIRECTORY OF WOMEN-OWNED BUSINESS FIRMS. *See* Yearbooks, Almanacs, Directories.

NATIONAL MINORITY BUSINESS INFORMATION SYSTEM. *See* Yearbooks, Almanacs, Directories.

NATIONAL NOW TIMES. Main/Corp National Organization for Women. VAT National Organization for Women Times. V. 10, No. 12- Dec. 1977-. 0149-4740. Periodical. US. English. bm. $2.00 Members, $25.00 Nonmembers. National Now Times, National Organization for Women Inc, 1401 New York Avenue NW/Suite 800, Washington DC 20005-2102. Ind/Abst Pop. Mag. Rev., Altern. Press Index. *Do It Now.*

NATIONAL WOMEN'S HEALTH NETWORK NEWS. (NETWORK NEWS). 0277-0385. Periodical. US. English. bm. National Womens Health Network, 224 7th Street SE, Washington DC 20003. **Tel** (202)543-9222. DD 362.

NATIVE WOMEN'S NEWS. *See* Ethnic.

NCJW JOURNAL. Main/Corp National Council of Jewish Women. VAT National Council of Jewish Women Journal. V. 1- Dec. 1979/Jan. 1980-. 0161-2115. Periodical. US. English. qt. National Council of Jewish Women, 15 East 26th Street, New York NY 10010. **Tel** (212)875-4562. *NCJW Journal, 0161-2115.*

NEW DIRECTIONS FOR WOMEN.
0160-1075. Periodical. US. English. bm. $36.00. New Directions for Women, 108 West Palisade Avenue, Englewood NJ 07631. **Tel** (201)568-0226. Ed Phyllis Kriegel. Ind/Abst Women Stud. Abstr., Altern. Press Index. bk rev. adv acc. **Circ** 50,000. (ctrl). National feminist newspaper. News coverage extends to virtually all political, economic, medical, cultural and social issues addressed by the movement. *New Directions for Women in New Jersey.*

NEW WOMAN. V. 1- June 1971-. 0028-6974. US. English. mo. $35.00. University Microfilms International, 300 North Zeeb Road, Ann Arbor MI 48106, (subscription address: Neodata, PO Box 2606, Boulder CO 80322). **Tel** (212)685-4790.

NEWS - FEMINIST PARTY OF CANADA. Main/Corp Feminist Party of Canada. VFOAT Nouvelles - Parti Feministe du Canada. V. 1- July 1979-. 0226-1944. Periodical. CN. English (French). qt. Feminist Party of Canada, PO Box 5117 Station A, Toronto Ontario M5W 1N8 Canada. DD 305.42.

NEWS LETTER - WOMEN'S HEALTH CLINIC. (NEWS LETTER). Dec. 1983-. 0822-7586. Periodical. CN. English. sa. Free to Members. Women's Health Clinic, 304-414 Graham Avenue, Winnipeg Manitoba R3C 0L8 Canada. DD 613.0424405.

NEWSLETTER - ASSOCIATION FOR WOMEN IN MATHEMATICS. *See* Mathematics.

NEWSLETTER- ASSOCIATION OF AMERICAN LAW SCHOOLS SECTION ON WOMEN IN LEGAL EDUCATION. *See* Law.

NEWSLETTER - ASSOCIATION OF CANADIAN WOMEN COMPOSERS. *See* Music.

NEWSLETTER - CAMPUS MINISTRY WOMEN (ORGANIZATION). (CAMPUS MINISTRY WOMEN NEWSLETTER). Main/Corp Campus Ministry Women (Organization). Nov./Dec. 1976-. 0276-9565. Periodical. US. English. bm. $15.00. Campus Ministry Women, 802 Monroe, Ann Arbor MI 48104. **Tel** (313)662-5189. Ed Ann Marie Coleman. **Circ** 200. Offers support and exchange of ideas, and raises women's issues within the wider state and national campus ministry circle of organizations. *Interim.*

NEWSLETTER - CANADIAN RESEARCH INSTITUTE FOR THE ADVANCEMENT OF WOMEN.
(NEWSLETTER). VFOAT Bulletin de Nouvelles. VAT Bulletin de Nouvelles - Institut Canadien de Recherches pour l'Avancement de la Femme. Mar. 1979-. 0229-7256. Periodical. CN. English (with French text on inverted pages). ir. Canadian Research Institute for the Advancement of Women, Suite 415/151 Slater Street, Ottawa Ontario K1P 5H3 Canada. DD 362.8306071.

NEWSLETTER - COUNCIL FOR EXCEPTIONAL CHILDREN. MANITOBA BRANCH CEASED. (BULLETIN DE LA FEDERATION DES FEMMES DU QUEBEC). Main/Corp Federation des Femmes du Quebec. No longer published after V. 10, No. 3, March 1980-. 0700-4621. CN. French. ir. Federation des Femmes du Quebec, Bureau 3115/1600 rue Berri, Montreal Quebec H2L 4E4 Canada. DD 301.412062714.

NEWSLETTER - INTERNATIONAL WOMEN'S YEAR SECRETARIAT.
Main/Corp Canada. International Women's Year Secretariat. VFOAT Bulletin - Secretariat de l'Annee Internationale de la Femme. V. 1- June 1974-. Periodical. CN. text in English and French. ir. Free. International Women's Year Secretariat, Privy Council Office, Ottawa Ontario K1A 0A3 Canada.

NEWSLETTER - NATIONAL COUNCIL OF WOMEN OF CANADA.
(NEWSLETTER). 0712-3035. Periodical. CN. English. qt. $3.00. National Council of Women of Canada, 20-270 MacLaren, Ottawa Ontario K2P 0M3 Canada. DD 305.406071.

NEWSLETTER - NEWFOUNDLAND STATUS OF WOMEN COUNCIL CEASED. Main/Corp Newfoundland Status of Women Council. Jan./Feb. 1974-June 1984. 0315-2324. Periodical. CN. English. ir. Newfoundland Status of Women Council, PO Box 6072, St John's Newfoundland A1C 5X8 Canada. *Women's Place Newsletter, 0829-1217.*

NEWSLETTER OF THE CPA SECTION ON WOMEN & PSYCHOLOGY. VAT Newsletter of the Canadian Psychological Association Section on Women & Psychology. Vol. 5, No. 1 (Sept. 1980)-. 0826-1989. Periodical. CN. English. ir. Free to Members. Newsletter of the CPA Section on Women & Psychology, c/o Dr Lorna Larsen, Student Counseling Services, University of Calgary, 2500 University Drive NW, Calgary Alberta T2N 1N4 Canada. DD 155.63305. *Newsletter of the CPA Interest Group on Women and Psychology, 0229-2386.*

NEWSLETTER - ONTARIO COMMITTEE ON THE STATUS OF WOMEN. (NEWSLETTER). VAT Ontario Committee on the Status of Women Newsletter, Ontario Committee on the Status of Women News. 0227-6879. Periodical. CN. English. ty. Free to Members, $10.00 Others. Ontario Committee on the Status of Women, PO Box 188, Station Q, Toronto Ontario M4T 2M1 Canada. DD 305.4209713.

NEWSLETTER - OTTAWA WOMEN'S CENTRE. Main/Corp Ottawa Women's Centre. VFOAT Ottawa Women's Centre Newsletter. Began with June 1972 issue. 0382-8271. Periodical. CN. English. ir. $3.00. Ottawa Women's Centre, 821 Somerset Street West, Ottawa Ontario K1R 6R4 Canada. DD 301.41206271384.

NEWSLETTER - PROVINCIAL COUNCIL OF WOMEN OF BRITISH COLUMBIA. Main/Corp Provincial Council of Women of British Columbia. Sept. 1977-. 0707-0195. Periodical. CN. English. ir. Free to Members. Provincial Council of Women of British Columbia, Apartment 101, 1315-7th Avenue, New Westminster British Columbia V3M 2J9 Canada. DD 301.412062711.

NEWSLETTER - WOMEN'S EQUAL RIGHTS ASSOCIATION. (WOMEN'S EQUAL RIGHTS ASSOCIATION : NEWSLETTER). VAT W.E.R.A. Women's Equal Rights Association, Women's Equal Rights Association. 0711-4478. Periodical. CN. English. Women's Equal Rights Association, 1306-17th Avenue, Prince George Vatican City V2L 3P1 Canada. DD 305.420607112. *Women's Collective Newsletter, 0711-446X.*

NEWSMAGAZINE - CENTRE FOR WOMEN. HUMBER COLLEGE OF APPLIED ARTS AND TECHNOLOGY. CENTRE FOR CONTINUOUS LEARNING. *See* Education (General) - Higher Education.

NEWTWORK OF SASKATCHEWAN WOMEN (1983). (NETWORK OF SASKATCHEWAM WOMEN). Sept. 1983-. 0826-4929. Periodical. CN. English. ir. Free to Members, Membership $5.00 per year. Saskatchewan Action Committee on the Status of Women, 3rd Floor/2204 McIntyre Street, Regina Saskatchewan S4P 2R9 Canada. DD 305.42097124. *Network (Saskatoon, Sask.), 0712-5925.*

NEXUS (ST. CATHARINES, ONT.).
(NEXUS). 0821-6401. Periodical. CN. English. mo. $12.00. Nexus c/o YWCA, Pen Centre, St Catharines Ontario L2T 2K9 Canada. **Tel** (416)688-3912. Ed Mary Stewart and Diane Newman. DD 305.40971338. bk rev. adv acc. **Circ** 5,000. Is a not-for-profit community service publication, published by a volunteer staff for the Saint Catharines YWCA. Its purpose is to facilitate networking for women in the Niagara Region.

NOK LAPJA. 1948. Periodical. NU. Hungarian. wk. $18.58. Pannonia Books, PO Box 1017, Postal Station B, Toronto Ontario M5T 2T8 Canada. **Tel** (416)535-3963. Ed Iren Nemeti. LC HQ1104. adv acc. **Circ** 800,000. Magazine for women including short stories, fashion, cooking, embroidery, health childcare and miscellaneous news for women.

NORTH CAROLINA COUNCIL OF WOMEN'S ORGANIZATIONS ANNUAL DIRECTORY. *See* Yearbooks, Almanacs, Directories.

NORTHERN WOMAN CEASED. (THE NORTHERN WOMAN). Ceased publication in 1976?. 0319-1966. CN. English. ir. $7.74. The Northern Woman, 316 Bay Street, Thunder Bay Ontario Canada P7B 1S1. DD 301.412097131. bk rev adv acc. **Circ** 1,000. Feminist-issues concerning women.

NORTHERN WOMAN JOURNAL.
0824-4081. Periodical. CN. English. ir. Northern Woman's Centre, 316 Bay Street, Thunder Bay Ontario P7B 1S1 Canada. DD 305.4097131. *Northern Woman, 0319-1966.*

NOTICIERO (INTER-AMERICAN COMMISSION OF WOMEN) CEASED. (NOTICIERO). VFOAT Noticiero de la Comision Interamericana de Nujeres. V. 1, No. 1, (Dec. 1951/Jan. 1952)-No. 33 (Nov. 1980). 0538-2920. US. Spanish. ir. LC HQ1239.

NOUVEAU TABLIER DEPOSE. (LE NOUVEAU TABLIER DEPOSE). Vol. 3, No. 1 (Mar. 1982)-. 0820-9294. Periodical. CN. French. ir. Nouveau Tablier Depose, 1964 rue Laurier, Rockland Ontario K0A 3A0 Canada. DD 305.4097137. *Tablier Depose, 0704-4852.*

NOUVELLE FEMME (MONTREAL, QUEBEC). (NOUVELLE FEMME). No. 1, (Dec. 1983)-. 0824-0671. Periodical. CN. French. bm. $12,00. Nouvelle Femme, C P 51 Succursale D, Montreal Quebec H3K 3B9 Canada. DD 054.1.

NOUVELLES QUESTIONS FEMINISTES. No 1 (Mar. 1981)-. 0248-4951. Periodical. FR. French (summaries in English). qt. 280. Association Nouvelles Questions Feministes, 34 Passage du Ponceau, 75002 Paris France. LC HQ1102. DD 305.4205.

NOW L.A. VFOAT N.O.W. LA. VAT National Organization for Women Los Angeles. Vol. 1, No 1-2 (Feb./Mar. 1983)-. 0741-9627. Periodical. US. English. ir. $10.00. Los Angeles Chapter of the National Organization for Women, 1242 South la Cienega Boulevard, Los Angeles CA 90035. **Tel** (213)652-5572. Ed Jean Stapleton. bk rev. adv acc. **Circ** 2,500. (ctrl). Covers news of activities, legislation and events related to women's rights as well as features and reviews of topics relating to equality of the sexes.

N.Y. AFFIRMATIVE ACTION WOMEN'S STUDIES NEWS. (NY AFFIRMATIVE ACTION WOMEN'S STUDIES NEWS : A PUBLICATION FROM THE AFFIRMATIVE ACTION/ WOMEN'S STUDIES OFFICE OF THE BOARD OF EDUCATION FOR THE CITY OF NORTH YORK). VFOAT Affirmative Action Women's Studies News.

Women

VAT North York Affirmative Action Women's Studies News. Vol. 1, No. 1 (Oct. 1982)-. 0712-595X. Periodical. CN. English. ir. Free. Affirmative Action, Womens Studies Department, North York Board of Education, Yonge Street, Willowdale Ontario M2N 5N8 Canada. DD 305.4209713541. (ctrl)

NY LITTERATUR OM KVINNOR : EN BIBLIOGRAFI. See Bibliographies.

OCCASIONAL PAPERS OF THE MCMASTER UNIVERSITY SOCIOLOGY OF WOMEN PROGRAMME. See Sociology: General Works, Theory.

OCCUPATIONAL STATUS OF WOMEN IN NEW YORK STATE. See Economics - Labor.

OFF OUR BACKS. V. 1- Feb. 1970-. 0030-0071. Periodical. US. English. ir $25.00. Off Our Backs, 1841 Columbia Road NW/Room 212, Washington DC 20009. Tel (202)234-8072. Ed OFF OUR BACKS COLLECTIVE. Ind/Abst Women Stud. Abstr., Altern. Press Index. bk rev. adv acc. Circ 20,000. Women's liberation news journal: health, labor, law, abortion rights, lesbians, international and national news, reviews, interviews, conferences, letters and bulletin board.

OFFICE GUIDE FOR WORKING WOMEN. See Business.

ON CAMPUS WITH WOMEN. See Education (General) - Higher Education.

ON YOUR OWN, A DIRECTORY FOR WOMEN. See Yearbooks, Almanacs, Directories.

ONE WOMAN. VFOAT 1 Woman. Winter 1983-. 0739-6708. Periodical. US. English. qt. $10.00. One Woman Publishing, 36 East 12th Street, New York NY 10003.

OPTIMST. (THE OPTIMST). VFOAT Newsletter. Began publication in 197-. 0384-5230. Periodical. CN. English. Victoria Faulkner Women's Centre, 4051 4th Avenue, Whitehorse, Yukon Y1A 1H1 Canada. DD 301.412097191.

OUTLOOK. Periodical. US. English. ty. Iowa State University at Ames, 127 Press Building, Ames IA 50012. Tel (515)294-5980. Outlook for Today's Woman.

OUTSTANDING YOUNG WOMEN OF AMERICA. See Biographies.

PAMPHLET - U.S. DEPARTMENT OF LABOR, EMPLOYMENT STANDARDS ADMINISTRATION, WOMEN'S BUREAU. See Economics - Labor.

PARITY. See Economics - Labor.

PEDESTAL. V. 7- 1975-. 0319-1001. CN. English. $3. Domestic, $3.50 US, $4. Foreign, $10. Institutions. Pedestal, 6854 Inverness, Vancouver British Columbia V5X 4G2 Canada. DD 301.4120971133. Women Can, 0319-0994.

PENELOPE (PARIS, FRANCE). (PENELOPE : POUR L'HISTOIRE DES FEMMES). No. 1 June 1979-. 0240-9453. Periodical. FR. French. sa. 80.00. Groupe d'Etudes Feminstes de l'Universite Paris, 54 Boulevard Raspail, 75270 Paris Cedex France. LC HQ1121. DD 305.409.

PENNSYLVANIA WOMEN ANNUAL REPORT. Main/Corp Pennsylvania. Commission for Women. 0149-2225. US. English. an. LC KFP91.W6. DD 342.748087.

THE PERFORMING WOMAN. See Music.

PERSPECTIVAS ANTROPOLOGICAS DA MULHER. VFOAT Mulher. 1-. Periodical. Portuguese. ir. Zahar Editores, Caixa Postal 207, ZC-00 Rio de Janeiro Brazil. LC HQ1104. DD 305.405.

PHU N VIET NAM. VM. Vietnamese. ir. Hoi Lien Hiep Phu N Viet Nam, 47 Hang Chuoi, Ha-Nai Viet Nam. LC HQ1749.V5.

PHU NU DIEN DAN. VM. Vietnamese. mo. $51.95. Bay Vietnamese Books Distribution, PO Box 703, La Puente CA 91747. Tel (818)810-4738. Ed Hanh Ngoc. LC AP95.V5. adv acc. Circ 3,000. (ctrl). Women's magazine. Helpful articles on various aspects of practical life (family, marriage, health, beauty care, etc.). Also literary contributions by contemporary Vietnamese authors.

PIONEER WOMAN. See Religion, Mythology, Rationalism - Judaism.

PLACES OF INTEREST TO WOMEN. (PLACES OF INTEREST TO WOMEN : WOMEN'S GUIDE USA & CANADA). VFOAT Lieux d'Interets pour les Femmes. 1982-. 0731-0951. US. English (French). an. $5.25 Single Issue. Ferrari Publications, PO Box 16054, Phoenix AZ 85011.

PLAINSWOMAN. V. 1- Oct. 1977-. 0148-902X. Periodical. US. English. ir. $10.00. Plainswoman, Box 8027, Grand Forks ND 58202. Tel (701)746-8043. Ed Elizabeth Hampsten. bk rev. Circ 500. A regional magazine featuring reminiscenses, interviews, essays, poetry and fiction which reflects political and social issues of women, and their historical development.

PLENARIA NACIONAL. Main/Corp Federacion de Mujeres Cubanas. Periodical. Spanish. ir.

PLEXUS. 1974. 0274-5526. Periodical. US. English. mo. $38.00. Plexus, 545 Athol Avenue, Oakland CA 94606. Tel (415)451-2585. Ed Karen Schiller. bk rev. adv acc. Circ 12,000. News and articles by, for and about women. Includes reviews, news, sports and a monthly calendar of events.

PODER Y LIBERTAD : REVISTA TEORICA DEL PARTIDO FEMINISTA DE ESPANA. Periodical. SP. Spanish. an. Partit Feminista de Catalunya Bailen, 18 3O La, Barcelona 13 Spain. LC HQ1693. DD 305.420946.

PRAIRIE WOMAN. 0229-5059. Periodical. CN. English. bm. $4.00. Prairie Woman, PO Box 4021, Saskatoon Saskatchewan Canada. DD 305.4205. Saskatoon Women's Liberation Newsletter, 0381-8764.

PRAKIZAH INTIRNASHINAL. (PAKIZAH INTIRNASHINAL). VFOAT Pakeeza. V. 2, No. 9 September 1980. 0711-4222. Periodical. CN. English (text in Urdu). mo. $5.00, Individuals. Pakizah International, 21 Lexington Avenue, Rexdale Ontario M9V 2G4 Canada. DD 059.91439. Pakizah, 0711-4214.

THE PRESS WOMAN. See Journalism.

PRIMAVERA. See Literature.

PRO SE. See Law.

PROBE (CHICAGO, ILL.). See Religion, Mythology, Rationalism - Theology.

PROGRESSIVE WOMAN. 0033-0833. Periodical. US. English. mo. Progressive Woman, Box 510, Middleburg IN 46540. LC HQ1101. DD 335.4305.

PROSVETENA ZENA. Periodical. Serbo-Croatian -C. ir. LC HQ1104.

PSYCHOLOGY OF WOMEN QUARTERLY. V. 1- Fall 1976-. 0361-6843. Periodical. US. English. qt. Cambridge University Press, Journals Department, 150 North Avenue, New Rochelle NY 10801. Tel (914)235-0300. Ind/Abst Sociol. Abstr., Soc. Welf. Soc. Plan./Policy Soc. Dev., Women Stud. Abstr., Curr. Index J. Educ., Psychol. Abstr., Soc. Sci. Index, Soc. Sci. Citation Index. LC HQ1206. DD 155.63305. NLM W1 PS746UN. CODEN PWOQDY.

PUBLICATION - SASKATCHEWAN ADVISORY COUNCIL ON THE STATUS OF WOMEN. Main/Corp Saskatchewan. Advisory Council on the Status of Women. No. 1- 1974-. 0380-8297. Monographic Series. CN. English. Saskatchewan Advisory Council on the Status of Women, 214-230 22nd Street East, Saskatoon Saskatchewan S7K 0E9 Canada. DD 301.420971.

QUEST. (QUEST : A FEMINIST QUARTERLY). Began with Summer 1974 issue. 0098-955X. Periodical. US. English. qt $7.00. Quest: A Feminist Quarterly, 1909 Que Street Northwest, Washington DC 20009. LC HQ1101. DD 301.41205.

R A I F. RESEAU D'ACTION ET D'INFORMATION POUR LES FEMMES. (R A I F). Main/Corp Reseau d'Action et d'Information pour les Femmes. VAT Reseau d'Action et d'Information pour les Femmes. First issue, Dec. 1973. 0705-3762. Periodical. CN. French. bm. $17.79. Reseua d'Act Information Femmes, C P 5, Sillery Quebec G1T 2P7 Canada. Tel (418)658-1973. DD 322.4409714. Circ 1,000. Feminist subjects pertaining to everyday rights and life, evolution of society, of laws, with a strong basis on human rights. Includes book reviews and a column on health.

RADICAL REVIEWER. See Literature.

RAIDA. Began with May 1976 issue. Periodical. LE. English. qt. $18.00. Institute for Women's Studies in the Arab World, PO Box 11-4080, Beirut University College, Beirut Lebanon. Tel 811 968. Ed Aida Arashoghli. LC HQ1726.5. DD 305.409174927. bk rev. Circ 1,000. (ctrl). Covers the news of Arab women and all conferences and projects relating to improving the conditions of Arab women and that world, and enhancing their integration in economic development.

RAPPORT ANNUEL - CONSEIL DU STATUT DE LA FEMME. Main/Corp Quebec (Province). Conseil du Statut de la Femme. 1974/75-. CN. French. an. LC KEQ234.A72. DD 354.71400996. Rapport Annuel - Conseil du Statut de la Femme, 0705-6435.

REFRACTORY GIRL. No. 1- Summer 1973-. 0310-4168. AT. English. ir $7.38. Refractory Girl, 62 Regent Street, Chippendale New South Wales 2008 Australia. Ind/Abst APAIS, Aust. Public Aff. Inf. Serv.

REPERTOIRE (VIDEO FEMMES). See Yearbooks, Almanacs, Directories.

REPORT AND RECOMMENDATIONS TO THE GOVERNOR AND THE GENERAL ASSEMBLY - ILLINOIS. COMMISSION ON THE STATUS OF WOMEN. Main/Corp Illinois. Commission on the Status of Women. US. English. an. Commission on the Status of Women, 1166 Debbie Lane, Macomb IL 61455. LC HQ1438.I3. DD 301.41209773. Women - Agents of Change.

REPORT OF THE IDAHO COMMISSION ON WOMEN'S PROGRAMS. See Law.

REPORT - WOMEN'S DEVELOPMENT PROGRAMME (BANGLADESH). Main/Corp Women's Development Programme (Bangladesh Academy for Rural Development). English. ir.

RESEARCH REPORTS - NAGWS. See Recreation, Leisure - Sports.

THE RESOURCEFUL WOMAN. V.1- July 1978-. Periodical. US. English. mo. Women's Resource Center, 1961 Government Street, Baton Rouge LA 70806.

RESOURCES FOR FEMINIST RESEARCH : RFR. VFOAT RFR., Documentation sur la Recherche Feministe : DRF. Began with Mar. 1979 issue. 0707-8412. Periodical. CN. English (French). qt. $27.86. RFR/DRF, 252 Bloor Street West, Toronto Ontario M5S 1V6 Canada. Tel (416)923-6641. Ed Frances Rooney. Ind/Abst Int. Labour Doc., Am. Hist. Life, Women Stud. Abstr., Sociol. Abstr., Soc. Welf. Soc. Plan./Policy Soc. Dev., Hist. Abst., Part B, Twent. Century Abstr., Hist. Abstr., Hist. Abst., Part B, Twent. Century Abstr. LC HQ1101. DD 305.405. bk rev. adv acc. Circ 2,000. Research on women and sex roles. Canadian Newsletter of Research on Women, 0319-4477.

RESOURCES FOR FEMINIST RESEARCH. SPECIAL PUBLICATION. VFOAT Documentation sur la Recherche Feministe. Special Publication. 5 (Spring) 1979-. 0820-9677. CN. English (includes some text in French). ir. 40.00 Domestic, 50.00 Foreign. Resources for Feminist Research Special Publication, 252 Bloor Street West, Toronto Ontario M5S 1V6 Canada. Tel (416)923-6641. Ed Melanie Randall, Mary Louise Adams, and Frances Rooney. DD 305.405. bk review. adv acc. Circ 1,200. Canadian journal of women's studies. Includes book reviews, abstracts, and lists of work in progress. Interdisciplinary. Canadian Newsletter of Research on Women. Special Publication.

REVUE DES FERMIERES. (LA REVUE DES FERMIERES). VFOAT Fermieres. V. 1- Nov./Dec. 1974-. 0381-8225. Periodical. CN. French. bm. $6.19. Revue des Fermieres, 3945 St Martin Boulevard West, Laval Quebec H7T 1B7 Canada. Tel (514)688-6380. Ed Pierratte Pare Walsh. DD 054.1. bk rev. adv acc. Circ 100,000. (ctrl). Deals with everyday concerns of women, their lifestyle, marriage, arts and crafts, and the traditional values of French Canada and Franco-Americans with French-Canadian ancestry.

RISK MANAGEMENT FOR EXECUTIVE WOMEN. See Business - General Management.

ROCHESTER WOMEN. Vol. 1, Issue 1 (Oct. 1983)-. Periodical. US. English. mo $15.95. Rochester Women Magazine, 771 Ridge Road, Webster NY 14580. Tel (716)671-1490.

Women

ROOM OF ONE'S OWN. See Literature.

SAGE (ATLANTA, GA.). (SAGE). Vol. 1, No. 1 (Spring 1984)-. 0741-8639. Periodical. US. English. sa. $25.00. Sage, PO Box 42741, Atlanta GA 30311-0741. DD 305.

SAGE YEARBOOKS IN WOMEN'S POLICY STUDIES. See Yearbooks, Almanacs, Directories.

SALUT CHERIE. No. 1- April 1979-. 0708-5443. Periodical. CN. French. mo. $1.75 Per Number. DD 301.41205.

SAVVY. V. 1- Jan. 1980-. 0194-2581. Periodical. US. English. mo. $12.00. Savvy Company, 3 Park Avenue, New York NY 10016. **Tel** (212)340-9200. **Ind/Abst** Mag. Index, Pop. Mag. Rev. LC HF5500.3.U54. DD 331.4816580973. adv acc. **Circ** 400. Geared towards career oriented women. It is full of tips on how to succeed in the business world. Spells out some of the pitfalls which women with little experience in business should watch out for.

SCHWEIZER FRAUENBLATT, MIR FRAUE. Periodical. German. mo. 45.00. Verlag Schweizer Frauenblatt Mir Fraue, Postfach 8703, Erlanbach West Germany.

SHAPE. VFOAT Shape Magazine. 0744-5121. Periodical. US. English. mo. $20.00. Shape Magazine, 21100 Erwin Street, Woodland Hills CA 91367. **Tel** (213)603-0648. **Ed** Chris MacIntyre. adv acc. **Circ** 500,000. A women's magazine on health, nutrition, fitness and fashion for today's women on the go.

SHE. 1971/72-. 0037-3370. US. English. mo. $23.00. National Magazine Company Ltd, Oakfield House Perrymount Road, Haywards Heath Sussex England. **Tel** 01-874-1181.

SIGNS. V. 1- Autumn 1975-. 0097-9740. Periodical. US. English. qt. University of Chicago Press, 11030 South Langley Avenue, Chicago IL 60672. **Tel** (312)753-3347. **Ind/Abst** Am. Hist. Life, Soc. Sci. Index, Soc. Sci. Citation Index, Curr. Index J. Educ., Int. Labour Doc., MLA Int. Bibliogr. Books Artic. Mod. Lang. Lit., Psychol. Abstr., Recent Publ. Artic., Sociol. Abstr., Women Stud. Abstr., Writ. Am. Hist., ABC Pol Sci, Hist. Abstr., Part A, Mod. Hist. Abstr., Hist. Abstr. Part B, Twent. Century Abstr., Hist. Abstr. LC HQ1101. DD 301.41205.

SING HEAVENLY MUSE. See Literature.

SINISTER WISDOM. See Literature.

SISTER; WEST COAST FEMINIST NEWSPAPER. V. 4- Jan. 1973-. Periodical. US. English. mo. Women's Center Newsletter.

SOCIALIST WOMAN. Periodical. UK. English. ir. Relgocrest Ltd, 32819 Upper Street, London England.

SOROPTIMIST OF THE AMERICAS. (THE SOROPTIMIST OF THE AMERICAS). V. 48- Aug./Sept. 1974-. 0097-9562. US. English. bm. Soroptimist International of the Americas, 1616 Walnut Street, Philadelphia PA 19103. LC HD6050. DD 369.5. American Soroptimist.

SOUTHERN CALIFORNIA WOMEN'S CAUCUS FOR ART. See The Arts (General).

SOUTHERN FEMINIST. Began publication in 1984. 8756-0569. Periodical. US. English. bm. $15.00. Southern Feminist Inc, PO Box 1846, Athens GA 30603. **Tel** (404)353-0312. **Ed** Sharron Hannon. DD 305. bk rev. adv acc. **Circ** 5,000. Newspaper covering women's rights issues and activities in 12 Southern states. Features include politics, work, health, arts and media, and more.

SOUTHWEST WOMAN. Vol. 2, No. 93 (May 1982)-. 0744-5938. Periodical. US. English. mo. Southwest Woman, 11824 Radium, San Antonio TX 78216. Southwest Secretary, 0274-8967.

SOVIET WOMAN. No. 1- 1945-. 0038-5913. Periodical. UR. English (Russian, Arabic, Bengali, Chinese, French, German, Hindi, Hungarian, Japanese, Korean and Spanish). mo. Soviet Woman, Anti Fashistskii Komitet Sovetskikh Zhenshehin, Moscow USSR. LC HQ1661. DD 396.

SPARE RIB (LONDON, ENGLAND). (SPARE RIB). No. 1- July 1972-. 0306-7971. Periodical. UK. English. mo. $13.80. Spare Rib, 27 Clerkenwell Close, London EC1R 0AT England. **Ind/Abst** Altern. Press Index. bk rev. adv acc. **Circ** 30,000. (ctrl). A 60-page magazine written by women for women- news, reviews, poetry, fiction, articles on law, work, sexuality, politics, health, the international women's movement.

THE SPOKESWOMAN CEASED. Began with June 1970 issue. Ceased with Dec. 1981 issue. 0038-7738. Periodical. US. English. mo. $27.00. **Ed** K Wellisch. **Ind/Abst** Ref. Source.

THE SPORTSWOMAN. See Recreation, Leisure - Sports.

SPRINGER SERIES. FOCUS ON WOMEN. (SPRINGER SERIES, FOCUS ON WOMEN). VFOAT Focus on Women. V. 1-. 0272-202X. Monographic Series. US. English. ir. Springer Publishing Company, 200 Park Avenue South, New York NY 10003. **Ed** V Franks. LC UNC. NLM W1 SP685KD.

STATUS OF WOMEN NEWS. V. 1- Summer 1973-. 0381-9418. Periodical. CN. English (includes some text in French). ir. National Action Committee on Status of Women, 40 St Clair Avenue East, Toronto Ontario M4T 1M9 Canada. **Tel** (416)922-3246. **Ed** Pat Daley and Andree Cote. bk rev. adv acc. **Circ** 3,000. News on matters of interest to Canadian women. Topics include pensions, equal pay, day care, reproductive choice, developments in the law, regional perspectives, interviews, and more.

STRENGTH. Began with V. 3, No. 1 (Sept. 1975). 0383-6940. Periodical. CN. English. ir. Free to Members. The Women's Place, 42-B King Street South, Waterloo Ontario N2J 1N8 Canada. DD 301.41206271344. Woman's Place, 0383-6932.

STUDIES ON WOMEN ABSTRACTS. See Indexes/Abstracts.

STUDYING WOMEN. V. 1-. US. English. an.

SUARA AISYIYAH. Main/Corp Aisyiyah (Association). Periodical. Indonesian. ir. 100 Each Issue. P P Aisyiyah Yogyakarta, Jalan Kha Dahlan 99, Yogyakarta Indonesia. LC HQ1170.

SUCCESSFUL SALESWOMAN. See Business.

SUCCESSFUL WOMAN. (SUCCESSFUL WOMAN : OFFICIAL PUBLICATION OF THE AMERICAN SOCIETY OF PROFESSIONAL AND EXECUTIVE WOMEN). Vol. 4, No. 9 (Feb. 1983)-. 0739-6945. Periodical. US. English. bm. $18.00. American Society of Professional & Executive Women, 1511 Walnut Street, Philadelphia PA 19102. **Tel** (215)563-4415. **Ed** Hennie Shore. bk rev. adv acc. Promotes a positive attitudinal environment for career women via practical information and benefits; focuses on commitment to personal achievement and societal contribution. Ascend Report, 0275-0260.

SWAG. STATUS OF WOMEN ACTION GROUP. (SWAG : VICTORIA STATUS OF WOMEN NEWS). VAT Status of Women Action Group. 0229-4982. Periodical. CN. English. mo. SWAG, PO Box 6296 Station C, Victoria British Columbia V8V 5L5 Canada. DD 305.4209711. Lysistrata, 0318-1480.

SWE NEWSLETTER. See Engineering.

TETES DE PIOCHE. (LES TETES DE PIOCHE). March 1976-. 0383-0837. Periodical. CN. French. ir. 0.50 Per No. Les Tetes de Pioche, CP 247 Succursale Ahuntsic, Montreal Quebec Montreal. DD 301.41205.

TEXAS WOMAN. V. 1- Feb. 1979-. 0160-0338. Periodical. US. English. mo. Paragon III Associates, 5551 Yale Boulevard/Suite 7, Dallas TX 75206.

TEXAS WOMAN. 1934. 0279-2443. Periodical. US. English. bm. $3.00. Texas Federation of Business and Professional Women's Clubs, 6100 Camp Bowie Boulevard, Room 115, Ft Worth TX 76116. **Ed** Gilda Murray. bk rev. adv acc. Articles of appeal to working Texas women, update on new laws, economic trends, political issues, high tech growth affecting women.

TIEN I. Ti 3 Chuan-Ti 19 Tse. Chinese. ir. LC HQ1104.

TIJDSCHRIFT VOOR VROUWENSTUDIES. Vol. 1, No. 1-. Periodical. Dutch. ir. 30.00. Sun Socialistiese Uitgeverij Nijmengen, Bijleidsingel 9, 6521 Am Nijmengen Netherlands. LC HQ1657.

TODAY'S CHRISTIAN WOMAN. See Religion, Mythology, Rationalism - Theology.

TOI. 1st- Yearly V. 0384-5249. Periodical. CN. French. mo. DD 054.1.

TOMIN FUJIN NO GONJO. JA. Japanese. ir. Tokyo-to Minseikyoku, 8-1 Marunouchi-3 chome, Chiyoda-ku, Tokyo Japan. LC HQ1765.T64.

TOMIN FUJIN NO ISHIKI TO JITTAI CHOSA HOKOKUSHO. Japanese. ir. Tokyo-To Minseikyoku Fujinbu, 8-1 Marunouchi 3 Chiyoda-Ku, Tokyo 100 Japan. LC HQ1765.T64.

TORONTO WOMEN & EDUCATION NEWS. Vol. 1, No. 1 (Oct. 1981)-. 0712-2675. Periodical. CN. English. ir. Toronto Women & Education News, c/o Board of Education for the City of Toronto, 155 Colllege Street, Toronto Ontario M5P 1T6 Canada. DD 305.4205.

TORONTO WOMEN'S YELLOW PAGES. 1974-. 0319-6917. CN. English. Toronto Women's Yellow Pages, Box 153 Station Q, Toronto Ontario M4T 2M1 Canada. DD 917.135410025.

THE TRIBUNE - INTERNATIONAL WOMEN'S TRIBUNE CENTRE. (THE TRIBUNE : A WOMEN AND DEVELOPMENT QUARTERLY). 0738-9779. Periodical. US. English. qt. $8.00. International Women's Tribune Centre, 305 East 46th Street, New York NY 10017. Newsletter (International Women's Tribune Centre).

TRIVIA. See Literary and Political Reviews.

TULSA STUDIES IN WOMEN'S LITERATURE. See Literature.

TW. TODAY'S WOMAN. (TW : TODAY'S WOMAN). VFOAT Today's Woman. VAT TW Magazine. Vol. 1, No. 1 (Winter 1980)-. 0711-7426. Periodical. CN. English. ir. Free. TW Magazine, 401 Richmond Street West, Toronto Ontario M5V 1X3 Canada. DD 051. (ctrl).

U OF T WOMAN'S NEWSMAGAZINE. VAT University of Toronto Woman's Newsmagazine. No. 1-. 0228-9024. CN. English. Free on University of Toronto Campuses. U of T Woman's Newsmagazine, 132 Medland Street, Toronto Ontario M6P 2N5 Canada. DD 305.4205.

UNION WOMAN. See Economics - Labor.

UPSTREAM. V. 1- Oct. 28, 1976-. 0700-9992. Periodical. CN. English. bw. $10.00. Feminist Publications of Ottawa, 227 Laurier Avenue West/Suite 207, Ottawa Ontario K1P 5J7 Canada. DD 301.4120971384.

VIDEO FEMMES. VFOAT Video Femmes. 1978-. 0225-0632. Periodical. CN. French. qt. $2.00 Each Number. Centre la Femme et le Film, #3875 10 rue McMahon, Quebec Quebec G1R 3S1 Canada. DD 016.3054.

VIE DE FEMME. Vol. 1, No 1 (22 Oct. 1977)-. 0703-9875. Periodical. CN. French. wk. $.50 Each Number. Vie de Femme, 4270 rue Papineau, Montreal Quebec H2H 1S9 Canada. DD 305.409714.

VIE EN ROSE. (LA VIE EN ROSE). Vol. 1, No. 1(March/April/May 1980)-. 0228-5479. Periodical. CN. French. mo. $14.70. La Vie en Rose, 3963 St Denis, Montreal Quebec H2W 2M4 Canada. **Ind/Abst** Point Repere. DD 305.409714.

VIEWPOINT. 0194-5289. Periodical. US. English. qt. $2.00 Domestic, $3.50 Canada. Viewpoint, 5211 Auth Road, Camp Springs MD 20023. Women's Viewpoint, 0164-8020.

VIP - LUTHERAN WOMEN'S MISSIONARY LEAGUE. WYOMING DISTRICT. See Religion, Mythology, Rationalism - Protestantism.

VIRGINIA DIVISION BULLETIN. Main/Corp American Association of University Women. Virginia Division. 0164-842X. Periodical. US. English. qt. $.97 Includes in Dues. Virginia Division Bulletin, 12816 Tewksbury Drive, Herndon VA 22071.

VIRTUE. See Religion, Mythology, Rationalism - Theology.

VIVA. V. 1- Dec. 1974-. Periodical. English. ir. 5.00 Single Issue. Trend Publishers, PO Box 44466, Nairobi Kenya. LC HQ1101. DD 301.412096762.

VIVRE. See Beauty & Cosmetics.

THE VOCAL MAJORITY. Began in 1970. 0148-4230. Periodical. US. English. mo. $15.00. National Organization for Women, 425 13th Street NW/Suite 1001, Washington DC 20004. **Tel** (202)3876895. LC HQ1. DD 301.41205.

VOILA. See Sociology: General Works, Theory.

Women

VOX BENEDICTINA. See Religion, Mythology, Rationalism - Roman Catholic Church.

VROUWEN EN HUN BELANGEN. Periodical. NE. Dutch. ir. Vrouwen en hun Belangen, Breestraat 126, Amsterdam The Netherlands.

WANITA DALAM PEMBANGUNAN. Began with Nov. 1980 issue. 0216-3209. Periodical. IO. Indonesian. ir. Kantor, Taman Merdeka Barat 3, Jakarta Pusat Indonesia. LC HQ1751.

WARM JOURNAL. See The Arts (General) - Art.

WEAL WASHINGTON REPORT. Main/Corp Women's Equity Action League. VAT Women's Equity Action League Washington Report. 1971. 0300-6867. US. English. bm. $50.00. WEAL Washington Report, 1250 Eye Street Northwest #305, Washington DC 20005. Tel (202)898-1588. Ed Char Mollison. bk rev. Publication focusing on issues, legislation, supreme court rulings, executive branch actions, etc.

WIDENING HORIZONS. 0049-7614. Periodical. UK. English (English, French and Spanish). ir. International Federation of Business & Professional Women, 54 Bloomsbury Street, London WCIB 3QU England. LC HD6050. *Independent Woman.*

WIFELINE. See Military Science.

WIN NEWS. (NEWS - WOMEN'S INTERNATIONAL NETWORK). Main/Corp Women's International Network. VFOAT Women's International Network News. V. 1- Jan. 1975-. 0145-7985. Periodical. US. English. qt. $30.00. Womens International Network, 187 Grant Street, Lexington MA 02173. Tel (617)862-9431. Ed Fran P Hosken. LC HQ1101. DD 301.41205. bk rev. adv acc. Circ 1,100. An open participatory by, for, and about women, it reports on the status of women and women's rights around the globe.

WINNIPEG WOMAN. V. 1- July/Aug. 1979-. 0709-6844. Periodical. CN. English. ir. $13.99. Pennex Ltd, 107 Paramount Road, Winnepeg Manitoba R2X 2W6 Canada. DD 301.412097127.

THE WISE WOMAN. 0883-119X. Periodical. US. English. qt. $6.00. The Wise Woman, 2441 Cordova Street, Oakland CA 94602. DD 305.

WLW JOURNAL. See Library and Information Science.

WOMAN CONSTITUTIONALIST. 0043-728X. Periodical. US. English. mo. Woman Constitutionalist, 310 West Robb Street, PO Box 220, Summit MS 39666.

THE WOMAN CPA. See Business - Accounting.

WOMAN IN HISTORY. Vol. 1-. 0195-9743. Monographic Series. US. English. mo. Monument Press, 513 South Rosemont Press, Dallas TX 75208. DD 306.

WOMAN LOCALLY. VFOAT Capitaland Woman. V. 1- Oct. 1978-. Periodical. US. English. mo. Captialand Woman Publishers, 97 Columbia Street, Albany NY 12210.

THE WOMAN MBA. See Business.

WOMAN OF POWER. Spring 1984-. 0743-2356. Periodical. US. English. sa. $18.00. Woman of Power Inc, PO Box 827, Cambridge MA 02238.

WOMANART. See The Arts (General) - Art.

WOMAN'S ART JOURNAL. See The Arts (General) - Art.

WOMAN'S DAY. 0043-7336. Periodical. US. English. ir. CBS Publications Ltd, PO Box 807, Mineaola MY 11501. Tel (203)622-2500. Ind/Abst Consum. Index Prod. Eval. Inf. Source, Bibliogr. Agric., Mag. Index, Access.

WOMAN'S HOME COMPANION. Periodical. PH. English. wk. $40.00. Woman's Home Companion, 70 18th Avenue Murphy, Quezon city Philippines.

THE WOMAN'S PULPIT. See Religion, Mythology, Rationalism - Theology.

WOMAN'S TOUCH. VFOAT Woman's Touch. Leader Edition. 0190-4620. Periodical. US. English (Spanish). bm. $4.50. Assemblies of God Inc, 1445 Boonville Avenue, Springfield MO 65802. Tel (417)862-2781. *Slant.*

WOMAN'S VOICE (NAIROBI, KENYA). (WOMAN'S VOICE : OFFICIAL JOURNAL OF MAENDELEO YA WANAWAKE). Vol. 1, No. 1 (Apr.-June 1979)-. Periodical. English. qt. 7.50 Each Issue. Peter Moll Africa Ltd, Richmond House, Mfangano Street, Box 40106, Nairobi Kenya. LC HQ1101. DD 305.4096762. *Sauti Ya Mabibi.*

THE WOMAN'S WORLD . . . CEASED. V. 1-3, Dec. 1887-Oct. 1890. Periodical. UK. English. mo. World Wide Subscription Services, Rosehill Ticehurst, East Sussex TN5 7AJ England. Ed Oscar Wilde.

WOMAN'S WORLD. V. 1- Oct. 14, 1980-. 0272-961X. Periodical. US. English. wk. $49.50. German Language Publications, 560 Sylvan Avenue, Englewood Cliffs NJ 07632. Tel (201)569-0006.

WOMANSPEAK. V. 1- 1974-. 0311-8479. Periodical. AT. English. qt. 10.00. Womanspeak, PO Box 103, Spit Junction News South Wales 2088 Australia. Ed Collective. bk rev. adv acc. Circ 1,500. Feminist publication, non-profit making, published by a small collective in New South Wales states.

WOMANSPIRIT CEASED. VFOAT Woman Spirit. Began with Autumn Equinox 1974. Ceased with Vol. 10, No. 40 (Summer Solstice). 0736-6930. Periodical. US. English. qt. $8.00. Womanspirit, 2000 King Mountain Trail, Wolf Creek OR 97497. Ind/Abst Altern. Press Index. LC HQ1101. DD 305.405. bk rev. Ten years of documenting women's spirituality. All back issues available.

WOMEN CEASED. Began with Fall 1969 issue. Ceased V. 8, 1983. 0043-7433. Periodical. US. English. ty. $15.00. Women, 3028 Greenmount Avenue, Baltimore MD 21218. Ind/Abst Altern. Press Index, Women Stud. Abstr. LC HQ1101. DD 301.41205. Available on microfilm from Bell & Howell to Oct. 1971.

WOMEN. Main/Corp United States. Citizens' Advisory Council on the Status of Women. 1970-. 0095-1536. US. English. an. Superintendent of Documents, US Government Printing Office, Washington DC 20402. LC HD6093. DD 301.4120973.

WOMEN ALONG BUSINESS LINES. See Business.

WOMEN AND ENVIRONMENTS. Vol. 4, No. 1/2 (June 1980)-. 0229-480X. Periodical. CN. English. ty. $15.00. Centre for Urban and Community Studies, Room 426/University of Toronto, 455 Spadina Avenue, Toronto Ontario M5S 2G8 Canada. Tel (416)978-4478. Ed Judith Kjellberg. DD 305.405. bk rev. Circ 1,000. A magazine that explores feminist perspectives on the natural and built environments. *Women and Environments International Newsletter, 0229-4796.*

WOMEN & HEALTH. See Medicine - Gynecology & Obstetrics.

WOMEN & HISTORY. VFOAT Women and History. No. 1 (Spring 1982)-. 0276-3885. Periodical. US. English. qt. $48.00 Institutions, $65.00 Libraries. Haworth Press, 28 East 22nd Street, New York NY 10010. Ind/Abst Am. Hist. Life, Hist. Abstr., Part A, Mod. Hist. Abstr., Hist. Abst., Part B, Twent. Century Abstr., Sociol. Abstr., Public Aff. Inf. Serv. Bull.

WOMEN AND LANGUAGE NEWS. See Linguistics.

WOMEN AND MINORITIES IN SCIENCE AND ENGINEERING. See Science (General).

WOMEN AND MINORITY MANPOWER STATISTICS. See Statistics.

WOMEN & POLITICS. VAT Women and Politics. V. 1- Spring 1980-. 0195-7732. Periodical. US. English. qt. $102.00. Haworth Press, 28 East 22nd Street, New York NY 10010. Tel (212)228-2800. Ed Sarah Slavin. Ind/Abst Sociol. Abstr., ABC Pol Sci, Public Aff. Inf. Serv. Bull. LC HQ1236. DD 305.42. bk rev. adv acc. Circ 485. This journal deals with description of the behavior, performance, and problems of women who participate in either mass or elite politics.

WOMEN AND THE LABOR FORCE : STATE OF ILLINOIS. See Economics - Labor.

WOMEN & WORK. See Economics - Labor.

WOMEN AND WORK (BEVERLY HILLS, CALIF.). See Economics - Labor.

WOMEN ARTISTS NEWS. See The Arts (General).

WOMEN AT WORK. See Economics - Labor.

WOMEN (BOCA RATON, FLA.). (WOMEN). Series/Titl Social Issues Resources Series. Vol. 1, Article 1-. 0273-0014. US. English. an. Social Issues Resources Series Inc, PO Box 2507, Boca Raton FL 33432. Ed Eleanor C Goldstein. LC HQ1101. DD 305.405.

WOMEN CAN. Began with Mar. 1974 issue. 0319-0994. Newspaper. CN. English. 3.00 Domestic, 3.50 US, 4.00 Others; 10.00 Institutions. Women Can, 6854 Inverness, Vancouver British Columbia V5X 4G2 Canada. DD 301.4120971133. *Pedestal, 0016-5476.*

WOMEN EXECUTIVES NEWSLETTER. See Business.

WOMEN IN A CHANGING WORLD. Periodical. SZ. English. ir. $1.00. Women's Desk, World Council of Churches, 150 Route de Ferney, 1211 Geneva 20 Switzerland.

WOMEN IN ACTION CEASED. -V. 11, No. 2 (July/Aug. 1981). 0090-2489. US. English. bm. Superintendent of Documents, US Government Printing Office, Washington DC 20402.

WOMEN IN BUSINESS. See Business.

WOMEN IN BUSINESS. See Business.

WOMEN IN DESIGN INTERNATIONAL COMPENDIUM. See The Arts (General) - Arts & Crafts, Handicrafts, Decorative Arts.

WOMEN IN FORESTRY. See Forestry.

WOMEN IN MEDICAL ACADEMIA. See Medicine.

WOMEN IN NEBRASKA; A LABOR FORCE ANALYSIS. See Economics - Labor.

WOMEN IN THE LABOR FORCE. See Economics - Labor.

WOMEN IN THE LABOUR FORCE. FACTS AND FIGURES. See Economics - Labor.

WOMEN IN THE UNIVERSITY GRADUATING POPULATION. See Education (General) - Higher Education.

WOMEN IN THE WORKING WORLD. See Economics - Labor.

WOMEN IN TRADES NEWS. See Economics - Labor.

WOMEN LAW REPORTER. See Law.

WOMEN LAWYERS' JOURNAL. See Law.

WOMEN LIKE ME. See Yearbooks, Almanacs, Directories.

WOMEN OF CHINA. VFOAT Chung-Kuo Fu Nu. Began in 1953. Periodical. English. mo. $33.00. China Books & Periodicals Inc, 2929 24th Street, San Francisco CA 94110. Tel (415)282-2994. LC HQ1736. DD 396.05.

WOMEN OF EUROPE. Periodical. English. bm. Commission of the European Communities, Directorate of General Information, Information for Women's Organizations and Press, rue de la Loi 200, B-1049 Brussels Belgium. LC HQ1101. DD 305.4094.

WOMEN OF KOREA. 0512-1817. Periodical. KO. English. qt. Korea Publications Export, Pyongyang DPRK Korea. LC HQ1765.6. DD 305.4095193.

WOMEN ORGANIZING. 0732-992X. Periodical. US. English. sa. $4.00. New American Research Institute, 3244 North Clark, Chicago IL 60657. LC HQ1402. DD 305.40973.

WOMEN STUDIES ABSTRACTS. See Indexes/Abstracts.

WOMEN TO BY OF FOR AND ABOUT. V. 1- 1970-. 0043-7492. Periodical. US. English. $1.00. New Moon Publication, Box 3488 Ridgeway Station, Stamford CT 06905. LC HQ1101. DD 301.4120973.

WOMEN TODAY CEASED. V. 1-12, No. 11. 0043-7506. Periodical. US. English. bw. Today Publications & News Service, National Press Building, Washington DC 20045. *Washington Newsletter for Women.*

WOMEN TODAY (BEETON, ONT.). (WOMEN TODAY). Vol. 1, No. 1 (June 2, 1980)-. 0711-4435. Periodical. CN. English. mo. $3.00. Women Today, PO Box 104, Beeton Ontario L0G 1A0 Canada. DD 051.

Yearbooks, Almanacs, Directories

WOMEN TODAY (WASHINGTON, D.C. : 1982). (WOMEN TODAY). Vol. 12, Issue #15 (Nov. 19, 1982)-. Periodical. US. English. mo $80.00. Triangle News Service Inc, National Press Building/Suite 801, Washington DC 20045. **Tel** (301)622-5677. (cum index). *Frontline News for Women.*

WOMENEWS. VAT Women News. Vol. 1, No. 1 (May, 1977)-. Periodical. US. English. bm. Free. Pennsylvania Commission for Women, Box 1323, Harrisburg PA 17105. **Tel** (717)787-8128. Ed Lisa Paige-Stone. bk rev. **Circ** 16,000. (ctrl). News and information concerning the women of Pennsylvania and the Pennsylvania Commission for Women. *News.*

WOMEN'S AD REVIEW. 0164-7911. Periodical. US. English. sm. $214.34. Retail Reporting Bureau, 101 Fifth Avenue, New York NY 10003. **Tel** (212)255-9595.

THE WOMEN'S ANNUAL : THE YEAR IN REVIEW. US. English. an. $50.00. G K Hall & Company, 70 Lincoln Street, Boston MA 02111. **Tel** (617)423-3990. Ed G K Hall. Focuses on key events and issues that involve and affect women, written by experts in their fields. Each chapter includes an annotated list of further reading and information on women's resources and organizations.

WOMEN'S COACHING CLINIC. *See* Recreation, Leisure - Sports.

WOMEN'S CONCERNS. *See* Religion, Mythology, Rationalism.

A WOMEN'S DIRECTORY FOR THE CEDAR RAPIDS AND IOWA CITY AREA. *See* Yearbooks, Almanacs, Directories.

THE WOMEN'S GUIDE TO BOOKS. No. 1- 1974-. US. English. MSS Information Corp, 133 East 58th Street, New York NY 10022. Ed S Strausberg.

WOMEN'S HEALTH. Vol. 1, No. 1 (Dec. 1983)-. 0741-2290. Periodical. US. English. mo. $24.95. Rodale Press, 33 East Minor Street, Emmaus PA 18049.

WOMEN'S HEALTH UPDATE. Vol. 1, No. 1 (Jan./Feb. 1985). 8756-7849. Periodical. US. English. bm. $22.00. Women's Health Update, PO Box 303, Hurley NY 12443. DD 618.

WOMEN'S HOUSEHOLD. 0510-7385. Periodical. US. English. mo. $18.00. House of White Birches-Tower Press, PO Box 337, Seabrook NH 03874. **Tel** (603)474-2404. adv acc. (ctrl). Discusses and offers help and gossip on all homemaking subjects such as sewing, recipes, hobbies, handicrafts, pen pals, etc.

WOMEN'S INVESTMENT NETWORK NEWSLETTER. *See* Business - Investments.

WOMEN'S LAW FORUM. *See* Law.

WOMEN'S LEAGUE OUTLOOK. *See* Religion, Mythology, Rationalism - Judaism.

THE WOMEN'S LEGAL DEFENSE FUND NEWSLETTER. *See* Law.

WOMEN'S NETWORK DIRECTORY. *See* Yearbooks, Almanacs, Directories.

WOMEN'S ORGANIZATIONS & LEADERS DIRECTORY. *See* Yearbooks, Almanacs, Directories.

WOMEN'S ORGANIZATIONS IN HAMILTON AND DISTRICT. 0700-5547. CN. English. DD 305.402571352.

WOMEN'S ORGANIZATIONS IN HAMILTON-WENTWORTH. 0823-9142. CN. English. an. Community Information Service Hamilton-Wentworth, Suite 601/155 James Street South, Hamilton Ontario L8P 2A4 Canada. DD 305.402571352. *Women's Organizations in Hamilton and District, 0700-5547.*

WOMEN'S POLITICAL REPORTER. *See* Political Science.

WOMEN'S POLITICAL TIMES. *See* Political Science.

WOMEN'S PROGRAM. Main/Corp Michigan. Women's Commission. 0360-4780. US. English. Women's Commission, 230 North Washington Avenue, Lansing MI 48993. LC HQ1438.M5. DD 353.977400996.

WOMEN'S QUARTERLY REVIEW. VFOAT W.Q. Review. Issue #1 (Fall 1984)-. 0882-1135. Periodical. US. English. qt. $8.00. Women's Quarterly Review, 900 West End Avenue, New York NY 10025. DD 305.

WOMEN'S REPORT. 0306-1426. Periodical. UK. English. Fawcett House, 27 Wilfred Street, London SW1 England. LC HQ1101. DD 301.41205.

WOMEN'S REPORT. (THE WOMEN'S REPORT). July 1982-. 0824-3875. Periodical. CN. English. ir. Free. Women's Report c/o New Democratic Party, House Of Commong, Ottawa Ontario K1A 0A6 Canada. DD 305.40971.

THE WOMEN'S REVIEW OF BOOKS. *See* Literary and Political Reviews.

WOMEN'S RIGHTS ALMANAC. *See* Yearbooks, Almanacs, Directories.

WOMEN'S RIGHTS BULLETIN. No. 1-. 0711-463X. Periodical. CN. English. ir. Free. Women's Rights Bulletin, c/o OFL, 15 Gervais Drive, Don Mills Ontario M3C 1Y8 Canada. DD 331.409713.

WOMEN'S RIGHTS LAW REPORTER. *See* Law.

WOMEN'S STUDIES. V. 1- 1972-. 0049-7878. Periodical. US. English. ty. $71.00. Gordon & Breach Science Publishers, 440 Park Avenue South, New York NY 10016. Ind/Abst Abstr. Engl. Stud., Am. Hist. Life, Hist. Abstr., Part A, Mod. Hist. Abstr., Hist. Abst., Part B, Twent. Century Abstr., MLA Int. Bibliogr. Books Artic. Mod. Lang. Lit., Women Stud. Abstr., Humanit. Index. LC HQ1101. DD 301.41205.

WOMEN'S STUDIES INTERNATIONAL FORUM. Vol. 5, No. 1-. 0277-5395. Periodical. UK. English. ir. Pergamon Press, 395 Sawmill River Road, Elmsford NY 10523. Ind/Abst Am. Hist. Life, Hist. Abstr., Part A, Mod. Hist. Abstr., Hist. Abst., Part B, Twent. Century Abstr., Int. Labour Doc., Psychol. Abstr., Writ. Am. Hist., Recent Publ. Artic. LC HQ1101. DD 305.405. CODEN WSINDA. Available on microfiche simultaneously with paper edition and on microfilm at end of subscription year. *Women's Studies International Quarterly, 0148-0685.*

WOMEN'S STUDIES INTERNATIONAL QUARTERLY. Vol. 2, No. 2-. US. English. qt. $61.00 Institutions, $30.00 Individuals affiliated with institutions. Pergamon Press Inc, Maxwell House, Fairview Park, Elmsford NY 10523. LC HQ1101. DD 305.405. *Women's Studies (Oxford), 0148-0685.*

WOMEN'S STUDIES NEWSLETTER CEASED. V. 1-8. 0363-1133. Periodical. US. English. qt. $12.00. Clearinghouse on Women's Studies, Box 334, Old Westbury NY 11568. Ind/Abst Women Stud. Abstr. (cum index).

WOMEN'S STUDIES REVIEW. Vol. 1, No. 1 (July 1979)-. 0195-6604. Periodical. US. English. bm. $6.00. Center for Womens Studies, 207 Dulles Hall, 230 West 17th Avenue, Columbus OH 43210. **Tel** (614)422-1021. *Women are Human.*

WOMEN'S TRACK & FIELD WORLD (1982). *See* Recreation, Leisure - Sports.

WOMEN'S TRAVEL CONNECTIONS. *See* Travel.

WOMEN'S WORK. *See* Economics - Labor.

WOMEN'S WORLD. 0043-759X. Periodical. US. English. bm. Womens World, 1640 Rhode Island Avenue NW, Washington DC 20036. DD 296.

THE WOMEN'S YELLOW PAGES. VFOAT New York Women's Yellow Pages. 1978/79-. US. English. St Martin's Press Inc, 175 Fifth Avenue, New York NY 10010.

WOMEN'S YELLOW PAGES (DENVER, COLO.). (WOMEN'S YELLOW PAGES). VFOAT Denver and Colorado Springs Women's Yellow Pages. 1st Ed. (1985)-. 0882-7184. US. English. an. $5.00. Women's Yellow Pages, PO Box 389, Denver CO 80201.

WOMENWISE : THE N. H. FEMINIST HEALTH CENTER QUARTERLY. Vol. 1, No. 1 (Winter 1978)-. Periodical. US. English. ir. $15.00. Womenwise, c/o NHFHC 38 South Main Street, Concord NH 03301. **Tel** (603)225-2739. Ed Susan Janicki. bk rev. adv acc. **Circ** 2,500. Women's health inforamtion and resources.

WORKING TOGETHER FOR YESTERDAY, TODAY, AND TOMORROW. 0733-4826. US. English. an. Nebraska Commission on the Status of Women, PO Box 94985, 301 Centennial Mall South, Lincoln NB 68509. LC HQ1905.N2. DD 305.4060782.

WORKING WOMAN. V. 1- Nov. 1976-. 0145-5761. Periodical. US. English. mo. Hal Publications, 342 Madison Avenue/22nd Floor, New York NY 10173, (subscription address: Communication Data Services PO Box 4966 Des Moines IA 50340). **Tel** (515)237-7500. Ind/Abst Pop. Mag. Rev., Read. Guide Period. Lit., Mag. Index, Manage. Contents. LC HQ1101. DD 301.4120973.

WORKING WOMEN IN CANADA. March 1973-. 0384-0654. Periodical. CN. English. Metropolitan Toronto Library Board, Business Library, 229 College Street, Toronto Ontario M5T 1R4 Canada. DD 016.33140971.

YEARBOOK - NATIONAL COUNCIL OF WOMEN OF CANADA. *See* Yearbooks, Almanacs, Directories.

YODAESAENG. *See* Education (General) - Higher Education.

YOSONG. Periodical. KO. Korean. mo. Hanguk Yosong Tanche Hyobuihoe, 40-427 3-ka Hanggang-ro Yongsan-ku, Seoul Korea. LC HQ1104. (ctrl).

YOSONG YONGU. VFOAT Women's Studies. Vol. 1- No. 1-(Winter 1983). Periodical. KO. Korean (summaries in English). qt. Hanguk Yosong Kaebarwon, 14-33 Youido-dong Yongdungpo-ku, Seoul 150 Korea. LC HQ1765.5. (ctrl).

YOUNG WOMAN. 1981-. 0278-3932. Periodical. US. English. 13-30 Corporation, 505 Market Street, Knoxville TN 37902. LC HQ1229. DD 305.23.

O ZHENSHCHINAKH. Began in 1970. Periodical. UR. Russian. an. 0.35. Izdatelstvo Iskusstvo, Sobinovskii Per 3, 103009 Moskva USSR.

ZHENSHCHINY MIRA. 1958-. 0044-4456. Periodical. UR. Russian. qt. $8.00. Victor Kamkin Inc (70281), 12224 Parklawn Drive, Rockville MD 20852. **Tel** (301)881-5973.

ZINOCYY SVIT. (ZHINOCHYI SVIT). VFOAT Woman's World. 1- Vol. 1- Jan. 1950-. 0513-9856. Periodical. CN. Ukranian (includes some text in English). mo. $6.00. Woman's World, 18 Leland Avenue, Toronto Ontario M8Z 2X5 Canada. LC HQ1104.

YEARBOOKS, ALMANACS, DIRECTORIES

18 ALMANAC. VAT Eighteen Almanac. 0163-1640. Periodical. US. English. an. $2.00. 505 Market Street, Knoxville TN 37902. LC LH1. DD 373.180973.

55,000 LARGEST U.S. CORPORATIONS. (WARD'S DIRECTORY OF 55,000 LARGEST U.S. CORPORATIONS). VFOAT Directory of . . . Largest U.S. Corporations. VAT Ward's Directory of . . . Largest United States Corporations. 1981-. 0730-3122. US. English. an. Baldwin H Ward Publications, Box 380, Petaluma CA 94952. *50,000 Leading U.S. Corporations, 0270-1804.*

A. A.'S FAR EAST BUSINESSMAN'S DIRECTORY. Main/Corp Artists Associates. VFOAT Far East Businessman's Directory. 0532-9175. HK. English. ir. Artists Associates, GPO 1623, Hong Kong. LC HF3763. DD 380.10255.

A.A.E.P. DIRECTORY. Main/Corp American Association of Equine Practitioners. US. English. an. $15.00. Directory of American Association of Equine Practitioners, 22363 Hillcrest Circle, Golden CO 80401. **Tel** (303)526-0820. Ed Wayne Kester. **Circ** 5,000. Names of equine practitioners in the USA, Canada and international countries.

AAG DIRECTORY. Main/Corp Association of American Geographers. VFOAT A.A.G. Directory. VAT Association of American Geographers Directory. 0740-6681. US. English. Association of American Geographers, 1710 Sixteenth Street Northwest, Washington DC 20009. **Tel** (202)234-1450. LC G64. DD 910.2573. adv acc. **Circ** 5,500. Listing of Association of American Geographers including their topical and area proficiencies and employment. *Directory of the Association of American Geographers, 0571-5962.*

Yearbooks, Almanacs, Directories

AAHA DIRECTORY OF MEMBERSHIP. Main/Corp American Animal Hospital Association. VFOAT Directory of Approved Hospitals, Hospitals' Directors and Affiliate Members. VAT American Animal Hospital Association Directory of Membership. US. English. an. $6.00. 3612 East Jefferson Boulevard, South Bend IN 46615. Tel (202)296-5960. *Directory of Membership.*

AAMC CURRICULUM DIRECTORY. Main/Corp Association of American Medical Colleges. VAT Association of American Medical Colleges Curriculum Directory. Began 1972/73. 0092-0371. US. English. an. Association of American Medical Colleges, One DuPont Circle NW, Washington DC 20036. LC R745. DD 610.71173. NLM W 19.5 AA1 A11.

AAMC DIRECTORY OF AMERICAN MEDICAL EDUCATION. Main/Corp Association of American Medical Colleges. VAT Association of American Medical Colleges Directory of American Medical Education. 0360-7437. US. English. an. Association of American Medical Colleges, One DuPont Circle NW, Washington DC 20036. LC R712.A1. DD 610.71173. NLM W 22 AA1 A8D. *AAMC Directory.*

AAMI MEMBERSHIP DIRECTORY. Main/Corp Association for the Advancement of Medical Instrumentation. VAT Association for the Advancement of Medical Instrumentation Membership Directory. 0883-4172. US. English. an. $100.00. Association for the Advancement of Medical Instrumentation, 1901 North Fort Meyer Drive/Suite 602, Arlington VA 22209. *Membership Directory, 0364-5150.*

AAOMS DIRECTORY. Main/Corp American Association of Oral and Maxillofacial Surgeons. VFOAT A.A.O.M.S. Directory. VAT American Association of Oral and Maxillofacial Surgeons Directory. 1982-. 0738-2375. US. English. an. American Association of Oral and Maxillofacial Surgeons, 211 East Chicago Avenue/Suite 930, Chicago IL 60611. LC RK37. DD 617.522006073. *Membership Directory, 0162-1483.*

AB BOOKMAN'S YEARBOOK. VFOAT A.B. Bookman's Yearbook. VAT Antiquarian Bookman Bookman's Yearbook. 0065-0005. US. English. sa. $15.00. A.B. Bookmans Yearbook, P.O. Box AB, Clifton, NJ 07015. Tel (201)772-0020. LC Z990. DD 010.58. (cum index).

ABAP ANUARIO. VFOAT A.B.A.P. Anuario. Vol. 1 (1981)-. BL. Portuguese. an. 1500. Associacao Brasileira de Agencias de Propaganda, ABAP R Jeronimo da Veiga 428-80., CFP 04536, Sao Paulo SP Brazil. LC HF6182.B6. DD 659.102581.

ABBOTSFORD-CLEARBROOK DIRECTORY. VFOAT Official City Directory of Abbotsford-Clearbrook. Began with 1970 issue. 0380-5301. CN. English. an. Henderson Directories Ltd, 419 MacMillan Avenue, Winnipeg Manitoba R3L 0N3 Canada. DD 917.1133.

ABC AIR CARGO GUIDE AND DIRECTORY. VFOAT Air Cargo Guide and Directory. No. 1- Jan. 1958-. UK. English. mo. LC TL720.7.

ABC DIRECTORY. US. English. LC TH12. *ABC Construction Directory.*

ABD. VAT AVIATION BUSINESS DIRECTORY. V.10, No. 4- Oct. 1958-. 0001-0502. US. English. qt. $20.00. Air Service Directory, 400 Main Street, Stamford CT 06901. Tel (203)325-2647. LC TL512. DD 338.47629102573. *Aviation Business Directory.*

ABMS DIRECTORY OF CERTIFIED ALLERGY/IMMUNOLOGY PHYSICIANS. VFOAT Directory of Certified Allergy and Immunology Physicians. 1st Ed.-. 0883-2994. US. English. be. $34.95. American Board of Medical Specialties, 1 American Plaza/Suite 805, Evanston IL 60201. Tel (312)491-9091. DD 610.

ABMS DIRECTORY OF CERTIFIED ANESTHESIOLOGISTS. VFOAT Directory of Certified Anesthesiologists. 1st Ed. (1985)-. 0883-122X. US. English. be. $39.95. American Board of Medical Specialties, 1 American Plaza/Suite 805, Evanston IL 60201. Tel (312)491-9091. LC RD78.62.U6. DD 617.9602573.

ABMS DIRECTORY OF CERTIFIED COLON AND RECTAL SURGEONS. VFOAT Directory of Certified Colon and Rectal Surgeons. 1st Ed.-. US. English. $24.95. American Board of Medical Specialties, 1 American Plaza Suite 805, Evanston IL 60201. Tel (312)491-9091. Circ 250. (ctrl). Biographical listing of certified medical specialists.

ABMS DIRECTORY OF CERTIFIED DERMATOLOGISTS. VFOAT Directory of Certified Dermatologists. VAT American Board of Medical Specialties Directory of Certified Dermatologists. 1st Ed.-. 0084-1489. US. English. be. $29.95. American Board of Medical Specialties, 1 American Plaza/Suite 805, Evanston IL 60201. Tel (312)491-9091. LC RL43. DD 616.5002573. Circ 600. (ctrl). Hardbound. Biographical listing of certified medical specialists.

ABMS DIRECTORY OF CERTIFIED EMERGENCY PHYSICIANS. VFOAT A.B.M.S. Directory of Certified Emergency Physicians. 1st Ed.-. 0742-0366. US. English. $24.95. American Board of Medical Specialties, 1 American Plaza Suite 805, Evanston IL 60201. LC RC86. DD 616.02502573.

ABMS DIRECTORY OF CERTIFIED FAMILY PRACTITIONERS. VAT American Board of Medical Specialties Directory of Certified Family Physicians. 1985-. 0884-643X. US. English. be. American Board of Medical Specialties, 1 American Plaza/Suite 805, Evanston IL 60201-4889. Tel (312)491-9091. DD 610.

ABMS DIRECTORY OF CERTIFIED INTERNISTS. VFOAT Directory of Certified Internists. 1985-. 0884-6448. US. English. be. American Board of Medical Specialties, 1 American Plaza/Suite 805, Evanston IL 60201-4889. LC PAR. DD 610.

ABMS DIRECTORY OF CERTIFIED NEUROLOGICAL SURGEONS. VFOAT Directory of Certified Neurological Surgeons. 1st Ed.-. 0882-2832. US. English. $24.95. American Board of Medical Specialties, One American Plaza/Suite 805, Evanston IL 60201. LC RD592.5. DD 617.48002573. Hardbound.

ABMS DIRECTORY OF CERTIFIED NEUROLOGISTS. VFOAT Directory of Certified Neurologists. 1st Ed.-. 0884-1500. Periodical. US. English. be. American Board of Medical Specialties, 1 American Plaza/Suite 805, Evanston IL 60201. Tel (312)491-9091. LC RC335. DD 616.802573.

ABMS DIRECTORY OF CERTIFIED NUCLEAR MEDICINE SPECIALISTS. VFOAT Directory of Certified Nuclear Medicine Specialists. 1st Ed.-. 0884-1454. US. English. be. American Board of Medical Specialties, 1 American Plaza/Suite 805, Evanston IL 60201. Tel (312)491-9091. LC R895.A4. DD 616.075702573.

ABMS DIRECTORY OF CERTIFIED OPHTHALMOLOGISTS. VFOAT Directory of Certified Ophthalmologists. 1st Ed.-. 8756-9175. US. English. $39.95. American Board of Medical Specialties, 1 American Plaza/Suite 805, Evanston IL 60201. LC RE22. DD 617.700273. Hardbound.

ABMS DIRECTORY OF CERTIFIED ORTHOPAEDIC SURGEONS. VFOAT Directory of Certified Orthopaedic Surgeons. VAT American Board of Medical Specialties Directory of Certified Orthopaedic Surgeons. 1st Ed.-. 0883-1211. US. English. be. $39.95. American Board of Medical Specialties, 1 American Plaza/Suite 805, Evanston IL 60201. Tel (312)491-9091. DD 610.

ABMS DIRECTORY OF CERTIFIED OTOLARYNGOLOGISTS. VFOAT Directory of Certified Otolaryngologists. 0883-3001. US. English. be. $39.95. American Board of Medical Specialties, 1 American Plaza/Suite 805, Evanston IL 60201. Tel (312)491-9091. DD 610.

ABMS DIRECTORY OF CERTIFIED PATHOLOGISTS. VFOAT Directory of Certified Pathologists. 0883-1203. US. English. be. $44.95. American Board of Medical Specialties, 1 American Plaza/Suite 805, Evanston IL 60201. Tel (312)491-9091. DD 610.

ABMS DIRECTORY OF CERTIFIED PEDIATRICIANS. VFOAT Directory of Certified Pediatricians. 1st Ed.-. 0884-1497. US. English. be. American Board of Medical Specialties, 1 American Plaza/Suite 805, Evanston IL 60201. Tel (312)491-9091. LC RJ29. DD 618.920023202573.

ABMS DIRECTORY OF CERTIFIED PHYSICAL MEDICINE & REHABILITATION PHYSICIANS. VFOAT Directory of Certified Physcial Medicine and Rehabilitation Physiatrists. 1st Ed.-. 0883-2986. US. English. be. $29.95. American Board of Medical Specialties, 1 American Plaza/Suite 805, Evanston IL 60201. Tel (312)491-9091. DD 610.

ABMS DIRECTORY OF CERTIFIED PLASTIC SURGEONS. VFOAT A.B.M.S. Directory of Certified Plastic Surgeons. 1st Ed.-. 0749-839X. US. English. $24.95. American Board of Medical Specialties, 1 American Plaza/Suite 805, Evanston IL 60201. Tel (312)491-9091. LC RD10.U6. DD 617.95002573. Circ 600. (ctrl). Hardbound. Biographic listings of certified medical specialists.

ABMS DIRECTORY OF CERTIFIED PREVENTIVE MEDICINE PHYSICIANS. VFOAT Directory of Certified Preventive Medicine Physicians. VAT American Board of Medical Specialties Directory of Certified Preventive Medicine Physicians. 1st Ed.-. 0883-2978. US. English. be. $29.95. American Board of Medical Specialties, 1 American Plaza/Suite 805, Evanston IL 60201. Tel (312)491-9091. DD 610.

ABMS DIRECTORY OF CERTIFIED PSYCHIATRISTS. VFOAT Directory of Certified Psychiatrists. VAT American Board of Medical Specialties Directory Psychiatrists. 1st Ed.-. 0884-1519. US. English. be. American Board of Medical Specialties, 1 American Plaza/Suite 805, Evanston IL 60201. Tel (312)491-9091. LC RC335. DD 616.89002573.

ABMS DIRECTORY OF CERTIFIED RADIOLOGISTS. 1985-. 5044-1238. US. English. be. $49.95. American Board of Medical Specialties, 1 American Plaza/Suite 805 Evanston IL 60201. Tel (312)491-9091. DD 610.

ABMS DIRECTORY OF CERTIFIED SURGEONS. VAT American Board of Medical Specialties Directory of Certified Surgeons. 1985-. 0884-1527. US. English. be. American Board of Medical Specialties, 1 American Plaza/Suite 805, Evanston IL 60201. Tel (312)491-9091. DD 617.

ABMS DIRECTORY OF CERTIFIED THORACIC SURGEONS. VFOAT Directory of Certified Thoracic Surgeons. 1st Ed.-. 0884-1462. US. English. be. American Board of Medical Specialties, 1 American Plaza/Suite 805, Evanston IL 60201. Tel (312)491-9091. LC PAR. DD 617.

ABMS DIRECTORY OF CERTIFIED UROLOGISTS. VFOAT A.B.M.S. Directory of Certified Urologists. 1st Ed.-. 0742-0374. US. English. $34.95. American Board of Medical Specialties, 1 American Plaza/Suite 805, Evanston IL 60201. Tel (312)491-9091. LC RC870. DD 616.6002573. Circ 1,250. Hardbound. Biographical listing of certified medical specialists.

ABSTRACTING AND INDEXING SERVICES DIRECTORY. 1st Ed., Issue No. 1 (July 1982)-. 0732-8583. US. English. ty. $170.00. Gale Research Company, Book Tower, Detroit MI 48226. Tel (800)521-0707. Ed John Schmittroth Jr. LC Z695.93. DD 025.4028. NLM Z 695.93 A164. Lists and describes more than 2,000 current and continuing publications, including abstracts, indexes, digest, bibliographies, catalogs and similar works in all fields.

ACADEMY PLAYERS DIRECTORY. VFOAT Players Directory. Began in 1943. US. English. ty. LC PN1998.A1. *Players Directory Bulletin.*

ACC DIRECTORY OF CRAFT COURSES. Main/Corp American Crafts Council. Research & Education Dept. US. English. an. 44 West 53rd Street, New York NY 10019. LC TT1. DD 745.5071073.

ACCESS : NATIONAL ASSOCIATION OF PERSONNEL CONSULTANTS MEMBERSHIP DIRECTORY. Main/Corp National Association of Personnel Consultants (U.S.). VFOAT Membership Directory. US. English. an. $12.50. National Association of Personnel Consultants, 1432 Duke Street, Alexandria VA 22314. Tel (703)684-0180. *Membership Directory.*

ACEL, ANUARIO DEL COMERCIO EXTERIOR LATINOAMERICANO. VFOAT Anuario Del Comercio Exterior Latinoamericano. VAT Anuario del Comercio Exterior Latinoamericano, Anuario del Comercio Exterior Latinoamericano. English, French, German, Portuguese and Spanish. ir. EPISA, Apartado Postal No 293, San Jose Puerto Rico. LC HF3236.5. DD 382.098.

ACHEMA JAHRBUCH. German. ir. Dechema Deutsche Gesellschaft, Postfach 970746, D-6000 Frankfurt West Germany.

Yearbooks, Almanacs, Directories

ACI DIRECTORY. Main/Corp American Concrete Institute. VAT American Concrete Institute Directory. 0363-2296. US. English. be. PO Box 4754, Redford Station, Detroit MI 48219. LC TA680. DD 624.183406273.

ACSUS MEMBERSHIP DIRECTORY. Main/Corp Association For Canadian Studies in the United States. VFOAT Membership Directory. 1984-1985-. US. English. $40.00. Association for Canadian Studies in the United States, One Dupont Circle/Suite 620, Washington DC 20036. Tel (202)887-6375. LC F1025. DD 971.002573. adv acc. Circ 1,200. (ctrl) Listing of ACSUS members by discipline and area of Canadian studies and also alphabetically and by state.

ADAM FILM WORLD GUIDE. ADAM FILM WORLD DIRECTORY OF ADULT FILMS. VFOAT Adam Film World Directory of Adult Films. 1984-. 0743-6335. US. English. $4.95. Knight Pub Corporation, 8060 Melrose Avenue, Los Angeles CA 90046.

ADCA. AMERICAN DIRECTORY OF COLLECTION AGENCIES AND ATTORNEYS. (ADCA, AMERICAN DIRECTORY OF COLLECTION AGENCIES AND ATTORNEYS). VFOAT American Directory of Collection Agencies and Attorneys. 1918. 0148-5350. US. English. an. $30.95. Service Publishing Company, Park Lane Building, 2025 I Street NW, Washington DC 20006. Tel (202)872-0082. LC HF5559.U5. DD 332.7. adv acc. (ctrl). A directory of firms and individuals throughout the United States, Canada and some European countries whose profession or business is to collect delinquent accounts. ADCA, American Directory of Collection Agencies, 0360-3806.

ADDRESS DIRECTORY - SOCIETY OF VERTEBRATE PALEONTOLOGY. (ADDRESS DIRECTORY. DELETE). Main/Corp Society of Vertebrate Paleontology. 0276-444X. US. English. Society of Vertebrate Paleontology, Florida State Museum, University of Florida, Gainesville FL 32611. LC QE841. DD 566.0601.

ADHESIVES AGE DIRECTORY. VFOAT Adhesives Age. Vol. 26, No. 6 (May 31, 1983)- – 15th (1983)-. Periodical. US. English. an. $32.50. Communication Channels Inc, 6255 Barfield Road, Atlanta GA 30328. Adhesives Red Book, 0065-1931.

ADIRONDACK ALMANACK. V. 1-2. 0198-7291. Periodical. US. English. sa. Adirondack Almanack, Box 11A Road 2, Corinth NY 12822. Tel (518)654-9825.

ADMINISTRATIVE DIRECTORY OF COLLEGE AND UNIVERSITY COMPUTER SCIENCE DEPARTMENTS AND COMPUTER CENTERS. VFOAT ACM Administrative Directory. 1976-. 0190-6607. US. English. an. $12.00. Association For Computing Machinery, P O Box 9209 Church Street Station, New York NY 10249. Tel (212)265-6300. LC QA76.27. DD 001.64071173.

ADMINISTRATIVE DIRECTORY OF THE PROVISIONAL MILITARY GOVERNMENT OF SOCIALIST ETHIOPIA. English. ir. Institut of Management and Training, Research and Documentation Branch, ATSE Teodros Street, PO Box 51, Addis Ababa Ethiopia. LC JQ3757. DD 354.6300025. Administrative Directory of the Imperial Ethiopian Government.

ADRESSBUCH DES DEUTSCHSPRACHIGEN BUCHHANDEL. (ADRESSBUCH FUR DEN DEUTSCHSPRACHIGEN BUCHHANDEL). 1977/78-. 0065-2032. GW. German. be. Buchhandler Vereinigung GMBH, Grosser Hirschgraben 17-21, D6000 Frankfurt 1 West Germany. LC Z317. NLM Z 317 A243. Adressbuch des Deutschsprachigen Buchhandels, 0065-2032.

ADVANCED TECHNOLOGY IN WASHINGTON STATE. (ADVANCED TECHNOLOGY IN WASHINGTON STATE, ... INDUSTRY DIRECTORY). 1983-. 0749-4874. US. English. an. $10.00. Economic Development Council of Puget Sound, 1218 3rd Avenue/19th Floor, Seattle WA 98101. LC T12.3.W2. DD 338.7616025797.

ADVERTISING AGE YEARBOOK. 1981-. 0276-9751. US. English. an. Crain Books, 740 Rush Street, Chicago IL 60611. LC HF5802. DD 659.105.

A.E.A. DIRECTORY OF TRACTORS AND AGRICULTURAL MACHINERY. Main/Corp Agricultural Engineers Association. VFOAT Directory of Tractors and Agricultural Machinery. 1972-. UK. English. an.

AECT MEMBERSHIP DIRECTORY AND DATA BOOK. Main/Corp Association For Educational Communications and Technology. 1970/71-. US. English. an. $10.00. AECT, 1126 Sixteenth Street, Washington DC 20036. Davi Membership Directory and Data Book, 0547-6305.

THE AEE DIRECTORY OF ENERGY PROFESSIONALS. Main/Corp Association of Energy Engineers. VFOAT Directory of Energy Professionals. VAT Association of Energy Engineers Directory of Energy Professionals. 1979-1980-. 0164-0917. US. English. an. Fairmont Press, P O Box 14227, Atlanta GA 30324. LC TJ163.165. DD 621.04202573.

THE AERO COLLEGE AVIATION DIRECTORY. VFOAT Aviation College Directory. 0747-797X. US. English. $24.95. Aero Publishers Inc, 329 West Aviation Road, Fallbrook CA 92028.

AEROSPACE CONSULTANTS DIRECTORY. June 1984-. 0747-8151. US. English. an. Society of Automotive Engineers, 400 Commonwealth Drive, Warrendale PA 15096. DD 629.

AETS YEARBOOK. Main/Corp Association for the Education of Teachers in Science. Vol. 1- 1974-. US. English. an. SMEAC Information Reference Center, 1200 Chambers Road, 3rd Floor, Columbus OH 43212. Tel (614)422-6717. Circ 1,000. This is an annual publication produced on a topic related to science education.

AFRICA, ASIA, & EUROPE DIRECTORY. VFOAT Dalil Afriqiya, Asiya, Urubba. UA. Arabic (English). ir. International Agency for Publicity, 117 Ahmed Abdel Salam St Helwan, PO Box 1312, Cairo Egypt. LC HF54.E3. DD 380.10294.

AFRICA-MIDDLE EAST PETROLEUM DIRECTORY. VAT Africa Middle East Petroleum Directory. 1st- Ed. 0197-7830. US. English. an. not sold separately. Pennwell Publishing Company, PO Box 1260, Tulsa OK 74101. Tel (918)835-3161. LC TN867. DD 338.762233802556.

AFRICA YEAR BOOK AND WHO'S WHO. 1977-. 0141-3341. UK. English. an. Africa Journal Ltd, 54 A Tottenham Court Road, London W1P 0BT Englsna. Tel (212)916-1600. LC DT1. DD 960.03. NLM DT 2 A260.

AFRICAN BOOK TRADE DIRECTORY. 1971-. Periodical. US. English. ir. R R Bowker, P O Box 1807, Ann Arbor MI 48106. Tel (800)521-8110.

THE AFRICAN BOOK WORLD & PRESS : DIRECTORY. VFOAT Repertoire du Livre et de la Presse en Afrique. VAT The African Book World and Press: A Directory. 1977-. UK. English (and French). ir. $78.00. Gale Research Company, Book Tower, Detroit MI 48226. Tel (800)521-0707. Ed Hanz M Zell. LC Z857.A1. DD 021.00256. Furnishes details on a variety of institutions and enterprises concerned with the book trade and press in Africa.

AFRICAN DIRECTORY OF STATISTICIANS. VFOAT Repertoire Africain des Statisticiens. English (French). ir. Economic Commission for Africa, PO Box 3001, Addis Ababa Ethiopia. LC HA37.A33. DD 310.256.

AFRICAN STATISTICAL YEARBOOK. VFOAT Annuaire Statistique pour l'Afrique. 1974-. SA. English. qt. United Nations Economic Commission of Africa, Box 3001, Addis Ababa Ethiopia. LC HA1955. DD 330.9600212. Circ 3,500. Data arranged on a country basis for 52 countries (African). Statistical Yearbook. Annuaire Statistique.

AFRICAN/AMERICAN DIRECTORY. VAT African American Directory. 1981-82-. 0275-2875. Periodical. US. English. an. Cooper/Lang Communications Inc, Watergate Suite 812/600 New Hampshire Avenue NW, Washington DC 20037. LC HF3132. DD 338.8897306025.

AFRIKA UND DIE DEUTSCHEN : JAHRBUCH DER DEUTSCHEN AFRIKA-STIFTUNG. 1981-. 0721-3107. Periodical. German (French). an. Verlag Gunther Neske, Pfullingen West Germany. LC DT1. DD 960.05.

AFTERMARKET STATISTICAL YEARBOOK. VFOAT Aftermarket Yearbook. 1st Ed. (1984)-. 0740-8676. US. English. an. $250.00. National Aftermarket Audit Company, PO Box 1509, Duxbury MA 02331. Tel (617)934-6577. Ed A C McKendry. LC HE5623. DD 388.34220973021. Car and truck registration statistics by make and year at state level. Also product replacement potentials for all SMSA counties.

AGENCY DIRECTORY - AMERICAN HUMANE ASSOCIATION. Main/Corp American Humane Association. VFOAT American Humane Agency Directory. 0147-4383. US. English. American Humane, 5351 South Roslyn Street, Englewood CO 80110. LC HV4763. DD 179.302573.

AGENTS ECONOMIQUES DU ZAIRE : ANNUAIRE. 1976-. CG. French. ir. Societe MYK Service, BP 5502, Kinshasa Gombe Zaire. LC HE9559. DD 384.60256751.

AGMA DIRECTORY. Main/Corp American Gear Manufacturers Association. VAT American Gear Manufacturers Association Directory. 0572-502X. US. English. American Gear Manufacturers Association, 1330 Massachusetts Avenue Northwest, Washington DC 20005. LC TJ184. DD 338.4762183302573.

AGRICULTURAL ALMANAC. VFOAT Baer's Agricultural Almanac. 0732-5932. US. English. an. $2.00. John Baers Sons, PO Box 328, Lancaster PA 17604. Tel (717)392-0733. Ed Gerald S Lestz. bk rev. adv acc. Circ 85,000. A folksy compendium on weather, gardens and history.

AGRICULTURAL ENGINEERS YEARBOOK CEASED. 1954-1982/83. 0065-4477. US. English. an. $16.00. American Society of Agricultural Engineers, 2950 Niles Road, St Joseph MI 49085. LC S671. DD 631.06273.

AGRICULTURE TEACHERS DIRECTORY. VFOAT Agriculture Teachers. 1977-. US. English. an. $10.00. Charles M Henry PRTO OC c/o Sarah Henry, P O Box 68, Greensburg PA 15601. Tel (412)834-7600. Ed Sarah Henry. adv acc. Circ 14,368. (ctrl). A directory of teachers of agriculture as furnished by the 50 state departments of education with editorial matter and advertising. Agriculture Teachers Directory and Handbook.

AIA DIRECTORY OF HELIPORTS & HELISTOPS IN THE UNITED STATES, CANADA, PUERTO RICO, AND DIRECTORY OF HOSPITAL HELIPORTS & HELISTOPS. VFOAT A.I.A. Directory of Heliports and Helistops In the United States, Canada, Puerto Rico, and Directory of Hospital Heliports & Helistops. 1984-. 0882-3367. US. English. $7.95. Aerospace Industries Association, Suite 700/1725 Desales Street NW, Washington DC 20036. DD 387.7362. AIA Directory of Heliports in the United States, Canada, Puerto Rico and Directory of Hospital Heliports.

AIAW HANDBOOK-DIRECTORY. Main/Corp Association for Intercollegiate Athletics for Women. VAT Association for Intercollegiate Athletics for Women Handbook-Directory. 0361-5898. US. English. $6.00. Association for Intercollegiate Athletics for Women, 1201 16th Street Northwest, Washington DC 20036. LC GV439. DD 796.0194. Directory, Charter Member Institutions, AIAW Handbook of Policies and Operating Procedures.

AIC DIRECTORY. Main/Corp American Institute For Conservation of Historic and Artistic Works. VFOAT Membership Directory - American Institute For Conservation of Historic and Artistic Works. US. English. $10.00. American Institute for the Conservation of Historic and Artistic Works, 1522 K Street Northwest, Washington DC 20005. LC N8554. DD 701.8.

AIC MEMBERSHIP DIRECTORY. Main/Corp Agricultural Institute of Canada. 1982-. 0820-8360. CN. English (prefatory material also in French). be. DD 630.2571. Membership Directory, 0515-7196.

AIR ALMANAC. Main/Corp Great Britain. Nautical Almanac Office. UK. English. sa. Her Majestys Stationery Office, P O Box 276, London SW8 5DT England. Tel 01-622 3316.

AIR ALMANAC (WASHINGTON, D.C.). (THE AIR ALMANAC). Began with Jan./Apr. 1953. 0400-8456. US. English. sa. Superintendent of Documents, US Government Printing Office, Washington DC 20402. LC TL587. DD 528.05. American Air Almanac, British Air Almanac.

A.I.R. DIRECTORY OF RADIO PROGRAMMING. VFOAT AIR Directory of Radio Programming. VAT Association of Independent Radioproducers Directory of Radio Programming. Winter 1981-. 0278-4467. US. English. $14.95. Association of Independent Radio Producers, Box 8888, Universal City CA 91608. LC PN1991.3.U6. DD 791.4402573. Directory of Radio Programming.

AIR FREIGHT DIRECTORY. 0092-2870. US. English. Air Cargo Inc, 1730 Rhode Island Avenue Northwest, Washington DC 20036. LC HE9788.5.U5. DD 387.7440973.

Yearbooks, Almanacs, Directories

AIR NEWS YEARBOOK. 1st-. US. English. an. Ed Phillip Andrews.

AIR TAXI CHARTER & RENTAL DIRECTORY OF NORTH AMERICA. VAT Air Taxi Charter and Rental Directory of North America. 1st- Ed. 0270-5079. US. English. $15.00. Aircraft Charter & Rental Tariff Information Service of North America Inc, Box 1412, Springfield IL 62705. LC HE9803.A2. DD 387.742.

AIRCRAFT CERTIFICATION DIRECTORY. Main/Corp United States. Federal Aviation Administration. Office of Airworthiness. Began with Vol. for 1983. 0747-5586. US. English. an. Federal Aviation Administration, Office of Airworthiness, 800 Independence Avenue SW, Washington DC 20591. LC TL671.1. DD 363.1246602573.

AIRLINE INDUSTRY DIRECTORY. VFOAT Aid, Airline Industry Directory. V. 1- Spring/Summer 1979-. 0194-0961. Periodical. US. English. sa. $35.00 Per Copy. Airline Pub Group, Suite 420 818/18th Street NW, Washington DC 20006. LC HE9768. DD 387.7025.

AIRPORT DIRECTORY. US. English. an. New Jersey Department of Transportation, Division of Aeronautics, 1035 Parkway Avenue, Trenton NJ 08625. LC TL726.3.N5. DD 387.736025749. *New Jersey Airport Directory, 0091-6978.*

AIRPORT DIRECTORY OF THE STATE OF COLORADO. VFOAT Colorado Airport Directory. 1st- Ed. 0145-4633. US. English. G A H Aviation Ltd, Box 2811, Littletown CO 80122. LC TL726.3.C7. DD 387.736.025788.

AKAD DIRECTORY OF BUSINESSES, TRADES, AND THE PROFESSIONS. VFOAT Akad Directory of Businesses, Trades, & the Professions. Began with 1974. English. an. Akad Directory Co Ltd, PO Box 30, Lagos Niberia Africa. LC HF3931.A48. DD 380.10294669.

AL-TAQRIR AL-IHSAI AL-TARBAWI AL-SANAWI AN AL-TALIM FI JAMI MADARIS AL-URDUN. VFOAT Taqrir Al-Ihsai Al-Sanawi Al-Tarbawi, The Statistical Yearbook of Education in All Schools of Jordan. 1974/75-. Arabic and English. ir. LC L633.

ALA HANDBOOK OF ORGANIZATION AND MEMBERSHIP DIRECTORY. Main/Corp American Library Association. VAT American Library Association Handbook of Organization and Membership Directory. 1980/1981-. 0273-4605. US. English. an. American Library Association, 50 East Huron Street, Chicago IL 60611. LC Z673.A5. DD 020.62202573. *ALA Handbook of Organization, 0084-6406; A.L.A. Membership Directory.*

ALA MEMBERSHIP DIRECTORY. (A. L. A. MEMBERSHIP DIRECTORY). Main/Corp American Library Assocaition. VAT American Library Association Membership Directory. 1949-. 0278-9019. US. English. an. $20.00. American Library Association, 50 East Huron Street, Chicago IL 60650. LC Z720.A4. DD 020.622. *ALA Handbook.*

ALA WORLDWIDE DIRECTORY & FACT BOOK. *See* Business - Marketing.

THE ALA YEARBOOK CEASED. Main/Corp American Library Association. VAT American Library Association Yearbook. 1976-1983. 0364-1597. US. English. an. American Library Association, 50 East Huron Street, c/o Bob Hershman, Chicago IL 60611. LC Z673.A5. DD 020.62273.

THE ALA YEARBOOK OF LIBRARY AND INFORMATION SERVICES. VFOAT Ala Yearbook of Library and Information Services. VAT American Library Association Yearbook of Library and Information Services. Vol. 9 (1984)-. 0740-042X. US. English. an. American Library Association, 50 East Huron Street, Chicago IL 60611. DD 020. *Ala Yearbook, 0364-1597.*

THE ALABAMA AND GEORGIA LEGAL DIRECTORY. US. English. an. LC KF190. DD 340.02573.

ALABAMA DIRECTORY OF MINING AND MANUFACTURING. 1976-. 0145-4048. US. English. an. $56.00. Manufacturers News Inc, 4 East Huron Street, Chicago IL 60611. Tel (312)337-1084. LC T12. DD 338.0025761. Contains alphabetical, SIC, product, geographical, resources, parent company, product index and international breakdowns of 5,000 companies. *Industrial Alabama, 0073-7321.*

THE ALABAMA LEGAL DIRECTORY. 1975/76-. 0145-4390. US. English. an. $16.50. Legal Directories Publication Company, 2122 Kidwell Street PO Box 140200, Dallas Tx 75214. Tel (214)824-8092. LC KF192.A5. DD 340.025761. adv acc. A digest of federal and state officals, law firms and individual lawyers, with pertinent information on county offices and jurisdiction of the courts at all levels.

ALABAMA PLANNING AND DEVELOPMENT COORDINATION DIRECTORY. 2nd- Ed. 0364-7684. US. English. LC JK4530. DD 309.25025761. *Planning and Development Coordination Directory, 0094-4009.*

THE ALASKA ALMANAC. VFOAT More Facts About Alaska, The Alaska Almanac. 1981 ed.-. 0270-5370. US. English. an. $3.95 Domestic, $4.95 Foreign. Alaska Northwest Publishing Company, Box 4-EEE, Anchorage AK 99509. LC F902.3. DD 979.8005. *Facts About Alaska.*

ALASKA DIRECTORY OF ATTORNEYS. 0275-1895. US. English. sa. $30.00. Todd Communications, 360 K Street/Suite 202, Anchorage AK 99501. Tel (907)274-8633. Ed Lisa Dunavin. LC KF192.A55. DD 349.798025, 347.980025. adv acc. Circ 2,600. Alphabetical listing of all members of Alaska Bar Associations business address and phone. Alaska Judicial Court System, law enforcement, agencies, process servers, court reporters, and title companies.

ALASKA EDUCATION DIRECTORY. 0733-236X. US. English. an. Alaska Department of Education, Pouch F, Juneau AK 99811. LC L903.A4. DD 370.25798. *Alaska Educational Directory, 0733-236X.*

ALASKA LIBRARY DIRECTORY. 0146-1028. US. English. Alaska State Library Division of State Libraries & Museums, Department of Education Pouch G, Juneau AK 99811.

ALASKA MARINE RADIO DIRECTORY. 8755-3422. US. English. Alascom Inc, Marketing Department/Marine Service, H-280 Pouch 6607, Anchorage AK 99502.

ALASKA PETROLEUM & INDUSTRIAL DIRECTORY. VAT Alaska Petroleum and Industrial Directory. V. 10- 1970/71-. 0065-5813. US. English. an. Howell Publishing Company, P O Box 104139, Anchorage AK 99510. Tel (907)276-5825. Ed Lalla Howell. LC HC107.A45. DD 338.0025798. bk rev. adv acc. Circ 1,800. Directory listing of 25,000 Alaska businesses and their branch offices and personnel. Full index for 240 categories, company names and personnel. *Alaska Petroleum Directory.*

ALBERTA. (ALBERTA : BUSINESS TO BUSINESS : COMMERCIAL DIRECTORY). VFOAT Alberta Commercial/Industrial Directory. 1980/1981-. 0228-8931. CN. English. an. $10.00. GTE Directories, 205-7710 5th Street South East, Calgary Alberta T2H 2L9 Canada. DD 380.10257123.

ALBERTA CATHOLIC DIRECTORY. VFOAT Official Alberta Catholic Directory. 1971-. 0316-473X. CN. English. an. $4.65. Alberta Catholic Directory, 10562 109th Street, Edmonton Alberta T5H 3B2 Canada. Tel 420-1330. DD 282.0257123. adv acc. Circ 3,000. (ctrl) Official ecclesiastical directory for Province of Alberta and Diocese of Mackenzie, Ft Smith. *Alberta Catholic Directory Edmonton Ed., 0316-4748; Alberta Catholic Directory Calgary Ed, 0316-4756.*

ALBERTA CO-OPERATIVE AND FARM ORGANIZATION DIRECTORY. 0822-7209. CN. English. an. $7.00. Rural Education and Development Association, 14815-119 Avenue, Edmonton Alberta T5L 2N9 Canada. DD 630.607123.

ALBERTA CONSTRUCTION & RESOURCE INDUSTRIES DIRECTORY/PURCHASING GUIDE. 1982-. 0713-4045. CN. English. an. 20.00. Sanford Evans Communications Ltd, PO Box 6900, 1077 St James Street, Winnipeg Manitoba M5W 3B1 Canada. DD 338.476900257123. Dedicated to contractors and firms engaged in construction, mining, forestry and oil and gas industries. Provides names, addresses and telephone numbers of suppliers, contractors and subcontractors. *Alberta Construction Industry Directory, Purchasing Guide, 0381-9663.*

ALBERTA CONSTRUCTION INDUSTRY DIRECTORY. PURCHASING GUIDE CEASED. (ALBERTA CONSTRUCTION INDUSTRY DIRECTORY, PURCHASING GUIDE). 1975/76-1981. 0381-9663. CN. English. an. DD 338.476900257123.

ALBERTA INSURANCE DIRECTORY. 1st Ed. (1982)-. 0712-9343. CN. English. an. $17.00 Per Volume. Arbutus Publications, PO Box 35070/Station E, Vancouver British Columbia V6M 4G1 Canada. DD 368.00257123.

ALBERTA LEGAL TELEPHONE DIRECTORY. 0823-2350. Periodical. CN. English. $7.00 Per Vol. Alberta Legal Telephone Directory, 240 Edward Street, Aurora Ontario L4G 3S9 Canada. DD 340.0257123.

ALBERTA LIBRARY DIRECTORY . . . . 2nd Ed. (1973)-. 0710-3123. CN. English. DD 027.00257123. *A Directory of Libraries in Alberta, 0714-7201.*

ALBERTA MOTOR TRANSPORT DIRECTORY. 1970-. 0084-6171. CN. English. an. 25.00. Alberta Trucking Association, 5112 3rd Street SE, PO Box 5520 A, Calgary Alberta T2H 1X9 Canada. Tel (403)253-8401. Ed Jim Bradbury. DD 388.3240257123. adv acc. Circ 1,500. Includes updated carrier points of service index, revised tariffs for general freight, bill of lading information, list of provincial and territorial transport boards, list of trucking associations across Canada, etc. *Alberta Shippers' Guide, 0318-0190.*

THE ALCOHOL AND DRUG ABUSE YEARBOOK/DIRECTORY. 1979/80-. 0193-3981. US. English. an. Van Nostrand Reinhold Company, 135 West 50th Street, New York NY 10020. Ed J Norback. LC HV5279. DD 362.29202573. NLM WM 22 AA1 A2.

ALCOHOLISM TREATMENT FACILITIES DIRECTORY. UNITED STATES AND CANADA. (ALCOHOLISM TREATMENT FACILITIES DIRECTORY : UNITED STATES AND CANADA). 1973/74-. 0092-3826. US. English. ir. $7.50. Alcohol & Drug Problems Association of America, 1130 17th Street Northwest, Washington DC 20036. Tel (202)468-2600. LC HV5279. DD 362.2920973. *Directory of Alcoholism Treatment Facilities, Domiciliary Houses and State and Provincial Alcoholism.*

ALLENSBACHER JAHRBUCH DER DEMOSKOPIE. 6.- Vol. GW. German. ir. $32.38. Verlag Fritz Molden GMBH, Stievestrasse 8, D8000 Munchen 19 West Germany. LC HN460.P8. *Jahrbuch der Offentlichen Meinung, 0075-2347.*

ALLIED HEALTH EDUCATION DIRECTORY. 7th- Ed. 0194-3766. US. English. an. $19.95. American Medical Association, 535 North Dearborn Street, Chicago IL 60610. Tel (312)645-4695. Ed John Boberg. LC R847. DD 610.71073. NLM W 22 AA1 D5. *Allied Medical Education Directory, 0163-2590.*

ALLIED LANDSCAPE INDUSTRY MEMBER DIRECTORY. 0098-793X. US. English. American Association of Nurserymen, 230 Southern Building, 15th and H Street Northwest, Washington DC 20005. LC SB44. DD 338.175902573.

ALMANAC. VFOAT Almanac Turkey. 1977-. English. ir. LC AY1038.T8. DD 052.

ALMANAC, CYPRUS IN 400 PAGES. 1980-. English. an. Target Publishers Ltd, PO Box 5419, Nicosia Cyprus. LC DS54. DD 956.45.

ALMANAC FOR COMPUTERS (WASHINGTON, D.C. : 1980). (ALMANAC FOR COMPUTERS). VFOAT A/C. 1980-. 0191-3867. US. English. an. $9.25. Superintendent of Documents, US Government Printing Office, Washington DC 20402. Tel (202)783-3238. LC QB12. DD 528. *Almanac for Computers for the Year . . ., 0191-3867.*

THE ALMANAC OF AMERICAN POLITICS. 1972-. 0362-076X. Periodical. US. English. be. National Journal Inc, 1730 M Street Northwest/11th Floor, Washington DC 20036. Tel (202)857-1400. Ed Julia M Romero. LC JK1012. DD 328.73005. Circ 40,000. A biography of every member of Congress and each governor. The almanac is published approximately 6 months after each national election. The next edition will be published in July 1987 after the 1986 elections. 1986 edition currently available.

ALMANAC OF CHINA'S ECONOMY. 1981-. 0731-1257. Periodical. US. English. an. Cheng & Tsui Company, 25 West Street, Boston MA 02111. Tel (617)426-6074. Ind/Abst Int. Labour Doc. LC HC427.92.A1. DD 330.951.005.

ALMANAC OF FEDERAL PACS. 0886-2567. Periodical. US. English. be. $49.50. Amward Publications, 824 National Press Building, Washington DC 20045.

Yearbooks, Almanacs, Directories

THE ALMANAC OF SEAPOWER. VFOAT Almanac of Sea Power. 1983-. 0736-3559. US. English. an. $12.95. Navy League of the United States, 2300 Wilson Boulevard PO Box 400, Arlington VA 22210. **LC** V1. **DD** 359.005.

THE ALMANAC OF THE CANNING, FREEZING, PRESERVING INDUSTRIES. 1st- 1916-. US. English. an. $32.50. The Almanac, PO Box 866, Westminster MD 21157. **Tel** (301)876-2052. Ed D P Judge. adv acc. US Food and Drug laws regulations, labeling law and regulations, USDA, quality grade standards, FDA product standards. US canned and frozen pack-statistics, imports, exports, crop statistics and conversions.

THE ALMANAC OF THE CANNING, FREEZING, PRESERVING INDUSTRIES : ... ANNUAL COMPILATION OF BASIC REFERENCES FOR THE CANNING, FREEZING, PRESERVING AND ALLIED INDUSTRIES. Began with 1958?. US. English. an. $20.00. Edward E Judge & Sons Inc, 79 Bond Street, Westminster MD 21157. **LC** TX599. **DD** 338.476640280973. *Canning Trade Almanac.*

THE ALMANAC OF VIRGINIA POLITICS. 1st Ed. (1977)-. 0276-9980. US. English. be. Woman Activist Fund Inc, Falls Church VA 22046. Ed Flora Crater, Elizabeth Vantrease, Meg Williams. **LC** JK3968. **DD** 328.75507345.

ALMANAC. SPORTS AND GAMES. VFOAT Sports and Games. 1979-. 0193-8088. US. English. an. $19.95. Facts On File, 119 West 57th Street, New York NY 10019. Ed N L Smith. **LC** GV571. **DD** 796.09.

ALMANACCO DELLO SPECCHIO. Began with 1972 Vol. English, French, Italian or Spanish. ir. 2800. **LC** PN6099.

ALMANACCO (MILAN, ITALY). (ALMANACCO). 1-. Periodical. Italian (Italian and English). an. Almanacco, 25 Hollinger Road, Toronto Ontario M4B 3G2 Canada. **Tel** (416)751-4520.

ALMANACCO MUSICA. Periodical. IT. Italian. ir. Edizioni Il Formichiere, Via Del Lauro 3, 20121 Milano Italy. **LC** ML3469. **DD** 780.4205.

ALMANACCO NAVALE. 1937-. Italian. ir. **LC** V9. **DD** 359.058.

ALMANACCO PIEMONTESE. VFOAT Armanach Piemonteis. Italian (Vols. for 1974- include material in Piemontese dialect). ir. 2.500. A Viglongo, Conto Corrente Postale N 2-31467 Casella Postale 412, Torino 10100 Italy. **LC** DG610.

L'ALMANACH AFRICAIN. FR. French. ir. Agence de Cooperation Culturelle et Technique, 170 rue de Grenelle, 7E Paris France. **LC** DT1. **DD** 960.05.

ALMANACH CHASSE ET PECHE. 1978-. 0704-7061. CN. French. an. $4.95 Per No. Librairie Beauchemin Limitee, 450 Avenue Beaumont, Montreal Quebec H3N 1T8 Canada. **DD** 799.09714.

ALMANACH DE KUYPER DE CHASSE ET PECHE. (L'ALMANACH DE KUYPER DE CHASSE ET PECHE). 1972-. 0381-8233. CN. French. an. John de Kupyer & Fils Ltd, 950 Chemin de l'Adacport, Montreal Quebec H3C 3W5 Canada. **DD** 799.9714. *Petit Almanach du Chasseur et du Pecheur, 0555-991X.*

ALMANACH DE LA FEMME. 81-. 0710-0884. CN. French. an. $4.95 Per Volume. Messageries Dynamiques, 775 Boulevard Lebeau, Ville Saint-Laurent Quebec H4N 1S4 Canada. **DD** 305.409714.

ALMANACH DE L'AUTO (MONTREAL, QUEBEC). (ALMANACH DE L'AUTO). 0821-7505. CN. French. an. $5,95 Per Vol. Almanach de l'Auto, 225 rue Roy, Montreal Quebec H2W SN6 Canada. **DD** 629.222205.

ALMANACH DER OSTERREICHISCHEN FORSCHUNG CEASED. 1978-. Periodical. German. ir. Verband der Wissenschaftlichen Gesellschaften Osterreichs, Lindengasse 37, A-1070 Wien Austria. **LC** DB30. **DD** 943.6.

ALMANACH DES VEDETTES. Ed. 1978-. 0704-7487. CN. French. an. $2.50 Per No. Bert-Hold les Distributions Eclair Ltee, 8320 Place de Lorraine Anjou, Montreal Quebec H1J 1E6 Canada. **DD** 790.209714. *Encyclopedie Artistique, le Monde du Spectacle, 0381-8063.*

ALMANACH DU BAS-DU-FLEUVE. 1980-. 0228-1422. CN. French. an. $4. Per No. Enterprises Castelriand Inc, CP 997, Riviere-du-Loup Quebec G5R 3Z5 Canada. **DD** 054.1. *Almanach Castelriand, 0708-9244.*

ALMANACH DU CRIME. 1980-. FR. French. an. 37 rue de Montholon, 75009 Paris France. **LC** PN3448.D4. **DD** 809.387205.

ALMANACH DU PEUPLE. Published since 1857. 0065-650X. Periodical. CN. French. an. $3.48. les Editions Societaires, 1280 Ouest rue Bernard Bur 6, Outremont Quebec H2V 1V9 Canada. **Tel** (514)274-3639. **DD** 034.1.

ALMANACH FUR LITERATUR UND THEOLOGIE. 1-. 0569-0927. GW. German. an. Peter Hammer Verlag, Postfach 200415, Wuppertal 1 West Germany.

ALMANACH-GRAPHIQUE - CENTRE DE QUEBEC. SOCIETE ROYALE D'ASTRONOMIE DU CANADA. (ALMANACH-GRAPHIQUE - CENTRE DE QUEBEC, SOCIETE ROYALE D'ASTRONOMIE DU CANADA). **Main/Corp** Societe Royale d'Astronomie du Canada. Centre de Quebec. 1973-. 0384-7691. Periodical. CN. French. an. Centre de Quebec, Societe Royale D Astronomie du Canada, CP 9396 Ste-Foy, Quebec Quebec G1V 4B5 Canada. **DD** 520.5. *Almanach Astronomique, 0384-7683.*

ALMANACH - K.K.L. STRASBOURG. **Main/Corp** KKL Strasbourg. VFOAT Almanach du K.K.L., Strasbourg. Periodical. FR. French. an. K K L Strasbourg, 1A rue Rene Hirschler, Strasbourg France. **LC** DS101.K17A. **DD** 909.04924.

ALMANACH MODERNE. 17- 1973. 0315-2898. Periodical. CN. French. an. $3.05. Almanach Moderne Eclair, 5701 Christopher Colomb, Montreal Quebec H2S 2E9 Canada. **Tel** (514)274-2501. Ed Denis Levesque. **DD** 034.1. bk rev. adv acc. **Circ** 150,000. (ctrl). Most of the subjects covered are the Olympics, sports, theatres, automobiles, house beautiful, health, science, psychology, travel, calendar of events, post scriptum, the universe, business, astrology, small business and motion picture. *Almanach Moderne Eclair, 0569-096X.*

ALMANACH - OSTERREICHISCHE AKADEMIE DER WISSENSCHAFTEN. (ALMANACH). **Main/Corp** Osterreichische Akademie der Wissenschaften. Vol. 1. 0378-8644. AU. German. an. Osterreichischen Akad Wissenschaften, Dr Inez-Spiel-Pltz 2, A-1010 Wien Austria. **Ind/Abst** GeoRef. **LC** AS142. **CODEN** OAWABT. (cum index).

ALMANACH POLONII. 1969-. PL. chiefly in Polish with selected articles translated into English, French and Spanish. ir. Wydawnictwo Interpress, Ul Bagatela 12 PO Box 388, 00-585 Warsaw Poland. **Tel** 28-22-21. Ed F Laszkiewicz & E Trzeciak. **LC** AY1039.P7. adv acc. **Circ** 30,000. Illustrated publication for Poles and residents abroad. *Kalendarz Polonii.*

ALMANACH POPULAIRE CATHOLIQUE. 1982-. 0821-4034. CN. French. an. $4,95 Per Vol. Revue Sainte Anne de Beaupre, C P 1000, Sainte-Anne-de-Beaupre Quebec G0A 3C0 Canada. **DD** 282.7105.

AN ALMANACK . . . . 0083-9256. UK. English. an. $50.00. Gale Research, Book Tower, Detroit MI 48226. **Tel** (313)961-2242. Contents include information on public affairs, government, industry, finance, commerce, social uses and the arts. Also contains detailed reporting of current events and social, political, and economic developments in Great Britain.

ALMANACK FOR THE YEAR OF OUR LORD. . . (LONDON, ENGLAND). (AN ALMANACK). VFOAT Whitaker's Almanack. Publication began in 1869. 0083-9256. UK. English. an. Whitaker's Almanack, 12 Dyott Street, London WC1A 1DF England. **LC** AY754. **DD** 314.2. **NLM** AY 754 W577A.

ALMANAH STVARNOST. 1975/76-. Serbo-Croatian(R). ir. **LC** AY1038.Y6.

ALMANAK ANTARA. **Main/Corp** Antara (News Agency). 1978/79-. Indonesian. ir. Badan Penerbit Non-Buletin LKBN Antara, J1 Antara No 53-57-61, Jakarta Kotak Pos 257 Indonesia. **LC** AY1165.I5. *Almanak Pers Antara.*

ALMANAK EKUIN. VFOAT Almanak E.K.U.I.N. Edition 2 (1983)-. English (Indonesian). be. **LC** HF3803. **DD** 382.025598. *Almanak Perdagangan Dan Koperasi.*

ALMANAK (INDONESIA). BADAN METEOROLOGI DAN GEOFISIKA). (ALMANAK). 1982-. IO. Indonesian. an. Badan Meteorologi dan Geofisika, J1 Arief Rakhman Hakim, No 3, Jakarta Indonesia. **LC** QC993.I5. *Almanak - Pusat Meteorologi dan Geofisika.*

ALMANAK INSA. **Main/Corp** Persatuan Pelayaran Niaga Indonesia. VFOAT Almanak I.N.S.A. 1981-. IO. English (Indonesian). ir. Persatuan Pelayaran Niaga Indonesia, Jl. Tanah Abang III No. 10, Jakarta Pusat Indonesia. **LC** HE887.

ALMANAK JAKARTA. 0301-7621. Indonesian. ir. 2500. Badan Penerbit Almanak Jakarta P T, Pentja Jakarta Jl Gajahmada No 25, Jakarta Indonesia. **LC** DS646.29.D5. *Almanak Djakarta.*

ALMANAK KEPOLISIAN REPUBLIK INDONESIA. VFOAT Almanak Kepolisian R.I. Indonesian. an. P T Dutarindo Adv, JL Pramuka Kav 72 Indonesia. **LC** HV8254.A2.

ALMANAK MUHAMMADIYAH. **Main/Corp** Muhammadiyah (Organization). Indonesian. ir. Pimpinan Pusat Muhammadiyah Majlis Pustaka, Jl Kha Dahlan 99, Jogyakarta Indonesia. **LC** BP10. *Almanak Muhammadijah.*

ALMANAK PERHUBUNGAN DAN PARIWISATA INDONESIA. 1982-. IO. Indonesian. an. Cv. Sandaan, JL. Cipinang Sodong Raya, No. 27, Jakarta-Timur Indonesia. **LC** HE275.

ALMANAK PERUMAHAN DAN KOMPONEN BAHAN BANGUNAN. 1983-. Indonesian. ir. **LC** HD9715.8.I5.

ALMANAKH GOMONU UKRAJINY. (ALMANAKH HOMONU UKRAINY). VFOAT Alamac of Homin Ukrainy. 1956-. 0441-1196. CN. Ukrainian. Homin Ukrainy Publishing Company, 140 Bathurst Street, Ontario Toronto M5V 2R3 Canada. **DD** 057.91.

AL'MANAKH VYDAVNYTSTVA TRYZUB. VFOAT Almanac of Trident Press. 1976-. 0824-5908. CN. Ukrainian. an. Almanac of Trident Press, 840 Main Street, Winnipeg Manitoba R2W 3N8 Canada. **DD** 057.91. *Kalendar-Al'Manakh Vydavnytstva Tryzub, 0319-5678.*

ALMANAQUE DA PARAIBA. 1973-. Portuguese. ir. Editora Almanaque da Pariba Ltd, rua Duque de Caixias 400, Joao Pessoa Brazil. **LC** F2591.

ALMANAQUE DE CHIAPAS. VFOAT Chiapas. MX. Spanish. an. Almanaque de Mexico S A, Gabriel Mancera 43 Col de Valle, Mexico 03100 DF Mexico. **LC** F1256. **DD** 972.75005.

ALMANAQUE DO TCHE. Periodical. BL. Portuguese. ir. Tche Editora Jornalistica Ltda, Salgado Filho, 359 Porto Alegre Brazil. **LC** AP111. **DD** 056.9.

ALMANAQUE MINO. No. 1- June 1975-. Portuguese. ir. Mino Criacoes, rua Casimiro Montenegro 50 Sao Gerardo, Fortaleza Brazil. **LC** AP111. **DD** 056.1.

ALMANAQUE MUNDIAL. Spanish. ir. **LC** AY515. **DD** 056.1.

ALMANAQUE NAUTICO. Periodical. Spanish. ir. 1200 Domestic, $80.00 Foreign. Instituto y Observatorio de Marina, San Fernando (Cadiz), San Fernando Spain. **Tel** 883548. **LC** QB8.S73. adv acc. **Circ** 5,000. Contains astronomical data as needed for navigation.

ALMANAQUE PUERTORRIQUENO. 1978. PR. Spanish. an. Editorial Edil, Box 23088-UPR Station, Rio Piedras PR 00931. **LC** F1951. General information about PR, relevant news, history, maps, documents, literature, music, origin of sports, etc.

ALPHABETICAL DIRECTORY OF ATTORNEYS IN NEW YORK STATE. VFOAT Directory of Attorneys in New York State. 1982-. 0738-8152. US. English. New York Lawyers Diary and Manual, Box 1226, Neward NJ 07101. **LC** KF192.N45. **DD** 349.747025, 347.470025.

ALPHABETIZED DIRECTORY OF AMERICAN JOURNALISTS. (ALPHABETIZED DIRECTORY OF AMERICAN JOURNALISTS : ASSOCIATED PRESS, UNITED PRESS INTERNATIONAL, AMERICA'S DAILY NEWSPAPERS). 0149-5186. US. English. $7.95. PO Box 231, Kokomo IN 46901. **LC** PN4871. **DD** 071.3025.

ALUMNAE DIRECTORY - BENNETT COLLEGE (GREENSBORO, N.C.). (ALUMNAE DIRECTORY). **Main/Corp** Bennett College (Greensboro, N.C.). VFOAT Bennett College Alumnae Directory. 1981-. 0731-4140. US. English. College & University Press, 1 Bell Road, Box 17940, Montgomery AL 36141. **LC** LD7045. **DD** 378.75662.

ALUMNAE DIRECTORY - BREARLEY SCHOOL. (ALUMNAE DIRECTORY). **Main/Corp** Brearley School. VFOAT Brearley School Alumnae Directory. 0742-5007. US. English. Bernard C Harris

Yearbooks, Almanacs, Directories

Publishing Company, 3 Barker Avenue, White Plains NY 10601. LC LD7501.N494. DD 373.7471.

ALUMNAE DIRECTORY - COLUMBIA COLLEGE (COLUMBIA, S.C.). (ALUMNAE DIRECTORY). **Main/Corp** Columbia College (Columbia, S.C.). VFOAT Columbia College Alumnae Directory. 1981-. 0731-9584. US. English. College & University Press, One Bell Road/PO Box 17940, Montgomery AL 36141. LC LD1205. DD 378.75771.

ALUMNAE DIRECTORY - MOUNT VERNON COLLEGE. **Main/Corp** Mount Vernon College. VFOAT Mount Vernon College Alumnae Directory. US. English. College & University Press, One Bell Road, Box 17940, Montgomery AL 36141. LC LD3561.M868. DD 378.753.

ALUMNAE DIRECTORY - QUEENS COLLEGE (CHARLOTTE, N.C.). (ALUMNAE DIRECTORY). **Main/Corp** Queens College (Charlotte, N.C.). VFOAT Queens College Alumnae Directory. 0731-9010. US. English. College & University Press, One Bell Road, Montgomery AL 36141. LC LD4863. DD 378.75676.

ALUMNAE DIRECTORY - RANDOLPH-MACON WOMAN'S COLLEGE (LYNCHBURG, VA.). **Main/Corp** Randolph-Macon Woman's College. VFOAT Randolph-Macon Woman's College Alumnae Directory. US. English. College & University Press, One Bell Road/PO Box 17940, Montgomery AL 36141. LC LD7251.L852. DD 378.755671.

ALUMNAE DIRECTORY - STEPHENS COLLEGE. (ALUMNAE DIRECTORY). **Main/Corp** Stephens College. 0738-6842. US. English. B C Harris Publishing Company, 3 Barker Avenue, White Plains NY 10601. LC LD5171.S524. DD 378.77829.

ALUMNAE DIRECTORY - WESLEYAN COLLEGE (MACON, GA.). (ALUMNAE DIRECTORY). **Main/Corp** Wesleyan College (Macon, GA.). VFOAT Wesleyan College Alumnae Directory. 0731-9002. US. English. College & University Press, One Bell Road/PO Box 17940, Montgomery AL 36141. LC LD7251.M18. DD 378.758552.

ALUMNAE/I DIRECTORY - LAKE ERIE COLLEGE. (ALUMNAE/I DIRECTORY). **Main/Corp** Lake Erie College. VFOAT Lake Erie College Alumnae/I Directory. 0738-2510. US. English. Bernard C Harris Publishing Company, 3 Barker Avenue, White Plains NY 10601. LC LD2897. DD 378.771334.

ALUMNAE/I DIRECTORY - RUTGERS LAW SCHOOL (NEWARK, N.J.). (ALUMNAE/I DIRECTORY). **Main/Corp** Rutgers Law School (Newark, N.J.). VFOAT Rutgers School of Law Newark Alumnae/I Directory. 0738-6672. US. English. B C Harris Publishing Company, 3 Barker Avenue, White Plains NY 10601. LC KF292.R87. DD 340.071174932.

ALUMNI AND ALUMNAE DIRECTORY - HOBART COLLEGE. (ALUMNI AND ALUMNAE DIRECTORY). **Main/Corp** Hobart College. VFOAT Hobart and William Smith Colleges. 0738-6796. US. English. Bernard C Harris Publishing Company, 3 Barker Avenue, White Plains NY 10601. LC LD2262.3. DD 378.74786.

ALUMNI & ASSOCIATES DIRECTORY - SAN DIEGO STATE UNIVERSITY. **Main/Corp** San Diego State University. VFOAT Alumni and Associates Directory. 0739-3644. US. English. One Bell Road, PO Box 17940, Montgomery AL 36141. LC LD729.6.S3. DD 378.79498.

ALUMNI ASSOCIATION MEMBERSHIP DIRECTORY - WVU ALUMNI ASSOCIATION. **Main/Corp** WVU Alumni Association. VFOAT West Virginia University Alumni Association Membership Directory. 1982-. 0736-8984. US. English. Bernard C Harris Publishing Company, 3 Barker Avenue, White, Plains NY 10601. LC LD5929. DD 378.95453.

ALUMNI DIRECTORY - ALBANY LAW SCHOOL. **Main/Corp** Albany Law School. VFOAT Albany Law School of Union University Alumni Directory. 1981-. US. English. B C Harris Publishing Company, 3 Barker Avenue, White Plains NY 10601. LC KF292.A52. DD 340.071174743.

ALUMNI DIRECTORY - ALBANY STATE COLLEGE. (ALUMNI DIRECTORY). **Main/Corp** Albany State College. VFOAT Albany State College Alumni Directory. 1983-. 0740-1620. US. English. Office of Alumni Affairs, Albany State College, Albany GA 31705. LC LD91.A55. DD 378.74743.

ALUMNI DIRECTORY - ALFRED UNIVERSITY. ALUMNI OFFICE. **Main/Corp** Alfred University. Alumni Office. VFOAT Alfred University Alumni Directory. US. English. Alfred University, PO Box 1165, Alfred NY 14802. LC LD131. DD 378.74784.

ALUMNI DIRECTORY AND NEWSLETTER - UNIVERSITY OF NORTH CAROLINA AT CHAPEL HILL. DEPT. OF GEOLOGY. **Main/Corp** University of North Carolina at Chapel Hill. Dept. of Geology. US. English. ir. University of North Carolina at Chapel Hill, Department of Geology, Mitchell Hall 029 A, Chapel Hill NC 27514.

ALUMNI DIRECTORY - BELMONT ABBEY COLLEGE. (ALUMNI DIRECTORY). **Main/Corp** Belmont Abbey College. VFOAT Belmont Abbey College Alumni Directory. 0740-1752. US. English. Belmont Abbey College, Belmont NC 28012. LC LD371.B6651A. DD 378.756773.

ALUMNI DIRECTORY - BETHEL COLLEGE (MCKENZIE, TENN.). (ALUMNI DIRECTORY). **Main/Corp** Bethel College (McKenzie, Tenn.). VFOAT Bethel College Alumni Directory. 1981-. 0731-4159. US. English. College & University Press, One Bell Road/PO Box 17940, Montgomery AL 36141. LC LD451.B31A. DD 378.76825.

ALUMNI DIRECTORY - BOSTON UNIVERSITY. SCHOOL OF MEDICINE. ALUMNI ASSOCIATION. (ALUMNI DIRECTORY). **Main/Corp** Boston University. School of Medicine. Alumni Association. 0743-5533. US. English. Alumni Association Boston University School of Medicine, 80 East Concord Street, Boston MA 02118. LC R747. DD 610.71174461.

ALUMNI DIRECTORY - BRYANT COLLEGE. (ALUMNI DIRECTORY). **Main/Corp** Bryant College. VFOAT Bryant College Alumni Directory. 0738-1158. US. English. Bernard C Harris Publishing Company, 3 Barker Avenue, White Plains NY 10601. LC LD649.8. DD 378.7451.

ALUMNI DIRECTORY - BUENA VISTA COLLEGE. **Main/Corp** Buena Vista College. VFOAT Buena Vista College Alumni Directory. US. English. College & University Press, One Bell Road/PO Box 17940, Montgomery AL 36141. LC LD701.B31. DD 378.77718.

ALUMNI DIRECTORY - CALIFORNIA COLLEGE OF ARTS AND CRAFTS (OAKLAND, CALIF.). (ALUMNI DIRECTORY). **Main/Corp** California College of Arts and Crafts (Oakland, Calif.). VFOAT California College of Arts and Crafts Alumni Directory. 1981-. 0731-8928. US. English. College & University Press, One Bell Road PO Box 17940, Montgomery AL 36141. LC N330.O352. DD 707.1179466.

ALUMNI DIRECTORY - CALIFORNIA STATE COLLEGE (PA.). (ALUMNI DIRECTORY). **Main/Corp** California State College (Pa.). VFOAT California State College Alumni Directory. 0732-426X. US. English. College & University Press, One Bell Road/PO Box 17940, Montgomery AL 36141. LC LD729.C9845. DD 378.74882.

ALUMNI DIRECTORY - CALIFORNIA STATE UNIVERSITY, NORTHRIDGE. (ALUMNI DIRECTORY). **Main/Corp** California State University, Northridge. VFOAT California State University, Northridge Alumni Directory. 1982-. 0736-6426. US. English. College and University Press, One Bell Road/PO Box 17940, Montgomery AL 36141. LC LD729.6.N6. DD 378.79494.

ALUMNI DIRECTORY - CANISIUS COLLEGE. **Main/Corp** Canisius College. VFOAT Canisius College Alumni Directory. 1982-. US. English. College and University Press, One Bell Road/PO Box 17940, Montgomery AL 36141. LC LD791.C51A. DD 378.74797.

ALUMNI DIRECTORY - CATAWBA COLLEGE. (ALUMNI DIRECTORY). **Main/Corp** Catawba College. VFOAT Catawba College Alumni Directory. 0732-345X. US. English. $27.45 Alumni and Staff. College & University Press, One Bell Road/PO Box 17940, Montgomery AL 36141. LC LD801.C41. DD 378.75671.

ALUMNI DIRECTORY - CHOATE ROSEMARY HALL. (ALUMNI DIRECTORY). **Main/Corp** Choate Rosemary Hall. VFOAT Choate Rosemary Hall Alumni Directory. 0738-680X. US. English. Bernard C Harris Publishing Company, 3 Barker Avenue, White Plains NY 10601. LC LD7501.W253. DD 373.222097467.

ALUMNI DIRECTORY - CHRISTIAN BROTHERS COLLEGE (MEMPHIS, TENN.). (ALUMNI DIRECTORY). **Main/Corp** Christian Brothers College (Memphis, Tenn.). VFOAT Christian Brothers College Alumni Directory. 0740-1779. US. English. Christian Brothers College, Alumni Association, 650 East Parkway South, Memphis TN 38104. LC LD961.C31A. DD 378.76819.

ALUMNI DIRECTORY - COKER COLLEGE. **Main/Corp** Coker College. VFOAT Coker College Alumni Directory. US. English. College & University Press, One Bell Road/PO Box 17940, Montgomery AL 36141. LC LD1061.C62. DD 378.75766.

ALUMNI DIRECTORY - COLUMBIA COLLEGE (COLUMBIA UNIVERSITY). (ALUMNI DIRECTORY). **Main/Corp** Columbia College (Columbia University). 0738-9817. US. English. Bernard C Harris Publishing Company, 3 Barker Avenue, White Plains NY 10601. LC LD1269.5.C6. DD 378.7471.

ALUMNI DIRECTORY - CORNELL COLLEGE (MOUNT VERNON, IOWA). (ALUMNI DIRECTORY). **Main/Corp** Cornell College (Mount Vernon, Iowa). VFOAT Cornell College Alumni Directory. 1981-. 0731-891X. US. English. College & University Press, One Bell Road/PO Box 17940, Montgomery AL 36141. LC LD1312.3. DD 378.77762.

ALUMNI DIRECTORY - CREIGHTON PREPARATORY SCHOOL. (ALUMNI DIRECTORY). **Main/Corp** Creighton Preparatory School. VFOAT Creighton Preparatory School Alumni Directory. 0740-1787. US. English. 7400 Western Avenue, Omaha NE 68114. LC LD7501.O657. DD 373.782254.

ALUMNI DIRECTORY - CULINARY INSTITUTE OF AMERICA. (ALUMNI DIRECTORY). **Main/Corp** Culinary Institute of America. VFOAT Culinary Institute of America Alumni Directory. 0738-1557. US. English. Bernard C Harris Publishing Company, 3 Barker Avenue, White Plains NY 10601. LC TX661. DD 641.502573.

ALUMNI DIRECTORY - CUSHING ACADEMY. (ALUMNI DIRECTORY). **Main/Corp** Cushing Academy. VFOAT Cushing Academy Alumni Directory. 0738-6664. US. English. Bernard C Harris Publishing Company, 3 Barker Avenue, White Plains NY 10601. LC LD7501.A77. DD 373.7443.

ALUMNI DIRECTORY - EASTERN NEW MEXICO UNIVERSITY (PORTALES, N.M.). **Main/Corp** Eastern New Mexico University (Portales, N.M.). VFOAT Eastern New Mexico University Alumni Directory. 1981-. US. English. an. College & University Press, One Bell Road/PO Box 17940, Montgomery AL 36141. LC LD3781.N3. DD 378.78932.

ALUMNI DIRECTORY - EMORY AND HENRY COLLEGE. (ALUMNI DIRECTORY). **Main/Corp** Emory and Henry College. VFOAT Emory and Henry College Alumni, Emory & Henry College Alumni Directory, Emory and Henry College Alumni Directory. 0738-3738. US. English. Bernard C Harris Publishing Company, 3 Barker Avenue, White Plains NY 10601. LC LD1751.E371A. DD 378.755725.

ALUMNI DIRECTORY - FLORIDA SOUTHERN COLLEGE. **Main/Corp** Florida Southern College. VFOAT Florida Southern College Alumni Directory. 1981-. US. English. College & University Press, One Bell Road PO Box 17940, Montgomery AL 36141. LC LD1771.F81. DD 378.75967.

ALUMNI DIRECTORY - GEORGE PEABODY COLLEGE FOR TEACHERS. (ALUMNI DIRECTORY). **Main/Corp** George Peabody College for Teachers. VFOAT Peabody College of Vanderbilt Alumni Directory. 0738-1581. US. English. College & University Press, One Bell Road PO Box 17940, Montgomery AL 36141. LC LB2193.N293. DD 378.76855.

ALUMNI DIRECTORY - GEORGE WASHINGTON UNIVERSITY. **Main/Corp** George Washington University, Washington, D.C. US. English. College and University Press, 803 West

Yearbooks, Almanacs, Directories

Broad Street, Falls Church VA 22046. LC LD1921. DD 378.753.

ALUMNI DIRECTORY - GLENVILLE STATE COLLEGE. (ALUMNI DIRECTORY). **Main/Corp** Glenville State College. **VFOAT** Glenville State College Alumni Directory. 0732-040X. US. English. College & University Press, One Bell Road/PO Box 17940, Montgomery AL 36141. LC LD2001.G43. DD 378.75427.

ALUMNI DIRECTORY - GRAMBLING STATE UNIVERSITY. (ALUMNI DIRECTORY). **Main/Corp** Grambling State University. **VFOAT** Grambling State University Alumni Directory. 1981-. 0738-6818. US. English. Bernard C Harris Publishing Company, 3 Barker Avenue, White Plains NY 10601. LC LD3091.L367. DD 378.76391.

ALUMNI DIRECTORY - GROVE CITY COLLEGE. (ALUMNI DIRECTORY). **Main/Corp** Grove City College. **VFOAT** Grove City College Alumni Directory. 0743-4405. US. English. B C Harris Publishing Company, 3 Barker Avenue, White Plains NY 10601. LC LD2072.3. DD 378.74895.

ALUMNI DIRECTORY - HAMPSHIRE COLLEGE. (ALUMNI DIRECTORY). 0278-887X. US. English. Free to Alumni. Hampshire College, Amherst MA 01002. LC LD2101.H662. DD 378.74423.

ALUMNI DIRECTORY - HAWKEN SCHOOL (LYNDHURST, OHIO). **Main/Corp** Hawken School (Lyndhurst, Ohio). **VFOAT** Hawken School Alumni Directory. US. English. College & University Press, 1 Bell Road/PO Box 17940, Montgomery AL 36141. LC LD7501.L97. DD 373.77131.

ALUMNI DIRECTORY - HUNTINGDON COLLEGE (MONTGOMERY, ALA.). (ALUMNI DIRECTORY). **Main/Corp** Huntingdon College (Montgomery, Al.). **VFOAT** Huntingdon College Alumni Directory. 1981-. 0731-4167. US. English. College & University Press, 1 Bell Road, Box 17940, Montgomery AL 36141. LC LD2281.H89. DD 378.76147.

ALUMNI DIRECTORY - JOHNSON C. SMITH UNIVERSITY. (ALUMNI DIRECTORY). **Main/Corp** Johnson C. Smith University. **VFOAT** Johnson C. Smith University Alumni Directory. 1983-. 0738-2006. US. English. Bernard C Harris Publishing Company, 3 Barker Avenue, White Plains NY 10601. LC LD2645. DD 378.75676.

ALUMNI DIRECTORY - LIVINGSTON UNIVERSITY. **Main/Corp** Livingston University. **VFOAT** Livingston University Alumni Directory. US. English. College & University Press, One Bell Road/PO Box 17940, Montgomery AL 36141. LC LD3071.L971. DD 378.76141.

ALUMNI DIRECTORY - LOOMIS CHAFFEE SCHOOL. (ALUMNI DIRECTORY). **Main/Corp** Loomis Chaffee School. **VFOAT** Loomis Chaffee School Alumni Directory. 0738-5897. US. English. Bernard C Harris Publishing Company, 3 Barker Avenue, White Plains NY 10601. LC LD7501.W75. DD 373.7462.

ALUMNI DIRECTORY - LSU SCHOOL OF MEDICINE, NEW ORLEANS. **Main/Corp** LSU School of Medicine, New Orleans. **VFOAT** L.S.U. School of Medicine, New Orleans Alumni Directory. 1981-. US. English. College and University Press, 1 Bell Road/PO Box 17940, Montgomery AL 36141. LC R747.L95. DD 610.2576.

ALUMNI DIRECTORY - MARSHALL UNIVERSITY. **Main/Corp** Marshall University. **VFOAT** Marshall University Alumni Directory. US. English. College & University Press, One Bell Road/PO Box 17940, Montgomery AL 36141. LC LD3231.M631. DD 378.75442.

ALUMNI DIRECTORY - MICHIGAN STATE UNIVERSITY. COLLEGE OF AGRICULTURE AND NATURAL RESOURCES. (ALUMNI DIRECTORY). **Main/Corp** Michigan State University. College of Agriculture and Natural Resources. 1983-. 0739-6147. US. English. Michigan State University, College of Agriculture and Natural Resources Alumni Association Agriculture Hall, East Lansing Mi 48824. LC S537.M716. DD 630.71177427.

ALUMNI DIRECTORY - NEW MEXICO MILITARY INSTITUTE. (ALUMNI DIRECTORY). **Main/Corp** New Mexico Military Institute. **VFOAT** Directory of Alumni. 1981-. 0738-8160. US. English. Bernard C Harris Publishing Company, 3 Barker Avenue, White Plains NY 10601. LC U430.N5. DD 378.78943.

ALUMNI DIRECTORY - NEW YORK MILITARY ACADEMY. (ALUMNI DIRECTORY). **Main/Corp** New York Military Academy. **VFOAT** New York Military Academy Alumni Directory. 8755-6952. US. English. B C Harris Publishing Company, 3 Barker Avenue, White Plains NY 10601. LC U430.N7. DD 355.0071173.

ALUMNI DIRECTORY - NICHOLS SCHOOL (BUFFALO, N.Y.). (ALUMNI DIRECTORY). **Main/Corp** Nichols School (Buffalo, N.Y.). **VFOAT** Nichols School Alumni Directory. 0732-0388. US. English. College & University Press, One Bell Road/PO Box 17940, Montgomery AL 36141. LC LD3914. DD 373.74797.

ALUMNI DIRECTORY - NORTHEAST LOUISIANA UNIVERSITY. (ALUMNI DIRECTORY). **Main/Corp** Northeast Louisiana University. **VFOAT** Northeast Louisiana University Alumni Directory. 1981-. 0732-0744. US. English. College & University Press, One Bell Road/PO Box 17940, Montgomery AL 36141. LC LD4005. DD 378.76387.

ALUMNI DIRECTORY - PEPPERDINE UNIVERSITY. (ALUMNI DIRECTORY). **Main/Corp** Pepperdine University. **VFOAT** Pepperdine University Alumni Directory. 1982-. 0737-1101. US. English. College & University Press, PO Box 17940, Montgomery AL 36141. LC LD4561.P428. DD 378.79494.

ALUMNI DIRECTORY - POPULATION COUNCIL. **Main/Corp** Population Council (New York, N.Y.). US. English. The Population Council, One Dag Hammarskjold Plaza, New York NY 10017. LC HB848. DD 304.606.

ALUMNI DIRECTORY - QUEENS COLLEGE (FLUSHING, N.Y.). (ALUMNI DIRECTORY). **Main/Corp** Queens College (New York, N.Y.). **VFOAT** Queens College Alumni Directory. 0738-5196. US. English. College and University Press, 1 Bell Road, Montgomery AL 36141. LC LD4685. DD 378.747243.

ALUMNI DIRECTORY - SAINT MARGARET'S-MCTERNAN (SCHOOL). **Main/Corp** Saint Margaret's-McTernan (School). **VFOAT** Saint Margaret's-McTernan Alumni Directory. US. English. College & University Press, One Bell Road PO Box 17940, Montgomery AL 36141. LC LD4819.S43. DD 373.7467.

ALUMNI DIRECTORY - SHAW UNIVERSITY. (ALUMNI DIRECTORY). **Main/Corp** Shaw University. **VFOAT** Shaw University Alumni Directory. 1982-. 0740-9362. US. English. College & University Press, One Bell Road P O Box 17940, Montgomery AL 36141. LC LD4931.S37. DD 378.75655.

ALUMNI DIRECTORY - SIENA COLLEGE. (ALUMNI DIRECTORY). **Main/Corp** Siena College. 1982-. 0738-8179. US. English. Bernard C Harris Publishing Company, 3 Barker Avenue, White Plains NY 10601. LC LD4933. DD 378.74742.

ALUMNI DIRECTORY - SOUTHERN METHODIST UNIVERSITY. (ALUMNI DIRECTORY). **Main/Corp** Southern Methodist University. **VFOAT** S.M.U. Alumni Directory. 1978-. 0738-1174. US. English. ir. B C Harris Publishing Company, 3 Barker Avenue, White Plains NY 10601. LC LD5101. DD 378.7642812. *SMU Alumni Directory.*

ALUMNI DIRECTORY - SPRINGFIELD COLLEGE. **Main/Corp** Springfield College. US. English. College & University Press, One Bell Road P O Box 17940, Montgomery AL 36141. LC LD5171.S48. DD 378.74426.

ALUMNI DIRECTORY - STATE UNIVERSITY OF NEW YORK AT ALBANY. (ALUMNI DIRECTORY). **Main/Corp** State University of New York at Albany. **VFOAT** State University of New York at Albany Alumni Directory. 1980-. 0733-1541. US. English. College & University Press, One Bell Road, PO Box 17940, Montgomery AL 36141. LC LD3841. DD 378.74743.

ALUMNI DIRECTORY - TEXAS A & I UNIVERSITY. (ALUMNI DIRECTORY). **Main/Corp** Texas A & I University. **VFOAT** Texas A and I University Alumni Directory. 0738-2219. US. English. College & University Press, One Bell Road, PO Box 17940, Montgomery AL 36141. LC LD5308. DD 378.764472.

THE ALUMNI DIRECTORY - TEXAS CHRISTIAN UNIVERSITY. **Main/Corp** Texas Christian University. 0147-4898. US. English. Texas Christian University, Office of Alumni, Fort Worth TX 76129.

ALUMNI DIRECTORY - TRI-STATE UNIVERSITY (U.S.). **Main/Corp** Tri-State University (U.S.). **VFOAT** Tri-State University Alumni Directory. US. English. College & University Press, One Bell Road/PO Box 17940, Montgomery AL 36141. LC LD5361.T31. DD 378.77278.

ALUMNI DIRECTORY - TRINITY COLLEGE (HARTFORD, CONN.). (ALUMNI DIRECTORY). **Main/Corp** Trinity College (Hartford, Conn.). **VFOAT** Trinity College Alumni Directory. 0740-1671. US. English. Trinity College, Hartford CT 06106. LC LD5361.T41A. DD 378.7463.

ALUMNI DIRECTORY - TROY STATE UNIVERSITY. **Main/Corp** Troy State University. **VFOAT** Troy State University Alumni Directory. US. English. College & University Press, One Bell Road, Montgomery AL 36141. LC LD5361.T7. DD 378.76135.

ALUMNI DIRECTORY - UNIVERSITY OF CALIFORNIA, BERKELEY. GRADUATE SCHOOL OF BUSINESS ADMINISTRATION. (ALUMNI DIRECTORY). **Main/Corp** University of California, Berkeley. Graduate School of Business Administration. **VFOAT** Berkeley Business School Alumni Directory. 1983-. 0742-4353. US. English. B C Harris Publishing Company, 3 Barker Avenue, White Plains NY 10601. LC HF1134.C3. DD 650.071179467.

ALUMNI DIRECTORY - UNIVERSITY OF CALIFORNIA, DAVIS. (ALUMNI DIRECTORY). **Main/Corp** University of California, Davis. **VFOAT** University of California Davis, Alumni Directory. 0742-4345. US. English. B C Harris Publishing Company, 3 Barker Avenue, White Plains NY 10601. LC LD781.D3. DD 378.79451.

ALUMNI DIRECTORY - UNIVERSITY OF CALIFORNIA, LOS ANGELES. GRADUATE SCHOOL OF MANAGEMENT. (ALUMNI DIRECTORY). **Main/Corp** University of California, Los Angeles. Graduate School of Management. **VFOAT** U.C.L.A. G.S.M. Alumni Directory. 0738-1182. US. English. Bernard C Harris Publishing Company, 3 Barker Avenue, White Plains NY 10601. LC HD30.42.U5. DD 658.0071179494.

ALUMNI DIRECTORY - UNIVERSITY OF CHICAGO LAW SCHOOL. (ALUMNI DIRECTORY - THE UNIVERSITY OF CHICAGO LAW SCHOOL). **Main/Corp** University of Chicago. Law School. 0162-0371. US. English. $15.00. University of Chicago, Law School, Chicago IL 60637. LC KF292.C45. DD 340.071177311.

ALUMNI DIRECTORY - UNIVERSITY OF COLORADO, BOULDER. COLLEGE OF BUSINESS AND ADMINISTRATION. **Main/Corp** University of Colorado, Boulder. College of Business and Administration. **VFOAT** University of Colorado, Boulder College of Business and Administration Alumni Directory. US. English. Bernard C Harris Publishing Company, 3 Barker Avenue, White Plains NY 10601. LC HF1134.U54. DD 650.071178863.

ALUMNI DIRECTORY - UNIVERSITY OF DENVER. (ALUMNI DIRECTORY). **Main/Corp** University of Denver. 0738-3630. US. English. B C Harris Publishing Company, 3 Barker Avenue, White Plains NY 10601. LC LD1562.3. DD 378.78883.

ALUMNI DIRECTORY - UNIVERSITY OF EVANSVILLE. (ALUMNI DIRECTORY). **Main/Corp** University of Evansville. **VFOAT** University of Evansville Alumni Directory. 0738-078X. US. English. Bernard C Harris Publishing Company, 3 Barker Avenue, White Plains NY 10601. LC LD1761.E61A. DD 378.77233.

ALUMNI DIRECTORY - UNIVERSITY OF MINNESOTA. MEDICAL SCHOOL. (ALUMNI DIRECTORY). **Main/Corp** University of Minnesota. Medical School. **VFOAT** University of Minnesota Medical School Alumni Directory. 0739-6899. US. English. College & University Press, One Bell Road, PO Box 17940, Montgomery AL 36141. LC R747. DD 610.711776579.

ALUMNI DIRECTORY - UNIVERSITY OF NORTH CAROLINA AT CHAPEL HILL. (ALUMNI DIRECTORY - THE ALUMNI OFFICE OF THE GENERAL ALUMNI ASSOCIATION). **Main/Corp** University of North Carolina at Chapel

Yearbooks, Almanacs, Directories

Hill. General Alumni Association. Alumni Office. 0146-7433. US. English. University of North Carolina at Chapel Hill, Alumni Office, Chapel Hill NC 27514. LC LD3942.3. DD 378.756565.

ALUMNI DIRECTORY - UNIVERSITY OF PITTSBURGH, SCHOOL OF MEDICINE. (ALUMNI DIRECTORY). Main/Corp University of Pittsburgh. School of Medicine. VFOAT University of Pittsburgh School of Medicine Alumni Directory. 0738-0240. US. English. College & University Press, One Bell Road/PO Box 17940, Montgomery AL 36141. LC R747.P77. DD 610.2573.

ALUMNI DIRECTORY - UNIVERSITY OF REDLANDS. (ALUMNI DIRECTORY). Main/Corp University of Redlands. VFOAT University of Redlands Alumni Directory. 0739-1366. US. English. Bernard C Harris Publishing Company, 3 Barker Avenue, White Plains NY 10601. LC LD4701.R6641A. DD 378.79495.

ALUMNI DIRECTORY - UNIVERSITY OF ROCHESTER. SCHOOL OF MEDICINE AND DENTISTRY. (ALUMNI DIRECTORY). Main/Corp University of Rochester. School of Medicine and Dentistry. VFOAT University of Rochester School of Medicine & Dentistry Alumni Directory. 0736-6671. US. English. College & University Press, One Bell Road, Montgomery AL 36141. LC R747.U6838. DD 610.71174789.

ALUMNI DIRECTORY - UNIVERSITY OF TORONTO. Main/Corp University of Toronto. 1979/80-. 0225-2333. Periodical. CN. English. Department of Alumni Affairs, Alumni House, 47 Willcocks Street, University of Toronto, Toronto Ontario M5S 1A1 Canada. DD 378.713541. *Directory, Alumni Officers, Varsity Fund Board, University of Toronto, 0381-999X.*

ALUMNI DIRECTORY - UNIVERSITY OF VIRGINIA. ALUMNI ASSOCIATION. (ALUMNI DIRECTORY). Main/Corp University of Virginia. Alumni Association. VFOAT Alumni Association of the University of Virginia Alumni Directory. 0738-0852. US. English. Bernard C Harris Publishing Company, 3 Barker Avenue, White Plains NY 10601. LC LD5675.3. DD 378.755481.

ALUMNI DIRECTORY - UNIVERSITY OF VIRGINIA. ALUMNI ASSOCIATION. (ALUMNI DIRECTORY). Main/Corp University of Virginia. Alumni Association. 1981-. 0738-3762. US. English. $20.00. University of Virginia Alumni Association, PO Box 3446 University Station, Charlottesville VA 22903. Tel (804)971-9721. Ed Bill Sublette. LC LD5675.3. DD 378.755481. bk rev. adv acc. Circ 50,000. (ctrl). The alumni news covers all aspects of the university community. All our stories have a University Virginia Alumni tie-in. We cover faculty, student and alumni activities.

ALUMNI DIRECTORY - VIRGINIA INTERMONT COLLEGE. (ALUMNI DIRECTORY). Main/Corp Virginia Intermont College. VFOAT Virginia Intermont College Alumni Directory. 0738-5250. US. English. Bernard C Harris Publishing Company, 3 Barker Avenue, White Plains NY 10601. LC LD7251.B7868. DD 378.755725.

ALUMNI DIRECTORY - VIRGINIA UNION UNIVERSITY (RICHMOND, VA.). (ALUMNI DIRECTORY). Main/Corp Virginia Union University (Richmond, VA.). VFOAT Virginia Union University Alumni Directory. 1983-. 0740-1795. US. English. Virginia Union University, 1500 North Lombardy Street, Richmond VA 23220. LC LC2851.V7. DD 378.755451.

ALUMNI DIRECTORY - WEST GEORGIA COLLEGE. (ALUMNI DIRECTORY). Main/Corp West Georgia College. VFOAT West Georgia College Alumni Directory. 1980-. 0278-8845. US. English. College & University Press, One Bell Road/PO Box 17940, Montgomery AL 36141. LC LD5901.W44. DD 378.75839.

ALUMNI DIRECTORY - WEST LIBERTY STATE COLLEGE. (ALUMNI DIRECTORY). Main/Corp West Liberty State College. VFOAT West Liberty State College Alumni Directory. 1981-. 0732-0450. US. English. College & University Press, One Bell Road, PO Box 17940, Montgomery AL 36141. LC LD5901.W49. DD 378.75414.

ALUMNI DIRECTORY - WESTERN RESERVE COLLEGE. Main/Corp Western Reserve College. VFOAT Western Reserve College Alumni Directory. US. English. College & University Press, One Bell Road/PO Box 17940, Montgomery AL 36141. LC LD5962.3. DD 378.77175.

ALUMNI DIRECTORY - WILLIAMS COLLEGE. (ALUMNI DIRECTORY). Main/Corp Williams College. 0738-3517. US. English. te. $9.00. Alumni Office, PO Box 38, Williamstown MA 01267. LC LD6072.3. DD 378.7441.

ALUMNI DIRECTORY - WINSTON-SALEM STATE UNIVERSITY. Main/Corp Winston-Salem State University. VFOAT Winston-Salem State University Alumni Directory. 1981-. Periodical. US. English. College & University Press, 1 Bell Road/PO Box 17940, Montgomery AL 36141. LC LD6093. DD 378.75667.

AMA DIRECTORY OF OFFICIALS AND STAFF - AMERICAN MEDICAL ASSOCIATION. Main/Corp American Medical Association. VFOAT A.M.A. Directory of Officials and Staff Association. Began with issue for 1979?. 0748-5557. US. English. ir. American Medical Association, 535 North Dearborn Street, Chicago IL 60610. Tel (312)645-4927. LC R15. DD 610.6073. *Directory of Officials and Staff.*

AMATEUR RADIO CALL DIRECTORY. UNITED STATES LISTINGS, GEOGRAPHICAL INDEX. (AMATEUR RADIO CALL DIRECTORY. UNITED STATES LISTINGS. GEOGRAPHICAL INDEX). VFOAT Radio Call Directory. 1982-83 Ed.-. 0737-7185. US. English. an. $25.00. Buckmaster Publishing, 70 Florida Hill Road, Ridgefield CT 06888.

AMERICAN ACADEMY OF OPHTHALMOLOGY DIRECTORY. VFOAT Ophthalmology Directory. 1978-. 0190-0293. US. English. an. American Academy of Ophthalmology and Otolaryngology, 15 2nd Street SW, Rochester MN 55901. LC RE22. DD 617.7002573. NLM WW 22 AA1 A4D. *Directory - American Academy of Ophthalmology and Otolarynology, Division of Ophthalmology, 0190-2032.*

AMERICAN ARCHITECTS DIRECTORY. 1st- 1956-. 0065-695X. US. English. ir. R R Bowker Company, 205 East 42nd Street, New York NY 10017. LC NA53. DD 720, 920.

AMERICAN ART DIRECTORY. V. 1- 1898-. 0065-6968. US. English. ir. $88.00. R R Bowker Company, PO Box 1807, Ann Arbor MI 48106. Tel (800)521-0600. Ed F N Levy. LC N50. DD 705.8.

AMERICAN ARTIST DIRECTORY OF ART SCHOOLS & WORKSHOPS. (AMERICAN ARTIST DIRECTORY OF ART SCHOOLS AND WORKSHOPS). VFOAT Art School Directory. VAT American Artist Directory of Art Schools and Workshops. 1977-. 0146-9606. US. English. $2.50. American Artist Reprints, 1515 Broadway, New York NY 10036. Tel (212)-581-6279. LC N328. DD 707.073. *American Artist Art School Directory, 0002-7375.*

AMERICAN BANK DIRECTORY. Began with: 1954?. 0569-292X. Periodical. US. English. sa. $130.00. McFadden Business Publications, 6195 Crooked Creek Road, Norcross GA 30092. Tel (404)448-1011. LC HG2441. *American Bank Reporter.*

AMERICAN BANKER DIRECTORY OF U.S. BANKING EXECUTIVES. VFOAT Directory of U.S. Banking Executives. VAT American Banker Directory of United States Banking Executives. 1st. Ed.-. 0277-819X. US. English. an. $93.00. American Banker, One State Street Plaza, New York NY 10004. Tel (212)943-8675. LC HG2463.A2. DD 332.10922, B.

AMERICAN BLACK DIRECTORY. 0364-0833. US. English. an. $3.00 Single Issue. Quiz-Set Publishing Company, P O Box 8084, Chicago IL 60680. LC HF5036.A47. DD 381.02573.

AMERICAN BOOK TRADE DIRECTORY. 12th Ed.-. 0065-759X. US. English. an. R R Bowker Company, PO Box 1807, Ann Arbor MI 48106. *American Booktrade Directory.*

AMERICAN BUSINESS IN ARGENTINA ... DIRECTORY. English. an. The American Chamber of Commerce in Argentina, Av Pte R Sanez Pena 567 6th Floor Office 603, Buenos Aires Argentina. *AMCHAM Argentina.*

THE AMERICAN CAMELLIA YEARBOOK. 1st- 1946-. 0065-762X. US. English. an. $7.50. American Camellia Society, PO Box 1217, Ft Valley GA 31030. Tel (912)967-2358. Ed Milton H Brown. Ind/Abst Bibliogr. Agric. LC SB413.C18. DD 635.933166. bk rev. adv acc. Circ 4,000. (ctrl). Articles promoting interest in the genus Camellia, including its culture. New varieties and events of interest to camellia growers.

THE AMERICAN CHAMBER OF COMMERCE IN HONG KONG : DIRECTORY. VFOAT Directory. English. an. $40.00 Members, $200.00 Nonmembers. American Chamber of Commerce in Hong Kong, 10/F Sire House, Hong Kong China. LC HF331.H6. DD 382.0951250730255125.

AMERICAN CONSTRUCTION INDUSTRY DIRECTORY. 0195-9484. US. English. an. $14.75 Post Publication. Studio 4 Products, 4439 Village Road, Long Beach CA 90808. LC HD9715.U5.

AMERICAN DANCE DIRECTORY. 1979/80-. 0197-6869. US. English. $10.00. AADC Publications, 162 West 56th Street, New York NY 10019. LC GV1587.5. DD 793.32.

AMERICAN DENTAL DIRECTORY. 1947-. 0065-8073. US. English. an. American Dental Association, Bureau of Data Processing and Membership Records, 211 East Chicago Avenue, Chicago IL 60611. LC RK37. DD 617.6002573. NLM WU 22 AA1 A513.

AMERICAN DIRECTORY OF OBSTETRICIANS AND GYNECOLOGISTS. See Medicine - Gynecology & Obstetrics.

AMERICAN DROP-SHIPPERS DIRECTORY. VFOAT Drop-Shippers Directory. VAT American Drop Shippers Directory. 0065-8103. Periodical. US. English. ir. World Wide Trade Service, Medina, WA 98039. LC HF5421. DD 318.202573.

THE AMERICAN EPHEMERIS AND NAUTICAL ALMANAC CEASED. Main/Corp United States Naval Observatory. Nautical Almanac Office. 1855-1980. 0065-8189. US. English. an. LC QB8. DD 52873.

THE AMERICAN FARM & HOME ALMANAC. V. 1- 1966-. 0065-8278. US. English. an. $1.50. Almanac Publishing Company, PO Box 1609, Lewiston ME 04240. LC AY64.

THE AMERICAN FISHERIES DIRECTORY AND REFERENCE BOOK. (THE AMERICAN FISHERIES DIRECTORY & REFERENCE BOOK). 2nd Ed. (1981)-. 0162-6728. US. English. be. National Fisherman, 21 Elm Street, Camden ME 04843. LC SH203. DD 338.37202573. *American Fisheries Directory and Reference Book, 0162-6728.*

AMERICAN FRANCHISE & BUSINESS OPPORTUNITY DIRECTORY. 0098-7328. US. English. $2.95. Bapi Services, 880 Boston Road, Billerica MA 01866. LC HF5429. DD 381.

AMERICAN INDIAN MEDIA DIRECTORY. 1974-. 0093-2094. US. English. an. American Indian Press Association, 1346 Connecticut Avenue NW, Washington DC 20036. LC E98.M33. DD 301.161025701.

AMERICAN INDIAN TALENT DIRECTORY. 0882-4495. US. English. American Indian Registry for the Performing Arts, 330 Barham Boulevard/Suite 208, Los Angeles CA 90068. DD 790.

AMERICAN INSTITUTE OF ARCHITECTS MEMBERSHIP DIRECTORY. (MEMBERSHIP DIRECTORY). VFOAT AIA Membership Directory. 1973-. 0276-668X. US. English. an. $75.00. American Institute of Architects, 1735 New York Avenue Northwest, Washington DC 20006. *AIA Membership Directory.*

AMERICAN JEWISH YEAR BOOK. V. 1- 1899/1900-. 0065-8987. US. English. an. LC E184.J5. NLM E 184.J5 A512. (cum index).

AMERICAN LIBRARY DIRECTORY. 1923-. 0065-910X. US. English. an. $119.95. R R Bowker Company, PO Box 1807, Ann Arbor MI 48106. Tel (212)916-1600. LC Z731. DD 021.002573. NLM Z 731 A512. The only professional reference with the latest information on public, academic and other libraries, as well as library personnel. *American Library Annual.*

AMERICAN LIBRARY DIRECTORY UPDATING SERVICE. V. 1- Jan. 1969-. 0002-9793. US. English. bm. $65.00. R R Bowker Company, PO Box 1807, Ann Arbor MI 48106. Tel (800)521-0600.

Yearbooks, Almanacs, Directories

AMERICAN MCD. NATIONAL EDITION. (AMERICAN MCD : AMERICAN MOTOR CARRIER DIRECTORY). **VFOAT** ATA American Motor Carrier Directory. **VAT** American Motor Carrier Directory. National Edition, American Trucking Associations American Motor Carrier Directory. 0569-6356. US. English. sa. $65.00. Guide Services Inc, National Edition, PO Box 13446, 2161 Monroe Drive, Atlanta GA 30324. **LC** HE5623.A45. **DD** 338.32402573.

AMERICAN MCD. NEW ENGLAND EDITION. (AMERICAN MCD : AMERICAN MOTOR CARRIER DIRECTORY). **VFOAT** American Motor Carrier Directory. **VAT** American Motor Carrier Directory. New England Edition, American Trucking Associations American Motor Carrier Directory. 0146-0811. US. English. an. $15.00. Guide Services Inc, New England Edition, PO Box 13446, Monroe Drive, Atlanta GA 30324.

AMERICAN MCD. PACIFIC STATES EDITION. (AMERICAN MCD : AMERICAN MOTOR CARRIER DIRECTORY). **VFOAT** American Motor Carrier Directory. **VAT** American Motor Carrier Directory. Pacific States Edition, American Trucking Associations American Motor Carrier Directory. 0146-082X. US. English. an. $15.00. Guide Services Inc, Pacific States Edition, PO Box 13446, 2161 Monroe Drive, Atlanta GA 30324.

AMERICAN MEDICAL DIRECTORY. 1st-Ed. 0065-9339. US. English. ir. American Medical Association, 535 North Dearborn Street, Chicago IL 60610. **Tel** (312)645-5129. Ed Annette Van Veen Daigle. **LC** R712.A1. **DD** 610.257. **NLM** W 22 AA1 A512. **Circ** 5,000. Directory of all physicians in US, indexed alphabetically and geographically by state, county, and city. Contains address, medical school, speciality, type of practice, license year, and board certification.

AMERICAN MEDICAL DIRECTORY UPDATE. 1981-. US. English. ir.

AMERICAN MILITARY INSTITUTE DIRECTORY OF MEMBERS. 0272-4480. US. English. Editor of Military Affairs, Eisenhower Hall/Kansas State University, Manhattan KS 66506. **LC** U1. **DD** 355.0071173.

AMERICAN PEACE DIRECTORY. 1st Ed. (1984)-. 0740-9885. US. English. an. Ballinger Publishing Company, Cambridge MA 02138. **LC** JX1905.5. **DD** 327.17206.

AMERICAN PEDIATRIC DIRECTORY. 1st- Ed. US. English. be. American Pediatric Directory, 7217 Kingston Pike, Knoxville TN 37919. **LC** R712.A1. **DD** 618.920002573. **NLM** WS 22 AA1 A55.

AMERICAN POLITICS YEARBOOK. 1982-83-. 0730-7594. Periodical. US. English. an. $9.95. Longman Inc, 19 West 44th Street, New York NY 10036. **LC** JK1. **DD** 320.973.

AMERICAN SHOEMAKING DIRECTORY OF SHOE MANUFACTURERS. 0146-6437. US. English. an. $7.00. Shoe Trades Publishing Company, 15 East Street, Boston MA 02111. Ed F E Atwood. **LC** TS945. **DD** 338.47685310257.

THE AMERICAN STATESMEN'S YEARBOOK : FROM OFFICIAL REPORTS OF THE UNITED STATES GOVERNMENT, STATE REPORTS, CONSULAR ADVICES, AND FOREIGN DOCUMENTS. US. English. an. Ed J Walker McSpadden. **LC** JA51.

AMERICAN SWIMMING COACHES ASSOCIATION WORLD CLINIC YEARBOOK. **VFOAT** World Clinic Yearbook. 1974-. 0747-5853. US. English. an. $25.00. ASCA, 1 Hall of Fame Drive, Fort Lauderdale FL 33316. **Tel** (305)462-6267. Ed John Leonard. adv acc. **Circ** 1,5000. Serials of international swim coaches talks.

AMERICA'S CORPORATE FAMILIES, THE BILLION DOLLAR DIRECTORY. **VFOAT** Billion Dollar Directory. 0733-1592. US. English. $385.00. Dun's Marketing Services, 49 Old Bloomfield Road, Mountain Lakes NJ 07046. **Tel** (201)299-8016. **LC** HG4057. **DD** 338.8202573. Comprehensive source detailing more than 8,000 US ultimate parent companies and their 44,000 US subsidiaries and divisions throughout the US.

ANAHEIM BUSINESS AND INDUSTRIAL DIRECTORY. (ANAHEIM ... BUSINESS AND INDUSTRIAL DIRECTORY). **VFOAT** Business and Industrial Directory. 0742-7298. US. English. an. $10.00 Member, $20.00 Non-Member. Anaheim Chamber of Commerce, 130 South Lemon Street POB 969, Anaheim CA 92805. **LC** HF5068.A5. **DD** 338.002579496.

ANALES - ACADEMIA DE FARMACIA, MADRID. **Main/Corp** Academia de Farmacia, Madrid. Year 1- 1932-. 0034-0618. Periodical. SP. Spanish. qt. 3.700. Instituto de Espana, Farmacia 11, Madrid Spain. **Tel** 231 03 07. **Ind/Abst** Ringdoc, Excerpta Med., Pestdoc, GeoRef, Vetdoc, Biol. Abstr., Chem. Abstr. **NLM** W1 AC156. **CODEN** ARAFAY. bk rev. **Circ** 1,200. Research works on problems concerning synthesis, analysis and pharmacological effects of drugs; farmacognosy, pharmaceutical chemistry, clinical biochemistry, microbiology, physiology, nutrition, botany, pharmaceutical history.

ANALES - ACADEMIA NACIONAL DE CIENCIAS MORALES Y POLITICAS. **Main/Corp** Acadmeia Nacional de Ciencias Morales y Politicas. Began with Vol. for 1972. Spanish. ir. Academia Nacional de Ciencias Morales Y Politicas, Avda Corrientes, Buenos Aires 1723 Argentina. **LC** H19.

ANALES - ARGENTINE REPUBLIC. INSTITUTO NACIONAL DE MICROBIOLOGIA. **Main/Corp** Argentine Republic. Instituto Nacional de Microbiologia. V.1- 1962-. Periodical. Spanish. ir. **LC** QR1.

ANALES CERVANTINOS. V. 1 (1951)-. 0569-9878. SP. Spanish. an. $16.35. Consejo Super de Invest Cienti, Vitruvio 8, Apartado 14 458, 28006 Madrid Spain. **Ind/Abst** MLA Int. Bibliogr. Books Artic. Mod. Lang. Lit.

ANALES CHILENOS DE HISTORIA DE LA MEDICINA. Yearly V. 1- 1959-. 0569-9886. Periodical. Spanish. ir. **LC** WMLC L 83/326. **NLM** W1 AN1287M.

ANALES. CIENCIAS - UNIVERSIDAD DE MURCIA. **Main/Corp** Universidad de Murcia. V. 13- 1954/55-. 0463-9847. Periodical. SP. Spanish. sa. Universite de Murcia, Murcia Spain. **Ind/Abst** Am. Hist. Life, Hist. Abstr., Chem. Abstr. Anales.

ANALES CIENTIFICOS - UNIVERSIDAD NACIONAL DEL CENTRO DEL PERU. **Main/Corp** Universidad Nacional del Centro del Peru. 1- 1971-. Spanish. ir. Departamento de Publicaciones e Impresiones, Calle Ferrocarril 469, Huancago Peru. **LC** Q183.4.P5. **DD** 505.

ANALES DE ANTROPOLOGIA. I, ARQUEOLOGIA Y ANTROPOLOGIA FISICA. **VFOAT** Arqueologia y Atropologia Fisica. Vol. 18 (1981)-. Periodical. MX. Spanish. an. Ciudad Universitaria, Mexico 20 DF Mexico. **Tel** 5-50-52-15. Ed andres Medina. **LC** GN49. **DD** 972.00497. bk rev. **Circ** 2,000. (ctrl). Specialized articles in archaeology, ethnology, linguistics, and physical anthropology. Anales de Antropologia. Tomo I, Arqueologia y Antropologia Fisica.

ANALES DE ANTROPOLOGIA. II, ETNOLOGIA Y LINGUISTICA. **VFOAT** Etnologia y Linguistica. Vol. 18 (1981)-. Periodical. MX. Spanish. an. Instituto de Investigaciones Antropologicas, Ciudad Universitaria, Mexico 20 DF Mexico. **LC** GN301. **DD** 972.0049705. Anales de Antropologia. Tomo II, Etnologia y Linguistica.

ANALES DE BROMATOLOGIA. Began in 1949. 0003-2492. Periodical. SP. Spanish (summaries in English). ir. Consejo Super Invest Cientific, Vitruvio 8 Apartado 14 458, 28006 Madrid Spain. **Ind/Abst** Chem. Abstr., Bibliogr. Agric. **LC** TX341. **NLM** W1 AN135. **CODEN** ANBRAD. (cum index).

ANALES DE CIENCIAS HUMANAS. No. 1- Dec. 1971-. Periodical. Spanish. ir. 2.50 Single Issue. Editorial Universitaria, Apartado 3368, Panama 4 Panama. **LC** HC147.A1.

ANALES DE CIRUGIA. V. 1- Jun. 1935-. 0066-1465. Periodical. Spanish. an. Calle Paraguay No 40, Rosario Argentina. **NLM** W1 AN142L.

ANALES DE DERECHO. No. 1-. Periodical. SP. Spanish. ir. Secretariado de Publicaciones e Intercambio Cientifico, Universidad de Murcia, Murcia Spain. **LC** K1. **DD** 340.0946.

ANALES DE EDAFOLOGIA Y AGROBIOLOGIA. V. 19-. 0365-1797. SP. Spanish. mo. Consejo Super Invest Cientific, Vitruvio 8 Apartado 14 458, 28006 Madrid Spain. **Ind/Abst** Excerpta Med., GeoRef, Biol. Abstr., Chem. Abstr., Bibliogr. Agric. **CODEN** AEDAAB.

ANALES DE FISICA CEASED. Began with V. 64, No. 1 & 2 (Jan./Feb. 1968). Ceased with V. 76, (Oct./Dec. 1980). 0365-4818. Periodical. SP. Spanish. qt. **Ind/Abst** GeoRef, Chem. Abstr., Nucl. Sci. Abstr. **LC** QC1. **DD** 530.05. **CODEN** ANFIA6. Anales de la Real Sociedad Espanola de Fisicia y Quimica. Serie A, Fisica.

ANALES DE GEOGRAFIA DE LA UNIVERSIDAD COMPLUTENSE. 1-. Periodical. Spanish. ir. Editorial de la Universidad Complutense, Edificio de Estomatologia Bajos, Madrid 3 Spain. **LC** G1. **DD** 910.5.

ANALES DE HISTORIA CONTEMPORANEA. 1 (1982)-. Periodical. Spanish. an. Patronato Angel Garcia Rogel, Pl/ Marques de Rafal 1 Y 3, Orihuela (Alicante) Spain. **LC** DP160.9. **DD** 946.05405.

ANALES DE INGENIERIA. V. 1- August 1887-. Periodical. Spanish. mo. **LC** TA4.

ANALES DE JURISPRUDENCIA. MX. Spanish. qt. Direccion Anales Jurisprudenci, Conjunto Pino S Torre E 3 Piso, Mexico 1 DF Mexico.

ANALES DE LA ACADEMIA DE GEOGRAFIA E HISTORIA DE GUATEMALA. **Main/Corp** Academia de Geografia e Historia de Guatemala. Vol. 53 (Jan/Dec 1980)-. Periodical. GT. Spanish. an. $10.00. Academia de Geografia e Historia de Guatemala, 3A Avenida 8-35, Zona 1 Guatemala. **Tel** 23544-535141. **LC** F1461. **DD** 972.81005. (cum index). bk rev. adv acc. **Circ** 1,000. Anales de la Sociedad de Geografia e Historia.

ANALES DE LA ACADEMIA NACIONAL DE CIENCIAS. CUADERNO 2 : SERIE CIENCIAS DE LA NATURALEZA. **VFOAT** Publicacion - Academia Nacional de Ciencias de Bolivia. No. 1- 1961-. 0567-5911. Periodical. Spanish (summaries in English). ir. **NLM** W1.

ANALES DE LA ACADEMIA NACIONAL DE CIENCIAS ECONOMICAS. **Main/Corp** Academia de Ciencias Economicas, Buenos Aires. V. 1-4, 1927-38. 0567-5804. AG. Spanish. ir. Academic Nacional de Ciencias Economicas, Avda Alvear 1711 3 Piso, 1014 Buenos Aires Argentina. **LC** HB51. **DD** 330.6382.

ANALES DE LA ESCUELA NACIONAL DE CIENCIAS BIOLOGICAS. **Main/Corp** Mexico (City). Instituto Politecnico Nacional. Escuela Nacional de Ciencias Biologicas. V. 1- Oct./Dec. 1938-. 0365-1932. Periodical. MX. Spanish (some summaries in English and German). an. $800.00. Escuela Nacional de Ciencias Biologicas IPN, Depto de Publicaciones, Carpio y Plan de Ayala, Apartado Postal 42-186, 11340 Mexico DF Mexico. Ed Martha Eugenia Perez V. **Ind/Abst** Life Sci. Collect., GeoRef. **LC** QH301. **DD** 574.05. **NLM** W1 ES669P. **CODEN** AENBAU. **Circ** 1,000. (ctrl). Deals with subjects of zoology, botany, morphology, ecology and any biological technology such as fishing, reproduction, cultivation (crop), etc.

ANALES DE LA ESTACION EXPERIMENTAL DE AULA DEI. **Main/Corp** Estacion Experimental de Aula Dei. V. 1-. 0365-1800. Periodical. SP. Spanish. ir. Consejo Super Invest Cientific, Viturvio 8 Apartado 14 458, 28006 Madrid Spain. **Ind/Abst** Bibliogr. Agric. **LC** S15. **DD** 630.94655.

ANALES DE LA FACULTAD PONTIFICIA DE TEOLOGIA. **Main/Corp** Santiago de Chile Universidad Catolica. Facultad de Teologia. Periodical. CL. Spanish. an. $27.00. Facultad de Teologia, Avenida Bernardo Ohiggins 224, Santiago Chile. **Tel** 744041. **LC** BX805. (cum index). **Circ** 500. Makes known research works in the sciences in the area of theology done by students in Chile, and professors of the School of Theology.

ANALES DE LA FUNDACION JUAN MARCH. **Main/Corp** Fundacion Juan March. 1 (1956-1962)-. 0532-8500. SP. Spanish. ir. Fundacion Juan March, Castello 77, Madrid Spain. **LC** AS911.F816. **DD** 011.44.

ANALES DE LA LITERATURA ESPANOLA CONTEMPORANEA. **VFOAT** ALEC. Vol. 6 (1981)-. 0272-1635. US. English (articles also in Spanish). ir. $35.00. University of Nebraska, Department of Modern Language and Literature, Old Father Hall, Lincoln NE 68588. **Tel** (402)472-3842. Ed Luis Gonzalez-del-Valle. **Ind/Abst** MLA Int. Bibliogr. Books Artic. Mod. Lang. Lit. **LC** PQ6144. **DD** 860.9. bk rev. adv acc. **Circ** 1,000. (ctrl). Scholarly articles studing all aspects of twentieth century Spanish literature (from Modernismo and the Generation of 1898). Book reviews, bibliographies and panoramic studies are also standard features.

Yearbooks, Almanacs, Directories

Anales de la Narrativa Espanola Contemporanea, 0270-6334; Journal of Spanish Studies: Twentieth Century, 0092-1807.

ANALES DE LA REAL ACADEMIA DE CIENCIAS MORALES Y POLITICAS. Main/Corp Academia de Ciencias Morales V Politicas, Madrid. Yearly V. 1- 1949-. SP. Spanish. ir. Real Academia de Ciencias Morales y Politicas, Plaza de Villa 2, Madrid 12 Spain. *Anales de la Real Academia de Ciencias Morales y Politicas.*

ANALES DE LA REAL ACADEMIA NACIONAL DE MEDICINA, MADRID. (ANALES DE LA REAL ACADEMIA NACIONAL DE MEDICINA). Vol. 1- 1879-. 0034-0634. Periodical. SP. Spanish. qt. $18.00. Anales de la Real Academia, Arrieta 12, Madrid Spain. Tel 247-03-18. Ind/Abst Life Sci. Collect., Excerpta Med., Index Med. NLM W1 AN149J.

ANALES DE LA SOCIEDAD CIENTIFICA ARGENTINA. Main/Corp Sociedad Cientifica Argentina. V. 1- 1876-. 0037-8437. Periodical. AG. Spanish (with English summaries). ir. Librart Srl/Department of Public AC, Cientif Argent 1/127 Corrientes, Buenos Aires Argentina. Ind/Abst GeoRef, Chem. Abstr. LC Q33. DD 505. NLM W1 AN149T. CODEN ASCAA2. (cum index).

ANALES DE LA UNIVERSIDAD CATOLICA DE VALPARAISO. Main/Corp Valparaiso (City). Universidad Catolica. No. 1- 1954-. 0504-9903. CL. Spanish. ir. Universidad Catholica, Valparaiso 4059, Valparaiso Chile.

ANALES DE L'ACADEMIA NACIONAL DE CIENCIAS EXACTAS, FISICAS Y NATURALES, BUENOS AIRES. (ANALES). Main/Corp Academia Nacional de Ciencias Exactas, Fisicas y Naturales, Buenos Aires. Began in 1928. 0365-1185. Periodical. AG. Spanish. ir. Ind/Abst GeoRef, Chem. Abstr., Energy Res. Abstr. LC Q33. DD 506.282. CODEN ACFBAA.

ANALES DE LITERATURA HISPANOAMERICANA. 1972-. SP. Spanish. an. $8.00. Universidad Complutense, Ciudad Universitaria 3, Madrid Spain. LC PQ7081.A1.

ANALES DE MEDICINA. V. 54- Jan./Mar. 1971-. PE. Spanish. qt. Dr Raul Jeri, Apt 5281, Lima 100 Peru.

ANALES DEL CENTRO DE CULTURA VALENCIANA. (ANALES). Main/Corp Centro de Cultura Valenciana, Valencia. 1-9 (No. 1-26), Jan. 1928-April/June 1936. Periodical. SP. Spanish. ir. Consejo Super Invest Cientific, Vitruvio 8, Apartado 14 458, 28006 Madrid Spain.

ANALES DEL FORO. Periodical. Spanish. bw. Ituizaingo, 1495 Piso 2, Montevideo Uruguay. LC KHU72. DD 348.895026, 348.950826.

ANALES DEL INSTITUTO BELGRANIANO CENTRAL. No. 1-. Periodical. AG. Spanish. ir. Instituto Belgrano Central Convento de Santo Domingo, Defensa 422, Buenos Aires Argentina. LC F2845.B378. DD 982.03.

ANALES DEL INSTITUTO DE BIOLOGIA, UNIVERSIDAD NACIONAL AUTONOMA DE MEXICO. SERIE BOTANICA. Main/Corp Mexico (City). Universidad Nacional. Instituto de Biologia. V. 38- 1967-. 0374-5511. Periodical. MX. Spanish (articles in English and various other languages). ir. Instituto de Biologiia, Universidad Nacional Autonoma de Mexico, Apart Post 70-233, Mexico 20 DF Mexico. Ind/Abst Life Sci. Collect. *Anales del Instituto Biologia, 0076-7174.*

ANALES DEL INSTITUTO DE CIENCIAS DEL MAR Y LIMNOLOGIA, UNIVERSIDAD NACIONAL AUTONOMA DE MEXICO. Vol. 8, No. 1-. Spanish (English). an. Instituto de Ciencias del Mar y Limnologia, Universidad Nacional Autonoma de Mexico, Apartado Postal 70-305, 04510 Mexico DF Mexico. Ind/Abst Life Sci. Collect. LC QH91.A1. DD 574.9205. *Anales del Centro de Ciencias del Mar y Limnologia, Universidad Nacional Autonoma de Mexico.*

ANALES DEL INSTITUTO DE ESTUDIOS GERUNDENSES. Main/Corp Instituto de Estudios Gerundenses. 0211-2329. Periodical. SP. Spanish. ir. Consejo Super Invest Cientific, Vitruvio 8, Apartado 14 458, 28006 Madrid Spain. Ind/Abst Am. Hist. Life, Hist. Abstr., Part A, Mod. Hist. Abstr., Hist. Abst., Part B, Twent. Century Abstr. LC DP402.G4.

ANALES DEL INSTITUTO DE ESTUDIOS MADRILENOS. Main/Corp Spain. Consejo Superior de Investigaciones Cientificas. Instituto de Estudios Madrilenos. V. 1- 1966-. 0584-6374. SP. Spanish. an. Consejo Superior de Investigaciones Cientificas, Vitruvio 8, apartado 14 458, 28006 Madrid Spain. Ind/Abst Am. Hist. Life, Hist. Abstr., Part A, Mod. Hist. Abstr., Hist. Abst., Part B, Twent. Century Abstr. LC DP302.M1. DD 946.41005.

ANALES DEL INSTITUTO DE GEOFISICA. Main/Corp Universidad Nacional Autonoma de Mexico. Instituto de Geofisica. V. 1-. 0076-7182. MX. Spanish. ir. Universidad Nacional Autonoma, Torre Ciencias 3ER Piso, Mexico City 20 DF Mexico. Ind/Abst GeoRef, Chem. Abstr. LC QC801. DD 551.05. CODEN AIGMAM.

ANALES DEL INSTITUTO DE INVESTIGACIONES ESTETICAS. Main/Corp Universidad Nacional Autonomia de Mexico. Instituto de Investigaciones Esteticas. V. 1- (No. 1-). 0185-1276. Periodical. MX. Spanish. qt. Anales de Instituto de Investigaciones Esteticas, Torre I de Humanidades, 6 Piso CD Universitaria, Mexico City 04510 DF Mexico. Tel 548 41 17. Ed Lic Xavier Moyssen. Ind/Abst Am. Hist. Life, Hist. Abstr., Part A, Mod. Hist. Abstr., Hist. Abst., Part B, Twent. Century Abstr. LC N16. DD 706.272. bk rev. Circ 2,000. (ctrl). Prehispanic, colonial history contemporary art, modern art, literature, architecture, dance, cinema and folklore, etc.

ANALES DEL INSTITUTO DE INVESTIGACIONES MARINAS DE PUNTA DE BETIN. Main/Corp Instituto de Investigaciones Marinas de Punta de Betin. VFOAT Investigaciones Marinas: Punta de Betin. No. 9-. Periodical. English (Spanish). ir. LC Q33. DD 574.92. *Mitteilungen.*

ANALES DEL INSTITUTO DE INVESTIGACIONES VETERINARIAS. Main/Corp Instituto de Investigaciones Veterinarias. Began with V. 5. SP. Spanish. ir. Consejo Super Invest Cientific Vitrubio 8, Apartado 14 458, 28006 Madrid Spain. Ind/Abst Chem. Abstr. *Anales de la Facultad de Veterinaria de la Universidad de Madrid y del Instituto de Investigaciones Veterinarias.*

ANALES DEL INSTITUTO DE MATEMATICAS. V. 1- 1961-. MX. Spanish. ir. Ciudad Universitaria/Academic Section, Inst Matematicas UNAM, Mexico 20 DF Mexico. Ind/Abst Math. Rev. LC QA1.

ANALES DEL INSTITUTO NACIONAL DE INVESTIGACIONES AGRARIAS. SERIE, FORESTAL. VFOAT Serie Forestal. No. 5-. 0211-9102. Spanish. ir. Instituto Nacional de Investigaciones Agrarias, Jose Abascal 56, Madrid 4 Spain. LC SD209. DD 634.905.

ANALES DEL INSTITUTO NACIONAL DE INVESTIGACIONES AGRARIAS. SERIE RECURSOS NATURALES *CEASED*. (ANALES DEL INSTITUTO NACIONAL DE INVESTIGACIONES AGRARIAS. SERIE, RECURSOS NATURALES). VFOAT Anales del INIA. Serie, Recursos Naturales, Anales del I.N.I.A. Serie, Recursos Naturales, Recursos Naturales. Began in 1974. Ceased with No. 4. 0210-2471. Periodical. Spanish (with some summaries in English and French). ir. Ind/Abst Chem. Abstr. LC SD209. DD 634.905. CODEN ASRNDH.

ANALES DEL JARDIN BOTANICO DE MADRID (1979). (ANALES DEL JARDIN BOTANICO DE MADRID). V. 36-. 0211-1322. SP. Spanish. ir. Consejo Super Invest Cientific Vitruvio 8, Apartado 14 458, 28006 Madrid Spain. Ind/Abst Biol. Abstr. CODEN AJBMD7. *Anales del Instituto Botanico A.J. Cavanilles, 0365-0790.*

ANALES DEL MUSEO DE HISTORIA NATURAL DE VALPARAISO. Main/Corp Museo de Historia Natural de Valparaiso. No. 1- 1968-. Spanish. ir. $15.00. Avenida Valparaiso, 155 Casilla 925, Vina del Mar Chile. Tel 977300. LC QH119. DD 574.98305. Circ 350. (ctrl). Covers botany, ecology, zoology (invertebrate and vertebrate), and archaeology.

ANALES DEL SEMINARIO DE HISTORIA DE LA FILOSOFIA. Main/Conf Seminario de Historia de la Filosofia (Spain). 1 (1980)-. Spanish. ir. Editorial de la Universidad Complutense, Edificio de Estomatologia, Ciudad Universitaria, Madrid 3 Spain. LC B5. DD 109.

ANALES GALDOSIANOS. Vol. 1 1966. 0569-9924. US. English (Spanish). an. $5.00. Anales Galdosianos, 745 Commonwealth Avenue, Boston University, Boston MA 02215. Ind/Abst MLA Int. Bibliogr. Books Artic. Mod. Lang. Lit. LC PQ6555.Z5. DD 863.5.

ANALES - MEXICO (CITY). UNIVERSIDAD NACIONAL. INSTITUTO DE FISICA. Main/Corp Mexico (City). Universidad Nacional. Instituto de Fisica. V. 1- 1955-. Periodical. Spanish. ir. LC QC1.

ANALES - MEXICO. INSTITUTO NACIONAL DE ANTROPOLOGIA E HISTORIA. Main/Corp Mexico. Instituto Nacional de Antropologia e Historia. V. 1- 1939/40-. 0076-7557. MX. Spanish. ir. Instituto Nacional de Antropologia Historia, Apartado Postal 5-119, Mexico 5 DF Mexico. LC F1219. DD 913.72. (cum index). *Anales de Museo Nacional de Arquelogia, Historia y Etnografia.*

ANALES - MUSEO NACIONAL DE HISTORIA NATURAL (URUGUAY). Main/Corp Museo Nacional de Historia Natural (Uruguay). Spanish. ir. Museo Nacional de Historia Natural, Casilla de Correo 399, Montevideo Uruguay. LC QH7. *Anales del Museo de Historia Natural de Montevideo.*

ANALES OTORRINOLARINGOLOGICOS IBERO-AMERICANOS. Vol. 1- 1974-. 0303-8874. Periodical. SP. Spanish (summaries in English, French, and German). bm. 94.00 US, 75.20 Europe. Anales Otorrinolaringologicos, Provenza 319, Barcelona 08037 Spain. Tel 257.78.18. Ed Enrique Perello Scherdel. Ind/Abst Excerpta Med., Index Med., Biol. Abstr., Sociol. Abstr., Lang. Lang. Behav. Abstr. NLM W1 AN189D. CODEN AOIAA4. bk rev. adv acc. Circ 1,000. (ctrl). Study of ear, nose and throat in Latin America. *Acto Oto-Rino-Laringologica Ibero-Americana, 0001-6500.*

ANALES PARLAMENTARIOS. No. 1-. Periodical. UY. Spanish. ir. Republica Oriental Del Uruguay, Palacio Legislativo Biblioteca, Montevideo Uruguay. LC J251. DD 328.89501.

ANALES - SALA PROVINCIA. Main/Corp Sala Provincia. 1971/72-. Spanish. ir. Espana, Institucion Fray Bermadino de Sahagun La Reina S/N, Leon Spain. LC N16.

ANALES - SANTIAGO DE CHILE. FACULTAD LATINOAMERICANA DE CIENCIAS SOCIALES. Main/Corp Santiago de Chile. Facultad Latinoamericana de Ciencias Sociales. Yearly V. 1- Jan./Dec. 1964-. 0581-6319. Periodical. Spanish. ir. LC H8.

ANALES - UNIVERSIDAD NACIONAL AUTONOMA DE MEXICO, INSTITUTO DE GEOLOGIA. (ANALES - INSTITUTO DE GEOLOGIA). Main/Corp Universidad Nacional Autonoma de Mexico. Instituto de Geologia. V. 4- 1930-. Monographic Series. Spanish. ir. LC QE201.

ANALES VALENTINOS. Yearly V. 1- 1975-. Periodical. SP. Spanish. ir. Moncada Paseo Al Mar 17, Valencia 10 Spain. LC BX805. DD 230.205.

ANALES Y BOLETIN DE LOS MUSEOS DE ARTE DE BARCELONA. V. 1- 1941/43-. 0404-9365. Periodical. SP. Spanish. ir. Barcelona Spain. LC N7. DD 708.6.

ANALOG YEARBOOK. VFOAT Science Fiction Analog Yearbook. 0194-4002. US. English. an. $5.95. LC PS648.S3. DD 813.087605.

ANBAR YEARBOOK. 1- 1972-. 0307-0409. UK. English. an. 80.00. Anbar Publications, PO Box 23, Wembley HA9 8DJ England. Tel (01)902-4489. Ed A C Ede. LC HD28. DD 658.4. Abstracts of articles on accounting, data processing, personnel training, marketing, distribution, work study, O&M fully indexed with bibliography of books and audio-visual material.

ANCHORAGE . . . CHAMBER OF COMMERCE MEMBERSHIP DIRECTORY AND BUYERS GUIDE. VFOAT Anchorage. US. English. an. $10.00 Members, $20.00 Non-Members. Anchorage Chamber of Commerce, 415 F Street, Anchorage AK 99501. LC HF296.A56. DD 380.10257983.

ANDERSON'S CAMPGROUND DIRECTORY. VFOAT Campground Directory. 0163-268X. US. English. $3.95. Campground Directory Inc, Box 111, Herndon VA 22070. Tel (703)79-5190.

Yearbooks, Almanacs, Directories

Ed M Flues. **LC** GV191.42.M52. **DD** 647.9475. adv acc. **Circ** 18,000. A guide to camping in the Mid-Atlantic and Southeast. Each annual issue includes information on private, state and federal campgrounds including rates. *Campground Directory, Mid Atlantic, 0098-5236.*

ANEP. ANNUAIRE EUROPEEN DE PETROLE. (ANNUAIRE EUROPEEN DU PETROLE). **VFOAT** European Petroleum Yearbook, European Petroleum Year Book, ANEP, Jahrbuch der Europaischen Erdolindustrie, European Petroleum Year Book : ANEP. 1974-. 0342-6947. English (French and German). an. Urban Verlag, Graumannsweg 25, D2000 Hamburg 76 West Germany. **Ind/Abst** GeoRef, Bibliogr. Index Geol. *Annuaire de l'Europe Petroliere, 0066-1716.*

ANGLICAN YEARBOOK. (ANGLICAN YEAR BOOK). 1965-. 0317-8765. Periodical. **CN**. English. an. Anglican Book Centre, 600 Jarvis Street, Toronto Ontario M4Y 2J6 Canada. **DD** 283.71.

ANGLO-AMERICAN DIRECTORY OF MEXICO. 19 -. English. ir. $33.00. J E Smith, Barranca del Muerto 472, Col Alpes 01010 Mexico DF Mexico. **Tel** (905)593-8766. Ed John E Smith Jr. **LC** F1204.5. **DD** 917.2. adv acc. **Circ** 1,500. Informative and comprehensive directory of English speaking people residing in the Mexican Republic.

ANGLO AMERICAN TRADE DIRECTORY. 1962/63-. 0066-1813. UK. English. an. American Chamber of Commerce (United Kingdom), 75 Brook Street, London WIY 2EB England. **LC** HF54.G7. *Anglo-American Year Book.*

ANIMAL HEALTH YEARBOOK. **VFOAT** Annuaire de la Sante Animale, Anuario de Sanidad Animal. US. English (French, and Spanish). ir. Unipub, PO Box 1222, Ann Arbor MI 48106. **Tel** (212)686-4707. **LC** SF600. **DD** 636.08944. **NLM** W2 MU5 F2. *FAO/OIE Animal Health Yearbooks.*

ANIMAL ORGANIZATIONS & SERVICES DIRECTORY. **VFOAT** Animal Organizations and Services Directory. 0748-5069. US. English. $12.95. Animal Stories, 16783 Beach Boulevard PO Box 2700, Huntington Beach CA 92647. Ed Kathleen A Reece. adv acc. **Circ** 5,000. Directory of animal organizations and services in the United States.

THE ANIMAL PEOPLE'S DIRECTORY. (THE ANIMAL PEOPLE'S DIRECTORY : APD). **VFOAT** APD. 1982-. 0733-4710. US. English. an. $9.50. APD Publications, PO Box 95, Moapa NV 89025. **LC** SF25. **DD** 636.002573.

ANITAF DIRECTORY. **VFOAT** A.N.I.T.A.F. Directory. English (French, German, and Portuguese). ir. Associacao Nacional das Industrias Texteis, Algodoeiras E Fibras, rue de Goncalo Cristovao, 96-10 E 20, Porto Portugal. **LC** HD9865.P66. **DD** 677.00294469.

ANNAIRE OFFICIEL - ACADEMIE DE MEDECINE VETERINAIRE DU QUEBEC. (ANNUAIRE OFFICIEL). **Main/Corp** Academie de Medecine Veterinaire du Quebec. 1980-. 0226-238X. **CN**. French. an. Free to Members. Compagnie des Editions du St-Laurent Ltee/Suite 3235, Place Ville Marie, Montreal Quebec H3B 3M7 Canada. **DD** 636.089025714.

ANNALES DE LA PROPRIETE INDUSTRIELLE, ARTISTIQUE ET LITTERAIRE. V. 1- (1.- Yearly V.). Periodical. FR. French. qt. $37.25. Annales de la Propriete, 10 Square Henri Pate, 75016 Paris France.

ANNALES D'UROLOGIE. V. 1- Feb. 1967-. 0003-4401. Periodical. French (summaries in English, German and Spanish). bm. $135.69. Semaine des Hopitaux, 15 rue St Benoit, 75278 Paris Cedex 06 France. **Tel** 548-42-60. **Ind/Abst** Excerpta Med., Biol. Abstr., Index Med., Sci. Cit. Index, Abr. Ed. **NLM** W1 AN407. **CODEN** AUROAV. *Annales de Chirurgie, 0003-3944.*

ANNALES INTERNATIONALES DE CRIMINOLOGIE. **VFOAT** International Annals of Criminology, Anales Internationales de Criminologia. V. 1- 1962-. 0003-4452. Periodical. FR. French (text in English and Spanish). sa. $33.26. International Society of Criminology, 4 rue de Mondovi, 75001 Paris France. **Tel** 42618022. Ed Melun. **Ind/Abst** Public Aff. Inf. Serv. Bull., Foreign Lang. Index, PAIS Foreign Lang. Index. adv acc. **Circ** 700. Scientific articles and reports on criminology particularly reflecting the activities of the International Society of Criminology. *Bulletin de la Societe Internationale de Criminologie.*

ANNALI DI MATEMATICA PURA ED APPLICATA. See Mathematics.

ANNEXE A L'ANNUAIRE DIOCESAIN (SAINTE-ANNE-DE-LA-POCATIERE) CEASED. (ANNEXE A L'ANNUAIRE DIOCESAIN). **Main/Corp** Eglise Catholique. Diocese de Sainte-Anne-de-la-Pocatiere. -1980. 0820-9650. **CN**. French. an. M Coulombe, Eveche de Sainte-Anne, CP 430, La Pocatiere Quebec G0R 1Z0 Canada. **DD** 282.02571475.

ANNOTATED DIRECTORY OF SELF-PUBLISHED TEXTILE BOOKS. 1977-. 0162-7651. US. English. Sommertime Publications, PO Box E, Woodmere NY 11598. **LC** Z6153.T4, TT699. **DD** 016.746.

ANNUAIRE ABREGE DE STATISTIQUES AGRICOLES, REGION RHONE-ALPES. Began with 1966/67 Vol. French. ir. Service Regional de Statistique Agricole-Rhone-Alpes, 55 rue Mazenod, Lyon 9426 Cedex 3 France. **Tel** 78.95.25.64. **LC** S230.R49. **DD** 338.10944.

ANNUAIRE - ACADEMIE D'ATHENES. **Main/Corp** Akademia Athenon. 0302-6868. French. ir. Bureau des Publications de l'Academie d'Athenes, 28 Avenue E, Venizelos T T 143 Athenai Greece. **LC** LF3245.A83. **DD** 378.385.

ANNUAIRE - ACADEMIE DES SCIENCES. **Main/Corp** Academie des Sciences (France). Vol. 1 1917-. 0065-0552. French. ir. Gauthier-Villars, 70 rue de Saint Mande, 93100 Montreuil France. **LC** Q46. **DD** 506.044.

ANNUAIRE ADMINISTRATIF DU QUEBEC. 1973-. **CN**. French. an. $5.00. Ministere des Communications, l'Editeur Officiel du Quebec, 2 rue Saint-Jean, Quebec Canada. **LC** JL241.A1. **DD** 354.7140005. *Bottin Administratif du Quebec.*

ANNUAIRE ADMINISTRATIF ET JUDICIAIRE DE BELGIQUE. **VFOAT** Administratief en Gerechtelijk Jaarboek voor Belgie. 94.-Yeary Volume. 0066-2461. BE. Dutch (Flemish and French). an. 4.566. Etablissements Emile Bruylant, 67 rue de la Regence, 1000 Bruxells Belgium. **Tel** 2/512.98.45. **LC** JN6105. adv acc. **Circ** 3,800. Addresses public organizations, universities and the legal profession; administrative and legal yearbook of Belgium. *Annuaire Administratif et Judiciaire de Blegique et de la Capitale du Royaume. Pouvoir Legislatif - Pouvoir Executif - Pouvoir Judiciaire. Institutions Proviciales et Communales.*

ANNUAIRE - ARCHIDIOCESE DE SHERBROOKE. **Main/Corp** Eglise Catholique. Archidiocese de Sherbrooke. 1977-. 0706-9774. **CN**. French. an. $2.00 Per No. La Procure de l'Archeveche, C P 430, Sherbrooke Quebec J1H 5K1 Canada. **DD** 282.02571466. *Bottin, 0317-8455.*

ANNUAIRE - ASSOCIATION DES. (ANNUAIRE - QUEBEC CAMPING ASSOCIATION). **Main/Corp** Quebec Camping Association. **VFOAT** VAT Directory - Association des Camps du Quebec. 1981-. 0226-5877. **CN**. English (text also in French). an. $1,00 Per Vol. Annuaire, c/o Quebec Camping Association, 1415 Jarry Street East, Montreal Quebec H2E 2L7 Canada. **DD** 796.542025714. *Directory, 0226-5877.*

ANNUAIRE - ASSOCIATION DES COLLEGES DU QUEBEC (1979). (ANNUAIRE). **Main/Corp** Association des Colleges du Quebec. **VFOAT** ACQ Annuaire. 1978/1979-. 0228-7730. **CN**. French. an. Free. Annuaire Association des Colleges du Quebec, 1940 Est Boul Henri-Bourassa, Montreal Quebec H2B 1S2 Canada. **DD** 378.1543060714. *Annuaire, 0227-0269.*

ANNUAIRE - ASSOCIATION DES INGENIERUS ET TECHNICIENS AFRICAINS DE COTE D'IVCI. **Main/Corp** Association des Ingenierus et Techniciens Africains de Cote d'Ivoire. French. ir. Autoroute de Post-Bouet, Boite Postal 794, Abidjan Ivory Coast. **LC** TA2. **DD** 620.00626668.

ANNUAIRE - ASSOCIATION DES INSTITUTIONS DE NIVEAUX PRESCOLAIRE ET ELEMENTAIRE DU QUEBEC. **Main/Corp** Association des Institutions de Niveaux Prescolaire et Elementaire du Quebec. 1970/71-. 0315-8764. **CN**. French. Free. Centre d'Animation de Developpement et de Recherche en Education, 1940 Est Boul Henri-Bourassa, Montreal Quebec H2B 1S2 Canada. **DD** 372.025714.

ANNUAIRE - ASSOCIATION DES INSTITUTIONS D'ENSEIGNEMENT SECONDAIRE. **Main/Corp** Association des Institutions d'Enseignement Secondaire. 1968/69-. 0066-8990. Periodical. **CN**. French. an. Free. Centre d'Animation de Developpement et de Recherche en Education, 1940 Est Boul Henri-Bourassa, Montreal Quebec H2B 1S2 Canada. **Tel** (514)381-8891. **DD** 373.22062714. adv acc. **Circ** 6,000. (ctrl). *Annuaire, 0430-2249.*

ANNUAIRE - ASSOCIATION DES ROUTES ET TRANSPORTS DU CANADA. **Main/Corp** Roads and Transportation Association of Canada. **VFOAT** Directory - Roads and Transportation Association of Canada. 1976-. 0701-1636. Periodical. **CN**. English (French). an. Roads and Transportation Association of Canada, 1765 Saint-Laurent Boulevard, Ottawa Ontario K1G 3V4 Canada. **Tel** (613)521-4052. Ed Gilbert C Morier. **DD** 388.106271. **Circ** 550. (ctrl). Directory of RTAC members; also contains general information on the Association. *Membership Directory, 0382-4381.*

ANNUAIRE - ASSOCIATION GENERALE DES HYGIENISTES ET TECHNICIENS MUNICIPAUX (FRANCE). **Main/Corp** Association Generale des Hyigenistes et Techniciens Municipaux (France). FR. French. an. Association Generale des Hygienistes et Techniciens Municipaux (France), 9 rue de Phalsbourg, 75017 Paris France. **LC** RA713. **DD** 362.10944. *Annuaire des Membres.*

ANNUAIRE ASTRONOMIQUE DE L'AMATEUR. See Astronomy.

ANNUAIRE BANCAIRE. 1981-. FR. French. an. Dafsa, 7 rue Bergere, 75009 Paris France. **LC** HG3025. **DD** 332.102544.

ANNUAIRE - BRITTANY (FRANCE). **Main/Corp** Brittany (France). Feb. 1983-. French. an. 5 rue Martenot, 35031 Rennes France. **LC** HC277.B7. **DD** 354.440081809441.

ANNUAIRE CATHOLIQUE DE FRANCE. 1952-. 0066-2488. FR. French. be. Annuaire Catholique de France, 17 Bd Poissonniere, 75002 Paris France. **Tel** 261 51 26. **LC** BX1528.A1. bk rev. adv acc. **Circ** 6,000. (ctrl).

ANNUAIRE : CHIMIE. FR. French. ir. Editions du Centre National de la Recherche, 15 Quai Anatole France, 75700 Paris France. **LC** QD49.F72. **DD** 540.72044.

ANNUAIRE CNRS SCIENCES DE L'HOMME. **VFOAT** Annuaire Sciences de l'Homme. French. an. 150. Centre de Documentation Sciences Humaines, 54 Boulevard Raspail, 75006 Paris France. **LC** AZ651. **DD** 001.302544. *Annuaire Sciences de l'Homme.*

ANNUAIRE. COMMERCANTS ET PROFESSIONNELS QUI DONNENT UN SERVICE EN FRANCAIS EN SASKATCHEWAN. (ANNUAIRE : COMMERCANTS ET PROFESSIONNELS QUI DONNENT UN SERVICE EN FRANCAIS EN SASKATCHEWAN). No. 1-. 0822-9368. **CN**. French. be. Free. Conseil de la Cooperation de la Saskatchewan, 2243 rue Lorne, Regina Saskatchewan S4P 2M8 Canada. **Tel** (306)737-4452. Ed N Lepage. **DD** 380.10257124. adv acc. **Circ** 3,000. Directory of businesses and professionals offering services in French-Saskatchewan.

ANNUAIRE COMMERCIAL DU GRAND MONTREAL. **VFOAT** Greater Montreal Business Directory. 1975-. 0380-3953. **CN**. text in French and English. an. 210.00. J Lovell, 423 rue St Nicolas, Montreal Quebec H2Y 2P4 Canada. **Tel** (514)849-2578. Ed R W Lovell. **DD** 380.102571428. adv acc. Businesses, professionals and organizations showing executives, business description, size by employees and telephone in alphabetical and street sequences, addresses include postal code.

ANNUAIRE - COMMISSION SCOLAIRE REGIONALE LOUIS-FRECHETTE. (ANNUAIRE). **Main/Corp** Commission Scolaire Regionale Louis-Frechette. 1982/83-. 0823-566X. **CN**. French. an. Free. Commission Scolaire Regionale Louis-Frechette, 30 Ouest rue Champagnat, Levis Quebec G6V 6P5 Canada. **DD** 379.153102571459. *Bottin, 0706-9960.*

Yearbooks, Almanacs, Directories

ANNUAIRE - CONFERENCE DES EVEQUES CATHOLIQUES DU CANADA. Main/Conf Canadian Conference of Catholic Bishops. VFOAT Directory - Canadian Conference of Catholic Bishops. 1977-. 9672-7737. CN. English (French). an. Publications Service CCCB, 90 Parent Avenue, Ottawa Ontario K1N 7B1 Canada. Tel (613)236-9461. DD 282.02571. Lists names, addresses, phone, numbers and statistics for bishops, dioceses and CCB offices. *Annuaire, 0319-4396.*

ANNUAIRE - CORPORATION OF TRANSLATORS AND INTERPRETERS OF NEW BRUNSWICK. Main/Corp Corporation of Translators and Interpreters of New Brunswick. 1976-. 0227-5546. CN. English (French). be. Free to Members. Directory, Corporation of Translators and Interpreters of New Brunswick, PO Box 427, Fredericton New Brunswick E3B 4Z9 Canada. DD 418.02025715.

ANNUAIRE - CORPORATION PROFESSIONNELLE DES COMPTABLES GENERAUX LICENCIES DU QUEBEC. (ANNUAIRE). Main/Corp Corporation Professionnelle des Comptables Generaux Licencies du Quebec. May '81-. 0711-0790. CN. French. an. Corporation Professionnelle des Comptables Licencies au Quebec, 152 Est rue Notre Dame, Montreal Quebec H2Y 3P6 Canada. DD 657.025714. *Annuaire des Membres de la Corporation Professionnelle des Comptables Generaux Licencies du Quebec, 0226-3319.*

ANNUAIRE - CORPORATION PROFESSIONNELLE DES URBANISTES DU QUEBEC. (ANNUAIRE). Main/Corp Corporation Professionnelle des Urbanistes du Quebec. 0824-1430. CN. French. an. Corporation Professionnelle des Urbanistes du Quebec, 1825 Ouest Boul Dorchester, Montreal Quebec H3H 1R4 Canada. DD 711.4025714.

ANNUAIRE DE HULL, GATINEAU, AYLMER, QUEBEC. (HULL, GATINEAU, AYLMER, QUEBEC, CITY DIRECTORY). 0711-4982. CN. English (French). be. $85.00 Per Volume. Hull Gatineau Aylmer City Directory, c/o R L Polk, 220 Bartley Drive, Toronto Ontario M4A 2N4 Canada. DD 917.142210025. *Polk's Hull City Directory, 0316-7992.*

ANNUAIRE DE JURISPRUDENCE DU QUEBEC. 1938-. 0066-2496. Periodical. CN. French (text also in English). Barreau du Quebec, 84 Ouest rue Norte-Dame, Montreal Quebec H2Y 1S6 Canada. DD 348.714046.

ANNUAIRE DE LA BANDE DESSINEE DANS LA COMMUNAUTE FRANCAISE DE BELGIQUE. French. ir. LC PN6790.B42. DD 741.50922, B.

ANNUAIRE DE LA PRESSE ET DE LA PUBLICITE. Vol. 1 Ed. 1880-. French. an. Agence Diffusion & Publicite, 24 Place du Gal-Catroux, 75017 Paris France.

ANNUAIRE DE LA RECHERCHE. FR. French. an. 12 Place Du Pantheon, Paris France. LC AS158. DD 001.402544.

ANNUAIRE DE LA VOILE. Main/Corp Federation de Voile du Quebec. 0822-8302. Periodical. CN. French. $1.00 Per Vol. Federation de Voile du Quebec, 1415 Est rue Jarry, Montreal Quebec H2E 2Z7 Canada. Tel (514)252-3000. DD 797.124025714. adv acc. Circ 2,500. List of schools and clubs, information on where to go to follow a sailing course.

ANNUAIRE DE L'A.A.A. Main/Corp Hague. Academy of International Law. Association of Attenders and Alumni. VFOAT Yearbook of the A.A.A. V. 1- 1925-. articles in French and English. ir. Kluwer Boston Inc, 190 Old Derby Street, Hingham MA 02043. LC JX1295.

ANNUAIRE DE L'ADMINISTRATION DES MINES. FR. French. an. 4 rue Las Cases, 75700 Paris France. LC HD9506.F7. DD 338.202544. *Annuaire de l'Administration et du Corps des Mines.*

ANNUAIRE DE L'ADMINISTRATION LOCALE. Ed. 1980-. FR. French. an. Editions Cujas, 4 6 8 rue de la Maison-Blanche, 75013 Paris France. LC JS4801. DD 352.044.

ANNUAIRE DE L'AFRIQUE DU NORD. VFOAT Annuaire d'Afrique du Nord. Vol. 1 1962-. 0066-2607. FR. French. ir. Editions du Cnrs, 26 rue Boyer, 75971 Paris Cedex 20 France. LC DT181. (cum index).

ANNUAIRE DE L'AFRIQUE ET DU MOYEN-ORIENT. French. an. Groupe Jeune Afrique, 51 Avenue des Ternes, 75827 Paris Cedex 17 France. *Afrique & Moyen-Orient.*

ANNUAIRE DE L'AMENAGEMENT DU TERRITOIRE. V. 8- 1977-. Periodical. FR. French. an. Presses Universitaire Grenoble, BP 47, 38040 Grenoble France. LC HT395.F7. DD 361.60944. *Amenagement du Territoire et Developpement Regional.*

ANNUAIRE DE L'ARMEMENT A LA PECHE. 1.- Yearly V. 0066-2623. FR. French. an. $44.56. Annuaire del Armement a la Peche, 190 Boulevard Haussman, 75008 Paris France. LC SH269. *Annuaire de la Maree et de l'Armement a la Peche.*

ANNUAIRE DE L'ART INTERNATIONAL. 1963/64-. FR. French. be. $30.59. Sermadiras Publicite SA, 11 rue Arsene Houssaye, 75008 Paris France.

ANNUAIRE DE L'ARTISANAT AFRICAIN. VFOAT African Handcrafts Directory. Vol. 1-. English (French). an. 6 rue Thys, Bruxelles Belgium. LC NK1080. DD 745.096.

ANNUAIRE DE L'ASSOCIATION CANADIENNE DES PERIODIQUES CATHOLIQUES. (ANNUAIRE . . . DE L'ASSOCIATION CANADIENNE DES PERIODIQUES CATHOLIQUES). 1984-. 0828-5462. CN. French. an. Association Canadienne des Periodiques Catholiques, C P 1000, Sainte-Anne-De-Beaupre Quebec G0A 3C0 Canada. DD 016.28205.

ANNUAIRE DE L'AUTOMOBILE. (L'ANNUAIRE DE L'AUTOMOBILE . . .). 82-. 0713-5297. CN. French. an. $3.50 Per No. L'Annuaire de l'Automobile Formula Publications, Bureau 105/1255 rue Yonge, Toronto Ontario M4T 1W6 Canada. DD 629.222205.

ANNUAIRE DE LEGISLATION FRANCAISE ET ETRANGERE. New Series V. 5 (Yearly 1956)-. 0066-2658. FR. French. an. Editions du CNRS, 15 Quai Anatole France, F-75700 Paris France. Tel (212)683-4441. Evolution of law in the different countries and in France, with analytical table. *Annuaire de Legislation Etrangere.*

ANNUAIRE DE L'EGLISE CATHOLIQUE AU CANADA. VFOAT Canadian Catholic Church Directory. 1983-. 0821-9885. CN. English (text also in French). be. $23.00 Per Vol. B M Advertising, 85 de Castelnau West, Montreal Quebec H2R 2W3 Canada. DD 282.02571.

ANNUAIRE DE L'EGLISE CATHOLIQUE EN TERRE SAINTE. 1972-. French. ir. Franciscan Print Press, PO Box 14064, Jerusalem Israel. LC BX1628. DD 282.56.

ANNUAIRE DE L'EGLISE DU QUEBEC. 1977-. 0706-8328. CN. French. an. $6. Publicite B M Inc, 450 Av Beaumont, Montreal Quebec H3N 1T8 Canada. DD 282.714025.

ANNUAIRE DE L'INDUSTRIE ET DU COMMERCE DE LA REPUBLIQUE UNIE DU CAMEROUN. CM. French. an. Cograca, Angle rue Surcouf-rue de la Gare, BP 1555, Douala Cameroon. LC HC557.C3. DD 330.96711.

ANNUAIRE DE L'INSTITUT DE DROIT INTERNATIONAL. Main/Corp Institute of International Law. V. 1- 1874-. FR. French. ir. Editions A Pedone, 13 rue Soufflot, 75005 Paris France.

ANNUAIRE DE L'INSTITUT DE PHILOLOGIE ET D'HISTOIRE ORIENTALES ET SLAVES. Main/Corp Universite Libre de Bruxelles. Institut de Philologie et d'Historie Orientales et Slaves. V. 4 (1936)-. BE. French (articles in English and German). ir. Editions de University Bruxelles, Avenue Paul Heger 26, B-1050 Bruxelles Belgium. Tel 021642. Ind/Abst Am. Hist. Life, Hist. Abstr., Part A, Mod. Hist. Abstr., Hist. Abst., Part B, Twent. Century Abstr., MLA Int. Bibliogr. Books Artic. Mod. Lang. Lit. Circ 500. *Annuaire de l'Institut de Philologie et d'Histoire Orientales, 0773-6193.*

ANNUAIRE DE POCHE ALSACE : RESULTATS DEPARTEMENTAUX ET REGIONAUX. VFOAT Statistique Agricole, ALSACE: Resultats Departementaux et Regionaux. French. ir. Metz Ministere de l'Agriculture, 23 rue des Parmentiers 3, Paris France 57000. LC S230.A45. DD 338.10944383.

ANNUAIRE DE POCHE LORRAINE : RESULTATS DEPARTEMENTAUX ET REGIONAUX. VFOAT Statistique Agricole, Lorraine: Resultats Departementaux et Regionaux. French. ir. Metz Ministere de l'Agriculture, 23 rue des Parmentiers, Paris France 57000. LC S230.L68. DD 338.1094438.

ANNUAIRE DE STATISTIQUE AGRICOLE (FRANCE. SERVICE REGIONAL DE STATISTIQUE AGRICOLE, POITOU-CHARENTES). (ANNUAIRE DE STATISTIQUE AGRICOLE). VFOAT Annuaire Poitou-Charentes. 0243-6507. French. an. 30. 47 rue de la Cathedrale, 86020 Poitiers Cedex France. LC HD1950.P65. DD 338.109446.

ANNUAIRE DE STATISTIQUE AGRICOLE. GUADELOUPE. VFOAT Annuaire de Statistique Agricole de la Guadeloupe. FR. French. an. 4 Avenue de Saint-Mande, 75570 Paris Cedex France. LC S183.G85. DD 338.10972976021.

ANNUAIRE DE STATISTIQUE INDUSTRIELLE. Vol. 1-. French. an. $35.92. S E S S I, 85 Boulevard du Montparnasse, 75270 Paris Cedex 06 France. Tel 556 41 08. LC HC271. DD 338.0944. adv acc.

ANNUAIRE DE STATISTIQUES AGRICOLES. French. ir. LC S348.U65. DD 338.1096625.

ANNUAIRE DE STATISTIQUES REGIONALES. 1976-. BE. French. ir. 360 Domestic, 480 Foreign. Institut National de Statistique, rue de Louvain 44, Bruxelles 1000 Belgium. Tel (02)5139650. LC HA1393. DD 314.93. Circ 900. (ctrl). General statistics about the regions, provinces and arrondissements in Belgium.

ANNUAIRE DENTAIRE. 1936-). FR. French. an. $47.90. Les Editions de Chabassol S A, 30 rue de Gramont, Paris 2E France. Tel (1) 4297 50 30. Ed B Laloup. adv acc. Circ 10,000. Directory of all French dental professions.

ANNUAIRE DENTAIRE - ORDRE DES DENTISTES DU QUEBEC. (ANNUAIRE DENTAIRE). Main/Corp Ordre des Dentistes du Quebec. VFOAT Dental Directory. 0826-2233. Periodical. CN. English (French). an. Free. Ordre des Dentistes du Quebec, Suite 200/3565 Berri Street, Montreal Quebec H2L 4G3 Canada. DD 617.60060714. (ctrl).

ANNUAIRE DEPARTEMENTAL PRIVE : ILE DE LA REUNION. French. ir. Societe Les 4 Points Cardinaux, 15 Rue Marignan (8E), Paris France. LC JS4991.R34. *Reunion.*

ANNUAIRE DES ABONNES AU SERVICE TELEX. Bulgarian (French). an. 0.351. Durzhavno Izdatelstvo Tekhnika, Ruski 6, Sofiia Bulgaria. LC HE8313.

ANNUAIRE DES BIBLIOTHECAIRES-CONSEILS DU QUEBEC. 1984-. 0825-3927. CN. French. an. Annuaire des Bibliothecaires-Conseils du Quebec, a/s Corporation des Bibliothecaires Professionnelles du Quebec 360 Rue Lemoyne, Montreal Quebec H2Y 1Y3 Canada. Tel (514)845-3327. DD 023.2025714. List of consultant librarians of Quebec and how to choose a consultant.

ANNUAIRE DES BIBLIOTHEQUES D'ENSEIGNEMENT DU QUEBEC. COLLEGES ET UNIVERSITES. VFOAT Colleges et Universites. 1983-. 0225-1108. CN. French. an. Ministere de l'Education du Quebec, 600 rue Fullum, Montreal Quebec H2K 4L1 Canada.

ANNUAIRE DES COLLECTIVITES LOCALES. 0248-0573. FR. French. an. Librairies Techniques, 27 Place Dauphine, 75001 Paris France. LC JS4801. DD 352.044.

ANNUAIRE DES COMITES - ASTED. (ANNUAIRE DES COMITES - A S T E D). Main/Corp ASTED. Ceased publication with issue for 1979/80. 0226-3149. CN. French. an. Free to Members. Association pour l'Advancement des Sciences et des Techniques de la Documentation, 360 rue Lemoyne, Montreal Quebec H2Y 1Y3 Canada. DD 020.6234714. *Reglements, 0384-5095.*

ANNUAIRE DES COMMERCANTS, DES PROFESSIONNELS ET DES ORGANISMES FRANCOPHONES DE LA COLOMBIE-BRITANNIQUE. 1983/1984-. 0823-6968. CN. French. an. 2.00. Federation des Franco-Colombiens, 104-853 rue Richards,

Yearbooks, Almanacs, Directories

Vancouver British Columbia V6B 3B4 Canada. **Tel** (604)681-2973. Ed Claude Roberge. **DD** 380.1025711. adv acc. **Circ** 15,000. Business directory covering British Columbia.

ANNUAIRE DES COMMUNAUTES EUROPEENNES. VFOAT European Communities Yearbook. 1977-. BE. English (French). an. $37.94. Editions Delta, 92-94 Square E Plasky, B-1040 Bruxelles Belgium. **Tel** (2) 736 90 60. Ed G Francis Seingry. **LC** JN15. **DD** 341.242. bk rev. adv acc. **Circ** 8,000. (ctrl). A working tool for those needing accurate information on the European communities and on the bodies whether private or public which contribute to European integration.

ANNUAIRE DES CONCEPTEURS. French. ir. **LC** TS71. **DD** 745.202544.

ANNUAIRE DES DIPLOMES DE L'ECOLE NATIONALE D'ADMINISTRATION PUBLIQUE. **Main/Corp** Ecole Nationale d'Administration Publique (Quebec). Association des Diplomes. 1980-. 0229-7272. **CN**. French. an. Association des Diplomes de L Enap, 979 Av de Bourgogne, Sainte-Foy Quebec G1W 2L4 Canada. **DD** 378.71447.

ANNUAIRE DES ENTREPRISES DU GABON. French. ir. Chambre de Commerce d Agriculture d Institute, Poite Postale 2.234, Libreville Gabon. **LC** HF5282.5.A3. **DD** 338.00256721.

ANNUAIRE DES FEMMES DE MONTREAL. (L'ANNUAIRE DES FEMMES DE MONTREAL). 1982-. 0823-0188. **CN**. French (English). an. 7.95. Editions Communiquelles, 3585 rue St-Urbain, Montreal Quebec H2X 2N6 Canada. **Tel** (514)844-1871. **DD** 362.8302571427. adv acc. **Circ** 10,000. 250 page directory of groups and resources in the greater Montreal area. Contains over 2,500 groups. *Pages Jaunes des Femmes de Montreal, 0706-828X.*

ANNUAIRE DES GEOGRAPHES DE LA FRANCE ET DE L'AFRIQUE FRANCOPHONE. VFOAT Annuaire des Geographes. 1.- Ed. FR. French. ir. Geographers de la France, 1914 Hamilton St, Regina Saskatchewan S4P 4V4 Canada. **LC** G64. **DD** 910.2517541.

ANNUAIRE DES LOISIRS SCIENTIFIQUES. **Main/Corp** Federation Quebecoise du Loisir Scientifique. 1981-. 0229-6616. **CN**. French. an. Federation Quebecoise du Loisir Scientifique, 1415 Est rue Jarry, Montreal Quebec H2E 1A7 Canada. **DD** 502.3714.

ANNUAIRE DES MAREES. French. ir. **LC** VK645. **DD** 525.690944.

ANNUAIRE DES MEMBRES - ASSOCIATION DES BIBLIOTHEQUES DE LA SANTE DU CANADA. (ANNUAIRE DES MEMBRES - CANADIAN HEALTH LIBRARIES ASSOCIATION). **Main/Corp** Canadian Health Libraries Association. VFOAT Membership Directory. Dec. 1980-. 0228-9679. **CN**. English (text also in French). Free to Members. Canadian Health Libraries Association, 3655 Drummond Street, Montreal Quebec H3C 1Y6 Canada. **DD** 026.6102571.

ANNUAIRE DES MEMBRES - ASSOCIATION INTERNATIONALE DE PEDAGOGIE UNIVERSITAIRE. (ANNUAIRE DES MEMBRES). **Main/Corp** Association International de Pedagogie Universitaire. 0711-7574. **CN**. French. an. Association Internationale de Pedagogie Universitaire, Secretariat General, Universite de Montreal, CP 6128, Montreal Quebec H3C 3J7 Canada. **DD** 378.125025.

ANNUAIRE DES MEMBRES DE L'ASSOCIATION DES BIBLIOTHECAIRES FRANCAIS. **Main/Corp** Association des Bibliothecaires Francais. French. ir. 4 rue de Louvois, Paris France 75002. **LC** Z673.A1. **DD** 020.62244.

ANNUAIRE DES MUSEES ROYAUX DES BEAUX-ARTS DE BELGIQUE. **Main/Corp** Brussels. Musees Royaux des Beaux-Arts de Belgique. VFOAT Jaarboek der Koninkl. Museums voor Schoone Kunsten van Belge. 1- 1938-. Periodical. BE. French (articles in German, English and Flemish). ir. 1040 Bruxelles Belgium. Ed Leo Van Puyvelde. **LC** N6961. **DD** 708.9493.

ANNUAIRE DES ORGANISMES COOPERATIFS, REGION RHONE-ALPES. French. ir. Seervice Regional de Statistique Agricole Rhone-Alpes, 55 rue Mazenod, 69426 Lyon Cedex 3 France. **LC** HD1491.F72. **DD** 334.6830944582.

ANNUAIRE DES ORGANISMES SCOLAIRES PUBLICS. 0709-3551. Periodical. **CN**. French. Secretariat Generale, 1035 rue de la Chevrotiere Edifice G 6E Etage, Quebec Quebec G1R 5A5 Canada. **DD** 371.01025714.

ANNUAIRE DES PAYS DE L'OCEAN INDIEN. 1- 1974-. 0247-400X. FR. French (summaries in English). an. Presses Univ d'Aix Marseille, 3 Ave Robert Schumann, 13628 Aix Provence France. **LC** DT468. **DD** 969.005.

ANNUAIRE DES PETITES ET MOYENNES ENTREPRISES. French. ir. Edition Myk, Kinshasa Congo (Zaire). **LC** HE9559.

ANNUAIRE DES PRODUCTEURS ET EXPORTATEURS DU ZAIRE. French. ir. B P 16.498, Kinshasa 1 Zaire. **LC** HC591.C6. **DD** 338.00256751.

ANNUAIRE DES PRODUITS CHIMIQUES. Series/Titl Annuaires Internationaux Rousset. French. an. Sair, 4 rue Robert-Giraudineau, 94300 Vincennes France. **LC** TP12. **DD** 660.2029444. *Annuaire des Produits Chimiques et de la Droguerie.*

ANNUAIRE DES PROFESSIONS JUDICIAIRES ET JURIDIQUES. FR. French. sm. $70.51. Journal des Notaires et des Notaires et Avocats, 6 rue Meziers, 75006 Paris France. **DD** 340.02544.

ANNUAIRE DES RESSOURCES COMMUNAUTAIRES DU MONTREAL METROPOLITAIN. 0822-6318. **CN**. French. an. 19.95. Annuaire des Ressources Communautaires du Montreal Metropolitain a/s Onfo-Pop, 524 rue de Casteineau, Montreal Quebec H2R 1R5 Canada. **Tel** (514)270-9489. **DD** 061.1714281. bk rev adv acc. **Circ** 300. (ctrl). Contains articles on: public and safety, children and youth, consumers interest, drug abuse and alcoholism, education, ethnics, family, women, directories.

ANNUAIRE DES SERVICES FRANCAIS AU MANITOBA. VFOAT Annuaire Francophone. VAT Annuaire Francophone (1982). '82-. 0713-4584. **CN**. French. an. Free. Annuaire des Services Francais au Manitoba, c/o Maison Avant-Garde, 193 rue Dumoulin, St-Boniface Manitoba R3H 0E4 Canada. **DD** 380.10257127.

ANNUAIRE DES SOCIETES ET DES ADMINISTRATEURS. 1982-. FR. French. an. Dafsa, 7 rue Bergere, 75009 Paris France. **LC** HG4151. **DD** 338.7402544.

ANNUAIRE DES STATISTIQUES DU COMMERCE EXTERIEUR. 0304-5692. CG. French. ir. Institut National de la Statistique, Kinshasa Zaire. **LC** HF270.5. **DD** 382.096751.

ANNUAIRE DES STATISTIQUES DU COMMERCE EXTERIEUR DU TOGO. TG. French. an. 500.00. Secretariat d'Etat a la Presidence Charge du Plan, Direction du la Statistique, BP No 118, Lome Togo. **LC** HF169.T6. **DD** 382.096681.

ANNUAIRE DIOCESAIN - DIOCESE DE SAINT-JEROME. **Main/Corp** Eglise Catholique. Diocese de Saint-Jerome. 0709-6887. **CN**. French. an. $4.60 Per No. Eveche De Saint-Jerome, CP 580, St-Jerome Quebec J7Z 2V3 Canada. **DD** 282.02571424.

ANNUAIRE DIOCESAIN - EGLISE DE JOLIETTE. (ANNUAIRE DIOCESAIN). **Main/Corp** Eglise Catholique. Diocese de Joliette. VAT Eglise de Joliette. Annuaire Diocesain. 0712-3124. **CN**. French. an. Diocese de Joliette, CP 470, Joliette Quebec J6E 6H6 Canada. **DD** 282.02571442.

ANNUAIRE D'ORIENTATION PROFESSIONNELLE. 1980/1981-. 0229-604X. **CN**. French. an. Association de Placement, Universitaire et Collegial, 10E Etage 43 Est Av Eglinton, Toronto Ontario M4P 1A2 Canada. **DD** 331.70202571. *Annuaire Universitaire et Collegial d'Orientation Professionnelle, 0705-7741.*

ANNUAIRE DU BATIMENT. 1 Ed.(1982)-. Tl. French. an. 5.000. Agep 19 Avenue de Carthage, Tunis Tunisia. **LC** HD9715.T8. **DD** 338.4762409611.

ANNUAIRE DU CANADA. 1905-. Periodical. **CN**. French. an. Receiver General For Canada, Supply & Services, Ottawa Ontario K1A 0S9 Canada. **LC** HA744. **DD** 317.1.

ANNUAIRE DU CINEMA ET TELEVISION. 196 -. FR. French. an. Editions Belefaye, 1 Avenue de Labbe/Roussel, 75016 Paris France. *Annuaire du Cinema.*

ANNUAIRE DU CINEMA FRANCAIS ET DE L'AUDIOVISUEL. VFOAT Directory of the French Film and Audiovisual Industries. English (French). an. 114 Champs-Elysees, 75008 Paris France. **LC** PN1993.5.F7. **DD** 384.55029444. *Annuaire du Cinema Francais.*

ANNUAIRE DU COLLEGE DE FRANCE. **Main/Corp** Paris. College de France. 1.- Vol. FR. French. an. $344.00. College de France, 11 Place Marcelin Berthelot, 75231 Paris Cedex 05 France. **Tel** 43 29 12 11. **LC** LF2211. **Circ** 700. Brings together resumes of the teaching, given by the professors, and of the research activities of the chairs.

ANNUAIRE DU FILM BELGE. VFOAT Jaarboek van de Belgische Film. 1958-. Dutch (Flemish and French). ir. **LC** PN1993. **DD** 791.4309493. Each issue contains an index to its own contents - no vol index - loose.

ANNUAIRE DU LOISIR DE L'EST DU QUEBEC. CEASED. Published since 197-. 0228-2054. **CN**. French. an. Conseil des Loisirs de l'Est du Quebec, 100 Ouest rue de l'Eveche, Rimouski Quebec G5L 4H7 Canada. **DD** 790.02571477.

ANNUAIRE DU MARKETING. 1964/65-. Periodical. FR. French. an. 410. ADETEM, 30 Rud d'Astorg, 75008 Paris France. **Tel** (1) 42 55 51 13. adv acc. **Circ** 2,000. (ctrl). The French handbook of marketing professionals lists of ADETEM members (The French Marketing Association).

ANNUAIRE DU MONDE POLITIQUE, DIPLOMATIQUE, ADMINISTRATIF ET DE LA PRESSE. 0304-1344. French. an. 785. **LC** JQ3457. **DD** 354.691002.

ANNUAIRE DU MUSEUM NATIONAL D'HISTOIRE NATURELLE POUR L'ANNEE. **Main/Corp** Museum National d'Histoire Naturelle (France). Began with 1939 vol. FR. French. ir. Editions du Museum, 57 rue Cuvier, 75231 Paris Cedex 05 France.

L'ANNUAIRE DU PAPIER. 0337-4971. FR. French. an. $29.93. Papier Carton et Cellulose, 1 Cite Bergire, 75009 Paris France. **Tel** (1) 824 23 24. Ed Roger Esselin. bk rev. adv acc. **Circ** 2,500. (ctrl).

ANNUAIRE DU SPORT UNIVERSITAIRE QUEBECOIS ET CALENDRIERS DES ACTIVITES. (ANNUAIRE DU SPORT UNIVERSITAIRE QUEBECOIS ET CALENDRIERS DES ACTIVITIES . . .). **Main/Corp** Association Sportive Universitaire du Quebec. VFOAT Directory of University Sports in Quebec and Schedules of Activities . . . . VAT Annuaire - Association Sportive Universitaire du Quebec., Directory - Quebec University Athletic Association, Quebec University Athletic Association, Directory of University Sports in Quebec and Schedules of Activities. 0228-7005. **CN**. French (English). an. ASUQ, 1415 est rue Jarry, Montreal Quebec H3E 2Z7 Canada. **DD** 796.025714.

ANNUAIRE DU TIERS MONDE. 1- 1974/75-. 0396-2156. FR. French. an. **LC** HC59.7. **DD** 309.11724.

ANNUAIRE ECONOMIQUE DE LA TUNISIE. VFOAT Economic Yearbook of Tunisia. Tl. French, (1966/67). an. Union Tunisienne de l'Industrie du Commerce et de l'Artisanat, 32 rue Charles de Gaulle, Tunis Tunisia. **LC** HC820.A1. **DD** 330.9611005.

ANNUAIRE ECONOMIQUE DES PAYS MEMBRES DE L'ORGANISATION DE L'UNITE AFRICAINE. VFOAT Economic Yearbook of Member States of the Organization of African Unity. English (French). an. Editions Edica, B P 9850, Kinshasa Republique du Zaire. **LC** HC800.A1. **DD** 330.96005. *Economic Yearbook.*

ANNUAIRE - EGLISE DE MONTREAL. (ANNUAIRE : L'EGLISE DE MONTREAL). **Main/Corp** Eglise Catholique. Archidiocese de Montreal. 1984-. 0826-0338. **CN**. French. an. Free. La Chancellerie Archeveche de Montreal, 2000 Ouest rue Sherbrooke, Montreal Quebec H3H 1G4 Canada. **DD** 282.025714281. *Bottin, 0317-8463.*

ANNUAIRE EGYPTIEN DES ENTREPRISES, DES SERVICES, DE L'INDUSTRIE ET DU COMMERCE EXTERIEUR. VFOAT Directory of Service, Industrial, and Foreign Trade Companies in Egypt. English (French). an. International Trade Consulting Co, 459 Al-Ahram St, Giza Cairo Egypt. **LC** HF3886.A48. **DD** 382.4500029462.

Yearbooks, Almanacs, Directories

ANNUAIRE ET RAPPORT D'ACTIVITES - DEPARTEMENT DE DEMOGRAPHIE. UNIVERSITE DE MONTREAL. (ANNUAIRE ET RAPPORT D'ACTIVITES - DEPARTEMENT DE DEMOGRAPHIE, UNIVERSITE DE MONTREAL). **Main/Corp** Universite de Montreal. Departement de Demographie. First issue in 1971?. 0225-2716. CN. French. an. Dep de Demographie, Universite de Montreal, CP 6128 Succursale A, Montreal Quebec H3C 3J7 Canada. **DD** 304.60711714281. *Bulletin d'Information, 0700-3064.*

ANNUAIRE ET REGLES DE JEU - ASSOCIATION CANADIENNE DE VOLLEY-BALL. (ANNUAIRE ET REGLES DE JEU). 1978/79-. 0710-0604. CN. French (text also in English). an. Association Canadienne de Volley-Ball, 333 Chemin River, Vanier Ontario K1L 0B9 Canada. **DD** 796.325. *Livre Annuel et Regles, 0705-3142.*

ANNUAIRE EUROPEEN. VFOAT European Yearbook. V. 1- 1955-. 0071-3139. NE. French (French). an. 29.95. Martinus Nijhoff, Lange Voorhout 9-11, PO Box 269, The Hague Netherlands. **Tel** (78)334248. **Ed** A Kiss and J G Lammers. **LC** JN3. **DD** 341.242. **NLM** JN 3 A615. The AAA aims at maintaining intellectual and friendly attenders and alumni of the Hague Academy of International Law and at developing international consciousness.

ANNUAIRE EUROPEEN D'ADMINISTRATION PUBLIQUE. 1- 1978-. Periodical. French. Editions du CNRS, 15 Quai Anatole, 75700 Paris France. **LC** JN1. **DD** 351.004094.

ANNUAIRE - FEDERATION DES CEGEPS. (ANNUAIRE). **Main/Corp** Federation des Cegeps. **VAT** Annuaire - Association des Colleges du Quebec (1974). 1973/1974-. 0227-0269. Periodical. CN. French. La Federation des CEGEPS, 1940 Est Boul Henri-Bourassa, Montreal Quebec H2B 1S2 Canada. **DD** 378.1543060714. *Annuaire, 0820-9073.*

ANNUAIRE FRANCAIS DE DROIT INTERNATIONAL. Vol. 1 1955-. 0066-3085. FR. French. mo. $86.48. Editions du CNRS, 295 rue Street Jacques, 75005 Paris France. **Tel** 4 26 56 11. **Ind/Abst** Int. Labour Doc.

ANNUAIRE (FRANCE. MINISTERE DE LA JEUNESSE, DES SPORTS ET DES LOISIRS. DIVISION DES ETUDES ET DE LA STATISTIQUE). (ANNUAIRE). VFOAT Regards Sur les Statistiques Jeunesse et Sports. FR. French. an. 118 Avenue du President-Kennedy, 75775 Paris Cedex 16 France. **LC** GV79. **DD** 790.0944. *Statistiques Jeunesse, Sports et Loisirs.*

ANNUAIRE FRANCO-ONTARIEN. 1978-. 0706-1021. CN. French. an. Conseil des Affaires Franco-Ontanennes, 77 Ouest rue Bloor, 4E Etage, Toronto Ontario M7A 2R9 Canada. **LC** F1059.7.F83. **DD** 305.81140713. *Bottin des Organismes Franco-Ontariens, 0707-3356.*

ANNUAIRE - FRERES PRECHEURS. PROVINCE SAINT-DOMINIQUE DU CANADA. (ANNUAIRE - DOMINICAINS. PROVINCE CANADIENNE DE SAINT-DOMINIGUE). **Main/Corp** Dominicains. Province Canadienne de Saint-Dominique. **VFOAT** Province Saint-Dominique du Canada. **VAT** Province Saint-Dominique du Canada (1984). 1984-. 0826-5119. CN. French. an. Les Dominicains Administration Provinciale, 5353 Av Notre-Dame de Grace, Montreal Quebec H4A 1L2 Canada. **DD** 255.2002571.

ANNUAIRE GENERAL - FRANCE. MINISTERE DE L'ECONOMIE ET DES FINANCES. **Main/Corp** France. Ministere de l'Economie et des Finances. FR. French. ir. Impr Nationale, BP 637, 59506 Douai Cedex France. **LC** HC271. **DD** 354.440072.

ANNUAIRE HYDROLOGIQUE. 1964-. 0481-2735. Periodical. CN. French. an. **LC** GB708.Q4. **DD** 551.4809714.

ANNUAIRE HYDROMETRIQUE. French. an. **LC** GB1373.8.R4. **DD** 551.483096981.

ANNUAIRE INFORMATIQUE-PHYSIQUE. 1975/76-. French. ir. 80.00. 15 Quai Anatole, Paris France 75700. **LC** Q180.F7. **DD** 530.072044.

ANNUAIRE INTERNATIONAL : AUDIOVISUEL. VFOAT Audiovisuel. French. ir. Editions Candelmon, 1 rue de Turbigo, Paris France 75001. **LC** TS2301.A7. **DD** 338.4762138. *Annuaire Audiovisuel.*

ANNUAIRE INTERNATIONAL DES DIX-HUITIEMISTES. VFOAT International Directory of Eighteenth-Century Research, International Directory of Eighteenth-Century Studies. 1971-. FR. English (French). an. $13.00. Presses Universitaires de Grenoble, BP 47, 38040 Grenoble France. **LC** CB411.

L'ANNUAIRE INTERNATIONAL DES FOIRES-EXPOSITIONS & I.E. ET SALONS SPECIALISES. VFOAT Exposant International. FR. French. ir. 72.00. Societe Europeenne d'Etudes et de Relations Internationales, C.C.P., Paris 7002-76 France. **LC** T391. **DD** 607.34.

ANNUAIRE INTERNATIONAL DES VENTES. 1963-. French. an. Editions Publisol, PO Box 339, 235 East 85th Street, New York NY 10028. **Ed** E Mayer. **LC** N8640. **DD** 707.5.

ANNUAIRE : MAGNETISME TERRESTRE. VFOAT Naarboek : Aardmagnetisme. BE. French (Flemish (Dutch)). an. Institut Royal Meteorologique de Belgique, Avenue Circulaire 3, 1180 Bruxelles Belgium. **LC** QC830.D68.

ANNUAIRE MARITIME NATIONAL. French. an. CNCC, B P 1588, Douala Cameroun. **LC** HE905.4. **DD** 387.50256711.

ANNUAIRE MINEMET. **Main/Corp** Minemet. 1977-. FR. French. an. Societe Minemet Direction Market, 33 Avenue du Maine, 75755 Paris Cedex 15 France. **LC** HD9506.A1. **DD** 338.20212. *Minemet. Annuaire.*

ANNUAIRE MUNICIPAL DE ST. I.E. SAINT DENIS. **Main/Corp** Saint-Denis, Reunion. 1978/79-. French. ir. Societe Novodoc, Service des Relations Publiques, Mairie De St Denis, Paris France. **LC** DT469.R5. **DD** 916.981.

ANNUAIRE NATIONAL DE LA CONSERVE. VFOAT A.N.C., ANC. FR. French. an. Les Editions Comindus, 1 rue Descombes, Paris 75017 France. **LC** HD9323.3. **DD** 338.476640280944.

ANNUAIRE NATIONAL DE LA REPUBLIQUE GABONAISE. VFOAT Annuaire National et International. 1980-. French. an. Edition Inf Afrique, B P 3875, Libreville Gabon. **LC** DT546.1. **DD** 967.21005.

ANNUAIRE NATIONAL DE LA REPUBLIQUE MALAGACHE. **Main/Corp** Malagasy Republic. French. ir. **LC** DT469.M21.

ANNUAIRE NATIONAL OFFICIEL DE LA REPUBLIQUE GABONAISE. 1973-. French. ir. Agence Havas Gabon, B P 213, Liberville Gabon. **LC** JQ3407.A1. **DD** 916.721034.

ANNUAIRE NATIONALE DES DEBITS DE COURS D'EAU. 1969-. French. ir. **LC** GB1293. **DD** 551.4830944.

ANNUAIRE OFFICIEL D'ADMINISTRATION ET DE LEGISLATION. **Main/Corp** Luxembourg. Service Central de Legislation. French. an. **LC** JN6381. **DD** 354.4935000202.

L'ANNUAIRE OFFICIEL DE LA CHARCUTERIE. VFOAT AOC. FR. French. an. 1 rue Descombes, 75017 Paris France. **LC** HD9435.F7. **DD** 338.1764002544.

ANNUAIRE OFFICIEL DES ASSURANCES AFRICAINES. 1.- Ed. English (French). ir. B P 5287, Kinshasa Congo. **LC** HG8720.A6. **DD** 368.96.

ANNUAIRE OFFICIEL TELEX DU ZAIRE. VFOAT Annuaire Telex Officiel du Zaire. 1979-. French. ir. Snat, B P 15.598, Kinshasa Zaire. **LC** HE8501. **DD** 384.14.

ANNUAIRE PARIS & I.E. ET REGION. VFOAT ADP Region. 1978/79-. FR. French. ir. 17 Rue de Paradis, 75010 Paris France. **LC** JS4991.I37. **DD** 352.04434.

ANNUAIRE POLK DE BAIE-COMEAU. VFOAT Polk's Baie-Comeau City Directory. Began publication in 1968?. 0316-8271. Periodical. CN. English (French). R L Polk, 220 Bartley Drive, Toronto Ontario M4P 1G2 Canada. **DD** 917.1417.

ANNUAIRE POLK DE GRANBY QUEBEC. (POLK'S GRANBY, QUEBEC, CITY DIRECTORY). VFOAT Annuaire Polk de Granby, Quebec. Began publication with the 1958/59 issue. 0317-1515. Periodical. CN. English (text also in French, each with special title page). an. $70.00 Per No. R L Polk & Company Ltd, 2485 Ste-Anne Boulevard, Quebec Quebec G1J 1Y4 Canada. **DD** 917.1463. *Annuaire Marcotte de Granby, 0317-1531.*

ANNUAIRE POLK DE HULL. (POLK'S HULL CITY DIRECTORY). 1959-. 0316-7992. Periodical. CN. text in English and French, Each With Special T. P. an. R L Polk and Company Ltd, 2485 Ste-Anne Boulevard, Quebec Quebec G1J 1Y4 Canada. **DD** 917.14221. *Marcotte's Hull City Directory.*

ANNUAIRE POLK DE RIMOUSKI ET MONT-JOLI QUEBEC. (POLK'S RIMOUSKI AND MONT-JOLI, QUEBEC, CITY DIRECTORY). VFOAT Annuaire Polk de Rimouski et Mont-Joli, Quebec. 1971-. 0380-3961. Periodical. CN. text in English and French. qt. R L Polk & Company Ltd, 2485 Ste-Anne Boulevard, Quebec Quebec G1J 1Y3 Canada. **DD** 917.14771. *Polk's Rimouski, Quebec, City Directory, 0380-397X.*

ANNUAIRE POLK DE SEPT-ILES. (POLK'S SEPT-ILES CITY DIRECTORY). 1961-. 0380-3775. CN. text in English and French. an. R L Polk & Company Ltd, 2485 Ste-Anne Boulevard, Quebec Quebec G1J 1Y3 Canada. **DD** 917.1417.

ANNUAIRE POLK DE SOREL TRACY ET ST-JOSEPH. VFOAT Polk's Sorel Tracy and St-Joseph City Directory. V. 1- 1965-. 0700-7272. CN. French (text in English and French). an. R L Polk & Ltd, 2485 Boul Ste Anne, Quebec Quebec G1J 1Y4 Canada.

ANNUAIRE POLK DE THETFORD MINES. VFOAT Annuaire de Thetford Mines City Directory. V. 1- 1962-. 0703-3354. Periodical. CN. French (text also in English). an. $55. Per V. R L Polk & Company LTD 1396 Avenue Maguire, Sillery Quebec G1T 1Z3 Canada.

ANNUAIRE PROFESSIONNEL FRANCAIS. (ANNUAIRE PROFESSIONEL FRANCAIS). First Issue in 1953. 0315-9019. Periodical. CN. French. Le Courrier Francais de Montreal, 429 Av Viger, Montreal Quebec H2L 2N9 Canada. **DD** 380.1025714281.

ANNUAIRE QUALITE DES EAUX (QUEBEC). **Main/Corp** Quebec (Province). Service Qualite des Eaux. 0388-557X. Periodical. CN. French. an. EOQ, Quebec (Province) Service des Eaux, Quebec Canada. **LC** TD227.Q42. **DD** 553.709714.

ANNUAIRE : RAYONNEMENT SOLAIRE. **Main/Corp** Institut Royal Meteorologique de Belgique. VFOAT Jaarboek: Zonnestraling. French (Flemish). ir. Institut Royal Meteorologique de Belgique, Avenue Circulaire 3, Brussels Belgium. **LC** QC911.82.B4.

ANNUAIRE REGIONAL DE STATISTIQUE AGRICOLE. French. ir. Ministere de l'Agriculture, 1 Bis rue Delavelle, Besancon France. **LC** S230.F7. **DD** 338.1094445.

ANNUAIRE REGIONAL - SERVICE CENTRAL DES ENQUETES ET ETUDES STATISTIQUES, REGION DE PROGRAMME BOURGOGNE. **Main/Corp** France. Service Central des Enquetes et Etudes Statistiques. Region de Programme Bourgogne. FR. French. ir. Service Central des Enquetes et Etudes Statistiques, 5 rue Casimir Perier, Paris France. **LC** S230.B87. **DD** 338.109444.

ANNUAIRE REGIONAL : STATISTIQUE AGRICOLE. VFOAT Statistique Agricole, Languedoc. Began with 1968 Vol. French. ir. Service Regional de Statistique Agricole/Region Languedoc, 16 rue de la Republique, Montpellier France. **LC** S230.L38. **DD** 338.109448.

ANNUAIRE RHONE-ALPES. FR. French. an. 12.00. Insee, 84 rue du 1er Mars 1943, Paris France 69525. **LC** HA1228.R55. **DD** 314.4582.

ANNUAIRE ROUMAIN D'ANTHROPOLOGIE. V. 1- 1964-. 0570-2259. RM. French. an. Ilexim Press Department, PO Box 1-136-1-137, Bucharest Romania. **Ind/Abst** Excerpta Med., Biol. Abstr. **LC** GN1. **CODEN** ARNAAG.

ANNUAIRE SCIENCES DE L'HOMME. FR. French. an. $10.00. Centre Documentation Sciences Humaines/54 Boulevard Raspail, 75260 Paris Cedex 06 France. **Tel** (1) 45 44 38 49. **Ed** Veronique Vincent. **LC** AZ651. **DD** 001.302544. **Circ** 2,000. Description of 600 French social sciences research centers, financed by National Center for Scientific Research.

Yearbooks, Almanacs, Directories

ANNUAIRE - SOCIETE DE DEVELOPPEMENT DU LIVRE ET DU PERIODIQUE. (ANNUAIRE). Main/Corp Societe de Developpement du Livre et du Periodique. 1980-. 0820-019X. Periodical. CN. French. an. Societe de Developpement du Livre et Duperiodique, 1151 rue Alexandre-Deseve, Montreal Quebec H2L 2T7 Canada. DD 070.5025714. *Annuaire, 0084-9197.*

ANNUAIRE - SOCIETE DE MUSIQUE DES UNIVERSITES CANADIENNES. (ANNUAIRE). VFOAT Directory. 1980/1981-. 0710-5398. CN. English (text also in French). an. Canadian University Music Society, c/o B J Ellard, School of Music, Universite de Sherbrooke, Sherbrooke Quebec J1K 2R1 Canada. DD 780.72971.

ANNUAIRE STATISTIQUE DE LA BELGIQUE. V. 81- 1960-. 0066-3646. BE. French (Flemish). an. 900 Domestic, 1050 Foreign. Institute national de Statistique, 44 rue de Louvaine, 1000 Bruxelles Belgium. Tel (02)513.96.50. LC HA1393. DD 314.93. NLM W2 GB4 I5AB. Circ 1,350. (ctrl). General statistics about Belgium. *Annuaire Statistique de la Belgique et du Congo Belge.*

ANNUAIRE STATISTIQUE DE LA FRANCE (INSTITUT NATIONAL DE LA STATISTIQUE ET DES ETUDES ECONOMIQUES (FRANCE)). (ANNUAIRE STATISTIQUE DE LA FRANCE). 66. Vol. (1961)-. FR. French. an. $57.20. Observatoire Economique Paris, 195 rud de Bercy/Tour Gamma A, 75582 Paris Cedex 12 France. NLM W2 GF7 I5A.

ANNUAIRE STATISTIQUE DE LA JUSTICE. 1978-. FR. French. an. La Documentation Francaise, 29-31 Quai Voltaire, 75340 Paris Cedex 07 France. DD 347.44013, 344.40713.

ANNUAIRE STATISTIQUE DE LA SECURITE SOCIALE. Main/Corp Belgium. Ministere de la Prevoyance Sociale. VFOAT Statistisch Jaarboek Van de Sociale Zekerheid. 1961-. 0067-5571. BE. French. an. Ministerie Sociale Voorzorg, Zwarte Lievevrouwstraat 3C, 1000 Brussels Belgium. LC HD7186.

ANNUAIRE STATISTIQUE DE LA TUNISIE. Main/Corp Tunisia. Institut National de la Statistique. 1967-. FR. French. ir. INSEE-CNGP, BP 2718, 80027 Amiens Cedex France. *Annuaire Statistique de la Tunisie.*

ANNUAIRE STATISTIQUE DE L'ALGERIE. Main/Corp Algeria. Bureau des Statistiques Generales. (1972-). Periodical. French. ir. Office of National Statistiques, 8 10 rue des Mousebilines, Algiers Algeria. *Annuaire Statistique de l'Algerie.*

ANNUAIRE STATISTIQUE DE L'ENSEIGNMENT. French. ir. Direction de la Planification et de la Programmation, BP 334, Libreville Gabon. LC LA1780. DD 370.96721.

ANNUAIRE STATISTIQUE DE L'INDUSTRIE FRANCAISE DU JUTE ET DES POLIOLEFINES TEXTILES. French. ir. General de I Industrie du Jute er des Textiles Associes, 33 rue de Moromesnil, 75008 Paris France. LC HD9156.J8. DD 338.47677130944.

ANNUAIRE STATISTIQUE DE POCHE - INSTITUT NATIONAL DE STATISTIQUE. (ANNUAIRE STATISTIQUE DE POCHE). Main/Corp Institut National de Statistique (Belgium). 1965-. 0067-5431. BE. French. an. 125 Domestic, 160 Foreign. Institut National de Statistique, rue de Louvain 44, 1000 Bruxelles Belgium. Tel (02)513.96.50. LC WMLC L 83/658. Circ 1,200. (ctrl). General statistics about Belgium.

ANNUAIRE STATISTIQUE DES TELECOMMUNICATIONS DU SECTEUR PUBLIC. VFOAT Yearbook of Common Carrier Telecommunication Statistics. 1963/72-. English, French and Spanish. ir. LC HE7601. DD 384.605.

ANNUAIRE STATISTIQUE DU LUXEMBOURG. VFOAT Annuaire Statistique. English. an. Service Central-Stats et Etudes Econ, 19-21 Boulevard Royal BP 305, Luxembourg 2013 Luxembourg. *Annuaire Statistique (Luxembourg. Service Central de la Statistique et des Etudes Economiques).*

ANNUAIRE STATISTIQUE DU MAROC (RABAT, MOROCCO : 1982). (ANNUAIRE STATISTIQUE DU MAROC). French. an. Direction de la Statistique, BP178, Rabat Morocco. *Nashriyah Al-Ihsaiyah Al-Sanawiyah Lil-Maghrib.*

ANNUAIRE STATISTIQUE DU TOGO. TG. French. ir. Secretariat la Presidence Charge du Commerce/de Industrie et du Plan Direction de la Statistique, BP 118, Lome Togo. LC HA2126. DD 316.681.

ANNUAIRE STATISTIQUE (HAITI.) DEPARTEMENT DE L'EDUCATION NATIONALE. SECTION DE STATISTIQUES). (ANNUAIRE STATISTIQUE). French. an. LC LA490. DD 371.207097294.

ANNUAIRE STATISTIQUE (INSTITUT NATIONAL DE LA STATISTIQUE ET DE L'ANALYSE ECONOMIQUE). (ANNUAIRE STATISTIQUE). VFOAT Annuaire Statistique de la Republique Populaire du Benin. No. 6 (1980)-. French. an. Direction Generale de L'INSAE, B P 323, Cotonou Dahomey. LC HA2111.D34. DD 316.683. *Annuaire Statistique de la Republique Populaire du Benin.*

ANNUAIRE STATISTIQUE (LUXEMBURG). Main/Corp Luxemburg. Service Central de la Statistique et des Etudes Economiques. 1964-. 0076-1575. LU. French. an. 1000. Statist et Etudes Econ Statec, 19-21 Boulevard Royal CP 304, L-2013 Luxembourg Luxembourg. Tel 4794-292. bk rev. (ctrl). Yearbook of all available statistics. *Annuaire Statistique.*

ANNUAIRE STATISTIQUE - NOUVELLE-CALEDONIE ET DEPENDANCES. SERVICE DE LA STATISTIQUE. (ANNUAIRE STATISTIQUE - NOUVELLE-CALEDONIE ET DEPENDANCES, SERVICE DE LA STATISTIQUE). Main/Corp New Caledonia. Service de la Statistique. VFOAT Annuaire Statistique de la Nouvelle-Caledonie. 0376-5598. NL. French. an. Service de la Statistique, BP C5, Noumea New Caldonia. LC HA4007.N4. DD 319.32.

ANNUAIRE STATISTIQUES. VFOAT Annuaire Statistique. French. an. Service National des Etudes et Statistiques, BP 1156, Bujumbura Republique du Burundi. LC HA2124.B86. DD 316.7572. *Annuaire Statistique (Burundi. Premier Ministere et Ministere du Plan. Departement des Etudes et Statistiques).*

ANNUAIRE SUISSE DE SCIENCE POLITIQUE. VFOAT Schweizerisches Jahrbuch fur Politische Wissenschaft. No. 5- 1965-. 0066-3727. French (and German). ir. Verlag Paul Haupt, Falkenplatz 14, 3001 Bern Switzerland. Tel 031/23 24 25. Ed Verlag Paul Haupt. Ind/Abst Am. Hist. Life, Hist. Abstr., Part A, Mod. Hist. Abstr., Hist. Abst., Part B, Twent. Century Abstr., ABC Pol Sci. bk rev. Circ 1,500. *Annuaire - Association Suisse de Science Politique. Jahrbuch - Schweizerische Vereinigung Fur Politische Wissenschaft.*

ANNUAIRE SUISSE DU FOLK : MUSICIENS. VFOAT Schweizer Folk-Kalendar : Musiker. 1-. Ed. SZ. English (French, and German). an. Peggy Moser Freigutstr, 22, 8002 Zurich Switzerland. LC ML3720. DD 781.70922.

ANNUAIRE SUISSE DU FOLK : ORGANISATEURS. VFOAT Schweizer Folk-Kalender : Veranstalter. 1-. Ed. English (French, and German). ir. Peggy Moser Freigutstrasse, 22, 8002 Zurich Switzerland. LC ML21.S9. DD 781.7025494.

ANNUAIRE SUISSE DU MONDE ET DES AFFAIRES. VFOAT Wer Ist Wer in der Schweiz?. 1972/73-. English, French, German, or Italian. ir. International Registry of Who's Who SA, 23 Chemin du Levant, CH-1005 Lausanne Switzerland. Tel 021/20 09 24. LC CT1383. DD 920.0494. bk rev. adv acc. Circ 5,000. Presents people important to the Swiss and Liechtenstein economy. A person may be listed by virtue of his position, or the market position of his company. Others have distinguished themselves by outstanding achievements and performance in their own fields.

ANNUAIRE SUISSE FOLK & CHANSON CHANSON. MUSICIENS, ORGANISATFURS. VFOAT Folk et Chanson, Schweizer Folk & Chanson Handbuch. Musiker, Veranstalter. English (French, and German). an. Edition CM Riedhofstrasse 106, 8408 Winterthur Switzerland. LC ML21.S9. DD 781.7025494.

ANNUAIRE SUISSE-TIERS MONDE. VFOAT Annuaire Suisse Tiers Monde, Jahrbuch Schweiz Dritte Welt. 1981-. Periodical. French (German). an. Institut Universitaire d'Etudes du Developpement, 24 rue Rothchild, 1202 Geneve Switzerland. LC HF1573. DD 337.4940172405.

ANNUAIRE TELEPHONIQUE - CENTRE DE CULTURE DIALOGUE ORIENTAL. Main/Corp Centre de Culture Dialogue Oriental. VFOAT Directory Book - Centre de Culture Dialogue Oriental. Began with 1972/73 issue?. 0703-2153. CN. English (text also in French). an. Centre de Culture Dialogue Oriental, Suite 5/5336 Queen Mary Road, Montreal Quebec H3X 1T8 Canada. DD 301.4511920714281. *L S C A.*

ANNUAIRE TELEPHONIQUE JUDICIAIRE DU QUEBEC. VFOAT The Quebec Legal Telephone Directory. 23rd- Ed. 0316-6120. Periodical. CN. text in French and English. an. $11.61. Annuaire Telephonique, CP 395-1495 del Eglise Stent, Montreal Quebec Canada. DD 340.025714. *Annuaire Telephonique Judiciaire de la Province de Quebec, 0316-6139.*

ANNUAIRE TOURISTIQUE ET DIPLOMATIQUE DU CAMEROUN. CM. French. an. Editions Stella, BP 1126, Yaounde Cameroon. LC DT561. DD 967.11.

ANNUAIRE - UNIVERSITE D'OTTAWA. Main/Corp University of Ottawa. VFOAT Directory - University of Ottawa. Began with 1958 issue. 0317-6142. Periodical. CN. text in French and English. University of Ottawa, Department of Public Relations, Ottawa Ontario K1N 6N5 Canada. DD 378.71384.

ANNUAIRE - UNIVERSITE PARIS 7. Main/Corp Universite de Paris VII. VFOAT Paris 7 Recherche. VAT Annuaire - Universite Paris Sept. French. ir. 10.00. Universite Paris 7, 2 Place Jussien, 75221 Paris Cedex 05 France. LC LF2161.C5.

ANNUAIRE - UNIVERSITE PARIS-SUD. INSTITUT DE PHYSIQUE NUCLEAIRE. Main/Corp Universite Paris-Sud. Institut de Physique Nucleaire. French (summaries in English). ir. Orsay, Institut de Physique Nucleaire, Paris 91406 France. LC QC789.4.F73. DD 539.7.

ANNUAL DIRECTORY - AMERICAN CHAMBER OF COMMERCE FOR BRAZIL. RIO DE JANEIRO CHAMBER. Main/Corp American Chamber of Commerce for Brazil. Rio de Janeiro Chamber. BL. English (Portuguese). an. American Chamber of Commerce for Brazil, Av Rio Branco 123, 21st Floor Rooms 2106/11, Rio de Janeiro Brazil. LC HF300. DD 382.09708103810258153.

ANNUAL DIRECTORY AND REPORT - AMERICAN DEFENSE PREPAREDNESS ASSOCIATION. (ANNUAL DIRECTORY AND REPORT). Main/Corp American Defense Preparedness Association. 1973/74-. 0092-7422. US. English. an. American Defense Preparedness Association, 819 Union Trust Building, Washington DC 20005. LC UF1. DD 623.06273.

ANNUAL DIRECTORY - CANADIAN ASSOCIATION OF FIRE CHIEFS. Main/Corp Canadian Association of Fire Chiefs. VFOAT Annuaire - Association Canadienne des Chefs de Pompiers. 1978/79-. 0706-1390. CN. English (French). an. Free to Members. Canadian Association of Fire Chiefs, 111-196 Bronson Avenue, Ottawa Ontario K1R 6H4 Canada. DD 363.378. *Annual Conference, 0706-1404.*

ANNUAL DIRECTORY - DEPARTMENT OF NATURAL RESOURCES. GEOLOGICAL SURVEY DIVISION. (ANNUAL DIRECTORY - GEOLOGICAL SURVEY DIVISION). Main/Corp Michigan. Geological Survey Division. VFOAT Michigan Mineral Producers. 1- 1966-. 0085-3372. US. English. an. Department of Natural Resources/Geological Department, Box 30028, Lansing MI 48909. Ind/Abst GeoRef. CODEN MGSDB4.

ANNUAL DIRECTORY - HAWAII STATE BAR ASSOCIATION. (ANNUAL DIRECTORY). Main/Corp Hawaii State Bar Association. 0277-0520. US. English. an. $10.00, Free to Hawaii Members of State Bar Association. Crossroads Press, PO Box 833, Honolulu HI 96808. LC KF192.H3. DD 349.969025, 349.690025. *Annual Directory.*

ANNUAL DIRECTORY, HOUSES OF PRAYER. VFOAT Directory Houses of Prayer. 1976-. 0363-5589. US. English. an. Clarity Publications Inc, 75 Champlain Street, Albany NY 12204. LC BX2438.5. DD 269.602573.

ANNUAL DIRECTORY - MINNESOTA STATE BOARD OF ACCOUNTANCY. Main/Corp Minnesota. State Board of Accountancy. US. English. Minnesota State Board of Accountancy, 5th Floor/Metro Square Building, St Paul MN 55101.

Yearbooks, Almanacs, Directories

ANNUAL DIRECTORY OF BOOKSELLERS IN THE BRITISH ISLES SPECIALISING IN ANTIQUARIAN AND OUT-OF-PRINT BOOKS. 1970-. 0066-3913. UK. English. an. Clique Ltd, 75 World End Road Handsworth, Birmingham B20 2NS England. LC Z327. DD 380.145070573.

THE ANNUAL DIRECTORY OF VEGETARIAN RESTAURANTS. (ANNUAL DIRECTORY OF VEGETARIAN RESTAURANTS). 1980-. 0270-031X. US. English. an. $8.95. Daystar Publishing Company, PO Box 707, Angwin CA 94508. LC TX907. DD 647.9573.

ANNUAL DIRECTORY - TEXAS RETAIL GROCERS ASSOCIATION. (ANNUAL DIRECTORY). Main/Corp Texas Retail Grocers Association. VFOAT TRGA . . . Annual Directory. 1st (1981)-. 0276-4458. US. English. an. Associated Business Publications Inc, Suite 921/41 East 42nd Street, New York NY 10017. LC HD9321.3. DD 381.456640025764.

ANNUAL MEETING MAGAZINE & MEMBERSHIP DIRECTORY - TENNESSEE FORESTRY ASSOCIATION. Main/Corp Tennessee Forestry Association. VFOAT Membership Directory. US. English. an. 1720 West End Avenue Suite 613, Nashville TN 37203.

ANNUAL MEMBERSHIP DIRECTORY - NORTH CAROLINA ASSOCIATION OF CONVENIENCE STORES. Main/Corp North Carolina Association of Convenience Stores. VFOAT N.C.A.C.S. . . . Annual Directory. 1st (Spring 1981)-. US. English. an. Associated Business Publishing Inc, 41 East 42nd Street/Suite 921, New York NY 10017. Tel (212)490-3999. LC HF5469.25. DD 381.1.

ANNUAL MEMBERSHIP TELEPHONE DIRECTORY - ASSOCIATION OF TRIAL LAWYERS OF AMERICA. Main/Corp Association of Trial Lawyers of America. 0270-1278. US. English. an. ATLA, 1050 31st Street Northwest, Washington DC 20007. LC KF195.L53. DD 347.737025.

ANNUAL OFFICE SALARIES DIRECTORY CEASED. VFOAT AMS Office Salaries Directory for United States and Canada, A.M.S. Office Salaries Directory for United States and Canada, AMS Annual Office Salaries Directory, Office Salaries Directory. 35th (1981-82)-. US. English. an. $115.00. Administrative Management Society, 2360 Maryland Road, Willow Grove PA 19090. *Office Salaries Directory for United States and Canada, 0731-4434.*

ANNUAL REPORT AND DIRECTORY OF ACCREDITED LABORATORIES. Main/Corp NVLAP (Program : U.S.). Series/Titl NBS Special Publication. 0883-3273. US. English. an. Office of Product Standards Policy, National Bureau of Standards, Washington DC 20234. CODEN XNBSAV. Vols. for (1983-) distributed to depository libraries in microfiche.

ANNUAL REPORT AND DIRECTORY OF MINES - WEST VIRGINIA. DEPT. OF MINES. Main/Corp West Virginia. Dept. of Mines. 1977-. US. English. an. State of West Virginia, Department of Mines, Charleston WV 25305. LC TN24.W4. DD 353.975400823806. *Annual Report, Directory of Mines, 0147-2798.*

ANNUAL REPORT & DIRECTORY OF OKLAHOMA LIBRARIES. Main/Corp Oklahoma. Dept. of Libraries. VFOAT Annual Report and Directory of Oklahoma Libraries. US. English. an. Free. Oklahoma Department of Libraries, 200 NE 18th Street, Oklahoma City OK 73105. Tel (405)521-2502. Ed Beverly Jones. LC Z732.O57. DD 027.07660212. Circ 419. Statistics of Oklahoma libraries. *Annual Report of Oklahoma Libraries.*

ANNUAL REPORT AND YEARBOOK - ADVERTISING RESEARCH FOUNDATION. (ANNUAL REPORT AND YEARBOOK). Main/Corp Advertising Research Foundation. 1982-. 0736-6752. US. English. an. Advertising Research Foundation, 3 East 54th Street, New York NY 10022. LC HF5815.U5. DD 659.1072073. *Yearbook, 0271-1400.*

ANNUAL REPORT - TYOTERVEYSLAITOS. See Industrial Health & Safety.

ANNUAL WHO'S IN CHARGE HERE YEARBOOK. VFOAT Who's In Charge Here Yearbook. 1st (1981)-. 0733-5229. US. English. an. $3.95. G P Putnam's Sons, 200 Madison Avenue, New York NY 10016. LC E839. DD 973.920207.

ANNUAL YEAR BOOK - UNITED STATES TROTTING ASSOCIATION, INC. (ANNUAL YEAR BOOK - UNITED STATES TROTTING ASSOCIATION). Main/Corp United States Trotting Association. 0083-3517. US. English. an. $11.09. US Trotting Association, 750 Michican Avenue, Columbus OH 43215. Tel (614)224-2291. LC SF325. DD 798.460973. *Year Book, Trotting and Pacing.*

ANNUARIO - BIENNALE DI VENEZIA. Main/Corp Biennale di Venezia. 1975-. Italian. ir. Archivio Storico Delle Arti Contemporanee Della Biennale di Venezia, Ca' Giustinian, S Maro 1344, 30100, Venezia Italy. LC NX430.I82.

ANNUARIO DE COMERCIO EXTERIOR (BOGOTA). (ANUARIO DE COMERCIO EXTERIOR). VFOAT Anuario de Comercio Exterior Colombia. 1939-. CK. Spanish. ir. Departamento Administrativo Nacional de Estadistica, Imprenta Nacional, Bogota CK. LC HF167. *Comercio Exterior de Colombia.*

ANNUARIO DE STATISTICHE INDUSTRIALI. V. 1- 1956-. 0075-1723. Italian. ir. LC HC301.

ANNUARIO DEGLI ARTISTI VISIVI ITALIANI. 1972-. Italian. ir. 12.000. LC N6922.

ANNUARIO DEI SERVIZI. V. 1, 1977/78-. Italian. ir. Via Aurelio Saffi 18, Torino 10138 Italy. LC HD9986.I8.

ANNUARIO DEL CINEMA ITALIANO. 1950/51-. Italian. ir. LC PN1993.5.I88.

ANNUARIO DEL COMMERCIO ESTERO. 0304-0364. IT. Italian. ir. 5000. F Angeli, Casella Postale 4294, Milano Italy. LC HF3586.5. DD 382.0945.

ANNUARIO DEL GRUPPO IRI. Main/Corp Istituto Per la Ricostruzione Industriale, Rome. Italian. ir. Istituto per la Ricostruzione Industriale, Via Vittorio Veneto 89, Roma 00187 Italy. LC HC301.

ANNUARIO DELLA ACCADEMIA DELLE SCIENZE DELL'ISTITUTO DI BOLOGNA : CLASSE DI SCIENZE FISICHE. Main/Corp Accademia Delle Scienze Dell'Istituto di Bologna. IT. Italian. ir. Palazzo Universitario, Via Zamboni, 31, Bologna Italy. LC QC1.

ANNUARIO DELLA SCUOLA ARCHEOLOGICA DI ATENE E DELLE MISSIONI ITALIANE IN ORIENTE. Main/Corp Athens. Scuola Archeologica Italiana. V. 1-15/16, 1914-1932/33. 0067-0081. IT. Italian. ir. L Erma di Bretschneider Spa, Via Cassiodoro 19, PO Box 6192, 00193 Rome Italy. Tel (06)353259. Ed L'Erma di Bretschneider. Ind/Abst Art Index, Avery Index Archit. Period. Second Ed. Revis. Enlarged Suppl. LC DF11. Circ 600. Archaeological reports, very often comprising acts, and proceedings of seminars or round tables.

ANNUARIO DELL'ABBIGLIAMENTO E DEL TEMPO LIBERO. Yearly V. 1- 1977/78-. Periodical. Italian. ir. Seat, Via Aurelio Saffi 18, Torino 10138 Italy. LC HD9940.I8.

ANNUARIO DELL'ALIMENTAZIONE E DELLE ATTIVITA RICETTIVE. Yearly V. 1-1977/78-. Italian. ir. Seat, Via Aurelio Saffi 18, Torino 10138 Italy. LC HD9015.I6.

ANNUARIO DELLE ATTIVITA GRAFICO-EDITORIALI, DEI TRASPORTI E DEI SERVIZI. IT. Italian. an. Edizioni Seat, Via Aurelio Saffi 18, 10138 Torino Italy. LC HF3583. DD 338.7402545.

ANNUARIO DELL'EDILIZIA E ARREDAMENTO. Yearly V. 1- 1977/78-. Italian. ir. Seat, Via Aurelio Saffi 18, Torino 10138 Italy. LC HD9715.I8.

ANNUARIO DELL'INDUSTRIA. Yearly V. 1-1977/78-. Italian. ir. Seat, Via Aurelio Saffi 18, Torino 10138 Italy. LC HC301.

ANNUARIO . . . DELL'INDUSTRIA ITALIANA DELLA MAGLIERIA E DELLA CALZETTERIA. VFOAT Annuaire de la Bonneterie Italienne, Yearbook of the Italian Knitting Industry. IT. English (French, German, Italian, and Spanish). an. 50.000. Gesto S R L, Via Cesare Battisti 21, 20122 Milano Italy.

ANNUARIO DI STATISTICA AGRARIA (ITALY). Main/Corp Istituto Centrale di Statistica (Italy). 0075-1669. IT. Italian. an. $5.35. Instituto Centrale di Statistica, Via A Depretis 82, 00100 Roma Italy. LC S235.

ANNUARIO DI STATISTICHE DEL LAVORO. V. 12- 1971-. Italian. ir. 6000. Istituto Centrale di Statistica, c/o Postale N L/9453, Roma 00100 Italy. LC HD8477. DD 331.0945. *Annuario di Statistiche del Lavoro e Dell'Emigrazione.*

ANNUARIO DI STATISTICHE GIUDIZIARIE (ITALY). Main/Corp Istituto Centrale di Statistica (Italy). V. 1- 1949-. 0075-1715. Italian. ir.

ANNUARIO DI STATISTICHE METEOROLOGICHE. V. 1- 1959-. 0075-1731. Italian. ir. 12000. Instituto Centrale di Statistica, c/c Postale N 1/9453, Rome Italy. LC QC851.

ANNUARIO ESTATISTICO (PARAIBA , BRAZIL). Main/Corp Paraiba, Brazil (State). Directoria Geral De Estatistica. Began publication with issue for 1930. BL. Portuguese. an. 50.00. Inst Brasileiro de Geog e Estat, Av Brasil 15-671 P de Lucas, 21241 Rio de Janeiro Brazil. Tel 2304747. LC HA988.P33. adv acc. Circ 8,000. It presents information and data on social, cultural, economic, physical, demographic, administrative and political aspects of the country.

ANNUARIO - INSTITUTO GIAPPONESE DI CULTURA IN ROMA. (ANNUARIO - ISTITUTO GIAPPONESE DI CULTURA). Main/Corp Japan Cultural Institute in Rome. 1- 1963/64-. 0080-391X. Periodical. Italian (French, with summaries in English). an. Instituto Giaponese di Cultura, Via Antonio Gramsci 74, 00197 Rome Italia. Tel (06)3609794. Ind/Abst Repert. Int. Litt. Art. LC DS834.95. DD 952.007045. Circ 1,000. Academic journal to introduce European studies by Japanese scholars.

ANNUARIO - ISTITUTO AGOSTINO GEMELLI PER LO STUDIO SPERIMENTALE DI PROBLEMI SOCIALI DELL'INFORMAZIONE VISIVA. Main/Corp Istituto Agostino Gemelli Per lo Studio Sperimentale di Problemi Sociali Dell'Informazione Visiva. 0544-1358. Italian. ir.

ANNUARIO POLITICO. IT. Italian. an. Unites SRL, Via Silvio Pellico 12, 20121 Milano Italy. LC JN5201.

ANNUARIO PONTIFICIO PER L'ANNO . . . . 1912-. IT. Italian. an. $38.74. Liberia Editrice Vaticana, Cilla del Vaticana, Rome Italy. Tel 06/698/48 34. Ed Segreteria di Stato. It contains the names and addresses of the Catholic Churches. *Gerarchia Cattolica.*

ANNUARIO SEAT. VOL. A, SIDERURGIA E MECCANICA. VFOAT Siderurgia e Meccanica. Italian. an. Casella Postale N 512, 10100 Torino Centro Italy.

ANNUARIO SEAT. VOL. B, ELETTROTECNICA, TERMOTECNICA E ATTREZZATURE INDUSTRIALI. VFOAT Annuario S.E.A.T. Italian. an. 20.000. Via Aurelio Saffi 18, 10138 Torino Italy.

ANNUARIO SEAT. VOL. C, CHIMICA, MATERIE PLASTICHE, MEDICINE. VFOAT Chimica, Materie Plastiche, Medicina. Italian. an. Casella Postale N 512, 10100 Torino Centro Italy.

ANNUARIO SEAT. VOL. D, EDILIZIA. VFOAT Edilizia. IT. Italian. an. 22.000. ILTE, Via Aurelio Saffi 18-10138, Torino Italy. LC HD9715.I8. DD 338.4762402545.

ANNUARIO SEAT. VOL. F, ABBIGLIAMENTO ED ESTETICA. VFOAT Annuario S.E.A.T. Italian. an. 22.000. Via Aurelio Saffi 18, 10138 Torino Italy. LC HD9940.I8. DD 338.4768702545.

ANNUARIO SEAT. VOL. G, TURISMO E TEMPO LIBERO. VFOAT Turismo e Tempo Libero. Italian. an. 22.000. Via Aurelio Saffi 18, 10138 Torino Italy. LC G155.I8. DD 914.504928025.

ANNUARIO SEAT. VOL. H, AGRICOLTURA ED ALIMENTAZIONE. VFOAT Agricoltura Ed Alimentazione. Italian. an. Casella Postale N 512, 10100 Torino Centro Italy.

Yearbooks, Almanacs, Directories

ANNUARIO SEAT. VOL. I, TRASPORTI, CARTOTECNICA ED EDITORIA. VFOAT Trasporti, Cartotecnica Ed Editoria. Italian. an. 22.000. Via Aurelio Saffi 18, 10138 Torino Italy.

ANNUARIO SEAT. VOL. L, CREDITO, ASSICURAZIONI E SERVIZI PER LE AZIENDE. VFOAT Annuario S.E.A.T. Italian. an. 22.000. Via Aurelio Saffi 18, 10138 Torino Italy. LC HG3729.I69. DD 332.102545.

ANNUARIO STATISTICO DEL COMMERCIO INTERNO E DEL TURISMO. 0075-1782. IT. Italian. an. 8500. Istituto Centrale di Statistica, Via Cesare Balbo 16 Sul C/C/ Postale N 619007, 00100 Roma Italy. LC HF199. *Anuario Statistico Del Commercio Interno.*

ANNUARIO STATISTICO DELL'ISTRUZIONE. Began with 1972 vol. Italian. an. 5.500. LC L421. DD 370.945. *Annuario Statistico dell'Istruzione Italiana.*

ANNUARIO STATISTICO ITALIANO. Main/Corp Istituto Centrale di Statistica (Italy). Ser. 3, 1927-1933. IT. Italian. an. $4.15. Istituto Centrale di Statistic, Via Centrale Balbo 168, 00100 Rome Italy. NLM W2 GI8 I5AU. *Annuario Statistico Italiano.*

ANNUARIO - UNIVERSITA CATTOLICA DEL SACRO CUORE. Main/Corp Universita Cattolica del Sacro Cuore. IT. Italian. ir. Universita Cattolica del Sacro Cuore Largo A Gemelli, 1 Biblioteca-Ufficio Scambi, 20123 Milano Italia.

ANTHOLOGY OF MAGAZINE VERSE AND YEARBOOK OF AMERICAN POETRY. VFOAT Anthology of Magazine Verse. 1980-. 0196-2221. Periodical. US. English. an. $37.86. Monitor Book Company, PO Box 3668, Beverly Hills CA 90212. Tel (213)271-5558. Ed Alan F Pater. LC PN6099.6. DD 811.008. Part I is a collection of the best poetry published in magazines during each year. Part II contains bibliographical material covering the world of poetry in all categories each year. *Anthology of Magazine Verse for . . . .*

ANTIOCH ALUMNI DIRECTORY. 1977-. 0148-0111. US. English. Marquis Who's Who Inc, 200 East Ohio Street, Chicago IL 60611. LC LD171.A51A. DD 378.77174.

ANUARIO - ABDIB. Main/Corp Associacao Brasileira Para o Desenvolvimento das Industrias de Base. VFOAT Annual - Abdib. VAT Anuario - Associacao Brasileira Para o Desenvolvimento das Industrias de Base. English, French, Portuguese and Spanish. ir. Diagrama Comunicacoes, rua Arthur de Azevedo 424, 05405 Sao Paulo Brazil. LC T12.5.B7.

ANUARIO (ACADEMIA DE LETRAS DO ESTADO DO RIO DE JANEIRO). (ANUARIO). VFOAT Anuario da Academia de Letras do Estado do Rio de Janeiro. V. 1 (1978-1979)- No. 1. Periodical. BL. Portuguese. an. Academia de Letras do Estado do Rio de Janeiro, Caixa Postal 40062, Rio de Janeiro Brazil. LC PQ9502. DD 869.08098153.

ANUARIO - ACADEMIA NACIONAL DE BELLAS ARTES. Main/Corp Academia Nacional de Bellas Artes, Buenos Aires. 1- 1973-. Spanish. ir. Academia Nacional de Bellas Artes, Bustamante 2663, Buenos Aires Argentina. LC N16.

ANUARIO ALLAN KARDEC. 1975-. Portuguese. ir. Livrarian Allan Kardec Editora, Cx Postal 15 190, Sao Paulo Brazil. LC BF1005.

ANUARIO BIBLIOGRAFICO COLOMBIANO. 1951-. 0570-393X. CK. Spanish. an. $15.00. Instituto Caro y Cuervo, Apartado Aereo 51502, Bogota Colombia. Tel 255-8289. LC Z1731. DD 015.861. Circ 1,300. (ctrl). National bibliography of Colombian culture.

ANUARIO BIBLIOGRAFICO PERUANO. 1943-. PE. Spanish. ir. Libros Antiguos Ref Am Lat Esp, Casilla 4640, Lima Peru. Tel 281979. LC Z1851. DD 015.85.

ANUARIO BIBLIOGRAFICO PUERTORRIQUENO. 1948-. Spanish. be. Universidad de Puerto Rico, Rio Piedras PR 00931. LC Z1551. DD 015.7295. NLM Z 1551 A636.

ANUARIO - BOLSA DE MADRID. Main/Corp Madrid. Bolsa. SP. Spanish. ir. Plaza de la Lealtad 1, Madrid Spain. LC HG5640.M33. DD 332.642094641.

ANUARIO BRASILEIRO DE CERAMICA. Began with vol. for 1978. BL. Portuguese. an. Associacao Brasileira de Ceramica, Caixa Postal 30327, Sao Paulo Brazil. LC HD9615.B7. DD 338.476660981.

ANUARIO BRASILEIRO DE ENTIDADES EM METALURGIA, MECANICA E AREAS CORRELATAS. 1982-. Portuguese. an. Editora E Consultoria Ltda, Av Paulista 2073 Horsa 1 CJ 907 9O Andar, CEP 01311 Sao Paulo SP Brazil.

ANUARIO BRASILEIRO DE MEDIA. 1974/75-. BL. Portuguese. ir. $50.00. Publicacoes Informativas, Direta S/C Ltda, rua Rosa e Silva 147, Sao Paula Brazil. LC P87.

ANUARIO BRASILEIRO DE MEDICINA VETERINARIA. 1976/77-. Periodical. Portuguese. ir.

ANUARIO BRASILEIRO DE MIDIA. BL. Portuguese. ir. $350. P I Publicacoes Informativas Ltda, rua Caetes, 139 CEP 05016, Sao Paulo SP Brazil. LC P87. DD 001.5502581. *Anuario Brasileiro de Media.*

ANUARIO BRASILEIRO DE PROPAGANDA. Portuguese. ir. Publinform, R Vitorino Carmilo 690, 01153 Sao Paulo Brazil. LC HF5802. DD 659.10981.

ANUARIO BRASILEIRO DE RECURSOS HUMANOS. 1984-. Periodical. BL. Portuguese. an. Embranews Publicacoes Especializadas Ltda, Av Sao Luis 258 1O Andar Conj 101, CEP 01046 Sao Paulo SP Brazil. LC HF5549.2.B7. DD 658.300981.

ANUARIO BRASILEIRO DE SUPERMERCADOS. BL. Portuguese. ir. Publinform, rua Cristiano Viana 78, Sao Paulo Brazil. LC HF5469.

ANUARIO BRASILEIRO DE TINTAS & I.E. E VERNIZES. Portuguese. ir. rua Jaceguai 438-2 Andar Cj 5, 01315 Sao Paulo Brazil. LC HF934.5.

ANUARIO BRASILEIRO DE TIPOS ALLTYPE. Main/Corp Alltype, Empresa de Tipos E Fotografias. 1974?. Portuguese. ir. Alltype, Empresa de Tipos E Fotografias, rua Augusta 283, Sao Paulo Brazil. LC Z250.

ANUARIO BRASILEIRO DE TRANSPORTES. 1974/75-. Portuguese. ir. $100.00. Publinform, rua Vitorino Carmilo 690, Sao Paulo Brazil. LC HE8.

ANUARIO BRASILEIRO DO FRIO. 1973-. BL. Portuguese. ir. Editar Publicacoes Tecnicas Ltda, Av Sao Joao 1113 Lo and CJ 5/6, Sao Paulo Brazil. LC TP490.

ANUARIO - CAMARA VENEZOLANO BRITANICA DE COMERCIO E INDUSTRIA. Main/Corp Camara Venezolano Britanica de Comercio E Industria. English or Spanish. ir. Edificio Blandin, Piso 1 Oficina 1 C Chacaito Apartado 5713, Caracas Venezuela. LC HF300.V3.

ANUARIO CASA DOS ARTISTAS. Periodical. BL. Portuguese. an. Casa dos Artistas rua Pedro I 7-GR 306, Rio de Janeiro Brazil. LC PN2470. DD 790.20981.

ANUARIO CIENTIFICO (BARRANQUILLA, COLOMBIA). (ANUARIO CIENTIFICO). Periodical. SA. Spanish. an. Universidad del Norte Centro de Investigaciones, Apartado Aereo 1569, Barranquilla Colombia S A.

ANUARIO COLOMBIANO DE HISTORIA SOCIAL Y DE LA CULTURA. V. 1- (No. 1-). 0066-5045. CK. Spanish. ir. Universite de Antioquia, Apartado Aereo 1226, Nal 229 Medellin Columbia. Ind/Abst Am. Hist. Life, Hist. Abstr., Part A, Mod. Hist. Abstr., Hist. Abst., Part B, Twent. Century Abstr.

ANUARIO CONSULTIVO DE TRABAJO. 1973-. 0304-8497. Spanish. ir. Arlaban 7 Dpchos 60, Y 69 Madrid Spain.

ANUARIO DA DIVISAO DE METEOROLOGIA AGRICOLA. Main/Corp Instituto de Investigacao Agronomica de Angola. Divisao de Meteorologia Agricola. 1972-. 0020-3904. Portuguese. ir. Centro de Estudios do Saccala Seccao de Publicacoes, C P 406, Nova Lisboa Angola. LC S600. DD 630.251509673.

ANUARIO DA INDUSTRIA BRASILEIRA DE AUTOPECAS. VFOAT Yearbook of the Brazilian Industry of Automotive Parts. 1976/77-. BL. Portuguese (English). ir. G & C Gomes, Av Paulista 807 9 Andar Conj 911, 01311 Sao Paulo Brazil. LC HD9710.3.B7. DD 338.4762920981.

ANUARIO DA LITERATURA BRASILEIRA. Yearly V. 1- 1960-. Portuguese. an. LC F2510.

ANUARIO DA PROPRIEDADE INDUSTRIAL. Yearl V. 1 (Ed. 1977)- No. 1-. Portuguese. an. DD 346.81048, 348.10648.

ANUARIO DAS INDUSTRIAS DO BRASIL : INDUSTRIAS, BANCO, FINANCEIRAS, TRANSPORTADORAS, SERVICOS. VFOAT Anuario das Industrias. Portuguese. an. LC HC188.S3. DD 338.0029481. *Anuario das Industrias.*

ANUARIO DAS INDUSTRIAS DO ESTADO DO RIO DE JANEIRO. 1980-. BL. Portuguese. an. JVS Publicidade e Representacoes Ltda, rua Sete de Setembro 98, 1O Andar CEP 20052, Rio de Janeiro RJ Brazil. LC HC188.R3. DD 380.102948153.

ANUARIO DE ARQUITECTURA, VENEZUELA. 1981-. VE. Spanish. an. Proimagen Editores C A Edif La Carlota, Piso 2 Ofic 1-B Ave Libertador, Los Caobos Caracas Venezuela. LC NA930. DD 720.987.

ANUARIO DE BIBLIOTECOLOGIA, ARCHIVOLOGIA E INFORMATICA. Spanish. ir.

ANUARIO DE CIENCIA ECONOMICA. 1971-. Spanish. ir. 400. CEU, Lecto Libreria, General Rodrigo, 5 Madrid Spain. LC HB9.

ANUARIO DE COMERCIO EXTERIOR DE MEXICO. 1972/1973-. 0185-1306. MX. Spanish. ir. Banco Nacional de Comercio Exterior S A, Venustiano Carranza 32, Mexico 1 D F Mexico. LC HF3236. *Comercio Exterior de Mexico (Annual).*

ANUARIO DE DADOS ESTATISTICOS DA EDUCACAO E CULTURA. VFOAT Anuario de Dados Estatisticos Educacionais. No. 1- 1975-. Portuguese. ir. LC LA559.B3.

ANUARIO DE DERECHO ADMINISTRATIVO. 1- 1975/76-. Periodical. Spanish. ir. Ediciones Revista de Derecho Publico, Universidad de Chile, Bernarda Morin 435, Santiago Chile. LC K1. DD 342.8306.

ANUARIO DE DERECHO AMBIENTAL. 1977-. VE. Spanish. ir. Editorial Juridica Venezolana, Apartado 62616 Chacao, Caracas 106 Venezuela. LC K1. DD 344.87046.

ANUARIO DE DERECHO CIVIL. SP. Spanish. qt. $52.00. Inst Nacl Estudios Juridicos, Duque de Medinaceli 6 y 8, Madrid-14 Spain.

ANUARIO DE DERECHO INTERNACIONAL. 1- 1974-. SP. Spanish. an. $30.00. Ed Universidad de Navarra SA, Apartado 396, Baranain Pamplona Spain. LC JX9. A scholarly publication whose aim is to provide students of international law and law scholars in general with a series of studies, chronicles and documentation dealing with legislative practice and Spanish jurisprudence, among other topics.

ANUARIO DE DIVULGACAO CIENTIFICA. Yearly V 1 1974-. Portuguese. ir. Gabinete de Arqueologia da Universidade Catolica de Goias, Caixa Postal 86, 74.000 Goiania Brazil. LC F2519.1.G68.

ANUARIO DE ESTADISTICA. Main/Corp Instituto Nacional De Estadistica (Ecuador). EC. Spanish. ir. Instituto Nacional de Estadistica Y, Censos 10 de Agosto, 229 Quito Ecuador. Tel 519-320. Circ 1,500. Summary of major statistics of The National Institute of Statistics and Census of Ecuador, especially important statistics on hospitals, industry, transport, internal commerce and services, price indexes and more.

ANUARIO DE ESTADISTICA AGRARIA. VFOAT Anuario Estadistica Agraria. 1972-. SP. Spanish. an. Secretaria General Tecnica Ser Publ Agrar, Pseo Infanta Isabel 1, Madrid 7 Spain. LC S253.

ANUARIO DE ESTADISTICAS DE TRANSPORTE. Spanish. ir. LC HE236. *Anuario de Estadistica de Transportes.*

ANUARIO DE ESTUDIOS AMERICANOS. V. 1- 1944-. 0210-5810. SP. Spanish. an. Consejo Super Invest Cientifico Vitruvio, 8 Apartado 14 458, 28006 Madrid Spain. Ind/Abst Am. Hist. Life, Hist. Abstr., Part A, Mod. Hist. Abstr., Hist. Abst., Part B, Twent. Century Abstr., Hist. Abstr. LC F1401. (cum index).

ANUARIO DE ESTUDIOS ATLANTICOS. No. 1- 1955-. 0570-4065. SP. Spanish. an. Consejo Super Invest Cientifico, Vitrubio 8 Apartado 14 458, 28006 Madrid Spain. Ind/Abst

Yearbooks, Almanacs, Directories

Am. Hist. Life, Hist. Abstr., Part A, Mod. Hist. Abstr., Hist. Abst., Part B, Twent. Century Abstr. **LC** DP302.C39. (cum index).

ANUARIO DE ESTUDIOS FILOLOGICOS. 1978-. Periodical. French (Spanish). ir. Facultad de Filosofia y Letras, Universidad de Extremadura, Caceres Spain. **LC** P1.A1. **DD** 410.

ANUARIO DE ESTUDIOS MEDIEVALES. Vol. 1 1964-. 0066-5061. Spanish. be. $58.87. Consejo Super Invest Cientifico, Virtruvio 8 Apartado 14 458, 28006 Madrid Spain. **Tel** 2612833. **Ind/Abst** Am. Hist. Life, Hist. Abstr., Part A, Mod. Hist. Abstr., Hist. Abst., Part B, Twent. Century Abstr. **LC** WMLC L 82/272.

ANUARIO DE ESTUDIOS MEDIEVALES. ANEJO. 1- 1972-. Monographic Series. Spanish. ir. Consejo Super Invest Cientific, Vitruvio 8 Apartado 14 458, 28006 Madrid Spain.

ANUARIO DE FAMILIAS CUBANAS. Spanish. ir. **LC** F1754.5.

ANUARIO DE FILOLOGIA. Began with: No. 1 (1962). 0066-507X. VE. Spanish. ir. Facultad Humanidades y Educa, Universidad del Zulia, Maracaibo Venezuela. **Ind/Abst** MLA Int. Bibliogr. Books Artic. Mod. Lang. Lit. **LC** P10. **DD** 410.5.

ANUARIO DE HISTORIA. V. 1 (1961)-. 0185-884X. Spanish. an. **Ind/Abst** Am. Hist. Life, Hist. Abstr., Part A, Mod. Hist. Abstr., Hist. Abst., Part B, Twent. Century Abstr. **LC** D1. **DD** 905.

ANUARIO DE HISTORIA CONTEMPORANEA. 8 (1981)-. 0210-9603. Periodical. Spanish. an. 800. Secretariado de Publicaciones, de la Universidad de Granada, Espana Granada Spain. **LC** DP160.9. **DD** 946.005. *Anuario de Historia Moderna Y Contemporanea.*

ANUARIO DE HISTORIA DEL DERECHO ESPANOL. V. 1- 1924-. 0304-4319. SP. Spanish. an. $50.00. Institute Nacl Estudios, Juridicos Duque de Medinaceli, 6 Y 8 Madrid-14 Spain. Ed L Diez Canseco. **Ind/Abst** Am. Hist. Life, Hist. Abstr., Part A, Mod. Hist. Abstr., Hist. Abst., Part B, Twent. Century Abstr., Hist. Abstr. **DD** 349.4609, 344.6009.

ANUARIO DE INFORMACAO COMERCIAL E INDUSTRIAL DE PORTUGAL E ILHAS ADJACENTES. PO. Portuguese. an. Anuario de Informacao Comercial E Industrial de Portugal E Ilhas Adjacentes, R Coelho da Rocha 66 R/C-ESQ, 1200 Lisboa Portugal. **LC** HF3693. **DD** 338.00294469.

ANUARIO DE INFORMATICA DN. VFOAT Anuario de Informatica D.N. 81/82-. Periodical. Portuguese. an. $324.00. Computerworld do Brasil Servicos E Publicacoes Ltda, rua Alcindo Guanabara, 25/100. Andar 20.031 Rio de Janeiro RJ Brazil. **Tel** (202)452-4200. Ed Deanne E Neuman. **LC** HD9696.C63. **DD** 338.76100402581. Extensive, fully indexed texts of import statutes, regulations, executive orders, forms and lists, plus analysis of important ongoing import issues.

ANUARIO DE JURISPRUDENCIA LABORAL. Series/Titl Biblioteca de Derecho Laboral. 1976-. Spanish. ir. Derecho Laboral, Cerrito 420 Esc 404, Montevideo Uruguay. **DD** 344.89501.

ANUARIO DE LA ACADEMIA NACIONAL DE LA HISTORIA. Main/Corp Academia Nacional de la Historia (Venezuela). VE. Spanish. an. Libreria Mundal T Forero & Co, Santa Cailla Mijares 26, Edif San Mauricio Venezuela. **LC** F2301. **DD** 987.005.

ANUARIO DE LA ARQUITECTURA EN COLOMBIA. CK. Spanish. ir. J Plazas S, Apartado Aereo 27765, Bogota Columbia. **Ind/Abst** Avery Index Archit. Period. Second Ed. Revis. Enlarged Suppl. **LC** NA875.

ANUARIO DE LA EDUCACION. 1974-. Spanish. ir. Santillana, Elfo 32, Madrid Spain. **LC** LA910.A4.

ANUARIO DE LA FACULTAD DE DERECHO. Yearly V. 1, No. 1, 1969-. Periodical. Spanish. ir.

ANUARIO DE LA INDUSTRIA Y COMERCIO DE ALIMENTACION. Spanish. ir. Publicaciones Tecnicas Periodicas A de la Hoz, Principe 9 Apartado 658, Madrid 12 Spain. **LC** HD9015.S8.

ANUARIO DE LA MINERIA DE CHILE. 0066-5096. CL. Spanish. an. **LC** HD9506.C5. **DD** 338.20983.

ANUARIO DE LA RELOJERIA PARA ESPANA E HISPANOAMERICA. SP. Spanish. ir. $50.00. Ediciones Cedel, Mallorca 257 10, Barcelona 1A Spain. **Tel** 2156088. Ed Jose Avilz. **LC** HD9999.C6. **DD** 380.1456811102546. bk rev. adv acc. **Circ** 4,000. Consists of more than 450 epigraphs, all of which have been prepared by the Promotion department together with the firms mentioned on the Directory.

ANUARIO DE LA SOCIOLOGIA ESPANOLA. Series/Titl Coleccion FF. Serie Sintesis. 1980-. SP. Spanish. an. 1250. Euramerica SA, Apartado 36.204, Madrid Spain. **LC** Z7164.S68, HM22.S72. **DD** 016.3010946.

ANUARIO DE LAS COMUNICACIONES. 1981-. SP. Spanish. an. Servicio de Publicaciones Ministerio de Transportes Turismo y Comunicaciones, c/o Augustin de Bethencourt, 25 Madrid 3 Spain.

ANUARIO DE LAS RELACIONES LABORALES EN ESPANA. 1975-. Spanish. ir. Ediciones de la Torre, Calle de Augusto Figueroa, Madrid 17 Spain. **LC** HD8582.

ANUARIO DE LETRAS. (ANUARIO DE LETRAS : REVISTA DE LA FACULTAD DE FILOSOFIA Y LETRAS). Vol. 1 (1961)-. 0539-6298. MX. Spanish. an. Universidad Nacional Autonoma de Mexico, Calle Porto Alegre 260, San Andres Tetepilco 13 DE Mexico. **Ind/Abst** Am. Hist. Life, Hist. Abstr., Part A, Mod. Hist. Abstr., Hist. Abst., Part B, Twent. Century Abstr., Hist. Abstr. **LC** PN508. **DD** 809.

ANUARIO DE POETAS DO BRASIL. 1976-. BL. Portuguese. Folha Carioca Editora, rua Joao Cardoso 23 Cep 20.000, Rio de Janeiro Brazil. **LC** PQ9650.

ANUARIO DE PORTOS E NAVIOS. BL. Portuguese. an. $3000. Revista Tecnica e Informativa Ltda, CX Postal 2791, Rio de Janeiro Brazil. **LC** HE803. **DD** 387.00981.

ANUARIO DE TRANSPORTES Y COMUNICACIONES *CEASED.* -1979-80. CK. Spanish. ir. **LC** HE235. *Anuario General de Estadistica.*

ANUARIO DEL ARTE ESPANOL. 1973-. Spanish. ir. Iberico Europea de Ediciones SA, Serrano 44, 1 Madrid Spain. **LC** N9.7.

ANUARIO DEL CENTRO DE ESTUDIOS MARTIANOS. Main/Corp Centro de Estudios Martianos (1977-). 1- 1978-. Periodical. CU. Spanish. ir. Apartado Postal 6640, Habana 6 Cuba. **LC** F1783.M38. **DD** 972.91050924. *Anuario Martiano, 0066-524X.*

ANUARIO DEL CINE. 1977-. AG. Spanish. ir. Ediciones Corregidor, Corriente 1585, Buenos Aires C 1042 Argentina. **LC** PN1993. **DD** 791.4305.

ANUARIO DEL EXPORTADOR. Spanish. ir. Instituto Mexicano de Comercio Exterior, Av Alfonso Reyes 30, Mexico City Mexico. **LC** HF1481.

ANUARIO DEL MINISTERIO DE JUSTICIA. Vol. 1-. UY. Spanish. an. Ministerio de Justicia, Av 18 de Julio 1865, Montevideo Uruguay. **LC** K1. **DD** 348.895025, 348.950825.

ANUARIO DEL PUERTO AUTONOMO DE BARCELONA. Main/Corp Puerto Autonomo de Barcelona. VFOAT Anuario Puerto Barcelona. Spanish. an. **LC** HE558.B3. **DD** 387.1094672.

ANUARIO DEL SERVICIO NACIONAL DE PRUEBAS. CK. Spanish. an. Instituto Colombiano Para el Fomento de la Educacion Superior, Carrera 4A. No. 17-40, Apartado Aero 6319 Nal 2868, Bogota de Colombia. **LC** L914.C6. **DD** 378.861.

ANUARIO DELTA-LAROUSSE. 1972-. BL. Portuguese. ir. Editora Delta, Av Almirante Barroso 63-26 Andar, Rio de Janeiro Brazil. **LC** AE37.

ANUARIO DO INSTITUTO DE ENGENHARIA. Main/Corp Instituto de Engenharia, Sao Paulo, Brazil. Portuguese. ir. $50.00. Instituto de Engenharia, Caixa Postal 9336, Sao Paulo CEP 01000 Brazil. **LC** TA4.

ANUARIO DO TEATRO BRASILEIRO. Periodical. Portuguese. ir. **LC** PN2471. **DD** 792.0981.

ANUARIO : EMPRESAS JAPONESAS NO BRASIL. VFOAT Empresas Japonesas No Brasil, Burajiru Nikkei Kigyo Nenkan. 1979-. Japanese and Portuguese. ir. **LC** HG4109. *Almanaque, Empresas Japonesas No Brasil.*

ANUARIO ENERGETICO. Portuguese. an. **LC** HD9502.B73. **DD** 333.79098142021.

ANUARIO ERNANI DE ARTE. 1984-. Portuguese. an. **LC** N8670. **DD** 707.5.

ANUARIO ESPANOL DE ACEITES Y GRASAS E INDUSTRIAS AUXILIARES. Spanish. ir. Edicion Oleo, Fernando VI 27 4, Madrid Spain. **LC** HD9490.S8.

ANUARIO ESPANOL DE EMPRESAS. SP. Spanish. ir. Editorial Financiera Alfa Omega, Castell O 45, 1 Madrid Spain. **LC** HG4216.Z5. **DD** 338.002546.

ANUARIO ESPANOL DE EMPRESAS. SUPLEMENTO AVANCE MENSUAL. Spanish. ir. Editorial Financiera Alfa Omega, Castello 45, 1 Madrid Spain. **LC** HG4216.

ANUARIO ESTADISTICO - ASOCIACION NACIONAL DE UNIVERSIDADES E INSTITUTOS DE ENSENANZA SUPERIOR. Main/Corp Asociacion Nacional de Universidades e Institutos de Ensenanza Superior. **Series/Titl** Serie—Consulta y Documentacion. MX. Spanish. an. $20.00. Asociacion Nacional de Universidades e Institutos de Ensenanza Superior, Ensananza Super 2133 3ER Piso, Mexico DF Mexico. **Tel** 5-48-42-16. **LC** LA428. **DD** 378.72. **Circ** 2,000. The undergraduated studies which are offered by the Mexican universities and technological institutions: the main admission requirements.

ANUARIO ESTADISTICO (AUTORIDAD PORTUARIA DE GUAYAQUIL). (ANUARIO ESTADISTICO). Spanish. ir. **LC** HE563.E2. **DD** 387.10986632.

ANUARIO ESTADISTICO DE ESPANA. Main/Corp Spain. Instituto Nacional de Estadistica. V. 1- 1912-. SP. Spanish. ir. Instituto Nacional de Estadistica, Avda Generalisimo 91, Madrid 91 Spain. **LC** HA1543. **DD** 314.6.

ANUARIO ESTADISTICO DE LA MINERIA MEXICANA. 0185-8696. MX. Spanish. an. **Ind/Abst** GeoRef. **LC** HD9506.M6. **CODEN** AEMMDR.

ANUARIO ESTADISTICO DE LA SIDERURGIA Y MINERIA DEL HIERRO DE AMERICA LATINA. VFOAT Statistical Yearbook of Steelmaking and Iron Ore Mining in Latin America. CL. Spanish (English). an. Instituto Latinoamericano del Fierro el Acero, Casilla 16065, Santiago 9 Chile.

ANUARIO ESTADISTICO DE SEGUROS. 0303-4763. MX. Spanish. ir. Comision Nacional Bancaria y de Seguros, Republica de el Salvador Num 47, Mexico City DF Mexico. **LC** HG8552.

ANUARIO ESTADISTICO DE TRANSPORTE. Yearly V. 1982-. Spanish. an. **LC** HE234.A15. **DD** 380.50983021.

ANUARIO ESTADISTICO DEL COMERCIO EXTERIOR DE LOS ESTADOS UNIDOS MEXICANOS. Main/Corp Mexico. Direccion General de Estadistica. 1920/22-. MX. Spanish. ir. Sec Indust y Comer Div de Adm, Direccion General Estadistica, Avenida Cuauhtemoc 80, Mexico 7DT Mexico. **LC** HF131. **DD** 382.0972.

ANUARIO ESTADISTICO - DEPTO ACTUARIAL Y ESTADISTICO. Main/Corp Caja Costarricense de Seguro Social. CR. Spanish. an. Caja Costarricense de Seguro Social, Apartado 10105, San Jose Costa Rica. **LC** HD7134. **DD** 368.40097286.

ANUARIO ESTADISTICO (INSTITUTO NACIONAL DE ESTADISTICA Y CENSOS (ARGENTINA)). (ANUARIO ESTADISTICO). VFOAT Anuario Estadistico de la Republica Argentina. 1979-1980-. AG. Spanish. ir. Inst Nacional Estad Y Censos, Hipolito Yrigoyen 250 Piso, 120 Buenos Aires Argentina. *Anuario Estadistico de la Republica Argentina.*

ANUARIO ESTADISTICO - INSTITUTO NACIONAL DE JUBILACIONES Y PENSIONES DE LOS EMPLEADOS Y FUNCIONARIOS DEL PODER EJECUTIVO. Main/Corp Instituto Nacional de Jubilaciones Y Pensiones de Los Empleados Y Funcionarios Del Poder Ejecutivo (Honduras). Spanish. ir. **LC** JL1532.Z2. **DD** 354.728300123.

2850

Yearbooks, Almanacs, Directories

ANUARIO ESTADISTICO PESQUERO (MEXICO. SECRETARIA DE PESCA. DIRECCION GENERAL DE INFORMATICA Y ESTADISTICA). (ANUARIO ESTADISTICO PESQUERO). VFOAT Anuario Estadistico de Pesca. Spanish. an. LC SH231. DD 338.37270972.

ANUARIO ESTADISTICO. Main/Corp Servuci Social do Comercio. Portuguese. ir. Servico Social do Comercio, Av General Justo 307, Rio de Janeiro Brazil. LC HV192.

ANUARIO ESTADISTICO. VFOAT Statistical Yearbook. English (text in Portuguese). an. Secretaria Ejecutiva Esplanada dos Ministerios, Bloco 6 5O Andar CEP 70 053, Brasilia DF Brazil. LC HD9506.B7. DD 338.4766900981021.

ANUARIO ESTADISTICO - COMISSAO DE FINANCIAMENTO DA PRODUCAO, DEPARTAMENTO DE PESQUISAS ECONOMICAS. Main/Corp Brazil. Comissao de Financiamento da Producao. Departamento de Pesquisas Economicas. BL. Portuguese. ir. Ministerio da Agricultura, Departamento de Pesquisas Economicas, Brasilia Brazil. LC HD9014.B8. DD 338.1881.

ANUARIO ESTATISTICO - CORREIOS E TELECOMUNICACOES DE PORTUGAL. Main/Corp Correios e Telecomunicacoes de Portugal. PO. Portuguese. ir. Correios e Telecomunicacoes de Portugal, rua Alexandre Herculano 100 - 2 Po S, Lisboa Portugal. LC HE7125.

ANUARIO ESTATISTICO DA UNIDADE CENTRAL DO SISTEMA DE INFORMACAO DE MERCADO AGRICOLA. Main/Corp Centro de Informacao de Mercado Agricola (Brazil). VFOAT Precos Nos Mercados Atacadistas. BL. Portuguese. ir. Ministerio de Agricultura, SCW, Q.02 No Andar Ed Ariston, 70.000 Brasilia Brazil. LC HD9014.B8. *Anuario Estatistico.*

ANUARIO ESTATISTICO DE ENERGIA ELECTRICA. BL. Portuguese. an. Av Angelica 2565, 150 Andar 01227, Sao Paulo SP Brazil. LC HD9685.B82.

ANUARIO ESTATISTICO DE TRANSITO NO ESTADO DO PARANA. Portuguese. ir. LC HE373.B72.

ANUARIO ESTATISTICO DO AMAPA. Portuguese. ir. Divisao de Geografia E Estatistica, Av Fab 1316, Mecape Brazil. LC HA988.A45. DD 318.11.

ANUARIO ESTATISTICO DO ARROZ. Safra 1944/45-. Periodical. Portuguese. ir. LC HD9066.B8. DD 338.17318.

ANUARIO ESTATISTICO DO ESTADO DE SAO PAULO. Vol. 56 (1979)-. 0100-8730. BL. Portuguese. an. Fundacao Sistema Estadual de Analise de Dados, Av Casper Libero 464, 01033 Sao Paulo SP Brazil. Tel (011)229-2433. LC HA988.S2. DD 318.161. Circ 1,200. Gathers tables and charts which characterize the state of Sao Paulo in its social, demographic and physical aspects. *Anuario Estatistico (Sao Paulo (Brazil : State). Departamento de Estatistica).*

ANUARIO ESTATISTICO DO ESTADO DO RIO DE JANEIRO. Series/Titl Serie Sipe. 1978-. BL. Portuguese. an. Secplan, Fiderj - Palacio Guanabara, Edificio Anexo 20. Andar, Rio de Janeiro Brazil. LC HA988.R6.

ANUARIO ESTATISTICO DOS TRANSPORTES. BL. Portuguese. ir. Pra Ca Duque de Caxias 86-9, Andar ZC-14, 20.224 Rio de Janeiro Brazil. LC HE48. DD 380.50981. *Anuario Estatistico dos Transportes.*

ANUARIO ESTATISTICO PARANA. VFOAT Anuario Estatistico Do Parana. Began with vol. for 1977. Portuguese. ir. Secretaria de Estado do Planejamento, Departamento Estadual de Estatistica, rua Barao do Rio Branco 45, 9O. Andar, 80.000 Curitiba Brazil. LC HA988.P35.

ANUARIO ESTATSITCO DAS FERROVIAS DO BRASIL. V. 1- 1977-. Portuguese. ir. Tel (021)233 45 41. LC HE2921. DD 385.0981. Circ 1,200. (ctrl) Rolling stone, railroad, transportation, permanent way, traffic accidents, revenues and expenses, statistics, etc. *Estatistica das Estradas de Ferro do Brasil.*

ANUARIO FINANCIERO DE MEXICO. V. 1- 1940-. MX. Spanish. ir. Asociacion de Banqueros de Mexico, Mexico DF Mexico. LC HG69.M6. DD 332.0972.

ANUARIO GERAL DE PORTUGAL. Began with vol. for 1977. Portuguese. ir. 700. Av da Liberadade 266, Lisboa Portugal. LC DP501. DD 946.9005.

ANUARIO GUIA DE SANTA CRUZ DE TENERIFE Y SU PROVINCIA. Spanish. ir. J.I.M. de Gardoqui, Santiago Beyro 12-1. A, Santa Cruz Spain. LC DP302.C36.

ANUARIO HIDROLOGICO. Spanish. ir. LC GB715.S26.

ANUARIO HISTORICO JURIDICO ECUATORIANO. 1-. Monographic Series. EC. Spanish. ir. Apartado 5314, Guayaquil Ecuador. LC K1. DD 340.09866.

ANUARIO IBEROAMERICANO DE CINE Y TELEVISION. 1 (1979)-. SP. Spanish. an. Equipo Cordillera S A, Apartado 2.420, Madrid 2 Spain. LC PN1993.5.L3. DD 384.8098.

ANUARIO INDUSTRIAL DO ESPIRITO SANTO. BL. Portuguese. ir. Federacao das Industries do Estados do Espirito Santo, Av Princesa Isabel 54-12 Andar, Victoria Brazil. LC HC188.E7.

ANUARIO (INSTITUTO DE INVESTIGACIONES HISTORICAS DR. JOSE GASPAR RODRIGUEZ DE FRANCIA). (ANUARIO). Yearly V. 1, No. 1 (May 1979)-. Periodical. Spanish. ir. LC F2686.F832. DD 989.2050924.

ANUARIO INTERAMERICANO DE DE INVESTIGACION MUSICAL *CEASED*. (ANUARIO INTERAMERICANO DE INVESTIGACION MUSICAL). VFOAT Yearbook for Inter-American Musical Research, Anuario Interamericano de Pesquisa Musical. V. 6-11. Periodical. US. Spanish (in English, or with English summaries). an. University of Texas, Department of Music, c/o E Thomas Stanford, Austin TX 78712. Ind/Abst RILM Abstr. LC ML1. DD 780.98. *Anuario - (Tulane University of Louisiana. Inter-American Institution for Musical Research).*

ANUARIO LATINOAMERICANO DE LAS ARTES PLASTICAS. Periodical. Spanish. an. Correo Editorial Arenales, 1131 P B 4 Capital Guatomala. LC N6502. DD 709.8.

ANUARIO MARITIMO ESPANOL. 1943-. Spanish. an. LC V10. DD 359.058.

ANUARIO MERCANTIL. Spanish. ir. Cetesa, Av Brasil 17, Madrid Spain. LC HF3683.

ANUARIO METEOROLOGICO DEL ISTMO CENTROAMERICANO. 1970-. Spanish. an. LC QC988.C3.

ANUARIO MINERAL BRASILEIRO. 1- 1972-. 0100-9303. BL. Portuguese. an. Av Pasteur, 404 20 Andar ZC 82, 20.000 Rio de Janeiro Brazil. Ind/Abst GeoRef. LC HD9506.B7. DD 338.20981. CODEN AMBRD9.

ANUARIO MUSICAL. Main/Corp Instituto Espanol de Musicologia. V. 1- 1946-. 0211-3538. SP. Spanish. an. $15.04. Consejo Super Invest Cientific, Vitruvio 8/Apartado 14 458, 28006 Madrid Spain. Ind/Abst Music Index, RILM Abstr. LC ML32.S7.

ANUARIO POSTAL Y TELEGRAFICO. Spanish. ir. P Martinez Del Rosal, Ayala 106 Planta 2 A, 6 Madrid Spain. LC HE7115.

ANUARIO PRENSA ECONOMICA. TENDENCIAS . . ., ARGENTINA . . . . VFOAT Tendencias . . ., Argentina . . . . 1978-. AG. Spanish. an. Editorial Lourdes, Pte Luis Saenz Pena 747, 1ER. Piso, Buenos Aires Argentina. LC HC171. DD 330.982005. *Prensa Economica. Tendencias . . ., Argentina . . . .*

ANUARIO SIMA : ESTADISTICAS REGIONALES BASICAS DEL MERCADO ARGENTINO. Main/Corp Servicio de Informaciones del Mercado Argentino. VAT Anuario Servicio de Informaciones del Mercado Argentino: Estadisticas Regionales Basicas del Mercado Argentino. AG. Spanish. an. Servicio de Informaciones del Mercado Argentino, Bolivar 177, Buenos Aires Argentina. LC HA954. DD 318.2.

ANUARIO TURISTICO DE PERNAMBUCO. V. 1- 1979-. Portuguese. ir. Avenida Marques de Olinda 55, 50.000 Recife Brazil. LC G155.B7.

ANUARIO (UNIVERSIDAD CENTRAL DE VENEZUELA. ESCUELA DE LETRAS). (ANUARIO). VFOAT Anuario Escuela de Letras U.C.V. 1979-. Spanish. ir. Escuela de Letras, Facultad de Humanidades y Educacion UCV, Ciudad Universitaria, Caracas Venezuela. LC P9. DD 410.5.

ANUARIO VERITAS. VFOAT Veritas. 1 (1982)-. Spanish (English). an. Universidad Regiomontana, Department de Publicaciones, Monterrey NL Mexico. LC AS63.M64. DD 056.1.

ANUARUL INSTITUTULUI DE ISTORIE SI ARHEOLOGIE CLUJ - NAPOCA. Main/Corp Institutul de Istorie si Arheologie, Cluj. 14- 1971-. RM. Romanian (summaries in French). an. Ilexim Press, PO Box 1-136-1-137, Bucharest Romania. *Anuarul Institutului de Istorie Din Cluj.*

A.P.C.A. DIRECTORY AND RESOURCE BOOK. (APCA DIRECTORY AND RESOURCE BOOK). Main/Corp Air Pollution Control Association. 0094-9191. US. English. an. Air Pollution Control Association, 4400 5th Avenue, Pittsburgh PA 15213. LC TD882. DD 363.6. *APCA Directory.*

APPLE SOFTWARE DIRECTORY. VFOAT P.C. Telemart/Vanloves Apple Software Directory. 1984-. US. English. PC Telemart Inc/ Vanloves, 11781 Lee-Jackson Highway, Fairfax VA 22033. *Vanloves . . . Apple II/III Software Directory,* 0732-0612.

APPLIANCE MANUFACTURER. DIRECTORY ISSUE. VFOAT Annual Directory Issue. Periodical. US. English. an. $10.00. Cahners Publishing, 270 St Paul Street, Denver CO 80206. Tel (303)388-4511.

APSA DIRECTORY OF DEPARTMENT CHAIRPERSONS. Main/Corp American Political Science Association. VAT American Political Science Association Directory of Department Chairpersons. 0196-5255. US. English. an. $20.-00. American Political Science Association, 1527 New Hampshire Avenue NW, Washington DC 20036. Tel (202)483-2512. LC JA28. DD 320.071173. adv acc. Circ 800. (ctrl). Names and addresses of chairpersons in departments offering political science at four-year institutions. Also includes phone numbers. *APSA Directory of Department Chairmen,* 0092-8658.

APSA DIRECTORY OF MEMBERS. Main/Corp American Political Science Association. US. English. 1527 New Hampshire Avenue NW, Washington DC 20036. Tel (202)483-2512. LC JA28. DD 320.06273. adv acc. Circ 3,500. Alphabetical listing of current APSA members, their training, affiliations and areas of specializations. Index for women, blacks, and Hispanics.

APTMA DIRECTORY OF MEMBERS. Main/Corp All Pakistan Textile Mills Association. VAT All Pakistan Textile Mills Association Directory of Members. PK. English. ir. 0.05. All Pakistan Textile Mills Association, Mohammedi House/3rd Floor, I I Chundrigar Road, Karachi Pakistan. LC HD9886.P14. DD 338.47677210255491.

ARAB AMERICAN ALMANAC. VFOAT Dalil Al-Arab, Arab Americans' Almanac, Dalil Al-Arab Al-Amrikiyin. 3rd Ed.-. 0742-9576. US. English. ir. $9.95. News Circle Publishing Co, PO Box 3684, Glendale CA 91201-0684. DD 973. *American Arabic Speaking Community Almanac,* 0094-8543.

THE ARAB BUSINESS YEARBOOK. 1976/77-. UK. English. an. $61.30. Graham & Trotman Ltd, Sterling House, 66 Wilton Road, London SW1V 1DE England. Tel 01 821 1123. LC HF3866.Z6. DD 338.09174927. adv acc. 5th edition provides business information on 20 countries of Arab world including economic matters, import and export, customs, national plus useful addresses and travel information.

ARAB OIL & GAS DIRECTORY. VAT Arab Oil and Gas Directory. 0304-8551. LE. English. an. $195.00. Arab Petroleum Research Center, 7 Avenue Angres, 75016 Paris France. Tel 4 524 33 10. Ed N Sarkis. LC HD9578.A55. DD 338.272809174927. adv acc. Circ 4,560. (ctrl). Surveys covering oil and gas in Algeria, Bahrain, Egypt, Iran, Iraq, Jordan, Kuwait, Lebanon, Libya, Morocco, Oman, Qatar, Saudi Arabia, Sudan, Syria, Turisia, United Arab Emirates, North and South Yemen.

ARABIAN GOVERNMENT AND PUBLIC SERVICES DIRECTORY. 1980-81-. 0261-6793. UK. English. an. $125.00. Learn Inc, Mt Laurel Plaza/ 113 Gaither Drive, Mt Laurel NJ 08054. LC JQ1825.S32. DD 351.0002553.

THE ARABIAN YEARBOOK. VFOAT Arabian Year Book, Commercial Directory: The Arabian Yearbook. 1st- Ed. KU. English. an. Dar Al Seyassah Press, Special Publications Division, PO Box 2270, Kuwait Kuwait. LC HF3762. DD 382.02553.

Yearbooks, Almanacs, Directories

ARABIAN YEARBOOK (INTERNATIONAL ARABIAN HORSE ASSOCIATION). (THE ARABIAN YEARBOOK). VFOAT Arabian Year Book. 1980-. US. English. an. $20.00. International Arabian Horse, 224 East Olive Avenue/PO Box 4502, Burbank CA 91503. **Tel** (213)846-5042. *Purebred Arabian Horse Yearbook.*

ARBETSMARKNADSSTATISTISK ARSBOK. VFOAT Yearbook of Labour Statistics. 1973-. 0347-6596. SW. English and Swedish. an. Allmanna Forlaget, PO Box 23116, 10435 Stockholm 23 Sweden. **LC** HD5801. **DD** 331.1109485.

ARBOG. Main/Corp Danmarks Radio. Danish. an. **LC** PN1991.1.

ARBOG FOR DANSK SKOLEHISTORIE. Vol. 1-17-. 0107-1661. Danish. ir. **LC** L46.

ARBOG FOR ERHVERVSUDDANNELSERNE I DANMARK. 1975-. Danish. ir. 84.00. Kroghs Skolehandbog, Gl Landeveg 13, Vejle 7100 Denmark. **LC** LC1047.D4.

ARBOG FOR KVINDESTUDIER VED AUC. Series/Titl Serie Om Kvindeforskning. VFOAT Arbog For Kvindestudier ved A.U.C. Danish. an. Aalborg Universitetsforlag, Postbox 159, 9100 Aalborg Denmark. **LC** HQ1672.

ARBOK. Main/Corp Bergen, Norway. Vestlandske Kunstindustrimuseum. 0405-4474. Periodical. NO. Norwegian. ir. Mohlensprisbk 3, Bergen Norway.

ARBOK FOR UNIVERSITETET I BERGEN., MATEMATISK-NATURVITENSKAPELIG SERIE. (ARBOK FOR UNIVERSITETET I BERGEN. MAT.-NATURV. SERIE). VFOAT Matematisk-Naturvitenskapelig Serie, Arbok for Universitetet I Bergen. Natematisk-Naturvitenskapelig, S Acta Universitatis Bergensis. Series Mathematica Rerumque Naturali, Acta Universitatis Bergensis. Series Mathematica Rerumque Naturalium. 1960-. 0522-9189. NO. Norwegian (English). ir. Universitetsforlaget, PO Box 2959-Toyen, Oslo 6 Norway. **Ind/Abst** Math. Rev., GeoRef. **LC** Q1. **DD** 505. **CODEN** ARBMAQ. *Arbok. Naturvitenskapelig Rekke.*

ARBOK - KRISTIANSUND OG NORDMRE TURISTFORENING. Main/Corp Kristiansund Og Nordmre Turistforening. Periodical. Norwegian. ir. **LC** DL596.K7. *Arbok.*

ARBOK - LANDSBOKASAFN ISLANDS. 1.-31, 1944-1974. 0254-1335. Icelandic. an. **NLM** Z 2590.A3 R457A.

ARBOK (NORDLAND FYLKESMUSEUM). (ARBOK). 1979-. Periodical. Norwegian. an. 45.00. Nordland Fylkesmuseum, Prinsensgt 116, 8000 Bod Norway. **LC** AM101.B537.

ARBOK - NORGES GEOLOGISKE UNDERSKELSE. Main/Corp Norway. Geologiske Underskelse. 1891-. Norwegian (summaries in English). ir. **LC** QE281.

ARBOK - NORSK POLARINSTITUTT. Main/Corp Norsk Polarinstitutt. 1960-. 0085-4271. NO. Norwegian. ir. Universitetsforlaget, PO Box 2959-Toyen, Oslo 6 Norway. **Ind/Abst** Life Sci. Collect., GeoRef, Bibliogr. Index Geol. **LC** G575. **CODEN** NPOAAE.

ARBOK OVER SKANDINAVISKE SKIPSREDERIER. VFOAT Year Book of Scandinavian Shipowners. Norwegian. an. **LC** HE563.N8. *Arbok Over Norske Skibsrederier.*

ARBOK - ROMSDALSMUSEET. Main/Corp Molde, Norway. Romsdalsmuseet. Norwegian. ir. **LC** N3135.M6.

ARBOK - UNIVERSITETETS OLDSAKSAMLING. Main/Corp Universitetet I Oslo. Universitetets Oldsaksamling. 1927-. Periodical. NO. Norwegian (with summaries in English). ir. Universitetets Oldsaksamlings, Frederiks GT 2, Oslo 1 Norway. **Tel** (02)416300. **Ind/Abst** Art Archaeol. Tech. Abstr. **LC** GN826.N8.

ARCHAOLOGISCHE BIBLIOGRAPHIE. (ARCHAOLOGISCHE BIBLIOGRAPHIE. BEILAGE ZUM JAHRBUCH DES DEUTSCHEN ARCHAOLOGISCHEN INSTITUTS). 1932-. 0341-8308. German. an. Walter de Gruyter & Company, 200 Sawmill River Road, Hawthorne NY 10532. **Tel** (914)747-0110. **LC** Z5132. *Bibliographie zum Jahrbuch des Deutschen Archaologischen Instituts.*

ARCHITECT'S YEAR BOOK. V. 1- 1945-. 0066-619X. UK. English. ir. Scientific Books Ltd, 54-58 Caledonian Road, London N1 9RN England. Ed Jane B Drew. **LC** NA9. **DD** 720.58.

ARD JAHRBUCH. Main/Corp Arbeitsgemeinschaft der Offentlich-Rechtlichen Rundfunkanstalten der Bundesrepublik Deutschland. VFOAT Ard-Jahrbuch. Began with: 1969. 0066-5746. GW. German. an. Verlag Hans-Bredow-Institut, Heimhuderstrasse 21, 2000 Hamburg 13 West Germany. **LC** HE8689.9.G4.

THE ARGENTINE-AMERICAN BUSINESS REVIEW DIRECTORY. Began with 1978. US. English. Motivational Communications Inc, 175 Fifth Avenue, New York NY 10010. **LC** HF3388.U5. **DD** 330.982.

ARGIEF-JAARBOEK VIR SUID-AFRIKAANSE GESKIEDENIS. VFOAT Archives Year Book For South African History. 1.- Vol. SA. Afrikaans (contributions in English, or Dutch). ir. Government Printer of South Africa, Pretoria South Africa.

ARIZONA DIRECTORY OF STATE REGULATORY AGENCIES FOR BUSINESSES AND OCCUPATIONS. 0098-9746. US. English. Office of Economic Planning and Development, Phoenix AZ 85007. **LC** JK8230. **DD** 353.9791091025.

ARIZONA EDUCATIONAL DIRECTORY. 1948/49-. 0095-005X. US. English. an. 1535 West Jefferson Street, Phoenix AZ 85007. **LC** LB2803.A6. **DD** 370.25791. *Arizona Educational Directory.*

ARIZONA, NEW MEXICO ZIP+4 STATE DIRECTORY. VFOAT Zip Plus Four State Directory. Arizona, New Mexico, Zip+4 State Directory. Arizona, New Mexico. VAT Arizona, New Mexico Zip Plus Four State Directory. 1985-. US. English. an. St Louis PDC Zip+4 State Directory Orders, PO Box 14921, St Louis MO 63180-9988.

THE ARKANSAS LEGAL DIRECTORY. VFOAT Legal Directory. US. English. an. 15.00. Legal Directories Publishing Company Inc, 700 Campbell Centre/PO Box 64805, Dallas TX 75206. **LC** KF192.A75. **DD** 349.767025, 347.670025. *Arkansas, Louisiana, and Mississippi Legal Directory.*

ARKANSAS, LOUISIANA, AND MISSISSIPPI LEGAL DIRECTORY. 1958/59-. US. English. Legal Directories Publishing, 2122 Kidwell Street/PO Box 140200, Dallas TX 75214.

ARKANSAS STATE DIRECTORY. US. English. an. $2.00. Heritage Publishing Company, PO Box 1371, North Little Rock AR 72203. **LC** JK5130. **DD** 353.976700025.

ARLIS/NA MEMBERSHIP DIRECTORY. Main/Corp Arlis/North America. US. English. Art Libraries Society/North America, Art Index H W Wilson Company, 950 University Avenue, Bronx NY 10452. **LC** Z5937.A74. **DD** 026.706273.

ARMENIAN TELEPHONE DIRECTORY. TORONTO. (ARMENIAN TELEPHONE DIRECTORY, TORONTO). Began with 1958 issue. 0700-4214. CN. English. be. Holy Trinity Armenian Church, 14 Woodlawn Avenue West, Toronto Ontario M4V 1G7 Canada. **DD** 917.135410025.

ARMSTRONG OIL DIRECTORIES, EASTERN UNITED STATES. 0732-0752. US. English. an. $40.00. Armstrong Oil Directories, 1606 South Jackson Street, Amarillo TX 79102. **Tel** (806)374-1818. Ed Alan Armstrong. **LC** HD9563. **DD** 338.7622338202574. *Oil directories.*

ARMSTRONG OIL DIRECTORIES. LOUISIANA, TEXAS GULF COAST, EAST TEXAS, ARK. AND MISS. (ARMSTRONG OIL DIRECTORIES, LOUISIANA, TEXAS GULF COAST, EAST TEXAS, ARK. AND MISS). VAT Armstrong Oil Directories. Louisiana, Texas Gulf Coast, East Texas, Arkansas and Mississippi. 1980-. 0273-4931. US. English. an. $40.00. Armstrong Oil Directories, 1606 Jackson Street, Amarillo TX 79102. **Tel** (806)374-1818. Ed Alan Armstrong. **LC** TN867. **DD** 338.762233802576. *Oil directories. Hank Seale Oil Directory: Louisiana, Texas Gulf Coast, East Texas, Ark. and Miss.*

ARMSTRONG OIL DIRECTORIES. ROCKY MOUNTAIN AND CENTRAL UNITED STATES. (ARMSTRONG OIL DIRECTORIES, ROCKY MOUNTAIN AND CENTRAL UNITED STATES). 1980-. 0273-5229. Periodical. US. English. an. $40.00. Armstrong Oil Directories, 1606 Jackson Street, Amarillo TX 79102. **Tel** (806)374-1818. Ed Alan Armstrong. **LC** TN867. **DD** 338.762233802578. *Oil directories. Hank Seale Oil Directory.*

ARMSTRONG OIL DIRECTORIES, TEXAS AND SOUTHEASTERN NEW MEXICO. New 1980 Ed.-. 0277-2280. US. English. an. $40.00. Alan Armstrong/Oil Men's Association of America, 1606 Jackson Street, Amarillo TX 79102. **Tel** (806)374-1818. Ed Alan Armstrong. **LC** TN867. **DD** 338.76223382025764. *Oil directories. Texas Oil Directory.*

THE ARNOLD ENCYCLOPEDIA OF REAL ESTATE. YEARBOOK. 1980-. 0270-921X. US. English. an. Warren Gorham & Lamont, 210 South Street, Boston MA 02111. Ed A L Arnold, J Kusnet and R M Lopati. **LC** HD1365. **DD** 333.330321.

ARNOLD G. RUDOFF'S TAX SHELTER DIRECTORY. 0732-491X. US. English. an. $87.00. Limited Partners Letter, PO Box 1146, Menlo Park CA 94025. **Tel** (415)321-9110. **LC** HJ4653.A3. **DD** 332.6042.

ARRL REPEATER DIRECTORY. Main/Corp American Radio Relay League. VFOAT Repeater Directory. VAT American Radio Relay League Directory. 0190-3632. US. English. an. $3.00. American Radio Relay League, 225 Main Street, Newington CT 06111. **Tel** (203)666-1541. Ed Bruce Jahnke. **Circ** 50,000. Published in April of each year and lists over 9,000 amateur radio repeater stations in the US and Canada by location and frequency. 180 pages.

ARSBOK. Main/Corp Sweden. Meteorologiska Och Hydrologiska Institutet. Vol. 1- 1919-. Swedish. ir. **LC** QC989.S77. *Arsbok.*

ARSBOK FOR KRISTEN HUMANISM. VFOAT Kristen Humanism. Vol. 1-. Swedish. ir. **LC** BR10.

ARSBOK FOR SVERIGES KOMMUNER. Series/Titl Sveriges Officiella Statistik. VFOAT Statistical Yearbook of Administrative Districts of Sweden. Vol. 1-. SW. Swedish. an. Statistiska Centralbyran, Aarsbok Foer Snerige, Stockholm Sweden. **LC** JS7. **DD** 352.0485.

ARSBOK - RIKSSKATTEVERKET. Main/Corp Sweden. Riksskatteverket. 1971-. Swedish. ir. Liberforlag, 171 94 Solna, Stockholm Sweden. **LC** HJ59.

ART SCHOOL DIRECTORY (WASHINGTON (D.C.)). (ART SCHOOL DIRECTORY). Vol. 1 (1939/40)-. US. English. an. $1.00. Billboard Publishers, 1 Color Court, Marion OH 43302. **LC** N330.A1.

ARTISTS IN EDUCATION DIRECTORY. US. English. an. Delaware State Arts Council, State Office Building, 820 North French Street, Wilmington DE 19801. **LC** NX396.5. **DD** 700.25751.

ARTS AND ACTIVITIES YEARBOOK. VFOAT Living Art Ideas. No. 1- 1960-. 0518-8172. US. English. an. $2.50. Publishers' Development Corporation, 8150 North Central Park Avenue, Skokie IL 60076. **LC** N81. **DD** 707.073.

ARTS REVIEW YEAR BOOK. VFOAT Arts Review Yearbook. 1982-. UK. English. an. $8.00. Starcity Ltd, 16 Saint James Gardens, London W11 England. **LC** N6761. **DD** 705. *Arts Review Yearbook, 0309-3611.*

ARTS REVIEW YEARBOOK. 1976-1981. 0309-3611. UK. English. an. $16.09. Arts Review Yearbook, 16 St James's Gardens, London W11 4RE England. Ed Graham Hughes. **LC** N9. **DD** 702.541. bk rev. adv acc. **Circ** 4,000. Essential reference book for all connected with visual arts. Comprehensive directory of London galleries and museums, regional museums and galleries, etc. *Arts Review Yearbook & Directory.*

ARTS REVIEW YEARBOOK & DIRECTORY CEASED. Began with vol. for 1974. UK. English. an. $5.00. R G Periodicals, 8 Wyndham Place, London W 1H2AY England. **LC** N9. **DD** 702.541.

AS, ANNUAIRE DU SPECTACLE. VFOAT Annuaire du Spectacle. VAT Annuaire Spectacle, Annuaire du Spectacle. FR. French. ir. 60. Editions Raouolt, 17 Faubourg Montamartre, 75009 Paris France. **LC** PN2620. **DD** 790.20944. *Annuaire du Spectacle, Theatre, Cinema, Musique, Radio, Television.*

Yearbooks, Almanacs, Directories

ASCOPE DIRECTORY. VFOAT ASEAN Council On Petroleum Directory. 1st Ed. (1984)-. 0217-5347. IO. English. be. P T Usaha Enterprises, Piola Building/2nd Floor, Jalan Kramat Raya 7/9, Jakarta Pusat Indonesia.

ASEAN PRESS YEARBOOK .... 1979-. English. ir. Confederation of Asean Journalists, 7-C Jalan Veteran Jakarta Indonesia. LC PN4699. DD 079.59.

ASHRAE HANDBOOK & PRODUCT DIRECTORY : APPLICATIONS. 1974-. Monographic Series. US. English. te. 345 East 47th Street, New York NY 10017. Each issue contains an index to its own contents - no vol index - loose. *ASRAE Guide and Data Book.*

ASIA-PACIFIC PETROLEUM DIRECTORY. VAT Asia Pacific Petroleum Directory. 1st- Ed. 0270-1235. US. English. an. Pennwell Publishing Company, PO Box 1260, Tulsa OK 74101. **Tel** (918)835-3161. LC HD9576.A68. DD 338.76223380255.

ASIA TRAVEL TRADE DIRECTORY. English. ir. $15.00. Interasia Publications Ltd, 5th Floor 257 Gloucester Road, Hong Kong Hong Kong. LC G155.A74. DD 338.479150442025.

ASIA YEARBOOK. VFOAT Far Eastern Economic Review. 1973-. HK. English. an. $23.95. Post Office Box 160, Hong Kong China. **Tel** 5-8911533. Ed Mike MacLachlan. LC HC411. DD 330.95042. adv acc. **Circ** 30,000. Covers events of Asian economic, political, social or strategic importance. *Far Eastern Economic Review . . . Yearbook, 0071-3821.*

ASIAN ALMANAC. V. 1- July 1/6 1963-. 0004-4520. Periodical. SI. English. wk. $148.17. Asian Almanac, PO Box 2737, Singapore 9047 Singapore. **Tel** 4816092. LC DS1. DD 950.05.

ASIAN COMPUTER YEARBOOK. VFOAT Computer Yearbook. V. 2-. HK. English. ir. Computer Yearbook, 302 Ivy Road, 20 Wyndham Street, Hong Kong Hong Kong. LC QA75.5. DD 001.6405. *Computer Yearbook.*

ASIAN PRESS AND MEDIA DIRECTORY. (THE ASIAN PRESS AND MEDIA DIRECTORY). 1974-. 0115-2254. English. an. $10.00. Press Foundation of Asia, PO Box 1843, Manila Philippines. LC HF5808.A7. DD 070.0255.

ASIS HANDBOOK & DIRECTORY. Main/Corp American Society for Information Science. VAT American Society for Information Science Handbook & Directory. 1968/69-. US. English. an. $10.00. American Society for Information Science, 1155 16th Street Northwest, Washington DC 20036. LC Z673. DD 020.5. *Handbook & Directory.*

THE ASSOCIATION OF AMERICAN UNIVERSITY PRESSES DIRECTORY. 19th Ed.-. 0193-8142. Periodical. US. English. an. $11.00. American University Press Service Inc, One Park Avenue/Suite 1102, New York NY 10016. **Tel** (212)889-3510. Directory of members and affiliates of the Association of American University Presses. *Directory - Association of American University Presses.*

ASSOCIATION OF COLLEGE, UNIVERSITY AND COMMUNITY ARTS ADMINISTRATORS, INC. (ASSOCIATION OF COLLEGE, UNIVERSITY AND COMMUNITY ARTS ADMINISTRATORS). DIRECTORY). 0097-7276. US. English. PO Box 2137, Madison WI 53701. LC NX110. DD 352.945402573.

THE ASSOCIATION OF CONSULTING ENGINEERS DIRECTORY .... VFOAT Directory. 1980/81-. English. ir. The Association of Consulting Engineers, 206 2nd Floor, Wisma MP1, Jalan Raja Chulan, Kuala Lumpur Malaysia. LC TA12. DD 620.0025595.

ASTM DIRECTORY. Main/Corp American Society for Testing and Materials. US. English. ir. American Society for Testing and Materials, 1916 Race Street, Philadelphia PA 19103.

THE ASTRONOMICAL ALMANAC. (THE ASTRONOMICAL ALMANAC FOR THE YEAR . . .). VFOAT Astronomical Almanac. 1981-. 0737-6421. US. English. an. Superintendent of Documents, United States Government Printing Office, Washington DC 20402. LC QB8.U6. DD 528. *American Ephemeris and Nautical Almanac, 0065-8189; Astronomical Ephemeris for the Year . . . .*

ASTRONOMICAL PAPERS. (ASTRONOMICAL PAPERS PREPARED FOR THE USE OF THE AMERICAN EPHEMERIS AND NAUTICAL ALMANAC). Began with V. 1, 1882. 0097-7055. US. English. ir. US Naval Observatory, Washington DC 20390. LC QB3.

ATLANTIC COMMUNICATION ARTS DIRECTORY. 1983-. 0822-4005. CN. English. an. $4.95 Per Vol. Atlantic Communication Arts Directory, PO Box 8748, Halifax Nova Scotia B3K 5M3 Canada. DD 791.025715.

THE ATTORNEY'S DIRECTORY OF FORENSIC PSYCHIATRISTS IN THE UNITED STATES AND CANADA. 1983 Ed.-. 0278-0879. US. English. an. $20.00. Amer College Forensic Psychiatrists, 26701 Quail Creek #295, Laguna Hills CA 92653. **Tel** (714)831-0236. Ed Ed Miller. LC RA1151. DD 614.1. **Circ** 1,000. A biographical professional and reference directory of psychiatrists who are expert witnesses in civil and criminal court cases.

ATTORNEYS' DIRECTORY OF SAN DIEGO COUNTY. VFOAT Attorneys' Directory. 0193-9300. US. English. an. Transcript Publishing Company, 861 Sixth Avenue, San Diego CA 92101. LC KF193.S24. DD 340.02579498.

ATTORNEYS' DIRECTORY OF SERVICES AND INFORMATION. (ATTORNEYS' DIRECTORY OF SERVICES AND INFORMATION : FEDERAL, CALIFORNIA STATE AND COUNTY GOVERNMENTS). 1977-. English. $20.00. California Continuing Education of the Bar, 2150 Shattuck Avenue, Berkeley CA 94704. Index in last issue of volume - attached.

AUDIO VISUAL DIRECTORY. UK. English. an. MacLaren Publishers, MacLaren House, Croydon Surrey England. LC HD9697.A843. DD 338.76213804402541.

THE AUDIO-VISUAL EQUIPMENT DIRECTORY CEASED. VAT Audio Visual Equipment Directory. Began with Mar. 1953. Ceased with 29th Ed. 1983-84. 0571-8759. US. English. an. National Audio-Visual Association Inc, 3150 Spring Street, Fairfax VA 22031. LC TS2301.A7. DD 621.380440294. NLM TS 2301.A7 A912.

AUSTRALIAN GAS INDUSTRY DIRECTORY. (THE AUSTRALIAN GAS INDUSTRY DIRECTORY). 1978/1979-. 0727-3525. AT. English. an. Australian Gas Association, Gas Industry House, 7 Moore Street, Canberra City Australian Capital Territory 2601 Australia. LC TP738. DD 665.702544. *Directory of the Australian Gas Industry.*

AUSTRALIAN GLIDING YEAR BOOK. 1969-. AT. English. an. 13.80. Gliding Federation Australia, GPO Box 1650, Adelaide South Australia 5001 Australia. **Tel** (08)211-8997. Ed Alan Ash. LC GV750. DD 797.550994. bk rev. adv acc. **Circ** 4,500. The sport of gliding world wide, but primarily Australian activities. Official journal of the Gliding Federation of Australia.

THE AUSTRALIAN KEY BUSINESS DIRECTORY. English. ir. LC HF3943. DD 338.002594.

AUSTRALIAN LEGAL DIRECTORY. 1979-. Periodical. AT. English. ir. Law Council of Australia, 155 Queen Street, Melbourne Victoria 3000 Australia. DD 349.94025, 349.4025.

AUSTRALIAN MINING AND PETROLEUM LAW ASSOCIATION YEARBOOK. VFOAT AMPLA Yearbook. 1983-. 0812-857X. AT. English. an. Australian Mining and Petroleum Law Association Limited, 160 Queen Street/8th Floor, Melbourne Victoria 3000 Australia. **Tel** (03)672544. Ed Alfreda Rosenthal. **Circ** 600. Articles covering the law relating to mining and petroleum exploration in Australia. *Australian Mining and Petroleum Law Journal, 0157-2083.*

AUSTRALIAN MINING YEARBOOK. VFOAT Australian Mining Year Book. English. an. Thomson Publications, PO Box 65, Chippendale New South Wales 2008 Australia.

AUSTRALIAN MUSIC DIRECTORY. 1st Ed. (1981)-. 0706-6678. AT. English. ir. $11.04. Australian Music Directory Party, 644 Victoria Street, North Melbourne Victoria 3051 Australia. LC ML21.A86. DD 338.477845002594.

THE AUSTRALIAN SUGAR YEAR BOOK. V. 1- 1940/41-. 0067-2173. AT. English. an. Publishing Marketing Australia (PMA), GPO Box 711, Brisbane 4001 Queensland Australia. **Tel** (07)832-2171. Ed Jenny Hallson. LC TP375.3. DD 664.1. adv acc. **Circ** 1,500. A directory of Australian sugar organizations and mills and a review of the year's events.

THE AUSTRALIAN WINE INDUSTRY DIRECTORY. Vol. 1, No. 1 (Mar. 1983)-. 0811-1324. English. an. Industrial Supplies Pty Ltd, 49 Port Road, Thebarton 503 South Australia. LC HD9388.A8. DD 338.476632002594.

AUSTRIAN HISTORY YEARBOOK. Vol. 1 (1965)-. 0067-2378. US. English. ir. Austrian History Yearbook, University of Minnesota, 715 Social Science Building, Minneapolis MN 55455. **Tel** (612)373-4670. Ed William E Wright. **Ind/Abst** Am. Hist. Life, Hist. Abstr., Part A, Mod. Hist. Abstr., Hist. Abst., Part B, Twent. Century Abstr., Writ. Am. Hist. LC DB1. bk rev. **Circ** 1,200. Includes book reviews, lists of recent books, articles, dissertations, and research in progress from North America and Europe on the Habsburg monarchy and on Austria and Hungary since 1018. *Austrian History News Letter.*

AUTOMOBILE ALMANAC. 1971-. 0067-2513. Periodical. US. English. an. Automobile Almanac, Box 160, Orangeburg NY 10962. **Tel** (914)359-5300. Ed David Ash. Each issue contains an index to its own contents - no vol index - loose.

AUTOMOTIVE, BURGLARY PROTECTION, MECHANICAL EQUIPMENT DIRECTORY. 1978-. US. English. an. $1.76. Underwriters Laboratories Inc, 333 Pfingsten Road, Northbrook IL 60062. **Tel** (312)272-8800. *Accident, Automotive, Burglary Protection Equipment Directory.*

AVIATION CONSUMER PILOTS' YEARBOOK. VFOAT Aviation Consumer. 1979-. 0192-6616. US. English. an. Belvoir Publications, 1111 East Putnam Avenue, Riverside CT 06878. LC TL721.4. DD 629.13252170973.

AWA MEMBERSHIP DIRECTORY. Main/Corp American Warehousemen's Association. VFOAT Roster of Members. 0569-9045. US. English. ir. American Warehousemen's Association, 222 West Adams Street, Chicago IL 60606.

AYER DIRECTORY OF PUBLICATIONS CEASED. 1972-1982. 0145-1642. US. English. an. $103.00. IMS Press, 426 Pennsylvania Avenue, Fort Washington PA 19034. **Tel** (215)628-4920. LC Z6951. DD 071.3025. NLM Z 6951 A976. *Ayer Directory, Newspapers, Magazines and Trade Publications, 0067-2696.*

B & CJ BUILDING DIRECTORY. VFOAT Building Directory. VAT B and CJ Building Directory. 1969-. UK. English. an. LC TH12. DD 690.02542.

BACK STAGE. TV FILM & TAPE PRODUCTION DIRECTORY. VFOAT Back Stage Film Directory. VAT Back State. Television Film and Tape Production Directory. 1982 Ed.-. 0734-9777. CN. an. $20.00. Back Stage Publications Inc, 330 West 42nd Street, New York NY 10036. **Tel** (212)947-0080. Ed Allen Znerdling. LC PN1998.A1. DD 384.8029473. bk rev. adv acc. **Circ** 7,000. (ctrl). Names, addresses, phones, execs. of TV commercial producers, suppliers, services, nationwide including ad agencies. *Back Stage. TV Film and Tape Syndication Directory.*

BACK STAGE. TV FILM & TAPE SYNDICATION DIRECTORY. VFOAT TV Film & Tape Syndication Directory. 1976 Ed.-. Periodical. US. English. an. $20.00. Backstage Publications Inc, 330 West 42nd Street, New York NY 10036. **Tel** (212)947-0020. *Backstage: TV Film, Tape & Syndicaton Directory.*

BACON'S NEWSPAPER DIRECTORY. U. S. EDITION. (BACON'S NEWSPAPER DIRECTORY). VAT Bacon's Newspaper Directory. United States Edition. 0360-1498. US. English. Bacon's Publishing Company, 14 East Jackson Boulevard, Chicago IL 60604. LC Z6951, PN4867. DD 071.3025.

BAHIA, ANUARIO DA MINERACAO. Yearly V. 1-1977-. Portuguese. ir. Secretaria das Minas e Energia Coordenacao da Producao Mineral, Centro Administrativo da Bahia, Av Luiz Viana Filho S/N, 40.000 Salvador Brazil. LC HD9506.B73.

BAHIA ANUARIO ENERGETICO. Vol. 1 (1982)-. Portuguese. an. LC TJ163.25.B6. DD 333.79098142.

BALANCE OF PAYMENTS STATISTICS YEARBOOK - INTERNATIONAL MONETARY FUND. (BALANCE OF PAYMENTS STATISTICS. YEARBOOK). Vol. 32, Pt. 1 (1981)-. 0252-3035. US. English. an. $12.00. International Monetary Fund, 700 19th Street North West, Washington DC 20431. **Tel** (202)477-7000. LC HG3882. DD 382.170212. *Balance of Payments Yearbook, 0378-2662.*

Yearbooks, Almanacs, Directories

BALANCE OF PAYMENTS YEARBOOK - INTERNATIONAL MONETARY FUND CEASED. (BALANCE OF PAYMENTS YEARBOOK). **Main/Corp** International Monetary Fund. V. 1-31. 0378-2662. US. English. mo. International Monetary Fund, Washington DC 20431. **DD** 382. *Balances of Payments.*

B&T YEAR BOOK. VFOAT B & T Year Book. Began with 17th Ed. (1974). AT. English. an. Greater Publications, Box 2608, Sydney 2001 Australia. **LC** HE8699.A8. **DD** 384.540994. *Broadcasting and Television Year Book.*

BANGLADESH DIRECTORY. 1978-. BG. English. ir. $10.00. Times Publications, 42-43 Purana Paltan, Dacca Bangladesh. **LC** DS393.3. **DD** 954.92.

BANGLADESH DIRECTORY & YEAR BOOK. II. English. an. $19.00. Associated Book Promoters, 912A Ekbalpur Lane, Calcutta 700023 India. **LC** HF3790.6. **DD** 380.10255492.

BANGLADESH EXPORTERS' DIRECTORY. English. ir. Export Promotion Bureau, 122 Motijheel Commercial Area, Dacca 2 Bangladesh. **LC** HF3790.6.A48. **DD** 382.602945492.

BANGLADESH SHIPPING DIRECTORY. English. ir. 46.00. Bangladesh Ocean Publications, 1314/A Bangabandhu Road PO Box 316, Chittagong Bangladesh. **LC** HE880.6. **DD** 387.50255492.

BANGLADESH YEARBOOK. 1983-. English. an. $20.00 US. Kabir Khan Prokashani, 144 Dhaka New Market, Dhaka Bangladesh. **LC** DS393. **DD** 954.92005.

BANK DIRECTORY OF CANADA CEASED. Began publication in 1907? Ceased with 1982 issue. 0045-1436. Periodical. CN. English. an. $12.00. Houston Standard Publications, 30 Duncan Street, Toronto Ontario M5V 2C3 Canada. **DD** 332.1202571.

THE BANKERS' ALMANAC AND YEAR BOOK . . . . 1845. UK. English. an. 175.00. Thomas Skinner Directories, Windsor Court, East Grinstead House, East Grinstead West Sussex England. **Tel** (0342)26972. Ed R L Phelps. adv acc. **Circ** 20,000. (ctrl). Contains entries for over 2,500 major banks worldwide with their branch locations in some 190 countries and 40,000 cities and towns. *London Bankers' Year-book.*

BANKERS DESK REFERENCE YEARBOOK. 1979?-. US. English. an.

BANKERS SCHOOLS DIRECTORY. 0145-5850. US. English. be. $9.00. American Bankers Association, 44-B Industrial Park Circle, Waldorf MD 20601. **Tel** (202)467-4028. **LC** HG1581. **DD** 332.1071173.

BANKER'S WORLD DIRECTORY. (THE BANKER'S WORLD DIRECTORY). 0376-6616. BE. English, French, German, and Spanish. ir. Common Market Publications, rue du Meridien 42, B 1030 Bruxelles Belgium. **LC** HG1536. **DD** 332.1025.

BANKS & FINANCIAL INSTITUTIONS IN SINGAPORE. See Business - Banking & Finance.

BAPTIST UNION DIRECTORY. (THE BAPTIST UNION DIRECTORY). 0302-3184. UK. English. an. $6.06. Baptist Church House, 4 Southampton Row, London WC1B 4AB England. **LC** BX6276.A1. **DD** 286.106242.

BAR CODE MANUFACTURERS & SERVICES DIRECTORY. VFOAT Bar Codes Manufacturers and Services Directory. 1982-. 8755-7851. US. English. an. $34.95. North American Technology Inc, 174 Concord Street, Peterborough NH 03458. **Tel** (603)924-7136. Ed Carl Helmers. **LC** HD9801.6.P763. **DD** 681.14. adv acc. The directory contains a complete listing of the companies which deliver bar code and related products/services. Name, type of product, notes. Indexed by company and product.

BARQUE'S PAKISTAN TRADE DIRECTORY AND WHO'S WHO. 1949/50-. 0083-9671. Periodical. PK. English. ir. PO Box 201, Lahore Pakistan. *All-India Trade Directory and Who's Who.*

BASEBALL AMERICA'S BASEBALL DIRECTORY. (BASEBALL AMERICA'S . . . BASEBALL DIRECTORY). VFOAT Baseball Directory. 0883-4415. US. English. an. $6.95. Baseball America, PO Box 2089, Durham NC 27702. **Tel** (919)682-9635. Ed Allan Simpson. adv acc. **Circ** 5,000. A Complete listing of baseball executives plus major and minor league schedules includes general information on many college programs.

BASLER JAHRBUCH FUR HISTORISCHE MUSIKPRAXIS : EINE VEROFFENTLICHUNG DER SCHOLA CANTORUM BASILIENSIS AN DER MUSIK-AKADEMIE DER STADT BASEL. 1 (1977)-. SZ. German. Amadeus Verlag, Gotzenwielerstrasse 8, CH 8405 Winterthur Switzerland. **Tel** (201)667-0956. **LC** ML5. **DD** 781.6309.

BAYERISCHES LANDWIRTSCHAFTLICHES JAHRBUCH. Yearly V. 32, No. 5- Oct. 1955-. 0375-8621. Periodical. GW. German. ir. 320. Bayerishcer Landwirtschaftsvg, Ludwigstr 2, 8 Munchen 22 West Germany. **Tel** (089)21820. Ed A Schuh and U Keymer. **Ind/Abst** Excerpta Med., GeoRef, Bibliogr. Agric., Chem. Abstr. bk rev. (ctrl). All agricultural disciplines: plant production, animal production, economics, soil, agriculture technical science, above all, but also horticulture, fish production and forest culture. *Landwirtschaftliches Jahrbuch Fur Bayern.*

B.C. DAIRY FARMERS' HANDBOOK & ALL BREEDS DIRECTORY. 1982 Ed.-. 0826-0893. CN. English. an. $5.00 Per Vol. Freyvogel Preiswerck Ltd, 208 West Hastings Street Suite 810, Vancouver B C V6B 1J8 Canada. **DD** 338.176244025711.

BC LABOUR DIRECTORY (1978). (BC LABOUR DIRECTORY). 0715-2574. CN. English. an. Ministry of Labour, Research and Planning Branch, Parliament Buildings, Victoria British Columbia V8V 1X4 Canada. **LC** HD6523. **DD** 331.88025711. *Labour Directory, 0702-0759.*

B.C. MUNICIPAL YEARBOOK. (B. C. MUNICIPAL YEAR BOOK). 1949-. 0068-161X. Periodical. CN. English. an. $7.74. JSB Productions Ltd, Box 46457 Station G, Vancouver British Columbia V6R 4G7 Canada. **Tel** (604)736-0205. **LC** HJ8514.B72. **DD** 336.711. *Red Book of British Columbia Municipal and Corporate Finance, 0317-4557.*

THE B.C. PROFESSIONAL ENGINEER ANNUAL DIRECTORY NUMBER. 1951-. Periodical. CN. English. mo. 11.61. The Association of Professional Engineers in British Columbia, 2210 West 12th Avenue Vancouver British Columbia V6K 2N6 Canada. **Tel** (604)736-9808. Ed M F Painter. **DD** 620.0062711. adv acc. **Circ** 12,000. (ctrl). Official publication of the Association of Professional Engineers of British Columbia.

BEHORDENVERZEICHNIS NORDRHEIN-WESTFALEN. **Main/Corp** Landesamt fur Datenverarbeitung und Statistik Nordrhein-Westfalen. 0522-6058. German. ir. Landsamt fur Datenverarbeitung und Statistik Nordrhein-Westfalen, Postfach 1105 Mauerstrasse 51, 4000 Dusseldorf West Germany.

BELIZE BUSINESS AND TRAVEL DIRECTORY. VFOAT Belize. US. English. ir. $4.00 US. Belize Tourist Board, PO Box 325, Belize City Belize C A. **LC** F1443.5. **DD** 917.2820453.

BELLEVUE KIRKLAND REDMOND (KING COUNTY WASHINGTON) POLK DIRECTORY. US. English. an. Polk & Company, 400 East Linwood Boulevard, Kansas City MO 04109. *Bellevue, Kirkland, Redmond (King County, Wash.) City Directory.*

BENN'S PRESS DIRECTORY. INTERNATIONAL. 131st Ed. (1983)-. Periodical. UK. English. an. Benn Publications Ltd, PO Box 20, Sovereign Way, Tonbridge Kent TN9 1RQ England. **Tel** (0732) 362666. Ed John Hedges. adv acc. **Circ** 2,000. The standard work of reference to the world's media. International volume covers overseas and international media with more than 28,000 titles in 195 countries. *Benn's Press Directory.*

BENRI CHO - BANKUBA IJUSHA NO KAI. (BENRI CHO). VFOAT Information & Directory for Greater Vancouver. 1978-. 0821-4735. CN. Japanese (includes some text in English). Japanese Immigrants' Association, Box 69012 Station K, Vancouver British Columbia V5K 4W3 Canada. **DD** 971.133.

BERKSHIRE TRAVELLER ALMANACK. (THE BERKSHIRE TRAVELLER ALMANACK). 1973-. 0090-1024. US. English. an. $1.95. Berkshire Traveller Press, Stockbridge MA 01262. Ed N T Simpson. **LC** AY64. **DD** 051.

BERRY ALUMNI DIRECTORY. 1983-. 0741-9112. Periodical. US. English. Bernard C Harris, 3 Barker Avenue, White Plains NY 10601. **LC** LD7501.M9275. **DD** 378.75835.

BEST OF SIR YEARBOOK. VFOAT Sir Yearbook. 0731-9886. Periodical. US. English. sa. $3.50 Per Issue. Histrionic Publishing Company Inc, 23 West 26th Street, New York NY 10010.

BEST'S DIRECTORY OF RECOMMENDED INSURANCE ADJUSTERS. VFOAT Directory of Recommended Insurance Adjusters. 50th- Ed. 0271-0927. US. English. an. A M Best Company, Ambest Road, Oldwick NJ 08858. **Tel** (201)439-2200. **LC** HG8525. **DD** 368.014. Includes nearly 1,000 pages with listings for more than 3,500 insurance adjusting firms throughout the world. Listings are arranged alphabetically by city within each state, Canadian province, and foreign country. *Best's Recommended Independent Insurance Adjusters, 0091-830X.*

BEST'S DIRECTORY OF RECOMMENDED INSURANCE ATTORNEYS. VFOAT Directory of Recommended Insurance Attorneys. 52nd Ed. (1981)-. 0277-1551. US. English. an. A M Best Company, Ambest Road, Oldwick NJ 08858. **Tel** (201)439-2200. **LC** KF195.I5. **DD** 346.74086025, 347.30686025. Contains more than 2,000 pages, listing over 4,000 top law firms. Listings are arranged alphabetically by city within each state, Canadian province and foreign country for ease of reference. *Best's Recommended Insurance Attorneys.*

BEST'S SAFETY DIRECTORY. 0090-7480. US. English. an. $15.00. A M Best Company, Ambest Road, Oldwick NJ 08858. **Tel** (201)439-2200. **LC** T55.A1. **DD** 338.47620860257. **NLM** W 26 B561. The most complete sourcebook for occupational safety-health needs. Contains information on regulatory standards, safety techniques, product descriptions, applications and purchase sources. *Best's Environmental Control and Safety Directory, 0067-6322.*

BETTER BOOK. (BETTER BOOK : MEMBERSHIP DIRECTORY & CONSUMER GUIDE). **Main/Corp** Better Business Bureau of the Mainland of British Columbia. July 1981-. 0711-3668. CN. English. an. Free. Better Business Bureau of the Mainland of British Columbia, 788 Beatty Street, Vancouver British Columbia V6B 2M1 Canada. **DD** 381.025711. (ctrl).

BHM SUPPORT. DIRECTORY OF GRANTS, AWARDS, AND LOANS. **Main/Corp** United States. Health Resources Administration. Bureau of Health Manpower. VAT Bureau of Health Manpower Support: Directory of Grants, Awards, and Loans. Periodical. US. English. an. Department of Health Education and Welfare, Public Health Service, Health Resources Administration, Bureau of Health Manpower, Program Management Information Section, 5600 Fishers Lane, Rockville MD 20852. **NLM** W 22 AA1 B106. *BHME Support, 0098-521X.*

BHPR SUPPORT. (BHPR SUPPORT : DIRECTORY OF GRANTS, AWARDS, AND LOANS). **Series/Titl** DHHS Publication. VFOAT B.H.P.R. Support. VAT Bureau of Health Professions Support. Fiscal year 79-. 0730-2452. US. English. an. **LC** R745. **DD** 610.7073. **NLM** W 22 AA1 B106. *BHM Support, 0273-2041.*

BIG TEN FOOTBALL ALMANAC. V. 1- 1978-. 0197-8128. US. English. an. $4.95. Alpine Book Company, 527 Madison Avenue, New York NY 10022. **LC** GV985.5.I55. **DD** 796.332630977.

BILLBOARD INTERNATIONAL AUDIO VIDEO TAPE DIRECTORY. VFOAT International Audio Video Tape Directory. 0736-7295. US. English. an. Billboard Subscription Department, PO Box 13808, Philadelphia PA 19108. *Billboard International Tape Directory, 009—645X.*

BILLBOARD INTERNATIONAL DIRECTORY OF RECORDING STUDIOS. VFOAT International Directory of Recording Studios. 0067-8627. US. English. an. 2160 Patterson Street, Cincinnati OH 45211. **LC** TS2301.P3. **DD** 621.38932.

BILLBOARD INTERNATIONAL RECORDING EQUIPMENT & STUDIO DIRECTORY. VFOAT Recording Equipment & Studios. VAT Billboard International Recording Equipment and Studio Directory. 0160-7790. US. English. an. Billboard Publishing Inc, 1515 Broadway, New York NY 10036. **Tel** (212)764-7300. Ed Sam

Yearbooks, Almanacs, Directories

Holdsworth. LC TK7881.4. DD 338.476213893025. adv acc. Circ 15,000. A complete directory of audio and video recording studios, studio equipment manufacturers and suppliers, presented by city and state as well as internationally by country. *Billboard International Directory of Recording Studios.*

BILLBOARD INTERNATIONAL TALENT & TOURING DIRECTORY. VFOAT International Talent & Touring Directory. 1981-1982-. 0732-0124. US. English. an. $25.00. Billboard Subscription Department, PO Box 13808, Philadelphia PA 19101. LC ML1. DD 780.42025. *Billboard International Talent Directory.*

BINSTED'S DIRECTORY OF FOOD TRADE MARKS AND BRAND NAMES. UK. English. an. 36.00. Food Trade Press Ltd, 29 High Street/Green St Green, Orpington Kent BR6 6LS England. Tel 44 689 50551. Ed Adrian Rinsted. adv acc. Circ 2,000. Trade marks and brand names used in the United Kingdom described. Plus company names and addresses.

BINTANG DIRECTORY. 1976-. English or Indonesian. ir. 3000. Bintang Advertising, Jl May Jend Sutoyo S 56, Medan Indonesia. LC HF5251.S85. DD 380.10255981. *Petunjuk Alamat Dagand Dan Industri Sumatera Utara, Indonesia.*

BIO-ENERGY DIRECTORY. 1978-. 0162-5713. US. English. ir. Bio Energy Council, 1625 Eye Street NW/Suite 825A, Washington DC 20006. Tel (703)276-9411. DD 333.7.

BIOGRAPHICAL DIRECTORY. Main/Corp American Political Science Association. 5th Ed. (1968)-. Periodical. US. English. be. $100.00. American Political Science Association, 1527 New Hampshire Avenue Northwest, Washington DC 20036. Tel (202)483-2512. Ed Samuel C Patterson and Catherine Rudder. bk rev. adv acc. Circ 12,000. *Biographical Directory of the American Political Science Association.*

BIOGRAPHICAL DIRECTORY - AMERICAN PSYCHIATRIC ASSOCIATION. (BIOGRAPHICAL DIRECTORY). Main/Corp Americah Psychiatric Association. 1983-. 0882-2506. US. English. ir. American Psychiatric Association, 1400 K Street Northwest, Washington DC 20005.

BIOGRAPHICAL DIRECTORY - AMERICAN PSYCHOLOGICAL ASSOCIATION CEASED. (BIOGRAPHICAL DIRECTORY OF THE AMERICAN PSYCHOLOGICAL ASSOCIATION). Main/Corp American Psychological Association. 1970-75. 0090-9076. US. English. ir. American Psychological Association, 1400 North Nule Street, Arlington VA 22201. Tel (703)247-7703. LC BF11. DD 150.2573. NLM BF 11 A51D. *Directory - American Psychological Association.*

BIOGRAPHICAL DIRECTORY OF THE AMERICAN ACADEMY OF PEDIATRICS. Main/Corp American Academy of Pediatrics. 1st Ed. (1980)-. 0275-1712. US. English. ir. R R Bowker Company, PO Box 1807, Ann Arbor MI 48106. Tel (313)761-4700. LC RJ43.A1. DD 618.92000922, B. NLM WS 22 AA1 A4B.

BIOGRAPHICAL DIRECTORY OF THE AMERICAN PODIATRY ASSOCIATION. Main/Corp American Podiatry Association. 1980-. 0272-3603. US. English. ir. R R Bowker, PO Box 1807, Ann Arbor MI 48106. LC RD563. DD 617.58500922, B. NLM WE 22 AA1 A556.

BIOGRAPHICAL DIRECTORY OF THE AMERICAN PUBLIC HEALTH ASSOCIATION. Main/Corp American Public Health Association. 1979-. US. English. ir. $54.50. R R Bowker, PO Box 1807, Ann Arbor MI 48106. Tel (313)761-4700. LC RA424.4. DD 614.0922, B.

BIOGRAPHICAL DIRECTORY OF THE FELLOWS & MEMBERS OF THE AMERICAN PSYCHIATRIC ASSOCIATION. Main/Corp American Psychiatric Association. VFOAT Biographical Directory of the American Psychiatric Association. 1973-. US. English. ir. R R Bowker Company, PO Box 1807, Ann Arbor MI 48106. Tel (202)682-6000.

BIOGRAPHICAL DIRECTORY OF THE MEMBERS OF THE CZECHOSLOVAK SOCIETY OF ARTS AND SCIENCES, INC. Main/Corp Czechoslovak Society of Arts and Sciences. VFOAT Biographical Directory. 0883-4849. US. English. Czechoslovak Society of Arts and Sciences, 2067 Park Road Northwest, Washington DC 20010. LC DB2043. DD 943.7002573. *Biographical Directory of the Members of the Czechoslovak Society of Arts and Sciences in America.*

BIOGRAPHY ALMANAC. 1st Ed-. 0738-0097. Periodical. US. English. an. Gale Research Company, Book Tower, Detroit MI 48226. Ed Annie Brewer. LC CT104. DD 920.02.

BIOLA COLLEGE ALUMNI DIRECTORY. 1979-. US. English. Biola College, 13800 Biola Avenue, La Mirado CA 90639. LC LD451.B564. DD 378.79493.

BIOTECHNOLOGY NEWS' DIRECTORY OF BIOTECHNOLOGY COMPANIES. VFOAT Directory of Biotechnology Companies. 1983-. 0736-4199. US. English. an. $150.00. CTB International Publishing Company, PO Box 218, Maplewood NJ 07040. LC HD9999.G45. DD 338.7615751025.

BIRMINGHAM & WEST MIDLANDS CHAMBERS OF COMMERCE DIRECTORY. VAT Birmingham and West Midlands Chambers of Commerce Directory. 0307-0158. UK. Multilingual (English, French, German, Spanish). Industrial Newspapers, Newhall Street, Birmingham B3 1LH England. LC HF302. DD 380.0624248.

BIRMINGHAM AREA INDUSTRIAL DIRECTORY. 0147-2097. US. English. $13.50. Birmingham Area Chamber of Commerce, PO Box 10127, Birmingham AL 35202. Tel (205)323-5461. LC HC108.B6. DD 338.402576178. adv acc. Circ 432. (ctrl). Listing of mining and manufacturing companies for the Birmingham Metropolitan area.

BLACK DIAL DIRECTORY. 1975/77-. 0701-0605. Periodical. CN. English. be. Black Dial Directory, 631A Bloor Street West, Toronto Ont M6G 1K8 Canada. DD 971.300496.

BLACK PRESS PERIODICAL DIRECTORY. (THE BLACK PRESS PERIODICAL DIRECTORY). 1973-. 0093-5697. US. English. $45.00. Systems Catalog Inc, 78 Merchant Street, Newark NJ 07105. LC Z6944.N39. DD 070.02573.

BLACK'S MEDICAL DICTIONARY. Began publication with 1st in 1906. UK. English. ir. Biblio Distribution Center, 81 Adams Drive, Totawa NJ 07512. Tel (201)256-8600. LC R121. DD 610.3.

BLUE JAYS YEARBOOK. (BLUE JAYS ... YEARBOOK). Main/Corp TORONTO BLUE JAYS (BASEBALL TEAM). VFOAT Toronto Blue Jays Yearbook. VAT Toronto Blue Jays Yearbook (1984). 1984-. 0828-6000. CN. English. an. $5.00 Per Vol. Blue Jays Yearbook, 160 Bedford Road, Toronto Ontario M5R 2K9 Canada. DD 796.3576409713541. *Toronto Blue Jays Yearbook, 0824-2720.*

THE BLUEGRASS DIRECTORY. 1st- Ed. 0148-7396. US. English. $2.50 Per Issue. Mike and Arlene Bailey, 4005 Lara Lane, Chattanooga TN 37416.

B.M.A.A. DIRECTORY AND HANDBOOK. Main/Corp Baptist Missionary Association of America. VFOAT Directory & Handbook. US. English. Baptist News Service, PO Box 97, Jacksonville TX 75766. Tel (214)586-8617. Ed Leon Gaylor. LC BX6209.B37. DD 266.6102573. Circ 5,000. Directory of churches, ministers and missionaries of the Baptist Missionary Association of America. Statistics included on these churches.

BOATING ALMANAC. 1966-. 0067-9356. Periodical. US. English. ir. G W Bromley & Co Inc, 325 Spring Street, New York NY 10013. LC GV771. DD 796. *Boating Almanac. New Jersey Edition, 0067-9372; Boating Almanac. New England Edition, 0520-3155.*

BOATING INDUSTRY STATISTICAL YEARBOOK. VFOAT Statistical Yearbook, Boating Industry. 1981-. 0277-8378. US. English. an. Business Projects Group, 7 Canterbury Lane, Nesconset NY 11767. LC HD9993.B633. DD 338.47623820973.

BODENDENKMALPFLEGE IN MECKLENBURG : JAHRBUCH. VFOAT Jahrbuch fur Bodendenkmalpflege in Mecklenburg. 1953-. 0067-9461. GE. German. an. 130,-. Deutscher Buch Export-Import, Leninstrasse 16, DDR-701 Leipzig East Germany. Tel 22900. Ed H Keiling. Mainly publishes the findings of the archaeological research work of the museum of prehistory and early history of the town of Schwerin achieved in the course of the respective current year.

BODY FASHIONS-INTIMATE APPAREL DIRECTORY. (BODY FASHIONS/INTIMATE APPAREL DIRECTORY). 0362-2452. US. English. $5.00. Harcourt Brace Jovanovich, 757 3rd Avenue, New York NY 10017. LC TT495. DD 338.476872502573. *Body Fashions Directory.*

BOISE (ADA COUNTY, IDAHO) CITY DIRECTORY. VFOAT Boise City Directory. US. English. an. $94.00. R L Polk, 400 East Linwood Boulevard, Kansas City MO 64109. Tel (816)756-0425. adv acc. Cross reference city directory.

BOLETIN ANUARIO - BANCO CENTRAL DEL ECUADOR. Main/Corp Banco Central del Ecuador. No. 1- 1978-. Spanish. ir. Banco Central del Ecuador Secretaria General, Quito Ecuador. LC HA1025.

BONNER JAHRBUCHER. No. 1- 1950-. Periodical. GW. German. ir. Verlag Butzon Bercker GMBH, Postfach 215/Neustrasse 7, D4178 Kevelaer West Germany. Ind/Abst Repert. Int. Litt. Art.

BONNER JAHRBUCHER. BEIHEFT. 1-. 0524-0441. Monographic Series. GW. German. ir. Rudolf Habelt GMBH, Am Buchenhang 1, D-5300 Bonn 1 West Germany.

BOOK PUBLISHERS DIRECTORY CEASED. 1st Ed (1977)-4th Ed. (1983). 0196-0903. US. English. an. Gale Research Company, Book Tower, Detroit MI 48226. LC Z475. DD 070.502573.

BOOK TRADE IN CANADA. *See* Publishing - Books and Bookmaking.

BORN-AGAIN CHRISTIAN DIRECTORY-CATALOG. (THE BORN-AGAIN CHRISTIAN DIRECTORY-CATALOG). No. 1-. 0824-555X. CN. English. an. $4.00. Born-Again Christian Directory-Catalog, PO Box 317 Station A, Ottawa Ontario K1N 9Z9 Canada. DD 248.05.

BOSTON BRUINS OFFICIAL YEARBOOK. 0361-6398. US. English. an. $2.50. RA Production Inc, PO Box 9100, Boston MA 02114. LC GV848.B6. DD 796.9620922 B.

BOTSWANA DIRECTORY. 1st- Issue. English. ir. 5,00. B & T Directories Ltd, PO Box 202, Francistown South Africa. LC DT790. DD 916.8110025.

BOTTIN - UNION CANADIENNE DES RELIGIEUSES COMTEMPLATIVES. (BOTTIN). Main/Corp Union Canadienne des Religieuses Contemplatives. VFOAT Directory. 0822-8949. CN. French. be. Free. Union Canadienne des Religieuses Contemplatives, CP 479, Berthierville Quebec J0K 1A0 Canada. DD 255.90102571.

BOWER'S METROPOLITAN TORONTO SYSTEMATIC DIRECTORY. VFOAT Metropolitan Toronto Systematic Directory. 1967-. 0317-6010. Periodical. CN. English. an. Metropolitan Cross-Reference Directory, 2 Ripley Avenue, Toronto Ontario M6S 3N9 Canada. LC DD 917.135410025. *Cross-Reference Directory of Metropolitan Toronto.*

BRABY'S CAPE PROVINCE DIRECTORY. Main/Corp A.C. Braby (Pty) Ltd. VFOAT Cape Province Directory. SA. Afrikaans (English). ir. 28.00. Braby Ltd, PO Box 1426, Pinetown 3600 South Africa. Tel 7017021. Ed I A W Gray. LC DT821. DD 916.870025. adv acc. Commerical directory with alphabetical and classified sections; also contains maps of the area.

BRABY'S NATAL DIRECTORY. VFOAT Natal Directory. Began with issue for 1902. SA. English. ir. 57.00. A C Braby Pty Ltd, Publishing House, 10 Caversham Road, PO Box 1426, Pinetown 3600 South Africa. Tel 7017021. Ed I A W Gray. adv acc. Contains maps of natal, post box listings for natal, alphabetical section and classified section. *Davis Natal Directory.*

BRABY'S ORANJE VRYSTAAT ADRESBOEK = ORANGE FREE STATE DIRECTORY. Main/Corp A.C. Braby (Pty) Ltd. SA. Afrikaans (English). an. 4.00. A C Braby, PO Box 731, Durban 4000, Natal South Africa. LC DT891. DD 968.50025. *Braby's Orange Free State and Northern Cape Directory.*

BRABY'S SOUTH WEST AFRICA DIRECTORY. VFOAT South West Africa Business Directory. Afrikaans or English. ir. A C Braby, PO Box 760, Durban South Africa. LC HF5283. DD 380.10294688.

BRABY'S S.W.A./NAMIBIA BUSINESS DIRECTORY. Main/Corp A.C. Braby (Pty) Ltd. VFOAT S.W.A./Namibia Business Directory. SA. English. ir. 14.50. A C Braby,

Yearbooks, Almanacs, Directories

Publishing House, 20 Caversham Road, PO Box 1426, Pinetown 3600 South Africa. Tel 7017021. Ed I A W Gray. LC HF5283. DD 380.10294688. adv acc. Contains maps, post box listing, numerical telephone numbers, alphabetical business listings and classified section for the whole of South West Africa/Nambia. *Braby's South West Africa Directory.*

BRABY'S TRANSKEI BUSINESS DIRECTORY. VFOAT Braby's Transkei Directory. English. ir. A C Braby Pty Ltd, Braby House 641 Ridge Road PO Box 731, Durban 4001 South Africa. LC HF5279.T7. DD 380.1029468791.

BRADDOCK'S FEDERAL-STATE-LOCAL GOVERNMENT DIRECTORY. Main/Corp Braddock Publications. VFOAT Federal-State-Local Government Directory. 1975-. 0363-6275. US. English. sa. $3.95. Braddock Publications, 1028 Connecticut Avenue NW/Suite 905, Washington DC 20036. LC JK6. DD 353.002. NLM JK 6 B798.

BRADFORD'S DIRECTORY OF MARKETING RESEARCH AGENCIES AND MANAGEMENT CONSULTANTS IN THE UNITED STATES AND THE WORLD. VFOAT Directory of Marketing Research Agencies and Management Consultants in the United States and the World. 11th- 1965/66-. 0068-063X. US. English. ir. $48.00. Bradfords Directory of Marketing Research Agencies, PO Box 276, Fairfax VA 22030. Tel (703)830-4646. Ed William W Denglinger. adv acc. Circ 3,000. Directory of marketing research and management consultants companies throughout the world. *Bradford's Directory of Marketing Research Agencies in the United States and the World.*

BRANCH DIRECTORY AND SUMMARY OF DEPOSITS FOR THE STATE OF NEW YORK. 0147-3131. US. English. an. $175.00. Decision Research Sciences Inc, 300 Axewood East Butler and Skipjack Pikes, Ambler PA 19002. LC HG2444.N6. DD 332.175209747.

BRANCH DIRECTORY AND SUMMARY OF DEPOSITS FOR THE STATE OF OHIO. 0147-1546. US. English. an. $175.00. Decision Research Sciences Inc, 300 Axewood East Butler and Skippack Pikes, Ambler PA 19002. LC HG2444.O3. DD 332.16.

BRANCH DIRECTORY AND SUMMARY OF DEPOSITS FOR THE STATE OF PENNSYLVANIA. 0148-3021. US. English. an. $225.00. Decision Research Sciences Inc, 300 Axewood East Butler and Skippac, Ambler PA 19002. Tel (215)542-9550. LC HG2444.P4. DD 332.175209748.

BRANCH DIRECTORY AND SUMMARY OF DEPOSITS FOR THE STATES OF CALIFORNIA, NEW MEXICO, ARIZONA. 0147-3115. US. English. an. $175.00. Decision Research Sciences Inc, 300 Axewood East on Butler and Skippack Pikes, Ambler PA 19002. LC HG2441. DD 332.175209789.

BRANCH DIRECTORY AND SUMMARY OF DEPOSITS FOR THE STATES OF CONNECTICUT, MAINE, MASSACHUSETTS, NEW HAMPSHIRE, RHODE ISLAND, VERMONT. 0147-5002. US. English. an. $175.00. Decision Research Sciences Inc, 300 Axewood East Butler and Skipjack Pikes, Ambler PA 19002. LC HG2441. DD 332.17520974.

BRANCH DIRECTORY AND SUMMARY OF DEPOSITS FOR THE STATES OF IDAHO, NEVADA, WASHINGTON, OREGON, UTAH. 0147-314X. US. English. an. $175.00. Decision Research Sciences Inc, 300 Axewood East Butler and Skipjack Pikes, Ambler PA 19002. LC HG2441. DD 332.17520979.

BRANCH DIRECTORY AND SUMMARY OF DEPOSITS FOR THE STATES OF INDIANA, MICHIGAN. 0147-1538. US. English. an. $175.00. Decision Research Sciences Inc, 300 Axewood East Butler and Skipjack Pikes, Ambler PA 19002. LC HG2444.I6. DD 332.16.

BRANCH DIRECTORY AND SUMMARY OF DEPOSITS FOR THE STATES OF MARYLAND, DISTRICT OF COLUMBIA, VIRGINIA. 8397-3123. US. English. an. $175.00. Decision Research Sciences Inc, 300 Axewood East Butler and Skipjack Pikes, Ambler PA 19002. LC HG2441. DD 332.175209752.

BRANCH DIRECTORY AND SUMMARY OF DEPOSITS FOR THE STATES OF NEW JERSEY, DELAWARE. 0147-3778. US. English. an. Decision Research Sciences, 300 Axewood East Butler and Skipjack Pikes, Ambler PA 19002. LC HG2444.N5. DD 332.175209749.

BRANCH DIRECTORY AND SUMMARY OF DEPOSITS FOR THE STATES OF SOUTH CAROLINA, NORTH CAROLINA. 0147-2836. US. English. an. $175.00. Decision Research Sciences Inc, 300 Axewood East Butler and Skipjack Pikes, Ambler PA 19002. LC HG2444.S68. DD 332.17509756.

BRAND GUIDE AND DIRECTORY. VFOAT Buying Guide & Directory. 1975/76-. 0362-9651. US. English. $3.95. Grocer's Advisor, 2416 West Whittier Boulevard, Montebello CA 90640. LC HD9007.A45. DD 381.4564130025794.

BRANDON DIRECTORY. (THE BRANDON DIRECTORY). 1978-. 0710-7676. CN. English. an. $4.00. Rural Community Resource Centre, Brandon University, Brandon Manitoba R7A 6A9 Canada. DD 917.1273.

THE BRECHT YEARBOOK. VFOAT Brecht Jahrbuch. Vol. 11 (1982)-. 0734-8665. US. English (French and German). an. $22.00. Wayne State University Press, 5959 Woodward Avenue, Detroit MI 48202. Tel (313)577-4602. Ed John Fuegi. Ind/Abst MLA Int. Bibliogr. Books Artic. Mod. Lang. Lit. LC PT2603.R397. DD 832.912. bk rev. Circ 750. Devoted to publishing solicited papers relating to the life and works of Bertold Brecht. *Brecht-Jahrbuch, 0341-9525.*

BREEDERS DIRECTORY - ALBERTA ARABIAN HORSE COUNCIL. (BREEDERS DIRECTORY). Main/Corp Alberta Arabian Horse Council. 1st Ed. (1981)-. 0714-4180. CN. English. an. Alberta Arabian Horse Council Breeders Directory, Box 101, Bowden Alberta T0M 0K0 Canada. DD 636.112.

BREWERS' ALMANAC. VFOAT Centennial Issue. 1940-. Periodical. US. English. an. US Brewers Association, 1759 K Street NW, Washington DC 20006. LC HD9397.U5. DD 338.476633.

BRICKER'S INTERNATIONAL DIRECTORY. 12th Ed. (1981)-. 0277-7312. US. English. an. $100.00. Brickers International Directory, 425 Family Farm Road, Woodside CA 94062. Tel (415)851-3090. Ed Samuel A Pond. LC HD20.15.U5. DD 658.40071173. A guide to some 300 general and functional management programs offered by Universities in the US and Canada plus UK, Europe and Australia. *0191-2682.*

BRIDGEPORT JAI-ALAI OFFICIAL SOUVENIR YEARBOOK. VFOAT OBJASY. 1977/78-. 0160-5542. US. English. an. 11 Soundview Avenue, Stamford CT 06902. LC GV1017.P4. DD 796.34.

BRIEF DIRECTORY OF MUSEUMS IN INDIA. VFOAT Museums in India. Began with 1969 Vol. II. English. ir. 5.00. Honorary Secretary, Museums Association of India c/o National Museum of Natural History, Barakhamba Road, New Delhi 110 001 India. LC AM73.A2. DD 069.02554.

BRITISH ALTERNATIVE THEATRE DIRECTORY. Began in 1979. 0142-5218. UK. English. an. $12.18. John Offord Publications, PO Box Eastbourne, East Sussex BN21 3LW England. Tel 0323 645871. Ed Cathy Itzin. LC PN2595. DD 792.029541. adv acc. Circ 2,000. Comprehensive guide to UK fringe and alternative theatre.

THE BRITISH ART & ANTIQUES YEARBOOK. 1978-. UK. English. an. $9.96. National Magazine House, 72 Broadwick Street, London W1V 2BP England. Tel 01-439-7144. Ed David Coombs. LC N8630. DD 380.1457002541. adv acc. Directory of approximately 5,000 antique and fine art dealers, auctioneers, restorers, etc. Throughout the British Isles indexed by speciality place and business name plus expert market analyses. *British Antiques Yearbook.*

THE BRITISH CLOTHING INDUSTRY YEAR BOOK. 5th Ed. (1978)-. UK. English. an. The Kemps Group, Federation House/2309 Coventry Road, Sheldon Birmingham B26 3PG England. LC HD9940.G78. DD 687.029441. *Clothing Export Council of Great Britain's Directory for the Clothing Industry.*

BRITISH COLUMBIA CHURCH DIRECTORY. 1971-. 0315-3282. CN. English. an. $3.95. BC Church Directory, Box 82011, Burnaby British Columbia V5C 5P2 Canada. DD 270.025711.

BRITISH COLUMBIA CONSTRUCTION & RESOURCE INDUSTRIES DIRECTORY, PURCHASING GUIDE. VFOAT British Columbia Directory. 1981/82-. 0711-3544. CN. English. an. 20.00. British Columbia Construction Guide, c/o Sanford Evans Publications, 4411-208th Street, Langley British Columbia V3A 2H7 Canada. DD 338.47690025711. *British Columbia Construction Industry Directory, Purchasing Guide, 0228-6785.*

BRITISH COLUMBIA LEGAL TELEPHONE DIRECTORY. (THE BRITISH COLUMBIA LEGAL TELEPHONE DIRECTORY). 1954-. 0521-0585. Periodical. CN. English. an. Canada Law Book, 240 Edward Street, Aurora Ontario Canada L4G 3S9. DD 340.025711.

BRITISH COLUMBIA PLASTICS DIRECTORY. 1982-. 0714-3486. CN. English. an. $10.00. Society of the Plastics Industry of Canada, Suite 104/1262 Don Mills Road, Don Mills Ontario M3B 2W7 Canada. DD 338.476684025711.

BRITISH COUNTRY MUSIC ASSOCIATION YEARBOOK. (YEARBOOK - BRITISH COUNTRY MUSIC ASSOCIATION). 0308-4698. UK. English. an. 1.00. British Country Music Association, PO Box 2, Newton Abot TQ12 4HT England. LC ML21. DD 784.

BRITISH DEFENCE DIRECTORY. Vol. 1, No. 1 (Mar. 1982)-. 0272-4782. UK. English. qt. Pergamon Press, 395 Saw Mill River Road, Elmsford NY 10523. LC UA647. DD 354.41066025.

BRITISH DIRECTORY OF LITTLE MAGAZINES AND SMALL PRESSES. 1st- Ed. 0307-434X. UK. English. ir. 38 York Avenue West, Kirby Wirral, Merseyside L48 3JF England. LC Z6944.L5, PN5124.P4. DD 052.025.

BRITISH FARMER AND STOCK BREEDER. YEARBOOK AND FARM DIARY. UK. English. sm. Business Press International Ltd, Perrymount Road Haywards Heath, W Sussex RH163BR England.

THE BRITISH GOAT SOCIETY'S YEAR BOOK FOR . . . . Main/Corp British Goat Society. UK. English. an. 2.50. British Goat Society, Roughman Bury Street, Edmunds Suffolk England. Tel (0359)70351. Ed L Worthy. bk rev. adv acc. Circ 3,200. (ctrl). Wide range of articles on goatkeeping and related issues together with photographs of livestock.

BRITISH RATE & DATA DIRECTORIES AND ANNUALS. UK. English. MacLean-Hunter Ltd, 30 Old Burlington Street, WI London England. LC Z5771.4.G7. DD 016.05.

BRITISH STANDARDS YEARBOOK CEASED. Began in 1959. 0068-2578. UK. English. an.

BRITISH THEATRE DIRECTORY. 1972-. 0306-4107. UK. English. an. Vance-Offord (Publications) Ltd, 1 Susan Road, Eastbourne England. LC PN2595. DD 792.0942.

THE BRITISH WATER SUPPLY YEAR BOOK. UK. English. Wheatlands Journals, 157 Hagden Lane, WD1 8LW Watford England. LC TD257.A1. DD 3636.10942. *British Waterworks Year Book and Directory with Statistical Tables.*

BRITISH YEAR BOOK OF INTERNATIONAL LAW. (THE BRITISH YEAR BOOK OF INTERNATIONAL LAW). Vol. 1 (1920-21)-. 0068-2691. UK. English. an. $120.00. Oxford University Press, Journals Department, Walton Street, Oxford OX2 6BP England. Tel (0865)56767. Ed Ian Brownlie. Ind/Abst Leg. Resour. Index, Index Leg. Period., Curr. Law Index. LC JX21. DD 341.05. (cum index). bk rev. Contains surveys of decisions of British courts, the Court of Justice of the EEC, the European Convention on Human Rights on questions of international law.

B.R.M.N.A. MEMBERSHIP DIRECTORY. (THE B.R.M.N.A. MEMBERSHIP DIRECTORY . . .). Main/Corp British Railway Modellers of North America. VAT British Railway Modellers of North America Membership Directory. 0229-7973. CN. English. an. B.R.M.N.A. Membership Directory, c/o J Jarrett, 666 Island Park Drive, Ottawa Ontario K1Y 0B7 Canada. DD 625.1902571.

BROADCASTING, CABLECASTING YEARBOOK. (BROADCASTING CABLECASTING YEARBOOK). 1982-. 0732-7196. US. English. an. $65.00. Broadcasting Publications Inc, 1735 DeSales Street NW, Washington DC 20036. LC HE8689. DD 384.540973. *Broadcasting Cable Yearbook, 0277-3678.*

Yearbooks, Almanacs, Directories

BROADCASTING YEARBOOK ISSUE. Main/Corp Broadcasting. Telecasting. 1935-. Periodical. US. English. an. $85.00. Broadcasting Publishing Inc, 1735 De Sales Street NW, Washington DC 20036. Tel (202)638-1022. Ed Lawrence B Taishoff. bk rev. adv acc. Circ 20,000. (ctrl). Source for details, facts, and figures for radio, television, and cable TV.

BROMINE IN . . . . See Economics - Economics: Industry & Production.

BROWNING DIRECTORY OF CANADIAN BUSINESS INFORMATION. (THE BROWNING DIRECTORY OF CANADIAN BUSINESS INFORMATION). VFOAT Browning Directory . . . . 1984-. 0824-0647. CN. English. an. $150.00. Browning Associates, 105 Browning Avenue, Toronto Ontario M4K 1W2 Canada. DD 016.3380971.

BROWN'S DIRECTORY OF NORTH AMERICAN AND INTERNATIONAL GAS COMPANIES. 92nd- Ed. 0197-8098. US. English. an. $145.00. Harcourt Brace Jovanich Publications, 1 East First Street, Duluth MN 55802. Tel (218)723-9200. Ed Dean Hale. LC TP714. DD 338.7622338502573. adv acc. Circ 1,500. Brown's Directory of North American Gas Companies, 0068-2888.

BUFFALO EVENING NEWS OFFICE ALMANAC. 1976-. US. English. an. Buffalo Evening News, 1 News Plaza, Buffalo NY 14240. Buffalo Evening News Almanac and Fact Book.

BUILDER DIRECTORY, HONG KONG. VFOAT Hong Kong Builder Directory. English. ir. $85.00. Far East Trade Press, 1913 Hanglund Centre, Causeway Bay Hong Kong. LC TH13.2.H6. DD 690.0255125.

BUILDING BOARD DIRECTORY. 1st- Ed. UK. English. ir. $25.00. Benn Electronics Publishing Ltd, Suite 9 Delaport House 57 Guilford, Luton LU1 2NE England.

BUILDING MATERIALS DIRECTORY. Began in 1972. US. English. an. Underwriter's Laboratories Inc, 333 Pfingsten Road, Northbrook IL 60062. Building Materials List, 0503-177X.

BUKU PENUNTUN PERUSAHAAN NEGARA. Series/Tlit Statistik Keuangan & I.E. Dan Perbankan. VFOAT Directory of Public Enterprises. Periodical. IO. English (Indonesian). ir. $2.60. Biro Pusat Statistik, Jalan Dr Sumoto No 8, Jakarta Indonesia. Tel 372808. LC HD4303. DD 338.74025598.

BUKU TAHUNAN . . . PROPINSI SUMATERA UTARA. VFOAT Year Book . . . Province of North Sumatra. 1984-. English (text in Indonesian). an. Pt Saguna Karya Graha Publisher & Designer, Jl Sei Blutu I/8A, Medan Indonesia. LC DS646.15.S8. DD 959.81.

BULLETIN DE LIAISON : INVENTAIRE DESCRIPTIF DES UNITES DE RECHERCHE ET DE FORMATION EN SCIENCES SOCIALES, AMERIQUE LATINE. VFOAT Liaison Bulletin : Directory of Social Science Research and Training Units, Latin America. US. Multilingual (English and French). ir. $6.50. OECD Publications Center, 1750 Pennsylvania Avenue NW/Suite 1207, Washington DC 20006.

BUMIPUTRA TRADE DIRECTORY OF MALAYSIA CEASED. 1978-. MY. English (Malay). ir. Berita Publishers, 31 Jalan Riong, Kuala Lumpur Malaysia. LC HF3800.6.A48. DD 380.10294595.

BURMASS' TEX-OK-KAN OIL DIRECTORY. VFOAT Tex Ok Kan Oil Directory. 8755-1489. US. English. an. $20.00. Burmass Publishing Company Inc, PO Box 1768, Midland TX 79702. LC HD9567.T3. DD 681.76.

BURNS CHRONICLE AND CLUB DIRECTORY. VFOAT Burns Chronicle. 3rd Ser., V. 1 (1952)-3rd Ser. V. 24 (1975). UK. English. an. Burns Federation-Dick Institute, Elmbank Avenue, Kilmarnock Scotland. Tel (0563) 26801. Ed James A Markay. LC PR4329. DD 821.6. bk rev. adv acc. Circ 3,000. Articles on life and works of Burns. Scottish studies, lists of affiliated clubs, reports of their activities and of federation activities. Scots Chronicle.

BURRELLE'S BLACK MEDIA DIRECTORY. VFOAT Black Media Directory. 1983-84-. 0748-4259. US. English. $50.00. Burrelle's Media Directories, 75 East Northfield Road, Livingston NJ 07039. LC P94.5.A37. DD 001.5108996073.

BURRELLE'S DELAWARE, MARYLAND, VIRGINIA, DISTRICT OF COLUMBIA MEDIA DIRECTORY. (BURRELLE'S . . . DELAWARE, MARYLAND, VIRGINIA, DISTRICT OF COLUMBIA MEDIA DIRECTORY). VFOAT Delaware, Maryland, Virginia, District of Columbia Media Directory. 0883-9794. US. English. ir. Burrelle's Media Directories, 75 East Northfield Road, Livingston NJ 07039. DD 071.

BURRELLE'S HISPANIC MEDIA DIRECTORY. VFOAT Hispanic Media Directory. 0748-1020. US. English. Burrell's Media Directories, 75 East Northfield Road, Livingston NJ 07073. LC P88.8. DD 001.5108968.

BURRELLE'S PENNSYLVANIA MEDIA DIRECTORY. (BURRELLE'S . . . PENNSYLVANIA MEDIA DIRECTORY). VFOAT Pennsylvania Media Directory. 1981-. 0276-7872. US. English. an. New England Newsclip Agency, 5 Auburn Street, Framingham MA 01701. Tel (617) 879-4460. LC P88.8. DD 070.1025748.

BURRELLE'S WOMEN'S MEDIA DIRECTORY. VFOAT Women's Media Directory. 0748-4240. US. English. $50.00. Burrelle's Media Directories, 75 East Northfield Road, Livingston NJ 07039. LC P94.5.W652. DD 001.51088042.

BURROUGHS SOFTWARE DIRECTORY. Began in 1984. 0743-9555. US. English. ty. $98.00. Burrows World, 12416 Hymeadow Drive/Suite 2, Austin TX 78750-1896. DD 001.

BUS RIDE. BUS INDUSTRY DIRECTORY. (BUS RIDE : BUS INDUSTRY DIRECTORY). VFOAT Bus Industry Directory. 1965. 0363-3764. US. English. ir. Friendship Publications Inc, PO Box 1472, Spokane WA 99210. Tel (509)328-9181. Ed William A Luke. LC HE5623.A45. DD 388.32202573. bk rev. adv acc. Circ 12,500. (ctrl). Bus industry trade journal.

BUSINESS 1000 DIRECTORY. VAT Business One Thousand Directory. 1980-. 0194-2654. US. English. an. RSC Book Publishers, Division of Research Services Corporation, PO Drawer 16549, 5280 Trail Lake Drive, Ft Worth TX 76133. LC HG4057. DD 338.740973.

BUSINESS & STREET DIRECTORY FOR . . . ADELAIDE CITY & SUBURBS, INCLUDING ELIZABETH & SALISBURY. VFOAT Business and Street Directory for . . . Adelaide City and Suburbs, Including Elizabeth and Salisbury. English. an. Universal Business Directories Pty, 21 Wright Street, Adelaide Australia. LC HF5308.A3. DD 919.42310405. Universal Business Directory for Adelaide City & Suburbs.

BUSINESS & STREET DIRECTORY FOR PERTH CITY & SUBURBS. VFOAT Business and Street Directory for Perth City and Suburbs. English. an. Universal Business Directoires Pty Ltd, 20 Milford Street, East Victoria Park, Perth 6101 Australia. LC HF5293.P47. DD 919.4110405.

BUSINESS BROKERAGE DIRECTORY. No. 1-. 0277-9234. US. English. an. $30.00. National Business Clearinghouse, PO Box 327, Croton Plaza, Croton-on-Hudson NY 10520.

BUSINESS DIRECTORY. English. ir. Thai Chamber of Commerce, 150 Rajbopitre Road, Bangkok Thailand. LC HF3850.5. DD 380.1025593.

BUSINESS DIRECTORY. 1976-. English. ir. Interafrica Publishers, PO Box 75024, Narobi Kenya. LC HF3892. DD 380.102567.

BUSINESS DIRECTORY - COMMERCIAL AND INDUSTRIAL DEVELOPMENT CORPORATION OF OTTAWA-CARLETON. (BUSINESS DIRECTORY). VFOAT Annuaire du Commerce. Apr. 30, 1981-. 0711-6098. CN. English (summaries in French). be. $10.00. Commercial and Industrial Development Corporation of Ottawa-Carleton, 222 Queen Street/Suite 700, Ottawa Ontario K1P 5V9 Canada. DD 380.102571383. Business Directory, Regional Municipality of Ottawa-Carleton, 0708-0972.

A BUSINESS DIRECTORY FOR KANO STATE. V. 1- 1973-. English. ir. $1.00. Rota Publishing Company, Lagos Street, PO Box 497, Kaduna Nairobi. LC HF5278.N52. DD 381.0256695.

BUSINESS DIRECTORY - GUAM. DEPARTMENT OF COMMERCE. Main/Corp Guam. Department of Commerce. 1 -. 0072-7865. Periodical. GU. English. ir. Department of Commerce, Agana Guam 96910. LC HF5319.G8. DD 338.

THE BUSINESS DIRECTORY, KERALA. 1968-. English. ir. LC HC437.K4. DD 338.40255483.

BUSINESS DIRECTORY - NATIONAL FOOTBALL LEAGUE RETIRED PLAYERS ASSOCIATION (U.S.). Main/Corp National Football League Retired Players Association (U.S.). VFOAT NFLRPA Business Directory. Sept. 1984-. US. English. National Football League Retired Player Association, 1300 Connecticut Avenue NW, Washington DC 20036. LC GV955.5.N36. DD 796.3320922.

BUSINESS DIRECTORY OF HONG KONG. English. ir. Current Publications Company, GPO Box 9848, Hong Kong Hong Kong. LC HF3851. DD 338.40255125.

BUSINESS DIRECTORY - PASADENA CHAMBER OF COMMERCE. Main/Corp Pasadena Chamber of Commerce. US. English. $10.00. Pasadena Chamber of Commerce and Civic Association, 11 West Del Mar Boulevard/Suite 201, Pasadena CA 91105-2567. LC HF5068.P3. DD 338.7402579493.

BUSINESS FIRMS DIRECTORY OF THE DELAWARE VALLEY. 16th- Ed. 0091-2581. US. English. ir. $60.00. Greater Philadelphia Chamber of Commerce, 1346 Chestnut Street/Suite 800, Philadelphia PA 19107. Tel (215)545-1234. Ed Robert S Barr. LC HF5041. DD 380.1025749. adv acc. Circ 2,000. Business Firms List of Greater Philadelphia.

BUSINESS INSURANCE. DIRECTORY OF CORPORATE BUYERS OF INSURANCE, BENEFIT PLANS AND RISK MANAGEMENT SERVICES. VFOAT Directory of Corporate Buyers of Insurance, Benefit Plans and Risk Management Services. 1st Ed. (July 1983-). 0747-7937. US. English. $50.00. Business Insurance, 740 North Rush Street, Chicago IL 60611. Tel (312)649-5279. Ed Marilou C Jones. LC HG4057. DD 368.8100973. adv acc. Circ 1,500. Names, and titles of financial, insurnace and employee benefits executives for over 2,000 major corporations.

BUSINESS MINI/MICRO SOFTWARE DIRECTORY. VFOAT Business Mini Micro Software Directory. 1-. 0000-0809. US. English. $75.00. R R Bowker Company, PO Box 1807, Ann Arbor MI 48106.

BUSINESS ORGANIZATIONS AND AGENCIES DIRECTORY. 1st- Ed. 0749-0801. Periodical. US. English. ir. $245.00. Gale Research, Book Tower, Detroit MI 48226. Tel (313)961-2242. Ed A Kruzas. Entries are arranged in nearly 25 separate sections covering business organizations, agencies, association, trade centers, and offices that furnish up-to-date information in their special business-related fields.

BUSINESS REFERRAL DIRECTORY (GREATER SAN DIEGO CHAMBER OF COMMERCE). (BUSINESS REFERRAL DIRECTORY). 1982-. US. English. an. Greater San Diego Chamber of Commerce, 110 West C Street/Suite 1600, San Diego CA 92101. Business Directory (San Diego Chamber of Commerce).

BUSINESS TELEPHONE & EQUIPMENT DIRECTORY OF THE INTERCONNECT INDUSTRY. VFOAT NATA Business Telephone and Equipment Directory. VAT Business Telephone and Equipment Directory of the Interconnect Industry. 1979/80-. 0275-8903. US. English. North American Telephone Association Inc, 1030 15th Street/Suite 360, Washington DC 20005. LC HD9697.T453. DD 381.4562138502573.

BUSINESSMAN'S DIRECTORY, THE REPUBLIC OF CHINA. VFOAT Chung-Hua Min Kuo Kung Shang Chi Yeh Chih Nan. CH. chiefly in English. an. $25.00. Taiwan Enterprise Press Ltd, Box 73-4 Taipei 25 Foo Shou Street, Taipei 1135 Taiwan. LC HF5237.5. DD 380.102551249.

BUTCE GELIRLERI YLLG (TURKEY). Main/Corp Turkey. Gelirler Umum Mudurlugu. VFOAT Budget Revenues Yearbook. English and Turkish. ir. LC HJ75. Devlet Gelirleri Bulteni.

BUYER'S DIRECTORY OF SUPPLIERS FOR GENERAL MERCHANDISE BUYERS. (BUYER'S DIRECTORY OF SUPPLIERS). 0361-4247. US. English. $5.00. Lebhar-Friedman, 2 Park Avenue, New York NY 10016. LC HF1040.8. DD 380.102573.

Yearbooks, Almanacs, Directories

BUYERS' GUIDE & DEALER DIRECTORY. NORTHEASTERN AREA. (BUYERS' GUIDE & DEALER DIRECTORY : NORTHEASTERN AREA). **VAT** Buyer's Guide and Dealer Directory. Northeastern Area. No. 1- 1976/77-. 0145-5915. US. English. $10.00 Member, $15.00 Nonmembers. Lumber Co-Operator, 339 East Avenue, Rochester NY 14604. **Tel** (716)325-1626. Ed James E Dunbar. **LC** HD9753. **DD** 381.4568. adv acc. **Circ** 3,400. (ctrl). Designed to various segments of the building materials industry. Magazine for retailer and distributors serving the Northeast area. Trade publication.

BUYING DIRECTORY & WHO'S WHO. **VFOAT** Buying Directory and Who's Who. 0749-0550. US. English. an. American Firearms Industry Communications Group Inc, 2801 East Oakland Park Boulevard, Ft Lauderdale FL 33306. **LC** HD9743.U5. **DD** 381.4568340029473.

BYOIN YORAN. **VFOAT** Japanese Hospital Directory. Japanese. ir. 8500. Igaku Shoin, 24-3 Hongo - 5, Bunkyo-ku (113-91), Tokyo Japan. **LC** RA990.J3. **NLM** WX 22 JJ3 QB9.

C D A DIRECTORY CEASED. Main/Corp Canadian Dental Association. **VFOAT** Annuaire de l'A D C. 1976-1978. 0381-5706. CN. English (text in French). an. Canadian Dental Association, 234 St George Street, Toronto Ontario M5R 2P2 Canada. **DD** 617.6006271. *C D A Membership Directory*, 0317-1647.

C E A HANDBOOK. See Education (General) - School Organization and Administration.

CABELL'S DIRECTORY OF PUBLISHING OPPORTUNITIES IN EDUCATION. **VFOAT** Directory of Publishing Opportunities in Education. 1st Ed. (1984)-. US. English. Cabell Publishing Co, Box 7173, Tobe Hahn Station, Beaumont TX 77706. Ed David W E Cabell.

CABLE COMMUNICATIONS. ANNUAL DIRECTORY AND BUYERS' GUIDE. 1974-. CN. English. an. $6.00 Per Number. Cable Communications, 30 Bloor Street West, Toronto Ontario M4W 1A2 Canada. **DD** 384.65025. *Canadian Telephone and Cable Television Journal. Annual Directory and Buyers' Guide*.

CAD/CAM INDUSTRY DIRECTORY. **VFOAT** C.A.D./C.A.M. Industry Directory. **VAT** Computer Aided Design Computer Aided Manufacturing Industry Directory. 1983-. 0736-1823. US. English. ir. $35.00. Technical Database Corporation, PO Box 720, Concroe TX 77305. **Tel** (409)529-9688. Ed Philip C Flora. **LC** HD9696.C6. **DD** 629.8920294. **Circ** 5,000. Highly detailed, contains detailed specifications with information on: price, warranty, and delivery time, plus the name, address, and phone number of a knowledgeable company representative.

CALGARY, ALBERTA, CITY DIRECTORY. **VFOAT** Calgary City Directory, Henderson's Calgary City Directory. **VAT** Henderson's Calgary City Directory (1979). 1979-. 0226-000X. CN. English. an. 115.00. Henderson Directories, 100 East 4th Avenue, Vancouver British Columbia V5T 1G3 Canada. **DD** 917.1233. *Henderson's Calgary, Alberta, City Directory*, 0318-5702.

CALGARY & AREA AIRPORT BUSINESS DIRECTORY. **VFOAT** Calgary Airport Business Directory. **VAT** Calgary and Area Airport Business Directory, Calgary Airport Business Directory (1984). 1984-. 0823-8219. CN. English. an. 3.50 Each Copy. Calgary & Area Airport Business Directory, Suite 158 158/1224-53rd Avenue Northeast, Calgary Alberta T2E 7E2 Canada. **Tel** (403)275-9457. Ed Paul J Skinner. **DD** 387.736402571233. adv acc. **Circ** 7,000. (ctrl). Descriptive listings of all activities of all companies that provide services for aviation in the Calgary area. *Calgary Airport Business Directory*, 0227-1672.

CALGARY COMMUNITY SERVICES DIRECTORY. 0824-5444. CN. English. an. Aid Centre, 205 8th Avenue SE/3rd Floor, Calgary Alberta T2P 2M5 Canada. **DD** 361.002571233.

CALGARY EVANGELICAL DIRECTORY. 0228-9229. CN. English. an. $2.00 Per Issue. Christian Info, 1623-3rd Street North West, Calgary Alberta T2M 2X9 Canada. **DD** 280.02571233.

CALIFORNIA AGRICULTURAL DIRECTORY. 1965-. 0575-5298. US. English. an. California Service Agency, 1601 Exposition Boulevard, Sacramento CA 95815. **Tel** (916)924-4360. Ed Clark Biggs. **Circ** 1,000. (ctrl). Lists individuals, agencies, associations, cooperatives, and organizations concerned with California agriculture. *California Agriculture Cooperative Directory*.

CALIFORNIA AGRICULTURAL EXPORT DIRECTORY. 1982-1983-. Periodical. US. English. ir. California Crop and Livestock Reporting Service, PO Box 1258, Sacramento CA 95806. **Tel** (916)445-6076. Ed Mark Woerner. **LC** HD9007.C2. **DD** 630.294794. **Circ** 1,500. Agricultural products/service suppliers listed by business name and products supplied. Food and fiber products available from California, and over 1,300 suppliers, and 100 product lists included.

CALIFORNIA ALMANAC. 1984/85-. 0748-4402. US. English. $12.95. Presidio Press, 31 Pamaron Way, Novato CA 94947. **LC** HA261. **DD** 317.94.

CALIFORNIA AVOCADO SOCIETY YEARBOOK. **VFOAT** Yearbook - California Avocado Society. 0096-5960. US. English. an. California Avocado Society, PO Box 4816, Saticoy CA 93003. **LC** SB379.A9. **DD** 634.653032794.

CALIFORNIA COMMUNITY SERVICE CABLE DIRECTORY. 1984 Ed.-. 0743-0930. US. English. Foundation for Community Service Cable Television, 5616 Geary Boulevard/Suite 212, San Francisco CA 94121. **LC** TK6675. **DD** 384.5556025794.

CALIFORNIA ENVIRONMENTAL DIRECTORY. 2D- Ed. 0148-0324. US. English. ir. $18.50. California Institute of Public Affairs, PO Box 10, Claremont CA 91711. **Tel** (714)624-5212. **LC** HC107.C23. **DD** 301.3109794. Describes more than 1,300 agencies and citizens' groups. User's guide identifies groups interested in 40 broad subject categories. *California Environment Yearbook & Directory*, 0092-1343.

CALIFORNIA JOURNAL ALMANAC OF STATE GOVERNMENT AND POLITICS. **VFOAT** Almanac of State Government and Politics, California Almanac. 1st- Ed. 0190-969X. US. English. be. California Journal Press, 1714 Capitol Avenue, Sacramento CA 95814. **Tel** (916)444-2840. **LC** JK8701. **DD** 320.9794. **Circ** 6,000. Statistical and biographical information on California's elected and appointed officials, election data, population, education, finance, legislative districts lobbyists, press and much more.

THE CALIFORNIA LEGAL DIRECTORY. US. English. an. $20.53. Legal Directory Publishing Company, 2122 Kidwell Street, PO Box 140200, Dallas TX 75214. **Tel** (214)824-8092. **LC** KF192.C3. **DD** 340.025794. *Pacific Coast Legal Directory*.

CALIFORNIA LEGISLATIVE DIRECTORY AND REFERENCE GUIDE. US. English. Career Publishing Inc, Box 5486, Orange CA 92667. **LC** JK8730. **DD** 328.7940922.

CALIFORNIA LIBRARY DIRECTORY. 1983-. 0740-7688. US. English. an. **LC** Z732.C2. **DD** 027.0025794. *California Library Statistics and Directory*.

CALIFORNIA LIBRARY DIRECTORY. (CALIFORNIA LIBRARY DIRECTORY : LISTINGS FOR PUBLIC, ACADEMIC, SPECIAL, STATE AGENCY AND COUNTY LAW LIBRARIES). 1983-. US. English. an.

CALIFORNIA LIBRARY TRUSTEES DIRECTORY. 1984-. 8755-7711. US. English. an. **LC** Z681.5. **DD** 021.82025794. *California Public Library Trustees and Commissioners State Directory*, 0885-7938.

CALIFORNIA MINORITY BUSINESS ENTERPRISES DIRECTORY CEASED. Mar. 1976-Spring 1980. 0146-9010. US. English. an. Source Publications Inc, 1900 Powell Street/Suite 1145, Emeryville CA 94608. **LC** HD2346.U52. **DD** 338.6422025794.

CALIFORNIA PRIVATE POSTSECONDARY EDUCATION DIRECTORY. 1983-. US. English. an. $2.00. California State Department of Education, PO Box 271, Sacramento CA 95802. **LC** L903.C2. **DD** 378.794.

CALIFORNIA PRIVATE SCHOOL DIRECTORY. 0098-5147. US. English. an. $9.00. California State Department of Education, Box 271, Sacramento CA 95802. **Tel** (916)445-1260. **LC** L903.C2. **DD** 371.02025794.

CALIFORNIA PUBLIC LIBRARY OUTLET DIRECTORY. 1st Ed.-. US. English. an.

CALIFORNIA PUBLIC SCHOOL DIRECTORY. 1970-. 0068-5771. US. English. an. California State Department of Education, PO Box 271, Sacramento Ca 95802. **Tel** (916)445-1260. **LC** L903.C2. **DD** 371.01025794. *Directory of Administrative and Supervisory Personnel of California Public Schools*.

CALIFORNIA ZIP+4 STATE DIRECTORY. **VFOAT** Zip Plus Four State Directory. **VAT** California Zip Plus Four State Directory. 1985-. US. English. an. St Louis PDC Zip+4 State Directory Orders, PO Box 14921, St Louis MO 63180-9988.

CAMA ENCYCLOPEDIA; DIRECTORY & BUYERS GUIDE. 1967-. 0315-8462. Periodical. CN. English (includes some text in French). an. $8.00 Including 3 other issues of CAMA. Children's Apparel Manufacturers' Association, Suite 304/8235 Mountain Sights, Montreal Quebec H4P 2B4 Canada. **DD** 338.476871302571.

CAMERART PHOTO TRADE DIRECTORY. Periodical. JA. English. an. $32.00. Camerart Inc, Hinode Building 5-4/2-chome, Kyobashi Chuo-ku Tokyo Japan. **Tel** (03)563-4871. Ed Kunika Todoriki. adv acc. **Circ** 13,000. The source of information on the Japanese photography trade and industry for importers, exporters and dealers.

CAMEROON YEAR BOOK. English. ir. United Publishers, PO Box 200, Victoria Cameroon. **LC** DT561. **DD** 916.71103405.

CAMP DIRECTORY. 0383-0985. CN. English. an. Social Planning and Research Council of Hamilton and District 153, 1/2 King Street East, Hamilton Ontario L8N 1B1 Canada. **DD** 796.54220257135.

CAMPBELL RIVER DIRECTORY. **VFOAT** Official City Directory of Campbell River. 1965-. 0319-5058. CN. English. an. Home Supplement Ed. Free to Homes in Canvass Area. B C Directories, 100 East 4th Avenue, Vancouver British Columbia V5T 1G3 Canada. **DD** 917.1134.

CAMPGROUND & TRAILER PARK DIRECTORY. UNITED STATES, CANADA, MEXICO. **VFOAT** Campground and Trailer Park Directory. 1984-. US. English. an. $12.95. Rand McNally & Company Campground Publications, PO Box 728, Skokie IL 60076. *Rand McNally Campground and Trailer Park Guide: United States, Canada, Mexico*, 0272-0663.

CAMPING DIRECTORY - ONTARIO PRIVATE CAMPGROUND ASSOCIATION. (CAMPING DIRECTORY). Main/Corp Ontario Private Campground Association. 1981-. 0827-4223. CN. English. an. Ontario Private Campground Association, 55 Nugget Avenue/Suite 224, Scarsborough Ontario M1S 3L1 Canada. **DD** 796.542025713. *Camp . . . Ontario*, 0827-4231.

CANADA A-Z. (CANADA A-Z : OIL, GAS, MINING DIRECTORY). **VFOAT** Oil, Gas, Mining Directory. 1983/1984-. 0824-4766. CN. English. an. $70.00. Canadian Trade & Industry Publishing Group, PO Box 597 Station M, Calgary Alberta T2P Canada. **DD** 338.272802571.

CANADA CALENDAR. (DER CANADA CALENDER). First published in 1841. 0383-7947. CN. German. an. McLaren Micropublishing, PO Box 972 Station F, Toronto Ontario M4Y Canada. **DD** 053.1.

CANADA LEGAL DIRECTORY. 1911-. 0315-8322. CN. English. an. Canada Legal Directory, 120 Eglinton Avenue East 7th Floor, Toronto Ontario M4P 1H1 Canada. **Tel** (416)488-0755. Ed R A Wharton. **DD** 340.02571. adv acc. (ctrl). Lists practicing lawyers and court officials plus synopsis and comparisons of law.

CANADA MISSION DIRECTORY. 0714-2358. CN. English. be. $4.00 Per Vol. Canada Mission Directory, c/o Christian Information, 1623-3rd Street West, Calgary Alberta T2M 2X9 Canada. **DD** 266.002571.

CANADA NORTH ALMANAC. V. 1 - V. 3. 0319-583X. Periodical. CN. English. Mr D Wood, PO Box 188 Professional Building, Yellowknife Northwest Territories X0E 1H0 Canada. **LC** F1090.5. **DD** 971.90305.

Yearbooks, Almanacs, Directories

CANADA SKI DIRECTORY. 1981/82-. 0713-6757. CN. English. an. $3.95 Per Vol. Canada Ski Directory, 2065 West 4th Avenue, Vancouver British Columbia V6J 1N3 Canada. **DD** 796.9302571.

CANADA WATER YEAR BOOK. 1975-. 0708-4285. CN. English. ir. Receiver General for Canada, Supply & Services Canada, Ottawa Ontario K1A 0S9 Canada. **LC** GB707. **DD** 333.9100971.

CANADA YEARBOOK. (CANADA YEAR BOOK). 1905-. 0068-8142. CN. English. be. $6.00. Statistics Canada, Publication Distribution, Ottawa Ontario K1A 0T6 Canada. **LC** HA744. **DD** 317.1. **NLM** HA 744 S81. *The Statistical Yearbook of Canada.*

CANADIAN ALMANAC & DIRECTORY. 101st- Year. 0068-8193. Periodical. CN. English. an. $64.00. Gale Research Company, Book Tower, Detroit MI 48226. **Tel** (313)961-2242. **Ed** S Bracken. **DD** 971.0025. The standard authoritative reference enables users to answer virtually any question on Canada, either directly from the book itself or from any of the thousands of bodies listed in its directory. *Canadian Almanac and Legal and Court Directory, 0316-277X.*

CANADIAN ANTIQUES & ART DEALERS YEARBOOK. VFOAT Antiques & Art, Canadian Dealers Yearbook. 1979/80-. 0709-809X. CN. English. an. $2.95 Per No. Left Bank Publications, 2227 Granville Street, Vancouver British Columbia V6H 3G1 Canada. **DD** 381.45745102571.

CANADIAN ARCHITECT YEARBOOK. (THE CANADIAN ARCHITECT YEARBOOK). 1964-. 0068-8231. Periodical. CN. English. an. Southam Communications Ltd, 1450 Don Mills Road, Don Mills Ontario M3B 1X2 Canada. **Tel** (403)269-3161. **DD** 720.971.

CANADIAN CONSERVATION DIRECTORY. VFOAT Guide de la Conservation du Canada. 1973-. 0318-2789. Periodical. CN. Multilingual (French). ir. Canadian Nature Federation, 75 Albert Street/Suite 203, Ottawa Ontario K1P 6G1 Canada. **Tel** (613)238-6154. **Ed** Christine van Zwamen. **LC** QH77.C2. **DD** 333.7206271. adv acc. **Circ** 5,000. A guide to governmental and non-governmental organizations in the environmental field in Canada.

CANADIAN CONSTRUCTION PRODUCT DIRECTORY CEASED. 1974-1980. 0316-6376. Periodical. CN. English. an. $48.00 Per Vol. Canadian construction Product Directory/Hume Publishing, Suite 400/150 Consumers Road, Willowdale Ontario M2J 1P9 Canada. **LC** TH13.2.C2. **DD** 620.029471.

CANADIAN DIRECTORY OF AWARDS FOR GRADUATE STUDY. VFOAT Awards for Graduate Study, Repertoire Canadien des Bourses d'Etudes Superieures. 1981-. 0711-8635. CN. English (French). be. 11.00 Domestic, 12.00 US, 13.00 Others. Association Universities and Colleges of Canada, 151 Slater, Ottawa Ontario K1P 5N1 Canada. **Tel** (613)563-1236. **Ed** Kimberley Allen. **LC** LB2338. **DD** 378.402571. **Circ** 2,000. A detailed reference guide to sources of financial aid and proves to be an invaluable tool to both Canadian and foreign students planning to pursue a master's or doctoral program. *Awards for Graduate Study and Research, 0576-6311.*

CANADIAN DIRECTORY OF INDUSTRIAL DISTRIBUTORS. 1979/80-. 0708-7241. CN. English. an. $49.00 Per Number. **DD** 381.456702571. *Manufacturers' Distributor Directory.*

CANADIAN DIRECTORY OF SHOPPING CENTRES. 0822-7799. CN. English. an. 196.00. Canadian Directory of Shopping Centres, 777 Bay Street MacLean Hunter Building, Toronto Ontario M5W 1A7 Canada. **Tel** (416)596-5939. **Ed** Jaimie Hubbard. **DD** 381.102571. Includes owner/developer, list of tenants, number of stores, sizes, rents and common area costs.

CANADIAN DIRECTORY TO FOUNDATIONS AND OTHER GRANTING AGENCIES. (A CANADIAN DIRECTORY TO FOUNDATIONS AND OTHER GRANTING AGENCIES). VAT Canadian Directory to Foundations and Granting Agencies. 3rd Ed. (1973)-. 0820-7682. CN. English. ir. 32.50. A Canadian Directory to Foundations and Other Granting Agencies, c/o Canadian Centre for Philanthropy, 185 Bay Street/Suite 504, Toronto Ontario M5J 1K6 Canada. **Ed** Allan Arlett and Ingrid van Rotterdam. **DD** 001.4402571. bk rev. **Circ** 4,000. Gives comprehensive information on all Canadian foundations and American foundations granting in Canada. *Canadian Universities' Guide to Foundations and Granting Agencies, 0820-7674.*

CANADIAN FARM & HOME ALMANAC. VFOAT Canadian Farm and Home Almanac. VAT Canadian Farm and Home Almanac. Began in 1978. 0704-9412. US. English. an. $1.75 Single Issue. Paperjacks Ltd, 330 Steelcase Road East, Markham Ontario L3R 2M1 Canada. **LC** AY413. **DD** 051. *Farm & Home Almanach, 0317-1124.*

CANADIAN FILM DIGEST YEARBOOK. -1972/73. 0820-6031. CN. English. an. $16.25. Canadian Film Digest, 950 Yonge Street/Suite 501, Toronto Ontario M4W 2J4 Canada. **Tel** (416)961-4581. **Ed** Patricia Thompson. **LC** PN1993.5.C2. **DD** 338.47791430971. adv acc. Comprehensive reference volume relating to exhibition, production, distribution, television, video, awards, and allied areas. Includes a directory of members of unions and guilds. *Year Book, Canadian Entertainment Industry, 0513-5141.*

CANADIAN FILM DIGEST YEARBOOK. (YEARBOOK). VFOAT Canadian Film Digest. 1977-. 0316-5515. CN. English. an. **DD** 338.4779143029571. *Year Book of Exhibition, Distribution and the Most Comprehensive Collection of Data ever Assembled on Canadian Film Production, 0820-6023; Canadian Professional Film Directory, 0382-8603.*

CANADIAN FINANCIAL E-Z DIRECTORY CEASED. VFOAT E-Z Telephone Directory. 1st-18th Ed. 0380-2221. CN. English. an. Canadian Dairy Quotation Service, Box 100 Terminal A, Toronto Ontario M5W 1A7 Canada. **DD** 332.102571.

CANADIAN FISHERIES AND OCEAN INDUSTRIES DIRECTORY. (THE CANADIAN FISHERIES AND OCEAN INDUSTRIES DIRECTORY). No. 1-. 0710-7641. Periodical. CN. English. be. $55.00 Per No. Maritime Ocean Resources Ltd, PO Box 2101 Station M, Halifax Nova Scotia B3J 3B7 Canada. **DD** 338.3727002571.

CANADIAN FISHING AND MARINE DIRECTORY. (THE CANADIAN FISHING AND MARINE DIRECTORY). No. 1-. 0710-2399. CN. English. an. $30.00 Per Vol. Canadian Fishing Report, Gough Communications Ltd, PO Box 818 Station B, Ottawa Ontario K1P 5P9 Canada. **DD** 338.3727002571.

CANADIAN FLORIST GREENHOUSE AND NURSERY DIRECTORY, HORTICULTURAL AND BUYER'S GUIDE. VFOAT Canadian Florist Directory and Horticultural Guide. Periodical. CN. English. an.

CANADIAN FOLK FESTIVAL DIRECTORY. 1984-. 0827-2492. Periodical. CN. English. an. Free. Canadian Folk Festival Directory, 1314 Shelbourne Street West, Calgary Alberta T3C 2K8 Canada. **DD** 780.7971.

CANADIAN FURNITURE & FURNISHINGS DIRECTORY. (CANADIAN FURNITURE AND FURNISHINGS DIRECTORY). 0826-6204. CN. English. an. 27.00 Domestic, $45.00 Foreign. Sentinel Business Publications, Unit 8 6420 Victoria Avenue, Montreal Quebec H3W 2S7 Canada. **Tel** (514)731-3523. **Ed** Carole Clifford. **DD** 338.47684102571. adv acc. **Circ** 7,412. (ctrl). Comprehensive listings by product category of suppliers to the furniture and home furnishings industries. *Lloyd's Canadian Furniture and Furnishings Directory, 0068-8789.*

CANADIAN GAS ASSOCIATION. MANUFACTURERS' PRODUCT DIRECTORY. (MANUFACTURERS' PRODUCT DIRECTORY). VFOAT Manufacturers' Directory. VAT Canadian Gas Association. Manufacturers' Directory (1970). 1969/70-. 0703-5934. Periodical. CN. English. be. Free. Canadian Gas Association, 55 Scarsdale Road, Don Mills Ontario M3B 2R3 Canada. **DD** 338.47665702571. *Manufacturers Directory, 0068-8797.*

CANADIAN HORSESHOE PITCHERS YEAR BOOK. No. 1- 1977-. 0703-7074. CN. English. an. $3.50 Per No. E H Murray, Canadian Horseshoe Pitchers Year Book, Delmas Saskatchewan S0M 0P0 Canada. **DD** 796.2405.

CANADIAN HOSPITAL DIRECTORY. VFOAT Annuaire des Hopitaux du Canada. V. 1- 1953-. 0068-8932. Periodical. CN. English (French). an. $46.43. Canadian Hospital Association, 17 York Street, Suite 100, Ottawa Ontario K1N 9J6 Canada. **Tel** (613)238-8005. **Ed** Eleanor Sawyer. **DD** 362.1102571. **NLM** WX 22 DC2 C2. bk rev. adv acc. **Circ** 4,500. Lists over 1,200 hospitals, health centers and nursing stations, 1,000 companies who manufacture or distribute to health, a statistical compendium, bed distribution tables, etc.

CANADIAN HOTEL & RESTAURANT. SOURCES DIRECTORY. VFOAT Foodservice & Lodging Directory. 1974-. CN. English. an. MacLean Hunter, Circulation & Accounting Department, PO Box 100 Station A, Toronto Ontario M5W 1A7 Canada. **DD** 338.47647941028. *Canadian Hotel & Restaurant. Annual Directory Issue.*

CANADIAN HUMAN RIGHTS YEARBOOK. VFOAT Annuaire Canadien des Droits de la Personne. 1983-. 0824-5266. CN. French (text also in English). an. **DD** 323.405.

CANADIAN INDUSTRY SHOWS AND EXHIBITIONS. VFOAT Canada's Directory of Convention & Meeting Facilities. 1965-. 0068-8967. CN. English. an. $19.87. MacLean Hunter/ Circulation/ Accounting Department, PO Box 100 Station A, Toronto Ontario M5W 1A7 Canada. **DD** 607.3471.

CANADIAN INSURANCE CLAIMS DIRECTORY. Began with 1933 issue. 0318-0352. Periodical. CN. English. an. University of Toronto Press, Front Campus, Toronto Ontario M5S 1A6 CN. **DD** 368.01402571.

CANADIAN INTERCONNECT DIRECTORY. (THE CANADIAN INTERCONNECT DIRECTORY). Oct. 1981-. 0828-0150. CN. English. an. $35.00 Per Vol. Northern Business Information, 287 MacPherson Avenue, Toronto Ontario M5V 1A4 Canada. **DD** 384.06571.

CANADIAN ISBN AGENCY. (CANADIAN ISBN PUBLISHERS' DIRECTORY). VFOAT Repertoire des Prefixes ISBN des Editeurs Canadiens. VAT Canadian International Standard Book Number Publisher's Directory. Jan. 1981-. 0228-8753. CN. English (text also in French). an. National Library of Canada, Public Relations Office, 395 Wellington Street, Ottawa Ontario K1A 0N4 Canada. **LC** Z485. **DD** 070.502571.

CANADIAN KEY BUSINESS DIRECTORY. 0315-0879. Periodical. CN. English. ir. Duns Marketing Services, 3 Century Drive Attn M Berger, Parsippany NJ 07054. **Tel** (800)526-0651. **Ed** Dun and Bradstreet Canada. **LC** HF3223. **DD** 338.002571. Two-volume directory with information on the top 14,000 top Canadian establishments. also, includes 60,000 executives, officers and managers' names, their titles, and job functions.

CANADIAN MEDICAL DIRECTORY. 1st- 1955-. 0068-9203. Periodical. CN. English. an. Secombe House, 443 Mount Pleasant Road, Toronto Ontario Canada. **DD** 610.695202571. **NLM** W 22 DC2 C22.

CANADIAN MINERALS YEARBOOK. Series/Titl Mineral Report. 1962-. 0068-9270. CN. English. an. Energy Mines and Resources Canada Minerals, 1 Observatory Cresent, Ottawa Ontario Canada K1A 0E4. **DD** 338.20971. *Canadian Mineral Industry, 0382-2443.*

CANADIAN MINES HANDBOOK. See Engineering - Mining Engineering.

CANADIAN MUSIC INDUSTRY DIRECTORY. 1st- 1965-. 0068-9335. Periodical. CN. English. an. RPM Music Publications Ltd, 6 Brentcliffe Road, Toronto Ontario M4G 3Y2 Canada. **DD** 780.65.

CANADIAN OIL INDUSTRY DIRECTORY. 1st- Ed. 0195-590X. US. English. an. $35.00. Pennwell Publishing Company, Box 1260, Tulsa OK 74101. **Tel** (918)835-3161. **Ed** William R Leek Jr. **LC** HD9574.C2. **DD** 338.2728202571. adv acc. **Circ** 2,000.

CANADIAN OPERA COMPANY. (CANADIAN OPERA COMPANY : YEARBOOK). 1980/81-. 0710-2666. CN. English. an. $5.00 Per No. Controlled Media Communications, 43 Madison Avenue, Toronto Ontario M5R 2S2 Canada. **DD** 782.105.

CANADIAN PALLIATIVE CARE DIRECTORY. (THE CANADIAN PALLIATIVE CARE DIRECTORY). 1983-. 0715-9471. Periodical. CN. English. ir. $12.00 Canada, $15.00 Foreign.

Yearbooks, Almanacs, Directories

Palliative Care Foundation, 228 Bloor Street West, Toronto Ontario M5S 1V8 Canada. **DD** 362.17502571.

CANADIAN PLASTICS DIRECTORY & BUYER'S GUIDE. **VFOAT** Plastics Directory. 1971/72-. 0068-9459. Periodical. CN. English. an. 25.00. Southam Communications Ltd, 1450 Don Mills Road, Don Mills Ontario M3B 2X7 Canada. **Tel** (416)445-6641. **Ed** Judith Nancekivell. **DD** 338.47668402571. adv acc. **Circ** 11,000. (ctrl). Annual directory of Canadian plastics processors, raw material suppliers, equipment suppliers, moldmakers and consultants. 0554-2944.

CANADIAN PLASTICS STATISTICAL YEAR BOOK. **VFOAT** Canadian Plastics Industry. 1981-. 0828-5810. Periodical. CN. English. an. $35.00 Per Vol. Society Of The Plastics Industry Of Canada, Suite 104/ 1262 Don Mills Road, Don Mills Ontario M3B 2W7 Canada. **DD** 338.4766840971.

CANADIAN PORTS AND SEAWAY DIRECTORY. 19th-. Ed. 0068-9467. CN. English. an. $21.63. Southam Communications Ltd, 1450 Don Mills Road, Don Mills Ontario M3B 1X2 Canada. **Tel** (416)445-6641. **DD** 387.002571. Canadian Ports and Shipping Directory, 0381-8241.

CANADIAN PROFESSIONAL REAL ESTATE DIRECTORY FOR THE PROVINCE OF BRITISH COLUMBIA. 1979-. 0709-0757. CN. English. an. $6. Per No. **DD** 333.33025711.

CANADIAN RODEO NEWS. (CANADIAN RODEO NEWS. YEARBOOK). 1968-. 0317-7785. Periodical. CN. English. Canadian Rodeo Cowboys' Association, 315 A 36th Avenue SE, Calgary Alberta T2H 1W1 Canada. **DD** 791.8. Reference Yearbook, 0317-7777.

CANADIAN SOLAR DIRECTORY. **VFOAT** Annuaire de l'Energie Solaire au Canada. 1983-. 0823-0226. CN. English (text also in French). an. $4.00 Per Volume. Solar Energy Society of Canada, 303-870 Cambridge Street, Winnipeg Manitoba R3M 3H5 Canada. **DD** 338.476214702571. SESCI Canadian Solar Directory, 0710-1384.

CANADIAN SPORTS ALMANAC AND DIRECTORY. (THE CANADIAN SPORTS ALMANAC AND DIRECTORY). 1974-. 0317-9702. Periodical. CN. English. an. Copp Clark, 35 Ames Circle, Don Mills Ontario M3B 3B9 Canada. **DD** 796.02571.

CANADIAN TOURIST ASSOCIATION MEMBERSHIP DIRECTORY. **VFOAT** Annuaire de l'Association Canadienne du Tourisme. 1st- 1964-. 0576-6281. Periodical. CN. English. Canadian Tourist Association, Suite 1704, 8 King Street East, Toronto Ontario M5C 1B7 Canada. **DD** 338.4791710406271.

CANADIAN WELDER AND FABRICATOR. DIRECTORY AND BUYERS' GUIDE. Began with 1961 issue. CN. English. an. Sanford Evans Communications Ltd, PO Box 6900/1077 St James Street, Winnipeg Manitoba R3C 3B1 Canada. **DD** 338.4767152028. Provides a comprehensive listing of products and supplies available for all welding and fabrications operations. Includes complete lists of names and addresses for manufacturers and distributors.

CANADIAN YEARBOOK OF INTERNATIONAL LAW. (THE CANADIAN YEARBOOK OF INTERNATIONAL LAW). **VFOAT** Annuaire Canadien de Droit International. V. 1- 1963-. 0069-0058. Periodical. CN. text in English and French. an. University of British Columbia Press, 6344 Memorial Road/Suite 303, Vancouver British Columbia VT6 1W5 Canada. **Tel** (604)228-3259. **Ed** C B Bourne. **Ind/Abst** Leg. Resour. Index, Index Leg. Period., Curr. Law Index. **LC** JX21. **DD** 341.05. bk rev. **Circ** 1,000. An authoritative annual survey of important and topical issues in international law including recent legal and policy changes of countries and of multinational organizations.

THE CANDY BUYERS' DIRECTORY. US. English. an. $25.00. Manufacturing Confectioner Publishing, 175 Rock Road, Glen Rock NJ 07452. **LC** TX784.

CANSIM. CANADIAN SOCIO-ECONOMIC INFORMATION MANAGEMENT SYSTEM. MINI BASE SERIE DIRECTORY. (CANSIM, CANADIAN SOCIO-ECONOMIC INFORMATION MANAGEMENT SYSTEM. MINI BASE SERIES DIRECTORY). **VFOAT** Canadian Socio-Economic Information Management System. **VAT** Canadian Socio-Economic Information Management System. Mini Base Series Directory. 1977-. 0706-0831. CN. English. ir. Receiver General for Canada, Statistics Canada Publications, Ottawa Ontario K1A 0T6 Canada. **Tel** (613)992-3155. **LC** HA741. **DD** 016.3171. Provides detailed information on the data contained in the CANSIM Mini Base. For each series, the series title, start date, source of data and other descriptive material are provided.

CAPITAL REGION CREATIVE SERVICES DIRECTORY. (THE CAPITAL REGION CREATIVE SERVICES DIRECTORY). **VFOAT** Directory. 1983-. 0822-918X. CN. English. an. $15.00 Per Volume. Local Association of Media Professionals, PO Box 220/Station A, Ottawa Ontario K1P 6C4 Canada. **DD** 700.29471384. Creative Services Directory, 0822-9171.

CAPT. LILLIE'S BRITISH COLUMBIA COAST GUIDE AND RADIOTELEPHONE DIRECTORY. **VFOAT** Capt. Lillie's British Columbia, Puget Sound & S.E. Alaska Coast Guide and Radiotelephone Directory. **VAT** Capt. Lillie's British Columbia, Puget Sound & S.E. Alaska Coast Guide and Radiotelephone Directory (1984). 24th (1983/84 Ed.)-. 0822-9481. CN. English. be. $14.00 Per Volume. Captain Lillie's British Columbia Coast Guide and Radiotelephone Directory, C-310 Marine Building/355 Burrard Street, Vancouver British Columbia V6C 2G6 Canada. **LC** WMLC L 83/272. **DD** 623.89229711. Capt. Lillie's Coast Guide and Radiotelephone Directory, 0318-3742.

CAPT. LILLIE'S COAST GUIDE AND RADIOTELEPHONE DIRECTORY CEASED. **VFOAT** Capt. Lillie's British Columbia, Puget Sound & S. E. Alaska Coast Guide and Radiotelephone Directory. 1st-23rd Ed. 0318-3742. Periodical. CN. English. be. **LC** WMLC L 83/272. **DD** 623.894.

CAR-PUTER'S NEW CAR YEARBOOK. (NEW CAR YEARBOOK). 0160-6883. Periodical. US. English. an. $1.50. 229 Park Avenue South, New York NY 10003. **LC** TL5. **DD** 629.222205.

CARAVAN CAMPING DIRECTORY. 0162-2803. AT. English. ir. 151 Clarence Street, Sydeny New South Wales Australia. **LC** GV191.48.A8. **DD** 647.9494.

THE CARDINAL YEARBOOK. **VFOAT** Whole University Catalogue. 0098-2598. US. English. an. Catholic University of America, 620 Michigan Avenue NE, Washington DC 20064. **LC** LD817. **DD** 378.753.

CAREER SCHOOL DIRECTORY. Began with 1973 Vol. 0278-1034. US. English. an. EDFAC Publishing Company, 2211 Broadway, Pekin IN 61554.

CARIBBEAN AMERICAN DIRECTORY. 0275-2883. Periodical. US. English. an. Cooper Lang Communications, 600 New Hampshire Avenue NW/Suite 812, Washington DC 20037.

CARIBBEAN ECONOMIC ALMANAC. 1962-. 0069-0481. Periodical. English. ir. **Ed** Max b Ifill. **LC** WMLC L 82/262.

CARIBBEAN YEAR BOOK. (THE CARIBBEAN YEAR BOOK). 48th- Ed. 0705-2731. CN. English. an. Caribook Ltd, 1255 Yonge Street, Toronto Ontario MT4 1W6 Canada. **LC** F2131. **DD** 972.9005. **NLM** F 1601 W517. West Indies & Caribbean Year Book, 0083-8233.

THE CARIBBEAN YEARBOOK OF INTERNATIONAL RELATIONS. 1975-. NE. English. ir. Sijthoff & Noordhoof, International Publishers BV, PO Box 4, Alphen an der Rijn Leyden Netherlands. **Ed** L F Manigat. **LC** F2155. **DD** 327.09729.

CARIBBEAN/AMERICAN DIRECTORY. 1983-84-. 0275-2883. US. English. an. $100.00. Caribbean/American Directory, 1377 K Street NW/Suite 663, Washington DC 20005. **Tel** (202)547-8024. **Ed** Herbert L Cooper. **LC** HG4093. **DD** 338.8897301821025. bk rev. adv acc. **Circ** 2,000. Listings of 4,500 American business organizations with activities throughout the Caribbean basin. Includes SIC personnel country operations and contact identification.

CARMICHAEL'S ANNUAL FRANCHISE DIRECTORY. 0164-0208. US. English. an. $9.95. Carmichael Associates Inc, 287 Lexington Avenue, Jersey City NJ 07304. **LC** HF5429.3. **DD** 381.

CAROLINAS GENEALOGICAL SOCIETY YEARBOOK. 0363-1826. US. English. an. 306 South Thompson Street, Monroe NC 28110. **LC** F253. **DD** 929.109756.

CASSELL AND PUBLISHERS ASSOCIATION DIRECTORY OF PUBLISHING IN GREAT BRITAIN, THE COMMONWEALTH, IRELAND, SOUTH AFRICA & PAKISTAN. **VFOAT** Directory of Publishing in Great Britain, the Commonwealth, Ireland, South Africa & Pakistan. 9th Ed. UK. English. be. Holt Saunders Ltd, 1 St Annes Road, Eastbourne East Sussex BN21 3UN England. Index in last issue of volume - attached. Cassell's Directory of Publishing in Great Britain, The Commonwealth, Ireland, South Africa and Pakistan, 0308-7018.

CATHOLIC ALMANAC. 65th- 1969-. 0069-1208. US. English. an. $13.95. Our Sunday Visitor, PO Box 920, Huntington IN 46750. **Tel** (219)356-8400. **Ed** Felician Foy and Rose Avato. **LC** AY81.R6. **DD** 282. bk rev. adv acc. Only single volume encyclopedic annual reference on Catholic church. National Catholic Almanac.

CATHOLIC DIRECTORY. RH. English. ir. Mambo Press, Senga Road, PO Box 779, Gwelo Rhodesia. **LC** BX1682.R5. **DD** 282.0256891. Catholic Directory of Rhodesia.

CATHOLIC DIRECTORY FOR SCOTLAND. (THE CATHOLIC DIRECTORY FOR SCOTLAND). 0306-5677. UK. English. an. J S Burns, 25 Finlas Street, Glasgow G22 5DS Scotland. **LC** BX1497.A3. **DD** 282.02541. Catholic Directory for the Clergy and Laity in Scotland, 0069-1232.

THE CATHOLIC DIRECTORY OF ENGLAND AND WALES. **VFOAT** Catholic Directory. UK. English. an. The Universe, 18 Crosby Road North, Waterloo Liverpool L22 4QF England. **LC** BX1491.A1. **DD** 282.42025. Catholic Directory.

CATHOLIC HOSPITAL ASSOCIATION OF CANADA DIRECTORY CEASED. **VFOAT** Annuaire de l'Association des Hopitaux Catholiques du Canada. Began with 1968 issue. 0380-8475. CN. English (French). an. Catholic Hospital Association of Canada, 312 Daly Street, Ottawa Ontario K1N 6G7 Canada. **DD** 362.1106271.

CATHOLIC PRESS DIRECTORY. 1923-. 0008-8307. US. English. an. $25.00. Catholic Press Association, 119 North Park Avenue, Rockville Centre NY 11570. **Tel** (516)766-3400. **Ed** Regina Salzmann. **LC** Z6951. **DD** 071.3. adv acc. **Circ** 2,200. (ctrl). A reference book for the Catholic press and members of the Catholic Press Association.

CATV DIRECTORY OF EQUIPMENT, SERVICES, & MANUFACTURERS. US. English. $6.95. Communications Publishing Corporation, 1900 West Yale, Englewood CO 80110. **LC** TK6675. **DD** 384.5547.

C.A.T.V. SYSTEMS DIRECTORY, MAY SERVICE & HANDBOOK. (CATV SYSTEMS DIRECTORY, MAP SERVICE & HANDBOOK). 0091-1984. US. English. $8.95. Communications Publishing Corporation, 1900 West Yale, Englewood CO 80110. **LC** TK6675. **DD** 384.55.

CB YEARBOOK. **VAT** Citizens Band Yearbook. 0270-5052. US. English. an. $1.75. Davis Publications Inc, 380 Lexington Avenue, New York NY 10017. **LC** TK6570.C5. **DD** 621.3845405.

C.B.A. ANUARIO. (CBA; ANUARIO). **VFOAT** CBA Anuario. **VAT** Comentarios Bibliograficos Americanos. 0301-6579. UY. Spanish. ir. CBA Annual Edition, CBA Casilla de Correo 1677, Montevideo Uruguay. **LC** Z1601.

CDE STOCK OWNERSHIP DIRECTORY. AGRIBUSINESS. (CDE STOCK OWNERSHIP DIRECTORY : AGRIBUSINESS). **Main/Corp** Corporate Data Exchange, Inc. **Series/Titl** CDE Stock Ownership Series. **VFOAT** Stock Ownership Directory: Agribusiness. **VAT** Corporate Data Exchange Stock Ownership Directory: Agribusiness. 1976-. 0277-5646. US. English. $75.00 Individuals and non-profit organizations, $250.00 Corporations. CDE, Room 707, 198 Broadway, New York NY 10038. **LC** HD9003. **DD** 338.740973.

CDE STOCK OWNERSHIP DIRECTORY : BANKING & FINANCE. **Series/Titl** CDE Stock Ownership Series. **VFOAT** C.D.E. Stock Ownership Directory. **VAT** Corporate Data Exchange Stock Ownership Directory. Banking and Finance. 1980-. 0197-0313. US. English. be.

Yearbooks, Almanacs, Directories

$250.00 Profit Institutions, $75.00 Nonprofit Institutions. Corporate Data Exchange Inc, 198 Broadway/7th Floor, New York NY 10038. **LC** HG65. **DD** 332.10973.

CDE STOCK OWNERSHIP DIRECTORY: ENERGY. (CDE STOCK OWNERSHIP DIRECTORY : ENERGY). **Series/Titl** CDE Stock Ownership Series. **VFOAT** C.D.E. Stock Ownership Directory. **VAT** Corporate Data Exchange Stock Ownership Directory: Energy. 1980-. 0197-0321. US. English. ir. $75.00. 198 Broadway 7th Floor, New York NY 10038. **LC** HD9502.U5. **DD** 338.76210420973.

CDE STOCK OWNERSHIP DIRECTORY : FORTUNE 500. **Series/Titl** CDE Stock Ownership Series. **VFOAT** Fortune 500. **VAT** Corporate Data Exchange Stock Ownership Directory. Fortune Five Hundred. 1981-. 0276-7775. US. English. be. Corporate Data Exchange Inc, 198 Broadway 7th Floor, New York NY 10038. **LC** HG4057. **DD** 338.740973.

CDE STOCK OWNERSHIP DIRECTORY : TRANSPORTATION INDUSTRY. **Main/Corp** Corporate Data Exchange, Inc. **Series/Titl** CDE Stock Ownership Series. **VFOAT** Stock Ownership Directory: Transportation Industry. 1976-. 0162-8275. US. English. Room 707, 198 Broadway, New York NY 10038. **LC** HE196.5. **DD** 338.76138050973.

CED DIRECTORY OF ENGINEERING AND ENGINEERING TECHNOLOGY CO-OP PROGRAMS. **VFOAT** Directory of Engineering and Engineering Technology CO-OP Programs. 1983-. US. English. be. $20.00. Mississippi State University Cooperative Education Program, PO Box M, Mississippi State MS 39762. **Tel** (601)325-3823. **Ed** Luther Epting. **Circ** 300. (ctrl). A directory of educational institutions offering engineering and engineering technology cooperative education programs with pertinent data included.

CENTRAL AFRICA . . . BUSINESS DIRECTORY. 27th Issue (1982)-. English. an. $20.00. B & T Directories Ltd, PO Box 1027, Bulawayo Zimbabwe. **LC** HC501. **DD** 380.1029467. *Directory of Central Africa.*

CENTRAL AFRICAN CHAMBER OF COMMERCE AND INDUSTRY DIRECTORY. **VFOAT** Annuaire des Chambres de Commerce et d'Industrie d'Afrique Centrale. 1st Ed.-. English (French and Spanish). an. Panaf, BP 1439, Douala Cameroon. **LC** HF3909.A48. **DD** 382.025.

CENTRAL CONFERENCE OF AMERICAN RABBIS ANNUAL CONVENTION. **VFOAT** Central Conference of American Rabbis Yearbook. 0069-1607. US. English. an. $17.50. Central Conference of American Rabbis, 21 East 40th Street, New York NY 10016. **Tel** (212)684-4990. **Ed** Elliot Stevens. **Circ** 1,350. Substantial, indexed reference on reform thought including the annual summary of proceedings of the Central Conference of American Rabbi's Convention, conferences, papers and addresses.

CENTRAL ONTARIO CONSTRUCTION INDUSTRY DIRECTORY, PURCHASING GUIDE. (CENTRAL ONTARIO CONSTRUCTION INDUSTRY DIRECTORY/ PURCHASING GUIDE). **VAT** Annual Central Ontario Construction Industry Directory, Purchasing Guide. 1978-. 0704-7436. CN. English. an. $4.00 Per No. Directory Division, Sanford Evans Publishing Ltd, 1077 Sainte-James Street, PO Box 6900, Winnipeg Manitoba R3C 3B1 Canada. **DD** 338.476900257137.

CERTIFIED PROTECTION PROFESSIONAL DIRECTORY. 0734-9114. US. English. an. American Society for Industrial Security, 2000 K Street NW/Suite 651, Washington DC 20006. **LC** HV8290. **DD** 363.28902573.

CERTIFIED SEED DIRECTORY. Winter 1979-. US. English. sa. *Directory (Indiana Crop Improvement Association).*

CHAEMI HANGUK KWAHAK KISUL KINUNG INSA CHONGNAM. **VFOAT** Directory. 0749-128X. US. English (Korean). Korean Scientists and Engineers Association in America Inc, 6261 Executive Boulevard, Rockville MD 20852. **LC** Q145.

CHAGRIN VALLEY DIRECTORY. 0749-6834. US. English. an. Chagrin Valley Chamber of Commerce, 13 1/2 North Franklin Street, PO Box 225, Chagrin Falls OH 44022. **LC** F499.C33. **DD** 977.1310025.

CHAMBER OF COMMERCE MEMBERSHIP DIRECTORY AND BUYER'S GUIDE (NEW ORLEANS). (MEMBERSHIP DIRECTORY AND BUYER'S GUIDE). **Main/Corp** Chamber of Commerce of the New Orleans Area. 0093-3783. US. English. an. $25.00. Windsor Publications, 301 Camp Street, New Orleans LA 70130. **LC** HF296. **DD** 380.102576335.

CHAMBERS OF COMMERCE DIRECTORY, ZIMBABWE. **Main/Corp** Associated Chambers of Commerce of Zimbabwe. 1981-. English. ir. Associated Chambers of Commerce of Zimbabwe, Equity House/Rezonde Street, Salisbury Rhodesia. **LC** HF336.Z54. **DD** 380.10256891.

CHAMBER'S TRADE DIRECTORY. 1976-. English. ir. Chamber of Commerce and Industry, Aiwan-E-Tijarat Road, PO Box No 4158, Karachi-2 Pakistan. **LC** HF5240.5.K35. **DD** 380.10255491. *Trade Directory.*

CHAMPIONSHIP WRESTLING YEARBOOK. 0364-2526. US. English. an. $2.00. Capital Wrestling, PO Box 557, Newark NJ 07101. **LC** GV1198.12.A2. **DD** 796.81205.

CHAO CHI SHIH CHANG SHIH PIN PAI HUO TSAI KOU NIEN CHIEN. **VFOAT** Modern Super Market Operation and Almanac. 1981-1982-. Chinese. an. $1,900.00. Chao Chi Chu Pan She, PO Box 8-198, Tai-Pei Shin China. **LC** HF5469.23.T28. **DD** 658.8780951249.

CHARITABLE TRUST DIRECTORY, OFFICE OF ATTORNEY GENERAL (WASHINGTON STATE)). **Main/Corp** Washington (State). Office of the Attorney General. 0148-3188. US. English. $3.00. Office of the Attorney General, Temple of Justice, Olympia WA 98504. **Tel** (206)753-6299. **Ed** Jeanette Dieckman. **LC** HV98.W3. **DD** 361.76025797. **Circ** 500. Brief description of registered organizations and sample grants. *Directory of Charitable Organizations and Trusts Registered with the Office of Attorney General (Olympia), 0093-6693.*

CHARTER FLIGHT DIRECTORY. **VFOAT** Jens Jurgen's Charter Flight Directory. 0147-4030. US. English. an. $3.95. Travel Information Bureau, PO Box 105, Kings Park NY 11754. **LC** HE9803.A2. **DD** 387.742.

CHARTERED BANKS & TRUST COMPANIES, SAVINGS BRANCHES, TELEPHONE DIRECTORY, METRO TORONTO & VICINITY. (CHARTERED BANKS & TRUST COMPANIES (SAVINGS BRANCHES) TELEPHONE DIRECTORY, METRO TORONTO & VICINITY). **VAT** Chartered Banks and Trust Companies, Savings Branches, Telephone Directory, Metro Toronto & Vicinity. 0822-5354. CN. English. Chartered Banks & Trust Companies (Savings Branches) Telephone Directory Metro Toronto & Vicinity, 60 Gervais Drive, Don Mills Ontario M3C 1Z3 Canada. **DD** 332.12025713541. *Chartered Banks & Trust Companies Telephone Directory, Metro Toronto & Vicinity, 0822-5346.*

CHASE ALMANAC & FACT BOOK CEASED. **VFOAT** Dr. A. W. Chase's Almanac and Fact Book. 1969-1981. 0316-747X. CN. English. an. A W Chase Corporation, PO Box 4444, Pointe Claire Quebec H9R 4R1 Canada. **DD** 051. *Dr A W Chase's Almanac, 0316-7488.*

CHASE ALMANAC. CANADIAN EDITION. (THE CHASE ALMANAC). 1982-. 0227-0900. CN. English. an. $0.25 Per No. Chase Almanac, c/o A W Chase, PO Box 4444, Pointe Claire Quebec H9R 4R1 Canada. **DD** 051. *Chase Almanac & Fact Book, 0316-747X.*

CHATHAM INDUSTRIAL DIRECTORY. 1980/81-. 0229-6004. CN. English. an. Economic Development Department, Box 640, Chatham Ontario N7M 5K8 Canada. **DD** 338.022571333. *Industrial & Services Directory, 0229-5997.*

CHATTANOOGA AND TRI-STATE AREA DIRECTORY OF MANUFACTURERS. **VFOAT** Manufacturers Directory, Chattanooga and Tri-State Area. 0160-4716. US. English. $10.00. 819 Broad Street, Chattanooga TN 37402. **LC** T12. **DD** 338.4767102576882.

THE CHEMICAL NEW PRODUCT DIRECTORY. Jan. 1976/July 1977-. 0160-6360. Periodical. US. English. 402 Border Road, Concord MA 01742. **LC** HD9650.3. **DD** 381.4566002573.

CHEMISCH JAARBOEK. **VFOAT** Kncv Chemisch Jaarboek. NE. Dutch. an. 29,50. Secretariat en Ledenadministratie KNCV, Burnierstraat L Postbus 90163, Den Haag 2509 Netherlands. **LC** QD1. *Chemisch Jaarboekje.*

CHEMIST & DRUGGIST DIRECTORY AND TABLET & CAPSULE IDENTIFICATION GUIDE. **VFOAT** Chemist and Druggist Directory and Tablet and Capsule Identification Guide. Began with Vol. for 1972. Periodical. UK. English. an. $61.30. Benn Business Information Services Ltd, PO Box 20 Sovereign Way, Tonbridge Kent TN9 1RQ England. **Tel** (0732) 362666. **Ed** John Hedges. **LC** HD9667.3. **DD** 615.1029441. adv acc. **Circ** 2,600. The directory of the pharmaceutical, drug, essential oil and cosmetic industries of the United Kingdon including the unique tablet and capsule identification guide. *Chemist and Druggist Tablet and Capsule Identification Guide, Chemist and Druggist Yearbook.*

CHESA TONGGYE YONBO. **VFOAT** Year Book of Raw Silk Statistics. KO. English (Korean). mo. Hanguk Saengsa Suchul Chohap, 1-426 Youido-dong, Yongdungpo-ku, Seoul South Korea. **LC** HD9926.K6. **DD** 338.47677391095195.

CHICAGO, COOK COUNTY, AND ILLINOIS INDUSTRIAL DIRECTORY. **VFOAT** Big Green Book. Ceased with 28th Ed. (1983). 0069-3251. US. English. an. $82.25. National Publishing Corporation, 2720 Des Plaines Avenue, Des Plaines IL 60018. **Tel** (312)297-5115. **LC** HC107.I3. **DD** 338.0029477311.

THE CHICAGO CREATIVE DIRECTORY. 0193-7596. US. English. $15.00. Creative Directory Inc, 33 North Michigan Avenue/ Suite 311, Chicago IL 60601. **LC** PN1993.5.U74. **DD** 384.5502577311.

CHICAGO GEOGRAPHIC EDITION OF THE ILLINOIS MANUFACTURERS DIRECTORY. 1985-. 0748-8548. US. English. an. $59.95. Manufacturers' News, 4 East Huron Street, Chicago IL 60611. **LC** T12. **DD** 670.2577311. *Chicago Geographic Zip-Coded Edition of the Illinois Manufacturers Directory, 0069-3383.*

CHICAGO GEOGRAPHIC ZIP-CODED EDITION OF THE ILLINOIS MANUFACTURERS DIRECTORY. 0069-3383. US. English. be. $59.95. Manufacturers News Inc, 4 East Huron Street, Chicago IL 60611. **Tel** (312)337-1084. **LC** T12. **DD** 338.767025773.

CHIEF COUNSEL OFFICE DIRECTORY (INTERNAL REVENUE SERVICE). **Main/Corp** United States. Internal Revenue Service. Office of the Chief Counsel. 0882-9926. US. English. sa. Internal Revenue Service, Office of the Chief Counsel, Washington DC 20224.

CHILDREN'S LITERARY ALMANAC. 1973-. 0093-0431. US. English. be. $6.95. G Kurian Reference Books, Box 154, Pelham NY 10803. **LC** PN1009.A1. **DD** 809.89282.

CHILTON'S JEWELERS' CIRCULAR/ KEYSTONE THE GREAT ALL IN ONE DIRECTORY. **VFOAT** Jewelers' Circular-Keystone Directory, Jewelers' Directory. **VAT** Chilton's Jewelers' Circular Keystone The Great All in One Directory. 1980-. 0886-1382. US. English. an. Chilton Company, Chilton Way, Radnor PA 19089. **Ind/Abst** Trade Ind. Index. **LC** TS720. **DD** 739.2702573. *Chilton's Jewelers' Circular/Keystone Directory.*

CHINA COAL INDUSTRY YEARBOOK. **VFOAT** Chung-Kuo Mei Tan Kung Yeh Nien Chien. 1982-. English. ir. $40.00. Economic Information & Agency, 342 Hennessy Road, Hong Kong. **Tel** 5-738217. **LC** TN809.C47. **DD** 338.27240951. bk rev. adv acc. **Circ** 1,500. Past, present and future development of China's coal industry with statistics support.

THE CHINA DIRECTORY OF INDUSTRY AND COMMERCE, AND ECONOMIC ANNUAL. 1982-. 0734-1725. US. English (Chinese). ir. Van Nostrand Reinhold, 5211 NE Sandy, Portland OR 97213. **Tel** (503)288-1255. **LC** HF3833. **DD** 382.029451.

Yearbooks, Almanacs, Directories

CHINA PHONE BOOK & ADDRESS DIRECTORY. (THE CHINA PHONE BOOK & ADDRESS DIRECTORY). VFOAT China Phone Book and Address Directory, Chung-kuo Tien Hua Pu. Began with 1978. 0250-4170. English (Chinese). an. $43.00. Tradelinks International Trade, 8119 NE 131st Street, Kirkland WA 98034. **Tel** (206)821-0774. **NLM** TK 6011 C536. adv acc. **Circ** 15,000. 616 page bi lingual reference listing address, phone, telex and cable numbers of the Chinese and foreign enterprises in China. Indispensable to anyone involved in China.

CHINA YEARBOOK CEASED. 1937/43-1980. CH. English. an. **LC** DS777.53. **DD** 915.1. **NLM** DS 701 C537.

CHINESE DIRECTORY & TELEPHONE BOOK. MANITOBA. WINNIPEG AND VICINITY. (CHINESE DIRECTORY & TELEPHONE BOOK, MANITOBA, WINNIPEG AND VICINITY). VFOAT Manitoba Chinese Directory & Telephone Book. V. 23- 1974/75-. 0316-716X. Periodical. CN. English (includes some text in Chinese). an. Chinese Publicity Bureau Ltd, 459 East Hastings Street, Vancouver British Columbia V6A 1P5 Canada. **DD** 971.27004951. *Chinese Directory and Telephone Book, Winnipeg and Vicinity, 0316-7178.*

CHINESE DIRECTORY, ONTARIO. VFOAT Ontario Chinese Directory. VAT NE, NW & SW Ontario Chinese Directory. 0711-3072. CN. English (includes some text in Chinese). Chinese Publicity Bureau, 459 East Hastings Street, Vancouver V6A 1P5 British Columbia Canada. **DD** 971.3004951025.

CHINESE YEARBOOK OF INTERNATIONAL LAW AND AFFAIRS. VFOAT Chinese Yearbook. Vol. 1 (1981)-. 0731-0854. US. English. an. $7.00. Oprscas Inc, 500 West Baltimore Street, Baltimore MD 21201. **LC** JX18. **DD** 341.05. *Annals of the Chinese Society of International Law.*

CHINHAE SANGGONG MYONGGAM. VFOAT Jinhae Business Directory. KO. Korean. ir. Chinhae Saggong Hoeuiso, 2-1 Kwangwha-dong, Chinhae-si Korea. **LC** HF5258.C47.

CHINOOK REGIONAL LIBRARY DIRECTORY. 1977-. 0705-2480. CN. English. an. Free. Chinook Regional Library, 1240 Chaplin Street West, Swift Current Saskkatchewan S9H 0G8 Canada. **DD** 027.402571243.

CHOLTO TONGGYE YONBO. VFOAT Statistical Yearbook of Railroad. Korean (English). ir. **LC** HE3360.5. **DD** 385.095195.

CHONGI KONGSAOP TONGGYE CHARYO. VFOAT Electrical Construction Statistics Yearbook. English. ir. Hanguk Chongi Kongsa Hyophoe, 533-2 Tungchon-dong Kangso-ku, Seoul Korea. **LC** HD9695.K82.

CHRISTIAN DIRECTORY. VFOAT Christian Thailand Directory. English (Thai). ir. 15.00. Suthep Chaviwan, PO Box 1405, Bangkok Thailand. **LC** BR1195. **DD** 275.93025.

CHRISTIAN INFO DIRECTORY. 1984/85-. CN. English. an. Christian Information Directory, #206-602 16 Avenue NW, Calgary Alberta T2M Canada. **DD** 280.02571233. *Calgary Evangelical Directory.*

CHUNG-HUA MIN KUO CHI CHI YU TIEN KUNG CHI TSAI NIEN CHIEN. VFOAT R.O.C. Machinery & Electrical Apparatus Industry Year Book. chiefly Chinese. ir. $40.00. World Enterprise, 247 San Ming Road Section 3, Tai-Chung China. **LC** HD9705.T3.

CHUNG-HUA MIN KUO CHING CHI NIEN CHIEN. VFOAT Economic Yearbook of the Republic of China. CH. chiefly Chinese. ir. $1,000.00 Single Issue. Ching Chi Jih Pao She Tsung Ching Hsias Nien Chung Chu Pan Shih yen Kung Ssu, 555 Chunghsian East Road, Section 4, Tai-pei Taiwan 105 Republic of China.

CHUNG-HUA MIN KUO ... LAN I NIEN CHIEN. VFOAT Lan I Nien Chien. 1983-. CH. Chinese. an. $600.00. Lan Hua Shih Chien Tsa Chih SHe, 138 Lo-Ssu-Fu Road, 3 Section Fourth Floor, Tai-Pei Shih Taiwan. **LC** SB409.A1. **DD** 635.94150951249.

CHUNG-KUO CHU KOU SHANG PIN HUI PIEN. VFOAT Directory of China's Export Commodities. Chinese (English). ir. $15.00. Wen Wei Po, 197-199 Wanchai Road, Hsiang-Kang Honk Kong.

CHUNG-KUO CHU PAN NIEN CHIEN. VFOAT Zhongguo Chuban Nianjian. 1980-. CC. Chinese. an. 8.00. Hsin Hua Shu Tien, Pei-Ching Fa Hsing So, Peking China.

CHUNG-KUO HO TSO NIEN PAO. VFOAT Co-Operative Yearbook Republic of China. CH. Chinese (English). ir. Chung-Kuo Ho Tso Shih Yeh Hsieh Hui, No 11-2 Fu-Chow Street, Taipei Taiwan. **LC** HD3092.

CHUNG-KUO TUI WAI CHING CHI MAO I NIEN CHIEN. VFOAT Almanac of China's Foreign Economic Relations and Trade, The Editorial Board of the Almanac of China's Foreign Economic Relations and Trade. 1984-. Chinese (English). an. Joint Publishing Company/Hong Kong Branch, 9 Queen Victoria Street, Central District Hong Kong.

THE CHURCH OF ENGLAND YEAR BOOK. 88th (1971-72)-. UK. English. an. Church House Publishing, Church House Westminster/Great Smith Street, London SW1P 3NZ England. **Tel** (01)222 9011. **Ed** Jo Linzey. adv acc. **Circ** 3,000. Official yearbook of the Church of England containing detailed information on dioceses throughout the Anglican communion with an extensive who's who and list of organisations. *Church of England Year Book.*

CHURCH RESOURCE DIRECTORY. US. English. an. Keener Marketing Inc, 124 East Main, Dayton TN 37321. **LC** TS2301.C5. **DD** 202.9473.

CIC'S SCHOOL DIRECTORY. ALABAMA. Began with 1978/79?. 0162-9646. US. English. an. $32.00. Curriculum Information Center, Box 510, Westport CT 06881.

CIC'S SCHOOL DIRECTORY. ARKANSAS. VFOAT Arkansas. VAT Curriculum Information Center's School Directory. Began with: school year 1978/1979. 0162-9646. US. English. an. $32.00. Curriculum Information Center, Box 510, Westport CT 06881. *School Universe Data Book. Library Edition, 0146-4329.*

CIC'S SCHOOL DIRECTORY. DISTRICT OF COLUMBIA. VFOAT C.I.C.'s School Directory. 0162-9646. US. English. an. Market Data Retrieval Inc, Ketchum Place, Westport CT 06880. **LC** L903.W27. **DD** 375.00025753.

CIC'S SCHOOL DIRECTORY. FLORIDA. VFOAT Florida. VAT Curriculum Information Center School Directory. Florida. 0162-9646. US. English. an. $32.00. Curriculum Information Center, Box 510, Westport CT 06881.

CIC'S SCHOOL DIRECTORY. IDAHO. VFOAT Idaho. US. English. an. Market Data Retrieval Inc, Ketchum Place, Westport CT 06880.

CIC'S SCHOOL DIRECTORY. INDIANA. US. English. an. Curriculum Information Center Inc, Ketchum Place, Westport CT 06880.

CIC'S SCHOOL DIRECTORY. MASSACHUSETTS. VFOAT Massachusetts. 0162-9646. Monographic Series. US. English. an. Market Data Retrieval Inc, Ketchum Place, Westport CT 06880.

CIC'S SCHOOL DIRECTORY. MINNESOTA. VFOAT Minnesota. US. English. an. Market Data Retrieval Inc, Ketchum Place, Westport CT 06880.

CIC'S SCHOOL DIRECTORY. MISSISSIPPI. VFOAT Mississippi. US. English. an. Market Data Retrieval Inc, Ketchum Place, Westport CT 06880.

CIC'S SCHOOL DIRECTORY. NORTH CAROLINA. VFOAT C.I.C.'s School Directory. 0162-9646. US. English. an. Curriculum Information Center, Box 510, Westport CT 16881.

CIC'S SCHOOL DIRECTORY. PENNSYLVANIA. 0162-9646. US. English. an. $38.00. Curriculum Information Center, Ketchum Place, Westport CT 06880.

CIC'S SCHOOL DIRECTORY. VIRGINIA. VFOAT Virginia. 0743-8222. US. English. an. $32.00. Curriculum Information Center, Box 510, Westport CT 06881. **LC** L903.V8. **DD** 370.9755.

CIC'S SCHOOL DIRECTORY. WISCONSIN. Periodical. US. English. an. Curriculum Information Center, Box 510, Westport CT 06881.

CIM DIRECTORY. Main/Corp Canadian Institute of Mining and Metallurgy. VAT Canadian Institute of Mining and Metallurgy Directory. V. 2- 1968-. 0068-9009. CN. English. an. 90.00 US. Canadian Institute of Mining & Metallurgy, 1130 Sherbrooke Street West/Suite 400, Montreal Quebec H3A 2M8 Canada. **Tel** (514)842-3461. **Ed** P Michaud. **Ind/Abst** Coal Abstr. adv acc. **Circ** 13,000. (ctrl). The directory reviews institute activities for the previous year, lists all current members, and carries special feature articles.

CITIZENS MEDIA DIRECTORY. April 1977-. 0363-843X. US. English. an. Telecommunications Research & Action Center, PO Box 12038, Washington DC 20005. **Tel** (202)466-8407. **LC** P88.8. **DD** 301.1602573.

CITY ALMANAC. V. 1- Jan. 1966-. 0009-7683. Periodical. US. English. qt. $24.00. New School for Social Research, 66 Fifth Avenue, New York NY 10011. **Tel** (212)741-5956. **Ed** Marilyn Rubin and Arley Bondarin. **Ind/Abst** Public Aff. Inf. Serv. Bull., Avery Index Archit. Period. **DD** 323, 11. **Circ** 1,000. Each issue usually focuses from different perspectives on an economic or social questions of particular relevance to New York City and urban areas generally.

THE CITY AND COUNTRY AMERICAN ELSEWHEN ALMANAC. 0147-6270. US. English. Pyramid Communications Inc, 919 Third Avenue, New York NY 10022.

CITY AND REGIONAL MAGAZINE DIRECTORY. 1977-. 0192-5040. US. English. an. $19.95. Conference Management Corporation, 500 Summer Street, Stamford CT 06901. **LC** Z6951, PN4877. **DD** 051.

CITY OF COTE SAINT-LUC HOUSEHOLDER'S DIRECTORY. VFOAT City of Cote Saint-Luc Annuaires des Residents. 1973-. 0318-2339. Periodical. CN. English and French. J Lovell, 423 rue St Nicolas, Montreal Quebec H2Y 2P4 Canada. **DD** 917.14281.

CITY OF TORONTO INDUSTRIAL DIRECTORY. Aug. 1984-. 0828-6280. CN. English. an. City of Toronto Industrial Directory, c/o Planning and Development Department, Economic Development Division, 18th Floor/East Tower City Hall, Toronto Ontario M5H 2N2 Canada. **DD** 338.0025713541.

CIVIL RIGHTS DIRECTORY. Series/Titl Clearinghouse Publication. 0360-1587. US. English. US Commission on Civil Rights, Washington DC 20425. **LC** KF4755, JC599.U45. **DD** 323.40973 S.

THE CIVIL SERVICE YEAR BOOK. 1974-. UK. English. ir. $19.92. Her Majestys Stationery Office, PO Box 276, London SW8 5DT England. **Tel** 01-622 3316. **LC** JN106. **DD** 354.42. *British Imperial Calendar and Civil Service List.*

CIVIL WAR COLLECTOR'S DEALER DIRECTORY. (THE CIVIL WAR COLLECTORS' DEALER DIRECTORY). Series/Titl The Military Collectors' Dealer Directory Series. 1st- Ed. 0094-1182. US. English. C L Batson, 10453 Medina Road, Richmond VA 23235. **LC** NK1127. **DD** 745.102573.

CIVITAS; JAHRBUCH FUR SOZIALWISSENSCHAFTEN. V. 1-. 0529-8695. German. ir. Matthias Grunewald Verlag, Bischofs Platz 6, D65 Mainz West Germany. **LC** HN37.C3.

CLA HANDBOOK AND MEMBERSHIP DIRECTORY. Main/Corp Catholic Library Association. US. English. ir. $35.00. Catholic Library Association, 461 Lancaster Avenue, Haverford PA 19041. **Tel** (215)649-5251. **Ed** John T Corrigan. **DD** 020.622. adv acc. **Circ** 3,000. (ctrl). Each issue focuses on a specific area of current concern to the library/information community.

CLARK'S DIRECTORY OF SOUTHERN HOSPITALS. 0069-4428. US. English. ir. $33.50. Clark Publishing Co, PO Box 88, Greenville SC 29602. **Tel** (404)955-5656. **Ed** Jeanine Glinski. **LC** RA977. **DD** 362.1102575. adv acc. **Circ** 4,000. Directory of (16 Southeastern states) hospitals, number of beds, key personnel and titles, average daily census; number of outpatient visits.

CLARK'S DIRECTORY OF SOUTHERN TEXTILE MILLS. US. English. an. $18.00. Clarks Publishing, PO Box 88, Greenville SC 29602. **Tel** (404)955-5656. **Ed** Jeanine Glinski. adv acc. **Circ** 2,000. Southern Textile Mill Directory list names,

Yearbooks, Almanacs, Directories

personnel, titles, products manufactured and, phone numbers.

CLASS DIRECTORY - HARVARD. 1913. (CLASS DIRECTORY). Main/Corp Harvard University. Class of 1913. 0092-122X. US. English. Harvard University(Class 1913), 79 Garden Street, Cambridge MA 02138. LC LD2147 1913B. DD 378.7444.

THE CLASSIC MG YEARBOOK. Began with Vol. for 1973. 0098-2741. US. English. an. $13.95. R L Knudson, 21 Franklin Street, Oneonta NY 13820. LC TL215.M2. DD 629.2222.

CLASSIFIED BUSINESS DIRECTORY OF THE STATE OF CONNECTICUT. VFOAT State Of Connecticut Classified Business Directory. 1957/58-. 0529-908X. US. English. an. $45.95. Connecticut Directory Inc, 400 Main Street, Stamford CT 06901. Tel (203)324-1222. Ed H Lisbon. LC HF5065.C8. adv acc. Classified business directory of Connecticut contains sales, purchasing, and marketing information.

CLASSIFIED DIRECTORY (NIAGARA FALLS, N.Y.). (CLASSIFIED DIRECTORY). Began in 1980. 0743-8419. US. English. an. $97.00. Niagara Directory Publishing Inc, MPO Box 1440, Niagara Falls NY 14302. Ed Joan Alalouf. LC HF5035. DD 381.029473. adv acc. Circ 100,000. (ctrl). Contains a cross section of businesses from coast to coast. Also a general interest reference section. Electronic database will be available free to computer users in 1986. *NDPI Classified Directory.*

CLASSIFIED DIRECTORY OF MEMBERS - LAHORE CHAMBER OF COMMERCE & INDUSTRY. Main/Corp Lahore Chamber of Commerce & Industry. English. ir. Lahore Chamber of Commerce and Industry, 11 Race Course Road, Lahore Pakistan. LC HF5240.5.L33. DD 380.1062549143.

CLASSIFIED DIRECTORY OF WISCONSIN MANUFACTURERS. 1st-Ed. 0069-4525. US. English. an. Manufacturers News Inc, 4 East Huron Street, Chicago IL 60611. Tel (312)337-1084. LC T12. DD 670.25775. Lists 8,700 manufacturers and processors. List 5 sections: alphabetical, geographical, by product, SIC and computer.

CLASSIFIED TRADE DIRECTORY OF MEMBERS (LEEDS CHAMBER OF COMMERCE). Main/Corp Leeds, England. Chamber of Commerce. 19 -. UK. English. mo. Leeds Chamber of Commerce & Industry, Commerce House, 2 St Albans Place, Wade Lane, Leeds LS2 8HZ England.

CLASSROOM COMPUTER LEARNING DIRECTORY OF EDUCATIONAL COMPUTING RESOURCES. Vol. 4, No. 1 (Fall 1983-84)-. Periodical. US. English. bm. Classroom Computer Learning, 19 Davis Drive, Belmont CA 94002. Tel (415)592-7810.

CLE DIRECTORY OF THE IRISH BOOK TRADE. VFOAT Directory of the Irish Book Trade. 1983-. English. ir. 12.00. Irish Book Publisher's Association, 65 Middle Abbey Street, Dublin 1 Ireland. LC Z331.5. DD 070.5025415.

CLEVELAND EAST SUBURBAN DIRECTORY (CUYAHOGA COUNTY, OHIO). Periodical. US. English. ir. R L Polk, 6400 Monroe Boulevard, Box 500, Taylor MI 48180.

THE CLOTHING INSTITUTE YEAR BOOK & MEMBERSHIP REGISTER. (YEAR BOOK & MEMBERSHIP REGISTER - CLOTHING INSTITUTE). Main/Corp Clothing Institute. VAT Clothing Institute Year Book and Membership Register. 0307-8515. UK. English. an. Sterling Professional Publications Ltd, 86-88 Edgware Road, London N2 2HP England. LC HD9940.G78. DD 338.4768706241. *Annual Report and Year Book.*

CO-OP SOURCE DIRECTORY. (CO-OP SOURCE DIRECTORY : A PUBLICATION OF STANDARD RATE & DATA SERVICE, INC) Vol. 1 (1981)-. 0736-0878. Periodical. US. English. sa. Standard Rate & Data Service Inc, 5201 Old Orchard Road, Skokie IL 60077. LC HF5827.4. DD 659.102573.

CO-OPERATORS' YEAR BOOK. UK. English. mo. $265.00. Pasha Publications, 1401 Wilson Boulevard/Suite 910, Arlington VA 22209. Tel (703)528-1244. Ed D Gump and Harry Baisden. Monitors utility stock piles and burn on a plant by plant basis, consumption reports and predicts when new coalfired plants are coming on line.

COAST MARINE & TRANSPORTATION DIRECTORY. Periodical. US. English. an. $37.00. Pacific Shipper, 1139 Howard, San Francisco CA 94103. Tel (415)981-7171. Ed Barbera Krueger. adv acc. Circ 2,500. The directory has the most concise and accurate listing of the regional transportation markets on the West Coast including British Columbia, Hawaii and Alaska. *Pacific Coast Directory of Transportation.*

CODE NAME DIRECTORY. INTERNATIONAL. VFOAT International Code Name Directory. 3rd Ed. (1984)-. 0883-2803. US. English. an. DMS Inc, 100 Northfield Street, Greenwich CT 06830. *International Code Name Handbook : Aerospace, Defense, Technology.*

CODE NAME DIRECTORY. US. VFOAT US Code Name Directory. 12th Ed. (1984)-. 0882-7621. US. English. an. Defense Marketing Services, 100 Northfield Street, Greenwich CT 06830. *Code Name Handbook : Aerospace, Defense, Technology.*

COIN. A DIRECTORY OF COMPUTERIZED INFORMATION IN CANADA. (COIN, A DIRECTORY OF COMPUTERIZED INFORMATION IN CANADA). VFOAT COIN Directory. 1st- Ed. 0226-7519. CN. English. an. $55. Per No. Alberta Information Retrieval Association, Alberta Research Council, 11315-87th Avenue, Edmonton Alberta T6G 2C2 Canada. DD 025.0402571.

COIN WORLD ALMANAC. 1st- 1976-. 0361-0845. US. English. $10.00. PO Box 150, Sidney OH 45365. LC CJ1. DD 737.405.

COIN YEAR BOOK. (COIN YEARBOOK). 1970-. 0307-6571. UK. English. an. -/-/80. Numismatic Publishing Company, Sovereign House High Street, Essex Brentwood England. LC CJ2471. DD 737.4942. *Coin Monthly Year Book.*

COLLECTORS' MARKETPLACE DIRECTORY. NEW YORK CITY DESIGN. (COLLECTORS' MARKETPLACE DIRECTORY). 1981-1982-. 0735-9357. US. English. Artrepreneur/Boritz M A F, 945 Fifth Avenue, New York NY 10021. LC AM311.N5. DD 300.0257471.

COLLEGE AND ADULT READING. (YEARBOOK). 1st- 1962-. 0069-553X. US. English. an. North Central Reading Association, 190 Coffey Hall, 1420 Eckles Avenue, St Paul MN 55108. Tel (612)373-1140. Ed Joe Fisher. bk rev. Circ 500. Reports of research on reading improvement for college and adult readers. Programs of study skills improvement.

COLLEGE & CAREER DIRECTORY. MARYLAND, DELAWARE. VFOAT Maryland-Delaware College & Career Directory. VAT College and Career Directory. Maryland, Delaware. 1979/80-. 0190-6445. US. English. an. $6.95. College & Career Directory, Box 3689, Baltimore MD 21214. Tel (301)254-0273. Ed Robert A Wittman. LC L903.M3. DD 378.752. adv acc. Circ 25,000. (ctrl). Directory of colleges, careers and schools of Maryland, Delaware and Washington DC financial programs and aid admissions information. *College & Career Directory. Maryland, 0147-8338.*

COLLEGE & CAREER DIRECTORY. PENNSYLVANIA. VFOAT Pennsylvania College & Career Directory. VAT College and Career Directory. Pennsylvania. 1979/80-. 0190-6429. US. English. an. $4.95. R R Bowker Company, 1180 Avenue of the Americas, New York NY 10036. LC L903.P4. DD 378.748.

COLLEGE OF SCIENCE ALUMNI DIRECTORY, THE PENNSYLVANIA STATE UNIVERSITY. Main/Corp Pennsylvania State University. College of Science. 0740-462X. US. English. Penn State Alumni Association, 105 Old Main, University Park PA 16802. LC Q183.3.P43. DD 507.1174853.

COLLIER'S YEAR BOOK. 1963-. US. English. an. Index in last issue of volume - attached. *Collier's Encyclopedia Yearbook.*

COLORADO EDUCATION DIRECTORY. 1956. 0588-4349. US. English. an. Colorado Department of Education, 201 East Colfax Avenue, Room 532, Denver CO 80203. Tel (303)534-8871. Ed Doug Bassett. adv acc. Directory of Colorado public schools and state education groups, organizations.

COLORADO HIGH TECHNOLOGY DIRECTORY. VFOAT Colorado High Technology Directory Update. 1985-. 0883-8208. US. English. an. $80.00. Leading Edge Communications, 1919 14th Street/Suite 606, Boulder CO 80302.

COLORADO LEGISLATIVE ALMANAC. 1981-. 0277-3708. US. English. be. $25.00. Ackerman-Rorex Corporation, 2888 Bluff/Suite 208, Boulder CO 80301. LC JK7830. DD 328.7880720202.

COLORADO MEDICINE. DIRECTORY OF PHYSICIANS. Main/Corp Colorado Medical Society. VFOAT Directory of Physicians. 1980-. 0743-5037. US. English. NLM W 22 AC6 C718C. *Directory of Physicians, 0420-0640.*

COLORADO ZIP+4 STATE DIRECTORY. VFOAT Zip Plus Four State Directory. VAT Colorado Zip Plus Four State Directory. 1985-. US. English. an. St Louis PDC, Zip+4 Directory Orders, PO Box 14921, St Louis MO 63180-9988.

COLUMBIA, S.C. CITY DIRECTORY. Series/Titl United States City Directories. 18-. Periodical. US. English. an.

COMENTARIOS BIBLIOGRAFICOS AMERICANOS. ANUARIO. VAT CBA Anuario. 1968-. 0010-2237. UY. Spanish. qt. $50.00. E Darino, PO Box 1496, Grand Central Station, New York NY 10163. Tel (212)228-4024. Ed Eduardo Darien. bk rev. (ctrl). Bibliographic service that reviews new books from the spanish publishing market. Also includes essays on bibliographical works of specific areas, articles, etc.

COMERCIO EXTERIOR (LA PAZ). (COMERCIO EXTERIOR; ANUARIO). 1934/35-. 0520-4712. Periodical. Spanish. an. LC HF161. DD 382. *Comercio Exterior de Bolivia.*

COMMERCE YEARBOOK OF PORTS, SHIPPING AND SHIPBUILDING. 1973/74-. English. ir. 1.75. D B Mahatme, 90 Veer Nariman Road 400 020, Bombay India. LC HE561. DD 387.0954. *Commerce Yearbook of Shipping and Shipbuilding.*

COMMERCE YEARBOOK OF PUBLIC SECTOR. VFOAT Yearbook of Public Sector. Began in 1970. 0591-1710. English. ir. $117.00. Commerce Publications Ltd, Manek Mahal 6th Floor, /90 Veer Nariman Road, Bombay 400 020 India. Tel 2024505. Ed D B Mahatme. LC HF3782.5. DD 380.10954. bk rev. adv acc. Circ 7,000. Authoritative source of information on economic and financial developments in India and abroad. Its bumper annual is devoted to a theme and serves as reference source. It also brings out directories.

COMMERCE YEARBOOK OF ROAD TRANSPORT. II. English. an. 50.00. Commerce Publications Ltd, Manek Mahal 90 Veer Nariman Road, Bombay 400 020 India.

THE COMMERCIAL DIRECTORY OF MALAYSIA. English. an. Darat Publications SDN BHD, 22A J1 SS2/24 Sungei Way, Subang Selangor Malaysia. LC HF3800.6.A48. DD 380.10294595.

COMMERCIAL DIRECTORY OF PUERTO RICO, VIRGIN ISLANDS. (THE COMMERCIAL DIRECTORY OF PUERTO RICO - VIRGIN ISLANDS). 1973/74-. 0092-1297. PR. English. an. Witcom Group Inc, El Caribe Building, 15th Floor, San Juan Puerto Rico 00901. Tel (809)725-8075. LC HF3353. DD 380.10257295.

COMMERCIAL FERTILIZER AND PLANT FOOD INDUSTRY. (YEARBOOK). US. English. an. W W Brown Publishing Company, 75 3rd Avenue NW, Atlanta GA 30328. LC TP963. DD 631.8058.

COMMERCIAL NEWS USA. ANNUAL DIRECTORY. (COMMERCIAL NEWS USA. ANNUAL DIRECTORY FOR . . .). VFOAT Commercial News USA. VAT Commercial News United States of America. Annual Directory for . . . . 1982-. 0738-0992. US. English. an. Commercial News USA Room H2106, Office of Event Management & Support Services, International Trade Administration, US Department of Commerce, Washington DC 20230. LC HF1040.8. DD 382.6029473. *Commercial News USA. U.S. Products for Export, 0732-846X.*

THE COMMERCIAL REAL ESTATE BROKERS DIRECTORY. 1985-. 0882-7664. US. English. an. $77.00. Whole World Publishing Inc, 400 Lake Cook Road, Deerfield IL 60015. DD 333.

Yearbooks, Almanacs, Directories

COMMERCIAL TELEVISION AND RADIO YEAR BOOK. VFOAT TV & Radio Year Book. 0306-7718. UK. English. an. Mercury House Business Publications, Waterloo Road, London SE1 8W England. LC HE8700.9.G7. DD 384.55402541. *Commercial Television Yearbook, 0069-6668.*

COMMERCIAL WEST BANK DIRECTORY OF THE UPPER MIDWEST. 1979-. US. English. an. *Bank Directory of the Upper Midwest.*

COMMITTEE DIRECTORY OF THE SECTION OF CORPORATION, BANKING AND BUSINESS LAW OF THE AMERICAN BAR ASSOCIATION. Main/Corp American Bar Association. Section of Corporation, Banking and Business Law. VFOAT Committee Directory. 0738-4823. US. English. American Bar Association, 1155 East 60th Street, Chicago IL 60637. LC KF195.C57. DD 346.7307025, 347.3067025. *Directory, 0091-8288.*

COMMODITY MONEY MANAGEMENT YEARBOOK. (COMMODITY MONEY MANAGEMENT . . . YEARBOOK). Vol. 1 (1979)-. 0734-2039. US. English. an. LC HG6046. DD 332.64405.

COMMONWEALTH GOVERNMENT DIRECTORY. 1977-. AT. English. an. Australian Government Publishing Service, PO Box 84, Canberra 2600 Australia. Tel (062) 95 4411. LC JQ4021. DD 354.9400025. *Australian Government Directory.*

COMMONWEALTH OFFICE YEAR BOOK. 1967-1968. Monographic Series. UK. English. ir. Her Majestys Stationery Office, PO Box 276, London SW8 5DT England. LC JN248. DD 354.42. *Colonial Office List, and the Commonwealth Relations Office Year Book.*

COMMONWEALTH UNIVERSITIES YEARBOOK. 1958-. 0069-7745. UK. English. an. Association of Commonwealth Universities, Gale Research Company, Book Tower, Detroit MI 48226. Tel (01)387-8572. Ed A Christodoulou and T Craig. LC LB2310. DD 378.42. NLM LB 2310 Y39. Guide to faculty programmes, organisation and activities of universities of good standing in commonwealth countries. *Yearbook of the Universities of the Commonwealth.*

COMMUNICATIO SOCIALIS YEARBOOK. 1981-1982-. English. an. 6.50. Rev Clarence Srambical, Sat Prachar Press, Indore MP 452 001 India. Tel 21 22 6. Ed Tomy Luiz. LC BV652.95. DD 260. bk rev. adv acc. Circ 1,000. Journal of Christian communication in the third world, containing articles, reports, documentation, chronicle, innovation, personality and review. It provides and sustains a scientific basis for all questions connected with Christian communications.

COMMUNICATION DIRECTORY. 1973/74-. 0094-2588. US. English. ir. Council of Communication Societies, PO Box 1074, Silver Spring MD 20910. Tel (301)953-7100. LC HE9.U5. DD 380.302573. *Directory of Communications Organizations.*

COMMUNICATION YEARBOOK. No. 1-. 0147-4642. US. English. an. $45.00. Sage Publications Inc, 275 South Beverly Drive, Beverly Hills CA 90212. LC P87. DD 001.505. NLM W1 CO4273M.

COMMUNICATIONS DIRECTORY & YEARBOOK. IE. English. ir. Mount Salus Press, Tritonville Road Sandymount, Dublin 4 Ireland. LC HE8123. DD 380.3025415.

COMMUNITY AFFAIRS AND PLANNING DIRECTORY. VFOAT State of Oklahoma Community Affairs and Planning Directory. 0094-5382. US. English. Office Of Community Affairs & Planning, 4901 North Lincoln, Oklahoma City OK 73105. LC HT393.O45. DD 309.212025766.

COMMUNITY DEVELOPMENT BLOCK GRANT PROGRAM. DIRECTORY OF ALLOCATIONS. (COMMUNITY DEVELOPMENT BLOCK GRANT PROGRAM. DIRECTORY OF ALLOCATIONS FOR FISCAL YEARS . . .). 0363-1613. US. English. US Department of Housing and Urban Development, Washington DC 20410. LC HN90.C6. DD 309.2620973. Vols. for 1976-81- distributed to depository libraries in microfiche.

COMMUNITY, JUNIOR, AND TECHNICAL COLLEGE DIRECTORY CEASED. 1975-1982. US. English. an. $7.00. One Dupont Circle/Suite 410, Washington DC 20036. LC L901. DD 378.154302573. *Community and Junior College Directory.*

COMMUNITY SERVICES DIRECTORY. 1976-. 0228-0817. CN. English. be. $3.00 Per No. Information Lethbridge, c/o Yates Memorial Centre, 4th Avenue & 10th Street South, Lethbridge Alberta T1J 0P6 Canada. DD 361.002571234. *Community Directory, 0228-0809.*

COMMUNITY, TECHNICAL, AND JUNIOR COLLEGE DIRECTORY. 1983-. 0749-9205. US. English. an. $25.00. American Association of Community & Junior Colleges, 80 South Early Street, Alexandria VA 22304. Tel (703)823-6966. DD 378. *Community, Junior, and Technical College Directory.*

COMMUTER DIRECTORY. US. English. an. PO Box 32486, San Antonio TX 78284.

COMPACT DIRECTORY OF KOREAN EXPORTERS. '82-'83-. English. ir. Buyers Guide Ltd, CPO Box 4922, Seoul Korea. LC HF3830.5.A48. DD 382.602945195.

COMPANIES HANDBOOK OF THE KUALA LUMPUR STOCK EXCHANGE BERHAD. Main/Corp Kuala Lumpur Stock Exchange. V. 1- 1974-. MY. English. ir. 35.00. Kuala Lumpur Stock Exchange, PO Box 1023, Kuala Lumpar 0102 Malaysia. Tel (03)2546662. Ed Qua Gek Kim. LC HG4244.66. DD 332.67. adv acc. Circ 4,000. It provides a comprehensive writeup on all listed companies' background, principal activities, shareholding analysis, statistical and graphical analyses of operations for 5 years.

THE COMPLETE GUIDE TO GOSPEL MUSIC. (THE COMPLETE GUIDE TO GOSPEL MUSIC : THE GOSPEL MUSIC ASSOCIATION'S OFFICIAL RESOURCE DIRECTORY). 1981-. 0733-4133. US. English. an. The Gospel Music Association, PO Box 23201, Nashville TN 37202. *Gospel Music, 0197-2715.*

THE COMPREHENSIVE DIRECTORY OF SPORTS ADDRESSES. 1st Ed.-. 0743-4561. US. English. $14.95. Ed Kobak Jr, 1015 Granville, Los Angeles CA 90049. Tel (213)826-2145. Ed Edward T Kobak Jr. LC GV853. DD 796.02573. bk rev. adv acc. Circ 15,000. A valuable reference guide listing over 3,500 addresses, telephone numbers and contact persons from the field of sports from around the globe.

COMPUTER DIRECTORY AND BUYERS' GUIDE. 1st (1955)- Annual Ed. Periodical. US. English. an. $31.00. Berkeley Enterprises Inc, 815 Washington Street, Newtonville MA 02160. Tel (617)332-5453. Ed Edmond C Berkeley. Circ 2,500. A basic buyers' guide to the organizations available for supplying, designing and using data processing and computing systems.

COMPUTER DIRECTORY FOR SCHOOLS. VFOAT Instructor . . . Computer Directory for Schools. 1982-83-. US. English. an. $9.95. Instructor Publications Inc, 757 3rd Avenue, New York NY 10017. Tel (212)503-2888. Ed John Lent. LC LB1028.43. DD 371.3944502573. adv acc. Circ 82,000. (ctrl). Comprehensive guide to educational software, computers, peripherals, and periodicals. Complete product lists and reports on how to select and use latest software and hardware.

COMPUTER GRAPHICS DIRECTORY. '84-. 0743-2836. US. English. an. Pennwell Directories, Division of Pennwell Publishing Company, PO Box 1260, Tulsa OK 74101. LC T385. DD 001.6443.

COMPUTER YEARBOOK. 1972-. 0163-4003. US. English. an. International Electronics Information Service, 200 Park Avenue/Suite 303 East, New York NY 10017. LC QA76. DD 001.6405. NLM Z 699.A1 C743. *Computer Yearbook and Directory.*

COMPUTER YEARBOOK. VFOAT Hong Kong Computer Directory. V. 1-. English. ir. Diamond Publications, 302 Ivy House, 20 Wyndam Street, Hong Kong Hong Kong. LC QA75.5. DD 001.6405.

CONCISE STATISTICAL YEARBOOK OF POLAND. Began with: V. 4 (1962). 0554-436X. PL. English. an. Central Statistical Office, ARS Polona Krakowskie Przedmiescie 7, 068 Warsaw Poland. LC HA1451. DD 314. *Concise Statistical Year Book of the Polish People's Republic.*

CONCRETE INDUSTRIES YEARBOOK. 0069-827X. Monographic Series. US. English. an. $25.00 Single Issue. Pit and Quarry Publications Inc, 105 West Adams Street, Chicago IL 60603. LC TA680. DD 693.5058.

CONGRESSIONAL QUARTERLY ALMANAC. Vol. 4 (1948)-. 0095-6007. US. English. an. Congressional Quarterly Inc, 1414 22nd Street NW, Washington DC 20037. Ind/Abst Nexis, Relig. Index One, Period. *Congressional Quarterly.*

CONGRESSIONAL STAFF DIRECTORY. 1959-. 0589-3178. US. English. an. $45.00. Congressional Staff Directory, PO Box 62, Mt Vernon VA 22121. Tel (703)765-3400. Ed Charles B Brownson. LC JK1012. DD 328.738. NLM JK 421 C749. Circ 32,000. Congress, its members, their staffs, its committees and subcommittees and staffs, 9,900 cities and towns with congressmen and districts, 3,200 biographies of key staff, 5,500 top officials in the executive branch.

CONGRESSIONAL STAFF DIRECTORY. ADVANCE LOCATOR FOR CAPITOL HILL. VFOAT C.S.D. Advance Locator. 1963-. 0069-8938. US. English. an. $45.00. Congressional Staff Directory, PO Box 62, Mt Vernon VA 22121. Tel (703)765-3400. Ed Charles B Brownson and Anna L Brownson. NLM JK 421 C7494. Circ 30,000. Congress, its members and their staffs, committees and subcommittees and their staffs, 9,900 cities and towns with congressmen and districts, 3,200 biographies of key staff.

CONN-CEPT VIII. CONNECTICUT'S PROGRMMING FOR THE GIFTED AND TALENTED : A SAMPLE LIST AND DIRECTORY OF STATE APPROVED PROGRAMS FOR THE GIFTED AND TALENTED. VFOAT Sample List and Directory of State Approved Programs for the Gifted and Talented. US. English. an. Connecticut State Department of Education, Bureau of Pupil Personnel and Special Educational Services, Hartford CT 06115. LC L903.C8. DD 371.95025746.

CONNECTICUT EDUCATION DIRECTORY. 1968-. US. English. an. Connecticut State Department of Education, Box 2219, Hartford CT 06115. LC L903.C8. DD 370.25746. *Educational Directory of Connecticut.*

CONNECTICUT FOUNDATION DIRECTORY. 1979-. 0734-4694. US. English. Ed Michael E Burns. LC AS911.A2. DD 001.44.

THE CONNECTICUT LEGAL DIRECTORY. 1977/78-. 0195-6809. US. English. an. Legal Directories Publishing Company Inc, 700 Campbell Center, PO Box 64805, Dallas TX 75206. LC KF192.C6. DD 340.025746.

CONNECTICUT MANUFACTURING DIRECTORY. 0099-0124. US. English. $5.00 Per Copy. Connecticut Labor Department, 200 Folly Brook Boulevard, Wethersfield CT 06109. LC HD9727.C8. DD 338.0025746. *Directory of Connecticut Manufacturing and Mechanical Establishments, 0197-3002.*

CONNECTICUT, RHODE ISLAND DIRECTORY OF MANUFACTURERS. 1979-. 0193-5909. US. English. $62.50. Commerce Registe Inc, 190 Godwin Avenue, Midlind Park NJ 07432. Tel (201)445-3000. Ed Joel Rosano. LC HD9727.C8. DD 338.4025746. adv acc. Circ 3,000. Detailed listings of all manufacturing companies, including top executives, annual sales, number of employees, address, phone, and more. Available in machine readable format and on mailing lists.

CONSERVATION DIRECTORY. 1956-. 0069-911X. US. English. an. National Wildlife Federation, 1412 16th Street NW, Washington DC 20036. Tel (703)790-4402. Ed Rue Gordon. LC S920. DD 333.9502573. adv acc. Circ 8,000. (ctrl). Extensive listing of government agencies and private organizations in US and Canada concerned with conservation and natural resource management. *Directory of Organizations and Officials Concerned with the Protection of Wildlife and other Natural Resources.*

CONSOLIDATED DEVELOPMENT DIRECTORY. 0362-7586. US. English. an. Department of Housing & Urban Development, 451 Seventh Street SW, Washington DC 20410. LC HD7293.A49. DD 301.5402573.

CONSORTIUM DIRECTORY. 0091-701X. US. English. an. $9.00. Council Inter-institutional Leadership, 1 Dupont Circle/Suite 800, Washington DC 20036. Tel (202)833-4993. LC L901. DD 378.10402573. Circ 1,000. Directory of cooperative ventures in higher education.

CONSTABULARY LIST AND DIRECTORY. 0376-7973. UK. English. an. -/-/ 50. Constabulary Gazette, 112 Lisburn Road, Belfast BT9 6AH Ireland. LC HV8197.N67. DD 363.2025416.

CONSTRUCTION STATISTICS YEARBOOK. 1982-. US. English. an. $30.00. Publishing Division, United Nations, New York NY 10017. Tel (212)754-8302. International statistics on

Yearbooks, Almanacs, Directories

dwelling. Construction is given with data for each country over a ten-year period. *Yearbook of Construction Statistics.*

CONSULTANTS AND CONSULTING ORGANIZATIONS DIRECTORY. 2nd Ed. (1973)-. 0196-1292. US. English. te. $310.00. Gale Research Company, Book Tower, Detroit MI 48226. **Tel** (800)521-0707. **Ed** J McLean. **LC** HD69.C6. **DD** 658.46025. **NLM** HD 69.C6 C758. Furnishes details on about 8,500 firms, individuals, and organizations active in 116 special fields. Entries include names, addresses, phone numbers and details on services performed. *Consultants and Consulting Organizations, 0589-4859.*

THE CONSULTING ENGINEERS WHO'S WHO & YEAR BOOK. UK. English. an. TPL Magazines Ltd, Northwood House, 93-99 Goswell Road, London EC1V 7QA England.

THE CONSUMER AFFAIRS LETTER. COMPUTERIZED DIRECTORY OF CONSUMER/PUBLIC INTEREST GROUPS. **VFOAT** Computerized Directory of Consumer/Public Interest Groups. Directory Issue No. 1(Nov. 1983)-. 0741-9902. US. English. sa. $60.00. Sklar Idelson, 800 18th Street NW #403, Washington DC 20006. **LC** JK1118. **DD** 322.4302573.

CONSUMERS ALMANAC & CALENDAR. (CONSUMER ALMANAC & CALENDAR). 0094-7652. US. English. National Consumers League, 1715 Massachusetts Avenue Northwest, Washington DC 20036. **LC** HC110.C63. **DD** 381.

CONSUMERS DIRECTORY CEASED. Began with Vol. for 1969. 0069-9284. English. ir. International Organization of Consumers Union, 8 Emmastraat, Hague Netherlands. **LC** HC79.C63. **DD** 381.

CONTACTS INFLUENTIAL. CLEVELAND METRO WEST. (CONTACTS INFLUENTIAL. CLEVELAND METRO WEST : COMMERCE AND INDUSTRY DIRECTORY). **VFOAT** Cleveland Metro West. 1984-1985-. 0748-5794. US. English. an. Contacts Influential, 20950 Center Ridge Road #103, Cleveland OH 44116. **LC** HF5068.C55. **DD** 338.7402577132.

CONTACTS INFLUENTIAL COMMERCE AND INDUSTRY DIRECTORY. FORT WORTH, TARRANT COUNTY. **VFOAT** Contacts Influential. 1982/1983-. 0743-0582. US. English. an. Contacts Influential International Corporation, 20950 Center Ridge Road 106, Cleveland OH 44116. **LC** HF5068.F67. **DD** 338.74025764531.

CONTACTS INFLUENTIAL. PENINSULA. (CONTACTS INFLUENTIAL COMMERCE AND INDUSTRY DIRECTORY. PENINSULA). **VFOAT** Peninsula. 8756-582X. US. English. an. Contacts Influential, 20950 Center Ridge Road #106, Cleveland OH 44116.

CONTACTS INFLUENTIAL. ST. PAUL. (CONTACTS INFLUENTIAL. ST. PAUL : COMMERCE AND INDUSTRY DIRECTORY). **VFOAT** St. Paul. **VAT** Contacts Influential. Saint Paul. 1983-. 0743-2631. US. English. an. Contacts Influential, 220 Robert Street South, St Paul MN 55107. **LC** HF5068.S352. **DD** 338.74025776581. *Contacts Influential Commerce and Industry Directory, St. Paul Metro.*

CONTACTS INFLUENTIAL. SUBURBAN MARYLAND (WASHINGTON, D.C. METRO AREA). (CONTACTS INFLUENTIAL. SUBURBAN MARYLAND (WASHINGTON, D.C. METRO AREA) : COMMERCE AND INDUSTRY DIRECTORY). **VFOAT** Suburban Maryland (Washington, D.C. Metro Area). 0741-0670. US. English. an. Contacts Influential, Weatherly Building 10th Floor, 516 SE Morrison, Portland OR 97214. **LC** HF5065.M25. **DD** 338.740257521.

CONTACTS INFLUENTIAL. TAMPA BAY. (CONTACTS INFLUENTIAL. TAMPA BAY : COMMERCE AND INDUSTRY DIRECTORY : CI). **VFOAT** Tampa Bay. Began publication with 1981/82-. 0748-4437. US. English. an. Contacts Influential, 3500 East Fletcher Avenue/Suite 423, Tampa FL 33612. **LC** HF5065.F6. **DD** 338.7402575965.

CONTACTS INFLUENTIAL. WASHINGTON, D.C. (CONTACTS INFLUENTIAL. WASHINGTON, D.C. : COMMERCE AND INDUSTRY DIRECTORY). **VFOAT** Washington, D.C. 0743-264X. US. English. an. Contacts Influential, Weatherly Building, 10th Floor, 516 SE Morrison, Portland OR 97214. **LC** HF5068.W3. **DD** 338.74025753.

CONTAINERISATION INTERNATIONAL YEARBOOK. UK. English. an. $29.89. Michael Joseph Ltd, 44 Bedford Square, London WC1B England. **Tel** (441)439-7144. **LC** TA1215. *Container Guide.*

CONTEMPORARY MUSIC ALMANAC. **VFOAT** Music Almanac. 0196-6200. Periodical. US. English. Schirmer Books, 806 Third Avenue, New York NY 10022. **LC** ML3533.8. **DD** 784.5400973.

CONTINENTAL DIRECTORY NMF. STANDARD POINT LOCATION CODES SPLC. (CONTINENTAL DIRECTORY : STANDARD POINT LOCATION CODES, SPLC). **VFOAT** Standard Point Location Codes SPLC. **VAT** Continental Directory National Motor Freight. Standard Point Location. NMF 102 A-. 0363-9983. US. English. ir. National Motor Freight Traffic Association, 1616 P Street, Washington DC 20036.

CONVERSE BASKETBALL YEARBOOK. US. English. an. Converse Rubber Company, 55 Fordham Road, Wilmington MA 01887. **Tel** (617)657-5500. **LC** GV885.

COORDINATION DIRECTORY OF STATE AND FEDERAL AGENCY WATER AND LAND RESOURCES OFFICIALS. 0363-8170. US. English. Missouri River Basin Commission, 10050 Regency Circle/Suite 403, Omaha NE 68114. **LC** HD1694. **DD** 333.91002573.

CORNWALL, ONTARIO CITY DIRECTORY. **VFOAT** Cornwall City Directory. 1980-. 0229-1991. CN. English. $80.00 Per Vol. Might Directories, 220 Bartley Drive, Toronto Ontario M4A 2N4 Canada. **DD** 917.1376. *Might's Cornwall (United Counties, Stormont, Dundas, and Glengarry, Ontario) Ontario City Directory, 0381-744X.*

CORO, DIRECTORIO DE ACTIVIDADES ECONOMICAS. **VFOAT** Directorio de Actividades Economicas de Coro. 1972-. Periodical. Spanish. ir. Fundacion Para el Desarrollo de la Region Centro Occidental de Venezuela, Rudeco Biblioteca, Barquisimeto Venezuela.

CORPORATE 500. THE DIRECTORY OF CORPORATE PHILANTHROPY. **VFOAT** Corporate Five Hundred. **VAT** Corporate Five-Hundred. The Directory of Corporate Philanthropy. 1980-. 0197-937X. US. English. an. $282.23. Public Management Institute, 358 Brannan Street, San Francisco 94110. **Tel** (415)896-1900. **Ed** J Isamu Yamamoto. **LC** HV97.A3. **DD** 361.76502573. **Circ** 3,000. (ctrl). Profile giving programs on top 500 US corporations. Detailed analysis and information on each corporation's direct and foundation contributions. Includes twelve indexes. All information verified by corporations.

CORPORATE DIRECTORY. 0093-545X. US. English. an. Department of Commerce, Corporations Section, Pouch D, Juneau AK 99801. **LC** HD2776.A4. **DD** 338.0025798. *Alaska Corporate Directory, 0568-8272.*

CORPORATE FINANCING DIRECTORY CEASED. **VFOAT** Corporate Directory, CF Directory. -March 1982. Periodical. US. English. sa.

CORPORATE TECHNOLOGY DIRECTORY. 0887-1930. US. English. an. $750.00. Corporate Technology Information Services Inc, 2 Laurel Avenue, Wellesley Hills MA 02181.

CORPUS ALMANAC & CANADIAN SOURCEBOOK. **VFOAT** Corpus Almanac and Canadian Sourcebook. 18th Ed. (1983)-. 0823-1133. CN. English. an. 119.00. Corpus Information Services, 1450 Don Mills Road, Don Mills Ontario M3B 2X7 Canada. **Tel** (416)445-6641. **Ed** Marilyn Hryciuk. **LC** F1004.7. **DD** 971.0025. **Circ** 4,500. Covers a range of Canadian topics from astronomy to a review of the economy, with special attention to government (federal, provincial and municipal governments are listed). *Corpus Almanac of Canada, 0315-7083.*

CORPUS ALMANAC OF CANADA CEASED. (THE CORPUS ALMANAC OF CANADA). 1974-1982. 0315-7083. CN. English. an. Corpus Publishers Service Ltd, 6 Crescent Road, Toronto Ontario M4W 1T1 Canada. **LC** F1004.7. **DD** 971.003. **NLM** F 1004.7 C822. *Corpus Directory and Almanac of Canada, 0315-5102.*

THE CORRECTIONS YEARBOOK. 1981-. 0273-4230. US. English. an. $1.75. Criminal Justice Institute, 60 East 42nd Street/Suite 956, New York NY 10165. **LC** HV8482. **DD** 365.973. *Instant Answers to Key Questions in Corrections.*

COST EFFECTIVENESS RESOURCE PERSONNEL DIRECTORY. **VFOAT** A.M.A. Cost Effectiveness Resource Personnel Directory. 0735-6188. US. English. $3.00. AMA Department of Health Care and Financing Organization, 535 North Dearborn Street, Chicago IL 60610. **LC** R712.A1. **DD** 610.681.

LA COTE D'IVOIRE : ANNUAIRE INTERNATIONAL. **VFOAT** La Cote d'Ivoire : International Directory. IV. French. an. **LC** JQ3386.A4.

COUNTRIES OF THE WORLD AND THEIR LEADERS YEARBOOK. *See* Geography.

COUNTRY SONG ROUNDUP YEARBOOK. (COUNTRY SONG ROUNDUP. YEARBOOK). **VFOAT** CSR Yearbook. 0277-1292. US. English. an. $1.75. Charlton Publications Inc, Charlton Building, Derby CT 06418. **LC** ML3523. **DD** 784.52005.

COUNTRYSIDE PLANNING YEARBOOK. Vol. 1 (1980)-. 0143-8190. UK. English. an. GEO Abstracts Ltd, University of East Anglia, Norwich NR4 7TJ England.

COUNTRYWIDE ANNUAL YEARBOOK. (COUNTRYWIDE ANNUAL YEAR BOOK). V. 1- 1973/74-. 0092-5454. US. English. ir. Country Publishing Company, PO Box 186, Fairfax VA 22030. **Tel** (703)521-6431. **LC** ML1. **DD** 784.

COUNTY AGENTS DIRECTORY. US. English. an. $18.95. Century Communications Inc, 5520 G Touhy Avenue, Skokie IL 60077. **Tel** (312)676-4060.

THE COUNTY & MUNICIPAL YEAR BOOK FOR SCOTLAND. LOCAL TAXATION SUPPLEMENT. UK. English. ir. WM Culross & Son Ltd, Queen Street, Coupar Angus, Perthshire Scotland. **LC** JS4101. **DD** 352.1309411.

COUNTY EXECUTIVE DIRECTORY. Winter/Spring 1984-. 0742-1702. US. English. sa. $125.00. Carroll Publishing Company, 1058 Thomas Jefferson Street NW, Washington DC 20007. **Tel** (202)333-8620. **Ed** Nancy Cahill. **LC** JS414. **DD** 352.00520973. Organizational listing county population, county seat, locator phone and address.

COURSE ANNOUNCEMENT - DIVISION OF TRAINING. NATIONAL INSTITUTE FOR OCCUPATIONAL SAFETY AND HEALTH. (DIRECTORY OF AIR QUALITY MONITORING SITES). 0093-5476. US. English. Air Pollution Technical Information Center, Durham NC 27711. **LC** TD883.2. **DD** 363.6.

THE CREATIVE DIRECTORY OF THE SUN BELT. 1979-. US. English. 1103 South Shepherd Drive, Houston TX 77019.

CREDIT UNION DIRECTORY. **VFOAT** National Credit Union Directory. 0196-3678. US. English. an. National Credit Union Administration, 2025 M Street NW, Washington DC 20456. **LC** HG2037. **DD** 334.2202573.

CREDIT UNION DIRECTORY AND BUYERS' GUIDE. V. 1- 1973-. 0092-4954. US. English. an. $39.00. National Institute for Public Services, 7315 Wisconsin Avenue/Suite 210W, Washington DC 20014. **LC** HG2037. **DD** 334.2.

CRIMINAL JUSTICE EDUCATION DIRECTORY. 0160-8215. US. English. International Association of Chiefs of Police, 11 Firstfield Road, Gaithersburg MD 20760. **LC** HV8143. **DD** 364.071173.

CRITTENDEN MORTGAGE DIRECTORY. **VFOAT** Mortgage Directory. 0271-3942. US. English. $195.00. Crittenden Financing Inc, POB 128, Nevada City CA 95959. **LC** HG2040.5.U5. **DD** 332.102573.

CROCKFORD'S CLERICAL DIRECTORY. 1st (1858)-. UK. English. ir. Oxford University Press, 16-00 Pollitt Drive, Fairlawn NJ 07410. *Clergy List, Clerical Guide and Ecclesiastical Directory.*

CSCM YEARBOOK. Main/Corp Valparaiso University. Center for the Study of Campus Ministry. 1975-. US. English. an. The Center for the Study of Campus Ministry, Valparaiso University, Valparaiso IN 46383.

CSP DIRECTORY OF SUPPLIERS OF EDUCATIONAL FOREIGN LANGUAGE MATERIALS. **VAT** Cruzada Spanish Publications Directory of Suppliers of Educational Foreign Language Materials. 0162-5977.

Yearbooks, Almanacs, Directories

US. English. be. $5.00. Cruzada Spanish Publications, PO Box 605909, Miami FL 33165. **LC** HD9999.I53. **DD** 338.470002573.

CT DIRECTORY OF SOUTHERN AFRICA. VFOAT Directory of Southern Africa. 1982-. SA. English. an. C T Directories, 504 Buitenkloof Centre, Kloof Street, Cape Town 8001, PO Box 11071, Vlaeberg 8018, Cape Town South Africa. **LC** HF3873. **DD** 338.7402568. *CAPE TIMES DIRECTORY OF SOUTHERN AFRICA.*

CU DIRECTORY. Main/Corp Chicago Unlimited, Inc. VAT Chicago Unlimited Directory. 0363-745X. US. English. sa. $3.00. Chicago Unlimited Inc, 203 North Wabash Avenue/Suite 1020, Chicago IL 60601. **LC** PN2277.C4. **DD** 790.202577311. *Chicago Directory.*

CULTURAL DOCTORATE DIRECTORY. Main/Corp World University Roundtable. VFOAT Annual Directory of Doctoral Memberships. 0731-406X. US. English. an. World University Roundtable, POB 40638 Sun Station, Tucson AZ 85717.

CURACAO TRADE AND INDUSTRY DIRECTORY. NE. Dutch, English or Spanish. an. Citroen-daal, Malmokweg 2, Aruba Netherlands Antilles. **LC** HF3368.C8. **DD** 380.102572986. *Curacao Trade Directory.*

CURRENT AFRICAN DIRECTORIES. 1972-. Monographic Series. UK. English. an. International Publishers Service, Taylor 7 Francis Inc, 242 Cherry Street, Philadelphia PA 19106. **Tel** (800)821-8312.

CURRENT BIBLIOGRAPHIC DIRECTORY OF THE ARTS & SCIENCES. VFOAT CBD, Current Bibliographic Directory of the Arts & Sciences. VAT Current Bibliographic Directory of the Arts and Sciences. 1978-. 0190-6003. Periodical. US. English. an. Institute for Scientific Information, 325 Chestnut Street, Philadelphia PA 19106. **LC** Q145. **DD** 001.43025. **NLM** Q 145 C976. *ISI'S Who is Publishing in Science, 0360-8174.*

CURRENT BIOGRAPHY YEARBOOK. 1955-. 0084-9499. US. English. an. Ind/Abst Biogr. Index. **LC** CT100. **DD** 920.00904. **NLM** CT 120 C9761. Index in last issue of volume - attached. (cum index). *Current Biography.*

CURRENT EUROPEAN DIRECTORIES. 1969-. Periodical. UK. English. ir. $145.00. CBD Research Ltd, 154 High Street, Beckenham Kent BR3 1EA England. **Tel** 01-650 7745. Ed G P Henderson. A guide to international, national city and specialised directories and similar reference works for all countries of continental Europe.

C.U.S.I.P. DIRECTORY. (THE CUSIP DIRECTORY). Main/Corp American Bankers Association. Committee on Uniform Security Identification Procedures. 0091-2212. US. English. an. Standard & Poors Corporation, 25 Broadway, New York NY 10004. **Tel** (212)208-8772. **LC** HG4907. **DD** 332.63202573.

C.U.S.I.P. DIRECTORY. CORPORATE DIRECTORY. (THE CUSIP DIRECTORY : CORPORATE DIRECTORY). Main/Corp American Bankers Association. Committee on Uniform Security Identification Procedures. 0091-3804. US. English. an. Standard & Poor's Corporation, 345 Hudson Street, New York NY 10014. **LC** HG4907. **DD** 332.63202573.

CWLA DIRECTORY OF MEMBER AND ASSOCIATE AGENCIES. Main/Corp Child Welfare League of America. VFOAT C.W.L.A. Directory of Member and Associate Agencies. 1982-. 0737-786X. US. English. an. $10.00. Child Welfare League of America Inc, 67 Irving Place, New York NY 10003. **Tel** (202)638-2952. Ed Eve Klein. **LC** HV741. **DD** 362.702573. **Circ** 2,500. Lists all affiliated agencies of CWLA. *Directory of Member Agencies, 0147-9180; Directory of Associate Agencies (1981), 0277-7177.*

T D C PROJECT DIRECTORY. Main/Corp Canada. Transport Canada. Research and Development Centre. Technology Branch. VFOAT C D T Repertoire des Projects. 1978-. 0225-6436. CN. English. an. Transportation Development Agency, 2085 Union, Montreal Quebec K3A 2C3 Canada. **DD** 629.040720971. *Project Directory, 0704-0962.*

DACCA DIRECTORY. 1976-. English. ir. 30.00. Times Publication, 166 Shantinagar, Dacca Bangladesh. **LC** DS396.9.D3. **DD** 954.9220025.

DAILY MAIL YEAR BOOK. V. 1- 1901-. UK. English. an. Associated Newspapers Group, Carmelite House, London EC4 YJA England. **Tel** 01-353 6000. Ed Mary Jenkins. **LC** AY755.L8. **DD** 032.02. adv acc. **Circ** 25,000. Covers royal family religion, education, biographies, taxation parliament, sport, entertainment, United Nations Gazetteer, current affairs, and armed forces.

THE DAILY PLANET ALMANAC. 0148-5369. US. English. an. $2.95. AND/OR Press, PO Box 2246, Berkeley CA 94702.

THE DAILY RECORDER'S SACRAMENTO COUNTY LEGAL DIRECTORY. VFOAT The Daily Recorder's Legal Directory. Spring, 1983-. Periodical. US. English. qt. (A Supplement to the Daily Recorder). Sacramento Legal Press Inc, 1115 H Street, Sacramento CA 95814.

DALIL AL-MUSADDIRIN FI JUMHURIYAT MISR AL-ARABIYAH. VFOAT Egyptian Exporters Directory. Arabic (English). ir. Al-Ittihad Al-Amm Lil-Ghuraf Al-Tijariyah Al- Misriyah, 4 Midan Al-Falaki, Al-Qahirah United Arab Republic. **LC** HF3886.A48.

DALIL AL-TAAWUN AL-IQTISADI. VFOAT Economic Co-Operation Directory. SJ. Arabic. ir. 5.00. Al-Maktab Al-Watani Lil-Nashr Wa-Al-Ilan Wa-Al-Alaqat Al-Ammah, S B 2413, Al-Khartum Sudan. **LC** HF1611.8.Z4.

DALTON'S DELAWARE VALLEY DIRECTORY. 18th Ed. (1982)-. 0733-2416. US. English. an. $72.50. Daltons Directory of Business & Industry, 410 Lancaster Avenue, Haverford PA 19041. **Tel** (215)649-2680. Ed Patrick F Dalton. **LC** HF3163.P5. **DD** 338.74025749. Lists over 10,000 companies and over 50,000 executives and key personnel in Philadelphia and suburbs including South Jersey and Delaware. *Dalton's Directory, Business and Industry, 0732-6955.*

DAN BROCK'S HISTORICAL ALMANAC OF LONDON CEASED. Spring-Autumn 1975. 0316-1404. CN. English. qt. $3.95 Per No. Applegarth Follies, 156 Albert Street, London Ontario N6A 1M1 Canada. **DD** 971.326005.

DARTMOUTH BUSINESS DIRECTORY. VAT Dartmouth Chamber of Commerce Business Directory. 1984-. 0827-2786. CN. English. an. Free to Members. Dartmouth Chamber of Commerce, 12 Portland Street, Dartmouth Nova Scotia B2Y 1G9 Canada. **DD** 380.102571622.

DATA BASE DIRECTORY. VFOAT Database Directory. 1984-85-. 0749-6680. US. English. an. $120.00. Knowledge Industry Publications, 701 Westchester Avenue, White Plains NY 10604. **DD** 025.

DATAPRO DIRECTORY OF MICROCOMPUTER SOFTWARE. VFOAT Directory of Microcomputer Software. Began in 1981?. 0730-8795. Periodical. US. English. mo. $643.26. Datapro Research Corporation, Attn: Director of Customer Service, 1805 Underwood Boulevard, Delran NJ 08075. **Tel** (609)764-0100.

DATAPRO DIRECTORY OF ON-LINE SERVICES. VFOAT Directory of On-Line Services. Began in Apr. 1982. 0730-7071. Periodical. US. English. mo. $479.00. Datapro Research Corporation, Attention Director Customer Service, 1805 Underwood Boulevard, Delran NJ 08075. **Tel** (609)764-0100. Ed Al Sakianas. **Circ** 900. (ctrl). An 1,800 page directory, listing profiled and detailed reports on companies offering information retrieval and timesharing services.

DATAPRO DIRECTORY OF SMALL COMPUTERS. 0276-1866. Periodical. US. English. mo. $643.26. Datapro Research Corporation, Attention Director of Customer Service, 1805 Underwood Boulevard, Delran NJ 08075. **Tel** (609)764-0100.

DATAPRO DIRECTORY OF SOFTWARE. 1975-. 0730-8779. Periodical. US. English. mo. $586.22. Datapro Research Corporation, Attn Director Customer Service, 1805 Underwood Boulevard, Delran NJ 08075. **Tel** (609)764-0100. Each issue contains an index to its own contents - no vol index - loose. (cum index).

DAWSON CREEK DIRECTORY, INCLUDING POUCE COUPE. (DAWSON CREEK DIRECTORY (INCLUDING POUCE COUPE)). VFOAT Dawson Creek Directory. VAT Dawson Creek Directory (1965). 1965-. 0712-1679. CN. English. an. Henderson Directories, 100 East 4th Avenue, Vancouver British Columbia V5T 1G3 Canada. **DD** 917.111. *Dawson Creek Directory, 0415-0848.*

DAY CARE DIRECTORY CEASED. VFOAT Day Care Directory for Hamilton and District. Ceased publication in 1980?. 0382-0645. CN. English. Central Information Service, Suite 609/42 James Street, North Hamilton Ontario L8R 2K2 Canada. **DD** 362.71.

D.C. DIRECTORY OF NATIVE AMERICAN FEDERAL AND PRIVATE PROGRAMS. VFOAT DC Directory of Native American Federal and Private Programs. VAT District of Columbia Directory of Native American Federal and Private Programs. Began in 1979. 0740-3984. US. English. $5.00, $25.00 includes update. American Indian Program, 1029 Vermont Avenue Northwest/Suite 1100, Washington DC 20005.

D.C. DIRECTORY OF NATIVE AMERICAN FEDERAL AND PRIVATE PROGRAMS / NATIVE AMERICAN-PHILANTHROPIC NEWS SERVICE. US. English. an. $25.00. Native American Philanthropic News Service, 1029 Vermont Avenue NW/Suite 1100, Washington DC 20005.

DEFENSE SURVEY & DIRECTORY. VFOAT Defense Survey and Directory. Began with Issue for Sept. 1975. 0099-166X. US. English. mo. Government Business, Worldwide Reports, PO Box 5651, Washington DC 20016. **LC** UA10. **DD** 355.005.

DELAWARE DIRECTORY OF COMMERCE AND INDUSTRY. VFOAT Directory of Commerce and Industry. 0272-8117. US. English. $20.00. One Commerce Circle/Suite 200, Wilmington DE 19801. **Tel** (302)655-7221. **LC** HD9727.D3. **DD** 338.0025751. adv acc. **Circ** 2,500. *Directory of Commerce and Industry, State of Delaware.*

DELAWARE STATE MINORITY BUSINESS DIRECTORY. 0098-6755. US. English. Office of Minority Business Enterprises, State House Annex 3rd Floor, Dover DE 19901. **LC** HD2346.U52. **DD** 338.4025751.

DEMOCRATIC PARTY. YEAR BOOK. *See* Political Science.

DEMOGRAPHIC YEARBOOK. VFOAT Annuaire Demographique. 1st- 1948-. 0082-8041. US. English (French). an. $80.00. United Nations Publications, Sales Section/Room A-3315, New York NY 10017. **Tel** (212)754-8302. **LC** HA17. **DD** 312.058. **NLM** W2 MU5 S7D. International demographic statistics covering 220 countries or areas. Tables give world summaries and country data on population, natality, infant mortality, nuptiality and divorce.

DENISON UNIVERSITY ALUMNI DIRECTORY. US. English. Alumni Office, PO Box A, Granville OH 43023. **LC** LD1522.3. **DD** 378.77154.

THE DENVER DOWNTOWN DIRECTORY. 1983-. 0736-7562. US. English. an. Downtown Data Company, Box 11605, Denver CO 80211. **LC** HF5068.D4. **DD** 338.002578883.

DENVER METROPOLITAN MEDIA DIRECTORY. 1st- Ed. 0196-8491. US. English. an. Kelly Communications, 6872 South Clearmont Drive, Littleton CO 80122. **Tel** (303)740-9670.

DEPARTMENT OF HEALTH AND HUMAN SERVICES TELEPHONE DIRECTORY. 1980-. US. English. ir.

DESERET NEWS CHURCH ALMANAC. 1974-. 0093-786X. US. English. an. Deseret News, 143 South Main Street, Salt Lake City UT 84110. **Tel** (801)524-2800. **LC** BX8606. **DD** 289.33.

THE DESIGN DIRECTORY. 1979/80-. 0195-4326. US. English. an. $41.00. Wefler and Associates, PO Box 1591, Evanston IL 60204. **Tel** (312)454-1940. Ed W Daniel Wefler. **LC** TS23. **DD** 745.202573. A listing of firms and consultants in industrial, graphic and commercial interior design.

DESIGN NEWS. FLUID POWER DIRECTORY. VFOAT Fluid Power Directory. 1978-. US. English. an. $25.00. Cahners Publishing Co, 270 St Paul Street, Denver CO 80206. **LC** TJ836. **DD** 621.2029473. *Design News. Fluid Power, 0164-2871.*

DESIGN NEWS SPECIFIER'S ANNUAL DIRECTORY. V. 1- 1970-. US. English. an. Rogers Publishing Company, 270 St Paul Street, Denver CO 80206. **LC** TA175. **DD** 621.81502573.

Yearbooks, Almanacs, Directories

DESIGNERS WEST RESOURCE DIRECTORY. 1970-. US. English. an. $5.00. Designers West, 9220 Sunset Boulevard, Los Angeles CA 90069. LC NK2004. DD 747.02578.

DESK-REFERENCE DIRECTORY. VAT Guide de l'Acheteur (Toronto), Guide de l'Acheteur (Collingwood). 1979-. 0711-3331. CN. English (French). an. $15.00. Jim Rennie's Sports Letter, Box 1000, Collingwood Ontario L9Y 4L4 Canada. DD 338.4779602571.

DEUTSCHER KUSTEN-ALMANACH. German. ir. Krogers, Bush. und Verlagsdruckerei Abt. Fauchbuch, Blankenser Bahnhofstrasse 17 2 55, Hamburg West Germany. LC QB8.G3.

DEUTSCHES METEOROLOGISCHES JAHRBUCH, BUNDESREPUBLIK. Began publication in 1953. 0417-3562. Periodical. GW. German. ir. Deutscher Wetterdienst, Frankfurter Strasse 135, 6050 Offenbach West Germany. *Deutsches Meteorologisches Jahrbuch (Britische Zone), Deutsches Meteorologisches Jahrbuch, US-Zone.*

DEUTSCHES METEOROLOGISCHES JAHRBUCH, BUNDESREPUBLIK DEUTSCHLAND. 1978-. 0417-3562. Periodical. GW. German. an. $48.69. Deutscher Wetterdienst, Frankfurter Strasse 135, 6050 Offenbach West Germany. Meteorological data and observations in the Federal Republic of Germany on a yearly basis. *Deutsches Meteorologisches Jahrbuch, Bundesrepublik.*

DIA YEARBOOK. Main/Corp Design and Industries Association, London. VAT Design and Industries Association Yearbook. UK. English. an. 1.00. Design and Industries Association, Nash House, 12 Carlton House Terrace, London SW1Y 5AL England. LC T177.G7. DD 745.206241.

DIAMOND'S JAPAN BUSINESS DIRECTORY. Main/Corp Diamond Lead Company. VFOAT Japan Business Directory. JA. English. ir. Diamond Lead Company, 4 2 Kasumi Gaseki I chome, Chiyoda ku Tokyo 100 Japan. LC HC461. DD 332.67. *Diamond Japan Business Directory.*

DICTIONARY OF LITERARY BIOGRAPHY YEARBOOK. 1980-. 0731-7867. US. English. an. $90.00. Gale Research Company, Book Tower, Detroit MI 48226. **Tel** (800)521-0707. LC PS221. DD 810.9, B. Focuses on a specific literary movement or period, so that the entire series will ultimately encompass all who have contributed to the greatness of literature in America, England, and elsewhere.

DIESEL FUEL DIRECTORY. 0272-3611. US. English. an. H M Gousha Company, PO Box 6227, San Jose CA 95150. LC TL153. DD 629.286029473. *Edna Connelly's Diesel Fuel and Truck Stop Guide, 0098-2172.*

DIPLOMATE DIRECTORY - AMERICAN BOARD OF FAMILY PRACTICE. (DIPLOMATE DIRECTORY). Main/Corp American Board of Family Practice. VFOAT Directory of Diplomates. 1981-. 0732-8982. US. English. an. American Board of Family Practice, 2228 Young Drive, Lexington KY 40505. LC R712.A1. DD 610.

DIPLOMATIC AND CONSULAR DIRECTORY (LILONGWE, MALAWI). (DIPLOMATIC AND CONSULAR DIRECTORY). English. ir. Ministry of External Affairs, PO Box 30315, Lilongwe 3 Malawi. LC JX1865.M3. DD 351.892096897. *Diplomatic and Consular List (Zomba, Malawi).*

DIPLOMATIC PRESS DIRECTORY OF THE REPUBLIC OF CYPRUS INCLUDING TRADE INDEX AND BIOGRAPHICAL SECTION. VFOAT Directory of the Republic of Cyprus including Trade Index and Biographical Section. Began with 1962/63 issue. 0417-5131. UK. English. Diplomatic Press & Publ Co, 29 March Lane, London NW7 England.

THE DIPLOMATIC PRESS SUDAN TRADE DIRECTORY. VFOAT Trade Directory of the Republic of the Sudan. 1st- Ed. 0082-5735. UK. English. an. Arthur H Thrower Ltd, 44-46 South Ealing Road, Ealing London W5 England.

THE DIPLOMATIC PRESS TRADE DIRECTORY OF TRINIDAD AND TOBAGO, INCLUDING ALPHABETICAL AND CLASSIFIED TRADE INDEX. VFOAT Trinidad and Tobago Trade Directory. 1963/64-. 0082-657X. UK. English. an. Arthur H Thrower Ltd, 44-46 South Ealing Road, Ealing London W5 England. LC F2122. DD 917.2983.

DIRECTION OF TRADE STATISTICS. YEARBOOK - INTERNATIONAL MONETARY FUND. (DIRECTION OF TRADE STATISTICS. YEARBOOK). 1981-. 0252-3019. US. English. an. $6.00. Publications Unit, International Monetary Fund, Washington DC 20431. LC HF91. DD 382.0212. *Direction of Trade Yearbook, 0250-7358.*

DIRECTORIES AND ASSOCIATIONS OF THE BOOK TRADE AND LIBRARIANSHIP. ADRESSBUCHER UND VERBANDE DES BUCH- UND BIBLIOTHEKSWESENS. VFOAT Adressbucher und Verbande des Buch- und Bibliothekswesens. Periodical. US. English (German). Gale Research Company, Book Tower, Detroit MI 48226. *Bibliographie der Bibliotheksadressbucher.*

DIRECTORIES OF HAWAII. 0094-209X. US. English. Office of Information & Public Services/Dept of Planning & Economic Development, State Capitol, Honolulu HI 96813. LC Z7165.U5. DD 016.91969034025.

DIRECTORIO AGROPECUARIO DE COLOMBIA. Began in 1979. Spanish. an. $500.00. Editores Y Distribuidores Asociados, Av Jimenez No 4-49 Of 617, Bogota Colombia. LC S410.C7. DD 338.1025861.

DIRECTORIO & GUIA DEL SECTOR FINANCIERO. VFOAT Directorio Y Guia del Sector Financiero. CK. Spanish. an. Medios & Medios Publicidad, Cia Ltda, Calle 14 No 8-79 of 703, Bogota Colombia. LC HG69. DD 332.1025861.

DIRECTORIO - COLEGIO DE PSICOLOGOS DE VENEZUELA. Main/Corp Colegio de Psicologos de Venezuela. 1977-. VE. Spanish. ir. Colegio de Psicologos de Venezuela, Apartado Postal, Caracas Venezuela. LC BF80.7.V4.

DIRECTORIO COLOMBIANO DE UNIDADES DE INFORMACION. 1976-. Spanish. ir. Impr Nacioanl, Carrera 13 No 60-34 (4 Piso), Apartado Aereo 051580, Bogota Colombia. LC Z773.A1.

DIRECTORIO COMERCIAL E INDUSTRIAL DE EL SALVADOR. EL SALVADOR'S COMMERCIAL AND INDUSTRIAL DIRECTORY. ES. Spanish. ir. Camara de Comercio e Industria de el Salvador, 9A Av Norte Y 5A Calle Pontente, San Salvador El Salvador. LC HF3303.

DIRECTORIO DE DESPACHOS PUBLICOS. Began in 1974. Spanish. ir. $50.00 Single Issue. Carrera 13 No 10-41 - OF. 606, BCO de la Costa Apartado Aereo 718, Bogota Columbia. LC JL2821.

DIRECTORIO DE EDITORES Y DISTRIBUIDORES LATINOAMERICANOS. VFOAT Latin American Directory of Publishers and Distributors. UY. Spanish. an. CBA, Casilla de Correo, 1677 Montevideo Uruguay.

DIRECTORIO DE EMPRESAS Y EJECUTIVOS. 1978-. CL. Spanish. ir. Comercial I.T.V. Ltd, Ebro 2734, Santiago Chile. LC HC191. DD 338.7402583.

DIRECTORIO DE ESTABLECIMIENTOS INDUSTRIALES DE PRIMERA Y SEGUNDA CATEGORIA. VFOAT Directorio Industrial. BO. Spanish. ir. Departamento de Estadistica Industrial, La Paz Bolivia. LC HC181. DD 338.470002584.

DIRECTORIO DE EXPORTADORES DE PANAMA. 1982-. Periodical. English (Spanish). an. LC HF3291.8. DD 382.6097287.

DIRECTORIO DE INSTITUCIONES FINANCIERAS. 1978-. CK. Spanish. ir. Avenida Jimenez No. 4-49, Oficina 617 Apdo. Aereo 14965, Bogota Colombia. LC HG185.C6.

DIRECTORIO DE LA ADMINISTRACION PUBLICA CENTRALIZADA Y PARAESTATAL. 1978-. MX. Spanish. ir. Presidencia de la Republica, Coordinacion General de Estudios Administrativos, Palacio Nacional, Mexico 1 DF Mexico. LC JL1221. DD 354.7204025. *Directorio de la Administracion Publica Centralizada.*

DIRECTORIO DE LA INDUSTRIA DE LAS ARTES GRAFICAS. Spanish. ir. Eidtores Internacionales, Bolivar No 235-237, Apartado Postal 99 Bis, Mexico City Mexico. LC Z244.6.M6.

DIRECTORIO DE LA INDUSTRIA TURISTICA DE EL SALVADOR. ES. English (Spanish). an. $1.00. Felicitaciones Centroamericanas, Apartado Postal 1642, San Salvador El Salvador. LC G155.E4. DD 917.2840452.

DIRECTORIO DE LA INDUSTRIA Y COMERCIO DE CENTROAMERICA Y PANAMA. Spanish. ir. Servicios de Anuario Telefonico Internacional, Aptdo 5272, San Jose Costa Rica. LC HC141.A1.

DIRECTORIO DE MEDIOS. MX. Spanish. ir. $500. Mediro Publicitarios Mexicanos, Av Mexico 99-303 11, Mexico City Mexico. LC P92.M45.

DIRECTORIO DE MIEMBROS - SOCIEDAD INTERAMERICANA DE PSICOLOGIA. Main/Corp Interamerican Society of Psychology. VFOAT Directory of Members - Interamerican Society of Psychology, Catalogo de Membros - Sociedade Interamericana de Psicologia. 0149-4368. US. English, Portuguese or Spanish. Interamerican Society of Psychology, De Paul University, 2323 North Seminary Avenue, Chicago IL. LC BF15. DD 150.621.

DIRECTORIO DE PERIODISTAS PROFESIONALES DE COLOMBIA. 1-1979-. Spanish. ir. Servicios de Comunicacion Social Ltda, Apartado Aereo 12003, Bogota DE Colombia. LC PN5053.

DIRECTORIO DE PRODUCTORES Y EXPORTADORES DE EL SALVADOR. VFOAT El Salvador, Directorio de Productores y Exportadores. English (Spanish). ir. LC HF3303. DD 382.602947284. *Directorio de Exportadores (Instituto Salvadoreno de Comercio Exterior).*

DIRECTORIO DE SERVICIOS DE INFORMACION Y DOCUMENTACION EN EL URUGUAY. LA. Ed.-. UY. Spanish. ir. Centro Nacional de Documentacion Cientifica Tecnica y Economica, 18 de Julio 1790 AP Postal 452, Montevideo Uruguay.

DIRECTORIO DE SOCIOS. Main/Corp American Chamber of Commerce Spain. VFOAT Membership Directory. English (Spanish). an. $30.00. Camara de Comercio Americana in Espana, Avda Diagonal 477, Barcelona 36 Spain. LC HF322. DD 382.094607302944672. *Membership Directory.*

DIRECTORIO . . . DE TIENDAS DEL SECTOR PUBLICO Y ASOCIADAS. Spanish. ir. LC JL1279. DD 354.7200712025.

DIRECTORIO DEL ABOGADO. 1976-. Spanish. ir. Libreria Atlantida Oscar Cuenca J Martinez, Av Colmena 287, Lima Peru.

DIRECTORIO FINANCIERO NACIONAL. 1970-. 0120-0755. CK. Spanish. ir. Editorial Accion, Apartado Aereo 17816, Bogota Columbia. LC HG185.C6. DD 332.1025861.

DIRECTORIO INDUSTRIAL. Main/Corp SIP (Panama). VFOAT Directorio Industrial de Panama. PN. Spanish. ir. Sindicato de Industriales de Panama, Apartado 6-4798, Estafeta El Dorado, Panama Panama. LC HC147.A1. DD 338.740257287.

DIRECTORIO INDUSTRIAL AZUCARERO. 1972-. VE. Spanish. ir. 50.00. Edificio Luz Electrica de Venezuela, Piso 7 Ave Urdaneta, Esquina de Urapal Venezuela. LC HD9114.V4.

DIRECTORIO INDUSTRIAL, CENTROAMERICA-PANAMA. 1973-. GT. Spanish. ir. Sieca, A Partado Postal 1237, Guatemal Guatemala. LC HC141.A1. DD 338.0025728.

DIRECTORIO INDUSTRIAL DE LATINO AMERICA. Spanish. ir. Directorio Industrial Internacional, Ave Insurgentes Sur 299 Pent-House, Mexico Mexico. LC HC122.

DIRECTORIO INDUSTRIAL U.S.A. 1974/75-. 0094-5595. US. Spanish. $30.00. America Latina Connection Cooporation of Florida, 2745 Ponce de Leon Boulevard, Coral Gables FL 33134. LC HC102. DD 338.402573.

DIRECTORIO INDUSTRIAL Y COMERCIAL DE HONDURAS. 1981-. 0331-0639. English (Spanish). ir. Servicopiax Editores Detras de la Catedral, Metropolitana Apartado Postal No 1178, Tegucigalpa DC Honduras CA. LC HF3273. DD 338.740257283.

DIRECTORIO INTERAMERICANO DE INSTITUCIONES DE INVESTIGACION Y DESARROLLO. 1979-. US. Spanish. 1735 Eye Street/Suite 1127, Washington DC 20006. LC Q180.L37. DD 507.208.

Yearbooks, Almanacs, Directories

DIRECTORIO LATINOAMERICANO DE INSTITUCIONES FINANCIERAS DE DESARROLLO. PE. Spanish. ir. Apartado 1230, Jiron Huancavelica 279, Lima Peru. **LC** HG2710.5.

DIRECTORIO MEDICO PANAMENO. 1961-. 0417-5433. Periodical. PN. Spanish. ir. Directorio Medico Panameno, Apartado 761, Panama 1 Panama.

DIRECTORIO MINERO NACIONAL. CK. Spanish. ir. Ministerio de Minas y Energia, Ave el Dorado - Can- A A 80319 Oficina No 417, Bogota de Columbia. **LC** TN45.

DIRECTORIO MPM : MEDIOS AUDIO/ VISUALES; INFORMACION Y TARIFAS. VFOAT Audio/Visuales. Periodical. MX. Spanish. ir. $600.00. Medios Publicitarios Mexicanos, AV Mexico 99-303, 11 Mexico City Mexico. **LC** HF5808.M6. **DD** 659.102572.

DIRECTORIO MUSICAL VENEZOLANO. VE. Spanish. an. Instituto Autonomo Biblioteca Nacional y de Services de Bibliotecas, Oficina de Informacion Calle Paris con Caroni, Edif. Macanao, 4O Piso Las Mercedes, Caracas Venezuela.

DIRECTORIO NACIONAL DE CURSOS DE POSTGRADO. Spanish. ir. Consejo Nacional de Investigaciones Cientificas y Tecnologic As, Departamento de Educacion, Apartado 70617 los Ruices, Caracas Venezuela. **LC** L914.V4.

DIRECTORIO NACIONAL DE INSTITUCIONES PRIVADAS FILANTROPICAS Y DE DESARROLLO SOCIAL. 1974-. Spanish. ir. Accion en Colombia, Carrera 6 No 69-A-23, Bogota Colombia. **LC** HV203.A2. **DD** 361.76025866.

DIRECTORIO NACIONAL DE PROFESIONALES. 0302-6876. Spanish. ir. ECOC Ltda, Calle 31 No 10-41 Of 702 Apartado Aereo 15964, Bogota Colombia. **LC** HD8038.C6.

DIRECTORIO POSTAL DE PANAMA. Spanish. an. Publicaciones Panamenas SA (PUPSA), Calle 65 No 23, Edificio Bazarebi Apdo 9-103 Zona 9, Panama Republic de Panama. **Tel** 63-5190-63-5286. **LC** HE6723. **DD** 383.0257287. bk rev. adv acc. **Circ** 50,000. (ctrl). Contains an information section, alphabetical section, numberical section, and commercial section.

DIRECTORIO PROFESIONAL HISPANO. 0147-5657. US. Spanish. an. Directorio Profesional Hispano, PO Box 408, Flushing NY 11352. **LC** HD8038.U5.

DIRECTORIO PROVISIONAL DE EXPORTADORES. VFOAT Directorio Provisional de Exportadores de Nicaragua Libre. Spanish (English). ir. El Ministerio, Apartado 2412, Managua Nicaragua.

DIRECTORIO TELEX (SAN SALVADOR, EL SALVADOR). (DIRECTORIO TELEX). Spanish. ir. Antel Edif T Roble, Metrocentre Nte, San Salvador El Salvador.

DIRECTORIO TURISTICO. VFOAT Tourism Directory. US. English (Spanish). sa. OAS, International Trade and Tourism Division, 1889 F Street NW/2nd Floor, Washington DC 20006. **LC** G155.L3. **DD** 380.1459104091812.

DIRECTORY. **Main/Corp** Canadian Psychological Association. VFOAT Repertoire des Membres. 1960-. 0068-9475. CN. English (French). **LC** BF30. **DD** 150.6271.

DIRECTORY - AAMC GROUP ON MEDICAL EDUCATION. (DIRECTORY). **Main/Corp** AAMC Group on Medical Education. VAT Directory - Association of American Medical Colleges Group on Medical Education. 1981-1982-. 0732-3468. US. English. AAMC Group on Medical Education, One Dupont Circle NW/Suite 200, Washington DC 20036. **LC** R735.A4. **DD** 610.71173. Membership Roster.

DIRECTORY - AGRICULTURAL COMMUNICATORS IN EDUCATION (U.S.). (DIRECTORY). **Main/Corp** Agricultural Communicators in Education (U.S.). 8755-5972. US. English. an. Ace Headquarters, 11500 Fairway Drive #308, Reston VA 22090. **DD** 630.

DIRECTORY AKOMODASI JAWA, BALI DAN SUMATERA UTARA. Series/ **Titl** Statistik Perhubungan. Indonesian. ir. Biro Pusat Statsitik, Jl Dr Sutomo 8, Jakarta Indonesia. **LC** TX910.I6.

DIRECTORY - AMERICAN ACADEMY OF DERMATOLOGY. (DIRECTORY). **Main/ Corp** American Academy of Dermatology. 0278-9000. US. English. American Academy of Dermatology, 820 Davis Street, Evanston IL 60201. **LC** RL43. **DD** 616.500607. **NLM** WR 22.1 A512R. Roster: Bylaws, Officers, Committees, 0162-0037.

DIRECTORY - AMERICAN BAR ASSOCIATION. **Main/Corp** American Bar Association. US. English. an. American Bar Association, 750 North Lake Shore Drive, Chicago Il 60611. **Tel** (312)988-5555.

DIRECTORY - AMERICAN BAR ASSOCIATION. FORUM COMMITTEE ON COMMUNICATIONS LAW. (DIRECTORY). **Main/Corp** American Bar Association. Forum Committee on Communications Law. 1980-81-. 0731-8766. US. English. **LC** KF195.C573. **DD** 343.73099025, 347.30399025.

DIRECTORY - AMERICAN BAR ASSOCIATION. FORUM COMMITTEE ON THE CONSTRUCTION INDUSTRY. (DIRECTORY - FORUM COMMITTEE ON THE CONSTRUCTION INDUSTRY, AMERICAN BAR ASSOCIATION). **Main/Corp** American Bar Association. Forum Committee on the Construction Industry. 0273-5180. US. English. American Bar Association, 1155 East 60th Street, Chicago IL 60637. **LC** KF195.C58. **DD** 343.73078690025, 347. 30378690025.

DIRECTORY - AMERICAN BAR ASSOCIATION. FORUM COMMITTEE ON THE ENTERTAINMENT AND SPORTS INDUSTRIES. (DIRECTORY - FORUM COMMITTEE ON THE ENTERTAINMENT AND SPORTS INDUSTRIES). **Main/Corp** American Bar Association. Forum Committee on the Entertainment and Sports Industries. 0273-5172. US. English. American Bar Association, 750 North Lake Shore Drive, Chicago IL 60611. **LC** KF195.E58. **DD** 340.02573.

DIRECTORY - AMERICAN BAR ASSOCIATION. SECTION OF TORT AND INSURANCE PRACTICE. (DIRECTORY). **Main/Corp** American Bar Association. Tort and Insurance Practice Section. VFOAT Section of Tort and Insurance Practice Directory. 0732-9857. US. English. A.B.A., 1155 East 60th Street, Chicago IL 60637. **LC** KF195.I5. **DD** 340.02573.

DIRECTORY - AMERICAN BAR ASSOCIATION. YOUNG LAWYERS DIVISION. (DIRECTORY). **Main/Corp** American Bar Association. Young Lawyers Division. 1981-1982-. 0731-6496. US. English. an. American Bar Association, 1155 East 60th Street, Chicago IL 60637. **LC** KF325.26. **DD** 340.06073. Directory.

DIRECTORY - AMERICAN BAR ASSOCIATION. YOUNG LAWYERS DIVISION. **Main/Corp** American Bar Association. Young Lawyers Division. US. English. an. American Bar Association, Young Lawyers Division, 1155 East 60th Street, Chicago IL 60637.

DIRECTORY - AMERICAN BELL ASSOCIATION. (DIRECTORY). **Main/Corp** American Bell Association. 0093-1330. US. English. an. American Bell Association, PO Box 5, Indiana PA 15701. **LC** ML27.U5. **DD** 789.506273.

DIRECTORY - AMERICAN CHAMBER OF COMMERCE IN FRANCE. **Main/Corp** American Chamber of Commerce in France. VFOAT Directory of the American Chamber of Commerce in France. English. an. American Chamber of Commerce in France, 21 Avenue George-V, 5008 Paris France. **LC** HF306.A452A. **DD** 382.094407302544361.

DIRECTORY - AMERICAN CHAMBER OF COMMERCE IN ITALY. **Main/Corp** American Chamber of Commerce in Italy. 1983-. English (Italian). an. 12 Via Agnello, 20121 Milano Italy. **LC** HF312. **DD** 382.09450730254521. Annual Directory.

DIRECTORY - AMERICAN COLLEGE OF HOSPITAL ADMINISTRATORS. **Main/Corp** American College of Hospital Administrators. VFOAT ACHA Directory. 1938-. 0065-7794. US. English. ir. $60.00. American College of Hospital Administrators, 840 North Lake Shore Drive, Chicago IL 60611. **Tel** (312)943-0544. Ed ACHA. **LC** RA977. **DD** 658.91362110922, B. **NLM** WX 22 AA1 A5D. **Circ** 4,000. (ctrl). Comprehensive listing of nearly 16,000 biographical profiles of leaders in the healthcare field.

DIRECTORY - AMERICAN CONSULTING ENGINEERS COUNCIL. **Main/Corp** American Consulting Engineers Council. 1973/74-. 0147-3484. US. English. an. $50.00. American Consulting Engineers Council, 1015 15th Street NW/Suite 802, Washington DC 20005. **Tel** (202)347-7474. Ed Teresa Y Peterson. **LC** TA12. **DD** 620.002573. adv acc. **Circ** 6,500. (ctrl). Most complete directory available of consulting engineering firms, alphabetically by state, listing firm services, principals and addresses. Directory - Consulting Engineers Council, 0589-4883; Engineering Consultants, 0569-549X.

DIRECTORY - AMERICAN COUNCIL OF INDEPENDENT LABORATORIES. **Main/Corp** American Council of Independent Laboratories. 1982-. US. English. be. $5.00. American Council of Independent Laboratories Inc, 1725 K Street NW, Washington DC 20006. **Tel** (202)887-5872. **Circ** 7,000. (ctrl). Describes services of each member laboratory of ACIL. Includes detailed index of services and geographical index.

DIRECTORY - AMERICAN GROUP PRACTICE ASSOCIATION. **Main/Corp** American Group Practice Association. VFOAT AGPA Directory. 17th- Ed. 0098-2377. US. English. ir. American Group Practice Association, 20 South Quaker Lane, Alexandria VA 22313. **LC** RA977. **DD** 362.1202573. **NLM** WX 22 AA1 A45D. Directory - American Association of Medical Clinics, 0569-2679.

DIRECTORY - AMERICAN GROUP PSYCHOTHERAPY ASSOCIATION. (DIRECTORY). **Main/Corp** American Group Psychotherapy Association. 0733-2920. US. English. $10.00 Members, $20.00 Nonmembers. American Group Psychotherapy Association, 1995 Broadway/ 14th Floor, New York NY 10023. **LC** RC488. **DD** 616.8915202573.

DIRECTORY - AMERICAN NUCLEAR SOCIETY. **Main/Corp** American Nuclear Society. 0092-8518. US. English. American Nuclear Society, PO Box 4957, Chicago IL 60680. **LC** QC16.2. **DD** 539.702573. **NLM** QC 774.2 A512D. Membership Directory - American Nuclear Society, 0517-4015.

DIRECTORY - AMERICAN POLITICAL SCIENCE ASSOCIATION. **Main/Corp** American Political Science Association. 1945-. US. English. Ed 1945-F L Burdette. **LC** JA28.

DIRECTORY - AMERICAN RECOVERY ASSOCIATION, INC. **Main/Corp** American Recovery Association. VAT Directory - American Recovery Association, Incorporated. 0149-5216. Periodical. US. English. 4040 West 70 Street, Minneapolis MN 55435. **LC** HF5585.R46. **DD** 338.7613327.

DIRECTORY - AMERICAN SOCIETY FOR CLINICAL PHARMACOLOGY AND THERAPEUTICS. **Main/Corp** American Society For Clinical Pharmacology and Therapeutics. 1970/71-. 0191-2550. US. English. an. American Society For Clinical Pharmacology and Therapeutics, 1718 Gallagher Road, Norristown PA 19401. **NLM** WB 22.1 A512.

DIRECTORY - AMERICAN SOCIETY FOR PSYCHOPROPHYLAXIS IN OBSTETRICS. **Main/Corp** American Society for Psychoprophylaxis in Obstetrics. 1974/75-. 0161-1240. US. English. an. American Society for Prophylaxis in Obstetrics, 1523 L Street NW, Washington DC 20005. **NLM** WQ 22 AA1 A6D.

DIRECTORY - AMERICAN SOCIETY JOURNALISTS AND AUTHORS. (DIRECTORY). **Main/Corp** American Society of Journalists and Authors. 0278-8829. US. English. ir. $50.00. Grenoble Books, 1931 Vernier, Grosse Pointe Woods MI 48236. **Tel** (313)874-1059. **LC** PN4841. **DD** 070.02573. Directory of Professional Writers.

DIRECTORY - AMERICAN SOCIETY OF CIVIL ENGINEERS. **Main/Corp** American Society of Civil Engineers. 0569-7883. US. English. be. $8.00 Single Issue. United Engineering Center, 345 East 47th Street, New York NY 10017. **LC** TA12. **DD** 624.06273.

DIRECTORY - AMERICAN SOCIETY OF ICHTYOLOGISTS AND HERPETOLOGISTS. (DIRECTORY). **Main/ Corp** American Society of Ichthyologists and Herpetologists. 0747-7317. US. English. **LC** QL614.9. **DD** 597.002573.

Yearbooks, Almanacs, Directories

DIRECTORY - AMERICAN VETERINARY MEDICAL ASSOCIATION. Main/Corp American Veterinary Medical Association. VFOAT AVMA Directory. VAT American Veterinary Medical Association Directory. 0066-1147. US. English. an. $40.00. American Veterinary Medicine Association, 930 North Meacham Road, Schaumburg IL 60196. **Tel** (312)885-807. Ed Jan LaFrana. LC SF611. DD 636.089, 619.06273. NLM SF 611 A512. adv acc. **Circ** 43,000. Annual directory of AVMA listing veterinarians alphabetically and geographically with reference section of organizational, school, governmental and materials information.

DIRECTORY & CONSUMER GUIDE - BETTER BUSINESS BUREAU, GREATER TORONTO. (DIRECTORY & CONSUMER GUIDE - BETTER BUSINESS BUREAU GREATER TORONTO). Main/Corp Better Business Bureau Greater Toronto. 1980-. 0225-2686. CN. English. an. Free. Better Business Bureau of Greater Toronto, Suite 901/321 Bloor Street, Toronto Ontario M4W 3K6 Canada. DD 381.025713541. (ctrl). *Directory, 0708-9759.*

DIRECTORY AND GUIDE - BUILDING CONSTRUCTION EMPLOYERS' ASSOCIATION OF CHICAGO, INC. Main/Corp Building Construction Employers' Association of Chicago. VFOAT BCEA Directory. 0190-4787. US. English. Building Construction Employers' Association of Chicago, 228 North Lasalle Street, Chicago IL 60601. LC KFX1238.1.C64. DD 344.77311018819.

DIRECTORY & GUIDE - FLORIDA INSTITUTE OF CONSULTING ENGINEERS. (DIRECTORY & GUIDE). Main/Corp Florida Institute of Consulting Engineers. VFOAT Directory and Guide. 0742-3381. US. English. $6.00 Members, $12.00 Non-Members. Florida Institute of Consulting Engineers, PO Box 750, Tallahassee FL 32302.

DIRECTORY & HANDBOOK - ONTARIO LIBRARY ASSOCIATION. Main/Corp Ontario Library Association. VFOAT Directory and Handbook. CN. English. an. Ontario Library Association, 73 Richmond Street West/Suite 402, Toronto Ontario M5H 1Z4 Canada. LC Z673.O353. DD 020.6234713. *Directory and Handbook, 0711-2017.*

DIRECTORY AND INDEX OF STANDARDS. SUPPLEMENT. (DIRECTORY AND INDEX OF STANDARDS). VFOAT Repertoire des Normes. No. 1- 1978-. 0226-0026. CN. French (text in English). an. Service d'Information sur les Normes, Conseil Canadien des Normes, 350 rue Sparks, Ottawa Ontario K1R 7S8 Canada. DD 389.60971.

A DIRECTORY AND LISTING OF PAINTINGS AS SHOWN IN THE MAGAZINE ANTIQUES. 1968-. 0747-4997. US. English. an. $3.00. Paul J Fredyma, 999 Lyme Road, Hanover NH 03755. **Tel** (603)643-4276. Ed Paul J Fredyma. DD 745. Soft cover, facsimile print, 20-25 pages listing oil paintings and artists in Antiques Magazine for the years 1968-1984.

DIRECTORY AND NEWSLETTER - FORESTRY ALUMNI ASSOCIATION. UNIVERSITY OF TORONTO. (DIRECTORY AND NEWSLETTER - FORESTRY ALUMNI ASSOCIATION, UNIVERSITY OF TORONTO). Main/Corp University of Toronto. Forestry Alumni Association. Began with 1962 issue?. 0705-1875. Periodical. CN. English. Department of Alumni Affairs, University of Toronto, 47 Willcocks Street, Toronto Ontario M5S 1A1 Canada. DD 634.90711713541.

DIRECTORY AND REGISTER - ROLLS ROYCE OWNERS' CLUB. (DIRECTORY AND REGISTER). Main/Corp Rolls-Royce Owners' Club. 0485-3695. US. English. Rolls-Royce Owners' Club, Box 2001, Mechanicsburg PA 17055. LC TL215.R6. DD 629.2222.

DIRECTORY AND REPORT - CARPET AND RUG INSTITUTE. (DIRECTORY AND REPORT). Main/Corp Carpet and Rug Institute. 1969/70-. 0069-0740. US. English. an. $10.00. LC HD9937.U5. DD 338.4767764302573.

DIRECTORY AND RULES - NEW YORK FUTURES EXCHANGE. Main/Corp New York Futures Exchange. VFOAT New York Futures Exchange Guide. 0271-9770. US. English.

$6.00. 4025 West Peterson Avenue, Chicago IL 60646. LC HG6024.U6. DD 332.644.

DIRECTORY AND STATISTICS OF OREGON LIBRARIES. 1977-. 0162-0290. US. English. an. Oregon State Library, State Library Building, Salem OR 97310. LC Z732.O8. DD 027.0795. *Directory of Oregon Libraries.*

DIRECTORY AND WHO IS WHO OF FARIDABAD INDUSTRIAL COMPLEX. English. ir. Institute of Sciences and Industrial Publications, 656 Sector 15A, Faridabad— 121007. LC HD2346.I52. DD 338.64202554558.

DIRECTORY AND YEAR BOOK OF AMERICAN BUSINESS IN IRELAND. VFOAT Directory and Yearbook of American Business in Ireland. English. an. 5.00 Members, 10.00 Non-Members. United States Chamber of Commerce in Ireland, 20 College Green, Dublin Ireland. LC HD2848. DD 338.889730417025. *Directory of American Business in Ireland.*

DIRECTORY AND YEARBOOK - HUMAN FACTORS SOCIETY. Main/Corp Human Factors Society. 0270-5311. US. English. an. $20.00. Human Factors Society, Box 1369, Santa Monica CA 90406. **Tel** (213)394-1811. LC TA166. DD 620.8206073. adv acc. An alphabetical and geographical listing of people engaged in human factor design, education, and research and development and their areas of expertise.

DIRECTORY, AREAWIDE PLANNING ORGANIZATIONS, STATE OF IOWA. (DIRECTORY : AREAWIDE PLANNING ORGANIZATIONS, STATE OF IOWA). VFOAT Areawide Planning Organizations, State of Iowa. 0363-0013. US. English. 523 East 12th Street, 50319. LC HT393.I8. DD 309.212025777.

DIRECTORY - ASSOCIATED CHURCH PRESS. (DIRECTORY). Main/Corp Associated Church Press. VFOAT Associated Church Press Directory. 0066-8710. US. English. an. The Associated Church Press, PO Box 306, Geneva IL 60134-0306. LC Z7753, BR1. DD 291.05.

DIRECTORY - ASSOCIATION OF ACADEMIC HEALTH CENTERS (U.S.). (DIRECTORY). Main/Corp Association of Academic Health Centers (U.S.). 1981-. 0276-6590. US. English. an. Association of Academic Health Centers, 11 Dupont Circle/Suite 210, Washington DC 20036. **Tel** (202)265-9600. LC RA977. DD 610.71173. NLM WX 22.

DIRECTORY - ASSOCIATION OF AMERICAN UNIVERSITY PRESSES. (DIRECTORY). Main/Corp Association of American University Presses. VFOAT AAUP Directory. 0739-3024. US. English. an. Association of American University Presses, One Park Avenue, New York NY 10016. LC Z475. DD 070.594.

DIRECTORY - ASSOCIATION OF AMERICAN UNIVERSITY PRESSES. Main/Corp Association of American University Presses. 1980/81-. US. English. an. Association of American University Presses Inc, One Park Avenue, New York NY 10016. *Association of American University Presses Directory.*

DIRECTORY - ASSOCIATION OF CANADIAN PUBLISHERS. (DIRECTORY). Main/Corp Association of Canadian Publishers. VFOAT ACP Directory. VAT ACP Directory (1984), Association of Canadian Publishers Directory (1984). 1983/84-. 0821-6096. CN. English. an. Free. Association of Canadian Publishers, 3rd Floor/70 The Esplanade, Toronto Ontario M5E 1R2 Canada. **Tel** (416)361-1408. DD 070.502571. Publication listing the members of the Association of Canadian Publishers. The ACP is a trade association for Canadian-owned book publishers. *ACP Directory, 0229-6918.*

DIRECTORY - ASSOCIATION OF EXECUTIVE RECRUITING CONSULTANTS. Main/Corp Association of Executive Recruiting Consultants (New York, N.Y.). 1980-. 0195-6981. US. English. an. R R Bowker Company, 1180 Avenue of the America, New York NY 10036. LC HF5500.3.U54. DD 658.40711102573.

DIRECTORY - ASSOCIATION OF HALFWAY HOUSE ALCOHOLISM PROGRAMS OF NORTH AMERICA, INC. (DIRECTORY - ASSOCIATION OF HALFWAY HOUSE ALCOHOLISM PROGRAMS OF NORTH AMERICA). Main/Corp Association of Halfway House Alcoholism Programs of North America. 0145-2401.

US. English. 786 East 7th Street, St Paul MN 55106. LC HV5275. DD 362.2920257.

DIRECTORY - ASSOCIATION OF THEOLOGICAL SCHOOLS IN THE UNITED STATES AND CANADA. Main/Corp Association of Theological Schools in the United States and Canada. 1975-. US. English. Association of Theological Schools in the United States and Canada, PO Box 396, Vandalia OH 54337. **Tel** (513)898-4654. **Circ** 2,000. Lists graduate schools of theology in the US and Canada which are members of the Association. Members may be accredited, candidates, or affiliates. *AATS Directory of Theological Schools.*

DIRECTORY - ASSOCIATION OF TRANSLATORS AND INTERPRETERS OF ONTARIO. (REPERTOIRE). Main/Corp Association of Translators and Interpreters of Ontario. VFOAT Directory. VAT Repertoire - Association des Traducteurs et Interpretes de l'Ontario. 0226-8868. CN. English (French). ir. Association of Translators and Interpreters of Ontario, Suite 1406/1 Nicholas Street, Ottawa Ontario K1N 7B7 Canada. DD 418.02025713. *Association of Translators and Interpreters, 0226-8868.*

DIRECTORY. ATLANTIC POSTAL REGION. POSTAL CODE. (DIRECTORY : ATLANTIC POSTAL REGION, POSTAL CODE). VFOAT Repertoire : Region Postale de l'Atlantique, Code Postal. 0317-4174. Periodical. CN. English (French). an. Free. Directory Unit, Suite 224, Sir Alexander Campbell Building, Ottawa Ontario K1A 0BL Canada. LC HE6656.M37. DD 383.14.

DIRECTORY, AVIATION MEDICAL EXAMINERS. VFOAT Aviation Medical Examiners. US. English. Federal Aviation Administration, Office of Aviation Medicine, 800 Independence Avenue SW, Washington DC 20591.

DIRECTORY : BANKS AND FINANCIAL INSTITUTIONS. US. English. an. Department of Commerce and Economic Development, Pouch D, Juneau AK 99811. LC HG2444.A4. DD 332.1025798.

THE DIRECTORY - BELGIAN AMERICAN CHAMBER OF COMMERCE IN THE UNITED STATES, INC. (THE DIRECTORY - BELGIAN AMERICAN CHAMBER OF COMMERCE IN THE UNITED STATES). Main/Corp Belgian American Chamber of Commerce in the United States. 0196-7622. US. English. be. $42.00. Belgian American Chamber of Commerce in the United States, 437 Madison Avenue/Suite 2009, New York NY 10022. **Tel** (212)832-1211. Ed C F Raick. LC HD2868. DD 338.889730493. adv acc. **Circ** 1,500. Directory of chamber membership contains information on US/Belgium trade exchanges.

DIRECTORY. BOROUGH & CITY OFFICIALS. (DIRECTORY OF BOROUGH AND CITY OFFICIALS). **Series/Titl** Alaska Local Government. 1973-. 0361-2910. US. English. an. Department of Community & Regional Affairs, Pouch B, Juneau AK 99811. LC JS3.A4. DD 320.209798 S, 352. 005209798. *Borough and City Officials.*

DIRECTORY - BRITISH COLUMBIA MOTOR TRANSPORT ASSOCIATION. (DIRECTORY). Main/Corp British Columbia Motor Transport Association. VFOAT British Columbia Motor Transport Directory. VAT British Columbia Motor Transport Directory (1981). 1981-. 0714-8658. CN. English. an. 34.95. B C Motor Transport Association Directory, 4090 Gravely Street, Burnaby British Columbia V5C 3T6 Canada. **Tel** (604)299-7407. DD 388.324025711. adv acc. **Circ** 1,700. Shippers guide to truck transportation services available in BC. *B.C. Motor Transport Directory, 0714-8666.*

DIRECTORY - BROOKHAVEN NATIONAL LABORATORY. Main/Corp Brookhaven National Laboratory. US. English. an. Brookhaven National Laboratory, Upton Long Island NY 11973.

DIRECTORY, CALIFORNIA CAMPAIGN CONTRIBUTORS. VFOAT California Campaign Contributors. 1982-. 0731-7263. US. English. an. ABC-Clio Inc, POB 4397, Santa Barbara CA 93103. LC JK1991.5.C2. DD 324.7809794.

DIRECTORY - CAMBRIDGE & DISTRICT CHAMBER OF COMMERCE & INDUSTRY (CAMBRIDGESHIRE). Main/Corp Cambridge & District Chamber of Commerce & Industry (Cambridgeshire). UK. English. Owen Webb

Yearbooks, Almanacs, Directories

House, 1 Gresham Road, Cambridge CB1 2EP England. **LC** HF302. **DD** 338.7402542659.

DIRECTORY - CANADA STUDIES FOUNDATION. Main/Corp Canada Studies Foundation. **VFOAT** Repertoire. 1977-. 0703-7066. **CN.** English (text in French, with French text on inverted pages). an. $1.00. Canada Studies Foundation, Suite 300A 151 Slater Street, Ottawa Ontario K1P 5H3 Canada. **DD** 370.6271.

DIRECTORY - CANADIAN ASSOCIATION OF GEOGRAPHERS. Main/Corp Canadian Association of Geographers. **VFOAT** Annuaire - Association Canadienne des Geographes. 1977-. 0707-3844. **CN.** English (French). an. $7.74. McGill University, 805 Sherbrooke Street West, Montreal Province of Quebec H4A 2K6 Canada. **Tel** (514)392-5496. **Ed** William Barr. **LC** G4. **DD** 910.2571, 910.72071. **Circ** 1,500. (ctrl). Directory of the staff, research activities and current publications for Canadian departments of geography and government departments. In geography related work. *Newsletter and Membership List - Canadian Association of Geographers, 0068-8312.*

DIRECTORY - CANADIAN ASSOCIATION OF LAW LIBRARIES. (DIRECTORY). **Main/Corp** Canadian Association of Law Libraries. **VAT** Annuaire - Association Canadienne des Bibliotheques de Droit. July 1982-. 0821-4638. **CN.** English (French). an. Canadian Association of Law Libraries, PO Box 220 Adelaide Street Postal Station, Toronto Ontario M5C 2J1 Canada. **DD** 026.34. *List of Members, 0707-5219.*

DIRECTORY - CANADIAN ASSOCIATION OF PATHOLOGISTS. (DIRECTORY). **Main/Corp** Canadian Association of Pathologists. **VFOAT** Annuaire. 0712-1997. **CN.** English. an. c/o K Pritzker, Mount Sinai Hospital, Department of Laboratories, Toronto Ontario M5G G1X5 Canada. **DD** 616.0706071.

DIRECTORY - CANADIAN BAND DIRECTORS' ASSOCIATION, ALBERTA CHAPTER. (DIRECTORY). **Main/Corp** Canadian Band Directors' Association. Alberta Chapter. 1982/1983-. 0826-0923. **CN.** English. an. Free to Members. Alberta Chapter/Canadian Band Directors Association, 911 Library Tower 2500 University Drive, Calgary Alberta 2TN 1N4 Canada. **DD** 785.067123.

DIRECTORY - CANADIAN GAS ASSOCIATION. (DIRECTORY). **Main/Corp** Canadian Gas Association. 1980/1981-. 0229-1142. **CN.** English. an. $5.00. Canadian Gas Association, 55 Scarsdale Road, Don Mills Ontario M3B 2R3 Canada. **DD** 363.6302571. *Canadian Gas Utilities Directory, 0576-5269.*

DIRECTORY - CANADIAN INTERUNIVERSITY ATHLETIC UNION. Main/Corp Canadian Interuniversity Athletic Union. **VFOAT** Repertoire - UnionSportive Interuniversitaire Canadienne. 1978/79-. 0706-697X. **CN.** English (French). an. Free to members. Canadian Interuniversity Athletic Union, 333 River Road, Vanier Ontario K1L 8B9 Canada. **DD** 796.02571.

DIRECTORY - CANADIAN LIFE AND HEALTH INSURANCE ASSOCIATION. (DIRECTORY). **Main/Corp** Canadian Life and Health Insurance Association. **VFOAT** Repertoire. **VAT** Repertoire - Association Canadienne des Compagnies d'Assurances de Personnes. 1981/82-. 0710-2429. **CN.** English (French). Canadian Life and Health Insurance Association, 55 University Avenue, Toronto Ontario M5J 2K7 Canada. **DD** 368.3002571. *Directory, 0707-6150.*

DIRECTORY - CANADIAN PAYMENTS ASSOCIATION. (DIRECTORY - CANADIAN PAYMENTS ASSOCIATION). **Main/Corp** Canadian Payments Association. **VFOAT** Repertoire. 1983-. 0822-7152. **CN.** English. an. V. 1, $24.83, V. 2 $21.33, V. 3 $15.83. Directory Canadian Payments Association, c/o Plow and Waters Printing Canada Ltd, 60 Gervais Drive, Don Mills Ontario M3C 1Z3 Canada. **DD** 332.102571. *Bank Directory of Canada, 0045-1436; Routing Numbers of Deposit-Taking Institutions in Canada other than Chartered Banks, 0708-9988.*

DIRECTORY - CANADIAN PSYCHOLOGICAL ASSOCIATION. (DIRECTORY OF THE CANADIAN PSYCHOLOGICAL ASSOCIATION). **Main/Corp** Canadian Psychological Association. **VFOAT** Repertoire de la Societe Canadienne de Psychologie. 1981 Ed.-. 0068-9475. **CN.** English (French). te. Free to Members. Canadian Psychological Association, 558 King Edward Avenue, Ottawa Ontario K1N 7N6 Canada. **DD** 150.6071. *Directory, 0068-9475.*

DIRECTORY - CANADIAN REAL ESTATE ASSOCIATION. Main/Corp Canadian Real Estate Association. **VFOAT** C R E A Directory. 1974-. 0319-0005. Periodical. **CN.** English. an. Canadian Real Estate Association Directory, 99 Duncan Mills Road, Don Mills Ontario M3B 1Z2 Canada. **DD** 333.3306271. *C R E A Directory, 0318-9996; FIABCI/Canada Roster, 1980, 0225-8099.*

DIRECTORY - CANADIAN RELIGIOUS CONFERENCE. Main/Corp Canadian Religious Conference. **VFOAT** Bottin - Conference Religieuse Canadienne. Began with 1970 issue. 0705-3118. **CN.** English (text in French). Free. Canadian Religious Conference, 324 Laurier Street East, Ottawa K1N 6P6 Canada. **DD** 255.002571. (ctrl).

DIRECTORY - CANADIAN ROOFING CONTRACTORS' ASSOCIATION. Main/Corp Canadian Roofing Contractors' Association. **VFOAT** Annuaire - Association Canadienne des Entrepreneurs en Couverture. 1980-. 0228-1619. **CN.** English (French). an. Canadian Roofing Contractors' Association, Suite 710/116 Albert Street, Ottawa Ontario K1P 5G3 Canada. **DD** 690.1506071. *CRCA Directory, 0228-0876.*

DIRECTORY - CANADIAN SOCIETY OF CINEMATOGRAPHERS. (DIRECTORY). **Main/Corp** Canadian Society of Cinematographers. 1980-. 0229-6985. **CN.** English. an. Free to Members. Canadian Society of Cinematographers, 22 Front Street West, Toronto Ontario M5J 1C4 Canada. **DD** 778.5302571.

DIRECTORY - CANADIAN STAMP DEALERS' ASSOCIATION. (DIRECTORY). **Main/Corp** Canadian Stamp Dealers' Association. **VFOAT** Canadian Stamp Dealers' Association Directory. 1984-. 0827-2034. Periodical. **CN.** English. an. Free. Canadian Stamp Dealers' Association, PO Box 1123 Adelaide Street PO, Toronto Ontario M5C 2K5 Canada. **DD** 769.5602571. adv acc. **Circ** 10,000. Members of Canadian Stamp Dealers' Association, listed by name and philatelic specialty.

DIRECTORY - CANADIAN TESTING ASSOCIATION. Main/Corp Canadian Testing Association. **VFOAT** Repertoire - Association Canadienne des Laboratoires d'Essais. 2d Ed.- 1965-. 0703-1742. **CN.** English (French, 1971?). be. Free. Canadian Testing Association, Suite 640/220 Laurier Avenue West, Ottawa Ontario K1P 5Z9 Canada. **DD** 658.5602571. *Directory, 0703-1734.*

DIRECTORY - CASLIS, CALGARY CHAPTER. (DIRECTORY). **Main/Corp** Canadian Association of Special Libraries and Information Services. Calgary Chapter. **VFOAT** Calgary Special Libraries Directory. **VAT** Calgary Special Libraries Directory (1982), Directory - Canadian Association of Special Libraries and Information Services, Calgary Chapter. 0821-3046. Periodical. **CN.** English. ir. Free to Members. CASLIS Calgary Chapter, 40 Research Place NW, Calgary Alberta T2L 1Y6 Canada. **DD** 027.602571233. *Calgary Special Libraries Directory, 0821-3135.*

DIRECTORY - CENTRAL ONTARIO REGIONAL LIBRARY SYSTEM. Main/Corp Central Ontario Regional Library System. 1975-. 0702-8350. Periodical. **CN.** English. an. Central Ontario Regional Library System, 129 Church Street, Richmond Hill Ontario L4C 1W4 Canada. **DD** 027.402571354.

DIRECTORY, CERTIFIED APPLIANCES AND ACCESSORIES. VFOAT Directory of Certified Appliances and Accessories. 1935. US. English. mo. $15.00. American Gas Association, 8501 East Pleasant Valley Road, Cleveland OH 44131. **Tel** (216)524-4990. **Circ** 4,500. (ctrl). Lists appliances and controls, the designs of which have been found by the American Gas Association laboratories to comply with applicable national standards. *Directory, Approved Appliances, Listed Accessories.*

DIRECTORY. CLASSIFIED TRADE INDEX. (DIRECTORY : CLASSIFIED TRADE INDEX). **VFOAT** Classified Trade Index, Directory: Trade Commerce Index: Kenya, Uganda, Tanzania, East African Community. 0376-8422. KE. English. ir. East Africa Directory Company, PO Box 31237, Nairobi Kenya. **LC** HF3893. **DD** 380.10256. *Directory Trade-Commerce and Local Manufacturers.*

DIRECTORY. COMMUNITY DEVELOPMENT EDUCATION AND TRAINING PROGRAMS THROUGHOUT THE WORLD. (DIRECTORY : COMMUNITY DEVELOPMENT EDUCATION AND TRAINING PROGRAMS THROUGHOUT THE WORLD). **VFOAT** Community Development Education and Training Programs Throughout the World. 0362-4366. US. English. $2.00. Community Development Society, 720 Clark Hall, Columbia MO 65201. **LC** HN49.C6. **DD** 301.350711.

DIRECTORY - COUNCIL OF PETROLEUM ACCOUNTANTS SOCIETIES (U.S.). Main/Corp Council of Petroleum Accountants Societies (U.S.). **VFOAT** C.O.P.A.S. Directory. US. English. Council of Petroleum, Accountants Societies, PO Box 13117, Arlington TX 76013. **LC** HF5686.P3. **DD** 657.862.

DIRECTORY - COUNCIL OF SCOTTISH CLAN ASSOCIATIONS. (DIRECTORY). 0747-6434. US. English. Council of Scottish Clan Associations, 7 Wyndmoor Drive, Convent Station NJ 07961. **LC** E184.S3. **DD** 973.049163025.

DIRECTORY - COUNCIL OF SPECIALISTS IN PSYCHIATRIC AND MENTAL HEALTH NURSING. Main/Corp American Nurses' Association. Council of Specialists in Psychiatric and Mental Health Nursing. 1979-. 0272-5940. US. English. be. Ana, 2420 Pershing Road, Kansas City MO 64108. **NLM** WY 22 AA1 A3D.

DIRECTORY DATABASE. 0741-5915. Periodical. US. English. mo. $50.00. Directory Database, Box J, Navesink NJ 07752.

DIRECTORY : DEPARTMENT STORE WINE SHOPS & WINE STORES IN MAJOR U.S. CITIES. VAT Directory: Department Store Wine Shops & Wine Stores in Major United States Cities. 1976-. US. English. International Wine Society, 304 East 45th Street, New York NY 10017. **LC** HD9373. **DD** 381.456632002573.

DIRECTORY, DEPARTMENTS OF ANATOMY OF THE UNITED STATES AND CANADA. (DIRECTORY : DEPARTMENTS OF ANATOMY OF THE UNITED STATES AND CANADA). Began with Vol. For 1968. 0364-7765. US. English. te. **LC** QM17. **DD** 611.0071173.

DIRECTORY. DIOCESAN AGENCIES OF CATHOLIC CHARITIES. UNITED STATES, PUERTO RICO AND CANADA. (DIRECTORY : DIOCESAN AGENCIES OF CATHOLIC CHARITIES, UNITED STATES, PUERTO RICO, AND CANADA). 0091-1003. US. English. an. $2.00. National Conference of Catholic Charities, 1346 Connecticut Avenue Northwest, Washington DC 20036. **LC** HV89. **DD** 361.75.

DIRECTORY - EASTERN ONTARIO LIBRARY SYSTEM. ANNUAIRE - FEDERATION DES BIBLIOTHEQUES DE L'EST DE L'ONTARIO. Main/Corp Eastern Ontario Library System. Began with 1970? issue. 0318-1502. Periodical. **CN.** English (includes some text in French, 1980/81-). Eastern Ontario Regional Library System, Suite 6/200 Cooper Street, Ottawa Ontario K2P 0G1 Canada. **DD** 027.40257138.

DIRECTORY : EASTERN ONTARIO, POSTAL CODE. VFOAT Repertoire:. **CN.** English and French. Information Canada/Receiver General Canada, Statistics Pub Canada, Ottawa Ontario K1A 0T6 Canada. **LC** HE6656.O5. **DD** 383.14.

DIRECTORY - EDITORIAL FREELANCERS ASSOCIATION (U.S.). (DIRECTORY). **Main/Corp** Editorial Freelancers Association (U.S.). 8755-285X. US. English. an. Editorial Freelancers Association, 175 Fifth Avenue/Suite 1101, New York NY 10010. **LC** PN149.8. **DD** 070.4102573.

DIRECTORY - EUROPEAN COIL COATING ASSOCIATION. Main/Corp European Coil Coating Association. **VFOAT** European Coil Coating Directory. UK. English, French, and German. 2.25. John Adam House, John Adam Street, London WC2N 6JN England. **LC** TS203. **DD** 671.73.

DIRECTORY - FEDERAL COMMUNICATIONS BAR ASSOCIATION. (DIRECTORY). **Main/Corp** Federal Communications Bar Association. 0093-1780. US. English. $1.00. Federal Communications Bar Association, 1815 H Street Northwest, Washington DC 20006. **LC** KF190. **DD** 343.73099402573.

Yearbooks, Almanacs, Directories

DIRECTORY. FEDERALLY FUNDED COMMUNITY MENTAL HEALTH CENTERS. (DIRECTORY, FEDERALLY FUNDED COMMUNITY MENTAL HEALTH CENTERS). **Series/Titl** DHHS Publication. **VFOAT** Directory of Federally Funded Community Mental Health Centers. 0272-4162. US. English. be. Superintendent of Documents, US Government Printing Office, Washington DC 20402. **LC** RA790.6. **DD** 362.202573. **NLM** WM 22 AA1 D26.

DIRECTORY. FLORIDA PORTS AND WATERWAYS. (DIRECTORY : FLORIDA PORTS AND WATERWAYS). **VFOAT** Florida Ports and Waterways Directory. 1972-. 0091-8458. US. English. Florida Department of Commerce Division of Economic Development, 107 West Gaines Street, Room 401, Tallahassee FL 32301. **Tel** (904)488-9553. Ed Wayne Mixson. **LC** HE554.A4. **DD** 387.1025759. **Circ** 10,000. (ctrl). Florida's major seaports are among the most sophisticated and cost effective in the world. Mode RN ports build for modern shipping needs. The better bottom line.

DIRECTORY FOR A NEW WORLD. US. English. an. 8570 Wilshire Boulevard, Beverly Hills CA 90211. *World Directory -International Cooperation Council.*

THE DIRECTORY FOR BOATS, ACCESSORIES AND FISHING TACKLE. Vol. 2 (1982)-. 0277-9528. US. English. an. $3.75. Salt Water Sportsman Inc, 10 High Street, Boston MA 02110. **LC** VM341. **DD** 623.82310294. *Directory for Motorboats, Accessories, and Fishing Tackle, 0272-376X.*

THE DIRECTORY FOR EXCEPTIONAL CHILDREN. 1st- Ed. 0070-5012. US. English. be. $41.44. Porter Sargent Publisher, 11 Beacon Street, Boston MA 02108. **Tel** (617)523-1670. Ed E N Hayes. **LC** L4007. **DD** 371.92058. **NLM** WS 22 AA1 D5. A single volume reference which provides a vital stepping stone for parents and professionals seeking the optimal environment for special needs of children.

DIRECTORY FOR MEMBERS ONLY - NATIONAL SCHOOL SUPPLY & EQUIPMENT (U.S.). **Main/Corp** National School Supply & Equipment Association (U.S.). 0741-2789. US. English. an. National School Supply & Equipment Association, 1500 Boulevard/Suite 609, Arlington VA 22209. **LC** L901. **DD** 338.4737162025. *Directory of Members, Officers, Committees, Bylaws, 0147-2577.*

DIRECTORY FOR MEMBERS - SOCIETY OF MOTION PICTURE AND TELEVISION ENGINEERS, INC. **Main/Corp** Society of Motion Picture and Television Engineers. **VFOAT** SMPTE Directory For Members. **VAT** Directory For Members - Society of Motion Picture and Television Engineers, Incorporated. 0364-8788. US. English. Society of Motion Picture and Television Engineers Inc, 862 Scarsdale Avenue, Scarsdale NY 10583. **LC** TR847.5. **DD** 621.36.

DIRECTORY FOR THE EASTERN ASSOCIATION OF STUDENT FINANCIAL AID ADMINISTRATORS. **Main/Corp** Eastern Association of Student Financial Aid Administrators. 1973-. 0091-7168. US. English. an. House of Printing, 8833 Brookville Road, Silver Spring MD 20910. **LC** L901. **DD** 378.302573.

DIRECTORY FOR THE ILLINOIS PUBLIC COMMUNITY COLLEGE SYSTEM. Began in 1977. US. English. an. Illinois Community College Board, 3085 Stevenson Drive, Springfield IL 62703. **LC** L903.I3. **DD** 378.1011. *Illinois Community College Board Directory for the Illinois Public Community College System.*

DIRECTORY FOR THE NATIONAL CLEARINGHOUSE LIFELINE PROGRAM OF THE AMERICAN ASSOCIATION OF BLOOD BANKS. **VFOAT** A.A.B.B. Directory for the National Clearinghouse Lifeline Program of the American Association of Blood Banks. 0748-7703. US. English. American Association of Blood Banks National Clearinghouse Office, Suite 401/1117 North 19th Street, Arlington VA 22209. **LC** RM172. **DD** 362.178402573. *Directory for the National Clearinghouse Program of the American Association of Blood Banks, 0160-0605.*

THE DIRECTORY FOR ZAMBIA, MALAW, BOTSWANA AND ADJACENT TERRITORIES. English. an. 10.00. Directory Publishers of Zambia, PO Box 1659, Ndola Zambia. **Tel** 212650/53. **LC** DT729. **DD** 968.06025. adv acc.

DIRECTORY - FORUM COMMITTEE ON FRANCHISING. **Main/Corp** American Bar Association. Forum Committee on Franchising. 0272-1198. US. English. American Bar Association, 750 North Lake Shore Drive, Chicago IL 60611. **LC** KF195.F73. **DD** 349.73025.

DIRECTORY - FORUM COMMITTEE ON HEALTH LAW, AMERICAN BAR ASSOCIATION. **Main/Corp** American Bar Association. Forum Committee on Health Law. 0271-0196. US. English. American Bar Association, 1155 East 60th Street, Chicago IL 60637. **LC** KF195.M43. **DD** 340.02573.

DIRECTORY. GOVERNMENTAL AIR POLLUTION CONTROL AGENCIES. (DIRECTORY : GOVERNMENTAL AIR POLLUTION CONTROL AGENCIES). **VFOAT** Directory of Governmental Air Pollution Control Agencies. 1977-. 0161-4991. US. English. an. $4.00. Air Pollution Control Association, PO Box 2861, Pittsburgh PA 15230. **LC** TD882. **DD** 353.008232. **NLM** WA 22 AA1 D4. *Directory. Governmental Air Pollution Agencies, 0090-807X.*

DIRECTORY - GRAPHIC ARTISTS GUILD (U.S.). (DIRECTORY). Began with 1977. 0733-9216. US. English. $35.00. Graphic Artists Guild, 30 East 20th Street, New York NY 10003. **LC** NC999. **DD** 741.602573.

DIRECTORY, HANDBOOK - CALIFORNIA STATE PSYCHOLOGICAL ASSOCIATION. **Main/Corp** California State Psychological Association. **VFOAT** CSPA Directory, Handbook. 0193-7561. US. English. $10.00. California State Psychological Association, 2365 Westwood Boulevard, Los Angeles CA 90064. **LC** BF30. **DD** 150.62794.

DIRECTORY, HANDBOOK - PENNSYLVANIA PSYCHOLOGICAL ASSOCIATION. **Main/Corp** Pennsylvania Psychological Association. 0147-3840. US. English. $10.00. Pennsylvania Psychological Association, 209 North Craig Street, Pittsburgh PA 15213. **Tel** (412)682-8220. Ed Zita Levin. **LC** BF30. **DD** 150.62748. adv acc. **Circ** 2,400. (ctrl). A directory of members of the state psychological association and licensed psychologists in Pennsylvania. Includes addresses, credentials, and health services offered.

DIRECTORY HOTEL, LOSMEN DAN PENGINAPAN. **Series/Titl** Statistik Perhubungan. 1973-. Indonesian. ir. Biro Pusat Statistik, Jln Dr Sutomo No 8, Jakarta Indonesia. **Tel** 372808. **LC** TX910.I6.

DIRECTORY HOTEL PARIWISATA & TRAVEL BUREAU. **Series/Titl** Statistik Perhubungan. 1973-. 0304-1484. Indonesian. ir. Biro Pusat Statistik, Jl Dr Sutomo No 8, Jakarta Indonesia. **LC** G155.I6.

DIRECTORY - INDEPENDENT CANADIAN BUSINESSMEN ASSOCIATION OF BRITISH COLUMBIA. **Main/Corp** Independent Canadian Businessmen Association of British Columbia. **VFOAT** I.C.B.A. Directory. **VAT** ICBA Directory (1979) Independent Canadian Businessmen Association of British Columbia Directory. 1979-. 0225-9583. CN. English. an. Independent Canadian Businessmen Association of British Columbia, 12202B-86th Avenue, Surrey British Columbia V3W 3H7 Canada. **DD** 338.642025711. *Directory, 0225-9575.*

DIRECTORY, INDIANA STATE-AIDED COMMUNITY AGENCIES FOR THE MENTALLY RETARDED AND OTHER DEVELOPMENTALLY DISABLED AND AGENCIES RECEIVING DEVELOPMENTAL DISABILITY PROJECT GRANTS CEASED. 0098-5171. US. English. Department of Mental Health, 3989 Meadows Drive/Suite 1, Indianapolis IN 46205. **LC** HV3006.I6. **DD** 362.3025773. *Directory, Indiana State Aided SIC Community Centers for the Mentally Retarded.*

DIRECTORY - INDUSTRIAL DEVELOPERS ASSOCIATION OF CANADA. (DIRECTORY). **Main/Corp** Industrial Developers Association of Canada. 1980/81-. 0711-6047. CN. English (French). Industrial Developers Association of Canada, 350 Sparks Street/Suite 602, Ottawa Ontario K1R 7S8 Canada. **DD** 338.006071. *Roster, 0708-9236.*

DIRECTORY INFORMATION SERVICE. No. 1 (Nov. 1980)-. 0146-7085. Periodical. US. English. ir. $110.00. Gale Research Company, Book Tower, Detroit MI 48226. **Tel** (800)521-0707. Ed J Ethridge. Keeps subscribers informed of new editions of established directories and brand-new directories. The DIS will cover well over 1,000 directories.

DIRECTORY : INSTITUTIONS AND LEADERSHIP PERSONNEL - OKLAHOMA STATE REGENTS FOR HIGHER EDUCATION. **Main/Corp** Oklahoma State Regents for Higher Education. US. English. an. **LC** LB2341.6.O5. **DD** 378.11025766.

DIRECTORY - INTERNATIONAL ASSOCIATION OF LAW LIBRARIES. **Main/Corp** International Assoication of Law Libraries. 0376-8430. GW. English (Multilingual). ir. $5.00. International Association of Law Libraries, D 35 Marburg Universitatsstr, D 6200 Marburg West Germany. **LC** Z675.L2. **DD** 026.340025.

DIRECTORY - INTERNATIONAL DOCUMENTARY ASSOCIATION. (DIRECTORY). **Main/Corp** International Documentary Association. **VFOAT** IDA Directory. Vol. 1, No. 1 (1984)-. 8755-8947. Periodical. US. English. an. $10.00. International Documentary Association, 8489 West Third Street, Los Angeles CA 90048. **DD** 070.

DIRECTORY - INTERNATIONAL FEDERATION OF COTTON AND ALLIED TEXTILE INDUSTRIES. **Main/Corp** International Federation of Cotton and Allied Textile Industries. 1st Ed. (1964)-. Periodical. English. be. International Textile Manufacturers Federation, Postfach 289, CH-8039 Zurich Switzerland.

DIRECTORY - INTERNATIONAL MONETARY FUND. (DIRECTORY). **Main/Corp** International Monetary Fund. 0250-7390. US. English. International Monetary Fund, 19th and H Streets, Washington DC 20431.

DIRECTORY - INTERNATIONAL READING ASSOCIATION. (DIRECTORY). **Main/Corp** International Reading Association. **VFOAT** IRA Directory. 0090-8975. US. English. an. International Reading Association, 800 Barksdale Road, PO Box 8139, Newark DE 19711. **Tel** (302)731-1600. **LC** L900. **DD** 428.4025.

DIRECTORY - INTERNATIONAL REAL ESTATE FEDERATION. **Main/Corp** International Real Estate Federation. FR. English (French, German, and Spanish). an. Editions Hervas, 123 Av Philippe-Auguste, 75011 Paris France. **LC** HD1361. **DD** 333.33025. *FIABCI International Directory.*

DIRECTORY - INTERNATIONAL REHABILITATION MEDICINE ASSOCIATION. **Main/Corp** International Rehabilitation Medicine Association. English. ir.

DIRECTORY - INTERSTATE OIL COMPACT COMMISSION. (DIRECTORY). **Main/Corp** Interstate Oil Compact Commission. 8755-5956. US. English. an. Interstate Oil Compact Commission, PO Box 53127, Oklahoma City OK 73152. **LC** TN867. **DD** 338.2728202573. *Directory of the Interstate Oil Compact Commission and Oil and Gas Agencies.*

DIRECTORY : JEWISH FEDERATIONS, WELFARE FUNDS AND COMMUNITY COUNCILS. **Main/Corp** Council of Jewish Federations and Welfare Funds. **VFOAT** Directory of Jewish Federations, Welfare Funds, Community Councils. US. English. an. Council of Jewish Federations & Welfare Funds, 575 Lexington, New York NY 10022. **LC** HV3191. **DD** 361.7.

DIRECTORY : JUVENILE AND ADULT CORRECTIONAL DEPARTMENTS, INSTITUTIONS, AGENCIES AND PAROLING AUTHORITIES, UNITED STATES AND CANADA. 1975/76-1978. Periodical. US. English. an. $35.00. American Correctional Association, 4321 Hartwick Road/Suite L-208, College Park MD 20740. **Tel** (301)699-7600. bk rev. adv acc. **Circ** 6,000. Lists administrative personnel, state level institutions, federal military in US and Canada, statistics on inmate populations, etc. *Directory. Juvenile and Adult Correctional Institutions and Agencies of the United States of America, Canada, and Great Britain.*

DIRECTORY, KOREA ELECTRONICS MANUFACTURERS. (DIRECTORY : KOREA ELECTRONICS MANUFACTURERS). **VFOAT** Directory of Korea Electronics Manufacturers. 0376-8384. English and Korean. ir. Korea Electronics and Manufacturers, Fine Instruments Center, 222-13 Kuro-dong, Seoul Korea. **LC** HD9696.A3.

Yearbooks, Almanacs, Directories

DIRECTORY - LAKE ONTARIO REGIONAL LIBRARY SYSTEM. Main/Corp Lake Ontario Regional Library System. Began with 1967 issue. 0315-2774. Periodical. CN. English. an. Lake Ontario Regional Library System, 88 Wright Crescent, Kingston Ontario K7L 4T9 Canada. **DD** 027.40257135.

DIRECTORY - LIBRARY OF CONGRESS. Main/Corp Library of Congress. VFOAT Library of Congress Directory. US. English. Library of Congress, Washington DC 20540.

DIRECTORY, LICENSED & CERTIFIED HEALTH CARE FACILITIES. (DIRECTORY : LICENSED & CERTIFIED HEALTH CARE FACILITIES). VAT Directory, Licensed and Certified Health Care Facilities. 0363-2563. US. English. Minnesota Department of Health, 717 Delaware Street Southeast, Minneapolis MN 55440. **LC** RA981.M6. **DD** 362.1025776. **NLM** WX 22 AM6 D4M. *Directory: Licensed Hospitals and Related Institutions.*

DIRECTORY. LICENSED HOSPITALS AND AMBULATORY SURGICAL TREATMENT CENTERS IN TENNESSEE. (DIRECTORY : LICENSED HOSPITALS AND AMBULATORY SURGICAL TREATMENT CENTERS IN TENNESSEE). **VF** Licensed Hospitals and Ambulatory Surgical Treatment Centers in Tennessee. 1978-. 0272-0892. US. English. Board for Licensing Health Care Facilities, 283 Plus Park Boulevard, Nashville TN 37217. **NLM** WX 22 AT2 D6LA. *Directory: Licensed Hospitals in Tennessee.*

DIRECTORY, LICENSED NURSING HOMES AND HOMES FOR AGED IN TENNESSEE. VFOAT Licensed Nursing Homes and Homes for Aged in Tennessee. Sept. 1, 1978-. 0730-1669. US. English. an. Board Licensing Health Care Facilities, 283 Plus Park Boulevard, Nashville TN 37217. **Tel** (615)741-6393. **NLM** WX 22 AT2 D6L. *Directory, Licensed Nursing Homes in Tennessee, Directory, Licensed Homes for Aged in Tennessee.*

DIRECTORY, LICENSED REAL ESTATE BROKERS AND SALES ASSOCIATES. VFOAT Directory of Oklahoma Licensed Real Estate Brokers and Sales Association. 0730-7357. US. English. Oklahoma Real Estate Commission, Suite 100/4040 North Lincoln Boulevard, Oklahoma City OK 73105. **LC** HD266.O5. **DD** 333.33025766.

DIRECTORY, LICENSED REAL ESTATE BROKERS AND SALESMEN - (SOUTH CAROLINA). Main/Corp South Carolina. Real Estate Commission. 1972-. US. English. ir. 2221 Devine Street, Columbia SC 29205. *Directory, Licensed Real Estate Brokers and Salesmen.*

DIRECTORY LISTING CURRICULUMS OFFERED IN THE COMMUNITY COLLEGES OF PENNSYLVANIA. 0092-8526. US. English. Department of Education, Box 911, Harrisburg PA 17126. **LC** L903.P4. **DD** 378.199025748.

DIRECTORY - LOUISIANA STATE BOARD OF EXAMINERS FOR SPEECH PATHOLOGY AND AUDIOLOGY. Main/Corp Louisiana. State Board of Examiners for Speech Pathology and Audiology. US. English. Louisiana State Board of Examiners for Speech Pathology and Audiology, 712 Bath Street, Metairie LA 70001. **LC** RC428.5. **DD** 6168506025763.

DIRECTORY : LUTHERAN CHURCHES IN CANADA. VFOAT Lutheran Churches in Canada. 0316-800X. Periodical. CN. English. Suite 500/Hargrave Street, R3B 2K3 Winnipeg Canada. **LC** BX8063.C2. **DD** 284.102571.

DIRECTORY. LUTHERAN CHURCHES IN CANADA. (LUTHERAN CHURCHES IN CANADA; DIRECTORY). 0316-800X. Periodical. CN. English. an. Lutheran Council in Canada, Division of Information Services, 365 Hargrave Street/Suite 500, Winnipeg Manitoba R3B 2K3 Canada. **DD** 284.102571.

DIRECTORY - MANITOBA DENTAL ASSOCIATION. (DIRECTORY). Main/Corp Manitoba Dental Association. 0711-2238. CN. English. an. Free. Manitoba Dental Association, 308 Kennedy Street, Winnipeg Manitoba R3B 2M6 Canada. **DD** 617.600607127. (ctrl).

DIRECTORY, MARYLAND MANUFACTURERS. VFOAT Maryland Manufacturers. 1969/70-. 0070-5802. US. English. an. $18.00. Department of Economic and Community Development, 45 Calvert Street, Annapolis MD 21401. **Tel** (312)337-1084. **LC** T12. **DD** 338.476025752. Provides names, addresses, zip codes, phone numbers, officers and employees. Contains 2,773 manufacturers and 11,000 executives. *Directory of Maryland Manufacturers, 0070-5802.*

DIRECTORY, MARYLAND MANUFACTURERS. (DIRECTORY OF MARYLAND MANUFACTURERS). VFOAT Maryland Manufacturers. 11th (1983-84)-. 0070-5802. US. English. be. 45 Calvert Street, Annapolis MD 21401. **Tel** (301)269-2041. **Ed** Marilyn Corbett. **LC** T12. **DD** 338.476025752. **Circ** 6,000. (ctrl). Manufacturers are listed alphabetical, geographical and by industry (SIC). Geographical section includes company address, telephone number, total employment, key executives, and products manufactured. *Directory, Maryland Manufacturers, 0070-5802.*

DIRECTORY, MARYLAND PUBLIC AND INDEPENDENT COLLEGES AND UNIVERSITIES. VFOAT Maryland Public and Independent Colleges and Universities. US. English. State Board for Higher Education, 16 Frances Street, Annapolis MN 21401. **LC** L903.M3. **DD** 378.752.

DIRECTORY - MASSACHUSETTS DEPARTMENT OF FOOD AND AGRICULTURE. Main/Corp Massachusetts. Dept. of Food and Agriculture. 0145-661X. US. English. 100 Cambridge Street, Boston MA 02202. **LC** HD1775.M4. **DD** 338.1025744.

DIRECTORY - MEDICAL LIBRARY ASSOCIATION. Main/Corp Medical Library Association. 1950-. US. English. an. $35.00. Medical Library Association Inc, 919 North Michigan Avenue, Chicago IL 60611. **Tel** (312)266-2456. **LC** Z675.M4. adv acc. **Circ** 5,500. Reference for general association information, including committee charges; section and chapter officers and alphabetical listing of current membership.

DIRECTORY. MEDICARE/MEDICAID PROVIDERS AND SUPPLIERS OF SERVICES. (DIRECTORY : MEDICARE/MEDICAID PROVIDERS AND SUPPLIERS OF SERVICES). VFOAT Medicare/Medicaid Providers and Suppliers of Services. Nov. 1975-. 0162-0614. US. English. an. $5.45. Superintendent of Documents, US Government Printing Office, Washington DC 20402. **LC** RA977. **DD** 362.102573. *Directory. Medicare Providers and Suppliers of Services, 0363-0390.*

DIRECTORY, MEMBER LIBRARIES, GEORGIAN BAY REGIONAL LIBRARY SYSTEM. Main/Corp Georgian Bay Regional Library System. Began with 1968 issue. 0380-8068. CN. English. ir. Georgian Bay Regional Library System, 30 Morrow Road, Barrie Ontario L4N 3V8 Canada. **DD** 027.402571317.

DIRECTORY, MEMBERS AND ASSOCIATE MEMBERS - AMERICAN APPAREL MANUFACTURERS ASSOCIATION. Main/Corp American Apparel Manufacturers Association. VFOAT A.A.M.A. Directory. 1983-. 0738-520X. US. English. an. $100.00. American Apparel Manufacturers Association, 1611 North Kent Street/Suite 800, Arlington VA 22209. **Tel** (703)524-1864. **DD** 687.029473. *AAMA Directory.*

DIRECTORY : MUNICIPAL BOND DEALERS OF THE UNITED STATES. US. English. The Bond Buyer, 77 Water Street, New York NY 10005. **LC** HG4907. **DD** 332.6202573. *Directory of Bond Dealers of the United States.*

DIRECTORY - NATIONAL ASSOCIATION OF REGIONAL COUNCILS. Main/Corp National Association of Regional Councils. 1974-. 0095-1455. US. English. an. National Association of Regional Councils, 1700 K Street NW, Washington DC 20006. **LC** HT392. **DD** 309.2502573. *Regional Council Directory, 0190-2334.*

DIRECTORY - NATIONAL ASSOCIATION OF SCHOOLS OF MUSIC. (DIRECTORY). Main/Corp National Association of Schools of Music. VFOAT NASM Directory. 1967-. 0547-4175. US. English. an. $8.00. National Association of Music, 11250 Roger Bacon Drive, Reston VA 22090. **Tel** (703)437-0700. **Ed** Michael Yaffe. **LC** ML27.U5. **DD** 780.72973. **Circ** 1,500. List accredited institutions and approved major degree programs. Includes address, telephone numbers and music executives for each member institution. *List of Members.*

DIRECTORY - NATIONAL BAND ASSOCIATION. Main/Corp National Band Association (U.S.). 0196-9757. US. English. PO Box 6, Ada OH 45810. **LC** ML17. **DD** 785.1206073.

DIRECTORY: NATIONAL BLACK ORGANIZATIONS. US. English. ir. AFRAM Associates Inc, 68-72 East 131st Street, harlem NY 10037.

DIRECTORY - NATIONAL COUNCIL OF SAVINGS INSTITUTIONS (U.S.). (DIRECTORY). Main/Corp National Council of Savings Institutions (U.S.). 1984-. 0882-1941. US. English. an. $50.00. National Council of Savings Institutions, 1101 Fifteenth Street NW, Washington DC 20005. **DD** 332. *Directory of the Savings Banks of the United States and Membership of NAMSB, 0737-1799.*

DIRECTORY - NATIONAL FLUID POWER ASSOCIATION. Main/Corp National Fluid Power Association. 0145-3866. US. English. an. $150.00. National Fluid Power Association, 3333 North Mayfair Road, Milwaukee WI 53222. **Tel** (414)778-3344. **Ed** Cynthia Peck. **LC** TJ843. **DD** 621.206273. **Circ** 2,000. (ctrl). Lists manufacturers of fluid power products.

DIRECTORY - NATIONAL RESEARCH COUNCIL (U.S.). DIVISION OF BIOLOGY AND AGRICULTURE. Main/Corp National Research Council (U.S.). Division of Biology and Agriculture. VFOAT Directory of Members and Committees. US. English. an.

DIRECTORY. NEW JERSEY AGRICULTURAL ORGANIZATIONS. (DIRECTORY : NEW JERSEY AGRICULTURAL ORGANIZATIONS). VFOAT New Jersey Agricultural Organizations. 0095-5205. US. English. New Jersey Department of Agriculture, PO Box 1888, Trenton NJ 08625. **LC** S409.5.N5. **DD** 630.62749.

DIRECTORY - NIAGARA REGIONAL LIBRARY SYSTEM. Main/Corp Niagara Regional Library System. Began with 1969 issue. 0316-6589. Periodical. CN. English. an. Free. Niagara Regional Library, System 15 Lloyd Street, St Catherines Ontario L2S 2N7 Canada. **DD** 027.47133.

DIRECTORY, NON-OPERATING LIBRARY BOARDS - GEORGIAN BAY REGIONAL LIBRARY SYSTEM. (DIRECTORY, NON-OPERATING LIBRARY BOARDS). Main/Corp Georgian Bay Regional Library System. 0712-9777. CN. English. an. Free. Georgian Bay Regional Library System, 30 Morrow Road, Barrie Ontario L4N 3V8 Canada. **DD** 021.8202571315. (ctrl).

DIRECTORY - NORTH CENTRAL REGIONAL LIBRARY SYSTEM. Main/Corp North Central Regional Library System (Ont.). VFOAT Annuaire. Began with 1970 issue. 0319-7972. CN. English (only, 1970-1982). an. North Central Regional Library System, 334 Regent Street South, Sudbury Ontario P3C 4E2 Canada. **DD** 027.402571313.

DIRECTORY - NORTH CENTRAL REGIONAL LIBRARY SYSTEM. (DIRECTORY). Main/Corp Federation des Bibliotheques du Centre-Nord (Ont.). 0319-7972. CN. French (text in English only, 1970?-1982). an. Free. North Central Regional Library System, 334 Regent Street South, Sudbury Ontario P3C 4E2 Canada. **DD** 027.402571313.

DIRECTORY. NORTH DAKOTA CITY OFFICIALS. (DIRECTORY : NORTH DAKOTA CITY OFFICIALS). 0090-1989. US. English. $5.00. North Dakota League of Cities, 217 North Third Street, Box 578, Fargo ND 58501. **LC** JS451.N93. **DD** 352.0784. *Directory of North Dakota Municipal Officials, 0740-6428.*

DIRECTORY - NORTHEASTERN REGIONAL LIBRARY SYSTEM. Main/Corp Northeastern Regional Library System (Ont.). VFOAT Annuaire - Federation des Bibliotheques du Nord-Est. Began with 1967 issue?. 0316-7003. Periodical. CN. English (text French, 1976). an. Free. Northeastern Regional Library System, 6 A1 Wende, Kirkland Lake Ontario P2N 3G9 Canada. **DD** 027.4025713142.

DIRECTORY - NORTHWESTERN ONTARIO REGION. MINISTRY OF EDUCATION. (DIRECTORY - NORTHWESTERN ONTARIO REGION, MINISTRY OF EDUCATION). Main/Corp Ontario. Education Administration

Yearbooks, Almanacs, Directories

Division. Northwestern Ontario Regional Office. 0228-3441. Periodical. CN. English. an. Free. Ministry of Education, Mowat Blk Queens Park-14th Floor, Toronto Ontario M7A 1L2 Canada. **DD** 370.2571311.

DIRECTORY. OCCUPATIONAL PROGRAMS - CANADIAN ADDICTIONS FOUNDATION. (DIRECTORY, OCCUPATIONAL PROGRAMS). **VFOAT** Repertoire, Programmes Industriels. 1977-. 0705-5587. Periodical. CN. English (French). Canadian Addictions Foundation, 303 Kendal Road, Vanier Ontario K1L 7S7 Canada. **DD** 362.29302571.

DIRECTORY OF AAAS FELLOWS. Main/Corp American Association for the Advancement of Science. 1979-. US. English. an. American Association for the Advancement of Science, 1776 Massachusetts Avenue NW, Washington DC 20036.

DIRECTORY OF ACCREDITED CAMPS. VFOAT Annuaire des Camps Membres Accredites. 1973-. 0316-1226. CN. text in English and French, each with special title page and separate paging. French text on inverted pages. an. Free. Quebec Camping Association, 952 Cherrier Street, Montreal Quebec H2L 1H7 Canada. **DD** 796.5422025714. Directory of Accredited Camps.

DIRECTORY OF ACCREDITED INSTITUTIONS. 1972?-. US. English. an. $2.50. Association of Independent College, One Dupont Circle NW/Suite 350, Washington DC 20036. Tel (202)659-2460. Directory of Business Schools.

DIRECTORY OF ACCREDITED INSTITUTIONS, CANDIDATES FOR ACCREDITATION. Main/Corp Western Association of Schools and Colleges (U.S.). VFOAT Directory. 1984-1985-. 0882-6870. US. English. an. WASC, Box 9990, Mills College, Oakland CA 94613. LC L903.C2. **DD** 378.78. Directory, 8755-982X.

DIRECTORY OF ACTIVE MINES IN ARIZONA. 0273-0553. US. English. Arizona Department of Mineral, Resources Mineral Building, Fairgrounds Phoenix AZ 85007. Tel (602)255-3791. Ed No No No. Listing of all the mines that were active in Arizona in a given year. Names, address and telephone numbers are provided along with commodities produced and number of employees.

DIRECTORY OF ADDRESSES - FEDERATION INTERNATIONALE DE FOOTBALL ASSOCIATION. Main/Corp Football Association International Federation. SZ. English. ir. Fifa-House, Hitzlwet 11, CH-8032 Zurich Switzerland. LC GV943.55.F65. **DD** 796.3320601.

DIRECTORY OF ADMINISTRATORS OF COMMUNITY, TECHNICAL, AND JUNIOR COLLEGES. 1984-. 8756-4254. US. English. $30.00. AACJC Publication Sales, 80 South Early Street, Alexandria VA 22304. **DD** 378.

DIRECTORY OF ADMINISTRATORS OF DEPARTMENTS OF ALUMNI AFFAIRS, INFORMATION, AND DEVELOPMENT IN CANADIAN UNIVERSITIES AND COLLEGES. LES UNIVERSITES, ET LES COLLEGES CANADIENS. 2nd Ed. (Dec. 1980)-. 0820-0688. CN. English (French). an. Free. Association of Universities and Colleges of Canada, 151 Slater Street, Ottawa Ontario K1P 5N1 Canada. **DD** 378.71. (ctrl). Directory of Administrators of Departments of Alumni Affairs, Development and Information in Canadian Universities and Colleges.

DIRECTORY OF ADULT DAY CARE CENTERS. 1977-. 0195-9859. US. English. Department of Health Education and Welfare, Health Care Financing Administration, Health Standards and Quality Bureau Parklawn Building, 5600 Fishers Lane, Rockville MD 20857. NLM WT 22 AA1 D4.

DIRECTORY OF AFRICAN & AFRO-AMERICAN STUDIES IN THE UNITED STATES. VAT Directory of African and Afro-American Studies in the United States. 1976-. 0147-9466. US. English. an. Africa Studies Association, 218 Shiffman Center Brandeis University, Waltham MA 02154. LC DT19.9.U5. **DD** 960.071173. Directory of African Studies in the United States.

DIRECTORY OF AGENCIES EMPLOYING COMMUNITY HEALTH NURSES IN MICHIGAN. VFOAT Agencies Employing Community Health Nurses in Michigan. 1978/79-. 0193-9440. US. English. an. Michigan Department of Public Health, Bureau of Personal Health Services, 3500 North Logan, Box 30035, Lansing MI 48909. **NLM** WY 22 AM5 D4N. Nurses Employed in Community Health Work in Michigan, 0091-4193.

DIRECTORY OF AGENCIES : U.S. VOLUNTARY, INTERNATIONAL VOLUNTARY, INTERGOVERNMENTAL. US. English. ir. National Association of Social Workers, 7981 Eastern Avenue, Silvers Springs MD 20910. Tel (301)565-0333.

DIRECTORY OF ALASKA COMMERCIAL ESTABLISHMENTS. 1974-. US. English. Department of Economic Development, Division of Economic Enterprise, Pouch EE, Juneau Alaska 99801. LC HF5065.A4. **DD** 338.0025798.

DIRECTORY OF ALBERTA GOVERNMENT LIBRARIES. Began with Sept. 1975. 0382-3482. CN. English. 6.00. Alberta Legislature Library, 216 Legislature Building, Edmonton Alberta T5K 2B6 Canada. Tel 427-3837. LC Z735.A45. **DD** 027.50257123. Listing of all government (provincial) libraries in the province of Alberta. Directory of Alberta Government Libraries, Edmonton, 0317-8188.

DIRECTORY OF ALCOHOLISM COUNCILS IN AMERICA. 0148-9771. US. English. American Council on Alcoholism, 200 East Joppa Road, Baltimore MD 21204. LC HV5279. **DD** 362.29202573.

DIRECTORY OF ALLIED DENTAL EDUCATORS. 0883-3591. US. English. an. 1619 Massachusetts Avenue NW, Washington DC 20036. Directory of Dental and Allied Dental Educators, 0271-8677.

DIRECTORY OF ALTERNATIVE PERIODICALS. 0302-3303. UK. English. Smoothie Publications, 67 Vere Road, BN1 4NQ Brighton England. LC Z6944.L5. **DD** 016.052. Directory of Alternative Media Periodicals.

DIRECTORY OF ALTERNATIVE SCHOOLS. 1970?-. US. English. an. New Schools Exchange, Pettigrew AR 72752.

DIRECTORY OF ALUMNI - DICKINSON COLLEGE. (DIRECTORY OF ALUMNI). Main/Corp Dickenson College. VFOAT Alumni Directory. 0738-1999. US. English. Bernard C Harris Publishing Company, 3 Barker Avenue, White Plains NY 10601. LC LD1662.3. **DD** 378.74843.

DIRECTORY OF ALUMNI - NATIONAL SCHOLARSHIP CENTER (PHILIPPINES). Main/Corp National Scholarship Center (Philippines). English. ir. National Scholarship Center, Ministry of Education and Culture Arroceros Street, Manila 2801 Philippines. LC L961.P4. **DD** 378.5991.

DIRECTORY OF ALUMNI - PENNSYLVANIA STATE UNIVERSITY. COLLEGE OF EARTH AND MINERAL SCIENCES. (DIRECTORY OF ALUMNI). Main/Corp Pennsylvania State University. College of Earth and Mineral Sciences. VFOAT Pennsylvania State University College of Earth and Mineral Sciences Directory of Alumni. 1980-. 0739-1331. US. English. Bernard C Harris Publishing Company, 3 Barker Avenue, White Plains NY 10601. LC QE47.P42. **DD** 550.71174853.

DIRECTORY OF AMERICAN BOOK SPECIALISTS. VFOAT American Book Specialists. Began publication in 1972. 0095-2869. US. English. Continental Publishing Company, 1261 Broadway, New York NY 10001. LC Z286.A55. **DD** 380.1450705730973.

DIRECTORY OF AMERICAN BUSINESS IN AUSTRIA. VFOAT Handbuch der Amerikanischen Geschaftsverbindungen in Osterreich. English and German. ir. $12.00. American Chamber of Commerce in Austria, Severingasse 1, A-1090 Vienna Austria. LC HF3543. **DD** 338.0025436.

DIRECTORY OF AMERICAN BUSINESS IN GERMANY. VFOAT Handbuch der Amerikanischen Wirtschaftsverbindungen in Deutschland. Began in 1967. GW. English (German). an. Siebt-Verlag, Rosenheimer Strasse 145A, D-8000 Munich 80 West Germany. Seibt Directory of American Business in Germany.

DIRECTORY OF AMERICAN BUSINESS IN HONG KONG. English. an. GTE Directories (HK), 205-7710 5th Street SE, Calgary Alberta T2H 2L9 Canada. LC HG4252. **DD** 338.88905125025.

DIRECTORY OF AMERICAN BUSINESS IN MALAYSIA. English. an. Embassy Publication SDN BHD, 93-2 Jalan Mega Mandung Kompleks, Bandar 5th Mile Jalan Kelang Lama, Kuala Lumpur Malaysia. LC HF3800.6.A48. **DD** 338.889730595025.

DIRECTORY OF AMERICAN BUSINESS IN SINGAPORE. 1981-. SI. English. an. $30.00. 617 Lorong 4 Toa Payoh, Singapore 1231, PO Box 211, Singapore 913 Singapore. LC HF3800.67.A48. **DD** 338.889730595725025.

DIRECTORY OF AMERICAN COLLEGE THEATRE. 1st- Ed. 0070-5063. US. English. ir. American Theatre Association, 1010 Wisconsin Avenue NW/Suite 630, Washington DC 20007. Tel (202)342-7530.

DIRECTORY OF AMERICAN FIRMS OPERATING IN FOREIGN COUNTRIES. 1st- Ed. 0070-5071. US. English. ir. World Trade Academy Press Inc, 50 East 42nd Street, New York NY 10017. Tel (212)697-4999. Ed J L Angel. LC HG4538.A1. **DD** 338.88025. Lists US firms with affiliates overseas. Address and product/service here and abroad. Foreign operations grouped by country.

DIRECTORY OF AMERICAN FULBRIGHT SCHOLARS. (DIRECTORY OF AMERICAN FULBRIGHT SCHOLARS : UNIVERSITY LECTURING & ADVANCED RESEARCH ABROAD). 1982-83-. 0883-0975. US. English. Council for International Exchange of Scholars, 11 Dupont Circle, Washington DC 20036. American Fulbright Scholars.

DIRECTORY OF AMERICAN PHILOSOPHERS. Vol. 1 (1962/63)-. 0070-508X. US. English. be. $37.00. Philosophy Documentation Center, Bowling Green University, Bowling Green OH 43403-0189. Tel (419)372-2419. Ed Archie J Bahm. LC B935. Circ 1,000. Handbook of philosophy covering the US and Canada. Information on faculties of philosophy, names, addresses, and specialties of philosophers, journals, societies, institutions, publishers, etc.

A DIRECTORY OF AMERICAN POETS AND FICTION WRITERS. 1980-81-. 0734-0605. US. English. ir. $19.95. Poets & Writers Inc, 201 West 54th Street, New York NY 10019. Tel (212)757-1766. LC PS129. **DD** 810.2573. Circ 5,000. Names, addresses, telephone numbers and representative publications of 6,020 contemporary poets and fiction writers who publish in the United States. Directory of American Poets, Directory of American Fiction Writers.

DIRECTORY OF AMERICAN PRESERVATION COMMISSIONS. 0732-5827. US. English. The Preservation Press, National Trust for Historic Preservation 1785 Massachusetts Avenue Northwest, Washington DC 20036. LC E151. **DD** 363.6902573.

DIRECTORY OF AMERICAN RESEARCH AND TECHNOLOGY. 20th Ed. (1986)-. 0886-0076. US. English. an. R R Bowker Company, 205 East 42nd Street, New York NY 10017. **DD** 607. Industrial Research Laboratories of the United States, including Consulting Research Laboratories, 0073-7623.

DIRECTORY OF AMERICAN SAVINGS AND LOAN ASSOCIATIONS. 1st- Ed. 0070-5098. US. English. an. $25.00. T K Sanderson Organizations, 200 East Twenty-Fifth Street, Baltimore MD 21218. Tel (301)235-3383. Ed T K Sanderson. LC HG2441. Contains names of associations including addresses, zip codes and telephone numbers.

DIRECTORY OF AMERICAN SCHOLARS. (DIRECTORY OF AMERICAN SCHOLARS : A BIOGRAPHICAL DIRECTORY). Began with: 1st. Ed. 0070-5101. US. English. ir. R R Bowker Co, PO Box 1807, Ann Arbor MI 48106. LC LA2311. **DD** 923.733, 920. NLM LA 2311 D598.

DIRECTORY OF AMERICAN WATER WORKS ASSOCIATION. ONTARIO SECTION. (DIRECTORY - AMERICAN WATER WORKS ASSOCIATION, ONTARIO SECTION). Main/Corp American Water Works Association. Ontario Section. 1977-. 0704-7878. CN. English. an. American Water Works Association, Ontario Section, 3190 Mavis Road, Mississauga Ontario L5C 1T9 Canada. **DD** 628.1062713. (ctrl).

DIRECTORY OF ANIMAL DISEASE DIAGNOSTIC LABORATORIES. 0146-1621. US. English. Superintendent of Documents, US Government Printing Office,

2873

Yearbooks, Almanacs, Directories

Washington DC 20402. **LC** SF769. **DD** 636.08960072073.

DIRECTORY OF AQUARIUM SPECIALISTS. 1974/75-. 0098-4469. US. English. Waikiki Aquarium, 2777 Kalakaua Avenue, Honolulu HI 96815. **LC** QH35. **DD** 574.074.

DIRECTORY OF ARCHITECTS FOR HEALTH FACILITIES. 0192-2297. US. English. ir. American Hospital Association, PO Box 99376, Chicago IL 60693. **Tel** (312)280-6029. **LC** RA969. **DD** 725.50922. **NLM** WX 22.1 D41.

DIRECTORY OF ARCHITECTURAL FIRMS. 0363-4531. US. English. $88.32. American Institute Architects, 1735 New York Avenue NW, Washington DC 20006. **LC** NA53. **DD** 720.5573.

DIRECTORY OF AREA WAGE SURVEYS. 0566-7801. US. English. US Department of Labor, Bureau of Labor Statistics, Washington DC 20212. **LC** Z7164.W1, HD4973. **DD** 016.3312973.

DIRECTORY OF ARKANSAS MANUFACTURERS. 1976-. 0363-5139. US. English. an. Arkansas Industrial Development Foundation, PO Box 1784, Little Rock AR 72203. **Tel** (501)371-1121. **LC** T12. **DD** 338.4767025767. *Directory of Manufacturers in Arkansas*.

DIRECTORY OF ARTS LIBRARIES AND RESOURCE COLLECTIONS IN AUSTRALIA. Aug. 1983-. 0811-6253. English. ir. $10.00. James Bennett Pty Ltd, 4 Collaroy Street, Collaroy New South Wales 2097 Australia. **LC** Z675.A85. **DD** 026.7002594.

DIRECTORY OF ARTS ORGANIZATIONS IN MISSISSIPPI. 1974/75-. 0098-4477. US. English. PO Box 1341, 301 North Lamar Street, Jackson MS 39205. **LC** NX24.M7. **DD** 700.62762.

DIRECTORY OF ASSOCIATIONS IN CANADA. VFOAT Repertoire des Associations du Canada. 1st - Ed. 0316-0734. Periodical. CN. English (text also in French). ir. $110.00. Micromedia Limited, 158 Pearl Street, Toronto Ontario M5H 1L3 Canada. **Tel** (416)593-5211 or (800)387-2689. **Ed** Brian Land and Diane Gallagher. **LC** AS40. **DD** 061.1. Circ 2,000. This comprehensive directory, an authoritative listing of associations in Canada, provides an indispensable tool for business, government, researchers, librarians, the tourism industry and the media.

DIRECTORY OF AUSTRALIAN ACADEMIC LIBRARIES. 1st- Ed. 0155-1027. AT. English. ir. $6.00. Orders Unit Library, Footscray Institute of Technology, PO Box 64, Footscray Victoria 3011 Australia. **LC** Z870.A1. **DD** 027.702594.

DIRECTORY OF AUSTRALIAN ASSOCIATIONS. 1st- Ed. English. ir. Australasia Reference Research Publications Ltd, 13 Pimento Place, New Lynn Auckland 7 New Zealand. **LC** AS718. **DD** 068.94. **NLM** HD 2429.A8 D598. Index in last issue of volume - attached.

DIRECTORY OF AUSTRALIAN MUSIC ORGANIZATIONS. VFOAT Australian Music Organizations. 1978-. AT. English. ir. $13.00. The Australia Music Centre, PO Box 9, Grosvenor Street, Sydney New South Wales 2000 Australia.

DIRECTORY OF AUTO AFTERMARKET SUPPLIERS. VFOAT Chain Store Guide, Auto Aftermarket Suppliers. 1983/84-. 0736-0452. US. English. be. $149.00. Chain Store Guide, Lebhar-Friedman, 425 Park Avenue, New York NY 10022. **Tel** (212)371-9400. **Ed** Paul Smith. **LC** HD9710.3.U5. **DD** 629.2029473. Complete company profiles on 1,900 jobber/retailers operating 17,500 stores, 800 warehouse distributors and their branch offices, and 20 distribution groups serving 45,000 stores. *Directory of Auto Supply Chains, 0730-2533*.

DIRECTORY OF AUTOMATED CRIMINAL JUSTICE INFORMATION SYSTEMS. Began with 1972. 0882-9993. US. English. ir. US Department of Justice, Bureau of Justice Statistics, Washington DC 20531. **Tel** (202)724-7770. **Ed** J R Jones. Circ 4,000. (ctrl). Indexed listings of the automated criminal justice information systems used by police, courts, corrections and other justice agencies. Over 900 systems are listed.

DIRECTORY OF AUTOMOTIVE CONSULTANTS. May 1981-. 0737-7835. US. English. sa. $10.00 per copy. Society of Automotive Engineers, 400 Commonwealth Drive, Warrendale PA 15096. **LC** TL12. **DD** 629.202573.

DIRECTORY OF BANK ECONOMISTS. US. English. an. $4.00. Economic & Policy Research, 1120 Connecticut Avenue NW, Washington DC 20036. **Tel** (202)467-4022.

DIRECTORY OF BANKING INSTRUCTORS. 1973-. 0092-4717. US. English. American Bankers Association, 1120 Connecticut Avenue Northwest, Washington DC 20036. **LC** HG1581. **DD** 332.1071073.

DIRECTORY OF BAR ACTIVITIES. **Main/Corp** American Bar Association. Division of Bar Services. 0273-494X. US. English. ABA Press, 1155 East 60th Street, Chicago IL 60637. **LC** KF330.A15. **DD** 340.060073.

DIRECTORY OF BAR ASSOCIATIONS. 8756-1565. US. English. an. ABA/Division of Bar Services, 33 West Monroe 7th Floor, Chicago IL 60690. **LC** KF330.A15. **DD** 340.060073.

DIRECTORY OF BARBERS AND BARBER INSTRUCTORS. 1977-. US. English. an. Informative Data Company, 3546 Watson Road, St Louis MO 63139. **LC** TT954.5. **DD** 646.74025778.

DIRECTORY OF BARTER ASSOCIATIONS AND ORGANIZATIONS BASED IN COLORADO. 0736-3109. US. English. te. $9.95. Barter Publishing, Box B-216, 323 Franklin Building/Suite 804, Chicago IL 60606-7093.

DIRECTORY OF BARTER ASSOCIATIONS AND ORGANIZATIONS BASED IN CONNECTICUT. 0736-3117. US. English. te. $9.95. Barter Publishing, Box B-216, 323 Franklin Building/Suite 804, Chicago IL 60606-7093.

DIRECTORY OF BARTER ASSOCIATIONS AND ORGANIZATIONS BASED IN MINNESOTA. 0736-3206. US. English. te. $9.95. Barter Publishing, Box B-216, 323 Franklin Building/Suite 804, Chicago IL 60606-7093.

DIRECTORY OF BARTER ASSOCIATIONS AND ORGANIZATIONS BASED IN MONTANA. 0736-3176. US. English. te. $9.95. Barter Publishing, Box B-216, 323 Franklin Building/Suite 804, Chicago IL 60606-7093.

DIRECTORY OF BARTER ASSOCIATIONS AND ORGANIZATIONS BASED IN NEBRASKA. 0736-3184. US. English. te. $9.95. Barter Publishing, Box B-216, 323 Franklin Building/Suite 804, Chicago IL 60606-7093.

DIRECTORY OF BARTER ASSOCIATIONS AND ORGANIZATIONS BASED IN NEVADA. 0736-3214. US. English. te. $9.95. Barter Publishing, Box B-216, 323 Franklin Building/Suite 804, Chicago IL 60606-7093.

DIRECTORY OF BARTER ASSOCIATIONS AND ORGANIZATIONS BASED IN NEW HAMPSHIRE. 0736-3168. US. English. te. $9.95. Barter Publishing, Box B-216, 323 Franklin Building/Suite 804, Chicago IL 60606-7093.

DIRECTORY OF BARTER ASSOCIATIONS AND ORGANIZATIONS BASED IN NEW JERSEY. 0736-3842. US. English. te. $9.95. Barter Publishing, Box B-216, 323 Franklin Building/Suite 804, Chicago IL 60606-7093.

DIRECTORY OF BILINGUAL SPEECH-LANGUAGE PATHOLOGISTS AND AUDIOLOGISTS. **Main/Corp** American Speech-Language-Hearing Association. 1982/1983-. 0743-5096. US. English. ir. $3.00. American Speech Language and Hearing Association, 10801 Rockville Pike, Rockville MD 20852. **Tel** (301)897-5700. **NLM** WV 22 AA1 A55. Directory of bilingual speech-language pathologists and audiologists for thirty-four languages.

DIRECTORY OF BIOMEDICAL ENGINEERS. 2nd Ed. (1983)-. 0740-6843. US. English. be. Directory of Biomedical Engineers, Suite 402/4405 East-Way Highway, Bethesda MD 20814. **LC** R856.A4. **DD** 610.28025. *International Directory of Biomedical Engineers, 0190-9282*.

DIRECTORY OF BLACK FILM/TV TECHNICIANS AND ARTISTS, WEST COAST. (DIRECTORY OF BLACK FILM/TV TECHNICIANS & ARTISTS, WEST COAST). VAT Directory of Black Film/Television Technicians and Artists, West Coast. 0277-1500. US. English. $16.00. Togetherness Productions, Box 75796 Sanford Station, Los Angeles CA 90075. **LC** PN1995.9.N4. **DD** 384.808996073.

DIRECTORY OF BLOOD ESTABLISHMENTS REGISTERED UNDER SECTION 510 OF THE FOOD, DRUG, AND COSMETIC ACT. 1976-. 0163-6065. US. English. an. Bureau of Biologics, Food and Drug Administration, Bethesda MD 20014. **LC** RM172. **DD** 362.1. **NLM** WH 22 AA1 D4.

DIRECTORY OF BRITISH ASSOCIATIONS. 1st-3rd. 0070-5152. UK. English. ir. $140.00. Gale Research, Book Tower, Detroit MI 48226. **Tel** (800)521-0707. **Ed** G P Henderson. **LC** AS118. The new edition of this standard work lists in alphabetical order about 9,000 national organizations of England, Wales, Scotland, and Ireland. Also includes local and regional organizations of national significance.

DIRECTORY OF BRITISH BRASS BANDS. UK. English. 1.00. British Federation of Brass Bands, 28 Marigold Street, Rochdale Lancs England. **LC** ML27.G7, B73 1978. **DD** 785.0671.

DIRECTORY OF BROADCAST EXECUTIVES. 1963/64-. 0419-2273. Periodical. CN. English. R C Ellis, 17 Dundonald Street, Toronto Ontario Canada. **LC** HE8689.9.C3. **DD** 384.5402571.

DIRECTORY OF BUSINESS AND FINANCIAL SERVICES. VFOAT Commercial Information Services Handbook. 1st-. US. English. ir. Special Libraries Association, 1700-18th Street NW, Washington DC 20009. **Tel** (202)234-4700. **LC** HF5353. **DD** 027.69025.

DIRECTORY OF BUSINESS AND INDUSTRY, FAIRFAX COUNTY, VIRGINIA. Periodical. US. English. be. Fairfax County Economic Development Authority, 8330 Old Courthouse Road/Suite 800 Tysons Corner, Vienna VA 22180. **LC** HC107.V82. **DD** 338.74025755291.

DIRECTORY OF BUSINESS AND ORGANIZATIONAL COMMUNICATORS. 8756-4645. US. English. ir. $40.00. International Association of Business Communicators, 870 Market Street/Suite 940, San Francisco CA 951-2. **DD** 658.

DIRECTORY OF BUSINESS CAPITAL SOURCES. Began with 1982-83?. 0734-6832. US. English. ir. $29.95. Interfinance Corporation, 2215 Pillsbury Avenue South, Minneapolis MN 55404. **LC** HG65. **DD** 332.6602573.

DIRECTORY OF BUYING OFFICES & ACCOUNTS. (DIRECTORY OF BUYING OFFICES AND ACCOUNTS). 1968-. 0070-5195. US. English. an. $45.00. Salesman's Guide Inc, 1140 Broadway, New York NY 10001. **Tel** (212)684-2985. **Ed** Edward R Blank. **LC** HF5429.3. **DD** 658.87002573. adv acc. Circ 5,000. Directory of all retail resident buying offices and all the accounts they represent.

DIRECTORY OF CALIFORNIA JUSTICE AGENCIES SERVING JUVENILES AND ADULTS. 0361-7327. US. English. $1.60. Department of the Youth Authority, PO Box 20191, Sacramento CA 95820. **LC** HV9503.C2. **DD** 364.6025794. *Directory of California Services for Juvenile and Adult Offenders*.

DIRECTORY OF CAMPUS MINISTRY. 0070-5209. US. English. United States Catholic Conference, 1312 Massachusetts Avenue NW, Washington DC 20005. **LC** BV4376. **DD** 253.02573.

DIRECTORY OF CANADIAN ARCHIVES. VFOAT Annuaire des Depots d'Archives Canadiens. 1981-. 0711-0413. Periodical. CN. English (French). an. 27. Domestic, 30. Foreign. Assn Archivistes du Quebec, 7243 St Denis, Montreal Quebec H2R 2E3 Canada. **Tel** (514)277-4090. **DD** 026.025171402571. adv acc. (ctrl). This directory is the first project to be coordinated by the Bureau. It is a good step about enlarging the horizons of the archival profession within and without the boundaries of the country. *Directory of Canadian Records and Manuscript Repositories, 0700-4850*.

DIRECTORY OF CANADIAN CHARTERED ACCOUNTANTS. VFOAT Annuaire des Comptables Agrees Canadiens. 1957/58-. 0527-9275. CN. English (French). an. Canadian Institute of Chartered Accountants, 150 Bloor Street West, Toronto Ontario M5S 2Y2 Canada. **LC** HF5616.C2. **DD** 657.02571. *Directory of Chartered Accountants in Canada, 0703-4490*.

Yearbooks, Almanacs, Directories

DIRECTORY OF CANADIAN COMMERCIAL AIR SERVICES. Main/Corp Canadian Transport Commission. CN. English. ir. $55.99. Receiver General for Canada, Supply and Services, Ottawa Ontario K1A 0S9 Canada.

DIRECTORY OF CANADIAN ENVIRONMENTAL EXPERTS. VFOAT Repertoire des Specialistes Canadiens de l'Environnement. 1978-. 0704-1497. CN. English (French). Receiver General for Canada, Supply and Services Canada, Ottawa Ontario K1A 0S9 Canada. Tel (819)997-2560. LC TD182. DD 363.7002571.

DIRECTORY OF CANADIAN GAS UTILITIES. Ceased with 1965 issue. 0315-8349. CN. English. an. $1.63. Canadian Gas Association, 55 Scarsdale Road, Don Mills Ontario Canada. DD 363.6302571.

DIRECTORY OF CANADIAN GRADUATE PROGRAMMES IN LAW. Began with 1st Ed., published in 1980. 0228-3395. CN. English (French). be. $7. Per No. W Angus, Osgoode Hall Law School, York University, Downsview Ontario M3J 2R5 Canada. LC KE280. DD 340.071171.

DIRECTORY OF CANADIAN HUMAN SERVICES. VFOAT Repertoire, Directory, Repertoire des Services Sociaux au Canada. 1982/83-. 0714-4687. CN. English (French). be. Canadian Council on Social Development, 55 Parkdale, Box 3505 Station C, Ottawa Ontario K1Y 4G1 Canada. LC HV105. DD 362.02571. *Directory of Canadian Welfare Services, 0084-9871.*

DIRECTORY OF CANADIAN MAP COLLECTIONS. VFOAT Repertoire des Collections de Cartes Canadiennes. 1969-. 0070-5217. Periodical. CN. text in English and French. Association of Canadian Map Libraries, c/o National Map Collection Public Archives of Canada, Ottawa Ontario K1A 0N3 Canada. DD 026.91202571.

DIRECTORY OF CANADIAN MUSEUMS AND RELATED INSTITUTIONS = REPERTOIRE DES MUSEES CANADIENS ET INSTITUTIONS CONNEXES. VAT Directory of Canadian Museums (1978), Repertoire des Musees Canadiens (1978). 1978-. 0714-2188. CN. French (English). ir. $30.00 Per Volume. Association des Musees Canadiens, Centre de Documentation Museale, Bureau 400/331 rue Cooper, Ottawa Ontario K2P 0G5 Canada. DD 069.02571. *Directory of Canadian Museums, 0714-2161.*

DIRECTORY OF CANADIAN NON-GOVERNMENTAL ORGANIZATIONS ENGAGED IN INTERNATIONAL DEVELOPMENT. VFOAT Repertoire des Organismes Non-Gouvernementaux Canadiens Engages Dans le Developpement International. 1971-74- Sept. 1974-. Periodical. Multilingual (English and French). ir.

DIRECTORY OF CANADIAN ORCHESTRAS AND YOUTH ORCHESTRAS. VFOAT Annuaire Canadien des Orchestres et Orchestres des Jeunes. 1975/76-. 0705-6249. CN. English. an. $3.00. ACO/OFSO Secretariat, Suite 503/151 Bloor Street West, Toronto Ontario M5S 1T6 Canada. DD 785.066102571.

A DIRECTORY OF CANADIAN PEACE ORGANIZATIONS WITH INTERNATIONAL CONCERNS. VFOAT Peace Unearth Directory. 1983-. CN. English (French). LC JX1905.5. DD 327.17206.

DIRECTORY OF CANADIAN PLAYS AND PLAYWRIGHTS. (A DIRECTORY OF CANADIAN PLAYS AND PLAYWRIGHTS). 0707-5456. Periodical. CN. English. be. Free. The Playwright's Canada, 6th Floor 8 York Street, Toronto Ontario Canada. LC PR9196.35. DD 812.009971. (ctrl).

DIRECTORY OF CANADIAN SCHOLARS AND UNIVERSITIES INTERESTED IN LATIN AMERICAN STUDIES. VFOAT Repertoire des Universitaires et Universites se Specialisant dans les Etudes Latino-Americaines au Canada. 1974/75-. 0382-9073. CN. English (French). an. Canadian Association of Latin American Studies, 151 Slater Street, Ottawa Ontario K1P 5H3 Canada. DD 980.0072. *Directory of Scholars in Latin American Teaching and Research in Canada, 0382-9081.*

DIRECTORY OF CANADIAN THEATRE SCHOOLS. (A DIRECTORY OF CANADIAN THEATRE SCHOOLS). 1979-. 0709-8421. CN. English. be. $2.50 per vol. Canadian Theatre Review Publications, 4700 Keele Street, Downsview Ontario M3J 1P3 Canada. DD 792.071071.

DIRECTORY OF CANADIAN UNIVERSITIES. VFOAT Repertoire des Universites Canadiennes. 1977-. 0706-2338. CN. English (text in French). an. $6. Association of Universities and Colleges of Canada, 151 Slater Street, Ottawa Ontario K1P 5N1 Canada. Tel (613)563-1236. LC L905. DD 378.71. Circ 3,000. Lists the names, titles, degrees and individual telephone numbers of senior university administrators, deans, directors of research institutes and department heads for the 1985-86 academic year. *Universities and Colleges of Canada, 083-3932.*

DIRECTORY OF CANADIAN UNIVERSITY RESOURCES FOR INTERNATIONAL DEVELOPMENT. VFOAT Repertoire des Ressources des Universites Canadiennes pour le Developpement International. 1st Ed. (1983). 0822-1502. CN. English (text in French). an. $10.00 Canada, $12.00 US. Association of Universities and Colleges of Canada, 151 Slater Street, Ottawa Ontario K1P 5N1 Canada. Tel (613)563-1236. DD 378.19902571. Lists information on the areas of specialization and research as well as past experience in international development of Canadian universities.

DIRECTORY OF CANADIAN URBAN INFORMATION SOURCES CEASED. 1974-1977. 0318-7276. CN. English. an. LC HT101. DD 301.36072071.

DIRECTORY OF CANADIAN WELFARE SERVICES CEASED. (DIRECTORY OF CANADIAN WELFARE SERVICES). VFOAT Repertoire des Services Sociaux Canadiens. -1980. 0084-9871. Periodical. CN. English (French). an. Box 3505 Station C, Ottawa Ontario K1Y 4G1 Canada. LC HV105. DD 362.02571. *Directory of Canadian Family and Child Welfare Agencies.*

DIRECTORY OF CANCER RESEARCH INFORMATION RESOURCES. 1977-. Periodical. US. English. be. NLM QZ 22.1 D598. Each issue contains an index to its own contents - no vol index - loose.

DIRECTORY OF CARDAMOM PLANTERS. 1974-. English. ir. 50.00. Cardamon Board, Chittoor Road, Ermakulam India 682018. LC SB307.C3. DD 633.83.

DIRECTORY OF CEMENT PRODUCERS. (DIRECTORY OF CEMENT PRODUCERS IN . . .). Series/Titl Mineral Industry Surveys. 0731-4132. US. English. an. US Department of the Interior, Bureau of Mines, Washington DC 20241. LC TP876.U4. DD 338.76669402573.

DIRECTORY OF CENTRAL ATLANTIC STATES MANUFACTURERS. 1st- Ed. 0070-5241. US. English. be. $76.90. George D Hall Company, 50 Congress Street, Boston MA 02109. Tel (617)523-3745. Ed George D Hall. LC T12. DD 670.58. adv acc. 20,000 manufacturers covering some southeastern states listed alphabetically, geographically and by product, company name, address, telephone number, number of employees, key personnel by name, title and product description.

DIRECTORY OF CERTIFICATES OF AUTHORIZATION HOLDERS AUTHORIZED TO PRACTISE PROFESSIONAL ENGINEERING IN THE PROVINCE OF ONTARIO. Vol. 8 (Aug. 1981)-. 0712-7499. CN. English. an. Free. Directory of Certificates of Authorization Holders . . ., c/o Association of Professional Engineers of Ontario, 1027 Yonge Street, Toronto Ontario M4W 3E5 Canada. DD 620.0060713. (ctrl). *Directory of Firms and Corporations Authorized to Practice Professional Engineering in the Province of Ontario, 0316-8123.*

DIRECTORY OF CERTIFIED NURSES. Main/Corp American Nurses' Association. Series/Titl ANA Publication Code, CR-21 2500 12/77, etc. VFOAT ANA Directory of Certified Nurses. 1975?-. Periodical. US. English. ir. American Nurses Association, Publ Orders/2420 Pershing Road, Kansas City MO 64108.

DIRECTORY OF CERTIFIED PETROLEUM GEOLOGISTS. VFOAT Certified Petroleum Geologists of AAPG. 0272-1309. US. English. an. $40.00. American Association of Petroleum Geologists, Division of Professional Affairs, Box 979, Tulsa OK 74101. Tel (918)584-2555. LC TN867. DD 553.2802573.

DIRECTORY OF CERTIFIED PSYCHIATRISTS AND NEUROLOGISTS. 1st- Ed. 0196-6421. US. English. Marquis Who's Who Inc, 200 East Ohio Street, Chicago IL 60611. Tel (312)787-2008. NLM WM 22 AA1 D28.

DIRECTORY OF CERTIFIED PUBLIC ACCOUNTANTS AND PUBLIC ACCOUNTANTS OF OKLAHOMA. (DIRECTORY OF CERTIFIED PUBLIC ACCOUNTANTS AND PUBLIC ACCOUNTANTS OF OKLAHOMA REGISTERED IN ACCORDANCE WITH OKLAHOMA STATUTES AND RULES OF THE OKLAHOMA STATE BOARD OF PUBLIC ACCOUNTANCY). Main/Corp Oklahoma State Board of Public Accountancy. 0361-4115. US. English. Oklahoma State Board of Public Accountancy, 265 West Court, 4545 Lincoln Boulevard, Oklahoma City OK 73105. LC HF5616.U5. DD 657.61025766. *Directory and Rules of General Application, Certified Public Accountants and Public Accountants of Oklahoma Registered in Accordance with Oklahoma Statutes and Rules.*

DIRECTORY OF CHAIN RESTAURANT OPERATORS. VFOAT Chain Restaurant Operators. 0411-7085. US. English. an. $179.00. Chain Store Guide Lebhar-Friedman Attn Priscilla G Jimenez, 425 Park Avenue, New York NY 10022. Tel (212)371-9400. Ed Jim Ticrney. LC TX907. DD 647.957305. Provides company profiles on 3,000 or more unit chain restaurant companies operating or franchising 160,000 restaurants, drive-ins, cafeterias, etc.

DIRECTORY OF CHAMBERS OF COMMERCE IN TEXAS. 0737-5573. US. English. ty.

DIRECTORY OF CHEMICAL ABSTRACTS REGISTRY NUMBERS AND EPA NUMBERS FOR COMMON PETROLEUM CHEMICALS. VAT Directory of Chemical Abstracts Registry Numbers and Environmental Protection Agency Numbers for Common Petroleum Chemicals. 0149-3485. US. English. American Petroleum Institute, 275 Madison Avenue, New York NY 10016.

DIRECTORY OF CHEMICAL DEPENDENCY PROGRAMS IN MINNESOTA. VFOAT Chemical Dependency Programs in Minnesota. 0734-0192. US. English. an. Department of Public Welfare, Centennial Office Building, 658 Cedar Street, St Paul MN 55155. LC HV5831.M6. DD 362.29.

DIRECTORY OF CHEMICAL ENGINEERING RESEARCH IN CANADIAN UNIVERSITIES. VFOAT Compte Rendu de la Recherche en Genie Chimique Dans les Universites Canadiennes. 18th- 1978/79-. 0709-3438. CN. English (French). an. Canadian Society for Chemical Engineering, Suite 906/151 Slater Street, Ottawa Ontario K1P 5H3 Canada. DD 660.2072071. *Annual Directory of Chemical Engineering Research in Canadian Universities, 0315-9752.*

DIRECTORY OF CHEMICAL PRODUCERS OF ASIA AND AUSTRALASIA. 1976/77-. 0362-3785. US. English. Chemical Information Services, Box 61, Oceanside NY 11572. LC TP12. DD 338.476600255.

DIRECTORY OF CHEMICAL PRODUCERS. UNITED STATES OF AMERICA. (DIRECTORY OF CHEMICAL PRODUCERS : UNITED STATES OF AMERICA). 1961-. 0012-3277. Periodical. US. English. an. $835.00. Stanford Research Institute, Research Information Center, Menlo Park CA 94025. Tel (415)859-3627. Ed Janet R Hardy. LC HD9651.3. (ctrl). Lists chemical producers, plant locations, products manufactured at each site. Subscription includes inquiry service and updates.

DIRECTORY OF CHEMICAL PRODUCERS, WESTERN EUROPE. 1978-. US. English. an. SRI International, 333 Ravenswood Avenue, Menlo Park CA 94025. Tel (415)859-3627. Ed Janet R Hardy. LC TP12. DD 338.47660025. Circ 600. (ctrl). Detailed description of more than 3,000 companies. Lists more that 1,300 chemical products and includes some 200 capacity tables. Subscription includes inquiry service.

DIRECTORY OF CHILD CARE CENTERS. 0147-4405. US. English. Department of Social Services, 300 South Capitol Avenue, Lansing MI 48926. LC HV857.M5. DD 362.71.

Yearbooks, Almanacs, Directories

DIRECTORY OF CHINESE OFFICIALS. NATIONAL LEVEL ORGANIZATIONS. July 1980-. US. English. an. Docex Project, Exchange and Gift Division, Library of Congress, Washington DC 20540. **LC** JQ1507. **DD** 354.51002. *Directory of Officials of the People's Republic of China.*

DIRECTORY OF CHINESE OFFICIALS. PROVINCIAL ORGANIZATIONS. Dec. 1981-. 0733-2025. US. English. Document Expediting Project, Exchange & Gift Division, Library of Congress, Washington DC 20540. **LC** JQ1507. **DD** 354.51002. Vols. for 1981- distributed to depository libraries in microfiche.

DIRECTORY OF CHINESE OFFICIALS. SCIENTIFIC AND EDUCATIONAL ORGANIZATIONS. VFOAT Scientific and Educational Organizations. Dec. 1982-. 0741-1901. US. English. National Technical Information Service, 5285 Port Royal Road, Springfield VA. 22161. **LC** Q149.C5. **DD** 502.551. *Directory of Chinese Scientific and Educational Officials.*

DIRECTORY OF CITY AND COUNTY HEALTH OFFICERS AND DISTRICT DIRECTORS. US. English. **LC** RA7.6.T4. **DD** 362.1025764.

DIRECTORY OF CLIENTS' SECURITY FUNDS. US. English. an. American Bar Association, 77 South Wacker Drive/6th Floor, Chicago IL 60606.

DIRECTORY OF CLINICAL FELLOWSHIPS IN MEDICINE. UNITED STATES AND CANADA. (DIRECTORY OF CLINICAL FELLOWSHIPS IN MEDICINE : UNITED STATES AND CANADA). 0161-5793. US. English. $12.00. Graduate Publications, PO Box 6610, Ventura CA 93003. **LC** R840. **DD** 610.79.

DIRECTORY OF CLINICAL LABORATORIES, CLINICAL LABORATORY PERSONNEL. VFOAT California Clinical Laboratory Technology. 0095-3725. US. English. $2.00. Laboratory Program Department of General Services, PO Box 20191, Sacramento CA 95820. **LC** RB37.6. **DD** 616.075025794.

DIRECTORY OF CLUB OFFICERS - HARVARD ALUMNI ASSOCIATION. Main/Corp Harvard Alumni Association. 0736-637X. US. English. Harvard Alumni Association, Wadsworth House, Cambridge MA 02138. *Directory of Officers, 0736-8828.*

DIRECTORY OF CO-OPERATIVE PRESS. 8th- Ed. UK. English. an. 2.00. International Co-Operative Alliance, 11 Upper Grosvenor Street, Longon W1X 9PA England. **LC** HD2951. **DD** 016.33405.

DIRECTORY OF COLLEGE SEMINARS AND SHORT COURSES IN ENGINEERING AND MANAGEMENT. No. 1-. 0278-1182. US. English. qt. $9.95. Stratford Publications Inc, 8614 Camden Street, Alexandria VA 22308.

DIRECTORY OF COLLEGES & UNIVERSITIES OFFERING DEGREES IN LEARNING DISABILITIES. VAT Directory of Colleges and Universities Offering Degrees in Learning Disabilities. 1st- Ed. 0161-5467. US. English. an. Academic Therapy Publications, 28 Commercial Boulevard, Novato CA 94947. **LC** LC4705. **DD** 371.9071173.

DIRECTORY OF COLLEGES OFFERING COURSES AND DEGREES BY MAIL. 0196-4704. US. English. Vocational Guidance Inc, 1391 Grandview Avenue/Box 12500, Columbus OH 43212. **LC** L901. **DD** 378.155402573.

DIRECTORY OF COLORADO LIBRARIES . . . & LIBRARY STATISTICS. VFOAT Directory of Colorado Libraries . . . and Library Statistics. 1980-. US. English. an. Colorado State Library, 1362 Lincoln Street, Denver CO 80203. **LC** Z732.C6. **DD** 027.0025788. *Directory of Colorado Libraries.*

DIRECTORY OF COLORADO MANUFACTURERS. 0084-9898. US. English. be. Manufacturers News Inc, 4 East Huron Street, Chicago IL 60611. **Tel** (312)337-1084. **LC** T12. **DD** 338.4767025788. Includes address, zip, telephone, year established; officers and number of employees, 397 pages. *Colorado Manufacturers Directory.*

DIRECTORY OF COMMERCE AND INDUSTRY. STATE OF DELAWARE. (DIRECTORY OF COMMERCE AND INDUSTRY, STATE OF DELAWARE). VFOAT Delaware Directory of Commerce and Industry. 0091-0740. US. English. wk. Long Island Association of Commerce and Industry, 303 Sunnyside Boulevard, Plainview NY 11803. **LC** HF3161.D3. **DD** 338.0025751. *Directory of Manufacturers, State of Delaware.*

DIRECTORY OF COMMUNICATIONS MANAGEMENT. Summer 1980-. 0270-4870. US. English. sa. $150.00. Applied Computer Research, PO Box 9280, Phoenix AZ 85068. **Tel** (602)995-5929. **LC** HF5548.125. **DD** 338.7402573.

DIRECTORY OF COMMUNICATORS IN AGRICULTURE. US. English. $5.00. Agricultural Relations Council, 18 South Michigan Avenue, Chicago IL 60603. **LC** S494.5.C6. **DD** 630.141.

DIRECTORY OF COMMUNITY-BASED MENTAL RETARDATION SERVICES. 0096-3054. US. English. Office of Mental Retardation, State House Station, Box 94728, Lincoln NE 68509. **LC** HV3006.N2. **DD** 362.3025782.

DIRECTORY OF COMMUNITY BLOOD BANKS. Main/Corp American Association of Blood Banks. 1982-. 0741-2304. US. English. an. American Association of Blood Banks, 1117 North 19th Street/Suite 600, Arlington VA 22209. **Tel** (703)528-8200. **NLM** WH 22 AA1 D52.

DIRECTORY OF COMMUNITY CARE FACILITIES. Mar. 1975-. 0361-6282. US. English. Sacramento Department of Health Facilities Licensing Section, 744 P Street Room 440, Sacramento CA 95814. **LC** HV742.C2. **DD** 362.025794. **NLM** WA 22 AC2 D4D.

DIRECTORY OF COMMUNITY EDUCATION PROJECTS. 1976/77-. 0161-9047. US. English. Superintendent of Documents, US Government Printing Office, Washington DC 20402. **LC** LB2820. **DD** 370.19402573. *Community Education Project Descriptions, 0148-7116.*

DIRECTORY OF COMMUNITY SERVICE ORGANIZATIONS IN THE WASHINGTON METROPOLITAN AREA. 1978-. 0162-3311. US. English. an. United Black Fund Inc of Greater Washington DC, 1343 H Street Northwest, Washington DC 20005. **LC** HV99.W29. **DD** 361.8025753.

DIRECTORY OF COMMUNITY SERVICES. 1966/67-. 0316-1099. Periodical. CN. English. Social Planning and Research Council of Hamilton and District 153, King Street East, Hamilton Ontario L8N 1B1 Canada. **DD** 361.002571352. *Directory of Community Services of Hamilton and District, 0316-1102.*

DIRECTORY OF COMMUNITY SERVICES. Ceased with 1981 issue. 0318-6474. Periodical. CN. English. Social Services Council of Greater Saint John, 10 King Street, Saint John New Brunswick E2L 1G2 Canada. **DD** 361.002571532.

DIRECTORY OF COMMUNITY SERVICES. Began with 1973 issue?. 0381-629X. CN. English. an. United Good Neighbour Fund, 105-26 Lorne Street, New Westminister British Columbia V3M 3L7 Canada. **DD** 361.002571133. *Introduction to Agency Services.*

DIRECTORY OF COMMUNITY SERVICES. VFOAT Repertoire des Services Communautaires. Began with 1975 issue. 0709-0749. CN. English (text in only, 1975-1977). an. 10.00. Information and Reference Department, Sudbury Public Library, Civic Square West Tower, 200 Brady Street, Sudbury Ontario P3E 5K3 Canada. **Tel** (705)675-1155. **Ed** Michaele Mueller. **DD** 361.0025713133. **Circ** 500. A list of social service agencies. Covers health, housing, counselling, legal employment, and vocational services, in the regional municipality of Sudbury.

DIRECTORY OF COMMUNITY SERVICES FOR EDMONTON & DISTRICT. Began publication in 1964?. 0380-805X. CN. English. an. $11.61. Aid Service of Edmonton, 10711-107th Avenue/Suite 203, Edmonton Alberta T5H 0W6 Canada. **Tel** (403)426-3242. **DD** 361.002571234. **Circ** 3,000. A directory of community services for the Edmonton region providing information on approximately 1,000 social service agencies.

DIRECTORY OF COMMUNITY SERVICES FOR GREATER WINDSOR. VFOAT Community Services Windsor-Essex. VAT Community Services, Windsor-Essex. 0710-4316. CN. English. be. $8.00 Per Volume. Windsor-Essex Community Information Service, 65 Wyandotte Street West, Windsor Ontario N9A 5W6 Canada. **DD** 361.002571316.

DIRECTORY OF COMMUNITY SERVICES FOR WATERLOO REGION. 0713-4681. CN. English. an. $12.50. Directory of Community Services, c/o Community Information Centre, 18 Queen Street North, Kitchener Ontario N2H 2G8 Canada. **DD** 361.002571344.

DIRECTORY OF COMMUNITY SERVICES IN MARYLAND. 0070-5306. US. English. be. Directory Office, 200 East Lexington Street, Baltimore MD 21202. **LC** HV98.M3. **DD** 361.0025752.

DIRECTORY OF COMMUNITY SERVICES IN REGIONAL NIAGARA. VFOAT Regional Niagara Directory of Services. 0823-6046. CN. English. be. 16.50. Information Niagara, 5017 Victoria Avenue, Niagara Falls Ontario L2E 4C9 Canada. **Tel** (416)356-4636. **DD** 361.002571338. **Circ** 1,000. Directory of human service agencies in the Niagara Region, Ontario Canada including special sections on mental health, addiction treatment service, long-term care services and services for children with special needs.

DIRECTORY OF COMMUNITY SERVICES (LONDON, ONT.). (DIRECTORY OF COMMUNITY SERVICES). 0828-5586. CN. English. an. $13.00. Information London, 388 Dundas Street, London Ontario NB6 1V8 Canada. **DD** 361.002571326. *Directory of Community Services for London and Area, 0820-8433.*

DIRECTORY OF COMMUNITY SERVICES (NEW YORK PUBLIC LIBRARY). (DIRECTORY OF COMMUNITY SERVICES). VFOAT Directorio de Servicios Para la Comunidad. 1980-. US. English. an. $26.00. Office of Branch Libraries, The New York Public Library, 455 Fifth Avenue, New York NY 10016. **LC** F128.18. **DD** 917.470025. *New York Public Library Directory of Community Services, 0191-6629.*

DIRECTORY OF COMMUNITY SERVICES. OTTAWA-CARLETON. (DIRECTORY OF COMMUNITY SERVICES, OTTAWA-CARLETON). VFOAT Ottawa-Carleton, Repertoire des Services Communautaires. 1976/77-. 0705-7075. CN. French (English). an. **DD** 361.002571384. *Directory of Social Services, Ottawa-Carleton, 0318-9686.*

DIRECTORY OF COMMUNITY SERVICES - THUNDER BAY. Main/Corp Thunder Bay, Ont. Began with 1973 issue. 0705-419X. CN. English. an. **DD** 361.002571312.

DIRECTORY OF COMPANIES OFFERING DIVIDEND REINVESTMENT PLANS. VFOAT Dividend Reinvestment Plans. 1982-. US. English. an. $18.95. Evergreen Enterprises, PO Box 763, Laurel MD 20707. **Tel** (301)953-1861. **Ed** S Kinoshita. Annual directory.

DIRECTORY OF COMPANIES PRODUCING SALT IN THE UNITED STATES. Series/Titl Mineral Industry Surveys. Began with 1977. 0272-3891. US. English. an. US Department of the Interior, 2410 E Street Northwest, Washington DC 20241. **Tel** (202)634-1177. **Ed** Dennis S Kostick. **LC** HD9213.U4. **DD** 338.7661402573. **Circ** 3,000. Directory of salt producing companies (rock, solar, brine, vacuum-pan) in the United States.

DIRECTORY OF COMPANIES REQUIRED TO FILE ANNUAL REPORTS WITH THE SECURITIES AND EXCHANGE COMMISSION UNDER THE SECURITIES EXCHANGE ACT OF 1934, ALPHABETICALLY AND BY INDUSTRY GROUPS. Began with 1976. 0149-6581. US. English. an. Superintendent of Documents, US Government Printing Office, Washington DC 20402. **LC** HG4057. **DD** 338.7402573. *Directory of Companies Filing Annual Reports with the Securities and Exchange Commission under the Securities Exchange Act of 1934.*

DIRECTORY OF COMPUTER DEALERS. INTERNATIONAL EDITION. (DIRECTORY OF COMPUTER DEALERS). VFOAT CEIB Directory of Computer Dealers. 0277-3694. US. English. $12.00. **LC** HD9696.C6. **DD** 621.3819580294.

Yearbooks, Almanacs, Directories

DIRECTORY OF COMPUTER EDUCATION AND RESEARCH. 1st- ed. US. English. bm. Scinece and Technology Press, PO Box 614, Latham NY 12110. **Ed** T C Hsiao.

DIRECTORY OF COMPUTER PROGRAMS AVAILABLE FROM C.O.S.M.I.C CEASED. (DIRECTORY OF COMPUTER PROGRAMS AVAILABLE FROM COSMIC). V. 1- 1967-. 0090-9793. US. English. University of Georgia, Computer Center, Athens GA 30602. **LC** QA76.6. **DD** 381.450016425.

A DIRECTORY OF COMPUTER SOFTWARE. 1983-. 0748-1543. US. English. NTIS, 5285 Port Royal Road, Springfield VA 22161. **LC** QA76.6. **DD** 001.6425029473. *Directory of Computer Software & Related Technical Reports, 0278-257X.*

A DIRECTORY OF COMPUTER SOFTWARE APPLICATIONS. ATMOSPHERIC SCIENCES. VFOAT Atmospheric Sciences. US. English. NTIS, 5285 Port Royal Road, Springfield VA 22161.

A DIRECTORY OF COMPUTER SOFTWARE APPLICATIONS. ENERGY. VFOAT Energy. 1977-. US. English. National Technical Information Service, 5285 Port Royal Road, Springfield VA 22161.

A DIRECTORY OF COMPUTER SOFTWARE APPLICATIONS. ENVIRONMENTAL POLLUTION AND CONTROL. (A DIRECTORY OF COMPUTER SOFTWARE APPLICATIONS. ENVIRONMENTAL POLLUTION & CONTROL). VFOAT Environmental Pollution & Control. VAT Environmental Pollution and Control. US. English. wk. $30.00. National Technical Information Service 5285 Port Royal Road, Springfield VA 22161. **Tel** (703)487-4650.

A DIRECTORY OF COMPUTER SOFTWARE APPLICATIONS. MARINE ENGINEERING. VFOAT Marine Engineering. 1970/Apr. 1979-. US. English. National Technical Information Service, US Department of Commerce, 5285 Port Royal Road, Springfield VA 22161.

A DIRECTORY OF COMPUTER SOFTWARE APPLICATIONS. TRANSPORTATION. VFOAT Transportation. US. English. Department of Commerce, National Technical Information Service, 5285 Port Royal Road, Springfield VA.

THE DIRECTORY OF COMPUTER + SOFTWARE RETAILERS. (THE ... DIRECTORY OF COMPUTER + SOFTWARE RETAILERS). VFOAT Directory of Computer and Software Retailers. 1983-. 0738-839X. US. English. an. $389.00. Chain Store Guide, Lebhar Friedman, Attn Priscilla Gilla Jiminez, 425 Park Avenue, New York NY 10022. **Tel** (212)371-9400. **Ed** Torry Burdick. **LC** HD9696.C63. **DD** 381.450016402573. Complete company profiles on computer store companies, consumer electronic retailers, mass merchandisers and specialty retailers, office equipment and supply dealers, and computer and software distributors.

A DIRECTORY OF COMPUTERIZED DATA FILES. 1982-. 0738-4610. US. English. be. National Technical Information Service, 5285 Port Royal Road, Springfield VA 22161. **LC** QA76. **DD** 001.6425029473. *Directory of Computerized Data Files & Related Technical Reports, 0731-3322.*

DIRECTORY OF COMPUTERIZED INFORMATION IN SCIENCE AND TECHNOLOGY. 1968-. 0070-5330. US. English. ir. Science Associates International Inc, 1841 Broadway, New York NY 10023. **Tel** (201)536-0662.

DIRECTORY OF COMPUTING FACILITIES IN INSTITUTIONS OF HIGHER EDUCATION. VFOAT Directory of Computing Facilities in Higher Education. 1982-83-. 0749-1999. US. English. an. Seminars for Academic Computing, La Sells Stewart Center, Oregon State University, Corvallis OR 97331-3102. **LC** QA76.215. **DD** 001.6402573. *Directory of Computing Facilities in Institutions of Higher Education throughout North America.*

DIRECTORY OF CONSTITUENT ORGANIZATIONS - NATIONAL JEWISH COMMUNITY RELATIONS ADVISORY COUNCIL. **Main/Corp** National Jewish Community Relations Advisory Council (U.S.). 0161-2298. US. English. National Jewish Community Relations Advisory Council, 55 West 42nd Street, New York NY 10036. **LC** E184.J5. **DD** 301.451924073.

DIRECTORY OF CONSTRUCTION ASSOCIATIONS. 1978-. 0193-2764. US. English. $15.00. Professional Publications, PO Box 319, Huntington NY 11743. **LC** TH12. **DD** 624.02573.

DIRECTORY OF CONSULTANT MEMBERS - AMERICAN MANAGEMENT ASSOCIATION. **Main/Corp** American Management Association. 1956-. US. English. ir. American Management Association, PO Box 319, Saranac Lake NY 12983. **Tel** (518)891-1500. **LC** HD28.

THE DIRECTORY OF CONSULTANTS IN BIOTECHNOLOGY. 0882-6005. Periodical. US. English. ir. $85.00. Research Publications, 12 Lunar Drive Drawer AB, Woodbridge CT 06525.

DIRECTORY OF CONSULTANTS (WASHINGTON, D.C. : 1983). (DIRECTORY OF CONSULTANTS). 0741-9732. US. English. APPA, Eleven Dupont Circle/Suite 250, Washington DC 20036. **LC** HD69.C6. **DD** 658.46025.

DIRECTORY OF CONSULTING SPECIALISTS. VFOAT Consulting Specialists. 0090-4945. US. English. Stemm's Information Systems and Indexes, PO Box 42576, Los Angeles CA 90050. **LC** HD69.C6. **DD** 658.403.

DIRECTORY OF CONTINUING EDUCATION OPPORTUNITIES FOR LIBRARY, INFORMATION, MEDIA PERSONNEL CEASED. 1977-1979. 0162-847X. US. English. an. K G Saur Verlag, 175 Fifth Avenue, New York NY 10010. **LC** Z668. **DD** 020.71102573. *Continuing Education Courses and Programs for Library, Information, and Media Personnel.*

DIRECTORY OF CONTINUING EDUCATION OPPORTUNITIES IN NEW YORK CITY. 1974-. 0094-095X. US. English. $10.00. New York City Regional Center for Life-Long Learning, Pace Plaza, New York NY 10038. **LC** L903.N75. **DD** 374.00257471.

DIRECTORY OF CONTRACT SERVICE FIRMS. 0148-1819. US. English. an. $7.50. Contract Engineer, PO Box 97000, Kirkland WA 98083. **Tel** (206)823-2222. **Ed** Jerry A Erickson. **LC** TA12. **DD** 620.004202573. adv acc. **Circ** 15,000. A directory of employers for contract (temporary) engineering and technical positions.

DIRECTORY OF CONVENIENCE STORE COMPANIES AND PROFILE OF THE INDUSTRY. VFOAT Profile of the Convenience Store Industry. 1981-. 0278-9698. US. English. an. $65.00. MacLean Hunter Media Inc, 708 3rd Avenue, New York NY 10017. **LC** HF5469.25. **DD** 381.1. *Directory of Convenience Store Companies.*

DIRECTORY OF CONVENTIONS. 1952-. 0417-5751. US. English. an. $79.00. Bill Brothers Publishing Company, 633 3rd Avenue, New York NY 10017. **Tel** (212)986-4800. **LC** AS8. **DD** 061.3.

DIRECTORY OF COOPERATING AGENCIES. 8755-7118. US. English. ir. United States Department of Agriculture, Food and Nutrition Service, Alexandria VA 22302. **LC** HV696.F6. **DD** 363.88302573.

DIRECTORY OF COOPERATIVE EDUCATION. (A DIRECTORY OF COOPERATIVE EDUCATION). First Vol. published in 1968. 0070-5357. US. English. $35.00. College Directory of Cooperative Education, Box 282, Newtown Square PA 19073. **Tel** (215)566-8418. **Ed** Stewart B Collins. **LC** L901. **DD** 331.25922. Only comprehensive directory of all colleges offering cooperative programs work and study in US and Canada. 355 pages, 635 college descriptions, 165 college majors.

DIRECTORY OF CORPORATE AFFILIATIONS. VFOAT Corporate Affiliations. 1973-. 0736-9778. US. English. an. $318.00. National Register Publishing Company Inc, 3004 Glenview Road, Wilmette IL 60091. **Tel** (800)323-4601. **Ed** R Weicherding. **LC** HG4057. **DD** 338.802573. adv acc. **Circ** 11,500. The 'Who Owns Whom' of American business: lists over 4,000 major public and privately-held companies with their divisions, subsidiaries and affiliates. *Directory of Corporate Affiliations of Major Corporations, 0737-3031.*

DIRECTORY OF CORPORATE ART COLLECTIONS. 1 (1982)-. 0732-7854. US. English. ir. $69.95. International Art Alliance, PO Box 1608, Largo FL 34294. **Tel** (813)581-7328. **Ed** S R Howarth. **LC** N5207. **DD** 708.002573. **Circ** 2,000. Descriptions of art collections owned by businesses and corporations in the US and Canada.

DIRECTORY OF CORPORATE FINANCING. 79th (Sept. 1982)-. 0882-7591. US. English. sa. $125.00 Single Issue. Subscription Department, Investment Dealer's Digest, 150 Broadway, New York NY 10038. *Corporate Financing Directory.*

DIRECTORY OF CORPORATE URBAN AFFAIRS OFFICERS. 0090-4066. US. English. $10.00. Public Affairs Council, 1601 Eighteenth Street Northwest, Washington DC 20009. **LC** HD60.5.U5. **DD** 361.8.

DIRECTORY OF COUNSELING SERVICES. 1973-. 0094-7512. US. English. an. American Association of Counseling Development, 5999 Stevenson Avenue, Alexandria VA 22304. **Tel** (703)823-9800. **LC** HF5381.A1. **DD** 378.1942502573. *Directory of Approved Counseling Agencies.*

DIRECTORY OF COUNTY OFFICERS OF KANSAS. 1953-. 0449-7864. Periodical. US. English. be. Kansas Secretary of State, Topeka KS 66612.

DIRECTORY OF COUNTY OFFICIALS (ANNAPOLIS, MD.). (DIRECTORY OF COUNTY OFFICIALS). US. English. Maryland Association of Counties, 169 Conduit Street, Annapolis MD 21401. **LC** JS451.M37. **DD** 352.0073.

DIRECTORY OF COURSE MATERIAL. 1984-. 0749-7458. US. English. an. HBS Case Services, Morgan Hall, Harvard Business School, Boston MA 02163. **LC** HD30.4. **DD** 650.071174461. *HBS Case Collection. Directory of Course Material, HBS Case Collection. Index to Course Material.*

DIRECTORY OF CRIMINAL JUSTICE AGENCIES IN ARIZONA. 1978-. US. English. an. Professional Plaza/4th Floor 4820 North Black Canyon Freeway, Phoenix AZ 85017. **LC** HV8145.A7. **DD** 350.74025791.

DIRECTORY OF CRIMINAL JUSTICE INFORMATION SOURCES. Began with 1976. 0191-4553. US. English. Superintendent of Documents, US Government Printing Office, Washington DC 20402. **LC** HV8138. **DD** 364.07.

DIRECTORY OF CROSS-CULTURAL RESEARCH AND RESEARCHERS. 0093-6251. US. English. Western Washington State College, Center for Cross-Cultural Research, Bellingham WA 98225. **LC** H62. **DD** 300.72.

DIRECTORY OF CULTURAL ORGANIZATIONS AND INSTITUTIONS IN ASIA AND THE PACIFIC. English. ir. Asian Cultural Centre for UNESCO, 6 Fukuromachi Shinjuku-ku, Tokyo 162 Japan. **LC** AS408. **DD** 068.5.

DIRECTORY OF CURRENT RESEARCH - NATIONAL UNIVERSITY OF SINGAPORE. **Main/Corp** National University of Singapore. 1982-3-. English. an. **LC** Q180.S5. **DD** 001.4095957.

DIRECTORY OF CUSTOM OPERATORS IN ALBERTA. 1984-. 0826-6530. CN. English. an. **LC** HD9014.C4. **DD** 630.20947123.

DIRECTORY OF CZECHOSLOVAK OFFICIALS. **Main/Corp** United States. Central Intelligence Agency. US. English. US Dept of State, Bureau of Intelligence & Research, Washington DC 20520. **LC** JN2217. **DD** 354.437002.

DIRECTORY OF DANCE COMPANIES. (DANCE TOURING PROGRAM. DIRECTORY OF DANCE COMPANIES). VFOAT Dance Touring Program: Directory of Dance Companies. 0363-972X. US. English. an. Charles Reinhart Management Inc, 1860 Broadway, New York NY 10023. **LC** GV1623. **DD** 338.477933202573.

DIRECTORY OF DATA FILES. **Main/Corp** United States. Bureau of the Census. Oct. 1979-. Periodical. US. English. ir. Department of Commerce, Bureau of the Census, Public Information Office, Washington DC 20233.

A DIRECTORY OF DEALERS IN SECONDHAND AND ANTIQUARIAN BOOKS IN THE BRITISH ISLES. VFOAT Dealers in Books. 1951/52-. 0070-5411. UK. English. ir. Sheppard Press Ltd, PO Box 42 Russell Chambers, London WC2E 8AX England. **Tel** (01) 240 0406. **Ed** T Rendall Davies. **LC** Z327. **DD** 655.5. adv acc. **Circ** 5,000. A directory of dealers in secondhand and antiquarian books in the British Isles- eleventh edition.

Yearbooks, Almanacs, Directories

THE DIRECTORY OF DEFENSE ELECTRONIC PRODUCTS AND SERVICES : UNITED STATES SUPPLIERS. 1975-. US. English. an. $20.00. Bermont Books, Suite 1108/815- 15th Street Northwest, Washington DC 20005. LC UG485. DD 623.04302573.

A DIRECTORY OF DELAWARE LIBRARIES. 0730-5222. US. English. ir. $5.00. Directory of Delaware Libraries, Box 1843, Wilmington DE 19899. LC Z732.D34. DD 027.0025751.

DIRECTORY OF DELAWARE SCHOOLS. 0362-5710. US. English. Department of Public Instruction, Townsend Building Federal Street at Loockerman Street, Dover DE 19901. LC L903.D3. DD 371.002573.

DIRECTORY OF DELAWARE VISUAL ARTISTS. 0736-1955. US. English. Delaware State Arts Council, State Office Building, 820 North French Street, Wilmington DE 19801. LC N52.D3. DD 720.5751.

DIRECTORY OF DENTAL EDUCATORS. 1966-. 0090-0141. US. English. be. $40.00. American Association of Dental Schools, 1619 Massachusetts Avenue NW, Washington DC 20036. Tel (202)667-9433. NLM WU22 AA1 A45N.

DIRECTORY OF DENTAL EDUCATORS (WASHINGTON, D.C. : 1983). (DIRECTORY OF DENTAL EDUCATORS). 1982/83-. 0882-1860. US. English. an. 1619 Massachusetts Avenue NW, Washington DC 20036. LC RK37. DD 617.6002573. *Directory of Dental and Allied Dental Educators, 0271-8677.*

DIRECTORY OF DENTISTS, DENTAL SPECIALISTS AND DENTAL HYGIENISTS. 1977-. 0162-4946. US. English. an. Informative Data Company, 3546 Watson Road, St Louis MO 63139.

DIRECTORY OF DEPARTMENT STORES. VFOAT Department Store Guide Directory. 1955-. 0419-2508. US. English. ir. $179.00. Chain Store Guide Lebhar-Friedman Attn Priscilla G Jimenez, 425 Park Avenue, New York NY 10022. Tel (212)371-9400. Ed Barbara Brown. Provides complete company profiles on 1,300 companies operating 9,000 stores. Separate sections feature listings on resident buying offices, 1,000 apparel and general merchandise mail order firms.

DIRECTORY OF DEPARTMENTAL INFORMATION CENTRES. (REPERTOIRE DES CENTRES D'INFORMATION DU MINISTERE). Main/Corp Canada. Ministere des Affaires Indiennes et du Nord Canadien. 1979-. 0225-3941. CN. text in French and English on inverted pages. DD 026.97100497.

DIRECTORY OF DEPARTMENTS OF GERMAN AT CANADIAN UNIVERSITIES AND COLLEGES. 1977/78-. 0703-3095. CN. English. an. 5.00. Prof R Farquharson, Germanic Languages & Literatures, University of Toronto, 97 Street George Street, Toronto Ontario M5S 1A1 Canada. Tel (416)978-4440. Ed R Farquharson. DD 830.02571. Circ 350. (ctrl). Directory of departments of German at Canadian universities and colleges, showing address, telephone, faculty, rank, degrees and scholarly interests. *Departments of German at Canadian Universities, Personalia, 0703-3087.*

DIRECTORY OF DESIGNATED MEMBERS - APPRAISAL INSTITUTE OF CANADA. (DIRECTORY OF DESIGNATED MEMBERS). Main/Corp Appraisal Institute of Canada. VFOAT Liste de Membres Designes. 1972-. 0316-9839. Periodical. CN. text in English and French. an. Free. Institut Canadien des Evaluateurs Bureau, 177 Avenue Lombard/Suite 502, Winnipeg Manitoba R3B 0W6 Canada. DD 333.33206271. *Directory, 0316-9820.*

A DIRECTORY OF DIESEL FUEL STATIONS COAST TO COAST. 1976-. 0360-9987. US. English. $5.95. Diesel Fuel Services Inc, 330 East 33rd Street, New York NY 10016. LC TL153. DD 381.45629286.

DIRECTORY OF DIETETIC PROGRAMS : ACCREDITED AND APPROVED. VFOAT Directory of Accredited and Approved Dietetic Programs. US. English. an. $6.00. American Dietetic Association, PO Box 91403, Chicago IL 60693.

DIRECTORY OF DIPLOMATES. Main/Corp The American Board of Orthopaedic Surgery. 1937. US. English. ir. American Board of Orthopaedic Surgery, 444 North Michigan Avenue/Suite 2970, Chicago IL 60611. Tel (312)822-9572. Circ 3,000. (ctrl). Names, addresses, certification and re-certification year for certified orthopaediests. Geographical list of deceased diplomats included.

DIRECTORY OF DIPLOMATIC CORPS AND INTERNATIONAL ORGANIZATIONS. Main/Corp Kenya. Protocol Dept. 0376-8465. English. ir. Protocol Department, PO Box 30551, Nairobi Kenya. LC JX1873.K42. DD 354.676200892. *Diplomatic Directory.*

DIRECTORY OF DIPLOMATIC MISSIONS. English. ir. LC JX1839. DD 354.5400892.

THE DIRECTORY OF DIRECTORIES. 1st Ed. 0275-5580. US. English. be. $160.00. Gale Research Company, Book Tower, Detroit MI 48226. Tel (313)961-2242. Ed J Ethridge. LC Z5771, AY2001. DD 300.02573. NLM AY 2001 D598. The fully revised and updated third edition thoroughly describes and indexes over 7,800 directories of all kinds. The detailed subject index, which employs more than 2,100 subject headings and many cross references, provides access to entires on a specific subject.

DIRECTORY OF DIRECTORS. VFOAT Financial Post Directory of Directors. 1947-. 0071-5042. Periodical. CN. English. an. The Financial Post, MacLean Hunter Building, 777 Bay Street, Toronto Ontario M5W 1A7 Canada. DD 658.420922. *Financial Post Directory of Canadian Directors and Officials, 0317-3658.*

DIRECTORY OF DIRECTORS. (THE DIRECTORY OF DIRECTORS). Began with: 1878. 0070-5438. UK. English. an. Business Press International USA, 205 East 42nd Street, New York NY 10017. Tel (212)867-2080. DD 658.

THE DIRECTORY OF DIRECTORS IN THE CITY OF BOSTON AND VICINITY. Periodical. US. English. an.

DIRECTORY OF DIRECTORS IN THE CITY OF NEW YORK AND TRI-STATE AREA. 1982 Ed.-. US. English. an. $155.00. Directory of Directors Company Inc, PO Box 462, Southport CT 06490. Tel (203)255-8525. Ed A M Dahl. bk rev. Circ 1,000. Lists approximately 15,000 executives address, company name, outside directorates, and approximately 2,500 firms and corporations indicating type of business in tri-state area. *Directory of Directors in the City of New York and Suburbs.*

DIRECTORY OF DISCOUNT STORES (NEW YORK, N.Y. : 1983). (DIRECTORY OF DISCOUNT STORES). VFOAT Chain Store Guide. 1983-. 0736-931X. US. English. an. $179.00. Chain Store Guide Information Services, 425 Park Avenue, New York NY 10022. Tel (212)371-9400. Ed Dick Rossini. LC HF5035. DD 381.1. Provides complete company profiles on 325 discount store companies operating 8,250 companies. Separate sections feature listings on 1,500 catalog showroom companies, 100 leased department operators, 4,300 CE audio and photo retailers operating 31,000 stores, and 375 CE distributors. *Directory of Discount Department Stores, 0070-5446.*

THE DIRECTORY OF DISTINGUISHED AMERICANS. 1st Ed.-. 0742-3349. US. English. 205 West Martin Street, PO Box 226, Raleigh NC 27602. LC CT220. DD 920.073.

DIRECTORY OF DISTRIBUTORS. (DIRECTORY OF DISTRIBUTORS : LATIN AMERICA, AFRICA, ASIA, MIDDLE EAST). 8755-3821. US. English. an. International Publications Inc, 15 Ketchum Street, Westport CT 06880. LC HF5421.5.L29. DD 382.025.

DIRECTORY OF DISTRIBUTORS IN METROPOLITAN TORONTO. CN. English. Province of British Columbia, Ministry of Economic Development, Suite 450/700 West Georgia Street, Pacific Center, Vancouver British Columbia V7Y 1C6 Canada. LC HF5421.5.C3. DD 380.102571355.

DIRECTORY OF DOCTORS OF MEDICINE, DOCTORS OF OSTEOPATHY, CLINICAL AUDIOLOGISTS, SPEECH PATHOLOGISTS, SPEECH PATHOLOGISTS & CLINICAL AUDIOLOGISTS, PROFESSIONAL PHYSICAL THERAPISTS, AND PSYCHOLOGISTS. VFOAT Directory, Doctors of Medicine, Doctors of Osteopathy, Clinical Audiologists, Speech Pathologists, Professional Physical Therapists, and Psychologists. 0732-5991. US. English. Informative Data Company, 3546 Watson Road, St Louis MO 63139. LC R712.A1. DD 610.25778.

DIRECTORY OF DOCTORS OF OSTEOPATHY LICENSED AND REGISTERED IN TENNESSEE. 1976-. 0149-3760. US. English. 352 Capitol Hill Building, Nashville TN 37219. LC RZ333. DD 615.533025768. NLM WB 22 AT2 D53. *Directory of Doctors of Osteopathy Licensed in Tennessee.*

A DIRECTORY OF DRUG ABUSE TREATMENT SERVICE UNITS AND ORGANIZATIONS OFFERING SPECIFIC SERVICES TO DRUG ABUSERS. VFOAT Directory of Drug Abuse Treatment Programs and Organizations Offering Specific Services to Drug Abusers. Began with: 8th Ed. (1978). US. English. MD Drug Abuse Administration, O'Conor Building/4th Floor, 201 West Preston Street, Balitmore MD 21201. LC HV5831.M3. DD 362.29386025752. NLM WM 22. *Directory of Drug Abuse Treatment Programs and Organizations Offering Specific Services to Drug Abusers.*

DIRECTORY OF DRUG INFORMATION AND TREATMENT ORGANIZATIONS. Began in 1972. 0361-1493. Periodical. US. English. mo. Stash, 118 South Bedford Street, Madison WI 53703. LC HV5825. DD 362.2902573. NLM WM 22 AA1 D3. *Directory of Drug Information Groups, 0098-4701.*

DIRECTORY OF DRUG STORE & HBA CHAINS INCLUDES DRUG WHOLESALERS. VFOAT Directory of Drug Store and Health and Beauty Aids Chains Includes Drug Wholesalers. 1982-. 0730-2703. US. English. an. $179.00. Chain Store Guide Lebhar-Friedman Attn Priscilla G Jimenez, 425 Park Avenue, New York NY 10022. Tel (212)371-9400. LC HD9666.3. DD 615.1029473. Complete company profiles on 2,000 2- or-more store chains operating 23,000 drug and HBA stores and 165 drug wholesale companies and their 275 divisions. *Directory of Drug, Health & Beauty Aid Chains, Drug Wholesalers, 0277-1977.*

DIRECTORY OF EAST ASIAN COLLECTIONS IN AMERICAN LIBRARIES. 0148-0065. US. English. Committee on East Asian Libraries, c/o Harvard-Yenching Library, Harvard University, 2 Divinity Avenue, Cambridge MA 02138. LC Z3001, DS504.5. DD 026.95002573.

DIRECTORY OF ECONOMIC DEVELOPMENT DISTRICTS AND AREA GRANTEES. US. English. US Department of Commerce, Economic Development Administration, Washington DC 20230. *Directory for Economic Development Districts.*

DIRECTORY OF ECONOMIC RESEARCH IN MISSISSIPPI. 1972/73-. 0094-1433. US. English. an. 3825 Ridgewood Road, Jackson MS 39205. LC Q180.U5. DD 330.0720762. *Directory of Research in Progress in Mississippi.*

DIRECTORY OF EDITORIAL RESOURCES. 1981-. 0731-4426. US. ENGLISH. an. Editorial Experts Inc, 4600 Duke St, Alexandria VA 22304. LC PN162. DD 070.4102573.

DIRECTORY OF EDUCATION. VFOAT Annuaire de l'Administration Scolaire. 1973/74-. 0316-8549. Periodical. CN. English (text in French, 1977/78-). an. Ministry of Education, Mowat Block, Queens Park, Toronto Ontario M7A 1L4 Canada. DD 370.25713.

DIRECTORY OF EDUCATION ASSOCIATIONS. Began with 1977. 0160-0508. US. English. an. US Government Printing Office, Superintendent of Documents, Washington DC 20402. LC L901. DD 370.6273. NLM L 901 D598. *Education Directory. Education Associations, 0083-2650.*

DIRECTORY OF EDUCATION STUDIES IN CANADA. VFOAT Annuaire d'Etudes en Education au Canada. 1st- Ed. 0070-5454. Periodical. CN. text in English and French. an. 30.00. The Canadian Education Association, 252 Bloor Street West, Toronto Ontario M5S 1V5 Canada. Tel (416)924-7721. Ed Maureen Davis. DD 016.37. Circ 400. (ctrl). Annotated directory of research studies and graduate theses from Canadian education institutions and organizations. *Education Studies Completed in Canadian Universities, 0424-5652.*

Yearbooks, Almanacs, Directories

DIRECTORY OF EDUCATIONAL FACILITIES FOR THE LEARNING DISABLED. CEASED. 5th-8th Ed. 0093-7703. US. English. Academic Therapy Publications, 1539 4th Street, San Rafael CA 94901. **LC** L901. **DD** 371.902573. **NLM** LC 4031 D598. *Directory of Facilities for the Learning Disabled, 0092-3257.*

DIRECTORY OF EDUCATIONAL INSTITUTIONS ACCREDITED BY THE ACCREDITING COMMISSION OF THE ASSOCIATION OF INDEPENDENT COLLEGES AND SCHOOLS. 1981-. 0733-2858. US. English. an. Accrediting Commission Association of Independent Colleges and Schools, Suite 600/1730 M Street NW, Washington DC 20036. **LC** L901. **DD** 378.73. *Directory of Institutions Accredited by the Accrediting Commission of the Association of Independent Colleges and Schools.*

DIRECTORY OF EDUCATIONAL INSTITUTIONS AND APPRENTICESHIP AND OTHER ON-THE-JOB TRAINING FACILITIES APPROVED BY THE WEST VIRGINIA DEPARTMENT OF EDUCATION FOR VETERANS EDUCATIONAL BENEFITS UNDER PUBLIC LAW 96-466. VFOAT Veterans Benefits. US. English. an. Office of Veterans Education & Training, Bureau of Services & Federal Programs, West Virginia Department of Education, Room 242/Building 6 Capitol Complex, Charleston WV 25314. **Tel** (304)348-2193. **Ed** Bob Siler. **LC** UB358.W4. **DD** 374.00880697. **Circ** 1,000. (ctrl). Institutions and businesses approved to train veterans.

DIRECTORY OF EDUCATIONAL INSTITUTIONS, HARYANA. English. ir. 3.70. **LC** L961.I4. **DD** 370.2554558.

A DIRECTORY OF EDUCATIONAL INSTITUTIONS IN OGUN STATE. 1977-. NR. English. ir. Ministry of Finance & Economic Development, Statistics Div, Abeokuta Nigeria. **LC** L971.N5. **DD** 370.256692.

DIRECTORY OF EDUCATIONAL INSTITUTIONS, RAJASTHAN. 1964/65-. 0420-0586. Periodical. II. English. ir. Education Department, Government of Rajasthan, Jaipur India.

DIRECTORY OF EDUCATIONAL OPPORTUNITIES IN GEORGIA. 0419-2559. US. English. be. Seven Hunter Street Building/ Room 656, Atlanta GA 30334. **LC** L903.G4. **DD** 374.013025758.

DIRECTORY OF EDUCATIONAL PROGRAMS. 1981-82-. 0275-9357. US. English. $4.00. National Registration Center for Study Abroad, 823 North Second Street, Milwaukee WI 53203. **Tel** (414)278-0631. **LC** L913. **DD** 370.258. **Circ** 10,000. Directory describes Spanish language study programs in Mexico. Includes program description, fees, dates, lodging, and registration information. All listed programs prescreened by US educators.

DIRECTORY OF EDUCATIONAL SPECIALISTS. 1972/73-. US. English. 3200 Southgreen Road, Baltimore MD 21207.

DIRECTORY OF ELECTRIC LIGHT AND POWER COMPANIES. 1973-. 0092-4970. US. English. an. Midwest Oil Register, PO Box 700597, Tulsa OK 74170. **LC** HD9685.U4. **DD** 363.6202573.

DIRECTORY OF ELEMENTARY AND SECONDARY SCHOOL DISTRICTS, AND SCHOOLS IN SELECTED SCHOOL DISTRICTS. Periodical. US. English.

DIRECTORY OF ENERGY DATA COLLECTION FORMS. Main/Corp United States. Energy Information Administration. Office of the NA. May 1981-. US. English. National Energy Information Center, Forrestal Building/ Room 1F048, Washington DC 20582. *EIA Data Collection Forms.*

DIRECTORY OF ENGINEERING SOCIETIES AND RELATED ORGANIZATIONS. VFOAT Directory of Engineering Societies. 0075-5470. US. English. be. $101.00. American Association of Engineering Societies, 415 Second Street Northeast/Suite 200, Washington DC 20002. **Tel** (202)546-2237. **Ed** Gordon Davis. **DD** 620.006. **Circ** 1,000. Contains detailed breakdown of engineers' salaries by industry group of employer, geographic location of employer, size of employer, years of experience, highest degree held, and supervisory status. *Engineering Societies Directory.*

DIRECTORY OF ENGINEERING UNITS IN PAKISTAN. 1974-. 0376-8473. English. ir. 10.00. Development Institute of Pakistan, Mohammadi House, I I Chundrigar Road. **LC** TJ104.5. **DD** 338.476210255491.

DIRECTORY OF ENGINEERS AND LAND SURVEYORS REGISTERED IN SOUTH CAROLINA. US. English. State Life Building, 710 Palmetto, Columbia SC 29201. **LC** TA12. **DD** 620.0025757. *Roster of Registered Professional Engineers and Land Surveyors.*

DIRECTORY OF ENVIRONMENTAL CONSULTANTS. 1972-. US. English. an. $4.00. Directory Press, PO Box 8002, St Louis MO 63108. **LC** TD12. **DD** 301.31025.

DIRECTORY OF ENVIRONMENTAL EDUCATION FACILITIES. US. English. ir. National Audubon Society, 950 Third Avenue, New York NY 10022.

DIRECTORY OF EQUIPMENT, SUPPLY AND SERVICE MEMBERS CEASED. Main/Corp British Columbia & Yukon Chamber of Mines. -1982. 0318-482X. CN. English. an. Free. British Columbia & Yukon Chamber of Mines, 840 West Hastings Street, Vancouver British Columbia V6C 1C8 Canada. **LC** HD9506.C23. **DD** 338.2025711. (ctrl). *Directory of Service, Supply and Equipment Members.*

DIRECTORY OF ERIC SEARCH SERVICES. Main/Corp Educational Resources Information Center (U.S.). VAT Directory of Educational Resources Information Center Search Service. US. English. be. Free. ERIC Processing and Reference Facility, 4833 Rugby Avenue/Suite 303, Bethesda MD 20814. **Tel** (301)656-9723. **Ed** Ted Brandhorst. **Circ** 10,000. The intent of this directory is to include all sites providing search services on a regular basis—irrespective of whether the service is available only to a circumscribed community.

DIRECTORY OF EUROPEAN ASSOCIATIONS. PART 1. NATIONAL INDUSTRIAL, TRADE & PROFESSIONAL ASSOCIATIONS. VFOAT Handbuch der Europaischen Verbande. Teil 1. Nationale Verbande im Bereich der Gewerblichen Wirtschaft und der Berufe. VAT Directory of European Associations. Part One. National Industrial, Trade and Professional Associations. 0070-5500. UK. Multilingual (English, French, German). ir. $195.00 Vol.1, $135.00 Vol.2. Gale Research, Book Tower, Detroit MI 48226. **Tel** (800)521-0707. **Ed** I G Anderson. **NLM** AS 98 D598. Vol.1 provides details on over 9,000 national organizations and regional organizations of national significance. Vol. 2 contains: natural sciences, technology, engineering, and architecture; economic sciences, finance and business managment; medicine; social sciences; law; history and archaeology.

DIRECTORY OF EVALUATION TRAINING. 0277-0873. US. English. Pintail Press Inc, 4122 Edmunds Street NW, Washington DC 20007. **LC** H62.5.U5. **DD** 361.61071073.

DIRECTORY OF EXECUTIVE RECRUITERS. 1971. 0090-6484. US. English. an. $21.00. Consultants News, Templeton Road, Fitzwilliam NH 03447. **Tel** (603)585-6544. **Ed** James A Kennedy. **LC** HF5549.5.R44. **DD** 658.3111. Identifies executive recruiters throughout North America - heavily cross indexed by function, industry, geography and key principals. Lists salary minimum, professional affiliation; 5-10 word description.

A DIRECTORY OF EXPANDED ROLE PROGRAMS FOR REGISTERED NURSES. Series/Titl Health Manpower References. US. English. US Department of Health Education and Welfare, Public Health Service, Bureau of Health Manpower, Division of Nursing, Washington DC 20402. *Directory of Programs Preparing Registered Nurses for Expanded Roles, 0160-4449.*

DIRECTORY OF EXPERT WITNESSES IN TECHNOLOGY. VFOAT Expert Witnesses in Technology. 1st Ed.-. 0749-9965. US. English. an. $125.00. Research Publications, 12 Lunar Drive Drawer AB, Woodbridge CT 06525. **LC** TA12. **DD** 620.002573. 9,000 profiles of top scientists and engineers available as expert witnesses. All profiles are indexes by 1,500 areas of technology and cross indexed by city/state.

DIRECTORY OF EXPORTERS. 1st- Ed. English. ir. 50.00. Federation of Pakistan, Chambers of Commerce & Industry, Bellasis Street, Karachi Pakistan. **LC** HF3790.5. **DD** 382.60255491.

DIRECTORY OF FACILITIES AND SERVICES FOR LEARNING DISABLED. 9th Ed. (1981-1982)-. Periodical. US. English. be. Free. Academic Therapy Publications, 20 Commercial Boulevard, Novato CA 94947. **Tel** (415)883-3314. **Ed** Betty Lou Kratoville. adv acc. **Circ** 40,000. For parents and professionals, list more than 500 private facilities and services serving the learning disabled. *Directory of Educational Facilities for the Learning Disabled, 0093-7703.*

DIRECTORY OF FACILITIES OBLIGATED TO PROVIDE UNCOMPENSATED SERVICES BY STATE AND CITY. (DIRECTORY OF FACILITIES OBLIGATED TO PROVIDE UNCOMPENSATED SERVICES BY STATE AND CITY AS OF JANUARY 1 . . .). 8755-593X. US. English. **LC** RA977. **DD** 362.1102573.

DIRECTORY OF FACULTY CONTRACTS AND BARGAINING AGENTS IN INSTITUTIONS OF HIGHER EDUCATION. Began with Vol. for 1976. 0276-7805. US. English. an. $15.00. National Center of Study of Collective Bargaining, 17 Lexington Avenue, New York NY 10010. **Tel** (212)725-3390. **Ed** Joel M Douglas. **LC** LB2335.885.U6. **DD** 331.890413781202573. **Circ** 325. A compilation and statistical analysis of faculty contracts and bargaining agents.

DIRECTORY OF FEDERAL AGENCY EDUCATION DATA TAPES. 1976-. US. English. an. 20402.

DIRECTORY OF FEDERAL AND STATE OFFICIALS ENGAGED IN WATER RESOURCES DEVELOPMENT. US. English. Missouri Basin Inter-Agency Committee, Suite 403/10050 Regency Circle, Omaha NE 68114. **LC** HD1694. **DD** 333.91002573.

DIRECTORY OF FEDERAL AUDIT AND INSPECTOR GENERAL ORGANIZATIONS. Apr. 1980-. US. English. qt. US General Accounting Office, Division of Financial and General Management Studies, Washington DC 20548. *Directory of Federal Audit Organizations.*

DIRECTORY OF FEDERAL DROUGHT ASSISTANCE. 0148-5091. Periodical. US. English. Institute for Policy Research, 2480 West 26th Avenue, Denver CO 80211. **LC** HD1759. **DD** 362.5.

DIRECTORY OF FEDERAL HEALTH/ MEDICINE GRANTS AND CONTRACTS PROGRAMS. VAT Directory of Federal Health Medicine Grants and Contracts Programs. 1st- Ed. 0744-0804. US. English. Science & Health Publications Inc, 6410 Rockledge Drive/Suite 208, Bethesda MD 20034. **LC** RA440. **DD** 610.79. **NLM** W 22 AA1 D58.

A DIRECTORY OF FEDERAL PROGRAMS ADMINISTERED BY THE NEW JERSEY DEPARTMENT OF EDUCATION. Main/Corp New Jersey. State Dept. of Education. Bureau of Grants Management. 0145-4374. US. English. New Jersey Department of Education, 225 West State Street, Trenton NJ 08625. **LC** LB2826.N5. **DD** 379.15209749.

A DIRECTORY OF FEDERAL PROGRAMS - (NEW JERSEY). Main/ Corp New Jersey. State Dept. of Education. US. English. State of New Jersey, Department of Education, 225 West State Street, Trenton NJ 08608. **LC** LB2826.N5. **DD** 379.12209749.

DIRECTORY OF FEDERAL SERVICES FOR THE HANDICAPPED AND DISABLED. VFOAT Repertoire des Services Federaux pour les Personnes Handicapees. Apr. 1984-. 0827-4002. CN. English (French). Centre for Service to the Public, Ottawa Ontario K1A 0S5 Canada. **LC** HV1559.C2. **DD** 362.404802571.

DIRECTORY OF FEDERAL STATISTICAL DATA FILES. March 1981-. 0731-3594. US. English. an. National Technical Information Service, 5285 Port Royal Road, Springfield VA 22161. **LC** HA37. **DD** 025.063102573.

Yearbooks, Almanacs, Directories

DIRECTORY OF FEDERAL STATISTICS FOR LOCAL AREAS. A GUIDE TO SOURCES. URBAN UPDATE. (DIRECTORY OF FEDERAL STATISTICS FOR LOCAL AREAS : A GUIDE TO SOURCES. URBAN UPDATE). 1977/78-. 0272-1317. US. English. LC HA37. DD 016.3173. *Directory of Federal Statistics for Local Areas. A Guide to Sources, 0272-1031.*

DIRECTORY OF FEDERAL TECHNOLOGY RESOURCES. 1984-. 0747-7880. US. English. be. $25.00. NTIS US Department of Commerce, 5285 Port Royal Drive, Springfield VA 22151. LC T21. DD 607.2073.

DIRECTORY OF FEDERALLY SUPPORTED INFORMATION ANALYSIS CENTERS. Series/Titl PB 233 582 PB 189 300. 1st- ed. US. English. ir. Superintendent of Documents, GPO, Washington DC 20402.

DIRECTORY OF FEDERALLY SUPPORTED RESEARCH IN UNIVERSITIES. VFOAT Repertoire de la Recherche dans les Universites Subventionnee par le Gouvernement Federal. 1972/73-. 0316-0297. Periodical. CN. French (English). an. $54. Bibliotheque Scientifique du Canada, Supply & Services, Ottawa Ontario K1A 0S9 Canada. DD 001.4402571.

THE DIRECTORY OF FEE-BASED INFORMATION SERVICES. 0147-1678. US. English. an. Information Alternatives, PO Box 657, Woodstock NY 12498. LC Z674.5.U5. DD 021.002573.

DIRECTORY OF FEMALE JAZZ PERFORMERS. VFOAT National Directory of Female Jazz Performers. Began with Vol. for 1979. 0275-9349. US. English. an. $2.50. Women's Jazz Festival Inc, Box 22321, Kansas City MO 64113. LC ML12. DD 785.420922.

DIRECTORY OF FIELD CONTACTS FOR THE COORDINATION OF THE USE OF RADIO FREQUENCIES. 0198-6422. US. English. Federal Communications Commission, 1919 M Street NW, Washington DC 20554. LC HE8698. DD 384.5452. Vols. for 1978- distributed to depository libraries in microfiche.

DIRECTORY OF FILM LIBRARIES IN NORTH AMERICA. 1971-. Periodical. US. English. be. LC PN1998.A1. DD 026.7914302957.

DIRECTORY OF FINANCIAL AIDS FOR INTERNATIONAL ACTIVITIES. 1978-. 0163-0199. US. English. ir. University of Minnesota, 201 Nolte West 315 Pillsbury Drive, Minneapolis MN 55455. Tel (612)373-3793. LC L900. DD 370.1965025. Circ 700. Contains information on individual opportunities for academic people for study, research, travel, and teaching abroad—this book is a listing of possible funding sources and their deadlines.

DIRECTORY OF FINANCIAL AIDS FOR MINORITIES. 1984-1985-. 0738-4122. US. English. be. $35.00. ABC-CLIO Information Services, Box 4397, Santa Barbara CA 93103. Each issue contains an index to its own contents - no vol. index - loose.

DIRECTORY OF FINANCIAL AIDS FOR WOMEN. Began with issue for 1978. 0732-5215. Periodical. US. English. American Bibliographical Center, Clio Press, PO Box 4397, Santa Barbara CA 93103.

DIRECTORY OF FINANCIAL INSTITUTIONS (MONETARY AUTHORITY OF SINGAPORE. (DIRECTORY OF FINANCIAL INSTITUTIONS). SI. English. ir. $2.50. Monetary Authority of Singapore, Sia Building/77 Robinson Road, Singapore 1 Singapore. LC HG86. DD 332.10255957.

DIRECTORY OF FINANCIAL SERVICES FOR STATE AND LOCAL GOVERNMENT. 1st (1982)-. Periodical. US. English. Municipal Finance Officers Association, 180 North Michigan Avenue/Suite 800, Chicago IL 60601.

DIRECTORY OF FIRMS AND CORPORATIONS AUTHORIZED TO PRACTISE PROFESSIONAL ENGINEERING IN THE PROVINCE OF ONTARIO. V. 1- 1970-. 0316-8123. Periodical. CN. English. an. Free. Association of Professional Engineers of the Province of Ontario, 236 Avenue Road, Toronto Ontario M5R 2J5 Canada. DD 620.0062713.

DIRECTORY OF FIRMS ENGAGED IN RESEARCH IN THE STATE OF NEW MEXICO. 0162-802X. US. English. University of New Mexico, Bureau of Business and Economic Research, Albuquerque NM 87131. LC Q180.U5. DD 001.43025789.

DIRECTORY OF FIRST DEGREE AND DIPLOMA OF HIGHER EDUCATION COURSES. 0308-8057. UK. English. Council for National Academic Awards, 344-354 Gray's Inn Road, London WC1X8BP England. LC L915. DD 378.41.

DIRECTORY OF FIRST DEGREE COURSES. Main/Corp Council for National Academic Awards (Great Britain). UK. English. an. Council for National Academic Awards, 344-354 Gray's Inn Road, London WC1X8BP Canada. Tel (01)278-4411. LC LB2362.G7. DD 378.15502541. Circ 25,000. Listing of first degree and diploma of higher education colleges of higher education in Britain. *Compendium of Degree Courses.*

DIRECTORY OF FLORIDA GOVERNMENT. US. English. an. Florida Department of State, Division of Elections/Room 801, Tallahassee FL 32301. Tel (904)488-7690. Ed Dorothy W Glisson. LC JK4430. DD 353.9759002. (ctrl). Names of public and elected officials in the state of Florida. *Directory of State Officers (Tallahassee, Fla.).*

DIRECTORY OF FLORIDA INDUSTRIES. US. English. an. $45.15. Florida Chamber of Commerce, PO Box 11309, Tallahassee FL 32302. Tel (904)222-2831. Ed The Florida Chamber. adv acc. Circ 9,000. Directory of Florida industries by county, SIC code or alphabetical. *Directory of Florida Manufacturers, Directory of Florida Manufacturers (Not in NAL).*

DIRECTORY OF FLORIDA MARKETS FOR WRITERS. 1982-. US. English. an. Ed Dana K Cassell.

DIRECTORY OF FOOD SERVICE DISTRIBUTORS. VFOAT Food Service Distributors. 1980-. 0271-7662. US. English. an. $169.00. Chain Store Guide, Lebhar-Friedman, Attn Priscilla G Jimenez, 425 Park Avenue, New York NY 10022. Tel (212)371-9400. Ed Jim Smethurst. LC HD9321.3. DD 380.145683802573. Provides complete company profiles on 4,000 distributors who supply food, equipment, supplies to restaurants and institutional accounts. *Food Service Distributors, 0091-9152.*

DIRECTORY OF FOREIGN FIRMS OPERATING IN THE UNITED STATES. Series/Titl Encyclopedia of International Information, V. 4. 1st- Ed. 0070-5543. US. English. ir. World Trade Academy Press Inc, 50 East 42nd St, New York NY 10017. Tel (212)697-4999. List of foreign firms owning or investing in United States businesses with addresses and products/services.

DIRECTORY OF FOREST INDUSTRIES IN MALAYSIA. 1974-. English. ir. $3.50. The Malaysian Forester, Forest Research Institute, Kepong Malaysia. LC TS803. DD 338.174982025595.

DIRECTORY OF FOUNDATIONS OF THE GREATER WASHINGTON AREA. 1984-. 0884-9056. Periodical. US. English. $10.00. Community Foundation of Greater Washington Inc, 3221 M Street NW, Washington DC 20007. LC HV99.W29. DD 361.7632025753.

DIRECTORY OF FRANCHISING ORGANIZATIONS. 0070-556X. US. English. an. $6.00. Pilot Books, 103 Cooper Street, Babylon NY 11702. Tel (516)422-2225. Ed Sam Small. A comprehensive listing of the top money-making franchises with concise description and approximate investment. Includes important facts about franchising and an evaluation checklist. *Directory of Franchising Organizations and a Guide to Franchising.*

THE DIRECTORY OF FREE PROGRAMS, PERFORMING TALENT AND ATTRACTIONS. 0736-7759. US. English. an. Pageant Publishing Company, PO Box 240334, Memphis TN 38124.

DIRECTORY OF FREELANCE TRANSLATORS IN THE NATIONAL CAPITAL REGION. 1982/1983-. 0714-3516. CN. English (French translation on opposite pages). an. Directory of Freelance Translators in the National Capital Region, c/o R Serre, 1057 Riviera Drive, Ottawa Ontario K1A 0N7 Canada. Ed Robert Serre. DD 418.0202571383.

DIRECTORY OF FREQUENT CONTACTS FOR INTERNATIONAL EDUCATIONAL, CULTURAL, SCIENTIFIC, AND TECHNICAL EXCHANGE PROGRAMS. US. English. Department of State, 2201 C Street NW, Washington DC 20520. LC LB2283. DD 370.196025.

DIRECTORY OF FROZEN FOOD PROCESSORS. VFOAT Quick Frozen Foods Processors Directory. 0417-5883. Periodical. US. English. an. $44.00. Harcourt Brace Jovanovich Publishers, 1 East First Street, Duluth MN 55802. Tel (218)723-9200. Ed Saul Beck. adv acc. Circ 1,200. *Directory of Frozen Food Processors & Products.*

A DIRECTORY OF FULL-TIME COUNTY AND URBAN HEALTH DEPARTMENTS. 0197-0704. US. English. qt. Office of Health Services and Local Health Administration, Department of Public Health, Springfield IL 62761. NLM WA 22 AI3 D7.

DIRECTORY OF FULL YEAR HEAD START PROGRAMS. 0092-6078. US. English. Project Head Start, PO Box 1182, Washington DC 20013. Tel (202)755-7405. LC L901. DD 372.2102573.

DIRECTORY OF FUNDED PROJECTS. Main/Corp United States. Bureau of Higher and Continuing Education. Division of Student Services and Veterans Programs. 0193-9084. US. English. US Department of Health, Education and Welfare, Office of Education, Washington DC 20202. LC LB2337.4. DD 378.302573.

DIRECTORY OF FURTHER EDUCATION. UK. English. an. 37.50. Hobsons Limited, Bateman Street, Cambridge CB2 1BR England. Tel 0223/3454551. Ed Denis Curtis. LC L915. DD 374.002542. adv acc. Circ 1,250. (ctrl). Covers 750 polytechnics and colleges with information on full-time and part-time courses, day release and block-release schemes. Useful for all school leavers, employers wishing to train or recruit personnel and adults who wish to return to work.

DIRECTORY OF GENERAL MERCHANDISE VARIETY CHAINS & SPECIALTY STORES. VFOAT General Merchandise Variety Chains & Specialty Stores, General Merchandise Variety Chains and Specialty Stores, Gen Mdse/Variety Chains and Specialty Stores, General Mdse/Variety Chains and Specialty Stores, General Merchandise/Variety Stores, Gen Mdse/Variety Chains & Specialty Stores. 1983-. 0741-6903. US. English. $169.00. Chain Store Guide, Lebhar-Friedman, 425 Park Avenue, New York NY 10022. Tel (212)371-9400. Ed Barbara Brown. LC HF5468. DD 381.1202273. Provides complete company profiles on 700 GM/Variety store companies operating 18,200 stores. Separate sections are featured on various specialty stores. *Directory of Gen Mdse/Variety Chains & Specialty Stores, 0731-6925.*

DIRECTORY OF GEOSCIENCE DEPARTMENTS, UNITED STATES AND CANADA. (DIRECTORY OF GEOSCIENCE DEPARTMENTS, UNITED STATES & CANADA). 0364-7811. US. English. an. $20.70. American Geological Institute, 4220 King Street, Alexandria VA 22302. Tel (800)336-4764. Ed Nicholas H Claudy. LC QE47.A1. DD 550.7117. adv acc. Lists US and Canadian geoscience departments, including addresses, telephone numbers, degrees offered, faculty with geologic specialty. Indices of faculty by specialty, alphabetically. *Directory of Geoscience Departments in the Colleges and Universities of the United States and Canada.*

DIRECTORY OF GOVERNMENT AGENCIES SAFEGUARDING CONSUMER AND ENVIRONMENT. 1st- Ed. 0070-5586. US. English. an. Serina Press, 70 Kennedy Street, Alexandria VA 22305. LC HC110.C6. DD 339.4702573. NLM WA 22 AA1 D3.

DIRECTORY OF GOVERNMENT AND PUBLIC SECTOR IN A.R.E. English. ir. Arab Modern House for Foreign Trade, 11 Abd El Khalek Tharwat Street, Cairo Egypt. LC HF3886. DD 354.62092025.

DIRECTORY OF GOVERNMENT OFFICIALS. FEDERAL, STATE, COUNTY, CITY, TOWNSHIP AND SPECIAL DISTRICT OFFICIALS IN NORTH DAKOTA. (DIRECTORY OF GOVERNMENT OFFICIALS . . . FEDERAL, STATE, COUNTY, CITY, TOWNSHIP AND SPECIAL DISTRICT

Yearbooks, Almanacs, Directories

OFFICIALS IN NORTH DAKOTA). 1982-. 0736-6183. US. English. an. $6.00. Bureau of Governmental Affairs, Box 7176, University of North Dakota, Grand Forks ND 58202. **LC** JK6430. **DD** 353.9784002. *Federal, State, County, City and Special District Officials in North Dakota.*

DIRECTORY OF GOVERNMENTAL OFFICES AND SERVICES IN NORTH CAROLINA. Periodical. US. English. Division of the State Library, 109 East Jones Street, Raleigh NC 27611. **LC** JK4130. **DD** 353.975600025.

DIRECTORY OF GOVERNMENTS IN METROPOLITAN TORONTO. 1970/71-. 0084-9944. Periodical. CN. English. be. Bureau of Municipal Research, 2 Toronto Street/Suite 306, Toronto Ontario M5C 2B6 Canada. **DD** 352.0713541. *Directory of Municipal Governments.*

DIRECTORY OF GOVERNORS AND STATE OFFICIALS RESPONSIBLE FOR DISASTER OPERATIONS. US. English. Department of Housing and Urban Development, 451-7th Street SW, Washington DC 20410. **LC** HV555.U6. **DD** 361.502573.

DIRECTORY OF GRADUATE PROGRAMS. VFOAT Official G.R.E./C.G.S. Directory of Graduate Programs. 9th Ed. (1984 & 1985)-. 0743-0566. US. English. be. Graduate Record Examinations Educational Testing Service, Box 2930, Princeton NJ 08541. **LC** L901. **DD** 378.155302573. *Graduate Programs and Admissions Manual, 0733-4729.*

DIRECTORY OF GRADUATE PROGRAMS IN CHEMICAL ENGINEERING IN CANADIAN UNIVERSITIES. VFOAT Annuaire des Programmes aux Etudes Anvancees en Genie Chimique dans les Universites Canadiennes. 1974/75-. 0317-1590. CN. English (French). Canadian Society for Chemcial Engineering, 151 Slater Street, Ottawa Ontario K1P 5H3 Canada. **LC** TP173. **DD** 660.2071171. *Directory of Graduate Programs in Canadian Universities, 0315-4971.*

DIRECTORY OF GRADUATE PROGRAMS IN THE COMMUNICATION ARTS AND SCIENCES. VFOAT Directory of Graduate Programs: Communication Arts and Sciences. 1979-1980-. 0732-2755. US. English. be. Speech Communication Association, 5105-E Backlick Road, Annandale VA 22003. **LC** P95. **DD** 001.54071173. *Directory of Graduate Programs in the Speech Communication Arts and Sciences, 0070-5616.*

DIRECTORY OF GRADUATE RESEARCH. Main/Corp American Chemical Society. Committee on Professional Training. VFOAT American Chemical Society Directory of Graduate Research. 1953-. US. English. be. American Chemical Society, PO Box 57136, West End Station, Washington DC 20037. **Tel** (202)872-4589. **LC** Z5525.U5. **DD** 016.54. **CODEN** ACDGA. **Circ** 5,000. Listing of US and Canadian schools with master's and doctoral programs in chemistry, chemical engineering, and related fields. *Titles of Theses Submitted for Doctoral Degrees in Chemistry and Chemical Engineering at American Educational Institutions.*

DIRECTORY OF GRANT-MAKING TRUSTS. Began with Vol. for 1968. UK. English. 32.50. CAF Publications, 48 Pembury Road, Tonbridge Kent TN9 2JD England. **LC** AS911.A2. **DD** 001.4402541.

DIRECTORY OF HALFWAY HOUSES AND GROUP HOMES FOR TROUBLED CHILDREN. 0149-0788. US. English. $1.00. Journal of Drug Issues, PO Box 4021, Tallahassee FL 32303. **LC** HV9091. **DD** 362.74.

DIRECTORY OF HANDWRITING ANALYSTS. 0731-3886. US. English. an. $10.95. Marjorie Westergaard, 31246 Wagner, Warren MI 48093. **Tel** (313)977-8942. Ed Marjorie Westergaard. **LC** BF901. **DD** 155.28202573. **Circ** 500. Academic background and specialties of graphologists; history of graphology. List of schools and professional organizations.

THE DIRECTORY OF HARDWARE & HOUSEWARES DISTRIBUTORS. (DIRECTORY OF HARDWARE AND HOUSEWARES DISTRIBUTORS). 1985/86-. 0882-536X. US. English. be. $149.00. Business Guides Inc, 425 Park Avenue, New York NY 10022. **LC** HD9745.U4. **DD** 381.456802573. Provides complete company profiles of 2,750 houseware, paint and paint sundries, electrical, heating, cooling, plumbing, lumber, building supplies and lawn and garden distributors serving 6,500,000 retailer, contractor and commercial accounts. *Directory of Hardware Distributors, 0736-9573.*

DIRECTORY OF HEALTH CARE FACILITIES. 0098-6135. US. English. an. Illinois Department of Public Health, 535 West Jefferson, Springfield IL 62706. **LC** RA981.I4. **DD** 362.1025773. **NLM** WX 22 AI3 B8DA. *Directory of Health Care Facilities and Approved Schools of Nursing, 0536-3942.*

DIRECTORY OF HEALTH SCIENCES LIBRARIES IN THE UNITED STATES. 1969-. 0095-7925. Periodical. US. English. ir. Medical Library Association, 919 North Michigan Avenue/Suite 3208, Chicago IL 60611. Ed F L Schick and S Crawford. **NLM** Z 675.M4 D598.

DIRECTORY OF HEALTH, WELFARE AND RECREATION SERVICES FOR GREATER DALLAS. 1969-. US. English.

DIRECTORY OF HEALTH, WELFARE, VOCATIONAL AND RECREATIONAL SERVICES IN LOS ANGELES CITY AND COUNTY. (DIRECTORY OF HEALTH, WELFARE, VOCATIONAL AND RECREATION SERVICES IN LOS ANGELES CITY AND COUNTY). 0360-408X. US. English. ir. Information Referral Service of Los Angeles, 3035 Tyler Road, El Monte CA 91713. **Tel** (213)444-2635. **LC** HV98.C3. **DD** 362.02579493.

DIRECTORY OF HELICOPTER OPERATORS IN THE UNITED STATES, CANADA, MEXICO, AND PUERTO RICO. VFOAT A.I.A. Directory of Helicopter Operators. 0741-0166. US. English. $6.95. Aerospace Industries Association of America, 1725 De Sales Street NW, Washington DC 20036. *AIA Directory of Helicopter Operators.*

DIRECTORY OF HIGH-ENERGY RADIOTHERAPY CENTERS. 1968-. English. ir. **NLM** WN 22 D597. Index in last issue of volume - loose - separately paged.

DIRECTORY OF HIGHER EDUCATION. 0094-8322. US. English. Board of Higher Education, 119 South Fifth Street/500 Reisch Building, Springfield IL 62701. **LC** L903.I3. **DD** 378.773.

DIRECTORY OF HIGHER EDUCATION COURSES. AT. English. an. Australian Government Public Service, PO Box 84, Wentworth Avenue, Canberra Australian Capital Territory 2600 Australia. **Tel** 062-95 4411. **LC** L981. **DD** 378.94.

DIRECTORY OF HIGHER EDUCATION INSTITUTIONS IN MISSOURI. 1978/79-. 0196-9307. US. English. 600 Monroe, Jefferson City MO 65101. **LC** L903.M8. **DD** 378.778.

DIRECTORY OF HISTORIANS OF LATIN AMERICAN ART. 1979-. 0196-8475. US. English. ir. University of Texas at San Antonio, Research Center for Arts and Humanities, San Antonio TX 78285. **Tel** (512)691-4358. **LC** N50. **DD** 709.22.

DIRECTORY OF HISTORICAL SOCIETIES AND AGENCIES IN THE UNITED STATES AND CANADA. VFOAT Directory, Historical Societies and Agencies in the United States and Canada. 1956-. 0070-5659. US. English. be. American Association for State and Local History, PO Box 40983, Nashville TN 37204. **LC** E172. **DD** 970.62. **NLM** E 172 D597.

DIRECTORY OF HISTORICAL SOCIETIES OF NEW JERSEY. 1972-. US. English. $1.00. League of Historical Societies of New Jersey, 44 East Oak Street, Basking Ridge NJ 07920. **LC** F131. **DD** 917.490025.

DIRECTORY OF HISTORICALLY BLACK COLLEGES AND UNIVERSITIES IN THE UNITED STATES. 0736-6868. US. English. an. National Alliance of Business, 1015-15th Street NW, Washington DC 20005. **LC** LC2781. **DD** 378.73. *Directory of Predominantly Black Colleges and Universities in the United States.*

DIRECTORY OF HOME CENTER OPERATORS & HARDWARE CHAINS. VFOAT Home Center Operators & Hardware Chains. VAT Directory of Home Center Operators and Hardware Chains. 0272-0167. US. English. an. $179.00. Chain Store Guide, Lebhar-Friedman, Attn Priscilla G Jimenez, 425 Park Avenue, New York NY 10022. **Tel** (212)371-9400. Ed Paul Smith. **LC** HD9745.U4. **DD** 381.4568302573. Profiles on 6,300 home centers, lumber/building material companies and hardware chains, 200 specialty paint/home decorating chains serving 22,700 units, Also covers 22 buying groups serving 85,000 stores. *Directory: Home Centers & Hardware Chains, Auto Supply Chains, 0094-8667.*

DIRECTORY OF HOME CENTERS. 0093-8718. US. English. an. $90.00. Vance Publishing Company, 300 West Adams, Chicago IL 60606. **LC** HD9745.U4. **DD** 381.4568302573.

DIRECTORY OF HOME HEALTH AGENCIES CERTIFIED AS MEDICARE PROVIDERS. 0360-5183. US. English. $4.95. National League for Nursing, 10 Columbus Circle, New York NY 10019. **LC** RA445. **DD** 362.1402573.

DIRECTORY OF HONG KONG INDUSTRIES. VFOAT Hsian-Kang Kung Yeh Chih Nan. Began with Vol. for 1976. HK. English (some captions in Chinese). an. Hong Kong Productivity Centre, PO Box 6123, General Post Office, Hong Kong Hong Kong. **LC** HD9736.H6. **DD** 338.40255125.

DIRECTORY OF HOSPITALITY EDUCATORS. VFOAT Directory. 0742-3306. US. English. $30.00. 1407 South Harrison Road, East Lansing MI 48823. **LC** TX911.3.M27. **DD** 647.94071073.

DIRECTORY OF HOSPITALS AND RELATED HEALTH SERVICES LICENSED OR CERTIFIED BY MISSOURI DIVISION OF HEALTH. US. English. an. Division of Health, 1511 Christy Lane/PO Box 570, Jefferson City MO 65102. **LC** RA977.5.M8. **DD** 362.11025778.

DIRECTORY OF HOSPITALS IN INDIA. English. ir. $9.90. Central Bureau of Health Intelligence, Directorate General of Health Services Nirman Bhavan, New Delhi 110011 India. **LC** RA978.I4. **DD** 362.1102554. **NLM** WX 22 JI4 D5.

DIRECTORY OF HOTEL & MOTEL SYSTEMS. US. English. an. $29.50. American Hotel & Motel Association, 888 7th Avenue, New York NY 10106. **Tel** (212)265-4506. Ed Richard Turner. adv acc. **Circ** 7,000. Lists companies that own, operate or manage three or more properties. Gives address, phone number, officers, property names, total number of rooms and properties. *Directory of Hotel Systems.*

DIRECTORY OF HOTELS: CENTRAL AMERICA, PANAMA, AND THE WEST INDIES. Periodical. US. English. an. **LC** TX907. **DD** 647.94058.

DIRECTORY OF HOTELS IN KENYA. VFOAT Kenya Directory of Hotels. KE. English. ir. Kenya Marketing & Publications Company, Biashara Street, Raja Building/PO Box 10304, Nairobi Kenya. **LC** TX910.K4. **DD** 647.946762.

DIRECTORY OF HOUSING CO-OPERATIVES. June 1978-. 0226-8558. Periodical. CN. English. sa. Free to Members. Co-Operative Housing Foundation of Canada, 237 Metcalfe Street, Ottawa Ontario K2P 1R2 Canada. **DD** 334.102571.

THE DIRECTORY OF HUMAN RESOURCE SERVICES & PRODUCTS. 0732-4723. US. English. an. $12.00. Human Resource Communications Group, 2355 East Stadium Boulevard, Ann Arbor MI 48104. **LC** HD69.C6. **DD** 338.7616584602573.

DIRECTORY OF HUMAN SERVICE AGENCIES IN RHODE ISLAND. VFOAT Human Service Agencies in Rhode Island. 0739-3083. US. English. Council for Community Services, 229 Waterman Street, Providence RI 02906. **LC** HV98.R4. **DD** 361.0025745. Each issue contains an index to its own contents - no vol index - loose. *CCS Directory.*

DIRECTORY OF HUMAN SERVICE ORGANIZATIONS. 0364-4766. US. English. Legislative Council, State Capitol, Juneau AK 99811. **LC** HV98.A4. **DD** 361.0025798.

DIRECTORY OF HUMAN SERVICES. 197 -. US. English. PO Box 152, 1800 Main Street, Columbia SC 29202.

DIRECTORY OF HUMAN SERVICES IN SASKATCHEWAN. 1975-. CN. English. be. Vocational Rehabilitation Division, Core Services Administration, 2708-12th Avenue, Regina Saskatchewan S4T 1J2 Canada. **LC** HV109.S3. **DD**

Yearbooks, Almanacs, Directories

362.0257124. *Directory of Health, Education, Recreation, Rehabilitation, Social Services.*

DIRECTORY OF HUMAN SERVICES IN THE KALAMAZOO AREA. US. English. $5.50. Library Office of Publications Desk, Kalamazoo Public Library 315 South Rose Street, Kalamazoo MI 49007. **Tel** (616)342-9837. **Ed** Margean Gladysz. **LC** HV99.K27. **DD** 362.02577417. Each issue contains an index to its own contents - no vol index - loose. **Circ** 1,000. Contains area providers of non-profit human services; that is health and medical care plus financial and other aid sources.

DIRECTORY OF HUNGARIAN RESEARCH INSTITUTIONS. HU. English. ir. Hungarian Central Technical Library and Documentation Centre, POB 12, H-1428 Budapest Hungary. **LC** Q180.H8. **DD** 001.43025439.

DIRECTORY OF ILLINOIS VISUAL ARTISTS. 0277-0164. US. English. $2.00. Illinois Arts Council, 111 North Wabash, Chicago IL 60602. **LC** N6530.I4. **DD** 702.5773.

DIRECTORY OF IMPORTERS AND MANUFACTURERS AGENTS IN BRITISH COLUMBIA. (DIRECTORY OF IMPORTERS AND MANUFACTURERS' AGENTS IN BRITISH COLUMBIA). 1976-. 0704-1004. CN. English. an. Free. Ministry of Economic Development, Box 10111/700 West Georgia Street, Vancouver British Columbia V7Y 1C6 Canada. **LC** HF5072.B75. **DD** 380.1025711.

DIRECTORY OF INCENTIVE TRAVEL INTERNATIONAL. VFOAT DITI. 0732-6572. Periodical. US. English. Directory of Incentive Travel, One East First Street, Duluth MN 55802. **LC** HD5260. **DD** 910.202.

THE DIRECTORY OF INDEPENDENT IBM PERSONAL COMPUTER HARDWARE AND SOFTWARE. VFOAT Directory of Independent I.B.M. Personal Computer Hardware and Software. 0735-617X. US. English. an. $31.95. Infopro Inc, 6048 Edge Avenue, Be Salem PA 19020. **Tel** (215)750-1023.

DIRECTORY OF INDIAN ECONOMIC JOURNALS. 1st- Ed. II. English. ir. Information Research Academy, 37 Syed Amir Ali Avenue, Calcutta 700018 India.

DIRECTORY OF INDIAN ENGINEERING EXPORTERS. English. ir. $10.50. Engineering Export Promotion Council/World Trade Center, 3rd Floor 14/1-B Ezra Street, Calcutta-1 India. **LC** HD9736.I5. **DD** 382.45620002554.

DIRECTORY OF INDIAN SCIENTIFIC PERIODICALS. 1st- Ed., 1964-. 0419-2745. II. English. ir. INSDOC, 14 Statsang Vihar Marg, New Delhi 11067 India. **Tel** 665837. **LC** Z7403. **DD** 016.505.

A DIRECTORY OF INDIANA LOCAL AND REGIONAL PLANNING AND DEVELOPMENT COMMISSIONS. US. English. State Planning Services Agency, Suite 300/Harrison Building, 143 West Market Street, Indianapolis IN 46204. **LC** HT393.I6. **DD** 352.96025772.

DIRECTORY OF INDONESIAN IMPORTERS. English. ir. World-Wide Import-Export Promotion Centre, PO Box 503, Marine Parade Post Office, Singapore 15 Singapore.

DIRECTORY OF INDUSTRIAL ENTERPRISES AND PRODUCTS IN TANZANIA. 1981-. English. an. Tisco, PO Box 2650, Dar-Es-Salaam Tanzania. **LC** HF3897.A48. **DD** 380.102946782.

DIRECTORY OF INDUSTRIAL ESTABLISHMENTS. VFOAT Directory of Industries. English. ir. Bureau of Statistics Tanzania, PO Box 1801, Dar Es Salaam Tanzania. **LC** HC557.T3. **DD** 338.0025678.

THE DIRECTORY OF INDUSTRIAL HEAT PROCESSING AND COMBUSTION EQUIPMENT. UNITED STATES MANUFACTURERS. 0738-0887. US. English. be. $38.50. Information Clearinghouse, 500 Fifth Avenue, New York NY 10036. **Tel** (212)354-2424. **LC** TH7213. **DD** 338.47621402502573. *Directory of Industrial Heating and Combustion Equipment. United States Manufacturers, 0146-6836.*

DIRECTORY OF INDUSTRIAL RELATIONS LIBRARIES IN CANADA. Began with 1979. 0225-5472. CN. English. Alberta Department of Labour, 10808-99th Avenue, Edmonton Alberta Canada. **LC** Z675.I53. **DD** 027.6902571.

DIRECTORY OF INDUSTRIAL UNITS. 1977-. English. ir. 30.00. Directorate General of Technical Development and Directorate of Publications and Public Relations, Udyong Bhavan Maulana Azad Road, New Delhi 110011 India. **LC** HC432. **DD** 338.002554.

DIRECTORY OF INDUSTRY : ADDIS ABABA, AKAKI, DEBRE ZEIT, MOJO, NAZRETH & DIRE DAWA, HARAR, ASMARA, GONDAR & JIMMA. ET. English. ir. Ethiopian Chamber of Commerce, Box 517, Addis Ababa Ethiopia. **LC** HC591.A3. **DD** 338.402563.

DIRECTORY OF INDUSTRY DATA SOURCES. THE UNITED STATES OF AMERICA AND CANADA. 1981, V. 1-. 0278-0119. US. English. ir. Ballinger Publishing Company, 54 Church Street, Cambridge MA 02138. **LC** Z7165.U5, HC101. **DD** 016.3380973.

DIRECTORY OF INDUSTRY DATA SOURCES. WESTERN EUROPE. 0732-7358. US. English. an. Ballenger Publishing Company, 54 Church Street, Cambridge MA 02138.

DIRECTORY OF INFORMATION AGE NEWSLETTERS. 1st Ed-. 0742-6755. US. English. ir. $95.00. Frank Communications Group, PO Box 144, Mont Vernon NH 03057. **LC** Z5641, QA76. **DD** 016.0016405.

DIRECTORY OF INFORMATION AND REFERRAL SERVICES IN THE UNITED STATES AND CANADA. 1975-. 0749-050X. US. English. ir. AIRS, 12 East Exchange Street, Akron OH 44308. **LC** HV89. **DD** 361.02573.

DIRECTORY OF INPATIENT FACILITIES FOR THE MENTALLY RETARDED. 1976-. 0147-3921. US. English. an. US Directory Service Inc, 655 Northwest 128 Street PO Box 68-1700, Miami FL 33168. **Tel** (305)769-1700. **NLM** WM 22 AA1 D36.

DIRECTORY OF INSTITUTIONAL INVESTORS. Oct. 1982-. 8755-0318. US. English. sa. $75.00. Vickers Associates, 226 New York Avenue, Huntington NY 11743. **Tel** (516)423-7710. **Ed** Jim Van Dyke. **DD** 332. (ctrl). List 3,500 domestic and foreign investment companies, banks, insurance firms, colleges and pension funds, money managers; lists name, address, phone, type of institution, and approximate assets.

DIRECTORY OF INSTITUTIONAL MEMBERS AND ASSOCIATION OFFICERS - AMERICAN ASSOCIATION OF DENTAL SCHOOLS. Main/Corp American Association of Dental Schools. US. English. an. $5.00. American Association of Dental Schools, 1619 Massachusetts Avenue Northwest, Washington DC 20036. **Tel** (202)667-9433. **Circ** 4,000. Lists names, addresses, telephone numbers and principal administrators of member institutions. Also included are names of AAOS officers, council members, section officers and staff. *Directory of Institutional Members and Section Officers.*

DIRECTORY OF INSTITUTIONS. Main/Corp Association of Independent Colleges and Schools. Accrediting Commission. VFOAT ACIS Directory. 19 -. US. English. an.

DIRECTORY OF INSTITUTIONS OF ORIENTAL STUDIES IN OVERSEAS COUNTRIES. 1974-. 0377-6948. II. English. ir. $3.00. Lord International, 2/6 Canal Road Vijay Nagar, 110009 Delhi India. **LC** DS32.8. **DD** 915.030711.

THE DIRECTORY OF INSURANCE BROKERS, LOSS ADJUSTORS AND CLAIMS ASSESSORS. UK. English. an. 0.80. A P Crawley, 13/14 Charterhouse Square, London EC1M 6AY England. **LC** HG8596. **DD** 368.002542. *Directory of Insurance Brokers and Claims Assessors.*

DIRECTORY OF INSURANCE COMPANIES. 0732-1767. US. English. an. **LC** HG8526.N6. **DD** 368.0025789.

DIRECTORY OF INSURANCE COMPANIES LICENSED IN NEW YORK STATE. US. English. New York Insurance Department, 2 World Trade Center, New York City NY 10047. **LC** HG8526.N7. **DD** 368.0025747. *Names and Addresses of Insurance Companies Listed in New York State Issued by the New York Insurance Dept.*

DIRECTORY OF INTERCULTURAL EDUCATION NEWSLETTERS. VFOAT Annual Directory of Intercultural Education Newsletters. Began in 1981. 0278-4084. US. English. an. $8.00. Information Consulting Associates, 303 West Pleasantview Avenue, Hackensack NJ 07601. **Tel** (201)343-8833. **Ed** Muriel Wall. **LC** L901. **DD** 370.115. Source of free and relatively low cost listing of newsletters, which provide information on fostering, intercultural and understanding pertaining to one or more ethnics or bilingual groups.

DIRECTORY OF INTERNSHIP AND RESIDENCIES MATCHING PROGRAM FOR . . . . VFOAT Veterinary Internship and Residency Matching Program. US. English. an.

DIRECTORY OF INTERNSHIP, WORKS EXPERIENCE PROGRAMS, AND ON-THE-JOB TRAINING OPPORTUNITIES. 1st- Ed. US. English. **Ed** A Renetzky.

THE DIRECTORY OF INTERPRETERS FOR THE DEAF. 3rd Ed. (1982)-. US. English. an. Illinois Department of Rehabilitation Services, 623 East Adams, PO Box 1587, Springfield IL 62705. **LC** HV2402. **DD** 362.4283. *Directory of Sign Language Interpreters, 0732-1147.*

DIRECTORY OF INTERPRETERS FOR THE DEAF IN TEXAS. 1982/1983-. 0741-8140. US. English. an. Texas Commission for the Deaf, PO Box 12904 Capitol Station, Austin TX 78711. **LC** HV2402. **DD** 362.4283. *Directory of Commission-Qualified Interpreters for the Deaf.*

DIRECTORY OF INVESTOR-OWNED HOSPITALS AND HOSPITAL MANAGEMENT COMPANIES. (DIRECTORY, INVESTOR-OWNED HOSPITALS AND HOSPITAL MANAGEMENT COMPANIES). 1982-. 0095-5191. US. English. an. $40.00. Federation of American Hospitals, 1045 North Pierce/Suite 311, Little Rock AR 72207. **Tel** (501)661-9555. **Ed** Maurice Moore. **LC** RA977. **DD** 362.1102573. **NLM** WX 22 AA1 D6. adv acc. **Circ** 18,000. (ctrl). Listing of name, address, phone, beds and administrator for investor-owned hospitals by state and by company ownership. *Directory of Investor-Owned Hospitals and Hospital Management Companies, 0095-5191.*

DIRECTORY OF IOWA MANUFACTURERS. VFOAT Iowa Manufacturers. 0095-4446. US. English. an. $47.52. Manufacturers News Inc, 4 East Huron Street, Chicago IL 60611. **Tel** (312)337-1084. **LC** T12. **DD** 338.476702577. List 4,837 manufacturing and processing companies, names and titles of 9,500 officers. Information on annual sales, plant size, number of employees, type of in-house computer and language used. *Directory, Iowa Manufacturers, A Buyer's Guide.*

DIRECTORY OF IOWA MUNICIPALITIES. 0363-1842. US. English. 444 Insurance Exchange Building, Des Moines IA 50309. **LC** JS451.I85. **DD** 352.008025777.

DIRECTORY OF IRON AND STEEL WORKS OF THE UNITED STATES AND CANADA. US. English. te. *Directory to the Iron and Steel Works of the United States.*

THE DIRECTORY OF ISRAEL. VFOAT Shenaton Ha-Yisraeli. 1970-. English. an. Directory of Israel, PO Box 815, Tel-Aviv 61 007 Israel. **LC** HF3861.P2. **DD** 380.102945694. *Directory of Israeli Merchants and Manufacturers (Commercial & Industrial Directory).*

DIRECTORY OF JAPANESE SCIENTIFIC PERIODICALS. VFOAT Nihon Kagaku Gijutsu Kankei Chikuji Kankobutsu Mokuroku. 1962-. JA. English (Japanese). ir. Maruzen Company Ltd, PO Box 5050, 100-31 Tokyo Japan. **NLM** ZQ 1 N691. *Directory of Japanese Learned Periodicals.*

DIRECTORY OF JEWISH FAMILY & CHILDREN'S AGENCIES. VFOAT AJFCA Directory of Jewish Family & Children's Agencies. VAT Directory of Jewish Family and Children's Agencies. 0271-0277. US. English. $3.50. Association of Jewish Family and Children's Agencies, 200 Park Avenue South, 6th Floor, New York NY 10003. **LC** HV3191. **DD** 362.849240273.

DIRECTORY OF JEWISH RESIDENT SUMMER CAMPS. 0732-0132. US. English. **LC** BM135. **DD** 296.67.

Yearbooks, Almanacs, Directories

DIRECTORY OF JUSTICE RELATED SERVICES, CAPITAL REGION DISTRICT. VFOAT Justice Services Directory. Began with 1976 issue. 0225-2759. CN. English. an. $3.50. Law Centre, 510 Fort Street, Victoria British Columbia V8W 1E6 Canada. **DD** 340.0257711334.

DIRECTORY OF KANSAS PUBLIC OFFICIALS. 0196-7681. US. English. an. $30.00. League of Kansas Municipalitie, 112 West 77 Street, Topeka KS 66603. **LC** JK6830. **DD** 353.9781002. *Kansas Directoty of Public Officials.*

DIRECTORY OF KEY CONTACTS AND SERVICES. VFOAT Commerce Department Directory of Key Contacts and Services. 1980-. US. English. an. Commerce Department, Washington DC 20230. *Commerce Department Resources and Services for Economic Development.*

DIRECTORY OF KOREAN ELECTRONICS EXPORTERS. KO. English (Korean). ir. World Trade Center Korea, 10-1 2-ka Hoehyun-dong, Chung-ku Seoul South Korea. **LC** HD9696.A3. **DD** 382.4562138102945195.

DIRECTORY OF KOREAN PHYSICIANS. DISTRICT OF COLUMBIA, MARYLAND, AND VIRGINIA. (DIRECTORY OF KOREAN PHYSICIANS : DISTRICT OF COLUMBIA, MARYLAND, AND VIRGINIA). 0271-9851. US. English (Korean). 4412 Powder Mill Road/Suite 200 Beltsville MD 20705. **LC** R712.W3. **DD** 610.6952025753.

DIRECTORY OF LABOR MARKET AND OCCUPATIONAL INFORMATION. 1980-. US. English. be. Job Service North Dakota, Box 1537, Bismark ND 58505. **LC** HD5725.N84. **DD** 016.331109784.

DIRECTORY OF LABOR MARKET INFORMATION. 0190-3217. US. English. an. Employment Security Commission, Manpower Research Division, 20 Union Street, Augusta ME 04330. **LC** Z7164.L1, HD5725.M3. **DD** 016.3311209741.

DIRECTORY OF LABOR MARKET INFORMATION (COLUMBIA, S.C.). (DIRECTORY OF LABOR MARKET INFORMATION). US. English. an. South Carolina Employment Security Commission, Research and Analysis, PO Box 995, Columbia SC 29202. **LC** HD8083.S5. **DD** 016.3311209757.

DIRECTORY OF LABOR MARKET INFORMATION REPORTS AND PUBLICATIONS. 1977-. 0149-4961. US. English. Department of Employment Security, 32 South Main Street, Concord NH 03301. **LC** Z7164.L1, HD5725.N4. **DD** 016.3311209742.

DIRECTORY OF LABOR MARKET INFORMATION REPORTS AND PUBLICATIONS. US. English. Labor Market Information Section, Labor and Industry Building/Room 1210, Harrisburg PA 17121. **LC** HD5725.P4. **DD** 331.12025748.

DIRECTORY OF LABOR ORGANIZATIONS (KENTUCKY. DEPT. OF LABOR). (DIRECTORY OF LABOR ORGANIZATIONS). VFOAT Kentucky Directory of Labor Organizations. US. English. an. Kentucky Department of Labor, Division of Management Information Systems and Research, 1923 Capitol Plaza Trail, Frankfort KY 40601. **LC** HD6504. **DD** 331.88025769.

DIRECTORY OF LABOUR ORGANIZATIONS IN CANADA. VFOAT Repertoire des Organisations de Travailleurs au Canada. 1980-. 0711-1703. CN. English (French). an. $5.00 Domestic, $6.00 Foreign. Labour Canada, Publications Distribution, Ottawa Ontario K1A 0J6 Canada. **LC** HD6521. **DD** 331.8802571. *Labour Organizations in Canada, 0075-7578.*

DIRECTORY OF LABOUR ORGANIZATIONS IN NEW BRUNSWICK. VFOAT Annuaire des Syndicats Ouvriers au Nouveau-Brunswick. 0702-973X. CN. French (English (inverted pages, 1975-1977)). an. **DD** 331.88'025'715.

DIRECTORY OF LATIN AMERICANISTS. 1972/73-. 0091-3235. US. English. an. Arizona State University, Center for Latin American Studies, Tempe AZ 85281. **Tel** (602)965-5127. **Ed** Evelyn Smith de Galvez. **LC** F1409.9. **DD** 918.002579173. adv acc. **Circ** 1,000. Covers topics of interest to Latin Americanists.

DIRECTORY OF LAW ENFORCEMENT AND CRIMINAL JUSTICE EDUCATION. Began in 1966. 0097-6083. US. English. an. $1.00. Professional Standards Division, International Association of Chiefs of Police, 11 Firstfield Road, Gaithersburg MD 20760. **LC** HV8143. **DD** 363.2071073.

DIRECTORY OF LAW ENFORCEMENT PROFESSORS. 1970-. US. English. 646 Main Street, Cincinnati OH 45201. **LC** HV8143. **DD** 363.207.

DIRECTORY OF LAW LIBRARIES. US. English. an. $10.00. American Association of Law Libraries, 53 West Jackson Boulevard, Chicago IL 60604. **Tel** (312)939-4764.

DIRECTORY OF LAW-RELATED EDUCATION PROJECTS. 3d Ed.-. 0743-118X. US. English. American Bar Association, 115 East Sixteenth Street, Chicago IL 60637. **LC** KF266. **DD** 349.73071, 347.30071. *Directory of Law-Related Educational Activities.*

DIRECTORY OF LEADING CHAIN STORES IN THE UNITED STATES. VFOAT Chain Stores. 0415-9594. US. English. be. $112.00. Chain Store Business Guide, 425 Park Avenue, New York NY 10022. **LC** HF5468. **DD** 381.1202573.

DIRECTORY OF LEARNING RESOURCES FOR READING. VFOAT Learning Resources for Reading. Began publication with issue for 1978/79. US. English. Croft Nei Publications, 24 Rope Ferry Road, Waterford CT 06386. Each issue contains an index to its own contents - no vol index - loose.

THE DIRECTORY OF LEGAL AID AND DEFENDER OFFICES IN THE UNITED STATES. (THE . . . DIRECTORY OF LEGAL AID AND DEFENDER OFFICES IN THE UNITED STATES). 0276-5365. US. English. an. $7.50 Members, $15.00 Non-members. National Legal Aid & Defender Association, 1625 K Street NW/8th Floor, Washington DC 20006. **LC** KF336. **DD** 347.7317025, 347.30717025. *Directory.*

DIRECTORY OF LEGAL EMPLOYERS (1985). (DIRECTORY OF LEGAL EMPLOYERS). VFOAT NALP Directory of Employers. 6th Ed. (1984-85- Academic Year)-. 0882-5033. US. English. an. $35.00 Members, $70.00 Non-Members. National Association for Law Placement, 6325 Freret Street, New Orleans LA 70118. **DD** 340. *Directory of Employers.*

DIRECTORY OF LEGISLATIVE LOBBYISTS. VFOAT Legislative Lobbyists. 1980-. US. English. Secretary of State Capitol, 2nd Floor, Topeka KS 66612. **LC** JK6874.5. **DD** 328.781078025. *Kansas Legislative Lobbyists.*

DIRECTORY OF LENDING & LEASING INSTITUTIONS. VFOAT Directory of Lending and Leasing Institutions. Began with 1982-83?. 0734-6840. US. English. ir. $29.95. Interfinance Corporation, 2215 Pillsbury Avenue South, Minneapolis MN 55404. **LC** HG65. **DD** 332.302573.

DIRECTORY OF LIBRARIES AND ARCHIVAL INSTITUTIONS IN PRINCE EDWARD ISLAND. CN. English. Provincial Library, University Avenue, Charlottetown Prince Edward Island Canada. **LC** Z735.P73. **DD** 027.0025717.

DIRECTORY OF LIBRARIES AND INFORMATION SERVICES IN THE PHILADELPHIA AREA. 15th Ed. (1980)-. 0278-5684. US. English. Jean Denio, Apartment C-2 209 West Montgomery Avenue, Haverford PA 19041. **LC** Z732.P6. **DD** 027.002574811. adv acc. **Circ** 900. Bibliography of holdings and personnel of corporate and academic libraries in mid-Atlantic area. *Directory of Libraries and Information Sources in the Philadelphia Area.*

DIRECTORY OF LIBRARIES IN MANITOBA. 1972/73-. 0317-8536. Periodical. CN. English. be. Department of Tourism Recreation & Cultural Affairs, Legislative Building/Room 313, Edmonton Alberta T5K 2B6 Canada. **LC** Z735.M3. **DD** 021.00257127.

DIRECTORY OF LIBRARIES IN NEWFOUNDLAND AND LABRADOR. (A DIRECTORY OF LIBRARIES IN NEWFOUNDLAND AND LABRADOR). 1975-. 0317-2465. Periodical. CN. English. 10. Memorial University of NFL, NFL Library Association, Newfoundland A1C 5S7 CN. **Tel** (709)737-7427. **DD** 021.0025718. A directory of libraries in New Foundland and Labrador.

DIRECTORY OF LIBRARIES IN NORTHWESTERN ONTARIO. 1971-. 0319-2377. CN. English. an. Free. Northwestern Regional Library System, 910 Victoria Avenue, Thunder Bay "F" Ontario P7C 1B4 Canada. **DD** 027.40257131. (ctrl).

DIRECTORY OF LIBRARY AND INFORMATION CONSULTANTS IN METROPOLITAN WASHINGTON. 1st Ed. (1983)-. 0743-4995. US. English. be. Metropolitan Washington Council of Governments, 1875 Eye Street NW/Suite 200, Washington DC 20006. **LC** Z682.4.C65. **DD** 023.2025753.

DIRECTORY OF LIBRARY ASSOCIATIONS IN CANADA. VFOAT Repertoire des Associations de Bibliotheques au Canada. 1st- Ed. 0380-1187. CN. English (French). an. National Library of Canada Library Documentation Centre, 395 Wellington Street, Ottawa Ontario K1A 0N4 Canada. **LC** Z673.A1. **DD** 020.6271.

DIRECTORY OF LIBRARY RELATED ORGANIZATIONS IN THE ATLANTIC PROVINCES. 1983-. 0715-5964. CN. English. an. School of Library Service, Dalhousie University, Halifax Nova Scotia B3H 4H8 Canada. **LC** Z673.A1. **DD** 020.25715.

DIRECTORY OF LIBRARY REPROGRAPHIC SERVICES; A WORLD GUIDE. 5th- 1973-. 0160-6077. US. English. ir. American Library Association, 50 East Huron Street, Chicago IL 60611. *Directory of Institutional Photocopying Services.*

A DIRECTORY OF LIBRARY SYSTEMS IN NEW YORK STATE. Fall 1976-. US. English. an. *Directory of New York State Public Library Systems, 0070-5950; Directory of Reference and Research Library Resources Systems in New York State.*

DIRECTORY OF LICENSED AUCTIONEERS, APPRENTICE AUCTIONEERS, AND FIRMS ENGAGED IN THE AUCTION BUSINESS IN NORTH CAROLINA. US. English. North Carolina Auctioneer Licensing Board, 3509 Haworth Drive, Raleigh NC 27609. **LC** HF5477.U5. **DD** 381.18.

DIRECTORY OF LICENSED HOSPITALS AND RELATED FACILITIES. 1979-. 0193-7456. US. English. an. Oklahoma State Department of Health, NE 10th Street & Stonewall, Oklahoma City OK 73152. **LC** RA981.O5. **DD** 362.11025766. **NLM** WX 22 AO5 H8D. *Directory of Licensed Hospitals, 0471-444X.*

DIRECTORY OF LICENSED NURSING HOMES, STATE OF LOUISIANA. Main/Corp Louisiana. State Dept. of Hospitals. 1958-. 0456-698X. US. English. State of Louisiana, PO Box 44125, Baton Rouge LA 70804. **LC** RT25.U5. **DD** 362.1609763. **NLM** WX 22 AL6 S7DI.

DIRECTORY OF LICENSED REAL ESTATE APPRAISERS. 0361-4980. US. English. Nebraska Real Estate Commission, 600 South 11th Street/Suite 200, Lincoln NE 68508. **LC** HD266.N2. **DD** 333.332025782.

DIRECTORY OF LICENSED REAL ESTATE BROKERS AND SALESMEN, STATE OF NEBRASKA. US. English. Nebraska Real Estate Commission, 6th Floor State Capitol, Lincoln NE 68509. **LC** HD266.N2. **DD** 333.33. *Roster of Licensed Real Estate Brokers and Salesmen in the State of Nebraska.*

DIRECTORY OF LICENSED REAL ESTATE BROKERS AND SALESPERSONS. US. English. Oregon Real Estate Division, Commerce Building, Salem OR 97310. **LC** HD266.O7. **DD** 333.33. *Directory of Licensed Real Estate Brokers and Salesmen.*

DIRECTORY OF LICENSED REAL ESTATE BROKERS AND SALESPERSONS. 1981-. US. English. an. New Mexico Real Estate Commission, 4000 San Pedro NE/Suite A, Albuquerque NM 87110. **LC** HD266.N6. **DD** 333.33025789. *Directory of Licensed Real Estate Brokers and Salesmen.*

DIRECTORY OF LICENSED VETERINARIANS. US. English. Board of Examiners in Veterinary Medicine, Consumers Affairs Building, 1020 N Street, Sacramento CA 95814. **LC** SF611. **DD** 636.0890922. *Directory.*

Yearbooks, Almanacs, Directories

DIRECTORY OF LICENSED VOCATIONAL NURSES IN TEXAS. Main/Corp Texas. State Board of Vocational Nurse Examiners. US. English. an. Board of Vocational Nurse Examiners, 5555 North Lamar, Building H #131, Austin TX 78751. Tel (512)458-1203. LC RT25.U5. DD 610.73058. NLM WY 22 AT4 D5.

DIRECTORY OF LICENSED YACHT AND SHIP BROKERS AND SALESPERSONS. VFOAT Directory, Licensed Yacht and Ship Brokers and Salespersons. US. English. an. Department of Boating and Waterways, 1629 S Street, Sacramento CA 95814-7291. *Directory of Licensed Yacht and Ship Brokers and Salesmen.*

DIRECTORY OF LICENSEES - OREGON STATE BOARD OF RADIOLOGIC TECHNOLOGY. Main/Corp Oregon State Board of Radiologic Technology. VFOAT Radiologic Technologists. US. English. an. Oregon State Board of Radiologic Technology, Box 231, Portland OR 97207. LC R895.A4. DD 362.177.

DIRECTORY OF LICENSEES - TEXAS STATE BOARD OF PUBLIC ACCOUNTANCY. (DIRECTORY OF LICENSEES). Main/Corp Texas State Board of Public Accountancy. 0731-2415. US. English. Texas State Board of Public Accountancy, 3301 Northland Drive/Suite 500, Austin TX 78731. LC HF5616.U5. DD 657.025764. *Permit Holders.*

DIRECTORY OF LICENSES. US. English. North Carolina Board of Physical Therapy Examiners, 2426 Tryon Road, Durham NC 27705. LC RM697.U5. DD 615.82025756.

DIRECTORY OF LICENTIATES AND REGISTRATION LAW. 1956-. US. English. Joe Verser, PO Box 102, Harrisburg AR 72432. LC R712.A2. DD 610.6952025767.

DIRECTORY OF LIFE INSURANCE LAWYERS. 0092-9573. US. English. LC KF195.I5. DD 346.73086025.

DIRECTORY OF LIFESTYLE CHANGE SERVICES. 1977/78-. 0707-0047. CN. English. an. Free. Healthful Lifestyle Program of Vancouver Health Department, 1060 West 8th Avenue, Vancouver British Columbia V6H 1C4 Canada. DD 362.102571133.

DIRECTORY OF LIMITED MEMBERS - COUNCIL OF PETROLEUM ACCOUNTANTS SOCIETIES (U.S.). Main/Corp Council of Petroleum Accountants Societies (U.S.). US. English. Council of Petroleum Accountants Societies, PO Box 13117, Arlington TX 76013. LC HF5686.P3. DD 657.862.

DIRECTORY OF LOCAL AGENCIES, HOUSING, COMMUNITY DEVELOPMENT, REDEVELOPMENT. (DIRECTORY OF LOCAL AGENCIES : HOUSING, COMMUNITY DEVELOPMENT, REDEVELOPMENT). 1980-. 0272-2283. US. English. National Association of Housing and Redevelopment Officials, 2600 Virginia Avenue Northwest, Washington DC 20037. LC HD7293.A1. DD 352.941802573. *NAHRO Directory, 0145-7209.*

DIRECTORY OF LOCAL CHIEF EXECUTIVES. Feb. 1985-. Periodical. US. English. sm. Tel (202)626-3115. Circ 1,500. Mayors, city managers, addresses, phone numbers of members and other cities over 30,000 in population. *Directory of Local Officials.*

DIRECTORY OF LOCAL EMPLOYMENT SECURITY OFFICES. 1967-. 0160-6239. US. English. an. US Department of Labor, Employment and Trainig Administration/Room 802, 711-14th Street, Washington DC 20210. LC HD5873. DD 331.11502573.

DIRECTORY OF LOCAL HOUSING AUTHORITIES. 0098-1095. US. English. Housing Management, US Department of Housing and Urban Development, Washington DC 20410. LC HD7293.A49. DD 352.750973.

DIRECTORY OF LOCAL OFFICIALS. VFOAT N.L.C. Directory of Local Officials. Began with: Jan. 1981. Periodical. US. English. sa. $25.00. National League of Cities Publications Sales, 1301 Pennsylvania Avenue Northwest, Washington DC 20004. Tel (202)626-3000. Circ 2,000. Directory of mayors, council members, and city managers. Listing names, titles, and term expiration dates for officials, and city hall address and phone numbers.

DIRECTORY OF LONDON PUBLIC LIBRARIES. 0419-2915. UK. English. LC Z791.

DIRECTORY OF LONG TERM CARE CENTRES IN CANADA. VFOAT Repertoire des Centres de Services de Sante A Long Terme au Canada. V. 1- 1980-. 0226-5419. Periodical. CN. English (French). be. $49.68. Canadian Hospitals Association, 17 York Street/Suite 100, Ottawa Ontario K1N 9J6 Canada. Tel (613)238-8005. Ed Eleanor Sawyer. DD 362.1602571. adv acc. Circ 2,000. Lists definitions of special long-term care, information on 3,500 facilities, a buyers' guide, association list and educational programs for long-term care personnel.

DIRECTORY OF LOUISIANA MANUFACTURERS. 1981-. 0275-1089. US. English. an. $20.00. Louisiana Department of Commerce, PO Box 44185, Baton Rouge LA 70804. LC T12. DD 670.25763. *Louisiana Directory of Manufacturers, 0076-1028.*

DIRECTORY OF MAILING LIST HOUSES - KLEIN (B.) AND COMPANY. Main/Corp Klein (B.) and Company. 1958-. US. English. be. $50.00. B Klein Publs, PO Box 8503, Coral Springs FL 33065. LC HF5805.

DIRECTORY OF MAINE INDUSTRIAL ARTS AND TRADE & INDUSTRY TEACHERS. Periodical. US. English. State Department of Educational and Cultural Services, Augusta ME 04333. LC TT163. DD 607.741.

DIRECTORY OF MAINE INDUSTRIAL EDUCATION TEACHERS. 1980-81-. US. English. State Department of Educational and Cultural Services, Augusta ME 04333. LC TT163. DD 607.741. *Directory of Maine Industrial Arts and Trade & Industry Teachers.*

DIRECTORY OF MAJOR MALLS. 0732-5983. US. English. an. $200.00. MJJTM Publ Corporation, PO Box 2, Suffern NY 10901. Tel (914)357-7690. Ed Murray Shor. LC HF5430.3. DD 381.102573. adv acc. Publication listing all major malls in the United States and Canada. Also lists tenants, site plans, contacts, leading retailers, etc.

DIRECTORY OF MAJOR U.S. CORPORATIONS INVOLVED IN AGRIBUSINESS. VFOAT AGBIZ Directory. 1976-. Monographic Series. US. English. ir. Agribusiness ACCT Project, 3410-19th Street/PO Box 5646, San Francisco CA 94101. Tel (415)626-1266. Ed 1976-A V Krebs.

DIRECTORY OF MANAGEMENT CONSULTANTS. Began in 1977. 0743-6890. US. English. Consultants News, Templeton Road, Fitzwilliam NH 03447. LC HD69.C6. DD 658.4602573.

DIRECTORY OF MANAGEMENT EDUCATION PROGRAMS. 1st- Ed. 0734-8002. US. English. ir. American Management Association, PO Box 319, Saranac Lake NY 12983. Tel (518)891-1500. Each issue contains an index to its own contents - no vol index - loose.

DIRECTORY OF MANUFACTURERS AND PROCESSORS. VFOAT SD Manufacturers and Processors Directory, S.D. Manufacturers & Processors Directory. 1983-1984-. 0743-5940. US. English. be. $23.50. State of South Dakota, Department of State Development, 221 South Central, Pierre SD 57501. LC HC107.S8. DD 338.00294783. *South Dakota Manufacturers & Processors Directory, 0094-2758.*

DIRECTORY OF MANUFACTURERS OF LUMBER, PLYWOOD, AND BUILDING MATERIALS ... MADE IN B.C. English. ir. Ministry of Economic Development, 315 Robson Square, 800 Hornby Street, Vancouver British Columbia B6Z 2C5 Canada. LC HD9764.C4. DD 338.76740025711.

DIRECTORY OF MANUFACTURERS, STATE OF HAWAII. 1967/68-. 0190-3047. US. English. be. $22.00. Chamber of Commerce of Hawaii, 735 Bishop Street, Honolulu HI 96813. Tel (808)531-4111. Ed Tatsuko Horjo. LC HD9727.H3. DD 338.0025969. Circ 500. Manufacturers listed by SIC classification, alphabetically listed by island and contains trade names of products.

DIRECTORY OF MANUFACTURING INDUSTRIES OF ROCHESTER AND MONROE COUNTY, NEW YORK : INFORMATION AS SUPPLIED BY THE FIRMS LISTED, OR COMPILED FROM AVAILABLE SOURCES. VFOAT Industrial Directory, Rochester and Monroe County, New York. Began with: 1979. US. English. ir. 55 St Paul Street, Rochester NY 14604. *Industrial Directory of Rochester, N.Y. and Monroe County.*

DIRECTORY OF MARINE SCIENTISTS IN CANADA. VFOAT Repertoire des Experts des Sciences de la Mer au Canada. 0710-863X. Periodical. CN. French (English). an. DD 551.46002571.

DIRECTORY OF MARYLAND EXPORTERS-IMPORTERS. 0070-5799. US. English. $10.00. Maryland Department of Economic Development, State Office Building, Annapolis MD 21401. LC HF5065.M25. DD 382.09752.

DIRECTORY OF MAYORS. 0146-8650. US. English. Department of Community Affairs, 363 West State Street, Trenton NJ 08625. Tel (609)633-7212. Ed Karen M Asunmaa. LC JS451.N55. DD 352.0082025749. Circ 1,000. (ctrl). An update of list of mayors' names, addresses, and phone numbers for every municipality in New Jersey.

DIRECTORY OF MEDICAL FACILITIES. ALL REGIONS. VFOAT Medicare/Medicaid Directory of Medical Facilities. 0272-4049. US. English. Superintendent of Documents, US Government Printing Office, Washington DC 20402. LC RA977. DD 362.1102573.

DIRECTORY OF MEDICAL FACILITIES. REGION VIII, DENVER. Oct. 1, 1984-. US. English.

DIRECTORY OF MEDICAL MANUFACTURER'S REPRESENTATIVES. US. English. $45.00. McKnight Medical Communications Inc, 550 Frontage Road, Northfield IL 60093. Tel (312)446-1622. Ed Jill Newman. adv acc. Circ 100. A directory listing approximately 275 manufacturers, representatives for health care products.

DIRECTORY OF MEDICAL PRODUCTS DISTRIBUTORS. 4th Ed. (1984)-. 8755-7037. US. English. $165.00. McKnight Medical Communications Inc, 550 Frontage Road, Northfield IL 60093. Tel (312)446-1622. Ed Jill Newman. LC HD9994.U5. DD 380.145681760294. adv acc. Circ 1,000. A directory listing 5,000 distributors, product lines carried, annual sales volume, and key executives. *MPS Directory of Medical Products Distributors.*

DIRECTORY OF MEDICAL SCHOOLS WORLDWIDE. 0160-6468. US. English. an. $26.95. US Directory Service, PO Box 68-1700, Miami FL 33168. Tel (305)769-1700. LC R735.A1. DD 610.711. NLM W 22.1 U58D. A detailed introduction provides vital facts and information on admissions, statistics, language and curricula.

DIRECTORY OF MEDICAL SPECIALISTS. 16th- Ed. 0070-5829. US. English. be. Marquis Whos Who Inc, 200 East Ohio Street, Chicago IL 60611. Tel (800)621-9669. LC R712.A1. DD 610.2573. NLM W 22 DA2 D5982. Valued by both the medical and reference communities. An essential information source to specialists, hospitals, medical schools libraries, clinics, insurance agencies, and research foundations. *Directory of Medical Specialists Holding Certification by American Specialty Boards.*

DIRECTORY OF MEMBER AGENCIES - FAMILY SERVICE ASSOCIATION OF AMERICA. Main/Corp Family Service Association of America. Began publication in 1910?. US. English. an. $18.00. Family Service of America, 44 East 23rd Street, New York NY 10010. Tel (212)674-6100. LC HV89.

DIRECTORY OF MEMBER ARCHIVES. UK. English. International Association of Sound Archives, Secretariate: D G Lance, Imperial War Museum, Lambeth Road, London SE1 6HZ England. LC CD941. DD 027.5025.

DIRECTORY OF MEMBER FIRMS - AMERICAN INSTITUTE OF CERTIFIED PUBLIC ACCOUNTANTS. DIVISION FOR CPA FIRMS. (DIRECTORY OF MEMBER FIRMS). Main/Corp American Institute of Certified Public Accountants. Division for CPA Firms. 0743-3948. US. English. an. AICPA Division for CPA Firms, 1211 Avenue of the Americas, New York NY 10036-8775. LC HF5616.U5. DD 338.76165702573.

DIRECTORY OF MEMBER INSTITUTIONS AND PROFESSIONAL STAFF. 0198-6724. US. English. c/o Bureau of Labor Education, 128 College Avenue, Orono ME 04473. LC HD4824.5.U5. DD 331.07117.

Yearbooks, Almanacs, Directories

DIRECTORY OF MEMBERS. VFOAT ASA Directory of Members. 1st- Ed. 0569-7808. US. English. an. American Society of Anesthesiologists, 515 Busse Highway, Parkridge IL 60068. Tel (312)825-5586.

DIRECTORY OF MEMBERS - ACADEMY OF PARISH CLERGY. Main/Corp Academy of Parish Clergy. US. English. Academy of Parish Clergy, PO Box 86, Princeton NJ 08540. LC BV4000. DD 253.06273.

DIRECTORY OF MEMBERS - ACME, INC. Main/Corp Acme, Inc. US. English. an. Acme Inc, 230 Park Avenue, New York NY 10169. Tel (212)697-9693. Circ 20,000. Lists member firms, their areas of practice, branch offices, addresses and phone numbers. Also includes ACME's code of ethics and standards of professional practice.

DIRECTORY OF MEMBERS - AMERICAN ASSOCIATION FOR CANCER RESEARCH. (DIRECTORY OF MEMBERS). Main/Corp American Association for Cancer Research. VFOAT A.A.C.R. Directory of Members. 1980-1981-. 0277-3414. US. English. LC RC261.A1. DD 616.99402702573. NLM QZ 22 AA1 A51D. *Annual Meeting of the American Association for Cancer Research. Proceedings,* 0197-106X.

DIRECTORY OF MEMBERS - AMERICAN FEDERATION OF CLINICAL ONCOLOGIC SOCIETIES. Main/Corp American Federation of Clinical Oncologic Societies. Began with: Vol. for 1973/74. US. English. 777 Third Avenue, New York NY 10017. LC RC276. DD 616.992002573. NLM QZ 22 AA1 A52.

DIRECTORY OF MEMBERS - AMERICAN HOLISTIC MEDICAL ASSOCIATION. (DIRECTORY OF MEMBERS). Main/Corp American Holistic Medical Association. Began with: Aug. 1979. 0732-9571. US. English. $5.00. American Holistic Medical Association, 6932 Little River Turnpike, Annandale VA 22003. Tel (703)642-5880. Ed Ron Goode. NLM W 22.1 A512D. adv acc. Circ 1,000. (ctrl). Membership directory of association including specialty codes, cross referenced geographically.

DIRECTORY OF MEMBERS - AMERICAN INSTITUTE OF REAL ESTATE APPRAISERS. Main/Corp American Institute of Real Estate Appraisers. 0569-5821. US. English. an. American Institute of Real Estate Appraisers, 155 East Superior Street, Chicago IL 60611. LC HD251.

DIRECTORY OF MEMBERS - AMERICAN PHILOLOGICAL ASSOCIATION. Main/Corp American Philological Association. 1970-. 0044-779X. US. English. ir. Scholars Press, PO Box 2268, Chico CA 95927. Tel (404)329-6950. LC P11. DD 480.06273.

DIRECTORY OF MEMBERS - AMERICAN SOCIETY FOR MICROBIOLOGY. Main/Corp American Society for Microbiology. 1977-. 0196-8254. US. English. American Society for Microbiology, 1913 I Street Northwest, Washington DC 20006. LC QR1.A47. DD 576.06073. NLM QW 22 AA1 A5D. *Directory and Constitution - American Society for Microbiology,* 0272-5142.

DIRECTORY OF MEMBERS - AMERICAN SOCIETY OF MAMMALOGISTS. (DIRECTORY OF MEMBERS, AMERICAN SOCIETY OF MAMMALOGISTS). Main/Corp American Society of Mammalogists. US. English. LC QL700. DD 599.006273.

DIRECTORY OF MEMBERS - AMERICAN SOCIOLOGICAL ASSOCIATION. Main/Corp American Sociological Association. 0093-898X. US. English. be. American Sociological Association, 1722 N Street Northwest, Washington DC 20036. Tel (202)833-3410. NLM HM 51 A512. Circ 2,500. A listing of 13,000 members of the American Sociological Association, including name, address, and interests. Also includes indexes by state and interest. *Directory - American Sociological Association.*

DIRECTORY OF MEMBERS AND FRIENDS. Main/Corp Royal School of Church Music (Warren, Conn.). VFOAT R.S.C.M. Directory of Affiliated Choirs and Friends in the U.S.A. 1983-. US. English. LC MT4.W28. DD 783.802573.

DIRECTORY OF MEMBERS AND LIBRARIES - INDIAN LIBRARY ASSOCIATION. (DIRECTORY OF MEMBERS AND LIBRARIES). Main/Corp Indiana Library Association. VFOAT Membership Directory. 0148-6454. US. English. Indiana Library Association, 1100 West 42nd Street, Indianapolis IN 46208. LC Z673. DD 020.6234772.

DIRECTORY OF MEMBERS & MUSEUMS. Main/Corp Musical Box Society International, Morgantown, Ind. VAT Directory of Members and Museums. 0197-9949. US. English. Hughes M Ryder, 495 Springfield Avenue, Summit NJ 07901. LC ML26, M873. DD 789.8025.

DIRECTORY OF MEMBERS AND SUBSCRIBERS - AMERICAN MUSICOLOGICAL SOCIETY. Main/Corp American Musicological Society. 1978-. 0192-8368. US. English. an. American Musicological Society, 201 South 34th Street, Philadelphia PA 19104. LC ML27.U5. *List of Members and Subscribers.*

DIRECTORY OF MEMBERS - ART LIBRARIES SOCIETY OF NORTH AMERICA CEASED. (DIRECTORY OF MEMBERS). Main/Corp Art Libraries Society of North America. 0364-121X. US. English. LC Z5937.A74. DD 026.7.

DIRECTORY OF MEMBERS - ASSOCIATION OF CANADIAN UNIVERSITY PRESSES. (DIRECTORY OF MEMBERS). Main/Corp Association of Canadian University Presses. VFOAT Repertoire des Membres. VAT Repertoire des Membres - Association des Presses Universitaires Canadiennes. 1980-. 0711-3056. CN. English (text in French). be. Free. Secretary of the Association of University Presses, c/o Editorial Department, University of Toronto Press, Toronto Ontario M5S 1A6 Canada. DD 070.594.

DIRECTORY OF MEMBERS - ASSOCIATION OF FEMINIST CONSULTANTS. Main/Corp Association of Feminist Consultants. 0362-2908. US. English. $1.00. Association of Feminist Consultants, 222 Rawson Road, Brookline MA 02146. LC HQ1402.A93. DD 301.41206273.

DIRECTORY OF MEMBERS - AUSTRALASIAN UNIVERSITIES LAW SCHOOLS ASSOCIATION. Main/Corp Australasian Universities Law Schools Association. AT. English. ir. Law Book Company, 4450 Waterloo Road, North Ryde New South Wales 2113 Australia. DD 340.071194.

DIRECTORY OF MEMBERS - BIBLIOGRAPHICAL SOCIETY OF CANADA. (DIRECTORY OF MEMBERS). Main/Corp Bibliographical Society of Canada. 0826-8541. CN. English. LC Z1008. DD 010.922.

DIRECTORY OF MEMBERS - CALIFORNIA SOCIETY, CERTIFIED PUBLIC ACCOUNTANTS. Main/Corp California Society of Certified Public Accountants. 0364-5703. US. English. 1000 Welch Road, Palo Alto CA 94304. LC HF5616.U5. DD 657.61062794. *Directory of the California Society of Certified Public Accountants.*

DIRECTORY OF MEMBERS - DIRECTORS GUILD OF AMERICA. Main/Corp Directors Guild of America. 1st- Ed. 0419-2052. US. English. an. Directors Guild of America, 7950 Sunset Boulevard, Hollywood CA 90046. Tel (213)656-1220. LC PN1998.A1. DD 791.430922. adv acc. Circ 10,000. A roster of members and their credits.

DIRECTORY OF MEMBERS - DIRECTORS GUILD OF GREAT BRITAIN. Main/Corp Directors Guild of Great Britain. 1984-. UK. English. $10.00. The Directors Guild of Great Britain, 3rd Floor 56 Whitfield Street, London W1 England.

DIRECTORY OF MEMBERS - DISTRICT OF COLUMBIA PSYCHOLOGICAL ASSOCIATION. Main/Corp District of Columbia Psychological Association. VFOAT Directory - District of Columbia Psychological Association. 0145-7292. US. English. District of Columbia Psychological Association, 2943 McKinley Street Northwest, Washington DC 20014. LC BF30. DD 150.25753.

DIRECTORY OF MEMBERS - ELECTROCHEMICAL SOCIETY. (DIRECTORY OF MEMBERS). Main/Corp Electrochemical Society. VFOAT Electrochemical Society Directory. 0735-8687. US. English. be. Electrochemical Society, 10 South Main Street, Pennington NJ 08534. LC QD551. DD 541.370601.

DIRECTORY OF MEMBERS - FEDERATION OF INDIAN PUBLISHERS. Main/Corp Federation of Indian Publishers. English. an. Federation of Indian Publishers, 18/1-C Institutional Area Jnu Road, New Delhi 110067 India. Tel 654847. LC Z455. DD 070.502554. adv acc. Circ 500. (ctrl). Contains names, addresses and subjects of specialisation of major publishers and also details of the Executive Committee members of the Federation.

DIRECTORY OF MEMBERS' FIRMS - SOUTH AFRICAN ASSOCIATION OF CONSULTING ENGINEERS. Main/Corp South African Association of Consulting Engineers. VFOAT Gids Van Lede Se Firmas. SA. Afrikaans and English. ir. Associated Scientific and Technical Societies of SA, Kelvin House 2 Holland Street, Johannesburg South Africa. LC TA12. DD 620.

DIRECTORY OF MEMBERS - FREELANCE EDITORS' ASSOCIATION OF CANADA. (DIRECTORY OF MEMBERS). Main/Corp Freelance Editors' Association of Canada. VFOAT Repertoire des Membres. VAT FEAC Directory, Freelance Editors' Association of Canada Directory. 0226-9031. CN. English. an. Freelance Editors' Association of Canada, Box 296, Quill & Quire, 59 Front Street East, Toronto Ontario M5E 1B3 Canada. DD 808.0202571.

DIRECTORY OF MEMBERS - INDIAN ARTS & CRAFTS ASSOCIATION (U.S.). Main/Corp Indian Arts & Crafts Association (U.S.). US. English. Indian Arts and Crafts Association, 4301 Lead SE/PO Box 40013, Albuquerque NM 87108. Tel (505)265-9149. Ed Dave Lewis. LC E98.A7. DD 745.08997. adv acc. Circ 550. (ctrl). Newsletter covers broad spectrum of handmade native American Indian creations and related government regulations.

DIRECTORY OF MEMBERS - INSTITUTE OF MANAGEMENT CONSULTANTS. Main/Corp Institute of Management Consultants, New York. 0097-6547. US. English. ir. Institute of Management Consultants, 19 West 44th Street/Suite 810-811, New York NY 10036. Tel (212)921-2885. LC HD69.C6. DD 658.4606273. Circ 2,000. (ctrl). Alphabetical listing of approximately 1,700 certified management consultants with geographical cross-reference. No cross-reference by skills.

DIRECTORY OF MEMBERS - INTERNATIONAL ASSOCIATION OF SURVEY STATISTICIANS. Main/Corp International Association of Survey Statisticians. VFOAT Liste des Membres - Association Internationale des Statisticiens d'Enquetes. English and French. ir. International Association of Survey Statisticians, 18 Boulevard A Pinard, Paris 75675 France. LC HA1. DD 310.621.

DIRECTORY OF MEMBERS - INTERNATIONAL BAR ASSOCIATION, SECTION ON BUSINESS LAW. Main/Corp International Bar Association. Section on Business Law. UK. English. International Bar Association, 2 Harewood PL Hanover Square, London W1R 9HB England. LC K70.C65. DD 346.070621.

DIRECTORY OF MEMBERS - INTERNATIONAL CITY MANAGEMENT ASSOCIATION. Main/Corp International City Management Association. 1975/76-. 0362-4420. US. English. an. International City Management Association, 1140 Connecticut Avenue Northwest, Washington DC 20036. LC JS344.C5. DD 352.00825. *Membership Roster.*

DIRECTORY OF MEMBERS - LOS ANGELES COUNTY MEDICAL ASSOCIATION. Main/Corp Los Angeles County Medical Association. 1935. US. English. an. $100.00. Los Angeles County Medical, PO Box 3465 Terminal Annex, Los Angeles CA 90054. Tel (213)483-1581. adv acc. Circ 13,000. (ctrl). Membership directory of Los Angeles County Medical Association's 10,000 members, including biographic and geographic data.

DIRECTORY OF MEMBERS, LOT EXCHANGE, MAUSOLEUM CRYPT EXCHANGE, DOLLAR CREDIT PLANS. Main/Corp National Association of Cemeteries. 0272-2674. US. English. National Association of Cemeteries, 1911 North Fort Meyer Drive/Suite 409, Arlington VA 22209. LC RA626. DD

Yearbooks, Almanacs, Directories

363.7502573. *Membership Directory - National Association of Cemeteries, 0360-2095.*

DIRECTORY OF MEMBERS - MANUSCRIPT SOCIETY (U.S.). (DIRECTORY OF MEMBERS). **Main/Corp** Manuscript Society (U.S.). 0742-373X. US. English. $5.00. 350 North Niagrara Street, Burbank CA 91505. **LC** Z991. **DD** 091.02573. *MS Directory.*

DIRECTORY OF MEMBERS - MUNICIPAL FINANCE OFFICERS ASSOCIATION. Main/Corp Municipal Finance Officers Association of the United States and Canada. 0148-1762. US. English. an. Municipal Finance Officers Association, 1313 East 60th Street, Chicago IL 60637. **LC** HJ9145. **DD** 336.01406273.

DIRECTORY OF MEMBERS - NATIONAL ASSOCIATION OF REAL ESTATE INVESTMENT TRUSTS. (DIRECTORY OF MEMBERS). **Main/Corp** National Association of Real Estate Investment Trusts. **VFOAT** Membership Directory. 1981-. 0731-8553. US. English. sa. $75.00. National Association of Real Estate Boards, 1101-17th Street NW, Washington DC 20036. **LC** HG5095. **DD** 332.6324702573. *Membership Directory, 0097-8191.*

DIRECTORY OF MEMBERS - NATIONAL SOFT DRINK ASSOCIATION. (DIRECTORY OF MEMBERS). **Main/Corp** National Soft Drink Association. Began with Vol. for 1980. 0278-050X. US. English. an. $15.00. National Soft Drink Association, 1101-16th Street Northwest, Washington DC 20036. **LC** HD9348.U5. **DD** 338.476636206073. *Directory of Members and Services, 0190-0587.*

DIRECTORY OF MEMBERS, NEW YORK STATE LEGISLATURE, AND MEMBERS OF CONGRESS. 0415-9675. US. English. an. $1.25. NY State Legislature, RD Box 196 E, Albany NY 12203. **LC** JK3430. **DD** 328.7470922.

DIRECTORY OF MEMBERS, OFFICERS, COMMITTEES - AMERICAN VACUUM SOCIETY. Main/Corp American Vacuum Society. 0360-8794. US. English. an. American Vacuum Society, 335 East 45th Street, New York NY 10017. **LC** TJ940. **DD** 621.5506273.

DIRECTORY OF MEMBERS - PUBLICISTS GUILD OF AMERICA. (DIRECTORY OF MEMBERS). **Main/Corp** Publicists Guild of America. **VFOAT** Directory, The Publicists Guild of America. 1983-. 0742-4000. US. English. an. 1427 North La Brea Avenue, Hollywood CA 90028. **LC** PN1995.9.P79. **DD** 659.29384802573.

DIRECTORY OF MEMBERS. PUNJAB HARYANA & DELHI CHAMBER OF COMMERCE AND INDUSTRY. (DIRECTORY OF MEMBERS - PUNJAB HARYANA & DELHI CHAMBER OF COMMERCE AND INDUSTRY). **Main/Corp** Punjab, Haryana & Delhi Chamber of Commerce and Industry. **VAT** Directory of Members. Punjab Haryana and Delhi Chamber of Commerce and Industry. Began with Vol. for 1972. 0376-8511. English. ir. 20.00. Punjab Haryana & Delhi Chamber of Commerce and Industry, Phelps Building 9-A Connaught Place, New Delhi 110001 India. **LC** HF331.I4. **DD** 380.10625455.

DIRECTORY OF MEMBERS' RESEARCH. SUPPLEMENT - OXFORDSHIRE FAMILY HISTORY SOCIETY. Main/Corp Oxfordshire Family History Society. 1981-1982-. UK. English. an. Veronica Lee Speedwell, North Moreton, Oxon OX11 9BG England.

DIRECTORY OF MEMBERS - SINGAPORE BOOK PUBLISHERS ASSOCIATION. Main/Corp Singapore Book Publishers Association. English. ir. **LC** Z464.S55. **DD** 070.50255957.

DIRECTORY OF MEMBERS - SOCIETY FOR NEUROSCIENCE. Main/Corp Society for Neuroscience. 0098-9460. US. English. Society for Neuroscience, 9650 Rockville Pike, Bethesda MD 20014. **LC** QP351. **DD** 612.8025.

DIRECTORY OF MEMBERS - SOCIETY OF AMERICAN TRAVEL WRITERS. (DIRECTORY OF MEMBERS). **Main/Corp** Society of American Travel Writers. 0277-5301. US. English. $40.00. Society of American Travel Writers, 1120 Connecticut Avenue, Washington DC 20036. **LC** G149.S65. **DD** 910.402573. *Roster of Members, 0091-4991.*

DIRECTORY OF MEMBERS - STATE BAR OF ARIZONA. Main/Corp State Bar of Arizona. 0099-1643. US. English. 858 Security Building, Phoenix AZ 85004. **LC** KF192.A73. **DD** 340.025791.

DIRECTORY OF MEMBERS - THE SOCIETY OF PUBLIC TEACHERS OF LAW. Main/Corp Society of Public Teachers of Law, London. 1953-. UK. English. School of Oriental And African Studies, University of London Malet Street, London WC1E 7HP England. **LC** KD422. **DD** 340.0711. Each issue contains an index to its own contents - no vol index - loose.

DIRECTORY OF MEMBERS - TORONTO HOME BUILDERS' ASSOCIATION. (DIRECTORY OF MEMBERS). **Main/Corp** Toronto Home Builders' Association. 1984-. 0824-1929. CN. English. an. Free to Members. Toronto Home Builders' Association, 5218 Yonge Street, Willowdale Ontario M2N 5P6 Canada. **DD** 690.83025713541. *Association Directory, 0228-8125.*

DIRECTORY OF MEMBERS - UNITED STATES LEAGUE OF SAVINGS ASSOCIATIONS CEASED. **Main/Corp** United States League of Savings Associations. 0095-5841. US. English. an. United States League of Savings Associations, 111 East Wacker Drive, Chicago IL 60601. **LC** HG2121. **DD** 332.3202573.

DIRECTORY OF MEMBERS - UNITED WAY OF CANADA. Main/Corp United Way of Canada. **VFOAT** Annuaire des Membres - Centraide Canada. 1977-. 0705-1107. CN. English (French). an. $3.00 Per No. United Way of Canada, 55 Parkdale Avenue, Ottawa Ontario K1Y 1E5 Canada. **DD** 361.802571. *Directory, 0319-7182.*

DIRECTORY OF MEMBERS - VEHICLE BUILDERS & REPAIRERS ASSOCIATION. Main/Corp Vehicle Builders & Repairers Association. **VFOAT** V.B.R.A. Directory of Members. UK. English. Vehicle Builders and Repairers Association, Belmont House/102 Finkle Lane, Gildersome Leed LS27 7TW England. **LC** TL12. **DD** 629.206041. *Directory.*

DIRECTORY OF MEMBERSHIP AND SERVICES - ASSOCIATION OF CONSULTING MANAGEMENT ENGINEERS. Main/Corp Association of Consulting Managment Engineers. US. English. ir. Association of Consulting Management Engineers Inc, 347 Madison Avenue, New York NY 10017. *Membership and Services.*

DIRECTORY OF MEMBERSHIP - FLORIDA COUNCIL OF TEACHERS OF ENGLISH. Main/Corp Florida Council of Teachers of English. Began publication May, 1959-. 0426-5688. Periodical. US. English. ir. Florida Council, Teachers of English, University of Florida, Editor FCTE, Tampa FL 33620.

DIRECTORY OF MEMBERSHIP - INTERNATIONAL FRANCHISE ASSOCIATION. (DIRECTORY OF MEMBERSHIP). **Main/Corp** International Franchise Association. **VFOAT** I.F.A. Directory of Membership. 1982-1983-. 0735-0775. US. English. an. Free. International Franchise Association, 1025 Connecticut Avenue NW/Suite 1005, Washington DC 20036. **LC** HF5429.23. **DD** 381.13025.

DIRECTORY OF MEN'S & BOYS' WEAR SPECIALTY STORES. VFOAT Directory of Men's and Boys' Wear Specialty Stores. 1982-. 0277-9625. US. English. an. $139.00. Chain Store Guide, Lebhar-Friedman, c/o Priscilla G Jimenez, 425 Park Avenue, New York NY 10022. **Tel** (212)371-9400. **LC** HD9940.U3. **DD** 687. Complete company profiles on 3,600 men and boys' wear specialty store companies and sport shops/activewear retailers operating 21,500 stores. *Directory of Men's and Boy's Specialty Stores, 0272-1112.*

DIRECTORY OF MENTAL HEALTH AND ALCOHOLISM PROGRAMS IN MARYLAND. Series/Titl Community Mental Health Publication. 0361-9516. US. English. Maryland State Dept of Health and Mental Hygiene, 111 N Calvert St 204 A, Baltimore MA 21202. **LC** RA790.65.M33. **DD** 362.20425025752.

DIRECTORY OF MENTAL HEALTH SERVICES IN ILLINOIS. 0361-8455. US. English. Illinois Department of Mental Health and Development, 710 Reisch Building/Lincoln Square, Springfield IL 62701. **LC** RA790.65.I4. **DD** 362.2025773.

DIRECTORY OF METROPOLITAN PLANNING ORGANIZATIONS AND STATE TRANSPORTATION AGENCIES. VFOAT Metropolitan Planning Organizations & State Transportation Agencies, Directory. 1980-. US. English. an. US Department of Transportation, Office of the Secretary, Assistant Secretary for Governmental Affairs, Office of Community Planning Assistance, Washington DC 20590.

DIRECTORY OF MICHIGAN MUNICIPAL OFFICIALS. (DIRECTORY OF MICHIGAN MUNICIPAL OFFICIALS, WITH SELECTED LISTING OF STATE & FEDERAL OFFICES). 0148-7442. US. English. sa. $36.00. Michigan Municipal League, 1675 Green Rd Box 1487, Ann Arbor MI 48106. **Tel** (313)662-3246. **Ed** Judy Beitel. **LC** JS303.M5. **DD** 352.005209774. **Circ** 2,000. (ctrl). Listing of local government officials published twice a year. *Annual Directory of Michigan Municipal Officials.*

DIRECTORY OF MINE SUPPLY HOUSES, DISTRIBUTORS AND SALES AGENTS. VFOAT Mine Supply House Directory. 1961-. 0417-612X. US. English. $20.00. McGraw-Hill Mining Publications, 1221 Avenue of the Americas, New York NY 10020.

DIRECTORY OF MINES PERSONNEL. VFOAT Directory of Mining Companies and Personnel. 1965-. 0383-1779. CN. English. Alberta & Northwest Chamber of Mines & Resources, 9915 108 St Petroleum Plaza, Edmonton Alberta Canada. **DD** 338.2025719. *Mining Companies and Personnel, 0383-1760.*

DIRECTORY OF MINING PROGRAMS. 0884-917X. US. English. an. Gibbs Associates, PO Box 706, Boulder CO 80306. **LC** TN1. **DD** 622.028553.

DIRECTORY OF MINNESOTA BUSINESS & PROFESSIONAL ASSOCIATIONS. VFOAT Directory of Minnesota Business and Professional Associations. 1984-. US. English. an. **Ed** Patricia Ricci. **LC** HD2428.M5. **DD** 061.76.

DIRECTORY OF MINNESOTA CITY OFFICIALS. 1985-. US. English. an. $15.00. League of Minnesota Cities, 183 University Avenue East, St Paul MN 55101. **LC** JS451.M65. *Directory of Minnesota Municipal Officials.*

DIRECTORY OF MINNESOTA MUNICIPAL OFFICIALS. Main/Corp League of Minnesota Municipalities. US. English. League of Minnesota Cities, 183 University Avenue East, St Paul MN 55101. **Tel** (612)227-5600. **Ed** Jean Mehle. **LC** JS451.M65. **DD** 352.0776. adv acc. **Circ** 2,500. List of Minnesota cities, city officials, phone numbers and addresses of city halls, council meeting dates, legislative and congressional districts; city population, county and zip code.

DIRECTORY OF MINNESOTA'S AREA MENTAL HEALTH-MENTAL RETARDATION-INEBRIETY PROGRAMS. (DIRECTORY OF MINNESOTA'S AREA MENTAL HEALTH, MENTAL RETARDATION, INEBRIETY PROGRAMS). 1973-. 0095-4888. US. English. 658 Cedar Street, St Paul MN 55155. **LC** RA790.65.M53. **DD** 362.2025776. *Directory of Minnesota's Area Mental Health - Mental Retardation Programs.*

DIRECTORY OF MINORITY AND WOMEN-OWNED ARCHITECTURAL AND ENGINEERING FIRMS. 1981-. 0731-3209. US. English. ACEC Research and Management Foundation, 1015-15th Street Northwest/Suite 802, Washington DC 20005. **LC** NA53. **DD** 338.7617202573. Index in last issue of volume - attached. *Directory of Minority Architectural and Engineering Firms.*

DIRECTORY OF MINORITY BUSINESSES. 0732-1759. US. English. an. 100 Cambridge Street/13th Floor, Boston MA 02202. **LC** HD2346.U52. **DD** 338.642025744.

DIRECTORY OF MINORITY ENGINEERING PROGRAMS. 1982-83-. 0736-0029. US. English. an. $24.95. CPC Foundation, 62 Highland Avenue, Bethlehem PA 18017. **LC** TA157. **DD** 620.0071173.

DIRECTORY OF MINORITY OWNED BUSINESSES IN TEXAS. 1974-. 0094-8004. US. English. $1.00. Office of Minority Business Enterprise, Information Office, 1711 San

Yearbooks, Almanacs, Directories

Antonio St, Austin TX 78701. **LC** HD2346.U52. **DD** 338.76025764.

DIRECTORY OF MISSISSIPPI ELECTIVE OFFICIALS. 0540-3820. US. English. Secretary of State, State of Mississippi, Jackson MI 39205. **LC** JK4630. **DD** 353.97620022.

DIRECTORY OF MISSOURI LIBRARIES. 1965/66-. 0092-4067. US. English. ir. Missouri State Library, PO Box 387-308 High Street, Jefferson City MO 65101. **Tel** (910)760-1589. **LC** Z732.M82. **DD** 027.0025778.

DIRECTORY OF MISSOURI'S REGIONAL PLANNING SYSTEM. (A DIRECTORY OF MISSOURI'S REGIONAL PLANNING SYSTEM). 0090-7812. US. English. Missouri Department of Community Affairs, 505 Missouri Boulevard, Jefferson City MO 65101. **LC** HT393.M8. **DD** 309.25025778.

DIRECTORY OF MONTANA MANUFACTURERS CEASED. Began publication with 5th Ed. 1979-77. 0742-7891. US. English. ir. Montana Department of Commerce, Capitol Station, Helena MT 59620. **Tel** (406)444-3923. **LC** HD9727.M9. **DD** 338.0025786. *Montana Directory of Manufacturers.*

DIRECTORY OF MONTANA MINING ENTERPRISES. (DIRECTORY OF MONTANA MINING ENTERPRISES FOR . . .). 0741-4544. US. English. an. **LC** TN12. **DD** 338.2025786. *Directory of Mining Enterprises for . . ., 0741-4552.*

DIRECTORY OF MULTIHOSPITAL SYSTEMS. 1980 Ed.-. 0731-8510. US. English. an. $53.82. American Hospital Association, PO Box 99376, Chicago IL 60693. **Tel** (312)280-6392. **Ed** Dorothy Cobbs. **LC** RA977. **Circ** 3,000. Listing of not-for-profit and for-profit multihospital systems. Also includes multi-state alliances and networks.

DIRECTORY OF MUNICIPAL AND COUNTY OFFICIALS IN COLORADO. US. English. an. Colorado Municipal League, 4800 Wadsworth Boulevard/Suite 204, Wheat Ridge Co 80033. *Directory: Municipal and County Officials in Colorado.*

DIRECTORY OF MUNICIPAL AUTHORITIES IN PENNSYLVANIA. 0361-6924. US. English. an. PA Department of Community Affairs, Forum Building/Room 321 A, Harrisburg PA 17120. **LC** HD4606.P4. **DD** 338.74. *Pennsylvania Municipal Authorities Directory.*

DIRECTORY OF MUNICIPAL BOND DEALERS OF THE UNITED STATES. VFOAT Municipal Bond Dealers of the United States. US. English. sa. $70.00. The Bond Buyer, 1 State Street Plaza, New York NY 10004. **Tel** (212)943-9427. **Ed** Denis F McFeely. **adv acc. Circ** 10,000. (ctrl). Contains listings of municipal bond dealers of the United States as well as municipal finance consultants and municipal bond attorneys.

DIRECTORY OF MUNICIPAL MANAGEMENT ASSISTANTS. 1975-. 0363-0552. US. English. an. International City Management Association, 1140 Connecticut Avenue Northwest, Washington DC 20036. **LC** JS344.C5. **DD** 352.00802573. *Municipal Assistants Directory.*

DIRECTORY OF MUNICIPAL OFFICIALS OF NEW MEXICO. US. English. an. $25.00. New Mexico Municipal League, PO Box 846/Diane Lang, Sante Fe NM 87501. **Tel** (505)982-5573. **LC** JS451.N67. **DD** 352.00809789.

DIRECTORY OF MUSEUMS, ARCHIVES & ART GALLERIES OF BRITISH COLUMBIA. VFOAT Directory of Museums, Art Galleries & Archives of British Columbia. 3rd Ed. (1981)-. 0714-7023. CN. English. Province of British Columbia, Ministry of Provincial Secretary and Government Services, Provincial Secretary, Victoria British Columbia Canada. **LC** AM21.B7. **DD** 069.025711. *Museums & Art Galleries in British Columbia, 0318-4021.*

DIRECTORY OF MUSEUMS, ART GALLERIES, AND RELATED INSTITUTIONS CEASED. VFOAT Repertoire des Musees, Galeries d'Art, et des Establissements Connexes. 1972. 0828-3109. CN. English (French). an. Receiver General for Canada, Supply & Services Canada, Ottawa Ontario K1A 0S9 Canada. **Tel** (819)997-2560. **LC** AM21.A1. **DD** 069.02571.

DIRECTORY OF MUSIC FACULTIES IN COLLEGES AND UNIVERSITIES, U.S. AND CANADA. (DIRECTORY OF MUSIC FACULTIES IN COLLEGES AND UNIVERSITIES, U. S. AND CANADA). Began with Vol. for 1970/72. 0098-664X. US. English. be. $25.00. College Music Society, Department of Music, 1444 15th Street, Boulder CO 80303. **Tel** (303)449-1611. **LC** ML13. **DD** 780.922. *Directory of Music Faculties in American Colleges and Universities.*

DIRECTORY OF NATIONAL AND INTERNATIONAL UNIONS AND ASSOCIATIONS WITH EXCLUSIVE RECOGNITION IN THE FEDERAL SERVICE. 0097-8639. US. English. **LC** HD8008. **DD** 331.881135300025.

DIRECTORY OF NATIONAL DEFENSE EXECUTIVE RESERVISTS ON ASSIGNMENT TO OFFICE OF SECRETARY OF TRANSPORTATION, U.S. DEPARTMENT OF TRANSPORTATION. Main/Corp United States. Dept. of Transportation. Office of the Secretary. VFOAT Directory, National Defense Executive Reserve, Office of Secretary of Transportation. US. English. US Department of Transportation, Office of the Secretary, 400-7th Street SW, Washington DC 20590.

DIRECTORY OF NATIONAL MEMBER FIRMS AND MEMBER-ASSOCIATIONS - ASSOCIATION CANADIENNE DE LA CONSTRUCTION. Main/Corp Association Canadienne de la Construction. VFOAT Repertoire des Membres Nationaux et des Associatiojs-Membres. VAT Directory of National Member Firms and Member-Associations of the Canadian Construction Association. 1984-. 0828-7031. CN. French (English). an. Association Canadienne de la Construction, 85 rue Albert, Ottawa Ontario K1P 6A4 Canada. **DD** 690.02571. *Directory of Members, 0820-0785.*

DIRECTORY OF NATIONAL SCIENCE FOUNDATION PROGRAMS AND GUIDELINES. (A DIRECTORY OF NATIONAL SCIENCE FOUNDATION PROGRAMS AND GUIDELINES). 0092-9921. US. English. Western Michigan University, Office of Research Services, Kalamazoo MI 49001. **LC** Q180.U5. **DD** 507.2073.

DIRECTORY OF NATIONAL SOURCES OF DATA ON BLACKS IN HIGHER EDUCATION. 0364-6955. US. English. Institute for Study of Educational Policy Howard University, 2935 Upton Street Northwest, Washington DC 20007. **LC** L901. **DD** 378.006273.

DIRECTORY OF NATIVE COMMUNITIES AND ORGANIZATIONS IN ONTARIO. VFOAT Directory, Native Communities and Organizations in Ontario. VAT Directory. Native Communities and Organizations in Ontario. Began with 1980? issue. 0227-1109. CN. English. $2.50. Native Community Branch, Publications Services Section, 5th Floor 880 Bay Street, Toronto Ontario M7A 1N8 Canada. **LC** E78.O5. **DD** 971.3004970025.

DIRECTORY OF NEBRASKA MANUFACTURERS AND THEIR PRODUCTS. US. English. be. $22.00. Manufacturers News Inc, 4 East Huron Street, Chicago IL 60611. **Tel** (312)337-1084. Contains addresses, zip codes, chief officers, number of employees and the telephone numbers of about 2,700 firms. 190 pages. *Directory of Nebraska Manufacturers, 0070-5926.*

DIRECTORY OF NEW BRUNSWICK LIBRARIES. VFOAT Repertoire des Bibliotheques du Nouveau-Brunswick. 1st Ed. (Jan. 1976)-. 0713-6358. Periodical. CN. English (French). ir. Directory of New Brunswick Libraries, c/o Bibliotheque Champlain, Universite de Moncton, Moncton New Brunswick E1A 3E9 Canada. **DD** 027.0025715.

A DIRECTORY OF NEW ENGLAND SKI TOURING CENTERS. 1979-. 0270-3815. US. English. an. Puckerbrush Press, PO Box 28, East Longmeadow MA 01028. **LC** GV854.5.N35. **DD** 796.9302574.

DIRECTORY OF NEW JERSEY CERTIFIED NURSERIES AND PLANT DEALERS. 1983-84-. 8756-0178. US. English. an. New Jersey Department of Agriculture, CN 330, Trenton NJ 08625. **LC** SB118.487.N5. **DD** 381.415025749. *New Jersey Certified Nurserymen and Dealers.*

DIRECTORY OF NEW MEXICO MANUFACTURING & MINING. (THE DIRECTORY OF NEW MEXICO MANUFACTURING & MINING). VFOAT Directory of New Mexico Manufacturing and Mining. 1958-. Periodical. US. English. be. Manufacturers News Inc, 4 East Huron Street, Chicago IL 606111. **LC** HD9727.N6. **DD** 670. *Directory of New Mexico Manufacturers.*

DIRECTORY OF NEW MUSIC. VFOAT Composium Directory of New Music. 1971-. US. English. an. Crystal Record Co, 2235 Willida Lane, Sedro Woolley WA 98284. **LC** ML118. **DD** 016.78.

DIRECTORY OF NIGHTCLUBS, HOTELS, THEATRES, LOUNGES & DISCOTHEQUES. VFOAT Talent & Booking's Nightclub Directory. VAT Directory of Nightclubs, Hotels, Theatres, Lounges and Discotheques. 1980-. &— 4-178X. US. English. an. $25.00. Talent & Booking Pub Co, 7033 Sunset Boulevard/Suite 222, Los Angeles CA 90028. **LC** PN1968.U5. **DD** 792.7029573.

DIRECTORY OF NORTH AMERICAN CHEMICAL PRODUCERS. 1978/79-. 0161-7532. US. English. **LC** TP12. **DD** 338.47661002571.

DIRECTORY OF NORTH AMERICAN FAIRS & EXPOSITIONS CEASED. VAT Directory of North American Fairs and Expositions. 0361-4255. US. English. an. $15.00. Amusement Business, PO Box 2150, Radnor PA 19089. **LC** T391. **DD** 973.9207401. *Cavalcade and Directory of Fairs.*

DIRECTORY OF NORTH AMERICAN FAIRS AND EXPOSITIONS CHRONOLOGICAL SUPPLEMENT. (V. 2, No. 1- Spring 1977-). Periodical. US. English. an. $35.00. Amusement Business, Box 24970, Nashville TN 37202. **Tel** (615)748-8120. **Ed** Leslie Shaver. **adv acc. Circ** 1,000. A comprehensive directory of every fair and exposition in the US and Canada which run three or more days. Contains data on managers, demographics, size of grounds and budgets, plus chronological cross reference of fairs.

A DIRECTORY OF NORTH CAROLINA HISTORICAL ORGANIZATIONS. 1977-. 0194-2093. US. English. be. Federation of North Carolina Historical Societies, Division of Archives and History, 109 East Jones Street, Raleigh NC 27611. **LC** F251. **DD** 975.6006.

DIRECTORY OF NORTH CAROLINA MANUFACTURING FIRMS. 0095-8298. US. English. ir. $35.00. North Carolina Department of Commerce, 430 North Salisbury Street, Raleigh NC 27611. **Tel** (919)733-4151. **LC** T12. **DD** 338.4767025756. *North Carolina Directory of Manufacturing Firms.*

DIRECTORY OF NORTH DAKOTA MANUFACTURERS. Main/Corp North Dakota. Business and Industrial Development Department. US. English. be. $16.20. Manufacturers News Inc, 4 East Huron St, Chicago IL 60611. **Tel** (312)337-1084. Contains products of manufacturing firms listed by SIC number, firms listed alphabetically, and geographically by city. 58 pages.

DIRECTORY OF NURSERYMEN AND DEALERS REGISTERED TO SELL NURSERY STOCK IN VIRGINIA AND SUMMARY OF LAWS AND REGULATIONS. 0507-0937. US. English. an. Division of Product and Industry Regulation, Plant Pest Control Section, 203 North Governor Street/Room 308, Richmond VA 23219. **LC** SB44. **DD** 381.41. *Directory of Nurserymen, Dealers and Agents Registered to Sell Nursery Stock in Virginia and Summary of Laws and Regulations.*

DIRECTORY OF NURSERYMEN AND OTHERS LICENSED TO SELL NURSERY STOCK IN CALIFORNIA, AND SUMMARY OF LAWS AND REGULATIONS. VFOAT Directory of Nurserymen-Laws and Regulations. 0099-1589. US. English. Federal-State Market News Service, 1220 N Street, Sacramento CA 95814. **LC** SB44. **DD** 338.1759025794. *Directory of Nurserymen and Others Licensed to Sell Nursery Stock in California.*

DIRECTORY OF NURSES WITH DOCTORAL DEGREES. 0273-2084. US. English. ir. American Nurses Association, 2420 Pershing Road/Publ Orders, Kansas City MO 64108. **Tel** (816)474-5720. **LC** RT25.U5. **DD** 610.7302573. **NLM** WY 22 AA1 D62.

DIRECTORY OF NURSING HOME ADMINISTRATORS LICENSED AND REGISTERED IN TENNESSEE. 1976-. 0191-2879. US. English. an. **NLM** WX 22 AT2 D5. *Directory of Nursing Home Administrators Licensed in Tennessee, 0164-2596.*

Yearbooks, Almanacs, Directories

DIRECTORY OF NURSING HOMES IN THE UNITED STATES, U. S. TERRITORIES, AND CANADA CEASED. US. English. ir. $225.00. McKnight Medic' Communication, 550 Frontage Road, Morthfield IL 60093. **Tel** (312)446-1622. Ed Jill Newman. **LC** RA997.A2. **Circ** 17,000. Complete listing of all licensed nursing homes with addresses, phone numbers, administrator's name and bed size.

DIRECTORY OF NURSING HOMES IN THE UNITED STATES, U.S. POSSESSIONS AND CANADA. (MODERN NURSING HOME DIRECTORY OF NURSING HOMES IN THE UNITED STATES, U.S. POSSESSIONS AND CANADA). **VFOAT** Directory of Nursing Homes in the United States, U.S. Possessions and Canada. **VAT** Directory of Nursing Homes in the United States, United States Possessions and Canada. 0093-9900. US. English. McGraw Hill, 1221 Avenue of the Americas, New York NY 10020. **LC** RA997.A2. **DD** 362.1602573. Directory of Nursing Homes in the United States, U.S. Territories, and Canada.

DIRECTORY OF OBSOLETE SECURITIES. **VFOAT** Financial Stock Guide Service. 0085-0551. US. English. an. Financial Information Inc, 30 Montgomery Street, Jersey City NJ 07302. **Tel** (201)332-5400. **LC** HG4961. **DD** 332.67. adv acc. Listing of over 1,200 pages of old securities dating back from 1927.

DIRECTORY OF OCEAN CONTAINERSHIP SERVICES BETWEEN THE PORTS OF HALIFAX-SAINT JOHN AND WORLD PORTS. 1st Ed.- 1972-. 0319-0137. Periodical. CN. English. Atlantic Provinces Transportation Commission, PO Box 577, Moncton New Brunswick E1C 8L9 Canada. **DD** 387.544025715.

DIRECTORY OF O.C.U.L. LIBRARIES. **Main/Corp** Ontario Council of University Libraries. **VAT** Directory of Ontario Council of University Libraries. 0822-935X. CN. English. an. $5.00 Per Year, Members. Directory of OCUL Libraries c/o Mrs Peggy Budd, McMaster University Library, 1280 Main Street West, Hamilton Ontario L8S 4L6 Canada. **DD** 027.7025713.

DIRECTORY OF OFFICERS, COUNCIL AND COMMITTEES. **Main/Corp** American Bar Association. Section of Real Property, Probate and Trust Law. 0147-1325. US. English. an. American Bar Association, 1155 East 60th Street, Chicago IL 60637. **LC** KF195.P75. **DD** 346.73043062.

DIRECTORY OF OFFICIALS OF THE DEMOCRATIC PEOPLE'S REPUBLIC OF KOREA. US. English. Central Intelligence Agency, Document Expediting (DOCEX), Library of Congress, Washington DC 20540. **LC** JQ1729.5.A4. **DD** 354.5193002. Vols. for (1983-) distributed to depository libraries in microfiche.

DIRECTORY OF OFFICIALS OF THE GERMAN DEMOCRATIC REPUBLIC CEASED. -Mar. 1982. Periodical. US. English. ir. Docement Expediting (DOCEX) Project, Exchange and Gift Division, Library of Congress, Washington DC 20540. Directory of East German Officials.

DIRECTORY OF OFFICIALS OF THE POLISH PEOPLE'S REPUBLIC. Began with 1977. US. English. Central Intelligence Agency, National Foreign Assignment Center, Document Expediting (DOCEX), Library of Congress, Washington DC 20540. **LC** JN6757. **DD** 354.438002. Vols. for (Aug. 1983-) distributed to depository libraries in microfiche. Directory of Polish Officials, 0090-9955.

DIRECTORY OF OFFICIALS OF VIETNAM. Oct. 1983-. US. English. The Directorate: Document Expediting (DOCEX) Project, Library of Congress, 10 First Street SE, Washington DC 20540. **LC** JQ821. **DD** 354.597002. Vols. for 1983- distributed to depository libraries in microfiche. Directory of Officials of the Socialist Republic of Vietnam.

DIRECTORY OF OHIO LIBRARIES (COLUMBUS, OHIO : 1980). (DIRECTORY OF OHIO LIBRARIES). Began with 1980. 0734-0389. US. English. an. State Library of Ohio, 65 South Front Street/Room 1206, Columbus OH 43215. **LC** Z732.O5. **DD** 027.0025771. Ohio Directory of Libraries, 0196-3872.

DIRECTORY OF OKLAHOMA. 1973-. 0095-0920. US. English. $6.00. State Library, 200 Northeast 18th, Oklahoma City OK 73105. **Tel** (405)521-2502. Ed Patricia Lester. **LC** JK7192. **DD** 353.9766002. **Circ** 7,500. General information on Oklahoma, government, history, people and election results and elected officials. Directory and Manual of the State of Oklahoma.

DIRECTORY OF OKLAHOMA. 1983-. US. English. be. Ed Howard Lowell and Jan Blakely.

DIRECTORY OF OKLAHOMA AIRPORTS. 0094-5390. US. English. Oklahoma Aeronautics Commission, Box 25352, Oklahoma City OK 73125. **LC** HE9797.5.U52. **DD** 387.736025766. Oklahoma Airport Directory.

DIRECTORY OF OKLAHOMA'S CITY AND TOWN OFFICIALS. 0099-197X. US. English. an. $10.00. Oklahoma Municipal League, 201 NE 23rd Street, Oklahoma City OK 73105. **LC** JS451.O57. **DD** 352.008025766.

DIRECTORY OF ON-GOING RESEARCH IN CANCER EPIDEMIOLOGY. Series/Titl IARC Scientific Publications. 1976-. FR. English. an. **LC** RC267. **DD** 616.994071072. **NLM** W1 I21K.

DIRECTORY OF ON-GOING RESEARCH IN SMOKING AND HEALTH. (DIRECTORY, ON-GOING RESEARCH IN SMOKING AND HEALTH). **VFOAT** On-Going Research in Smoking and Health. 8th Ed. (1980)-. 0070-6000. US. English. be. Superintendent of Documents, US Government Printing Office, Washington DC 20402. **LC** RA1242.T6. **DD** 615.952374. **NLM** QV 22 AA1 D6. Directory of On-Going Research in Smoking and Health, 0070-6000.

DIRECTORY OF ONLINE DATABASES. V. 1- Fall 1979-. 0193-6840. US. English. qt. $210.00. Cuadra Associates Inc, 2001 Wilshire Boulshire/Suite 305, Santa Monica CA 90403. **Tel** (213)829-9972. Ed Orest Balaban. **LC** Z699.22. **DD** 025.04025. **CODEN** DODADF. Describes virtually all publicly available online databases worldwide. Includes name, producer, online services, address and telephone number, content, updates, etc., for each database.

DIRECTORY OF ONTARIO MUSEUMS. 1982-. CN. English. $5.00. Ontario Museum Association, 38 Charles Street East, Toronto Ontario M4Y 1T1 Canada. Directory of Ontario Museums and Related Institutions.

DIRECTORY OF OPERATING LIBRARIES - GEORGIAN BAY REGIONAL LIBRARY SYSTEM. (DIRECTORY OF OPERATING LIBRARIES). **Main/Corp** Georgian Bay Regional Library System. 0712-9785. CN. English. an. Free. Georgian Bay Regional Library System, 30 Morrow Road, Barrie Ontario L4N 3V8 Canada. **DD** 027.402571315. (ctrl).

DIRECTORY OF OPERATING SMALL BUSINESS INVESTMENT COMPANIES. 0736-2129. US. English. Small Business Administration, Washington DC 20416. **LC** HG3729.U49. **DD** 332.6722. List of Small Business Investment Companies.

DIRECTORY OF OPPORTUNITIES FOR GRADUATES. **VFOAT** Opportunities for Graduates. 1956-. 0070-6019. UK. English. an. VNU Business Publications, Freepost 38, London W1E 6QZ England.

DIRECTORY OF OPPORTUNITIES FOR GRADUATES (LONDON, ENGLAND : 1984). (THE DIRECTORY OF OPPORTUNITIES FOR GRADUATES). **VFOAT** D.O.G. 1984-. UK. English. an. 11.50. VNU Business Publications, 53-55 Frith Street, London W1A 2HG England. **LC** HF5382.5.G7. **DD** 331.7023. DOG . . . Employers.

DIRECTORY OF OPPORTUNITIES IN INTERNATIONAL LAW. 1968. 0148-7345. US. English. be. $14.00. John Bassett Moore Society of International Law, University of Virginia School of Law, Charlottesville VA 22901. **Tel** (804)924-3087. Ed Deborah M Awai. **LC** KF195.I54. **DD** 331.761341025. A guide to the possibilities for employment in this field.

DIRECTORY OF OREGON CRIMINAL JUSTICE AGENCIES. 0149-3477. US. English. Oregon Law Enforcement Council, 2001 Front Street NE, Salem OR 97310. **LC** HV8145.O7. **DD** 364.025795.

DIRECTORY OF ORGANIZATIONS AND INDIVIDUALS PROFESSIONALLY ENGAGED IN GOVERNMENTAL RESEARCH AND RELATED ACTIVITIES. **Main/Corp** Governmental Research Association. **VFOAT** GRA Directory. 1935-. 0072-520X. US. English. an. Governmental Research Association, PO Box 387, Ocean Gate NJ 08740. **LC** JK3. **DD** 350.6273.

DIRECTORY OF ORGANIZATIONS CONCERNED WITH ENVIRONMENTAL RESEARCH. 1970-. Periodical. US. English. ir. Lake Erie Environmental Studies, State University College, Fredonia NY 14063. Ed Wendall A Mordy and Phyllis A Sholtys. **DD** 574, 628.

DIRECTORY OF ORGANIZATIONS CONCERNED WITH SCIENTIFIC RESEARCH AND TECHNICAL SERVICES IN ZIMBABWE RHODESIA. English. ir. **LC** Q180.R5. **DD** 607.206891.

DIRECTORY OF ORGANIZATIONS INTERESTED IN THE HANDICAPPED. 197 -. Periodical. US. English. ir. $3.00. People to People Program, 1522 K Street NW #1130, Washington DC 20005. **Tel** (202)638-2487.

DIRECTORY OF ORGANIZATIONS PROMOTING EQUAL EMPLOYMENT OPPORTUNITIES FOR WOMEN, CALIFORNIA. US. English. Agriculture and Service Agency, 455 Golden Gate Avenue/Room 1193, San Francisco CA 94102. **LC** HD6058. **DD** 331.128.

DIRECTORY OF ORGANIZATIONS WORKING FOR WOMEN'S EDUCATIONAL EQUITY. 0272-1864. US. English. Women's Educational Equity Communications Network, 1855 Folsom Street, San Francisco CA 94103. **LC** HQ1883. **DD** 305.4202573.

DIRECTORY OF OSTEOPATHIC PHYSICIANS AND SURGEONS LICENSED BY THE STATE OF CALIFORNIA. 0163-478X. US. English. State of California, Board of Osteopathic Examiners, 921-11th Street/Suite 1201, Sacramento CA 95814. **LC** RZ333. **DD** 615.533025794.

DIRECTORY OF PARA MEDICAL INSTITUTIONS OF INDIA. (DIRECTORY OF PARA-MEDICAL INSTITUTIONS OF INDIA). 0253-7656. English. ir. **NLM** W 22 JI4 D56.

DIRECTORY OF PATHOLOGY TRAINING PROGRAMS. Began with 1969/70 issue. 0070-6086. US. English. an. $400.00. Intersociety Committee on Pathology Information, 4733 Bethesda Avenue/Suite 735, Bethesda MD 20814. **Tel** (301)656-2944. Ed Judy Graves. **NLM** QZ 22 AA1 D5. **Circ** 2,500. (ctrl). Listings of pathology residency training programs in the US and Canada, also fellowship programs in subspecialists of pathology.

DIRECTORY OF PENNSYLVANIA ACADEMIC AND RESEARCH LIBRARIES. 1970/71. US. English. ir. Pennsylvania State Library, Harrisburg PA 17105. **LC** Z732.P42. **DD** 027.0748.

DIRECTORY OF PERMITS, STATE OF ALASKA. **Main/Corp** Alaska. Dept. of Commerce and Economic Development. **VFOAT** Directory of Permits. 1978-. US. English. an. Juneau Permit Information and Regional Center, Department of Environmental Conservation Mail Pouch O, Juneau AK 99811. Each issue contains an index to its own contents - no vol index - loose.

DIRECTORY OF PERSONAL IMAGE CONSULTANTS. 0163-6537. US. English. an. $10.95. Editorial Services Co, 1140 Avenue of the Americas, New York NY 10036. **LC** HD59. **DD** 659.202573.

DIRECTORY OF PERSONNEL - CANADA DEPT. OF AGRICULTURE. (DIRECTORY OF PERSONNEL - CANADA DEPARTMENT OF AGRICULTURE). **Main/Corp** Canada. Dept. of Agriculture. Began publication in 1957?. 0576-033X. CN. English. an. Free. Agricultural Canada, 930 Carling Avenue/Room 124, Ottawa Ontario K1A 0C5 Canada. **DD** 354.71068233.

DIRECTORY OF PERSONNEL OF UNITED NATIONS ORGANIZATIONS AND THE INTERNATIONAL MONETARY FUND IN THE DEMOCRATIC REPUBLIC OF THE SUDAN. English. ir. Office of the Resident Representative of United Nations Development Program, PO Box 913, Khartoum Sudan.

DIRECTORY OF PERSONNEL RESPONSIBLE FOR RADIOLOGICAL HEALTH PROGRAMS. (DIRECTORY OF—PERSONNEL RESPONSIBLE FOR RADIOLOGICAL HEALTH PROGRAMS). 0149-8304. US. English. an.

Yearbooks, Almanacs, Directories

Bureau of Radiological Health, 5600 Fishers Lane, Rockville MD 20857. **LC** RA569. **DD** 363.179. **NLM** WN 22 AA1 D5.

DIRECTORY OF PHILIPPINE BANKS AND OTHER FINANCIAL INSTITUTIONS. English. an. **LC** HG3313. **DD** 332.1025599.

DIRECTORY OF PHYSICAL THERAPISTS AND PHYSICAL THERAPISTS ASSISTANTS LICENSED AND REGISTERED IN TENNESSEE. 0162-5543. US. English. 352 Capitol Hill Building, Nashville TN 37219. **LC** RM697.T4. **DD** 615.8025768. **NLM** WB 22 AT2 D55. *Directory of Physical Therapists Registered in Tennessee.*

DIRECTORY OF PHYSICS & ASTRONOMY STAFF MEMBERS. **Series/Titl** AIP Publication. **VFOAT** Directory of Physics and Astronomy Staff Members. 1975/76-. 0361-2228. US. English. an. $30.00. American Institute of Physics, 335 East 45th Street, New York NY 10017. **Tel** (516)349-7800. **LC** QC47.N75. **DD** 530.0257. *Directory of Physics & Astronomy Faculties in North American Colleges & Universities*, 0419-3253.

DIRECTORY OF PODIATRISTS LICENSED IN TENNESSEE. 1975-. 0148-4745. US. English. an. State Licensing Board for the Healing Arts, 352 Capitol Hill Building, Nashville TN 37219. **NLM** WE 22 AT2 D5.

DIRECTORY OF POST-PRIMARY INSTITUTIONS IN THE EAST-CENTRAL STATE OF NIGERIA. Began in 1970. 0331-0299. English. ir. **LC** L971.N5. **DD** 373.025669.

DIRECTORY OF POSTSECONDARY EDUCATIONAL INSTITUTIONS IN ALASKA. 0147-9113. US. English. Alaska Commission on Postsecondary Education, Pouch F State Office Building, Juneau AK 99811. **LC** L903.A4. **DD** 378.798.

DIRECTORY OF POSTSECONDARY OCCUPATIONAL EDUCATION OPPORTUNITIES IN LOUISIANA. **VFOAT** Postsecondary Occupational Education Opportunities in Louisiana. 0149-6697. US. English. Board of Regents State of Louisiana, Suite 1530/One American Place, Baton Rouge LA 70825. **LC** LA295.5. **DD** 370.113025763.

A DIRECTORY OF PRECEPTORSHIP PROGRAMS IN THE HEALTH PROFESSIONS. 1975-. 0162-9387. US. English. an. Manpower Distribution Project, National Health Council, 1740 Broadway, New York NY 10019. **NLM** W 22 AA1 D67.

DIRECTORY OF PREMIUM, INCENTIVE, AND TRAVEL BUYERS. 0196-8262. US. English. $130.00. The Salesman's Guide Inc, 1140 Broadway, New York NY 10001. **Tel** (212)684-2985. **Ed** Edward R Blank. **LC** HF6146.P7. **DD** 658.82. adv acc. **Circ** 1,000. (ctrl). Lists 17,500 executives responsible for buying premiums, incentives and incentive travel. *Directory of Premium and Incentive Buyers*, 0070-6124.

DIRECTORY OF PRINCIPAL SAND AND GRAVEL PRODUCERS IN THE UNITED STATES IN . . . . **Series/Titl** Mineral Industry Surveys. 1977-. 0735-5181. US. English. an. US Department of the Interior, Bureau of Mines, Washington DC 20241.

DIRECTORY OF PRIVATE ELEMENTARY AND SECONDARY SCHOOLS IN CANADA. **VFOAT** Repertoire des Ecoles Privees Elementaires et Secondaires au Canada. 1972/73-. CN. English and French. $0.75. Information Canada, Receiver General for Canada, Statistics Publication Canada, Ottawa Ontario K1A 0T6 Canada. **LC** L905. **DD** 371.0102571. *Directory of Private Schools in Canada.*

DIRECTORY OF PRIVATE ELEMENTARY SCHOOLS AND HIGH SCHOOLS IN CALIFORNIA THAT HAVE COMPLIED WITH EDUCATION CODE SECTION 29009.5. 0092-2404. US. English. California State Department of Education, 721 Capitol Mall, Sacramento CA 95814. **LC** L903.C2. **DD** 371.02025794.

DIRECTORY OF PRIVATE SCHOOLS AND INSTITUTIONS IN KENYA. English. ir. Nobel Printers, Raja Building Biashara Street/PO Box 10304, Nairobi Kenya. **LC** L971.K4. **DD** 371.020256762.

DIRECTORY OF PRIVATE SCHOOLS IN NEW YORK STATE. 0095-828X. US. English. an. University of the State of New York, State Education Dept, Divsion of Special Occupational Services, Albany NY 12210. **LC** L903.N7. **DD** 371.02025747.

DIRECTORY OF PRIVATE TRADE, TECHNICAL, AND ART SCHOOLS. 0092-4202. US. English. **LC** L903.N5. **DD** 373.24025749.

DIRECTORY OF PROFESSIONAL ENGINEERS OF ONTARIO. **VFOAT** Directory of the Association of Professional Engineers of Ontario (Title Varies Slightly). Began publication in 196-. 0701-1814. Periodical. **CN**. English. be. Free to Members. Association of Professional Engineers of Ontario, 1027 Yonge Street, Toronto Ontario M4W 3E5 Canada. **DD** 620.0062713. *List of Members.*

DIRECTORY OF PROFESSIONAL GENEALOGISTS AND RELATED SERVICES. 1979-. 0272-3387. US. English. $25.00. PO Box 11601, Salt Lake City UT 84147. **LC** CS5. **DD** 929.102573. bk rev. adv acc. **Circ** 600. Lists professional genealogists by specialty or service, with addresses, phone numbers and sometimes fees charged.

DIRECTORY OF PROFESSIONAL PHOTOGRAPHY. 0070-6132. US. English. an. $25.00. PPA Publications Inc, 1090 Executive Way, Des Plaines IL 60018. **Tel** (312)299-8161. **LC** TR12. **DD** 770.2573. adv acc. **Circ** 15,000. A annual directory of qualified portrait, commercial and industrial photographers, listed geographically and by photographic specialty and index of certified, master, and craftsman photographers.

DIRECTORY OF PROGRAMS AND PERSONNEL. (DIRECTORY OF PROGRAMS AND PERSONNEL - MASSACHUSETTS, DEPARTMENT OF EDUCATION). **Main/Corp** Massachusetts. Dept. of Education. 1974-. 0097-8647. US. English. Massachusetts Department of Education, 182 Tremont Street, Boston MA 02111. **LC** L160. **DD** 370.25744.

DIRECTORY OF PROGRAMS AND SERVICES FOR OLDER ADULTS. STATE OF OREGON BY COUNTIES. (DIRECTORY OF PROGRAMS AND SERVICES FOR OLDER ADULTS : STATE OF OREGON BY COUNTIES). 0090-5658. US. English. Portland State University, PO Box 751, Portland OR 97207. **LC** HV1468.O7. **DD** 362.609795.

DIRECTORY OF PROGRAMS IN LINGUISTICS IN THE UNITED STATES & CANADA. 1982-. US. English. Linguistic Society of America, 3520 Prospect Street NW, Washington DC 20007. *Directory of Programs in Linguistics in the U.S. and Canada.*

DIRECTORY OF PROGRAMS IN STATISTICS AND RELATED AREAS IN CANADIAN UNIVERSITIES. **VFOAT** Registre de Programmes de Statistique et Sujets Connexes Offerts par les Universites Canadiennes. 1980-. 0229-0081. **CN**. English (French). an. Statistical Society of Canada, c/o McMaster University Department of Clinical Epidemiology and Biostatistics, 1200 Main Street West, Hamilton Ontario L8N 3Z5 Canada. **DD** 519.5071171.

DIRECTORY OF PROVIDERS OF FAMILY PLANNING AND ABORTION SERVICES. 0148-6322. US. English. Alan Guttmacher Institute, 515 Madison Avenue, New York NY 10022. **LC** HQ763. **DD** 362.82.

DIRECTORY OF PSYCHIATRY RESIDENCY TRAINING PROGRAMS. **VFOAT** Psychiatry Residency Training Programs. 1st Ed. (1982)-. 0740-8250. US. English. an. **NLM** WM 22 AA1 D52.

DIRECTORY OF PSYCHOLOGISTS AND PSYCHOLOGICAL EXAMINERS LICENSED AND REGISTERED IN TENNESSEE. Began with: 19767. 0732-1333. US. English. an. State Licensing Board for the Healing Arts, TDPH State Office Building, Ben Allen Road, Nashville TN 37216. **NLM** BF 109 D615. *Directory of Psychologists and Psychological Examiners Licensed in Tennessee,* 0163-8556.

DIRECTORY OF PSYCHOLOGISTS REGISTERED IN THE PROVINCE OF ONTARIO CEASED. 1975-1981. 0316-0793. **CN**. English. an. Ontario Board of Examiners in Psychology, PO Box 221 Station M, Toronto Ontario M6S 4T3 Canada. **DD** 150.25713. *Directory of Registered Psychologists in the Province of Ontario,* 0419-3369.

DIRECTORY OF PSYCHOSOCIAL INVESTIGATORS. July 1975-. 0361-3771. US. English. Center for Psychosocial Studies, 233 North Michigan Avenue, Chicago IL 60601. **LC** BF30. **DD** 301.1025.

DIRECTORY OF PUBLIC ENTERPRISES IN INDIA. 1974-. 0376-8546. English. ir. S L Sharma, C-40 South Extension-11 49, New Delhi India. **LC** HD4293. **DD** 338.702554.

DIRECTORY OF PUBLIC HIGH TECHNOLOGY CORPORATIONS. 2nd Ed. (1984-1985)-. 0882-5076. US. English. $195.00. American Investor Information Services Inc, 311 Bainbridge Street, Philadelphia PA 19147. **Tel** (215)925-2761. **Ed** Ronald P Smolin. **Circ** 1,200. Profiles of high technology companies in computer, telecommunications, electronics, medical, biotechnology industries. Includes management names, sales, product information. Covers some 2,200 companies in the public sector. *Directory of Public High Technology Corporations and Products & Services Listing,* 0738-7369.

DIRECTORY OF PUBLIC HOUSING AGENCIES. 0160-4856. US. English. US Department of Housing and Urban Development, 451 7th Street SW, Washington DC 20410. **LC** HD7293.A1. **DD** 352.7502573.

DIRECTORY OF PUBLIC LIBRARY SERVICES IN VICTORIA. AT. English. ir. Library Council of Victoria Public Libraries Division, 328 Swanston Street, Melbourne 3000 Victoria. **LC** Z870.V5. **DD** 027.4945.

DIRECTORY OF PUBLIC LIBRARY SERVICES, WESTERN AUSTRALIA. English. ir. Library Board of Western Australia, 102 Beaufort Street, Perth Western Australia 6000 Australia. **LC** Z870.W4. **DD** 025.52774941.

DIRECTORY OF PUBLIC OFFICIALS IN THE LAKE ERIE REGION. 1976-. 0383-7599. **CN**. English. Lake Erie Regional Library System, 380 Saskatoon Street, London Ontario N5W 4R3 Canada. **DD** 350.000257133.

DIRECTORY OF PUBLIC REFRIGERATED WAREHOUSES. **VFOAT** Public Refrigerated Warehouses. Began publication in 1973. 0070-6167. US. English. an. International Association of Refrigerated Warehouses, 7315 Wisconsin Avenue, Washington DC 20014.

DIRECTORY OF PUBLIC SCHOOLS, APPROVED PRIVATE AND SPECIAL SCHOOLS. **Main/Corp** Tennessee. Dept. of Education. **VFOAT** Directory of Tennessee Public Schools. 0149-2527. US. English. **LC** L903.T2. **DD** 321.21025768.

DIRECTORY OF PUBLISHED PROCEEDINGS CEASED. **VFOAT** Interdok Directory of Published Proceedings. V.1-3, No. 4, Sept. 1965-Dec. 1967. Periodical. US. English. mo. (cum index).

DIRECTORY OF PUBLISHED PROCEEDINGS. SERIES PCE - POLLUTION CONTROL - ECOLOGY. (DIRECTORY OF PUBLISHED PROCEEDINGS. SERIES PCE : POLLUTION CONTROL/ECOLOGY). V. 1- March 1974-. 0093-5816. Periodical. US. English. sa. $100.00. Interdok Corp, PO Box 326, Harrison NY 10528. **Tel** (914)835-3506. **Ed** Rose Besada and Carol Hoffman. **LC** Z7916. **DD** 016.30131. **NLM** W 3.5 D597. (ctrl). Index to conference proceedings in pollution control and ecology on a world-wide basis.

DIRECTORY OF PUBLISHED PROCEEDINGS. SERIES SEMT-SCIENCE-ENGINEERING-MEDICINE-TECHNOLOGY. (DIRECTORY OF PUBLISHED PROCEEDINGS. SERIES SEMT : SCIENCE/ENGINEERING/MEDICINE/TECHNOLOGY). V. 3- Sept. 1967-. 0012-3293. US. English. mo. Interdok Corporation, PO Box 326, Harrison NY 10528. **Tel** (914)835-3506. **Ind/Abst** Mintec, Min. Technol. Abstr., Minproc. **LC** Z7409. **DD** 016.5. **NLM** W 3.5 D598. (cum index). *Directory of Published Proceedings.*

DIRECTORY OF PUBLISHED PROCEEDINGS. SERIES S.S.H.-SOCIAL SCIENCES-HUMANITIES. (DIRECTORY OF PUBLISHED PROCEEDINGS. SERIES SSH : SOCIAL SCIENCES/HUMANITIES). V. 1/4- 1968/71-. 0012-3307. US. English. qt. Interdok

Yearbooks, Almanacs, Directories

Corporation, PO Box 326, Harrison NY 10528. **Tel** (914)835-3506. **LC** Z7161. **DD** 300.25. **NLM** W 3.5 D599. *Directory of Published Proceedings.*

DIRECTORY OF PUBLISHING OPPORTUNITIES IN JOURNALS AND PERIODICALS. 4th Ed. (1979)-. 0275-3820. US. English. bm. Marquis Whos Who Inc, 200 East Ohio Street, Chicago IL 60611. **Tel** (800)621-9669. **LC** Z6944.S3, PN4836. **DD** 070.5025. Details thousands of publishing opportunities for the scholarly specialized writer. *Directory of Publishing Opportunities, 0733-0871.*

DIRECTORY OF QUARRIES AND PITS. UK. English. Quarry Managers Journal Ltd, 62-64 Baker Street, WIM 2BN London England. **LC** TN12. **DD** 338.27502542. *Directory or Quarries, Clayworks, Sand and Gravel Pits, etc.*

DIRECTORY OF REAL ESTATE AND BUSINESS CHANCE BROKERS AND SALESMEN. 0093-9439. US. English. PO Box 44095 Capitol Station, Baton Rouge LA 70804. **LC** HD266.L8. **DD** 333.33. *Roster of Real Estate and Business Chance Brokers and Salesmen.*

THE DIRECTORY OF REAL ESTATE INVESTORS. 1982-. 0277-9986. US. English. an. $121.00. Whole World Publishing Inc, 400 Lake Cook Road/Suite 207, Deerfield IL 60015. **Tel** (312)945-8050. **LC** HD1382.5. **DD** 332.632402573.

DIRECTORY OF RECOGNIZED LOCAL GOVERNMENTS. 0145-3602. US. English. 1140 Connecticut Avenue, Washington DC 20036. **LC** JS323. **DD** 352.0002573.

DIRECTORY OF REGIONAL SOCIAL WELFARE ACTIVITIES. Main/Corp United Nations. Economic Commission for Africa. Social Development Section. 1964-. English. ir. United Nations Economic Commission for Africa, PO Box 3001, Addis Ababa Ethopia. **LC** JX1977. **DD** 361.06.

DIRECTORY OF REGISTERED ARCHITECTS, PROFESSIONAL ENGINEERS, LAND SURVEYORS, AND ARCHITECTURAL, ENGINEERING AND LAND SURVEYING CORPORATIONS. US. English. an. Missouri Board of Architects, Professional Engineers and Land Surveyors, PO Box 184, Jefferson City MO 65101. **LC** TA12. **DD** 624.025778.

DIRECTORY OF REGISTERED FACTORIES IN THE PUNJAB. June 1975-. English. ir. Bureau of Statistics, Government of the Punjab, 2 Begum Road, Lahore Pakistan. **LC** HD9736.P143. **DD** 338.402554914.

DIRECTORY OF REGISTERED LICENSEES, BOARD OF MEDICAL EXAMINERS OF THE STATE OF OREGON. Main/Corp Board of Medical Examiners of the State of Oregon. US. English. an. **LC** R712.A2. **DD** 610.25795. *Directory of Board of Medical Examiners of the State of Oregon.*

DIRECTORY OF REGISTERED LICENTIATES IN NORTH DAKOTA. US. English. an. North Dakota State Board of Medical Examiners, 418 East Rosser Avenue, Bismark ND 58501. **LC** R712.A2. **DD** 610.6952025784.

DIRECTORY OF REGISTERED PATENT ATTORNEYS AND AGENTS. Main/Corp United States Patent Office. 0565-9582. US. English. ir. Pergamon International Information Corp, 1340 Old Chain Bridge Road, McLean VA 22101. **Tel** (703)442-0900. *Patent Attorneys and Agents Available to Represent Inventions Before the United States Patent Office.*

DIRECTORY OF REGISTERED PHARMACISTS AND PHARMACIES. US. English. Informative Data Co, 3546 Watson Road, St Louis MO 63139.

DIRECTORY OF REGISTERED PRIVATE VOCATIONAL SCHOOLS. *CEASED.* 1974-1982. 0318-8221. Periodical. CN. English. an. *Directory of Registered Private Trade Schools.*

DIRECTORY OF REGISTERED PROFESSIONAL ARCHITECTS, ENGINEERS AND LAND SURVEYORS. (DIRECTORY OF REGISTERED PROFESSIONAL ARCHITECTS, ENGINEERS, AND LAND SURVEYORS). 0732-782X. VI. English. ir. Virgin Islands Board for Architects, Engineers and Land Surveyors, PO Box 476, St Thomas Virgin Islands 00801. **LC** NA54.V57. **DD** 620.0025729722.

DIRECTORY OF REGISTERED PROFESSIONAL NURSES AND LICENSED PRACTICAL NURSES. VFOAT Directory, Registered Professional Nurses and Licensed Practical Nurses. Began with Vol. for 1977. 0275-9705. US. English. an. Informative Data Co, 3546 Watson Road, St Louis MO 63139. **LC** RT25.U5. **DD** 610.73025778.

DIRECTORY OF REGISTRATION FOR ARCHITECTS, ENGINEERS AND LAND SURVEYORS. Main/Corp Alaska. State Board of Registration for Architects, Engineers and Land Surveyors. Periodical. US. English. Department of Commerce and Economic Development, Architects Engineers & Land Surveyors Occupational Licensing, Pouch Y, Juneau AK 99811. **LC** TA12. **DD** 620.0025798. *Directory of Architects, Engineers, and Land Surveyors (Juneau), 0094-1786.*

A DIRECTORY OF REGULARLY SCHEDULED, FIXED ROUTE, LOCAL PUBLIC TRANSPORTATION SERVICE IN URBANIZED AREAS OVER 50,000 POPULATION. UMTA Technical Notice 2-80 (August, 1980)-. Periodical. English. an.

DIRECTORY OF REGULATED LOAN COMPANIES, PAWNBROKERS, INSURANCE PREMIUM FINANCE COMPANIES. 1973-75. 0145-3521. US. English. an. Consumer Credit Commissioner, 1011 San Jacinto Boulevard, Post Office Box 2107, Austin TX 78767. **LC** HG3729.U6. **DD** 332.7025764. *Directory of Regulated Lenders and Pawnbrokers, 0145-2266.*

DIRECTORY OF RELIGIOUS BROADCASTING (MORRISTOWN, N. J. : 1982). (THE DIRECTORY OF RELIGIOUS BROADCASTING). 1982-83 Ed.-. 0731-0331. US. English. an. National Religious Broadcaster, CN 1926, Morristown NJ 07960. **Tel** (201)428-5400. **Ed** Ben Armstrong. **LC** BV655. **DD** 384.545302573. bk rev. adv acc. **Circ** 2,500. The most comprehensive listing of religious broadcasters and related services. Radio, TV stations, program producers, suppliers of equipment, consultants, representatives, agencies, and many more. *Annual Directory of Religious Broadcasting, 0160-029X.*

DIRECTORY OF RESEARCH FUNDING SOURCES FOR WOMEN. VFOAT Repertoire des Sources de Financement de la Recherche a la Portee des Femmes. 2nd Ed.-. 0824-0361. CN. English (French). an. 3.00. Canadian Research Institute for the Advancement of Women, Suite 408/151 Slater Street, Ottawa Ontario K1P 5H3 Canada. **Tel** (613)563-0681. **DD** 001.4402571. **Circ** 300. A directory listing sources of funding for women researchers. *Canadian Directory of Funding Sources for Research for Women, 0820-7585.*

DIRECTORY OF RESEARCH GRANTS. VFOAT DRG. Began with 1975. 0146-7336. US. English. an. ORYX Press, 3930 East Camelback Road, Phoenix AZ 85018. **Ed** W K Wilson and B L Wilson. **LC** LB2338. **DD** 001.4402573. **NLM** LB 2338 D5986.

DIRECTORY OF RESEARCH INSTITUTES & INDUSTRIAL LABORATORIES IN ISRAEL. VFOAT Directory of Research Institutes and Industrial Laboratories in Israel. 3rd Ed.-. 0334-3197. English (Hebrew). ir. $35.00. National Centre of Scientific Technology Information, PO Box 20125, Tel Aviv Israel 61200. **LC** AS591.A7. **DD** 001.40255694. *Madrikh La-Agudot Veli-Mekhonim Madaiyim Ve-Tekhniyim Be-Yisrael.*

DIRECTORY OF RESEARCH INSTITUTIONS IN THAILAND. TH. English. ir. National Research Council of Thailand, 196 Phahon Yothin Road, Bangkok Thailand. **LC** Q180.T5. **DD** 300.720593.

DIRECTORY OF RESEARCH PERSONNEL. Main/Corp Universitat Ben-Guryon Ba-Negev. English. ir. Research and Development Authority, Universitat Ben-Guryon Ba-Negu, PO Box 1025, Beer-Sheva Israel. **LC** Z5055.I754, LG341.B4. **DD** 016.3785694.

DIRECTORY OF RESEARCH SERVICES PROVIDED BY MEMBERS OF THE MARKETING RESEARCH ASSOCIATION *CEASED.* **Main/Corp** Marketing Research Association (U.S.). **VFOAT** MRA Research Service Directory. -1980-1981 Ed. 0147-8036. US. English. $25.00. MRA Research Service Directory, c/o Callahan Research Associates Inc, 31 East 28th Street, New York NY 10016. **LC** HF5415.2. **DD** 658.8302573.

A DIRECTORY OF RESEARCH WHICH IS BEING CONDUCTED BY KENYATTA UNIVERSITY COLLEGE STAFF. Main/Corp Kenyatta University College. 1974/75-. English. ir. Nairobi Library, PO Box 43844, Nairobi Kenya. **LC** LG418.N25. **DD** 378.6762.

DIRECTORY OF RESIDENCY TRAINING PROGRAMS ACCREDITED BY THE ACCREDITATION COUNCIL FOR GRADUATE MEDICAL EDUCATION. VFOAT Green Book. 1981/82-. 0164-1670. US. English. an. Order Department OP-123, American Medical Association, PO Box 821, Monroe WI 53566. *Directory of Residency Training Programs Accredited by the Liaison Committee on Graduate Medical Education, 0165-1670.*

DIRECTORY OF RESIDENCY TRAINING PROGRAMS ACCREDITED BY THE LIAISON COMMITTEE ON GRADUATE MEDICAL EDUCATION. VFOAT Green Book. 1978/79-. 0164-1670. US. English. an. American Medical Association, 535 North Dearborn Street, Chicago IL 60610. **Tel** (312)645-4927. **LC** R840. **DD** 610.71173. *Directory of Accredited Residencies, 0147-2291.*

DIRECTORY OF RESIDENTIAL PROGRAMS FOR COURT-INVOLVED YOUTH. US. English. an. Committee on Criminal Justice, 110 Tremont Street/4th Floor, Boston MA 02108. **LC** HV9105.M4. **DD** 365.42025744.

DIRECTORY OF RESOURCE ORGANIZATIONS AND MEDIA SERVING MINORITY COMMUNITIES IN CONNECTICUT. 0362-9562. US. English. Connecticut Commission on Human Rights and Opportunities, 90 Washington Street, Hartford CT 06115. **LC** HD8083.C7. **DD** 362.84025746.

DIRECTORY OF RESOURCES FOR OLDER PEOPLE IN NEW HAMPSHIRE. 1st- Ed. 0094-1441. US. English. New Hampshire State Council on Aging, 71 South Main Street/PO Box 786, Concord NH 03301. **LC** HV1468.N4. **DD** 362.6025742.

DIRECTORY OF RESOURCES FOR SENIOR CITIZENS OF OTTAWA-CARLETON. VFOAT Repertoire des Services pour Personnes Agees d'Ottawa-Carleton. 0824-5398. CN. English (French text on inverted pages). be. Ottawa Senior Citizens Council, Room 16/53 Queen Street, Ottawa Ontario K1P 5C5 Canada. **DD** 362.602571383.

DIRECTORY OF RESTAURANT AND FAST FOOD CHAINS IN CANADA. VFOAT Restaurant and Fast Food Chains in Canada. 1980-. 0227-4302. CN. English. an. $49.00 Per Vol. Directory of Restaurants and Fast Food Chains, c/o Monday Report on Retailers, 481 University Avenue, Toronto Ontario M5W 1A7 Canada. **DD** 642.50971.

DIRECTORY OF RETAIL CHAINS IN CANADA. VAT Monday Report on Retailers. Directory Retail Chains in Canada. Began publication in 1976. 0225-9443. CN. English. an. $195.00. Directory Retail Chains in Canada, 777 Bay Street 5th Floor, Toronto Ontario M5W 1A7 Canada. **Tel** (416)596-5939. **Ed** Jaimie Hubbard. **DD** 381.1202571. A listing of retail chains including their head office address, management, number of stores, expansion plans, and the type of retailer they are.

DIRECTORY OF RETAILER OWNED COOPERATIVES, WHOLESALER SPONSORED VOLUNTARIES, WHOLESALE GROCERS, SERVICE MERCHANDISERS. 1981-. 0277-1969. US. an. $169.00. Chain Store Guide, Lebhar-Friedman, Attn Priscilla G Jimenez, 425 Park Avenue, New York NY 10022. **Tel** (212)371-9400. **Ed** Jim Smethurst. **LC** HD9321.3. **DD** 381.456413002573. Provides complete company profiles on 1,400 headquarters and divisions for 100 co-ops, 200 voluntary groups, 400 wholesale grocers, 400 cash-and-carry warehouse operations, and 350 service merchandisers. *Directory of Retailer Owned Cooperative Chains, Wholesaler Sponsored Voluntary Chains, Wholesale Grocers, 0271-8006.*

DIRECTORY OF RETIRED MEMBERS - AMERICAN FOREIGN SERVICE ASSOCIATION. Main/Corp American Foreign Service Association. 0093-7444. US. English. American Foreign Service Association, 2101 E Street

Yearbooks, Almanacs, Directories

Northwest, Washington DC 20037. **LC** JX1628. **DD** 327.202573.

DIRECTORY OF RURAL HEALTH CARE PROGRAMS. 1979-. 0270-9953. US. English. **NLM** WA 22 AA1 D65.

DIRECTORY OF SAN FRANCISCO ATTORNEYS. 0092-9174. US. English. $35.00. Bar Association of San Francisco, 483 Mills Building 230 Montgomery Street, San Francisco CA 94104. **Tel** (415)392-3960. **LC** KF193.S25. **DD** 340.02579461. adv acc. **Circ** 7,500. The directory includes the addresses and telephone numbers for over 11,000 attorneys as well as those of all ASF law firm, Bay area courts, and legal associations in San Francisco.

DIRECTORY OF SASKATCHEWAN LIBRARIES. 0228-7617. CN. English. Saskatchewan Provincial Library, 1325 Winnepeg Street, Regina Saskatchewan S4P 3V7 Canada. **LC** Z735.S27. **DD** 027.00257124.

DIRECTORY OF SCHOOLS AND ESTABLISHMENTS APPROVED FOR VETERANS TRAINING. VFOAT Directory of West Virginia Educational and Training Programs Approved for Veterans' Educational Benefits. 0146-2431. US. English. Stanley Building/Suite 214, Charleston WV 25301. **LC** UB358.W4. **DD** 355.115209754.

DIRECTORY OF SCHOOLS OFFERING LIBRARY SCIENCE. English. ir. Philippine Association of Teachers of Library Science, Room 301/The National Library Building, T M Kalaw Street, Manila 2801 Philippines. **LC** Z669.5.P45. **DD** 020.711599.

DIRECTORY OF SCIENTIFIC & TECHNICAL ASSOCIATIONS IN ISRAEL. 3d- Ed. 0334-2824. IS. English (Hebrew). ir. National Center for Scientific Technical Information, PO Box 20125, Tel Aviv 61200 Israel. *Madrikh La-Agudot Veli-Mekhonim Madaiyim Ve-Tekhniyim Be-Yisrael.*

DIRECTORY OF SCIENTIFIC AND TECHNICAL PERIODICALS PUBLISHED IN SOUTH AFRICA CEASED. VFOAT Gids van Wetenskaplike en Tegniese Tydskrifte in Suid-Afrika Uitgegee. 1971-. SA. English (Afrikaans). be. CSIR-Publishing Division, PO Box 395, Pretoria 0001 South Africa. **Tel** 86-9211. **LC** Z7403. **DD** 016.505. *Scientific and Technical Periodicals Published in South Africa.*

DIRECTORY OF SCIENTIFIC AND TECHNICAL PERSONNEL OF SRI LANKA. English. ir. National Science Council of Ceylon, 47/5 Maitland Place, Colombo 7 Ceylon (Sri Lanka). **LC** Q149.S75. **DD** 502.55493.

DIRECTORY OF SCIENTIFIC & TECHNICAL RESEARCH CENTRES IN MALAYSIA. VAT Directory of Scientific and Technical Research Centres in Malaysia. 1977-. 0126-5776. English. ir. $5.00. **LC** T177.M3. **DD** 607.2595. Each issue contains an index to its own contents - no vol index - loose.

DIRECTORY OF SCIENTIFIC AND TECHNICAL SOCIETIES IN SOUTH AFRICA. VFOAT Gids van Wetenskaplike en Tegniese Verenigings in Suid-Afrika. 1971-. SA. English (Afrikaans). be. South African Council of Scientific and Industrial Organizations, PO Box 395, Pretoria 0001 South Africa. **Tel** 27 12 86-9211. Ed Marian de Wind. **LC** Q85. **DD** 506.268. **Circ** 800. Comprehensive listing of societies in South Africa active in the field of science or technology, stating office bearers, objectives, conditions for membership, publications, etc. *Scientific and Technical Societies in South Africa.*

THE DIRECTORY OF SCIENTIFIC RESEARCH INSTITUTIONS IN INDIA. 1969-. 0419-3482. II. English. ir. Indian National Scientific Documentation Centre, 14 Satsang Vihar Marg, New Delhi 110067 India. **LC** Q183.43.I5. **DD** 507.20954.

DIRECTORY OF SCIENTIFIC RESEARCH INSTITUTIONS IN THE CENTO REGION. Main/Corp Central Treaty Organization. VAT Directory of Scientific Research Institutions in the Central Treaty Organization Region. 1976-. IR. English. ir. Free. Central Treaty Organization, PO Box 1828, Tehran Iran. **LC** Q180.A74. **DD** 507.205.

DIRECTORY OF SCIENTIFIC RESEARCH ORGANIZATIONS IN SOUTH AFRICA. VFOAT Gids van Wetenskaplike Navorsingsorganisasies in Suid-Afrika. 1971-. 0584-2921. SA. English (Afrikaans). be. CSIR Publishing Division, PO Box 395, Pretoria 0001 South Africa. **Tel** 27 12 86-9211. Ed Marian De Wind. **LC** Q180.A55. **DD** 507.2068. **Circ** 800. Listings of organized research undertaken in South Africa indicating research body, its executive, address, type of research undertaken, special facilities used, library, publications, affiliations. *Scientific Research Organizations in South Africa.*

DIRECTORY OF SCIENTIFIC RESOURCES IN GEORGIA. 1st- Ed. 0417-6480. US. English. ir. Georgia Institute of Technology, 225 North Avenue SW, Atlanta GA 30322. **LC** T176. **DD** 607.2758.

DIRECTORY OF SCOTTISH SPORTS. UK. English. **LC** GV605.2. **DD** 796.06025411.

DIRECTORY OF SECONDARY SCHOOLS AND TERTIARY INSTITUTIONS. English. an. Department of Education/Head Office, Private Bag, Wellington New Zealand. **LC** L985. **DD** 370.25931.

DIRECTORY OF SECURITY ANALYST SOCIETIES, ANALYST SPLINTER GROUPS, STOCKBROKER CLUBS. 0160-404X. US. English. an. Burson-Marsteller, 866 Third Avenue, New York NY 10022. **LC** HG4621. **DD** 332.6706273.

DIRECTORY OF SENIOR CENTERS AND CLUBS. 0098-2709. US. English. National Council on the Aging, 1828 L Street Northwest, Washington DC 20036. **LC** HQ1060. **DD** 362.6302573. *National Directory of Senior Centers.*

DIRECTORY OF SERVICES, ARKANSAS MENTAL HEALTH SERVICES. VFOAT Mental Health Services in Arkansas, Directory. US. English. an. Mental Health Services, 4313 West Markham Street, Little Rock AR 72201. **LC** RA790.65.A8. **DD** 362.2025767. Index in last issue of volume - loose - separately paged.

DIRECTORY OF SERVICES FOR GREATER VANCOUVER. Began publication with 1974 issue?. 0319-0242. Periodical. CN. English. an. $30.00. Info Services Vancouver, Suite 105/1956 West Broadway, Vancouver British Columbia V6J 1Z2 Canada. **Tel** (604)736-3661. Ed Cynthia Crampton. **DD** 361.002571133. **Circ** 2,500. Contact information and service descriptions for 1,600 government and private non-profit, human and community services in the metropolitan Vancouver area. *Directory of Services: Health, Welfare, Recreation in the Lower Mainland, 0319-0250.*

DIRECTORY OF SERVICES FOR MIGRANT FAMILIES. VFOAT Directorio de Servicios Para Familias Migrantes. 1975-. 0362-7179. US. English AND Spanish. Illinois Office of Education, 100 East Edwards Street, Springfield IL 62704. **LC** HV98.I15. **DD** 362.85.

DIRECTORY OF SERVICES FOR THE CITY OF TORONTO. (A DIRECTORY OF SERVICES FOR THE CITY OF TORONTO). Mar. 1982-. 0714-8542. CN. English. an. Free. Department of the City Clerk, City Hall, Toronto Ontario M5H 2N2 Canada. **DD** 352.0713541. (ctrl). *Municipal Handbook, 0316-9006.*

DIRECTORY OF SERVICES. PORT OF SAINT JOHN, NEW BRUNSWICK. (DIRECTORY OF SERVICES, PORT OF SAINT JOHN, NEW BRUNSWICK). 15th- Ed. 0225-4646. Periodical. CN. English. Saint John Port Development Commission, PO Box 1971, Saint John New Brunswick E2L 4L1 Canada. **DD** 387.10971532. *Port Directory, Saint John, New Brunswick, Canada, 0225-4646.*

DIRECTORY OF SERVICES - TEXAS DEPARTMENT OF MENTAL HEALTH AND MENTAL RETARDATION. 0164-0550. Periodical. US. English. **NLM** WM 22 AT4 D5. *Directory of Mental Health and Mental Retardation Services for Texas.*

DIRECTORY OF SHARED SERVICES ORGANIZATIONS AND CONSORTIA OF HEALTH CARE INSTITUTIONS. 1984 Ed.-. 8756-8659. US. English. American Hospital Publishing Inc, 211 East Chicago Avenue, Chicago IL 60611. **LC** RA977. **DD** 362.1102573. **NLM** WX 22. *Directory of Shared Services Organizations for Health Care Institutions, 0733-091X.*

DIRECTORY OF SHIPOWNERS, SHIPBUILDERS, & MARINE ENGINEERS. UK. English. an. $38.31. Business Press International Ltd, Perrymount Road/Haywards Heath, W Sussex RH163AR England. **LC** HE565.A3.

DIRECTORY OF SHOPPING CENTERS IN THE UNITED STATES. VFOAT Shopping Center Directory. V. 18-. US. English. an. National Research Bureau, 424 North 3rd Avenue, Chicago IL 62220. **LC** HF5035. **DD** 381.02573. *Directory of Shopping Centers in the United States and Canada, 0419-3512.*

DIRECTORY OF SMALL MAGAZINE-PRESS EDITORS AND PUBLISHERS CEASED. (DIRECTORY OF SMALL MAGAZINE PRESS EDITORS AND PUBLISHERS). VFOAT Directory: Small Press Editors. Began in 1970. 0095-6414. US. English. an. $14.95. Dustbooks, Box 100, Paradise CA 95969. **Tel** (916)877-6110. Ed Len Fulton. **LC** PN4820. **DD** 070.4025. **Circ** 500. The companion volume to the International Directory of Little Magazines and Small Presses.

THE DIRECTORY OF SMALL PRESS & MAGAZINE EDITORS & PUBLISHERS. VFOAT Directory of Small Press and Magazine Editors and Publishers. 11th Ed. (1980-81)-. 0277-1519. US. English. an. $22.00. Dustbooks, PO Box 100, Paradise CA 95969. **Tel** (916)877-5435. Ed Len Fulton. **LC** PN4820. **DD** 070.41025. bk rev. adv acc. **Circ** 2,500. (ctrl). A running document containing news, reviews, features and updates on the listing in the International Directory. *Directory of Small Magazine Press Editors and Publishers, 0095-6414.*

DIRECTORY OF SMALL SCALE INDUSTRIAL UNITS EMPLOYING FIVE OR MORE PERSONS IN THE UNORGANISED SECTOR IN HARYANA. 0376-8570. II. English. ir. Economic and Statistical Organization, Government of Haryan, Chandigarn India. **LC** HD2346.I52. **DD** 338.64202554558.

DIRECTORY OF SOCIAL SERVICE ADMINISTRATORS OF LOCAL MUNICIPALITIES. Began publication in 1976?. 0226-0905. Periodical. CN. English. an. Ontario Ministry of Community & Social Services, 12th Floor 700 Bay Street, Toronto Ontario M7A 1E9 Canada. **DD** 352.944025713.

DIRECTORY OF SOCIAL SERVICES. OTTAWA-CARLETON. (DIRECTORY OF SOCIAL SERVICES, OTTAWA-CARLETON). VFOAT Repertoire des Oeuvres, Ottawa-Carleton. First issue in 1971. 0318-9686. Periodical. CN. French (text in English). an. Centre d'Information Communautaire, 377 rue Rideau, Ottawa Ontario K1N 5Y6 Canada. **DD** 361.002571383. *Directory of Social Services.*

DIRECTORY OF SOCIAL WELFARE ACTIVITIES IN AFRICA. English. ir. Association for Social Work Education in Africa, PO Box 1176, Addis Abeba Ethiopia. **LC** HV438.A2. **DD** 362.0256.

DIRECTORY OF SOLAR ENERGY RESEARCH ACTIVITIES IN THE UNITED STATES. 1st- Ed. 0273-1525. US. English. an. Solar Energy Research Institute, Academic and University Programs Branch, 5285 Port Royal Road, Springfield VA 22161. **LC** TJ810. **DD** 621.47072073.

DIRECTORY OF SOUTH CAROLINA PORT SERVICES. VFOAT Directory of Services. 0732-5975. US. English. South Carolina State Ports Authority, 176 Concord Street, PO Box 817, Charleston SC 29402. **LC** HE553. **DD** 387.16025757.

DIRECTORY OF SOUTH CAROLINA SCHOOLS. 1977/78-. 0190-6283. US. English. an. $2.00 Each. Education Products Center, 1209 Rutledge Building, 1429 Senate Street, Columbia SC 29201. **LC** L903.S6. **DD** 370.25757. *South Carolina School Directory, 0363-9495.*

DIRECTORY OF SOUTH DAKOTA REGISTERED NURSES AND LICENSED PRACTICAL NURSES. US. English. South Dakota State Board of Nursing, 301 Western Building, Mitchell SD 57301. **LC** RT5.S8. **DD** 610.73025783. **NLM** WY 22 AS8 D5.

DIRECTORY OF SOUTHERN BAPTIST CHURCHES. 0740-9915. US. English. Sunday School Board, 127 Ninth Avenue North, Nashville TN 37234. **LC** BX6462. **DD** 286.13202573.

DIRECTORY OF SOVIET OFFICIALS. -1980. 0734-810X. US. English. ir. **LC** JN6521. **DD** 354.47002. **NLM** JN 6521 D598.

DIRECTORY OF SOVIET OFFICIALS. NATIONAL ORGANIZATIONS. VFOAT National Organizations. May 1981-. 0742-2830. US. English. Document Expediting (DOCEX) Project,

Yearbooks, Almanacs, Directories

Exchange and Gift Division, Library of Congress, Washington DC 20540. **LC** JN6521. **DD** 354.47002. Vols. for Aug. 1983- distributed to depository libraries in microfiche. *Directory of Soviet Officials, 0734-810X.*

DIRECTORY OF SOVIET OFFICIALS. REPUBLIC ORGANIZATIONS. VFOAT Republic Organizations. Oct. 1981-. 0743-5371. US. English. DOCEX Project, Exchange and Gift Division, Library of Congress, Washington DC 20540. **LC** JN6521. **DD** 354.47002. *Directory of Soviet Officials, 0734-810X.*

DIRECTORY OF SOVIET OFFICIALS. SCIENCE AND EDUCATION. US. English. Document Expediting Project, Exchange and Gift Division, Library of Congress, Washington DC 20540. *Directory of Soviet Officials, 0734-810X.*

DIRECTORY OF SPECIAL LIBRARIES AND INFORMATION CENTERS. 1st Ed.-. 0731-633X. US. English. ir. $320.00. Gale Research Company, Book Tower, Detroit MI 48226. **Ed** Brigitte Darnay. **LC** Z731. **DD** 026.002573. Contains some 17,500 entries offering full descriptions of special libraries, information centers, and similar units. 850 entries are brand new.

DIRECTORY OF SPECIAL LIBRARIES AND INFORMATION CENTERS IN TEXAS. 1981-. 0082-3163. US. English. be.

DIRECTORY OF SPECIAL LIBRARIES IN AUSTRALIA. Main/Corp Library Association of Australia. Special Libraries Section. 1952-. Monographic Series. AT. English. ir. $33.20. Library Association of Australia, 376 Jones Street, Ultimo New South Wales 2007 Australia. **Tel** 02/6929233.

DIRECTORY OF SPECIAL LIBRARIES IN THE MONTREAL AREA. VFOAT Repertoire des Bibliotheques Specialisees de la Region de Montreal. 11th- Ed. 0319-2563. Periodical. CN. text in English and French. ir. Miss E MacLean, Blacker-Wood Library, McGill University, 3459 McTabish Street, Montreal Quebec H3A 1Y1 Canada. **DD** 026.0002571428. *Directory of Special Libraries in Montreal, 0070-6396.*

DIRECTORY OF SPECIAL LIBRARIES (SEMMON TOSHOKAN KYOGIKAI). (DIRECTORY OF SPECIAL LIBRARIES). 1969-. JA. English (Japanese). an. Maruzen Co Ltd, PO Box 5050, 100-31 Tokyo Japan. *Chosa Kikan Toshokan Soran.*

DIRECTORY OF SPECIAL PROGRAMS FOR MINORITY GROUP MEMBERS. (DIRECTORY OF SPECIAL PROGRAMS FOR MINORITY GROUP MEMBERS. CAREER INFORMATION SERVICES, EMPLOYMENT SKILLS BANKS, FINANCIAL AID SOURCES). 2nd-. 0093-9501. Periodical. US. English. ir. Garrett Park Press, Garrett Park MD 20896. **Tel** (301)946-2553. **Ed** Willis L Johnson. Directory of special programs for minority group members: career information, services, employment skills, banks, and financial aid sources. *Directory of Special Programs for Minority Group Members, 0093-9501.*

DIRECTORY OF SPECIAL PURPOSE FACILITIES FOR THE EDUCATION OF THE HANDICAPPED. 1978-1979-. 0731-289X. US. English. an. Office of Special Concerns, Office for Civil Rights US Department of Education, 400 Maryland Avenue NW, Washington DC 20202. **LC** L901. **DD** 371.90450973.

DIRECTORY OF SPECIFIC LEARNING DISABILITY SERVICES. 1973-. 0092-2455. US. English. an. $2.00. PO Box 6495, Savannah GA 31405. **LC** L901. **DD** 362.402573.

DIRECTORY OF SPOKEN-VOICE AUDIO-CASSETTES. 1972-. Monographic Series. US. English. an. **LC** ML157.32. **DD** 011.

DIRECTORY OF STAFF ASSISTANTS TO THE GOVERNORS. Main/Corp National Governors' Association. US. English. an. $3.00. National Governors Association, Center of Policy Research, 444 North Capitol Street, Washington DC 20001. *Directory of Staff Assistants to the Governors.*

A DIRECTORY OF STATE AGENCIES, COUNCILS OF GOVERNMENTS, UNIVERSITIES AND COLLEGES, TECHNICAL COLLEGES, AND ASSOCIATIONS. VFOAT Local Government Resources. 1981-. US. English. an. South Carolina Advisory Commission on Intergovernmental Relations, 1205 Pendelton Street/Room 474, Columbia SC 29201. **LC** JK4230. **DD** 353.975704025.

DIRECTORY OF STATE AND PROVINCIAL ARCHIVES. 1975-. 0361-5529. US. English. Society of American Archivist, 600 South Federal/Suite 504, Chicago IL 60605. **LC** CD3000. **DD** 027.502573.

DIRECTORY OF STATE CORPORATIONS. English. ir. 10.00. 380 Bauddhaloka Mawatha, Colombo 7. **LC** HD4285.8. **DD** 338.740255493.

DIRECTORY OF STATE, COUNTY AND FEDERAL OFFICIALS. (DIRECTORY OF STATE, COUNTY, AND FEDERAL OFFICIALS). 1973-. 0440-4947. US. English. an. 2.00. Legislative Reference Bureau, State Capitol, Honolulu HI 96813. **Tel** (808)548-7853. **LC** JK9330. **DD** 353.9969002. **Circ** 1,000. Names, titles, addresses, telephone numbers of officials in the state, county and federal governments in Hawaii. *Directory of State, County, Federal Officials.*

DIRECTORY OF STATE ENVIRONMENTAL AGENCIES. Began in 1977. 0733-6128. US. English. ir. $22.50. Environmental Law Institute, 1616 P Street Northwest/Suite 200, Washington DC 20036. **Ed** Kathryn Hubler and Timothy Henderson. **LC** HC110.E5. **DD** 353.9382321025. Gives you the fast, accurate information you need when searching for the right contact in environmental agencies in the states or US territories.

DIRECTORY OF STATE GOVERNMENT ENERGY-RELATED AGENCIES. 0361-3445. US. English. National Energy Information Center, Room 2109/12th & Pennsylvania Avenue NW, Washington DC 20461. **LC** HD9502.U5. **DD** 353.9382. *Catalogue of State Energy Organizations.*

DIRECTORY OF STATE PUBLICATIONS. V. 10- 1959-. 0093-3147. US. English. ir. Department of Property & Supplies, Bureau of Topographic Geology Survey, PO Box 2357, Harrisburg PA 17120. **LC** Z1223.5.P4. **DD** 015.748. *List of State Publications.*

DIRECTORY OF STATE, REGIONAL AND COMMERCIAL ORGANIZATIONS. 0098-5368. US. English. $7.00. Pennsylvania Chamber of Commerce, 222 North Third Street, Harrisburg PA 17101. **LC** HF295. **DD** 061.48.

DIRECTORY OF STATE, TERRITORIAL, AND REGIONAL HEALTH AUTHORITIES. 1968-. 0083-1190. US. English. $0.65. Superintendent of Documents, US Government Printing Office, Washington DC 20402. **LC** RA7.5. **DD** 362.1042506173. **NLM** WA 22 AA1 D8. *Directory of State and Territorial Health Authorities.*

DIRECTORY OF STATE-U.S.D.A. RURAL DEVELOPMENT COMMITTEES. (DIRECTORY OF STATE - USDA RURAL DEVELOPMENT COMMITTEES). 0091-7672. US. English. US Department of Agriculture, Washington DC 20250. **LC** HN90.C6. **DD** 309.26302573.

DIRECTORY OF STUDENTS - HARVARD UNIVERSITY. (DIRECTORY OF STUDENTS). Main/Corp Harvard University. 0145-6539. US. English. Harvard University, 79 Garden Street, Cambridge MA 02138. **LC** LD2125. **DD** 378.7444. *Directory of Faculty, Professional and Administrative Staff, and Students (Cambridge), 0090-2365.*

DIRECTORY OF SUBSPECIALTY FELLOWSHIP TRAINING PROGRAMS. 0192-8104. US. English. Association of Professors of Medicine, One Dupont Circle, Washington DC 20036. **LC** R840. **DD** 616.026079.

A DIRECTORY OF SUMMER CHAMBER MUSIC WORKSHOPS, SCHOOLS & FESTIVALS. Periodical. US. English. $3.00. Chamber Music America, 1372 Broadway, New York NY 10018.

THE DIRECTORY OF SUMMER JOBS IN BRITAIN. VFOAT Summer Jobs in Britain. 1970-. UK. English. an. 2.25. Writer's Digest Books, 9933 Alliance Road, Cincinnati OH 45242. **LC** HF5382.5.G7. **DD** 331.12.

DIRECTORY OF SUPERMARKET, GROCERY AND CONVENIENCE STORE CHAINS. (DIRECTORY OF SUPERMARKET, GROCERY & CONVENIENCE STORE CHAINS). VFOAT Chain Store Guide, Guide to the Supermarket and Grocery Chains, Supermarket and Grocery Chains, Supermarket. 1981-. 0196-1845. US. English. an. $179.00. Chain Store Guide, Lebhar-Friedman, Attn Priscilla G Jimenez, 425 Park Avenue, New York NY 10022. **Tel** (212)371-9400. **Ed** Jim Smithurst. **LC** HD9321.3. **DD** 381.45664002573. Provides company profiles on 3,700 or more store chains operating 75,000 units. *Directory of Supermarket, Grocery, and Convenience Store Chains, 0196-1845.*

DIRECTORY OF SURNAMES - ONTARIO GENEALOGICAL SOCIETY. (DIRECTORY OF SURNAMES). Main/Corp Ontario Genealogical Society. May 1982-. 0823-7891. CN. English. an. $3.00. Ontario Genealogical Society, Box 66 Station Q, Toronto Ontario M4T 2L7 Canada. **DD** 929.3713.

DIRECTORY OF SYSTEMS HOUSES AND COMPUTER OEM'S. -1982 Ed. 0733-4516. US. English. an. $397.00. Sentry Database Publishing, 5 Kane Industrial Drive, Heedson MA 01749. **Tel** (617)562-9308. **LC** HD9696.C63. **DD** 001.64029473. *Directory of Systems House & Minicomputer OEM's, 0194-1852.*

THE DIRECTORY OF TALENT & MODELING AGENCIES & SCHOOLS INTERNATIONAL. VFOAT Directory of Talent and Modeling Agencies and Schools International. 6th Ed. (1984)-. 0742-5570. US. English. Peter Glenn Publications, 17 East 48th Street, New York City NY 10017. *Directory of Modeling/Talent Agencies & Schools International.*

DIRECTORY OF TEACHERS OF LIBRARY SCIENCE IN THE PHILIPPINES. PH. English. ir. Philippine Association of Teachers of Library Science, National Library Building/Room 301/T M Kalaw Street, Manila 2801 Philippines. **LC** Z669.5.P58. **DD** 020.711599.

DIRECTORY OF TECHNICAL AND FURTHER EDUCATION. 17th Ed.- 1977-. 0309-5290. UK. English. ir. Nichols Publishing Company, PO Box 96, New York NY 10024. **Ed** Paul J Edmonds. *Year Book of Technical Education and Training for Industry.*

DIRECTORY OF TENNESSEE COUNTY OFFICIALS. Sept. 1974-. 0160-0273. US. English. an. 580 Capitol Hill Building, Seventh and Union, Nashville TN 37219. **LC** JS451.T35. **DD** 352.00520968. *Directory, Tennessee County Officials.*

DIRECTORY OF TENNESSEE MANUFACTURERS. 0070-6450. US. English. an. $75.00. 162 Fourth Avenue North, PO Box 2678, Nashville TN 37219. **Tel** (615)256-7808. **Ed** Mary Ellen Henry. adv acc. **Circ** 5,000. A complete and easy-to-use reference guide to over 5,000 manufacturers in Tennessee. *Tennessee Directory of Manufacturers, 0196-5360.*

DIRECTORY OF TENNESSEE MINING, OIL, AND GAS OPERATIONS. 0271-9665. US. English. **LC** TN12. **DD** 338.2025768. *Directory of Tennessee Mining and Oil and Gas Operations, 0271-9665.*

DIRECTORY OF TEXAS MANUFACTURERS. Began in 1932. US. English. ir. $110.00. Bureau of Business Research, University of Texas at Austin, Box 7459, Austin TX 78713. **Tel** (512)471-1616. **Ed** Ida Lambeth. **LC** HD9727.T4. **DD** 338.4767025764. **Circ** 5,000. Directory of manufacturers including chief officers, products, sales figures, addresses and phone numbers. Also indicates type of company and width of goods distribution.

THE DIRECTORY OF TEXTILE PLANT PROCESSES. 1969/70-. US. English. $65.00. Textile World, 330 West 42nd Street, New York NY 10036. **LC** HD9853. **DD** 338.47677002573.

DIRECTORY OF THE AGRICULTURAL RESEARCH SERVICE. Main/Corp United States. Agricultural Research Service. 0196-3511. US. English. US Department of Agriculture, Washington DC 20250. **LC** S21. **DD** 630.72073.

DIRECTORY OF THE AMERICAN BAPTIST CHURCHES IN THE U.S.A. Main/Corp American Baptist Churches in the U.S.A. VAT Directory of the American Baptist Churches in

Yearbooks, Almanacs, Directories

the United States of America. 1973-. 0091-9381. US. English. an. American Baptist Churches USA, Office of General Secretary, Valley Forge PA 19481. **LC** BX6207. **DD** 286.13102573.

DIRECTORY OF THE AMERICAN LEFT. 0733-9623. US. English. an. Editorial Research Service, PO Box 1832, Kansas City MO 64141. Ed L M Wilcox.

DIRECTORY OF THE AMERICAN OPTOMETRIC ASSOCIATION. Main/Corp American Optometric Association. 1st- Ed. 0091-4258. US. English. **LC** RE940. **DD** 617.7506273. **NLM** WW 22 AA1 A7D.

DIRECTORY OF THE AMERICAN PSYCHOLOGICAL ASSOCIATION. Main/Corp American Psychological Association. 1981-. US. English. ir. American Psychological Association, 1200-17th Street NW, Washington DC 20036. **Tel** (703)247-7705. adv acc. **Circ** 10,000. Lists names and addresses of American Psychological Association (APA) members, home and office phone number, current major field, areas of specialization, licensure as a psychologists, ABPP and ABPH diplomate status.

DIRECTORY OF THE AMERICAN RIGHT. 0163-7541. Periodical. US. English. an. Editorial Research Service, PO Box 1832, Kansas City MO 64141. Ed Laird M Wilcox.

DIRECTORY OF THE AMERICAN SOCIETY OF PLANT PHYSIOLOGISTS. Main/Corp American Society of Plant Physiologists. 0271-9789. US. English. 9650 Rockville Pike, Bethesda MD 20014. **LC** QK710. **DD** 581.106073.

DIRECTORY OF THE AMERICAN THEATRE ASSOCIATION, INC CEASED. (DIRECTORY - AMERICAN THEATRE ASSOCIATION). Main/Corp American Theatre Association. **VAT** Directory of the American Theatre Association, Incorporated. 1972-80. 0145-3955. US. English. an. $6.00. American Theater Association Inc, 1029 Vermont Avenue NW, Washington DC 20005. **LC** PN2289. **DD** 792.0973. Directory of Members.

DIRECTORY OF THE ASSOCIATION OF AMERICAN GEOGRAPHERS. Main/Corp Association of American Geographers. 1967-. 0571-5962. US. English. ir. Association of American Geographers, 1710-16th Street NW, Washington DC 20009. **Tel** (202)234-1450. **LC** G64. **DD** 910.6073. adv acc. **Circ** 5,600. Listing of members of the Association of American Geographers. Handbook-Directory.

DIRECTORY OF THE ASSOCIATION OF PROFESSIONAL ENGINEERS OF THE PROVINCE OF BRITISH COLUMBIA. Main/Corp Association of Professional Engineers of the Province of British Columbia. 1959-. 0316-490X. Periodical. CN. English. an. Association of Professional Engineers of the Province of British Columbia, 2210 West 12th Avenue, Vancouver British Columbia V6K 2N6 Canada. **DD** 620.0062711. Yearbook of the Engineering Profession in British Columbia, 0316-4918.

DIRECTORY OF THE BUSINESS RESEARCH ADVISORY COUNCIL TO THE BUREAU OF LABOR STATISTICS. Main/Corp United States. Bureau of Labor Statistics. Business Research Advisory Council. US. English. an. U S Department of Labor, Bureau of Labor Statistics, Washington DC 20212. **LC** HD8051. **DD** 330.02573.

DIRECTORY OF THE CANADIAN ASSOCIATION OF UNIVERSITY SCHOOLS OF MUSIC. Main/Corp Canadian Association of University Schools of Music. **VFOAT** Annuaire de l'Association Canadienne des Ecoles Universitaires de Musique. 1974/75-. 0317-2155. Periodical. CN. English and French. Free. Mr B Ellard/Dep de Musique, Ottawa Ontario K1S 5B6 Canada. **DD** 780.72971.

DIRECTORY OF THE CANADIAN BOTANICAL ASSOCIATION & CANADIAN SOCIETY OF PLANT PHYSIOLOGISTS. Main/Corp Canadian Botanical Association. 1984-. 0824-1996. Periodical. CN. English. be. Free to Members. S Taylor, c/o Office of the Botanical Garden, University of British Columbia, 6501 North West Marine Drive, Vancouver British Columbia V6T 1W5 Canada. **DD** 580.2571.

THE DIRECTORY OF THE CANNING, FREEZING, PRESERVING INDUSTRIES. 1st- Ed. 0419-3717. US. English. be. Directory of Canning Freezing, PO Box 550, Westminster MD 21157. **Tel** (301)876-7150. **LC** TX600. **DD** 338.47664.

DIRECTORY OF THE CARIBBEAN FREE TRADE ASSOCIATION. Main/Corp Caribbean Free Trade Association. 1973/74-. TR. English. an. $7.00. International Publications Ltd, Fernandes Industrial Centre, Eastern Main Road, Laventille Trinidad. **LC** HF3311. **DD** 372.025729.

DIRECTORY OF THE COLLEGE STUDENT PRESS IN AMERICA. 1967/68-. 0085-0020. US. English. ir. $40.00. Oxbridge Communications Inc, 150 5th Avenue/Suite 301, New York NY 10011. **Tel** (212)741-0231. Ed Margie Domenech. **LC** Z6944.S8, LB3621. **DD** 378.1989702573. Listing of colleges in the US.

DIRECTORY OF THE COMMISSION OF THE EUROPEAN COMMUNITIES. Main/Corp Commission of the European Communities. 0591-1745. BE. English. ty. European Communities Commission, Case Postale 1003, Luxembourg Luxembourg. **DD** 341.11.

DIRECTORY OF THE DIPLOMATIC CORPS AND INTERNATIONAL ORGANIZATIONS. English. ir. Department of Foreign Affairs, PO Box 518, Mbabane Swaziland. **LC** JX1865.S8. **DD** 351.892096813. Directory of the Diplomatic Corps.

THE DIRECTORY OF THE EUROPEAN COUNCIL OF INTERNATIONAL SCHOOLS. Main/Corp European Council of International Schools. **VFOAT** ECIS Directory. 0307-9430. UK. English. an. European Council of International Schools Inc, 19 Claremont Road, Surbiton Surrey KT6 4QR England. **LC** L900. **DD** 370.254.

DIRECTORY OF THE HIGHWAY RESEARCH BOARD. US. English. $10.00. National Research Council, 2101 Constitution Avenue NW, Washington DC 20418. **LC** TE12. **DD** 625.702573.

DIRECTORY OF THE KANSAS BAR ASSOCIATION. Main/Corp Kansas Bar Association. **VFOAT** K.B.A. Directory. 1982-83-. 0742-1273. US. English. an. Office of the Kansas Bar Association, 1200 Harrison, PO Box 1037, Topeka KS 66601. **Tel** (913)234-5696. Ed Patti Slider. **LC** KF192.K3. **DD** 340.025781. adv acc. **Circ** 4,600. (ctrl). A list of Kansas Bar Association members and phone catalog of member services.

DIRECTORY OF THE LABOR RESEARCH ADVISORY COUNCIL TO THE BUREAU OF LABOR STATISTICS. (DIRECTORY). Main/Corp United States. Labor Research Advisory Council. 0091-9497. US. English. US Department of Labor, Labor Research Advisory Council, Washington DC 20212. **LC** HD8061. **DD** 331.8802573.

DIRECTORY OF THE LEADING FIRMS IN THE JOB PLATING AND ENAMELING INDUSTRY. (DIRECTORY OF THE LEADING FIRMS IN THE JOB PLATING AND ENAMELING INDUSTRY WHO ARE MEMBERS OF THE NATIONAL ASSOCIATION OF METAL FINISHERS, INC). Main/Corp National Association of Metal Finishers. **VFOAT** N.A.M.F. Directory of Electro Plating and Enameling Firms. 0092-6418. US. English. Dime Building, Detroit MI 48226. **LC** TS670.A1. **DD** 671.706273.

DIRECTORY OF THE MINERAL INDUSTRY IN PENNSYLVANIA. **VFOAT** Mineral Industry Directory. 3d- Ed. US. English. State Book Store, PO Box 1365, Harrisburg PA 17125. **LC** QE157, HD9506. U63P4. **DD** 557.4808 S, 338.2025748. Directory of the Mineral Industry in Pennsylvania.

DIRECTORY OF THE MINERAL INDUSTRY IN VIRGINIA. 0419-3776. US. English. an. Virginia Division of Mineral Resources, Box 3666 University Station, Charlottesville VA 22903. Ed D C Le Van and R F Pharr. **LC** HD9506.U63. **DD** 338.2025755. Directory of Rock and Mineral Producers in Virginia, 0163-5522.

DIRECTORY OF THE MUTUAL SAVINGS BANKS OF THE UNITED STATES CEASED. **VFOAT** Mutual Savings Banks of the United States. -1981/82. 0092-6132. US. English. an. $17.00. New York National Association of Mutual Savings Bank, 200 Park Avenue, New York NY 10017. **LC** HG2441. **DD** 332.21. Directory and Guide to the Mutual Savings Banks of the United States.

DIRECTORY OF THE NEW MEXICO BENCH AND BAR. 8756-1611. US. English. an. State Bar of New Mexico, 1117 Stanford NE/PO Box 25883, Albuquerque NM 87125. Attorney Directory.

DIRECTORY OF THE NEW YORK METROPOLITAN REFERENCE AND RESEARCH LIBRARY AGENCY, METRO AND METROPOLITAN NEW YORK REGIONAL INTERSYSTEM COOPERATIVE LIBRARY NETWORK, INTERSHARE. **VFOAT** Directory of Metro Libraries and Buyers Guide. 1983-84-. 0748-2566. US. English. an. $23.95. LDA Publishers, 4236-209 Street, Bayside NY 11361.

DIRECTORY OF THE OFFICERS, BOARD OF MANAGERS, COMMITTEES AND SECTIONS AFFILIATED AND COOPERATING ORGANIZATIONS. Main/Corp Indiana State Bar Association (Founded 1896). 0363-4930. US. English. an. Indiana State Bar Association, 230 East Ohio Street, Indianapolis IN 46204. **LC** KF192.I5. **DD** 340062772.

DIRECTORY OF THE RESEARCH ESTABLISHMENTS IN PAKISTAN. English. ir. 20.00. National Science Council, 63 School Road Shalimar 7/4, Islamabad Pakistan. **LC** Q180.P25. **DD** 507205491.

DIRECTORY OF THE SAVINGS BANKS OF THE UNITED STATES AND MEMBERSHIP OF NAMSB. Main/Corp National Association of Mutual Savings Banks. 1982-1983-. 0737-1799. US. English. an. $15.00 Bank Members, $40.00 Others. National Association of Mutual Savings Banks, 200 Park Avenue, New York NY 10017. **LC** HG2441. **DD** 332.2102573. Directory of the Mutual Savings Banks of the United States, 0092-6132.

DIRECTORY OF THE SCIENTISTS, TECHNOLOGISTS, AND ENGINEERS OF THE PCSIR. Main/Corp Pakistan Council of Scientific and Industrial Research. **VAT** Directory of the Scientists, Technologists, and Engineers of the Pakistan Council of Scientific and Industrial Research. English. ir. **LC** T177.P18. **DD** 607.25491.

DIRECTORY OF THE STATE AND COUNTY OFFICIALS OF NORTH CAROLINA. US. English. an. Secretary of State, Director of Publications, Raleigh NC 27602. Ed John L Cheney.

DIRECTORY OF THE TRANSPORTATION RESEARCH BOARD. Main/Corp National Research Council (U.S.). Transportation Research Board. 1974-. 0360-5078. US. English. an. $20.00. Transportation Research Board, 2101 Constitution Avenue, Washington DC 20418. **Tel** (202)334-2000. Ind/Abst Eng. Index. **LC** TE12. **DD** 380.502573. Directory of the Highway Research Board.

DIRECTORY OF THE UNITED NATIONS ORGANIZATION AND SPECIALIZED AGENCIES IN IRAQ. **VFOAT** Dalil Al-Uman Al-Muttahida Fi Al-Iraq. 0303-1594. English. ir. United Nations den Programme, P O B 2048 (Alwiyah), Baghdad Iraq. **LC** JX1977.2.I7. **DD** 341.23567.

DIRECTORY OF TOLL BRIDGES, FERRIES, DOMESTIC STEAMSHIP LINES AND AUTO-PASSENGER LAND CARRIERS. (DIRECTORY OF TOLL BRIDGES, FERRIES, DOMESTIC STEAMSHIP LINES AND AUTO/PASSENGER LAND CARRIERS). **VFOAT** Auto/Passenger Land Carriers. 0149-757X. US. English. an. American Automobile Association, Highway Information Services, National Travel Department, 8111 Gatehouse Road, Falls Church VA 22042. **LC** HE5773. **DD** 380.5.

DIRECTORY OF TOP COMPUTER EXECUTIVES. 0193-9920. US. English. sa. $275.00 Domestic, $325.00 Foreign. Applied Computer Research, PO Box 9280, Phoenix AZ 85068. **Tel** (602)995-5929. Ed Alan S Howard. **LC** HD9696.C63. **DD** 338.47001602573. Includes key DP and MIS decision makers from the Fortune 500 industrials, the seven non-industrial classifications, and thousands of other large end-user organizations.

Yearbooks, Almanacs, Directories

DIRECTORY OF TOXICOLOGY TESTING INSTITUTIONS IN THE UNITED STATES. 1st Ed. (1983)-. US. English. an. $55.00. NLM QV 605.

DIRECTORY OF TRADE AND INDUSTRIAL EDUCATION. SOUTH CAROLINA. (DIRECTORY OF TRADE AND INDUSTRIAL EDUCATION : SOUTH CAROLINA). VFOAT Trade and Industrial Education Teachers Directory. 0146-5341. US. English. State Department of Education, Office of Vocational Education, 1009 Rutledge Building, Columbia SC 29201. LC L903.S6. DD 371.10025757.

DIRECTORY OF TRUST INSTITUTIONS. 1969/70-. 0093-951X. US. English. an. $19.50. Communication Channels Inc, 6255 Barfield Road, Atlanta GA 30328. Tel (404)256-9800. LC HG4347. DD 332.178. *Directory of Trust Institutions of United States and Canada.*

DIRECTORY OF UNDERGRADUATE POLITICAL SCIENCE FACULTY. 1984-. 0884-5859. US. English. $8.00 Members, $12.00 Nonmembers. American Political Science Association, 1527 New Hampshire Avenue NW, Washington DC 20036. Tel (202)483-2512. LC JA28. DD 320.071173. adv acc. Circ 2,500. Lists nearly 500 separate departments of political science with names, addresses, phone numbers, and specializations of faculty members.

DIRECTORY OF UNIONS AND ASSOCIATIONS WITH EXCLUSIVE RECOGNITION IN THE FEDERAL SERVICE. 0193-385X. US. English. US Civil Service Commission, 1900 E Street NW, Washington DC 20415. LC HD8005.2.U5. DD 331.881135300025.

DIRECTORY OF UNIT TRUSTS. VFOAT Unit Trusts. UK. English. Association of Unit Trust Managers, 306/308 Salisbury House Finsbury Circus, EC2 London England. LC HG5436.5. DD 332.6.

DIRECTORY OF U.S. AND CANADIAN MARKETING SURVEYS AND SERVICES. 1976-. 0364-8966. US. English. an. $167.00. Rauch Associates Inc, PO Box 6802, Bridgewater NJ 08807. Tel (201)231-9548. Ed James A Rauch. LC HF5415.3. DD 658.8350257. Contains market studies and services.

DIRECTORY OF UNITED STATES CEMETERIES. V. 1- 1974-. 0095-1862. US. English. Cemetery Research Inc, PO Box 6616, San Jose CA 95150. LC RA626.3. DD 363.

DIRECTORY OF U.S. FIRMS AND ORGANIZATIONS IN INDONESIA. VAT Directory of United States Firms and Organizations in Indonesia. 0149-7553. English. ir. Directory of United States Firms and Organizations in Indonesia, Medan Merdeka Selatan 5, Jakarta Indonesia. LC HD2904 B .D57. DD 338.88025598. *Directory of United States Firms in Indonesia.*

DIRECTORY OF U.S. GOVERNMENT AUDIOVISUAL PERSONNEL. VFOAT U.S. Government Audiovisual Personnel. VAT Directory of United States Government Audiovisual Personnel. Began with 1970. 0098-1109. US. English. ir. National Audiovisual Center, National Archives & Records Services, Washington DC 20408. LC JK849. DD 353.0081. NLM JK 849.A24 DI517.

DIRECTORY OF UNITED STATES IMPORTERS. 1967-. 0070-6531. US. English. bm. Journal of Commerce, 445 Marshall Street, Phillipsburg NJ 08865. Tel (201)859-1300. LC HF3012. DD 382.502573. *Directory of United States Import Concerns.*

DIRECTORY OF U.S. LABOR ORGANIZATIONS. VFOAT Directory of US Labor Organizations. 1982-83 Ed.-. 0734-6786. US. English. an. $15.00. BNA Books, 1321 25th Street NW, Washington DC 20037. Tel (202)452-4531. Ed Courtney D Gifford. LC HD6504. DD 331.8802573. Contains an extensive labor organization listing of headquarters' addresses and telephone numbers, key officers, membership statistics and other information. *Directory of National Unions and Employee Associations.*

DIRECTORY OF UNITED STATES POISON CONTROL CENTERS AND SERVICES. 1983-. US. English. an. US Department of Health and Human Services, Food and Drug Administration, Office of Drug Poisoning Surveillance and Epidemiology Branch, 5600 Fishers Lane, Rockville MD 20857. LC RA1193.7. DD 363.179. NLM QV 605. *Directory (National Clearinghouse for Poison Control Centers (U.S.)), 0740-1256.*

DIRECTORY OF UNITED STATES PROBATION OFFICERS. VFOAT United States Probation Officers. 0731-8790. US. English. an. Probation Division, Administrative Office of the United States Courts, Washington DC 20544. LC HV9304. DD 364.6302573.

DIRECTORY OF UNITED STATES TRADITIONAL AND ALTERNATIVE COLLEGES AND UNIVERSITIES. 1984-1986-. 0882-7745. US. English. $30.00. NASACU, PO Box 9478, Washington DC 20016. Ed Jean-Maximillien.

DIRECTORY OF UNIVERSITY ATHLETICS. VFOAT Ontario Directory of University Athletics. Intercollegiate Ed. 1982/83-. 0820-8441. CN. English. an. Free. Ontario Universities Athletic Association-Ontario Women's Intercollegiate Athletic Association, Room 110/Athletic Centre, University of Guelph, Guelph Ontario N1G 2W1 Canada. DD 796.0711713. (ctrl). *Ontario Directory of University Athletics, 0225-6908.*

DIRECTORY OF UNPUBLISHED EXPERIMENTAL MENTAL MEASURES. V. 1- 1974-. 0731-8081. US. English. ir. Human Sciences Press, 72 5th Avenue, New York NY 10011. Tel (212)243-6000. Ed J L Saunders. LC BF431. DD 152.8. NLM Z 5814.P8 D598.

DIRECTORY OF USSR FOREIGN TRADE ORGANIZATIONS AND OFFICIALS. VFOAT Directory of U.S.S.R. Foreign Trade Organizations and Officials. 0742-9118. US. English. Documents Expediting DOCEX Project Exchange and Gift Division, Library of Congress, Washington DC 20540. LC HF3623. DD 354.4700827025. Vols. for (Jan. 1984-) Distributed to depository libraries in microfiche. *Directory of Soviet Foreign Trade Organizations and Officials.*

DIRECTORY OF U.S.S.R. MINISTRY OF DEFENSE AND ARMED FORCES OFFICIALS. (DIRECTORY OF USSR MINISTRY OF DEFENSE AND ARMED FORCES OFFICIALS). 0096-9990. US. English. Central Intelligence Agency, Washington DC 20201. LC UA770. DD 355.30947. Vols. for April 1980 distributed to depository libraries in microfiche.

DIRECTORY OF USSR MINISTRY OF FOREIGN AFFAIRS OFFICIALS. VFOAT Directory of U.S.S.R. Ministry of Foreign Affairs Officials. VAT Directory of Union of Soviet Socialist Republics Ministry of Foreign Affairs Officials. 0191-8621. US. English. Central Intelligence Agency, Document Expediting (DOCEX) Project, Exchange and Gift Division, Library of Congress, Washington DC 20540. LC JX1807. DD 354.4700892. Vols. for June 1983- distributed to depository libraries in microfiche.

DIRECTORY OF UTAH LOCAL OFFICIALS. VFOAT Directory of Local Government Officials. US. English. Utah League of Cities and Towns, 10 West Broadway/Suite 305, Salt Lake City UT 84101. LC JS451.U87. DD 352.005209792. *Directory of Utah Municipal Officials.*

DIRECTORY OF UTILITIES, TRANSMISSION AND PRODUCTION COMPANIES. Main/Corp Canadian Gas Association. 1982-. 0820-604X. CN. English. an. $8.00 Per Vol. Canadian Gas Association Directory, 55 Scarsdale Road, Don Mills Ontario M3B 2R3 Canada. LC TP714. DD 363.6302571. *Directory.*

THE DIRECTORY OF VARS. (THE . . . DIRECTORY OF VARS). VFOAT Directory of Value Added Resellers. 1985-. 0884-8300. US. English. an. $289.00. Business Guides Inc, 425 Park Avenue, New York NY 10022. DD 004. Provides complete company profiles on 3,500 VARs, including Value Added Dealers, Systems Houses, Systems Integrators, Turkey System Specialists and OEMs serving a wide variety of end users.

DIRECTORY OF VETERANS ORGANIZATIONS. 1984-. 0743-3166. US. English. an. Veterans Service Organization, Coordination Administrator, 810 Vermont Avenue NW/Room 1018, Washington DC 20420. LC UB357. DD 355.11506073. *Directory of Veterans Organizations and State Departments of Veterans Affairs.*

DIRECTORY OF VIRGINIA PROPRIETARY SCHOOLS. US. English. an. Commonwealth of Virginia, Department of Education, Division of Vocational Research and Adult Services, PO Box 6-Q, Richmond VA 23216.

DIRECTORY OF VIRGINIA'S POSTSECONDARY EDUCATION AND TRAINING OPPORTUNITIES. 1976/77-. 0148-0782. US. English. Virginia's Postsecondary Education Planning Commission, The State Council of Higher Education for Virginia, 700 Fidelity Building, Ninth and Main Streets, Richmond VA 23219. LC L903.V8. DD 378.755.

DIRECTORY OF VISITING FULBRIGHT SCHOLARS & OCCASIONAL LECTURER PROGRAM. VAT Directory of Visiting Fulbright Scholars and Occasional Lecturer Program. 1982-83—. US. English. an. *Directory of Visiting Fulbright Scholars.*

DIRECTORY OF VOLUNTARY AGENCIES. 1984 Y-. 0743-9725. US. English. be. Immigration and Naturalization Service, INS Outreach Program, 425 I Street NW, Washington DC 20536. LC HV89. DD 362.8.

DIRECTORY OF WASHINGTON BUSINESS ASSOCIATIONS. 0098-5635. US. English. an. Trade Development Division, General Administration Building, Olympia WA 98504. LC HD2428.W35. DD 381.062797. *Directory of Business Associations in the State of Washington, 0417-5573.*

DIRECTORY OF WASHINGTON CREATIVE SERVICES. 1st- Ed. 0191-3719. US. English. LC NX110. DD 700.25753.

DIRECTORY OF WATER RESOURCES EXPERTISE. 1st Ed.- 1974-. 0364-9296. US. English. LC TC424.C2. DD 333.910025794.

DIRECTORY OF WESTCHESTER LIBRARIES AND MEDIA CENTERS AND BUYERS GUIDE CEASED. 0741-2053. US. English. an. $18.95 Members, $23.95 Non-Members. Library Directory Associates, 42-36-209 Street, Bayside NY 11361. LC Z732.N7. DD 027.0747277. *Directory of Westchester Libraries and Media Centers, 0275-214X.*

DIRECTORY OF WOMEN ATTORNEYS IN THE UNITED STATES. 1972-. 0092-1416. US. English. $10.00. Ford Associates, 701 South Federal Avenue, Butler IN 46721. LC KF190. DD 340.02573.

DIRECTORY OF WOMEN HISTORIANS. VFOAT Women Historians. 1st-1975-. US. English. American Historical Association, 400 A Street SE, Washington DC 20003. Tel (202)544-2422. Ed J A Justice.

DIRECTORY OF WOMEN IN MARQUIS WHO'S WHO PUBLICATIONS. 1984-. 8756-422X. US. English. Marquis Who's Who Inc, 200 East Ohio Street, Chicago IL 60611. LC CT3260. DD 920.720973.

A DIRECTORY OF WOMEN IN PHILOSOPHY CEASED. Began with 1976/1977 Volumn. Ceased 1981/1982. 0148-3277. US. English. Bowling Green University, Philosophy Documentation Center, Bowling Green OH 43403. LC B105.W6. DD 102.573.

DIRECTORY OF WOMEN IN THE MATHEMATICAL SCIENCES. 0732-5967. US. English. AMS, PO Box 1571 Annex Station, Providence RI 02901. LC QA30. DD 510.922. *Directory of Women Mathematicians, 0091-7583.*

DIRECTORY OF WOMEN OWNED BUSINESSES AND PROFESSIONAL WOMEN : METRO ST. LOUIS AREA. 1981-. Periodical. US. English.

DIRECTORY OF WOMEN-OWNED BUSINESSES. WASHINGTON-BALTIMORE METROPOLITAN AREA. (DIRECTORY OF WOMEN-OWNED BUSINESSES : WASHINGTON/BALTIMORE METROPOLITAN AREA). 0147-4553. US. English. $10.00. National Association of Women Business Owners, 2000 P Street NW/Suite 511, Washington DC 20036. LC HD2346.U52. DD 338.0025753.

DIRECTORY OF WOMEN PHYSICIANS IN THE U.S. VAT Directory of Women Physicians in the United States. Began in 1973. US. English.

Yearbooks, Almanacs, Directories

DIRECTORY OF WOMEN'S & CHILDREN'S WEAR SPECIALTY STORES. VFOAT Directory of Women's and Children's Wear Specialty Stores. 1982-. 0277-9617. US. English. an. $139.00. Chain Store Guide, Lebhar-Friedman, c/o Priscilla G Jimenez, 425 Park Avenue, New York NY 10022. **Tel** (212)371-9400. **Ed** Barbara Brown and Elaine Kohlstein. **LC** HD9940.U3. **DD** 687.029473. Complete company profiles on 5,000 women's and children's wear specialty store companies and sport shops/activewear retailers operating 36,000 stores. *Directory of Apparel Specialty Stores, Women's & Children's, 0272-1104.*

DIRECTORY OF WOOL, HOSIERY & FABRICS. VAT Directory of Wool, Hosiery and Fabrics. 1972-. II. English. ir. $3.00. Manek Mahal, 6th Floor/90 Veer Nariman Road, Nhurchgate Bombay-20 India. **LC** HD9906.I4. **DD** 380.1456773102554. *India & Pakistan Wool, Hosiery & Fabrics.*

DIRECTORY OF WORD PROCESSING MANAGEMENT. Premier Issue 1981-. 0278-9663. US. English. sa. $160.00 per copy. Word Systems Division, Applied Management Services, Box 73, Massapequa Park NY 11762. **LC** HF5548.2. **DD** 652.

DIRECTORY OF WORKERS EDUCATION. Began with Vol. for 1979/80. 8755-4496. US. English. Workers Education Local 189, 4917 Morris Street, Philadelphia PA 19144. *Directory of Labor Education.*

DIRECTORY OF WORKING WOMEN. Began with 1979 Vol. 0197-5935. US. English. an. $6.00. A Jane Heim & Associates, 1228 Cardinal lane, Naperville IL 60540. **Ed** A J Heim. **LC** HD6093. **DD** 650.14024042.

DIRECTORY OF WORLD CHEMICAL PRODUCERS. 1980/81- Ed. 0196-0555. US. English. ir. Chemical Information Services, PO Box 61, Oceanside NY 11572. **LC** TP12. **DD** 338.476610025.

DIRECTORY - OFFICE OF THE SUPERINTENDENT, DEPARTMENT OF EDUCATION, STATE OF HAWAII. **Main/Corp** Hawaii. Dept. of Education. Office of the Superintendent. 0148-8929. US. English. an. Office of the Superintendent, PO Box 2360, Honolulu HI 96804. **LC** L903.H3. **DD** 370.25969.

DIRECTORY - OHIO EDUCATIONAL LIBRARY/MEDIA ASSOCIATION. **Main/Corp** Ohio Educational Library/Media Association. VAT Directory - Ohio Educational Library Media Association. 0198-6163. US. English. 3019 Muirfield Drive, Toledo OH 43614. **LC** Z675.S3. **DD** 027.0025771.

DIRECTORY - ONTARIO AMATEUR FOOTBALL ASSOCIATION. (DIRECTORY). **Main/Corp** Ontario Amateur Football Association. 0713-6781. CN. English. an. $5.00. Ontario Amateur Football Association Directory, 160 Vanderhoof Avenue, Toronto Ontario M4G 4B8 Canada. **DD** 796.335060713.

DIRECTORY - ONTARIO LIBRARY SERVICE, SAUGEEN. (DIRECTORY). **Main/Corp** Ontario Library Service, Saugeen. 1984-. 0828-7708. CN. English. an. Saugeen Library Service, 637 Victoria Street North, Kitchener Ontario N2H Canada. **DD** 027.40257134.

DIRECTORY. ONTARIO POSTAL REGION. POSTAL CODE. (POSTAL CODE DIRECTORY : ONTARIO POSTAL REGION). VFOAT Code Postal, Repertoire : Region Postale de l'Ontario. 0317-4271. CN. English (French). an. Free. Director of Coding and Mechanization, Post Office Department Sir Alexander Campbell Building Klaobl, Ottawa Ontario K1A 0B1 Canada. **LC** HE6656.O5. **DD** 383.14.

DIRECTORY. ONTARIO POSTAL REGION. POSTAL CODE. (POSTAL CODE DIRECTORY : ONTARIO POSTAL REGION = CODE POSTAL REPERTOIRE : REGION DE L'ONTARIO). VFOAT Code Postal, Repertoire: Region Postale de l'Ontario. 0317-4271. Periodical. CN. English (text also in French). Free. Postal Coding, Station 814, Ottawa Ontario K1A 0B1 Canada.

DIRECTORY - ONTARIO VETERINARY ASSOCIATION. (DIRECTORY). **Main/Corp** Ontario Vacation Farm Association. 0822-8248. CN. English. an. Free to members. Ontario Veterinary Association, Suite 24/25 340 Woodlawn Road West, Guelph Ontario N1H 2X1 Canada. **DD** 636.089025713.

DIRECTORY - ORGANIZATION OF AMERICAN STATES. (DIRECTORY). **Main/Corp** Organization of American States. Began with Nov. 1963 issue. 0250-6211. US. English. $1.00 Single Issue. General Secretariat of American States, Washington DC 20006. **LC** F1402. *Directory of Delegations.*

DIRECTORY, ORGANIZATIONS OFFERING LITERACY TRAINING COURSES. English. ir. International Institute for Adult Literacy Methods, PO Box 1555, Tehran Iran. **LC** L900. **DD** 370.194025.

DIRECTORY - OUTDOOR WRITERS ASSOCIATION OF AMERICA. **Main/Corp** Outdoor Writers Association of America. VFOAT OWAA Outdoor Writers Directory. 1979/80-. 0195-6124. US. English. an. Outdoor Writers Association of America Inc, 4141 West Bradley Road, Milwaukee WI 53209. **LC** PN4871. **DD** 070.4497965. *OWAA National Outdoor Writers Directory.*

DIRECTORY - PARENT COOPERATIVE PRESCHOOLS INTERNATIONAL. **Main/Corp** Parent Cooperative Preschools International. CN. English. International Office Whiteside Taylor Center for Cooperative Education, 20551 Lakeshore Road, Baie d'Urfe Quebec Canada. **LC** L900. **DD** 372.21025.

DIRECTORY - PERSEKUTUAN PEKILAND-PEKILANG MALAYSIA. **Main/Corp** Persekutuan Pekiland-Pekilang Malaysia. English. an. Federation of Malaysian Manufacturers, Angkasa Raya Building/8th Floor, PO Box 2194, Kuala Lumpur. **LC** T12.5.M4. **DD** 670.25595. *Federation of Malaysian Manufacturers' Directory.*

DIRECTORY PERUSAHAAN BIS (ANTAR PROPINSI). **Series/Titl** Statistik Perhubangan. 0126-4613. IO. Indonesian. ir. $3.20. Bagian Statistik Tahunan dan Peneritan Biro Pusat Statistik Jl Dr Sutomo No 8, PO Box 3, Jakarta Indonesia. **Tel** 372808. **LC** HE5695.A45. bk rev. adv acc. (ctrl)

DIRECTORY, POSTSECONDARY EDUCATIONAL OPPORTUNITIES IN ARKANSAS. (DIRECTORY : POSTSECONDARY EDUCATIONAL OPPORTUNITIES IN ARKANSAS). VFOAT Postsecondary Educational Opportunities in Arkansas. 1975/76-. 0147-166X. US. English. an. Planning Commission, 401 National Old Line Building, Little Rock AR 72201. **LC** L903.A8. **DD** 378.767.

DIRECTORY, PROFESSIONAL REAL ESTATE MANAGEMENT WHO'S WHO. 0161-3154. US. English. Institute of Real Estate Management, 155 East Superior Street, Chicago IL 60611. **LC** HD251. **DD** 658.9133333.

DIRECTORY, PROFESSIONAL WORKERS IN STATE AGRICULTURAL EXPERIMENT STATIONS AND OTHER COOPERATING STATE INSTITUTIONS. (DIRECTORY OF PROFESSIONAL WORKERS IN STATE AGRICULTURAL EXPERIMENT STATIONS AND OTHER COOPERATING STATE INSTITUTIONS). VFOAT Professional Workers in State Agricultural Experiment Stations and Other Cooperating State Institutions. 1980-81-. 0732-8524. US. English. an. Superintendent of Documents, US Government Printing Office, Washington DC 20402. **LC** S21, S530.52.U6. **DD** 630, 630.20573. *Directory, Professional Workers in State Agricultural Experiment Stations and Other Cooperating State Institutions, 0732-8524.*

DIRECTORY : PROGRAMS IN PUBLIC AFFAIRS AND ADMINISTRATION. VFOAT NASPAA Directory. 1978-. Periodical. US. English. $10.00. National Association of Schools of Public Affairs and Administration, 1225 Connecticut Avenue NW, Washington DC 20036. **LC** JF1338.A2. **DD** 350.00071173. *Graduate Programs in Public Affairs and Public Administration, 0272-7498.*

DIRECTORY, PROGRAMS SERVING THE MENTALLY RETARDED IN MAINE. VFOAT Programs Serving the Mentally Retarded in Maine. US. English. Bureau of Mental Retardation, State House Station 40, Augusta ME 04333. **LC** HV3006.M2. **DD** 362.38309741.

DIRECTORY, REGISTERED DENTISTS AND REGISTERED DENTAL HYGIENISTS IN CONNECTICUT. 0085-0004. US. English. $20.00. State Department of Health, State Office Building, 165 Capital Avenue, Hartford CT 06115. **LC** RK5. **DD** 617.60232025746. **NLM** WU 22 AC8 D4D. *Directory of Registered Dentists, Unlicensed Assistants and Dental Hygienists in Connecticut.*

DIRECTORY. REPUBLIC OF SENEGAL. (DIRECTORY OF THE REPUBLIC OF SENEGAL). 0376-8627. SG. French. ir. American Embassy, Republic of Senegal, Dakar Senegal. **LC** JQ3396.A4. **DD** 916.63035025.

DIRECTORY - ROYAL COLLEGE OF PHYSICIANS OF EDINBURGH. (DIRECTORY). **Main/Corp** Royal College of Physicians of Edinburgh. 0265-0118. UK. English. ir. **NLM** W 22.1 R888D. *Year Book and Calendar (Royal College of Physicians of Edinburgh).*

DIRECTORY - SINGAPORE INDIAN CHAMBER OF COMMERCE. **Main/Corp** Singapore Indian Chamber of Commerce. 1974-. 0376-8635. SI. English. ir. Singapore Indian Chamber of Commerce, 55-A Robinson Road/PO Box 1038, Singapore Singapore. **LC** HF3800.6.Z8. **DD** 382.0255952. *Trade Directory.*

DIRECTORY : SOCIAL AND HUMAN FORECASTING DOCUMENTATION. VFOAT Social and Human Forecasting Documentation. English. ir. Institute for Futures Research and Education, Edizioni Previsionali, Via G Paisiello 4, Roma Italy. **LC** CB158. **DD** 300.

DIRECTORY - SOCIETY OF INDEPENDENT PROFESSIONAL EARTH SCIENTISTS. **Main/Corp** Society of Independent Professional Earth Scientists. VFOAT SIPES Directory. US. English. Society of Independent Professional Earth Scientists, PO Box 3370, Midland TX 79702.

DIRECTORY - SOCIETY OF INDUSTRIAL REALTORS. **Main/Corp** Society of Industrial Realtors. VFOAT SIR Directory. 0560-6322. US. English. Society of Industrial Realtors, 925-15th Street North West, Washington DC 20005. **LC** HD251. **DD** 333.3302573.

DIRECTORY (SOUTH CAROLINA STATE BOARD OF REGISTRATION FOR PROFESSIONAL ENGINEERS AND LAND SURVEYORS). (DIRECTORY). US. English. $10.00. 2221 Devine Street/Suite 404, PO Drawer 50408, Columbia SC 29250. **LC** TA12. **DD** 620.0025757. *Directory (South Carolina State Board of Engineering Examiners).*

DIRECTORY - SOUTH CENTRAL REGIONAL LIBRARY SYSTEM. **Main/Corp** South Central Regional Library System (Ont.). Began with 1968 issue. 0319-0293. Periodical. CN. English. an. South Central Regional Library System, 220 Dundurn Street South, Hamilton Ontario L8P 4K7 Canada. **DD** 027.40257135.

DIRECTORY - SOUTH DAKOTA REAL ESTATE BOARD. (DIRECTORY). 1981-. 0731-9525. US. English. an. $3.00. South Dakota Real Estate Board, PO Box 490, Pierre SD 57501. **LC** HD266.S8. **DD** 333.33025783. *Directory (South Dakota Real Estate Commission).*

DIRECTORY - SPECTROSCOPY SOCIETY OF CANADA. (DIRECTORY). **Main/Corp** Spectroscopy Society of Canada. VFOAT Annuaire. Began with V. for 1979. 0709-8448. CN. English. an. $80.00. Multiscience Publications, 1253 Avenue, McGill College/Suite 111, Montreal Quebec H3B 2Y5 Canada. **Tel** (514)866-8236. **Ed** I S Butler and T Theophanides. **LC** QC450. **DD** 535.8406071. bk rev. adv acc. **Circ** 1,200. (ctrl). An international bilingual journal published for all branches of fundamental and applied spectroscopy.

DIRECTORY - SPORTS FEDERATION OF CANADA. (DIRECTORY). **Main/Corp** Sports Federation of Canada. VFOAT Repertoire Sports = Recreation Directory. VAT Recreation Directory - Sports Federation of Canada, Directory - Federation des Sports du Canada, Repertoire Sports - Federation des Sports du Canada. 0229-3161. CN. English (French). an. Sports Federation of Canada, 333 River Road, Vanier Ontario K1L 8B9 Canada. **DD** 796.02571.

DIRECTORY - STATE BAR OF GEORGIA. **Main/Corp** State Bar of Georgia. US. English. an. $8.00. State Bar of Georgia, Georgia Justice Center, 84 Peachtree Street 11th Floor, Atlanta GA 30303. **Tel** (404)522-6255. **LC** KF192.G46. **DD** 349.758025. adv acc. **Circ** 17,000. (ctrl). Lists the names, addresses and telephone numbers of the

Yearbooks, Almanacs, Directories

members of the State Bar of Georgia. Also lists committees and related organizations. *Handbook and Directory.*

DIRECTORY - STATE BOARD OF ACCOUNTANCY, STATE OF FLORIDA. **Main/Corp** Florida. State Board of Accountancy. 1979-. US. English. State Board of Accountancy, PO Box 13475, Gainesville FL 32604. *Register - Florida State Board of Accountancy.*

DIRECTORY - STATE BOARD OF MEDICAL EXAMINERS OF SOUTH CAROLINA. **Main/Corp** South Carolina. State Board of Medical Examiners. 0194-0554. US. English. State Board of Medical Examiners of South Carolina, Nathaniel B Heyward/Executive Director, 1315 Blanding Street, Columbia SC 29201. **LC** R712.A2. **DD** 610.25757.

DIRECTORY. SUB-STATE PLANNING DISTRICTS IN OKLAHOMA. (DIRECTORY : SUB-STATE PLANNING DISTRICTS IN OKLAHOMA). **VFOAT** Sub-State Planning Districts in Oklahoma. 0094-5994. US. English. Office of Community Affairs & Planning, 4901 North Lincoln, Oklahoma City OK 73105. **LC** HT393.O45. **DD** 309.25025766.

DIRECTORY SUPPLEMENT - AMERICAN SPEECH-LANGUAGE-HEARING ASSOCIATION. (DIRECTORY SUPPLEMENT). **Main/Corp** American Speech-Language-Hearing Association. 1981-. 0737-2043. US. English. $35.00. American Speech Language Hearing Association, 10801 Rockville Pike, Rockville MD 20852. **Tel** (301)897-5700. **Ed** Frederick T Spahr. adv acc. **Circ** 3,500. Members, names, address and job titles listed alphabetically and geographically. *Directory.*

DIRECTORY - TECHNICAL ASSOCIATION OF THE PULP AND PAPER INDUSTRY CEASED. Main/Corp Technical Association of the Pulp and Paper Industry. **VFOAT** TAPPI Directory. 1973-1981. 0091-7737. US. English. 1 Dunwoody Park, Atlanta GA 30341. **LC** TS1088. **DD** 676.0621. *Yearbook - Technical Association of the Pulp and Paper Industry, 0092-3737.*

DIRECTORY - TEXAS LIBRARY ASSOCIATION. **Main/Corp** Texas Library Association. 1984-. Periodical. US. English. an. 3355 Bee Cave Road/Suite 603, Austin TX 78746. *Directory for Members.*

DIRECTORY - TEXAS OSTEOPATHIC MEDICAL ASSOCIATION. **Main/Corp** Texas Osteopathic Medical Association. 1978/79-. 0196-6340. US. English. an. Texas Osteopathic Medical Association, 512 Bailey, Fort Worth TX 76107. **NLM** WB 22 AT4 T4D. *Membership Directory - Texas Osteopathic Medical Association, 0190-7026.*

DIRECTORY - THE NEW YORK SOCIETY OF CLINICAL PSYCHOLOGISTS, INC. Main/Corp New York Society of Clinical Psychologists. Feb. 1950-. 0545-6371. US. English. an. New York Society of Clinical Psychologists, 30 West 60th Street, New York NY 10023. **NLM** WM 22 AA1 N5D.

DIRECTORY - THE SECTION OF LITIGATION. **Main/Corp** American Bar Association. Section of Litigation. 0192-9798. Periodical. US. English. Section of Litigation Staff Liaison, American Bar Association, 1155 East 60th Street, Chicago IL 60637. **LC** KF195.L53. **DD** 340.02573.

DIRECTORY TO CO-OPERATIVE NATURALISTS' PROJECTS IN ONTARIO. Began publication in 1976. 0707-0942. CN. English. an. 50. Long Point Bird Observatory, PO Box 160, Port Rowan Ontario N0E 1M0 Canada. **DD** 598.207309713.

DIRECTORY - TOY TRAIN OPERATING SOCIETY. (DIRECTORY). **Main/Corp** Toy Train Operating Society. 0732-9873. US. English. an. $20.00. Toy Train Operating Society National Business Office, 25 West Walnut Street, Pasadena CA 91103. **Tel** (818)578-0673. **Ed** David Otth. **LC** TF197. **DD** 625.1902573. bk rev. adv acc. **Circ** 5,000. (ctrl) A newsletter of classified toy train advertisements.

DIRECTORY - U. S. COAST GUARD ACADEMY ALUMNI ASOCIATION. **Main/Corp** United States. Coast Guard, Academy, New London, Conn. Alumni Association. 1978-. US. English. an. PO Box 31-A, US Coast Guard Academy, New London CT 06320. **LC** V437. **DD** 359.9707117465. *Annual Directory - U. S. Coast Guard Academy Alumni Association.*

DIRECTORY (UNITARIAN UNIVERSALIST ASSOCIATION : 1965). (DIRECTORY). 1965-. US. English. an. $15.00. Unitarian Universalist Association, 25 Beacon Street, Boston MA 02108. **Tel** (617)742-2100. adv acc. **Circ** 2,000. (ctrl) A directory of all Unitarian Universalist churches, ministers, offices and related organizations. *Directory . . . of the Unitarian Universalist Association.*

DIRECTORY - UNITED STATES. FOOD AND DRUG ADMINISTRATION. **Main/Corp** United States. Food and Drug Administration. **VFOAT** FDA Location Directory. June 1983-. US. English. Superintendent of Documents, US Government Printing Office, Washington DC 20402. Vols. for 1983- distributed to depository libraries in Microfiche. *Location Directory.*

DIRECTORY : UNITED STATES, TERRITORIES, AND CANADA. US. English. National Center for Health Statistics, 3700 East-West Highway, Hyattsville MD 20782. **LC** RA407.3. **DD** 362.10973. *Directory: United States and Canada.*

DIRECTORY, UNITED WAY AFFILIATED INFORMATION AND REFERRAL SERVICES. **VFOAT** United Way Affiliated Information and Referral Services. 0731-9509. US. English. United Way of America, United Plaza, Alexandria VA 22314. **LC** HV97.U553. **DD** 361.802573.

DIRECTORY : UNIVERSITIES AND INSTITUTES OFFERING LITERACY TRAINING PROGRAMMES. English. ir. International Institute for Adult Literacy Methods, PO Box 1555, Tehran Iran. **LC** L900. **DD** 370.194025.

DIRECTORY - VIRGINIA HIGH SCHOOL LEAGUE. **Main/Corp** Virginia High School League. US. English. an. Virginia High School League Inc, PO Box 3597, Charlottesville VA 22903. **LC** L903.V8. **DD** 373.189025755. *League Directory.*

DIRECTORY: WESTERN POSTAL REGION, POSTAL CODE. **VFOAT** Repertoire: Region Postale de l'Ouest, Code Postal, Western Postal Region, Postal Code, Code Postal Repertoire. CN. Multilingual (English and French). an. Canada Post, Station 224 Sir Alexander Campbell Building, Ottawa Ontario K1A 0B7 Canada. **LC** HE6653. **DD** 383.14.

DIRECTORY. WESTERN POSTAL REGION. POSTAL CODE. (POSTAL CODE DIRECTORY : WESTERN POSTAL REGION = CODE POSTAL, REPERTOIRE : REGION POSTAL DE L'OUEST). **VFOAT** Code Postal, Repertoire: Region Postale de l'Ouest. 0317-4239. Periodical. CN. English (text also in French). Free. Postal Coding, Station 814, Ottawa Ontario K1A 0B1 Canada.

DIRECTOY OF DCAA OFFICES. **Main/Corp** United States. Defense Contract Audit Agency. **Series/Titl** DCAAP. **VAT** Directory of Defense Contract Audit Agency Offices. Periodical. US. English. ty. Superintendent of Documents, US Government Printing Office, Washington DC 20402.

DIREKTORI PERUSAHAAN TRUK (ANTAR PROPINSI) DI JAWA. 1981-. 0216-700X. IO. Indonesian. an. Biro Pusat Statistik, JL DR Sutomo No 8, jakarta Indonesia. **LC** HE5695.A1. *Directory Perusahaan Truck (Antar Propinsi) di Jawa.*

DIRETORIO LITURGICO. **Main/Corp** Catholic Church. Conferencia Nacional dos Bispos do Brasil. Portuguese. ir. Comissao Nacional de Liturgia, Caixa Postal 13-2067, 70401 Brasilia DF Brazil. **LC** BX1466.A4. **DD** 264.021.

THE DISCOVERAMERICARD DIRECTORY OF CITIES & HOTELS. (THE . . . DISCOVERAMERICARD DIRECTORY OF CITIES & HOTELS). **VFOAT** Directory of Cities & Hotels. 1980-1981-. 0277-8416. US. English. $29.95. Discoveramericard, Box 1984 New England Station, Hartford CT 06101. **LC** TX907. **DD** 647.947301.

DISNEY'S YEAR BOOK. 1981-. 0273-1274. US. English. an. $5.90. Grolier Enterprises, Sherman Turnpike, Danbury CT 68816.

DISPUTE RESOLUTION PROGRAM DIRECTORY. **VFOAT** Dispute Resolution Directory. 1981-. 0731-4833. US. English. $18.00. Special Committee on Dispute Resolution, ABA 1800 M Street NW/Suite 200, Washington DC 20036. **Tel** (202)331-2258. **Ed** Larry Ray. **LC** KF9084.A15. **DD** 347.739, 347.3079. **Circ** 3,000. A listing of dispute resolution programs with focus on median and on a list of resources.

DISPUTE RESOLUTION RESOURCE DIRECTORY. Jan. 1984-. 0741-8442. US. English. an. National Institute for Dispute Resolution, 1901 L Street Northwest/Suite 600, Washington DC 20036. **LC** KF9084.A15. **DD** 347.739, 347.3079.

DISTRICT EXPORT COUNCILS MEMBERSHIP DIRECTORY. **VFOAT** Membership Directory. US. English. be. Department of Commerce, International Trade Administration, Washington DC 20230.

DISTRICT OF COLUMBIA AND VIRGINIA ZIP+4 STATE DIRECTORY. **VFOAT** Zip+4 State Directory. 1985-. US. English. an.

DIVER'S ALMANAC. (DIVER'S ALMANAC : SCUBA DIVING ON THE WEST COAST). **VFOAT** Scuba Diving on the West Coast. 1st Ed. (1984-)-. 8755-5573. US. English. $11.95. Adventure Series Productions, Diver's Almanac, PO Box 1119, Jacksonville OR 97530. **LC** GV840.S78. **DD** 797.23.

DM. JAHRBUCH. 1970-. German. ir. Wofgang Kruger Verlag, Frankfurt Am Main West Germany. **LC** TX335.

DOANE'S AGRICULTURAL COMPUTING DIRECTORY. **VFOAT** Agricultural Computing Directory. 1985-. 0882-4282. US. English. an. $10.00. Doane Publishing, 11701 Borman Drive, St Louis MO 63146. **DD** 630.

DOCUMENT RETRIEVAL, SOURCES & SERVICES. **VFOAT** Document Retrieval, Sources and Services. Began with 1981. 0742-8375. US. English. ir. $60.00. The information Store, 140-2nd St, San Francisco CA 94105. **Tel** (415)543-4636. **Ed** Katharine T Alvord. **NLM** Z 674.3 D637. Comprehensive directory listing worldwide public and private document suppliers in over 100 countries. Source for journal articles, conference, papers, government documents, any kind of published material.

D.O.D. DIRECTORY OF CONTRACT ADMINISTRATION SERVICES COMPONENTS. (DOD DIRECTORY OF CONTRACT ADMINISTRATION SERVICES COMPONENTS). **VAT** Department of Defense Directory of Contract Administration Services Components. 0095-4349. Periodical. US. English. sa. HQ Defense Logistics Agency, Attn: DLA-XPD, Cameron Station, Alexandria VA 22314. **LC** UC263. **DD** 355.621102573.

DOD'S PARLIAMENTARY COMPANION. See Public Administration.

DOE TELEPHONE DIRECTORY. **Main/Corp** United States. Dept. of Energy. **VAT** Department of Energy Telephone Directory. Oct. 1977-. Periodical. US. English. qt. US Department of Energy, Directorate of Administration, Office of Computer Services and Telecommunications Management, Washington DC 20402.

DON CLEARY'S RECORD COLLECTORS DIRECTORY. 0197-2626. US. English. PO Box 16265, Ft Lauderdale FL 33318. **LC** ML12. **DD** 789.912075.

DONOGHUE'S MUTUAL FUNDS ALMANAC. **VFOAT** Mutual Funds Almanac. 13th Annual Ed. (1982)-. 0737-0369. US. English. an. Donoghue's Mutual Funds Almanac, PO Box 540, Holliston MA 01746. **Ed** William E Donoghue. **LC** HG4930. **DD** 332.6327. *Mutual Funds Almanac.*

DORLAND'S MEDICAL DIRECTORY OF PHILADELPHIA AND METROPOLITAN AREA. **VFOAT** Dorland's Medical Directory. Philadelphia and Metropolitan Area. -20th. US. English. an. Dorlands Medical Directory of Philadelphia & Metropolitan Area, 10th & Spring Garden, Philadelphia PA 19123. **Tel** (215)236-2000. **Ed** Charlene Goldstein. adv acc. **Circ** 6,000. Contains listings of over 7,200 physicians. Also hospital staff rosters, special service hospitals, health agencies and boards of medical specialties. *Medical Directory of Philadelphia and Metropolitan Area.*

THE DOW JONES-IRWIN BUSINESS ALMANAC CEASED. 1977-1981. 0146-6534. US. English. an. Dow Jones-Irwin, Homewood IL 60430. **LC** HF5003. **DD** 330.9005.

THE DOW JONES-IRWIN MUTUAL FUND YEARBOOK. **VFOAT** Dow Jones Irwin Mutual Fund Yearbook. 1984-. 0742-0919. US. English. an. **LC** HG4930. **DD** 332.6327.

Yearbooks, Almanacs, Directories

THE DOW JONES-IRWIN BUSINESS AND INVESTMENT ALMANAC. (THE ... DOW JONES-IRWIN BUSINESS AND INVESTMENT ALMANAC). VFOAT Dow Jones Irwin Business and Investment Almanac. 1982-. 0733-2610. US. English. an. Dow Jones-Irwin, Homewood IL 60430. Ed Sumner N Levine. LC HF5003. DD 330.9005. *Dow Jones-Irwin Business Almanac, 0146-6534.*

DP DIRECTORY. VFOAT D.P. Directory. VAT Data Processing Directory. 1981. 0730-6806. US. English. mo. $48.00. DP Directory, PO Box 562, Bloomfield CT 06002. The tables of contents of dozens of other data processing magazines are published each month.

DRG : DIRECTORY OF RESEARCH GRANTS. VFOAT Directory of Research Grants. 1981-. 0146-7336. US. English. an. $74.50. Oryx Press, 2214 North Central at Encanto/Suite 103, Phoenix AZ 85004. Tel (602)254-6516. This directory provides essential information for applicants who need to apply for funds for sponsored projects. *Directory of Research Grants, 0146-7336.*

DRUG STORE AND HEALTH & BEAUTY AIDS CHAINS CEASED. (CHAIN STORE GUIDE DIRECTORY : DRUG STORE AND HEALTH & BEAUTY AIDS CHAINS). VFOAT Directory of Drug Store and Health & Beauty Aids Chains. VAT Drug Store and Health and Beauty Aids Chains. 0092-0029. US. English. ir. Lebhar-Friedman Attn Priscilla G Jimenez, 425 Park Avenue, New York NY 10022. Tel (212)371-9400. Ed Jim Tierney. LC HD9666.3. DD 615.1029473. Provides complete company profiles on 2,000 or more store chains operating 23,000 drug and HBA stores and 165 drug wholesale companies and their 275 divisions. *Directory of Chain Drug Stores.*

DRUG TOPICS HEALTH & BEAUTY AIDS DIRECTORY. VFOAT Health & Beauty Aids Directory. VAT Drug Topics Health and Beauty Aids Directory. 1970?-. US. English. LC RS355. *Drug Topics Pink Book.*

DUKE'S WASHINGTON POCKET DIRECTORY. Series/Titl Know Your Government Series. VFOAT Washington Pocket Directory. 0732-068X. US. English. an. $5.95. Want Publishing Company, 1511 K Street NW, Washington DC 20005. Tel (202)783-1887. LC JK6. DD 353.00025.

DUNHILL GOLF YEARBOOK. 1979-. US. English. an. Ed M H McCormack. LC GV961. DD 796.3526405. *World of Professional Golf.*

DUN'S INDUSTRIAL GUIDE, THE METALWORKING DIRECTORY. 1981, V. 1-. 0278-8799. US. English. an. $590.00. Duns Marketing Service, 3 Century Drive, Attention M Berger, Parsippany NJ 07054. Tel (800)624-0324 inside NJ, (800)526-0651 outside NJ. LC TS203. DD 671029473. Source that identifies the products, processes and purchases of more than 65,000 plants and distributors throughout the US. A comprehensive source to the multi-billion dollar metalworking industry. *Dun & Bradstreet Metalworking Directory.*

EADI EAST TRADE DIRECTORY. VFOAT East Trade Directory. 1st- Ed. SP. English, French and Spanish. ir. Eadi East Trade Directory, Apartado 14-126, Madrid Spain. LC HF54.S7. DD 382.0255.

E&MJ INTERNATIONAL DIRECTORY OF MINING. VFOAT E & MJ. VAT Engineering and Mining Journal International Directory of Mining. 1981-. US. English. an. $80.00. Engineering and Mining Journal, 1221 Avenue of the Americas, New York NY 10020. Tel (212)512-6158. LC HD9506.A1. DD 338.7622025. adv acc. Circ 2,500. *E & MJ International Directory of Mining and Mineral Processing Operations.*

EARLY AMERICAN LIFE. YEARBOOK. 0094-7083. US. English. an. Early American Society, 3300 Walnut Street, Boulder CO 80302. LC E162. DD 917.3032.

EASTERN HEMISPHERE PETROLEUM DIRECTORY. VFOAT Petroleum Directory: Eastern Hemisphere. 0070-8224. US. English. an. Petroleum Publ Co, 1421 South Sheridan Road, Tulsa OK 74112. LC TN867. DD 338.4766550251811.

EASTERN KENTUCKY UNIVERSITY ALUMNI DIRECTORY. (ALUMNI DIRECTORY). Main/Corp Eastern Kentucky University. 0278-8780. US. English. an. College & University Press, One Bell Road, PO Box 17940, Montgomery AL 36141. LC LD1741.E463. DD 378.76953.

EASTERN ONTARIO CONSTRUCTION INDUSTRY DIRECTORY, PURCHASING GUIDE. (EASTERN ONTARIO CONSTRUCTION INDUSTRY DIRECTORY/ PURCHASING GUIDE). VAT Annual Eastern Ontario Construction Industry Directory, Purchasing Guide. 1978-. 0705-3045. CN. English. an. $4. Per No. Sanford Evans Publications Ltd, Directory Division, PO Box 6900, 1077 Sainte James Street, Winnipeg Manatoba R3C 3B1 Canada. DD 338.476900257137.

ECCLESIASTICAL PROVINCE OF NEWFOUNDLAND DIRECTORY. Main/Corp Catholic Church. Province of Newfoundland. 1980-. 0712-6654. CN. English. an. Free. Archdiocese of St John's Chancery Office, PO Box 1363, St John's Newfoundland A1C 5N5 Canada. DD 282.025718. (ctrl).

ECHO DE LA COUR. BOTTIN. VFOAT Court House Echo. Directory. Began with 1973 issue?. 0317-3410. Periodical. CN. French and English. an. Court House Echo, 1484 Fleury Street East, Montreal Quebec H2C 1S3 Canada. DD 348.714048.

ECONOMIC WORLD DIRECTORY OF JAPANESE COMPANIES IN USA. VFOAT Directory of Japanese Companies in USA. 1978-. 0163-4682. US. English. an. $150.00. Economic Salon Ltd, 60 East 42nd Street/Room #734, New York NY 10017. Tel (212)986-1588. Ed Yashimasa Takagi. LC HG4057. DD 338.88. bk rev. adv acc. Circ 45,000. (ctrl). A business magazine dedicated to covering Japanese and American industry in the United States and expanding economic horizons between the US and Japan.

ECUMENICAL DIRECTORY OF RETREAT AND CONFERENCE CENTERS. 1st- Ed. 0361-2236. US. English. an. $15.00. Jarrow Press, 552 DeHaro Street, San Francisco CA 94107. LC BV1652. DD 269.602573.

EDITOR & PUBLISHER INTERNATIONAL YEAR BOOK. VFOAT Editor and Publisher International Year Book. 1959-. 0424-4923. US. English. an. Editor & Publisher Co, 11 West 19th Street, New York NY 10011. LC PN4700. DD 070.5025. *Editor & Publisher. International Year Book Number.*

EDITOR & PUBLISHER. SYNDICATE DIRECTORY. VFOAT Syndicate Directory. Periodical. US. English. an. $6.00. Editor and Publisher, 11 West 19th Street, New York NY 10011. Tel (212)675-4380. Ed Robert U Brown. adv acc. Circ 30,000. Complete listing of all newspaper syndicates and syndicated writers and services.

EDMONTON & AREA AIRPORT BUSINESS DIRECTORY. VFOAT Edmonton Airport Business Directory. VAT Edmonton Airport Business Directory (1984), Edmonton and Area Airport Business Directory. 1984-. 0823-8200. CN. English. an. 3.50 Each Copy. Edmonton & Area Airport Business Directory, Suite 158 158/1224-53rd Avenue Northeast, Calgary Alberta T2E 7E2 Canada. Tel (403)475-9457. Ed Paul J Skinner. DD 387.736402571233. adv acc. Circ 7,000. (ctrl). Descriptive listing of all activities of all companies providing services for aviation in the Edmonton area. *Edmonton Airport Business Directory, 0227-1664.*

EDMONTON BUSINESS DIRECTORY. 1978-. 0707-378X. CN. English. an. Edmonton Business Directory & Information Services, 10053A Jasper Avenue, Edmonton Alberta T5J 1T8 Canada. DD 917.1233.

THE EDUCATION ALMANAC. 1984-. 0747-5772. US. English. an. $14.95. National Association of Elementary School Principals, 1920 Association Drive, Reston VA 22091. Tel (703)620-6100. LC LA210. DD 370.973.

THE EDUCATION AUTHORITIES DIRECTORY AND ANNUAL. 0070-9131. UK. English. an. School Government Publications Company, Darby House/Bletchingley Road, RH1 3 DN Redhill England.

EDUCATION DIRECTORY. Main/Corp New Hampshire. State Dept. of Education. Division of Administration. 1974/75-. 0362-6709. US. English. an. New Hampshire State Department of Education, 103 North State Street, Concord NH 03301. LC L903.N4. DD 390.25742. *Directory - New Hampshire, State Department of Education.*

EDUCATION DIRECTORY. COLLEGES & UNIVERSITIES. VFOAT Education Directory. 1975-76-. 0730-7896. US. English. an. LC L901. DD 378.73. NLM L 901 E24. *Education Directory. Higher Education, 0083-2669.*

EDUCATION DIRECTORY. LOCAL EDUCATION AGENCIES. (EDUCATION DIRECTORY : LOCAL EDUCATION AGENCIES). VFOAT Local Education Agencies. 19 -. Periodical. English. ir.

EDUCATIONAL DIGEST. BUYERS' GUIDE, DIRECTORY OF SUPPLIERS. 1974-. CN. English. an. $4.65. MacLean Hunter, PO Box 100 Station A, Toronto Ontario M5W 1A7 Canada. DD 338.473716702571.

EDUCATIONAL DIRECTORY. US. English. Department of Educational & Cultural Affairs, Division of Elementary & Secondary Education, Pierre SD 57501. LC L903.S8. DD 370.25783.

EDUCATIONAL DIRECTORY OF MISSISSIPPI SCHOOLS. Series/Titl Mississippi School Bulletin. 0363-874X. US. English. an. State Superintendent of Education, State Department of Education, Jackson MS 39205. LC L166. DD 370.25762. *Mississippi Educational Directory, 0092-7899.*

EDUCATIONAL DIRECTORY. STATE & DISTRICT OFFICES. (EDUCATIONAL DIRECTORY : STATE & DISTRICT OFFICE). Main/Corp Hawaii. Dept. of Education. 0092-1777. US. English. State of Hawaii, Department of Education, PO Box 2360, Honolulu HI 96804. Tel (808)548-6583. Ed Kathleen Jones. LC L903.H3. DD 370.25969. Circ 14,000. (ctrl). Listing of schools, officials and offices within the Department of Education. Demographic and contact information provided. Also included are 1985-86/1986-87 school calendars. *Directory - State of Hawaii, Department of Education.*

EDUCATIONAL MEDIA AND TECHNOLOGY YEARBOOK. (EDUCATIONAL MEDIA & TECHNOLOGY YEARBOOK). Vol. 11 (1985)-. 8755-2094. US. English. an. $47.50. Libraries Unlimited Inc, PO Box 263, Littleton CO 80160. Tel (303)770-1220. LC LB1028.3. DD 371.3078. Directory listings of organizations and associations, graduate programs in educational technology and educational computing at all levels, and funding sources will be included as well as a mediagraphy. *Educational Media Yearbook, 0000-037X.*

EDUCATIONAL MEDIA YEARBOOK. Periodical. US. English. an. $47.50. Libraries Unlimited Inc, Box 263, Littleton CO 80160. Tel (303)770-1220. Ed Elwood Miller. Continues the broad coverage of its predecessors, providing educational media/technology communications professionals with an indispensable reference tool.

EDUCATIONAL MEDIA YEARBOOK CEASED. Began in 1973. 0000-037X. US. English. R R Bowker, 1180 Avenue of the Americas, New York NY 10036. LC LB1028.3. DD 001.5. NLM W1 ED85E.

EDUCATIONAL RESOURCES DIRECTORY. 1980/81-. 0193-8622. US. English. be. $8.20. Museums Collaborative Inc, 15 Gramercy Park South, New York NY 10003. LC AM13.N5. DD 069.0257471. *Educational Resources Directory of New York City's Museums, Zoos, Botanical Gardens.*

EDUCATIONAL STATISTICS YEARBOOK CEASED. V. 1- 1974-. 0376-9135. FR. English. an. $3.75. Organization for Economic Co-Operation and Development, 2 rue Andre-Pascal, 75775 Paris Cedex 16 France. LC L11. DD 370.

EDUCATIONAL YEARBOOK. UK. English. an. British Computer Society, 29 Portland Place, London W1N 4HU England. LC QA76. DD 001.64071041. *BCS Educational Yearbook.*

EEO YEARBOOK. VAT Equal Employment Opportunity Yearbook. 0147-5339. US. English. an. Department of Defense, Defense Supply Agency, Cameron Station, Alexandria VA 22314. LC UC263.

EGLISE DE CHICOUTIMI. ANNUAIRE DIOCESAIN. (EGLISE DE CHICOUTIMI ... ANNUAIRE DIOCESAIN). Main/Corp Eglise Catholique. Diocese de Chicoutimi. VAT Annuaire Diocesain (Chicoutimi). 1981. 1981-. 0710-6238. CN. French. an. $5,00 Per Volume. Eveche de Chicoutimi, CP 278, Chicoutimi Quebec G7H 5C3 Canada. DD 282.0257471. *Repertoire, 0381-6710.*

EGYPT INVESTMENT & BUSINESS DIRECTORY. VFOAT Egypt Investment and Business Directory. UA. English. ir. Fiani & Partners Egypt, 143 El Tahrir Street, Dokki Cairo Egypt. *Egypt Investment Directory.*

EGYPTIAN COMPANIES DIRECTORY, PUBLIC & PRIVATE SECTORS. VFOAT Dalil Al-Sharikat Lil-Qitaayn Al-Amm Wa-Al-Khass. Began with Vol. for 1976. UA. English. an. 8

Yearbooks, Almanacs, Directories

Chawarby Street, Cairo Egypt. **LC** HF3886.A48. **DD** 338.7402562.

EIA PUBLICATIONS DIRECTORY, A USER'S GUIDE. VFOAT E.I.A. Publications Directory, A User's Guide. **VAT** Energy Information Administration Publications Directory, A User's Guide. 1979-. US. English. an. Superintendent of Documents, US Government Printing Office, Washington DC 20402. *EIA Publications Directory, EIA Publications Directory. Supplement.*

EIC ENERGY DIRECTORY UPDATE SERVICE CEASED. VFOAT Energy Directory Update Service, Energy Directory. **VAT** Environment Information Center Energy Directory Update Service. Began with Sept. 1975. Ceased with Dec. 1980. 0147-653X. US. English. an. Environment Information Center Inc, 292 Madison Avenue, New York NY 10017. *Energy Directory, 0096-3062.*

EINWOHNER-ADRESSBUCH DES LANDKREISES BREISGAU-HOCHSCHWARZWALD. BD. 3, TITISEE-NEUSTADT UND HOCHSCHWARZWALD. VFOAT Einwohner Adressbuch des Landkreises Breisgau Hochschwarzwald. German. an. Rombach + Co GMBH Druck- und Verlagshaus, Postfach 1349, D-7800 Freiburg I West Germany.

EIS DIRECTORY. (EIS . . . DIRECTORY). VFOAT E.I.S. . . . Directory. 0732-2445. US. English. an. Center for Disease Control, Attn: EIS Coordinator, Epidemiology Program Office, Atlanta GA 30333. **LC** RA650.5. **DD** 614.402573.

EIS DIRECTORY OF TOP 1500 COMPANIES. VFOAT Directory of Top 1500 Companies. US. English. an. $120.00. Economic Information Systems, 310 Madison Avenue, New York NY 10017. **Tel** (212)697-6080.

EISS YEARBOOK. VFOAT Annuaire Eiss. Periodical. US. English (French). ir. Kluwer Law and Taxation Publishers, 190 Old Derby Street, Hingham MA 02043. **LC** HD7164. **DD** 368.40094.

E.I.T.D. ELECTRONIC INDUSTRY TELEPHONE DIRECTORY. (EITD : ELECTRONIC INDUSTRY TELEPHONE DIRECTORY). VFOAT Electronic Industry Telephone Directory. 0422-9053. US. English. an. $38.00. Harris Publishing Company, 2057-2 Aurora Road, Twinsburg OH 44087. **LC** HD9696.A3. **DD** 384.6.

ELECTION DIRECTORY (WASHINGTON, D.C.). (ELECTION DIRECTORY). VFOAT Directory of Election Officials. 0163-5441. US. English. an. Superintendent of Documents, US Government Printing Office, Washington DC 20402. **LC** JK2021. **DD** 329.002573.

ELECTRICAL WORLD DIRECTORY OF ELECTRIC UTILITIES IN LATIN AMERICA, BERMUDA AND THE CARIBBEAN ISLANDS. VFOAT Directory of Electric Utilities in Latin America, Bermuda and the Caribbean Islands. 0092-2501. US. English. McGraw Hill, 1221 Avenue of the Americas, New York NY 10020. **LC** HD9685.S6. **DD** 363.6202572.

ELECTRICAL WORLD INTERNATIONAL DIRECTORY OF ELECTRICITY SUPPLIERS. VFOAT International Directory of Electricity Suppliers. 0092-1467. US. English. McGraw Hill, 1221 Avenue of the Americas, New York NY 10020. **LC** HD9685.A1. **DD** 382.4562131025.

ELECTRONIC MAIL EXECUTIVES DIRECTORY. Began with Jan. 1980 issue. 0735-2379. US. English. an. $595.00. International Resource Development Inc, 30 High Street, Norwalk CT 06851. **Tel** (203)866-7800. **Ed** Diam Tomck. **LC** HE6239.E54. **DD** 384.14. Results of primary survey of approximately 1,000 major US corporations. (All raw survey data provided). Plans for procurement of microcomputers and software. Centralized/decentralized procurement policies, etc.

ELECTROSOURCE. (ELECTROSOURCE : PRODUCT REFERENCE GUIDE AND TELEPHONE DIRECTORY). '84-. 0826-192X. CN. English. an. $30.00 Domestic, $40.00 Foreign. Lakeview Publications Inc, Unit 28/1200 Aerowood Drive, Mississauga Ontario L4W 2S7 Canada. **DD** 338.47621380971.

E/MJ INTERNATIONAL DIRECTORY. MINING ACTIVITY DIGEST. (E/MJ INTERNATIONAL DIRECTORY MINING ACTIVITY DIGEST). VFOAT E/MJ Mining Activity Digest, Mining Activity Digest. 0149-5275. Periodical. US. English. mo. $96.00. McGraw-Hill E/MJ Mining Information, 1221 Avenue of the Americas, New York NY 10020. **Tel** (212)512-6158. **Ind/Abst** GeoRef, Nexis, Bibliogr. Index Geol. **Circ** 1,000. Worldwide mining and mineral update.

E/MJ INTERNATIONAL DIRECTORY OF MINING AND MINERAL PROCESSING OPERATIONS. VFOAT International Directory of Mining and Mineral Processing Operations. Began in 1968. 0579-3831. US. English. an. McGraw-Hill Inc, 1221 Avenue of the Americas, New York NY 10020. **Tel** (212)512-6158. **LC** HD9506.A1. **DD** 338.2025. adv acc. **Circ** 3,000. Metals and non-metallics worldwide.

ENCYCLOPAEDIA JUDAICA YEAR BOOK. 1973-. 0303-7819. US. English. an. American Comm Shaare Zedek, Hospital 49 West 45th Street, New York NY 10036. **LC** DS102.8. **DD** 909.04924. **NLM** DS 102.8 E561.

ENERGISTATISTISK ARBOG. VFOAT Jahrbuch Energiestatistik, Energy Statistics Yearbook. 1970/75-. LU. Danish (Dutch, English, French, German, or Italian). an. European Community Information Inc, 2100 M Street NW/Suite 707, Washington DC 20037. **Tel** (202)862-9500. **LC** HD9502.E79. *Energistatistisk.*

ENERGY CONSERVATION RESOURCE DIRECTORY. US. English. an. Washington State Energy Office, 400 East Union Avenue/Mail Drop ER-11, Olympia WA 98504. **LC** HD9502.U53. **DD** 333.7916025797.

ENERGY DIRECTORY. (THE ENERGY DIRECTORY). 1974-. Periodical. US. English. qt. EIC/Order Processing, 48 West 38th Street, New York NY 10018. **Tel** (212)944-8500.

ENERGY EXECUTIVE DIRECTORY. Began with Spring 1980 issue. 0275-2905. US. English. ty. $60.00. Carroll Publishing Co, 1058 Thomas Jefferson Street NW, Washington DC 20007. **LC** HD9502.U5. **DD** 350.82302573.

ENERGY INFORMATION DIRECTORY. 1st Quarter 1981-. 0278-1581. Periodical. US. English. sa. National Energy Information Center, EI-20 Energy Information Administration, Forrestal Building/Room 1F-048, Washington DC 20585. **LC** HD9502.U5. **DD** 025.49333790973. *Energy Infomration Referral Directory, 0270-0026.*

ENERGY STATISTICS YEARBOOK (UNITED NATIONS. STATISTICAL OFFICE). (ENERGY STATISTICS YEARBOOK). VFOAT Energy Statistics Year Book, Annuaire des Statistiques de l'Energie. 1982-. US. English (French). an. $45.00. United Nations Publications, Sales Section/Room A-3315, New York NY 10017. **Tel** (212)754-8302. **LC** HD9502.A1. **DD** 333.79021. Provides a global framework of comparable data on trends and developments in the supply of all forms of energy. *Yearbook of World Energy Statistics.*

ENERGY YEAR BOOK. Began with Vol. for 1978/79. PK. English. an. Free. **LC** HD9502.P27. **DD** 353.79095491.

ENGINEERING & CONTRACT RECORD. PRODUCT DISTRIBUTION DIRECTORY. 1974-. CN. English. an. Southam Business Publications, 1450 Don Mills Road, Don Mills Ontario Canada. **DD** 338.47690028. *Construction and Aggregates Production Industries Directory, Buyers' Guide.*

ENR DIRECTORY OF CONTRACTORS. VFOAT Contractors, Engineering News-Record, Directory of Contractors, Directory of Contractors. 1974/75-. 0098-6453. US. English. an. $32.50. McGraw-Hill Inc, 1221 Avenue of the Americas, New York NY 10060. **Tel** (212)512-4634. **Ed** James Webber and John Drury. **LC** TA12. **DD** 338.47624. adv acc. **Circ** 13,000. (ctrl). Reference guide to construction contractors. 90 firms take descriptive spreads, includes top 400 US firms and top 250 international firms with addresses and phone numbers.

ENR DIRECTORY OF DESIGN FIRMS. VFOAT Design Firms, Directory of Design Firms. **VAT** Engineering News-Record, Directory of Design Firms. 1974/75-. 0098-6305. US. English. an. $32.50. McGraw-Hill Inc, 1221 Avenue of the Americas, New York NY 10020. **Tel** (202)512-4634. **Ed** James Webber and John Drury. **LC** TA12. **DD** 620.0042. adv acc. **Circ** 13,000. (ctrl). Directory of engineering and design firms for the construction industry.

THE ENTERTAINMENT INDUSTRY DIRECTORY. 0271-8014. US. English. an. $11.95. 6255 Sunset Boulevard, Hollywood CA 90028. **LC** PN2289. **DD** 381.457902029479493.

ENVIRONMENTAL INFORMATION SYSTEMS DIRECTORY. 0094-3231. US. English. ir. US Environmental Protection Agency, Room 3101/401 M Street NW, Washington DC 20460. **LC** TD169.5. **DD** 026.3636.

EPISTEME : ANUARIO DE FILOSOFIA. 1-. VE. Spanish. ir. University of Central Venezuela, Apartada 47342 Institute of Filosofia, Caracas 1041-A Venezuela. **LC** B25.

EQUINE VETERINARY AND RESEARCH DIRECTORY. VFOAT Evard. 1981/82-. 0278-9361. Periodical. US. English. an. $18.95. Fleet Street Corporation, 656 Quince Orchard Road, Gaithersburg MD 20760.

ERASMUS OF ROTTERDAM SOCIETY YEARBOOK. 1 (1981)-. 0276-2854. Periodical. US. English. an. $35.00. Erasmus of Rotterdam Society, 2217 Old Fort Hills Drive, Fort Washington MD 20744. **Tel** (302)292-7598. **Ed** Richard L DeMolen. **LC** B785.E64. **DD** 199.492. bk rev. **Circ** 600. Contains scholarly articles and book reviews which deal with the life and works of Erasmus, the leading humanist of the Renaissance.

ERC DIRECTORY. Main/Corp Employee Relocation Council. **VAT** Employee Relocation Council Directory. 0160-9629. US. English. an. $20.00. Employee Relocation Council, 1627 K Street NW, Washington DC 20006. **Tel** (202)857-0857. **Ed** Patricia Whric. **LC** HD255. **DD** 333.33. bk rev. adv acc. **Circ** 16,000. (ctrl). Listing of real estate services that assist with relocating transferred employees of corporations. *ERREAC Directory of Employee Relocation Real Estate Services.*

ERIE, PA. CITY DIRECTORY. Series/Titl United States City Directories. 18 -. Periodical. US. English. an. R L Polk & Co, 600 Washington Street, Boston MA 02111. **Tel** (617)426-6309.

ERISA BENEFIT FUNDS. DIRECTORY OF PENSION FUNDS. STATE OF ILLINOIS, CHICAGO AREA. (ERISA BENEFIT FUNDS. DIRECTORY OF PENSION FUNDS, STATE OF ILLINOIS, CHICAGO AREA). VFOAT Directory of Pension Funds, State of Illinois, Chicago Area. 1st- Ed. 0148-1312. US. English. an. 533 National Press Building, Washington DC 20045. **LC** HD7106.U6. **DD** 332.6327.

ERISA BENEFIT FUNDS. DIRECTORY OF PENSION FUNDS. STATE OF ILLINOIS, EXCLUDING CHICAGO AREA. (ERISA BENEFIT FUNDS. DIRECTORY OF PENSION FUNDS, STATE OF ILLINOIS, EXCLUDING CHICAGO AREA). VFOAT Directory of Pension Funds, State of Illinois, Excluding Chicago Area. 1st- Ed. 0148-1592. US. English. an. 533 National Press Building, Washington DC 20045. **LC** HD7106.U6. **DD** 332.6327.

ERISA BENEFIT FUNDS. DIRECTORY OF PENSION FUNDS. STATE OF MASSACHUSETTS. (ERISA BENEFIT FUNDS. DIRECTORY OF PENSION FUNDS, STATE OF MASSACHUSETTS). VFOAT Directory of Pension Funds, State of Massachusetts. 1st- Ed. 0148-1304. US. English. an. 533 National Press Building, Washington DC 20045. **LC** HD7106.U6. **DD** 332.6327.

ERISA BENEFIT FUNDS. DIRECTORY OF PENSION FUNDS. STATE OF NEW YORK, NEW YORK CITY AREA. (ERISA BENEFIT FUNDS. DIRECTORY OF PENSION FUNDS, STATE OF NEW YORK, NEW YORK CITY AREA). VFOAT Directory of Pension Funds, State of New York, New York City Area. 1st- Ed. 0148-124X. US. English. an. 533 National Press Building, Washington DC 20045. **LC** HD7106.U6. **DD** 332.6327.

ERISA BENEFIT FUNDS. DIRECTORY OF PENSION FUNDS. STATE OF VIRGINIA. (ERISA BENEFIT FUNDS. DIRECTORY OF PENSION FUNDS, STATE OF VIRGINIA). VFOAT Directory of Pension Funds, State of Virginia. 1st- Ed. 0148-1193. US. English. an. Insurance Research Inc, 533 National Press Building, Washington DC 20045. **LC** HD7106.U6. **DD** 332.6327.

ERISA BENEFIT FUNDS. DIRECTORY OF PENSION FUNDS. STATE OF WYOMING. (ERISA BENEFIT FUNDS. DIRECTORY OF PENSION FUNDS, STATE OF WYOMING). VFOAT Directory of Pension Funds,

Yearbooks, Almanacs, Directories

State of Wyoming. 0148-1576. US. English. an. Insurance Research Inc, 533 National Press Building, Washington DC 20045. LC HD7106.U6. DD 332.67254.

ERISA BENEFIT FUNDS. FINANCIAL DIRECTORY OF PENSION FUNDS. NORTHERN NEW JERSEY. (ERISA BENEFIT FUNDS - FINANCIAL DIRECTORY OF PENSION FUNDS, NORTHERN NEW JERSEY). **VAT** Employee Retirement Income Security Act Benefit Funds. Financial Directory of Pension Funds. Northern New Jersey. 1978/79-. 0190-6046. US. English. an. 533 National Press Building, Washington DC 20045. **LC** HD7106.U6. **DD** 332.6327. *ERISA Benefit Funds. Directory of Pension Funds. Northern New Jersey, 0148-1231.*

ERISA BENEFIT FUNDS. FINANCIAL DIRECTORY OF PENSION FUNDS. NORTHERN TEXAS, EXCLUDING DALLAS AREA. (ERISA BENEFIT FUNDS. FINANCIAL DIRECTORY OF PENSION FUNDS, NORTHERN TEXAS, EXCLUDING DALLAS AREA). 1978/79-. 0190-8634. US. English. an. 533 National Press Building, Washington DC 20045. **LC** HD7106.U6. **DD** 332.67254. *ERISA Benefit Funds. Directory of Pension Funds. Northern Texas, 0148-1436.*

ERISA BENEFIT FUNDS. FINANCIAL DIRECTORY OF PENSION FUNDS. NORTHERN VIRGINIA. (ERISA BENEFIT FUNDS. FINANCIAL DIRECTORY OF PENSION FUNDS, NORTHERN VIRGINIA). **VFOAT** Financial Directory of Pension Funds, Northern Virginia. **VAT** Employee Retirement Income Security Act Benefit Funds. Financial Directory of Pension Funds. Northern Virginia. 0192-2440. US. English. ir. Erisa Benefit Funds Inc, 1012- 14th Street NW/Suite 700, Washington DC 20005. **Tel** (800)368-5818. **LC** HD7106.U6. **DD** 332.67254.

ERISA BENEFIT FUNDS. FINANCIAL DIRECTORY OF PENSION FUNDS. SOUTHERN CALIFORNIA, EXCLUDING LOS ANGELES. (ERISA BENEFIT FUNDS. FINANCIAL DIRECTORY OF PENSION FUNDS, SOUTHERN CALIFORNIA, EXCLUDING LOS ANGELES). 1978/79-. 0190-9568. US. English. an. 533 National Press Building, Washington DC 20045. **LC** HD7106.U6. **DD** 332.67254. *ERISA Benefit Funds. Directory of Pension Funds. Southern California, 0148-1398.*

ERISA BENEFIT FUNDS. FINANCIAL DIRECTORY OF PENSION FUNDS. SOUTHERN CALIFORNIA, LOS ANGELES SURROUNDING AREA. (ERISA BENEFIT FUNDS. FINANCIAL DIRECTORY OF PENSION FUNDS, SOUTHERN CALIFORNIA, LOS ANGELES SURROUNDING AREA). **VAT** Employee Retirement Income Security Act Benefit Funds. Directory of Pension Funds. Southern California. 1978/79-. 0190-8650. US. English. an. 533 National Press Building, Washington DC 20045. **LC** HD7106.U6. **DD** 332.67254. *ERISA Benefit Funds. Directory of Pension Funds. Southern California, 0148-1398.*

ERISA BENEFIT FUNDS. FINANCIAL DIRECTORY OF PENSION FUNDS. STATE OF ILLINOIS, CHICAGO SURROUNDING AREA. (ERISA BENEFIT FUNDS. FINANCIAL DIRECTORY OF PENSION FUNDS, STATE OF ILLINOIS, CHICAGO SURROUNDING AREA). **VFOAT** Financial Directory of Pension Funds. State of Illinois, Chicago Surrounding Area. **VAT** Employee Retirement Income Security Act Benefit Funds. Financial Directory of Pension Funds. State of Illinois, Chicago Surrounding Area. 0192-7620. US. English. an. 533 National Press Building, Washington DC 20045. **LC** HD7106.U6. **DD** 336.185.

ERISA BENEFIT FUNDS. FINANCIAL DIRECTORY OF PENSION FUNDS. STATE OF MARYLAND. (ERISA BENEFIT FUNDS. FINANCIAL DIRECTORY OF PENSION FUNDS, STATE OF MARYLAND). 1978/79-. 0190-8316. US. English. an. 533 National Press Building, Washington DC 20045. **LC** HD7106.U6. **DD** 332.6327. *ERISA Benefit Funds. Directory of Pension Funds. State of Maryland, 0148-1460.*

ERISA BENEFIT FUNDS. FINANCIAL DIRECTORY OF PENSION FUNDS. STATE OF WASHINGTON. (ERISA BENEFIT FUNDS. FINANCIAL DIRECTORY OF PENSION FUNDS, STATE OF WASHINGTON). **VAT** Employee Retirement Income Security Act Benefit Funds. Financial Directory of Pension Funds. State of Washington. 1978/79-. 0190-7964. US. English. an. 533 National Press Building, Washington DC 20045. **LC** HD7106.U6. **DD** 332.6327. *ERISA Benefit Funds. Directory of Pension Funds. State of Washington, 0148-1215.*

ERISA BENEFIT FUNDS. FINANCIAL DIRECTORY OF PENSION FUNDS. STATE OF WISCONSIN, MILWAUKEE AREA. (ERISA BENEFIT FUNDS. FINANCIAL DIRECTORY OF PENSION FUNDS, STATE OF WISCONSIN, MILWAUKEE AREA). **VAT** Employee Retirement Income Security Act Benefit Funds. Financial Directory of Pension Funds. State of Wisconsin, Milwaukee Area. 1978/79-. 0191-0019. US. English. an. Insurance Research Inc, 533 National Press Building, Washington DC 20045. **LC** HD7106.U6. **DD** 332.67254. *ERISA Benefit Funds. Directory of Pension Funds. State of Wisconsin, 0148-1622.*

ESA DIRECTORY OF OFFICES. Main/Corp United States. Employment Standards Administration. Series/Titl ESA Publication. **VAT** Employment Standards Administration Directory of Offices. US. English. Employment Standards Administration, Washington DC 20210.

ESPIAL DATA BASE DIRECTORY. Began in 1979. 0706-1781. CN. English. $12.50 per vol. Espial Productions, PO Box 624 Station K, Toronto Ontario M4P 2H1 Canada. Ed H C Campbell. **LC** Z699.5.C27. **DD** 025.06971.

ESPOON KAUPUNGIN TILASTOLLINEN VUOSIKIRJA. Began with Vol. for 1970. 0357-6825. Finnish (Swedish). an. Espoonkatu 3, 02770 Espoo 77 Finland. **LC** HA1450.5.Z9.

ESTABLECIMIENTOS QUE PROCESAN PRODUCTOS DE ORIGEN AGROPECUARIO, DIRECTORIO. Began in 1978. MX. Spanish. ir. Carolina No. 132-120 Piso, Mexico 18 DF Mexico. **LC** HD9014.M6. **DD** 338.476640029472.

ESTADISTICA PANAMENA. SERIE K : ANUARIO DE COMERCIO EXTERIOR. Main/Corp Panama. Direccion de Estadistica y Censo. **VFOAT** Estadistica Panamena: Anuario de Comerico Exterior. PN. Spanish. an. $4.84. Contraloria Gen Republica, Apartado 5213, Pananma 5 Panama. **LC** HF142. **DD** 382.097287. *Estadistica Panamena. Serie K. 1: Anuario de Comercio Exterior.*

ESTADO DA PARAIBA, ANUARIO ESTATISTICO. **VFOAT** Anuario Estatistico P.B. Portuguese. an. Fundacao Instituto de Planejamento da Paraiba, rua 1O de Maio 417, Joao Pressoa PB Brazil. **Tel** (083)221-4430. **LC** HA988.P33. **DD** 318.133. Statistical yearbook of the state of Paraiba, cost of living index, social indicatores of Paraiba and others.

ETAT DU MONDE. (L'ETAT DU MONDE : ANNUAIRE ECONOMIQUE ET GEOPOLITIQUE MONDIAL). Ed. 1981-. 0712-1180. CN. French. an. $14.95 Per Volume. L'Etat du Monde, Boreal Express, CP 418 Station Youville, Montreal Quebec H2P 2V6 Canada. **DD** 909.82805.

ETHNIC AND CULTURAL DIRECTORY. 1975-. 0384-0441. CN. English. Central Information Service, 42 James Street North/Suite 609, Hamilton Ontario L8R 2K2 Canada. **DD** 917.1352.

ETHNIC DIRECTORY. 1977-. 0705-3177. CN. English. an. Thunder Bay Multicultural Association, PO Box 2334, Thunder Bay Ontario P7B 5E8 Canada. **DD** 301.45102571312. *Thunder Bay Ethnic Groups, 0318-8744.*

ETHNIC DIRECTORY OF ALASKA, HAWAII, OREGON AND WASHINGTON. CN. English. 10.00. Western Publishers, PO Box 30193/Station B, Calgary Alberta Canada. **Tel** 289-3301. Ed Vladimir Markotic. **LC** F915.A1. **DD** 301.4502579. **Circ** 300. Religious, social, cultural, archives, bookshops, newspapers, embassies, libraries, restaurants, etc.

ETHNIC DIRECTORY OF CALIFORNIA. CN. English. Western Publishers, PO Box 30193/Station B, Calgary Alberta Canada. **Tel** 289-3301. Ed Vladimir Markotic. **LC** F870.A1. **DD** 979.405025. **Circ** 500. Business, churches, archives, libraries, bookshops, clubs, newspapers, publishers, ethnic societies etc.

ETHNIC DIRECTORY OF CANADA. 1976-. CN. English. Western Publishers, Dr Vladimir Markotic, University of Calgary, Calgary Alberta T2N 1N4 Canada. **Tel** 289-3301. Ed V Markotic. **LC** F1035.A1. **DD** 971.004. **Circ** 1,000. Societies, churches, stores, newspapers, and other ethnic organization addresses.

ETHNIC DIRECTORY OF WINDSOR & ESSEX COUNTY. 1976-. 0703-8348. CN. English. Free. Multicultural Council of Windsor and Essex County, 737 Ouellette Avenue, Windsor Ontario N9A 6T5 Canada. **DD** 971.331004. (ctrl).

ETHNIC MINORITY AFFAIRS DIRECTORY. 0095-0548. US. English. State of Washington/Council on Higher Education, 908 East 5th Street, Olympia WA 98504. **LC** L903.W3. **DD** 378.797.

THE EUROPA YEARBOOK. 0071-2302. UK. English. an. $210.00. UNIPUB, Box 433 Murray Hill Station, New York NY 10157. **Tel** (212)916-1650.

EUROPEAN ACCOMMODATIONS DIRECTORY. 0146-5171. US. English. American Automobile Association, 8111 Gatehouse Road, Falls Church VA 22042. **LC** TX910.A1. **DD** 647.944.

EUROPEAN DESIGN DIRECTORY. 1974-. UK. English. an. 42.00. Engineering Materials and Design, Quadrant House, The Quadrant, Sutton Surrey SM2 5AS England. **Tel** (01)661-3174. Ed R Narraway. **LC** TA402.5.E85. **DD** 338.47620002541. adv acc. (ctrl). Covers technical features, new products, data, technology transfer, manufacturing technique and news relating to product, machine and equipment design.

EUROPEAN GLASS DIRECTORY & BUYERS' GUIDE. (EUROPEAN GLASS DIRECTORY & BUYERS GUIDE). **VFOAT** European Glass Directory and Buyers' Guide. 0306-204X. UK. English. 28.00. Fuel and Metallurgical Journals Ltd, Queensway House, 2 Queensway, Redhill RH1 1QS England. **Tel** (0737)68611. Ed Bob Sanson. **LC** HD9623.E8. **DD** 380.14566610254. adv acc. Information on manufacturers, processors, and users of glass and the companies who supply them with plant equipment and services.

EUROPEAN PETROLEUM DIRECTORY. Began with 1980 Vol. 0275-3871. US. English. an. $55.00. Pennwell Publishing Co, PO Box 1260, Tulsa OK 74101. **Tel** (918)663-4220. Ed William R Leeks. **LC** HD9575.A12. **DD** 338.272820254. adv acc. **Circ** 2,000. Lists all countries in all phases of oil industry operating in Europe. Listings organized by country with company index.

EUROPEAN RUBBER DIRECTORY. 1st- Ed. 0306-414X. UK. English, French, German, and Italian. an. 27.-. MacLaren Publishers, PO Box 109 Davis House High Street, Croydon CR9 10H England. **Tel** (01)831-9511. Ed Robert C Grace. **LC** TS1877. **DD** 338.4767830254. bk rev. adv acc. **Circ** 8,000. (ctrl). Provides news and analyses of technical and commercial developments in the rubber and related end-user industries. Also, details new equipment materials, processes and applications.

EUROPLASTICS YEARBOOK. UK. English, French, German, Italian and Spanish. ir. Business Press International Ltd, Perrymount Road/Haywards Heath, West Sussex RH163BR England. **LC** TP1103. **DD** 338.476684094.

EUROSTAT, ACP: ANNUAIRE DES STATISTIQUES DU COMMERCE EXTERIEUR. (ACP : YEARBOOK OF FOREIGN TRADE STATISTICS). **VFOAT** Annuaire des Statistiques du Commerce Exterieur. 0255-397X. LU. English (French). an. $9.88. European Community Information Service, 2100 M Street NW/Suite 707, Washington DC 20037. **LC** HF91. **DD** 382.0904. *ACP : Annuaire des Statistiques du Commerce Exterieur, Synthese.*

EVERY WOMAN'S ALMANAC. (EVERYWOMAN'S ALMANAC). 1976-. 0319-7530. CN. English. an. Canadian Women's Educational Press, Suite 305/280 Bloor Street West, Toronto Ontario M5S 1W1 Canada. **DD** 301.41205.

EVERYBODY'S MONEY COMPLAINT DIRECTORY FOR CONSUMERS. **VFOAT** Complaint Directory for Consumers. 0732-0485. US. English. $2.50. Everybody's Money, Box 431, Madison WI 53701. **LC** HC110.C63. **DD** 381.3302573. *Em Complaint Directory for Consumers, 0363-2083.*

THE EXECUTIVE BIO-PICTORIAL DIRECTORY. 1980-. 0272-345X. US. English. Braddock Publications, 1001 Connecticut Avenue NW, Washington DC 20036. **LC** JK723.E9. **DD** 353.0023.

Yearbooks, Almanacs, Directories

EXECUTIVE DIRECTORY OF THE U. S. PHARMACEUTICAL INDUSTRY. 1st- Ed. 0071-3309. US. English. ir. Chemical Economic Services, PO Box 468, Princeton NJ 08540. **Tel** (609)921-8468. **Ed** K R Kern. NLM QV 22 AA1 E9.

EXHIBITION DIRECTORY. US. English. an. LC N6512. **DD** 709.73074013.

EXHIBITS DIRECTORY - ASSOCIATION OF AMERICAN PUBLISHERS. **Main/Corp** Association of American Publishers. **VFOAT** National, State, Regional Exhibits Directory. 0147-0310. US. English. an. $45.00. Association of American Publishers Inc, One Park Avenue, New York NY 10016. **Tel** (212)689-8920. **Ed** Ray George. adv acc. **Circ** 700. Directory of educational, library, and technical associations at which publishers may wish to exhibit their books. *Joint Directory of Exhibit Opportunities. National, State and Region.*

EXHIBITS SCHEDULE; ANNUAL DIRECTORY OF TRADE AND INDUSTRIAL SHOWS. 0531-5360. US. English. an. $90.00. Bill Communications Inc, 633- 3rd Avenue, New York NY 10017. **Tel** (212)986-4800. LC HF5438.8.M4. **DD** 607.34. **Circ** 4,000. A listing of exhibits, trade shows and fairs in the US and abroad.

EXPORT CANADA : THE MARKETING DIRECTORY FOR CANADIAN EXPORTS. **VFOAT** Marketing Directory for Canadian Exports. 1980-. 0708-1332. CN. English (French and Spanish). an.

EXPORT DIRECTORY CHILE. **VFOAT** Directorio de la Exportacion. CL. English (French, German, and Spanish). ir. 1.500. Direccion de Promocion de Exportaciones Prochile, Av Pedro de Valdivia 0193-Piso 2, PO Box 16587, Correo 9 Chile. **Tel** 2317108. LC HF3413. **DD** 382.6029483. adv acc. **Circ** 15,000. (ctrl). Lists Chilean exporters. *Directorio de la Exportacion Chilena.*

EXPORT DIRECTORY OF BRAZIL. **VFOAT** Guia Brasileiro de Exportacao. 6th- Ed. BL. English, French, German, Portuguese, and Spanish. ir. Editora de Guisa Ltb Sa, rua Desembar Gador Viriato, 20000 Rio de Janeiro RJ Brazil. **Tel** 288-7667. **Ed** Gilberto Huber. LC HF3403. **DD** 382.602581. adv acc. A collection of catalogues which products are divided by market segments to promote Brazilian exportations. *GBE.*

EXPORT DIRECTORY OF NEPAL. English. ir. Post Box No 825, Kathmandu Nepal. LC HF3770.9. **DD** 382.6095496.

EXPORT DIRECTORY OF PARANA, BRAZIL. 1st Ed. (1982/83)-. BL. English (Spanish). ir. $25.00. EBIS - Empreendimentos Brasileiros de Informacoes, Dirigidas Av Paulista 326- 6 Andar, PO Box 4724, 01310 Sao Paulo SP-Brazil. LC HF5126.P37. **DD** 382.602948162.

EXPORT DIRECTORY OF SANTA CATARINA, BRAZIL. 1982/83-. English. an. Brazilian Foreign Trade Publications, Cecesc Office, PO Box D-87, 88000 Florianopolis SC Brazil. LC HF5126.S22. **DD** 382.602948164.

EXPORTERS GUIDE & KEY BUSINESS DIRECTORY - CARIBBEAN & LATIN AMERICA. **VFOAT** Guia del Exportador y Director de Empresas Claves - Caribe y America Latina. **VAT** Exporters Guide and Key Business Directory - Caribbean and Latin America. 2nd- Ed. Periodical. PR. English (Spanish). an. $60.00. Witcom Group Inc, El Caribe Building/15th Floor, San Juan Puerto Rico 00901. **Tel** (809)725-8075. LC HC121. *Exporters Guide.*

FAA DIRECTORY. **Main/Corp** United States. Federal Aviation Administration. **VFOAT** Federal Aviation Administration Directory. 0192-057X. Periodical. US. English. sa. Superintendent of Documents, US Government Printing Office, Washington DC 20402. LC HE9803.A1. **DD** 353.00877025.

FACILITIES DIRECTORY. US. English. Texas Parks & Wildlife Department, 4200 Smith School Road, Austin TX 78744. LC GV54.T59. **DD** 790.025764.

THE FACTS ON FILE SCIENTIFIC YEARBOOK. **VFOAT** Scientific Yearbook. 1985-. 0883-0800. US. English. an. $21.95. Facts on File Publications, 460 Park Avenue South, New York NY 10016. LC Q9. **DD** 505. *Young Students Science Yearbook.*

FACTS ON FILE YEARBOOK. V. 1- 1941-. 0196-2981. US. English. an. Facts on File Inc, 119 West 57th Street, New York NY 10019. LC D410. **DD** 905. (cum index).

FAIRCHILD'S TEXTILE & APPAREL FINANCIAL DIRECTORY. **VFOAT** Textile and Apparel Financial Directory, Fairchild's Textile and Apparel Financial Directory, Textile & Apparel Financial Directory. 1974-. US. English. an. $50.00. Fairchild Publishing Company, 7 East 12th Street, New York NY 10003. **Tel** (212)741-4280. **Ed** Robert Benjamin. **Circ** 1,000. (ctrl). Financial profiles of over two hundred publicly owned textile and apparel manufacturers. *Fairchild's Textile & Apparel Financial Fact Book & Directory.*

FAIRPLAY WORLD SHIPPING YEAR BOOK. 1978-. 0140-5047. UK. English. an. Financial Times Business Division, Minster House Arthur Street, London EC4R 9AX England. LC HE561. **DD** 387.505. *Financial Times World Shipping Year Book.*

FAMILY STUDIES REVIEW YEARBOOK. Vol. 1 (1983)-. 0734-2926. US. English. ir. $37.50. Sage Publications Incorporated, 275 South Beverly Drive, Beverly Hills CA 90213. **Tel** (213)274-8003. LC HQ518. **DD** 306.85. NLM W1.

FAO FERTILIZER YEARBOOK. **Main/Corp** Food and Agriculture Organization of the United Nations. **VFOAT** Annuaire FAO des Engrais, Anuario FAO de Fertilizantes. **VAT** Food and Agriculture Organization of the United Nations Fertilizer Yearbook. 1978-. English (French and Spanish). an. $26.00. UNIPUB, PO Box 1062, Ann Arbor MI 48106. **Tel** (800)521-8110. LC HD9483.A1. **DD** 338.47668620212. *Annual Fertilizer Review, 0084-6546.*

FAO PRODUCTION YEARBOOK. **Main/Corp** Food and Agriculture Organization of the United Nations. **VFOAT** Annuaire FAO de la Produccion, Anuario FAO de Produccion. V. 30- 1976-. English (French and Spanish). an. UNIPYB, PO Box 1222, Ann Arbor MI 48106. **Tel** 212-686-4707/800/521-8110. LC HD1421. **DD** 338.10212. *Production Yearbook.*

FAO TRADE YEARBOOK. **Main/Corp** Food and Agriculture Organization of the United Nations. **VFOAT** Annuaire FAO du Commerce, Annuario FAD de Commercio. **VAT** Food and Agriculture Organization Trade Yearbook. V. 30- 1976-. IT. text in English, French, and Spanish. an. UNIPUB, PO Box 1222, Ann Arbor MI 48106. **Tel** (800)521-8110. LC HD9000.4. **DD** 380.1410212. *Trade Yearbook.*

FAR EASTERN ECONOMIC REVIEW .. . ASIA YEARBOOK. 1973-. HK. English. an. $23.95. Far Eastern Economic Review, GPO Box 160, Hong Kong. **Tel** 5-8911533. **Ed** Mike MacLachlan. adv acc. **Circ** 30,000. Hardbound. Covers events of Asian economic, political, social or strategic importance.

FARM EQUIPMENT DIRECTORY. **VFOAT** Canadian Farm Equipment Dealer. Directory. 1965/66-. 0071-3899. CN. English. an. Southam Business Publications, 1450 Don Mills Road, Don Mills Ontario Canada. **DD** 338.476313025.

FARMER AND STOCK-BREEDER YEAR BOOK AND DESK DIARY. 80- 1956-. Periodical. UK. English. an. *Farmer and Stockbreeder Yearbook.*

FARMERS' ALMANAC FOR CANADA AND THE UNITED STATES CEASED. (FARMERS' ALMANAC FOR THE YEAR . . . FOR CANADA AND THE UNITED STATES). V. 158-165. 0737-0644. US. English. an. Victoria and Grey Trust, Lindsay Ontario Canada. **DD** 051. *Farmers' Almanac for the Year . . . for the United States and Canada.*

FAX/NET, PUBLIC ACCESS FACSIMILE STATION DIRECTORY. **VFOAT** F.A.X./N.E.T., Public Access Facsimile Station Directory. 0749-2715. US. English. Perimeter Inc, 12 South 6th Street, PO Box 27222, Minneapolis MN 55402. LC TK6710. **DD** 384.14.

FEDERAL AND STATE JUDICIAL CLERKSHIP DIRECTORY. **VFOAT** Judicial Clerkship Directory. Began with: 1983. 0882-5041. US. English. an. $35.00 Members, $70.00 Non-Members. NALP Administrative Office, 6325 Freret Street, New Orleans LA 70118. **DD** 340. *Judicial Clerkship Survey.*

FEDERAL CAREER DIRECTORY; A GUIDE FOR COLLEGE STUDENTS. 1962-. US. English. ir. Superintendent of Documents, US Government Printing Office, Washington DC 20402. *Federal Careers in the Sixties.*

THE FEDERAL DIRECTORY. 3D.- Ed. 0360-3512. US. English. sa. Consolidated Directories, 1133 15th Street Northwest, Washington DC 20005. LC JK6. **DD** 353.002. *Federal Telephone Directory, 0093-674X.*

FEDERAL EDUCATION GRANTS DIRECTORY. 1978/79. 0164-0690. US. English. an. Capitol Publications, 1300 North 17th Street, Arlington VA 22209. **Tel** (703)528-1100. LC LB2336. **DD** 37912102573. *Federal Education Program Guide, 0145-4854.*

FEDERAL EMPLOYEES ALMANAC. Began in 1954. 0071-4127. US. English. an. $3.50. Federal Employees' Almanac, PO Box 457, Merrifield VA 22116. **Tel** (703)533-3031. **Ed** Joseph Young. LC JK671. **DD** 353.001. **Circ** 160,000. Contains benefits and job rights of federal and postal employees and retirees, plus listings of government unions and professional organizations, key committees of Congress, etc.

THE FEDERAL EMPLOYMENT INFORMATION DIRECTORY. 1st Ed.-. 0194-1704. US. English. an. $5.00. National Employment Listing Service, Texas Criminal Justice Center, Sam Houston State University, Huntsville TX 77341. LC HV8130. **DD** 364.02373.

FEDERAL EVALUATIONS. (FEDERAL EVALUATIONS : A DIRECTORY). Series/Titl Congressional Sourcebook Series. 1980-. 0277-4224. US. English. an. US General Accounting Office, Washington DC 20548. LC H62.5.U5. **DD** 353.076025. NLM Z 1223.A12 F294. *Federal Program Evaluations, 0148-8708.*

FEDERAL EXECUTIVE DIRECTORY. Mar./Apr. 1980-. 0270-563X. Periodical. US. English. bm. Carroll Publishing Co, 812 Pennsylvania Avenue NW, Washington DC 20007. LC JK6. **DD** 353.002. *Federal Executive Telephone Directory, 0363-5384.*

FEDERAL FINANCIAL MANAGEMENT DIRECTORY. 0092-0126. US. English. an. Joint Financial Management Improvement Program, Superintendent of Documents, US Government Printing Office, Washington DC 20402. LC JK723.E9. **DD** 353.0072025.

FEDERAL HOTEL/MOTEL DISCOUNT DIRECTORY. **VFOAT** Federal Hotel Motel Discount Directory. Sept. 1981-. 0747-6442. US. English. an. US General Services Administration, Federal Supply and Services, Washington DC 20406.

FEDERAL REGIONAL EXECUTIVE DIRECTORY. Winter/Spring 1984-. 0742-1729. US. English. sa. $125.00. Carroll Publishing Company, 1058 Thomas Jefferson Street Northwest, Washington DC 20007. **Tel** (202)333-8620. **Ed** Nancy Cahill. LC JK723.E9. **DD** 353.04025. The only directory that gives you rapid access to the field office of executive branch agencies, including regional maps showing agency service areas.

FEDERAL REGULATORY DIRECTORY. **VFOAT** Congressional Quarterly's Federal Regulatory Directory. 1979/80-. 0195-749X. US. English. an. $22.50. Congressional Quarterly Inc, 1414 22nd Street NW, Washington DC 20037. LC KF5406.A15. **DD** 353.00025.

FEDERAL STAFF DIRECTORY. 1982-. 0735-3324. US. English. an. Congressional Staff Directory Ltd, PO Box 62, Mt Vernon VA 22121. **Tel** (703)765-3400. **Ed** Charles B and Anna L Brownson. LC JK723.E9. **DD** 353.002. **Circ** 12,000. United States government executive branch, with 27,000 key staff by department and agency including building, room, and extension for each inside and out of Washington. 2,2000 biographies.

FEDERAL TRAVEL DIRECTORY (WASHINGTON, D.C. : 1981). (FEDERAL TRAVEL DIRECTORY). Issue No. 6 (Oct. 1981)-. 0278-0941. Periodical. US. English. mo. Superintendent of Documents, US Government Printing Office, Washington DC 20402. *Federal Contract Air Service and Travel Directory, 0279-6066.*

FEDERATION OF CHILDREN'S BOOK GROUPS YEARBOOK. UK. English. an. Federation of Children's Book Groups, Owston Ferry Doncaster Yorks, Owston Ferry 220, Doncaster England. LC Z1037.A1. **DD** 028.5.

FELLOWSHIP YEARBOOK. (THE FELLOWSHIP YEAR BOOK). 1969-. 0317-266X. CN. English. an. Fellowship of Evangelical Baptist Churches in Canada, 74 Sheppard Avenue West, Willowdale Ontario M2N 1M3 Canada. **DD** 286.106271. *Missions Digest and Year Book, 0544-439X.*

Yearbooks, Almanacs, Directories

FERGUSON'S CEYLON DIRECTORY. VFOAT Ceylon Directory. 1920/21-1979/81. English. an. DD 915.4930025. *Ceylon Handbook & Directory and Compendium of Useful Information.*

FERGUSON'S SRI LANKA DIRECTORY. VFOAT Sri Lanka Directory. 121st Ed. (1981-83)-. English. an. 20.00. Associated Newspapers of Ceylon Ltd, Lake House D R Wijewardene Mawatha, PO Box 1198, Colombo 10 Sri Lanka. **Tel** (01)23119. **Ed** T C L Ferdinando. **LC** DS488.9. **DD** 954.930025. adv acc. **Circ** 10,000. (ctrl). Geographical description of the island, history, islands elective franchise, staff officers, diplomatic representation, local government, postal information, tourism, banks, business, commerce, finance, professions, institutions, hospitals, education, sports, trade, estates, and agriculture. *Ferguson's Ceylon Directory.*

FERNALD CLUB YEARBOOK. Main/Corp Massachusetts. University. Fernald Entomological Club. V. 1- 1932-. 0196-2140. US. English. an. Department of Entomology, Fernald Hall, University of Massachusetts, Amherst MA 01002.

FIABCI INTERNATIONAL DIRECTORY. Main/Corp International Real Estate Federation. English (French, German, and Spanish). ir. Federation Internationale des Professions Inmobilieres, Clayton Promotion, 99 rue de Fichelieu, 75002 Paris France. **LC** HD1361. **DD** 333.33025.

FIBER OPTICS DIRECTORY UPDATE SERVICE. 0270-3068. Periodical. US. English. bm. $43.50. Patent Data Publications, 901 North President Street, Wheaton IL 60187.

FID DIRECTORY .... Main/Corp International Federation for Documentation. VFOAT F.I.D. Directory. 0379-3680. NE. English. be. 25.00. International Federation Documentation, PO Box 90402, 2509 LK The Hague Netherlands. **LC** Z1008. **DD** 025.0601. Supersedes the "FID Yearbook" which was published through 1977 as FID 526. *FID Yearbook, 0077-5839.*

THE FIFTY BILLION DOLLAR DIRECTORY. VFOAT 50 Billion Dollar Directory. 1984 Ed.-. 0741-8892. US. English. an. $65.00. Publishers Services, 6318 Vesper Avenue, Van Nuys CA 91411-2378. **LC** HF5465.5. **DD** 381.1402573.

THE FILIPINO DIRECTORY OF CALIFORNIA. 0739-4802. US. English. FIL-AM Enterprises Inc, 46060 Hollywood Boulevard, Los Angeles CA 90028. **LC** F870.F4. **DD** 979.4053025.

THE FILM AND VIDEO MAKERS DIRECTORY. 0270-3289. US. English. be. $5.00. Carnegie Institute, 4400 Forbers Avenue, Pittsburgh PA 15213. **Tel** (412)622-3212. **Ed** Lisa Mertz. **LC** PN1993.5.U6. **DD** 384.8025. adv acc. **Circ** 2,000. Lists screening and lecture tours of independent filmmakers and other information relevent to independents and their exhibitors in the United States and abroad.

FILM YEAR BOOK. (THE FILM YEAR BOOK). 1983-. 0739-6856. US. English. $12.95. Grove Press Inc, 196 West Houston Street, New York NY 10014. **Ed** Al Clark. **LC** PN1993.3. **DD** 791.4305.

FINANCIAL & INVESTMENT YEARBOOK ROC. VFOAT Financial and Investment Year Book Roc. 1983/84-. CH. English. an. China Economic News Service, 555 Chunghsiao East Road/ Section 4, Taipei Taiwan. **LC** HG187.T28. **DD** 332.0951249. *Financial Yearbook Roc.*

FINANCIAL DIRECTORY OF NON-PROFIT GROUPS. 0747-8755. US. English. an. ERISA Benefit Funds Inc, Suite 610/1341 G Street Northwest, Washington DC 20005. **LC** HG4057. **DD** 338.7402573.

FINANCIAL DIRECTORY OF PENSION FUNDS. ALABAMA. 0742-0072. US. English. an. ERISA Benefit Funds Inc, 1341 G Street NW/Suite 610, Washington DC 20005. **LC** HD7106.U6. **DD** 332.67254. *ERISA Benefit Funds. Financial Directory of Pension Funds, State of Alabama, 0190-6259.*

FINANCIAL DIRECTORY OF PENSION FUNDS. ALASKA. 0742-0099. US. English. an. ERISA Benefit Funds Inc, 1341 G Street NW, Washington DC 20005. **LC** HD7106.U6. **DD** 332.67254. *ERISA Benefit Funds. Financial Directory of Pension Funds, State of Alaska, 0190-6038.*

FINANCIAL DIRECTORY OF PENSION FUNDS. ARIZONA. 0742-0110. US. English. an. ERISA Benefit Funds Inc, Suite 610/1341 G Street Northwest, Washington DC 20005. **LC** HD7106.U6. **DD** 332.67254. *ERISA Benefit Funds. Financial Directory of Pension Funds, State of Arizona, 0190-6550.*

FINANCIAL DIRECTORY OF PENSION FUNDS. ARKANSAS. 0742-0102. US. English. an. ERISA Benefit Funds Inc, Suite 610/1341 G Street Northwest, Washington DC 20005. **LC** HD7106.U6. **DD** 332.67254. *ERISA Benefit Funds. Financial Directory of Pension Funds, State of Arkansas, 0190-6534.*

FINANCIAL DIRECTORY OF PENSION FUNDS. CALIFORNIA, NORTHERN, EXCLUDING SAN FRANCISCO. OAKLAND, SAN JOSE, FRESNO & OTHERS. (FINANCIAL DIRECTORY OF PENSION FUNDS. CALIFORNIA, NORTHERN, EXCLUDING SAN FRANCISCO (OAKLAND, SAN JOSE, FRESNO & OTHERS)). 0739-2737. US. English. an. ERISA Benefit Funds Inc, 1341 G Street NW/Suite 610, Washington DC 20005. **LC** HD7106.U6. **DD** 332.67254. *ERISA Benefit Funds. Financial Directory of Pension Funds, Northern California, excluding San Francisco, 0190-8677.*

FINANCIAL DIRECTORY OF PENSION FUNDS. CALIFORNIA, NORTHERN. SAN FRANCISCO AREA. (FINANCIAL DIRECTORY OF PENSION FUNDS. CALIFORNIA, NORTHERN (SAN FRANCISCO AREA)). 0739-2699. US. English. an. ERISA Benefit Funds Inc, 1341 G Street NW/Suite 610, Washington DC 20005. **LC** HD7106.U6. **DD** 332.67254. *ERISA Benefit Funds. Financial Directory of Pension Funds, Northern California, San Francisco Area, 0190-9878.*

FINANCIAL DIRECTORY OF PENSION FUNDS. CALIFORNIA, SOUTHERN, EXCLUDING LOS ANGELES AREA (SAN DIEGO, SANTA ANA, SANTA BERNARDINO & OTHERS). 0739-3385. US. English. an. ERISA Benefit Funds Inc, 1341 G Street NW/Suite 610, Washington DC 20005. **LC** HD7105.35.U6. **DD** 332.67254.

FINANCIAL DIRECTORY OF PENSION FUNDS. CALIFORNIA, SOUTHERN. LOS ANGELES CITY PROPER. (FINANCIAL DIRECTORY OF PENSION FUNDS. CALIFORNIA, SOUTHERN (LOS ANGELES CITY PROPER)). 0739-2591. US. English. an. ERISA Benefit Funds Inc, 1341 G Street NW/Suite 610, Washington DC 20005. **LC** HD7106.U6. **DD** 332.67254. *ERISA Benefit Funds. Financial Directory of Pension Funds, Southern California, Los Angeles Proper, 0190-8669.*

FINANCIAL DIRECTORY OF PENSION FUNDS. CALIFORNIA, SOUTHERN, NO. SUBURBAN LOS ANGELES. VENTURA, PASADENA, ALHAMBRA & OTHERS. (FINANCIAL DIRECTORY OF PENSION FUNDS. CALIFORNIA, SOUTHERN, NO. SUBURBAN LOS ANGELES (VENTURA, PASADENA, ALHAMBRA & OTHERS)). 0739-2729. US. English. an. ERISA Benefit Funds Inc, 1341 G Street NW/Suite 610, Washington DC 20005. **LC** HD7105.45.U6. **DD** 332.67254.

FINANCIAL DIRECTORY OF PENSION FUNDS. CALIFORNIA, SOUTHERN. SO. SUBURBAN LOS ANGELES. INGLEWOOD, WHITTIER, LONG BEACH & OTHERS. (FINANCIAL DIRECTORY OF PENSION FUNDS. CALIFORNIA, SOUTHERN, SO. SUBURBAN LOS ANGELES (INGLEWOOD, WHITTIER, LONG BEACH & OTHERS)). 0739-2672. US. English. an. ERISA Benefit Funds Inc, 1341 G Street NW/Suite 610, Washington DC 20005. **LC** HD7105.45.U6. **DD** 332.67254.

FINANCIAL DIRECTORY OF PENSION FUNDS. CALIFORNIA, UPPER NORTHERN (STOCKTON, SACRAMENTO & OTHERS). VFOAT Financial Directory of Pension Funds. 0278-2405. US. English. an. ERISA Benefit Funds Inc, 1341 G Street Northwest/Suite 909, Washington DC 20005. **LC** HD7106.U6. **DD** 332.67254.

FINANCIAL DIRECTORY OF PENSION FUNDS. COLORADO. 0741-4714. US. English. ERISA Benefit Funds Inc, Suite 610/1341 G Street Northwest, Washington DC 20005. **LC** HD7106.U6. **DD** 332.67254. *ERISA Benefit Funds. Financial Directory of Pension Funds, State of Colorado, 0190-6542.*

FINANCIAL DIRECTORY OF PENSION FUNDS. CONNECTICUT, NORTHERN. HARTFORD, WILLIMANTIC, WATERBURY & OTHERS. (FINANCIAL DIRECTORY OF PENSION FUNDS. CONNECTICUT, NORTHERN (HARTFORD, WILLIMANTIC, WATERBURY & OTHERS)). 0739-280X. US. English. an. ERISA Benefit Funds Inc, 1341 G Street NW/Suite 610, Washington DC 20005. **LC** HD7106.U6. **DD** 332.67254. *0190-9312.*

FINANCIAL DIRECTORY OF PENSION FUNDS. CONNECTICUT, SOUTHERN. STAMFORD, NEW HAVEN, NEW LONDON & OTHERS. (FINANCIAL DIRECTORY OF PENSION FUNDS. CONNECTICUT, SOUTHERN (STAMFORD, NEW HAVEN, NEW LONDON & OTHERS)). 0739-2621. US. English. an. ERISA Benefit Funds Inc, 1341 G Street NW/Suite 610, Washington DC 20005. **LC** HD7106.U6. **DD** 332.67254. *ERISA Benefit Funds. Financial Directory of Pension Funds, Southern Connecticut, 0190-9304.*

THE FINANCIAL DIRECTORY OF PENSION FUNDS. DELAWARE. 1984-85-. 0882-2980. US. English. an. ERISA Benefit Funds, Suite 700/1012-14th Street NW, Washington DC 20005. *Financial Directory of Pension Funds. State of Delaware, 0731-7387.*

FINANCIAL DIRECTORY OF PENSION FUNDS. DISTRICT OF COLUMBIA. 0742-0080. US. English. an. ERISA Benefit Funds Inc, Suite 610/1341 G Street Northwest, Washington DC 20005. **LC** HD7106.U6. **DD** 332.67254. *ERISA Benefit Funds. Financial Directory of Pension Funds, District of Columbia, 0190-6291.*

FINANCIAL DIRECTORY OF PENSION FUNDS. FLORIDA, CENTRAL (TAMPA, LAKELAND, ORLANDO & OTHERS). VFOAT Financial Directory of Pension Funds. 0278-0348. US. English. an. ERISA Benefit Funds Inc, 1341 G Street Northwest/Suite 909, Washington DC 20005. **LC** HD7106.U5. **DD** 332.67254.

FINANCIAL DIRECTORY OF PENSION FUNDS. FLORIDA, NORTHERN. JACKSONVILLE, TALLAHASSEE, GAINESVILLE & OTHERS. (FINANCIAL DIRECTORY OF PENSION FUNDS. FLORIDA, NORTHERN (JACKSONVILLE, TALLAHASSEE, GAINESVILLE & OTHERS)). 0739-2656. US. English. an. ERISA Benefit Funds Inc, 1341 G Street NW/Suite 610, Washington DC 20005. **LC** HD7106.U6. **DD** 332.67254. *ERISA Benefit Funds. Financial Directory of Pension Funds, Northern Florida, 0190-6308.*

FINANCIAL DIRECTORY OF PENSION FUNDS. FLORIDA, SOUTHERN. WEST PALM BEACH, MIAMI, FT. MYER & OTHERS. (FINANCIAL DIRECTORY OF PENSION FUNDS. FLORIDA, SOUTHERN (WEST PALM BEACH, MIAMI, FT. MYER & OTHERS)). 0739-2664. US. English. an. ERISA Benefit Funds Inc, 1341 G Street NW/Suite 610, Washington DC 20005. **LC** HD7106.U6. **DD** 332.67254. *ERISA Benefit Funds. Financial Directory of Pension Funds, Southern Florida, 0190-6267.*

FINANCIAL DIRECTORY OF PENSION FUNDS. GEORGIA, ATLANTA AREA. 0739-3245. US. English. an. ERISA Benefit Funds Inc, 1341 G Street NW/Suite 610, Washington DC 20005. **LC** HD7106.U6. **DD** 332.67254. *ERISA Benefit Funds. Financial Directory of Pension Funds, State of Georgia, Atlanta Area, 0192-2947.*

FINANCIAL DIRECTORY OF PENSION FUNDS. GEORGIA, EXCLUDING ATLANTA AREA. 0731-7328. US. English. an. ERISA Benefit Funds Inc, 1341 G Street NW/Suite 909, Washington DC 20005. **LC** HD7106.U5. **DD** 332.67254. *ERISA Benefit Funds. Directory of Pension Funds, State of Georgia, 0148-1614.*

THE FINANCIAL DIRECTORY OF PENSION FUNDS. HAWAII. 1984-85-. 0882-2956. US. English. an. ERISA Benefit Funds, Suite 700/1012-14th Street NW, Washington DC 20005. *Financial Directory of Pension Funds. State of Hawaii, 0731-7352.*

FINANCIAL DIRECTORY OF PENSION FUNDS. IDAHO. 0742-5139. US. English. an. ERISA Benefit Funds Inc, Suite 610/1341 G Street Northwest, Washington DC 20005. **LC** HD7106.U6. **DD** 332.67254. *ERISA Benefit Funds. Financial Directory of Pension Funds, State of Idaho, 0190-7131.*

FINANCIAL DIRECTORY OF PENSION FUNDS. ILLINOIS, CENTRAL DOWNSTATE (KANKAKEE, ROCKFORD, PEORIA & OTHERS). VFOAT Financial Directory of Pension Funds. 0732-6963. US. English. an. ERISA Benefit Funds Inc, 1341 G Street NW/Suite 909, Washington DC 20005. **LC** HD7106.U5. **DD** 332.67254.

Yearbooks, Almanacs, Directories

FINANCIAL DIRECTORY OF PENSION FUNDS. ILLINOIS, CHICAGO CITY PROPER. 0739-2834. US. English. an. ERISA Benefit Funds Inc, 1341 G Street NW/Suite 610, Washington DC 20005. LC HD7106.U6. DD 332.67254. *ERISA Benefit Funds. Financial Directory of Pension Funds, State of Illinois, Chicago Proper, 0192-3463.*

FINANCIAL DIRECTORY OF PENSION FUNDS. ILLINOIS, NO. SUBURBAN CHICAGO (OAK PARK, SKOKIE, EVANSTON & OTHERS). VFOAT Financial Directory of Pension Funds. 0731-3748. US. English. an. ERISA Benefit Funds Inc, 1341 G Street NW/#909, Washington DC 20005. LC HD7106.U6. DD 332.67254.

FINANCIAL DIRECTORY OF PENSION FUNDS. ILLINOIS, NORTHERN, EXCLUDING CHICAGO AREA. KANKAKEE, ROCKFORD, PEORIA & OTHERS. (FINANCIAL DIRECTORY OF PENSION FUNDS. ILLINOIS, NORTHERN, EXCLUDING CHICAGO AREA (KANKAKEE, ROCKFORD, PEORIA & OTHERS)). 0739-2818. US. English. an. ERISA Benefit Funds Inc, 1341 G Street NW/Suite 610, Washington DC 20005. LC HD7105.45.U6. DD 332.67254.

FINANCIAL DIRECTORY OF PENSION FUNDS. ILLINOIS, SO. SUBURBAN CHICAGO (EVERGREEN PARK, CHICAGO HEIGHTS, JOLIET & OTHERS). VFOAT Financial Directory of Pension Funds. 0731-3756. US. English. an. ERISA Benefit Funds Inc, 1341 G Street NW/#909, Washington DC 20005. LC HD7106.U6. DD 332.67254.

FINANCIAL DIRECTORY OF PENSION FUNDS. ILLINOIS, SOUTHERN DOWNSTATE (CHAMPAIGN, SPRINGFIELD, EAST ST. LOUIS & OTHERS). VFOAT Financial Directory of Pension Funds. 0732-7145. US. English. an. ERISA Benefit Funds Inc, 1341 G Street NW/Suite 909, Washington DC 20005. LC HD7106.U5. DD 332.67254.

FINANCIAL DIRECTORY OF PENSION FUNDS. INDIANA, NORTHERN. SOUTH BEND, FT. WAYNE, MUNCIE & OTHERS. (FINANCIAL DIRECTORY OF PENSION FUNDS. INDIANA, NORTHERN (SOUTH BEND, FT. WAYNE, MUNCIE & OTHERS)). 0739-2583. US. English. an. ERISA Benefit Funds Inc, 1341 G Street NW/Suite 610, Washington DC 20005. LC HD7106.U6. DD 332.67254. *ERISA Benefit Funds. Financial Directory of Pension Funds, Northern Indiana, 0190-8251.*

FINANCIAL DIRECTORY OF PENSION FUNDS. INDIANA, SOUTHERN (INDIANAPOLIS, TERRE HAUTE, EVANSVILLE & OTHERS). 0739-2869. US. English. an. ERISA Benefit Funds Inc, 1341 G Street NW/Suite 610, Washington DC 20005. LC HD7106.U6. DD 332.67254. *ERISA Benefit Funds. Financial Directory of Pension Funds, Southern Indiana, 0190-9894.*

FINANCIAL DIRECTORY OF PENSION FUNDS. IOWA. 0742-0129. US. English. an. ERISA Benefit Funds Inc, Suite 610/1341 G Street Northwest, Washington DC 20005. LC HD7106.U6. DD 332.67254. *ERISA Benefit Funds. Financial Directory of Pension Funds, State of Iowa, 0190-7123.*

THE FINANCIAL DIRECTORY OF PENSION FUNDS. KANSAS. 1984-85-. 0882-083X. US. English. an. ERISA Benefit Funds, Suite 700/1012-14th Street NW, Washington DC 20005. LC HD7106.U6. DD 332.67254. *ERISA Benefit Funds. Financial Directory of Pension Funds, State of Kansas, 0190-7719.*

FINANCIAL DIRECTORY OF PENSION FUNDS. LOUISIANA. 0742-0137. US. English. an. ERISA Benefit Funds Inc, Suite 610/1341 G Street NW, Washington DC 20005. LC HD7106.U6. DD 332.67254. *ERISA Benefit Funds. Financial Directory of Pension Funds, State of Louisiana, 0190-7700.*

FINANCIAL DIRECTORY OF PENSION FUNDS. MAINE. 0741-8663. US. English. an. ERISA Benefit Funds Inc, 1341 G Street NW/Suite 601, Washington DC 20005. LC HD7106.U6. DD 332.67254. *ERISA Benefit Funds. Financial Directory of Pension Funds. State of Maine, 0190-7239.*

FINANCIAL DIRECTORY OF PENSION FUNDS. MARYLAND, EASTERN (BALTIMORE, ANNAPOLIS, EASTERN SHORE & OTHERS). VFOAT Financial Directory of Pension Funds. 0278-0283. US. English. an. ERISA Benefit Funds Inc, 1341 G Street Northwest/Suite 909, Washington DC 20005. LC HD7106.U5. DD 332.67254.

FINANCIAL DIRECTORY OF PENSION FUNDS. MARYLAND, WESTERN (FREDERICK, ROCKVILLE, WALDORF & OTHERS). VFOAT Financial Directory of Pension Funds. 0278-2162. US. English. an. ERISA Benefit Funds Inc, 1341 G Street Northwest/Suite 909, Washington DC 20005. LC HD7106.U6. DD 332.67254.

FINANCIAL DIRECTORY OF PENSION FUNDS. MASSACHUSETTS, BOSTON CITY PROPER. VFOAT Financial Directory of Pension Funds. 0278-2081. US. English. an. ERISA Benefit Funds Inc, 1341 G Street Northwest/Suite 909, Washington DC 20005. LC HD7106.U6. DD 332.67254.

FINANCIAL DIRECTORY OF PENSION FUNDS. MASSACHUSETTS, EXCLUDING BOSTON & SUBURBS. WORCESTER, SPRINGFIELD, PITTSFIELD & OTHERS. (FINANCIAL DIRECTORY OF PENSION FUNDS. MASSACHUSETTS, EXCLUDING BOSTON & SUBURBS (WORCESTER, SPRINGFIELD, PITTSFIELD & OTHERS)). 0739-2648. US. English. an. ERISA Benefit Funds Inc, 1341 G Street NW/Suite 610, Washington DC 20005. LC HD7106.U6. DD 332.67254. *ERISA Benefit Funds. Financial Directory of Pension Funds, State of Massachusetts, excluding Boston Area, 0192-3226.*

FINANCIAL DIRECTORY OF PENSION FUNDS. MASSACHUSETTS, SUBURBAN BOSTON (LYNN, FRAMINGHAM & OTHERS). VFOAT Financial Directory of Pension Funds. 0278-209X. US. English. an. ERISA Benefit Funds Inc, 1341 G Street Northwest/Suite 909, Washington DC 20005. LC HD7106.U6. DD 332.67254.

FINANCIAL DIRECTORY OF PENSION FUNDS. MICHIGAN, CENTRAL AND NORTHERN (SAGINAW, TRAVERSE CITY, IRON MOUNTAIN & OTHERS). VFOAT Financial Directory of Pension Funds. 0278-2138. US. English. an. ERISA Benefit Funds Inc, 1341 G Street Northwest/Suite 909, Washington DC 20005. LC HD7106.U6. DD 332.67254.

FINANCIAL DIRECTORY OF PENSION FUNDS. MICHIGAN, DETROIT CITY PROPER. 0731-7379. US. English. an. ERISA Benefit Funds Inc, 1341 G Street NW/Suite 909, Washington DC 20005. LC HD7106.U6. DD 332.67254. *ERISA Benefit Funds. Directory of Pension Funds, Detroit Area, 0148-1479.*

FINANCIAL DIRECTORY OF PENSION FUNDS. MICHIGAN, SOUTHERN, EXCLUDING DETROIT & SUBURBS (FLINT, GRAND RAPIDS, KALAMAZOO & OTHERS). 0731-7484. US. English. an. ERISA Benefit Funds Inc, 1341 G Street NW/Suite 909, Washington DC 20005. LC HD7106.U6. *ERISA Benefits Funds. Directory of Pension Funds, State of Michigan, excluding Detroit Area, 0148-1185.*

FINANCIAL DIRECTORY OF PENSION FUNDS. MICHIGAN, SURBURBAN DETROIT (PONTIAC, ANN ARBOR, MONROE & OTHERS). VFOAT Financial Directory of Pension Funds. 0278-2170. US. English. an. ERISA Benefit Funds Inc, 1341 G Street Northwest/Suite 909, Washington DC 20005. LC HD7106.U5. DD 332.67254.

FINANCIAL DIRECTORY OF PENSION FUNDS. MINNESOTA (EXCLUDING MINNEAPOLIS-ST. PAUL AREA). 0731-7301. US. English. an. ERISA Benefit Funds Inc, 1341 G Street NW/Suite 909, Washington DC 20005. LC HD7106.U5. *ERISA Benefit Funds. Directory of Pension Funds. State of Minnesota, 0148-1223.*

FINANCIAL DIRECTORY OF PENSION FUNDS. MINNESOTA, MINNEAPOLIS-ST. PAUL AREA. (FINANCIAL DIRECTORY OF PENSION FUNDS. MINNESOTA (MINNEAPOLIS-ST. PAUL AREA)). 0739-5787. US. English. an. ERISA Benefit Funds Inc, 1341 G Street NW/Suite 610, Washington DC 20005. LC HD7106.U6. DD 332.67254. *ERISA Benefit Funds. Financial Directory of Pension Funds, State of Minnesota, Minneapolis-St. Paul Area, 0192-2556.*

FINANCIAL DIRECTORY OF PENSION FUNDS. MISSISSIPPI. 0741-868X. US. English. an. ERISA Benefit Funds Inc, 1341 G Street Northwest/Suite 601, Washington DC 20005. LC HD7106.U6. DD 332.67254. *ERISA Benefit Funds. Financial Directory of Pension Funds. State of Mississippi, 0190-8308.*

FINANCIAL DIRECTORY OF PENSION FUNDS. MISSOURI, EASTERN. ST. LOUIS, JEFFERSON CITY & OTHERS. (FINANCIAL DIRECTORY OF PENSION FUNDS. MISSOURI, EASTERN (ST. LOUIS, JEFFERSON CITY & OTHERS)). 0739-2877. US. English. an. ERISA Benefit Funds Inc, 1341 G Street NW/Suite 610, Washington DC 20005. LC HF7106.U6. DD 332.67254. *ERISA Benefit Funds. Financial Directory of Pension Funds, Eastern Missouri, 0192-7582.*

FINANCIAL DIRECTORY OF PENSION FUNDS. MISSOURI, WESTERN. KANSAS CITY, ST. JOSEPH, SPRINGFIELD & OTHERS. (FINANCIAL DIRECTORY OF PENSION FUNDS. MISSOURI, WESTERN (KANSAS CITY, ST. JOSEPH, SPRINGFIELD & OTHERS)). 0739-2826. US. English. an. ERISA Benefit Funds Inc, 1341 G Street NW/Suite 610, Washington DC 20005. LC HD7106.U6. DD 332.67254. *ERISA Benefit Funds. Financial Directory of Pension Funds, Western Missouri, 0197-3614.*

FINANCIAL DIRECTORY OF PENSION FUNDS. MONTANA. 0742-0153. US. English. an. ERISA Benefit Funds Inc, Suite 610/1341 G Street Northwest, Washington DC 20005. LC HD7106.U6. DD 332.67254. *ERISA Benefit Funds. Financial Directory of Pension Funds, State of Montana, 0190-7263.*

FINANCIAL DIRECTORY OF PENSION FUNDS. NEBRASKA. 0741-5117. US. English. ERISA Benefit Funds Inc, Suite 610/1341 G Street NW, Washington DC 20005. LC HD7106.U6. DD 332.67254. *ERISA Benefit Funds. Financial Directory of Pension Funds, State of Nebraska, 0190-7271.*

FINANCIAL DIRECTORY OF PENSION FUNDS. NEVADA. 0741-8671. US. English. an. ERISA Benefit Funds Inc, 1341 G Street Northwest/Suite 610, Washington DC 20005. LC HD7106.U6. DD 332.67254. *ERISA Benefit Funds. Financial Directory of Pension Funds. State of Nevada, 0190-7247.*

FINANCIAL DIRECTORY OF PENSION FUNDS. NEW HAMPSHIRE. 0741-4706. US. English. ERISA Benefit Funds Inc, Suite 610/1341 G Street NW, Washington DC 20005. LC HD7106.U6. DD 332.67254. *ERISA Benefit Funds. Financial Directory of Pension Funds, State of New Hampshire, 0190-8014.*

FINANCIAL DIRECTORY OF PENSION FUNDS. NEW JERSEY, NORTHERN, EXCLUDING NEWARK AND ENVIRONS (HACKENSACK, PATTERSON, SUMMIT & OTHERS). VFOAT Financial Directory of Pension Funds. 0278-6001. US. English. an. ERISA Benefit Funds Inc, 1341 G Street NW/Suite 909, Washington DC 20005. LC HD7106.U5. DD 332.67254.

FINANCIAL DIRECTORY OF PENSION FUNDS. NEW JERSEY, NORTHERN, NEWARK AND ENVIRONS (NEWARK, PASSAIC, JERSEY CITY & OTHERS). VFOAT Financial Directory of Pension Funds. 0278-579X. US. English. an. ERISA Benefit Funds Inc, 1341 G Street NW/Suite 909, Washington DC 20005. LC HD7106.U5. DD 332.67254.

FINANCIAL DIRECTORY OF PENSION FUNDS. NEW JERSEY, SOUTHERN. TRENTON, CAMDEN, ATLANTIC CITY & OTHERS. (FINANCIAL DIRECTORY OF PENSION FUNDS. NEW JERSEY, SOUTHERN (TRENTON, CAMDEN, ATLANTIC CITY & OTHERS)). 0739-2567. US. English. an. ERISA Benefit Funds Inc, 1341 G Street NW/Suite 610, Washington DC 20005. LC HD7106.U6. DD 332.67254. *ERISA Benefit Funds. Financial Directory of Pension Funds, Southern New Jersey, 0190-6240.*

THE FINANCIAL DIRECTORY OF PENSION FUNDS. NEW MEXICO. 1984-85-. 0882-2964. US. English. an. ERISA Benefit Funds, Suite 700/1012-14th Street NW, Washington DC 20005. *Financial Directory of Pension Funds. State of New Mexico, 0731-7360.*

FINANCIAL DIRECTORY OF PENSION FUNDS. NEW YORK. BROOKLYN, S.I., BRONX, QUEENS. (FINANCIAL DIRECTORY OF PENSION FUNDS. NEW YORK (BROOKLYN, S.I., BRONX, QUEENS)). 0739-2680. US. English. an. ERISA Benefit Funds Inc, 1341 G Street NW/Suite 610, Washington DC 20005. LC HD7106.U6. DD 332.67254. *ERISA Benefit Funds.*

Yearbooks, Almanacs, Directories

Financial Directory of Pension Funds, State of New York, Brooklyn, S.I., Bronx, Queens, L.I., 0191-0442.

FINANCIAL DIRECTORY OF PENSION FUNDS. NEW YORK, EASTERN UPDATE. POUGHKEEPSIE, ALBANY, GLENS FALLS & OTHERS. (FINANCIAL DIRECTORY OF PENSION FUNDS. NEW YORK, EASTERN UPSTATE (POUGHKEEPSIE, ALBANY, GLENS FALLS & OTHERS)). 0739-2761. US. English. an. ERISA Benefit Funds Inc, 1341 G Street NW/Suite 610, Washington DC 20005. LC HD7106.U6. DD 332.67254. *ERISA Benefit Funds. Financial Directory of Pension Funds, State of New York, Eastern Upstate, 0190-9290.*

FINANCIAL DIRECTORY OF PENSION FUNDS. NEW YORK, MANHATTAN-DOWNTOWN. WALL ST. TO 40 ST. (FINANCIAL DIRECTORY OF PENSION FUNDS. NEW YORK, MANHATTAN-DOWNTOWN (WALL ST. TO 40 ST.)). 0739-2605. US. English. an. ERISA Benefit Funds Inc, 1341 G Street NW/Suite 610, Washington DC 20005. LC HD7106.U6. DD 332.67254. *ERISA Benefit Funds. Financial Directory of Pension Funds, State of New York Manhattan-Downtown Wall St. to 40 St.), 0191-0345.*

FINANCIAL DIRECTORY OF PENSION FUNDS. NEW YORK, MANHATTAN-MIDTOWN, 41 ST. TO 50 ST. (FINANCIAL DIRECTORY OF PENSION FUNDS. NEW YORK, MANHATTAN-MIDTOWN (41 ST. TO 50 ST.)). 0739-2745. US. English. an. ERISA Benefit Funds Inc, 1341 G Street NW/Suite 610, Washington DC 20005. LC HD7106.U6. DD 332.67254. *ERISA Benefit Funds. Financial Directory of Pension Funds, State of New York, Manhattan-Midtown (41 St. to 50 St.), 0190-9932.*

FINANCIAL DIRECTORY OF PENSION FUNDS. NEW YORK, MANHATTAN-UPTOWN. 51 ST. TO HARLEM RIVER. (FINANCIAL DIRECTORY OF PENSION FUNDS. NEW YORK, MANHATTAN-UPTOWN (51 ST. TO HARLEM RIVER)). 0739-2842. US. English. an. ERISA Benefit Funds Inc, 1341 G Street NW/Suite 610, Washington DC 20005. LC HD7106.U6. DD 332.67254. *ERISA Benefit Funds. Financial Directory of Pension Funds, State of New York, Manhattan-Uptown (51 St. to Harlem River), 0191-0493.*

FINANCIAL DIRECTORY OF PENSION FUNDS. NEW YORK (NASSAU & SUFFOLK COUNTIES ONLY). VFOAT Financial Directory of Pension Funds. 0278-0305. US. English. an. ERISA Benefit Funds Inc, 1341 G Street NW Suite 909, Washington DC 20005. LC HD7106.U5. DD 332.67254.

FINANCIAL DIRECTORY OF PENSION FUNDS. NEW YORK, WEST CENTRAL UPSTATE (UTICA, SYRACUSE, BINGHAMTON & OTHERS). VFOAT Financial Directory of Pension Funds. 0278-0291. US. English. an. ERISA Benefit Funds Inc, 1341 G Street Northwest Suite 909, Washington DC 20005. LC HD7106.U5. DD 332.67254.

FINANCIAL DIRECTORY OF PENSION FUNDS. NEW YORK, WESTCHESTER COUNTY AREA (YONKERS, WHITE PLAINS, MIDDLETOWN & OTHERS). VFOAT Financial Directory of Pension Funds. 0278-0356. US. English. an. ERISA Benefit Funds Inc, 1341 G Street NW Suite 909, Washington DC 20005. LC HD7106.U5. DD 332.67254.

FINANCIAL DIRECTORY OF PENSION FUNDS. NEW YORK, WESTERN UPSTATE. ROCHESTER, BUFFALO, ELMIRA & OTHERS. (FINANCIAL DIRECTORY OF PENSION FUNDS. NEW YORK, WESTERN UPSTATE (ROCHESTER, BUFFALO, ELMIRA & OTHERS)). 0739-2850. US. English. an. ERISA Benefit Funds Inc, 1341 G Street NW/Suite 610, Washington DC 20005. LC HD7106.U6. DD 332.67254. *ERISA Benefit Funds. Financial Directory of Pension Funds, State of New York, Western Upstate, 0190-9908.*

FINANCIAL DIRECTORY OF PENSION FUNDS. NORTH CAROLINA, EASTERN. RALEIGH, FAYETTEVILLE, WILMINGTON & OTHERS. (FINANCIAL DIRECTORY OF PENSION FUNDS. NORTH CAROLINA, EASTERN (RALEIGH, FAYETTEVILLE, WILMINGTON & OTHERS)). 0739-2796. US. English. an. ERISA Benefit Funds Inc, 1341 G Street NW/Suite 610, Washington DC 20005. LC HD7106.U6. DD 332.67254. *ERISA Benefit Funds.*

Financial Directory of Pension Funds, North Carolina, Eastern, 0190-8324.

FINANCIAL DIRECTORY OF PENSION FUNDS. NORTH CAROLINA, WESTERN. WINSTON-SALEM, LEXINGTON, GREENSBORO, CHARLOTTE & OTHERS. (FINANCIAL DIRECTORY OF PENSION FUNDS. NORTH CAROLINA, WESTERN (WINSTON-SALEM, LEXINGTON, GREENSBORO, CHARLOTTE & OTHERS)). 0739-263X. US. English. an. ERISA Benefit Funds Inc, 1341 G Street NW/Suite 610, Washington DC 20005. LC HD7106.U6. DD 332.67254. *ERISA Benefit Funds. Financial Directory of Pension Funds, North Carolina, Western, 0190-9886.*

FINANCIAL DIRECTORY OF PENSION FUNDS. NORTH DAKOTA. 0741-479X. US. English. ERISA Benefit Funds Inc, Suite 610/1341 G Street Northwest, Washington DC 20005. LC HD7106.U6. DD 332.67254. *ERISA Benefit Funds. Financial Directory of Pension Funds, State of North Dakota, 0190-8022.*

FINANCIAL DIRECTORY OF PENSION FUNDS. OHIO, MIDEASTERN (AKRON, YOUNGSTOWN, ZANESVILLE, CANTON & OTHERS). VFOAT Financial Directory of Pension Funds. 0278-0321. US. English. an. ERISA Benefit Funds Inc, 1341 G Street Northwest Suite 909, Washington DC 20005. LC HD7106.U5. DD 332.67254.

FINANCIAL DIRECTORY OF PENSION FUNDS. OHIO, NORTHERN, CLEVELAND AREA. 0731-7026. US. English. an. ERISA Benefit Funds Inc, 1341 G Street NW, Washington DC 20005. LC HD7106.U5. DD 332.67254. *ERISA Benefit Funds. Directory of Pension Funds, Northern Ohio, 0148-1371.*

INANCIAL DIRECTORY OF PENSION FUNDS. OHIO, NORTHWESTERN (TOLEDO, MANSFIELD, LIMA & OTHERS). VFOAT Financial Directory of Pension Funds. 0278-0275. US. English. an. ERISA Benefit Funds Inc, 1341 G St NW Suite 909, Washington DC 20005. LC HD7106.U5. DD 332.67254.

FINANCIAL DIRECTORY OF PENSION FUNDS. OHIO, SOUTHERN, CINCINNATI AREA. 0731-700X. US. English. an. ERISA Benefit Funds Inc, 1341 G Street NW, Washington DC 20005. LC HD7106.U5. DD 332.67254. *ERISA Benefit Funds. Directory of Pensions, Southern Ohio, 0148-1665.*

FINANCIAL DIRECTORY OF PENSION FUNDS. OHIO, SOUTHERN, EXCLUDING CINCINNATI AREA (COLUMBUS, DAYTON, ATHENS & OTHERS). 0731-7018. US. English. an. ERISA Benefit Funds Inc, 1341 G Street NW, Washington DC 20005. LC HD7106.U5. DD 332.67254. *ERISA Benefit Funds. Directory of Pensions, Southern Ohio, 0148-1665.*

FINANCIAL DIRECTORY OF PENSION FUNDS. OKLAHOMA. 0741-8698. US. English. an. ERISA Benefit Funds Inc, 1341 G Street NW/Suite 610, Washington DC 20005. LC HD7106.U6. DD 332.67254. *ERISA Benefit Funds. Financial Directory of Pension Funds. State of Oklahoma, 0190-8332.*

FINANCIAL DIRECTORY OF PENSION FUNDS. OREGON. 0742-0161. US. English. an. ERISA Benefit Funds Inc, Suite 610/1341 G Street NW, Washington DC 20005. LC HD7106.U6. DD 332.67254. *ERISA Benefit Funds. Financial Directory of Pension Funds, State of Oregon, 0190-7816.*

FINANCIAL DIRECTORY OF PENSION FUNDS. PENNSYLVANIA, EASTERN, EXCLUDING PHILADELPHIA AREA. HARRISBURG, WILKESBARRE & OTHERS. (FINANCIAL DIRECTORY OF PENSION FUNDS. PENNSYLVANIA, EASTERN, EXCLUDING PHILADELPHIA AREA (HARRISBURG, WILKESBARRE & OTHERS)). 0739-2575. US. English. an. ERISA Benefit Funds Inc, 1341 G Street NW/Suite 610, Washington DC 20005. LC HD7106.U6. DD 332.67254. *ERISA Benefit Funds. Financial Directory of Pension Funds, Eastern Pennsylvania, excluding Philadelphia Area, 0190-955X.*

FINANCIAL DIRECTORY OF PENSION FUNDS. PENNSYLVANIA, EASTERN, PHILADELPHIA CITY PROPER. Series/Titl Book / ERISA Benefit Funds, Inc. 0739-5779. US. English. an. ERISA Benefit Funds Inc, 1341 G Street NW/Suite 610, Washington DC 20005. LC

HD7106.U6. DD 332.67254. *ERISA Benefit Funds. Financial Directory of Pension Funds, Eastern Pennsylvania, Philadelphia Area, 0190-8278.*

FINANCIAL DIRECTORY OF PENSION FUNDS. PENNSYLVANIA, EASTERN, SUBURBAN PHILADELPHIA (UPPER DARBY, WEST CHESTER, KING OF PRUSSIA & OTHERS). VFOAT Financial Directory of Pension Funds. 0278-0364. US. English. an. ERISA Benefit Funds Inc, 1341 G Street Northwest Suite 909, Washington DC 20005. LC HD7106.U5. DD 332.67254.

FINANCIAL DIRECTORY OF PENSION FUNDS. PENNSYLVANIA, WESTERN, EXCLUDING PITTSBURGH AREA. ERIE, NEW CASTLE, GREENSBURG & OTHERS. (FINANCIAL DIRECTORY OF PENSION FUNDS. PENNSYLVANIA, WESTERN, EXCLUDING PITTSBURGH AREA (ERIE, NEW CASTLE, GREENSBURG & OTHERS)). 0739-2710. US. English. an. ERISA Benefit Funds Inc, 1341 G Street NW/Suite 610, Washington DC 20005. LC HD7106.U6. DD 332.67254. *Financial Directory of Pension Funds, Western Pennsylvania, excluding Pittsburgh Area, 0190-9916.*

FINANCIAL DIRECTORY OF PENSION FUNDS. PENNSYLVANIA, WESTERN (PITTSBURGH AREA). 0741-5427. US. English. ERISA Benefit Funds Inc, 1341 G Street NW/Suite 610, Washington DC 20005. LC HD7106.U6. DD 332.67254. *ERISA Benefit Funds. Financial Directory of Pension Funds. Western Pennsylvania, Pittsburgh Area, 0190-9924.*

THE FINANCIAL DIRECTORY OF PENSION FUNDS. PUERTO RICO. 1984-85-. 0882-2972. US. English. an. Erisa Benefit Funds, Suite 700/1012-14th Street NW, Washington DC 20005. *Financial Directory of Pension Funds. Puerto Rico & Other Foreign, 0739-2702.*

FINANCIAL DIRECTORY OF PENSION FUNDS. RHODE ISLAND. 0741-871X. US. English. an. ERISA Benefit Funds Inc, 1341 G Street NW/Suite 610, Washington DC 20005. LC HD7106.U6. DD 332.67254. *ERISA Benefit Funds. Financial Directory of Pension Funds. State of Rhode Island, 0190-8006.*

THE FINANCIAL DIRECTORY OF PENSION FUNDS. SOUTH CAROLINA. 1984-85-. 0882-293X. US. English. an. Erisa Benefit Funds, Suite 700/1012-14th Street NW, Washington DC 20005. *Financial Directory of Pension Funds. State of South Carolina, 0731-731X.*

FINANCIAL DIRECTORY OF PENSION FUNDS. SOUTH DAKOTA. 0741-8701. US. English. an. ERISA Benefit Funds Inc, 1341 G Street NW/Suite 610, Washington DC 20005. LC HD7106.U6. DD 332.67254. *ERISA Benefit Funds. Financial Directory of Pension Funds. State of South Dakota, 0190-8219.*

FINANCIAL DIRECTORY OF PENSION FUNDS. STATE OF KENTUCKY. 0731-7395. US. English. an. ERISA Benefit Funds Inc, 1341 G Street NW/Suite 909, Washington DC 20005. LC HD7106.U6. DD 332.67254. *ERISA Benefit Funds. Directory of Pension Funds, State of Kentucky, 0148-1401.*

FINANCIAL DIRECTORY OF PENSION FUNDS. TENNESSEE. 0742-017X. US. English. an. ERISA Benefit Funds Inc, Suite 610/1341 G Street Northwest, Washington DC 20005. LC HD7106.U6. DD 332.67254. *ERISA Benefit Funds. Financial Directory of Pension Funds, State of Tennessee, 0190-7980.*

FINANCIAL DIRECTORY OF PENSION FUNDS. TEXAS, NORTH CENTRAL & EASTERN, EXCLUDING DALLAS AREA (LONGVIEW, FORT WORTH, WACO, SAN ANGELO & OTHERS). VFOAT Financial Directory of Pension Funds. 0278-2189. US. English. an. ERISA Benefit Funds Inc, 1341 G Street Northwest Suite 909, Washington DC 20005. LC HD7106.U6. DD 332.67254.

FINANCIAL DIRECTORY OF PENSION FUNDS. TEXAS, NORTHERN, DALLAS AREA. (FINANCIAL DIRECTORY OF PENSION FUNDS. TEXAS, NORTHERN, DALLAS AREA). 0739-3237. US. English. an. ERISA Benefit Funds Inc, 1341 G Street NW/Suite 610, Washington DC 20005. LC HD7106.U6. DD 332.67254. *ERISA Benefit Funds. Financial Directory of Pension Funds, Northern Texas, Dallas Area, 0190-8642.*

Yearbooks, Almanacs, Directories

FINANCIAL DIRECTORY OF PENSION FUNDS. TEXAS, NORTHWESTERN (AMARILLO, LUBBOCK, ABILENE & OTHERS). VFOAT Financial Directory of Pension Funds. 0278-2103. US. English. an. ERISA Benefit Funds Inc, 1341 G Street Northwest Suite 909, Washington DC 20005. LC HD7106.U6. DD 332.67254.

FINANCIAL DIRECTORY OF PENSION FUNDS. TEXAS, SOUTHERN, EXCLUDING HOUSTON AREA (BEAUMONT, SAN ANTONIO, CORPUS CHRISTI & OTHERS). 0731-7484. US. English. an. ERISA Benefit Funds Inc, 1341 G Street NW, Washington DC 20005. LC HD7106.U5. DD 332.67254. *ERISA Benefit Funds. Directory of Pension Funds, Southern Texas, 0148-1495.*

FINANCIAL DIRECTORY OF PENSION FUNDS. TEXAS, SOUTHERN, HOUSTON AREA. 0739-2788. US. English. an. ERISA Benefit Funds Inc, 1341 G Street NW/Suite 610, Washington DC 20005. LC HD7106.U6. DD 332.67254. *ERISA Benefit Funds. Financial Directory of Pension Funds, Southern Texas, Houston Area, 0192-5520.*

FINANCIAL DIRECTORY OF PENSION FUNDS. UTAH. 0742-0188. US. English. an. ERISA Benefit Funds Inc, Suite 610/1341 G Street Northwest, Washington DC 20005. LC HD7106.U6. DD 332.67254. *ERISA Benefit Funds. Financial Directory of Pension Funds, State of Utah, 0190-7999.*

FINANCIAL DIRECTORY OF PENSION FUNDS. VERMONT. 0742-0196. US. English. an. ERISA Benefit Funds Inc, Suite 610/1341 G Street NW, Washington DC 20005. LC HD7106.U6. DD 332.67254. *ERISA Benefit Funds. Financial Directory of Pension Funds, State of Vermont, 0190-7972.*

FINANCIAL DIRECTORY OF PENSION FUNDS. VIRGINIA, NORTHERN. ARLINGTON, WINCHESTER, HARRISONBURG & OTHERS. (FINANCIAL DIRECTORY OF PENSION FUNDS. VIRGINIA, NORTHERN (ARLINGTON, WINCHESTER, HARRISONBURG & OTHERS)). 0739-2613. US. English. an. ERISA Benefit Funds Inc, 1341 G Street NW/Suite 610, Washington DC 20005. LC HD7106.U6. DD 332.67254. *ERISA Benefit Funds. Financial Directory of Pension Funds. Northern Virginia, 0192-2440.*

FINANCIAL DIRECTORY OF PENSION FUNDS. VIRGINIA, SOUTHERN (RICHMOND, NORFOLK, ROANOKE & OTHERS). VFOAT Financial Directory of Pension Funds. 0278-212X. US. English. an. ERISA Benefit Funds Inc, 1341 G Street Northwest Suite 909, Washington DC 20005. LC HD7106.U6. DD 332.67254.

FINANCIAL DIRECTORY OF PENSION FUNDS. WASHINGTON, EASTERN (SPOKANE, YAKIMA, PASCO & OTHERS). VFOAT Financial Directory of Pension Funds. 0278-0313. US. English. an. ERISA Benefit Funds Inc, 1341 G Street Northwest Suite 909, Washington DC 20005. LC HD7106.U5. DD 332.67254.

FINANCIAL DIRECTORY OF PENSION FUNDS. WASHINGTON, WESTERN, EXCLUDING SEATTLE AREA (TAKOMA, OLYMPIA & OTHERS). VFOAT Financial Directory of Pension Funds. 0278-2073. US. English. an. ERISA Benefit Funds Inc, 1341 G Street Northwest Suite 909, Washington DC 20005. LC HD7106.U6. DD 332.67254.

FINANCIAL DIRECTORY OF PENSION FUNDS. WASHINGTON, WESTERN (SEATTLE AREA ONLY). VFOAT Financial Directory of Pension Funds. 0278-2111. US. English. an. ERISA Benefit Funds Inc, 1341 G Street Northwest Suite 909, Washington DC 20005. LC HD7106.U6. DD 332.67254.

THE FINANCIAL DIRECTORY OF PENSION FUNDS. WEST VIRGINIA. 1984-85-. 0882-0821. US. English. an. Erisa Benefit Funds, Suite 700/1012-14th Street NW, Washington DC 20005. *Financial Directory of Pension Funds. State of West Virginia, 0731-7344.*

FINANCIAL DIRECTORY OF PENSION FUNDS. WISCONSIN, MILWAUKEE CITY PROPER. 0739-277X. US. English. an. Erisa Benefit Funds Inc, 1341 G Street NW/Suite 610, Washington DC 20005. LC HD7105.45.U6. DD 332.67254.

FINANCIAL DIRECTORY OF PENSION FUNDS. WISCONSIN, MILWAUKEE SUBURBAN (SHEBOYGAN, WAUWATOSA, RACINE & OTHERS). VFOAT Financial Directory of Pension Funds. 0278-2154. US. English. an. ERISA Benefit Funds Inc, 1341 G Street Northwest Suite 909, Washington DC 20005. LC HD7106.U5. DD 332.67254.

FINANCIAL DIRECTORY OF PENSION FUNDS. WISCONSIN, NORTHERN (GREENBAY, WAUSAU, EAU CLAIRE & OTHERS). VFOAT Financial Directory of Pension Funds. 0278-033X. US. English. an. Erisa Benefit Funds Inc, 1341 G Street Northwest Suite 909, Washington DC 20005. LC HD7106.U5. DD 332.67254.

FINANCIAL DIRECTORY OF PENSION FUNDS. WISCONSIN, SOUTHERN, EXCLUDING MILWAUKEE AREA. MADISON, LACROSSE, OSHKOSH & OTHERS. (FINANCIAL DIRECTORY OF PENSION FUNDS. WISCONSIN, SOUTHERN, EXCLUDING MILWAUKEE AREA (MADISON, LACROSSE, OSHKOSH & OTHERS)). 0739-2753. US. English. an. ERISA Benefit Funds Inc, 1341 G Street NW/Suite 610, Washington DC 20005. LC HD7106.U6. DD 332.67254. *0191-0000.*

THE FINANCIAL DIRECTORY OF PENSION FUNDS. WYOMING. 1984-85-. 0882-2948. US. English. an. Erisa Benefit Funds, Suite 700/1012-14th Street NW, Washington DC 20005. *Financial Directory of Pension Funds. State of Wyoming, 0731-7336.*

FINANCIAL INDUSTRY NUMBER STANDARD DIRECTORY. 1976. 0362-1405. US. English. 55 Water Street, New York NY 10041. LC HG4512. DD 332.10257.

FINANCIAL MANAGEMENT DIRECTORY. Main/Corp United States. Joint Financial Management Improvement Program. VFOAT Directory. 1982-1983-. 0736-2749. US. English. an. Joint Financial Management Improvement Program, 666 11th Street NW, Washington DC 20001. LC HJ267.2. DD 353.0072025. *Directory (United States. Joint Financial Management Improvement Program), 0731-5104.*

THE FINANCIAL PLANNER'S TAX ALMANAC. 1984-. 0741-3297. US. English. an. Dow Jones-Irwin, 1820 Riggs Road, Homewood IL 60430. LC KF6297. DD 343.7304, 347.3034.

FINANCIAL SERVICES SOFTWARE DIRECTORY, THE BUYER'S GUIDE. 0882-7303. US. English. qt. Longman Financial Services Publishing, A Longman Group Company, 500 North Dearborn Street, Chicago IL 60610. LC HG1709. DD 332.17.

FINANCIAL STOCK GUIDE SERVICE. DIRECTORY OF ACTIVE STOCKS. (DIRECTORY OF ACTIVE STOCKS). 0364-0752. US. English. Financial Information Inc, PO Box 473, Jersey City NJ 07303. LC HG4512. DD 332.67.

FINANCIAL TIMES MINING INTERNATIONAL YEAR BOOK. Series/Titl Financial Times International Year Books. VFOAT Mining International Year Book. 1983-. 0141-3244. UK. English. an. LC TN13. DD 338.7622025. *Mining International Year Book.*

FINANCIAL TIMES OIL AND GAS INTERNATIONAL YEAR BOOK. (OIL AND GAS INTERNATIONAL YEAR BOOK). Began with Vol. for 1978/79. 0141-3228. UK. English. an. $99.50. Longman Group Limited, 95 Church Street, White Plains NY 10601. Tel 0279 442601. Ed Diana Russell. Ind/Abst Life Sci. Collect. LC HG4821. DD 338.7622338025. adv acc. Company information worldwide. Lists operations key personnel, and company reports. *Walter R. Skinner's Oil and Gas International Year Book.*

THE FINANCIAL TIMES WORLD HOTEL DIRECTORY. Main/Corp Financial Times Limited. VFOAT FT World Hotel Directory. 1975/76-. 0308-8464. UK. English. an. 35.00. Longman Group Ltd, Fourth Avenue, Harlow Essex CM19 5AA England. Tel (0279)442601. LC TX907. DD 647.94. adv acc. Circ 3,000. Includes extensive details of over 43,600 top quality hotels in more than 130 countries which have been specially selected for the business traveller.

THE FINANCIAL TIMES WORLD INSURANCE YEARBOOK. VFOAT FT, World Insurance Yearbook. 1976/77-. UK. English. an. $65.90. Longman Group Ltd, Fourth Avenue, Harlow Essex CM19 5AA England. Tel (0279)442601. LC HG8019. DD 368.005. adv acc. Circ 1,200. Presents detailed corporate and financial information on over 1,200 insurance companies worldwide.

FINANCIAL TREND'S CORPORATE DIRECTORY SERVICE FOR TEXAS, OKLAHOMA, LOUISIANA, ARKANSAS, NEW MEXICO. VFOAT Corporate Directory Service for Texas, Oklahoma, Louisiana, Arkansas, New Mexico. 1972. US. English. mo. $75.00. Equity Media Inc, 7616 LBJ Freeway, Suite 115, Dallas TX 75251. Tel (214)239-0161. Ed William H Bradfield. Circ 1,000. Listing of all publicly-held companies in the southwest. company names, top officers' names, addresses, telephone numbers, latest sales and earnings.

FINDER BINDER. ARIZONA'S UPDATED MEDIA DIRECTORY. VAT Finderbinder. Arizona's Updated Media Directory. 1st Ed. 0196-8548. US. English. mo. $107.00. Arizonas Updated Media Directory, 432 East Southern Avenue, Tempe AZ 85282. Tel (602)967-8714. Ed Pam MacMillan. Media Directory.

FINDER BINDER. DETROIT AREA UPDATED MEDIA DIRECTORY. VAT Finderbinder. Detroit Area Updated Media Directory. 1st- Ed. 0276-2196. US. English. an. $70.00. Tom McPhail Associates Inc, 17321 Telegraph/Suite 301, Detroit MI 48219. Tel (313)535-6377. Ed Tom McPhail. (ctrl). Detroit area media directory and updating service. Details key people, deadlines, interview shows PSA'a for nearly 400 media indexes.

FINDER BINDER. NEW MEXICO'S UPDATED MEDIA DIRECTORY. VFOAT New Mexico's Updated Media Directory, Finderbinder. 0084-0261. US. English. an. Rick Johnson & Company Inc, PO Box 4770, Albuquerque NM 87196. LC P88.8. DD 001.51025789.

FINDER BINDER, (NEW ORLEANS, LA.). (FINDER BINDER. LOUISIANA'S UPDATED MEDIA DIRECTORY). Premier Ed.-. 0739-8190. Periodical. US. English. an. R H Mehaffey and Associates, 6001 Winchester Park Drive, New Orleans LA 70128. LC P88.8. DD 001.51025763.

FINDER BINDER. OKLAHOMA CITY METROPOLITAN UPDATED MEDIA DIRECTORY. VAT Finderbinder. Oklahoma City Metropolitan Updated Media Directory. 1st- Ed. 0196-8734. US. English. mo. $60.00. Finderbinder of Oklahoma, PO Box 3093, Edmond OK 63083. Tel (405)348-1779.

FINDER BINDER. SAN DIEGO COUNTY'S UPDATED MEDIA DIRECTORY. VAT Finderbinder. 1974. 0196-853X. US. English. mo. $78.25. G Geals, Public Relations and Advertising Agency, 4141 Fairmont Avenue, San Diego CA 92105. Tel (619)284-1145. Ed James Tuck. Circ 500. (ctrl). Media directory plus six detailed updating newsletters.

FINDER BINDER. WILLAMETTE VALLEY'S UPDATED MEDIA DIRECTORY. VAT Finderbinder. Willamette Valley's Updated Media Directory. 1st.- Ed. 0196-8513. US. English. mo. $45.00. Hauser Webb Wykoff, 30 NW 23rd Place, Portland OR 97210. Tel (503)221-0284.

FINDERBINDER. ARIZONA'S UPDATED MEDIA DIRECTORY. 0196-8548. US. English. an. $45.00. Arizonas Updated Media Directory, 432 East Southern Avenue, Tempe AZ 58282. DD 23025791. Each issue contains an index to its own contents - no vol index - loose.

FINDEX. See Business - Marketing.

FINDEX : THE DIRECTORY OF MARKET RESEARCH REPORTS, STUDIES AND SURVEYS. 1979-. US. English. an. $139.00. Index in last issue of volume - attached.

FINE PAPER DIRECTORY. VFOAT Grade Finders Fine Paper Directory. 1st- Ed. 0147-8095. US. English. $60.00. Grade Finders Incorporated, PO Box 444, Bala-Cynwyd PA 19004. Tel (215)644-4159. Ed Bill Subers. LC HD9823. DD 380.145676202573. adv acc. (ctrl). A guide for paper buyers, paper salesmen, paper mills, printers, publishers, converters, advertising agencies, purchasing agencies, in-plant printers, schools, municipalities, and other government agencies.

THE FIRE ALMANAC. (THE . . . FIRE ALMANAC). 1983-. 0736-6027. US. English. an. $8.95 Members, $9.95 Nonmembers. National Fire

Yearbooks, Almanacs, Directories

Protection Association, Batterymarch Park Quincy MA 02269. **LC** TH9150. **DD** 628.920973.

FIRE PROTECTION REFERENCE DIRECTORY CEASED. **VFOAT** Annual Fire Protection Reference Directory. 1975-1982. 0361-8382. US. English. an. National Fire Protection Association, Battery March Park, Quincy MA 02269. **Tel** (617)770-3000. **Ed** Denise L Babcock. **LC** TH9116.5. **DD** 628.92029473. adv acc. **Circ** 90,000. (ctrl). Names, addresses, telephone numbers, products and trade names of manufacturers who produce fire protection systems, controls, equipment and services.

FIRE PROTECTION REFERENCE DIRECTORY AND BUYER'S GUIDE. **VFOAT** N.F.P.A. Fire Protection Reference Directory and Buyer's Guide. 8th Ed. (1983)-. 0738-3754. US. English. an. National Fire Protection Association, Batterumarch Park, Quincy MA 02269. **LC** TH9116.5. **DD** 628.92029473. *Fire Protection Reference Directory, 0361-8382.*

FIRE RESISTANCE DIRECTORY. US. English. an. $6.08. Underwriters Laboratories Inc, 333 Pfingsten Road, Northbrook IL 60062. **Tel** (312)272-8800. *Fire Resistance Index.*

FISCHER FILM ALMANACH. 1980-. German. an. **LC** PN1997.8. **DD** 791.4305.

FISH DIRECTORY. 1973-. 0090-7081. US. English. Jarrow Press Inc, 552 de Haro Street, San Francisco CA 94107. **LC** HV7. **DD** 361.8.

FISKERISTATISTISK ARBOG. **VFOAT** Fischereistatistisches Jahrbuch, Yearbook of Fishery Statistics. 1983-. Danish (Multilingual). an. $14.00. European Community Information Service, 2100 M Street NW/Suite 707, Washington DC 20037. *Fiskeri, Produkter og Fladen, Fiskeri, Fangster Efter Omrader.*

FLIGHT DIRECTORY OF BRITISH AVIATION. 0071-5700. UK. English. be. 21.00. Transport Press, Division of Business Press International Ltd, Quadrant House/The Quadrant, Sutton Surrey SM25A5 England. **Tel** 01 661. **Ed** David Mason. adv acc. **Circ** 1,800. A who's who of everyone and everything in the United Kingdom flying scene. It puts thousands of facts at your fingertips about airports, heliports, cargo equipment manufacturers.

FLORAL MARKETING DIRECTORY & BUYERS GUIDE. **VFOAT** Floral Marketing Directory and Buyer's Guide. US. English. be. Produce Marketing Association, 1500 Casho Mill Road, Newark DE 19711.

FLORIDA AIRPORT DIRECTORY. 0097-9260. US. English. Department of Transportation, Bureau of Aviation, Burns Building/605 Suwannee Street, Tallahassee FL 32304. **Tel** (904)488-8444. **LC** HE9813.F6. **DD** 387.736025759. **Circ** 3,000. (ctrl). Airport information: diagrams, manager, description, services for public airports plus lists of private airports, seaplane bases and helistops.

FLORIDA ALMANAC. 1972-. 0361-9796. US. English. $2.95. West Coast Productions Inc, PO Box 1577, St Petersburg FL 33731. **LC** F311. **DD** 917.59.

FLORIDA BUILDERS AND CONTRACTORS DIRECTORY. 0276-8208. US. English. Florida Builders and Contractors Directory Inc, The Gulfstream Building, 8751 West Broward Boulevard, Fort Lauderdale FL 33324. **LC** TH13.F6. **DD** 690.025759.

FLORIDA FOLK ARTS DIRECTORY. 0162-5616. US. English. Stephen Foster Center, White Springs FL 32096. **Tel** (904)397-2192. **LC** NX510.F6. **DD** 700.25759. (ctrl). Lists artists, interpreters, scholars, and others related to the folklife field.

FLORIDA GOLF DIRECTORY. 1983-. 0737-6847. US. English. an. $10.20. Florida Golfweek, POB 1458, Winter Haven FL 33882-1458. **Tel** (813)294-5511. **Ed** Larry Kieffer. **LC** WMLC L 83/104. adv acc. **Circ** 16,000. (ctrl). A directory of Florida Golf courses in detail; locator index over 1,000 individuals, tournament records, touring pros, publications and organizations.

THE FLORIDA LEGAL DIRECTORY. 1974/75-. 0145-7829. US. English. an. $9.00. Legal Directories Publishing Co, 1314 Westwood Boulevard, Los Angeles CA 90024. **LC** KF192.F54. **DD** 340.025759.

FLORIDA LIBRARY DIRECTORY. US. English. ir. Florida State Library, R A Gray Building, Tallahassee FL 32301.

FLORIDA MEDICAL DIRECTORY. 1938-. US. English. an. $15.00. Florida Medical Association Inc, PO Box 2411, Jacksonville FL 32203. **Tel** (904)356-1571. **Ed** R G Lacsamana. **LC** R712.A2. bk rev. adv acc. **Circ** 15,500. (ctrl). Scientific material targeted towards the medical profession in Florida.

FLORIDA NEWS MEDIA DIRECTORY. **VFOAT** News Media Directory. 1978/79-. US. English. an. $29.50. Gail E West, PO Box 316, Mount Dora FL 32757. *Dahne's Florida News Media Directory, 0161-231X.*

FLORIDA ZIP+4 STATE DIRECTORY. **VFOAT** Zip Plus Four State Directory. **VAT** Florida Zip Plus Four State Directory. 1985-. US. English. an. St Louis PDC, Zip+4 State Directory Orders, PO Box 14921, St Louis MO 63180-9988.

FLUID POWER HANDBOOK & DIRECTORY. 0428-7738. Periodical. US. English. an. Penton/IPC, PO Box 95759, Cleveland OH 44101. **Tel** (216)696-0300. **LC** TJ950. *Fluid Power Directory.*

FLYING BUYERS' GUIDE. (FLYING BUYERS' GUIDE : COMPLETE DIRECTORY OF AIRCRAFT AND AVIONICS). No. 1 (1982)-. 0738-3800. Periodical. US. English. $3.95. One Park Avenue, New York NY 10016. **Tel** (212)503-4212. **Ed** Richard L Collins. **LC** TL512. **DD** 629.13334042205. adv acc. **Circ** 185,000. Buyers guide including specifications for all current production models of general aviation, aircraft, avionics and accessories.

FLYING YEARBOOK. 1979-. 0190-6526. US. English. an. **LC** TL721.4. **DD** 629.13252170973.

FOLIO'S MEDICAL DIRECTORY OF MASSACHUSETTS. **VFOAT** Medical Directory of Massachusetts. Began with 1980 issue. 0741-241X. US. English. an. $32.00. Folio Associates Inc, 581 Boylston Street, Boston MA 02116. **LC** R712.A2. **DD** 610.25744. *Datawell's Medical Directory of Massachusetts, 0192-5091.*

FOLK DANCE DIRECTORY. 0163-528X. US. English. an. $3.00. Folk Dance Directory, PO Box 500/Midwood Station, Brooklyn NY 11230.

THE FOLK DIRECTORY. 1965-. 0430-876X. UK. English. English Folk Dance & Song Society, 2 Regents Park Road, London NW1 England. **DD** 780.

FOLKLORE VERZEICHNIS FUR EUROPA. English (German). ir. 1.50. Floricica News, Dorrei Schafer Danziger Str 17, D-6113 Babenhausen West Germany. **LC** GV1643. **DD** 793.3194.

FOOD CO-OP DIRECTORY. **VAT** Food Co-Operative Directiry. 0271-5880. US. English. an. $3.00 Individual, $6.00 Institution. Food Co-Operative Directory, 106 Girard Se, Albuquerque NM 87106.

FOOD ENGINEERING'S DIRECTORY OF U.S. FOOD & BEVERAGE PLANTS. (FOOD ENGINEERING'S . . . DIRECTORY OF U.S FOOD & BEVERAGE PLANTS). **VFOAT** Food Engineering's . . . Directory of US Food & Beverage Plants. **VAT** Food Engineering's Directory of United States Food and Beverage Plants. 0730-1413. US. English. be. Chilton Publishing Company, PO Box 1412, Riverton NJ 08077. **Tel** (215)964-4000. **LC** HD9003. **DD** 338.47664002573.

FOOD IN CANADA. BUYERS' DIRECTORY & SERVICES INDEX. (FOOD IN CANADA BUYERS' DIRECTORY & SERVICES INDEX). 1973-. 0317-3364. Periodical. CN. English. an. $5.00 Per Number. MacLean-Hunter, 777 Bay Street, Toronto Ontario M5W 1A7 Canada. **DD** 338.47664002571. *Food in Canada. Buyers' Guide, 0317-3372.*

THE FOOD INDUSTRY DIRECTORY. **VFOAT** Washington Food Industry Directory. 0145-3610. US. English. $3.00 Single Issue. Washington State Food Dealers Association, 120 Sixth Avenue North, Seattle WA 98109. **LC** HD9007.W2. **DD** 338.4764130025797.

FOODSERVICE DIRECTORY. **VFOAT** Food Service Directory. 1985-. 0883-1912. US. English. $25.00 Single Copy. C-Store Business Foodservice Directory, 1351 Washington Boulevard, Stamford CT 06902.

FOODSERVICE EQUIPMENT DEALER. BUYERS GUIDE AND PRODUCT DIRECTORY. 1975-. 0363-1303. US. English. an. $10.00. Circulation Office, 270 St Paul Street, Denver CO 80206. **LC** TX912. **DD** 338.47642502573. *Foodservice Equipment Product Directory.*

FOODSERVICE EQUIPMENT SPECIALIST. BUYERS GUIDE AND PRODUCT DIRECTORY. 1978-. US. English. an. $40.00. Foodservice Equipment Specialist Circulation Office, 270 St Paul Street, Denver CO 80206. **Tel** (312)635-8800. **Ed** Robin Ashton. adv acc. **Circ** 16,600. (ctrl). The standard journal of the foodservice equipment industry intended for buyers, specifiers and distributors of foodservice equipment for commercial and institutional use. *Foodservice Equipment Dealer. Buyers Guide and Product Directory.*

THE FOOKIEN TIMES PHILIPPINES YEARBOOK. **VFOAT** Philippines Yearbook. 1975-. PH. English. ir. 20.00, $10.00 US. Fookien Times Publishing Company Ltd, 13th & Railroad Streets, Port Area, Manila Philippines. **LC** DS666.C5. **DD** 959.9005. (cum index). *Year Book.*

FOREIGN COUNSEL DIRECTORY. 0748-9943. US. English. American Corporate Counsel Association, 1747 Pennsylvania Avenue Northwest/Suite 701, Washington DC 20006. **LC** K68. **DD** 340.025.

FOREIGN FORUM YEARBOOK INTERNATIONAL. **VFOAT** Foreign Forum. **VAT** Foreign Forum Year Book International. 0732-1384. US. English. Success Publishing, PO Box 296, Estero FL 33928. **LC** Z7164.C8, HF54.U5. **DD** 016.382025.

FORENSIC SERVICES DIRECTORY. 1980-. 0192-3145. Periodical. US. English. an. $69.50. Forensic Services Directory, PO Box 305, Fair Lawn NJ 07410. **Tel** (201)797-4343. **LC** KF195.E96. **DD** 363.2502573.

FOREST INDUSTRIES DIRECTORY, BUYERS' AND SELLERS' GUIDE. Periodical. English. be. Australian Forest Industries Journal, 203 Castlereagh Street, Sydney New South Wales 2000 Australia.

FOREST PRODUCTS DIRECTORY FOR THE STATE OF WASHINGTON. US. English. Department of Natural Resources, Division of Geology and Earth Resources, Olympia WA 98504. **LC** TS803. **DD** 333.7509797 S, 338. 47674009797.

FOREST SERVICE ORGANIZATIONAL DIRECTORY. Main/Corp United States. Forest Service. **VFOAT** Organizational Directory. 0160-9904. US. English. US Department of Agriculture, Forestry Service, PO Box 2417, Washington DC 20013. **LC** SD11. **DD** 353.0082338025. *Directory, Forest Service.*

FORTSCHRITT UND FORTBILDUNG IN DER MEDIZIN : JAHRBUCH. Main/Corp Interdisziplinares Forum der Bundesaerztekammer. **VFOAT** Jahrbuch. 1. (1976/77)-. 0170-3331. German. an. **NLM** W3.

FORTUNE WORLD BUSINESS DIRECTORY. 0197-7792. US. English. an. $7.00. Fortune Directories, Time/Life Building, Rockerfeller Center, New York NY 10020. **Tel** (212)586-1212. **LC** HG4009. **DD** 338.74025. *Fortune Directory.*

THE FOUNDATION DIRECTORY. 1st- Ed. 0071-8092. US. English. ir. Foundation Center, 79 Fifth Avenue, New York NY 10003. **Tel** (212)620-4230. **Ed** Loren Renz. **LC** AS911.A2. **DD** 061. **NLM** AS 911 F771. Detailed descriptions of over 4,400 of the largest US foundations, including address, contact person, and complete financial data. Subject, personnel geographic, and type of support indexes. *American Foundations and Their Fields.*

THE FOUNDATION DIRECTORY. SUPPLEMENT. No. 1- 1975-. US. English. an. Foundation Center, 79 Fifth Avenue, New York NY 10003. **Tel** (212)620-4230. **Ed** Loren Renz. Detailed updates to foundation directory entries, describing important changes in foundation names, addresses, programs, giving limitations, application guidelines, and fiscal data.

FOUNDATION GRANTS TO INDIVIDUALS. 1st Ed.-. US. English. an. $18.00. Foundation Center, 79 Fifth Avenue, New York NY 10003. **Tel** (212)620-4230. **Ed** Claude Barrilleaux. Directory describing over 950 foundations that have programs for or make grants to individual applicants. Includes address and telephone, contact person, application procedures, limitations on giving, etc.

FOUNDATIONS IN WISCONSIN. (FOUNDATIONS IN WISCONSIN : A DIRECTORY). 1975-. 0360-8042. US. English. be. Foundation Collection, Marquette University Library, Milwaukee WI 53233. **LC** AS911.A2. **DD** 001.44025775.

FOUNDRY YEAR BOOK. Began with issue for 1972. UK. English. an. Fuel & Metallurgical Journals Ltd, Queensway House, 2 Queensway,

Yearbooks, Almanacs, Directories

Redhill Surrey RHI 105 England. **LC** TS229. **DD** 671.20941.

THE FRANCHISE ANNUAL. Began publication in 1969. 0318-8752. CN. English. an. $22.95. Info Press, 728 Center Street, Box 550, Lewiston NY 14092. **Tel** (716)754-4669. Ed Edward L Dixon Jr. **LC** HF5429.3. **DD** 658.87002573. adv acc. **Circ** 10,000. (ctrl). Directory list over 2,500 business format franchisors (McDonalds etc.) with complete descriptions. Handbook section details pros and cons of franchising.

DE FRANSE NEDERLANDEN : JAARBOEK. **VFOAT** Les Pays-Bas Francais : Annales. Dutch (French, with summaries in other languages). ir. 1.100. Stichting ons Erfdeel, B-8530 Rekkem, Murissonstraat 60, Rekkem Belgium. **Tel** (056)411201. **LC** DC611.N821. **DD** 944.28. bk rev. **Circ** 2,000. (ctrl).

FRASER'S CANADIAN TRADE DIRECTORY. **VFOAT** Canadian Trade Directory. 1913-. 0071-9277. Periodical. CN. English. an. 110.00. MacLean Hunter, PO Box 100 Station A, Toronto Ontario M5W 1A7 Canada. **Tel** (416)596-5086. **DD** 338.402571. adv acc. **Circ** 10,000. Industrial Directory.

FRASER'S CONSTRUCTION AND BUILDING DIRECTORY CEASED. 1st-6th. 0318-0344. Periodical. CN. English. an. Fraser's Trade Directories, 481 University Avenue, Toronto Ontario M5G 1W8 Canada. **DD** 338.4769002571.

THE FREE STOCK PHOTOGRAPHY DIRECTORY. 0190-1567. Periodical. US. an. $10.00. Infosource Business Publications, 1600 Lehigh Parkway East, Allentown PA 18103. **LC** TR12. **DD** 779.074013.

FREIGHT SERVICE DIRECTORY. CHICAGO EDITION. (FREIGHT SERVICE DIRECTORY). Vol. No. 1 (Aug. 1981)-. 0278-5404. US. English. sa. $26.00. Equipment Interchange Association, 1616 P Street Northwest, Washington DC 20036. **LC** HE5623. **DD** 388.32402573.

FRENCH COMPANY HANDBOOK. 1981-. US. English. an. $42.00. Addor Associates Inc, PO Box 2128, Westport CT 06880. **Tel** (203)226-9791. Ed Barton Reichert and Irving Sedar. **LC** HD2853. **DD** 338.740944. **Circ** 15,000. Guide to the French corporate world published in English. Up-to-date information on major companies, evaluations, introductions to Paris Stock Exchange, practical dictionary of English-French business and financial terminology.

FRIENDLY FAIRWAYS OF MICHIGAN. See Recreation, Leisure - Sports.

FROZEN FOOD FACTBOOK AND DIRECTORY. 0071-9684. US. English. an. $10.00. National Frozen Food Association Inc, PO Box 398, One Chocolate Avenue, Hershey PA 17033. **Tel** (717)534-1601. Ed Tracy Fellin. adv acc. **Circ** 4,000. An annual desktop work listing all member companies of the National Frozen Food Association. NFF represents all facets of the frozen food industry.

FSL. FRENCH SECOND LANGUAGE DIRECTORY FOR CANADA. (FSL : FRENCH SECOND LANGUAGE DIRECTORY FOR CANADA). **VFOAT** French Second Language Directory for Canada. '83-. 0822-5834. CN. English (includes some text in French). an. $19.50 Per Number. FSL Publications, PO Box 184, Douglastown New Brunswick E0G 1H0 Canada. **DD** 440.7071.

FUNPARKS DIRECTORY. 0147-5606. US. English. an. $35.00. Amusement Business, 14 Music Circle East, Nashville TN 37203. **Tel** (615)748-8120. Ed Leslie Shaver. **LC** GV1851. **DD** 790.06802573. adv acc. **Circ** 6,500. (ctrl). A directory of over 2,000 amusement parks, theme parks, water parks and tourist attractions in the US and Canada.

FUR DIE SICHERHEIT IM BERGLAND; JAHRBUCH. **VFOAT** Sicherheit in den Bergen. AU. German. ir. Prinz-Eugen-Strasse 12, 1040 Wien Austria. **LC** GV199.8. **DD** 614.877.

FURASUCHIKKU GAIDO; GENTAIRYE FUKUZAIRYO HEN. PLASTICS YEARBOOK. **VFOAT** Plastics Yearbook. JA. Japanese. ir. Kogyo Chosakai, 14-7 Hongo 2, Bunkyo-ku 113, Tokyo Japan. **LC** TP1103.

FURMAN UNIVERSITY ALUMNI DIRECTORY. Main/Corp Furman Alumni Association. 1976-. 0148-2580. US. English. College & University Press, Furman University, PO Box 28884, Greenville SC 29405. **LC** LD1871. **DD** 378.75727.

FURNITURE AND FURNISHINGS. DIRECTORY. 1973/74-. CN. English. an. $5.00 Per Number. Southam Business Publications Ltd, 1450 Don Mills Road, Don Mills Ontario M3B 2X7 Canada. **DD** 338.476841002571. Furniture and Furnishings. Buyers' Guide and Directory.

FUTURE SURVEY ANNUAL. See Indexes/Abstracts.

FUTURES MARKET SERVICE. See Business - Investments.

GARTNER GROUP TOP 100 DP ALMANAC. **VFOAT** Gartner Group Top One Hundred DP Almanac. 1984-. 0883-8674. US. English. an. $300.00. Gartner Group Inc, 72 Cummings Point Road, Stamford CT 06902. **Tel** (203)964-0096. Collection of market statistics on the computer industry. Gartner Group Top 100 Almanac, 0883-7430.

GAS DIRECTORY AND WHO'S WHO. **VFOAT** Gas Directory. Began with 1975 issue. 0307-3084. UK. English. an. 40.00. Benn Business Info Services Ltd, PO Box 20/Sovereign Way, Tonbridge Kent TN9 1RQ England. **Tel** (0732) 362666. Ed John Hedges. **LC** TP714. **DD** 338.47665702541. adv acc. **Circ** 1,500. The standard reference guide to the United Kingdom gas industry-suppliers to the industry, classified buyers guide, British gas statistics, trade name and trade associations. Gas Directory and Undertakings of the World, Who's Who in the Gas Industry.

GAYELLOW PAGES. See Sexual Life.

GAY/LESBIAN MEDIA DIRECTORY WORLDWIDE. **VFOAT** Lesbian Media Directory Worldwide. **VAT** Gay Lesbian Media Directory Worldwide. 1981-82-. 0730-3297. US. English. Vox Populi Publications, PO Box 59154, Chicago IL 60659. **LC** HQ76.25. **DD** 016.30676605.

GAZETTE YEARBOOK. 1972-. UK. English. 113 Chancery Lane, London WC2 England. **LC** KD345. **DD** 340.05.

GEBBIE PRESS ALL-IN-ONE DIRECTORY. **VFOAT** All-in-One Directory. 1st-Ed. 0097-8175. US. English. an. $72.25. Gebbie Press, Box 1000, New Paltz NY 12561. **Tel** (914)255-7560. Ed Amalia Gebbie. **LC** P88.8. **DD** 301.16102573. Lists daily, weekly newspapers; radio, TV stations; consumer magazines, business publications, farm press nationwide. Separate black press, radio.

GEGENBAURS MORPHOLOGISCHES JAHRBUCH. V. 30- 1902/03-. 0016-5840. Periodical. Multilingual. Kunst & Wissen Erich Bieber, Dufourstrasse 51, CH-8008 Zurich Switzerland. **Ind/Abst** Index Med., Hospit. Lit. Index, Bibliogr. Index Geol. (cum index). Morphologisches Jahrbuch, Beitrage zur Anatomie Funktioneller Systeme.

GENEALOGICAL RESEARCH DIRECTORY. **VFOAT** Australasian Genealogical Research Directory. 1981 , Pt. 1-. AT. English. ir. Library of Australian History, 17 Mitchell Street, New South Wales 2060 Australia. **LC** CS2000. **DD** 929.1025931.

GENEESKUNDIG JAARBOEK MEDICIJNEN. **VFOAT** Geneeskundig Jaarboek. 0302-6752. Dutch. ir. H W Blok/Uitgeverij BV, Schiedamsevest 51, Rotterdam Netherlands. **LC** R101. Geneeskundig Jaarboekje voor Nederland.

GENERAL INSURANCE REGISTER. See Insurance.

GENERAL PRACTICE SECTION DIRECTORY. Main/Corp American Bar Association. Section of General Practice. 0741-0913. US. English. American Bar Association, Section of General Practice, 1155 East 60th Street, Chicago IL 60637. **LC** KF190. **DD** 340.02573. Directory, 0149-9491.

GENETIC ENGINEERING AND BIOTECHNOLOGY FIRMS WORLDWIDE DIRECTORY. 1983/1984-. US. English. an. $200.00. Sittig and Noyes, PO Box 592, Kingston NJ 08528. **Tel** (609)924-5722. Ed Marshall Sittig. **NLM** QH 442. Directory of Genetic Engineering & Biotechnology Firms, U.S.A.

GENETIC ENGINEERING AND BIOTECHNOLOGY YEARBOOK. US. English. ir. Elsevier Science Publishing Company, 52 Vanderbilt Avenue, New York NY 10017. **LC** TP248.2. **DD** 660.605. **NLM** TP 248.2.

GEOGRAPHICAL INDEX TO THE DIRECTORY OF CORPORATE AFFILIATIONS. (DIRECTORY OF CORPORATE AFFILIATIONS. GEOGRAPHICAL INDEX). 1978-. 0161-6013. US. English. an. $318.00. National Register Publishing Company, 3004 Glenview Road, Wilmette IL 60091. **Tel** (312)441-2200. Ed Robert Weicherding. **LC** HG4057. **DD** 338.802573. adv acc. **Circ** 10,000. (ctrl). The 'Who Owns Whom' of corporate America.

GEOGRAPHISCHES JAHRBUCH. V. 1-. GE. German. ir. Deutscher Buch Export-Import, Leninstrasse 16, DDR-701 Leipzig East Germany. **Tel** 3872. (cum index). bk rev. Bibliography about geographical literature.

GEOGRAPHISCHES JAHRBUCH BURGENLAND. 1977-. German. ir. Vereinigung Burgenlandischer Geographen, Hautplata 50, Neusiedl Am See Austria. **LC** DB785.B8.

GEOGRAPHISCHES TASCHENBUCH. See Geography.

GEOLOGISCHE JAHRBUCH. REIHE A. ALLGEMEINE UND REGIONALE GEOLOGIE BR DEUTSCHLAND UND NACHBARGEBIETE, TEKTONIK, STRATIGRAPHIE, PALHAONTOLOGIE. (GEOLOGISCHES JAHRBUCH, REIHE A : ALLGEMEINE UND REGIONALE GEOLOGIE BR DEUTSCHLAND UND NACHBARGEBIETE, TEKTONIK, STRATIGRAPHIE, PALAONTOLOGIE). Vol. 1-. 0341-6399. German (summaries in English, French, and Russian). ir. **Tel** 0711/625001. **Ind/Abst** GeoRef, Chem. Abstr. **LC** QE269. **DD** 554.305. **CODEN** GJRABD. Geology, mineralogy, geophysics, paleontology. Geologisches Jahrbuch, 0016-7851; Beihefte zum Geologischen Jahrbuch, 0005-8017.

GEOLOGISCHES JAHRBUCH HESSEN. V. 104-. 0341-4027. GW. German. an. Hessisches Landesmat fur Bodenforschung, Leberberg 9, 6200 Wiesbade West Germany. **Ind/Abst** GeoRef, Chem. Abstr. **CODEN** GJHEDB. Notizblatt des Hessischen Landesamtes fur Bodenforschung zu Wiesbaden.

GEOLOGISCHES JAHRBUCH. REIHE B. REGIONALE GEOLOGIE AUSLAND. (GEOLOGISCHES JAHRBUCH, REIHE B : REGIONALE GEOLOGIE, AUSLAND). 0341-6402. German (summaries in English, French, Portuguese, Russian, Spanish, or Turkish). ir. **Tel** 0711/625001. **Ind/Abst** GeoRef, Chem. Abstr. **LC** QE1. **DD** 550.85. **CODEN** GJRBAF. Geology, mineralogy, geophysics, paleontology. Geologisches Jahrbuch, 0016-7851; Geologische Jahrbuch. Beihefte, 0005-8017.

GEOLOGISCHES JAHRBUCH. REIHE C. HYDROGEOLOGIE, INGENIEURGEOLOGIE. (GEOLOGISCHES JAHRBUCH, REIHE C : HYDROGEOLOGIE, INGENIEURGEOLOGIE). 0341-6410. Monographic Series. German (summaries in English, French, and Russian). ir. **Tel** 0711/625001. **Ind/Abst** GeoRef, Chem. Abstr. **LC** GB651. **CODEN** GJRCAI. Geology, mineralogy, geophysics, paleontology. Geologisches Jahrbuch, 0016-7851; Beihefte zum Geologischen Jahrbuch, 0005-8017.

GEOLOGISCHES JAHRBUCH. REIHE D. MINERALOGIE, PETROGRAPHIE, GEOCHEMIE, LAGERSTATTENKUNDE. (GEOLOGISCHES JAHRBUCH, REIHE D : MINERALOGIE, PETROGRAPHIE, GEOCHEMIE, LAGERSTATTENKUNDE). 0341-6429. English (German with summaries in French and Russian). ir. **Tel** 0711/625001. **Ind/Abst** Life Sci. Collect., Coal Abstr., GeoRef, Chem. Abstr. **LC** QE351. **CODEN** GJRDAL. Covers geology, mineralogy, geophysics, paleontology. Geologisches Jahrbuch, 0016-7851; Beihefte zum Geologischen Jahrbuch, 0005-8017.

GEOLOGISCHES JAHRBUCH. REIHE E. GEOPHYSIK. (GEOLOGISCHES JAHRBUCH, REIHE E : GEOPHYSIK). Vol. 1-. 0341-6437. German (summaries in English, French, and Russian). ir. **Tel** 0711/625001. **Ind/Abst** Int. Aerosp. Abstr., GeoRef, Chem. Abstr. **LC** QE500. **CODEN** GJREAO. Covers geology, mineralogy, geophysics and paleontology. Geologisches Jahrbuch, 0016-7851; Beihefte zum Geologischen Jahrbuch, 0005-8017.

GEOLOGISCHES JAHRBUCH. REIHE F. BODENKUNDE. (GEOLOGISCHES JAHRBUCH. REIHE F, BODENKUNDE). Vol. 1- 1973-. 0341-6445. German (summaries in English, French, and Russian). ir. E Schweizerbartsche Verlagsbuchhandlung In Kommission, Johannesstrasse 3A, D7000 1 Stuttgart West Germany. **Tel** 0711/625001. **Ind/Abst** GeoRef, Chem.

Yearbooks, Almanacs, Directories

Abstr. LC S599.4.G3. DD 631.4943. **CODEN** GJRFAR. Geology, mineralogy, geophysics, paleontology. *Geologisches Jahrbuch, 0016-7851; Beihefte zum Geologishen Jahrbuch, 0005-8017.*

THE GEOPHYSICAL DIRECTORY. 1946. US. English. an. Geophysical Directory, Box 13508, Houston TX 77019. **Tel** (713)529-8789. adv acc. **Circ** 12,000. Compilation of geophysical and oil companies listings.

GEORG BRANDES ARBOG. 1975-. DK. Danish. ir. Georg Brandes Biblioteket, Smallegade 43, 2000 Kbenhavn F Denmark. LC PT8125.B8.

GEORGE D. HALL'S CONNECTICUT SERVICE DIRECTORY. VFOAT Connecticut Service Directory. 1983-1984-. 0743-4502. US. English. $35.00. George D Hall Company, 20 Kilby Street, Boston MA 02109. LC HD9981.7.C8. DD 338.46025746.

GEORGE D. HALL'S DIRECTORY OF CONNECTICUT MANUFACTURERS. **Main/Corp** Hall, George D., Company, Boston. VFOAT Directory of Connecticut Manufacturers. 0196-8270. US. English. $25.00. George D Hall Company, 20 Kilby Street, Boston MA 02109. LC HD9727.C8. DD 338.0025746.

GEORGE D. HALL'S DIRECTORY OF MASSACHUSETTS MANUFACTURERS. VFOAT Directory of Massachusetts Manufacturers. 0149-6913. US. English. $39.00. George D Hall Company, 20 Kilby Street, Boston MA 02109. **Tel** (617)523-3745. LC HD9727.M4. DD 338.4700025744. adv acc. Approximately 22,000 manufacturing companies in New England listed alphabetically, geographically by product, company name, address, telephone number, number of employees, key executive (by name and title), and product description.

GEORGE D. HALL'S MASSACHUSETTS SERVICE DIRECTORY. **Main/Corp** Hall, George D., Company. VFOAT Directory of Massachusetts Services. 1979/80-. 0196-7185. US. English. ir. $60.90. George D Hall Company, 50 Congress Street, Boston MA 02109. **Tel** (617)523-3745. LC HD9981.7.M4. DD 338.46025744. adv acc. Alphabetically, geographically and by product service, the company name, address, telephone number, number of employees and key executives by name, title and product or service.

GEORGE D. HALL'S NEW JERSEY MANUFACTURERS DIRECTORY. VFOAT New Jersey Manufacturers Directory. 0278-9124. US. English. an. $55.95. George D Hall Company, 50 Congress Street, Boston MA 02109. **Tel** (617)523-3745. LC HD9727.N5. DD 338.47000294749. adv acc. 19,000 New Jersey manufacturers listed alphabetically, geographically by product, company name, address, telephone number, number of employees, key personnel by name and title, and product description.

GEORGE D. HALL'S NEW YORK MANUFACTURERS DIRECTORY. VFOAT New York Manufacturers Directory. 0272-1074. US. English. an. $55.90. George D Hall Company, 50 Congress Street, Boston MA 02109. **Tel** (617)523-3745. LC HD9727.N7. DD 380.145000294747. adv acc. 20,000 New York manufacturers listed alphabetically, geographically and by product, company name, address, telephone number, number of employees, key personnel by name and title and product description.

GEORGE D. HALL'S THE NEW ENGLAND INDUSTRIAL SERVICE DIRECTORY. (THE NEW ENGLAND INDUSTRIAL SERVICE DIRECTORY). 1st- 1976-. 0147-2356. US. English. $49.00. G D Hall Co, 20 Kilby Street, Boston MA 12109. LC HD9981.7.A1. DD 338.402574.

GEORGIA COURTS DIRECTORY. US. English. Judicial Council of Georgia, 2220 Parklake Drive NE/Suite 335, Atlanta GA 30345. LC KFG508.A19. DD 347.75801025.

THE GEORGIA LEGAL DIRECTORY. 0145-2991. US. English. an. $6.00. Legal Directions Publishing Company, 1314 Westwood Boulevard, Los Angeles CA 90024. LC KF192.G46. DD 340.025758.

GEORGIA MANUFACTURING DIRECTORY. 0435-5482. US. English. be. $50.00. Manufacturers News Inc, 4 East Huron Street, Chicago IL 60611. **Tel** (312)337-1084. Lists manufacturing, mining, agricultural and processing plants and wholesalers. Address, zip code, phone, officers, number of employees included. Alphabetically and SIC and geographic sections. 612 pages.

THE GEORGIA MUNICIPAL YEARBOOK. 0146-5295. US. English. an. 10 Pryor Street Building/Suite 220, Atlanta GA 30303. LC HD4606.G4. DD 363.5.

GEOTHERMAL WORLD DIRECTORY. 1972-. 0094-9779. US. English. an. $55.00. Geothermal World Inc, 5762 Firebird Ct, Camarillo CA 93010. **Tel** (805)482-6288. **Ed** Tratner. LC TJ280.7. DD 338.2. bk rev. adv acc. **Circ** 19,000. Covers all aspects of international geothermal energy development. Current edition is 1984-85; listings, articles, news reports from over 100 countries.

GERMAN-CANADIAN YEARBOOK. VFOAT German Canadian Yearbook. V. 1- 1973-. 0316-8603. Periodical. CN. text in English and German. an. Historical Society of Mecklenburg Upper Canada Inc, 42 Noranda Drive, Toronto Ontario M6M 2X9 Canada. **Ind/Abst** MLA Int. Bibliogr. Books Artic. Mod. Lang. Lit. DD 917.10631.

GERMAN TRADE DIRECTORY. VFOAT Directory: German Trade. 1st Ed. (1976)-. GW. English. Interpress Obersee Verlag-GMBH, Schoene Aussicht 23, D-2000 Hamburg 76 West Germany. LC HF3563. DD 382.029443.

GERMAN YEARBOOK OF INTERNATIONAL LAW. VFOAT Jahrbuch fur Internationales Recht. V. 19- 1976-. 0344-3094. GW. English (French or German). an. Duncker und Humblot Verlag, Dietrich-Schafer Weg 9, 1000 Berlin 41 West Germany. **Ind/Abst** Am. Hist. Life, Hist. Abstr., Part A, Mod. Hist. Abstr., Hist. Abst., Part B, Twent. Century Abstr. LC JX201. DD 341.05. *Jahrbuch fur Internationales Recht.*

GERMAN YEARBOOK ON BUSINESS HISTORY. 1981-. 0722-2416. English. an. LC HC14. DD 330.9005.

GERONTOLOGY GRADUATE PROGRAM DIRECTORY. Periodical. US. English. an. $49.00. Warren Research, PO Box 1771, Decatur IL 62525.

GEWERKSCHAFTS JAHRBUCH. VFOAT Gewerkschaftsjahrbuch. 1984-. German. an. Bund Verlag GMBH, Postfach 90 08 40, 5000 Koln 90 West Germany. LC HD6691. DD 331.870943.

GEZINSSOCIOLOGISCHE DOCUMENTATIE JAARBOEK. English. ir. Uitgeverij Acco, Tiensestraat 134-136, 3000 Leuven Belgium. LC HQ728.

THE GIANTS NEWSWEEKLY. See Recreation, Leisure - Sports.

GIDS VOOR HET AANVRAGEN VAN Z. W.O.-STEUN. VFOAT Gids voor het Aanvragen van Zwo-Steun. NE. Dutch. ir. Free. Nederlandse Organisatie voor Zuiver-Wetenschappelijk Onderzoek, Juliana van Stolberglaan 148 Postbus 93138, 2509 AC 'S-Gravenhage Netherlands. **Tel** (070)4966 49. **Circ** 9,500. (ctrl). Directory for applicants to Zuiver Wetenschappelijk Onderzoek, subsides, fellowships, and scholarships.

GIFAP DIRECTORY. **Main/Corp** International Group of National Associations of Agrochemical Manufacturers. VFOAT G.I.F.A.P. Directory. English. ir. International Group of National Associations of Agrochemical Manufacturers, Avenue Hamoir 12, 1180 Brussels Belgium. LC HD9482.A1. DD 338.76686025.

GIFT AND DECORATIVE ACCESSORY BUYERS DIRECTORY. (THE GIFT AND DECORATIVE ACCESSORY BUYERS DIRECTORY). 0072-4505. US. English. Geyer-McAllister Publications, 51 Madison Avenue, New York NY 10010. LC T12. DD 338.47745502573. *Gift and Art Buyers Directory.*

THE GIRLS' SCHOOL YEAR BOOK. VFOAT Girls' School Year Book, Public Schools. UK. English. an. 7.50. Adam & Charles Black, 35 Bedford Row, London WC1R 4JH England. **Tel** 01-242 0946. **Ed** J F Burnet. adv acc. Official handbook of the Girls' Schools Association, listing major public and preparatory schools.

GLABC DIRECTORY. **Main/Corp** Government Libraries Association of British Columbia. VAT Government Libraries Association of British Columbia Directory. 0821-5693. CN. English. an. Free. Ministry of Human Resources Library, 800 Cassiar Street, Vancouver British Columbia V5K 4N6 Canada. DD 027.5025711.

GLAD DIRECTORY OF RESOURCES AVAILABLE TO DEAF & HARD-OF-HEARING PERSONS IN THE SOUTHERN CALIFORNIA AREA. **Main/Corp** Greater Los Angeles Council on Deafness. VFOAT Directory of Resources Available to Deaf & Hard-of-hearing Persons in the Southern California Area. VAT Greater Los Angeles Council on Deafness Directory of Resources Available to Deaf and Hard-of-Hearing Persons in the Southern California Area. 0146-8340. US. English. Greater Los Angeles Council on Deafness, 621 South Virgil Avenue, Los Angeles CA 90005. LC HV2561.C2. DD 362.420257949.

THE GLADIOLUS ANNUAL : BEING THE YEARBOOK OF THE BRITISH GLADIOLUS SOCIETY. Began in 1927. 0072-4580. UK. English. an. LC SB413.G5.

GLASGOW CHAMBER OF COMMERCE AND MANUFACTURES REGIONAL DIRECTORY. UK. English. Kemps Group Printers & Publishers Ltd, Federation House 2309 Coventry Road, Birmingham B26 3PG England. LC HF302.G52. DD 380.106041443.

GLASS ART SOCIETY PHOTOGRAPHIC DIRECTORY. VFOAT Photographic Directory. 1983-1984-. 0740-8889. US. English. an. $7.50. Glass Art Society, PO Box 1364, Corning NY 14830. LC NK5112. DD 748.0973.

GLASS FACTORY DIRECTORY. VFOAT Directory of Glass Factories in the United States and Canada. 1917. US. English. an. $12.00. National Glass Budget, Box 7138, Pittsburgh PA 15213. **Tel** (412)362-5136. **Ed** Liz Scott. bk rev. adv acc. **Circ** 1,650. (ctrl). News of glass manufacturing worldwide, including products, financial and production reports, personnel, uses and patents. Also annual directory of US and Canadian glass plants.

THE GLASS INDUSTRY DIRECTORY ISSUE. US. English. an. Magazines for Industry, 777 Third Avenue, New York NY 10017. LC HD9623.A1. DD 338.47666025. *Glass Industry International Directory, 0436-0494.*

GLOBAL AUTOVON AUTOMATIC VOICE NETWORK, DEFENSE COMMUNICATIONS SYSTEM DIRECTORY. **Main/Corp** United States. Defense Communications Agency. VFOAT Global Autovon Directory. 0747-7651. US. English. sa. Superintendent of Documents, US Government Printing Office, Washington DC 20402. LC UA23.2. DD 353.6025.

GLOBAL AUTOVON TELEPHONE DIRECTORY. **Main/Corp** Defense Communications Agency. VFOAT Global Autovon Directory. Periodical. US. English. ty.

GLOBAL BANKING DIRECTORY CEASED. US. English. an. Institutional Investor, 488 Madison Avenue, New York NY 10022. LC HG1536. DD 332.1025.

GLOBAL DIRECTORY OF GAS COMPANIES. VFOAT Gas Global Directory. 1973-. 0094-6303. US. English. $90.00. 4151 Southwest Freeway/Suite 735, Houston TX 77027. LC TP714. DD 338.47665702573.

GODISEN ZBORNIK (UNIVERZITET KIRIL I METODIJ—SKOPJE. BIOLOSKI FAKULTET). (GODISEN ZBORNIK). VFOAT Annuaire. No. 32-. Macedonian (summaries in English, French, and German). an. Bioloski Fakultet, Postenski Fah 107, Cair-Skopje Yugoslavia. LC QH301. *Godisen Zbornik. Biologija, 0560-2270.*

GOETHE-ALMANACH. 1967-. 0436-1156. German. ir. Ed H Holtzhauer and H Henning. LC AY856. DD 830.5.

GOETHE-JAHRBUCH. JA. German. ir. Goeth-Gesellschaft, c/o Nippon-Universitat, 156 Sakurajousi 3-25-40, Setagaya-Ku, Tokyo Japan. LC PT2046.

GOETHE YEARBOOK. (GOETHE YEARBOOK : PUBLICATIONS OF THE GOETHE SOCIETY OF NORTH AMERICA). Vol. 1-. 0734-3329. US. English. an. $25.00. Camden House, Drawer 2025, Columbia SC 29202. **Tel** (803)788-8689. **Ed** Thomas Saine. LC PT2046. DD 831.6. bk rev. adv acc. Literary criticism and book reviews on Goethe and the Goethe period.

GOLF & CLUB YEARBOOK. 0092-6914. US. English. an. $1.00. Werner Book Corp, Box 1136, Santa Monica CA 90406. LC GV961.

THE GOLF DIGEST ALMANAC. 1984-. 0742-4485. US. English. an. $19.95. Golf Digest/Tennis Inc, 495 Westport Avenue, PO Box 5350, Norwalk CT 06856. LC GV981. DD 796.3520973.

Yearbooks, Almanacs, Directories

GOLF DIRECTORY. (GOLF . . . DIRECTORY). 0275-5734. US. English. $2.95. Jiff-Davis Publishing Company, One Park Avenue, New York NY 10016. **LC** GV961. **DD** 796.35205.

GOMER'S BUDGET TRAVEL DIRECTORY. 0163-6227. US. English. Gomer Guides, PO Box 310, Maplewood NJ 07040. **LC** E158. **DD** 917.304926.

GOOD SAM CLUB'S RECREATIONAL VEHICLE OWNERS DIRECTORY. (THE GOOD SAM CLUB'S RECREATIONAL VEHICLE OWNERS DIRECTORY). **VFOAT** Recreational Vehicle Owners Directory. 0090-3256. US. English. $5.45 Single Issue. PO Box 500, Calabasas CA 91302. **LC** SK601.3. **DD** 647.947.

GOODHUE COUNTY RURAL IDENTIFICATION DIRECTORY. 0148-8104. US. English. Public Safety Building, Goodhue County Civil Defense Sixth Street, Red Wing MN 55066.

GOSPEL MUSIC ASSOCIATION ANNUAL DIRECTORY & YEARBOOK. **VAT** Gospel Music Association Annual Directory and Yearbook. 0362-7330. US. English. an. Gospel Music Association, PO Box 23201, Nashville TN 37202. **LC** ML19. **DD** 783.7. *Gospel Music Directory & Yearbook.*

GOSPEL MUSIC OFFICIAL DIRECTORY. 1982/1983-. 0739-604X. US. English. $5.00. Gospel Music Association, Box 23201, Nashville TN 37202. **LC** ML3186.8. **DD** 783.702573.

GOVERNANCE DIRECTORY. Main/Corp National Association of College Admissions Counselors. 0735-0201. US. English. an. National Association of College Admissions Counselors, 9933 Lawler Avenue/Suite 500, Skokie IL 60077. **LC** L901. **DD** 378.73.

GOVERNMENT ASSISTANCE ALMANAC. 1985-86-. 0883-8690. Periodical. US. English. an. Foggy Bottom Publications, PO Box 57150 West End Station, Washington DC 20037. **DD** 353.

GOVERNMENT CONTRACTS DIRECTORY. US. English. an. $79.50. Government Data Publications, 1120 Connecticut Avenue NW, Washington DC 20036. **Tel** (718)627-0819. **Ed** Siegfried Lobel. Contains government contract listing and is organized by product category. Within each product category, the contracts are further organized in alphabetical order by contractor.

GOVERNMENT DIRECTORY FOR BRITISH COLUMBIA WITH SELECTED FEDERAL CONTACTS. June 1983-. 0822-8620. Periodical. CN. English. sa. Employers' Council of British Columbia, Suite 1130/800 West Pender Street, Vancouver British Columbia V6C 2V6 Canada. **DD** 354.71100025. *Departmental and Staff Directory, Government of British Columbia, 0710-2798.*

GOVERNMENT FINANCE STATISTICS YEARBOOK. INTERNATIONAL MONETARY FUND. (GOVERNMENT FINANCE STATISTICS YEARBOOK). V. 1- 1977-. 0250-7374. US. English (introduction, data fund codes, yearbook line numbers, and titles of yearbook lines also in French and Spanish). an. $20.00 Regular, $15.00 Other. International Monetary Fund, 700 19th Street NW, Washington DC 20431. **Tel** (202)477-7000. **LC** HJ101. **DD** 336.0212.

GOVERNMENT HOTEL DIRECTORY CEASED. **VFOAT** Repertoire Gouvernemental des Hotels. Jan. 1976-July 1980. 0381-3703. Periodical. CN. English (French). sw. *Government Hotel Index, 0706-4373.*

GOVERNMENT OF CANADA. TELEPHONE DIRECTORY. NATIONAL CAPITAL REGION. (TELEPHONE DIRECTORY, NATIONAL CAPITAL REGION). **VFOAT** Annuaire Telephonique, Region de la Capitale Nationale. Spring 1975-. 0382-1846. Periodical. CN. English (French). sa. 20.00 Domestic, 24.00 Foreign. Receiver General for Canada, Statistics Canada Publications, Ottawa Ontario K1A 0T6 Canada. **Tel** (800)268-1151. *Government Directory, National Capital Region, 0318-3343.*

THE GOVERNMENT OF NEW SOUTH WALES DIRECTORY OF ADMINISTRATION AND SERVICES. **VFOAT** New South Wales Government Directory. 1st- Ed. Periodical. AT. English. ir. Government of New South Wales, Department of Services, Box 30, Government Printing Office, Sydney 2001 Australia. **LC** JQ4521. **DD** 354.94400025.

GOVERNMENT OF ONTARIO. TELEPHONE DIRECTORY. (GOVERNMENT OF ONTARIO TELEPHONE DIRECTORY). **VFOAT** Telephone Directory. **VAT** Telephone Directory - Government of Ontario, Government Telephone Directory (Toronto). Began with V. for 1973. 0701-9599. CN. English. an. Ministry of Government Services, 880 Bay Street, 5th Floor, Toronto Ontario M7A 1N8 Canada. **LC** JL267. **DD** 354.71300025. *Ontario Government Telephone Directory.*

GOVERNMENT OFFICIALS DIRECTORY AS ON . . . . Began in 1981. II. English. ir. PHD Chamber of Commerce and Industry, PHD House 4/2 Siri Fort Institutional Area Panchsheel Marg, New Delhi 110016 India.

GOVERNMENT PRODUCTION PRIME CONTRACTORS DIRECTORY. (DIRECTORY OF GOVERNMENT PRIME CONTRACTORS). **VFOAT** Directory of Government Production Prime Contractors. 1968-. 0887-4107. US. English. an. Government Data Publications, 1661 McDonald Avenue, Brooklyn NY 11230. **Tel** (718)627-0819. **DD** 351. This valuable two-part directory lists the names and addresses of organizations which received government production prime contracts. alphabetically by firm name. Directory II is organized in zip code number sequence.

GOVERNMENT PROGRAMS AND PROJECTS DIRECTORY. 1st Ed., Issue No. 1 (May 1983)-. 0737-5255. US. English. ir. Gale Research Company Book Tower, Detroit MI 48226. **LC** JK404. **DD** 353.078025. Provides facts and figures on hundreds of programs implemented, managed, and supported by executive departments and independent agencies of the Federal Government.

GOVERNMENT PUBLICATIONS DIRECTORY. **VFOAT** Cheng Fu Kan Wu Mu Lu. Periodical. English (Chinese). ir. Free. Government Publications Centre, General Post Office Building, Ground Floor Connaught Place, Hong Kong Hong Kong. **LC** Z3107.H7, J613. **DD** 015.5125. **Circ** 8,000. Lists all saleable government publications which include laws of Hong Kong, maps, trade forms, statistical periodicals and miscellaneous reports. *List of Government Publications.*

GOVERNMENT RESEARCH CENTERS DIRECTORY. 1st- Ed. 0270-4811. US. English. $72.00. Gale Research Co, Book Tower, Detroit MI 48226. **LC** Q179.98. **DD** 001.402573. **NLM** Q 179.98 G721.

GOVERNMENT YEARBOOK. Main/Corp Israel. Periodical. IS. English. an. State of Israel, Ministry of Defence/Publishing House, Tel-Aviv Israel.

GRADUATE ASSISTANTSHIP DIRECTORY IN THE COMPUTER SCIENCES. 0072-5234. US. English. an. $10.00. Association for Computing Machinery, PO Box 9209 Church Street Station, New York NY 10249. **Tel** (212)265-6300. Contains information about assistantships and fellowships available in university computing science departments and university computing centers for graduate study.

GRAND ALMANACH CEASED. (LE GRAND ALMANACH LA PRESSE). 1974-1981. 0317-0853. CN. French. Les Messageries Internationales du Livre Inc, 4550 rue Hochelaga, Montreal Quebec Canada. **LC** AY417. **DD** 054.1.

GRANDE PRAIRIE, ALBERTA, CITY DIRECTORY. **VAT** Grande Prairie Directory Grande Prairie City Directory. 1979-. 0715-4127. CN. English. an. $75.00 Per Vol. Grande Prairie Alberta City Directory, 100 East 4th Avenue, Vancouver British Columbia V5T 1G3 Canada. **DD** 917.1231. *Henderson's Grande Prairie, Alberta, City Directory, 0316-8344.*

GRANITE & MARBLE DIRECTORY . . . . **VFOAT** Granite and Marble Directory. 0731-4094. US. English. American Monument Association, 6902 North High Street, Worthington OH 43085. **LC** TN970. **DD** 338.275202573.

GRAPH-AGRI : ANNUAIRE DE GRAPHIQUES AGRICOLES. **VFOAT** Graph Agri. 79-. 0242-2085. FR. French. an. 60. SCEES, 4 Avenue de Saint-Mande, 75570 Paris Cedex 12 France. **LC** HD1941. **DD** 338.10944.

GRAPHIC ARTS TRADE DIRECTORY & REGISTER. 0072-5498. US. English. an. $50.00. Publishers Advertising Co, 220 South State Street, Chicago IL 60604. **LC** Z244.6.U5. **DD** 686.2025773.

THE GREAT METROPOLIS, OR NEW-YORK ALMANAC. **VFOAT** Great Metropolis. US. English. wk. $18.00. New York Almanac, 799 Broadway, New York NY 10003. **Tel** (212)673-3930. **Ed** Marvin Tabak. adv acc. **Circ** 8,000. Day-by-day listings of cultural and special events in New York City area. *Great Metropolis, or Guide to New York.*

GREAT SOUTHERN MANUFACTURERS DIRECTORY. AT. English. ir. Department of Industrial Development, 63 Serpentine Road, Albany Western Australia 633 Australia.

GREATER BOSTON MEDIA DIRECTORY. 1981-. 0275-8369. US. English. $17.50. Media Directories Division, New England Newsclip, 5 Auburn Street, Framingham MA 01701. **LC** P88.8. **DD** 302.23.

THE GREATER NEW YORK DIRECTORY. **VFOAT** Directory. 0743-6904. US. English. an. Dental Insurance Services Inc, PO Box 485, Belmont MA 02178. **LC** HD7104.5.U52. **DD** 368.382300257471.

GREECE'S WEEKLY FOR BUSINESS & FINANCE YEARBOOK. **VFOAT** Greece's Weekly for Business and Finance Yearbook. 1982-. English. wk. $120.00. Coronakis Press Ltd, 10 Fokidos Street, Athens 115 26 Greece. **Tel** 770-7280. **LC** HC291. **DD** 330.9495005.

GROUP HQ DIRECTORY. **VFOAT** Group Headquarters Directory. 1982-. 0277-108X. US. English. an. $95.00. Group HQ Directory, 633 Third Avenue, New York NY 10017. **LC** AS29.5. **DD** 061.3.

GROUP INSURANCE STANDARD DIRECTORY. 1983-84-. 0741-9201. US. English. an. 1341 G Street Northwest/#610, Washington DC 20005. **LC** HG8058. **DD** 368.3002573.

GROUP INSURANCE STANDARD DIRECTORY : OHIO, SOUTHERN (CINCINNATI AREA). Periodical. US. English. ir. ERISA Benefit Funds Inc, 1012 14th Street NW/Suite 700, Washington DC 20005. **Tel** (202)737-0666.

GUIA COMERCIAL Y TELEFONICA DEL DEPARTAMENTO DE SORIANO. Periodical. Spanish. ir. Talleres Graficos Moyano, Del Departamento de Soriano, Roosevelt 602 Al 610, Mercedes Uruguay.

GUIA DE ABONADOS : PARANA, VICTORIA, GUALEGUAY. Main/Corp Compania Entrerriana de Telefonos. **VFOAT** Guia Telefonica: Parana, Gualeguay, Victoria. Spanish. ir. Compania Entrerriana de Telefonos, Buenos Aires 156, Parana Argentina.

GUIA DE EXPORTADORES DEL URUGUAY. **VFOAT** Uruguayan Export Directory. 1974-. UY. English (Spanish). ir. Ministerio de Economia y Finanzas, Colonia 1013 Piso 8, Montevideo Uruguay. **LC** HF3473. **DD** 382.6025895.

GUIA DE LA PAZ : ANUARIO POSTAL (GUIA DE CASILLAS). Spanish. ir. Editorial Sanabria, Casilla 2767 Indaburo No 1184 Altos, Lapez Bolivia. **LC** HE6826.L3.

GUIDA NAZIONALE DEL COMMERCIO CON L'ESTERO : ANNUARIO DI CONSULTAZIONE PER IMPORTATORI ED ESPORTATORI. **VFOAT** Italian Directory for Foreign Trade. IT. English (French, German, Italian, and Spanish). an. Istituto Editorale Pubblicazioni Internazionali, Piazza Ruggero di Sicilia 1, 00162 Roma Italy. **LC** HF3583. **DD** 380.1029445.

GUIDE TO AMERICAN DIRECTORIES. Began publication in 1954. 0533-5248. US. English. B Klein Publications, PO Box 8503, Coral Springs FL 33065. **Ed** B Klein. **LC** Z5771. **DD** 016.380102573.

GUIDE TO AMERICAN DIRECTORIES. Began with: 4th Ed., 1960. 0533-5248. US. English. ir. B Klein Publications, PO Box 8503, Coral Springs FL 33065. **Tel** (313)961-2242. *Guide to American Directories for Compiling Mailing Lists.*

GUIDE TO AMERICAN EDUCATIONAL DIRECTORIES. 1st Ed. (1963)-. 0072-8225. US. English. ir. B Klein Publications, PO Box 8503, Coral Springs FL 33065. **Tel** (914)967-4340. **LC** Z5813. **DD** 016.3702573.

Yearbooks, Almanacs, Directories

GUIDE TO DEPARTMENTS OF SOCIOLOGY, ANTHROPOLOGY, AND ARCHAEOLOGY IN UNIVERSITIES AND MUSEUMS IN CANADA. CN. English (French). an. LC HM47.C2. DD 301.071171. *Annuaire de Departments de Sociologie, d'Anthropologie, d'Archeologie des Universites et des Musees du Canada, 0707-9214.*

GUIDE TO JEWISH CHICAGO AND YEARBOOK. (GUIDE TO JEWISH CHICAGO, AND YEARBOOK). Main/Corp American Jewish Congress. 4th- Ed. 0272-1066. US. English. $2.50. American Jewish Congress, 22 West Monroe Street/Suite 2102, Chicago IL 60603. LC F548.9.J5. DD 305.8924077311.

GUIDE TO MICROFORMS IN PRINT. SUPPLEMENT. Began in 1979. 0164-0739. US. English. an. $65.00. Meckler Publishing, 11 Ferry Lane West, Westport CT 06880. Tel (203)226-6967. Ed Ardis Carleton. LC Z1033.M5. DD 011.36. adv acc. Circ 1,000. Bibliographic access to microform titles. *Microlist, 0362-1014.*

GUIDE TO MINORITY BUSINESS DIRECTORIES. 0362-3459. US. English. $2.25 Single Issue. 1016 Plymouth Avenue, Minneapolis MN 55411.

GULF COAST OIL DIRECTORY. 1981/82-. 0739-3547. US. English. an. $35.00 Domestic, $45.00 Foreign. Resource Publications, 3210 Marquart, Houston TX 77027. LC HD9567.A13. DD 622.338029476. *Original Gulf Coast Oil Directory.*

GULF STATES OIL AND GAS DIRECTORY. 0191-9849. US. English. an. $25.00. Gulf States Oil and Gas Directory of LA Inc, 3810 Lakeshore Drive, Shreveport LA 71109. LC TN867. DD 338.272802576.

GUYANA YEAR BOOK. 1963-. 0533-6961. SA. English. ir. Guyana Graphic, Lama Avenue, Belair Park, East Demerara, Georgetown Guyana South Africa.

HAEOE HANIN KANHOWON CHONGNAM. 1983-. US. English (Korean). Chaemi Kahno Sinbosa, 10568 Magnolia Avenue/#102, Anaheim CA 92804. LC RT25.A2.

HAEUN PYOLLAM. VFOAT Shipping Directory. KO. English (Korean). ir. 9,000. Hanguk Haesa Munje Yonguso, 163-3 2-ka Ulchi-ro, Chung-ku, Seoul South Korea. LC HE892.5.

HALLE YEARBOOK. Main/Corp Halle Concerts Society. VFOAT Halle Year Book. 81/82-. UK. English. an. 1.50. Halle Concerts Society, 30 Cross Street, Manchester M2 7BA England. LC ML28.M19. DD 785.06242733.

HALLESCHES JAHRBUCH FUR MITTELDEUTSCHE ERDGESCHICHTE. V. 1-. German. an. Ind/Abst GeoRef. LC QE269. CODEN HAJEAY.

THE HAMBRO EUROMONEY DIRECTORY. 1972. 0306-3933. UK. English. an. 95.00. Euromoney Publishing Ltd, 92 Queensway, Bletchley Milton Keynes MK2 2QU England. Tel (01)236 3288. Ed I Swanton. LC HG3851. DD 332.45025. adv acc. Circ 10,000. Contains the names of 4,000 financial institutions across the globe, it lists a wide range of job functions at each institution.

HAMBURGER JAHRBUCH FUR WIRTSCHAFTS- UND GESELLSCHAFTSPOLITIK. Vol. 1- 1956-. 0072-9566. German. ir. (cum index).

HAMILTON AND NIAGARA PENINSULA DIRECTORY. VFOAT Directory for Hamilton and Niagara Peninsula. 1979- Ed. 0225-5685. CN. English. an. $55. Routing Services Ltd, Unit #2 185 Gibson Drive, Markham Ontario L3R 3K7 Canada. DD 380.102571338.

HAMILTON-WENTWORTH CANADA, BUSINESS DIRECTORY. (HAMILTON-WENTWORTH CANADA BUSINESS DIRECTORY). VAT Business Directory - Hamilton-Wentworth, Ont. 1982/1983-. 0712-5909. CN. English. be. Economic Development Department, Regional Municipality of Hamilton Wentworth, PO Box 910, Hamilton Ontario L8N 3V9 Canada. DD 380.102571352. *Hamilton Wentworth Canada, 0710-0264.*

HAMMOND ALMANAC (MAPLEWOOD, N.J. : 1983). (THE HAMMOND ALMANAC). 14th Ed. (1983)-. 0734-9092. US. English. an. $7.95. Hammond Almanac Inc, 515 Valley Street, Maplewood NJ 07040. LC AY64. DD 051. *Hammond Almanac of a Million Facts, Records, Forecasts, 0191-3883.*

HANDBOOK AND DIRECTORY - AMERICAN SOCIETY FOR INFORMATION SCIENCE. Main/Corp American Society for Information Science. 0066-0124. US. English. an. $50.00. American Society for Information Science, 1010 16th Street NW/2nd Floor, Washington DC 20036. Tel (202)659-3644.

HANDBOOK AND DIRECTORY - ASSOCIATION FOR EDUCATIONAL DATA SYSTEMS. (HANDBOOK AND DIRECTORY). Main/Corp Association for Educational Data Systems. 0092-6280. US. English. Association for Educational Data Systems, 1201 16th Street Northwest, Washington DC 20036. LC L901. DD 370.2854.

HANDBOOK AND DIRECTORY - CANADIAN FIELD HOCKEY ASSOCIATION. Main/Corp Canadian Field Hockey Association. Began publication in 1972?. 0225-0314. CN. English. an. Free to Members. Canadian Field Hockey Council, 333 River Road, Vanier Ontario K1L 8B9 Canada. DD 796.35502571.

HANDBOOK AND DIRECTORY - CANADIAN WOMEN'S FIELD HOCKEY ASSOCIATION. Main/Corp Canadian Women's Field Hockey Association. Began publication in 1972?. 0225-0306. CN. English. an. Free to Members. Canadian Field Hockey Council, 333 River Road, Vanier Ontario K1L 8B9 Canada. DD 796.35502571.

HANDBOOK AND DIRECTORY - CLASSIC CAR CLUB OF AMERICA. Main/Corp Classic Car Club of America. 0163-1055. Periodical. US. English. an. Classic Car Club of America, PO Box 443, Madison NJ 07940.

HANDBOOK AND DIRECTORY - NATIONAL UNIVERSITY EXTENSION ASSOCIATION CEASED. Main/Corp National University Extension Association. 0097-0255. US. English. ir. National University Extension Association, One Dupont Circle/Suite 360, Washington DC 20036. Tel (202)659-3130. LC LC6201. DD 378.155402573. Circ 1,500. (ctrl). Listing of all institutional and professional National University Extension Association members, NUCEA organizational chart, officers, staff, by-laws, and other association information.

HANDBOOK & DIRECTORY OF THE ARTS IN THE NORTH WEST. 1972-. UK. English. an. 2.00. North West Arts Association, 44 Sackville Street, M1 3NE Manchester England. LC NX120.G7. DD 702.542.

HANDBOOK AND MEMBERSHIP DIRECTORY - SOUTHERN COLLEGE PLACEMENT ASSOCIATION. (HANDBOOK AND MEMBERSHIP DIRECTORY). Main/Corp Southern College Placement Association. 0092-1718. US. English. 985 Lincoln Circle, Winter Park FL 32789. LC L903.S84. DD 378.002575.

HANDBOOK - ESOMAR. Main/Corp Esomar. VFOAT Annuaire - Esomar, Handbuch - Esomar. English. ir. 175.00. ESOMAR, Raadhuisstraat 15, Amsterdam Netherlands. LC HF5415.2. DD 658.83025.

HANDBUCH DES SCHWEIZER EXPORTES. Ed. 13 (1978-80)-. English (French, and German). ir. LC HF3703. DD 382.6025494. *Swiss Export Directory.*

HANDICAPPED FUNDING DIRECTORY. 1978-79 Ed.-1980-81 Ed. 0733-4753. US. English. be. $23.50. Research Grant Guides, PO Box 10726, Marina Del Rey CA 90295. Tel (213)306-2931. Ed Richard M Eckstein. LC HV1553. DD 338.4336240480973. A major resource of information for fund seekers for the handicapped. Listing over 700 foundations, corporations, government agencies and associations which grant funds to handicapped programs.

HANDY POCKET DIRECTORY OF TELEVISION STATIONS IN OPERATION. US. English. ir. Television Digest, 1836 Jefferson Place Northwest, Washington DC 20036.

HAN'GUK CHONJA KONGOP TONGGYE YON'GAM. VFOAT Korean Electronic Industry Statistics Yearbook. 1978-. KO. English (Korean). ir. Hanguk Chongmil Kigi Sento, 222-13 Kuro-dong, Yongdungpo-ku, Seoul South Korea. LC HD9696.A3.

HANGUK KUMHYONG KONGOP CHONGNAM. VFOAT Korea Mould Industrial Directory. KO. Korean. ir. Hanguk Kumhyong Kisul Chongbo Sento, 54-34 Munnae-dong 3-ka Yongdungpo-ku, Seoul Korea. LC TS229.

HANGUK TAEHAK YONGUM. VFOAT Korean University Yearbook. V. 1-. Korean. ir. 50.000. Aedu Yong Chulp Anbu, 1-537 Youido-dong Yongdungpo-ku, Seoul Korea. LC LA1333.

HARBOUR & SHIPPING. ANNUAL SHIPPING DIRECTORY. VFOAT Annual Shipping Directory. 1975-. CN. English. Progress Publishing Co, Marine Building, 355 Burrard Street, Vancouver British Columbia 1 Canada. DD 387.102571133.

HARBOUR NET DIRECTORY. (THE HARBOUR NET DIRECTORY). 1974-. 0703-8429. Periodical. CN. English. Toronto Power Squadron, PO Box 968 Station F, Toronto Ontario M4Y 2N9 Canada. DD 384.530257135. *Harbour Net, 0703-8410.*

HARDWARE AND HOME IMPROVEMENT CENTER CHAINS. AUTO SUPPLY CHAINS. (DIRECTORY : HARDWARE AND HOME IMPROVEMENT CENTER CHAINS, AUTO SUPPLY CHAINS). VFOAT Hardware and Home Improvement Center Chains, Auto Supply Chains. 1973-. 0092-1483. US. English. an. $54.00. Business Guides Inc, 2 Park Avenue, New York NY 10016. LC HD9745.U4. DD 381.45629202573. *Directory: Auto Supplies and Hardware Chains.*

HARPERS DIRECTORY. UK. English. an. 8.50. Harper Trade Journals Ltd, Harling House, 47-51 Great Suffolk Street, London SE1 England. LC TP500.5. DD 380.1456631025. *Harpers Directory and Manual.*

HARRIS ILLINOIS INDUSTRIAL DIRECTORY. VFOAT Illinois Industrial Directory. 0734-3256. US. English. an. $97.20 Ohio Only, $93.00 Others. Harris Publishing Co, 2057-2 Aurora Road, Twinsburg OH 44087. *Harris Illinois Marketers Industrial Directory.*

HARRIS INDIANA INDUSTRIAL DIRECTORY. VFOAT Indiana Industrial Directory, IID. 1984-. US. English. an. $69.50. Harris Publishing Company, 2057-2 Aurora Road, Twinsburg OH 44807. Tel (216)425-9000. Ed Irene Amick. Circ 3,000. Industrial manufacturers in city order for state. Also address and phone, employment manufactured products and key personnel. products and key personnel. *Harris Indiana Marketers Industrial Directory, 0734-844X.*

HARRIS MICHIGAN INDUSTRIAL DIRECTORY (TWINSBURG, OHIO : 1984). (HARRIS MICHIGAN INDUSTRIAL DIRECTORY). VFOAT Michigan Industrial Directory. 1984-85-. US. English. an. $89.00. Harris Publishing Company, 2057-2 Aurora Road, Twinsburg OH 44087. Tel (216)425-9000. Ed Maryellen Smith. Manufacturers listed by alpha, geo, products and SIC codes. Shows key personnel, annual SIS, EMPL, EST, import/export, research, major manufactured products, SIC code. Statistical section and maps. *Harris Michigan Marketers Industrial Directory.*

HARRIS MICHIGAN MARKETERS INDUSTRIAL DIRECTORY. VFOAT Michigan Marketers Industrial Directory. 1982/83-. 0734-8568. US. English. an. $83.00. Harris Publishing Company, 2057-2 Aurora Road, Twinsburg OH 44087. Tel (216)425-9000. Ed Mary Ellen Smith. LC HD9727.M5. DD 380.10294774. Circ 3,800. Lists 14,000 manufacturers and importers in city order for Michigan sections: geographical products, SIC. Lists available for customized mailings. *Harris Michigan Industrial Directory, 0271-146X.*

HARRIS OHIO INDUSTRIAL DIRECTORY. VFOAT Ohio Industrial Directory. 1984-. 0733-4664. US. English. an. $89.00. Harris Publishing Company, 2057-2 Aurora Road, Twinsburg OH 44087. Tel (216)425-9000. Ed Fran Carlsen. Circ 4,000. Lists over 11,600 manufacturers in 5 sections: alpha, geographical, by product, SIC and statistical sections. Lists personnel, year est., annual sig., import/export, research facilities. Lists available customized labels. *Harris Ohio Marketers Industrial Directory, 0733-4664.*

HARRIS PENNSYLVANIA INDUSTRIAL DIRECTORY. VFOAT Pennsylvania Industrial Directory. 1st (1982/83)-. 0734-8541. US. English. an. $83.00. Harris Publishing Company, 2057-2 Aurora Road, Twinsburg OH 44087. Tel (216)425-9000. Ed Fran Segulin. Circ 3,500. Contains over 15,000 manufacturers listings with complete company data: key personnel, year established, annual sales, products, export/import. Six sections: alphabetically, geographically by city, by product, SIC and statistically. *Industrial Directory of the Commonwealth of Pennsylvania.*

Yearbooks, Almanacs, Directories

THE HARRIS SURVEY YEARBOOK OF PUBLIC OPINION. 1970-. 0085-1442. US. English. an. Louis Harris and Associates, 630 5th Avenue, New York NY 10020. LC HN90.P8. DD 306.0973.

HART'S ROCKY MOUNTAIN MINING DIRECTORY. 0736-2366. US. English. an. Hart Publications Inc, PO Box 1917, Denver CO 80201. LC HD9506.U63. DD 338.762202578.

HARVARD ALUMNI DIRECTORY. Began in 1919. US. English. ir. Harvard University, Alumni Record Office, 1350 Massachusetts Avenue/Room 671, Cambridge MA 02138. Tel (617)495-2371. LC LD2138. *Harvard University Directory, Quinquennial Catalog of the Officers and Graduates.*

HAWAII AGRICULTURAL EXPORT PRODUCTS DIRECTORY. 0160-6530. US. English. Hawaii Department of Agriculture/Division of Marketing and Consumer Service, 1428 South King Street, Honolulu HI 96814. Tel (808)548-4251. LC HD9007.H3. DD 380.141025969. Circ 6,000. (ctrl). Hawaii agricultural and food products export directory. Contains companies which export Hawaiian agricultural and food products in wholesale quantities to overseas domestic and foreign markets.

HAWAII BUSINESS DIRECTORY. Began with 1975/76. US. English. ir. $10.00 Mainland, $20.00 Foreign. Hawaii Business Directory Inc, 1164 Bishop Street, Suite 1007, Honolulu HI 96813. Tel (808)526-2287. Ed John L Witwer. adv acc. Hawaii's business and professional people, by island, address, phone, kind of business, names of key officers, number of employees, annual sales volume, date established, and more. *State of Hawaii Business Directory,* 0081-4547.

HAYES DIRECTORY OF PHYSICIAN AND HOSPITAL SUPPLY HOUSES. (HAYES DIRECTORY OF PHYSICIAN & HOSPITAL SUPPLY HOUSES). VFOAT Directory of Physician & Hospital Supply Houses. US. English. ir. Edward N Hayes, 4429 Birch Street, Newport Beach CA 92660. Tel (714)756-9063. Ed James E Hayes. Lists all dealers of physician hospital and medical supplies and equipment in US with address, financial strength, credit rating, and telephone number. Association members specially indicated.

HAYES DRUGGIST DIRECTORY. US. English. an. $190.00. Edward N Hayes Publisher, 4229 Birch Street, Newport Beach CA 92660. Tel (714)756-9063. Ed James E Hayes and Jay D Hayes. Lists all retail drug stores in US with address, financial strength, and credit rating. Separate listings of all larger wholesale druggists. Mailing labels available by individual selection. *Hayes' Druggists' Directory.*

HDS TELEPHONE DIRECTORY. Main/Corp United States. Office of Human Development Services. VAT Human Development Services Telephone Directory. Periodical. US. English. qt. US Department of Health and Human Services, Office of Human Development Services, Washington DC 20201.

HEADQUARTERS TELEPHONE DIRECTORY. Main/Corp United States. National Aeronautics and Space Administration. 0364-2488. US. English. qt. Superintendent of Documents, US Government Printing Office, Washington DC 20402. Tel (202)783-3238.

HEALTH AND ENVIRONMENT DEPARTMENT RESOURCE DIRECTORY. Main/Corp New Mexico. Health and Environment Dept. 1978-. 0195-9042. US. English. an. Health & Environment Planning Bureau, PO Box 968 Southwest Plaza Building, 809 St Michaels Drive, Sante Fe NM 87503. LC RA7.6.N6. DD 362.109789.

THE HEALTH CARE DIRECTORY. 0147-7846. US. English. Medical Economics, Book Division, Oradell NJ 07649. LC RA977. DD 362.102573.

HEALTH DEVICES SOURCEBOOK. See Medicine.

HEALTH FACILITIES DIRECTORY. VFOAT Directory of Health Facilities. March 1975-. 0361-2929. US. English. qt. Sacramento Department of Health Facilities Licensing Section, 744 P Street/Room 440, Sacramento CA 95814. LC RA981.C3. DD 362.1025794. NLM WX 22 AC2 H4.

HEALTH GROUPS IN WASHINGTON, A DIRECTORY. See Public Health and Safety.

HEALTH MANPOWER DIRECTORY. Periodical. English (text in Nepali). ir. NLM W 22 JN4 H4.

THE HEALTH SCIENCES VIDEOLOG : A DIRECTORY OF VIDEO CASSETTE PROGRAMS. 1981-. Periodical. English. ir.

HEALTH SERVICES DIRECTORY. 1st Ed. (1981)-. 0731-6607. US. English. ir. Gale Research Company, Book Tower, Detroit MI 48226. Tel (800)521-0707. Ed Anthony T Kruzas. LC RA977. DD 362.102573. NLM W 22 AA1 H55.

HEALTH SYSTEMS REPORT ALMANAC ON FEDERAL HEALTH ISSUES, PROPOSALS, ADMINISTRATIVE ACTIONS, LEGISLATION, PUBLIC LAWS. 1978-. 0194-3049. US. English. an. $105.00. Morris Associates, 1346 Connecticut Avenue Northwest, Washington DC 20036. LC KF3821.A15. DD 344.73041. NLM W1 HE589F.

HEARTLAND OF SOUTHERN ONTARIO DIRECTORY. 1979- Ed. 0225-5677. CN. English. an. $55. Routing Services Ltd, Unit #2, 185 Gibson Drive, Markham Ontario L3R 3K7 Canada. DD 380.1025713.

HEBBEL JAHRBUCH. Began publication in 1939. 0073-1560. GW. German. an. Westholsteinische Verlag, Postfach 1880, D-2240 Heide West Germany. Tel 0481/691-138. Ed Dieter Lohmeier. Ind/Abst MLA Int. Bibliogr. Books Artic. Mod. Lang. Lit. LC PT2296.A1. DD 832.77. Circ 600. The yearbook contents are what international Germanistic scientists have found about literature and reception of Hebbel-Literature.

HEIDELBERGER JAHRBUCHER. 1-1957-. 0073-1641. GW. German. an. Springer Verlag-New York Inc, 175 5th Avenue, New York NY 10010. Tel (212)460-1584. Ind/Abst Biol. Abstr., Am. Hist. Life, Hist. Abstr., Part A, Mod. Hist. Abstr., Hist. Abstr., Part B, Twent. Century Abstr., Hist. Abstr. LC AS181. CODEN HDJBAC.

HEIMATKALENDER FUR DAS PIRMASENSER UND ZWEIBRUCKER LAND. 1973-. German. ir. LC AY860.P57.

HEINE-JAHRBUCH. 1962-. 0073-1692. GW. German. an. Hoffmann und Campe Verlag, Havestehuder Weg 45, 2000 Hamburg 13 West Germany. Ind/Abst MLA Int. Bibliogr. Books Artic. Mod. Lang. Lit. LC PT2328.

HELPING THE EXOFFENDER. (HELPING THE EXOFFENDER . . . . A TEXAS DIRECTORY). 1975/76-. 0364-3441. US. English. State Bar of Texas, PO Box 12487, Austin TX 78711. LC HV9305.T4. DD 364.8025764.

THE HEP HIGHER EDUCATION DIRECTORY. (THE HEP . . . HIGHER EDUCATION DIRECTORY). VFOAT H.E.P. Higher Education Directory. VAT Higher Education Publications Higher Education Directory. 1983-. 0736-0797. US. English. an. $31.00. Higher Education Publishing Inc, 1920 North Street NW/Suite 520, Washington DC 20036. Tel (202)296-9106. Ed Constance Torregrosa. LC L901. DD 378.73. Circ 10,000. Directory of all accredited colleges and universities in the country, plus institutional characteristics and top administrators.

HIGHER EDUCATION DIRECTORY. Began in 1979. 0740-9230. US. English. $4.00 Each. Council for Advancement and Support of Education, Suite 400/11 Dupont Circle, Washington DC 20036. LC L901. DD 378.002573.

HIGHER EDUCATION IN MONTANA DIRECTORY. 0145-2207. US. English. an. Montana University Systems, 1231 11th Avenue, Helena MT 59601. LC L903.M9. DD 378.786.

THE HIGHER EDUCATION PUBLIC ADMINISTRATION DIRECTORY. (THE . . . HIGHER EDUCATION PUBLIC ADMINISTRATION DIRECTORY). 0747-9743. US. English. Terry L Johnson Author, 1185 Meadow Lane - #107, Concord CA 94520. LC JF1338.A2. DD 350.0007073.

HILBORN'S FAMILY NEWSLETTER DIRECTORY. VFOAT Family Newsletter Directory. VAT Family Newsletter Directory (1984). 3rd Ed. (Aug. 1984)-. 0828-4466. CN. English. an. 5.00. Hilborn's Family Newsletter Directory, 42 Sources Boulevard #11, Pointe-Claire Quebec H9S 2H9 Canada. DD 016.92910973. An alphabetical list, by surname, of 1,509 newsletters, each devoted to the history and genealogy of one family name. *Family Newsletter Directory,* 0227-5317.

HIMA DIRECTORY. VFOAT H.I.M.A. Directory. VAT Health Industry Manufacturers Association Directory. 0741-8191. US. English. be. Health Industry Manufacturers Association, 1030 15th Street Northwest, Washington DC 20005. LC HD9994.U5. DD 338.768176102573.

HINE'S DIRECTORY OF INSURANCE ADJUSTERS. VFOAT Directory of Insurance Adjusters. US. English. an. $10.00. Hine's Legal Directory Inc, Professional Center Building/PO Box 71, Glen Ellyn IL 60137. Tel (312)469-3983. Ed J R Collins. adv acc. Circ 7,000. (ctrl). Directory of independent insurance claim adjusters. *Hine's Insurance Adjusters.*

THE HISTORIC PRESERVATION YEARBOOK. 1st Ed/ 1984/1985-. 0748-8823. US. English. an. 78.00. Adler & Adler, 4550 Montgomery Avenue/Suite 705, Bethesda MD 20814. DD 363.

HISTORISCHES JAHRBUCH. Vol. 1-. 0018-2621. Periodical. GW. German. sa. 58.00. Verlag Karl Alber, Hermann-Herder-Strasse 4, 7800 Freiburg IM Breisgau West Germany. LC D1. (cum index).

HOFSTRA UNIVERSITY YEARBOOK OF BUSINESS. VFOAT Yearbook of Business. Ser. 1, V. 1 (Mar. 1964)-. 0073-2907. Monographic Series. US. English. ir. Hofstra University, 1000 Fulton Avenue, Hempstead NY 11550. Tel (516)560-5678. Each volume in this series has a distinctive title. Topics are selected from the areas of business and industrial research.

HOKKYOKUSEI HOIKAKU HYO. VFOAT Polaris Almanac for Azimuth Determination. Japanese. ir. 400. Heiwa No Umi Kyokai, 48 Kanda Jinboku 2 Chiyida-ku (101-91), Tokyo Japan. LC VK563.

HOLLIS PRESS & PUBLIC RELATIONS ANNUAL. See Business - Advertising & Public Relations.

THE HOLLYWOOD REPORTER STUDIO BLU-BOOK DIRECTORY. (THE HOLLYWOOD REPORTER STUDIO BLU-BOOK . . . DIRECTORY). 0278-419X. US. English. an. $45.00. Hollywood Reporter, 6715 Sunset Boulevard, Hollywood CA 90028. Tel (213)464-7411. Ed Brenda Marshall. LC PN1998.A1. DD 384.8025794. adv acc. *Studio Blu-Book Directory.*

HOLMESTED AND GALE ONTARIO PRACTICE YEAR BOOK. 1969-. 0441-6821. Periodical. CN. English. an. Carswell Company Ltd, 2330 Midland Avenue, Agincourt Ontario M5S 1P7 Canada. Ed W J Hemmerick. DD 347.71305.

THE HOME VIDEO YEARBOOK. 1981-. 0278-1336. US. English. an. $7.00. Applause Publications, 2234 South Sandy Hills Drive, Diamond Bar CA 91765. LC PN1992.95. DD 011.37.

HOMPO KOGYO NO SUSEI. VFOAT Mining Year Book. 1906-. JA. Japanese (with captions in English or Japanese). ir. 42.00. Tsusho Sangyo Chosaki, c/o Tsusansho Ginza Shosha, 15-1 Ginza 6-chome Chuo-ku, Tokyo Japan. LC HD9506.J29.

HONG KONG BUILDER DIRECTORY. HK. English. ir. Far East Trade Press, Toppan Building/22 Westlands Road, Quarry Bay Hong Kong. LC HD9715.H6. DD 338.476240255125.

HONG KONG INTERBANK DIRECTORY. English. an. Asia Trade Journals Ltd, PO Box 20014, Hennessy Road, Hong Kong. LC HG3351. DD 332.10255125.

HORIZON. (HORIZON : DIRECTORY OF ASSOCIATIONS IN THE FINANCIAL SERVICES INDUSTRY). VFOAT Horizon, Directory of Associations. 1983-. 0741-7241. US. English. an. $50.00. International Association for Financial Planning, Suite 120-C/5775 Peachtree-Dunwoody Road, Atlanta GA 30342. Tel (404)921-6579. Ed Cheryl King DuVall. LC HG65. DD 332.102573. adv acc. Circ 40,000. (ctrl). Directory of financial planning products and services (including associations and educational institutions in the financial service industry).

HORSE & RIDER ALL-WESTERN YEARBOOK. VAT Horse and Rider All-Western Yearbook. No 5 1975-. 0193-2950. US. English. an. $2.95. Rich Publishing Company, 41919 Moreno Road, Temecula CA 92390.

Yearbooks, Almanacs, Directories

HORSE INDUSTRY DIRECTORY. 1976-. US. English. an. $2.75. American Horse Council, 1700 K Street NW #300, Washington DC 20001. Tel (202)296-4031. Circ 5,000. Comprehensive listing of major breed groups, health and humane organizations, racetracks and related groups, sporting organizations, and government information sources. Also listings for horse publications. *Horse Industry Trade Press Directory.*

HORSE INDUSTRY DIRECTORY OF CANADA. 1984-. 0828-4679. CN. English. an. $10.00 Per No. Whitehouse Publishing, 10205 Venables Drive, Vernon British Columbia V1B 2K4 Canada. DD 636.1002571.

HOSPITAL AND NURSING YEAR BOOK OF SOUTHERN AFRICA (JOHANNESBURG (SOUTH AFRICA) : 1971)). (HOSPITAL AND NURSING YEAR BOOK OF SOUTHERN AFRICA). VFOAT Hospital & Nursing Year Book. SA. English. an. $18.59. Thomson Publishing Sa Pty Ltd, PO Box 8308, Joannesburg 2000 South Africa. Tel 789-2144. LC RA991.S7. DD 362.110968. NLM W1 HO73E. *Hospital and Nursing Year Book of South Africa.*

HOSPITAL DIRECTORY OF INDIA. 1st-Ed. II. English. ir. $13.00. Kay Jay Publications, 85-A Ashok Vihar, Delhi 110052 India. LC RA979. DD 362.1102554.

HOSPITAL PURCHASING GUIDE. (HOSPITAL PURCHASING GUIDE : HPG). VFOAT HPG. Began in 1978. 0741-2975. US. English. an. $105.00. IMS Communications Inc, 426 PA Avenue, Ft Washington PA 19034. Tel (215)628-4920. Ed C S Risley. LC HD9995.H63. DD 681.761029473. adv acc. Circ 1,500. Compendium of hospital equipment and supplies. Lists manufacturers address and phone number.

HOSPITALS & HEALTH SERVICES YEARBOOK AND DIRECTORY OF HOSPITAL SUPPLIERS. (THE HOSPITALS & HEALTH SERVICES YEAR BOOK AND DIRECTORY OF HOSPITAL SUPPLIERS). VFOAT Hospitals and Health Services Year Book and Directory of Hospital Suppliers. 1973-. 0300-5968. UK. English. an. $68.89. Institute Health Service Management, 75 Portland Place, London W1N 4AN England. Tel 01-580-5041. Ed N W Chaplin. LC RA986. DD 362.1102541. NLM WX 22 FA1 H9. adv acc. Circ 5,000. A comprehensive annual directory of health authorities in the UK, and the hospitals they manage, government departments, statutory bodies and other organizations concerned with health care and other related information. *Hospitals Year Book and Directory of Hospitals Suppliers, 0300-8479.*

HOSPITALS & HEALTH SERVICES YEARBOOK AUSTRALIA. VAT Hospitals and Health Services Yearbook Australia. AT. English. an. 70 Domestic. Peter Isaacson Publishing Pty Ltd, 46-50 Porter Street/Box 172, Prahran Victoria 3181 Australia. Tel 520-5555. Ed John Ross. adv acc. Circ 2,500. An indispensible source of information for anyone connected with hospitals and health services. *Australian Hospitals and Health Services Yearbook.*

HOT ROD PERFORMANCE AND CUSTOM DIRECTORY. VFOAT Hot Rod Directory. 0196-7010. US. English. an. $4.95 Single Copy. Petersen Publishing Company, 6725 Sunset Boulevard, Los Angeles CA 90028. LC TL12. DD 338.47629202573.

HOTEL & MOTEL DIRECTORY. AT. English. sa. 45. Peter Isaacson Publications Private Ltd, 46-50 Porter Street/Box 172, Prahran Victoria 3181 Australia. Tel 520555. Ed John Ross. LC TX907. DD 647.949. adv acc. Circ 3,000.

HOUSTON BUILDING & CONSTRUCTION DIRECTORY. VFOAT Houston Building and Construction Directory. 1982/83-. 0747-7430. US. English. an. Resource Publications, 3210 Marquart, Houston TX 77027. LC TH13.T4. DD 690.0257641411.

HOUSTON CORPORATE DIRECTORY. 0278-4963. US. English. Houston Chamber of Commerce, 1100 Milam Building/25th Floor, Houston TX 77002. LC HG4058.H68. DD 338.74025764235.

HOUSTON INTERNATIONAL BUSINESS DIRECTORY. 0197-3630. US. English. $27.84 Members, $34.80 Nonmembers. Houston Chamber of Commerce, 1100 Milam Building/25th Floor, Houston TX 77002. LC HF3163.H8. DD 338.88025764235.

HOUSTON OIL DIRECTORY. 0739-3555. US. English. an. $32.00 US, $44.00 Foreign. Resource Publications, 3210 Marquart, Houston TX 77027. LC TN867. DD 338.272820257641411.

HOW TO FIND INFORMATION ABOUT COMPANIES. See Business.

HSIANG-KANG KUNG YEH CHIH PIN NIEN CHIEN. VFOAT Hong Kong Industrial Products Directory. 1973/74-. Chinese or English. ir. $50.00. Handicrafts Manufacturers Development Association, PO Box K-880, Kowloon Hong Kong. LC T12.5.H6.

HSIN-CHIA-PO CHING CHI NIEN CHIEN. VFOAT Almanac of Singapore Economy. 1975/76-. Chinese. ir. $36.00 Per Copy. Shih Li Pao Yeh Chi Kou, 78-B Robinson Road 1, Hsin-Chia-Po China Mainland. LC HC445.8.A1.

HU-PEI TUAN PIEN HSIAO SHUO NIEN KAN. VFOAT Hubei Duan Pian Xiaoshuo Nian Kan. 1982-. Periodical. CC. Chinese. an. 1.30. Hsin Hua Shu Tien, Hu-Pei Sheng China.

HUDSON HOME PRODUCTS DIRECTORY. VFOAT Home Products Directory. 1980-. 0195-8941. US. English. an. $2.95. Hudson Home Publications, 175 South San Antonio Road, Los Altos CA 94022. LC TH455. DD 690.029473.

HUDSON'S STATE CAPITAL NEWS MEDIA CONTACTS DIRECTORY. VFOAT State Capitals News Media Contacts Directory. 1985-. 0885-1328. US. English. an. Hudson's State Capitals, 7315 Wisconsin Avenue #1200 North, Bethesda MD 20814. Tel (301)340-2100. Ed H P Hudson. LC P88.8. DD 001.5102573. Index each issue contains an index to its own contents - No Vol. index - loose. adv acc. Listing of news media, editors and correspondents in the 50 state capitals.

HUDSON'S WASHINGTON NEWS MEDIA CONTACTS DIRECTORY. VFOAT Washington News Media Contacts Directory. 1968-. 0441-389X. US. English. an. $95.00. 7811 Montrose Road, Potomac MD 20854. Tel (301)340-2100. Ed Howard Penn Hudson. LC Z6953.W2. DD 071.53. adv acc. Comprehensive listing of Washington DC Press Corporation's, 3,500 publications, radio, television, magazines, editors and correspondents.

HUI YUAN MING LU. Main/Corp Singapore Chinese Chamber of Commerce & Industry. Began with 1978 issue. Chinese (English). ir. Singapore Chinese Chamber of Commerce and Industry, 47 Hill Street, Singapore 0617 Singapore. LC HF5246.6.S55. DD 380.10255957. *Hsin-Chia-Po Chung-Hua Tsung Shang Hui Hui Yuan Hang Yeh Ming Tse.*

HUMAN RIGHTS DIRECTORY WESTERN EUROPE. (HUMAN RIGHTS DIRECTORY. WESTERN EUROPE). VFOAT Human Rights Europe. No. 1-. 0732-0906. US. English. be. Human Rights Internet, 1502 Ogden Street NW, Washington DC 20010. LC JC599.E9. DD 323.40604.

HUMAN RIGHTS ORGANIZATIONS & PERIODICALS DIRECTORY. 0098-0579. US. English. be. $22.00. Legal Publications, PO Box 673, Berkeley CA 94701. LC KF4741. DD 323.402573.

HUMAN SERVICES DIRECTORY. 1979-. 0821-9893. CN. English. be. DD 361.00257124.

HUMAN SERVICES DIRECTORY (SAINT JOHN, N.B.). (HUMAN SERVICES DIRECTORY). No. 1-. 0823-8480. CN. English. an. $5.00. Saint John Human Development Council, PO Box 6125 Station A, 3rd Floor/City Market, St John British Columbia E2L 4R6 Canada. DD 361.002571532. *Directory of Community Services, 0318-6474.*

HURRIYET ANSIKLOPEDIK YLLG. Turkish. ir. LC AY1187.A3.

I.A.A.F. DIRECTORY. Main/Corp International Amateur Athletic Federation. VFOAT IAAF Directory. UK. English (Multilingual). International Amateur Athletic Federation, 3 Hans Crescent Knightsbridge, London SW1X OLN England. LC GV563. DD 796.0601.

IASSW DIRECTORY; MEMBER SCHOOLS AND ASSOCIATIONS. Main/Corp International Association of Schools of Social Work. VAT International Association of Schools of Social Work Directory. 0098-8278. US. Multilingual (English). International Association of Schools of Social Work, 345 East 46th Street, New York NY 10017. LC HV6. DD 361.0071. *Directory of Members and Constitution.*

IBM SOFTWARE DIRECTORY (NEW YORK, N.Y.). (IBM SOFTWARE DIRECTORY). 1984-. 0000-0795. US. English. an. R R Bowker Company, 205 East 42nd Street, New York NY 10017. LC QA76.753. DD 001.6425029473.

IBS YEARBOOK. Main/Corp Instituto Brasileiro de Siderurgia. VFOAT Anuario Estatistico da Industria Siderurgica Brasileira. VAT Instuteto Brasileiro de Siderurgia Yearbook. Anuario Estatistico da Industria Siderurgica Brasileira. 1974-. BL. English (Portuguese). ir. Instituto Brasileiro de Siderurgia, rua Sao Jose, 90-Grupo 2001/2/5, Rio de Janeiro Brazil. LC HD9524.B8. *Anuario (Instituto Brasileiro de Siderurgia).*

ICCH COMMODITIES AND FINANCIAL FUTURES YEARBOOK. VFOAT I.C.C.H. Commodities and Financial Futures Yearbook. 1982. UK. English. an. $63.00. Landell Mills Commodities, 50-51 Wells Street, London W1P 3FD England. Tel 01-580-6886. Ed Michael Atkin. LC HG6046. DD 332.64405. adv acc. Circ 530. Directory and chapters on commodities and financial instruments and futures.

ICP REFERENCE SERIES SOFTWARE DIRECTORY. Main/Corp International Computer Programs, Inc. VFOAT ICP Software Directory. Periodical. US. English. sa.

ICP SOFTWARE DIRECTORY (1981). (ICP SOFTWARE DIRECTORY). VAT International Computer Programs Software Directory. Oct. 1981-. 0736-282X. US. English. ir. $758.00. International Computer Programs, 9000 Keystone Crossing, Indianapolis IN 46240. Tel (800)428-6179. Ed Dennis Hamilton. LC QA76. DD 001.6425029473. adv acc. Circ 3,500. Seven volume set-leading source of software information in the market. *ICP Directory, 0272-1171.*

ID HANDBOOK OF FOODSERVICE DISTRIBUTION. See Food & Drink.

IDAHO EDUCATIONAL DIRECTORY. VFOAT Educational Directory. US. English. an. LC L903.I2. DD 370.25796. *Educational Directory and Textbook Adoptions List.*

IDEA. (IDEA : JAHRBUCH DER HAMBURGER KUNSTHALLE). 1 (1982)-. GW. German. an. Prestel Verlag, Mandlstrasse 26, D-8000 Munich 40 West Germany. Tel 089/33-30-55. Ind/Abst Repert. Int. Litt. Art. LC N2305.H3. DD 708.3515. *Jahrbuch der Hamburger Kunstsammlungen.*

IDEA ANNUAL DIRECTORY. Main/Corp International Dance-Exercise Association. VFOAT I.D.E.A. Annual Directory. 1984-. 8755-7789. US. English. an. $15.00. Internatioanl Dance-Exercise Association, 4501 Misson Bay Drive/Suite 2F, San Diego CA 92109. LC RA781.15. DD 613.71.

IEA. INSTRUMENTS, ELECTRONICS, AUTOMATION PURCHASING DIRECTORY. (IEA : INSTRUMENTS, ELECTRONICS, AUTOMATION PURCHASING DIRECTORY). VFOAT Instruments, Electronics, Automation Purchasing Directory. -11th Ed. 0074-0578. UK. English. an. Morgan Grampian, Royal Sovereign House, 40 Beresford, London SE18 6BQ England. Tel 01-854 2200. LC TJ213. DD 338.4762138102542. *Instruments, Electronics, Automation Year Book and Buyers Guide, 0538-2483.*

IFLA DIRECTORY. Main/Corp International Federation of Library Associations and Institutions. 1977-. Periodical. NE. English. be. 35.00. International Federation Library Association, POB 95312, 2509 CH Hague Netherlands. Tel (70) 140884. Circ 2,000. (ctrl). Addrss list of IFLA officers and IFLA members. *IFLA Directory.*

THE IFT WORLD DIRECTORY & BUYERS' GUIDE. (THE IFT . . . WORLD DIRECTORY & BUYERS' GUIDE : A PUBLICATION OF THE INSTITUTE OF FOOD TECHNOLOGISTS). VFOAT I.F.T. . . . World Directory and Buyers' Guide. VAT Institute of Food Technologists World Directory and Buyers' Guide. 0737-4380. US. English. an. Institute of Food Technologists, 221 North La Salle Street, Chicago IL 60601. LC TP373. DD 664.002573. *IFT World Directory & Guide.*

ILLINOIS AIRPORT DIRECTORY. 1953-. US. English. Capital Airport, PO Box 218, Springfield IL 62705. LC TL726.3.I3. DD 387.736025773.

THE ILLINOIS ARCHITECTURE REFERENCE DIRECTORY. VFOAT Architecture Reference Directory. 1984-. 0747-6345. US. English. an. Metropolitian Press Publications Inc, PO Box 3680/Merchandise Mart Plaza, Chicago IL 60654.

ILLINOIS HANDCRAFTS DIRECTORY. 1973-. 0095-5337. US. English. an. $1.50. PO Box 157, Bondville IL 61815. LC TT12. DD 745.5025773.

ILLINOIS LEGISLATIVE DIRECTORY. US. English. be. $3.14. Center for Business Management, 20 North Wacker Drive, Chicago IL

Yearbooks, Almanacs, Directories

60606. **Tel** (312)372-7373. **Circ** 25,000. Alpha list of members of the Illinois general assembly, office numbers, committee assignments, seating plans and Illinois legislative and congressional districts maps.

ILLINOIS MANUFACTURERS DIRECTORY. VFOAT Where to Buy, Where to Sell. 1976-. 0160-3302. US. English. an. $123.00. Manufacturers News Inc, 4 East Huron Street, Chicago IL 60611-2793. **Tel** (312)337-1084. **Ed** Louise West. **LC** T12. **DD** 338.4767025773. adv acc. A guide to major non-manufacturing prospects in Illinois, including wholesalers, jobbers, contractors, retailers, finance, service businesses, etc. *Directory of Manufacturers of the State of Illinois.*

ILLINOIS MINORITY VENDORS DIRECTORY. US. English. an. **DD** 338.4025773.

ILLINOIS MUNICIPAL DIRECTORY. US. English. ir. Illinois Municipal League, PO Box 3387, Springfield IL 62708. **LC** JS451.I35.

ILLINOIS POLICE & LAW ENFORCEMENT DIRECTORY. VFOAT Illinois Police and Law Enforcement Directory. Began in 1977/1978. US. English. $22.50. Illinois Police and Law Enforcement Directory, 625 North Michigan Avenue/Suite 500, Chicago IL 60622. **LC** HV9475.I3. **DD** 363.2025773.

ILLINOIS REGIONAL PLANNING AGENCY DIRECTORY. 0361-6932. US. English. Department of Local Government Affairs, 303 East Monroe, Springfield IL 62701. **LC** HT393.I4. **DD** 309.25025773.

ILLINOIS SERVICES DIRECTORY. 1974-. 0092-3818. US. English. an. $109.00. Manufacturers News Inc, 4 East Huron Street, Chicago IL 60611-2793. **Tel** (312)337-1084. **Ed** Louise West. **LC** HC107.I3. **DD** 338.0025773. adv acc. 24,800 companies employing over 2 million people are described in detail, showing address, phone, zip, names of 55,000 key executives, number of employees, in-house computer, SIC number.

ILLINOIS SMALL PRESS DIRECTORY. 1984 Ed.-. 0743-2925. US. English. an. $3.00. Red Herring Press, 1209 West Oregon, Urbana IL 61801. **LC** Z231.5.L5. **DD** 070.5025773.

ILLINOIS SOLAR ENERGY DIRECTORY. 1978-. US. English. Illinois Institute of Natural Resources, 325 West Adams Street/Room 300, Springfield IL 62706. **Ed** G W Mielke.

THE ILLUSTRATED ENCYCLOPAEDIA YEARBOOK. 0145-1790. US. English. an. $6.95. Encyclopaedia Britannica Inc, 425 North Michigan Avenue, Chicago IL 66611. **LC** AY12. **DD** 031.

ILPA DIRECTORY OF MEMBER PUBLICATIONS. 1st- 1957-. Periodical. US. English. ir. International Labor Press Association, AFL-CIO/CLC, 815 16th Street NW, Washington DC 20006. **LC** PN4888.L3. *Labor Press Directory.*

IMPACT YEARBOOK. VFOAT Impact Year Book. 1985-. 0749-7946. US. English. an. M Shanken Communications, 400 East 51st Street, New York NY 10002. **Ed** Marvin R Shanken. **LC** HD9353. **DD** 338.7663102573. adv acc. A directory of people and companies in the wine and spirits industry.

IMPRIMATUR; EIN JAHRBUCH FUR BUCHERFREUNDE. 1-12, 1930-55. 0073-5620. English. ir. Bahnofstrasse 18 13, 8900 Augsburg West Germany. **Ind/Abst** MLA Int. Bibliogr. Books Artic. Mod. Lang. Lit. **LC** Z1008. **DD** 655.058. (cum index).

IMPROVING COLLEGE AND UNIVERSITY TEACHING YEARBOOK. 1975-. 0363-2598. US. English. an. $8.00. Oregon State University Press, PO Box 689, Corvallis OR 97330. **LC** LB2331. **DD** 378.12.

THE IMS AYER DIRECTORY OF PUBLICATIONS. (THE IMS . . . AYER DIRECTORY OF PUBLICATIONS). VFOAT I.M.S. . . . Ayer Directory of Publications. 1983-. 0738-372X. US. English. an. IMS Press, 426 Pennsylvania Avenue, Fort Washington PA 19034. **LC** Z6951, PN4841.A1. **DD** 071.3025. *Ayer Directory of Publications, 0145-1642.*

INCHON KYOYUK TONGGYE YONBO. VFOAT Statistical Year Book of Education. KO. Korean. an. Inchon Chikhalsi Kyoyik, Wiwonhoe San 50, Kuwol-dong Nam-ku, Inchon Korea. **LC** L614.I53.

INCLUSIVE DIRECTORY OF INDEPENDENT OPERATING TELEPHONES. 0361-3437. US. English. an. $5.00. Missouri Public Service Commission Office of Economic Research, PO Box 360, Jefferson City MO 65101. **LC** HE8805.M8. **DD** 384.6309773.

INCOLA, ANUARIO DE JURISPRUDENCIA. VFOAT Anuario de Jurisprudencia Incola. Portuguese. ir. Edicoes Incola, Rua Dr Rodrigo Silva 70 32 Conj 32, Sao Paulo Brazil.

INDEPENDENT MERCEDES BENZ BUSINESS DIRECTORY. 1983-. 0743-5932. US. English. an. Silver Star Executive, Enterprises/Box 975, Highland CA 92346. **LC** HD9710.U54. **DD** 381.4562922202573.

INDIA LEATHER & LEATHER PRODUCTS DIRECTORY. VAT India Leather and Leather Products Directory. 0376-978X. English. ir. 45.00. Export India Journal Publications, 8 Peters Road, Madras 600014 India. **LC** HD9780.I62. **DD** 338.47685202554.

INDIA-WEST GUIDE AND BUSINESS DIRECTORY. VFOAT India-West Guide. 0740-2589. US. English. India-West Publications Inc, 5082 Appian Way, El Sobrante CA 94803. **LC** HD2346.U52. **DD** 380.14500029478.

INDIAN ECONOMIC ALMANAC. Vol. 1, No. 1 (Dec. 1980)-. Periodical. II. English. qt. 10.00. Delhi Research and Statistics Bureau Pvt Ltd, B-6 Asaf Ali Road, New Delhi 110002 India. **LC** HC435.2. **DD** 330.954005.

INDIAN MARINE DIRECTORY. Began with Vol. for 1981. English. ir. Daily Shipping Times, 5 Gunbow Street, Bombay 400001 India. **Ed** Nikhil N Modi. **LC** HE879. **DD** 387.502554.

INDIAN MOTION PICTURE ALMANAC. English. ir. 40.00. Shot Publications, 3-B Madan Street, Calcutta 700013 India. **LC** PN1993.3. **DD** 791.430954.

INDIAN NURSING YEAR BOOK. 1982-. English. an. **NLM** W1 IN258.

THE INDIAN YEAR BOOK OF INTERNATIONAL AFFAIRS. V. 1- 1952-. 0537-2704. II. English. ir. $5.72. University of Madras Registrar, University Buildings, Chepauk Madras 600 005 India.

INDIANA GENERAL ASSEMBLY LEGISLATIVE DIRECTORY. VFOAT Legislative Directory. US. English. Indiana State Chamber of Commerce, 1 North Capital/Suite 200, Indianapolis IN 46204. **Tel** (317)634-6407. Information regarding Indiana legislators, committees, districts, etc.

THE INDIANA INDUSTRIAL DIRECTORY. US. English. be. $20.00. Indiana State Chamber of Commerce, 1 North Capital/Suite 200, Indianapolis IN 46204. **LC** T12. **DD** 670.9772. Each issue contains an index to its own contents - no vol index - loose.

INDIANA MANUFACTURERS DIRECTORY. 1st Ed (1982)-. 0735-2417. US. English. an. $85.00. Manufacturers News Inc, 4 East Huron Street, Chicago IL 60611-2793. **Tel** (312)337-1084. **Ed** Louise West. **LC** HD9727.I6. **DD** 380.10294772. adv acc. Information on more than 9,211 firms in the state. Company addresses, phone numbers, year established, annual sales, plant, square footage, model and language of in-house computer.

INDIANA NEWSPAPER DIRECTORY AND RATE BOOK. Periodical. US. English. an. $13.60. Hoosier State Press Association, 1542 Consolidate Building/115 North Pen, Indianapolis IN 46204. **Tel** (317)637-3966.

INDIANA ZIP+4 STATE DIRECTORY. VFOAT Zip+4 State Directory. VAT Indiana Zip Plus Four state Directory. 1985-. US. English. an. St Louis PDC, Zip+4 State Directory Orders, PO Box 14921, St Louis MO 63180-9988.

THE INDIANAPOLIS 500 YEARBOOK. VFOAT Carl Hungness Presents the Indianapolis 500 Yearbook. 1973-. US. English. an. Carl Hungness Publishing, Box 24308, Speedway IN 46224. **Tel** (317)244-4792. **Ed** Carl Hungness.

INDICE DO BRASIL. VFOAT Brazilian Index Yearbook. English (Portuguese). ir. Indice-O Bankode Dados, Rua Alcindo Guanabara 24-19 Andar, Rio de Janeiro Brazil. **LC** HC186.

INDONESIA HOTEL DIRECTORY. 1976. English. ir. Jakarta Directorate General of Tourism, Jalan Kramat Raya 81, Jakarta Indonesia. **LC** TX910.I6.

INDUSTRIAL AND BUSINESS DIRECTORY OF TENNESSEE, ARKANSAS AND MISSISSIPPI. 0362-1286. US. English. 1037 East Parkway, Memphis TN 38104. **LC** HC107.T3. **DD** 338.002576.

INDUSTRIAL AND TRADE DIRECTORY. VFOAT Industrial & Trade Directory. 1982 Ed.-. English. ir. Industrial and Trade Directory Company, PO Box 44169, Nairobi Kenya. **LC** HF3893.A48. **DD** 380.102946762.

INDUSTRIAL AND TRADE DIRECTORY OF MALAWI. VFOAT Industrial Directory and Brand Names Index of Malawi. 0377-0028. English. ir. 2.00 Per Copy. Chamber of Commerce and Industry of Malawi, PO Box 258, Blantyre Malawi. **LC** HF3899.M25. **DD** 338.00256897.

INDUSTRIAL DIRECTORY. 1970-. English. ir. Western Nigeria Development Corporation, PMB 5085/Cocoa House Ibadan Nigeria. **LC** HC517.N52. **DD** 338.00256692.

INDUSTRIAL DIRECTORY. 1974/75-. 0300-1687. English. ir. Manufacturers Association of Nigeria, 37 Marina PO Box 3835, Lagos Nigeria. **LC** HC517.N48. **DD** 338.4025669. *Industrial Directory.*

INDUSTRIAL DIRECTORY FOR THE KENT COUNTY REGION. (INDUSTRIAL DIRECTORY FOR THE KENT COUNTY REGION . . .). VFOAT Repertoire des Industries de la Region du Comte de Kent. 1980-. 0229-8996. CN. English (French). an. Free. Kent Industrial Commission, PO Box 490, Bouctouche New Brunswick E0A 1G0 Canada. **DD** 338.002571522.

INDUSTRIAL DIRECTORY FOR THE RESTIGOUCHE REGION. VFOAT Repertoire Industriel Pour la Region du Restigouche. 0710-0507. CN. English. an. Restigouche Development Corporation, PO Box 825, Campbellton New Brunswick E3N 3H2 Canada. **DD** 338.002571511.

INDUSTRIAL DIRECTORY — NIAGARA FALLS AREA. VFOAT City of Niagara Falls, King of Power/Queen of Beauty. US. English. an. $10.00. Niagara Falls Area Chamber of Commerce, Carborundum Center/345 Third Street, Niagara Falls NY 14303.

INDUSTRIAL DIRECTORY OF SOUTH CAROLINA. VFOAT South Carolina . . . Industrial Directory. US. English. an. South Carolina State Development Board, PO Box 927, Columbia SC 29202. **LC** HC107.S7.

INDUSTRIAL DIRECTORY OF WALES. UK. English. 4.00. Development Corporation of Wales, 15 Park Place, Cardiff CF1 3DQ Wales. **LC** HC257.W3. **DD** 338.76025429.

INDUSTRIAL POLLUTION CONTROL YEARBOOK. (INDUSTRIAL POLLUTION CONTROL YEAR BOOK). 1974-. 0306-8285. UK. English. an. 3.75. Fuel & Metallurgical Journals Ltd, John Adam House/John Adam Street, WC2N 6IH London England. **LC** TD186.5.G7. **DD** 363.6.

INDUSTRIAL SENSOR DIRECTORY. Series/Titl Intelligent Factory Library. 1st Ed.-. 0736-1831. US. English. an. $45.00. Technical Database Corporation, PO Box 720, Conroe TX 77305. **Tel** (409)539-9688. **Ed** Philip C Flora. **Circ** 3,000. Provides detailed specifications on hundreds of sensors designed for monitor and control of industrial products, equipment and processes.

INDUSTRY'S DIRECTORY OF TECHNICAL CONSULTANTS. 1981-82 Ed.-. 0277-2043. US. English. an. Technology Recognition Corporation, 1382 Old Freeport Road, Pittsburg PA 15238. **LC** TA12. **DD** 620.002573.

INFORMATIC ANNUAIRE. VFOAT Informatic. BE. French. an. 995. DDC Publications, 122 Avenue de Tervuren 1040 Bruxelles Belgium.

INFORMATION AND LIBRARY SERVICES DIRECTORY. 1981-. US. English. ir. US Department of the Interior, Office of Information Resources Management, Center for Information and Library Services, Washington DC 20240. *Libraries and Information Services Directory, 0191-8672.*

INFORMATION CHICAGO. Vol. 1, No. 1 (Fall 1979)-. 0196-3643. US. English. sa. $25.00. Information Chicago, 26 East Huron Street, Chicago

Yearbooks, Almanacs, Directories

IL 60611. **Tel** (312)787-2677. Ed Arnie Matanky. LC F548.18. **DD** 977.311025. adv acc. **Circ** 5,000. (ctrl). Most comprehensive listing of names, addresses and telephone numbers of Chicago area government, transportation, media, clubs and other organizations.

INFORMATION GUIDE AND DIRECTORY OF OCCUPATIONAL-TECHNICAL PROGRAMS IN POST-SECONDARY INSTITUTIONS IN TEXAS CEASED. 0145-1944. US. English. Education Agency, 201 East 11th Street, Austin TX 78701. **LC** LC1046.T4. **DD** 378.013025764.

INFORMATION PLEASE ALMANAC, ATLAS AND YEARBOOK. 34th- Ed. US. English. an. Information Please Almanac, 502 Park Avenue, New York NY 10022.

INFORMATION SOURCES. (INFORMATION SOURCES : THE ANNUAL DIRECTORY OF THE INFORMATION INDUSTRY ASSOCIATION). **Main/Corp** Information Industry Association. 1982-83-. 0734-9637. US. English. an. Information Industry Association, 316 Pennsylvania Avenue SE/Suite 400, Washington DC 20003. **LC** HC102. **DD** 020.62273. Membership Directory of the Information Industry Association, 0148-1053.

INFORMATION SOURCES : THE MEMBERSHIP DIRECTORY OF THE INFORMATION INDUSTRY ASSOCIATION. **Main/Corp** Information Industry Association. **VFOAT** Membership Directory of the Information Industry Association. 1978/79-. US. English. an. Information Industry Association, 316 Pennsylvania Avenue/Suite 400, Washington DC 20003. **Tel** (202)544-1969. Membership Directory of the Information Industry Association, 0148-1053.

INFORMATOR I SKAD OSOBOWY NA ROK AKADEMICKI . . . . **Main/Corp** Politechnika Poanasnka. Polish. an. Wydawnictwo Politechniki Poznanskiej, Pl M Skodowskiej-Curie, 60-965 Poznan Poland.

INFORMATOR ROBOTNICZY. 1973-. Polish. ir. 35.00. Ksiazka I Wiedza, Ul Nowy Swiat 27, Warzsawa Poland. **LC** HD8537. Kalendarz Robotniczy.

INNOVATIVE GRADUATE PROGRAMS DIRECTORY. See Education (General) - Higher Education.

INSIDE RADIO RATINGS REPORT & DIRECTORY. US. English. sa. Inside Radio Inc, 125 Gaither Drive/Suite 1, Mt Laurel NJ 08054.

THE INSIDER'S BANKING & CREDIT ALMANAC. **VAT** Insider's Banking and Credit Almanac. 1977-. 0195-3311. US. English. an. Kephart Communications, 901 North Washington Street, Alexandria VA 22314. **LC** HG1601. **DD** 332.024.

INSTA-MATCH DIRECTORY OF MINORITY OWNED BUSINESSES IN TEXAS. **VFOAT** Insta Match Directory. 0730-3521. US. English. $15.00. Texas Office of Minority Business Enterprise, PO Box 12728 Capitol Station, Austin TX 78711. **LC** HD2346.U52. **DD** 338.74025764.

THE INSTITUTE OF HOUSING YEAR BOOK. 0260-7239. UK. English. an. The Institute of Housing, 12 Upper Belgrave Street, London SW1X 8BA England. **LC** HD7333.A3. **DD** 363.506041. Year Book and List of Members (Institute of Housing (Great Britain)).

THE INSTITUTE OF MATHEMATICAL STATISTICS DIRECTORY. **VFOAT** IMS Directory. 0883-444X. US. English. Institute of Mathematical Statistics, 3401 Investment Boulevard #7, Hayward CA 94545.

INSTITUTIONAL DIRECTORY OF HIGHER EDUCATION IN TENNESSEE CEASED. 0148-9259. US. English. 501 Union Building/Suite 300, Nashville TN 37219. **Tel** (615)741-3605. Ed Matte Campbell. **LC** LA226. **DD** 378.0025768. **Circ** 1,800. (ctrl). Administration, facts, admission and financial aid information, deadlines and cost of education for both public and private institutions in Tennessee.

INSTITUTIONAL INVESTOR DIRECTORY. 1982-. 0735-9098. US. English. $150.00 Single Issue. Institutional Investor Directory, 488 Madison Avenue, New York NY 10022. **LC** HG4907. **DD** 332.6202573.

INSTITUTO DE INVESTIGACIONES BIOQUIMICAS, ANUARIO. Spanish. ir. Instituto de Investigaciones Bioquimicas, Calle Obligado 2490, Buenos Aires Argentina. **LC** QP518. **DD** 574.192072082.

INSURANCE ALMANAC (UNDERWRITER PRINTING AND PUBLISHING COMPANY). (THE INSURANCE ALMANAC). 0074-0675. US. English. an. $65.00. Underwriter Printing and Publishing Company, 50 East Palisade Avenue, Englewood NJ 07631. **Tel** (201)569-8808. Ed Donald Wolff. adv acc. **Circ** 10,000. The who, what, when and where of insurance. Listings of agencies, companies, adjusters, appraisers, auditors, insurance officials and organizations. Insurance Almanac and Who's Who in Insurance, 0363-4108.

INSURANCE DIRECTORY. US. English. an. **LC** HG8511.A2. **DD** 368.9761.

INTERACTIVE VIDEO. See Computers and Computer Science.

INTERAVIA AEROSPACE DIRECTORY ABC. **VFOAT** Aerospace Directory ABC. 32nd Ed. (1984)-. English. an. $296.48. Interavia, Avenue Louis-Casai 86, Ch-1216 Geneva Switzerland. **Tel** 022/98-05-05. Ed J Didelot. adv acc. **Circ** 5,000. Contains essential information on governmental authorities, organizations, aerospace industries and allied companies throughout the world, classified both geographically and by field of activity. Interavia ABC.

THE INTERIOR DECORATORS' HANDBOOK, A NATIONAL DIRECTORY OF INTERIOR FURNISHINGS. 19 -. US. English. **LC** NK1127.

INTERNATIONAL A.A. DIRECTORY. (INTERNATIONAL A. A. DIRECTORY). **VAT** International Alcoholics Anonymous Directory. 1975-. 0361-7459. US. English. Alcoholics Anonymous World Services Inc, Box 459/Grand Central Station, New York NY 10017. **LC** HV5275. **DD** 362.292.

INTERNATIONAL AEROSPACE DIRECTORY. 1985-1986—. 0882-6730. US. English. an. $50.00. Eclipse Publishing Company, PO Box 1796, Centreville VA 20020. **Tel** (703)549-2138. **DD** 629. adv acc. **Circ** 10,000. 2,000 companies that provide space related services and products. Indexes by service. Includes government agencies; glossary.

INTERNATIONAL ART & ANTIQUES YEARBOOK. **VAT** International Art and Antiques Yearbook. 1977-. UK. English (Multilingual). an. $50.00. Gale Research, Book Tower, Detroit MI 48226. **Tel** (313)961-2242. Ed M D'Argy Smith. **LC** NK1125. **DD** 380.1457025. Furnishes names, addresses, and descriptions of 13,000 antique shops, antiquarian booksellers, and picture dealers located throughout the world. International Antiques Yearbook, International Antiques Yearbook, Encyclopedia & Directory.

INTERNATIONAL ART MATERIAL DIRECTORY AND BUYERS' GUIDE. **VFOAT** Art Material Trade News International Directory. '83-. 0742-7387. US. English. an. $15.00. **LC** HD9791.A1. **DD** 702.8. International Art Material Directory & Buyers Guide, 0742-7387.

INTERNATIONAL BANK DIRECTORY. **VFOAT** MCF International Bank Directory. 1985 Ed-. US. English. an. $50.00. McFadden Business Publications, 6195 Crooked Creek Road, Norcross GA 30092.

INTERNATIONAL BIBLIOGRAPHY OF DIRECTORIES. **VFOAT** Internationale Bibliographie der Fachadressbucher. 0074-9672. US. Multilingual (English and German). ir. K G Saur Verlag, PTFCH 711009/Possenbacherstr 2B, D8000 Muenchen 71 West Germany. **Tel** (089) 798901.

INTERNATIONAL BIO-ENERGY DIRECTORY AND HANDBOOK. 1984-. US. English. an. Bio-Energy Council, Suite 825A/1625 Eye Street Northwest, Washington DC 20006. International Bio-Energy Directory, 0730-4854.

THE INTERNATIONAL BIOTECHNOLOGY DIRECTOR. 1984-. 0265-3877. US. English. an. $140.00. Stockton Press, 15 East 26th Street, New York NY 10010. **Tel** (212)481-1334. Ed J Coombs. adv acc. Worldwide directory of biotechnology-companies and products, services, research organizations, associations, country porfiles.

INTERNATIONAL BOOK COLLECTORS ALMANAC/NEWSLETTER. Vol. 1, Issue 1 (Feb. 1984)-. 0741-9953. Periodical. US. English. mo. $36.00. Pegasus Publishing Inc, PO Box 1350, Vashon Island WA 98070. **DD** 002.

INTERNATIONAL BOOK TRADE DIRECTORY. 1st- Ed. US. English. ir. R R Bowker, 205 East Forty Second Street, New York NY 10017. **Ed** Peter Found. **LC** Z282. **DD** 070.5025.

INTERNATIONAL BUSINESS TRAVEL AND RELOCATION DIRECTORY. 2nd Ed. (1981)-. US. English. an. $350.00. Gale Research Company, Book Tower, Detroit MI 48226. Individual country-by-country sections provide essential information for the employee on a long term overseas assignment as well as for the international traveler. Directory of International Business Travel and Relocation.

INTERNATIONAL COMMISSION FOR THE NORTHWEST ATLANTIC FISHERIES. SAMPLING YEARBOOK. (SAMPLING YEARBOOK - INTERNATIONAL COMMISSION FOR THE NORTHWEST ATLANTIC FISHERIES). V. 1- 1955/56-. 0074-2686. Periodical. CN. English. an. International Commission for the Northwest Atlantic Fisheries, PO Box 638, Dartmouth Novia Scotia B2Y 3Y9 Canada. **DD** 639.22091634.

INTERNATIONAL DENDROLOGY SOCIETY YEARBOOK. (YEAR BOOK). **VFOAT** Yearbook - International Dendrology Society. 0307-322X. UK. English. an. $13.80. International Dendrology Society, Whistley Green Farmhouse, Hurst Reading Berkshire RG100DU England. **Tel** 0734-341065. Ed K Beckett. **LC** QK475. **DD** 582.16005. bk rev. **Circ** 1,100. (ctrl). Book contains articles on tours made by members and their study of trees throughout the world.

INTERNATIONAL DIATOMIST DIRECTORY. 0882-2093. US. English. Environmental Research and Technology Inc, PO Box 2150, 1716 Heath Parkway, Fort Collins CO 80522.

INTERNATIONAL DIRECTORY. **Main/Corp** United Way of America. **VFOAT** Directory. Began with 1974-75 issue. 0730-5354. US. English. an. United Way of America, 801 North Fairfax Street, Alexandria VA 22314. **LC** HV97.U553. **DD** 361.8025.

INTERNATIONAL DIRECTORY OF ACCESS GUIDES. Series/Titl Rehabilitation World. 1978-79 -. Monographic Series. US. English. an.

INTERNATIONAL DIRECTORY OF BEHAVIOR AND DESIGN RESEARCH. 1974-. 0094-4084. US. English. sa. $12.00. PO Box 57, Orangeburg NY 10962. **LC** H57. **DD** 300.25.

INTERNATIONAL DIRECTORY OF BOOKSELLERS. Series/Titl Handbook of International Documentation and Information. 1st- Ed. 0161-6617. US. English. ir. K G Saur Inc, 175 5th Avenue, New York NY 10010. **Tel** (313)961-2242. **LC** Z282. **DD** 380.145070573025.

INTERNATIONAL DIRECTORY OF CENTERS FOR ASIAN STUDIES. HK. English. an. $40.00 US. Asian Research Service, PO Box 2232, GPO Hong Kong. **Tel** 5-733641. Ed Nelson Leung. **LC** DS32.8. **DD** 950.072. **Circ** 2,000. Provides important information about major research centers and institutions concerned with Asian studies in various countries of the world.

INTERNATIONAL DIRECTORY OF CONSULTING ENVIRONMENTAL AND CIVIL ENGINEERS. **VFOAT** Directory of Consulting Environmental and Civil Engineers. 0191-9636. US. English. International Research Service, PO Box 225, Blue Bell PA 19422. **LC** TD169.6. **DD** 625.025.

INTERNATIONAL DIRECTORY OF CORPORATE AFFILIATIONS. See Business.

THE INTERNATIONAL DIRECTORY OF ENERGY ECONOMISTS. 8756-9183. US. English. $17.50 Members. International Association of Energy Economists, 1133 15th Street, Washington DC 20005.

INTERNATIONAL DIRECTORY OF ENERGY MEETINGS & TRADE SHOWS. **VFOAT** Energy Meetings and Trade Shows. 4th Ed. (1984)-. 0742-4337. US. English. an. $75.00 US and Canada, $93.50 Foreign. Penwell Publishing Company, PO Box 1260, Tulsa OK 74101. **Tel** (918)835-3161. Ed William R Leek Jr. **LC** TN867. **DD** 621.04206. adv acc. **Circ** 1,500. International Directory of Petroleum Meetings and Trade Shows, 0272-8672.

INTERNATIONAL DIRECTORY OF EXECUTIVE RECRUITERS. 1st- Ed. 0092-4989. US. English. ir. $27.95. Consultants News, Templeton Road, Fitzwilliam NH 03447. **Tel** (603)525-2200. Ed James H Kennedy. **LC** HF5500.2. **DD** 658.40711102573. bk rev. (ctrl). Lists international

Yearbooks, Almanacs, Directories

executive recruiting firms by geographic location cross indexed by functions and industries.

INTERNATIONAL DIRECTORY OF LITTLE MAGAZINES AND SMALL PRESSES. (INTERNATIONAL DIRECTORY OF LITTLE MAGAZINES & SMALL PRESSES). 9th- Ed. 0092-3974. US. English. an. $19.95. Dustbooks, Box 100, Paradise CA 95969. Tel (916)877-6110. Ed Len Fulton. LC Z6944.L5. DD 051.025. adv acc. Circ 6,000. Used as the standard reference worldwide by writers, librarians, contemporary literature students and the trade for the past twenty years. *Directory of Little Magazines and Small Presses, 0363-2016.*

INTERNATIONAL DIRECTORY OF MARKETING RESEARCH HOUSES AND SERVICE. VFOAT Green Book. 1962-. 0074-459X. US. English. an. $50.00. American Marketing Association, 420 Lexington Avenue/Suite 1733, New York NY 10170. Tel (212)687-3280. Ed Pat Ryan. adv acc. Circ 6,000. Over 1,200 marketing research companies, company names and descriptions listed alphabetically by company name-indexed geographically, by principals, computer programs, and company services.

INTERNATIONAL DIRECTORY OF MEMBERS. 0149-2039. US. English. St Louis Homes for Living Headquarters International, 2632 Woodson Road, St Louis MO 63114. LC HD251. DD 333.33.

INTERNATIONAL DIRECTORY OF NUCLEAR UTILITIES. 1983-1984-. 0742-5821. US. English. an. $235.00. Lotte Ltd, Box 237/Contract Station 27, Lakewood CO 80215. Ed Joseph H Bach. LC TK9012. DD 621.483025.

INTERNATIONAL DIRECTORY OF NURSES WITH DOCTORAL DEGREES. 1973- Ed. 0091-9462. US. English. an. American Nurses Foundation, 10 Columbus Circle, New York NY 10019. LC RT25.A2. DD 610.730922, B. NLM WY 22 I613.

INTERNATIONAL DIRECTORY OF PHILOSOPHY AND PHILOSOPHERS. *See Philosophy.*

INTERNATIONAL DIRECTORY OF SCHOLARLY PUBLISHERS. 1977-. English. ir. UNESCO, 7 Place de Fontenoy, 75700 Paris France. LC Z286.S37. DD 070.594025.

INTERNATIONAL DIRECTORY OF SOCIAL SCIENCE ORGANIZATIONS. VFOAT Social Science Organizations. 1981-1982-. English. Almqvist and Wiksell International, 108 Drottninggatan, PO Box 45150, S-104 30 Stockholm Sweden. LC H62.A1. DD 300.25. *International Directory of Social Science Research Councils, 0193-337X.*

INTERNATIONAL DIRECTORY OF SOFTWARE. 1983-84. UK. English (text in French and German). be. Cuyb Publications Ltd USA, 1st Federal Building/Suite 401, Pottstown PA 19464.

INTERNATIONAL DIRECTORY OF SYSTEMS HOUSES & COMPUTER OEM'S. 0887-4921. US. English. an. $345.00. Technical Pub Co, 199 Wells Avenue, Newton Center MA 02159. *International Directory of Computer & Software Sales Agents & Distributors, 0882-3324.*

INTERNATIONAL DIRECTORY OF THE NONWOVEN FABRICS INDUSTRY. 0095-683X. US. English. be. $35.00. Association Nonwoven Fabrics Industry, 1700 Broadway, New York NY 10019. LC HD9869.N64. DD 338.47677. *Directory for the Nonwoven Fabrics and Disposable Soft Goods Industries, 0070-5020.*

INTERNATIONAL DIRECTORY - ROYAL BANK OF CANADA. (INTERNATIONAL DIRECTORY). Main/Corp Royal Bank of Canada. 0823-1362. CN. English. an. Royal Bank of Canada, PO Box 6001/Station A, Montreal Quebec H3C 3A9 Canada. DD 332.15025.

INTERNATIONAL DIRECTORY TO CANADIAN STUDIES. VFOAT Repertoire International des Etudes Canadiennes. 1980-1981-. CN. English (French). 6.00. Association for Canadian Studies, 544 King Edward Avenue, Ottawa Ontario K1N 6N5 Canada. Tel (613)564-3905. LC F1025. DD 971.007. adv acc. Circ 1,000. The reference book gives information on: Canadian Studies Associations around the world on Canadian Studies Centres, Programmes, Instituts in Canada and abroad.

INTERNATIONAL ENGINEERING DIRECTORY. 0074-5774. US. English. be. $15.00. American Consulting Engineers Council, 1015 15th Street NW/Suite 802, Washington DC 20005. Tel (202)347-7474. Ed Terry Griffith. LC TA12. DD 620.002573. Circ 2,000. A directory listing U.S. consulting engineering firms that provide international services. Each listing describes the firm and the types of engineering services offered.

INTERNATIONAL FILM AND TV YEAR BOOK *CEASED.* VFOAT International Film and TV Yearbook, Screen International Film and TV Year Book, Film and TV Year Book. VAT International Film and Television Yearbook. Began with 31st, 1976/77. Ceased with 37th, 1982/83. UK. English. an. 142 Wardour Street, London W1V 4BR England. Ed P Noble. LC PN1993.3. DD 791.430280922 B. *British Film and TV Year Book.*

INTERNATIONAL FINANCIAL STATISTICS ANUARIO. 1979-. 0250-7471. US. Spanish. an. $13.00. International Monetary Fund, Washington DC 20431. *International Financial Statistics.*

INTERNATIONAL FINANCIAL STATISTICS YEARBOOK - INTERNATIONAL MONETARY FUND. (INTERNATIONAL FINANCIAL STATISTICS YEARBOOK). 1979-. 0250-7463. US. English. an. $25.00. International Monetary Fund, 700 19th Street Northwest, Washington DC 20431. Tel (202)477-7000. LC HG61. DD 332.0212.

THE INTERNATIONAL GOLF DIRECTORY. 0272-1775. US. English. sa. $12.50 Per Copy. International Golf Directory, 444 Burchett Street, Glendale CA 91203. LC GV962. DD 796.352068025.

INTERNATIONAL MARINE SAFETY DIRECTORY. 0263-7618. UK. English. an. Industrial and Marine Publications Ltd, Queensway House 2 Queensway, Redhill Surrey RH1 1QS England. LC VK200. DD 623.893029.

INTERNATIONAL MAURITIUS DIRECTORY. English (French). an. 50.00 Per Issue. PO Box 287, Port Louis Mauritius. LC DT469.M4. DD 969.8203025.

INTERNATIONAL MEALS ON WHEELS DIRECTORY. 1978-. 0161-2522. US. English. an. Capitol Hill United Methodist Church, 421 Seward Square SE, Washington DC 20003. LC HV696.F6. DD 362.63.

INTERNATIONAL MINICOMPUTER SOFTWARE DIRECTORY. 0732-362X. US. English. qt. $72.90. Imprint Editions, 1520 South College, Ft Collins CO 80524.

INTERNATIONAL MONETARY MARKET YEAR BOOK. 1972/73-. 0195-9980. US. English. an. $10.00. Chicago Mercantile Exchange, 30 South Wacker Drive, Chicago IL 60606. Tel (312)930-3454. LC HG3853.F6. DD 332.45.

INTERNATIONAL MUSIC EDUCATION. (ISME YEARBOOK). Main/Corp International Society for Music Education. VFOAT I.S.M.E. Yearbook. V. 1- 1973-. 0172-0597. UK. English. ir. $10.00. International Society for Music Education, 7 Townsend Drive, St Albans Herfordshire AL3 5RB England. Tel 58296. Ed Jack Dobbs. Ind/Abst Music Index, RILM Abstr. LC ML5. DD 780.7. Circ 2,000. Selected papers from conferences and seminars of the International Society for Music Education. *International Music Educator.*

INTERNATIONAL NUMISMATIC DIRECTORY. 1st- Ed. UK. English. J J Krasnodebshi, 9 St Lawrence Road, SW9 GPW London England. LC CJ63. DD 737.025.

INTERNATIONAL OMBUDSMAN INSTITUTE DIRECTORY OF OMBUDSMEN AND OTHER COMPLAINT-HANDLERS. (THE INTERNATIONAL OMBUDSMAN INSTITUTE DIRECTORY OF OMBUDSMEN AND OTHER COMPLAINT-HANDLERS). 0715-576X. CN. English. an. Free. International Ombudsman Institute Law Centre, c/o University of Alberta, Edmonton Alberta T6G 2H5 Canada. DD 351.91025. (ctrl).

INTERNATIONAL ORGANISATIONS IN WORLD POLITICS YEARBOOK. 0363-7123. US. English. an. $27.50. Westview Press, 1898 Flatiron Court, Boulder CO 80301. LC JX1995. DD 341.205.

INTERNATIONAL POLITICAL ECONOMY YEARBOOK. Vol. 1-. 8755-8335. US. English. an. $30.00 Hardback, $12.95 Paperback. Westview Press, 5500 Central Avenue, Boulder CO 80301.

INTERNATIONAL PRINT BUYER'S DIRECTORY. 1983-. UK. English. Metal Bulletin Books, Park House/Park Terrace-Worcester Park, Surrey KT4 7HY Great Britain. LC Z282. DD 686.2025.

INTERNATIONAL PULP & PAPER DIRECTORY. 1975/76-. 0097-2509. US. English. ir. Miller Freeman Publications, 500 Howard Street, San Francisco Ca 94105. LC HD9820.3. DD 338.47676025.

INTERNATIONAL QUILT GUILD DIRECTORY. VFOAT Quilt Guild Directory. 1983-. 0883-203X. US. English. $5.00. Leman Publications Inc, Box 394, Wheatridge CO 80033. Tel (303)420-4272. Ed Bonnie Leman. LC TT835. DD 746.46025. adv acc. Circ 1,000. (ctrl). International listing of quilt guilds. Includes names, addresses, contact person, phone, times and dates for meetings. Quilt supply companies and shops listed by state.

INTERNATIONAL RESEARCH CENTERS DIRECTORY. 1981-. US. English. Each issue contains an index to its own contents - no vol index - loose.

INTERNATIONAL ROBOTICS INDUSTRY DIRECTORY. 4th Ed.-. US. English. an. Technical Database Corporation, PO Box 720, Conroe TX 77305. Tel (409)539-9688. Detailed listings are provided on each robot model with photo and work envelope drawing if available. *Robotics Industry Directory, 0278-159X.*

THE INTERNATIONAL ROBOTICS YEARBOOK. 1st Ed.-. 0739-1595. US. English. an. 50.00. Ballinger Publishing Company, 54 Church Street, Cambridge MA 02138. Ed I Aleksander. LC TJ210.5. DD 629.89205. A comprehensive guide to contemporary industrial and academic activity in the field of robotics. Detailed specifications are included on all the robot models available at present, and information given on the manufacturers, suppliers and distributors of these systems.

INTERNATIONAL SCHOLARS' DIRECTORY. VFOAT International Directory of Scholars. US. English. ir. Marquis Whos Who Inc, 200 East Ohio Street, Chicago IL 60611. Tel (317)298-5400.

INTERNATIONAL SECURITY YEARBOOK (NEW YORK, N.Y.). (INTERNATIONAL SECURITY YEARBOOK). VFOAT International Security Year Book. 1983/84-. 0265-4369. US. English. an. St Martin's Press, 175 5th Avenue, New York NY 10010. LC UA10. DD 355.0330047.

INTERNATIONAL SOCIAL SCIENCE COUNCIL : DIRECTORY. FR. English. ir. UNESCO, House 1 rue Miollis, 75015 Paris France.

INTERNATIONAL SOLID FUEL BUYER'S GUIDE DIRECTORY. 1980-. 0277-870X. US. English. an. $4.50 US, $19.95 Foreign. Circulation Manager, 10221 Slater Avenue/Suite 104, PO Box 8006, Fountain Valley CA 92708. LC HD9971.5.S76. DD 697.02029473.

INTERNATIONAL TELEPHONE DIRECTORY OF THE DEAF. 0160-7472. US. English. an. PO Box 28332, Dublin NC 28332. LC HV2510. DD 362.42025.

INTERNATIONAL TELEVISION ALMANAC. Began in 1956. 0539-0761. US. English. an. Quigley Publications, 159 West 53rd Street, New York NY 10019. Tel (212)247-3100. Ed Richard Gertner. adv acc. Contains comprehensive information about the television industry. Detailed listing of company networks, major producer-distributors personnel, network program listings, equipment and supply companies and state by state listing of TV stations.

INTERNATIONAL WHO'S WHO IN MUSIC AND MUSICIANS' DIRECTORY. 7th- Ed. UK. English. Melrose Press, International Biographical Centre, Cambridge CB2 3QP England. LC ML106.G7. DD 780.922, B. Circ 5,000. Detailed biographical entries on leading contemporary musicians, composers, singers, critics, conductors, etc. throughout the world. *Who's Who in Music.*

Yearbooks, Almanacs, Directories

THE INTERNATIONAL YEAR BOOK AND STATESMEN'S WHO'S WHO. 1953-. UK. English. an. $180.00. International Publishing Service, Taylor and Francis Inc, 242 Cherry Street, Philadelphia PA 19106. **Tel** (800)821-8312. **LC** JA51.

INTERNATIONAL YEARBOOK - NAVAL STORES REVIEW. Main/Corp Naval Stores Review. US. English. an. Naval Stores Review, PO Box 2406, New Orleans LA 70176. **Tel** (504)524-2119.

INTERNATIONAL YEARBOOK OF CARTOGRAPHY. VFOAT Annuaire International de Cartographie, Internationales Jahrbuch fur Kartographie. 1- 1961-. 0341-0986. GW. English (French or German, with summaries in languages other than the language of the article). an. Kirschbaum Verlag, Slegfriedstrasse 28 Postfach 210209, D-5300 Bonn 2 West Germany. **Tel** 02281 343057. **Ind/Abst** GeoRef. **LC** GA101. **CODEN** IYCTAJ.

INTERNATIONAL YEARBOOK OF EDUCATIONAL AND INSTRUCTIONAL TECHNOLOGY. Main/Corp Association for Educational and Training Technology. 1980/81-. UK. English. be. $38.50. Nichols Publishing Company, PO Box 96, New York NY 10024. **Tel** (212)580-8079. **Ed** Linda Kahn. **LC** LB1028.7. **DD** 370.777. Provides overview of educational technology and gives detailed lists of where information relating to theory and practice can be found worldwide. *International Yearbook of Educational and Instructional Technology.*

INTERNATIONAL YEARBOOK OF FOREIGN POLICY ANALYSIS. (THE INTERNATIONAL YEARBOOK OF FOREIGN POLICY ANALYSIS). V. 1- 1974-. 0095-1471. US. English. ir. MacMillan of Canada, 70 Bond Street, Toronto Ontario M5B 1X3 Canada. **LC** JX21. **DD** 327.0904.

INTERNATIONALES BODENSEE JAHRBUCH DER SPORTSCHIFFAHRT. German. ir. Internationaler Verlag H Mann, Friedrichstrasse 53, Postfach 17 26, 7990 Friedrichshafen 1 West Germany. **LC** GV771.

INTERNATIONALES JAHRBUCH FUR GESCHICHTS- UND GEOGRAPHIE- UNTERRICHT. Vol. 1- 1951-. 0074-9834. Periodical. German. ir.

INTERNATIONALES VERLAGSADRESSBUCH. VFOAT Publishers' International Directory. 1st - 7th Ed. 0074-9877. US. English (German). ir. Gale Research, Book Tower, Detroit MI 48226. **Ed** K G Saur. **LC** Z282. **NLM** Z 282 P976. Volume 1 lists some 150,000 publishers' names, addresses and areas of interest. Volume 2 is an ISBN registry of some 70,000 publishers and their ISBN prefixes.

INTERSTATE ACCOMMODATION DIRECTORY. AT. English. ir. Free to Members. Royal Automobile Club of Queensland, C Nr Ann and Boundary Streets, Brisbane Queensland Australia. **LC** TX907. **DD** 647.9494.

INVESTMENT ADVISER DIRECTORY. 0091-2328. US. English. qt. Superintendent of Documents, US Government Printing Office, Washington DC 20402. **LC** HG4907. **DD** 332.6202573.

INVESTMENT COMPANIES INTERNATIONAL YEARBOOK. 0091-4533. US. English. Scheinman Ciaramella International, 505 Park Avenue, New York NY 00122. **LC** HG4530. **DD** 332.6327.

INVESTMENT DECISIONS DIRECTORY OF WALL STREET RESEARCH. VFOAT Directory of Wall Street Research, Investment Decisions' Directory. 10th Annual Ed. (1985)-. 0740-8714. US. English. an. W R Nelson and Company 11 Elm Place, Rye NY 10580. *Nelson's Directory of Wall Street Research, 0740-8714.*

INVESTOR'S FRANCHISE DIRECTORY. 1980-. 0198-8913. US. English. **LC** HF5429.3. **DD** 658.8700973.

INVESTOR'S YEARBOOK. 1984-. 0741-9813. Periodical. US. English. an. $75.00. Newsletter Digest, 2335 Pansy Street, Huntsville AL 35801. **Tel** (205)536-0901. **Ed** Al Owen. **LC** HG4501. **DD** 332.60973. bk rev. **Circ** 5,000. A timely digest of more than 300 investment advisory and economic newsletters, with editorial commentary and current recommendations. All investments. Emphasis on timing.

IOWA AIRPORT DIRECTORY. 1st 1975-. 0578-6541. US. English. an. $2.00. 610 Guaranty Bank Building, Subscription Department, Cedar Rapids IA 52401. **LC** TL522.I8. **DD** 387.736025777.

IOWA AIRPORT DIRECTORY (DES MOINES, IOWA). (IOWA AIRPORT DIRECTORY). US. English. an. **LC** TL726.3.I8. **DD** 629.136025777.

IOWA BUSINESS DIRECTORY. US. English. American Directory Publishing Company, 5639 South 86t Circle, Omaha NB 68127.

IOWA CAPITOL COMPLEX TELEPHONE DIRECTORY. US. English. The Department, Core Depository, Des Moines IA 50319. *Iowa State Government Telephone Directory, Capitol Complex.*

IOWA EDUCATIONAL DIRECTORY. Main/Corp Iowa. Department of Public Instruction. US. English. an. $2.06. Grimes State Office Building, Department of Public Instruction, Urban Education Section, Des Moines IA 50319.

IOWA PEACE DIRECTORY. 8755-5948. US. English. United Nations Association of Iowa, 26 East Market Street, Iowa City IA 55240.

IRAMANATAPURAM PANCANKAM. Tamil. an. M Palaniyanti Cervai Son, Putumantapam Madurai 625001. **LC** AY1051.

IRAN BANKING ALMANAC. 0377-0214. English. an. Iranian Banking Association, 41 Daraye Noor Street, Tehran Iran. **LC** HG3333. **DD** 332.10955.

IRAN YEARBOOK. English. ir. Kayhan Research Association, Tehran Iran. **LC** DS251. **DD** 955.05.

IRELAND : A PARLIAMENTARY DIRECTORY. 1973/74-. IE. English. ir. 9.00. Institute of Public Administration, 57-62 Lansdowne Road, Dublin Ireland. **LC** JN1468. **DD** 328.4170025.

THE IRI GROUP YEARBOOK. Main/Corp Istituto per la Richostruzione Industriale (Italy). VAT Istituto per la Richostruzione Industriale Group Yearbook. 0390-6272. Multilingual (English). ir. **LC** HC301. **DD** 338.40945.

THE IRIS YEAR BOOK. 1930-. UK. English. an. $7.96. British Iris Society, c/o Neville Watkins, 31 Larkfield Road, Farnham Surrey FU9 7DE England. *Bulletin (London, England).*

IRREGULAR SERIALS & ANNUALS; AN INTERNATIONAL DIRECTORY. VAT Irregular Serials and Annuals. 1st- Ed. 0000-0043. US. English. an. $124.00. R R Bowker, PO Box 1807, Ann Arbor MI 48106. **Ed** E Koltay. **LC** Z6941. **DD** 016.05. **NLM** Z 6941 I71.

ISA DIRECTORY OF INSTRUMENTATION (TRADE EDITION). (ISA DIRECTORY OF INSTRUMENTATION). VFOAT Directory of Instrumentation. VAT Instrument Society of America Directory of Instrumentation. 1980/81-. 0272-8141. US. English. an. $115.00. Instrument Society of America, PO Box 12277, Research Triangle Park NC 27709. **Tel** (919)549-8411. **Ed** Robin M Christopher. **LC** HD9706.6.U6. **DD** 681.20294. adv acc. **Circ** 37,500. (ctrl) Products, manufacturers, and sales representatives for industrial process instrumention and control are arranged for easy reference. *ISA Directory of Instrumentation. International Volume, 0193-7243; ISA Directory of Instrumentation. North American Volume, 0191-9008.*

THE ISBA BLUE BOOK. See Law.

ISRAEL BOOK TRADE DIRECTORY. 5th- Ed. IS. English. be. Free. Publishers and Printers of Israel, PO Box 50084, Tel Aviv Israel. **Tel** 03-630-830. **LC** Z449.5. **DD** 070.508855694. adv acc. **Circ** 3,000. Publication listing Israeli publishers and printing services with a special emphasis on Israeli export in this area. Each listing has a comprehensive description. *Publishers and Printers of Israel, 0079-7820.*

THE ISRAEL YEARBOOK. 0075-1413. IS. English. an. 30.00. Israel Yearbook, PO Box 17130, Tel Aviv 61171 Israel. **Tel** 03-416881. **Ed** Menachem Knaan. adv acc. Contains articles and commentary by prominent analysts and experts in political, economic and cultural affairs of the Middle East in general and the state of Israel in particular.

ISRAEL YEARBOOK ON HUMAN RIGHTS. V. 1- 1971-. 0333-5925. IS. English. an. 25.00. Tel Aviv University, Faculty of Law, Tel Aviv 69978 Isreal. **Tel** (03)420361. **Ed** Yoram Pinstein. **Ind/Abst** ABC Pol Sci. bk rev. **Circ** 1,000. Devoted to studies on human rights in peace and war, with particular emphasis on problems relevant to the State of Israel and the Jewish people.

ISS DIRECTORY OF OVERSEAS SCHOOLS. VFOAT Directory of Overseas Schools. VAT International Schools Services Directory of Overseas Schools. 1981/82-. 0732-7862. Periodical. US. English. an. $25.00. International Schools Service, PO Box 5910-8, Princeton NJ 08540. **Tel** (609)452-0990. **Ed** Mea Johnston. **LC** L900. **DD** 371.02025. adv acc. **Circ** 5,000. Information pertaining to overseas schools. A complete list of these schools is geographically referenced. *Directory of Overseas Schools.*

THE ITALIAN YEARBOOK OF INTERNATIONAL LAW. V. 1- 1975-. IT. English. an. Oceana Publications, 75 Main Street, Dobbs Ferry NY 10522. **LC** JX7. **DD** 341.05.

IUCN YEARBOOK. Main/Corp International Union for Conservation of Nature and Natural Resources. VFOAT Yearbook - International Union for Conservation of Nature and Natural Resources. 1970-. English and French. ir. International Union for Conservation of Nature and Natural Resources, 1110 Morges Switzerland. **DD** 333.7. *Annual Report - International Union for Conservation of Nature and Natural Resources, 0074-9265.*

IUI YEARBOOK. VFOAT I.U.I. Yearbook. English. an. Industriens Utredningsinstitut, Grevgatan 34 5TR S-11453 Stockholm Sweden. **LC** HC371. **DD** 338.54409485. *IUI Research Program.*

IWSA YEAR BOOK : AN OFFICIAL PUBLICATION OF THE INTERNATIONAL WATER SUPPLY ASSOCIATION. Main/Corp International Water Supply Association. VFOAT IWSA Yearbook, Annuaire de l'AIDE. UK. English (Multilingual). an. 17.00. International Water Supply Association, 1 Queen Anne's Gate, London SW1H 9BT England. **Tel** (01)222-8111. **Ed** L R Bays. **LC** TD201. **DD** 363.61025. adv acc. **Circ** 3,000. (ctrl). List of members of Association and addresses of water supply organisations in the world.

JAARBERICHT VAN HET VOORAZIATISCH-EGYPTISCH GENOOTSCHAP EX ORIENTE LUX. ANNUAIRE DE LA SOCIETE ORIENTALE EX ORIENTE LUX. Main/Corp Vooraziatisch-Egyptisch Genootschap ex Oriente Lux. VFOAT Annuaire de la Societe Orientale ex Oriente Lux. No. 1- 1933-. NE. various European languages. ir. $32.00. Ex Oriente Lux, Postbus 9615, Witte Sinel 24, 2300 Ra Leiden The Netherlands.

JAARBOEK. Main/Corp Academie voor Nederlandse taal- en Letterkunde. 1972-. Dutch. ir. Koningstraat 18, 9000 Gent The Netherlands. **LC** PF1001. *Jaarboek.*

JAARBOEK. Main/Corp Maatschappij der Nederlandse Letterkunde te Leiden. NE. Dutch. an. Maatschappy der Ned Letterkund Rapenburg 70-74, Leiden The Netherlands. **LC** AS244. (cum index).

JAARBOEK. Main/Corp University of Pretoria. SA. Afrikaans. qt. Suid Afrikakao Wetens Kuns, Box 53 8, Pretoria South Africa. **LC** LG471. **DD** 378.68.

JAARBOEK (AMSTERDAM (NETHERLANDS). BESTUURSINFORMATIE. AFDELING STATISTIEK). (JAARBOEK : UITGAVE VAN BESTUURSINFORMATIE, AFDELING STATISTIEK). 11. (1980)-. NE. Dutch. an. Bestuursinformatie Afdeling Statistiek, Singel 250-256, 1016 AB Amsterdam Netherlands. **LC** HA1388.A5. *Jaarboek (Amsterdam (Netherlands). Bureau van Statistiek).*

JAARBOEK - GEWESTELIJKE ONTWIKKELINGSMAATSCHAPPIJ. Main/Corp Gewestelijke Ontwikkelingsmaatschappij (Limburg, Belgium). Dutch. ir. Gewestelijke Ontwikkelingsmaatschappij, 3500 Hasselt Kunstlaan 18, Hasselt Belgium. **LC** HC317.L4.

JAARBOEK - KAMER VAN KOOPHANDEL EN NIJVERHEID VAN ANTWERPEN. Main/Corp Chambre de Commerce et d'Industrie d'Anvers. VFOAT Annuaire - Chambre de Commerce et d'Industrie d'Anver. 1972/73-. English, Flemish, French and German. ir.

Yearbooks, Almanacs, Directories

Markgracestraat 12, B-2000 Antwerpen Belgium. **LC** HF21.

JAARBOEK OPENBARE BIBLIOTHEKEN. NE. Dutch. an. $12.57. NBLC, Postbus 93054, 2509 AB Den Haag Netherlands. **LC** Z815.A1.

JAARBOEK VAN DE HAVEN VAN ANTWERPEN. Main/Corp Port d'Anvers. **VFOAT** Annuaire du Port d'Anvers, Antwerp Port Annual. Dutch (English, French, and German). ir. 500.00. Antwerpse Lloyd, Eiermarkt 23, B-2000 Antwerpen Belgium. **LC** HE558.A6. **DD** 387.1094932.

JAARBOEK VAN DIE CHRISTELIJKE GEREFORMEERDE KERKEN IN NEDERLAND. Main/Corp Christelijke Gereformeerde Kerk. NE. Dutch. ir. Uitgeverij D J van Brummen B V, Dordrecht Netherlands. **LC** BX9470.

JAARBOEK VAN HET DEPARTEMENT VAN BUITENLANDSE ZAKEN CEASED. **Main/Corp** Netherlands (Kingdom, 1815-) Departement van Buitenlandse Zaken. 1949/50-. 0466-9371. Dutch. ir. **LC** JX741. **DD** 327.492.

JAARBOEK VAN HET KATHOLIEK DOCUMENTATIE CENTRUM. Main/Corp Katholiek Documentatie Centrum. 1971-. Dutch (summaries in English and French). an. 27.50. Katholiek Documentatie Centrum, Erasmuslaan 36, 6525 GG Nijmegen Netherlands. **Tel** 080-512412. **LC** BX1549.A1. **Circ** 500. (ctrl). Report of activities by the Katholiek Documentatie Centrum. Scientific articles about the history of the Catholic life, Catholic people and the Catholic church in the Netherlands in the 19th and 20th century.

JAARBOEK (VLAAMS INSTITUUT VOOR AMERIKAANSE KULTUREN). (JAARBOEK). **VFOAT** Annales, Yearbook. 1982-. Periodical. Dutch (English, French, and Spanish). an. 500. Vlaams Instituut voor Amerikaanse Kulturen, Nieuwe Beggaardenstraat 15, B 2800 Mechelen Belgium. **Tel** 015/21 87 86. **LC** E51. bk rev. adv acc. **Circ** 500. American anthropology, archaeology and astronomy.

JAHRBUCH. Main/Corp Deutsche Gesellschaft fur Luft- und Raumfahrt. **VFOAT** DGLR Jahrbuch. 1-1968-. GW. German. ir. Goethestrasse 10, D-5 Koln 51 West Germany. **LC** TL503. **DD** 629.105. *Jahrbuch der Wissenschaftliche Gesellschaft.*

JAHRBUCH. Main/Corp Ruhr-Universitat Bochum. German. ir. Gesllschaft der Freunde der Ruhr-Universitat Bochum EV, 463 Bochum Postfach 21148, Bochum West Germany. **LC** LF3094.

JAHRBUCH. Main/Corp Opernhaus Zurich. German. ir. **LC** ML1749.8.Z8.

JAHRBUCH. Main/Corp Gesellschaft fur die Geschichte und Bibliographie des Brauwesens (Berlin, Germany). Began in 1928. 0072-422X. WB. German. an. Gesellschaft fur die Geschichte und Bibliographie des Brauwesens, E V, D-1000 West Berlin 65 Germany. **LC** HD9397.G2. **DD** 338.4766330943.

JAHRBUCH ASIEN-AFRIKA-LATEINAMERIKA. 1973-. GE. German. ir. Redaktion, Karl-Marx-Platz 9, 701 Leipzig East Germany. **LC** D839. **DD** 320.91724. *Asien, Afrika, Lateinamerika.*

JAHRBUCH DER ABSATZ- UND VERBRAUCHSFORSCHUNG. 0021-3985. GW. German. qt. Duncker & Humbolt Verlag, Dietrich-Schaefer-Weg 9, 1000 Berlin 41 West Germany. **Ind/Abst** Foreign Lang. Index. **LC** HC79.C6.

JAHRBUCH DER AKADEMIE DER WISSENSCHAFTEN DER DDR. Main/Corp Akademie der Wissenschaften der DDR. 0304-2154. GE. German. an. Deutscher Buch Export-Import, Leninstrasse 16, DDR-701 Leipzig East Germany. **Ind/Abst** Bibliogr. Index Geol. **LC** AS182. **DD** 063.

DAS JAHRBUCH DER BAUTECHNIK. August 1, 1982-. Periodical. GW. German. an. Expert Verlag, 7031 Grafenau, 1/Wurttemburg West Germany. **LC** TH3. **DD** 690.05.

JAHRBUCH DER BERLINER MUSEEN. Vol. 1- 1959-. 0075-2207. WB. German. an. Gebrueder Mann Verlag, Lindenstrasse 76, 1000 Berlin 61 West Germany. **Tel** 03/25913589. **Ind/Abst** Avery Index Archit. Period., Art Index, Repert. Int. Litt. Art. **LC** N3. adv acc. **Circ** 700. Contributions to art (paintings, sculpture, etc.). *Jahrbuch der Preussischen Kunstsammlungen.*

JAHRBUCH DER DEUTSCHEN BUNDESPOST. V. 28-. German (summaries in English and French). ir. **LC** HE6995. **DD** 383.0943. *Jahrbuch des Elektrischen Fernmeldewesens, Jahrbuch des Postwesens.*

JAHRBUCH DER DEUTSCHEN GESELLSCHAFT FUR LUFT- UND RAUMFAHRT. Main/Corp Deutsche Gesellschaft fur Luft-und Raumfahrt. 1968-. GW. German. an. Deutsche Gesellschaft Luft Raw, Postfach 51 06 45, 5 Koln 51 West Germany.

JAHRBUCH DER DEUTSCHEN MUSIKORGANISATION. 1931-. German. ir. **LC** ML21.

JAHRBUCH DER DEUTSCHEN SCHILLERGESELLSCHAFT. Main/Corp Deutsche Schillergesellschaft. Vol. 1-. 0070-4318. Periodical. GW. German. an. $21.06. Alfred Kroner Verlag, Postfach 1109, Reinsburgstr 56, D-7000 Stuttgart 1 West Germany. **Ind/Abst** MLA Int. Bibliogr. Books Artic. Mod. Lang. Lit. **LC** PT105. **DD** 830. (cum index).

JAHRBUCH DER DISSERTATIONEN - RUPRECHT-KARLS-UNIVERSITAT HEIDELBERG, MEDIZINISCHE FAKULTAT. (JAHRBUCH DER DISSERTATIONEN - RUPRECHT-KARL-UNIVERSITAT HEIDELBERG, MEDIZINISCHE FAKULTAT). 0441-795X. GW. German. ir. **NLM** ZW 4 J25.

JAHRBUCH ... DER GEWERKSCHAFT OFFENTLICHER DIENST. German. an. Gewerkschaft Offentlicher Dienst, Teinfaltstrasse 7, 1010 Wien 1 West Germany. **LC** HD8013.A9. **DD** 354.43600205. *Jahrbuch (Gewerkschaft der Offentlich Bediensteten).*

JAHRBUCH DER GRAPHISCHEN UNTERNEHMUNGEN OSTERREICHS. 0075-2266. AU. German. an. Jahrbuch der Graphischen, Grunangergasse 4, 1010 Wein Austria. **LC** Z119.

JAHRBUCH DER HAFENBAUTECHNISCHEN GESELLSCHAFT. Main/Corp Hafenbautechnische Gesellschaft. 0340-4838. Monographic Series. German. ir. Springer Verlag-New York Inc, 175 5th Avenue, New York NY 10010. **Tel** (212)460-1584. **LC** TC203. **DD** 627.2.

JAHRBUCH DER HAMBURGER KUNSTSAMMLUNGEN CEASED. V. 1-25 1948-1980. 0075-2274. GW. German. an. **Ind/Abst** Avery Index Archit. Period., Avery Index Archit. Period. Second Ed. Revis. Enlarged Suppl., Repert. Int. Litt. Art. **LC** N9.

JAHRBUCH DER HEIDELBERGER AKADEMIE DER WISSENSCHAFTEN. Main/Corp Heidelberger Akademie der Wissenschaften. 1962/63-. 0341-2865. GW. German. an. Carl Winter Universitatsverlag, Postfach 1886, Lutherstrasse 59, D6900 Heidelberg West Germany. **Ind/Abst** Math. Rev., GeoRef. *Sitzungsberichte der Heidelberger Akademie der Wissenschaften. Jahresheft.*

JAHRBUCH DER HISTORISCHEN FORSCHUNG IN DER BUNDESREPUBLIK DEUTSCHLAND. GW. German. an. $64.93. W E Saarbach GMBH, Postfach 101610, D 5000 Koeln 1 West Germany. **LC** DD86.

JAHRBUCH DER JEAN-PAUL-GESELLSCHAFT. Main/Corp Jean-Paul-Gesellschaft. 1- Volume. 0075-3580. German. an. Emil Muehl, Richard Wagner Street 21/858 Bayreuth BRD Germany. **Ind/Abst** MLA Int. Bibliogr. Books Artic. Mod. Lang. Lit. **LC** PT2456. **DD** 838.609. *Hesperus.*

JAHRBUCH DER KAMMER FUR ARBEITER UND ANGESTELLTE FUR NIEDEROSTERREICH. Main/Corp Kammer fur Arbeiter und Angestellte fur Niederostereeich. German. ir. Kammer fur Arbeiter und Angestellte fur Niederostereeich, Windmuhlgasse 28 1060, Wien Austria. **LC** HD8419.N53. *Jahresbericht.*

JAHRBUCH DER KARL-MAY-GESELLSCHAFT. (JAHRBUCH). **Main/Corp** Karl-May-Gesellschaft. **VFOAT** Jahrbuch der Karl-May-Gesellschaft. 1970-. 0300-1989. GW. German. ir. Hansa-Verlag, Hamburg 63 West Germany. **Ind/Abst** MLA Int. Bibliogr. Books Artic. Mod. Lang. Lit. **LC** PT2625.A848.

JAHRBUCH DER KUNSTHISTORISCHEN SAMMLUNGEN IN WIEN. V. 35-36. AU. German. an. $51.29. Verlag Anton Schroll and Company, Spengergasse 39, A-1051 Vienna 1 Austria. **Tel** 0222/ 55 56 41. **Ind/Abst** Art Index, Repert. Int. Litt. Art. *Jahrbuch der Kunsthistorischen Sammlungen des Allerhochsten Kaiserhauses.*

JAHRBUCH DER LUFT- UND RAUMFAHRT. V. 1- 1951/52-. 0447-256X. GW. German. an. $25.53. Sudwestdeutsche Verlagsanstalt Presseehaus Am Markt, 6800 Mannheim West Germany.

JAHRBUCH DER MARINE. Series 12- 1976/77-. German. an. Wehr und Wissen, Heilsbachstrasse/Postfach 87, 5300 Bonn Duisdorf Germany. **LC** V10. *Jahrbuch der Deutschen Marine.*

JAHRBUCH DER MUSIKBIBLIOTHEK PETERS. V. 1-. Periodical. German. ir. **LC** ML5.

JAHRBUCH DER OSTERREICHISCHEN BYZANTINISTIK. Vol. 18-. 0378-8660. AU. German (French, Greek or Italian). an. Osterreichischen Akademie Wissenschaften, Dr Inez-Spiel-Pltz 2, A-1010 Wien Austria. **Tel** 52 96 81. **Ind/Abst** MLA Int. Bibliogr. Books Artic. Mod. Lang. Lit., Avery Index Archit. Period. Second Ed. Revis. Enlarged Suppl., Repert. Int. Litt. Art. **LC** DF501. *Jahrbuch der Osterreichischen Byzantinischen Gesellschaft.*

JAHRBUCH DER PSYCHOANALYSE. Vol. 1- 1960-. 0075-2363. GW. German. an. 82.-. Fromman-Holzboog Verlag, Postfach 500460G, 7 Stuttgart 50 West Germany. **Tel** 0711/569039. Ed Gunther Holzboog. **Ind/Abst** Psychol. Abstr. **NLM** W1 JA18. adv acc. **Circ** 1,000.

JAHRBUCH DER RHEINISCHEN DENKMALPFLEGE. Began with V. 21 (1957). 0341-924X. Periodical. GW. German. ir. Rheinland-Verlan GMBH, Koln West Germany. **Ind/Abst** Repert. Int. Litt. Art. **LC** N6879. **DD** 709.4355. *Jahrbuch der Rheinischen Denkmalpflege in Nord-Rheinland.*

JAHRBUCH DER SCHIFFBAUTECHNISCHEN GESELLSCHAFT. Main/Corp Schiffbautechnische Gesellschaft. 1.- 1900-. 0374-1222. US. German. ir. Springer Verlag-New York Inc, 175 5th Avenue, New York NY 10010. **Tel** (212)460-1584. **Ind/Abst** Eng. Index. **LC** VM3. **DD** 623.8105. Numbered series.

JAHRBUCH DER SCHLESIER. V. 1- (1979)-. German. an. Helmut Preussler Heimatverlag, Rothernburger Strasse 25, 85 Nurnberg West Germany. **LC** DK4600.S42. **DD** 943.85005.

JAHRBUCH DER SCHWEIZERISCHEN NATURFORSCHENDEU GESELLSCHAFT. VFOAT Wissenschaftlicher Teil. 1978-. English (French and German). an. **Ind/Abst** Life Sci. Collect. **LC** Q67. **DD** 505. *Verhandlungen der Schweizerischen Naturforschenden Gesellschaft, 0080-7362.*

JAHRBUCH DER SOZIALDEMOKRATISCHEN PARTEI DEUTSCHLANDS. Main/Corp Sozialdemokratische Partei Deutschlands. GW. German. ir. Vorwaerts Verlag, AM Michaelshof 8-10, D-53 Bonn 2 West Germany. **LC** JN3926.S8.

JAHRBUCH DER TURNKUNST. V. 72-. Periodical. GW. German. ir. Pohl-Verlag, Postfach 103, 3100 Celle West Germany. **LC** GV204.G4. **DD** 613.70943. *Amtliches Jahrbuch des Deutschen Turner-Bundes.*

JAHRBUCH DER UHRENINDUSTRIE UND IHRER VERWANDTEN ZWEIGE. VFOAT Annuaire de l'Industrie de la Montre et de Ses Branches Annexes. French or German. ir. 11.00. Vogt-Schild SA, 4500 Soleure 2, Soleure Switzerland. **LC** HD9999.C6.

JAHRBUCH DER WEHRTECHNIK. Series 1- 1966-. 0075-2428. GW. German. an. Wehr und Wissen, Heilsbachstrasse/Postfach 87, 5300 Bonn Duisdorf Germany. **LC** UF530.

JAHRBUCH DER WIENER GESELLSCHAFT FUR THEATERFORSCHUNG. 18-20-. 0377-0354. AU. German. an. Vervand Wissen Gesellschaften, Osterreichs/Lindengasse 37, A 1070 Wien Austria. **Tel** 93 47 56. Ed Otto Schindler. **LC** PN2616.V5. **DD** 792.0943613. **Circ** 500. Articles about different details

Yearbooks, Almanacs, Directories

of the history of theatre, about playwriters or actors; listings of performances in Austria. *Jahrbuch der Gesellschaft fur Wiener Theaterforschung.*

JAHRBUCH DER WIRTSCHAFT OSTEUROPAS. VFOAT Yearbook of East-European Economics. Vol. 1- 1970-. 0449-5225. GW. English (German). sa. $34.09. Guenter Olzog Verlag GMBH, Thierschstrasse 11, D-8000 Munchen 22 West Germany. **Ind/Abst** GeoRef, Public Aff. Inf. Serv. Bull., Bibliogr. Index Geol. LC HC244.

JAHRBUCH DES ARCHIVS DER DEUTSCHEN JUGENDBEWEGUNG. **Main/Corp** Archiv der Deutschen Jugendbewegung. Began publicaiton in 1969. 0587-5277. GW. German. ir. 25.00. Burg Ludwigstein, c/o M Mogge, D-3430 Witzenhausen 1 West Germany. Tel (5542)1862. Ed Winfried Mogge. LC HN19. DD 305.230943. bk rev. Circ 2,000. Contains history of the youth movement in the Third Reich from beginning to present, youth and national socialism, alternate lifestyles among the young, book reviews and bibliographies.

JAHRBUCH DES DEUTSCHEN ARCHAOLOGISCHEN INSTITUTS. V. 33.- -1918-. 0070-4415. German. an. Walter de Gruyter and Company, 200 Saw Mill River Road, Hawthorne NY 10532. Tel (914)747-0110. **Ind/Abst** Art Index, Avery Index Archit. Period. (cum index). *Jahrbuch des Kaiserlich Deutschen Archaologischen Instituts.*

JAHRBUCH DES EISENBAHNFREUNDES. German. ir. Roster and Zimmer Verlag, 8900, Augsburg West Germany. LC TF73.

JAHRBUCH DES EISENBAHNWESENS. 1950-. 0075-2479. GW. German. an. Hestra Verlag Hernichel and Dr, Postfach 4244/Holzhofallee 33, 836100 Darmstadt 1 West Germany. **Ind/Abst** Energy Res. Abstr. LC HE3071.

JAHRBUCH DES FREIEN DEUTSCHEN HOCHSTIFTS. **Main/Corp** Freies Deutsches Hochstift (Frankfurt Am Main, Germany). 1902-. 0071-9463. GW. German. an. Max Niemeyer Verlag, Postfach 21 40, 7400 Tuebingen 1 West Germany. Ed Christoph Perels. **Ind/Abst** MLA Int. Bibliogr. Books Artic. Mod. Lang. Lit. LC AS182. Yearbook with contributions on German literature of the the 19th century (especially Goethe, Brentano, Von Arnim). *Berichte.*

JAHRBUCH DES HEERES. 0075-2282. GW. German. an. Wehr und Wissen, Heilsbachstrasse, Postfach 87, 5300 Bonn Duisdorf Germany.

JAHRBUCH DES HISTORISCHEN VEREINS DILLINGEN AN DER DONAU. **Main/Corp** Historischer Verein Dillingen an der Donau. Began with Vol. for 1896. Periodical. German. ir. 30.00. Historischer Verein Dillingen, Postcheckamt Munchen, Nr 29089-809, Dillingen West Germany. LC DD901.D485. DD 943.37. *Jahresbericht.*

JAHRBUCH DES INSTITUTS FUR DEUTSCHE GESCHICHTE. **Main/Corp** Tel-Aviv. University. Institute for German History. V. 1-. 0334-4606. German (summaries in Hebrew). an. $20.00. Tel Aviv University, Ramat Aviv, Tel Aviv Israel. Tel 03-420731. Ed Prof Walter Grab. **Ind/Abst** Am. Hist. Life, Hist. Abstr., Part A, Mod. Hist. Abstr., Hist. Abst., Part B, Twent. Century Abstr. LC DD4. DD 943.005. bk rev. adv acc. Circ 800. Geman social history and history of ideas; German-Jewish relations; relations between Germany and the Middle East.

JAHRBUCH . . . DES INSTITUTS FUR DEUTSCHE SPRACHE. Series/Titl Sprache der Gegenwart. 1975-. German. an. LC PF3003. DD 430.5. *Jahrbuch (Institut fur Deutsche Sprache).*

JAHRBUCH DES KREISES DUREN. 1973-. GW. German. ir. Eifelverein, 516 Duren, Surtzstrasse Postfach 646, Duren West Germany. LC DD491.R51. DD 914.355. *Heimatjahrbuch Kreis Duren, Heimatjahrbuch Kreis Julich.*

JAHRBUCH DES MARKISCHEN MUSEUMS. **Main/Corp** Markisches Museum. 1- 1975-. GE. German. an. Markisches Museum, AM Kollnischen Park 5, 102 Berlin East Germany. LC DD853.

JAHRBUCH DES MUSEUMS FUR KUNST UND GEWERBE HAMBURG. New Series, V. 1 (1982)-. 0723-7871. GW. German. an. **Ind/Abst** Avery Index Archit. Period., Repert. Int. Litt. Art. LC N9. DD 705. *Jahrbuch der Hamburger Kunstsammlungen.*

JAHRBUCH DES MUSEUMS FUR VOLKERKUNDE ZU LEIPZIG. **Main/Corp** Museum fur Volkerkunde zu Leipzig. V. 10 (1926/1951)-. 0075-8663. GE. German. ir. Deutscher Buch Export-Import Leninstrasse 16, DDR-701 Leipzig East German. *Jahrbuch des Stadtischen Museums fur Volkerkunde zu Leipzig.*

JAHRBUCH DES OFFENTLICHEN RECHTS DER GEGENWART. Vol. 1-25, 1907-38. 0075-2517. GW. German. an. JCB Mohr-Paul Siebeck, Postfach 2040, 7400 Tuebingen West Germany. Tel 0 70 71/2 60 64. LC JF13.

JAHRBUCH DES OO. MUSEALVEREINES GESELLSCHAFT FUR LANDESKUNDE. VFOAT Jahrbuch des O.O. Periodical. German. an. Verlag Oberosterreichischer Musealverein, Linz Austria. **Ind/Abst** Am. Hist. Life, Hist. Abstr., Part A, Mod. Hist. Abstr., Hist. Abst., Part B, Twent. Century Abstr. *Jahrbuch des Oberosterreichischen Musealvereines.*

JAHRBUCH DES ROMISCH-GERMANISCHES ZENTRALMUSEUM MAINZ. 1. Volume (1954)-. 0076-2741. GW. German. ir. Dr Rudolf Habelt GMBH, Am Buchenhang 1, 5300 Bonn 1 West Germany.

JAHRBUCH DES SOZIALRECHTS DER GEGENWART. V. 1 (1979)-. German. an. LC KK3270.5.A63. DD 344.43, 344.304. *Sozialordnung der Gegenwart.*

JAHRBUCH DES VEREINS FUR GESCHICHTE DER STADT WIEN. **Main/Corp** Verein fur Geschichte der Stadt Wien. Vol. 1-. AU. German. an. Verlag Strasse 21 23, A 3580 Horn Austria. **Ind/Abst** Am. Hist. Life, Hist. Abstr., Part A, Mod. Hist. Abstr., Hist. Abst., Part B, Twent. Century Abstr. LC DB843. DD 943.613. *Mitteilungen.*

JAHRBUCH DES VEREINS ZUM SCHUTZ DER BERGWELT. **Main/Corp** Verein zum Schutz der Bergwelt. V. 42-. 0171-4694. German. ir. Verein Zum Schutz der Bergwelt, 8000 Munchen 22 Praterinsel 5, Munchen West Germany. **Ind/Abst** GeoRef. LC QH77.A46. DD 333.95094947. *Jahrbuch.*

JAHRBUCH DES WIENER GOETHE-VEREINS. **Main/Corp** Wiener Goethe-Verein. Vol. 1- 1886/87-. 0250-443X. AU. German. an. 150. Wiener Goethe Verien, Stallburggasse 2, Vienna 1 Austria. Ed Herbert Zeman. **Ind/Abst** MLA Int. Bibliogr. Books Artic. Mod. Lang. Lit. LC PT2045. DD 832.62. (cum index). bk rev. Circ 750. (ctrl). Deals with 18th century German literature, Australian literature, and especially the works of Goethe.

JAHRBUCH DEUTSCH ALS FREMDSPRACHE. V. 1-. GW. German. an. 25.80. J Groos Verlag, D-6900 Heidelberg West Germany. LC PF3066.

JAHRBUCH - DEUTSCHE AKADEMIE FUR SPRACHE UND DICHTUNG DARMSTADT. (JAHRBUCH - DEUTSCHE AKADEMIE FUR SPRACHE UND DICHTUNG). **Main/Corp** Deutsche Akademie fur Sprache und Dichtung. 1953/54-. 0070-3923. Periodical. GW. German. an. 36.-. Verlag Lambert Schneider, Hauackerweg 16, 69 Heidelberg West Germany. Tel 06151/44823. Ed Marie-Luise Hubscherbitter. **Ind/Abst** MLA Int. Bibliogr. Books Artic. Mod. Lang. Lit. LC PF3013. Circ 600. (ctrl). Yearbook of the German Academy of Language and Poetry. Contribution to language and literature, speeches of prize winning authors of the academy, commemorations of dead members, bibliography, list of members and notices.

JAHRBUCH - DEUTSCHE SHAKESPEARE-GESELLSCHAFT WEST. **Main/Corp** Deutsche Shakespeare-Gesellschaft West. 1965-. 0070-4326. GW. German. ir. Verlag Ferdinand Kamp GMBH, Postfach 101309, Widumestrasse 6-8, 4630 1 Bochum 1 West Germany. Tel 234/15071. **Ind/Abst** Mather. Engl. Stud., MLA Int. Bibliogr. Books Artic. Mod. Lang. Lit., Annu. Bibliogr. Engl. Lang. Lit. bk rev. Essays on Shakespeare research, critical book reviews, theatre discussions, interpretations, Shakespeare on film and TV, reports on Shakespeare institutions and events, bibliography. *Shakespeare Jahrbuch.*

JAHRBUCH - DEUTSCHER BUNDESJUGENDRING. **Main/Corp** Deutscher Bundesjugendring. German. ir. Deutscher Bundesjugendring, Haager Weg 44, 5400 Bonn 1 West Germany. LC HQ799.8.G4.

JAHRBUCH DEUTSCHER DICHTUNG. 1977-. German. ir. LC PT1141.A2. *Jahrbuch - der Karlsruher Bote.*

JAHRBUCH DRITTE WELT. 1-. 0724-4762. Periodical. German. an. LC D880. DD 909.09724.

JAHRBUCH FUR AFRIKANISCHES RECHT. VFOAT Annuaire de Droit Africain, Yearbook of African Law. V. 1 (1980)-. English (French and German). an. C F Muller Juristischer Verlag GMBH, Heidelberg West Germany. DD 349.6, 346.

JAHRBUCH FUR ANTIKE UND CHRISTENTUM. Vol. 1- 1958-. 0075-2541. GW. German (English and French). an. Aschendorffsche Verlagsbuchhan Dlung, Postfach 1124, 4400 Munster West Germany. Tel 251/6901. Ed Theodor Klauser, Ernst Dassmann and Klaus Thraede. **Ind/Abst** New Testam. Abstr., Repert. Int. Litt. Art. LC BR128.A2. Study of antiquity and christianity. *Antike und Christentum.*

JAHRBUCH FUR DIE GESCHICHTE MITTEL- UND OSTDEUTSCHLANDS. V. 2- 1953-. 0075-2614. German. an. Walter de Gruyter & Company, 200 Saw Mill River Road, Hawthorne NY 10532. Tel (914)747-0110. **Ind/Abst** Am. Hist. Life, Hist. Abstr., Part A, Mod. Hist. Abstr., Hist. Abst., Part B, Twent. Century Abstr., Hist. Abstr. (cum index). *Jahrbuch fur Geschichte des Deutschen Ostens.*

JAHRBUCH FUR ERZIEHUNGS- UND SCHULGESCHICHTE. Vol. 1- 1961-. 0075-2622. GE. German. an. Deutscher Buch Export-Import, Leninstrasse 16, DDR-701 Leipzig East Germany. Tel 20430. LC L101.G3. (ctrl).

JAHRBUCH FUR FINNISCH-DEUTSCHE LITERATURBEZIEHUNGEN. No. 13 (1979)-. Fl. German. an. Deutsche Bibliothek, Pohj Makasiinikatu 7, SF-00131 Helsinki 13 Finland. LC PH300. DD 894.54109. *Mitteilungen aus der Deutschen Bibliothek.*

JAHRBUCH FUR FRANKISCHE LANDESFORSCHUNG. 1- 1935-. 0446-3943. GW. German. ir. Verlag Degener and Company, Postfache 1340, Neuinberger Street 27, D8530 Neustadt, West Germany. **Ind/Abst** MLA Int. Bibliogr. Books Artic. Mod. Lang. Lit., Recent Publ. Artic. LC DD801.B465. DD 943.3. (cum index).

JAHRBUCH FUR GEOLOGIE. V. 1- 1965-. 0448-1518. Periodical. GE. German (summaries in English and Russian). an. Deutscher Buch Export-Import, Leninstrasse 16, DDR-701 Leipzig East Germany. **Ind/Abst** GeoRef. LC QE269. DD 550.5. CODEN JBGEBF.

JAHRBUCH FUR GESCHICHTE DER SOZIALISTISCHEN LANDER EUROPAS. Vol. 13/1-. GE. German. an. 68.-. Deutscher Buch Export-Import, Leninstrasse 16, DDR-701 Leipzig East Germany. Tel 22900. **Ind/Abst** Am. Hist. Life, Hist. Abstr., Part A, Mod. Hist. Abstr., Hist. Abst., Part B, Twent. Century Abstr., Hist. Abstr. Contains articles such as papers, short items, publications of documents and reviews on the history and culture of the people of East and South-East Europe. *Jahrbuch fur Geschichte der Udssr und der Volksdemokratischen Lander Europas.*

JAHRBUCH FUR GESCHICHTE DES FEUDALISMUS. 1-. GE. German. an. 48.00. LC D131. DD 321.02.

JAHRBUCH FUR GESCHICHTE VON STAAT, WIRTSCHAFT UND GESELLSCHAFT LATEINAMERIKAS. 0075-2673. GW. Multilingual (German, French, and Spanish). an. $41.03. W E Saarbach GMBH, Postfach 101610, D-5000 Koeln 1, West Germany. Tel 02 21-23 46 31. **Ind/Abst** Am. Hist. Life, Hist. Abstr.

DAS JAHRBUCH FUR INGENIEURE. SZ. German. an. $19.54. Verlag Industrielle Organization, Zurichbergstrasse 18, Zurich 8028 Switzerland.

JAHRBUCH FUR INTERNATIONALE GERMANISTIK. Vol. 1- No. 1-. 0449-5233. Periodical. WB. German. sa. $45.52. Peter Lang Publishers Inc, Jupiterstrasse 15/PO Box 277, CH-3000 Berne Switzerland. Tel 031/32 11 22. **Ind/Abst** MLA Int. Bibliogr. Books Artic. Mod. Lang. Lit. LC PD3. bk rev. adv acc. Circ 14,000. Yearbook of international German philology. Published in connection with the International Association for German Language and Literature.

Yearbooks, Almanacs, Directories

JAHRBUCH FUR INTERNATIONALE GERMANISTIK. REIHE B, GERMANISTISCHE DISSERTATIONEN IN KURZFASSUNG. VFOAT Germanistische Dissertationen Kurzfassung. V. 1- 1975-. Dutch, English, French, or German. ir. H Lang, Munzgraben 2, CH-3000 7 Bern Switzerland. **LC** PF3010.

JAHRBUCH FUR INTERNATIONALES RECHT. VFOAT German Yearbook of International Law. 1- 1948-. 0021-3993. GW. German (English). an. Duncker und Humblot, Dietrich-Schaefer-Weg 9-BX 330, 1000 Berlin 41 West Germany. **Tel** (030)7912026. Ed J Delbiuck, W Fiedler and W A Kewluig. **Ind/Abst** Am. Hist. Life, Hist. Abstr. Yearbook of international law.

JAHRBUCH FUR LITURGIK UND HYMNOLOGIE. 1.- Volume. 0075-2681. GW. German. an. Baerenreiter Music Corporation, 224 King Street, Englewood, NJ 07631. **Tel** 561-30011. Ed Konrad Ameln and Alexander Volker. **Ind/Abst** RILM Abstr. **LC** ML3168. bk rev. Essays and miscellany on liturgy and hymn by international and ecumenical authors. Comprehensive reports on international literature.

JAHRBUCH FUR OPTIK UND FEINMECHANIK. 0075-272X. GW. German. an. Fachverlag SChiele and Schoen Markgrafenstrasse 11, 1 Berlin 61 West Germany. **Tel** 030/251 60 29. **LC** Q185.

JAHRBUCH FUR OSTDEUTSCHE VOLKSKUNDE. Vol. 7 (1962/1963)-. 0075-2738. GW. German. an. N G Elwert Verlag, Postfach 1128, Reitgasse 7+9, D-3550 Marburg West Germany. **Ind/Abst** MLA Int. Bibliogr. Books Artic. Mod. Lang. Lit. *Jahrbuch fur Volkskunde der Heimatvertriebenen.*

JAHRBUCH FUR OSTRECHT. Vol. 1- April 1960-. 0075-2746. GW. German. ir. 86.00. Deutscher Bundes-Verlag GMBH, Postfach 12 03 80, D-5300 Bonn 1 West Germany. Annual of eastern law, analyses, reports, comparisons of laws, translations, documnets and discussions on eastern European laws. Forum for the complete German and international research on Eastern Europe.

JAHRBUCH FUR REGIONALGESCHICHTE. V. 1 (1965)-. 0085-2341. Periodical. GE. German. ir. 28.00 Domestic. Deutscher Buch Export-Import, Leninstrasse 16, DDR-701 Leipzig East Germany. **LC** DD280. **DD** 943.1005. Contains proceedings, literary reports and reviews on the history of German national territories, the history of towns and settlements, the archaeology of the Middle Ages and the comparative regional history.

JAHRBUCH FUR REGIONALWISSENSCHAFT. V. 1, (1980)-. 0173-7600. GW. German (English). an. $21.43. Vandenhoeck and Ruprecht, Postfach 3753, Theaterstr 13, D 3400 Goettingen West Germany. **Tel** 0551/65061.

JAHRBUCH FUR SOZIALWISSENSCHAFT. V. 1, No. 1 (1950)-. 0075-2770. Periodical. GW. German. ty. $66.68. Vandenhoeck and Ruprecht, Postfach 3753, Theaterstr 13, D 3400 Goettingen West Germany. **Tel** 0551/65061. **Ind/Abst** PAIS Foreign Lang. Index, Foreign Lang. Index, Sociol. Abstr., Lang. Lang. Behav. Abstr., Recent Publ. Artic. **LC** H9. **NLM** W1 JA196P.

JAHRBUCH FUR SOZIOLOGIE UND SOZIALPOLITIK. 1980-. Periodical. GE. German (summaries in English, French, and Russian). an. Academie-Verlag, Leipziger Str 3-4, DDR-1080 Berlin West Germany. **LC** HM5.

JAHRBUCH FUR UMWELTSCHUTZ. 1973-. German. ir. Keller and Company, Druckerei und Verlag, Baselstrasse 11-13 6002, Luzern Switzerland. **LC** TD169.

JAHRBUCH FUR VOLKSKUNDE UND KULTURGESCHICHTE. Vol. 16-. GE. German. ir. Deutscher Buch Export-Import, Leninstrasse 16, DDR-701 Leipzig East Germany. **Ind/Abst** Am. Hist. Life, Hist. Abstr., Part A, Mod. Hist. Abstr., Hist. Abstr., Part B, Twent. Century Abstr., Recent Publ. Artic., Hist. Abstr. **LC** GR165. *Deutsches Jahrbuch fur Volkskunde.*

JAHRBUCH FUR VOLKSLIEDFORSCHUNG. Began publication in 1928. GW. German. ir. Erich Schmidt Verlag GMBH, PO Box 7330-40/Viktoriastr 44-A, D4800 Bielefeld 1 West Germany. **Tel** 0521/66061. **Ind/Abst** MLA Int. Bibliogr. Books Artic. Mod. Lang. Lit. bk rev. Folk song research.

JAHRBUCH FUR WESTDEUTSCHE LANDESGESCHICHTE. Volume 1-. German. ir. Selbstverlag der Landesarchivverwaltung Rheinland-Pfalz, Karmeliterstr 1/3, D 54 Koblenz West Germany. **LC** DD259. **DD** 943.

JAHRBUCH FUR WIRTSCHAFTSGESCHICHTE. 1960-. 0075-2800. GE. German. ir. Deutscher Buch Export-Import, Leninstrasse 16, DDR-701 Leipzig East Germany. **Ind/Abst** Am. Hist. Life, Hist. Abstr., Part A, Mod. Hist. Abstr., Hist. Abstr., Part B, Twent. Century Abstr., PAIS Foreign Lang. Index, Foreign Lang. Index, Hist. Abstr., Recent Publ. Artic. **LC** HC281. (cum index).

JAHRBUCH - JUNGE UNION DEUTSCHLANDS. **Main/Corp** Junge Union Deutschlands. German. ir. Junge Union Deutschlands, Annaberger Str 283, Bonn-Bad Godesberg West Germany. **LC** HQ799.G5.

JAHRBUCH - MAX-PLANCK-GESELLSCHAFT. (MAX-PLANCK-GESELLSCHAFT JAHRBUCH). **Main/Corp** Max-Planck-Gesellschaft. 1975-. 0341-0218. GW. German. an. Vandenhoeck & Ruprecht, Postfach 3753, Theaterstr 13, D 3400 Goettingen West Germany. **Tel** (0551)65061. **Ind/Abst** Biol. Abstr., Chem. Abstr. **CODEN** MPJADF. adv acc. *Jahrbuch der Max-Planck-Gesellschaft zur Forderung der Wissenschaften.*

JAHRBUCH OBERFLACHENTECHNIK. Began publication with Vol. for 1939. 0075-2819. GW. German. an. Jahreszeiten Verlag GMBH, Possmoorweg 1, 2000 Hamburg 60 West Germany. **Ind/Abst** Chem. Abstr., Eng. Index Annu., Eng. Index Mon., Eng. Index Bioeng. Abstr., Eng. Index Energy Abstr., Am. Hist. Life, Hist. Abstr., Eng. Index. **LC** TS670. **CODEN** JBOFAN.

JAHRBUCH PETERS / HERAUSGEGEBEN VON EBERHARDT KLEMM. 1. Vol. (1978)-. Periodical. German. an. $25.00. C F Peters Corporation, 373 Park Avenue South, New York NY 10016. **Tel** (212)686-4147. Ed Klemm. **Circ** 31. German yearbook of musicology. *Deutsches Jahrbuch der Musikwissenschaft.*

JAHRBUCH POLITIK. German. ir. K Wagenbach, Jenaer Strasse 6 31, Berlin West Germany. **LC** JA55.

JAHRBUCH PREUSSISCHER KULTURBESITZ. 0342-0124. GW. German. an. Gebr Mann Verlag, Lindenstrasse 76, D-1000 Berlin 61 West Germany. **Ind/Abst** Avery Index Archit. Period., Repert. Int. Litt. Art, Recent Publ. Artic. **LC** AM51.B4. **DD** 069.0943. *Jahrbuch (Stiftung Preussischer Kulturbesitz).*

JAHRBUCH - SACHSISCHE AKADEMIE DER WISSENSCHAFTEN ZU LEIPZIG. **Main/Corp** Sachsische Akademie der Wissenschaften zu Leipzig. 0080-5262. GE. German. ir. Deutshcer Buch Export-Import Leninstrasse 16, DDR-701 Leipzig East Germany. **Ind/Abst** Am. Hist. Life, Hist. Abstr., Part A, Mod. Hist. Abstr., Hist. Abst., Part B, Twent. Century Abstr. **LC** AS182. **NLM** W1 SA122.

JAHRBUCH (SCHWEIZERISCHE NATURFORSCHENDE GESELLSCHAFT. (JAHRBUCH). VFOAT Annuaire. French (German). an. Schweizerische Naturforschende Gesellschaft, Laupenstrasse 10, Berne 3001 Switzerland. **LC** QH5. **DD** 508.0720494.

JAHRBUCH (THOMAS-MORUS-GESELLSCHAFT). (JAHRBUCH). VFOAT Thomas-Morus-Jahrbuch. 0723-0516. Periodical. GW. German. an. Triltsch Druck und Verlag GMBH & Company KG, Dusseldorf West Germany. **LC** PR2322. **DD** 828.209.

JAHRBUCH - WIENER GEBIETSKRANKENKASSE FUR ARBEITER UND ANGESTELLTE. **Main/Corp** Wiener Gebietskrankenkasse fur Arbeiter und Angestellte. German. ir. Wiener Gebietskrankenkasse fur Arbeiter und Angestellte, Wipplingerstrasse 28, Wien 1 Austria. **LC** HD7102.A9.

JAHRBUCH ZUR MEDIENSTATISTIK UND KOMMUNIKATIONSPOLITIK. 1971-. GW. German. ir. Verlag V Spiess, Postfach 147, 1000 Berlin 62 West Germany. **LC** P92.G4. **DD** 301.1610943. *Jahresbibliographie: Massenkommunikation.*

JAHRBUCHER DER ZENTRALANSTALT FUR METEOROLOGIE UND GEODYNAMIK. **Main/Corp** Austria. Zentralanstalt fur Meteorologie und Geodynamik. 1.- Vol., 1848/49-. AU. German. ir. 500.- Domestic. Hohe Warte 38, 1190 Vienna Austria. **Tel** 0222 36 44 53. **Ind/Abst** GeoRef. (cum index). adv acc. **Circ** 500. Meteorological and geophysical yearly data measured in Austria.

JAHRBUCHER FUR STATISTIK UND LANDESKUNDE VON BADEN-WURTTEMBERG. **Main/Corp** Statistisches Landesamt Baden-Wurttemberg. V. 1-. 0408-1706. GW. German. ir. St Landesamt Baden Wurttemberg, Postfach 898, 7 Stuttgart Germany.

JAKARTA BUSINESS DIRECTORY. 1973/74-. English or Indonesian. ir. Badan Registrasi Perusahoan, Kamar Dagang Dan Industri Jakarta, Jalan W - Jakarta Fair, Tromol Post 3077, Jakarta Indonesia. **LC** HF5251.J3. **DD** 338.760255982.

THE JAMAICAN EXPORTER : OFFICIAL YEARBOOK AND MEMBERSHIP DIRECTORY OF THE JAMAICA EXPORTERS' ASSOCIATION. Periodical. English. an. Jamaica Exporters' Association, 3 Dominica Drive, Kingston 5 Jamaica. **LC** HF3341. **DD** 382.60607292.

JAPAN AVIATION DIRECTORY. JA. English. ir. $45.00. Wings Aviation Press Inc, 1-14-5 Ginza, Chuo-ku Tokyo 104 Japan. **Tel** (03)561-8305. Ed H Ohashi. **LC** TL501. **DD** 387.702552. adv acc. **Circ** 5,000. Yearbook of Japan's military, aerospace and air transport world. Also it contains directory listings for government organizations and companies plus personnel listings. *Japanese Aerospace Directory*, 0304-1654.

JAPAN CHEMICAL DIRECTORY. 0075-3203. JA. English. an. The Chemical Daily Company Ltd, 19-16 Shibaura 3 chome, Minato-ku Tokyo 108 Japan. **LC** TP12. **DD** 660.02552.

JAPAN DIRECTORY. JA. English. an. $265.00. Japan Press Ltd, 12-8 Kita Aoyama, 2-chome Minato-ku, Tokyo 107 Japan. **Tel** (03)404-5161. Ed Yoshio Wads. **LC** HF3823. **DD** 380.102552. adv acc. **Circ** 25,000. Complete coverage of firms and foreign residents in Japan.

JAPAN DIRECTORY OF PROFESSIONAL ASSOCIATIONS. VFOAT JDPA. 1st ED. (1984-1987)-. 0287-9530. Periodical. English. ir.

JAPAN ENGLISH MAGAZINE DIRECTORY. JA. English. ir. $70.00. International Marketing Corporation, 19-8 Nihonbashi Kakigaracho 1 Chuo-ku, Tokyo 103 Japan. **LC** Z6958.J3, PN5407.F62E5. **DD** 052.

JAPAN PETROLEUM & ENERGY YEARBOOK. VAT Japan Petroleum and Energy Yearbook. Began with 1975. JA. English. an. Maruzen Company Ltd, PO Box 5050, 100-31 Tokyo Japan. **LC** HD9576.J3. **DD** 338.4766550952.

JAPAN PETROLEUM INDUSTRY YEARBOOK. 1st Ed. (1983)-. English. an. **LC** HD9576.J3. **DD** 338.272820952.

JAPAN SUGAR YEARBOOK. JA. English. ir. Mitsiu & Company Ltd, 2-9 Nishi Shimbashi Ltchome Minato-ku Tokyo Japan. **LC** HD9116.J2. **DD** 338.4766410942.

JAPAN TRADE DIRECTORY (NIHON BOEKI SHINKOKAI). (JAPAN TRADE DIRECTORY). 1982-. English. ir. $170.00 Southeast Asia and Oceania, $180.00 North and Central America, $190.00 Europe, Africa, Middle East and South America. JETRO Publications Department, 2-2-5 Toranomon Minato-ku, Tokyo 105 Japan. **Tel** 03-582-5511. **LC** HF3823. **DD** 382.029452. Balanced and informative - the indispensable reference guide to dynamic trade with Japan.

JAPANESE AEROSPACE DIRECTORY. 0304-1654. English. ir. $8.50. Kohu Shimbun Sha, 4-18 Ginza 5-chome Chuo-ku, Tokyo Japan. **LC** TL501. **DD** 338.4762910952.

JAPAN'S WATERWORKS YEARBOOK. JA. English. ir. $6.00. Journal of Waterworks Industry, Osaka Godo Building 33 Taiyuji-cho Kita-ku, Osaka Japan. **LC** TD305.A1. **DD** 363.610952.

JAPTA LIST; JAPANESE DRUG DIRECTORY. **Main/Corp** Nihon Yakugyo Boeki Kyokai. VFOAT Japanese Drug Directory. Began in 1968. JA. English. ir. Japan Pharmaceutical Traders'

Association, 1 Kanda Izumicho Chiyoda-ku, Tokyo Japan. **LC** RS141.7. **DD** 615.1152.

JAZZ FESTIVALS INTERNATIONAL DIRECTORY. **VFOAT** Festivals International Directory. 0882-0368. US. English. an. Jazz World Society, PO Box 777/Times Square Street, New York NY 10108. **DD** 785. *World Jazz Calendar of Festivals & Events, 0275-973X.*

JEPPESEN SANDERSON AVIATION YEARBOOK. **VFOAT** Aviation Yearbook. 0364-331X. US. English. an. Jeppersen Sanderson Inc, 8025 East 40th Avenue, Denver CO 80207. **LC** TL501. **DD** 629.13005.

JEWISH EDUCATION DIRECTORY. Began in 1971. 0276-6310. US. English. ir. $8.50. American Association of Jewish Studies, 114 Fifth Avenue, New York NY 10011. **Tel** (212)675-5656. **LC** LC741. **DD** 370.89924073. *Jewish Education Register and Directory.*

JIDO BUNGAKU ANYUARU. **VFOAT** Yearbook of Children's Literature. Began with issue for 1982. Periodical. JA. Japanese. an. 7500. Kaiseisha 3-5, Ichigaya Sadohara-cho Shinjuku-ku, Tokyo-to 162 Japan. **LC** PN1008.2.

JOBSON'S MINING YEAR BOOK. **VFOAT** Jobson's Investment Digest Mining Year Book. Began with: 1957. 0075-3777. AT. English. an. The Publications Division of Dun & Bradstreet Pty Ltd, GPO Box 425G, Melbourne Victoria 3001 Australia. **Tel** (03)698-9400. **Ed** David M Newbold. **LC** HG5899.M4. **DD** 338.2. adv acc. **Circ** 6,600. Directory of mining and petroleum companies in Australia and New Zealand plus extensive articles and features relating to both industries.

JOBSON'S YEAR BOOK : PUBLIC COMPANIES OF AUSTRALIA AND NEW ZEALAND. **Main/Corp** Jobson's Financial Services. **VFOAT** Jobson's Investment Digest Year Book. 1967-. 0075-3785. AT. English. an. Dun & Bradstreet Australian Pty Ltd, 13 Wentworth Avenue, GPO Box 5338, Sydney New South Wales 2001 Australia. **Tel** 03 699 2500. **Ed** David Newbold. **LC** HG5891. **DD** 332.6302594. adv acc. Lists 1,600 major public private companies in Australia and New Zealand. Details structure, finance, history operations and management. *Digest Yearbook of Public Companies of Australia & New Zealand.*

JOBSON'S YEAR BOOK. PUBLIC COMPANIES OF AUSTRALIA & NEW ZEALAND. (JOBSON'S YEAR BOOK). **Main/Corp** Jobson's Publications. **VFOAT** Jobson's Year Book of Public Companies. AT. English. ir. The Publications Division of Dun & Bradstreet Pty Ltd, GPO Box 425G, Melbourne Victoria 3001 Australia. **Tel** (03)698 9400. **Ed** David M Newbold. Provides Australian and international business, government, academics and investors with the most in-depth, comprehensive and relevant analysis of the ever changing nature of commerce and industry throughout Australia and the world. *Jobson's Yearbook: Public Companies of Australia & New Zealand.*

JOINT MEMBERSHIP DIRECTORY - AMERICAN SOCIETY OF HUMAN GENETICS. (JOINT MEMBERSHIP DIRECTORY). **Main/Corp** American Society of Human Genetics. 1983-. 0883-4709. US. English. American Society of Human Genetics, PO Box 6015, Rockville MD 20850. **LC** QH429.5. **DD** 575.106073. **NLM** QH 429.5.

JOURNAL-BULLETIN RHODE ISLAND ALMANAC. **VFOAT** Providence Journal-Bulletin Almanac. **VAT** Journal Bulletin Rhode Island Almanac. 87th Ed. (1973)-. 0364-2909. Periodical. US. English. an. $4.13. Providence Journal Company, 75 Foundation Street, Providence RI 02902. **Tel** (401)277-7393. **Ed** Joseph O Mehr. Information on Rhode Island and its 39 cities and towns. *Journal-Bulletin Almanac, 0731-5511.*

JOURNALISM DIRECTORY. (JOURNALISM DIRECTORY : JD). **VFOAT** JD. Vol. 1 (Feb. 1983)-. 0735-3103. US. English. an. $15.00 Domestic, $25.00 Foreign. Association for Education in Journalism and Mass Communication, 1621 College Street University of South Carolina, Columbia SC 29208-0251. **Tel** (803)777-2005. **Ed** Fred L Williams. **LC** PN4788. **DD** 070.02573. adv acc. **Circ** 2,500. Guide to 300, plus journalism and mass communication programs, information on multitude of subjects related to the field, complete AEJMC membership roster with brief biographical sketches.

JUDICIAL & LEGAL DIRECTORY. **VFOAT** Judicial and Legal Directory. English. ir. Mayalsian Law Publishers Sdn, Bhd Room 201/2nd Floor Lee Yan Lian Building Jalan Tun Perak, Kuala Lumpur Malaysia.

JURONG INDUSTRIES DIRECTORY. English. ir. Business Media, 39 Stamford Road/Unite 136 Stamford House, Singapore 0617 Singapore. **LC** HC445.8.A1. **DD** 338.740255957.

KAIYO SANGYO JIMMEIROKU. **VFOAT** Japan Oceanology Directory. JA. Multilingual (English and Japanese). ir. 4300. Kaiyo Sangyo Kenkyukai, c/o Marufuji Building/3-1-10 Shimbashi Manato-ku, Tokyo 105 Japan. **LC** GC10.

KALENDAR GOLOSU SPASYTELJA. (KALENDAR HOLOSU SPASYTELIA). **VFOAT** Redeemer's Voice Almanac. Began with 1939 issue. 0381-5110. CN. Ukrainian. an. 6.00. Redeemer's Voice Press, Yorkton Saskatchewan S3N 3V7 Canada. **Tel** (306)783-4487. **Ed** Roman Chomiak. **DD** 281.971. bk rev. adv acc. **Circ** 1,200. Interspersed with English and Ukrainian; has Ukrainian Catholic liturgical calendar.

KALENDAR HRVATSKI GLAS. **VFOAT** Croation Voice Almanac. Began with 1930 issue?. 0319-5244. CN. Serbo-Croatian(R) (text in Croatian). sm. $23.21. Croatian Voice Hrvatski Glas, Box 596, Nanaimo British Columbia V9R 5L5 Canada. **Tel** (604)754-8282. **DD** 057.82.

KALENDAR SLOVO. **VFOAT** Free Word Almanac. V. 1-. 0318-1596. Periodical. CN. Ukrainian. an. 196 Bathurst Street, Toronto Ontario Canada. **DD** 957.91.

KALENDAR SVITLA. THE LIGHT ALMANAC. **Main/Corp** Svilto. **VFOAT** Light Almanac. CN. Ukrainian. an. **LC** BX1695.U5.

KALENDARZ BESKIDZKI. 0451-257X. Polish. ir. **LC** AY1039.P7.

KALENDARZ LUDOWY. Began with issue for 1984. Periodical. Polish. an. 130.00. **LC** AY934.

KALENDARZ POLSKI NA ROK. Periodical. US. Polish. an. Wydawn Promyk, 4566 Bermuda Street, Philadelphia PA 19137. **Ed** Antoni Gadysz. **LC** AY934.

KAN-NICHI KANKO HOTERU SORAN. **VFOAT** Korea-Japan Tourist Hotel Directory. Japanese. ir. 7500. Towa Shinjusha, Tonghwa Chunchu Sa 28-1 Sam Gag dong, Chung-ku Seoul Korea. **LC** TX910.K6.

KANON : YEARBOOK OF THE SOCIETY OF THE LAW OF THE ORIENTAL CHURCHES. 1-. Monographic Series. AU. German (English, French, Italian or Latin). ir. Verband Wissen Gesellschaften, Oesterreichs/Lindengasse 37, A-1070 Vienna Austria. **Tel** 63 98 62. **LC** UNC. **Circ** 200. Publishes the main lectures and speeches of the bi-annual congress of the society for the law of the Eastern Christian Churches.

KANSAS DIRECTORY. SUPPLEMENT. 0360-6252. US. English. Secretary of State, Jack H Brier/2nd Floor, Topeka KS 66612. **LC** JK6830. **DD** 353.978104.

KANSAS EDUCATIONAL DIRECTORY. 0099-0728. US. English. an. Kansas State Education Building, 120 East 10th Street, Topeka KS 66612. **LC** L150. **DD** 370.9781 S, 370.25781. *Kansas Educational Directory.*

KANSAS MINORITY INDUSTRIAL DIRECTORY. 1978-. US. English. Kansas Department of Economic Development, 503 Kansas Avenue/6th Floor, Topeka KS 66603. **Tel** (913)296-3805. **LC** HD2346.U52. **DD** 338.6422025781. **Circ** 1,000. (ctrl). Listing of minority business enterprises and women business enterprises in the state of Kansas, and minority business development resources in Kansas and Missouri.

KANSAS, NEBRASKA ZIP+4 STATE DIRECTORY. **VFOAT** Zip Plus Four State Directory. **VAT** Kansas, Nebraska Zip Plus Four State Directory. 1985-. US. English. an. St Louis PDC, Zip+4 State Directory Orders, PO Box 14921, St Louis MO 63180-9988.

KARLSRUHER ALMANACH FUR LITERATUR. 1977-. German. ir. Atelier Paysage, Agathenstrasse 7, 7500 Karlsruhe West Germany. **LC** PT3807.K27. **DD** 830.8.

KEITHWOOD DIRECTORY OF HOSPITAL & SURGICAL SUPPLY DEALERS. **VFOAT** Directory of Hospital & Surgical Supply Dealers. **VAT** Keithwood Directory of Hospital and Surgical Supply Dealers. 0162-9840. US. English. $45.00. Keithwood Company, 18th and Courtland Streets, Philadelphia PA 19140.

KEIZAI TOKEI NENKAN. **VFOAT** Economic Statistics Year Book, Year Book of Economic Statistics. 1952-. JA. Japanese. an. Tokyo Keizai Shimpo Sha, 1-4 Nihonbashi Hongokucho Chuo-ku (103), Tokyo Japan. **LC** HC461.

KELLY'S MANUFACTURERS AND MERCHANTS DIRECTORY. 82nd- 1968/69-. UK. English. an. $99.61. Kellys Directory Ltd, Windsor Court East/Grinstead House, East Grinstead West Sussex England. **Tel** 0342 26972. **LC** HF54.G7. **DD** 380.1025. bk rev. adv acc. **Circ** 11,250. The number one buyers guide, purchased every year by more decision makers and found in more buying offices than any other national directory. *Kelly's Directory of Manufacturers and Merchants including Industrial Services.*

KELLY'S POST OFFICE LONDON DIRECTORY. **VFOAT** Post Office London Directory. 0075-5389. Periodical. UK. English. an. 46. Kellys Directories E Grinstad, Windsor Court East/Grinstead, West Sussex England RH19 1XB. **Tel** 0342-26972. **LC** DA679. **DD** 914.210025. bk rev. adv acc. **Circ** 6,000. Provides a more comprehensive coverage of business in London than any other business-to- business guide. *Post Office London Directory.*

KELOWNA CITY DIRECTORY. **VFOAT** Official City Directory of Kelowna. 1958-. 0319-0013. Periodical. CN. English. an. B C Directories, 287 Bernard Avenue, Kelowna British Columbia V1Y 6N2 Canada. **DD** 917.1142. *Kelowna City and Central Okanagan Directory, 0319-0021.*

KEMPE'S ENGINEER'S YEAR-BOOK. 1st- Ed. 0075-5400. Periodical. UK. English. 40.00. Morgan Grampian, Royal Sovereign House/40 Beresfd, London SE18 6BQ England. **Tel** (01)855-7777. **Ed** J Quale. **LC** TA151.A1. adv acc. **Circ** 5,000. Typifies everyone's ideal of the classic engineering reference work.

KEMPS INTERNATIONAL FILM & TELEVISION YEAR BOOK. **VFOAT** International Film & Television Year Book. **VAT** Kemps International Film and Television Year Book. 1978/79-. UK. English. an. $50.00. R R Bowker, PO Box 1385, Ann Arbor MI 48106. **Tel** (212)916-1600. Yearbook/directory for international film and TV industries. *Kemp's Film and Television Yearbook (International).*

KEMP'S MUSIC & RECORDING INDUSTRY YEARBOOK. **VFOAT** Music & Recording Industry Yearbook. Began in 1965. 0075-5451. UK. English. Kemps Group Ltd, 5 Bath Street/City Road, London England. **LC** ML21. **DD** 338.4778025.

KEMP'S MUSIC & RECORDING INDUSTRY YEARBOOK INTERNATIONAL. **VFOAT** Music & Recording Industry Yearbook International. Began in 1965. Periodical. UK. English. The Kemps Group Ltd, 1-5 Bath Street, London EC1V 9QA England. *Kemp's Music & Recording Industry Yearbook, 0075-5451.*

KENT DIRECTORY. **VFOAT** Kent County Directory. May 1984/85-. 0828-5543. CN. English. an. $2.00. Kent County Directory, c/o Leader Publications, PO Box 490, Dresden Ontario N0P 1M0 Canada. **DD** 917.13330025.

KENTUCKY AIRPORT DIRECTORY. **Main/Corp** Kentucky. Dept. of Aeronautics. US. English. Free. Kentucky Department of Aeronautics, State Office Building, Frankfort KY 40601. **Tel** (502)564-4480. **Ed** Ben Prewitt. **LC** TL726.3.K4. **DD** 629.136058. **Circ** 3,000. Directory of public use airports. Lists runway length and width radio frequencies, phone numbers, fuels, lighting, repairs, and navigation. Also location and layout maps.

THE KENTUCKY AND TENNESSEE LEGAL DIRECTORY. 0450-089X. US. English. an. Legal Directories Publisher Company, 2122 Kidwell Street/PO Box 1402000, Dallas TX 75214. **LC** KF192.K4. **DD** 347.069.

THE KENTUCKY COAL DIRECTORY. US. English. Coal and Gas Computer Services Inc, 10405 Laurel Ridge Road, Ashland KY 41101. **LC** TN805.A4. **DD** 622.334025769.

KENTUCKY DIRECTORY OF BLACK ELECTED OFFICIALS. **Main/Corp** Kentucky Commission on Human Rights. **VFOAT** Directory of Black Elected Officials. 1st- 1969-. US. English. Kentucky Commission on Human Rights, 828 Capital Plaza Tower, Frankfort KY 40601.

THE KENTUCKY LEGAL DIRECTORY. 0145-658X. US. English. an. $7.00. Legal Directories Publisher Company, 1314 Westwood Boulevard, Los Angeles CA 90024. **LC** KF192.K4. **DD** 340.025769.

Yearbooks, Almanacs, Directories

KENTUCKY SCHOOL DIRECTORY. (THE KENTUCKY SCHOOL DIRECTORY). **Series Corp** Kentucky. Dept. of Education. Educational Bulletin. 0091-0775. US. English. an. LC L152.

KENTUCKY, WEST VIRGINIA ZIP+4 STATE DIRECTORY. VFOAT Zip Plus Four State Directory. VAT Kentucky, West Virginia Zip Plus Four State Directory. 1985-. US. English. an. St Louis PDC, Zip+4 State Directory Orders, PO Box 14921, St Louis MO 63180-9988.

KENYA BUSINESS DIRECTORY. 1982-. English. an. Peter Evans Musira Managing Director/ Editor Beaver Marketing Company, PO Box 26218, Nairobi Kenya. LC HF3893.A48. DD 380.102946762.

KENYA EXPORT DIRECTORY. Began with Vol. for 1977. KE. English. ir. Kenya External Trade Authority, PO Box 43137, Nairobi Kenya. LC HF3893.A48. DD 382.602946762.

KENYA POST OFFICE DIRECTORY OF PRIVATE BOX AND PRIVATE BAG RENTERS. English. ir. 3. LC HE7343.A4. DD 383.145.

KENYAN PERIODICALS DIRECTORY. VFOAT KPD. 1984-85-. KE. English. be. $9.50. Kenya National Library Service, National Reference and Bibliographic Department, PO Box 30573, Nairobi Kenya.

KENYA'S ... TRADE DIRECTORY : DOUGHARTY AND ASSOCIATES' DIRECTORY OF LOCAL AND OVERSEAS OPERATING COMPANIES. 1st Ed. (1981)-. English. ir. Dougharty and Associates, PO Box 55040, Nairobi Kenya. LC HF3893.A48. DD 380.10256762.

KEPES EVKONYV. Hungarian. ir. 16.00. LC AY814.

KEY COMPANY DIRECTORY MANUFACTURING. (KEY COMPANY DIRECTORY; MANUFACTURING). **Main/Corp** The Conference Board. US. English. sa. $350.00. Conference Board, 845 Third Avenue, New York NY 10022.

KEY COMPANY DIRECTORY, U.S. MANUFACTURING. VFOAT Key Company Directory, US Manufacturing, Key Company Directory, United States Manufacturing. Mar. 1980-. US. English. an. The Conference Board, 845 Third Avenue, New York NY 10022. *Key Company Directory, Manufacturing.*

KEY PERSONNEL DIRECTORY. (KEY PERSONNEL DIRECTORY : A GENERAL PUBLIC INFORMATION PUBLICATION). **Main/Corp** Law Society of Alberta. 0229-9089. CN. English. Canadian Bar Association, Alberta Branch, 610-8th Avenue SW/ Suite 640, Calgary Alberta T2P 1H1 Canada. DD 349.712306.

KEY TO NORTH YORK. (THE KEY TO NORTH YORK). VFOAT Key to North York, Directory of Community and Social Services. 1982-. 0821-0748. Periodical. CN. English. be. Link Community Information and Referral Service, 5126 Yonge Street, Willowdale Ontario M2N 5N9 Canada. DD 061.13541.

KIMBERLY DIRECTORY. AT. English. ir. Office of Regional Administration and the North West, PO Box 185, Kununurra Western Australia 6743. LC HF5293.K55. DD 338.002949414.

KIME'S INTERNATIONAL LAW DIRECTORY. VFOAT International Law Directory. Began in 1892. 0075-6040. UK. English. an. Kimes International Law Directory Ltd, 170 Sloan Street, London SW1X 9QG England. Tel 6977 3445. Ed James Matthews. DD 340.025. List of legal practitioners in principal cities throughout the world plus useful legal information for each country.

KIOPCHE YONGAM. VFOAT Korean Industry Directory. Began with Vol. for 1975. KO. Korean. an. 38.000. Kyongje Tongsinsa, 111 Chinghak-dong, Chongno-ku, Seoul South Korea. LC HC466.

KIRCHENMUSIKALISCHES JAHRBUCH. Began with 1886. 0075-6199. GW. German. an. Allgemeiner Caecilien Verband, Andreasstrasse 9, D-8400 Regensburg West Germany. Ind/Abst Music Index, RILM Abstr. *Caecilienkalendar.*

KIRCHLICHES JAHRBUCH FUR DIE EVANGELISCHE KIRCHE IN DEUTSCHLAND. GW. German. an. Guetersloher Verlagshaus, Postfach 1343/ Koenigstrasse 23-25, 4830 Guetersloh West Germany. Tel 5241/8620. Ed Wolf D Hauschild, Erwin Wilkins, Georg Kretschmar, and Eduard Lonse. LC BX8020.A2. Church annual of the Protestant church in West Germany.

KLA MEMBERSHIP DIRECTORY. (KLA ... MEMBERSHIP DIRECTORY). **Main/Corp** Kentucky Library Association. VFOAT Membership Directory. 0883-4520. US. English. Tom Sutherland, KLA Executive Secretary, 555 Washington Street, Paducah KY 42001.

KNITTING TIMES BUYERS' GUIDE DIRECTORY. US. English. an. Salzburg O Muller, 51 Madison Avenue, New York NY 10010. LC TT695. DD 338.4767702824. *Knitted Outerwear Times Buyers' Guide Directory.*

KOKU UCHU KOGYO NENKAN. VFOAT Aerospace Industry Yearbook. 1974-. JA. Japanese. ir. Nihon Koku Uchu Kogyokai, c/o Chiyda Building 1-2, Marunouchi 2-chome, Chiyoda-ku 100, Tokyo Japan. LC HD9711.5.J3. *Koku Kogyo Nenkan.*

KOLNER DOMBLATT. (KOLNER DOMBLATT; JAHRBUCH DES ZENTRAL-DOMBAUVEREINS). 0450-6413. German. ir. Ind/Abst Avery Index Archit. Period. Second Ed. Revis. Enlarged Suppl. LC NA5586.C7.

KOLNER JAHRBUCH FUR VOR- UND FRUHGESCHICHTE. 1.- Volume. 0075-6512. GW. German. ir. Gebrueder Mann Verlag, Lindenstrasse 76, D-1000 Berlin 61 West Germany. Tel 30-25913589. Ind/Abst Avery Index Archit. Period. LC DD901.C745. adv acc. Circ 800. Contributions to the prehistoric period and early history.

KONSTRUKSI: DIRECTORY PERUSAHAAN DKI JAKARTA. 1977-. IO. Indonesian. ir. Kantor Sensus dan Statistik DKI Jakarta, Jl Medan Merdeka Selatan No 8-9 Lantai XX, Jakarta Indonesia. LC TH13.2.I5.

KOREA PRODUCTS & CATALOGUES DIRECTORY. VAT Korea Products and Catalogues Directory. 1977-. English. ir. CPO Box 4890, Seoul Korea. LC HF3830.5. DD 382.450009519.

KOREAN BUSINESS DIRECTORY. 0454-4102. English. ir. Chamber of Commerce of Korea, 45 Namdaemunno 4 GA, Chung Gu Seoul Korea. LC HF3861.K8.

KOREAN CHURCH DIRECTORY OVERSEAS. VFOAT Hoeoe Hanin Kyohoe (Kidokkyo Kigwan) Chusorok. 0197-7776. US. English (Japanese). c/o Clarendon Presbyterian Church, 1305 North Jackson Street, Arlington VA 22201.

KOREAN TRADE DIRECTORY. Began in 1959. 0075-698X. KO. English. an. $35.00. Korean Trade Directory, 10-1 2KA Hoehyon-Dong Box 1117, Seoul Korea. Tel (02)771-41. Ed Duck-Woo Nam. LC HF3865. DD 380.10255195. adv acc. Circ 20,000. (ctrl). Lists of member firms and their lines of business.

KUALA LUMPUR BANKERS DIRECTORY. 1978-. MY. English. ir. $15.00. PO Box 233, Kual Lumpur 01-01 Malaysia. LC HG3300.6. DD 332.10255951.

KULTURNO POLITICKY KALENDAR. 1968-. CS. Slovak. an. LC AY829.S55. *Kulturne Politicky Kalendar.*

KUNSTHISTORISCHES JAHRBUCH GRAZ. 13-. AU. German. an. Akademische Druck U Verlagsanstalt, Neufeldweg 75 POB 598, A 8011 Graz Austria. Ind/Abst Avery Index Archit. Period., Repert. Int. Litt. Art. LC N386.G7. DD 709. *Jahrbuch des Kunsthistorischen Institutes der Universitat Graz.*

KUO WAI KUNG SSU FEN LEI CHIH NAN. VFOAT Classified International Business Directory for China. Chinese (English (1983-1984)). ir. Wen Hua Chu Pan She, 345 des Voeux Road West, Hong Kong. LC HD2709. DD 338.74025.

KYONGBUK KYOYUK TONGGYE YONBO. VFOAT Statistical Yearbook of Education. English (Korean). an. LC L614.K95. DD 370.95195.

KYONGGI KYOYUK TONGGYE YONBO. VFOAT Statistic Year Book of Gyeong Gl Education. Korean. an. LC L614.K94.

KYONGNAM KYOYUK TONGGYE YONBO. VFOAT Statistical Year Book of Gyeong Nam Education. Korean. an. LC LA1334.K93.

LABOR ARBITRATION CUMULATIVE DIGEST AND INDEX WITH CONTRACT TERMS INTERPRETED, TABLE OF CASES, DIRECTORY OF ARBITRATORS. US. English. Bureau of National Affairs Inc, 1231 25th Street Northwest, Washington DC 20037.

LABOR MARKET INFORMATION DIRECTORY FOR VIRGINIA EMPLOYMENT COMMISSION. Main/ Corp Virginia Employment Commission. 0149-9254. US. English. Virginia Employment Commission, PO Box 1358, Richmond VA 23211. LC HD5725.V8. DD 016.3311209755.

LABOR RELATIONS YEARBOOK. 1965-. 0075-7489. US. English. an. Bureau of National Affairs Inc, 1231 25th Street NW, Washington DC 20037. Tel (301)258-1033. LC HD8059. DD 331.1973.

LABOR YEAR BOOK. 1973-. 0310-5296. AT. English. an. Mass Communications Australia Pty Ltd, 377 Sussex Street, Sydney 2000 Australia. LC JQ4098.L3. DD 329.994.

LABORATORY DIRECTORY, ARTICLES OF INCORPORATION, BY-LAWS, STATEMENTS OF COMPETENCE. Main/Corp Association of Cytogenetic Technologists. 0732-8753. US. English. an. Association of Cytogenetic Technologists, Department of Pediatrics, 677-S, University of California, San Francisco CA 94143.

LABORATORY EQUIPMENT DIRECTORY. UK. English. an. 20.00. Morgan-Grampian Book Publishing Co Ltd, 30 Calderwood Street, London SE18 6QH England. Tel 01-855-7777. Ed P Brown. LC Q183.A1. DD 681.7502541. adv acc. Circ 2,000. *Laboratory Equipment Directory & Buyers Guide.*

LABORATORY EQUIPMENT DIRECTORY & BUYERS GUIDE. UK. English. an. 6.00. Gerard Mann Ltd, 1 - 3 Astoria Parade, London SW16 1PF England. LC Q183.A1. DD 338.475028.

LABRADOR WEST HAS SOMETHING FOR EVERYONE . (LABRADOR WEST HAS SOMETHING FOR EVERYONE; COMMUNITY DIRECTORY). Jan./May 1978-. 0705-6974. Periodical. CN. English. ty. Labrador City Recreation Commission, Labrador City Newfoundland Canada. DD 790.0257182.

LAGOS CITY DIRECTORY. Began with Vol. for 1967. English. ir. Lagos City Directory, PO Box 603, Lagos Nigeria. LC DT515.9.L3. DD 916.6910025.

LAMBERT'S COMMUNICATIONS DIRECTORY, WASHINGTON-BALTIMORE. VFOAT Communications Directory, Washington-Baltimore. 0741-689X. US. English. $25.00. Lambert Publications, 1000 Connecticut Avenue NW, Washington DC 20036. LC P88.8. DD 001.51025753.

LAMBERT'S WORLDWIDE DIRECTORY OF DEFENSE AUTHORITIES WITH INTERNATIONAL DEFENSE ORGANIZATIONS AND TREATIES. VFOAT Worldwide Directory of Defense Authorities with International Defense Organizations and Treaties. 1984-. US. English. an. Lambert Publications Inc, 1030 15th Street NW, Washington DC 20009.

LAMBERT'S WORLDWIDE GOVERNMENT DIRECTORY WITH INTER-GOVERNMENTAL ORGANIZATIONS. (LAMBERT'S WORLDWIDE GOVERNMENT DIRECTORY, WITH INTER-GOVERNMENTAL ORGANIZATIONS). VFOAT Worldwide Government Directory, with Inter-Governmental Organizations. 1981-. 0276-900X. US. English. an. $330.00. Lambert Publications Inc, 1030 15th Street NW/Suite 408, Washington DC 20005. Tel (202)682-1111. Ed Patrica Nelson. LC JF37. DD 351.2025. adv acc. Circ 5,000. International directory of government contacts. Covers personnel in all aspects of government in 173 countries.

LAMBTON COUNTY'S COMMUNITY SERVICE DIRECTORY. 1980-. 0711-5415. CN. English. an. Free. Lambton County Library, PO Box 100, Wyoming Ontario N0N 1T0 Canada. DD 361.002571327. (ctrl).

LANARK, LEEDS AND GRENVILLE COMMUNITY INFORMATION DIRECTORY. 1st Ed. (Jan. 1982)-. 0715-4739. Periodical. CN. English. te. $10.70 Per Vol. Lanark/ Leeds & Grenville Information Bank, Box 172, Smiths Falls Ontario K7A 4T1 Canada. DD 361.002571373.

LAND INFORMATION DIRECTORY. 1981-. AT. English. ir. Government Computing, 22 Saint George's Terrace, Perth 6000 Australia. LC HD1039.W47. DD 333.7313025941.

LAPORAN TAHUNAN. Main/Corp Indonesia. Direktorat Jenderal Perhubungan Laut. Kantor Wilayah II. Pelabuhan Dumai. 1980-. Indonesian. ir. *Laporan Tahunan.*

Yearbooks, Almanacs, Directories

LATIN AMERICA PETROLEUM DIRECTORY. VFOAT Petroleum Directory: Latin America, Latin America Directory. 1st- Ed. 0193-8738. US. English. an. $35.00. Pennwell Publishing CO, Box 1260, Tulsa OK 74101. **Tel** (918)835-3161. **Ed** William R Leek Jr. **LC** HD9574.L28. **DD** 338.272820258. Each issue contains an index to its own contents - no vol index - loose. adv acc. **Circ** 2,000.

THE LATIN AMERICAN CONSTRUCTION INDUSTRY DIRECTORY. 8756-5749. US. English. an. $180.00 Domestic, $205.00 Foreign. Aurora International, PO Box 668, Norwalk CT 06856. **Tel** (203)368-0579. adv acc. Major manufacturers, importers, exporters, distributors Latin America, Caribbean, US firms in Latin America. Firms, products cross-referenced alphabetically, geographically, SIC, BTN. Address, telephone, telex, contact, more.

THE LATIN AMERICAN INTERNATIONAL FOOD INDUSTRY DIRECTORY. 8756-5757. US. English. an. $180.00 Domestic, $205.00 Foreign. Aurora International, PO Box 668, Norwalk CT 06856. **Tel** (203)368-0579. adv acc. Major manufacturers, importers, exporters, and distributors in Latin America and the Caribbean, and US firms in Latin America. Firms and products cross-referenced alphabetically and geographically; SIC, BTN, address, telephone, telex, contact, more.

THE LATIN AMERICAN TEXTILE INDUSTRY DIRECTORY. 8756-5765. US. English. an. $180.00 Domestic, $205.00 Foreign. Aurora International, PO Box 668, Norwalk CT 06856. **Tel** (203)368-0579. adv acc. Major manufacturers, importers, exporters, distributors Latin America, Caribbean, US firms in Latin America. Firms, products cross-referenced alphabetically, geographically, SIC, BTN. Address, telephone, telex, contact, more.

THE LATIN MUSIC YEARBOOK. 1981-. 0278-7989. US. English. an. $6.50. Applause Publications, 2234 South Shady Hills Drive, Diamond Bar CA 91765. **LC** ML3486.5. **DD** 789.91361726805.

LAW ALMANAC. AT. English. Methuen Law Book Co Ltd, 35 Mitchell Street, c/o Bennett EBSCO, North Sydney New South Wales Australia.

LAW & BUSINESS DIRECTORY OF CORPORATE COUNSEL. (DIRECTORY OF CORPORATE COUNSEL). **VAT** Law and Business Directory of Corporate Counsel. 1980/81-. 0272-4065. US. English. an. $175.00. Law & Business Inc, 855 Valley Road, Clifton NJ 07013. **Tel** (201)472-7400. **Ed** Robert J Fox. **LC** KF195.C6. **DD** 340.02573. **Circ** 5,000. Directory includes coverage of corporate law departments at over 5,000 parent companies and subsidiaries. Included are listings of 25,000 attorneys with job titles and biographies, contains 1,700 pages.

LAW AND LEGAL INFORMATION DIRECTORY. 1st Ed.-. 0740-090X. US. English. ir. $260.00. Gale Research Company, Book Tower, Detroit MI 48226. **Ed** P Wasserman and S Wasserman. **NLM** KF 190 L415. Covers national and international organizations, bar associations, federal court system federal regulatory agencies, law schools, para-legal education, scholarships and grants, special libraries, research centers, legal periodical publications.

LAW ENFORCEMENT AND CRIMINAL JUSTICE EDUCATION DIRECTORY. US. English. $9.75. International Association of Chiefs of Police, 11 Firstfield Road, Gaithersburg MD 20760. **LC** HV8143. **DD** 364.071073.

LAWYER DIRECTORY (BAR ASSOCIATION OF MONTGOMERY COUNTY, MARYLAND). (LAWYER DIRECTORY). VFOAT Bar Association of Montgomery County Lawyer Directory. 0276-6108. US. English. $1.00. Lawyer Directory, 17 West Jefferson Street/Suite 105, Rockville MD 20850. **LC** KF193.M65. **DD** 349.75284025, 347.52840025.

LAWYER GUIDE & DIRECTORY, LOS ANGELES COUNTY. VFOAT Los Angeles County Lawyer Guide. 1st- Ed. US. English. Lawyer Guide & Directory Publishing Co, 7045 Hawthorne Avenue, Los Angeles CA 90028. **LC** KF193.L65. **DD** 340.02579493.

THE LAWYER'S ALMANAC. 1981-82-. 0277-9544. US. English. an. $25.00. Law & Business Inc, 757 3rd Avenue, New York NY 10017. **Tel** (201)472-7400. **LC** KF190. **DD** 349.73025, 347.30025.

LAWYERS' DESKBOOK AND DIRECTORY. Main/Corp Oregon State Bar. 1980-. 0272-9725. US. English. an. Oregon State Bar, 1776 SW Madison Street, Portland OR 97205. **Tel** (503)224-4280. **LC** KF192.O7. **DD** 349.795025, 347.950025. adv acc. **Circ** 8,000. (ctrl). Lawyers' names and addresses. Membership Directory.

LAWYERS DIARY AND MANUAL INCLUDING BAR DIRECTORY OF MASSACHUSETTS. VFOAT Massachusetts Lawyers Diary and Manual. US. English. an. $30.50. New Jersey Law Journal Publishing Co, PO Box 50, Newark NJ 07101. Massachusetts Lawyers Diary for . . . .

LAWYERS DIARY AND MANUAL INCLUDING BAR DIRECTORY OF NEW JERSEY. VFOAT Bar Directory of New Jersey. US. English. an. New York Lawyers Diary & Manual, 240 Mulberry Street, Newark NJ 07101. **LC** KF192.N4. **DD** 340.025749.

THE LEARNING RESOURCES DIRECTORY FOR HEALTHCARE EXECUTIVES : LRD. VFOAT LRD. Vol. 1 (1984-85)-. 8755-2922. Periodical. US. English. an. $115.00. ACHA, 840 North Lake Shore Drive, Chicago IL 60611. **Tel** (312)943-9544. **Ed** Lydia S Clary. **DD** 658. bk rev. **Circ** 600. A comprehensive listing of learning and informational resources for hospital and health care executives. Health care topics covered include financial management, marketing, law and ethics, etc.

LEGAL DIRECTORY FOR SOUTHERN NEVADA (THREE TIMES A YEAR). (LEGAL DIRECTORY FOR SOUTHERN NEVADA). US. English. ty. $1.00 Single Issue. Nevada Legal News, 516 South Fourth, Las Vegas NV 89101.

LEGAL DIRECTORY OF WASHINGTON STATE. 1984-. 0741-5036. US. English. an. $14.95. Vector Associates, PO Box 6215, Bellevue WA 98008. **LC** KF192.W37. **DD** 340.025797.

LEMKIVSKYJ KALENDAR. (LEMKIVS'KYI KALENDAR). VFOAT Lemko Almanac. 1965-. 0317-2910. Periodical. CN. Ukrainian. an. Organization for Defence of Lemkivshchyna, 310 Dupont Street, Toronto Ontario M5R 1V9 Canada. **DD** 971.00491791.

LEN BUCKWALTER'S NORTH AMERICAN CB CHANNEL DIRECTORY. VFOAT North American CB Channel Directory. **VAT** Len Buckwalter's North American Citizen's Band Channel Directory. 1st- Ed. US. English. an. $2.95. Grosset & Dunlap, 51 Madison Avenue, New York NY 10010. **LC** TK6570.C5. **DD** 384.53.

LESOTHO BUSINESS DIRECTORY. English. ir. AC Braby Lesotho Ltd, Business Extension Service, Department of Commerce & Industry, PO Box 747, Maseru Lesotho South Africa. **LC** HC517.L4. **DD** 380.1025686.

LESSING YEARBOOK. 1- 1969-. 0075-8833. US. English (German). an. $40.00. Wayne State University Press, 5959 Woodward Avenue, Detroit MI 48202. **Tel** (313)577-4602. **Ed** Edward P Harris and Richard Schade. **Ind/Abst** MLA Int. Bibliogr. Books Artic. Mod. Lang. Lit. **LC** PT2405.5. **DD** 838.609. bk rev. **Circ** 1,000. Devoted to studies of German culture, literature, and thought of the Eighteenth Century.

LEVNADSFORHALLANDEN ARSBOK. Series/Titl Sveriges Officiella Statistik. VFOAT Living Conditions Yearbook. 1975-. Swedish (English). an. Statistiska Centralbyran, Liber Distribution, Forlagsorder 162, 89 Vallingby Stockholm Sweden. **LC** HN572.5.

LIA MEMBERSHIP DIRECTORY & BUYERS' GUIDE. Main/Corp Long Island Association of Commerce & Industry. VFOAT L.I.A. Membership Directory and Buyers' Guide. 1982-83-. US. English. Long Island Association, 80 Hauppauge Road, Commack Long Island NY 11725. Directory of Commerce & Industry, Nassau and Suffolk Counties.

LIBER ANNUUS. Main/Corp Studium Biblicum Franciscanum. VFOAT Studii Biblici Franciscani. 1- 1950/51-. 0334-455X. Periodical. IS. Latin (English, French, German, Italian and Spanish). an. Franciscan Printing Press, PO Box 14064, Jerusalem 91140 Israel. **Tel** (02)28 65 94. **Ind/Abst** Old Testam. Abstr., New Testam. Abstr., Repert. Int. Litt. Art. **LC** BS410. (cum index). bk rev. adv acc. (ctrl). Theological, biblical, archaeological books.

THE LIBRARIES, MUSEUMS AND ART GALLERIES YEAR BOOK. UK. English. J Clarke, 1180 Avenue of the Americas, New York NY 10036. **LC** Z791.

LIBRARY DIRECTORY. Main/Corp South Central Research Library Council. 1968-. 6531-2722. US. English. South Central Research Library Council, Sheldon Court, Ithaca NY 14850.

LICENSED & CERTIFIED HEALTH CARE FACILITIES : DIRECTORY. Main/Corp Minnesota. Department of Health. Monographic Series. US. English. an. Minnesota Directory of Licensed Hospitals and Related Institutions.

THE LILY YEARBOOK OF THE NORTH AMERICAN LILY SOCIETY, INC. 0741-9910. Periodical. US. English. an. $12.50. North American Lily Society Inc, PO Box 476, Waukee IA 50263. **Tel** (515)987-1371. **Ed** John A Montgomery. **Ind/Abst** Bibliogr. Agric. **Circ** 1,475. Information on the propagation and culture of true (bulb) lilies and the research being done with them around the world. Lily Yearbook.

LINENS DOMESTICS BATH - ANNUAL DIRECTORY. US. English. an. $10.00. Columbia Communications Inc, 370 Lexington Avenue, New York NY 10017.

LINN'S U.S. STAMP YEARBOOK. (LINN'S U.S. STAMP YEARBOOK : A COMPREHENSIVE RECORD OF TECHNICAL DATA, BACKGROUND AND STORIES BEHIND ALL OF THE STAMPS . . .). VFOAT Linn's US Stamp Yearbook. 1983-. 0748-996X. US. English. an. Linn's Stamp News, PO Box 29, Sidney OH 45365. **LC** HE6185.U6. **DD** 769.56973.

LINN'S WORLD STAMP ALMANAC. 1st- Ed. 0146-6887. US. English. PO Box 129, Sidney OH 45365. **LC** HE6194. **DD** 769.56075.

LINSCOTT'S DIRECTORY OF IMMUNOLOGICAL AND BIOLOGICAL REAGENTS. VFOAT Linscott's. 3rd Ed. (1984-1985)-. US. English. be. $50.00. Linscott's Directory of Immunological & Biological Reagents, 40 Glen Drive, Mill Valley CA 94941. **Tel** (415)383-2622. **Ed** William D Linscott. adv acc. **Circ** 5,000. (ctrl). Lists sources for 20,000 reagents used in bio-medical and immunological research. world-wide in scope. Linscott's Directory (Formerly Catalog) of Immunological and Biological Reagents, 0740-7394.

LIQUEFIED GAS DIRECTORY OF AMERICA INC. WESTERN REGION. VFOAT Western Region. 8756-7091. US. English. $5.95. Liquified Gas Directory of America Inc, 1108 East 33rd South, Salt Lake City UT 84106. **LC** HD579.P43. **DD** 381.45665773.

LISTE DES MEMBRES - ASSOCIATION DES FABRICANTS DE MEUBLES DU QUEBEC. Main/Corp Association des Fabricants de Meubles du Quebec. 0318-1456. Periodical. CN. French (text in English). an. Association des Fabricants de Meubles de Quebec, CP 1002, Place Bonaventure, Montreal Quebec H5A 1E9 Canada. **DD** 338.4768410062714.

LISTING OF WOMEN'S GROUPS, CANADA. VFOAT Liste des Groupes de Femmes, Canada. 1981-. 0710-7080. Periodical. CN. French (text in English). Secretary of State, Women's Program, Ottawa Ontario K1A 0M5 Canada. **DD** 362.8302571.

LITERATURWISSENSCHAFTLICHES JAHRBUCH. 1.-9 Volume, 1926-39. 0075-997X. GW. German. an. Duncker & Humblot Verlag, Dietrich-Schaefer-Weg 9, 1000 Berlin 41 West Germany. **Tel** (030)7912026. **Ed** Kunisch, Berchem, Heftrich, Link, and Wolf. **Ind/Abst** MLA Int. Bibliogr. Books Artic. Mod. Lang. Lit., Years Work Eng. Stud. **LC** PT13. Yearbook of literary sciences.

LITURGISCHES JAHRBUCH. 1.- Yearly, 1951-. 0024-5100. Periodical. GW. German. qt. Aschendorffsche Verlagsbuchhan Dlung, Postfach 1124, 4400 Muenster West Germany. **Tel** 251/6901. **Ind/Abst** Relig. Index One, Period. (cum index). adv acc. **Circ** 1,400. Discussions of current questions of the worship service, attempts to analyze today's worship based on anthropological, historical and theological foundations, background information on liturgy and reform.

THE LIVELY ARTS INFORMATION DIRECTORY. 1st Ed. (1981)-. US. English. **Ed** Steven T Wasserman.

LIVING HISTORY OF THE WORLD; YEARBOOK. 0076-0072. US. English. an. Stravon Educational Press, 845 3rd Avenue, New York NY 10022. **Ed** G D Stoddard. **LC** D410. **DD** 905.

LIVRE DE L'ANNEE - ASSOCIATION DES HOMMES D'AFFAIRES ET PROFESSIONNELS CANADIENS-ITALIENS INC. (LIVRE DE L'ANNEE). Main/Corp Canadian Italian Business and Professional Men's Association. VFOAT Year Book. 1979/80-.

Yearbooks, Almanacs, Directories

0711-6144. CN. English (French and Italian). Canadian/Italian Business and Professional Men's Association, 892 Cremazie West, Montreal Quebec H3N 1A4 Canada. **DD** 650.06071. *Year Book, 0225-8552.*

LIVRES D'ETRENNES. VFOAT Etrennes. FR. French. ir. Cercle de la Librairie, 117 Boulevard Saint-Germain, Paris 6E France. **LC** Z2165.B58, Z6520.G4, AY16. **DD** 016.0252. *Livres d'Etrennes et Publications Periodicals.*

LLOYD'S CANADIAN CHEMICAL, PHARMACEUTICAL AND PRODUCT DIRECTORY. (LLOYD'S CANADIAN CHEMICAL, PHARMACEUTICAL, AND PRODUCT DIRECTORY). VFOAT Canadian Chemical, Pharmaceutical, and Product Directory. 0068-8452. Periodical. CN. English. an. $38.69. Sentinel Business Publications, 6420 Victoria Street/Suite 8, Montreal Quebec H3W 2S7 Canada. **Tel** (514)731-3523. **Ed** Carole Clifford. **LC** HD9655.C2. **DD** 338.4766002571. adv acc. **Circ** 5,000. (ctrl). A directory of product listings and suppliers to Canada's chemical and pharmaceutical industries. *Lloyd's Canadian Chemical Directory, 0381-5749.*

LLOYD'S CANADIAN ENGINEERING AND INDUSTRIAL YEARBOOK. (LLOYD'S CANADIAN ENGINEERING & INDUSTRIAL YEAR BOOK). Began with 1961 issue. 0068-8665. CN. English. an. 30.00. Sentinel Business Publications, 6420 Victoria Street/Suite 8, Montreal Quebec H3W 2S7 Canada. **Tel** (514)731-3523. **Ed** Carole Clifford. **DD** 338.476218. adv acc. **Circ** 9,000. (ctrl). A directory of product listing and suppliers to the engineering and general manufacturing markets. *Lloyd's Canadian Engineering & Machinery Year Book, 0456-3859.*

LLOYD'S CANADIAN FOOTWEAR AND LEATHER DIRECTORY. VAT Canadian Footwear and Leather Directory (1965). 41st- Ed. 0068-8762. CN. English. an. 27.00. Sentinel Business Publications, 6420 Victoria Street/Suite 8, Montreal Quebec H3W 2H7 Canada. **Tel** (514)731-3523. **Ed** Carola Clifford. **DD** 338.4768502571. adv acc. **Circ** 4,800. (ctrl). A directory of product listings and suppliers to the footwear and leather industries in Canada. *Willson's Canadian Footwear and Leather Directory, 0510-498X.*

LLOYD'S CANADIAN FURNITURE AND FURNISHINGS DIRECTORY. 40th ed. 0068-8789. Periodical. CN. English. an. $27.00. Sentinel Business Publications, 6420 Victoria Street/Suite 8, Montreal Quebec H3W 2S7 Canada. **Tel** (514)731-3523. **Ed** Carola Clifford. **DD** 338.47684102571. adv acc. **Circ** 6,300. (ctrl). A directory of product listings and suppliers of machinery, equipment and suppliers for the furniture manufacturing and woodworking industries. *Willson's Canadian Furniture and Furnishings Directory.*

LLOYD'S CANADIAN HARDWARE, ELECTRICAL AND BUILDING SUPPLY DIRECTORY. VFOAT Canadian Hardware, Electrical & Building Supply Directory. 0456-3867. CN. English. an. $23.21. Sentinel Business Publications, 6420 Victoria Street Suite 8, Montreal Quebec H3W 2S7 Canada. **Tel** (514)731-3523. **Ed** Carole Clifford. **LC** TS26. adv acc. **Circ** 13,000. (ctrl). Detailed product listings of companies supplying hardware, electrical, building supply retailers, wholesalers, distributors and contractors.

LLOYD'S CANADIAN JEWELLERY AND GIFTWARE DIRECTORY. 41st ed. 0068-9041. Periodical. CN. English. 27.00. Sentinel Business Publications, 6420 Victoria Street/Suite 8, Montreal Quebec H3W 2S7 Canada. **Tel** (514)731-3523. **Ed** Carola Clifford. **DD** 338.47688. adv acc. **Circ** 5,500. (ctrl). A directory of product listings and suppliers of jewelry and giftware for retailers. *Willson's Canadian Jewellery and Giftware Directory.*

LLOYD'S CANADIAN MUSIC DIRECTORY. 40th- Ed. 0381-5730. Periodical. CN. English. an. 23.21. Sentinel Business Publications, 6420 Victoria Street/Suite 8, Montreal Quebec H3W 2S7 Canada. **Tel** (514)731-3523. **Ed** Carola Clifford. **DD** 338.47681802571. adv acc. **Circ** 3,800. (ctrl). A directory of product listings and suppliers to the retail and wholesale music trade in Canada. *Willson's Canadian Music Directory.*

LLOYD'S CANADIAN TEXTILE DIRECTORY. 41st- Ed. 0068-9858. CN. English. an. $23.21. Sentinel Business Publications, 6420 Victoria Street/Suite 8, Montreal Quebec H3W 2S7 Canada. **Tel** (514)731-3523. **Ed** Carole Clifford. **DD** 338.47677. adv acc. **Circ** 4,500. (ctrl). A directory of product listing and suppliers to Canada's textile industry. *Wilson's Canadian Textile Directory.*

LLOYD'S CANADIAN VARIETY MERCHANDISE DIRECTORY. VFOAT Canadian Variety Merchandise Directory. 43rd ed. 0068-9955. Periodical. CN. English. an. $23.21. Sentinel Business Publications, 6420 Victoria Street/Suite 8, Montreal Quebec H3W 2S7 Canada. **Tel** (514)731-3523. **Ed** Carola Clifford. **DD** 338.47688. adv acc. **Circ** 3,500. (ctrl). A directory of product listings and suppliers of general merchandise for retailers. *Lloyd's Canadian Toy, Notion and Stationery Directory, 0381-5757.*

LLOYD'S MARITIME DIRECTORY. VFOAT I.S.S.D. 1982-. UK. English. an. Lloyd's of London Press Ltd, Sheepen Place Colchester, Essex CO3 3LP United Kingdom. **LC** HE951. **DD** 387.2025. *International Shipping and Shipbuilding Directory.*

LLOYD'S NAUTICAL YEAR BOOK. 1979-. UK. English. an. **LC** VK8. **DD** 623.8905. *Lloyd's Calendar.*

THE LOCAL AREA NETWORKING DIRECTORY. US. English. an. $127.00. Phillips Publishing, 7811 Montrose Road, Potomac MD 20854. **Tel** (301)340-2100. **Ed** Mark R Kimmel. **Circ** 1,000. Everything you need to know about local area networks, names, addresses and phone numbers of 500 major figures, along with detailed network profiles describing products and services.

LOCKWOOD'S DIRECTORY OF THE PAPER AND ALLIED TRADES. 1st- Ed. 0076-0277. US. English. an. $85.00 Domestic, $95.00 Foreign. Vance Publishing Corporation, 122 East 42nd Street/Room 1903, New York NY 10168. **Tel** (212)682-7777. **Ed** Harry Dyer. **LC** TS1088. **DD** 676.058. adv acc. Lists head office, statistics, products, equipment, personnel of US and Canadian pulp and paper mills, converters, merchants; buyer's guide to vendors of equipment, supplies, and services.

THE L.O.H. CENTRAL CALIFORNIA INDUSTRIAL DIRECTORY. VFOAT LOH Central California Industrial Directory. VAT Larsen, Ohlinger, Hill Central California Industrial Directory. 8756-5102. US. English. Larsen Ohlinger & Hill Inc, 2325 M Street, Box 2127, Merced CA 95340. **LC** HC107.C2. **DD** 338.740257944.

THE LONDON CHAMBER OF COMMERCE DIRECTORY. 1968-. UK. English. an. Guardian Communications Ltd, Albany House Hurst Street, Birmingham B54 4BD England. **Tel** 021-622 4011. **LC** HF302. **DD** 380.1025421. adv acc. **Circ** 13,000. General trade and commercial directory, covering commerce and industry membership in London area.

THE LONDON DIRECTORY. UK. English. an. 6.50. Kemps Group Ltd, 1-5 Bath Street, London EC1V9QA England. **LC** HC258.L6. **DD** 338.0025421. *Trades Register of London.*

THE LONDON DIRECTORY & INTERNATIONAL REGISTER OF COMMERCE. 1973-. UK. English. an. 338 Kilburn High Road, London NW6 2QR England. **LC** DA679. **DD** 338.0025421. *London Directory and International Register of Manufacturers, Wholesalers, and Shippers.*

THE LONDON DIRECTORY OF INDUSTRY AND COMMERCE. UK. English. The Kemps Group Printers & Publishers Ltd, 1-5 Bath Street, London EC1V 9QA England. **LC** HF3520.L65. **DD** 380.1025421.

LONG ISLAND ASSOCIATION DIRECTORY OF DIVERSIFIED SERVICES. 1985-1986-. 0882-3626. US. English. be. $49.95. The Long Island Association Inc, 80 Hauppauge Road, Commack Long Island NY 11725. **Tel** (516)499-4400. adv acc. **Circ** 10,000. More than 3,500 Long Island service companies listed alphabetically, geographically and by SIC code and classification. Includes names, address, phone, revenue, employees, officers, import/export, additional locations.

LONG ISLAND DIRECTORY OF MANUFACTURERS. 1981-. 0882-3618. US. English. be. $49.95. Macrae's Blue Book Inc, 817 Broadway, New York NY 10003. Each issue contains an index to its own contents - no vol index - loose.

LOS ANGELES COMMERCIAL DIRECTORY. 0736-1971. US. English. an. G A & A E Kurtz Publishers, 1902 South Pacific Avenue, San Pedro CA 90731. **LC** HF5068.L6. **DD** 333.338.

LOS ANGELES COUNTY ALMANAC; A GUIDE TO GOVERNMENT. 11th- Ed. 0092-1882. US. English. an. $20.00. Republican Central Committee, 1045 S Byran, Los Angeles CA 90015. **Tel** (213)746-2394. **Ed** Joe Irvin. **LC** JS451.C29. **DD** 352.079493. adv acc. **Circ** 5,600. (ctrl). A non-partisan guide to city, county, state and Federal government. *Los Angeles County Almanac and Buyers' Guide.*

A LOT OF BUNKUM. YEARBOOK. Vol. 1 (1980)-. 0882-2425. US. English. an. Old Buncombe County Genealogical Society, PO Box 2122, Asheville NC 28802. **LC** F262.B94. **DD** 929.1072075688.

LOUISIANA ALMANAC. US. English. be. $12.62. Pelican Publishing Co, 1101 Monroe Street, Gretna LA 70053. **Tel** (504)258-1175. **Ed** David Calhoun. Invaluable for those interested in Louisiana's government, natural resources, history, and people. With charts, maps, graphs, and tables. Over 500 pages at your fingertips. *Louisiana Almanac and Fact Book.*

LOUISIANA DIRECTORY OF CITIES, TOWNS, AND VILLAGES. VFOAT Directory of Cities, Towns, and Villages. 0741-0867. US. English. Office of Public Works, Internal Services Section, PO Box 44155, Baton Rouge LA 70804. **LC** F379.A15. **DD** 976.30025. *Directory of Louisiana Cities, Towns and Villages, 0092-0614.*

LOUISIANA DIRECTORY OF MANUFACTURERS. 1942-. Periodical. US. English. ir. $66.96. Manufacturers News Inc, 4 East Huron Street, Chicago IL 60611. **Tel** (312)337-1084. Lists address, zip, phone, year established, chief officer, purchasing agent, and number of employees. 546 pages.

LOUISIANA INTERNATIONAL TRADE DIRECTORY. 1st- ed. 0147-4464. US. English. $25.00. International Marketing Institute, University of New Orleans, Lake Front, New Orleans LA 70122. **Tel** (504)286-6963. **Ed** Thomas S O'Connor. **LC** HF5065.L8. **DD** 382.025763. adv acc. **Circ** 2,500. (ctrl). We publish a directory of Louisiana based manufacturers, importers, exporters, and others involved in international trade.

THE LOUISIANA LEGAL DIRECTORY. (THE LOUISIANA LEGAL DIRECTORY : OFFICIAL DIRECTORY OF THE LOUISIANA STATE BAR ASSOCIATION). 1980-. 0278-4734. US. English. an. Legal Directories Pub Co Inc, 700 Campbell Centre/PO Box 64805, Dallas TX 75206. **LC** KF192.L8. **DD** 349.763025, 347.630025. *Arkansas, Louisiana, and Mississippi Legal Directory.*

LOUISIANA PLANNING DIRECTORY. 1976-. 0148-6160. US. English. be. Louisiana State Planning Office, 4528 Bennington Avenue, Baton Rouge LA 70803. **LC** JK4730. **DD** 353.9763002.

LOUISVILLE AREA DIRECTORY OF MANUFACTURERS. US. English. Research Department, Louisville Area Chamber of Commerce, 300 West Liberty Street, Louisville KY 40202.

LOWER BUCKS COUNTY REAL ESTATE DIRECTORY. 0146-3438. US. English. Philadelphia Real Estate Directories Inc, 1010 Arch Street, Philadelphia PA 19107. **LC** HD266.P4. **DD** 333.33.

LUDAS MATYI EVKONYVE. HU. Hungarian. ir. Hirlapkiado Vallalat, Budapest VIII/Gyulai Palu 14, Budapest Hungary. **LC** AY814.

LUFTFARTSVERKET : ARBOK. Main/Corp Norway. Luftfartsverket. 1982-. English (Norwegian). an. Luftfartsverket, Storgt 10, Oslo 1 Norway. **Tel** (02)429280. **Ed** Elsc Frisell. **Circ** 4,000. *Luftfartsverkets Arbok.*

LUSK'S ANNE ARUNDEL COUNTY REAL ESTATE DIRECTORY, PROPERTY TRANSFERS. 0099-1686. US. English. R S Lusk, 1824-26 Jefferson Place Northwest, Washington DC 20036. **LC** HD266.M3. **DD** 333.33.

LUSK'S BALTIMORE COUNTY REAL ESTATE DIRECTORY, PROPERTY TRANSFERS. 0099-104X. US. English. R S Lusk, 1824 Jefferson Place Northwest, Washington DC 20036. **LC** HD266.M3. **DD** 333.3302575271.

Yearbooks, Almanacs, Directories

LUSK'S CARROLL COUNTY REAL ESTATE DIRECTORY. 0360-0874. US. English. R S Lusk, 1824 Jefferson Place Northwest, Washington DC 20036. LC HD266.M3. DD 333.33.

LUSK'S DISTRICT OF COLUMBIA REAL ESTATE DIRECTORY SERVICE. VFOAT District of Columbia Real Estate Directory Service. 0196-4119. US. English. an. LC HD268.W3. DD 333.337025753. *Lusk's District of Columbia Assessment Directory Service.*

LUSK'S EAST SUFFOLK COUNTY REAL ESTATE DIRECTORY. 0363-0668. US. English. R S Lusk, 1824 Jefferson Place Northwest, Washington DC 20036. LC HD266.N72. DD 333.33.

LUSK'S FAIRFAX COUNTY, VIRGINIA REAL ESTATE DIRECTORY SERVICE. VFOAT Fairfax County, Virginia Real Estate Directory Service. 1930. 0197-0305. US. English. qt. $400.00. Rufus S Lusk and Son Inc, 1824 Jefferson Place Northwest, Washington DC 20036. Tel (202)331-9696. Ed Rufus S Lusk III. LC HD266.V82. DD 333.305875529. We publish real estate information for the Washington metropolitan areas, Baltimore and surrounding counties.

LUSK'S MONTGOMERY COUNTY, MARYLAND, ASSESSMENT DIRECTORY. VFOAT Montgomery County, Maryland, Assessment Directory. 0557-4447. US. English. $400.00. R S Lusk, 1824 Jefferson Place Northwest, Washington DC 20036. Tel (202)331-9696. Ed Rufus S Lusk III. LC HJ9253.M65. DD 336.2202575284. We publish real estate information for the Washington metropolitan areas, Baltimore and surrounding counties.

LUSK'S PRINCE WILLIAM COUNTY REAL ESTATE DIRECTORY SERVICE. 0094-8713. US. English. ir. $400.00. R S Lusks & Sons Inc c/o Burns, 1824-26 Jefferson Place NW, Washington DC 20036. Tel (202)331-9696. Ed Rufus S Lusk III. LC HD266.V82. DD 333.33025755273. adv acc. We publish real estate information for the Washington metro area, Baltimore and surrounding counties, New York, Richmond and New Orleans.

LUTHERAN CHURCH DIRECTORY FOR THE UNITED STATES. 1971-. 0363-4051. US. English. ir. $3.00. Lutheran Council in the USA, 360 Park Avenue South, New York NY 10010. Tel (212)532-6350. Ed Benjamin A Bankson. LC BX8009. DD 284.102573. Circ 25,000. (ctrl). The directory contains a state-by-state listing of the names and addresses of all US Lutheran congregations and Inter-Lutheran organizations. *Lutheran Church Directory for the United States and Canada, 0460-0096.*

LYCHNOS : LARDOMSHISTORISKA SAMFUNDETS ARSBOK. VFOAT Annual of the Swedish History of Science Society. 1936-. 0076-1648. SW. the contributions are chiefly in Swedish, with occasional articles in English, French, or German, and summary in one of these languages for each of the Swedish papers. ir. 80. Laerdomshistoriska Samfundetid, Labygatan 24, S-752 39 Uppsala Sweden. Tel 0171/76089. Ed Gunnar Eriksson. LC Q64. NLM W1 LY51E. bk rev. Circ 2,000. Yearbook devoted to history of science; ideas and general culture.

LYNX JAHRBUCH. German. ir. 10.00. Club Lynx, Hallerplatz 14/11, Hamburg West Germany. LC AY18.

MCCA CORRECTIONS DIRECTORY. US. English. MCCA Corrections Directory, 1025 Portland, Minneapolis MN 55404.

MCD. MIDDLE ATLANTIC EDITION. (MCD). VFOAT M.C.D. VAT Motor Carrier Directory. Middle Atlantic Edition. 0733-6012. US. English. an. $40.00 single issue. American Motor Carrier Directory, PO Box 720455, Atlanta GA 30328.

MCD WAREHOUSING DISTRIBUTION DIRECTORY. VFOAT Warehousing Distribution Directory. US. English. an. $51.50. American Motor Carrier, PO Box 720455, Atlanta GA 30328. Tel (404)955-3000. LC HF5415.6. DD 381.02573. *National Distribution Directory of Local Cartage-Short Haul Carriers Warehousing, 0364-9539.*

MCGRAW-HILL YEARBOOK OF SCIENCE AND TECHNOLOGY. VFOAT Yearbook of Science and Technology. 1962-. 0076-2016. US. English. an. $45.96. McGraw Hill, PO Box 404, Hightstown NJ 08520. LC Q121. DD 505. NLM Q 121 M1471. (cum index).

MACHINE AND TOOL DIRECTORY. V. 1- 1952-. US. English. an. $30.00. Hitchcock Publication Company, Hitchcock Building, Wheaton IL 60188. Tel (312)665-1000. LC TJ1180.A1. DD 621.90202573.

MACRAE'S ALABAMA STATE INDUSTRIAL DIRECTORY. VFOAT Alabama State Industrial Directory. 0733-5016. US. English. an. Macraes Blue Book, 817 Broadway, New York NY 10003. Tel 800 622 7237. LC HD9727.A35. DD 338.0025761. *Alabama State Industrial Directory, 0161-8563.*

MACRAE'S ARKANSAS STATE INDUSTRIAL DIRECTORY. VFOAT Arkansas State Industrial Directory. 1982-. 0732-6351. US. English. an. Macraes Blue Book, 817 Broadway, New York NY 10003. Tel (212)673-4700. Ed Harry P Dedyo. LC HD9727.A8. adv acc. Listings and important facts about manufacturing firms in Arkansas. *Arkansas State Industrial Directory, 0197-3800.*

MACRAE'S CALIFORNIA STATE INDUSTRIAL DIRECTORY. VFOAT California State Industrial Directory. 1982-. 0195-7090. US. English. an. Macrae's Blue Book, 817 Broadway, New York NY 10003. Tel (800)622-7237. LC HD9727.C2. DD 338.0025794.

MACRAE'S CONNECTICUT STATE INDUSTRIAL DIRECTORY. VFOAT Connecticut State Industrial Directory. 1981-. 0732-8672. US. English. an. Macraes Blue Book, 817 Broadway, New York NY 10003. Tel (212)673-4700. Ed Harry P Dedyo. LC T12. DD 338.4767025746. adv acc. Listings and descriptions of manufacturing firms in Connecticut. *Connecticut State Industrial Directory, 0098-6186.*

MACRAE'S DIRECTORY OF FIRMS MARKETING THROUGH MANUFACTURERS' REPRESENTATIVES. VFOAT Directory of Firms Marketing through Manufacturers' Representatives. 15th ed.-. 0749-1093. US. English. an. Macraes Blue Book Inc, 817 Broadway, New York NY 10003. Tel (212)673-4700. Ed Harry P Dedyo. adv acc. Nine thousand manufacturers of industrial and consumer products who market through representatives. *Macrae's Manufacturers' Agents' Guide, 0737-4372.*

MACRAE'S FLORIDA STATE INDUSTRIAL DIRECTORY. VFOAT Florida State Industrial Directory. 1982-. 0733-5008. US. English. ir. Macraes Blue Book, 817 Broadway, New York NY 10003. Tel (212)673-4700. Ed Harry P Dedyo. LC HD9727.F6. DD 338.0025759. adv acc. Listings and important facts about manufacturing firms in Florida. *Florida State Industrial Directory, 0163-4712.*

MACRAE'S GEORGIA STATE INDUSTRIAL DIRECTORY. VFOAT Georgia State Industrial Directory. US. English. an. Macraes Blue Book, 817 Broadway, New York NY 10003.

MACRAE'S IDAHO STATE INDUSTRIAL DIRECTORY. VFOAT Idaho State Industrial Directory. 1982-. 0732-4200. US. English. an. Macraes Blue Book Inc, 817 Broadway, New York NY 10003. LC HD9727.I2. DD 338.0025796.

MACRAE'S ILLINOIS STATE INDUSTRIAL DIRECTORY. VFOAT Illinois State Industrial Directory. 1982-. 0731-521X. US. English. an. Macraes Blue Book, 817 Broadway, New York NY 10003. Tel (212)673-4700. Ed Harry P Dedyo. LC HD9727.I3. DD 338.0025773. adv acc. Listings and important facts about manufacturing firms in Illinois.

MACRAE'S INDIANA STATE INDUSTRIAL DIRECTORY. VFOAT Indiana State Industrial Directory. 1981-. 0733-4168. US. English. an. Macraes Blue Book, 817 Broadway, New York NY 10003. Tel (212)673-4700. Ed Harry P Dedyo. LC HD9727.I6. DD 338.0025772. adv acc. Listings and important facts about industrial firms in Indiana. *Indiana State Industrial Directory, 0190-1362.*

MACRAE'S INDUSTRIAL DIRECTORY. 92 Ed. (1985)-. 0749-5986. US. English. an. Macraes Blue Book Inc, 817 Broadway, New York NY 10003. DD 338. *Macrae's Blue Book, 0076-2067.*

MACRAE'S INDUSTRIAL DIRECTORY. ALABAMA. VFOAT Alabama. 1984-. 0740-431X. US. English. an. $70.00. Macraes Blue Book Inc, 817 Broadway, New York NY 10003. LC HD9727.A35. DD 338.0025761. *Macrae's Alabama State Industrial Directory, 0733-5016.*

MACRAE'S INDUSTRIAL DIRECTORY ARIZONA, NEW MEXICO. 1984-. 0739-8476. US. English. an. Macraes Blue Book, 817 Broadway, New York NY 10003. Tel (21)673-4700. Ed Harry P Dedyo. adv acc. Listings and important facts about manufacturing firms in Arizona and New Mexico. *Macrae's Arizona State Industrial Directory, 0731-6704; Macrae's New Mexico State Industrial Directory, 0275-1836.*

MACRAE'S INDUSTRIAL DIRECTORY. ARKANSAS. VFOAT Industrial Directory. 1985-. 0740-4670. US. English. an. $85.00. Macraes Blue Book Inc, 817 Broadway, New York NY 10003. LC HD9727.A8. DD 338.0025767. *Macrae's Arkansas State Industrial Directory, 0732-6351.*

MACRAE'S INDUSTRIAL DIRECTORY. CALIFORNIA. VFOAT California. 1985-. 0740-4638. US. English. an. Macraes Blue Book Inc, 817 Broadway, New York NY 10003. LC HD9727.C2. DD 338.0025794. *Macrae's California State Industrial Directory, 0195-7090.*

MACRAE'S INDUSTRIAL DIRECTORY. COLORADO, UTAH, NEVADA. VFOAT Colorado, Utah, Nevada. 1985-. 0740-6126. US. English. an. $95.00. Macraes Blue Book Inc, 817 Broadway, New York NY 10003. LC HC107.C7. DD 338.002579. *Macrae's Colorado State Industrial Directory, 0732-4197; Macrae's Utah State Industrial Directory, 0733-446X; Macrae's Nevada State Industrial Directory, 0734-015X.*

MACRAE'S INDUSTRIAL DIRECTORY CONNECTICUT. (MACRAE'S INDUSTRIAL DIRECTORY. CONNECTICUT). VFOAT Connecticut. 1984-. 0740-2937. US. English. an. Macraes Blue Book Inc, 817 Broadway, New York NY 10003. LC T12. DD 670.294746. *Macrae's Connecticut State Industrial Directory, 0732-8672.*

MACRAE'S INDUSTRIAL DIRECTORY. FLORIDA. VFOAT Industrial Directory. 1985-. 0740-4697. US. English. an. $85.00. Macraes Blue Book Inc, 817 Broadway, New York NY 10003. LC HD9727.F6. DD 338.0025759. *Macrae's Florida State Industrial Directory, 0733-5008.*

MACRAE'S INDUSTRIAL DIRECTORY. GEORGIA. VFOAT Georgia. 1984-. 0740-2910. US. English. an. Macraes Blue Book Inc, 817 Broadway, New York NY 10003. LC HD9727.G4. DD 338.0025758. *Macrae's Georgia State Industrial Directory, 0733-4982.*

MACRAE'S INDUSTRIAL DIRECTORY. ILLINOIS. 1984-. 0740-4336. US. English. an. $97.00. Macraes Blue Book Inc, 817 Broadway, New York NY 10003. LC HD9727.I3. DD 338.0025773. *Macrae's Illinois State Industrial Directory, 0731-521X.*

MACRAE'S INDUSTRIAL DIRECTORY. INDIANA. VFOAT Industrial Directory. 1985-. 0740-6045. US. English. an. $85.00. Macraes Blue Book Inc, 817 Broadway, New York NY 10003. LC HD9727.I6. DD 338.0025772. *MacRae's Indiana State Industrial Directory, 0733-4168.*

MACRAE'S INDUSTRIAL DIRECTORY. IOWA, NEBRASKA. 1984-. 0740-428X. US. English. an. $90.00. Macraes Blue Book Inc, 817 Broadway, New York NY 10003. Ed Harry P Dedyo. LC HD9727.I8. DD 338.0025777. adv acc. Listings and important facts about manufacturing firms in Iowa and Nebraska. *Macrae's Iowa State Industrial Directory, 0732-4170; Macrae's Nebraska State Industrial Directory, 0731-6720.*

MACRAE'S INDUSTRIAL DIRECTORY. KANSAS. VFOAT Industrial Directory. 1985-. 0740-6118. US. English. an. $85.00. Macraes Blue Book Inc, 817 Broadway, New York NY 10003. LC HD9727.K2. DD 338.0025781. *Macrae's Kansas State Industrial Directory, 0732-636X.*

MACRAE'S INDUSTRIAL DIRECTORY. LOUISIANA. 1984-. 0740-4301. US. English. an. Macraes Blue Book Inc, 817 Broadway, New York NY 10003. LC T12. DD 338.4767025763. *Macrae's Louisiana State Industrial Directory, 0733-3234.*

MACRAE'S INDUSTRIAL DIRECTORY. MAINE, NEW HAMPSHIRE, VERMONT. 1984-. 0740-2945. US. English. an. Macraes Blue Book Inc, 817 Broadway, New York NY 10003. *Macrae's Maine State Industrial Directory,*

Yearbooks, Almanacs, Directories

0731-6739; Macraes' New Hampshire State Industrial Directory, 0733-4974; Macraes' Vermont Industrial Directory, 0731-6747.

MACRAE'S INDUSTRIAL DIRECTORY. MARYLAND, D.C., DELAWARE. 1984-. 0740-2929. US. English. an. $70.00. Macraes Blue Book Inc, 817 Broadway, New York NY 10003. LC T12 .3.M3. DD 670.294752. Macrae's Maryland State Industrial Directory, 0732-9695; Macrae's Delaware State Industrial Directory, 0733-2947.

MACRAE'S INDUSTRIAL DIRECTORY. MASSACHUSETTS, RHODE ISLAND. VFOAT Massachusetts, Rhode Island. 1985-. 0740-4689. US. English. an. $97.00. Macraes Blue Book Inc, 817 Broadway, New York NY 10003. LC HD9727.M4. DD 338.0025744. Macrae's Massachusetts State Industrial Directory, 0732-1112; Macrae's Rhode Island State Industrial Directory, 0733-4451.

MACRAE'S INDUSTRIAL DIRECTORY. MICHIGAN. VFOAT Michigan. 1985-. 0740-6096. US. English. an. Macraes Blue Book Inc, 817 Broadway, New York NY 10003. LC HD9727.M5. DD 338.0025774. Macrae's Michigan State Industrial Directory, 0733-4958.

MACRAE'S INDUSTRIAL DIRECTORY. MINNESOTA. VFOAT Minnesota. 1985-. 0740-6061. US. English. an. $65.00. Macraes Blue Book Inc, 817 Broadway, New York NY 10003. LC HD9727.M6. DD 338.0025776. Macrae's Minnesota State Industrial Directory, 0732-9687.

MACRAE'S INDUSTRIAL DIRECTORY. MISSISSIPPI. VFOAT Mississippi. 1985-. 0740-4654. US. English. an. Macraes Blue Book, 817 Broadway, New York NY 10003. LC HD9727.M7. DD 338.0025762. Macrae's Mississippi State Industrial Directory, 0733-4591.

MACRAE'S INDUSTRIAL DIRECTORY. MISSOURI. VFOAT Industrial Directory. 1985-. 0740-607X. US. English. an. $85.00. Macraes Blue Book Inc, 817 Broadway, New York NY 10003. LC HC107.M8. DD 338.0025778. MacRae's Missouri State Industrial Directory, 0275-1828.

MACRAE'S INDUSTRIAL DIRECTORY NEW JERSEY. 1984-. 0739-8492. US. English. an. $97.00. Macraes Industrial Directories, 817 Broadway, New York NY 10003. LC HC107.N5. DD 380.10294749. Macrae's New Jersey State Industrial Directory, 0733-3684.

MACRAE'S INDUSTRIAL DIRECTORY NEW YORK STATE. (MACRAE'S INDUSTRIAL DIRECTORY. NEW YORK STATE). VFOAT Industrial Directory New York State. 1984-. 0740-2953. US. English. an. $110.00 Hardbound, $97.00 Softbound. Macraes Blue Book Inc, 817 Broadway, New York NY 10003. LC HC107.N7. DD 338.0025747. Macrae's New York State Industrial Directory, 0733-3552.

MACRAE'S INDUSTRIAL DIRECTORY NORTH CAROLINA. 1984-. 0739-845X. US. English. an. Macraes Industrial Directories, 817 Broadway, New York NY 10003. LC HC107.N8. DD 338.0025756. Macrae's North Carolina State Industrial Directory, 0733-4966.

MACRAE'S INDUSTRIAL DIRECTORY. OHIO. 1985-. 0740-6037. US. English. an. $99.00. Macraes Blue Book Inc, 817 Broadway, New York NY 10003. DD 338. Macrae's Ohio State Industrial Directory, 0733-4176.

MACRAE'S INDUSTRIAL DIRECTORY. OKLAHOMA. VFOAT Industrial Directory. 1985-. 0740-4662. US. English. an. Macraes Blue Book Inc, 817 Broadway, New York NY 10003. LC HC107.O5. DD 338.0025766. Macrae's Oklahoma State Industrial Directory, 0197-3819.

MACRAE'S INDUSTRIAL DIRECTORY. OREGON. VFOAT Oregon. 1985-. 0740-610X. US. English. an. $70.00. Macraes Blue Book Inc, 817 Broadway, New York NY 10003. LC HD9727.O7. DD 338.0025795. Macrae's Oregon State Industrial Directory, 0733-4990.

MACRAE'S INDUSTRIAL DIRECTORY. PENNSYLVANIA. VFOAT Pennsylvania. 1984-. 0740-4298. US. English. an. $97.00. Macraes Blue Book Inc, 817 Broadway, New York NY 10003. LC HC107.P4. DD 338.0025748. Macrae's Pennsylvania State Industrial Directory, 0732-1104.

MACRAE'S INDUSTRIAL DIRECTORY SOUTH CAROLINA. 1984-. 0739-8441. US. English. an. $58.75 U.S., $61.25 Foreign. Macraes Blue Book Inc, 817 Broadway, New York NY 10003. LC HD9727.S6. DD 380.10294757. Macrae's South Carolina State Industrial Directory, 0733-4931.

MACRAE'S INDUSTRIAL DIRECTORY. TENNESSEE. VFOAT Tennessee. 1985-. 0740-4646. US. English. an. Macraes Blue Book Inc, 817 Broadway, New York NY 10003. LC HD9727.T2. DD 338.0025768. Macrae's Tennessee State Industrial Directory, 0733-494X.

MACRAE'S INDUSTRIAL DIRECTORY TEXAS. 1984-. 0739-8484. US. English. an. Macraes Industrial Directories, 817 Broadway, New York NY 10003. LC HD9727.T4. DD 338.0025764. Macrae's Texas State Industrial Directory, 0731-5228.

MACRAE'S INDUSTRIAL DIRECTORY. VIRGINIA. VFOAT Virginia. 1984-. 0740-2902. US. English. an. $70.00. Macraes Blue Book Inc, 817 Broadway, New York NY 10003. LC HD9727.V8. DD 338.0025755. Macrae's Virginia State Industrial Directory, 0732-4154.

MACRAE'S INDUSTRIAL DIRECTORY. WASHINGTON STATE. 1985-. 0740-6134. US. English. an. $85.00. Macraes Blue Book Inc, 817 Broadway, New York NY 10003. DD 338. Macrae's Washington State Industrial Directory, 0275-1844.

MACRAE'S INDUSTRIAL DIRECTORY. WISCONSIN. VFOAT Industrial Directory. 1985-. 0740-6053. US. English. an. $85.00. Macraes Blue Book Inc, 817 Broadway, New York NY 10003. LC HD9727.W6. DD 338.0025775. Macrae's Wisconsin State Industrial Directory, 0734-4554.

MACRAE'S KANSAS STATE INDUSTRIAL DIRECTORY. VFOAT Kansas State Industrial Directory. 1982-. 0732-636X. US. English. an. Macraes Blue Book Inc, 817 Broadway, New York NY 10003. Tel (212)673-4700. Ed Harry P Dedyo. LC HD9727.K2. DD 338.0025781. adv acc. Listings and important facts about manufacturing firms in Kansas. Kansas State Industrial Directory, 0197-3843.

MACRAE'S KENTUCKY STATE INDUSTRIAL DIRECTORY. 0733-5024. US. English. an. Macraes Blue Book Inc, 817 Broadway, New York NY 10003. Tel (502)564-4886. LC HD9727.K4. DD 338.0025769. Kentucky State Industrial Directory, 0190-1354.

MACRAE'S LOUISIANA STATE INDUSTRIAL DIRECTORY. VFOAT Louisiana State Industrial Directory. 1981-. 0733-3234. US. English. an. Macraes Blue Book Inc, 817 Broadway, New York NY 10003. Tel (212)673-4700. Ed Harry P Dedyo. LC T12. DD 338.0025763. adv acc. Listings and important facts about manufacturing firms in Louisiana. Louisiana State Industrial Directory, 0190-129X.

MACRAE'S MARYLAND STATE INDUSTRIAL DIRECTORY. VFOAT Maryland State Industrial Directory. 0732-9695. US. English. an. Macrae's Blue Book Inc, 817 Broadway, New York NY 10003. Tel (800)622-7237. LC HD9727.M3. DD 338.0025752. Maryland State Industrial Directory, 0148-5660.

MACRAE'S MICHIGAN STATE INDUSTRIAL DIRECTORY. VFOAT Michigan State Industrial Directory. 0733-4958. US. English. an. Macraes Blue Book Inc, 817 Broadway, New York NY 10003. Tel (212)673-4700. Ed Harry P Dedyo. LC HD9727.M5. DD 338.0025774. adv acc. Listings and important facts about manufacturing firms in Michigan. Michigan State Industrial Directory, 0190-1338.

MACRAE'S MINNESOTA STATE INDUSTRIAL DIRECTORY. VFOAT Minnesota State Industrial Directory. 0732-9687. US. English. an. Macraes Blue Book Inc, 817 Broadway, New York NY 10003. Tel (212)673-4700. Ed Harry P Dedyo. LC HD9727.M6. DD 338.0025776. adv acc. Listings and important facts about manufacturing firms in Minnesota. Minnesota State Industrial Directory, 0195-7112.

MACRAE'S MISSISSIPPI STATE INDUSTRIAL DIRECTORY. VFOAT Mississippi State Industrial Directory. 1981-. 0733-4591. US. English. an. Macrae's Blue Book, 817 Broadway, New York NY 10003. Tel (800)622-7237. LC HD9727.M7. DD 338.0025762. Mississippi State Industrial Directory, 0190-1346.

MACRAE'S MISSOURI STATE INDUSTRIAL DIRECTORY. VFOAT Missouri State Industrial Directory. 1982-. 0275-1828. US. English. an. Macraes Blue Book, 817 Broadway, New York NY 10003. Tel (212)673-4700. Ed Harry P Dedyo. LC HC107.M8. DD 338.0025778. adv acc. Listings of and important facts about manufacturing firms in Missouri.

MACRAE'S MONTANA STATE INDUSTRIAL DIRECTORY. VFOAT Montana State Industrial Directory. 1982-. 0732-4189. US. English. an. $43.50. Macraes Blue Book Inc, 817 Broadway, New York NY 10003. LC HC107.M9. DD 338.0025786. Montana State Industrial Directory, 0195-7120.

MACRAE'S NEBRASKA STATE INDUSTRIAL DIRECTORY. VFOAT Nebraska State Industrial Directory. 1982-. 0731-6720. US. English. an. Macraes Blue Book Inc, 817 Broadway, New York NY 10003. Tel (800) 622 7237. LC HD9727.N2. DD 338.0025782. Nebraska State Industrial Directory, 0197-3835.

MACRAE'S NEW JERSEY STATE INDUSTRIAL DIRECTORY. VFOAT New Jersey State Industrial Directory. 1982-. 0733-3684. US. English. an. Macraes Blue Book Inc, 817 Broadway, New York NY 10003. Tel (212)673-4700. Ed Harry P Dedyo. LC HC107.N5. DD 380.10294749. adv acc. Listings and important facts about manufacturing firms in New Jersey. New Jersey State Industrial Directory, 0098-6224.

MACRAE'S NEW YORK STATE INDUSTRIAL DIRECTORY. VFOAT New York State Industrial Directory. 1982-. 0733-3552. US. English. an. Macraes Blue Book Inc, 817 Broadway, New York NY 10003. Tel (212)673-4700. Ed Harry P Dedyo. LC HC107.N7. DD 380.145000294747. adv acc. Listings and important facts about manufacturing firms in New York. New York State Industrial Directory, 0548-9067.

MACRAE'S NORTH CAROLINA STATE INDUSTRIAL DIRECTORY. VFOAT North Carolina State Industrial Directory. 1982-. 0733-4966. US. English. an. Macraes Blue Book Inc, 817 Broadway, New York NY 10003. Tel (212)673-4700. Ed Harry P Dedyo. LC HD9727.N8. DD 338.0025756. adv acc. Listings and important facts about manufacturing firms in North Carolina. North Carolina State Industrial Directory, 0161-4738.

MACRAE'S OKLAHOMA STATE INDUSTRIAL DIRECTORY. VFOAT Oklahoma State Industrial Directory. 1982-. 0197-3819. US. English. an. Macraes Blue Book Inc, 817 Broadway, New York NY 10003. Tel (212)673-4700. Ed Harry P Dedyo. LC HC107.O5. DD 338.0025766. adv acc. Listings of and important facts about manufacturing firms in Oklahoma.

MACRAE'S OREGON STATE INDUSTRIAL DIRECTORY. VFOAT Oregon State Industrial Directory. 0733-4990. US. English. an. Macraes Blue Book Inc, 817 Broadway, New York NY 10003. Tel (212)673-4700. Ed Harry P Dedyo. LC HD9727.O7. DD 338.0025795. adv acc. Listing and important facts about manufacturing firms in Oregon. Oregon State Industrial Directory, 0195-7147.

MACRAE'S PENNSYLVANIA STATE INDUSTRIAL DIRECTORY. VFOAT Pennsylvania State Industrial Directory. 1981-. 0732-1104. US. English. an. Macraes Blue Book Inc, 817 Broadway, New York NY 10003. Tel (212)673-4700. Ed Harry P Dedyo. LC HC107.P4. DD 338.0025748. adv acc. Listings and descriptions of manufacturing firms in Pennsylvania. Pennsylvania State Industrial Directory, 0553-6065.

MACRAE'S SOUTH CAROLINA STATE INDUSTRIAL DIRECTORY. VFOAT South Carolina State Industrial Directory. 1982-. 0733-4931. US. English. an. $47.00. Macraes Blue Book Inc, 817 Broadway, New York NY 10003. Tel (312)337-1084. LC HD9727.S6. DD 380.10294757. adv acc. Consists of alphabetical, geographical, SIC sections, index of cities and towns, name of company, address, phone number, total employees, officers, products, importers and exporters. South Carolina State Industrial Directory, 0162-0878.

MACRAE'S STATE INDUSTRIAL DIRECTORY. NORTH CAROLINA, SOUTH CAROLINA, VIRGINIA. 0888-3793. US. English. ir. Macres Blue Book Inc, 817 Broadway, New York NY 10003. Macrae's Industrial Directory, North Carolina, 0739-845X; Macrae's Industrial Directory, South Carolina, 0739-8441; Macrae's Industrial Directory, Virginia, 0740-2902.

MACRAE'S TENNESSEE STATE INDUSTRIAL DIRECTORY. VFOAT Tennessee State Industrial Directory. 1981-. 0733-494X. US. English. an. Macrae's Blue Book Inc,

Yearbooks, Almanacs, Directories

817 Broadway, New York NY 10003. **Tel** (800)622-7237. **LC** HD9727.T2. **DD** 338.0025768. *Tennessee State Industrial Directory, 0190-1311.*

MACRAE'S TEXAS STATE INDUSTRIAL DIRECTORY. VFOAT Texas State Industrial Directory. 1982-. 0731-5228. US. English. an. Macraes Blue Book Inc, 817 Broadway, New York NY 10003. **Tel** (212)673-4700. **Ed** Harry P Dedyo. **LC** HD9727.T4. **DD** 338.0025764. adv acc. Listings and important facts about manufacturing firms in Texas.

MACRAE'S VERIFIED DIRECTORY OF MANUFACTURERS' REPRESENTATIVES. VFOAT Verified Directory of Manufacturers' Representatives. 1984-. 0738-4599. US. English. be. $75.00. Macrae's Blue Book Inc, 817 Broadway, New York NY 10003. **Tel** (800)622-7237. **Ed** Teresa Schnabel. **LC** HD9723. **DD** 381.02573. Lists over 15,000 top manufacturers' representatives, organized both geographically and by product lines. *Verified Directory of Manufacturers' Representatives (Agents).*

MACRAE'S VIRGINIA STATE INDUSTRIAL DIRECTORY. VFOAT Virginia State Industrial Directory. 1982-. 0732-4154. US. English. an. Macraes Blue Book Inc, 817 Broadway, New York NY 10003. **Tel** 800 622 7237. **LC** HD9727.V8. **DD** 338.0025755. *Virginia State Industrial Directory, 0190-132X.*

MACRAE'S WASHINGTON STATE INDUSTRIAL DIRECTORY. VFOAT Washington State Industrial Directory. 1982-1984. 0275-1844. US. English. ir. Macraes Blue Book Inc, 817 Broadway, New York NY 10003. **Tel** (212)673-4700. **Ed** Harry P Dedyo. **LC** HD9727.W2. **DD** 338.0025797. adv acc. Listings and important facts about manufacturing firms in Washington State.

MACRAE'S WISCONSIN STATE INDUSTRIAL DIRECTORY. VFOAT Wisconsin State Industrial Directory. 1981-. 0734-4554. Periodical. US. English. an. Macraes Blue Book Inc, 817 Broadway, New York NY 10003. **Tel** (212)673-4700. **Ed** Harry P Dedyo. **LC** HD9727.W6. **DD** 338.0025775. adv acc. Listings and important facts about manufacturing firms in Wisconsin. *Wisconsin State Industrial Directory, 0195-7155.*

MACRAE'S WYOMING STATE INDUSTRIAL DIRECTORY. VFOAT Wyoming State Industrial Directory. 1982-. 0275-1852. US. English. an. $35.00. Macraes Blue Book Inc, 817 Broadway, New York NY 10003. **Ed** Harry P Dedyo. **LC** HD9727.W8. **DD** 338.0025787. adv acc. Listings and important facts about manufacturing firms in Wyoming.

MADISON'S CANADIAN LUMBER DIRECTORY. Began publication with 1952 issue. 0316-6414. Periodical. CN. English. an. Madisons Canadian Lumber Directory, PO Box 2486, Vancouver British Columbia V6B 3W7 Canada. **Tel** 604 681-6838. **Ed** Laurence Cater. **DD** 338.4767402571. bk rev. adv acc. A single authoritative guide to Canada's lumber industry. Includes wholesalers, lumber and plywood manufacturers, wood preservers, remanufacturers, statistics, price graphs, personnel and a mill product guide.

THE MAGIC DIRECTORY. (THE . . . MAGIC DIRECTORY). 0736-704X. US. English. an. Monson Productions, PO Box 5324, Madison WI 53705. **LC** GV1541. **DD** 793.8028.

THE MAGICK CIRCLE DIRECTORY OF OCCULT GOODS AND SERVICES. 1984/85 ed.-. 0742-8898. US. English. ir. $5.00. Technology Group, PO Box 93124, Pasadena CA 91109. **Tel** (818)794-6013. **Ed** Rev White. **DD** 133. adv acc. **Circ** 1,000. Directory of occult shops, suppliers, and practitioners.

MAGYAR KEVE. 1978-. US. Hungarian. an. 1739 Mehoning Avenue, Youngstown Ohio 44509. **LC** AY78.H8.

MAGYAR NAPTAR. 0094-1484. US. Hungarian. $3.00. Amerikai Magyar Szo, 130 East 16th Street, New York NY 10003. **LC** AY78.H8.

MAGYAR NEMZETI GALERIA EVKONYVE. VFOAT Annales de la Galerie Nationale Hongroise. No. 1- 1970-. Periodical. HU. French and Hungarian. ir. PO Box 149, 1389 Budapest Hungary. **Ind/Abst** Repert. Int. Litt. Art. *Magyar Nemzeti Galeria Kozlemenyei.*

A MAGYAR SZO NAPTARA. Hungarian. ir. 10.00. Forum Nyomda, Novi Sad Vojvode Misica 1, Ujvidek Yugoslavia. **LC** AY1038.Y6.

MAIL ORDER BUSINESS DIRECTORY : A COMPLETE GUIDE TO THE MAIL ORDER MARKET. Began in 1955. 0085-2953. US. English. ir. B Klein Publishing, PO Box 8503, Coral Springs FL 33065. **Tel** (305)752-1708. **LC** HF5466. **DD** 381.14025.

MAINE DIRECTORY OF NATURAL RESOURCE ORGANIZATIONS. 1977-. 0148-0359. US. English. an. State Planning Office, 184 State Street, Augusta ME 04333. **LC** HC107.M2. **DD** 333.

MAINE EDUCATIONAL DIRECTORY. 0460-6949. English. ir. **LC** LB2803.M2. *Directory of Secondary Schools.*

MAINE MARKETING DIRECTORY. 1976-. 0145-9007. US. English. be. $5.00. Tower Publishing Company, 163 Middle Street, Portland ME 04111. **LC** HD9727.M2. **DD** 381.4500025741. *Maine Buyer's Guide and Directory of Maine Manufacturers.*

MAINE, NEW HAMPSHIRE, VERMONT ZIP+4 STATE DIRECTORY. VFOAT Zip Plus Four State Directory. VAT Maine, New Hampshire, Vermont Zip Plus Four State Directory. 1985-. 8756-9841. US. English. an. St Louis PDC, Zip+4 State Directory Orders, PO Box 14921, St Louis MO 63180-9988. **LC** HE6363.M2. **DD** 383.145.

MAINE REGISTER, STATE YEAR-BOOK AND LEGISLATIVE MANUAL. VFOAT Annual Register of Maine, Maine Register. 1887/88-. 0145-9597. US. English. an. Tower Publishing Company, 34 Diamond Street/PO Box 7220, Portland ME 04112. **Tel** (207)774-9813. **Ed** Esther Peison. **LC** JK2830. **DD** 974.10025. adv acc. **Circ** 1,500. The single most comprehensive, one volume, reference work on the state of Maine. *Maine State Year-Book, and Legislative Manual.*

MAINE STATE INDUSTRIAL DIRECTORY CEASED. Began in 1975. 0098-6194. US. English. be. $19.50. State Industrial Directories Inc, 2 Penn Plaza, New York NY 10002. **LC** T12. **DD** 338.4767025741.

MAINE, VERMONT, NEW HAMPSHIRE DIRECTORY OF MANUFACTURERS. 0197-1220. US. English. an. $52.50. Commerce Register Inc, 190 Godwin Avenue, Midland Park NJ 07432. **Tel** (201)445-3000. **Ed** Joel Rosano. **LC** T12. **DD** 338.470002574. adv acc. **Circ** 3,000. Detailed listings of all manufacturing companies, including top executives, annual sales, number of employees, addresses, phone numbers and more. Available in machine readable formats and on mailing labels.

MAINICHI NYUSU JITEN. V. 1-. JA. Japanese. ir. 7900. Mainichi Shimbun Sha, 1-1-1 Hitotsubashi Chiyoda-ku, Tokyo Japan. **LC** AY1155.T6.

MALAWI STATISTICAL YEARBOOK. 1972-. English. an. $8.50. National Statistical Office, PO Box 333, Zomba Malawi. **LC** HA1977.M3. **DD** 316.897. *Compendium of Statistics for Malawi.*

MALAYSIA AGRICULTURAL DIRECTORY & INDEX. VFOAT Malaysia Agricultural Directory and Index. 84/85-. MY. English. ir. Pantai Maju Sdn Bhd, 78B Jalan SS22, 21 Damansara Jaya Petaling, Jaya Selangor Malaysia. **Tel** 7195272. adv acc. **Circ** 4,000. Complete guide to Malaysian agriculture. Includes about 4,000 key personnel, both government and commercial agriculture organizations. *Agricultural Directory of Malaysia, 0376-5644.*

MALTA TRADE DIRECTORY. UK. English. ir. Malta Chamber of Commerce/ Arthur H Thrower Ltd, 4446 South Ealing Rd, Ealing London W5 England. **LC** HF328.M3. **DD** 380.10254585.

MALTESE DIRECTORY. CANADA-UNITED STATES. (MALTESE DIRECTORY : CANADA, UNITED STATES). Series/Titl Ethnic Directories. 1974-. 0317-6983. CN. English (includes some text in Maltese). Free. Maltese Service Bureau, PO Box 826 Station B, Ottawa Ontario K1P 5P9 Canada. **Ed** G Bonavia. **LC** E184.M34. **DD** 971.0049277.

MANA MEMBERSHIP DIRECTORY OF MANUFACTURER'S SALES AGENCIES. Main/Corp Manufacturers' Agents National Association (U.S.). VFOAT Directory of Manufacturers' Agents National Association. VAT Manufacturers' Agents National Association Membership Directory. 1984-. US. English. an. $65.00. Manufacturers Agents National Association, 23016 Mill Creek Road/PO Box 3467, Laguna Hills CA 92654. *MANA Directory of Manufacturers' Agents, 0732-5843.*

MANCHESTER CHAMBER OF COMMERCE AND INDUSTRY YEARBOOK. VFOAT Annuaire de la Chambre de Commerce et Industrie de Manchester. 0306-5758. UK. English (French and German). an. Rex Buildings Wilmslow Cheshire, Manchester SK9 1HZ England. **LC** HF302. **DD** 380.106242733.

MANCHESTER FOLK DIRECTORY. UK. English. an. 0.20. T & C Hicks, 12 Winster Avenue, Stretford M32 95E England. **LC** ML21. **DD** 781.742.

MANHATTAN DIRECTORY OF COMMERCIAL & INDUSTRIAL PROPERTIES. (THE MANHATTAN DIRECTORY OF COMMERCIAL & INDUSTRIAL PROPERTIES). 0095-0688. US. English. Standard Abstract Corporation, 132 Nassau Street, New York NY 10038. **LC** HF5068.M3. **DD** 338.00257471.

MANHATTAN LAND USE DIRECTORY. VFOAT Manhattan, New York Land Use Directory. Vol. 1 (1982-83)-. US. English. Real Estate Data Inc, 12 East 41st Street, New York NY 10017. **LC** HJ9289.N4. **DD** 336.222.

MANITOBA CAMPING DIRECTORY. 0823-8588. CN. English. an. Free. Manitoba Camping Association, 1700 Ellice Avenue, Winnipeg Manitoba R3H 0B1 Canada. **DD** 796.5420257127.

MANITOBA FOOD PRODUCTS DIRECTORY. 1980-81-. 0228-8966. CN. English. an. Manitoba Agriculture Marketing Branch, Norquay Building, 916-411 York Avenue, Winnipeg Manitoba Canada. **LC** HD9014.C4. **DD** 381.45641300257127. *Listing of Manitoba Food Products for . . ., 0228-8974.*

MANITOBA HIGH SCHOOLS ATHLETIC DIRECTORY. 1978/79-. 0225-9273. Periodical. CN. English. be. Manitoba High Schools Athletic Association, 1301 Ellice Avenue, Winnipeg Manitoba R3G 0G1 Canada. **DD** 796.0257127. *Contact Personnel in Sport Recreation & Schools, 0225-9265.*

MANITOBA PLASTICS DIRECTORY. 1980-. 0714-3478. CN. English. an. $5.00 Each Volume. The Society, Suite 104/1262 Don Mills Road, Don Mills Ontario M3B 2W7 Canada. **DD** 338.476684025712.

MANITOBA TRADE DIRECTORY. 1st- ed. 0076-390X. Periodical. CN. English. an. 20.00. Sanford Evans Communications Ltd, Box 6900/1077 St James Street, Winnipeg Manitoba R3C 3B1 Canada. **Tel** (204)775-0201. **DD** 338.40257127. adv acc. **Circ** 12,500. (ctrl). Provides an alphabetical listing of manufacturers and distributors. Includes addresses, telephone numbers, head office identification, branches, range of products, names and titles of management personnel, and number of employees.

MANITOBA WINNIPEG BUILDING AND CONSTRUCTION TRADES COUNCIL YEARBOOK. Series/Titl Building Trades in Canada. 0714-3222. CN. English. an. Free. Manitoba Winnipeg Building and Construction Trades Council Yearbook, c/o Naylor Communications, 1494 Regent Street West, Winnipeg Manitoba R2C 3A8 Canada. **DD** 331.76900257127.

MANORAMA YEAR BOOK. Began in 1965?. 0542-5778. II. English. an. 15.00. Foreign. Manorama Publishing House, PO Box 26, Kottayam 1 Keral India. **Tel** 3615. **Ed** K M Mathew. **LC** DS401. **DD** 315.4. adv acc. **Circ** 60,000. A general reference publication of four parts, viz. science and technology, world panorama, India and states, and the world of sports.

MANUAL & DIRECTORY - ONTARIO JOINT FICTION RESERVE. Main/Corp Ontario Joint Fiction Reserve. 1972-. 0319-406X. CN. English. be. Ontario Joint Fiction Reserve, Box 100, Wyoming Ontario N0N 1T0 Canada. **DD** 025.26.

MANUFACTURED HOUSING DEALER. ANNUAL DIRECTORY & BUYER'S GUIDE. VFOAT Manufactured Housing Dealer. Began with Vol. for 1979. 0277-7924. US. English. an. $9.00. TL Enterprises Inc, 29901 Agoura Road, Agoura CA 91301. **LC** HD9715.7.U6. **DD** 381.4569087902573. *Mobile-Modular Housing Dealer. Annual Directory and Buyer's Guide, 0097-7233.*

MANUFACTURERS & PROCESSORS DIRECTORY CEASED. (SOUTH DAKOTA MANUFACTURERS & PROCESSORS DIRECTORY). VAT Manufacturers and Processors Directory. 1974/75-. 0094-2758. US. English. be. $25.38. Manufacturers News Inc, 4 East Huron Street, Chicago IL 60611. **Tel** (312)337-1084. **LC** HC107.S8.

Yearbooks, Almanacs, Directories

DD 338.00294783. Lists addresses, zip codes, telephone numbers, employees, name of chief executive, products manufactured and market area. Contains 1,000 firms and 3,000 executives. *Directory of South Dakota Manufacturers and Processors.*

MANUFACTURERS DIRECTORY. Main/Corp Health Industry Distributors Association (U.S.). VFOAT Hida Manufacturers Directory. 28th Ed. (1984-85)-. US. English. an. NLM W 22. *Official Buyers Directory.*

MANUFACTURERS DIRECTORY (SAINT JOHN, N.B.). (MANUFACTURERS DIRECTORY : SAINT JOHN FUNDY REGION, NEW BRUNSWICK). 0713-5556. CN. English. an. Manufacturers Directory, c/o Saint John Fundy Region Development Commission, PO Box 1971, Saint John New Brunswick E2L 4L1 Canada. DD 338.002571532.

MANUFACTURERS DIRECTORY, WINDSOR-ESSEX COUNTY, ONTARIO, CANADA. (MANUFACTURERS DIRECTORY). VFOAT Repertoire des Fabricants. 1984-. 0826-7413. CN. English (includes some text in French). an. Windsor-Essex County Development Commission, Place Goyau, Windsor Ontario N9A 2W1 Canada. DD 338.402571332. *Repertoire des Fabricants, Windsor-Essex, Ontario, Canada, 0822-5036.*

MANUFACTURING DIRECTORY OF IDAHO. 0199-9710. US. English. bm. Center for Business Development & Research, University of Idaho, Moscow ID 83843. Tel (208)885-6611. Ed Joy Passanante Williams. LC HD9727.I2. DD 338.4025796. Circ 2,000. Listing of high technology and manufacturers in the state of Idaho. Listed by city, by alphabet, and by standard industrial classifications. *Idaho Directory of Manufacturers.*

MARBURGER JAHRBUCH FUR KUNSTWISSENSCHAFT. V. 1-. 0342-121X. GW. German. an. Verlag des Kunstgeschichtlich, 3550 Marburg/Law, Ernst-von-Hulsen-Haus Germany. Ed Richard Hamann and others. Ind/Abst Avery Index Archit. Period. Second Ed. Revis. Enlarged Suppl., Repert. Int. Litt. Art. LC N9. DD 705.

MARDOM NAMEH. JAHRBUCH ZUR GESCHICHTE UND GESELLSCHAFT DES MITTLEREN ORIENTS. VFOAT Jahrbuch zur Geschichte und Gesellschaft des Mittleren Orients. 1980-. Periodical. GW. German. ir. Syndikat Autoren und Verlagsgesellschaft, Frankfurt Am Main, Frankfurt West Germany. LC DS41. DD 956.005.

MARIGOLD LIBRARY SYSTEM DIRECTORY. VFOAT Directory. VAT Directory - Marigold Library System. Jan. 1982-. 0714-895X. Periodical. CN. English. sa. Free. Marigold Library System Directory, PO Box 1830, Strathmore Alberta T0J 3H0 Canada. DD 027.402571233. (ctrl).

MARINA YEARBOOK. 0302-0983. UK. English. an. 1.00. LC VK369.8.G7. DD 797.1.

MARINE BUYERS' DIRECTORY. 1974-. 0318-3017. Periodical. CN. English. MacLean-Hunter, PO Box 100 Station A, Toronto Ontario M5W 1A7 Canada. DD 338.476238602571. *Marine Equipment, Buyers' Directory, 0318-3033.*

MARINE DIRECTORY. US. English. an. Marine Engineering, 508 Birch Street, Bristol CT 06010. LC HE565.U5. DD 338.476238025. *Simmons-Boardman Marine Directory.*

MARINE EQUIPMENT DIRECTORY. Nov./Dec. 1972-. 0824-8729. CN. English. an. $19.35. Shipping Register Publications, 2050 Mansfield/Suite 601, Montreal Quebec H3A 1Y9 Canada. Tel (514)842-5263. Ed Olaf J Silva. LC VM470. DD 338.4762386025. adv acc. Circ 3,000. Directory of marine products and services offered.

MARKETS YEAR BOOK. Periodical. English. ir. Worlds Fair Ltd, PO Box 54, 2 Daltry Street, Shaw Road, Oldham Lancs OL1 4BB England.

MARQUIS WHO'S WHO DIRECTORY OF COMPUTER GRAPHICS. VFOAT Who's Who Directory of Computer Graphics. 1st Ed. (1984)-. 8756-0690. US. English. LC T385. DD 006.6025.

MARQUIS WHO'S WHO DIRECTORY OF ONLINE PROFESSIONALS. VFOAT Directory of Online Professionals. 1st Ed.-. 0884-044X. US. English. Marquis Who's Who Inc, 200 East Ohio Street, Chicago IL 60611. LC QA76.55. DD 004.330257.

MARTINDALE-HUBBELL LAW DIRECTORY. 1868. 0191-0221. US. English. an. $175.00. Martindale-Hubbell Inc, PO Box 1001, Summit NJ 07901. Tel (201)464-6800. Contains information on lawyers of the United States, Canada, and other countries of the world as well as authoritative digests of laws. *Martindale's American Law Directory, Hubbell's Legal Directory.*

MARYLAND ASSOCIATION, BUSINESS , CHAMBER OF COMMERCE, PROFESSIONAL SOCIETY, AND TRADE ASSOCIATION DIRECTORY. V. 1- 1977/78-. 0163-237X. US. English. an. PO Box 67, Annapolis MD 21401. LC HF5065.M25. DD 061.3.

MASS COMMUNICATION REVIEW YEARBOOK. Vol. 1 (1980)-. 0196-8017. US. English. an. $40.00. Sage Publications Inc, PO Box 5024, Beverly Hills CA 90210. Tel (213)274-8003. LC P87. DD 302.23.

MASSACHUSETTS DIRECTORY OF MANUFACTURERS. 0195-5810. US. English. an. $62.50. Commerce Register Inc, 190 Godwin Avenue, Midland Park NJ 07432. Tel (201)445-3000. Ed Joel Rosano. LC HD9727.M4. DD 338.4700025744. adv acc. Circ 3,000. Detailed listings of all manufacturing companies, including top executives, annual sales, number of employees, addresses, phone numbers and more. Available in machine readable format and on mailing lists.

MASSACHUSETTS FOUNDATION DIRECTORY. 0739-1315. US. English. Associated Grantmakers of Massachusetts Inc, 294 Washington Street/Suite 417, Boston MA 02108. LC HV98.M39. DD 361.7632025744.

MASSACHUSETTS LEGAL DIRECTORY, WITH RHODE ISLAND SECTION. VFOAT Massachusetts Legal Directory. 1977/78-. 0195-5845. US. English. an. Legal Directories Publishing Company, 700 Campbell Center, PO Box 64805, Dallas TX 75206. LC KF192.M38. DD 340.025744.

MASSACHUSETTS LEGISLATIVE DIRECTORY. US. English. Free. Massachusetts Taxpayers Foundation Inc, One Federal Street, Boston MA 02110.

MASSACHUSETTS MUNICIPAL DIRECTORY. 0361-2090. US. English. $15.00. Massachusetts Municipal Association, 131 Tremont Street, Boston MA 02111. Tel (617)426-7272. Ed Noni Flanagan. LC JS451.M47. DD 352.005209744. adv acc. Includes regional planning agencies, statewide municipal organizations, state map and Massachusetts municipal officials in every city and town.

THE MASSACHUSETTS POLITICAL ALMANAC. 1981-1982-. 0277-1314. US. English. be. $15.00. The Almanac, 18 Trement Street/Suite 816, Boston MA 02108. LC JK3130. DD 353.9744002. *Almanac: Massachusetts State Officials, 0147-5029.*

MASSACHUSETTS ZIP+4 STATE DIRECTORY. VFOAT Zip+4 State Directory. VAT Massachusetts Zip Plus Four State Directory. 1985-. US. English. an. St Louis PDC, Zip+4 State Directory Orders, PO Box 14821, St Louis MO 63180-9988.

MASTERGUIDE. CENTRAL. (MASTERGUIDE. CENTRAL : THE OFFICIAL SPECIFYING AND BUYING DIRECTORY OF THE AMERICAN INSTITUTE OF ARCHITECTS). 8756-2812. Periodical. US. English. an. Pactel Publishing, 1600 South Main/Suite 290, PO Box 8124, Walnut Creek CA 92696.

MASTERGUIDE. NORTHEAST. (MASTERGUIDE. NORTHEAST : THE OFFICIAL SPECIFYING AND BUYING DIRECTORY OF THE AMERICAN INSTITUTE OF ARCHITECTS). VFOAT Master Guide Northeast. 1985-. 8756-2715. US. English. an. Pactel Publishing, 1600 South Main/Suite 290, PO Box 8124, Walnut Creek CA 94596. DD 721.

MATERIAL CULTURE DIRECTORIES. 0743-7528. US. English. ir. Greenwood Press, PO Box 5007, 88 Post Road West, Westport CT 06881.

MATHEMATICAL SCIENCES ADMINISTRATIVE DIRECTORY CEASED. 0543-0895. US. English. an. American Mathematical Society, PO Box 1571 Annex Station, Providence RI 02901. LC QA1. DD 510.06073.

MATHEMATICAL SCIENCES PROFESSIONAL DIRECTORY. 1983-. 0737-4356. US. English. an. American Mathematical Society, Box 6248, Providence RI 02940. LC QA1. DD 510.2573. *Mathematical Sciences Administrative Directory, 0543-0895.*

MAURITIUS AND SEYCHELLES BUSINESS DIRECTORY. 1984-. English. an. B & T Directories (MTS) Ltd, PO Box 322, Port Louis Mauritius. LC HF5291.A3. DD 380.10294698. *Business Directory of Mauritius, Reunion, and Seychelles.*

MAURITIUS DIRECTORY OF THE DIPLOMATIC CORPS. Main/Corp Mauritius. English. ir. 25. LC JX1865.M45. DD 351.892096982.

THE MEANS COLORADO DIRECTORY. 0273-3803. Periodical. US. English. $15.00. The Means Ltd, 521 South Washington, Denver CO 80209. LC PN1993.U72. DD 791.43025788.

MEAT AND POULTRY INSPECTION DIRECTORY. July/Dec. 1977-. 0740-8609. US. English. sa. US Government Printing Office, Superintendent of Documents, Washington DC 20402. Tel (202)783-3238. *APHIS Program Services Directory.*

MECHANO BUYERS DIRECTORY. NORTHERN CALIFORNIA. US. English. an. $16.95. Mechano Buyers Directory, PO Box 70460, Sunnyvale CA 94086. Tel (408)738-3020. Ed Gerald Willis. adv acc. Circ 7,000. (ctrl). Nationwide listings of manufacturers cross-referenced to Northern California sources for electronic, electrical and mechanical goods and services.

MEDALS YEARBOOK. VFOAT Medals Year Book. Began in 1979/80. 0737-6529. US. English. ir. Cobra Publications Ltd, Contract Station 22, 9297 Federal Building, Box 327, Denver CO 80221. Tel (303)467-1400. Ed J Brant. adv acc. Circ 6,000. Photographic, illustrated price guide on British and Colonial military medals. Over 450 photographs with over 2,300 price valuations.

MEDIA DIRECTORY. VFOAT Pittsburgh & Tristate Media Directory. 1st-. Ed. 0196-8521. US. English. an. Thompson Matelan & Hawbaker Inc, Gateway Towers/Suite 318, Pittsburgh PA 15222.

MEDIA DIRECTORY : SINGAPORE, MALAYSIA & BRUNEI. VAT Media Directory: Singapore, Malaysia and Brunei. 1976/77-. English. ir. $11.50. LC P92.M3. DD 301.16109595. *Malaysia Singapore Media-Annual.*

MEDICAL ALMANAC. 1961/62-. 0543-2480. Periodical. US. English. Ed P S Nagan. LC R104. DD 610.82.

MEDICAL AND HEALTH INFORMATION DIRECTORY. 1st Ed.-. 0749-9973. US. English. ir. $390.00. Gale Research, Book Tower, Detroit MI 48226. Ed A Kruzas, K Jill and K Bachus. LC R118.4.U6. DD 610.72073. NLM W 22. Volumes contain information about medical organizations, agencies, institutions, libraries, publications, audiovisuals, and database services.

MEDICAL DIRECTORY. V. 1- 1845-. 0305-3342. UK. English. an. 62.00. Churchill Livingstone, 43/45 Annandale Street, Edinburgh EH7 4AT Scotland. Tel (0279)442601. LC R713.29. DD 614.240942. adv acc. The medical directory gives an alphabetical listing of over 100,000 doctors registered to practice in the UK as well as other health care coverage.

MEDICAL DIRECTORY. (MEDICAL DIRECTORY - COLLEGE OF PHYSICIANS AND SURGEONS OF B.C.). Main/Corp College of Physicians and Surgeons of British Columbia. 1956/57-. 0069-5726. Periodical. CN. English. an. College of Physicians and Surgeons of British Columbia, 1807 West 10th Avenue, Vancouver British Columbia V6J 2A9 Canada. DD 610.6952025711. NLM W 22 DC2.1B8M. *Council. Directory, 0315-2294.*

MEDICAL DIRECTORY. 0145-5583. US. English. Board of Registration in Medicine, 100 College Avenue, Waterville ME 04901. LC R712.A2. DD 610.25741.

MEDICAL DIRECTORY - COLLEGE OF PHYSICIANS AND SURGEONS OF ALBERTA. (MEDICAL DIRECTORY). Main/Corp College of Physicians and Surgeons of Alberta. 1976-. 0702-7826. Periodical. CN. English. be. Free to Registered Physicians in Alberta, $10.00 Each

2926

Yearbooks, Almanacs, Directories

Number Others. College of Physicians and Surgeons, 9901-108th Street, Edmonton Alberta T5K 1G9 Canada. DD 610.69520257123. *Alberta Physicians and Surgeons, Province of Alberta, 0319-5031.*

MEDICAL DIRECTORY OF AUSTRALIA. Periodical. AT. English. ir. Australasian Medical Publishing Company, PO Box116, Glebe New South Wales 2037 Australia. Alphabetical list of doctors in Australia, New Zealand and Papau New Guinea. Includes health authorities, gazeteer hospitals, organizations, universities, colleges, societies and research institutes. *Medical Directory of Australia, New Zealand, etc.*

MEDICAL DIRECTORY OF NEW YORK STATE. 0273-0561. US. English. be. $70.20. Medical Society of New York, 420 Lakeville Road, Lake Success NY 11040. **Tel** (516)488-6100. **Ed** Michael Martino. **NLM** W 22 AN6 M4. **Circ** 30,000. (ctrl). Directory listing New York State doctors and staff lists of New York State hospitals. *Medical Directory of New York, New Jersey and Connecticut.*

MEDICAL EXAMINING BOARD. (MEDICAL EXAMINING BOARD : DIRECTORY). **Main/Corp** Wisconsin. Medical Examining Board. 1978-79-. 0748-0849. US. English. be. Department of Regulation and Licensing, Medical Examining Board, 1400 East Washington Avenue, Madison WI 53702. **LC** RA396.A4. **DD** 610.25775. *List of Registered Doctors of Medicine and Surgery . . . .*

MEDICAL PRODUCTS MARKETERS DIRECTORY. (MEDICAL PRODUCTS MARKETERS DIRECTORY : MPMD). **VFOAT** MPMD. 1st Ed. (1981)-. 0275-4940. US. English. an. $44.95. Fisher-Stevens Publications, Campus Road, Totowa NJ 07512. **LC** HD9994.U5. **DD** 681.761029473.

MEDICAL STAFF DIRECTORY. **Main/Corp** National Institutes of Health (U.S.). Clinical Center. Began with 1970?. 0730-1448. US. English. an. Office of Medical Staff Affairs, The Clinical Center Room 1N-205, Bethesda MD 20205. **NLM** W 22 AA1 N2745M.

THE MEDICARE DIRECTORY OF PREVAILING CHARGES. Began with 1976. 0743-1252. US. English. Superintendent of Documents, US Government Printing Office, Washington DC 20402. **LC** R728.5. **DD** 338.4336210973. **NLM** W2.

THE MEED MIDDLE EAST FINANCIAL DIRECTORY. **VFOAT** M.E.E.D. Middle East Financial Directory. **VAT** Middle East Economic Digest Middle East Financial Directory. 1983. UK. English. an. $60.00. Meed Ltd, 21 John Street Meed House, London WC1N 2BP England. **Tel** 01-242-8. **Ed** Anna Krajewska. **LC** HG3256.A5. **DD** 332.102556. adv acc. The most comprehensive reference work on the subject of banking and finance in the Middle East. *Middle East Financial Directory.*

MEGHALAYA YEAR BOOK. (THE MEGHALAYA YEAR BOOK). 0377-127X. English. an. 5.00. Northeast India News and Feature Service, Jaiaw Langsnin, 793002 Shillong India. **LC** DS485.M58. **DD** 954.16.

MEMBER DIRECTORY. **Main/Corp** Financial Executives Institute. US. English. Financial Executives Institute, 10 Madison Avenue PO Box 1938, Morristown NJ 07960. **LC** HF5001. **DD** 650.6273. *Member Directory.*

MEMBERS' DIRECTORY. **Main/Corp** Federation of Hong Kong Industries. **VFOAT** Hsiang-Kang Kung Yeh Tsung Hui Hui Yuan Ming Lu. HK. Chinese (English). ir. 100 Domestic, 35.00 Foreign. Federation of Hong Kong Industries, 12/F 21A Ma Tau Wei Rd, Hung Hom Kowloon Hong Kong. **LC** HD9736.H6. **DD** 380.102945125.

MEMBERS DIRECTORY - INSTITUTION OF ENVIRONMENTAL HEALTH OFFICERS. (MEMBERS DIRECTORY). **Main/Corp** Institution of Environmental Health Officers (London, England). Began in 1981?. 0264-5947. Periodical. UK. English. 56.00 Foreign. Institution of Environmental Health Officers, Chadwick House, Rushworth Street, London SE1 ORB England. **Tel** (01)928-6006. **Ed** A M Tanner. **NLM** WA 22 FA1 I4M. bk rev. adv acc. **Circ** 7,500. (ctrl). Covers all areas of public health, housing, food hygiene, air and water pollution, health and safety, legislation, book reviews, etc.

MEMBER'S YEAR BOOK - AMERICAN SOCIETY OF CORPORATE SECRETARIES. (MEMBER'S YEAR BOOK). **Main/Corp** American Society of Corporate Secretaries. **VFOAT** Member's Yearbook. 0742-986X.

US. English. an. American Society of Corporate Secretaries Inc, 1270 Avenue of the Americas, New York NY 10020. **LC** HD2709. **DD** 658.4. *Year Book.*

MEMBERSHIP AND STATISTICAL DIRECTORY - NEW ENGLAND GAS ASSOCIATION. (MEMBERSHIP AND STATISTICAL DIRECTORY). **VFOAT** New England Gas Association. 0741-112X. US. English. be. New England Gas Association, 1427 Statler Office Building, Boston MA 02116. **LC** TP723. **DD** 363.6302574.

MEMBERSHIP DIRECTORY - AATG. **Main/Corp** American Association of Teachers of German. **VAT** Membership Directory - American Association of Teachers of German. 1976-. US. English. ir. $4.00. American Association of Teachers of German 523 Building Route 38/Suite 201, Cherry Hill NJ 08034. **Tel** (609)663-5264. *German Quarterly, 0016-8831.*

MEMBERSHIP DIRECTORY - ADULT EDUCATION ASSOCIATION. (MEMBERSHIP DIRECTORY). **Main/Corp** Adult Education Association. **VFOAT** A.E.A. Membership Directory. 0732-2372. US. English. Free to Members, $20.00 Nonmembers. Adult Education Association of the USA, 810 18th Street Northwest, Washington DC 20006. **LC** LC5201. **DD** 374.06073.

MEMBERSHIP DIRECTORY - ALASKA STATE CHAMBER OF COMMERCE. (MEMBERSHIP DIRECTORY). **Main/Corp** Alaska State Chamber of Commerce. 0091-8873. US. English. State Chamber of Commerce, 310 2nd Street, Juneau AK 99801. **Tel** (907)586-2323. **LC** HF295. **DD** 380.1062798. adv acc. Businesses who are members with the state Chamber of Commerce.

MEMBERSHIP DIRECTORY - ALBERTA ASSOCIATION OF LIBRARY TECHNICIANS. (MEMBERSHIP DIRECTORY). **Main/Corp** Alberta Association of Library Technicians. 0228-7447. CN. English. an. Free to Members. Alberta Association of Library Technicians, PO Box 700, Edmonton Alberta T5J 2L4 Canada. **DD** 020.62347123.

MEMBERSHIP DIRECTORY - AMERICAN ACADEMY OF FORENSIC SCIENCES. **Main/Corp** American Academy of Forensic Sciences. **VFOAT** AAFS Membership Directory. 0192-7086. US. English. an. $25.00. American Academy of Forensic Sciences, 11400 Rockville Pike, Rockville MD 20852. **LC** HV8073. **DD** 364.1202573.

MEMBERSHIP DIRECTORY - AMERICAN ACADEMY OF NEUROLOGY. **Main/Corp** American Academy of Neurology. US. English. ir. American Academy of Neurology, 4015 West 66th Street, Minneapolis MN 55435.

MEMBERSHIP DIRECTORY - AMERICAN ASSOCIATION FOR ARTIFICIAL INTELLIGENCE. **Main/Corp** American Association for Artificial Intelligence. **VFOAT** AAAI Membership Directory. US. English. American Association for Artificial Intelligence (AAAI), 445 Burgess Drive, Menlo Park CA 94025.

MEMBERSHIP DIRECTORY - AMERICAN ASSOCIATION FOR CLINICAL CHEMISTRY. **Main/Corp** American Association for Clinical Chemistry. US. English. **NLM** QD 23. *Membership Directory and Handbook - American Association of Clinical Chemists, 0095-1773.*

MEMBERSHIP DIRECTORY - AMERICAN ASSOCIATION OF HOMES FOR THE AGING. **Main/Corp** American Association of Homes for the Aging. **VFOAT** AAHA Directory of Members. 0160-2055. US. English. American Association of Homes for the Aging, 1051 17th Street Northwest/Suite 770, Washington DC 20036. **LC** HV1461. **DD** 362.61502573.

MEMBERSHIP DIRECTORY - AMERICAN ASSOCIATION OF PETROLEUM LANDMEN. **Main/Corp** American Association of Petroleum Landmen. 0272-8370. US. English. an. American Association of Petroleum Landmen, 2408 Continental Life Building, Fort Worth TX 76102. **LC** HD9563. **DD** 338.2728025. *Official Directory.*

MEMBERSHIP DIRECTORY - AMERICAN ASSOCIATION OF PHYSICISTS IN MEDICINE. **Main/Corp** American Association of Physicists in Medicine. US. English. American Institute of Physics, 335 East 45 Street, New York NY 10017. **LC** R895.A1. **DD** 610.153.

MEMBERSHIP DIRECTORY - AMERICAN ASSOCIATION OF TEACHERS OF FRENCH. (MEMBERSHIP DIRECTORY). **Main/Corp** American Association of Teachers of French. 0737-8890. Periodical. US. English. American Association of Teachers of French, National Office, 57 East Armory Avenue, Champaign IL 61820. **LC** PC2068.U7. **DD** 448.002573.

MEMBERSHIP DIRECTORY - AMERICAN CHAIN OF WAREHOUSES, INC. **Main/Corp** American Chain of Warehouses Inc. 0360-5965. US. English. an. American Chain of Warehouses Inc, 250 Park Avenue, New York NY 10017.

MEMBERSHIP DIRECTORY - AMERICAN CHAMBER OF COMMERCE IN EGYPT. **Main/Corp** American Chamber of Commerce in Egypt. 1983/84-. UA. English. ir. Cairo Marriott Hotel, Suite 1537, Zamalek Cairo Egypt. **LC** HF336.E3. **DD** 382.09620730256216.

MEMBERSHIP DIRECTORY - AMERICAN CHAMBER OF COMMERCE OF GUATEMALA. **Main/Corp** American Chamber of Commerce of Guatemala. English. ir. Apartado Postal 832 9A Calle 5-54, Zona 1, Guatemala Republica de Guatemala.

MEMBERSHIP DIRECTORY - AMERICAN CHIROPRACTIC ASSOCIATION. (MEMBERSHIP DIRECTORY). **Main/Corp** American Chiropractic Association. 1983-. 0747-8372. US. English. an. American Chiropractic Association, 1916 Wilson Boulevard, Arlington VA 22201. **LC** RZ233. **DD** 615.53402573. *Official Membership Directory - American Chiropractic Association, 0569-3837.*

MEMBERSHIP DIRECTORY - AMERICAN COLLEGE OF SPORTS MEDICINE. (MEMBERSHIP DIRECTORY). **Main/Corp** American College of Sports Medicine. Began with 1977. 0732-7056. US. English. $15.00 Members, $30.00 Nonmembers. American College of Sports Medicine, 401 West Michigan Street, Indianapolis IN 46202. **Tel** (317)637-9200. **NLM** QT 22.1 A512M. A membership directory of the American College of Sports Medicine.

MEMBERSHIP DIRECTORY - AMERICAN COMPENSATION ASSOCIATION. **Main/Corp** American Compensation Association. US. English. American Compensation Association, PO Box 1176, Scottsdale AZ 85252. **LC** HF5549.5.C67. **DD** 658.3206273.

MEMBERSHIP DIRECTORY - AMERICAN CRYSTALLOGRAPHIC ASSOCIATION. **Main/Corp** American Crystallographic Association. 0362-4390. US. English. American Crystallographic Association, 335 East 45th Street, New York NY 10017. **LC** QD901. **DD** 548.06273.

MEMBERSHIP DIRECTORY - AMERICAN FIRST DAY COVER SOCIETY. (MEMBERSHIP DIRECTORY). **Main/Corp** American First Day Cover Society. 0732-2348. US. English. an. $6.00. American First Day Cover Society, PO Box 23, Cranford NJ 07016. **Ed** Sol Koved. **LC** HE6184.F57. **DD** 769.5650750973. bk rev. adv acc. **Circ** 4,000. Covers a branch of philately concerned with the issue of stamps. Current news, research, auction, services, and do-it-yourself.

MEMBERSHIP DIRECTORY - AMERICAN FOLKLORE SOCIETY. (MEMBERSHIP DIRECTORY). **Main/Corp** American Folklore Society. 0275-1747. US. English. American Folklore Society, 1703 New Hampshire Avenue Northwest, Washington DC 20009. **LC** GR1. **DD** 398.02573.

MEMBERSHIP DIRECTORY - AMERICAN IMPORTERS ASSOCIATION. (MEMBERSHIP DIRECTORY). **Main/Corp** American Importers Association. 0090-4562. US. English. American Importers Association, Graybar Building, Room 2626, 420 Lexington Avenue, New York NY 10170. **LC** HF3012. **DD** 382.502573.

MEMBERSHIP DIRECTORY - AMERICAN INDUSTRIAL DEVELOPMENT COUNCIL, INC. (MEMBERSHIP DIRECTORY). **Main/Corp** American Industrial Development Council. 0093-8734. US. English. an. $2.00. American Industrial Development Council, 215 West Pershing Road/Suite 707, Kansas City MO 64108. **LC** HC95.Z9. **DD** 338.0973.

Yearbooks, Almanacs, Directories

MEMBERSHIP DIRECTORY - AMERICAN INSTITUTE OF ARCHITECTS. Main/Corp American Institute of Architects. VFOAT AIA Membership Directory. US. English. an. American Institute of Architects, 1735 New York Avenue NW, Washington DC 20006. LC NA11.A42. DD 720.6273.

MEMBERSHIP DIRECTORY - AMERICAN INSTITUTE OF CHEMISTS. Main/Corp American Institute of Chemists. US. English. American Institute of Chemists, 7315 Wisconsin Avenue, Washington DC 20014.

MEMBERSHIP DIRECTORY - AMERICAN INSTITUTE OF PROFESSIONAL GEOLOGISTS. (MEMBERSHIP DIRECTORY). Main/Corp American Institute of Professional Geologists. VFOAT AIPG ... Membership Directory. 0275-4991. US. English. an. $15.00. American Institute of Professional Geologist, 7827 Vance Drive/Suite 103, Arvada CO 80003. Tel (303)431-0831. LC QE1. DD 550.607.

MEMBERSHIP DIRECTORY - AMERICAN MEDICAL WOMEN'S ASSOCIATION. Main/Corp American Medical Women's Association. 1978-. US. English. mo. $20.00. American Medical Womens Association, 465 Grand Street, New York NY 10002. Tel (212)533-5104.

MEMBERSHIP DIRECTORY - AMERICAN METEOROLOGICAL SOCIETY. Main/Corp American Meteorological Society. 0162-7988. US. English. 45 Beacon Street, Boston MA 02108. LC QC851. DD 551.506273.

MEMBERSHIP DIRECTORY - AMERICAN OCCUPATIONAL MEDICAL ASSOCIATION. Main/Corp American Occupational Medical Association. 1975/76-. 0190-1664. US. English. $20.00. American Occupational Medical Association, 150 North Wacker Drive, Chicago IL 60606. NLM WA 22 AA1 A53M. Membership Directory - Industrial Medical Association.

MEMBERSHIP DIRECTORY - AMERICAN ORTHOPSYCHIATRIC ASSOCIATION. (MEMBERSHIP DIRECTORY). Main/Corp American Orthopsychiatric Association. Began in 1977. 0164-2669. US. English. ir. American Orthopsychiatric Association, 1775 Broadway, New York NY 10019. LC RC326. DD 616.89. NLM WM 22 AA1 A58M. Membership Directory, Constitution, and By-Laws - The American Orthopsychiatric Association.

MEMBERSHIP DIRECTORY - AMERICAN POLITICAL SCIENCE ASSOCIATION. (THE AMERICAN POLITICAL SCIENCE MEMBERSHIP DIRECTORY). Main/Corp American Political Science Association. VFOAT Membership Directory. 1980-. 0730-6385. US. English. $10.00 Members, $12.00 Nonmembers. American Political Science Association, 1527 New Hampshire Avenue NW, Washington DC 20036. Tel (202)483-2512. Lists nearly 9,500 individual Association members with information on their current position, institutional affiliation, address, phone number, highest degree (including data and granting institution), and fields of specialization. APSA Directory of Members.

MEMBERSHIP DIRECTORY - AMERICAN PREPAID LEGAL SERVICES INSTITUTE. (MEMBERSHIP DIRECTORY). Main/Corp American Prepaid Legal Services Institute. 0732-3557. US. English. an. $7.50. American Prepaid Legal Services Institute and the American Bar Center, 750 North Lake Shore Drive, Chicago IL 60611. Tel (312)988-5751. LC KF310.G7. DD 331.255. Circ 500. Directories list members by self-designated specialty categories to enable members to refer business, seek consultants, plan sponsors and legal service providers.

MEMBERSHIP DIRECTORY - AMERICAN RHEUMATISM ASSOCIATION. (MEMBERSHIP DIRECTORY). Main/Corp American Rheumatism Association. VFOAT ARA/AHP Membership Directory. 0278-0496. US. English. $35.00 Noncommercial Use. Arthritis Foundation, 3400 Peachtree Road Northeast, Atlanta GA 30326. LC RC927. DD 616.723006073.

MEMBERSHIP DIRECTORY - AMERICAN SOCIETY FOR PUBLIC ADMINISTRATION, NATIONAL CAPITAL AREA CHAPTER. Main/Corp American Society for Public Administration. National Capital Area Chapter. 0145-2223. US. English. an. $2.00. American Society for Public Administration, National Capital Area Chapter, Box 1384, Washington DC 20036. LC JA28. Membership Directory - American Society for Public Administration, Washington D.C. Chapter, 0360-0459.

MEMBERSHIP DIRECTORY - AMERICAN SOCIETY OF HOSPITAL PHARMACISTS. Main/Corp American Society of Hospital Pharmacists. 0084-6449. US. English. American Society of Hospital Pharmacists, 4630 Montgomery Avenue, Washington DC 20014. LC RS75.

MEMBERSHIP DIRECTORY - AMERICAN SOCIETY OF INTERNAL MEDICINE. Main/Corp American Society of Internal Medicine. 1967-. 0569-8170. US. English. be. American Society of Internal Medicine, 535 Central Tower Building, 703 Market Street, San Francisco CA 94103. NLM W 22 AA1 A55. Directory of Members - American Society of Internal Medicine.

MEMBERSHIP DIRECTORY - AMERICAN SOCIETY OF ORAL SURGEONS. (MEMBERSHIP DIRECTORY). Main/Corp American Society of Oral Surgeons. 0093-6529. US. English. American Society of Oral Surgeons, 211 East Chicago Avenue, Chicago IL 60611. LC RK37. DD 617.6002573.

MEMBERSHIP DIRECTORY - AMERICAN SOLAR ENERGY SOCIETY. (MEMBERSHIP DIRECTORY). Main/Corp American Solar Energy Society. 1982-83-. 0743-958X. US. English. an. American Solar Energy Society Inc, 1230 Grandview Avenue, Boulder CO 80302. LC TJ810. DD 621.4702573. Membership Directory, 0278-1271.

MEMBERSHIP DIRECTORY - AMERICAN STAMP DEALERS' ASSOCIATION. (MEMBERSHIP DIRECTORY). Main/Corp American Stamp Dealers' Association. VFOAT ASDA Membership Directory. 0736-6035. US. English. an. American Stamp Dealers' Association, 5 Dakota Drive/Suite 102, Lake Sucess NY 11042.

MEMBERSHIP DIRECTORY - AMERICAN STATISTICAL ASSOCIATION. MONTREAL CHAPTER. (MEMBERSHIP DIRECTORY - AMERICAN STATISTICAL ASSOCIATION, MONTREAL CHAPTER AND STATISTICAL SOCIETY OF CANADA, MONTREAL REGIONAL ASSOCIATION. MONTREAL DE L'A S A). Main/Corp American Statistical Association. Montreal Chapter. VFOAT Liste des Membres - Association Regionale de Montreal, Societe Statistique du Canada et Section de Montreal de l'A S A. VAT Liste des Membres - Section de Montreal de l'ASA, Liste des Membres - Association Regionale de Montreal. Societe Statistique du Canada. 1978/79-. 0225-2805. CN. English (French). an. Statistical Society of Canada, Montreal Regional Association, PO Box 1433 Station B, Montreal Quebec H38 3L2 Canada. DD 519.5060714.

MEMBERSHIP DIRECTORY - AMERICAN TOPICAL ASSOCIATION. Main/Corp American Topical Association. US. English. ir. $3.00 Members, $25.00 Non-members. American Topical Association, PO Box 630, Johnstown PA 15907. Tel (814)539-6301. Ed Donald W Smith. LC HE6188. DD 769.56406273. adv acc. Circ 2,000. (ctrl). Listing of members and services of American Topical Association.

MEMBERSHIP DIRECTORY AND AMERICAN CORRESPONDENTS OVERSEAS. Main/Corp Overseas Press Club of America. 0360-5752. US. English. $10.00. Overseas Press Club of America, 55 East 43rd Street, New York NY 10017. LC PN4871. DD 070.402573. Directory of the Overseas Press Club of America and American Correspondents Overseas.

MEMBERSHIP DIRECTORY AND ANNUAL REPORT - SWEDISH-AMERICAN CHAMBER OF COMMERCE. (MEMBERSHIP DIRECTORY AND ANNUAL REPORT). Main/Corp Swedish-American Chamber of Commerce. VFOAT Annual Report and Membership Directory. 0740-1000. US. English. an. Swedish-American Chamber of Commerce, One Dag Hammarskjold Plaza, New York NY 10017. LC HF296.A29. DD 382.094850730601.

MEMBERSHIP DIRECTORY AND BUYERS GUIDE - AMALGAMATED CONSTRUCTION ASSOCIATION OF B.C. (MEMBERSHIP DIRECTORY AND BUYERS GUIDE). Main/Corp Amalgamated Construction Association of British Columbia. 0712-6204. CN. English. an. Free to Members. Amalgamated Construction Association of British Columbia, 2675 Oak Street, Vancouver British Columbia V6H 2K3 Canada. Tel (604)736-6311. DD 338.47690025711. adv acc. Circ 3,000. (ctrl). Contains names and addresses of all major construction contractors in British Columbia by region, and by trade classification as well as members of all consultants' associations.

MEMBERSHIP DIRECTORY AND BUYERS' GUIDE - AMERICAN FROZEN FOOD INSTITUTE. Main/Corp American Frozen Food Institute. 0361-0888. US. English. an. $100.00. American Frozen Food Institute, 1764 Old Meadow Lane #350, McLean VA 22102. Tel (703)821-0770. Ed Kathleen A Larsen. LC TP493.5.A1. DD 338.47664028502573. adv acc. Circ 2,800. Buyers guide containing complete cross referenced information on products, services, plant locations, key personnel, etc. for AFFI processor, supplier, marketing associate members.

MEMBERSHIP DIRECTORY AND BUYERS GUIDE - BEDDING PLANTS, INC. Main/Corp Bedding Plants, Inc. 1982-. 0748-9811. US. English. an. Bedding Plants Inc, PO Box 286, Okemos MI 48864. Membership Directory, 0748-9803.

MEMBERSHIP DIRECTORY & BUYERS' GUIDE - BRITISH COLUMBIA CONSTRUCTION ASSOCIATION. (MEMBERSHIP DIRECTORY AND BUYERS' GUIDE). Main/Corp British Columbia Construction Association. VFOAT British Columbia Construction Association Directory. 1983-. 0822-9155. CN. English. an. $55.00 Each Volume. British Columbia Construction Association, 40-10551 Shallbridge Way, Richmond British Columbia V6X 2W9 Canada. DD 338.47690025711.

MEMBERSHIP DIRECTORY & BUYER'S GUIDE - GREATER BOSTON CHAMBER OF COMMERCE. Main/Corp Greater Boston Chamber of Commerce. VFOAT Membership Directory and Buyer's Guide. US. English. an. Greater Boston Chamber of Commerce, 125 High Street, Boston MA 02110.

MEMBERSHIP DIRECTORY AND BUYERS GUIDE - GREATER MINNEAPOLIS CHAMBER OF COMMERCE. (MEMBERSHIP DIRECTORY AND BUYERS GUIDE). Main/Corp Greater Minneapolis Chamber of Commerce. 0145-2983. US. English. an. $5.00. 15 South Fifth Street, Minneapolis MN 55402. LC HF296.M714. DD 380.1062776579.

MEMBERSHIP DIRECTORY & BUYER'S GUIDE - HAMILTON AND DISTRICT CHAMBER OF COMMERCE. Main/Corp Hamilton and District Chamber of Commerce. 0226-6474. CN. English. an. Free to Members, $10.00 Nonmembers. Hamilton and District Chamber of Commerce, James Street South, Hamilton Ontario L8P 3A5 Canada. DD 380.102571352.

MEMBERSHIP DIRECTORY AND BUYERS' GUIDE - MANITOBA RESTAURANT & FOODSERVICES ASSOCIATION. (MEMBERSHIP DIRECTORY AND BUYERS' GUIDE). Main/Corp Manitoba Restaurant & Foodservices Association. 1983/1984-. 0824-0930. CN. English. an. Free to Members, $10.00 Nonmembers. Manitoba Restaurant and Foodservices Association, 203-897 Corydon Avenue, Winnipeg Manitoba R3M 0W7 Canada. DD 381.4564250257127.

MEMBERSHIP DIRECTORY AND BUYERS' GUIDE - OTTAWA-CARLETON BOARD OF TRADE. (MEMBERSHIP DIRECTORY AND BUYERS' GUIDE). Main/Corp Ottawa-Carleton Board of Trade. 1981/1982-. 0712-4201. CN. English. an. Membership Directory, c/o Ottawa-Carleton Board of Trade, 27th Floor/100 Kent Street, Ottawa Ontario K1P 5R7 Canada. DD 380.06071383. Membership Directory and Buyers' Guide, 0226-0204.

MEMBERSHIP DIRECTORY & BUYER'S GUIDE - THUNDER BAY CHAMBER OF COMMERCE. (MEMBERSHIP DIRECTORY & BUYER'S GUIDE). Main/Corp Thunder Bay Chamber of Commerce. VFOAT Thunder Bay Chamber of Commerce Membership/Buyer's Guide. 1983/84-. 0826-4821. CN. English. an. Thunder Bay Chamber of Commerce, PO Box 2000, Thunder Bay Ontario P7C 4Y4 Canada. DD 380.06071312. Membership Directory, 0229-3145.

Yearbooks, Almanacs, Directories

MEMBERSHIP DIRECTORY & BUYERS GUIDE - TUCSON METROPOLITAN CHAMBER OF COMMERCE. Main/Corp Tucson Metropolitan Chamber of Commerce. VFOAT Membership Directory and Buyers Guide. 1983-84-. US. English. an. $10.00. Blake Publishing Company, 365 West Bradley Avenue/Suite D, PO Box 2606, El Cajon CA 92020. LC HF296.T78. DD 380.106079177. *Tucson Buyer's Guide.*

MEMBERSHIP DIRECTORY AND BUYERS' GUIDE - WINNIPEG CHAMBER OF COMMERCE. Main/Corp Winnipeg Chamber of Commerce. 0707-0039. CN. English. an. $25.00. Winnipeg Chamber of Commerce, 700-177 Lombard Avenue, Winnipeg Manitoba R3B 0W7 Canada. DD 380.06271274.

MEMBERSHIP DIRECTORY AND CERTIFICATION REGISTRY. Main/Corp Wildlife Society. 0271-5082. US. English. an. $2.95. Wildlife Society, 7101 Wisconsin Avenue NW/Suite 611, Washington DC 20014.

MEMBERSHIP DIRECTORY AND CONSTRUCTION BUYERS GUIDE - NORTHERN B.C. CONSTRUCTION ASSOCIATION. (MEMBERSHIP DIRECTORY AND CONSTRUCTION BUYERS GUIDE). Main/Corp Northern B.C. Construction Association. 0714-3109. CN. English. an. Free to Members. Northern B C Construction Association Membership Directory c/o Naylor Communications, 1494 Regent Avenue West, Winnipeg Manitoba R2C 3A8 Canada. DD 338.47690025711.

MEMBERSHIP DIRECTORY AND HANDBOOK - AMERICAN FISHERIES SOCIETY. (MEMBERSHIP DIRECTORY AND HANDBOOK). Main/Corp American Fisheries Society. VFOAT AFS Membership Directory and Handbook. Began with 1979. 0736-475X. US. English. an. American Fisheries Society, 5410 Grosvenor Lane/Suite 110, Bethesda MD 20814-2199. LC SH203. DD 639.202573. *Membership Directory.*

MEMBERSHIP DIRECTORY AND INDUSTRY BUYERS' GUIDE - IRRIGATION ASSOCIATION. Main/Corp Irrigation Association. VFOAT Irrigation Association . . . Directory and Industry Buyer's Guide. 0277-6529. US. English. Irrigation Association, 13975 Connecticut Avenue, Silver Spring MD 20906. LC HD1720. DD 681.7631.

MEMBERSHIP DIRECTORY AND INTERNATIONAL BUYERS' GUIDE TO MARKETING SERVICES. Main/Corp American Marketing Association. 1984-. 0748-7037. US. English. an. $62.00. American Marketing Association, 250 South Wacker Drive, Chicago IL 60606. Tel (312)648-0536. Ed Ginger Spitzer. LC HF5410. DD 338.76165883025. adv acc. Circ 25,000. (ctrl). Buyer's guide to marketing services. *Membership Roster and International Buyers' Guide to Marketing Services.*

MEMBERSHIP DIRECTORY & RESOURCE MANUAL - AMERICAN ACADEMY OF OPHTHALMOLOGY. Main/Corp American Academy of Ophthalmology. VFOAT Membership Directory and Resource Manual. 1981-1982-. US. English. be. American Academy of Ophthalmology, PO Box 45524, Rincon Annex, San Francisco CA 94145. LC RE22. DD 617.7002573. *American Academy of Ophthalmology Directory, 0190-2093.*

MEMBERSHIP DIRECTORY AND SOURCE BOOK FOR GREENHOUSE GARDENERS. Main/Corp Hobby Greenhouse Association. VFOAT Hobby Greenhouse Association Membership Directory and Source Guide. 1979-. Periodical. US. English.

MEMBERSHIP DIRECTORY - APPRAISERS ASSOCIATION OF AMERICA, INC. Main/Corp Appraisers Association of America. 0148-9348. US. English. be. $3.00. Appraisers Association of America, 60 East 42nd Street, New York NY 10017. Tel (212)867-9775. LC HF5681.V3. DD 333.332.

MEMBERSHIP DIRECTORY - ASSOCIATION FOR ADVANCEMENT OF BEHAVIOR THERAPY. (MEMBERSHIP DIRECTORY). Main/Corp Association for Advancement of Behavior Therapy. VFOAT AABT . . . Membership Directory. 8756-8993. US. English. Association for Advancement of Behavior Therapy, 15 West 36th Street, New York NY 10018.

MEMBERSHIP DIRECTORY - ASSOCIATION FOR CREATIVE CHANGE WITHIN RELIGIOUS AND OTHER SOCIAL SYSTEMS (U.S.). (MEMBERSHIP DIRECTORY). Main/Corp Association for Creative Change Within Religious and Other Social Systems (U.S.). 0733-9887. US. English. Association for Creative Change Within Religious and Other Social Systems, PO Box 2212, Syracuse NY 13220. LC BV4012. DD 253.

MEMBERSHIP DIRECTORY - ASSOCIATION OF COLLEGE, UNIVERSITY AND COMMUNITY ARTS ADMINISTRATORS. Main/Corp Association of College, University and Community Arts Administrators. US. English. $10.00 Members, $75.00 Nonmembers. Association of College University & Community Arts Administrators, 6225 University Avenue, Madison WI 53705-1099. LC NX765. DD 700.2573. *ACUCAA Membership Directory.*

MEMBERSHIP DIRECTORY - ASSOCIATION OF DIESEL SPECIALISTS. (MEMBERSHIP DIRECTORY). Main/Corp Association of Diesel Specialists. 0278-0461. US. English. an. Diesel Progress North American, PO Box 26308, 11225 West Bluemound Road, Milwaukee WI 53226. LC TJ619. DD 621.4360601.

MEMBERSHIP DIRECTORY - ATLANTIC PROVINCES LIBRARY. (MEMBERSHIP DIRECTORY - ATLANTIC PROVINCES LIBRARY ASSOCIATION). Main/Corp Atlantic Provinces Library Association. VAT APLA. Membership Directory, Atlantic Provinces Library Association. Membership Directory. 1978/79-. 0707-3895. CN. English. an. Free to Members, $5.00 Each Number to Libraries. Atlantic Provinces Library Association, School of Library Services, Dalhousie University, Halifax Nova Scotia B3H 4H8 Canada. DD 020.25715.

MEMBERSHIP DIRECTORY - BETTER BUSINESS BUREAU OF SOUTHEASTERN VIRGINIA. Main/Corp Better Business Bureau of Southeastern Virginia. VFOAT Membership Directory (Better Business Bureau of Southeastern Virginia). US. English. Better Business Bureau of Southeastern Virginia Inc, 2019 Llewellyn Avenue, PO Box 11133, Norfolk VA 23517. LC HF5065.V8. DD 338.740257555.

MEMBERSHIP DIRECTORY - BURLINGTON CHAMBER OF COMMERCE. (MEMBERSHIP DIRECTORY). Main/Corp Burlington Chamber of Commerce. 0227-6666. CN. English. an. Free. Burlington Chamber of Commerce, 1340 Lakeshore Road, PO Box 103, Burlington Ontario L7R 3X8 Canada. DD 380.060713533.

MEMBERSHIP DIRECTORY - CANADA-JAPAN TRADE COUNCIL. (MEMBERSHIP DIRECTORY). Main/Corp Canada-Japan Trade Council. 0822-9899. CN. English. an. Canada-Japan Trade Council, Suite 903/Fuller Building, 75 Albert Street, Ottawa Ontario K1P 5E7 Canada. LC HF298. DD 382.0621. *Members of the Canadian Trade Council and Their Business Classification, 0822-9880.*

MEMBERSHIP DIRECTORY - CANADIAN ASSOCIATION FOR INFORMATION SCIENCE. Main/Corp Canadian Association for Information Science. VFOAT Annuaire des Membres - Association Canadienne des Sciences de l'Information. 1976/77-. 0705-6834. Periodical. CN. English (French). Free to Members. Canadian Association for Information Science, PO Box 158 Station A, Ottawa Ontario K1N 8V2 Canada. DD 020.62271.

MEMBERSHIP DIRECTORY - CANADIAN PSYCHIATRIC ASSOCIATION. Main/Corp Canadian Psychiatric Association. VFOAT Repertoire des Membres - Association des Psychiatres du Canada. 0576-5986. CN. text in English and French. ir. Canadian Psychiatric Association/Suite 103, 225 Lisgar Street, Ottawa Ontario K2P 0C6 Canada. Tel (416)297-2030. DD 616.89006271. NLM WM 22 DC2 C3M.

MEMBERSHIP DIRECTORY - CANADIAN URBAN TRANSIT ASSOCIATION. (MEMBERSHIP DIRECTORY). Main/Corp Canadian Urban Transit Association. 1983-. 0821-2988. CN. English. an. $15.00 Each Number Members Only. Canadian Urban Transit Association, Suite 220/Union Station 140 Bay Street, Toronto Ontario M4P 1K5 Canada. DD 388.406071. *Transit Fact Book and Membership Directory, 0706-7658.*

MEMBERSHIP DIRECTORY - CHAMBER MUSIC AMERICA. (MEMBERSHIP DIRECTORY). Main/Corp Chamber Music America. 1980-. 0277-4054. US. English. $5.00. Chamber Music of America, 1372 Broadway/14th Floor, New York NY 10018. Ed Lillian Helmen. LC ML19. DD 785.7002573.

MEMBERSHIP DIRECTORY CLASSIFIED BY SPECIALTY. Main/Corp Financial Analysts Federation. 0147-1953. US. English. $30.00 Nonmembers. Financial Analysts Federation, Tower/Suite 219, East 42nd Street, New York NY 10017. LC HG4907. DD 332.6202573.

MEMBERSHIP DIRECTORY - COMMUNITY DEVELOPMENT SOCIETY. Main/Corp Community Development Society. Periodical. US. English. an. Community Development Society, Anderson 43 Fellogg Center, East Lansing MI 48823.

MEMBERSHIP DIRECTORY - COUNCIL FOR ADVANCEMENT AND SUPPORT OF EDUCATION. Main/Corp Council for Advancement and Support of Education. 1976-. 0146-583X. US. English. $50.00. Council for Advancement and Support of Education, One Dupont Circle/Suite 530, Washington DC 20036. LC L900. DD 370.2575. *Directory - Council for Advancement and Support of Education, 0099-1805.*

MEMBERSHIP DIRECTORY - DIPLOMATIC AND CONSULAR OFFICERS, RETIRED. (MEMBERSHIP DIRECTORY). Main/Corp Diplomatic and Consular Officers, Retired. 0092-010X. US. English. Diplomatic and Consular Officers Retired, 1718 H Street, Washington DC 20006. LC JX1705. DD 327.202573.

MEMBERSHIP DIRECTORY - EARLY AMERICAN INDUSTRIES ASSOCIATION. (MEMBERSHIP DIRECTORY). Main/Corp Early American Industries Association. 0424-0316. US. English. $18.00 Domestic, $20.00 Foreign. Early American Industries Association, PO Box 2128, Empire State Plaza Station, Albany NY 12220. Tel (518)439-2215. Ed Elliot Sayward. bk rev. Circ 2,800. (ctrl). The Association is composed of collectors of tool and other artifacts related to early American crafts and industries.

MEMBERSHIP DIRECTORY - FEDERAL HOME LOAN BANK OF GREENSBORO. Main/Corp Federal Home Loan Bank of Greensboro. 0430-1749. US. English. ir. Federal Home Loan Bank of Greensboro, Greensboro NC 27420. DD 332.1.

MEMBERSHIP DIRECTORY - FINANCIAL ANALYSTS FEDERATION. (MEMBERSHIP DIRECTORY - THE FINANCIAL ANALYSTS FEDERATION). Main/Corp Financial Analysts Federation. 0430-4756. US. English. an. Financial Analysts Federation, Tower/Suite 219, East 42nd Street, New York NY 10017. LC HG4907. DD 332.6206273. *Directory of Memberships.*

MEMBERSHIP DIRECTORY - FINANCIAL MANAGERS SOCIETY FOR SAVINGS INSTITUTIONS, INC. Main/Corp Financial Managers Society for Savings Institutions. VFOAT Directory of Members - Financial Managers Society for Savings Institutions. US. English. an. $75.00. Financial Managers Inc, 111 East Wacker Drive/Suite 2221, Chicago IL 60601. Tel (312)938-2576. Ed Marilyn Helfers. LC HG2121. DD 658.15933. adv acc. Circ 5,000. (ctrl). Directory of members and affiliates of the Financial Managers Society Inc., geographically and alphabetically. *Directory of Members - Financial Managers Society for Savings Institutions, Inc., 0097-2517.*

MEMBERSHIP DIRECTORY - FLA. (MEMBERSHIP DIRECTORY). Main/Corp Foothills Library Association. VAT Membership Directory - Foothills Library Association (1984). 1983/1984-. 0826-7006. CN. English. an. Foothills Library Association, c/o Calgary Board of Education, 3610-36 Street South East, Calgary Alberta T2A 1N4 Canada. DD 020.62471233. *Directory, 0822-6628.*

MEMBERSHIP DIRECTORY - FLORIDA INSTITUTE OF CERTIFIED PUBLIC ACCOUNTANTS. Main/Corp Florida Insititue of Certified Public Accountants. US. English. Florida Institute of Certified Public Accountants, 1320 Executive Center Drive/Suite 100, PO Box 5437, Tallahassee FL 32301. LC HF5627. DD 657.025759.

Yearbooks, Almanacs, Directories

MEMBERSHIP DIRECTORY - FLORIDA LIBRARY ASSOCIATION. Main/Corp Florida Library Association. 1959-. 0270-4595. US. English. Florida Library Association, 2020 West Fairbanks Avenue, Winter Park FL 32789. LC Z720.A45. DD 020.922, B.

MEMBERSHIP DIRECTORY - FOREST HISTORY SOCIETY. Main/Corp Forest History Society. (Summer 1975-). Periodical. US. English.

MEMBERSHIP DIRECTORY - GEOLOGICAL SOCIETY OF AMERICA. (MEMBERSHIP DIRECTORY). Main/Corp Geological Society of America. Began in 1978. 0277-5816. US. English. an. Geological Society of America Inc, PO Box 9140, Boulder CO 80301. LC QE1. DD 550.6073. *Yearbook - Geological Society of America, 0095-3547.*

MEMBERSHIP DIRECTORY - GREATER WASHINGTON BOARD OF TRADE. (MEMBERSHIP DIRECTORY). Main/Corp Greater Washington Board of Trade. VFOAT Greater Washington Board of Trade Membership Directory. 0731-4418. US. English. an. $35.00. The Greater Washington Board of Trade, 1129 20th Street Northwest, Washington DC 20036. LC HF296.W43. DD 381.060753.

MEMBERSHIP DIRECTORY - GYPSY LORE SOCIETY, NORTH AMERICAN CHAPTER. Main/Corp Gypsy Lore Society., North American Chapter. 0193-1598. US. English. $2.00. Gypsy Lore Society, 2104 Dexter Avenue, Silver Spring MD 20902. Tel (301)681-3123. Ed Sheila Salo. LC DX101. DD 909.0491497. adv acc. Circ 250. (ctrl) *Aid to communication among scholars and others interested in gypsy studies. Lists members, their areas of interest, their contributions to the field.*

MEMBERSHIP DIRECTORY - HAMILTON CONSTRUCTION ASSOCIATION. (MEMBERSHIP DIRECTORY). Main/Corp Hamilton Construction Association. 0714-3141. CN. English. an. Free. Hamilton Construction Association, 1494 Regent Avenue West, Winnipeg Manitoba R2C 3A8 Canada. DD 338.4769006071352.

MEMBERSHIP DIRECTORY - INDONESIAN PETROLEUM ASSOCIATION. PROFESSIONAL DIVISION. Main/Corp Indonesian Petroleum Association. Professional Division. English. an. Indonesia Petroleum Association, JL. Menteng Raya 3, Jakarta Pusat Indonesia. LC HD9576.I5. DD 338.27282025598.

MEMBERSHIP DIRECTORY - INDUSTRIAL DESIGNERS SOCIETY OF AMERICA. (MEMBERSHIP DIRECTORY). Main/Corp Industrial Designers Society of America. 0741-2916. US. English. an. Industrial Designers Society of America, 1717 North Street NW, Washington DC 20036. LC TS171.A1. DD 745.20607.

MEMBERSHIP DIRECTORY - INSTITUTE OF INTERNAL AUDITORS. (MEMBERSHIP DIRECTORY). Main/Corp Institute of Internal Auditors. 0276-1424. US. English. Institute of Internal Auditors Inc, 249 Maitland Avenue, Altamonte Springs FL 32701. LC HF5668. DD 657.45802573.

MEMBERSHIP DIRECTORY - INSTITUTE OF MATHEMATICAL STATISTICS. (MEMBERSHIP DIRECTORY). Main/Corp Institute of Mathematical Statistics. VFOAT Directory of I.M.S. Members. 0736-8402. US. English. an. The Institute of Mathematical Statistics, 3401 Investment Boulevard/Suite 6, Hayward CA 94545. LC QA276.A1. DD 519.50601.

MEMBERSHIP DIRECTORY - INSTITUTE OF RESIDENTIAL MARKETING. Main/Corp Institute of Residential Marketing. 0193-094X. US. English. National Association of Home Builders, Marketing Department, 15th and M Streets NW, Washington DC 20005. LC HD9715.U5. DD 381.45690802573.

MEMBERSHIP DIRECTORY - INSTITUTE OF TRANSPORTATION ENGINEERS. Main/Corp Institute of Transportation Engineers. 0161-9462. US. English. Institute of Transportation Engineers, PO Box 9234, Arlington VA 22209. LC TA1001. DD 629.0406273.

MEMBERSHIP DIRECTORY - INTERNATIONAL ASSOCIATION OF ASSESSING OFFICERS. Main/Corp International Association of Assessing Officers. VFOAT Members Only. Began with 1977. 0538-446X. US. English. ir. International Association of Assessing Officers, PO Box 94573, Chicago IL 60690. *IAAO Membership Directory.*

MEMBERSHIP DIRECTORY - INTERNATIONAL ASSOCIATION OF ASSESSING OFFICERS. PERSONAL PROPERTY SECTION. (MEMBERSHIP DIRECTORY). Main/Corp International Association of Assessing Officers. Personal Property Section. 0737-4267. US. English. International Association of Assessing Officers, 1313 East 60th Street, Chicago IL 60637. LC HD1387. DD 350.7243102573.

MEMBERSHIP DIRECTORY - INTERNATIONAL ASSOCIATION OF MARINE SCIENCE LIBRARIES AND INFORMATION CENTERS. (MEMBERSHIP DIRECTORY). Main/Corp International Association of Marine Science Libraries and Information Centers. 1983/1984-. 0255-8114. CN. English. an. International Association of Marine Science Libraries and Information Centers c/o Bedford Institute of Oceanography The Library, P O Box 1006, Dartsmouth Nova Scotia B2Y 4A2 Canada. DD 026.551460025.

MEMBERSHIP DIRECTORY - INTERNATIONAL BANK NOTE SOCIETY. Main/Corp International Bank Note Society. 0198-9057. US. English. an. International Bank Note Society, M Alusic/General Secretary, 4910 Biscane Avenue 13, Racine WI 53406. LC HG353. DD 0769.550601.

MEMBERSHIP DIRECTORY - INTERNATIONAL COUNCIL FOR TRADITIONAL MUSIC. (MEMBERSHIP DIRECTORY). Main/Corp International Council for Traditional Music. 1982-. 0739-3954. US. English. International Council for Traditional Music, Department of Music, Columbia University, New York NY 10027. Tel (212)678-0332. LC ML3798. DD 781.70601. Circ 1,000. *Address list of International Council for Traditional Music members and institution subscribers. Members.*

MEMBERSHIP DIRECTORY - INTERNATIONAL COUNCIL OF SHOPPING CENTERS. (MEMBERSHIP DIRECTORY). Main/Corp International Council of Shopping Centers. 8756-9337. US. English. an. International Council of Shopping Centers, 665 5th Avenue, New York NY 10022. LC HF5429.7. DD 381.10601.

MEMBERSHIP DIRECTORY - INTERNATIONAL FRANCHISE ASSOCIATION. Main/Corp International Franchise Association. 1981/82-. Periodical. US. English.

MEMBERSHIP DIRECTORY - INTERNATIONAL SOCIETY OF APPRAISERS. (MEMBERSHIP DIRECTORY). Main/Corp International Society of Appraisers. VFOAT Official . . . Membership Directory. 1984-. 8755-4356. US. English. an. International Society of Appraisers, PO Box 726, Hoffman Estates IL 60195. DD 332. *Official . . . Membership Directory.*

MEMBERSHIP DIRECTORY - INTERNATIONAL SOCIETY OF HYPNOSIS. (MEMBERSHIP DIRECTORY). Main/Corp International Society of Hypnosis. Began in 1976. 0277-4151. US. English. 111 North 49th Street, Box 144, Philadelphia PA 19139. NLM WM 22.1 161M.

MEMBERSHIP DIRECTORY - INTERNATIONAL TRUMPET GUILD. (MEMBERSHIP DIRECTORY). Main/Corp International Trumpet Guild. 8755-5964. US. English. Bryan Goff/Treasurer, International Trumpet Guild, School of Music, Florida State University, Tallahassee FL 32306. DD 788.

MEMBERSHIP DIRECTORY - INVESTMENT DEALERS' ASSOCIATION OF CANADA. (MEMBERSHIP DIRECTORY). Main/Corp Investment Dealers' Association of Canada. No. 1-. 0711-4885. Periodical. CN. English. sa. Free to Members. Membership Directory, Investment Dealers' Association of Canada, PO Box 217, Commerce Court South, Toronto Ontario M5L 1E8 Canada. DD 332.6202571. *Blue Book.*

MEMBERSHIP DIRECTORY - KOREA-UNITED STATES ECONOMIC COUNCIL. Main/Corp Korea-U.S. Economic Council. KO. English (Korean). ir. Korea US Economic Council, CPO Box 6754 10-1, 2-KA Hoehyun-dong, Chung-ku Seoul. LC HF1602.5. DD 382.0951950730601.

MEMBERSHIP DIRECTORY - LIBRARY ASSOCIATION OF ALBERTA. Main/Corp Library Association of Alberta. 1977/78-. 0705-4025. Periodical. CN. English. ir. Library Association of Alberta, 9505 99B Street, Edmonton Alberta T6E 3X1 Canada. DD 020.62347123. *Directory of Members.*

MEMBERSHIP DIRECTORY - MEETING PLANNERS INTERNATIONAL. (MEMBERSHIP DIRECTORY). Main/Corp Meeting Planners International. VFOAT M.P.I.-Membership Directory. 0731-292X. US. English. $100.00. 3719 Roosevelt Boulevard, Middletown OH 45042. LC AS6. DD 658.4560601.

MEMBERSHIP DIRECTORY - METALLURGICAL SOCIETY OF AIME. (MEMBERSHIP DIRECTORY - THE METALLURGICAL SOCIETY OF AIME). Main/Corp Metallurgical Society of AIME. 0539-4589. Periodical. US. English. The Society, 233 Spring Street, New York NY 10013.

MEMBERSHIP DIRECTORY - METROPOLITAN WASHINGTON BOARD OF TRADE. Main/Corp Metropolitan Washington Board of Trade. 0362-3807. US. English. an. $25.00. Metropolitan Washington Board of Trade, 1129 20th Street NW/Suite 200, Washington DC 20036. LC HF296. DD 381.062753.

MEMBERSHIP DIRECTORY - MICHIGAN SPEECH-LANGUAGE-HEARING ASSOCIATION. (MEMBERSHIP DIRECTORY). Main/Corp Michigan Speech-Language-Hearing Association. 0742-1400. US. English. Michigan Speech-Language-Hearing Association, 855 Grove Street, East Lansing MI 48823. LC HV2561.M5. DD 362.4260774.

MEMBERSHIP DIRECTORY - MICHIGAN SPEECH-LANGUAGE-HEARING ASSOCIATION. Main/Corp Michigan Speech-Language-Hearing Association. US. English. Michican Speech-Language-Hearing Association, 855 Grove Street, East Lansing MI 48823. LC HV2522. DD 362.42060774.

MEMBERSHIP DIRECTORY - MINNESOTA LIBRARY ASSOCIATION. (MEMBERSHIP DIRECTORY). Main/Corp Minnesota Library Association. VFOAT Minnesota Library Association Directory. 1981-. 0737-8572. US. English. an. Minnesota Library Association, Membership Services, Box 863, Lake Crystal MN 56055. LC Z673.M66. DD 020.6234776. *Directory.*

MEMBERSHIP DIRECTORY - NATIONAL ABORTION FEDERATION. Main/Corp National Abortion Federation (U.S.). 0196-3163. US. English. National Abortion Federation, 110 East 59th Street/Suite 1019, New York NY 10022. LC HQ767.5.U5. DD 363.4602573.

MEMBERSHIP DIRECTORY - NATIONAL ASSOCIATION FOR MUSIC THERAPY. (MEMBERSHIP DIRECTORY). Main/Corp National Association for Music Therapy. 8755-2892. US. English. an. National Association for Music Therapy, 1001 Connecticut Avenue NW/Suite 800, Washington DC 20036. DD 615.

MEMBERSHIP DIRECTORY - NATIONAL ASSOCIATION OF CHURCH BUSINESS ADMINISTRATION (U.S.). (MEMBERSHIP DIRECTORY). Main/Corp National Association of Church Business Administration (U.S.). 0882-0031. US. English. National Association of Church Business Administration, 7001 Grapevine Highway/Suite 324, Fort Worth TX 76118. LC BV652.A1. DD 254.002573.

MEMBERSHIP DIRECTORY - NATIONAL ASSOCIATION OF COLLEGE ADMISSIONS COUNSELORS. (MEMBERSHIP DIRECTORY). Main/Corp National Association of College Admissions Counselors. 0090-3965. US. English. an. $10.00. NACAC Membership Directory, 9933 Lawler Avenue/Suite 500, Skokie IL 60076. Tel (312)676-0500. LC LB2343. DD 378.19402573. *Membership Directory.*

MEMBERSHIP DIRECTORY - NATIONAL ASSOCIATION OF COSMETOLOGY SCHOOLS. Main/Corp National Association of Cosmetology Schools. 0360-3490. US. English. National Association of

Yearbooks, Almanacs, Directories

Cosmetology Schools, 599 South Livingston Avenue, Livingston NJ 07039. LC TT954.5. DD 646.72071073.

MEMBERSHIP DIRECTORY - NATIONAL ASSOCIATION OF RECYCLING INDUSTRIES. (MEMBERSHIP DIRECTORY). Main/Corp National Association of Recycling Industries. 0275-1704. US. English. National Association of Recycling Industries, 330 Madison Avenue, New York NY 10017. LC TD794.5. DD 604.602573.

MEMBERSHIP DIRECTORY - NATIONAL ASSOCIATION OF SUGGESTION SYSTEMS. (MEMBERSHIP DIRECTORY). Main/Corp National Association of Suggestion Systems. 0733-9747. US. English. an. National Association of Suggestion Systems, 435 North Michigan Avenue, Chicago IL 60611. LC HF5549.5.S8. DD 658.314.

MEMBERSHIP DIRECTORY - NATIONAL COUNCIL FOR RESOURCE DEVELOPMENT. Main/Corp National Council for Resource Development. VFOAT NCRD Membership Directory. 0162-0339. US. English. an. $60.00. National Council for Resource Development, Suite 410/One Dupont Circle Northwest, Washington DC 20036. Tel (202)293-7050. Ed Terri Fawcett. LC L901. DD 370.2573. Circ 650. (ctrl).

MEMBERSHIP DIRECTORY - NATIONAL COUNCIL OF UNIVERSITY RESEARCH ADMINISTRATORS. Main/Corp National Council of University Research Administrators. 0272-4073. US. English. National Council of University Research Administrators, 1100 17th Street NW, Washington DC 20036. LC Q11. DD 001.4068.

MEMBERSHIP DIRECTORY - NATIONAL PEANUT COUNCIL. Main/Corp National Peanut Council. 0748-982X. US. English. an.

MEMBERSHIP DIRECTORY - NATIONAL SOCIETY FOR PERFORMANCE AND INSTRUCTION. (MEMBERSHIP DIRECTORY). Main/Corp National Society for Performance and Instruction. VFOAT N.S.P.I. Membership Directory. 0730-7675. US. English. an. National Society for Performance and Instruction, 1126 Sixteenth Street Northwest/Suite 315, Washington DC 20036. LC LB1028.5. DD 371.3944502573.

MEMBERSHIP DIRECTORY - NATIONAL SOCIETY OF FUND RAISING EXECUTIVES. Main/Corp National Society of Fund Raising Executives. 0195-6795. US. English. National Society of Fund Raising Executives, Investment Building, 1511 K Street NW/Suite 831, Washington DC 20005. LC HG177. DD 361.702573.

MEMBERSHIP DIRECTORY - NEW ENGLAND FOLK FESTIVAL ASSOCIATION. Main/Corp New England Folk Festival Association. 0160-483X. US. English. $2.00. New England Folk Festival Association, Mrs Julie Keith, 269 Harvard Street, Cambridge MA 02139. LC GR106. DD 390.02574.

MEMBERSHIP DIRECTORY - NEW YORK STATE LAND TITLE ASSOCIATION. Main/Corp New York State Land Title Association. 1967-. US. English. an. New York State Land Title Association, 233 Broadway, New York NY 10007. *Directory - New York State Land Title Association*.

MEMBERSHIP DIRECTORY. NEWFOUNDLAND AND LABRADOR. (MEMBERSHIP DIRECTORY : NEWFOUNDLAND AND LABRADOR). Main/Corp Newfoundland Library Association. 1974/75-. 0319-7638. CN. English. an. $5. Newfoundland Library Association, Arts & Culture Centre Allandale Centre, St John's Newfoundland A1B 3A3 Canada. DD 020.6234718. *Membership Directory, 0319-7646*.

MEMBERSHIP DIRECTORY - NORTHAMERICAN HEATING AND AIRCONDITIONING WHOLESALERS ASSOC. (MEMBERSHIP DIRECTORY). Main/Corp Northamerican Heating and Airconditioning Wholesalers Assoc. 0278-4041. US. English. Northamerican Heating and Airconditioning Wholesalers Association, 1661 West Henderson Road, Columbus OH 43220. LC HD9683.N67. DD 381.456214002573.

MEMBERSHIP DIRECTORY OF THE AMERICAN SOCIETY FOR HOSPITAL PUBLIC RELATIONS. Main/Corp American Hospital Association. American Society for Hospital Public Relations. 8756-4904. US. English. American Society for Hospital Public Relations of the American Hospital Association, 840 North Lake Shore Drive, Chicago IL 60611.

MEMBERSHIP DIRECTORY OF THE BIOFEEDBACK SOCIETY OF AMERICA. Main/Corp Biofeedback Society of America. 0739-5280. US. English. an. $16.00. Biofeedback Society of America, 4301 Owens Street, Wheat Ridge CO 80003. Tel (303)422-8436. Ed Francine Butler. LC BF319.5.B5. DD 152.188. Circ 2,100. (ctrl). A listing of all members, their clinical and research interests.

MEMBERSHIP DIRECTORY OF THE FEDERAL STATISTICS USERS' CONFERENCE. Main/Conf Federal Statistics Users' Conference. VFOAT Membership Directory - Federal Statistics Users' Conference. Mar. 1977-. 0148-320X. US. English. $5.00 Members, $10.00 Nonmembers. Federal Statistics Users' Conference, 1030 15th Street NW, Washington DC 20005. LC HA37.U55. DD 310.6273.

MEMBERSHIP DIRECTORY OF THE GOLF COURSE SUPERINTENDENTS ASSOCIATION OF AMERICA. (MEMBERSHIP DIRECTORY). Main/Corp Golf Course Superintendents Association of America. VFOAT GCSAA Membership Directory. 0436-1474. US. English. Golf Course Superintendents Association of America, 1617 St Andrews Drive, Lawrence KS 66044. LC GV975. DD 658.91796352068606273.

THE MEMBERSHIP DIRECTORY OF THE INFORMATION INDUSTRY ASSOCIATION CEASED. Main/Corp Information Industry Association. VFOAT Information Sources. 0148-1053. US. English. an. $21.00. Information Industry Association, 316 Pennsylvania Avenue SE/Suite 400, Washington DC 20003. LC HC102. DD 020.62.

MEMBERSHIP DIRECTORY OF THE PHOTOGRAPHIC HISTORICAL SOCIETY OF N.Y. (MEMBERSHIP DIRECTORY). Main/Corp Photographic Historical Society of New York. 0093-254X. US. English. $3.00. Photographic Historical Society of New York, 244 Fifth Avenue, New York NY 10001. LC TR1. DD 770.627471.

MEMBERSHIP DIRECTORY - ONTARIO MORTGAGE BROKERS ASSOCIATION. (MEMBERSHIP DIRECTORY). Main/Corp Ontario Mortgage Brokers Association. 0826-0559. CN. English. an. Free. Ontario Mortgage Brokers Association, 8 King Street East Suite/1710, Toronto Ontario M5C 1B5 Canada. DD 332.72060713. (ctrl). *Membership Roster, 0227-258X*.

MEMBERSHIP DIRECTORY - ONTARIO SPEECH AND HEARING ASSOCIATION. (MEMBERSHIP DIRECTORY). Main/Corp Ontario Speech and Hearing Association. 0821-4921. CN. English. an. Free. Ontario Speech and Hearing Association, 170 St George Street/Suite 504, Ottawa Ontario M5R 2M8 Canada. DD 616.8550060713.

MEMBERSHIP DIRECTORY - ONTARIO SWIMMING POOL ASSOCIATION CEASED. Main/Corp Ontario Swimming Pool Association. Ceased with 1982 issue. 0316-6937. Periodical. CN. English. Ontario Swimming Pool Association, Suite 210/61 Alness Street, Downsview Ontario M3J 2H2 Canada. DD 690.574062713.

MEMBERSHIP DIRECTORY - PACIFIC TROLLERS' ASSOCIATION. Main/Corp Pacific Trollers' Association. 1973-. 0319-194X. CN. English. an. Pacific Trollers' Association, PO Box 94336, Richmond British Columbia V6Y 2A8 Canada. DD 639.2062711.

MEMBERSHIP DIRECTORY - PROFESSIONAL CONVENTION MANAGEMENT ASSOCIATION. (MEMBERSHIP DIRECTORY). Main/Corp Professional Convention Management Association. VFOAT PCMA . . . Membership Directory. 0743-8583. US. English. an. Professional Convention Management Association, 2027 First Avenue North/Suite 1007, Commerce Center, Birmingham AL 35203.

MEMBERSHIP DIRECTORY - PSYCHONOMIC SOCIETY. (MEMBERSHIP DIRECTORY). Main/Corp Psychonomic Society. VFOAT Psychonomic Society Membership Directory. 0748-9951. US. English. an. The Psychonomic Society, 2904 Guadalupe Street, Austin TX 78705. LC BF11. DD 150.2573.

MEMBERSHIP DIRECTORY - SAVINGS INSTITUTIONS MARKETING SOCIETY OF AMERICA. (MEMBERSHIP DIRECTORY). Main/Corp Savings Institutions Marketing Society of America. 0278-5773. US. English. an. Savings Institutions Marketing Society of America, 111 East Wacker Drive, Chicago IL 60601. LC HG1536. DD 332.3202573.

MEMBERSHIP DIRECTORY - SIGMA CHI FRATERNITY. (MEMBERSHIP DIRECTORY - THE SIGMA CHI FRATERNITY). Main/Corp Sigma Chi. VFOAT Sigma Chi Directory. 3571-6501. US. English. 1714 Hinman Avenue, Box 469, Evanston IL 60204.

MEMBERSHIP DIRECTORY - SOCIETY FOR NUTRITION EDUCATION. Main/Corp Society for Nutrition Education. 0192-3714. US. English. $5.00. Society for Nutrition Education, 2140 Shattuck Avenue/Suite 1110, Berkeley CA 94704. LC TX341. DD 641.1071073.

MEMBERSHIP DIRECTORY - SOCIETY FOR THE ADVANCEMENT OF MATERIAL AND PROCESS ENGINEERING. (MEMBERSHIP DIRECTORY). Main/Corp Society for the Advancement of Material and Process Engineering. 0092-1017. US. English. Society for the Advancement of Material and Process Engineering, 668 South Azusa Avenue, PO Box 613, Azusa CA 91702. LC TA12. DD 620.1106273.

MEMBERSHIP DIRECTORY - SOCIETY OF AMERICAN ARCHIVISTS. Main/Corp Society of American Archivists. 0145-6490. US. English. ir. Society of American Archivists, 600 South Federal/Suite #504, Chicago IL 60605. Tel (312)922-0140. LC CD3020. DD 020.62273.

MEMBERSHIP DIRECTORY - SOCIETY OF COSMETIC CHEMISTS (U.S.). (MEMBERSHIP DIRECTORY). Main/Corp Society of Cosmetic Chemists (U.S.). 0730-7756. US. English. Society of Cosmetic Chemists, Suite 1701/1995 Broadway, New York NY 10023. LC TP983.A6. DD 668.5506073.

MEMBERSHIP DIRECTORY - SOCIETY OF NEMATOLOGISTS. Main/Corp Society of Nematologists. 0091-276X. US. English. Secretary: Dr B Y Endo, USDA Plant Industry Station, Beltsville MD 20705. LC QL35. DD 595.1820621.

MEMBERSHIP DIRECTORY - STATISTICAL SOCIETY OF CANADA. Main/Corp Statistical Society of Canada. VFOAT Liste des Membres - Societe Statistique du Canada. 1978/79-. 0709-5953. CN. English (French). $9.67. Statistical Society of Canada, McGill University, 805 Ouest rue Sherbrooke, Montreal Quebec H3A 2K6 Canada. DD 519.506271.

MEMBERSHIP DIRECTORY - SUBURBAN NEWSPAPERS OF AMERICA. Main/Corp Suburban Newspapers of America, Chicago, Ill. 0270-4641. US. English. Suburban Newspapers of America, 111 East Wacker Drive, Chicago IL 60610. LC Z6944.C64, PN4888.C594. DD 071.3.

MEMBERSHIP DIRECTORY - TECHNICAL SECTION, CANADIAN PULP AND PAPER ASSOCIATION. (MEMBERSHIP DIRECTORY). Main/Corp Canadian Pulp and Paper Association. Technical Section. VFOAT Annuaire des Membres. 1983-. 0821-1396. CN. English (French). an. Free to Members. Canadian Pulp and Paper Association, 23rd Floor/1155 Metcalfe Street, Montreal Quebec H3B 2X9 Canada. DD 676.02571. *Membership Directories, 0714-3540*.

MEMBERSHIP DIRECTORY - UCPA. (MEMBERSHIP DIRECTORY). Main/Corp University and College Placement Association. VAT Membership Directory - University and College Placement Association, Repertoire d'Adresses - Association de Placement Universitaire et Collegial. 1981/82-. 0713-5041. CN. English (text in French). an. $5.00 Per Volume. UCPA Membership Directory, 10th Floor/43

Yearbooks, Almanacs, Directories

Eglinton Avenue, Toronto Ontario M4P 1A2 Canada. **DD** 378.1942502571. *Handbook and Membership Directory, 0228-0701.*

MEMBERSHIP DIRECTORY - UNIVERSITY FILM ASSOCIATION. **Main/Corp** University Film Association. 0094-3010. US. English. University of Iowa/TV Center, F Dennis Lynch UFA Membership Chairman, Iowa City IA 52240. **LC** PN1993.U616. **DD** 791.4306273.

MEMBERSHIP DIRECTORY - VANCOUVER ISLAND CONSTRUCTION ASSOCIATION. (MEMBERSHIP DIRECTORY). **Main/Corp** Vancouver Island Construction Association. **VFOAT** Membership Directory & Construction Buyers Guide. 0712-5623. CN. English. an. Free to members. Vancouver Island Construction Association, 1075 Alston Street, Victoria British Columbia V5W 3T9 Canada. **DD** 338.4769002571134.

MEMBERSHIP DIRECTORY - WATER POLLUTION CONTROL FEDERATION. **Main/Corp** Water Pollution Control Federation. 1983-. US. English. **NLM** WA 22.1 W324M.

MEMBERSHIP DIRECTORY - WOMEN'S CAUCUS FOR ART. **Main/Corp** Women's Caucus for Art. 1984-1985-. US. English. $30.00 Membership. Women's Caucus for Art, National Office, Moore College of Art, 20th & The Parkway, Philadelphia PA 19103. **Tel** (215)854-0922. Ed Janet Miller. bk rev. adv acc. **Circ** 3,500. (ctrl). A membership magazine which summarizes NCA annual activities. Our directory is a listing of all current members, with address, phone number and area of specialization.

MEMBERSHIP DIRECTORY - WORLD MARICULTURE SOCIETY. **Main/Corp** World Mariculture Society. 1981-. US. English. an.

MEMBERSHIP ROSTER AND CHAPTER DIRECTORY - CANSPA/OSPA. (MEMBERSHIP ROSTER AND CHAPTER DIRECTORY). **Main/Corp** Ontario Swimming Pool Association. **VAT** Membership Roster and Chapter Directory - Canadian Swimming Pool Association/Ontario Swimming Pool Association. 1982-. 0822-8582. CN. English. an. Free. Ontario Swimming Pool Association, Suite 217/6 Lansing Square, Willowdale Ontario M2J 1T5 Canada. **DD** 338.4769089. *Membership Directory, 0316-6937.*

MEMBERSHIP ROSTER AND DIRECTORY OF INFORMATION - WESTERN PENNSYLVANIA GENEALOGICAL SOCIETY. (MEMBERSHIP ROSTER AND DIRECTORY OF INFORMATION). **Main/Corp** Western Pennsylvania Genealogical Society. 0275-1925. Periodical. US. English. Western Pennsylvania Genealogical Society, 4338 Bigelow Boulevard, Pittsburgh PA 15213. **LC** F148. **DD** 929.1060748.

MEMBERSHIP-TEAM DIRECTORY - AMERICAN CLEFT PALATE ASSOCIATION. (MEMBERSHIP-TEAM DIRECTORY). **Main/Corp** Americna Cleft Palate Association. 0733-8120. US. English. an. $6.00. American Cleft Palate Association, University of Pittsburgh, 331 Salkhal, Pittsburgh PA 15261. **Tel** (412)681-9620. *Membership Directory.*

MEMBERSHIP/COMMITTEE DIRECTORY - BUILDING OWNERS AND MANAGERS ASSOCIATION INTERNATIONAL. **Main/Corp** Building Owners and Managers Association International. 0192-9909. US. English. an. Building Owners and Managers Association International, 1221 Massachusetts Avenue NW, Washington DC 20005. **LC** TX955. **DD** 643.0621.

MEMBERSHIP/COMMITTEE DIRECTORY - NATIONAL ASSOCIATION OF MEAT PURVEYORS (U.S.). (MEMBERSHIP/COMMITTEE DIRECTORY). **Main/Corp** National Association of Meat Purveyors (U.S.). US. English. an. National Association of Meat Purveyors, 8365-B Greensboro Drive, McLean VA 22102.

THE MEMPHIS MUSIC DIRECTORY. 1980-. 0272-8214. US. English. an. $5.00 Each Copy. Ward Archer Jr, Memphis Music Directory, PO Box 41072, Memphis TN 38104. **LC** ML19. **DD** 780.2576819.

MENNONITE BUSINESS AND PROFESSIONAL PEOPLE'S DIRECTORY. Began in 1974. US. English. $12.50. Office of Executive Director, 2000 South 15th Street Walnut Court D4-2, Goshen IN 46526. **LC** HC102. **DD** 338.002573.

MENNONITE YEARBOOK AND DIRECTORY. (MENNONITE YEARBOOK & DIRECTORY). **VFOAT** Mennonite Yearbook. **VAT** Mennonite Year Book and Directory. V. 1- 1910-. 0275-1178. US. English. be. $6.95. Mennonite Publishing House, 616 Walnut Avenue, Scottsdale PA 15683. **Tel** (412)887-8500. Ed James E Horsch. **LC** BX8107. **DD** 289.7. **Circ** 5,000. Information concerning the ministers, congregations, boards and institutions of the Mennonite Church in North America.

MENTAL HEALTH SYSTEMS SOFTWARE DIRECTORY. 1985 Ed.-. 0883-3443. Periodical. US. English. $5.00 Members, $10.00 Nonmembers. American Association for Medical Systems & Informatics, 1101 Connecticut Avenue Northwest/Suite 700, Washington DC 20036. **DD** 362.

THE MENTAL HEALTH YEARBOOK/DIRECTORY. **VAT** Mental Health Yearbook Directory. 1979/80-. 0195-766X. US. English. Van Nostrand Reinhold, 135 West 50th Street, New York NY 10020. Ed J Norback. **LC** RA790.6. **DD** 362.202573. **NLM** WM 22 AA1 M62.

THE MENTAL MEASUREMENTS YEARBOOK. 1st- 1938-. 0076-6461. Periodical. US. English. ir. Buros Institute of Mental Measurements, University of Nebraska Press, 901 North 17th Street, Lincoln NE 68588-0520. **Tel** (402)472-1739. Ed James V Mitchell Jr. **LC** Z5814.P8. **DD** 016.1512, 016.159928. Descriptive information, references, and critical reviews by professionals for new and revised commercially published tests in English. Extensive multiple indexes. *Mental Measurements Yearbook of the School of Education, Rutgers University.*

THE MERCHANDISER MASS RETAILER BUYERS DIRECTORY. US. English. $75.00. Merchandiser Publishing Company, 419 Park Avenue South, New York NY 10016. **LC** HD9723. **DD** 381.02573.

MERSEYSIDE CHAMBER OF COMMERCE AND INDUSTRY DIRECTORY. (DIRECTORY). 0302-4148. UK. English. Industrial Newspapers, Albany House Hurst Street, B5 4BD Birmingham England. **LC** HF302. **DD** 380.1062427.

METAL PROGRESS. HEAT TREATING BUYERS GUIDE AND DIRECTORY. **VFOAT** Heat Treating Buyers Guide and Directory. 0277-1284. Periodical. US. English. an. $14.00 Domestic, $15.00 Foreign. American Society for Metals, Metals Park, OH 44073. **LC** TN672. **DD** 671.36029473.

METALLURGY-MATERIALS EDUCATION YEARBOOK. (METALLURGY/MATERIALS EDUCATION YEARBOOK). **VFOAT** Materials Education Yearbook. 0094-5447. US. English. an. $20.00. American Society for Metals, Metals Park OH 44073. **Tel** (216)338-5151. Ed Kali Mukherjee. **LC** TN675.3. **DD** 669.0071173. **Circ** 2,000. Directory of schools in USA, Canada and Mexico with metallurgy materials science faculties. Also schools with faculties of ceramics and polymer science as well as foreign schools.

METODISTKYRKANS I SVERIGE ARSBOK. **Main/Corp** Methodist Church (Sweden). Swedish. ir. NYA Bokforlaags AB, Sibyllegatan 18 III, 114 42 0, Stockholm Sweden. **LC** BX8310.S87.

METRIC YEARBOOK. Series/Titl Metric System Guide, V. 1- Supplement 3-. 1975-. 0363-2652. US. English. an. $10.00. J J Keller & Associates, 145 West Wisconsin Avenue, Neenah WI 54956. **LC** QC92.U54. **DD** 389.1520973.

METRO NEW YORK DIRECTORY OF MANUFACTURERS. 0731-7417. US. English. ir. $82.50. Commerce Register Inc, 190 Godwin Avenue, Midlind Park NJ 07432. **Tel** (201)445-3000. Ed Joel Rosano. **LC** HD9728.N4. **DD** 338.47000257471. adv acc. **Circ** 3,000. Detailed listings of all manufacturing companies, including top executives, annual sales, number of employees, address, phone, and more.

METROPOLITAN AREA BUSINESS DIRECTORY. 0821-0136. CN. English. an. $15.00 Per Volume. Halifax Board of Trade, Duke Tower/4th Floor, Halifax Nova Scotia B3J 1P3 Canada. **DD** 380.102571622.

METROPOLITAN ATLANTA BUSINESS DIRECTORY. 0091-9756. US. English. an. $83.20. Terminus Media, 1720 Peachtree Road NW, Atlanta GA 30309. **LC** HF5068.A75. **DD** 338.0025758231.

METROPOLITAN WASHINGTON REGIONAL DIRECTORY. 1971-. 0076-7115. US. English. an. Metropolitan Washington Council of Governments, Washington DC 20036. **LC** JS1512.A3. **DD** 352. *Regional Directory - Metropolitan Washington Council of Governments.*

METUKALENDORIUS - PRISIKELIMO PARAPIJA. EKONOMINE SEKCIJA. (METU KALENDORIUS - PRISIKELIMO PARAPIJA, EKONOMINE SEKCIJA). **VFOAT** Lithuanian Calendar - Prisikelimo Parapija, Ekonomine Sekcija. 1975-. 0380-1373. CN. Lithuanian. $6.00. Parish of the Resurrection, 1011 College Street, Toronto Ontario M6H 1A8 Canada. **Tel** (416)233-4486. Ed Stan Prakapas. **DD** 059.9192. bk rev. adv acc. **Circ** 3,000. Poetry, jokes, cooking, travel, educational items, and advertising.

MEYER'S DIRECTORY OF GENEALOGICAL SOCIETIES IN THE U.S.A. AND CANADA. **VAT** Meyer's Directory of Genealogical Societies in the United States of America and Canada. 4th Ed.-. 0732-3395. US. English. be. $15.00. Libra Publications, 297 Cove Road, Pasadena MD 21122. **LC** CS44. **DD** 929.102573. *Directory of Genealogical Societies in the U.S.A. and Canada, 0734-6867.*

MICHIGAN CENTENNIAL FARMS DIRECTORY. 0092-2250. US. English. Michigan History Division, Department of State, Lansing MI 48918. **LC** S409.5.M5. **DD** 631.025774.

MICHIGAN EDUCATION DIRECTORY AND BUYER'S GUIDE. 0741-7942. US. English. an. Michigan Education Directories, 925 East Kalamazoo Street, Lansing MI 48912. **Tel** (517)482-8467. **LC** LB2803.M5. **DD** 370.25774.

MICHIGAN FOUNDATION DIRECTORY. Ed. 1- 1976-. 0362-1561. US. English. be. Michigan League Human Services, 200 Mill Street, Lansing MI 48933. **Tel** (517)487-5436. **LC** HV98.M5. **DD** 361.76025774.

THE MICHIGAN HOLISTIC HEALTH DIRECTORY. 1983 Ed.-. US. English. Michigan Holistic Health Association, PO Box 20082, Ferndale MI 48220.

MICHIGAN LIBRARY AUTOMATION DIRECTORY. 1983-. 0739-8174. US. English. an. $22.95 Members, Prepaid, $24.00 Members, Invoice, $27.95 Others Prepaid, $29.95 Others, Invoice. Michigan Library Consortium, 6810 South Cedar Street/Suite 8, Lansing MI 48910. **LC** Z678.9.A3. **DD** 027.0025774.

MICHIGAN LIBRARY DIRECTORY. US. English. an. **LC** Z732.M6. **DD** 027.4025774.

MICHIGAN MANUFACTURERS DIRECTORY. 1937. 0736-2889. Periodical. US. English. an. $113.50. Pick Publications, 8543 Puritan Avenue, Detroit MI 48238. **Tel** (313)864-9388. adv acc. **Circ** 8,000. Michigan manufacturers by geographic location, alphabet and product. Includes names, addresses, officers, phone sales volume, square footage, date of established employment, import/export, TWX, cable code, telex, affiliations. *Directory of Michigan Manufacturers.*

MICHIGAN MINERAL PRODUCERS : ANNUAL DIRECTORY. 1966-. 0580-6143. US. English. an. **LC** HD9506.U53. **DD** 338.209774. *Directory of Mineral Producers.*

MICHIGAN PURCHASING DIRECTORY. 1983-. 0736-2870. US. English. an. $15.00. Pick Publications Inc, 8543 Puritan Avenue, Detroit MI 48238. **LC** HD9727.M5. **DD** 380.10294774.

MICHIGAN YEARBOOK OF INTERNATIONAL LEGAL STUDIES. V. 1-. 8756-0615. Monographic Series. US. English. ir. Clark Boardman Company Ltd, 495 Hudson Street, New York NY 10014. **Ind/Abst** Leg. Resour. Index, Index Leg. Period., Curr. Law Index. **LC** K13.I36. **DD** 341.

Yearbooks, Almanacs, Directories

MICROCOMPUTER SOFTWARE DIRECTORY, TRANSPORTATION APPLICATIONS. VFOAT Canadian Directory of Microcomputer Transportation Applications Software. Jan. 1984-. 0828-4091. Periodical. CN. English. sa. Microcomputer Transportation Applications Resource Centre, c/o Roads and Transportation Association of Canada, 1765 St Laurent Boulevard, Ottawa Ontario K1G 3V4 Canada. DD 380.50285.

MICROCOMPUTER VENDOR DIRECTORY. 0747-511X. US. English. $9.95. Auerbach Publishers Inc, 6560 North Park Drive, Pennsauken NJ 08109. LC HD9696.C63. DD 001.64.

MICROGRAPHIC EQUIPMENT DIRECTORY AND BUYING GUIDE. VFOAT IRM Micrographic Equipment Directory and Buying Guide. (1977-). Periodical. US. English. an.

MICROWAVES PRODUCT DATA DIRECTORY. 0194-7397. Periodical. US. English. an. Hayden Publishing Company, 10 Moulholand Drive, Hasbrouck Heights NJ 07604. Tel (201)393-6000.

MIDDLE MONEY MARKET DIRECTORY. 1977-. 0148-0022. US. English. an. Money Market Directories Inc, 370 Lexington Avenue, New York NY 10017. LC HD7106.U5. DD 331.25202573.

THE MIDWEST DIRECTORY OF COMPUTER INSTALLATIONS. US. English. an. $125.00. C I I Publications, Suite 2010/ Harris Tower, 233 Peachtree Street NE, Atlanta GA 30303. LC QA74. DD 001.6402577.

MIGHT'S CHARLOTTETOWN PRINCE EDWARD ISLAND CITY DIRECTORY. (MIGHT'S CHARLOTTETOWN, PRINCE EDWARD ISLAND, CITY DIRECTORY). VFOAT Charlottetown City Directory. Began with 1973 issue?. 0318-1146. Periodical. CN. English. an. Might Directories, PO Box 1005 Station O, Toronto Ontario M4A 2N4 Canada. DD 917.1750025.

MIGHT'S COBOURG PORT HOPE ONTARIO CITY DIRECTORY. (MIGHT'S COBOURG, PORT HOPE, ONTARIO, CITY DIRECTORY). VFOAT Cobourg, Port Hope, City Directory. Began with 1973 issue?. 0317-6487. Periodical. CN. English. Might Directories, 220 Bartley Drive, Toronto Ontario M4A 2N4 Canada. DD 917.1357.

MIGHT'S OAKVILLE ONTARIO CITY DIRECTORY. VFOAT Oakville Ontario City Directory. 1971-. 0381-8578. Periodical. CN. English. $70.00. Might Directories, 220 Bartley Drive, PO Box 1005 Station O, Toronto Ontario M4A 2N4 Canada. DD 917.13533. *Might's Oakville Directory, 0381-8586.*

MILITARY ASSISTANCE PROGRAM ADDRESS DIRECTORY. 0278-3029. US. English. mo. Superintendent of Documents, US Government Printing Office, Washington DC 20402.

MILITARY DEALERS AND COLLECTORS DIRECTORY AND HANDBOOK. US. English. an. HAAS Publications, PO Box 775, Worthington OH 43085.

MILKING SHORTHORN YEAR BOOK. Main/Corp American Milking Shorthorn Society. V. 28- 1943-. US. English. an. American Milking Shorthorn, 1722 JJS Glenstone, Springfield MO 65804. *Milking Shorthorn Year Book.*

MILWAUKEE AREA MEDIA DIRECTORY. 1st-. Ed. 0196-8505. US. English. an. Bishea Meili & Associates Inc, 312 East Wisconsin Avenue, Milwaukee WI 53202.

MIME DIRECTORY. V. 1- 1977-. 0148-6942. US. English. International Mimes and Pantomimists, The Valley Studio, Route 3, Spring Green WI 53588. LC PN1985. DD 792.30295. *Directory - International Mimes & Pantomimists, 0095-2087.*

MINERALS YEARBOOK. Began with 1932/33. 0076-8952. US. English. an. Superintendent of Documents, US Government Printing Office, Washington DC 20402. Ind/Abst GeoRef, Chem. Abstr. LC TN23. DD 338.20973. CODEN MYEAAG. *Mineral Resources of the United States.*

MINES DIRECTORY. 0197-9965. US. English. an. $20.00 US and Canada. CSM Alumni Association, Colorado School of Mines, Guggenheim Hall, Golden CO 80401. Tel (303)273-3291. Ed Patricia Curtis Petty. LC TN210.C7. DD 553.02578. bk rev. adv acc. Publishes articles on mineral policy, political and world issues, business, and technological developments affecting the nation's basic industries. Emphasis on alumni affairs.

MINING INTERNATIONAL YEAR BOOK. 1979-1982. 0076-9002. UK. English. an. 64.36. Longman Group Ltd, Fourth Avenue Harlow, Essex CM19 5AA England. Tel 0279 442601. Ed Diana Russell. LC TN13. DD 338.2025. Index each issue contains an index to its own contents - no volume index - loose. adv acc. Company information worldwide. Lists operations key personnel, company reports. *Walter R Skinner's Mining International Year Book.*

MINING YEAR BOOK. VFOAT Mining Year Book of the Inter-Mountain Region. 1933-. 0197-1409. US. English. an. The Colorado Mining Association, 1515 Cleveland P330 Denver HI, Denver CO 80202. Ind/Abst Eng. Index Annu., Eng. Index Mon., Eng. Index Bioeng. Abstr., Eng. Index Energy Abstr., Coal Abstr., GeoRef, Energy Res. Abstr., Chem. Abstr. LC TN24.C6. DD 622.058. CODEN MYBODC.

THE MINNESOTA ALMANAC. 1977-. 0363-289X. US. English. $4.95. The Minnesota Almanac, 2409 West 66th Street, Minneapolis MN 55423. LC F606. DD 977.6.

MINNESOTA AND ENVIRONS WEATHER ALMANAC. VFOAT Minnesota Weather Almanac. 1975-. 0095-7348. US. English. an. Freshwater Biological Research Foundation, 2500 Shadywood Road, Box 90, Novarre MN 55392. LC QC999. DD 551.6977605.

MINNESOTA DIRECTORY OF MANUFACTURERS. Periodical. US. English. an. 537 Plymouth Building/12 South 6th Street, Minneapolis MN 55402. *Directory of Minnesota Manufacturers and Guide Book to Minnesota Industry.*

MINNESOTA DIRECTORY OF MINORITY ENTERPRISES. 1977-. 0160-0397. US. English. Suite 370/Hennepin Square, 2021 East Hennepin Avenue, Minneapolis MN 55413. LC HD2346.U52. DD 338.04025776.

MINNESOTA INDUSTRIAL MINERALS DIRECTORY. 1979-. 0272-8583. US. English. an. $5.00. Minerals Resources Research Center, University of Minnesota, 56 East River Road, Minneapolis MN 55655. Tel (612)373-3341. Ed Rodney J Lipp. LC TN799.6.M6. DD 622.025776. Provides listing of names, addresses, and telephone numbers of Minnesota producers of natural abrasives, clays, shale, peat, construction sand and gravel, industrial sand, crushed stone, and diminsion stone.

MINNESOTA INTERNATIONAL TRADE DIRECTORY. US. English. Minnesota Department of Economic Development, International Trade Division, 480 Cedar Street, St Paul MN 55101. LC HF3161.M6. DD 382.6025776.

THE MINNESOTA LEGAL DIRECTORY. 1982-1983-. 0749-0224. US. English. an. Legal Directories Publishing Company Inc, 2122 Kidwell Street, Box 140200, Dallas TX 75214. LC KF192.M55. DD 340.025776. *Minnestoa, Nebraska, North Dakota and South Dakota Legal Directory.*

MINNESOTA MINING DIRECTORY. 1979-. 0276-6191. US. English. an. $6.00. Mineral Resources Research Center, University of Minnesota, 56 East River Road, Minneapolis MN 55455. Tel (612)373-3341. Ed Rodney J Lipp. Ind/Abst GeoRef. LC TN12. DD 622.025776. Circ 1,000. Provides statistical and historical overview of iron ore industry of Minnesota, lake superior region, Canada, and U.S.A. Lists Minnesota's taconite plants and current copper-nickel lease holders. *Mining Directory of Minnesota, 0196-3937.*

MINNESOTA REAL ESTATE DIRECTORY. 0360-8077. US. English. Metro Square Building/5th Floor, St Paul MN 55101. LC HD266.M6. DD 333.33.

MINNESOTA WOMAN'S YEARBOOK. 1978/79-. 0198-9898. US. English. an. $6.70. Sprague Publications, 430 Oak Grove Street/Suite B-10, Minneapolis MN 55403. LC HV1446.M6. DD 362.838025776.

MINORITY BIOMEDICAL SUPPORT PROGRAM : A DIRECTORY OF THE RESEARCH PROJECTS. Main/Corp Research Resources Information Center. Series/Titl DHEW Publication HE 20.3002:M 66. US. English. Department of Health Education and Welfare, National Institutes of Health, Division of Research Resources, 9000 Rockville Pike, Bethesda MD 20014. Each issue contains an index to its own contents - no vol index - loose.

MINORITY ORGANIZATIONS : A NATIONAL DIRECTORY. VFOAT Minority Organizations. 1st- 1978-. 0162-9034. US. English. ir. $30.00. Garrett Park Press, Garrett Park MD 20896. Tel (301)946-2553. Ed Robert Calvert Jr. LC E184.A1. DD 301.45106173. Lists over 7,100 organizations including minority membership organizations or programs developed by other groups to serve minority group members.

MINORITY/WOMEN'S BUSINESS ENTERPRISES DIRECTORY. VFOAT Minority Women's Business Enterprises Directory. 0743-7366. US. English. an. M/WBE Coordinator, 116 New Montgomery Street/Room 421, San Francisco CA 94105. LC HD2346.U5. DD 338.642202573.

THE MISSISSIPPI LEGAL DIRECTORY. 0738-2235. US. English. an. 15.00. Legal Directories Publishing Company, 700 Campbell Centre, PO Box 64805, Dallas TX 75206. LC KF192.M57. DD 349.762025, 347.620025. *Arkansas, Louisiana and Mississippi Legal Directory.*

MISSISSIPPI MANUFACTURERS DIRECTORY. Began Publication in 1962. US. English. an. $60.00. Manufacturers News Inc, 4 East Huron Street, Chicago IL 60611. Tel (312)337-1084. Provides a readily available source of information about 2,580 Mississippi manufacturers and 5,000 executives. Provides address, zip, phone, products manufactured, home office information. 302 pages. *Encyclopedia of Mississippi Manufacturers.*

MISSOURI AIRPORT DIRECTORY. 0160-4562. US. English. LC TL726.3.M8. DD 629.13254778.

MISSOURI DIRECTORY OF MANUFACTURING AND MINING. VFOAT Directory of Manufacturing and Mining. US. English. an. $86.40. Manufacturers News Inc, 4 East Huron Street, Chicago IL 60611. Tel (312)337-1084. LC T12. DD 670.25778. Contains an alphabetical listing of manufacturers with address, zip code and phone number, a geographic listing by city and county and a product listing of manufacturers. 640 pages. *Missouri Directory of Manufacturers and Mining Operations, 0076-9584.*

THE MISSOURI LEGAL DIRECTORY. US. English. an. $29.42. Legal Directories Publishing Company, 2122 Kidwell Street, PO Box 104200, Dallas TX 75124. LC KF192.M58. DD 340.025778.

MISSOURI STATE EXECUTIVE BRANCH DIRECTORY. US. English. an. Missouri Office of Administration, State Capitol/Room 125, Jefferson City MO 65102. LC JK5430. DD 353.977800025.

MITGLIEDER-VERZEICHNIS. Main/Corp Deutsche Orient-Gesellschaft. VFOAT Mitglieder Verzeichnis. German. ir. Deutsche Orient-Gesellschaft EV, 1 Berlin 19, Schloss Charlottenburg Langhansbau Museum fur Vor und Fruhgeschichte.

MITGLIEDERVERZEICHNIS DER GESELLSCHAFT FUR SCHLESWIG-HOLSTEINISCHE GESCHICHTE. Main/Corp Gesellschaft fur Schleswig-Holsteinische Geschichte. GW. German. ir. Gesellschaft fur Schleswig-Holsteinische, Geschichte Schloss Gottorf, 2380 Schleswig West Germany.

MITTELLATEINISCHES JAHRBUCH. 1.- Yearly Volume. 0076-9762. GW. German (Latin). ir. Anton Hiersemann Verlag, Rosenbergstasse 113, 7 Stuttgart 1 West Germany. Tel (711)63-82-64. Ed F Wagner. Ind/Abst MLA Int. Bibliogr. Books Artic. Mod. Lang. Lit. LC PA2802. bk rev. adv acc. Circ 1,000. Editions of and monographs about late Latin texts.

MJSA ARBOK. Norwegian. an. Totens Bokhandel, 2850 Lena, Minnesund Norway.

MLA DIRECTORY OF PERIODICALS. (MLA DIRECTORY OF PERIODICALS : A GUIDE TO JOURNALS AND SERIES IN LANGUAGES AND LITERATURES). Main/Corp Modern Language Association of America. VFOAT Modern Language Association Directory of Periodicals. 1978/79-. 0197-0380. Periodical. US. English. ir. $30.00. Modern Language Association of America, 62 5th Avenue, New York NY 10011. Tel (212)475-9500. Ed Eileen M Mackesy and Janet G Nottenburg. LC P1.A1. DD 016.405.

Yearbooks, Almanacs, Directories

Companion volume to MLA International Bibliography with data on 3,000 journal and series regularly searched for the bibliography.

MONCTON, NEW BRUNSWICK, CITY DIRECTORY (1980). (MONCTON, NEW BRUNSWICK, CITY DIRECTORY). VFOAT Moncton City Directory. VAT Moncton City Directory (1980). 1980-. 0229-7302. CN. English. an. $90.00. Might Directories, 220 Bartley Drive, Toronto Ontario 375 Canada. DD 917.1523. *Mights Greater Moncton (Westmorland County) New Brunswick, City Directory, 0318-9570.*

THE MONEY MARKET DIRECTORY OF PENSION FUNDS AND THEIR INVESTMENT MANAGERS. (DIRECTORY OF PENSION FUNDS AND THEIR INVESTMENT MANAGERS). 1983-. 0736-6051. US. English. an. $345.00. Money Market Directories Inc, 300 East Market Street, Charlottesville VA 22901. LC HG4509. DD 332.67254. *Money Market Directory, 0077-0388.*

MONEY MARKET FUND SURVEY'S COMPLETE DIRECTORY OF MONEY MARKET FUNDS. VFOAT Complete Directory of Money Market Funds. 0730-949X. US. English. Money Market Fund Survey, 51 East 42nd Street, New York NY 10017. *Performance Report & Directory of Money Market Funds, 0271-7751.*

MONTANA DIRECTORY OF TRADE, TECHNICAL, AND SELECTED PROFESSIONAL ASSOCIATIONS. US. English. Montana Department of Community Affairs, Research and Information Systems Division, Capitol Station, Helena MT 59601. LC HD2428.M6. DD 380.1025786. *Montana Directory of Trade and Technical Associations.*

MONTANA ENERGY ALMANAC. 1978-. 8755-2736. US. English. an. Energy Division and Facility Siting Division, Department of Natural Resources and Conservation, 32 South Ewing, Helena MT 59620. LC HD9502.U53. DD 333.7909786.

MONTANA HUMAN SERVICES DIRECTORY. 0160-595X. US. English. Montana State University, Montana Human Service Directory, Bozeman MT 59717. LC HV98.M85. DD 361.0025786. *Montana Social Service, Health and Recreational Directory, 0096-3151.*

MONTHLY DIRECTORY OF S. ASIAN ASSOCIATIONS & BUSINESSES. (THE MONTHLY DIRECTORY OF S. ASIAN ASSOCIATIONS & BUSINESSES). VFOAT Directory of S. Asia Associations & Businesses. Began publication in 1974 or 1975. 0700-3471. Periodical. CN. English. mo. Directory Monthly, 1433 Bloor Street West, Toronto Ontario M6P 3L6 Canada. DD 301.4519140713541. *Directory of S. Asian Associations & Businesses, 0700-3463.*

MOTEL/HOTEL MANAGEMENT DIRECTORY. US. English. an. ATCOM Publishers Inc, ATCOM Building, 2315 Broadway, New York NY 10024. LC TX911.3.M27. DD 647.947301068.

MOTOR CYCLE AND CYCLE TRADER YEARBOOK. 0306-4867. UK. English. an. Wheatland Journals, 157 Hagden Lane, Watford WD1 8W England. LC HD9710.5.G7. DD 381.4562922702541.

MOTOR INDUSTRY YEAR BOOK. NZ. English. an. New Zealand Motor Trade Federation, PO Box 390, Wellington New Zealand. Tel 735094. Ed R C Morpeth. LC HD9710.N5. DD 338.47629209931. adv acc. Circ 1,100. Reference book covering statistics related to the motor industry. Taxes, sales, import duties, licenses transport law, etc. *New Zealand Motor Trade Year Book.*

MOTOR SPORT YEARBOOK. 0091-8822. US. English. $4.95. Collier Books, 866 Third Avenue, New York NY 10022. LC GV1029. DD 796.7205.

MS DIRECTORY. Main/Corp Manuscript Society. 1953-. Periodical. US. English. ir. Manuscript Society, 350 N Niagara Street, Burbank CA 91505. DD 091.058.

MULTINATIONAL MARKETING & EMPLOYMENT DIRECTORY. VAT Multinational Marketing and Employment Directory. 7th- Ed. 0363-4426. US. English. ir. World Trade Academy Press Inc, 50 East 42nd Street, New York NY 10017. Tel (212)697-4999. LC HG4057. DD 338.88. US multinational companies, address and product/service. Location (country) of foreign operations (where known). *Angel's National Directory of Personnel Managers, Multinational Corporations Operating Overseas; National & International Employment Handbook for Specialized Personnel.*

MULTISTATE CORPORATE TAX ALMANAC. 1984 ed.-. 0747-718X. US. English. an. $110.00. Panel Publishers, 14 Plaza Road, Greenvale NY 11548. Tel (516)484-0006. LC HD2753.U6. DD 343.730526705, 347.303526705. Circ 2,000. A fact book containing over 45 detailed charts summarizing each states position on the key issues in corporate income taxation. Plus an inside look behind the states key developments.

MUNCHNER JAHRBUCH DER BILDENDEN KUNST. Vol. 1-13, 1906-23. 0077-1899. German. ir. **Ind/Abst** Avery Index Archit. Period., Repert. Int. Litt. Art, Art Index. LC N9. (cum index).

MUNICIPAL DIRECTORY. CN. English. $1.50. Ministry of Treasury, Economics and Intergovernmental Affairs, Government Bookstore, 880 Bat Street, Toronto M7A 1Y7 Canada. LC JS1721.O58. *Municipal Directory.*

MUNICIPAL DIRECTORY. 1948-. 0318-0743. Periodical. CN. English. an. Provincial-Municipal Affairs Secretariat, 130 Adelaide Street West/Suite 1900, Toronto Ontario M5H 3P5 Canada. DD 352.00025713.

MUNICIPAL DIRECTORY. (MUNICIPAL DIRECTORY - MAINE MUNICIPAL ASSOCIATION). **Main/Corp** Maine Municipal Association. 0272-4596. Periodical. US. English. an. $20.00 Each Copy. Maine Municipal Association, Community Drive, Augusta ME 04330. LC JS451.M25. DD 352.005209741.

MUNICIPAL EXECUTIVE DIRECTORY. Winter/Spring 1984-. 0742-1710. US. English. sa. $125.00. Carroll Publishing Company, 1058 Thomas Jefferson Street NW, Washington DC 20007. Tel (202)333-8620. Ed Nancy Cahill. LC JS363. DD 352.00520973. It lists approximately 19,000 elected, appointed, and career officials with their addresses an phone numbers.

MUNICIPAL MANAGEMENT DIRECTORY. US. English. an. International City Management Association, 1120 G Street NW, Washington DC 20005. LC JS344.C5. DD 352.00840973. *City-Manager Directory.*

THE MUNICIPAL YEAR BOOK. 1st- Ed. 0077-2186. US. English. an. International City Management Association, 1140 Connecticut Avenue NW, Washington DC 20036. Ed C E Ridley and O F Nolting. LC JS344.C5. NLM JS 342 M966. *City Manager Yearbook.*

THE MUNICIPAL YEAR BOOK AND PUBLIC SERVICES DIRECTORY. 1973-. 0305-5906. UK. English. an. $65.12. Municipal Group, 178-202 Great Portland Street, London W1N 6NH England. Tel (01)637-2400. LC JS3003. DD 352.041. *Municipal Year Book and Public Utilities Directory.*

THE MUNICIPAL YEAR BOOK DIRECTORIES. Vol. 1 (1981)-. 0276-489X. US. English. an. $19.75. International City Management Association, 1120 G Street Northwest, Washington DC 20005. Tel (202)626-4600. Ed Mary A Schellinger. LC JS39. DD 352.007202573. Circ 3,500. Handy desk-to-reference containing the names and phone numbers of over 70,00 local government officials.

MUNICIPAL YEAR BOOK, KERALA. English. ir. Government of Kerala, Bureau of Economics & Statistics, Trivandrum India. LC HA4587.K47. DD 315.483.

MUNICIPAL/COUNTY EXECUTIVE DIRECTORY. VFOAT Municipal County Executive Directory. 1984-. 0743-6211. US. English. an. $98.00. Carroll Publishing Company, 1058 Thomas Jefferson Street NW, Washington DC 20007. Tel (202)333-8620. Ed Nancy Cahill. DD 352. The first and only directories of all federal, state, municipal and county officials. This vital resource provides rapid access to government officials at all level.

MUSEUMS YEARBOOK. 1976-. UK. English. an. $44.00. Museums Association, 34 Bloomsbury Way, London WC1A 2SF England. Tel 01-404-4767. Ed Gilliam Bromley. LC AM1. DD 069.0941. adv acc. Circ 1,500. Directory of museums, their administering authorities, members of the Museums Association, for the UK, and other useful addresses and information. *Museums Calendar.*

MUSIC BUSINESS DIRECTORY. 1st Ed. (1983-84)-. 0747-6655. US. English. sa. Music Business Directory, 1100 16th Avenue South, Nashville TN 37212. LC ML15.N2. DD 338.477802576855.

MUSIC DIRECTORY CANADA. 83-. 0820-0416. CN. English. an. 19.95. c/o CM Books, 832 Mount Pleasant Road, Toronto Ontario M4P 2L3 Canada. Tel (416)485-8284. Ed Ted Burles. LC ML21.C3. DD 780.2571. The guide to Canadian music. A comprehensive guide book containing invaluable information for anyone involved in music in Canada.

MUSIC INDUSTRY DIRECTORY. 7th (1983)-. 0740-476X. US. English. ir. Marquis Professional Publications, 200 East Ohio Street, Chicago IL 60611. *Musician's Guide, 0580-3160.*

MUSIC TRADES INTERNATIONAL DIRECTORY. (MTI, MUSIC TRADES INTERNATIONAL DIRECTORY). 0307-8523. UK. English. an. Trade Papers London Ltd, 902 High Road, London N12 9SB England. LC ML12. DD 338.4778025.

MUSIC TRADES INTERNATIONAL YEARBOOK. 3d- Ed. UK. English. Trade Papers, 157 Hagden Lane, Watford Herts WD1 8LW London England. LC ML21. DD 380.1457802542. *Piano World and Music Trades Review Yearbook.*

MUSIC WEEK INDUSTRY YEAR BOOK. UK. English. an. 2.75 per issue. 7 Carnaby Street, London W1V 1PG England. LC ML21. DD 338.47780942.

MUSIC WORLD YEAR BOOK. VFOAT Music World Yearbook. 1985-. UK. English. an. Turret-Wheatland, Penn House, Penn Place, Herts WD3 1SN England. *Music World Directory.*

MUSIKBRANCHENS ARBOG. 1. Issue (1982)-. Danish. an. Danplay APS, Kroghsgade 1 2100 Denmark. LC ML1.D29.

MUTUAL FUND DIRECTORY. Began in 1938. Periodical. US. English. sa. $95.00. Dealers Digest Inc, 150 Broadway, New York NY 10038. Tel (212)227-1200.

MUTUAL FUNDS ALMANAC. 12th Ed. (1981). 0076-4175. US. English. an. $23.00. Donohue's Mutual Funds Almanac, PO Box 540, Holliston MA 01746. Tel (617)429-5930. Ed Connie Bugbee. adv acc. The most complete source of information on mutual funds available anywhere. Includes directory, toll-free numbers and ten-year performance on over 850 funds. *Mutual Funds Almanac.*

MUYOK TAERIJOM CHONGNAM. VFOAT Trading Agents Directory. English (Korean). ir. Hanguk Muyok Taerijom Hyophoe, 1-537 Youido-dong Yongdungpo-ku, Seoul South Korea. LC HF3830.5.A48.

MYSORE STATE TRADE AND INDUSTRIAL DIRECTORY. II. English. ir. 12.00. Allied Business Enterprises, 94 9th Cross Hanumanthanagar, Bangalore 19 India. LC HF5239.M9. DD 338.40255487.

N. W. AYER & SON'S DIRECTORY, NEWSPAPERS AND PERIODICALS. MID-YEAR SUPPLEMENT. 1917-32. Periodical. US. English.

NAFED DIRECTORY. Main/Corp National Association of Fire Equipment Distributors. VAT National Association of Fire Equipment Distributors Directory. 0363-7131. US. English. National Association of Fire Equipment Distributors, 111 East Wacker Drive, Chicago IL 60601. LC HD9999.F53. DD 381.4568.

NAFSA DIRECTORY OF INSTITUTIONS AND INDIVIDUALS IN INTERNATIONAL EDUCATIONAL EXCHANGE. VFOAT N.A.F.S.A. Directory of Institutions and Individuals in International Educational Exchange. VAT National Association for Foreign Student Affairs Directory of Institutions and Individuals in International Educational Exchange. 1983-. 0736-4660. US. English. be. $15.00 Members, $20.00 Non-members. National Association for Foreign Student Affairs, 1860 19th Street Northwest, Washington DC 20009. Tel (202)462-4811. Ed Carole Robertson Fenn. LC LA203. DD 370.1962025. bk rev. adv acc. Circ 8,000. A comprehensive listing of who's who in US foreign student and scholarly interests which lists more than 7,000 institutions and

Yearbooks, Almanacs, Directories

individuals in international educational exchange. *NAFSA Directory of Institutions and Individuals in International Educational Interchange.*

NAMA KONKURITO TOKEI NEMPO. VFOAT Year Book of Readymixed Concrete Statistics. 1971-. JA. Japanese. ir. 700. Zenkoku Konkurito Jigyota Dantai Rengokai, 1-7-5 Uchikanda Chiyoda-ku, Tokyo Japan. **LC** HD9622.J3.

NANAIMO DIRECTORY. VFOAT Nanaimo City Directory. 1959-. 0317-8838. Periodical. CN. English. an. B C Directories, Box 486, Nanaimo British Columbia V9R 5L5 Canada. **DD** 917.1134.

NAPSAC DIRECTORY OF ALTERNATIVE BIRTH SERVICES AND CONSUMER GUIDE. Main/Corp National Association of Parents & Professionals for Safe Alternatives in Childbirth. **VAT** National Association of Parents & Professionals for Safe Alternatives in Childbirth Directory of Alternative Birth Services and Consumer Guide. 2nd- Ed. 0273-3730. US. English. $5.95. NAPSAC International, PO Box 429, Marble Hill MO 63764. **Tel** (314)238-2010. **Ed** Lee Stewart. **LC** RG661. **DD** 362.19840973. bk rev. adv acc. **Circ** 2,000. (ctrl). Covers birth, pregnancy, nutrition, midwifery, obstetrics, homebirth, breastfeeding, parenting, pediatrics, medical politics, legal issues, health rights, legislation.

NARODNOE KHOZIAISTVO SSSR: STATISTICHESKII EZHEGODNIK. (NARODNOE KHOZIAISTVO SSSR. STATISTICHESKII EZHEGODNIK). 0469-5941. UR. Russian. ir. Geological Map Service, PO Drawer 920, Sag Harbor NY 11963. **Tel** (516)725-0780. **LC** HA1432. **DD** 330. **NLM** W2 GR9 T8N.

NASHVILLE AREA CHAMBER OF COMMERCE BUSINESS DIRECTORY. VFOAT Nashville Business Directory. 0278-3223. US. English. an. $15.00. Nashville Area Chamber of Commerce, 161 Fourth Avenue North, Nashville TN 37219. **LC** HF5068.N2. **DD** 381.029476855.

NASSAU COUNTY BAR ASSOCIATION ANNUAL DIRECTORY. Main/Corp Bar Association of Nassau County, N.Y. 0197-0968. US. English. an. Bar Association of Nassau County New York, 15th and West Streets, Mineola NY 11501. *Nassau County Bar Directory, 0197-095X.*

THE NASW PROFESSIONAL SOCIAL WORKERS' DIRECTORY. Main/Corp National Association of Social Workers. VFOAT Professional Social Workers' Directory. **VAT** National Association of Social Workers Professional Social Workers' Directory. 1978-. 0163-8823. US. English. ir. National Association of Social Workers, 7981 Eastern Avenue, Silver Springs MD 20910. **Tel** (301)565-0333. **LC** HV89. **DD** 361.002573. *NASW Directory of Professional Social Workers.*

NATIONAL ALUMNI DIRECTORY - ITHACA COLLEGE. (NATIONAL ALUMNI DIRECTORY). **Main/Corp** Ithaca College. VFOAT Alumni Directory. 1980-. 0737-6596. US. English. B C Harris Publishing Company, White Plains NY 10601. **LC** LD2594. **DD** 378.74771.

NATIONAL ASSOCIATION FOR LAW PLACEMENT MEMBERSHIP DIRECTORY. 0272-6025. US. English. $5.00. National Association for Law Placement, 6325 Freret Street, New Orleans LA 70118. **LC** KF297.A1. **DD** 340.02573.

NATIONAL BEVERAGE MARKETING DIRECTORY. VFOAT Beverage Marketing Directory. 1979/80-. 0197-3061. US. English. an. Beverage Marketing Corporation, 2670 Commercial Avenue Ming O, Junction OH 43938. **Tel** (614)598-4133. **Ed** Terry L Welling. **LC** HD9348.U5. **DD** 381.4566302573. adv acc. *National Beverage Marketing Directory of Telephone Numbers & Addresses, 0160-9580.*

NATIONAL BUSINESS ASSOCIATION. (NATIONAL BUSINESS ASSOCIATION. DIRECTORY). 0191-5223. US. English. an. $50.00. National Business Association Directory, 230 Congress Street/Suite 206, Boston MA 02110. **LC** HF5035. **DD** 338.002573.

NATIONAL BUSINESS EDUCATION YEARBOOK. No. 1-. 0547-4728. Monographic Series. US. English. an. National Business Education Association, 1906 Association Drive, Reston VA 22091. **Ed** T Woodward. **LC** HF1101. **DD** 658.0071073. *American Business Education Yearbook.*

NATIONAL CATTLE FEEDLOT, MEAT PACKER & GRAIN DEALERS DIRECTORY. (NATIONAL CATTLE FEEDLOT, MEAT PACKER AND GRAIN DEALERS DIRECTORY). 1970-. 0882-5149. Periodical. US. English. be. $45.00. Tara Publishing Company, 2143 50th Street/PO Box 3614, Lubbock TX 79412. **DD** 338.

THE NATIONAL CONSUMER MONEY MARKET DIRECTORY. 3rd Quarter 1984-. 8755-6197. Periodical. US. English. qt. National Consumer Money Market Directory, PO Box 105195, Atlanta GA 30348. **DD** 332.

NATIONAL DEFENSE AND DIRECT STUDENT LOAN PROGRAM DIRECTORY OF DESIGNATED LOW-INCOME SCHOOLS FOR TEACHER CANCELLATION BENEFITS. (NATIONAL DEFENSE AND DIRECT STUDENT LOAN PROGRAM DIRECTORY OF DESIGNATED LOW- INCOME SCHOOLS FOR TEACHER CANCELLATION BENEFITS FOR . . .). 0742-1443. US. English. an. Department of Education Office of Postsecondary Education, Office of Student Financial Assistance, Washington DC 20202. **LC** L901. **DD** 378.302573.

NATIONAL DIRECTORY AND ATLAS OF BUDGET MOTELS. 1981-. 0272-8699. US. English. an. $4.95. Michael West Inc, PO Box 520, East Setauket NY 11733. **LC** TX907. **DD** 647.947302.

NATIONAL DIRECTORY - CANADIAN INSTITUTE OF FOOD SCIENCE AND TECHNOLOGY. (NATIONAL DIRECTORY). **Main/Corp** Canadian Institute of Food Science and Technology. VFOAT Registre National. 0823-2717. CN. English (French). an. $45.00-$50.00 Membership. Canadian Institute of Food Science and Technology, Suite 48-46 Elgin Street, Ottawa Ontario K1P 5K6 Canada. **DD** 664.006071.

NATIONAL DIRECTORY FOR THE PERFORMING ARTS AND CIVIC CENTERS. (THE NATIONAL DIRECTORY FOR THE PERFORMING ARTS AND CIVIC CENTERS). 1st- Ed. 0092-0738. US. English. an. John Wiley & Sons, 605 Third Avenue, New York NY 10158. **LC** PN2289. **DD** 790.20973.

NATIONAL DIRECTORY, HOME HEATING PRODUCTS. VFOAT Repertoire National, Produits de Chauffage Residentiel. 1983/84-. 0825-8260. CN. English (French in parallel columns). an. $4.00. Canadian Institute of Energy, Suite 1802/181 University Avenue, Toronto Ontario M5H 3M7 Canada. **DD** 697.070216.

NATIONAL DIRECTORY OF ADDRESSES AND TELEPHONE NUMBERS (NEW YORK, N.Y.). (THE NATIONAL DIRECTORY OF ADDRESSES AND TELEPHONE NUMBERS). Began in 1977. 0740-7203. US. English. be. $24.95. Concord Reference Books Inc, 830 3rd Avenue, New York NY 10022. **Tel** (212)223-5100. **Ed** Steven Spaeth. **LC** E154.5. **DD** 384.602573. adv acc. **Circ** 100,000. Contains the name, address and telephone number of the nation's leading 75,000 private and public corporations - listed both alphabetically and by industry (SIC) classification.

NATIONAL DIRECTORY OF BLIND TEACHERS. (NATIONAL DIRECTORY OF BLIND TEACHERS : A PROJECT OF THE NATIONAL ASSOCIATION OF BLIND TEACHERS). 1983-. 0743-4081. US. English. National Association of Blind Teachers, Suite 506/1211 Connecticut Avenue NW, Washington DC 20036. **LC** HV1790. **DD** 371.1008808161.

NATIONAL DIRECTORY OF BUDGET MOTELS. 1975-. 0146-3950. US. English. an. $4.95. Pilot Industries Inc, 347 Fifth Avenue, New York NY 10016. **LC** TX907. **DD** 647.9473.

NATIONAL DIRECTORY OF CATHOLIC HIGHER EDUCATION. 1983-. 0736-9476. US. English. an. $10.00. Catholic News Publishing Company, 80 West Broad Street, Mt Vernon NY 10552. **LC** L901. **DD** 378.73.

THE NATIONAL DIRECTORY OF CERTIFIED PUBLIC ACCOUNTANTS. VFOAT National Directory of Certified Public Accountants. 1st Ed.-. 0731-0625. US. English. Peter Norback Publishing Co, 621 Alexander Road, Princeton NJ 08540. **LC** HF5627. **DD** 657.02573.

NATIONAL DIRECTORY OF CHILD ABUSE SERVICES AND INFORMATION. 1st- Ed. 0097-479X. US. English. $4.00. National Committee for Prevention of Child Abuse, Room 510 111 West Wacker Drive, Chicago IL 60601. **LC** HV741. **DD** 362.7.

NATIONAL DIRECTORY OF CHILDREN & YOUTH SERVICES. VFOAT Child Protection Report's National Directory of Children & Youth Services, National Directory of Children and Youth Services. 1979-. 0190-7476. US. English. be. $49.00. Bookmakers Guild Inc, 1430 Florida Avenue/Suite 202, Longmont CO 80501. **Tel** (303)442-5774. **LC** HV741. **DD** 362.702573. **NLM** WA 22 AA1 N22. adv acc. **Circ** 80,000. A reference handbook for child care professionals. Includes names, addresses, phone numbers and managers of every social service agency, health department and juvenile courts in the country plus 2,500 private providers.

NATIONAL DIRECTORY OF COLLEGE ATHLETICS (WOMEN'S ED.). (THE NATIONAL DIRECTORY OF COLLEGE ATHLETICS). 1976/77-. 0092-5489. US. English. an. $14.00. Ray Franks Publishing Ranch, PO Box 7068, Amarillo TX 79109. **Tel** (806)355-6417. **Ed** Ray Franks. adv acc. Pertinent information about athletic departments of 2,100 senior and junior colleges in US and Canada, such as addresses, enrollment, athletic personnel, coaches, phone numbers, etc. *National Directory of Women's Athletics.*

THE NATIONAL DIRECTORY OF COMMUNICATION CUSTOMER PREMISE EQUIPMENT WIRING & EQUIPMENT INSTALLERS, WITH RATE INFORMATION BY CITY, STATE & REGION. 0743-7072. US. English. an. Carl D Southard Associates Inc, PO Box 30033, Raleigh NC 27622. **LC** TK6011. **DD** 621.38602573.

NATIONAL DIRECTORY OF CORPORATE PUBLIC AFFAIRS. VFOAT Corporate Public Affairs. 1st Ed. (1983)-. 0749-9736. Periodical. US. English. an. $53.00. Columbia Books Inc Publishers, 1350 New York Avenue NW/Suite 207, Washington DC 20005. **Tel** (202)737-3777. **Ed** Arthur C Close. **LC** HD59. **DD** 659.28502573. **Circ** 1,800. Directory of approximately 9,500 public affairs offices and officers from 1,600 companies. Includes corporate public information, political activity, and philanthropy.

NATIONAL DIRECTORY OF COUNTY PARK AGENCIES. 1981-82 Ed.-. US. English. ir. Dr D M Knudson, Department of Forestry and Natural Resources, Purdue University, West Lafayette IN 47907.

NATIONAL DIRECTORY OF DECOY COLLECTORS. 0196-3902. US. English. **LC** SK335. **DD** 745.593.

NATIONAL DIRECTORY OF EDUCATIONAL PROGRAMS IN GERONTOLOGY. 1st- Ed. 0148-4508. US. English. US Department of Health Education & Welfare, Washington DC 20220. **LC** HQ1060. **DD** 362.6042071173. **NLM** WT 22 AA1 S7N.

NATIONAL DIRECTORY OF FREE TOURIST ATTRACTIONS. 1977-. US. English. be. $3.50. Pilot Books, 103 Cooper Street, Babylon NY 11702. **Tel** (516)422-2225. **Ed** Raymond Carlson. **LC** E158. Lists free gardens, restored villages, ships, museums and other interesting presentations of history, science and fine art throughout the United States.

NATIONAL DIRECTORY OF GRADUATE PROGRAMS IN FAMILY STUDIES. NATIONAL DIRECTORY OF POST DOCTORAL OPPORTUNITIES IN FAMILY STUDIES. NATIONAL ROSTER OF ONGOING RESEARCH IN FAMILY STUDIES. VFOAT National Directory of Post Doctoral Opportunities in Family Studies. 1970- Ed. 0094-811X. US. English. National Council on Family Relations, 1219 University Avenue South, Minneapolis MN 55414. **NLM** HQ 728 N277.

NATIONAL DIRECTORY OF HEALTH PROFESSIONS ADVISORS. Main/Corp National Association of Advisors for the Health Professions. VFOAT N.A.A.H.P. Directory of Health Professions Advisors. 1981-1982-. 0737-1616. US. English. NAAHP, PO Box 5017, Champaign IL 61820. **Tel** (217)344-6013. **Ed** Sherri N Weidemann. adv acc. **Circ** 750. (ctrl). A publication designed to provide the names, school addresses, and telephone numbers of advisors who are current members of the national association and its regional affiliates.

NATIONAL DIRECTORY OF HEALTH/MEDICINE ORGANIZATIONS. **VAT** National Directory of Health Medicine Organizations. 1980/81-. 0270-8191. US. English. be. $25.00.

Yearbooks, Almanacs, Directories

Science and Health Publications Inc, Suite 208/6410 Rockledge Drive, Bethesda MD 20034. **LC** R712.A1. **DD** 610.6073. **NLM** WA 22 AA1 N224.

THE NATIONAL DIRECTORY OF HIGH SCHOOL COACHES. **VFOAT** High School Coaches. 1963-. US. English. an. $32.95. Athletic Publishing Company, PO Box 931, Montgomery AL 36102. **Tel** (205)263-4436. **Ed** John Allen Dees. **LC** GV697.A1. **DD** 796.07702573. bk rev. adv acc. (ctrl). Nationwide listing of high schools, coaches addresses, sport the coach teaches and telephone numbers. *Directory of High School Coaches.*

NATIONAL DIRECTORY OF HISPANIC ELECTED AND APPOINTED OFFICIALS. 1981-. US. English. an. The Caucus, House Annex II Room 557, Washington DC 20515.

THE NATIONAL DIRECTORY OF HOLISTIC HEALTH PROFESSIONALS. **Main/Corp** Association for Holistic Health (U.S.). 1st Vol. -. 0739-6724. US. English. Association for Holistic Health, PO Box 9532, San Diego CA 92109. **LC** R723. **DD** 613.

THE NATIONAL DIRECTORY OF INVESTMENT NEWSLETTERS. 1982 Ed.-. 0735-035X. US. English. be. $35.00. Idea Publishing Corporation, 55 East Afton Avenue, Yardley PA 19067. **Tel** (215)493-1810. **Ed** George T Schlieben Jr. **LC** Z7164.F5,HG4501. **DD** 016.332605. **Circ** 4,000. Lists over 1,250 investment publications and services.

NATIONAL DIRECTORY OF LANDSCAPE ARCHITECTURE FIRMS. **VFOAT** Landscape Architecture. 1980-. 0272-247X. US. English. an. American Society of Landscape Architects, 1900 M Street NW/Suite 750, Washington DC 20036. **LC** SB469.33. **DD** 338.7617120973.

NATIONAL DIRECTORY OF LAW ENFORCEMENT ADMINISTRATORS AND CORRECTIONAL INSTITUTIONS. 1964?-. 0547-6224. US. English. an. $34.85. National Police Chief & Sheriffs, PO Box 92007, Milwaukee WI 53202. **Tel** (414)272-3853. **Ed** Martin E Wyrick. **Circ** 11,000. (ctrl). Directory of law enforcement and correctional agencies. Police Chiefs, Sheriffs, Prosecutors, Courts, and State Federal criminal investigation agencies, covering all areas of criminal justice systems.

NATIONAL DIRECTORY OF LOCAL RESEARCHERS. **VFOAT** Family Tree National Directory of Local Researchers. 0742-9045. US. English. sa. $1.00. The Family Tree, 450 Potter Street, Wauseon OH 43567. **Tel** (419)335-6485. **Ed** Howard V Fausey. **LC** CS44. **DD** 909.102573. bk rev. adv acc. (ctrl). Names of people doing local genealogical research.

NATIONAL DIRECTORY OF MEDICARE HOME HEALTH AGENCIES. 0147-3476. Periodical. US. English. 6401 Security Boulevard, Baltimore MD 21235. **LC** RA445. **DD** 362.611402573.

NATIONAL DIRECTORY OF MINORITY MANUFACTURERS. 0094-9663. US. English. US Department of Commerce, Office of Minority Business Enterprises, Washington DC 20230. **LC** HD2346.U5. **DD** 338.002573.

NATIONAL DIRECTORY OF MODULAR BUILDING MANUFACTURERS. 1974-. 0092-668X. US. English. Reference Development Corporation, PO Box 2331, Princeton NJ 08540. **LC** TH12.5. **DD** 338.4769.

NATIONAL DIRECTORY OF NEWSLETTERS AND REPORTING SERVICES. 1st- Ed. 0547-6232. US. English. ir. $130.00. Gale Research Company, Book Tower, Detroit MI 48226. **Ed** R Thomas and B Darnay. **LC** Z6941. **DD** 011. Provides detailed information on newsletters issued regularly by business firms, associations, societies, clubs, government agencies, finanical institutions, etc.

NATIONAL DIRECTORY OF PRIVATE SOCIAL AGENCIES. Began in 1964. US. English. mo. $54.90. Croner Publications Inc, 211-05 Jamaica Avenue, Queens Village NY 11428. **Tel** (718)464-0866. **Ed** Helga B Croner. Private social agencies listed by field of service.

THE NATIONAL DIRECTORY OF PROFESSIONAL CONSULTANTS AND CONSULTING ORGANIZATIONS. 0735-1119. US. English. **LC** HD69.C6. **DD** 658.4602573.

NATIONAL DIRECTORY OF PROGRESSIVE AND RANK & FILE LABOR LAWYERS. **VAT** National Directory of Progressive and Rank and File Labor Lawyers. 1977-. 0160-2586. US. English. $2.50. 712 South Grand View Street, Los Angeles CA 90057. **LC** KF195.L3. **DD** 344.7301025.

NATIONAL DIRECTORY OF PROVIDERS OF PSYCHIATRIC SERVICES TO RELIGIOUS INSTITUTIONS. 1972-. 0090-4074. US. English. American Psychiatric Association, Task Force on Religion and Psychiatry, Washington DC 20037. **LC** RC443. **DD** 616.8900922.

NATIONAL DIRECTORY OF SAFETY CONSULTANTS. 3d- Ed. 0361-7904. US. English. $25.00. American Society of Safety Engineering, 1800 East Oakton Highway, Des Plaines IL 60018-2187. **Tel** (312)692-4121. **LC** T55.A1. **DD** 338.47614802573. **NLM** WA 22 AA1 N23. **Circ** 1,200. (ctrl). Qualifications/credentials of about 300 of the nation's best safety and health consultants available to work with lawyers and corporate executives.

NATIONAL DIRECTORY OF SHOPS/GALLERIES, SHOWS/FAIRS. (NATIONAL DIRECTORY OF SHOPS/GALLERIES/SHOWS/FAIRS). **VFOAT** Shops/Galleries/Shows/Fairs. 1982/83-. 0730-9309. US. English. an. $12.95. Writer's Digest Books, 9933 Alliance Road, Cincinnati OH 45242. **LC** HD2346.U5. **DD** 381.45745502573. *Craftworker's Market.*

NATIONAL DIRECTORY OF SHORTHAND REPORTERS. 0271-1133. US. English. National Directory of Shorthand Reporters, Bank of Idaho, PO Box 1758, Boise ID. **LC** KF8700.A19. **DD** 347.7316.

NATIONAL DIRECTORY OF STATE AGENCIES. (THE NATIONAL DIRECTORY OF STATE AGENCIES). 1974/75-. 0095-3113. US. English. be. $85.00. National Standards, 5161 River Road, Bethesda MD 20816. **Tel** (301)951-1389. **LC** JK2443. **DD** 353.9025. **NLM** JK 2443 N277. A two-part index to state agencies. The first half lists all agencies within each state. The second half lists all agencies by function. All entries include contact name, address and phone number.

NATIONAL DIRECTORY OF STATE & LOCAL GOVERNMENT TRAINERS. **VAT** National Directory of State and Local Government Trainers. 1978-. 0192-4273. US. English. an. Trainer's Resource Service, c/o National Training and Development Service, 5028 Wisconsin Avenue NW, Washinton DC 20016. **LC** JK2480.I6. **DD** 350.1502573.

NATIONAL DIRECTORY OF SUMMER INTERNSHIPS FOR UNDERGRADUATE STUDENTS. 0098-1451. US. English. Career Planning Offices of Bryn Mawr and Haverford Colleges, Summer Internship Research Project/Career Planning Office, Bryn Mawr PA 19019. **LC** LC5751. **DD** 378.14202573.

NATIONAL DIRECTORY OF WEEKLY NEWSPAPERS, INCLUDING SEMI-WEEKLY AND TRI-WEEKLY NEWSPAPERS. Began publication with the 34th Ed. in 1954. US. English. an. $42.50. America Newspaper Reps, 186 Joralemon Street, Brooklyn NY 11201. **Tel** (718)522-4600. adv acc. **Circ** 2,000. National directory of weekly newspapers. *Annual Directory of Country and Suburban Home Town Newspapers.*

NATIONAL DIRECTORY OF WOMEN ELECTED OFFICIALS. 1981-. 0740-2813. US. English. National Women's Political Caucus, 1411 K Street Northwest, Washington DC 20005. **LC** HQ1236. **DD** 320.973088042.

NATIONAL DIRECTORY OF WOMEN-OWNED BUSINESS FIRMS. **VFOAT** National Directory of Women Owned Business Firms. 0886-389X. Periodical. US. English. an. Business Research Services, 2 East 22nd Street, Lombard IL 60148. *National Directory of Minority & Women-Owned Business Firms, 8756-6532.*

NATIONAL DIRECTORY OF WOMEN'S ATHLETICS. (THE NATIONAL DIRECTORY OF WOMEN'S ATHLETICS). 0092-5489. US. English. an. $10.00. R Franks Publishing Ranch, Box 7068, Amarillo TX 79114. **Tel** (806)355-6417. **Ed** Ray Franks. **LC** GV439. **DD** 796.0194. adv acc. **Circ** 6,500. Pertinent information and records on all senior and junior college intercollegiate athletic programs, including scholarship information.

THE NATIONAL FACULTY DIRECTORY. 1970-. 0077-4472. US. English. an. $450.00. Gale Research Company, Book Tower, Detroit MI 48226. **Tel** (800)521-0707. **LC** L901. **DD** 378.1202573. **NLM** L 901 N277. An alphabetic listing of nearly 600,000 names and addresses of teaching faculty members at 3,030 US and selected Canadian junior colleges, colleges, and universities. Includes a list of schools covered.

THE NATIONAL FACULTY DIRECTORY. SUPPLEMENT. 1984-. US. English. $160.00. Gale Research Company, Book Tower, Detroit MI 48226. This inter-edition supplement to the main directory furnishes updated information on faculty addresses and locations.

NATIONAL FIVE DIGIT ZIP CODE AND POST OFFICE DIRECTORY. 1982-. 0731-9185. US. English. an. Superintendent of Documents, US Government Printers Office, Washington DC 20402. **LC** HE6361. **DD** 383.145. *National Zip Code & Post Office Directory, 0191-6971.*

NATIONAL GUARD ALMANAC. 1977-. 0363-8618. US. English. an. Uniformed Services Almanac, PO Box 76 Department G, Washington DC 20044. **Tel** (703)532-1631. **Ed** Sol Gordon. **LC** U9. **DD** 355.370973. bk rev. **Circ** 25,000,000. (ctrl). Reference volume on pay and allowances for guardesmen including state and federal benefits, organization, taxes, and other important articles of the Army and Air National Guard. *Uniformed Services Almanac. National Guard Edition, 0363-8588.*

THE NATIONAL GUARDIAN DIRECTORY OF THE SCOTTISH LICENSED TRADE. UK. English. an. 2.50. Muro-Barr Publications, 113 St Vincent Street, Glasgow Scotland. **LC** HD9361.7.A3. **DD** 381.45663102541. *Scottish Licensed Trade Directory.*

NATIONAL HEALTH DIRECTORY. 1st- Ed. 0147-2771. US. English. an. $55.00. Aspen Systems Corporation, PO Box 6018, Gaithersburg MD 20760. **Tel** (301)424-7410/(800)638-8437. **LC** RA7.5. **DD** 353.0084102573. **NLM** WA 22 AA1 N32.

NATIONAL INDUSTRIAL COUNCIL DIRECTORY. **Main/Corp** National Industrial Council. **VFOAT** NIC Directory. 0194-0686. US. English. $10.00. National Industrial Council, 1776 F Street NW, Washington DC 20006. **LC** HD2425. **DD** 338.002573.

NATIONAL JAIL AND ADULT DETENTION DIRECTORY. 1978-. 0192-8228. US. English. $35.00. American Correctional Association, 4321 Hartwick Road/Suite L 208, College Park MD 20740. **Tel** (301)699-7600. **LC** HV9463. **DD** 365.02573. bk rev. adv acc. **Circ** 4,000. List county jail with names of administrators, addresses, phone, statistical information on capacities, level of security, personnel, etc.

NATIONAL MALL MONITOR INC'S. RETAIL TENANT DIRECTORY. (NATIONAL MALL MONITOR INC'S RETAIL TENANT DIRECTORY). **VFOAT** Retail Tenant Directory. 5th Ed. (1981)-. 0277-9331. US. English. an. $95.00. National Mall Monitor, Arbor Center Suite 500-1321 US 19 South, Clearwater FL 33516. **LC** HF5429.3. **DD** 381.102573. *Retail Tenant Prospect Directory, 0270-2568.*

NATIONAL MEMBERSHIP DIRECTORY - NATIONAL ASSOCIATION OF STUDENT FINANCIAL AID ADMINISTRATORS. (NATIONAL MEMBERSHIP DIRECTORY). **Main/Corp** National Association of Student Financial Aid Administrators. **VFOAT** NASFAA Directory. 0196-3279. US. English. an. $10.00. National Association of Student Financial Aid Administrators, 910 17th Street Northwest, Washington DC 20006. **LC** LB2337.4. **DD** 378.302573.

NATIONAL MEMBERSHIP DIRECTORY - WOMEN IN COMMUNICATIONS, INC. **Main/Corp** Women in Communications, Inc. 0360-3296. US. English. $5.00. Women in Communications Inc, 8305 A Shoal Creek Boulevard, Austin TX 78758. **LC** P87. **DD** 001.502573.

NATIONAL MINORITY BUSINESS INFORMATION SYSTEM. (NATIONAL MINORITY BUSINESS INFORMATION SYSTEM : A NATIONAL DIRECTORY OF MINORITY AND WOMEN OWNED FIRMS). **VFOAT** Minority Business Information System. 1981 Ed.-. 0730-6334. US. English. an. Source Publications Inc, 1900 Powell Street/Suite 1145, Emeryville CA 94608. **Tel**

Yearbooks, Almanacs, Directories

(415)547-6670. LC HD2346.U52. DD 338.6422025794. *California Minority Business Enterprises Directory, 0146-9010.*

NATIONAL MOBILE TELEPHONE SERVICE DIRECTORY. 0882-4215. US. English. $8.00. Communications Publishing Service, 3790 El Camino Road/Suite 300, Palo Alto CA 94306-3389. Tel (415)968-9358. Ed Steven S Brown. LC TK6570.M6. DD 384.5302573. adv acc. Circ 20,000. Car telephone guide for 2,000 US and Canadian cities. Lists channel numbers, rooming instructions and level of public-cellular service provided by telephone companies.

NATIONAL NETWORK DIRECTORY. Main/Corp Women's Caucus for Art. Fall 1982-. 0736-7341. US. English. WCA National Business Office, 1301 East Monte Vista Road, Phoenix AZ 85006.

NATIONAL NEWS MEDIA DIRECTORY. MEDICINE/HEALTH. (NATIONAL NEWS MEDIA DIRECTORY : MEDICINE/HEALTH). VFOAT Media Directory. 1980/81-. 0270-7896. US. English. $25.00. Science and Health, Suite 208, 6410 Rockledge Drive, Bethesda MD 20034. LC R118.4.U6. DD 362.107. NLM WA 22 AA1 N39.

NATIONAL NEWSPAPER ASSOCIATION DIRECTORY. 0147-7528. US. English. $2.00. Washington DC 20045. LC JK1010. DD 070.06273.

NATIONAL POULTRY IMPROVEMENT PLAN DIRECTORY OF PARTICIPANTS HANDLING EGG-TYPE AND MEAT-TUPE CHICKENS AND TURKEYS. (NATIONAL POULTRY IMPROVEMENT PLAN. DIRECTORY OF PARTICIPANTS HANDLING EGG-TYPE AND MEAT-TYPE CHICKENS AND TURKEYS). VFOAT Directory of Participants Handling Egg-type and Meat-type Chickens and Turkeys. 0271-793X. US. English. an. Animal and Plant Health Inspection Service-Veterinary Services, US Department of Agriculture, Room 828/FCB #1, Hyattsville MD 20782. LC SF481.25. DD 635.5002573. Vols. for (1984-) distributed to depository libraries in microfiche. *Directory of Participants Handling Egg-type and Meat-type Chickens and Turkeys.*

NATIONAL POULTRY IMPROVEMENT PLAN DIRECTORY OF PARTICIPANTS HANDLING WATERFOWL, EXHIBITION POULTRY, AND GAME BIRDS. (NATIONAL POULTRY IMPROVEMENT PLAN. DIRECTORY OF PARTICIPANTS HANDLING WATERFOWL, EXHIBITION POULTRY, AND GAME BIRDS). VFOAT Directory of Participants Handling Waterfowl, Exhibition Poultry, and Game Birds. 0271-7948. US. English. an. Free. Animal and Plant Health Inspection Service, Veterinary Services U S Department of Agriculture, Room 828 FCB #1 Hyattsville MD 20782. Tel (301)436-5140. Ed Irvin L Peterson. LC SF481.25. DD 636.5002573. Circ 3,000. (ctrl). Vols. for (1981, 1984-) distributed to depository libraries in microfiche. *Directory of Participants Handling Egg-type and Meat-type Chickens and Turkeys.*

THE NATIONAL PRISON DIRECTORY : ORGANIZATIONAL PROFILES OF PRISON REFORM GROUPS IN THE UNITED STATES. 1975-. US. English. Urban Information Interpreters, PO Box AH, College Park MD 20740. Ed M L Bundy and K R Harmon. DD 365.706273. Each issue contains an index to its own contents - no vol index - loose.

NATIONAL RADIO PUBLICITY DIRECTORY. 1972. 0276-4520. Periodical. US. English. bm. $95.00. PO Box 1197 33 Wittlesey Avenue, New Milford CT 06776. Tel (800)223-1254. Ed Ronald T Robinson. bk rev. adv acc. (ctrl). This comprehensive directory covers all of the fifty states in the USA as well as key Canadian cities, with special attention paid to major markets.

NATIONAL REAL ESTATE INVESTOR. DIRECTORY ISSUE. VFOAT National Real Estate Investor Directory. 0731-8693. US. English. an. $43.00. National Real Estate Investor Directory, 6255 Barfield Road, Atlanta GA 30328. Tel (404)256-9800. Ed Paula S Stephens. adv acc. Circ 28,000. (ctrl). News, market reports and trend articles about the investment in and development of income-producing property. *National Real-Estate Investor Directory, 0547-8383.*

NATIONAL SALES TAX RATE DIRECTORY. 1976-. 0735-6684. US. English. an. Vertex Systems Inc, 222 Lancaster Avenue, Devon PA 19333. LC HJ5715.U6. DD 343.73055205, 3476.30355205.

NATIONAL SOFT DRINK BOTTLERS AND CANNERS DIRECTORY. 6th Ed., 1974/75-. Periodical. US. English. ir.

NATIONAL SOLAR ENERGY EDUCATION DIRECTORY. Began with issue for 1979. 0197-3142. US. English. an. Superintendent of Documents, US Government Printing Office, Washington DC 20402. LC TJ810. DD 621.47071073.

NATIONAL SQUARE DANCE DIRECTORY. 0196-0040. US. English. $4.00. National Square Dance Directory, PO Box 54055, Jackson MS 39208. LC GV1623. DD 793.3402573.

NATIONAL TANK TRUCK CARRIER DIRECTORY. 1st- Ed. 0077-586X. US. English. an. $21.50. National Truck Carriers Inc, 2200 Mill Road, Alexandria VA 22314. Tel (703)838-1960. LC E5623.A45. DD 388. adv acc. Circ 3,000. Listing of for hire Bulk Carriers (tank truck carriers) in the US, Canada, and several other nations.

NATIONAL TELEPHONE DIRECTORY. Main/Corp United States. Dept. for Energy. Office of the Assistant Secretary for Management and Administration. Jan. 1982-. US. English. an. US Department of Energy, Assistant Secretary, Management and Administration, Washington DC 20585. *National Telephone Directory.*

NATIONAL TELEPHONE DIRECTORY FOR BROKERS, DEALERS, BANKS, MUTUAL FUNDS. 1927. 0730-3823. US. English. sa. E Z Telephone Directory of Brokers & Banks, 106 7th Street, Garden City NY 11530. Tel (212)422-9492. Ed A A Gentile. LC HG65. DD 332.102573. adv acc. Telephone directory of stock brokers and banks.

THE NATIONAL TRUST YEAR BOOK. Main/Corp National Trust (Great Britain). 1975/76-. UK. English. an. Europa Publishing Ltd, 18 Bloomsbury Square, London WC1B 3JN England. LC NX28.G72. DD 700.941.

NATIONAL ZIP CODE & POST OFFICE DIRECTORY. 1980-. Periodical. US. English. an. $24.95. National Information Data Center, PO Box 2977, Washington DC 20013. Tel (301)565-2539. adv acc. Circ 125,000. (ctrl). Listing of all zip codes and post offices in the U.S. Comes with free 22" X 30" zip code wall map. *Post Office Directory, National Zip Code Directory.*

NATIONWIDE DIRECTORY BUYERS FOR EXPORT. APPAREL EDITION. (NATIONWIDE DIRECTORY BUYERS FOR EXPORT). 1982-. 0730-5494. US. English. an. The Saleman's Guide Inc, 1140 Broadway, New York NY 10001. LC HD9940.U3. DD 687.029473.

NATIONWIDE DIRECTORY. MAJOR MASS MARKET MERCHANDISERS. (NATIONWIDE DIRECTORY. MAJOR MASS MARKET MERCHANDISERS : EXCLUSIVE OF NEW YORK METROPOLITAN AREA). VFOAT Major Mass Market Merchandisers. 0737-061X. US. English. $65.00. Salesman's Guide Inc, 1140 Broadway, New York NY 10001. LC HD9940.U4. DD 381.4568702573.

NATIONWIDE DIRECTORY OF CORPORATE MEETING PLANNERS. VFOAT Directory of Corporate Meeting Planners. 0735-4444. US. English. $180.00. Salesman's Guide Inc, 1140 Broadway, New York NY 10001. Tel (212)685-2985. Ed Edward R Blank. LC HD2743. DD 658.456302573. adv acc. Circ 1,500. (ctrl). Lists 15,200 corporate meeting planners who elect hotel space for their companies.

NATIONWIDE DIRECTORY SPORTING GOODS BUYERS. VFOAT Salesman's Guide Sporting Goods Buyers Nationwide Directory. 0148-2734. US. English. an. $75.00. Salesman's Guide Inc, 1140 Broadway, New York NY 10001. LC HD99992 .U5. DD 381.456887602573.

NATO SCIENCE COMMITTEE YEAR BOOK. VFOAT N.A.T.O. Science Committee Year Book, Annuaire du Comite Scientifique de l'Otan. English, (1976). an. Nato Scientific Affairs Division, 1110 Brussels Belgium. LC Q10. DD 354.1855091821.

NATURAL RESOURCES INFORMATION DIRECTORY. Series/Titl ENR References Report. 1981-. 0711-5369. Periodical. CN. English. an. Alberta Map and Air Photo Distribution Centre, Alberta Energy and Natural Resources, North Tower Petroleum Plaza/2nd Floor, Edmonton Alberta T5K 2G6 Canada. LC HC117.A6. DD 333.70257123. *Natural Resources Inventory Information Index, 0708-5826.*

NATURAL RESOURCES INFORMATION DIRECTORY FOR THE STATE OF CONNECTICUT AND LIST OF PUBLICATIONS FOR THE CONNECTICUT GEOLOGICAL AND NATURAL HISTORY SURVEY. VFOAT Natural Resources Information Directory and List of Publications. 0748-481X. US. English. an. LC HC107.C8. DD 333.709746. *List of Publications, Natural Resources Information Directory for the State of Connecticut, 0748-481X.*

THE NATURALISTS' DIRECTORY AND ALMANAC INTERNATIONAL. SUPPLEMENT. 1980-1981-. US. English. World Natural History Publications, PO Box 505, Kinderhook NY 12106.

NATURE. DIRECTORY OF BIOLOGICALS. VFOAT Directory of Biologicals. 1982-. UK. English. an. $198.50 US and Canada. Nature Directory of Biologicals, 15 East 26th Street, New York NY 10010. LC RM270. DD 660.6025.

NATURVETENSKAPLIGA FORSKNINGSRADETS ARSBOK. 1976/77-. SW. Swedish. ir. Naturvetenskapliga Forskningsradet, Wenner-Gren Center Box 6711, S-113 Stockholm 85 Sweden. LC Q180.S8. DD 001.409485. Index received separately bound from publisher. *Svensk Naturvetenskap.*

NAUTISCHES JAHRBUCH; ODER, EPHEMERIDEN URED TAFELN. VFOAT Ephemeriden und Tafeln. Began with 1852. German. ir. LC QB8. DD 528.3.

NAUTISK ALMANAK. DK. Danish. an. I C Weilbach & Company, c/o PO Box 2051, 1253 K Benhavn K Denmark. LC QB8. DD 623.89. *Dansk Nautisk Almanak.*

NAVAJO YEARBOOK. (THE NAVAJO YEARBOOK). Began with No. 6, in 1957. 0466-6658. US. English. an. US Bureau of Indian Affairs, Navajo Agency, Education Division, Window Rock AZ 86515. *Navajo Yearbook of Planning in Action.*

NAWGA DIRECTORY OF MEMBERS. Main/Corp National-American Wholesale Grocers' Association. VAT National-American Wholesale Grocers' Association Directory of Members. 0145-4218. US. English. National-American Wholesale Grocers' Association, 51 Madison Avenue, New York NY 10010. LC HD9321.3. DD 381.

NCAA DIRECTORY. Main/Corp National Collegiate Athletic Association. VFOAT NCAA Membership Directory. VAT National Collegiate Athletic Association Directory. 1976/77-. 0162-1467. US. English. an. $6.00. National Collegiate Athletic Association, PO Box 1906, Shawnee Mission KS 66222. Tel (913)384-3220. LC GV347. DD 796.071102573. Contains roster of members by district and by division as well as listing of NCAA committees and Association's structure.

NCFA MEMBERSHIP DIRECTORY. Main/Corp National Consumer Finance Association. VFOAT N.C.F.A. Membership Directory. 1980-. 0732-359X. US. English. an. National Consumer Finance Association, 1000-16th Street NW, Washington DC 20036. LC HG3756.U54. DD 332.3502573.

NCOBPS BIOGRAPHICAL DIRECTORY. 1972-. US. English. LC JA28. DD 320.0922.

THE NEA ALMANAC OF HIGHER EDUCATION. (THE NEA . . . ALMANAC OF HIGHER EDUCATION). VFOAT N.E.A. Almanac of Higher Education. VAT National Education Association Almanac of Higher Education. 1984-. 0743-670X. US. English. an. National Education Association, 1201 16th Street NW, Washington DC 20036. LC LA227.3. DD 378.73.

NEA GOVERNANCE AND COMMITTEE DIRECTORY. Main/Corp National Education Association of the United States. VAT National Education Association of the United States Governance and Committee Directory. 1977-. 0148-1126. US. English. an. NEA Executive Office, 1201 16th Street NW, Washington DC 20036. *NEA Governance Directory.*

THE NEBRASKA LEGAL DIRECTORY. VFOAT Legal Directory. 1982-1983-. 0748-2744. US. English. an. Legal Directories Publishing Company

Yearbooks, Almanacs, Directories

Inc, 2122 Kidwell Street, PO Box 140200, Dallas TX 75214. **LC** KF192.N39. **DD** 349.782025, 347.820025. *Minnesota, Nebraska, North Dakota and South Dakota Legal Directory.*

NEDERLANDS KUNSTHISTORISCH JAARBOEK. VFOAT Netherlands Yearbook for History of Art. Vol. 1- 1947-. 0169-6726. NE. Dutch (summaries in English). an. 145. Uniboek BV, PO Box 185, 1380 AD Weesp Netherlands. **Tel** 02940-80480. **Ind/Abst** Art Index, Repert. Int. Litt. Art. **LC** N5. **DD** 705. **Circ** 600. Yearbook for the history of art.

NEDERLANDS THEATER- EN TELEVISIE JAARBOEK. NE. Dutch. an. 20.00. Theater Institute, Postbus 19304, 1000 GH Amsterdam Netherlands. **Tel** 020-235104. **LC** PN2714. bk rev. adv acc. **Circ** 5,000. (ctrl). *Nederlands Theater Jarrboek.*

THE NEGRO ALMANAC. 1st Ed.-. US. English. ir. John Wiley & Sons Inc, 1 Wiley Drive, Somerset NJ 08873. **Tel** (212)850-6418. Each issue contains an index to its own contents - no vol index - loose.

NEGRO DIRECTORY. V. 1- Mar. 1966-. 0381-9477. Periodical. CN. English. sa. McLaren Micropublishing, PO Box 972 Station F, Toronto Ontario M4Y Canada. **DD** 338.0025713541.

NETHERLANDS-BRITISH TRADE DIRECTORY. UK. English. an. Netherlands Chamber of Commerce in the United Kingdom, 307/308 High Holborn, WCJ London England. **LC** HF302. **DD** 382.0942.

NETHERLANDS YEARBOOK OF INTERNATIONAL LAW. V. 1- 1970-. Periodical. English. an. Kluwer Academic Publisher, 190 Old Derby Street, Hingham MA 02043. **Ind/Abst** Contents Curr. Leg. Period. **LC** JX21. (cum index).

NEU-BRAUNFELSER JAHRBUCH. Series/Titl German-Texan Folkways Series. 0273-0359. US. English. an. Folkways Publishing Co, New Braunfels TX 78130. **LC** F395.G3. **DD** 976.400431.

NEUE ASPEKTE RADIOLOGISCHER DIAGNOSTIK UND THERAPIE : JAHRBUCH . . . DER SCHWEIZERISCHEN GESELLSCHAFT FUR RADIOLOGIE UND NUKLEARMEDIZIN. Periodical. SZ. articles in English, French, or German. ir. **NLM** W1.

NEUE PREUSSISCHE JAHRBUCHER. 1.-. German. ir. Preussen-Verlag A Boldt, 2420 Eutin, Eutin West Germany. **LC** AP30.

NEUES JAHRBUCH FUR GEOLOGIE UND PALAONTOLOGIE. ABHANDLUNGEN. Vol. 92-. 0077-7749. Periodical. German. English (or French). ir. E Schweizerbart'sche Verlagsbuchhandlung (Nagele U Obermiller), Johannestrasse 3A, D-7000 Stuttgart 1 Germany. **Tel** 0711/62 50 01. Ed Klans Schmidt. **Ind/Abst** GeoRef, Energy Res. Abstr. **CODEN** NEJPAP. Index in last issue of volume - attached. adv acc. Covers geology and paleontology. *Neues Jahrbuch fur Mineralogie, Geologie und Palaontologie. Abhandlungen. ABT. B: Geologie - Palaontologie.*

NEUES JAHRBUCH FUR GEOLOGIE UND PALAONTOLOGIE. MONATSHEFTE. 1950-. 0028-3630. Periodical. GW. German. mo. E Schweizerbart'sche Verlag, Johannesstrasse 3-A, D7000 Stuttgart 1 West Germany. **Tel** 0711/62 50 01. Ed Klaus Schmidt. **Ind/Abst** GeoRef, Energy Res. Abstr., Chem. Abstr., Bibliogr. Index Geol., Pet. Abstr. **LC** QE1. **CODEN** NJGMA2. adv acc. Contains information on geology and paleontology. *Neues Jahrbuch fur Mineralogie, Geologie und Palaontologie. Monatshefte. Abt. B: Geologie - Palaontologie.*

NEUES JAHRBUCH FUR MINERALOGIE. ABHANDLUNGEN. Vol. 81-. 0077-7757. Periodical. GW. German. ir. E Schweizerbart'sche Verlag, Johannesstrasse 3-A, D7000 Stuttgart 1 West Germany. **Tel** 0711/62 50 01. Ed H Saalfeld and K R Mehnert. **Ind/Abst** Int. Aerosp. Abstr., GeoRef, Energy Res. Abstr., Chem. Abstr. **LC** QE351. **CODEN** NJMIAK. adv acc. Mineralogy, crystallography. *Neues Jahrbuch fur Mineralogie, Geologie und Palaontologie. Abt. A: Mineralogie, Gesteinskunde.*

NEUES JAHRBUCH FUR MINERALOGIE. MONATSHEFTE. 1950-. 0028-3649. GW. German. mo. E Schweizerbart'sche Verlag, Johannesstrasse 3-A, D7000 Stuttgart 1 West Germany. **Tel** 0711/62 50 01. Ed H Saalfeld. **Ind/Abst** GeoRef, Art Archaeol. Tech. Abstr., Chem. Abstr., Sci. Cit. Index, Abr. Ed., Bibliogr. Index Geol. **LC** QE351. **CODEN** NJMMAW. bk rev. adv acc. Mineralogy, crystallography. *Neues Jahrbuch fur Mineralogie, Geologie und Palaontologie. Monatshefte. Abt. A: Kristallographie, Mineralogie, Gesteinskunde.*

NEW ALBANY (FLOYD COUNTY, IND). VFOAT Caron's New Albany-Jeffersonville City Directory. US. English. an. $90.00. Caron Directory Co, 6400 Monroe Boulevard, Box 500, Taylor MI 48186.

THE NEW COLLECTOR'S DIRECTORY. Began with Vol. for 1976. 0363-3284. US. English. $4.00. Padre Production Inc, Box 1275, San Luis Obispo CA 93406.

THE NEW DIRECTORY OF MEDICAL SCHOOLS. 1962-. US. English. Ed A S White and E Pokress. **NLM** W 22 N525.

NEW ENGLAND DIRECTORY FOR COMPUTER PROFESSIONALS. 0739-6120. US. English. Bradford Company, PO Box 256, Scituate MA 02066. **LC** QA76.215. **DD** 001.642502574.

THE NEW ENGLAND FOLK DIRECTORY. 0732-4820. US. English. an. $7.50. New England Folk Directory, c/o Alcazar Inc, PO Box 429, Waterbury VT 05676. **LC** ML14.N33. **DD** 781.702574.

THE NEW ENGLAND HUMAN RIGHTS DIRECTORY. VFOAT Human Rights Directory. 1982-1983-. 0732-748X. US. English. be. $4.50. New England Human Rights Network, c/o American Friends Service Committee, 2161 Massachusetts Avenue, Cambridge MA 02140. **LC** JC599.U52. **DD** 323.402574.

THE NEW ENGLAND MEDIA DIRECTORY. 1978-. 0195-7619. US. English. $24.00. New England Newsclip Agency Inc, 5 Auburn Street, Framingham MA 01701. **LC** P92.U5. *Directory of New England Newspapers, College Publications, Periodicals, and Radio and Television Stations.*

NEW ENGLAND TALK SHOW DIRECTORY. (NEW ENGLAND TALK SHOW DIRECTORY : RADIO STATIONS, TELEVISION STATIONS). 1982-83-. 0741-7225. US. English. an. $30.00. New England Newsclip Agency, 5 Auburn Street, Framingham MA 01701. **LC** PN1990.9.T34. **DD** 791.447502574.

NEW HAMPSHIRE COMMUNITY MENTAL HEALTH AGENCIES, DIRECTORY OF STAFFS AND BOARD OF DIRECTORS. 0362-7950. US. English. New Hampshire Division of Mental Health, 105 Pleasant Street, Concord NH 03301. **LC** RA790.65.N4. **DD** 362.22025742.

NEW HAMPSHIRE LAW DIRECTORY & DAYBOOK. VFOAT New Hampshire Law Directory and Daybook. 0730-6210. US. English. an. $16.25. New Hampshire Law Directory and Daybook, 795 Elm Street, Manchester NH 03101. **LC** KF192.N395. **DD** 349.742025, 347.420025.

NEW HAMPSHIRE MARKETING DIRECTORY. 1980-. 0276-2110. US. English. be. $18.38. Tower Publishing Company, PO Box 7220, Portland ME 04112. **Tel** (207)774-9813. Ed Esther Peison. **LC** HF5065.N4. **DD** 381.45000294742. **Circ** 2,500. Complete listings of all manufacturers in the state of New Hampshire. Contains complete address, telephone numbers, top management, number of employees, gross sales and SIC codes.

NEW HAMPSHIRE MEDIA DIRECTORY. 0278-3177. US. English. an. New England Newsclip Agency, 5 Auburn Street, Framingham MA 01701. **Tel** (617)879-4460. **LC** P88.8. **DD** 001.51.025742.

THE NEW HAMPSHIRE POLITICAL ALMANAC. 1981-1982-. 0276-9778. US. English. $15.00. Almanac Research Services, PO Box 2010, Concord NH 03301. **LC** JK2930. **DD** 328.742073025.

NEW HAMPSHIRE REGISTER, STATE YEAR-BOOK AND LEGISLATIVE MANUAL. 1869-. 0545-1671. US. English. an. $67.50. Tower Publishing Company, 34 Diamond Street, PO Box 7220, Portland ME 04112. **Tel** (207)774-9813. Ed Esther Peison. **LC** JK2930. adv acc. **Circ** 750. The single most comprehensive, one volume reference work on the state of New Hampshire.

NEW JERSEY AREA LIBRARY DIRECTORY. 0362-2967. US. English. New Jersey Department of Education, 185 West State Street, Trenton NJ 08625. **LC** Z732.N6. **DD** 021.0025749.

NEW JERSEY DIRECTORY OF MANUFACTURERS. 0195-9352. US. English. $82.50. Commerce Register Inc, 190 Godwin Avenue, Midland Park NJ 07432. **Tel** (201)445-3000. Ed Joel Rosano. **LC** HD9727.N5. **DD** 338.0025749. adv acc. **Circ** 3,000. Detailed listings of all manufacturing companies, including top executives, annual sales, number of employees, address, phone, and more. Available in machine readable formats and on mailing labels.

THE NEW JERSEY ECONOMIC ALMANAC. 1983-. 0736-4210. US. English. an. $29.95. New Jersey Associates, Box 505, Montclair NJ 07042. **LC** HC107.N5. **DD** 330.9749005.

THE NEW JERSEY MEDIA DIRECTORY. (NEW JERSEY MEDIA DIRECTORY). 1978-. 0195-6817. US. English. an. New Jersey Clipping Services, 75 East Northfield Avenue, Livingston NJ 07039. **Tel** (201)992-7070. **LC** PN4897.N49. **DD** 071.49. *New Jersey Newspapers and Periodicals.*

NEW JERSEY POLITICAL ALMANAC. Began in 1978. 8756-2618. US. English. $25.00. The Center for Analysis of Public Issues, 16 Vandeventer Avenue, Princeton NJ 08542. **Tel** (609)924-9570. Ed Rick Sinding. **LC** JK3568. **DD** 328.74907305. bk rev. **Circ** 3,000. A journal of New Jersey public issues.

NEW JERSEY PUBLIC LIBRARY DIRECTORY. VFOAT Public Libraries in New Jersey Directory. 1977-. US. English. an. New Jersey State Library, Library Development Bureau 185 West State Street, Trenton NJ 08625. **LC** Z732.N6. **DD** 027.4025749. *Public Library Directory, 0364-0345.*

NEW JERSEY ZIP+4 STATE DIRECTORY. VFOAT Zip Plus Four State Directory. VAT New Jersey Zip Plus Four State Directory. 1985-. US. English. an. St Louis PDC, Zip + 4 State Directory Orders, PO Box 14921, St Louis MO 63180-9988.

THE NEW MEXICO ALMANAC. 1975-. 0360-1048. US. English. an. $2.00. J R Spencer, 2921 Axtell Street, Clovis NM 88101. **LC** JK8030. **DD** 354.72.

NEW MEXICO EDUCATIONAL PERSONNEL DIRECTORY. Began with Vol. for 1962/63. US. English. an. State Department of Education, Statistical Services, Santa Fe New Mexico 87503. **LC** LB2803.N6. **DD** 371.2011025789. *Educational Directory.*

NEW MEXICO FOREST PRODUCTS DIRECTORY. 0094-2782. US. English. Department of State Forestry, PO Box 2167, Santa Fe NM 87501. **LC** HD9757.N65. **DD** 338.17498025789.

NEW MEXICO LIBRARY DIRECTORY. US. English. New Mexico State Library, 325 Don Gaspar, Santa Fe NM 87503. **LC** Z732.N65. **DD** 027.0025789.

NEW MEXICO MANUFACTURING DIRECTORY. 1983-. 0742-7204. US. English. bm. $38.00. Manufacturers News Inc, 4 East Huron Street, Chicago IL 60611. **Tel** (312)337-1084. **LC** HD9727.N6. **DD** 338.47670294789. adv acc. Consists of two major sections, manufacturing and high technology. Includes address, zip code, county, telephone, date established, number of employees, owner or manager. 177 pages. *New Mexico Directory of Manufacturing.*

NEW ORLEANS (ORLEANS PARISH, LA.) DIRECTORY. 1974-. US. English. R L Polk, Attn Mrs E Glenn, 7168 Envoy Court, Dallas TX 75247. **Tel** (214)631-8210.

NEW ORLEANS SUBURBAN (JEFFERSON AND ST. BERNARD PARISHES, LA.) DIRECTORY. 1974-. US. English. an. R L Polk, Attn Mrs E Glenn, 7168 Envoy Court, Dallas TX 75247. **Tel** (214)631-8210. *Polk's New Orleans Suburban (Jefferson and St. Bernard Parishes, La.) Directory.*

NEW PRODUCT DIRECTORY OF NEW YORK STOCK EXCHANGE LISTED COMPANIES. (THE NEW PRODUCT DIRECTORY OF NEW YORK STOCK EXCHANGE LISTED COMPANIES). 0094-8918. US. English. 402 Border Road, Concord MA 01742. **LC** HD69.N4. **DD** 338.002573.

Yearbooks, Almanacs, Directories

NEW SOUTH WALES YEARBOOK. No. 66 (1981)-. 0085-4441. English. be. **Tel** (02)268 4611. **LC** DU150. **DD** 994.4. **Circ** 1,500. Provides a comprehensive statistical, legislative and administrative survey of the social, demographic and economic structure and growth of New South Wales. *Official Year Book of New South Wales.*

NEW SPECIAL LIBRARIES : A PERIODIC SUPPLEMENT TO THE SEVENTH EDITION OF DIRECTORY OF SPECIAL LIBRARIES AND INFORMATION CENTERS. No.1 (Oct. 1982)-. 0193-4287. Periodical. US. English. ir. $275.00. Gale Research, Book Tower, Detroit MI 48226. Ed B Darnay. Periodical supplement to Volume 1, keeps subscribers informed of new information facilities.

THE NEW STRAITS TIMES DIRECTORY OF MALAYSIA CEASED. **VFOAT** New Straits Times Directory (Buku Merah) of Malaysia. Multilingual (English or Malay). ir. 31 Jalan Riong, Kuala Lumpur Malaysia. **LC** HF5239.M36. **DD** 338.0025595. *Straits Times Directory of Malaysia.*

NEW TRAINING ORGANIZATIONS. **VFOAT** Training and Development Organizations Directory. No. 1 (Mar. 1981)-. 0278-5749. US. English. sa. $150.00. Gale Research Company, Book Tower, Detroit MI 48226. Ed Paul Wasserman and Janice McLean. **LC** HD30.42.U5. **DD** 658.0071073. Two supplements of training and development organizations which keep subscribers informed of newly formed or newly identified services.

NEW YORK AND SURROUNDING TERRITORY CLASSIFIED BUSINESS DIRECTORY. US. English. an. $59.95. New York Directory Company, 358 New York Avenue, Huntington NY 11743. **Tel** (516)549-1344. **LC** F128.24. **DD** 380.102947471. adv acc. **Circ** 500. *Buyer's Blue Book.*

NEW YORK METROPOLITAN DIRECTORY OF COMPUTER INSTALLATIONS. **VFOAT** Directory for Computer Users and Vendors. 4th Ed.-. 8756-999X. US. English. an. $465.00. Computer Management Research Inc, 20 Waterside Plaza, New York NY 10010. **LC** HF5548.125. **DD** 338.47001640257471. *New York Metropolitan Directory of Data Processing, 0738-3673.*

THE NEW YORK PUBLIC LIBRARY DIRECTORY OF COMMUNITY SERVICES. **VFOAT** Directorio de Servicios para la Comunidad. 1978-. 0191-6629. US. English (Spanish). $20.00. Community Information Project, Office of Adult Services, 8 East 40th Street, New York NY 10016. **LC** F128.18. **DD** 917.470025.

THE NEW YORK STATE DIRECTORY. 1983 Ed.-. 0737-1314. US. English. an. $27.50. Empire State Report Inc, 17 Elk Street, Albany NY 12207. **LC** JK3430. **DD** 353.9747002.

THE NEW YORK STATE MEDIA DIRECTORY. Began with Vol. for 1971. 0195-8607. US. English. an. New York State Clipping Service, 75 East Northfield Avenue, Livingston NJ 07039. **Tel** (212)233-1373. **LC** Z6952.N57, PN4897.N56. **DD** 071.3.

NEW YORK STATE STATISTICAL YEARBOOK. 10th Ed.- 1983-84-. 0077-9334. Periodical. US. English. an. $19.00. The Nelson A Rockefeller Institute of Government, Publications Department, 411 State Street, Albany NY 12203. **Tel** (518)472-1300. adv acc. **Circ** 5,000. Over 450 pages of statistical tables perpared with cooperation of 70 state agencies. Also contains maps and graphics; user notes provide background information. *New York State Statistical Yearbook, 0077-9334.*

THE NEW YORK TIMES DIRECTORY OF THE FILM. **VFOAT** Directory of the Film. 1971-. Periodical. US. English. an. Arno Press, 3 Park Avenue, New York NY 10016. **LC** PN1995. **DD** 791.43.

NEW YORK ZIP+4 STATE DIRECTORY. Series/Tlt Zip + 4 State Directory. 1985-. Monographic Series. US. English. an.

THE NEW ZEALAND COMPANY REGISTER. First published June, 1963. English. ir. Mercantile Gazette of N Z, 8 Sheffield Crescent GPO Box 20034, Bishopdale Christchurch New Zealand. **LC** HG4274.6. **DD** 338.7409931.

NEW ZEALAND MEDICAL REGISTER. English. ir. Medical Council of New Zealand, PO Box 5135, Wellington New Zealand. **LC** R713.93. **DD** 610.6952025931. **NLM** W 22 KN4 M4.

NEW ZEALAND REGISTER OF SPECIALISTS. *See* Medicine.

NEWFOUNDLAND AND LABRADOR BUSINESS DIRECTORY AND BUYERS' GUIDE. (NEWFOUNDLAND AND LABRADOR BUSINESS DIRECTORY AND BUYERS GUIDE). **VFOAT** Newfoundland Business Directory and Buyers' Guide. 1968-. 0316-7798. CN. English. an. Maritime Directories, PO Box 2039, St John's New Foundland A1C 5R6 Canada. **LC** HF3229.N5. **DD** 380.1025718. *Newfoundland Business Directory and Buyers' Guide, 0549-088X.*

NEWFOUNDLAND MEDICAL DIRECTORY. 1961-. 0078-0316. Periodical. CN. English. an. Free. Newfoundland Medical Board, 47 Queen's Road, St Johns Newfoundland A1C Y2B Canada. **LC** 610.6952025718. **NLM** W 22 DC2 N4N. *Newfoundland Medical Register, 0317-8374.*

THE NEWSLETTER YEARBOOK/ DIRECTORY. Began with Vol. for 1977. 0270-5990. US. English. an. $60.00. Newsletter Clearinghouse, PO Box 311, Rhinebeck NY 12572. **Tel** (914)876-2081. Ed Howard Penn Hudson. **LC** PN4784.N5. **DD** 070.025. Each issue contains an index to its own contents - no vol index -loose. (cum index). adv acc. (ctrl). Directory of subscription newsletters; annual; by subject category, geographically, and alphabetically.

NEWSROOM DIRECTORY & GUIDE TO THE ILLINOIS ENVIRONMENTAL PROTECTION AGENCY. **Main/Corp** Illinois Environmental Protection Agency. **VFOAT** Illinois EPA Directory/Guide. 1980-. US. English. an. Illinois Environmental Protection Agency, 2200 Churchill Road, Springfield IL 62706. **LC** HC107.I33. **DD** 353.97730082321025. Index in last issue of volume - attached.

NIGERIA YEAR BOOK. 1952-. 0078-0685. NR. English. an. Daily Times of Nigeria, PO Box 1198 Surulere, Lagos Nigeria West Africa. **LC** DT515. **DD** 916.69.

NIGERIAN OFFICE & RESIDENTIAL DIRECTORY. **VAT** Nigerian Office and Residential Directory. No. 2- 1977-. NR. English. ir. 12.00. ICIC, PMB 3204 Suru-Lere, Lagos Nigeria. **LC** HF5286.5.A3. **DD** 380.1025669. *Nigerian Office & Quarters Directory.*

NIGERIAN YELLOW PAGES : AN A TO Z TRADE DIRECTORY. **VFOAT** A to Z Trade Directory. 1979-. English. ir. Directory House, 28 Taoridi Street Opposite Census Office P M B 3204, Suru-Lere Lagos Nigeria.

NIH ALMANAC. **Main/Corp** National Institutes of Health (U.S.). Division of Public Information. **VAT** National Institutes of Health Almanac. 1978-. 8756-601X. US. English. an. US Department of Health Education and Welfare, Public Health Service, 3700 East/West Highway, Hyattsville MD 20782. **LC** RA11. **DD** 353.007705. **NLM** W2 A N221. *National Institutes of Health Almanac.*

NIHON TOKEI NENKAN. **VFOAT** Japan Statistical Yearbook. Began in 1949. 0389-9004. English (Japanese). an. Taylor & Francis Inc, 242 Cherry Street, Philadelphia PA 19106. **Tel** (800)821-8312. **LC** HA1832. *Dai Nihon Teikou Tokei Nenkan.*

NOISE CONTROL DIRECTORY. 0164-0895. US. English. Fairmont Press, 134 Peachtree Street/Suite 918, Atlanta GA 30303. **LC** TD891.5. **DD** 363.7402573.

NONGOP KIBAN CHOSONG SAOP TONGGYE YONBO. **VFOAT** Yearbook of Land and Water Development Statistics. KO. English (Korean). an. Agricultural Development Corporation, 487 Poli-ri, Euiwangeub Siheung-gun, Gyeonggi-do South Korea. **LC** HD2095.5.

NONGOP KIGYE YONGAM. **VFOAT** Agricultural Machinery Yearbook, Republic of Korea. KO. English (Korean). an. Hanguk Nonggigu Kongop Hyoptong Chohap, 19-6 1-ka To-dong Yongsan-ku, Seoul Korea. **LC** S760.K6.

NORDISK HANDELSKALENDER, SKANDINAVIASK ADRESSEBØG. 0549-6233. DK. Danish. ir. Nordisk Handelskalender, Sydvestvej 49, 2600 Glostrup Denmark.

NORIN SUISANSHO TOKEIHYO. **Main/Corp** Japan. Norin Suisansho. Keizaikyoku. Tokei Johobu. **VFOAT** Statistical Yearbook of Ministry of Agriculture, Forestry and Fisheries. 1977/78-. JA. English and Japanese. ir. 5000. Norin Tokei Kyokai, c/o Otori Building, 11-14 Meguro 2-chome, Meguro-ku 153 Tokyo Japan. **LC** HD2091. *Norinsho Tokeihyo.*

NORSK LITTERR ARBOK. 1966-. 0078-1266. NO. Norwegian. ir. $20.66. Forlagsentralens Tidsskriftaud, Postboks 6079 Etterstad, N-0601 Oslo 6 Norway. **Tel** (02)687600. **Ind/Abst** MLA Int. Bibliogr. Books Artic. Mod. Lang. Lit. **LC** PT8301.

NORSK NAUTISK ALMANAKK OG SJFARTSKALENDER. **VFOAT** Nautical Almanac and Shipping Review. Norwegian (English). ir. **LC** QB8. **DD** 528.8481.

NORSK UTENRIKSPOLITISK ARBOK. 1973-. NO. Norwegian. an. 165.-. Norsk Utenrikspolitisk Institute, Postboks 8159, Dep Oslo 1 Norway. **Tel** 44 58 20. **LC** DL458. **Circ** 1,000. (ctrl). Comprehensive collection of materials, articles and documentation on Norwegian foreign policy.

NORTH AMERICA TRAVEL AGENCY DIRECTORY. V. 1- 1977-. 0147-0159. US. English. an. $22.00. 11411 Cumpston Street, North Hollywood CA 91601. **LC** G154. **DD** 338.761910257.

NORTH AMERICAN DIRECTORY & REFERENCE GUIDE OF ASIAN INDIAN BUSINESSES AND INDEPENDENT PROFESSIONAL PRACTITIONERS ALONG WITH COMMUNITY REFERENCE GUIDE & TRAVEL INFORMATION. *See* Business.

NORTH AMERICAN DIRECTORY OF FEDERAL, PROVINCIAL AND STATE WEED SCIENTISTS. 0099-202X. US. English. Weed Science Society of America, 309 West Clark Street, Champaign IL 61820. **LC** SB613.N67. **DD** 632.5802573.

NORTH AMERICAN DIRECTORY OF MONTESSORI SCHOOLS. 1977/78-. 0193-9874. US. English. an. $15.00. Montessori International Directory Services, PO Drawer 1047, Huntsville AL 35807. **LC** L901. **DD** 371.39202573.

NORTH AMERICAN FILM AND VIDEO DIRECTORY. **VFOAT** Film and Video Directory. 1976-. 0362-7802. US. English. ir. R R Bowker Company, 1180 Avenue of the Americas, New York NY 10036.

NORTH AMERICAN FOREST PRODUCTS EXPORT DIRECTORY. 1st- Ed. 0145-7225. US. English. 4077 Viscount, Memphis TN 38118. **LC** HD9753. **DD** 382.45674002573.

NORTH AMERICAN HUMAN RIGHTS DIRECTORY. **VFOAT** Human Rights Internet. 1980-. 0270-2282. US. English. ir. $30.00. Garrett Park Press, Garrett Park MD 20896. **Tel** (301)946-2553. Ed Robert Calver Jr. **LC** JC571. **DD** 323.406073. Lists organizations in North and South America concerned with human rights and social justice. *Human Rights Directory, 0197-8101.*

NORTH AMERICAN LIBRARY EDUCATION DIRECTORY AND STATISTICS. **Main/Corp** Indiana. University. Graduate Library School. 1971/73-. 0090-0605. US. English. **LC** Z668. **DD** 020.71173. **NLM** Z 668 N864. *North American Library Education Directory and Statistics, 0090-0605.*

NORTH AMERICAN RETAIL FURRIERS DIRECTORY. 0740-9117. US. English. an. $50.00. Directory Enterprises, 141 West 28th Street, New York NY 10001. **LC** HD9944.U44. **DD** 685.24029473.

NORTH & CENTRAL AMERICAN DIRECTORY. **Main/Corp** Amateur Chamber Music Players. **VFOAT** North and Central American Directory. 27th (1982)-. 0734-1741. US. English. Amateur Chamber Music Players Inc, Box 547, Vienna VA 22180. **LC** ML26. **DD** 785.700257. *North American Directory, 0364-5975.*

NORTH AUSTRALIA RESEARCH DIRECTORY. 1974-. English. ir. North Australia Research Unit, PO Box 39448, Willellie NT 5789 Australia. **LC** Q180.A8. **DD** 001.430994.

NORTH CAROLINA COUNCIL OF WOMEN'S ORGANIZATIONS ANNUAL DIRECTORY. 23rd- Ed. US. English. an. $15.00. North Carolina Council of Women's Organizations, PO Box 17712, Raleigh NC 27619. **Tel** (919)876-2165. Ed Shirley Willis. **LC** HS61. **DD** 366.0088042. adv acc. **Circ** 1,000. (ctrl). Directory of North Carolina Organizations, listing their officers and boards of directors, and prinicpal meeting dates.

Yearbooks, Almanacs, Directories

Includes description of organizations purposes and program interests. *Annual Directory of North Carolina Organizations.*

NORTH CAROLINA DIRECTORY OF LICENSED AUCTIONEERS, APPRENTICE AUCTIONEERS, AND AUCTION FIRMS. 7th Ed. (1980-81 Fiscal Year)-. US. English. an. North Carolina Auctioneer Licensing Board, 3509 Haworth Drive, Raleigh NC 27609. LC HF5477.U5. DD 381.18. *Directory of Licensed Auctioneers, Apprentice Auctioneers, and Firms Engaged in the Auction Business in North Carolina.*

NORTH CAROLINA EDUCATION DIRECTORY. 0278-4971. US. English. an. State Deparment of Public Instruction, Education Building, Raleigh NC 27602. LC LB2803.N8. DD 379.756. *Educational Directory of North Carolina.*

NORTH CAROLINA MINORITY BUSINESS DIRECTORY. 0148-0839. US. English. Office of Minority Business Enterprise, PO Box 27687, Raleigh NC 27611. LC HD2346.U52. DD 338.642025756.

NORTH CAROLINA ZIP+4 STATE DIRECTORY. VFOAT Zip Plus Four State Directory. VAT North Carolina Zip Plus Four State Directory. 1985-. US. English. an. St Louis PDC Zip + 4 State Directory Orders, PO Box 14921, St Louis MO 63180-9988.

THE NORTH DAKOTA AND SOUTH DAKOTA LEGAL DIRECTORY. VFOAT South Dakota Legal Directory. 1982-1983-. 0748-2752. US. English. an. $14.00. PO Box 140200, Dallas TX 75214. LC KF192.N69. DD 340.025783. *Minnesota, Nebraska, North and South Dakota Legal Directory.*

NORTH SEA OIL & GAS DIRECTORY. VFOAT North Sea Oil and Gas Directory. UK. English. an. 32.95. Spearhead Publications, Rowe House 55/59 Fife Road, Kingston-Upon-Thames Surrey KT1 1TA England. Tel 01 549 5831. Ed Judith Patten. LC TN874.N78. DD 338.272802516336. adv acc. Circ 3,500. Comprehensive guide to operating companies, official organizations, and manufacturers and suppliers in the oil and gas industries in and around the North Sea.

NORTH WEST ENGLAND INDUSTRIAL CLASSIFIED DIRECTORY. 0260-0587. UK. English. an. Kemps Group (Printer & Publishers), 1-5 Bath Street, City Road, London EC1V 9QA England. LC HF257.E5. DD 338.00294427.

NORTH-WESTERN STATE SCHOOL DIRECTORY. English. ir. LC L971.N5. DD 371.01025669.

THE NORTHERN NEW ENGLAND LEGAL DIRECTORY, MAINE, NEW HAMPSHIRE, AND VERMONT. 1977/78-. 0194-0015. US. English. an. $14.00. Legal Directories Publishing Company, 2122 Kidwell Street, PO Box 140200, Dallas TX 75214. Tel (214)692-5825. LC KF190. DD 340.02574.

NORTHERN ONTARIO CONSTRUCTION & RESOURCE INDUSTRIES DIRECTORY, PURCHASING GUIDE. 1981-. 0229-1983. Periodical. CN. English. an. $10.00. DD 338.4769002571313. 0704-688X.

NORTHERN ONTARIO DIRECTORY. (DIRECTORY : NORTHERN ONTARIO). 1978-. 0714-0541. CN. English. Ministry of Northern Affairs, Information Services Branch, 10 Wellesley Street/9th Floor, Toronto Ontario M4Y 1G2 Canada. LC HT127. DD 361.00257131.

NRCP DIRECTORY. VFOAT N.R.C.P. Directory. 1981-. English. ir. NRCP General Santos Avenue, Bicutan Tagig, Metro Manila Philippines. LC Q141. DD 502.5599.

NRCSA DIRECTORY OF SPECIAL INTEREST PROGRAMS, BRITAIN-IRELAND. (NRCSA ... DIRECTORY OF SPECIAL INTEREST PROGRAMS, BRITAIN-IRELAND). VFOAT N.R.C.S.A. ... Directory of Special Interest Programs, Britain-Ireland. 1982-1983-. 0731-2822. US. English. be. $7.95. NRCSA, 823 North Second Street, Milwaukee WI 53203. LC L915. DD 300.2541.

NRCSA PROGRAM DIRECTORY. EUROPE. VFOAT N.R.C.S.A. Program Directory. Europe. 1982-83-. 0278-3789. US. English. be. $6.00. NRCSA, 823 North 2nd Street, Milwaukee WI 53203.

Tel (414)278-0631. LC L914.5. DD 370.254. Circ 10,000. Four brochures describe foreign language programs in Spain, France, Switzerland, Germany, Austria and Italy. Includes program description, fees, dates, lodging and registration information.

NURSING CAREER DIRECTORY. 1979-. 0192-2394. US. English. an. Free. Customer Service, 132 Welsh Road, Horsham PA 19044. LC RT82. DD 610.7302473. NLM WY 22 AA1 N9.

NYSAC COUNTY DIRECTORY. Main/Corp New York State Association of Counties. VFOAT N.Y.S.A.C. County Directory. Began with Vol. for 1980. US. English. an. $5.00. New York State Association of Counties, 150 State Street, Albany NY 12207. *Roster - New York State Association of Counties.*

OCEAN YEARBOOK. 1- 1978-. 0191-8575. US. English. ir. University of Chicago Press, PO Box 37005, Chicago IL 60637. Ind/Abst Life Sci. Collect., GeoRef, Bibliogr. Index Geol. LC GC1000. DD 333.9164.

O'DWYER'S DIRECTORY OF CORPORATE COMMUNICATIONS. VFOAT Directory of Corporate Communications. 1976-. 0149-1091. US. English. an. $90.00. O'Dwyers Directory of Corporate Communications, 271 Madison Avenue, New York NY 10016. Tel (212)679-2471. Ed Jack O'Dwyer. LC HD59. DD 338.761659202573. adv acc. Circ 2,000. Listings of 3,150 corporate public relations departments and 500 association public relations departments including names and titles of public relations executives and staff members, direct dial phone numbers for many addresses and phones of corporate headquarters and divisional offices.

O'DWYER'S DIRECTORY OF PUBLIC RELATIONS EXECUTIVES. 1979-. 0191-0051. US. English. te. $70.00. Jack O'Dwyer Company Inc, 271 Madison Avenue, New York NY 10016. Tel (212)679-2471. Ed Jack O'Dwyer. LC HD59. DD 659.202573. adv acc. Biographical data on more than 6,000 public relations executives.

O'DWYER'S DIRECTORY OF PUBLIC RELATIONS FIRMS. VFOAT Directory of Public Relations Firms. 0078-3374. US. English. an. $90.00. Jack O'Dwyers Company Ltd, 271 Madison Avenue, New York NY 10016. Tel (212)679-2471. Ed Jack O'Dwyer. LC HM263. DD 338.761659202573. adv acc. Listings on more than 1,600 public relations firms throughout the US accounts, executives, branch offices.

OFFICE DIRECTORY - DEPT. OF ESTABLISHMENT & TRAINING. Main/Corp Swaziland. Dept. of Establishment & Training. VAT Office Directory - Department of Establishment and Training. English. ir. Department of Establishment & Training Office Directory, PO Box 170, Mbabane Swaziland. LC JQ2721.A4. DD 354.683002.

OFFICE DIRECTORY : LAGOS AREA. Main/Corp Nigeria. Printing Division. English. ir. 25. Federal Ministry of Information, Printing Division, 9 Yakubu Gowon Street, Lagos Nigeria. LC JQ3087. DD 354.669002.

OFFICE SALARIES DIRECTORY FOR UNITED STATES AND CANADA CEASED. VFOAT AMS Office Salaries Directory for United States and Canada. Began with 1965/66. Ceased 34th (1980-81). 0731-4434. US. English. an. Administrative Management Society, Willow Grove PA 19090. LC HD4966.M4. DD 331.281651370973. *Directory of Office Salaries.*

OFFICER AND WARRANT OFFICER DIRECTORY. Main/Corp United States. Army. Corps of Engineers. VFOAT Directory, Corps of Engineers Officers and Warrant Officers. Began with 1982. 0732-7587. US. English. Adjutant General Headquarters, Department of the Army, Washington DC 20310. LC UG23. DD 358.202573. *Officer Directory.*

OFFICERS AND COMMITTEE DIRECTORY INCLUDING POLICY STATEMENTS AND OFFICIAL DOCUMENTS. Main/Corp American Water Works Association. VFOAT AWWA Officers & Committee Directory, Policy Statements & Official Documents. 0160-6867. US. English. $4.00. 6666 West Quincy Avenue, Denver CO 80235. LC TD1. DD 363.6106273.

OFFICIAL CONGRESSIONAL DIRECTORY. Main/Corp United States. Congress. VFOAT Congressional Directory. 50th Congress, 1st Session-. 0160-9890. US. English. an.

$17.00. US Government Printing Office, Superintendent of Documents, Washington DC 20402. Tel (202)783-3238. LC JK1011. DD 328.73073025. NLM JK 1011 A1. *Congressional Directory.*

OFFICIAL DIRECTORY - FIJI TRADES UNION CONGRESS. Main/Corp Fiji Trades Union Congress. VFOAT Fiji Trade Union Directory. English. ir. LC HD6937.7. DD 331.88099611.

OFFICIAL DIRECTORY - INTERNATIONAL NARCOTIC ENFORCEMENT OFFICERS ASSOCIATION. Main/Corp International Narcotic Enforcement Officers Association. US. English. International Narcotic Enforcement Officers Association, 178 Washington Avenue, Albany NY 12210. LC HV5801. DD 363.45.

OFFICIAL DIRECTORY - NEW JERSEY STATE BAR ASSOCIATION. Main/Corp New Jersey State Bar Association. 1972/73-. US. English. an. New Jersey State Bar Association, 172 West State Street, Trenton NJ 08608. LC KF192.N4. DD 340.062749. *Directory - New Jersey State Bar Association.*

THE OFFICIAL DIRECTORY OF CANADIAN MUSEUMS AND RELATED INSTITUTIONS. VFOAT Directory of Canadian Museums and Related Institutions. 1984-85-. 0829-0474. CN. English (text in French). an. Canadian Museums Association, 280 Metcalfe Street/Suite 202, Ottawa Ontario K2P 1R7 Canada. LC AM21.A1. DD 069.02571. *Directory of Canadian Museums and Related Institutions,* 0714-2188.

OFFICIAL DIRECTORY OF DATA PROCESSING. COMPUTER USERS EASTERN USA. (OFFICIAL DIRECTORY OF DATA PROCESSING, COMPUTER USERS EASTERN USA). VFOAT Official Directory of Data Processing, Eastern Computer Users. 0276-6442. US. English. an. $120.00. Official Directories and Services Inc, Gresham OR 97030. LC QA76.215. DD 001.6402574.

OFFICIAL DIRECTORY OF DATA PROCESSING. COMPUTER USERS SOUTHERN USA. (OFFICIAL DIRECTORY OF DATA PROCESSING, COMPUTER USERS SOUTHERN USA). VFOAT Official Directory of Data Processing, Southern Computer Users. 0276-6434. US. English. an. $120.00. Official Directories and Services Inc, Box 488, Gresham OR 97030. LC QA76.215. DD 001.642575.

OFFICIAL DIRECTORY OF DATA PROCESSING. COMPUTER USERS WESTERN USA. (OFFICIAL DIRECTORY OF DATA PROCESSING, COMPUTER USERS WESTERN USA). VFOAT Computer Users Western USA. 1981-82 Ed.-. 0278-5889. US. English. an. $195.00 Each Volume. Box 488, Gresham OR 97030. Tel (503)667-4669. Ed R F Knudson. Circ 5,000. USA end-user computer sites with in-depth information on computer installations including computer manufacturer and model number, computer, executives' names and titles plus programming languages. *Official Directory of Data Processing, EDP Systems Users Western U.S.A.,* 0278-6109.

OFFICIAL DIRECTORY OF DATA PROCESSING, EDP SYSTEM USERS MIDWESTERN USA. VFOAT Official Directory of Data Processing, Midwestern System Users. 0276-6450. US. English. an. $90.00. Offical Directories and Services Inc, 620 North Cleveland Street, Gresham OR 97030. LC QA76.215. DD 001.642577.

THE OFFICIAL DIRECTORY OF INDUSTRIAL AND COMMERCIAL TRAFFIC EXECUTIVES. VFOAT Directory of Industrial and Commercial Traffic Executives. 0192-2629. US. English. an. $75.00. Traffic Service Corporation, 1435 G Street/Suite 815, Washington DC 20005. Tel (202)626-4500. LC HF5780.U6. *Official Directory of Commercial Traffic Executives, with an Appendix of Transportation Commissions and Organizations.*

OFFICIAL DIRECTORY OF NEW JERSEY LIBRARIES AND MEDIA CENTERS. See Library and Information Science.

OFFICIAL DIRECTORY OF REGISTERED DOCTORS OF MEDICINE, MEDICAL CORPORATIONS AND DOCTORS OF CHIROPODY-PODIATRY. 0148-3579. US. English. Medical Licensing Board of West Virginia, State Office Building, 1800 Washington Street,

Yearbooks, Almanacs, Directories

Charleston WV 25305. LC R712.A2. DD 610.25754. *Official Directory of Registered Doctors of Medicine.*

OFFICIAL DIRECTORY OF REGISTERED NURSES AND LICENSED PRACTICAL NURSES. 0360-2850. US. English. State Board of Nursing, 100 Vassar, Reno NV 89502. LC RT5.N3. DD 610.73025793. *Official Directory of Registered Professional Nurses and Licensed Practical Nurses Holding Licenses Permitting Practice in the State of Nevada.*

OFFICIAL DIRECTORY OF THE LEGISLATURE, STATE OF IOWA. Main/Corp Iowa. General Assembly. US. English. an. General Assembly, Core Depository, 707 Savings and Loan Building, Des Moines IA 50309. LC JK6330. DD 328.7770025. *Legislative Directory (Iowa. Secretary of State).*

OFFICIAL DIRECTORY - UNITED STATES. ARMY. CORPS OF ENGINEERS. (OFFICIAL DIRECTORY). Main/Corp United States. Army. Corps of Engineers. 0278-6559. US. English. Superintendent of Documents, Government Printing Office, Washington DC 20402. LC UG23. DD 358.202573. *Directory of Regular Army Officers.*

OFFICIAL DIRECTORY - VIRGINIA BANKERS ASSOCIATION. Main/Corp Virginia Bankers' Association. 0160-5267. US. English. 700 East Main Street/Suite 1411, Richmond VA 23203. LC HG1507. DD 332.122062755.

OFFICIAL HELLENIC YEAR BOOK (1984). (OFFICIAL HELLENIC YEAR BOOK). VFOAT Hellenic Community of Ottawa. VAT Hellenic Community of Ottawa (1984). 1984-. 0823-8596. CN. English (text in Greek). an. Free. Hellenic Canadian Community of Ottawa and District, 1315 Prince of Wales Drive, Ottawa Ontario K2C 1N2 Canada. DD 971.38400489. (ctrl). *Year Book (Hellenic Canadian Community of Ottawa and District), 0822-5958.*

OFFICIAL INTERNATIONAL BUSINESS DIRECTORY OF THE SPANISH SPEAKING WORLD. 1982-1983-. 0735-5513. US. English (Spanish). an. $200.00 US and Canada. Aurora International Consulting, PO Box 668, Norwalk CT 06856. LC HF3230.5.A48. DD 338.7402517561.

THE OFFICIAL INTERNATIONAL DIRECTORY OF SPECIAL EVENTS & FESTIVALS. (THE OFFICIAL ... INTERNATIONAL DIRECTORY OF SPECIAL EVENTS & FESTIVALS). VFOAT International Directory of Special Events & Festivals. VAT Official International Directory of Special Events and Festivals. 1st Ed. (1984-1985)-. 0743-4170. US. English. an. $100.00. The Official International Directory of Special Events & Festivals, 213 West Institute Place/Suite 303, Chicago IL 60610. LC GT3930. DD 791.6025.

OFFICIAL MANITOBA SHIP-BY-TRUCK DIRECTORY. (THE OFFICIAL MANITOBA SHIP-BY-TRUCK DIRECTORY). VFOAT Manitoba Ship-by-Truck Directory. 1982/83-. 0713-8776. CN. English. an. 15.00. Official Manitoba Ship-by-Truck Directory, c/o Manitoba Trucking Association, 25 Bunting Street, Winnipeg Manitoba R2X 2P5 Canada. Tel (204)632-6600. Ed Bob Wilks. DD 388.3240257127. adv acc. Directory containing complete information on shipping and truck services in Manitoba for carriers, shippers, receivers and traffic managers. SBTD : *Manitoba Ship-by-Truck Directory, 0228-7315.*

OFFICIAL MOTOR CARRIER DIRECTORY. Began in Autumn 1958. 0472-6243. US. English. sa. $31.50. Official Motor Carrier Directory Inc, 1130 South Canal Street, Chicago IL 60607. Tel (312)939-1434 800/621-4650. Ed Sheila K Levine. LC HE5623.A45. DD 388.32402573. adv acc. Circ 5,000. Alphabetical listing of motor and air carriers. Provides general office information, terminals etc. Also lists organizations related to transportation.

OFFICIAL MUSEUM DIRECTORY. (THE OFFICIAL MUSEUM DIRECTORY). Began in 1971. 0090-6700. US. English. an. National Register Publishing Company, 3004 Glenview Road, Wilmette IL 60091. LC AM10.A2. DD 069.02257. NLM AM 10 M986. *Museums Directory of the United States and Canada, 0090-6697.*

THE OFFICIAL MUSEUM PRODUCTS AND SERVICES DIRECTORY. VFOAT Products and Services. 1981-. 0276-637X. US. English. American Association of Museums, 1055 Thomas Jefferson Street NW, Washington DC 20007. LC AM127. DD 069.302573.

OFFICIAL MUSIC & RECORD DIRECTORY. VAT Official Music and Record Directory. 0162-3540. US. English. 45 Oakland Street, Irvington IL 07111. LC ML18. DD 338.47780973.

OFFICIAL SOUTH AFRICAN MUNICIPAL YEARBOOK. VFOAT Amptelike Suid-Afrikaanse Munisipale Jarrbook. Began publication in 1909. English. an. Ed W P Henderson and F G Pay. LC JS7531.

OFFICIAL SOUTHERN CALIFORNIA PORTS MARITIME DIRECTORY AND GUIDE. 1st- Ed. 0094-8454. US. English. $10.00. 404 South Bixel Street, Los Angeles CA 90051. LC HE554.A6. DD 387.109794.

THE OFFICIAL STEAMSHIP SERVICE DIRECTORY. June July/Aug. 1981-. 0734-1016. US. English. qt. $75.00. Official Steamship Service Directory, 21st Century Pub Company, PO Box 1148, San Carlos CA 94070. LC HE945.A2. DD 387.5025.

OFFICIAL TRADE UNION DIRECTORY AND INDUSTRIAL RELATIONS HANDBOOK. VFOAT Trade Union Directory. English. an. Trade Union Council of South Africa (TUCSA), 90 Anderson Street, Trades Hall East/4th Floor, PO Box 5592, Johannesburg 2000 South Africa. *Official Trade Union Directory (Johannesburg, South Africa).*

OFFICIAL TRADE UNION DIRECTORY (JOHANNESBURG, SOUTH AFRICA). (OFFICIAL TRADE UNION DIRECTORY). VFOAT Trade Union Directory. 1975-. SA. English. an. Trade Union Council of South Africa (TUCSA), 90 Anderson Street, Trades Hall East/4th Floor, PO Box 5592, Johannesburg 2000 South Africa. LC HD6870.5. DD 331.880968.

THE OFFICIAL UNITED STATES TENNIS ASSOCIATION YEARBOOK AND TENNIS GUIDE WITH THE OFFICIAL RULES. Main/Corp United States Tennis Association. VFOAT Tennis Yearbook. 0196-5425. US. English. an. $11.00. US Tennis Association, 729 Alexander Road, Princeton NJ 08540. Tel (609)452-2580. Ed Miles Dumont. Circ 50,000. Up-to-date information on tournaments, committees, rankings, members, records, tournament regulations, and the official rules of tennis and cases and decisions. *Official United States Lawn Tennis Association Yearbook and Tennis Guide with the Official Rules.*

OFFICIAL YEAR BOOK. Main/Corp Nairobi Stock Exchange. English. ir. 10/-. Nairobi Stock Exchange, PO Box 30127, Nairobi Kenya. LC HG5850.K454. DD 332.6420967625.

OFFICIAL YEAR BOOK - MALAYSIA. Main/Corp Malaysia. VFOAT Buku Rasmi Tahunan. Official Yearbook. V. 1- 1961-. 0076-3373. MY. English. ir. Government Printing Press, Jalan Chan Sow Ling, Kuala Lumpur Malaysia. LC DS591. DD 915.95005.

OFFICIAL YEAR BOOK OF THE COMMONWEALTH OF AUSTRALIA. VFOAT Year Book of Australia. VAT Official Yearbook of the Commonwealth of Australia. No. 1-58. 0078-3927. AT. English. an. Australian Government Printing Office, PO Box 84, Canberra Australian Capital Territory 2600 Australia. Tel 062-954411. LC HA3001. DD 319.4. NLM W2 KA8 B9O.

OFFICIAL YEARBOOK AND BUYERS GUIDE. Main/Corp Southern Nurserymen's Association. (1975-). Periodical. US. English. an.

OFFSHORE CONTRACTORS AND EQUIPMENT DIRECTORY. VFOAT Worldwide Directory Offshore Contractors and Equipment. 0475-1310. US. English. an. $106.50. Pennwell Publishing Company, PO Box 1260, Tulsa OK 74101. Tel (918)835-3161. Ed William R Leek Jr. LC TN871.3. DD 338.7622338028. adv acc. Circ 2,500. For offshore and oil gas contractors. Sections include drilling, construction, diving, transportation (marine and air), geophysical service-supply-manufacturing, equipment index. Has drilling platforms, construction barges.

OFFSHORE INDUSTRIAL DIRECTORY. 1979-. 0712-0745. CN. English. Department of Development, Confederation Building, Saint John's Newfoundland A1C 5T7 Canada. LC HD9574.C23. DD 681.76.

OFFSHORE OIL & GAS YEARBOOK. VFOAT Offshore Oil & Gas Yearbook: UK & Continental Europe. 1978/79-. 0260-6437. UK. English. an. Benn Technical Books, 17 Scarbrook Road, Tolley House, Croydon Surrey CR0 1SQ England. Tel (01)686 9141. Ed Michael Gale. Ind/Abst Life Sci. Collect. LC TN874.A1. DD 338.2728094. Circ 650. A reference work with comprehensive coverage of the European offshore oil and gas industry, country by country, in words, maps and statistics. Includes a directory of the industry's suppliers. *European Offshore Oil & Gas Yearbook, U. K. Offshore Oil & Gas Yearbook, 0305-4691.*

OFFSHORE TECHNOLOGY YEARBOOK. 0094-9124. US. English. Energy Communications, PO Box 1589, Dallas TX 75221. LC TN871.3. DD 622.338.

OFICIALA JARLIBRO DE LA ESPERANTO-MOVADO. Main/Corp Universala Esperanto-Asocio, Geneve. Began publication with 1908 issue. 0083-3851. NE. Esperanto. ir. 28.00. Universala Esperanto-Asocio, Nieuwe Binnenweg 176, 3015 BJ Rotterdam Netherlands. Tel (010)4361539. Ed Simo Milojevic. LC PM8201. DD 408.92058. adv acc. Circ 8,000. (ctrl).

O'HARA'S INTERNATIONAL SPORT FISHING TOURNAMENT DIRECTORY. (O'HARA'S ... INTERNATIONAL SPORT FISHING TOURNAMENT DIRECTORY). VFOAT International Sport Fishing Tournament Directory. 1st Ed. (1984)-. 0740-4883. US. English. LC SH455.2. DD 799.12.

OHIO ALMANAC. 1st- Ed. 0473-9760. US. English. an. Ohio Almanac, PO Box 562, Forest Park Station, Dayton OH 45405. LC AY271.L6. DD 917.71'005.

THE OHIO FARMER COUNTY LINE RURAL DIRECTORY. CRAWFORD COUNTY. (THE OHIO FARMER COUNTY LINE RURAL DIRECTORY : CRAWFORD COUNTY). VFOAT County Line Rural Directory. Crawford County. 1976-. 0149-2934. US. English. 9800 Detroit Avenue, Cleveland OH 44102. LC F497.C8. DD 977.12704025.

THE OHIO FARMER COUNTY LINE RURAL DIRECTORY. HURON COUNTY. (THE OHIO FARMER COUNTY LINE RURAL DIRECTORY : HURON COUNTY). VFOAT County Line Rural Directory. Huron County. 1976-. 0148-981X. US. English. 9800 Detroit Avenue, Cleveland OH 44012. LC F497.H8. DD 977.12504025.

OHIO INDUSTRIAL BUYERS DIRECTORY. 0197-1190. US. English. an. Harris Publishing Company, State Directory Division, 2057-2 Aurora Road, Twinsburg OH 44087. LC T12. DD 670.25771.

OHIO MANUFACTURERS DIRECTORY. 1st Ed. (1983)-. 0737-7495. US. English. an. $98.00. 4 East Huron Street, Chicago IL 60611. Tel (312)337-1084. Ed Louise West. LC HD9727.O3. DD 338.47000294771. adv acc. Contains data on Ohio's 17,833 manufacturing plants: names of 43,391 executives. Five sections: city, product, SIC name and computer. Gives number of employees, year established, phone, and up to 27 facts.

THE OHIO REGIONAL ART DIRECTORY. 1983-. 0736-9824. US. English. an. Ohio Regional Art Directory, 1861 West 25th, Cleveland OH 44113. LC NC975. DD 741.6025771.

OIKONOMIKOS HODEGOS TON HELLENIKON HETAIRION. VFOAT Hodegos I.C.A.P., Financial Directory of Greek Companies. 1979-. GR. English (Greek). an. ICAP Hellas S A, Vas Sophias 64, Athena 115 28 Greece. LC HF5175. DD 338.74025495. *Oikonomikos Hodegos Ton en Helladi Anonymon Hetareion Kai Hetareion Periorismenes Euthynes.*

THE OIL AND GAS DIRECTORY. (THE OIL & GAS DIRECTORY). VFOAT Oil and Gas Directory. Began with issue for 1970/71. US. English. an. $42.46. Oil & Gas Directory, 2200 Welch Avenue, Houston TX 77019. Tel (713)529-8789. LC TN867. DD 338.2728025. adv acc. Circ 5,000. List of contractors, suppliers and oil and gas companies engaged in petroleum exploration, drilling and producing.

OIL DIRECTORY OF ALASKA. 1945-. 0471-3850. US. English. an. $9.25. Midwest Oil Register Inc, PO Box 700597, Tulsa OK 74170. Tel (918)742-9925. Ed Ross Sloan. LC TN867. DD 338.27282.

OIL DIRECTORY OF LOUISIANA AND PRODUCTION SURVEY. VFOAT Oil and Gas Directory and Production Survey of Louisiana. US. English. $18.00. R W Byram & Company, PO

Yearbooks, Almanacs, Directories

Drawer 1867, Austin TX 78767. LC HD9567.L8. DD 338.2728025763.

OIL DIRECTORY OF TEXAS. VFOAT Oil Directory of Texas and Production Survey. 0471-3893. US. English. an. $30.00. R W Byram & Company, PO Drawer 1867, Austin TX 78767. Tel (512)478-2551. Oil and gas producers in Texas. Includes production for one month.

OIL, GAS, MARINE DIRECTORY OF THE GULF SOUTH/ATLANTIC COAST. 0162-5675. US. English. an. PO Box 8313, Metairie LA 70011. LC TN867. DD 338.4762233802573.

OIL SCOUTS DIRECTORY. Main/Corp International Oil Scouts Association. 0742-7263. US. English. $35.00. International Oil Scouts Association, PO Box 2121, Austin TX 78768. LC HD9560.3. DD 622.182802573.

OILFIELD SERVICE, SUPPLY AND MANUFACTURERS WORLDWIDE DIRECTORY. VFOAT Worldwide Oilfield Service, Supply and Manufacturers Directory. 1983-. 0736-038X. US. English. an. $65.00. Pennwell Publishing Company, PO Box 1260, Tulsa OK 74101. Tel (918)835-3161. Ed William R Leek Jr. LC HD9560.3. DD 338.768176. adv acc. Circ 1,500. USA based oilfield manufacturing, supply and service companies. Divided into these three sections and has a company index.

OKLAHOMA DIRECTORY OF MANUFACTURERS AND PRODUCTS. VFOAT Oklahoma Directory of Manufacturers. US. English. be. $35.00. Oklahoma Manufacturers, 4024 North Lincoln Boulevard, Oklahoma City OK 73105. Tel (405)521-2181. LC HD9727.O5. DD 338.4767025766. Index in last issue of volume - attached. *Directory of Oklahoma Manufacturers.*

THE OKLAHOMA LEGAL DIRECTORY. US. English. an. Legal Directories Publishing Company Inc, 2122 Kidwell Street, PO Box 140200, Dallas TX 75214. LC KF192.O38. DD 340.025766.

OKLAHOMA STATE INDUSTRIAL DIRECTORY. US. English. an. State Industrial Directories Corporation, 2 Penn Plaza, New York NY 10001.

OKLAHOMA UTILITIES DIRECTORY. US. English. Oklahoma Department of Industrial Development, 500 Will Rogers Building, Oklahoma City OK 73105. LC HD2767.O5. DD 363.6025766.

THE OLD FARMER'S ALMANAC. SPECIAL CANADIAN EDITION. (THE OLD FARMER'S ALMANAC). VFOAT Old Farmer's Almanack. 1792. 0276-3060. US. English. an. $1.95. Yankee Publishing Inc, Dublin NH 03444. Tel (603)563-8111. Ed Jud Hale. DD 032.02. adv acc. Circ 2,500,000. In its 193rd year, this American tradition is an interesting collection of facts, entertaining features, astrological information and weather predictions.

THE OLD FARMER'S ALMANACK. VFOAT Thomas's Old Farmer's Almanac. No. 1- 1793-. 0075-4516. US. English. an. LC AY81.F3. DD 051.

ON LOCATION, THE NATIONAL FILM & VIDEOTAPE PRODUCTION DIRECTORY. VFOAT On Location National Film & Videotape Production Directory. V. 2- 1978/79-. 0740-1159. US. English. an. $49.00 Each Issue. On Location Publishing Inc, 6777 Hollywood Boulevard, Los Angeles CA 90028. LC PN1998.A1. DD 338.470002573. *On Location Film and Videotape Production Directory, 0160-5933.*

ON YOUR OWN, A DIRECTORY FOR WOMEN. Sept. 1982-. 0827-8717. CN. English. an. $0.50 Each Volume. Young Women's Christian Association of Metropolitan Toronto, 80 Woodlawn Avenue East, Toronto Ontario M4T 1B1 Canada. DD 362.793025713541.

ON YOUR OWN, A DIRECTORY FOR YOUNG MEN. Sept. 1983-. 0827-8725. CN. English. an. $0.50 Each Volume. Young Women's Christian Association of Metropolitan Toronto, 80 Woodlawn Avenue East, Toronto Ontario M4T 1C1 Canada. Tel (416)961-8100. Ed Rochelle Rabinowicz. DD 362.792025713541. Directory of services for young men on their own in Toronto.

ONLINE DATABASE SEARCH SERVICES DIRECTORY. 1st Ed., Part 1 of 2 parts (Dec. 1983)-. 0741-0077. US. English. sa. Gale Research Company, Book Tower, Detroit MI 48226. LC QA76.55. DD 026.524.

ONLINE MICRO-SOFTWARE GUIDE & DIRECTORY. VFOAT Micro-Software Guide & Directory. 1983-84-. 0734-5097. Periodical. US. English. an. $40.00. Online Inc, Department S-D/ Tannery Lane, Weston CT 06883.

ONLINE MICRO-SOFTWARE GUIDE & DIRECTORY. SUPPLEMENT. VFOAT Online Micro Software Supplement. 1983-. 0734-5097. US. English. an. Online Inc, Department S/D, 11 Tannery Lane, Weston CT 06883.

ONLINE TERMINAL/ MICROCOMPUTER GUIDE & DIRECTORY. VFOAT Online Terminal Microcomputer Guide and Directory. 1982-83-. 0734-5100. US. English. te. $40.00. Online Inc, 11 Tannery Lane, Weston CT 06883. LC HD9696.C63. DD 380.145621381958. *Online Terminal Guide & Directory, 0198-697X.*

ONTARIO ASSOCIATION OF ART GALLERIES WHO'S WHO DIRECTORY OF ART GALLERIES AND SERVICE ORGANIZATIONS IN ONTARIO. VFOAT Who's Who Directory of Art Galleries and Service Organizations in Ontario. 1984-. 0827-2360. CN. English. an. $10.00 Each Volume Members, $15.00 Each Volume Nonmembers. Ontario Association of Art Galleries, 38 Charles Street East, Toronto Ontario M4Y 1T1 Canada. DD 069.97025713.

ONTARIO CATHOLIC DIRECTORY CEASED. 1959-1980. 0078-4702. Periodical. CN. English. an. Ontario Catholic Directory, 89 St George Street, Toronto Ontario M5S 2E8 Canada. DD 282.025713. *Ontario Catholic Year Book and Directory, 0315-2820.*

ONTARIO CRAFTS DIRECTORY. No. 1-. 0712-306X. CN. English. be. $3.00 Each Number. Ontario Crafts Directory, c/o Ontario Crafts Council Resource Centre, 346 Dundas Street West, Toronto Ontario M5T 1G5 Canada. DD 338.477455025713. *Ontario Craft Directory, 0317-1256.*

ONTARIO GOLDEN HORSESHOE CONSTRUCTION INDUSTRY DIRECTORY, PURCHASING GUIDE. (ONTARIO GOLDEN HORSESHOE CONSTRUCTION INDUSTRY DIRECTORY/PURCHASING GUIDE). VAT Annual Ontario Golden Horseshoe Construction Industry Directory, Purchasing Guide. 1977-. 0704-6898. CN. English. an. $4.00 Each Number. Sanford Evans Publishing Ltd, Construction Directory Division, PO Box 6900, Winnipeg Manitoba R3C 3B1 Canada. DD 381.456900257133.

ONTARIO HOSPITALS DIRECTORY. CN. English. Ontario Government Bookstore, 880 Bay Street, Toronto Ontario M7A 1N8 Canada. LC RA978.C2. DD 362.11025713.

ONTARIO HYDRO STATISTICAL YEARBOOK. (STATISTICAL YEARBOOK). 0382-2834. CN. English. an. Ontario Hydro, 620 University Avenue, Toronto Ontario Canada. LC HD9685.C3. DD 363.609713.

OPD CHEMICAL BUYERS DIRECTORY. VFOAT Chemical Buyers Directory. VAT Oil, Paint, Drug Chemical Buyers Directory. 1968/69-. 0276-539X. US. English. an. Schnell Publishing Company Inc, 100 Church Street, New York NY 10007. LC TP12. DD 660.029473. *Chemical Buyers Directory.*

OPERATIONS RESEARCH/ MANAGEMENT SCIENCE YEARBOOK. VFOAT Operations Research Yearbook. 1961-. 0473-0496. US. English. an. $128.00. Executive Sciences Institute, Whippany NJ 07981. Tel (201)887-1233. Ed Arnold J Rosenthal. LC HD20. DD 658.403405. Circ 1,000. An international literature digest service covering the methods of operations research and their applications in management of industry and government.

THE OPTICAL INDUSTRY & SYSTEMS PURCHASING DIRECTORY. VAT The Optical Industry and Systems Purchasing Directory. 25th- ed. 0191-0647. US. English. an. $68.00. Optical Publication Company Inc, Box 1146, Pittsfield MA 01202. Tel (413)499-0514. LC TS511.U6. DD 338.476213602573. *Optical Industry & Systems Directory, 0078-5474.*

ORAL AND MAXILLOFACIAL SURGERY DIRECTORY OF THE WORLD. VFOAT Oral Maxillofacial Surgeons Directory of the World. 0147-1449. US. English. 761 Osage Road, Pittsburgh PA 15243. LC RD523. DD 617.5220025. *Oral Surgery Directory of the World.*

ORANGE COUNTY BUSINESS AND INDUSTRIAL DIRECTORY. 19-. Periodical. US. English. an. $47.70. Orange County Chamber of Commerce, 1 City Boulevard West 401 Bank Amer Tower, Orange CA 92668. Tel (714)634-2900.

ORBIS GEOGRAPHICUS. *See* Geography.

THE OREGON BLUE BOOK. 1933/34-. US. English. be. Secretary of State, Department of State, Salem OR 97310. Tel (503)378-4144. *Blue Book and Official Directory.*

OREGON DIRECTORY OF AMERICAN INDIAN RESOURCES. VFOAT American Indian Resources. 1981-82-. 0733-477X. US. English. an. $9.00. Commission on Indian Services, 454 State Capitol, Salem OR 97310. Tel (503)378-5481. Ed Peggy Walker. LC E78.O6. DD 305.8970795. Circ 2,000. Lists all American Indian tribes, organizations, interest groups, programs, etc. in the state of Oregon. Contains addresses, phone numbers and program or organization descriptions.

OREGON GENEALOGICAL SOCIETY DIRECTORY. VFOAT Directory. 0749-1271. US. English. Oregon Genealogical Society, PO Box 10306, Eugene OR 97440. LC F875. DD 929.10720785.

OREGON INTERNATIONAL TRADE DIRECTORY. 1978-79-. 0731-9096. US. English. an. $25.00. State of Oregon, 155 Cottage Street NE, Salem OR 97310. Tel 229-5625. Ed Douglas V Frengle. LC HF3161.O7. DD 382.025795. Circ 3,000. (ctrl). Lists Oregon companies engaged in exporting and importing. Information is cross-indexed by company, product, country of activity, and geographic location of the firm.

OREGON LABOR MARKET INFORMATION DIRECTORY. 0732-6084. US. English. ir. State of Oregon Employment Division, Department of Human Resources, 875 Union Street, Salem OR 97311. LC HD5725.O7. DD 016.331109795.

OREGON SCHOOL COMMUNITY COLLEGE DIRECTORY. 0090-5623. US. English. Oregon Board of Education, 700 Pringle Parkway SE, Salem OR 97310. LC L903.O7. DD 370.25795.

THE OREGON SCHOOL DIRECTORY. US. English. an. $5.00. Oregon Department of Education, 700 Pringle Parkway SE, Salem OR 97310. Tel (503)378-3569. LC L903.O7. DD 370.58.

THE ORGAN YEARBOOK. V. 1- 1970-. English. an. 49-. Uitgeverij Frits Knuf B V, PO Box 720, 4116 ZJ Buren Netherlands. Tel 03447-1691. Ed Peter Williams. Ind/Abst Music Index, RILM Abstr. LC ML5. DD 786.505. bk rev. adv acc. Circ 1,000. (ctrl). A journal for the players and historians of keyboard instruments.

ORGANIZATIONAL DIRECTORY - NATIONAL SCIENCE FOUNDATION (U.S.). (ORGANIZATIONAL DIRECTORY). Main/ Corp National Science Foundation (U.S.). 0737-0792. US. English. 1800 G Street NW, Washington DC 20550. NLM Q 11 N278O. *Organizational Directory of the National Science Foundation.*

THE ORIENTAL ECONOMIST'S JAPAN ECONOMIC YEARBOOK. VFOAT Japan Economic Yearbook. Began in 1954. Ceased with 1981/82 issue. 0075-3246. JA. English. an. LC HC461. DD 330.952005.

ORSA/TIMS MEMBERSHIP DIRECTORY. Main/Corp Operations Research Society of America. VAT Operations Research Society of America/The Institute of Management Sciences Membership Directory. 0271-2008. US. English. an. Operations Research Society of America, 428 East Preston Street, Baltimore MD 21202. LC Q175. DD 001.42406073. *Combined Membership Directory - Operations Research Society of America. Institute of Management Sciences, 0160-2535.*

ORTHODONTIC DIRECTORY OF THE WORLD. US. English. be. $20.00. 1915 Broadway, Nashville TN 37203. Tel (615)383-5152. Ed William H Oliver. NLM WU22 O77. adv acc. Circ 5,000. Includes names, addresses, and training.

OTTAWA CITY DIRECTORY (TORONTO, ONT.). (THE OTTAWA CITY DIRECTORY MICROFORM). VFOAT Boyd and M'Donald's Ottawa City Directory. 1861/2-. CN. English. Ottawa Public Library Business Office, 120 Metcalfe Street, Ottawa Ontario K1P 5M2 Canada. DD 917.13840025.

OTTAWA CO-OPERATIVE DIRECTORY. (THE OTTAWA CO-OPERATIVE DIRECTORY). VFOAT Repertoire Cooperatif de l'Est de l'Ontario. No. 1-. 0228-8656. CN. English (French).

Yearbooks, Almanacs, Directories

an. $0.50 Each Number. Potential Co-Op Society, PO Box 5 Station B, Ottawa Ontario K1P 6C3 Canada. **DD** 334.097138.

OTTAWA. DIRECTORY OF MUNICIPAL SERVICES. (OTTAWA; DIRECTORY OF MUNICIPAL SERVICES). **VFOAT** Ottawa. 1979/80-. 0225-2090. **CN**. English (text in French with French text on inverted pages). be. Free. Information and Public Relations Division, Ottawa City Hall, 111 Sussex Drive, Ottawa Ontario K1N 5A1 Canada. **DD** 352.071384.

OTTAWA ETHNIC GROUPS DIRECTORY *CEASED*. Series/Titl Ethnic Directories. Began with 1971 issue. 0315-0771. **CN**. English (includes some text in French). an. Free to Government Departments and Organizations. G Bonavia, PO Box 826 Station B, Ottawa Ontario K1P 5P9 Canada. **Tel** (613)521-5285. **Ed** George Bonavia. **LC** F1059.5.O9. **DD** 971.384004. bk rev.

OTTAWA JEWISH REFERENCE TELEPHONE DIRECTORY *CEASED*. Began with issue for 1975? Ceased in 1983. 0317-2988. Periodical. **CN**. English. an. **DD** 971.384004924. *Ottawa Jewish Reference Book and Telephone Directory, 0316-4950.*

OTTAWA JEWISH TELEPHONE DIRECTORY. 5744/1984-. 0828-4652. **CN**. English. an. $12.00 Per Vol. Ottawa Jewish Telephone Directory, PO Box 288 Station A, Ottawa Ontario K1N 8V2 Canada. **DD** 971.3884004924025. *Ottawa Jewish Reference Telephone Directory, 0828-4652.*

OUA/DATA'S GUIDE TO CORPORATE GIVING IN MAINE. (OUA/DATA'S ... GUIDE TO CORPORATE GIVING IN MAINE). **VFOAT** OUADATA'S ... Guide to Corporate Giving in Maine. 1984-. 0883-2730. US. English. be. $7.50. OUA/DATA, 81 Saltonstall Avenue, New Haven CT 06513. **Tel** (203)278-4271. **LC** HV98.M2. **DD** 001.44025741. **Circ** 500. (ctrl). A directory of 300 Maine corporation philanthropic policies, practices and procedures.

OUTDOOR LIFE DEER HUNTER'S YEARBOOK. **VFOAT** Outdoor Life Deerhunter's Yearbook. 1983-. 0734-2918. US. English. an. $16.95. Stackpole Books, Cameron and Kelker Streets, PO Box 1831, Harrisburg PA 17105. **LC** SK301. **DD** 639.117357.

OVERSEAS ASSIGNMENT DIRECTORY SERVICE. 1977-. 0735-231X. US. English. mo. Overseas Assignment Directory Service, 701 Westchester Avenue, White Plains NY 10604. **Tel** (914)328-9157. **Ed** Alison Lanier.

OXBRIDGE DIRECTORY OF NEWSLETTERS. 1979-. 0163-7010. US. English. be. $98.00. Oxbridge Communications Inc, 150 Fifth Avenue, New York NY 10011. **Tel** (212)741-0231. **Ed** Margie Domenech. **LC** Z6944.N44, PN4784.N5. **DD** 071.3025. adv acc. Contains over 15,000 newsletter listings in general categories from A to Z. *Standard Directory of Newsletters.*

OXBRIDGE DIRECTORY OF RELIGIOUS PERIODICALS. 0191-4502. Periodical. US. English. ir. $25.00. Oxbridge Communications Inc, 150 5th Avenue/Suite 301, New York NY 10011. **Tel** (212)741-0231. **Ed** Margie Domenech. **LC** Z7753. **DD** 016.2005. Listing of religious directories covering all religions.

OYO STATE YEAR BOOK AND WHO'S WHO. 1981-. English. an. Ayinda Brothers Ltd, N4/815B Yemetu-Agip, Box 7583, Secretariat, Ibadan Nigeria. **LC** DT515.9.O9. **DD** 966.92.

PAC-FINDER SYSTEM 34/36 SOFTWARE DIRECTORY. **VFOAT** Pac-Finder System Thirty-Four, Thirty-Six Software Directory. 1984-. 0741-4978. US. English. an. $79.00. Elsevier Science Publishing Co, 52 Vanderbilt Avenue, New York NY 10017. **DD** 001.

PACIFIC BOATING ALMANAC. NORTHERN CALIFORNIA & NEVADA. **VAT** Pacific Boating Almanac. Northern California and Nevada. 0193-3515. US. English. an. $5.95. Western Marine Enterprises Inc, Box Q, Ventura CA 93001. **Ed** William Berssen. **LC** GV776.C2. **DD** 797.1097941. *Sea Boating Almanac. Northern California & Nevada, 0363-7700.*

PACIFIC BOATING ALMANAC. OREGON, WASHINGTON, BRITISH COLUMBIA AND SOUTHEASTERN ALASKA EDITION. **VFOAT** Pacific Boating Almanac. 1981-. 0276-8771. US. English. an. $6.95. Western Marine Enterprises Inc, Box Q, Ventura CA 93002. **LC** GV776.N76. **DD** 797.109795. *Pacific Boating Almanac. Pacific Northwest & Alaska, 0148-1177.*

PACIFIC BOATING ALMANAC. SOUTHERN CALIFORNIA, ARIZONA & BAJA. **VAT** Pacific Boating Almanac. Southern California, Arizona and Baja. 0193-3507. US. English. an. $5.95 Single Issue. Western Marine Enterprises Inc, Box Q, Ventura CA 93001. **Ed** William Berssen. **LC** GV776.C22. **DD** 797.1097949. *Sea Boating Almanac. Southern California, Arizona, Baja, 0363-6712.*

PACIFIC HOTEL DIRECTORY AND TRAVEL GUIDE. 1957-. Periodical. US. English. sa. Pacific Area Travel Association, 274 Brannan Street, San Francisco CA 94107.

PACIFIC ISLANDS YEAR BOOK. 11th- Ed. AT. English. ir. Pacific Publication Pty Ltd, GPO Box 3408, Sydney New South Wales 2000 Australia. **Ed** John Carter. **LC** DU1. *Pacific Islands Year Book and Who's Who.*

PACIFIC NORTHWEST TRADE DIRECTORY. 1984-. US. English. be. $65.00. Robinson Publishing Company Inc, 207 SW 150th Street, Seattle WA 98166. **Tel** (206)241-2700. **Ed** Howard Hirshman. bk rev. adv acc. **Circ** 20,000. (ctrl). International trade, 3,000 importers and exporters. Also trade statistics.

PACKAGE ENGINEERING. BUYERS GUIDE & DIRECTORY. **VFOAT** Buyers Guide & Directory. US. English. an. Cahners Publications, PO Box 668, Englewood CO 80110. **Tel** (303)388-4511. *Modern Packaging Encyclopedia and Buyers Guide.*

PACKAGING DIRECTORY. UK. English. an. $31.41. Wheatland Journals Limited, Penn House Penn Place, Rickmanoworth Herts WD3 1SN England. **LC** TS195.A3. **DD** 688.8029441.

EL PAIS, ANUARIO .... **VFOAT** Anuario el Pais. Spanish. an. Promotora de Informaciones Sociedad Anonima (Prisa). **LC** D839. **DD** 909.0805.

PAKISTAN DIRECTORY OF TRADE AND INDUSTRY. English. ir. 25.00. 11 Race Course Road, Lahore West Pakistan.

THE PAKISTAN INSURANCE YEAR BOOK. Began with 1948 issue. English. ir. **LC** HG8704.5. **DD** 368.95491.

PAKISTAN STATISTICAL YEARBOOK. 1st- 1952-. 0078-8023. English. an. **LC** HA1730.5.

PAKISTAN TRADE DIRECTORY. Series/Titl Pakistan Economic Development Series. **VFOAT** Trade Directory, Exporters & Manufacturers. 9th Ed. (1983-1984)-. English. ir. Publishers International, Bandukwala Building No 4, I I Chundrigar Road, Karachi Pakistan. This directory has been published to introduce Pakistan's exports and manufacturers to the world where such factors exist. *Directory of Exporters and Manufacturers.*

PAKISTAN YEAR-BOOK. (PAKISTAN YEAR BOOK). 1969-. 0552-9263. English. ir. **LC** DS376. **DD** 052.

THE PAN AMERICAN YEARBOOK. 1945-. US. English. ir. Pan American Associates, 1150 Avenue of the Americas, New York NY 10036. **LC** E11. **DD** 917.

PANDUAN BANDARAYA KUALA LUMPUR. **VFOAT** Kuala Lumpur City Directory. English. ir. Syarikat Yellow Pages, 11 Jalan Telawi Tiga, Bangsar Baru, Kuala Lumpur Malaysia. **LC** HF5246.6.K8.

THE PAPER YEAR BOOK. 1945-. 0162-8844. US. English. an. $50.00. Paper Year Book, 1-East First Street, Duluth MN 55802. **Tel** (218)723-9200. **Ed** Roy Wirtzfeld. **Ind/Abst** Abstr. Bull. Inst. Paper Chem. **LC** TS1080. **DD** 676.205. Each issue contains an index to its own contents - no vol index - loose. adv acc. **Circ** 2,000. A directory of principal paper, plastic and related products, giving encyclopedia entries on the products, plus a list of manufacturers, converters of each, plus additional sales articles, charts and tables, etc. *Paper Sales Year Book.*

PAPERBOARD PACKAGING'S INTERNATIONAL CONTAINER DIRECTORY. **VFOAT** International Container Directory. 0741-4129. US. English. an. Magazines for Industry Inc, 1 East First Street, Duluth MN 55802. **LC** HD9999.C74. **DD** 688.80294. *International Container Directory.*

PAPERBOARD PACKAGING'S OFFICIAL CONTAINER DIRECTORY. **VFOAT** Official Container Directory. 0198-8867. US. English. sa. Official Container Directory, 1 East First Street, Duluth MN 55802. **Tel** (218)723-9555. **Ed** Mark Arzoumanian. **LC** HD9820.1. **DD** 380.145676302947. adv acc. **Circ** 4,000. Each issue carries the information about almost all converters of corrugated and solid fibre containers, folding cartons, rigid boxes, fibre drums, fibre cans and tubes, plus packaging machinery.

PARENTS' GUIDE. EDMONTON & ENVIRONS EDITION. (PARENTS' GUIDE : THE BABYSITTER DIRECTORY). **VFOAT** Babysitter Directory, Liste de 'Babysitters'. **VAT** Babysitter Directory. Edmonton & Environs Edition. No. 1 (Summer/Fall 1981)-. 0711-2033. Periodical. **CN**. English. ir. $2.95 Per Number. Edmonton Babysitting Registry Ltd, 6811/12 Avenue, Edmonton Alberta T6K 3J6 Canada. **DD** 649.102571233.

PARENTS' GUIDE. TORONTO & VICINITY EDITION. (PARENTS' GUIDE : THE BABYSITTER DIRECTORY). **VFOAT** Liste de 'Babysitter'. **VAT** Babysitter Directory. Toronto & Vicinity Edition. No. 1 (Summer/Fall 1981)-. 0713-0260. Periodical. **CN**. English. sa. $2.95 Per No. Toronto Babysitter Directory, 8 Killarney Road, Toronto Ontario M5P 1L8 Canada. **Tel** (416)486-9386. **DD** 649.1025713541.

PARENTS' GUIDE. VANCOUVER, VICTORIA AND LOWER MAINLAND EDITION. (PARENTS' GUIDE : THE BABYSITTER DIRECTORY). **VFOAT** Babysitter Directory, Liste de 'Babysitters'. **VAT** Babysitter Directory. Vancouver, Victoria and Lower Mainland Edition. No. 4 (Winter/Spring 81)-. 0711-2106. Periodical. **CN**. English. sa. $5.42. The Parents Guide, 8 Killarney Road, Toronto Ontario M5P 1L8 Canada. **Tel** (416)486-9386. **DD** 649.10257113. *Parents' Guide (Vancouver and Lower Mainland Edition), 0711-2068.*

PARKER DIRECTORY OF CALIFORNIA ATTORNEYS. 1980-. 0196-6138. US. English. an. $20.94. Parker & Sons Inc, PO Box 60001, Los Angeles CA 90060. **Tel** (213)727-1088. **Ed** Yvonne A Anderson. **LC** KF192.C3. **DD** 340.025794. adv acc. Lists attorneys, firms, court reporters and courts alphabetically by county (only in state of California). *Parker Directory of Attorneys, 0079-0044.*

PARLEMENT EN KIEZER : JAARBOEK. Began with Vol. for 1911/12. NE. Dutch. Martinus Nijhoff Publishers, PO Box 163, Spul Boulevard 50, 3300AD Dordrecht Netherlands. **LC** JN5873.

PARLIAMENTARY HISTORY. (PARLIAMENTARY HISTORY : A YEARBOOK). Vol. 1 (1982)-. 0264-2824. UK. English. an. Alan Sutton Publishing Ltd, 30 Brunswick Road, Gloucester GL1 1JJ England. **Ind/Abst** Recent Publ. Artic. **LC** JN500. **DD** 328.41005.

PASAULIO LIETUVIU KATALIKU ZINYNAS. **VFOAT** World Lithuanian Roman Catholic Directory. US. English of Lithuanian. 213 South 4th Street, Brooklyn NY 11211. **LC** BX845. **DD** 282.02573.

PC CLEARINGHOUSE DIRECTORY. **VFOAT** PC Directory. 7th Ed.-. 0736-4180. Periodical. US. English. sa. $32.45. PC Clearinghouse Inc, Publishers Department, 11781 Lee Jackson Highway, Fairfax VA 22033. **LC** HD9696.C63. **DD** 001.6425029473. *Software Vendor Directory.*

PEACE CORPS DIRECTORY, FORMER VOLUNTEERS AND STAFF. **VFOAT** Peace Corps Directory of Former Volunteers and Staff. 1981-. US. English. ir. One Bell Road, PO Box 17940 Montgomery AL 36141. **LC** HC60.5. **DD** 361.2606073.

PENNSYLVANIA AMISH DIRECTORY : LANCASTER & CHESTER COUNTY DISTRICTS. US. English. ir. **LC** F157.L2. **DD** 929.374813.

THE PENNSYLVANIA ANTI-MASONIC ALMANAC. US. English. an. **LC** HS537.P2.

PENNSYLVANIA DIRECTORY OF MANUFACTURERS (HOHOKUS, N.J.). (PENNSYLVANIA DIRECTORY OF MANUFACTURERS). Began with 1980/81 issue. 0733-5237. US. English. an. $82.50. Commerce Register Inc, 190 Godwin Avenue, Midland Park NJ 07432. **Tel** (201)445-3000. **Ed** Joel Rosano. **LC** HD9727.P4. **DD** 338.4700025748. adv acc. **Circ** 3,000.

Yearbooks, Almanacs, Directories

Detailed listings of all manufacturing companies, including top executives, annual sales, number of employees, address, phone, and more. Available in machine readable format and on mailing lists.

PENNSYLVANIA DIRECTORY OF RECREATION, PARK, AND CONSERVATION AGENCIES. 0146-7018. US. English. Department of Community Affairs, Room 106 South Office Building, Harrisburg PA 17120. LC GV54.P4. DD 333.78025748.

PENNSYLVANIA EDUCATION DIRECTORY. 1975-76-. 0738-3983. US. English. an. Applied Arts Publishers, PO Box 479, Lebanon PA 17042. LC L194. DD 370.25748. *Education Directory, 0146-6860.*

PENNSYLVANIA EXPORTERS DIRECTORY. VFOAT Pennsylvania Exporters. 0360-8859. US. English. Pennsylvania Department of Commerce, 222 North Third Street, Harrisburg PA 17101. LC HD9727.P4. DD 382.6025748. *Pennsylvania Manufacturing Exporters.*

PENNSYLVANIA HIGH SCHOOL ATHLETIC YEARBOOK. Vol. 1 (1978-79)-. 0734-0230. US. English. an. $19.95. Sportron Publications, 3162 Glenwood Park Avenue, Erie PA 16508. LC GV346. DD 796.0712748.

PENNSYLVANIA RECREATION & PARKS YEARBOOK & DIRECTORY. (PENNSYLVANIA RECREATION & PARKS... YEARBOOK & DIRECTORY). VFOAT Pennsylvania Recreation and Parks... Yearbook and Directory. 0743-6696. US. English. an. $6.00 (Members, and Included in Membership), $7.00 (Non-Members). PRPS, 723 South Atherton Street, State College PA 16801. LC GV54.P4. DD 333.783025748.

PENNSYLVANIA ZIP+4 STATE DIRECTORY. VFOAT Zip Plus Four State Directory. VAT Pennsylvania Zip Plus Four State Directory. 1985-. US. English. an. St Louis PDC, Zip+4 State Directory Orders, PO Box 14921, St Louis MO 63180-9988.

PENSION FUND DIRECTORY. 0731-5619. US. English. $69.95 (Single Issue). Public Data Corporation, 420 South Beverly Drive/Suite 207, Beverly Hills CA 90212. LC HD7106.U5. DD 332.67254.

PENSIONS DIRECTORY. VFOAT Annual Pensions Directory. US. English. an. Institutional Investor Systems, 488 Madison Avenue, New York NY 10022. Tel (212)832-8888.

PEOPLE'S FOLK DANCE DIRECTORY. 1977/78-. 0160-5550. US. English. $1.25. PO Box 8575, Austin TX 78713. LC GV1595. DD 793.31973.

THE PERFORMING RIGHT YEARBOOK. 1977-. UK. English. an. Performing Right Society, 29/33 Berners Street, London W1P 4AA England. LC ML27.G7. DD 780.6241.

PERSONNEL DIRECTORY - NEW BRUNSWICK DEPARTMENT OF AGRICULTURE AND RURAL DEVELOPMENT. (PERSONNEL DIRECTORY). Main/Corp New Brunswick. Dept. of Agriculture and Rural Development. VFOAT Annuaire Personnel. VAT Annuaire Personnel - Ministere de l'Agriculture et l'Amenagement Rural du Nouveau-Brunswick. 0229-852X. CN. English (French). an. New Brunswick Department of Agriculture & Rural Development, PO Box 6000, Fredericton New Brunswick E3B 5H1 Canada. DD 354.715068233025.

PERSONNES C.L.E.F. *See* Law.

PERTAMINA, PETUNJUK TELEPON. VFOAT Pertamina Telephone Directory. 1974/75-. IO. English and Indonesian. ir. Usaha Advertising Co, Jalan Kemiri No 22, Jakarta Indonesia. LC HE9443. DD 384.6025598.

PERU, DIRECTORIO DE EXPORTADORES. VFOAT Peru Export Directory. PE. Spanish. ir. Asociacion de Export Adores del Peru, Las Flores 346, Lima 27 Peru. LC HF3463. *Peru Exporta (Asociacion de Exportadores del Peru).*

PETERSON DIRECTORY. 0882-8296. US. English. be. Peterson Cipher Code Company, 37 West Fort Lee Road, Bogata NJ 07603. LC HE7677.B2. DD 332.1025. *Peterson Cable Address Directory.*

PETIT ALMANACH DES LETTRES. (LE PETIT ALMANACH DES LETTRES). No. 1- Nov. 1976-. 0700-9194. Periodical. CN. French. bm. Le Petit Almanach des Lettres, 1651 rue Sainte-Denis, Montreal Quebec H2X 3K4 Canada. DD C840.5.

PETROLEUM SOFTWARE WORLDWIDE DIRECTORY. VFOAT Petroleum Software Directory. 1st Ed. (1985)-. 0743-6750. US. English. an. $95.00 US and Canada, $118.00 all other countries. Pennwell Books, 1421 South Sheridan PO Box 1260, Tulsa OK 74101. Tel (918)835-3161. Ed William R Leek Jr. LC TN860. DD 665.502854. adv acc. Circ 1,500. Details software specifically for the petroleum industry, from accounting to well log interpretation.

PETROMIN ASIA DIRECTORY. 1st Ed. (1976)-. Periodical. English. ir.

PHARMACISTS DIRECTORY. 0739-375X. US. English. LC RS75. DD 615.4025791. *Arizona Pharmacist Directory.*

PHILIPPINE ALMANAC & HANDBOOK OF FACTS. 1973-. PH. English. ir. 1 Makatarungan St, U P Village, Quezon City D505 Philippines. LC DS651. DD 915.99034.

PHILIPPINE BUILDER DIRECTORY. English. ir. Trend Publishing Company, 402 Campos Rueda Building 101 Tindalo Street, Makati Philippines. LC HD9715.P6. DD 338.47690025599.

PHILIPPINE CONSTRUCTION DIRECTORY. 1981-82-. English. ir. Asean Journals, Warner Building/Mahesak Road, Bangkok Thailand. LC HD9715.P6. DD 338.7624025599.

PHILIPPINE DIRECTORY OF FINANCIAL INSTITUTIONS. PH. English. ir. Sinag-Tala Publishers Inc, Greenhills, PO Box 536, Manila 3113 Phillipines. LC HG187.P6. DD 332.1025599.

PHILIPPINE OVERSEAS EMPLOYMENT ANNUAL-DIRECTORY. VFOAT Philippine Overseas Employment Annual Directory. PH. English. an. Projects Division, Metrocolor Services 6th Floor, Medalla Building, EDSA Cubao Q C Philippines. LC HF5549.5.E45. DD 650.14.

PHILIPPINE STATISTICAL YEARBOOK. Began in 1977. Periodical. PH. English. ir. National Economy & Development Authority, PO Box 419 Greenhills, Metro Manila Philippines. LC HA1821. DD 315.99. Circ 1,000. *NEDA Statistical Yearbook of the Philippines.*

PHILIPPINE YEARBOOK. 1971-. PH. English. an. National Census & Statistics Office, PO Box 779, Manila Philippines. *Philippine Statistics Yearbook.*

THE PHILIPPINE YEARBOOK OF INTERNATIONAL LAW. V. 1- 1966/68-. Periodical. PH. English. ir. LC JX18.

PHILIPPINES BUSINESS DIRECTORY. VFOAT Business Directory. 1978-. PH. English. an. $70.00. Philippines Editors and Publishers, PO Box 3199, Manila D 406 Philippines. Tel 79-86-33. Ed J C Borja. LC HF3813. DD 338.74025599. adv acc. Circ 10,000. Listing alphabetically firms, corporate or personal entities in business or industry with addresses, activities, products, services, etc. and affiliated chamber, professional, and trade groups.

PHILIPPINES' DIRECTORY OF BANKS, INSURANCE & INVESTMENT HOUSES. VAT Philippines' Directory of Banks, Insurance and Investment Houses. 2nd - Ed. English. ir. Jamel Information and Business Assistance, PO Box 2014, Manila Philippines. LC HG3313. DD 332.1025599. *Directory of Banks in the Philippines.*

PHILLIPS PAPER TRADE DIRECTORY. 1974-. UK. English. 10.50. Benn Brothers Ltd, 25 New Street Square, London EC4A 3JA England. LC TS1088. DD 338.476762025. *Phillips' Paper Trade Directory of the World, Paper Makers' & Merchants' Directory of all Nations.*

PHILOSOPHISCHES JAHRBUCH. Vol. 1-. 0031-8183. Periodical. GW. German. bm. $25.16. Verlag Herder Freiburg, Hermann Herder Strasse 4, D7800 Freiburg West Germany. Tel (0761)273495. Ed Hermann Krings. Ind/Abst Math. Rev., MLA Int. Bibliogr. Books Artic. Mod. Lang. Lit., Philos. Index, Index Book Rev. Humanit. LC B3. (cum index). bk rev. Circ 800. Philosophy.

PHOTO INFORMATION ALMANAC. 0093-1365. US. English. an. $3.95. ABC Leisure Magazine Inc, 8th Floor/825 7th Avenue, New York NY 10019. Tel (212)265-8360. LC TR150. DD 770.5. adv acc. Circ 125,000. Report and articles on lenses, film and darkroom equipment.

THE PHOTOGRAPH COLLECTORS' RESOURCE DIRECTORY. 1983-. US. English. be. $125.00. The Photographic Arts Center, 127 East 59th Street, New York NY 10022. Tel (212)838-8640. Ed Robert S Persky. bk rev. adv acc. Circ 2,500. The newsletter for collectors of, and dealers in, fine art photography. Gallery, museum, and university exhibitions, dealer news, auction coverage, and conservation news.

PHOTOGRAPHIC PROCESSING EQUIPMENT DIRECTORY & BUYING GUIDE. VFOAT Photographic Processing Equipment Directory and Buying Guide. 0748-0911. US. English. an. $15.00. PTN Publishing Corporation, 101 Crossways Park West, Woodbury NY 11797. LC TR12. DD 771.1.

PHOTOGRAPHY DIRECTORY & BUYING GUIDE *CEASED.* VAT Photography Directory and Buying Guide. Ceased with 1982. 0079-1857. Periodical. US. English. an. Ziff-Davis Service Division, 1 Park Avenue, New York NY 10016.

PIT & QUARRY DIRECTORY OF THE U.S. NONMETALLIC MINING INDUSTRIES. VFOAT Pit and Quarry Directory of the U.S. Nonmetallic Mining Industries, Pit and Quarry Directory, Nonmetallic Minerals Industries, Pit and Quarry Directory, Pit & Quarry Directory, Nonmetallic Minerals Industries, Pit & Quarry Directory. 1982 Ed.-. 0732-4898. US. English. $175.00. Pit and Quarry Publications Inc, 205 West Wacker Drive, Chicago IL 60606. LC TN12. DD 553.602573. *Pit and Quarry Directory of the Nonmetallic Minerals Industries.*

PLASTICS DIRECTORY OF CANADA. 1959-1970/71. 0554-2944. Periodical. CN. English. an. Southam Communications Ltd, 1450 Don Mills Road, Don Mills Ontario, M3B 1X2 Canada. Tel (403)269-3161.

PMD. PHARMACEUTICAL MARKETERS DIRECTORY. (PMD, PHARMACEUTICAL MARKETERS DIRECTORY). VFOAT Pharmaceutical Marketers Directory. 1977-. 0149-0885. US. English. an. $87.30. Fisher Stevens Publications, Campus Road, Totawa NJ 07512. Tel (201)890-1122. LC HD9666.3. DD 381.45615102573.

POCKET DIRECTORY OF THE CALIFORNIA LEGISLATURE. 1975-. 0163-3333. US. English. an. $5.95. Capitol Enquiry, PO Box 22246, Sacramento CA 95822. Tel (916)428-3271. Ed Ruth Pritchard. Circ 15,000. Directory of the legislature.

POCKET YEAR BOOK, AUSTRALIA. VFOAT Australian Pocket Year Book. No. 64- 1979-. AT. English. an. 3.50. Australian Bureau of Statistics, PO Box 84, Canberra Australian Capital Territory 3001 Australia. Tel (062)52 6778. LC HA3001. DD 319.4. A pocket year book emulating Year Book Australia in comprehensiveness without the detail. Emphasis is on basic statistics. *Pocket Compendium of Australian Statistics.*

POCKET YEAR BOOK - EDUCATION DEPARTMENT OF WESTERN AUSTRALIA. Main/Corp Western Australia. Australia. Education Dept. No. 1- 1975-. AT. English. ir. LC LA2172. DD 370.9941.

THE POCKET YEAR BOOK OF TASMANIA. 1920-. 0314-1640. AT. English. an. 3.50. Australian Bureau of Statistics, Commonwealth Government Centre 3rd Floor, 188 Collins Street, Hobart Tasmania 7000 Australia. Tel (002)20 9409. Contains the majority of the Tasmanian Year Book statistics but in less detail. Presents a basic summary of Tasmania. *Statesman's Pocket Year Book of Tasmania.*

POETRY OTTAWA YEARBOOK. 1977/78-. 0704-4801. CN. English. an. $3. Per No. C S P World News, PO Box 2608, Station D, Ottawa Ontario K1P 5W7 Canada. Ed Guy F Claude Hamel. DD C811.5406271384.

POHOM TONGGYE YONBO. VFOAT Insurance Statistics Yearbook. KO. English (Korean). an. Taehan Sonhae Pohom Hyophoe, 1-614 Youido-dong, Yongdungpo-ku, Seoul South Korea. LC HG8707. DD 368.95195.

Yearbooks, Almanacs, Directories

POHOM TONGGYE YON'GAM. VFOAT Insurance Statistics Yearbook. 1977- Nyondo. KO. Korean. ir. Hanguk Pohom Kongsa, C P O Box 2838, Seoul South Korea. LC HG8707.A4.

POLICE CALL, FIRE EMERGENCY RADIO DIRECTORY. 0098-177X. US. English. an. $3.95. Hollins Radio Data, PO Box 35002, Los Angeles CA 90035. LC TK6555. DD 621.38416.

THE POLICE YEARBOOK. Main/Corp International Association of Chiefs of Police. 1894-. 0079-2950. US. English. an. $8.00. International Association of Chiefs of Police, 13 Firstfield Road, Gaithersburg MD 20878. Tel (301)948-0922. LC HV8143. DD 363.2076.

POLICY PUBLISHERS AND ASSOCIATIONS DIRECTORY. 1980-. 0272-0671. US. English. $3.00 Individuals, $5.00 Libraries. Policy Studies Organization, 361 Lincoln Hall, University of Illinois, Urbana IL 61801. LC H61. DD 070.5.

POLICY RESEARCH CENTERS DIRECTORY. 1978-. 0270-1200. US. English. $10.00 Individuals, $20.00 Libraries. University of Illinois, 361 Lincoln Hall, Urbana IL 61801. LC H62.5.U5. DD 361.61072073.

THE POLICY STUDIES DIRECTORY. 1973-. 0362-6016. US. English. $1.00. University of Illinois, 361 Lincoln Hall, Urbana IL 61801. LC H62.5.U5. DD 309.212071173.

POLICY STUDIES PERSONNEL DIRECTORY CEASED. 1979-. 0275-4002. US. English. Free to Members, $3.00 Individuals, $5.00 Institutions. Policy Studies Organization, 361 Lincoln Hall, University of Illinois, Urbana IL 61801. LC H62.5.U5. DD 361.6102573.

POLISH YEARBOOK OF INTERNATIONAL LAW. (THE POLISH YEARBOOK OF INTERNATIONAL LAW). 1- 1966/67-. 0554-498X. PL. English. an. Ars Polona, Krakowskie Przedmiescie 7, 00-068 Warsaw Poland. LC JX21. DD 341.05.

THE POLITICAL SCIENCE UTILIZATION DIRECTORY. 1975-. 0362-4765. US. English. $1.00. University of Illinois, 361 Lincoln Hall, Urbana IL 61801. LC JA88.U6. DD 353.

POLITIE-ALMANAK. NE. Dutch. an. Schaafsma & Brouwer, Postbus 10, 9100 AA Dokkum Netherlands. Tel 05190-3322. Ed Schaafsma & Brouwer. LC HV8220. adv acc. Police yearbook.

POLITISCHES JAHRBUCH DER CHRISTLICH - DEMOKRATISCHEN UNION DEUTSCHLANDS. Main/Corp Christlich-Demokratische Union Deutschlands (Germany : East). V. 1-. 0578-0225. Periodical. GW. German. ir. Union Verlag, HeidelBerger Platz 3, 1000 Berlin 33 West Germany. LC JN3971.5.A98. DD 324.243108.

POLK'S ALBANY (ALBANY COUNTY, N.Y.). VFOAT Albany City Directory. US. English. an. $92.00. R L Polk Company, 6400 Monroe Boulevard, Taylor MI 48180. Tel (313)292-3200.

POLKS CHARLESTON S.C. CITY DIRECTORY. Series/Titl United States City Directories. 17-. Periodical. US. English. an.

POLK'S MINNEAPOLIS SUBURBAN CITY DIRECTORY. US. English. an. $149.00. R L Polk, 400 E Linnwood Boulevard, Kansas City MO 64109-9983. Tel (816)756-0425. adv acc. Cross reference city directory.

POLK'S MISHAWAKA-SOUTH BEND SUBURBAN (ST. JOSEPH COUNTY, IND.) DIRECTORY. VFOAT Polk's Mishawaka - South Bend Suburban Directory. 1973. US. English. an. R L Polk Co, 6400 Monroe Boulevard, Box 500, Taylor MI 48180. Tel (313)292-3200. Polk's South Bend Suburban (St. Joseph County, Inc.) Directory.

POLK'S SAGUENAY DIRECTORY. VFOAT Annuaire Polk du Saguenay. 1960-. 0316-0556. Periodical. CN. English (text also in French). R L Polk and Company, 2485 Ste-Anne Boulevard, Quebec Quebec G1J 1Y4 Canada. DD 917.1416.

POLK'S ST. PETER (NICOLLET COUNTY, MINNESOTA). 19 -. US. English. an. $72.08. R L Polk Co, 400 E Linwood Boulevard, Kansas City MO 64109. Tel (816)756-0425. adv acc. Cross reference city directory.

POLYMER YEARBOOK. 1st Edition. 0738-1743. Periodical. US. English. an. Harwood Academic Publishers, PO Box 786 Cooper Station, New York NY 10276. LC QD380. DD 547.7.

POLYMERS PAINT COLOUR YEAR BOOK. VFOAT Polymers Paint & Colour Year Book. UK. English. an. $26.05. Fuel & Metallurgical Journals Ltd, Queensway House 2 Queensway, Redhill Surrey RHI 105 England. Tel 68611. Ed R Robin. LC TP934.5. DD 338.476676025. bk rev. adv acc. Circ 1,126. Journal for the surface coatings industry keeping readers abreast of technical and commercial developments.

POOL & SPA NEWS DIRECTORY ISSUE. US. English. an. $14.75. Leisure Publications Inc, 3923 West 6th Street, Los Angeles CA 90020. Tel (213)385-3926. Ed David Dickman. LC HD9993.S953. DD 381.4569089. bk rev. adv acc. Circ 12,000. (ctrl). Pool and spa magazine going to pool and spa trade. Pool News Directory, 0194-1380.

POOR JOE'S CALIFORNIA ALMANACK. US. English. $1.25. Crabapple Press, 300 North Street, Meadville PA 16335. LC AY121.M4. DD 051.

POOR JOE'S COLORADO ALMANACK. US. English. $1.25. Crabapple Press, 300 North Street, Meadville PA 16335. LC AY126.M4. DD 051.

POOR JOE'S INDIANA ALMANACK. VFOAT Indiana Almanack. 0160-8193. US. English. an. $1.00. Crabapple Press, 300 North Street, Meadville PA 16335.

POOR JOE'S MISSOURI ALMANACK. US. English. an. $1.25. Crabapple Press, 300 North Street, Meadville PA 16335. LC AY221.M4. DD 051.

POOR JOE'S NORTH CAROLINA ALMANACK. US. English. $1.25. Crabapple Press, 300 North Street, Meadville PA 16335. LC AY261.M4. DD 051.

POOR JOE'S OHIO STATE ALMANACK. VFOAT Ohio State Almanack. 0160-8185. US. English. an. $1.00. Crabapple Press, 300 North Street, Meadville PA 16335.

POOR JOE'S PENNSYLVANIA FARM ALMANACK. VFOAT Poor Joe's Pennsylvania Almanack. 0362-8523. US. English. an. $0.75. Crabapple Press, 300 North Street, Meadville PA 16335. LC AY81.F3. DD 051.

POOR JOE'S WASHINGTON ALMANACK. VFOAT Washington Almanack. 0160-8207. US. English. an. $1.00. Crabapple Press, 300 North Street, Meadville PA 16335. LC AY331.M4. DD 051.

POP DIRECTORY. V. 1- Summer 1970-. 0556-5189. US. English. $1.00 Single Issue. Daisy Publishing Company, Box 154, Encino CA 91316. LC ML17. DD 780.4202573.

POPULAR MECHANICS DO-IT-YOURSELF YEARBOOK. 0360-2273. US. English. an. Hearst Magazines, 224 West 57th Street, New York NY 10019. LC TT155. DD 605.

POPULAR SCIENCE DO-IT-YOURSELF YEARBOOK. VFOAT Do-It-Yourself Yearbook. VAT Popular Science Do it Yourself Yearbook. 1983-. 0733-1894. US. English. an. Times-Mirror Magazines Inc, 380 Madison Avenue, New York NY 10017. LC TT1. DD 643.705.

PORT ALBERNI DIRECTORY. VFOAT Official City Directory of Port Alberni. 1968-. 0318-2940. Periodical. CN. English. B C Directories, 4918 Napier Street, Port Alberni British Columbia Canada. DD 917.1134. 0318-2959.

PORT OF NEW ORLEANS ANNUAL DIRECTORY. 0085-5030. US. English. an. Free. Public Information Department, Board of Commissioners of the Port of New Orleans, 2600 International Trade Mart, 2 Canal Street, PO Box 60046, New Orleans LA 70160. Tel (504)528-3249. Ed Russ Greenbaum. LC HE554.N4. DD 387.102576335. adv acc. Circ 15,000. (ctrl). A description of operations of the port of New Orleans with a list of more than 1,000 companies and organizations associated with the local maritime community.

POST OFFICE DIRECTORY OF PRIVATE BOX AND PRIVATE BAG RENTERS, UGANDA. UG. English. ir. LC HE7350.U43.

POST-PRIMARY SCHOOLS DIRECTORY OF MID-WESTERN STATE OF NIGERIA. Main/Corp Mid-Western State, Nigeria. Ministry of Education. Planning Division. English. ir. LC L971.N5. DD 373.6693025.

POSTAL ADDRESSES AND INDEX TO POSTCODE DIRECTORIES. Nov. 1974-. UK. English. 0.10. Post Office, 2 12 Gresham Street/ Room 120, London EC2V 7A0 England. LC DD 383.4941. Postal Addresses, United Kingdom and the Irish Republic Excluding the London Postal Area, Index to Postcode Directories.

POTATO REFERENCE YEARBOOK. Main/Corp Potato Growers Association of California. VFOAT Potato Reference Book. 25th- 1969-. Periodical. US. English. an. Yearbook.

POTATO STATISTICAL YEARBOOK. 0739-0238. US. English. an. $5.00. National Potato Council, 4685 Peoria Street/Suite 101, Denver CO 80239. Tel (303)373-5639. Ed Mary Ramsey Humann. LC HD9235.P82. DD 338.174210973. adv acc. Circ 11,800. Contains all statistics on potatoes—from prouction to varieties to costs to per capital consumption. The 52-page book combines historical and current data on the potato industry.

POTOMAC ALMANAC. 0194-2182. Newspaper. US. English. sm. Potomic Almanac Inc, 9812 Falls Road, Potomac MD 20854.

THE POULTRY INDUSTRY DIRECTORY. (THE ... POULTRY INDUSTRY DIRECTORY). VFOAT S.E.P.E.A. Industry Directory. Began with 1968 issue. 0740-2821. US. English. an. Southeastern Poultry & Egg Association, 1456 Church Street, Decatur GA 30030. LC HD9437.U6. DD 636.50029473. Southeastern Poultry Directory.

PRAYER GROUP DIRECTORY. Began publication in 1971. 0747-5748. US. English. an. Charismatic Renewal Services, 237 North Michigan Street, South Bend IN 46601. LC BX2350.57. DD 248.02573.

PRENTICE-HALL ACCOUNTING FACULTY DIRECTORY. VFOAT Accounting Faculty Directory. VAT Prentice Hall Accounting Faculty Directory. Began with 1978-79 Vol. 0277-6618. US. English. an. Prentice-Hall Inc, Englewood Cliffs NJ 07632. LC HF5630. DD 657.02573.

PREP ALL-AMERICA BASKETBALL YEARBOOK. 0098-2490. US. English. an. 200 South Hull Street, Montgomery AL 36104. LC GV884.A1. DD 796.32362.

PREP ALL-AMERICA FOOTBALL YEARBOOK. 0095-3229. US. English. an. 200 South Hull Street, Montgomery AL 36104. LC GV939.A1. DD 796.332620973.

PREPRINT FROM THE BUREAU OF MINES MINERALS YEARBOOK. Main/Corp United States. Bureau of Mines. 1934-. Periodical. US. English. an. Bureau of Mines, 4800 Forbes Avenue, Pittsburgh PA 15213.

PREPRINT FROM THE ... BUREAU OF MINES MINERALS YEARBOOK. LEAD. VFOAT Lead. US. English. an. Publications Distribution, Bureau of Mines, 4800 Forbes Avenue, Pittsburgh PA 15213.

PREPRINT FROM THE ... BUREAU OF MINES MINERALS YEARBOOK. SALT. VFOAT Salt. US. English. an. Publications Distribution, Bureau of Mines, 4800 Forbes Avenue, Pittsburgh PA 15213.

PREPRINT FROM THE ... BUREAU OF MINES MINERALS YEARBOOK. THE MINERAL INDUSTRY OF BULGARIA. VFOAT Mineral Industry of Bulgaria. US. English. an. Bureau of Mines, Publication Distribution Branch, 4800 Forbes Avenue, Pittsburgh PA 15213.

PREPRINT FROM THE ... BUREAU OF MINES MINERALS YEARBOOK. THE MINERAL INDUSTRY OF GHANA. VFOAT Mineral Industry of Ghana. US. English. an. Publications Distribution, Bureau of Mines, 4800 Forbes Avenue, Pittsburgh PA 15213.

PREPRINT FROM THE ... BUREAU OF MINES MINERALS YEARBOOK. VANADIUM. VFOAT Vanadium. US. English. an. Publications Distribution, Bureau of Mines, 4800 Forbes Avenue, Pittsburgh PA 15213.

Yearbooks, Almanacs, Directories

PRESS AND ADVERTISERS YEAR BOOK. VFOAT INFA. II. English. an. INFA Publications, Parliament Street-Jeevandeep, New Delhi India. **Tel** 343330. Ed Vunil Satyajit. **LC** PN4709. **DD** 079.54. adv acc. **Circ** 3,000. (ctrl). Complete information on media for advertisers, advertising agencies and communication managers. *INFA . . . Press and Advertisers Year Book.*

PRESSENS ARBOG. Series/Titl Skrifter Udgivet Af Dansk Pressehistorisk Selskab. Began in 1974. Periodical. DK. Danish. an. 75.00. Dag Hammerskjolds, Alle 33, 2100 Kbenhavn Denmark. **LC** PN4705. **DD** 078. *Pressehistorisk Arbog.*

PRESTEL DIRECTORY. (THE PRESTEL DIRECTORY). 0266-0288. Periodical. UK. English. qt. $30.65. Directel Ltd, 54 Hagley Road/12th Floor Edgbaston, Birmingham B16 8PE England. **Tel** 021-455-6585. Ed Dawn Howell. **Ind/Abst** Predicasts. bk rev. adv acc. **Circ** 65,000. (ctrl). News and views on the world of viewdata. Prestel directory of information and advertisements about products, and services on prestel in a classified subject index format. *Prestel Magazine, Viewdata and TV User.*

PRIESTHOOD AND BROTHERHOOD. (PRIESTHOOD AND BROTHERHOOD : DIRECTORY OF VOCATIONS FOR MEN). VFOAT Directory of Vocations for Men. 0161-0090. US. English. 1865 Broadway, New York NY 10023. **LC** BX2505. **DD** 255.002573.

PRIME SOURCE MINI REFERENCE DIRECTORY. MOST WANTED NAMES AND ADDRESSES OF: FOREIGN CONSULATE IN U.S.A. (PRIME SOURCE MINI REFERENCE DIRECTORY. MOST WANTED NAMES AND ADDRESSES OF— FOREIGN CONSULATE I.E. CONSULATES IN U.S.A). Series/Titl Mail Order Opportunity Library. VFOAT Most Wanted Names and Addresses of—Foreign Consulate in U.S.A. 1983 Ed.-. 0742-4191. US. English. an. $19.95 Domestic, $24.95 Foreign. EGW International Corporation, 1300 Galaxy Way/Suite 8, Concord CA 94520. **LC** JX1705. **DD** 351.8920973.

PRIME SOURCE MINI REFERENCE DIRECTORY. MOST WANTED NAMES AND ADDRESSES OF : MAGAZINES IN U.S.A. (WITH MAIL ORDER ADVERTISING SECTION). Series/Titl Mail Order Opportunity Library. VFOAT Magazines in U.S.A. (with Mail Order Advertising Section), Weekly Newspaper, Publications (with Variety of Shopping News). 1983 Ed.-. 0742-4205. US. English. an. $19.95 Domestic, $24.95 Foreign. EGW International Corporation, 1300 Galaxy Way/Suite 8, Concord CA 94520.

PRIMITIVE BAPTIST YEARBOOK. V. 1- 1972-. 0092-4415. US. English. PO Box 235, Rainsville AL 35986. **LC** BX6380. **DD** 286.4.

PRINCE GEORGE DIRECTORY. VFOAT Official City Directory of Prince George. 1955-. 0317-3186. Periodical. CN. English. an. B C Directories, PO Box 5700, Prince George V2L 5K9 Canada. **DD** 917.112. *Prince George City and Northern British Columbia Directory, 0478-2208.*

PRINTERS YEARBOOK : THE COMPREHENSIVE GUIDE TO THE PRINTING INDUSTRY. 1982/83-. UK. English. an. British Printing Industries Federation, 11 Bedford Row, London WC1R 4JH England. **LC** Z119.5. **DD** 686.20941. *Printing Industries Annual.*

PRINTING TRADES DIRECTORY. UK. English. an. $72.03. Benn Business Information Service Ltd, PO Box 20, Sovereign Way, Tonbridge Kent TN9 1RQ England. **Tel** (0732) 362666. Ed John Hedges. **LC** Z327. **DD** 686.202541. adv acc. **Circ** 2,800. Covers every aspect of the British printing industry. Suppliers of equipment, materials and services together with a buyers guide to their products and ancillary services.

PRINTWORLD DIRECTORY OF CONTEMPORARY PRINTS AND PRICES. VFOAT Printworld Directory. 1st Ed. (1982)-. 0734-2721. US. English. an. $59.95. Printworld Inc, PO Box 785, Bala Cynwyd PA 19004. **Tel** (215)649-5140. Ed Selma L Smith. **LC** NE491. **DD** 769.922. adv acc. **Circ** 20,000. (ctrl). Complete reference research manual of limited edition fine art, prints with full documentation photos, prices, comprehensive articles, biography publisher galleries, institutional, corporate, and private collectors.

PROBATION AND PAROLE DIRECTORY. (PROBATION AND PAROLE DIRECTORY : ADULT AND JUVENILE PROBATION AND PAROLE SERVICES, UNITED STATES AND CANADA). 1st Ed. (1981)-. 0732-0965. US. English. be. $25.00. American Correctional Association, 4321 Hartwick Road/Suite L-208, College Park MD 20740. **LC** HV9304. **DD** 350.849302573.

PROBE DIRECTORY OF FOREIGN DIRECT INVESTMENT IN THE UNITED STATES. 0094-3134. US. English. be. Probe International Inc, PO Box 3364, Stamford CT 06905. **Tel** (203)329-42615. **LC** HG4907. **DD** 332.6730973.

THE PROCEEDINGS, DIRECTORY AND HANDBOOK OF THE NATIONAL ASSOCIATION OF ACADEMIES OF SCIENCE. Main/Corp National Association of Academies of Science (U.S.). VFOAT Proceedings, Directory and Handbook. 0739-361X. US. English. an. $15.00. Archivist, Ohio Academy of Sciences, 445 King Avenue, Columbus OH 43201. **LC** Q11. **DD** 506.073. *Directory and Handbook of the National Association of Academies of Science.*

PROCOF MEDICAL : ANNUAIRE MEDICAL ET PHARMACEUTIQUE DE FRANCE. VFOAT Annuaire Medical et Pharmaceutique de France. Ed. 1981/82-. French. ir. **NLM** W 22.

PRODUCT DIRECTORY OF THE REFRACTORIES INDUSTRY IN THE UNITED STATES. 1958-. 0196-2388. US. English. Refractories Institute, 1102 One Oliver Plaza, Pittsburg PA 15222. **LC** TP789. **DD** 338.476667202573.

PRODUCTS FINISHING DIRECTORY. Periodical. English. an. $10.00. Gardner Publications, 6600 Clough Pike, Cincinnati OH 45244. **Tel** (513)231-8020. Ed Gerard H Poll Jr. adv acc. **Circ** 12,000. (ctrl). Electroplating, painting and other finishing operations. Also articles on pollution control, etc.

PRODUCTS LIABILITY AND TRANSPORTATION LEGAL DIRECTORY. 1978-79-. 0272-1767. US. English. an. Products Liability and Transportation Legal Directory, 8396 Mississippi Street, Merrillville IN 46410. **LC** KF195.T7. **DD** 346.730382025, 347.306382025. *Transportation and Products Legal Directory, 0092-6175.*

PROFESSIONAL AND SERVICE DIRECTORY, GREATER METRO TORONTO AREA. VFOAT Greater Toronto Area, Professional & Service Directory. 0828-5845. CN. English. ir. Routing Services Ltd, 185 Gibson Drive/Unit 2, Markham Ontario L3R 3K7 Canada. **DD** 338.4700025113541. *Professional and Service Directory, Metro Toronto, 0821-2619.*

PROFESSIONAL ENGINEERS' ACT, LAND SURVEYORS' ACT, WITH RULES AND REGULATIONS AND DIRECTORY CEASED. (THE PROFESSIONAL ENGINEERS' ACT, LAND SURVEYORS' ACT, WITH RULES AND REGULATIONS AND DIRECTORY). Main/Corp California. Board of Registration for Professional Engineers. VFOAT Directory of Professional Engineers and Land Surveyors. 0092-2072. US. English. $1.05. **LC** TA24.C2. **DD** 620.0025794. *Civil and Professional Engineers and Surveyors' Roster.*

PROFESSIONAL MEMBERSHIP DIRECTORY. Main/Corp American Diabetes Association. US. English. an. American Diabetes Association, Two Park Avenue, New York NY 10016. **Tel** (212)683-7444. **LC** RC660.A1. **DD** 616.46200621. *Membership Directory, Constitution and Bylaws.*

PROFESSIONAL PREPARATION DIRECTORY FOR ELEMENTARY SCHOOL PHYSICAL EDUCATION. 1st-ed. 0193-5747. US. English. be. American Alliance for Health Physical Education and Recreation, 1201 Sixteenth Street NW, Washington DC 20036. **LC** GV365. **DD** 613.70973.

PROFESSIONAL SERVICES DIRECTORY OF THE AMERICAN TRANSLATORS ASSOCIATION. Main/Corp American Translators Association. Began with 3rd Ed. (1976). US. English. ir. $22.50. American Translators Association, 109 Croton Avenue, Ossining NY 10562. **Tel** (914)941-1500. *ATA Professional Services Directory.*

PROFESSIONAL VIDEO INTERNATIONAL YEARBOOK. 1984/85-. 0261-1910. UK. English. an. *International Video Yearbook.*

PROGRAM DIRECTORY - ARKANSAS DEPARTMENT OF PLANNING. Main/Corp Arkansas. Dept. of Planning. 0360-2869. US. English. Arkansas Department of Planning, 400 Train Station Square/Victory at Markham, Little Rock AR 72201. **LC** HC107.A8. **DD** 353.97670082.

PROPRIETARY SCHOOL DIRECTORY. Main/Corp Virginia. Proprietary School Service. 0145-4609. US. English. State Department of Education, Proprietary School Service, PO Box 6Q, Richmond VA 23216. **LC** L903.V8. **DD** 371.02025755.

PROVINCIAL BUILDING & CONSTRUCTION TRADES COUNCIL OF ONTARIO. (PROVINCIAL BUILDING & CONSTRUCTION TRADES COUNCIL OF ONTARIO : YEARBOOK). Series/Titl Building Trades in Canada. VFOAT Building Trades Council of Ontario. VAT Provincial Building and Construction Trades Council of Ontario. 0714-3206. CN. English. an. Free to Members. Building Trades Council of Ontario Yearbook, c/o Naylor Communications, 1494 Regent Street West, Winnipeg Manitoba R2C 3A8 Canada. **DD** 338.4769009713.

PRSA DIRECTORY. Main/Corp Public Relations Society of America. VFOAT P.R.S.A. Directory. 1981-. US. English. an. Public Relations Society of America Inc, 845 Third Avenue, New York NY 10022. *Public Relations Handbook and Register.*

PSYCHOLOGISTS REGISTERED IN ONTARIO. (PSYCHOLOGISTS REGISTERED IN ONTARIO, DIRECTORY). VFOAT Directory of Psychologists Registered in the Province of Ontario. 1982-. 0713-5750. CN. English. an. Free to Registered Psychologists in Ontario. Ontario Board of Examiners in Psychology, 37 Prince Arthur Avenue, Toronto Ontario M5R 1B2 Canada. **DD** 150.25713. *Directory of Psychologists Registered in the Province of Ontario, 0316-0793.*

PUBLIC & PREPARATORY SCHOOLS YEARBOOK. VFOAT Public and Preparatory Schools Yearbook. 1979-. UK. English. an. 10.95. Adam and Charles Black, 35 Bedford Row, London WC1R 4JH England. **Tel** 01-242-0946. Ed J F Burnet. adv acc. Official handbook of the Headmasters Conference, the Incorporated Association of Preparatory Schools, the Society of Headmasters of Independent Schools, listing major public and preparatory schools. *Public and Preparatory Schools Yearbook.*

PUBLIC AUTHORITIES DIRECTORY. UK. English. an. 12.00. Brown Knight & Truscott Holdings Ltd, Publications Division, 11-12 Bury Street, London EC3A 5AP England. **LC** JS3001. **DD** 352.041.

PUBLIC CONTINUING AND ADULT EDUCATION ALMANAC CEASED. Began 1970. Ceased with 1982 issue. 0091-0791. US. English. an. $10.00. 1201 Sixteenth Street NW, Washington DC 20036. **LC** LC5201. **DD** 374.003. *Public School Adult Education Almanac.*

PUBLIC EDUCATION DIRECTORY. 1977/78-. 0160-8126. US. English. an. Tomi Publications, 746 East 79th Street, Lock Box 95, Chicago IL 60619. **LC** L901. **DD** 371.0102573.

PUBLIC MANAGEMENT RESEARCH DIRECTORY. Vol. 1 (1980-81)-. 0749-775X. US. English. an. National Association of Schools of Public Affairs & Administration, 1120 G Street NW/#520, Washington DC 20005. **DD** 350.

THE PUBLIC RELATIONS ALMANAC FOR EDUCATORS. V. 1-. 0273-3757. Periodical. US. English. Educational Communication Center, Camp Hill PA 17011. **LC** LB2847. **DD** 659.2937100973.

PUBLIC WELFARE DIRECTORY. (THE PUBLIC WELFARE DIRECTORY). 1940-. 0163-8297. US. English. an. $50.00. American Public Welfare Association, 1125 15th Street NW/Suite 300, Washington DC 20005. **Tel** (202)293-7550. Ed Amy Weinstein. **LC** HV89. **DD** 360.58. **NLM** HV 89 P976. **Circ** 6,000. A resource book that describes public welfare programs and agencies in the US and Canada.

PUBLISHERS DIRECTORY. 5th Ed.-. 0742-0501. US. English. an. $240.00. Gale Research Company, Book Tower, Detroit MI 48226. **LC** Z475. **DD** 070.502573. **NLM** Z 475. Included in the expanded edition are producers of books, classroom materials, reports, databases, software, and other print as well as nonprint publications. *Book Publishers Directory, 0196-0903.*

PUBLISHERS' INTERNATIONAL DIRECTORY WITH ISBN INDEX. VFOAT Internationales Verlagsadressbuch mit ISBN-Register. 9th Ed., 1-2-. US. English (Multilingual). ir.

Yearbooks, Almanacs, Directories

$1451.00. Gale Research Company, Book Tower, Detroit MI 48226. **Tel** (800)521-0707. **LC** Z282. **DD** 070.5025. Lists over 160,000 publishers' names, addresses, and areas of interest, both trade and non-trade publishers including private individuals, newspapers, and journal publishers. *Publishers International Directory, 0556-4328.*

THE PUBLISHING & BOOKSELLING DIRECTORY. VFOAT Publishing and Bookselling Directory. UK. English.

PUERTO RICO OFFICIAL INDUSTRIAL DIRECTORY. 1967. 0090-3612. US. English or Spanish. an. $85.00. Whitney Marketing Inc, Apdo 2631, Old San Juan Puerto Rico 00903. **Tel** (809)765-7373. **LC** HC157.P8. **DD** 380.10257295. adv acc. **Circ** 5,000. Cross-referenced, detailed directory of the public relations industrial community including representatives and their lines.

PUGET SOUND MEDIA DIRECTORY. 1st- Ed. 0196-8572. US. English. mo. $60.00. McConnell Country Public Relations Council, 220 West Mercer Street/Suite 505, Seattle WA 98119. **Tel** (206)285-0140. **Ed** Jane B McConnell. **LC** P88.8. **DD** 302.23. **Circ** 300. (ctrl). A publicist's guide to Washington state news media.

PULP & PAPER CANADA ANNUAL AND DIRECTORY. VFOAT Pulp and Paper Canada Annual and Directory. 1980-. 0709-2563. CN. English. an. Southam Communications Ltd, 1450 Don Mills Road, Don Mills Ontario M3B 1X2 Canada. **Tel** (416)445-6641. **Ind/Abst** Abstr. Bull. Inst. Paper Chem. **DD** 338.4767602571. *Pulp & Paper Canada Directory, 0708-501X; Pulp & Paper Canada Reference Manual & Buyer's Guide, 0316-6716.*

PYTTERSEN'S NEDERLANDSE ALMANAK. 1963-. NE. Dutch. an. 121. Postbus 23, 7400 GA Deventer Netherlands. **Tel** 05700-10011. bk rev. adv acc. **Circ** 5,000. (ctrl). Approximately 850 pages with more than 55,000 names and over 15,000 addresses of the most important social, political and educational institutions in the Netherlands. *Pyttersen's Nederlandse Almanak voor Iedereen.*

QUALIS. (QUALIS : THE YEARBOOK OF HUNTER PUBLISHING COMPANY). 1981-. 0735-6854. US. English. Hunter Publishing Company, PO Box 5867, Winston Salem NC 27113. **LC** Z286.Y43. **DD** 070.50975667.

QUEENSLAND ACCOMMODATION AND CARAVANNING DIRECTORY. **Main/Corp** Royal Automobile Club of Queensland. English. ir. Royal Automobile Club of Queensland, Corner Ann and Boundary Streets, Brisbane Australia. **LC** GV198.67.A8. **DD** 649.94943.

THE QUEENSLAND POCKET YEAR BOOK. No. 1- 1950-. AT. English. an. 3.50. Australian Bureau of Statistics, Ground Floor Statistics House, 345 Ann Street, Brisbane Queensland 4000 Australia. **Tel** (07)222 6351. **LC** HA3072. **DD** 319.43. **Circ** 2,000. A pocket-sized reference to the state's official statistics. Covers most areas of statistics in concise tabular form.

QUEENSLAND YEAR BOOK. No.1- 1937-. 0085-5359. AT. English. an. 22.70. Australian Bureau of Statistics, Ground Floor Statistics House, 345 Ann Street, Brisbane Queensland 4000 Australia. **Tel** (07)222 6351. adv acc. A general reference book for any person who wishes to acquire a broad knowledge of the State of Queensland.

QUESTOR REAL ESTATE SYNDICATION YEARBOOK. VFOAT Real Estate Syndication Yearbook. 1983-. 0749-3819. US. English. an. Questor Information Services, PO Box 3274, San Francisco CA 94119. **DD** 332. *Questor Real Estate Investment Yearbook.*

QUICK FROZEN FOODS. PROCESSORS DIRECTORY AND BUYER'S GUIDE. VFOAT Directory of Frozen Food Processors. 36th Annual Ed. (1984)-. US. English. an. $55.00. Harcourt Brace Jovanovich, 1 East First Street, Duluth MN 55802. *Directory of Frozen Food Processors.*

RADIO CONTROL PRODUCTS DIRECTORY. VFOAT RC Products Directory. 1973-. 0090-9157. US. English. an. $2.25. Potomac Aviation Publications, 733 Fifteenth Street Northwest, Washington DC 20005. **LC** TT154.5. **DD** 338.476881.

RADIOPHARMACY AND RADIOPHARMACOLOGY YEARBOOK. 0748-6111. US. English. an. $47.00. Gordon & Breach Science Publishers, 50 West 23rd Street, New York NY 10016.

RAIL TRANSIT DIRECTORY. 0360-5272. US. English. an. Rail Ways of the Americas Inc, Box 1437, Washington DC 20013. **LC** HE1009. **DD** 385.0974.

RAND MCNALLY INTERNATIONAL BANKERS DIRECTORY. VFOAT International Bankers Directory. 158th Ed. (1955)-. Periodical. US. English. sa. $150.00. Rand McNally & Company, 23 East Madison, Chicago IL 60602. **Tel** (312)673-9100. adv acc. Comprehensive banking industry reference. Four volumes detailing all US and major international banks. Addresses, phone numbers, officers, routing numbers, financial figures, correspondents, and more. *Rand McNally Bankers Directory.*

RANDOM LENGTHS . . . YEARBOOK. V. 1 (1964?)-. Periodical. US. English. an. $24.75. Random Lengths Yearbook, PO Box 867, Eugene OR 97440. **Tel** (503)686-9925. **Ed** Terri Richards. **Circ** 2,700. Price histories of lumber and panel products.

READER'S DIGEST ALMANAC AND YEARBOOK. (READER'S DIGEST . . . ALMANAC AND YEARBOOK). VFOAT Almanac and Yearbook. Began in 1967. 0079-9831. US. English. an. Random House, 400 Hahn Road, Westminster MD 21157. **Tel** (914)241-5798. **Circ** 12,000. General and statistical one volume reference source for the year 1985 - a wealth of facts at your fingertips. *Reader's Digest Almanac.*

READING AND LITERATURE. GENERAL INFORMATION YEARBOOK. (READING AND LITERATURE : GENERAL INFORMATION YEARBOOK). VFOAT General Information Yearbook. 1972-. 0097-5214. US. English. an. Education Commission of States, Suite 300/1860 Lincoln Street, Denver CO 80203. **LC** LB1576. **DD** 420.7.

REAL. (THE YEARBOOK OF RESEARCH IN ENGLISH AND AMERICAN LITERATURE : REAL). VFOAT R.E.A.L. Vol. 1 1982-. 0723-0338. English. an. **Ind/Abst** MLA Int. Bibliogr. Books Artic. Mod. Lang. Lit. **LC** PR13. **DD** 820.9.

REAL ESTATE DIRECTORY OF MANHATTAN. 0098-8936. US. English. Real Estate Directories Company, 12 East 41st Street, New York NY 10017. **LC** HD268.N5. **DD** 333.33. *Real Estate Directory of the Borough of Manhattan.*

RECREATION AND OUTDOOR LIFE DIRECTORY. 1st Ed.-. US. English. ir. $140.00. Gale Research Company, Book Tower, Detroit MI 48226. **Ed** S Wasserman. Part I covers general sources such as organizations, federal and state agencies, etc. Part II covers details on outdoor recreational facilities provided by state and federal governments.

RECREATION AND PARK YEARBOOK. Periodical. US. English. ir. National Recreation and Park Association, 3101 Park Center Drive/12th Floor, Alexandria VA 22302. **LC** GV185. *Yearbook -Playground and Recreation Association of America.*

THE RECREATION MANAGEMENT YEARBOOK. Periodical. English. ir.

RED BOOK DIRECTORY OF MAJOR BAKERIES. **Main/Corp** Bakery Production and Marketing. US. English. an. $85.00. Gorman Publishing Company, 5725 East River Road, Chicago IL 60631. **Tel** (312)693-3200.

RED DEER, ALBERTA, CITY DIRECTORY. VFOAT Henderson's Red Deer City Directory. VAT Henderson's Red Deer City Directory(1984). 1983/84-. 0826-4686. CN. English. an. $75.00 Each Volume. Henderson Directories, 100 East 4th Avenue, Vancouver British Columbia V5T 1G3 Canada. **DD** 917.1233. *Red Deer, Alberta, Directory, 0712-3078.*

THE REEL DIRECTORY. Began with Vol. 1, 1979. 8755-786X. US. English. an. $10.00. The Reel Directory, PO Box 866, Cotati CA 94928. **LC** PN1993.5.U718. **DD** 384.8025794.

REFINING, PETROCHEMICAL & GAS PROCESSING WORLDWIDE DIRECTORY. 0749-6443. US. English. an. Pennwell Directories Division of Pennwell Books, 1421 South Sheridan Road, Box 1260, Tulsa OK 74101. **Tel** (918)835-3161. *Refining & Gas Processing Worldwide Directory (Tulsa, Okla. : 1981), Petrochemical Worldwide Directory, 0084-2583.*

REGINA BUSINESS DIRECTORY. 1978-. 0706-8131. CN. English. an. $10.00 Each Number. The Regina Chamber of Commerce, 2145 Albert Street, Regina Saskatchewan S4P 2 Canada. **DD** 380.06271244.

REGIONAL DIRECTORY - CAPITAL AREA PLANNING COUNCIL. (REGIONAL DIRECTORY). **Main/Corp** Capital Area Planning Council. 1976-. 0740-4611. US. English. Capital Area Planning Council, 2520 Interstate Highway, 35 South/ Suite 100, Austin TX 78704. **LC** JS451.T45. **DD** 352.00025764. *Regional Directory for the Capital State Planning Region, 0092-3958.*

REGIONAL NIAGARA INDUSTRIAL DIRECTORY. VAT Niagara Region Industrial Directory. (1983). 1983-. 0826-5046. CN. English. an. Niagara Falls Business and Industrial Growth Agency, Chamber of Commerce Building, 4616 Ontario Avenue, Niagara Falls Ontario L2E 3P9 Canada. **DD** 338.002571338. *Niagara Region Industrial Directory, 0714-3389.*

REGISTER OF ON-GOING LABOUR RESEARCH. VFOAT Annuaire de la Recherche en Cours sur le Travail. Issue No. 1- 1978-. 0708-1065. CN. English (French). an. Free. Centre for Developing-Area Studies, McGill University MacDonald-Harrington Building Building/815 Sherbrooke Street West, Montreal Quebec H3A 2K6 Canada. **Tel** (514)392-5327. **Ed** Rosalind Boyd. **DD** 331.091724. **Circ** 1,000. (ctrl). Lists contemporary research on labour questions in Third World countries, and their funding sources.

REGISTRE-ANNUAIRE - MENSA CANADA. (REGISTRE-ANNUAIRE). **Main/Corp** Mensa Canada Society. 1975-. 0714-4261. CN. English (French). Mensa Canada Registre Annuaire, 10240 Olympia Boulevard, Montreal Quebec H2C 2V9 Canada. **DD** 367.02571. *Directory, 0714-4253.*

REINSURANCE DIRECTORY. 0747-5276. US. English. an. $29.50. College of Insurance, 123 William Street, New York NY 10038. **LC** HG8083. **DD** 368.012.

RELATORIO ANUAL DA DIRETORIA - CETESB. **Main/Corp** Companhia Estadual de Tecnologia de Saneamento Basico e de Defesa do Meio Ambiente. Portuguese. ir. Av Professor Fredico Hermann Jr, 345 CEP, 05459 Sao Paulo Brazil. **LC** TD171.5.B6.

REMOTE COMPUTING DIRECTORY. 0098-0722. US. English. Quantum Science Corporation, 245 Park Avenue, New York NY 10017. **LC** QA76.53. **DD** 001.64404.

THE REP DIRECTORY. 1984-. 0882-7354. US. English. an. Lin Berla Enterprises, 27 East 63rd Street, New York NY 10021.

THE REPAIR CAR/NEW CAR DIRECTORY. VFOAT Repair Car, New Car Directory. 0885-1638. US. English. AD/CAL Publishing Company, 2206 Fairway Drive, Michigan City IN 46360. **DD** 625. *Repair Car Directory.*

REPERTOIRE - CANADIAN SOCIETY FOR RENAISSANCE STUDIES. **Main/Corp** Canadian Society for Renaissance Studies. 1983-. 0822-6369. CN. English (includes some text in French). an. Free. c/o Department of English, University of Windsor, Windsor Ontario N9B 3P4 Canada. **Tel** (519)253-4232. **Ed** W H Herenden. **DD** 940.21071171. **Circ** 2,000. (ctrl). Biographical and bibliographical directory of renaissance scholars and members of Canadian Society for Renaissance Studies and interdisciplinary in scope.

REPERTOIRE - CHAMBRE DE COMMERCE DE LA PROVINCE DE QUEBEC. (REPERTOIRE). **Main/Corp** Province of Quebec Chamber of Commerce. VFOAT Directory. 0822-5389. CN. English (French). an. $12.00. Province of Quebec/Chamber of Commerce, 500 St-Francois-Xavier, Montreal Quebec H2Y 2T6 Canada. **DD** 380.1025714.

REPERTOIRE COMMERCIAL DE LA REGION DU SUD-EST. **Main/Corp** South East Economic Commission (N.B.). 1982-. 0820-8522. CN. English (French). be. Free. Southeast Economic Commission, PO Box 578 Main Street, Shediac New Brunswick E0A 3G0 Canada. **DD** 380.102571523. (ctrl).

REPERTOIRE - COMMISSION INDUSTRIELLE DU NORD-OUEST. (REPERTOIRE). VFOAT Directory. 1982-. 0822-7454. CN. English (French). be. Free. Northwest Industrial Commission, PO Box 490, Edmundston New Brunswick E3V 3L2 Canada. **DD** 338.7602571554. *Repertoire (Northwest Regional Development Commission (N.B.)), 0822-7446.*

Yearbooks, Almanacs, Directories

REPERTOIRE D'ADRESSES - CONSEIL SUPERIEUR DU SPORT EN AFRIQUE. Main/Corp Supreme Council for Sport in Africa. VFOAT Address Directory - Supreme Council for Sport in Africa. CM. English (French). ir. Conseil Superieur du Sport en Afrique, PO Box 1363, Yaounde Cameroon. LC GV665. DD 796.02568.

REPERTOIRE D'AYLMER. (LE REPERTOIRE D'AYLMER). VFOAT Aylmer's Directory. 0711-401X. CN. English (French). be. Free. Aylmer's Directory, c/o Aylmer's Professional Industrial Commercial Association, CP 24, Aylmer Quebec J9H 5E4 Canada. DD 381.025714221. (ctrl).

REPERTOIRE DES ANCIENS - UNIVERSITE D'OTTAWA. Main/Corp University of Ottawa. Alumni Association. VFOAT Alumni Directory - University of Ottawa. 1977-. 0702-6722. Periodical. CN. English (French). ir. Alumni Association, University of Ottawa, 550 Cumberland Street, Ottawa Ontario K1N 6N5 Canada. DD 378.71384. *Bottins des Anciens, 0319-4752.*

REPERTOIRE DES ETABLISSEMENTS MANUFACTURIERS. VFOAT Directory of Manufacturing Establishments. CN. English and French. Bureau of Statistics, 117 rue Saint Andre, Quebec Quebec G1K 3Y3 Canada. LC HD9734.C3. DD 338.0025714.

REPERTOIRE DES INDUSTRIES - COMMISSION INDUSTRIELLE DE LA REGION DE GRAND-SAULT, INC. (REPERTOIRE DES INDUSTRIES). 1981/1982-. 0820-621X. CN. English (French). an. Grand Falls Region Development Commission, PO Box 576, 272 Broadway Street, Grand Falls New Brunswick E0J 1M0 Canada. DD 338.7602571553. *Area Industrial and Commercial Directory, 0713-3510.*

REPERTOIRE DES INGENIEURS-MEMBRES, NON-RESIDENTS ET MEMBRES A VIE. Main/Corp Order of Engineers of Quebec. VAT Repertoire des Membres - Ordre des Ingenieurs du Quebec (1981), Membership Directory - Ordre des Ingenieurs du Quebec. 1981-. 0820-0181. CN. English (French). te. $25.00 Each Volume. Directory of Engineers-Members, c/o Order of Engineers of Quebec, 11th Floor/2075 University Avenue, Montreal Quebec H3A 1K8 Canada. DD 620.0060714. *Liste Officielle des Membres, 0316-0467.*

REPERTOIRE DES LABORATOIRES D'ESSAIS ET D'ANALYSES DU QUEBEC .... 0229-9534. CN. French. $9.67. Centre de Recherche Industrielle Quebec, CP 9038/333 Rue Franquet, Ste Foy Quebec G1V 4C7 Canada. Tel (418)659-1550. DD 620.0044025714. adv acc. Circ 1,000. Directory of testing laboratories located in province of Quebec, Canada.

REPERTOIRE DES MANUFACTURES DE LA PROVINCE DE QUEBEC. VFOAT Directory of Quebec Manufactures. CN. Multilingual (English and French). $3.00. Bureau de la Statistique du Quebec/Division de la Production, 117 rue Saint Andre, Quebec Quebec G1K 3YE Canada. LC HD9734.C3. DD 338.0025714.

REPERTOIRE DES SERVICES COMMUNAUTAIRES DU GRAND MONTREAL. BIEN-ETRE. SANTE. LOISIRS. (DIRECTORY OF COMMUNITY SERVICES OF GREATER MONTREAL). VFOAT Repertoire des Services Communautaires du Grand Montreal. 0319-258X. CN. English (text also in French, each with special title page and separate paging. French text on inverted pages, 1974-). be. 1800 Dorehester Boulevard West, Montreal Quebec H3H 2H2 Canada. LC HV110.M6. DD 362.025714281, 361. 0025714281.

REPERTOIRE INTERNATIONAL DE LA LITTERATURE DE L'ART. (RILA, REPERTOIRE INTERNATIONAL DE LA LITTERATURE DE L'ART). VFOAT RILA, RILA, International Repertory of the Literature of Art. V. 1- 1975-. 0145-5982. US. French (Multilingual). sa. RILA, College Art Association, Clark Art Institution, Williamstown MA 01267. Tel (413)458-8260. LC Z5937, N7510. DD 016.7.

REPERTOIRE : MONTREAL METROPOLITAIN, CODE POSTAL. VFOAT Directory. CN. English and French. an. Sir Alexander Campbell Building, Klaobl, Ottawa Ontario Canada. LC HE6656.M65. DD 383.14.

REPERTOIRE. REGION POSTALE DE QUEBEC. CODE POSTAL. (CODE POSTAL, REPERTOIRE : REGION POSTALE DU QUEBEC). VFOAT Postal Code Directory : Quebec Postal Region. 0317-5146. Periodical. CN. English (French). an. Free. Post Office Department, Director of Coding and Mechanization, Sir Alexander Campbell, Ottawa Ontario K1A 0B1 Canada. LC HE6656.Q4.

REPERTOIRE - SOCIETE DES TRADUCTEURS DU QUEBEC. Main/Corp Translators' Society of Quebec. VFOAT Directory - Translators' Society of Quebec. 1977-. 0707-6169. CN. English (French). an. Translators' Society of Quebec, Suite 841/1010 St Catherine Street West, Montreal Quebec H3B 3R5 Canada. DD 418.02062714. *Repertoire des Membres Agrees, 0381-6087.*

REPERTOIRE (VIDEO FEMMES). (REPERTOIRE). 1984-. CN. French. te. Video Femmes, Bureau 3875/10 McMahon, Quebec Quebec G1R 3S1 Canada. DD 016.3054. *Repertoire Video Femmes.*

REPERTORIO DE LAS EMPRESAS SIDERURGICAS Y FERROMINERAS LATINOAMERICANAS. Ed. 1-6. CL. Spanish. an. $50.00. Instituto Latinoamericano del Fierro el Acero, Casilla 16065, Santiago 9 Chile.

REPORT ON OHIO MINERAL INDUSTRIES. (REPORT ON OHIO MINERAL INDUSTRIES : WITH DIRECTORIES OF REPORTING COAL AND INDUSTRIAL MINERAL OPERATORS). VFOAT Ohio Mineral Industries. 1981-. 0747-7333. US. English. an. LC TN24.O3. DD 338.209771. *Report with Coal and Industrial Mineral Directories of Reporting Firms.*

REPUBLICAN ALMANAC. 0363-9290. US. English. National Republican Committee, 310 First Street Northeast, Washington Dc 20003. LC JK1967. DD 329.00973.

REPUBLIQUE UNIE DU CAMEROUN : ANNUAIRE INTERNATIONAL. VFOAT United Republic of Cameroon. English or French. ir. Les 4 Points Cardinaux, B P 513, Doula Cameroon. LC DT563. DD 967.11.

RESEARCH & DEVELOPMENT DIRECTORY. (UNIQUE 3-IN-1 RESEARCH & DEVELOPMENT DIRECTORY). VAT Unique Three-in-One Research and Development Directory. 1963-. 0080-1461. US. English. an. $15.00. Government Data Publications, 1120 Connecticut Avenue NW, Washington DC 20036. Tel (718)627-0819. Ed Siegfried Lobel. LC Q180.U5. DD 507.2073. This 3-part directory contains research and development contracts awarded over the previous 12-month period. Each listing contains awardee, address, agency, description of work, dollar amount of contract, etc.

RESEARCH & DEVELOPMENT. TELEPHONE DIRECTORY. VFOAT Telephone Directory. 1984-. US. English. an. Research & Development, 1301 South Grove Avenue, PO Box 1030, Barrington IL 60010. *Industrial Research & Development Telephone Directory.*

RESEARCH AND PROFESSIONAL ACTIVITIES DIRECTORY. Main/Corp University of Regina. Faculty of Graduate Studies and Research. 1980/1982-. 0823-9479. CN. English. te. Free. Faculty of Graduate Studies and Research, University of Regina, Regina Saskatchewan S4S 0A2 Canada. DD 378.71244. *Research Directory, 0229-5180.*

RESEARCH CENTERS DIRECTORY. Began with 2nd edition. 0080-1518. US. English. ir. $310.00. Gale Research Center, Book Tower, Detroit MI 48226. Tel 1(800)521-0707. Ed M Watkins and J Ruftner. LC AS25. NLM Q 180.U5 D598A. Contains 7,500 unduplicated listings of university-related and other nonprofit research organizations throughout the United States and Canada. *Directory of University Research Bureaus and Institutes.*

RESEARCH DIRECTORY - MEMORIAL UNIVERSITY OF NEWFOUNDLAND. OFFICE OF RESEARCH. Main/Corp Memorial University of Newfoundland. Office of Research. 1977-. 0704-7452. CN. English. an. Office of Research, Memorial University of Newfoundland, St John's Newfoundland A1C 5S7 Canada. DD 001.4309718.

RESEARCH DIRECTORY OF THE REHABILITATION RESEARCH AND TRAINING CENTERS. Began with 1968/69. 0096-1531. US. English. an. National Institute of Handicapped Research, Department of Education, 330 C Street Southwest, Washington DC 20202. LC RM930.5.U6. DD 362.1786072073. NLM HD 7256.U5 R432.

RESEARCH DIRECTORY OF THE REHABILITATION RESEARCH AND TRAINING CENTERS : FISCAL YEAR .... 1968/69-. 0096-1531. Periodical. US. English. an. Department of Health, Education and Welfare, Washington DC 20201.

RESEARCH SERVICE DIRECTORY. VFOAT M.R.A. Research Service Directory. 0748-089X. US. English. MRA, 171 Madison Avenue, New York NY 10016. LC HF5415.2. DD 658.8302573. *Directory of Research Services Provided by Members of the Marketing Research Association, 0147-8036.*

RESEARCH SERVICES DIRECTORY. Issue No. 1 (Sept. 1981)-. 0278-1743. Periodical. US. English. ir. $260.00. Gale Research Company, Book Tower, Detroit MI 48226. Tel (313)961-2242. LC Q179.98. DD 001.402573. NLM Q 179.98 R431. Covers about 2,000 for-profit organizations providing research services on a contract or fee-for-service basis to a wide range of clients.

RESERVE FORCES ALMANAC. 3D- Ed. 0363-860X. US. English. an. Uniformed Services Almanac, PO Box 76, Department R, Washington DC 20044. Tel (703)532-1631. Ed Sol Gordon. LC U9. DD 355.370973. bk rev. Circ 50,000,000. (ctrl). Deals with drill pay, organizations, promotions, retirement, taxes, and many more subjects to all military forces. *Uniformed Services Almanac. Reserve Forces Edition, 0363-8596.*

RESIDENCY DIRECTORY. US. English. an. American Society of Hospital Pharmacists, 4630 Montgomery Avenue, Bethesda MD 20814. *Directory of Pharmacy Residency Programs in Hospitals Accredited by the American Society of Hospital Pharmacists and Directory of Pharmacy Residency Programs Participating in the ASHP Resident Matching Program.*

RESOURCE DIRECTORY. Main/Corp University of New Brunswick. VFOAT UNB Resource Directory. VAT University of New Brunswick Resource Directory. 1983-. 0824-3697. CN. English. an. University of New Brunswick, PO Box 4400, Fredericton New Brunswick E3B 5A3 Canada. DD 001.202571551.

THE RESOURCE DIRECTORY FOR THE APPLE COMPUTER. 0740-7866. US. English. $9.95. Widl Video Chicago, 5245 West Diversey Avenue, Chicago IL 60639. LC QA76.8.A66. DD 001.64.

RESOURCE DIRECTORY, HEALTH INFORMATION SHARING PROJECT. VFOAT Health Information Sharing Project Resource Directory. 1978-. 0190-3527. US. English. NLM W 22 AN6 R434.

RESOURCE DIRECTORY OF DOE INFORMATION ORGANIZATIONS. Main/Corp United States. Dept. of Energy. Technical Information Center. VFOAT Resource Directory of D.O.E. Information Organizations. Jan. 1982-. 0748-7231. US. English. an. US Department of Energy, Technical Information Center, Cataloging and Bibliographic Support Division, Oak Ridge TN 37830. LC HD9502.U52. DD 026.3337902573. *Directory of Librarians and Information Specialists in DOE and its Contractor Organizations.*

RESOURCE DIRECTORY (TORONTO, ONT.). (RESOURCE DIRECTORY). 1984-. 0822-2479. CN. English (includes some text in French). an. Source Handbook Publishers, Suite 1200 1/St Clair Avenue West, Toronto Ontario M4K 1V4 Canada. Tel (416)489-2470. Ed Joanne Maxwell. DD 338.4774702571. adv acc. Circ 10,000. (ctrl). Provides a comprehensive list of sources available to the design trade.

RESOURCE DIRECTORY. TOURING PERFORMING COMPANIES. 1982-83-. 0738-3681. US. English. Great Lakes Arts Alliance, 11424 Bellflower Road, Cleveland OH 44106. LC PN2273.G73. DD 790.202577.

RESOURCE GUIDE AND MEMBERSHIP DIRECTORY - ALBERTA CHAMBER OF RESOURCES. (RESOURCE GUIDE AND MEMBERSHIP DIRECTORY). VFOAT Membership Roster and Resource Guide. 1981/82-. 0714-718X. CN. English. an. $10.00 Each Volume. Alberta Chamber of Resources, #1403 10025-106 Street, Edmonton Alberta T5J 1G4 Canada. DD 338.20257123. *Membership Directory, 0710-7293.*

Yearbooks, Almanacs, Directories

RETAIL BANK CREDIT REFERRAL DIRECTORY. 0272-0000. US. English. ir. American Bankers Association, 44-B Industrial Park Circle, Waldorf MD 20601. Tel (202)467-4028. LC HG2441. DD 332.102573.

THE RETAIL BANKER'S YEARBOOK. 1983-84-. UK. English. an. Lafferty Publications Ltd, 2 Pear Tree Court, London EC1R 0DS England. Tel (01)251-5545. Ed Michael Lafferty. adv acc. Circ 12,000. (ctrl). Review of past year's events in retail banking worldwide. Includes key interviews and a directory of associations.

RETAIL TENANT PROSPECT DIRECTORY. 0270-2568. Periodical. US. English. an. $5.00. National Mall Monitor Inc, Arbor Center/Suite 500, 1321 US 19 South, Clearwater FL 33516.

RETAIL YEARBOOK. Began with 1st ed. 8755-3015. US. English. an. Management Horizons Inc, 450 West Wilson Bridge Road, Columbus OH 43085-2299. LC HF5429.3. DD 381.10973021.

RETIRED MILITARY ALMANAC. 1978-. 0149-7197. US. English. an. $4.25. Uniformed Services Almanac Inc, PO Box 76, Department M, Washington DC 20044. Tel (703)532-1631. Ed Sol Gordon. LC UB357. DD 355.114. bk rev. Circ 40,000,000. Vital information for retired military personnel including listings of military installations, health care, benefits, entitlements, restrictions, survivor benefits and many other interesting and important subjects.

THE RETREAT DIRECTORY. (THE... RETREAT DIRECTORY). 0749-0593. US. English. $3.00. Norma Down, 7201 16th Place, Hyattsville MD 20783. LC BV5068.R4. DD 269.602575.

REVUE MUNICIPALE. ANNUAIRE. (LA REVUE MUNICIPALE. ANNUAIRE). 1975-. 0317-5510. Periodical. CN. French. an. La Revue Municipale, 6841 rue St-Hubert, Bureau 203, Montreal Quebec H2S 2M8 Canada. DD 338.476025714.

RHODE ISLAND DIRECTORY OF MANUFACTURERS. 0361-5103. US. English. be. $18.00. Manufacturers News Inc, 4 East Huron Street, Chicago IL 60611. Tel (312)337-1084. Lists 2,500 firms by name, location, SIC telephone, total employees, and chief executive officer listed. Includes geographical, alphabetical and SIC sections. 267 pages. *Rhode Island Directory of Manufacturers and List of Commercial Establishments.*

RHODE ISLAND EDUCATIONAL DIRECTORY. US. English. an. Rhode Island Department of Education, 199 Promenade Street, Providence RI 02908.

RHODE ISLAND MEDIA DIRECTORY. 1980-. 0275-1909. US. English. an. $15.00. New England Newsclip Agency Inc, 5 Auburn Street, Framingham MA 01701. LC P88.8. DD 302.23.

RHODES' DIRECTORY OF BLACK DENTISTS REGISTERED IN THE UNITED STATES. VFOAT Directory of Black Dentists Registered in the United States. 0090-7995. US. English. ir. $7.50. 501 E Brambleton Avenue, Norfolk VA 23501. LC RK37. DD 617.6002573. NLM WU 22 AA1 R476.

RIBA DIRECTORY OF PRACTICES. VFOAT Practices. 1973-. UK. English. an. Royal Institute of British Architects, 66 Portland Place, London W1N 4AD England. *RIBA Directory.*

RICE UNIVERSITY ALUMNI DIRECTORY. Main/Corp William Marsh Rice University, Houston, Tex. Office of Development. Periodical. US. English. Rice University, PO Box 1892, Houston TX 77001. LC LD6053. DD 378.7641411.

RICHMOND, VA. CITY DIRECTORY. Series/Titl United States City Directories. 18 -. Periodical. US. English. Hill Directory Company, 2910 Clay Street, Richmond VA 23230. Tel (804)359-6001.

RIVERS STATE TRADE DIRECTORY. English. ir. Ministry of Trade and Industry, Trade Division, 8 Yakubu Gowan Drive, P M B-5084, Port Harcourt Nigeria. LC HF5278.N52. DD 380.10256694.

ROBINSON'S HOWARD COUNTY, INDIANA RURAL DIRECTORY. US. English. Robinson Directories Inc, Hillsdale MI 49249.

ROCKY MOUNTAIN ENERGY DIRECTORY. 0730-0891. US. English. $22.00. Golden Bell Press, 2403 Champa Street, Denver CO 80205. LC TJ163.165. DD 338.762104202578.

ROCKY MOUNTAIN HIGH TECHNOLOGY DIRECTORY. 0883-8046. US. English. an. Leading Edge Communications, 1919 14th Street/Suite 606, Boulder CO 80302.

ROCKY MOUNTAIN PETROLEUM DIRECTORY. VFOAT Rocky Mountain Petroleum Sales and Service Directory. 0278-9299. US. English. an. $32.00. Hart Publishing Inc, PO Box 1917, Denver CO 80201. Tel (303)837-1917. Ed Jennifer Valentine. LC TN867. DD 338.762233802578. adv acc. Circ 18,000. Directory of Rockies exploration, production and land companies, pipelines, refiners, gas processors, supply and service companies, locations, field locations, key personnel, business activity description. *Kirkland's Rocky Mountain Petroleum Directory.*

ROCZNIK INSTYTUTU RYNKU WEWNETRZNEGO I KONSUMPCJI. Periodical. PL. Polish. ir. 300.00. Instytut Rynku Wewnetrznego I Konsumpcji, Plac Trzech Kyzyzy 16, 00-950 Warszawa Poland.

ROCZNIK STATYSTYCZNY. PL. Polish (English). an. ARS Polano, Krakowski Przedmiescie 7, 00 068 Warsaw Poland. NLM W2 GP6 G5RC. *Maly Rocznik Statystyczny.*

RODRIGUES ALMANACH. Periodical. French. an. 15.00. Maurice Almanach Ltee, rue Auguste Esnouf, Curepipe Mauritius. LC DT469.M492. DD 969.82.

ROMANISTISCHES JAHRBUCH. Vol. 1-. 0080-3898. German. ir. Walter de Gruyter & Company, 200 Saw Mill River Road, Hawthorne NY 10532. Tel (914)747-0110. Ind/Abst MLA Int. Bibliogr. Books Artic. Mod. Lang. Lit. LC PC3. DD 440.05. (cum index).

ROMISCHES JAHRBUCH FUR KUNSTGESCHICHTE. Vol. 1-. 0342-2046. GE. German. be. Verlag Ernst Wasmuth, Postfach 2728, Furststrasse 133, D-7400 Tubingen West Germany. Tel 07071/33658. Ind/Abst Avery Index Archit. Period. Second Ed. Revis. Enlarged Suppl., Art Index, Repert. Int. Litt. Art. LC N6911.A1. DD 709.45. Circ 400. Art history, especially of Italy and a collection of specialists, edited by the Max-Planck-Institut in Rome. (Bibliothece Hertziana).

THE ROSETTE: A JUVENILE ANNUAL. 1846-. Periodical. US. English. an. LC AY11.

ROSTER/INDUSTRY DIRECTORY. Main/Corp Wine and Spirits Wholesalers of America. VAT Roster, Industry Directory. 24th Ed.- 1973-. 0197-1565. US. English. an. Wine & Spirits Wholesalers of America, Suite 400/2033 M Street NW, Washington DC 20036. Tel (202)293-9220. *Blue Book, Industry Directory, 0364-751X.*

ROTHMANS FOOTBALL YEARBOOK. VFOAT Football Yearbook. UK. English. 1.20. Queen Ann Press Ltd, Paulton House Shepherdess Walk, London N1 England. LC GV942. DD 796.3340942.

ROYAL CANADIAN MILITARY INSTITUTE YEARBOOK. (YEAR BOOK - ROYAL CANADIAN MILITARY INSTITUTE). Began publication in 1947. 0315-6451. Periodical. CN. English. Free. Royal Canadian Military Institute, 426 University Avenue, Toronto Ontario M5G 1S9 Canada. Tel (416)960-5588. Ed David E C Hugigns. DD 369.271. bk rev. adv acc. Circ 7,000. (ctrl) Items on military with Canadian emphasis. The purpose is to stimulate and educate serving and retired officers in military matters.

RULES AND DIRECTORY. Main/Corp Kansas. Legislature. House of Representatives. US. English. Kansas Legislature, House of Representatives, Topeka KS 66612. LC JK6878. DD 328.7815.

THE RUNNER YEARBOOK. 1980-. 0272-0353. US. English. $1.95. New Times Communications Corporation, One Park Avenue, New York NY 10016. LC GV1061. DD 796.426.

THE RUNNER'S ALMANAC USA-CANADA. VFOAT Runners Almanac. VAT The Runner's Almanac United States of America Canada. 1980-. 0194-0821. US. English. an. LC GV1061.2. DD 796.426.

RUNNING TIMES YEARBOOK. 0164-0720. Periodical. US. English. Davis Publications Inc, 380 Lexington Avenue, New York NY 10017. LC GV1061. DD 796.42605.

RURAL INDUSTRY DIRECTORY. English. ir. Australian Government Publishing Service, PO Box 84, Canberra Australian Capital Territory 2600 Australia. LC HD2152. DD 338.102594.

R.U.S.I. AND BRASSEY'S DEFENCE YEARBOOK. Main/Corp Royal United Services Institute for Defence Studies. VFOAT Brassey's Defence Yearbook. VAT Royal United Services Institute and Brassey's Defence Yearbook. 85th-1974-. UK. English. an. $52.50. Pergamon Press, 395 Sawmill River Road, Elmsford NY 10523. Tel (914)592-7700. *Brassey's Annual.*

RUSSKII ALMANAKH. VFOAT Almanach Russe. FR. Russian (table of contents also in French). ir. l'Almanach Russe, 37 rue du Fort, 92130 Issy-les-Moulineaux France.

RVBUSINESS. ANNUAL DIRECTORY AND BUYER'S GUIDE. US. English. an. $9.00. TL Enterprises, 29901 Agoura Road, Agoura CA 91301. LC HD9710.37.U6. DD 338.4762922602573.

RYLAND'S: THE DIRECTORY OF THE ENGINEERING INDUSTRY. VFOAT Ryland's Directory. UK. English. 10/-/-. Fuel and Metallurgical Journals Ltd, John Adams House, 17/19 John Adam Street, London WC2N 6JH England. LC TN12. DD 338.476702541. *Ryland's Coal, Iron, Steel, Tinplate, Metal, Engineering, Foundry, Hardware and Allied Trades Directory, with Brands and Trade Marks.*

THE S. KLEIN DIRECTORY OF COMPUTER GRAPHICS SUPPLIERS. VFOAT Directory of Computer Graphics Suppliers. 1982-83 Ed.-. 0732-9199. US. English. an. $65.00. Technology and Business Communications Inc, 730 Boston Post Road/Suite 27, Sudbury MA 01776. Tel (617)443-4671. Ed Stanley Klein. adv acc. A comprehensive reference tool listing suppliers of computer graphics equipment and services, grouped by product type and application, market research firms, conference organizers and consultants. *Directory of Computer Graphics Suppliers.*

SACRAMENTO METROPOLITAN CHAMBER OF COMMERCE MEMBERSHIP DIRECTORY AND BUYERS' GUIDE. (SACRAMENTO... METROPOLITAN CHAMBER OF COMMERCE MEMBERSHIP DIRECTORY AND BUYERS' GUIDE). VFOAT Metropolitan Chamber of Commerce Membership Directory and Buyers' Guide. 8756-4289. US. English. an. Blake Publishing Company, 365 W Bradley/Suite D, El Cajon CA 92027. LC HF296.S142. DD 380.106079453.

SAENGMYONG POHOM TONGGYE YONBO. VFOAT Life Insurance Statistics Yearbook. English (Korean). ir. 84-18 5-Ka Namdae Moon-ro, Choong-ku, Seoul South Korea. LC HG9167.

SAGE INTERNATIONAL YEARBOOK OF FOREIGN POLICY STUDIES. VFOAT International Yearbook of Foreign Policy Studies. V. 1- 1973-. 0094-0658. US. English. ir. $14.00. Sage Publications Inc, 275 South Beverly Drive, Beverly Hills CA 90212. LC JX1291. DD 327.072.

SAGE YEARBOOKS IN POLITICS AND PUBLIC POLICY. V. 1- 1975-. 0275-5297. Monographic Series. US. English. an. Sage Publications Inc, 275 South Beverly Drive, Beverly Hills CA 90212.

SAGE YEARBOOKS IN WOMEN'S POLICY STUDIES. Vol. 1- 1976-. 0275-5300. Monographic Series. US. English. ir. Sage Publishing Inc, 275 South Beverly Drive, Beverly Hills CA 90212.

SAILBOAT & EQUIPMENT DIRECTORY. VAT Sailboat and Equipment Directory. 0148-8732. US. English. an. $3.50 Single Issue. United Marine Publishing Inc, 38 Commercial Wharf, Boston MA 02110.

SAINT JOHN, NEW BRUNSWICK, CITY DIRECTORY. VFOAT Saint John City Directory. VAT Saint John City Directory (1980). 1980-. 0713-8962. CN. English. an. Saint John New Brunswick City Directory, c/o Might Directories, 220 Barleu Drive, Toronto Ontario M4A 1N4 Canada. DD 917.1532. *Might's Saint John (Saint John County, N.B.) City Directory, 0316-0939.*

ST. LAWRENCE NEIGHBOURHOOD NEWS AND DIRECTORY. (THE ST. LAWRENCE NEIGHBOURHOOD NEWS AND DIRECTORY). 14th Ed. (Nov. 1, 1983)-. 0822-9821. CN. English. an. St Lawrence Neighbourhood News and Directory, 77 Front Street East/Suite 301, Toronto Ontario M5E 1C1 Canada. DD 971.3541. *St. Lawrence Neighbourhood News, 0822-9813.*

SAISEKI TOKEI NENPO. 1980-. JA. Japanese. an. Tsusan Tokei Kyokai, c/o Kobikikan Bekkan, 15-2 Ginza 6, Chuo-ku Tokyo 104 Japan. LC HD9621.J3.

Yearbooks, Almanacs, Directories

SAL VUOSIKIRJA. Main/Corp Suomen Aikakauslehdentoimittajain Liitoo. VFOAT S.A.L. Vuosikirja. FI. Finnish. an. Yrjonkau 11 C 16, 00120 Helsinki 12 Finland.

THE SALESMAN'S GUIDE NATIONWIDE DIRECTORY. GIFT, HOUSEWARES & STATIONERY BUYERS. VFOAT Gift, Housewares & Stationery Buyers. 0734-8932. US. English. $95.00. Salesman's Guide Inc, 1140 Broadway, New York NY 10001. Tel (212)684-2985. Ed Edward R Blank. LC HD9773.U4. DD 380.102573. adv acc. Circ 500. (ctrl). Lists 6,000 major retail stores in the US with names of buyers of housewares, gifts and stationery. Nationwide Directory. Gift and Housewares Buyers, 0193-7006.

THE SALESMAN'S GUIDE NATIONWIDE DIRECTORY: MAJOR MASS MARKET MERCHANDISERS (EXCLUSIVE OF NEW YORK METROPOLITAN AREA). VFOAT Nationwide Directory: Major Mass Market Merchandisers (Exclusive of New York Metropolitan Area). US. English. an. $75.00. The Salesmans Guide Inc, 1140 Broadway, New York NY 10001. Tel (212)684-2985. Ed Edward R Blank. LC HF5468. DD 380.102573. adv acc. Circ 5,000. Directory of mass merchandisers with executives and buyers for all apparel.

SALZBURGER JAHRBUCH FUR PHILOSOPHIE. l- 1957-. 0080-5696. AU. German. ir. Universitatsverlag Anton Pustet, Postfach 144, A-5021 Salzburg Austria. Tel 06621763P2. Ed Paus, Vohler, Neidl. Ind/Abst Philos. Index. bk rev. adv acc. Circ 250.

SAMPLING YEARBOOK. V. 1- 1955/56-. 0074-2686. CN. English. an. International Commission for the Northwest Atlantic Fisheries, PO Box 638, Dartmouth Nova Scotia B24 349 Canada. DD 639.

SAN BERNARDINO, RIVERSIDE COUNTIES STREET ATLAS AND DIRECTORY (ZIP CODE EDITION). (SAN BERNARDINO, RIVERSIDE COUNTIES STREET ATLAS AND DIRECTORY). VFOAT San Bernardino County, Riverside County. Updated 1984 Ed.-. 0883-0118. US. English. an. $25.00. Thomas Brothers Maps, 17731 Cowan, Irvan CA 92714. Tel (714)863-1984. adv acc. Street maps and index for San Bernardino and Riverside County in California. San Bernardino, Riverside Counties Popular Street Atlas, 0733-7183.

SAN DIEGO COUNTY DIRECTORY OF MANUFACTURERS AND INDUSTRIAL DISTRIBUTORS. VFOAT San Diego Industrial Directory. 1981-. 0273-3447. US. English. an. Shaver & Debth Inc, 9420 Activity Road/Suite C, San Diego CA 92126. LC HD9727.C2. DD 338.470002579498.

SANITATION INDUSTRY YEARBOOK. Began with 1st Ed., published in 1963. 0080-6021. US. English. an. $10.00. Communication Channels Inc, 6255 Barfield Road, Atlanta GA 30328. Tel (404)256-9800.

SAS YEARBOOK. Main/Corp Scandinavian Airlines System. VAT Scandinavian Airlines System Yearbook. Periodical. US. English. ir. 630 Fifth Avenue/Suite 242, New York NY 10020. LC HE9856.S3. DD 387.7065485.

SASKATCHEWAN CHINESE DIRECTORY & TELEPHONE BOOK. VFOAT Saskatchewan Chinese Directory. V. 23- 1972-. 0316-7054. Periodical. CN. English (includes some text in Chinese). an. Chinese Publicity Bureau Ltd, 459 East Hastings Street, Vancouver British Columbia V6A 1P5 Canada. DD 971.24004951. Saskatchewan Chinese Directory, 0317-1426.

SASKATCHEWAN CONSTRUCTION & RESOURCE INDUSTRIES DIRECTORY PURCHASING GUIDE. See Building and Construction.

SASKATCHEWAN DIRECTORY OF PROFESSIONAL CONSULTANTS. VFOAT Directory of Professional Consultants. Periodical. CN. English. an. Saskatchewan Industry and Commerce, 7th Floor Saskatchewan Power Building, Regina Saskatchewan S4P 3V7 Canada. LC HD69.C6. DD 658.460257124.

SASKATCHEWAN MUNICIPAL DIRECTORY. 1958-. 0581-8435. CN. English. an. $2.32. Saskatchewan Urban Affairs, 2151 Scarth Street, Regina Saskatchewan S4P 3V7 Canada. Tel (306)787-2664. Ed Debbie Wilkie. LC JS1721.S3. DD 352.000257124. Circ 5,500. Listing of municipal offices, officials and populations in Saskatchewan. Municipal Directory, 0318-143X.

SASKATOON BUSINESS DIRECTORY. 1st Ed. (1980/81)-. 0714-8607. CN. English. an. Free. Saskatoon Board of Trade, 601 Spadina Crescent, Saskatoon Saskatchewan S7K 3L6 Canada. DD 380.102571242. (ctrl).

SASKATOON, SASKATCHEWAN, CITY DIRECTORY. VFOAT Henderson's Saskatoon Directory. VAT Henderson's Saskatoon Directory (1980). 1980-. 0228-9695. CN. English. an. $85.00 Per Number. Henderson Directories, 100 East 4th Avenue, Vancouver British Columbia V5T 1G3 Canada. DD 917.1242. Henderson's Saskatoon, Saskatchewan City Directory, 0316-0491.

THE SATELLITE DIRECTORY. (THE ... SATELLITE DIRECTORY). Began with 1979 issue. 0731-0293. US. English. an. $197.00. Phillips Publishing Inc, 7811 Montrose Road, Potomac MD 20854. Tel (301)340-2100. LC TK5104. DD 621.380422. The one desktop database on prospects, products, companies, contacts, and connections that can help your business thrive.

SAUDI ARABIA TRADE DIRECTORY. English. an. Saudi Advertising, PO Box 6557, Jeddah Saudi Arabia. LC HF3763.A48. DD 338.74025538.

SAUDI TRADE DIRECTORY FOR RIYADH. 1980-. English. an. $25.00. Directory Bureau, A-799 Block 12 Gulberg, Federal 'B' Area, Karachi-38 Pakistan. LC HF3763.Z9. DD 380.1025538.

SAVE ON SHOPPING DIRECTORY. VFOAT S.O.S. 7th Ed.-. 0276-6701. US. English. SOS Directory Inc, Box 10482, Jacksonville FL 32207. LC HF5421. DD 381.1. Save on Shopping, 0092-8003.

SBTD. SHIP-BY-TRUCK DIRECTORY CEASED. (SBTD : MANITOBA SHIP-BY-TRUCK DIRECTORY). VAT SBTD. Ship-by-Truck Directory, Ship-by-Truck Directory (1981), Official Manitoba Ship-by-Truck Directory, Manitoba Ship-by-Truck Directory. 80/81-81/82. 0228-7315. CN. English. an. 13.00. Manitoba Trucking Association, 25 Bunting Street, Winnipeg Manitoba R2X 2P5 Canada. Tel (204)632-6600. Ed Bob Wilks. DD 388.3240257127. adv acc. Circ 1,500. A directory containing complete information on Manitoba for hire trucking with tariffs, mileages and complete operating authority terms. Official Ship by Truck Directory, 0705-6664.

SCHAAK JAARBOEK. Dutch. ir. Spectrum, Uitgeverij Het Spectrum, Utrecht Netherlands. LC GV1313. DD 794.15.

SCHMOLLERS JAHRBUCH FUR GESETZGEBUNG, VERWALTUNG UND VOLKSWIRTSCHAFT IM DEUTSCHEN REICH. V. 37, No. 1, (1913)-V. 87, No. 6, (1967). Periodical. GW. German. bm. Dunker & Humblot, Dietrich-Schaefer-Weg 9, 1000 Berlin 41 West Germany. Jahrbuch fur Gesetzgebung, Verwaltung und Volkswirtschaft im Deutschen Reich.

SCHOOL DIRECTORY (TRENTON, N.J.). (SCHOOL DIRECTORY). US. English. an. New Jersey Department of Education, 225 West State Street/CN 500, Trenton NJ 08625. LC L903.N5. DD 370.25749. New Jersey Education School Directory.

SCHOOL DIRECTORY, U.S. VIRGIN ISLANDS. VFOAT School Directory, US Virgin Islands. English. ir. LC L912.V5. DD 371.0025729722. Directory.

SCHWALMER JAHRBUCH. German. ir. LC DD491.K397.

SCHWEIZER ALMANACH. German. ir. Transbooks Inc, 13 East 16th Street, New York NY 10003.

SCHWEIZERISCHES IDIOTIKON. WORTERBUCH DER SCHWEIZERDEUTSCHEN SPRACHE. V. 1-. SZ. German. ir. 32-. J Huber and Company, Promenadenstrasse 16, CH-8500 Frauenfeld Switzerland. Tel (054)271111. LC PF5146. Circ 1,000. Dictionary of the Swiss German dialects.

SCHWEIZERISCHES JAHRBUCH FUR INTERNATIONALES RECHT. VFOAT Annuaire Suisse de Droit International. Vol. 1- 1944-. SZ. Multilingual (German, French, and English). an. $58.38. Schulthess Polygraph Verlag Ag, Zwingiplatz 2, CH-8022 Zuerich Switzerland. Tel 01/251 93 36. LC JX21. DD 341.058. Each issue contains an index to its own contents - no vol index - loose. (cum index).

SCHWENDEMAN'S DIRECTORY OF COLLEGE GEOGRAPHY OF THE UNITED STATES. VFOAT Directory of College Geography of the United States. Vol. 30, No. 1 (Apr. 1979)-. 0734-8185. US. English. an. $4.00. Geographical Studies and Research Center, Department of Geography and Planning, Eastern Kentucky University, Richmond KY 40475-0953. Tel (606)622-1424. Ed Dale R Monsebroten. LC G77. DD 910.71173. adv acc. Circ 1,000. The directory lists over 600 college departments. The listing includes faculty and student enrollments in 69 topical areas in geography. Directory of College Geography of the United States.

SCIENCE & GOVERNMENT REPORT INTERNATIONAL ALMANAC. VAT Science and Government Report International Almanac. 1977-. 0192-4052. US. English. an. $185.00. Science & Government Report Inc, 3736 Kanawha Street NW, Washington DC 20015. Tel (202)244-4135. Ed Daniel S Greenberg. LC Q127.U6. DD 509. NLM W1 SC668R. bk rev. Circ 1,100. Covers government activities of importance to University governments and industrial scientists and research administrators.

SCIENCE AND TECHNOLOGY YEARBOOK. 0377-7901. English. an. Services de Programmation de la Politique Scientifique, rue de la Science 8, 1040 Bruxelles Belgium. LC Q127.B4. DD 509.493.

SCIENTIFIC DIRECTORY ... ANNUAL BIBLIOGRAPHY .... Main/Corp National Institutes of Health (U.S.). VFOAT Scientific Directory and Annual Bibliography. US. English. an. National Institutes of Health, Bethesda MD 20014. NLM ZWA 4 N277S. Scientific Directory and Annual Bibliography, 0083-2197.

SCOTT DIRECTORY OF ARGENTINE EXPORTERS & IMPORTERS. VFOAT Scott Directory of Argentine Exporters and Importers. AG. English (Spanish). an. $50.00. Editorial Scott S A, Guemes 3440 P B A, 1425 Buenos Aires Argentina. LC HF3383. DD 382.602582. Guia Scott de Exportadores Argentinos.

THE SCOTTISH ARCHITECTS DIRECTORY. UK. English. an. Royal Incorporation of Architects in Scotland, 15 15 Rutledge Square, Edinburgh EH1 2BE Scotland. LC NA60.G7. DD 720.25411.

SCOTTISH FOLK DIRECTORY. 1st- 1973-. UK. English. S Douglas, 12 Mansfield Road, Perth Scotland. LC ML21. DD 781.7411025411.

SCOTT'S DIRECTORIES, WESTERN MANUFACTURERS. VFOAT Scott's Directory of Western Manufacturers. 7th Ed. (1985/1986)-. 0829-2248. CN. English. be. Scott's Directories, 75 Thomas Street, PO Box 365, Oakville Ontario L6J 5M5 Canada. DD 338.4025712. Scott's Industrial Directory. Western Manufacturers, 0317-879X.

SCOTT'S INDUSTRIAL DIRECTORY. ATLANTIC MANUFACTURERS. (SCOTT'S INDUSTRIAL DIRECTORY, ATLANTIC MANUFACTURERS). VAT Industrial Directory. Atlantic Manufacturers. 1st Ed.- 1977-. 0706-5167. Periodical. CN. English. be. Scotts Directories, PO Box 365/75 Thomas Street, Oakville Ontario L6J 5M5 Canada. Tel (416)845-8881. Ed Muriel Throop. DD 338.0025715. Industrial and trade directories of information on Canadian manufacturers (Ontario, Quebec, Western Provinces, and Atlantic Provinces).

SCOTT'S INDUSTRIAL DIRECTORY. ONTARIO MANUFACTURERS CEASED. VFOAT Industrial Directory. Ontario Manufactures, Scott's Ontario ... Ed., Industrial Directory. Began with 8th Ed. for 1972/73. 0316-7879. CN. English. be. Scott's Industrial Directories, 75 Thomas Street, Oakville Ontario L6J 3A3 Canada. LC HC117.O6. DD 338.74025713. Scott's Industrial Directory. Ontario Section, 0316-7860.

SCOTT'S INDUSTRIAL DIRECTORY. WESTERN MANUFACTURERS. VFOAT Scott's Western. 2nd Ed. 0317-879X. Periodical. CN. English. ir. $110.27. Scotts Directories, PO Box 365, 75 Thomas Street, Oakville Ontario L6J 5M5 Canada. Tel (416)845-8881. Ed Muriel Throop. DD 338.4025712. Sure-fire marketing strategies based on the most accurate and complete compilation of information on Canadian manufacturers available.

Yearbooks, Almanacs, Directories

Scott's Industrial Directory, Western Section, 0317-8781.

SCOTT'S QUEBEC INDUSTRIAL DIRECTORY. VFOAT Quebec Industrial Directory, Scott's Repertoire Industriel du Quebec. 1st- Ed. 0582-3080. CN. English (French). be. $110.27. Scotts Directories, PO Box 365, 75 Thomas Street, Oakville Ontario L5J 5M5 Canada. **Tel** (416)845-8881. **LC** T12.5.C2. **DD** 338.4025714.

SCOTT'S TRADE DIRECTORY. VFOAT Scott's Trade Directory-Metropolitan Toronto. 1st Ed. (1980)-. 0228-6920. CN. English. ir. $68.87. Scott's Directories, PO Box 365/75 Thomas Street, Oakville Ontario L6J 5M5 Canada. **DD** 338.4025713541.

SCREEN INTERNATIONAL FILM AND TV YEAR BOOK. 38th Year (1983-84)-. UK. English. an. $50.00. King Publications, 6/7 Great Chapel Street, London W1 England. *International Film and TV Yearbook.*

SCROGGINS NATIONAL LAW ENFORCEMENT DIRECTORY. 1984-. 0882-1909. US. English. an. $41.85. Scroggins National Law Enforcement Directory, PO Box 945, Montrose CA 91020.

SD. PACIFIC COAST STUDIO DIRECTORY. VFOAT Pacific Coast Studio Directory. 1919. Periodical. US. English. qt. $18.00. Pacific Coast Studio Director, 6331 Hollywood Boulevard/Room 603, Hollywood CA 90028. **Tel** (213)467-2920. Ed Harry C Reitz. adv acc. **Circ** 25,000. (ctrl)

SEA TECHNOLOGY. HANDBOOK, DIRECTORY. (SEA TECHNOLOGY : HANDBOOK, DIRECTORY). VFOAT ST Handbook/Directory. 0145-6121. US. English. an. $14.00. Compass Publications, 1117 North 19th Street, Arlington VA 22209. **LC** TC1550. **DD** 338.47620416202573.

SEAISI DIRECTORY. Main/Corp South East Asia Iron and Steel Institute. VFOAT S.E.A.I.S.I. Directory. English. an. South East Asia Iron And Steel Institute, P O Box 7759, Airmail Distribution Center, Manila International Airport M I A, Manila Philippines.

SEATRADE US YEARBOOK. (SEATRADE U.S. YEARBOOK). VAT Seatrade United States Yearbook. Began with Vol. for 1979. 0142-5056. UK. English. an. Whitehall Building, 17 Battery Place, New York NY 10004. **LC** HE561. **DD** 387.00973.

SEATTLE-KING COUNTY CONVENTION AND VISITORS' GUIDE AND MEMBERSHIP DIRECTORY. (SEATTLE-KING COUNTY ... CONVENTION AND VISITORS' GUIDE AND MEMBERSHIP DIRECTORY). VFOAT Seattle King County ... Convention and Visitors' Guide and Membership Directory. 8756-4297. US. English. an. Blake Publishing Company, 365 West Bradley, El Cajon CA 92929. **LC** F899.S43. **DD** 979.777.

SEAWAY MARITIME DIRECTORY. 1960. 0582-3668. US. English. an. $20.00. Fourth Seacoast Publishing Company Inc, PO Box 145, St Clair Shores MI 48080. **Tel** (313)779-5570. Ed Roger J Buysse. adv acc. **Circ** 8,000. (ctrl). General description of entire Great Lakes and St. Lawrence Seaway system. Services and facilities of 35 seaway ports on seaway route. Description lock system, and container services at all ports. *Official Seaway Maritime Directory.*

SECTION OF ADMINISTRATIVE LAW DIRECTORY. Main/Corp American Bar Association. Section of Administrative Law. 0749-6613. US. English. an. American Bar Association, 1155 East 60th Street, Chicago IL 60637. **LC** KF195.A4. **DD** 342.7306025, 347.3026025. *Directory,* 0569-308X.

SEIBT EXPORT DIRECTORY OF GERMAN INDUSTRIES. GW. English (French or German). an. 98. Seibt Verlag, Rosenheimer Strasse 145 A, D8000 Munich 80 West Germany. **Tel** (089)662064. adv acc. Buyers' guide listing 30,000 products of 130 sectors broken down by product categories.

SEKAI DAI HYAKKA NENKAN. 1956-. JA. Japanese. ir. 4000. 4 Yobancho Chiyoda-ku, Tokyo Japan. **LC** AY1152. *Sekai Bunka Nenkan.*

SEKAI KONPYUTA NENKAN. VFOAT Computer Yearbook. JA. Japanese. an. 6800. Konpyuta Ejisha, c/o Kasumigaseki Building, 2-5 Kasumigaseki 3, Chiyoda-ku 100 Japan. **LC** HD9696.C6.

SEKIYU TO SHOHI DOTAI TOKEI NENPO, SHO-KO- KOGYO. VFOAT Yearbooks of the Current Survey of Oil Consumption in Commerce, Mining and Manufacturing. 1983-. JA. Japanese. an. Tsusan Tokei Kyokai 8-9, Ginza 2 Chuo-ku, Tokyo-to 104 Japan. *Enerugi Shohi Dotai Tokei Nenpo. Sho-Ko-Kogyo.*

SELF-HELP GROUP DIRECTORY. (THE SELF-HELP GROUP DIRECTORY). VFOAT Self Help Group Directory. 1984-. 0740-7548. US. English. an. New Jersey Self-Help Clearinghouse, Saint Clare's Hospital CMHC Pocono Road, Denville NJ 07834. **Tel** (201)625-7101. Ed Edward J Madara. **DD** 361. **Circ** 4,000. Comprehensive guide to self-help groups in New Jersey and national organizations.

SELL'S BRITISH EXPORTERS' REGISTER & NATIONAL DIRECTORY. UK. English. an. $25.65. Sell's Publications Ltd, Sell's House 39 East Street, Epsom Surrey KT17 1BQ England. **Tel** (212)879-6577.

SELL'S DIRECTORY OF PRODUCTS & SERVICES. VAT Sell's Directory of Products and Services. 87th-95th. 0300-5046. UK. English. bm. $68.94. Sell's Publications Ltd, Sells House, 39 East Street, Epsom Surrey KT17 1BQ England. **LC** HC252. **DD** 338.002542. *Sell's Directory of British Industry and Commerce.*

SENATE ISSUES YEARBOOK. 0271-4280. US. English. an. $3.50. Conservative Caucus Research Analysis & Education Foundation, 422 Maple Avenue, East Vienna VA 22180. **LC** JK1161. **DD** 328.730775.

SENSOR AND TRANSDUCER DIRECTORY. VFOAT Sensor & Transducer Directory. 1984-. 8755-5999. US. English. an. $39.95. North American Technology Inc, 174 Concord Street, Peterborough NH 03458. **Tel** (603)924-7261. Ed Carl Helmers. **LC** TA165. **DD** 681.2. adv acc. Contains a complete listing of all the manufacturers of sensors and transducers including company information, type of sensor, etc. Completely indexed by type of sensor.

THE SERIALS DIRECTORY. (THE SERIALS DIRECTORY : AN INTERNATIONAL REFERENCE BOOK). 1st ed.- 1986-. 0886-4179. US. English. an. $249.00. EBSCO Publishing, PO Box 1943, Birmingham AL 35201. **Tel** (800)826-3024. Ed Emmy S. Carmichael. Over 113,000 international serials listed with information such as LC, DD, and NLM classes, CODEN, title statement, key title, varying titles, former titles, and current and former ISSN.

SERVICE CORPORATION DIRECTORY. 0272-3484. US. English. United States League of Savings Associations, 111 East Wacker Drive, Chicago IL 60601. **LC** HG2150. **DD** 332.3.202573.

SHAKESPEARE JAHRBUCH. V. 1-99, 1865-1963. 0080-9128. GE. German. an. $16.23. Herman Boehlaus Nachfolger, Meyerstr 500, 53 Weimar East Germany.

SHAW'S DIRECTORY OF COURTS IN ENGLAND AND WALES. 0307-3343. UK. English. an. Shaw and Sons, Shaway House Lower Sydenham, London SE26 5AE England. **LC** KD7302.3. **DD** 347.4202025. *Shaw's Directory of Magistrates' Courts and Crown Courts,* 0085-6061.

SHAW'S DIRECTORY OF COURTS IN THE UNITED KINGDOM. UK. English. **Tel** 01-778-5131. **Circ** 2,500. Names, addresses and telephone numbers of the High Court and Crown Courts, County Courts, Courts of Summary, Jurisprudence and Prison Department establishments.

SHEET METAL INDUSTRIES YEARBOOK. 0305-7798. UK. English. an. 4.00. 17-19 John Adam Street, London NC2N 6JH England. **LC** TS250. **DD** 671.82305.

SHELDON'S RETAIL DIRECTORY OF THE UNITED STATES AND CANADA AND PHELON'S RESIDENT BUYERS AND MERCHANDISE BROKERS. 1864-. 0094-0453. US. English. an. $90.00. Phelon Sheldon & Marsar Inc, 15 Industrial Avenue, Fairview NJ 07022. **Tel** (201)473-2590. Ed Kenneth W Phelon. **LC** HF5429.3. **DD** 381. **Circ** 5,000. (ctrl). Department stores and chains; womens stores; womens chains; home furnishing chains; all resident buying offices. Address, phone numbers, number of stores operated; sales volumes, executives, titles; merchandise managers and buyers. *Sheldon's Retail Directory of the United States and Canada, Phelon's Resident Buyers and Merchandise Brokers of Department Store Merchandise, Ready to Wear, Millinery.*

SHIP-BY-TRUCK OFFICIAL ONTARIO DIRECTORY AND BUYER'S GUIDE. VFOAT Official Ontario Directory and Buyer's Guide. VAT Official Ontario Ship-By-Truck- Directory and Buyers' Guide. Vol. 38 (1981)-. 0711-303X. CN. English. an. $34.95 Per No. Ontario Trucking Association, 555 Dixon Road, Rexdale Ontario M9W 1H8 Canada. **DD** 388.324025713. *O T A Official Ontario Ship-by-Truck Directory,* 0226-5680.

S.H.S.A.A. DIRECTORY OF SCHOOLS. Main/Corp Saskatchewan High Schools Athletic Association. VAT Saskatchewan High Schools Athletic Association Directory of Schools. Feb. 1984-. 0824-1775. CN. English. be. Free to Member Schools. Saskatchewan High Schools Athletic Association, 2220 College Avenue, Regina Saskatchewan S4P 3V7 Canada. **DD** 796.0257124. *Directory,* 0709-7816.

SIGMA ALPHA EPSILON ALUMNI DIRECTORY. VFOAT Alumni Directory. 1980-. 0730-4757. US. English. College & University Press, One Bell Road, PO Box 17940, Montgomery AL 36141. **LC** LJ75. **DD** 378.19855025757.

THE ... SILVER SPRUCE YEARBOOK. US. English. an. $18.00. Charles A Lory Student Center, Colorado State University, Fort Collins CO 80523. **LC** LD1150. **DD** 378.78868.

SIMMS' BLUE BOOK AND NATIONAL NEGRO BUSINESS AND PROFESSIONAL DIRECTORY. 1923-. US. English. **LC** E185.82. **DD** 338.002573.

SIMON'S DIRECTORY OF THEATRICAL MATERIALS, SERVICES & INFORMATION. VFOAT Simon's Directory of Theatrical Materials, Services & Information Covering the Entire United States & Canada. VAT Simon's Directory of Theatrical Materials, Services and Information. 1st Ed. (1955)-. US. English. ir. Package Publications City Service, 27 West 24th Street, New York NY 10010. **Tel** (212)255-2872. Ed Avivah Simon. **LC** PN2289. **DD** 792.058. bk rev. adv acc. **Circ** 10,000. (ctrl). A listing, in city-state order, in 97 categories, of manufacturers and vendors of supplies and services for the theatre, lighting, scenery, props, costumes, advertising, B.O. supplies, etc.

SINGAPORE BUILDERS DIRECTORY. English. an. Far East Media Representatives, 57B 2D Floor President Building, 320 Serangoon Road, Singapore 8 Singapore. **LC** HD9715.S5. **DD** 338.76240255957. *Singapore Builder Directory.*

SINGAPORE BUSINESS YEARBOOK. 1978-. Periodical. SI. English. ir. $6.00. Tiems Periodicals, 422 Thomson Road, Singapore 11 Singapore. **LC** HF3800.67. **DD** 330.9595205. *Singapore Trade & Industry Year Book.*

SINGAPORE DIRECTORY OF ADULT EDUCATION AGENCIES. 1975-. SI. English. ir. Statistics and Evaluation Unit, Adult Education Board, 126 Cairnhill Road, Singapore 9 Singapore. **LC** L961.S5. **DD** 374.00255952.

SINGAPORE GOVERNMENT DIRECTORY. SI. English. ir. $8.00. Publicity Division, Ministry of Culture, Singapore 0617 Singapore. **LC** JQ745.S5. **DD** 354.5952002.

SINGAPORE MANUFACTURERS AND PRODUCTS DIRECTORY. 1971-. English. ir. Straits Times Press, Press Times House River Valley Road, Singapore 9 Singapore. **LC** HD9736.S54. **DD** 338.00255952.

SINGAPORE SHIPBUILDING & REPAIRING DIRECTORY. VFOAT Singapore Shipbuilding and Repairing Directory. Periodical. SI. English. ir. $25.00. Singapore Association of Shipbuilders and Repairers, World Trade Centre No 1 Maritime Square #09-50, Singapore 0409 Singapore. **LC** VM299.7.S55. **DD** 623.830255957.

SINGAPORE SHIPPING & AIR TRANSPORTATION INDUSTRIES DIRECTORY. 1974/75-. English. bm. $46.00. Victor Kamkin Inc, 12224 Parklawn Drive, Rockville MD 20852. **Tel** (301)881-5973. Ind/Abst Math. Rev., Int. Aerosp. Abstr., Appl. Mech. Rev. **LC** HE884.6.S52. **DD** 387.5440255952.

Yearbooks, Almanacs, Directories

SINGAPORE STANDARDS YEARBOOK. 0129-6256. English. an. Singapore Institute of Standards and Industrial Research, 179 River Valley Road, Singapore 0617 Republic of Singapore. LC TA368. DD 389.6095957.

SINGAPORE TELEX & TELEFAX DIRECTORY. VFOAT Singapore Telex and Telefax Directory. Oct. 1984-. English. an. Telecommunication Authority of Singapore Comcentre, 31 Exeter Road, Singapore 0923 Singapore. LC HE8390.67. DD 384.10255957. *Singapore Telex Directory.*

SINGAPORE YEAR BOOK CEASED. 19 -68. 0441-5787. Periodical. SI. English. an. $16.29. Singapore National Printers, 303 Upper Serangdon Road, Singapore 13 Singapore. Tel 28-20611. LC DS598.S7. DD 915.952005.

SINGAPORE'S JUDICIAL & LEGAL DIRECTORY. VFOAT Singapore's Judicial and Legal Directory. English. ir. Legal Publications, Box 673, Berkeley CA 94701.

THE SISKIYOU PIONEER IN FOLKLORE, FACT AND FICTION AND YEARBOOK. VFOAT Siskiyou Pioneer. V. 3- 1957-. 0196-0725. US. English. an. $7.00. Siskiyou County Historical Society, 910 South Main Street, Yreka CA 96097. Ind/Abst Am. Hist. Life, Hist. Abstr., Part A, Mod. Hist. Abstr., Hist. Abst., Part B, Twent. Century Abstr.

SJFARTSHISTORISK ARBOK. VFOAT Norwegian Yearbook of Maritime History. English or Norwegian. ir. 10. LC V5.

SKIERS DIRECTORY. (SKIERS . . . DIRECTORY). Began with 1973. 0730-2150. US. English. an. $3.95. Ziff-Davis Publishing Company, One Park Avenue, New York NY 10016. Tel (212)503-3923. Ed William Grout. LC GV854.4. DD 796.930973. bk rev. adv acc. Circ 100,000. An comprehensive introduction to the sport of snow skiing including listings on equipment, clothing, and ski areas, both cross country and downhill.

SKINNER'S DIRECTORY OF SECURITY DEALER NAME AND ADDRESS CHANGES INCLUDING MERGERS, ABSORPTIONS, LIQUIDATIONS, AND NAMES OF TRUSTEES IN LIQUIDATION. VFOAT Directory of Security Dealer Name and Address Changes. 0163-6502. US. English. Skinner and Company, 110 Sutter Street/Suite 1003, San Francisco CA. LC HG4621. DD 332.62.

SLAM, TRADE YEAR BOOK OF AFRICA. VFOAT Trade Year Book of Africa, SLAM, Annuaire Commercial de l'Afrique. 7th- Ed. English (French, Italian, and/or Spanish). ir. Slam, Apartado 14-013, Madrid 20 Spain. LC HF54.S7. DD 380.102946. *Spanish-Lusitanian-American Trade Directory.*

SLOVO NA STOROZHI. See Linguistics.

THE SMA DIRECTORY. Main/Corp Singapore Manufacturers Association. VAT Singapore Manufacturers Association Directory. English. ir. Singapore Manufacturers Association, Kompass Singapore Pte Ltd, 704 Supreme House, Penang Road 9, Singapore Singapore. LC HD9736.S54. DD 338.00255952.

SMALL BUSINESS SUBCONTRACTING DIRECTORY. 0741-4811. US. English. US S B A, Office of Procurement and Technical Assistance, Washington DC 20416. LC HG4057. DD 338.64202573.

SMAR'S INDUSTRIAL DIRECTORY OF PAKISTAN. English. ir. $5.00. Smar International, 6 Afshan Chambers, Tariq Road P E C H S, Karachi Pakistan. LC HC440.5.Z7. DD 338.00255491. *Smar's Industrial Directory of West Pakistan.*

SOCIAL DIRECTORY OF HOUSTON. 0489-2593. US. English. The Social Directory of Houston, PO Box 22454, Houston TX 77027. DD 917.64.

SOCIETY OF CHRISTIAN POETS DIRECTORY. VFOAT Directory. Periodical. US. English. Society of Christian Poets, Box 214, Van Buren AR 72956. LC PS5. DD 811.006073.

SOLAR ENERGY AND NONFOSSIL FUEL RESEARCH. (SOLAR ENERGY AND NONFOSSIL FUEL RESEARCH : A DIRECTORY OF PROJECTS RELATED TO AGRICULTURE). Began with 1976/79. 0741-5419. US. English. an. US Department of Agriculture, Cooperative State Research Service, Washington DC 20250. LC S21., TJ811. DD 630, 016.621042. Vols. for 1981- distributed to depository libraries in microfiche.

SOLAR ENERGY & RESEARCH DIRECTORY. VAT Solar Energy and Research Directory. 0148-0871. US. English. Ann Arbor Science Publishers Inc, PO Box 1425, Ann Arbor MI 48106. LC TJ810. DD 621.47025.

SOMETHING ELSE YEARBOOK. 1974-. 0093-0776. US. English. $3.95. PO Box 26, West Glover VT 05875. LC NX1. DD 705.

THE SOONER; YEARBOOK OF THE UNIVERSITY OF OKLAHOMA. 0038-1497. US. English. bm. University Oklahoma Alumni Association, 900 Asp Avenue, Norman OK 73019. Tel (405)325-5711. Each issue contains an index to its own contents - no vol index - loose.

SORKINS' DIRECTORY OF BUSINESS & GOVERNMENT (ST. LOUIS EDITION). (SORKINS' DIRECTORY OF BUSINESS & GOVERNMENT). VFOAT Sorkins' Directory of Business and Government. 1984/1985-. 0748-0458. US. English. an. $19.95. Town Publications Inc, 300 Chesterfield Center/Suite 190, St Louis MO 63017. LC HC108.S2. DD 338.740257786. *Who's Who of St. Louis Business.*

SOURCE DIRECTORY : NATIVE AMERICAN OWNED AND OPERATED ARTS AND CRAFTS BUSINESSES. Main/Corp United States. Indian Arts and Crafts Board. VFOAT Native American Owned and Operated Arts and Crafts Businesses. 1979-. US. English. be. Indian Arts and Crafts Board, Room 4004, US Department of the Interior, Washington DC 20240.

SOURCE DIRECTORY OF PREDICASTS, INC. (THE SOURCE DIRECTORY OF PREDICASTS, INC). Main/Corp Predicasts, Inc. V. 1- June 1973-. 0092-7767. Periodical. US. English. qt. $135.00 Domestic, $150.00 Foreign. Predicasts Inc, 11001 Cedar Avenue, Cleveland OH 44106. Tel (800)321-6388. LC Z7164.C81. DD 016.338. Names and addresses of publications abstracted and indexed in Predicasts' hardcopy publications and online databases.

SOURCES OF INFORMATION AND SERVICES FOR THE HEARING IMPAIRED IN TEXAS. (SOURCES OF INFORMATION AND SERVICES FOR THE HEARING IMPAIRED IN TEXAS : A DIRECTORY). 1974-. 0098-0595. US. English. Texas Commission for the Deaf, PO Box 12904 Capitol Station, Austin TX 78711. LC HV2561.T6. DD 362.42025764. NLM WV 22 AT4 S7.

SOUTH AFRICAN YEARBOOK OF INTERNATIONAL LAW. VFOAT Suid-Afrikaanse Jaarboek vir Volkereg. V. 1- 1975-. 0379-8895. SA. English. an. $20.00. University of South Africa Institute of Foreign & Comparative Law, POB 392, Pretoria 0001 South Africa. Tel 325-4450. Ed D H Van Wyk. LC JX21. DD 341.05. Each issue contains an index to its own contents - no vol index - loose. bk rev. adv acc. Circ 700. Articles, case discussions, book reviews, notes, and comments on international law, with particular reference to the Republic of South Africa and the international community.

SOUTH AUSTRALIAN YEAR BOOK. No.1- 1966-. 0085-6428. AT. English. an. 27.20. Australian Bureau of Statistics, Ground Floor Annexe, City Mutual Centre, 10-20 Pulteney Street, Adelaide South Australia 5000 Australia. Tel (08)228 9439. LC HC636. DD 309.1942. A general reference work providing a comprehensive statistical and descriptive portrayal of South Australia's physiography, history, institutions and social and economic conditions.

SOUTH BEND (ST. JOSEPH COUNTY, IND.) CITY DIRECTORY. VFOAT Polk's South Bend City Directory. 1974-. US. English. an. R L Polk Company, 6400 Monroe Boulevard, Box 500, Taylor MI 48180. *Polk's South Bend (St. Joseph County, Ind.) City Directory.*

SOUTH CAROLINA FOOD AND AGRICULTURAL PRODUCTS EXPORT DIRECTORY. (SOUTH CAROLINA FOOD AND AGRICULTURAL PRODUCTS : EXPORT DIRECTORY). 0145-5796. US. English. Wade Hampton State Office Building, PO Box 11280, Columbia SC 29211. LC HD9007.S6. DD 382.41025757.

SOUTH CAROLINA METALWORKING DIRECTORY. 0363-5090. US. English. Free. South Carolina State Development Board, PO Box 927, Columbia SC 29202. Tel (803)758-3046. LC TS203. DD 338.97671025757. Circ 2,000. Listing of metalworking job shops in South Carolina including a complete equipment breakdown.

SOUTH CAROLINA ZIP+4 STATE DIRECTORY. VFOAT Zip+4 State Directory. VAT South Carolina Zip Plus Four State Directory. 1985-. US. English. an. St Louis PDC, Zip + 4 State Directory Orders, PO Box 14921, St Louis MO 63180-9988.

SOUTH DAKOTA EDUCATIONAL DIRECTORY. 1972/73-. 0363-0137. US. English. Department of Education & Cultural Affairs, Division of Elementary & Secondary Education, State Capitol Building, Pierre SD 57501. LC L903.S8. DD 370.25783. *Educational Directory of South Dakota Schools.*

SOUTH DAKOTA LIBRARY DIRECTORY. US. English. South Dakota State Library & Archives, 800 North Illinois, Pierre SD 57501. *Directory of South Dakota Libraries.*

SOUTH EAST ASIA OIL DIRECTORY, SINGAPORE. 1976/77-. SI. English. ir. LC HD9576.A23. DD 338.2728202559.

THE SOUTHEAST CREATIVE DIRECTORY. VFOAT South East Creative Directory. 8756-5544. US. English. Southeast Creative Directory, 382 Golfview Road Northwest, Atlanta GA 30309. LC F207.3. DD 975.0025.

THE SOUTHERN AFRICAN AND INDIAN OCEAN ISLANDS TRAVEL INDUSTRY'S YEARBOOK, DIRECTORY AND WHO'S WHO. VFOAT Southern Africa's Travel Industry. 1976/77-. English. ir. 10.00. World Freight & Markets Pty Ltd, PO Box 6202, 200 Johannesburg South Africa. LC G155.S57. DD 338.47916804025.

SOUTHERN BANKERS DIRECTORY. (SOUTHERN BANKERS DIRECTORY, CONTAINING COMPLETE ALPHABETICAL LIST OF COMMERCIAL BANKS IN ALABAMA, ARKANSAS, DIST. OF COLUMBIA ETC). 0734-7812. US. English. McFadden Business Publications, 6264 Warren Drive, Norcross GA 30093. LC HG2441.

SOUTHERN CALIFORNIA BUSINESS DIRECTORY AND BUYERS GUIDE. 1964. 0093-3090. US. English. an. $85.00. Civiv Data Corporation, 523 Superior Avenue, Newport Beach CA 92663. Tel (714)646-1626. Ed Milo E Rodich. LC HF5065.C2. DD 380.10257949. adv acc. Circ 6,000. (ctrl). Directory of business in 13 Southern California counties. Lists manufacturers, distributors, major retailers and service companies. Lists statistical data on the market area and a general business reference.

SOUTHERN CALIFORNIA GROUP LEGAL SERVICES DIRECTORY. Periodical. US. English. an.

SOUTHERN PACIFIC LOCOMOTIVE DIRECTORY. VFOAT Locomotive Directory. 84-. 8756-8853. US. English. Wordways, PO Box 2592, Menlo Park CA 94026. LC TJ603.3.S6. DD 625.260978.

SOUTHERN PROGRESSIVE PERIODICALS DIRECTORY. 0271-5961. US. English. $4.00. Progressive Education, PO Box 120574, Nashville TN 37212. Ed C T Canan. LC Z6952.S6, PN4893. DD 051. adv acc. Circ 1,500. Over 100 periodicals published in the Southern United States which the author describes as progressive. Includes topics such as peace, religion, labor and health.

SOUTHWEST DIRECTORY OF ADVERTISING AND PUBLIC RELATIONS AGENCIES. 1976-. 0361-3593. US. English. Cordovan Corp, 5314 Bingle Road, Houston TX 77018. LC HF6182.U5. DD 338.761659102576. *Southwest Directory of Ad & PR Agencies, 0360-1854.*

THE SOYFOODS INDUSTRY AND MARKET, DIRECTORY AND DATABOOK. VFOAT Directory and Databook. 1983-. 8755-1683. US. English. an. $75.00. The Soyfoods Center, PO Box 234, Lafayette CA 94549. Tel (415)283-2991. Ed William Shurtleff. LC

Yearbooks, Almanacs, Directories

HD9235.S6. **DD** 338.4766480565505. **Circ** 300. Analysis of the soyfoods industry and market; plus a directory of all manufacturers of tofu soymilk, tempeh soy sauce, miso, and soy protein products. *Soyfoods Industry Directory & Databook.*

SOZIALPOLITISCHES JAHRBUCH. 1.- 1954-. 0490-1894. German. ir. **LC** HD28.

SPEAKERS BUREAU INTERNATIONAL. (SPEAKERS BUREAU INTERNATIONAL : DIRECTORY). **VFOAT** Directory. 1982/83-. 0820-6074. CN. English. an. $5.00 Each Volume. Speakers Bureau International Directory, c/o The Bureau, 961 Eglinton Avenue East/Suite 200, Toronto Ontario M4G 4B5 Canada. **DD** 808.5102571.

SPECIAL EDUCATION DIRECTORY. 0364-0035. US. English. an. Department of Education, Division of Special Education, 933 High Street, Worthington OH 43085. **Tel** (614)466-3641. **LC** L903.O3. **DD** 371.91025771.

SPEECH COMMUNICATION DIRECTORY. Began in 1973/74. 0190-2075. US. English. an. $12.00 Each Copy. Speech Communication Association, 5105 Backlick Road, Annandale VA 22003. **LC** PN4073. **DD** 001.542025. **NLM** WV 22 AA1 S8. *Directory of the Speech Communication Association, 0091-0589.*

SPORT MEDICINE DIRECTORY. **VFOAT** Repertoire de la Medecine Sportive. 1980-. 0229-1541. CN. English (includes some text in French). an. Sport Medicine Council of Canada, 333 River Road, Ottawa Ontario K1L 8B9 Canada. **DD** 617.1027.

SPORT ONTARIO DIRECTORY OF SPORTS, RECREATION AND PHYSICAL EDUCATION. (DIRECTORY OF SPORTS, RECREATION AND PHYSICAL EDUCATION). 1977/78-. 0708-6113. CN. English. an. Sport Ontario, 559 Jarvis Street, Toronto Ontario M4Y 2J1 Canada. **DD** 796.025713.

SPORTING GOODS CANADA. DIRECTORY ISSUE. 1975-. CN. English. an. **DD** 338.476887602571. *Sporting Goods Canada. Annual Directory for Canadian Sporting Goods Buyers.*

THE SPORTING NEWS BASEBALL YEARBOOK. (THE SPORTING NEWS . . . BASEBALL YEARBOOK). **VFOAT** Baseball Yearbook. 1981-. 0275-0732. US. English. an. $3.50. The Sporting News Publishing Co, 1212 North Lindbergh Boulevard, St Louis MO 63166. **Tel** (314)997-7111. **LC** GV863.A1. **DD** 796.3570973. adv acc. **Circ** 300,000.

THE SPORTING NEWS COLLEGE AND PRO BASKETBALL YEARBOOK. (THE SPORTING NEWS COLLEGE AND PRO . . . BASKETBALL YEARBOOK). **VFOAT** College and Pro Basketball Yearbook. 1982-83-. 0733-6047. US. English. an. $2.95. Sporting News Publishing Company, PO Box 56, St Louis MO 63166. **LC** WMLC L 83/112.

THE SPORTING NEWS COLLEGE FOOTBALL YEARBOOK. (THE SPORTING NEWS . . . COLLEGE FOOTBALL YEARBOOK). **VFOAT** College Football Yearbook. 1982-. 0733-2823. US. English. an. $2.95 Each Issue. Sporting News Publishing Company, 1212 North Lindbergh, PO Box 56, St Louis MO 63166. **LC** WMLC L 83/138.

THE SPORTING NEWS PRO FOOTBALL YEARBOOK. (THE SPORTING NEWS . . . PRO FOOTBALL YEARBOOK). **VFOAT** Pro Football Yearbook. 1981-. 0276-2307. US. English. an. $2.95 Each Issue. Sporting News, 1212 North Lindbergh, St Louis MO 63132. **LC** GV937. **DD** 796.332640973.

THE SPORTS AFIELD OUTDOOR ALMANAC. 0190-1249. US. English. The Hearst Corporation, 57th Street Eighth Avenue, New York NY 10019. **LC** SK1. **DD** 799.05. *Sports Afield Almanac, 0092-7082.*

THE SPORTS COLLECTORS DIRECTORY. 1979-. 0198-6597. US. English. an. Urban Publications, 4928 North 85th Street, Milwaukee WI 53225. **LC** GV568.5. **DD** 796.028.

SPORTS DIRECTORY. 1st- Ed. 0380-5751. CN. English. an. Northwestern Ontario Sports Council, 189 Arthur Street, Thunder Bay "P" Ontario P7B 1A2 Canada. **DD** 796.0257131.

THE SPOTLIGHT CASTING DIRECTORY. Periodical. UK. English. an. $41.14. Spotlight Casting Directory, 43 Cranbourn Street, London WC2H 7AP England.

SRI LANKA YEAR BOOK. 1975-. CE. English. ir. 24.00. Department of Census and Statistics, PO Box 563, Colombo Sri Lanka. **Tel** 595291. **LC** DS488. **DD** 315.493. **Circ** 4,990. Contains salient facts on the historical background, geographical features, social and economic conditions of Sri Lanka and the various development activities of the government. *Ceylon Year Book. The Official Statistical Annual of the Social, Economic and General Conditions of the Island.*

STAATS-HEROLD ALMANACH. **VFOAT** Delikatessen, Geschenke, Schallplatten aus Europa und der Ganzen Welt. US. German. an. Staats-Herold Corporation, 36-30 37th Street, Lond Island City NY 11101. *Deutsche in Amerika.*

STADTADRESSBUCH JEVER. **VFOAT** Adressbuch Jever. German. ir. Kommunikation und Wirtschaft GMBH, 2900 Oldenburg, Ammergaustrasse 7 West Germany.

STAFF DIRECTORY - INSTITUT PERTANIAN BOGOR. Main/Corp Institut Pertanian Bogor. English. ir. **LC** S539.I45. **DD** 630.205598.

STAMM LEITFADEN DURCH PRESSE UND WERBUNG. **VFOAT** Leitfaden Durch Presse und Werbung, Annual Directory Through Press and Advertising. Aug. 29 (1976)-. 0341-7093. GW. English (German and French). an. 121.-. Stamm Verlag GMBH, Goldammerweg 16, 4300 Essen West Germany. **Tel** 0201/41757. **LC** Z6956.G3, PN5208. **DD** 073. **NLM** Z 6956.G3 L718. adv acc. **Circ** 8,500. *Stamm Leitfaden fur Presse und Werbung, 0341-7093.*

STANDARD AND POOR'S DIRECTORY OF BOND AGENTS. Main/Corp Standard and Poor's Corporation. **VFOAT** Directory of Bond Agents. 1974/75- Ed. US. English. ir. Standard & Poors Corporation, 25 Broadway, New York NY 10004. **Tel** (212)208-8772. **LC** HG4907. **DD** 332.67.

STANDARD COMMERCIAL DIRECTORY. V. 1- 1976/77-. 0147-8486. US. English. Liberty Publications, 11906 Wilshire Boulevard/Suite 8, Los Angeles CA 90025. **LC** HF5035. **DD** 380.102573.

STANDARD DIRECTORY OF ADVERTISERS. 1964-. US. English. ir. $471.04. National Register Publishing Company Inc, 3004 Glenview Road, Wilmette IL 60091. **Tel** (312)256-6067. *Standard Advertising Register, McKittrick Directory of Advertising.*

STANDARD DIRECTORY OF ADVERTISING AGENCIES. 1964-. 0085-6614. US. English. ty. NaitoanI Register Publishing Company Inc, 20 East 46 Street, New York NY 10017. *Standard Advertising Register, Agency List, McKittrick Directory of Advertisers, Agency List.*

STANDARD EDUCATION ALMANAC. 1968-. 0081-4237. US. English. an. Marquis Who's Who Inc, 200 East Ohio Street, Chicago IL 60611. **Tel** (317)298-5484. Ed A Renetzky and P A Kaplan. **LC** L101.U6. **DD** 370.5. **NLM** L 101.U6 S785.

STANDARD MEDICAL ALMANAC. 1st- Ed. 0162-2544. US. English. an. Marquis Academic Media, Marquis Who's Who Inc, 200 East Ohio Street, Chicago IL 60611. **NLM** W1 ST139M.

THE STANDARD PERIODICAL DIRECTORY. 1- Ed., 1964/65-. 0085-6630. US. English. be. $225.00. Oxbridge Communications Inc, 150 Fifth Avenue, New York NY 10011. **Tel** (212)741-0231. Ed Margie Domenech. **LC** Z6951. **DD** 016.051. **NLM** Z 6941 S785. adv acc. Largest directory of periodicals in the US and Canada. Over 67,000 listings by general categories from A-Z.

STANDARD TRADE DIRECTORY OF INDONESIA. 1979-. IO. English. ir. $100.00. Indonesian Chamber of Commerce & Industry, Jl Hayam Wuruk 4TX, Jakarta PO Box 4556, Jakarta Indonesia. **Tel** 373707. Ed Freddy Sutesi. **LC** HF3803. **DD** 380.1025598. adv acc. **Circ** 15,000. (ctrl). List of companies in Indonesia and other important functionaries and their adresses.

STANGER'S DRILLING FUND YEARBOOK. 0739-5205. US. English. an. Robert A Stanger & Company, 623 River Road, Fair Haven NJ 07701. **LC** HD9561. **DD** 338.23.

STANGER'S PARTNERSHIP SPONSOR DIRECTORY DIRECTORIES BUSINESS. (STANGER'S PARTNERSHIP SPONSOR DIRECTORY : A GUIDE TO SPONSORS OF PUBLIC AND PRIVATE LIMITED PARTNERSHIPS). **VFOAT** Partnership Sponsor Directory. 1984-. US. English. an. $49.95. Robert A Stanger & Company, 1129 Broad Street, Shrewsbury NJ 07701.

STANGER'S TAX SHELTER YEARBOOK. **VFOAT** Tax Shelter Yearbook. 1983-. 8756-4319. US. English. an. Dow Jones-Irwin, Homewood IL 60430. **LC** HJ4653.T38. **DD** 336.206.

THE STAR ALMANAC FOR LAND SURVEYORS. 0481-4377. UK. English. Her Majesty's Stationery Office, PO Box 276, London SW8 5DT England. **Tel** (01)622 3316. **DD** 528.2.

STATE DIRECTORY OF HIGHER EDUCATION INSTITUTIONS AND AGENCIES IN MARYLAND. 0098-4132. US. English. an. Maryland Council for Higher Education, 93 Main Street, Annapolis MD 21401. **LC** L903.M3. **DD** 378.752.

STATE DIRECTORY OF KENTUCKY. 1965. 0585-1173. US. English. an. $11.00. Directories Inc, PO Box 187, Pewee Valley KY 40056. **Tel** (502)241-8256. Ed Mary M Wright. **LC** JK5330. **DD** 353.9769002. **Circ** 4,500. City, county and state elected and appointed officials including practicing attorneys, news media and school superintendants, courts, judicial, and vital statistics.

STATE DIRECTORY OF PUBLIC OFFICIALS IN GEORGIA. (THE STATE DIRECTORY OF PUBLIC OFFICIALS IN GEORGIA). V. 1- 1975-. 0099-0175. US. English. an. $10.00. PO Box 125, Richmond Hill GA 31324. **LC** JK4330. **DD** 353.9758002.

STATE EXECUTIVE DIRECTORY. Began with Spring/Summer 1980. 0276-7163. Periodical. US. English. ty. $50.00. Carroll Publishing Company, 1058 Thomas Jefferson Street NW, Washington DC 20007. **Tel** (202)333-8620. **LC** JK2482.E94. **DD** 353.932. Current alphabetic name and organizational directory of 27,000 state executive branch officials, with subject index, fully cross-referenced.

STATE OF CALIFORNIA TELEPHONE DIRECTORY. Main/Corp California. Dept. of General Services. **VFOAT** State Offices Telephone Directory. Apr. 1969-. US. English. an. State of California, Department of General Services Publication Division, PO Box 1015 North Highlands CA 95660. **Tel** (916)445-1020. *State Offices Telephone Directory.*

THE STATESMAN'S YEAR-BOOK. 1st- ed. 0081-4601. US. English. an. $45.00. St Martins Press Inc, 175 Fifth Avenue, New York NY 10010. **Tel** (212)674-5151. Ed John Paxton. **LC** JA51. **NLM** JA 51 S797. Listing of political, social and economic institutions and structures by country, covering every part of the present-day world.

STATISTICAL SERVICES DIRECTORY. **VFOAT** Directory to Statistical Services. First Ed., Issue No. 1(June 1982)-. 0732-6971. US. English. ir. $180.00. Gale Research Company, Book Tower, Detroit MI 48226. **LC** HA37. **DD** 310.2573. The new edition of this directory provides over 2,000 detailed entries leading researchers to the primary gatherers and disseminators of statistics in numerous industries and areas of interest.

STATISTICAL SOURCE DIRECTORY FOR NEW JERSEY STATE GOVERNMENT. 1977-. 0147-5525. US. English. NJ Department of Labor & Industry, Division of Planning & Research, Trenton NJ 08625. **LC** HA37.U7. **DD** 310.61749.

STATISTICAL YEAR BOOK - CENTRAL BUREAU OF STATISTICS. Main/Corp Ghana. Central Bureau of Statistics. 1st- 1961-. 0435-8899. Periodical. GH. English. ir. Central Bureau of Statistics, PO Box 1098 Accra Ghana. **LC** HA1977.G6. **DD** 316. **NLM** W2 HG6 C3S.

STATISTICAL YEAR BOOK, THAILAND. Main/Corp Thailand. National Statistical Office. No. 1-21. 1916-1939/44. TH. Beginning with 1933/35, English and Thai. ir. National Statistical Office, Larn Luang Road, Bangkok 10100, Thailand 1407/244. **Tel** 2818618. **Circ** 1,000. (ctrl). Area population, public health, and vital statistics on immigration, education, public justice, agriculture, fisheries, forestry, mining industry, business enterprises, transport and communication.

STATISTICAL YEAR BOOK - THE AUSTRALIAN GAS INDUSTRY. Main/Corp National Gas Association of Australia. **VFOAT** The Australian Gas Industry: Statistical Year Book.

Yearbooks, Almanacs, Directories

1958-. 0466-2865. Periodical. AT. English. ir. National Gas Association of Australia, Melbourne Victoria 3000 Australia. **LC** TP738. *Statistical Year Book of the Gas Industry in Australia.*

STATISTICAL YEAR BOOK. TIN, TINPLATE, CANNING. (STATISTICAL YEAR BOOK : TIN, TINPLATE, CANNING). **VFOAT** Statistical Year Book: Tin. 1952-. 0074-9117. UK. English. be. International Tin Council, Haymarket House, 1 Ovendon Street, London SW1Y 4EQ England. **DD** 338.2. *Statistical Year Book -International Tin Study Group.*

STATISTICAL YEARBOOK. Main/Corp United Nations. Statistical Office. **VFOAT** Annuaire Statistique. 1st- issue. 0082-8459. US. English (French). ir. $60.00. United Nations Publications, Sales Section Room A-3315, New York NY 10017. **Tel** (212)754-8302. **LC** HA12.5. **DD** 310.5. Provides a wealth of statistical data for more than 270 countries and territories on economic and social subjects.

STATISTICAL YEARBOOK (ARAB MEMBER STATES). VFOAT Annuaire Statistique (Etats Membres Arabes). 1982-. Periodical. Arabic (English and French). an. UNESCO, 7 Place de Fontenoy, 75700 Paris France. **LC** DS36.88. **DD** 310.9174927.

STATISTICAL YEARBOOK - CENTRAL STATISTICAL OFFICE. Main/Corp Zambia. Central Statistical Office. 1967-. 0084-4551. ZA. English. ir. Central Statistical Office, Box 1908, Lusaka Zambia. **LC** HA1977.R48. **DD** 316.894.

STATISTICAL YEARBOOK FOR ASIA AND THE PACIFIC. VFOAT Annuaire Statistique pour l'Asie et le Pacifique. 1973-. US. Multilinugal (English and French). an. $54.00. United Nations Publications, Sales Section/Room A-3315, New York NY 10017. **Tel** (212)754-8302. **LC** JX1977, HA1665.S73. **DD** 300.8 S, 315. Contains a wealth of statistics covering population, manpower, national accounts, agriculture, forestry and fishing, industry, energy supplies, consumption, transport and communication, internal and external trade, wages and banking. *Statistical Yearbook for Asia and The Far East.*

STATISTICAL YEARBOOK FOR LATIN AMERICA. VFOAT Anuario Estadistico de America Latina. 1979-. Periodical. US. Spanish (English). $40.00. United Nations Publications, Sales Section/Room A-3315, New York NY 10017. **Tel** (212)754-8302. Over-all and individual country tables covering population, national accounts, agriculture, industry, import-export of goods and services, balance of payments and transports. *Anuario Estadistico de America Latina.*

STATISTICAL YEARBOOK. GOLD OPTIONS DATA. VFOAT Gold Options Data. 1983-. 0883-4156. US. English. an. Commodity Exchange Inc, Four World Trade Center, New York NY 10048. *Statistical Yearbook (Commodity Exchange, Inc.), 0162-4970.*

STATISTICAL YEARBOOK - INTERNATIONAL NORTH PACIFIC FISHERIES COMMISSION. (STATISTICAL YEARBOOK). 0535-1588. CN. English. an. International North Pacific Fisheries Commission, 6640 Northwest Marine Drive, Vancouver British Columbia V6T 1X2 Canada. **DD** 639.22091644.

STATISTICAL YEARBOOK. METALS FUTURES DATA. VFOAT Metals Futures Data. 1983-. 0883-4164. US. English. an. Commodity Exchange Inc, Four World Trade Center, New York NY 10048. *Statistical Yearbook (Commodity Exchange, Inc.), 0162-4970.*

STATISTICAL YEARBOOK - NEW YORK MERCANTILE EXCHANGE. Main/Corp New York Mercantile Exchange. **VFOAT** New York Mercantile Exchange Yearbook. 0090-8991. US. English. an. Publications Department, New York Mercantile Exchange, 4 World Trade Center, New York NY 10048. **LC** HD9275.U8. **DD** 332.63280973.

STATISTICAL YEARBOOK OF BANGLADESH. VFOAT Bamladesa Parisamkhyana Barshagrantha. 1975-. BG. English. an. $30.00. Bangladesh Bureau of Statistic, Bangladesh Secretariat, Dacca Bangladesh. **LC** HA4590.6. **DD** 315.492. *Statistical Digest of Bangladesh.*

STATISTICAL YEARBOOK OF CHINA. 1981-. English. an. Economic Information & Agency Hong Kong, 342 Hennessy Road, Hong Kong China. **LC** HA4631. **DD** 315.1.

STATISTICAL YEARBOOK OF MEMBER STATES OF THE COUNCIL FOR MUTUAL ECONOMIC ASSISTANCE. Main/Corp Sovet Ekonomicheskoi Vzaimopomoshchi. UK. English (Russian). an. $38.31. Business Press International Ltd, Perrymount Road, Haywards Heath, West Sussex RH16 3DH England. **LC** HA1107. **DD** 314.7.

STATISTICAL YEARBOOK OF MUNICIPAL FINANCE. 1979-. 0740-5790. US. English. an. $61.50. Public Securities Association, One World Trade Center, New York NY 10048. **Tel** (212)466-1900. *Statistical Yearbook: Municipal Securities Data Base.*

STATISTICAL YEARBOOK OF THE NETHERLANDS. 1969/70-. English. ir. 25.00. Central Bureau of Statistics, PO Box 959 2270 AZ Voorburg, The Hague Netherlands. **LC** HA1381. **DD** 314.92. **NLM** W2 GN4 C3J. *Jaarcijfers voor Nederlanden.*

STATISTICAL YEARBOOK OF THE SOCIALIST FEDERAL REPUBLIC OF YUGOSLAVIA. VFOAT Statistical Yearbook of the SFRY. 1963-. 0585-1858. YU. English (Serbo-Croatian(R)). an. $40.00. Federal Institute for Statistics, Kneza Milosa 20, 11000 Beograd Yugoslavia. *Statistical Yearbook of the Federal People's Republic of Yugoslavia.*

STATISTICAL YEARBOOK OF THE SOCIALIST REPUBLIC OF ROMANIA. 1966-. 0377-5739. Periodical. RM. English (Romanian). ir. Socialist Republic of Romania, Central Statistical Board, Bucharest Romania. **DD** 314. **NLM** W2 GR8 D5AA. *Statistical Yearbook of the R.P.R., 0485-6147.*

STATISTICAL YEARBOOK OF THE WESTERN LUMBER INDUSTRY. 0195-931X. US. English. an. $12.50. Western Wood Products Association, 1500 Yeon Building, Portland OR 97204. **Tel** (503)224-3930. **LC** HD9757.A17. **DD** 338.476740978. *Statistical Yearbook (Western Wood Products Association), 0511-8301.*

STATISTIK ARSBOK FOR SVERIGE. VFOAT Statistical Abstract of Sweden. V. 1 - 1914-. Periodical. SW. Swedish and French 1941-51. Swedish and English, No. 39- 1952-. Liber Foerlag, Fack S 182, 89 Vaellingby Sweden. **LC** HA1523. *Sveriges Officiella Statistiki Sammandrag.*

STATISTIK INDONESIA. VFOAT Statistical Yearbook of Indonesia. 1975-. IO. English and Indonesian. ir. 14.500.-. Biro Pusat Statistik, Jalan Dr Sumoto No 8, Jakarta Indonesia. **Tel** 372808. **LC** HA1811. bk rev.

STATISTIKE EPETERIS DEMOSION OIKONOMIKON. VFOAT Statistical Yearbook of Public Finance. English and Greek. ir. National Statistical Service of Greece, Ethnike Statistike Hyperesia Hellados, Athens Greece. **LC** HJ50. **DD** 336.495.

STATISTIKE EPETERIS TES HELLADOS / STATISTICAL YEARBOOK OF GREECE / HELLENIC REPUBLIC, NATIONAL STATISTICAL SERVICE OF GREECE. VFOAT Statistical Yearbook of Greece. Began in 1955. Periodical. GR. English (Greek). an. 12.00. National Statistical Service, Greece 14-16 Lycourgou Street, Athens Greece. **Tel** 3244-746. **NLM** W2 GG6 G8S. **Circ** 3,500. Concise statistical data on population, employment, education, agriculture, industry, external trade, public finance, etc. *Sunoptine Statostike Epeteris Tes Hellados.*

STATISTIQUES AGRICOLES, ANNUAIRE. French. ir. **LC** HD2135.M25. **DD** 338.109691.

STATISTISCHES JAHRBUCH BERLIN. GW. German. an. Kulturbuch-Verlag, Passauer Strasse 4 1 30, Berlin West Germany. **Tel** (030)2136071. **LC** HA1330. **Circ** 1,500. Statistical numbers of the growth in Berlin: economy, peoples, culture, law and security, etc. *Statistisches Jahrbuch der Stadt Berlin.*

STATISTISCHES JAHRBUCH DER NORDRHEIN-WESTFALISCHEN INDUSTRIE- UND HANDELSKAMMERN. Began publication with Vol. for 1954. German. an. 30.00. Gemeinsamen Statistischen Stelle der Nordrhein-Westfalischen Industrie- und Handelskammern, Marktische Strasse 120, 4600 Dortmund 1 West Germany. **LC** HC287.N6. Yearbook of economical statistics for the Chambers of Commerce in Nordrhein-Westfalen.

STATISTISCHES JAHRBUCH DER SCHWEIZ. 0081-5330. German (French). an. $41.40. Birkhauser Boston Inc, 380 Green Street, PO Box 3005, Cambridge MA 02139. **Tel** (617)876-2333.

STATISTISCHES JAHRBUCH ... FUR DIE BUNDESREPUBLIK DEUTSCHLAND. Began in 1952. 0081-5357. German. an. W Kohlhammer, Postfach 747, Urbanstrasse 12-16, Stuttgart West Germany. **LC** HA1232. **DD** 314.3.

STATISTISCHES JAHRBUCH NORDRHEIN-WESTFALEN. Vol. 16- 1974-. 0468-656X. German. ir. 39.-. Landesamt fur Datenverarbeitung und Statistik Nordrhein-Westfalen, Postfach 1105 Mauerstrasse 51, 4000 Dusseldorf 30. West Germany. **Tel** (0211)44971. adv acc. **Circ** 2,000. Statistical returns about a lot of different areas. *Statistisches Jahrbuch Nordrhein-Westfalen.*

STATISTISK ARBOG. Main/Corp Danmarks Statistik. **VFOAT** Statistical Yearbook. V. 71-1967-. 0070-3567. DK. Danish (English). an. Danmarks Statistik, Sejrogade 11, PO Box 2550, 11 Copenhagen 0 Denmark. **DD** 314. *Statistisk Arbog.*

STATISTISK ARBOG. Main/Corp Denmark. Danmarks Statistik. DK. Multilingual (Danish and English). an. 80.33. Danmarks Statistik, Sejrogade 11, PO Box 2550, 21 Copenhagen 0 Denmark. **Tel** (01)29 82 22. **Circ** 15,000. Population, housing, agriculture, manufacturing external trade, social security, elections, public finance, national accounts, Denmark, Faeroe Islands, Greenland.

STATISTISK ARBOG FOR NORGE. Main/Corp Norway. Statistisk Sentralbyra. **VFOAT** Annuaire Statistique de la Norvege, Statistical Yearbook of Norway. V. 1-. UK. Norwegian (French or English). $5.33. Central Bureau of Statistics, PO Box 8131, Oslo 1 Norway. **Tel** (47 02) 41 38 20. bk rev. **Circ** 45,000. Main statistical data on population, socioeconomic topics, labour, mining and manufacturing, trade, transport and communication, national accounts, finance, education, agriculture.

STATISTISK ARBOK. Main/Corp Norway. Statistisk Sentralbyra. **VFOAT** Statistical Yearbook of Norway. 1964-. 0078-1932. text in English and Norwegian. ir. **NLM** W2 GN6 S6SA. *Statistisk Arbok for Norge.*

STATISTISK ARSBOK FOR FINLAND. VFOAT Annuaire Statistique de Finlande, Statistical Yearbook of Finland. 1879-. 0081-5063. Fl. Finnish (English and Swedish). an. 148. Finland Central Statistisk Office, T1 1 Astokeskus Annankatu 44, SF-00100 Helsinki Finland. **Tel** 3580-17341. **Circ** 4,000. Covers statistics of demography, agriculture, forestry, industry, construction, trade, banking, insurance transport communications, finances, income, wages, national accounts, consumption, prices, labour, social and cultural affairs justice, and elections.

STATISZTIKAI EVKONYV. (STATISTICAL YEARBOOK / S TATISTICHESKII EZHEGODNIK). **VFOAT** Statisticheskii Ezhegodnik. 0441-4748. Periodical. US. English (English and Russian summaries in Hungarian). ir. Arthur Vanous, PO Box 650279, Vero Beach FL 32965. **Tel** (305)562-9186. Ed Allan Benz. **NLM** W2 GH8 K7SW.

STEAM PASSENGER SERVICE DIRECTORY. 0081-542X. US. English. an. $6.00. Empire State Railway Museum, PO Box 666, Middletown NY 10940. **Tel** (914)343-4219. Ed Marvin H Cohen. **LC** TA6.U5. **DD** 385.2202573. adv acc. **Circ** 15,000. Illustrated directory of all tourist type railroads, trolley museums and railway museums in the United States and Canada.

STEREO DIRECTORY & BUYING GUIDE. VAT Stereo Directory and Buying Guide. 0090-6786. US. English. an. $1.50. Ziff Davis Publishing Company, One Park Avenue, New York NY 10016. **LC** TK7881.8. **DD** 338.47621393302573. *Stereo/Hi-Fi Directory.*

STEREO/HI-FI DIRECTORY. US. English. an. Ziff-Davis, One Park Avenue, New York NY 10016.

STEWART ANNE ARUNDEL COUNTY CRISS-CROSS DIRECTORY. VFOAT Stewart Anne Arundel County Criss Cross Directory. 8756-8837. US. English. Stewart Directories Inc, 304 West Chesapeake Avenue, Baltimore MD 21204. **LC** F187.A6. **DD** 975.2550025.

STEWART BALTIMORE CITY CRISS-CROSS DIRECTORY. VFOAT Stewart Baltimore City Criss Cross Directory. 8756-9159. US. English. Stewart Directories Inc, 304 West Chesapeake Avenue, Baltimore MD 21204. **LC** F189.B13. **DD** 917.52600321.

Yearbooks, Almanacs, Directories

STEWART BALTIMORE COUNTY CRISS-CROSS DIRECTORY. VFOAT Stewart Baltimore County Criss Cross Directory. 8756-9167. US. English. Stewart Directories Inc, 304 West Chesapeake Avenue, Baltimore MD 21204. LC F187.B2. DD 975.2710025.

THE STOCK EXCHANGE OFFICIAL YEAR-BOOK. VAT Stock Exchange Official Year Book. Began in 1934. UK. English. an. $176.45. IPC Business Press Ltd, 205 East 42nd Street, New York NY 10017. Tel (212)867-2080. LC HG5431. DD 332.6424212. *Stock Exchange Year-Book, Stock Exchange Official Intelligence; Register of Defunct and Other Companies Removed from the Stock Exchange Official Year-Book.*

THE STOCK TRADER'S ALMANAC. US. English. an. Hirsch Organization Inc, 6 Deer Trail, Old Tappan NJ 07675. Tel (201)664-3400.

THE STORAGE BATTERY MANUFACTURING INDUSTRY. YEARBOOK. 1970-. US. English. an. Battery Council International, 1801 Murchison Drive, Burlingame CA 94010. LC HD9695.U5. DD 338.4762135405. *Storage Battery Manufacturing Industry. Yearbook.*

STORES, SHOPS, HYPERMARKETS RETAIL DIRECTORY. VFOAT Retail Directory. UK. English. an. Newman Books Ltd, 48 Poland Street, London W1V 4PP England. LC HF5155. DD 381.102541. *Stores, Shops, Supermarkets Retail Directory.*

THE STRAITS TIMES DIRECTORY OF SINGAPORE. SI. English. an. Strait Times Press Ltd, Times House, 390 Kim Seng Road, Singapore 9 Singapore. LC HF3800.6.Z8. DD 338.740255957. *Straits Times Directory of Malaysia & Singapore.*

STREET AND SMITH'S OFFICIAL YEARBOOK. BASEBALL. VFOAT Baseball. 0161-2018. Periodical. US. English. an. $5.25. Conde Nast Publications Inc, 304 East 45 Street, New York NY 10017. Tel (212)880-8800. LC GV877. DD 796.3570973.

STREET AND SMITH'S OFFICIAL YEARBOOK. COLLEGE FOOTBALL. (STREET AND SMITH'S OFFICIAL YEARBOOK : COLLEGE FOOTBALL). VFOAT Street and Smith's College Football. 0091-9977. US. English. an. $0.75. Conde Nast Publications Inc, 350 Madison Avenue, New York NY 10017. LC GV956.8. DD 796.332630973.

STREET AND SMITH'S OFFICIAL YEARBOOK. PRO FOOTBALL. (STREET AND SMITH'S OFFICIAL YEARBOOK : PRO FOOTBALL). VFOAT Street and Smith's Pro-Football Yearbook. 0092-3214. US. English. an. $5.25. Conde Nast Publications Inc, 304 East 45 Street, New York NY 10017. LC GV937. DD 796.332640973.

STRUCTURAL FOAM PLASTICS. (STRUCTURAL FOAM PLASTICS : DIRECTORY & MARKETING GUIDE). 1983-. 8755-7371. US. English. LC HD9662.P53. DD 381.456684930973.

SUBJECT DIRECTORY OF SPECIAL LIBRARIES AND INFORMATION CENTERS. VFOAT Subject Directory of Special Libraries. 1st Ed.- 1975-. 0732-927X. US. English. ir. $625.00. Gale Research Company, Book Tower, Detroit MI 48226. Ed B Darnay. LC Z675.A2. DD 026.0002573. Five volumes contain the same information found in Vol. 1 of DSL, conveniently rearranged under 27 subject sections in five volumes.

SUBSCRIBERS DIRECTORY - TELEFLORA CANADA. (SUBSCRIBERS DIRECTORY). Main/Corp Teleflora Canada. VFOAT Annuaire des Abonnes. Dec. 1983/Jan. 1984-. 0824-0442. Periodical. CN. English (French). bm. Free to subscribers of Teleflora Canada, 350 Bay Street, Toronto Ontario M5H 3N9 Canada. DD 338.175902571. *Membership and Delivery Directory, 0830-9537.*

SUBURBAN METRO TORONTO CRISS-CROSS DIRECTORY. VFOAT Might's Suburban Metro Toronto Criss Cross Directory. 1981-. 0710-0728. CN. English. an. $100.00 Each Volume. Might Directories, 220 Bartley Drive, Toronto ON Ontario Canada. DD 917.135. *Might's Metro Toronto Satellite Cities Directory, 0318-4471.*

SUFFOLK UNIVERSITY LAW SCHOOL ALUMNI DIRECTORY. Main/Corp Suffolk University, Boston. Law School. Suffolk Law Alumni Association. VFOAT Alumni Directory of Suffolk University Law School. 0196-318X. US. English. $5.00. Alumni Office, Suffolk University, Beacon Hill, Boston MA 02114. LC KF292.S84. DD 340.071174461.

SUGAR INDUSTRY'S WHO'S WHO AND DIRECTORY. V. 1- 1976-. II. English. ir. V K Publications, 36 Todarmal Road, New Delhi India. LC HD9116.I39. DD 338.173610954.

SUGAR Y AZUCAR. YEARBOOK. V. 36- 1968-. 0081-9212. US. English (Spanish). an. Palmer Publication, 2050 Center Avenue, Fort Lee NJ 07024. Tel (212)461-8660. LC TP375.3.

SUGAR YEAR BOOK. UK. English. an. LC HD9100.2. DD 338.476641.

SUMMER EMPLOYMENT DIRECTORY OF THE UNITED STATES. 0081-9352. US. English. an. Writers Digest, 9933 Alliance Road, Cincinnati OH 45242. Tel (513)984-0717. Ed Rand Ruggebers. LC HF5382.5.U5. DD 331.1280973. bk rev. 50,000 summer job opportunities throughout the United States. Each listing tells who to contact and where, pay, benefits, qualifications needed.

SUOMEN TILASTOLLINEN VUOSIKIRJA. VFOAT Statistisk Arsbok for Finland, Statistical Yearbook for Finland. New Series, 49- 1953-. Fl. English (Finnish and Swedish). an. 215. Central Statistical Office of Finland, Annankatu 44, SF-00100 Helsinki Finland. Tel 358-0-17341. Ed Eila Laakso. LC HA1448. DD 314.71. NLM W2 GF5 T5SA. Circ 4,000. Covers the general interest in Finland, demography, agriculture, forestry, industry, construction, trade, banking, transport, communications, national accounts, prices, labour, education, social affairs, and elections. *Suomen Tilastollinen Vuosikirja.*

SUPPLEMENT TO THE DIRECTORY OF THE AMERICAN RIGHT. (DIRECTORY OF THE AMERICAN RIGHT. SUPPLEMENT). 0164-2510. US. English. be. $3.95. Laird M Wilcox, Editorial Research Service, PO Box 1832, Kansas City MO 64141.

SUPPLEMENT TO THE STATISTICAL YEARBOOK AND THE MONTHLY BULLETIN OF STATISTICS. Main/Corp United Nations. Statistical Office. 1967-. 0503-4019. US. English. ir. $29.00. United Nations Publications, Sales Section Room A-3315, New York NY 10017. Tel (212)754-8302. LC HA36. DD 310.5. Possibly the most complete statistical reference book in existence, it provides a wealth of statistical data for more than 270 countries and territories on economic and social subjects. *Monthly Bulletin of Statistics.*

SUPPLEMENTAL DIRECTORY OF CERTIFIED APPLIANCES AND ACCESSORIES. Periodical. US. English. mo. 8501 East Pleasant Valley Road, Cleveland OH 44131.

SUPPLEMENTAL YEARBOOK - FLORIDA STATE BOARD OF PROFESSIONAL ENGINEERS AND LAND SURVEYORS. (SUPPLEMENTAL YEAR BOOK - STATE BOARD OF PROFESSIONAL ENGINEERS AND LAND SURVEYORS). Main/Corp Florida. State Board of Professional Engineers and Land Surveyors. 0095-0416. US. English. Suite 100, 6900 Lake Ellenor Drive, Orlando FL 32809. LC TA12. DD 620.00922.

SUPPLEMENTARY DIRECTORY OF THE AMERICAN BAPTIST CHURCHES IN THE U.S.A. (SUPPLEMENTARY DIRECTORY). Main/Corp American Baptist Churches in the U.S.A. 1972/73-. 0090-9459. US. English. Judson Press, Box 851, Valley Forge PA 19481. LC BX6207. DD 286.173. *Year Book, Containing Historical Documents and Tables.*

SURFACE WATER YEAR-BOOK OF GREAT BRITAIN. 1935/36-1966/70. 0081-959X. UK. English. ir. Her Majesty's Stationery Office, PO Box 276, London SW8 5DT England. Tel (01)622-3316.

SURINAME DIRECTORY OF COMMERCE, INDUSTRY AND TOURISM. 1st- 1975/76-. SR. English. ir. Publico, PO Box 129, Paramaribo Surinamen SA. LC HF3450.5.A48. DD 380.1025883.

SURNAME RESEARCH DIRECTORY. 0277-366X. US. English. Guildord County Genealogical Society, PO Box 9693, Greensboro NC 27408. LC F253. DD 929.375662.

SURVEYS, POLLS, CENSUSES, AND FORECASTS DIRECTORY. VFOAT Surveys, Polls, Censuses & Forecasts Directory. Issue No. 1 (Oct. 1983)-. 0737-545X. Periodical. US. English. ty. Gale Research Company, Penobscot Building, Detroit MI 48226. LC Z7554.U5, HA203. DD 016.0014330973. Provides access to a wide range of surveys, polls censuses, and forecasts that are available through public and private organizations.

SVENSK EXEGETISK ARSBOK. Began with Vol. for 1936. SW. Multilingual (English and Swedish). an. 100. Liber International, S-205 10 Malmo Sweden. Tel 46-40-70650. Ind/Abst Old Testam. Abstr., New Testam. Abstr. LC BS410. bk rev.

SVENSK FORSAKRINGS-ARSBOK. VFOAT Swedish Insurance Year-Book. Began with Vol. for 1916. Swedish. ir. 50.00. Svenska Forsakringsforeningen, Kungsgatan 4B I1 111 43, Stockholm Sweden. LC HG5621.

SVENSK GEOGRAFISK ARSBOK. VFOAT Swedish Geographical Yearbook. Vol. 1- 1925-. 0081-9808. SW. Swedish. ir. Gleerupska Univ Bokhandelns, Forlag AB Fack, 221 01 Lund 1 Sweden. Ind/Abst GeoRef. CODEN SGGAAY. (cum index).

SVENSK INDUSTRIKALENDER. VFOAT Swedish Industrial Directory. English or Swedish. ir. P A Norstedt Etc, Box 2052, 103 12 2 Stockholm Sweden. LC HF3673.

SWEDISH EXPORT DIRECTORY. VFOAT Annuaire de l'Exportation Suedoise. Began with 28th Ed. in 1946. 0280-4344. SW. English. an. Swedish Trade Council, Box 551 3, S-11485 Stockholm Sweden. Tel 4687838500. LC HF3673. DD 382.6025485. Circ 20,000. Directory of Swedish manufacturers and exporters with indices in English, French, German and Spanish. *Svensk Exportkalender.*

SWIFT'S . . . EDUCATIONAL SOFTWARE DIRECTORY. VFOAT Educational Software Directory. 1982-83-. US. English. an. Sterling Swift Publishing Company, 7901 South I-35, Austin TX 78744. Each issue contains an index to its own contents - no vol index - loose. *Educational Software Directory.*

SWISS EXPORT DIRECTORY. 12th- Ed. English. ir. *Directory of Swiss Manufacturers and Producers.*

SYNDICATED COLUMNISTS DIRECTORY. 1982 Ed.-. US. English. an. $30.00. Public Relations Publishing Company Inc, 888 Seventh Avenue, New York NY 10106. Tel (212)582-7373. *Syndicated Columnists.*

SYNERJY; A DIRECTORY OF ENERGY ALTERNATIVES. V.1-. 0163-2183. Periodical. US. English. sa. $15.00. J Twine, PO Box 4790, Grand Central Station, New York NY 10017. Ind/Abst Energy Res. Abstr. LC TJ163.2. DD 333.7.

SYNFUELS PROJECT DIRECTORY. 1981-. 0735-8067. US. English. ir. $125.00. Pasha Publications, 1401 Wilson Boulevard/Suite 910, Arlington VA 22209. Tel (703)528-1244.

SYNTHETIC FUELS AND ALTERNATE ENERGY WORLDWIDE DIRECTORY. (WORLDWIDE SYNTHETIC FUELS AND ALTERNATE ENERGY DIRECTORY). 1st Ed. (1982)-. 0731-2369. US. English. ir. $60.00. Pennwell Publishing Company, PO Box 1260, Tulsa OK 74101. Tel (918)835-3161. Ed William R Leek Jr. LC TP360. DD 333.79025. adv acc. Circ 1,250. Engineering, construction companies and companies that operate synthetic fuels and or alternate energy projects. Divided into education, government and industry. Subject and company index.

TAE NYUYOK CHIGU HANILLOK. VFOAT The Korean Directory of Greater New York. 1980-81-. US. English (Korean). an. Dong-A Daily News Inc, 1261 Broadway/Room 608, New York NY 10001. LC F128.9.K6.

TAFT CORPORATE GIVING DIRECTORY. 1985 Ed.-. 0882-7176. US. English. an. Taft Corporation, 5125 MacArthur Boulevard NW, Washington DC 20016. DD 361. *Taft Corporate Directory, 0732-8958.*

TAI-WAN CHU KUNG SHANG CHI YEH PAO TIEN. VFOAT Mercantile Directory of Taiwan. CH. Chinese (English). an. Hua Weng Chi Yeh Yu Hsien Kung SSU, Taipei Taiwan. LC HC430.5.A1. DD 338.0951249.

TAI-WAN MAO I YAO LAN. VFOAT Taiwan Trade Directory. Began in 1963. Chinese (with appendix in English). ir. Importers & Exporters Association of Taipei, PO Box 598, Tai-pei 104 China. LC HF5237.5.

TAI-WAN NUNG YEH NIEN PAO. VFOAT Taiwan Agricultural Yearbook. 1920-. 0429-1255. English and Chinese. ir. Taiwan Department of

Yearbooks, Almanacs, Directories

Agriculture & Fisheries, Chung Hsing New Villa, Nantou Taiwan. LC S304.F6.

TAIWAN TRADE DIRECTORY. VFOAT Tai-Wan Mao I Yao Lan. Began in 1963. CH. Chinese and English, (1969/70-). ir. Importers & Exporters Association of Taipei, PO Box 598, Taipei 104 China. LC HF5237.5. DD 382.02551249.

TAIWAN YELLOW PAGES. VFOAT Republic of China Business Telephone Directory. CH. English (Chinese). ir. $65.00. Croner Publishing Company, 211-05 Jamaica Avenue, Queens Village NY 11428. Tel (718)464-0866. LC HF3846.8. DD 380.1029451249. Similar to US yellow pages, it lists manufacturers, traders, agents, exporters, importers, service firms. Includes name, address, executives, telex numbers, products handled.

TALK SHOW DIRECTORY. VFOAT Talk Show Directory for Radio and Television. 0731-9134. US. English. LC PN1990.9.T34. DD 791.445.

TALLASU HANIN CHUSO MIT OPSOROK. VFOAT The Korean Directory of Dallas. 0742-7352. US. English (Korean). an. Hanguk Chilsong Inswae, 1701 North Greenville Avenue/#1001, Richardson TX 75081. LC E184.K6.

TALON (WASHINGTON, D.C.). (TALON). US. English. $20.00. Editor-in-Chief of the Talon, American University/Room 228 Mary Graydon Center, Washington DC 20016. Tel (202)885-1420. Ed Denise DiStefano. LC LD131.A85. DD 378.753. adv acc. Circ 600. Comprehensive coverage of the year's events at the American University. Includes exceptional photography and copy.

THE TAMPA BAY SUNCOAST BUSINESS DIRECTORY. 1983-84 Ed.-. 0736-4652. US. English. an. $120.00. ABC-CLIO Information Services Inc, 2040 Alameda Padre Serra, PO Box 4397, Santa Barbara CA 93103. LC HF5065.F6. DD 380.102947596.

TANZANIA IMPORT, EXPORT DIRECTORY. 1st- 1975-. TZ. English. ir. Tanzania National Bank of Commerce, City Drive, PO Box 9062, Dar Es Salaam Tanzania. LC HF3914.T3. DD 382.025678.

TAPION VUOSIKIRJA. Main/Corp Keskusemtsalautakunta Tapio. VFOAT Tapio's Yearbook. Finnish (summaries in English). ir. LC SD217.F5. DD 333.7509471.

TASMANIAN YEAR BOOK. No. 1- 1967-. 0082-2116. AT. English. ir. 22.70. Australian Bureau of Statistics, Commonwealth Government Centre 3rd Floor, 188 Collins Street, Hobart Tasmania 7000 Australia. Tel (002)29 9409. LC HA3111. DD 319.46. Contains information on history and chronology, physical environment, public finance, demography, agriculture, government and administration.

TEA DIRECTORY. 1966-. II. English. ir. 16.00. Tea Board, 14 Brabourne Road, Calcutta 1 India. LC HD9195.A1. DD 380.14137202554. All-India Tea Directory.

THE TEACHER BROTHERS MODERN-DAY ALMANAC. 1979- Ed. 0733-6136. US. English. an. Running Press, 125 South 22nd Street, Philadelphia PA 19103.

TECHNICAL MANUAL AND YEAR BOOK OF THE AMERICAN ASSOCIATION OF TEXTILE CHEMISTS AND COLORISTS. Vol. 24 (1947/48)-V. 33. US. English. an. $63.00. American Association of Textile Chemists Color, PO Box 12215, Research Triangle Park NC 27709. Tel (919)549-8141. Circ 1,400. Compilation of AATCC test methods plus AATCC research and administrative committee rosters and reports. Year Book of the American Association of Textile Chemists and Colorists.

TECHNICIAN EDUCATION YEARBOOK. 1963/64-. 0082-2353. US. English. be. Prakken Publications, PO Box 8623, Ann Arbor MI 48107. Tel (313)769-1211. LC T73. DD 607.1073.

TEKSTIILITEOLLISUUDEN VUOSIKIRJA. TEXTILINDUSTRINS ARSBOK. VFOAT Textilindustrins Arsbok, The Textile Industry Yearbook. Finnish (Swedish, with summaries in English). ir. Tekstiiliteollisuuden Tyonantajialiitio, Aleksis Kivenkatu 10 33210, Tampere 21 Finland. LC TS1395.F5.

TELECOMMUNICATIONS SYSTEMS AND SERVICES DIRECTORY. Issue No. 1 (July 1983)- 1st Ed.-. 0738-3045. US. English. ir. $240.00. Gale Research Company, Book Tower, Detroit MI 48226. Tel (800)521-0707. Ed Martin Connors. LC TK5102.5. DD 384.025. Detailed descriptions and complete contact information on today's high technology communications systems and services.

THE TELECONFERENCING DIRECTORY. US. English. an. $30.00. Center Interactive Programs, 610 Langdon Street, Howell Hall, Madison WI 53703. Tel (608)262-4554.

TELEGEN INDEX AND YEARBOOK. VFOAT Index and Yearbook. 1982-. 8755-2493. Periodical. US. English. an. EIC/Intelligence, 48 West 38th Street, New York NY 10018. Tel (212)944-8500. Ed Laura Weiss. DD 574. (cum index). A biotechnology information system including a database, monthly journal and annual index, and covering the biotech field through abstracts of research articles, conferences and patents.

TELEPHONE AND SERVICE DIRECTORY. Main/Corp National Institutes of Health (U.S.). VFOAT NIH Telephone and Service Directory. Periodical. US. English. ty. National Institutes of Health, 9000 Rockville Pike, Bethesda MD 20014.

TELEPHONE DIRECTORY CEASED. Main/Corp United States. Congress. Senate. VFOAT Senate Telephone Directory. Ceased with May 1982. US. English. sa. Superintendent of Documents, US Government Printing Office, Washington DC 20402.

TELEPHONE DIRECTORY. Main/Corp U.S. Nuclear Regulatory Commission. US. English. sa. Superintendent of Documents, US Government Printing Office, Washington DC 20402. Tel (202)783-3238.

TELEPHONE DIRECTORY. Main/Corp World Bank. US. English. qt. $20.00. World Bank Publications, 1818 H Street NW, Washington DC 20433. Tel (202)473-2937. A key guide to world bank staff and organization, as well as to embassies and legislations in Washington, D.C.

TELEPHONE DIRECTORY. Main/Corp United States. Dept. of State. Began with Spring 1980. US. English. an. Superintendent of Documents, US Government Printing Office, Washington DC 20402. Telephone Directory. Department of State, International Development Cooperation Agency, Agency for International Development, Arms Control and Disarmament Agency, Overseas Private Investment C.

TELEPHONE DIRECTORY. Main/Corp United States. Dept. of Health and Human Services. VFOAT Directory. Began with Spring 1980. US. English. an. Superintendent of Documents, US Government Printing Office, Washington DC 20402. Telephone Directory (United States. Dept. of Health, Education, and Welfare), 0276-1238.

TELEPHONE DIRECTORY. Main/Corp Geological Survey (U.S.). Central Region. US. English. US Geological Survey Central Region, Box 25046 Denver Federal Center, Denver CO 80225.

TELEPHONE DIRECTORY. Main/Corp United States Postal Service. US. English. US Postal Service Headquarters, Washington DC 20260.

TELEPHONE DIRECTORY (BRITISH COLUMBIA : GREATER VANCOUVER AND AREA). (TELEPHONE DIRECTORY). VFOAT Telephone Directory for Greater Vancouver and Area. Oct. 1981 Ed. -. 0710-8265. Periodical. CN. English. Province of British Columbia, 1450 Government Street, Information Service, Victoria British Columbia V8W 3E7 Canada. DD 354.71100025.

TELEPHONE DIRECTORY, CENTRAL OFFICE AND NATIONAL CAPITAL REGION. Main/Corp United States. General Services Administration. 1980-. US. English. an. General Services Administration, Automated Data and Telecommunications Service, Washington DC 20402. Telephone Directory, Central Office, National Capital Region, and Region 3.

TELEPHONE DIRECTORY CENTRAL OFFICE AND REGION 3. Main/Corp United States. General Services Administration. VFOAT Telephone Directory - General Services Administration:. US. English. ir. US General Services Administration, Automated Data and Telecommunications Service, Washington DC 20402.

TELEPHONE DIRECTORY - DEPARTMENT OF DEFENSE. (TELEPHONE DIRECTORY). Main/Corp United States. Department of Defense. 0363-6844. US. English. ty. $24.00. Superintendent of Documents, US Government Printing Office, Washington DC 20402. Tel (202)783-3238. LC UA23.2. DD 353.6.

TELEPHONE DIRECTORY - ENVIRONMENTAL PROTECTION AGENCY CEASED. (TELEPHONE DIRECTORY). Main/Corp United States. Environmental Protection Agency. Began with 1971. Ceased with supplemental summer 1983 updated alphabetical directory. Periodical. US. English. sa. US Environmental Protection Agency, 401 M Street SW, Washington DC 20460.

TELEPHONE DIRECTORY. MANITOBA GOVERNMENT. (MANITOBA GOVERNMENT TELEPHONE DIRECTORY). VFOAT Telephone Directory - Manitoba Government. Began with Feb. 1974 issue?. 0318-0255. Periodical. CN. English. sa. Winnepeg Department of Public Works, Box 6666, Winnipeg Manitoba R3C 3V6 Canada. DD 354.712700025.

TELEPHONE ENGINEER & MANAGEMENT DIRECTORY. VFOAT Telephone Engineer's Composite Catalog & Buyers' Directory. Began publication in 1936?. US. English. an. Harcourt Brace Jovanovich Publications, 402 West Liberty Drive, Wheaton IL 60187. LC TK6195.

TELEPHONY'S DIRECTORY & BUYERS' GUIDE FOR THE TELEPHONE INDUSTRY. VAT Telephony's Directory and Buyers' Guide for the Telephone Industry. 0196-139X. US. English. an. Telephony Publishing Corporation, 55 East Jackson Boulevard, Chicago IL 60604. LC TK6011. DD 338.47621385025. Telephony's Directory of the Telephone Industry.

TELEX DANMARK. VFOAT Annuaire des Abonnes Telex du Danemark. DK. Danish. ir. Generaldirektoratet for Postog Telegrafvaesenet, Teletjeneste Farvergade 17, 1007 Kbenhavn K Denmark. LC HE8233.

TELEX DIRECTORY. VFOAT RCA Telex Directory. 0091-3170. US. English, French, German, and Spanish. RCA Global Communications, 60 Broad Street, New York NY 10004. LC HE7621. DD 384.102573.

TELEX DIRECTORY (WELLINGTON, N.Z.). (TELEX DIRECTORY). English. ir. LC HE8620.5. DD 384.14.

TENNESSEE ATTORNEYS DIRECTORY. 1982-. 0742-4329. US. English. an. $24.50. M Lee Smith Publishers & Printers, PO Box 2678, Arcade Station, Nashville TN 37219. Tel (615)242-7395. Ed Mary Ellen Henry. LC KF192.T4. DD 340.025768. adv acc. Circ 2,000. A complete, accurate, and east-to-use listing of all Tennessee attorneys and law firms.

TENNESSEE DIRECTORY OF MANUFACTURERS. 1978-. 0196-5360. US. English. an. $75.00. Manufacturers News Inc, 4 East Huron Street, Chicago IL 60611. Tel (312)337-1084. Contains an alphabetical guide, country-town index, city guide, SIC index, address, telephone number, officers names and employee figure. Tennessee Manufacturers Directory, 0360-5477.

TENNESSEE DIRECTORY OF SERVICES FOR THE DEVELOPMENTALLY DISABLED. VFOAT Directory of Services for the Developmentally Disabled. 0146-5732. US. English. Tennessee-Peabody Referral and Information Center, Box 40, Peabody College 37203. LC HV3006.T35. DD 362.3025768.

TENNESSEE EXPORT/IMPORT TRADE DIRECTORY. VFOAT Tennessee Export Import Trade Directory. 1979-. Periodical. US. English. ir. 1018 Andrew Jackson State Office Building, Nashville TN 37219.

TENNESSEE LABOR MARKET INFORMATION DIRECTORY. VFOAT Labor Market Information Directory. 0749-9930. US. English. 519 Cordell Hull Building, Nashville TN 37219. DD 331.

TERMINUS BUSINESS DIRECTORY. V. 1- 1976-. 0362-1995. US. English. an. $156.00. 1720 Peachtree Road NW, Atlanta GA 30309. LC HF5068.A75. DD 381.025758231.

TESOL MEMBERSHIP DIRECTORY. Main/Corp Teachers of English to Speakers of Other Languages. Began with Issue for 1972. 0730-9325. US. English. an. Tesol, 202 D C Transit Building, Georgetown University, Washington DC 20057. LC PE1128.A2. DD 428.24025.

Yearbooks, Almanacs, Directories

TEXAS AGRICULTURAL EXPORT DIRECTORY. 0735-1542. US. English. Texas Department of Agriculture, PO Box 12847, Austin TX 78711. LC HD9007.T4. DD 382.410294764.

TEXAS AIRPORT DIRECTORY. US. English. an. Free. Aeronautics Commission, Box 12607/Capitol Station, Austin TX 78711. LC TL726.3.T4. DD 629.136025764. *Directory of Texas Airports.*

TEXAS ALMANAC AND STATE INDUSTRIAL GUIDE. VFOAT Texas Almanac. 1857-. 0363-4248. US. English. be. $8.95. Dallas Morning News, PO Box 225237, Dallas TX 75265. Tel (214)977-8261. Ed Mike Kingston. LC AY311.G3. adv acc. Circ 100,000. The almanac strives to present an accurate statistical picture of Texas.

TEXAS BUILDERS AND CONTRACTORS DIRECTORY. 0731-4035. US. English. Gulfstream Publishing Company, 8751 West Broward Boulevard, Fort Lauderdale FL 33324. LC TH13.T4. DD 338.47690025764.

TEXAS BUSINESS EDUCATION ASSOCIATION YEARBOOK. 0196-3198. US. English. an. Texas Business Education Association, 6534 Lindy Ann Lane, Houston TX 77008. LC HF1101. DD 658.0070764.

TEXAS CERTIFIED SEED DIRECTORY. 1971-. 0095-1927. US. English. an. LC SB113.4. DD 338.17. *Texas Seed Directory.*

TEXAS COLLEGIATE EDUCATION DIRECTORY. 1976/77-. 0145-4242. US. English. CSPS Foundation, 359 East Hildebrand, San Antonio TX 78212. LC L903.T4. DD 378.764.

TEXAS HUNTER'S DIRECTORY. 0748-9854. US. English. an. Ourtood Worlds of Texas Inc, 1647 South Alameda, Corpus Christi TX 78404. Tel (512)882-2953.

TEXAS LEGAL DIRECTORY. 1935-. US. English. ir. Texas Legal Directory, 700 Campbell Center, PO Box 64805, Dallas TX 75206. LC KF192.T45. DD 340.025764.

TEXAS PUBLISHERS & PUBLICATIONS DIRECTORY. VAT Texas Publishers and Publications Directory. V. 1- 1980-. 0197-5358. US. English. an. $6.95. S & S Press, PO Box 5931, Austin TX 78763. LC PN161. DD 070.5209764.

TEXAS SAVINGS & LOAN DIRECTORY. VFOAT Savings & Loans. US. English. sa. $19.95. Legislative Associates, PO Box 12186/Capitol Station, Austin TX 78711. Tel (512)477-5698. Ed Scott Sayers. adv acc. Listing of all savings and loans in Texas with addresses and phone numbers. Lists all their financial information.

TEXAS SCHOOL DIRECTORY. 1975/76-. 0363-4566. US. English. an. $5.26. Texas Education Agency, 201 East 11th Street, Austin TX 78701. Tel (512)475-2268. Ed Barbara Walters. LC L903.T4. DD 371.01025764. Texas ISD addresses, superintendent, principal, enrollment statistics, telephone numbers, all Texas education agency personnel phone numbers, all accredited private schools. *Public School Directory.*

TEXAS STATE DIRECTORY. 0363-7530. US. English. an. $21.95. Texas State Directory, Box 12186, Capitol Station, Austin TX 78711. Tel (512)477-5698. Ed Scott Sayers. LC JK4830. DD 328.764. adv acc. Circ 12,000. (ctrl). We publish Texas savings and loan directory, Texas legislative handbook, and Texas legislative manual.

TGC TYPEFACE DIRECTORY. Main/Corp Typographics Communications, Inc. VFOAT Typeface Directory. US. English. ir. Typographers Association of New York Inc, 461 Eigth Avenue, New York NY 10001.

THAI BUILDER DIRECTORY. VFOAT Khum Sathapanik Witsawakon L Naichang. TH. English (Thia). an. $18.00. Gemini International Services, 116/340 Mooban Pricha Soi 1, Bangkok 10110 Thailand. Tel 2519016. LC HD9715.T48. DD 380.145624025593.

THAI INDUSTRIAL DIRECTORY. VFOAT Thai Indatsatrian Dairekthori. English (and Thai). an. $18.00. Gemini International Services, 116/340 Mooban Pricha Soi 1, Bangkok 10110 Thailand. Tel 25119016. LC HC497.S5. DD 380.1025593.

THAILAND INVESTMENT HANDBOOK AND DIRECTORY OF PROMOTED COMPANIES. Periodical. English. an. Business Information and Research Company Ltd, 2948A Soi Somprasong 3, Petchburi Road, Bangkok Thailand. LC HG5750.55.A2. DD 332.6732259305. *Thailand Investment Handbook.*

THAILAND MANUFACTURERS AND PRODUCTS DIRECTORY. 1977-. TH. English. ir. 300.00. Fareast Media Center, Suite 202 Asvahem Building 179 Suriwongse Road, Bangkok Thailand. LC T12.5.T47. DD 338.4767025593.

THAILAND TRAVEL TRADE YEARBOOK. VFOAT Travel Trade Yearbook. English. ir. Media Transasia Thailand Ltd, 3rd Floor Sarasia Building, 14 Surasak Road, Bangkok Thailand. LC DS566.2. DD 915.93044405.

THAILAND'S COMMODITY EXPORTS DIRECTORY. English (Thai). an. Sarnprachachon Company, 150/19 Lanluang Road, Bangkok Thailand. LC HF3800.55.A48. DD 382.60294593.

THE ROCK YEAR BOOK. VFOAT Rock Yearbook. 1981-. 0275-9187. US. English. an. $12.95. Grove Press, 80 University Place, New York NY 10003. LC ML3533.8. DD 784.54005.

THEATRE CRAFTS DIRECTORY. 1979/80-. US. English. an. National Fulfillment Services, 100 Pine Street, Holmes PA 19043. Tel (212)677-5997. bk rev. adv acc. Circ 27,500. Covers theatre, film and video for the professional with the emphasis on how things get done: lighting, sound, costume design, make-up, construction, etc. *Theatre Crafts.*

THEATRE DIRECTORY. 1973. 0271-3136. US. English. an. $5.64. Theatre Communication Group, 355 Lexington Avenue, New York NY 10017. Tel (212)697-5230. LC PN2289. DD 792029575. Circ 4,000. Contact information for nearly 300 nonprofit professional theatres and related art organizations across the US.

THEATRE DIRECTORY OF THE SAN FRANCISCO BAY AREA. 1983-84-. 0737-0172. Periodical. US. English. be. $9.00. Theatre Communications Center of the Bay Area, 2940 16th Street/Suite 102, San Francisco CA 94103. LC PN2275.C3. DD 790.2097946. *Theatre Directory of the Bay Area, 0730-9260.*

THEOLOGIA VIATORUM (BERLIN, GERMANY) CEASED. (THEOLOGIA VIATORUM : JAHRBUCH DER KIRCHLICHEN HOCHSCHULE BERLIN). Began with 1 (1948/49)-. Ceased with V. 15 (1979/80). German. ir. LC BR10. DD 230.05.

THOMAS HARDY YEAR BOOK. (THE THOMAS HARDY YEAR BOOK). VAT Thomas Hardy Yearbook. No. 1- 1970-. 0082-416X. UK. English. an. Toucan Press, Birling Mt Durand, St Peter Port Guernsey CI England. Ind/Abst MLA Int. Bibliogr. Books Artic. Mod. Lang. Lit., Years Work Eng. Stud. LC PR4752. DD 823.8.

THE THORNDIKE ENCYCLOPEDIA OF BANKING AND FINANCIAL TABLES. YEARBOOK. (THORNDIKE ENCYCLOPEDIA OF BANKING AND FINANCIAL TABLES. YEARBOOK). VFOAT Encyclopedia of Banking and Financial Tables. 0196-7762. US. English. an. Warren Gorham & Lamont, 210 South Street, Boston MA 02111. LC HG1626. DD 332.820212.

TIDEWATER EVENTS CALENDAR/ALMANAC. 0740-0616. Periodical. US. English. an. Design Initiatives, PO Box 1101, Virginia Beach VA 23451.

TIDINGS INTERNATIONAL BUSINESS DIRECTORY. VFOAT Tidings Directory. 1982-. English. ir. 20.00. Tidings Publications, PO Box 425, New Delhi 110001 India. Tel (0)352045. Ed K Srinivasan. LC HC435.2. DD 330.954005. adv acc. Circ 3,000. Projects strength of Indian economy treated in publication are budget, taxation, industry, commerce, nonresident Indian interests, recent liberalisation steps, procedures for industry formation and guidelines.

TIMBER MART-SOUTH YEARBOOK. (TIMBER MART-SOUTH ... YEARBOOK). VFOAT Timber Mart South ... Yearbook. 1983-. 0882-732X. US. English. an. $125.00. Data Resources Inc, Attn J Hussey, 24 Hartwell Avenue, Lexington MA 02173. LC HD9757.A13. DD 338.134980975.

TIMES BUSINESS DIRECTORY OF SINGAPORE. 1984-. English. an. 60.00. Times Periodicals Pte Ltd, Times Centre 1 New Industrial Road, Singapore 1953 Singapore. Tel 284-8844. LC HF3800.6.Z8. DD 338.740255957. adv acc. Circ 45,000. (ctrl). *Straits Times Directory of Singapore.*

THE TIMES OF INDIA DIRECTORY AND YEAR BOOK INCLUDING WHO'S WHO. 1914-. 0082-4445. UK. English. an. Bennett Coleman & Company Ltd, 26 Station Approach, Sudbury Wembley Middlesex HA0 2LA England. Tel (01)903-9696. LC DS405. DD 915.4.

THE TIMES YEARBOOK OF WORLD AFFAIRS. VFOAT Yearbook of World Affairs. 1978-. UK. English. an. Times Books, Golden Square, London W1R 4BN England. Ed D Hunt. LC D839. DD 909.82.

TM, TRADEMARK DIRECTORY. VFOAT Trademark Directory. 0148-3498. US. English. National Paint and Boatings Association, Trademark Bureau, 1500 Rhode Island Avenue NW, Washington DC 20005. LC T223.V4. DD 929.

TOLL FREE SHOP-AT-HOME PHONE DIRECTORY. (TOLL-FREE SHOP-AT-HOME PHONE DIRECTORY). 0734-550X. US. English. an. $6.95. Celebrity Publishing Inc, PO Box 98, Suffern NY 10901. LC HF5465.5. DD 381.1402573.

TOLL-FREE TRAVEL/VACATION PHONE DIRECTORY. VFOAT Travel/Vacation Phone Directory. 0739-1420. US. English. an. $6.95. Celebrity Publications Inc, PO Box 98, Suffern NY 10901. LC G155.U6. DD 381.4591730402573.

TONGGYE YONBO (SUNCHON-SI, KOREA). (TONGGYE YONBO). VFOAT Sun Cheon Statistical Year Book. Korean. an. Sunchon-si, 5-5 Changchon-dong, Sunchon-si Korea. LC HA4630.5.Z9.

TORONTO & AREA AIRPORT BUSINESS DIRECTORY. VFOAT Toronto Airport Directory. VAT Airport Business Directory (1984). 1983/84-. 0822-7748. CN. English. an. 3.50. Toronto & Area Airport Business Directory, Suite 158/1224-53 Avenue Northeast, Calgary Alberta T2E 7E2 Canada. Tel (403)275-9457. Ed Paul J Skinner. DD 387.7364025713541. adv acc. Circ 7,000. (ctrl). *Toronto Airport Business Directory, 0714-8593.*

TORONTO & AREA CONSTRUCTION INDUSTRY DIRECTORY PURCHASING GUIDE. (TORONTO & AREA CONSTRUCTION INDUSTRY DIRECTORY, PURCHASING GUIDE). VAT Annual Toronto & Area Construction Industry Directory Purchising Guide. 1979-. 0707-5251. CN. English. an. $8.00. Sanford Evans Publishing Ltd, 1077 St James Street, Winnipeg Manitoba R3C 3B1 Canada. DD 338.47690025713541.

TORONTO LEGAL DIRECTORY. VFOAT Toronto Legal Directory (Metropolitan List) and Tariff guide. Began with 1925 issue. 0317-588X. Periodical. CN. English. an. University of Toronto Press, University of Toronto Front Campus, Toronto Ontario M5S 1A6 Canada. DD 340.025713541.

TOSHO SHINYOROKU. KANTO-BAN. *See Business.*

TOURS AND VISITS DIRECTORY. 2nd Ed.-. 0278-467X. US. English. Gale Research Company, Book Tower, Detroit MI 48226. LC T49.5. DD 917.304927. Over 2,500 entries describe free and low-cost tours available on-site from business, industry, and government. *Behind the Scenes, 0270-3416.*

TOXICOLOGY RESEARCH PROJECTS DIRECTORY CEASED. Series/Titl DHEW Publication. Began with V. 1, No. 1 (Jan. 1976). Ceased with V. 5, No. 12 (Dec. 1980). 0362-3211. US. English. mo. National Technical Information Service, 5285 Port Royal Road, Springfield VA 22161. LC RA1199. DD 615.90072073. NLM QV 22 AA1 T7. Each issue contains an index to its own contents - no vol index - loose. (cum index).

TOY AND DECORATION FAIR. (DIRECTORY - CANADIAN TOY & DECORATION FAIR). Main/Corp Canadian Toy and Decoration Fair. 33d- 1973-. 0317-9443. Periodical. CN. English (includes some text in French). an. Canadian Toy Manufacturing Association, Box 294, Kleinburg Ontario Canada. Tel (416)893-1689. DD 338.476887202571. *Official Directory, 0068-9890.*

TOY TRADER YEAR BOOK. UK. English. 3.10. 157 Hagden Lane, Watford WD1 8LW England. LC HD9999.T7. DD 338.476887202541.

TRACTION YEARBOOK. 1981-. 0730-5400. US. English. an. Traction Slides International, Box 123, Bank Plaza Station, Merrick NY 11566. Ed

Yearbooks, Almanacs, Directories

Joseph P Saitta. **LC** TF701. **DD** 388.4205. *Traction Fan's Directory, 0496-0076.*

TRADE AND INDUSTRIAL DIRECTORY OF NEPAL. English. ir. Adri Trade Link, 355 Gucha Tole, Kathmandu Nepal. **LC** HF3861.N42. **DD** 380.10255496.

TRADE AND PROFESSIONAL ASSOCIATIONS IN CALIFORNIA : A DIRECTORY. 1st-. US. English. ir. $22.50. California Institute of Public Affairs, PO Box 10, Claremont CA 91711-0010. **Tel** (714)625-5527. **LC** HD2428.C3. Each issue contains an index to its own contents - no vol index - loose. A unique guide to sources of help and information on hundreds of topics ranging from accounting and banking to yachts and zoologists.

TRADE DIRECTORIES OF THE WORLD. 1st- Ed. 0564-0482. US. English. ir. $69.85. Croner Publications, 211-05 Jamaica Avenue, Queens Village NY 11428. **Tel** (718)464-0866. **LC** Z5771. **DD** 016.38. Directory listing trade, industrial and professional directories. Valuable information for importers and exporters.

TRADE DIRECTORY. **VFOAT** Malta Chamber of Commerce—Trade Directory. 1978/79-. English. an. 3.50. Malta Chamber of Commerce, Exchange Buildings, Republic Street, Valletta Malta. **Tel** 624183,627233. **Ed** J G Vassallo. **LC** HF328.M3. **DD** 380.10254585. adv acc. **Circ** 1,500. Exclusive reference source on the Malta economy and the Maltese business community. *Malta Trade Directory.*

TRADE DIRECTORY - COMMERCIAL BANK OF ETHIOPIA S. C. **Main/Corp** Yaityopya Negd Bank. English. ir. Commercial Bank of Ethiopia, Haile Selassie I Square, PO Box 255, Addis Ababa Ethiopia. **LC** HF3931.E8. **DD** 380.102563.

TRADE DIRECTORY OF PAKISTAN. English. ir. Lahore Chamber of Commerce & Industry, 11 Sharae Aiwan-I-Tijarat, PO Box No 597, Lahore Pakistan. **LC** HF3790.5.A48. **DD** 380.10255491.

TRADESHOW WEEK'S MAJOR EXHIBIT HALL DIRECTORY. **VFOAT** Major Exhibit Hall Directory. US. English. an. $25.00. Tradeshow Week, PO Box 716, Back Bay Annex, Boston MA 02117. **LC** NA6750.A2. **DD** 725.9102573. *Annual Major Exhibit Hall Directory, 0160-8630.*

TRADESHOW WEEK'S NATIONAL TRADESHOW SERVICES DIRECTORY. **VFOAT** National Tradeshow Services Directory. 0733-8767. US. English. an. $35.00. Tradeshow Week, 12233 West Olympic Boulevard/Suite 236, Los Angeles CA 90064. **LC** AS6. **DD** 061.3.

TRADO, ASIAN AFRICAN DIRECTORY OF EXPORTERS-IMPORTERS & MANUFACTURERS. US. English. ir. Taylor & Francis Inc, 242 Cherry Street, Philadelphia PA 19106. **Tel** (215)238-0939. *Trade Asian Directory of Exporters, Importers & Manufacturers.*

TRAILER LIFE'S RV CAMPGROUND & SERVICES DIRECTORY. **VFOAT** RV Campground & Services Directory. **VAT** Trailer Life's Recreational Vehicle Campground and Services Directory. 9th- 1975-. 0099-0191. US. English. an. $5.95. Trailer Life Publishing Company, 23945 Craftsman Road, Calabasas CA 91302. **LC** GV198.56. **DD** 647.947. *Trailer Life's Recreational Vehicle Campground and Services Guide.*

TRAINING AND DEVELOPMENT ORGANIZATIONS DIRECTORY. See Business - Personnel Management.

TRANSACTIONS AND DIRECTORY. **Main/Corp** Ohio College Association. English. ir. *Transactions of the Annual Meeting of the Ohio College Association, 0731-793X.*

TRANSLATION SERVICES DIRECTORY. 0738-4750. US. English. American Translators Association, 109 Croton Avenue, Ossining NY 10562. **Tel** (914)941-1500. **Ed** Justus Ernst. adv acc. **Circ** 1,000. Names, addresses, background and services available of 600-700 translators and interpreters. *Professional Services Directory of the American Translators Association.*

TRANSLATOR REFERRAL, TRANSLATION SERVICES DIRECTORY. **VAT** Translator Referral/Translation Services Directory. 1982-. 0730-3327. US. English. an. $12.50. Translation Research Institute, 5914 Pulaski Avenue, Philadelphia PA 19144. **LC** P306.A1. **DD** 418.0202573. *Translator Referral Directory, 0096-3259.*

TRAVEL INDUSTRY PERSONNEL DIRECTORY. **VFOAT** Travel Agent Personnel Directory. Began publication in 1954?. 0082-6146. US. English. an. $12.00. Travel Industry Personnel, 2 West 46th Street, New York NY 10036.

TRAVEL INDUSTRY WORLD YEARBOOK. **VFOAT** Big Picture. Vol. 27 (1983)-. 0738-9515. US. English. ir. $52.00. Child & Waters, 516 5th Avenue, New York NY 10036. **Tel** (212)840-1935. **Ed** Somerset R Waters. **LC** G155.A1. **DD** 380.1459104. Travel industry statistics for US and foreign countries. Latest trend information for airlines, hotels, rental cars, cruise ships, travel agencies, ad country receipts. *Big Picture (New York, N.Y.).*

TRAVEL TRADE DIRECTORY. 1982-. UK. English. an. 18.00. Morgan Grampian, 30 Calderwood Street, London SE18 6QH England. **Tel** (01)855-7777. **LC** G155.G7. **DD** 380.145910402541. adv acc. **Circ** 5,000. A complete single-volume guide to the travel trade. *United Kingdom & Ireland Travel Trade Directory.*

TRAVELER'S ALMANAC. 2D- Ed. 0161-8075. US. English. an. $7.95. B Muster, 6900 Santa Monica Boulevard, Los Angeles CA 90038. **LC** G153.4. **DD** 910.202. *World Traveler's Almanac, 0161-8083.*

TRAVELER'S TOLL-FREE TELEPHONE DIRECTORY. **VAT** Traveler's Toll Free Telephone Directory. 0146-5988. US. English. $2.25. Landmark Publishers, Box 3287, Burlington VT 05401. **LC** TX907. **DD** 647.9473.

TRINIDAD & TOBAGO BUSINESS & INDUSTRIAL CLASSIFIED DIRECTORY. **VFOAT** Trinidad and Tobago Business and Industrial Classified Directory. English. ir. Graphic Design Ltd, PO Box 591 3 Keate Street, Port-of-Spain Trinidad West Indies. **LC** HF3364.T7. **DD** 380.1029472983. *Trinidad and Tobago Directory of Commerce, Industry & Tourism.*

TRINIDAD AND TOBAGO BUSINESS DIRECTORY AND GUIDE TO THE LOME CONVENTION. **VFOAT** Guide to Lome Convention. TR. English. an. Trinidad and Tobago Manufacturers Association, 20 Herbert Street, St Clair Port-of-Spain, Trinidad West Indies. **LC** HF3365. **DD** 338.7402572983.

TRUCK BROKER DIRECTORY. 0362-5737. US. English. ir. J J Keller & Associates Inc, 145 West Wisconsin Avenue, Neenah WI 54956. **LC** HE5623.A1. **DD** 388.32402573.

TRUCKER'S ALMANAC. 1984-. 0743-5525. US. English. an. $7.95. J J Keller & Associates Inc, 145 West Wisconsin Avenue, Neenah WI 54956. **LC** HE5623. **DD** 388.3240973.

TRURO AND DISTRICT, NOVA SCOTIA, CITY DIRECTORY. **VFOAT** Truro and District, Including Bible Hill, Onslow and Salmon River, City Directory. **VAT** Truro and District Including Bible Hill, Onslow and Salmon River City Directory. 1980-. 0227-8464. Periodical. CN. English. ir. $55.00 Each Number. Might Directories, 220 Bartley Drive, Toronto Ontario M4A 2N4 Canada. **DD** 917.1612. *Might's Truro and District, Nova Scotia, City Directory, 0700-4575.*

TRY US : NATIONAL MINORITY BUSINESS DIRECTORY. 1981-. US. English. an. $31.00. National Minority Business Campaign, 65 22nd Avenue NE, Minneapolis MN 55418. **Tel** (612)781-6819. adv acc. **Circ** 8,000. National directory of minority businesses; approximately 5,000 firms organized under 83 product/service categories. *Try Us.*

TTG ASIA YEARBOOK. **VFOAT** Asia Yearbook. 1st- Ed. English. ir. $4.50. TTG Asia Ltd, 7th Floor Willington Building, 20 Bideford Road, Singapore 9 Singapore. **LC** G154. **DD** 338.7619150442025.

TURKEY YEAR BOOK. **VAT** Turkey Yearbook. 0161-8903. US. English. an. $10.00. D Uluc, 18 West 56th Street, New York NY 10019. **LC** DR401. **DD** 949.61005.

TURKIYE ISTATISTIK YLLG. **VFOAT** Statistical Yearbook of Turkey. English and Turkish. ir. Turkish State Institute of Statistics, Necatibey Cadessi 114, Ankara Turkey. **LC** HA1911. **NLM** W2 GT8 I8T. *Annuaire Statistique.*

TYOKANSAN KALENTERI. CN. Finnish.

TZU JAN KO HSUEH NIEN CHIEN. **VFOAT** Science Yearbook. CH. Chinese. an. 3.85. Hsin Hua Shu Tien, Shang-Hai fa Hsing so Shang-Hai China. **LC** Q127.C5. **DD** 509.51.

U. S. FOOD PRODUCTS DIRECTORY, THE BLUE BOOK OF FOOD PACKERS AND DISTRIBUTORS. US. English. ir. Gorman Publishing Company, 5725 East River Road, Chicago IL 60631. **LC** HD9003. **DD** 664.058. *California Food Products Directory.*

U/B SPEAKERS BUREAU DIRECTORY. **VFOAT** Speakers Bureau Directory. US. English. an. Speakers Bureau, State University of New York at Buffalo, 516 Capen Hall, Amherst Campus, Buffalo NY 14260. *Speakers' Bureau Directory.*

UBD AUSTRALIA WIDE BUSINESS AND STREET DIRECTORY : BUNDABERG. **Main/Corp** Universal Business Directories (Aust.) Pty. Ltd. AT. English. ir. Universal Business Directories Pty Ltd, Manning and Boundary Streets, South Brisbane 4101 Australia. **LC** HF5293.B86. **DD** 919.432.

UBD AUSTRALIA WIDE BUSINESS AND STREET DIRECTORY : GLADSTONE. **Main/Corp** Universal Business Directories (Aust.) Pty. Ltd. AT. English. ir. Universal Business Directories Pty Ltd, Manning and Boundary Streets, South Brisbane 4101 Australia. **LC** HF5293.G55. **DD** 919.435.

UBD AUSTRALIA WIDE BUSINESS AND STREET DIRECTORY : GOLD COAST. **Main/Corp** Universal Business Directories (Aust.) Pty. Ltd. English. ir. Universal Business Directories Pty Ltd, Manning and Boundary Streets, South Brisbane 4101 Australia. **LC** HF5293.G64. **DD** 919.43.

UBD AUSTRALIA WIDE BUSINESS AND STREET DIRECTORY, NORTH WESTERN QUEENSLAND. **Main/Corp** Universal Business Directories (Aust.) Pty. Ltd. **VFOAT** Business and Street Directory, North Western Queensland. AT. English. ir. Universal Business Directories Pty Ltd, Brisbane Australia. **LC** HF5293.Q43. **DD** 919.4370405.

UBD AUSTRALIA-WIDE BUSINESS AND STREET DIRECTORY. SOUTH AUSTRALIA, SOUTH AND EAST. **VFOAT** U.B.D. Australia-Wide Business and Street Directory. English. an. Universal Business Directories Pty Ltd, 21 Wright Street, South Adelaide Australia. *UBD Australia-Wide Business Guide. South Australia.*

UBD AUSTRALIA-WIDE BUSINESS AND STREET DIRECTORY. TASMANIA. **VFOAT** U.B.D. Australia-Wide Business and Street Directory. English. an. Universal Business Directories Pty Ltd, 24 Thomson Street, South Melbourne 3205 Australia. **LC** HF5310. **DD** 919.460405. *Universal Business Directory for Tasmania.*

UBD AUSTRALIA WIDE BUSINESS AND STREET DIRECTORY : TOOWOOMBA DISTRICT. **Main/Corp** Universal Business Directories (Aust.) Pty. Ltd. AT. English. ir. Universal Business Directories Pty Ltd, Manning and Boundary Streets, South Brisbane 4101 Australia. **LC** HF5293.T66. **DD** 919.433.

UBD AUSTRALIA WIDE BUSINESS AND STREET DIRECTORY : WARWICK, STANTHORPE, GOONDIWINDI, ST. GEORGE. **Main/Corp** Universal Business Directories (Aust.) Pty. Ltd. AT. English. ir. Universal Business Directories Pty Ltd, Manning and Boundary Streets, South Brisbane 4101 Australia. **LC** HF5293.Q43. **DD** 919.433.

UBD BUSINESS & STREET DIRECTORY : BRISBANE, CITY & SUBURBAN. **Main/Corp** Universal Business Directories (Aust.) Pty. Ltd. **VFOAT** Brisbane Business & Street Directory. 45th- Ed. AT. English. an. $18.45. Universal Business Directories, 64 Talavera Road, North Ryde New South Wales 2112 Australia. **LC** HF5305.B7. **DD** 919.4310405. *Universal Business Directory for Brisbane City & Suburbs.*

UBD BUSINESS & STREET DIRECTORY, WESTERN AUSTRALIAN COUNTRY TOWNS. **Main/Corp** Universal Business Directories (W.A.) Pty. Ltd. **VFOAT** Western Australian Country Business and

Yearbooks, Almanacs, Directories

Street Directory. **VAT** Universal Business Directories Business and Street Directory. Western Australian Country Towns. English. ir. Universal Business Directories, 44 Hill Street, Perth 6000 Western Australia. **LC** HF3949.W47. **DD** 919.410405. *Universal Business Directory: Western Australian Country Business Directory.*

UK OFFSORE OIL & GAS DIRECTORY. VFOAT U.K. Offshore Oil & Gas Directory. UK. English. an. Thomas Telfor Ltd, Telford House, PO Box 101, 26/34 Old Street, London EC1P 1JH England. **LC** TN874.G7. **DD** 622.338029441.

ULRICH'S INTERNATIONAL PERIODICALS DIRECTORY. Began with 11th Ed., 1965. 0000-0175. US. English. an. $139.95. R R Bowker Company, PO Box 1807, Ann Arbor MI 48106. **Tel** (212)916-1640. **NLM** Z 6941 U45. Complete directory of all serials and periodicals published worldwide. Full information. *Ulrich's Periodicals Directory.*

UNDERSEA TECHNOLOGY HANDBOOK, DIRECTORY. VFOAT UST Handbook/Directory. 1968-. 0503-1702. US. English. an. Compass Publications Inc, 1117 North 19th Street, Arlington VA 22209. **LC** GC10. **DD** 551.460025.

UNESCO YEARBOOK ON PEACE AND CONFLICT STUDIES. VFOAT Yearbook on Peace and Conflict Studies. 1980-. 0250-779X. US. English. an. Greenwood Press, 88 Post Road West, Westport CT 06881. **LC** JX1904.5. **DD** 327.172072.

UNIFORMED SERVICES ALMANAC. 0503-1982. US. English. an. $2.00. Uniformed Services Almanac, PO Box 76 Department A, Washington DC 20044. **Tel** (703)532-1631. **Ed** Lee E Sharff. **LC** U9. **DD** 355.00973. bk rev. **Circ** 50,000,000. (ctrl). Reference volume on military pay, allowances, entitlements, and benefits for active duty members and their families.

UNIREA. ALMANAC. VFOAT Calendarul. Unirea. US. English (Romanian). an. $3.75. Association of Romanian Catholics of America Inc, 4309 Olcott Avenue, East Chicago IL 46312. **LC** BX4711.41. **DD** 281.5.

UNITED KINGDOM & IRELAND TRAVEL TRADE DIRECTORY CEASED. **VFOAT** Travel Trade Directory. UK. English. an. 4.50. Morgan-Grampian House, Calderwood Street, London SE18 6QH England. **LC** G155.G7. **DD** 338.479102542. *United Kingdom & Eire Travel Trade Directory.*

THE UNITED KINGDOM, THE COMMONWEALTH OF NATIONS, A DIRECTORY OF GOVERNMENTS. VFOAT United Kingdom, The Commonwealth of Nations. V. 1- 1979/81-. 0193-4783. US. English. te. $340.00. Political Research Inc, 16850 Dallas Parkway, Dallas TX 75248. **Tel** (214)931-8827. **Ed** John Clements. **LC** JN248. **DD** 351.00025171241. Comprehensive resource of current facts on 49 member nations of commonwealth, current governer of each in depth coverage includes updates, monthly publication of world events a matching binder.

THE UNITED NATIONS DISARMAMENT YEARBOOK. V. 1- 1976-. US. English. an. $35.00. United Nations Publications, Room A-3315, New York NY 10017. **Tel** (212)754-8302. **LC** JX1974. **DD** 327.17405. Reviews the main developments and negotiations during the year. Covers disarmament, nuclear arms limitations, prohibition of chemical, biological and radiological weapons and reduction of military budget.

UNITED NATIONS JURIDICAL YEARBOOK. 1962-. 0082-8297. US. English. an. $25.00. United Nations Publications, Sales Section/Room A-3315, New York NY 10017. **Tel** (212)754-8302. **LC** JX1977. **DD** 341.2305. Documentary texts of treaties and other materials concerning the legal status and activities of the United Nations and related inter-governmental organizations.

U.S. BIOTECHNOLOGY COMPANY INTELLIGENCE REPORT. *See* Biology.

UNITED STATES COURT DIRECTORY (UNITED STATES. ADMINISTRATIVE OFFICE OF THE UNITED STATES COURTS). (UNITED STATES COURT DIRECTORY). 0162-8674. US. English. sa. Superintendent of Documents, US Government Printing Office, Washington DC 20402. **LC** KF8700.A19. **DD** 347.731025.

U.S. CUSTOMS DIRECTORY. Main/Corp United States. Customs Service. US. English. Customs Service, 1301 Constitution Avenue Northwest, Washington DC 20229.

U.S. DEPARTMENT OF LABOR ADVISORY COMMITTEE DIRECTORY. Main/Corp United States. Dept. of Labor. Periodical. US. English. an. US Department of Labor, Room S1032/200 Constitution Avenue, Washington DC 20210.

THE UNITED STATES DIRECTORIES OF MINORITY CONTRACTORS, YELLOW PAGES. VFOAT US Directories of Minority Contractors. 1981-. 0731-5643. US. English. an. The United States Directories of Minority Contractors, PO Box 82, Brentwood TN 37027. **LC** HD2346.U5. **DD** 338.6422.

UNITED STATES DIRECTORY OF FEDERAL REGIONAL STRUCTURE. 1979-. 0730-1332. US. English. an. $8.75. Superintendent of Documents, Government Printing Office, Washington DC 20402. **Tel** (202)783-3238. **LC** JK404. **DD** 353.00025. **NLM** JK 404 U58.

U.S. DIRECTORY OF POULTRY & EGG PROCESSING PLANTS. (1976-). Periodical. US. English.

U.S. DIRECTORY OF RENDERERS. (1976-). Periodical. US. English.

U.S. FACILITIES AND PROGRAMS FOR CHILDREN WITH SEVERE MENTAL ILLNESSES. DIRECTORY. (U.S. FACILITIES AND PROGRAMS FOR CHILDREN WITH SEVERE MENTAL ILLNESSES : DIRECTORY). 0160-676X. US. English. US Department of Health Education and Welfare, Public Health Service, Alcohol Drug Abuse and Mental Health Administration, National Institute of Mental Health, 5600 Fishers Lane, Rockville MD 20857. **LC** RJ111. **DD** 362.7820973.

U.S. FIRMS IN TAIWAN : DIRECTORY. VFOAT US Firms in Taiwan. 1981-. English. an. $6.00. PO Box 68-328, Taipei Taiwan Republic of China. **LC** HF3130. **DD** 338.88973051249025.

U.S. FOAMED PLASTICS MARKETS & DIRECTORY. 1978-. 0083-0968. US. English. an. $40.00. Technomic Publishing Company, 851 New Holland Avenue, Box 3535, Lancaster PA 17604. **Tel** (717)291-5609. **LC** TP1183.F6. **DD** 338.4766849302573. adv acc. Lists what companies provide what services and products related to foamed plastics. A description of each company's products or markets for rigid and flexible foamed plastics. *International Foamed Plastic Markets & Directory.*

UNITED STATES GOVERNMENT DIRECTORY. Series/Titl Lawyer's Telephone Directory Series. **VFOAT** U.S. Government Directory. 0277-0210. US. English. an. $9.25. Want Publishing Company, 1511 K Street Northwest, Washington DC 20005. **LC** JK661. **DD** 353.00025.

U.S. GOVERNMENT OFFICES IN CALIFORNIA : A DIRECTORY. 1979?-. Periodical. US. English. **Tel** (714)624-5212. Lists names, addresses, and phone numbers of well over a thousand federal government offices in California.

UNITED STATES GOVERNMENT TELEPHONE DIRECTORY. REGION 1. (UNITED STATES GOVERNMENT . . . TELEPHONE DIRECTORY. REGION 1). 0276-7457. US. English. Superintendent of Documents, US Government Printing Office, Washington DC 20402. **LC** JK7.5.N36. **DD** 353.9320974.

UNITED STATES GOVERNMENT TELEPHONE DIRECTORY. UTAH. US. English. General Services Administration, Region 8, Automated Data & Telecommunications Service, Denver CO 80225.

U.S. INDUSTRIAL DIRECTORY. VFOAT Industrial Telephone/Address Directory, Industrial Trade Name Directory, Industrial Product Directory, Industrial Literature Directory. **VAT** United States Industrial Directory. 0095-7046. US. English. an. US Industrial Directory, 270 St Paul Street, Denver CO 80206. **Tel** (303)388-4511. **LC** T12. **DD** 338.476702573. *Conover-Mast Purchasing Directory.*

UNITED STATES LAWYERS REFERENCE DIRECTORY. 1967-. US. English. ir. Legal Directories Publishing Company Inc, 2122 Kidwell Street, Box 140220, Dallas TX 75214. **Tel** (213)478-1919. **LC** KF190. **DD** 340.02573.

U.S. MEDICAL DIRECTORY. 1972-. 0091-8393. US. English. be. $94.45. US Directory Service, PO Box 86-1700, Miami FL 33168. **Tel** (305)769-1700. **LC** R712.A1. **DD** 610.2573. **NLM** W 22 AA1 U57. Gives you accurate detailed information on thousands of medical doctors, hospitals, nursing facilities, laboratories, medical information sources, poison control centers, US medical school and buyers guide.

U.S. MILITARY AND GOVERNMENT INSTALLATION DIRECTORY SERVICE. VAT United States Military and Government Installation Directory Service. 19 -. Periodical. US. English. ty. $235.00. US Organization Chart Service, PO Box 1335, La Jolla CA 92038. **Tel** (619)454-3711. Lists every military and federal government installation in the United States with full addresses, telephone number and key personnel.

U.S. NON-PROFIT ORGANIZATIONS IN DEVELOPMENT ASSISTANCE ABROAD. TAICH DIRECTORY SUPPLEMENT. VFOAT Taich Directory Supplement. 1 (Aug. 1980)-. US. English. ir. 200 Park Avenue South, New York NY 10003. *U.S. Non-Profit Organizations, Voluntary Agencies, Missions, and Foundations in Technical Assisance Abroad. Supplement.*

U.S. PROGRESSIVE PERIODICALS DIRECTORY. VFOAT US Progressive Periodicals Directory. 1st Ed. (1982-83)-. 0743-4138. US. English. $8.00. Progressive Education Service of the South Inc, PO Box 120574, Nashville TN 37212. **Ed** C T Canan. **LC** Z6951, PN4877. **DD** 051.025. adv acc. **Circ** 1,500. About 500 periodicals, which author describes as "progressive". Includes such titles as "Nutrition Action" and "Solidarity," subjects such as peace, religion, labor and health.

U.S. PUBLICITY DIRECTORY. BUSINESS & FINANCE. VAT United States Publicity Directory. Business and Finance. 0196-5093. US. English. sa. $65.00. John Wiley and Sons Inc, 1 Wiley Drive, Somerset NJ 08873. **Tel** (201)469-4400. **LC** Z6951, PN4888.C59. **DD** 070.59202573.

U.S. PUBLICITY DIRECTORY. COMMUNICATION SERVICES. VFOAT USPD, U.S. Publicity Directory. Communications Services. **VAT** United States Publicity Directory. Communication Services. Summer 1980-. 0196-5107. US. English. sa. John Wiley & Sons Inc, 605 Third Avenue, New York NY 10016. **LC** P88.8. **DD** 071.3.

U.S. PUBLICITY DIRECTORY. MAGAZINES. VFOAT USPD. U.S. Publicity Directory. Magazines. **VAT** United States Publicity Directory. Magazines. Summer 1980-. 0196-5085. US. English. sa. John Wiley & Sons Inc, 605 Third Avenue, New York NY 10016. **LC** Z6951, PN4877. **DD** 051.

U.S. PUBLICITY DIRECTORY. NEWSPAPERS. VFOAT USPD, U.S. Publicity Directory. Newspapers. **VAT** United States Publicity Directory. Newspapers. Summer 1980-. 0196-5077. US. English. sa. John Wiley & Sons Inc, 605 Third Avenue, New York NY 10016. **LC** Z6951, PN4867. **DD** 071.3.

U.S. PUBLICITY DIRECTORY. RADIO & TV. VAT United States Publicity Directory. Radio and Television. 0196-5069. Periodical. US. English. sa. $65.00. John Wiley and Sons, 1 Wiley Drive, Somerset NJ 08873. **Tel** (201)469-4400. **LC** TK6555. **DD** 384.5402573.

THE U.S. SAVINGS AND LOAN DIRECTORY. VFOAT US Savings and Loan Directory. **VAT** United States Savings and Loan Directory. Vol. 1 (1982)-. 0734-9203. US. English. an. Rand McNally & Company, 23 East Madison, Chicago IL 60602. **Tel** (312)332-4627. **LC** HG2150. **DD** 332.3202573.

UNITED STATES SENATE TELEPHONE DIRECTORY. Main/Corp United States. Congress., Senate. **VFOAT** Senate Telephone Directory. May 1983-. US. English. ir. Superintendent of Documents, US Government Printing Office, Washington DC 20402. *Telephone Directory.*

U.S. TENNIS TOURNAMENT DIRECTORY. SUPPLEMENT. VFOAT Official U.S. Tennis Tournament Directory. Supplement. **VAT** United States Tennis Tournament Directory. Supplement. 0160-1113. US. English. sa. United States Tennis Survey Inc, 1013 Cornwell Place, Ann Arbor MI 48104.

Yearbooks, Almanacs, Directories

UNIVERSAL BUSINESS DIRECTORY FOR SOUTH AUSTRALIAN COUNTRY. VFOAT South Australian Country Business & Trade Directory. AT. English. an. Universal Business Directories, 45 Talavera Road, North Ryde New South Wales 2113 Australia. Tel 888 1877. LC HF5307. DD 919.4230405.

UNIVERSALIA. 1st- 1974-. FR. French. ir. $30.92. Encyclopaedia Universalis, PO Box 2249, 175 Holiday Inn Drive, Cambridge Ontario N3C 3N4 Canada. Index in first issue of next- volume- loose - separately paged. This is a yearbook for Encyclopedaedia Universalis.

UNIX PRODUCTS DIRECTORY. 0886-2575. Periodical. US. English. sa. Free to Members, $100.00 Nonmembers. USR Group, 4655 Old Ironsides Drive/Suite 200, Santa Clara CA 95054. *Unix Products Catalog, 0886-2583.*

U.P. LAW ALUMNI YEARBOOK. VFOAT UP Law Alumni Yearbook. 1980-. Periodical. English. an. LC K25. DD 349.59905, 345.99005.

UPASI PLANTING DIRECTORY. Main/Corp United Planters' Association of Southern India. VFOAT Planting Directory. Periodical. English. ir. *Planting Directory of Southern India.*

UPSTATE NEW YORK DIRECTORY OF MANUFACTURERS. 1st Ed. (1982-1983)-. 0732-2860. US. English. ir. $52.50. Commerce Register Inc, 190 Godwin Avenue, Midlind Park NJ 07432. Tel (201)445-3000. Ed Joel Rosano. LC HD9727.N7. DD 381.45000294747. adv acc. Circ 3,000. Detailed listings of all manufacturing companies, including top executives, annual sales, number of employees, address, phone, and more.

URAL-ALTAISCHE JAHRBUCHER (BLOOMINGTON, IND.). (URAL-ALTAISCHE JAHRBUCHER). VFOAT Ural-Altaic Yearbook. Vol. 50 (1978)-. Periodical. US. German (English). an. $48.00. Eurolingua, PO Box 101, Bloomington IN 47402. Tel (812)332-8918. Ed Gynn Decsy. bk rev. adv acc. Circ 500. (ctrl). Languages and cultures of people in East Eurasia from the point of view of genetic and area comparative research. *Ural-Altaische Jahrbucher (Wiesbaden : 1952-1977).*

URBAN HISTORY YEARBOOK. 1974-. 0306-0845. UK. English. an. 17.95. Leicester University Press, Fielding Johnson Building, Building/University Road, Leicester LE1 7RH England. Tel 0533 551860. Ed D Reeder. Ind/Abst Am. Hist. Life, Hist. Abstr., Part A, Mod. Hist. Abstr., Hist. Abst., Part B, Twent. Century Abstr. LC HT101. DD 301.3609. bk rev. Circ 700. bibliography, reports on conferences and theses in urban history.

URISA DIRECTORY OF MEMBERS. Main/Corp Urban and Regional Information Systems Association. VFOAT U.R.I.S.A. Directory of Members. VAT Urban and Regional Information Systems Association Directory of Members. Began in 1980. 0733-0634. US. English. an. URISA, 2033 M Street NW/Suite 300, Washington DC 20036.

URNER BARRY'S MEAT & POULTRY DIRECTORY. VFOAT Urner Barry's Meat and Poultry Directory. 1984-. 0738-6745. US. English. $34.10. Urner Barry Publications Inc, PO Box 389, Toms River NJ 08753. Tel (201)240-5330. Ed Paul B Brown Jr. LC HD9413. DD 381.456649202573. adv acc. Circ 1,000. A national directory of meat and poultry traders with over 5,000 listings of current, relative information, Many listings contain phone numbers, key personnel, sales territory, products handled, and product form.

U.S.A. OIL INDUSTRY DIRECTORY. VAT United States of America Oil Industry Directory. 1970-. 0082-8599. US. English. an. $95.00. Pennwell Publishing Company, PO Box 1260, Tulsa OK 74101. Tel (918)835-3161. Ed William R Leek Jr. LC HD9563. DD 338.272802573. adv acc. Circ 6,000. Includes major integrated oil companies, independent oil producers, fund companies, government agencies, associations listed geographically. Cross-referenced with subject index and company index. *Personnel Directory of U.S.A. Oil Industry.*

U.S.A. OILFIELD SERVICE, SUPPLY, AND MANUFACTURERS DIRECTORY. VFOAT U.S.A. Oilfield Service, Supply & Manufacturers Directory. 1985-. US. English. an. Pennwell Directories, Pennwell Pub Co, Box 1260, Tulsa OK 74101. LC HD9560.5. DD 338.768176. *Oilfield Service, Supply and Manufacturers Worldwide Directory, 0736-038X.*

USDA SOFTWARE DIRECTORY. Main/Corp United States. Dept. of Agriculture. Automated Data Systems. 1977-. Periodical. US. English.

USDF DRESSAGE INSTRUCTORS, CLINICIANS, TRAINERS, TECHNICAL DELEGATOS DIRECTORY. VFOAT USDF Dressage Directory. 0882-4991. US. English. be. $5.00. USDF, PO Box 80668, Lincoln NE 68501.

U.S.H.L. YEARBOOK. Main/Corp United States Hockey League. VAT United States Hockey League Yearbook. 1975/76-. 0363-7050. US. English. an. $1.00. PO Box 1093, Green Bay WI 54305. LC GV847.8.U53. DD 796.9620973.

UTAH DIRECTORY OF BUSINESS AND INDUSTRY. VFOAT Directory of Utah Business and Industry. 1983-. 8755-2841. US. English. an. $15.00. Utah Department of Employment Security, 174 Social Hall Avenue/PO Box 11249, Salt Lake City UT 84147. Tel (801)533-2296. Ed Kris Beckstead. LC HD9727.U8. DD 338.00294792. adv acc. Circ 2,500. This directory includes statistical information showing Utah economic and industry growth by planning district counties and lists Utah businesses and firms by alphabetical, SIC, geographical and product index. *Directory of Utah Manufacturers.*

UTAH MINERAL INDUSTRY OPERATOR DIRECTORY. 0146-6186. US. English. $3.00. Utah Geological and Mineral Survey, 606 Black Hawk Way, Salt Lake City UT 84108. LC QE169. DD 557.9208 S, 338.7622025792.

UTAH SCHOOL DIRECTORY. US. English. Utah State Board of Education, 250 East 5th Street South, Salt Lake City UT 84111. LC L903.U7. DD 370.25792.

UTAH STATE BAR DIRECTORY. 0737-9277. US. English. Utah State Bar Office, 425 East First South, Salk Lake City UT 84111. LC KF192.U8. DD 340.025792.

UTBILDNINGSSTATISTISK ARSBOK. Series/Titl Sveriges Officiella Statistik. VFOAT Yearbook of Educational Statistics. 1978-. English (Swedish). an. LC LA902.

VALIS-EESTLASE KALENDER. US. English. an. LC AY78.E6.

VANCOUVER & AREA AIRPORT BUSINESS DIRECTORY. VFOAT Vancouver Airport Business Directory. 1984-. 0828-4504. CN. English. an. 3.50. Vancouver & Area Airport Business Directory, Suite 158/1224 53rd Avenue Northeast, Calgary Alberta T2E 7E2 Canada. Tel (403)275-9457. Ed Paul J Skinner. DD 387.7364025711. adv acc. Circ 7,000. (ctrl). Descriptive listing of all aviation related companies and services in the Vancouver area. *Vancouver Airport Business Directory, 0227-1680.*

VANCOUVER ARTS DIRECTORY. 1984/85-. 0827-3081. CN. English. an. Community Arts Council of Vancouver, 314 West Cordova Street, Vancouver British Columbia V6B 1E8 Canada. DD 700.2571133. *Community Arts Directory (Vancouver, B.C.), 0712-1393.*

VANCOUVER B.C. CITY DIRECTORY. VFOAT Vancouver Directory. VAT Vancouver Directory (1979), Vancouver British Columbia City Directory. 1979-. 0712-1881. CN. English. an. British Columbia Directories, 1000 East 4th Avenue, Vancouver British Columbia V5T 1G3 Canada. DD 917.1133. (ctrl). *Vancouver City Directory, 0316-1498.*

VANDERBILT MEDICAL ALUMNI DIRECTORY. Main/Corp Vanderbilt University. School of Medicine. VFOAT Alumni Directory. 0740-901X. US. English. an. College & University Press, One Bell Road, PO Box 17940, Montgomery AL 36141. LC R747.V36. DD 610.71176147.

VENTURE CAPITAL JOURNAL YEARBOOK. (VENTURE CAPITAL JOURNAL . . . YEARBOOK). 1983-. 8756-8896. US. English. an. Venture Economics Inc, PO Box 348, 16 Laurel Avenue, Wellesley Hills MA 02181. LC HG4028.C4. DD 332.041505.

THE VERMONT ECONOMIC ALMANAC. 1980-. 0270-3955. US. English. an. $9.95. Vermont Business World, On the Square, Bellows Falls VT 05101. Ed G M Bright. LC HC107.V5. DD 330.9743005.

VERMONT LEGISLATIVE DIRECTORY AND STATE MANUAL. Main/Corp Vermont. Secretary of State. 1867-. 0363-3225. US. English. an. $11.44. Vermont Department of Libraries, c/o State Office Building, Montpelier VT 05602. Tel (802)828/3261. LC JK3031. DD 328.7430025.

VERMONT LIBRARY DIRECTORY. 0364-7382. US. English. State of Vermont, Department of Libraries, Montpelier VT 05602. LC Z732.V5. DD 021.0025743.

VERMONT STATE INDUSTRIAL DIRECTORY. 1975/76-. 0098-6208. US. English. be. $20.00. Vermont State Industrial Directory, 2 Pennsylvania Plaza, New York NY 10001. LC HC107.V5. DD 338.0025743.

VERMONT YEAR BOOK. VFOAT Vermont Yearbook. 1818. 0083-5781. US. English. an. The National Survey, Chester VT 05143. Tel (802)875-2121. Ed Cecil Waldo. adv acc. Circ 3,000. (ctrl). The only complete business directory covering the entire state of Vermont. It is a source for general Vermont information, directory of Vermont products and manufacturers, local information and business directory. *Vermont Year-Book & Guide.*

VERNON'S BURLINGTON AND HAMILTON SUBURBAN DIRECTORY. 20th- Ed. 0701-8665. CN. English. an. Vernon's Directories Ltd, 29 Rebecca Street, Hamilton Ontario L8R 1B3 Canada. DD 917.1353. *Vernon's Hamilton Suburban Directory, 0316-1773.*

VERNON'S CITY OF BELLEVILLE ONTARIO DIRECTORY. (VERNON'S CITY OF BELLEVILLE (ONTARIO) DIRECTORY). VFOAT City of Belleville (Ontario) Directory, Vernon's Belleville Directory, Vernon's Belleville City Directory. Began publication in 1963. 0383-0063. Periodical. CN. English. be. Vernon Directories Ltd City Directory Publishers, 29 Rebecca Street, Hamilton Ontario L8R 1B3 Canada. DD 917.13585. *Vernon's City of Belleville Ontario Miscellaneous, Business, Alphabetical and Street Directory, 0383-0071.*

VERNON'S CITY OF BRANTFORD (ONTARIO) DIRECTORY. VFOAT Brantford Directory. Began with 1912 Ed. 0317-2880. Periodical. CN. English. an. Vernon Directories, 29 Rebecca Street, Hamilton Ontario L8R 1B3 Canada. DD 917.13480025. (ctrl).

VERNON'S CITY OF CAMBRIDGE (ONTARIO) DIRECTORY. VFOAT Vernon's Cambridge City Directory. 43d- Ed. 0317-2899. Periodical. CN. English. an. Vernon Directories, 29 Rebecca Street, Hamilton Ontario L8R 1B3 Canada. DD 971.344. (ctrl). *Vernon's Galt-Preston, Ontario Directory, 0317-2902.*

VERNON'S CITY OF HAMILTON (ONTARIO) DIRECTORY. VFOAT Vernon's Hamilton Directory. 1958-. 0316-1765. Periodical. CN. English. an. Vernon Directories, 29 Rebecca Street, Hamilton Ontario L8R 1B3 Canada. DD 917.1352. (ctrl). *Vernon's . . . City of Hamilton Miscellaneous, Business, Alphabetical and Street Directory.*

VERNON'S CITY OF NIAGARA FALLS (ONTARIO) DIRECTORY. (VERNON'S CITY OF NIAGARA FALLS, ONTARIO, DIRECTORY). VFOAT Vernon's Niagara Falls Directory. Began with 1924 issue?. 0316-1676. Periodical. CN. English. an. Vernon Directories, 29 Rebecca Street Hamilton Ontario L8R 1B3 Canada. DD 917.13390025. (ctrl).

VERNON'S CITY OF NORTH BAY (ONTARIO) DIRECTORY. VFOAT Vernon's North Bay (Ontario) Directory. Began between 1931 and 1935 (16th-20th Eds.). 0316-1692. Periodical. CN. English. be. Vernon Directories, 29 Rebecca Street, Hamilton Ontario L8R 1B3 Canada. DD 917.13147. (ctrl). *Vernon's North Bay (Ontario) Directory.*

VERNON'S CITY OF OSHAWA AND TOWN OF WHITBY (ONTARIO) DIRECTORY. VFOAT Vernon's Oshawa and Whitby City Directory. 37th- 1960-. 0317-2856. CN. English. an. Vernon Directories, 29 Rebecca Street, Hamilton Ontario L8R 1B3 Canada. DD 917.13'55. *Vernon's City of Oshawa (Ontario) Directory, 0317-3232.*

VERNON'S CITY OF TIMMINS (ONTARIO) DIRECTORY. (VERNON'S CITY OF TIMMINS, ONTARIO, DIRECTORY). VFOAT Timmins, Ontario, Directory. VAT Timmins City Directory. 1st- ed. 0706-5035. CN. English. an. $95.00. Vernon Directories, 29 Rebecca Street, Hamilton Ontario L8R 1B3 Canada. DD 917.13142.

VERNON'S KITCHENER WATERLOO (ONTARIO) DIRECTORY. VFOAT Vernon's Kitchener and Waterloo Directories. 1958-. 0316-179X. Periodical. CN. English. an. Vernon Directories, 29 Rebecca Street, Hamilton Ontario L8R

Yearbooks, Almanacs, Directories

1B3 Canada. **DD** 917.13450025. (ctrl). *Vernon's Kitchener-Waterloo City Directories (Ontario), 0229-7329.*

VERNON'S TOWN OF LINDSAY ONTARIO DIRECTORY CEASED. (VERNON'S TOWN OF LINDSAY (ONTARIO) DIRECTORY). **VFOAT** Lindsay, Ontario, Directory. Began publication in 1934. Ceased 5th Ed. 1981. 0380-898X. **CN**. English. be. **DD** 917.1364.

VERNON'S WELLAND AND PORT COLBORNE (ONTARIO) DIRECTORY. Began publication in 1966?. 0317-283X. Periodical. **CN**. English. Vernon Directories, 29 Rebecca Street, Hamilton Ontario L8R 1B3 Canada. **DD** 971.1338. *Vernon's City of Welland and Town of Port Colborne (Ontario) Directory, 0317-2872.*

VERZEICHNIS DER LAND- UND ERNAHRUNGSWIRTSCHAFTLICHEN VERBANDE ZUSAMMENGESCHLOSSEN IM RAHMEN DER EG. **VFOAT** Directory of Non-Governmental Agricultural Organizations Set Up at European Community Level. 1980-. German (English and French). ir.

VICTORIAN GOVERNMENT DIRECTORY. 0158-1589. **AT**. English. an. Government Printing Office/Victoria, PO Box 203, North Melbourne Victoria 3051 Australia. **LC** JQ5321. **DD** 354.945002.

VICTORIAN TRADES HALL COUNCIL OFFICIAL TRADE UNION DIRECTORY & DIGEST. **VAT** Victorian Trades Hall Council Official Trade Union Directory and Digest. English. ir. Box 93 Trades Hall, Victoria and Lygon Streets, 3053 Carlton South Australia. **LC** HD6895.V52. **DD** 331.88025945.

VICTORIAN YEAR-BOOK. **VFOAT** Victorian Year Book. 0067-1223. **AT**. English. an. $19.92. Australian Government Publications Service, PO Box 84, Canberra Australian Capital Territory 2600 Australia. **Tel** 062-95 4411. **NLM** W2 KA8.1 V6.

VIDEO INDUSTRY DIRECTORY. Vol. 1, No. 1 (80/81)-. 0730-6180. US. English. an. $25.00. Reese Publishing Company, 235 Park Avenue South, New York NY 10003. **LC** HD9696.T463. **DD** 338.762138802573.

VIDEO YEARBOOK. Began in 1977. 0140-2277. UK. English. an. $37.50. Sterling Publishing Company Inc, 2 Park Avenue, New York NY 10016. **LC** TK6650. **DD** 621.38830294.

VIDEOTEX DIRECTORY. (VIDEOTEX DIRECTORY : A GUIDE TO THE VIDEOTEX/TELETEXT INDUSTRIES). 1982-83-. 0737-7916. US. English. an. Arlen Communications Inc, 7315 Wisconsin Avenue/Suite 600E, Bethesda MD 20814. **Tel** (301)656-7940. Ed Gary H Arlen and Richard Adler. **LC** HD9696.D38. **DD** 384. adv acc. Comprehensive information on all aspects of videotex, teletext, cabletext, online banking, and brokerage, electronic publishing, public access and transactional services.

VIETNAM EXPORT DIRECTORY. **VM**. English. Vietnam Export Development Center, 16-18 Hai BA Trung, Saigon Vietnam. **LC** HF3799.V5. **DD** 382.6025597.

VILLE DE HAMPSTEAD REPERTOIRE. **VFOAT** Town of Hampstead Directory. V. 9- 1980-. 0227-8626. **CN**. English (includes some text in French). an. J Lovell, 423 rue St Nicolas, Montreal Quebec H2Y 2P4 Canada. **DD** 917.142810025. *Town of Hampstead Directory, 0316-7836.*

THE VINEYARD ALMANAC & WINE GAZETTEER. **VFOAT** Vineyard Almanac and Wine Gazetteer. 0276-4687. US. English. an. $2.25. Gene Tartt, 960 N San Antonia Road/Suite 125, Los Altos CA 94303. **LC** TP557. **DD** 641.22205.

VINTAGE AIRCRAFT DIRECTORY. UK. English. an. 0.85. G Riley, 3 New Plaistow Road, London England. **LC** TL506.G7. **DD** 629.13334075.

VINTAGE AUTO ALMANAC CEASED. 1977-. 0363-4639. US. English. an. $4.50. **LC** TL12. **DD** 629.2222075.

VIRGIN ISLANDS DIRECTORY OF SERVICES FOR THE AGING. **VFOAT** Directory of Services for the Elderly. VI. English. ir. PO Box 5138, St Thomas US Virgin Islands 00801. **LC** HV1478.V5. **DD** 362.6042.

VIRGINIA EDUCATIONAL DIRECTORY. 0083-6354. US. English. State Department of Education, Box 6Q, Richmond VA 23216. **LC** L903.V8. **DD** 370.25755.

VIRGINIA HORSE INDUSTRY YEARBOOK. No. 1- 1976-. Periodical. US. English. be. Virginia Horse Council, Box 1191, Middleburg VA 22117. **Ind/Abst** Bibliogr. Agric. Program/Proceedings - National Horsemen's Seminar.

VIRGINIA INDUSTRIAL DIRECTORY. See Manufacturing.

THE VIRGINIAS, MARYLAND, DELAWARE AND DISTRICT OF COLUMBIA LEGAL DIRECTORY. 0507-1348. US. English. an. Legal Directories Publishing Company, 2122 Kidwell Street, PO Box 140200, Dallas TX 75214. **Tel** (214)692-5825. **LC** KF190. **DD** 340.02575.

VIVLIO TES CHRONIAS. **VFOAT** Year Book. Vol. 1 (1979)-. Greek, Modern. an. 500. Amerikes 4, Athena 133 Greece.

VOCATIONAL EDUCATION DIRECTORY. **Main/Corp** Kentucky. Dept. of Education. US. English. an. **LC** L903.K4. **DD** 373.246025769.

VOCATIONAL EDUCATION PROGRAM DIRECTORY, SECONDARY, POSTSECONDARY, ADULT. US. English. State Board of Vocational and Technical Education, 401 Illinois Building, 17 West Market Street, Indianapolis IN 46204. **LC** LC1046.I4. **DD** 379.1552025772.

VOLKS-CALENDAR FUR DIE DEUTSCHEN IN WEST-CANADA. First published 18—. 0383-1930. **CN**. German. an. McLaren Micropublishing, PO Box 972 Station F, Toronto Ontario M4Y 2N9 Canada. **DD** 053.1.

WALDEN'S ABC GUIDE AND PAPER PRODUCTION YEARBOOK. **VFOAT** ABC Guide and Paper Production Yearbook. 1885. 0731-2571. US. English. an. $75.00. Walden-Mott Corporation, 475 Kinderkamack Road, Oradell NJ 07649. **Tel** (201)261-2630. Ed Michael Balbian. adv acc. Circ 3,125. Buying guide for people responsible for buying paper. Includes names, addresses, etc. of paper manufacturers, converters, paper merchants in US and Canada. Classified section of paper items.

WARD'S AUTOMOTIVE YEARBOOK. 1st- Ed. 0083-7229. US. English. an. Ward's Communication Inc, 28 West Adams Street/Suite 1805, Detroit MI 48226. **Tel** (313)962-4433.

WASHBURN UNIVERSITY SCHOOL OF LAW ALUMNI DIRECTORY. 0278-7652. US. English. ir. College & University Press, One Bell Road, PO Box 17940, Montgomery AL 36141. **LC** KF292.W20. **DD** 340.071178163.

THE WASHINGTON-AREA MICROCOMPUTER DIRECTORY. (THE WASHINGTON-AREA MICROCOMPUTER DIRECTORY : A BUYERS/USERS GUIDE TO MICROCOMPUTER-RELATED GOODS AND SERVICES IN THE WASHINGTON METROPOLITAN AREA). **VFOAT** Washington Area Microcomputer Directory. 0882-8962. US. English. $8.95. New Local Resources Inc, PO Box 2133, Silver Spring MD 20902.

THE WASHINGTON D.C. METROPOLITAN AREA FOUNDATION DIRECTORY. (THE WASHINGTON D. C. METROPOLITAN AREA FOUNDATION DIRECTORY). 0192-5342. US. English. Management Communications, Publications Division, 4416 Edmunds Street NW, Washington DC 20007. **LC** AS911.A2. **DD** 001.44025753.

WASHINGTON EDUCATION DIRECTORY. US. English. $10.75. B Krohn & Associates, 835 Securities Building, Seattle WA 98101. *Washington Educational Directory.*

WASHINGTON ENERGY DIRECTORY : AN ENERGY RESEARCH AND DEVELOPMENT RESOURCE. 1975-1976- 1975-. Periodical. US. English. an. Ed Rowan Wakefield.

WASHINGTON INFORMATION DIRECTORY. **VFOAT** Congressional Quarterly's Washington Information Directory. 1975/76-. US. English. an. $18.35. Congressional Quarterly, 1414 22nd Street NW, Washington DC 20037. **LC** F192.3. **DD** 975.30025. **NLM** F 192.3 W318B.

THE WASHINGTON LOBBYISTS & LAWYERS DIRECTORY. **VFOAT** Washington Lobbyists and Lawyers Directory. 4th Ed. (1981)-. 0741-9295. US. English. an. $34.50. Communications Services, Benjamin Franklin Station, PO Box 137, Washington DC 20044. Ed Ed Zuckerman. **LC** KF195.L6. **DD** 328,73078025753. *Washington Lobbyists/Lawyers Directory, 0741-9295.*

WASHINGTON LOBBYISTS/ LAWYERS DIRECTORY. **Main/Corp** Am Ward Publications, Inc. US. English. $36.00. Communications Services Inc, 121 4th Street SE, Washington DC 20003. **Tel** (202)544-8792. Ed E Zuckerman.

THE WASHINGTON PHYSICIANS DIRECTORY. 0161-7176. US. English. $10.00. National Directories Inc, 2626 Pennsylvania Avenue Northwest, Washington DC 20037.

THE WASHINGTON PSYCHIATRIC SOCIETY DIRECTORY. 14th- Ed. 0196-6537. US. English. Washington Psychiatric Society, 1700 18th Street NW, Washington DC 20009. **NLM** WM 22 AD6 D5.

WASHINGTON STATE RESOURCE DIRECTORY FOR LOCAL JURISDICTIONS. US. English. 400 Capitol Center Building, Olympia WA 98504. **LC** HJ755. **DD** 336.185.

WASHINGTON STATE YEARBOOK. **VFOAT** Washington State Year Book. 1983-. 0736-3850. US. English. an. Information Press, PO Box 957, Sisters OR 97759. **LC** JK9230. **DD** 320.979705.

WASHINGTON TELECOM DIRECTORY. **VFOAT** Washington Telecommunications Directory. 8755-2876. US. English. Dawson-Butwick Publishing, 1001 Connecticut Avenue NW/Suite 1128, Washington DC 20036. **DD** 384.

WATER QUALITY MANAGEMENT DIRECTORY. 0148-1797. US. English. an. US Environmental Protection Agency, Room 3101/401 M Street SW, Washington DC 20460. **LC** TD223. **DD** 363.61.

WATER RESOURCES COORDINATION DIRECTORY. 0270-0034. US. English. United States Water Resources, Council 2120 L Street NW, Washington DC 20037. **LC** TC423. **DD** 333.91002573.

THE WEATHER ALMANAC. 1st Ed.-. 0731-5627. US. English. $100.00. Gale Research, Book Tower, Detroit MI 48226. Ed James A Ruffnev and Frank E Bair. **LC** QC983. **DD** 551.6973. In addition to many new features, the fouth edition includes updated climatic data based on the 1951-1980 period; updated climatological narratives for cities; a list of every earthquake in U.S. history.

WENCO INTERNATIONAL TRADE DIRECTORY. (THE WENCO INTERNATIONAL TRADE DIRECTORY). 1973/74-. 0091-9705. US. English. $125.00. Wenco Enterprises, PO Box 4263, Portland OR 97208. **LC** HF54.U5. **DD** 382.025.

WEST BENGAL INFORMATION DIRECTORY. 1979/80-. II. English. an. 15.00. Hony Executive Director, Eastern India Centre for Mass Communication Studies, Nicco House 2 Hare Street, Calcutta 700 001 India. **LC** DS485.B493. **DD** 915.414.

WEST VIRGINIA MANUFACTURING DIRECTORY. 1962-. 0511-6708. US. English. be. West Virginia Department of Commerce, Industrial Development Division, State Office Building 6, 1900 Washington Street East, Charleston WV 25305. **LC** HD9727.W4.

WEST VIRGINIA MINERAL PRODUCERS DIRECTORY. 0195-6493. US. English. an. West Virginia Geological and Economic Survey, PO Box 879, Morgantown WV 26507-0879. **Tel** (304)594-2331. Ed Fred Schroyer. **Ind/Abst** GeoRef. **LC** HD9506.U63. **DD** 338.2025754. Circ 1,000. Directory of West Virginia mineral producers and processors.

WEST VIRGINIA MINING DIRECTORY. **VFOAT** Mining Directory. 1983 Ed.-. 0743-5282. US. English. an. $29.95. Coal & Gas Computer Services Inc, P O Box 989, Blackburg VA 24061. **LC** HD9506.U63. **DD** 338.7622334025754.

WESTCHESTER HUMAN SERVICES DIRECTORY. 8755-4534. US. English. Westchester Community Services Council, 175 Clearbrook Road, Elmsford NY 10523. **LC** HV98.N7. **DD** 361.9747277.

WESTERN AUSTRALIAN MANUFACTURERS DIRECTORY. Periodical. English. ir. **LC** HD9738.A83. **DD** 338.4025941.

2961

Yearbooks, Almanacs, Directories

WESTERN AUSTRALIAN POCKET YEAR BOOK. No. 48- 1966-. AT. English. an. $1.79. Australian Bureau of Statistics, 1-3 St Georges Terrace, Perth WA 6000 Australia. LC HA3153. DD 319.41. *Pocket Year Book of Western Australia.*

WESTERN AUSTRALIAN PRODUCTS DIRECTORY. AT. English. ir. Department of Industrial Development and Commerce, 32 St George's Terrace, Box D 160 GPO, Perth Western Australia 6001. LC T12.5.A8. DD 670.294941.

WESTERN AUSTRALIAN YEAR BOOK. No. 6 (1967)-. AT. English. an. Australian Government Publishing Service, PO Box 84, Canberra Australian Capital Territory 2600 Australia. Tel (062)95-4411. *Official Year Book of Western Australia.*

WESTERN BANK DIRECTORY. 0272-5371. US. English. an. Western Banker Publications, 49 Geary Street/Suite 210, San Francisco CA 94102. Tel (415)392-5452. LC HG2609. DD 332.102578.

WESTERN CANADA OIL & GAS DIRECTORY. 83-. 0823-115X. CN. English. an. Western Canada Oil & Gas Directory, 4135 Edmonton Trail NE, Calgary Alberta T2E 3V5 Canada. DD 338.27280257123. *Alberta Oil & Gas Directory, 0711-2793.*

WESTERN CANADA STALLION DIRECTORY. 0826-0850. CN. English. an. $15.00 Each Volume. Canadian Thoroughbred Horse Society, British Columbia Division, 4023 East Hastings Street, Burnaby British Columbia V5C 2J1 Canada. DD 636.13209712.

WESTERN CANADIAN ANTIQUE & ART DEALERS YEARBOOK. VAT Antique and Art Dealers Yearbooks. Began publication in 1976. 0705-310X. CN. English. an. $1.25 Per No. Left Bank Publications, 148 East 1st Avenue, Vancouver British Columbia V5T 1A4 Canada. DD 381.457451025712. *B.C. Antique Dealers Yearbook, 'Where-to-Find' on B.C. Art Dealers, 0714-8968.*

WESTERN CANADIAN STEAM LOCOMOTIVE DIRECTORY. Began with 1969 issue. 0085-8188. Periodical. CN. English. be. $1.00 Each Number. Richard L Coulton, Bentley Alberta T0C 0J0 Canada. DD 625.26109712.

WESTERN HUMOR AND IRONY MEMBERSHIP SERIAL YEARBOOK. (WESTERN HUMOR AND IRONY MEMBERSHIP SERIAL YEARBOOK : WHIMSY : PROCEEDINGS OF THE . . . WHIM CONFERENCE). Main/Conf Whim Conference. VFOAT Whimsy. 1 (1983)-. 0737-0342. US. English. an. Don L F Nilsen, Department of English, Arizona State University, Tempe AZ 85281. LC PN6146.5. DD 809.7005.

WESTERN MACHINERY AND STEEL WORLD. BUYERS DIRECTORY. VFOAT Western Machinery . . . Buyers Directory. Vol. 65 (1975). 0732-8559. US. English. an. Cardinal Publishing Company, 1098 Harrison Street, San Francisco CA 94103. Tel (415)864-1234. LC HD9703.U52. DD 621.902029478.

WESTERN MINING DIRECTORY. V. 1- 1978-. 0162-9026. US. English. an. $45.00. Howell Publishing Company, 311 Steele Street/Suite 208, Denver CO 80206. Tel (303)355-5202. Ed Don E Howell. Ind/Abst GeoRef. LC TN12. DD 338.202578. adv acc. Circ 8,000. Mines and mining companies in the Western U.S. listed geographically and alphabetically. Equipment and suppliers listed alphabetically by company and product.

WESTERN ROUNDUP COUNTRY MUSIC TRADE DIRECTORY & NEWS REPORT. VAT Western Roundup Country Music Trade Directory and News Report. Summer 1974-. 0273-1991. US. English. LC ML19. DD 784.52002573. *Western Roundup Country Music Trade Directory, 0273-2009.*

WESTERN UNITED STATES A.A. DIRECTORY. (WESTERN UNITED STATES A. A. DIRECTORY). VAT Western United States Alcoholics Anonymous Directory. 0362-1359. US. English. Alcoholics Anonymous World Services Inc, 468 Park Avenue South, New York NY 10016. LC HV5287.A48. DD 362.292.

WHO IS WHO IN MANAGEMENT : SINGAPORE INSTITUTE OF MANAGEMENT DIRECTORY OF MANAGERS. Main/Corp Singapore Institutue of Management. 1981-. SI. English. an. Singapore Institute of Management, 3rd Floor, Thong Teck Building, Scotts Road, Singapore 0922 Singapore. LC HF5500.3.S55. DD 658.400255957.

THE WHOLE WORLD OIL DIRECTORY. Began in 1979. 0148-3609. US. English. an. Whole World Publishing Ltd, 400 Lake Cook Road, Deerfield IL 60015. Tel (312)945-8050. *Whole Oil World Oil Directory, 0276-1068.*

WHO'S WHO DIRECTORY OF SPORTS, RECREATION AND PHYSICAL EDUCATION. (ANNUAIRE DES SPORTS, DES LOISIRS, ET DE L'EDUCATION PHYSIQUE). VFOAT Directory of Sports, Recreation and Physical Education. 1983-. 0229-611X. CN. English (text also in French). an. Sport New Brunswick, 65 Brunswick Street, Fredericton New Brunswick E3B 1G5 Canada. DD 796.025715. *Who's Who Directory of Sports, Recreation and Physical Education, 0229-611X.*

WHO'S WHO IN LANDSCAPE CONTRACTING. (WHO'S WHO IN LANDSCAPE CONTRACTING : MEMBERSHIP DIRECTORY). Main/Corp Associated Landscape Contractors of America. 0730-7225. US. English. an. $25.00. Assocated Landscape Contractors, 405 North Washington Street, Falls Church VA 22046. Tel (703)241-4004. LC SB472.55. DD 338.76171202573. adv acc. Circ 4,000. Membership listing of landscape contracting firms located throughout the country.

WHO'S WHO IN NORTH DAKOTA. (WHO'S WHO IN NORTH DAKOTA : A BIOGRAPHICAL DIRECTORY OF NORTH DAKOTA ACHIEVERS). VFOAT Biographical Directory of North Dakota Achievers. 1st- Ed. US. English. te. Dakota West Enterprises Inc, 303 NE 1st Street, Mandan ND 58554.

WHO'S WHO IN UNITED STATES POLITICS AND AMERICAN POLITICAL ALMANAC. VFOAT American Political Almanac, Who's Who in U.S. Politics. 1st Ed.-. Periodical. US. English. ir. Ed R Nowinson. LC E747. DD 973.273.

WIENER JAHRBUCH FUR KUNSTGESCHICHTE. Vol. 1- 1921/22-. 0083-9981. AU. German. ir. Hermann Boehlaus Nachfolger, Postfach 200, A-1014 Wein Austria. Tel (0222)63 87 35-0. Ind/Abst Avery Index Archit. Period. Second Ed. Revis. Enlarged Suppl., Repert. Int. Litt. Art. LC N9. *Jahrbuch des Kunsthistorischen Institutes.*

WIENER JAHRBUCH FUR PHILOSOPHIE. V. 1- 1968-. 0083-999X. AU. German. an. Universitats Verlagsbuchhand, Servitengasse 5, 1092 Wien Austria. Tel 02 22-34 81 24. Ed Wilhelm Braumuller. LC B31. DD 105. bk rev. adv acc. Circ 500. Yearbook of the Institute of Philosophy of the University of Vienna. *Wiener Zeitschrift fur Philosophie, Psychologie, Padagogik.*

WIENER SLAVISTISCHES JAHRBUCH. V. 1- 1950-. 0084-0041. AU. German. ir. Osterreichischen Akad Wissenschaften, Dr Ignaz-Seipelpl 2, A-1010 Wien Austria. Tel 52-96-81. Ind/Abst MLA Int. Bibliogr. Books Artic. Mod. Lang. Lit. LC PG1. DD 491.805. bk rev. Circ 500. Scientific treatises on Slavic philology (language, literature, folklore).

WILMINGTON CENTREX DIRECTORY. VFOAT Wilmington, Del., New Castle, Del., Dover, Del. US. English. General Services Administration, 600 Arch Street, Philadelphia PA 19106.

WINDSOR & ESSEX COUNTY MANUFACTURERS DIRECTORY. 1973-. 0316-1145. CN. English. an. Greater Windsor Industrial Commission, 500 Riverside Drive West, Windsor Ontario N9A 5K6 Canada. DD 338.402571332. *Greater Windsor Manufacturers Directory, 0316-1153.*

WINDSOR YEARBOOK OF ACCESS TO JUSTICE. (THE WINDSOR YEARBOOK OF ACCESS TO JUSTICE). VFOAT Access to Justice, Recueil Annuel de Windsor d'Acces A la Justice. Vol. 1 (1981)-. 0710-0841. CN. English (French). an. $25.00. Windsor Yearbook of Access to Justice, c/o Faculty of Law University of Windsor, Windsor Ontario N9B 3P4 Canada. Ind/Abst Index Leg. Period., Index Can. Leg. Period. Vit. LC K27. DD 347.005, 342.7005.

WINES & VINES DIRECTORY. VFOAT Wines and Vines Directory. Vol. 45 (1964-65). 0749-9434. US. English. an. $35.00. Wines & Vines Directory, 1800 Lincoln Avenue, San Rafael CA 94901. Tel (415)453-9700. Ed Philip E Hiaring. LC TP557. DD 338.76632202573. adv acc. Circ 5,200. (ctrl). A technical trade publication for the wine industry. *Wines & Vines Annual Directory Issue, 0084-0351.*

WINKLER PRINS JAARBOEK. 1970-. Periodical. Dutch. ir. $25.60. Elseiver Science Publishing Company Ltd, PO Box 1663 Grand Central Station, New York NY 10163. *Winkler Prins Boek van Het Jaar.*

WINNIPEG CONSTRUCTION ASSOCIATION DIRECTORY. 0712-6093. CN. English. an. Free. Winnipeg Construction Association, 290 Burnell Street, Winnipeg Manitoba R3G 2A7 Canada. DD 338.4769002571274. (ctrl).

WINTER RECREATION DIRECTORY. 1982/83-. 0825-4044. Periodical. CN. English. Sasktravel, 3211 Albert Street, Regina Saskatchewan S4S 5W6 Canada. DD 796.90257124. *Winter Events, 0715-724X; Welcome to Winter, 0825-4036.*

WINTERTHURER JAHRBUCH. Periodical. SZ. German. ir. Amt fur Kulturelles der Stadt Winterthur, Sruckerei Winterthur Ag, Winterthur Switzerland. LC DQ851.W63. DD 949.45.

WIRE JOURNAL DIRECTORY-CATALOG. (WIRE JOURNAL DIRECTORY/CATALOG). 0091-3162. US. English. an. $50.00. Wire Association International, 1570 Boston Post Road, Guilford CT 06437. LC TS571.A1. DD 338.4767184.

THE WISCONSIN ALMANAC. Began with 1981. 0734-0982. US. English. an. $6.95. J L Brekke, Route 1 Box 83, Taylors Falls MN 55084. LC F576. DD 977.5005.

WISCONSIN DENTISTRY EXAMINING BOARD DIRECTORY. 1979-. US. English. an. LC RK37. DD 617.60025775.

THE WISCONSIN LEGAL DIRECTORY. US. English. an. $29.49. Legal Directories Publishing Company, 2122 Kidwell, Box 140200, Dallas TX 75214. Tel (214)824-8092. LC KF192.W57.

WISCONSIN NONPUBLIC SCHOOL DIRECTORY. 0149-7855. US. English. an. $1.00. Wisconsin Department of Public Instruction 126 Langdon Street, Madison WI 53702.

WISCONSIN PUBLIC SCHOOL DIRECTORY. 0148-5059. US. English. an. $1.50. Wisconsin Department of Public Instruction, 126 Langdon Street, Madison WI 53702. LC L216, L903.W6. DD 370.9775 S, 370.25775. *Wisconsin Official School Directory.*

WISCONSIN ZIP+4 STATE DIRECTORY. VFOAT Zip Plus Four State Directory. VAT Wisconsin Zip Plus Four State Directory. 1985-. US. English. an. St Louis PDC, Zip + 4 State Directory Orders, PO Box 14921, St Louis MO 63180-9988.

WOMEN LIKE ME. (WOMEN LIKE ME : THE WOMEN'S BUSINESS DIRECTORY). VFOAT Women's Business Directory. 1982-. 0821-4794. CN. English. an. $5.00 Each Volume. Women Like Me, c/o K Fraser, 124 Cumberland Street, Toronto Ontario M5R 1A3 Canada. DD 331.4025713541. *Women's Business Directory, 0821-4786.*

WOMEN'S AND CHILDREN'S WEAR AND FASHION ACCESSORIES BUYERS NATIONWIDE DIRECTORY. English. ir. *Nationwide Directory of Women's and Children's Wear Buyers.*

A WOMEN'S DIRECTORY FOR THE CEDAR RAPIDS AND IOWA CITY AREA. VFOAT Women's Directory. 1st Ed. (1982)-. 0736-4784. US. English. an. PRN Corporation, 397 Forest Drive SE, Cedar Rapids IA 52403. LC HQ1439.C4. DD 061.7762.

WOMEN'S NETWORK DIRECTORY. (THE WOMEN'S NETWORK DIRECTORY). Main/Corp Vancouver Women's Network. VFOAT Vancouver Women's Network Directory. VAT Vancouver Women's Network Directory (1984). 1983/84-. 0824-2755. CN. English. Vancouver Women's Network, c/o University of British Columbia, Centre for Continuing Education, Vancouver British Columbia V6T 2A4 Canada. DD 305.4302571133. *Vancouver Women's Network Directory, 0711-4168.*

WOMEN'S ORGANIZATIONS & LEADERS DIRECTORY. VAT Women's Organizations and Leaders Directory. 1973-. 0092-6639. US. English. be. Today News Service Inc, National Press Building, Washington DC 20045. Tel (202)347-7777. LC HQ1883. DD 301.41206273. NLM HQ 1883 W872.

Yearbooks, Almanacs, Directories

WOMEN'S RIGHTS ALMANAC. 1974-. 0363-5082. US. English. an. $4.95. Elizabeth Cady Stanton Publishing Company, 5857 Marbury Road, Bethesda MD 20034. LC HQ1406. DD 301.4120973.

WOODALL'S CAMPGROUND DIRECTORY. EASTERN EDITION. (WOODALL'S CAMPGROUND DIRECTORY). **VFOAT** Campground Directory. 5th- Ed. 1977-. 0162-7406. US. English. an. $12.95. Woodall Publishing Company, 500 Hyacinth Place, Highland Park IL 60035. **Tel** (312)433-4550. Ed Linda Profaizer. **DD** 647.9473. adv acc. **Circ** 450,000. Directory contains complete listings of campgrounds in the United States; public and private campgrounds, inspection rated.

WOODALL'S CAMPGROUND DIRECTORY. NORTH AMERICAN EDITION. (WOODALL'S CAMPGROUND DIRECTORY). **VFOAT** Campground Directory. 11th Ed. (1977)-. 0146-1362. US. English. an. 6.95. Woodall Publishing Company, 500 Hyacinth Place, Highland Park IL 60035. **Tel** (312)433-4550. **LC** GV198.56. **DD** 647.9473. adv acc. Includes full color US map, interesting travel section, at front of each state, containing information about climate, time zone, and most popular attractions, etc. Woodall's Trailering Parks & Campgrounds. North American Ed.

WOODALL'S CAMPGROUND DIRECTORY. WESTERN EDITION. (WOODALL'S CAMPGROUND DIRECTORY). **VFOAT** Campground Directory. 6th- Ed. 1977-. 0162-7414. US. English. an. $4.95. Woodall Publishing Company, 500 Hyacinth Place, Highland Park IL 60035. **DD** 647.9473.

WOODALL'S DIRECTORY OF MOBILE HOME COMMUNITIES. 24th- Ed. 0094-1891. US. English. an. $5.95. Woodall Publishing Company, 500 Hyacinth Place, Highland Park IL 60035. **LC** TX907. **DD** 647.9473. Woodall's Mobile Home Park Directory.

WOODALL'S FLORIDA CAMPGROUND DIRECTORY. **VFOAT** Florida Campground Directory. 1st- 1973-. 0090-5151. US. English. an. $1.95. Woodall Publishing Company, 500 Hyacinth Place, Highland Park IL 60035. **LC** SK601.5.F6. **DD** 917.59046.

WOODALL'S MISSOURI/ARKANSAS CAMPGROUND DIRECTORY. **VFOAT** Missouri/Arkansas Campground Directory. 0163-5328. US. English. an. Woodall Publishing Company, 500 Hyacinth Place, Highland Park IL 60035. **Tel** (312)433-4550. adv acc. Contain expanded listings for all campgrounds listed in each state or group of states.

WOODALL'S RETIREMENT DIRECTORY. (WOODALL'S . . . RETIREMENT DIRECTORY). 1982-. 0731-6526. Periodical. US. English. an. Woodall Publishing Company, 500 Hyacinth Place, Highland Park IL 60035. **Tel** (312)433-4550. **LC** HQ1063. **DD** 646.79. adv acc. A complete, illustrated directory featuring all leisure living opportunities for those people contemplating active retirement. Woodall's . . . Sunbelt Retirement Directory, 0731-5635.

WOODALL'S THE TENTING DIRECTORY. (WOODALL'S THE TENTING DIRECTORY. WESTERN REGION). **VFOAT** Tenting Directory. 1st Ed. (1984)-. 0742-3950. US. English. an. $7.80 Domestic, $7.95 Canada. Woodall Publishing Company, 500 Hyacinth Place, Highland Park IL 60035. **LC** GV191.42.W47. **DD** 647.9478. Designed exclusively for the tent camping families. Easily identifiable symbols at the beginning of the listings indicate whether the campground has a special tenting area.

WOODALL'S THE TENTING DIRECTORY. (WOODALL'S THE TENTING DIRECTORY. EASTERN REGION). **VFOAT** Tenting Directory. 1st Ed. (1984)-. 0742-3969. US. English. an. $7.80 Domestic, $7.95 Canada. Woodall Publishing Company, 500 Hyacinth Place, Highland Park IL 60035. **Tel** (312)433-4550. **LC** GV191.42.A84. **DD** 647.9474. Lists campgrounds in the Southern and Eastern states, as well as the Canadian Provinces of Quebec, New Foundland, Brunswick, Nova Scotia, and the Prince Edward Islands.

WOODALL'S THE TENTING DIRECTORY. (WOODALL'S THE TENTING DIRECTORY. CENTRAL REGION). **VFOAT** Tenting Directory. 1st Ed. (1984)-. 0742-3977. US. English. an. $7.80 Domestic, $7.95 Canada. Woodall Publishing Company, 500 Hyacinth Place, Highland Park IL 60035. **Tel** (312)433-4550. **LC** GV191.42.M525. **DD** 647.9477. Lists campgrounds in the Mid-Western states as well as the Canadian Provinces of Ontario and Manitoba.

WOODALL'S TRAILERING PARKS AND CAMPGROUNDS DIRECTORY. **VFOAT** Trailering Parks and Campgrounds Directory. US. English. Woodall Publishing Company, 500 Hyacinth Place, Highland Park IL 60035. **LC** GV191.35. **DD** 647.9473.

WOODBINE ANGLING YEARBOOK. 1st- Ed. UK. English. MacDonald & Company Ltd, Maxwell House 74 Worship Street, London EC24 2EN England. **LC** SH439. **DD** 799.120942.

WOODSTOVE FIREPLACE AND EQUIPMENT DIRECTORY. 0160-3299. US. English. an. $2.00. Mitchell Associates Inc, 106 Market Street, PO Box 4474, Manchester MA 03108. **LC** TH7438. **DD** 338.4769722.

WOODSTOVE, WOOD, COAL AND SOLAR EQUIPMENT DIRECTORY. (WOODSTOVE, WOOD, COAL, AND SOLAR EQUIPMENT DIRECTORY). **VFOAT** Woodstove Directory. Vol. 5 (1982)-. 0744-0820. US. English. an. $3.50 Domestic, $5.00 Canada. Energy Communications Press Inc, 105 West Merrimack Street, PO Box 4474, Manchester NH 03108. **LC** TH7438. **DD** 683.88. Woodstove, Coalstove, Fireplace & Equipment Directory, 0271-5090.

THE WORLD ALMANAC & BOOK OF FACTS. (THE WORLD ALMANAC AND BOOK OF FACTS). **VAT** World Almanac and Book of Facts. 1923-. 0084-1382. US. English. an. World Almanac c/o Lisa Scott, 1278 West 9th Street, Cleveland OH 44113. **Tel** (216)621-7300. Ed Hana Umlauf Lane. **LC** AY67.N5. **DD** 317.3. **NLM** AY 67.N5 W927. **Circ** 1,000,000. (ctrl). The reference book to have on hand for all the up-to-date facts, statistics, events and information about the past year. World Almanac and Encyclopedia.

WORLD ALMANAC GUIDE TO PRO HOCKEY. (THE WORLD ALMANAC GUIDE TO PRO HOCKEY). 0095-7240. US. English. $1.95. Bantam Books Inc, 666 Fifth Avenue, New York NY 10019. **LC** GV847.5. **DD** 796.962097.

WORLD ARMAMENTS AND DISARMAMENT. (WORLD ARMAMENTS AND DISARMAMENT : SIPRI YEARBOOK). **VFOAT** SIPRI Yearbook, S.I.P.R.I. Yearbook. 1972-. 0347-2205. SW. English. an. 28.00. SIPRI, Pipers Vag 28, S-171 73 Solna Sweden. **Tel** (08)55 97 00. **LC** UA10. **DD** 355.0330047. (cum index). **Circ** 5,000. Armament and disarmament analyses of and statistics on negotiations. New weapons, technologies, arms trade, military expenditure, etc., and their implications. SIPRI Yearbook of World Armaments and Disarmament.

WORLD AVIATION DIRECTORY. V. 1 (No. 1-). 0043-826X. US. English. sa. $150.00. Ziff Davis Publishing Company, 1156 15th Street NW, Washington DC 20005. **Tel** (202)822-4600. **LC** TL512. American Aviation World Wide Directory.

THE WORLD BOOK YEAR BOOK. 1962-. 0084-1439. US. English. an. $18.95. World Book Encyclopedia Inc, PO Box 3405, Chicago IL 60654. **Tel** (800)621-8202. **LC** AE5. World Book Encyclopedia Annual Supplement.

WORLD CEMENT DIRECTORY. English. ir. The European Cement Association, 2 rue Saint-Charles, 75740 Paris Cedex 15 France. **LC** TP876.A2. **DD** 338.476668.

WORLD CLINIC YEARBOOK. Main/Corp American Swimming Coaches Association. 1974-. Periodical. US. English. an. American Swimming Coaches Association, 1 Hall of Fame Drive, Fort Lauderdale FL 33316. **Tel** (305)462-6267.

WORLD COAL INDUSTRY REPORT AND DIRECTORY. V. 1- 1979/80-. 0193-5453. US. English. be. $20.00. Miller Freeman Publications Inc, Circulation Department, 500 Howard Street, San Francisco CA 94105. **LC** HD9540.3. **DD** 338.272025.

WORLD CURRENCY YEARBOOK. **VFOAT** World Currency Year Book. 1984-. 0743-5363. US. English. an. $180.00. World Currency Yearbook, 7239 Avenue North, Brooklyn NY 11234. **Tel** (718)531-3685. Ed Philip Cowitt. **DD** 332. **Circ** 1,000. (ctrl). Complete source of monetary information analyses 146 currency units. Pick's Currency Yearbook, 0079-2063.

WORLD DIRECTORY : CARPETS, SPORTS, SURGICAL. English. ir. $20.00. National Publication Company, 4/35 New Mustafabad, Lahore Pakistan. **LC** HD9937.A1. **DD** 381.4568.

WORLD DIRECTORY OF AL-ANON FAMILY GROUPS AND ALATEENS. Main/Corp Al-Anon Family Group Headquarters, Inc. **VFOAT** Al-Anon World Directory. 0512-2716. US. English. an. $3.00. Al-Anon Family Groups HQ, Box 182 Madison Square Station, New York NY 10010. **LC** HV5001. **DD** 362.292025.

WORLD DIRECTORY OF DEALERS IN ANTIQUARIAN MAPS. 1977-. 0190-4728. US. English. **LC** Z286.M3. **DD** 658.809912.

WORLD DIRECTORY OF ENGINEERING SCHOOLS. 1st- Ed. Periodical. English. ir.

WORLD DIRECTORY OF ENVIRONMENTAL ORGANIZATIONS. **VFOAT** Annuaire Mondial des Organismes de l'Environnement. 1973-. US. English or French. ir. $27.44. California Institute of Public Affairs, PO Box 10, Claremont CA 91711. **Tel** (714)624-5212. **LC** S920. **DD** 333.72025.

WORLD DIRECTORY OF HISTORIANS OF MATHEMATICS. 1st- Ed. 0315-1700. Periodical. CN. English. ir. $7.00. Historia Mathematica, University of Toronto, Toronto Ontario M5S 1K7 Canada. **Tel** (416)978-5047. Ed C E Scriba. **LC** QA30. **DD** 510.9. A list of historians of mathematics and their addresses.

WORLD DIRECTORY OF MATHEMATICIANS. Began with 1958. 0512-2740. II. English. ir. **LC** QA30. **DD** 510.25.

WORLD DIRECTORY OF MEDICAL SCHOOLS. **VFOAT** Repertoire Mondial des Ecoles de Medecine. Began publication with 1953. 0512-2759. US. English (French). ir. World Health Organization, 49 Sheridan Avenue, Albany NY 12210. **Tel** (518)436-9686. **LC** R711. **DD** 610.71. **NLM** W 22 W927.

WORLD DIRECTORY OF NEUROLOGICAL SURGEONS. PART 1, UNITED STATES OF AMERICA AND CANADA. **VFOAT** Directory of Neurological Surgeons in the United States of America and Canada. **VAT** World Directory of Neurological Surgeons. Part One, United States of America and Canada. 0276-5306. US. English. be. Free. World Directory Committee, 324-10th Avenue Suite 140, Salt Lake City, UT 84103. **LC** RD592.5. **DD** 617.480025. (ctrl).

WORLD DIRECTORY OF PHYSIOLOGISTS. **VFOAT** IUPS World Directory. 1977-. US. English. te. IUPS World Directory, American Physiological Society, 9650 Rockville Pike, Bethesda MD 20014.

WORLD DIRECTORY OF SCHOOLS FOR ANIMAL HEALTH ASSISTANTS. 1971-. 0303-7509. SZ. English. ir. $12.00. World Health Organization, 1211, Geneva 27 Switzerland. **Tel** (022)91 24 94. **LC** SF775. **DD** 636.0890711. **NLM** SF 23 W925. A directory providing details of systems of education for animal health assistants and lists of schools in 52 countries throughout the world.

WORLD DIRECTORY OF SCHOOLS FOR MEDICAL ASSISTANTS. **VFOAT** Repertoire Mondial des Ecoles d'Assistants Medicaux. 0378-8598. English (French). ir. **NLM** W 22.1 W927.

WORLD DIRECTORY OF VETERINARY SCHOOLS. 1963-. 0512-2791. Periodical. English. ir. **LC** SF779.A1. **NLM** SF 23 W927.

WORLD DIRECTORY OF WOOD-BASED PANEL PRODUCERS. 1st- Ed. 0160-869X. US. English. be. $55.00. Miller Freeman Publishing, 500 Howard Street, San Francisco CA 94105. **LC** HD9750.1. **DD** 338.456748.

WORLD LEASING YEARBOOK. **VFOAT** World Leasing Year Book. Began with V. For 1980. 0264-0732. UK. English. an. Davsell Ltd, 33 Gold Street L-2, New York NY 10038.

WORLD LEGAL DIRECTORY. 1974-. US. English. World Peace through Law Center, 400 Hill Building, Washington DC 20006. **DD** 340.025. World Law Directory.

WORLD MUSEUM PUBLICATIONS. (WORLD MUSEUM PUBLICATIONS : A DIRECTORY OF ART AND CULTURAL MUSEUMS, THEIR PUBLICATIONS AND AUDIO-VISUAL MATERIALS). 1982-. 0000-0698. US. English. ir. R R Bowker & Company, 205 East Forty-Second Street, New York NY 10017. **Tel** (212)916-1600. **LC** AM1. **DD** 069.025. **NLM** Z 5931 W919.

Yearbooks, Almanacs, Directories

WORLD NUCLEAR DIRECTORY (HARLOW, ESSEX). (WORLD NUCLEAR DIRECTORY). Series/Titl Reference on Research. 6th Ed.-. UK. English. ir. $180.00. Gale Research Company, Book Tower, Detroit MI 48226. Ed C W J Wilson. LC QC770. DD 539.7025. Provides a comprehensive worldwide guide to 2,500 organizations in over 90 countries that conduct, promote, and encourage research and development work in the field of pure and applied atomic energy. *Nuclear Research Index.*

WORLD PHARMACEUTICALS DIRECTORY. 1980-. 0276-2277. US. English. Unlisted Drugs, PO Box 401, Chatham NJ 07928. NLM QV 22.1 W928.

WORLD PROGRESS YEARBOOK. 0091-1852. US. English. Standard Educational Corporation, 200 West Monroe, Chicago IL 60606. LC D410. DD 909.82.

WORLD STATISTICAL DIRECTORY OF VOLUNTEER AND DEVELOPMENT SERVICE ORGANISATIONS. VFOAT Repertoire Statistique Mondial des Organisations de Volontaires et de Service pour le Developpement. English, French, and Spanish. ir. International Secretariat for Volunteer Service, 10 Chemin de Surville, Geneve 1213 Switzerland. LC HV7. DD 361.0025.

WORLD TELECOMMUNICATIONS DIRECTORY. 0364-3360. US. English. World Telecommunications, PO Box Y, Montclair NJ 07042. LC HE7621. DD 384.025.

WORLD TOPICS YEAR BOOK. 1956-. US. English. LC D410. DD 905.8.

WORLD TRAVEL DIRECTORY. V. 1-1970-. US. English. an. $85.00. Ziff-Davis, PO Box 5840, Cherry Hill NJ 08034. Tel (212)725-3500. LC G154. DD 380.14591025.

WORLD-WIDE CHAMBER OF COMMERCE DIRECTORY. VFOAT Johnson's World Wide Chamber of Commerce Directory. VAT World Wide Chamber of Commerce Directory. July 1981-. 0733-1509. US. English. an. $21.00. US International Marketing Company, 17057 Bellflower Boulevard/Suite 205, Bellflower CA 90706. Tel (213)925-2918. Ed R M Meadow. Circ 2,000. Lists US and major overseas chambers of commerce consulates, embassies, in US and abroad. *World Wide Chamber of Commerce Directory (1979), 0733-1509.*

WORLD-WIDE GOLF DIRECTORY. 1973-. 0093-2477. US. English. an. $9.75. World Sports Publishers, 1511 K Street Northwest/Suite 1036, Washington DC 20005. LC GV975. DD 796.35206025.

WORLD-WIDE SUMMER PLACEMENT DIRECTORY. 1952-. 0512-3879. Periodical. US. English. an. Advancement and Placement Institute, 169 North 9th Street, Brooklyn NY 11211. Ed Beth Dobson. DD 371.4.

WORLD WINE ALMANAC & WINE ATLAS. (WORLD WINE ALMANAC & WINE ATLAS COMPLETE WINE BUYING GUIDE & CATALOGUE OF WINE LABELS). VAT World Wine Almanac and Wine Atlas Complete Wine Buying Guide and Catalogue of Wine Labels. 1976-. 0145-9848. US. English. International Wine Society, 304 East 45th Street, New York NY 10017. LC TP544. DD 641.220275.

WORLDWIDE DIRECTORY OF NATURAL AND HOT SPRINGS. 0736-3249. Periodical. US. English. te. $39.95. Alpha Pyramis Publishing Company, 153 South Bradford, Dover DE 19901.

WORLDWIDE DIRECTORY OF PLACES TO LOCATE RECYCLABLE SCRAP. 0736-329X. US. English. te. $59.95. Alpha Pyramis Publishing Company, 153 South Bradford, Dover DE 19901.

WORLDWIDE EDUCATIONAL DIRECTORY. English. ir. International Educational Services, PO Box No 11119, Karachi 47 Pakistan. LC L900. DD 371.0025.

WORLDWIDE PETROCHEMICAL DIRECTORY. VFOAT Petrochemical Worldwide Directory, Petrochemical Directory. 11th Ed. (1973)-. 0084-2583. US. English. an. $85.00 US/Canada, $106.50 Others. Penwell Publishing Company, PO Box 1260, Tulsa OK 74101. Tel (918)835-3161. Ed William R Leek Jr. LC TP692.3. DD 338.47661804025. adv acc. Circ 2,500. Directory of petrochemical plant operators worldwide. Included is a survey of plant feedstocks and the products produced from these feedstocks. *Petrochemical Directory, 0090-9904.*

WORLDWIDE PIPELINE AND CONTRACTORS DIRECTORY. (WORLDWIDE PIPELINE & CONTRACTORS DIRECTORY). 7th Ed. (1982)-. 0146-3349. US. English. an. $50.00 US and Canada, $62.00 Others. Pennwell Directories, A Division of Pennwell Publishing Company, Box 1260, Tulsa OK 74101. Tel (918)835-3161. Ed William R Leek Jr. LC TN879.5. DD 338.7665544025. bk rev. adv acc. Circ 1,500. *0146-3349.*

WORLDWIDE PIPELINES AND CONTRACTORS DIRECTORY. VFOAT Worldwide Directory Pipelines and Contractors. 1st-6th Ed. 0146-3349. US. English. an. Pennwell Publishing Company, PO Box 1260, Tulsa OK 74101. Tel (918)835-3161. Ed William R Leek Jr. LC TN879.5. DD 338.4766554. adv acc. Circ 1,250. Directory of gas, crude oil, petroleum products, and coal slurry pipeline operators. Additional section of engineering and construction firms.

WORLDWIDE REFINING AND GAS PROCESSING DIRECTORY (TULSA, OKLA. : 1978). (WORLDWIDE REFINING AND GAS PROCESSING DIRECTORY). VFOAT Worldwide Directory, Refining and Gas Processing, Refining and Gas Processing, Directory, Refining and Gas Processing. 36th Ed. (1978/79)-. 0277-0962. US. English. an. $85.00 Domestic, $106.50 Foreign. Pennwell Publishing Company, PO Box 1260, Tulsa OK 74101. Tel (918)835-3161. Ed William R Leek Jr. adv acc. Circ 2,500. Directory of refining and gas processing companies worldwide. Includes plant operators, engineering and construction companies, several surveys for refinery, and gas capacities, etc. *Gas Processing, Refining, and Worldwide Directory.*

WRIGLEY'S HOTEL DIRECTORY. 18th-1928-. 0316-8298. Periodical. CN. English. an. Wrigley Directories, 1104 Hornby Street/Suite 203, Vancouver British Columbia V6Z 1V9 Canada. DD 647.947. *Wrigley's Hotel Red Book, 0316-8301.*

WRITERS' & ARTISTS' YEARBOOK. 0084-2664. US. English. an. Writers Digest, 9933 Alliance Road, Cincinnati OH 45242. Tel (513)984-0717. Writers, artists, photographers and songwriters can sell their work in English-speaking countries world-wide with this handy directory.

WRITERS' & ARTISTS' YEARBOOK (LONDON, ENGLAND : 1984). (WRITERS' & ARTISTS' YEARBOOK). VFOAT Writers' and Artists' Yearbook. 1984-. UK. English. an. $5.36. Adam and Charles Black, 35 Bedford Row, London WC1R 4JH England. Tel (01)242-0946. Handbook and directory for writers, artists, publishers, photographers, designers, and composers. *International Writers' & Artists' Yearbook.*

THE WRITERS DIRECTORY. 1971/73-. 0084-2699. UK. English. be. $35.00. St Martins Press, 175 Fifth Avenue, New York NY 10010. LC PS1. DD 808.

WRITERS GUILD DIRECTORY. 0196-5611. US. English. an. $10.00. Writers Guild of America West Inc, 8955 Beverly Boulevard, Los Angeles CA 90048. LC PS5. DD 810.2573.

WRITER'S YEARBOOK. US. English. an. $2.95. Writer's Digest Books, 9933 Alliance Road, Cincinnati OH 45242. *Writer's Year Book.*

WU YU NIEN CHIEN. VFOAT Housing Directory. 1983-. Periodical. HK. Chinese. an. $50.00. Wu Yu Kuan Li Yu Hsien Kung SSU, 23/F Wu Sang House, 655 Nathan Road, Kowloon Hong Kong.

WURZBURGER JAHRBUCHER FUR DIE ALTERTUMSWISSENSCHAFT. 1.-4 Yearly Vol. 1946-1950. Periodical. GW. German (English, or Italian). an. 70.-. Ferdinand Schoeningh Kommissionsverlag, Postfach 129, D-8700 Wurzburg 11 West Germany. Tel 0931/12044. Ed Joachim Latacz and Gunter Neumann. LC PA25. adv acc. Circ 600.

WYOMING DIRECTORY OF MANUFACTURING AND MINING. 1956-. 0511-0289. US. English. ir. $15.00. Manufacturers News Inc, 4 East Huron Street, Chicago IL 60611. Tel (312)337-1084. LC HD9727.W8. DD 338.0025787. Each listing includes firm name, address, chief officer, employee figure, phone, and product and market areas. Alphabetical, geographical and SIC sections.

WYOMING MINERAL YEARBOOK. 0096-9842. US. English. an. Wyoming Department Economic Planning & Development, Barrett Building, Cheyenne WY 82002. Tel (307)777-7284. LC HD9506.U63. DD 338.209787.

WYOMING OFFICIAL DIRECTORY. See Public Administration.

THE Y-NOT ANTIQUE & FLEA MARKET DIRECTORY. VAT Y-Not Antique and Flea Market Directory, Why-Not Antique and Flea Market Directory. 0192-8821. US. English. an. $3.00. Y-Not, PO Box 8561, Fort Lauderdale FL 33310. LC NK1127. DD 381.45745102573.

YACHTING YEARBOOK OF NORTHERN CALIFORNIA. (YACHTING YEAR BOOK OF NORTHERN CALIFORNIA). 0094-8136. US. English. an. $8.20. Yachting Year Book of Northern California, 582 Market Street, San Francisco CA 94104. LC GV825. DD 797.109794.

YACHTING'S BOAT BUYERS GUIDE. (YACHTING'S BOAT BUYERS GUIDE : DIRECTORY OF BOATS AND EQUIPMENT). VFOAT Boat Buyers Guide. 0740-7483. Periodical. US. English. an. $3.95. Ziff-Davis Publishing Company, One Park Avenue, New York NY 10016. LC VM333. DD 623.82230294. *Yachting Boat Owners Buyers Guide.*

THE YACHTSMAN'S POCKET ALMANAC. 0276-8917. US. English. an. Simon and Schuster Building, Rockefeller Center, 1230 Avenue of the Americas, New York NY 10020. LC GV811.8. DD 797.105.

YEAR BOOK. Main/Corp Banaras Hindu University. Centre of Advanced Study in Philosophy. II. English. ir. Banaras Hindu University, Centre of Advanced Study in Philosophy, Varanasi 5 India. LC B130. DD 107.11542.

YEAR BOOK. Main/Corp Clothing Institute. 1967-72. UK. English. Clothing Institute, 17/18 Henrietta Street, London England. LC TT490.C65. DD 687.06242.

YEAR BOOK. Main/Corp Ittihad Al-Sinaat Al-Misriyah. 1971-. English. ir. 26 A Sherif Street Immobilia, Cairo United Arab Republic Egypt. LC HC531. DD 338.0962.

YEAR BOOK. Main/Corp Society of Actuaries. VFOAT Yearbook. US. English. an. $55.00. Society of Actuaries, 500 Park Boulevard, Itasca IL 60143. Tel (312)773-3010. Ed Linda M Delgadillo. LC HG8754. DD 368.0106073. Circ 13,000. (ctrl). *Year Book.*

YEAR BOOK. Main/Corp Norske Handelskammer i London. VFOAT Year Book and Directory of Members. 0305-0998. UK. English. an. Norwegian Chamber of Commerce, 21-24 Cockspur Street, London SW1Y 5BN England. LC HF302.

. . . YEAR BOOK. Main/Corp Institute of Actuaries (Great Britain). UK. English. an. Alden Press Ltd, Osney Road, Oxford OX2 OEF England. Tel (0865)49071. LC HG8754. DD 368.306242.

YEAR BOOK. Main/Corp Faculty of Actuaries in Scotland. Began with 1938-39 issue. UK. English. an. $1.53. Faculty of Actuaries, 23 Saint Andrew Square, Edinburgh EH2 1AQ Scotland. LC HG8602. DD 368.9411.

YEAR BOOK. Main/Corp Library Association. VFOAT Library Association Year Book. UK. English. an. Library Association Publishing Ltd, 7 Ridgemount Street, London WCIE 7A England. LC Z673. DD 020.62241. *Library Association Year Book.*

YEAR BOOK. Main/Corp Dr. S. Radhakrishnan Institute for Advanced Study in Philosophy. 1976-77-. English. ir. Free. University of Madras, Madras 600005 India. LC B130. DD 181.405. *Year Book.*

YEAR BOOK. Main/Corp Owsley Family Historical Society. US. English. an. Owsley Family Historical Society, L5 Greenbriar Drive, Tchefuncta Club Estates, Covington LA 70433. LC CS71. DD 929.20973.

YEAR BOOK. Main/Corp California Community Foundation. VFOAT Yearbook. 1981-. Periodical. US. English. an. California Community Foundation, 1151 West 6th Street, Los Angeles CA 90017. *Report - California Community Foundation.*

YEAR BOOK - AMERICAN ACADEMY OF ACTUARIES. Main/Corp American Academy of Actuaries. 1967-. 0569-2032. US. English. an. American Academy of Actuaries, PO Box 95991, Chicago IL 60694. LC HG8754. DD 368.006273.

Yearbooks, Almanacs, Directories

YEAR BOOK - AMERICAN PHILOSOPHICAL SOCIETY. (YEAR BOOK - THE AMERICAN PHILOSOPHICAL SOCIETY). **Main/Corp** American Philosophical Society. **VAT** Yearbook - American Philosophical Society. 1937-. 0065-9762. US. English. an. American Philosophical Society, PO Box 493, Canton MA 02021. **Tel** (617)232-9885. **Ind/Abst** GeoRef, Bibliogr. Index Geol., Hist. Abstr., Part A, Mod. Hist. Abstr., Hist. Abst., Part B, Twent. Century Abstr. **LC** Q11. **DD** 506.273. **NLM** W1 YE102D. **CODEN** YAPSAL.

YEAR BOOK - AMERICAN SOCIETY OF BOOKPLATE COLLECTORS AND DESIGNERS. (YEAR BOOK). **VFOAT** Yearbook. Vol. 34 (1967/1968)-. 0275-1569. English. an. American Society of Bookplate Collectors and Designers, 605 North Stoneman Avenue #F, Alhambra CA 91801. **DD** 769.

YEAR BOOK AND CLERICAL DIRECTORY. **Main/Corp** Church of the Province of South Africa. SA. English. an. Ecumenical Distribution Trust, PO Box 2115, 2000 Literature, Johannesburg South Africa. **LC** BX5700.6.A1. **DD** 283.68025. *South African Church Yearbook and Clerical Directory.*

THE YEAR-BOOK AND DIGEST. 1979-. II. English. an. Taxation Publishers Private Limited, 174 Jor Bagh, New Delhi 110003 India. **DD** 343.540402638, 345.403402638. *Taxation's Year Book and Digest.*

YEAR BOOK & DIRECTORY. **Main/Corp** Society of Airway Pioneers. **VFOAT** Airway Pioneer. Periodical. US. English. Society of Airway Pioneers, PO Box 17020, San Diego CA 92117. **LC** TL501. **DD** 629.13006273.

YEAR BOOK AND DIRECTORY OF MEMBERS. **Main/Corp** Institution of Structural Engineers (London, England). UK. English. 0.75 each issue. J Morris Publicity Ltd, Publicity House Streatham Hill, London SW2 4TP England. **LC** TA680. **DD** 624.170621. *Year Book and List of Members.*

YEAR BOOK AND DIRECTORY OF MEMBERS. **Main/Corp** Institute of Building. 1967/68-. UK. English. an. 10.00 single issue. J Morris Publicity Ltd, Englemer Kings Ride Ascot Berks, London SL5 8BJ England. **LC** TH13.2.G7. **DD** 690.06242.

YEAR BOOK AND PROCEEDINGS OF THE GENERAL ASSEMBLY - PRESBYTERIAN CHURCH OF NEW ZEALAND. (YEAR BOOK AND PROCEEDINGS OF THE GENERAL ASSEMBLY). **Main/Corp** Presbyterian Church of New Zealand. General Assembly. 1970-. 0110-0416. NZ. English. an. $1.00. Otago Daily Times, Dundeon Ci, New Zealand. **LC** BX9165. **DD** 285.2931. *Proceedings of the General Assembly of the Presbyterian Church of New Zealand, 0551-9845; Year Book - Presbyterian Church of New Zealand, 0551-9853.*

YEAR BOOK & REGISTER OF MEMBERS. **Main/Corp** Clarinet & Saxophone Society (Great Britain). **VFOAT** Year Book and Register of Members. 0260-1702. UK. English. an. Clarinet & Saxophone Society of Great Britain, Honorary Secretary, 26 Monks Orchard, Wilmington Kent DA1 2TB England. **LC** ML27.G7. **DD** 788.602541.

YEAR BOOK - ANDHRA PRADESH AKADEMI OF SCIENCES. **Main/Corp** Andhra Pradesh Akademi of Sciences. II. English. ir. Andhra Pradesh Akademi of Sciences, Osmanian University, Hyderabad India. **LC** Q73. **DD** 506.25484.

YEAR BOOK - ASSOCIATION OF COUNTY COUNCILS. **Main/Corp** Association of County Councils. UK. English. an. 2.00. Association of County Councils, Eaton House/66A Eaton Square, London SW1W 9BH England. **Tel** (01)235-1200. **Circ** 3,000. Details the association's aims and constitution; information on member counties, Association County Councils committees and other national and local organizations. *Year Book - County Councils Association.*

YEAR BOOK, AUSTRALIA. Began with No. 62 for 1977/78. 0312-4746. AT. English. an. $32.10. Australian Bureau of Statistics, 8th Floor Commonwealth Banks Building, Cnr Elizabeth and Flinders Streets, Melbourne Victoria 3000 Australia. **Tel** (03)652-6490. **Ind/Abst** Energy Res. Abstr. **LC** HA3001. **DD** 319.4. **NLM** W2 KA8 B9O. The principal general reference work of the ABS Central Office. Includes statistical material, illustrated by maps, pictures and graphs. *Official Year Book of Australia, 0312-4746.*

YEAR BOOK - CARNEGIE INSTITUTION OF WASHINGTON. **Main/Corp** Carnegie Institution of Washington. No. 1-1902-. 0069-066X. US. English. an. $8.00. Carnegie Institution of Washington, 1530 P Street Northwest, Washington DC 20005. **Tel** (202)387-6411. **Ed** Ray Bowers. **Ind/Abst** GeoRef, Biol. Abstr., Bibliogr. Agric. **LC** AS32. **DD** 505. **NLM** W1 YE102P. **CODEN** CIWYAO. (cum index). **Circ** 700. Describes for the nonspecialist reader the year's work by the institution's scientists in biology, astronomy, and the earth sciences. Includes opening commentary by the President.

YEAR BOOK - CHICAGO MERCANTILE EXCHANGE. **Main/Corp** Chicago Mercantile Exchange. 1952/53-. 0577-7259. US. English. an. $10.00. Chicago Mercantile Exchange, 30 South Wacker Drive, Chicago IL 60606. **Tel** (312)930-3454. **LC** HG6046. **DD** 338.5. *Dairy and Poultry Yearbook.*

YEAR BOOK COLOR ATLAS SERIES. 0147-9784. Monographic Series. US. English. ir. Yearbook Medical Publishers, 35 East Wacker Drive, Chicago IL 60601. **Tel** (312)726-9733. **LC** UNC.

YEAR BOOK - DUTCHESS COUNTY HISTORICAL SOCIETY. (YEAR BOOK). **Main/Corp** Dutchess County Historical Society. **VFOAT** Yearbook. 0739-8565. US. English. an. $15.00. Dutchess County Historical Society, Box 88, Poughkeepsie NY 12602. **Tel** (914)471-1630. **Ed** John and Mary Lou Jeanneney. bk rev. adv acc. **Circ** 1,000. Scholarly and folk articles concerning the local history of Dutchess County New York from precolonial days through the present. *Year Book of the Dutchess County Historical Society, 0739-8565.*

YEAR BOOK - FLORIDA GENEALOGICAL SOCIETY, TAMPA, FLA. **Main/Corp** Florida Genealogical Society, Tampa, Fla. 0428-7282. US. English. ir. $7.00. Florida Genealogical Society, PO Box 18624, Tampa FL 33679. **Tel** (813)839-0810. **Ed** Helen Norris Byrd. bk rev. adv acc. **Circ** 315. (ctrl). Genealogical and historical material, primarily but not restricted to Florida, queries and book reviews.

YEAR BOOK - FLORIDA STATE BOARD OF ENGINEER EXAMINERS. **Main/Corp** Florida. State Board of Engineer Examiners. US. English. ir. Florida State Board of Engineer Examiners, Gainesville FL 32611. **LC** TA24.F6.

YEAR BOOK FOR NORWEGIAN PETROLEUM SOCIETY. **Main/Corp** Norsk Petroleumsforening. 1979-. English. ir. Norwegian Information Publishers AS, PO Box 873, Sentrum Oslo 1 Norway. **LC** TN860.

YEAR BOOK - HISTORICAL SOCIETY OF HOPKINS COUNTY. **Main/Corp** Historical Society of Hopkins County (Kentucky). V. 1-1975-. 0197-0291. US. English. an. Free for Life and Endowment Members. Historical Society of Hopkins County, 107 Union Street, Madisonville KY 42431. **LC** F457.H8. **DD** 976.9823005.

YEAR BOOK - INSURANCE ACCOUNTING AND STATISTICAL ASSOCIATION. **Main/Corp** Insurance Accounting and Statistical Association. 0534-4352. US. English. an. Edwin C Carlson, Insurance Accounting and Statistical Association, 406 West 34th Street, Kansas City MO 64111. **LC** HG8019. **DD** 657.836.

YEAR BOOK (LEO BAECK INSTITUTE). (YEAR BOOK). **Series/Titl** Publications of the Leo Baeck Institute. Began with Vol. 5 (1960). UK. English (German). an. **Ind/Abst** Am. Hist. Life, Hist. Abstr., Part A, Mod. Hist. Abstr., Hist. Abst., Part B, Twent. Century Abstr. **LC** DS135.G3. **DD** 305.8924043. (cum index). *Year Book (Leo Baeck Institute of Jews from Germany).*

YEAR BOOK - NATIONAL AURICULA & PRIMULA SOCIETY (SOUTHERN SECTION). **Main/Corp** National Auricula and Primula Society. Southern Section. UK. English. an. $4.60. National Auricula & Primula Society, 146 Queens Road, Cheadle Cheshire SK8 5HY England.

YEAR BOOK OF ADULT CONTINUING EDUCATION : YEAR BOOK OF THE NATIONAL INSTITUTE OF ADULT CONTINUING EDUCATION (ENGLAND AND WALES). 1983-84-. 0265-1726. UK. English. an. National Institute of Adult Continuing Education, 19B de Montfort Street, Leicester LE1 7GE England. **LC** LC5201. **DD** 374.005. *Year Book of Adult Education.*

YEAR BOOK OF ADULT EDUCATION. **VFOAT** Yearbook of the National Institute of Adult Education. 1961-. 0084-3601. UK. English. an. $6.89. National Institute of Adult Continuing Education, 19B de Montfort Street, Leicester LE1 7GE England. **Tel** (0533)551451. **DD** 374.005. adv acc. **Circ** 2,000. A comprehensive directory of adult education in the UK-organizations, addresses, information, contacts, publications, etc. *Guide to Studies in Adult Education.*

THE YEAR BOOK OF ANESTHESIA. **Series/Titl** Practical Medicine Year Books. 1963/64-. 0084-3652. US. English. an. Yearbook Medical Publishers, 35 East Wacker Drive, Chicago IL 60601. **NLM** W1 YE106. *Year Book of General Surgery, 0084-3776.*

THE YEAR BOOK OF CANCER. **Series/Titl** The Practical Medicine Year Books. 1956/57-. 0084-3679. US. English. an. Yearbook Medical Publishers, 35 East Wacker Drive, Chicago IL 60601. **LC** RC261. **DD** 616.994058. **NLM** W1 YE112.

THE YEAR BOOK OF CARDIOLOGY. 1976-. 0145-4145. US. English. an. Yearbook Medical Publishers, 35 East Wacker Drive, Chicago IL 60601. **LC** RC681.A1. **DD** 616.12005. **NLM** W1 YE113. *Year Book of Cardiovascular Medicine, 0360-6023.*

THE YEAR BOOK OF CLINICAL PHARMACY. **VAT** Yearbook of Clinical Pharmacy. 1981-. 0271-7956. US. English. an. $29.95. Year Book Medical Publishers Inc, 35E Wacker Drive, Chicago IL 60601. **LC** RM300. **DD** 615.705. **NLM** W1 YE114B.

THE YEAR BOOK OF CRITICAL CARE MEDICINE. **VFOAT** Critical Care Medicine. **VAT** Yearbook of Critical Care Medicine. 1983-. 0734-3299. Periodical. US. English. an. $39.95. Year Book Medical Publishers, 35 Wacker Drive, Chicago IL 60601. **Tel** (312)726-9733.

THE YEAR BOOK OF DENTISTRY. **Series/Titl** The Practical Medicine Year Books. 1936-. 0084-3717. US. English. an. Yearbook Medical Publishers, 35 East Wacker Drive, Chicago IL 60601. **LC** RK16. **DD** 610.58 S. **NLM** W1 YE117.

THE YEAR BOOK OF DERMATOLOGY AND SYPHILOLOGY CEASED. **Series/Titl** The Practical Medicine Year Books. 1933-58/59. 0093-3627. US. English. an. Brown & Connolly Inc, 1399 Boylston Street, Boston MA 02215. **NLM** W1 YE121. *Dermatology and Syphilis. Urology, 0093-3554.*

THE YEAR BOOK OF DIAGNOSTIC RADIOLOGY. 1975-. 0098-1672. US. English. an. Yearbook Medical Publishers, 35 East Wacker Drive, Chicago IL 60601. **LC** RC78. **DD** 616.0757205. **NLM** W1 YE122. *Year Book of Radiology, 0084-3989.*

YEAR BOOK OF DIGESTIVE DISEASES. (THE YEAR BOOK OF DIGESTIVE DISEASES). 1984-. 0739-5930. Periodical. US. English. an. $39.95. Year Book Medical Publishers, 35 East Wacker Drive, Chicago IL 60601. **LC** RC799. **DD** 616.33005.

THE YEAR BOOK OF DRUG THERAPY. **Series/Titl** Practical Medicine Year Books. 1949-. 0084-3733. US. English. an. Yearbook Medical Publishers, 35 East Wacker Drive, Chicago IL 60601. **Ed** H Beckman. **NLM** W1 YE126. *Year Book of General Therapeutics, 0270-0638.*

THE YEAR BOOK OF EMERGENCY MEDICINE. **VAT** Yearbook of Emergency Medicine. 1981-. 0271-7964. US. English. an. Yearbook Medical Publishers, 35 East Wacker Drive, Chicago IL 60601. **LC** RC86. **DD** 616.02505. **NLM** W1 YE143.

THE YEAR BOOK OF ENDOCRINOLOGY. **Series/Titl** The Practical Medicine Year Books. 1950-. 0084-3741. US. English. an. Yearbook Medical Publishers, 35 East Wacker Drive, Chicago IL 60601. **Ed** W O Thompson. **LC** RC648. **DD** 616.4058. **NLM** W1 YE144. *Yearbook of Endocrinology, Metabolism and Nutrition, 0196-836X.*

THE YEAR BOOK OF FAMILY PRACTICE. 1977-. 0147-1996. US. English. an. Yearbook Medical Publishers, 35 East Wacker Drive, Chicago IL 60601. **LC** R101. **DD** 616.005. **NLM** W1 YE155.

YEAR BOOK OF INFECTIOUS DISEASES. **VFOAT** Yearbook of Infectious Diseases. 0743-9261. US. English. an. $42.95. Year Book Medical Publishers, 35 East Wacker Drive, Chicago IL 60601.

Yearbooks, Almanacs, Directories

YEAR BOOK OF LABOUR STATISTICS. VFOAT Annuaire des Statistiques du Travail, Anuario de Estadisticas del Trabajo / International Labour Office. 10th issue (1947/48)-. 0084-3857. English (text in French and Spanish). an. A comprehensive survey of annual data from all parts of the world, relating to economically active population, employment, unemployment, hours of work, wages, labour cost, industrial disputes, etc. Annuaire des Statistiques du Travail. Anuario de Estadisticas del Trabajo. Year Book of Labour Statistics.

YEAR BOOK OF MEDICINE. (THE YEAR BOOK OF MEDICINE). 1901-. 0084-3873. US. English. an. Yearbook Medical Publishers, 35 East Wacker Drive, Chicago IL 60601. **LC** R101. **NLM** W1 YE26.

THE YEAR BOOK OF NEUROLOGY AND NEUROSURGERY. 1969-. 0513-5117. US. English. an. Yearbook Medical Publishers, 35 East Wacker Drive, Chicago IL 60601. **LC** RC329. **DD** 616.8. **NLM** W1 YE276N. Yearbook of Neurology, Psychiatry and Neurosurgery (Chicago, Ill. : 1953).

THE YEAR BOOK OF NUCLEAR MEDICINE. VFOAT Nuclear Medicine. V. 1-1966-. 0084-3903. US. English. an. Yearbook Medical Publishers, 35 East Wacker Drive, Chicago IL 60601. **LC** RC93.A1. **DD** 616. **NLM** W1 YE279. **CODEN** YNUMA.

THE YEAR BOOK OF OBSTETRICS AND GYNECOLOGY. (THE . . . YEAR BOOK OF OBSTETRICS AND GYNECOLOGY). **Series/Titl** Practical Medicine Year Books. Began with 1933. 0084-3911. US. English. an. Yearbook Medical Publishers, 35 East Wacker Drive, Chicago IL 60601. **LC** RG26. **DD** 610.58 S. **NLM** W1 YE282. Obstetrics. Gynecology.

THE YEAR BOOK OF OPHTHALMOLOGY. 1957/58-. 0084-392X. US. English. an. Yearbook Medical Publishers, 35 East Wacker Drive, Chicago IL 60601. **LC** RE6. **DD** 617.7058. **NLM** W1 YE285. Yearbook of the Eye, Ear, Nose and Throat.

THE YEAR BOOK OF ORTHOPEDICS. 1980-. 0276-1092. US. English. an. Year Book Medical Publishers Inc, 35 East Wacker Drive, Chicago IL 60601. **LC** RD711. **DD** 617.3005. **NLM** W1 YE287Z. Year Book of Orthopedics and Traumatic Surgery, 0084-3938.

THE YEAR BOOK OF ORTHOPEDICS AND TRAUMATIC SURGERY. **Series/Titl** Practical Medicine Yearbooks. 1969-79. 0084-3938. US. English. an. Yearbook Medical Publishers, 35 East Wacker Drive, Chicago IL 60601. **NLM** W1 Y3228B. **CODEN** YOTSA. Year Book of Orthopedics, Traumatic and Plastic Surgery, 0190-3713.

THE YEAR BOOK OF OTOLARYNGOLOGY. 1976-. 0146-7247. US. English. an. Yearbook Medical Publishers, 35 East Wacker Drive, Chicago IL 60601. **Ed** M M Paparella and M S Strong. **LC** RF11. **DD** 616.21. **NLM** W1 YE29. Yearbook of the Ear, Nose & Throat and Maxillofacial Surgery.

THE YEAR BOOK OF PATHOLOGY AND CLINICAL PATHOLOGY. **Series/Titl** Practical Medicine Year Books. 1947-. 0084-3946. US. English. an. Yearbook Medical Publishers, 35 East Wacker Drive, Chicago IL 60601. **NLM** W1 YE293. Year Book of Pathology and Immunology.

THE YEAR BOOK OF PEDIATRICS. **Series/Titl** Practical Medicine Year Books. 1933-. 0084-3954. US. English. an. Yearbook Medical Publishers, 35 East Wacker Drive, Chicago IL 60601. **NLM** W1 YE297. Pediatrics.

THE YEAR BOOK OF PLASTIC AND RECONSTRUCTIVE SURGERY. **Series/Titl** The Practical Medicine Year Books. VFOAT Plastic and Reconstructive Surgery. 1970-. 0084-3962. US. English. an. Yearbook Medical Publishers, 35 East Wacker Drive, Chicago IL 60601. **Tel** (800)621-9262. **LC** RD118.A1. **DD** 617.95. **NLM** W1 YE21. **CODEN** YPRSA.

THE YEAR BOOK OF PSYCHIATRY AND APPLIED MENTAL HEALTH. **Series/Titl** The Practical Medicine Year Books. VFOAT Psychiatry and Applied Mental Health. VAT Yearbook of Psychiatry and Applied Mental Health. 1970-. 0084-3970. US. English. an. $43.50. Yearbook Medical Publishers, 35 East Wacker Drive, Chicago IL 60601. **LC** RC329. **DD** 616.89005. **NLM** W1 YE316K.

Yearbook of Neurology, Psychiatry and Neurosurgery (Chicago, ILL. : 1953), 0364-5126.

YEAR BOOK OF SOCIAL POLICY IN BRITAIN. (THE YEAR BOOK OF SOCIAL POLICY IN BRITAIN). 1971-. 0307-0476. UK. English. an. Routledge & Kegan Paul Ltd, 9 Park Street, Boston MA 02108. **Tel** (617)742-5863. **Ind/Abst** Int. Labour Doc. **LC** HV248. **DD** 361.942.

THE YEAR BOOK OF SPORTS MEDICINE. 1979-. 0162-0908. US. English. an. $30.00. Year Book Medical Publishers, 35 East Wacker Drive, Chicago IL 60601. **LC** RC1200. **DD** 617.102705. **NLM** W1 YE333M.

THE YEAR BOOK OF SURGERY. 1971-. 0090-3671. US. English. an. Yearbook Medical Publishers, 35 East Wacker Drive, Chicago IL 60601. **LC** RD9. **DD** 617.005. **NLM** W1 YE182. Year Book of General Surgery, 0084-3776.

YEAR BOOK OF THE (COLLEGIATE). **Main/Corp** Collegiate Reformed Protestant Dutch Church of the City of New York. VFOAT Yearbook of the (Collegiate) Reformed Protestant Dutch Church of the City of New York. Began in 1880. US. English. an. Free. Reformed protestant Dutch Church of the City of New York, 45 John Street, New York 10038. **Tel** (212)233-1960. **Ed** Catharine Gallagher. **LC** BX9531.N5. **Circ** 3,000. (ctrl). Mission and service of the collegiate church of New York City.

YEAR BOOK OF THE INDIAN NATIONAL SCIENCE ACADEMY. (THE YEAR BOOK OF THE INDIAN NATIONAL SCIENCE ACADEMY). **Main/Corp** Indian National Science Academy. 0073-6619. II. English. an. Asia Books & Periodicals Company, 1/3 Darya Ganj Ansari Road, New Delhi-110002 India. **LC** Q73. **DD** 506.254. Year Book of the National Institute of Sciences of India, 0375-5193.

THE YEAR BOOK OF THE INTERNATIONAL COUNCIL OF SCIENTIFIC UNIONS. **Main/Corp** International Council of Scientific Unions. Began publication in 1954. 0074-4387. English. an. $5.00. ICSTI, 51 Bd de Montmorency, Paris 75016 France.

YEAR BOOK OF THE ROYAL SOCIETY OF EDINBURGH. **Main/Corp** Royal Society of Edinburgh. 1940/41-. 0080-4576. UK. English. an. $15.00 US. Royal Society of Edinburgh, 22 George Street, Edinburgh EH2 2PQ England. **Tel** 031-225-6054. **Ed** William H Rutherford. **Ind/Abst** GeoRef, Bibliogr. Index Geol. **LC** Q41. **DD** 068.41. **NLM** W1 YE374E. **CODEN** RSEYAX. **Circ** 1,500. Proceedings of meetings, obituaries, list of fellows, prizes, awards and annual report.

YEAR BOOK OF TRANSPORT STATISTICS. Began with 1973 Vol. English. ir. **LC** HE273.6. **DD** 380.509595.

YEAR BOOK OF UROLOGY. 1933-. 0084-4071. US. English. an. Yearbook Medical Publishers, 35 East Wacker Drive, Chicago IL 60601. Urology.

THE YEAR BOOK OF WORLD AFFAIRS CEASED. V. 1-38. 0084-408X. UK. English. an. **Ed** G W Keeton and Georg Schwarzenberger. **LC** JX21. **DD** 341.058. (cum index).

YEAR-BOOK OF WORLD PROBLEMS AND HUMAN POTENTIAL. 1st- ed. 0304-0089. English. ir. Union of International Associations, Rue Washington 40, B-1050 Bruxelles Belgium. **Tel** (01)32026404109. **Ed** A Judge, O Victor, and Nebel. **LC** AS2.5. **DD** 050. **NLM** WA 22.1 Y39. **Circ** 5,000. Concordance to international and national social, political, economic and military problems and the various means to overcome them.

YEAR BOOK - PERQUIMANS COUNTY HISTORICAL SOCIETY. **Main/Corp** Perquimans County Historical Society. 1958/59-. 0196-8866. US. English. an. Secretary of Perquimans County Historical Society, PO Box 652, Hertford NC 27944. **LC** F262.P4. **DD** 975.6144005. Each issue contains an index to its own contents - no vol index - loose.

YEAR BOOK - ROYAL INSTITUTION OF CHARTERED SURVEYORS. (YEAR BOOK - THE ROYAL INSTITUTION OF CHARTERED SURVEYORS). **Main/Corp** Royal Institution of Chartered Surveyors. 1974/75-. 0308-1451. UK. English. an. 9.00. Thomas Skinner Directories, Rac House, Lansdowne Road, Croydon CR9 2HE England. **LC** TA501. **DD** 624.

YEAR BOOK - ROYAL SOCIETY OF TROPICAL MEDICINE AND HYGIENE. 1920-. 0080-4711. Periodical. UK. English. an. 7.50. Royal Society of Tropical Medicine and Hygiene, Manson House, 26 Portland, London W1N 3EY England. **Tel** (01)580-2127. **NLM** W1 YE375. adv acc. **Circ** 3,500. Covers laws of the society. Contains a list of members, alphabetically and by country. Year Book - Society of Tropical Medicine and Hygiene, London.

YEAR BOOK - ROYAL YACHTING ASSOCIATION. **Main/Corp** Royal Yachting Association. 0307-868X. UK. English. an. Royal Yachting Association, 5 Buckingham Gate, London SW1 England. **LC** GV814. **DD** 797.125.

YEAR BOOK - TIRE AND RIM ASSOCIATION INC. (YEARBOOK - TIRE AND RIM ASSOCIATION). **Main/Corp** Tire and Rim Association. 0362-6725. US. English. an. $18.00. Tire & Rim Association, 3200 West Market Street/Suite 304, Akron OH 44313. **Tel** (216)836-5553. Airplane Handbook.

YEAR BOOK - TORONTO HISTORICAL BOARD. **Main/Corp** Toronto Historical Board. 1975-. 0226-7209. CN. English. an. Toronto Historical Board, General Office, Stanley Barracks, Toronto Ontario M6K 3C3 Canada. **DD** 352.945909713541. Annual Report, 0226-7217.

YEAR BOOK - ULSTER FOLK AND TRANSPORT MUSEUM. **Main/Corp** Ulster Folk and Transport Museum. 1973/74-. UK. English. ir. Ulster Folk Museum, Cultra Manor Holywood Co Down, Northern Ireland. Yearbook.

YEAR BOOK - UNITED REFORMED CHURCH. **Main/Corp** United Reformed Church. 1973/74-. UK. English. an. 86 Travistock Place, London SC1H 9RT England. **LC** BX9890.U25. **DD** 285.2.

YEAR BOOK - VENEZUELAN-AMERICAN CHAMBER OF COMMERCE & INDUSTRY. **Main/Corp** Venezuelan-American Chamber of Commerce & Industry. VFOAT Venamcham Year Book. VAT Year Book - Venezuelan-American Chamber of Commerce and Industry. English. an. $30.00. Venezuelan-American Chamber of Commerce and Industry, Apartado 5181, Caracus Venezuela. **Tel** 31.30.07. **Ed** Michael E Heggie. **LC** HF296.A29. **DD** 380.106287. adv acc. **Circ** 3,000. The most comprehensive guide to businesses available in Venezuela. This membership directory contains the names, addresses, officers, and other vital data pertaining to our 520 member companies. Year Book - American Chamber of Commerce of Venezuela.

YEAR BOOK . . . (. . . YEAR OF ISSUE). **Main/Corp** Church of Scotland. 1966-. 0069-3995. UK. English. an. Church of Scotland Publishers Department, 121 George Street, Edinburgh EH2 4YN Scotland. Church of Scotland Year-Book.

YEAR-END REPORT - HERITAGE CONSERVATION AND RECREATION SERVICE. **Main/Corp** United States. Heritage Conservation and Recreation Service. **Series/Titl** HCRS Publication. 1978-. 0192-6621. US. English. an. US Department of the Interior, Heritage Conservation & Recreation Service, Washington DC 20240. **LC** E151. **DD** 353.0085.

YEARBOOK. **Main/Corp** American Goat Society. 0065-8456. US. English. ir. American Goat Society Inc, Route 2 Box 112, Deleon TX 76444.

YEARBOOK. **Main/Corp** American Society of Sanitary Engineering. 0066-068X. US. English. an. $10.00. American Society of Sanitary Engineering, PO Box 40362, Bay Village OH 44140. **Tel** (216)835-3040.

YEARBOOK. **Main/Conf** Claremont Reading Conference. 25th-. US. English. an. $16.00. Claremont Reading Conference, Claremont Graduate School, Harper Hall, Claremont CA 91711. **Tel** (714)621-3750. **Ed** Malcolm P Douglass. **Ind/Abst** Educ. Index. **Circ** 1,500. Reports of the annual Claremont Reading Conference. Focuses on the nature of the reading (and writing) process and its relationship to thinking, learning, and knowing. Yearbook - Claremont College Reading Conference.

YEARBOOK. **Main/Corp** Lutheran Church in America. US. English. an. $5.95. Fortress Press, 2900 Queen Lane, Philadelphia PA 19129. **Tel** (215)848-6800. **Ed** R T Swanson. adv acc. **Circ** 15,000. Directory of clergy, congregations, and

Yearbooks, Almanacs, Directories

church wide in America including colleges, seminaries and institutions.

YEARBOOK. Main/Corp International Court of Justice. 1946/47-. NE. English. an. $10.00. United Nations Publications, Sales Section/Room A-3315, New York NY 10017. Tel (212)754-8302. LC JX1971.6. DD 341.63. Discusses the cases before the court pertaining to subjects such as territorial rights, law of the sea and treaty interpretation.

YEARBOOK. Main/Corp New York Society for the Experimental Study of Education. US. English. an. Society for Experimental Study of Education, 110 Livingston Street, Brooklyn NY 11201.

YEARBOOK. Main/Corp States of Malaya Chamber of Mines. 1966-. English. ir. States of Malaya Chamber of Mines, 130 Jalan Belfield, Ipoh Malaysia. LC HD9506.M3. DD 338.209595.

YEARBOOK. Main/Corp Water Pollution Control Federation. 1960-. US. English. ir. Water Pollution Control Federation, 2626 Pennsylvania Avenue NW, Washington DC 20037. Tel (202)337-2500.

YEARBOOK. Main/Corp International Maritime Committee. VFOAT Annuaire - Comite Maritime International, Annuaire. English (French). ir. c/o Messrs Henry Voet-Genicot, 17 Borzestraat, B2000 Antwerp Belgium.

YEARBOOK. Main/Corp Independent Schools Association. 1957-. Periodical. UK. English. be. Independent Schools Association, Max Gate Etchingham, Sussex TN19 7PF England.

YEARBOOK. Main/Corp Illinois Credit Union League. VFOAT Illinois Credit Union League . . . Yearbook. US. English. an. Illinois Credit Union League, 2D11 Swift Drive, Oak Park IL 6052.

YEARBOOK. Main/Conf Citadel Reading Conference. VFOAT Annual Citadel Reading Conference Yearbook. US. English. an. LC LB1049.9. DD 371.3028205.

YEARBOOK - AFRICANA SOCIETY OF PRETORIA. Main/Corp Africana Society of Pretoria. VFOAT Jaarboek - Africana Vereiging van Pretoria. 1- 1975-. SA. Afrikaans (English). ir. Africana Society of Pretoria, Post Box 3239, Pretoria 0001 South Africa. LC DT766. DD 968.005.

YEARBOOK - AMERICAN COUNCIL ON INDUSTRIAL ARTS TEACHER EDUCATION. Main/Corp American Council on Industrial Arts Teacher Education. VFOAT Inventory-Analysis of Industrial Arts Teacher Education Facilities, Personnel and Programs. 1st- 1952-. 0084-6333. Monographic Series. US. English. an. McKnight & McKnight Publishing Company, PO Box 854, Bloomington IL 61701. Tel (309)663-1341. Ind/Abst Educ. Index. LC T61. DD 607.73. Available in microform from Xerox University Microfilms.

YEARBOOK - AMERICAN SOCIETY OF PENSION ACTUARIES. Main/Corp American Society of Pension Actuaries. 0194-3979. US. English. an. American Society of Pension Actuaries, 1700 K Street NW/Suite 404, Washington DC 20006. LC HD7106.U5. DD 331.252.

YEARBOOK AND CHURCH DIRECTORY OF THE ORTHODOX CHURCH IN AMERICA. Main/Corp Orthodox Church in America. 22d- Ed. 0145-7950. US. English. an. $9.50. Route 25A PO Box 675, Syosset NY 11791. Tel (516)922-0550. LC BX496.A5. DD 281.90251812. adv acc. Directory of dioceses, parishes, organizations, institutions and clergy, organized geographically by states. Covers US and Canada, plus foreign OCA parishes. Year Book and Church Directory.

YEARBOOK AND DIRECTORY - CANADIAN ORNAMENTAL PHEASANT & GAME BIRD ASSOCIATION. (YEARBOOK AND DIRECTORY). Main/Corp Canadian Ornamental Pheasant and Game Bird Association. 83-. 0822-8566. CN. English. ir. Free. Canadian Ornamental Pheasant and Game Bird Association, c/o Mrs Inge Neuman, PO Box 1161 Rural Route #1, Uxbridge Ontario L0C 1R0 Canada. DD 636.59406071. (ctrl). Yearbook and Directory of Members (1978), 0712-8738.

YEARBOOK AND DIRECTORY OF OSTEOPATHIC PHYSICIANS. VFOAT Directory of Osteopathic Physicians. VAT Association of Osteopathic Physicians Directory of Osteopathic Physicians. 0084-358X. US. English. an. $35.00. American Osteopathic Association, 212 East Ohio Street, Attn Order Department, Chicago IL 60611. Tel (312)280-5800. DD 615. NLM WB 22 DA2 D5983. Directory of Osteopathic Physicians.

YEARBOOK & DIRECTORY OF THE CHRISTIAN CHURCH (DISCIPLES OF CHRIST). Main/Corp Christian Church (Disciples of Christ). VFOAT Yearbook and Directory of the Christian Church (Disciples of Christ). 0731-5392. US. English. an. General Office of the Christian Church, Disciples of Christ, 222 South Downy Avenue, Indianapolis IN 46206. LC BX7307. DD 286.63.

YEARBOOK AND MINUTES OF THE ANNUAL CONFERENCE - EVANGELICAL FREE CHURCH OF AMERICA. (YEARBOOK AND MINUTES OF THE ANNUAL CONFERENCE). Main/Corp Evangelical Free Church of America. 0092-4660. US. English. an. Evangical Free Church of America, 1515 East 66th Street, Minneapolis MN 55423. LC BX7548.A1. DD 289.9.

YEARBOOK AND PHILATELIC SOCIETIES' DIRECTORY. 0260-1265. UK. English. an. 2.50. British Philatelic Federation Ltd, 1 Bell Yard, London WC2A 2JP England. LC HE6188. DD 769.5606041. B. P. F. Yearbook and Philatelic Societies' Directory.

YEARBOOK & REGISTER MEMBERS. Main/Corp Incorporated Society of Musicians (Great Britain). VFOAT Yearbook and Register of Members. UK. English. an. Incorporated Society of Musicians, 10 Stratford Place, London W1N 9AE England.

YEARBOOK - BAPTIST CONVENTION OF ONTARIO AND QUEBEC. (YEAR BOOK - BAPTIST CONVENTION OF ONTARIO AND QUEBEC). Main/Corp Baptist Convention of Ontario and Quebec. 106th- 1960/61-. 0316-9472. Periodical. CN. English. an. Baptist Convention of Ontario and Quebec, 217 St George Street, Toronto Ontario M5R 2M2 Canada. DD 286.1713.

YEARBOOK - BAPTIST UNION OF WESTERN CANADA. (YEAR BOOK - BAPTIST UNION OF WESTERN CANADA). Main/Corp Baptist Union of Western Canada. Began with 1907 issue. 0067-4087. Periodical. CN. English. an. Baptist Union of Western Canada, 4404-16th Street Southwest, Calgary Alberta T2T 4H9 Canada. DD 286.1712.

YEARBOOK - CANADIAN INSTITUTE OF ACTUARIES. (YEAR BOOK - CANADIAN INSTITUTE OF ACTUARIES). Main/Corp Canadian Institute of Actuaries. VFOAT Annuaire - Institut Canadien des Actuaires. 1966-. 0068-8975. Periodical. CN. text in English and French. Canadian Institute of Actuaries, Suite 506, 116 Alberta Street, Ottawa Ontario K1P 5G3 Canada. DD 368.0106271.

YEARBOOK - CANADIAN LADIES' GOLF ASSOCIATION. (YEAR BOOK - CANADIAN LADIES' GOLF ASSOCIATION). Main/Corp Canadian Ladies' Golf Association. Began with 1967 issue. 0084-8565. Periodical. CN. English (includes some text in French). Canadian Ladies' Golf Association, National Office, 333 River Road, Ottawa Ontario K1L 8B9 Canada. DD 796.35206271.

YEARBOOK - CANADIAN SOCIETY FOR THE STUDY OF EDUCATION CEASED. Main/Corp Canadian Society for the Study of Education. V. 1 began in 1974. Ceased with Vol. 9. 0315-727X. CN. English (summaries in French). 3.00. Canadian Society for the Study of Education, University of Alberta, Faculty of Education, PO Box 1000, Edmonton Alberta T6G 2G5 Canada. LC L13.C37. DD 370.971.

YEARBOOK : COMMERCIAL ARBITRATION. VFOAT Commercial Arbitration. V. 1- 1976-. US. English. an. $37.50. American Arbitration Association, 140 West 51 Street, New York NY 10020. Tel (212)484-4000. Ed Pieter Sanders. LC K2400.A53. DD 346.070269. The foremost guide to commercial arbitration law and practice throughout the world.

YEARBOOK - CONFERENCE OF MENNONITES IN CANADA. Main/Corp Conference of Mennonites in Canada. 1966-. 0543-467X. Periodical. CN. English (includes some text in German). an. Conference of Mennonites in Canada, 600 Shaftesbury Boulevard, Winnipeg Manitoba R3P 0M4 Canada. DD 289.771. Jahrbuch der Konferenz der Mennoniten in Kanada, 0318-028X.

YEARBOOK - CUNA. Main/Corp Credit Union National Association. 1978-. Periodical. US. English. ir. $5.00. Credit Union National Association, PO Box 431, Madison WI 53701. Tel (608)231-4048. Ed Terri Hanke. Circ 5,000. Statistical reports on US credit unions by state. CUNA Yearbook.

YEARBOOK, DIRECTORY & BUYERS' GUIDE. Main/Corp United Synagogue of America. VFOAT Yearbook, Directory and Buyers' Guide. 0747-5152. US. English. an United Synagogue of America, 155 5th Avenue, New York NY 10010. LC BM197.5. DD 296.6705.

YEARBOOK - ENSIGN CLASS ASSOCIATION. Main/Corp Ensign Class Association. 0146-2458. US. English. an. $3.50. 96 Washington Street, Newport RI 02840. LC GV810.5. DD 797.12406273.

YEARBOOK - FIRE MARSHALS ASSOCIATION OF NORTH AMERICA. (YEAR BOOK). Main/Corp Fire Marshals Association of North America. 0090-5313. US. English. 60 Batterymarch Street, Boston MA 02110. LC TH9502. DD 628.9206273.

YEARBOOK - FLORIDA STATE BOARD OF PROFESSIONAL ENGINEERS AND LAND SURVEYORS. (YEAR BOOK - FLORIDA STATE BOARD OF PROFESSIONAL ENGINEERS AND LAND SURVEYORS). Main/Corp Florida. State Board of Professional Engineers and Land Surveyors. 0094-1778. US. English. State Board of Professional Engineers and Land Surveyors, 6990 Lake Eleanor Drive, Orlando FL 32809. LC TA24.F6. DD 620.0025759.

YEARBOOK FOR TRADITIONAL MUSIC. Vol. 13 (1981)-. 0740-1558. US. English (includes some text in French and German). sa. $22.00. International Council of Traditional Music, Columbia University, Music Department, New York NY 10027. Tel (212)678-0332. Ed Dieter Christensen. Ind/Abst MLA Int. Bibliogr. Books Artic. Mod. Lang. Lit., Music Index. LC ML1. DD 781.705. bk rev. Circ 1,000. Scholarly journal for Ethnorusicologists. Yearbook of the International Folk Music Council, 0316-6082.

YEARBOOK - FUTURE TEACHERS OF AMERICA. FLORIDA ASSOCIATION. Main/Corp Future Teachers of America. Florida Association. 1- 1953/54-. 0427-7902. US. English. ir. Florida Association, Future Teachers of America, Tallahassee FL 32304. Ed Margaret Ann Nash. DD 370.

YEARBOOK - GEOLOGICAL SOCIETY OF AMERICA CEASED. Main/Corp Geological Society of America. 0095-3547. US. English. an. Geological Society of America, PO Box 9140, Boulder CO 80301. LC QE1. DD 550.6273.

YEARBOOK - IFA. (YEARBOOK - INTERNATIONAL FISCAL ASSOCIATION). Main/Corp International Fiscal Association. 0377-6662. English. ir. General Secretariat, PO Box 1738, Burg Oudlaan 50, 3016 Rotterdam Netherlands. DD 341.75. Annual of the International Fiscal Association.

YEARBOOK - INSTITUTION OF CIVIL ENGINEERS. Main/Corp Institution of Civil Engineers, London. UK. English. ir. Thomas Telford, 26-34 Old Street, PO Box 101, London EC1P 1JH England. Tel (01)253-9999. LC TA1. DD 624.06242. List of Members.

YEARBOOK - INSTITUTION OF ENGINEERS, SRI LANKA. (YEAR BOOK). Main/Corp Institution of Engineers, Sri Lanka. 1973-. 0302-8062. English. ir. Institution of Engineers Sri Lanka, Lower Chatham Street, Colombo 1 Ceylon. LC TA1.I729. DD 620.00625493.

YEARBOOK - INTER-MENNONITE CONFERENCE, ONTARIO. (YEARBOOK). Main/Corp Inter-Mennonite Conference (Ontario). 8th Ed. (1981)-. 0710-4707. CN. English. an. Inter-Mennonite Conference, Conrad Grebel College, Waterloo Ontario Canada. DD 289.7713. Yearbook, 0319-0218.

YEARBOOK. MANITOBA AGRICULTURE. (YEARBOOK MANITOBA AGRICULTURE). 1963-. 0084-3865. CN. English. an. LC S147. DD 338.1097127.

YEARBOOK - MONTGOMERY COUNTY GENEALOGICAL & HISTORICAL SOCIETY. (YEARBOOK). Main/Corp Montgomery County Genealogical & Historical Society. 1984-. 8755-8432. US. English. an.

Yearbooks, Almanacs, Directories

Montgomery County Genealogical & Historical Society, PO Box 751, Conroe TX 77305-0751. **LC** F392.M7. **DD** 929.1060764153. *Yearbook.*

THE YEARBOOK - NATIONAL ASSOCIATION OF CONGREGATIONAL CHRISTIAN CHURCHES. Main/Corp National Association of Congregational Christian Churches. 1972/73-. 0272-5339. US. English. an. $8.00. Editorial Office/ National Association of Congregational Churches, 87473 South Howell Avenue Box 1620, Oak Creek WI 53154. **Tel** (414)764-1620. Ed J Fred Rennebohm. **LC** BX7113. **DD** 285.83302573. **Circ** 2,400. (ctrl) A directory of membership of Congregational Christian Churches. *Handbook.*

YEARBOOK - NATIONAL COUNCIL FOR THE SOCIAL STUDIES. Main/Corp National Council for the Social Studies. 1st- 1931-. 0085-3720. US. English. an. Free to members. National Council for the Social Sciences, 1515 Wilson Boulevard/Suite 101, Arlington VA 22209. **Ind/Abst** Educ. Index. **LC** H62.A1. **DD** 307.

YEARBOOK - NATIONAL COUNCIL OF TEACHERS OF MATHEMATICS. 1926-. 0077-4103. US. English. an. National Council of Teachers Mathematics, 1906 Association Drive, Reston VA 22091. **Tel** (703)620-9840. **Ind/Abst** Educ. Index. **LC** QA1.

YEARBOOK - NATIONAL COUNCIL OF WOMEN OF CANADA. Main/Corp National Council of Women of Canada. 1- 1894-. CN. English. an. National Council of Women, 270 MacLaren Street, Ottawa Ontario K2P 0M3 Canada. **Tel** (613)233-4953. **DD** 301.41206271.

YEARBOOK - NATIONAL ICE CREAM RETAILERS ASSOCIATION (U.S.). (YEARBOOK). Main/Corp National Ice Cream Retailers Association (U.S.). 8756-1719. US. English. an. National Ice Cream Retailers Association, 1800 Pickwick Avenue, Glenview IL 60025. **LC** TX795.A1. **DD** 381.4563740973.

YEARBOOK - NATIONAL SOCIETY OF PUBLIC ACCOUNTANTS. Main/Corp National Society of Public Accountants. 0547-9193. US. English. an. **LC** HF5601. **DD** 657.606273.

YEARBOOK - NATIONAL TRUST FOR SCOTLAND. (YEARBOOK). Main/Corp National Trust for Scotland. 0077-5916. UK. English. National Trust for Scotland, 5 Charlotte Square, EH2 4DU Edinburgh Scotland. **LC** DA873. **DD** 914.1.

YEARBOOK - NEW YORK COUNTY LAWYERS' ASSOCIATION. Main/Corp New York County Lawyers' Association. 1909-. 0548-8729. US. English. an. New York County Lawyers Association, 14 Vesey Street, New York NY 10007. **Tel** (212)267-6646. Ed Jan Levy. adv acc. **Circ** 10,000. (ctrl). Lists members, officers, past officers, directors, past and present, committees, by-laws of New York County Lawyers' Association.

YEARBOOK OF ADULT AND CONTINUING EDUCATION *CEASED*. 1st-6th Ed. 0146-0927. US. English. an. Marquis Academic Media, 200 East Ohio Street, Chicago IL 60611. **LC** LC5251. **DD** 374.973.

YEARBOOK OF AGRICULTURE. 1926-. 0084-3628. US. English. an. Superintendent of Documents, US Government Printing Office, Washington DC 20402. **Ind/Abst** Biol. Abstr. **LC** S21. **DD** 630.58. **CODEN** YAXAA7. (cum index) *Agriculture Yearbook.*

YEARBOOK OF AMERICAN AND CANADIAN CHURCHES. 41st- 1973-. 0195-9034. US. English. an. $16.64. Abingdon Press, 201 Eighth Avenue South, Nashville TN 37202. **Tel** (615)749-6457. **LC** BR513. **DD** 277.05. *Yearbook of American Churches.*

YEARBOOK OF ASTRONOMY. 1962-. 0084-3660. US. English. mo. W W Norton & Company Inc, 500 Fifth Avenue, New York NY 10110. **Tel** (212)354-5500. Ed J G Porter and P Moore. **LC** QB1. **DD** 523.058. Information for the amateur astronomer, with articles on topical astronomical events and research.

YEARBOOK OF BROADCASTING ARTICLES. VFOAT Broadcasting Articles. V.1- 1959/78-. 0271-3934. Periodical. US. English. an. Federal Publications Inc, 1725 K Street NW, Washington DC 20006. **LC** K29. **DD** 343.7309945.

YEARBOOK OF COMPARATIVE AND GENERAL LITERATURE. 1- 1952-. 0084-3695. US. English. ir. Indiana University, Comparative Literature Program, Ballantine Hall 402, Bloomington IN 47405. **Tel** (812)335-2140. **Ind/Abst** Abstr. Engl. Stud., MLA Int. Bibliogr. Books Artic. Mod. Lang. Lit., Index Book Rev. Humanit. **LC** PN851. adv acc. **Circ** 1,400. Comparative literature, translation theory, East-West literary relations, and comparative arts, including film.

YEARBOOK OF COMPARATIVE CRITICISM. V. 1-. 0084-3709. US. English. ir. Pennsylvania State University Press, 215 Wagner Building, University Park PA 16802. **Tel** (814)865-1327. Ed Joseph P Strelka. **Ind/Abst** MLA Int. Bibliogr. Books Artic. Mod. Lang. Lit. Books on literary criticism.

YEARBOOK OF CONSTRUCTION ARTICLES. VFOAT Construction Articles. Vol. 1 (1931-1982)-. 0747-8399. US. English. Federal Publications Inc, One Lafayette Centre, Washington DC 20036. **Tel** (202)337-7000. Ed Justin Sweet. **LC** K29. **DD** 343.7307869, 347.3037869. adv acc.

YEARBOOK OF CONSTRUCTION STATISTICS *CEASED*. 1963/72-1974/81. 0377-6689. US. English. an. United Nations Publications, Room A-3315, New York NY 10017. **LC** HD9715.A1. **DD** 338.4762405.

THE YEARBOOK OF CONTEMPORARY POETRY. 1936-. English. ir. Avon House, 1790 Broadway, New York NY 10019. Ed Margaret Nelson. **LC** PS614. **DD** 811.50822.

THE YEARBOOK OF CORPORATE MERGERS, JOINT VENTURES AND CORPORATE POLICY. (YEARBOOK ON CORPORATE MERGERS, JOINT VENTURES AND CORPORATE POLICY). 3rd Ed. (1980)-. 0732-5320. US. English. an. Cambridge Corporation, PO Drawer K, Ipswich MA 01938. **Tel** (617)356-0072. Ed Andrew Clapp. **LC** HD2746.5. **DD** 338.8305. adv acc. Reports on mergers, acquisitions, joint ventures, and LBO's, plus analysis by industry, and fully indexed by companies. Used by corporate acquisition executives. *Yearbook of Merger Activity.*

YEARBOOK OF DERMATOLOGY. (THE YEAR BOOK OF DERMATOLOGY). 1902-. 0093-3619. US. English. an. Yearbook Medical Publishers, 35 East Wacker Drive, Chicago IL 60601. **LC** RL26. **DD** 616.5005. **NLM** W1 YE121.

YEARBOOK OF ENGLISH STUDIES. (THE YEARBOOK OF ENGLISH STUDIES). V. 1- 1971-. 0306-2473. UK. English. an. $48.00. Modern Humanities Research Association, Kings College Strand, London WC2R 2LS England. **Ind/Abst** Abstr. Engl. Stud., MLA Int. Bibliogr. Books Artic. Mod. Lang. Lit., Index Book Rev. Humanit., Years Work Eng. Stud. **LC** PE1.

YEARBOOK OF EUROPEAN LAW. 1 (1981)-. UK. English. an. $90.00. Oxford University Press, 16-00 Pollitt Drive, Fairlawn NJ 07410. Ed F G Jacobs. **LC** K29. **DD** 349.405, 344.005. Each issue contains an index to its own contents - no vol index - loose.

YEARBOOK OF FINNISH FOREIGN POLICY. 1973-. 0355-0079. English. ir. Finnish Institute of International Affairs, Museokatu 18 A 9, SF-00100 Helsinki Finland. **Ind/Abst** ABC Pol Sci. **LC** DK451.7. **DD** 327.471.

YEARBOOK OF FISHERY STATISTICS. VFOAT Annuaire Statistique des Peches. V. 1- 1947-. 0084-375X. English, French and Spanish. ir. **LC** SH1. **DD** 338.3727.

YEARBOOK OF FOREIGN TRADE STATISTICS, THIRD COUNTRIES. VFOAT Annuaire des Statistiques du Commerce Exterieur, Pays Tiers. English (and French). ir. European Community Information Service, 2100 M Street Northwest/Suite 707, Washington DC 20037. **LC** HF3871. **DD** 382.0212.

YEARBOOK OF GERMAN-AMERICAN STUDIES. VFOAT Yearbook of German American Studies. Vol. 16 (1981)-. 0741-2827. US. English, 1981. an. $15.00. C Richard Beam Treasurer, 406 Spring Drive, Millersville PA 17551. **Tel** (717)872-8506. Ed J Anthony Burzle. **Ind/Abst** MLA Int. Bibliogr. Books Artic. Mod. Lang. Lit., Writ. Am. Hist. **LC** E184.G3. **DD** 973.0431. bk rev. **Circ** 500. Scholarly articles on all aspects of German culture in America. *Journal of German-American Studies,* 0195-5381.

YEARBOOK OF HIGHER EDUCATION. 1969-. 0084-3784. US. English. an. Marquis Whos Who Inc, 200 East Ohio Street, Chicago IL 60611. **Tel** (800)621-9669. **LC** LB2300. **DD** 378.73. **NLM** LB 2300 Y39. The most comprehensive, convenient and current reference book of its kind. Details more than 3,500 degree-granting institutions of post-secondary education throughout the US and Canada.

YEARBOOK OF INTERNATIONAL ORGANIZATIONS. Series Corp Union of International Associations. Publication -. VFOAT Annuaire des Organisations Internationales. 1st- 1948-. 0084-3814. US. English (French with instructions in various other languages). ir. $420.00. Gale Research, Book Tower, Detroit MI 48226. **Tel** (313)961-2242. **LC** JX1904. Vol.1 contains a comprehensive directory of nearly 20,000 international organizations. Vol. 2 is a country-by-country arrangement of secretariats and memberships. Vol. 3 contains organizations which are classified by subject and region. *Who's Who in International Organizations.*

YEARBOOK OF INTERNATIONAL TRADE STATISTICS. 1st- issue. 0498-0204. US. English. an. $80.00. United Nations Publications, Sales Section/Room A 3315, New York NY 10017. **Tel** (212)754-8302. **LC** JX1977. **DD** 382.058. Gives international coverage of foreign trade statistics through summary tables showing overall trade by regions and countries, world exports by origin and area of destination as well as by product. *International Trade Statistics.*

YEARBOOK OF INVESTMENT STATISTICS. VFOAT Ezhegodnik po Kapitalnym Vlozheniiam. 0230-418X. Hungarian (with explanatory data in English and Russian). an. **LC** HG5470.5.A2. **DD** 332.609439.

YEARBOOK OF ITALIAN STUDIES. 1971-. IT. English. an. Casalini Libri, Via Benedetto da Malano 3, 50014 Fiesole Italy. **Ind/Abst** MLA Int. Bibliogr. Books Artic. Mod. Lang. Lit. **LC** DG401.

YEARBOOK OF JEHOVAH'S WITNESSES. 0084-3849. US. English. an. Watchtower Bible and Track Society, 117 Adams Street, Brooklyn NY 11201.

YEARBOOK OF LABOR STATISTICS. (YEAR BOOK OF LABOR STATISTICS). 1973-. 0115-1851. US. English. an. International Labor Office, 1750 New York Avenue NW, Suite 330, Washington DC 20006. **Tel** (202)376-2315. **LC** HD8713. **DD** 331.1109599.

THE YEARBOOK OF LANDSCAPE ARCHITECTURE. 1983-. 0747-9581. US. English. an. Ed Richard L Austin. **LC** SB469. **DD** 712.05.

YEARBOOK OF NATIONAL ACCOUNTS STATISTICS *CEASED*. Main/Corp United Nations. Statistical Office. VFOAT Annuaire de Statistiques des Comptabilites Nationales. 1957-1981. 0084-3881. US. English (French). an. Publishing Service, United Nations, New York NY 10017. **LC** HC79.I5. **DD** 339.30212. *Statistics of National Income and Expenditure.*

YEARBOOK OF NORDIC STATISTICS. VFOAT Nordisk Statistisk Arsbok. Began with the Yearbook for 1962. 0078-1088. SW. English (Swedish). an. Almqvist & Wiksell, 108 Drottninggatan/PO Box 45150, S-104 30 Stockholm Sweden. **Tel** 85413160. **LC** DL1, HA1465. **DD** 314.8. **NLM** W1 YE278.

YEARBOOK OF PHYSICAL ANTHROPOLOGY. 0096-848X. US. English. ir. Alan R Liss, 41 East 11th Street, New York NY 10003. **Tel** (212)475-7700. **Ind/Abst** Biol. Abstr., Soc. Sci. Citation Index. **NLM** W1 YE312. **CODEN** YANTAE.

YEARBOOK OF PODIATRIC MEDICINE AND SURGERY. 1981-. 0276-6744. US. English. an. Futura Publishing Company, 295 Main Street, Mt Kisco NY 10549. Ed T H Clarke. **LC** RD563. **DD** 617.58505. **NLM** W1 YE316F. *Yearbook of Podiatry.*

YEARBOOK OF PROCUREMENT ARTICLES. V. 1- 1940/61-. US. English. an. **DD** 340. (cum index).

THE YEARBOOK OF PSYCHOANALYSIS AND PSYCHOTHERAPY. (YEARBOOK OF PSYCHOANALYSIS AND PSYCHOTHERAPY). VFOAT Year Book of Psychoanalysis and Psychotherapy. Vol.

Yearbooks, Almanacs, Directories

1-. 8756-4998. US. English. an. $49.95. Newconcept Press Inc, PO Box 124, Emerson NJ 07630. **DD** 616.

YEARBOOK OF RAILROAD FACTS CEASED. 1965-82. 0084-3997. US. English. an. **LC** HE2713. **DD** 385.0973. *Yearbook of Railroad Information, Railroad Information; Railroad Facts.*

YEARBOOK OF ROMANIAN STUDIES. No. 1- 1976-. 0149-7219. Periodical. US. English. an. $5.00. University of South Florida, c/o Edward J Neugaard, Department of Foreign Languages, Tampa FL 33620. **Ind/Abst** MLA Int. Bibliogr. Books Artic. Mod. Lang. Lit. **LC** DR201. **DD** 949.80305.

THE YEARBOOK OF SCHOOL LAW. 1950-. 0084-4004. US. English. an. $29.95. National Organization on Legal Problems on Education, 3601 SW 29th Street, Topeka KS 66614. **Tel** (913)273-3550. Ed L O Garber. **Ind/Abst** Educ. Index. **LC** KF4102.5. **DD** 379.1473. A convenient and concise reference to latest court decisions affecting policy and management in the US, includes subject index/table of cases. *Yearbook of School Law (1933), 0084-4004; Yearbook of Higher Education Law.*

YEARBOOK OF SCIENCE AND THE FUTURE. 1975-. 0096-3291. US. English. an. $10.95. Encyclopedia Britannica Inc, 425 North Michigan Avenue, Chicago IL 60611. **LC** Q9. **DD** 505. *Britannica Yearbook of Science and the Future.*

YEARBOOK OF SPECIAL EDUCATION CEASED. 1st-6th Ed. 0146-2040. US. English. an. Marquis Academic Media, 200 East Ohio Street, Chicago IL 60611. **LC** LC3993.9. **DD** 371.90973. Each issue contains an index to its own contents - no vol index - loose.

YEARBOOK OF STATISTICS: SINGAPORE. 1967-. 0583-3655. SI. English. an. $3.11. Singapore National Printers, 303 Upper Serangdon Road, Singapore 13 Singapore. **LC** HA1797.S5. **DD** 315.957. **NLM** W2 JS6 D4Y.

THE YEARBOOK OF SUBSTANCE USE AND ABUSE. V. 2- 1980-. 0273-3722. US. English. ir. Human Sciences Press, 72 5th Avenue, New York NY 10011. Ed L Brill and C Winick. **LC** HV5825. **DD** 362.2930973. **NLM** W1 YE334. *Yearbook of Drug Abuse, 0090-662X.*

YEARBOOK OF TESTIMONY. 0361-3755. US. English. an. Herald Pub House, Drawer HH, Independence MO 64055. **LC** BX8674. **DD** 289.33.

YEARBOOK OF THE AMERICAN BAPTIST CHURCHES IN THE U.S.A. (YEARBOOK). **Main/Corp** American Baptist Churches in the U.S.A. 0092-3478. US. English. The Judson Book Stores, Valley Forge PA 19481. **LC** BX6207. **DD** 286.173.

YEARBOOK OF THE AMERICAN COUNCIL ON INDUSTRIAL ARTS TEACHER EDUCATION. **Main/Corp** American Council on Industrial Arts Teacher Education. Vol. 1 1952—. Periodical. US. English.

YEARBOOK OF THE AMERICAN LUTHERAN CHURCH. **Main/Corp** American Lutheran Church (1961-). 1961-. 0401-9636. US. English. an. $7.94. Augsburg Publishing House, 426 South Fifth Street, Minneapolis MN 55415. **Tel** (800)328-4648. **LC** BX8009. *Yearbook of the American Lutheran Church, 0401-9636; Lutheran Yearbook of the Evangelical Lutheran Church.*

YEARBOOK OF THE ARIZONA STATE UNIVERSITY READING CONFERENCE. **Main/Conf** Arizona State University Reading Conference. V. 10- 1978-. 0197-4130. US. English. an. $2.00. Graduate Students in Reading Education, Payne B-112, Arizona State University, Tempe AZ 85281. **LC** LB1049.95. **DD** 428.4.

YEARBOOK OF THE ASSOCIATION FOR EDUCATION AND REHABILITATION OF THE BLIND AND VISUALLY IMPAIRED. VFOAT Alliance Yearbook. 1983-. 0748-9714. US. English. an. $15.50. AER, 206 North Washington Street, K Room 320, Alexandria VA 22314. **Tel** (703)548-1884. Ed Gregory Goodrich. **LC** HV1788. **DD** 362.418. **Circ** 6,000. (ctrl). Research papers, reviews of research, legislation, and litigation in the fields of blindness and low vision.

YEARBOOK OF THE ASSOCIATION OF PACIFIC COAST GEOGRAPHERS. Vol. 27 (1965)-. US. English. ir. Oregon State University Press, 101 Waldo Hall, Corvallis OR 97331. **Tel** (503)754-3166. *Yearbook (Association of Pacific Coast Geographers).*

YEARBOOK OF THE CALIFORNIA AVOCADO SOCIETY. **Main/Corp** California Avocado Society. US. English. an. $25.00. California Avocado Society, PO Box 4816, Saticoy CA 93004. **Tel** (805)644-1184. Ed J L Shepherd. **Ind/Abst** Bibliogr. Agric. adv acc. **Circ** 2,500. Compendiums of information on every aspect of avocado industry: culture, marketing, pests and diseases, economics, basic research reports and applied research "how-to" articles, popular and technical. *Yearbook of the California Avocado Association.*

YEARBOOK OF THE CANADIAN BAR ASSOCIATION AND THE MINUTES OF PROCEEDINGS OF ITS ANNUAL MEETING. (YEARBOOK OF THE CANADIAN BAR ASSOCIATION AND THE MINUTES OF PROCEEDINGS OF THE . . . ANNUAL MEETING). **Main/Corp** Canadian Bar Association. VFOAT Annuaire de l'Association du Barreau Canadien et le Proces-Verbal de sa . . . Assemblee Annuelle. 28th (1946)-. 0318-4935. CN. English (French). an. Canadian Bar Association, #320 90 Sparks Street, Ottawa Ontario K1P 5B4 Canada. **DD** 340.06271. *Proceedings of the Council of the Canadian Bar Association, 0318-4919.*

YEARBOOK OF THE EUROPEAN CONVENTION ON HUMAN RIGHTS, THE EUROPEAN COMMISSION AND EUROPEAN COURT OF HUMAN RIGHTS. VFOAT Annuaire de la Convention Europeenne des Droits de l'Homme, Commission et Court Europeennes des Droits de l'Homme. 1958/1959-. Periodical. English. ir. Kluwer Boston Inc, 190 Old Derby Street, Hingham MA 02043. **Tel** (617)749-5262. *Documents and ET Decisions.*

YEARBOOK OF THE INTERNATIONAL ASSOCIATION FOR CHILD AND ADOLESCENT PSYCHIATRY AND ALLIED PROFESSIONS. Vol. 6-. 0277-6790. Monographic Series. US. English. an. John Wiley & Sons Inc, 1 Wiley Drive, Somerset NJ 08873. Ed E James Anthony. **NLM** W1 YE42. Index in last issue of volume - attached. *Yearbook of the International Association for Child Psychiatry and Allied Professions, 0090-6719.*

YEARBOOK OF THE INTERNATIONAL FOLK MUSIC COUNCIL CEASED. V. 1-12. 0316-6082. Periodical. CN. English. an. International Folk Music Council, Queen's University, Music Department, Kingston Ontario Canada. **Ind/Abst** RILM Abstr. **DD** 781.705.

YEARBOOK OF THE INTERNATIONAL LAW COMMISSION. **Main/Corp** United Nations. International Law Commission. 1949-. 0082-8289. US. English. an. $68.50. United Nations Publications, Sales Section/Room A-3315, New York NY 10017. **Tel** (212)754-8302. **LC** JX1977. **DD** 341.0611. Contains summary records of International Law Commission sessions and documents relating to the subjects discussed, including the report to the General Assembly.

YEARBOOK OF THE NATIONAL CONFERENCE OF STATE LEGISLATIVE LEADERS. **Main/Corp** National Conference of State Legislative Leaders. VFOAT State Legislature: Winds of Change. Began with issue for 1966. 0547-521X. US. English. an. Office of the Secretariat, National Conference of State Legislative Leaders, 5215 North Ironwood Road, Milwaukee WI 53217. **LC** JS301. **DD** 328.73.

YEARBOOK OF THE NATIONAL READING CONFERENCE. **Main/Conf** National Reading Conference. 10th- 1961-. 0547-8375. US. English. an. National Reading Conference Inc, 1070 Sibley Tower, Rochester NY 14604. **Tel** (716)546-7241. Ed Jerome A Niles. **Circ** 1,800. Selected papers from the preceding conference. *Yearbook -The National Reading Conference for College and Adults.*

YEARBOOK OF THE NATIONAL SCIENCE TEACHERS ASSOCIATION. VFOAT NSTA Yearbook. 1983-. 0739-1986. US. English. an. $6.50. National Science Teachers Association, 1742 Connecticut Avenue NW, Washington DC 20009. **LC** Q183.3.A1. **DD** 507.1073.

THE YEARBOOK OF THE NATIONAL SOCIETY FOR THE STUDY OF EDUCATION. **Main/Corp** National Society for the Study of Education. 9th-. 0077-5762. Monographic Series. US. English. ir. University of Chicago Press, PO Box 37005, Chicago IL 60637. **Ind/Abst** Educ. Index. **LC** LB5. *Yearbook of the National Society for the Scientific Study of Education.*

YEARBOOK OF THE NEGRO HISTORICAL ASSOCIATION OF COLORADO SPRINGS. 1982-. 0743-4375. US. English. an. NHACS Inc, PO Box 16123, Colorado Springs CO 80935. **LC** F784.C7. **DD** 978.856.

YEARBOOK OF THE UNITED BAPTIST CONVENTION OF THE ATLANTIC PROVINCES. (YEAR BOOK OF THE UNITED BAPTIST CONVENTION OF THE ATLANTIC PROVINCES). **Main/Corp** United Baptist Convention of the Atlantic Provinces. VFOAT United Baptist Yearbook. 1963-. 0082-7843. Periodical. CN. English. United Baptist Convention of the Atlantic Provinces, PO Box 1053, Saint John Newfoundland E2L 4E7 Canada. **DD** 286.1715.

YEARBOOK OF THE UNITED NATIONS. **Main/Corp** United Nations. 1946/47-. 0082-8521. US. English. an. International Publishing Service, Taylor & Francis Inc, 242 Cherry Street, Philadelphia PA 19106. **Tel** (800)821-8312. **LC** JX1977.A37.

YEARBOOK OF U.S.-JAPAN ECONOMIC RELATIONS. VAT Yearbook of United States-Japan Economic Relations. 1978-. 0197-3223. US. English. an. Japan Economic Institute of America, 1000 Connecticut Avenue Northwest, Washington DC 20036. **LC** HF1456.5.J3. **DD** 337.5207305.

YEARBOOK OF WORLD ENERGY STATISTICS CEASED. VFOAT Annuaire des Statistiques Mondiales de l'Energie. 1979-1981. US. English (French). ir. United Nations Publications, Sales Section Room A-3315, New York NY 10017. **Tel** (212)754-8325. **LC** HD9502.A1. **DD** 333.790212. *World Energy Supplies.*

YEARBOOK ON HUMAN RIGHTS FOR . . . . (YEARBOOK ON HUMAN RIGHTS). VFOAT Human Rights Yearbook. 1946-. 0084-4098. US. English. ir. $39.00. United Nations Publications, Sales Section Room A-3315, New York NY 10017. **Tel** (212)754-8302. **LC** JC571. **DD** 323.4058. Contains extracted texts and summaries of significant constitutional, legislative and judicial developments on personal, civil, political, economic, social and cultural rights throughout the world.

YEARBOOK ON INDIA'S FOREIGN POLICY. 1982-83-. 8756-5307. US. English. an. 250.00. Sage Publications, 275 South Beverly Drive, Beverly Hills CA 90212.

YEARBOOK. PROCEEDINGS AND APPOINTMENTS. NEW YORK YEARLY MEETING, RELIGIOUS SOCIETY OF FRIENDS. (YEARBOOK - NEW YORK YEARLY MEETING, RELIGIOUS SOCIETY OF FRIENDS). **Main/Corp** Society of Friends. New York Yearly Meeting. 0148-3013. US. English. an. Society of Friends, 15 Rutherford Place, New York NY 10003. **LC** BX7607.N5. **DD** 289.605.

YEARBOOK - PUBLIC RELATIONS SOCIETY OF AMERICA. (PRSA YEARBOOK). **Main/Corp** Public Relations Society of America. 1st- Ed. 0092-2420. US. English. $2.00. Public Relations Society of America, 845 Third Avenue, New York NY 10022. **LC** HM263. **DD** 659.206273.

YEARBOOK - ROYAL CANADIAN COLLEGE OF ORGANISTS. (YEARBOOK). **Main/Corp** Royal Canadian College of Organists. No. 21 (Oct. 1978)-. 0228-9539. CN. English. an. Royal Canadian College of Organists, Suite 300A/212 King Street West, Toronto Ontario M5H 1K5 Canada. **DD** 786.506071. *Royal Canadian College of Organists Quarterly, 0380-8424.*

YEARBOOK, SHIPYARDS, BOATBUILDERS, AND MARINE ENGINEERS. VFOAT Shipyards, Boatbuilders, and Marine Engineers. English. an. K/S Selvig Publishing A S, PO Box 9070 Vaterland Chr Krohsgst 16A, Oslo Norway. **LC** VM86.5. **DD** 623.8302548.

YEARBOOK - SOCIETY OF COLONIAL WARS (U.S.). (YEARBOOK). **Main/Corp** General Society of Colonial Wars (U.S.). **Series/Titl** Publications of the General Society of Colonial Wars. 1976-. 0882-2328. US. English. an. Society of Colonial Wars, Office of the Secretary General, Lawson Ewing Whitesides, 840 Woodbine Avenue, Glendale OH 45246. **LC** E186.3. *General Society of Colonial Wars.*

YEARBOOK - SUPREME COURT HISTORICAL SOCIETY. **Main/Corp** Supreme Court Historical Society. 1976-. 0362-5249. US. English. an. Supreme Court Historical Society,

Zoology-Vertebrate and Invertebrate

1629 K Street NW, Washington DC 20006. **Tel** (202)785-0298. **Ind/Abst** Leg. Resour. Index, Writ. Am. Hist., Index Leg. Period. **LC** KF8741. **DD** 347.732609.

YEARBOOK - SWAZILAND NATIONAL MUSEUM. Main/Corp Swaziland National Museum. 1976-. English. ir. Swaziland National Museum, PO Box 100, Lobamba Swaziland. **LC** DT971.A2. **DD** 069.09683. *Yearbook - Swaziland National Centre.*

YEARBOOK - UNITED CHURCH OF CANADA. (YEAR BOOK - UNITED CHURCH OF CANADA). **Main/Corp** United Church of Canada. 1927-. 0082-7886. Periodical. CN. English. sa. $10.83. The United Church House, 85 St Clair Avenue E, Toronto Ontario M4T 1M8 CANADA. **Tel** (416)925-5931. Ed Douglas L Flanders. **DD** 287.9205. **Circ** 5,000. (ctrl). A publication of reports, mailing address listings, directories, church statistics, and other reference for The United Church of Canada.

YEARBOOK - UNITED NATIONS. COMMISSION ON INTERNATIONAL TRADE LAW. (YEARBOOK - UNITED NATIONS COMMISSION ON INTERNATIONAL TRADE LAW). **Main/Corp** United Nations Commission on International Trade Law. **Series Corp** United Nations. Document. **VFOAT** International Trade Law Yearbook. V. 1- 1968/70-. US. English. an. United Nations Publications, Room A 3315, New York NY 10017. **LC** JX1977. **DD** 300 S, 341.754.

YEARBOOK - UNITED STATES POLO ASSOCIATION. Main/Corp United States Polo Association. US. English. ir. **LC** GV1011.A1. **DD** 796.353058.

YEARBOOK (WORLD CONFEDERATION OF JEWISH COMMUNITY CENTERS). (YEARBOOK). **VFOAT** Year Book. English (French, Hebrew, and Spanish). an. **LC** DS102.9. **DD** 305.8924.

YEARBOOK - WORLD COUNCIL OF CREDIT UNIONS. Main/Corp World Council of Credit Unions. 0147-7803. Periodical. US. English. an. World Council of Credit Unions, PO Box 431, Madison WI 53701. **LC** HG2033. **DD** 334.2.

YEARBOOK/ANNUAL REPORT. Main/Corp Illinois Credit Union League. US. English. an. Illinois Credit Union League, 2011 Swift Drive, Oak Brook IL 60521. **LC** HG2038.I5. **DD** 334.2209773. *Yearbooks.*

YMCA YEAR BOOK AND OFFICIAL ROSTERS. Main/Corp National Council of the Young Men's Christian Associations of the United States of America. US. English. an. **LC** BV1005.

YMER. ARSBOK. 0044-0477. SW. Swedish. ir. Garvargatan 9, Box 22069, 104 22 Stockholm 22 Sweden. **Ind/Abst** GeoRef. **LC** GN1. **DD** 301. **CODEN** YMERAD. *YMER.*

YOKSO (KUNGNIP CHONMUNDAE (KOREA)). (YOKSO). **VFOAT** Korean Almanac for . . . . KO. Korean. ir. 500. Namsandang 18-1, 1-Ka Namsan-Dong Chung-ku Seoul Korea. **LC** QB4.9.K8.

YORKTON, SASKATCHEWAN, CITY DIRECTORY. VFOAT Henderson's Yorkton City Directory. **VAT** Henderson's Yorkton City Directory (1980). 1980-. 0228-9733. CN. English. an. $60.00. Yorkton Saskatchewan City Directory, Henderson Directories, 419 MacMillan Avenue, Winnipeg Manitoba R3L 0N3 Canada. **DD** 917.1242. *Henderson's Yorkton, Saskatchewan, City Directory, 0319-2490.*

YOUTH CONSERVATION CORPS. (YOUTH CONSERVATION CORPS : YEARBOOK). 1979-. 0276-9271. US. English. an. Division of State Parks, Capital Complex, Carson City NV 89710. **LC** S932.N4. **DD** 333.78309793. *YCC Program, 0276-9263.*

YOUTH GROUP TRAVEL DIRECTORY. 1981-82-. 0817-4127. US. English. an. $7.95. Group Books, Box 481, Loveland CO 80537. **LC** BV4447. **DD** 647.947307.

YOUTH-SERVING ORGANIZATIONS DIRECTORY. VAT Youth Serving Organizations Directory. 1st- Ed. 0196-9668. Periodical. US. English. ir. $72.00. Gale Research Company, Book Tower, Detroit MI 48226. **Tel** (312)961-2242. Ed A Brewer. **LC** HS17. In a single alphabetic sequence, detailed entries, describe relevant special libraries and information centers, research centers, and national associations in the United States.

YUGOSLAVIA; HOTEL AND TOURIST DIRECTORY. VFOAT Hotelsko-Turisticki Adresar. English, French, German, and Serbo-Croatian. ir. Privredni Pregled, Marsala Birjuzova 3-5, Beograd Yugoslavia. **LC** TX910.Y8.

YUSHUTSU HOKEN GYOMU GAIKYO. Main/Corp Japan. Kobe Tsusho Jimusho. No. 10- Oct. 1977-. Japanese. ir. **LC** HG4538.

ZAINICHI GAISHI KIGYO YORAN. VFOAT Directory of Foreign Business in Japan. '84-. JA. Japanese. ir. 6400. Nihon Kogyo Shinbunsha 7-2 Otemachi 1 Chiyoda-ku, Tokyo-to 10 Japan.

THE ZAMBIA DIRECTORY. ZA. English. ir. 10.00. Directory Publishers of Zambia, PO Box 1659, Ndola Zambia. **LC** DT963.A2. **DD** 916.8940025.

ZAMBIA MINING YEAR BOOK. English. ir. Copper Industry Service Bureau, PO Box 2100, Kitwe Zambia. **LC** TN119.Z34. **DD** 338.2096894.

ZAMBIAN INDUSTRIAL DIRECTORY. English. ir. 1.00. Associated Reviews Ltd, Lufunsa Avenue Box 717, Ndole Zambia. **LC** HC517.R42. **DD** 380.10256894.

ZENKOKU DAIGAKU SHOKUINROKU. Began in 1958. Japanese. an. **LC** L961.J3.

ZENKOKU KOGAKU SHOTOKUSHA MEIBO. *See* Business - Public Finance.

ZENKOKU RYOKO GYOSHA MEIBO. JA. Japanese. ir. 2500. Zenkoku Ryokogyo Kyokai, c/o Sanshi Kaikan, 7 Yurakucho 1-chome Chiyoda-ku, Tokyo 100 Japan. **LC** G155.J27. *Zenkoku Ryoko Assen Gyosha Meibo.*

ZIONIST YEAR BOOK. 1951/52-. 0084-5531. UK. English. an. $18.75. Zionist Federation Great Britain & Ireland, 741 High Road Finchley, London N12 OBQ England. **Tel** (01)446-1477. Ed E Salmon. **LC** DS149. **DD** 956.94. adv acc. **Circ** 800. Comprehensive reference and information about Israeli and Jewish institutions and organisations; who is who in Israel and world Jewry.

ZIP+4 STATE DIRECTORY. VFOAT Zip Plus Four State Directory. 1985-. US. English. an. Saint Louis PDC, Zip + 4 State Directory Orders, PO Box 14921, Saint Louis MO 63180-9988.

ZOSEN YEAR BOOK. 1968-. JA. English. ir. Tokyo News Service, Kosoku Doro Building 10 Ginza Nishi 8-Chrome/Chuo-Ku, Tokyo Japan. **LC** VM105. **DD** 338.476238200952.

ZOOLOGY- VERTEBRATE AND INVERTEBRATE

AAZPA ANNUAL CONFERENCE PROCEEDINGS. (AAZPA . . . ANNUAL CONFERENCE PROCEEDINGS). **Main/Corp** American Association of Zoological Parks and Aquariums. **VFOAT** A.A.Z.P.A. . . . Annual Conference Proceedings. 0731-0390. US. English. an. $12.00. American Association of Zoological Parks and Aquariums, Oglebay Park, Wheelin WV 26003. **LC** QL76.5.U6. **DD** 636.0889905.

AAZPA REGIONAL CONFERENCE PROCEEDINGS. Main/Corp American Association of Zoological Parks and Aquariums. **VFOAT** A.A.Z.P.A. Regional Conference Proceedings. **VAT** American Association of Zoological Parks and Aquariums Regional Conference Proceedings. 0731-0439. US. English. an. American Association of Zoological Parks and Aquariums, Oglebay Park, Wheeling WV 26003. **LC** QL76.5.U6. **DD** 636.0889905. *AAZPA Regional Workshop Proceedings, 0731-0420.*

ABEILLE. (L'ABEILLE : ORGANE DE LA FEDERATION DES ASSOCIATIONS APICOLES DU QUEBEC). Vol. 1, No. 1 (July. 1980)-. 0821-5111. Periodical. CN. French. ir. Free. Federation des Associations Apicoles du Quebec, C P 656, St-Hyacinthe Quebec J2S 7P5 Canada. **DD** 638.109714. *Bulletin Apicole (Saint-Hyacinthe, Quebec), 0821-5103.*

L'ABEILLE DE FRANCE ET L'APICULTEUR. No. 1- 1920-. 0373-4625. Periodical. FR. French. mo. Abeille de France, 5 rue Copenhague, 75008 Paris France.

ABSTRACTS OF ENTOMOLOGY. *See* Indexes/Abstracts.

ACAROLOGIA. V. 1- Jan. 1959-. 0044-586X. Periodical. French (English and German). ir. Dawson France, BP 40 F-91, Palaiseau France. **Tel** 842600394. **Ind/Abst** Pestdoc, Ringdoc, Vetdoc, Biol. Abstr., Nuci. Sci. Abstr., Index Med., Sci. Cit. Index, Abr. Ed. **LC** QL458.A2. **NLM** W1 AC585. **CODEN** ACRLAW. (cum index).

ACHATINA. No. 1- 1970-. Periodical. French (English). ir.

ACRIDA. V. 1-10. 0300-4686. Periodical. English, French, or Spanish, with summaries in English or French. ir. **Ind/Abst** Life Sci. Collect., Biol. Abstr., Bibliogr. Agric. **CODEN** ACRDCA.

ACTA ANATOMICA. V. 1-. 0001-5180. Periodical. English (French or German with summaries in English, French and German). mo. $450.00. S Karger AG, PO Box 352, White Plains NY 10602. **Tel** (061)39 08 80. Ed W Lierse and R O'Rahilly. **Ind/Abst** Life Sci. Collect., Excerpta Med., Int. Aerosp. Abstr., Curr. Contents, Index Med., Nuci. Sci. Abstr., Biol. Abstr., Chem. Abstr., Bibliogr. Agric., Sci. Cit. Index, Abr. Ed., Abstr. Anthropol. **LC** QL801. **DD** 611.05. **NLM** W1 AC752. **CODEN** ACATA5. Index in last issue of volume - attached. (cum index). adv acc. Available on microfilm. Concise reports from major laboratories throughout the world present original findings on the macro and microscopic anatomy, ultrastructure, embryology and histochemistry of mammals, in particular man. *Bio-Morphosis.*

ACTA ARACHNOLOGICA. V. 1- 1936-. 0001-5202. Periodical. Japanese (text also in English). an. $1.10. Sunset Shoin Post 113, 22-19 2-chome Hishikata, Sunkyoku Tokyo Japan. **Ind/Abst** Biol. Abstr., Bibliogr. Agric. **CODEN** AACHBY.

ACTA ENTOMOLOGICA BOHEMOSLOVACA. Vol. 62- 1965-. 0001-5601. Periodical. English (and German). bm. 210.00 Domestic, $85.00 US. Kluwer Academic Publishing, PO Box 322, 3300 AH Dordrecht The Netherlands. **Tel** 521041. Ed I Hrdy. **Ind/Abst** Life Sci. Collect., Biol. Abstr., Chem. Abstr., Bibliogr. Agric., Sci. Cit. Index, Abr. Ed. **NLM** W1 AC8013. **CODEN** AEBOA9. bk rev. **Circ** 1,200. General and experimental arachnoentomology, morphology, ecology, physiology, ethology, toxicology and pathology of insects. Taxonomy, faunistics, biographies, and reviews. The fauna of the Palaearctic region. *Casopis.*

ACTA ENTOMOLOGICA FENNICA. No. 1-. 0001-551X. Monographic Series. Fl. English (Finnish). ir. Akakeeminen-Kirjakuppa, PO Box 128, 00101 Helsinki Finland. **Ind/Abst** Life Sci. Collect., Biol. Abstr., Bibliogr. Agric. **LC** QL462. **DD** 595.709471. **NLM** W1 AC8014. **CODEN** AEFEAX.

ACTA MORPHOLOGICA NEERLANDO-SCANDINAVICA. V. 1- 1956-. 0001-6225. NE. English (French; or German). qt. 100.-. Swets & Zeitlinger BV, 347 Heereweg, 2161 Ca Lisse The Netherlands. **Tel** 02521-19113. Ed J Drukker. **Ind/Abst** Life Sci. Collect., Excerpta Med., Biol. Abstr., Chem. Abstr., Index Med., Nuci. Sci. Abstr., Sci. Cit. Index, Abr. Ed. **LC** QL799. **DD** 591.405. **NLM** W1 AC865. **CODEN** AMNSAZ. bk rev. adv acc. **Circ** 800. The journal contains the results of anatomical, histological, icytological, embryological and anthropological research from laboratories of many countries. *Acta Neerlandica Morphologicae Normalis Et Pathologicae.*

ACTA ORNITHOLOGICA. V. 5- Apr. 1955/ 1960-. 0001-6454. Monographic Series. PL. articles in Polish, English, or German, summaries in French and Russian. ir. ARS Polona, Krakowskie Przedmiescie 7, 00-068 Warsaw Poland. **Ind/Abst** Biol. Abstr., Life Sci. Collect., Ref. Z., Zool. Rec. **CODEN** AORNAK. *Acta Ornithologica Musei Zoologici Polonici.*

ACTA ORNITHOLOGICA. (ACTA ORNITHOLOGICA). **Series/Titl** TT. US. English. ir. US Department of Commerce, Clearing House for Federal Scientific & Technical Information, Springfield VA 22161. **LC** QL671. **DD** 598.05.

ACTA PROTOZOOLOGICA. V. 1- 1963-. 0065-1583. Periodical. PL. English (articles in French, German, or Russian with summaries in two of the following: English, French, German, Polish, or Russian). qt. ARS Polona, Krakowskie Przedmiescie 7, 00-068 Warsaw Poland. **Ind/Abst** Life Sci. Collect., Excerpta Med., GeoRef, Biol. Abstr., Chem. Abstr., Bibliogr. Agric., Bibliogr. Index Geol., Sci. Cit. Index, Abr. Ed. **NLM** W1 AC929D. **CODEN** ACPZAU.

ACTA THERIOLOGICA. Vol. 1- 1955-. 0001-7051. PL. English, German, and Polish (summaries in Russian). ir. ARS Polona, Krakowskie Przedmiescie 7, 00-068 Warsaw Poland. **Ind/Abst** Life Sci. Collect., Biol. Abstr., Curr. Contents. Life Sci., Wildl. Rev., Sci. Cit. Index, Abr. Ed. **LC** QL700. **DD** 599. **NLM** W1 AC95R. **CODEN** ATRLAF. Index in last issue of volume - attached.

ACTA ZOOLOGICA BULGARICA. 1- 1975-. 0324-0770. BU. Multilingual (Bulgarian with summaries in French, German, and Russian). ir. 1.131 Per Issue. Izd-vo na Bulgarskata Academiia Na Naukite, 13 Ul Akad G Bonchev, Sofia Bulgaria. **Ind/Abst** Life Sci. Collect., Biol. Abstr., Chem. Abstr., Bibliogr. Agric. **LC** QL298.B8. **CODEN** AZBUD7. *Izvestiia na Zoologicheskiia Institut S Muzei, 0068-3981.*

ACTA ZOOLOGICA CRACOVIENSIA. V. 1Sept. 15, 1956-. 0065-1710. Monographic Series. PL. English (English, French, German or Polish, with summaries in Polish and Russian). ir. ARS Polona, Krakowskie Przedmiescie 7, 00-068 Warsaw Poland. **Ind/Abst** Life Sci. Collect., GeoRef, Biol. Abstr., Bibliogr. Agric., Bibliogr. Index Geol. **LC** QL1. **CODEN** AZCRAY.

ACTA ZOOLOGICA ET PATHOLOGICA ANTVERPIENSIA. No. 39-. 0001-7280. Periodical. BE. Dutch, English, French or German with some summaries in Dutch, English, French and German. ir. Societe Royale de Zoologie, Danvers Koningin Astridplein, Antwerp Belgium Europe. **Ind/Abst** Life Sci. Collect., Chem. Abstr., Biol. Abstr., Bibliogr. Agric., Index Med., Sci. Cit. Index, Abr. Ed. **NLM** W1 AC957E. **CODEN** AZPAAE. *Bulletins de la Societe Royale de Zoologie D'Anvers.*

ACTA ZOOLOGICA FENNICA. Began with Vol. 1- 1926. 0001-7299. Periodical. FI. English (text in English or German). ir. Akakeeminen-Kirjakuppa, PO Box 128, 00101 Helsinki Finland. **Ind/Abst** Life Sci. Collect., GeoRef, Biol. Abstr., Ref. Z., Sel. Water Resour. Abstr., Bibliogr. Index Geol. **LC** QH7. **DD** 591.94897. **NLM** W1 AC957J. **CODEN** AZFEAA. (cum index).

ACTA ZOOLOGICA (KUNGLIGA SCENSKA VETENSKAPSAKADEMIEN). (ACTA ZOOLOGICA). Vol. 62, No. 1-. Periodical. US. English. qt. Pergamon Press, 395 Sawmill River Road, Elmsford NY 10523. *Acta Zoologica (Statens Naturvetenskapliga Forskningsrad (Sweden)), 0001-7272; Zoon, 0346-508X.*

ACTA ZOOLOGICA LILLOANA. V. 1-. 0065-1729. Monographic Series. AG. English (Spanish, with summaries in French or German). ir. Ministerio de Cultura, Educacion Instituto, Minguel Lillo 205, 4000 San Miguel de Tucuman Republica Argentina. **Ind/Abst** Life Sci. Collect., Biol. Abstr., Chem. Abstr., Bibliogr. Agric. **LC** QL1. **DD** 591.05. **CODEN** AZOLA8.

ACTA ZOOLOGICA MEXICANA. V. 1, No. 1- (July 1955)-. 0185-5476. MX. Spanish (English). ir. $20.00. Instituto de Ecologia, Apartado Postal 18-845, 11800 Mexico DF Mexico. **Tel** 271-03-50. **Ed** Instituto de Ecodogin AC. **Ind/Abst** Life Sci. Collect. (ctrl). Topics include behavior, zoogeography, ecology and systematic of terrestrial fauna.

ACTAS Y TRABAJOS DEL . . . ENCUENTRO VENEZOLANO DE ENTOMOLOGIA. **Main/Corp** Encuentro Venezolano de Entomologia. 1, 1976-. Spanish. an. Apartado 4579, Maracay Venezuela.

ADVANCES IN INSECT PHYSIOLOGY. V. 1- 1963-. 0065-2806. UK. English. ir. Academic Press, 4805 Sand Lake Road, Orlando FL 32887. **Tel** (305)345-4100. **Ed** J W L Beament J E Treherne and V B Wigglesworth. **Ind/Abst** Life Sci. Collect., Biol. Abstr., Chem. Abstr., Bibliogr. Agric., Biol. Agric. Index, Sci. Cit. Index, Abr. Ed. **LC** QL495. **DD** 595.7. **NLM** W1 AD651. **CODEN** AIPYAZ.

ADVANCES IN INVERTEBRATE REPRODUCTION. **Main/Corp** International Society of Invertebrate Reproduction. International Symposium. 2nd 1979-. US. English. **LC** QL364.15. **DD** 592.016. *Advances In Invertebrate Reproduction.*

ADVANCES IN ODONATOLOGY. **VFOAT** Proceedings of the Sixth International Symposium of Odonatology. Vol. 1 (1982)-. Monographic Series. English. ir. Dr W Junk, PO Box 3713, The Hague Netherlands. Book series on entomology.

ADVANCES IN PRIMATOLOGY. V. 1-. Monographic Series. US. English. Appleton-Century-Crofts, 25 Van Zant Street, East Norwalk CT 06855. **LC** QL737.P9. **DD** 599.8.

AFRICAN JOURNAL OF ECOLOGY. *See* Veterinary Medicine, Animal Culture.

AFRICANA. V. 1- Mar. 1962-. 0002-0281. Periodical. English. qt. East African Wildlife Society, PO Box 20110, Nairobi Kenya. **LC** QL337.E25. **DD** 591.967605.

ALAUDA. Ser. 1, Vol. 1, No. 1-. 0002-4619. Periodical. FR. French (English and German summaries). qt. $38.58. Soc d'Etudes Ornithologiques, 46 rue d'Ulm, 75230 Paris Cedex 05 France. **Ind/Abst** Life Sci. Collect., Biol. Abstr. **CODEN** ALUDAI. bk rev. adv acc. Ornithology and ecology.

ALEXANOR. V. 1- 1959-. 0002-5208. Periodical. FR. French. qt. 150.00 Domestic, 160.00 Foreign. Revue des Lepidopteristes Francais, 45 rue de Buffon, F-75005 Paris France. **Tel** (1).43.36.04.06. **Ed** Gerard Chr Luquet. **Ind/Abst** Life Sci. Collect., Biol. Abstr., Bibliogr. Agric. **CODEN** ALEXBX. bk rev. adv acc. **Circ** 1,250. (ctrl). General lepidopterology; systematics, nomenclature, biology, ecology, ethology, biogeography, capture and preservation methods, rearing.

ALLATTANI KOZLEMENYEK. V. 63- 1976-. Periodical. HU. Hungarian (some summaries in English or German). an. 52.-. Akademiai Kiado, POB 24, 1363 Budapest Hungary. **Tel** 189-883. **Ed** I Andrassy. **Ind/Abst** Biol. Abstr. **CODEN** ALLKAS. bk rev. **Circ** 400. Different articles of the zoological sciences; neurologies, memorials; book reviews; proceedings of the Hungarian Zoological Society.

AMERICAN ARACHNOLOGY. Began in 1973. 0364-9504. US. English. American Arachnology Society, 940 Poly Drive, Billings MT 59102. **LC** QL453.1.U6. **DD** 595.405. **CODEN** AMARD4.

AMERICAN BIRDS. V. 25- Feb. 1971-. 0004-7686. Periodical. US. English. ir. $32.00. National Audubon Society, 950 Third Avenue, New York NY 10022. **Tel** (212)546-9189. **Ed** Susan Roney Drennan. **Ind/Abst** Can. Environ., Biol. Abstr., Biol. Agric. Index. **LC** QL671. **DD** 598.297. **CODEN** ABRDAZ. bk rev. adv acc. **Circ** 10,000. A seasonal journal devoted to the birds of Americas; their changing distribution, population, migration, rare occurrence, ecology and behavior. Includes field identification, site guides and centers of learning. *Audubon Field Notes, 0097-7144.*

AMERICAN CAGE-BIRD MAGAZINE. **VFOAT** American Cage Bird Magazine. 1935. 0002-7782. Periodical. US. English. mo. $15.00. American Cage Bird Magazine, One Glamore Court, Smithtown NY 11787. **Tel** (516)979-7962. **Ed** Arthur Freud. **LC** SF461.A1. **DD** 636.68605. bk rev. adv acc. **Circ** 13,000. (ctrl). Authoritative articles dealing with the care, breeding and training of parrots, cockatiels, canaries, budgies, finches and other cage birds. *American Canary Magazine.*

AMERICAN HAWKWATCHER. No. 1 (Aug. 1982)-. 0748-8319. Monographic Series. US. English. ir. American Hawkwatcher, 629 Green Street, Allentown PA 18102.

AMERICAN JOURNAL OF PRIMATOLOGY. **VFOAT** Primatology. Vol. 1, No. 1-. 0275-2565. Periodical. US. English. ir. Alan R Liss Inc, 41 East 11th Street, New York NY 10003. **Tel** (212)741-2515. **Ind/Abst** Life Sci. Collect., Excerpta Med., Biol. Abstr., Chem. Abstr., Psychol. Abstr. **LC** QL737.P9. **NLM** W1 AM51F. **CODEN** AJPTDU.

AMERICAN MALACOLOGICAL BULLETIN. Vol. 1 (July 1983)-. 0740-2783. Periodical. US. English. sa. $28.00. University of Southern Mississippi, Department of Biology, Hattiesburg MS 39406-5018. **Tel** (601)266-4751. **Ed** Robert S Prezant. **LC** QL401. **DD** 594.005. adv acc. **Circ** 800. Original research, detailed reviews, and symposia dealing with molluses. *Bulletin of the American Malacological Union, Inc., 0096-5537.*

AMERICAN MUSEUM NOVITATES. Began in 1921. 0003-0082. Monographic Series. US. English. ir. American Museum of Natural History, Central Park West at 79th Street, New York NY 10024. **Tel** (212)873-1300. **Ed** Brenda Jones. **Ind/Abst** Int. Aerosp. Abstr., GeoRef, Biol. Abstr., Bibliogr. Index Geol. **DD** 505. **CODEN** AMUNAL. Index published separately - free - automatically sent. **Circ** 1,500. Contains descriptions of new forms and reports in zoology, paleontology, geology and mineralogy.

AMERICAN PIGEON JOURNAL. V. 1- 1912-. 0003-0511. Periodical. US. English. mo. $14.00. American Pigeon Journal, PO Box 278, Warrenton MO 63383. **Tel** (314)456-2122. *American Pigeon Keeper, Pigeon Loft.*

AMERICAN TAXIDERMIST MAGAZINE. Periodical. US. English. bm. $11.00. American Taxidermist Magazine, PO Box 11186, Albuquerque NM 87112. **Tel** (505)298-3734. **Ed** T E Kelly. bk rev. adv acc. **Circ** 2,700. (ctrl). Trade journal devoted to the technical and commercial aspects of taxidermy.

AMERICAN ZOOLOGIST. V. 1- Feb. 1961-. 0003-1569. Periodical. US. English. qt. American Society of Zoologists, Box 2739, California Lutheran College, Thousand Oaks CA 91360. **Tel** (805)492-3585. **Ed** Milton Fingerman. **Ind/Abst** Sociol. Abstr., GeoRef, Biol. Abstr., Chem. Abstr., Bibliogr. Agric., Gen. Sci. Index, Biol. Agric. Index, Life Sci. Collect., Sci. Cit. Index, Abr. Ed., Bibliogr. Index, Bibliogr. Index Geol. **LC** QL1. **DD** 590.5. **NLM** W1 AM874. **CODEN** AMZOAF. bk rev. adv acc. **Circ** 6,300. Symposia presented at the annual meetings in the biological sciences field.

AMPHIBIA-REPTILIA. V. 1- Aug. 1980-. 0173-5373. Periodical. GW. English (French, German, or Spanish). Uitgeverij E J Brill, Oude Rijn 33A, Postbus 9000, NL-2300 PA Leiden The Netherlands.

ANALES DEL INSTITUTO DE BIOLOGIA, UNIVERSIDAD NACIONAL AUTONOMA DE MEXICO. SERIE ZOOLOGIA. **Main/Corp** Mexico (City). Universidad Nacional. Instituto de Biologia. V. 38- 1967-. 0368-8720. Periodical. MX. Spanish (articles in English and various other languages). ir. Instituto de Biologia Universidad Nacional Autonoma de Mexico, Apartado Post 70-233, Mexico 20 DF Mexico. **Ind/Abst** Life Sci. Collect. *Anales del Instituto de Biologia, 0076-7174.*

ANGEWANDTE PARASITOLOGIE. Vol. 1-. 0003-3162. Periodical. German (summaries in English, Russian, and German). qt. $30.00. VCH Publishers Inc, 303 12th Avenue NW, Deerfield Beach FL 33442. **Tel** (305)428-5566. **Ind/Abst** Life Sci. Collect., Excerpta Med., Index Med., Biol. Abstr., Bibliogr. Agric. **LC** QL757. **DD** 591.524905. **NLM** W1 AN223M. **CODEN** AWPAAR.

ANIMAL BEHAVIOUR. V. 6- Jan./Apr. 1958-. 0003-3472. Periodical. UK. English. qt. 76.50. Bailliere Tindall, 1 St-Annes Road, Eastbourne East Sussex BN21 3UN England. **Tel** (01)630-7881. **Ed** T R Halliday. **Ind/Abst** Life Sci. Collect., Biol. Abstr., Chem. Abstr., Psychol. Abstr., Bibliogr. Agric., Gen. Sci. Index, Biol. Agric. Index, Ringdoc, Pestdoc, Vetdoc, Bibliogr. Index, Index Med., Sci. Cit. Index, Abr. Ed., MLA Int. Bibliogr. Books Artic. Mod. Lang. Lit. **LC** QL750. **DD** 591.51. **NLM** W1 AN228E. **CODEN** ANBEA8. bk rev. adv acc. Examines all aspects of behaviour study. Original papers and critical reviews are published. *British Journal of Animal Behaviour.*

ANIMAL BEHAVIOUR ABSTRACTS. *See* Indexes/Abstracts.

ANIMAL KINGDOM. *See* Conservation & Natural Resources.

ANIMAL LEARNING & BEHAVIOR. **VAT** Animal Learning and Behavior. V. 1- Feb. 1973-. 0090-4996. Periodical. US. English. qt. $48.00. The Psychonomic Society Inc, 2904 Guadalupe Street, Austin TX 78705. **Tel** (512)476-9687. **Ed** Russell Church. **Ind/Abst** Life Sci. Collect., Excerpta Med., Biol. Abstr., Psychol. Abstr., Gen. Sci. Index, Sci. Cit. Index, Abr. Ed., Soc. Sci. Citation Index. **LC** QL785. **DD** 591.5. **NLM** W1 AN228TE. **CODEN** ALBVAB. adv acc. Deals with broad categories of animal learning motivation, emotion and comparative animal behavior. Examples of more specific topics are classical and operant conditioning, habituation. *Psychonomic Science, 0033-3131.*

ANIMALAND. 0019-3127. US. English. Staten Island Zoological Society, 614 Broadway, Staten Island NY 10310. **LC** QL1. **DD** 590.5. *In Animaland with the Staten Island Zoological Society, Inc.*

ANNALEN - KONINKLIJK MUSEUM VOOR MIDDEN-AFRICA, ZOOLOGISCHES WETENSCHAPPEN. (ANNALES - MUSEE ROYALE DE L'AFRIQUE CENTRAL. SERIE IN 8 : SCIENCES ZOOLOGIQUES). **Main/Corp** Musee

Zoology-Vertebrate and Invertebrate

Royale de l'Afrique Centrale. **VFOAT** Annalen - Koninklijk Museum Voor Midden-Afrika. Reeks in 8 : Zoologisches Wetenschappen. No. 91-. Monographic Series. English (French, German, and Italian). Musee Royal de l'Afrique Centr Steenweg OP, Leuven 13, 1980 Tervuren Belgium. **Ind/Abst** Biol. Abstr. **CODEN** MRAZBN. bk rev. **Circ** 350. (ctrl). The annals of the tervuren museum are various papers published in several series: zoology, geology, and cultural anthropology. *Annales du Musee Royale du Congo Belge. Serie in 8 : Sciences Zoologiques.*

ANNALES BIOLOGIE ANIMALE. **Main/Corp** Universite de Clermont-Ferrand. Faculte des Sciences. 1- 1963?-. 0069-4681. Periodical. FR. French. ir. Clermont-Ferrand, Docs BP 6009, 45060 Orleans Cedex France. **DD** 591.

ANNALES DE LA SOCIETE ENTOMOLOGIQUE DE FRANCE. **Main/Corp** Societe Entomologique de France. V. 1 (1832)-V. 11 (1842). 0037-9271. Periodical. FR. French. qt. Annales de la Societe, 45 rue de Buffon, Paris F-75005 France. **Tel** (212)683-4441. **Ind/Abst** GeoRef, Biol. Abstr., Sci. Cit. Index, Abr. Ed. **NLM** W1 AN342. **CODEN** ASEQAQ. (cum index). bk rev. General entomology, systematics (taxonomy, biotaxonomy, phylogeny, comparative morphology). *Revue de Pathologie Vegetale et d'Entomologie Agricole de France.*

ANNALES DE LA SOCIETE ENTOMOLOGIQUE DU QUEBEC **CEASED. Main/Corp** Entomological Society of Quebec. **VFOAT** Annals of the Entomological Society of Quebec. V. 1-28, No. 2/3. 0037-9301. Periodical. CN. English (text also in French). ty. $11.61. Societe Entomologique du Quebec, 2700 Einstein, Ste-Foy Quebec 12 Province of Quebec Canada. **Tel** (418)643-2354. **Ind/Abst** Environ., Biol. Abstr., Bibliogr. Agric. **CODEN** AETQA3.

ANNALES DES SCIENCES NATURELLES. ZOOLOGIE ET BIOLOGIE ANIMALE. **VFOAT** Zoologie et Biologie Animale. 2nd Ed. Ser. V. 1-20, 1834-43. 0003-4339. Periodical. French (with summaries in English and French). qt. Masson Publishing USA Inc, 211 East 43rd Street/Room 1306, New York NY 10017. **Tel** (212)370-1937. **Ind/Abst** Life Sci. Collect., GeoRef, Biol. Abstr. **LC** QH3. **DD** 574.05. **CODEN** ASNBAQ. (cum index). *Annales des Sciences Naturelles, Annales des Sciences Geologiques.*

ANNALES ENTOMOLOGICI FENNICI. **VFOAT** Suomen Hyonteistieteellinen Aikakauskirja. Vol. 26- 1960-. 0003-4428. Periodical. FI. English (Finnish, French or German). ir. Department of Agricultural and Forest Zoology, University of Helsinki, SF-00710 Helsinki Finland. Ed Anna-Liisa Varis. **Ind/Abst** Life Sci. Collect., Chem. Abstr., Biol. Abstr., Bibliogr. Agric. **NLM** W1 AN408. **CODEN** AETFA4. bk rev. **Circ** 700. (ctrl). Concerns entomology-Finland, taxonomic entomology, insect biogeography, insect ecology, insect physiology, acarology, arachnology, and applied entomology. *Suomen Hyonteistieteellinen Aikakauskirja.*

ANNALES ZOOLOGICI. Vol. 16- May 29, 1954-. 0003-4541. Periodical. PL. English (text in French, or German). ir. ARS Polona, Krakowskie Przedmiescie 7, 00-068 Warsaw Poland. **Ind/Abst** Biol. Abstr. **CODEN** AZOGAR. Index in last issue of Volume - attached. *Annales Musei Zoologici Polonici.*

ANNALES ZOOLOGICI FENNICI. V. 1- 1964-. 0003-455X. Periodical. FI. Finnish (English and German). qt. 250.-. Akakeeminen-Kirjakuppa, PO Box 128, 00101 Helsinki Finland. **Tel** (90)651 122. **Ind/Abst** Life Sci. Collect., Excerpta Med., GeoRef, Biol. Abstr., Bibliogr. Agric., Chem. Abstr., Nuci. Sci. Abstr., Sel. Water Resour. Abstr., Sci. Cit. Index, Abr. Ed., Ocean. Abstr., Bibliogr. Index Geol. **CODEN** AZOFAO. *Annales Zoologici Societatis Zoologicae-Botanicae Fennicae Vanamo, 0365-8627; Archivum Societatis Zoologicae-Botanicae Fennicae Vanamo, 0365-7280.*

ANNALI, NUOVA SERIE : SEZIONE 3, BIOLOGIA ANIMALE. SUPPLEMENTO. Main/Corp Universita di Ferrara. **VAT** Annali, Nuova Serie : Sezione Tre, Biologia Animale. Supplemento. French. ir. VIA Festa del Perdono 7, Milano 20122 Italy. **LC** QL368.A22. **DD** 591.05.

ANNALS OF THE ENTOMOLOGICAL SOCIETY OF AMERICA. **Main/Corp** Entomological Society of America. V. 1- Mar. 1908-. 0013-8746. Periodical. US. English. bm. $60.00. Entomological Society of America, 4603 Calvert Road, College Park MD 20740. **Tel** (301)864-1334. Ed C W Schaefer and R W Howard. **Ind/Abst** Life Sci. Collect., Pestdoc, Ringdoc, Vetdoc, Energy Inf. Abstr., Environ. Abstr., Bibliogr. Agric., Biol. Abstr., Chem. Abstr., Nuci. Sci. Abstr., Sel. Water Resour. Abstr., Biol. Agric. Index, Sci. Cit. Index, Abr. Ed. **LC** QL461. **DD** 595.7005. **NLM** W1 AN626S. **CODEN** AESAAI. adv acc. **Circ** 2,000. (ctrl). Available on microfilm from University Microfilms International. Reports on basic aspects of the biology of insects, including taxonomy, systematics, techniques, morphology, behavior, karyology, and reproduction.

ANNALS OF ZOOLOGY. (THE ANNALS OF ZOOLOGY). V. 1- Jan. 1955-. 0003-5009. Periodical. II. English. qt. $30.00. Academy of Zoology, Khandari Road, Agra India. **Tel** 26 86 45. Ed Beni Charan Mahendra. **Ind/Abst** Biol. Abstr., Chem. Abstr., Index Med., Bibliogr. Agric. **LC** QL1. **DD** 590.5. **CODEN** AZLGAC. bk rev. **Circ** 1,500. Taxonomy, anatomy, physiology, cytology and other branches of zoology, both fundamental and applied.

ANNOTATIONES ZOOLOGICAE JAPONENSES **CEASED. VFOAT** Nihon d'Obutsugaku Iho. Vol. 1, Pt. 1 and 2-V. 56, No. 4 (Dec. 1983). 0003-5092. Periodical. JA. English (German, French, and Italian). qt. **Ind/Abst** Life Sci. Collect., GeoRef, Biol. Abstr., Chem. Abstr., Bibliogr. Agric. **LC** QL1. **NLM** W1 AN682. **CODEN** NPDIAH. (cum index).

ANNUAL JOB COMPLETION REPORT. MIGRATORY BIRDS, WATERFOWL. **VFOAT** Migratory Birds, Waterfowl. 1983-. US. English. an. **LC** QL696.A52. **DD** 639.9784109787.

ANNUAL PERFORMANCE REPORT, FEDERAL AID PROJECT E-1, SEGMENT 4. US. English. an. PO Box 7961, Madison WI 53707. **LC** QL84.22.W6. **DD** 591.04209775.

ANNUAL PROGRESS REPORT, CHILKAT RIVER COOPERATIVE BALD EAGLE STUDY. 8755-4690. US. English. an. National Audubon Society, 950 Third Avenue, New York NY 10022. **DD** 598.

ANNUAL REPORT AND ACCOUNTS - BRITISH TRUST FOR ORNITHOLOGY. See Conservation & Natural Resources.

ANNUAL REPORT - COOPERATIVE PARK STUDIES UNIT (MOSCOW, IDAHO). See Forestry.

ANNUAL REPORT - INTERNATIONAL CENTRE OF INSECT PHYSIOLOGY AND ECOLOGY. (ANNUAL REPORT - THE INTERNATIONAL CENTRE OF INSECT PHYSIOLOGY AND ECOLOGY). **Main/Corp** International Centre of Insect Physiology and Ecology. 1st- 1973-. 0304-8314. English. ir. PO Box 30772, Nairobi Kenya. **LC** QL495. **DD** 595.70105.

ANNUAL REPORT - INTERNATIONAL COUNCIL FOR BIRD PRESERVATION, BRITISH SECTION. **Main/Corp** International Council For Bird Preservation. British Section. 1959-. UK. English. an. c/o British Museum of Natural History, Cromwell Road, London England. **LC** QL671. **DD** 333.9505.

ANNUAL REPORT - NATIONAL ZOOLOGICAL PARK (U.S.). **Main/Corp** National Zoological Park (U.S.). **VFOAT** National Zoological Park Annual Report. Began with 1976. US. English. an. National Zoological Park, 3001 Connecticut Avenue NW, Washington DC 20008. *National Zoological Park Three-Year Report.*

ANNUAL REPORT OF THE MARINE MAMMAL COMMISSION : A REPORT TO CONGRESS. 1st (1973)-. US. English. an. Marine Mammal Commission, 1625 I Street NW, Washington DC 20006.

ANNUAL REPORT OF THE NEW ZEALAND BIRD BANDING SCHEME. **Main/Corp** New Zealand Bird Banding Scheme. 13th- 1962/63-. 0549-0162. Periodical. NZ. English. ir. Ornithological Society of New Zealand, PO Box 22 23D, Auckland New Zealand. **LC** QL693. **DD** 598.2. *Annual Report of the Banding Committee.*

ANNUAL REPORT ON THE ZOOLOGICAL SURVEY OF INDIA. **Main/Corp** India (Republic). Zoological Survey. II. English. ir. 10. Indian Books and Periodicals Syndicate, B-5/62 Dev Nagar P L Road Karol Bagh, New Delhi 110005 India. **LC** QL309. **DD** 591. bk rev. *Report on the Zoological Survey of India, 0537-0744.*

ANNUAL REPORT - PRIMATE RESEARCH CENTERS ADVISORY COMMITTEE, NATIONAL INSTITUTES OF HEALTH. **Main/Corp** National Institutes of Health. Primate Research Centers Advisory Committee. US. English. an. National Institutes of Health, 9000 Rockville Pike, Bethesda MD 20014.

ANNUAL REPORT TO THE LEGISLATURE - MINNESOTA ZOOLOGICAL GARDEN. **Main/Corp** Minnesota Zoological Garden. US. English. an. Minnesota Zoological Garden, Apple Valley MN 55124. **LC** QL76.5.U62. **DD** 353.97760085590744.

ANNUAL REPORT - WESTERN SOCIETY OF MALACOLOGISTS. **Main/Corp** Western Society of Malacologists. V. 7- 1974-. 0361-1175. US. English. an. $7.50. Western Society of Malacologists, c/o Ms Mulliner, 5283 Vickie Drive, San Diego CA 92109. **Ind/Abst** Biol. Abstr., GeoRef. **LC** QL401. **DD** 594.005. **CODEN** ARWMDW. **Circ** 250. (ctrl). Abstracts of papers given at the annual meeting of society. Roster of members and addresses. *Echo, 0147-2674.*

ANNUAL REPORT - WESTERN STATES EXOTIC GAME BIRD COMMITTEE. **Main/Corp** Western States Exotic Game Bird Committee. V. 5- 1957/58-. 0511-8158. US. English. an. *Chukar Committee Semi-Annual Report.*

ANNUAL REVIEW OF ENTOMOLOGY. V. 1- 1956-. 0066-4170. US. English. an. $31.00 Domestic, $34.00 Foreign. Annual Reviews Inc, 4139 El Camino Way, Palo Alto CA 94306. **Tel** (415)493-4400. Ed Thomas E Mittler. **Ind/Abst** Life Sci. Collect., Pestdoc, Ringdoc, Vetdoc, Excerpta Med., Energy Inf. Abstr., Environ. Abstr., Index Med., Biol. Abstr., Chem. Abstr., Biol. Agric. Index, Sci. Cit. Index, Abr. Ed. **LC** QL461. **DD** 595.7. **NLM** W1 AN771. **CODEN** ARENAA. Comprehensive, thorough coverage of latest advances in entomology, written by acknowledged experts in the field. Extensive literature citations included.

ANNUAL SPRING MIGRATION REPORT, POINT PELEE NATIONAL PARK & VICINITY. (ANNUAL . . . SPRING MIGRATION REPORT, POINT PELEE NATIONAL PARK & VICINITY). 0712-5437. CN. English. an. **DD** 598.25250971331.

ANNUAL UPLAND GAME BIRD REPORT (IDAHO). **Main/Corp** Idaho. Fish and Game Department. 0445-1953. US. English. an. **LC** SK387.

ANTENNA. V. 1- July 1977-. 0140-1890. Periodical. UK. English. qt. 10.00 Domestic, 10.50 Foreign. Royal Entomological Society, 41 Queens Gate, London SW7 5HU England. **Tel** 01-584 8361. **LC** QL461. **DD** 595.7005. Contains reports of all Society meetings, workshops, symposia and other activities. Also contains scientific articles, readers' correspondence, an important diary section, and other items of interest to all entomologists. *Proceedings of the Royal Entomological Society of London. Journal of Meetings.*

ANTHUS. Periodical. German. ir. 14.00. Kilda Verlag, Munsterstrasse 71, 4402 Greven West Germany. **LC** QL671.

ANZEIGER DER ORNITHOLOGISCHEN GESELLSCHAFT IN BAYERN. (ANZEIGER DER ORNITHOLOGISCHE GESELLSCHAFT IN BAYERN). **Main/Corp** Ornithologische Gesellschaft in Bayern, Munich. Vol. 1- 1919-. 0030-5715. Periodical. GW. English. ty. 40. Ornithologische Gesellschaft in Bayern, c/o Zoologische Staatssammlung, Muenchhausenstr 21, D-8000 Muenchen 60 West Germany. **Tel** 89-8107-123. Ed Josef Reichholf. **Ind/Abst** Life Sci. Collect., Biol. Abstr., Sel. Water Resour. Abstr. **LC** QL671. **CODEN** AOGBAV. bk rev. **Circ** 1,200. (ctrl). Ornithology and ecology.

APICULTURA IN ROMANIA. V. 50, No. 12- Dec. 1975-. 0378-2425. Periodical. RM. Romanian. mo. Ilexim Press Department, PO Box 1-136/1-137, Bucharest Romania. **Ind/Abst** Chem. Abstr., Biol. Abstr., Nuci. Sci. Abstr., Bibliogr. Agric. **CODEN** APRODX. *Apicultura.*

APIDOLOGIE. V. 1, 1-. 0044-8435. Periodical. FR. French (summaries in English, French, and German). ir. 350. Service des Publications INRA, Rte de St Cyr,

Zoology-Vertebrate and Invertebrate

7800 Versailles France. **Tel** 30217622. **Ind/Abst** Life Sci. Collect., GeoRef, Biol. Abstr., Chem. Abstr., Nuci. Sci. Abstr., Bibliogr. Agric., Sci. Cit. Index, Abr. Ed., Bibliogr. Index Geol. **CODEN** APDGB5. bk rev. **Circ** 600. *Annales de l'Abeille, Zeitschrift fur Bienenforschung.*

APPLIED ANIMAL ETHOLOGY *CEASED.* Began with V. 1 Dec. 1974. Ceased with V. 11 1984. 0304-3762. Periodical. English. qt. **Ind/Abst** Psychol. Abstr., Bibliogr. Agric.

APPLIED ENTOMOLOGY AND ZOOLOGY. Began in June 1966. 0003-6862. Periodical. JA. English (text in French or German). qt. Japan Publishing Trading Company Limited, PO Box 5030, Tokyo International, Tokyo 100-31 Japan. **Ind/Abst** Life Sci. Collect., Pestdoc, Ringdoc, Vetdoc, Energy Inf. Abstr., Environ. Abstr., Biol. Abstr., Art Archaeol. Tech. Abstr., Curr. Contents Agric. Food Vet. Sci., Sci. Cit. Index, Abr. Ed., Chem. Abstr., Bibliogr. Agric. **LC** QL461. **CODEN** APEZAW.

AQUATIC INSECTS. Vol. 1, No. 1 (Jan. 1979)-. 0165-0424. Periodical. English. qt. $62.00. Swets & Zeitlinger BV, 347 Heereweg, 2161 Ca Lisse The Netherlands. **Tel** 02521-19113. **Ed** Peter Zwich. **Ind/Abst** Life Sci. Collect., Abstr. Bull. Inst. Paper Chem., Biol. Abstr. **CODEN** AQINDQ. bk rev. adv acc. **Circ** 800. Aquatic entomology is a well established line of research with a growing number of students, important for entomology as well as limnology.

AQUATIC MAMMALS. V. 1- Jan. 1972-. Periodical. UK. English (articles in French or German). sa. 35. Zoological Society of London, Whipsnade Park, Dunstable Beds LU6 2LF England. **Tel** 872171. **Ed** V J A Manton. **Ind/Abst** Life Sci. Collect. bk rev. **Circ** 110. (ctrl). Papers dealing with catching, transport, husbandry, medical care, conservation and original investigation in aquatic mammals.

AQUILO. SER. ZOOLOGICA. V. 1- 1963-. 0570-5177. Finnish (German or English). ir. **Ind/Abst** Life Sci. Collect., Biol. Abstr., ASTIS Bibliogr., ASTIS Curr. Aware. Bull. **CODEN** AQZOA9.

ARCHIV FUR PROTISTENKUNDE. *See* Genealogy and Heraldry - Archives.

ARDEA. Vol. 1- Apr. 1912-. 0373-2266. Periodical. NE. English (French, or German with some summaries in Dutch). sa. Nederlandse Ornithologische, Sportlaan 13, 2225 Jn Katwijk Z the Netherlands. **Tel** 01718-13296. **Ind/Abst** GeoRef, Biol. Abstr., Life Sci. Collect., Sci. Cit. Index, Abr. Ed., Bibliogr. Index Geol. **LC** QL671. **DD** 598.2949205. **CODEN** ADEAA9. Index published separately - free - automatically sent.

ARDEOLA. V. 1- 1954-. 0570-7358. SP. Spanish (summaries in English). ir. Sociedad Espanola Ornithologia, Nuseo Nacl Cien Nat Castell 84, Madrid Spain. **CODEN** ARDEDF.

ARQUIVOS DE ZOOLOGIA DO ESTADO DE SAO PAULO. V. 1-14. 0066-7870. Periodical. BL. Portuguese (English). ir. $25.00. Universidade de Sao Paulo, Avenida Nazare 481 Caixa 7172, Sao Paulo Brazil Z C 01051. **Tel** (011)274 3455. bk rev. adv acc. **Circ** 458. (ctrl). Zoological paper.

ARQUIVOS DO MUSEU BOCAGE *CEASED.* (ARQUIVOS DO MUSEU BOCAGE : PUBLICACAO DO MUSEU E LABORATORIO ZOOLOGICO E ANTROPOLOGICO, FACULDADE DE CIENCIAS DE LISBOA). 2A. Ser., V. 1, No. 1-2A. Ser., V. 7. 0027-3988. Monographic Series. PO. Portuguese (summaries in English, French or German). ir. **Ind/Abst** Life Sci. Collect. **LC** QL1. **DD** 590.5. Index published separately free - automatically sent. *Revista Protuguesa de Zoologia e Biologia Geral.*

ARTHROPODS OF FLORIDA AND NEIGHBORING LAND AREAS. V. 1-. 0066-8036. Monographic Series. US. English. ir. Florida Department of Agriculture & Consumer Services, Division of Plant Industry, PO Box 1269, Gainesville FL 32602. **LC** QL434. **DD** 595.209759.

ATALA. V. 1- Apr. 1973-. 0160-5674. Periodical. US. English. sa. Xerces Society, 235 East 73rd Street, New York NY 10021. **Ind/Abst** Life Sci. Collect. **LC** QL541. **DD** 595.7005.

ATALANTA. V. 1- March 1964-. 0171-0079. Periodical. GW. German. ir. $12.18. Deutsche Forschung fur Schmett, Humboldstrasse 13, D-8688 Marktleuthen West Germany. **Tel** 09285 6587. **Ed** Ulf Eitschberger. **Ind/Abst** Life Sci. Collect., Biol. Abstr. **CODEN** ATLNDS. bk rev. adv acc. **Circ** 1,200. (ctrl). Insect migration, lepidoptera: description of new species, faunistic, ecology, etc.

THE AUK. V. 1- 1884-. 0004-8038. Periodical. US. English. qt. **Ind/Abst** Life Sci. Collect., Can. Environ., GeoRef, Ref. Source, Nuci. Sci. Abstr., Biol. Abstr., Chem. Abstr., Psychol. Abstr., Bibliogr. Agric., Biol. Agric. Index. **LC** QL671. **DD** 598. **CODEN** AUKJAF. (cum index). *Bulletin of the Nuttall Ornithological Club.*

THE AUSTRALASIAN BEEKEEPER. V. 1- 1899-. 0004-8313. Periodical. AT. English. mo. $12.60. Pender Beekeeping Supplies, PL P M B 19, Maitland New South Wales 2320 Australia.

AUSTRALIAN BEE JOURNAL. V. 1- 1918-. 0045-0294. Periodical. AT. English. mo. $11.07. Victorian Apiarists's Association, PO Box 426, Benalla Victoria 3672 Australia. **Ed** L Desailly. bk rev. adv acc. **Circ** 1,000. Honey industry news, reviews, and practical information.

AUSTRALIAN ENTOMOLOGICAL MAGAZINE. V. 1- July 1972-. 0311-1881. Periodical. AT. English. bm. $15.00. Australian Entomological Press, 14 Chisholm Street, Greenwich New South Wales 2065 Australia. **Tel** (02)43 3972. **Ed** M S Moulds. **Ind/Abst** Life Sci. Collect., Biol. Abstr., Bibliogr. Agric. **CODEN** AEMZAT. bk rev. adv acc. **Circ** 500. Original research papers in entomology biased towards Australian region.

AUSTRALIAN JOURNAL OF HERPETOLOGY. Vol. 1, No. 1 (Mar. 1981)-. Periodical. AT. English. ir. 20.00 Domestic, 30.00 Foreign. Australian Journal of Herpetology, PO Box 409, Katoomba New South Wales 2780 Australia. **Tel** 02 3398392. **Ed** Richard W Wells. bk rev. adv acc. **Circ** 1,000. All aspects of the study of reptiles and amphibians world-wide.

AUSTRALIAN JOURNAL OF ZOOLOGY. V. 1- Jan. 1953-. 0004-959X. Periodical. AT. English. ir. 120.00. CSIRO, PO Box 89, East Melbourne Victoria 3002 Australia. **Tel** 418-7333. **Ed** Meredith Dobbie and Susan Ingham. **Ind/Abst** Life Sci. Collect., GeoRef, Biol. Abstr., Chem. Abstr., Nuci. Sci. Abstr., Bibliogr. Agric. **LC** QL1. **DD** 591.05. **NLM** W1 AU626. **CODEN** AJZOAS. adv acc. **Circ** 355. Reports of original research in all branches of zoology. Taxonomic supplements are issued from time to time to subscribers.

AUSTRALIAN MAMMALOGY. V. 1- Dec. 1972-. 0310-0049. Periodical. AT. English. an. 16.00. Geoffrey A Ross NSW NPWS Scientific Services, PO Box N189 Grosvenor Street, Sydney New South Wales 2000 Australia. **Tel** 02 237-6687. **Ed** M Archer. **Ind/Abst** GeoRef, Biol. Abstr., Aust. Sci. Index. **CODEN** AUMACY. bk rev. The journal publishes original research articles and notes on all aspects of Australian mammals. A notes section provides opportunity for publication of observations about Australian mammals.

AUSTRALIAN ZOOLOGIST. (THE AUSTRALIAN ZOOLOGIST). V. 1- June 13, 1914-. 0067-2238. Periodical. English. ir. **Tel** 969.7336. **Ind/Abst** Life Sci. Collect., Biol. Abstr., Bibliogr. Agric. **LC** QL1. **DD** 591.994. **CODEN** AUZOA3. bk rev. adv acc. **Circ** 3,000. (ctrl). A magazine presenting a blend of scientific reports of interest to general zoologists and naturalists with news, feature articles and book reviews. *Koolewong.*

AVES. V. 1- Feb. 1964-. 0005-1993. Periodical. FR. French (with summaries in Dutch, English and German). ir. 290. Societe d' Etudes Ornithologiques, 46 rue d'Ulm, Paris 5E France. **Tel** 329 12 25. **Ind/Abst** Life Sci. Collect., Biol. Abstr. **CODEN** AVESAJ. bk rev. adv acc. **Circ** 1,000. (ctrl).

AVIAN BIOLOGY. Vol. 1-. US. English. ir. Academic Press, 4805 Sand Lake Road, Orlando FL 32887. **Tel** (305)345-4100. **DD** 598.2.

AVICOLTURA. Yearly V. 1-46. 0005-2213. Periodical. IT. Italian. mo. Edagricole, PO Box 2157, 40100 Bologna Italy. **Ed** A Ghigi.

L'AVICULTEUR. 0150-939X. Periodical. FR. French. ir. $37.65. Editions du Boisbaudry, 35 rue Carnot, 35000 Rennes France. **Ind/Abst** Bibliogr. Agric.

AVICULTURA BRASILEIRA. V. 1- 1964-. Periodical. BL. Portuguese. mo. Avicultura Brasileira, Editora Brasilerio Agricultura, Sao Paulo Brazil.

AVICULTURAL BULLETIN. 0567-2856. Periodical. US. English. mo. Avicultural Society of America, Doris Mayfield/6606 Enfield, Reseda CA 91335.

AVICULTURAL JOURNAL. (THE AVICULTURAL JOURNAL). May 1975-. 0317-5650. CN. English. 12.00. Avicultural Advancement Council of Canada, 3631 Cedar Hill Road, Victoria British Columbia V8P 3Z3 Canada. **Tel** (604)477-9982. **Ed** Doreen E Albion. **DD** 636.68606271. bk rev. adv acc. **Circ** 310. (ctrl). Contains articles on all types of birds, their genetics and health of birds. Articles by knowledgable veterinarians for our readers. Many writers from all over the world.

THE AVICULTURAL MAGAZINE. V. 1-8, Nov. 1894-Oct. 1902. 0005-2256. Periodical. UK. English. qt. $30.00. Avicultural Magazine, Windsorforest Stud Mill Road, Berkshire SL5 8 LT England. **LC** QL671. **DD** 636.606242. (cum index).

BANGLADESH JOURNAL OF ZOOLOGY. V. 1- Dec. 1973-. 0304-9027. Periodical. English. ir. $4.00 Per Copy. Zoological Society of Bangladesh, c/o Department of Zoology, University of Dacca, 2, Dacca Bangladesh. **Ind/Abst** Life Sci. Collect., Biol. Abstr. **LC** QL334.B34. **DD** 591.05. **CODEN** BJZOA5.

BASTERIA. V. 1- Feb. 1936-. 0005-6219. Periodical. NE. Dutch (contributions in English and German). bm. 17.97. Nederlandse Malacologische ver, c/o Zoolmus, Postbox 20125, 1000 HC Amsterdam The Netherlands. **Tel** 020-5223473. **Ed** A C van Bruggen. **Ind/Abst** Biol. Abstr. **LC** QL401. **DD** 594.05. **CODEN** BSTRAD. (cum index). bk rev. **Circ** 600. The science of malacology, dealing with shells and the mollusks.

B.C. SHELLFISH MARICULTURE NEWSLETTER. (THE B.C. SHELLFISH MARICULTURE NEWSLETTER). Vol. 1, No. 1 (Jan. 1981)-. 0713-2557. Periodical. CN. English. ir. Province of British Columbia, 1450 Government Street Information Service, Victoria British Columbia V8w 3E7 Canada. **DD** 639.409711.

BEAUFORTIA. V. 1- (No. 1-). 0067-4745. Periodical. NE. English (articles in French, German or Dutch). an. Zoological Museum Universitei, Plantage Middenlaan 53, Amsterdam Netherlands. **Ind/Abst** Life Sci. Collect., Can. Environ., GeoRef, Biol. Abstr., Bibliogr. Agric., Bibliogr. Index Geol. **CODEN** BUFOAG. *Amsterdam Naturalist.*

BEE CRAFT. V. 1- 1919-. 0005-7703. Periodical. UK. English. mo. $7.81. Bee Craft, 15 Westway Copthrn Bk, Crawley W Sussex RH10 3QS England. **Tel** 0342 712119. **Ed** Robert C Young. bk rev. adv acc. **Circ** 9,000. Information for bee keepers, articles of general interest, advertisements, legislation.

BEE WORLD. V. 1- June 1919-. 0005-772X. Periodical. UK. English. qt. $26.50 US. International Bee Research Association, Hill House Gerrards Cross, Bucks SL9 ONR United Kingdom. **Ed** Margaret Adey. **Ind/Abst** Life Sci. Collect., Chem. Abstr., Bibliogr. Agric. **CODEN** BEWOAN. (cum index). bk rev. adv acc. **Circ** 2,000. Provides the international beekeeping community with news and articles on recent developments in practical and scientific work.

BEEKEEPING. V. 1- May 1935-. Periodical. UK. English. ir. $7.66. Devon Beekeepers Association, Wrenwell Farm, Newton Abbot, Devon TW12 6EE England.

BEEKEEPING, AUSTRALIA. **Main/Corp** Australian Bureau of Statistics. 1974/75-. AT. English. an. **LC** SF522. **DD** 338.17810994. *Bee Farming, Australia, 0587-5781.*

BEHAVIOR OF NON-HUMAN PRIMATES. (BEHAVIOR OF NONHUMAN PRIMATES : MODERN RESEARCH TRENDS). V. 1- 1965-. 0090-8592. US. English. ir. Academic Press, 4805 Sand Lake Road, Orlando FL 32887. **Tel** (305)345-4100. **Ed** A Schrier. **Ind/Abst** Life Sci. Collect. **LC** QL737.P9. **DD** 156. **NLM** W1 BE125K.

BEHAVIORAL ECOLOGY AND SOCIOBIOLOGY. V. 1-. 0340-5443. Periodical. US. English. mo. $307.00. Springer Verlag New York Inc, 175 5th Avenue, New York NY 10010. **Tel** (212)460-1500. **Ed** H Markl, B Holldobler, P Marler, J Maynard Smith and E O Wilson. **Ind/Abst** Life Sci. Collect., Psychol. Abstr., Bibliogr. Agric., Sci. Cit. Index, Abr. Ed. **LC** QL750. **DD** 591.505. **NLM** W1 BE13C. **CODEN** BESOD6. Original contributions and short communications dealing with quantitative studies and the experimental analysis of animal behavior.

BEHAVIORAL PRIMATOLOGY. V. 1- 1977-. 0148-3781. Periodical. US. English. ir. John Wiley & Sons, One Wiley Drive, Somerset NJ 08873. **Tel** (212)867-9800. **LC** QL737.P9. **DD** 599.8045. **NLM** W1 BE13P.

Zoology-Vertebrate and Invertebrate

BEHAVIOURAL PROCESSES. V. 1- July 1976-. 0376-6357. Periodical. NE. English (summaries in French and German). qt. Elsevier Science Publishers, PO Box 211, 1000 AE Amsterdam Netherlands. **Tel** (020)5803911. **Ind/Abst** Life Sci. Collect., Excerpta Med., Biol. Abstr., Ref. Source, Chem. Abstr., Psychol. Abstr., Sci. Cit. Index, Abr. Ed. **LC** QL750. **DD** 591.5. **NLM** W1 BE135F. **CODEN** BPRODA. *Behaviour Analysis Letters, 0166-4779.*

BEILEI XUEHUI HUIZHI. (PEI LEI HSUEH HUI HUI CHIH). **Main/Corp** Chung-Hua Min Kuo Pei Lei Hsueh Hui. **VFOAT** Bulletin of the Malacological Society of China. V. 1-. 0254-671X. Chinese or English. ir. $5.00. Malacological Society of China, Taiwan Museum, Tai-Pei China. **Ind/Abst** Life Sci. Collect. **LC** QL401.

BEITRAGE ZUR ENTOMOLOGIE. V. 1, No. 1 (Oct. 1951)-. 0005-805X. Periodical. German. sa. Kunst & Wissen Erich Bieber, Dufourstrasse 51, CH-8008 Zurich Switzerland. **Tel** 01/69 44 20. **Ind/Abst** Life Sci. Collect., Biol. Abstr., Bibliogr. Agric. **LC** QL461. **DD** 595.7005. **CODEN** BEIEAP.

BEITRAGE ZUR VOGELKUNDE. Began in 1949. 0005-8211. Periodical. US. German. ir. $40.00. VCH Publishers Inc, 303 NW 12th Avenue, Deerfield Beach FL 33442. **Tel** (305)428-5566. **Ind/Abst** Life Sci. Collect., Biol. Abstr. **CODEN** BEVOAI.

BERICHTE DER ARBEITSGEMEINSCHAFT FUR OKOLOGISCHE ENTOMOLOGIE IN GRAZ. **Main/Corp** Arbeitsgemeinschaft fur Okologische Entomologie In Graz. No. 1-. Periodical. German. ir. Arbeitsgemeinschaft fur Okologische Entomologie in Graz, Heinrichstr 5/III, Graz Austria. **LC** QL482.A9.

BERICHTE DER BOTANISCH-ZOOLOGISCHE GESELLSCHAFT. *See* Biology - Botany.

BERLINER UND MUNCHENER TIERARZTLICHE WOCHENSCHRIFT. *See* Veterinary Medicine, Animal Culture.

BESTIMMUNGSBUCHER ZUR BODENFAUNA EUROPAS. V. 1- 1963-. 0067-6314. Periodical. GE. German. ir. Deutscher Buch Export-Import, Leninstrasse 16, DDR-701 Leipzig East Germany.

BIBLIOGRAFIA BRASILEIRA DE ZOOLOGIA. V. 1- 1950/55-. 0067-6691. BL. Portuguese. ir. Instituto Brasileira de Informacao em Ciencia e Tecnologia, Ave General Justo 171-3, Rio de Janeiro Brazil. **Tel** 242-2915. **LC** WMLC L 83/479.

BIBLIOGRAPHY OF INDIAN ZOOLOGY. *See* Bibliographies.

BIENNIAL REPORT - COMMONWEALTH SCIENTIFIC AND INDUSTRIAL RESEARCH ORGANIZATION (AUSTRALIA). DIVISION OF ENTOMOLOGY. **Main/Corp** Commonwealth Scientific and Industrial Research Organization (Australia). Division of Entomology. 1981-1983-. English. be. *Annual Report - Commonwealth Scientific & Industrial Research Organization, Division of Entomology.*

BIJDRAGEN TOT DE DIERKUNDE. **VFOAT** Contributions to Zoology, Contributions to Zoology, Amsterdam. No. 1- 1848-. 0067-8546. Periodical. NE. English (French and German). sa. 120. Commissie Artis-Bibliotheek, 1018 DC Plantage, Middenlaan 45A, Amsterdam Netherlands. **Tel** 20-5223614. Ed J H Stock, B M Lensink and F F Pieters. **Ind/Abst** Life Sci. Collect., Biol. Abstr., GeoRef, Sci. Cit. Index, Abr. Ed. **LC** QL1. **CODEN** BJDIAD. **Circ** 600. (ctrl). Articles in the field of any branch of zoology. Preferred language is English but French and German are also permitted. Topics include ecology, ethology, morphology, physiology and taxonomy.

BIOLOGY OF BATS. *See* Biology.

BIOLOGY OF BEHAVIOUR. **VFOAT** Biologie du Comportement. V. 1-. 0397-7153. Periodical. English (French, with summary in the other language). qt. Masson Publishing USA Inc, 211 East 43rd Street/Room 1306, New York NY 10017. **Tel** (212)370-1937. **Ind/Abst** Life Sci. Collect., Biol. Abstr., Bibliogr. Agric. **LC** QL751. **DD** 591.5. **NLM** W1 BI852K. **CODEN** BIBEDL.

BIOLOGY OF THE REPTILIA. *See* Biology.

BIOSCIENCE RESEARCH REPORTS. RESEARCH NOTES IN ANIMAL BEHAVIOUR. **VFOAT** Research Notes in Animal Behaviour. 1-. 0741-5699. Monographic Series. US. English. ir. Pitman Publishing Inc, 1020 Plain Street, Marshfield MA 02050. **DD** 591.505. **NLM** W1 BI91W.

BIRD STUDY. V. 1- March 1954-. 1706-3657. Periodical. UK. English. ty. British Trust for Ornithology, Beech Grove, Tring Herts HP23 5NR England. **Ind/Abst** Life Sci. Collect., Biol. Abstr., Ref. Source. **LC** QL671. **DD** 598.205. **CODEN** BISTAC. *Bird Migration, 0523-6894.*

BIRD WATCHER'S DIGEST. V. 1- Sept. 1978-. 0164-3037. Periodical. US. English. bm. $11.00. Pardson Inc, PO Box 110, Marietta OH 45750. **Tel** (614)373-5285. Ed Mary Bowers. **LC** QL677.5. **DD** 598.07234705. bk rev. adv acc. **Circ** 43,000. Sparkling fact-filled articles on attracting and feeding birds, identification, bird behavior, unusual birding adventures. Also humor, art, poetry, birding tips-column by Roger Troy Peterson.

BIRD WORLD. 0199-5979. Periodical. US. English. bm. $12.00. Bird World, PO Box 70, Hollywood CA 91603. **Tel** (818)769-6111. Ed Kathy Lyon. bk rev. adv acc. **Circ** 12,500. (ctrl). Birds in your home or aviary.

BIRDFINDING IN CANADA. Jan. 1981-. 0229-5024. Periodical. CN. English. G Bennerr, Rural Route 2/10780 Pine Valley Drive, Woodbridge Ontario L4L 1A6 Canada. **DD** 598.0723471.

BIRDING. Began with Jan./Feb. 1969 issue. 0161-1836. Periodical. US. English. bm. $20.00. American Birding Association, PO Box 4335, Austin TX 78765. **Tel** (512)474-4804. Ed Ron Naveen. **Ind/Abst** Can. Environ. **LC** QL677.5. **DD** 598.2073. bk rev. adv acc. **Circ** 6,000. Where, when, how, and what kind of bird. This magazine tells all there is to know about birds.

BIRDING NEWS SURVEY. V. 1- Fall 1978-. 0162-0738. Periodical. US. English. qt. Avian Publications Inc, PO Box 310, Elizabethtown KY 42701.

BIRDS. V. 1- Jan./Feb. 1966-. 0006-3665. Periodical. UK. English. qt. *Bird Notes.*

BIRDS IMPORTED INTO THE UNITED STATES. **Main/Corp** Bird and Mammal Laboratories. **Series/Titl** Special Scientific Report—Wildlife. 0094-4068. US. English. $1.25. Superintendent of Documents, US Government Printing Office, Washington DC 20402. Ed R B Clapp and R C Banks. **LC** SK361, QL685. **DD** 598.2973.

BOLETIM DE ZOOLOGIA. 1-. BL. English (Portuguese). ir. Instituto de Biociencias, Caixa Postal 20.520, Sao Paulo 01000 Brazil. **Ind/Abst** Life Sci. Collect. **LC** QL242. *Boletim de Zoologia e Biologia Marinha.*

BOLETIM DO MUSEU NACIONAL. NOVA SERIE, ZOOLOGIA. **Main/Corp** Brazil. Museu Nacional. **VFOAT** Zoologia. No. 1 (30. Jan. 1942)-. 0080-312X. BL. Portuguese (summaries in English, French, and German). ir. Museu Nacional Boletin NS Zoo, Rio de Janeiro ZC-08 Brazil. **Tel** 264-8262. **Ind/Abst** Biol. Abstr., Life Sci. Collect. **LC** QL1. **CODEN** BMJZAD. **Circ** 1,000. (ctrl). It contains works due to research developed by the researchers of the Museu Nacional. *Boletim do Museu Nacional.*

BOLETIN DE LA SOCIEDAD ENTOMOLOGICA DEL PERU. **Main/Corp** Sociedad Entomologica del Peru. Spanish. ir. $1.50. Sociedad Entomologica del Peru, Apartado 4796 Local Fermin Tanguis Av Arequipa 8Va Cuadra, Lima Peru. **LC** QL461.

BOLLETTINO DELLA SOCIETA ENTOMOLOGICA ITALIANA. **Main/Corp** Societa Entomologica Italiana. V. 1-. 0373-3491. Monographic Series. IT. Italian. ir. 30.000 Domestic, 45.000 Foreign. Societa Entomologica Italiana, Via Brigata Liguria 9, NR 16121 Genoa Italy. **Tel** 010-564567. **Ind/Abst** Life Sci. Collect., Biol. Abstr., Bibliogr. Agric. **LC** QL461. **DD** 595.7005. **CODEN** BENIAS. (cum index). bk rev. adv acc. **Circ** 1,500. (ctrl). Works only on entomology.

BOLLETTINO DI ZOOLOGIA. V. 1- Feb. 1930-. 0373-4137. Periodical. IT. Italian. qt. Unione Zoologica Italiana, Via Loredan 10, 35100 Padua Italy. **Ind/Abst** Life Sci. Collect., GeoRef, Biol. Abstr., Bibliogr. Agric. **LC** QL1. **DD** 590.5. **CODEN** BZOOAS.

BONNER ZOOLOGISCHE BEITRAGE. 1.- Yearly Volume. 0006-7172. Periodical. GW. German (articles in English or Spanish with summaries in English and German and occasionally in French). ir. 80-. Zoologisches Forschungs Institut U Museum, A Koenig Bibliothek, D-5300 Bonn West Germany. **Tel** (0228)211026. **Ind/Abst** Life Sci. Collect., GeoRef, Biol. Abstr., Bibliogr. Index Geol. **CODEN** BZOBAN. bk rev. **Circ** 500. (ctrl). Scientific periodical for zoology. Topics: anatomy, animal geography, ecology, ethology, morpholoy, systematics, According to the museum collections, it mainly contains papers on vertebrates and insects.

BOOKS ABOUT BIRDS. V. 1- Sept. 1974-. Periodical. US. English. ir. $9.00. Books About Birds, PO Box 106 Kew Gardens, Jamaica NY 11415. **Tel** (718)544-3279. Ed Jessie Kitching. bk rev. News of bird books, books just published, auction news, reviews, dealers' prices, collectors' items.

BRAIN, BEHAVIOR AND EVOLUTION. *See* Medicine - Neurology.

BREVIORA. No. 1- Feb. 8, 1952-. 0006-9698. US. English. ir. Harvard University, Museum of Comparative Zoology, Cambridge MA 02138. **Tel** (617)495-2988. Ed Elizabeth Campbell Elliott. **Ind/Abst** Life Sci. Collect., GeoRef, Biol. Abstr., Bibliogr. Index Geol. **LC** QL1. **DD** 590.5. **CODEN** BRVRAG. Index published separately free - automatically sent. (cum index). **Circ** 900. Covers systematics and evolution.

BRIMLEYANA. No. 1- Mar. 1979-. 0193-4406. US. English. sa. North Carolina State Museum, PO Box 27647, Raleigh NC 27611. **Tel** (919)733-7450. Ed John E Cooper. **Ind/Abst** Biol. Abstr. **LC** QL155. **DD** 591.97505. **CODEN** BRIMD7. bk rev. **Circ** 300. (ctrl). Taxonomy and systematics, ecology, zoogeography, evolution, and behavior of vertebrate and invertebrate animals of the southeastern United States.

BRITISH BEE JOURNAL. V. 80- (Whole No. 3652-). Periodical. UK. English. mo. 9.00 Foreign. British Bee Publishing Ltd, 46 Queen Street Geddington Kettering, Northamptonshire N141 AZ England. **Tel** (0536)742250. Ed C C Tonsley. **Ind/Abst** Bibliogr. Agric. bk rev. adv acc. **Circ** 3,500. *British Bee Journal & Bee-Keepers Advisor.*

BRITISH BIRDS. V. 1- June 1907-. 0007-0335. Periodical. UK. English. mo. $55.41. British Birds Ltd, Fountains Park Lane/Blunham, Bedford MK44 3NJ England. **Tel** 0767-40340. Ed J T R Sharrock. **Ind/Abst** Life Sci. Collect., Can. Environ., Energy Inf. Abstr., Environ. Abstr., Biol. Abstr., Sci. Cit. Index, Abr. Ed. **CODEN** BRBIAP. Index published separately - free - automatically sent. bk rev. adv acc. **Circ** 9,000. Papers and notes by amateur and professional birdwatchers on the ornithology of Britain, Europe, North Africa and the Middle East. Identification, breeding, biology, migration, news, etc.

BRITISH JOURNAL OF HERPETOLOGY. V. 1- June 1948-. 0007-1056. Periodical. English. sa. $40.00. British Herpetological Society, c/o Zoological Society of London, Regents Park, London WC1 England. **Tel** 01 205 7635. Ed T Beebee. **Ind/Abst** Life Sci. Collect. bk rev. adv acc. **Circ** 800. Deals with only reptiles and amphibians.

BROOKFIELD ZOO BISON. **VFOAT** Bison. Vol. 1, No. 1 (Nov./Dec. 1983)-. 8756-3479. Periodical. US. English. qt. $7.50 (Zoo Members), $10.00 others. Chicago Zoological Society, Brookfield Zoo, Brookfield IL 60513. **DD** 590. *Brookfield Bison.*

BROWSE (SCARBOROUGH, ONT.). (BROWSE). July 16, 1981-. 0225-5413. Periodical. CN. English. ir. Metro Toronto Zoo, PO Box 280, West Hill Ontario M1E 4R5 Canada. **DD** 590.74471354105. *Your-Browse, 0225-5413.*

B.T.O. NEWS. **Main/Corp** British Trust for Ornithology. **VAT** British Trust for Ornithology News. No. 1- Jan. 1964-. 0005-3392. Periodical. UK. English. bm. 10.00. British Trust for Ornithology, Beech Grove Station Road, Tring Herts HP23 5NR England. **Tel** (044282)3461. Ed T J Davis. **LC** QL690.G7. **DD** 598.20730941. bk rev. adv acc. **Circ** 8,000. (ctrl). Contains news, reviews, letters, and up-to-the-minute information on trends in British bird populations.

BULLETIN & I.E. ET ANNALES DE LA SOCIETE ROYALE BELGE D'ENTOMOLOGIE. **Main/Corp** Societe Royale Belge d'Entomologie. **VFOAT** Bulletin et Annales de la Societe Royale Belge d'Entomologie. V. 108- June 30 1972-. BE. Dutch (French). ir. Societe Royale Belge Entomologie, rue Vautier 31, 1040 Bruxelles Belgium. **Ind/Abst** Life Sci. Collect., Biol. Abstr. **LC** QL461. **DD** 595.7005. **CODEN** BASEBE. *Bulletin & I.E. et Annales de la Societe Royale d'Entomologie de Belgique.*

Zoology-Vertebrate and Invertebrate

BULLETIN (BRITISH ARACHNOLOGICAL SOCIETY). (BULLETIN). V. 1- Jan. 1969-. 0524-4994. Periodical. UK. English. ir. $19.16. British Arachnological Society Institute, Terrestrial Eco/Furzebrook Research Station, Wareham Dorset BH20 5AS England. **Ed** P Merrett. **Ind/Abst** Life Sci. Collect., Bibliogr. Agric. **LC** QL451. **DD** 595.405. bk rev. **Circ** 600. (ctrl). Papers, reviews and notes concerned with the study of arachnology, excluding acari. *Bulletin of the British Spider Study Group.*

BULLETIN - CANADIAN SOCIETY OF ZOOLOGISTS. **Main/Corp** Canadian Society of Zoologists. Began with Feb. 1974 issue. 0319-6674. Periodical. CN. English. 30.00. Editor CSZ Bulletin, Institute of Parasitology, 21 111 Lakeshore Road, Ste Anne de Bellevue H9X 1C0 Canada. **Tel** (514)457-2000. **Ed** Gaetan Faubert. bk rev. adv acc. **Circ** 1,000. (ctrl). Activities of the Society, articles on institutions, policies and topical issues in Canadian zoology.

BULLETIN - CHUNG YANG YEN CHIU YUAN. TUNG WE YEN CHIU, SO NANKANG, FORMOSA. **Main/Corp** Chung Yang Yen Chiu Yuan. Tung Wu Yen Chiu So, Nankang, Formosa. V. 1- June 1962-. 0001-3943. Periodical. CH. English (summaries in Chinese). ir. Academia Sinica, Nankang, Taipei Taiwan China. **Ind/Abst** Biol. Abstr., Chem. Abstr. **LC** QL307.2. **CODEN** BIZYAS. *Sinensia.*

BULLETIN - COLLEGE OF FORESTRY, WILDLIFE AND RANGE SCIENCES. *See* Forestry.

BULLETIN DE LA SOCIETE ENTOMOLOGIQUE DE FRANCE. **Main/Corp** Societe Entomologique de France. Began in 1896. 0037-928X. Periodical. FR. French. 390,000. Society Entomologique de France, 45 rue de Buffon, Paris 5 France. **Tel** (1)4336 04 06. **Ind/Abst** Life Sci. Collect., Bibliogr. Agric. **LC** QL461. **NLM** W1 BU516M. bk rev. adv acc. **Circ** 1,200. Taxonomy and biology of insects. *Annales de la Societe Entomologique de France.*

BULLETIN DE LA SOCIETE ZOOLOGIQUE DE FRANCE. **Main/Corp** Societe Zoologique de France. V. 1- 1876-. 0037-962X. Periodical. FR. French (English summaries). qt. $47.90. Societe Zoologique de France, 195 rue Saint-Jacques, 75005 Paris France. **Ind/Abst** Life Sci. Collect., Excerpta Med., GeoRef, Biol. Abstr., Chem. Abstr., Bibliogr. Agric., Sci. Cit. Index, Abr. Ed. **CODEN** BZOFAZ. (cum index).

BULLETIN D'INVENTAIRE DES INSECTES DU QUEBEC. **VFOAT** Quebec Insect Survey Bulletin. V. 1- Mar. 1979-. 0704-4666. Periodical. CN. French (English). qt. $4.00. Societe d'Inventaire des Insectes du Quebec, College Bourget CP 1000, Rigaud Quebec Canada. **DD** 595.709714.

BULLETIN - ENTOMOLOGICAL SOCIETY OF CANADA. **Main/Corp** Entomological Society of Canada (1950-). V. 1- Mar. 1969-. 0071-0741. CN. English. qt. 1320 Carling Avenue, Ottawa Ontario K1Z 7K9 Canada. **Ind/Abst** Life Sci. Collect. **LC** QL461. **DD** 595.7006271. **NLM** W1 BU651U.

BULLETIN - ENTOMOLOGICAL SOCIETY OF NEW ZEALAND. **Main/Corp** Entomological Society of New Zealand. 1-1972-. Monographic Series. NZ. English. ir. Lincoln College/Department of Entomology, c/o R R Scot, Christchurch New Zealand. **Tel** (03)252-811. **Ed** T K Crosby. **Ind/Abst** Biol. Abstr. **CODEN** BESZD5. adv acc. **Circ** 700. Comprises occasional publications on the Entomology of New Zealand, the offshore sub-antarctic islands, published at irregular intervals as suitable material is written.

BULLETIN - INSTITUT ROYAL DES SCIENCES NATURELLES DE BELGIQUE. ENTOMOLOGIE. **Main/Corp** Institut Royal des Sciences Naturelles de Belgique. **VFOAT** Bulletin. Entomologie, Entomologie, Bulletin. V. 48- 1972-. 0303-9129. Periodical. BE. French (German). ir. Institut Royal des Sciences Naturelles de Belgique, 31 rue Bautier, B1050 Brussels Belgium. **Ind/Abst** GeoRef, Biol. Abstr. **CODEN** BIETBB. *Bulletin - Institut Royal des Sciences Naturelles de Belgique.*

BULLETIN - INTER-AMERICAN TROPICAL TUNA COMMISSION. **Main/Corp** Inter-American Tropical Tuna Commission. **VFOAT** Boletin - Comision Interamericana del Atun Tropical. V. 1- 1954-. 0074-0993. Periodical. US. text in English and Spanish. ir. Inter-American Tuna Commission, Scripps Institute of Oceanography, La Jolla CA 93207. **Ind/Abst** Life Sci. Collect., Biol. Abstr. **LC** QL614. (cum index).

BULLETIN - INTERNATIONAL WATERFOWL RESEARCH BUREAU. **Main/Corp** International Waterfowl Research Bureau. **VFOAT** Bulletin du Bureau International de Recherche sur la Sauvagine. No. 33- July 1972-. Periodical. UK. English (summaries in French or German). sa. 2. International Waterfowl Research Bureau, New Grounds, Slimbridge GL2 7BX England. **Tel** (045 389) 333. **Ed** M Smart. bk rev. **Circ** 800. Worldwide research on water birds and conservation of their wetland habitats. Reports on international meetings and wetland conservation agreements. *Bulletin -International Wildfowl Research Bureau.*

BULLETIN - KANSAS ORNITHOLOGICAL SOCIETY. **Main/Corp** Kansas Ornithological Society. V. 1- Apr. 1950-. 0022-8729. Periodical. US. English. qt. $6.00. Kansas Ornithological Bulletin, E R Lewis Treasurer, 1285 Macvicar, Topeka KS 66604. **Ed** John Zimmerman. bk rev. **Circ** 400. (ctrl). The study of birds with emphasis on their occurence, nesting and population dynamics applied to Kansas.

BULLETIN LA SOCIETE ENTOLMOLOGIQUE D'EGYPTE. (BULLETIN DE LA SOCIETE ENTOMOLOGIQUE D'EGYPTE). **VFOAT** Majalat Al-Jamiyah Al-Misriyah Li-Ilm Al-Hasharat. 39E V.- V. 59 (1975). 0373-3289. Periodical. French (English, German, and Italian). an. Sirovic Bookshop, POB 615, Cairo-R A E Egypt. **Ind/Abst** Life Sci. Collect. **LC** QL461. *Bulletin de la Societe Fouad 1er d'Entomologie.*

BULLETIN OF ENTOMOLOGICAL RESEARCH. **Main/Corp** Commonwealth Institute of Entomology. V. 1- Apr. 1910-. 0007-4853. Periodical. UK. English. qt. $281.20. Commonwealth Agricultural Bureau, Farnham House/ Farnham Royal, Slough SL2 3BN England. **Tel** (02814) 2662. **Ed** J R Metcalfe. **Ind/Abst** Life Sci. Collect., Pestdoc, Ringdoc, Vetdoc, Energy Inf. Abstr., Environ. Abstr., Biol. Abstr., Chem. Abstr., Biol. Agric. Index, Sci. Cit. Index, Abr. Ed. **NLM** W1 BU76. **CODEN** BEREA2. adv acc. Devoted to papers dealing with original research concerning insects, mites or ticks of economic importance in the agricultural, medical or veterinary fields in any part of the world.

BULLETIN OF ENTOMOLOGY. V. 1- 1960-. 0013-8762. Periodical. II. English. ir. $30.00. Entomological Society of India, Indian Agricultural Research Institute, New Delhi 110012 India.

BULLETIN OF THE BRITISH ORNITHOLOGISTS' CLUB. **Main/Corp** British Ornithologists' Club. Vol. 1 (1892/93)-. Periodical. UK. English. qt. $29.00. The Honorable Treasurer or the British Ornithologists' Club, 53, Osterley Road, Isleworth Middlesex TW7 4PW England. **Ed** James Monk. **Ind/Abst** Biol. Abstr. **CODEN** BBOCAS. (cum index). bk rev. **Circ** 650. Short papers on taxonomy including descriptions of new forms, nests and eggs, papers on field studies, anatomy, ethology, food, moult, nomenclature parasitology and voice worldwide coverage.

BULLETIN OF THE CALIFORNIA INSECT SURVEY. Vol. 1, No. 1 (June 30, 1950)-. 0068-5631. Monographic Series. US. English. ir. University California Press, 2223 Fulton Street/ Judy Taylor, Berkeley CA 94720. **Tel** (415)642-0061. **Ind/Abst** Biol. Abstr. **LC** QL475.C3. **DD** 595.7097494. **CODEN** BCINA4. **Circ** 800.

BULLETIN OF THE ENTOMOLOGICAL SOCIETY OF AMERICA. V. 1- Mar. 1955-. 0013-8754. Periodical. US. English. qt. $15.00. Entomological Society of America, 4603 Calvert Road, College Park MD 20740. **Tel** (301)864-1334. **Ed** P A Opler. **Ind/Abst** Life Sci. Collect., Energy Inf. Abstr., Environ. Abstr., Bibliogr. Agric. **NLM** W1 BU846I. (cum index). bk rev. adv acc. **Circ** 8,000. (ctrl). Presents information to general audiences about entomology. Includes feature articles, book reviews, and ESA notes.

BULLETIN OF THE ENTOMOLOGICAL SOCIETY OF EGYPT. ECONOMIC SERIES. **Main/Corp** Jamiyah Al-Misriyah Li-Ilm Al-Hasharat. 0081-0991. Periodical. UA. English. an. Entomological Society of Egypt, PO Box 430, Cairo Egypt. **Ind/Abst** Chem. Abstr. **CODEN** BEGEBG.

BULLETIN OF THE GEORGIA HERPETOLOGICAL SOCIETY. **Main/Corp** Georgia Herpetological Society. V. 2, No. 2- June 1976-. 0363-2172. Periodical. US. English. $8.00. John C Zegel, 5341 Smoke Rise Drive, Stone Mountain GA 30083. **LC** QL640. **DD** 598.105. *Bulletin of the Southeastern Herpetological Society.*

BULLETIN OF THE INTERNATIONAL COUNCIL FOR BIRD PRESERVATION. **Main/Corp** International Council for Bird Preservation. 8th- 1962-. US. text in English, French, German and Japanese. ir. 10. International Council for Bird Preservation, 219 East Huntingdon Road, Cambridge CB3 09L England. **Tel** 0223-177318. **Ed** T Urpuhart. bk rev. **Circ** 21,500. (ctrl). Report on annual activity to further cause of world bird conservation, including education, research and field projects. *Bulletin of the International Committee for Bird Preservation.*

BULLETIN OF THE MARYLAND HERPETOLOGICAL SOCIETY. **Main/Corp** Maryland Herpetological Society. **VFOAT** Bulletin of the MDHS. V. 1- Nov. 1965-. 0025-4231. Periodical. US. English. qt. $10.00. Natural Historical Society of Maryland, 2643 North Charles Street, Baltimore MD 21218. **Tel** (301)235-6116. **Ed** Herbert S Harris Jr. **Ind/Abst** Biol. Abstr. **LC** QL653.M3. **CODEN** MHSBB5. bk rev. **Circ** 300. Original articles on biology, taxonomy, distribution, etc., of amphibians and reptiles international.

BULLETIN OF THE MUSEUM OF COMPARATIVE ZOOLOGY. **Main/Corp** Harvard University. Museum of Comparative Zoology. V. 130- 1964-. 0027-4100. Periodical. US. English. ir. Harvard University, Museum of Comparative Zoology, 26 Oxford Street, Cambridge MA 02138. **Tel** (617)661-3721. **Ed** Elizabeth Campbell Elliott. **Ind/Abst** Life Sci. Collect., GeoRef, Biol. Abstr., Bibliogr. Agric., Bibliogr. Index Geol. **LC** QL1. **CODEN** MCZBA4. **Circ** 900. Covers systematics and evolution. *Bulletin of the Museum of Comparative Zoology.*

BULLETIN OF THE NATIONAL SCIENCE MUSEUM. SERIES A. ZOOLOGY. (BULLETIN OF THE NATIONAL SCIENCE MUSEUM. SERIES A, ZOOLOGY). **VFOAT** Zoology. V. 1- March 1975-. 0385-2423. Periodical. English. ir. Library/National Science Museum, Ueno Park, Tokyo 110 Japan. **Ind/Abst** Biol. Abstr. **LC** QL325. **DD** 591.05. *Bulletin of the National Science Museum.*

BULLETIN OF THE PHILADELPHIA HERPETOLOGICAL SOCIETY. V. 1- 1953-. 0553-9587. Periodical. US. English. an. $6.00. Philadelphia Herpetological Society, 2103 Solly Avenue, Philadelphia PA 19152. **Tel** (215)353-1223. **Ed** Robert C Feuer. **DD** 597. bk rev. adv acc. **Circ** 300. Concerns any phase of herpetology (amphibians and reptiles). *Philadelphia Herpetological Society Bulletin, 0884-0113.*

BULLETIN OF THE TEXAS ORNITHOLOGICAL SOCIETY. **Main/Corp** Texas Ornithological Society. **VFOAT** TOS Bulletin. **VAT** Texas Ornithological Society Bulletin. V. 1- Apr. 1967-. 0040-4543. US. English. sa. $10.00. Texas A & M University, Department Wildlife and Fisheries Science, Dr D Slack, College Station TX 77843. **Tel** (915)942-2189. **Ed** Terry C Maxwell. **Ind/Abst** Zool. Rec. **Circ** 500. (ctrl). Natural history, conservation and history of the study of Texas birds. *Newsletter.*

BULLETIN OF THE ZOOLOGICAL SURVEY OF INDIA. **Main/Corp** Zoological Survey of India. V. 1- 1978-. 0255-9587. Periodical. II. English. ir. $10.00. Controller of Publications, New Delhi India. **Ind/Abst** Bibliogr. Agric. **LC** QL309. **DD** 591.05.

THE BULLETIN OF ZOOLOGICAL NOMENCLATURE. **Main/Corp** International Commission on Zoological Nomenclature. V. 1- May 1943-. 0007-5167. Periodical. UK. English. qt. $193.80. Commonwealth Agricultural Bureau, Farnham House, Farnham Royal, Slough S12 3BN England. **Tel** (02814) 2662. **Ed** J R Metcalfe. **Ind/Abst** Life Sci. Collect., GeoRef, Biol. Abstr., Bibliogr. Agric., Bibliogr. Index Geol. **NLM** W1 BU899K. **CODEN** BZONAP. Contains applications to the international commission in zoological nomenclature on particular problems in nomenclature, and comments on them by zoologists. Also contains the commission's rulings on these problems. *Opinions and Declarations Rendered by the International Commission on Zoological Nomenclature.*

BULLETIN - OFFICE DES RECHERCHES SUR LES PECHERIES DU CANADA. **Main/Corp** Canada. Office des Recherches sur les Pecheries. Monographic Series. CN. French (English). Office des Recherches sur les

Pecheries du Canada, Ottawa Ontario Canada. **DD** 591. *Bulletin - Office de Biologie.*

BULLETIN - ORNITHOLOGICAL SOCIETY OF THE MIDDLE EAST. **Main/Corp** Ornithological Society of the Middle East. No. 1- Autumn 1978-. Periodical. UK. English. ir. 7.00. Ornithological Society of the Middle East, c/o The Lodge, Sandy Bedfordshire England. **Ed** David Fisher. bk rev. adv acc. **Circ** 600. (ctrl). Short papers, book reviews, details of meetings and expeditions and lists of current literature concerning ornithology in the Middle East. *Bulletin - Ornithological Society of Turkey.*

BULLETIN ORNITHOLOGIQUE. First issue in 1956. 0007-5256. Periodical. CN. French. qt. Club des Ornitho de Quebec Inc, 8191 Avenue du Zoo, Orsainville Quebec G1G 4G4 Canada.

BULLETIN - PACIFIC SEABIRD GROUP. (BULLETIN). **Main/Corp** Pacific Seabird Group. **VFOAT** P.S.B. Bulletin. Vol. 1, No. 1 (Jan. 1974)-. 0740-3771. Periodical. US. English. sa. $10.00. c/o Dr D Siegel-Causey, Museum of Natural History KU, Lawrence KS 66045. **Tel** (912)982-2767. **Ed** Malcolm Coulter. **LC** QL683.P37. **DD** 598.40979. bk rev. **Circ** 400. (ctrl). Informs select international readership about current research on seabirds, conservation issues, legislation and policy decisions.

BULLETIN SIGNALETIQUE. 364, PROTOZOAIRES ET INVERTEBRES, ZOOLOGIE GENERALE ET APPLIQUEE. **VFOAT** Protozoaires et Invertebres, Zoologie Generale et Appliquee. V. 40-. 0181-0006. Periodical. FR. French. ir. Centre National de la Recherche Scientifique, 26 rue Boyer, 75971 Paris Cedex 20 France. **LC** Z7993, QL1. **DD** 016.592. **NLM** ZQ 1 B936. *Bulletin Signaletique. 360, Biologie Animale, Physiologie et Pathologie des Invertebres, Ecologie, 0397-7722.*

BULLETIN - ZOOLOGISCH MUSEUM, UNIVERSITEIT VAN AMSTERDAM. (BULLETIN ZOOLOGISCH MUSEUM, UNIVERSITEIT VAN AMSTERDAM). Vol. 1, No. 1 (Aug. 31, 1966)-. 0066-1325. Monographic Series. NE. English. ir. Universitei van Amsterdam, Plantage Middenlasn 53, Amsterdam Netherlands. **Ind/Abst** Life Sci. Collect., GeoRef, Biol. Abstr., Bibliogr. Agric. **LC** QL1. **CODEN** BZMAAA.

BUTTERFLIES OF EUROPE. English. AULA-Verlag GMBH, Verlag fur Wissenschaft und Forschung, Luisenplatz 2, Postfach 1366, D-6200 Wiesbaden West Germany. **Tel** 06121/373060. **Ed** Otakar Kudrna. Deals in 8 volumes with systematics, taxonomy, distribution and biology of all European butterflies.

CAHIERS O.R.S.T.O.M. SERIE ENTOMOLOGIE MEDICALE ET PARASITOLOGIE. **VFOAT** Serie Entomologie Medicale et Parasitologie. 0029-7224. Periodical. French (summaries and bibliographies in English). qt. $33.26. Service Central Documentation, 70-74 Route d'Aulnay, 93140 Bondy France. **Ind/Abst** Life Sci. Collect., Biol. Abstr. **CODEN** CAOEA4.

CANADIAN FIELD-NATURALIST. (THE CANADIAN FIELD-NATURALIST). V. 33- April 1919-. 0008-3550. Periodical. CN. English. ir. $30.00. Ottawa Field Naturalist Club, Box 3264 Postal Station C, Ottawa Ontario K1Y 4J5 Canada. **Tel** (613)996-1665. **Ed** F R Cook. **Ind/Abst** Life Sci. Collect., Environ., Can. Environ., GeoRef, ASTIS Bibliogr., ASTIS Curr. Aware. Bull., Sel. Water Resour. Abstr., Nuci. Sci. Abstr., Biol. Abstr., Bibliogr. Agric., Energy Inf. Abstr., Environ. Abstr., Sci. Cit. Index, Abr. Ed., Bibliogr. Index Geol. **CODEN** CAFNAK. bk rev. **Circ** 2,200. (ctrl). Natural history-scientific. *Ottawa Naturalist, 0316-4411.*

CANADIAN JOURNAL OF ZOOLOGY. **VFOAT** Journal Canadien de Zoologie. V. 29- Jan. 1951-. 0008-4301. Periodical. CN. English (includes some text in French). mo. $41.02. Receiver General for Canada, National Research Council, Ottawa Ontario K1A 0R6 Canada. **Tel** (613)993-0362. **Ed** G O Mackie. **Ind/Abst** Sel. Water Resour. Abstr., Excerpta Med., Nuci. Sci. Abstr., Abstr. Bull. Inst. Paper Chem., Biol. Abstr., Chem. Abstr., Bibliogr. Agric., Index Med., Biol. Agric. Index, Sci. Cit. Index, Abr. Ed., Bibliogr. Index Geol. **NLM** W1 CA624. **CODEN** CJZOAG. adv acc. **Circ** 1,600. Available on microfiche from: Toronto, Micromedia, 197—, Available on microfiche from: Ann Arbor, Mich., University Microfilms International. Papers, notes, rapid communications, and reviews in all aspects of zoology including animal ecology, biochemistry and physiology, parasitology, systematics and evolution. *Canadian Journal of Research.*

THE CARDINAL NEWS. V. 21, No. 1 (March 1982)-. Periodical. US. English. qt. Illinois Audubon Society, PO Box 608, Wayne IL 60184. *Audubon Newsletter.*

CARNETS DE ZOOLOGIE. (LES CARNETS DE ZOOLOGIE). V. 20, No. 2- April 1960-. 0008-669X. Periodical. CN. French. qt. 15.00. Societe Zoologique de Quebec, 9141 Aveneu du Zoo, Charlesbourg Quebec G1G HGH Canada. **Tel** (418)627-3072. **Ind/Abst** Point Repere, Biol. Abstr. **CODEN** CZOOA5. bk rev. **Circ** 1,500. Our publication contributes to a better knowledge of the zoo and the natural sciences. *Carnets, 0319-4531.*

CATALOGUE OF AMERICAN AMPHIBIANS AND REPTILES. Began in 1963 with 1. Periodical. US. English. Society for the Study of Amphibians, c/o Milwaukee Public Museum, Eighth and Wells, Milwaukee WI 53233. **LC** QL651. **DD** 598.10973.

CECIDOLOGIA INTERNATIONALE. Vol. 1, No. 1, 2, 3-. Periodical. II. English. ty. $103.00. Cecidological Society of India, 14 Park Road, Allahabad 211002 India. **Ind/Abst** Life Sci. Collect., Biol. Abstr. **CODEN** CEINEX. *Cecidologia Indica, Marcellia.*

CENTZONTLE : REVISTA DE LA SOCIEDAD MEXICANA DE ORNITOLOGIA. Began in Sept. 1979. Periodical. MX. Spanish (English). bm. $40.00. Sociedad Mexicana Ornitologia, Apartado Postale 70-581, Mexico 20 DF Mexico. **Tel** 550-59-14. **Ed** Salvador Avila Beltran. bk rev. **Circ** 1,000. (ctrl). Original works of research in ornitology as well as of all aspects related to this specialty.

CETOLOGY. No. 1-. 0097-031X. Monographic Series. US. English. ir. Biological Systems Inc, PO Box 26, St Augustine FL 32086. **Tel** (904)797-5057. **Ed** David K Caldwell. **Ind/Abst** Life Sci. Collect., Biol. Abstr., Ocean. Abstr. **LC** QL737.C4. **DD** 599.505. **CODEN** CTGYAL. Biology of marine mammals.

C.F.O. JOURNAL. **Main/Corp** Colorado Field Ornithologists. **VAT** Colorado Field Ornithologists Journal. No. 23- Spring 1975-. 0362-9902. Periodical. US. English. qt. $8.00. Colorado Field Ornithologists, 1917 South Quitman, Denver CO 80219. **Tel** (303)297-1192. **Ed** Ann Hodgson. **LC** QL684.C6. **DD** 598.2978805. bk rev. **Circ** 450. A journal of Colorado field ornithology containing articles on distribution, behavior, and occurrence of birds. Also book reviews, seasonal Colorado reports and records committee decisions. *Colorado Field Ornithologist.*

CHAMP CHANNELS. Vol. 1, No. 1 (April 1983)-. 0747-9840. Periodical. US. English. qt. $9.00. Lake Champlain Phenomena Investigation, PO Box 2134, Wilton NY 12866. **Tel** (518)587-7638. **Ed** Joseph W Zarzynski. **DD** 001. bk rev. **Circ** 200. Focus on cryptozoology-specifically the 'Loch Ness and Lake Champlain Monsters.'.

CHECK-LIST OF BIRDS OF THE WORLD. US. English. ir. Harvard University, Museum of Comparative Zoology, Cambridge MA 02138. **Tel** (617)495-2471. **Ed** R A Painter Jr. **Circ** 2,000. Scientific compilation of bird names and distribution of species and subspecies.

CHEMICAL ZOOLOGY. V. 1- 1967-. Monographic Series. US. English. ir. Academic Press, 4805 Sand Lake Road, Orlando FL 32819. **Ed** M Florkin and B T Scheer. **LC** QP514. **DD** 591.192.

CHO TO GA. TYO TO GA. **VFOAT** Nihon Rinshi Gakkai Kaiho : Transactions of the Lepidopterological Society of Japan. V. 1- 1945-. English (Japanese). ir. Nihon Rinshi Gakkai, c/o Ogata Byoin 18 Imabashi 3 chome Higashi-ku, 541 Osaka Japan. **LC** QL541. **DD** 595.7805.

CICINDELA. Began in March 1969. 0590-6334. Periodical. US. English. qt. $7.00. R L Huber, 4637 West 69th Terrace, Prairie Village KS 66203. **Tel** (913)661-4279. **Ed** Ronald L Huber. **Ind/Abst** Life Sci. Collect., Bibliogr. Agric. bk rev. **Circ** 150. Studies on tiger beetles.

CLADISTICS. (CLADISTICS : THE INTERNATIONAL JOURNAL OF THE WILLI HENNIG SOCIETY). Vol. 1, No. 1 (Winter 1985)-. 0748-3007. Periodical. US. English. qt. $95.00. Meckler Publishing, 11 Ferry Lane West, Westport CT 06880. **Tel** (203)226-6967. **Ed** N Platnick. **DD** 574. bk rev. adv acc. **Circ** 425. Papers on theory, method and applications of a systematic method of characterizing groups and naming them. Contains reports of Willi Hennig Society.

THE COLEOPTERISTS BULLETIN. (THE COLEOPTERISTS' BULLETIN). V. 1- April 1947-. 0010-065X. Periodical. US. English. qt. $30.00. Coleopterists Society c/o Terry L Erwin-Treasurer, Department of Entomology NHB, 169 Smithsonian Institution, Washington DC 20560. **Tel** (202)357-2209. **Ind/Abst** Life Sci. Collect., Biol. Abstr., Bibliogr. Agric. **CODEN** COBLAO. Object is the advancement of the science of coleopterology in all its aspects of theory, principles, methodology and practice, for both living and fossil beetles.

COLEOPTERORUM CATALOGUS SUPPLEMENTA *CEASED.* V. 1-. Monographic Series. NE. Latin. ir. Dr W Junk, PO Box 3713, The Hague Netherlands. **Tel** (904)371-9858. **Ed** Ross Arnett.

COLONIAL WATERBIRDS. (COLONIAL WATERBIRDS : JOURNAL OF THE COLONIAL WATERBIRD GROUP). Vol. 4 (1981). 0738-6028. US. English. an. $25.00. Im Price Treasurer CWG, 563 Fairview Avenue, Ottawa Ontario K1M 0X4 Canada. **Tel** (819)997-1362. **Ed** James Kushlan. **LC** QL671. **DD** 598.29240973. adv acc. **Circ** 350. Biology, management, conservation of colonial nesting waterbirds; research heron, stork, ibis, cormorant, gull, tern seabird. *Proceedings.*

COMPTES-RENDUS. **Main/Corp** Colloque d'Arachnologie d'Expression Francaise. French (summaries in English and Spanish). ir. Eunibar S A, Diputacion 216, Barcelona-11 Spain. **LC** QL451. **DD** 595.405.

THE CONDOR. Began in 1900. 0010-5422. Periodical. US. English. qt. $25.00. Ornithological Society of North America, PO Box 21618, Columbus OH 43221. **Tel** (617)422-0639. **Ed** Keith L Bildstein. **Ind/Abst** Life Sci. Collect., Can. Environ., GeoRef, Biol. Abstr., Ref. Source, Biol. Agric. Index. **DD** 598. **CODEN** CNDRAB. bk rev. adv acc. **Circ** 3,500. Articles deal with all aspects of ornithology, including ecology, behavior, natural history, physiology, anatomy, taxonomy and biogeography. *Bulletin of the Cooper Ornithological Club of California.*

CONIGLICOLTURA. (RIVISTA DI CONIGLICOLTURA). Yearly V. 15, No. 1-. 0010-5929. Periodical. IT. Italian. mo. Edagricole, PO Box 2157, 40100 Bologna Italy. **Ind/Abst** Bibliogr. Agric.

CONTINENTAL BIRDLIFE. Vol. 1, No. 1 (Feb. 1979)-. 0270-2894. Periodical. US. English. bm. $12.00. Continental Birdlife, 2416 East Adams, Tucson AZ 85719. **Tel** (602)795-4924. **LC** QL681. **DD** 598.297.

CONTRIBUTIONS DE L'INSTITUT DE BIOLOGIE DE L'UNIVERSITE DE MONTREAL. **Main/Corp** Universite de Montreal. Institut de Biologie. No. 21- 1948-. Monographic Series. CN. text in French and English. ir. Institut de Biologie de Universite de Montreal, CP 6128, Montreal Quebec H3C 3J7. **LC** QL1. **DD** 590.82. *Contributions de l'Institut de Biologie Generale et de Zoologie de l'Universite de Montreal.*

CONTRIBUTIONS OF THE AMERICAN ENTOMOLOGICAL INSTITUTE. **Main/Corp** American Entomological Institute. V. 1-. 0569-4450. Monographic Series. US. English. ir. $40.00. American Entomological Institute, 3005 56th Avenue, Gainesville FL 32806. **Tel** (904)377-6458. **Ed** H Townes. **Ind/Abst** Life Sci. Collect., Bibliogr. Agric. **LC** QL461. **Circ** 140. Taxonomy of insects.

CONTRIBUTIONS TO PRIMATOLOGY. V. 1-. 0301-4231. Monographic Series. English. ir. S Karger AG, PO Box, CH-4009 Basel Switzerland. **Tel** (061)390880. **Ed** F S Szalay. **Ind/Abst** Life Sci. Collect., GeoRef, Index Med., Bibliogr. Index Geol. **NLM** W1 CO778UP. **CODEN** CPMYAN. A series that has established scientific standards for evolutionary biology. *Bibliotheca Primatologica, 0067-8139.*

CONTRIBUTIONS TO VERTEBRATE EVOLUTION. V. 1- 1977-. 0376-4230. Monographic Series. English. ir. S Karger Ag, PO Box, CH-4009 Basel Switzerland. **Ed** M K Hecht and F S Szalay. **Ind/Abst** GeoRef, Biol. Abstr., Bibliogr. Index Geol. **NLM** W1 CO778XE. **CODEN** CVEVDJ. Studies covering the phylogeny, taxonomy, adaptions and biogeography of vertebrate groups.

COPEIA. No. 1-173, Dec. 27, 1913-Oct./Dec. 1929. 0045-8511. Periodical. US. English. qt. $50.00 Domestic, $55.00 Foreign. Copeia, Florida State Museum A S I H, Gainesville FL 32611. **Tel**

(904)392-6572. **Ind/Abst** Life Sci. Collect., Sel. Water Resour. Abstr., Energy Inf. Abstr., Environ. Abstr., GeoRef, Biol. Abstr., Biol. Agric. Index, Sci. Cit. Index, Abr. Ed., Ocean. Abstr., Bibliogr. Index Geol. **LC** QL1. **DD** 579.005. **NLM** W1 CO826. **CODEN** COPAAR. (cum index). Scientific articles dealing with the natural history, physiology and systematics of cold-blooded vertebrates, fishes, amphibians and reptiles.

CORAX. Periodical. GW. German. ir. Schleswig-Holstein und Hamburg, Von Melle Park, 2 Hamburg 13 West Germany. **LC** QL690.G3. *Mitteilungen.*

CORDULIA. V. 1- Jan. 1975-. 0700-4966. Periodical. CN. French (English). qt. $2.00. R Hutchinson Ou a Larochelle, College Bourget, CP 1000, Rigaud Quebec J0P 1P0 Canada. **DD** 591'.9'714.

CORELLA. V. 1- Mar. 1977-. 0155-0438. Periodical. AT. English. qt. $13.28. Australian Bird Study Association, PO Box 313, Sydney New South Wales 2000 Australia. **Ed** G R Cam. bk rev. **Circ** 600. Publication of results of ornithological research especially those studies which have involved bird ringing.

CRYPTOZOOLOGY. (CRYPTOZOOLOGY : INTERDISCIPLINARY JOURNAL OF THE INTERNATIONAL SOCIETY OF CRYPTOZOOLOGY). Vol. 1 (Winter 1982)-. 0736-7023. Periodical. US. English. an. $35.00. ISC, PO Box 43070, Tucson AZ 85733. **Tel** (602)884-8369. **Ed** J Richard Greenwell. bk rev. **Circ** 800. (ctrl). Material on the present or recent occurrence of 'unexpected' animals not recognized by contemporary zoology, but which are known through native accounts, historical or archaeological evidence, works of art, and oral traditions.

CSIRO DIVISION OF ENTOMOLOGY REPORT. **VFOAT** Division of Entomology Report. **VAT** Commonwealth Scienfific and Industrial Research Organization, Division of Entomology Report. Monographic Series. English. ir.

CURRENT ORNITHOLOGY. Vol. 1-. 0742-390X. Periodical. US. English. an. Plenum Press, 233 Spring Street, New York NY 10013. **Ed** Richard F Johnston. **LC** QL671. **DD** 598.05.

CYBIUM. *See* Fish Culture and Fisheries.

DANIRUI KENKYUKAI KAIHO. JA. Japanese. ir. Danirui Kenkyukai, c/o Kokuritsu Kagaku Hakubutsukan d'Obutsu, Kenkyubu 23-1 Huakunin-cho 3, Shinjuku-ku Tokyo-to 160 Japan. **LC** QL458.

DANSK ORNITHOLOGISK FORENINGS TIDSSKRIFT. Vol. 1-. 0011-6394. Periodical. DK. Danish (summaries in English). sa. 100.-. Dansk Ornithologisk Forening, Vesterbrogade 140, DK-1620 Kobenhaven Denmark. **Tel** 01-318106. **Ed** Kay Kampp. **Ind/Abst** Life Sci. Collect., Biol. Abstr., ASTIS Bibliogr., ASTIS Curr. Aware. Bull. **LC** QL671. **CODEN** DOFTAB. Index published separately - free - automatically sent. (cum index). bk rev. Ornithological research in Denmark and Greenland.

DANSKE FUGLE. Vol. 1- 1920-. Periodical. DK. English summaries. ir. Danske Ornitologisk Central, Box 55, DK-6900 Skjern Denmark.

DEUTSCHE ENTOMOLOGISCHE ZEITSCHRIFT (1881). (DEUTSCHE ENTOMOLOGISCHE ZEITSCHRIFT). Vol. 25, Nos. 1 & 2 May and Oct. 1881 -Vol. 1943, Vol. 3/4. 0012-0073. Periodical. GE. German. mo. $57.89. Kunst & Wissen Erich Bieber, Dufourstrasse 51, CH-8008 Zurich Switzerland. **Tel** (01)694420. **Ind/Abst** Life Sci. Collect., Bibliogr. Agric., Sci. Cit. Index, Abr. Ed. **LC** QL461. **DD** 595.7005. **NLM** W1 DE627. (cum index). *Zeitschrift fur Systematische Hymenopterologie und Dipterologie, Berliner Entomologische Zeitschrift.*

DEVELOPMENT IN MAMMALS. V. 1- 1977-. 0165-2168. Periodical. English. ir. Elsevier Science Publishing Company Inc, PO Box 1663/ Grand Central Station, New York NY 10163. **Ind/Abst** Chem. Abstr. **NLM** W1 DE997PI. **CODEN** DMAMDM.

DINNY'S CALGARY DIGEST. **VFOAT** Dinny's Digest. V. 1- Oct. 1969-. 0046-029X. Periodical. CN. English. qt. 10.00. Calgary Zoological Society, St George's Island, Calgary Alberta T2G3H4 Canada. **Tel** (403)265-9310. **Ed** David Banks. **Circ** 10,000. (ctrl). Includes articles concerning vertebrate zoology and horticultural interest at the Calgary Zoo as well as current events at the zoo.

DIRECTORY OF NORTH AMERICAN ENTOMOLOGISTS AND ACAROLOGISTS. 0198-9332. US. English. $8.95. Entomological Society of America, PO Box 4104, Hyattsville MD 20781. **LC** QL35. **DD** 595.700257.

DIRECTORY OF THE PUBLIC AQUARIA OF THE WORLD. 1st - Ed. 0085-0039. US. English. Waikiki Aquarium, 2777 Kalakaua Avenue, Honolulu HI 96826. **Tel** (808)923-9741. **Ed** Charles DeLuca. **LC** QL78. **DD** 590.74. adv acc. **Circ** 200. A directory of aquariums of the world, covering address, attendence, specimens, directory, and educational facilities.

DOBUTSU BUNRUI GAKKAI SHI. **VFOAT** Proceedings of the Japanese Society of Systematic Zoology. Periodical. English (Japanese). sa. Dobutsu Bunrui Gakkai, c/o Kokuritsu Kagaku Hakubursukan Bunkan Doobutsu Kenkyubu, 23-1 Hyakunin-cho Shinjuku-ku, Tokyo-to 160 Japan. **LC** QL352.

DOCUMENTATION ZOOLOGIQUE. **VFOAT** Zoologische Docementatie. No. 1- 1961-. 0563-1750. Monographic Series. French and English. ir. Musee Royal de Afrique Centrale, Stenweg OP Leuven 13, 1980 Tervuren Belgium. **Ind/Abst** Life Sci. Collect. **LC** QH71.T4. **DD** 591.

THE DODO: JOURNAL OF THE JERSEY WILDLIFE PRESERVATION TRUST. No. 14- 1977-. Periodical. UK. English. an. Jersey Wildlife Preservation Trust, Les Augres Manor, Trinity Jersey Channel Islands. **Ind/Abst** Life Sci. Collect., Psychol. Abstr. **LC** QL76.5.C55. **DD** 636.0899. *Annual Report.*

DOKLADY NA EZHEGODNOM CHTENII PAMIATI N. A. KHOLODKOVSKOGO. **VFOAT** Chteniia Pamiati Nikolaia Aleksandrovicha Kholodkovskogo. Began publication with 1948 issue. Monographic Series. UR. Russian. **LC** QL461.

DOKMAKIERIE. Began in 1950. Periodical. Afrikaans or English. ir. South African Ornithological Society, PO Box 9081, Johannesburg South Africa. **LC** QL692.S6. **DD** 598.296805.

E. Monographic Series. US. English. ir. US Department of Agriculture, Entomology Research Branch, SW 14th and Independence Avenue, Washington DC 20250. **LC** SB823.

ECHINODERM STUDIES. Vol. 1-. US. English. be. MBS, 99 Main Street, Salem NH 03079. **LC** QL381. **DD** 593.905.

THE ECHINODERMS NEWSLETTER. 0735-7494. Periodical. US. English. ir. Smithsonian Institution National Museum of Natural History, Department of Invertebrate Zoology (Echinoderms), Washington DC 20560. *Echinoderm Newsletter.*

ECOLOGICAL ENTOMOLOGY. V. 1- Feb. 1976-. 0307-6946. Periodical. UK. English. qt. 55.00 Domestic, 66.00 Foreign. Blackwell Scientific Publishing Ltd, PO Box 88, Oxford OX2 0EL England. **Tel** 0865-240201. **Ed** J H Lawton. **Ind/Abst** Life Sci. Collect., Pestdoc, Ringdoc, Vetdoc, Energy Inf. Abstr., Environ. Abstr., Biol. Abstr., Ref. Source, Bibliogr. Agric., Biol. Agric. Index, Sci. Cit. Index, Abr. Ed. **LC** QL461. **DD** 595.705. **NLM** W1 EC911G. **CODEN** EENTDT. bk rev. adv acc. Field biology and natural history of terrestrial and aquatic insects. *Transactions of the Royal Entomological Society of London.*

EISEI DOBUTSU. **VFOAT** Japanese Journal of Sanitary Zoology. Began in April 1950. 0424-7086. Periodical. JA. Japanese (English). ir. 10.000. Business Center Academic Society, 16-3 Hongo 6 chome, Bunkyo ku Tokyo 113 Japan. **Tel** 817-5811. **Ed** Nobuo Kumado. **Ind/Abst** Life Sci. Collect., Biol. Abstr., Chem. Abstr., Bibliogr. Agric. **NLM** W1 EI555. **CODEN** ESDBAK. (cum index). bk rev. adv acc. **Circ** 1,100. (ctrl).

EKOLOGICHESKAIA I EKSPERIMENTAL'NAIA PARAZITOLOGIIA. Vol. 1- 1975-. 0136-9121. Periodical. UR. Russian (summaries in English). 1.29 Single Issue. IZD-VO Leningradskogo Universiteta, Universitetskaia Nab 7/9, Leningrad Russia. **LC** QL757.

ELEPHANT. (ELEPHANT : THE PUBLICATION OF THE ELEPHANT INTEREST GROUP). 0737-108X. Periodical. US. English. H Shoshani, Department of Biological Sciences, Wayne State University, Detroit MI 48202. **LC** QL737.P98. **DD** 599.6105. *Elephant Newsletter.*

ENGELHARDTIA. V. 1- 1968-. Periodical. US. English. qt. $20.00. Northeastern Field Naturalist Society, PO Box 6, Central Islip Long Island NY 11722. *Bulletin - Long Island Herpetological Society, Journal - Long Island.*

ENGLISH TRANSLATIONS OF SELECTED TAXONOMIC PAPERS IN NEMATOLOGY. Vol. 1-. Periodical. US. English (French).

ENTOMOGRAPHY. Vol. 1 (1982)-. 0734-9874. Periodical. US. English. an. $40.00. Entomography Publications, 1722 J Street/Suite 19, Sacramento CA 95814. **Tel** (916)444-9133. **Ed** T D Eichlin and C S Papp. **Circ** 500. (ctrl). Larger papers (more than 10 printed pages) dealing with biosystematics of insects. Illustrations are welcome.

ENTOMOLOGIA EXPERIMENTALIS ET APPLICATA. V. 1, No. 1- Feb. 1958-. 0013-8703. Periodical. English. ir. 600.00 Domestic, $227.00 US. Kluwer Academic Publishing Group, PO Box 322, AH Dordrecht Netherlands. **Ed** A K Minks, L M Schoonhoven and P A van der Laan. **Ind/Abst** Life Sci. Collect., Pestdoc, Ringdoc, Vetdoc, Biol. Abstr., Chem. Abstr., Nuci. Sci. Abstr., Bibliogr. Agric., Sci. Cit. Index, Abr. Ed. **NLM** W1 EN923H. **CODEN** ETEAAT. bk rev. adv acc. **Circ** 200. Covers the field of experimental biology and ecology, both pure and applied, of insects and other land arthropods.

ENTOMOLOGICA BASILIENSIA. Vol. 1-. 0253-2484. SZ. German (articles in German, English, and French). an. $34.64. Naturhistoriches Museum Entom, Augustinergasse 2, CH-4001 Basel Switzerland. **Tel** (061)258282. **Ind/Abst** Life Sci. Collect. Taxonomy, systematics and faunistic of insects and other arthropods.

ENTOMOLOGICA SCANDINAVICA. V. 1- Feb. 1970-. 0013-8711. Periodical. SW. English (with some articles in French or German). qt. $46.58. Forlagstjansten Publishing House, PO Box 6710, S-113 85 Stockholm Sweden. **Ed** C H Lindroth. **Ind/Abst** Life Sci. Collect., GeoRef, Biol. Abstr., Nuci. Sci. Abstr., Sel. Water Resour. Abstr., Bibliogr. Agric., Sci. Cit. Index, Abr. Ed. **LC** QL461. **DD** 595.705. **CODEN** ENTSBF.

ENTOMOLOGICAL NEWS. V. 36- 1925-. 0013-872X. Periodical. US. English. bm. **Tel** (215)561-3978. **Ind/Abst** Life Sci. Collect., Coal Abstr., GeoRef, Ref. Source, Biol. Abstr., Chem. Abstr., Index Med., Bibliogr. Agric. **NLM** W1 EN923R. **CODEN** ETMNA6. bk rev. adv acc. **Circ** 700. Classification, taxonomy, systematics, and ecology of insects. *Entomological News and Proceedings of the Entomological Section of the Academy of Natural Sciences of Philadelphia.*

ENTOMOLOGICAL REVIEW. V. 37- 1958-. 0013-8738. Periodical. US. English (translation of the original work in Russian). qt. John Wiley & Sons Inc, 605 Third Avenue, New York NY 10158. **Tel** (800)526-5368. **Ind/Abst** Life Sci. Collect., Chem. Abstr., Biol. Abstr., Nuci. Sci. Abstr., Bibliogr. Agric. **NLM** W1 EN923V. **CODEN** ENREBV.

THE ENTOMOLOGICAL REVIEW OF JAPAN. V. 1- Jan. 1946-. Periodical. JA. English and Japanese. sa. Japan Publishing Trading Co Ltd, PO Box 5030 Tokyo International, Tokyo 100-31 Japan. (cum index). *Entomological Review of Japan.*

ENTOMOLOGICESKOE OBOZRENIE. (ENTOMOLOGICHESKOE OBOZRENIE). **VFOAT** Revue d'Entomologie de l'URSS. V. 25, No. 1/2-. Periodical. Russian (text in English, French or German). qt. $60.00. Victor Kamkin Inc, 12224 Parklawn Drive, Rockville MD 20852. **Tel** (301)881-5973. **Ind/Abst** Life Sci. Collect., Biol. Abstr., Bibliogr. Agric., Pestdoc, Ringdoc, Vetdoc. **CODEN** ETOBAE. *Russkoe Entomologicheskoe Obozrenie.*

ENTOMOLOGICKE PROBLEMY. **VFOAT** Entomological Problems. 1.- 1961-. 0071-0792. Monographic Series. Czech (summaries in Russian, and English or German). ir. **Ind/Abst** Life Sci. Collect. **LC** QL461.

ENTOMOLOGISCHE ABHANDLUNGEN. **Main/Corp** Dresden. Staatliches Museum fur Tierkunde. Vol. 26- 1961/62-. 0070-7244. German (summaries in English). ir. Deutscher Buch Export-Import, Leninstrasse 16, DDR-701 Leipzig East Germany. **Tel** 4952503. bk rev. **Circ** 550. (ctrl). Taxonomy, systematics, morphology, biology, ecology, zoogeography of the invertebrate groups insecta and arachnida in global range. *Abhandlungen und Berichte aus dem Staatlichen Museum fur Tierkunde in Dresden.*

ENTOMOLOGISCHE BERICHTEN. V. 1 No. 1- Sept. 1, 1901-. 0013-8827. Periodical. text in Dutch, English, French or German. mo. Nederlandse Entomologische, Plantage Middenlaan 64, Amsterdam 1018 DH Netherlands. **Ind/Abst** Life Sci. Collect., Biol. Abstr., Bibliogr. Agric. **NLM** W1. **CODEN** ETBRAV.

ENTOMOLOGISCHE BLATTER FUR BIOLOGIE UND SYSTEMATIK DER KAFER. Began publication in 1945. 0013-8835. Periodical. German (summaries in English). ir. Verlag Goecke & Evers, Durerstrasse 13, 4150 Krefeld West Germany. **Ind/Abst** Life Sci. Collect., Bibliogr. Agric., Biol. Abstr. **CODEN** EBBSAA. *Entomologische Blatter, 0342-412X.*

L'ENTOMOLOGISTE. V. 1- 1944-. 0013-8886. Periodical. FR. French. bm. $25.00. L'Entomologiste Revue, 45 Bis rue de Buffon, 75005 Paris France. **Ind/Abst** Life Sci. Collect., Biol. Abstr. **NLM** W1 EN931J. **CODEN** ETMGAJ.

ENTOMOLOGIST'S GAZETTE. V. 1- Jan. 1950-. 0013-8894. Periodical. UK. English. qt. E W Classey Ltd, PO Box 93, Faringdon Oxon SN7 7DR England. **Ed** W G Tremewan. **Ind/Abst** Life Sci. Collect., Sel. Water Resour. Abstr., Bibliogr. Agric., Biol. Abstr. **NLM** W1 EN931K. **CODEN** ETGAA5. bk rev. adv acc. **Circ** 750. A quarterly periodical of paleartic entomology.

THE ENTOMOLOGIST'S MONTHLY MAGAZINE. V. 1- (No. 1-). 0013-8908. Periodical. UK. English. ty. 20.00 Domestic, $41.00 Foreign. GEM Publishing Company, Brightwood Bell Lane, Wallingford Oxon OX10 OQD England. **Tel** (0491)33882. **Ed** K G V Smith. **Ind/Abst** Life Sci. Collect., Biol. Abstr. **LC** QL461. **DD** 595.7005. **CODEN** ENMMAT. bk rev. adv acc. **Circ** 600. Caters for articles on all orders of insects and terrestrial anthropods, specialising in the British Fauna and groups other than Lepidoptera.

THE ENTOMOLOGIST'S RECORD AND JOURNAL OF VARIATION. V. 1- Apr. 1890-. 0013-8916. Periodical. UK. English. bm. $30.65. 31 Oakdene Road, Brockham Betchworth Surrey RH3 7JV England. **Tel** 073786-3151. **Ed** P A Sokoloff. **Ind/Abst** Life Sci. Collect., Biol. Abstr., Bibliogr. Agric., Ref. Source. **NLM** W1 EN933. **CODEN** ERJVAZ. bk rev. adv acc. **Circ** 700. General entomology emphasising British and European Lepidoptera.

ENTOMOLOGY ABSTRACTS. *See* Indexes/Abstracts.

ENTOMON. Began in 1976. 0377-9335. Periodical. II. English. qt. $50.00. University Kerala Department Zoology, Association for the Advancement of Entomology, Trivandrum 695581 India. **Tel** 8306. **Ed** V K K Prabhli. **Ind/Abst** Life Sci. Collect., Biol. Abstr., Chem. Abstr., Sci. Cit. Index, Abr. Ed. **LC** QL461. **DD** 595.7005. **CODEN** ENTOD5. bk rev. adv acc. **Circ** 400. Covers entomology.

ENTOMOPHAGA. V. 1- July 1956-. 0013-8959. Periodical. text in English, French, German, Italian, or Spanish with summaries in English, French or German. qt. **Tel** 42.65.71.67. **Ind/Abst** Life Sci. Collect., Pestdoc, Ringdoc, Vetdoc, Chem. Abstr., Bibliogr. Agric. **NLM** W1 EN939. **CODEN** ETPGAY. (cum index). **Circ** 1,250. (ctrl). Official periodical of the International Organization for Biological Control of Noxious Animals and Plants. Includes original research papers on the biological control of crops, forests, and stored products.

ENVIRONMENTAL ENTOMOLOGY. V. 1- Feb. 1972-. 0046-225X. Periodical. US. English. bm. $60.00 Domestic, $72.00 Canada, Mexico and others. Entomological Society of America, 4603 Calvert Road, College Park MD 20740. **Tel** (301)864-1334. **Ed** R R Chapman and W A Bell. **Ind/Abst** Life Sci. Collect., Pestdoc, Ringdoc, Vetdoc, Excerpta Med., Coal Abstr., Energy Inf. Abstr., Environ. Abstr., Chem. Abstr., Biol. Abstr., Nuci. Sci. Abstr., Sel. Water Resour. Abstr., Bibliogr. Agric., Energy Res. Abstr., Biol. Agric. Index, Sci. Cit. Index, Abr. Ed., Pollut. Abstr. Indexes. **LC** SB599. **DD** 632.705. **NLM** W1 EN981Q. **CODEN** EVETBX. adv acc. **Circ** 2,000. Devoted to research on the interaction of insects with the biological, chemical, and physical aspects of their environments.

ENVOL. **VFOAT** Flight. **VAT** Flight (Montreal). April 1978-. 0707-7165. Periodical. CN. French (English). Free to Members. Club d'Amateurs d'Oiseaud de Montreal, 228 de la Salle, Mont St-Hilaire Quebec J3H 3C2 Canada. **DD** 598.205.

ENYO : SUISAN KENKYUJO NYUSU. *See* Fish Culture and Fisheries.

ERGEBNIS DER WASSER- UND WATVOGELZAHLUNGEN . . . IN NIEDERSACHSEN UND AN DER WESTKUSTE VON SCHLESWIG-HOLSTEIN. **Series/Titl** Veroffentlichungen des Niedersachsischen Landesverwaltungsamtes, Naturschutz, Landschaftspflege, Vogelschutz. 1980/81-. German. ir. 8.00. Niedersachsisches Landesverwaltungsamt Naturschutz Landschaftspflege Vogelschutz, Richard-Wagner-Strasse 22, D-3000 Hannover 1 West Germany. **LC** QL690.G3. **DD** 912.15984094359.

ESA NEWSLETTER. **VAT** Entomological Society of America Newsletter. V. 1- Feb. 1978-. 0273-7353. Periodical. US. English. mo. $6.50. Entomological Society of America, 4603 Calvert Road, College Park MD 20740. **Tel** (301)864-1334. **Ed** C Miro. **Circ** 8,500. (ctrl). Newsletter containing ESA business, current topics in entomology.

ETHOLOGY. Vol. 71, 1 (Jan. 1986)-. 0179-1613. Periodical. English (German). mo. Paul Parey Scientific Publishing, 35 West 38th Street #3W, New York NY 10018. **Tel** (212)730-0518. **NLM** W1. bk rev. adv acc. **Circ** 1,500. Descriptions of behavior of animals. Basis of discussions concerning their adaptability and onto- and phylogenesis. Function and interplay of their sense organs, neural and hormone systems. *Zeitschrift fur Tierpsychologie, 0044-3573.*

FABRERIES. V. 1- Jan. 1975-. 0318-6725. Periodical. CN. French. ir. $2. Association des Entomologistes Amateurs du Quebec, 2400 Chemin Sainte-Foy, Quebec Quebec G1V 1T2 Canada. **DD** 595.7005.

FAUNA. Vol. 1- (No. 1-). 0014-8881. Periodical. NO. Norwegian (summaries in English). qt. 125.-. Norsk Zoologisk Forening, Zoologisk Museum, Sarsgaten 1 N 0562 Oslo 5 Norway. **Tel** 02 68 69 60. **Ed** Lauritz Somme. **Ind/Abst** Bibliogr. Agric., Biol. Abstr., Life Sci. Collect., Sel. Water Resour. Abstr., Nuci. Sci. Abstr., Energy Res. Abstr. **LC** QL289. **CODEN** FUNAAO. bk rev. adv acc. **Circ** 1,500. Review articles and original papers in all fields of zoology with emphasis on Norwegian fauna.

FAUNA. No. 1-4, Jan./Feb. 1971-July/Aug. 1972. 0046-337X. Periodical. US. English. bm. **LC** QL1. **DD** 590.5.

FAUNA NA BULGARIIA. **VFOAT** Fauna Bulgarica. V.1- 1950-. 0428-0636. Bulgarian. ir.

FAUNA NORVEGICA. SER. B. **VFOAT** Norwegian Journal of Entomology. Began in 1979 with Vol. 26. 0332-7698. Periodical. English. sa. $9.32. Fauna Norvefica Zoologisk Museum, Sarsgt 1, Oslo 5 Norway. **Ind/Abst** Life Sci. Collect., Biol. Abstr., Bibliogr. Agric. **LC** QL461. **CODEN** FNSBD6. *Norwegian Journal of Entomology.*

FAUNA OF MASSACHUSETTS SERIES. Monographic Series. US. English. Massachusetts Division of Fisheries and Wildlife, Boston MA 02203. **LC** UNC. **DD** 591.9744.

FAUNA OF NEW ZEALAND. No. 1-. 0111-5383. Monographic Series. English. ir. Science Info Publ Centre, PO Box 9741/DSIR, Wellington New Zealand. **Tel** Wellington 858 939. **Ed** C T Duval. **Ind/Abst** Life Sci. Collect. **Circ** 700. Monograph series on taxonomy of New Zealands insects or other terrestrial invertebrates, with text keys and illustrations.

FAUNA OF THE NATIONAL PARKS OF THE UNITED STATES. FAUNA SERIES. (FAUNA OF THE NATIONAL PARKS OF THE UNITED STATES : FAUNA SERIES). **VFOAT** Fauna Series. No. 1- 1932-. Monographic Series. US. English. ir. **LC** QL155.

FAUNA OF THE U.S.S.R.: ARACHNIDA. V. 1- 1956?-. 0428-0660. US. English (translation of Fauna S.S.S.R). ir. American Institute of Biological Sciences, 1401 Wilson Boulevard, Arlington VA 22209.

FAUNA OF THE U.S.S.R.: ORTHOPTERA. V. 1- 1962?-. 0430-1242. IS. English (translation of Fauna SSSR: Priamokryle, of the An SSSR Zoologicheskii Institut). ir. Israel Program for Scientific Translations, PO Box 7145, Jerusalem Israel.

FAUNE DE L'EUROPE ET DU BASSIN MEDITERRANEEN. Vol. 1-. Monographic Series. FR. French. ir. Scientific and Medical Publications of France, 16 East 34th Street, New York NY 10016. **Tel** (212)683-4441.

FELTORNITHOLOGEN *CEASED.* Vol. 1-22. 0046-3647. Periodical. DK. Danish. ir. **LC** WMLC L, #/1217. Index in last issue of volume - attached.

FEUILLE DE CONTACT - CLUB DES ORNITHOLOGUES DE QUEBEC. (FEUILLE DE CONTACT). 0710-2356. Periodical. CN. French. mo. Club des Ornithologues du Quebec Inc, 8191 Av du Zoo, Orsainville Quebec G1G 4G4 Canada. **DD** 598.060714.

FIELDIANA: ZOOLOGY. Vol. 1 1895-. 0015-0754. Periodical. US. English. ir. Field Museum of Natural History, Roosevelt Road and Lake Shore Drive, Chicago IL 60605. **Tel** (312)922-9410. **Ed** Timothy Plowman. **LC** QL1. **Circ** 550. Systematics and geographical distribution studies.

FIELDIANA. ZOOLOGY MEMOIRS. **VFOAT** Zoology Memoirs. Vol. 1 (Feb. 28, 1950)-. 0430-3776. Monographic Series. US. English. ir. Chicago Natural History Museum, Roosevelt Road & Lake Shore Drive, Chicago IL 60605. **LC** QL3. **DD** 590.

FINS AND FEATHERS (CONNECTICUT EDITION). (FINS AND FEATHERS). **VFOAT** Connecticut Fins and Feathers. 0741-3866. Periodical. US. English. mo. $12.95 U.S., $15.95 Canada. Fins and Feathers, PO Box 1318, Hartford CT 06143.

FINS AND FEATHERS (INDIANA EDITION). (FINS AND FEATHERS). **VFOAT** Indiana Fins and Feathers. Began in 1981?. 0741-4064. Periodical. US. English. mo. $12.95 US, $15.95 Canada. Fins and Feathers, PO Box 2083, Indianapolis IN 46206.

FINS AND FEATHERS (KANSAS EDITION). (FINS AND FEATHERS). **VFOAT** Kansas Fins and Feathers. 0741-3874. Periodical. US. English. mo. $12.95 U.S., $15.95 Canada. Fins and Feathers, PO Box 12648, Wichita KS 67277.

FINS AND FEATHERS (SOUTH DAKOTA EDITION). (FINS AND FEATHERS). **VFOAT** South Dakota Fins and Feathers. 0741-4005. Periodical. US. English. mo. $12.95 U.S., $15.95 Canada. Fins and Feathers, PO Box 727, Pierre SD 57501.

FINS AND FEATHERS (VERMONT EDITION). (FINS AND FEATHERS). **VFOAT** Vermont Fins and Feathers. Began in 1982?. 0741-3858. Periodical. US. English. mo. $12.95 U.S., $15.95 Canada. Fins and Feathers Publishing Company, PO Box 942, Montpelier VT 05602.

FINS AND FEATHERS (VIRGINIA EDITION). (FINS AND FEATHERS). **VFOAT** Virginia Fins and Feathers. 0741-7101. Periodical. US. English. mo. $12.95 U.S., $15.95 Foreign. Fins and Feathers, PO Box 27706, Richmond VA 23261.

FLORA OG FAUNA. V. 1-. 0015-3818. Periodical. DK. Danish (summaries in English). $12.00. Naturhistorisk Forening for Jylland, c/o Natural History Museum Universitetsparken Building 210, 8000 Aarhus C Denmark. **Tel** 06-129777. **Ed** Birger Jensen and Bernt Lojtnant. **Ind/Abst** Life Sci. Collect., Biol. Abstr., Bibliogr. Agric., Energy Res. Abstr. **CODEN** FLFAAN. (cum index). bk rev. **Circ** 700. Original contributions to Danish faunistic and floristic and to the biology, ecology and systematics of Danish animal and plant species.

THE FLORIDA ENTOMOLOGIST. (THE FLORIDA ENTOMOLOGIST : OFFICIAL ORGAN OF THE FLORIDA ENTOMOLOGICAL SOCIETY). Vol. 4, No. 1 (July 1920)-. 0015-4040. Periodical. US. English. qt. $30.00. Florida Entomological Society, 4628 NW 40th Street, Gainesville FL 32606. **Tel** (813)324-5502. **Ed** John McLaughlin. **Ind/Abst** Life Sci. Collect., Pestdoc, Ringdoc, Vetdoc, Excerpta Med., Bibliogr. Agric., Biol. Abstr., Chem. Abstr., Nuci. Sci. Abstr., Sci. Cit. Index, Abr. Ed. **LC** QL461. **CODEN** FETMAC. bk rev. **Circ** 1,000. General entomological and related sciences relating to subtropical US, Caribbean Islands, Central and South America. *Florida Buggist.*

FLORIDA FIELD NATURALIST. V. 1- Spring 1973-. 0738-999X. Periodical. US. English. qt. $25.00. Florida Ornithological Society, 1701 NW 24th Street, Gainesville FL 32611. **Tel** (214)886-5377. **Ed** James A Kushlan. **Ind/Abst** Biol. Abstr. **CODEN** FFNADO. bk rev. adv acc. **Circ** 500. Biology and natural history of vertebrate animals in and near Florida and Caribbean.

THE FLORIDA NATURALIST. *See* Conservation & Natural Resources.

FOLIA PARASITOLOGICA. V.13 (1966)-. 0015-5683. Periodical. English (with summaries in Russian and English). qt. Kluwer Academic Publishing Group, PO Box 322, 3300 AH Dordrecht Netherlands. **Tel** 411 58. **Ed** Jan Prokopic. **Ind/Abst** Life Sci. Collect., Index Med., Biol. Abstr., Chem. Abstr., Bibliogr. Agric. **NLM** W1 FO277R. **CODEN** FRARA9. bk rev. adv acc. Publishes original papers from all branches of general medical and veterinary parasitology. *Ceskoslovenska, Parasitologie.*

FOLIA PRIMATOLOGICA. V. 1- 1963-. 0015-5713. Periodical. SZ. English (French or German). mo. $176.00. S Karger AG, PO Box 352,

White Plains NY 10602. **Tel** (061)39 08 80. **Ed** J Biegert. **Ind/Abst** Life Sci. Collect., GeoRef, Int. Aerosp. Abstr., Biol. Abstr., Chem. Abstr., Index Med., Nuci. Sci. Abstr., Psychol. Abstr., Sci. Cit. Index, Abr. Ed., Bibliogr. Index Geol. **LC** QL737.P9. **NLM** W1 FO282J. **CODEN** FPRMAB. adv acc. Gives access to key investigations on human primates. Topics range from physiology, biochemistry and pathology, through taxonomy, phylogeny and paleontology, to behavior, psychology and ecology.

FOLIA ZOOLOGICA. V. 26-. 0139-7893. Periodical. CS. English (German, with summaries in the other language). qt. 100.00. Dr W Junk, B V Publishers, PO Box 3713, The Hague Netherlands. **Tel** 331144. **Ind/Abst** Life Sci. Collect., Biol. Abstr., Bibliogr. Agric. **LC** QL1. **CODEN** FOZODJ. bk rev. **Circ** 1,000. Brings articles on research in mammalogy, ornithology, ichthyology, and morphology. *Zoologicke Listy.*

FORAMINIFERA. V. 1-. 0140-0010. Periodical. US. English. ir. Academic Press Inc, 4805 Sand lake Road, Orlando FL 32819. **Ed** R H Hedley and C G Adams. **Ind/Abst** Chem. Abstr. **LC** QL368.F6. **DD** 593.12. **CODEN** FORAD5.

FOREIGN COMPOUND METABOLISM IN MAMMALS. V. 1- 1960/69-. 0300-3493. UK. English. be. 159.00 Vols. 2-6. Royal Society of Chemistry, Blackhorse Road, Letchworth Herts SG6 1HN England. **Ind/Abst** Life Sci. Collect., Chem. Abstr. **LC** QL739.2. **DD** 599.0133. **NLM** W1 FO558K. **CODEN** FCMMAV.

FRAGMENTA FAUNISTICA. V. 7, No. 1 (Oct. 25, 1954)-. 0015-9301. Periodical. PL. Polish (English, French and German with summaries in Russian). ir. ARS Polona, Krakowskie Przedmiescie 7, 00-068 Warsaw Poland. **Ind/Abst** Life Sci. Collect., Biol. Abstr., Bibliogr. Agric. **LC** QL1. **CODEN** FRGFAH. *Fragmenta Faunistica Musei Zoologici Polonici.*

FRESHWATER INVERTEBRATE BIOLOGY. Vol. 1, No. 1 (Feb. 1982)-. 0738-2189. Periodical. US. English. qt. Freshwater Invertebrate, PO Box 413, Department of Zoology, Milwaukee WI 53201. **Tel** (414)963-4214. **Ind/Abst** Life Sci. Collect., Biol. Abstr. **CODEN** FIBID9.

GAME BIRD BREEDERS, AVICULTURISTS, AND CONSERVATIONISTS' GAZETTE. (GAME BIRD BREEDERS, AVICULTURISTS AND CONSERVATIONISTS' GAZETTE). V. 15, No. 8-. 0435-1061. Periodical. US. English. mo. $28.00. Allen Publishing Co, 1155 East 4780 South, Salt Lake City UT 84117. **Tel** (801)262-4852. **Ed** George A Allen. bk rev. adv acc. **Circ** 7,000. Every issue is highly illustrated with articles on keeping and raising waterfowl, pheasants, quail, partridge, and other ornamental birds. Instructive, informative. Also contains a classified section. *Game Bird Breeders, Pheasant Fanciers and Aviculturists' Gazette.*

GAME BIRD BREEDERS, AVICULTURISTS, ZOOLOGISTS AND CONSERVATIONISTS GAZETTE. **VFOAT** Gazette. Jan. 1970-. 0164-3711. Periodical. US. English. mo. Allen Publishing Company, 1155 East 4780 South, Salt Lake City UT 84117. **DD** 598. *Game Bird Breeders, Aviculturists and Conservationists' Gazette.*

GASTROPODIA. V. 1- (No. 1-). 0435-1363. Periodical. US. English. ir. Glenn R Webb, Route 1 Box 158, Fleetwood PA 19522. **Tel** (215)682-7291. **Ed** Glenn R Webb. **Ind/Abst** Biol. Abstr. **CODEN** GSTPAS. bk rev. **Circ** 53. An irregular journal for the publication of original papers on mollusks.

GAYANA. ZOOLOGIA. **VFOAT** Zoologia. No. 1, 1961-. 0016-531X. Monographic Series. CL. Spanish. ir. Universidad de Concepcion, Instituto de Biologia, Ongolmo 196 Casilla 1557, Concepcion Chile. **Ind/Abst** Life Sci. Collect., GeoRef, Biol. Abstr. **LC** 591.983/05. **CODEN** GBCZAO.

DIE GEFIEDERTE WELT. V. 1- 1872-. 0016-5816. Periodical. GW. German. mo. Verlag Omnia Serrice Gesellsch, Witsbaddenerstr 63, D-6503 Mainz West Germany.

GEGENBAURS MORPHOLOGISCHES JAHRBUCH. Began publication in 1953?. 0016-5840. Periodical. German. ir. $131.41. Kunst & Wissen Erich Bieber, Dufourstrasse 51, CH-8008 Zurich Switzerland. **Tel** 011-41-1-69 44 20. **Ind/Abst** Life Sci. Collect., Index Med., GeoRef, Bibliogr. Agric. **LC** QL801. **NLM** W1 GE107. *Gegenbaurs Morphologisches Jahrbuch und Beitrage zur Anatomie Funktioneller Systeme.*

GENERAL AND APPLIED ENTOMOLOGY. V. 10- July 1978-. 0158-0760. Periodical. AT. English. an. Entomological Society of Australia, PO Box 22, Five Dock New South Wales 2046 Australia. **Ind/Abst** Life Sci. Collect., Chem. Abstr. **LC** QL487. **DD** 595.7005. **CODEN** GAENDS. *Journal of the Entomological Society of Australia (N.S.W.), 0071-0725.*

LE GERFAUT. **VFOAT** Giervalk, De Giervalk. Vol. 1-. 0251-1193. Periodical. BE. Dutch (summaries in English and French, text in German). qt. $16.00. Patrimoine de Institut Science Belgique, 31 rue Vautier, B-1040 Bruxelles Belgium. **Ind/Abst** Biol. Abstr., GeoRef. **LC** QL671. **CODEN** GRFTAV. Index published separately - free - automatically sent.

GLADYS PORTER ZOO NEWS. **VFOAT** Zoo News. Periodical. US. English. qt. Gladys Porter Zoo, 500 Ringgold Street, Brownsville TX 78520. **Tel** (512)546-7187. **Ed** Sandra Skrei. **Circ** 2,000. (ctrl). Information on animals in zoo's collection, new arrivals, happenings at the Gladys Porter Zoo.

GLEANINGS IN BEE CULTURE. **VFOAT** Bee Culture. V. 2- Jan. 1, 1874-. 0017-114X. US. English. mo. $10.75. A I Root Company, PO Box 706/ 623 West Liberty Street, Medina OH 44258. **Tel** (216)725-6677. **Ed** John Root. **Ind/Abst** Biol. Agric. Index, Biol. Abstr., Chem. Abstr., Bibliogr. Agric. **LC** SF521. **CODEN** GLBCAK. bk rev. adv acc. **Circ** 20,000. Available on microfilm from Universtiy Microfilms. Geared for hobbiest beekeeper. Containing articles on honey production, nectar and pollen, how-to and everything the hobbiest beekeeper would want to know about beekeeping. *Novices' Gleanings in Bee Culture.*

GRAELLSIA. Began in 1943. 0367-5041. Periodical. Spanish. ir. Consejo Super Investment Scientific Vitruvio, 8 Apartado, 14 458 28006 Madrid Spain. **Ind/Abst** Life Sci. Collect., Biol. Abstr. **LC** QL461. **DD** 595.7005. **CODEN** GRAEAT.

GREAT LAKES ENTOMOLOGIST. (THE GREAT LAKES ENTOMOLOGIST). V. 5- Spring 1972-. 0090-0222. Periodical. US. English. qt. $15.00. Michigan Entomology Society, Michigan State University, East Lansing MI 48824. **Tel** (517)373-1950. **Ed** David C L Gosling. **Ind/Abst** Life Sci. Collect., Energy Inf. Abstr., Environ. Abstr., Biol. Abstr., Bibliogr. Agric., Sci. Cit. Index, Abr. Ed. **LC** QL461. **DD** 595.70977. **CODEN** GRLEAG. bk rev. **Circ** 600. Scientific papers dealing with all aspects of the study of insects, their life history, behavior, distribution, habits and habitat- mainly of the Great Lakes region. *Michigan Entomologist, 0026-2145.*

GUILLEMOT. (LE GUILLEMOT). Vol. 1, No. (Winter 1981)-. 0714-8283. Periodical. CN. French. qt. $2.50 Per No. Guillemot, c/o Club des Ornithologues de la Gaspesie, C P 245, Perce Quebec G0C 2L0 Canada. **DD** 598.2971477.

GYORUIGAKU ZASSHI. **VFOAT** Japanese Journal of Ichthyology. V. 1- 1950-. 0021-5090. Periodical. JA. Japanese (with English summaries). qt. $50.00. Kyowa Book Company Inc, 1-38 Kanda Jinbocho/Chiyoda-ku, Tokyo 101 Japan. **Tel** 293-0727. **Ind/Abst** Sci. Cit. Index, Abr. Ed., Biol. Abstr., Chem. Abstr., Zool. Rec., Life Sci. Collect. **CODEN** GYOZA7.

HA-OZNIYAH. **VFOAT** Torgos. 0333-7383. Periodical. Hebrew (with summaries in English). ir. **LC** QL696.F3.

HALIOTIS. Vol. 1, No. 1-. 0397-765X. Periodical. FR. French. ir. $13.30. Societe Francaise Malacologie, 55 rue de Buffon, Paris 75005 France. **Tel** 331-38-95. Scientific papers on molluscs.

HANDBOOK SERIES (ZOOLOGICAL SURVEY OF INDIA). (HANDBOOK SERIES). No. 1-. Monographic Series. English. ir.

HANDBOOKS FOR THE IDENTIFICATION OF BRITISH INSECTS. Began with Vol. 1, published in 1949?. Monographic Series. UK. English. ir. E W Classey Ltd, Park Road, Faringdon Berks, Faringdon Berks England. **LC** QL482.G8.

HANDBUCH DER PALAOHERPETOLOGIE. **VFOAT** Encyclopedia of Paleoherpetology. Periodical. English (German). ir. VCH Publishers Inc, 303 NW 12th Avenue, Deerfield Beach FL 33442. **Tel** (305)428-5566.

HANDBUCH DER ZOOLOGIE. V. 1- 1923-. Monographic Series. German. ir. Walter de Gruyter & Company, 200 Sawmill River Road, Hawthorne NY 10532. **Tel** (914)747-0110. **Ind/Abst** Bibliogr. Agric.

HANGUG JAMSA HAGNOI JI. (HANGUK CHAMSA HAKHOE CHI). **VFOAT** Sericultural Journal of Korea. 0440-2332. Periodical. KO. Korean (summaries in English). ir. Hanguk Chamsa Hakhoe, 103 Sodun-dong, Suwon-si South Korea. **Ind/Abst** Chem. Abstr. **LC** SF553.K6. **CODEN** HCHCAW.

HERD BOOK - BRITISH GOAT SOCIETY. **Main/Corp** British Goat Soceity. No. 1- 1875-. UK. English. an. $5.00. British Goat Society, Roughman Bury Street, Edmunds Suffolk England.

HERP. **VFOAT** N.Y.H.S. Bulletin. 0440-7296. Periodical. US. English. sa. NY Herpetological Society, Central Park West at 79th Street, New York NY 10024. **LC** QL640. **DD** 598.1'05.

HERPETOLOGICA. V. 1- July 1936-. 0018-0831. Periodical. US. English. qt. Herpetologist's League, 1041 New Hampshire Street, Lawrence KS 66044. **Ind/Abst** Life Sci. Collect., GeoRef, Biol. Abstr., Chem. Abstr., Nuci. Sci. Abstr. **LC** QL640. **DD** 598.105. **CODEN** HPTGAP. (cum index).

HERPETOLOGICAL MONOGRAPH. No. 1-. 0733-1347. Monographic Series. US. English. ir. W Ronald Heyer, Publications Secretary, Herpetologists' League, Smithsonian Institution/Natural History Building, Washington DC 20560.

HERPETOLOGICAL REVIEW. V. 1- Sept. 1967-. 0018-084X. Periodical. US. English. qt. Dr Henri Seibert, Zoology Department, Ohio University, Athens OH 45701. **Ind/Abst** Biol. Abstr. **LC** QL640. **CODEN** HEPRB. *Newsletter of the Ohio Herpetological Society.*

HERPETOLOGY. Began With V. 1, No. 1, Apr. 1967?. 0441-666X. Periodical. US. English. ty. $10.00. Southwestern Herpetologists, Society, PO Box 7469, Van Nuys CA 91409. **Tel** (818)982-8520. **Ed** H F DeLisle. **DD** 597. bk rev. **Circ** 200. (ctrl). General interest topic in natural history of reptiles and amphibians.

HERPETON. 0090-5410. Periodical. US. English. qt. South Western Herpetologists, Society, Box 2054 D, Pasadena CA 91105. **LC** QL640. **DD** 597.

HERPETON. (HERPETON : THE JOURNAL OF THE SOUTHWESTERN HERPETOLOGISTS SOCIETY). Began in Aug. 1966. 0440-7326. Periodical. US. English. ir. Herpeton, PO Box 7469, Van Nuys CA 91409. **Tel** (818)982-8520. **Ed** H F Delisle. **DD** 597. **Circ** 200. (ctrl). Original research in herpetology.

H.I.S.S. TITLES AND REVIEWS *CEASED.* (HISS TITLES AND REVIEWS). **Main/Corp** Herpetological Information Search Systems. Began in Feb. 1973. Ceased in 1973. 0092-2307. Periodical. US. English. qt. $6.00. American Museum of Natural History, Central Park West 79 Street, New York NY 10024. **LC** Z7996.R4. **DD** 016.5981. *Herpteological Review.*

HOGLE ZOO NEWS. 0275-4584. US. English. Hogle Zoological Garden, 2600 East Sunneyside Avenue, PO Box 8475, Salt Lake City UT 84108.

EL HORNERO. V. 1- 1917/19-. 0073-3407. AG. Spanish. ir. $8.00. Association Ornitologica del Plata, Del Plata-25 de Mayo 749, P 2-6 BS AS Argentina. **Ind/Abst** Biol. Abstr. **CODEN** HRNOAX.

IHERINGIA. SERIE ZOOLOGIA. Began with issue for Sept. 6, 1967. 0073-4721. Periodical. BL. Portuguese (German with summaries in English, French, and German). ir. Fundacao Zoobotanica do Rio, Grande do Sul Biblioteca, Caixa Postal 1188, 90.000 Porto Alegre RS Brasil. **Tel** (0512)36-15-11. **Ed** Arno Antonio Lise. **Ind/Abst** Life Sci. Collect., GeoRef, Biol. Abstr., Bibliogr. Agric. **LC** QL1. **DD** 590.5. **CODEN** IHZOAY. **Circ** 600. (ctrl). Zoology, systematics of invertebrates and vertebrates, Rio Grande of Brazil. *Iheringia. Zoologia.*

ILAR NEWS. **Main/Corp** Institute of Laboratory Animal Resources (U.S.). **VAT** Institute of Laboratory Animal Resources News. V. 10- Oct. 1966-. 0018-9960. Periodical. US. English. qt. Institute of Laboratory Animal Resources, 2101 Constitution Avenue NW, Washington DC 20418. **LC** QL55. **DD** 591.0724. **NLM** W1 I245. *Information on Laboratory Animals for Research.*

INDEX OF ENTOMOPHAGOUS INSECTS. *See* Indexes/Abstracts.

INDIAN BEE JOURNAL. V. 1- 1939-. 0019-4425. Periodical. II. English. qt. $10.00. All India Bee Keepers Association, 1325 Sadashiv Peth, Poona 411 030 India. **Tel** 4434444. **Ed** S G Shende. **Ind/Abst** Bibliogr. Agric. bk rev. adv acc. **Circ** 800. (ctrl). Only journal of India useful to beekeepers and bee scientists. Gives information on beekeeping and bee research in India and abroad.

INDIAN JOURNAL OF ACAROLOGY. Periodical. English. sa. $30.00. Acarological Society of India, Department of Entomology, University of Agricultural Sciences, Hebbal Bangalore 560 024 India. **Ind/Abst** Life Sci. Collect., Biol. Abstr. **CODEN** IJACDQ.

INDIAN JOURNAL OF ENTOMOLOGY. (THE INDIAN JOURNAL OF ENTOMOLOGY). V. 1- June 1939-. 0367-8288. Periodical. II. English. qt. $40.00. Entomological Society of India, Indian Agricultural Research Institute, New Delhi 12 India. **Ind/Abst** Life Sci. Collect., Excerpta Med., Biol. Abstr., Chem. Abstr., Bibliogr. Agric. **LC** QL461. **DD** 595.705. **NLM** W1 IN208L. **CODEN** IJENA8.

INDIAN JOURNAL OF HELMINTHOLOGY. Vol. 1, No. 1 (Oct. 1948)-. 0019-5227. Periodical. II. English. sa. $40.00. Asia Books and Periodicals Company, 11 Darya Ganju Ansari Road, New Delhi 110002 India. **NLM** W1 IN209.

INDIAN JOURNAL OF NEMATOLOGY. V. 1- Mar. 1971-. 0303-6960. Periodical. II. English. sa. $32.00. Asia Books and Periodicals Company, 11 Darya Ganj, New Delhi 110002 India. **Ind/Abst** Biol. Abstr., Chem. Abstr., Bibliogr. Agric. **CODEN** IJNEDT.

INDIAN JOURNAL OF SERICULTURE. Vol. 1- July 1962-. 0445-7722. II. English. an. $0.88. Central Silk Board, 95 B Marine Drive, Bombay 2 India. **Tel** 292413. **Ind/Abst** Nuci. Sci. Abstr., Biol. Abstr., Chem. Abstr. **LC** SF541. **DD** 638.20954. **CODEN** IJSEAH.

INDIAN JOURNAL OF ZOOLOGY. V. 1- 1973-. 0302-7562. English. ir. $48.00. c/o Department of Zoology, Saifia College, Bhopal India. **Ind/Abst** Life Sci. Collect., Biol. Abstr., Chem. Abstr. **LC** QL1. **DD** 591.05. **CODEN** IJZLA5.

INDO-PACIFIC MOLLUSCA. V. 1- Mar. 1959-. 0073-7240. Monographic Series. US. English. ir. Delaware Museum of Natural History, Box 3937, Greenville DE 19807. **Ind/Abst** Life Sci. Collect., GeoRef, Biol. Abstr. **LC** QL401. **DD** 591, 562. **CODEN** IPMOAP.

EL INFORMADOR APICOLA. (V. 3, No. 31- Oct. 1972-). Periodical. Spanish. ir.

INFORMATIONS. Serie 1 (1972)-. Periodical. French. ir. Monsieur J Buyle, Av Maurice Maeterlinck 56 Bte 8, B-1030 Bruxelles Belgium. **Ind/Abst** GeoRef. **CODEN** ISBMDM.

INLAND BIRD BANDING. Vol. 51, No. 1 (Spring 1979)- Vol. 53, No. 4 (Winter 1981). Periodical. US. English. qt. $15.00. Inland Bird Banding Association, 6305 Cumberland Road SW, Sherrodsville OH 44675. **Tel** (815)594-2259. **Ed** Terrance Ingram. **LC** QL677.5. **DD** 598.07232. (cum index). bk rev. adv acc. **Circ** 1,500. (ctrl). For bird banders and others interested in ornithology. *Inland Bird Banding News (1968), 0197-5862.*

INSECT SCIENCE AND ITS APPLICATION. Vol. 1, No. 1-. 0191-9040. Periodical. UK. English (text in French). bm. Pergamon Press, 395 Sawmill River Road, Elmsford NY 10523. **Ind/Abst** Life Sci. Collect., Pestdoc, Ringdoc, Vetdoc, Biol. Abstr., Chem. Abstr., Bibliogr. Agric. **NLM** W1 IN456W. **CODEN** ISIADL.

INSECTA HELVETICA. CATALOGUS. Vol. 1- 1966-. Monographic Series. SZ. German. ir. Schweizische Entomol Gesell, Entomol Inst Eth Zentrum, CH-8092 Zurich Switzerland. **Tel** 01-256 22 11. **Circ** 600. List and distribution of insect species in Switzerland.

INSECTS OF MICRONESIA. (INSECTS OF MICRONESIA BERNICE P. BISHOP MUSEUM). Vol. 1-. 0073-8115. Monographic Series. US. English (French and German). ir. Bishop Museum Press, PO Box 19000-A, Honolulu HI 96819. **Ind/Abst** Biol. Abstr. **LC** QL489.M5. **DD** 595.7. **CODEN** IMICAG.

THE INSECTS OF VIRGINIA. No. 1- Sept. 1969-. 0098-1222. US. English. Virginia Polytechnic Institute and State University, 225 Norris Hall, Blacksburg VA 24061. **LC** AS36, QL475.V5. **DD** 081 S, 595.709755.

INTERNATIONAL JOURNAL FOR PARASITOLOGY. *See* Biology.

INTERNATIONAL JOURNAL OF ACAROLOGY. V. 1- June 1975-. 0164-7954. Periodical. US. English. qt. $90.00. Indira Publishing House, PO Box 37256, Oak Park MI 48033. **Tel** (313)661-2529. **Ed** V Prasad. **Ind/Abst** Biol. Abstr. **CODEN** IJOADM. adv acc. A journal of mites and ticks, agriculture, general, medical, veterinary, and aquatic biology, ecology, control, morphology, histology, genetics and taxonomy.

INTERNATIONAL JOURNAL OF ENTOMOLOGY. V. 25, 1 (26 Apr. 1983)-. 0735-6250. Periodical. US. English. qt. Bishop Museum Press, PO Box 19000-A, Honolulu HI 96819. **Ind/Abst** Life Sci. Collect. **LC** QL461. **DD** 595.7099. Available on microfilm from University Microfilms International. *Pacific Insects, 0030-8714.*

INTERNATIONAL JOURNAL OF INSECT MORPHOLOGY & EMBRYOLOGY. **VFOAT** Insect Morphology & Embryology. **VAT** International Journal of Insect Morphology and Embryology. V. 1- Sept. 1971-. 0020-7322. Periodical. UK. English. bm. Pergamon Press, 395 Sawmill River Road, Elmsford NY 10523. **Tel** (914)592-7700. **Ind/Abst** Life Sci. Collect., Biol. Abstr., Chem. Abstr., Sci. Cit. Index, Abr. Ed. **LC** QL494. **DD** 595.70405. **NLM** W1 IN769E. **CODEN** IJIMBQ.

INTERNATIONAL JOURNAL OF INVERTEBRATE REPRODUCTION AND DEVELOPMENT. Vol. 7, No. 1 (Mar. 1984)-. 0165-1269. Periodical. English (French). bm. Elsevier Science Publishers, PO Box 211, 1000 AE Amsterdam Netherlands. **Tel** (020)5803.911. **Ind/Abst** Curr. Contents, Life Sci. Collect. *International Journal of Invertebrate Reproduction, 0165-1269.*

INTERNATIONAL JOURNAL OF PRIMATOLOGY. V. 1- Mar. 1980-. 0164-0291. Periodical. US. English. bm. $110.00 Domestic, $124.00 Foreign. Plenum Publishing Corporation, 233 Spring Street, New York NY 10013. **Tel** (212)620-8000. **Ed** G A Doyle and Matt Cartmill. **Ind/Abst** Curr. Contents, Life Sci. Collect., Chem. Abstr., Ref. Z., Psychol. Abstr., Sci. Cit. Index, Abr. Ed. **LC** QL737.P9. **DD** 599.805. **NLM** W1 IN775K. **CODEN** IJPRDA. bk rev. adv acc. This is a multi-disciplinary journal devoted to basic primatology, i.e., studies in which the primate is featured. Brings together field and lab studies, also publishes articles in fundamental primatology.

INTERNATIONAL PEST CONTROL. *See* Agriculture.

INTERNATIONAL QUARTERLY OF ENTOMOLOGY. Vol. 1, No. 1 (Jan. 1985)-. Periodical. TU. English (French or German). qt. 70.00. Genel Basin Limited, PO Box 100 Konak, Izmir Turkey. **Ed** Tahsin Yazicioglu. bk rev. adv acc. Covers entomology, arthropids, insects, systematic zoology, ecology, zoogeography, paleontology, agricultural and medical entomology.

INTERNATIONAL REVIEW OF GENERAL AND EXPERIMENTAL ZOOLOGY. V. 1- 1964-. 0074-7734. US. English. ir. Academic Press, 4805 Sand Lake Road, Orlando FL 32819. **Ed** W J LFelts and R J Harrison. **LC** QL1. **DD** 591. **NLM** W1 IN832R.

INTERNATIONAL SERIES OF MONOGRAPHS ON PURE AND APPLIED BIOLOGY. DIVISION : ZOOLOGY. Monographic Series. US. English. ir. Pergamon Press, c/o Cashier, 395 Sawmill Road, Elmsford NY 10523.

INTERNATIONAL ZOO-NEWS. 0020-9155. Periodical. UK. English. bm. 15.00 Domestic, 62.50, $40.00. Zoo Centrum, Worthyvale Manor Farm, Camelford Cornwall England. **Tel** (0840)212711. **Ed** Peter Bunyard. bk rev. adv acc. **Circ** 500. A magazine providing news from and about the zoos of the world.

INTERNATIONAL ZOO YEARBOOK. V. 1- 1959-. 0074-9664. UK. English. an. $34.48. Zoological Society of London, Regents Park, London NW1 4RY England. **Tel** 01-722-3333. **Ed** C Jarvis and D Morris. **Ind/Abst** Biol. Abstr., Chem. Abstr. **LC** QL76. **DD** 591. **NLM** QL 76 I61. **CODEN** IZYBAE. (cum index).

IOWA BIRD LIFE. 1931. 0021-0455. Periodical. US. English. qt. $12.00. Hank Zalatel, Treasurer of Iowa Ornothlogist Union, 715 West Street, Colo IA 50056. **Tel** (515)377-2889. **Ed** Peter Petersen. **LC** QL671. **CODEN** IOBLAM. bk rev. **Circ** 500. Promotes and encourages enjoyment and study of birds in Iowa. Includes summary of bird sightings, Christmas counts, research, book reviews, meetings.

IPR ANNUAL REPORT. **Main/Corp** Institute of Primate Research (Kenya). **VFOAT** I.P.R. Annual Report. English. an. Institute of Primate Research, PO Box 114, Limuru Kenya. **LC** QL737.P9. **DD** 599.807206762. *Annual Progress Report.*

IRISH BIRDS. Vol. 1- 1977-. 0332-0111. IE. English. 5.00. Irish Wildbird Conservancy, Southview Church Road, Greystones Company, Wicklow Ireland. **Tel** (01)875759. **Ed** Hugh Brazier. **Ind/Abst** Biol. Abstr. **LC** QL690.I7. **DD** 598.2941835. **CODEN** IBIRDL. bk rev. adv acc. **Circ** 1,500. Scientific papers, short notes and articles on all aspects of birds and ornithology in Ireland. *Irish Bird Report.*

ISRAEL JOURNAL OF ENTOMOLOGY. V. 1- 1966-. 0075-1243. IS. English. an. 20.00. Entomological Society of Israel, PO Box 6, Bet Dagan 50200 Israel. **Ind/Abst** Life Sci. Collect., Pestdoc, Ringdoc, Vetdoc, Biol. Abstr., Chem. Abstr., Bibliogr. Agric. **LC** QL461. **DD** 595.7'005. **CODEN** IJENB9. **Circ** 250. Original contributions on all aspects of entomology, e.g. systematics, faunistic, physiology, control.

ISRAEL JOURNAL OF ZOOLOGY. V. 1, No. 1/4 (Dec. 1963)-. 0021-2210. Periodical. IS. articles in English, French or German. qt. $37.00. Weizmann Science Press Israel, POB 801, Jerusalem 91007 Israel. **Ind/Abst** Life Sci. Collect., Biol. Abstr., GeoRef, Bibliogr. Agric. **NLM** W1 IS63V. **CODEN** IJZOAE. Index in last issue of volume - attached. *Bulletin of the Research Council of Israel. Section B, Zoology, 0375-9156.*

THE JACK-PINE WARBLER. **VAT** Jack Pine Warbler. Began with Vol. 5, published in 1927?. 0021-3845. Periodical. US. English. qt. $10.00. Michigan Audubon Society, 409 West East Avenue, Kalamazoo MI 49006. **Tel** (616)344-8648. **Ed** Thomas Howes. **Ind/Abst** Biol. Abstr., Ref. Source, Biol. Abstr. **LC** QL671. **CODEN** JPWBAD. bk rev. adv acc. **Circ** 4,000. Natural history and ornithology journal articles on birds, mammals, plants and others. *Michigan Audubon Society Quarterly News Letter.*

JOHNSONIA. Vol. 1-. Periodical. US. English. ir. Harvard University, Department of Mollusks/Museum of Comparative Zoology, Cambridge MA 02138.

JOURNAL DE CONCHYLIOLOGIE, COMPRENANT L'ETUDE DES MOLLUSQUES VIVANTS ET FOSSILES . . . . V. 1-4. Feb. 1850-Nov. 1853. Periodical. AT. French. ir. Dr P H Fischer, 18/55 Prince Albert Street, Nosman New South Wales 2088 Australia. **Ed** S Petit de la Saussaye.

JOURNAL FUR ORNITHOLOGIE. Volume 1- Jan. 1853-. 0021-8375. Periodical. GW. German. qt. 232.00. R Friedlander and Sohn, Dessauer Strasse 28/29, D-1000 Berlin 61 West Germany. **Tel** 030/262 23 28. **Ind/Abst** Life Sci. Collect., GeoRef, Biol. Abstr., Chem. Abstr., Bibliogr. Index Geol. **LC** QL671. **CODEN** JORNAH. (cum index). bk rev. Articles on scientific ornithology, mostly in German language.

JOURNAL OF ADVANCED ZOOLOGY. Began in 1980. 0253-7214. Periodical. II. English. sa. $20.00. Association for the Advancement of Zoology, 1 Kamla Kuteer Raiganj, Gorakhpur-273001 India. **Tel** 4680. **Ed** S P Tripathi. **Ind/Abst** Biol. Abstr., Chem. Abstr. **LC** QL1. **DD** 591.05. **CODEN** JAZODX. bk rev. adv acc. **Circ** 1,000. (ctrl). This is a research journal which publishes twice in a year high quality scientific papers on different aspects of zoology from foreign and Indian workers.

THE JOURNAL OF ANIMAL ECOLOGY. Periodical. UK. English. ty. $155.00. Blackwell Scientific Publisher, PO Box 88, Oxford OX2 OEL England. **Tel** (0865)240201. **Ed** L R Taylor and J M Elliott. **Ind/Abst** Biol. Agric. Index, Math. Rev., Sci. Cit. Index, Abr. Ed. bk rev. adv acc. **Circ** 3,700. Publishes original research papers on any aspect of animal ecology, but prefers an experimental, analytical or theoretical approach to real data.

JOURNAL OF ANIMAL MORPHOLOGY AND PHYSIOLOGY. (THE JOURNAL OF ANIMAL MORPHOLOGY AND PHYSIOLOGY). V. 1- June 1954-. 0021-8804. Periodical. II. English. sa. $20.00. Society Animal Morphology and Physiology, University of Baroda, c/o Department of Zoology, Baroda 390 002 India. **Ed** R V Shah. **Ind/Abst** Life Sci. Collect., Excerpta Med., Nuci. Sci. Abstr., Biol. Abstr., Chem. Abstr., Bibliogr. Agric. **LC** QL801. **NLM** W1 JO536F. **CODEN** JAMPA2. bk rev. adv acc. **Circ** 300. (ctrl). Morphology and physiology of animals.

JOURNAL OF APICULTURAL RESEARCH. V. 1-. 0021-8839. Periodical. UK. English. qt. 30. International Bee Research Association, Hill House, Gerrards Cross Bucks SL9 ONR United Kingdom. **Tel** (0753)885011. **Ed** R W

Shuel. **Ind/Abst** Life Sci. Collect., Bibliogr. Agric., Biol. Abstr., Chem. Abstr. **CODEN** JACRAQ. adv acc. **Circ** 585. Publishes original research papers on beekeeping subjects.

THE JOURNAL OF ARACHNOLOGY. V. 1- Jan. 1973-. 0161-8202. Periodical. US. English. ty. $35.00. American Arachnological Society, Central Park West at 79th, New York NY 10024. **Tel** (212)873-1300. **Ed** O F Francke. **Ind/Abst** Life Sci. Collect., Biol. Abstr., Bibliogr. Agric. **LC** QL451. **DD** 595.405. **CODEN** JARCDP. bk rev. **Circ** 600. Systematics, phylogenetics, biogeography, morphology, physiology, behavior and ecology of arachnids (spiders, scorpions, etc.).

JOURNAL OF CONCHOLOGY. 0022-0019. Periodical. UK. English. sa. $26.05. Conchological Society of Great Britain and Ireland, 88 Peperharow Road, Godalming Surrey GU7 2PN England. **Ed** Bran Coles. **Ind/Abst** Life Sci. Collect. Index published separately - free - automatically sent. **Circ** 900. (ctrl). Scientific journal related to molluses. *Quarterly Journal of Conchology.*

JOURNAL OF CRUSTACEAN BIOLOGY. (JOURNAL OF CRUSTACEAN BIOLOGY : A QUARTERLY OF THE CRUSTACEAN SOCIETY FOR THE PUBLICATION OF RESEARCH ON ANY ASPECT OF THE BIOLOGY OF CRUSTACEA). Vol. 1, No. 1 (Feb. 1981)-. 0278-0372. Periodical. US. English. qt. $60.00. Crustacean Society Smithsonian Institute IZ-NBH-W323, Washington DC 20560. **Tel** (212)357-2964. **Ed** Arthur Humes. **Ind/Abst** Electron. Commun. Abstr. J., ISMEC Bull., Pollut. Abstr. Indexes, Saf. Sci. Abstr. J., Life Sci. Collect., Biol. Abstr., Chem. Abstr. **LC** QL435.A1. **DD** 595.305. **CODEN** JCBIDB. **Circ** 1,000. Seeks to provide international exchange of information among all those interested in any aspect of the biology of crustaceans.

JOURNAL OF ECONOMIC ENTOMOLOGY. Periodical. US. English. bm. $60.00 Domestic, $74.00 Foreign. Entomological Society of America, 4603 Calvert Road, College Park MD 20740. **Tel** (301)864-1334. **Ed** J Robertson. **Ind/Abst** Biol. Agric. Index, Chem. Abstr., Index Med., Sci. Cit. Index, Abr. Ed. adv acc. **Circ** 3,300. (ctrl). Contains research reports on the economic effects of insects. Pest management biological control, and crop protection are among the topics.

JOURNAL OF ECONOMIC ENTOMOLOGY. V. 1- Feb. 1908-. 0022-0493. Periodical. US. English. bm. $66.00 Domestic, $78.00 Foreign. Entomological Society of America, 4603 Calvert Road, Box AJ, College Park MD 20740. **Tel** (301)864-1334. **Ed** J A Robertson. **Ind/Abst** Life Sci. Collect., Pestdoc, Ringdoc, Vetdoc, Excerpta Med., Energy Inf. Abstr., Environ. Abstr., Index Med., Biol. Abstr., Chem. Abstr., Biol. Agric. Index, Energy Res. Abstr. **LC** SB599. **DD** 632.705. **NLM** W1 JO627. **CODEN** JEENAI. adv acc. **Circ** 3,400. (ctrl). Provides vital information for all libraries serving the agricultural community. Each volume contains over 200 original and significant research reports on the economic effects of insects.

JOURNAL OF ENTOMOLOGICAL SCIENCE. Vol. 1, No. 1 (Jan. 1985)-. 0749-8004. Periodical. US. English. qt. $15.00. Secretary-Treasurer, Georgia Entomological Society, PO Box 748, Insect Biology and Population Management Research Laboratory, USDA, Tifton GA 31793. **Ind/Abst** Chem. Abstr. **DD** 595. **CODEN** JESCEP. *Journal of the Georgia Entomological Society, 0016-8238.*

THE JOURNAL OF EXPERIMENTAL ZOOLOGY. V. 1- May 1904-. 0022-104X. Periodical. US. English. $90.00 Domestic $94.00 Foreign. Alan R Liss Inc, 150 5th Avenue, New York NY 10011. **Ind/Abst** Excerpta Med., Energy Inf. Abstr., Environ. Abstr., Biol. Abstr., Chem. Abstr., Nuci. Sci. Abstr., Index Med., Sel. Water Resour. Abstr., Bibliogr. Agric., Biol. Agric. Index, Energy Res. Abstr. **LC** QL1. **DD** 591.0724. **NLM** W1 JO644Y. **CODEN** JEZOAO.

JOURNAL OF FIELD ORNITHOLOGY. Vol. 51, No. 1 (Winter 1980)-. 0273-8570. Periodical. US. English. qt. $20.00. The Allen Press, 1041 New Hampshire Street, PO Box 368, Lawrence KS 66044. **Tel** (913)843-1234. **Ed** Edward Burtt. **Ind/Abst** Can. Environ., Life Sci. Collect., Biol. Abstr. **CODEN** JFORDM. **Circ** 1,000. (ctrl). This journal publishes scientific findings from ornithological endeavors across the United States. *Bird-Banding, 0006-3630.*

JOURNAL OF FISH BIOLOGY. V. 1- Jan. 1969-. 0022-1112. Periodical. UK. English. mo. Academic Press, 4805 Sand Lake Road, Orlando FL 32819. **Tel** (305)345-4100. **Ind/Abst** Electron. Commun. Abstr. J., ISMEC Bull., Pollut. Abstr. Indexes, Saf. Sci. Abstr. J., Can. Environ., Life Sci. Collect., Excerpta Med., Coal Abstr., Energy Inf. Abstr., Environ. Abstr., GeoRef, Biol. Abstr., Chem. Abstr., Sel. Water Resour. Abstr., Bibliogr. Index Geol., Sci. Cit. Index, Abr. Ed., Ocean. Abstr. **LC** QL614. **DD** 598.205. **NLM** W1 JO65K. **CODEN** JFIBA9.

JOURNAL OF FISH DISEASES. V. 1- Jan. 1978-. 0140-7775. Periodical. UK. English. bm. 96 Domestic, 115 Foreign, $190.00 US. Blackwell Scientific Publishers Ltd, PO Box 88, Oxford OX2 OEL England. **Tel** (031)226-7232. **Ed** R J Roberts and R Wootten. **Ind/Abst** Can. Environ., Life Sci. Collect., Excerpta Med., Biol. Abstr., Chem. Abstr., Bibliogr. Agric. **CODEN** JFIDDI. bk rev. adv acc. **Circ** 600. The remit of the journal covers all aspects of disease in wild and cultured fish and shellfish.

JOURNAL OF FORAMINIFERAL RESEARCH. V. 1- Jan. 1971-. 0096-1191. Periodical. US. English. qt. $20.00. US National Museum/Room E-501, Washington DC 20560. **Ind/Abst** GeoRef, Biol. Abstr., Sel. Water Resour. Abstr. **LC** QL368.F6. **DD** 593.1205. **CODEN** JFARAH.

JOURNAL OF HELMINTHOLOGY. Began with Vol. 1, published in 1923. 6232-149X. Periodical. UK. English. qt. $78.50. Bureau of Hygiene and Tropical Diseases, Keppel Street, London WCZE 7H7 England. **Ind/Abst** Life Sci. Collect., Pestdoc, Ringdoc, Vetdoc, Excerpta Med., Biol. Abstr., Bibliogr. Agric., Chem. Abstr., Index Med., Nuci. Sci. Abstr., Sci. Cit. Index, Abr. Ed. **NLM** W1 JO67C. **CODEN** JOHLAT.

JOURNAL OF HERPETOLOGY. V. 1- Mar. 1968-. 0022-1511. Periodical. US. English. qt. $40.00. Society for the Study of Amphibians and Reptiles, Irvine Hall, Ohio University, c/o H C Seibert, Athens OH 45701. **Tel** (614)593-5185. **Ed** Rodolfo Ruibal. **Ind/Abst** Life Sci. Collect., GeoRef, Biol. Abstr., Chem. Abstr. **LC** QL640. **DD** 598.1. **CODEN** JHERAH. **Circ** 2,200. Research results concerning reptiles and amphibians. *Journal of the Ohio Herpetological Society, 0473-9868.*

JOURNAL OF INSECT PHYSIOLOGY. V. 1- Mar. 1957-. 0022-1910. UK. English (French or German, with English abstracts). mo. Pergamon Press, 395 Sawmill River Road, Elmsford NY 10523. **Ind/Abst** Life Sci. Collect., Pestdoc, Ringdoc, Vetdoc, Biol. Abstr., Chem. Abstr., Index Med., Bibliogr. Agric., Nuci. Sci. Abstr., Biol. Agric. Index, Sci. Cit. Index, Abr. Ed. **LC** QL461. **DD** 595.705. **NLM** W1 JO714. **CODEN** JIPHAF.

JOURNAL OF INVERTEBRATE PATHOLOGY. V. 7- Mar. 1965-. 0022-2011. Periodical. US. English. bm. Academic Press, 4805 Sand Lake Road, Orlando FL 32819. **Tel** (305)345-4100. **Ind/Abst** Life Sci. Collect., Excerpta Med., Pestdoc, Ringdoc, Vetdoc, Energy Inf. Abstr., Environ. Abstr., Int. Aerosp. Abstr., Biol. Abstr., Chem. Abstr., Index Med., Nuci. Sci. Abstr., Bibliogr. Agric., Energy Res. Abstr., Sci. Cit. Index, Abr. Ed. **LC** SB942. **NLM** W1 JO727. **CODEN** JIVPAZ. *Journal of Insect Pathology, 0095-9049.*

JOURNAL OF MAMMALOGY. Periodical. US. English. qt. $28.00. American Society of Mammalogists, Vertebrate Museum, Shippensburg PA 17257. **Tel** (717)532-1407. **Ed** Clyde Jones. **Ind/Abst** Gen. Sci. Index, Biol. Agric. Index, Sci. Cit. Index, Abr. Ed., Index Med., Bibliogr. Index Geol. bk rev. adv acc. **Circ** 4,500. Publishes results of original research on terrestrial and marine mammals. All aspects of biology of mammals are covered in the worldwide scope of this journal.

JOURNAL OF MEDICAL ENTOMOLOGY. *See* Public Health and Safety.

JOURNAL OF MEDICAL PRIMATOLOGY. V. 1- 1972-. 0047-2565. Periodical. US. English. bm. Alan R Liss Inc, 41 East 11th Street, New York NY 10003. **Tel** (212)741-2515. **Ind/Abst** Life Sci. Collect., Excerpta Med., Biol. Abstr., Chem. Abstr., Nuci. Sci. Abstr., Index Med., Sci. Cit. Index, Abr. Ed. **LC** QL737.P9. **DD** 599.804205. **NLM** W1 JO754. **CODEN** JMPMAO.

JOURNAL OF MOLLUSCAN STUDIES. (THE JOURNAL OF MOLLUSCAN STUDIES). V. 42- April 1976-. 0260-1230. Periodical. UK. English (French). ty. 70.00. Oxford University Press, Walton Street, Oxford OX2 6DP England. **Tel** (0865)56767. **Ed** John Taylor and Peter Newell. **Ind/Abst** Life Sci. Collect., Biol. Abstr., GeoRef, Bibliogr. Index Geol., Sci. Cit. Index, Abr. Ed. **LC** QL401. **DD** 594.005. **CODEN** JMSTDT. adv acc. *Proceedings of the Malacological Society of London, 0025-1194.*

JOURNAL OF NEMATOLOGY. V. 1- Jan. 1969-. 0022-300X. Periodical. US. English. qt. $30.00. Society of Nematologists, c/o D Schmitt, North Carolina State Universtiy, 3127 Ligon Street/Box 7631, Raleigh NC 27694-7631. **Tel** (919)737-2734. **Ed** Lorin R Krusberg. **Ind/Abst** Life Sci. Collect., Excerpta Med., Pestdoc, Ringdoc, Vetdoc, Bibliogr. Agric., Biol. Abstr., Chem. Abstr., Sel. Water Resour. Abstr., Biol. Agric. Index, Sci. Cit. Index, Abr. Ed. **LC** QL386.A1. **DD** 595.105. **CODEN** JONEB5. **Circ** 1,350. The official organ of the Society of Nematologists. Papers deal with pathogenicity, ecology, physiology, taxonomy, and biology of nematodes.

JOURNAL OF PLANKTON RESEARCH. *See* Biology.

THE JOURNAL OF PROTOZOOLOGY. V. 1- Feb. 1954-. 0022-3921. Periodical. US. English (French and German). qt. $60.00 Domestic, 85.00 Canada, 97.00 Others. Journal of Protozoology, PO Box 368, Lawrence KS 66044. **Tel** (913)823-1234. **Ed** Phyllis Bradbury. **Ind/Abst** Life Sci. Collect., Excerpta Med., Pestdoc, Ringdoc, Vetdoc, Int. Aerosp. Abstr., GeoRef, Biol. Abstr., Chem. Abstr., Nuci. Sci. Abstr., Index Med., Bibliogr. Agric., Sel. Water Resour. Abstr., Biol. Agric. Index, Energy Res. Abstr., Sci. Cit. Index, Abr. Ed., Bibliogr. Index Geol., Ocean. Abstr. **LC** QL366. **DD** 593.105. **NLM** W1 JO853. **CODEN** JPROAR. bk rev. adv acc. **Circ** 2,000. (ctrl). Publishes original work-descriptive or experimental-in protozoology sinsu lato. Common medium for the cell biologist, taxonomist, physiologist, biochemist, ecologist, parasitologist, geneticist immunologist, morphogeneticist, and phylogeneticist working with protozoan material.

THE JOURNAL OF RESEARCH ON THE LEPIDOPTERA. V. 1- Aug. 1962-. 0022-4324. Periodical. US. English. ir. $25.00. Santa Barbara Museum of Natural History, 2559 Puesta del Sol Road, Santa Barbara CA 93105. **Tel** (805)964-8934. **Ed** R H T Mattoni. **Ind/Abst** Life Sci. Collect., Chem. Abstr., Biol. Abstr., Bibliogr. Agric. **CODEN** JRLPAE. bk rev. **Circ** 700. (ctrl). Purpose is to combine the work in the Lepidoptera field for the aid of students who study this group of insects in a way not presently available. Publishes primarily critical papers.

JOURNAL OF SHELLFISH RESEARCH. *See* Fish Culture and Fisheries.

JOURNAL OF THE AUSTRALIAN ENTOMOLOGICAL SOCIETY. V. 6- June 1967-. 0004-9050. Periodical. AT. English. qt. $39.10. Australian Entomology Branch, Department of Prim Ind, Meiers Road, Indooroopilly Queensland 4068 Australia. **Ed** N W Heather. **Ind/Abst** Life Sci. Collect., Pestdoc, Ringdoc, Vetdoc, Biol. Abstr., Chem. Abstr., Bibliogr. Agric. **LC** QL487. **DD** 595.7005. **CODEN** AESJBC. bk rev. **Circ** 900. (ctrl). General entomology especially in an Australian setting or to the fauna of the Australian region. *Journal of the Entomological Society of Queensland.*

JOURNAL OF THE ENTOMOLOGICAL SOCIETY OF BRITISH COLUMBIA. **Main/Corp** Entomological Society of British Columbia. V. 63- Dec. 1, 1966-. 0071-0733. Periodical. CN. English. an. $9.28. Entomological Society of British Columbia, 506 Burnside Road, Victoria British Columbia V8Z 1M5 Canada. **Ed** H R MacCarthy. **Ind/Abst** Life Sci. Collect., Bibliogr. Agric., Biol. Abstr., Chem. Abstr. **DD** 595.709711. **CODEN** JEBCA4. **Circ** 400. Available on microfiche from University Microfilms International. Papers on entomological research. *Proceedings, 0316-9049.*

JOURNAL OF THE ENTOMOLOGICAL SOCIETY OF SOUTHERN AFRICA. **Main/Corp** Entomological Society of Southern Africa. V. 1- Mar. 30, 1939-. 0013-8789. Periodical. SA. English. sa. 50.00. Entomological Society of South Africa, PO Box 103, Pretoria South Africa. **Ed** R M Crewe. **Ind/Abst** Life Sci. Collect., Energy Inf. Abstr., Environ. Abstr., Biol. Abstr., Sci. Cit. Index, Abr. Ed. **LC** QL461. **NLM** W1 JO92P. **CODEN** JESAAF. bk rev. **Circ** 600. (ctrl).

JOURNAL OF THE GEORGIA ENTOMOLOGICAL SOCIETY *CEASED.* **Main/Corp** Georgia Entomological Society. V. 1-19. 0016-8238. Periodical. US. English. qt. $10.00. Forestry Sciences Laboratory, USFS, Carlton Street, Athens GA 30602. **Ind/Abst** Life Sci. Collect., Energy Inf. Abstr., Environ. Abstr., Biol. Abstr., Nuci. Sci. Abstr., Chem. Abstr. **LC** SB818. **DD** 632.705. **CODEN** GENSAB.

JOURNAL OF THE HERPETOLOGICAL ASSOCIATION OF AFRICA. **Main/Corp** Herpetological Association of Africa. **VFOAT** H.A.A. No. 1- 1965-. 0441-6651. Periodical. SA. English. ir.

Zoology-Vertebrate and Invertebrate

$10.00 Foreign 15.00 Domestic. H A A, c/o National Museum, PO Box 266, 9300 Bloemfontein Republic of South Africa. **Tel** RAS 051 79609. **Ed** W Branch. **Ind/Abst** Biol. Abstr. **CODEN** HAAJA4. bk rev. **Circ** 250. All aspects of herpetology, primarily African herpetology, but also overseas. Regular listing of new literature on African herpetology. *Journal of the Herpetological Association of Rhodesia.*

JOURNAL OF THE KANSAS ENTOMOLOGICAL SOCIETY. **Main/Corp** Kansas Entomological Society. V. 1- Jan. 1928-. 0022-8567. Periodical. US. English. qt. $50.00. Journal of the Kansas, PO Box 368, Lawrence KS 66044. **Tel** (913)843-1234. **Ed** Leonard C Ferrington Jr. **Ind/Abst** Life Sci. Collect., Bibliogr. Agric., Biol. Abstr., Chem. Abstr., Sci. Cit. Index, Abr. Ed. **LC** QL461. **CODEN** JKESA7. **Circ** 800. (ctrl). The journal of the Kansas Entomological Society is a publication of the central states (Kansas) Entomological Society and publishes research on all aspects of the science of entomology.

JOURNAL OF THE LEPIDOPTERISTS' SOCIETY. *See* Biology.

JOURNAL OF THE MALACOLOGICAL SOCIETY OF AUSTRALIA. **Main/Corp** Malacological Society of Australia. V. 1- 1957-. 0085-2988. AT. English. ir. 25.00. c/o Dr R C Willar, Department of Zoology/University of Queensland, St Lucia Queensland 4067 Australia. **Tel** (07)377-2510. **Ed** F E Wells. **Ind/Abst** Life Sci. Collect., Biol. Abstr., GeoRef. **LC** QL401. **DD** 594.0994. **CODEN** JMLAA2. (cum index). bk rev. **Circ** 1,000. Scientific papers on malacology: molluscan taxonomy, biology, ecology, and biogeography.

THE JOURNAL OF THE MAMMALOGICAL SOCIETY OF JAPAN. **Main/Corp** Nihon Honyu Dobutsu Gakkai. **VFOAT** Honyu Dobutsu Zasshi. V. 1- Apr. 1952-. 0546-0670. Periodical. JA. Japanese (English). ir. $37.50. Japan Publishers Trading Company Ltd, PO Box 5030, Tokyo International, 100-31 Tokyo Japan.

JOURNAL OF THE ZOOLOGICAL SOCIETY OF INDIA. **Main/Corp** Zoological Society of India. V. 1- Jan. 1949-. 0049-8769. Periodical. II. English. sa. $20.00. Zoological Society of India, Utkal University, Bhubaneswan 4 Orissa India. **Ind/Abst** Life Sci. Collect., GeoRef, Biol. Abstr. **LC** QL1. **DD** 590.6254. **CODEN** JZSIAG.

JOURNAL OF ZOOLOGY. (THE JOURNAL OF ZOOLOGY). V. 146- Sept. 1965-. 0022-5460. Periodical. UK. English. mo. $410.00. Oxford University Press, Journals Department, Walton Street, Oxford 0X2 6DP England. **Tel** 0865-56767. **Ed** Marcia A Edwards. **Ind/Abst** Life Sci. Collect., Excerpta Med., Energy Inf. Abstr., Environ. Abstr., GeoRef, Bibliogr. Agric., Biol. Abstr., Chem. Abstr., Nuci. Sci. Abstr., Sel. Water Resour. Abstr., Biol. Agric. Index, Sci. Cit. Index, Abr. Ed., Ocean. Abstr., Bibliogr. Index Geol. **NLM** W1 JO974Z. **CODEN** JZOOAE. adv acc. This journal, being the proceedings of the Zoological Society of London, contains original papers within the general field of experimental and descriptive zoology. *Proceedings of the Zoological Society of London.*

K.C. ZOO BOOMERANG. **VFOAT** Zoo Boomerang. **VAT** Kansas City Zoo Boomerang. 0276-5195. Periodical. US. English. Kansas City Zoo, Swope Park, Kansas City MO 64132.

THE KENTUCKY WARBLER. V. 1- 1925-. 0160-5070. Periodical. US. English. qt. $5.00. Kentucky Ornithological Society, c/o Dr Blaine Ferrell, Department of Biology, Western Kentucky University, Bowling Green KY 42101. **Tel** (502)425-1635. **Ed** Blaine Ferrell. **Ind/Abst** Ref. Source. **CODEN** KEWAA. bk rev. **Circ** 500. (ctrl). Subjects deal primarily with studies on birds of Kentucky, Christmas counts, annual eagle censuses reports of spring, and fall meetings, review of ornithology books.

KIKAN ANIMA. **VFOAT** Anima Quarterly. 1- Summer 1975. Periodical. JA. Japanese. ir. 1700. Heibon Sha, 4 Yonbancho, Chiyoda-ku (102) Tokyo Japan. **LC** QL1.

THE KINGBIRD. V. 1- Nov./Dec. 1950-. 0023-1606. Periodical. US. English. qt. $18.00. Federation of New York State Bird Association, c/o C N Wilkins, 4000 West Road, Cortland NY 13045. **Tel** (607)753-3131. **Ed** Paul de Benedictis. **Ind/Abst** Biol. Abstr. **LC** QL671. **DD** 598.205. **CODEN** KNGBAW. bk rev. **Circ** 1,000. Organized to further the study of bird life and to disseminate knowledge thereof to educate the public in the need of conserving natural resources and to encourage the establishment and maintenance of sanctuaries.

KISTENYESZTOK LAPJA. V. 20, No. 8- (Aug. 1976)-. 0133-4565. Periodical. HU. Hungarian. mo. **Ind/Abst** Bibliogr. Agric.

KLUCZE DO OZNZCZANIA KREGOWCOW POLSKI. Vol. 1 1962-. 0075-6342. Monographic Series. PL. Polish (preface and explanations in English and Russian). ir.

KOEDOE. *See* Conservation & Natural Resources.

KOLEOPTEROLOGISCHE RUNDSCHAU. AU. German. an. $9.85. Zoologisch Botanische, Brugring 7, 1010 Vienna Austria. *Coleopterologische Rundschau.*

KOMBA. Periodical. English. ir. Wildlife Clubs of Kenya Association, PO Box 40658, Nairobi Kenya. **Tel** 742564. **Ed** Nathaniel Arap-Chumo. **LC** QL84.6.K4. **DD** 333.95416096762. bk rev. adv acc. **Circ** 6,000. (ctrl). A magazine for wildlife club members.

KONCHU. **VFOAT** Kontyu. Began in 1926. 0013-8770. Periodical. Japanese (summaries in English). qt. $56.00. Japan Publishers Trading Company Inc, PO Box 5030, Tokyo International, Tokyo 100-31 Japan. **Ind/Abst** Bibliogr. Agric.

KOOLEWONG. V. 1- Mar. 1972-. 0310-9682. AT. English. ir. 8.00. Honorary Secretary/Taronga Zoo, PO Box 20, Mosman 2088 New South Wales. **Ind/Abst** Life Sci. Collect. **LC** QL1. **DD** 591.05. *Proceedings of the Royal Zoological Society of New South Wales.*

KOREAN ARACHNOLOGY. **VFOAT** Korean Arachnol. Periodical. Korean (English). ir. Arachnology Institute of Korea, 42 Dosun Dong/ Songdong GU, Seoul 133 Korea. **Ind/Abst** Biol. Abstr. **LC** PAR. **CODEN** KOARER.

KOREAN JOURNAL OF PARASITOLOGY. (KISAENGCHUNGHAK CHAPCHI). Began in 1963. 0023-4001. Periodical. KO. Korean (English). sa. $15.00. Department of Parasitology, 28 Yeon-Keon Dong Chong-Ro Ku, Seoul Korea. **Tel** 7601-3317. **Ed** Seung-Yull Cho. **Ind/Abst** Excerpta Med., Biol. Abstr., Chem. Abstr. **LC** QL757. **NLM** W1 KI839. **CODEN** KSCHAV. **Circ** 700. (ctrl). Includes original and/or reviews articles on current research of parasites and diseases of animals and man.

KUN CHUNG CHIH SHIH. **VFOAT** Kunchong Zhishi. 0452-8255. Periodical. CH. Chinese. bm. Chung-kuo Kuo Chi-shu Tien, PO PO Box 2820, Peking China. **Ind/Abst** Chem. Abstr. **LC** QL461. **DD** 595.7005. **CODEN** KCCSAK.

KUN CHUNG FEN LEI HSUEH PAO. **VFOAT** Entomotaxonomia. V. 1, First published in (Oct. 1979)-. Periodical. CC. Chinese (abstracts in English). ir. 1.50. Entomotaxonomia, c/o NW College of Agriculture, Wukung Shensi China. **Ind/Abst** Biol. Abstr. **LC** QL468. **DD** 595.70012. **CODEN** KFXUDJ.

KUN CHUNG HSUEH PAO. **VFOAT** Acta Entomologica Sinica. Began in 1950. 0454-6296. Periodical. CC. Chinese (text in Chinese with summaries in English). qt. $17.28. China Publication Centre, PO Box 2820, Beijing China. **Ind/Abst** GeoRef, Biol. Abstr., Chem. Abstr., Bibliogr. Agric., Sci. Cit. Index, Abr. Ed. **LC** QL461. **DD** 595.7005. **NLM** W1 KU701J. **CODEN** KCHPA2.

KUN CHUNG HSUEH YEN CHIU CHI KAN. V. 1, (1980)-. Chinese (summaries in English). ir. 1.95. Hsin Hua Shu Tien, Shang-hai Fa Hsing So Shanghai China. **LC** QL461. **DD** 595.7.

LACERTA. Began in 1943. 0023-7051. Periodical. Dutch (English summaries). ir. **Tel** 31-34973043. **Ind/Abst** Biol. Abstr. bk rev. adv acc. **Circ** 2,000. (ctrl). Publication for the Dutch Society for Herpetology. Articles on amphibians and reptiles (ecology, ethology, reproduction).

LEPIDOPTERA. V. 1- June 1967-. 0075-8787. Periodical. DK. Danish. sa. 150. Lepidopterologisk Forening, Sandtoften 37, 2800 Lyngby Denmark. **Ind/Abst** Biol. Abstr., Bibliogr. Agric. **CODEN** LEPDAV. About Danish butterflies.

LIFE SCIENCES CONTRIBUTIONS. ROYAL ONTARIO MUSEUM. *See* Museums.

LIFE SCIENCES MISCELLANEOUS PUBLICATION. 0082-5093. Monographic Series. CN. English. ir. Royal Ontario Museum, Publishing Services, 100 Queens Park, Toronto Ontario M5S 2C6 Canada. **Tel** (416)978-3641. **Ind/Abst** GeoRef, Bibliogr. Index Geol. **DD** 591.05. **CODEN** ROLMB5.

LIFE SCIENCES OCCASIONAL PAPER. No. 29 (June 15, 1977)-. 0082-5107. Monographic Series. CN. English. ir. Royal Ontario Museum, 100 Queen's Park, Toronto Ontario M5S 2C6 Canada. **LC** QL1. **DD** 574.05. *Life Sciences Occasional Papers, 0082-5107.*

LIMOSA. Vol. 1- Oct. 1928-. 0024-3620. Periodical. NE. Dutch (summaries in English). qt. $24.03. Nederlandse Ornithologische, Sportlaan 13, 2225 JN Katwijk The Netherlands. **Tel** 01718-132996. **Ind/Abst** Biol. Abstr. **CODEN** LIMOA9. (cum index). *Jaarbericht - Club Van Nederlandsche Vogelkundigen.*

LINTUMIES. Began in 1965. 0357-3524. Periodical. FI. Finnish (summaries in English). qt. 35. Lintumies-Lehit/Heikki Lokki, Huovitie 10 A 9, SF-00400 Helsinki 40 Finland. **LC** QL690.F6. **DD** 598.294897.

LISTE DES MEMBRES DU CLUB DES ORNITHOLOGUES DE QUEBEC. (LISTE DES MEMBRES DU CLUB DES ORNITHOLOGUES DE SIC QUEBEC). **Main/Corp** Club des Ornithologues du Quebec. 0228-2151. CN. French. an. Free to Members. Club des Ornithologues du Quebec, 8191 av du Zoo, Orsainville Quebec G1G 4G4 Canada. **DD** 598.025714.

LISTE DES TRAVAUX ARACHNOLOGIQUES PARUS EN . . . OU ACTUELLEMENT SOUS PRESSE. French. ir. 61 rue de Buffon, Paris France 75005. **LC** Z7996.A6, QL451. **DD** 016.5954. *Liste des Travaux Arachnologiques Mondiaux.*

LITTLEFOOT CLUB NEWSLETTER. Vol. 1, No. 1 (June 1979)-. 0229-723X. Periodical. CN. English. mo. Free to Members, Membership $5.00. Littlefoot Club Newsletter, Metro Toronto Zoo, PO Box 280, West Hill Ontario M1E 4R5 Canada. **DD** 590.74471354106.

THE LIVING BIRD *CEASED.* 1st-19th. 0459-6137. US. English. an. **Ind/Abst** Biol. Abstr. **LC** QL671. **CODEN** LIBIA4.

THE LIVING BIRD QUARTERLY. Vol. 1, No. 1 (Summer 1982)-. 0732-9210. Periodical. US. English. qt. Free to Members of the Laboratory. Laboratory of Ornithology at Cornell University, 159 Sapsucker Woods Road, Ithaca NY 14850. **LC** QL671. **DD** 598.05. *Living Bird.*

THE LOON. 1929. 0024-645X. Periodical. US. English. qt. Minnesota Ornithologists Union, Bell Museum of Natural History, University of Minnesota, 10 Church Street SE, Minneapolis MN 55455. **Ind/Abst** Biol. Abstr. **CODEN** LOONAO. bk rev. adv acc. **Circ** 1,000. *Flicker, 0199-9672.*

LOZANIA. **VFOAT** Acta Zoologica Colombiana. No. 1-. 0085-2899. Monographic Series. CK. Spanish (summaries in English). ty. University Nacional de Colombia, Facutad Ciencia/Aereo 14490, Bogota Colombia. **Ind/Abst** Biol. Abstr. **LC** QL244. **CODEN** LZNAAN.

LUTRA. No. 19-20, 1958/59-59. 0024-7634. Periodical. NE. Dutch (summaries in French, English, or German). ir. EJ Brill, POB 9000, 2300 PA Leiden The Netherlands. **Ind/Abst** Biol. Abstr., GeoRef, Bibliogr. Index Geol. **CODEN** LUTAAI.

LYMAN ENTOMOLOGICAL MUSEUM AND RESEARCH LABORATORY MEMOIR. *See* Museums.

MAINE BIRDLIFE. **VFOAT** Birdlife. 8756-9620. Periodical. US. English. qt. $10.00 Domestic, $12.50 Foreign. Maine Birdlife, PO Box 18, Winthrop ME 04364. **DD** 508. Articles and columns on the natural history of the Northeast for professionals and serious amateurs. Also ornithological field notes.

MAINE QUARTERLY AUDUBON. 0192-6799. Periodical. US. English. qt. MAS, Gilsland Farm Old Route 1, Falmouth ME 04105. **LC** QL684.M2. **DD** 598.29741.

MALACOLOGIA. V. 1-. 0076-2997. US. English (articles in French, German, Russian, or Spanish, with summaries in the other languages). ir. $27.00. Academy of Natural Science of Philadelphia, Nineteenth and the Parkway, Philadelphia PA 19103. **Tel** (215)299-1130. **Ed** G M Davis and R Robertson. **Ind/Abst** Life Sci. Collect., GeoRef, Energy Res. Abstr., Biol. Abstr., Nuci. Sci. Abstr., Sel. Water Resour. Abstr., Index Med., Chem. Abstr., Sci. Cit. Index, Abr. Ed., Bibliogr. Index Geol. **LC** QL401. **DD**

Zoology-Vertebrate and Invertebrate

594.005. NLM W1 MA495. **CODEN** MALAAJ. **Circ** 700. An international journal of Malacology. It publishes original research on the Mollusca that is of high quality and of broad international interest.

MALACOLOGICAL REVIEW. 1- 1968-. 0076-3004. US. English. ir. Malacological Review, PO Box 637, Niwot CO 80544. **Tel** (303)492-7359. **Ed** J B Burch. **Ind/Abst** Life Sci. Collect., GeoRef, Biol. Abstr., Sel. Water Resour. Abstr. **LC** QL401. **DD** 594.605. NLM W1 MA496. **CODEN** MLGRBL. bk rev. **Circ** 500. (ctrl). Original or review articles on various aspects of Malacology, information on current publications.

MALAKOLOGISCHE ABHANDLUNGEN. V. 1- 1964-. 0070-7260. German (some articles in English or French). ir. Deutscher Buch Export-Import, Leninstrasse 16, DDR-701 Leipzig East Germany. **Tel** 4952503. **Ind/Abst** Biol. Abstr. **LC** QL401. **CODEN** SMTMB8. bk rev. **Circ** 250. (ctrl). Taxonomy, systematics, morphology, biology, ecology, zoogeography, faunistics of the invertebrate group mollusca in global range. Abhandlungen und Berichte aus dem Staatlichen Museum fur Tierkunde in Dresden.

MAMMAL REVIEW. V. 1- Feb. 1970-. 0305-1838. Periodical. UK. English. qt. $70.00. Blackwell Scientific Publishers Ltd, PO Box 88, Oxford 0X2 0EL England. **Tel** (0865)24021. **Ed** D W Yalden and G R Hosey. **Ind/Abst** Life Sci. Collect., Art Archaeol. Tech. Abstr., Biol. Abstr. **LC** QL700. **DD** 599.005. NLM W1 MA534. **CODEN** MMLRAI. bk rev. adv acc. **Circ** 1,500. Reviews and reports on any aspect of mammalogy (not the results of original research), reports on status and distribution of mammalian species.

MAMMALIA, MORPHOLOGIE, BIOLOGIE, SYSTEMATIQUE DES MAMMIFERES. V. 1, No. 1- September 1936-. Periodical. FR. French. qt. $73.17. Museum National d'Historie Naturelle, 55 rue Buffon, 75005 Paris France. **Tel** 337 89 56. **Ed** Jean Dorst. bk rev. **Circ** 550. Morphology, biology (ecology, behavior physiology) systematics, biogeography of mammals.

MAMMALIAN PROTEIN METABOLISM. US. English. ir. Academic Press, 4805 Sand Lake Road, Orlando FL 32887. **Tel** (305)345-4100. **Ed** H N Munro and J B Allison.

MAMMALIAN SPECIES. See Biology.

MARINE BEHAVIOUR AND PHYSIOLOGY. See Biology - Physiology.

MARINE INVERTEBRATES OF SCANDINAVIA. Series/Titl Scandinavian University Books. **VFOAT** M. I. O. S. No. 1- 1966-. 0542-6987. Monographic Series. NO. English. ir. Universitetsforlaget, PO Box 2959, Toyen Oslo 6 Norway. **Ind/Abst** Biol. Abstr. **LC** QL128. **DD** 574. **CODEN** MAISBP.

THE MARINE MAMMAL PROTECTION ACT OF 1972 ANNUAL REPORT. Began with 1977/78. 0196-4690. US. English. an. US Department of Commerce, Washington DC 20230. **LC** QL713.2. **DD** 333.95909162. Vols. for Apr. 1980-Mar. 1981- distributed to depository libraries in microfiche. Administration of the Marine Mammal Protection Act of 1972, 0148-186X.

MARINE MAMMAL SCIENCE. Vol. 1, No. 1 (Jan. 1985)-. 0824-0469. Periodical. US. English. qt. $60.00 Membership $45.00 Nonmembers Domestic, $50.00 Nonmembers, Foreign. Society for Marine Mammology, 1041 New Hampshire Street, Lawrence KS 66044. **Tel** (913)843-1234. bk rev. Publishes the results of original research and observations on marine mammals, their evolution, form, function, husbandry, health, populations, and ecological relationships.

MARYLAND ENTOMOLOGIST. V. 1- Feb. 1977-. 0275-8652. Periodical. US. English. ir. Maryland Entomological Society, 1215 Stella Drive, Baltimore MD 21207. **Tel** (301)944-4630.

MATSYA. No. 1- 1975-. 0253-9314. Periodical. II. English. an. $30.00. Indian Society of Ichthyologists, 100 Santhome High Road, Madras 60028 India. **Ind/Abst** Chem. Abstr. **CODEN** MTSYDO.

MAURI ORA. V. 1- 1973-. 0302-086X. English. an. 6. University of Cantebury/Editor, Department of Zoology, Private Bag, Christchurch New Zealand. **Tel** 482-009. **Ed** Craig E Franklin and William Davison. **Ind/Abst** Life Sci. Collect., Excerpta Med., Biol. Abstr., Zool. Rec., Bibliogr. Agric. **LC** QH320.N45. **DD** 574.9931. **CODEN** MAUOA4. bk rev. **Circ** 350. (ctrl). A wide variety of papers are published encompassing such areas as physiology, ecology, taxonomy marine biology, entomology and paleoecology, volume 12 special edition: EPFS Marine Laboratory Research.

MEDITERRANEA. No. 1- Sept. 1976-. Periodical. Spanish (summaries in English). ir. 200 Each issue. Departamento de Biologia, Facultad de Ciencias de Alicante, Universidad de Valencia, Apartado 99, Alicante Spain. **Tel** (965)66511. **LC** QL254. Mediterranean terrestrial ecology.

MEGADRILOGICA. See Biology.

MELSHEIMER ENTOMOLOGICAL SERIES. No. 1- Sept. 1967-. 0076-6321. US. English. sa. Entomological Society of Pennsylvania, 107 Patterson Building, University Park PA 16802. **Tel** (814)865-1895. **Ind/Abst** Biol. Abstr., Bibliogr. Agric. **CODEN** MLESBE.

MEMOIRES DE BIOSPEOLOGIE. See Biology.

MEMOIRES DE LA SOCIETE ENTOMOLOGIQUE DU QUEBEC. Main/Corp Societe Entomologique du Quebec. **VFOAT** Memoirs of the Entomological Society of Quebec. 0071-0784. Periodical. CN. French (summaries in English). ir. Societe Entomologique du Quebec, c/o M Michele Letendre, Complex Scientifique D-1-59, 2700 rue Einstein, Ste-Foy Quebec G1A 1E6 Canada. **Ind/Abst** Biol. Abstr. **LC** QL461. **DD** 595.7. **CODEN** SEQMA4. Memoires de la Societe Entomologique du Quebec, 0071-0784.

MEMOIRS OF THE AMERICAN ENTOMOLOGICAL INSTITUTE. Main/Corp American Entomological Institute. No. 1-. 0065-8162. Monographic Series. US. English. ir. American Entomological Association, 3005 56th Avenue, Gainesville FL 32608. **Tel** (904)377-6458. **Ed** H Townes. **Ind/Abst** Life Sci. Collect., Biol. Abstr. **LC** UNC. **CODEN** MAEIA8. **Circ** 180. Taxonomy of insects.

MEMOIRS OF THE AMERICAN ENTOMOLOGICAL SOCIETY. Main/Corp American Entomological Society. No. 1- 1916-. 0065-8170. US. English. ir. American Entomological Society, Academy of Natural Sciences, Philadelphia PA 19103. **Tel** (215)561-3978. **Ed** Selwyn S Roback. **Ind/Abst** Life Sci. Collect., Biol. Abstr. **LC** QL461. **DD** 595.7082. **CODEN** AESMAK. **Circ** 400. Classification, taxonomy, systematics, and ecology of insects.

MEMOIRS OF THE ENTOMOLOGICAL SOCIETY OF CANADA. (MEMOIRES DE LA SOCIETE ENTOMOLOGIQUE DU CANADA). No 43 (1965)-. 0071-075X. Monographic Series. CN. French. ir. Societe Entomologique du Canada, 1322 Carling Avenue, Ottawa Ontario K1Z 7K9 Canada. **DD** 595.7005.

MEMOIRS OF THE PACIFIC COAST ENTOMOLOGICAL SOCIETY. Main/Corp Pacific Coast Entomological Society. 0475-3208. Monographic Series. US. English. qt. California Academy of Science, Golden Gate Park, San Francisco CA 94118. **Tel** (415)221-5100. **Ed** J A Chemsak. **Ind/Abst** Biol. Abstr. **CODEN** PCEMBY. (ctrl). Monographic works on entomology.

MEMOIRS OF THE ZOOLOGICAL SURVEY OF INDIA. Main/Corp Zoological Survey of India. V. 15- Dec. 1970-. Monographic Series. English. ir. Indian Books & Periodicals Syndicate, B-5/62 Dev Nagar P L Road Karol Bagh, New Delhi 110005 India. **Tel** 565444. **Ind/Abst** Life Sci. Collect. bk rev. Memoirs of The Indian Museum.

MEMORABILIA ZOOLOGICA. V. 1- 1958-. 0076-6372. Monograph. PL. Polish. ir. Zaklad Narodowy Im Ossolinskch, Ul Szewska 37, Wroclaw Poland. **Ind/Abst** Biol. Abstr., Bibliogr. Agric. **CODEN** MEZOAN.

MEMORIE DELLA SOCIETA ENTOMOLOGICA ITALIANA. Main/Corp Societa Entomologica Italiana. V. 1- 1922-. 0037-8747. Italian. an. **Tel** 010-564567. **Ind/Abst** Life Sci. Collect., Bibliogr. Agric. **LC** WMLC L 83/1131. (cum index). bk rev. adv acc. **Circ** 1,500. (ctrl). Works only on entomology.

M.H.S. REVIEW. (MHS REVIEW). Main/Corp Massachusetts Herpetological Society. **VAT** Massachusetts Herpetological Society Review. 0093-9560. Periodical. US. English. sa. Massachusetts Herpetological Society, PO Box 263, Byfield MA 01922. **LC** QL640. **DD** 598.105.

THE MIGRANT. Began with June 1930 Issue. 0026-3575. Periodical. US. English. qt. $6.00. Tennessee Ornithological Society, PO Box 17317, Memphis TN 38187-0317. **Tel** (901)767-3933. **Ed** Charles P Nicholson. **Ind/Abst** GeoRef, Biol. Abstr., Bibliogr. Index Geol. **CODEN** MGNTAQ. bk rev. **Circ** 1,000. Records and encourages the study of ornithology in Tennessee with focus on field observations and records of birdlife in the state.

MIKROFAUNA DES MEERESBODENS. 1- 1970-. 0342-3247. Monographic Series. GW. German (French or English with English or Spanish summaries). ir. Franz Steiner Verlag GMBH, Postfach 347, D7000 Stuttgart 1 West Germany. **Ind/Abst** Life Sci. Collect., Biol. Abstr., Sel. Water Resour. Abstr. **CODEN** AWMMAE.

MISCELLANEOUS PUBLICATIONS - MUSEUM OF ZOOLOGY, UNIVERSITY OF MICHIGAN. (MISCELLANEOUS PUBLICATIONS). No. 1-. 0076-8405. Monographic Series. US. English. ir. University of Michigan, Museum of Zoology, Ann Arbor MI 48109. **Tel** (313)764-0476. **Ind/Abst** Life Sci. Collect., Biol. Abstr. **LC** UNC. **CODEN** MUZPA2.

MISCELLANEOUS PUBLICATIONS OF THE ENTOMOLOGICAL SOCIETY OF AMERICA. Vol. 1, No. 1 (Oct. 1959)-. 0071-0717. Periodical. US. English. ir. $17.50. Entomological Society of America, 4603 Calvert Road, College Park MD 20740. **Tel** (301)864-1334. **Ed** Morris Rockstein. **Ind/Abst** Bibliogr. Agric., Biol. Abstr., Chem. Abstr. **LC** QL461. NLM W1 MI791G. **CODEN** MPEAAL. **Circ** 200. (ctrl). Topics are discrete, entomological.

MISCELLANEOUS PUBLICATIONS OF THE ENTOMOLOGICAL SOCIETY OF AMERICA. Main/Corp Entomological Society of America. V. 1- 1959-. Periodical. US. English. ir. $7.50. Entomological Society of America, 4603 Calvert Road, College Park MD 20740. **Tel** (301)864-1334. **Ed** Morris Rockstein. **Circ** 150. (ctrl). Monograph on insects or related organisms.

MISCELLANIA ZOOLOGICA. Vol. 5 (1979)-. 0211-6529. Periodical. SP. Catalan (English, Italian, and Spanish). ir. Museu de Zoologia, Biblioteca, Ap de Correus 593, Barcelona 3 Spain. **Ind/Abst** Life Sci. Collect., Biol. Abstr. **CODEN** MZOODG. Miscelanea Zoologica (Museo de Zoologia (Barcelona, Spain)).

MITTEILUNGEN AUS DEM HAMBURGISCHEN ZOOLOGISCHEN MUSEUM UND INSTITUT. See Museums.

MITTEILUNGEN DER MUNCHNER ENTOMOLOGISCHEN GESELLSCHAFT. Main/Corp Munchner Entomologische Gesellschaft. Began in 1910. 0340-4943. GW. German. au. R Friediander & Sohn, Dessauer Strasse 28 29, 1000 Berlin 61 West Germany. **Ind/Abst** Life Sci. Collect., Bibliogr. Agric. **LC** QL461. **DD** 595.706243. Entomologisches Nachrichtenblatt.

MITTEILUNGEN DER SCHWEIZERISCHEN ENTOMOLOGISCHEN GESELLSCHAFT. Main/Corp Schweizerische Entomologische Gesellschaft. **VFOAT** Bulletin de la Societe Entomologique Suisse. Began publication with Feb. 1862 issue. 0036-7575. Periodical. SZ. German (French). qt. $44.53. Schweizerische Entomologische Gesellschaft, Eth-Zentrum, CH-8092 Zurich Switzerland. **Tel** 01/256 39 19. **Ed** Georg Benz. **Ind/Abst** Life Sci. Collect., Biol. Abstr., Bibliogr. Agric. NLM W1 SC46. **CODEN** MSEGAQ. Covers systematic and applied entomology.

MONITORE ZOOLOGICO ITALIANO. MONOGRAFIA. **VFOAT** Italian Journal of Zoology. Monograph. V. 1- 1975-. 0026-9786. IT. Italian. ir. 65.000 Vol.1, 102.000 Vol.2. Monitore Zoologico Italiano, Via Romana 17, 50125 Firenze Italy. **Tel** (055)222448-229289-220507. **Circ** 500. The series regards monographic subjects on zoology and/or biology.

MONOGRAPHS - ACADEMY OF NATURAL SCIENCES OF PHILADELPHIA. See Biology.

MONOGRAPHS IN PRIMATOLOGY. Vol. 1-. 0740-9729. Monographic Series. US. English. ir. Alan R Liss, 41 East 11th Street, New York NY 10003. **Tel** (212)475-7700. **Ed** Clarkson, J Erwin, Edward Goldsmith, G Mitchell, Moor-Jankkowski, Leonard Rosenblum, Charles Southwick, and Robert A Whitney. **Ind/Abst** Biol. Abstr. **LC** UNC. **DD** 599.8. NLM W1 MO568N. **CODEN** MONPD5. A scholarly book series covering areas of primatology-human and non-human.

MONOGRAPHS OF MARINE MOLLUSCA. No. 1- Dec. 15, 1978-. 0162-8321. Monographic Series. US. English. ir. American Malacologists Inc, PO Box 2255, Melbourne FL 32901. **Tel** (305)725-2260. **Ed** R T Abbott. **Ind/Abst** GeoRef. **Circ** 1,200. (ctrl). Definitive illustrated monographs of marine mollusks of the world and fossil shells.

MONOGRAPHS OF THE WESTERN FOUNDATION OF VERTEBRATE ZOOLOGY. **Main/Corp** Western Foundation of Vertebrate Zoology. No. 1-. 2097-0387. Monographic Series. US. English. ir. Western Foundation for Vertebrate Zoology, 1100 Glendon Avenue, Los Angeles CA 90024. **Tel** (213)208-8003. **Ed** Jack C Von Bloeker Jr. **LC** UNC. **DD** 596. **Circ** 1,000. Papers of intermediate length reporting original research in vertebrate zoology with emphasis on ornithology.

MONOGRAPHS. STUDIES IN ENTOMOLOGY. **Main/Corp** Oregon State University. **VFOAT** Studies in Entomology. No. 1- 1939-. 0078-5806. Monographic Series. US. English. ir. Oregon State University Press, 101 Waldo Hall, Corvallis OR 97331.

MOS NEWSLETTER. **Main/Corp** Mississippi Ornithological Society. Periodical. US. English.

MURRELET. (THE MURRELET). V. 1- May 1920-. 0027-3716. Periodical. US. English. ty. $15.00. Pacific Northwest Bird & Mammal Society, University of Puget Sound Museum of Natural History, Tacoma WA 98416. **Tel** (206)756-3189. **Ed** Eric Yensen. **Ind/Abst** ASTIS Bibliogr., ASTIS Curr. Aware. Bull., Biol. Abstr. **LC** QL1. **CODEN** MRLTAP. **Circ** 650. (ctrl). Scientific articles of birds and mammals of the Pacific Northwest.

MYOTIS. 0580-3896. German (English and French). an.

MZG NEWSLETTER. **VAT** Minnesota Zoological Garden Newsletter. Vol. 2, No. 5 (May 1970- Vol. 6, No. 3-4 (Mar.-Apr. 1976). Periodical. US. English. bm. Minnesota Zoological Garden, 12101 Johnny Cake and Ridge Road, Apple Valley MN 55124. **Tel** (612)432-9000. *Newsletter (Minnesota State Zoological Board).*

NATURA JUTLANDICA. 1.- Bind. 0077-6033. Periodical. Danish (English). ir. 100. Natural History Museum, Universitetsparken Building 210, 8000 Aarhus C Denmark. **Tel** 06-129777. **Ed** Birger Jensen. **Ind/Abst** Life Sci. Collect., Biol. Abstr., GeoRef. **LC** QH7. **DD** 574.05. **CODEN** NAJUAC. **Circ** 700. Scientific publication in zoology (systematics, biology, ecology).

NATUREZA EM REVISTA. No. 1- Dec. 1976-. Periodical. Portuguese. ir. 40.00. Fundacao Zoobotanica do Rio Grande do Sul, C P 1188, 90.000 Porto Alegre Brazil. **LC** QL242.

THE NAUTILUS. V. 3- 1889-. 0028-1344. Periodical. US. English. qt. $20.00. American Malacologists Inc, PO Box 2255, Melbourne FL 32901. **Tel** (305)725-2260. **Ed** R Tucker Abbott. **Ind/Abst** Life Sci. Collect., Biol. Abstr., GeoRef, Sel. Water Resour. Abstr., Sci. Cit. Index, Abr. Ed., Ocean. Abstr. **LC** QL401. **CODEN** NUTLA5. (cum index). bk rev. adv acc. **Circ** 800. (ctrl). Original scientific contributions on mollusks and shells. *Conchologists' Exchange.*

THE NEBRASKA BIRD REVIEW. V. 1- 1933-. 0028-1816. Periodical. US. English. qt. $10.00. Nebraska Ornithologist Union, c/o Lona Shafer-Treasurer, Route 2 Box 61, Wood River NE 68883. **Tel** (402)556-7489. **Ed** R G Cortelyou. **Ind/Abst** Ref. Source, Biol. Abstr. **CODEN** NBBRA4. bk rev. **Circ** 375. A magazine of ornithology of the Nebraska region.

NEOTROPICA. V. 1- (No. 1-). 0548-1686. Periodical. Spanish (English summaries for some articles). ir. **Ind/Abst** Life Sci. Collect., GeoRef. **LC** QL235. **DD** 591.98. **CODEN** NTRPAY.

NETHERLANDS JOURNAL OF ZOOLOGY. **VFOAT** Archives Neerlandaises de Zoologie. V. 18- May 1968-. 0028-2960. Periodical. English. qt. 125.-. E J Brill, PO Box 9000, 2300 PA Leiden The Netherlands. **Tel** (071)312624. **Ed** J J M van Alphen and C D N Barel. **Ind/Abst** Life Sci. Collect., GeoRef, Bibliogr. Agric., Biol. Abstr., Chem. Abstr., Nucl. Sci. Abstr., Sci. Cit. Index, Abr. Ed., Bibliogr. Index Geol. **CODEN** NEJZAL. bk rev. **Circ** 1,300. Covers the entire field of zoology and is open for publications of scientific papers on zoology in its widest sense. *Archives Neerlandaises de Zoologie.*

NEUE ENTOMOLOGISCHE NACHRICHTEN. 0722-3773. Periodical. GW. German (summaries in English). ir. 75.00. Verlag Erich Bauer, Seidlung 15, D-7538 Keltern West Germany. **Ind/Abst** Biol. Abstr. **CODEN** NENAD3.

NEW ENTOMOLOGIST. **VFOAT** NYU Entomorojisuto. Vol. 1, No. 1 (Apr. 1, 1951)-. 0028-4955. JA. Japanese (with titles of some articles in English). ir. $30.50. Japan Publishing Trading Company Ltd, PO Box 5030 Tokyo International, Tokyo 100-31 Japan. **Ind/Abst** Biol. Abstr., Bibliogr. Agric. **CODEN** NENTAN.

THE NEW ZEALAND BEEKEEPER. V. 1- 1939-. Periodical. NE. English. qt. $10.00. National Beekeepers of New Zealand, PO Box 4048, Wellington New Zealand. **Ed** M Burgess. bk rev. adv acc. **Circ** 1,400. General beekeeping; disorders in New Zealand honey bees, hive maintenance; reports from regions, and general matters pertaining to beekeepers.

NEW ZEALAND ENTOMOLOGIST. (THE NEW ZEALAND ENTOMOLOGIST). V. 1- Dec. 1951-. 0077-9962. Periodical. NZ. English. an. $11.82. Lincoln College, Department of Entomology, c/o R R Scott, Christchurch New Zealand. **Tel** (03)252-811. **Ed** T K Crosby. **Ind/Abst** Life Sci. Collect., Biol. Abstr., Chem. Abstr., Bibliogr. Agric., Sci. Cit. Index, Abr. Ed. **LC** QL487.5. **CODEN** NEZEA4. adv acc. **Circ** 1,000. (ctrl). Papers cover all aspects of New Zealand entomology from taxonomy to chemical control and occasionally include material on the southwest Pacific region.

NEW ZEALAND JOURNAL OF ZOOLOGY. V. 1- Feb. 1974-. 0301-4223. Periodical. NZ. English. qt. 50.00. Science Information Publishing Center, Box 9741, Wellington New Zealand. **Tel** 858 939. **Ed** Craig W Matthews. **Ind/Abst** Life Sci. Collect., Biol. Abstr., Chem. Abstr., Bibliogr. Agric., Sci. Cit. Index, Abr. Ed. **LC** QL340. **DD** 591.05. **NLM** W1 NE975. **CODEN** NZJZAW. bk rev. adv acc. **Circ** 800. Publishes papers on original research in all branches of zoology, pertinent to New Zealand and associated territories.

NEWS - AMERICAN REGISTRY OF PROFESSIONAL ENTOMOLOGISTS. (NEWS). **Main/Corp** American Registry of Professional Entomologists. **VFOAT** APRE News. 0882-8431. Periodical. US. English. qt. $5.00. American Registry of Professional Entomologists, Entomological Society of America, 4603 Calvert Road, PO Box AJ, College Park MD 20740. **Tel** (301)864-1336. **Ed** William H Wymer. **DD** 595. bk rev. **Circ** 1,800. (ctrl). Provides information on insects, insect management and persons studying or applying same. News of activities of registered professional entomologist.

NEWS FROM THE PHILADELPHIA ZOO. Periodical. US. English. 34th Street and Girard Avenue, Philadelphia PA 19104.

NEWSLETTER - LONG POINT BIRD OBSERVATORY. **Main/Corp** Long Point Bird Observatory. **VFOAT** L P B O Newsletter. Began with Spring 1969 issue. 0317-9575. CN. English. ir. $15.48. Long Point Bird Observatory, PO Box 160/Port Rowan, Ontario Canada N0E IM0. **Tel** (519)586-2909. **Ed** Martin K McNicholl. **DD** 598.107230971336. bk rev. **Circ** 800. Observatory activities and people, locally and provincially. Articles on birds and other nature, biographies of naturalists, profiles of related organizations.

NEWSLETTER - MINNESOTA ORNITHOLOGISTS' UNION. **Main/Corp** Minnesota Ornithologists' Union. V. 1-. Periodical. US. English. qt. MOU Newsletter, Bell Museum of Natural History, 10 Church Street, Minneapolis MN 55455.

NEWSLETTER - NOVA SCOTIA BIRD SOCIETY. **Main/Corp** Nova Scotia Bird Society. V. 1- Mar. 1959-. 0383-9567. Periodical. CN. English. ir. Nova Scotia Museum, 1747 Summer Street, Halifax Nova Scotia B3H 3A6 Canada.

NEWSLETTER - THE WILDLIFE CLUBS OF KENYA ASSOCIATION. **Main/Corp** Wildlife Clubs of Kenya Association. Periodical. English. ir. Wildlife Clubs of Kenya Association, PO Box 40658, Nairobi Kenya. **LC** QL337.K4. **DD** 591.9605.

NIGERIAN JOURNAL OF ENTOMOLOGY. V. 1- Dec. 1974-. 0331-0094. Periodical. English. ir. Entomological Society of Nigeria, University of Ibadan, Ibadan Oyo State Nigeria. **Ind/Abst** Chem. Abstr., Biol. Abstr., Bibliogr. Agric. **LC** QL461. **DD** 595.7005. **CODEN** NJENDW. *Bulletin of the Entomological Society of Nigeria, 0425-1067.*

NIHON DOBUTSUEN SUIZOKUKAN NENPO. Japanese. an. **LC** QL76.5.J3.

NIHON OYO DOBUTSU KONCHU GAKKAISHI. **VFOAT** Japanese Journal of Applied Entomology and Zoology. V. 1 No. 1 (Mar. 1957)-. 0021-4914. Periodical. JA. Japanese (summaries and table of contents in English). qt. 56.00. Maruzen Company Ltd, PO Box 5050, 100-31 Tokyo Japan. **Tel** 03-943-6021. **Ed** Toshiaki Ikeshoji. **Ind/Abst** Life Sci. Collect., Excerpta Med., Pestdoc, Ringdoc, Vetdoc, Biol. Abstr., Chem. Abstr., Curr. Contents, Bibliogr. Agric., Sci. Cit. Index, Abr. Ed. **CODEN** NIPTAR. adv acc. **Circ** 2,300. (ctrl). An organ paper of the Japanaese Society of Applied Entomology and Zoology. *Oyo Dobutsu Zasshi, Oyo Konchu.*

NIHON SENCHU KENKYUKAI SHI. **VFOAT** Japanese Journal of Nematology. V. 1- June 1972-. Periodical. JA. Japanese (summaries in English). an. National Institute of Agricultural Sciences, Nishigahara Kita-ku, Tokyo 114 Japan. **Ind/Abst** Bibliogr. Agric.

NIPPON CHIKUSAN GAKKAI-HO. (THE JAPANESE JOURNAL OF ZOOTECHNICAL SCIENCE). 0021-5309. Periodical. JA. Japanese (English). mo. 90.00. Maruzen Company Ltd, PO Box 5050, 100-31 Tokyo Japan. **Tel** 03-82808409. **Ind/Abst** Biol. Abstr., Chem. Abstr., Bibliogr. Agric. **CODEN** NICKA3. adv acc. **Circ** 2,500. (ctrl). An organ magazine of the Japanese Society of Zoological Technical Science.

NOMENCLATOR ZOOLOGICUS. 0078-0952. UK. English. ir. Zoological Society of London, Regents Park, London NW1 4RY England. **Tel** 722-3333. **Ed** M Edwards. Lists names of genera and subgenera with bibliographical reference for the original description of each.

NOTATKI ORNITOLOGICZNE. Vol. 1 1960-. 0550-0842. PL. Polish (summaries in English). ir. ARS Poland, Kackowskie Przedmiescie 7, 00 068 Warsaw Poland. **DD** 598.2.

NOTORNIS. V. 4- July 1950-. 0029-4470. Periodical. NZ. English. qt. Ornithological Society of New Zealand, PO Box 22-23 D, Auckland New Zealand. **Ind/Abst** Biol. Abstr., GeoRef, Bibliogr. Index Geol. **LC** QL671. **DD** 598.05. **CODEN** NTNSAN. *New Zealand Bird Notes.*

NOTULAE ENTOMOLOGICAE. **VFOAT** Entomologisk Tidskrift. Vol. 1- 1921-. 0029-4594. Periodical. FI. English (Finnish and Swedish). qt. $20.00. Societas Entomolog Helsingfor, Zoological Museum N Jarnv 13, Helsinki Finland. **Tel** 4027259. **Ed** Martin Meinander. **Ind/Abst** Life Sci. Collect., Biol. Abstr., Bibliogr. Agric. **LC** QL461. **DD** 595.705. **CODEN** NOENAU. bk rev. adv acc. **Circ** 800. (ctrl). Covers entomology, faunistics, ecology, and systematics.

NOUVELLE REVUE D'ENTOMOLOGIE. V. 1- 1971-. 0374-9797. Periodical. FR. French (articles in English, German, Italian or Spanish). qt. $29.80. Laboratoire de Etres Organises, 105 Boulevard Raspail, 75006 Paris France. **Ind/Abst** Life Sci. Collect., Biol. Abstr., Chem. Abstr. **CODEN** NRETAZ.

NOVITATES ARTHROPODAE. V. 1- Jan. 1979-. 0278-3274. Monographic Series. US. English. ir. J B Publishing Company, 430 Ivy Avenue, Crete NE 68333. **Tel** (402)826-3356. **Ed** William F Rapp. **Ind/Abst** Biol. Abstr. **CODEN** NOARDP. **Circ** 100. Comprehensive treatment of the American species of Dacnusinae. The Dacnusiane are parasites of diptera, mainly stem boring and leaf mining maggots.

OCCASIONAL BULLETIN - ZOOLOGICAL SOCIETY OF SOUTHERN AFRICA. **Main/Corp** Zoological Society of Southern Africa. SA. Afrikaans (English). ir. **LC** QL337.S66.

OCCASIONAL PAPERS IN ENTOMOLOGY. No. 21- 1975-. 0362-2622. Monographic Series. US. English. ir. Free. California Department of Food and Agriculture, 1220 N Street, Sacramento CA 95814. **Tel** (916)445-4521. **Ed** Fred G Andrews. **LC** QL461. **DD** 595.70012. **Circ** 1,000. (ctrl). Insect systematics.

OCCASIONAL PAPERS OF THE MUSEUM OF ZOOLOGY. *See* Museums.

OCCASIONAL PAPERS OF THE MUSEUM OF ZOOLOGY, UNIVERSITY OF MICHIGAN. *See* Museums.

OCCASIONAL PAPERS OF THE WESTERN FOUNDATION OF VERTEBRATE ZOOLOGY. Main/Corp Western Foundation of Vertebrate Zoology. No. 1- June 1968-. 0511-7542. Monographic Series. US. English. ir. Western Foundation for Vertebrate Zoology, 1100 Glendon Avenue, Los Angeles CA 90024. **Tel** (213)208-8003. **Ed** Jack C von Bloeker Jr. **LC** QL1. **DD** 596.008. **Circ** 1,000. Papers of short length reporting original research in vertebrate zoology.

OCCASIONAL PAPERS ON MOLLUSKS. Main/Corp Harvard University. Museum of Comparative Zoology. Dept. of Mollusks. V. 1- (No. 1-). 0073-0807. Monographic Series. US. English. ir. The Department of Mollusks, Harvard University, Museum of Comparative Zoology, Cambridge MA 02138. **Ind/Abst** Biol. Abstr. **CODEN** OPMOAN.

ODONATOLOGICA. V. 1- Mar. 1972-. 0375-0183. Periodical. NE. English, French, German or Italian. qt. Societas Internationalis Odonatologica, Universite Utrecht, Padualaan 8, Utrecht The Netherlands. **Ed** B Kiauta. **Ind/Abst** Life Sci. Collect., Biol. Abstr. **CODEN** ODTGAI. bk rev. **Circ** 600. (ctrl). Original research papers on biology of dragonflies and damselflies and their conservation-odon. Abstracts section covers world literature.

OECOLOGIA. V. 1- Apr. 1968-. 0029-8549. Periodical. English (French and German, with summaries in English). mo. $698.00. Springer Verlag-New York Inc, 175 5th Avenue, New York NY 10010. **Tel** (212)460-1500. **Ed** H Remmert and E D Schulze. **Ind/Abst** Can. Environ., Life Sci. Collect., Excerpta Med., Coal Abstr., Energy Inf. Abstr., Environ. Abstr., GeoRef, Energy Res. Abstr., Biol. Abstr., Nuci. Sci. Abstr., Bibliogr. Agric., Sel. Water Resour. Abstr., Sci. Cit. Index, Abr. Ed., Ocean. Abstr. Indexes, Ocean. Abstr. **LC** QH540. **DD** 591.5. **NLM** W1 OE28. **CODEN** OECOBX. Presents articles on developments in research on the functional relationships between plant and animal organisms and their environment. *Zeitschrift fur Morphologie und Okologie der Tiere.*

OF SEA AND SHORE. 0030-0055. Periodical. US. English. qt. Of Sea & Shore, Box 219, Port Gambles WA 98364. **CODEN** OSSHDM. Available in microform from Xerox University Microfilms.

OISEAU ET LA REVUE FRANCAISE D'ORNITHOLOGIE. (L'OISEAU ET LA REVUE FRANCAISE D'ORNITHOLOGIE). V. 1- Jan./Feb. 1931-. 0030-1531. Periodical. FR. French. qt. $46.57. Societe Ornithologique France, 55 rue Buffon, 75005 Paris France. **Tel** 43 31 02 49. **Ed** Jean Louis Mougin. **Ind/Abst** Life Sci. Collect. bk rev. **Circ** 1,000. (ctrl). Studies on wild birds. *Revue d'Histoire Naturelle. Deuxieme Partie: l'Oiseau et la Revue Francaise d'Ornithologie.*

ONTARIO BIRD BANDING. V. 1- June 1965-. 0475-025X. Periodical. CN. English. ty. $10.00. Ontario Bird Banding Association, 10 Paulson Court, St Thomas Ontario N5R 1M9 Canada. **Tel** (519)821-2549. **Ed** David Lamble. **Ind/Abst** Can. Environ., Biol. Abstr. **CODEN** ONBBAH. bk rev. **Circ** 250. (ctrl). Articles promote understanding of native bird species as well as techniques in capturing and banding these birds.

ONTARIO NEST RECORDS SCHEME. VFOAT ONRS. Began publication in 1961?. 0228-0787. CN. English. an. Free. Department of Ornithology, Royal Ontario Museum, 100 Queen's Park Crescent, Toronto Ontario M5S 2C6 Canada. **Ed** G K Peck. **DD** 598.0720713. (ctrl).

OPHELIA. V. 1- May 1964-. 0078-5326. Periodical. DK. English. sa. 980. Marine Biological Labatory, University of Copenhagen, DK-3000 Helsingor Denmark. **Ed** Kirsten Muus. **Ind/Abst** Life Sci. Collect., Energy Res. Abstr., Biol. Abstr., Chem. Abstr., Ocean. Abstr., Pollut. Abstr. Indexes, Sel. Water Resour. Abstr., Bibliogr. Agric., Soc. Sci. Citation Index, Sci. Cit. Index, Abr. Ed. **LC** QH91.A1. **CODEN** OPHLAN. adv acc. **Circ** 500. Marine biology and ecology.

OPUSCULA ZOOLOGICA - INSTITUTUM ZOOSYSTEMATICUM UNIVERSITATIS BUDAPESTINENSIS. (OPUSCULA ZOOLOGICA). V. 1-. 0473-1034. Periodical. HU. German (articles in English and French). sa. Akademiai Kiado, POB 24, 1363 Budapest Hungary. **Ind/Abst** Biol. Abstr. **CODEN** OPUZAS.

ORIENTAL INSECTS. V. 1- Sept. 1967-. 0030-5316. Periodical. US. English. an. $46.00. Oriental Insects, PO Box 13148, Gainesville FL 32604. **Tel** (904)372-3505. **Ed** V K Gupta. **Ind/Abst** Life Sci. Collect., Biol. Abstr., Bibliogr. Agric., Sci. Cit. Index, Abr. Ed. **LC** QL461. **DD** 595.7095. **CODEN** ORINAE. bk rev. adv acc. **Circ** 250. An international journal of taxonomic entomology of insects and other land anthropods of the Old World tropics. Faunistics and ecological works also published. Both original and review articles are accepted for publication.

ORIENTAL INSECTS MONOGRAPH. US. English. ir. $45.00. Oriental Insects, PO Box 13148, Gainesville FL 32604. **Tel** (904)372-3505. **Ed** V K Gupta. **Circ** 100. Monographic works on insects and other land arthropods of old world tropics. Irregular series-published as works available.

ORIENTAL INSECTS SUPPLEMENT. No. 1- 1971-. Periodical. US. English. ir. Oriental Insects, PO Box 13148, Gainesville FL 32604-1148.

ORNIS FENNICA. 1.- Vol. 0030-5685. Periodical. Fl. English (Finnish and Swedish). qt. 18.00. Finnish Ornithological Society, P Rautatiek 13, SF-00100 Helsinki 10 Finland. **Ind/Abst** Life Sci. Collect., Biol. Abstr., Chem. Abstr. **LC** QL671. **CODEN** ORFEA6. bk rev. adv acc. **Circ** 1,250. Covers ornithology.

ORNIS SCANDINAVICA. Vol. 1-. 0030-5693. Periodical. NO. English (occasional articles in French and German). sa. Munksgaard Ltd, 35 Norre Sogade, DK-1370 Copenhagen K Denmark. **Tel** 1.12.70.30. **Ed** Sven-Axel Bengtson. **Ind/Abst** Can. Environ., Life Sci. Collect., Biol. Abstr., Sci. Cit. Index, Abr. Ed. **LC** QL671. **DD** 598.205. **CODEN** ORSCAV. bk rev. adv acc. **Circ** 570. Original work in all aspects of ornithology.

ORNITHOLOGICAL MONOGRAPHS. Began with No. 1, 1964-. 0078-6594. Monographic Series. US. English. ir. American Ornithologists Union, c/o Glen E Woolfenden, University of South Florida, Department of Biology, Tampa FL 33620. **LC** QL671. **DD** 598.05. **CODEN** ORMNBZ.

ORNITHOLOGICAL NEWSLETTER. 0274-564X. Periodical. US. English. bm. $1.50. Ornithological Societies of NA, PO Box 21618, Columbus OH 43221. **Tel** (614)422-0639. **Ed** Richard Banks. **DD** 598. **Circ** 7,000. News and information about meetings, people and events in the American Ornithologists Union, Cooper Ornithological Society and Wilson Ornithological Society.

ORNITHOLOGISCHE BEOBACHTER. (DER ORNITHOLOGISCHE BEOBACHTER). Yearly 1- 1902-. 0030-5707. Periodical. German (summaries in English and French). qt. $19.79. Geschaftsstelle Muri-, Geschaftsstelle: Frau K Kunz, CH-2543 Lengnau BE Switzerland. **Tel** 65 52 58 95. **Ed** ALA. **Ind/Abst** Biol. Abstr. **CODEN** ORBEAK. Index in first issue of next volume - attached. bk rev. adv acc. Study of birds.

ORNITHOLOGISCHE MITTEILUNGEN. V. 1- 1948-. 0030-5723. Periodical. GW. German. ir. Biologie-Verlag, Postfach 1649, D 62 Wiesbaden West Germany. **Ind/Abst** Biol. Abstr. **LC** QL671. **DD** 598. **CODEN** ORMIAJ.

ORNITOLOGIIA. Vol. 2-. 0474-7313. UR. Russian. ir. **LC** QL671. *Uchenye Zapiski.*

EL ORNITORRINCO. No. 1- Oct./Nov. 1977-. Periodical. Spanish. ir. Talleres Graficos Alemann y Cia, Gral Enrique Martinez 813 10 B, Buenos Aires Argentina. **Ed** A Castillo.

ORYX. *See* Biology - Botany.

OSTRICH. (THE OSTRICH). V. 1- Mar. 1930-. 0030-6525. Periodical. SA. English. qt. $35.00. South African Ornithological Society, PO Box 87234, Houghton Johannesburg 2041 South Africa. **Tel** (011)782-1547. **Ed** A J F K Craig. **Ind/Abst** Life Sci. Collect., Biol. Abstr., Wildl. Rev. **LC** QL671. **DD** 598.05. **CODEN** OSTHAO. bk rev. **Circ** 4,000. (ctrl).

THE OSTRICH. SUPPLEMENT. No. 1- 1941-. Monographic Series. SA. English. ir. $35.00. South African Ornithologic Society, PO Box 87234/ 2041 Hoghton, Johannesburg South Africa. **Tel** 011 782.1547. **Ed** A Craig. **Ind/Abst** Sci. Cit. Index, Abr. Ed. bk rev. **Circ** 4,500.

OTAN NEWSLETTER. Main/Corp Organization of Tropical American Nematologists. VFOAT Carta Informativa Onta. Periodical. US. English. sa. Organization of Tropical American Nematologists, Box 5690 College Street, N Acosta, Mayaguez Puerto Rico 00708. **Ind/Abst** Bibliogr. Agric.

OTTAWA BANDING GROUP. (THE OTTAWA BANDING GROUP : NEWSLETTER). Vol. 1, No. 1 (1983)-. 0827-2298. Periodical. CN. English. ty. $10.00. Ottawa Banding Group, PO Box 3633/Station C, Ottawa Ontario K1Y 4J7 Canada. **Tel** (614)728-0695. **Ed** Colin Griffiths. **DD** 598.0723206071384. bk rev. **Circ** 50. (ctrl). Informative articles on birds caught during bird-banding activities in the Ottawa area; mainly small passerine birds, but also larger owls, ducks and hawks.

OUR FOURFOOTED FRIENDS. 0030-6851. Periodical. US. English. qt. $4.00. Animal Rescue League of Boston, PO Box 265, Boston MA 02117. **Tel** (617)426-9170.

OXYTOCIN. Series/Titl Annual Research Reviews. V. 1- 1977-. 0706-3520. Periodical. CN. English. ir. Eden Press, 4626 St Catherine Street West, Montreal Quebec H3Z 1S3 Canada. **Ed** J S Roberts. **Ind/Abst** Life Sci. Collect. **DD** 591.1927. **NLM** W1 OX64.

PACIFIC FLYWAY WATERFOWL REPORT. Began with No. 79 (May 1978) issue. 0740-6940. Periodical. US. English. sa. USFWS, 500 NE Multnomah Street, Portland OR 97232. **LC** QL696.A52. **DD** 598.410978. *Pacific Waterfowl Flyway Report.*

PACIFIC INSECTS *CEASED.* V. 1-24. 0030-8714. Periodical. US. English. qt. **Ind/Abst** Energy Inf. Abstr., Environ. Abstr., Biol. Abstr., Bibliogr. Agric. **LC** QL461. **DD** 595.7099. **CODEN** PFISAO.

PACIFIC INSECTS MONOGRAPH. 1-. 0078-7515. Monographic Series. US. English. ir. Bishop Museum, Box 6047, Kalin Street, Honolulu HI 96818. **Ind/Abst** Life Sci. Collect., Biol. Abstr. **LC** QL461. **DD** 595.7005. **CODEN** PIMOBK.

PAKISTAN JOURNAL OF ZOOLOGY. V. 1- Jan. 1969-. 0030-9923. Periodical. English. sa. $50.00. University of Punjab, New Campus, Zoology Society of Pakistan, c/o Department of Zoology, Lahore Pakistan. **Tel** 854096. **Ed** Muzaffer Ahmad. **Ind/Abst** Life Sci. Collect., Excerpta Med., Curr. Contents, Agric. Biol. Environ. Sci., Biol. Abstr., Chem. Abstr., Zool. Rec., Ocean. Abstr., Pollut. Abstr. Indexes. **LC** QL1. **DD** 591.05. **NLM** W1 PA358T. **CODEN** PJZOAN. **Circ** 600. Publishes research papers in the fields of biochemistry, cell biology, entomology, endocrinology, fisheries, genetics, morphology, physiology, taxonomy, vertebrate and invertebrate zoology.

THE PAN-PACIFIC ENTOMOLOGIST. V. 1- July 1924-. 0031-0603. Periodical. US. English. qt. $20.00. Pacific Coast Entomological Society, California Academy of Sciences/Golden Gate Park, San Francisco CA 94118. **Tel** (415)221-5100. **Ed** J A Chemsak and Duzee. **Ind/Abst** Life Sci. Collect., Energy Inf. Abstr., Environ. Abstr., Bibliogr. Agric., Biol. Abstr., Chem. Abstr. **LC** QL461. **DD** 595.705. **CODEN** PPETA9. bk rev. **Circ** 670. (ctrl). Systematic and biological aspects of entomology.

PAPEIS AVULSOS DE ZOOLOGIA. V. 20- 1967-. 0031-1049. BL. English (with summaries in Portuguese). ir. $15.00. Universidade de Sao Paulo, Museu Zoologia Caixa Post 7172, Sao Paulo Brazil Z C 01051. **Tel** (011)274-3455. **Ind/Abst** Life Sci. Collect., Biol. Abstr., Bibliogr. Agric. **LC** QL1. **DD** 591.8. **CODEN** PAZOAS. bk rev. adv acc. **Circ** 458. (ctrl). Zoological papers. *Papeis Avulsos do Departamento de Zoologia.*

PAPERS - QUEENSLAND. UNIVERSITY, BRISBANE. DEPT. OF ENTOMOLOGY. Main/Corp Queensland., University, Brisbane., Dept. of Entomology. V. 1- 1955-. 0079-8916. AT. English. ir. University of Brisbane, Department of Entomology, Queensland Australia.

THE PASSENGER PIGEON. Began with Vol. 1 in Jan. 1939. 0031-2703. Periodical. US. English. qt. Wisconsin Society for Ornithology Inc, W330 N8275 West Shore Drive, Hartland WI 53029. **Tel** (414)966-1072. **Ed** Charles Kemper. **Ind/Abst** Biol. Abstr. **LC** QL671. **DD** 598.29775. **CODEN** PPGNAZ. (cum index). bk rev. adv acc. **Circ** 1,200. (ctrl). Study of Wisconsin birds including preservation of species and habitats.

PAW PRINTS. 0163-562X. Periodical. US. English. bm. $2.50. Friends of the National Zoo, C/O National Zoo-Mary Matthews, Washington DC 20009. **Tel** (202)673-4711. **Ed** Bettina Conner. bk rev. **Circ** 26,000. Children's newsletter highlighting animals and events at the National Zoo, Washington, DC.

LE PETIT JOURNAL DU BRASSEUR. Periodical. BE. Dutch. mo. $62.25. Conf des Brasseries Belgique, Broquevillelaan 23, B-8430 Middelkerke Belgium. **Tel** 02-531-8324. adv acc. News and articles about the world of bears.

Zoology-Vertebrate and Invertebrate

PHILIPPINE ENTOMOLOGIST. V. 1- Apr. 1968-. 0369-9536. Periodical. PH. English. sa. 3.78. Philippine Association Entomologists, University of Philippines, Los Banos Laguna 3720 Philippines. Ed Virginia R Ocampo. Ind/Abst Life Sci. Collect., Chem. Abstr. CODEN PHETBM. adv acc. Circ 400. This journal publishes papers dealing with systematic, economic and industrial entomology insect physiology, biochemistry and toxicology.

PHYSIOLOGICAL ENTOMOLOGY. V. 1- Mar. 1976-. 0307-6962. Periodical. UK. English. qt. 55.00 Domestic, 66.00 Foreign. Blackwell Scientific Publishing Ltd, PO Box 88, Oxford OX2 0EL England. Tel 0865-240201. Ed G J Goldsworthy. Ind/Abst Life Sci. Collect., Biol. Abstr., Chem. Abstr., Energy Inf. Abstr., Environ. Abstr., Sci. Cit. Index, Abr. Ed. LC QL495. DD 595.70105. CODEN PENTDE. bk rev. adv acc. Physiology of insects. *Journal of Entomology. Series A. Physiology & Behaviour, 0308-5007.*

PHYSIOLOGICAL ZOOLOGY. V. 1- Jan. 1928-. 0031-935X. Periodical. US. English. bm. $38.00. University of Chicago Press, PO Box 37005, Chicago IL 60637. Tel (312)753-3347. Ind/Abst Life Sci. Collect., Biol. Abstr., Chem. Abstr., Nuci. Sci. Abstr., Sel. Water Resour. Abstr., Bibliogr. Agric., Biol. Agric. Index, Sci. Cit. Index, Abr. Ed. LC QL1. DD 591.05. NLM W1 PH932. CODEN PHZOA9. Available on microfilm from University Microfilms.

PHYSIS. V. 36- (No. 92-). Periodical. AG. Spanish (summaries in English). sa. $65.00. Cuidad Universitatia de Nunez, Ciencias Biologicas, 1428 Buenos Aires Argentina. Ed Juan Carlos Giacchi. Ind/Abst Life Sci. Collect., Bibliogr. Index Geol. bk rev. Circ 700. A semestral journal devoted to zoology and botany systematics, physiology, distribution, ecology, histology, embriology, anatomy, etc. mainly of South America. *Physis. Seccion A. Los Oceanos y Sus Organismos, 0325-0342; Physis. Seccion B. Los Aguas Continentales y Sus Organismos, 0325-0350; Physis. Seccion C. Los Continentes y Los Organismos Terrestres, 0325-0369.*

POLSKIE PISMO ENTOMOLOGICZNE. VFOAT Bulletin Entomologique de Pologne. V. 1- 1922-. 0032-3780. Periodical. PL. English (French, German or Polish). ir. 45.00. ARS Polona, Krakowskie Przedmiescle 7, 00 068 Warsaw Poland. Ind/Abst Life Sci. Collect., Biol. Abstr., Chem. Abstr. LC QL461. DD 595.7005. CODEN PEBEA8. *Polskie Pismo Entomologiczne. Seria B: Entomologia Stosowana.*

PRACE ZOOLOGICZNE. Main/Corp Krakow. Wyzsza Szkoa Pedagogiczna. Began in 1967. Polish (summaries in English and Russian). ir. 12.00 Each Issue. Naukowe Szkoy Pedagogicznej, Ksiegarnia Naukowa Komu Ksiazki, 31-118 Ul Pod Wale 6, Krakow Poland. LC AS142.K66, QL1.

PRIMATE NEWS. Began in 1963. 0032-8324. Periodical. US. English. ir. $5.00. Oregon Regional Primate, 505 NW 185th Avenue, Beaverton OR 97006. Tel (503)645-1141. Ind/Abst Chem. Abstr. NLM W1 PR522D. CODEN PRNWBA.

PRIMATE RECORD. Began with Vol. 3 (Spring 1972) issue. 0093-2744. Periodical. US. English. Free. Public Information Officer of Wisconsin Regional Primate Research Center, 1223 Capitol Court, Madison WI 53706. LC QL737.P9. DD 599.805. NLM W1 PR522DK. CODEN PMRCB. Mainly Monkeys.

PRIMATES. V. 1- Sept. 1957-. 0032-8332. Periodical. JA. English (French or German). qt. $100.00. Japan Monkey Centre, 26 Kanrin, Inuyama Aichi Japan. Ind/Abst Biol. Abstr., Life Sci. Collect., Psychol. Abstr., Chem. Abstr. LC QL737.P9. NLM W1 PR522F. CODEN PRMTBU. (cum index).

PRIMATES IN MEDICINE. V. 1-. 0079-5119. English. ir. Ind/Abst Excerpta Med., Biol. Abstr., Chem. Abstr. LC QL55. NLM W1 PR522E. CODEN PRIMBN.

PRIRODOVEDNE PRACE USTAV CESKOSLOVENSKE AKADEMIE VED V BRNE. VFOAT Acta Scientiarum Naturalium Academiae Scientiarum Bohemoslovacae Brno. New Series 1- 1967-. 0032-8758. Periodical. CS. Czech (articles in English or German with summaries in English and Russian). mo. Artia, VE Smecky 30, Praha 1 Czechoslovakia. Tel 331143. Ind/Abst Life Sci. Collect., GeoRef, Biol. Abstr. CODEN PPUCA4. Circ 700. (ctrl). Brings articles on research in zoology, archaeology, botany, and geography. *Prace Brnenske Zakladny Ceskoslovenske Akademie Ved.*

PROBLEMY ZOOLOGII. Periodical. UR. Russian. 0.38. B-164 Mendeleevskaia Lin D 1, Liningrad Russian SFSR. LC QL281.

PROCEEDINGS AND TRANSACTIONS OF THE BRITISH ENTOMOLOGICAL AND NATURAL HISTORY SOCIETY. Main/Corp British Entomological and Natural History Society. V. 1- Oct. 1968-. 0525-5252. Periodical. UK. English. qt. Ind/Abst Life Sci. Collect., Bibliogr. Agric. LC QL461. DD 595.7005. *Proceedings and Transactions of The South London Entomological and Natural History Society.*

PROCEEDINGS. ANNUAL A.A.Z.P.A. CONFERENCE. (PROCEEDINGS; ANNUAL AAZPA CONFERENCE). Main/Corp American Association of Zoological Parks and Aquariums. VAT Proceedings. Annual American Association of Zoological Parks and Aquariums Conference. 0090-4473. US. English. an. $5.00. American Association of Zoological Parks & Aquariums, Oglebay Park, Wheeling WV 26003. LC QL77.5. DD 590.74405.

PROCEEDINGS - BIRD CONTROL SEMINAR. Main/Conf Bird Control Seminar. 1st- 1962-. 0067-8945. US. English. an. Ind/Abst Chem. Abstr., Biol. Abstr. CODEN PBCNBK.

PROCEEDINGS - INTERNATIONAL CONGRESS OF ZOOLOGY. Main/Conf International Congress of Zoology. 1st- 1889-. Monographic Series. English (French, German, Italian, or Spanish). ir. LC QL1. DD 590.82.

PROCEEDINGS OF SYMPOSIUM - DESERT TORTOISE COUNCIL. Main/Corp Desert Tortoise Council. 1st- 1976-. 0191-3875. US. English. an. Desert Tortoise Council, 5319 Cittitos Avenue, Long Beach CA 90805. Tel (213)422-6172. Ed Mary Trotter and K S Hashagen. LC QL666.C584. DD 598.13. Scientific papers on desert tortoise studies.

PROCEEDINGS OF THE ALL-INDIA CONGRESS OF ZOOLOGY. Main/Conf All-India Congress of Zoology. 1st- 1959-. 0569-0242. II. English. ir. Zoological Society of India, Utkal University, Dr BK Behura, Bhubaneswar 4 Orissa India.

PROCEEDINGS OF THE ANNUAL MEETING - FLORIDA STATE BEEKEEPERS ASSOCIATION. Main/Corp Florida. State Beekeepers Association. US. English. ir.

PROCEEDINGS OF THE ... ANNUAL MEETING OF THE ACADIAN ENTOMOLOGICAL SOCIETY. (PROCEEDINGS OF THE ... ANNUAL MEETING). Main/Corp Acadian Entomological Society. Meeting. VAT Proceedings of the ... Annual Meeting - Acadian Entomological Society. 0822-5915. CN. English. an. Free to Members. G Boiteau, Agriculture Canada Research Station, PO Box 20280, Fredericton New Brunswick E3B 4Z7 Canada. DD 595.70060715. *Proceedings of the Acadian Entomological Society, 0701-2101.*

PROCEEDINGS OF THE ANNUAL MEETING OF THE ENTOMOLOGICAL SOCIETY OF ALBERTA. Main/Corp Entomological Society of Alberta. V. 1- 1953-. 0071-0709. CN. English. an. 6.00. Entomological Society of Alberta, c/o Department of Entomology 255 University of Alberta, Edmonton Alberta T6G 2E3 Canada. Tel (403)432-3237. DD 595.7005. adv acc. Circ 120. Abstracts of scientific papers presented at annual meetings, plus general information about the Entomological Society.

PROCEEDINGS OF THE CANADIAN SOCIETY OF ZOOLOGISTS ANNUAL MEETING. Main/Corp Canadian Society of Zoologists. Meeting. 1974-. 0225-090X. Periodical. CN. English. $4.99 Each Number to Members. Canadian Society of Zoologists, Department of Biology, 4700 Keele Street, Downsview Ontario M3J 1P3 Canada. DD 591.

PROCEEDINGS OF THE ... ENTOMOLOGICAL CONGRESS. Main/Conf Entomological Congress. SA. English (Afrikaans). ir. 50. Entomological Society South Africa, PO Box 103, Pretoria South Africa. Ed R M Crewe. bk rev. Circ 600. (ctrl). Covers entomology and ecology. *Proceedings of the ... Congress of the Entomological Society of Southern Africa.*

PROCEEDINGS OF THE ENTOMOLOGICAL SOCIETY OF MANITOBA. Main/Corp Entomological Society of Manitoba. V. 1- 1945-. 0315-2146. CN. English. ir. Entomological Society of Manitoba, Research Statistics, 195 Dafoe Road, Winnipeg Manitoba R3T 2M9 Canada. *Manitoba Entomologist.*

PROCEEDINGS OF THE ENTOMOLOGICAL SOCIETY OF ONTARIO. Main/Corp Entomological Society of Ontario. V. 90- 1959-. 0071-0768. Periodical. CN. English. an. Entomological Society of Ontario, Universtiy of Guelph, Guelph Ontario Canada. Ind/Abst Life Sci. Collect., Bibliogr. Agric., Biol. Abstr., Chem. Abstr., Energy Inf. Abstr., Environ. Abstr., Sci. Cit. Index, Abr. Ed. DD 595.7005. CODEN PESOAL. *Proceedings of the Entomological Society of Ontario, 0317-1914.*

PROCEEDINGS OF THE ENTOMOLOGICAL SOCIETY OF WASHINGTON. Main/Corp Entomological Society of Washington. V. 1- Feb. 1884-. 0013-8797. Periodical. US. English. qt. $9.00. Entomological Society of Washington, c/o Department of Entomology, Smithsonian Institution, 10th and Constitution, Washington DC 20560. Ind/Abst Life Sci. Collect., Bibliogr. Agric., Biol. Abstr., Chem. Abstr., Energy Inf. Abstr., Environ. Abstr. LC QL461. DD 595.7005. NLM W1 PR585HN. CODEN PESWAB.

PROCEEDINGS OF THE HAWAIIAN ENTOMOLOGICAL SOCIETY. Main/Corp Hawaiian Entomological Society. V. 1- 1905/07-. 0073-134X. US. English. an. $10.00. Hawaiian Entomological Society, 3050 Maileway, Honolulu HI 96822. Tel (808)948-7054. Ed C R Joyce. Ind/Abst Life Sci. Collect., Energy Inf. Abstr., Environ. Abstr., Bibliogr. Agric., Biol. Abstr., Chem. Abstr., Nuci. Sci. Abstr., Sci. Cit. Index, Abr. Ed. CODEN PHESAI. adv acc. Circ 250. General entomology with special interest in Hawaiian insects.

PROCEEDINGS OF THE HELMINTHOLOGICAL SOCIETY OF WASHINGTON. Main/Corp Helminthological Society of Washington. V. 1- Mar. 1934-. 0018-0130. Periodical. US. English. sa. $30.00 Domestic, $33.00 Foreign. PO Box 368, Lawrence KS 66044. Tel (913)843-1234. Ed J Ralph Lichtenfels. Ind/Abst Excerpta Med., Pestdoc, Ringdoc, Vetdoc, Bibliogr. Agric., Biol. Abstr., Chem. Abstr., Nuci. Sci. Abstr., Sel. Water Resour. Abstr., Sci. Cit. Index, Abr. Ed. LC QL386. DD 595.105. NLM W1 PR585IM. CODEN PHSWAW. Circ 1,000. (ctrl). Publishes original research papers on the biology, immunology, ecology, biochemistry, and systematics of all groups of parasites, particularly the protozoa, helminths, and anthropods.

PROCEEDINGS OF THE INTERNATIONAL ORNITHOLOGICAL CONGRESS. Main/Corp International Ornithological Congress. 1884-. 0074-7211. AT. English (French, German, or Italian). ir. 62.50. Australian Academy of Sciences, PO Box 783, Canberra Australian Capital Territory 2601 Australia. LC QL671. DD 598.2082. This free interchange of views enables scientists to keep abreast with the latest developments in their field.

PROCEEDINGS OF THE ROYAL ZOOLOGICAL SOCIETY OF NEW SOUTH WALES CEASED. Main/Corp Royal Zoological Society of New South Wales. 54th-89th. 0373-4129. AT. English. qt. Royal Zoological Society of NSW, PO Box 20, Mosman New South Wales 2088 Australia. Tel (02)969 7336.

PROCEEDINGS OF THE WESTERN FOUNDATION OF VERTEBRATE ZOOLOGY. V. 1- Apr. 1963-. 0511-7550. US. English. ir. Western Foundation for Vertebrate Zoology, 1100 Glendon Avenue, Los Angeles CA 90024. Tel (213)208-8003. Ed Jack C von Bloeker Jr. Ind/Abst Biol. Abstr. CODEN PWFVA2. Circ 1,000. Papers reporting original research in vertebrate zoology with emphasis on ornithology.

PROCEEDINGS - VERTEBRATE PEST CONFERENCE. Main/Conf Vertebrate Pest Conference. 0507-6773. US. English. be. $10.00. University of California Wildlife Extension, Vertebrate Pest Conference c/o Terrell Salmon, Davis CA 95616. Tel (916)752-6409. Ed Terrell P Salmon. Ind/Abst Pestdoc, Ringdoc, Vetdoc, Chem. Abstr., Bibliogr. Agric. CODEN PVPCBM. Circ 600. (ctrl). Articles dealing with research into and application of vertebrate pest management techniques.

PROCEEDINGS - WASHINGTON STATE ENTOMOLOGICAL SOCIETY. Main/Corp Washington State Entomological Society. VFOAT Proceedings of the Washington State Entomological Society. US. English. qt. Proceedings

Zoology-Vertebrate and Invertebrate

of the Smithsonian Institute, Department of Entomology, NHB 168, Washington DC 20560. Tel (202)382-1800.

PROCEEDINGS - ZOOLOGICAL SOCIETY OF BENGAL. Main/Corp Zoological Society of Bengal. V. 1- Mar. 1948-. Periodical. II. English. ir. Zoological Society of Bengal, 35 Ballygunge Circular Road, Calcutta 700019 India. LC QL1. DD 590.5.

PROTEINS OF ANIMAL CELL PLASMA MEMBRANES. Series/Titl Annual Research Reviews. V. 1-2. 0705-4726. CN. English. ir. Eden Press, 4626 St Catherine Street West, Montreal Quebec H3Z 1S3 Canada. Ed D F H Wallach. DD 591.875. NLM W1 PR791.

PROTOZOOLOGICAL ABSTRACTS. See Indexes/Abstracts.

PRZEGLAD ZOOLOGICZNY. V. 1-. 0033-247X. Periodical. PL. Polish (some have summaries and added table of contents in English). qt. ARS Polona, Krakowskie Przedieście 7, 00-068 Warsaw Poland. Ind/Abst Life Sci. Collect., GeoRef, Biol. Abstr., Chem. Abstr. LC QL1. DD 591.05. NLM W1 PR94. CODEN PZOOAC.

PSYCHE. Began in 1874. 0033-2615. Periodical. US. English. qt. Psyche Editorial Office, 16 Divinity Avenue, Cambridge MA 02138. Ind/Abst Life Sci. Collect., Excerpta Med., GeoRef, Biol. Abstr., Chem. Abstr., Index Med., Psychol. Abstr., Bibliogr. Agric. LC QL461. NLM W1 PS229. CODEN PYCHAQ.

PUBL HERPETOL. VFOAT Publications in Herpetology. VAT Publications in Herpetology. 1-. 0161-5009. Monographic Series. US. English. ir. Herpetological Information Search Systems of the American Museum of Natural History, Central Park West at 79th Street, New York NY 10024. CODEN PUHEDH. Publications in Herpetology.

PUBLIC EDUCATION SERIES. No. 1-. 0272-2658. Monographic Series. US. English. ir. Publications Secretary Museum of Natural History, University of Kansas, Lawrence KS 66045. Tel (913)864-4540. Ed Joseph T Collins. LC UNC. Circ 1,500. (ctrl). Each number is on a different zoological subject, ichthyology, herpetology, mammalogy and archeology.

PUBLICACIONES. Main/Corp Chile. Universidad, Santiago. Centro de Estudios Entomologicos. No. 1- 1960-). 0577-8298. Periodical. CL. Spanish. ir. Av Bernardo O Higgins 1058, Casilla 10 D Santiago Chile.

PUBLICACIONES DEL DEPARTMENTO DE ZOOLOGIA. Main/Corp Barcelona. Universidad. Facultad de Biologia. 1- 1976-. Periodical. SP. Spanish (summaries in English, French, or German). ir. Departmento del Zoologia, Facultad de Biologia, Universidad de Barcelona, Barcelona 7 Spain.

PUBLICATION E. Main/Corp Purdue University. Cooperative Extension Service. 1950-. US. English. ir. Ind/Abst Bibliogr. Agric.

PUBLICATIONS IN ZOOLOGY CEASED. VFOAT Publications de Zoologie. Began with No. 1-17, 1969-1982. 0068-8037. Monographic Series. CN. English (includes abstracts in French). ir. Ind/Abst Biol. Abstr., Life Sci. Collect. CODEN NMPZA5.

PUBLICATIONS OF THE NUTTALL ORNITHOLOGICAL CLUB. No. 1- 1957-. 0550-4082. Monographic Series. US. English. ir. Nuttall Ornithological Club, Harvard University, Cambridge MA 02138. Tel (617)495-2471. Ed R A Paynter, Jr. LC UNC. CODEN NUOPAQ. Circ 1,000. Scientific studies of birds.

QUARTERLY - MIAMI MALACOLOGICAL SOCIETY. (QUARTERLY). Main/Corp Miami Malacological Society. V. 1- April/June 1967-. 0090-323X. Periodical. US. English. qt. $1.50. Mrs M Ellen Crovo Corresponding Secretary, 2915 SW 102nd Avenue, Miami FL 33165. LC QL401. DD 594.005.

RAOU NEWSLETTER. See Conservation & Natural Resources.

RAPPORT DES INVENTAIRES AERIENS DU GROS GIBIER. Main/Corp Quebec (Province). Comite des Inventaires Aeriens du Gros Gibier. CN. French. Gouvernement du Quebec, 150 Est Boul, Saint-Cyrille Quebec Quebec G1R 4Y3 Canada. Tel (418)644-8114. LC QL721.5.Q4. DD 333.95909714. Circ 100. (ctrl).

RATEL. (RATEL : JOURNAL OF THE ASSOCIATION OF BRITISH WILD ANIMAL KEEPERS). 0305-1218. Periodical. UK. English. ty. 4.00. Ratel Editorial Office, 67 Reedley Road, Westbury-on-Trym Bristol B59 3TD England. Ind/Abst Life Sci. Collect. LC QL77.5. DD 636.0889905.

RECORDS OF NEW JERSEY BIRDS. Vol. 8, No. 4 (Winter 1982/83)-. US. English. qt. NJ Audubon : Records of New Jersey Birds.

RECORDS OF THE ZOOLOGICAL SURVEY OF INDIA. Main/Corp India (Republic). Zoological Survey. VFOAT India Records. V. 61- June 1963-. 0375-1511. II. English. qt. Controller of Publications, Civil Lines, Delhi 110006 India. Ind/Abst GeoRef. CODEN RZSIA2. Records of the Indian Museum.

RECORDS OF VERMONT BIRDS. 0197-3169. Periodical. US. English. qt. $5.00. Vermont Institute of Natural Sciences, Church Hill Road, Woodstock VT 05091. Tel (802)457-2779.

REFERATIVNYI ZHURNAL : PCHELOVODSTVO, SHELKOVODSTVO. VFOAT Pchelovodstvo, Shelkovodstvo. 1978, No. 1- Jan. 1978-. Periodical. UR. Russian. mo. Referativnyi Zhurnal: Pchelovodstvo, Shelkovodstvo, Rybovodstvo.

REICHENBACHIA. V. 1- 1962-. 0080-0767. Periodical. GE. German. ir. Deutscher Buch Export-Import, Leninstrasse 16, DDR-701 Leipzig East Germany. Tel 4952503. Ind/Abst Life Sci. Collect., Biol. Abstr. LC QL461. CODEN RCHBA3. bk rev. Circ 350. (ctrl). Taxonomy and systematics of the invertebrate groups insecta and archnida in global range.

REPORT - AUDUBON SOCIETY OF RHODE ISLAND. Main/Corp Audubon Society of Rhode Island. VFOAT Audubon Society of Rhode Island Report. 0274-502X. Periodical. US. English. ir. $5.00. Audubon Society of Rhode Island, 40 Bowen Street, Providence RI 02903. Tel (401)521-1670. Ed Eugenia Marks. bk rev. adv acc. Circ 4,000. (ctrl). Birdlife, bird records, natural history, environmental issues in Rhode Island. Refuge programs and events for members and general public. Society affairs.

REPORT OF THE INTERNATIONAL WHALING COMMISSION. Main/Corp International Whaling Commission. 28th- 1976/77-. 0143-8700. Periodical. UK. English. an. International Whaling Commission, The Red House, Station Road, Histon, Cambridge CB4 4NP England. Tel 022023 3971. Ed G P Donovan. Ind/Abst Life Sci. Collect. Circ 500. Report of management actions taken by the IWC, the report of its scientific committee and over 50 scientific papers on cetacean biology and management. Report of the Commission, 0074-9591.

REPORT ON THE BIRDS OF THE DONCASTER DISTRICT. Main/Corp Doncaster and District Ornithological Society. VFOAT Doncaster Bird Report. 1951-. UK. English. an. LC N1219.5.

THE REVIEW OF APPLIED ENTOMOLOGY. SERIES A : AGRICULTURAL. V. 1- Jan. 1913-. 0305-0076. UK. English. mo. $296.00. CAB International Central Sales, Farnham House, Farnham Royal Slough SL2 3BN England. Tel (02814)2662. Ed J M B Harley. LC SB599. DD 632.705. CODEN RAEAA5. Index published separately - free - automatically sent. (cum index). bk rev. adv acc. Circ 1,200. Deals with insects and other anthropod pests of cultivated plants, forest trees and stored products; beneficial anthropods such as parasites and predators are included.

REVISTA BRASILEIRA DE ENTOMOLOGIA. V. 1- 1954-. 0085-5626. Monographic Series. BL. text in Portuguese or English. qt. $30.00. Soc Brasileira de Entomologia, Caixa Postal 9063, Sao Paulo Brazil. Tel 274-3455. Ind/Abst Life Sci. Collect., Biol. Abstr. CODEN RBREAL. bk rev. Circ 650. Original papers on entomology (systematic, ecology, morphology, agricultural entomology, medical entomology).

REVISTA BRASILEIRA DE ZOOLOGIA. Vol. 1, No. 1-. 0101-8175. Periodical. English (Portuguese). ir. $20.00. Presidente da SBZ a/c Departamento de Zoologia Instituto de Biociencias Universidade de Sao Paulo, C P 20.520, Sao Paulo SP Brazil. LC QL242. DD 591.05.

REVISTA CHILENA DE ENTOMOLOGIA. V. 1, 1951-. 0034-740X. Monographic Series. CL. Spanish. $15.00. Revista Chilena de Entomologia, Casilla 21132, Santiago Chile. Tel 90011. Ind/Abst Life Sci. Collect. LC QL461. bk rev. adv acc. Circ 500. Taxonomy and systematic of Chilean and neotropical insects; including agricultural and forestal pests.

REVISTA DE BIOLOGIA MARINA (VALPARAISO (CHILE) : 1965). See Earth Sciences - Oceanography.

REVISTA DE LA SOCIEDAD MEXICANA DE LEPIDOPTEROLOGIA. Main/Corp Sociedad Mexicana de Lepidopterologia. V. 1, No. 1- June 1975-. Periodical. Spanish (summaries in English). sa. Sociedad Mexicana de Lepidopterologia, Apdo Postal 70-153, Mexico DF Mexico. Ind/Abst Biol. Abstr., Bibliogr. Agric. LC QL553.M4. CODEN RSMLD3.

REVISTA DEL MUSEO DE LA PLATA. SECCION ZOOLOGIA. See Museums.

REVISTA IBERICA DE PARASITOLOGIA. V. 1- Jan. 1941-. 0034-9623. Periodical. SP. Spanish. qt. Consejo Super Invest Cientific, Vitruvio 8, Apartado 14 458, 28006 Madrid Spain. Ind/Abst Life Sci. Collect., Excerpta Med., Biol. Abstr., Chem. Abstr., Bibliogr. Agric. LC QL757. DD 595.1105. NLM W1 RE5927. CODEN RIPAAE.

REVISTA PERUANA DE ENTOMOLOGIA. V. 1- June 1958-. 0080-2425. PE. Spanish. mo. $8.00. Sociedad Entomologica del Peru, Apartado 4796, Lima 100 Peru. Ed Pedro G Aguilar. (cum index). bk rev. adv acc. Circ 1,000. Pure and applied entomology (medical, agricultural and veterinary aspects of insects and related arthropods).

REVUE DE NEMATOLOGIE. V. 1- 1978-. 0183-9187. Periodical. FR. French (English). sa. 96 Domestic, $20.00 US. Service des Publications de l'Orstom, 70-74 Route d'Aulnay, 93140 Bondy France. Ind/Abst Life Sci. Collect., Excerpta Med., Biol. Abstr., Chem. Abstr. LC QL391.N4. DD 595.182005. CODEN RNEMDX.

REVUE DE ZOOLOGIE AFRICAINE. Began with Mar. 1974 issue. 0771-0488. Periodical. French. qt. $60.00. Revue de Zoologie Africaine, B-1980 Musee Royal l'Afriq Cen, Tervuren Belgium. Tel 32 2 7675401. Ed H M Andre. Ind/Abst Life Sci. Collect., Biol. Abstr., GeoRef, Bibliogr. Agric. LC QL1. DD 591.9605. CODEN RZOABR. Index in last issue of volume - attached. bk rev. adv acc. Original contributions and short communications dealing with the study of African fauna, especially that of Central Africa in all aspects. Revue de Zoologie et de Botanique Africaines.

REVUE D'ENTOMOLOGIE DU QUEBEC. Vol. 29, No. 1 (Jan. 1984)-. 0825-1215. Periodical. CN. French (text also in English). ir. $20.00. Societe d'Entomologie du Quebec, a/s Claude Bouchard, Complexe Scientifique D-1-54, 2700 rue Einstein, Ste-Foy Quebec G1P 3W8 Canada. DD 595.709714. Annales de la Societe Entomologique du Quebec, 0037-9301.

REVUE FRANCAISE D'ENTOMOLOGIE. V. 1-31, 1934-64. 0181-0863. Periodical. FR. French. qt. 420 Domestic. AALEM, 45 rue de Buffon, F-75005 Paris France. Tel (1) 43 36 06 06. Ind/Abst Biol. Abstr. LC QL461. DD 595.7005. CODEN RFENDE. bk rev. adv acc. Circ 300. (ctrl). Entomology, taxonomy, biogeography.

REVUE SUISSE DE ZOOLOGIE. Vol. 1- 1893-. 0035-418X. Periodical. SZ. French. ir. $113.79. Museum d'Histoire Naturelle, 1 Route de Malagnou, Boite Postale 434, 1211 Geneva Switzerland 6. Ind/Abst Life Sci. Collect., Biol. Abstr., Chem. Abstr., Index Med., Sci. Cit. Index, abr. Ed. LC QL1. DD 590.5. NLM W1 RE969. CODEN RSZOA6. (cum index). Recueil Zoologique Suisse.

RINGING & MIGRATION. VAT Ringing and Migration. V. 1- 1975-. 0307-8698. Periodical. UK. English. sa. $13.80. British Trust for Ornithology, Beech Grove, Tring Herts HP23 5NR England. Ind/Abst Life Sci. Collect., Biol. Abstr. LC QL671. DD 598.20723. CODEN RIMIDQ.

RSPB BIRD LIFE. Main/Corp Royal Society for the Protection of Birds. VAT Royal Society for the Protection of Birds Bird Life. UK. English. an. 1.50. Royal Society for the Protection of Birds, Berkshire House Queen Street, Maidenhead England. LC QL690.G7. DD 598.294105.

SALAMANDRA. V. 1- Sept. 1965-. 0036-3375. Periodical. GW. German (with English summaries). qt. $20.00. Museum Alexander Konig, Adenduerallee 150,

Zoology-Vertebrate and Invertebrate

D-53000 Bonn 1 West Germany. **Ind/Abst** Biol. Abstr., Life Sci. Collect. **LC** QL640. **CODEN** SALAAH. bk rev. **Circ** 4,000. Reports and scientific news regarding herpetology (natural history of reptiles and amphibians).

SANCTUARY ASIA. *See* Conservation & Natural Resources.

SAUGETIERKUNDLICHE MITTEILUNGEN. *See* Biology.

SBORNIK TRUDOV ZOOLOGICHESKOGO MUZEIA. **Main/Corp** Moskovskii Universitet. Zoologicheskii Muzei. **VFOAT** Archives du Musee Zoologique de l'Universite de Moscou. V. 8- 1961-. Periodical. UR. Russian. ir. **Ind/Abst** Chem. Abstr. **CODEN** SZMMAT. *Sbornik Trudov Gosudarstvennogo Zoologicheskogo Muzeia.*

SCHWEIZERISCHE BIENEN-ZEITUNG. Vols. 1-9, 1869-77. 0036-7540. Periodical. SZ. German. mo. $12.37. Sauerlaender AG, CH-5001 Aarau Switzerland. **Ind/Abst** Bibliogr. Agric. (cum index).

THE SCIENTIFIC REPORTS. **Main/Corp** Tokyo. Whales Research Institute. 1948-. Periodical. English. ir.

SCOTTISH BEEKEEPER. V. 1- July 1924-. 0370-8918. Periodical. UK. English. mo. 5.00. Scottish Beekeepers Association, 97 Old Edinburg Road, Inverness IV2 3HT Scotland. **Tel** 0682 2028. **Ed** A Ferguson. **Ind/Abst** Bibliogr. Agric. adv acc. **Circ** 1,500. (ctrl). All about beekeeping.

SCOTTISH BIRDS. V. 1- Autumn 1958-. 0036-9144. Periodical. UK. English. qt. $19.16. Scottish Ornithologists Club, 21 Regent Terrace, Endinburgh EH7 5BT Scotland. **Ind/Abst** Life Sci. Collect., Biol. Abstr., Ref. Source. **LC** QL690.S4. **CODEN** SCTBB7.

SEA PEN. Began with V. 20, No. 1, Jan. 1976. 0700-9275. Periodical. CN. English. mo. Vancouver Public Aquarium, PO Box 3232, Vancouver British Columbia V6B 3X8 Canada. **Tel** (604)685-3364. **Ed** Stefani I Hewlett. **DD** 590.744971133. bk rev. **Circ** 14,000. (ctrl). Membership news and activities, marine biology, new exhibits, field trips, photographs, research projects and new specimens. *0042-2495.*

LE SECTEUR AVICOLE EN . . . . **Series/Titl** Production Animale. FR. French. an. 4 Avenue de Saint-Mande, 75570 Paris Cedex 12 France.

SEITAI NO KAGAKU. *See* Biology.

SERIE DIDACTICA - FACULTAD DE AGRONOMIA Y ZOOTECNIA. UNIVERSIDAD NACIONAL TUCUMAN. (SERIE DIDACTICA). No. 1-. 0325-2493. Monographic Series. AG. Spanish. ir. **Ind/Abst** Life Sci. Collect., Bibliogr. Agric.

SERIES ENTOMOLOGICA. V. 1-. 0080-8954. Monographic Series. English. ir. Kluwer Boston Inc, 190 Old Derby Street, Hingham MA 02043. **Ind/Abst** Biol. Abstr. **CODEN** SEENAF.

SHELLFISH DIGEST. **VFOAT** Shellfish Digest Series. 0732-9180. US. English. Shellfish Digest Series, 115 North Race Street, PO Box 469, Georgetown DE 19947. **LC** QL401. **DD** 591.92.

SHOU LEI HSUEH-PAO. **VFOAT** Acta Theriologica Sinica. Vol. 1, No. 1 (June 1981)-. Chinese (with abstracts in English). sa. 1.30. Chung-kuo Chi Shu Tien, PO Box 2820, Peking Ching Mainland. **LC** QL700. **DD** 599.

SHRIKE. (THE SHRIKE). V. 1- Jan./Feb. 1976-. 0382-9618. Periodical. CN. English. ir. $2.00. Ottawa Field Naturalists Club, Box 3264 Postal Station C, Ottawa Ontario K1Y 4J5 Canada. **DD** 598.2971384.

SKAGEN FUGELSTATION. **Main/Corp** Dansk Ornithologisk Forening. Danish. ir. Dansk Ornithologisk Forening, Hojen Station Flagbakkevej, Kbenhavn Denmark. **LC** QL690.D3.

SMITHSONIAN CONTRIBUTIONS TO ZOOLOGY. No. 1-. 0081-0282. Monographic Series. US. English. Smithsonian Institute Press, PO Box 1579, Washington DC 20013. **Ind/Abst** Life Sci. Collect., GeoRef, Bibliogr. Agric., Biol. Abstr. **LC** QL1. **DD** 591.08 S. **NLM** W1 SM454N. **CODEN** SMCZBU.

SNAKE. (THE SNAKE). V. 1- Aug. 1969-. 0386-3425. Periodical. JA. English (articles in English or Japanese). sa. $27.00. Japan Snake Institute, Yabuzuka-honmachi/Nittagun, Gunma Prefecture 379-23 Japan. **Tel** 0277(78) 5193. **Ed** Y Sawai. **Ind/Abst** Biol. Abstr., Chem. Abstr. **LC** QL640. **DD** 615.942. **NLM** W1 SN105. **CODEN** NJGKBV. bk rev. adv acc. The journal of the Japan Snake Institute and publishes general papers on the biology of snakes, snake venom and snakebites.

SOUTH AFRICAN ANIMAL LIFE. V. 1- 1955-. Periodical. text mostly in English. ir. Swedish Natural Science Research Council, Editorial Service, PO Box 2316, S104 35 Stockholm Sweden. **Ed** Bertil Hamstrom, Per Brinck and Gustaf Rudebeck. **LC** QL337.S65.

SOUTH AFRICAN BEE JOURNAL. **VFOAT** Suid Afrikaanse Byetydskrif. V. 1- April 1921-. 0038-2019. Periodical. SA. English. bm. $4.96. South African Federation of Bookeepers, PO Box 47198, Parklands 2121, Johannesburg South Africa.

SOUTH AFRICAN JOURNAL OF ZOOLOGY. **VFOAT** Suid-Afrikaanse Tydskrif vir Dierkunde. V. 14-. 0254-1858. Periodical. SA. English (Afrikaans). qt. 20.00. Bureau for Scientific Publications, PO Box 1758, Pretoria 0001 South Africa. **Tel** (012)260207. **Ed** H R Hepburn. **Ind/Abst** Life Sci. Collect., Biol. Abstr., Chem. Abstr., Sci. Cit. Index, Abr. Ed. **LC** QL337.S65. **NLM** W1 SO9058. **CODEN** SAJZDH. bk rev. **Circ** 800. Original research articles on any aspect of zoology in Africa, especially ecology, ethology, physiology and taxonomy. *Zoologica Africana, 0044-5096.*

SOUTH AUSTRALIAN ORNITHOLOGIST. V. 1- 1914-. 0038-2973. Periodical. AT. English. sa. $9.60. South Australian Ornithological Association, c/o South Australian Museum, North Terrace, Adelaide SA 5000 Australia. **Ed** Leo Joseph. **Ind/Abst** Life Sci. Collect. **CODEN** SAORAF. bk rev. **Circ** 700. (ctrl). General ornithology (Australian).

SOUTH DAKOTA BIRD NOTES. V. 1- (No. 1-). 0038-3252. Periodical. US. English. qt. $6.00. South Dakota Ornithologists Union, Route 4 Box 252, Brookings SD 57006. **Tel** (605)693-4572. **Ed** Dan Tallman. **Ind/Abst** Biol. Abstr. **CODEN** SDBNAR. (cum index). bk rev. **Circ** 350. Publication devoted to biology and ecology of South Dakota birds. A seasonal report is included.

SOUTHEASTERN AREA SOUTHERN PINE BEETLE OUTBREAK STATUS. Jan.1974-. Periodical. English. ir.

THE SOUTHWESTERN ENTOMOLOGIST. V. 1- Mar. 1976-. 0147-1724. Periodical. US. Multilingual (English, Spanish). qt. $20.00. Southwestern Entomologist, Department of Entomology, c/o Dr W Scott Fargo, Oklahoma State University, Stillwater OK 74078. **Ed** Don Rummel. **Ind/Abst** Life Sci. Collect., Pestdoc, Ringdoc, Vetdoc, Biol. Abstr., Chem. Abstr., Sci. Cit. Index, Abr. Ed. **CODEN** SENTDD. **Circ** 500. Research reports on insects impacting on agricultural production.

SPECIAL PUBLICATION - AMERICAN SOCIETY OF MAMMALOGISTS. (SPECIAL PUBLICATION). No. 1-. 0569-8219. Monographic Series. US. English. ir. American Society of Mammalogists, Shippensburg University, Shippensburg PA 17257. **Tel** (717)532-1407. **Ed** Timothy E Lawlor. **Ind/Abst** Biol. Abstr. **CODEN** AMAMBL. Monographs which deal with selected topics in mammalogy.

SPECIAL PUBLICATION - CUSHMAN FOUNDATION FOR FORAMINIFERAL RESEARCH. **Main/Corp** Cushman Foundation for Foraminiferal Research. No. 1-. 0070-2242. Monographic Series. US. English. ir. Cushman Foundation, F Collier, E-501 US National Museum, Washington DC 20560. **Ind/Abst** GeoRef. **CODEN** SPCFAO. *Cushman Laboratory for Foraminiferal Research Special Publication, 0197-548X.*

SPECIAL PUBLICATION - ENTOMOLOGICAL SOCIETY OF AMERICA. **Main/Corp** Entomological Society of America. 0363-8634. Monographic Series. US. English. $3.50. Entomological Society of America, 4603 Calvert Road, College Park MD 20740. **Ind/Abst** Chem. Abstr. **LC** UNC. **CODEN** SPEADM.

THE SPEEDY BEE. (SPEEDY BEE). V. 1- Feb. 1972-. 0190-6798. Periodical. US. English. mo. $10.75. The Speedy Bee, PO Box 998, Jesup GA 31545. **Tel** (912)427-4018. **Ed** Troy Fore. bk rev. adv acc. **Circ** 9,000. Tabloid newspaper for beekeepers and honey industry. News, how-to's, features, advertising.

SPIXIANA. 1/1 (1 Aug. 1977)-. 0341-8391. Periodical. English (French or German). ty. 40.00 Members, 100.00 Others. Zoologische Staatssammlung Munchen, Maria-Ward-Strasse 1B, D-8000 Munchen 19 West Germany. **Ind/Abst** Life Sci. Collect., Biol. Abstr., Bibliogr. Agric. **LC** QL1. **DD** 590.5. **CODEN** SPIXD9. *Opuscula Zoologica, 0030-4158; Veroffentlichungen der Zoologischen Staatssammlung Munchen, 0077-2135.*

SPRINGER SERIES IN EXPERIMENTAL ENTOMOLOGY. 1-. 0172-6188. Monographic Series. US. English. Springer Verlag-New York Inc, 175 5th Avenue, New York NY 10010. **Tel** (212)460-1584. Topics include techniques in pheromone research, and neurochemical techniques in insects.

STEENSTRUPIA. Vol. 1, No. 1 (Nov. 2, 1970)-. 0375-2909. Monographic Series. DK. English (English). ir. Steenstrupia, Universitetsparken 15, DK-2100 Copenhagen Denmark. **Ind/Abst** Life Sci. Collect., Biol. Abstr. **LC** QL1. **DD** 591.05. **CODEN** STRUB3.

STROITEL'STVO GEL'MINTOLOGICHESKOI NAUKI I PRAKTIKI V SSSR. Vol. 1- 1962-. Periodical. UR. Russian. ir.

STUDIA ENTOMOLOGICA. (STUDIA ENTOMOLOGICA : REVISTA INTERNACIONAL DE ENTOMOLOGIA). 1-3, 1952-55. 0585-5098. English (French, Portuguese or Spanish). ir. $12.00. Editoras Vozes Ltda, Caixa Postal 23, Petropolis Brazil. **Ind/Abst** Life Sci. Collect. **LC** QL461.

STUDIES ON NEOTROPICAL FAUNA AND ENVIRONMENT. V. 11- June 1976-. 0165-0521. Periodical. NE. English (articles in French, Spanish, Portuguese or German with English summaries). qt. 100.-. Swets & Zeitlinger BV, 347 Heereweg, 2161 Ca Lisse The Netherlands. **Tel** 02521-19113. **Ed** E J Fittkau. **Ind/Abst** Life Sci. Collect., Biol. Abstr., Bibliogr. Agric. **LC** QL235. **DD** 591.98. **CODEN** SNFEDP. bk rev. adv acc. **Circ** 600. International journal dealing with the ecology, systematics and distribution of the neotropical fauna. *Studies on the Neotropical Fauna.*

STUDIES ON THE FAUNA OF CURACAO AND OTHER ISLANDS. (STUDIES ON THE FAUNA OF CURACAO AND OTHER CARIBBEAN ISLANDS). **Series Corp** Natuurwetenschappelijke Studiekring voor Suriname en de Nederlandse Antillen Uitgaven - Natuurwetenschappelijke Studiekring voor Suriname en de Nederlandse Antillen. V. 4- June 1953-. 0166-5189. Periodical. NE. English. ir. Foundation for Scientific Research in Surinam and the Netherlands Antilles, c/o Zoology Lab, Plomptorengrachi 9 11, Utrecht Netherlands. **Tel** 030-392478. **Ed** L J Westermann-Van der Steen and P Wagenaar Hummelinck. **Ind/Abst** Bibliogr. Agric. **LC** QH7. **DD** 591.9428. **Circ** 500. Zoological research on the Caribbean Islands, emphasis on the Netherlands Antilles, but also includes tropical American mainland. The articles deals with species occuring also on the islands. *Studies of the Fauna of Curacao, Aruba, Bonaire and the Venezuelan Islands.*

STUDIES ON THE FAUNA OF SURINAME AND OTHER GUYANAS. V. 1- 1957-. English. ir. Foundation for Scientific Research in Surinam and the Netherlands, c/o Zool Lab Plompetorengrachi, 9-11 3512 CA Utrecht Netherlands. **Tel** 030-392478. **Ed** P Wagenaar Hummelinck and D C Geijskes. **LC** QH7, QL246.2. **DD** 500.108 S, 591.9883. **Circ** 800. The fauna of the northern part of South America with emphasis on Surinam.

STUDIES ON THE MORPHOLOGY AND SYSTEMATICS OF SCALE INSECTS. No. 1- Mar. 1969-. 0271-6348. Monographic Series. US. English. ir. **LC** AS36. **DD** 081 S.

A SUMMARY OF THE MID-WINTER BALD EAGLE SURVEY IN WASHINGTON. 1979-. 0731-3535. US. English. an. **LC** QL696.F32. **DD** 598.96.

SWARA. Vol. 1, No. 1 (July-Aug. 1978)-. Periodical. English. bm. $15.00 Foreign. Keith Tucker Chief American Representative, PO Box 82002, San Diego CA 92139. **LC** QL337.E25. **DD** 333.954160968.

SYMPOSIA OF THE ZOOLOGICAL SOCIETY OF LONDON. No. 1-. 0084-5612. UK. English. ir. Academic Press, 24-28 Oval Road, London NW1 7DX England. **Ind/Abst** Life Sci. Collect., GeoRef, Chem. Abstr., Biol. Abstr., Bibliogr. Index Geol. **LC** QL1. **DD** 591. **NLM** W1 SY432Q. **CODEN** SZSLAM.

SYNOPSES OF THE BRITISH FAUNA. NEW SERIES. No. 1-. 0082-1101. Monographic Series. UK. English. ir. Linnean Society, Burlington House/Piccadilly, London W1 England. **Ind/Abst** Biol.

Abstr., GeoRef. **CODEN** SBFSDH. *Synopses of the British Fauna.*

SYNOPSIS OF THE HERPETOFAUNA OF MEXICO. V. 1- 1971-. Monographic Series. US. English. ir. John Johnson Books, Rural Free Delivery 2, North Bennington VT 05257. **Tel** (802)442-6738. Ed Hobart M Smith and Rozella B Smith. A series of books intended for the serious herpetologist.

SYSTEMA HELMINTHUM. 1958-. English. ir. Interscience Publishers, 605 3rd Avenue, New York NY 10016. **LC** QL386. **DD** 595.1.

SYSTEMATIC ENTOMOLOGY. V. 1- Jan. 1976-. 0307-6970. Periodical. UK. English. qt. 55.00 Domestic, 66.00 Foreign. Blackwell Scientific Publishing Ltd, PO Box 88, Oxford OX2 0EL England. **Tel** 0865-240201. **Ed** I Gauld and J Cox. **Ind/Abst** Life Sci. Collect., Energy Inf. Abstr., Environ. Abstr., Biol. Abstr., GeoRef, Ref. Source, Bibliogr. Agric., Sci. Cit. Index, Abr. Ed., Bibliogr. Index Geol. **LC** QL461. **DD** 595.70012. **CODEN** SYENDM. bk rev. adv acc. Taxonomy and systematics of insects. *Journal of Entomology. Series B: Taxonomy & Systematics.*

SYSTEMATIC PARASITOLOGY. V. 1- Sept. 1979-. 0165-5752. Periodical. NE. English. qt. 245.00 Domestic, $93.00. Kluwer Academic Publishers Distribution Center, PO Box 322, 3300 AH Dordrecht Netherlands. **Ed** D I Gibson. **Ind/Abst** Biol. Abstr., Sci. Cit. Index, Abr. Ed. **LC** QL757. **DD** 591.5249. **NLM** W1 SY696. **CODEN** SYPAD4. adv acc. **Circ** 350. Publishes papers on the systematics, taxonomy and nomenclature of the nematoda, monogenea, digenea, cestoda, acanthocephala, aspidobothria, cestodaria, anthropoda, hymenopterans, mites, ticks, etc.

SYSTEMATIC ZOOLOGY. V. 1- Spring 1952-. 0039-7989. Periodical. US. English. qt. $26.00. Systematic Zoology, National Museum of Natural History, Washington DC 20560. **Tel** (202)357-2964. **Ed** Gary Schnell. **Ind/Abst** Life Sci. Collect., GeoRef, Biol. Abstr., Chem. Abstr., Index Med., Nucl. Sci. Abstr., Bibliogr. Agric., Biol. Agric. Index, Sci. Cit. Index, Abr. Ed., Comput. Rev., Bibliogr. Index Geol. **LC** QH83. **DD** 591.012. **NLM** W1 SY69. **CODEN** SYZOAP. (cum index). bk rev. **Circ** 2,500. (ctrl).

TAXIDERMY REVIEW. 0199-2988. Periodical. US. English. bm. $15.00. Taxidermy Review, 747 Santa Fe, Denver CO 80204. **LC** QL63. **DD** 579.405. *Wide World of Taxidermy.*

TAXIDERMY TODAY. 0279-9731. Periodical. US. English. qt. $18.00. Taxidermy Today, 229 Gadsden Street, Chester SC 29706. **Tel** (803)-377-7211. **Ed** Terry Ehrlich. **LC** QL63. **DD** 579.405. bk rev. adv acc. **Circ** 3,000. Trade journal for taxidermists and related artists, both professional and hobbiest. Contains how-to articles, product and services reviews, introductions and sources of supplies.

TECHNICAL COMMUNICATION OF THE COMMONWEALTH INSTITUTE OF HELMINTHOLOGY. **Main/Corp** Commonwealth Institute of Helminthology. No. 42- 1971-. Monographic Series. UK. English. Commonwealth Agricultural Bureaux, Farnham House, Farnham Royal Slough SL2 3BN England. **LC** QL386.A1. **DD** 595.108. *Technical Communication of the Commonwealth Bureau of Helminthology.*

TECHNICAL MONOGRAPH - ZOOLOGICAL SURVEY OF INDIA. **Main/Corp** Zoological Survey of India. No. 1- 1978-. Monographic Series. English. ir.

TECHNICAL NOTE - BUREAU OF LAND MANAGEMENT, U.S. DEPARTMENT OF THE INTERIOR. (TECHNICAL NOTE). **VAT** Technical Note - Bureau of Land Management, United States Department of the Interior. 0098-6860. Monographic Series. US. English. Denver Service Center, Federal Center Building 50, Denver CO 80225. **LC** QL84.2. **DD** 639.90973.

TECHNIQUES IN PROTEIN BIOSYNTHESIS. Ceased with V. 3, 1973. US. English. ir. Academic Press, 4805 Sand Lake Road, Orlando FL 32819. **Tel** (305)345-4100. **LC** QP551. **DD** 591.19296.

TENNEN KINENBUTSU NARA NO SHIKA CHOSA HOKOKU. **VFOAT** Nara No Shika Chosa Hokoku. 1974-. JA. Japanese. ir. Kasuga Kenshokai, 160 Kasugano, Nara 630 Japan. **LC** QL737.U55.

TENNESSEE COOPERATIVE ECONOMIC INSECT SURVEY REPORT : ANNUAL SUMMARY. **Main/Corp** Tennessee. Division of Plant Industries. Insect Survey Committee. US. English. an. Survey Entomologist/Tennnessee Department of Agriculture, Box 40627, Melrose Station, Nashville TN 37204. **LC** SB824.T2. **DD** 632.709768.

TENNESSEE ECONOMIC PEST REPORT, ANNUAL SUMMARY. *See* Agriculture.

TERRA. Periodical. BE. Dutch. ir. Verenigning voor Terrariumkunde en Herpetologie, Neptunusstraat 62, 2600 Berchem Belgium.

THALASSIA JUGOSLAVICA. V. 1- 1956-. 0495-4025. Periodical. YU. Serbo-Croatian -R (English or German). ir. **Ind/Abst** Life Sci. Collect., Energy Res. Abstr., Chem. Abstr. **LC** QL1. **CODEN** THJUAP.

TIEG. **Main/Corp** Teen International Entomology Group. **VAT** Teen International Entomology Group. V. 9- Sept. 1974-. 0272-3077. Periodical. US. English. sa. $7.00. Tieg Editor, Department of Entomology/ Michigan State University, East Lansing MI 48824. **Tel** (517)353-3890. **Ed** Gary A Dunn. bk rev. adv acc. **Circ** 450. Entomological information: life histories, collecting, reading, identification, illustrations, poems, cartoons, field notes, book reviews, trading post, specimen exchange network, awards programs and games. *Tieg Newsletter.*

TIER (BERN, SWITZERLAND : 1960). (TIER). Oct. 1960-June 1981. 0040-7291. Periodical. SZ. German. mo. 62.40. Hallwag AG, Nordring 4, CH-3001 Bern Switzerland. **Tel** (031)42 31 31. **Ed** Peter V Kulig and Bernhard Grzimek. bk rev. adv acc. **Circ** 220,000. The international magazine for animals, men and nature.

TIJDSCHRIFT VOOR ENTOMOLOGIE. Vol. 1-. 0040-7496. Periodical. NE. Multilingual. ir. Nederlandsche Entomol Vereen, Plantage Middenlaan 64, Amsterdam 1004 Netherlands. **LC** QL461. *Handelingen.*

TRAITE DE ZOOLOGIE. Vol. 1-. Monographic Series. French. ir. **Ed** Pierre P Grasse.

TRANSACTIONS OF THE AMERICAN ENTOMOLOGICAL SOCIETY. **Main/Corp** American Entomological Society. V. 17- 1890-. 0002-8320. Periodical. US. English. qt. $18.00. American Entomological Society, Academy of Natural Sciences, Philadelphia PA 19103. **Tel** (215)561-3978. **Ed** Daniel Otte. **Ind/Abst** Life Sci. Collect. **DD** 595. **Circ** 500. Classification, taxonomy, systematics, and ecology of insects. *Transactions of the American Entomological Society and Proceedings of the Entomological Section of the Academy of Natural Sciences.*

TRANSACTIONS OF THE SHIKOKU ENTOMOLOGICAL SOCIETY. **VFOAT** Shikoku Konchu Gakkai Kaiho. Began with issue for Jan. 1950. 0037-3680. JA. English. sa. Japan Publications Trading Company, PO Box 5030, Tokyo International, Tokyo 100-31 Japan. **Ind/Abst** Life Sci. Collect., Biol. Abstr., Bibliogr. Agric. **LC** QL461. **CODEN** TSHEAA.

TRANSPORT IN HIGH RESISTANCE EPITHELIA. **Series/Titl** Annual Research Reviews. V. 1- 1977-. 0705-4734. CN. English. ir. Eden Press, 4626 St Catherine Street West, Montreal Quebec H3Z 1S3 Canada. **Ed** T W Ziegler. **DD** 596.0875. **NLM** W1 TR235R.

TRAVAUX DE LA STATION MARINE DE VILLEFRANCHE-SUR-MER. **Main/Corp** Station Marine de Villefranche-Sur-Mer. No. 40- 1975-. FR. French (with added explanation in English). ir. Station Marine de Villefranche-sur-Mer, La Station Marine, 06230 Villefranche-sur-Mer France. *Travaux de la Station Zoologique de Villefranche-sur-Mer.*

TRUBUS. *See* Agriculture.

TSETSE AND TRYPANOSOMIASIS INFORMATION QUARTERLY. *See* Veterinary Medicine, Animal Culture.

TULANE STUDIES IN ZOOLOGY AND BOTANY. Vol. 15, No. 1 (Oct. 16, 1968)-. 0082-6782. Periodical. US. English. ir. $12.50 Domestic, $13.50 Foreign. Tulane University, Department of Botany, 6823 St Charles Avenue, New Orleans LA 70118. **Tel** (504)865-5546. **Ed** Alfred E Smalley. **Ind/Abst** Life Sci. Collect., Biol. Abstr. **LC** QL1. **DD** 574.05. **CODEN** TSZBAN. Botany and zoology of Gulf Coast and Middle America. Invertebrate taxonomy and ecology and plant taxonomy. *Tulane Studies in Zoology, 0090-9246.*

TUNG WU FEN LEI HSUEH PAO. **VFOAT** Acta Zootaxonomica Sinica. Began in 1976. Periodical. CC. Chinese (summaries in English). qt. $15.84. China Publication Centre, PO Box 2820, Beijing China. **LC** QL35L. **DD** 590.12. Index in last issue of volume - attached.

TUNG WU HSUEH CHI KAN. **VFOAT** Sinozoologia. Vol. 1- (May 1981)-. Periodical. Chinese (with summaries in English). ir. Hsin Hua Shu Tien Pei-Ching Fa Hsing so Peking China. **LC** QL1. **DD** 591.

TUNG WU HSUEH PAO. **VFOAT** Acta Zoologica Sinica. 0001-7302. Periodical. CC. Chinese (added tables of contents and summaries in English, French and Russian, (V. 23, No. 2)). qt. China Publication Centre, PO Box 2820, Beijing China. **Ind/Abst** Life Sci. Collect., GeoRef, Biol. Abstr., Chem. Abstr., Bibliogr. Agric., Bibliogr. Index Geol., Sci. Cit. Index, Abr. Ed. **LC** QL1. **DD** 591.05. **NLM** W1 TU724H. **CODEN** TWHPA3.

TUNG WU HSUEH TSA CHIH. **VFOAT** Dongwuxue Zazhi. 0250-3263. Periodical. CC. English. bm. $10.80. China Publication Centre, PO Box 2820, Beijing China. **Ind/Abst** Chem. Abstr., Bibliogr. Agric. **LC** QL1. **CODEN** TWHCDZ.

UNIVERSITY OF CALIFORNIA PUBLICATIONS IN ENTOMOLOGY. V. 1-. 0068-6417. Monographic Series. US. English. ir. University of California Press, 2120 Berkeley Way, Berkeley CA 94720. **Tel** (415)642-4191. **Ind/Abst** Biol. Abstr., GeoRef. **LC** QL461. **CODEN** UCPEAH. **Circ** 900. *University of California Publications. Entomology.*

UNIVERSITY OF CALIFORNIA PUBLICATIONS IN ZOOLOGY. V. 1- Nov. 1902-. 0068-6506. Monographic Series. US. English. ir. University of California Press, 1428 Harbour Way South, Richmond CA 94804. **Tel** (415)642-0061. **Ind/Abst** Biol. Abstr., Chem. Abstr. **CODEN** UCPZAC. **Circ** 1,250.

VAR FAGELVARLD. Vol. 1- 1942-. 0042-2649. Periodical. SW. Swedish. ir. $19.97. Sveriges Ornitologiska Forenin, Box 26011, S-10041 Stockholm Sweden. **LC** QL671. **DD** 598.05.

THE VASCULUM. *See* Biology - Botany.

THE VELIGER. V. 1- June 1958-. 0042-3211. Periodical. US. English. qt. California Malacozoological Society, PO Box 9977, Berkeley CA 94709-9977. **Ed** D W Phillips. **Ind/Abst** Life Sci. Collect., Sel. Water Resour. Abstr., Biol. Abstr., GeoRef, Sci. Cit. Index, Abr. Ed., Bibliogr. Index Geol., Ocean. Abstr. **LC** QL401. **DD** 594.09164. **NLM** W1 VE15K. **CODEN** VLGHAL. bk rev. **Circ** 1,000. Any aspect pertaining to mollusks, such as ecology, reproduction, distribution, taxonomy, paleontology, microbiology, conchology, etc.

VENOMOUS ANIMALS AND THEIR VENOMS. Periodical. US. English. ir. Academic Press, 4805 Sand Lake Road, Orlando FL 32887. **Tel** (305)345-4100. **Ed** W Bucherl, E E Buckley and V Deulofeu.

VENUS. KAIRUIGAKU ZASSHI. **VFOAT** Kairuigaku Zasshi. V. 15, No. 5/8- Oct. 1949-. 0042-3580. Periodical. JA. Japanese (English). qt. $40.00. Malacological Society, 23-23-1 Hyakunin Shinjuku ku, Tokyo 160 Japan. **Tel** 03(364)2311. **Ed** T Okutani & S Nishiwaki. bk rev. **Circ** 1,000. (ctrl). The journal is devoted to publishing original research papers, short notes, book reviews and miscellaneous relation to any field of sciences on the Mollusce. *Japanese Journal of Malacology.*

VERHANDLUNGEN DER DEUTSCHEN ZOOLOGISCHEN GESELLSCHAFT. **Main/Corp** Deutsche Zoologische Gesellschaft. **VFOAT** Proceedings of the German Zoological Society. 0070-4342. German (with English summaries). ir. VCH Publishers Inc, 303 NW 12th Avenue, Deerfield Beach FL 33442. **Tel** (305)428-5566. **Ind/Abst** Life Sci. Collect., GeoRef, Bibliogr. Agric. **CODEN** VDZGAN.

VERHANDLUNGEN DER ORNITHOLOGISCHE GESELLSCHAFT IN BAYERN. **Main/Corp** Ornithologische Gesellschaft in Bayern, Munich. Vol. 1- 1897/98-. Periodical. German. ir. Zoologische Staatssammlung, Maria-Ward-Strasse 1B, D-8000 Munich West Germany. **Ind/Abst** Life Sci. Collect. Index in last issue of volume - attached.

VERKSAMHETEN VID KVISMARE FAGELSTATION. **Main/Corp** Kvismare Fagelstation. **Series Corp** Its Meddelande. Began with Report for 1962. Swedish. ir.

VEROFFENTLICHUNGEN AUS DEM NATURHISTORISCHEN MUSEUM WIEN. *See* Earth Sciences.

Zoology-Vertebrate and Invertebrate

VESTNIK CESKOSLOVENSKE ZOOLOGICKE SPOLECNOSTI. Main/Corp Ceskoslovenska Spolecnost Zoologicka. **VFOAT** Memoires de la Societe Zoologique Tchecoslovaque de Prague. Vol. 2-. Periodical. English (Czech, French, and German). qt. 99.-. Kubon and Sagner, Postfach 34 01 08, D8 Muenchen 34 West Germany. **Tel** (089)52 20 27. Ed M Kunst and K Hurka. **DD** 590.62437. bk rev. **Circ** 850. Publishes articles devoted to reporting recent Czech studies in zoology. Subjects discussed are: invertebrate and vertebrate zoology, morphology, anatomy, physiology, bionomics, phylogeny, taxonomy, zoogeography. *Zprava o Cinnosti Ceskoslovenske Zoologicke Spolecnosti.*

VESTNIK ZOOLOGII. **VFOAT** Zoological Record. 1967-. 0084-5604. Periodical. UR. Russian (table of contents and summaries in English). bm. $19.00. Victor Kamkin Inc (74084), 12224 Parklawn Drive, Rockville MD 20852. **Tel** (301)881-5973. **Ind/Abst** Life Sci. Collect., Biol. Abstr., GeoRef, Chem. Abstr., Bibliogr. Agric. NLM W1 VE845B. **CODEN** VEZOAK.

VIDENSKABELIGE MEDDELELSER FRA DANSK NATURHISTORISK FORENING. See Natural History.

LA VIE DES BETES. Periodical. French. ir. B P 559-8020293, Versailles France. LC QL1. **DD** 591.05. *Betes et Nature.*

VIE ET MILIEU (PARIS, FRANCE : 1980). *See* Earth Sciences - Oceanography.

VIRGINIA AVIFAUNA. No. 1- Dec. 1957-. 0505-7043. Monographic Series. US. English. ir. Virginia Society of Ornithology, 520 Rainbow Forest Drive, Lynchburg VA 24502. **DD** 598.2.

DIE VOGELWARTE. V. 15- Dec. 1948-. 0049-6650. Periodical. GW. German. sa. Vogelzug-Verlag, Duerren Hofstr 16, D-776 Moeggingen West Germany.

DIE VOGELWELT. 70.- Yearly Volume. 0042-7993. Periodical. GW. German. bm. Duncker & Humblot Verlag, Dietrich-Schafer Weg 9, PO 330, 1 Berlin 41 West Germany. **Tel** (030)7912026. Ed R Berndt, E Bezzel, K Haarmann and C Koinig MA. **Ind/Abst** Life Sci. Collect., Biol. Abstr. **CODEN** VGLWAM. adv acc. **Circ** 1,300. The study of birds and protection of birds. *Deutsche Vogelwelt.*

VOGELWELT. BEIHEFT. No. 1- 1968-. Periodical. GW. German. ir. Duncker und Humblot Verlag, Dietrich-Schafer-Weg 9, 1000 Berlin 41 West Germany.

DIE VOGELWELT; ZEITSCHRIFT FUR VOGELSCHUTZ UND VOGELKUNDE. Began publication in 1876. 0042-7993. Periodical. German. ir. LC QL671.

WAS. WESTERN APICULTURAL SOCIETY JOURNAL. (WAS, WESTERN APICULTURAL SOCIETY JOURNAL). Main/Corp Western Apicultural Society of North America. **VFOAT** Western Apicultural Society Journal. V. 1- Apr. 1978-. 0199-221X. Periodical. US. English. bm. $15.00 Members, $5.00 Nonmembers. WAS, 115 Court Street, Woodland CA 95695.

WATASHITACHI NO SHIZEN. NATURE. See Conservation & Natural Resources.

WATERFOWL STATUS REPORT. See Conservation & Natural Resources.

DIE WELT DER TIERE. Periodical. German. ir. 23.40. Kilda-Verlag, D-4402 Greven, Munsterstrasse 71, Greven West Germany. **Ind/Abst** Life Sci. Collect. LC QL81.5.

WESTERN BIRDS. V. 4-. 0160-1121. Periodical. US. English. qt. $14.00. WFO/Garth Alton, 17 Camino Lenada, Orinda CA 94563. Ed Alan M Craig. **Ind/Abst** Biol. Abstr. **CODEN** WSBDAA. bk rev. adv acc. **Circ** 1,100. A journal of field ornithology for active birders and professional ornithologists. Articles on Avian ecology, biology, identification. *California Birds,* 0045-3897.

THE WHALE REPORT. 0270-2851. Periodical. US. English. qt. Center for Environmental Education Inc, 1925 K Street NW/Suite 206, Washington DC 20006.

WILDFOWL CARVING AND COLLECTING. **VFOAT** Wildfowl Carving & Collecting. 0886-3407. Periodical. US. English. qt. PO Box 1831, Harrisburg PA 17105.

WILDLIFE MONOGRAPHS. No. 1- Mar. 1958-. 0084-0173. Monographic Series. US. English. ir. Wildlife Society, 5410 Grosvenor Lane, Bethesda MD 20814. **Ind/Abst** Life Sci. Collect., Can. Environ., Energy Inf. Abstr., Environ. Abstr., Biol. Abstr. LC QL1. **DD** 690.05. **CODEN** WLMOAF.

THE WILSON BULLETIN. V. 6- 1894-. 0043-5643. Periodical. US. English. qt. Ornithological Society North America, PO Box 21618, Columbus OH 43221. **Tel** (603)488-4655. Ed Peter Stettenheim. **Ind/Abst** Biol. Abstr., Can. Environ., GeoRef, Life Sci. Collect., Ref. Source, Gen. Sci. Index, Sci. Cit. Index, Abr. Ed., Bibliogr. Index Geol. **DD** 598. **CODEN** WILBAI. bk rev. adv acc. **Circ** 3,500. Also available on microfilm from University Microfilms. Articles are based on original studies of birds and general notes that describe observations of particular interest. Contributions are of interest both to professional and advanced amateurs. *Journal of the Wilson Ornithological Chapter of the Agassiz Association.*

WINGTIPS (LANSING, N.Y.). (WINGTIPS). Began in 1984. 8756-4505. Periodical. US. English. qt. $10.00. Bluestone Publishing, Box 226, Lansing NY 14882. **DD** 598.

WOODCOCK STATUS REPORT. Main/Corp United States. Fish and Wildlife Service. Series/Ttl Special Scientific Report—Wildlife. US. English. an. US Department of Interior Fish & Wildlife Service, Washington DC 20240. LC SK361, QL696.C48. **DD** 639.990973 S, 333.95. *Woodcock Status Report.*

YADORIGA. **VFOAT** Yadoriga. 0513-417X. Japanese. ir. LC QL541.

YANGBONGGYE. **VFOAT** Korean Bee Journal. Periodical. Korean. mo. 2.500. Yangbonggye SA, 29 Pongsan-Dong, Taegu Korea 630. LC SF521.

YEARBOOK OF HERPETOLOGY. **VFOAT** HISS Yearbook of Herpetology. V. 1- 1974-. 0098-2644. US. English. an. American Museum of Natural History, Central Park West at 79th Street, New York NY 10024. LC QL640. **DD** 598.105.

YONGU POGO (KORYO TAEHAKKYO. PUSOL HANGUK KONCHUNG YONGUSO). (YONGU POGO). **VFOAT** Entomological Research Bulletin. Began with Vol. for 1965. Periodical. KO. English (Korean). ir. Korean Entomological Institute Korea University, 126-1 5 Anam-dong Sungbuk-ku, Seoul 132 Korea. LC QL461.

ZBORNIK RADOVA O ENTOMOFAUNI SR SRBIJE. **VFOAT** Recueil des Travaux sur la Faune d'Insectes de la Serbie. Vol. 1-. Periodical. Serbo-Croatian -C (summaries in English, French, or German). ir. LC QL482.Y8.

ZEITSCHRIFT DER ARBEITSGEMEINSCHAFT OSTERRICHISCHER ENTOMOLOGEN. Vol. 1- 1949-. GW. German. qt. $6.08. W E Saarbach GMBH, Postfach 101610, C-5000 Koln 1 West Germany. **Tel** 02 21 23 46 31.

ZEITSCHRIFT FUR ANGEWANDTE ENTOMOLOGIE. **VFOAT** Journal of Applied Entomology. Volume 1-. 0044-2240. Periodical. US. English (German). ir. $394.70. Paul Parey Scientific Publishing, 35 West 38th Street #3W, New York NY 10018. **Tel** (212)730-0518. Ed Wolfgang Schwenke. **Ind/Abst** Life Sci. Collect., Pestdoc, Ringdoc, Vetdoc, Curr. Contents, Agric. Biol. Environ. Sci., Bibliogr. Agric., Biol. Abstr., Energy Res. Abstr., Chem. Abstr. LC SB599. **DD** 632.705. NLM W1 ZE231N. **CODEN** ZANEAE. bk rev. adv acc. **Circ** 1,000. Presents original articles on current research in entomology applied to agriculture, forestry, biomedical areas, food and feed storage.

ZEITSCHRIFT FUR ANGEWANDTE ZOOLOGIE. BEIHEFTE. No. 1-. 0514-2563. Monographic Series. German (summaries in English). ir. Duncker & Humblot Verlag, Dietrich Schafer Weg 9, 1000 Berlin 41 West Germany. Ed H Kemper.

ZEITSCHRIFT FUR SAUGETIERKUNDE. See Biology.

ZEITSCHRIFT FUR TIERPHYSIOLOGIE, TIERERNAHRUNG UND FUTTERMITTELKUNDE. **VFOAT** Journal of Animal Physiology and Animal Nutrition. Vo. 1- 1938-. 0044-3565. Periodical. US. English, German, French with summaries in English and French. ir. 267.30. Paul Parey Scientific Publisher, 35 West 38th Street #3W, New York NY 10018. **Tel** (212)730-0518. Ed K D Guenther and M Kirchgessner. **Ind/Abst** Biol. Abstr., Index Med., Chem. Abstr., Nutr. Abstr Rev., Index Vet., Vet. Bull., Vetdoc, Curr. Contents, Agric. Biol. Environ. Sci., Chem. Abstr., Sci. Cit. Index, Abr. Ed. bk rev. adv acc. **Circ** 500. *Landwirtschaftlichen Versuchs-Stationen.*

ZEITSCHRIFT FUR ZOOLOGISCHE SYSTEMATIK UND EVOLUTIONSFORSCHUNG. Vo. 1- May 1963-. 0084-5418. Periodical. German (articles and summaries in English, French or German). qt. $129.00. Paul Parey Scientific Publishing, 35 West 38th Street #3W, New York NY 10018. **Tel** (212)730-0518. Ed W Herre, N Kristensen, G Osche, and D Sperlich. **Ind/Abst** Life Sci. Collect., GeoRef, Biol. Abstr., Curr. Contents, Agric. Biol. Environ. Sci., Sci. Cit. Index, Abr. Ed. LC QL351. **DD** 590.12. **CODEN** ZZSEAA. bk rev. adv acc. Publishes original articles on systematic zoology interlined with research on evolution. The aim is to synthesize the results from research in anatomy, morphology, animal geography, ecology, physiology, and genetics.

ZESZYTY NAUKOWE. AKADEMIA ROLNICZA W KRAKOWIE, ZOOTECHNIKA. (ZESZYTY NAUKOWE. ZOOTECHNIKA). Main/Corp Akademia Rolnicza w Krakowie. No. 13-. 0137-1916. Periodical. PL. Polish. ir. **Ind/Abst** Bibliogr. Agric. *Zootechnika.*

ZESZYTY NAUKOWE AKADEMII ROLNICZEJ WE WROCAWIU. ZOOTECHNIKA. **VFOAT** Zootechnika. Monographic Series. Polish (with added tables of contents and summaries in English and Russian). ir. *Zeszyty Naukowe Wyzszej Szkoy Rolniczej We Wrocawiu.*

ZOO. Began in 1935. 0044-5029. Periodical. BE. English. qt. Societe Royale de Zoologie, 26 Koningin Astridplein, Antwerpen 1 Belgium. **Tel** (03)231-1640. LC QL77.A6. **CODEN** ZOOAB4. bk rev. adv acc. Zoo news, general articles on animal care, behaviour, breeding, animals in art, book revisions, botany, nature-conservation and education.

ZOO ANVERS. Began with Oct. 1971 issue. Periodical. French. qt. Societe Royale de Zoologie D'Anvers, Koningin Astridplein 26, 2000 Antwerpen Belgium. **Ind/Abst** Bibliogr. Agric. *Zoo d'Anvers.*

ZOO BIOLOGY. Vol. 1, No. 1-. 0733-3188. Periodical. US. English. qt. Alan R Liss Inc, 41 East 11th Street, New York NY 10003. **Tel** (212)741-2515. **Ind/Abst** Life Sci. Collect., Chem. Abstr., Psychol. Abstr. LC QL77.5. **DD** 591. **CODEN** ZOBIDX.

THE ZOO GOER. (THE ZOOGOER). 0163-416X. Periodical. US. English. bm. $7.50. Friends of the National Zoo, National Zoological Park, Washington DC 20009. **Tel** (202)673-4711. Ed Bettina Conner. bk rev. **Circ** 26,000. A color magazine that highlights the animals and people of the National Zoological Park in Washington DC.

ZOO ONE. (ZOO ONE : THE MAGAZINE OF AMERICA'S FIRST ZOO). **VFOAT** Zoo 1. Fall 1982-. 0745-1555. Periodical. US. English. qt. Membership Department, Zoological Society of Philadelphia, 34th Street and Grand Avenue, Philadelphia PA 19104.

ZOO VIEW. 0276-3303. Periodical. US. English. qt. $5.25. Greater Los Angeles Zoo Association, 5333 Zoo Drive, Los Angeles CA 90027. **Tel** (213)661-2184.

ZOOBOOKS 2. **VFOAT** Zoo Books 2. Vol. 1, No. 1 (Oct. 1984)-. 8755-0601. Periodical. US. English. mo. $14.00. Wildlife Education, 930 West Washington Street, San Diego CA 92103. **Tel** (619)299-5034. Ed John Wexo. **DD** 591. **Circ** 350,000. Each issue gives basic information on one animal or group of animals. Full color, describing anatomy, habitat, reproduction, food, locomotion, sociology, and future.

ZOOBOOKS (SAN DIEGO, CALIF.). (ZOOBOOKS). **VFOAT** Zoo Books. Vol. 1, No. 1 (Nov. 1983)-. 0737-9005. Monographic Series. US. English. mo. $14.00 10 issues. Wildlife Education Ltd, 930 West Washington Street, San Diego CA 92103. **DD** 591.

ZOOLOGICA. Issue 1- (Vol. 1-). 0044-5088. Monographic Series. GW. German. ir. E Schweizerbartsche Verlag, Johannesstrasse 3-A, D7000 Stuttgart 1 West Germany. **Tel** 0711/625001. Ed F Schaller. **Ind/Abst** Bibliogr. Index Geol. **CODEN** ZLGAAA. Original zoological contributions.

ZOOLOGICA GOTHOBURGENSIA. 1. 0084-5590. Monographic Series. English. ir. University of Goteborg, Department of History, Goteborg Sweden. LC QL1. **DD** 591.08.

Zoology-Vertebrate and Invertebrate

ZOOLOGICA POLONIAE; ARCHIVUM SOCIETATIS ZOOLOGORUM POLONIAE. See Genealogy and Heraldry - Archives.

ZOOLOGICA SCRIPTA. V. 1- 1971-. 0300-3256. Periodical. SW. English (French or German). qt. Pergamon Press, 395 Sawmill River Road, Elmsford NY 10523. Tel Telex 85413160. Ind/Abst Sci. Cit. Index, Abr. Ed., Bibliogr. Index Geol. LC QL1. DD 574.05. NLM W1 ZO606BJ. CODEN ZLSCA8. *Arkiv for Zoologi, Norwegian Journal of Zoology, 0029-6864.*

ZOOLOGICAL JOURNAL OF THE LINNEAN SOCIETY. Main/Corp Linnean Society of London. V. 48- Feb. 1969-. 0024-4082. Periodical. UK. English. mo. Academic Press, 4805 Sand Lake Road, Orlando FL 32819. Tel (305)345-4100. Ind/Abst Life Sci. Collect., Excerpta Med., GeoRef, Biol. Abstr., Bibliogr. Agric., Bibliogr. Index, Sci. Cit. Index, Abr. Ed., Bibliogr. Index Geol. LC QH1. DD 591.05. NLM W1 ZO607. CODEN ZJLSA7. *Journal of the Linnean Society of London. Zoology.*

ZOOLOGICAL PARKS AND AQUARIUMS IN THE AMERICAS. Began with 1978-79. 0740-7610. US. English. be. $50.00. American Association of Zoological Parks and Aquariums, Oglebay Park, Wheeling WV 26003. LC QL76. DD 590.7447. *Zoos & Aquariums in the Americas.*

ZOOLOGICAL RECORD. 7th- 1870-. 0144-3607. UK. English. an. Ind/Abst GeoRef. LC Z7991, QL1. DD 016.59. NLM ZQL 15 Z88. CODEN ZOREAU. *Record of Zoological Literature.*

ZOOLOGICAL RECORD : BEING RECORDS OF ZOOLOGICAL LITERATURE, SECTION 7. BRACHIOPODA. Periodical. UK. English. an. $45.00. Bioscience Information Service, 2100 Arch Street, Philadelphia PA 19103. Tel (215)587-4800. Index of brachiopoda literature.

ZOOLOGICAL RECORD: BEING RECORDS OF ZOOLOGICAL LITERATURE, SECTION 10. CRUSTACEA. Periodical. UK. English. an. $105.00. Bioscience Information Services, 2100 Arch Street, Philadelphia PA 19103. Tel (215)587-4800. Index of crustacea literature.

ZOOLOGICAL SCIENCE. Vol. 1, No. 1 (Feb. 1984)-. 0289-0003. Periodical. JA. English. bm. 411. VNU Science Press BV, Park Voorn 4, 3454 Jr de Meern, PO Box 2073, 3500 GB Utrecht The Netherlands. Tel (0)3406 63737. Ed N Ecami. Ind/Abst Life Sci. Collect., Chem. Abstr. adv acc. The official journal of the Zoological Society of Japan. Publishes articles from the many subspecialities within zoology. *Dobutsugaku Zasshi, 0044-5118; Annotationes Zoologicae Japonenses, 0003-5092.*

ZOOLOGICESKIJ ZURNAL. (ZOOLOGICHESKII ZHURNAL). Vol. 11, No. 1-. 0044-5134. Periodical. UR. Russian (summaries in English and German). mo. $99.00. Victor Kamkin Inc (70333), 12224 Parklawn Drive, Rockville MD 20852. Tel (301)881-5973. Ind/Abst Life Sci. Collect., Sel. Water Resour. Abstr., GeoRef, Biol. Abstr., Bibliogr. Agric. CODEN ZOLZAT. *Russkii Zoologicheskii Zhurnal.*

ZOOLOGICKE LISTY. VFOAT Folia Zoologica. Vol. 1-25. 0139-7893. Periodical. Czech (table of contents also in Russian, German and English). qt. 220.00 Domestic, $83.00 US. Kluwer Academic Publishing Group, Distribution Center, PO Box 322, 3300 AH Dordrecht Netherlands. Tel 33 11 44. Ed Josef Kratochvil. Ind/Abst Sci. Cit. Index, Abr. Ed. LC QL1. bk rev. Circ 1,200. Brings comprehensive articles on the results of original research in vertebrate zoology (mammalogy, ornithology, ichthyology, morphology, etc.). *Entomologicke Listy.*

ZOOLOGISCHE ABHANDLUNGEN. Main/Corp Dresden. Staatliches Museum fur Tierkunde. Vol. 26- 1961/62-. 0070-7287. German (summaries in English). ir. Deutscher Buch Export-Import, Leninstrasse 16, DDR-701 Leipzig East Germany. Tel 4952503. Ind/Abst Biol. Abstr., Life Sci. Collect. CODEN ZASMAT. bk rev. Circ 750. (ctrl). Taxonomy, systematics, morphology, anatomy, bionomics, ecology, zoogeography of the vertebrate groups in global range. *Abhandlungen und Berichte aus dem Staatlichen museum fur Tierkunde in Dresden.*

ZOOLOGISCHE BEITRAGE. Volume 1-. 0044-5150. Periodical. English summaries. ir. Duncker & Humblot, Dietrich Schafer Weg 9, 1 Berlin 41 West Germany. Tel (030)7912026. Ed W Dohle, G Weigmann and I Zerbst-Boroffka. Ind/Abst Life Sci. Collect., Biol. Abstr. LC QL1. CODEN ZOBEAI. Circ 300. Study of zoology. *Zoologische Beitrage.*

ZOOLOGISCHE GARTEN; ZEITSCHRIFT FUR DIE GESAMTE TIERGARTNEREI. Vol. 1-63, 1860-1922. 0044-5169. Periodical. German. bm. $48.00. VCH Publishers Inc, 303 Northwest 12th Avenue, Deerfield Beach FL 33442. Tel (305)428-5566.

ZOOLOGISCHE JAHRBUCHER. ABTEILUNG FUR ALLGEMEINE ZOOLOGIE UND PHYSIOLOGIE DER TIERE. Began with Vol. for 1910. 0044-5185. Periodical. US. English (German). ir. 107.00. VEB Gustav Fischer Verlag Jena, Villengang 2/Postfach 176, DDR 69 Jena East Germany. Tel 27332. Ed Heinz Penzlin. Ind/Abst Bibliogr. Agric., Chem. Abstr., Life Sci. Collect., Curr. Contents. LC QL1. DD 590.5. NLM W1 ZO612E. CODEN ZJZPAY. bk rev. Founded in 1886, belongs to the oldest German zoological special journals. Contains generally zoology and physiology of animals. *Zoologische Jahrbuecher.*

ZOOLOGISCHE JAHRBUCHER. ABTEILUNG FUR ANATOMIE UND ONTOGENIE DER TIERE. Began with Vol. for 1888. 0044-5177. Periodical. English (German articles). ir. $107.00. VCH Publishers Inc, 303 Northwest 12th Avenue, Deerfield Beach FL 33442. Tel (305)428-5566. Ind/Abst Life Sci. Collect., Excerpta Med., Bibliogr. Agric. LC QL1. DD 590.5. NLM W1 ZO612G. CODEN ZJAOA8.

ZOOLOGY PUBLICATIONS FROM VICTORIA UNIVERSITY OF WELLINGTON. Main/Corp Victoria University of Wellington. No. 22- Nov. 1957-. 0083-6060. Monographic Series. NZ. English. ir. Victoria University of Wellington, Department of Zoology, Wellington New Zealand. Tel 721-000. Ed J A F Garrick. Ind/Abst Life Sci. Collect., Biol. Abstr. LC QL1. DD 591. CODEN ZPVWA9. Circ 325. (ctrl). Mainly systematic zoology dealing principally with the New Zealand fauna. *Zoology Publications from Victoria University College, Wellington.*

ZOOMORPHOLOGY. Vol. 96, No. 1/2 (Oct. 1980)-. 0720-213X. Periodical. US. English. ir. Springer Verlag-New York Inc, 175 5th Avenue, New York NY 10010. Tel (212)460-1500. Ed O Kraus. Ind/Abst Life Sci. Collect., Biol. Abstr. LC QL1. DD 591.405. CODEN ZMPHDI. Research in animal morphology at all levels of ontogeny and organization, including ultrastructure of invertebrates and vertebrates. *Zoomorphologie.*

ZOONOOZ. V. 1- Jan./Feb. 1926-. Periodical. US. English. mo. San Diego Zoological Society, PO Box 551, San Diego CA 92112. LC QL1. DD 590.74.

ZOOPHYSIOLOGY. V. 11-. 0720-1842. Monographic Series. English. ir. Springer Verlag-New York Inc, 175 5th Avenue, New York NY 10010. Tel (212)460-1500. Ind/Abst Life Sci. Collect., Biol. Abstr. LC UNC. NLM W1 ZO615M. CODEN ZOOPDH. Number series on zoophysiology. *Zoophysiology and Ecology, 0084-5663.*

ZUCHTHYGIENE. V. 1-. 0044-5371. Periodical. German (table of contents and summaries in English). ir. $107.80. Paul Parey Scientific Publishing, 35 West 38th Street 3 West, New York NY 10018. Tel (212)730-0518. Ed R Hahn. Ind/Abst Life Sci. Collect., Pestdoc, Ringdoc, Vetdoc, Chem. Abstr., Biol. Abstr., Curr. Contents, Index Vet., Vet. Bull. LC S494. DD 631.5305. NLM W1 ZU655. CODEN ZUCYAN. bk rev. adv acc. Circ 500. Of interest to veterinarians, animal breeders and zoologists concerned with animal reproduction and insemination, their institutions and libraries.

JUN 1 5 1987

Z
6941
S464
1st ed.
1986
v.2